Who's Who in American Education®

Who's Who in American Education®
2004-2005

6th Edition

121 Chanlon Road
New Providence, NJ 07974 U.S.A.
www.marquiswhoswho.com

Who's Who in American Education
Marquis Who's Who

Chief Executive Officer	Gene M. McGovern
President	James A. Finkelstein
Senior Managing Director	Fred Marks
Director, Editorial & Product Development	Robert Docherty
Research Director	Lisa Weissbard

Editorial

Managing Editor	Karen Chassie
Senior Editor	Danielle Netta
Associate Editor	Kate Spirito
Assistant Editors	Patricia Delli Santi
	Ryan Karwell
	Deanna Richmond
	Sandy Sauchelli

Editorial Services

Director	Debby Nowicki
Production Manager	Paul Zema
Production Editors	Daniel D. Crawford
	Jeffrey Uthaichai
Freelance Manager	Mary SanGiovanni
Editorial Services Assistant	Ann Chavis
Special Projects Supervisor	Sola Osofisan
Mail Processing Manager	Kara A. Seitz
Mail Processing Staff	Betty Gray
	Hattie Walker

Creative Services

Director, Marketing & Creative Services	Michael Noerr
Creative Services Manager	Rose Butkiewicz
Production Manager	Jeanne Danzig
Marketing Specialist	Jill Tarbell

Research

Managing Editor	Kerry Nugent Morrison
Senior Research Editors	Maria L. Izzo
	Jennifer Podolsky
Associate Research Editor	Todd Kineavy

Editorial Systems

Director	Jack Zimmerman
Technical Project Leader	Ben Loh
Composition Programmer	Tom Haggerty
Database Programmer	Latha Shankar
Senior Quality Assurance Analyst	Angela Sorrenti

Published by Marquis Who's Who LLC.

Copyright ©2003 by Marquis Who's Who LLC. All rights reserved.

No part of this publication may be reproduced, stored in a retrieval system, or transmitted, in any form or by any means—including, but not limited to, electronic, mechanical, photocopying, recording, or otherwise—or used for any commercial purpose whatsoever without the prior written permission of the publisher and, if publisher deems necessary, execution of a formal license agreement with publisher.

For information, contact:
   Marquis Who's Who
   121 Chanlon Road
   New Providence, New Jersey 07974
   1-908-673-1001
   www.marquiswhoswho.com

WHO'S WHO IN AMERICAN EDUCATION is a registered trademark of Marquis Who's Who LLC.

Library of Congress Card Catalog Number   89-649424
International Standard Book Number   0-8379-2706-4   (Classic Edition)
                                     0-8379-2707-2   (Deluxe Edition)

No payment is either solicited or accepted for the inclusion of entries in this publication. Marquis Who's Who has used its best efforts in collecting and preparing material for inclusion in this publication, but does not warrant that the information herein is complete or accurate, and does not assume, and hereby disclaims, any liability to any person for any loss or damage caused by errors or omissions in this publication, whether such errors or omissions result from negligence, accident, or any other cause.

Manufactured in the United States of America.

Table of Contents

Preface	vi
Board of Advisors	vii
Standards of Admission	viii
Key to Information	ix
Table of Abbreviations	x
Alphabetical Practices	xvii
Who's Who in American Education Biographies	1
Professional Index	1313
Adult Education	1313
Association Administration	1314
Counseling/Career Planning	1316
Education: Other	1317
Gifted and Talented/Special Education	1321
Government Administration	1328
Higher Education Administration	1329
Higher Education:	
Architecture and Design	1338
Education	1338
Engineering	1342
Finance and Business	1347
Healthcare	1353
Humanities	1363
Law	1373
Life Sciences	1376
Mathematics and Computers	1380
Media and Communications	1384
Physical Education	1386
Physical Sciences	1388
Social Sciences	1392
Visual and Performing Arts	1399
Libraries	1405
Preschool Education	1408
Primary/Elementary/Middle School Education	1409
Private/Parochial School Education	1425
School Administration	1426
School System Administration	1430
Secondary School Education	1434
Vocational School Education	1446

Preface

The sixth edition of Marquis *Who's Who in American Education* recognizes those individuals in the diverse field of education who are making a difference in today's society.

The Marquis researchers have drawn on a wide range of contemporary sources in the preparation of more than 23,000 sketches found in this edition: newspapers, periodicals, and professional associations rosters, among others. The result is broad coverage of personal and professional biographical facts concerning individuals from every area of the education community.

Listed in this volume are outstanding educators from all levels: secondary and elementary educators, university educators, administrators, chancellors, deans, school board members, librarians, program directors, and others. In most cases, Biographees have furnished their own data, thus assuring a high degree of accuracy. In some cases where individuals failed to supply information, Marquis staff members compiled the data through careful, independent research.

Sketches compiled in this manner are denoted by an asterisk (*). As in previous editions, Biographees were given the opportunity to review prepublication proofs of their sketches to make sure they were correct.

To supplement the efforts of Marquis researchers, and to ensure comprehensive coverage of important professionals, members of the distinguished Board of Advisors have nominated outstanding individuals for inclusion in this volume. The question is often asked, "How do people get into a Marquis Who's Who volume?" Name selection is based on one fundamental principle: reference value.

In the editorial evaluation that resulted in the ultimate selection of the names appearing in this directory, an individual's desire to be listed was not sufficient reason for inclusion; rather it was the person's achievement that ruled. Similarly, neither wealth nor social position was a criterion; only occupational stature or achievement in a field within the education profession influenced selection.

Following the biographical profiles is the Professional Index. Here the reader can locate each professional in the publication, categorized by state and city within their specialty. The specialties listed include primary/elementary/middle school education, secondary school education, vocational school education, school administration, school system administration, libraries, higher education, higher education administration, and others.

Marquis Who's Who editors exercise the utmost care in preparing each biographical sketch for publication. Occasionally, however, errors occur. Users of this directory are requested to draw the attention of the publisher to any errors found so that corrections can be made in a subsequent edition.

The sixth edition of *Who's Who in American Education* carries on the tradition of excellence established in 1899 with the publication of the first edition of *Who's Who in America*. The essence of that tradition is reflected in our continuing effort to produce reference works that are responsive to the needs of their users throughout the world.

Board of Advisors

Marquis Who's Who gratefully acknowledges the following distinguished individuals who have made themselves available for review, evaluation, and general comment with regard to the publication of the sixth Edition of *Who's Who in American Education*. The advisors have enhanced the reference value of this edition by the nomination of outstanding individuals for inclusion. However, the Board of Advisors, either collectively or individually, is in no way responsible for the selection of names appearing in this volume, nor does the Board of Advisors bear responsibility for the accuracy or comprehensiveness of the biographical information or other material contained herein.

Mindy Aloff
Freelance Writer

William C. Anderson
Executive Director
American Academy of
    Environmental Engineers
Annapolis, Maryland

Steven C. Beering
President Emeritus
Purdue University
West Lafayette, Indiana

Willard L. Boyd
President Emeritus
Field Museum of
    Natural History

Dr. Thomas C. Dolan
President and CEO
American College of Healthcare
    Executives

Charles C. Eldredge
Hall Distinguished Professor
    of American Art and Culture
University of Kansas
Lawrence, Kansas

Barbara Haskell
Curator
Whitney Museum of American Art

Thomas R. Horton
Former Chairman
American Management
    Association

Jill Krementz
Author and Photographer

Charles F. Larson
President
Innovative Research Intl.

Andrew Leckey
Syndicated Investment
Columnist
The Chicago Tribune

Judith P. Lotas
Founding Partner
Lotas Minard Patton
    McIver, Inc.

Martin E. Marty
Professor Emeritus
University of Chicago
    Divinity School

Robert G. McKinnell
Professor Emeritus
Department of Genetics, Cell Biology
    and Development
University of Minnesota
Minneapolis, Minnesota

Jeremiah P. Ostriker
Plumian Prof. Astronomy
    & Exptl. Philosphy
U. Cambridge, England

Louis Rukeyser
Economic Commentator
Host, Louis Rukeyser's
    Wall Street

James B. Sales
Former Senior Partner
Fulbright & Jaworski
Houston, Texas

John Fox Sullivan
President and Publisher
National Journal

Elie Wiesel
Author, Professor of Philosophy
Boston University

Standards of Admission

The foremost consideration in determining possible Biographees for Marquis *Who's Who in American Education* is the extent of an individual's reference value, as determined by either of two factors: (1) the position of responsibility held, or (2) the level of achievement attained by the individual.

The factor of position includes, but is not limited to, the following categories:

1. High ranking officers from major universities throughout the United States. This group includes, for example, presidents, chancellors, and deans of schools of education.

2. Professors from major universities.

3. Top education officials from various levels of jurisdiction.

Included in this category are selected officials from the United States Department of Education, including the Secretary of Education, state superintendents of education and presidents of state boards of education, and superintendents of school boards in the largest U.S. cities.

Admission by the second factor—significant achievement—is based on the application of objective criteria established for each educational level. A professor who has made important research contributions in his or her field is of reference interest because of outstanding achievements. Award-winning teachers of the primary, secondary, and college/university levels qualify for admission because of outstanding performance in the classroom. Qualitative standards determine eligibility for every field.

Key to Information

[1] SCHAFFER, STACY LYNN, [2] elementary school educator; **[3]** b. Skokie, Ill., Feb. 16, 1958; **[4]** d. Barry and Lorraine (Lebovitz) Lutz; **[5]** m. Bennett Shaffer, June 12, 1985; **[6]** children: Brandon, Bret, Alison. **[7]** Student U. Ill. Chgo, 1976-78; BE Nat. Louis U., 1980, MEd, 1984. **[8]** Cert. elem. tchr., Ill., learning disabilities. **[9]** Tchr. Edison Elem Sch., Skokie, 1980-81, primary tchr. learning disabilities, 1982—1987; ass't. supt. Learning Disabilities curriculum Skokie elementary schs., 1987—1998; supt., 1998— **[10]** tchr. remedial reading Madison Elem. Sch., Skokie, summers, 1980, 81, cons., lectr. in field. **[11]** Author: Beginning Reading Series for grades K-2, 1994; contbr. articles to profl. jours., mags., 2nd edit., 2001 **[12]** Vol. MADD, Am. Cancer Soc. **[13]** Capt. USAFR, 1985—2001; **[14]** Recipient Good Apple award. 1992. **[15]** Mem. NEA, Ill. Tchrs. Assn., Ill. Coun. Learning Disabilites (bd. dirs. 1989—), Internat. Reading Assn., Phi Beta Kappa. **[16]** Democrat. **[17]** Jewish. **[18]** Running, pottery. **[19]** Home: 1842 Willow Ln **[20]** Office: 22 Alexander Ave

KEY

- [1] Name
- [2] Occupation
- [3] Vital statistics
- [4] Parents
- [5] Marriage
- [6] Children
- [7] Education
- [8] Professional certifications
- [9] Career
- [10] Career-related
- [11] Writings and creative works
- [12] Civic and political activities
- [13] Military
- [14] Awards and fellowships
- [15] Professional and association memberships, clubs and lodges
- [16] Political affiliation
- [17] Religion
- [18] Avocations
- [19] Home address
- [20] Office address

Table of Abbreviations

The following abbreviations and symbols are frequently used in this book.

*An asterisk following a sketch indicates that it was researched by the Marquis Who's Who editorial staff and has not been verified by the Biographee.

A

A Associate (used with academic degrees only)
AA, A.A. Associate in Arts, Associate of Arts
AAAL American Academy of Arts and Letters
AAAS American Association for the Advancement of Science
AACD American Association for Counseling and Development
AACN American Association of Critical Care Nurses
AAHA American Academy of Health Administrators
AAHP American Association of Hospital Planners
AAHPERD American Alliance for Health, Physical Education, Recreation, and Dance
AAS Associate of Applied Science
AASL American Association of School Librarians
AASPA American Association of School Personnel Administrators
AAU Amateur Athletic Union
AAUP American Association of University Professors
AAUW American Association of University Women
AB, A.B. Arts, Bachelor of
AB Alberta
ABA American Bar Association
ABC American Broadcasting Company
AC Air Corps
acad. academy, academic
acct. accountant
acctg. accounting
ACDA Arms Control and Disarmament Agency
ACHA American College of Hospital Administrators
ACLS Advanced Cardiac Life Support
ACLU American Civil Liberties Union
ACOG American College of Ob-Gyn
ACP American College of Physicians
ACS American College of Surgeons
ADA American Dental Association
a.d.c. aide-de-camp
adj. adjunct, adjutant
adj. gen. adjutant general
adm. admiral
adminstr. administrator
adminstrn. administration
adminstrv. administrative
ADN Associate's Degree in Nursing
ADP Automatic Data Processing
adv. advocate, advisory
advt. advertising
AE, A.E. Agricultural Engineer
A.E. and P. Ambassador Extraordinary and Plenipotentiary
AEC Atomic Energy Commission
aero. aeronautical, aeronautic
aerodyn. aerodynamic
AFB Air Force Base
AFL-CIO American Federation of Labor and Congress of Industrial Organizations
AFTRA American Federation of TV and Radio Artists
AFSCME American Federation of State, County and Municipal Employees
agr. agriculture
agrl. agricultural
agt. agent
AGVA American Guild of Variety Artists
agy. agency
A&I Agricultural and Industrial
AIA American Institute of Architects
AIAA American Institute of Aeronautics and Astronautics
AIChE American Institute of Chemical Engineers
AICPA American Institute of Certified Public Accountants
AID Agency for International Development
AIDS Acquired Immune Deficiency Syndrome
AIEE American Institute of Electrical Engineers
AIM American Institute of Management
AIME American Institute of Mining, Metallurgy, and Petroleum Engineers
AK Alaska
AL Alabama
ALA American Library Association
Ala. Alabama
alt. alternate
Alta. Alberta
A&M Agricultural and Mechanical
AM, A.M. Arts, Master of
Am. American, America
AMA American Medical Association
amb. ambassador
A.M.E. African Methodist Episcopal
Amtrak National Railroad Passenger Corporation
AMVETS American Veterans of World War II, Korea, Vietnam
ANA American Nurses Association
anat. anatomical
ANCC American Nurses Credentialing Center
ann. annual
ANTA American National Theatre and Academy
anthrop. anthropological
AP Associated Press
APA American Psychological Association
APGA American Personnel Guidance Association
APHA American Public Health Association
APO Army Post Office
apptd. appointed
Apr. April
apt. apartment
AR Arkansas
ARC American Red Cross
arch. architect
archeol. archeological
archtl. architectural
Ariz. Arizona
Ark. Arkansas
ArtsD, ArtsD. Arts, Doctor of
arty. artillery
AS American Samoa
AS Associate in Science
ASCAP American Society of Composers, Authors and Publishers
ASCD Association for Supervision and Curriculum Development
ASCE American Society of Civil Engineers
ASHRAE American Society of Heating, Refrigeration, and Air Conditioning Engineers
ASME American Society of Mechanical Engineers
ASNSA American Society for Nursing Service Administrators
ASPA American Society for Public Administration
ASPCA American Society for the Prevention of Cruelty to Animals
assn. association
assoc. associate
asst. assistant
ASTD American Society for Training and Development
ASTM American Society for Testing and Materials
astron. astronomical
astrophys. astrophysical
ATLA Association of Trial Lawyers of America
ATSC Air Technical Service Command
AT&T American Telephone & Telegraph Company
atty. attorney
Aug. August
AUS Army of the United States
aux. auxiliary
Ave. Avenue
AVMA American Veterinary Medical Association
AZ Arizona
AWHONN Association of Women's Health Obstetric and Neonatal Nurses

B

B. Bachelor
b. born
BA, B.A. Bachelor of Arts
BAgr, B.Agr. Bachelor of Agriculture

Balt. Baltimore
Bapt. Baptist
BArch, B.Arch. Bachelor of Architecture
BAS, B.A.S. Bachelor of Agricultural Science
BBA, B.B.A. Bachelor of Business Administration
BBB Better Business Bureau
BBC British Broadcasting Corporation
BC, B.C. British Columbia
BCE, B.C.E. Bachelor of Civil Engineering
BChir, B.Chir. Bachelor of Surgery
BCL, B.C.L. Bachelor of Civil Law
BCLS Basic Cardiac Life Support
BCS, B.C.S. Bachelor of Commercial Science
BD, B.D. Bachelor of Divinity
bd. board
BE, B.E. Bachelor of Education
BEE, B.E.E. Bachelor of Electrical Engineering
BFA, B.F.A. Bachelor of Fine Arts
bibl. biblical
bibliog. bibliographical
biog. biographical
biol. biological
BJ, B.J. Bachelor of Journalism
Bklyn. Brooklyn
BL, B.L. Bachelor of Letters
bldg. building
BLS, B.L.S. Bachelor of Library Science
BLS Basic Life Support
Blvd. Boulevard
BMI Broadcast Music, Inc.
BMW Bavarian Motor Works (Bayerische Motoren Werke)
bn. battalion
B.&O.R.R. Baltimore & Ohio Railroad
bot. botanical
BPE, B.P.E. Bachelor of Physical Education
BPhil, B.Phil. Bachelor of Philosophy
br. branch
BRE, B.R.E. Bachelor of Religious Education
brig. gen. brigadier general
Brit. British, Brittanica
Bros. Brothers
BS, B.S. Bachelor of Science
BSA, B.S.A. Bachelor of Agricultural Science
BSBA Bachelor of Science in Business Administration
BSChemE Bachelor of Science in Chemical Engineering
BSD, B.S.D. Bachelor of Didactic Science
BSEE Bachelor of Science in Electrical Engineering
BSN Bachelor of Science in Nursing
BST, B.S.T. Bachelor of Sacred Theology
BTh, B.Th. Bachelor of Theology
bull. bulletin
bur. bureau
bus. business
B.W.I. British West Indies

C

CA California
CAA Civil Aeronautics Administration
CAB Civil Aeronautics Board
CAD-CAM Computer Aided Design–Computer Aided Model
Calif. California
C.Am. Central America
Can. Canada, Canadian
CAP Civil Air Patrol
capt. captain
cardiol. cardiological
cardiovasc. cardiovascular
CARE Cooperative American Relief Everywhere
Cath. Catholic
cav. cavalry
CBC Canadian Broadcasting Company
CBI China, Burma, India Theatre of Operations
CBS Columbia Broadcasting Company
C.C. Community College
CCC Commodity Credit Corporation
CCNY City College of New York
CCRN Critical Care Registered Nurse
CCU Cardiac Care Unit
CD Civil Defense
CE, C.E. Corps of Engineers, Civil Engineer
CEN Certified Emergency Nurse
CENTO Central Treaty Organization
CEO chief executive officer
CERN European Organization of Nuclear Research
cert. certificate, certification, certified
CETA Comprehensive Employment Training Act
CFA Chartered Financial Analyst
CFL Canadian Football League
CFO chief financial officer
CFP Certified Financial Planner
ch. church
ChD, Ch.D. Doctor of Chemistry
chem. chemical
ChemE, Chem.E. Chemical Engineer
ChFC Chartered Financial Consultant
Chgo. Chicago
chirurg. chirurgical
chmn. chairman
chpt. chapter
CIA Central Intelligence Agency
Cin. Cincinnati
cir. circle, circuit
CLE Continuing Legal Education
Cleve. Cleveland
climatol. climatological
clin. clinical
clk. clerk
C.L.U. Chartered Life Underwriter
CM, C.M. Master in Surgery
CM Northern Mariana Islands
CMA Certified Medical Assistant
cmty. community
CNA Certified Nurse's Aide
CNOR Certified Nurse (Operating Room)
C.&N.W.Ry. Chicago & North Western Railway
CO Colorado
Co. Company
COF Catholic Order of Foresters
C. of C. Chamber of Commerce
col. colonel
coll. college
Colo. Colorado
com. committee
comd. commanded
comdg. commanding
comdr. commander
comdt. commandant
comm. communications
commd. commissioned
comml. commercial
commn. commission
commr. commissioner
compt. comptroller
condr. conductor
Conf. Conference
Congl. Congregational, Congressional
Conglist. Congregationalist
Conn. Connecticut
cons. consultant, consulting
consol. consolidated
constl. constitutional
constn. constitution
constrn. construction
contbd. contributed
contbg. contributing
contbn. contribution
contbr. contributor
contr. controller
Conv. Convention
COO chief operating officer
coop. cooperative
coord. coordinator
CORDS Civil Operations and Revolutionary Development Support
CORE Congress of Racial Equality
corp. corporation, corporate
corr. correspondent, corresponding, correspondence
C.&O.Ry. Chesapeake & Ohio Railway
coun. council
CPA Certified Public Accountant
CPCU Chartered Property and Casualty Underwriter
CPH, C.P.H. Certificate of Public Health
cpl. corporal
CPR Cardio-Pulmonary Resuscitation
C.P.Ry. Canadian Pacific Railway
CRT Cathode Ray Terminal
C.S. Christian Science
CSB, C.S.B. Bachelor of Christian Science
C.S.C. Civil Service Commission
CT Connecticut
ct. court
ctr. center
ctrl. central
CWS Chemical Warfare Service
C.Z. Canal Zone

D

D. Doctor
d. daughter
DAgr, D.Agr. Doctor of Agriculture
DAR Daughters of the American Revolution
dau. daughter
DAV Disabled American Veterans
DC, D.C. District of Columbia
DCL, D.C.L. Doctor of Civil Law
DCS, D.C.S. Doctor of Commercial Science
DD, D.D. Doctor of Divinity

DDS, D.D.S. Doctor of Dental Surgery
DE Delaware
Dec. December
dec. deceased
def. defense
Del. Delaware
del. delegate, delegation
Dem. Democrat, Democratic
DEng, D.Eng. Doctor of Engineering
denom. denomination, denominational
dep. deputy
dept. department
dermatol. dermatological
desc. descendant
devel. development, developmental
DFA, D.F.A. Doctor of Fine Arts
D.F.C. Distinguished Flying Cross
DHL, D.H.L. Doctor of Hebrew Literature
dir. director
dist. district
distbg. distributing
distbn. distribution
distbr. distributor
disting. distinguished
div. division, divinity, divorce
divsn. division
DLitt, D.Litt. Doctor of Literature
DMD, D.M.D. Doctor of Dental Medicine
DMS, D.M.S. Doctor of Medical Science
DO, D.O. Doctor of Osteopathy
docs. documents
DON Director of Nursing
DPH, D.P.H. Diploma in Public Health
DPhil, D.Phil. Doctor of Philosophy
D.R. Daughters of the Revolution
Dr. Drive, Doctor
DRE, D.R.E. Doctor of Religious Education
DrPH, Dr.P.H. Doctor of Public Health, Doctor of Public Hygiene
D.S.C. Distinguished Service Cross
DSc, D.Sc. Doctor of Science
DSChemE Doctor of Science in Chemical Engineering
D.S.M. Distinguished Service Medal
DST, D.S.T. Doctor of Sacred Theology
DTM, D.T.M. Doctor of Tropical Medicine
DVM, D.V.M. Doctor of Veterinary Medicine
DVS, D.V.S. Doctor of Veterinary Surgery

E

E, E. East
ea. eastern
E. and P. Extraordinary and Plenipotentiary
Eccles. Ecclesiastical
ecol. ecological
econ. economic
ECOSOC Economic and Social Council (of the UN)
ED, E.D. Doctor of Engineering
ed. educated
EdB, Ed.B. Bachelor of Education
EdD, Ed.D. Doctor of Education
edit. edition
editl. editorial
EdM, Ed.M. Master of Education
edn. education
ednl. educational

EDP Electronic Data Processing
EdS, Ed.S. Specialist in Education
EE, E.E. Electrical Engineer
E.E. and M.P. Envoy Extraordinary and Minister Plenipotentiary
EEC European Economic Community
EEG Electroencephalogram
EEO Equal Employment Opportunity
EEOC Equal Employment Opportunity Commission
E.Ger. German Democratic Republic
EKG Electrocardiogram
elec. electrical
electrochem. electrochemical
electrophys. electrophysical
elem. elementary
EM, E.M. Engineer of Mines
EMT Emergency Medical Technician
ency. encyclopedia
Eng. England
engr. engineer
engring. engineering
entomol. entomological
environ. environmental
EPA Environmental Protection Agency
epidemiol. epidemiological
Episc. Episcopalian
ERA Equal Rights Amendment
ERDA Energy Research and Development Administration
ESEA Elementary and Secondary Education Act
ESL English as Second Language
ESPN Entertainment and Sports Programming Network
ESSA Environmental Science Services Administration
ethnol. ethnological
ETO European Theatre of Operations
Evang. Evangelical
exam. examination, examining
Exch. Exchange
exec. executive
exhbn. exhibition
expdn. expedition
expn. exposition
expt. experiment
exptl. experimental
Expy. Expressway
Ext. Extension

F

F.A. Field Artillery
FAA Federal Aviation Administration
FAO Food and Agriculture Organization (of the UN)
FBA Federal Bar Association
FBI Federal Bureau of Investigation
FCA Farm Credit Administration
FCC Federal Communications Commission
FCDA Federal Civil Defense Administration
FDA Food and Drug Administration
FDIA Federal Deposit Insurance Administration
FDIC Federal Deposit Insurance Corporation
FE, F.E. Forest Engineer
FEA Federal Energy Administration
Feb. February

fed. federal
fedn. federation
FERC Federal Energy Regulatory Commission
fgn. foreign
FHA Federal Housing Administration
fin. financial, finance
FL Florida
Fl. Floor
Fla. Florida
FMC Federal Maritime Commission
FNP Family Nurse Practitioner
FOA Foreign Operations Administration
found. foundation
FPC Federal Power Commission
FPO Fleet Post Office
frat. fraternity
FRS Federal Reserve System
FSA Federal Security Agency
Ft. Fort
FTC Federal Trade Commission
Fwy. Freeway

G

G-1 (or other number) Division of General Staff
GA, Ga. Georgia
GAO General Accounting Office
gastroent. gastroenterological
GATE Gifted and Talented Educators
GATT General Agreement on Tariffs and Trade
GE General Electric Company
gen. general
geneal. genealogical
geod. geodetic
geog. geographic, geographical
geol. geological
geophys. geophysical
geriat. geriatrics
gerontol. gerontological
G.H.Q. General Headquarters
GM General Motors Corporation
GMAC General Motors Acceptance Corporation
G.N.Ry. Great Northern Railway
gov. governor
govt. government
govtl. governmental
GPO Government Printing Office
grad. graduate, graduated
GSA General Services Administration
Gt. Great
GTE General Telephone and Electric Company
GU Guam
gynecol. gynecological

H

HBO Home Box Office
hdqs. headquarters
HEW Department of Health, Education and Welfare
HHD, H.H.D. Doctor of Humanities
HHFA Housing and Home Finance Agency
HHS Department of Health and Human Services

HI Hawaii
hist. historical, historic
HM, H.M. Master of Humanities
HMO Health Maintenance Organization
homeo. homeopathic
hon. honorary, honorable
Ho. of Dels. House of Delegates
Ho. of Reps. House of Representatives
hort. horticultural
hosp. hospital
H.S. High School
HUD Department of Housing and Urban Development
Hwy. Highway
hydrog. hydrographic

I

IA Iowa
IAEA International Atomic Energy Agency
IATSE International Alliance of Theatrical and Stage Employees and Moving Picture Operators of the United States and Canada
IBM International Business Machines Corporation
IBRD International Bank for Reconstruction and Development
ICA International Cooperation Administration
ICC Interstate Commerce Commission
ICCE International Council for Computers in Education
ICU Intensive Care Unit
ID Idaho
IEEE Institute of Electrical and Electronics Engineers
IFC International Finance Corporation
IGY International Geophysical Year
IL Illinois
Ill. Illinois
illus. illustrated
ILO International Labor Organization
IMF International Monetary Fund
IN Indiana
Inc. Incorporated
Ind. Indiana
ind. independent
Indpls. Indianapolis
indsl. industrial
inf. infantry
info. information
ins. insurance
insp. inspector
insp. gen. inspector general
inst. institute
instl. institutional
instn. institution
instr. instructor
instrn. instruction
instrnl. instructional
internat. international
intro. introduction
IRE Institute of Radio Engineers
IRS Internal Revenue Service
ITT International Telephone & Telegraph Corporation

J

JAG Judge Advocate General
JAGC Judge Advocate General Corps
Jan. January
Jaycees Junior Chamber of Commerce
JB, J.B. Jurum Baccalaureus
JCB, J.C.B. Juris Canoni Baccalaureus
JCD, J.C.D. Juris Canonici Doctor, Juris Civilis Doctor
JCL, J.C.L. Juris Canonici Licentiatus
JD, J.D. Juris Doctor
jg. junior grade
jour. journal
jr. junior
JSD, J.S.D. Juris Scientiae Doctor
JUD, J.U.D. Juris Utriusque Doctor
jud. judicial

K

Kans. Kansas
K.C. Knights of Columbus
K.P. Knights of Pythias
KS Kansas
K.T. Knight Templar
KY, Ky. Kentucky

L

LA, La. Louisiana
L.A. Los Angeles
lab. laboratory
L.Am. Latin America
lang. language
laryngol. laryngological
LB Labrador
LDS Latter Day Saints
LDS Church Church of Jesus Christ of Latter Day Saints
lectr. lecturer
legis. legislation, legislative
LHD, L.H.D. Doctor of Humane Letters
L.I. Long Island
libr. librarian, library
lic. licensed, license
L.I.R.R. Long Island Railroad
lit. literature
litig. litigation
LittB, Litt.B. Bachelor of Letters
LittD, Litt.D. Doctor of Letters
LLB, LL.B. Bachelor of Laws
LLD, L.L.D. Doctor of Laws
LLM, L.L.M. Master of Laws
Ln. Lane
L.&N.R.R. Louisville & Nashville Railroad
LPGA Ladies Professional Golf Association
LPN Licensed Practical Nurse
LS, L.S. Library Science (in degree)
lt. lieutenant
Ltd. Limited
Luth. Lutheran
LWV League of Women Voters

M

M. Master
m. married
MA, M.A. Master of Arts
MA Massachusetts
MADD Mothers Against Drunk Driving
mag. magazine
MAgr, M.Agr. Master of Agriculture
maj. major
Man. Manitoba
Mar. March
MArch, M.Arch. Master in Architecture
Mass. Massachusetts
math. mathematics, mathematical
MATS Military Air Transport Service
MB, M.B. Bachelor of Medicine
MB Manitoba
MBA, M.B.A. Master of Business Administration
MBS Mutual Broadcasting System
M.C. Medical Corps
MCE, M.C.E. Master of Civil Engineering
mcht. merchant
mcpl. municipal
MCS, M.C.S. Master of Commercial Science
MD, M.D. Doctor of Medicine
MD, Md. Maryland
MDiv Master of Divinity
MDip, M.Dip. Master in Diplomacy
mdse. merchandise
MDV, M.D.V. Doctor of Veterinary Medicine
ME, M.E. Mechanical Engineer
ME Maine
M.E.Ch. Methodist Episcopal Church
mech. mechanical
MEd., M.Ed. Master of Education
med. medical
MEE, M.E.E. Master of Electrical Engineering
mem. member
meml. memorial
merc. mercantile
met. metropolitan
metall. metallurgical
MetE, Met.E. Metallurgical Engineer
meteorol. meteorological
Meth. Methodist
Mex. Mexico
MF, M.F. Master of Forestry
MFA, M.F.A. Master of Fine Arts
mfg. manufacturing
mfr. manufacturer
mgmt. management
mgr. manager
MHA, M.H.A. Master of Hospital Administration
M.I. Military Intelligence
MI Michigan
Mich. Michigan
micros. microscopic, microscopical
mid. middle
mil. military
Milw. Milwaukee
Min. Minister
mineral. mineralogical
Minn. Minnesota
MIS Management Information Systems
Miss. Mississippi
MIT Massachusetts Institute of Technology
mktg. marketing
ML, M.L. Master of Laws
MLA Modern Language Association
M.L.D. Magister Legnum Diplomatic
MLitt, M.Litt. Master of Literature, Master of Letters

xiii

MLS, M.L.S. Master of Library Science
MME, M.M.E. Master of Mechanical Engineering
MN Minnesota
mng. managing
MO, Mo. Missouri
moblzn. mobilization
Mont. Montana
MP Northern Mariana Islands
M.P. Member of Parliament
MPA Master of Public Administration
MPE, M.P.E. Master of Physical Education
MPH, M.P.H. Master of Public Health
MPhil, M.Phil. Master of Philosophy
MPL, M.P.L. Master of Patent Law
Mpls. Minneapolis
MRE, M.R.E. Master of Religious Education
MRI Magnetic Resonance Imaging
MS, M.S. Master of Science
MS, Ms. Mississippi
MSc, M.Sc. Master of Science
MSChemE Master of Science in Chemical Engineering
MSEE Master of Science in Electrical Engineering
MSF, M.S.F. Master of Science of Forestry
MSN Master of Science in Nursing
MST, M.S.T. Master of Sacred Theology
MSW, M.S.W. Master of Social Work
MT Montana
Mt. Mount
MTO Mediterranean Theatre of Operation
MTV Music Television
mus. museum, musical
MusB, Mus.B. Bachelor of Music
MusD, Mus.D. Doctor of Music
MusM, Mus.M. Master of Music
mut. mutual
MVP Most Valuable Player
mycol. mycological

N

N. North
NAACOG Nurses Association of the American College of Obstetricians and Gynecologists
NAACP National Association for the Advancement of Colored People
NACA National Advisory Committee for Aeronautics
NACDL National Association of Criminal Defense Lawyers
NACU National Association of Colleges and Universities
NAD National Academy of Design
NAE National Academy of Engineering, National Association of Educators
NAESP National Association of Elementary School Principals
NAFE National Association of Female Executives
N.Am. North America
NAM National Association of Manufacturers
NAMH National Association for Mental Health
NAPA National Association of Performing Artists

NARAS National Academy of Recording Arts and Sciences
NAREB National Association of Real Estate Boards
NARS National Archives and Record Service
NAS National Academy of Sciences
NASA National Aeronautics and Space Administration
NASP National Association of School Psychologists
NASW National Association of Social Workers
nat. national
NATAS National Academy of Television Arts and Sciences
NATO North Atlantic Treaty Organization
NATOUSA North African Theatre of Operations, United States Army
nav. navigation
NB, N.B. New Brunswick
NBA National Basketball Association
NBC National Broadcasting Company
NC, N.C. North Carolina
NCAA National College Athletic Association
NCCJ National Conference of Christians and Jews
ND, N.D. North Dakota
NDEA National Defense Education Act
NE Nebraska
NE, N.E. Northeast
NEA National Education Association
Nebr. Nebraska
NEH National Endowment for Humanities
neurol. neurological
Nev. Nevada
NF Newfoundland
NFL National Football League
Nfld. Newfoundland
NG National Guard
NH, N.H. New Hampshire
NHL National Hockey League
NIH National Institutes of Health
NIMH National Institute of Mental Health
NJ, N.J. New Jersey
NLRB National Labor Relations Board
NM New Mexico
N.Mex. New Mexico
No. Northern
NOAA National Oceanographic and Atmospheric Administration
NORAD North America Air Defense
Nov. November
NOW National Organization for Women
N.P.Ry. Northern Pacific Railway
nr. near
NRA National Rifle Association
NRC National Research Council
NS, N.S. Nova Scotia
NSC National Security Council
NSF National Science Foundation
NSTA National Science Teachers Association
NSW New South Wales
N.T. New Testament
NT Northwest Territories
nuc. nuclear
numis. numismatic
NV Nevada

NW, N.W. Northwest
N.W.T. Northwest Territories
NY, N.Y. New York
N.Y.C. New York City
NYU New York University
N.Z. New Zealand

O

OAS Organization of American States
ob-gyn obstetrics-gynecology
obs. observatory
obstet. obstetrical
occupl. occupational
oceanog. oceanographic
Oct. October
OD, O.D. Doctor of Optometry
OECD Organization for Economic Cooperation and Development
OEEC Organization of European Economic Cooperation
OEO Office of Economic Opportunity
ofcl. official
OH Ohio
OK Oklahoma
Okla. Oklahoma
ON Ontario
Ont. Ontario
oper. operating
ophthal. ophthalmological
ops. operations
OR Oregon
orch. orchestra
Oreg. Oregon
orgn. organization
orgnl. organizational
ornithol. ornithological
orthop. orthopedic
OSHA Occupational Safety and Health Administration
OSRD Office of Scientific Research and Development
OSS Office of Strategic Services
osteo. osteopathic
otol. otological
otolaryn. otolaryngological

P

PA, Pa. Pennsylvania
P.A. Professional Association
paleontol. paleontological
path. pathological
PBS Public Broadcasting System
P.C. Professional Corporation
PE Prince Edward Island
pediat. pediatrics
P.E.I. Prince Edward Island
PEN Poets, Playwrights, Editors, Essayists and Novelists (international association)
penol. penological
P.E.O. women's organization (full name not disclosed)
pers. personnel
pfc. private first class
PGA Professional Golfers' Association of America
PHA Public Housing Administration
pharm. pharmaceutical

PharmD, Pharm.D. Doctor of Pharmacy
PharmM, Pharm.M. Master of Pharmacy
PhB, Ph.B. Bachelor of Philosophy
PhD, Ph.D. Doctor of Philosophy
PhDChemE Doctor of Science in Chemical Engineering
PhM, Ph.M. Master of Philosophy
Phila. Philadelphia
philharm. philharmonic
philol. philological
philos. philosophical
photog. photographic
phys. physical
physiol. physiological
Pitts. Pittsburgh
Pk. Park
Pky. Parkway
Pl. Place
P.&L.E.R.R. Pittsburg & Lake Erie Railroad
Plz. Plaza
PNP Pediatric Nurse Practitioner
P.O. Post Office
PO Box Post Office Box
polit. political
poly. polytechnic, polytechnical
PQ Province of Quebec
PR, P.R. Puerto Rico
prep. preparatory
pres. president
Presbyn. Presbyterian
presdl. presidential
prin. principal
procs. proceedings
prod. produced (play production)
prodn. production
prodr. producer
prof. professor
profl. professional
prog. progressive
propr. proprietor
pros. atty. prosecuting attorney
pro tem. pro tempore
PSRO Professional Services Review Organization
psychiat. psychiatric
psychol. psychological
PTA Parent-Teachers Association
ptnr. partner
PTO Pacific Theatre of Operations, Parent Teacher Organization
pub. publisher, publishing, published
pub. public
publ. publication
pvt. private

Q

quar. quarterly
qm. quartermaster
Q.M.C. Quartermaster Corps
Que. Quebec

R

radiol. radiological
RAF Royal Air Force
RCA Radio Corporation of America
RCAF Royal Canadian Air Force
RD Rural Delivery
Rd. Road
R&D Research & Development
REA Rural Electrification Administration
rec. recording
ref. reformed
regt. regiment
regtl. regimental
rehab. rehabilitation
rels. relations
Rep. Republican
rep. representative
Res. Reserve
ret. retired
Rev. Reverend
rev. review, revised
RFC Reconstruction Finance Corporation
RFD Rural Free Delivery
rhinol. rhinological
RI, R.I. Rhode Island
RISD Rhode Island School of Design
Rlwy. Railway
Rm. Room
RN, R.N. Registered Nurse
roentgenol. roentgenological
ROTC Reserve Officers Training Corps
RR Rural Route
R.R. Railroad
rsch. research
rschr. researcher
Rt. Route

S

S. South
s. son
SAC Strategic Air Command
SAG Screen Actors Guild
SALT Strategic Arms Limitation Talks
S.Am. South America
san. sanitary
SAR Sons of the American Revolution
Sask. Saskatchewan
savs. savings
SB, S.B. Bachelor of Science
SBA Small Business Administration
SC, S.C. South Carolina
SCAP Supreme Command Allies Pacific
ScB, Sc.B. Bachelor of Science
SCD, S.C.D. Doctor of Commercial Science
ScD, Sc.D. Doctor of Science
sch. school
sci. science, scientific
SCLC Southern Christian Leadership Conference
SCV Sons of Confederate Veterans
SD, S.D. South Dakota
SE, S.E. Southeast
SEATO Southeast Asia Treaty Organization
SEC Securities and Exchange Commission
sec. secretary
sect. section
seismol. seismological
sem. seminary
Sept. September
s.g. senior grade
sgt. sergeant
SHAEF Supreme Headquarters Allied Expeditionary Forces
SHAPE Supreme Headquarters Allied Powers in Europe
S.I. Staten Island
S.J. Society of Jesus (Jesuit)
SJD Scientiae Juridicae Doctor
SK Saskatchewan
SM, S.M. Master of Science
SNP Society of Nursing Professionals
So. Southern
soc. society
sociol. sociological
S.P.Co. Southern Pacific Company
spkr. speaker
spl. special
splty. specialty
Sq. Square
S.R. Sons of the Revolution
sr. senior
S S Steamship
SSS Selective Service System
St. Saint, Street
sta. station
stats. statistics
statis. statistical
STB, S.T.B. Bachelor of Sacred Theology
stblzn. stabilization
STD, S.T.D. Doctor of Sacred Theology
std. standard
Ste. Suite
subs. subsidiary
SUNY State University of New York
supr. supervisor
supt. superintendent
surg. surgical
svc. service
SW, S.W. Southwest
sys. system

T

TAPPI Technical Association of the Pulp and Paper Industry
tb. tuberculosis
tchg. teaching
tchr. teacher
tech. technical, technology
technol. technological
tel. telephone
Tel. & Tel. Telephone & Telegraph
telecom. telecommunications
temp. temporary
Tenn. Tennessee
Ter. Territory
Ter. Terrace
TESOL Teachers of English to Speakers of Other Languages
Tex. Texas
ThD, Th.D. Doctor of Theology
theol. theological
ThM, Th.M. Master of Theology
TN Tennessee
tng. training
topog. topographical
trans. transaction, transferred
transl. translation, translated
transp. transportation
treas. treasurer
TT Trust Territory
TV television

TVA Tennessee Valley Authority
TWA Trans World Airlines
twp. township
TX Texas
typog. typographical

U

U. University
UAW United Auto Workers
UCLA University of California at Los Angeles
UDC United Daughters of the Confederacy
U.K. United Kingdom
UN United Nations
UNESCO United Nations Educational, Scientific and Cultural Organization
UNICEF United Nations International Children's Emergency Fund
univ. university
UNRRA United Nations Relief and Rehabilitation Administration
UPI United Press International
U.P.R.R. United Pacific Railroad
urol. urological
U.S. United States
U.S.A. United States of America
USAAF United States Army Air Force
USAF United States Air Force
USAFR United States Air Force Reserve
USAR United States Army Reserve
USCG United States Coast Guard
USCGR United States Coast Guard Reserve
USES United States Employment Service
USIA United States Information Agency
USMC United States Marine Corps
USMCR United States Marine Corps Reserve
USN United States Navy
USNG United States National Guard
USNR United States Naval Reserve
USO United Service Organizations
USPHS United States Public Health Service
USS United States Ship
USSR Union of the Soviet Socialist Republics
USTA United States Tennis Association
USV United States Volunteers
UT Utah

V

VA Veterans Administration
VA, Va. Virginia
vet. veteran, veterinary
VFW Veterans of Foreign Wars
VI, V.I. Virgin Islands
vice pres. vice president
vis. visiting
VISTA Volunteers in Service to America
VITA Volunteers in Technical Assistance
vocat. vocational
vol. volunteer, volume
v.p. vice president
vs. versus
VT, Vt. Vermont

W

W, W. West
WA Washington (state)
WAC Women's Army Corps
Wash. Washington (state)
WATS Wide Area Telecommunications Service
WAVES Women's Reserve, US Naval Reserve
WCTU Women's Christian Temperance Union
we. western
W. Ger. Germany, Federal Republic of
WHO World Health Organization
WI Wisconsin
W.I. West Indies
Wis. Wisconsin
WSB Wage Stabilization Board
WV West Virginia
W.Va. West Virginia
WWI World War I
WWII World War II
WY Wyoming
Wyo. Wyoming

X, Y

YK Yukon Territory
YMCA Young Men's Christian Association
YMHA Young Men's Hebrew Association
YM & YWHA Young Men's and Young Women's Hebrew Association
yr. year
YT, Y.T. Yukon Territory
YWCA Young Women's Christian Association

Z

zool. zoological

Alphabetical Practices

Names are arranged alphabetically according to the surnames and under identical surnames according to the first given name. If both surname and the first given name are identical, names are arranged alphabetically according to the second given name.

Surnames beginning with De, Des, Du (however capitalized or spaced) are recorded with the prefix preceding the surname and arranged alphabetically under the letter D.

Surnames beginning with Mac and Mc are arranged alphabetically under M.

Surnames beginning with Saint or St. appear after names that begin Sains, and are arranged according to the second part of the name, e.g., St. Clair before Saint Dennis.

Surnames beginning with Van, Von, or von are arranged alphabetically under the letter V.

Compound surnames are arranged according to the first member of the compound.

Many hyphenated Arabic names begin Al-, El-, or al-. These names are alphabetized according to each Biographee's designation of last name. Thus Al-Bahar, Neta may be listed either under Al- or under Bahar, depending on the preference of the listee.

Also, Arabic names have a variety of possible spellings when transposed to English. Spelling of these names is always based on the practice of the Biographee. Some Biographees use a Western form of word order, while others prefer the Arabic word sequence.

Similarly, Asian names may have no comma between family and given names, but some Biographees have chosen to add the comma. In each case, punctuation follows the preference of the Biographee.

Parentheses used in connection with a name indicate which part of the full name is usually deleted in common usage. Hence Chambers, E(lizabeth) Anne indicates that the usual form of the given name is E. Anne. In such a case, the parentheses are ignored in alphabetizing and the name would be arranged as Chambers, Elizabeth Anne. However, if the name is recorded Chambers, (Elizabeth) Anne, signifying that the entire name Elizabeth is not commonly used, the alphabetizing would be arranged as though the name were Chambers, Anne. If an entire middle or last name is enclosed in parentheses, that portion of the name is used in the alphabetical arrangement. Hence Chambers, Elizabeth (Anne) would be arranged as Chambers, Elizabeth Anne.

Where more than one spelling, word order, or name of an individual is frequently encountered, the sketch has been entered under the form preferred by the Biographee, with cross-references under alternate forms.

Who'sWho in American Education®

Biographies

AANSTOOS, CHRISTOPHER MICHAEL, psychology educator; b. Saipan Island, U.S. Trust, Apr. 4, 1952; s. Anthony Matthew and Frances Henrietta (Jambrick) A.; children: Megan, Elizabeth, Lucas Matthew. BA, Mich. State U., 1974; MA, Duquesne U., 1976, PhD, 1982. Instr. Pa. State U., McKeesport, 1979—82; asst. prof. psychology State U. West Ga., Carrollton, 1982-87, assoc. prof., 1987-92, prof., 1992—, chmn., 1995-96. Contracted rschr. Pitts. Sch. Dist., 1979, Opaion, 2001; manuscript reviewer Harcourt, Brace, Jovanovich, NYC, 1983, New Ideas in Psychology, 1984—85, Saybrook Inst., 1986, Metaphor and Symbolic Activity, 1985—88, Sage, 1989, Guilford, 1990; nat. adv. panel Existential-Humanistic Inst.; adv. coun. Ctr. Study Psychology Psychiatry; program chmn. Symposium for Qualitative Rsch., Perugia, Italy, 1987, Perugia, 99; lectr. in field. Editor: Exploring the Lived World, 1984, The World of the Infant, 1987, The Humanistic Psychologist, 1985—2002, Human Growth and Development, 1990, Studies in Humanistic Psychology, 1991; editor: (assoc.) Jour. Theoretical Philos. Psychology, 1986—89; editor: (cons.) Jour. Phenomenological Psychology, 1982—, Jour. Humanistic Psychology, 1989, Jour. Psychology of Religion, 1991—94, Psychotherapy Patient, 1996—, Ethical Human Scis. and Svcs., 1999—; contbr. articles to profl. pubs. Vol. West Ga. Coll. Spkrs. Bur., 1983—; coord. fund drive Am. Heart Assn., State U. West Ga., 1985. Faculty Rsch. grantee State U. West Ga., 1983-85, 89-90, 92-93. Fellow APA (exec. bd. divs. 24, 32, program chmn. divsn. 24 1991, pres. divsn. 32 1997-98); mem. AAUP, Human Sci. Rsch. Assn. (program chmn. 1984), Southeastern Psychol. Assn., Assn. Qualitative Rsch. Psychology (chmn. program com. 1987-97), Chess Fedn. West Ga., Phi Beta Kappa. Home: 2175 Hog Liver Rd Carrollton GA 30117-9308 Office: State U West Ga Psychology Dept Carrollton GA 30118-0001

AARONSON, DAVID ERNEST, law educator, lawyer; b. Washington, Sept. 19, 1940; s. Edward Allan and May (Rosett) A.; m. Laura Dine, 1991; stepchildren: Dara Prushansky, Jared Prushansky. BA in Econs, George Washington U., 1961, MA, 1964, PhD, 1970; LL.B., Harvard U., 1964; LL.M. (E. Barrett Prettyman fellow), Georgetown U., 1965. Bar: D.C. bar 1965, Md. bar 1975, U.S. Supreme Ct. bar 1969. Research asst. Office of Commr., Bur. Labor Stats., U.S. Dept. Labor, Washington, 1961; staff atty. legal intern program Georgetown Grad. Law Ctr., Washington, 1964-65; rsch. assoc. patent rsch. project dept. econ. George Washington U., Washington, 1966; assoc. firm Aaronson and Aaronson, Washington, 1965-67, ptnr., 1967-70; prof., B.J. Tennery Scholar Am. U. Law Sch., Washington, 1970—; prof. Sch. Justice, Coll. Pub. and Internat. Affairs, 1981-92; dep. dir. Law and Policy Inst., Jerusalem, summer, 1978. Interim dir. clin. programs Md. Criminal Justice Clinic, 1971-73, founder prosecutor criminal litigation clinic, 1972, co-dir. trial practice litigation program, 1982—; vis. prof. Law Sch. of Hebrew U., Jerusalem, summer, 1978; trustee Montgomery-Prince George's Continuing Legal Edn. Inst., 1983—. Author: Maryland Criminal Jury Instructions and Commentary, 1975, (with N.N. Kittrie and D. Saari) Alternatives to Conventional Criminal Adjudication: Guidebook for Planners and Practitioners, 1977, (with B. Hoff, P. Jaszi, N.N. Kittrie and D. Saari) The New Justice: Alternatives to Conventional Criminal Adjudication, 1977, (with C.T. Dienes and M.C. Musheno) Decriminalization of Public Drunkenness: Tracing the Implementation of a Public Policy, 1981, Public Policy and Police Discretion: Processes of Decriminalization, 1984, (with R. Simon) The Insanity Defense: A Critical Assessment of Law and Policy in the Post-Hinckley Era, 1988, Maryland Criminal Jury Instructions and Commentary, 2d rev. edit., 1988; contbr. articles to legal and public policy jours. Mem. council Friendship Heights Village Council, 1979. Recipient Outstanding Community Service award, 1980; Outstanding Tchr. award Am. U. Law Sch., 1978, 81, Scholar/Tchr. of the Year award Am. U., 1989; Pauline Ruyle Moore scholar in Pub. Law, 1983 Mem. ABA (mem. criminal justice sect. rules of cr. prof. and evid. com. 1991—), D.C. Bar Assn. (chmn. criminal code rev. com. 1971-73), Md. State Bar Assn. (criminal law sect. coun. 1984—, chairperson 1989-90, Robert C. Heeney award 1999), Assn. Am. Law Schs. (elected to sect. coun., criminal justice sect. 1999—), Montgomery County (Md.) Bar Assn., Am. Law Inst., Phi Beta Kappa. Office: Am U Law Sch 4801 Massachusetts Ave NW Washington DC 20016-8196 E-mail: daarons@wcl.american.edu.

AARONSON, SHELDON, microbiology educator; b. N.Y.C., Oct. 9, 1922; s. Samuel and Dora Aaronson; m. Shirley Zepnick, Nov. 28, 1948; children: Naomi, Susan, Joshua, Beth. BS, CCNY, 1944; MA, U. Pa., 1948; PhD, NYU, 1953. Teaching fellow biology dept. CCNY, N.Y.C., 1943-44; rsch. assoc. Haskins Labs., N.Y.C., 1949-67; guest rsch. collaborator Brookhaven Nat. Lab., Upton, N.Y., 1957-58; vis. scientist Weizmann Inst., Rehovot, Israel, 1975; vis. prof. biol. dept. Ben Gurion U., Beersheba, Israel, 1975; lectr. UNEO/UNESCO/ICRO, Nairobi, Kenya, 1976; prof. Queens Coll., CUNY, Flushing, 1953—; prof. grad. sch. CUNY, N.Y.C., 1963—; prof. emeritus Queens Coll., CUNY, N.Y.C., 1995. Guest collaborator scientist U. Calif., Berkeley, 1963; cons. U. Calif., Laurence Livermore, 1967; Fulbright sr. med. lectr. Hacettepe U. Med. Sch., Ankara, Turkey, 1986-87. Author: Experimental Microbial Ecology, 1970, Molecular Communication in Microorganisms, 1982. Coord. Dem. Party, 3d Congl. Dist., 1972; mem. acad. affairs com. ACLU, N.Y.C., 1990-91; chmn. bd. Friends of Queens Coll. Library, Queens County, N.Y. Sgt. U.S. Army, 1944-46, PTO. Atomic Energy Commn. predoctoral fellow NYU, 1949-50, Sci. Faculty fellow NSF, 1959-60, Mellon fellow Queens Coll., 1982-84, fellow Am. Acad. Microbiology, 1991. Fellow AAAS; mem. Am. Soc. for Microbiology (Pres.'s fellowship 1957, fellow, 1991), Phycological Soc. Am., Soc. for Gen. Microbiology (Gt. Britain), Soc. Protozoologists, (emeritus 1998), Soc. of Ethnobotonists, (fellow 2000). Office: Queens Coll CUNY Biology Dept 6530 Kissena Blvd Flushing NY 11367-1575

AARSLEFF, HANS, linguistics educator; b. Rungsted Kyst, Denmark, July 19, 1925; came to U.S., 1948, naturalized, 1964; s. Einar Faber and Inger (Lotz) A. BA, U. Copenhagen, 1945; PhD, U. Minn., 1960. Instr. English U. Minn., 1952-56; instr. Princeton U., 1956-60, asst. prof., 1960-65, assoc. prof., 1965-72, prof., 1972-97. Author: The Study of Language in England 1780-1860, 1967, From Locke to Saussure: Essays on the Study of Language and Intellectual History, 1982, Introduction to Wilhelm von Humboldt, On Language, 1988; editor, translator: Condillac, Essay on the Origin of Human Knowledge, 2001; ; assoc. editor: The Historiography of Linguistics, bd. editors: Jour. History Ideas, 1979—; contbr. articles to jours. and books. Jr. fellow Council of Humanities Princeton U., fall 1962; fellow Am. Council Learned Socs., 1964-65, 72-73, NEH, 1975-76 Fellow Am. Acad. Arts and Scis.; mem. Am. Philos. Soc., Royal Danish Acad. Scis. and Letters (fgn.). Office: Princeton U Dept English Princeton NJ 08544-0001

AASEN-HULL, AUDREY AVIS, music educator; b. Coquille, Oreg., July 9, 1916; d. John Lawrence and Orra Amy (Kelley) Aasen; m. James Byrne Hull, Sept. 15, 1962. BA, U. Oreg., 1939; MA, Stanford U., 1946. Music tchr. Monroe (Oreg.) H.S., 1939-40, Estacada (Oreg.) Union Sch., 1940-41; performer of solo violin program Sta. KOOS, Coos Bay, Oreg., 1941-43; supr. instrumental music San Francisco Pub. Schs., 1944-45; tchr. violin and piano Menlo Sch. & Coll., Menlo Park, Calif., 1947-48, Sacred Heart Convent Sch., Menlo Park, Calif., 1948-49. Performances of string quartets, trios, quintets and sextets for San Francisco Musical Club and Palo Alto Fortnightly Music Club, 1947-89; performed with People's Symphony, San Francisco, 1945, Calif. Mfrs. Assn., San Francisco, 1950, Palo Alto String quartet, 1958, String Orch. Televised Concert, Innsbruck, Austria, 1982, Queen Elizabeth Hall, Belgium, Internat. String Tchrs. Workshop, Brussels, 1984, and numerous others; soloist at Soroptimist Internat. Conv. for Am. Fedn. Soroptimist Clubs, Can., 1954; concertmistress Penisula Symphony, 1958-59; most recent performances include recital Menlo Park, Calif., 1997, performances at Fortnightly Music Club, 1997, 98, U. Oreg., 1997. Adv. bd. mem. Calif. Summer Music at Pebble Beach, initiating mem., 1996—; patron San Francisco Symphony, underwriter violin chair position, 1989—. Recipient citation for Disting. Svc. USO, 1943-44, 45-46. Mem. Am. Fed. Musicians (life), Am. String Tchrs. Assn., Soroptimist Club (life), Fortnightly Music Club. Avocations: gardening, studying french, dancing, cooking.

AASLESTAD, HALVOR GUNERIUS, college dean, retired; b. Birmingham, Ala., Sept. 6, 1937; s. Knut and Geraldine (Dobson) Aaslestad; m. Barbara Wohn, July 30, 1960 (dec.); children: Katherine, Karen, Peter, Lauren; m. Peggy Smethie, Dec. 14, 2002. BS, La. State U., 1960, PhD, 1965; MS, Pa. State U., 1961. Asst. prof. U. Ga., Athens, 1968-70; rsch. scientist Wistair Inst., Phila., 1970-73; sr. scientist Frederick (Md.) Cancer Rsch. Ctr., 1973-76; exec. sec. NIH, Bethesda, Md., 1976-81, rev. chief, 1981-85; dir. rsch. grants Sch. Medicine Yale U., New Haven, 1985-95, asst. dean Sch. Medicine, 1987-89, assoc. dean, retired, 1989-96; sr. mem. Rsch. and Review Svcs., Staunton, Va., 1996-98; sr. assoc. United Info. Sys., Inc., Bethesda, Md., 1998-2001; sci. rev. mgr. Analytical Scis., Inc., Bethesda, Md., 2001—02, sr. sci., 2002—03; sr. rsch. sci. Constella Health Scis., Frederick, Md., 2003—. Cons. NIH, Bethesda, 1985—. NIH rsch. grantee and fellow, 1965—.

ABAD, ROSARIO DALIDA, elementary education educator; b. Ilocos Norte, The Philippines, Apr. 23, 1936; came to U.S., 1966; d. Primitivo Agoo and Adelaida (Cacal) Dalida; m. Domingo Abad, June 8, 1969; children: Eric, Jon, Jenny; 1 adopted child, Daniel Dalida. Grad., Philippine Normal Coll., 1954; BA in Edn., Far Eastern U., Manila, 1961; MA in Edn., Far Eastern U., 1966; grad., Our Lady of Holy Cross Coll., 1972. Educator Rizal Pub. Schs., Philippines, 1955-58, Manila Pub. Schs., 1958-66; instr. Mindoro Coll., Philippines, 1964-66; tchr. Sudbury (Ont., Can.) Schs., 1966-67, St. Bernard (La.) Schs., 1967-68, Jefferson Parish (La.) Schs., 1968-73, New Orleans Sch. Bd., 1973—. Contbr. articles to profl. jours.; free-lance writer. V.p. Kapit-Bahay Assn., 1984—, Philippine-Am. Sports Assn. New Orleans, 1987-93, pres., 1993—. Recipient Recognition award Kapit-Bahay Assn., 1984. Mem. ASCD, Internat. Reading Assn., La. Reading Assn., Our Lady of Holy Cross Alumni Assn., Our Lady of Holy Cross Alumni Assn., Our Lady of Holy Cross Friends of Libr., Philippine-Am. Women's Assn. La. (v.p. 1985-87, pres. 1989-91, 91-93, Recognition award 1986), Behrman Heights Neighborhood and Civic Club. Democrat. Roman Catholic. Home: 2612 Mercedes Blvd New Orleans LA 70114-6834

ABATA, DUANE, dean; BSME, MSME, PhD in Mech. Engring., U. Wis. Registered profl. engr., Wis.; lic. FAA instrument-rated pvt. pilot. Various positions including exec. assoc. dean Coll. Engring., assoc. dean for rsch., dept. head mining engring., interim dean Coll. Engring. Mich. Technol. U., prof. dept. mech. engring.; program dir. engring. edn. and ctrs. divsn. NSF; dean Coll. Engring. and Tech. No. Ariz. U., Flagstaff, 2003—. Evaluator Am. Bd. Engring.Tech. Recipient svc. award, Am. Soc. Automotive Engrs. Mem.: Am. Soc. for Engring. Edn. (pres. 2003—04). Office: No Ariz U Coll Engring and Tech S San Francisco St Flagstaff AZ 86011*

ABBOTT, BARBARA LOUISE, artist, educator; b. San Francisco, Calif., Oct. 16, 1941; d. C. Paige and Mary Ellen Abbott; m. Edward Michael Seman, Nov. 21, 1964 (div. June 1980); children: Jill, Janet, Michael Paige. BFA, U. Utah, 1982; MFA, Ariz. State U., 1986. Prof. art Edinboro U. Pa., Edinboro, Pa., 1989—90, La. State U., Shreveport, La., 1990—96; prin., owner Abbott Art Studio, San Jose, Calif., 1996—. Prin. works include Quilt Kiosks, Shreveport, La., 1993, Great Blue Herons, Santa Cruz, Calif., 2000, Perro Feliz, San Jose, Calif., 2002, exhibitions include Award Winning Prints, Phila. Print Club, Phila., 1986, Marking Time: Making Space, South of Mkt. Cultural Ctr., San Francisco, 2001, book, Twice Descending, 1991. Fellow Fulbright-Hays fellowship, U.S. Govt., 1993. Home and Studio: 778 Crestview Drive San Jose CA 95117

ABBOTT, H(ORACE) PORTER, English language educator; b. Balt., Nov. 21, 1940; s. Horace P. and Barbara Ann (Trueblood) A.; m. Anita Vaivods, June 25, 1966; children: Jason, Byram. BA, Reed Coll., Portland, Oreg., 1962; MA, U. Toronto, Ont., Can., 1964, PhD, 1968. From asst. prof. to assoc. prof. U. Calif., Santa Barbara, 1966-82, prof., 1982—, chair of English, 1983-87, 90, acting dean humanities and fine arts, 1992-94. Lectr., instr. Yeats Summer Sch., Sligo, Ireland, 1989. Author: The Fiction of Samuel Beckett, 1973, Diary Fiction, 1984, Beckett Writing Beckett, 1996, The Cambridge Introduction to Narrative, 2002; (poetry) Cold Certainties and Changes Beyond Measure, 1988; editor On the Origin of Fictions, 2001. Pres. Foothill Preservation League, Santa Barbara, 1996—. Recipient William Stafford award Poetry Assn. Wash., 1977. Mem. MLA, Samuel Beckett Soc. (pres. 1962-64). Office: U of Calif Dept English Santa Barbara CA 93106

ABBOTT, REGINA A. neurodiagnostic technologist, consultant, business owner; b. Haverhill, Mass., Mar. 5, 1950; d. Frank A. and Ann (Drelick) A. Student, Pierce Bus. Sch., Boston, 1967-70, Seizure Unit Children's Hosp. Med. Ctr. Sch. EEG Tech., 1970-71. Registered electroneurodiagnostic technologist Advanced Fuller Sch. Massage Therapy, 2001, nat. cert. massage therapist Nat. Cert. Bd. Therapeutic Massage and Bodywork. Tech. dir. electrodiagnostic labs. Salem Hosp., 1972-76; lab. dir. clin. neurophysiology Tufts U. New Eng. Med. Ctr., Boston, 1976-78; clin. instr. EEG program Laboure Coll., Boston, 1977-81; adminstrv. dir. dept. Neurology Mt. Auburn Hosp., Cambridge, Mass., 1978-81; tech. dir. clin. neurophysiology Drs. Diagnostic Service, Virginia Beach, Va.; tech. dir. neurodiagnostic ctr. Portsmouth Psychiatric Ctr., 1981-87; founder, pres., owner Commonwealth Neurodiagnostic Services, Inc., 1986—, Hands on Health-Care, 2001—. Co-dir. continuing edn. program EEG Tech., Boston, 1977-78; mem. adv. com. sch. neurodiagnostic tech. Laboure Coll., 1977-81, Sch. EEG Tech. Children's Hosp. Med. Ctr., Boston, 1980-81; assoc. examiner Am. Bd. Registration of Electroencephalographic Technologists, 1977-83; mem. guest faculty Oxford Medilog Co., 1986; cons. Nihon Kohden Am., 1981-83; cons., educator Teca Corp., Pleasantville, N.Y., 1981-87; allied health profl. staff mem. Virginia Beach Gen. Hosp., Humana Hosp. Bayside, Virginia Beach; clin. evaluator Calif. Coll. for Health Scis., 1995—. Contbr. articles to profl. jours. EIL scholar, Poland/USSR, 1970; recipient Internat. Woman of Yr. award in bus. and sci. Internat. Biographical Ctr., London, 1993-94, Woman of Yr. award Am. Biographical Inst., 1993. Mem.: NAFE, New Eng. Soc. EEG Technologists (bd. dirs., sec., tng. and edn. com., faculty tng. and edn.), Am. Massage Therapy Assn., Epilepsy Soc. Mass. Avocations: running, art collecting, photography, reading, investing.

ABBOTT, ROBERT DEAN, education scientist; b. Twin Falls, Idaho, Dec. 19, 1946; s. Charles Dean and Billie June (Moore) A.; m. Sylvia Patricia Keim, Dec. 16, 1967; children: Danielle, Matthew. BA, Calif. Western U., San Diego, 1967; MS, U. Wash., 1968, PhD, 1970. Asst. prof., assoc. prof. Calif. State U.-Fullerton, 1970-75; asst. prof., prof. ednl. psychology U. Wash., Seattle, 1975—; dir. Ctr. Inst. Devel. and Research, Seattle, 1983-92. Author: Elementary Multivariate Statistics, 1983; contbr. articles to profl. jours. Calif. State scholar, 1964-67 Fellow Am. Psychol. Assn.; mem. Am. Ednl. Research Assn., Am. Stats. Assn., Psychometric Soc. Methodist. Office: Ednl Psych 312 Miller PO Box 353600 Seattle WA 98195-3600

ABBOTT, SUSAN ALICIA, elementary education educator; b. Easton, Pa., July 8, 1947; d. Solomon and Edith Mae (Cooper) Bergstein; m. William Walter Wood, Aug. 28, 1971 (div. Mar. 1976); m. Karl Richard Abbott, Feb. 19, 1977 (div. July, 1996); 1 child, Tracie Ellen. BA in Psychology, Pa. State U., 1969; MS in Edn., Nazareth Coll. of Rochester, N.Y., 1976. Cert. nursery/elem. and spl. edn. tchr., N.Y. Tchr. Penn Yan (N.Y.) Cen. Schs., 1970; learning disabilities tchr. Wayne-Finger Lakes Bd. Coop. Schs., Stanley, N.Y., 1970-79; spl. edn. tchr. Victor (N.Y.) Cen. Schs., 1979—. Tchr. rep. com. on handicapped Com. Spl. Edn., Victor, 1987-91, coord. grades 4-6, 1991-94, chmn. grades 5-6, 1991-93. Bd. dirs. Genesee Valley Orch. and Chorus, 1994-96, Sta. WXXI, pub. TV, Rochester, 1978—; leader Girl Scouts Am., Fairport, N.Y., 1987-90; chmn. publicity program Seneca Zool. Soc., Rochester, 1974-77, bd. dirs., 1975-78, mem. 1982—; supt. ch. sch., asst. supt. Sunday sch. Ref. Ch. Women, 1990-94; mem. Trinity Reformed Ch., 1990—. Mem. ASCD, Coun. for Exceptional Children (divsn. learning disabilities), Am. Fedn. Tchrs., Nature Conservancy, Whale Adoption Project, Internat. Assn. Children and Adults with Learning Disabilities, N.Y. State Assn. Learning Disabilities, N.Y. State United Tchrs., Monroe County Learning Disabilities Assn., Greenpeace, Rochester Mus. Sci. Ctr., Pa. State U. Alumni Assn., Habitat for Humanity, Fairport PTSA, Nat. Coun. Tchrs. Math., Victor Tchrs. Assn., Psi Chi. Avocations: crafts, piano, reading, choir. Home: 58 Alina St Fairport NY 14450-2843 Office: Victor Cen Schs 953 High St Victor NY 14564-1168

ABBOUD, FRANCOIS MITRY, physician, educator; b. Cairo, Jan. 5, 1931; arrived in U.S., 1955, naturalized, 1963; s. Mitry Y. and Asma (Habac) Abboud; m. Doris Evelyn Khal, June 5, 1955; children: Mary Agnese, Susan Marie, Nancy Louise, Anthony Lawrence. Student, U. Cairo, 1948—52; MBBCh, Ein Chams U., 1955; D (hon.), U. Lyon, France, 1991; DSc (hon.), Med. Coll. Wis., 1994. Diplomate Am. Bd. Internal Medicine, Am. Bd. Cardiovasc. Disease (bd. govs. 1987-93). Intern Demerdash Govt. Hosp., Cairo, 1955; resident Milw. County Hosp., 1955—58; Am. Heart Assn. rsch. fellow cardiovasc. labs. Marquette U., 1958—60; Am. Heart Assn. advanced rsch. fellow U. Iowa, 1960—62, asst. prof., 1961—65, assoc. prof. medicine, 1965—68, prof. medicine, 1968—, prof. physiology and biophysics, 1975—, Edith King Pearson prof. cardiovascular rsch., 1988—, dir. cardiovasc. divsn., 1970—76, chmn. dept. internal medicine, 1976—2002, dir. cardiovasc. rsch. ctr., 1974—, assoc. v.p. for health affairs, 2002—. Attending physician U. Iowa Hosps., 1961—, VA Hosp., Iowa City, 1963—; chmn. rsch. rev. com. Nat. Heart, Lung and Blood Inst., 1978—80, adv. coun., 1995—99. Editor Circulation Rsch., 1981—86, Procs. Assn. Am. Physicians, 1995—, assoc. editor Advances in Internal Medicine, 1991—96, Physiology in Medicine, 2002—, editl. bd. Medicine, 1992—. Recipient European Traveling fellowship, French govt., 1948, NIH Career Devel. award, 1962—71. Master: ACP; mem.: AMA, Assn. Patient Oriented Rsch. (founding mem.), Am. Acad. Arts and Scis., Internat. Soc. Hypertension (Merck Sharp & Dohme Internat. award for rsch. in hypertension 1994), Am. Soc. Pharmacology and Exptl. Therapeutics (award exptl. therapeutics 1972), Am. Clin. and Climatol. Assn. (councillor 1992), Am. Physiol. Soc. (chmn. circulation group 1979—80, chmn. clin. physiology sect. 1979—83, publ. com. 1987—90, Wiggers award 1988), Assn. Am. Physicians (treas. 1979—84, councillor 1984—89, pres.-elect 1989—90, pres. 1990—91), Assn. Profs. Medicine (bd. dirs. 1993—97, Robert H. Williams Disting. Chmn. of Medicine award 1993), Assn. Univ. Cardiologists, Am. Fedn. Clin. Rsch. (pres. 1971—72), Am. Heart Assn. (bd. dirs. 1977—80, pres.-elect 1989—90, pres. 1990—91, past chmn. rsch. coms., award of merit 1982, Disting. Achievement award 1988, CIBA award for hypertension rsch. 1990, Gold Heart award 1995, Rsch. Achievement award 1999), Soc. Exptl. Biology and Medicine, Ctrl. Soc. for Clin. Rsch. (pres. elect 1984—85, pres. 1985—86), Am. Soc. Clin. Investigation, Inst. Medicine NAS, Alpha Omega Alpha (bd. dirs. 1989—), Sigma Xi. Achievements include research and publications in cardiovascular physiology on neurohumoral control of circulation and molecular mechanisms and gene regulation of baroreceptor activation. Home: 24 Kennedy Pky Iowa City IA 52246-2780 Office: Carver Coll Medicine Univ Iowa 318 CMAB VPHA Iowa City IA 52242-1101

ABDALJABBAR, ABDALHAMEED A. educational administrator; b. Falluja, Iraq, July 1, 1941; came to U.S., 1982; s. Abdullah A. Abdaljabbar and Baseirra (Saleh) Mustafah; m. Amal Abdalrazak, Feb. 1, 1971; children: Bushra, Nagam, Azaheer. BA, Almustansyriah U., Baghdad, Iraq, 1967; MA, Baghdad U., 1977; EdD, U. No. Colo., 1989. Tchr. Ramadi (Iraq) Sch. Dist., 1968-73, Baghdad-Risafa Sch. Dist., 1973-77; lectr. Mosel (Iraq) U., 1977-82; prin. Granada Sch., Santa Clara, Calif., 1991-93, 1993-94, dir. curriculum and staff devel., 1994-95. Postdoctoral fellow U. No. Colo., 1990-91. Avocations: swimming, volleyball, gymnastics, writing children's stories. Home: 1865 Cabrillo Ave Santa Clara CA 95050-3706

ABDELGHANI, ASSAF A. medical educator; b. Arrabeh, Jordan, Dec. 30, 1937;, U.S.1971; s. Assaf and Rukayya Arabi; m. Laila Abdelghani, Jan. 1, 1981; children: Ramsy, Samy. BS, Am. U., Beirut, Lebanon, 1967; MS, Tulane U., 1972, DS, 1978. Prof. Tulane U., New Orleans, 1975—, lab. dir., 1993—, chmn. dept. environ. health, 1999—. Office: Tulane U 1430 Tulane New Orleans LA 70112

ABDELSAYED, WAFEEK HAKIM, accounting educator; b. Fayoum, Egypt, Aug. 16, 1958; came to U.S., 1970; s. Fr. Gabriel H. and Tahani (Mikhael) A. BBA, Hofstra U., 1979; MBA, Adelphi U., 1983, MS, 1984; PhD, U. Conn., 1996. CPA Fla., N.Y.; cert. fraud examiner Assn. of Cert Fraud Examiners; cert. fin. mgr; cert. control assesment, cert. gov. auditing prof. Staff acct. KPMG Peat Marwick, L.I., N.Y., 1981-82, Deloitte & Touche, L.I., 1983-84; prof. acctg. dept. So. Conn. State U., New Haven, 1984—. Contbr. rsch. papers to profl. publs. (Competitive Paper award 1991, Becker's Outstanding Rsch. award 1991). Mem. bd. deacons Virgin Mary Coptic Orthodox Ch., treas. Recipient scholarship N.Y. State Soc. CPAs, 1983. Mem. AICPA, N.E. Bus. and Econs. Assn. (bd. dirs.), Am. Acctg. Assn., Inst. Mgmt. Accts. (cert. mgmt. acct., cert. fin. mgmt.), Inst. Internal Auditors (cert. internal auditor), Cert. Govt. Financial Mgr., Assn. of Govt. Accts, Conn. Soc. CPAs, Beta Gamma Sigma, Beta Alpha Psi. Egyptian/Christian Orthodox. Avocations: coin and stamp collecting, photography. Home: PO Box 170 North Haven CT 06473-0170 Office: So Conn State U Sch Bus 501 Crescent St New Haven CT 06515-1330

ABDOLALI, NASRIN, political scientist, educator, consultant; b. Tehran, Iran, June 28, 1957; came to U.S., 1983; d. Nematollah and Molouk Akram (Miraftab) A. BA in Polit. Sci., Tehran U., Iran, 1978; MA in Politics, NYU, 1986, PhD in Polit. Sci., 1990. Dir. devel. project. Simin Lang. Inst., Tehran, Iran, 1978-81; legal advisor Bur. D'Etude d'Avocat, Tehran, Iran, 1981-83; asst. prof. NYU, N.Y.C., 1989-92; analytical svcs. exec. Nielsen Mktg. Rsch., Wilton, Conn., 1992-93, analytical svcs. mgr. N.Y.C., 1993, analytical svcs. sr. mgr., 1994; asst. prof. C.W. Post Coll., Long Island U., 1994—; cons. Office for Internat. Students and Scholars NYU, 1995—. Recipient Grad. Studies award Pahlavi Found. Iran, 1978, Penfield Dissertation grant NYU, 1988, Best Paper award N.E. Polit. Sci. Assn., 1988, GFUSA Productivity award Kraft Gen. Foods, 1993. Mem. Am. Polit. Sci. Assn., Internat. Studies Assn., Asia Soc., Phi Eta Sigma (hon.). Avocations: tennis, swimming, horseback riding, books, plays. Home: 1 Washington Square Vlg Apt 11R New York NY 10012-1608 Office: Long Island U CW Post Coll Dept Polit Sci/Internat Studies Greenvale NY 11548

ABDULLAEV, YALCHIN, neuroscientist, physician, educator; b. Baku, Azerbaijan, Aug. 19, 1960; s. Gulhuseyn and Almas Abdullaev; m. Naida Velieva, Nov. 24, 1987 (div. June 2003); 1 child, Mikail. MS, Azerbaijan State U., Baku, 1982; PhD, Inst. Exptl. Medicine, St. Petersburg, Russia, 1987; MD, St. Petersburg Med. Acad., 1994. Rsch. asst. Inst. Physiology, Azerbaijan Acad. Scis., Baku, 1982-84; grad. stud. Inst. Exptl. Medicine, St. Petersburg, 1984-87, jr. rsch. scientist, 1987-89, sr. rsch. scientist, 1989-90, Brain Ctr., St. Petersburg, 1990-94; asst. prof. U. Oreg., Eugene, 1994-96; asst. prof. U. Louisville, 1996—. Mem. grad. faculty U. Louisville, 1996—; rsch. dir. Cognitive Neurosci. Lab., 1996—. Mem. editl. bd.: Internat. Jour. Psychophysiology, 1992—96; mem. editl. bd. The Scientific World, 2002—; contbr. more than 60 rsch. articles to profl. jours. Mem.: Internat. Orgn. Psychophysiology, Internat. Orgn. Human Brain Mapping, Soc. Neurosci., Am. Psychol. Soc. Avocations: swimming, running, reading. E-mail: yabdullaev@yahoo.com.

ABEL, ERNEST LAWRENCE, education educator; b. Toronto, Ont., Can., Feb. 10, 1943; s. Jack and Rose (Tarshes) A.; m. Barbara Ellen Buckley, Sept. 20, 1970; children: Jason Robert, Rebecca Rosanne. BA, U. Toronto, 1965, MA, 1967, PhD, 1971. Rsch. scientist Rsch. Inst. on Alcoholism, Buffalo, N.Y., 1971-83, acting dep. dir., 1983-84, rsch. scientist VI, 1984-85; prof. Wayne State U., Detroit, 1985—, dir. C.S. Mott Ctr. for human growth and devel., 1985—98, dir. reproductive toxicology, 1998—. Pres. Fetal Alcohol Study Group, 1985-86. Author: Marihuana, 1980, Alcohol Wordlore, 1987, Fetal Alcohol Syndrome, 1990, 2d edit., 1999, America's 25 Top Killers, 1991, Singing the New Nation, 2000, Jewish Genetic Disorders-A Layman's Guide, 2001, Arab Genetic Disorders-A Layman's Guide, 2003. Named Disting. Faculty fellow Bd. Govs., Wayne State U., 1989. Mem. Behavioral Teratology Soc. (pres. 1984-85). Office: CS Mott Ctr Human Growth 275 E Hancock St Detroit MI 48201-1415

ABEL, MARY ELIZABETH (BETTE), art educator, artist; b. Englishtown, N.J., Sept. 14, 1917; d. Charles Reid and Ethel Mae (Mount) English; m. Leon Arnold Abel, Dec. 27, 1952; 1 child, Craig Reid. BFA, Rollins Coll., 1939; student, Yale U., 1941-42, Monmouth Coll., 1964, 74-76, Rutgers U., 1970-72. Cert. tchr., N.J. Profl. artist, Little Silver, N.J., 1939—; asst. mgr. Lorstan Studios, Red Bank, N.J., 1943-49; instr. art AAUW, Monmouth, 1959—, Guild of Creative Art, Shrewsbury, N.J., 1970—. Art dir. Boro of Little Silver, 1970—; mem. adv. bd. Guild of Creative Art, 1975-80; cultural arts chmn. Little Silver PTA, 1961-69, chmn. Festival '67 and symphony concerts, 1967; bd. dirs. Monmouth Arts Gallery, Red Bank, 1960—; chair com. interviews and selection People to People Student Amb. Program Am. Soviet Youth Exch., 1991—. Artist working in oils, pastels, watercolors, ink, charcoal, and mixed media; sculptor; exhibited in group shows including Little Silver Boro Hall, New Sch. and Whitney Mus., N.Y.C.; one woman shows include Poets Inn, Matawan, N.J., Guild of Creative Arts, Shrewsbury, N.J., MidLantic Bank, Red Bank, N.J. Mem. com. Bicentennial Celebration, Little Silver, 1988; pres. Jersey Shore chpt. People to People, 1985—, homestay coord., 1964—, sec. bd. dirs. East Coast Coun., 1986-94; host Meet the Am. Program: People to People Internat.; hosting coll. students from Zimbabwe; hosting and coord. homestays and planning activities for 26 young people from Austria, 1993, Berlin, Germany, 1994, Kiev, Ukraine, Russia, China, Japan, 1995, Israel, 1996; hosting Argentine family, Belgian prof., Japanese coll. sr., 1996, Estonian and Japanese coll. students, 1997; coord. and activities dir. for 13 teenage children and 2 chaperons from Israel, 1998, Austrians, 1999, hosting and coordinating homestays, planning activities for 13 teenagers and one chaperone from Austria, 1999; homestay coord., planner activities 2 Japanese teenage girls, 2002, and 1 Japanese boy, 2003. With U.S. Army, 1949-55. Recipient Best in Show award Riverview Hosp., Red Bank, 1982, 85, 2d Pl. award, 1996; Second Pl. award Eaton Town Hist. Show, 1985; 1st prize State of Fla. Show, 1939, Exec. Ctr., Red Bank, 1996; Outstanding Vol. of Yr. award Monmouth Arts Gallery and Found., 1981, 1st prize gallery show, 1998, honorable mention, Monmouth Arts Gall. Show, Little Silver Borough Hall, 1st prize, 2000, 2001, 2d prize, 2002, appreciation cert. People to People Internat., 1993, Commendation award People to People Internat., 1993; Honorable Mention award Monmouth Arts Gallery. Mem. Art Alliance, Monmouth Arts Found. (bd. dirs.), AAUW (chmn. arts study group), Red Bank Hist. Soc., N.J. Symphony League, Monmouth Mus., Guild of Creative Arts (instr.). Presbyterian. Avocations: hosting foreign groups and individuals, reading, music, theater, bridge. Home: 107 Queens Dr Little Silver NJ 07739 Office: Guild Creative Art 620 Broad St Shrewsbury NJ 07702-4117

ABELL, DAWN GABBITAS, elementary school, high school educator, administrator; b. Detroit, Sept. 23, 1947; B of Art Edn., Ea. Mich. U., 1969; MEd in Sch. Adminstrn., Winthrop U., 1982. Tchr. 1st grade Learning Improvement Ctr. Melvindale (Mich.) Northern-Allen Park, 1969-79; interior designer, owner La Maison Magnifique, Dearborn, Mich., 1975-79; tchr. art, remedial reading and writing Clover (S.C.) Sch. Dist. 2, 1979-85; tchr. gifted Cherokee County Sch. Dist. I, Gaffney, S.C., 1985-87; dist. vocat. coord. for spl. populations Aiken (S.C.) County Pub. Schs., 1987-89; asst. dir. S.C. Coun. Vocat./Tech. Edn., Columbia, 1989-90; vocat. coord. Richland County Sch. Dist. 1, Columbia, 1990-92; curriculum supr. Beaufort-Jasper Career Edn. Ctr., Ridgeland, S.C., 1992-93; tech. prep. dir., tchr. art Gaston County Schs., Gastonia, N.C., 1993-96; asst. prin. Union County Schs., Monroe, N.C., 1996-97; elem. prin., spl. advisor vocat. edn. Wilson County Schs., Lebanon, Tenn., 1997-98; asst. prin. Midwood H.S. (alt. sch. and TAPS Teen Pregnancy Program), 1998-2000, Starmount Elem. Sch., Charlotte-Mecklenberg Sch. Sys., Charlotte, NC, 2000—01, Sedgefield Mid. Sch., 2001—02; tchr. Lake Wylie Elem. Sch., 2002—. Owner The Learner's Edge Inc., Gastonia, 1987-88; facilitator nat. career devel. teleconf./workshop, Dallas, N.C., 1994. Organizer/creator Focus: Special Populations 2000 Conf., 1990; contbr. articles to profl. jours. Mem. ASCD, Nat. Assn. Sec. Sch. Prins., Am. Vocat. Assn., S.C. Vocat. Dirs. Assn., N.C. Educators Assn., Internat. Tech. Edn. Prevention Network, Nat. Bus. Edn. Assn., Mktg. Edn. Assn., S.C. Network for Women in Adminstrn. Avocations: horseback riding, antiques, american history, painting, fishing. E-mail: dga901@aol.com.

ABELS, MICHAEL ALAN, university administrator; b. Newark, Dec. 16, 1957; BS, U. Alaska, Fairbanks, 1980. EMT; cert. tchr. Alaska. Field ops. mgr. Inst. Arctic Biology, Fairbanks, Alaska, 1976-90, program field ops. mgr., 1990—; sta. mgr. Toolik Field Sta., Toolik Lake, Alaska, 1990—98. Dir. ops. Wilderness Search & Rescue, Fairbanks, 1986—92; head instr. Sei Shin Kai Aikido (5th degree black belt 2003), Fairbanks, 1984—, Hakko Ryu Jujitsu (2d degree black belt 1996), IAI-TATE Do (2d degree black belt). Leader 4-H, Fairbanks, 1988—91; CPR instr. Am. Heart Assn., Fairbanks, 1991. Named Eagle Scout, 1976, Woodbadge Beads Boy Scouts Am., 1977, Outstanding Young Men of Am., 1988, Rifle Disting. Expert Nat. Rifle Assn., 1976; recipient U. Alaska Merit award, 1989, Support award Interior Fire Chief's Assn., 1992, State of N.J. Gen. Assembly commentation, Am. Legion Good Citizen citation, 1976, Dist. Award of Merit Midnight Sun Coun. Boy Scouts Am., 1980, U. Alaska Army ROTC Charles J. Keim award, 1976, Chancellor's medal, 1977. Mem. Am. Soc. Safety Engrs. (mem. svc. award Midnight Sun chpt. 1998), Nat. Assn. Search and Rescue, Am. Polar Soc., Internat. Shooting Coaching Assn. (founder, bd. dirs.), Nat. Eagle Scout Assn. (chpt. pres. 1978), Internat. Design Extreme Environ. Assembly, Interior Fire Chiefs Assn. (bd. dirs.), Soc. Rsch. Adminstrs., No. Region Critical Incident Stress Debriefing Team, Order of Arrow (vigal mem.), NRA (cert. rifle, pistol, shotgun instr.), Internat. Karate Assn., Kappa Alpha Mu (chpt. pres. 1978-80), Sigma Delta Chi. Avocations: yoshinkan aikido (2nd degree black belt), shihano ranno jujitsu (1st degree black belt), shudokan karate (2nd degree black belt), wu chin gung fu (yellow sash). Home: PO Box 80981 Fairbanks AK 99708-0981 Office: U Alaska Inst Artic Biology PO Box 757000 Fairbanks AK 99775-7000 E-mail: fnmaa@uaf.edu.

ABER, JOHN WILLIAM, finance educator; b. Canonsburg, Pa., Sept. 9, 1937; s. John William and Rose (Lauda) A.; m. Cynthia Louise Sousa, Nov. 24, 1962; children: John, Valerie, Alexander. BS, Pa. State U., 1959; MBA, Columbia U., 1965; DBA, Harvard U., 1972. Cons. Univ. Affiliates, Inc., Boston, 1969-71; asst. prof. fin. Ga. State U., Atlanta, 1971-72, Boston U., 1972-78, assoc. prof., 1978-97, prof., 1997—. Fin. and bank mgmt. cons.; dir. mgrs. funds Appleton Growth Fund, 1999—; dir. Third Ave. Funds, 2001—. McKinsey scholar Columbia U.; Bus. Sch. leadership fellow, Divsn. of Rsch. fellow. Home: 51 Columbia St Brookline MA 02446-2407 Office: Boston U 595 Commonwealth Ave Boston MA 02215-1704 E-mail: jackaber@bu.edu.

ABERCROMBIE, CHARLOTTE MANNING, reading specialist, supervisor; b. Swampscott, Mass., Oct. 25, 1915; d. Fredric Wilbur and Mary Sayer (Delano) Manning; m. Alexander Vaughan Abercrombie, Oct. 17, 1937; children: Lois A. Street, Paul M., David M., Lucia A. Harvilchuck. BA, Marietta Coll., 1937; MA, Columbia U., 1974, EdD, 1976. Cert. tchr. R.I., Wash., Wis., N.J.; cert. reading specialist, supr. N.J. Tchr. elem. schs. Tacoma (Wash.) Pub. Schs., 1958-62, Warwick (R.I.) Pub. Schs., 1957; tchr., reading specialist Milw. Pub. Schs., 1966-69; elem. tchr. and reading specialist, supr. East Orange (N.J.) Pub. Schs., 1969-79. Dir. Fla. Ctr. for Philosophy for Children, Pensacola, 1994—. Mem. Nat. Assn. Congregational Chs. (exec. com. 1980-84). Mem. AAUW (v.p. Marco Island, Fla. chpt. 1988-89, bd. dirs. State of Fla. 1990, bd. dirs. Pensacola br. Coll. Univ., 1992). Republican. Avocations: reading, swimming, walking the beach. Home: 10100 Hillview Rd Apt 616 Pensacola FL 32514-5460 E-mail: comaber@hotmail.com.

ABERNATHY, DIXIE FRIEND, elementary education educator; Sci. tchr. Southwest Jr. High Sch., Gastonia, NC; asst. principal Forest Heights Elementary; principal Belmont Middle Sch., 1998—2000, N. Belmont Elementary, Belmont, NC, 2000—. Named N.C. State Sci. Tchr. of Yr., 1993. Office: N Belmont Elementary 210 School St Belmont NC 28012*

ABERNATHY, MARY GATES, elementary school educator; b. Elmira, N.Y., May 6, 1945; d. Kenneth B. and Becky Jane (Jones) Gates; m. Mark Eugene Abernathy, Dec. 29, 1980; children: Kenetha Jane, Alan Wayne. AA, Bluefield (Va.) Coll., 1965; BS in Edn. with honors, Radford (Va.) Coll., 1967; postgrad., U. Va., 1977-78; MEd, George Mason U., 1982. Cert. elem. sch. educator, Va. 1st grade tchr. Battlefield Elem. Sch., Spotsylvania, Va., 1976-77; 2d grade tchr. Grafton Village Elem. Sch., Stafford, Va., 1977-78, Barden Elem. Sch., Fort Belvoir, Va., 1980-84, Woodlawn Elem. Sch., Alexandria, 1984-89; 1st and 4th grade tchr. Hybla Valley Elem. Sch., Alexandria, 1989-96; 4th grade tchr. Woodlawn Elem. Sch., 1996—. Pilot and tchr. trainer Amimal Life Sci., Fairfax County, Va., 1982-84; tchr. trainer elem. writing program phase III, Fairfax County, 1983-84; chairperson writing Woodlawn Elem. Writing Com., 1984-89; primary team leader Barden and Woodlawn Elem. Schs., 1981-84, 85-89; cooperating tchr. Woodlawn Elem. Sch., 1986-88. Sign lang. interpreter Groveton Bapt. Ch., Alexandria, 1982—, sign lang. instr., 1984—; interpreter Nat. Christian Choir, Rockville, Md., 1986—. Fellow Nat. Coun. Tchr. Math., Assn. for Supervision and Curriculum Devel., Nat. Coun. for Better Edn.; mem. Phi Theta Kappa, Kappa Delta Pi, Phi Kappa Phi. Avocations: sign language, cross-stitch, knitting, baking, sewing. Office: Woodlawn Elem Sch 8505 Highland Ln Alexandria VA 22309-1798

ABERNATHY, SUE EURY, physical education educator; b. Washington, N.C., July 28, 1947; d. Craig Stanford and Lelia Frances (McHarney) Eury; m. Dean Judson Abernathy Jr., Dec. 27, 1970; children: Kristan Joanna, Dean Judson III. BS in Health and Phys. Edn., Campbell U., 1969; MA in Tchg., U. N.C., 1970; DA in Phys. Edn., Middle Tenn. State U., 1995. Cert. tchr. Tchr. Lee County Schs., Lemon Springs, N.C., 1970-71, Weatherford County Schs., Reno, Tex., 1971-73, Prince George's County Schs., Suitland, Md., 1973-75, Duval County Schs., Jacksonville, Fla., 1975-84, Akiva Sch., Nashville, 1984-92, Metro Nashville (Tenn.) Schs., Lakeview Elem Sch., 1992—. 4th degree black belt World Tae Kwon Do Fedn., Seoul, Korea, 1987—; writer Tenn. Elem. Tae Kwon Do curriculum, 1993; mem. adv. team Lakeview Elem. Sch., 1993-94; presenter in field. Youth dir., tchr. Brentwood (Tenn.) Bapt. Sunday Sch., 1984—; active tchg. mission trip Brentwood Bapt. Ch., Scotland, 1990, 92. Tchr. award grantee Hosp. Corp. Am., 1994, 97, Eskind Edn. grantee, 1995, 96, Am. South Excellence in Edn. grantee, 1995; recipient Mayor's Acts of Excellence award Mayor of Nashville, 1994, 95, Letter of Commendation, World Tae Kwon Do Fedn., 1994. Mem. AAHPERD (presenter so. dist. 1994-95, sec. hist. coun. 1995-96), Tenn. AHPERD (presenter 1994, 95, 96), N.Am. Assn. Sport History, All-Am. Scholar, Phi Epsilon Kappa, Kappa Delta Pi, Phi Kappa Phi. Avocation: Tae Kwon Do. Home: 1020 Highland Rd Brentwood TN 37027-5528

ABERNETHY, ANN LAWSON, retired elementary school education educator; b. Pa., July 19, 1937; d. Samuel Chrisman Abernethy and Josephine Crozer Ludlow II. BS in Edn., SUNY, Oneonta, 1959. Cert. early childhood tchr., N.Y. Tchr. grade 1 Mineola (N.Y.) Sch. Dist., 1959-93, primary dir. summer recreation program, 1954-64, winter recreation dir., 1967, dir. sci. curriculum writing, 1972; strategic plan writer, 1990-91; chair grade level Mineola (N.Y.) Sch. Dist., 1985-93; substitute tchr., 1993-94; ret., 1993—. Staff liaison PTA, 1980-93; sec. Northville Beach Civic Assn., 1982—; vice chair elders Cmty. Ch. of East Williston, chair mem. personnel and relationships com. Recipient Jenkins Meml. award. Mem. AAUW, N.Y. State United Tchrs. (del. rep.), Mineola Tchrs. Assn. (bldg. rep., co-chmn. assn. ret. staff 1993—), ED19 Retiree Coun. (co-v.p.), Women's Club of the Willistons. Home: 371 Feather Ln East Williston NY 11596-2545

ABERNETHY, SHARRON GRAY, language educator; b. Tishomingo, Miss., Mar. 22, 1945; d. Dennis F. Gray (deceased) and Lyda Waddell Gray; m. Elliott Lee Abernethy, Jr.; children: Damon, Ryan (Deceased). BA, Secondary Edn., U. North Ala., Florence, 1966; MA in Latin and Am. Studies, U. Ala., Tuscaloosa, 1971, PhD, 1982, EdS, 1976; cert., U. Carlos III, Madrid, 2000. Cert. ESADE Barcelona, Spain, 1999. Spanish/Latin Am. history tchr. Deshler H.S., Tuscumbia, AL, Ala., 1966—68; Spanish/English tchr. Eastwood Jr. H.S., Tuscaloosa, 1968—68; rsch. asst. U. Ala., Tuscaloosa, 1969—70, tchg. asst., 1970—73, Spanish instr., 1977, Spanish prof. (part-time) Huntsville, 1988—90, 1994—96, Spanish prof., 1996—, departmental internat. internship coord., 2001—; Spanish/Am. history tchr. Eastwood Jr. H.S., Tuscaloosa, 1973—76; Spanish prof. Miss. State U., Meridian, 1982—84; Spanish instr. Meridian H.S., 1982—85; owner Sir Speedy Printing franchise, Pittsburg, 1986—87, Huntsville, 1988—93; reviewer John Wiley & Sons, Inc., New York, NY, 2002—. Faculty advisor Phi Sigma Iota, Huntsville, 1997—; participant numerous confs./workshops on curricular and instrnl. improvement, 1999—. Vol. St. Jude's Children's Hosp., Memphis, 1977—78, Riley Hosp., Meridian, 1981—83; bd. dirs. Harris Home for Children, Huntsville, 1990—92; supporter/vol. Chi-Ho Home for Children, Huntsville, 1988—2001; mem./officer Huntsville West Kiwanis, Huntsville, 1988—94; chair Huntsville West Kiwanis/Chi-Ho Benefit Golf Tournament, Huntsville, 1990—93; leader Cub Scouts, Meridian, 1981—84; mem. Rep. Women, Huntsville, 1988—89; tchr., deacon, com. mem. adminstrn., stewardship, fin., hospitality, pastoral search coms., co-editor 1993 ch. history/dire First Presbyn. Ch., Huntsville, 1988—2002. Mem.: Naita (UAH liaison to North Ala. Internat. Trade Assn. 1999—, bd. dirs. 2003, 1999—), Exec. Women Internat. (VIP award 2001). Republican. Presbyterian. Avocations: piano, travel, golf, culinary arts.

ABLIN, RICHARD JOEL, immunologist, educator; b. Chgo., May 15, 1940; s. Robert Benjamin and Minnie Edith (Gordon) A.; m. Linda Lee Lutwack; 1 son, Michael David. AB, Lake Forest Coll., 1962; PhD in Microbiology, SUNY, Buffalo, 1967. Diplomate Am. Bd. Clin. Immunology and Allergy; cert. specialist in pub. health and med. lab. microbiology Nat. Registry Microbiologists of Am. Acad. Microbiology. Grad. asst. dept. biology SUNY-Buffalo, 1963-65, research asst., summer 1963, research fellow, 1965-66; USPHS postdoctoral fellow dept. microbiology Sch. Medicine, lectr., lab instr., 1966-68; instr., research asst. Rosary Hill Coll., 1965-66; research cons. program med. edn. AID, Paraguay, 1968; dir. div. immunology Millard Fillmore Hosp. Rsch. Inst., Buffalo, 1968-70; head sect. immunology, renal unit Meml. Hosp. of Springfield, 1970-73; dir. sect. immunobiology div. urology dept. surgery Cook County Hosp. and Hektoen Inst. for Med. Research, Chgo., 1973-75, sr. sci. officer div. immunology, 1976-83; sr. mem. sci. staff, clin. immunologist Cook County Hosp., 1973-75; asst. prof. medicine So. Ill. U., 1971-73; assoc. prof. microbiology Univ. Health Sci. (Chgo. Med. Sch.), 1973-74; research assoc. prof. urology, dir. immunology unit dept. urology SUNY, Stony Brook, 1983-89; pres., dir. Robert Benjamin Ablin Found. for Cancer Rsch., Evergreen Park, Ill., 1979—; dir. sci. investigation Innapharma, Inc., Park Ridge, N.J., 1991—. Mem. Univ. Senate, 1986-89, 89-92, Univ. Governing Coms., 1984-92; acad. del. United Univ. Professions, 1986-88, 88-90; organizer, presenter, instr., participant numerous nat. and internat. profl. meetings, symposia, seminars. Editor: Allergologia et Immunopathologia, 1980—84; contbg. editor: Current Perspectives in Allergology and Immunopathology, 1974—84, Cancer Watch, 2001—, Seminars in Immunopathology and Oncology, Ill. Med. Jour., 1975—88; assoc. editor: Jour. Investigational Allergology and Clin. Immunology (formerly Allergologia et Immunopathologia), 1985—95, adv. editor: Jour. Cancer, 1976—89, assoc. editor: Low Temperature Medicine, 1975—; translator: Jour. Experimental Therapeutics and Oncology, 2003—; mem. editl. bd.: Medikon, 1974—80; mem. editl. bd. Advances in Therapy, 1999—, Am. Jour. Reproductive Immunology and Microbiology, 1980—91, Annals Clin. and Lab.Sci., 2000—, Bratislava Med. Jour., 1999—, Cancer Therapy, 2003—, Cellular and Molecular Biology, 1985—87, Clin. and Applied Immunology Revs., 2001—, Clin. and Diagnostic Lab. Immunology, 2002—, Current Oncology, 1998—, Early Pregnancy: Biology and Medicine, 1995—, Exptl. Biology and Medicine, 2000—, Immunology and Allergy Practice, 1979—95, Prostate Jour., 1999—2001, UroOncology, 2000—, mem. sci. bd. Chemistry Today, 1991—97, TumorDiagnostik und Therapie, 1980—98; mem. editl. acad.: Internat. Jour. Oncology, 1996—, mem. editl. adv. bd.: Med. Sci. Rsch., 1984—2000, mem. editl. bd.: Expert Rev. Anticancer Therapy, 2002—; contbr. articles to profl. jours. Chief Sangamo Nation Y-Indian Guides, Springfield, 1972-73; mgr. Skokie Indians' Boys' Baseball, Ill., 1973-74, 77, 80, 81, bd. dirs., 1979-83, exec. v.p., 1981-82; mgr. Little League Three Villages, Setauket, N.Y., 1986; cubmaster N.W. Suburban coun. Boy Scouts Am., 1974-78, asst. scoutmaster, 1975-77; mem. exploring divsn. Suffolk County coun. Boy Scouts Am., 1985-88; pres., dir. Spirit of Chgo. Hockey Club Found., Evergreen Park, Ill., 1982—. Recipient Nat. Pres. Leader's Dist. Boy Scouts Am., 1975; named Cubmaster of Yr. Boy Scouts Am., 1977 Fellow: Assn. Clin. Scientists, Am. Coll. Cryosurgery (adv. bd. 1977—78, v.p. 1977—79, parliamentarian 1977—79, adv. bd. 1980—81, 1984—99), Am. Coll. Allergy and Immunology, Indian Cryogenics Coun. (hon.); mem.: AAAS, Metastasis Rsch. Soc., Am. Assn. Cancer Rsch., Am. Assn. Immunologists, Am. Soc. Microbiology, Assn. Med. Lab Immunologists, Brit. Assn. Surg. Oncology, Buffalo Collegium Immunology, Internat. Soc. Andrology, Internat. Soc. Chronobiology, Internat. Soc. Cryosurgery (pres. 1977—80, bd. dirs. 1980—, hon. life pres.), Internat. Soc. Immunology Reprodn., Japan Soc. Low Temperature Medicine, N.Y. Acad. Scis., Soc. Cryobiology, Soc. Exptl. Biology and Medicine, Soc. Leukocyte Biology, Soc. Protozoologists, Soc. Study Reprodn., Transplantation Soc., Cryoimmunotherapeutic Study Group (chmn.), Witebsky Ctr. Microbial Pathogenesis and Immunology, Sigma Xi, Phi Beta Kappa (Theta of Ill. at Lake Forest Coll.). Achievements include identification of prostate specific antigen (PSA), used as tumor marker (diagnosis) in prostate cancer, and of human thymic specific antigen providing means for differentiation of thymic lymphocytes from other lymphoid cells and the development of antithymocyte globulin (selectively immunosuppressive for thymocytes) used in renal allograft (transplant) recipients; and development of concept of cryoimmunotherapy for treatment of cancer. Office: Innapharma Inc Ste 205 1 Maynard Dr Park Ridge NJ 07656 E-mail: rablin@innapharma.com.

ABOUSLEIMAN, YOUNANE NASSIB, civil engineer, researcher, educator; b. Beirut, Dec. 9, 1957; came to U.S., 1984; s. Nassib Younane and Alice (Hajj) A. B in Engring., Am. U., Beirut, 1982; MS, Columbia U., 1986; PhD, U. Del., 1991. registered profl. engr. Project engr. Min. Pub. Works, Beirut, 1982-84; rsch. scientist U. Okla., Norman, 1991-94, sr. rsch. scientist, mem. faculty, 1994-96, vis. scientist, 1996—; prof. Lebanese Am. U., Beirut, 1996—; Larry Brummett ONEOK chair, prof. Melbourne Sch. of Petrol. and Geol. Engring, 2001—. Office: U Okla 100 E Boyd St Norman OK 73019-1000

ABRAHAM, LAWRENCE DAGGER, kinesiology educator; b. Washington, Sept. 19, 1949; s. Stuart Broadus and Ida Jeanne (Dagger) A.; m. Dorothy Downing Lambdin, Aug. 16, 1975; children: Andrew Carson Lambdin-Abraham, Rebecca Diana Lambdin-Abraham. AB, Oberlin Coll., 1971; MS, Kans. State Tchrs. Coll., Emporia, 1972; EdD, Columbia U., 1975. Asst. prof. U. Tex., 1975-82, assoc. prof., 1982—2003, assoc. dean tchr. edn. and student affairs Coll. of Edn., 1998—2002, chair dept. curriculum and instrn., 2000—, prof., 2003—. Rsch. assoc. NIH, Bethesda, Md., 1980-81, Healthcare Rehab. Ctr., Austin, Tex., 1990-2000; vis. adj. U. Mass., 1987-88; vis. lectr. U. Otago, New Zealand, 1995; cons. biomechanics U.S. Modern Pentathlon Assn., San Antonio, 1986-87. Mem. editorial bd. QUEST, 1986-92; contbr. articles to profl. jours. Vol. leader Boy Scouts Am., 1966-75, 91-01; instr. ARC, 1969-71, Hagerstown, Md.; pres. PTA, Austin, 1989-90. Named W.D. Blunk prof., 1993-94; rsch. grantee (5) Univ. Rsch. Inst., U. Tex., 1977-86, instrnl. grantee IBM, U. Tex., 1985-87, rsch. grantee (6) Healthcare Rehab. Ctr., 1990-96, rsch. grantee (4) NASA, 1992-96. Mem. ASCD, AAHPERD, Nat. Assn. Phys. Edn. in Higher Edn., Am. Coll. Sport Medicine, North Am. Soc. Psychology of Sport and Phys. Activity, Internat. Soc. Biomechanics, Internat. Soc. Electrophysiol. Kinesiology, Soc. Neurosci. Avocations: camping, sports, reading. Home: 1708 Westmoor Dr Austin TX 78723-3410 Office: Univ Tex Austin Dept Curriculum and Instrn Austin TX 78712 E-mail: l.abraham@mail.utexas.edu.

ABRAHAM, REBECCA JACOB, finance educator; b. Calcutta, India, Nov. 4, 1962; came to U.S., 1986; d. Connayil Mani and Susan (Varugis) Jacob; m. Anthony Zikiye, May 10, 1989 (dec. Jan. 1994); 1 child, Mark. BS in Chemistry, Women's Christian Coll., Madras; MBA, U.S. Internat., San Diego, 1984, D in Bus. Adminstrn., 1989. Asst. prof. Nova S.E. Univ., Ft. Lauderdale, Fla., 1989-94, assoc. prof., 1994—. Corr. South Fla. Bus., Ft. Lauderdale, 1995, Broward Times, Ft. Lauderdale, 1995; contbr. articles to profl. jours. Recipient Nat. Collegiate Bus. award, 1987. Mem. Acad. Mgmt. Avocations: reading, traveling, badminton. Office: Nova SE Univ 3301 College Ave Fort Lauderdale FL 33314-7721 E-mail: abraham@nova.edu.

ABRAHAM, ROBERT PAUL, secondary education administrator; b. Harvey, Ill., Apr. 19, 1954; s. Herbert Albert and Mary Catherine Abraham; m. Laura Mann; 1 child, Barrett Mann. BS, Ea. Ill. U., 1976; MS, Ill. State U., 1978; EdD, No. Ill. U., 2000. Phys. edn. tchr. Twin Groves Jr. H.S., Buffalo Grove, Ill., 1979-89, asst. prin., 1989-95; dir. media & tech. St. Charles (Ill.) East H.S., 1995—. Coach St. Charles Boys Baseball, 2000, St. Charles Boys Basketball, 2001. Avocations: computers, travel. Office: St Charles East High Sch 1020 Dunham Rd Saint Charles IL 60174 E-mail: rabraham@d303.org.

ABRAHAM, TERRY, school librarian; b. Portland, Oreg., Oct. 6, 1944; BA, U. Washington, 1965; MFA, Washington State U., 1968; MLS, U. Oreg., 1970. Cert. archivist, 1989. Libr. Washington State U., Pullman, 1967-68, manuscript-archives libr., 1970-84; head, spl. collections and archives U. Idaho, Moscow, 1984—. Projects editor Soc. Am. Archivists, Chgo., 1981-85; program officer Nat. Endowment for Humanities, Washington, 1987-88. Author: Austin Mires, 1968, Selected Manuscript Resources in the Washington State University Library, 1974, A Union List of the Papers of Members of Congress from the Pacific Northwest, 1976; compiler (with R. Davis) Day to Day: A Guide to the Records of the Historic Day Mines Group in the university of Idaho Library, 1992. Adv. bd. mem. Washington State Hist. Records, Olympia, Washington, 1981-84, Idaho Hist. Records, Boise, Idaho, 1984-92, 97-2003, Idaho Ctr. for The Book, Boise, 1993—. Recipient Hard-Rock Mining in the Coeur d'Alenes Nat. Hist. Publs. and Records Commn., 1986-88, Idaho Archives and Manuscripts Database, 1989-91, Nat. Hist. Publs. and Records Commn., Mining Records Appraisal and Description U.S. Dept. Edn., 1991-92. Office: Special Collections University of Idaho Library Rayburn St Moscow ID 83844-2351 E-mail: tabraham@uidaho.edu.

ABRAHAMSON, WILLIAM GENE, retired school counselor; b. Billings, Mont., Dec. 14, 1936; s. John C. and Sarah (McNeil) A.; m. Elaine B. Abrahamson, Aug. 12, 1961; children: Donna Key, William Gene Jr. BS in Edn., Eastern Mont. Coll., Billings, 1958; MS in Sch. Counseling, Ind. State U., Terre Haute, 1969; diploma in Sch. Counseling, Auburn (Ala.) U., 1976. Nat. cert. counselor. Tchr. Lovell (Wyo.) Pub. Schs., 1958-59, 61-63, Ft. Benning (Ga.) Schs., 1963-68, sch. counselor, 1969-92, Muscogee County Sch. Dist., Columbus, Ga., 1992-2001; ret., 2001. Presenter local, dist. and state profl. meetings. Scout leader Boy Scouts Am., Chattahoochee Coun., 1984—; scouting coord. South Ga. Conf., United Meth. Ch., 1992-2000. With U.S. Army, 1959-61. Recipient experienced tchr. fellowship Ind. State U., 1968-69, Silver Beaver award Chattahoochee coun. Boy Scouts Am., 1988, Cross and Flame award for svc. to scouting St. Mark United Meth. Ch., 1988, Kappan of Yr. award Chattahoochee Valley Ga. chpt. Phi Delta Kappa, 1991, Svc. Key, 1994, Giwell award for svc. to scouting Boy Scouts Am., 1993, Torch award South Ga. Conf. United Meth. Ch., 2001. Mem. ACA, Am. Sch. Counselors Assn. (cert. of merit 1978), Ga. Sch. Counselors Assn. (sec. 1980-81, pres.-elect, membership chairperson 1981-82, pres. 1982-83, chairperson long range planning com. 1983-85, by-laws com. mem. 1990-91, past pres. action com. 1995—, Elem. Sch. Counselor of Yr. 1978, Mid. Sch. Counselor of Yr. 1998), Ga. Ret. Educators Assn., Masons. Avocations: scouting activities, reading, hiking, camping, Scottish cultural activities, travel. Home: 3104 Bellanca St Columbus GA 31909-5184 E-mail: wabemonty@aol.com.

ABRAHMS, SHAWNA K. special education services professional; b. Lynn, Mass., Jan. 7, 1938; d. Herbert Abrahms and Katherine McGinnity; m. Gilbert Riley, Oct. 15, 1960 (div. Dec. 1970). BS, U. Conn., 1967; MS, So. Conn. State U., New Haven, 1971. Tchr. special edn. Columbus Elem. Schs., Columbus, Ohio, 1972—76; mgr. Meriks Educational Facilities, Columbus, Ohio, 1977—. Office: Meriks Educational Facilities 4719 Reed Rd #402 Columbus OH 43220-3071

ABRAM, DARLENE RUTH SHEPPARD, education educator, consultant; b. Oklahoma City, May 25, 1938; d. James Wesley and Maggie F. (McCowan) Sheppard; m. James Baker Abram Jr., June 24, 1961; children: James Baker III, Carmelita Michelle. BS, Prairie View (Tex.) A&M U., 1960; MA, Hampton (Va.) U., 1973, 76; cert. advanced grad. studies, Va. Polytech. Inst. & State U., 1980, EdD, 1982. Asst. registrar and admissions clk. U. Md., Princess Anne, Md., 1963-70; adminstrv. asst. Hampton U., 1970-74, dir. student teaching, 1974-84; personnel staffing specialist Ft. Monroe (Va.), 1984-86; dir. div. edn. Paul Queen Coll., Waco, Tex., 1987-88; tchr. elem. Bradley Elem. Sch., New Orleans, 1988-89; cons. Darlene's Cons., Metairie, 1988-91; prof. edn. Xavier U., New Orleans, 1989-91; dean Sch. Edn. and Behavioral Scis. Langston (Okla.) U., 1991—. Cons. Fed. Women Program, Ft. Eustis, Va., 1986; edn. svc. specialist Army Edn. Ctr., Ft. Sill, Okla., summer 1983; employee devel. specialist Rock Island (Ill.) Arsenal, summer 1984, tng. specialist, summer 1987. Mem. NAACP. Mem. Assn. Tchr. Educators, ASCD, La. Assn. Supervision and Curriculum Devel., Am. Assn. Colls. for Tchr. Edn., Alpha Kappa Alpha, Inc., Kappa Delta Pi. Democrat. Baptist. Avocations: reading, tennis, travel, cooking. Home: 1113 Kenilworth Rd Oklahoma City OK 73114-1609

ABRAMOWICZ, JACQUES SYLVAIN, obstetrician, perinatologist, educator; b. Paris, Dec. 5, 1948; s. Theodore Dov and Sara Ethel (Cukiernik) A.; m. Annie Sternelicht, Aug. 1, 1972; children: Shelly, Ory. MD, Sackler Sch. Medicine, Tel-Aviv, 1975. Diplomate Israel Bd. Ob-Gyn., Am. Bd. Ob-Gyn. Rotating intern Tel-Aviv Mcpl. Med. Ctr., 1973-74; resident dept. ob-gyn. Sapir Med. Ctr., Kfar-Saba, Israel, 1978-85; rsch. registrar ultrasound dept. ob-gyn. King's Coll. Hosp., London, 1981; resident dept. gen. surgery Sapir Med. Ctr., 1982-83, resident dept. urology, 1983; cons. Timsit Inst. Reproductive Medicine, Tel-Aviv, 1986-87; dir. clin. rsch. Div. Maternal-Fetal Medicine, Ea. Va. Med. Sch., Norfolk, 1987-89; assoc. researcher Jones Inst. Reproductive Medicine, Norfolk, 1989; dir. perinatal ultrasound, asst. prof. dept. ob-gyn. U. Rochester Med. Ctr., 1990-93, assoc. prof., 1993-99, prof., 1999-2000, assoc. prof. radiology, 1995-99, prof. radiology, 1999-2000; prof. dept. ob-gyn. and dept. radiology U. Chgo., 2000—. Co-editor: Handbook of Ultrasound in Obstetrics and Gynecology, 1997, Imaging in Infertility and Reproductive Endocrinology, 1994; contbr. articles to profl. jours. including Am. Jour. Ob-Gyn., Obstet. Gynecology, Jour. Ultrasound Medicine, Prenatal Diagnosis, Am. Jour. Perinatology, Fetal Therapy, Jour. Perinatal Medicine, Jour. Clin. Ultrasound, Ultrasound Med. Biology, also chpts. to books; referee various jours. Maj. Israel Def. Forces, 1974-78. Fellow: ACOG, Am. Inst. Ultrasound in Medicine (sr.; internat. rels. com. 1988—91, stds. com. 1991—93, mfrs. commendation panel 1991—93, chair mfrs. commendation panel 1993—94, bioeffects com. 1994—, chair epidemiology subcom. 1999—); mem.: Internat. Soc. Ultrasound in Ob-Gyn. (chair bioeffects and safety com. 2001—), Internat. Fetal Med. and Surg. Soc., Internat. Perinatal Doppler Soc., Soc. Perinatal Obstetricians, N.Y. Acad. Scis. Jewish. Achievements include rsch. in prenatal diagnosis and therapy, ultrasound, Doppler velocimetry, ultrasound contrast media, placental perfusion, bioeffects of ultrasound. Office: U Chgo Dept Ob/Gyn MC 2050 5841 S Maryland Ave Chicago IL 60637-1463 E-mail: jsa@babies.bsd.uchicago.edu.

ABRAMS, NORMAN, law educator, university administrator; b. Chgo., July 7, 1933; s. Harry A. and Gertrude (Dick) A.; m. Toshka Alster, 1977; children: Marshall David, Julie, Hanna, Naomi. AB, U. Chgo., 1952, JD, 1955. Bar: Ill. 1956, US Supreme Ct. 1967. Assoc. in law Columbia U., 1955-57; rsch. assoc. Harvard U., 1957-59; sec. Harvard-Brandeis Coop. Rsch. for Israel's Legal Devel., 1957-58, dir., 1959; mem. faculty law sch. UCLA, 1959—, prof. law, 1964—, assoc. dean law, 1989-91, vice chancellor acad. pers., 1991-2001, interim exec. v. chancellor, spring 1998, co-dir. Ctr. for internat. and strategic studies, 1982-83, chmn. steering com., 1985-87, 88-89, interim dean law, 2003—; vis. prof. Hebrew U., 1969-70, Forchheimer vis. prof., 1986; vis. prof. Bar Ilan U., 1970-71, 78, U. So. Calif., 1972, Stanford U., Conn., 1977, U. Calif. at Berkeley, Calif., 1977, Loyola U., LA, summers 1974, 75, 76, 79; spl. asst. to US atty. gen., also prof.-in-residence criminal div. Dept. Justice, 1966-67. Reporter for So. Calif. indigent accused persons study Am. Bar Found., 1963; cons. Gov. Calif. Commn. L.A. Riots, 1965, Pres.'s Commn. Law Enforcement and Adminstrn. Justice, 1966-67, Nat. Commn. on Reform of Fed. Criminal Laws, 1967-69, Rand Corp., 1968-74, Ctr. for Adminstrv. Justice, ABA, 1973-77, Nat. Adv. Commn. on Criminal Justice Stds., Organized Crime Task Force, 1976; spl. hearing officer conscientious objector cases Dept. Justice, 1967-68; vis. scholar Inst. for Advanced Studies, Hebrew U., summer, 1994. Author: (with others) Evidence, Cases and Materials, 7th edit., 1983, 8th edit., 1988, 9th edit., 1997, Federal Criminal Law and Its Enforcement, 1986, 2d and 3d edits. (with S. Beale), 1993, 2000, Antiterrorism and Criminal Enforcement, 2003; mem. editl. bd. Criminal Law Forum, 1990—. Chmn. Jewish Conciliation Bd., LA, 1975-81; bd. dir. Bet Tzedek, 1975-85, LA Hillel Coun., 1979-82, Shalhevet HS, 1998—; chmn. So. Calif. region Am. Prof. for Peace in Middle East, 1981-83; bd. dir. met. region Jewish Fedn., 1982-88, v.p. 1982-83; pres. Westwood Kehillah Congregation, 1985. Mem. Internat. Soc. for Reform of Criminal Law (mem. exec. com. 1994—), Phi Beta Kappa. Office: UCLA Law School 405 Hilgard Ave Los Angeles CA 90095-9000 E-mail: abrams@law.ucla.edu.

ABRAMS, REID ALLEN, surgeon, educator; b. San Antonio, July 26, 1955; BA in Biology, Lawrence U., 1977; MD, U. Colo., 1982. Diplomate Am. Bd. Orthopaedic Surgery, with cert. of added qualifications in hand surgery; lic. physician, Calif., Colo., Washington. Intern then resident in orthopedic surgery U. Colo. Health Scis. Ctr., Denver, 1982-87; fellow pediatric orthopedics Children's Hosp. and Health ctr., San Diego, 1987-88; fellow hand and microvascular surgery Brigham and Women's Hosp., Boston, 1988-89; gen. orthopedist Group Health Coop. Puget Sound, 1989-90; assoc. prof. clin. orthopedics U. Calif. Med. Ctr., San Diego, 1990—, chief hand and microvascular surgery, 1990—, vice chair dept. orthopedics, 2000—. Contbr. numerous articles to profl. jours. Mem. Western Orthopedic Assn., Acad. Orthopaedic Soc., Am. Acad. Orthopedic Surgeons, Am. Soc. Surgery of the Hand, Kiros Soc., Phi Sigma. Avocations: music, back-packing, snow skiing. Office: U Calif Med Ctr Orthopedic Surgery 200 W Arbor Dr San Diego CA 92103-8894

ABRAMS, ROGER IAN, law educator, arbitrator; b. Newark, July 30, 1945; s. Avel S. and Myrna (Posner) A.; m. Frances Elise Kovitz, June 1, 1969; children: Jason, Seth. BA, Cornell U., 1967; JD, Harvard U., 1970. Bar: Mass. 1970, U.S. Dist. Ct. Mass. 1971, U.S. Ct. Appeals (1st cir.) 1971. Law clk. to Judge Frank M. Coffin U.S. Ct. Appeals (1st cir.), Boston, 1970-71; assoc. Foley, Hoag & Eliot, Boston, 1971-74; prof. law Sch. Case Western Res. U., Cleve., 1974-86; dean Law Ctr. Nova U., Ft. Lauderdale, Fla., 1986-93; dean Law Sch. Rutgers U., Newark, 1993-1998; prof. law sch. Rutger U., Newark, 1993-99; Herbert J. Hannuch scholar Rutgers U., Newark, 1998-99; dean Northeastern U., Boston, 1999—2002, Richardson prof. law, 1999—. Labor arbitrator Fed. Mediation Svc., 1975—; mem. gender bias report implementation com. Fla. Supreme Ct. Author: Legal Bases: Baseball and the Law, 1998, The Money Pitch: Baseball Free Agency and Salary Arbitration, 2000, The First World Scenes and the Baseball Fanatics of 1903, 2003; contbr. articles to law jours. Bd. dirs. Inst. for Continuing Legal Edn., N.J., 1993-98. Recipient Gen. Counsel's Advocacy award NAACP, Boston, 1974; inductee Union N.J. Hall of Fame, 1995. Mem. Am. Law Inst., Am. Bar Found., Am. Arbitration Assn. (labor arbitrator). Democrat. Jewish. Avocations: swimming, distance walking, reading. Office: Northeastern Univ Sch Law 400 Huntington Ave Boston MA 02115-5005 E-mail: rabrams@neu.edu.

ABRAMS, RONI, business education educator, communications consultant, trainer; b. N.Y.C. d. William and Edith Lillian (Monkarsh) Abrams. BA, U. Miami, 1971. Mng. editor Corset, Bra and Lingerie Mag., N.Y.C., 1972-75; assoc. advt. dir. TV World Mag., N.Y.C., 1976-80; pres. Roni Abrams Assoc., Ltd., Bklyn., 1981—; founder The Ctr. for Networking, Bklyn., 1982—. Design and conduct tng. programs in field of perception, interpersonal comm., negotiations, mgmt., sales, orgnl. devel. and personal transformation; spkr. in field. Contbg. author: (textbook) Basic Sales Skills Business to Business, 1995; contbr. articles to profl. jours. Asst. to dir. Impact on Hunger, N.Y.C, 1980; coord. campaign com. to elect Paul Wrablica for state assembly, N.Y.C., 1988. Mem. Sales and Mktg. Execs. of Greater N.Y. (faculty). Avocations: theater, opera, travel. Home and Office: Roni Abrams Assocs Ltd 2820 Avenue J Brooklyn NY 11210-3736

ABRAMSON, SARA JANE, radiologist, educator; b. New Orleans, La., May 12, 1945; m. Walter Squire; children: Harrison, Russell, Zachary, Andrew. BA, Sarah Lawrence Coll., 1967; postgrad., Tulane U., 1967-69; MD, Mt. Sinai Sch. Medicine, 1971. Diplomate Am. Bd. Radiology, cert. added qualifications pediat. radiology. Intern in pediatrics Mt. Sinai Hosp., N.Y.C., 1971-72, resident in pediatrics, 1972-73; resident in radiology St. Luke's Children's Mercy Hosp., Kansas City, Mo., 1973-76; asst. prof. radiology U. Mo., 1976-79, Harvard U. Med. Sch., Cambridge, Mass., 1979-81; fellow in pediatric radiology Children's Hosp., Boston, 1979-81; asst. prof. radiology Columbia Coll. Physicians & Surgeons, N.Y.C., 1981-88, assoc. prof. radiology, 1988-93; assoc. attending radiologist Babies Hosp. Columbia Presbyn. Med. Ctr., N.Y.C., 1981-93, dep. dir. divsn. pediatric radiology, 1992-93; assoc. prof. radiology Cornell U. Med. Coll., N.Y.C., 1993-99, prof., 1999—; assoc. attending radiologist, assoc. mem. Sloan-Kettering Cancer Ctr., Meml. Hosp., N.Y.C., 1993-98, attending radiologist, mem., 1999—. Mem. radiology elective program Columbia U. Med. Sch., N.Y.C., 1981-93, radiology residency program reevaluation, 1984-93, program coord. affiliated hosps. teaching program, 1991-93, med. student advisor, 1991-93; mem. faculty coun. Columbia U., 1987-93; cons. in pediatric radiology Blythedale Children's Hosp., 1982—, Bet Israel Hosp., N.Y.C., 1983—, Harlem Hosp., N.Y.C., 1983—, N.Y. Foundling Hosp., 1988—, Lenox Hill Hosp., 1990—, Morristown Meml. Hosp., 1990—; lectr., presenter in field. Contbr. over 40 articles to profl. jours., chpts. to books. Named Radiology Tchr. of Yr., Columbia Coll. Physicians and Surgeons, 1992. Fellow Am. Coll. Radiology (del. N.Y. chpt. 1991—, alt. del. 1984-91, co-chair nominating com. 2000—); mem. AMA, Soc. for Pediat. Radiology (bd. dirs. 2000—), Radiology Soc. N.Am., European Soc. for Pediat. Radiology, Soc. Thoracic Radiology, Am. Assn. Ultrasound in Medicine, Am. Assn. Women in Radiology, N.Y. Roentgen Soc. (exec. com. 1999—, sec.-treas. 1991-94, v.p. 1996-97, pres.-elect 1997-98, pres. 1998-99, moderator, pediat. program chair spring conf. 1991), N.Y. State Radiological Soc. (chmn. residents sect. 1998—, treas. 2002—, guest lectr. spring conf. 1990-98), Nat. Children's Cancer Study Group, Caffey Soc., Neuhauser Soc., Kirkpatrick Soc. Office: Sloan-Kettering Cancer Ctr 1175 York Ave New York NY 10021-7169

ABT, CLARK C. social scientist, executive, engineer, publisher, educator; b. Cologne, Germany, Aug. 31, 1929; came to U.S., 1937, naturalized, 1945; m. Wendy Peter, Nov. 3, 1971; children: Thomas, Emily. BS, MIT, 1951, PhD, 1965; MA, Johns Hopkins U., 1952. Instr. Johns Hopkins U., Balt., 1951-52; mgr. advanced systems dept. Raytheon Co., Bedford, Mass., 1957-64; pres., treas. Abt Assocs., Inc., Cambridge, Mass., 1965-86, chmn., 1986—; pres., publisher Abt Books Inc., Cambridge, 1987-94; prof., dir. Ctr. for Study of Small States Boston U., 1991-93, rsch. prof. internat. rels., 1991-94, dir. Def. Tech. Conversion Ctr., 1993-96. Vis. lectr. Harvard U., 1968-69; vis. prof. SUNY, Binghamton, 1975-76; adj. prof. mgmt. U. Mass., 1991-93; dir. Russian Am. Boston Workshop on Def. Tech. Conversion, 1992, dir. Moscow Workshop, 1993; faculty dir. Moscow Entrepreneurial Workshop, 1993, 95; assoc. Ctr. for Sci. and Internat. Affairs Harvard U., 1991—; mem. smallpox preparedness adv com. Mass. Dept. Pub. Health, 2002—. Author: Serious Games, 1970, The Evaluation of Social Programs, 1977, The Social Audit for Management, 1977, Applied Research for Social Policy: The U.S. and the Federal Republic of Germany Compared, 1978, Costs and Benefits of Applied Social Research, 1979, A Strategy for Terminating a Nuclear War, 1985, AIDS and the Courts, 1990, Drugs and Crime CD-ROM Library, 1990, International Drug Library CD-ROM, 1990, National Portrait Gallery Permanent Collection of Notable Americans on CD-ROM, 1990, Solar-Powered Economic Growth, 1999, The Future of Energy, 2001, Economic Impacts of Biological and Nuclear Terrorist Attacks on Seaport-Based Transport, 2003. Vol. tutor Boston Pub. High Schs., 1998—. Recipient grand prize Thoreau award for landscape architecture, 1975 Mem.: Internat. Inst. Strategic Studies, Old Cambridge Shakespeare Soc., Cosmos Club, Cambridge Tennis Club, Mt. Auburn Tennis Club. also: Abt Assocs Inc 55 Wheeler St Cambridge MA 02138-1192 E-mail: clarkabt@aol.com., clark_abt@abtassoc.com.

ABULARACH, GLORIA, special education educator; b. Cali, Colombia, Mar. 5, 1948; came to U.S., 1967; d. Manuel Salazar Valencia and Lyda (Garcia) de Salazar; m. Edgar R. Abularach, Jan. 7, 1975; children: Sandra, Henry Jr., Vanessa. BA in Edn., Nat. Coll. Edn., Chgo., 1975; MEd, Gov. State U., 1981; cert. in spl. edn., Northwestern U., 1986; EdD, No. Ill. U., 1990. Tchr. bilingual edn. Chgo. Bd. Edn., 1977-84, tchr. spl. edn., 1984-86, dist. officer learning disabilities program, 1987-89, citywide learning disabilities cons., 1989-90, citywide perceptual/motor cons., 1990-91, citywide edn. specialist, 1991—. Prof. psychology St. Augustine Coll., Northwestern U., Chgo., 1991—; ednl. therapist Profls. in Learning Disabilities, Winnetka, Ill., 1992—. Author curriculum materials. Mem. ASCD, Assn. Colombian Educators in Chgo. Roman Catholic. Avocations: reading, writing, church activities, sports. Home: 149 E Chewink Ct Palatine IL 60067-3549 Office: Chgo Bd Edn 1819 W Pershing Rd Chicago IL 60609-2338

ACCORDINO, BARBARA LYNN, elementary school educator; b. Louisville, June 28, 1953; d. Samuel D. and Juanita Lee (Carter) A. BA Elem. Edn., Morehead State U., 1975; MEd, U. Louisville, 1979, Diploma/6th Yr. Rank I, 1994. Spl. edn. tchr. Jefferson County Schs., Louisville, 1975-86, Fort Knox (Ky.) Schs., 1986-89, Dept. Def. Schs., Herbornseelbach, Germany, 1989-92, Meade County Schs., Brandenburg, Ky., 1992-94, Henry County Schs., New Castle, Ky., 1994-96, Charlestown (Ind.) H.S., 1996-97, Maryville (Ky.) Elem. Sch., 1997—. Mtg. planner Cath. Alumni Clubs, Washington, 1983-94; peer coach Fort Knox Schs., 1987-89; tchr. mentor Frankfurt Sch. Dist., 1989-92; curriculum chmn. Campbellsburg (Ky.) Sch., 1994-95. Pres. Cath. Alumni Clubs Internat., 1985, 86. Named to Outstanding Young Women of Am., 1985, 86. Mem. NEA, ASCD, Nat. Coun. Math. Tchrs., Coun. for Exceptional Children, Cath. Alumni Club Louisville (pres. 1994-95), Beta Sigma Phi. Roman Catholic. Avocations: travel, theatre, cooking. Home: 5710 Hasbrook Dr Louisville KY 40229-2944 E-mail: KyLADYBARB@aol.com.

ACETO, VINCENT JOHN, librarian, educator; b. Schenectady, N.Y., Feb. 5, 1932; s. Henry and Gilda (Maietta) A.; m. Jean Louise Rasey, Aug. 27, 1955 (div. 1974); children: David, Paul Andrew; m. Kveta Urbanova, June 16, 1993. AB, MA, SUNY, 1953, MLS, 1959; postgrad., Case Western Res. U., 1959, 62, 65-66. Tchr. Scotia (N.Y.)-Glenville Ctrl. Schs., 1956-57; high sch. libr. Burnt Hills (N.Y.)-Ballston Lake Ctrl. Schs., 1957-59; libr. dir. Town of Ballston Pub. Libr., Burnt Hills, 1958-60; Fulbright lectr. U. Dacca, East Pakistan, 1964-65; asst. prof. Sch. Libr. Sci., SUNY, Albany, 1959-62, assoc. prof. libr. sci., 1963-69, prof., 1969—, assoc. dean, 1987-93, interim dean, 1993-95, co-dir. film and TV documentation ctr., 1983—, Disting. Svc. prof., 2000—. Libr. cons. various pub. schs., N.Y. State Edn. Dept., U.S. Dept. Edn., USA Govt. of Bangladesh, 1965, Govt. of Cyprus, 1992, 94; dir. U.S. Office Edn. insts. and traineeships. Joint Editor: Film Lit. Index; contbr. articles to profl. jours. Prs., Filmdex Par II, Inc., 1973-90; bd. dirs. Freedom Forum, Schenectady, 1970-78, chmn., 1976-78; trustee Shenendehowa Pub. Libr., 1995—, v.p., 1996-97, 2000, pres., 1997-99, pres., 2002-; mem. Shenendehowa Ctrl. Pub. Schs. Bd. of Edn., 2002—. Served with AUS, 1954-56. Collins fellow U. Albany, 1997. Mem. ALA, NEA, Pakistan Libr. Assn., East Pakistan Libr. Assn. N.Y. Libr. Assn., Hudson-Mohawk Libr. Assn. (v.p. 1964-66), Am. Soc. Indexers, Am. Soc. Info. Scis., Soc. Cinema Studies, Idaka Forum, Clifton Park Rotary Club, Kappa Phi Kappa, Phi Delta Kappa. Democrat. Unitarian Universalist. Home: 46 Southbury Rd Clifton Park NY 12065 Office: SUNY Albany Sch Info Sci and Policy 1400 Washington Ave Albany NY 12222-0100 E-mail: vaceto1@nycap.rr.com., aceto@albany.edu.

ACEVEDO, ANGELIQUE MARIE, art educator; b. Houston, Dec. 11, 1953; Art cert. K-12, Metro. State Coll., Denver, 1987; vocat. edn. cert., U. N.Mex., 1982, MA, 1981; BFA, Va. Commonwealth U., 1975; doctoral studies in curriculum & instrn., U. Denver, 1992. Resource tchr. Profl. Arts Resource Team, Colo., 1988—; curriculum resource tchr. State Dept. Edn., Colo., 1988—; global exchange U. Denver, 1989-90; curriculum integration strategies resource tchr. Minn. Dept. Pub. Instrn., Stillwater, 1991; part time art and music methods classroom tchr. Metro. State Coll., Colo., 1991-92; artist and classroom curriculum developer Young Audiences, Colo., 1991—; tchr. researcher N.Y.U., 1991; classroom resource and tchr. trainer Pub. Edn. Coalition, Colo., 1991—; K-12 art instr. Jefferson County Sch. Dist., Colo., 1989—. Cons. Talamasca Integrated Arts,Lakewood, Colo., Binney and Smith Crayola Corp., Colo. Coun. on Arts and Humanities Indiv. Artists Program, Artist in Residence Program and Young Audiences, NYU Tchr. Rschr. Program, Geraldine Dodge Found., Ednl. Concepts, Atlanta, 1994, Nat. Endowment for the Arts in Edn. Program, 1994; coun. mem. arts ednl. consensus project Nat. Assessment Ednl. Progress, 1993—; bd. dirs. Nat. Bd. Profl. Teaching Standards; mem. Coun. Chief State Sch. Officers. Author: Collage, Colo., 1992, A Multicultural Resource Guide, Colo., 1991-92. Mem. Nat. History Mus., Denver Art Mus., Denver Botanic Gardens; mem. urban arts com. City of Lakewood; bd. mem. arts coun. City of Arvada, Colo., 1994; mem. Arts Task Force Colo. Dept. Edn., 1994. Named Colo. Art Educator of Yr., 1991-92; nominated Colo. Educator of Yr., 1992, finalist Colo. Educator of Yr., 1993; recipient Disney Am. Tchr. Visual Arts award, 1992, Excellence in Edn. award for Colo., 1992. Mem. NEA, Nat. Art Edn. Assn., Art Student League Denver, Colo. Alliance for Arts in Edn., Art Edn. Equity Network, Profl. Arts Resource Team, Colo. Art Edn. Assn. (rep. coun. exec. bd. mem. 1994). Democrat. Roman Catholic. Avocations: exploring cultures and continents, researching esoteric topics, visual and performing arts, camping, fishing. Home: 32 Ward Ct Lakewood CO 80228-5029 Office: Jefferson County Sch Dist 1829 Denver West Dr Bldg 27 Golden CO 80401-3120 also: Bear Creek Sr High Sch 3490 Kipling St Wheat Ridge CO 80033-5735

ACEVEDO, ELIZABETH MORRISON, special education educator; b. Kittanning, Pa., Apr. 22, 1938; d. Thomas L. and Ethel (Morrison) McKelvey; m. Ruben Acevedo, Oct. 11, 1963; children: Thomas B., Samantha Jo Acevedo-Fox, Holly Elizabeth. BA, Muskingum Coll., 1960; MS, Pepperdine U., 1980; postgrad., Claremont Grad. Sch., 1988-90, Azusa-Pacific U. Lifetime credentials in English and spl. edn., Calif., Pa.; credential in resource specialist, Calif.; cert. adminstr., Calif. Tchr. Armstrong Sch. Dist., Ford City, Pa., 1970-77, Glendora (Calif.) Unified Sch. Dist., 1979-80, resource specialist, 1980-97; adj. prof., field supervisor Grad. Sch. of Edn., Azusa-Pacific U., Azusa, Calif., 1997—. Cons. reading program The Acevedo Advantage, Glendora, 1986—. Contbr. articles to profl. jours. Bd. dirs. christian edn. Ch. Brethren, Glendora, 1989—. Grantee Claremont (Calif.) Grad. Sch., 1989. Mem. AAUW, ASCD, Calif.

Assn. Resource Specialists, Pi Lambda Theta (membership com.). Democrat. Mem. Ch. Brethren. Avocations: reading, jogging, sewing, refinishing antique wood pieces. Home: 643 N Wabash Ave Glendora CA 91741-2116 E-mail: eacevedo@apu.edu.

ACHENBACH, JAN DREWES, engineering educator, scientist; b. Leeuwarden, Netherlands, Aug. 20, 1935; came to U.S., 1959, naturalized, 1978; s. Johannes and Elizabeth (Schipper) A.; m. Marcia Graham Fee, July 15, 1961. Candidate engr., Tech. U. Delft, 1959; PhD, Stanford U., 1962. Preceptor Columbia U., 1962-63; asst. prof. Northwestern U., Evanston, Ill., 1963, assoc. prof., 1966-69, prof. dept. civil engring., 1969—, Walter P. Murphy prof. civil engring., mech. engring. and applied math., 1981—, dir. Ctr. for Quality Engring. and Failure Prevention, 1986—; vis. assoc. prof. U. Calif., San Diego, 1969; vis. prof. Tech. U. Delft, 1970-71; prof. Huazhong Inst. Sci. and Tech., 1981. Mem. at large U.S. Nat. Com. Theoretical and Applied Mechanics, 1972-78, 86—. Author: Wave Propagation in Elastic Solids, 1973, A Theory of Elasticity with Microstructure for Directionally Reinforced Composites, 1975, (with A.K. Gautesen and H. McMaken) Ray Methods for Waves in Elastic Solids, 1982, (with Y. Rajapakse) Solid Mechanics Research for Quantitative Non-Destructive Evaluation, 1987; editor: (with J. Miklowitz) Modern Problems in Elastic Wave Propagation, 1978 (with S.K. Datta and Y.S. Rajapakse) Elastic Waves and Ultrasonic Nondestructive Testing, 1990; editor-in-chief: Wave Motion, 1979—. Recipient award C. Gelderman Found., 1970, C.W. McGraw Rsch. award Am. Soc. Engring. Edn., 1975, Tempo All-Professor Team, Sciences, Chicago Tribune, 1993, Model of Excellence award McDonnell-Douglas, 1996, Disting. Svc. medal Am. Acad. Mechanics, 1997, Prager medal Soc. Engring. Sci., 2001. Fellow AAAS, ASME (hon., Timoshenko medal 1992), Soc. Engring. Sci., Am. Acad. Arts Scis., Acoustical Soc. Am., Soc. Engring. Sci.; mem. Royal Dutch Acad. Scis. (corres.), U.S. Nat. Acad. Scis., US Nat. Acad. Engring., Am. Soc. Nondestructive Testing. Home: 711 Roslyn Ter Evanston IL 60201-1721 Office: Northwestern U Room 324 2137 N Sheridan Catalysis Bldg Evanston IL 60208 E-mail: achenbach@northwestern.edu.

ACHOR, LOUIS JOSEPH MERLIN, psychology and neuroscience educator; b. Clarendon, Tex., Jan. 2, 1948; s. Merlin Farr and Aileen (Arneson) A.; m. Sharon Lyn Slack, Nov. 7, 1970; children: Shawn Joseph, Amy Christina. BA in Psychology, UCLA, 1971, MA in Zoology, 1972; PhD in Psychobiology, U. Calif., Irvine, 1977. NIMH predoctoral fellow U. Calif., Irvine, 1974-76, trainee, 1972-74, 76-77; asst. prof. in psychology Baylor U., Waco, Tex., 1978-85, assoc. prof. psychology, 1986-91, assoc. prof. neurosci. and psychology, 1991—, dir. undergrad. programs in neurosci. and psychology, 1992-94. Jour. and conf. reviewer; judge Ctrl. Tex. Regional Sci. Fair, 1979—, mem. sci. rev. com., 1991-92, mem. instnl. rev. bd., 1997-2002; instr. Baylor U. for Young People, 1991-93; mem. pre-med./pre-dental adv. com. Baylor U., 1994—. Contbr. articles to profl. jours. Chmn. nat. and internat. scholarships com. Baylor U., 1986-90; asst. scoutmaster Boy Scouts Am., 1989-93; trustee, tchr. Sunday sch., 2001—. Recipient Young Investigator award Baylor U., 1982; honoree Phi Beta Kappa, 2002; named Cir. of Achievement Outstanding Prof., Mortar Board, Baylor U., 2001. Mem. AAUP, Soc. for Neurosci., Faculty for Undergrad. Neurosci. (charter, funding sources com. 1992-93, councilor exec. com. 1993-94, sec. 1994-97, chmn. com. to establish nat. honor soc. in neurosci. 2001—, fellow 2002), Internat. Brain Rsch. Orgn., Tex. Assn. Advisors for Health Professions, Baylor Neurosci. Soc. (founder, advisor 1997—), Sigma Xi (Baylor U. chpt. sec.-treas. 1988-89, v.p. 1989-90, pres. 1990-92, nominating com. 2003, del. to nat. mtg.), Psi Chi (founder, advisor 1985—, scholarship established in his honor Baylor U. 1986, Prof. of Yr. 1996, 98), Nu Rho Psi (founder, advisor 2000—). Achievements include discovery that components of brainstem auditory evoked response have multiple generators. Home: 10005 Treeline Dr Waco TX 76712-8529 Office: Dept Psychology and Neurosci Baylor U Waco TX 76798

ACKER, LINDA BROWN, middle school educator; b. Dallas, Jan. 21, 1946; d. Donald Henry and Ruth Ilene (Duncan) Brown; m. James Leslie Acker, Feb. 14, 1976 (div. 1988); children: Vanessa Grace, Susanna Ruth. BFA, So. Meth. U., 1968; postgrad., U. Tex., 1969-70, North Tex. State U., 1973-75, So. Meth. U., 1973-75, Tex. Tech U., 1993. Salesperson Cokesbury Bookstore, Dallas, 1970-71; with Art Ctr. Studio, Dallas, 1971-72; tchr. upper art Amelia Earhart Elem. Sch.-Dallas Ind. Sch. Dist., 1972-75; tchr. art Hurst-Euless-Bedford (Tex.) Ind. Sch. Dist., 1975-77; tchr. Creative Alternatives or "Art After Sch." Programs, 1982-84; substitute tchr. Cypress-Fairbanks (Tex.) Ind. Sch. Dist., 1984-85; tchr. art 6th, 7th and 8th grades Arnold Jr. High, Nat. Exemplary Sch., 1985—. Cons. Massengil & Henderson Art Resources, Houston, 1992. Free-lance artist The Transit engring. jour. Mem. Art Scholarship Found./Cypress-Fairbanks, 1990—; treas., sec. Lake Cypress Estates Civic Club, 1988—. Mem. Water Art Soc. of Houston, Mus. of Fine Arts Houston, Tex. Art Edn. Assn., Nat. Art Edn. Assn. Republican. Methodist. Home: Lake Cypress Estates PO Box 1045 Decatur TX 76234-6045

ACKER, VIRGINIA MARGARET, nursing educator; b. Madison, Wis., Aug. 11, 1946; d. Paul Peter and Lucille (Klein) A. Diploma in nursing, St. Mary's Med. Ctr., Madison, 1972; BSN, Incarnate Word Coll., San Antonio, 1976; MS in Health Professions, S.W. Tex. State U., 1980; postgrad., U. Tex., 1992-93. RN, Tex. Staff nurse St. Mary's Hosp., Milw., 1972-73, Kenosha (Wis.) Meml. Hosp., 1973-74, S.W. Tex. Meth. Hosp., San Antonio, 1974-75, Met. Gen. Hosp., San Antonio, 1975-76; instr. Bapt. Meml. Hosp. Sys. Sch. Nursing, San Antonio, 1976-83; DON, Meml. Hosp., Gonzales, Tex., 1983-84; instr., DON, Victoria Coll., Cuero, Tex., 1984-86; DON, Rocky Knoll Health Care Facility, Plymouth, Wis., 1986-87, Unicare Health Facilities, Milw., 1987-88; coord. nursing edn. St. Nicholas Hosp., Sheboygan, Wis., 1989-90; instr. U. Wis., Oshkosh, 1990-92, St. David's Hosp., Austin, Tex., 1992-95; coord. quality improvement Bailey Square Surgery Ctr., Austin, 1995-98; coord. regulation compliance South Austin Hosp., 1998—2003; program dir. Prevent Inc., 2003—. Roman Catholic. Avocations: cross-stitching, reading, camping, fishing. Home: 129 Copano Cove Rd Rockport TX 78382

ACKERMAN, ANTHONY WAYNE, secondary school educator, band director; b. Lexington, Ky., June 28, 1971; s. James Anthony Ackerman and Patricia Sue Kirby; m. Carol Elizabeth Ackerman; children: Clay, Amelia, Elizabeth. BMus Edn., Ea. Ky. U., 1995; MMus Edn., U. Tenn., 1997; Rank I, Ea. Ky. U., 2002. Asst. band dir. Knox Ctrl. H.C., Knoxville, Tenn.; band dir. Russell County Schs., Russell Springs, Ky. Musician: performing with various groups, including Knoxville Symphony Orch., So. Brass Quintet, Oak Ridge Symphony, Oak Ridge Cmty. Band, 1997—. Mem.: ITG, Music Educators Nat. Conf., Ky. Music Educators Assn. (rep. dist. 10 Marching Band Bd. Control, Russell Springs, pres. dist. 10). Home: 2166 S Hwy 127 Russell Springs KY 42642

ACKERMAN, ARLENE, school system administrator; BA in Elem. Edn., Harris Stowe Tchrs. Coll.; MA in Edni. Adminstrn. an dpolicy, Washington U.; MA in Edn., EdD in Adminstrn., Planning and Social Policy, Harvard U. Supt. San Francisco United Sch. Dist., 1999—, Washington (D.C.) Pub. Schs., 1997—99. Bd. mem. WestEd Regional Edn. Lab., 2003—; mem. Bay Area Sch. Reform Collaboration; program advisor BROAD-Urban Supts. Acad. Trustee San Francisco Fine Arts; bd. govs. San Francisco Symphony; active San Francisco Workforce Investment Bd. Recipient Apple for the Tchr. award, Iota Lambda Sorority, Disting. Alumni award, Harris Stowe Tchrs. Coll.; McDonnell Douglas fellow. Mem.: ASCD, Presdl. Commn. on Hist. Black Colls. and Univs., Nat. Assn. Black Sch. Educators, Coun. of the Great City Schs., Am. Assn. Sch. Adminstrs., Phi Delta Kappa. Office: 555 Franklin St San Francisco CA 94102*

ACKERMAN, BRUCE ARNOLD, law educator, lawyer; b. N.Y.C., Aug. 19, 1943; s. Nathan and Jean (Rosenberg) A.; m. Susan Gould Rose, May 29, 1967; children: Sybil Rose, John Mill. BA summa cum laude, Harvard U., 1964; LLB with honors, Yale U., 1967. Bar: Pa. 1970. Law clk. U.S. Ct. Appeals (2d cir.), New York, 1967-68; law clk. to assoc. justice John M. Harlan U.S. Supreme Ct., Washington, 1968-69; prof. law and public policy analysis U. Pa., Phila., 1969-74; prof. law Yale U., New Haven, 1974-82, Sterling prof. law and polit. sci., 1987—; Beekman prof. law and philosophy Columbia U., N.Y.C., 1982-87. Author: Private Property and the Constitution, 1977, Social Justice in the Liberal State, 1980 (Gavel award ABA), (with Hassler) Clean Coal/Dirty Air, 1981, Reconstructing American Law, 1984, We the People: Foundations, 1991, The Future of Liberal Revolution, 1992, (with Golove) Is NAFTA Constitutional?, 1995, We the People: Transformations, 1998, (with others) The Uncertain Search for Environmental Quality, 1974 (Henderson prize Harvard Law Sch.). Guggenheim fellow, 1985. Fellow Am. Acad. Arts and Scis.; mem. Am. Law Inst. Office: Yale U Law Sch PO Box 208215 New Haven CT 06520-8215

ACKERMAN, FELICIA, philosophy educator, writer; b. Bklyn., June 23, 1947; d. Arthur and Zelda (Sondack) A. AB summa cum laude, Cornell U., 1968; PhD, U. Mich., 1976. Asst. prof. philosophy Brown U., Providence, 1974-79, assoc. prof., 1979-91, prof., 1991—. Vis. asst. prof. philosophy UCLA, 1976; vis. hon. lectr. logic and metaphysics U. St. Andrews, Scotland, 1983; sr. Fulbright lectr. Hebrew U., 1985. Contbr. articles and short stories to various mags. Recipient O. Henry award for short story pub. in Prize Stories, 1990; fellow Ctr. for Advanced Study in Behavioral Scis., NEH, 1988-89. Mem. Am. Philos. Assn., ACLU, NAACP. Office: Brown U Dept Philosophy PO Box 1918 Providence RI 02912-1918 Business E-Mail: felicia_ackerman@brown.edu.

ACKERMAN, JUDY KAY, English educator; b. Enid, Okla., Dec. 1, 1945; d. Alvin Corlett and Frances A. (Seigler) Carson; m. Arthur L. Palmer, Sept. 22, 1967 (div. June 1981); children: Christopher Carson Palmer, Jennifer Robyn Palmer; m. Andrew A. Ackerman, Aug. 7, 1984. BA in Edn., U. Cen. Okla., 1968, MA in Edn., 1976, MA in English, 1989. Tchr. of English and journalism Wheeler AFB, Hawaii, 1968-70, Edmond (Okla.) H.S., 1970-74, Cen. Mid. H.S., Edmond, 1974-82, Cimarron Mid. Sch., Edmond, 1982-93, North H.S., Edmond, 1993—. Seminar dir. in field. State Supt. scholar State of Okla. Fine Arts Inst., Quartz Mountain. Mem. Edmond Assn. of Classroom Tchrs. (bargaining team 1996-98), Okla. Edn. Assn., NEA, Okla. Interscholastic Press Advs. Assn. Avocations: reading, computers, rsch., writing. Home: 14109 Scott St Edmond OK 73013-7006 Office: Edmond N High Sch 215 W Danforth Rd Edmond OK 73003-5206

ACKERMAN, KENNETH EDWARD, lawyer, educator; b. Bronx, May 25, 1946; s. Kenneth L. and Anna (McCarthy) A.; m. Kathryn H. Hartnett, July 10, 1972; children: Andrew, Carl, Sheila, Edward, Daniel, Kenneth. Student, Talladega Coll., 1966; BA, Fordham Coll., 1968; JD, Cornell U., 1971. Bar: N.Y. 1972, Pa. 1994, U.S. Ct. Appeals (2d cir.) 1975, U.S. Supreme Ct. 1976; cert tchr., N.Y. State, 2002. Clk. legal dept. Port Authority N.Y. and N.J., 1969, IBM, 1970; ptnr. Mackenzie Hughes LLP, Syracuse, N.Y., 1971—. Adj. prof. banking law and negotiable instruments Am. Inst. Banking program Onondaga Community Coll., 1984—, Syracuse U. Coll., lectr.; adj. prof. white collar crime Ithaca Coll., 2002—. Author: Alcoholism-Prognosis for Recovery in the Reconstituted Soviet Republics, 1991; contbr. articles to profl. jours. Chmn. Ctrl. N.Y. chpt. March of Dimes, 1972-82; mem. A.A.-USSR Travel Group, 1987; bd. dirs. Ctrl. N.Y. Health Systems Agy., Inc., 1982-83, Syracuse Sr. Citizens Housing Corp., 1992—; trustee N.Y. State Lawyers Assistance Trust, 2003—; mem. Kaye Spl. Commn. Alcohol and Drug Abuse in the Profession, 1999-2001. Mem.: ABA, Onondaga County Bar Assn. (bd. dirs. 1990—93), N.Y. State Bar Assn. (chmn. com. lawyer alcoholism and drug abuse 1993—95). Office: 600 M & T Bldg PO Box 4967 Syracuse NY 13221-4967

ACKERT, MARY ANN, secondary school educator; b. Downers Grove, Ill., July 8, 1947; d. William George and Marguerite E. (O'Connell-Scanlan) Hoffert; m. William Joseph Ackert, Aug. 14, 1971; children: Andrea, Joseph, Benjamin. BA, Loretto Heights Coll., Denver, 1969; MS in Secondary Math. Edn., Emporia (Kans.) State U., 1970. Cert. master math. tchr., Kans., Wis., Ill. Colo. Tchr. math. Wichita (Kans.) Pub. Schs., 1970, Kenosha (Wis.) Pub. Schs., 1970, Lisle (Ill.) Community High Sch., 1970-71, St. Mary's Acad. High Sch., Denver, 1986-88; substitute tchr. Racine (Wis.) Pub. Schs., 1971; instr. math. Sauk Valley Coll., Dixon, Ill., 1973-74; tchr. math. and computer sci. Newman High and Mid. Schs., Sterling, Ill., 1981-86, Littleton (Colo.) Pub. Schs., 1988—2003, rep. to Powell mgmt. coun., 1990—2003; ret., 2003. Coach Mathcounts, 1988—. Mem. St. Mary's Elem. Sch. Bd., Sterling, 1977-83. Mem. NEA, Nat. Coun. Tchrs. Math., Colo. Coun. Tchrs. Math. (math dept. chmn. 1994-99), Colo. Edn. Assn., Littleton Edn. Assn. E-mail: meateach@yahoo.com.

ACOSTA, FRANK XAVIER, psychologist, educator; b. L.A., Apr. 2, 1945; s. Gilbert Lascurain and Virginia A.; m. MaryAnn Gonzales, June 30, 1979; children: Robert Xavier, Jeanette Marie. BS in Psychology magna cum laude, Loyola U., L.A., 1968; MA, UCLA, 1970, PhD in Clin. Psychology, 1974. Lic. psychologist, Calif. Rsch. asst. Neuropsychiat. Inst., UCLA, 1968-71, vis. assoc. prof., 1984-85; clin. psychology intern VA Outpatient Clinic, L.A., 1971-72, Didi Hirsch Cmty. Mental Health Ctr., Culver City, Calif., 1972-73, Long Beach VA Hosp., Calif., 1973-74; clin. psychologist L.A. County/U. So. Calif. Med. Ctr., L.A., 1974—; dir. Spanish-Speaking Clinic, Adult Psychiat. Clinic, 1975-2000; dir. Hispanic psychol. svcs. Los Angeles County/U. So. Calif. Med. Ctr., 1981—, from assoc. dir. to dir. clin. psychol. internship tng. prog, 1986-96; asst. prof. psychiatry Keck Sch. Medicine, U. So. Calif., L.A., 1974-80, assoc. prof. clin. psychiatry, 1980-84, assoc. prof. psychiatry and behaviorl scis., 1984—, mem. allied health profl. staff, 1991—; dir. clin. psychology advanced clerkship/pre-internship Hispanic Psychol. Svcs., 1997—. Cons. Spanish Speaking Mental Health Rsch. Ctr., L.A., 1974-88; cons., reviewer NIMH, 1977-2000; guest lectr. U. Nacional Autonoma de Mexico, Mexico City, 1985, Tulane U. Sch. Medicine, 1985. Author: (with J. Yamamoto and L. Evans) Effective Psychotherapy for Low-Income and Minority Patients, 1982 (Behavioral Sci. Book Club selection 1983); mem. editorial bd. Hispanic Jour. Behavioral Scis., 1981-85; contbr. chpts. to books, articles to profl. jours. Cons. Nat. Coalition Hispanic Mental Health and Human Svcs. Orgns., Washington, 1976—88; mem. psychol. rev. panel med. svcs. and occupl. health and safety divsns. pers. dept. City of L.A., 1986—93; asst. scoutmaster troop com. mem.troop 31 Boy Scouts Am., 1994—2003; chair NRC evaln. panel psychology Ford Found. Doctoral Fellowships Minorities Program, Washington, 1986—89. Rsch. grantee Social Sci. Rsch. Coun., L.A., 1976, NIMH, 1977-84; Ford Found. postdoctoral minorities fellow NRC, 1984; recipient faculty rsch. prize, dept. psychiatry U. So. Calif. Sch. Medicine, 1977; disting. scholar profl. devel. program U. Calif., Berkeley, 1985. Fellow APA (mem. accreditation com. 1977-80), Am. Assn. for Applied and Preventive Psychology; mem. Western Psychol. Assn., Calif. Psychol. Assn., Los Angeles County Psychol. Assn., Alpha Sigma Nu. Office: Dept Psychiat U So Calif Keck Sch Medicine IRD Bldg 2020 Zonal Ave Los Angeles CA 90089-0121

ACREE, WILMA KATHERYN, retired secondary school educator; b. Ripley, W.Va., July 16, 1942; d. Mote Jackson and Emma Roseanne (McHenry) Stanley; m. Frank H. Acree Sr., Sept. 26, 1975 (dec. Oct. 1990). BA in Edn., Glenville State Coll., 1965; MA in Edn., W.Va. U., 1971. Tchr. English Wood County Schs., Parkersburg, W.Va., 1965-97, ret., 1997. Adj. faculty mem. W.Va. U., Parkersburg, 1999—; presenter workshop W.Va. Writers' Conf., Ripley, 1995, 96. Author: About Bee Robbing and Other Things, 1995, Wilma Acree: Greatest Hits 1985-2000, 2001; contbr. poems in lit. publs.; editor children's poetry Gambit Lit. Mag., Parkersburg, W.Va., 1986. Citizen rep. Jackson Jr. H.S. Local Sch. Improvement Assn., Vienna, W.Va., 1997-2000; advisor Jackson Jr. H.S. Writers' Club, 1995-99; mem. adv. bd. Confluence lit. mag., Marietta (Ohio) Coll., 1996—, editor, 2000—. Mem. W.Va. Writers, Inc. (pres. 1997-99, 3rd pl. narrative poetry 1991), Ohio Valley Lit. Group (exec. dir. 1993—), Wood County Ret. Tchrs. Assn. Avocations: writing, reading, walking, dogs, computers. Home: 1024 28th St Vienna WV 26105-1475 E-mail: wilmaacree@charter.net.

ACUÑA-REYES, RITA, foreign language educator; b. Tantara, Peru, May 29, 1946; came to U.S., 1971; d. Teófilo Acuña and Juana Rosa Rojas; m. Robert Reyes. BA, Ctrl. U., Huancayo, Peru, 1967; MA, CCNY, 1977; PhD, Fordham U., 1987; postgrad., U. Nacional de Edn., Lima, Peru, 1968-71, Internat. Lang. Inst., Washington, 1973, Pan-Am. Schs., N.Y.C., 1976. Cert. bilingual supr., fgn. lang. tchr., elem. tchr. K-6. 4th grade tchr. Andino Elem. Sch., Huancayo, 1965-66; kindergarden and 1st grade tchr. Colegio Particular Maria Auxiliadora, Huancayo, 1967-68; tchr. history, geography, child psychology Escuela Secundaria Huancayo, Huancayo, 1969-71; tchr. Spanish and reading Pub. Schs. #57, N.Y.C., 1985-87; bilingual coord. and Spanish tchr. Graphic Comm. Arts H.S., N.Y.C., 1985-90; tchr. Spanish Martin Luther King Jr. H.S., N.Y.C., 1991-94; tchr. trainer N.Y.C., 1995—; tchr. Spanish Bayside H.S., Queens, N.Y., 1995—. Lectr. in field; adj. prof. Hunter Coll., N.Y.C., 1988—, Fordham U., 1984—; adult edn. tchr. conversational Spanish to tchrs. Graphic Comm. Arts H.S., Winter 1987; TESOL, Pan Am. Schs., 1980-86, tchr. ESL, 1979, others; coord. instructional workshops, lectr. Contbr. articles to profl. jours. Mem. Dist. 30 Adv. Com., Queens, bilingual edn. adv. com.; v.p. rsch. and pubs. The Latino Children's Ednl. Network, 1991—; mem. Hispanic Civic Assn. of N.Y., Inc. Recipient Plaque as Outstanding Tchr., Hispanic Assn. Journalists of N.Y.C., 1988, Tchr. of Yr. award Graphic Comm. Arts H.S., 1987; U.S. Dept. Edn. Office of Bilingual Edn. and Minority Lang. Affairs fellow, 1981. Mem. N.Y. State Assn. Bilingual Edn. (del.-at-large 1991—, regional rep. 1989-91, Tchr. of the Yr. 1989), Nat. Coun. Adminstrv. Women in Edn., Printing Tchrs. Guild of N.Y., N.Y. Assn. Fgn. Lang. Tchrs., N.Y. Assn. Tchrs. Spanish and Portuguese, Teaching English to Speakers of Other Langs. Democrat. Roman Catholic. Avocations: reading, writing. Home: 82-43 234th St Queens Village NY 11427

ADA, ALMA FLOR, education educator, writer; b. Camagüey, Cuba, Jan. 3, 1938; came to U.S., 1970; d. Modesto Arturo Ada and Alma Lafuente; children: Rosalma, Alfonso, Miguel, Gabriel Zubizarreta. Diploma in Spanish studies, U. Complutence, Madrid, 1960; B of Humanities, U. Cath., Lima, Peru, 1963, PhD, 1965. Assoc. prof. Emory U., Atlanta, 1970-72; prof. Mercy Coll. Detroit, 1972-75; prof. Sch. Edn. U. San Francisco, 1976—. Author: The Gold Coin (Christopher award 1991), My Name is María Isabel, 1993, The Unicorn of the West, 1994, Dear Peter Rabbit, 1994, Where the Flametrees Bloom, 1995, Gathering the Sun, 1997, Under the Royal Palms, 1998 (Pura Belpré award 2000), The Lizard and the Sun, 1997, The Malachite Palace, 1998, Yours Truly, Goldilocks, 2002, Three Golden Oranges, 1999, Friend Frog, 2000, With Love, Little Red Hen, 2003, I Love Saturdays...y domingos, 2003, A pesar del amor, 2003, A Magical Encounter: Latino Children's Literature in the Classroom, 2003; co-author: Authors in the Classroom. A Transformative Education Experience, 2003. Recipient Ann. award L.A. Bilingual Dirs. Assn., 1993, Calif. State PTA Assn., Simon Weisenthal Mus. of Tolerance award, 1998, Gold medal Parenting Mag., 1998, Purá Belpré, 2000; Fulbright scholar, 1966-68. Mem. Internat. Bd. Books for Young People, Nat. Assn. for Bilingual Edn., Calif. Assn. for Bilingual Edn. Home: 1459 18th St # 138 San Francisco CA 94107-2801 Office: U San Francisco Ignatian Heights San Francisco CA 94117

ADAMANY, DAVID WALTER, law and political science educator; b. Janesville, Wis., Sept. 23, 1936; s. Walter Joseph and Dora Marie (Mutter) Adamany. AB, Harvard U., 1958, JD, 1961; MS, U. Wis., 1963, PhD in Polit. Sci., 1967; LLD (hon.), Adrian Coll., 1984; AAS (hon.), Schoolcraft Coll., 1986; D. Engring. (hon.), Mich. Tech. U., 1987; D in Pub. Svc. (hon.), Eastern Mich. U., 1997. Bar: Wis. 1961. Spl. asst. to atty. gen. State of Wis., Madison, 1961—63, exec. pardon counsel, 1963; commr. Wis. Pub. Svc. Commn., 1963—65; instr. polit. sci. Wis. State U., Whitewater, 1965—67; asst. prof., then assoc. prof. Wesleyan U., Middletown, Conn., 1967—72, dean coll., 1969—71; assoc. prof., then prof. polit. sci. U. Wis., Madison, 1972—77; v.p. acad. affairs, prof. Calif. State U., Long Beach, 1977—80, U. Md., College Park, 1980—82; disting. prof. law and polit. sci. Wayne State U., Detroit, 1982—2000, pres., 1982—97, pres. emeritus, 1997; CEO Detroit Pub. Schs., 1999—2000; pres. Temple U., Phila., 2000—, Laura Carnall prof. law and polit. sci. Chmn. Wis. Coun. Criminal Justice, 1973—75, Wis. Elections Bd., 1976—77; sec. Wis. Dept. Revenue, 1973—75. Author: Financing Politics, 1969, Campaign Finance in America, 1972; co-author: Borzoi Reader in American Politics, 1972, American Government: Democracy and Liberty in Balance, 1975, Political Money, 1975; editl. bd.: Social Sci. Quarterly, 1973—, State and Local Govt. Rev., 1974—80; contbr. articles to profl. jours. Mem. exec. com. Detroit Med. Ctr., 1982—97; chmn. Mich. Bicentennial of U.S. Constrn. Commn., 1986—88; mem. Mich. Civil Svc. Commn., 1996—99; bd. dirs. Greater Phila. First, 2001—, African Am. Mus. Phila., 2001—; mem. Wis. Gov.'s Commn. on Campaign Fin. Reform, 1996—97; bd. dirs. Detroit Inst. Arts Founders Soc., 1983—92, Detroit Symphony Orch., 1983—89, Detroit Econ. Growth Corp., 1984—92, Karmanos Cancer Inst., 1982—97, New Detroit, 1982—95, Blue Cross Blue Shield Found. Mich., 1995—2000, Gilmour Fund, 1996—, HOPE Fund of Cmty. Found. of S.E. Mich., 1995—2000. Mem.: ABA (commn. on coll. and univ. legal studies 1992—95), ACLU, Pres.'s Coun. State Univs. (chmn. 1982—97), Am. Polit. Sci. Assn., Wis. Bar Assn., Greater Phila. C of C (exec. com. 2000—), Nat. Adv. Com. on Instl. Quality and Integrity (U.S. dept. edn. 1994—2000), Can.-U.S. Fulbright Commn. (bd. dirs. 1993—97). Democrat. Office: Temple U Rm 200 Sullivan Hall 1330 W Berks Street Philadelphia PA 19122-6087

ADAMO, JOSEPH FRANCIS, management educator; b. Syracuse, N.Y., Sept. 4, 1954; s. James F. and Monica M. (Catenzaro) A. BS, Oswego (N.Y.) State U., 1976; MS, Chapman U., 1988; PhD, Syracuse U., 1996. Prof. Cazenovia Coll., Cazenovia, NY, 1979—. Home: 5769 Innsbruck Rd East Syracuse NY 13057-3057 Office: Cazenovia Coll Dept Mgmt Cazenovia NY 13035 E-mail: jadamo@cazenovia.edu.

ADAMS, ALFRED HUGH, retired college president; b. Punta Gorda, Fla., Mar. 8, 1928; s. Alfred and Irene (Gatewood) A.; m. Joyce Morgan, Nov. 10, 1954; children: Joy, Al, Paul; m. Lynda K. Long, Apr. 20, 1999. AA, U. Fla., 1948; BS, Fla. State U., 1950, MS, 1956, Ed.D., 1962; L.H.D., Fla. Atlantic U., 1972. Asst. coach varsity football Fla. State U., 1955-58, asst. dir. housing, instr. edn., 1958-62, asst. dean men, asst. prof. edn., 1962-64; supt. pub. instrn. Charlotte County, Fla., 1965-68; pres. Broward Community Coll., Ft. Lauderdale, Fla., 1968-87; exec. dir. Performing Arts Ctr. Authority, Ft. Lauderdale, 1987-88; pres. Broward Performing Arts Found., Ft. Lauderdale, 1990-91. Bd. dirs. Am. Council on Edn.; vis. lectr. in higher edn. Inst. Higher Edn., U. Fla.; also mem. com. on internat. edn. relations, com. on mil-higher edn. relations; mem. adv. com. Inst. Internat. Edn.; dir. Sun Bank/South Fla., N.A.; Vice chmn. Gov. Fla. Commn. Quality Edn., 1968-70; mem. Gov.'s Adv. Com. Edn., 1966-70; mem. regional council Southeastern Edn. Corp., 1966-69; mem. commn. adminstrv. affairs Am. Council on Edn., 1973; pres. Pub. Instns. Higher Learning in So. States, 1975; mem. adv. com. Joint Council on Econ. Edn.; chmn. AACJC Internat./Intercultural Consortium, S.E. Fla. Ednl. Consortium; chmn. council pres. Fla. Community Colls.; Trustee South Fla. Edn. Center, Pub. Service TV Mem. editorial bd., Soc. for Coll. and Univ. Planning. Pres. United Way, 1973; bd. dirs. local chpt. ARC, 1971; bd. dirs. Opera Guild, Ft. Lauderdale, pres., 1983-85; bd. dirs. Coll. Consortium Internat. Studies; exec. dir. Performing Arts Ctr. Authority, Ft. Lauderdale; pres. Broward

Performing Arts Found., Ft. Lauderdale. Served to comdr. USNR, 1945-46, 52-55. Decorated knight Internat. Constantinian Order, 1971; recipient Liberty Bell award, 1975, Patriot award Freedoms Found., Disting. Alumnus award Fla. State U., A. Hugh Adams Coll. Gold Key. cert. of recognition Fla. Ho. of Reps., Disting Omicron Delta Kappa Alumnus of Yr., 1987; named Patriot Fla. Bicentennial Commn., Fla. State U. Sports Hall of Fame. Mem. Fla. Tchr. Edn. Adv. Council, Fla. Edn. Council Ethics Com. Sch. Adminstrs., Am. Assn. Sch. Adminstrs., Ft. Lauderdale C. of C. (v.p.), Profl. Practices Commn., Fla. Assn. Colls. and Univs. (pres. 1975), Naval Res. Assn., Res. Officers Assn., U.S. Naval Inst. (life), Broward Minutemen (pres.), Fla. Inter-agy. Law Enforcement Planning Council, Omicron Delta Kappa, Phi Theta Kappa. Clubs: Gulfstream Sailing, Fort Lauderdale; Tower (gov. 1985-86). Lodges: Kiwanis. Methodist. Home: 16723 Seagull Bay Ct Bokeelia FL 33922-1554

ADAMS, ARVIL VAN, economist, educator; b. Cape Girardeau, Mo., Jan. 31, 1943; s. Arvil V. and Evelyn G. (Liles) A.; m. Mary Benn Ammerman, May 26, 1968; children: Gregory Edwards, Christopher Conner, Cynthia Liles. Student, William Jewell Coll., 1961-63; BA, Memphis State U., 1965, MBA, 1966; MA, U. Ky., 1968, PhD, 1970. Asst. prof. U. Ky., Lexington, 1970-72, Ohio State U., Columbus, Ohio, 1972-73, rsch. assoc., 1972-74; prof., assoc. dir. Human Resources Inst. U. Utah, Salt Lake City, 1974-77; exec. dir. Nat. Commn. on Employment and Unemployment Statis., Washington, 1977-79; prof., dir. Grad. Inst. George Washington U., Washington, 1979-89; sr. adv. The World Bank, Washington, 1989—. Author: Lingering Crisis of Youth Employment, 1978; co-author: Skills for Productivity, 1993, Skills Develop. in Sub-Saharan Africa, 2003; contbr. articles over 50 to profl. jours. Vice chmn. bd. trustees Bluefield (Va.) Coll., 1987-2001; mem. officer various civic orgns. Mem. Am. Econ. Assn. Democrat. Baptist. Home: 6431 Eastleigh Ct Springfield VA 22152-2425 Office: The World Bank 1818 H St NW Ste J10-067 Washington DC 20433-0001

ADAMS, BARBARA, English language educator, poet, writer; b. N.Y.C., Mar. 23, 1932; d. David S. Block and Helen (Taxter) Block Tyler; m. Elwood Adams, June 6, 1952; (dec. 1993); children: Steven, Amy, Anne, Samuel. BS, SUNY, New Paltz, 1962, MA, 1970; PhD, NYU, 1981. Prof. English Pace U., N.Y.C., 1984-2000, dir. bus. comm., 1984-2001. Poet in residence Cape Cod Writers' Conf., 1988. Author: Double Solitaire, 1982, The Enemy Self: The Poetry & Criticism of Laura Riding, 1990, Hapax Legomena, 1990, Negative Capability, 1999 (1st Prize for Fiction), (play) God's Lioness and the Crow: Sylvia Plath and Ted Hughes, 2000; contbr. poems, stories, articles to various mags. and jours. Recipient 1st prize for poetry NYU and Acad. Am. Poets, 1975, 1st prize for fiction Negative Capability contest, 1999; Penfield fellow NYU, 1977. Mem. PEN, Poetry Soc. Am., Poets and Writers. Home: 59 Coach Ln Newburgh NY 12550-3818

ADAMS, BERNARD SCHRODER, retired college president; b. Lancaster, Pa., July 20, 1928; s. Martin Ray and Charlotte (Schroder) A.; m. Natalie Virginia Stout, June 2, 1951; children: Deborah Rowland, David Schroder. BA, Princeton, 1950; MA, Yale, 1951; PhD, U. Pitts., 1964; LL.D. (hon.), Lawrence U., 1967; cert., Inst. for Ednl. Mgmt., Harvard U., 1975. Asst. dir. admissions, instr. English Princeton, 1953-57; dir. admissions and student aid U. Pitts., 1957-60, spl. asst. to chancellor, 1960-64; dean students, lectr. English Oberlin (Ohio) Coll., 1964-66; pres. Ripon (Wis.) Coll., 1966-85, Ft. Lewis Coll., Colo., 1985-87; ednl. cons. pvt. practice, Colo. Springs, 1987-88; v.p. resources Goodwill Industries, Colorado Springs, Colo., 1988-96. Dir. Wis. Power & Light Co., Newton Funds, 1970-85; cons., examiner Commn. on Instns. Higher Edn., North Cen. Assn. Colls. and Secondary Schs., 1972-87, exec. commr., 1981-86; bd. dirs. Four Corners Opera Assn., 1985-87, pres., 1986-87. Contbr. articles to profl. jours. Bd. dirs. Keep Colorado Springs Beautiful, 1990—99; bd. dirs. Colo. chpt. Nat. Assn. Fundraising Execs., 1990—94; bd. dirs. Colorado Springs Symphony Vols., 1992—98, 2000—, Ctr. Prevention Domestic Violence, 1995—2001. 1st lt. USAF, 1951—53. Woodrow Wilson fellow, 1951 Mem. Assoc. Colls. Midwest (bd. dirs. 1966-85, pres. 1973-75), Wis. Assn. Ind. Colls. and Univs. (bd. dirs. 1966-85, pres. 1969-71, 83-85). Home: 90 Ellsworth St Colorado Springs CO 80906-7954

ADAMS, (ALFRED) BIRK, biochemistry educator, nutritionist; b. Steubenville, Ohio, Jan. 16, 1934; s. John Newmeyer and Lois Madden (White) A.; m. Jeanne Ann Ewing, Aug. 7, 1960; 1 child, William Birk. BS, Bethany Coll., 1955; MS, Mich. State U., 1959; PhD, Ohio State U., 1966. Rsch. instr. Coll. Dentistry Ohio State U., Columbus, 1959-64; rsch. assoc. Mich. State U., East Lansing, 1965-68; asst. prof. Coll. Dentistry U. Nebr., Lincoln, 1968-73, assoc. prof. biochemistry, 1973-99, ret., 1999, assoc. prof. emeritus, 1999—. Chair bd. dirs. Crestwood Christian Ch., Lincoln, 1989-91, 2000-02. With U.S. Army, 1956-58. Mem. AAAS, Assn. Psychol. Type (chpt. coord. 1987-91), Am. Assn. Oral Biologists, Am. Assn. Dental Schs. (sect. officer 1987-89). Home: 7200 S Wedgewood Dr Lincoln NE 68510-4265

ADAMS, CATHERINE HORN, secondary school educator; b. Morristown, N.J., Sept. 29, 1952; d. Fred Ernest and Mary Dolores (Anderson) Horn; m. Michael Wayne Adams, July 12, 1980; children: Rebecca, Daniel. AA, County Coll. Morris, Randolph, N.J., 1972; BA, Montclair State Coll., Upper Montclair, N.J., 1976; MEd, DeSales U., 2003. Elem. tchr. St. Mary's Sch., Bordentown, N.J., 1976; tchr. math. Passaic County Tech. and Vocat. High Sch., Wayne, N.J., 1976—. Mem. Nat. Coun. Tchrs. Math., Assn. Math. Tchrs. N.J. Home: 84 Vreeland Rd West Milford NJ 07480-2937

ADAMS, CRAIG DAVID, environmental engineering educator; b. St. Paul, Minn., Apr. 25, 1958; married; 4 children. BS in Chem. Engring., U. Kans., 1983, MS in Environ. Engring., 1988, PhD, 1991. Registered profl. engr., Kans. Product devel. engr. Optical Coating Lab., Inc., Santa Rosa, Calif., 1983-87; grad. rsch. asst. Dept. Environ. Engring. U. Kans., Lawrence, 1987-91; asst. prof. environ. sys. engring. Clemson (S.C.) U., 1991-95; John & Susan Mathers prof. environ. engring. U. Mo., Rolla, 1995—, assoc. prof. civil engring., 1995—. Dir. environ. rsch. ctr. U. Mo., 1995—, sr. investigator Ctr. Environ. Sci. & Tech., 1995—; cons. in field, 1993—. Contbr. articles to profl. jours. Recipient Young Investigator award NSF, Arlington, Va., 1992-97. Mem. AIChE, Am. Water Works Assn., Am. Soc. Civil Engring., Internt. Water Assn., Internat. Ozone Assn. (dir., internat. bd. dirs. 1993—), Water Environment Fedn., Assn. Environ. Engring. Profs. (membership com. 1991—), Tau Beta Pi (life), Chi Epsilon. Achievements include development of products and technology related to environmental chemistry, oxidation and sveption processes for air, water, wastewater and hazardous waste treatment, occurrance and control of antibiotics and endocrine disrupting compounds. Office: Univ Mo Rolla Dept Civil Arch & Environ Engring 220 Butler Carlton Hall Rolla MO 65409-0001

ADAMS, CYNTHIA ANN, librarian, media specialist, writing instructor; b. Thomaston, Ga., Nov. 27, 1942; d. Emory Ellis and Marian (Moseley) A. AB, Mercer U., 1964; MEd, U. Ga., 1972; EdS, Ga. State U., 1994. Cert. English tchr., career libr. media specialist, Ga. Libr. media specialist Walton County Bd. Edn., Monroe, Ga., 1972-74, Madison County Bd. Edn., Danielsville, Ga., 1974-80; tchr. English, libr. media specialist Westwood Bd. Trustees, Thomaston, 1981-82; libr. media specialist Harris County Bd. Edn., Hamilton, Ga., 1983—97; instr. writing, asst. computer lab. Gordon Coll., Barnesville, Ga., 1997—. Book reviewer Sch. Libr. Jour., 1973-74; contbr. poetry to anthologies; crafts accepted and displayed Nat. Mus. Women in the Arts, Washington. Mem. visual arts com. Thomaston Upson Arts Coun.; vol. Am. Heart Assn. Grad. study scholar. Mem. Kappa Delta Pi. Home: 630 S Center St Thomaston GA 30286-4133 Office: Gordon Coll 419 Coll Dr Barnesville GA 30204 E-mail: C_Adams@gdn.edu.

ADAMS, DARLENE AGNES, secondary education educator; b. Prague, Okla., Aug. 23, 1952; d. Carney and Bertha Ellen (Capps) A. AS, Murray State Coll., 1972; BA, East Ctrl. State Coll., 1974, MEd, 1978. Cert. libr. media specialist. Tchr., libr. Carney Pub. Schs., 1974-75, Paden (Okla.) Pub. Schs., 1975—2003. Staff devel com. Paden Pub. Schs., 1985-90, curriculum guidelines com., 1985—, career counseling com., 1990—, gifted and talented com., 1993—, sponsor jr. and sr. class plays and proms. Pres. The Chem. People, Paden, 1983—; sponsor Beta Club, 1990-91, 95-96. Mem. ALA, NEA, Okla. Library Asnn., Okla. Edn. Assn., Smithsonian, Phi Theta Kappa. Republican. Pentecostal. Avocations: photography, painting, fishing, hiking, reading. Home: 300 E Kerr Mcgee Rd Paden OK 74860-9007 Office: Paden Pub Schs PO Box 370 Paden OK 74860-0370

ADAMS, F. GERARD, economist, educator; b. Apr. 28, 1929; s. Walter and Margot Adams; m. Heidi Vernon; children: Leslie, Colin, Loren, Mark. BA, U. Mich., 1949, MA, 1951, PhD, 1956. Instr. dept. econs. U. Mich., Ann Arbor, 1952—56; economist Calif. Tex. Oil Corp., N.Y.C., 1956—59; cons. economist, mgr. gen. econs. dept. Compagnie Française des Pétroles, N.Y.C. and Paris, 1959—61; mem. faculty U. Pa., Phila., 1961—98, prof. econs. and fin.; McDonald prof. Northeastern U., Boston, 1998—; Freeman Disting. prof. Johns Hopkins U., Balt., 2002. Dir. Econs. Research Unit, 1961-98, chmn. Faculty Senate, 1987-88; chmn. profl. bd. WEFA Group, Phila., 1969-91. Author: (with others) An Econometric Analysis of International Trade, 1969, (with J.R. Behrman) Econometric Models of World Agricultural Commodity Markets, 1976, Commodity Exports and Economic Development, 1982, (with L.R. Klein) Industrial Policies for Growth and Competitiveness, 1983, The Business Forecasting Revolution, 1986; editor: (with S.A. Klein) Stabilizing World Commodity Markets - Analysis, Practice and Policy, 1978, The Macroeconomic Dimensions of Arm Reduction, 1992, Economic Activity, Trade and Industry in the U.S.-Japan-World Economy, 1993, East Asian Development: Will the Miracle Survive?, 1998; Public Policies in East Asian Development: Facing New Challenges, 1999, Macroeconomics for Business and Society, 2002, The E-Business Revolution and the New Economy,2003. Home: 39 Stafford Rd Newton Center MA 02459-1818 E-mail: adams@ssc.upenn.edu., f.adams@neu.edu.

ADAMS, FRANK, education specialist; b. Cleve., Sept. 11, 1948; s. Frank Albin and Helen (Coleman) Kovacevic. BS in Bus. Adminstrn., Bowling Green (Ohio) State U., 1970, MEd in Phys. Edn., 1978. Tech. writer Soldier Phys. Fitness Sch., Ft. Ben Harrison, Ind., 1983-85; edn. specialist Directorate of Tng. and Doctrine, Ft. Huachuca, Ariz., 1985-90, Dept. Tactics Intelligence Mil. Sci., Ft. Huachuca, 1990-93, 111th Mil. Intelligence Brigade, Ft. Huachuca, 1993-97; staff 112th Mil. Intelligence Brig. U.S. Army Intelligence Ctr., 1998—2003, staff, faculty devel. divsn., 2003—. Mem. steering com. tng. and doctrine command, staff and faculty devel. divsn., El Paso, Tex., 1987. Co-author: (field manual) Physical Fitness Training, 1984, (Internet site) Total Fitness; contbr. articles to profl. jours. and local newspapers. Recipient Civilian Achievement medal Dept. Army, Ft. Huachuca 1993, Comdr.'s award, 1995, 2003, Superior Civilian Svc. award, 1999. Mem. AAHPERD (life), Mil. Intelligence Corp. Avocations: internal martial arts, reading, reiki master-teacher. Home: 4838 Corte Vista Sierra Vista AZ 85635-5738 Office: Tng Devel & Support 112th Mil Intelligence Brig Fort Huachuca AZ 85613-6000

ADAMS, GAIL JACKSON, educational administrator; b. Balt., Dec. 22, 1946; d. Eugene and Mary S. (Wright) Jackson; m. Matthew Jerome Adams, June 27, 1970. BS, Coppin State Coll., Balt., 1969; MS, Morgan State U., Balt., 1974. Cert. advanced profl. tchr., Md. Sr. tchr., early childhood specialist, support tchr. Balt. City Pub. Schs., asst. prin. Supervising mentor for project site support urban tchr. edn. program U. Md. Baltimore County. Mem. ASCD, NASAP, Phi Delta Kappa. Home: 522 S Beechfield Ave Baltimore MD 21229-4326

ADAMS, JEANETTE BROWN, educational association administrator; b. MAcon, Miss., Oct. 28, 1941; d. Robert Earl and Verna Virginia (McBride) Brown; m. Jimmy Adams, June 4, 1961; children: Melanie Farmer, Angie. BS, Livingston U., 1972, MAT in English, 1982, MSED in K-12 Principalship, 1987. Tchr. English, guidance Patrician Acad., Butler, Ala., 1971-80; instr. English Livingston (Ala.) U., 1980-84; adminstr. Patrician Acad., 1984—. Cons. So. Assn. Colls. and Schs., Tuscaloosa, Ala., 1992; mem. accreditation team Ala. Ind. Sch., Montgomery (Ala.), 1985. Chair, v.p. curriculum Leadership Choctaw, Butler, 1993—; bd. found. bd. Ala. So. C.C., 1990-92. Recipient Achievement award U. West Ala. Coll. Edn., 1995. Mem. AISA (exec. bd. dirs. 1985—, pres., v.p., headmaster assoc. 1987-88), SAIA, AAIS, Vision 2020 S.W. Ala. (charter), Choctaw County C. of C., Delta Kappa Gamma (chair profl. affairs 1994-96, pres. 1998—, Choctaw County Beta Alpha Woman of Achievement 1999), Phi Delta Kappa (pres. 1992-93, v.p. 1993-94), U. West Ala. Alumni Assn., Blue Key Soc. Baptist. Avocations: organ, family.

ADAMS, JOSEPH BRIAN, operations research engineer, mathematics and computer science educator; b. Lancaster, Pa., Apr. 23, 1961; s. Laurence John and Ann (Onufrak) A. BS in Nuclear Engring., Pa. State U., 1983, M in Engring. Sci., 1987; M of Mech. Engring., U. Del., 1996, PhD in Ops. Rsch., 1997. Registered profl. engr., Pa. Radiol. engr. Phila. Electric Co., 1983-88; instr. math. U. Del., Newark, 1988-91; pres. J.B. Adams & Assocs., Lancaster, Pa., 1993—; asst. prof. math. scis. Lebanon Valley Coll., Annville, Pa., 1997-00. Lectr. math. and engring. Widener U., Chester, Pa., 1987-91; adj. prof. math., stats. and engring. Pa. State U., 1992-2001; lectr. in ops. rsch. U. Del., 1996; asst. prof. math. and computer sci. Franklin & Marshall Coll., Lancaster, Pa., 2000—. Mem. AAUP, Math. Assn. Am., Informs, Aircraft Owners and Pilots Assn. Roman Catholic. Home: 23 Ramsgate Ln Lancaster PA 17603-5975 Office: Franklin and Marshall Coll Dept Math PO Box 3003 Lancaster PA 17604-3003

ADAMS, LAVONNE MARILYN BECK, critical care nurse, nursing educator; b. Bridgeport, Conn., Feb. 22, 1965; d. Adolf and Hazel B. (Henderson) Beck. ASN, Kettering Coll. Med. Arts, 1985; BSN, Wright State U., 1988; MSN, Andrews U., 1992, PhD., 2003. CCRN. Staff nurse Kettering (Ohio) Med. Ctr., 1985-89, resource staff nurse, 1989-95, instr. in nursing, 1989-92; asst. prof. nursing Kettering (Ohio) Coll. Med. Arts, 1999—2003; assoc. prof. nursing Southwestern Adventist U., Keene, Tex., 2003—; PRN staff nurse Huguley Mem. Hosp., 2002—; assoc. prof. Southwestern Adventist U., 2003. Asst. leader kindergarten divsn. Seventh-day Adventist Ch., Kettering, 1987—93, Arlington SDA Ch., 2001—; mem. Southwestern Sem. Oratorio Chorus, 1999—. Mem.: Am. Assn. Critical Care Nurses, Nat. League Nursing, Pi Lambda Theta, Sigma Theta Tau, Phi Kappa Phi. Avocations: music, travel. Home: 7000 Welch Ct Fort Worth TX 76133-6726 Office: Southwestern Adventist Univ 100 W Magnolia Keene TX 76059

ADAMS, MARION RUTH ALLISON, special education educator; b. Boone, N.C., June 11, 1937; d. Robert Lee and Lena Ruth (Reid) Allison; m. David Thomas Greer, Sept. 10, 1959; children: David Thomas Jr., Allison Greer Neely; m. Edmund Ivan Adams, Oct. 24, 1981. BS, Appalachian State U., 1959, MA, 1989, cert. in adminstrn., 1990. Cert. tchr., N.C. Tchr. spl. edn. Alleghany County Bd. Edn., 1965—; now asst. prin. Glade Creek Elem. Sch. Mem. cub scout com. Boy Scouts Am., Alleghany County, 1992; mem. Dems. of Alleghany, 1992. Mem. NEA, N.C. Assn. Gifted and Talented, N.C. Assn. Educators (pres. Alleghany County 1989, bldg. rep. 1992), N.C. Assn. Retarded Citizens, Am. Assn. Sch. Adminstrs., Order Ea. Star (worthy matron 1970-71, dist. dep. 1980-81), Alleghany County C. of C. Methodist. Avocations: music, piano, organ, reading, hiking. Home: 405 Grayson St Sparta NC 28675-9200 Office: Glade Creek Elem Sch RR 1 Sparta NC 28675-9801

ADAMS, MICHAEL FRED, university president, political communications specialist; b. Montgomery, Ala., Mar. 25, 1948; s. Hubert W. and Jean (Taylor) A.; m. Mary Lynn Ethridge, June 7, 1969; children: David Winston, Stephen Taylor. BA, Lipscomb U., 1970; MA, Ohio State U., 1971, PhD, 1973. Asst. prof. Ohio State U., 1973-74; chief of staff for Sen. Howard Baker, Washington, 1975-79; advisor to gov. State of Tenn., Nashville, 1981-82; v.p. Pepperdine U., Malibu, Calif., 1982-88; pres. Centre Coll. Ky., Danville, 1988-97, U. Ga., Athens, 1997—. Chmn. Nat. Assn. Ind. Colls. and Univs., 1995-96, Assoc. Colls. of South; mem. coun. for advancement and support of edn. NCAA Pres. Commn., 1992-94; chmn. Commn. on Colls. of So. Assn. Colls. and Schs.; vice chmn. task force that founded Coun. for Higher Edn. Accreditation; chair Am. Coun. on Edn., 2000. Author: Rhetorical Strategies of Howard Baker, 1973; contbr. articles to various publs. Pres. Circle K Internat., Chgo., 1970; nominee for U.S. Congress, Nashville, 1980; mem. site host com. 1984 Olympiad, L.A.; elder Christian Ch. Recipient Bronze Quill award Internat. Assn. Bus. Communicators, 1986, Excellence award Nat. Sch. Pub. Relations Soc., 1985; Ohio State U. grad. fellow, 1970-73 Mem. Young Pres. Orgn., Speech Comm. Assn., Ctr. for Study of Presidency, Univ. Club (N.Y.C.), Coun. Fgn. Relations. Republican. Avocations: golf, reading, travel. Office: U Ga Adminstrn Bldg Athens GA 30602

ADAMS, NANCY CALHOUN, elementary education educator; b. Batavia, N.Y., Jan. 16, 1940; d. Arthur Charles and Lula Irene (Clark) Calhoun; m. Harold D. Adams, Nov. 6, 1959; children: Elizabeth, Bryan. BA, Roanoke Coll., Salem, Va., 1973. Cert. tchr., Va. Tchr. Roanoke County Sch. Bd., Salem, 1973—2000; ret., 2000. Mem. Roanoke County Edn. Assn. (faculty rep. 1989-91, 94-95), PTA, (life), Va. Ret. Tchrs. Assn., Roanoke County Ret. Tchrs. Lutheran. Avocations: sewing, crafts, ceramics, camping, walking.

ADAMS, PAMELA GRACE, primary school educator; b. Waukegan, Ill., Oct. 14, 1954; d. Margaret Grace (Koss) Lyons; m. Thomas Edward Adams, Feb. 12, 1977; children: Emily, Mary-Margaret, Douglas, Sarah, William. BA, Carthage Coll., Kenosha, Wis., 1990; MEd, Nat. Louis U., Evanston, Ill., 1994. Kindergarten tchr. Waukegan Sch. Dist. 60, 1991—. Clearview chairperson Waukegan Schoolathon, 1993, 94, 95, United Way, Waukegan, 1992, 93, 94, 95; leader 4-H, Waukegan, 1990—; asst. coach Park Dist. Pony Baseball, Zion, Ill., 1994. Fellow Pi Lambda Theta. Christian Ch. Avocations: piano, sewing, swimming, reading, computers. Home: 1308 20th St Zion IL 60099-1725 Office: Clearview School 1700 Delaware Rd Waukegan IL 60087-4622

ADAMS, PATRICIA MURPHY, special education educator; b. Mt. Kisco, NY, Aug. 12, 1947; d. John A. and Natalie (Coffey) Murphy; m. Gerald N. Adams, July 29, 1989; children: Frank R. Mattoni, Christopher T. Mattoni, Howard M. Adams, Melissa J. Adams. BA in Psychology, Mercy Coll., Dobbs Ferry, N.Y., 1978; MS in Reading, L.I. U., Dobbs Ferry, 1983. Cert. in elem. edn., reading, spl. edn., N.Y. Spl. edn. tchr. North Salem (N.Y.) Schs., 1980—. Bd. dirs., chair No. Westchester Tchr. Ctr., North Salem, 1982-89; tchr. critical thinking, effective teaching program N.Y. State United Tchrs., Albany, 1985-89; tchr. writing Fairfield (Conn.) U., 1985. Bd. dirs., sec. Mt. Kisco (N.Y.) Recreation Commn., 1987-89; mem. com. Mt. Kisco Meml. Day Com., 1985-89. Recipient Excellence in Tchg. award Mid-Hudson Sch. Study Coun., 1997; Coun. for Ednl. Children lending libr. grantee, 1980s; Danbury News Times/Union Carbide Learning Links grantee, 1994. Mem. Coun. for Exceptional Children, Internat. Reading Assn., Assn. for Learning Disabilities, Autism Soc. Am., Kappa Delta Pi. Democrat. Roman Catholic. Avocations: reading, writing, antiquing. Home: 117 Ives Farm Rd Brewster NY 10509 Office: Pequenakonck Elem Sch 173 June Rd North Salem NY 10560-1202

ADAMS, PHYLLIS CURL, nursing educator; b. Houston, Sept. 15, 1947; d. Kenneth H. and Helen (Phillips) Curl; m. Todd E. Adams, Aug. 28, 1982. BSN, Dillard U., 1969; MSN, Ohio State U., 1972; EdD, Tex. So. U., 1989; postmasters FNP, Tex. Woman's U., 1995. RN; cert family nurse practitioner. Charge nurse The Meth. Hosp., Houston, 1969-71, practitioner, asst. mgr., 1981—90, staff nurse, 1990—95; faculty coord. Columbus (Ohio) Tech. Inst., 1973-81; coord., asst. prof. Sch. Nursing U. Tex. Health Sci. Ctr., Houston, 1990-95, spl. asst. to pres. for Office of Campus Diversity, 1993—95; asst. prof. U. Tex. Sch. Nursing, Arlington, 1995—2001, asst. clin. prof., 2001—. FNP, Ft. Worth, 1997—2001, Cmty. Partnership of Tarrant County, Ft. Worth, 2001—; dir. FNP program U. Tex. Sch. Nursing, Arlington, 2000—. Contbr. articles to profl. jours. Mem. ANA (mem. adv. bd. ethics and human rights), Tex. Nurses Assn. (bd. dirs. 1994-95, mem. dist. 4), Minority Faculty Assn., Sickle Cell Assn. Ft. Worth (bd. dirs.), TEXGENE (mem. ethics and human rights com.), State Tex. Bd. Nursing (mem. adv. coun. on edn.), Nat. Black Orgn. Nurses, Sigma Theta Tau, Phi Delta Kappa. Avocations: frog collecting, aerobics, reading, skeet. Home: 1225 Chinkapin Pl Flower Mound TX 75028-3229 Office: U Tex-Arlington Sch Nursing PO Box 19407 411 S Nedderman Dr Arlington TX 76019 E-mail: pcadams@uta.edu.

ADAMS, RENEE BLEDSOE, retired elementary school educator; b. Louisville, Mar. 7, 1947; d. Charles Henry and Irene (Russell) Bledsoe; m. Neil Douglas Adams, Apr. 13, 1968; children: Krista Lynn, Shawnda Renee. BA, U. Ky., 1970; MA, Murray State U., 1980. Cert. rank I tchr., Ky. Tchr. 1st grade Anderson County Sch., Lawrenceburg, Ky.; tchr. sci. kindergarten through 6th grades Paducah Ind. Sch., Ky., ret. Presenter workshops on space and environ. edn., performance assessment. Publ. com. Childhood Edn. mag. Mem. NEA, Assn. Childhood Ednl. Internat. (pres. Ky. chpt. 1987-89, 92-94, pres. coun. 1998-2000), Assn. Childhood Edn. (pub. com. 1988-91), Nat. Sci. Tchr. Assn., Ky. Edn. Assn., Ky. Instrnl. Results Info. System (sci. cons. adv. com.), Ky. Ednl. Reform Act (assessment fellow), Partnership in Reform Initiative in Sci. and Math. (primary level curriculum devel. specialist), Alpha Delta Kappa, Phi Delta Kappa.

ADAMS, ROBERT MCCORMICK, anthropologist, educator; b. Chgo., July 23, 1926; s. Robert McCormick and Janet (Lawrence) Adams; m. Ruth Salzman Skinner, July 24, 1953; 1 child, Megan. PhB, U. Chgo., 1947, MA, 1952, PhD, 1956; DSc (hon.), U. Pitts., 1985, Dartmouth Coll., 1989; LHD (hon.), Hunter Coll., CUNY, 1986, Coll. William and Mary, 1989, Brandeis U., 1992; LD (hon.), Harvard U., 1992; PhD (hon.), U. Copenhagen, 2002. Archaeol. field tng. in, Jarmo, Iraq, 1950—51, 1953; field studies history irrigation and urban settlement, 1956—77; Homewood prof. dept. anthropology and near ea. studies, 1956—77, 1956—77; reconnaissance and excavation ancient Mayan settlement patterns, 1958—61; mem. faculty dept. anthropology, Oriental Inst. U. Chgo., 1955—84, assoc. prof. Oriental Inst., 1961—62, prof., 1962—84, dir. Oriental Inst., 1962—68, 1981—83, dean div. social scis., 1970—74, 1979—80, provost, 1982—84; sec. Smithsonian Instn., Washington, 1984—94; Homewood prof. dept. anthropology and near ea. studies Johns Hopkins U., 1984—94. Adj. prof. U. Calif., San Diego, 1993—; fellow Inst. for Advanced Study, Berlin, 1995—96; resident dir. Baghdad Sch., Am. Schs. Oriental Rsch., 1968—69; chmn. assembly behavioral and social scis. NRC, 1972—76, chmn. commn. on behavioral and social scis. and edn., 1987—93. Author: The Evolution of Urban Society, 1966; author: (with H.J. Nissen) The Uruk Countryside, 1972; author: Heartland of Cities, 1981, Paths of Fire: An Anthropologist's Inquiry into Western Technology, 1996; editor (with C.H. Kraeling): City Invincible: A Symposium on Urbanization and Cultural Development in the Ancient Near East, 1960; editor: (with C.S. Schelling) Corners of a Foreign Field, 1979; editor: (with N.J. Smelser and D.J. Treiman) Behavioral and Social Science Research: A National Resource, 1982; editor: Trends in

American and German Higher Education, 2002. Trustee Nat. Opinion Rsch. Ctr., 1970—94, Nat. Humanities Ctr., 1976—83, Russell Sage Found., 1978—91, Santa Fe Inst., 1984—, Am. U. Beirut, 1989—94, Morehouse Coll., 1989—94, German Am. Acad. Coun., 1993—99. Recipient UCLA medal, 1989, Great Cross of Vasco Nuñez de Balboa, Panama, 1993, Gold medal, Am. Inst. Archaeology, 2002, award of merit, Field Mus., 2003. Fellow: AAAS, Mid. East Studies Assn., Am. Acad. Arts and Scis., Iraqi Acad. (assoc.), Am. Anthrop. Assn.; mem.: NAS, Coun. Fgn. Rels., Am. Philos. Soc., German Archaeol. Inst., Soc. Am. Archaeology (Disting. Svc. award 1996), Sigma Xi. E-mail: rmadams@ucsd.edu.

ADAMS, RONALD G. middle school educator; b. Boston, July 7, 1948; s. Russell Lawrence and Alice Gertrude (LeCorn) A.; m. Patricia Marie Sullivan, Mar. 15, 1950; children: Ronald Patrick, Michael Joseph, Kevin Russell. BS, U. Mass., 1975; MEd, Cambridge Coll., 1992. Cert. tchr. English, reading, adult basic edn., Mass. Tchr. English Quincy (Mass.) Pub. Sch., 1975-81, tchr. grade 7, 1983—; tchr. grade 7/8 Lincoln (Mass.) Pub. Schs., 1981-83. Mem. adv. bd. Mass. Carnegie Coun.: Turning Points, Dept. Edn., Mass., 1991-93; founding mem. Internat. Space Educators Coun., Huntsville, Ala., 1992-93; on-air moderator PBS Annenberg documentary series Primary Sources in Teaching American History, 2001. Prodr. TV documentary Quincy Shipbuilding, 1989 (award Dept. Edn. 1990); co-author: (booklet) Not Me, I Can Handle It, 1985 (Gov.'s award 1986); cons. TV series A Century of Women, TBS, 1994 (A&E Cable award 1992). Founder Winnie the Welder Day, City of Quincy, 1991-93; coach Houghs Neck Women's Softball League, Quincy, 1980-85; vol. Cub Scouts, Weymouth, Mass., 1989-93; mem. edn. steering com. Amnesty Internat., Somerville, Mass., 1989-93; mem. adv. bd. U.S. Naval Shipbldg. Mus., Quincy, 1992-93. Recipient Nat. Ednl. award Cable in Classroom, 1992, George Washington medal Freedoms Found., 1992, Young Prodr.'s award Continental Cablevision, 1992, A World of Difference Tchr. award Anti-Defamation League, 1994, Giraffe award, Reebok Internat. Youth-in-Action Human Rights award, 1995, Minn. Advocates for Human Rights award, 1997, Domestic Partnership award US AID, 1998, Anti-defamation League's Global Activism award 1998, 99, Darryl Williams Human Rights Leadership award Northeastern U., 1999, Bearer of Light award Union of Am. Hebrew Congregations, 1999, Hero Among Us award Boston Celtics, 2000, Global Edn. award The Peace Corps, 2000; named Tchr. of Yr., Mass. Dept. Edn., 1992, Nat. Consumers League Trumpeter award, 1998, Citizen of the Yr. 2000, Quincy Sun Newspaper. Fellow Mass. Acad. Tchrs. (history coord. 1992-93), Boston Writing Project; mem. NEA (Human and Civil Rights award 2000Applegate/Dorros Peace and Global Edn. award 2000), Nat. State Tchrs. of Yr., Nat. Coun. Social Studies, Nat. Coun. Tchrs. English, Mass. Tchrs. Assn. (Human Rights award 1991), Quincy Edn. Assn. (exec. bd. 1980-81). Avocation: N.Y. Giants football. Home: 8 Coolidge Ave Weymouth MA 02188-3605 Office: Broad Meadows Middle Sch 50 Calvin Rd Quincy MA 02169-2516

ADAMS, STEWART LEE, special education educator; b. Moline, Ill., June 18, 1949; s. Robert Earl Jr and Henrietta Harriet (Jones) Adams; m. Ann Edwards, Oct. 12, 1985 (div. Nov. 1989). AA, Blackhawk Jr. Coll., Moline, Ill., 1969; BA, Ill. State U., 1971, MA, 1974, EdD, 2003. Cert. teacher elem K-9, spl. edn. K-12, educable mentally handicapped, learning disabled, behavior disabled. Spl. edn. tchr. Rock Island (Ill.)-Milan Sch. Dist. 41, 1972—; Master tchr., 1998—. Chair, vice chair Ill State Adv Coun Spec Educ, Springfield, 1984—92; Ill cong contact # 17 NEA, Washington, 1982—94; peer monitor spec educ Ill State Bd Educ, Springfield, 1992—; vpres Community Serv Options, Rock Island-Mercer County, 1994—97, pres, 1997—2002; app mem State Adv Coun Educ Children with Disabilities, 1996—99. Mem disabled transit comt Quad Cities Mass Transit Dist, Davenport, Iowa, 1993—; panel mem Gov Thompson's Educ Summits, Springfield, Ill., 1989—90. Mem.: NEA (caucus mem spec educ 1980—94), ASCD, Rock Island Educ Asn (vpres 1992—94, secy 1998—2000), Ill Educ Asn (chair region 18 1982—88, mem Ill Polit Act Comt Educ 1986—88, bd dirs, grassroots polit. activist for Region 18). Democrat. Presbyterian. Avocation: genealogy. Home: 3709 31st Ave Rock Island IL 61201-6548 E-mail: stewart.adams@mchsi.com.

ADAMS, SUSAN LOIS, music educator; b. New Albany, Ind., July 27, 1946; d. Frank Mitchell, Sr. and Dorothy Stalker Adams. BA, Smith Coll., 1968; MS in Edn., Ind. U., 1970, postgrad., 1994. Cert. tchr. Ind. Tchr. Lafayette (Ind.) Sch. Corp., 1969—70, New Albany-Floyd County Consol. Sch. Corp., 1970—. Mem. editl. com. (hymnal) Chalice Hymnal, 1995; co-editor: (hymnal companion) Chalice Hymnal Worship Leaders' Companion, 1998. Elder Ctrl. Christina Ch., New Albany, 1996—98, Ctrl. Christian Ch., New Albany, 2000—02. Recipient Honored Laywoman, Commn. Women-Ind. Region Christian Ch., 1998. Mem.: Ind. Music Educators, Music Educators Nat. Conf., Nat. Assn. Disciple Musicians (pres. 1988, chair workshop 1989, 2001). Mem. Christian Ch. (Disciples Of Christ). Avocations: travel, reading.

ADAMS, WAYNE VERDUN, pediatric psychologist, educator; b. Rhinebeck, N.Y., Feb. 24, 1945; s. John Joseph and Lorena Pearl (Munroe) A.; m. Nora Lee Swindler, June 12, 1971; children: Jennifer, Elizabeth. BA, Houghton Coll., 1966; MA, Syracuse U., 1969, PhD, 1970; postgrad., U. N.C., Chapel Hill, 1975. Hon. diplomate Am. Bd. Profl. Psychology; lic. psychologist, N.Y., Oreg. Asst. prof. Colgate U., Hamilton, N.Y., 1970-75; chief psychologist Alfred I. DuPont Inst., Wilmington, Del., 1976-86; dir. divsn. psychology, dept. pediat. DuPont Hosp. for Children (formerly Alfred I. DuPont Inst.), Wilmington, 1987-99; mem. Del. Bd. Licensure in Psychology, 1983-86, bd. pres., 1986; assoc. prof. pediat. Thomas Jefferson Coll. Medicine, Phila., 1995-99; prof. psychology George Fox U., Newberg, Oreg., 1999—, dept. chair grad. sch. clin. psychology, 2001—. Grant reviewer NIH, 1999—. Cons. editor Jour. Pediatric Psychology, 1980-83, guest reviewer, 1984—; co-author 4 nationally used psychol. tests in field; contbr. articles to profl. jours. Fellow APA, Nat. Acad. Neuropsychology; mem. Soc. Pediatric Psychology, Del. Psychol. Assn. (exec. com. 1979-82, pres. 1981-82), Oreg. Psychol. Assn. Office: George Fox U Grad Sch Clin Psychology 414 N Meridian St Newberg OR 97132-2697

ADAMS, WILLIAM D. academic administrator; b. Pontiac, Mich., Aug. 18, 1947; s. Waldemar Harmon Adams and Charlotte Elizabeth (Drea) Rising; m. Catherine Spaulding Bruce, Oct. 10, 1993; children: Sean Douglass Vallant, Carmen Milena. BA magna cum laude, The Colo. Coll., 1972; PhD, U. Calif., Santa Cruz, 1982. Vis. asst. prof. dept. polit. sci. U. N.C., Chapel Hill, 1983—84, U. Santa Clara, Calif., 1984—85; instr. great works in western culture program Stanford U., Calif., 1985—86, program coord. great works in western culture program, 1986—88; exec. asst. to pres. Wesleyan U., Middletown, Conn., 1988—93, v.p., sec., 1993—95; pres. Bucknell U., Lewisburg, Pa., 1995—2000, Colby Coll., Waterville, Maine, 2000—. Contbr. articles to profl. jours. 1st lt. U.S. Army, 1966—69. Office: Colby Coll Office of Pres 4601 Mayflower Hl Waterville ME 04901-8846 E-mail: wadams@colby.edu.

ADAMSHICK, PAMELA ZENZ, nursing educator; b. Monroe, Mich., Apr. 21, 1952; d. John Thomas and Helen (Strimbel) Zenz; m. George Adamshick, Aug. 30, 1975; children: Justin, Jacqueline. BSN cum laude, Univ. Detroit Mercy, 1974; MSN, U. Ill. Med. Ctr., Chgo., 1977; postgrad., Pa. State U., 2000—. RN, Pa. Staff nurse U. Chgo., Billings Hosp., 1974-76; instr. nursing Lewis U., Romeoville, Ill., 1978-79; clin. nurse specialist St.Jospeh Hosp., Joliet, Ill., 1979-80; asst. prof. nursing Northampton Community Coll., Bethlehem, Pa., 1988-91; instr. Sch. Nursing St. Luke's Hosp., Bethlehem, Pa., 1991—2001; asst. prof. nursing St. Luke's Sch. Nursing at Moravian Coll., Bethlehem, Pa., 2001—. Part-time staff nurse Lehigh Valley Hosp., Allentown, Pa., 1986-99; mem. mental health subcom., group facilitator for sch.-based suport and self-esteem groups Bethlehem Partnership for a Healthy Cmty. Chair BSN curriculum devel. team St. Luke's Sch. Nursing, 1995-97. Recipient M. H. Nursing Grad. fellow; St. Luke's faculty scholar, 1997. Mem.: Pa. State Nurses Assn. Dist 2 (Innovative Nursing Practice award 2000), Nat. Coun. State Bds. Nursing (computerized simulation testing com. 1996—99). Home: 972 Bridle Path Rd Allentown PA 18103-4680

ADAMSON, JANE NAN, retired elementary school educator; b. Amarillo, Tex., Feb. 5, 1931; d. Carl W. and Lydie O. (Martin) Ray (dec.); 1 child, Dave R. Student, Eastfield Coll., Amarillo Coll., Richland Coll. Univ. Dallas, U. North Tex.; BS, West Tex. A&M U., Canyon, 1953; MEd, Tex. A&M U., Commerce, 1975; diploma, Inst. Children's Lit., 1991; cert., Bur. Edn. and Rsch., 1995; PhD, Am. Coll. Metaphys. Theology, 2000. Cert. elem. tchr., Tex.; lic. real estate salesman. Tchr. Dallas Ind. Sch. Dist., ret. Avocations: music, traveling, decorating, writing, dog training.

ADAMS-PASSEY, SUELLEN S. elementary education educator; b. Cin. d. Raymond J. and Thelma P. (Munk)Sweany; m. Douglas Passey ; children; Amy, Jacqueline, James, Sarah, Kristina, Zoya. BS in Edn., Kent State U. Cert. elem. tchr., Wash. Tchr. 4th and 5th grades Chgo. Jr. Sch., Elgin, Ill.; gen. dir., program developer Courtyard Theatre, Edmonds, Wash.; tchr. 4th grade Edmonds (Wash.) Dist. 15; tchr. 4th, 5th and 6th grades combination class Martha Lake Elem. Sch., Lynnwood, Wash. Bd. dirs. Pub. Edn. Fund for Dist. 15, 1985-87; pres. Seattle Storytellers Guild, 1985-88; bd. dirs. Seattle Folklore Soc. 1998-, founder and chair, concert com. 1988-2002, dir. Crackerbarrel Mornings, 1982-87, co-chair, student subsidy program, 1998-2000, Seattle Opera Guild.

ADASKO, MARY HARDY, speech pathologist; b. Miss., Jan. 6, 1920; d. B.F. and Margaret Elizabeth (Walker) Hardy; m. Herbert I. Adasko, Sept. 21, 1944; children: H. Hardy, Laura A. Lenzner. BA, CUNY, 1969, MS, 1976. Berard cert. in Auditory Integration Tng. Tchr. speech improvement Day Elem. Schs., N.Y.C. Bd. Edn., 1972-92; pvt. practice speech/lang. cons. N.Y.C., from 1992. V.p. United Parents Assn., N.Y.C., 1960-64; pres. Madison High Sch. Parent Assn., 1962-64. Mem. Am. Speech-Hearing-Lang. Assn. (clin. competence cert./speech lang.), N.Y. State Speech-Hearing-Lang. Assn. (lic. speech lang. pathologist N.Y. state), N.Y.C. Speech-Hearing-Lang. Assn. (officer), Coun. for Exceptional Children, Bi-lingual Lang.-Speech-Hearing Assn., N.Y. Acad. Sci., Autism Rsch. Rev. Internat., Children and Adults with Attention Deficit Disorder, Autism Soc. Am., Soc. Auditory Integration Tng., Am. Tinnitus Assn., Orton Duslexic Soc. (del. and presenter Conf. on Exceptionality, Beijing 1995, South Africa 1996). Avocations: traveling, gardening. Home: Brooklyn, NY. Died July 29, 2000.

ADATO, LINDA JOY, artist, educator; b. London, Oct. 24, 1942; d. John and Renee (Katz) Falber; m. Albert Adato, June 26, 1966; 1 child, Vanessa. Student, Hornsey (Eng.) Coll. of Art, 1960-61; BA in Pictorial Arts, UCLA, 1966, MA in Art Edn., 1967. Adj. lectr. in art Manhattanville Coll., Purchase, NY, 1987—2000; printmaking tchr. Silvermine Sch. of Art, New Canaan, Conn., 1995—. Exhibitions include Achenbach Found. for Graphic Arts, Fine Arts Mus., San Francisco, 1987, Decordova Mus., Lincoln, Mass., 1990, Portland (Oreg.) Art Mus., 1994, Art Complex Mus., Duxbury, Mass., 1994, Newark Pub. Libr., 1994, Housatonic Mus. Art, Bridgeport, Conn., 1998, Old Print Shop, N.Y.C., 1998, 2002, De Cordova Mus., Lincoln, Mass., 1998-99; mem. travelling exhbn. Am. Print Alliance, 1998—. Recipient anonymous prize for prints NAD, 1990, Karlene Cusick Purchase award Print Club Albany, 1995; William Meyerowitz Meml. award Audubon Artists, 1996, Atlantic Papers award 1997; purchase award Internat. Miniature Print Exhibit, Conn. Graphic Arts Ctr., 1997, Alice Pauline Schafer Meml. purchase award Print Club, Albany, 1998, Gold medal of Honor Audubon Artists, 2000, Ralph Fabri medal of Merit Audubon Artists, 2002. Mem. Soc. Am. Graphic Artists (treas. 1995-2002, purchase award 1985). Home: 20 Pratt St New Rochelle NY 10801-4314

ADCOCK, MURIEL W. special education educator; b. Chgo. BA, U. Calif. Sonoma State, Rohnert Park, 1979. Cert. spl. edn. tchr., Calif., Montessori spl. edn. tchr. Tchr. The Concordia Sch., Concord, Calif., 1980-85; tchr., cons. Tenderloin Community Children's Ctr., San Francisco, 1985-86; adminstr. Assn. Montessori Internat.-USA, San Francisco, 1988, tchr., advisor, 1989—. Course asst. Montessori Spl. Edn. Inst., San Francisco, 1985-87, tchr. spl. edn., 1990, tchr. cons., 1991—, rschr. 1992—. Contbr. articles to profl. jour. Sec. Internat. Forum World Affairs Coun., San Francisco, 1990-95, program chair, 1993-95, pres./founder Club of Budapest, U.S., 2000—. Mem. ASCD, Am. Orthopsychiat. Assn., Internat. Soc. Sys. Scientists, Internat. Sys. Inst., Assn. Montessori Internat., N.Am. Montessori Tchrs. Assn., Assn. Childhood Edn. Internat., Smithsonian Assocs., N.Y. Acad. Scis., Internat. Sys. Inst. Avocations: general evolutionary systems theory, sustainable development, educational systems design, ethical leadership. Office: 4040 Civic Center Dr Ste 200 San Rafael CA 94903

ADDICOTT, BEVERLY JEANNE, retired elementary school educator; b. Youngstown, Ohio, Nov. 9, 1948; m. Gerald Leslie Addicott, Mar. 30, 1974; 1 child, Katherine Elizabeth. BS in Edn., Youngstown State U., 1971, cert. media specialist, 1978; cert. in ESL, 1995. Cert. tchr., Ohio, Fla. Tchr. Mathews Sch. Dist., Vienna, Ohio, 1972-75, media specialist, 1975-78, supr. media, 1978-79; media specialist Brevard County Schs., Melbourne, Fla., 1987-91, tchr., 1991—2000. Chef du jour Haven for Children, Melbourne, 1989-94; vol. Habitat for humanity, Melbourne, 1993, University Park PTO, Melbourne, 1989-2000. Mem. Melbourne Alumnae Panhellenic (chair fundraiser 1992), Jr. League of South Brevard (parent educator 1992-95). Avocations: cross-stitch, knitting, crocheting.

ADDIS, MARGUERITE CHRISTJOHN (CHRIS ADDIS), physical therapist; b. Pitts., Sept. 14, 1930; d. Preston Arthur and Marguerite Elizabeth (Shirley) Christjohn; m. Richard Barton Addis, Feb. 9, 1957 (div. Oct. 1989); children: Jacqueline Carol Addis, Barton David. BS in Phys. Therapy, Boston U., 1952. Phys. therapist Ohio State U. Hosp., Columbus, 1952-57, Pa. Easter Seals Camp, White Haven, 1954, 55, 56, Canton (Ohio) Rehab. Ctr., 1957-58, Tinken-Mercy Hosp., Canton, 1959-62, Lovelace Med. Ctr., Albuquerque, 1987-89, Ednl. Assessment Systems, Albuquerque, 1990-94, Rehab. Ctr. Inc., 1994-96, Ednl. Assessments Sys., 1996—2000. Mem. Am. Phys. Therapy Assn., N.Mex. Phys. Therapy Assn., Altura Addition Neighborhood Assn., Music Theater S.W., Xeric Garden Club of Albuquerque. Avocations: gardening, sewing, calligraphy, photography, walking. Home: 3708 Hannett Ave NE Albuquerque NM 87110-4914

ADE, BARBARA JEAN, secondary education educator; b. Youngstown, Ohio, Nov. 6, 1951; d. Donald Eugene Sr. and Louise Ann (Bodnark) Kihm; m. Robert Randal Ade, Mar. 17, 1973. BS in Edn., Youngstown State U., 1975, MS in Edn., 1987. High sch. media specialist Springfield Local High Sch., New Middletown, Ohio, 1975—. Active Youngstown Area YWCA. Grad. Sch. scholar Youngstown State U., 1986-87; named Woman of the Yr., Youngstown Area YWCA, 1993. Mem. NEA, AAUW, Ohio Ednl. Libr./Media Assn., Ohio Edn. Assn., Delta Kappa Gamma, Phi Delta Kappa. Democrat. Roman Catholic. Avocations: reading, antique collecting, golf, painting. Office: Springfield Local High Sch 11335 Youngstown Pittsburgh Rd New Middletown OH 44442-8724

ADEKSON, MARY OLUFUNMILAYO, therapist, counselor educator; b. Ogbomoso, Nigeria; came to U.S., 1988; d. Gabriel and Deborah Williams; children: Adedayo, Babatunde. BA in English and Am. Lit., Brandeis U., 1975; MEd in Guidance and Counseling, Obafemi Awolowo U., Ile-Ife, Nigeria, 1987; PhD, Ohio U., 1997. English tchr. Ctrl. Sch. Bd., Ibadan, Nigeria, 1968-88; acting prin. Abe Tech. Coll., Ibadan, Nigeria, 1978; coord. guidance svcs. Min. Edn., Ile-Ife, 1984-88; part-time lectr. Obafemi Awolowo U., Ile-Ife, 1986-88; vice prin. Olubuse Meml. HS, Ile-Ife, 1987-88; grad. asst. Ohio U., Athens, 1988-91. Vol. contract worker, trainer Careline, Tri-County Mental Health Ctr., Athens, 1988-92; vol. My Sister's Place, Athens, 1989, Good Works Athens, 1989, Montgomery County Hotline, 1994; contract worker Tri County Activity Ctr., Athens, 1989-92, therapist II Woodland Ctr., Gallipolis, Ohio, 1991-92; part-time lectr. U. Md., 1993, coord. tutorial svc.; dir. Christian Book Ctr., Ile-Ife; vol., part-time counselor DWI program Prince George's County Health Dept., Hyattsville, Md.; counselor Potomac Healthcare Fund. Mountain Manor Treatment Program; adj. prof. Bowie (Md.) State U. Counseling Program, 1997-98; asst. prof. St. Bonaventure U., 1998—; faculty adviser Chi Sigma Iota, Phi Rho chpt. Vol. Montgomery County Police Dept.; mem. Alcohol and Other Drug Abuse Adv. Coun., Montgomery County, Md.; mem. adv. com. Germantown (Md.) Libr.; mem. Gaithersburg (Md.) City Adv. Com.; chmn. bd. dir. Faith Enterprises; dir. Faith Consultancy Group. Recipient Gold medal West African Athletic Assn., 1965; Internat. Peace scholar P.E.O., 1990-91, Wien Internat. scholar Brandeis U., 1973-75. Mem. ACA, Am. Mental Health Counselors Assn. Network on Children and Teens (membership chair 1991-92, chair 1993-98), Am. Assn. Counseling and Devel. (award for internat. grad. students 1990), Counseling Assn. Nigeria (planning com. 1986), Oyo State Nigeria Assn. Guidance Counselors (chmn. Oranmiyan local govt. area 1986-88), Chi Sigma Iota (program coord. Ohio U. chpt. 1990, faculty advisor Phi Rho chpt.). Avocations: meeting people from around the world, jogging, walking, playing tennis, reading.

ADELMAN, PAMELA BERNICE KOZOLL, education educator; b. Milw., Dec. 26, 1945; d. Harry and Rebecca (Sharp) Kozoll; m. Steven H. Adelman, June 30, 1968; children: David, Robert. BS, U. Wis., Madison, 1967; MA, Northwestern U., 1972, PhD, 1982. Cert. tchr., Ill. Chair edn. dept. Barat Coll., Lake Forest, Ill., 1986-97; tchr. Peckham Jr. High Sch., Milw., 1967-68, Fairview Sch., Skokie, Ill., 1968-70; learning disabilities specialist Sch. Dist 28, Northbrook, Ill., 1971-77; instr., rsch. asst. Northwestern U., Evanston, Ill., 1977-80; lectr., asst. prof., then assoc. prof. Barat Coll., Lake Forest, Ill., 1977-90, prof. edn., 1990-99, dir. learning opportunities program, 1985-99, chmn. edn. dept., 1986-97, grad. dean, 1997-99, chmn. edn. dept., 1986-97; founding exec. dir. Hyde Park Day Sch., 1999—. Cons. Deerfield (Ill.) Pub. Schs., 1986-90; proposal reviewer State of N.J., Trenton, 1986-87; mem. Pres.'s Com. on Hiring of Disabled, 1990; higher edn. adv. coun. State of Ill.; mem. Coun. Chgo. Area Deans of Edn., 1992-99, chair, 1998-99; comprehensive sys. of pers. devel. adv. com. Ill. State Bd. Edn.; presenter in field. Co-author: Learning Disabilities, Graduate School, and Careers, 1990; co-editor: Success for College Students with Learning Disabilities, 1993; consulting editor Learning Disabilities Focus, 1989-92, Jour. Developmental Edn., 1990-98, Jour. of Postsecondary Edn. and Disabilities, 1991-95; contbr. articles to ednl. publs. Chair Sch. Dist. 107 Caucus, Highland Park, Ill., 1982; bd. dirs. Jewish Children's Bur., Chgo., 1985—, pres., 1994-96; co-author brochure for Ill. Dept. Human Rights, Chgo., 1986; bd. dirs. Jewish Fedn. Met. Chgo., 1996. Paul A. Witty fellow Northwestern U., 1978-80; grantee Lloyd A. Fry Found., 1985-86, McDonald's Corp., Chgo., 1986, Kraft Corp., Chgo., 1989, Thorn River Found., 1990—. Fellow Internat. Acad. for Rsch. in Learning Disabilities; mem. Internat. Dyslexia Assn. (bd. dirs. Ill. br. 2000—), Coun. Exceptional Children, Learning Disabilities Assn. Am., Coun. Learning Disabilities. Avocations: reading, walking, music, swimming. Office: Hyde Park Day Sch 1375 E 60th St Chicago IL 60637-2856

ADELMAN, RICHARD CHARLES, gerontologist, educator; b. Newark, Mar. 10, 1940; s. Morris and Elanor (Wachman) A.; m. Lynn Betty Richman, Aug. 18, 1963; children— Mindy Robin, Nicole Ann AB, Kenyon Coll., 1962; MA, Temple U., 1965, PhD, 1967. Postdoctoral fellow Albert Einstein Coll. Medicine, Bronx, N.Y., 1967-69; from asst. prof. to prof. Temple U., Phila., 1969-82, dir. Inst. Aging, 1978-82; prof. biol. chemistry U. Mich., Ann Arbor, 1982-2000, dir. Inst. Gerontology, 1982-97, prof. emeritus, 2001—; dir. univ. rels. University Assisted Living, Ann Arbor, 2002—. Mem. study sect. NIH, 1975-78; adv. coun. VA, 1981-85; chmn. Gordon Rsch. Conf. Biol. Aging, 1976; adv. com. VA, 1981-91; chmn. VA Geriatrics and Gerontology Adv. Com., 1987-91; dir. univ. rels. University Living, Inc., 2001—. Mem. various editorial bds. biomed. research jours., 1972—. Bd. dirs. Botsford Continuing Care Ctrs., Inc., Farmington Hills, Mich., 1984-88. Recipient Medalist award Intrasci. Research Found., 1977; grantee NIH, 1970—; established investigator Am. Heart Assn., 1975-78 Fellow Gerontol. Soc. Am. (v.p. 1976-77, pres. elect 1986-87, Kent award 1990); mem. Am. Soc. Biol. Chemists, Gerontol. Soc. Am. (pres. 1986-87), Am. Chem. Soc., AAAS, Phila. Biochemists (pres.), Practictioners in Aging. Jewish.

ADELMAN, SAUL JOSEPH, astronomy educator, researcher; b. Atlantic City, Nov. 18, 1944; s. Benjamin and Kitty (Sandler) A.; m. Carol Jeanne Sugerman, Mar. 28, 1970; children: Aaron, Barry, David. BS, U. Md., 1966; PhD, Calif. Inst. Tech., 1972. Postdoctoral rsch. assoc. NASA Goddard Space Flight Ctr., Greenbelt, Md., 1972-74; asst. prof. dept. astronomy Boston U., 1974-78; asst. prof. dept. physics The Citadel, Charleston, S.C., 1978-83, assoc. prof., 1983-89, prof., 1989—; sr. rsch. assoc. NASA Goddard Space Flight Ctr., Greenbelt, Md., 1984-86. Guest observer Dominion Astrophys. Obs., Victoria, B.C., Can., 1984—; guest investigator Internat. Ultraviolet Explorer Satellite, 1980, 82-87, 89-96, FUSE Satellite, 1999—; Guest Investigator Hubble Space Telescope, 20003, vis. astronomer Kitt Peak Nat. Obs., Tucson, 1972-82, 85, 89, 91, 93-95, Complejo Astronomico El Leonisto, 1994—; campus dir. S.C. Space Grant Consortium, 1997—. Assoc. producer TV show The Perfect Stargazer, 1990; author: (with Benjamin Adelman) Bound for the Stars, 1981; contbr. articles to profl. jours. Grantee NSF, NASA. Fellow Royal Astron. Soc., Brit. Interplanetary Soc.; mem. Internat. Astron. Union, Am. Astron. Soc., Astron. Soc. Pacific, Can. Astron. Soc., Phi Beta Kappa, Sigma Xi (pres. chpt. 2001-02), Phi Kappa Phi (pres. chpt. 1982-83, 90-92), Sigma Pi Sigma. Avocations: photography, genealogy, gardening. Office: The Citadel Dept Physics 171 Moultrie St Charleston SC 29409-0002

ADELSON, EDWARD, physicist, educator, musician; b. Bklyn., Aug. 19, 1934; s. Barnet and Sarah (Strongin) A.; m. Juliane A.W. Riedel, Aug. 5, 1961 (div. June 1982). BA, NYU, 1956; postgrad. (Woodrow Wilson fellow), Eastman Sch. Music, 1956-57; MS, Ohio State U., 1965, PhD, 1974. Prin. physicist Battelle Mem. Inst., Columbus, Ohio, 1957-71; lectr. Ohio State U., Columbus, 1974-88, acad. program specialist, 1988—. Cons. in field. Author: Student Companion for Reese's University Physics, vol. 2, 2001; contbr. articles to profl. jours. Organist, choirmaster emeritus St. Alban's Episcopal Ch., Bexley, Ohio. Mem.: AAAS, Am. Guild Organists, Am. Assn. Physics Tchrs., Am. Phys. Soc., Chrichton Club, Sigma Pi Sigma, Phi Beta Kappa. Home: 6384 Falkirk Pl Columbus OH 43229-2045 Office: Ohio State U Smith Lab Columbus OH 43210

ADELSTEIN, S(TANLEY) JAMES, physician, educator; b. NYC, Jan. 24, 1928; s. George and Belle (Schild) Adelstein; m. Mary Charlesworth Taylor, Sept. 20, 1957; children: Joseph Burrows, Elizabeth Dunster. BS, MS, MIT, 1949, PhD in Biophysics, 1957; MD, Harvard U., 1953. Med. house officer Peter Bent Brigham Hosp., Boston, 1953-54, sr. asst. resident physician, 1957-58, chief resident, 1959-60; fellow Howard Hughes Med. Inst., 1957-58, Henry A. and Camilus Christian fellow, 1959-60; Moseley travel fellow Harvard U. Med. Sch., Boston, 1958-59, instr. anatomy, then asst. prof., 1961-68, assoc prof. radiology, 1968-72, prof., 1972-89, Paul C. Cabot prof. med. biophysics, 1989-97, prof. pathology, Daniel S. Tosteson univ. prof., 1997—, dean for acad. program, 1978-97. Dir. Nat. Coun. for Radiation Protection Measurements, 1980—2002, v.p., 1982—2002, hon. v.p., 2002—; cons. Med. Found. fellow, 1960—63; Walter Dandy lectr. Johns Hopkins U., 1996; John Cameron lectr. U. Wis., 1998; Lauristen Taylor lectr. Nat. Coun. for Radiatide Protection, 2000; radiation rsch. bd.

NAS, 1999—2002, chair, 2002—; biol. rsch. adv. com. Dept. Energy, 2001—; John Cameron lectr. U. Wis., 1998; L. Taylor lectr. Nat. Coun. for Radiation Protection, 2000; rsch. coll. adv. bd. U. Tasmania, 2003—. Mem. editl. bd.: Investigative Radiology, 1972—80, Postgrad. Radiology, Radiology Rsch., 1990—94; editor (assoc. editor): Jour. Nuc. Medicine, 1975—81; contbr. articles to profl. jours. Trustee Am. Bd. Nuc. Medicine, 1972—78; mem. fellowship adv. com. Whitaker Found., 1991—97. Recipient Career Devel. award, NIH, 1965—68; fellow Nat. Found., MIT, 1957, Fogarty Sr. Internat., 1976. Fellow: AAAS, Am. Coll. Nuc. Physician; mem.: Inst. Medicine, Boylston Med. Soc., Soc. Nuc. Medicine (trustee 1970—74, Blumgart award 1983, Aebersold award 1986, Dr. Hevesy award 1999), Radiation Rsch. Soc. (councillor 1975—78), Assn. Radiation Rsch., Biophys. Soc., Am. Chem. Soc., Alpha Omega Alpha, Tau Beta Pi, Sigma Xi. Office: Harvard Med Sch 25 Shattuck St Boston MA 02115-6027

ADEWUYI, YUSUF GBADEBO, chemical engineering educator, researcher, consultant; b. Offa, Kwara, Nigeria, Nov. 26, 1952; came to U.S., 1975; s. Alhaji Kadiri and Sifawu (Oguntundun) A.; m. Janice Hughes, Jan. 16, 1987; 1 child, Kasim Adesegun. BSChemE, Ohio U., 1978; MSChemE, U. Iowa, 1980, PhD, 1985. Postdoc. resident assoc. Boston Coll., 1986-87; postdoc. resident fellow U. Ill., Urbana-Champaign, 1987-88; sr. staff engr. Mobil R & D Corp., Paulsboro, N.J., 1988-91, rsch. engr., 1991-93; assoc. prof. chem. engring. N.C. A & T State U., Greensboro, 1994—2002, prof. chem. engring., 2002—. Cons. Air Purification Inc., N.Y., 1996—; rev. panelist NSF, Washington, 1996—. Contbr. articles to I&E Chem. Rsch., Jour. Hazardous Materials, Atmospheric Environment, Environ. Sci. Tech., Jour. Geophysics Rsch., Chem. Engring. Comms., Applied Catalysis, others. Named to environ. del. to China by Citizen Ambassador's Program, Spokane, Wash., 1994. Mem. AAAS, AIChE (sec. Triad sect. 1996-97, pres. 1997, sec. environ. divsn. 1999-2001), Am. Chem. Soc., Am. Soc. Engring. Edn., Sigma Xi Sci. Rsch. Soc. Achievements include patent for Riser cracking for maximum C3 and C4 Olefin yields; for fluidized catalytic cracking. Home: 3916 Brass Cannon Ct Greensboro NC 27410-9229 Office: NC Agrl Tech State Univ Dept Chem Engring 1601 E Market St Dept Chem Greensboro NC 27401-3209 E-mail: adewuyi@ncat.edu.

ADICKES, SANDRA ELAINE, English language educator, writer; b. N.Y.C., July 14, 1933; d. August Ernst and Edythe Louise (Oberschlake) A.; children: Delores, Lily, Cynthia. BA, Douglass Coll., 1954; MA, CUNY, 1964; PhD, NYU, 1977. Asst. registrar NYU, 1954-55; sec. McCann Erickson, J. Walter Thompson Cos., N.Y.C., 1955-60; English tchr. N.Y.C. Bd. Edn., 1960-70, 1980-88; instr. edn. N.Y.C. Tech. Coll., 1970-72; asst. prof. English S.I. C.C., N.Y.C., 1972-77; dir. project chance Bklyn. Coll., 1977-80; from assoc. prof. to prof. English Winona (Minn.) State U., 1988-98, prof. emerita, 1998—. Cons. Antioch Coll. N.Y.C., 1970; guest tutor London U., 1979. Author: The Social Quest, 1991, Legends of Good Women, 1992, To Be Young Was Very Heaven, 1997; editor: By A Woman Writt, 1973; contbr. articles to profl. jours. Co-founder Tchrs'. Freedom Sch. Project, Miss., 1963-64, Tchrs'. Com. for Peace Vietnam, 1965-66. Named Woman of Yr. Nat. Assn. Negro Bus. Profl. Women, N.J., 1966. Mem. MLA, Midwest Modern Lang. Assn., Nat Coun. Tchrs. of English, Popular Culture Assn. Democrat. Home: 19 Davids Ct Dayton NJ 08810-1302 E-mail: s.adickes@att.net.

ADILETTO, JOHN J., JR., principal; married; 3 children. BS in Edn., Millersville U.; MA in Edn. Adminstrn., Villanova U. Tchr., adminstr. Upper Merion Area Middle Sch., King of Prussia, Pa., prin., 1995—. Recipient Pa. Secondary Sch. of Distinction award, 2001—02, U.S. Dept. Edn. Blue Ribbon Sch. of Excellence award, 2001—02. Mem.: Montgomery County Prins. and Suprs. Assn. (pres.). Office: Upper Merion Area Middle Sch King Of Prussia PA 19406*

ADISMAN, I. KENNETH, prosthodontist, educator; b. N.Y.C., Aug. 3, 1919; s. Joseph and Frances (Gertz) A.; m. Joan Sugarman, June 28, 1957 (dec. June 1998); children: Leslie, Kathryn. Student, Mich. State Coll., 1935-37; D.D.S., U. Buffalo, 1940; MS, NYU, 1960. Diplomate: Am. Bd. Prosthodontics (examiner; pres. 1980). Attending dentist NYU Med. Center, U. Hosp., N.Y.C., 1960-78; prof. dept. prosthodontics and occlusion, dir. maxillofacial prosthetics Dental Center, 1978-86, chmn. dept. removable prosthodontics, 1978-86, dir. advanced edn. program in prosthodontics, dir. implant dentistry; clin. prof. sch. dentistry U. N.C., Chapel Hill, 1992—. Attending dentist Meml. Hosp., N.Y.C., 1976-78; pres. Greater N.Y. Acad. Prosthodontics Rsch. Found., 1980; pres., dir. Internat. Cir. Courses, Inc. of Am. Prosthodontic Soc.; prof. emeritus Coll. Dentistry, NYU. Jour. Prosthetic Dentistry, 1985-98, cons., 1998-99. Served to maj. Dental Corps, U.S. Army, 1942-46. Recipient Alumni Achievement award Coll. of Dentistry, NYU, 1988, Sch. Dental Medicine, U. Buffalo, 1990, Carl O. Boucher Disting. Svc. award Fedn. Prosthodontic Orgns., 1992, Disting. Svc. award The Greater N.Y. Acad. of Prosthodontics, 1996. Fellow Acad. of Prosthodontics (pres. 1988-89), Acad. Maxillofacial Prosthetics; mem. Am. Coll. Prosthodontists (past pres. N.Y. sect.), Am. Coll. Dentists, Internat. Coll. Dentists, Nat. Acad. Practice, N.Y. Acad. Dentistry, N.Y. Acad. Sci. Clubs: The Carolina.

ADLER, BRIAN UNGAR, English language educator, program director; b. El Paso, Tex., May 28, 1957; s. Bernard Abraham and Helene Adler; m. Annette Louise Vaigneur, Sept. 6, 1988; children: Sarah, Noah. BA, U. S.C., 1978; MA, U. Ga., Athens, 1984; PhD, U. Tenn., Knoxville, 1988. Tchr. Allendale (S.C.) Mid. Sch., 1979-80; rsch. asst. U. Tenn., Knoxville, 1982-86, vis. asst. prof., 1986-89; asst. prof. English Marian Coll., Indpls., 1989-92, assoc. prof. English, head dept. English, 1992-94; assoc. prof. English, dir. honors program Valdosta (Ga.) State U., 1994—, prof., 1998. Evaluator Ford Found., Knoxville, 1985-88; cons. Ednl. Testing Svc., Princeton, N.J., 1989-93. Reviewer (evaluations) CHOICE, 1989—; contbr. poems to New Arts Rev., The Sun, 1982—. Leader Elderhostel/Geneva Bay Ctr., Lake Geneva, Wis., 1990—. Ind. Humanities Coun. grantee, 1990, Lilly Endowment Devel. grantee, 1992. Mem. MLA (sec. N.E. chpt. 1990—, chair psychology sect. N.E. chpt. 1995), Bernard Malamud Soc., Nat. Collegiate Honors Coun. Jewish. Office: Honors Program Valdosta State U Valdosta GA 31698-0001 E-mail: badler@valdosta.edu.

ADLER, LAUREL ANN, educational administrator, consultant; b. Sept. 6, 1948; d. Clarence Linsley and Margaret Ann (Roberts) Wheeler; children: David, Anthony, Jennifer. BA, U. Calif., Irvine, 1968; MA, UCLA, 1972; EdD, U. La Verne, 1980. Adult edn. adminstr. Hacienda La Puente Unified Sch. Dist., 1972—79; dir. career and vocat. edn. El Monte Union High Sch. Dist., 1979—83; sup. East San Gabriel Valley Regional Occupl. Ctr., West Covina, Calif., 1984—; instr. UCLA, 1989—, U. Calif. State U., Long Beach, 1999—. Cons. Trust Ty. Pacific Islands, 1979—, L.A. C.C.'s, 1993—. Author: A Self Evaluation Model for Micronesia Education Programs, 1987, Poor Readers, What Do They Really See on the Page?, 1987, Shedding Light on Reading Disabilities, 1989, How Students and Programs Benefit from Business/Education Partnerships, 1993, Design Based Learning, 1998; pub. Essential English for Microneians, Beginning, 1980, Essential English for Micronesians, 1980, Reading Exercises for Micronesians, 1980; contbr. articles. Named Citizen of Yr., La Puente C. of C., 1977, Outstanding Vocat. Educator, Hoffman Ednl. Sys., 1983; recipient Nat. Vol. Action award, 1974, Calif. Sch. Adminstrs. award, 1981, Calif. Consortium Ind. Study Recognition award, Outstanding Ednl. Program, 1983, Woman Achievement award, YWCA, 1991. Mem.: Calif. Consortium Ind. Study, Assn. Supervision and Curriculum Devel., Internat. Reading Assn., Assn. Calif. Sch. Adminstrs. (Outstanding Mech. Educator 1997, 1998), Phi Delta Kappa. Office: E San Gabriel Valley Regional Occupational Ctr 1501 Del Norte St West Covina CA 91790-2105 Address: 5831 Friends Ave Whittier CA 90601-3723

ADLER, MADELEINE WING, academic administrator; b. Ohio; d. George and Bette Wing; m. Frederick S. Lane; children: J. Peter Adler, Rand Lane, Cary Lane. BA in Polit. Sci., Northwestern U., 1962; MA in Polit. Sci., U. Wis., 1963, PhD in Polit. Sci., 1969. Asst. prof. polit. sci. Am. U., Washington, 1965-67; cons. Charles Nelson Assoc., N.Y.C., 1967-68; asst. prof. Queens Coll. CUNY, N.Y.C., 1969-74, assoc. prof. Queens Coll., 1974-86, assoc. dean, 1983-86; v.p. acad. affairs, prof. polit. sci. Framingham (Mass.) State Coll., 1986-92; pres. West Chester (Pa.) U., 1993—. Staff mem. Joint Com. Orgn. Congress, Washington, 1965-66; vis. asst. prof. Pa. State U., summers 1967-71; dir. profl. staff recruitment N.Y.C. Urban Acad., 1975-78; pres. Ctr. Applied Rsch. and Analysis Social Scis., Inc., 1976-86; mem. crosscutting rsch. panel, office rsch. and evaluation U.S. HEW, 1978-80; program coord. N.E. region Soc. Coll. and Univ. Planning, 1987-89; mem. exec. bd. Am. Coun. Edn./Nat. Identification Project, State of Mass., 1987-92, vice chair exec. bd., 1991—. Author: (with Harold Savitch) Decentralization at the Grassroots: Political Innovation in New York City and London, 1974; contbr. article to profl. jours. Mem. Comty. Bd. 14, Bklyn., 1978-81, Gov.'s Award Panel for Humanities, 1993—, Gov.'s Comty. Svc. Adv. Bd., 1994—. Chester County Comty. Found., 1994—; appointee Bklyn. Econ. Devel. Corp., 1982-86; bd. advisors Acad. Search Consultation Svcs., 1994—. Mem. Pa. Assn. Colls. and Univs. (com. acad. issues 1993—). Home: 100 E Rosedale Ave West Chester PA 19382-4927 Office: Office of Pres West Chester Univ Philips Meml Bldg West Chester PA 19383

ADMIRE, SHERILYNN, special education educator; b. Shawnee, Okla., Feb. 16, 1955; d. George Riley and Virginia Ann (McBride) Petty; div.; children: Heather Marie, Karen Elizabeth. Student, Oscar Rose Jr. Coll., Midwest City, Okla., 1975; BS in Spl. Edn./Emotionally Handicapped, Cen. State U., Edmond, Okla., 1977, MEd in Spl. Edn., 1986; grad., Midwest City Leadership Class, 1991. Cert. tchr. severely emotionally disturbed, educable handicapped. Tchr. spl. edn. Oklahoma City Schs./Hosp., 1977-81, Midwest City-Del City Schs., Midwest City, Okla, 1981—; instr. Okla. Aerospace Acad., Norman, 1990-91; adj. prof. East Ctrl. U., Ada, 1992-94; instr. Aerospace Sci. and Tech. Edn. Ctr., Oklahoma City U. Com. mem. North Ctrl. Accreditation Process, 1992, Sch. Effectiveness Com., Midwest City, Okla., 1983-84; staff devel. coord. Country Estates Elem., Midwest City, 1984-85, nat. children's book week coord., 1985-88; yearbook coord. Soldier Creek Elem., 1993; chpt. leader Young Astronauts Program, 1990—; workshop speaker Aerospace Teaching Methods, 1991-92; com. mem. Prent U. Com. mem., chmn. tchr. workshops NASA Cmty. Involvement Program; pub. rels. rep. PTA; crew coord. Balloon Festival, Okla. City, 1994. With USAF, 1977-80. Grantee Mid-Del. Schs. Found., 1990-92, Mission Flying Apple Site, 1991-92; McDonalds scholar, 2000; recipient Brewer award Okla. CAP, 1992; named one of Okla.'s Best Tchrs., Channel 5's Project Challenge, 1990-91 Mem. Coun. for Exceptional Children, Okla. Aerospace Educators Assn. (historian 1990-91, Flying Leather award 1991), Okla. Sci. Tchrs. Assn. Republican. Baptist. Avocations: quilting, sewing, water skiing, woodworking, teaching children aerospace skills. Office: Soldier Creek Elem Sch 9021 SE 15th St Oklahoma City OK 73130-5299 Home: 1813 Cherokee Trl Choctaw OK 73020-8069

ADRIAZOLA, ANA, Spanish and Latin American culture educator; b. Arequipa, Peru, July 7, 1945; came to U.S., 1990; d. Jorge-Roberto and María Adriazola; m. Jose O. Rodriguez, Dec. 6, 1974; children: Ana María, Aurora-Luz. EdD, Nat. U. San Agustin, Arequipa, 1985, D History and Anthropology, 1989. Cert. prof. secondary history and social scis. Prin. pvt. schs. So. Peru Cooper Co., Tacna, 1972-76, coord. ednl. and technol., 1976-81; conservator, curator Museo San Agustin U., Arequipa, 1982-83; prof. Colls. Edn. and History U. Nat. San Agustin, 1984-89; prof. Spanish and culture U. N.C., Charlotte, 1991-92, Fla. Atlantic U., Boca Raton, 1994—. Advisor textiles Kontisuyo Archaeol. Program, Moquegua, Peru, 1984-89. Mem. NAFE, MLA, Sigma Delta (pres. 1994-95). Avocation: writing fiction and literary criticism. Home: 2250 NW 8th St Boca Raton FL 33486-1450

ADROUNIE, V. HARRY, public health administrator, scientist, educator, environmentalist; b. Battle Creek, Mich., Apr. 29, 1915; s. Haroutune Asadour and Dorthy (Kalaidjian) A.; m. Emalea Riley, June, 1943 (div. Jan. 1980); children: Harry Michael, Vee Patrick; m. Agnes M. Slone, June 26, 1981. BS, St. Ambrose U., 1940, BA, 1959; MS in Environ. Health, PhD in Environ. Health, PhD in Pub. Health, Western States U. Profl. Studies, 1984. Diplomate Am. Bd. Indsl. Hygiene, Am. Acad. Sanitarians; registered sanitarian, Calif., Mich., Pa. Enlisted U.S. Army, 1941, commd. 2nd. lt., 1943; advanced through grades to lt. col. USAF, ret., 1968; founder, tech. dir. ARA Environ. Svcs., 1968—72; dir. environ. health div. Chester County (Pa.) Health Dept., 1972—75, Berrien County (Mich.) Health Dept., 1975-78; prof. environ. health Sch. Pub. Health U. Hawaii, Manoa, 1978-80; dean, prof. Sch. Pub. Health, Western States U. Profl. Studies, Mo., 1980-83; vis. prof. environ. and pub. health Am. U., Armenia, 1995. USAF rep. U.S. Interdepartmental Com. on Nutrition for Nat. Def., 1959—61; cons. Health Mobilization Program USPHS Surgeon Gen., 1957—61; mem. USAF Surgeon Gen.'s med. goodwill tour all S.Am. countries, 1960; chmn., vis. assoc. prof. dept. environ. health, faculty med. scis. Am. U. Beirut, 1963—66, chmn. dept. environ. health, 1964—66; charter mem. RSH-UN Welfare Relief Agy. Pub. Health Examining Bd. for Mid. East, 1963—66; cons. UN Welfare Relief Agy., 1964—66; founder, coord. 1st and 2nd Environ. Health Symposium of Mid. East, 1965—66; mem. Mich. Hazardous Waste Policy Com., 1990—91, Mich. Underground Storage Fin. Policy Bd., 1994—2001; adj. instr., adv. com. environ. health Ferris State Coll., Big Rapids, Mich., 1974—75, Big Rapids, 1977—78. Contbr. numerous articles to profl. jours.; author many manuals and tng. booklets for USAF and other orgns., several books. Chmn. Barry County Solid Waste Planning and Oversight com., 1981—; mem. Barry County Family Ind. Agy., 1996—, vice chmn., 1998—, Hastings City Planning Commn., 1984—; mem., vice chmn., co-founder sci. adv. and policy bd. Mich. Ground Water Survey, Inc., 1983—90, chmn., 1988—91; chmn. adv. coun. South Ctrl. Mich. Commn. on Aging, 1981—91; charter mem. UL Underwriters adv. coun. environ. and pub. health, 1996—; appointed mem. Vision 2020 Com. St. Ambrose U., 2000—01; past adult leader Boy Scouts Am. Decorated Legion of Merit, USAF; named Alumnus of Yr., Hastings H.S., 1961; recipient Walter S. Mangold award Nat. Environ. Health Assn., 1963, spl. recognition Mich. Environ. Health Assn., 1980, Concerned Citizen award World Safety Orgn., 1992, Safety Person of World Safety Orgn., 1991, State of Mich. White Pine award, 1998. Mem.: APHA (pres. 1995—97, emeritus conf., task force on aging 2002—), NRA (life; cert. rifle marksmanship instr.), VFW (life), Indonesian Environ. Health Assn. (co-founder 1979), World Safety Orgn. (bd. dirs. 1986—95, cert. bd. 1987—2000, editl. bd. 1988—2000), Global Health Assn., Internat. Pub. Health Soc. (charter-emeritus), Mich. Assn. Local Environ. Health Adminstrs. (pres., founder 1976, V. Harry Adrounie award named in his honor 2001), Mich. Environ. Health Assn. (life; pres. 1991—92), Assn. Mil. Surgeons (life), Nat. Environ. Health Assn. (life; pres. 1961—62), Am. Legion (comdr. post 45 1989—90), Air Force Assn., Mil. Officers Assn. Am. (life), Kiwanis (pres. Hastings, Mich. chpt. 1985—86), Moose, Elks (life), Lions (life). Home: 1905 N Broadway Hastings MI 49058-1086

ADWERE-BOAMAH, JOSEPH, school district administrator; b. Asokori, Ashanti, Ghana, May 20, 1937; came to U.S., 1965; s. Robert Adwere and Matha (Yaa) Boatemah; m. Norma Beaver, Aug. 15, 1967; children: Robert, Kwame. BS, U. Oreg., 1966, MS, 1967; PhD, U. Calif., Berkeley, 1970. Skills asst., cons. Sonoma County Schs., Sonoma, Calif., 1967-68; jr. supr. programs, rsch. asst., teaching asst. U. Calif., Berkeley, 1968-69, fgn. student advisor, program asst. and counselor, 1969-71; sr. program evaluator Dropout Program, Oakland (Calif.) Unified Sch Dist., 1971-75, dir. rsch., 1975—; adj. sr. faculty U. San Francisco, 1975. Author various publs. Bd. dirs. YMCA, Albany, Calif., 1987, NetWork, Oakland, 1992. Newhouse fellow U. Calif., Berkeley, 1969-70; Victor Ludorum fellow Abuakwa State Coll., Kibi, Ghana, 1958. Mem. Am. Statis. Assn., Am. Ednl. Rsch. Assn. (Svc. award 1992), Internat. Soc. Applied Psychology, Calif. Edn. Rsch. Assn., Nat. Coun. on Measurement, Phi Delta Kappa (pres. 1972). Avocations: jogging, reading, music. Home: 1310 Portland Ave Albany CA 94706-1428 Office: Oakland Pub Schs Dept Rsch and Evaluation 1025 2nd Ave Dept Rschand Oakland CA 94606-2212

ADY, LAURENCE IRVIN, academic administrator; b. Washington, Mar. 15, 1932; s. Laurence E. and Georgiana C. (Covington) A.; m. Jan. 10. 1959; children: Marc S., Lori L. BA, U. Md., 1956; MA in Tchg., Rollins Coll., 1964, Ednl. Specialist, 1974. Cert. ednl. adminstrn. & supervision, elem. edn., early childhood edn., drivers edn., history, adult edn.; lic. police officer. Police officer Orlando Police Dept., 1958-59, Ocoee (Fla.) Police Dept., 1959-64; constable Dist. #3, Orange County, Fla., 1964-66; tchr. H.S. Sch. Bd. Orange Ct., Fla., 1967-68, from supervisor adult basic edn. to sch. adminstr., 1968—. Dep. sheriff Orange County, 1971-80; elem. sch. tchr. Sch. Bd. Orange Ct., 1959-67; pres. Commn. on Adult Basic Edn., 1984-85, treas. 1979—. Commr. City of Belle Isle, Fla., 1977—; treas. Dem. exec. com., Orange County, 1982—. Named to Fla. Adult Edn. Hall of Fame Fla. Adult Edn. Assn., Cocoa Beach, 1985. Mem. Am. Assn. for Adult/Continuing Edn. (treas. 1987-91), Tiger Bay Orlando, Kiwanis (treas., dir. 1972—). Methodist. Avocations: boating, swimming, exercising. Home: 2495 Trentwood Blvd Orlando FL 32812-4833 Office: COABE PO Box 592053 Orlando FL 32859-2053

AFFLECK, STEPHEN BRUCE, chemical and civil engineer, educator; b. Logan, Utah, Oct. 6, 1937; s. Doyle Peter and Ruth (Dawson) A.; m. Carolyn Hall, Sept. 6, 1960; children: Erin, Adam, Jessica, Matthew, Jared, Anna, David, Sara. BSChE, U. Utah, 1960; MS in Sanitary Engring., Iowa State U., 1973, PhD in Chem. Engring./Water Resources, 1980. Registered profl. engr., Idaho. Project engr. Procter & Gamble Co., Cin., 1960-68; asst. prof. U. Utah, Salt Lake City, 1978-81; assoc. prof. Boise State U., 1981-91, prof., 1991—, dept. chair, 1994—. Civil engring. cons. various pvt. cos. and individuals, Boise, 1990-94. Patentee detergent filled disposable dishcloth. Mem. NSPE, Sigma Xi. Mem. Lds Ch. Avocation: gardening. Home: 9108 Burnett Dr Boise ID 83709-4008 Office: Boise State U 1910 University Dr Boise ID 83725-2075 E-mail: saffleck@boisestate.edu.

AFFLICK, CLIVE HENRY, minister, guidance counselor; b. Kingston, Jamaica, Oct. 26, 1933; came to U.S., 1977; s. Jabez Gilbert and Hattie Laura (Kennedy) A.; m. Deta Pauline Burrowes, June 11, 1960; 1 child, Clive Henry Jr. BS, Phila. Coll. Bible, 1959; MA, Temple U., 1965; DA, U. Miami, 1989; DDiv, Internat. Sem., 1982. Adminstrv. asst. Chase Manhattan Bank, N.Y.C., 1969-71; prin. Dunrobin High Sch., Kingston, Jamaica, 1971-79; head dept. history, guidance coord. Univ. Christian Sch., Jacksonville, Fla., 1979-82, dir. guidance, acad. advisor, counselor, 1990—; pres. Jamaica Theol. Sem., Kingston, 1983-90. Pres. Caribbean Evangel. Theol. Assn., Kingston, 1988-90. Min., teacher Bapt. Ch., Jacksonville, 1990—. Mem. Am. Assn. Christian Counselors, Orgn. Am. Historians, Fla. Christian Counselors Assn. Baptist. Avocations: reading non-fiction, swimming, writing. Office: Univ Christian Sch 5520 University Blvd W Jacksonville FL 32216-5557

AFOAKU, OYIBO HELISITA, academic administrator; b. Abakaliki, May 6, 1961; came to U.S., 1986; d. Nweke Samuel and Akunkwo Obijele Victoria (Chidumeh) Akpu; m. Osita George, Aug. 30, 1986; children: MmaChukwu, NzubeChukwu, OnyinyeChukwu, AmalaChukwu. Edn. cert., Fed. Coll. Edn., Katsina, Nigeria, 1984; nat. svc. cert., Fed. Republic of Nigeria, Benin-City, 1985; BA in History, Wash. State U., 1990, tchg. cert., 1991; MA, U. No. Colo., 2001. Libr. technician II/clerical asst. II Holland & Owen Librs. Wash. State U., Pullman, 1987-92, office asst. II Western Jour. Black Studies, 1992-93; asminstrv. asst. III Marcus Garvey Ctr. for Black Edn. U. No. Colo., Greeley, 1994-97, asst. dir., 1997—, mem. adv. bd. dirs., 1994—, co-founder, coord. Ann. Africana Night, 1994—. Co-founder, coord. Weld World Festival; spkr., presenter, and workshop condr. at spl. events promoting diversity and multiculturalism. Mem. Marcus Garvey Ctr. Cmty. Friends Program; city commr. Greeley Human Rels. Commn. Mem. AAUW, Internat. Friends and Families, Women Internat. League for Peace and Freedom, Greeley Interfaith Assn., Greeley Human Rela. Commn. (city commr.) Avocations: cultural exchanges, academic and cultural programmings, reading, cooking, volunteer services. Office: Marcus Garvey Ctr for Black Cultural Edn 928 20th St David House Greeley CO 80639-0001 Fax: 970 351-2337. E-mail: oyibo.afoadku@unco.edu.

AFTERMAN, ALLAN B. accountant, educator, researcher, consultant; b. Chgo., Jan. 25, 1944; s. Joseph and Ruth Gertrude (Jacobson) A.; m. Joan Elaine Hoffman, Apr. 30, 1974; children: Debra, Lori, Julie, Robin. BBA, Roosevelt U., 1964; PhD, U. Birmingham, Eng., 1989. CPA, Calif. Asst. dir. securities exchange com. practices Alexander Grant & Co., Chgo., 1967-70; nat. staff mgr. Touche Ross & Co., Chgo., 1970-73; nat. tech. dir. Practice Devel. Inst., Chgo., 1977-82; acctg. prof. U. Ill., Chgo., 1983-88, dir. exec. edn.; mem. faculty grad. sch. bus. U. Chgo., 1992-99. Cons. to govts. Author: Accounting and Auditing Disclosure Manual, 1982, Compilation and Review, 1983, Accounting and Auditing Update, 1984, SEC Accounting and Reporting Update, 1985, GAAP Practice Manual, 1985 (best loosleaf bus. reference award profl. and scholastic divsn. Assn. Am. Pubs. 1985), Accounting and Tax Highlights, 1986, Handbook of SEC Accounting and Disclosure, 1987, Credit Analyst's Report, 1988, Financial Reporting and Disclosure Manual in the United Kingdom, 1989, Public Accounting Practice Manual, 1990, Governmental Accounting & Auditing Disclosure Manual, 1991, Nonprofit Accounting and Auditing Disclosure Manual, 1992, Auditing Standards and Practices in Poland, 1993, SEC Regulation of Public Companies, 1994, International Financial Accounting, Reporting & Analysis, 1994, U.S. Securities Regulation of Foreign Issuers, 1995, Charities Accounting and Auditing Disclosure Manual in the United Kingdom, 1996, Nonprofit GAAP Practice Manual, 1998, Audit Committee Governance Report, 2000, Corporate Financial Management, 2001. Mem. AICPA, Am. Acctg. Assn., Practicing Law Inst., N.Y. Soc. CPAs. Jewish. Home: 3900 Mission Hills Rd Apt 302 Northbrook IL 60062-5721 Office: 3330 Dundee Rd Ste N6 Northbrook IL 60062-2329 E-mail: allan@ab-afterman.com.

AGARWAL, ANIL KUMAR, nephrologist, educator; b. Lucknow, India, Nov. 5, 1957; s. Harish Chandra and Kailash Wati Agarwal; m. Garima Suyal, Dec. 29, 1985; 1 child, Deepak. MBBS, Maharani Lakshmi Bai Coll, Jhansi, India, 1979, MD, 1983. Diplomate Am. Bd. Internal Medicine, Am. Bd. Nephrology. Intern Ohio State U. Hosp., Columbus, 1992-93, resident in internal medicine, 1993-94, fellow in nephrology, 1994-96, attending physician, 1996—; asst. prof. clin. medicine Ohio State U., 1996—. Fellow ACP; mem. Internat. Soc. Nephrology, Am. Soc. Nephrology, Nat. Kidney Found., Indian Med. Assn. Office: Ohio State U Hosp N210 Means 1654 Upham Dr Columbus OH 43210-1250

AGEE, BOB R. academic administrator, educator, minister; b. Brownsville, Tenn., Sept. 30, 1938; s. Edwin L. and Katie L. (Stewart) A.; m. Nelle Rose; children— Nancy Denise, Robyn Janelle BA, Union U., Tenn., 1960; M.Div., So. Bapt. Theol. Sem., 1964, D.Min., 1974; PhD, Vanderbilt U., 1986. Ordained to ministry Baptist Ch. Pastor Shively Heights Bapt. Ch., Louisville, 1964-70; pastor Ardmore Bapt. Ch., Memphis, 1970-75; dean, v.p. religious affairs Union U., Jackson, Tenn., 1975-82; pres. Okla. Bapt. U., Shawnee, 1982-98, pres. emeritus, 1998—. Mem. edn. commn. So. Bapt. Conv., 1985-93, chmn., 1987-90; bd. dirs. Co-op Svcs. Internat. Edn. Consortium, chmn., 1988-90; cons. evaluator North Ctrl. Assn. Colls. and Univs., 1987—; bd. dirs. Nat. Assn. Ind. Colls. and Univs., 1986-90, 93—. Author Bibl. study materials and articles Mem. human relations com.

Memphis Bd. Edn., 1972-74; mem. Memphis Mayor's Crime Commn., 1973-75; mem. Okla. Ind. Coll. Found., 1982-98, chmn., 1985-87. Inducted into Okla. Higher Edn. Hall of Fame, 1999. Mem. Soc. Coll. and Univ. Planning, Shawnee C. of C. (bd. dirs. 1983-98), So. Bapt. Theol. Sem. Alumni Assn. (nat. pres. 1985-86), AAUP, Am. Assn. Univ. Adminstrs., Nat. Assn. Ind. Colls. and Univs. (bd. dirs. 1988-97), Coun. for Christian Colls. and Univs. (bd. dirs. 1997-2003), Assn. So. Bapt. Colls. and Schs. (exec. dir. 1998—, exec. dir. consortium global edn. 1998-2002). Republican. Avocations: racquetball, golf, fishing, writing. Office: PO Box 11655 Jackson TN 38308-0127

AGEE, NELLE HULME, retired art history educator; b. Memphis, May 22, 1940; d. John Eulice and Nelle (Ray) Hulme; m. Bob R. Agee, June 7, 1958; children: Denise, Robyn. Student, Memphis State U., 1971—72; BA, Union U., Jackson, Tenn., 1978; postgrad., Seminole Okla. Col., 1982, Okla Bapt. U., 1984; MEd, Ctrl. State U., Edmond, Okla., 1989. Cert. tchr. art, history Ky., Tenn., Okla. Offices svcs. supr. So. Bapt. Theol. Sem., Louisville, 1961—64; kindergarten tchr. Shively Heights Bapt. Ch., Louisville, 1965—70; editl. asst. Little Publs., Memphis, 1973—75; tchr. art Humboldt HS, Tenn., 1978—82. Vis. artist-in schs. Tenn. Arts. Commn., Nashville, 1978, 81, 82; adj. prof. art history Seminole Col., Okla., 1985—86, 1989; asst. prof. art and edn. Okla. Bapt. U., 1989—98; spkr. art orgns, ch. groups; tchr. art workshops Humboldt City Sch. Sys.; tchr. Cultural Arts Day Camp, Jackson, Tenn., 1982. Exhibited in various shows. Nat. pres. ministers' wives conf. So. Bapt. Conv., 1988; vol. Mabee-Gerrer Mus., Shawnee; bd. dirs. Robert Dotson Foun., Mabee-Gerrer Mus., Family Resource Ctr., 1993—98; active vol. Salvation Army Aux., Shawnee. Recipient Disting. Classroom Tchr. award, Tenn. Edn. Assn., 1982. Mem.: Goals 2000, Alpha Delta Kappa, Delta Kappa Gamma. Republican. Baptist. Avocations: stained glass, pottery, travel. Home: 14 Woodmanor Pl Jackson TN 38305-1718

AGEE, WARREN KENDALL, journalism educator; b. Sherman, Tex., Oct. 23, 1916; s. Frederic M. and Minnie E. (Logsdon) A.; m. Edda Robbins, June 1, 1941; children: Kim Kendall, Robyn Kendall Ansley. BA cum laude, Tex. Christian U., 1937; MA, U. Minn., 1949, PhD, 1955. Mem. editorial staff Ft. Worth Star-Telegram, 1937-48; instr. journalism Tex. Christian U., 1948-50, asst. prof., 1950-55, asso. prof., 1955-57, prof., 1957-58, chmn. dept., 1950-58, faculty adviser student publs., 1949-58; prof. journalism, dean sch. journalism W.Va U., 1958-60; mem. ednl. adv. com. WJPB-TV, Fairmont and Weston, W.Va., 1959-60; nat. exec. officer Soc. Profl. Journalists, Sigma Delta Chi, 1960-62; prof. journalism, dean Evening Coll., Tex. Christian U., Ft. Worth, 1962-65; dean William Allen White Sch. Journalism, U. Kans., Lawrence, 1965-69, Henry W. Grady Coll. Journalism and Mass Communication U. Ga., 1969-75, prof. journalism, 1975-87, dean and prof. emeritus, 1987—; vis. scholar U. Tex., fall 1975; copy editor Atlanta Constn., summer 1977. Combat corr. USCG Res., 1941-44; pub. info. specialist USCG Res. Hdqrs., 1944-45; mem. adv. screening com. journalism, com. internat. exchange of persons Conf. Bd. Assn. Rsch. Couns., Washington, 1958-62; mem. Am. Coun. Edn. for Journalism and Mass Communication, 1958-60, 65-67, mem. accrediting com., 1969-76, vice chmn., 1973-74, chmn., 1974-76, chmn. appeals bd., 1977, 79, 81, 83; mng. dir. William Allen White Found., 1965-69, trustee, 1970—; mng. dir. George Foster Peabody Radio and TV awards, 1969-75, Sigma Delta Chi Nat. Journalism Awards, 1960-62; assoc. James M. Cox Jr. Ctr. Internat. Mass Comm. Tng. and Research, U. Ga., 1985—. Author: (with Edwin Emery and Phillip H. Ault) Introduction to Mass Communications, 1960, 12th rev. edit., 1997, Reporting and Writing the News, 1983, (with Dennis L. Wilcox, Ault) Public Relations: Strategies and Tactics, 1986, 8th edit., 2003, (with Nelson Traquina) O Quarto Poder Frustrado: Os Meios de Comunicação Social No Portugal Pós-Revolucionário, 1988; also articles.; editor: The Press and the Public Interest, 1968, Mass Media In A Free Society, 1969, (with Emery and Ault) Perspectives on Mass Communications, 1982, Maincurrents in Mass Communications, 1986, rev. edit., 1989; assoc. editor, bus. mgr.: The Quill, 1960-62; press rev. columnist, contbg. editor, 1977-82; adv. editl. bd. Journalism Quar, 1955-60. Mem. Athens (Ga.) Internat. Rels. Cmty. Coun., pres., 1980-82; pres. Friends of Mus. Art U. Ga., 1974-75; mem. Howard Blakeslee Media Awards judging com. Am. Heart Assn., 1976-94, chmn. judging com., 1980-94. Recipient Journalism award Fort Worth Press, 1936; Outstanding News Writing award Ft. Worth Profl. chpt. Sigma Delta Chi, 1946; Carl Towley award Journalism Edn. Assn., 1969; Outstanding Achievement award U. Minn., 1973; Wells Meml. key Sigma Delta Chi, 1978, Disting. Teaching award Soc. Profl. Journalists, 1987; Fulbright grantee to Portugal, 1982, 85. Mem.: Soc. Profl. Journalists, Southwestern Journalism Congress (sec. 1957—58), Am. Studies Assn., Am. Soc. Journalism Sch. Adminstrs. (pres. 1956), Assn. Edn. in Journalism and Mass Comm. (pres. 1958, Disting. Leadership award 2001), Gridiron Club (Ft. Worth), Rotary, Phi Beta Delta, Alpha Sigma Lambda, Phi Kappa Sigma, Alpha Chi, Kappa Tau Alpha (50 yr. journalism edn. svc. award 1987), Sigma Delta Chi (pres. Fort Worth profl. chpt. 1954—55, sec. Tex. 1957—58, nat. v.p. campus chpt. affairs 1966—69, leader coun. 1982—, v.p. N.E. Ga. profl. chpt. 1978—79, pres. 1979—80). Presbyterian. Home and Office: 130 Highland Dr Athens GA 30606-3212

AGGARWAL, JAGDISHKUMAR KESHORAM, electrical and computer engineering educator, research administrator; b. Amritsar, India, Nov. 19, 1936; came to U.S., 1960; s. Keshoram J. and Harkaur A.; m. Shanti Seth, July 1965; children: Mala, Raj. BS, U. Bombay, 1957; B in Engring., U. Liverpool, Eng., 1960; MS, U. Ill., 1961, PhD, 1964. Registered profl. engr., Tex. Rsch. asst. Marconi's Rsch. Lab., Chelmsford, Eng., 1959; fellow U. Ill., Urbana, 1960-61, rsch. asst. coordinated sci. lab., 1961-64; asst. prof. elec. engring. U. Tex., Austin, 1964-68, assoc. prof. elec. engring., 1968-72, prof. elec. and computer engring., 1972—, John J. McKetta Energy prof., 1981-90, Cullen Trust for Higher Edn. Endowed prof. No. 2, 1990—. Dir. Computer and Vision Rsch. Ctr., Austin, 1985—; cons. IBM Corp., Shell Devel. Corp. Co-author: Deconvolution of Seismic Data, 1982, Motion Understanding, 1988; editor: Multisensor Fusion for Computer Vision, 1993. Recipient Outstanding Contbn. award Pattern Recognition Soc., 1985, 86, Disting. Alumnus award U. Ill., 1986, Alumni Honor award U. Ill. Coll. Engring., 1987, Am. Soc. Engring. Edn. Sr. Rsch. award, 1992. Fellow IEEE (editor Expert jour. 1986-89, editor Trans. Parallel and Dist. Systems 1992-96), Internat. Assn. for Pattern Recognition (rep. 1985-2000, treas. 1989-92, pres. 1992-94, computer vision program chmn. 1990 conf.); mem. IEEE Computer Soc. (chmn. tech. com. on pattern recognition and machine intelligence 1987-89, gen. chmn. conf. on computer vision and pattern recognition 1993), Austin Yacht Club. Avocation: sailing. Office: U Tex Computer & Vision Rsch Ctr Austin TX 78712-1084 E-mail: aggarwaljk@mail.utexas.edu.*

AGGARWAL, SURESH KUMAR, mechanical and aerospace engineering educator; b. India, Aug. 22, 1949; came to U.S., 1973; m. Veena Gupta, Dec. 12, 1980; children: Sonal, Monika. PhD, Ga. Inst. Tech., 1979. Rsch. fellow Princeton (N.J.) U., 1978-79; rsch. engr. Carnegie-Mellon U., Pitts., 1979-82, sr. rsch. engr., 1983-84; asst. prof. mech. engring. U. Ill., Chgo., 1984-88, assoc. prof. mech. engring., 1989-94, prof. mech. engring., 1995—. Cons. NASA, Cleve., 1988. Assoc. editor AIAA; contbr. articles to profl. jours. Named one of the Outstanding Young Men of Am.; U. Ill. scholar; Am. Soc. Engring. Edn./USN sr. faculty fellow, 1994. Fellow AIAA (assoc., assoc. editor AIAA Jour.); mem. Gas Turbine Inst. Home: 6428 Waterford Ct Hinsdale IL 60521-5438 Office: U Ill Dept Mech Engring Chicago IL 60607

AGHAJANIAN, GEORGE KEVORK, medical educator; b. Beirut, Apr. 14, 1932; Am. parents; s. Ghevont M. and Araxi (Movsessian) A.; m. Anne E. Hammond, Jan. 10, 1959; children: Michael, Andrew, Carol, Laura. AB, Cornell U., 1954; MD, Yale U., 1958. Asst. prof. psychiatry Sch. of Medicine Yale U., New Haven, 1965-68, assoc. prof. psychiatry Sch. of Medicine, 1968-70, assoc. prof. psychiatry and pharmacology Sch. of Medicine, 1970-74, prof. psychiatry and pharmacology Sch. of Medicine, 1974—, founds. fund prof. Sch. of Medicine, 1985. Contbr. more than 300 articles to profl. jours. Capt. U.S. Army, 1963-65. Recipient Hoffheimer prize Am. Psychiat. Assn., 1981, Scheele medal Swedish Acad. Pharmacy, 1981, Merit award NIH, 1990-2000, Hillarp award Internat. Amine Group, 1996, Lieber prize NARSAD, 1998. Fellow Am. Coll. Neuropsychopharmacology (Efron award 1975); mem. Soc. for Pharmacology and Exptl. Therapeutics, Soc. for Neurosci., Internat. Brain Rsch. Orgn., Inst. of Medicine, Inst. of Medicine/Nat. Acad. Sci. Achievements include research in electrophysiological and pharmacological properties of brain serotonergic, noradrenergic, and dopaminergic neurons. Office: 34 Park St New Haven CT 06519-1109 E-mail: george.aghajanian@yale.edu.

AGICH, GEORGE JOHN, medical educator, educator; b. Rochester, Pa., May 27, 1947; s. Charles Albert and Mary (Mikovich) A.; m. Mary Kate Fredriksen; 1 child, Nicholas Carl. BA in English and Philosophy cum laude, Duquesne U., 1969; MA in Philosophy, U. Tex., 1971, PhD in Philosophy, 1976. Prof. med. ethics and psychiatry So. Ill. U., Springfield, 1976-97; F. J. O'Neil chair clin. bioethics, chmn. dept. bioethics Cleve. Clinic Found., 1997—, mem. transplant ctr., 1997—. Dir. clin. ethics ctr. Meml. Med. Ctr., Springfield, Ill., 1994-97, dir. ethics consultation svc., 1991-97; vis. scholar history and philosophy of sci. Cambridge U., 1982-83. Author: Autonomy and Long-Term Care, 1993; editor: Price of Health, 1986, Responsibility in Health Care, 1982. Bd. dirs. Friends of Lincoln Libr., Springfield. Recipient Nellie Westerman prize Am. Fedn. Clin. Rsch., Century Club Disting. Alumni Duquesne U., 1999. Mem. Assn. for Advancement Philosophy and Psychiatry (pres. 1994—, founding fellow 1989—), Am. Philos. Assn., Soc. Health and Human Values, Am. Soc. Law, Medicine, and Ethics, European Soc. Philosophy of Medicine and Health Care, Am. Soc. for Bioethics and Humanities (sec.-treas., bd. dirs. 1997-2000). Office: Cleve Clinic Found Dept Bioethics Cleveland OH 44195-0001 E-mail: agichg@ccf.org.

AGIN, DENNIS MICHAEL, aircraft manufacturer, orthodontist educator; b. Cleve., Nov. 13, 1942; s. Henry E. and Mintsy (Gutterman) A. Student, Toledo U., 1960-62; DDS, Western Res. U., 1966; postgrad., U. Rochester, 1966-67, 69-71, Ohio State U., 1988-91. Diplomate Am. Bd. Orthodontics; cert. flight instr. Instr. Case Western Res. U. Dental Sch., Cleve., 1972-84; clin. staff Cleve. VA Hosp., 1973-84; asst. prof. Ohio State U., Columbus, 1985-87; lectr. Columbus state Coll., 1993—. Flight instr. Firebird Aviation, Middlefield, Ohio, 1980-84; flight advisor Exptl. Aircraft Assn., Oshkosh, Wis., 1994—, ultralight flight instr.; mfr. Heath Aircraft, Columbus, 1994—; bd. dirs. Heath Found., Columbus, 1994—. LTCDR USN, 1962—88, ret. Decorated Ribbon of Combat Action, Nat. Defense medal, Vietnam Svc. medal (7 stars), Vietnam Cross of Gallantry with Palm, Vietnam Campaign medal. Mem. Nat. Flight Instrs. Assn., Exptl. Aircraft Assn., VFW, Jewish War Vets., Kiwanis, Am. Mensa, Intertel, Masons (32 deg.), Shriners, Alpha Epsilon Delta, Omicron Kappa Upsilon, Alpha Epsilon Pi, Alpha Zeta Omega. Republican. Jewish. Avocations: aviation, amateur radio, bicycling. Home: 438 Allenby Dr Marysville OH 43040-9354 Office: Heath Aerocraft Ltd 438 Allenby Dr Marysville OH 43040-9354

AGLI, STEPHEN MICHAEL, English language educator, literature educator; b. Yonkers, N.Y., Feb. 11, 1942; s. Michael Joseph and Pauline Joanna (Perrone) A. AB summa cum laude, Fordham Coll., 1965; AM, Harvard U., 1968, EdM, 1972; postgrad., CUNY, 1995—. Cert. secondary sch. English tchr., N.Y. Resident tutor Quincy House, Harvard Coll., Cambridge, Mass., 1968-73; instr. humanities Berklee Coll. Music, Boston, 1971-73; mem. curriculum devel. com., teaching fellow in expository writing Harvard U., Cambridge, 1973-77, tutor in expository writing Bur. of Study Counsel, 1977-81; tchr., chmn. English dept. Jewish H.S. South Fla., North Miami Beach, 1982-83, St. Sergius H.S., N.Y.C., 1983-84; tchr. secondary sch. English Columbia Grammar and Prep. Sch., N.Y.C., 1984-85; coll. counselor, ednl. adminstr. St. Sergius Acad., 1994-95. Bd. Freshman advisers Harvard Coll., 1970-77; counselor, ednl. cons., Cambridge, Mass., N.Y.C., 1977-82; ednl. rsch. and cons., N.Y.C., 1985—; adj. instr. English N.J. Inst. Tech., Newark, 1987-88, CUNY, 1992—; conf. session chmn. Soc. for Textual Scholarship, 1993; presenter rsch. papers Rockhurst Coll., Kansas City, Mo., 1989, St. Louis U., Gerard Manley Hopkins Centennial Celebration, 1989, Malone Soc. Centennial Conf., Stratford-upon-Avon, Eng., 1990; spkr. St. Sergius H.S. commencement, 1992-93; lectr. Gerard Manley Hopkins lecture series, various locations, U.S., 1999—. Alumni rep. Harvard U., 1982-90. Recipient Woodrow Wilson fellowship Woodrow Wilson Found. to Harvard U., 1965-66, CUNY travel and rsch. awards to confs. and librs. in U.S. and Europe, 1988-90, 95; fellow NDEA Dept. Celtic Langs. and Lit., Harvard U., 1967-70, CUNY, 1986-90, N.E. MLA, London and Oxford, 1990. Mem. MLA, N.E. MLA, Celtic Studies Assn. N. Am. (speaker annual meeting 1989), Phi Beta Kappa. Home: 65 Central Park Ave Apt 1M Yonkers NY 10705-4707

AGNEW, JANET BURNETT, secondary education educator; b. Spartanburg, S.C., Aug. 29, 1936; d. James and Ruby Evelyne (Burnett) A.; 1 child, James Gilmour. BA, U. N.C., Greensboro, 1958; MA in Teaching, Converse Coll., Spartanburg, S.C., 1966; postgrad., Clemson (S.C.) U., 1970-72, U. S.C., Columbia, 1990—97. Cert. tchr., prin., math. supr., gen. sci. and physics. Tchr. gen. math. for Tech. and algebra I & II Greensboro Schs.-Aycock, 1958-60; tchr. coll. prep. math. Air Force Dependent H.S., Stevenville, Nfld., Can., 1960-61; tchr. gen. math. and algebra Roebuck H.S. Spartanburg Schs. #6, 1962; tchr. gen. phys. and sci. Campobello Sch. Spartanburg Schs. #1, 1962-63; tchr. math. and algebra Spartanburg Schs. #7, 1965-68, substitute tchr., 1975-76; tchr. gen. math. for techs. and algebra I & II Pacolet & Broome H.S., Spartanburg Sch. #3, 1976-98; corp. sec. Delagrave Co., Spartanburg, 1963-75; instr. math. Spartanburg Meth. Coll., 1968-75; ret., 1998. Cons., 1998—. Contbr. articles to profl. jours. Pres. Gen. Fedn. Women's Clubs-S.C., Columbia, 1978—80, chmn. trustees, 1985—87, 1988—91, 1991—97, 1999—2000, 2001—03, chmn. scholarship com., 1991—93, 1995—97; sec.-treas. southern region Gen. Fedn. Women's Clubs, 1990—92; v.p. Gen. Fedn. Women's Clubs-S.C., 1992—94; pres. Gen. Fedn. Women's Clubs S.O. Region, 1994—96. Recipient Svc. award Spartanburg March of Dimes, 1967, 68. Mem.: NEA-R (life), Gen. Fedn. Women's Clubs Jubilee Club (pres. 1996—2000, sec. 2000—02), Spartanburg County Retired Educators Assn. (sec. 2000—01, v.p. 2001—03, pres. 2003—), Piedmond Jr. Woman's Clubs (pres. 1974, 1976, Clubwoman of Yr. 1974, 1974, 1976), Spartanburg County Assn. Educators (rep. to del. assembly 1987—98, dist. dir. 1988—91, NEA rep. assembly 1989—97, v.p., pres. elect 1991—92, pres. 1992—93), Nat. Coun. Tchrs. Maths., S.C. Tchrs. Math. (life), S.C. Edn. Assn.-R (life; Rep. dist. dir. #3 1999—2001, chmn. by-laws and politics com. 1999—2001, del. assembly 1999—, v.p. 2001—02, pres. 2002—03), Spartanburg Coun. Federated Women's Clubs (pres. 1989—92, 2000—), Spartanburg Country Club Women's Golf Assn., Delta Kappa Gamma (chpt. v.p. 2000—02, pres. 2002—). Democrat. Presbyterian. Avocations: crafts, travel. Home: 140 Burnett Dr Spartanburg SC 29302-3402 E-mail: janetag@yahoo.com.

AGNEW, JOHN A. education educator; b. Millom, Cumbria, Eng., Aug. 29, 1949; s. Herbert and Anne (MacPherson) A.; children: Katherine, Christine. BA, Exeter U., Eng., 1970; Cert. Edn., Liverpool U., Eng., 1971; MA, Ohio State U., 1973, PhD, 1976. From asst. prof. to prof. Syracuse (NY) U., 1975—96; prof. UCLA, 1996—, chair dept. geography, 1998—2002. Dir. social sci. program Syracuse U., 1981—88; vis. prof. U. Chgo., 1992, U. Durham, 2003; Hettner lectr. U. Heidelberg, 2000; chmn. dept. geography U. Chgo.; Guggenheim fellow UCLA, 2003—. Author: Place and Politics, 1987, The U.S. in World Economy, 1987, Rome: The Modern City, 1995, Geopolitics: Re-Visioning World Politics, 1998, 2d edit., 2003, Place and Politics in Modern Italy, 2002; co-author: The Geography of World Economy, 1989, 2d edit., 2003, Mastering Space, 1995; editor: The City in Cultural Context, 1984, The Power of Place, 1989, American Space/American Place, 2002, Companion to Political Geography, 2002; mem. editl. bd. Polit. Geography, Urban Geography, Soc. and Space, Nat. Identities, Global Networks, Scottish Geog. Jour., European Jour. Internat. Rels. Fellow: Royal Geog. Soc.; mem.: N.Y Acad. Sci., Am. Polit. Sci. Assn., Coun. European Studies, Social Sci. Hist. Assn., Assn. Am. Geographers. Office: UCLA 1255 Bunche Hl Los Angeles CA 90095-1524 E-mail: jagnew@geog.ucla.edu.

AGNEW, KATHLEEN DIANNE CROSBIE, language educator; b. Tulsa, Okla., June 16, 1946; d. James Conn and Madeline Madge (Baldwin) Crosbie; m. James Alford Tulley, Jan. 28, 1968 (div. 1991); children: Jennifer R., Scott A.; m. David Dutilh Agnew, June 21, 1997. BA, Butler U., 1968. Lic. secondary tchr. Educator East Ladue Jr. HS, 1968—74, Sweet Grass County HS, Big Timber, Mont., 1975—. Mem. Sweet Grass County Task Force At Risk Children, 1985-90; organist, vestry St. Mark's Episcopal Ch., Big Timber, 1991-98; mem. Mont. task force on tchr. edn. std., 1999. Recipient Milken Educator award Milken Family Found., 1997; Excellence in Tchg. English and Am. Studies award Am. Coun. Tchr. Russian and Am. Coun. Collaboration in Edn. and Lang. Study, 1998. Mem. NEA, Nat. Coun. Tchr. English, Mont. Assn. Tchr. English and Lang. Arts, Mont. Edn. Assn. (pres., sec), Sponsors Sch. Publ. (v.p., pres.); participant in NEH seminar "Shakespeare: Enacting the Text", 2003. Avocations: piano, writing, photography, painting. Office: Sweet Grass County HS PO Box 886 Big Timber MT 59011-0886

AGRANOFF, BERNARD WILLIAM, biochemist, educator; b. Detroit, June 26, 1926; s. William and Phyllis (Pelavin) A.; m. Raquel Betty Schwartz, Sept. 1, 1957; children: William, Adam. MD, Wayne State U., 1950; BS, U. Mich., 1954. Intern Robert Packer Hosp., Sayre, Pa., 1950-51; commd. surgeon USPHS, 1954-60; biochemist Nat. Inst. Neurol. Diseases and Blindness, NIH, Bethesda, Md., 1954-60; mem. faculty U. Mich., Ann Arbor, 1960—, prof. biochemistry, 1965—; R.W. Gerard prof. of neurosci. in psychiatry, 1991. Rsch. biochemist Mental Health Rsch. Inst., 1960—, assoc. dir., 1977-83, dir. 1983-95, dir. neurosci. lab., 1983-2000; vis. scientist Max Planck Inst. Zellchemie, Munich, 1957-58, Nat. Inst. Med. Rsch., Mill Hill, Eng., 1974-75; Henry Russel lectr. U. Mich., 1987; cons. pharm. industry, govt. Contbr. articles to profl. jours. Fogarty scholar-in-residence NIH, Bethesda, Md., 1989-95; named Mich. Scientist of Yr. Mus. of Sci., Lansing, 1992. Fellow AAAS (Am. Assn. Advanced Sci.), Am. Acad. Arts and Sci., N.Y. Acad. Sci., Am. Coll. Neuropsychopharmacology; mem. Am. Soc. Biochemistry and Molecular Biology, Am. Chem. Soc., Inst. Medicine of NAS, Internat. Soc. Neurochemistry (treas. 1985-89, chmn. 1989-91), Am. Soc. Neurochemistry (pres. 1973-75). Achievements include research in brain lipids, biochem. basis of learning, memory and regeneration in the nervous system, human brain imaging. Office: U Mich C 560 MSRB II 1150 W Medical Center Dr Ann Arbor MI 48109-0669 E-mail: agranoff@umich.edu.

AGRAWAL, GOVIND PRASAD, optics educator; b. Kashipur, India, July 24, 1951; came to U.S., 1977; s. Amarnath and Sushila (né Singhal) A.; m. Anne L. Frette-Damicourt, July 22, 1977; children: Sipra, Caroline, Claire. BS, U. Lucknow, 1969; MS, Indian Inst. of Tech., 1971, PhD, 1974. Rsch. assoc. Ecole Polytechnique, Palaiseau, France, 1974-76, CUNY, 1977-79; staff scientist Quantel, Orsay, France, 1980-81; tech. staff mem. AT&T Bell Labs., Murray Hill, N.J., 1982-88; assoc. prof. U. Rochester, 1989-91, prof., 1992—. Author: Semiconductor Lasers, 1986, 2d edit., 1993, Nonlinear Fiber Optics, 1989, 3d edit., 2001, Fiber Optic Communications, 1992, 3d edit., 2002, Applications of Nonlinear Fiber Optics, 2001, Optical Solitons, 2003; editor: Semiconductor Lasers, 1995; contbr. 300 articles to profl. jours. Fellow IEEE, Optical Soc. of Am. (topical editor 1993-98); mem. European Optical Soc. (editl. bd. 1995-98), Laser and Electro-optical Soc. (ednl. com. 1996-99). Office: The Inst of Optics U Rochester Rochester NY 14627 E-mail: gpa@optics.rochester.edu.

AGRAWAL, PIYUSH C. school system administrator; b. Khairagarh, Agra, India, June 26, 1936; arrived in U.S., 1976; s. Ram C. and Chameli (Kiran) Agrawal; m. Sudha Sita Bansal, May 18, 1963; children: Seema, Sukrit, Akhil. BSc, Agra (India) U., 1955, MSc, 1963; BEd, Delhi U., 1958; MS, SUNY, Albany, 1972, EdS, 1978, EdD, 1979. Tchr., dept. head Delhi Adminstrn., 1958-68; expert UNESCO, Liberia, 1968-76, 1968—76; dir. metric edn. Regional Planning Ctr., Albany, 1977-79; supr. math. Dade County Pub. Sch., Miami, Fla., 1979-94; assoc. supt. Piscataway Bd. Edn., 1992-94, dep. supt., 1994-97, acting supt., 1997-98; chmn. & CEO APS Tech., Inc., 2000. Cons. in field; Fla. state coord. nat. math. competition Am. Jr. HS Math. Exam., 1989—92; rev. panelist Am. 2000 proposals New Am. Schs. Devel. Corp., 1992; tchr. enhancement program NSF, 1992; mem. nat. adv. panel Md. Pub. TV, 1993—95; mem. nat. adv. coun. South Asian affairs, 1994—, vice chair, 1998—. Author: numerous books and booklets. Mem. U.S. Census 2000 Adv. Com. on Asian and Pacific Islander Populations, 1993—, chair, 1995, 1997, 1999, 2000, 2001; mem. Fla. House Spkr.'s Task Force on Math., Sci., and Computer Edn., 1982—83; nat. selection com. mem. Presdl. Awards for Excellence in Sci. and Math. Tchg., 1990, state selection com. mem., 1987, 1990, 1991; chmn. Secondary math. Fla. State Textbook Adoption Coun., 1984. Mem.: Asian Am. Cmty. Forum (founding Chair 2002), Asian Am. Found. (chair 2001—), Asian Am. Alliance (founding mem. 2001—, chair 2002—), Mid. States Assn. Colls. and Schs. (task force 1993—95), Fla. Leadership Alliance for Improving Math. Edn. (founder 1991), Dade County Sch. Adminstrs. Assn. (v.p. 1985—86), Fla. Assn. Instrnl. Supr. and Adminstrs. (bd. dirs. 1985—86), UNESCO Staff Assn. (pres. 1971—76), Fla. Assn. Math. Supr. (pres. 1986—87), Fla. Coun. Tchrs. Math. (pres. 1990—92), U.S. Metric Assn. (ann. conf. chmn. 1982), Assn. Indians in Am. (nat. v.p. 1984—88, 1992—94, trustee 1997—, nat. pres. 2000—). Home: 1625 Eagle Bnd Weston FL 33327-1615 Office: APS Techs Inc 630 W 84th St Hialeah FL 33014-3617 E-mail: sudhapca@aol.com.

AGRICOLA, DIANNE G. secondary education educator, tutor; b. Portsmouth, Va. d. James H. and Vermelle E. (Pinnix) Griffin; m. William Edward Agricola, Apr. 19, 1975; 1 child, William Edward Jr. AA, Chowan Coll., 1974; BA in Journalism, U. S.C., 1982; BA in English, Christopher Newport U., 1988. Cert. English, journalism educator. Asst. acct. Va. Nat. Bank, Norfolk, 1970-75; mortgage loan assoc. Bank of Va., Richmond, 1976, VNB Mortgage Corp., Richmond, Va., 1975; legal sec. Wilmeth & DeLoach, Hartsville, S.C., 1976-80; reporter Tidewater News, Franklin, Va., 1984; subs. tchr. Franklin Schs., 1984-85, Southampton County Schs., Courtland, Va., 1985-86; summer sch. tchr. Franklin H.S., 1988; tchr. English and journalism Greensville County H.S., Emporia, Va., 1988-98; tchr. English Hunt-Mapp Mid. Sch., Portsmouth, Va., 1998-99, Hidden Valley H.S., Grants Pass, Oreg., 1999—. Mem. Oreg. Educators Assn., Journalism Educators Assn., Chowan Coll. Alumni Assn. (v.p. 1989-94, pres. 1995), Christopher Newport U. Edn. Found. Alumni Assn., Sigma Tau Delta, Alpha Epsilon Rho, Beta Sigma Phi. Methodist. Avocations: reading, bowling, swimming, home decorating and design, shopping. Home: 109 Sweetbriar Cir Grants Pass OR 97527-5372 Office: Hidden Valley High Sch 3701 Willett Dr Grants Pass OR 97526

AGUERREBERE, JOSEPH A. academic administrator; b. E Los Angeles; BA in polit. sci, U. So. Calif.; M in edn. admin., U. So. Calif; Doctorate in ednl. admin., U. So. Calif. Pres. Nat. Bd. for Profl. Tchg. Standards,

Arlington, Va., 2003—; dep. dir. edn., sexuality and religion unit Ford Found., NYC; assoc. prof. to prof. Calif. State U., Grad Edn. Dept. Office: Nat Bd Profl Tchg Standards 1525 Wilson Blvd Ste 500 Arlington VA 22209*

AGUILAR, FÉLIX, public health physician, educator; b. Tegucigalpa, Honduras, Mar. 31, 1963; s. Felix and Orbelina Aguilar; m. Clare Marie Weber; 1 child, René Aguilar-Weber. BS, U. Calif., Irvine, 1986, MD, 1996; MPH, Tulane U., 1987. Diplomate Am. Bd. Family Medicine, Am. Bd. Preventive Medicine. Health educator Charles Drew U. Medicine and Sci., L.A., 1988—90; project coord. Tobacco Control Program, Los Angeles County Dept. of Health Svcs., 1990—91; acting city health officer Long Beach Dept. Health and Human Svcs., Calif., 2000, preventive health med. dir., 2000—01, dir. of child health and disability prevention program, 2001—; affiliate staff physician Long Beach Meml. Med. Ctr., 2000—; asst. clin. prof. U. Calif. at Irvine Coll. of Medicine, 2000—. Pres. Am. Cancer Soc. of Long Beach, 2000—; mem. edn. com. L.A. County Commn. on AIDS, 1989—90. Author: Palabra Vigente, 1990. Del. med. dir. and mem. bd. dirs. Witness for Peace, L.A., 1990—; co-chair People of Color AIDS Conf., L.A., 1990, Chicanos for Creative Medicine, Irvine, 1986—86; mem. bd. dirs. Physicians for Social Responsibility Nat., Washington, 2002—; pres., mem. bd. dirs. Physicians for Social Responsibility, L.A., 1994—, Monsignor Oscar Romero Clinic, L.A., 1990—93; pres., bd. mem. Irvine Students Housing, Inc, Irvine, 1985—86. Named Cancer Control Vol. of the Yr., Am. Cancer Soc., 2001, Breast Health Edn. Vol. of the Yr., 2000; recipient Outstanding Achievement award, City of Long Beach, 2001, Spl. Recognition award, Calif. State Senate, 1998, Sr. Humanitarian award, U. of Calif. Irvine Coll. of Medicine, 1996. Fellow: Am. Acad. Family Practice (pres. Long Beach subchpt. 2000—); mem.: APHA, Physicians for Social Responsibility (pres. L.A. chpt. 2000—), Am. Coll. Preventive Medicine, Audubon Soc. (newsletter editor 1990—91). Avocations: social justice, poetry, travel. Home: 771 Raymond Ave Long Beach CA 90804-4624 Office: Long Beach Dept of Health and Human Svcs 2525 Grand Ave Long Beach CA 90815-1765 Office Fax: 562-570-4310. Personal E-mail: felix.aguilar@earthlink.net. Business E-Mail: felix_aguilar@ci.long-beach.ca.us.

AGUILAR, GLADYS MARIA, counselor, educator; b. Mérida, Mexico, Mar. 16, 1965; came to the U.S., 1968; d. Francisco Javier and Gladys Maria (Salazar) Aguilar; children: Emmanuel, Daniel. BS cum laude, Loyola Marymount U., 1987; MS, Calif. State U., 1990. Cert. in pupil personnel svcs. Youth min. St. Francis of Assisi Parish, L.A., 1987-88; sch. counselor Concern Counseling Svcs., Fullerton, Calif., 1988-89; bilingual behavioral therapist Inst. for Applied Behavioral Analysis, L.A., 1988-89; sch. counselor, tchr. St. Lucy's Priory High Sch., Glendora, Calif., 1989-90; intern Cath. Psychol. Svcs. Cath. Charities of L.A., L.A., 1990-93; bilingual elem. sch. counselor L.A. Unified Sch. Dist., 1993-96; therapist Foothill Cmty. Mental Health Ctr., 1996-97; mental health cons. Plz. de la Raza Preschool Corp., 1996—; bilingual elem. sch. tchr. Ont.-Montclair Sch. Dist., 1997—2003, Azusa Unified Sch. Dist., 2003—. Marriage, family and child counseling intern Brown & Assocs., Whittier, Calif., 1989-93. Eucharistic min., lector St. Francis of Assisi Cath. Ch., 1986-92. Mem. Soc. Children Book Writers and Illustrators, Calif. Tchrs. Assn., Calif. Assn. Marriage and Family Therapists, Calif. Assn. Bilingual Educators, L.A. Sch. Counselors Assn., Psi Chi, Alpha Sigma Nu. Avocations: travel, folkloric dancing, reading. Home: 836 N Forest Hills Dr Covina CA 91724-3609

AGUILAR, ISABEL (CHAVELA), counselor, university official; b. Calexico, Calif., Nov. 5, 1936; d. Silbestre Macias Badajós and Petra (Soria) Badajós; m. Ruben Aguilar, Apr. 7, 1956; children: Ruben Anthony, John Xavier. AA, Imperial Valley Coll.; BA in Art, MS in Counseling, San Diego State U. Credentialed cmty. coll. counselor, adminstr., instr., pers. worker, Calif. Admissions and records officer Imperial Valley Campus, San Diego State U., Calexico, 1972-77; admissions officer San Diego State U.-Imperial Valley Campus, Calexico, 1977-80, admissions counselor and vet., 1980-83, outreach coordinator, counselor, alumni dir., scholarship coordinator-,campus staff senator disabled students services, student info. coordinator, student life advisor, new student orientation coord., 1978-93; supr. high schs., student intern counselors, 1987-93; outreach coordinator for local area, campus staff chair, coordinator ann. Women's Non-traditional Conf. for High Sch. Women, 15 years. San Diego State U.-Imperial Valley Campus, Calexico, 1987-93. Campus liaison Imperial Valley Coll., Imperial, Calif., 1980—. Sec. Tirado for County Supr., Dist. One polit. campaign, 1993-94; chmn. City Beautification Com., Calexico, 1980-93; past chmn. Affirmative Action Adv. Cons. to Bd. of Suprs., El Centro, 1983-92; trustee self-sufficiency adv. bd. Imperial Valley Housing Authority; trustee, v.p. Calexico Ednl. Found.; bd. dirs. Calexico Neighborhood House; commr. City of Calexico Sister Cities, 1993—. Recipient San Diego State U. Annual Alumna award, 1980; Delta Kappa Gamma scholar, 1978; named SER-Hispanic Woman of Yr., 1991. Mem. Advocated for Women in Academia, Imperial Valley Guidance Assn. (sec. 1985-90), Raza Advocates for Calif. Higher Edn., Western Assn. Ednl. Opportunity Pers., Hispanic Assn. Colls. and Univs., Soroptimists (pres. Calexico club 1983-84, v.p. 1982-83, sec. 1984-85, publicity mgr. 1981-82, alt. del. 1985-86). Democrat. Roman Catholic. Home: 814 Rockwood Ave Calexico CA 92231-2438 Office: San Diego State U Imperial Valley 720 Heber Ave Calexico CA 92231-2480

AGUIRRE-BATTY, MERCEDES, Spanish and English language and literature educator; b. Cd Juarez, Mex., Dec. 20, 1952; came to U.S., 1957. d. Alejandro M. and Mercedes (Péon) Aguirre; m. Hugh K. Batty, Mar. 17, 1979; 1 child, Henry B. BA, U. Tex., El Paso, 1974, MA, 1977. Cert. online tchr., Calif. Instr. ESL Paso del Norte- Prep Sch., Cd Juarez, 1973-74; tchg. asst. ESL and English U. Tex., El Paso, 1974-77; instr. ESL English Lang. Svcs., Bridgeport, Conn., 1977-80; instr. Spanish and English, coord. modern lang. Sheridan (Wyo.) Coll., 1980—, pres. faculty senate, 1989-90; pres. faculty senate, chair dist. coun. No. Wyo. C.C. Dist., 1995-96. Planning com. No. Wyo. C.C. Dist., 1996-97; mem. advanced placement faculty Spanish cons. Coll. Bd. Ednl. Testing Svc., 1996-99; adj. prof. Spanish, U. Autonoma Cd Juarez, 1975; adj. prof. Spanish and English, Sacred Heart U., Fairfield, Conn., 1977-80; spkr. in field. Bd. dirs. Wyo. Coun. for the Humanities, 1988-92; translator county and dist. cts., Sheridan; vol. Wmen's Ctr.; translator Sheridan County Meml. Hosp.; del. Citizen Ambassador Program, People to People-India, 1996. NEH fellow, 1991-92; Wyo. State Dept. Edn. grant, 1991. Mem. MLA (del. assembly 1998-2000), Wyo. Fgn. Lang. Tchrs. Assn. (pres. 1990-92), Am. Assn. Tchrs. Spanish and Portuguese (founder, 1st pres. Wyo. chpt. 1987-90), TESOL, Sigma Delta Mu (v.p. 1992-99, pres. 2000—), Sigma Delta Pi (Alpha Iota chpt. pres. 1974-75). Avocations: travel, reading, archeology, languages, geography. Office: Sheridan Coll NWCCD 3059 Coffeen Ave Sheridan WY 82801-9133

AHART-WALLS, PAMELA, elementary school principal; b. Sacramento, Calif., May 31, 1950; d. Eury Anthony and Mercedes (Brown) Ahart; children: Courtney Ahart James, Howell Burl Walls. BA in English, Edn., Our Lady of the Lake Coll., 1971; MA Comm. Disorders, Lrning. Disabilities, Our Lady of the Lake U., 1973. Tchr. H.K. Williams Elem. Sch. Edgewood Ind. Sch. Dist., San Antonio, Tex., 1971-73; cons. spl. edn. and materials specialist Edn. Svc. Ctr., Region 20, San Antonio, 1973-79, project mgr. metric edn., 1979-81; tchr. lang. and learning disabilites San Antonio Ind. Sch. Dist., 1981-88, peer tchr. evaluator, 1988-89, elem. prin., 1989-95. Cons., speaker on elem. edn., various cities, Tex., 1985—. Author: (edn. kit) Metric Education Made Easy, Kindergarten to 5th Grade, 1980. Mem. exec. com. Met. Alliance, San Antonio, 1994—; mem. Lit. Commn. of San Antonio, 1994—. School recognized as Smart Sch., Trinity Univ., San Antonio, 1991-95; grantee Tex. Edn. Agy., 1992-97. Mem. ASCD, Tex. Elem. Prins. and Suprs. Assn., Jack and Jill of Am., LINKS, Nat. Coalition of 100 Black Women. Home: 9626 Cloverdale San Antonio TX 78250-1703 Office: Samuel Houston Gates Elem San Antonio Ind Sch Dist 510 Morningview Dr San Antonio TX 78220-3220

AHLERS, GLEN-PETER, SR., law library director, educator, consultant; b. N.Y.C., Mar. 15, 1955; s. LeGrande Jacob and Joan (Stoltz) A.; m. Sondra Sue Wadley, May 17, 1987; children: Glen-Peter II, Sandia Marie, Gavin Patrick, Sierra Le Ann Rose, Stacia Camille, Sienna Catherine. BS, U. N.Mex., Albuquerque, 1979; MA, U. of South Fla., 1983; JD, Washburn U., 1987. Bar: Kans. 1987, U.S. Dist. Ct. Kans. 1987, U.S. Ct. Mil. Appeals 1988, D.C. 1990. Reference asst. U. N.Mex. Sch. Law, Albuquerque, 1979-83; asst. dir. Washburn Sch. Law Libr., Topeka, 1983-87; assoc. libr. dir. Wake Forest U., Winston-Salem, N.C., 1987-90; libr. dir., assoc. prof. D.C. Sch. Law, Washington, 1990-92, U. Ark., Fayetteville, 1992-2000, prof., 2001—02; assoc. dean info. services Barry U. Dwayne O. Andreas Sch. of Law, Orlando, Fla. Computer and libr. cons. Ctr. for R&D in Law-Related Edn., Winston-Salem, 1987-90; adj. prof. Sch. of Law Wake Forest U., Winston-Salem, N.C., 1987-90; Mid-Am. Law Sch. Libr. Consortium, 1992-2002, bd. dirs. Consortium of Southestern Law Librs., 1988-90, pres. 2000-02. Author: History of Law School Libraries in the United States, 2002, Election Laws of the United States, 1995; co-author: Notary Law and Practice, 1997; editor The Maall Newsletter, 1984-87, The Scrivener, 1992—; tech. editor Washburn Law Jour., 1985-86; contbr. articles to profl. jours. Mediator N.C. Neighborhood Justice Ctr., Winston-Salem, 1989-90. Mem. ABA, ALA, Fla. Bar Assn., Am. Assn. Law Librs., Southwestern Assn. Law Librs. (pres. 1995-97), Southeastern Assn. of Law Librs., Mid Am. Assn. Law Librs. (pres. 1999-2000), Scribes (exec. dir. 1997—), Phi Kappa Phi, Kappa Delta Pi, Beta Phi Mu. Avocation: writing. Home: 1069 Winding Waters Cir Winter Springs FL 32708-6326 Office: Barry U Dwayne O Andreas Sch of Law 6441 E Colonial Dr Orlando FL 32807-3650 E-mail: gahlers@mail.barry.edu.

AHLSTROM, CALLIS BLYTHE, university official; b. Oct. 1, 1933; BS, Utah State U., 1958; postgrad., Rutgers U., 1959-62; MA, Columbia U., 1961. Exec. asst. to pres. Calif. State U., Chico, 1971-79; asst. prof. history Utah State U., Logan, 1964-71, asst. to pres., 1979-86, asst. provost, 1986—2001, emeritus asst. provost, 2001—. Chmn. bd. dirs.; bd. dirs. Logan area Habitat for Humanity, Logan City Libr., Utah State U. Libr. Friends, Logan City Hist. Preservation Com. Served to capt. U.S. Army, 1962-64, U.S. Army Res., 1964-73. Home: 1661 E 1650 N Logan UT 84341-2912 Office: Utah State U Provost's Office Logan UT 84322-1435 E-mail: blythea@champ.usu.edu.

AHMAD, JAMEEL, civil engineer, researcher, educator; b. Lahore, Punjab, Pakistan, May 22, 1941; came to U.S. 1962; s. Naseer and Iftikhar (Dean) Bakhsh; m. Rosalba Quiroz, March 31, 1983; 1 child, Monica. BSc, Punjab U., Lahore, 1962; MS, U. Hawaii, 1964; PhD, U. Pa., 1967. East-west ctr. fellow U. Hawaii, Honolulu, 1962-65; rsch. fellow U. Pa., Phila., 1965-67; asst. prof. Widener U., Chester, Pa., 1967-68, Cooper Union, N.Y.C., 1968-71, assoc. prof., 1971-80, chmn. civil engrng., 1980—, prof. civil engring., 1979—; dir. rsch. Cooper Union Rsch. Found., N.Y.C., 1983—; sr. advisor Verdant Power, Arlington, Va., 2003—. Dir. High Techs., Inc., N.Y.C., 1986—; bd. dirs. Consortium of N.Y.C. Engring. Colls. and Univs., Mayor's Office of Constrn., 1994—, fellow Rsch. Inst. for the Study of Man, 2002. V.p. Vilmanor Community Assn., N.Y.C., 1992, West Side Community Assn., N.Y.C., 1976. Mem. ASCE (Outstanding Svc. award 1985), Am. Soc. Engring. Edn., Pakistan League of Am. (bd. dirs., Abdus Salam medal for disting. rsch. in engring. scis. 1993). Achievements include patents for fleximech reinforcement system, asphalt reinforcement system. Office: Cooper Union Coll 51 Astor Pl New York NY 10003-7132 E-mail: ahmad@cooper.edu.

AHMAD, SHARMIN, elementary education educator; b. Dhaka, Bangladesh, Feb. 29, 1960; came to U.S., 1984; d. Tajuddin Ahmad and Zohra (Khatun) Ahmad; children: Taj C., Aumrita. B in Liberal Arts, Navran Coll., 1980; MA, George Washington U., 1990. Tchr. Maple Leaf Internat. Sch., Dhaka, 1980-84; head counsellor Green Acre Sch. Summer Camp, Rockville, Md., 1986; elem. tchr. Muslim Community Sch., Potomac, Md., 1990-92. Advisor Primary Sch., Dhaka, 1987-91; sponsor, co-dir. Dardaria Primary Sch., Dhaka, 1987—. Contbr. poetry to lit. jours., books; writer, spkr. on spirituality and women's rights. Mem. SahHati Women's Orgn., Bethesda, Md., 1987—; bd. dirs. Minaret of Freedom Inst., 1995—. Fellow George Washington U., 1987, fellow, 1988; recipient Woman of Distinction award Soroptimist Internat. of Am., 1996. Mem. Muslim Women's Georgetown Study Project, Women of Vision, Lifeline Network: World Alliance for Humanitarian Assistance for Bosnia. Avocations: creative writing, reading, collecting info. on sci., women's issues and spiritual matters, walking, gardening. Office: Muslim Cmty Sch 7917 Montrose Rd Potomac MD 20854-3360

AHMED, GAIL R. music educator; b. Martins Ferry, Ohio, Oct. 2, 1953; d. Edgar Milton and Margaret Elizabeth Horner; m. Bashir Gakhru Ahmed, Aug. 25, 1979; 1 child, Aisha. BA, West Liberty State Coll., 1975; MEd, U. Dayton, 1991. Cert. music profl. K-12. Music educator Edison Local Schs., Ironton, Ohio, 1975—77, Tipp City (Ohio) Schs., Tipp City, 1977—. Music dir. Tippecanoe Cmty. Band, Tipp City, 1979—; gen. music rep. Ohio Music Educator's Nat. Conf., Columbus, 1985—90; mem. gifted com. Tipp City Schs., 1999—2002; cons. curriculum devel. Dayton Islamic Sch., Beavercreek, 1997—98; dist. gen. music rep. Ohio Music Educator's Nat. Conf., Columbus, 1985—90; orchestral dir. Tippecanoe H.S. Mus., Tipp City; presenter Lesson Plans that Work TRIAD OMEA State Conv., 1995. Dir. United Meth. Church Bell Choir, Tipp City, 1985—87. Grantee Environ. Edn. grantee, Miami County Park Dist., 2001—02. Mem.: NGAC, Music Educator's Nat. Conf. (dist. gen. music rep. 1985—90, Ohio chpt. dist. II treas. 2002—, 25-Yr. mem. 2001), Friends of Libr. Avocations: travel, music, needlework, reading. Home: 790 Shirley Dr Tipp City OH 45371 Office: Tipp City Schs 90 S Tippecanoe D Tipp City OH 45371 Personal E-mail: grahmed@hotmail.com.

AHMED, S. BASHEER, research company executive, educator; b. Kurnool, Andhra, India, Jan. 1, 1934; s. S. M. and K.A. (Bee) Hussain; m. Alice Cordelia Pearce; 1 child, Ivy Amina. BA, Osmania Coll., Kurnool, 1955; MA, Osmania U., Hyderabad, India, 1957; MS, Tex. A&M U., 1963, PhD, 1966. Asst. prof. Tenn. Tech. U., Cookeville, 1966-68, Ohio U., Athens, 1968-70; vis. fellow Princeton U., N.J., 1977-78; prof. Western Ky. U., Bowling Green, 1970-80; prof. Mgmt. Scis. Lubin Grad. Sch. Bus., dir. doctoral program Pace U., NYC, 1982-92, prof. emeritus, 1993—2003; pres. Princeton Econ. Rsch., Inc., 1980-99, Pearce Cons. Svcs., 2000—. Cons. Oak Ridge (Tenn.) Nat. Lab., 1969-77, Inst. for Energy Analysis, Oak Ridge, 1975, Honeywell Corp., Mpls., 1985. Author: Quantitative Methods for Business, 1974, Nuclear Fuel and Energy Policy, 1979; author, editor: Technology, International Stability, and Growth, 1984. Mem. cirs. bd. The Kennedy Ctr., 1997-2000. Recipient Achievement award Oak Ridge Nat. Lab., 1977, IEEE Centennial Medal, 1983, Millennium medal, 2000. Fellow AAAS, Systems, Man, and Cybernetics Soc. (pres. 1980-82). Home: 817 Albemarle Dr Bowling Green KY 42103 E-mail: sbahmed@aol.com.

AHRENHOLTZ, MARY MICKELSON, special education educator; b. Harlan, Iowa, July 17, 1951; d. Howard Gail and Dolores Beatrice (Wiig) Mickelson; m. Clark C. Ahrenholtz, Mar. 21, 1980; children: Tabitha Catherine, Camilla Christina. AA, N.E. C.C., Norfolk, Nebr., 1976; BA in Edn. cum laude, Wayne (Nebr.) State Coll., 1979; MA in Spl. Edn., Morningside Coll., Sioux City, Iowa, 1994. Lic. tchr. elem. edn., remedial reading, learning disabilities, multicategorical resource-mild. Tchr. 6th grade Irwin (Iowa)-Kirkman Cmty. Sch., 1979-82; substitute tchr. Shelby County Area Schs., Harlan and Irwin, 1982-88; resource rm. tchr. Harlan Cmty. Sch., 1988—. Mem. NEA, Iowa Cheerleaders Coaches Assn., Nat. Spirit Fedn., Iowa Assn. Mid. Level Edn., Womens Sports Found., Iowa State Edn. Assn., Harlan Edn. Assn. Republican. Avocations: genealogy, piano, quilting. Home: 1412 7th St Harlan IA 51537-1716 Office: Harlan Mid Sch 700 Baldwin St Harlan IA 51537-1612

AIELLO, ELIZABETH BLACKWELL, secondary school educator; b. Chgo., Nov. 24, 1946; d. William Thomas and Betty Louise (Landis) Blackwell; m. John William Aiello, Mar. 7, 1970; 1 child, Sarah Elizabeth. EdB, Ind. U., 1968; MS in Reading, Western Ill. U., 1992. Cert. tchr. 6-12 reading endorsement, Ill. Tchr. S.E. H.S., Springfield, Ill., 1968-69, St. Aloysius Sch., Springfield, 1971-72, St. Patrick Sch., Springfield, 1974-75, St. Agnes Sch., Springfield, 1977—. Mem. DAR, Internat. Reading Assn., Nat. Coun. English Tchrs., Ctrl. Ill. Reading Coun., Nat. Cath. Educators Assn., Alpha Upsilon Alpha. Home: 156 Maple Grv Springfield IL 62707-9567 Office: St Agnes Sch 251 N Amos Ave Springfield IL 62702-4792

AIKEN, DOROTHY LOUISE, secondary education educator; b. Washington, Apr. 27, 1924; d. Willard Ross and Gertrude (Rucker) Snyder; m. William David Aiken, May 22, 1948 (dec. 1988); children: Katherine Aiken Schwartz, Mary Aiken Fishback, Sally Aiken Fitterer, Jerome. BS, George Washington U., 1946; postgrad., Wash. State U., 1946-47. Teaching fellow Wash. State U., Pullman, 1946-47; tchr. secondary sch. D.C. Schs., Washington, 1947-50; tchr. Sunnyside (Wash.) Sch. Dist. 201, 1962-80. Sec. vestry Holy Trinity Ch., 1968-70; staff Evergreen Girls State, 1972-81; Dem. precinct committeeman, Sunnyside, 1980-86; mem. com. Margaret Rayburn Legislator campaign, Grandview, Wash., 1990; vice chair Yakima Valley C.C., 1994-95, trustee, chair, 1995-97; trustee Assn. Cmty. and Tech. Colls., mem. conf. com., 1992; co-producer Valley Mus. Comedy Co. Prodns., 1989-91; chmn. Hospice Light Up a Life, 1991; vol., program head ARC. Mem. Am. Legion Aux. (pres. 1974-76, meritorious svc. citation 1983, 88), Nouvella Federated Women's Club (2d v.p. 1984-86), Women's Golf Assn. (pres.). Episcopalian. Avocations: golf, swimming. Home: 1241 Sunset Pl Sunnyside WA 98944-1720

AIKEN, LINDA HARMAN, nurse, sociologist, educator; b. Roanoke, Va., July 29, 1943; d. William Jordan and Betty Philips (Warner) Harman; children: June Elizabeth, Alan James. BSN, U. Fla., 1964, M in Nursing, 1966; PhD in Sociology, U. Tex., 1973. Nurse Med. Ctr. U. Fla., Gainesville, 1964-65, instr. coll. nursing, 1966-67; instr. sch. of nursing U. Mo., Columbia, 1967-70, clin. nurse specialist sch. of nursing, 1967-70; program officer Robert Wood Johnson Found., Princeton, N.J., 1974-76, dir. rsch., 1976-79, asst. v.p., 1979-81, v.p., 1981-87; Claire M. Fagin Leadership prof. nursing, prof. sociology U. Pa., Phila., 1988—, dir. Ctr. for Health Svcs. and Policy Rsch., 1988—, rsch. assoc. population studies ctr. Mem. Sec. Health and Human Svcs. Commn. on Nursing, 1988, Pres. Clinton's Nat. Health Care Reform Task Force, 1993; commr. Physician Payment Rev. Commn. nat. adv. coun. U.S. Agy. for Health Care Policy and Rsch. Author: Health Policy and Nursing Practice, 1981, Nursing in the 1980s, 1982, Applications of Social Science to Clinical Medicine and Health Policy, 1986, Evaluation Studies Rev. Ann., 1985, Charting Nursing's Future, 1991, Hospital Restructuring in North America and Europe, 1997; contbr. articles to profl. jours. Mem. Adv. Council Social Security, 1982-83. Recipient Joint Secretarial commendation U.S. Dept. Health and Human Services and HUD, 1987; NIH Nurse Scientist fellow, 1970-73. Mem. ANA (Jessie M. Scott award 1984), Am. Acad. Arts and Scis., Assn. Health Svcs. Rsch. (Disting. Investigator), Inst. Medicine, Nat. Acad. Scis., Nat. Acad. Social Ins., Am. Acad. Nursing (pres. 1979-80), Am. Sociol. Assn. (chair med. sociology sect. 1983-84), Sociol. Rsch. Assn., Coun. Nurse Rschrs. (Nurse Scientist of Yr. 1991), Sigma Theta Tau, Phi Kappa Phi. Home: 2209 Lombard St Philadelphia PA 19146-1107 Office: U Pa 420 Service Dr Philadelphia PA 19104-4210

AIKEN, MICHAEL THOMAS, former academic administrator; b. El Dorado, Ark., Aug. 20, 1932; s. William Floyd and Mary (Gibbs) Aiken; m. Catherine Comet, Mar. 28, 1969; 1 child, Caroline R. BA, U. Miss., 1954; MA, U. Mich., 1955, PhD, 1964. Asst. prof. U. Wis., Madison, 1963—67, assoc. prof., 1967—70, prof., 1970—84, assoc. dean coll. arts and scis., 1980—82; prof. U. Pa., Phila., 1984—93, dean sch. arts and scis., 1985—87, provost, 1987—93; chancellor U. Ill., Urbana, 1993—2001, Champaign/Urbana, 1993—2001. Co-author: The Dynamics of Idealism, 1971, Economic Failure, Alienation, and Extremism, 1968; co-editor: Complex Organizations: Critical Perspectives, 1981, The Structures of Community Power, 1970. Mem.: Am. Sociol. Assn. (sec. 1986—89). E-mail: aiken@uiuc.edu.*

AIKENS, DONALD THOMAS, educational administrator, consultant; b. L.A., June 17, 1931; s. Clarence Beatty and Edith Grace (Crippin) A.; m. Marjorie Jane Conley, Aug. 6, 1960. AA, Glendale Coll., 1951; BS, U. So. Calif., 1953, MS, 1960. Cert. tchr., pupil pers., adminstr., Calif. Indsl. rels. mgr. Gen. Petroleum Corp., L.A., 1953-55; elem. tchr. Gallatin Elem. Dist., Downey, Calif., 1955-57; jr. high tchr. Burbank (Calif.) Unified Sch. Dist., 1957-59, Palm Springs (Calif.) Unified Sch. Dist., 1959-65, counselor, 1965-70, asst. prin., 1970-77, adminstr. The Ind. Study Program, 1977-94; trustee, pres. Palm Springs Unified Sch. Dist. Bd. Edn., 1995—; pres. Riverside County Sch. Bds. Assn., 2000—02. Creator The Ind. Study Program, Palm Springs Unified Sch. Dist., 1977. Chairperson, bd. dirs. United Way of the Desert, Palm Springs, 1987—. Named to Riverside County Edu. Hall of Fame, 2002. Mem. Nat. Assn. Secondary Sch. Prins. (cons., presentor 1980—), Calif. Consortium for Ind. Study (pres. 1983-85), Rotary Club (pres. 1987-88), Trojan Club of the Desert (pres. 1983-88). Methodist. Office: Palm Springs Unified Sch Dist 980 E Tahquitz Canyon Way Palm Springs CA 92262-6786 Fax: 760-416-8051.

AIKENS, ELAINE BOWER, secondary school educator; b. Roanoke, Va., Jan. 2, 1953; d. Carl Dove and Mildred (Hockett) Bower; m. Walter Harrison Aikens, Oct. 18, 1974; children: William Harrison, Jason Carl. B in Music Edn., Shenandoah U., 1975. Tchr. K-5 Warren County Pub. Schs., Front Royal, Va., 1975—79; pre-sch. tchr., dir. Sch. 1st Presbyn. Ch., Winchester, Va., 1985—88; music tchr. K-5 Frederick County Pub. Schs., Winchester, 1987—91; music tchr. grades 6,7, 8 Daniel Morgan Middle Sch., Winchester, 1991—2000; music tchr. grades 9-12 John Handley High Sch., Winchester, 2000—. V.p. Shenandoah Apple Blossom Festival, Winchester, 1985—; mem. alumni bd. Shenandoah U., Winchester, pres. libr. bd. Recipient Artie award, Shenandoah Arts Coun., 1998, Disting. Svc. award, Shenandoah U., 1998. Mem.: Va. Music Edn. Assn., Music Educators Nat. Conf., Delta Psi Omega. Baptist. Avocations: singing, acting. Home: 819 Armistead St Winchester VA 22601

AIKIN, JUDITH POPOVICH, languages educator, academic administrator; b. L.A., Aug. 6, 1946; d. Milosh and Jeanne (Hartman) Popovich; m. Roger Cushing Aikin, Dec. 27, 1966; 1 child, Thomas. BA, U. Oreg., 1968, MA, 1969; PhD, U. Calif., Berkeley, 1974. Asst. prof. U. Iowa, Iowa City, 1975-81, assoc. prof., 1981-88, prof., 1988—, assoc. dean liberal arts, 1990-92, interim dean liberal arts, 1992-93, dean liberal arts, 1993-97, prof. German, 1988—. Author: The Mission of Rome in the Dramas of Daniel Casper von Lohenstein: Historical Tragedy as Prophecy and Polemic, 1978, German Baroque Drama, 1982, Scaramutza in Germany: The Dramatic Works of Caspar Stieler, 1989, A Language for German Opera: The Development of Forms and Formulas for Recitative and Aria in Seventeenth-Century German Libretti, 2002; contbr. articles to profl. jours. Fellow NEH, 1988, Am. Coun. Learned Socs., 1988-89. Mem. MLA (chair exec. com. divsn. German lit. to 1700, 1989), Soc. for German Renaissance and Baroque Lit. (pres. 1985), Am. Assn. Tchrs. German. Office: U Iowa Dept German 528 PH Iowa City IA 52242 E-mail: judith-aikin@uiowa.edu.

AILLAUD, CINDY LOU VIRGINIA, elementary education educator; b. Renton, Wash., May 10, 1955; d. Ronald Delano and Lola May Virginia (Marberg) Petett;m. Whitney Lane Aillaud, June 11, 1976; children: Jason, Brian. BA in Edn., Wash. State U., 1977; spl. edn. endorsement, Ctrl. Wash. U., 1989. Lic. elem. and spl. edn. Tchr. 6th grade North Auburn (Wash.) Elem. Sch., 1977-78; tchr. K-5th grade Arctic Village (Alaska) Sch., 1978-79; tchr. 5th and 6th grades Delta Elem. Sch., Delta Junction, Alaska, 1979-82, tchr. 3rd grade, 1993-95, tchr. spl. edn. grades 4-6, 1995-97; kindergarten tchr., 1997-98; K-3 phys. edn./spl. edn. tchr., 1998—2001; tchr. 4th and 5th grade Ft. Greely (Alaska) Sch., 1989-90, tchr. spl. edn. K-6th grade, 1990-93, tchr. K-6 elem. phys. edn., 2001—. Developer district wide wellness program Seward Wellness, Delta Junction, 1991-94; dir., coord. elem. plays Delta/Greely Sch.Dist., Delta Junction, 1993-97; spirit and pride com. chair Delta Elem. Sch., Delta Junction, 1994. Mem., officer Delta/Greely Arts Coun., Delta Junction, 1980-84; clk. elections bd. State of Alaska, Delta Junction, 1984-98; dir. Miss Delta Pageant Deltana Fair, Delta Junction, 1993; cubmaster pack 76 Boy Scouts Am., Delta Junction, 1992-96. Fulbright scholar, 2000. Fellow Sci. Consortium; mem. NEA (Alaska Steeringard rules com. at del. assembly 1998—), AAHPERD, Delta/Greely Edn. Assn. (assoc. rep. del. assembly 1993-98, bldg. rep. 1993-97, Delta/Greely Sch. Dist. Tchr. of Yr. 1993, co-pres. 1999-2002). Avocations: hiking, photography, walking, travel. Office: Delta Elem Sch PO Box 647 Delta Junction AK 99737

AINSWORTH, JOAN HORSBURGH, university development director; b. Cleve., Dec. 30, 1942; d. Donald Francis and Elaine Mildred Horsburgh; m. Richard B. Ainsworth Jr., Oct. 30, 1965; children: Richard B. III, Alison. BA, Wells Coll., 1965; MBA, Case Western Res. U., 1986. Cert. fund raising exec. Social worker San Diego County (Calif.) Welfare Dept., 1966-68; social worker, vol. coord. Washtenaw County (Mich.) Juvenile Ct., Ann Arbor, 1968-70; adminstrv. asst. to pres. Med. Ventures, Ltd., Cleve., 1985-86; dir. Project MOVE, Office of Mayor City of Cleve., 1986-89; dir. devel. and pres.'s programs Case Western Res. U., Cleve., 1989-97, dir. spl. gifts and prin. projects, 1997-98, dir. devel. Coll. Arts and Scis., 1998-2001, asst. dean for devel. Coll. Arts and Scis., 2001—. Trustee, v.p. Children's Aid Soc., Cleve., 1989—, pres., 1997—; trustee, chair devel. Project: LEARN, Cleve., 1990-96; past trustee, cmty. vol. Jr. League Cleve., Inc., 1971—; mem. Vol. Ohio, 1987-96. Named Hon. Mayor City of Cleve., 1989. Mem.: Coun. for Advancement and Support of Edn., Nat. Assn. Fundraising Profls. (cert, chair publicity Greater Cleve. chpt. 1994—96). Avocations: flying, tennis, boating, travel. Home: 2023 Lyndway Rd Cleveland OH 44121-4265 Office: Case Western Res U 10900 Euclid Ave Cleveland OH 44106-1712 E-mail: jha@po.cwru.edu.

AIRD, ROBERT BURNS, neurologist, educator; b. Provo, Utah, Nov. 5, 1903; s. John William and Emily Dawn (McAuslan) A.; m. Ellinor Hill Collins, Oct. 5, 1935 (dec. 1988); children: Katharine (dec. 1992), Mary, John, Robert. BA, Cornell U., 1926; MD, Harvard Med. Sch., 1930. Diplomate Nat. Bd. Med. Examiners, Am. Bd. Psychiatry and Neurology. Intern Strong Meml. Hosp-U. Rochester (N.Y.) Sch. Medicine, 1930-31, resident, 1931-32; rsch. assoc. U. Calif., San Francisco, 1932-35, instr., 1935-39, from asst. to assoc. prof., 1939-49, prof. neurology, 1949-71, founder dept. neurology, 1947, chmn. dept. neurology, 1947-66, established Electroencephalographic Lab., 1940, dir. Electroencephalographic Lab., 1940-71. Neurology cons. 9 hosps., Calif.; trustee Deep Springs Coll., Inyo County, Calif., 1959-71, dir. coll., 1960-66, hon. trustee, 1971—; founder No. Calif. chpt. Multiple Sclerosis Soc.; mem. five coms. NIH, Washington, 1953-63; rep. of AMA on Residency Rev. Bd., 1967-73; lectr. in field, U.S. and 10 fgn. countries. Author: Foundations of Modern Neurology: A Century of Progress, 1993, Conversations with Dr. Robert B. Aird: The Origins of Neuroscience at University California, San Francisco, 1995, Deep Springs--Its Founder, History and Philosophy, with Personal Recollections; ; sr. author: Management of Epilepsy, 1974, The Epilepsies-A Critical Review, 1984; co-author: Clinical Neurology, 1955, Textbooks of Medicine, 1959, 62; editl. bd. Internat. Jour. Electroencephalography and Clin. Neurophysiology, 1945-65, Jour. Nervous and Mental Disorders, 1952-67; contbr. numerous articles to profl. jours. Founding chmn. William G. Lennox Trust Fund, 1961-69. Fulbright scholar, 1957-58; recipient Royer Significant Contbns. to Advancement of Neurology award, 1969, Hope Chest award Nat. Multiple Sclerosis Soc., 1962, 72, 82; founder vis. professorship in neurology U. Calif., San Francisco, 1949, endowed and named in his honor, 1973, professorship established, 1991, bldg. named in his honor Deep Springs Coll. (Medal of Honor, 1995), 1971, professorship, 1993. Mem. AAAS, Am. Episepsy Soc. (hon. pres. 1959-60, Lennox award 1970), Am. Electronecephalographic Soc. (charter mem., pres. 1953-54), Am. Neurol. Assn. (v.p. 1955, 69, 72, sr. mem.), Pan-Am. Med. Soc. (N.Am. v.p. 1966), Calif. Acad. Sci. (life), Calif. Acad. Medicine, San Francisco Neurol. Soc. (co-founder, pres. 1951-52), Am. Bd. Qualification in Electroencephalography (founding chair), Western Soc. Electroencephalography (founder pres. 1946), Swedish Soc. of Med. Scis. (hon.), Argentina Assn. Neurol. and Psychiatry (hon.), Gold Headed Care Soc. (hon.), San Francisco Med. Soc. (hon.), Calif. Med. Assn. (hon.), others. Achievements include establishment of importance of blood-brain barrier in cerebral concussions, EST and epileptogenesis of CNS lesions; identification and control of seizure-inducing mechanisms for comprehensive management of epilepsy; research on CNS effects of subarachnoid-injected agents, on the effect of thyrotropic hormone in production of malignant exophthalmos. Office: U Calif Dept Neurology M-798 PO Box 114 San Francisco CA 94143-0001

AISENBERG, ALAN C. physician, educator, researcher; b. N.Y.C., Dec. 7, 1926; s. Jacob and Celia (Able) A.; m. Nadya Margulies, Oct. 2, 1952 (dec. Apr. 1999); children: James, Margaret. SB, Harvard U., 1945, MD, 1950; PhD, U. Wis., 1956. Diplomate Am. Bd. Internal Med. Internship and resident Presbyn. Hosp., N.Y.C., 1950-53; instr. medicine Harvard Med. Sch., Boston, 1956-62, asst. prof., 1962-69, assoc. prof., 1969-84, prof., 1984—; asst. physician Mass. Gen. Hosp., Boston, 1959-69, assoc. physician, 1969-84, physician, 1984—. Mem. Clin. Trials Com. Nat. Cancer Inst., Bethesda, Md., 1977-82. Author: Glycolysis and Respiration of Tumors, 1961, Malignant Lymphoma: Biology, Natural History and Treatment, 1991; contbr. over 150 articles on rsch. in oncology to profl. jours. Recipient Guggenheim Fellowship, Guggenheim Found. Nat. Inst. for Med. Research, London, 1964-65. Mem. Am. Coll. of Physicians, Am. Soc. of Clin. Oncology, Am. Assn. Immunologists. Home: 124 Chestnut St Boston MA 02108-3318 Office: Mass Gen Hosp Fruit St Boston MA 02114-2620 E-mail: aaisenberg@partners.org.

AITCHISON, SUANN, elementary school educator; b. Paterson, N.J., Oct. 1, 1941; d. Archie Wilson and Isabell (Farrow) A. BA, William Paterson Coll., 1963, MEd, 1976; student, Fairleigh Dickinson U., 1991, St. Peter's Coll., 1996. Cert. elem. edn., reading tchr., elem. reading specialist. Tchr. 3d grade Fair Lawn (N.J.) Pub. Schs., 1963-64, 70-71, tchr. 2d grade, 1964-70, 71-87, tchr. reading, 1987-95, reading specialist, 1997—; tchr. reading and math. Fair Lawn (N.J.) Bd. Edn., 1996—; literacy specialist grades 6-8 Meml. and Thomas Jefferson Mid. Schs., Fair Lawn, 2003—. Adj. prof. William Paterson Coll., 1977; developer curriculum guides for remedial reading, 1989, lang. arts and reading for ESL children, 1989, lang. arts and reading for gifted children, 1989, libr. skills and lit. for neurologically impaired children, 1991; mem. Coun. Basic Edn., 1997; com. mem. Bergen County Celebrates Excellence and Pride in our Pub. Schs., 1997. Active Observation and Evaluation Revision Com., 1995, Cerebral Palsy Ctr.; choir Ch. in Radburn, 1993—95; mem. Garretson Forge Found., 1993—95; assoc. Cerebral Palsy Ctr., 1993—95; mem. com. Bergen County Celebrates Excellence and Pride in Edn., 1997; mem. Coun. for Basic Edn., 1997, Borough Fair Lawn Family Aquatic Study Com., 1997—; dist. reading tchr. family literacy reading take home program grades 1-2 elem. schs., 1999—; mem. 1st class Fair Lawn Police Dept.'s Citizen's Police Acad. Course, 2002; reapptd. mem. adv. com. Ams. with Disability Act, 2002—; com. mem. Fair Lawn Rep. County Com., 1986—98, rec. sec., 1994; vol. Gov. Whitman primary and gen. election campaigns, 1992; mem. Fair Lawn mayor and coun. adv. com. Ams. With Disabilities Act, 1996. Mem. AAHPERD, ASCD (premium mem. 1995—), AAUW, N.J. Reading Assn. (North Jersey coun. 1987-95), Coun. Exceptional Children, N.J. ASCD, Math. Assn. Am., Nat. Coun. Tchrs. of English, Coun. Ednl. Diagnostic Svcs., Fair Lawn Rep. Club (trustee 1997), Fair Lawn Pride Com. Assn., Nat. Assn. Secondary Prins. Baptist. Avocations: singing, reading, restaurant dining, theater, concerts. Home: 38-56 Van Duren Ave Fair Lawn NJ 07410-5018 Office: Fair Lawn Bd Edn 37-01 Fair Lawn Ave Fair Lawn NJ 07410-4919

AITKEN, RUTH ELAINE WILLSON, educational and career/job search consultant; BS in Secondary Edn., Indiana U. of Pa.; MS in Human Devel./Family Studies, postgrad., Pa. State U. Cert. tchr. Pa. Dir. field placements Pa. State U., University Park, 1972-83; edn./mktg./mgmt. cons. Aitken Assocs., State College, Pa., 1983—. Substitute tchr. in secondary edn., 1985—94; intstr. and substitute tchr. Dept. Continuing Edn. Pa. State U., 1985—94. Regional chair Am. Cancer Soc., Arthritis Found., Centre Region Health Coun.; membership com. Centre County Coun. on Human Svcs. Mem.: Chamber of Bus. and Industry of Centre County, Bus. and Profl. Women (state and dist. conv. del, newsletter editor, founds. chair), Coll. Human Devel. Alumni Assn. (bd. dirs. nominations com., chair), Pa. State Alumni Assn. (univ.-alumni-faculty task force com.), Soroptimist Club (youth scholarship com.), Alpha Kappa Delta (Nat. Woman of Excellence award), Omicron Nu. Avocation: community service projects. Office: Aitken Assocs 124 S Patterson St State College PA 16801-3911

AIZAWA, HERMAN, state agency administrator; m. Muriel Ogata; children: Lisa Chan, Lori, Linda. EdB in Edn./Biology, U. Hawaii, 1963; MAT in Biol. Sci., Wash. State U., 1970; PhD in Ednl. Adminstrn., Ohio State U., 1974. Cert. profl. secondary tchr., profl. sch. adminstr. Tchr. biol. scis. Kailua (Hawaii) High Sch., 1964-70, vice prin., 1970-72; summer sch. dir. Kailua Complex Summer Sch., 1971, 72; prin. Waimanalo (Hawaii) Elem. & Intermediate Sch., 1974-76, Farrington High Sch., 1976-80; asst. supt. Office of Instrnl. Svcs., 1980-82, 87-91; prin. Kaiser High Sch., 1982-84, Pearl City High Sch., 1985-87; dep. supt. Supt's Office, Honolulu, 1991-94, supt., 1994—1998; prin. McKinley Cmty. Sch. for Adults, Honolulu, 1998—. Mem. Western Regional Ctr. Drug Free Schs. & Cmtys., 1988-91, chair, 1989-90. Author: A Technique for Projecting Pupil Enrollments in Underdeveloped and Changing Areas by Utilizing Federal Census Data, 1974, (with others) A Study of School Building Needs for the Westerville City School District, 1972, Educational Facility Needs of the Tipp City Exempted Village School District, 1974. Bd. dirs. Boy Scouts Am., 1980-83, mem. long-range membership planning com., 1993—; mem. Waimanalo Edn. Task Force, 1974-75; bd. dirs. Kalihi-Palama Cmty. Coun., 1977-78, Kalihi YMCA, 1978—; mem. Kalihi Interagy. Coun., 1979-80; chairperson Leasehold Conversion Com., Pikailoa Tract, Kaneohe, 1979-82; bd. dirs. Troy Barboza Ednl. Fund, 1992—. NSF fellow Wash. State U., 1967, 68, 69; recipient Outstanding Young Educator award Jr. C. of C., Kaneohe, 1969; Cmty. scholar, State of Hawaii, 1972-74, Willis B. Coale scholar Phi Delta Kappa, 1972-74; NEH fellow U. Calif., San Diego, 1977; Leadership fellow U. So. Calif., 1988. Mem. Am. Assn. Sch. Adminstrs., Nat. Assn. Secondary Sch. Prins., Hawaii Cmty. Ednl. Assn. (treas. 1976-81, dir. 1986—), Phi Delta Kappa (pres.- elect Beta Tau chpt. 1971, pres. 1972, faculty rep. 1975-78). Avocations: golf, woodworking, coral carving, photography. Office: 634 Pensacola St Rm 216 Honolulu HI 96816*

AKANA, KEITH KALANI, elementary education educator, consultant; b. Honolulu, June 8, 1957; s. Arthur Kaheakulani and Iola Shinae (Hangai) A. BE, U. Hawaii, 1980; MEd, 1994. Resource tchr. Leeward Dist. Office, Manoa, 1984-89; lectr. Leeward Cmty. Coll., Pearl City, 1985-87; tchr. Waiau Elem. Sch., Pearl City, Hawaii, 1989—; lectr. U. Hawaii, Manoa, 1994. Cons. Ike Pono Cons., Honolulu, 1979—; dir. Ka Pa Hooheno Hawaii, Pearl City, 1984—, prodr., "Manaleo" TV series. Author: Pleiades, 1985; contbr. articles to profl. jours. V.p., 1980—, dir., 1992-94, pres. Ahahui Olelo Hawaii, Honolulu, 1996; pres. Ahahui Kapiolani, Honolulu, 1990-94. Recipient Chant Competition King Kamehameha Commn., 1975, 80, 85, Ke Kukui Malamalama, Office of Hawaiian Affairs, 1991; grantee Bishop Mus., 1990; named Tchr. of Yr. Leeward Dist. Office, 1994. Mem. ASCD, NAESP. Avocations: hawaiian chant, travel, crafts, norman rockwell memorabilia.

AKAY, ADNAN, mechanical engineer, educator; BS, N.C. State U., 1971, MME, 1972, PhD, 1976. Rsch. fellow Nat. Inst. Environ. Scis., Research Triangle Park, N.C., 1976-78; from asst. prof. to DeVlieg prof. Wayne State U., Detroit, 1978-92; Lord prof., head dept. mech. engring. Carnegie-Mellon U., Pitts., 1992—. Coun. chmn. United Engring. Found., 1998-2000. Contbr. articles to profl. jours. Fellow ASME, Acoustical Soc. Am. Office: Carnegie Mellon U Dept Mech Engring Pittsburgh PA 15213

AKERS, WILLIAM WALTER, chemical engineering educator; b. Panola County, Tex., Dec. 31, 1922; s. Oscar Walter and Lela (Malone) A.; m. Nancy Tressel, Mar. 1, 1947; children— Susan Elaine, Carol Lorraine. BS, Tex. Tech Coll., 1943; MS, U. Tex., 1944; PhD, U. Mich., 1951. With Atlantic Refining Co., 1947; mem. faculty Rice U., 1947-93, prof. chem. engring., 1956—93, prof. emeritus, 1993—, chmn. dept., 1955-66; dir. Bio-Med. Engring., Lab., 1963-69, asst. to pres. univ., 1973-74, dir. univ. relations, 1974, v.p. for external affairs, 1975-80, v.p. adminstrn., 1980-89. Cons. chem. industries, 1947-65; mem. coun. Oak Ridge Inst. Nuclear Studies, 1958-63, vice chmn., 1962, bd. dirs., 1963-69; tech. adviser to Yugoslavia, 1962; mem. U.S.-Afghanistan Ednl. Consortium, 1963-70; rshc. project dir. Baylor Coll. Medicine, 1965-70; mem. biomed. engring. fellowship com. NIH, 1967-70; mem. Sec.'s Adv. Coun. for Coal Mine Health Rsch., 1970-71; mem. adv. coun. Nat. Inst. Occupational Safety and Health, 1971-73; mem. adv. com. on nuclear energy Tex. Energy and Natural Resources Adv. Coun., 1980-88. Author papers in field. Trustee St. Luke's Hosp., Houston, 1975-79; bd. dirs. South Main Center Assn., 1976-87, Houston Symphony Soc., 1983-85; mem. adv. bd. Salvation Army, 1998—. Served with C.E., AUS, 1941-43. Recipient Disting. Engring. Alumnus award Tex. Tech U., 1967, Disting. Alumnus award, 1968 Mem. AAAS, Am. Chem. Soc., Am. Inst. Chem. Engrs. (Best Fundamental Paper award 1967, Distinguished lectr. 1969), Am. Soc. Artificial Organs, Council on Fgn. Relations, Houston Philos. Soc., Sigma Xi, Tau Beta Pi. Episcopalian. Home: 5214 Green Tree Rd Houston TX 77056-1309

AKIN, BARBARA JEAN, secondary educator; b. Monticello, Ark., Dec. 10, 1942; d. William Thomas and Agatha Mae (Linderman) Paschall; m. Joe Thomas Akin, Aug. 20, 1967; children: Kenneth Wayne, Joe Thomas Jr. BS in Edn., U. Ark., Monticello, 1964; MS in Edn., Memphis State U., 1968; postgrad., U. Ark., Fayetteville, 1979-90, U. Cen. Ark., 1989, Ark. State U., 1990-93. Bus. edn. vocat. endorsement, Ark. Tchr. bus. DeWitt (Ark.) High Sch., 1964-65, Bishop Bryne High Sch., Memphis, 1965-67, Monticello High Sch., 1967-96, ret., 1996. Instr. U. Ark., Monticello, 1979-94. Adviser Future Bus. Leaders Am., Monticello, 1967-96; team leader WalkAm., March of Dimes, Monticello, 1992. Mem. NEA, Ark. Edn. Assn., Monticello Edn. Assn. (sec. 1975, 95-96, bldg. rep. 1992), Am. Vocat. Assn., Ark. Vocat. Assn., Nat. Bus. Edn. Assn., So. Bus. Edn. Assn., Ark. Bus. Edn. Assn. (legis. action com. 1990), Classroom Bus. Office Educators, Beta Sigma Phi (svc. com. Monticello 1992), Delta Kappa Gamma (sec. Gamma Beta chpt. 1996-2001). Baptist. Avocations: reading, needlework. Home: PO Box 2 Monticello AR 71657-0002

AKIYAMA, TOSHIO, cardiologist, educator, researcher; b. Shimizu, Japan, Mar. 10, 1941; came to U.S., 1968; m. Akiko Okamura Akyama; children: Naoko, Sachiko. MD, Kyoto Prefectural U. Med., 1966. Cert. in internal medicine, specialty in cardiovasc. disease. Rotating intern U.S. Naval Hosp., Yokosuka, Japan, 1966—67; med. resident, 3d internal medicine dept. Kyoto Prefectural U. Medicine, 1967; staff physician Atomic Bomb Casualty Commn., Hiroshima, Japan, 1967—68; intern Rochester Gen. Hosp., 1968-69, resident in medicine, 1969-70, Strong Meml. Hosp.-U. Rochester, 1970-71, resident in cardiology, 1972-73; fellow in cardiology Emory U., Atlanta, 1971-72, U. Chgo., 1973-75; dir. heart sta. Strong Meml. Hosp., Rochester; prof. medicine with unltd. tenure U. Rochester Sch. Medicine, 1993—. Reviewer NIH study sect. Biomed. Tech. Spl. Emphasis Panel; cons. Exec. com. for Japanese Med. Specialist Joint commn. Mem. editl. bd. Jour. Electrocardiology, Japanese Circulation Jour., Acta Medica Mem. Biologica; contbr. over 150 articles to profl. jours. Chmn. Rochester Hamamatsu Sister City Com., chmn., 1998-2000. Fellow Am. Coll. Cardiology; mem. Am. Heart Assn., N.Am. Soc. of Pacing and Electrophysiology, Japanese Med. Soc. (exec. com. joint commn. med. specialist sys.), Japanese Clin. Cardiology Soc. Office: U Rochester Med Ctr Dept Cardiology 601 Elmwood Ave Box 679 Rochester NY 14642-8679 Office Fax: 585-242-9549. E-mail: toshio_akiyama@urmc.rochester.edu.

AKKARA, JOSEPH AUGUSTINE, chemist, educator; b. Feb. 22, 1938; came to U.S., 1964; naturalized, 1980; s. Augustine Aippu Akkara and Theresa Anthony Kolapran; m. Mary Ann Malaickel, Aug. 18, 1969; children: Augustine Viju, Jeena Theresa. PhD in Biochemistry, U. Mo., 1969. Med. rschr. Med. Coll. Trivandrum, Kerala, India, 1959-61; tech. asst. Ctrl. Food Technol. Rsch. Inst., Mysore, India, 1961-64; grad. asst., rsch. assoc. Sch. Medicine U. Mo., Columbia, 1964-69; rsch. assoc. Rockefeller U., N.Y.C., 1969-71, Brookdale Hosp. Med. Ctr., Bklyn., 1971-73, chief radioassay, 1973-80; sr. scientist Med. Rsch. Inst., Worcester, Mass., 1980-81; biochemist stat. Toxicology Svc. Boston, 1981-84; rsch. chemist U.S. Army Natick Rsch. and Engring. Ctr., 1984-99; program dir. NSF, 1999—. Adj. faculty Framingham State Coll., 1996-99; mem. biotechnology adv. bd. Mass. Bay Coll.; advisor NRC; bd. dirs. Invention Evaluation. Recipient R&D award U.S. Army, 1992, 96, Inventor of Yr. award U.S. Army Soldier Sys. commd., 1998. Mem. Materials Rsch. Soc., Am. Chem. Soc., N.Y. Acad. Scis., Kerala Assn. New Eng. (pres. 1986-87), Indian Assn. Greater Boston (sec. 1986-88, 1st v.p. 1988-89), Lions Club, Rotary, Sigma Xi (pres. Natick chpt. 1998-99). Roman Catholic. Achievements include patents and publications in synthesis, modification, characterization, and applications of polymers and materials for electro-optic and high performance multifunctional applications; enzymology, nutrition, endocrinology, analytical chemistry, and research program management. Home: 7520 Walnut Hill Ln Falls Church VA 22042-3539 E-mail: jakkara@nsf.gov., jaakkara@aol.com.

AKUBUILO, FRANCIS EKENECHUKWU, secondary school educator; b. Ebe-Udi, Enugu, Nigeria, Mar. 25, 1952; came to U.S., 1984; d. Robert O. and Regina N. (Agada) A.; m. Assumpta Ify Chinegwu, Aug. 22, 1987; children: Frank-Roberts, Olivia, Nneoma, Christopher-Daniel. AS, Fachhochschule, Stuttgart, Fed. Republic of Germany, 1983; MArch, Fachhochschule, Frankfurt, Fed. Republic of Germany, 1984; D in Bus., Pacific State U., 1985; M in Adminstrn., Nat. U., San Diego, 1989. BDB, Germany; cert. tchr. bus. & indsl. mgmt., basic edn., bus. edn., social sci., vocat. tng. Asst. archtl. engr. Albrecht Assocs., Stuttgart, 1978-83; asst. lectr. Fachhochschule, Frankfort, 1981-83; legal researcher Control Data, L.A., 1984; legal edn. researcher Am. Legal Systems, L.A., 1984-86; head para-lega litigation, supr. Chase, Rotchford, et. al., L.A., 1986—; adj. faculty prof. Coll. of Canyons, Valencia, Calif., 1990—; tchr. Calif. Youth Authority, Whittier, Calif., 1992—, Hacienda/ La Puente Sch., Whittier, Calif., 1992-93. Cons. Udi Div. Schs., Udi-Enugu, Nigeria, 1981-83, Frank's Consulting Svcs., L.A., 1988—; dir., pres. Okuli Enterprises, L.A., 1991—; dir. Enugu Cultural Assn., L.A., 1992—. Mem. German Architects Engrs. Assn. Roman Catholic. Avocations: table tennis, soccer, jogging. Home: 7122 Bon Villa Cir La Palma CA 90623-1167

AKUJUOBI, CAJETAN MADUABUCHUKWU, systems engineer, electrical engineering educator, researcher; b. Umuahia, Abia, Nigeria, Apr. 18, 1950; came to U.S., 1977; s. John Ohiri and Roseline (Amadi) A.; m. Caroline Chioma Njoku, May 8, 1982; children: Obinna Chukwuemeka, Chijoke Eze. BSEE, So. Univ., 1980; MSEE, Tuskegee (Ala.) Inst., 1983; MBA, Hampton U., 1987; PhD, George Mason U., 1995. Asst. prof. elec. engr. Norfolk State U., Va., 1983-96; R&D engr. Austin Product Ctr., Schlumberger Inc., 1996-97; engr. sr. design and devel. Data Race, Inc., San Antonio, 1997—; rsch./systems engr., cons. Advanced Hardware Architectures, Inc., Pullman, Wash., 1998—; assoc. prof., rschr. NASA ctr. space radiation Prairie View A&M U., Prairie View, Tex., 1998—; assoc. prof. electr. engrng. Praire View A&M Univ., Praire View, TX, 1998—, dir. mixed-signal DSP solutions and broadband access tech., 1999—; dir. Ctr. of Excellence for Comm. Systems Tech. Rsch., 2001—. Adj. assoc. prof. U. D.C., 1989-90; rsch. fellow NASA, Langley, Va., 1987; tech. staff AT&T Bell Labs., Holmdel, N.J., 1986, 88, 90, 91; prin. engr. Spectrum Engring. & Tech., Washington, 1991-92; rschr. George Mason U., Fairfax, Va., 1991-94; engr. Intelsat, Washington, 1993; session chmn. Modeling and Simulation Conf., Pitts., 1986-90; judge Tidewater Sci. Fair, Southampton H.S., Courtland, Va., 1994; chief judge sr. engring. design projects Tidewater Sci. Fair, 1996, head jusge, 1995; faculty rsch. participant Argonne Nat. Lab., 1995-96; dir. analog and mixed signals and DSP solutions programs Prairie View A&M U. Mem. SPIE, IEEE (award 1982, 83, counselor 1977—, judge 1986), Instrument Soc. Am. (chmn. digital sys. 1986, session organizer 1986—), Am. Soc. Engring. Edn. (campus rep. 1983—), Soc. Indsl. and Applied Math., Sigma Xi, Alpha Kappa Mu. Roman Catholic. Avocations: soccer, tennis, swinning, volleyball, table tennis. Home: 14826 Cascade Bend Ln Cypress TX 77429-4555 Office: A&M U Dept Elec Engring PO Box 2117 Prairie View TX 77446-2117

AKUTSU, HIDEO, biophysical chemist, educator; b. Tokyo, Mar. 21, 1944; s. Yashichi and Hideyo (Mashima) A.; m. Junko Sato, Mar. 26, 1973; children: Shiho, Miho, Chihiro. BS, U. Tokyo, 1967, MS, 1969, DS, 1973. Instr. Osaka (Japan) U., 1972, assoc. prof., 1985-86, vis. assoc. prof., 1987-88; assoc. prof. Yokohama (Japan) Nat. U., 1985, prof., 1991-2001, chmn. div. material scis. and chem. engring. Grad. Sch., 1994-96; prof. Osaka (Japan) U., 2000—. Vis. scientist U. Basel, Switzerland, Japan Soc. for Promotion Sci., 1978, European Molecular Biology Orgn. fellow, 1979-80; vis. prof. U. Ariz., Tucson, 1989. Contbr. articles to profl. jours. Grantee Japan Ministry Edn., Sci. and Culture, 1985-86, 89-94, 97—; rsch. grantee New Energy and Indsl. Tech. Devel. Orgn., Tokyo, 1995-97. Mem. Biophys. Soc. Japan (steering com. 1993-94, 2000-03), Japanese Biochem. Soc., Chem. Soc. Japan. Achievements include patents for a lipid membrane structure containing muramyldipeptide; determiniation of the polar head group of lipgid bilaryers by 2H-NMR; determination of microscopic redox potentials of tetraheme cytochromes by NMR. Home: 1-4-27-131 Nishimidorigaoka Toyonaka 560-0005 Japan Office: Osaka U Inst Protein Rsch 3-2 Yamadaoka Suita 565-0871 Japan E-mail: akutsu@protein.osaka-u.ac.jp.

ALADEEN, LARY JOE, secondary school educator; b. St. Joseph, Mo., Oct. 17, 1946; s. Joseph Harold and Hilda Marie (Bowman) A.; m. Donna Marlene Hill, July 1, 1972 (div.); 1 child, Juliana Hill; m. Robin Irene Williams, Dec. 19, 1999. BA, Calif. Bapt. Coll., Riverside, 1971; MA, Calif. State U., Hayward, 1989. Cert. secondary tchr., cmty. coll. tchr., Calif. Tchr. Norbridge H.S., Castro Valley, Calif., 1974-75, Foothill H.S., Pleasanton, Calif., 1975—. Cons. George Lucas Edn. Found., Mill Valley, Calif., 1992; reader Golden State exam. Calif. Dept. Edn., Sacramento, 1994—; mem. social studies curriculum rev. com. Pleasanton (Calif.) Unified Sch. Dist., 1989-90; presenter seminar workshop Calif. Coun. for Social Studies Conv., 1993. Editor: Supplemental Readings for A.P. U.S. History, 1994.

Media rep. Dem. Campaign Com., Riverside, 1972; vol. Dem. Election campaigns, Pleasanton, 1976-94, Love, Inc., San Mateo, Calif., 1992—. With USMC, 1967-70. Recipient Outstanding Svc. award Amador Valley Secondary Edn. Assn., Pleasanton, 1982-83; Mentor Tchr., Pleasanton Unified Sch. Dist., 1985-86, Master Tchr., 1988-91. Mem. Orgn. Am. Historians, Nat. Coun. for the Social Studies, Calif. Coun. for the Social Studies. Democrat. Presbyterian. Avocations: golf, writing, travel. Home: 855 La Playa St Apt 152 San Francisco CA 94121-3250 Office: Foothill High Sch 4375 Foothill Rd Pleasanton CA 94588-9720

ALAGHBAND, GITA, computer engineer, educator; b. Tehran, Iran, Jan. 15, 1955; d. Shodja Alaghband and Momtaz Majd-Teymoury; m. Hamid Z. Fardi, July 27, 1979; children: Nicole, Sara. BS in Physics, U. Tehran, 1976; MS in Computer Sci., U. Colo., 1980, PhD in Elec. Engring., 1986. Rsch. fellow NASA, Hampton, Va., 1985; postdoctoral rsch. assoc., adj. prof. Univ. Colo., Boulder, 1986; asst. prof. ECSE dept. Rensselaer Polytech. Inst., Troy, N.Y., 1987; asst. prof. computer sci. and engring. dept. U. Colo., Denver, 1987-94, assoc. prof. computer sci. and engring. dept., 1994—, dept. chair, 1996—, prof., 1997—. Contbr. articles to profl. jours. Recipient rsch. award NSF, 1993-96. Office: Univ Colo Dept Computer Sci PO Box 173364 Denver CO 80217-3364

ALANIS, FELIPE, education commissioner; b. Oct. 6, 1948; m. Gracie Alanis; 4 children. BS, MS, U.Tex.-Pan Am; D in Ednl. Adminstrn., U. Tex. From tchr. to prin. Pharr-San Juan-Alamo Schs., 1970—80; exec. dir. for secondary edn. Odessa's Ector County Ind. Sch. Dist., Tex., 1989—92, dep. supt., 1992—94; supt. San Benito Consolidated Ind. Sch. Dist., Rio Grande Valley, 1994—95; dep. commr. for programs and instruction Tex. Edn. Agy, 1995—99; vice chancellor acad. affairs U. Tex. Edn. System, Austin, 1999—2002; commr. of edn. Tex. Dept. Edn., Austin, 2002—. Mem. sr. staff Commr. Jim Nelson, Austin, 1999—2002. Office: Tex Edn Agy Wm B Travis Bldg 1701 N Congress Ave Austin TX 78701-1494

ALANIZ, THEODORA VILLARREAL, elementary education educator; b. Mercedes, Tex., Feb. 16, 1951; d. Alejandro and Maria (Villarreal) A. BS in Elem. Edn., Pan Am. U., 1979; MEd, Tex. A&I U., 1984; cert. in counseling, U. Tex., 1992. Cert. vocat. counselor, Level I and II lic. chem. dependency counselor, South Tex. C.C. Asst. tchr. Mercedes Ind. Sch. Dist., 1973-78; tchr. Pharr (Tex.)-San-Juan-Alamo Ind. Sch. Dist., 1979-91, Edcouch-Elsa (Tex.) Ind. Sch. Dist., 1991-93; counselor Donna Ind. Sch. Dist., 1993—. Census rep. Diocese of Brownsville, 1974-75; choir mem. Sacred Heart Ch., Mercedes, Tex., 1974-78, 3rd grade tchr., 1975-78; rep. Cancer Soc., Mercedes, 1980-81, Assn. Tex. and Profl. Educators to Pharr and Elsa Ind. Sch. Dists. Scholar Title VII Bilingual/Bicultural, 1978-79. Roman Catholic. Avocations: photography, pencil drawing, sight seeing. Address: RR 4 Box 161-c Mercedes TX 78570-9313

ALANO, ERNESTO OLARTE, secondary education educator; b. Naga City, Philippines, Aug. 2, 1948; s. Pedro Quirante and Nieves (Olarte) A.; m. Arsenia Paulino Monedera, June 18, 1972; children: Jose Paulo Monedera Alano, Dionessa Monedera Alano. BA, Ateneo de Naga Coll., Philippines, 1969; MA, Loyola Marymount U., L.A., 1979. Classroom tchr. Ateneo de Naga, Philippines, 1969-74, Xavier H.S., Truk, 1974-79; dir. Diocesan Catechetical Program, Caroline/Marshall Islands, 1979-81; classroom tchr. Acad. of Our Lady, Guam, 1981-83; social worker Cath. Social Svc., Guam, 1983-86; classroom tchr. Hopwood Jr. H.S., Northern Marianas, 1986-96; pastoral asst. San Juan Bautista Ch., Ordot, Guam, 1997—. Pres. Commonwealth Accreditation Network, Northern Marianas, 1994-95. Editor, advisor Book of Poems, Vols., 1, 2, 3, 1989-95. V.p. Filipino Cmty., Inc., No. Marianas, 1989-95; sec. Fedn. of Filipino Assns., No. Marianas, 1994-95. Recipient Nat. New Hero award Bagong Bayani Found., Philippines, 1994; named Outstanding Pacific Educator, Pacific Region Ednl. Lab., Hawaii, 1994. Mem. Nat. State Tchrs. of Yr. (state rep. 1994-95), Kappa Delta Pi. Roman Catholic. Avocations: reading, jogging, playing basketball. Office: San Juan Bautista Ch PO Box 49 Hagatna GU 96932-0049

ALAO, ADEKOLA OLATUNJI, psychiatrist, educator; b. Iwo, Nigeria, June 5, 1960; s. Joseph and Deyo Alao; m. Lola Ojo; children: Deyo, Dami. MD, U. Ibadan, Nigeria, 1983; MSc in Mental Health Studies, U. London, 1995; MRCPsych, U. Oxford, U.K., 1996. Diplomate Am. Bd. Psychiatry 2001, Am. Acad. Pain Mgmt., cert. psychiat. adminstrn. and mgmt. Asst. prof. psychiatry SUNY Upstate Med. U., Syracuse, NY, 1998—. Contbr. over 50 articles to profl. jours. Assoc. dir. Consultation Liaison Psychiatry, Syracuse. Recipient All Star award, 2000. Mem.: APA (treas. 2002), Am. Assn. Psychosomatic Medicine, Assn. Psychiatric Adminstrs. Avocations: travel, reading, dancing. Office: SUNY Upstate Med Univ 750 East Adams St Syracuse NY 13210

ALATIS, JAMES EFSTATHIOS, university dean emeritus; b. Weirton, W.Va., July 13, 1926; s. Efstathios and Vasiliki (Galanoudis) A.; m. Penelope Mastorides, Dec. 30, 1951; children: William, Stephen, Anthony. BA, W.Va. U., 1948; MA, Ohio State U., 1953; PhD, 1966. Fulbright lectr. English U., Athens, 1955-57; English testing and teaching specialist Dept. State, 1959-61; specialist for lang. research U.S. Office Edn., 1961-65, chief lang. sect., 1965-66; asso. dean Sch. Langs. and Linguistics, Georgetown U., Washington, 1966-73, dean, 1973-94; dean emeritus Georgetown U., Washington, 1994—, sr. advisor to exec. v.p. internat. lang. programs and rsch., 1994-96, sr. advisor to Dean of Georgetown Coll. for internat. langs. programs and rsch., 1996—; assoc. prof. linguistics Sch. Langs. and Linguistics, Georgetown U., Washington, 1966-75; disting. prof. linguistics and modern Greek Georgetown U., Washington, 1994—. Exec. sec. TESOL, 1966-87, exec. dir. emeritus, 1987—; pres. Joint Nat. Com. for Langs., 1980-88, bd. dirs. 1998—, TESOL Internat. Rsch. Found., 1999—; mem. Greek Orthodox Archbishop's commn., 1999; bd. advisors U.S. Dept. Agriculture Grad. Sch. Author: (with Peter Lowenberg) The Three Circles of English: A Conference in honor of Braj B. Kachru, 2002; editor: Studies in Honor of Albert H. Marckwardt, 1972, (with Kristie Twaddell) English as a Second Language in Bilingual Education, 1976, (with Ruth Crymes) Human Factors in ESL, 1977, (with Gerli and Brod) Language in American Life, 1978, Internat. Dimensions of Bilingual Education, 1978, (with G. R. Tucker) Language in Public Life, 1979, Current Issues in Bilingual Education, 1980, (with others) The Second Language Classroom: Directions for the 1980s, 1981, Applied Linguistics and the Preparation of Second Language Teachers: Toward a Rationale, 1983, (with John J. Staczek) Perspectives on Bilingualism and Bilingual Education, 1985, (with Deborah Tannen) Language and Linguistics: The Interdependence of Theory, Data, and Application, 1986, Language Teaching, Testing, and Technology: Lessons from the Past with a View Toward the Future, 1989, Linguistics, Language Teaching and Language Acquisition: The Interdependence of Theory, Practice, and Research, 1990, Quest for Quality: The First 21 Years of TESOL, 1991, Linguistics and Language Pedagogy: The State of the Art, 1991, Language, Communication and Social Meaning, 1993, Strategic Interaction and Language Acquisition: Theory, Practice and Research, 1993, Educational Linguistics, Cross-Cultural Communication, and Global Interdependence, 1994, (with others) Linguistics and the Education of Language Teachers: Ethnolinguistic, Psycholinguistic, and Sociolinguistic Aspects, 1995, (with others) Linguistics, Language Acquisition and Language Variation: Current Trends and Future Prospects, 1996, (with others) Aspects of Sociolinguistics in Greece, 1997, (with others) Language in Our Time: Bilingual Education and Official English, Ebonics and Standard English, Immigration and the Unz Initiative, 1999, (with others) Linguistics, Language, and the Professions: Education, Journalism, Law, Medicine and Technology, Georgetown Univ. Round table on Languages and Linguistics, 2000, Linguistics, Language, and the Real World: Discourse and Beyond, Georgetown Univ. Round Table on Languages and Linguistics, 2001 (with Deborah Tannen) Georgetown University Round Table on Language and Linguistics, 2001; mem. editl. bd. World Englishes, English Today. Served with USNR, 1944-46. Recipient N.E. Conf. award, 1985, Pres.'s award Nat. Assn. for Bilingual Edn., 1987. Mem. MLA, Am. Coun. on Teaching Fgn. Langs., Linguistic Soc. Am (del. 1966-69), Nat. Assn. Fgn. Student Affairs (dir. 1965-66), Def. Lang. Inst. (bd. visitors), Phi Beta Kappa. Home: 5108 Sutton Pl Alexandria VA 22304-2704 Office: Georgetown U Int'l Langs Prog & Rsch 37th & 0 St Washington DC 20057-0001

ALAUPOVIC, ALEXANDRA VRBANIC, artist, educator; b. Slatina, Yugoslavia, Dec. 21, 1921; d. Joseph and Elizabeta (Papp) Vrbanic; m. Peter Alaupovic, Mar. 22, 1947; 1 child, Betsy. Student Bus. Sch., Zagreb, Yugoslavia, 1940-41, Acad. Visual Arts, Zagreb, Yugoslavia, 1944-48; postgrad. Acad. Visual Arts, Prague, Czechoslovakia, 1949, Art Sch., U. Ill., 1959-60; MFA, U. Okla., 1966; came to U.S., 1958. Sec., Arko Liquer & Yeast Factory and Distillery, Zagreb, 1941-44; instr. U. Okla., Norman, 1964-66; instr. three dimensional design sculpture Oklahoma City U., 1969-77, Okla. Sci. Found., Oklahoma City, 1969-75; one-woman shows at Okla. Art Ctr., Oklahoma City, U. Okla. Mus. Art, Norman, La Mandragore Internat. Galerie d'Art, Paris, 1984; exhibited art in group shows retrospective 50 yrs. Struggle, Growth and Whimsy, 1987-88, Okla. Art Ctr., Springfield (Mo.) Art Mus., Okla. U. Mus., Norman, 7th Ann. Temple Emanuel Brotherhood Arts Festival, Dallas, Salon des Nation, Paris, 1983; since statehood twevle Okla. artists Art. Mus., Okla. 1996; represented in permanent collections Okla. U. Art Mus., Okla. State Art Collection, Okla. Art Ctr., Mercy Health Ctr. Recipient Jacobson award U. Okla., 1964; hon. mention in sculpture Philbrook Art Ctr., Tulsa, 1967; 1st sculpture award Philbrook Art Ctr., Tulsa, 1970; biography included in Virginia Watson Jones' Contemporary American Women Sculptors, 1986, Jules and Nancy Heller's North American Women Artists of 20th Century, 1995; State of Okla. Art commemdation, 1996. Mem. Internat. Sculpture Center, Lausanne, Suisse, Prestige de la Peinture et de la Sculpture d'Aujourd'hui dans le Monde, 1992, Paris, 1995. Home and Office: 11908 N Bryant Ave Oklahoma City OK 73131-4823

ALAYETO, OFELIA LUISA, writer, researcher, educator; b. Havana, Cuba, July 24; came to U.S., 1960; d. Pedro O. and Ofelia Luisa (Martínez-Torres) A.; m. Allan W. Solomonow, Oct. 16, 1967; children: Gregory Igal, Seth Rafael. BA, CUNY, 1973, MPhil, 1980, PhD, 1983. Spl. asst. to exec. dir. Sierra Club, San Francisco, 1984-90, assoc. dir. rsch., 1990-93; lectr. U. San Francisco, 1987—, 1987—; rsch. analyst U. Calif., San Francisco, 1994—. Author: Sofia Casanova: Spanish Poet, Journalist and Writer, 1992; contbr. articles to profl. jours. Recipient Humanities award Richmond Coll./CUNY, 1973, Arleigh Williamson award, 1973. Mem. MLA, Am. Assn. Tchrs. Spanish and Portuguese, Sierra Club. Democrat. Roman Catholic. Avocations: opera, ballet, film, modern and classical literatures. Office: Univ of San Francisco Presentation Campus 103 Ignatian Heights San Francisco CA 94117-1080

ALAZRAKI, JAIME, Romance languages educator; b. La Rioja, Argentina, Jan. 26, 1934; came to U.S., 1962, naturalized, 1971; s. Leon and Clara A. (Bolomo) A.; children: Daphne G., Adina L. BA, Hebrew U., Jerusalem, 1962; MA, Columbia U., 1964, PhD, 1967. Instr. Columbia U., N.Y.C., 1964-67; asst. prof. U. Calif.-San Diego, 1967-68, assoc. prof., 1968-71, prof., 1971-77; prof. dept. romance langs. Harvard U., Cambridge, Mass., 1977-87; prof. dept. Spanish and Portuguese Columbia U., N.Y.C., 1987—, chair, 1988-91. Vis. prof. U. Wis., 1972, UCLA, 1975-76, Autonomous U. Barcelona, Spain, 1985-86; spl. advisor Guggenheim Found., 1981-91. Author: Poética y poesía de P. Neruda, 1965, La prosa narrativa de J.L. Borges, 1968, 74, 84, En busca del unicornio: Los cuentos de J. Cortázar, 1983, Jorge Luis Borges, 1971, Versiones, inversiones, reversiones, 1977, Critical Essays on J.L. Borges, 1987, Borges and the Kabbalah and Other Essays on His Fiction and Poetry, 1988, Hacia Cortázar: Aproximaciones a su obra, 1994; editor: (with I. Ivask) The Final Island: The Fiction of J. Cortázar, 1978, J.L. Borges: el escritor y la critica, 1976, 84, 86, 87, Julio Cortazar, Obra critica/2, 1994, J. Cortázar, Final del Juego, 1995, Critical Essays on Julio Cortázar, 1999; co-editor: Revista Hispánica Moderna, 1988—; mem. editorial bd. Jour. Spanish Studies, 1973-76, Hispanic Review, 1977—, La Torre 1977-95, Revista Iberoamericana, 1977-81, Hispanic Jour., 1980—, Hispania, 1980-85, Confluencia, 1987—. Recipient Nieto gold medal Argentina, 1970; NEH fellow, 1976; Guggenheim Found. fellow, 1971-72, 82-83 Mem. MLA (mem. adv. bd. Publs. of MLA of Am. 1980-84), Internat. Inst. Ibero-Am. Lit., Am. Assn. Tchrs. Spanish and Portuguese (Huntington prize 1964), Internat. Assn. Hispanists. Office: Columbia U Dept Spanish and Portuguese 612 W 116th St New York NY 10027-7009

ALBACH, RICHARD ALLEN, microbiology educator; b. Chgo., Mar. 31, 1930; s. Maurice and Martha (Silverman) A.; m. Janice Elaine Boewe, Jan. 23, 1962; children: Michael, Karren, Kimala, David, Brian, Julie, Barry. BS, U. Ill., 1956, MS, 1958; PhD, Northwestern U., 1963. Asst. prof. U. Health Scis., Chgo. Med. Sch., North Chicago, Ill., 1968-69, assoc. prof., 1969-73, prof., 1973—, vice-chmn., 1975-82, acting chmn., 1982-83. Editl. cons. Yearbook Med. Pubs., Chgo., 1975-81; vis. prof. St. George's U. Sch. Medicine, Grenada, 1992—. Contbr. articles to profl. jours. With U.S. Army, 1953-55. Recipient Trustees Rsch. award Chgo. Med. Sch., 1968, Tchg. Prof. of Yr. award, 1976, 78, 82; fellow Abbott Found., 1961; grantee NIH, 1965-78. Fellow Am. Acad. Microbiology; mem. Am. Soc. Microbiology, Soc. Protozoologists (exec. com. 1984-89, chmn. awards com. 1995-1999), Am. Soc. Parasitologists, Ill. Soc. Microbiology (membership chmn. 1969-70). Achievements include research in biology of parasitic protozoa. Office: U Health Sci Chgo Med Sch 3333 Green Bay Rd North Chicago IL 60064-3037 E-mail: albachr@finchcms.edu

ALBAMONTE, MARY KAY, secondary education educator; b. Rockford, Ill., Aug. 19, 1960; d. Anthony Samuel and Ada Catherine (Nardini) Gugliuzza; m. Phillip Gerald Albamonte, July 5, 1991; children: Haley Victoria, Anthony John. BA in Speech, Marquette U., 1982; cert. type 9 secondary edn. tchr., No. Ill. U., 1984, MA in English, 1988; postgrad., various univs., 1992. Acad. advisor Office Clin. Edn., No. Ill. U., DeKalb, 1983-84; tchr. English, Grant H.S., Fox Lake, Ill., 1985, J.B. Conant H.S., Hoffman Estates, Ill., 1985—, peer coach, 1990—, mentor tchr., 1994—, jr. level leader, 2002—. Mem. AAUW, NOW, Ill. Assn. Tchrs. English, Ill. Fedn. Tchrs., Am. Fedn. Tchrs., Dist. 211 Tchrs. Union (bldg. rep. 1991-95, editor newsletter Union Focus 1992-99, local union sec. 2002—), Com. for Am. Studies Edn., Sigma Delta Chi. Democrat. Office: JB Conant HS 700 E Cougar Trl Hoffman Estates IL 60194-3659

ALBANESE, JAY SAMUEL, criminologist, educator; b. Mineola, N.Y., Feb. 10, 1953; s. Samuel S. and Doris (Mather) A.; m. Leslie Elizabeth King, July 12, 1980; children: Thomas, Kelsey. BA, Niagara U., 1974; MA, Rutgers U., 1976, PhD, 1981. Chief Internat. Ctr. Nat. Inst. Justice, 2002—; prof. Niagara U., Niagara Falls, NY, 1981-96; prof. govt. and pub. policy Va. Commonwealth U., Richmond, 1996—. Vis. prof. Simon Fraser U., Vancouver, B.C., Can., 1988. Author: Dealing with Delinquency, 2d edit., 1993, Organized Crime in America, 3d edit., 1996 Criminal Justice, 1999, 2nd. edit., 2002; co-author: Crime in America, 1993, White Collar Crime in America, 1995; editor: Contemporary Issues in Organized Crime, 1995, Organized Crime: World Perspectives, 2003; contbr. articles to profl. jours. Recipient Sears Found. Teaching Excellence award, 1989-90, Founder's Award, Acad. Criminal Justice Scis., 2000, Elske Smith District Lectr. Award, Virginia Commonwealth U., Coll. Humanities & Scis. (for outstanding contributions to teaching and scholarship), 2001. Fellow Acad. Criminal Justice Scis., 2002/ mem. Am. Soc. Criminology, Internat. Assn. Study Organized Crime (exec. dir. 2002—), Northeastern Assn. Criminal Justice Scis. (pres. 1988-89), Acad. Criminal Justice Scis.(pres. 1995-96), White Collar Crime Res. Consortium (pres. 2000-02), Phi Kappa Phi. Office: PO Box 50484 Washington DC 20091-0484

ALBANO, PASQUALE CHARLES, management educator, management and organization development consultant; b. Bayonne, N.J., Dec. 3, 1941; s. Armando and Marie (Fasulo) A.; m. Norma Agnes Eichholz, July 16, 1960; children: Donna, Nancy, Susan, Carol. BS in Edn.-Social Sci. cum laude, Monmouth U., 1967; postgrad., Rutgers U., 1969-70; MA in Mgmt. magna cum laude, Pepperdine U., 1976; cert. in orgnl. cons., U.S. Army Tng. Ctr., 1979; EdD in Leadership and Policy summa cum laude, Temple U., 1987. Cert. tchr. social scis., N.J.; orgn. devel. cons. Personnel-employee devel. specialist Hdqs. Army Comm.-Electronics Command, Ft. Monmouth, N.J., 1967-69; chmn. mgmt. devel. dept. army edn. ctr. Hdqs. Army Comm. Command, Ft. Monmouth, N.J., 1969-75, dir. northeastern U.S. regional tng. ctr., 1975-78, orgnl. effectiveness officer R & D ctr., 1978-81, chief orgnl. effectiveness office, 1981—85, chief leadership rsch. office, 1985-87, chief orgnl. consulting office, 1987—94; pvt. practice cons., 1993—. Tchr. U.S. Army Pers. Mgmt. Program, Ga., Wash., Pa., NJ, Ala., Ariz., Va., NY, Okla., SC, Panama, 1976—78, Internat. Assn. Quality Cirs., Internat. Pers. Mgmt. Assn., Info. Resource Mgmt. Assn., USAR, 1981—91, Am. Mgmt. Assn., 1995—, Ctr. for Bus. and Inds., Monmouth and Ocean Counties, 1995; adj. prof. mgmt. and social psychology small bus. mgmt. Kean Coll., Union, NJ, 1981—96, Brookdale C.C., NJ, 1975—93, Pepperdine U., L.A., 1977—81, Temple U., Phila., 1987—88, grad. sch. bus. Fairleigh Dickinson U., 1990—; adj. prof. tchr. mgmt. and orgnl. psychology in MBA and spl. corp. onsite edn. programs Rutgers U., 1997—, adj. prof. M of Adminstrv. Sci. program, Jewish and Israeli fgn. student program, 2002; adj. prof. orgnl. behavior St. Peter's Coll., Jersey City, 2003—; tchr. interpersonal rels. Ocean County Coll., 1971—73; creative thinking Brookdale C.C., 1972—73; mem. small bus. adv. coun., 1996; cons. Mut. UFO Network, 1998; global CEO Inst. Chartered Fin. Analysts, India, 2002—; adj. prof. global mgmt. N.J. City Univ., St. Peter's Coll., Jersey City, 2003—; reviewer coll. textbooks Prentice-Hall Pubs., 2003—; presenter Bayonne Hist. Soc., 2003; program instr. Brookdale Coll. Communiversity, Camp Evans, Belmar, NJ, 2003. Author: Transactional Analysis on the Job, 1974, Retention of Engineers and Scientists, 1983, The Effects of an Experimental Training Program on the Creative Thinking Abilities of Adults, 1987, Value-Adding Leadership, 1988, Tapping the Potential to Contribute, 1998, One Summer, A Thousand Days, 2001, The Cloud Shaman, 2001, Fires Burning Deep Inside, 2001, Turn the Sandglass Over, 2001, Skyline Drive: A Poetic Journey Through Business Life, 2001; contbr. poetry anthologies Anagram: Art and Literature of Asian Americans, 1998, Snow and Barn, The Golden Wings, Bytes of Poetry, 2001—02, Taj Mahal Rev., India, 2002, developer mgmt. tng. curriculum for Monmouth and Ocean County Adult Edn. Commn., 1996, also instnl. materials for tng. tel. crisis hotline ctr. workers Contact USA, ednl. programs for lab. software engrs. and orgnl. surveys of U.S. Army, 1995, merger, mgmt. and original design tng. programs, 1996—; contbr. world wide web articles to numerous publs., materials for use in tng. sr. officers, fgn. mil. officers U.S. Army and Command Gen. Staff Coll. Tchr. human rels. ednl. assns. Monmouth and Ocean Counties, 1970-74, Fed. Women's Program, 1980, ESL Cmty. and Family Svcs., Monmouth, 1990-93; pvt. tutor English Citizenship; vol. Habitat for Humanity Internat., 1995-96, Contact USA, 1995-96, Presbyn. Youth Program, 1965; mem. NAACP, 1963-64; mem. Small Bus. Adv. Coun., Ocean County Coll., 1996; vol. Sierra Club, Wilderness Soc., Save the Planet, Nat. Rsch. Def. Coun., Nat. Wildlife Fedn., CMove On.org, Common Cause, 2002—. With U.S. Army, 1958-60. Recipient Bernard Watson award William Penn Found., 1987, Quality Circle Devel. commendation U.S. Army, 1981, Devel. Sci. Pers. commendation, 1983, Creative Edn. Techniques commendation, 1988, ESL Textbooks commendation U.S. Army Materiel Command, 1992, Mgmt. Devel. Curriculum commendation, 1992, numerous World Wide Net awards for creative writing, 1998. Mem. ASTD, ACLU, Creative Edn. Found., Internat. Transactional Analysis Assn., Adult Edn. Assn., Nat. Assn. Retired Fed. Employees, Nat. Speleol. Soc., Archaeol. Inst. of Am., Soc. Advancement of Mgmt., Acad. Mgmt., World Future Soc., Assn. of U.S. Army, Internat. Platform Assn. (elected), Union Concerned Scientists,Jersey Shore Quality Coun., Nat. Space Soc., Inst. Noetic Sciences, Acad. of Am. Poets, Planetary Soc. (cons. mutual UFO network 1998), Search for Extraterrestrial Intelligence Inst., Mensa, Phi Alpha Theta, Phi Delta Kappa. Avocations: investigating mysteries, exploring caves and ancient ruins, digging fossils, inventing, writing poetry. Home and Office: Adaptive Leadership 805 Woodwild Dr Point Pleasant NJ 08742 E-mail: charlesalbano@webtv.net.

ALBARRACIN-NWOKE, LUZ G. adult education educator; b. Saavedra, Philippines, Sept. 27, 1947; d. Anatolia Tabotabo; m. Nicholas C. Nwoke. BA, Rizal Meml. Coll., 1967; BS in Edn., Holy Cross Coll. of Digos, 1971; MEd-ESL, U. Philippines System, 1978, MA in Urban and Regional Planning, 1983; MA in (Acad.) Guidance, Internat. Hawadian U., 1974, MA in (Acad.) Edn. Tech., 1976. Tchr., coord. MEC Philippines, Davao, Quezon City, Philippines, 1972-80; project trainer, basin cons. Metro Manila, Philippines, 1981-82; tchr. The Ascension, N.Y.C., 1987-90; instr. Met. Career Inst., N.Y.C., 1988-90, Berlitz Lang. Ctr., N.Y.C., Monroe Coll., N.Y.C., 1990—; ESL tchr. N.Y.C. Pub. Schs., 1991-93; assoc. in ednl. improvement svcs. N.Y. State Edn. Dept., 1994—. Recipient Outstanding Achievement award AFTA, 1997.

ALBAUM, JEAN STIRLING, psychologist, educator; b. Beijing, Jan. 11, 1932; came to U.S., 1936; d. Richard Henry and Emma Bowyer (Lueders) Ritter; m. B. Taylor Stirling, Aug. 15, 1953 (div. 1965); 1 child, Christopher Taylor Stirling; m. Joseph H. Albaum; stepchildren: Thomas Gary, Lauren Jean. BA, Beloit (Wis.) Coll., 1953; MS, Danbury (Conn.) State U., 1964, U. La Verne, Calif., 1983; PhD, Claremont (Calif.) Grad. Sch., 1985. Lic. ednl. psychologist, Calif. Spl. edn. tchr. Charter Oak (Calif.) Sch. Dist., 1966-80; psychologist, coord. elem. counseling Claremont Sch. Dist., 1980—2002; pvt. practice in ednl. psychology Encino, Calif., 1987—2003. Clin. supr. marriage, family and child counselor interns Claremont Grad. Sch., 1987—2002; sr. adj. prof. U. La Verne, 1988—; oral commr. Bd. Behavioral Sci. Examiners, Sacramento, 1989—2001. Contbr. articles to profl. jours. Hostess L.A. World Affairs Coun., 1980—; pres. Woodley Homeowner's Assn., Encino, 1986-89. Grantee Durfee Found., 1986, 92. Mem. Am. Psychol. Assn., Calif. Assn. Marriage, Family and Child Therapists, Calif. Assn. Lic. Ednl. Psychologists. Avocations: travel, international relations, history, sailing, skiing. Office: Edn Ctr 2080 N Mountain Ave Claremont CA 91711-2643

ALBAZZAZ, FAIQ JABER, physician, researcher, educator; b. Baghdad, Iraq, July 1, 1939; s. Jaber Mehdi and Fadela (Hassoun) Albazzaz; m. Thuraia Albazzaz; children: Alexandra Nesreen, Michael Basheer, Brian Senan, Samara Emily. M.B.Ch.B., U. Baghdad, 1962. Diplomate Am. Bd. Internal Medicine, Am. Bd. Pulmonary Diseases. Intern Tchg. Hosp., Mosul, Iraq, 1965—66; resident in medicine U. Miss. Med. Ctr., 1966—68, Mpls. VA Hosp.-U. Minn. Hosp., 1968—69; pulmonary fellow Mass. Gen. Hosp.-Harvard Med. Sch., Boston, 1969—71; asst. prof. medicine U. Ill.-Chgo., 1971—78, assoc. prof., 1978—86, prof. medicine, 1986—, prof. physiology and biophysics, 1993—. Dir. pulmonary lab. VA Westside Med. Ctr., Chgo., 1971—, chief respiratory and critical care sect., 1977—. Contbr. articles to profl. jours. Fellow: ACP, Am. Coll. Chest Physicians, Ctrl. Soc. Clin. Rsch., Am. Fedn. Clin. Rsch., Royal Coll. Physicians and Surgeons (Can.); mem.: Am. Thoracic Soc., Am. Physiol. Soc. Avocation: photography. Home: 1900 Berry Ln Des Plaines IL 60018 Office: VA 820 S Damen Ave (MP 111) Chicago IL 60612-3728

ALBERG, JONI YALE, special education educator, jewelry designer; b. Mpls., Nov. 26, 1955; d. Robert Elon and Marjory Louise (Champagne) Yale; m. Jarles Alberg, Sept. 11, 1982. BS in Spl. Edn. and MS, Fla. State

U., 1978; PhD in Spl. Edn., U. N.C., Chapel Hill, 1986. Cert. in reading, mentally handicapped, emotionally handicapped and learning disabilities teaching. Tchr. emotionally handicapped Leon County Schs., Fla., 1978; noncategorical resource tchr. Wake County Schs., N.C., 1978-81; interviewer Child Health Care Project, N.C. State U., Raleigh, 1981; instr. dept. curriculum and instrn. Sch. Edn., N.C. State U., Raleigh, 1981-82; intern Dept. Pub. Instrn., Div. Exceptional Children, Raleigh, 1982-83, cons. spl. projects, 1983-85, coord. planning, communication, statistics and rsch., 1985-87; sr. ednl. rsch. scientist Ctr. for Rsch. in Edn., Research Triangle Park, N.C., 1987-93; pres. Silhouettes, Inc., Raleigh, N.C., 1991—. Field editor Teaching Exceptional Children, 1986-88; contbr. articles to profl. jours, chpts. to books. Mem. Coun. for Exceptional Children (pres. 1990-91, gov.-at-large 1985-88, pres. N.C. Fedn. 1981-82), Nat. Assn. Women Bus. Owners, Found. for Exceptional Children (bd. dirs. 1990-91).

ALBERS, DOLORES M. secondary education educator; AA, Casper Coll., 1969; BS, U. No. Colo., 1972; postgrad., U. N.C., U. Wyo., Chadron State. Physical edn. instr. for grades K-12, 6th and 8th grade sci. tchr. Bent County Sch. Dist. 2, McClave, Colo., 1972-75; physical edn./health instr. Sweetwater County Sch. Dist. # 2, Green River, Wyo., 1972—. Mem. phys. edn. coun. Mid. and Secondary Schs., 1999—2003, chmn. phys. edn. coun., 2002—03. Mem., chmn. Green River Parks and Recreation Bd.; coord. Hoops for Heart; co-chmn. United Way Sweetwater County, 1999-2001. Named Tchr. of Yr., Ctrl. Dist., 1994—95, Nat. Assn. Sport and Phys. Edn., 1995. Mem. AAHPERD, AALR, ASCD/NFOIA, NEA, Wyo. Edn. Assn., Wyo. Assn. Health, Phys. Edn., Recreation and Dance (Tchr. of Yr. award 1994-95), Green River Edn. Assn., Nat. Assn. for Sport and Phys. Edn., Mid. and Secondary Sch. Phys. Edn. Coun. (chmn. 2002-03). Home: PO Box 868 1745 Massachusetts Ct Green River WY 82935-6229 Office: Green River HS 1615 Hitching Post Dr Green River WY 82935-5771

ALBERS, EDWARD JAMES, SR., retired secondary school educator; b. Centralia, Wash., July 6, 1922; s. Otto Johnson and Nell Genevieve Albers; m. Caroline Constance Cochran, July 30, 1944; 1 child, Edward James Jr. Student, Wash. State Coll., 1942, U. Ariz., 1949-51; BA, U. Nebr., Omaha, 1959; MA, Rollins Coll., 1966. Cert. tchr., Fla. Commd. 2d lt. USAF, 1944, advanced through grades to maj., 1961, pilot, 1944-65, served command pilot SAC, ret., 1965; tchr. social studies Winter Park (Fla.) H.S., 1966-96, chmn. dept. social studies, 1973-88, ret., 1996. Decorated Yun-Hui medal, Chinese pilot wings, Chinese medal of Honor, 2001. Mem. Air Force Assn., Burma Star (Eng.), Mil. Order of the World Wars (past comdr.), Exptl. Aircraft Assn. and Warbirds, Ret. Officers' Assn., China-Burma-India Vets. Assn., Santa Ana Calif. AAF Cadet Class 44G Alumni, Train Collectors Assn., Lionel Collectors Assn., Officers' Club, Patrick AFB, Hump Pilots' Assn., Daedalians, Sigma Phi Epsilon. Democrat. Episcopalian. Avocations: antique toy train collecting, golfing, scuba diving, snow and water skiing, flying.

ALBERT, CAROLE ANNETTE, elementary school educator; b. Bronx, N.Y., Jan. 15, 1944; d. Henry and Antoinette (Lamborghini) Busto; m. Russell Alger Albert, July 20, 1968; 1 child, Laura Lydia. BS, SUNY, New Paltz, 1965; MA in reading, U. N.H., 1992. life cert. elem. tchr., N.Y., Calif.; cert. elem. tchr., N.H. Tchr. 2d grade Port Washington (L.I., N.Y.) Pub. Schs., 1965-67; tchr. 1st grade Simi Valley Unified Sch. Dist., Santa Susanna, Calif., 1967-68, Huntington Beach (Calif.) Sch. Dist., 1969-75; tchr. Big Bird Kindergarten, Rochester, N.H., 1976-80; Chpt. I coord. Sch. Adminstrv. Unit 44, Farmington, N.H., 1981-88; Title I project mgr. Sch. Adminstrv. Unit 61, Farmington, 1981-2001. Bd. dirs., sec. Farmington Child Care Ctr. Recipient Cert. of Recognition, Commr. Edn., 1984. Fellow: NEA; mem.: Internat. Reading Assn., Delta Kappa Gamma (pres. 2002—03). Avocations: travel, reading, photography. Home: 230 Gonic Rd Rochester NH 03839-4923

ALBERT, JANYCE LOUISE, human resources specialist, retired business educator, banker, consultant, human resources specialist; b. Toledo, July 27, 1932; d. Howard C. And Glenola Mae (Masters) Blessing; m. John R. Albert, Aug. 7, 1954; children: John R., James H. Student, Ohio Wesleyan U., 1949-51; BA, Mich. State U., 1953; MS, Iowa State U., 1980. Asst. pers. mgr./tng. sup. Sears, Roebuck & Co., Toledo, 1953-56; tchr. adult edn. Tenafly Pub. Schs. (N.J.), 1966-70; pers. officer, tng. officer, tng. and edn. mgr. Iowa Dept. Transp., Ames, 1974-77; coll. recruiting coord. Rockwell Internat., Cedar Rapids, Iowa, 1977-79, engring. adminstrn. mgr., 1979-80; employee rels. and job evaluation analyst, recruiter Phillips Petroleum Co., Bartlesville, Okla., 1980-81; v.p., dir. pers. Rep. Bancorp, Tulsa, 1981-83; sr. v.p. and dir. human resources First Nat. Bank, Rockford, Ill., 1983-94; dir. bus. divsn. Rock Valley Coll., Rockford, Ill., 1994-99, ret., 1999; human resources cons. Furst Group, Rockford, 2000—. Advisor to Nat. Profl. Secs. Assn.; bd. dirs. Riverside Cmty. Bank, 1995—; mem. adv. com. Zion Devel. Corp., 1999—. Bd. dirs. Rocvale Children's Home, 1986-97, 99-2001, pres. 1991-94; bd. dirs. United Way of Ames, 1976-77; mem. employee svc. comm., Rockford Pub. Schs., 1988-92; account exec. United Way Rockford, 1993-98, account sec. head, 1996, allocations com., 2000-01; bd. dirs. Rockford Human Resources Cmty. Action Program; chair legis. com. Rockford Human Svcs. Dept., 1989-92; chair Rockford State of Ill. Job Svcs. Employers Coun., 1990-97; publicity chmn. Tenafly 300th Ann. Celebration, 1969; mem. task force Rockford Bd. Edn., 1993-94; mem. gala com. Janet Wattles Mental Health Ctr., 1990; deacon Collegiate Presbyn. Ch., Ames, 1972-75; mem. adv. coun. Rockford YWCA, 1986, mem. fund drive task force, 1998-99, co-chair YWCA Leader Luncheon, 1986-87; advisor Rockford chpt. ARC, 1991—; mem. Mayor's Task Force for Rockford Project Self-Sufficiency, 1986-89, chmn. adv. coun., 1991; chair info. and referral com., bd. dirs. Contact, 1994-2003; bd. dirs. Rockford Symphony Orch., 1992-95, sec. 1994-95; bd. dirs. Rockford Leadership Found., 1994-96; chair pers. com. Rockford Ctrl. Area Commn., 1997-99, v.p., bd. dirs.; mem. fund drive taskforce Blackhawk Day Nursery, 1998-99; bd. dirs. Rock Valley Coll. Found., 2000-03, co-chmn. governance com., 2001-03; mem. session 1st Presbyn. Ch., Rockford, 2000-01, chair mktg. task force; mem. ctrl. steering com. Ctr. for Learning in Retirement, 2000-01. Pres.'s scholar Mich. State U., 1951-53; recipient YWCA Kate O'Connor award for Women in Labor Force, 1984; named Bd. Mem. of Yr. Rockford Human Resources Community Action Program, 1992. Mem.: Ill. Consortium Internat. Travel (mentor The Netherlands 1997), Employee Benefits Assn. No. Ill. (membership chmn.), Am. Soc. Pers. Adminstrn., Crusader Clin. Found. (bd. dirs. 1997—, v.p. bd. dirs. 2000, pres. bd. 2001—02, chmn. 2001—), Rockford Pers. Assn. (adv. coun. 1983—91, co-chmn. programs 1985—86), Rockford C. of C. (leadership program 1989, pres. coun. 1991—94, mem. internat. bus. coun. 1993—99, transp. com., human resources com., Nat. Athena Found. award 1991, Woman of Yr.), Rockford Network (past chairperson 1985—86, awards com. 1995—97), World Trade Coun. (bd. dirs. 1994—97), Womenspace (bd. dirs. 1993—95, mktg. com. 1993—99, awards com. 1995, 1996—98, adv. bd. 1996—), Rockford Panhellenic Coun. (sec. 1992—93, treas. 1993—94, v.p. 1994—95, pres. 1995—96, Woman of Yr. award 1994, Rockford Lifescape Sr. of Yr. award 1999), P.E.O., Rotary Internat. (chair Rockford Athena chpt. 1991—, membership com. 1999—, chair steering com. 2000—01, co-chair membership com. 2001—), Phi Kappa Phi, Alpha Gamma Delta, Sigma Epsilon (Rockford award). Home and Office: 5587 Thunderidge Dr Rockford IL 61107-1756 Fax: 815-282-8248. E-mail: janycealbert@hotmail.com.

ALBERT, SUSAN WITTIG, writer, English educator; b. Maywood, Ill., Jan. 2, 1940; d. John H. and A. Lucille (Franklin) Webber; m. William Albert, 1986; children by previous marriage: Robert, Robin, Michael. BA, U. Ill., 1967; PhD, U. Calif.-Berkeley, 1972. Instr. U. San Francisco, 1969-71; asst. prof. to assoc. prof. U. Tex., Austin, 1971-79; assoc. dean Grad. Sch., U. Tex., Austin, 1977-79; dean Sophie Newcomb Coll., New Orleans, 1979-81; dean of faculty. grad. dean S.W. Tex. State U., San Marcos, 1981-82, v.p. acad. affairs, 1982-86, prof. English, 1981-87. Founder Story Circle Network, Inc., 1997. Author: Work of Her Own, 1992, Writing From Life, 1996; author: (China Bayles novels) Thyme of Death, 1992; author: Witch's Bane, 1993, Hangman's Root, 1994, Rosemary Remembered, 1995, Rueful Death, 1996, Love Lies Bleeding, 1997, Chile Death, 1998, Lavender Lies, 1999, Mistletoe Man, 2000, Bloodroot, 2001, Indigo Dying, 2003, An Unthymely Death, 2003; author: (Robin Paige novels) Death at Bishop's Keep, 1994; author: Death at Gallows Green, 1995, Death at Daisy's Folly, 1997, Death at Devil's Bridge, 1998, Death at Rottingdean, 1999, Death at Whitechapel, 2000, Epsom Downs, 2001, Death at Dartmoor, 2002, Death at Glamis Castle, 2003; contbr. articles to profl. jours.; editor: With Courage and Common Sense: Memoirs from the Older Women's Legacy Circles, 2003. Danforth grad. fellow, 1967-72 Home: PO Box 1616 Bertram TX 78605 E-mail: china@tstar.net.

ALBERTO, PAMELA LOUISE, oral and maxillofacial surgeon, educator; b. Somerville, Mass., Apr. 13, 1954; d. Louis Leon and Pamela Marie (Spera) A.; m. Gregory John Wroclawski, Aug. 4, 1979; children: Daniel Alberto, Catherine Marie. BS, Rensselaer Poly. Inst., 1976; DMD, U. Pa., 1980. Cert. oral and maxillofacial surgeon; diplomate Am. Bd. Forensic Dentistry. Clin. asst. prof. dept. oral/maxillofacial surgery N.J. Dental Sch., Newark, 1983-89, clin. assoc. prof. dept. oral/maxillofacial surgery, 1989—, dir. predoctoral edn. dept. oral/maxillofacial surgery, 1989—; pvt. practice Sparta, N.J., 1984—. Dir. CPR N.J. Dental Sch., Newark, 1985-90; dir. Dental Implant Ctr. Wallkill Valley Hosp., Sussex, N.J., 1988—; vice chief surgery Newton Meml. Hosp., 1998-2000, chief surgery, 2000-02. Recipient Outstanding Clin. Dentistry award Acad. Gen. Dentistry, 1980. Fellow Am. Assn. Oral and Maxillofacial Surgery, Am. Coll. Oral/Maxillofacial Surgery; mem. ADA, AAUP, Am. Assn. Dental Anesthesiology, Internat. Congress Oral Implantology, Psi Omega. Avocations: tennis, skiing, photography, scuba diving, jewelry making. Home: 14 Cherry Tree Ln Kinnelon NJ 07405-2229 Office: 171 Woodport Rd Sparta NJ 07871-2637

ALBERTS, BRUCE MICHAEL, research organization executive; b. Chicago, Ill., Apr. 14, 1938; s. Harry C. and Lillian (Surasky) A.; m. Betty Neary, June 14, 1960; children: Beth L., Jonathan B., Michael B. AB in Biochemical Scis. summa cum laude, Harvard Coll., 1960; PhD in Biophysics, Harvard U., 1965. Postdoctoral fellow NSF Institut de Biologie Moleculaire, Geneva, 1965-66; asst. prof. dept. chemistry Princeton (N.J.) U., 1966-73, assoc. prof. dept. biochemical scis., 1971-73, Damon Pfeiffer prof. life scis., 1973-76; prof., vice chmn. dept. biochemistry and biophysics U. Calif., San Francisco, 1976-81, Am. Cancer Soc. Rsch. prof., 1981-85, prof., chmn., 1985-90, Am. Cancer Soc. Rsch. prof. of biochemistry, 1990-93; pres. NAS, Washington, 1993—; chrm. NRC, Washington, 1993—. Trustee Cold Spring Harbor Lab., 1972-75; adv. panel human cell biology NSF, 1974-76; adv. coun. dept. biochemical scis. and molecular biology Princeton U., 1979-85; chmn. vis. com. dept. biochemistry and molecular biology Harvard Coll., 1983-86; chmn. mapping and sequencing the human genome Nat. Rsch. Coun. Com., 1986-88; bd. sci. couns. divsn. arthritis and metabolic diseases NIH, 1974-78, molecular cytology study sect. 1982-86, chmn. 1984-86; program adv. com. NIH Human Genome Project, 1988-91; sci. adv. bd. Jane Coffin Childs Meml. Fund for Med. Rsch., 1978-85, Markey Found., 1984—, Fred Hutchinson Cancer Rsch. Ctr., Seattle, 1988—; com. mem. corp. vis. dept. biology MIT, 1978—, dept. embryology Carnegie Inst., Washington, 1983—; faculty rsch. lectr. U. Calif., San Francisco, 1985; sci. adv. com. Marine Biological Lab., Woods Hole, Mass., 1988—; bd. dirs. Genentech Rsch. Found., Fed. Am. Socs. for Experimental Biology; adv. bd. Bethesda Rsch. Labs. Life Tech. Inc., Nat. Sci. Resources Ctr., Smithsonian Inst., 1990—; com. mem. adolescence and young adulthood/sci. standards, Nat. Bd. Profl. Teaching Standards, 1991—. Co-author: The Molecular Biology of the Cell, 1989; editor: Mechanistic Studies of DNA Replication and Genetic Recombination, 1980; editorial bd. Jour. Biological Chemistry, 1976-82, Jour. Cell Biology, 1984-87; assoc. editor Annual Reviews Cell Biology, 1984—; essay editor Molecular Biology of the Cell, 1991—; contbr. numerous articles to profl. jours. including Saunders Sci. Publ., Current Sci., Ltd. Fellow NSF, 1960-65; recipient Eli Lilly award in biological chemistry Am. Chemical Soc., 1972, Baxter award for Disting. Rsch. in Biomedical Scis. Assn. Am. Med. Colls., 1992; named Lifetime Rsch. Prof. Am. Cancer Soc., 1980, Outstanding Vol. Coord. Calif. Sch. Vol. Partnership, 1993. Gairdner Foundation International Award, 1995. Fellow AAAS; mem. NAS (commn. life scis. Nat. Rsch. Coun. 1988—, chmn. 1988-93, adv. bd. Nat. Sci. Resources Ctr. 1990—, Nat. Com. Sci. Edn. Standards and Assessment 1992—, com. mem. Nat. Edn. Support System for Tchrs. and Schs. 1992—, U.S. Steel Found. award 1975), Am. Chemical Soc., Am. Soc. for Cell Biology, Am. Soc. for Microbiology, Genetics Soc. Am., Am. Soc. Biochemistry and Molecular Biology (councilor 1984—), Am. Philos. Soc., European Molecular Biology Orgn. (assoc.), Phi Beta Kappa. Office: National Academy of Sciences/NRC Office of the President 500 Fifth St NW NAS215 Washington DC 20001*

ALBIN, LESLIE OWENS, biology educator; b. Spur, Tex., Jan. 8, 1940; s. John Leslie and Ottie Maude (Lassetter) A.; m. Monta Kay Gragg, Sept. 3, 1961 (div. 1982); children: Leslie Susan Albin Gann, Kimberly Ann Albin. BA, McMurry Coll., Abilene, 1962; MA, N. Tex. State U., 1969. Instr. biology E. Cen. State U., Ada, Okla., 1969-71; rsch. assoc. M.D. Andrson Hosp. & Tumor Inst., Houston, 1971; asst. prof. biology Western Tex. Coll., Snyder, 1971-74, assoc. prof. biology, 1974-77; prof. Austin (Tex.) C.C., 1977—, chmn. divsn. natural scis., 1978-95, head dept. biology, 1977-97. NDEA fellow, 1968. Mem. Am. Inst. Biol. Scis., Faculty Assn. Western Tex. Coll. (pres. 1973-74), Faculty Assn. Austin C.C. (pres. 1987-88), Faculty Senate Austin C.C., Tex. C.C. Tchrs. Assn., Tex. Acad. Sci., Am. Soc. for Microbiology, Alpha Chi. Office: Austin Community Coll Cypress Creek Campus 1555 Cypress Creek Rd Cedar Park TX 78613-3607 Business E-Mail: lesalbin@austincc.edu.

ALBINAK, MARVIN JOSEPH, chemistry educator; b. Detroit, June 21, 1928; s. Alfred S. and Katherine (Smulson) A.; m. Gloria Ann Galamb, Aug. 26, 1961; children: Stephen, Anne, Alexandra. AB, U. Detroit, 1949, MS, 1952; PhD, Wayne State U., 1959. Rsch. chemist Ethyl Corp., Detroit, 1952-54; instr. to asst. prof. U. Detroit, 1954-58, 59-61; rsch. fellow Wayne State U., Detroit, 1958-59; sr. rsch. scientist Elec. Autolite Corp., Toledo, Ohio, 1961-62; rsch. chemist Owens-Ill., Inc., Toledo, 1962-65; asst. to assoc. prof. Wheeling (W.Va.) Coll., 1965-68; assoc. prof. to prof. chemistry and adminstr. Essex Community Coll., Balt., 1968-96, prof. emeritus, 1997. 7 U.S. patents; contbr. articles to profl. jours. Mem. Am. Chem. Soc., Sigma Xi, Phi Lambda Upsilon. Democrat. Avocations: music, theatre, books, environmental activities. Home: 819 Providence Rd Baltimore MD 21286-2964

ALBINO, JUDITH ELAINE NEWSOM, university president; b. Jackson, Tenn. m. Salvatore Albino; children: Austin, Adrian. BJ, U. Tex., 1967, PhD, 1973. Mem. faculty sch. dental medicine SUNY, Buffalo, 1972-90, assoc. provost, 1984-87, dean sch. arch. and planning, 1987-89, dean grad. sch., 1989-90; v.p. acad. affairs and rsch, dean system grad. sch. U. Colo., Boulder, 1990-91, pres., 1991-95, pres. emerita, prof. psychiatry, 1995-97; pres. Calif. Sch. Profl. Psychology Alliant Internat. U., San Francisco, 1997—. Contbr. articles to profl. jours. Acad. Adminstrn. fellow Am. Coun. on Edn., 1983; grantee NIH. Fellow APA (treas., bd. dirs.); mem. Behavioral Scientists in Dental Rsch. (past pres.), Am. Assn. Dental Rsch. (bd. dirs.). Office: Calif Sch Profl Psychology Alliant Internat U Office Pres 2728 Hyde St Ste 100 San Francisco CA 94109-1251 Fax: 415-771-5908. E-mail: jalbino@alliant.edu.

ALBORES-SAAVEDRA, JORGE, pathologist, educator; b. La Concordia, Chiapas, Mex., Dec. 15, 1933; came to U.S., 1984; s. Enrique and Aurora (Saavedra) Albores; m. Blanca Gallo, Dec. 16, 1957; children: Lilia, Ruth. MD, Nat. U. Mex., Mexico City, 1957. Assoc. prof. pathology Nat. U. Mex., 1964-67, prof. pathology, 1968-84, U. Miami (Fla.) Sch. Medicine, 1984-90; prof. pathology, dir. divsn. anatomical pathology U. Tex. Southwestern Med. Ctr., Dallas, 1990—. Chmn. dept. pathology Gen. Hosp. Mexico City, 1968-83, Nat. U. Mex., 1976-83, Hosp. Ctrl. sur de PEMEX, Mexico City, 1983-84. Author: Tumors of the Gallbladder and Extrahepatic Bile Ducts and Ampulla of Vater, 2000; co-author: Pathology of Incipient Neoplasia, 3d edit., 2001; contbr. more than 230 sci. papers to profl. publs., 39 chpts. to books. Office: Dept Pathology LSU Health Sci Ctr 1501 Kings Hwy Shreveport LA 71130 E-mail: albore@LSUHSC.edu.

ALBRECHT, BEVERLY JEAN, special education educator; b. Dixon, Ill., Sept. 8, 1936; d. Harold Ivan Foster and Grace Gertrude Tracy Freed; m. Marvin Blackert Albrecht, Aug. 13, 1960; children: Bradley K., Brent D., Kimberly S. Albrecht Schluns. BS, Manchester Coll., North Manchester, Ind., 1958; MS, No. Ill. U., 1978. Cert. in elem. edn., educable mentally handicapped, learning disabled, supervision and early childhood edn., Ill. Kindergarten tchr. Sch. Dist. 300, Carpentersville, Ill, 1958-60; thcr. 5th grade Sch. Dist. 5, Sterling, Ill., 1960-61, 64-65, kindergarten tchr., 1962-64, substitute tchr., 1965-71, 97—; dir. nursery sch. Sterling YWCA, 1971-75; program dir. Ctr. for Human Devel., Sterling, 1975-76; family advocate Ill. Dept. Child and Family Svcs., Rock Falls, 1977-78; learning disablities and behavior disorders spl. edn. tchr. Sch. Dist. 289, Mendota, Ill., 1978-84, devel. pre-sch. tchr., 1984-89; clinician, case mgr., mental health provider Family Preservation Sinnissippi Ctrs. Inc., Sterling, 1989-97. Replication specialist PEECH project U. Ill., Champaign, 1985-88; supervisory faculty Ill. State U., Normal, 1983-85, Ill. Valley C.C., Oglesby 1985-89. Chair coun. on edn. United Meth. Ch., Rock Falls, 1973—75, supt., tchr. ch. sch., 1968—88; host family Rock River Valley Internat. Fellowships, Sterling, 1975—2003; vol. Rock River Valley Hospice United Ch. Women's Bd., 1998—2002; vol. Pub. Action to Deliver Shelter, 1997—99; vol. tutor Ill. Cmty. Sch. Dist. #5, 1997. Spl. Edn. fellow Ill. Office of Pub. Instrn., 1966; name grant honoree United Meth. Women, Rock Falls. Republican. Avocations: tennis, golf, travel. Home: 3254 Mineral Springs Rd Sterling IL 61081-4107 E-mail: marvbev@essex1.com.

ALBRECHT, KAY MONTGOMERY, early childhood educator, author, child advocate; b. Lafayette, La., Jan. 29, 1949; d. Michael H. and Imogene (McCallum) M.; m. Larry Steven Albrecht, June 23, 1973. BA, U. La., 1970; MS in Child Devel., U. Tenn., 1972, PhD in Family Studies, 1984. Head Start coordinator U. Tenn., Knoxville, 1972-75; instr. Incarnate Word Coll., San Antonio, 1976-77; instr. Southwest Tex. State U., San Marcos, 1977-80; tng. dir. Daybridge Learning Ctrs., Houston, 1984-85, v.p., 1985-86; v.p. Child Care Mgmt. Assocs., 1986-90, sr. ptnr., 1990-92; founder Hearts Home Early Learning Ctrs., Inc., 1986-2000; sr. ptnr. Innovations in Early Childhood Edn., 1992—; cons. Adminstrn. for Children, Youth and Families, HHS, Washington, 1982-83, Binney & Smith (author Crayola Creativity Program), Mervyn's, Angeles Toys, Houston Ind. Sch. Dist., Houston Mayor's Office, United Way of the Tex. Gulf Coast; mem. adv. bd. Nat. Acad. Early Childhood Programs, validator, commr., 1989—, 1986-91; scholarship chmn. Parrish Sch. Bd., 1990-93; dean Internat. Forum Early Edn., 1999, 2000, 2001, 2002-. Author staff orientation manual and consumer curriculum guide, 1980, 85, quality assurance manual for child care ctrs., 1987, School-Age Child Care Manual, Infant-Toddler Child Care Manual, Crayola Creativity Program Manual, Developmentally Appropriate Practice in School-Age Child Care, 1991, 2nd edit., 1993, Innovations: The Comprehensive Infant Curriculum, 2000, The Complete Toddler Curriculum and Associated Teacher and Trainer Guides, 2000, Infant and Toddler Development, 2001, The Right Fit: Recruiting and Selecting Staff, 2002; contbg. editor Child Care Information Exchange mag.; contbr. Pre-K Today/Scholastic mag.; contbr. Early Childhood News. Mem. Hayes County Child Welfare Bd. San Marcos, 1979-81, Houston Com. for Pvt. Sector Initiatives Child Care Com.; vol. Initiatives for Children, 1988-90; coord. Child Care Am. Campaign, 1988; pres. bd. dirs. Big Bros.-Big Sisters, Knoxville, 1981-83; vol. cons. Head Start, San Marcos and Knoxville, 1978-84; mem. com. Mayor's Task Force on Children, Houston, 1985; cons. Brown & Root Inc., Vinsin & Elkins, Baker & Botts, Table Toys Inc., 1982-83. Recipient Woman of Excellence award Houston Fedn. Profl. Women, 1993. Mem. Am. Home Econs. Assn. (section treas. 1984-86, project Home Safe Nat. Adv. bd. 1988-93), Nat. Assn. for Edn. Young Children, Nat. Council Family Relations, Nat. Acad. Early Childhood Programs (adv. bd. 1987-91), Houston Assn. Edn. Young Children (bd. dirs. 1984-86, 91—, Child Care Am. coordinator 1988, Educator of Yr. award 1993), Internat. Council on Women's Health Issues (bd. dirs. 1987-90). Democrat. Methodist. Avocations: water skiing, hiking, cooking, wild flower identification. Office: Innovations in Early Childhood Edn 11414 Cedar Creek Dr Houston TX 77077 E-mail: innovations-ka@houston.rr.com.

ALBRECHT, THOMAS BLAIR, microbiology educator, researcher, consultant; b. Phila., July 31, 1943; s. Edward Blair Robson and Deborah Hawley (Smedley) A.; m. Isis Galvao deAlencar, July 28, 1967 (div. 1982); children: Christine deAlencar, Thomas Edward, Alan Wayne. BS, Brigham Young U., 1967, MS, 1969; PhD, Pa. State U., Hershey, 1973. Asst. prof. U. Tex. Med. Br., Galveston, 1976-80, assoc. prof., 1980-86, prof., 1986—. Mem. U.S. EPA Sci. Rev. Panel for Health Effects, 1981-93, 95—. Rsch. fellow Harvard U., 1974-75; recipient several awards NIH, U.S. EPA. Mem. Am. Soc. for Microbiology, Am. Soc. for Cell Biology, Am. Soc. Virology, Soc. Exptl. Biology and Medicine, Environ. Mutagen Soc., Sigma Xi. Achievements include nine patents for anti-viral and anti-proliferative drugs; investigation of the relationship of virus induction of proliferative signals to cell cycle perturbation, the induction of chromosome damage, the priming of cells to injury (particularly neoplastic transformation) by environmental chemicals and drugs; research on the relationship of viral induction of signal transduction and cell activation responses to the pathogenesis of virus infections. Home: 1905 Back Bay Dr Galveston TX 77551-1210 Office: U Tex Med Br Route J-19 11th And Texas Ave Galveston TX 77555-1019

ALBRECHT, TIMOTHY EDWARD, musician, educator; b. Mpls., May 11, 1950; s. James Henry and Helen Josephine (Sweeney) Albrecht; m. Tamara Makdad, Apr. 28, 1955; 1 child, Esther Allison. BA, MusB, Oberlin Coll., 1973; MusM, Eastman Sch. Music, Rochester, N.Y., 1975, D in Mus. Arts, 1978. Prof. Lebanon Valley Coll., Annville, Pa., 1978-82; organist, assoc. prof. music Emory U., Atlanta, 1982-97, prof., 1997—. Vis. assoc. Cambridge (Eng.) U., 1985. Musician: (organ recitals) N.Y., Boston, Vienna, Austria, Berlin, Lima, Peru, Taipei, Taiwan; author: (organ compositions) Grace Notes, I-X, 1982—2002. Lutheran. Office: Emory U Dept Music Atlanta GA 30322-0001 E-mail: talbrec@emory.edu.

ALBRIGHT, ANNAROSE M. secondary school educator; b. Norton, Va., May 8, 1944; d. Joseph Paul and Dorothy Mae (Woody) Cooch; m. William J. Albright, Mar. 28, 1975; children: Angela Rose, Marisa Rose. BS in Edn., Millersville (Pa.) U., 1965; MS in Edn., Temple U., 1968. Cert. English and history tchr., supr., Pa. Tchr. Eastern Lancaster County Sch. Dist., New Holland, Pa., 1965-67, Lancaster County Sch. Dist., 1967-70, Conestoga Valley Sch. Dist., Lancaster, Pa., 1970-84, chief negotiator for union, 1978-80; supr. English dept. Hempfield Sch. Dist., Landisville, Pa., 1984-91, tchr., 1992—. Rep. People to People, 1981-90; chairperson Christian edn. adv. com. St. John Neumann Cath. Ch., 1991-96; tchr., catechism, 1987—; mem. pub. policy com. YWCA, Pa., 1991-95. Recipient journalistic recognition from local and state edn. assns. Mem. NEA, Pa. Edn. Assn., HEA, AAUW (chair local chpt. pub. policy com.), ASCD, Nat. Coun. Tchrs. English (hospitality com. 1990), Conf. on English Leadership (program com. 1991), Pa. Coun. Tchrs. English, Landis Valley Mus. Assn. (chmn. Christmas program, bd. dirs.), Mission Hills Civic Assn. Home: 2636 Breezewood Dr Lancaster PA 17601-4804

ALCALAY, ALBERT S. artist, design educator; b. Paris, Aug. 11, 1917; came to U.S., 1951, naturalized, 1956; s. Samuel and Lepa (Afar) A.; m. Vera Eskenazi, Nov. 11, 1950; children: Leor, Ammiel. Student in Paris, Rome. Lectr. design Carpenter Center, Harvard U., 1960—. One man shows, De Cordova and Dana Mus., Lincoln, Mass., 1968, Swetzoff Gallery, Pucker-Safrai Gallery, Pace Gallery, others; retrospective, Carpenter Ctr., Harvard U., 1982; group shows, Inst. Contemporary Art, Boston, 1960, Venice (Italy) Biennale, Mus. Modern Art., 1955, Whitney Mus. Am. Art, 1956, 58, 60, U. Ill., Urbana, Pa. Acad. Fine Arts, 1960; represented in permanent collections, Mus. Modern Art, N.Y.C., Boston Mus. Fine Arts, Fogg Art Mus., DeCordova and Dana Mus., Phillips Acad., Mus. Am. Art, Brandeis U. Rose Art Mus., U. Mass. Mus., Wellesley Coll. Mus., Colby Coll. Mus., Smith Coll., Rome Mus. Modern Art, U. Rome, Brockton Art Mus., Tufts U., Medford, Mass., Boston Pub. Library, Smithsonian Inst. Archives of Am. Artists. Guggenheim fellow, 1959-60; recipient prize Boston Arts Festival, 1960 Home: 66 Powell St Brookline MA 02446-3929 Office: Harvard U Carpenter Ctr Cambridge MA 01238

ALCAMO, FRANK PAUL, retired educational administrator; b. South Fork, Pa., May 25, 1920; s. Carmelo and Antonia (Trifiro) A.; m. Josephine Giusto, June 22, 1944; 1 child, Antoinette. Student, Johnstown Coll., 1938-39; BS, Indiana U. Pa., 1942; MEd, Pa. State U., 1954. Tchr. math. and sci. Wilmore (Pa.) H.S., 1942-54, Beaverdale (Pa.)-Wilmore H.S., 1954-56; tchr. math. South Fork-Croyle H.S., 1956-61, Triangle Area H.S., Sidman, Pa., 1961-62; asst. prin. Windber (Pa.) Area H.S., 1962-63, prin., 1963-81; ret., 1981. Bd. dirs. Allegheny Ridge Corp. Author: The Windber Story, 1983, The South Fork Story, 1987, The Summerhill Story, 1992. Treas. Windber Summer Playground Assn., 1963; chmn. Windber Police CSC, 1964-81; bd. dirs., pres. Mid-State Automobile Club Johnstown, Pa., 1965—; bd. dirs. Johnstown-Windber Indsl. Devel. Assn., Cambria County Hist. Soc., 1988-93, Sr. Activities Ctr. Cambria County, Inc., 1994-98; founder, dir. CBW Schs. Fed. Credit Union, 1956—; v.p. Windber Pub. Libr., 1976-81; bd. dirs. Windber Recreation Assn., treas., 1974-80; bd. dirs., v.p. Johnstown Area Heritage Assn., 1985—; instr., site coord. counselor IRS Tax Counseling for Elderly, 1984-96. Lt. (j.g.) USNR, 1944-46. Named to Windber Hall of Fame, 1984. Mem. NEA (life), ARC (historian Keystone chpt.), Pa. Edn. Assn. (local br. com. 1966-70, dept. adminstrn. pres. 1971-75, pres. Windber 1965-66), Somerset County Secondary Prins. Assn. (pres. 1965-66), Nat. Secondary Sch. Prins. Assn., Pa. Secondary Sch. Prins. Assn., Pa. Insterscholastic Athletic Assn. (dist. treas. 1970-80), Greater Johnstown Assn. Sch. Retirees (pres. 1983-85, 88-91, 95-96), Sons of Italy, Pa. Assn. Sch. Retirees, Automobile Club So. Pa. (bd. dirs. 1988—), Rotary (dir. Windber 1964-69, pres. 1968-69), Phi Delta Kappa, Sigma Tau Gamma. Democrat. Roman Catholic. Avocations: playing the trombone swing city johnstown, model railroading. Home: 603 Harshberger St Johnstown PA 15905-3129

ALCORN, KAREN ZEFTING HOGAN, artist, art educator, journalist; b. Hartford, Conn., Sept. 29, 1949; d. Edward C. and Doris V. (Anderson) Zefting; m. Wendell R. Alcorn, Apr. 12, 1985. BS, Skidmore Coll., 1971; MFA, Boston U., 1976. Secondary art tchr. Scituate (Mass.) High Sch., 1971-73, Milton (Mass.) High Sch., 1973-79; engr. VEDA, Inc., Arlington, Va., 1979-80; analyst Info. Spectrum, Inc., Arlington, Va., 1980-82, Pacer Systems, Inc., Arlington, Va., 1982-84; dir. ops., mgr. tng. program Starmark Corp., Arlington, Va., 1984; sr. systems analyst VSE Corp., Arlington, Va., 1984-85; analyst, tech. writer Allen Corp., Las Vegas and Fallon, Nev., 1987-88; mem. faculty Western Nev. C.C., 1989, 97-2000; instr. Newport (R.I.) Art Mus., 1990-92; dir. North Tahoe (Calif.) Art Ctr. Dir. Artward Bound, 1994; instr. Sierra Nevada Coll., 1995-98; acting edn. dir., instr. Brewery Arts Ctr., 1996-97; dir. Art Gallery Western Nevada C.C., Carson City, 1999-2000; trustee Western Nev. C.C. Found., 2000—. Exhibitions include Am. Artists Profl. League Grand. Nat., N.Y.C., 1995, 1998, Nev. Biennial, 1996, Catharine Lorillard Wolfe Art Club, N.Y.C., 1996, 2000, Nat. Oil and Acrylic Painters Soc., 1996, 1998, 2000, Nev. State Libr. and Archives, 1997, Salmagundi Club, N.Y.C., 1997, 1998, 2000, 2002, Allied Artists Am., N.Y.C., 1997, Butler Inst. Am. Art, Youngstown, Ohio, 2001, Audubon Artists Inc., 2001, Great Still Life Adventure II, 2002; columnist, writer: Artifacts Mag., 1998—2001. Finalist Artists' Mag., 1994; recipient Silver medal, Calif. Discovery Awards, 1994, Coun. Am. Artist Socs. award, Graphic Am. Artists Profl. League, 1995, 1998, Sarah Marshall and Ida Kaminski Meml. award, Salmagundi Club, 2000, award, Art Calendar Centerfold Contest, 1999; grantee Sierra Arts Found., 1996. Mem.: Capital Arts Coalition, Nat. Oil and Acrylic Painters Soc. (signature mem.), Am. Artists Profl. League, Catharine Wolfe Art Club (assoc.). Address: PO Box 8000 PMB 360 Mesquite NV 89024 E-mail: alcornart@att.net.

ALDAG, RAMON JOHN, management and organization educator; b. Beccles, Suffolk, Eng., Feb. 11, 1945; came to U.S., 1947; s. Melvin Frederick and Joyce Evelyn (Butcher) A.; m. Hollis Maura Jellinek, June 11, 1977; children— Elizabeth, Katherine BS, Mich. State U., 1966, MBA, 1968, PhD, 1974. Thermal engr. Bendix Aerospace div., Ann Arbor, Mich., 1966-70; teaching asst., instr. Mich. State U., East Lansing, Mich., 1966-73; asst. prof. mgmt. U. Wis., Madison, 1973-78, assoc. prof., 1978-82, prof. mgmt. and orgn., 1982—, chmn. dept. mgmt., 1986-88, assoc. dir. Indsl. Rels. Rsch. Inst., 1977-83, co-dir. Ctr. for Study of Orgnl. Performance, 1982—, faculty senator, 1980-84, Pyle Bascom prof. leadership, 1992—, student advisor, 1979—, Glen A. Skillrud Family chair in bus., 2001—, chmn. dept. mgmt. and human resources Sch. Bus., 1995—, co-dir. Weinert Ctr. for Entrepreneurship, 2000—, exec. dir. Weinert Ctr. Entrepreneurship, 2002—. Mgmt. cons. various businesses and industries, 1973— Author: Task Design and Employee Motivation, 1979, Managing Organizational Behavior, 1981, Introduction to Business, 1984, (now titled Business in a Changing World), 3d edit., 1993, 4th edit., 1996, Management, 1987, 2d edit., 1991, Leadership and Vision, 2000, Organizational Behavior and Management, 2002; contbr. articles to profl. jours.; cons. editor for mgmt. South-Western Pub. Co., 1987—; assoc. editor Jour. Bus. Rsch., 1988—, Decision Scis., 2002-; essays co-editor Jour. Mgmt. Inquiry. Bd. dirs. Family Enhancement Program, Madison, 1981— Grantee U. Wis., HEW, 1975-85; recipient Adminstrv. Rsch. Inst. award, 1976, Jerred Disting. Svc. award, 1993, NSF, 2000—; U. Wis. faculty rsch. fellow, 1985-88 Fellow. Acad. of Mgmt. (div. chmn. 1971—, bd. govs. 1986—, v.p. and program chair 1989—, pres. elect 1990, pres. 1991, past pres. 1992—, recipient Disting Svc. award, 1995); mem. Midwest Acad. Mgmt. (pres. 1973—), Decision Scis. Inst. (track chmn. 1975—), Indsl. Rels. Rsch. Assn. (elections commn. 1980—), Found. Adminstrn. Rsch. (pres. 1992—), Pi Tau Sigma, Tau Beta Pi, Sigma Iota Epsilon, Beta Gamma Sigma, Alpha Iota Delta. Avocations: gardening, fishing. Home: 2818 Van Hise Ave Madison WI 53705-3620 Office: U Wis 3112 Grainger Hall 975 University Ave Madison WI 53706-1323 E-mail: raldag@bus.wisc.edu.

ALDCROFT, GEORGE EDWARD, guidance counselor; b. Toronto, Nov. 29, 1941; s. George and Margaret Aldcroft; m. Bernadette M. Cartoski, Nov. 27, 1971; children: Allison Marie, Bonnie Christine. BS in Edn., Wayne State U., 1966; MS in Guidance and Counseling, U. Mich., 1971; postgrad., Gestalt Ctr. L.I. Nat. cert. counselor, nat. cert. sch. counselor; cert. leader Developing Capable Young People. Elem. and jr. h.s. tchr. Center Line (Mich.) Pub. Sch. Sys., 1967-72; summer camp counselor, vol. worker Boys' Clubs Met. Detroit, 1967-69; guidance dir. Shelter Island (N.Y.) Union Free Sch. Dist., 1972-83; sch. counselor Westhampton Beach (N.Y.) Union Free Sch. Dist., 1983-89, Mattituck Cutchogue Sch. Dist., 1989—2002. Part-time employee Mattituck Cutchogue Sch. Dist., Cutchogue, NY, 2002—; facilitator parenting program. Mem. Shelter Island Drug Edn. Com., 1974, Southold Union Free Sch. Dist. Bd. Edn., 1983-86; bd. dirs. Human Understanding and Growth Seminars, 1985—, pres. bd. dirs., 1991-92. Recipient Outstanding Vol. Leader award Boys' Clubs Detroit, 1968. Mem. N.Y. State Counseling Assn., N.Y. State Sch. Counselors Assn., East End Counselors Assn. (pres. 1995-97), Am. Sch. Counselors Assn., U. Mich. Aumni Assn., N.Y. State United Tchrs. Roman Catholic. Home and Office: PO Box 431 Peconic NY 11958-0431 E-mail: galdcroft@aol.com.

ALDEA, GABRIEL S. cardiothoracic surgeon, educator; b. Bucharest, Romania, Nov. 7, 1956; came to U.S., 1970; s. Adrian and Blanche (Fainaru) A.; m. Susan Arnold, May 8, 1988; children: Alexander, Daniel. BA in Biochemistry summa cum laude, Columbia Coll., 1977; MD, Columbia U., 1981. Diplomate Am. Bd. Surgery, Am. Bd. Thoracic Surgery, Nat. Bd. Med. Examiners. Resident in gen. surgery N.Y. Hosp., Cornell Med. Ctr., N.Y.C., 1981—86, adminstrv. chief resident Dept. Surgery, 1985-86; cardiothoracic residency Dept. Cardiothoracic Surgery N.Y. Hosp., Cornell Med. Ctr. & Meml. Sloane Kettering Hosp., N.Y.C., 1988-90; cardiovasc. rsch. fellowship Cardiovasc. Rsch. Inst.-U. Calif. San Francisco, 1986-88; asst. vis. surgeon in cardiothoracic surgery Boston U. Med. Ctr., 1990-98; assoc. vis. surgeon in thoracic surgery Boston City Hosp., 1990-98; thoracic surgeon Jamaica Plain VA Hosp., Boston; assoc. prof. cardiothoracic surgery Boston U. Sch. Medicine, 1990-98; chief adult cardiac surgery, prof. surgery U. Wash., Seattle, 1998—; cardiac surgeon N.W. Hosp., Seattle, 1998—, Puget Sound VA Hosp., Seattle, 1998—. Contbr. articles to profl. jours. and chpts. to books. Recipient Nat. Rsch. Svc. award in heart & vascular diseases NIH, 1986-88. Fellow New Eng. Oncologic Soc.; mem. AAAS, AMA, ACS, Am. Coll. Chest Physicians, Am. Coll. Cardiology, Am. Heart Assn., Soc. for Thoracic Surgeons, Am. Assn. for Thoracic Surgery, Assn. Acad. Surgery, Am. Surg. Assn., Mass. Med. Soc., Rsch. Assocs. Southwestern Oncology Group, Western Thoracic Assn. Home: The Highlands Seattle WA 98177 Office: U Wash Dept Cardiothorasic Surgery PO Box 356310 Seattle WA 98195-6310

ALDERDICE, DOUGLAS ALAN, secondary education educator; b. Buffalo, May 26, 1964; s. Lawrence Gilchrist and Carol Isabelle (Maas) A. BA, Susquehanna U., 1986; MS in Edn., Canisius Coll., 1993. Cert. secondary math. tchr., N.Y. Tchr. computers, tech. integration specialist Buffalo Bd. Edn., 1986—. Mem. Am. Radio Relay League, Antique Telephone Collectors Assn., Buffalo Amateur Radio Repeater Assn. (v.p. 1988-89, pres. 1989-94, editor jour. 1994—, v.p. 2000—), Greenkeys Teleprinter Collectors Assn., Lafayette High Sch. Alumni Assn. (alumni liaison 1987—), Morse Telegraph Club. Republican. Lutheran. Avocations: amateur radio, photography, model railroading, classical organ playing. Office: Lafayette High Sch 370 Lafayette Ave Buffalo NY 14213-1494 E-mail: dalderdice@buffalo.k12.ny.us.

ALDERFER, CLAYTON PAUL, organizational consultant, educator, writer, administrator; b. Sellersville, Pa., Sept. 1, 1940; s. Joseph Paul and Ruth Althea (Buck) A.; m. Charleen Judith Frankenfield, July 14, 1962; children: Kate, Benjamin. BS with high honors, Yale U., 1962, PhD, 1966. Cert. Am. Bd. Profl. Psychology. Asst. prof. Cornell U., Ithaca, N.Y., 1966-68, Yale U., New Haven, 1968-70, assoc. prof., 1970-78; prof. Sch. Orgn. Mgmt., Yale U., New Haven, 1978-92, assoc. dean, 1982-84; prof. II Grad. Sch. Applied and Profl. Psychology Rutgers U., 1992—, dir. Orgnl. Psychology program, 1992—. Author: Existence, Relatedness and Growth, 1972, Learning from Changing, 1975; contbr. articles to profl. jours.; mem. editl. bd. Jour. Applied Behavioral Sci., 1978-89, editor, 1990-93; mem. editl. bd. Family Bus. Rev., 1987—, Jour. Orgnl. Behavior, 1988-92; editor: Advances in Experiential Social Processes, vol. 1, 1979, vol. 2, 1980. Bd. dirs. NTL Inst., Arlington, Va., 1975-78, DATA, New Haven, 1989-92. Grantee Office Naval Research, 1970-74, 79-80, 82-86; recipient Cattell award, 1972, McGregor award, 1979, Levinson award, 1997, Helms award, 1999. Fellow Am. Psychol. Assn., Soc. Applied Anthropology, Am. Psychol. Soc.; mem. Sigma Xi, Tau Beta Pi. Independent. Lutheran. Office: Rutgers Grad Sch Applied Profl Psychology 152 Frelinghuysen Rd Piscataway NJ 08854-8020 E-mail: alderfer@rci.rutgers.edu.

ALDERMAN, MINNIS AMELIA, psychologist, educator, small business owner; b. Douglas, Ga., Oct. 14, 1928; d. Louis Cleveland Sr. and Minnis Amelia (Wooten) A. AB in Music, Speech and Drama, Ga. State Coll., Milledgeville, 1949; MA in Supervision/Counseling Psychology, Murray State U., 1960; postgrad., Columbia Pacific U., 1987—. Tchr. music Lake County Sch. Dist., Umatilla, Fla., 1949-50; instr. vocal/instrumental music, dir. band, orch., choral Fulton County Sch. Dist., Atlanta, 1950-54; instr. English, speech, debate, vocal and instrumental music Elko County Sch. Dist., Wells, Nev., 1954-59, dir. drama, band, choral and orchestra, 1954-59; tchr. English and social studies Christian County Sch. Dist., Hopkinsville, Ky., 1960; instr. psychology, counselor critic prof. Murray (Ky.) State U., 1961-63, U. Nev., Reno, 1963-67; owner Minisizer Exercising Salon, Ely, Nev., 1969-71, Knit Knook, Ely, 1969—, Minimimeo, Ely, 1969—, Gift Gamut, Ely, 1977—; prof. dept. fine arts Wassuk Coll., Ely, 1986-91, assoc. dean, 1986-87, dean, 1987-90; counselor White Pine County Sch. Dist., Ely, 1960-68; dir. Child and Family Ctr. Ely Indian Tribe, 1988-93. Supr. testing Ednl. Testing Svc., Princeton, N.J., 1960-68, Am. Coll. Testing Program, Iowa, 1960-68, U. Nev., Reno, 1960-68; chmn. bd. White Pine Sch. Dist. Employees Fed. Credit Union, Ely, 1961-69; psychologist mental hygiene div. Nev. Pers., Ely, 1969-75, dept. employment secrity, 1975-80; sec.-treas. bd. dirs. Gt. Basin Enterprises, Ely, 1969-71; speaker at confs.; rep. Ely/East Ely Bus. Coun., 1997—; mem. Econ. Devel. Bd., 1998—; prof. Great Basin C.C., 1999—. Author various news articles, feature stories, pamphlets, handbooks and grants in field. Pvt. instr. piano, violin, voice and organ, Ely, 1981—. Dir. Family Resource Ctr. (Great Basin Rural Nev. Youth Cabinet), 1996—; bd. dirs. band Sacred Heart Sch., Ely, 1982-99; mem. Gov.'s Mental Health State Commn., 1963-65, Ely Shoshone Tribal Youth Camp, 1991-92, Elys Shoshone Tribal Unity Conf., 1991-92, Tribal Parenting Skills Coord., 1991, White Pine C. of C., 2000-; bd. dirs. White Pine County Sch. Employees Fed. Credit Union, 1961-68,, pres., 1963-68; 2d v.p. White Pine Community Concert Assn., 1965-67, pres., 1967, 85—, treas., 1975-79, dr. chmn., 1981-85; chmn. of bd., 1984; bd. dirs. White Pine chpt. ARC, 1978-82; mem. Nev. Hwy. Safety Leaders Bd., 1979-82; mem. Gov.'s Commn. on Status Women, 1968-74, Gov.'s Nevada State Juvenile Justice Adv. Commn., 1992-94; mem. White Pine C. of C.; dir. White Pine Legisl. Coalition, 2002—; mem. White Pine Overall Econ. Devel. Plan Coun., 1992-99; sec.-treas. White Pine Rehab. Tng. Ctr. for Retarded Persons, 1973-75; mem. Gov.'s Commn. on Hwy. Safety, 1979-81, Gov's. Juvenile Justice Program; sec.-treas. White Pine County Juvenile Problems Cabinet, 1994—; dir. Ret. Sr. Vol. Program, 1973-74; vice chmn. Gt. Basin Health Coun., 1973-75, Home Extension adv. Bd., 1977-80; sec.-treas. Great Basin chpt. Nev. Employees Assn.; bd. dirs. United Way, 1970-76; vice chmn. White Pine Coun. on Alcoholism and Drug Abuse, 1975-76, chmn., 1976-77, White Pine County Bus. Coun., 1998—; dir. White Pine Coalation; grants author 3 yrs. Indian Child Welfare Act, State Hist. Preservation, Fair and Recreation Bd. Centennial Fine Arts Ctr.; originator Community Tng. Ctr. for Retarded People, 1972, Ret. Sr. Vol. Program, 1974, Nutrition Program for Sr. Citizens, 1974, Sr. Citizens Ctr., 1974, Home Repairs for Sr. Citizens, 1974, Sr. Citizens Crafters Assns., 1976, Inst. Current World Affairs, 1989, Victims of Crime, 1990-92, grants author Family Resource Ctr., 1995; bd. dirs. Family coalition, 1990-92, Sacred Heart Parochial Sch., 1982—, dir. band, 1982—; candidate for diaconal ministry, 1982-93; dir. White Pine Cmty. Chior, 1962— invited performer Branson Jubilee Nat. Ch. Chior Festival, Mo., Ely Meth. Ch. Choir, 1960-84; chior dir., organist Sacred Heart Ch., 1984—; Precinct reporter ABC News, 1966; speaker U.S. Atty. Gen. Conf. Bringing Nev. Together; bd. dirs. White Pine Juvenile Cabinet, 1993—, Ely/East Ely Bus. Coun., 1997—, Econ. Devel. Bd., 1998—. Named scholar, Nat. Trust for Hist. Preservation, 2000; recipient Recognition rose, Alpha Chi State Delta Kappa Gamma, 1994, Recognition Rose, 2002, Perserving America's Treasures in the 21st Century, 2001; grantee, Nat. Trust for Historic Preservation, L.A., 2000. Fellow Am. Coll. Musicians, Nat. Guild Piano Tchrs.; mem. NEA (life), UDC, DAR, Nat. Fedn. Ind. Bus. (dist. chair 1971-85, nat. guardian coun. 1985—, state guardian coun. 1987—), AAUW (pres. Wells br. 1957-58, pres. White Pine br. 1965-66, 86-87, 89-91, 93—, bd. dirs. 1965-87, rep. edn. 1965-67, implementation chair 1967-69, area advisor 1969-73, 89-91), Nat. Fedn. Bus. and Profl. Women (1st v.p. Ely chpt. 1965-66, pres. Ely chpt. 1966-68, 74-76, 85—, bd. dirs. Nev. chpt. 1966—, 1st v.p. Nev. Fedn. 1970-71, pres. Nev. chpt. 1972-73,nat. bd. dirs. 1972-73), White Pine County Mental Health Assn. (pres. 1960-63, 78—), Mensa (supr. testing 1965—), White Pine C. of C., Delta Kappa Gamma (br. pres. 1968-72, 94—99, state bd. 1967—, chpt. parliamentarian 1974-78, 99—, state 1st v.p. 1967-69, state pres. 1969-71, nat. bd. 1969-71, state parliamentarian 1971-73, 95—, chmn. state nominating com. 1995-97, chmn. bylaws com. 2003—, workshop presenter on aging 1995, presenter 1998-99), White Pine Knife and Fork Club (1st v.p. 1969-70, pres. 1970-71, bd. dirs. 1979—), Soc. Descs. of Knights of Most Noble Order of Garter, Nat. Soc. Magna Charta Dames. Office: PO Box 150457 Ely NV 89315-0457

ALDERSON, MARGARET NORTHROP, arts administrator, educator, artist; b. Washington, Nov. 28, 1936; d. Vernon D. and Margaret (Lloyd) Northrop; m. Donald Marr Alderson, Jr., June 4, 1955; children: Donald Marr III, Barbara Lynn Hennessy, Brian Keith, Graham Dean. Student, George Washington U., 1954-55; AA, Monterey Peninsula Jr. Coll., 1962. Staff, tchr. Galerie Jaclande, Springfield, Va., 1972-73; artist, tchr. Studio 7 Torpedo Factory Art Ctr., Alexandria, Va., 1974—, dir. ctr., 1979-85; tchr. Fairfax County Recreation, 1972-73, Art League Schs., Alexandria, 1978—92. Tchr. ann. Feb. Workshops Accapulco, Mex., 1985-2000, English painting workshop, 1989-91, 93, 95, 98, Santa Fe workshop, 1991-92, 95-96, 98, 2000, Italian Watercolor workshop, 1996-97, Provence France workshop, 1995, Day of Dead workshop, Mex., 2000, Andalusian workshop, 2000, Bali Painting workshop, 2000, Irish Painting Workshop, 2002; ptnr. Soho Hubris Art Gallery, N.Y., 1977-78; pres. Touchstone Gallery, Washington; cons. in field. One woman shows include Way Up Gallery, Livermore, Calif., 1971, Lynchburg (Va.) Coll., 1978, Farm House Gallery, Rehobeth, Del., 1979, Art League Gallery, Alexandria, 1980, 86, 93, Lyceum Mus., Alexandria, 1987, Alexandria Mus., 1987-88, William Ris Gallery, Stone Harbor, N.J., 1988, Touchstone Gallery, Washington, 1992, 94, 96, 98, 2000, 2002, 20th Century Gallery, Williamsburg, Va., 1996, Mus. Southwest, Midland, Tex., 1998; exhibited in group shows at Art League Gallery, Alexandria, 1972—, Lynchburg Coll., 1978, Montgomery (Ala.) Mus., 1980, Art Barn, 1989, Moscow-Washington Art Exch. Exhibit Internat., Moscow, 1990, Washington, 1991, Fernbank Mus. Natural History Mus., 1997-98, Bennet Gallery, Knoxville, Tenn., 1998; represented in permanent collections Texaco, Inc., Phillip Morse Collection, United Va. Bank, CSX Corp., Fannie Mae Corp., Acacia Fin. Group, Office U.S. Atty. Gen., Office Ins. Gen., EPA, Aerospace Corp., Texaco Corp.; traveling shows include Chrysler Mus. Biennial, 1988, Audubon Artists Nat. Show, 1989, Balt. Regional Watercolor Ann., 1989. Project supr. City Alexandria for Torpedo Factory Art Ctr., 1978-83; festival chmn. City Festival Cultural Arts, Livermore, Calif., 1971; bd. dirs. Cultural Alliance Greater Washington, 1982—, Torpedo Factory Art Ctr., 1978—; mem. Ptnrs. Liveable Places, 1979—, Catherine Llorilard Wolfe Art Soc.; pres. Touchstone Art Coop.; mem. Virginians for the Arts. Recipient Balt. watercolor regional ann. Md. Foun. award, 1989, Elgie and David Ject Kay award Audubon Artists ann., 1989, 1st pl. award in watercolor Arts League, 1975, 76, 77, 82, 84-85, numerous purchase awards, Jane Morton Norman award Ky. Nat. Watercolor Show, 1986, Adirondack Nat. Watercolor Show, 1987, 3d award Catherine Lorillard Show, N.Y.C., 1987, Albert Ehringer award, 1989, Holbein award Mid Atlantic Watercolor Regional show, 1992, Pruchase award d'Arches Paer Co., Knickerbocker Exhibit, Best in Show award Deland Mus. Art, 1993, Catherine Lovell award, 1993; nominated Woman of Yr. Alexandria C. of C., 1992, 93, Living Legend award City Alexandria Commn. Women, 1999. Mem. Fed. Nat. Mortgage Assn., Va. Watercolor Assn. (pres. 1982, 1st place award ann. exhibit 1980, 82, excellence award 1989, 94), Potomac Valley Watercolorists (pres. 1978), Torpedo Factory Artists Assn. (pres. 1977-78), Springfield Art Guild (pres. 1977), Artists Equity, Am. Coun. Arts., Am. Watercolor Soc., Am. Coun. Univ. & Community Arts Ctrs., Phila. Watercolor Club, Watercolor West, Soc. Layerists Multi-Media, Va. Watercolor Soc. Am. Profl. Artists' League, Am. Mgmt. Assn., Nat. Hist. Trust, Ga. Watercolor Soc., Miss. Watercolor Soc., La. Watercolor Soc., Ky. Watercolor Soc., Catherine Llorilard Wolfe Club. Republican. Home: 2204 Windsor Rd Alexandria VA 22307-1018 Studio: Torpedo Factory Art Ctr 105 N Union St # 7 Alexandria VA 22314-3217 E-mail: margalderson@worldnet.att.net.

ALDRIDGE, LINDA ANN, retired elementary education educator, librarian; b. Columbus, Ga., July 27, 1931; d. Carey Curry and Jimmie Allie (Brown) Willis; m. R. Franklynn Van Stralen, Aug. 5, 1950 (div. Mar. 1974); children: Errol, Daved, Cary; m. Charles Ray Aldridge, Dec. 22, 1974. BA, Calif. State U., L.A., 1966, MA, 1972. Tchr. Bellflower (Calif.) Unified Schs., 1966-71, L.A. Unified Schs., 1971-81, Pinellas Sch. Dist., St. Petersburg, Fla., 1983—2003. Instr. St. Petersburg Jr. Coll., 1983—. Libr. info. specialist Pinellas County, 1997, 2003. Mem. Fla. Assn. Media Edn., Fla. Storytellers Guild, Pinellas Assn. Libr.-Media Specialists (Libr. Info. Specialist of Yr. 1998). Baptist. Avocations: composing and writing children's music and plays, storytelling, musician. E-mail: aldridge@aldridges.com.

ALDROW-LIPUT, PRISCILLA REESE, retired elementary education educator; b. Kingston, Pa., Apr. 10, 1951; d. Thomas Edward and Martha Mae (Hadsall) Reese; children: Colin Michael, Justin John; m. Willard C. Aldrow. BS, Bloomsburg State Coll., 1973. Cert. instructional II. Tchr. grade 5 Dallas (Pa.) Sch. Dist., ret., 2001; homebound tchr., pre-K-12 Williamsburg-James City County Sch. Dist., Va. Homebound tchr. Williamsburg-James County Sch. Dist., Va. Mem. NEA, Pa. State Edn. Assn., Dallas Edn. Assn. Home: 109 Rondane Pl Williamsburg VA 23188 E-mail: aldrow@bznt.com.

ALESSE, JUDITH, special education educator; b. N.Y.C., Apr. 16, 1953; d. Joseph and Rose Alesse. BA cum laude, Hofstra U., 1977; MS, Adelphi U., 1979. Cert. spl. edn. tchr. N.Y. Spl. edn. tchr. Malverne (N.Y.) Sch. dist., 1980—. V.p. Nassau Reading Coun., NY, 2001—. Office: HT Herber Mid Sch 75 Ocean Ave Malverne NY 11565

ALEXAKOS, FRANCES MARIE, counselor, business owner, psychology educator, researcher, producer, editor; b. Fitchburg, Mass., Dec. 29, 1947; d. Samuel Rosario and Mary (Cucchiara) Sciabarrasi; m. Haritos Kyniacou Agadakos, June 5, 1988 (dec. Feb. 1987); m. Demetrios P. Alexakos, June 5, 1988 (dec. Dec. 1999); children: Katerina, Demetra, Artemis, Alexis. BA in Psychology, U. Mass., 1970; MA in Psychology, Assumption Coll., 1972; BA in Studio Art, U. R.I., 1994; cert. in humanities, Salve Regina U., 1996, PhD, 2003. Social worker, Mass.; psychologist, Mass.; cert. tchr., R.I.; cert. sch. counselor, R.I. Sr. med. social worker Roger William Hosp., Providence, 1972-78; prof. psychology Johnson & Wales U., Providence, 1991—96, C.C. R.I., Warwick; dir. mktg. Oak Internat. Academies, Guadelahara, Mex., 1996-97. Mem. vis. faculty summer ethics inst. Dartmouth Coll., 1998. Editor, Mediterranean bur. chief Slugfest lit. mag., 1997-2002; author: Medicine and Health, Rhode Island Physicians' Attitudes Toward Genetic Testing and Breast Cancer, 1999. Active Zoning Bd. of Rev., Wakefield, RI, 2001—; trustee U. R.I. Found.; health com. R.I. Women's Commn., 2001—. Daus. of Penelope scholar, 1994; NIH grantee, 1998; named Person of Yr., Wakefield C. of C., 1987, Leadership R.I. award 1995. Mem. LWV (chair ednl. grants com.), Rotary (chmn. charitable gifts 2003), Golden Key Honor Soc. Greek Orthodox.

ALEXANDER, EDNA M. DEVEAUX, elementary education educator; d. Richard and Eva (Musgrove) DeVeaux. BBA, Fla. A & M U., 1943; BS in Elem. Edn., Fla. A&M U., 1948; MS in Supervision and Adminstrn., U. Pa., 1954; cert., U. Madrid, 1961; postgrad., Dade Jr. Coll., U. Miami. Sec. Dunbar Elem. Sch., 1943-46, tchr., 194-55, Orchard Villa Elem., 1959-66; prin. A. L. Lewis Elem. Sch., 1955-57; reading specialist North Cen. Dist., 1966-69; tchr. L. C. Evans Elem. Sch., 1969-71. First black woman newscaster in Miami, Sta. WBAY, 1948. V.p. Fla. Coun. on Human Rels. Dade County, Coun. for Internat. Visitors Greater Miami; vice chmn. Cmty. Action Agy. Dade County; chmn. Dade County Minimum Housing Appeals Bd.; active Vol. Unltd. Project Nat. Coun. Negro Women; sponsor Am. Jr. Red Cross, Girl Scouts U.S.; trustee Fla. Internat. U. Found., 1974—79; mem. Jacksonville Symphony Assn. Guild Bd., Salvation Army Women's Aux., Jacksonville U. Friends of Libr. Bd.; past pres. Episcopal Church-women of Christ Ch., Miami; bd. dirs. YWCA. Named to Miami Centennial Women's Hall of Fame, 1996. Mem. AAUW (life, Edna M. DeVeaux Alexander fellowship named in her honor Miami br., del. seminar 1977), NEA (life), LWV, Fla. Edn. Assn., Classroom Tchrs. Assn., Dade County Edn. Assn. (chmn. pub. rels. com.), Dade County Reading Assn., Assn. for Childhood Edn., Internat. Reading Tchr. Assn., U. Pa. Alumni Assn., Alpha Kappa Alpha. Avocations: composing lyrics and music, gardening, travel, golf, photography. Home: 805 Blue Gill Rd Jacksonville FL 32218-3660

ALEXANDER, GREGORY STEWART, law educator, educator; b. 1948; BA, Ill. U., 1970; JD, Northwestern U., 1973; postgrad., U. Chgo., 1974-75. Law clk. to chief judge U.S. Ct. Appeals, 1972-74; asst. prof. law U. Ga., 1975-78, assoc. prof., 1978-84; prof. Cornell U., Ithaca, N.Y., 1984—, A. Robert Noll prof. law, 2000—. Vis. prof. Harvard Law Sch., 1997—. Bigelow fellow U. Chgo., 1974-75; fellow Max-Planck Inst. (Germany), 1995-96, Ctr. for Advanced Study in Behavioral Scis., Palo Alto, Calif., 2003-2004. Fellow Ctr. Advanced Study in Behavioral Scis.; mem. Am. Soc. Politics and Legal Philosophy, Am. Soc. Legal History. Office: Cornell U Law Sch Myron Taylor Hall Ithaca NY 14853 E-mail: gsa9@cornell.edu.

ALEXANDER, JEFFREY CHARLES, sociology educator; b. Milw., May 30, 1947; s. Frederick Charles and Esther Leah (Schlossman) A.; m. Morel Morton; children: Aaron, Benjamin. BA, Harvard Coll., 1969; PhD, U. Calif., Berkeley, 1978. Lectr. U. Calif., Berkeley, 1974-76; asst. prof. UCLA, 1976-81, prof., 1981-2001, chair dept. sociology, 1989—92, prof. emeritus, 2001—; prof. sociology Yale U., 2001—, chair dept. sociology, 2002—, dir. grad. program, acting chair, 2001—02, dir. Ctr. for Cultural Sociology, 2002—. Prof. U. Bordeaux, France, 1994; vis. prof. Inst. Advanced Studies, Vienna, Austria, 1995. Author: Theoretical Logic in Sociology, vols. I-IV, 1982-83, Twenty Lectures: Sociological Theory Since World War Two, 1987, Action and Its Environments: Towards a New Synthesis, 1988, Structure and Meaning: Relinking Classical Sociology, 1989, Teoria Sociologia E Mutamento Sociales, Un Analisi Multidemensionale della Modernita, 1990, Soziale Differenzierung und Kultureller Wandel Studien zur Neofunktionalistischen Gesellschafstheorie, 1993, Fin-de-Siecle Social Theory: Relativism, Reduction and the Problem of Reason, 1995, Neofunctionalism and After, 1998, (Japanese trans.) Neofunctionalism and Civil Society, 1996, Cultural Trauma and Collective Identity, 2003, The Meanings of Social Life: A Cultural Sociology, 2003; editor: Neofunctionalism, 1985, Durkheimian Sociology: Cultural Studies, 1988, Real Civil Societies, 1997; co-editor: The Micro-Macro Link, 1987, Differentiation Theory and Social Change: Historical and Comparative Perspectives, 1990, Rethinking Progress: Movements, Forces and Ideas at the End of the Twentieth Century, 1990, Culture and Society: Contemporary Debates, 1990, Diversity and Its Discontents, 1999, The New Social Theory, 2001; The Sociological Traditions, 2001 (8 vols.), 2001. Guggenheim fellow, 1979-80; Travel and Study fellow Ford Found., 1980; Princeton Inst. for Advanced Studies fellow, 1985-86; Swedish Colloquium for Advanced Study in the Social Scis., 1992, 96; Ctr. for Advanced Studies in the Behavioral Scis., 1998-99. Mem. Am. Sociol. Assn., Internat. Sociol. Assn. (founder, co-chair rsch. com. sociol. theory 1990-94), Sociol. Rsch. Assn. Democrat. Jewish. Avocations: art, photography, tennis, skiing. Office: Dept Sociology Yale U New Haven CT 06511

ALEXANDER, JOHN KURT, history educator; b. Vancouver, Wash., Oct. 25, 1941; s. Eugene Victor and Marta T. Alexander; m. June Granatir, Dec. 29, 1973. BS in Edn. with honors, Western Oreg. U., Monmouth, 1964; MA in History, U. Chgo., 1965, PhD in History, 1973. From asst. prof. to prof. history U. Cin., 1969—2002, Disting. tchg. prof., 2003—. Author: Render Them Submissive, 1980, The Selling of the Constitutional Convention, 1990, Samuel Adams, 2002; assoc. editor Am. Nat. Biography, Oxford U. Press, 1989-99; contbr. articles to profl. jours. Mem. Orgn. Am. Historians, Hist. Soc. Pa., Pa. Hist. Soc., Ohio Acad. History (Outstanding Tchr. award 2002), Soc. for Historians of Early Am. Republic. Home: 3410 Bishop St Cincinnati OH 45220-1831 Office: Univ Cin Dept History Ml 0373 Cincinnati OH 45221-0373 E-mail: John.K.Alexander@uc.edu.

ALEXANDER, KATHRYN JEAN (KAY ALEXANDER), retired art education consultant, art curriculum writer; b. Oakland, Calif., July 31, 1924; d. Haskell Seward Bennett and Ruth (Simpson) Bennett Macaulay; m. Earl Bryan Alexander, Aug. 12, 1945; children: Steven Bryan, Lauren Alexander Hildebrand, Douglas Brandon. BA in Art with honors, U. Calif., Berkeley, 1946; MA in Edn. Adminstr. with honors, Calif. State U., Long Beach, 1959; postgrad., Oxford (Eng.) U., 1984. Cert. tchr., adminstr., supr. Elem. tchr. Anaheim (Calif.) Sch. Dist., 1956-60, coord. gifted edn., 1960-63, art edn. coord., 1963-67, Palo Alto (Calif.) Unified Sch. Dist., 1967-85; ind. art edn. cons. Los Altos, Calif., 1984—. Adj. prof. Hayward (Calif.) State U., 1971-73; chair interdisciplinary com. State of Calif. Arts Framework, Sacramento, 1980-82; dir. Curriculum Devel. Inst., Getty Ctr. for Edn., L.A., 1986-89. Author: (series of 9 books) Learning to Look and Create: The SPECTRA Program, 1986-94, (40 annotated posters) Take Five, 1988-90, (6 video-filmstrip sets) The Skills of Art, 1987; editor (handbook) Discipline Based Art Education, A Curriculum Sampler, 1990, (multimedia H.S. program) Native American Arts & Crafts, 1995, Who is the Artist? (impressionism), Who is the Artist? (post-impressionism), 2000, Who is the Artist? Painters of the American Scene, 2002, Who is the Artist? Painters of Fantasy and Imagination, 2002, Who is the Artist? Painters of Line and Color, 2003, Who is the Artist? Pop Art, 2003; online Internet series: (72 art lessons for children), At Home with Art, 2000; writer curriculum materials in field; contbg. editor Arts and Activities, 1988—. Assoc. dir. J. Paul Getty Ctr. for Edn. in Arts Curriculum Devel. Inst., 1987-89; vol. Stanford Com. for Art, 1971-; docent Cantor Art Ctr., Stanford U., 1996-2000, docent trainer, 2000. Recipient Humanities award Calif. Humanities Assn., 1984, Emerson award Cultural Arts Peninsula Area, Calif., 1986. Mem. Nat. Art Edn. Assn. (chair publs. com. 1974-78, Outstanding Art Educator award 1983, Pacific Region Outstanding Art Supr. 1984), Pacific Art League (sec. bd. trustees 1983-85), Calif. Art Edn. Assn. (various exec. positions 1964—, Disting. Art Educator 1988), Photog. Soc. Am., Phi Beta Kappa. Avocations: photography, painting, sculpture, printmaking, flying. Home and Office: 800 El Monte Ave Los Altos CA 94022-3960 E-mail: donkay@earthlink.net.

ALEXANDER, MICHELE YERMACK, private school educator; b. Pitts., Sept. 16, 1947; d. Michael and Bernadette (Vogel) Yermack; m. Michael Allen Alexander, Aug. 14, 1971; children: Alexia Michele, Aaron Michael, Adam Mikhail. BS in Biology, George Mason U., 1969; MA in Sci. Edn., Ohio State U., 1975, postgrad., 1975-79. Cert. sci. tchr., Va., Ohio, Pa. 8th grade sci. tchr. Fred M. Lynn Mid. Sch., Woodbridge, Va., 1969-71, 7th grade sci. tchr. Orange (Va.) Intermediate Sch., 1971-72; sci.-biology tchr. Groveport (Ohio) Madison H.S., 1972-77; biology tchr. Sewickley (Pa.) Acad., 1980-87; substitute tchr. Corpus Christi Sch., Wilmington, Del., 1991-92, full-time sci. tchr., sci. coord., 1993—. Quality monitor Stream Watch of Del., Hockessin, 1989—; state co-dir. Del. Sci. Olympiad, 2002—, bd. dirs.; mem. com. to write Wilmington Diocesan Sci. Curriculum Guidelines, 1995-96. Editor: Energy Activities for the Classroom, 1976. Mem. Sewickley Watershed Assn., 1980-87; nature guide Sewickley Nature Guides, 1980-87; bd. dirs. Conservation Consultants, Sewickley, 1980-87; sec. Bon Ayre Civic Assn., Hockessin, 1981-88, treas., 1988-89; co-leader Girl Scouts U.S., Wilmington, 1989-90; mem. St. Mary of the Assumption Parish Coun., Hockessin, 1990-93. Mem. Nat. Sci. Tchrs.' Assn., Corpus Christi Home and Sch. Assn. (bd. dirs., v.p. 1989-91, pres.-elect 1991-92, pres. 1992-93), Del. Tchrs. Sci., Del. Adv. Coun. Sci. and Environ. Edn., Del. Nature Soc., Phi Delta Kappa. Roman Catholic. Avocations: ballet, baseball, photography, reading. Home: 803 Ciderbrook Rd Hockessin DE 19707-1325

ALEXANDER, PATRICK BYRON, university administrator; b. Texas City, Tex., May 11, 1950; s. Alvin Wesley and Mabel Bernice Alexander; m. Linda Graham, May 7, 1975. BA in Econs., George Mason Coll., U. Va., 1972. Publs. dir. George Mason U., Fairfax, Va., 1973-75, U. Okla. Health Scis. Ctr., Okla. City, 1975-78, Presbyn. Hosp. Inc., Okla. City, 1978-79; mng. dir. Okla. Symphony Orch., Okla. City, 1979-88; exec. dir. Allied Arts Found., 1988-92, Okla. Zool. Soc., 1992—2001; exec. dir. advancement Okla. City U., 2001—03, cons., 2003—. Bd. dirs. Ambassador's Concert Choir, Okla. Philharm. Found., English-Speaking Union Okla., Possibilities, Red Earth Indian Ctr. Recipient Gov.'s award for excellence in arts, 1987, Okla. Fundraiser of Yr. award, 1991; English-Speaking Union Okla. Kerr Found. fellow, 1981. Home: 1515 Glenwood Ave Oklahoma City OK 73116-5206 Office: Oklahoma City U 2501 N Blackwelder Oklahoma City OK 73106 E-mail: palexander@okcu.edu.

ALEXANDER, RALPH WILLIAM, JR., physics educator; b. Phila., May 17, 1941; s. Ralph William and Gladys (Robin) A.; m. Janet Erdien Bradley, Sept. 4, 1965; children: Ralph III, Margaret. BA, Wesleyan U., Middletown, Conn., 1963; PhD, Cornell U., Ithaca, N.Y., 1968; postdoctoral study, U. of Freiburg, Fed. Republic Germany, 1968-70. From asst. to assoc. prof. physics U. Mo., Rolla, 1970-80, prof., 1980—, chmn. dept., 1983-92. Contbr. articles to profl. jours. Mem. Am. Phys. Soc., Assn. Am. Physics Tchrs. Office: U Mo Dept Physics Rolla MO 65409-0640 E-mail: ralexand@umr.edu.

ALEXANDER, ROBERT EARL, university chancellor, educator; b. Kinston, N.C., Oct. 21, 1939; s. Joseph Culbreath and Pauline (Fussell) A.; m. Leslie Johnson, Mar. 11, 1971; children— Lara, Robert BA in Polit. Sci., Duke U., 1962, M.Div., 1966; D. in Higher Edn., U. S.C., 1977. Ordained to ministry United Methodist Ch., 1967. Assoc. chaplain N.C. State U., Raleigh, 1965-66; assoc. chaplain U. S.C., Columbia, 1966-68, dir. vol. services, 1969-70, adminstrv. asst. to v.p. student affairs, 1970-71, dean student activities, 1971-75, dean students, asst. v.p. student affairs, 1975-78, assoc. prof., 1981-83, assoc. v.p. for 2-year campuses and continuing edn., 1978-83, chancellor Aiken, 1983-2000, chmn. systems rev. panel, 1981-83, chancellor emeritus, disting. prof. emeritus Sch. of Edn., 2000—. Bd. dirs. Security Fed. Bank S.C. Contbr. articles to profl. jours. Nat. observer White House Conf. on Youth, Denver, 1971; bd. dirs. United Way, Aiken, S.C., Bus. Tech. Ctr. of N. Augusta, S.C., 1984-89, Strom Thurmond Found., Inc., Aiken, 1985—, now sec. Econ. Devel. Partnership, 1984—, sec., 1989—; mem. Commn. on Future S.C., 1987-89, Commn. on Future of Aiken County, 1987-89, chmn., 1989-90; trustee Hopeland Gardens, Aiken, 1984-88; mem. S.C. Coun. Econ. Edn., 1988-96; chmn. Peach Belt Athletic Conf., 1989-91; mem. regional adv. bd. SCANA, 1990—; mem. nat. adv. com. on Student Fin. Assistance, 1991-97, chair 1996-97; bd. trustees Aiken Regional Med. Ctrs., 1992—; vice chmn., chmn. exec. com. Savannah River Regional Diversification Initiative, 1993-96. Named Man of Yr., Greater Aiken C. of C., 1985; Kellog grantee, 1981; NEH grantee, 1982, 85— Mem. S.C. Assn. Higher Continuing Edn. (pres. 1980-81, Outstanding Pres.'s award 1987), S.C. Assn. for Comty. Edn., Nat. Comty. Edn. Assn., Assn. Higher Continuing Edn., Nat. Entertainment and Campus Activities Assn. (bd. dirs. 1973-79), Inst. for Continuing Edn. Nat. Univ. Continuing Edn. Assn. (bd. dirs. 1981-83), S.C. Coun. Pub. Coll. and Univ. Pres. (chmn. 1996—), S.C. 2000 (bd. dirs. 1989-91), Greater Aiken C. of C. (pres. 1987), Am. Assn. State Colls. and Univs. (com. on sci. and tech. 1987-90, state rep. 1990-95, fins. in higher edn. 1991—, fed./state rels. com. 1984-94), Rotary (Aiken bd. dirs. 1984—, scholarship com. Internat. chpt. 1993—), Houndslake Country Club, Woodside Plantation Country Club, Green Boundary Country Club, Phi Delta Kappa, Alpha Kappa Psi, Gamma Beta Phi, Omicron Delta Kappa. Methodist. Avocations: woodworking; winemaking; reading. Office: Univ SC 471 University Pkwy Aiken SC 29801-6389

ALEXANDER, ROBERT JACKSON, economist, educator; b. Canton, Ohio, Nov. 26, 1918; s. Ralph S. and Ruth (Jackson) A.; m. Joan O. Powell, Mar. 26, 1949; children: Anthony, Margaret. BA, Columbia U., 1940; MA, Columbia U., 1941; PhD, Columbia U., 1950. Asst. economist Bd. Econ. Warfare, 1942, Office Inter-Am. Affairs, 1945-46; mem. faculty Rutgers U., 1947—, prof. econs., 1961-89, prof. emeritus, 1989—. Mem. Pres.-elect Kennedy's Latin Am. Task Force, 1960-61 Author 41 books including Juan Domingo Peron: A History, 1979, Romulo Betancourt and the Transformation of Venezuela, 1982, Bolivia: Past, Present and Future of Its Politics, 1982, Biographical Dictionary of Latin American and Caribbean Politics, 1988, Juscelino Kubitschek and the Development of Brazil, 1991, International Trotskyism 1929-85, 1991, The ABC Presidents, 1992, The Bolivarian Presidents, 1994, The Presidents of Central America, Mexico, Cuba and Hispaniola, 1995, Presidents, Prime Ministers and Governors of the English Speaking West Indies and Puerto Rico, 1997, The Anarchists in the Spanish Civil War, 1999, International Maoism in the Developing World, 1999, Hava de la Torre Man of the Millennium: His Life, Ideas and Continuing Relevance, 2001, A History of Organized Labor in Cuba, 2002. Mem. nat. bd. League Indsl. Democracy, 1955—; mem. nat. exec. com. Socialist Party-Social Dem. Fedn., 1957-66; bd. dirs. Rand Sch. Social Sci., 1951-56; mem. exec. com. Open Door Student Exch., 1970-94. Decorated officer Order Condor of the Andes Bolivia Mem. Am. Econ. Assn., Latin Am. Studies Assn., Mid. Atlantic Coun. Latin Am. Studies (v.p. 1986-87, pres. 1987-88), Coun. Fgn. Rels., Interam. Assn. Democracy and Freedom (chmn. N.Am. com. 1970-87), Phi Gamma Delta. Home: 944 River Rd Piscataway NJ 08854-5504 Office: Rutgers U Dept Econs New Brunswick NJ 08903

ALEXANDER, ROBERTA SUE, history educator; b. N.Y.C., Mar. 19, 1943; d. Bernard Milton and Dorothy (Linn) Cohn; m. John Kurt Alexander, 1966 (div. Sept. 1972); m. Ronald Burett Fost, May 7, 1977. BA, UCLA, 1964; MA, U. Chgo., 1966, PhD, 1974; JD, U. Dayton, 2000. Instr. Roosevelt U., Chgo., 1967-68; prof. U. Dayton, Ohio, 1969—. Author: North Carolina Faces the Freedman: Race Relations During Presidential Reconstruction, 1985; mem. editl. bd. Cin. Hist. Soc., 1973—; contbr. chpt. to book and articles to law revs. Recipient summer stipend NEH, Washington, 1975, Tchg. Excellence and Campus Leadership award Sears-Roebuck Found, 1990, Tchg. Excellence in History award Ohio Acad. History, 1991, Michael and Elissa Cohen Writing award, 1999; fellow in residence NEH, 1976-77, fellow Inst. for Legal Studies, NEH, 1982, summer rsch. fellow U. Dayton, 1972, 74, 76, 80. Mem. Am. Hist. Assn., Orgn. Am. Historians, Am. Soc. Legal History, Midwest Assn. Prelaw Advisors (pres.), So. Hist. Soc., Mortar Bd., Am. Contract Bridge Assn. (life master 1983), Phi Beta Kappa, Phi Alpha Theta. Avocations: bridge, golf. Home: 7715 Legendary Ln West Chester OH 45069-4605 Office: U Dayton Dept History Dayton OH 45469-0310 Fax: (937) 229-4298. E-mail: roberta.alexander@notes.udayton.edu.

ALEXANDER, THOMAS GLEN, history educator; b. Logan, Utah, Aug. 8, 1935; s. Glen M. and Violet Bird Alexander; m. Marilyn Johns; children: Brooke Ann, Brenda Lynn, Tracy Lee, Mark Thomas, Paul Johns. AS, Weber State Coll., 1955; BS, Utah State U., 1960, MS, 1961; PhD, U. Calif., Berkeley, 1965. Asst. prof. history Brigham Young U., Provo, Utah, 1964-68, assoc. prof., 1968-73, prof., 1973—, assoc. dir. Charles Redd Ctr., 1973-80, dir. Charles Redd Ctr., 1980-92, Lemuel Hardison Redd Jr. Prof. Western Am. History, 1992—. Adj. assoc. prof. history, So. Ill. U., Carbondale, 1970-71; vis. prof. Utah State U., Logan, 1965; vis. instr. NDEA, U. Nebr., Kearney, 1966; instr. Salzburg, Austria, 1968. Author: Clash of Interests, 1977, Mormonism in Transition, 1986, 2d edit., 1996, Things in Heaven and Earth: The Life and Times of Wilford Woodruff, 1991, 2d edit., 1993, Utah, The Right Place, 1995, 2d edit., 1996, rev. edit., 2003; co-author: Mormons and Gentiles, 1985, Grace and Grandeur: A History of Salt Lake City, 2001. Mem. Provo City Landmarks Commn., 1995—, chair, 1996-99. Grantee Utah Endowment for Humanities, 1975, 76, 70-80, 90; recipient David L. and Beatrice C. Evans Biography award, 1992. Fellow Utah State Hist. Soc.; mem. Am. Hist. Assn. Pacific Coast Br. Am. Hist. Assn.(coun. 2000—, pres. 2001-02), Orgn. Am. Historians (membership com. 1972-95), Mormon History Assn. (pres. 1974-75, Best Article award 1968, 76, 80, Best Book award 1987, 92), Assn. Utah Historians (pres. 1983-85), Western History Assn. (parliamentarian 1978—), Utah Bd. State History (chmn. 1985-89, bd. editors 1968-79), Utah Acad. Scis., Arts and Letters (pres.-elect 1987-89, pres. 1989-91), Utah Humanities Coun. (bd. dirs. 1996—, chair 2001-03), Am. Soc. for Environ. History (Rachel Carson Prize Com. 1992-95, chair 1994-95), Nat. Soc. DAR (Am. History medal award 1997), Phi Alpha Theta (internat. coun. 1997-2000, bd. advisors 2000—). Democrat. Mem. Lds Ch. Home: 3325 Mohican Ln Provo UT 84604-4854 Office: Brigham Young U Dept History 410 KMB Provo UT 84602

ALEXANDER, VERA, dean, marine science educator; b. Budapest, Hungary, Oct. 26, 1932; came to U.S., 1950; d. Paul and Irene Alexander; div.; children: Graham Alexander Dugdale, Elizabeth Alexander. BA in Zoology, U. Wis., 1955, MS in Zoology, 1962; PhD in Marine Sci., U. Alaska, 1965; LLD, Hokkaido U., Japan, 1999. From asst. prof. to assoc. prof. marine sci. U. Alaska, Fairbanks, 1965-74, prof., 1974—, dean Coll. Environ. Scis., 1977-78, 80-81, dir. Inst. Marine Sci., 1979-93, acting dean Sch. Fisheries and Ocean Scis., 1987-89, dean, 1989—. Mem. adv. com. to ocean scis. divsn. NSF, 1980-84, chmn. adv. com., 1983-84; mem. com. to evaluate outer continental shelf environ. assessment program Minerals Mgmt. Svc., Bd. Environ. Sci. and Tech. NRC, 1987-91, mem. com. on geophys. and environ. Data, 1993-98; mem. adv. com. Office Health and Environ. Rsch., U.S. Dept. Energy, Washington, 1987-90; vice chmn. Arctic Ocean Scis. Bd., 1988-89; commr. U.S. Marine Mammal Commn., 1995—; U.S. del. North Pacific Marine Sci. Orgn., 1991-2002, vice-chmn., 1999-2002, chmn., 2002—; bd. dirs. Western Regional Aquaculture Ctr.; mem. sci. adv. bd. NOAA, 1998—; bd. govs. consortium for oceanographic rsch. and edn.; mem. ocean rsch. adv. panel Nat. Oceans Leadership Coun., 1998-2002; mem. internat. steering com. Census of Marine Life, 1999—; mem. Pres.'s Panel on Ocean Exloration, 2000; pres. Arctic Rsch. Consortium U.S., 2003—. Editor: Marine Biological Systems of the Far North (W.L. Rey), 1989. Sec. Fairbanks Light Opera Theatre Bd., 1987-88; chair Rhodes Scholar Selection Com., Alaska, 1986-95; pres. Arctic Rsch. Consortium U.S., 2003—. Research grantee U. Alaska. Fellow AAAS, Arctic Inst. N.Am., Explorers Club (sec., treas. Alaska/Yukon chpt. 1987-89, 91-99, pres. 1990-91); mem. Am. Soc. Limnology and Oceanography, Am. Geophys. Union, Oceanography Soc., Am. Fisheries Soc., Nature Conservancy of Alaska (bd. dirs.), Rotary (pres. 1999-2000). Avocations: classical piano, horsemanship. Home: 3875 Geist Rd Ste E Fairbanks AK 99709 Office: U Alaska PO Box 707220 Fairbanks AK 99775 E-mail: veraialex@aol.com., vera@sfos.uaf.edu.

ALEXANDROV, VLADIMIR EUGENE, Russian literature educator; b. Germany, May 9, 1947; married; 2 children. BA in Geology magna cum laude, CUNY, 1968, MA in Geology, 1971; MA in Comparative Lit., U. Mass., Amherst, 1973, Princeton U., 1976, PhD, 1979. Instr. dept. geology CUNY, 1970-71; lectr. Slavic dept. Princeton (N.J.) U., 1978-79; asst. prof. Slavic dept. Harvard U., 1979-84, dir. undergraduate studies in Russian lit. and Soviet studies Slavic dept., 1979-86, assoc. dir. Slavic and East European Lang. and Area Ctr., 1980-86, assoc. prof. Slavic dept., 1984-86, Yale U., New Haven, Conn., 1986-90, dir. grad. studies Slavic dept., 1987, 89-91, dir. undergrad. studies Slavic dept., 1989, prof. Russian lit. Slavic dept., 1990—, chmn. Slavic dept., 1991-97. Coord. Eastern European area Federally Funded Fgn. Lang. Area Studies Fellowships, Harvard U., 1980-86; vis. assoc. prof. Slavic dept. Yale U., 1985, coun. on Soviet and Easter European studies, 1986—, com. on fgn. lang. proficiency, 1987-88, Whiting and Traveling Lurcy fellowship com. grad sch., 1988-90, tenure appointments com. in humanitites, 1990-91, adv. com. divsn. humanities, 1990-91, mem. quorum joint bds. permanent officers grad. sch., 1990—, exec. com. grad sch., 1990-92, mem. prize tchg. fellowship com. Yale Coll., 1991; coord for fgn. participants Internat. Conf. on Vladimir Nabokov, Moscow, 1990; evaluator NEH Scholarly Grants Program, Harvard-Radcliffe Bunting Inst. Fellowship Program, NEH Program for Scholarly Transition; outside referee on appointments, promotion and tenure U. Calif., Davis, Bryn Mawr Coll., Middlebury coll., U. Wis., Madison, Stanford U., U. Kans., Pa. State U., Dartmouth Coll., Columbia U., Cornell U., U. Va., Brown U., U. Wash., Seattle; lectr., spkr., presenter in field Author: Andrei Bely: The Major Symbolist Fiction, 1985, Nabokov's Otherworld, 1991; referee Slavic and East European Jour., Slavic Rev., Russian Rev., Mosaic, Nabokov Studies, UCLA Slavic Studies, Northwestern U. Press, Princeton U. Press, Doubleday, Garland Pub.; editor: The Garland Companion to Vladimir Nabokov; contbr. articles and book revs. to profl. publs. Fellow Am. Coun. Learned Socs., 1982, Travel grantee, 1984; Harvard Russian Rsch. Ctr. fellow, 1983-84; Ind. Study and Rsch. fellow NEH, 1986; Com. Faculty Rsch. Support grantee Harvard U., 1981-83, 83-85, 85-86; Travel grantee Internat. Rsch. and Exchs. Bd., 1992. Mem. Am. Assn. for Advancement Slavic Studies (com. on lang. tng. 1991-93), Modern Lang. Inst. Am., Russian-Am. Inst. (steering com. 1990—). Office: Yale Univ Slavic Dept PO Box 208236 New Haven CT 06520-8236

ALFANO, EDWARD CHARLES, JR., elementary education educator; b. Bklyn, NY, Mar. 20, 1945; s. Edward Charles and Victoria Helen (Fanti) A.; m. Mary Fien, Aug. 27, 1983; children: Elizabeth Anne, Christina Irene. BA in Philosophy, Cathedral Coll., 1967; post grad., Bklyn. Coll., NY, 1967-70; MS in Edn., LI U., 1972, post grad., 1976, Oxford U., UK, 1973, Bklyn. Mus., NY, 1990, Pastoral Inst., 2001—03. Cert. elem. tchr., NY. Tchr. English St. Mark Sch., Bklyn., 1968-69; tchr. NYC Pub. Sch. Sys., Bklyn., 1969—2000; math. specialist Pub. Sch. 15, Bklyn., 1976-78; tchr. English as 2d lang. Pub. Sch. 169, Bklyn., 1985-86, tchr. art, 1986-94, tchr. sci., 1994-95, tchr. English, 1995-96, tchr. music movement/phys. edn. Early Childhood Learning Ctr, 1996-99, sr. sci. tchr., 1999—2000; tchr. 4th grade St. Simon and Jude Sch., Bklyn., 2000—01. Del. United Fedn. Tchr., Bklyn., 1977-78; faculty rep. policy consultation com. Pub. Sch. 169, 1979-92, dir. summer recreation program, 1989-97; presenter workshops and symposia; tchr. Murals in Park Project, Bklyn., 1990, summer literacy program, 1998-99; mem. Dist. 15 Sci. Focus Group, 1999-2000. Narrator video The Passion of Our Lord According to Saint John, 1993; contbr.poetry and articles to various publs. Pres. Friends of LI U. Libr., 1977-80; mem. vis. com. LI U., Bklyn., 1978-80; bd. dir. Hispanic Young People's Alternatives, Bklyn., 1990-95; lector Good Shepherd Ch., Bklyn., parish coord. Sanctity of Life com., 1993—; mem. Bklyn. Diocesan Pastoral Team for Charismatic Renewal, 1995—. Commissioned as a Lay Ecclesial Minister for the Diocese of Bklyn, May 2, 2003; recipient cmty. svc. award Cmty. Bd. 7, Bklyn., 1990, 91, Sanctity of Life Recognition award Roman Cath. Diocese of Bklyn., 1997, Pro-Life award Flatbush Coun. 497 KC, 1998. Mem. Cath. Tchr. Assn. (Educator of Yr. award 1992), So. Poetry Assn., Charismatic Prayer Group, Sanctity of Life Com., LI U. Alumni Assn. Democrat. Avocations: poetry, art, swimming, music, dramatics.

ALFIERI, FRANCIS JOSEPH, physical education educator; b. Boston, Dec. 25, 1955; s. John Charles and Nancy Ann (Mendolia) A. BS, Boston State Coll., 1977; MS, U. Mass., 1990. Recreation dir. Mattahunt Cmty. Sch., Boston, 1977-78; phys. edn. instr. Don Bosco H.S., Boston, 1978-80, Milton (Mass.) Pub. Schs., 1980-82; phys. edn./health instr. Whitingham Sch., Jacksonville, Vt., 1982—. Pres. Deerfield Valley Health Adv. Bd., Wilmington, Vt., 2001—. Mem. Zoning Bd., Wilmington, Vt., 1994-97. Recipient Outstanding Tchr. Recognition, U. Vt., Burlington, 1994. Mem. AAHPERD, Vt. Assn. Health, Phys. Edn., Recreation and Dance. Roman Catholic. Avocations: community chorus, tennis, skiing, guitar, landscaping. Home: 348 Ray Hill Rd Wilmington VT 05363-9772 Office: Whitingham Sch PO Box 199 Jacksonville VT 05342-0199 E-mail: falfieri@whitingham.k12.vt.us.

ALFIERI, JOHN CHARLES, JR., educational administrator; b. Passaic, N.J., Dec. 25, 1949; s. John C. and Anne (Zangara) A.; m. Theresa Meskis, Oct. 26, 1974; children: Christopher, Carlea. BA in Elem. Edn., William Paterson Coll., Wayne, N.J., 1971, MA in Edn., 1975, MA in Adminstrn., 1979. Tchr. grade 6 Bergenfield (N.J.) Bd. Edn., 1971-82, 90-91, math/sci. resource tchr., 1982-90, grade 7 writing lab/study skills tchr., 1991-95, adminstrv. intern, 1971-91, mem. tech. com., 1993—; dir. Bergenfield Cmty. Sch., 1991-95; prin. Lincoln Sch., 1995—. Coach soccer, basketball, track Saddle Brook (N.J.) Recreation, 1985-92; advancement chmn. Boy Scouts Am., Troop 213, Pack 222, Saddle Brook, 1985—; past pres. and co-founder Friends of Saddle Brook Libr., 1990—. Staff sgt. N.J. Army N.G., 1971-77. Named Tchr. of Yr., Bergenfield Optimist Club, 1992; A Plus for Tchrs. grantee Channel 9 TV, 1991. Mem. ASCD, Nat. Assn. Elem. Sch. Prins., N.J. Prins. and Suprs. Assn., N.J. Coun. Edn., Bergen County Elem. and Mid. Sch. Adminstrs. Assn., Saddle Brook Main Lions Club. Avocations: computers/technology, photography, sports. Office: Lincoln Sch 115 Highview Ave Bergenfield NJ 07621-3400

ALFORD, BOBBY RAY, physician, educator, university official; b. Dallas, May 30, 1932; s. Bryant J. and Edith M. (Garrett) A.; m. Othelia Jerry Dorn, Aug. 28, 1953; children: Bradley Keith, Raye Lynn, Alan Scott. AS, Tyler Jr. Coll., 1951; postgrad., U. Tex., 1951-52; MD, Baylor U., 1956. Diplomate Am. Bd. Otolaryngology (dir. 1972-90, pres. 1985-86, exec. v.p. 1986-90). Intern Jefferson Davis Hosp., Houston, 1956-57; resident Baylor U. Coll. Medicine Affiliated Hosps. Program, 1957-60; mem. faculty Baylor U. Coll. Medicine, 1962—, prof. otolaryngology, 1966—, chmn. dept., 1967-95, 96—, v.p. and dean acad. and clin. affairs, 1984-88, exec. v.p., dean medicine, 1988—, disting. service prof., 1985—, interim chmn. dept. surgery, 1993-94; pres., CEO BaylorMedCare, Houston, 1994-96; chmn., CEO Nat. Space Biomed. Rsch. Inst., 1997—. Mem. rev. panel surgeon gen. on neurol. and sensory disease USPHS, 1965-67; cons. Nat. Inst. Neurol. Disease and Stroke, 1970-74; cons. to surgeon gen. U.S. Army, 1963-73; mem. nat. adv. coun. Neurol. and Communicative Disorders and Stroke, NIH, 1977-80, Deafness and Other Communicative Disorders, 1991-95; chmn. aerospace medicine adv. con. NASA, 1993-94, mem. nat. adv. coun., 1992-95, chmn. life microgravity scis. and applications adv. com., 1993-95. Author: Neurological Aspects of Auditory and Vestibular Disorders, 1964, Electrophysiologic Evaluation in Otolaryngology, 1997; Chief editor: A.M.A. Archives of Otolaryngology, 1970-79. Bd. dirs. Houston Acad. Medicine Tex. Med. Ctr. Libr., 1983-94. Recipient Herman Johnson award Baylor U. Coll. Medicine, 1956, NASA Disting. Pub. Svc. award, 1992, 95, Jeffries Aerospace Medicine and Life Scis. Rsch. award Am. Inst. Aeronautics and Astronautics, 2003; spl. NIH fellow Johns Hopkins Hosp., 1961-62. Fellow ACS (bd. govs. 1977-82); mem. AIAA (Jeffries Aerospace Medicine and Life Scis. Rsch. award 2003), NAS Inst. Medicine, Am. Laryngol. Assn., Soc. Univ. Otolaryngologists-Head and Neck Surgeons (sec. 1965-69), Am. Otol. Soc., Assn. Acad. Dept. Otolaryngology-Head and Neck Surgery, Am. Laryngol., Rhinol. and Otol. Soc., Am. Soc. Head and Neck Surgery (councillor 1978-80) Am. Acad. Otolaryngology-Head and Neck Surgery (pres. 1981), Am. Coun. Otolaryngology-Head and Neck Surgery (pres. 1980-81), Am. Bronchoesophagological Assn., Soc. Head and Neck Surgeons, Acoustical Soc. Am., Collegium Oto-Rhino-Laryngologicum Amicitiae Sacrum, Johns Hopkins U. Soc. Scholars, Univ. Space Rsch. Assn. (bd. dirs. 1991-95), Tex. Corinthian Yacht Club (bd. dirs. 1978-80, 94-95), Doctors Club (bd. govs. 1967-70, 91-93), Petroleum Club, Lakewood Yacht Club, Alpha Omega Alpha. Office: Baylor Coll Medicine One Baylor Plz Houston TX 77030

ALFORD, ELISABETH M. technical communication educator; b. Columbia, S.C., May 18, 1936; d. Thomas F. Murphy and Rhetta W. Smith; m. James W. Alford, Apr. 11, 1960; 1 child, James W. Jr. PhD, U. S.C., 1993. Exec. v.p. S.C. Hosp. Assn., West Columbia, 1961-78; dir. Elec. and Computer Engring. Writing Ctr. U. S.C. Coll. Engring. and Info. Tech., Columbia, 1995-98, dir. Profl. Comms. Ctr., 1998—; dir. Rsch. Coms. Studio, 2000—. Chair emergency med. svcs. adv. bd. S.C. Dept. Health and Environ. Control, Columbia, 1970-73. Author: (book chpt.) Worlds of Writing, 1984. Fellow WHO, 1974, Mass. Media Awards, Fund for Adult Edn., Harvard U., 1958. Office: U S C Coll Engring & Info Tech Columbia SC 29208

ALFORD, PAUL LEGARE, college and religious foundation administrator; b. Tampa, Fla., Mar. 16, 1930; s. Louis Emerson and Mary (Alderman) A.; m. Grace Alford, Dec. 29, 1951; children: Rebecca Grace, Sharon Ann. Student, U. Fla., 1947; diploma, Nyack Coll., 1948-51; DD (hon.), Trinity Coll., 1964, Asbury Coll., 1978; LLD (hon.), Toccoa Falls Coll., 1976. Supt. Ind. Life, Columbus, Ga., 1951-53; founding pastor Christian & Missionary Alliance, Columbus, 1951-56; missionary Ecuador, 1956-60; dir. Spanish ministries Christian Missionary Alliance, Nyack, N.Y., 1960-70; dist. supt. Christian & Missionary Alliance, Orlando, Fla., 1970-79, v.p., 1976-86; pres. Toccoa Falls (Ga.) Coll., 1979—, chancellor, 2002—. Chmn. DeLand (Fla.) Retirement Bd., 1970-79; bd. mgrs. Christian and Missionary Alliance, Colorado Springs, Colo., 1993-99; trustee Asbury Coll., Wilmore, Ky.; chmn. bd. dirs. Lake Swan Conf. Grounds, Melrose, Fla., Shell Point Village, Ft. Myers, Fla., Trans World Radio, 1995-99; del. Congress on Edn., 1971, 86. Mem. editorial bd. New King James Bible; producer daily radio broadcast, 1975—. Mem. leadership coun. Stephens County, Toccoa, 1982—; bd. dirs. Salvation Army, Toccoa, 1986-93; pres. Ga. Assn. Colleges and Univs., 1997-98. Served with USNR, 1947-54. Honored by Ga. State Senate for outstanding contbn. to edn. in State of Ga., 2002; named to Hillsborough High Sch. Hall of Fame, Tampa, 1994. Mem. Am. Assn. Bible Colls. (bd. dirs. 1987-92), So. Assn. Colls. and Schs. (evaluation com.), Rotary. Republican. Avocations: golf, tennis. Home: 380 Carlyle Cir Toccoa Falls GA 30598 Office: Toccoa Falls Coll Chapel Dr Toccoa Falls GA 30598

ALFORD, SANDRA ELAINE, university official; b. Steubenville, Ohio, Oct. 26, 1944; d. Island Lee and Katherine (Agee) Johnson; m. Roger Kent Alford, Aug. 17, 1968 (dec.); children: Deidre Shannon, Jarrett Anthony. BS in Edn., West Chester (Pa.) U., 1971; MS in Child Devel., U. Pitts., 1973, PhD in Higher Edn., 1982. Tchr. kindergarten Pitts. Bd. Edn., 1971-72; adj. asst. prof. dept. child devel. and child care U. Pitts., 1974-79, child devel. specialist Arsenal Family and Children's Ctr., 1974-75, 76-79; edn. specialist CETA child care Urban League, Pitts., 1975-76; rsch. asst. Ctr. for Urban Studies, Wayne State U., Detroit, 1980-82, rsch. assoc., 1982-85, dir. Project 350, 1985-90, dir. div. community edn., 1990—; assoc. dean for student svcs., 1991—. Chmn. Met. Detroit Teen Conf., 1989-90; cons. U.S. Dept. Edn., Washington, 1998—. Editl. asst., reviewer Jour. Ednl. Opportunity, 1989-90. Recipient Provost Devel. award U. Pitts., 1976, Outstanding Female Faculty and Staff award Wayne State U., 1989, Presdl. Bonus award, 1990, '91, Spirit of Detroit award, Detroit City Coun., 1990,'91, Appreciation award Met. Detroit Teen Conf., 1990; grantee NIMH, 1972-75. Mem. Mid-Am. Assn. Ednl. Opportunity Program Pers. (regional bd. dirs. 1988-90, bd. dirs. Mich. chpt., pres. 1989-90, validation facilitator exemplary program 1988—, Distinctive Leadership award 1989). Democrat. Office: Wayne State U Coll Lifelong Learning 5700 Cass Ave Detroit MI 48202-3629 E-mail: aa3994@wayne.edu.

ALFRED, R. See BEATTY, ROBERT ALFRED

ALFREY, LYDIA JEAN, musician educator; b. Kingsport, Tenn., July 16, 1954; d. Milburn Flay and Betty Jo (Sensabaugh) Brooks; m. Charles Leonard Alfrey, Oct. 2, 1987; children: Benjamin Daniel, Tyler Nathaniel, Ryan Daniel. BA, Anderson (Ind.) U., 1977. Music tchr. Huntington Sch., Ferriday, La., 1978-80; elem. tchr. Warner Christian Acad., Daytona Beach, Fla., 1982-83; pvt. instr. Eustis, Fla., 1993—; prin. pianist First Bapt. Ch., Eustis, 1994—98, Mt. Dora, 2003—. Adjudicator piano competitions Lake County Music Tchrs., Eustis, 1994-97; dir., coord. Summer Music Camps, Eustis, 1994, 95, 97; pianist jazz orch.; guest artist numerous recitals. Mem.: Music Tchrs. Nat. Assn. (publicity chairperson, Fla. chpt. rec. sec. 1994—2001), Nat. Guild Piano Tchrs., Delta Omicron, Kappa Delta Pi, Pi Kappa Lambda. Baptist. Avocations: floral arranging, interior designing, oil painting. Home: 1375 Old Mount Dora Rd Eustis FL 32726-7949

ALICEA, YVETTE, special education educator; b. Bronx, Aug. 27, 1962; d. Gregorio and Lucia Alicea; m. Leontitsis Eleftherios, Sept. 19, 1997. BA in Modern Langs., U. P.R., 1987; MS in Spl. Edn., CUNY, 1995. Cert. tchr. N.Y. Tchr. English José de Choudens, Arroyo, PR, 1983—84; tchr., asst. prin. St. Patrick's Bilingual Sch., Guayama, 1987—91; tchr. bilingual spl. edn. P.S. 26, N.Y.C. Bd. Edn., 1991—95; tchr. English Betsis Lang. Sch., Athens, Greece, 1996—99; tchr. spl. edn. P.S./M.S. 306, N.Y.C. Bd. Edn., 1999—2000, P.S. 46, N.Y. C. Bd. Edn., 2000—. Recipient Appreciation plaque, Parents Assn. of P.S. 26, Bronx, 1995. Avocations: reading, literature, movies. Home: 266 Bedford Park Blvd 2H Bronx NY 10458

ALKER, HAYWARD ROSE, political scientist, educator; b. N.Y.C., Oct. 3, 1937; s. Hayward Rose and Dorothy (Fitzsimmons) Alker; m. Judith Ann Tickner, June 3, 1961; children: Joan Christina, Heather Jane, Gwendolyn Ann. BS, MIT, 1959; MS, Yale U., 1960, PhD, 1963. From instr. to assoc. prof. Yale U., New Haven, 1963-68; prof. polit. sci. MIT, 1968-95; John A. McCone prof. internat. rels. U. So. Calif., L.A., 1995—. Vis. prof. U. Mich., 1968; Olaf Plame vis. prof. U. Stockholm, U. Uppsala, 1989; vis. prof., scholar Brown U., 1996, 1997—2000; chmn. Math. Social Scis. Bd., 1970—71; mem. exec. com. Internat. Social Sci. Coun., 1990—92. Author: (non-fiction) Mathematics and Politics, 1965; co-author: World Handbook of Political and Social Indicators, 1966; co-author: (with Russett) World Politics in the General Assembly, 1966; co-author: (with Bloomfield and Choucri) Analyzing Global Interdependence, 1974; co-author: (with Hurwitz) Resolving Prisoner's Dilemmas, 1981; co-editor, co-author: non-fiction Journeys Through Conflict, 2001; author: Rediscoveries and Reformations, 1996; editor (mem. bd.): (jour.) Jour. Interdisciplinary History, 1969—71, Internat. Orgn., 1970—76, Quality and Quantitiy, 1974—, Internat. Studies Quar., 1980—89, European Jour. Internat. Rels., 1995—99, Internat. Rels. of Asia Pacific, 2000—. Congl. intern Office of Chester Bowles, 1960. Fellow, Ctr. Advanced Studies in Behavioral Scis., 1967—68. Mem.: Internat. Studies Assn. (v.p. 1990—91, pres. 1992—93), Internat. Peace Rsch. Assn., Internat. Polit. Sci. Assn., Am. Polit. Sci. Assn. E-mail: alker@usc.edu.

ALLAIRE, GLORIA KAUN, Italian language educator; b. Reedsburg, Wis., Feb. 20, 1954; d. Robert W. and Arlowene Marie (Wolter) Kaun. MusB with honors, U. Wis., 1976, MA in Italian, 1986, PhD, 1993. Italian lang. coach Madison Opera, 1985—87; vis. lectr. in Italian lang. and lit. Univs. Mich. and Wis. Studies Abroad Program, Florence, Italy, 1987-88; grad. teaching asst. dept. French and Italian U. Wis., Madison, 1988-93, 84-87; vis. asst. prof. dept. modern langs. and linguistics Fla. State U., Tallahassee, 1993-94; vis. asst. prof. dept. modern langs. Ohio U., Athens, 1994—97; vis. instr. dept. fgn. langs. and lits. Purdue U., West Lafayette, Ind., 1997-98; asst. prof. Italian studies Gettysburg Coll., 1999—2001; Italian program coord. divsn. French and Italian U. Ky., Lexington, 2001—. Vis. asst. prof. modern langs. U. Miami, Coral Gables, 1998-99. Author: Andrea da Barberino and the Language of Chivalry, 1997; editor: Modern Retellings of Chivalric Texts, 1999, The Italian Novella, 2003; editor, translator, Il Tristano Panciatichiano, 2002; contbr. articles to profl. jours. Fulbright grantee, 1990-91, Am. Philosophy Soc. grantee, 1996; summer fellow UCLA Ctr. for Medieval and Renaissance Studies, 1994, NEH Summer Inst., 1995. Mem. MLA, Am. Assn. Tchrs. Italian, Am. Assn. for Italian Studies, Medieval Acad. Am., Soc. Rencesvals. Avocations: bicycling, cats, equitation. Home: 249 Elmwood Dr Lexington KY 40505-1911

ALLAIRE-CURTIS, MARY, dance instructor; b. Ft. Stockton, Tex., Jan. 14, 1955; d. Howard J. Sr. and Lavine M. (Sommerlautte) Colson; m. Edward James Allaire, June 25, 1973 (div. 1991); children: Shane Allaire, Theresa Allaire-Wirtz; m. Robert Leewane Curtis, July 5, 1998; Sharika Curtis, Isaac Curtis. BS cum laude, cert. in dance, physic. edn., English, Sul Ross State U., Alpine, Tex., 1984. Cert. aerobics tchr., Tex. Owner, instr. Mary Allaire's Sch. Dance, Ft. Stockton, 1972-91; owner, trainer Body Building Fitness Ctr., Ft. Stockton, 1987—91; owner, instr. dance studio Tex., 1988-91; tchr. dance Mountain View H.S., El Paso, 1998—. Instr. jazz Sul Ross State U., 1982; instr. Ft. Stockton High Sch. Twirlers, 1983, Midland Coll., 1987; judge various pageants, 1984—; performer, choreographer, instr. Mary Allaire Dancers, Internat. Dance Festival, Innsbruck, Austria, 1987; sponsor Lobo Strutters Dance Team, 1998—. Mem. Meml. Hosp. Candystripers, Ft. Stockton, 1972; fundraiser Muscular Dystrophy Found., Ft. Stockton, 1973; sec. St. Agnes Parish Council, Ft. Stockton, 1983; jazz instr. Round Rock Repertory Dance Ctr., 1991, also aerobic instr. Recipient 1st and 2d place awards Showcase Modeling and Talent, Las Vegas, Nev., 1986, 87, 1st place award Showcase U.S.A Talent Competition, Houston, 1986, 5 1st place trophies All Am. Talent Showcase, San Antonio, 1987. Mem. NAFE, Ft. Stockton C. of C., Ft. Stockton Downtown Assn., Sigma Tau Delta, Epsilon Sigma Alpha (pres. 1973). Clubs: Future Homemakers Am. (Ft. Stockton) (pres. 1973). Roman Catholic. Avocations: weight lifting, bicycling, skating, swimming, writing. Office: 3710 Oxford Ave El Paso TX 79903-1719

ALLAN, ROBERT MOFFAT, JR., corporate executive, educator; b. Detroit, Dec. 8, 1920; s. Robert M. and Jane (Christman) A.; m. Harriet Spicer, Nov. 28, 1942; children: Robert M. III, Scott, David, Marilee. BS, Stanford U., 1941; postgrad., Stanford Grad. Sch. Bus., 1941-42; MS, UCLA, 1943; postgrad., Loyola Law Sch., 1947-50. Economist rsch. dept. Security First Nat. Bank, 1942; exec. Marine Ins., 1946-53; asst. to pres., work mgr. Zinsco Elec. Products, 1953-55, v.p., dir., 1956-59; asst.to pres. The Times-Mirror Corp., 1959-60, corp. v.p., 1961-64; pres., dir. Cyprus Mines Corp., 1964-67; pres. Litton Internat., 1967-69, U.S. Naval Postgrad. Sch. Found., prof. internat. mgmt., 1969-85. Bd. dirs., advisor U.S. Naval Acad.; trustee Boys Republic, Pomona Grad. Sch., Claremont Grad. Sch., Del Monte Forest Homeowners; vis. prof. of internat. mgmt. grad. schs. of bus. MBA Stanford, Harvard, U. of Chgo., UCLA, USA and Internat. Inst. Fgn. Studies, Monterey; adv. trustee Monterey County Sheriff, 1982—. Capt. USAF, 1942-45. Recipient award Helms Athletic Found., 1947, 49, Navy Cross of Merit, 1976, Plaque of Merit USCG, 1990, Medal for Heroism, 1990; named Outstanding Businessman of Yr., L.A., Nat. Assn. Accts., 1966; elected to U.S. Intercollegiate Sailing Hall of Fame, 2000; named Monterey Inst. Fgn. Studies trustee and sr. fellow, 1976. Mem. Mchts. and Mfrs. Assn. (dir.), Intercollegiate Yachting Assn. (dir.), Intercollegiate Yachting Assn. (regional dir. 1940-55), Newport Harbor Yacht Club (commodore 1962), Trans-Pacific Yacht Club, Carmel Valley Country Club, Phi Gamma Delta, Phi Delta Phi. Home: 167 Del Mesa Carmel CA 93923

ALLAND, ALEXANDER, JR., anthropology educator; b. Newark, Sept. 23, 1931; s. Alexander Sr. and Alexandra Sarah A.; m. Sonia Louise Feldman, Aug. 26, 1956; children: David, Julie. BS, U. Wis., 1954; MS, U. Conn., 1958; PhD, Yale U., 1963. Asst. prof. Vassar Coll., Poughkeepsie, N.Y., 1962-63; asst. prof. Hunter Coll., Bronx, N.Y., 1963-64, Columbia U., N.Y.C., 1964-68, assoc. prof., 1968-73, prof. anthropology, 1973—. Chair dept. anthropology Columbia U., N.Y.C., 1981-87. Author: La Dimension Humain, 1974, Playing with Form, 1983, La Danse de Araignée, 1985, Human Nature: Darwin's View, 1986, (with Sonia Alland) Crisis and Commitment, 1994, Race in Mind: Race, IQ, & Other Racisms, 2002. J.S. Guggenheim fellow Guggenheim Found., 1977. Fellow AAAS, Am. Anthrop. Assn., Sigma Xi. Office: Columbia U Dept Anthropology New York NY 10027

ALLARD, JUDITH LOUISE, secondary education educator; b. Rutland, Vt., Feb. 21, 1945; d. William Edward and Orilla Marion (Trombley) A. BA, U. Vt., 1967, MS, 1969. Nat. bd. cert. tchr. in adolescent and young adulthood sci., 1999. Tchr. math., sci. Edmunds Jr. H.S., Burlington, Vt., 1969-73, biology tchr., 1973-78, sci. dept. chair, 1975-78; biology tchr. Burlington (Vt.) H.S., 1978—; instr. edn. St. Michaels Coll., Winooski, Vt., 2001—02; lectr. U. Vt., 2003—. Bd. dirs. Vt. Creative Imagination, Inc., 1998—; instr. environ. studies U. Vt., Burlington, 1988-89, 2001. Edn. U. of Vt., 2002—; adviser Nat. Honor Soc., 1986—. Co-author Favorite Labs of Outstanding Tchrs., 1991. Active Amnesty Internat., 1985—; mem. Lake Champlain Com., Burlington, 1987—, Vt. Goals 2000 Panel, 1995—99, Vt. State Licensing Commn., 1995—96, Vt. Stds. Bd. for Profl. Educators, 1996—2002, co-vice chair, 2000—01, chmn., 2001—02; state bd. dirs. Odyssey of the Mind, 1986—98. Named Outstanding Vt. Educator, U. Vt., 1983, Outstanding Vt. Sci. Tchr., Sigma Xi Soc., 1984, Vt. Tchr. Yr., 1998, Outstanding Vt. Sci. Tchr., Vt. Acad. Sci. and Engring., 2000, Tandy Tech. scholar, 1990, Genentech Access Excellence fellow, 1995, 1996, Access Excellence Retro fellow, 1996, Tchr. of Yr., Biol. Scis. Curriculum Study, 2001; recipient Presdl. Sci. Tchg. award, NSF, 1983, Tech. award, Tandy, 1998, Siemens award for Advanced Placement, 2000. Mem. NEA (bd. dirs. Vt. chpt., 1990-98), Vt. Sci. Tchrs. Assn. (bd. dirs. 1980-92, treas. 1985-92), Burlington Profl. Stds. Bd. (chair 1991-2001), Parents and Friends of Edn. (trustee), Nat. Assn. Biology Tchrs. (dir. Vt. Outstanding Biology Tchr. award program 1977—, Outstanding Biology Tchr. award 1975), Assn. Presdl. Awardees in Sci., Phi Delta Kappa. Roman Catholic. Avocations: needlework, fishing, music. Home: 221 Woodlawn Rd Burlington VT 05401-5722

ALLAWAY, WILLIAM HARRIS, retired university official; b. Oak Park, Ill., Mar. 31, 1924; s. William Horsford and Helen Margaret (Harris) A.; m. Olivia Woodhull Foster, June 28, 1952; children: William Harris Jr., Ben Foster, Eve Olivia. BS, U. Ill., 1949; postgrad., U. Grenoble, France, 1950-51; MA, U. Ill., 1951; EdD, U. Denver, 1957. Traveling sec. World Student Svc. Fund, 1947-48; spl. asst. to chmn. U.S. Nat. Commn. for UNESCO, 1949; asst. to field dir. World U. Svc. attached to Internat. Refugee Orgn., Salzburg, Austria, 1951; field rep. Inst.of Internat. Edn., Chgo. and Denver, 1952-54; gen. sec. U. Kans. YMCA, 1954-57; asst. dean of men and dir. Wilbur Hall Stanford (Calif.) U., 1957-61; dir. edn. abroad program U. Calif., Santa Barbara, 1961-89, spl. asst. to chancellor, 1990-93. Cons. and lectr. in field; mem. ednl. assoc. adv. com. Inst. Internat. Edn., 1984-87; mem. Pres.'s Coun. for Internat. Youth Exch., 1982-85; mem. U.S. Del. to conf. on ednl. exch. between U.S. and U.K., 1970, 1974. Co-chair Peace and Justice Com., Goleta Presbyn. Ch., 1991-2000, mem. Nuclear Age Peace Found., Santa Barbara, Internat. Peace Rsch. Assn., Yellow Springs, Ohio; mem. Coun. on Internat. Ednl. Exch., 1961—, chmn. bd. dirs. 1978-83; past bd. dirs., hon. trustee Am. Ctr. for Students and Artists, Paris; bd. advisors Hariri Found., 1987—; exec. sec. Internat. Com. for Study of Edn. Exch., 1970-95, exec. com. Inter-Univ. Ctr. Postgrad. Studies, Dubrovnik, 1988-96, bd. dirs., 1996—; del. Hague Appeal for Peace, 1999; chair PAX 2100 Found., PAX 2100 Forum. With USAAF, 1943-46. Hon. DHC, U. Sussex, Eng., 1992; PhD h.c. U. Bergen, Norway, 1990; DHC, U. Bordeaux, France, 1988; Hon. Dr. of U. of Stirling, Scotland, 1981; recipient Scroll of Appreciation Leningrad State U., 1989, Award for Svc. to Internat. Ednl. Exch. Council on Internat. Ednl. Exch., 1989, Silver medal U. Lund, Sweden, 1990, Alumni Achievement award Coll. Liberal Arts and Sci. Alumni Assn. U. Ill., 1990, Gold Medal of Honor of the Complutense U. of Madrid, Spain, 1991. Mem. NAFSA Assn. Internat. Educators (hon. life mem.), Internat. Assn. Univs. (dep. mem., adminstrv. bd. 1995-2000, chair task force on internationalization of higher edn.), La Cumbre Country Club. Democrat. Presbyterian. Avocations: golf, skiing, choir, reading. Home: 2661 Tallant Rd C-871 Santa Barbara CA 93105 Fax: 805-687-5779. E-mail: boallaway@aol.com.

ALLBEE, TERESA JO, elementary school educator; b. Indpls., Sept. 20, 1961; d. Jack M. and Sally J. (Sipe) Roach; m. D. Scott Allbee, May 4, 1985; children: Justin, Joshua, Courtney. BA, North Cen. Coll., Naperville, Ill., 1984; postgrad., Northestern Ill. U., Chgo. Cert. elem. educator. Tchr. Sipley Elem. Sch., Woodridge, Ill., summer 1985, Jane Addams Middle Sch., Bolingbrook, Ill., 1986-88, John R. Tibbott Elem. Sch., Bolingbrook, 1989-95, Indian Trace Elem. Sch., Weston, Fla., 1995—2000, Walter C. Young Mid. Sch., Pembroke Pines, Fla., 2000—. Mem. PEO. Home: 16311 NW 19th St Pembroke Pines FL 33028-1742 Office: Walter C Young Mid Sch 901 NW 129th Ave Pembroke Pines FL 33026

ALLCOCK, HARRY R. chemistry educator; b. Loughborough, Eng., Apr. 8, 1932; naturalized U.S. citizen; s. Claud Leonard and Nora (Clarke) A.; m. Noreen Raworth, Nov. 14, 1959. BSc, U. London, 1953, PhD, 1956. Cert. chemist. Postdoctoral fellow Purdue U., West Lafayette, Ind., 1956-58, Can. Nat. Rsch. Coun., Ottawa, Ont., 1958-60; rsch. scientist Cen. Rsch. Labs. Am. Cyanamid Co., Stamford, Conn., 1961-66; assoc. prof. chem. Pa. State U., University Park, 1966-70, prof. chem., 1970-85, Evan Pugh Prof. Chem., 1985—. Author: (books) Heteroatom Ring Systems and Polymers, 1967, Phosphorus-Nitrogen Compounds, 1972, (monograph) Chemistry and Applications of Polyphosphazenes, 2003; author: (with F.W. Lampe) (books) Contemporary Polymer Chemistry, 1981; author: (with F.W. Lampe and J.E. Mark), 2003; author: (with M. Zeldin & K.J. Wynne) Inorganic and Organometallic Polymers, 1988; author: (with P. Wisian-Neilson and K.J. Wynne) Inorganic and Organometallic Polymers II, 1994, editor Inorganic Syntheses Vol. XXV, (jours.) Phosphorous, 1973—77, Macromolecules, 1974—79, Chem. Revs., 1974—79, Biomaterials, 1980—82, Jour. of Polymer Sci., 1987—, Inorganic Chem., 1988—91, Chem. of Materials, 1988—, Heteroatom Chem., 1988—93, Jour. Inorganic and Organometallic Polymers, 1990—. Guggenheim fellow 1986-87. Fellow Am. Inst. Chemists (Chem. Pioneer award 1989); mem. Am. Chem. Soc. (nat. award polymer chemistry 1984, nat. award chemistry of materials 1992, Herman Mark award polymer chemistry 1994), Royal Soc. Chemistry (various coms.), Corp. Inorganic Syntheses. Office: Pa State U Dept Chemistry 152 Davey Lab University Park PA 16802-6300

ALLCORN, TERRY ALAN, principal, educator; b. Springfield, Mo., Dec. 7, 1952; s. Calbert and Bonnie Lee (Taylor) A.; m. Rhonda Gay Martens, May 24, 1974; children: Eric Alan, Nathan Scott. ThG, Bapt. Bible Coll., 1974, BS, 1977; MA, S.W. Mo. State U., 1980. Assoc. pastor Prairie Garden Bapt. Ch., Houston, 1974-76; purchasing agt. Fed. Enterprises, Inc., Nixa, Mo., 1976-80; prin. Christian Schs. of Springfield, 1980-85, 89—; pastor Mt. Calvary Bapt. Ch., Richmond, Mo., 1985-89. Tchr. Pisgah Christian Sch., Excelsior Springs, Mo., 1987-88, adminstr., 1988-89; prof. U.S. history Bapt. Bible Coll., Springfield, 1990—. Mem. Police Pers. Bd., Richmond, 1987-89; election judge Ray County, Richmond, 1985-89; dep. registrar Greene County Clk., Springfield, 1983-85, 89—; deacon Bapt. Temple, 1977-80; bd. dirs. Tri-State Christian Conf., 1998—. Mem. Mo. Assn. Christian Schs., Mo. Christian Schs. Athletic Assn. (bd. dirs. 1996—),

Northside Springfield Betterment Assn. (bd. dirs. 2000). Avocations: softball, golf. Home: PO Box 8464 Springfield MO 65801-8464 Office: Christian Schs Springfield 739 W Talmage St Springfield MO 65803-1117 E-mail: allcorns@cnonline.com.

ALLEN, B. JANICE, elementary educator; b. Athens, Ga., May 20, 1951; d. Herman Charles and Hazel (Pruett) A.; children: Joy Cooper, Andy Cooper, Van Cooper. AS, Gainesville Coll., 1971; BS in Edn., U. Ga., 1973, MEd, 1990, EdS in Supervision and Adminstrn., 1993. Cert. tchr., Ga. Tchr. Bethlehem (Ga.) Elem. Sch., 1973-77, Winder (Ga.) Elem. Sch., 1980-88, Kennedy Elem. Sch., Winder, 1988-89, County Line Elem. Sch., Winder, 1989-90, instnl. lead tchr., counselor, 1990—; prin. County Line Elem., Winder, 1995—. Mem. ASCD, Ga. Assn. Curriculum and Supervision, Ga. Assn. Educators, Phi Delta Kappa, Alpha Delta Kappa. Methodist. Avocations: reading, postgraduate studies, music, crafts. Office: County Line Elem Sch 905 Mulberry Rd Winder GA 30680-2831

ALLEN, BARBARA ANN, musician, educator, personnel contractor; b. Abilene, Tex., Apr. 18, 1956; d. Ira James Jr. and Doris Mae (Reid) A. MusB with spl. honors, U. Tex., 1979; MusM, So. Meth. U., 1984. Cert. elem. and secondary tchr., Tex. Orch. instr., condr. Richardson (Tex.) Ind. Sch. Dist., 1979-81; violinist, violist Ft. Worth Symphony Orch., 1979-81; condr. U. Tex. Summer String Inst., Dallas, 1980, 81; violinist, violist AIMS Symphony Orch., Graz, Austria, 1980—; violinist Innsbruck (Austria) Symphony and Opera Orch., 1981-82, Münchner Instrumental Ensemble, Munich, 1981-82; faculty, dir. Am. Inst. of Mus. Studies, Graz, 1982—; violinist Dallas Ballet Orch., 1984-87; violinist, tenured core mem. Dallas Opera Orch., 1986—. 2d violinist Eger Artist-In-Residence String Quartet, Graz, Austria, 1983-87; rec. artist Profl. Rec. Studios, Dallas, 1984—; 1st violinist Lone Star String Quartet, Dallas, 1985-90; instr. violin and viola Arapaho Music Studios, Dallas, 1985-90; founder Studio of Barbara Allen-Violin and Viola, 1988—, The Classic Strings Ensembles, Musical Entertainment Booking, 1990—;instrumental pers. contr.Wichita Falls Symphony Orch., 2000—. Author: Auditioning in Europe for the Instrumentalist-A Guide to Professionalism in Music, 1987, Musicians' Tax Records - An Organizational Guide, 1997. Assoc. concertmaster Wichita Falls Symphony Orch., 2000—. Scholar Meadows Found. Scholar, So. Meth. Univ., 1982—84. Mem. Am. Fedn. Musicians. Methodist. Avocations: creative arts, tennis, travel, swimming, gardening. Home and Office: 2514 Muret St Irving TX 75062-7182 E-mail: barbara@classicstrings.us.

ALLEN, BARBARA JILL, educator; b. Syracuse, N.Y., Nov. 4, 1962; d. James Matthew and Barbara Lou (Hine) O.Brien; m. David Barry, Oct. 24, 1987; 1 child Matthew. BS in Sociology, SUNY, Brockport, 1985; cert. in elem. edn., SUNY, Cortland, 1982; MEd, Loyola Coll., 1995. Cert. elem. edn.; cert. Wilson Reading Sys. tchr. Tchr. Our Lady Pompei, Archdiocese Balt., 1986-92; owner, dir. in-home daycare, 1993—; tchr. spl. edn. Jacksonville Elem. Sch., 1995—. Summer sch. tchr.; pvt. tutor 1986—; home and hosp. tchr. Baltimore County, 2002—. Moderator Student govt. 1988-92; facilitator Rainbows for All God's Children, 1989; vol. for homeless, Balt., 1991-92. Republican. Episcopalian. Avocations: wreath making, camping. Office: 10416 Greenside Dr Cockeysville Hunt Valley MD 21030-3328

ALLEN, BETTY JEAN, assistant principal; b. Madison, Ga., Sept. 20, 1943; d. Jesse Banks and Madeline (Colbert) Davis; m. James Adams Allen, Dec. 26, 1972; children: James Adams II, Shannon Denise. BS in Elem. Edn., Ft. Valley (Ga.) State Coll., 1965; MEd in Early Childhood Edn., U. Ga., 1973, EdS in Ednl. Adminstrn., 1993; student, DeKalb Coll., Atlanta, 1985. Tchr. 3d grade Blackwell Elem. Sch., Elberton, Ga., 1966-70; tchr. 5th grade Falling Creek Elem. Sch., Elberton, 1970-76; tchr. adult edn. Morgan County Sch. System, Madison, 1979-82; tchr. Chpt. I Morgan County Primary Sch., Madison, 1976-79, tchr. 2d grade, 1979-85, tchr., lead tchr., 1985-86, asst. prin., 1986—. Coord. In-Sch. Suspension, Madison, 1992—; evaluator Ga. Leadership Evaluation, Madison, 1989—; advisor Paraprofls., Madison, 1986—. Sunday sch. tchr., usher, sec. Calvary Bapt. Ch., Madison; treas., asst. treas. Christian Women In Action, Madison, 1993—; sec. Pearl/Burney Alumni Assn., 1990—. Named Parent of the Yr. HeadStart, 1986; Tchr. of Yr., Morgan County Primary Sch., 1984. Mem. ASCD, NAACP, Ga. Assn. Educators, Ga. Assn. Elem. Sch. Prins., HeadStart Parent Orgn. (pres.), Order Eastern Star (Worthy Matron 1991-93, treas. 1994—). Democrat. Avocations: reading, listening to music, researching materials for students' improvement. Home: PO Box 345 Madison GA 30650-0345 Office: Morgan County Bd Edn 1065 East Ave Madison GA 30650-1497

ALLEN, BRENDA KAY, elementary school educator; b. Poplar Bluff, Mo., Dec. 11, 1957; d. Harold Alan and Earline Smith Robertson; m. Thomas Franklin Allen, Dec. 31, 1978; children: Joshua Sutherland, Silas Wright, Emily Harper. B Music Edn., Murray State U., 1983; MA, S.E. Mo. State U., 2000. Cert. tchr. Mo. Tchr. Poplar Bluff Sch. Dist., 1986—. Dir. R-1 Schs. Safe Schs. Healthy Students, Poplar Bluff, Mo., 2002—. Mem.: Mo. Music Educators Assn., Nat. Assn. Music Edn., Mo. State Tchrs. Assn. Avocations: sailing, scuba diving, aviation. Office: Poplar Bluff 5th and 6th Grade Ctr 3209 Oak Grove Rd Poplar Bluff MO 63901

ALLEN, CAROL LINNEA OSTROM, art educator; b. Phila., Apr. 23, 1936; d. Gustaf Adolph Ostrom and Anne Marie (Scheib) Heckman; m. David Wilford Allen Sr., Mar. 8, 1932; children: Jonathan Ostrom, David Wilford. BS in Art Edn. with honors, Kutztown U., 1958; MA in Art Edn., U. of the Arts, 1991. Cert. tchr., supr. art, English. Jr. H.S. art tchr. West York (Pa.) Sch. Dist., 1958-60; elem. art supr. Colonial Sch. Dist., Plymouth Meeting, Pa., 1960-62; substitute tchr., art tchr., English tchr. Phoenixville (Pa.) Area Sch. Dist., 1968—, art dept. head, yearbook advisor, 1991—, mem. strategic planning com., 1992-94. Presenter at state and nat. art confs., 1986—. Exhibited in group shows at Nat. Art Edn. Assn. Electronic Gallery, 1989, 95. Mem. LWV, Valley Forge, 1992—. Mem. AAUW, NOW, Nat. Art Edn. Assn., Pa. Art Edn. Assn., Phoenixville Area Edn. Assn. (polit. action com. for edn. chair 1992—). Office: Phoenixville Area Sch Dist 1120 Gay St Phoenixville PA 19460-4417

ALLEN, CHARLES EUGENE, university administrator, agriculturist, educator; b. Burley, Idaho, Jan. 25, 1939; s. Charles W. and Elsie P. (Fowler) A.; m. Connie J. Block, June 19, 1960; children: Kerry J., Tamara S. BS, U. Idaho, 1961; MS, U. Wis., 1963, PhD, 1965. NSF postdoctoral fellow, Sydney, Australia, 1966-67; asst. prof. agr. U. Minn., St. Paul, 1967-69, assoc. prof., 1969-72, prof., 1972—, dean Coll. Agr., assoc. dir. Agrl. Expt. Sta., 1984-88, acting v.p., 1988-90, v.p. agriculture, forestry and home econs., dir. Minn. Agr. Expt. Sta., 1990-95, provost prof. studies, dir. Minn. Agr. Expt. Sta., 1995-97, dir. global outreach, 1997-98, exec. dir. internat. programs, 1998—. Vis. prof. Pa. State U., 1978; cons. to industry; C. Glen King lectr. Wash. State U., 1981; Univ. lectr. U. Wyo., Laramie, 1984; adj. prof. Hassan II U., Rabat, Morocco, 1984 Recipient Horace T. Morse-Amoco Found. award in undergrad. edn. U. Minn., 1984, Disting. Tchr. award U. Minn. Coll. Agr., 1984, Disting. Alumni award U. Idaho, 1989. Fellow AAAS, Inst. Food Tech.; mem. Am. Meat Sci. Assn. (dir. 1970-72; Research award 1980, Signal Service award, 1985), Am. Soc. Animal Sci. (Exceptional Research Achievement award 1972, Research award 1977), Sigma Xi. Avocations: photography, reading, outdoor sports, golf.

ALLEN, CHARLOTTE, secondary education educator; BS in Edn., Athens State Coll. Tchr. sci. East Lawrence High Sch., Trinity, Ala., 1988—. Coach cheerleading; camp dir. Nat. Cheerleading Assn. Named Outstanding Sci. Tchr., 1992. Mem. Nat. Assn. Geology Tchrs. Avocations: church activities, hiking.*

ALLEN, CLARENCE RODERIC, geologist, educator; b. Palo Alto, Calif., Feb. 15, 1925; s. Hollis Partridge and Delight (Wright) A. BA, Reed Coll., 1949; MS, Cal. Inst Tech., 1951, PhD, 1954. Asst. prof. geology U. Minn., 1954-55; mem. faculty Calif. Inst. Tech., 1955—, prof. geology and geophysics, 1964-91, prof. emeritus, 1991—; interim dir. Seismological Lab., 1965-67, acting chmn. division of geological scis., 1967-68. Phi Beta Kappa Disting. lectr., 1978; chmn. cons. bd. earthquake analysis Calif. Dept. Water Resources, 1965-74; chmn. geol. hazards adv. com. for program Cal. Resources Agy., 1965-66; mem. earth scis. adv. panel NSF, 1965-68, chmn., 1967-68, mem. adv. com. environmental scis., 1970-72; mem. U.S. Geol. Survey adv. panel to Nat. Center Earthquake Research, Calif. Cal. Mining and Geology Bd., 1969-75, chmn., 1975; mem. task force on earthquake hazard reduction Office Sci. and Tech., 1970-71; mem. Can. Earthquake Prediction Evaluation Council, 1983-88; vice-chmn. Nat. Acad. Sci. Com. on Advanced Study in china, 1981-85; chmn. geology sect. Nat. Acad. Sci., 1982-85, Com. on Scholarly Communication with People's Republic China, 1984-89, chmn., 1987-89; mem. Nat. Acad. Sci. Commn. on Phys. Scis., Math. and Resources; mem. Pres.'s Nuclear Waste Tech. Rev. Bd., 1989-97. Served to 1st lt. USAAF, 1943-46. Recipient G.K. Gilbert award seismic geology Carnegie Instn., 1960. Fellow Am. Geophys. Union, Geol. Soc. Am. (counselor 1968-70, pres. 1973-74), Am. Acad. Arts Scis.; mem. Nat. Acad. Scis., Earthquake Engring. Research Inst. (bd. dirs. 1985-88, Housner medal 2001), Seismological Soc. Am. (dir. 1970-76, pres. 1975-76, medal 1995), Nat. Acad. Engring., Phi Beta Kappa. Office: Calif Inst Tech Dept Geology Pasadena CA 91125-0001 E-mail: allen@gps.caltech.edu.

ALLEN, DENSIL E., JR., retired agricultural studies educator; Prof. agriculture Ctrl. Mo. State U., Warrensburg, 1979—2002, ret., 2002. Fellow Nat. Assn. Colls. Tchrs. Agriculture, 1992.*

ALLEN, DOROTHEA, secondary education educator; b. Rockaway, NJ, Apr. 30, 1919; d. Harrison Engleman and Caroline (Tierney) Allen. AB, Montclair U., 1941, MA, 1949. Cert. secondary, sci., math. tchr., counselor, supr., prin. N.J. Tchr. sci. and math. Denville (N.J.) Jr. High Sch., 1942-46; tchr. sci. Boonton (N.J.) High Sch., 1946-94, supr. sci. dept., 1978-94. Lab. technician Drew Chem. Corp., Boonton, 1942—47; tech. asst. Bell Telecom. Lab., Whippany, NJ, 1956; rsch. scientist Warner Lambert Rsch. Inst., Morris Plains, NJ, 1959—62; tchr. sci. enrichment Boonton Summer Sch., 1963—85; curriculum developer Morris County Vocat.-Tech. Sch., Denville, 1987; project evaluator Mid. States Assn., 1973, 79; facilitator Ptnrs. in Edn. Program; promoter Media Ctr. Open House; cons., reviewer Am. Biol. Tchr. Mag., 1975—; com. mem. Sch. Articulation Program Boonton Schs., 1991—94; media ctr. spkr. Meet the Author; sponsor Student Showcase of Excellence in Sci., 1990—94; faculty sponsor, mentor h.s. students, 1966—94; mentor Alt. Rt. Program Tchrs. N.J. Organizer Am. Dental Health Clinic, Boonton, 1968—72; presenter, spkr. in field. Author: Research Projects for High School Biology, 1971, Biology Teacher's Desk Book, 1979, Science Activities for Every Month of the School Year, 1981, Science Demonstrations for Elementary Classrooms, 1988, Hands-on Science, 1991; contbr. articles to profl. jours., including Am. Biology Tchr. Mem. career com. N.J. divsn. Theobald Smith Soc., 1975—76, mentoring program, 1992—; fundraiser Am. Hemophilia Found., Rockaway, NJ, 1985—, Am. Heart Assn., 1995—, Muscular Dystrophy Found., 1995—, Nat. Children's Cancer Soc., 1996—; mothers march vol. March of Dimes, 1990—; cons. Cmty. Mid. Sch. Planning Com., Boonton, 1988—90; bd. advisors ABI Rsch., 1995—. Named Outstanding Biology Tchr., Nat. Assn. Biology Tchrs., 1972, Outstanding Sci. Tchr., Rsch. Assn. N.Am., 1980, Woman of the Yr., 1993—98; named to Sci. Edn. Hall of Fame, 1994—98, Boonton H.S. Wall of Fame, 1996, 1997, 1998; recipient Disting. Citizen's award, Town of Rockaway, 1984, Gov.'s and Edn. award, N.J. Dept. Edn., 1984, Morris County Tchr. of the Yr. award, 1990, Presdl. award, NSF, 1984, Cert. of Honor, State of N.J., 1985, World Lifetime Achievement award, 1994, Internat. Order of Merit, 1994, Spotlight award, Boonton Bd. Edn., 1980—86, Tchr. of Yr., 1984, 1990, Women's Inner Cir. of Achievement award, 1995. Mem.: NSTA, ASCD, NEA, NEA Ret., Morris Area Sci. Alliance, N.J. Dept. Edn. Exec. Acad., N.J. Dept. Edn. Exec. Acad., N.J. Alliance for Math. and Sci., N.J. Prins. And Suprs. Assn., N.J. Edn. Assn., Assn. Presdl. Award Winners in Sci. Tchg., Nat. Assn. Secondary Sch. Prins., Morris County Ret. Educators Assn. Avocations: reading, propagating plants, collecting gold coins. Home: 115 Jackson Ave Rockaway NJ 07866-3039

ALLEN, ELIZABETH JEAN JACKSON, associate headmaster, language arts specialist, educator; b. Balt., May 31, 1945; d. John Henry and Nannie Dorothea (Logan) Jackson; m. Reginald Emerson Allen, Nov. 22, 1967; children: Reginald Marcus-Emerson, Leslie Kathleen. MS, Copping State U., 1967; postgrad., Coppin State U., Morgan State U., Johns Hopkins U. Cert. advanced profl. tchr., Md. Tchr. elem. grades 1-6 Balt. Pub. Schs., 1967-88; lang. arts specialist McDonogh Sch., Owings Mills, Md., 1988-92, asst. to assoc. headmaster, 1992-96; middle sch. head The Langley Sch., 1996—. Mem. evaluation team Nat. Assn. Ind. Schs., Washington, 1991, mem. accreditation team, Md., 1992. Contbr. chpt. to Cookbook for Schools, 1992, What's Whole in Whole Language. Mem. ASCD, Nat. Alliance of Black Sch. Educators (pres. 1992—), Phi Delta Kappa. Democrat. Roman Catholic. Avocations: ballroom dancing, reading, travel. Home: Apt 1E 1900 Sulgrave Ave Baltimore MD 21209-4531

ALLEN, GARY CURTISS, geology educator; b. Stockton, Calif., July 18, 1939; s. Curtiss Wright and Helen Lucille (McElroy) A.; m. Ruth Lee Mayeux, June 5, 1965; children: Adrienne Lucille, Christopher Gary. BS in Chemistry, Stanford U., 1961; MA in Geology, Rice U., 1963; PhD in Geochemistry, U. N.C., 1968. Head geochemistry and petrology dept. Mineral Resources div. State of Va., Charlottesville, 1966-68; asst. prof. earth scis. La. State U., New Orleans, 1968-78; assoc. prof. earth scis. U. New Orleans, 1972-78, prof. geology, 1978—, dir. environ. tng. program, 1993-94, coord. environ. sci. and policy degree program, 2000—. Coord. for radiation safety La. State U. System, 1989—, chair coun. faculty advisors, 1995-97; pres. Sunbelt Assocs. Inc., New Orleans 1978—; bd. dirs. Holocene Rsch. Inst.; pres. Assn. La. Faculty Senates, 1997-99; chair La. Bd. Regents Faculty Adv. Coun., 1997-2000 Contbr. articles to profl. jours. Mem. St. Frances Cabrini Sch. Bd., New Orleans, 1979-82. NASA fellow, 1963-66. Mem. Geol. Soc. Am., New Orleans Geol. Soc., U. New Orleans Fedn. Tchrs. (pres. 1985-87, treas. 1987—), Sigma Xi (pres. New Orleans chpt. 1977-78, v.p. 1991—). Home: 180 Devon Dr Mandeville LA 70448-3406 Office: U New Orleans Dept Geology And Geoph New Orleans LA 70148-0001

ALLEN, HAROLD (JIM), secondary school English educator; b. Cleve., Apr. 15, 1938; s. Harold and Hazel May (Zacasky) A.; m. Elaine Frances Riechenstein, Jan. 30, 1965 (div. July 1992); 1 child, Jill Ann; m. Martha Ellen Gioia, July 10, 1993; stepchildren: Deborah Burke, Patrick Burke. AA, Coll. of San Mateo, 1960; AB, San Francisco State U., 1968; MA, U. Redlands, 1982. Cert. secondary tchr., Calif. Reading, lang. arts tchr. San Benito H.S., Hollister, Calif., 1969-71, English and drama dir., 1971-84, English tchr., 1985—, U.S. history tchr., 1992-95. Mentor tchr. San Benito H.S., 1983, 84, 94, 96. Mem. San Benito County Dem. Ctrl. Com., 1980-91. Lance cpl. USMCR, 1956-65. Recipient 5 Superior Play awards Amador Drama Festival, Best Play award Stanislaus Drama Festival, 1975. Mem. Calif. Tchrs. Assn. (pres. San Benito H.S. chpt. 1978-91, We Honor Ours award 1985), Phi Delta Kappa. Avocations: reading, travel, study of world war ii, hiking. Home: 522 Humes Ave Aptos CA 95003-5241

ALLEN, HENRY LEE, sociology educator, consultant; b. Joiner, Ark., July 7, 1955; s. John Henry Jr. and Mahalie (Moore) A.; m. Juliet Eugenia-Agnes Cooper, July 7, 1979; children: Jonathan, Jessica, Janice, Justin, Julia, Janel, Joseph, Judith. BA cum laude, Wheaton Coll., 1977; MA, U. Chgo., 1979, PhD, 1988. Sociology instr., adminstrv. asst. to pres. Bethel Coll., St. Paul, 1982-87; assoc. prof. sociology Calvin Coll., Grand Rapids, Mich., 1987-91; asst. prof. edn. Grad. Sch. Edn., U. Rochester, N.Y., 1991-97; assoc. prof. sociology Rochester N.Y.) Inst. Tech., 1997-98, Wheaton (Ill.) Coll., 1998—. Cons. NEA, Washington, 1992—, Am. Bible Soc., 2001—, Inst. for the Black Family, Detroit, 1984—, among others. Contbr. articles to profl. jours. Bd. dirs. Genessee Settlement House, Rochester, 1993-96, Koinonia House, 2000—, African-Am. Leadership Roundtable of Dupage County, 2000—; mem. Kettering Found. Cmty. Leadership Program; mem. adv. com. United Way, Rochester, 1995-96; African-Am. Leadership Roundtable, Rochester, 1993-96; mem. Jubilee Bapt. Ch., 2002. Fellow Danforth Found., 1978-81. Mem. ASCD, Wilson Ctr. for Scholars, N.Y. Acad. Scis. Avocations: science fiction, archery, astronomy, football, museums. Home: 111 W Lincoln Ave Wheaton IL 60187-4114 Office: Wheaton Coll Dept Sociology Wheaton IL 60187 E-mail: henry.l.allen@wheaton.edu.

ALLEN, HERBERT ELLIS, environmental chemistry educator; b. Sharon, Pa., July 19, 1939; s. Jacob Samuel and Florence (Safier) A.; m. Deena Wilner, 1962 (dec. 1983); children: Francine Joy, Julie Michelle; m. Ronnie Magil, 1984 BS in Chemistry, U. Mich., 1962; MS, Wayne State U., 1967; PhD, U. Mich., 1974. Chemist U.S. Bur. Comml. Fisheries, Ann Arbor, Mich., 1962-70; lectr. U. Mich., Ann Arbor, 1970-74; asst. prof. Ill. Inst. Tech., Chgo., 1974-76, assoc. prof., 1976-80, prof. environ. engring., 1980-83; dir. Environ. Studies Inst., Drexel U., Phila., also prof. chemistry, 1983-89; prof. civil engring. U. Del., Newark, 1990—, dir. Ctr. for Study of Metals in the Environment, 2002—; dir. Del. Waste Reduction Assistance Program, 1991-95. Vis. prof. Water Rsch. Ctr., Medmenham, Eng., 1980-81, Nankai U., Tianjin, People's Republic of China, 1993—; cons. WHO, U.S. EPA. Editor: Nutrients in Natural Waters, 1972, Analysis and Effects of Metal Speciation, Applications to Water, Waste, Soil, 1988, Metals in Groundwater, 1993, Metal Speciation and Contamination of Soil, 1994, Metal Contaminated Aquatic Sediments, 1995, Metals in Surface Water, 1998, Bioavailability of Metals in Terrestrial Ecosystems, 2002. Fellow, WHO, 1981. Mem. Am. Chem. Soc. (chmn. divsn. environ. chemistry 1972-75), Water Environment Fedn., Soc. for Environ. Toxicology and Chemistry, Internat. Water Assn. Home: 21 E Levering Mill Rd Bala Cynwyd PA 19004-2251 Office: Univ Delaware Dept Civil & Environ Engring Newark DE 19716 E-mail: allen@ce.udel.edu.

ALLEN, HOWARD NORMAN, cardiologist, educator; b. Chgo., Nov. 19, 1936; s. Herman and Ida Gertrude (Weinstein) Allen; children: Michael Daniel, Jeffrey Scott. BS, U. Ill., Chgo., 1958, MD, 1960. Diplomate Am. Bd. Internal Medicine, Am. Bd. Cardiovasc. Disease, Nat. Bd. Med. Examiners. Intern Los Angeles County Gen. Hosp., L.A., 1960—61; resident in internal medicine Wadsworth VA Med. Ctr., L.A., 1961, 1964—66; fellow in cardiology Cedars-Sinai Med. Ctr., L.A., 1966—67, dir. cardiac care unit Cedars of Lebanon Hosp. div., 1968—74, dir. Pacemaker Evaluation Ctr., 1968—89, dir. Cardiac Noninvasive Lab., 1972—88; Markus Found. fellow in cardiology St. George's Hosp., London, 1967—68; attending physician cardiology svc. Sepulveda (Calif.) VA Med. Ctr., 1972—86; pvt. practice Beverly Hills, Calif., 1988—. Asst. prof. medicine UCLA, 1970—76, assoc. prof., 1976—84, adj. prof., 1984—88, clin. prof., 1988—; cons. Sutherland Learning Assocs., Inc., L.A., 1970—75; cardiology cons. Occidental Life Ins. Co., L.A., Calif., 1972—86. Contbr. articles to profl. jours., chapters to books. Commr. L.A. County Emergency Med. Svcs., 1989—91. Capt. M.C. U.S. Army, 1962—63, Korea. Fellow, NSF, 1958, NIH, 1966—67. Fellow: ACP, Am. Coll. Cardiology (Calif. chpt. dist. councilor 1999—2003); mem.: Am. Heart Assn. (bd. dirs. 1979—94, fellow coun. clin. cardiology, pres. Greater L.A. affiliate 1987—88, Heart of Gold award 1994), U. Ill. Alumni Assn. (Life; Loyalty award 1996), Cedars-Sinai Alumni Assn. (life; exec. bd. 1999—, sec., treas. 2000, pres. 2001—02), Big Ten Club So. Calif. (bd. dirs.), Pi Kappa Epsilon, Alpha Omega Alpha. Office: 414 N Camden Dr Ste 1100 Beverly Hills CA 90210-4532 E-mail: allen@cvmg.com.

ALLEN, JOHN LYNDON, social studies educator; b. Boston, June 7, 1934; s. Lyndon Ball and Irene Butterfield (Roys) A.; children: Jennifer, Geoffrey, Jason Allen. BA, Northeastern U., 1957, MEd, 1966. Social studies tchr. jr. and h.s. Kennedy Jr. H.S., Randolph, Mass., 1965-71; social studies tchr. sr. h.s. Randolph (Mass.) H.S., 1971-94; supr. student tchrs. Bridgewater State Coll. Sch. Edn., 1996—. Mem. vestry Episcopal ch., Whitman, Mass., 1980-84, edn. adv. com., 1981-82, govt. study com., 1979-81, fin. com., 1986-87. Recipient Disting. Svc. cert. Mass. Tchrs. Assn., 1994, Plaque of Appreciation, Football Boosters Club, 1993. Mem. RAndolph Tchrs. Assn. (v.p. jr. h.s. 1967-70, v.p. sr. h.s. 1971-74, profl. policies com. 1974-76, bldg. rep. h.s. 1976-82), South Shore Coun. for Social Studies. Avocations: photography, fishing, hiking.

ALLEN, JUDITH MARCHESE, special education educator; b. Atlanta, June 15, 1952; d. Alvin D. Jr. and Cecelia L. (Henderson) Jones; m. Frank J. Marchese, Aug. 26, 1972 (div. Nov. 1988); children: Michael Duane, Andrea Michelle; m. Patrick R. Allen, Nov. 27, 1992 (dec. Mar. 1993). BS in Edn., Ga. State U., 1974, MEd, 1980; EdS, U. Ga., 1991. Cert. tchr., Ga. Elem. tchr. DeKalb County Pub. Schs., Decatur, Ga., 1974-77, Gwinnett County Pub. Schs., Lawrenceville, Ga., 1978-80, spl. edn. tchr., 1980-82, 84—. Grad. asst. U. Ga., Athens, 1991. Scout leader Boy Scouts Am. Pack 100, Lilburn, Ga., 1986-90. Recipient Cub Scouter award Boy Scouts Am., Lilburn, 1989. Mem. NEA, Ga. Assn. Educators, Gwinnett County Assn. Educators, Coun. for Exceptional Children. Republican. Methodist. Avocations: cross stitch crafts. Office: Parkview High Sch 998 Cole Rd SW Lilburn GA 30047-5499

ALLEN, JUDITH MARTHA, nursing administrator, educator, career officer; b. Syracuse, N.Y., Feb. 4, 1942; d. Bernard J. and Genevieve R. (Greene) Arndt; m. Anthony S. Allen, Nov. 1984. Diploma, Champlain Valley Sch. Nursing, Plattsburg, N.Y., 1964; BSN, D'Youville Coll., 1974; postgrad., U. N.C., 1976; MS, U. San Francisco, 1984. Cert. cardiovascular nurse clinician; CPR instr. trainer; CCM. Head nurse CCU Millard Fillmore Hosp., Buffalo, 1974-80; commd. officer U.S. Army, 1976, advanced through grades to col., 1998; chief surg. nursing Ireland Army Cmty. Hosp., Ft. Knox, Ky., 1985-87, chief nursing edn. and staff devel., 1987-88; clin. coord. ICU, CCU, asst. chief spl. projects officer Letterman Army Med. Ctr., San Francisco, 1980-85, head nurse post operative cardiovascular/neurosurg. unit, 1988-89, asst. chief nursing edn., staff devel. svc., 1989-91, asst. chief evenings/nights, 1991-92, asst. quality improvement nurse, 1992, chief nursing adminstrn., days, med. surg. sect. chief, 1992-94; rev. coord. State Indsl. Ins. Sys. Universal Health Network, Sparks, Nev., 1994—96. Case mgr. and adminstr. Home Care Plus; dir. profl. svcs. The Helping Angels, 2002. Contbr. articles to profl. jours. Mem. AACCN, Nev. State Nurses Assn. Home: PO Box 1026 Virginia City NV 89440-1026 Office: 1311 N McCarran Blvd Ste 101 Sparks NV 89431

ALLEN, LAYMAN EDWARD, law educator, research scientist; b. Turtle Creek, Pa., June 9, 1927; s. Layman Grant and Viola Iris (Williams) A.; m. Christine R. Patmore, Mar. 29, 1950 (dec.); children: Layman G., Patricia R.; m. Emily C. Hall, Oct. 3, 1981 (div. 1992); children: Phyllip A. Hall, Kelly C. Hairston; m. Leslie A. Olsen, June 10, 1995. Student, Washington and Jefferson Coll., 1945-46; AB, Princeton U., 1951; MPub. Admnstrn., Harvard U., 1952; LLB, Yale U., 1956. Bar: Conn. 1956. Fellow Ctr. for Advanced Study in Behavioral Scis., 1961-62; sr. fellow Yale Law Sch., 1956-57, lectr., 1957-58, instr., 1958-59, asst. prof., 1959-63, assoc. prof., 1963-66; assoc. prof. law U. Mich. Law Sch., Ann Arbor, 1966-71, prof., 1971—. Chmn. bd. trustees Accelerated Learning Found., 1998—; sr. rsch. scientist Mental Health Rsch. Inst., U. Mich., 1966-99; cons. legal drafting Nat. Life Ins. Co., Mich. Blue Cross & Blue Shield (various law firms); mem. electronic data retrieval com. Am. Bar Assn.; ops. rsch. analyst

McKinsey & Co.; orgn. and methods analyst Office of Sec. Air Force.; trustee Ctr. for Study of Responsive Law. Editor: Games and Simulations, Artificial Intelligence and Law Jour., Theoria; author: WFF 'N Proof: The Game of Modern Logic, 1961, latest rev. edit., 1990, (with Robin B.S. Brooks, Patricia A. James) Automatic Retrieval of Legal Literature: Why and How, 1962, WFF: The Beginner's Game of Modern Logic, 1962, latest rev. edit., 1973, Equations: The Game of Creative Mathematics, 1963, latest rev. edit., 1994, (with Mary E. Caldwell) Reflections of the Communications Sciences and Law: The Jurimetrics Conference, 1965, (with J. Ross and P. Kugel) Queries 'N Theories: The Game of Science and Language, 1970, latest rev. edit., 1973, (with F. Goodman, D. Humphrey and J. Ross), On-Words: The Game of Word Structures, 1971, rev. edit., 1973; contbr. articles to profl. jours.; co-author/designer: (with J. Ross and C. Stratton) DIG (Diagnostic Instrnl. Gaming) Math; (with C. Saxon) Normalizer Clear Legal Drafting Program, 1986, MINT System for Generating Dynamically Multiple-Interpretation Legal Decision-Assistance Systems, 1991, The Legal Argument Game of Legal Relations, 1997, (with Sandra Bartlett) LawToe: the Game to Learn the Game Rules of The Legal Argument Game of Legal Relations, 2003, The New Legal Argument of Legal Relations, 2003. With USNR, 1945-46. Mem. ABA (coun. sect. sci. and tech.), AAAS, ACLU, Assn. Symbolic Logic, Nat. Coun. Tchrs. Math. Democrat. Unitarian Universalist. Home: 2114 Vinewood Blvd Ann Arbor MI 48104-2762 Office: U Mich Sch Law 625 S State St Ann Arbor MI 48109-1215 E-mail: laymanal@umich.edu.

ALLEN, LEE NORCROSS, historian, educator; b. Shawmut, Ala., Apr. 16, 1926; s. Leland Norcross and Dorothy (Whitaker) A.; m. Catherine Ann Bryant, Aug. 24, 1963; children— Leland Norcross, Leslie Catherine. BS, Auburn U., 1948, MS, 1949; PhD, U. Pa., 1955. From instr. to prof. history Ea. Bapt. Coll., St. Davids, Pa., 1952-61; prof. history Samford U., Birmingham, Ala., 1961-2001, grad. dean, 1965-86; dean Howard Coll. Arts and Scis., 1975-90, rsch. prof., 2001—. Author: (with Mrs. E.S. Bee) History of Ruhama, 1969, The First One Hundred Fifty Years: First Baptist Church of Montgomery, 1979, Born for Missions, 1984; Southside Baptist Church: A Centennial History, 1985, Woodlawn Baptist Church: The First Century, 1886-1986, 1986; (with Catherine B. Allen) Courage to Care, 1988; Expanding the Dream, Montgomery Baptist Hospital, 1988, Notable Past, Bright Future: First Baptist Church 1893-1993, 1993, Born for Missions, 16th Decade, 1993, Ralph W. Beeson: A Biography, 2001, Outward Focus: Mountain Brook Baptist Church, The First Fifty Years, 1994, The First 150 Years Supplement: 1980-1995, 1996, (with Catherine B. Allen) Christ Is Our Salvation: Paul Piper, 1998, (with Catherine B. Allen) The Boaz Heritage: A Centennial History, Boaz, Alabama, 1897-1997, 1999. Served with AUS, 1944-46. Recipient Commendation cert. Am. Assn. State and Local History, Thomas Jefferson award, 1995, disting. svc. award Ala. Baptist Hist. Commn., 1996; Auburn U. rsch. fellow, 1948-49; Harrison fellow U. Pa., 1949-52. Mem. Am. Hist. Assn., Am. Bapt. Hist. Assn. (editor The Ala. Bapt. Historian 1989—), So. Bapt. Hist. Assn. (pres. 1987-88), So. Hist. Assn., Ala. Hist. Assn. (editor newsletter 1989-2001, pres. 1994-95), So. Bapt. Club, Rotary (pres. Shades Valley chpt. 1969-70), Omicron Delta Kappa, Phi Alpha Theta, Phi Kappa Phi, Pi Gamma Mu. Baptist. Home: 5025 Wendover Dr Birmingham AL 35223-1631

ALLEN, LINDA, secondary education educator; b. Harlan, Iowa, Apr. 16, 1941; d. Jens Gordon and Iris Maude (Martin) Mark; m. Charles L. Allen, Apr. 20, 1965; 1 child, Kevin. BA, Graceland Coll., 1963; MA, East Tex. State U., 1981. Cert. secondary tchr., Tex. Tchr. Taipei Am. Sch., Taiwan, Dept of Def., Washington; clinician Academic Clin. Svc., Dallas; tchr., reading specialist Dallas Ind. Sch. Dist. NSF grantee. Mem. ASCD, Nat. Reading Assn., Nat. Middle Sch. Assn., Tex. Reading Assn., Tex. Middle Sch. Assn., Phi Delta Kappa. Office: O W Holmes Middle Sch 2001 E Kiest Blvd Dallas TX 75216-3300

ALLEN, MARY LOUISE HOOK, secondary education educator; b. Ironwood, Mich., July 18, 1930; d. Frank Eugene and Elsie Clara (Schneider) Hook; m. Dale Sanson Allen, June 30, 1955; children: Jack Eugene, Bradley Arthur. BS in Phys. Edn. cum laude, U. Mich., 1951; MA in Phys. Edn., U. Minn., 1970, postgrad., 1987—. Life teaching cert., coaching lic., Minn. Secondary edn. tchr. New Trier Twp. High Sch., Winnetka, Ill., 1951-55, Richfield (Minn.) Sch. Dist., 1955-59; teaching assoc. U. Minn., Mpls., 1969-70, part-time lectr., 1985-86; tchr. Bloomington (Minn.) Sch. Dist., 1961-85. Adj. prof. Concordia Coll., St. Paul, Minn., 1987-92; officiator U.S. Synchro Minn. Assn., Minn. State High Sch. League, Pan-Am. Trials Swimming Co-Chair, others; past officiating bd. chmn. North Shore (Winnetka) Basketball/Volleyball, Ill. State Basketball com., others. Co-author: Soccer/Speedball Rule Book - Creative Game, 1952; dir. Aqua Debs Synchronized swim shows, 1962-82. Mem. Atonement Luth. Ch., Bloomington, 1956—; worker Dem. Party, Bloomington, 1988—; dir. Synchronized Swimming Camp, 1980-87. Recipient numerous athletic awards, Minn. Pathfinder award Nat. Assn. Girls and Women in Sport, 1996, U. Mich. Kinesiology Alumni Achievement award, 1996. Mem. AAHPERD (mem. com. 1949—), Minn. Assn. Health, Phys. Edn., Recreation and Dance (sec. 1982-83, pres.-elect 1984, pres. 1985, past pres. 1986, conv. chmn. 1984, 86, student confs. 1988-92), Synchronized Swim Coaches Assn. (state chmn. 1980-82), Athletic Fedn. Coll. Women (chmn. nat. conv. 1951), Mortarboard, Phi Beta Kappa, Phi Kappa Phi, Pi Lambda Theta, also others. Avocations: athletics, camping, politics, gardening. Home: 10312 Wentworth Ave Bloomington MN 55420-5249 E-mail: mlhauofm@usfamily.net.

ALLEN, MICHAEL JOHN BRIDGMAN, English educator; b. Lewes, Eng., Apr. 1, 1941; came to U.S., 1966; m. Elena Hirshberg; children: William, Benjamin. BA, Oxford (Eng.) U., 1964, MA, 1966, DLitt, 1987; PhD, U. Mich., 1970. Asst. prof. UCLA, 1970-74, assoc. prof., 1974-79, prof. English, 1979—, assoc. dir. Ctr. for Medieval and Renaissance Studies, 1978-88, dir. Ctr. for Medieval and Renaissance Studies, 1988-93, 2003—. Editor Renaissance Quar., 1993-2001; faculty rsch. lectr. UCLA, 1998. Author: Marsilio Ficino: The Philebus Commentary, 1975, Marsilio Ficino and the Phaedran Charioteer, 1981, The Platonism of Marsilio Ficino, 1984, Icastes: Marsilio Ficino's Interpretation of Plato's "Sophist," 1989, Nuptial Arithmetic, 1994, Plato's Third Eye: Studies in Marsilio Ficino's Metaphysics and Its Sources, 1995, Synoptic Art: Marsilio Ficino on the History of Platonic Interpretation, 1998; co-author: Sources and Analogues of Old English Poetry, 1976, Marsilio Ficino: Platonic Theology, Vol. I, Books I-IV, 2001, Vol. 2, Books V-VIII, 2002, Vol. 3, Books IX-XI, 2003; co-editor: First Images of America, 1976, Shakespeare's Plays in Quarto, 1984, Sir Philip Sidney's Achievements, 1990, Marsilio Ficino: His Theology, His Philosophy, His Legacy, 2002. Recipient Eby award for disting. teaching UCLA, 1977; Guggenheim fellow, 1977; disting. vis. scholar Center for Reformation and Renaissance Studies, U. Toronto, 1997, Ludwig Maximilians U., Munich, 1999, Ariz. Ctr. for Medieval & Renaissance Studies, 2002. Office: UCLA 2225 Rolfe Hall 405 Hilgard Ave Los Angeles CA 90095-9000 E-mail: mjballen@humnet.ucla.edu.

ALLEN, NANCY, vocational rehabilitation counselor; b. Louisville, Oct. 16, 1945; d. James William and Genevieve (Hambrick) A. BA, U. Miami, 1968; MA, Spalding U., 1969. Counseling supervisor Fla. Job Svc., Miami, 1969-76; dir. rehab. Crawford & Co., Miami, 1976-85; admissions rep. South Miami Hosp., 1985-89; sr. vocat. rehab. counselor State Fla. Dept. Labor, Miami, 1989—. Treas. Project YES, Miami, 1996. V.p. Fla. Rehab. Assn. Avocations: gardening, cats. Home: 6770 SW 59th St Miami FL 33143-1906

ALLEN, NORMA ANN, librarian, educator; b. Balt., Jan. 22, 1951; d. James Crawley and Thelma Agusta (Keaton) Ghee; children: Lamont Ricardo Ghee, Alissa S. Allen, Avery O. Allen. BA in Adminstrn. Mgmt., Sojourner Douglass Coll., Balt., 1987; MS in Instrnl. Tech., Towson State U., 1999. Instr. data processing PSI Inst., Balt., 1987-88; acquisition technician Social Security Adminstrn., Balt., 1987-89, reference librarian, 1989-91, acquisitions librarian, 1991—. Instrnl. developer Computer Asst. Instrn., Towson U., 1995—; bus. computer tech. instr. Balt. City C.C., 2000—; freelance floral designer/arranger, freelance instr. basic writing skills and computer literacy; instr. bus. computer tech. Balt. City C.C., 2000—. Sec., bd. dirs. New Image Child Care Facility, Balt., 1992, chmn. bd. dirs., 2001-02; instr. active reading literacy program Enoch Pratt Libr., Balt., 1992; instr. United Missionary Bapt. Conv., 1997, libr., 2003. Multicultural scholar Towson U., 1995-96. Mem. ALA, Spl. Librs. Assn., Horizon User Group. Office: Social Security Adminstrn 6401 Security Blvd Rm 571 Baltimore MD 21235-0001 E-mail: norma.allen@ssa.gov.

ALLEN, PAUL ALFRED, lawyer, educator; b. New Canaan, Conn., Feb. 18, 1948; s. Alfred J. and Wilma T. (DeWaters) A. BA, Johns Hopkins U., 1970; JD, NYU, 1974; MBA, U. Colo., 1989. Bar: Md. 1974, D.C. 1978, Colo. 1984, Calif. 1992. Exec. dir. Md. Environ. Trust, Balt., 1974-75; assoc. Bergson, Borkland, Margolis & Adler, Washington, 1975-79, ptnr., 1980-82; gen. counsel Plus System, Inc., Denver, 1983-91; counsel Visa USA, Inc., San Francisco, 1991-92, exec. v.p., gen. counsel, 1992—. Lectr. Grad. Sch. of Banking, Boulder, Colo., 1984-86, U. Denver Law Sch., 1985-90. Editor: How to Keep Your Company Out of Court, 1984; contbr. articles to profl. jours. Recipient Svc. award Supreme Ct. Colo. Mem. ABA, Calif. Bar Assn., Colo. Bar Assn., Am. Corp. Counsel Assn. Democrat. Office: Visa USA Inc PO Box 194607 San Francisco CA 94119-4607

ALLEN, ROCELIA J. retired special education educator; b. Cin., Oct. 19, 1924; married; 1 child BS cum laude in Instrumental Mus., Chgo. Conservatory Music, 1948; MEd in Spl. Edn., U. Del., Newark, 1966; PhD, Union Grad. Sch., Newark, 1979. Certified in spl. and elementary edn., music, Del.; specialist in lang. arts, behavior modification, using the operatta to teach lang. arts to educable mentally retarded. Tchr. exceptional children Colonial Sch. Dist., New Castle, Del., 1960-85; chmn. dept. spl. edn. George Read Sch., New Castle, Del., to 1985. Asst. prof. English and reading Del. Tech. Community Coll., Stanton, 1967—. Recipient Another Dream award, 1986, spl. award for Outstanding and Significant Contbn. in Edn., 1987. Mem. AAUW, NEA, Del. Edn. Assn., Nat. Music Educators Assn., Del. Music Educators Assn., Coun. Exceptional Children, Nat. Assn. Univ. Women (Woman of Yr. 1989, Wilmington Woman of Yr. 1989), Phi Delta Kappa (Book award 1991), Zeta Phi Beta. Home and Office: Tanglewood 4322 Bedrock Cir Apt 104 Baltimore MD 21236-5637

ALLEN, RONALD JAY, law educator; b. Chgo., July 14, 1948; s. J. Matteson and Carolyn L. (Latchum) A.; m. Debra Jane Livingston, May 25, 1974 (div. 1982); children: Sarah, Adrienne; m. Julie O'Donnell, Sept. 2, 1984; children: Michael, Conor. BS, Marshall U., 1970; JD, U. Mich., 1973. Bar: Nebr. 1974, Iowa 1979, U.S. Ct. Appeals (8th cir.) 1980, U.S. Supreme Ct. 1981, Ill. 1986. Prof. law SUNY, Buffalo, 1974-79, U. Iowa, Iowa City, 1979-82, 83-84, Duke U., Durham, N.C., 1982-83, Northwestern U., Chgo., 1984—, John Henry Wigmore prof., 1992—. Pres. faculty senate U. Iowa, 1980-81. Author: Constitutional Criminal Procedure, 1985, 91, 95, An Analytical Approach to Evidence, 1989, Evidence: Text, Cases and Problems, 1997, Arthritis of the Hip and Knee: The Active Person's Guide to Taking Charge, 1998, Comprehensive Criminal Procedure, 2001, Evidence: Text, Problems, Cases, 2002; contbr. articles to profl. jours. Mem. ABA (rules com. criminal justice sect.), Am. Law Inst. Office: Northwestern U Sch Law 357 E Chicago Ave Chicago IL 60611-3059 E-mail: rjallen@northwestern.edu.

ALLEN, ROSE LETITIA, special education educator; b. Dayton, Ohio, Oct. 10, 1960; d. Billie Wesley and Elisabeth Julia (Coler) Taylor; m. Randolph Eugene Allen, June 27, 1987; 1 child, Michelle Elisabeth. BSN, Wright State U., 1982; MS in Edn., U. Bridgeport, 1987. Cert. elem., K-12 handicapped edn., developmentally handicapped and specific LD tchr. Tchr. Hawaii Dept. of Edn., Honolulu, 1989-91; substitute tchr. Montgomery County Bd. Mental Retardation and Devel. Disabilities, Dayton, Ohio, 1993; tchr. Dayton Pub. Schs., 1994—. Mem. Faculty Coun., Dayton, 1994-95. 2d lt. USAF, 1983-84. Mem. AAUW, Alpha Xi Delta. Home: 2421 Orange Ave Dayton OH 45439-2839 E-mail: rose@joyrose.com.

ALLEN, STEVEN GLEN, economics and business educator; b. Louisville, Mar. 17, 1952; s. Charles Freeman and Lois (Crask) A.; m. Linda L. Pattison, May 19, 1978. BA in Math., Mich. State U., 1973, MA in Econs., 1974; PhD in Econs., Harvard U., 1978. Asst. prof. econs. and bus. N.C. State U., Raleigh, 1978—83, assoc. prof., 1983—87, prof., 1987—, dir. MS mgmt. program, 1993—2002, dir. MBA program, 2002—, assoc. dean grad. programs and rsch., 2003—. Rsch. economist Nat. Bur. Econ. Rsch., Cambridge, Mass., 1983-86, rsch. assoc., 1986—; mem. bd. reviewers Indls. Rels., Berkeley, Calif., 1989—. Contbr. articles to profl. jours. Recipient Allyn Young award Harvard Coll., 1975, 76, Disting. Rsch. and Lit. Publ. award Sch. Humanities and Social Scis., N.C. State U., 1986, Outstanding Rsch. award Coll. Mgmt., 1993; NSF grantee, 1984-86, 87-92, five-time U.S. Dept. Labor grantee; Fulbright scholar, 1991, 93. Mem. Am. Econ. Assn., Soc. Labor Economists, Econometric Soc. Office: NC State U PO Box 7229 Raleigh NC 27695-7229

ALLEN, SUZANNE, financial planning executive, insurance agent, writer; b. Santa Monica, Calif, May 31, 1963; d. Raymond A. and Ethel Allen; m. Steve Milstein Roth, Dec. 27, 1992, (div. 2000). BA, U. Calif., Santa Cruz, 1986; MA in Edn., Calif. State U., L.A., 1990; postgrad., Art Ctr. Sch. Design, Pasadena, Calif., 1994—. Cert. tchr., Calif.; lic. real estate agt., Calif. Interviewer LA Times Newspaper, 1986-88; educator LA Unified Sch. Dist., 1987-90, Burbank Unified Sch. Dist., Calif., 1990-94, 1994—; ptnr. fin. svc. Roth & Assoc./NY Life, LA, 1993-2000; educator Pasadena Unified Sch. Dist., 2001—02; ptnr. fin. svc. Pacific Life Ins. Co.; v.p. Jarvis & Mandell LLC Estate Planning Svc., Mass. Mut. Ins. Co., 2001—; agt. Mass. Mut. Ins., Beverly Hills, Calif. Ptnr. Retirement Educators Fin. Svc.; agt.-cons. Frasier Fin. Group, 2001—02. Model, actor :, 1998—; author: End of Days, 2001—; author: (pen name Quinn Allen) I Will Serve You All My Days, Black Dahlia, Alone, 2002, I Miss Him, 2003, (poem) Waiting for Godot, 2003. Mem. PTA, United Tchr. Pasadena, Civil War Trust; vol. SPCA/Humane Soc., 1999—; mem. Nat. Trust Hist. Preservation, Honor Roll mem.; bd. mem. Bungalow Heaven Neighborhood Assn.; hon. mem. Top Bus. Rep. Party for Sen. Tom Delany. Recipient 3 Silver Cups, Internat. Poet of Merit, 5 Bronze medal, Internat. Poets Soc., Silver Outstanding Achievement in Poetry Trophy, 2003, 2 silver trophies for outstanding achievement in poetry, 2003, Piece of the Roof award, N.Y. Life Ins. Co. for Roth & Assocs., 1994, Nat. Leadership award, Nat. Rep. Congl. Com., 2003. Mem.: NEA, Libr. of Congress, Nat. Soc. for Hist. Preservation, Burbank Tchrs. Union, Internat. High IQ Soc., Abraham Lincoln Assn., Internat. Soc. Poets (hon.). Avocations: painting, illustrating, writing, weight training, old house renovation. Office: Jarvis & Mandell LLC 1875 Century Park E # 1550 Los Angeles CA 90067 also: Michael's Agy Mass Mut Beverly Hills Office 1875 Century Park E # 1550 Los Angeles CA 90067

ALLEN, THOMAS WESLEY, medical educator, dean; b. Chgo., Sept. 13, 1938; s. Thomas and Helen Irene (Spitler) A.; m. Annette Faye Power, June 23, 1962 (div. 1988); children: Roderick Nelson, Andrea Jane; m. Keith Mayo Capen, Oct. 16, 1988; 1 stepchild, Hilary Tate Cox. BA, Ottawa (Kans.) U., 1960; DO, Midwestern U., Chgo., 1964; DHL (hon.), U. New Eng., Biddeford, Maine, 1989. Diplomate internal medicine with subspecialty in pulmonary medicine, Am. Osteo. Bd. Internal Medicine. Intern Met. Hosp., Grand Rapids, Mich., 1964-65; resident in internal medicine Hosps. Chgo. Coll. Osteo Medicine, 1965-68; fellow in pulmonary medicine Northwestern U., 1969-70; from asst. to prof. medicine Chgo. Coll. Osteo. Medicine, 1968-87; pvt. practice Chgo., 1970-78; dean and v.p. acad. affairs and prof. medicine Midwestern U. Coll. Osteo. Medicine, Chgo., 1978-87; assoc. dean for acad. and clin. affars, prof. medicine U. Medicine and Dentistry of N.J. Coll. of Osteo. Medicine, 1987-91; provost, dean, prof. medicine Okla. State U. Coll. Osteo. Medicine, Tulsa, 1991-99, v.p. for health affairs, dean, 1999—. Mem. Nat. Adv. Coun. on Nat. Health Service Corps, Washington, 1994-97, Nat. Adv. Coun. on Health Professions Edn., Washington, 1986-90. Editor-in-chief Jour. Am. Osteo. Assn., 1987-98. Civic unit chair Tulsa Area United Way, 1995, health unit chair, 2000; trustee Village of Western Springs, Ill., 1981—85. Col. USAR, 1988—. Recipient Outstanding Achievement award, Chgo. Coll. Osteo. Medicine Alumni Assn., 1993, Phillips medal, Ohio U., 2001. Fellow Am. Coll. Osteo. Internists, Am. Coll. Chest Physicians; mem. Am. Osteo. Assn., Am. Assn. Colls. Osteo. Medicine, Am. Osteo. Acad. Sports Medicine, Am. Coll. Sports Medicine, Phi Kappa Phi. Episcopalian. Avocations: running, horseback riding. Home: 8911 S Florence Pl Tulsa OK 74137-3333 Office: Okla State Univ College Osteopathic Med 1111 W 17th St Tulsa OK 74107-1800

ALLEN, VICKI LYNETTE, physical education educator; b. Denver, Oct. 27, 1952; d. Donald Joseph and Jacqueline (Jones) Roth; m. Robert Craig Allen, Aug. 14, 1976; children: Jeffrey, Gregory, Stacy. BA magna cum laude, Calif. State U., Northridge, 1974; MEd summa cum laude, U. Nev., Las Vegas, 1987. Cert. tchr., Nev. Tchr. phys. edn., jr. varsity basketball coach Beverly Hills (Calif.) Unified Sch. Dist., 1975-78; tchr. secondary phys. edn. Clark County Sch. Dist., Las Vegas, 1978-89, elem. tchr. phys. edn., 1989-96, 2001—, basketball coach, 1988-89, tchr. on spl. assignment in phys. edn., 1997—2001. Adj. instr. U. Nev., Las Vegas, 1993-97; mem. phys. fitness task force Clark County Sch. Dist., 1990-91, integrated curriculum task force, 1992-93, task force on assessment, 1996-97. task force on curriculum revision, 1998-2000; mem. Nev. State Bd. Edn. team to write Stds. for Phys. Edn., 1999; mem. Nev. State Dept. Edn. com. to set stds. for phys. edn. tchr. licensure, 1993. Author phys. fitness and multicultural games publs.; mem. editl. bd. Teaching Elem. Phys. Edn., 1995-97. Coach Nev. State Youth Soccer Orgn., Las Vegas, 1988-91, Am. Youth Soccer Orgn., 1992; eucharistic min. St. Thomas More Cath. Ch., Las Vegas, 1991—; core leader for youth group, Las Vegas, 1994-95; mem. Nat. Charity League, 1998-02. Named Nev. Elem. Phys. Educator of Yr., 1996-97; Jr. League Nev. grantee, 1991. Mem. NEA, AAHPERD, Nev. Assn. Health, Phys. Edn., Recreation and Dance (pres. 2000-02), So. Nev. Assn. for Health, Phys. Edn., Recreation and Dance (bd. dirs. 1988-2003), Nat. Charity League, Phi Kappa Phi. Avocations: camping, weight lifting, reading, crafts, hiking. Office: Walter Bracken Magnet Sch 1200 N 27th St Las Vegas NV 89101

ALLEN, WANDA RUTH, secondary school educator; b. Savannah, Tennesse, Sept. 16, 1957; d. Curtis Eugene and Vada Ruth (Gilham), Waller; m. Ricky Lee Allen, May 25, 1980; 1 child, Tyler Lee. BA in English, BA in history, U. Tenn., Martin, 1979; MA in history, Murray State U., 1992. Cert. secondary tchr., history, English, polit. sci., and psychology, Tenn. Tchr. Big Sandy HS, Benton County Bd. Edn., Tenn., 1980-81, Briarwood Jr. HS, Benton County Bd. Edn., 1981-83; tchr., chair social studies dept. Camden Ctrl. HS, Benton County Bd. Edn., 1984—. Author: Benton County's Sesquicentennial, 1986. Pres. Cumberland Presbyn. Women, 1990—; Benton County Arts Coun., Camden, 1992—. Named Outstanding History Tchr., DAR, 1992, 2003. Mem. NEA, Nat. Coun. Social Studies (com. on nat. conv.), Tenn. Edn. Assn., Tenn. Coun. Social Studies, Benton County Geneal. Assn. (Outstanding Tenn. Social Studies Tchr. 1998), Benton County Reading Assn., Lions (sec. Camden 1985—, Lioness of the Decade 1995), Phi Kappa Phi. Republican. Avocations: travel, reading, photography, writing, sewing. Home: 530 Kelly Rd Holladay TN 38341-2432

ALLEN, WILLIAM CECIL, physician, educator; b. LaBelle, Mo., Sept. 8, 1919; s. William H. and Viola O. (Holt) A.; m. Madge Marie Gehardt, Dec. 25, 1943; children: William Walter, Linda Diane Allen Deardeuff, Robert Lee, Leah Denise Rogers. AB, U. Nebr., 1947, MD, 1951; M.P.H., Johns Hopkins U., 1960. Diplomate Am. Bd. Preventive Medicine. Intern Bishop Clarkson Meml. Hosp., Omaha, 1952; practice medicine specializing in family practice Glasgow, Mo., 1952-59; specializing in preventive medicine Columbia, Mo., 1960—; dir. sect. chronic diseases Mo. Div. Health, Jefferson City, 1960-65; asst. med. dir. U. Mo. Med. Ctr., 1965-75; assoc. coordinator Mo. Regional Med. Program, 1968-73, coordinator health programs, 1969—, clin. asst. prof. community health and med. practice, 1962-65, asst. prof. community health and med. practice, 1965-69, assoc. prof., 1969-75, prof., 1975-76, prof. dept. family and community medicine, 1976-87, prof. emeritus, 1987—. Cons. Mo. Regional Med. Program, 1966-67, Norfolk Area Med. Sch. Authority, Va., 1965-66; governing body Area II Health Systems Agy., 1977-79, mem. coordinating com., 1977-79; founding dir. Mid-Mo. PSRO Corp., 1974-79, dir., 1976-84. Contbr. articles to profl. jours. Mem. Gov.'s Adv Council for Comprehensive Health Planning, 1970-73; trustee U. Mo. Med. Sch. Found., 1976— . Served with USMC, 1943-46. Fellow Am. Coll. Preventive Medicine, Am. Acad. Family Physicians (sci. program com. 1972-75, commn. on edn. 1975-80), Royal Soc. Health; mem. Mo. Acad. Family Physicians (dir. 1956-59, 76-82, alt. del. 1982-87, pres. 1985-86, chmn. bd. 1986-87), Mo. Med. Assn., Howard County Med. Soc. (pres. 1958-59), Boone County Med. Soc. (pres. 1974-75), Am. Diabetes Assn. (pres. 1978, dir. 1974-77), Mo. Diabetes Assn. (pres. 1972-73), Soc. Tchrs. Family Medicine, AMA, Mo. Public Health Assn., Am. Heart Assn. (program com. 1979-82), Am. Heart Assn. of Mo. (sec. 1980-81), Mo. Heart Assn. (sec. 1979-82, pres.-elect 1982-84, pres. 1984-86). Methodist. Office: U Mo M218 Medical Ctr Columbia MO 65203

ALLEN, YVONNE, principal; Elem. sch. tchr.; vocat.-tech. instr.; adj. prof. Lambrith U.; prin. Whiteville (Tenn.) Elem. Sch. Recipient Nat. Educator award, Milken Family Found., 1996. Mem.: West Tenn. Assn. Elem. Schs. (past pres.), Nat. Assn. Elem. Sch. Prins., Nat. Bd. for Profl. Tchg. Stds. (bd. mem., past pres.). Office: Whiteville Elem Sch Hwy 100 Box 659 Whiteville TN 38075*

ALLENSWORTH, DIANE DEMUTH, academic association director; b. Defiance, Ohio, Nov. 14, 1941; d. Joseph Gordon and Edith Geraldine (Smith) DeMuth; m. John Michael Allensworth, Aug. 25, 1962; children: Elizabeth, Elaine. Diploma, Parkview Meth. Sch. Nursing, Ft. Wayne, Ind., 1962; BS in Health Edn., Kent State U., 1973, MA in Health Edn., 1975, PhD in Health Edn., 1983. Cert. health edn. specialist, RN, Ohio. Staff nurse operating rm. Robinson Meml. Hosp., Ravenna, Ohio, 1962-64, 69-71, operating rm. insvc. educator, 1971-72; vol. rural health edn. Peace Corps., Panama, 1964-66, cons., staff mem. tng. program Brockport, N.Y., 1967-69; sch. health nurse Pub. Health Dept. Paulding, Ohio, 1966-67; instr., asst. prof. Kent (Ohio) State U., 1975-85, assoc. prof. health edn., 1986-95; assoc. exec. dir. programs Am. Sch. Health Assn., Kent, 1990-94, exec. dir., 1995—97; br. chief program devel. divsn. adolescent and sch. health Ctr. for Disease Control, Atlanta, 1997—2001; exec. dir. Kids Health, Atlanta, 2002—. Co-author: Schools & Health, 1977, Building Effective Coalitions, 1994, Healthy Students 2000, 1994, School Health in America, 1981, 3d edit., 1989; editor Jour. Sch. Health, 1987. Vol. instr. ARC, Kent, 1975-79, Amigos de Las Americas, Kent, 1973-76. Mem. APHA, ASCD, Am. Sch. Health Assn. (pres. 1986), Internat. Union Health Educators (membership com. 1992-93), Assn. Advancement Health Edn. (bd. dirs. 2002—), Phi Delta Kappa. Avocations: gardening, cafe sitting, reading, traveling. Office: Kids Health 1655 Tullie Cir NE Atlanta GA 30329

ALLEY, MARY DEAN BREWER, medical foundation executive; b. Columbia, S.C., Oct. 23, 1942; d. Barney Frank and Mary Mattie (Mathis) B.; m. George Thayer Alley. BA, Winthrop U., 1963; MA, U. S.C., 1971; EdD, U. Rochester, 1988. English tchr., dept. chmn. Irmo (S.C.) High Sch.,

1963-72; sch. dir. Columbia (S.C.) Jr. Coll., 1972-74; instr. Rochester (N.Y.) Inst. of Tech., 1975-78, asst. prof. mktg. and dir. career edn., 1978-84, dir. of devel., 1984-88, Boston U., 1988-89; v.p. of devel. Elmira (N.Y.) Coll., 1989-94; corp. v.p. McLeod Health, Florence, SC, from 1994; CEO McLeod Found., Florence, SC, from 1994. Ednl. cons. ITT, Bobbs-Merrill Pub., 1974-78; pres. Organizational Devel. Assocs., 1985—. Editorial Bd. mem. Jour. of Co-operative Edn., 1981-83, book reviewer, 1982; editor Pub. The Bottom Line, 1975-77, CareerLine, 1979. Dir. women's com. Rochester Philharm. Orch., Rochester, 1976—78; dir. Women's Career Ctr., Rochester, 1980—84, Women's Ctr. The So. Tier, 1993—94; active Arnot Art Mus., 1990—94; bd. dirs. Girl Scout Coun. Pee Dee Region, Inc., from 1996, pres., from 2001; active Susan B. Anthony Rep. Women, Rochester, 1975—77; bd. dirs. S.C. Planned Giving Coun., from 1997. Named to Women's Hall of Fame, 2000; recipient Mary Mildred Sullivan award, Winthrop U., 2001. Mem. Women's Studies Adv. Coun., N.Y. State Assn. Women in Higher Edn., Co. for Advancement and Support of Edn., Women in Devel., Nat. Commn. on Planned Giving S.C. Hosp. Assn., Assn. Healthcare Philanthropy, S.C. Women in Higher Edn., Leadership S.C. Class 1998, Rotary (Florence), Kappa Delta Pi, Omicron Delta Kappa. Episcopalian. Avocations: writing, reading, theatre, travel, antiques. Home: Florence, SC. Died Feb. 26, 2002.

ALLGOOD, MARILYN JANE, mathematics educator; b. Nebraska City, Nebr., Nov. 11, 1939; d. William Andrew and Margaret M. (Parriott) Tynon; m. Clyde Eldon Allgood, July 23, 1960; children: Steven, Teresa, Mark, Bret. BS in Edn., Peru (Nebr.) State Coll., 1960. Math/sci. tchr. Bratton-Union H.S., Humboldt, Nebr., 1960-62; math./physics tchr. Johnson (Nebr.) Brock H.S., 1963-64; math./sci. tchr. Lourdes Ctrl. H.S., Nebraska City, Nebr., 1968-72; math./computer tchr. Fremont-Mills Cmty. Sch., Tabor, Iowa, 1972—2002; substitute tchr. Nebraska City and Omaha, 2002—. Mem. NEA, Nat. Coun. Tchrs. Math., Iowa State Edn. Assn., Fremont-Mills Edn. Assn. Democrat. Roman Catholic. Avocations: cooking, sewing, gardening. E-mail: eallgood@neb.rr.com.

ALLIGOOD, ELIZABETH ANN HIERS, retired special education educator; b. W Palm Beach, Fla, Dec. 7, 1931; d. Hubert Victor and Ethel Ruth (Palmer) Hiers; m. Jesse LeRoy Alligood, Aug. 24, 1952; children: Stephen Leon, Larry Lamar, Miriam Ruth, Julia Ann, Carol Beth. AA, Norman Coll., 1951; BS in Edn., Valdosta State, 1978; postgrad., Columbus Coll., 1987, 92. Cert. tchr., Ga. Resource educator Irwin County Bd. Edn., Ocilla, Ga., 1969-71; dir. Sunny Dale Tng. Ctr., Ocilla, Ga., 1971-78, Green Oaks Tng. Ctr., Moultrie, Ga., 1978-81; tchr. Calhoun County Bd. Edn., Edison, Ga., 1978; cons. Am. Heart Assn., Columbus, Ga., 1984-86; tchr. Thomas County Bd. Edn., Thomasville, Ga., 1987-89, Muscogee County Bd. Edn., Columbus, Ga., 1989-94, Colquitt County Bd. Edn., Moultrie, Ga., 1994-97; ret., 1997. Founder Sunny Dale Tng. Ctr., 1969; mem. adv. bd. Columbus Specialized Preschool, 1985. Chairperson W. Ga. area Mental Health Adv. Coun., Columbus, 1986-87. Named to Honors Day, Sunny Dale Tng. Ctr., 1992. Mem. Civitan, 1980, (treas. 1997-1999), Assn. Retarded Citizens Ga. (bd. dir. at large 1977-78, state sec. 1980-81,), Ga. Assn. Educators, Norman Coll. Alumni Assn. (editor Normanlite 1998—). Democrat. Baptist. Avocations: bowling, computers, writing.

ALLIGOOD, MARY SALE, special education educator; b. Richmond, Va., Oct. 28, 1942; d. Charles Latané and Virginia Carter (Elmer) Sale; m. Frederick Marvin Alligood, Jr., June 12, 1965; children: Anne Hassell Alligood Tadlock, Frederick Carter. BA in Psychology, Mary Washington Coll., 1965; MEd in Spl. Edn./Learning Disabilities, Va. Commonwealth U., 1982. 2d grade tchr. West Columbia-Cayce Schs., Columbia, S.C., 1965-67; 3d/4th grade tchr. Riverside Sch., Richmond, Va., 1972-79; 1st/2d grade tchr. Steward Sch., Richmond, Va., 1979-83; learning disabilities tchr. Chesterfield County Schs., Richmond, Va., 1983-85; spl. edn. educator Powhatan (Va.) County Schs., 1985-96. Bd. dirs., sec., chair Redeemer Episcopal Day Sch., Midlothian, Va., 1992-97; mem., treas. Episcopal Ch. Women, Richmond, 1967—; mem. vestry Episcopal Ch. of Redeemer, Midlothian, 1975-78, 81-83, mem. search com., 1994, stewardship co-chair, 1996—. Mem. ASCD, Coun. for Learning Disabilities, Assn. for Children/Adults with Learning Disabilities, Powhatan County Edn. Assn. (pres. 1989-91), Delta Kappa Gamma (membership com., programs 1989-92, pres. 1996-98). Home: 2841 River Oaks Dr Midlothian VA 23113-2226

ALLING, NORMAN LARRABEE, mathematics educator; b. Rochester, N.Y., Feb. 8, 1930; s. Harold Lattimore and Merle (Kolb) A.; m. Katharine McPherson Page, Aug. 20, 1957; children: Elizabeth Larrabee, Margaret Tilden. BA, Bard Coll., 1952; MA, Columbia U., 1954, PhD, 1958. Lectr. math. Columbia U., 1955-57; asst. prof. math. Purdue U., 1957-62, assoc. prof., 1962-65; assoc. prof. math. U. Rochester, 1965-70, prof., 1970-93, prof. emeritus, 1993—. Lectr. math. MIT, Cambridge, 1962-64; vis. prof. U. Wüzburg, Fed. Republic Germany, 1971; rsch. on ordered groups and fields, surreal numbers, valuation theory, extensions of meromorphic function fields, Banach algebras of analytic functions and real algebraic curves. Author: Real Elliptic Curves, 1981, Analysis Over Surreal Number Fields, 1987; co-author: Foundations of the Theory of Klein Surfaces, 1971; contbr. articles to profl. jours. Postdoctoral fellow NSF, 1961-62; sr. postdoctoral fellow, 1964-65 Mem. Am. Math. Soc. Home: 215 Sandringham Rd Rochester NY 14610-3450

ALLIO, ROBERT JOHN, management consultant, educator; b. N.Y.C., Sept. 1, 1931; s. Albert Joseph and Helen (Gerbereux) A.; m. Barbara Maria Littauer, Oct. 3, 1953; children: Mark, Paul, David, Michael. BMetE, Rensselaer Poly. Inst., 1952; MS, Ohio State U., 1954; PhD, Rensselaer Poly. Inst., 1957. Mgr. advanced materials Gen. Electric Co., Schenectady, 1957-60; sr. staff AEC, Washington, 1962; engring. mgr. atomic power div. Westinghouse Corp., Pitts., 1962-68; dir. corp. planning Babcock & Wilcox, N.Y., 1968-75; v.p. Can. Wire Co., Toronto, Ont., 1975-78; pres. Canstar Communications, Toronto, 1976-78; sr. staff mem. Arthur D. Little Co., Cambridge, Mass., 1978-79; dean Rensselaer Poly. Inst. Sch. Mgmt., Troy, N.Y., 1981-83; pres. Robert J. Allio and Assoc., Providence, 1979—; prof. mgmt. Babson Coll, Wellesley, Mass., 1984—; mng. dir. Anasazi Group, 2000—. Bd. dirs. Fourth Shift, Springboard Software, GardenWay, NICON, TBS Funding Corp., Infantelligence; chmn. bd. TracRac Inc. Author: Corporate Planning: Techniques and Applications, 1979, Corporate Planning, 1985, The Practical Strategist, 1988, Leadership Myths and Realities, 1999, The Seven Faces of Leadership, 2003; editor Planning Rev. Jour.; contbg. editor Strategy and Leadership Jour. Mem.: Planning Forum (pres. 1976—77). Office: 150 Chestnut St Providence RI 02903

ALLISON, BRENDA KAYE, special education educator, administrator; b. Clover, S.C., Dec. 19, 1952; d. Waddell and Georgia Elois (McDaniel) A. BA cum laude, Johnson C. Smith U., 1975; MEd, Coppin State Coll., 1978. Cert. educator, guidance counselor/adminstrn., pupil pers. worker, Md. Diagnostic/prescriptive tchr. Balt. City Pub. Schs., 1978-82, resource tchr., 1982-88, spl. edn. tchr., 1988-90, Balt. County Pub. Schs., Towson, Md., 1990-92; spl. edn. outreach tchr. Balt. County Pub. Schs., 1992—94, spl. edn. inclusion tchr., 1994—2000, mentor tchr., 2000—01, spl. edn. math tchr., 2001—, spl. edn. tchr., 1992—. GED testing proctor Md. State Dept. Edn., Balt., 1988—; home/hosp. tutor Balt. County Pub. Schs., 1991—. Notary Pub., Md. With USAF, 1990-91; with Md. Air N.G., 1991-95; USAFRES, 1995-. Mem. ASCD, Baltimore County Tchrs. Assn., Nat. Tchrs. Assn., Les Gemmes, Inc. Democrat. Methodist. Avocations: theater, reading, furniture refinishing, attending cultural arts events. Home: 1421 Druid Hill Ave Baltimore MD 21217-3423

ALLISON, GENEVIEVE J. business educator; b. Hot Springs, Ark., Apr. 13, 1939; d. Lester J. and Elva (Burdwell) Killingsworth; m. Gary G. Allison, July 7, 1962 (div. 1975); 1 child, Gary G. Allison, Jr.; m. John H. Wedin, Dec. 22, 1979. AA, Altus Jr. Coll., Okla., 1965; BS in Sec. Edn., S.W. Tex. State U., 1974; MBE, N. Tex. State U., 1979; postgrad., Tex. A&M. Clerical cluster instr. San Antonio Skill Ctr., 1974, 75; bus. tchr. E. Cen. High Sch., San Antonio, 1976-84; prof. adminstrv. computer tech. San Antonio Coll., 1984—; pres. V & G Contracting, Inc., 1988—. Cons. McGraw-Hill Pub. Co., 1986-87, Southwestern Pub. Co.; tutor San Antonio Literacy Coun., 1989-92; lead instr. microcomputers OCSTP, 1992-93, lead instr. microcomputer data entry, 1992—, lead instr. coop. work and keyboarding II and III. Contbg. editor: Grassroots, 1988. Treas. Trailwood Homeowners' Assn., 1994-96, v.p. 2001-; exec. bd. dirs. Leon Springs Vol. Fire Dept., 1996-99. Grantee LCD Visual Project, 1988-89, Can-Write Project, 1989-90; named Outstanding Collegiate Bus. Tchr. of the Yr. of Dist. 20, 1989-90, 99-2000; nominated for Minnie Piper Outstanding Teacher award, 1996. Mem. ASCD, AAUP (treas. 1989-92), Dist. 20 Tex. Bus. Educators Assn. (pres. 1985-86, dist. rep. 1990-2001), Tex. Cmty. Coll. Tchrs. Assn., Nat. Bus. Edn. Assn., Tex. Bus. Tchrs. Assn., Internat. Soc. Bus. Educators, Gold Key Club, Delta Pi Epsilon, Kappa Delta Pi. Republican. Baptist. Avocations: reading, gardening, square dancing, traveling, bowling. Office: San Antonio Coll 1300 San Pedro Ave San Antonio TX 78212-4201

ALLISON, HELEN THOMAS, retired primary school educator, author; b. Capleville, Tenn., June 2, 1916; d. Robert Younger Thomas and Bertha Frances Douglass; m. William W. Allison (div.). Student, U. Memphis. Cert. tchr. Tenn. Kindergarten tchr. Memphis Schs. Author: (book) Small Miracles, 1962, Little Elf Men and Fairies, 1984, Right Down Middle of Highway, 1994, P.S., 1996, Passenger Pigeons, 1997, Billy Butler, 1997, The Elf Man's Joke, 2000, Nine Lives of Midnite, 2001, Tendrils of Honeysuckle, 2001, Hatties Garden, 2002, The Jeweled Moments, 2003; contbr. short stories, poetry to numerous pubs. Active United Meth. Women, Memphis; vol. Womens Health Initiative, Memphis, 1993-99. Recipient Golden Owl award for versatility Tenn. State Nat. League Am. Pen Women, 1977, Poetry awards Writers Unltd., 1981, Fedn. Women's Clubs, 1980, 89, Miss. Poetry Soc., 1991, 92, numerous others. Mem. DAR, World Poetry Soc., Nat. League Am. Pen Women, Poetry Soc. of Tenn. (historian, Poetry awards 1959, 60, 61, 62, 65, 82, 88, Poet Laureate of Tenn. 1992-93), Wildflower Soc. Memphis, Huguenot Soc., Plantagent Soc., 17th Century Colonial Dames, N.Am. Royal Descent. Avocations: genealogy, gardening, sewing, needlepoint. Home: 3628 E Mallory Ave Memphis TN 38111-5204

ALLISON, JOAN KELLY, music educator, pianist; b. Denison, Iowa, Jan. 25, 1935; d. Ivan Martin and Esther Cecelia (Newborg) K.; m. Guy Hendrick Allison, July 25, 1954 (div. Apr. 1973); children: David, Dana, Douglas, Diane. MusB, St. Louis Inst. of Music, 1955; MusM, So. Meth. U., 1976. Korrepetitor Corpus Christi (Tex.) Symphony, 1963-85; staff pianist Am. Inst. Mus. Studies, Graz, Austria, 1974-89; prof. Del Mar Coll., Corpus Christi, 1976—2002. Adj. prof. Del Mar Coll., 1959-75, Corpus Christi State U., 1978-93, Tex. A&M U., Corpus Christi, 1993—; program dir. Corpus Christi Chamber Music Soc., 1986—; piano chmn. Corpus Christi Young Artists' Competition, 1987—; chmn. Del Mar Coll. Student Programs Com., 1986-88, 91-92, 94-95, 2001-02; chmn. radio com., S.Tex. Pub. Broadcasting Svc., Corpus Christi, 1987-88; asst. mus. dir. Little Theater, Corpus Christi, 1970-74; judge, Houston Symphony Auditions, 1988, S.C. Young Artist Competition, Columbia, 1990; freelance accompanist, 1955—, adjudicator, 1960—; v.p. united fac., Del Mar Coll., 1986-88; pianist with Del Mar Trio, 1965-95, Young Audiences, Inc., 1975-83; recital tours in U.S., Mex., Austria, 1954-88. Piano soloist, St. Louis Symphony, 1956, 57, Bach Festival Orch., St. Louis, 1955, Corpus Christi Symphony; recipient Artist Presentation award, Artist Presentation Soc., St. Louis, 1956; contbr. articles to profl. jours., including Internat. Piano Quar. Co-chmn. Mayor's Com. on Recycling, Corpus Christi, 1989-91; bd. dirs. Corpus Christi Symphony; adv. bd. Corpus Christi Concert Ballet; mem. steering com. cultural devel. plan City of Corpus Christi, 1995-96. Recipient Women in Careers award YWCA, 1985. Mem. Music Tchrs. Nat. Assn., Tex. Music Tchrs. Assn., Corpus Christi Music Tchrs. Assn., Liszt Soc. (contbr. to jour.). Avocations: foreign travel, water-skiing, hiking, acting in community theatre. Home: 4709 Curtis Clark Dr Corpus Christi TX 78411-4801 E-mail: Jallison@the-i.net.

ALLISON, LAIRD BURL, business educator; b. St. Marys, W.Va., Nov. 7, 1917; s. Joseph Alexander and Opal Marie (Robinson) A.; m. Katherine Louise Hunt, Nov. 25, 1943 (div. 1947); 1 child: William Lee; m. Genevieve Nora Elmore, Feb. 1, 1957 (dec. July 1994). BS in Personnel and Indsl. Relations magna cum laude, U. So. Calif., 1956; MBA, UCLA, 1958. Chief petty officer USN, 1936-51, PTO; asst. prof. to prof. mgmt. Calif. State U., L.A., 1956-83; asst. dean Calif. State U. Sch. Bus. and Econs., L.A., 1971-72, assoc. dean, 1973-83, emeritus prof. mgmt., 1983—. Vis. asst. prof. mgmt. Calif. State U., Fullerton, 1970. Co-authored the Bachelors degree program in mgmt. sci. at Calif. State U., 1963. Mem. U.S. Naval Inst., Navy League U.S. Ford Found. fellow, 1960. Mem. Acad. Mgmt., Inst. Mgmt. Sci., Western Econs. Assn. Internat., World Future Soc., Am. Acad. Polit. Social Sci., Calif. State U. Assn. Emeriti Profs., Calif. State U. L.A. Emeriti Assn. (program v.p. 1986-87, v.p. adminstrn. 1987-88, pres. 1988-89, exec. com. 1990-91, treas. 1991—), Am. Assn. Individual Investors, Am. Assn. Ret. Persons, Ret. Pub. Employees Assn. Calif. (chpt. sec. 1984-88, v.p. 1989, pres. 1990-92), Am. Legion, Phi Kappa Phi, Beta Gamma Sigma, Alpha Kappa Psi. Avocations: history, travel, photography, hiking. Home: 2176 E Bellbrook St Covina CA 91724-2346 Office: Calif State U Dept Mgmt 5151 State University Dr Los Angeles CA 90032-4226

ALLISON, MICHAEL DAVID, space scientist, astronomy educator; b. Salem, Ill., Oct. 11, 1951; s. James M. and Claudine K. A.; m. Siri Wannamaker, Feb. 4, 1984; children: Hilary Kirstyn, Christopher Caleb. AB in Physics and English, Wittenberg U., 1973; SM in Physics, U. Chgo., 1976; PhD in Space Physics and Astronomy, Rice U., 1982. Resident rsch. assoc. Nat. Rsch. Coun. NASA/Goddard Inst for Space Studies, N.Y.C., 1981-83, space scientist, 1984—. Guest lectr. Am. Mus. Natural History, Hayden Planetarium, N.Y.C., 1984-88, 94—; mem. joint sci. working group for the NASA/ESA assessment study of the Cassini mission to Saturn and Titan, 1984-89; adj. prof. astronomy Columbia U., N.Y.C.- 1987—; co-investigator Huygens, Titan Doppler Wind Expt., U. Bonn., Germany, 1990—, team mem. Cassini Radar investigation, NASA, 2000—; rsch. assoc. Am. Mus. Dept. Astronomy, 1997-99. Co-editor: (conf. proceedings) The Jovian Atmospheres, 1986; contbr. articles to profl. jours. including Science, Icarus, Jour. of Atmospheric Scis., Geophys. Rsch. Letters, Planetary and Space Sci. Participating scientist Mars Observer and Surveyor '98 Missions, NASA, 1992-99. Mem. Am. Astron. Soc. (divsn. for planetary scis.), Am. Meteorol. Soc. Achievements include research in planetary atmospheric dynamics and meteorology, application of potential vorticity homogenization to planetary zonal circulation studies, first identification of Saturn's polar hexagon as a planetary Rossby wave, inference of a probable super-solar abundance of water on Jupiter based on the diagnostic analysis of equatorial waves. Home: 81 Teller Ave Beacon NY 12508-3067 Office: NASA/Goddard Inst Space Studies 2880 Broadway New York NY 10025-7848 E-mail: mallison@giss.nasa.gov.

ALLISON, ROBERT HARRY, school counselor; b. Hazleton, Pa., Oct. 26, 1952; s. Harry John and Loretta Ida (Henry) A. m. Barbara Joyce Ent, Oct. 28, 1978; 1 child, Diane Amy. BS in Rehab. Edn., Pa. State U., 1974; MS in Counselor Edn., U. Scranton, 1976; supervisory cert., Shippensburg (Pa.) U., 1981; principal's cert., Pa. State U., 1992, cert. in coop. edn., 1999. Work experience coord. Carbon County Area Vocat.-Tech. Sch., Jim Thorpe, Pa., 1974-75; rehab. counselor R.B. Nipon Assn., Phila., 1975-76; career svcs. coord. Sleighton Sch., Lima, Pa., 1976-77; sch. counselor West Perry Sch. Dist., Loysville, Pa., 1977-79; counselor/coord. Alternative Sch. Mifflin County Sch. Dist., Lewistown, Pa., 1979-80; elem. counselor Jersey Shore (Pa.) Sch. Dist., 1980-82; mid. sch. counselor, spl. edn. liaison, career edn. coord. Brandywine Heights Sch. Dist., Topton, Pa., 1982-90, mid.-elem. counselor, 1990-93, sch.-to-work transition/elem. counselor, 1994-2000; career counselor, sch.-to-work transition coord., 2000—; regional mgr. Primorica Fin. Svcs., 1985—. Bd. dirs. Weatherly Area Jaycees, 1974-75; asst. dist. commr. Boy Scouts Am., 1977-83, asst. dist. commr. for exploring, 1990-94, dist. com. mem. 1994-96. Mem. Am. Sch. Counselors Assn., Assn. for Career and Tech. Edn., Pa. Coop. Edn. Assn., Pa. Sch. Counselors Assn., Phi Kappa Phi. Lutheran. Home: 104 W Jackson St Fleetwood PA 19522-1706 Office: Brandywine Heights HS PO Box 98 Mertztown PA 19539 E-mail: rha1952@ptdprolos.net., roball@bhasd-k12.pa.us.

ALLOTTA, JOANNE MARY, elementary education educator; b. Bklyn., Dec. 8, 1962; d. Joseph and Adela (Castagna) A.; m. Edward James Cirminiello, Mar. 23, 1991. BA in Child Study, St. Joseph's Coll., 1984; MS in Edn., Bklyn. Coll., 1987; postgrad., 1987-88; advanced cert., Bklyn. Coll. Cert. tchr., NY, sch. dist. adminstr., NY; provisional cert. sch. adminstr. and supr., NY. Tchr. Holy Family Sch., Bklyn., 1984—85; elem. tchr. Pub. Sch. 97, Bklyn., 1985—2001, cooperating tchr. for srs. majoring in edn., 1985—2001; curriculum writer for profl. devel. Sch. Dist. 21, N.Y.C., 1991—, program facilitator gifted program Bklyn., 2001—. Workshop presenter; reviewer N.Y.C. Bd. Edn., Bklyn, 1992; mem. task force com. N.Y. Partnership for Statewide Systems Change-Dist. 21, 1993-95; textbook reviewer grade 4 social studies Scott Forseman, 2002-03. Active Pub. Sch. 97 PTA, 1985-2001; fund raiser St. Jude's Children's Hosp., 1990-2001. Recipient Tchr. of Yr. award Phi Delta Kappa, 1994, Tchr. of Yr. award Pub. Sch. 97, 1999. Mem. ASCD, Am. Fedn. Tchrs., United Fedn. Tchrs., N.Y. State of United Tchrs., Kappa Delta Pi. Roman Catholic. Avocations: reading, writing, needlepoint. Office: Cmty Sch Dist 21 521 West Ave Brooklyn NY 11224

ALLRED, RACHEL HALL, retired nurse, educator; b. Siler City, N.C., June 3, 1930; d. Homer Glenn and Artis (Brewer) Hall Sr.; m. Harold Hearthy Allred, June 28, 1952. Diploma, Watts Hosp. Sch. Nursing, 1951; BSN, The U. N.C., 1964, MPH, 1972; PhD, Walden U., 1991. Cert. occupational health nurse. Pub. health nurse Dist. Health Dept., Siler City, N.C., 1963-67; supr. oper. rm. Chatham Hosp., Siler City, 1955-61, 67-70; supr., inservice instr. Moore Meml. Hosp., Pinehurst, N.C., 1971; lectr. The U. N.C., Greensboro, 1972-74, asst. prof. nursing, 1974-95, ret., 1995. Recipient Schering award, 1987. Mem. ANA, Am. Assn. Occupational Health Nurses (One of Great 100 Nurses N.C. 1991), Sigma Theta Tau, Alpha Delta Kappa. Home: 1611 W Raleigh St Siler City NC 27344-4226

ALLRED, RUEL ACORD, education educator; b. Spring City, Utah, Mar. 30, 1929; s. Reid Henderson and Anna Elizabeth (Acord) A.; m. Betty Brown Best, Sept. 3, 1954; children: Anita, Chad R., Lynette, Eileen, Brent B., Marie, Reid R. AA, Snow Jr. Coll., Ephraim, Utah, 1949; BS in Elem. Edn. with honors, Brigham Young U., 1954, MS in Pers. and Guidance with honors, 1958; EdD in Elem. Edn., U. Oreg., 1965. Elem. sch. tchr. Provo City (Utah) Sch. Dist., 1958-61; elem. tchr. lab. sch. Brigham Young U., Provo, 1961-62, writer curriculum materials lab. sch., 1962-63, prin. elem. lab. sch., 1963-64, clin. instr. elem. edn., 1965-66, asst. prof., 1966-68; assoc. prof., 1968-73; prof. Brigham Young U., Provo, Utah, 1973-94, prof. emeritus, 1994—; grad. coord. elem. edn., 1971-78; assoc. dean coll. edn. Brigham Young U., Provo, 1988-92. Test adminstr. Provo City Sch. Dist., 1958; vis. asst. prof. U. Mo., St. Louis, 1966; vis. lectr. U. Alaska, Anchorage, 1974, 76; cons. in field, 1967—. Author: Spelling: The Application of Research Findings, 1977, Spelling Trends, content, and Methods, 1984, 2nd edit., 1987; co-author: The Sucher-Allred Reading Placement Inventory, 1972, 2nd edit., 1981, Continuous Progress in Spelling: An Individualized Spelling Program, 1972, 2nd edit., 1977, 3rd edit., 1982, Keys to Spelling Mastery: A Basal Spelling Program for Schools: Grades 1-8, 1981, 2nd edit., 1984. Microspell: A Comprehensive Computer Spelling Program for Schools: Grades 2-8, 1984, AEC Spelling: A Spelling Program for the Home: Grades 2-8, 1984, The Computer and Education, 1984, 2nd edit., 1991, McGraw Hill Spelling Grades 1-8, 1990. Missionary Netherlands Mission LDS Ch., 1949-52, Hawaii Honolulu Mission, 1998—; mission pres. Belgium Antwerp Mission LDS Ch., 1978-81; bd. dirs. Provo City Libr., 1984-89. Lt. USAF, 1955-57. Recipient Disting. Svc. award Brigham Young U. Alumni Assn., 1976, Karl G. Maeser Disting. Teaching award, 1977; Outstanding Alumnus award Snow Jr. Coll., 1988. Mem. Phi Kappa Phi, Phi Delta Kappa. Home: 1067 N Grand Ave Provo UT 84604-3009

ALLSBROOK, OGDEN OLMSTEAD, JR., retired economics educator; b. Wilmington, NC, July 1, 1940; s. Ogden Olmstead Sr. and Elizabeth Barringer (Warren) A. BA, Wake Forest U., 1962; PhD, U. Va., 1966. Ops. rsch. analyst Dep. Def., Washington, 1966-68; asst. prof. econs. U. Ga., Athens, 1968-73, dir. grad. studies econs., 1971-81, assoc. prof., 1974-96, ret., 1996. Author: Utilization of Military Resources, 1969; contbr. articles to profl. jours. Capt. U.S. Army, 1966-68. Mem. AAUP, Nat. Soc. SAR (pres. Athens chpt. 1992-94), Cape Fear Club, So. Econ. Assn. Lutheran. Avocations: motor sports, philately, turned wood objects, numismatics, Japanese cloisonne. Home: 115 Tillman Ln Athens GA 30606-4115 E-mail: ooalls1@wmconnect.com.

ALLSHOUSE, ROBERT HAROLD, history educator; b. Erie, Pa., Apr. 30, 1940; s. Harold and Anne Marie (Dranzek) A.; m. Marcia Catherine Windsor, Aug. 17, 1963; children: Lisa Catherine, Heather A. Kenny, Todd Anthony. BBA, Cleve. State U., 1963; MA, Case Western Res. U., 1965, PhD, 1967. Instr. Russian history Alliance Coll., Cambridge Springs, Pa., 1966-67, Gannon U., Erie, 1967-70, asst. prof., 1970-77, assoc. prof., 1977-82, prof., 1982—, chmn. dept. history, 1981-89, grad. dir. social sci., 1977-96, faculty senate, v.p., 2001—02, pres., 2002—; sec., treas. Gt. Lakes Pen Sales, Inc., Erie, 1976-98; pres. Allegheny Internat. Devel. Inc., Erie, 1990—; sec., treas. Pennfoil Tech. Inc., Erie, 1993—2001. Vis. prof. Latvian State U., Riga, 1991; mem. fgn. trade com. Erie Excellence Coun., 1992—2002. Author: Aleksander Izvolskii and Russian Foreign Policy, 1910-1914, 1977; editor: A Select Bibliography of Military History Since 1715, 1977, Photographs for the Tsar, 1980 (Photog. Soc. N.Y. Merit award 1980); gen. editor A Centennial History of the Erie Yacht Club, 1996. Mem. adv. bd. United Way, Erie, 1989-1996, Erie County Historic Preservation Bd., 1983-1990; pres. Erie Mus. Authority, 1985-87; bd. trustees Flagship Niagara League, 1998-2003, sec., 1999-2000, v.p., 2000-2002; v.p. faculty senate Gannon U., 1001-02, pres., 2002-03, trustee, 2002-03. Recipient Cmty. Edn. award Erie Sch. Dist., 1986, All Russian State TV award Russian State TV Co., Moscow, 1991, cert. of honor Assn. Ind. Video Prodrs., Russia, 1991, cert. of leadership All Union Inst. TV/Radio Broadcasting, Moscow, 1991, cert. of appreciation SAR, 1992. Fellow Phi Alpha Theta, Pi Gamma Mu; mem. Internat. Order Blue Gavel, Erie C. of C., Rotary Internat., Erie Yacht Club (fleet capt. 1988-89, rear commodore 1989-90, vice commodore 1990-91, commodore 1991-92, svc. award 1992). Avocations: sailing, travel. Office: Gannon U Perry Sq Erie PA 16541

ALLUMS, HENRIENE, elementary education educator; b. Jackson, Miss., July 30, 1945; d. Henry and Annie (Johnson) A. BA, Calif. State U., Long Beach, 1967; MA, U. San Francisco, 1978. Cert. elem., secondary tchr., Calif., ESL tchr., cross cultural, language and acad. devel. tchr. Tchr., grades 1-3 L.A. Unified Sch. Dist. Mem. Calif. Assn. bilingual Edn., Calig. Tchrs. English to Speakers of Other Langs., Internat. Reading Assn., Tchrs. English to Speakers of Other Langs. Home: 1522 E 123rd St Los Angeles CA 90059-2920

ALLWOOD, RHONDA MARIE, middle school educator; b. Boston, July 23, 1961; d. Kenneth Dudley and Lena Theodosia (Stewart) A.; 1 child, Hashabiah Y.O. Nelson. BA in Psychology, Coll. of the Holy Cross, 1982; MA in Indsl. Orgnl. Psychology, U. New Haven, 1986. Cert. elem. tchr., cert. tchr. psychology, N.J. Client relation mgr. People Express Airlines,

Newark, N.J., 1987; owner, operator Just Hearts Internat., West Haven, Conn., 1988-91; substitute tchr. West Haven Bd. of Edn., 1990-91, Newark Bd. of Edn., 1991-92, 8th grade math. tchr., 1992—. Cons. Homeschoolers, East Orange, N.J., 1993—. Mng. bd. dirs. YMCA, East Orange, 1994—. Recipient Very Important Parent award Clark Sch., 1993. Mem. Nat. Coun. Tchrs. Math., Assn. Math. Tchrs. N.J., Assn. Supervision and Curriculum Devel., Psi Chi. Avocations: reading, traveling, calistenics, textile-related crafts, cooking. Office: Thirteenth Ave Elem Sch 359 13th Ave Newark NJ 07103-2125

ALMAN, EMILY ARNOW, lawyer, sociologist; b. N.Y.C., Jan. 20, 1922; d. Joseph Michael and Cecilia (Greenstone) Arnow; B.A., Hunter Coll., 1948; Ph.D., New Sch. for Social Research, 1963; J.D., Rutgers U., Newark, 1977; m. David Alman, Aug. 1, 1940; children: Michelle Alman Harrison, Jennifer Alman Michaels. Bar: N.J. 1978, U.S. Supreme Ct. 1987. Probation officer, N.Y.C., 1945-48; assoc. prof. sociology Douglass Coll. Rutgers U., Newark, 1960-86, prof. emeritus, 1986—; sr. ptnr. Alman & Michaels, Highland Park, N.J., 1978—. Candidate for mayor, City of East Brunswick, 1972; chmn. Concerned Citizens of East Brunswick, 1970-78; pres. bd. trustees Concerned Citizens Environ. Fund., East Brunswick, 1977-78. Mem. ABA (com. family law) N.J. Bar Assn. (bd. dirs. legal svcs), Middlesex County Bar Assn. (Ann. Aldona Appleton award women lawyers sect. 1990, Ann. Svc. to Families award 1993), Am. Sociol. Assn., Assn. Fed. Bar State of N.J., Assn. Trial Lawyers Am., Trial Lawyers Assn. Middlesex County, Law and Soc. Assn., Am. Judicature Soc., Nat. Assn. Women Lawyers, N.J. Assn. Women Lawyers, ACLU, AAUP, Women Helping Women. Author: Ride The Long Night, 1963; screenplay, The Ninety-First Day, 1963. Home: 48 Timber Trace Ballston Spa NY 12020-3720

ALMEIDA, ARTIE N. music specialist; Music spec. Bear Lake Elem. Sch., Apopka, Fla., 1985—; tchr. U Ctrl. Fla., 1997—98, Seminole Cmty. Coll., 1995—, Valencia Cmty. Coll., 1992; dir. U. Ctrl. Fla., 1997—98. Music instr. four-day seminar, Taiwan. Author various music instruction books. Finalist Fla. Tchr. of Yr., 1998; named Music Educator of Yr., Fla., 1999, Seminole County Tchr. of Yr., 1999, School Level Tchr. of Yr., six times. Mem.: nat. Bd Profl. Tchg. Standards. Office: Bear Lake Elem Sch Music Dept 3399 Gleaves Ct Apopka FL 32703 Office Fax: 407-320-5599.

ALMEIDA, EVELYN, retired elementary education educator; b. Fall River, Mass., Nov. 21, 1924; d. Amelia (Enos) Almeida. BS in Edn., Bridgewater State Coll., 1946; attended graduate courses, R.I. Coll., 1950's; postgrad., Bridgewater State Coll., 1970's. Cert. elem. tchr., Mass. Elem. tchr. Swansea (Mass.) Sch. Dept., 1946-94; dir. elem. sch., glee club and drama dir. Luther and Stevens, Swansea, 1948-68; tchr. Brown Sch., Swansea, 1968-94. English as second lang. tchr. Fall River Diocesan Clergy, 1970—. Contbr. articles to profl. publs. Sec., treas. parish socs., St. Michael's Ch., Fall River, 1953-67, also pres., fundraising, dir. activities, parish sec. 1945-67, co-chairman golden jubilee Cath. Charities, sec., lector, 1986—, choir mem., tchr. spl. needs children Christian Doctrine Class; fundraiser Assn. for Devel. of Cath. U. of Portugal, Fall River, 1982-2000; bd. dirs. Swansea PTA, 1946-94; cons. Sch. Coun. Assn., Swansea, 1990-93; mem. Fall River Hist. Soc., 1990—; corr. sec. North End. Cmty. Devel. Assn., Fall River, 1987-94; bd. dirs. ednl. com. St. Michael's Fall River Credit Union, 1950's; instr. Fall River Playground, 1940's. Recipient Commonwealth of Mass. Ho. of Reps. citation, 1991, Portuguese Am. Fedn. citation, Classroom Excellence citation State House, Boston, Bristol County Commrs. of Mass. citation, Town of Swansea, proclamation, Hon. Mayor City of Fall River, citation, PTO Brown Sch. citation, Outstanding Tchg. citation City Coun. Fall River, Marian Medal, Bishop of Fall River, Mass. Diocese for Outstanding involvement is St. Michael's Parish activities Eucharistic Minister and Lector in Parish. Mem. AAUW (edn. role group 1970's), NEA, Mass. Tchrs. Assn., Portuguese Am. Fedn. (sec. 1987-90, bd. dirs. 1990-93, 94-97, Advancement of Portuguese Culture citation), Portuguese Am. Hist. Found. of Fall River (founding mem. bd. dirs. 1991-1998), Coimbra U. Club (v.p.), Cath. Woman's Club (mem. bd., auditor, scholarship com.), Arts Unltd., Bristol County Ret. Tchrs. Assn. of Mass., Friends of Fall River Pub. Libr., Bridgewater Coll. Alumni Assn., Sacred Heart Acad. Alumni Assn., Woman's Club, Fall River Garden Club, Delta Kappa Gamma. Roman Catholic. Avocations: U.S. and European travel, classical theatre, plays, musicals, piano, collecting foreign dolls, singing, directing glee clubs and plays.

ALMORE-RANDLE, ALLIE LOUISE, special education educator; b. Jackson, Miss, Apr. 20; d. Thomas Carl and Theressa Ruth (Garrett) Almore; m. Olton Charles Randle, Sr., Aug. 3, 1974. BA, Tougaloo (Miss.) Coll., 1951; MS in Edn., U. So. Calif., L.A., 1971; EdD, Nova Southeastern U., 1997. Recreation leader Pasadena Dept. Recreation, Calif., 1954-56; demonstration tchr. Pasadena Unified Sch., 1956-63; cons. spl. edn. Temple City Sch. Dist., Calif., 1967; supr. tchr. edn. U. Calif., Riverside, 1971; tchr. spl. edn. Pasadena Unified Sch. Dist., 1955-70, dept. chair spl. edn. Pasadena H.S., 1972-98, also adminstrv. asst. Pasadena HS, 1993-98, surrogate parent, 2001—; ind. rep. Am. Comm. Network, Inc., 1997—; surrogate parent Pasadena Unified Sch., Pasadena, Calif., 2001. Supr. Evelyn Frieden Ctr., U. So. Calif., LA, 1970; mem. Coun. Exceptional Children, 1993—; ednl. cons. Shelby Renee Ednl. Ctr., Gardena, Calif., 2000—. Organizer Northwest Project, Camp Fire Girls, Pasadena, 1963; leader Big Sister Program, YWCA, Pasadena, 1966; organizer, dir. March on The Boys' Club, the Portrait of a Boy, 1966; organized Dr. Allie's Book Mobile Project, 2002; pub. souvenir jours. Women's Missionary Soc., AME Ch., State of Wash. to Mo.; mem. NAACP, Ch. Women United, Afro-Am. Quilters LA, established Dr. Allie Louise Almore-Randle Scholarship Award, Pasadena HS, 1998; co-established Theressa Garrett Almore Music Scholarsip award Jackson State U., Jackson, Miss., 1989; founding mem. Cmty. Women of San Gabriel Valley, 1998, Women of Pasadena, 2002. Recipient Cert. of Merit, Pasadena City Coll., 1963, Outstanding Achievement award Nat. Coun. Negro Women, Pasadena, 1965, Earnest Thompson Seton award Campfire Girls, Pasadena, 1968, Spl. Recognition, Outstanding Cmty. Svc. award The Tuesday Morning Club, 1967, Dedicated Svc. award AME Ch., 1983, Educator of Excellence award Rotary Club of Pasadena, 1993, Edn. award Altadena NAACP, 1994; named Tchr. of Yr., Pasadena Masonic Bodies, 1967, Woman of the Yr. for Community Svc. and Edn., Zeta Phi Beta, 1992, Commendation, City of Pasadena; grad. fellow U. So. Calif., LA, 1970, recognition Uniformly Excellent Work and Exceptional Commitment and Dedication to Altadena/Pasadena Communities, Pasadena African Amer. Sch. Administr., 1998, Cert. Achievment in Educational Leadership, First AME Ch., 1998, Fran Cook Salute Great Inspiring Educator Award, United Tchr. of Pasadena, 1998, Named Outstanding Educator, Nat. Sorority Phi Delta Kappa, 1998. Mem. NAACP (life; bd. mem., chmn. ch. workers com. 1955-63, Fight for Freedom award West Coast region 1957, NAACP Edn. award Altadena, Calif. chpt. 1994), ASCD, Calif. Tchrs. Assn., Calif. African Am. Geneal. Soc., Nat. Coun. Negro Women, African Pan Am. Doctoral Scholars, L.A. World Affairs Coun., Phi Delta Gamma (hospitality chair 1971—), U. So. Calif. Alumni Assn. (life), Tougaloo Coll. Nat. Alumni Assn. (life), Phi Delta Kappa, Alpha Kappa Alpha (life, membership com.), Phi Delta Phi (founder, organizer 1961), Phi Delta Kappa. Democrat. Mem. Ame Ch. Avocations: wedding director, photography, gardening, family history. Home: 1710 La Cresta Dr Pasadena CA 91103-1261 Fax: 626-797-5549. E-mail: akainger@acninc.net.

ALMOUR, VICKI LYNN, elementary education educator; b. Oak Ridge, Tenn., May 22, 1954; d. Victor Glynnwood and Beverly Jane Harness; m. Gary Bruce Palmer, Sept. 5, 1981 (div. July 1989); m. Ralph Almour, Jan. 2, 1997. BA, E. Tex. State U., 1976; MEd, Seattle U., 1989. Cert. tchr. ESL, history, gifted edn., early childhood edn., elem. edn., Tex. Tchr. elem. Killeen (Tex.) Ind. Sch. Dist., 1979—84, specialist ESL, 1994—99; specialist child devel. U.S. Dept. of Def., Seoul, Republic of Korea, 1984-86; specialist gifted edn. Clover Park Sch. Dist., Tacoma, 1987-92, Round Rock (Tex.) Ind. Sch. Dist., 2000—. Recipient Outstanding ESL Tchr. award, Tex. TESOL, 1999. Mem. ASCD, Tex. Assn. Talented and Gifted (staff devel. presenter 1997—, Awareness cert. 1998). Methodist. Avocations: creative writing, aerobics, arts and crafts, travel, cultural studies. Home: 614 Thrush Dr Leander TX 78641-2963

ALOFSIN, ANTHONY, art historian, writer, educator; b. Memphis, June 22, 1949; s. Frederick Benjamin and Eleanor (Brodsky) A.; m. Patricia Tierney, June 5, 1993. AB magna cum laude, Harvard U., 1971, MArch with distinction, 1981; MPhil, Columbia U., 1983, PhD, 1987. Assoc. chmn. divsn. hist. preservation Columbia U., N.Y.C., 1983-84, adminstrv. dir., founder Ctr. Preservation Rsch., 1984-85; scholar-in-residence The Frank Lloyd Wright Found., 1984-85; asst. prof. architecture Columbia U., N.Y.C., 1984-86; from assoc. prof. to prof. architecture U. Tex., Austin, 1987—99, prof. art and art history, Roland Roessner Centennial prof., 1999—. Curator, organizer A Tense Alliance: Arch. Cen. Europe, Internat. Travelling Exhbn., 1993-96; dir. MS in archtl. studies, history and theory program and PhD program, U. Tex., Austin, 1987-97; cons., lectr., spkr. in field. Author: Frank Lloyd Wright: Lost Years 1910-1922, 1993, The Struggle for Modernism: Architecture Landscape Architecture and City Planning At Harvard, 2002; editor: Frank Lloyd Wright: An Index to the Taliesin Correspondence, 1988, Frank Lloyd Wright: Europe and Beyond, 1999; contbr. articles to lit. and profl. jours. Recipient Vasari award Dallas Mus. Art, 1989; Graham Found. for Visual Arts grantee, 1993; Santa Fe Workshop Contemporary Art scholar, 1971; Fulbright Professorship fellow Acad. Fine Arts, Vienna, Austria, 1989-90, fellow Internationales Forschungzentrum Kulterwissenshaften, Vienna, 1995, Ailsa Mellon Bruce Sr. fellow Casva Nat. Gallery Art, Washington, 2003—. Mem. Soc. Archtl. Hists., (nat. chpt., N.Y. chpt., Tex. chpt.), Coll. Art Assn., Fulbright Assn., U.S. Internat. Coun. Monuments and Sites, Phi Kappa Phi. Avocation: gardening. Home: 2207 Camino Alto Austin TX 78746-2436 Office: U Tex Sch Architecture Goldsmith Hall 2 308 Austin TX 78712-1160

ALOIA, ROLAND CRAIG, scientist, administrator, educator; b. Newark, Dec. 21, 1943; s. Roland S. and Edna M. (Mahan) A. BS, St. Mary's Coll., 1965; PhD, U. Calif., Riverside, 1970. Postdoctoral fellow City of Hope, Duarte, Calif., 1971-75; research biologist U. Calif., Riverside, 1975-76; asst. prof. Sch. of Medicine Loma Linda (Calif.) U., 1976-79; assoc. prof. Loma Linda (Calif.) U., 1979-89, prof. anesthesiology and biochemistry, 1989—. Chemist VA, Loma Linda, 1979-94, chief rsch. ops., 1994-99; pres., chmn. Loma Linda VA for Rsch. and Edn., 1988-94, pres., CEO, 1994-99. Editor: Membrane Fluidity in Biology, Vols. 1-4, 1983, 85; sr. editor: (series) Advanced in Membrane Fluidity vols. 1-3, 1988, vol. 4, 1989, vol. 5, 1991, vol. 6, 1992. Pres. Riverside chpt. Calif. Heart Assn., 1979-80, 1984-86, exec. com. mem., 1973-86, bd. dirs. 1978-86, v.p. 1984-86. Calif. Heart Assn. fellow, 1971-73. Mem. N.Y. Acad. Scis., Sigma Xi (pres. Loma Linda chpt. 1991-92, pres.-elect 1990-91). Avocations: flying, jogging, reading. Office: Dept Biochemistry Loma Linda U Loma Linda CA 92350

ALOTTA, ROBERT IGNATIUS, historian, educator, writer; b. Feb. 26, 1937; s. Peter Philip and Jean (Sacchetti) A.; m. Alice J. Danley, Oct. 1, 1960; children: Peter Anthony, Amy Louise. BA, LaSalle Coll., Phila., 1959; MA, U. Pa., 1981; PhD, Temple U., 1984. With Triangle Publs., Phila., 1956-67, merchandising mgr. Inquirer divsn., 1959-63, mgr. customer svc. Inquirer-Daily News, 1963-66, new bus. coord. Daily News, 1966-67; mgr. spl. projects Penn Cen. Transp. Co., Phila., 1967-72; dir. pub. info. Phila. Housing Authority, 1972-81; asst. prof. comms. Grand Valley State Coll., Allendale, Mich., 1981-84; from asst. prof. comm. to assoc. prof. Miss. State U., 1984-92; pres. Alotta Ink, 1992—. Prof., dean Sr. U., Ctr. Mil. Studies, 1996—; dir. edn. and info. svcs. Rockingham County Sheriff's Office, 1996—; adj. assoc. prof. Blue Ridge C.C., 1999—. Exec. prodr.: (TV series) The Kids Show, 1985-86; scriptwriter: (radio series) A Philadelphia Moment, 1982, Past/Prolog, 1976, other radio, TV series, 1969—; host: (TV series) Perceptions of War, 1988-89; co-host TV series Midweek, 1989, (radio show) Midday; narrator: (radio series) A Minute of Your Time, 1977-78; host, prodr.: (radio show) Point of View, 1996-98; Gimme a Break (radio show), 2001-. author: Street Names of Philadelphia, 1975, Stop the Evil, 1978, Old Names and New Places, 1979, A Look at the Vice President, 1981, Military Executions of the Union Army, 1861-1866, 1984, Civil War Justice, 1989, Mermaids, Monasteries Cherokees and Custer: The Story Behind Philadelphia's Street Names, 1990, Another Part of the Field: Philadelphia's Revolution, 1777-78, 1991, Signposts and Settlers: The History Behind the Place Names Beyond the Rockies, 1993, The Last Voyage of the Henry Bacon, 2001 (with Donald R. Foxvog), Margaret "Peggy" Eaton: The Innkeeper's Daughter, 2004; contbr. articles, book revs. to pubs. Pres. Shackamaxon Soc., 1967—; mem. pres.'s coun. LaSalle Coll., 1976-81. With Security Agy., AUS, 1960-61. chmn., Rockingtom Regional Triad, 1999-. Recipient Freedom Found. at Valley Forge awards, 1970, 73, 74, 76, Legion of Honor award Chapel of 4 Chaplains, 1975, Colonial Dames, DAR awards, 1976, Americanism award County Detectives Assn. Pa., 1977, 17 Web site design awards; Comdr.'s award and medal for pub. svc. U.S. Dept. Army, 2000. Mem. Am. Name Soc. (trustee 1982-84), Coun. on Am.'s Mil. Past (bd. dirs. 1984-88, 89-92), Mil. History Inst., Orgn. Am. Historians, Am. Hist. Assn., Cross Keys, Order of Sons of Italy (trustee 1983-84), Nat. Press Club (Washington), KC, Sigma Delta Chi (bd. dirs. Golden Triangle chpt. 1984-86), Tau Alpha Pi, Alpha Phi Omega. Home: 283 Newman Ave Harrisonburg VA 22801-4027 Office: Rockingham Co Sheriff 25 S Liberty St Harrisonburg VA 22801 E-mail: bob@alottaink.com.

ALPEN, EDWARD LEWIS, biophysicist, educator; b. San Francisco, May 14, 1922; s. Edward Lawrence and Margaret Catherine (Shipley) A.; m. Wynella June Dosh, Jan. 6, 1945; children: Angela Marie, Jeannette Elise. BS, U. Calif., Berkeley, 1946, PhD, 1950. Br. chief, then dir. biol. and med. scis. Naval Radiol. Def. Lab., San Francisco, 1952-68; mgr. environ. and life scis. Battelle Meml. Inst., Richland, Wash., 1968-69, assoc. dir., then dir. Pacific N.W. div., 1969-75; dir. Donner Lab., U. Calif., Berkeley; also assoc. dir. Lawrence Berkeley Lab., 1975-87; prof. biophysics emeritus U. Calif., Berkeley, 1975—, prof. radiology emeritus San Francisco, 1976—, dir. study ctr. London, 1988-90; councillor, dir. Nat. Council Radiol. Protection, 1969-92; exec. v.p., tech. dir. Neutron Tech. Corp., Berkeley, 1990-93. Mem. Gov. Wash. Council Econ. Devel., 1973-75; bd. dirs. Wash. Bd. Trade, 1973-76. Author books, papers, abstracts in field. Served to capt. USN, 1942-46, 50-61. Recipient Navy Sci. medal, 1962, Disting. Service medal Dept. Def., 1963, Sustaining Members medal Assn. Mil. Surgeons, 1971; fellow Guggenheim Found., 1960-61; sr. fellow NSF, 1958-59 Fellow: Calif. Acad. Scis.; mem.: Biophys. Soc., Radiation Rsch. Soc., Am. Philat. Soc., Bioelectromagnetics Soc. (pres. 1979—80), Sigma Xi (nat. lectr. 1994—96). Episcopalian. Home: 1101 Ivy Ct El Cerrito CA 94530-2745 E-mail: e.alpen@attbi.com.

ALPER, STEVEN IRA, principal; b. Phila., June 3, 1946; s. Norman and Regina (Silverman) A.; m. Sheila M. Sherlis; children: Randi, Adam. BS, Bloomsburg U., 1968; MA, Rider Coll., 1975. Head tchr. N.E. Bradford Sch. Dist., Rome, Pa., 1968-69; tchr. elem. sch. North Pa. Sch. Dist., Lansdale, 1969-72, Sch. Dist. Phila., 1972-76, adminstrv. asst., 1976-80, prin. elem. sch., 1980—. Camp dir. Variety Club, Phila., 1976-88; mem. tech. adv. bd. Sch. Dist. Phila., 1992-93. Mem. task force Am. St. Corridor, Phila., 1989—. Mem. Am. Camping Assn., Pa. Assn. Sch. Adminstrs., Bustleton Civic Assn., Bustelton Youth Assn., Golden Slipper Club and Charities (camp dir. 1988—), B'nai B'rith Educators Lodge (NYSA Youth award 1988). Avocations: tennis, baseball, camping. Home: 9981 Sandy Rd Philadelphia PA 19115-1706 Office: John Welsh Sch 2331 N 4th St Philadelphia PA 19133-2933

ALPERT, JOEL JACOBS, medical educator, pediatrician; b. New Haven, May 9, 1930; s. Herman Harold and Alice (Jacobs) A.; m. Barbara Ellen Wasserstrom, July 13, 1957; children: Norman, Mark, Deborah. AB, Yale U., 1952; MD, Harvard U., 1956. Diplomate Am. Bd. Pediatrics. Intern in medicine Children's Hosp. Med. Ctr., Boston, 1956-57, jr. asst. resident in medicine, 1957-58, chief resident for ambulatory svcs., fellow in medicine, 1961-62, from asst. to sr. assoc., 1962-72; exch. registrar St. Mary's Hosp. Med. Sch., London, 1958-59; from instr. to assoc. prof. Med. Sch., Harvard U., Boston, 1962-72, lectr., 1972; pediatrician in chief Boston City Hosp., 1972-92; prof. pediatrics and pub. health Boston U. Sch. Medicine, 2002—02, chmn. dept. pediatrics, 1972-93, also prof. sociomed. scis. and pub. health law, 1980—2002, prof. emeritus pediats. cmty. medicine and sociomed. scis., chmn. pediats., 2002—, prof. emeritus pub. health and health law, 2002—. Dozer vis. prof. Ben. Gurion Sch. Medicine, Beersheva, Israel, 1979; Raine Found. vis. prof. U. Western Australia, Perth, 1983; James and Jean Davis Prestige visitor U. Otago, Dunedin, New Zealand, 1995; cons. USPHS, 1972—, Children's Hosp., Boston, 1972; spl. cons. pres. N.Y.C. Health and Hosps. Corp., 1989; vis. prof. pediatrics Columbia Coll. Phys. and Surg., NYU Sch. Medicine; mem. med. adv. com. N.Y.C. Health and Hosps. Corp., 1989—. Author books, including: The Education of Physicians For Primary Care, 1974; also numerous papers Mem. Town Meeting, Winchester, Mass., 1970-72; mem. exec. com. Mass. Com. for Children and Youth, Boston, 1975-82; chmn. adv. com. Mass. Poison Info. System, Boston, 1980-92; bd. dirs. Med. Found., Boston, 1992—; cons. Commonwealth Fund and MEM Assocs., 1996—. Capt. U.S. Army, 1959-61. Recipient lifetime achievement award Mass. Poison Info. System, 1992, Hon. Mention Pub. Health Svc. award Pew Found., 1999, Pew Found. award for Achievement in Primary Care Edn.; numerous grants, 1965—; spl. fellow Nat. Ctr. Health Svcs. Rsch., London, 1971. Fellow: Royal Coll. Pediat. and Child Health (hon. 2000, U.K.), Am. Acad. Pediat. (v.p. 1997—98, pres. 1998—99, Job Lewis Smith award 1992); mem.: Mass. Assn. Pediat. Dept. Chmn. (chmn. 1976—78, 1981—93), Ambulatory Pediat. Assn. (pres. 1969, George Armstrong medal 1989, Lifetime Career Achievement award 2000, Pub. Policy and Advocacy award 2002), Philippine Ambulatory Pediat. Assn. (hon.), Soc. Pediat. Rsch., Am. Pediat. Soc., Inst. Medicine NAS (mem. governing coun. 1993—95, mem. bd. families and children 1993—95, mem. task force on future of primary care 1994—96), St. Botolph Club, Aescalapian Club, Harvard Club, Yale Club, Lancet Club, Alpha Omega Alpha. Jewish. Office: Boston U Sch Medicine Boston Med Ctr 91 E Concord St Boston MA 02118-2335 Home: 1802 Wisteria Way Wayland MA 01778

ALSBRO, DONALD EDGAR, health educator; b. Detroit, May 20, 1940; s. Oscar Edgar and Alice Eleanor (Roberts) A.; m. Sharon Marie Gildea, May 18, 1963; children: Laura Lynn, Steven Dieter, Alan Keith. BA, Western Mich. U., 1963; MA, Roosevelt U., 1973; MS, Ea. Mich. U., 1973; EdS, Western Mich. U., 1980; EdD, Wayne State U., 1988. Cert. health edn. specialist. Commd. 2d lt. U.S. Army, 1963, advanced through grades to col., 1989; instr. health Lake Michigan Coll., Benton Harbor, Mich., 1973-92. Developer "Dump Your Plump" nat. worksite wellness program; bd. dirs. Rainbow Wellness, Benton Harbor. With USAR, 1972-94. Named to Western Mich. U. ROTC Hall of Fame, 1991, Lake Michigan Coll. Hall of Fame, 2001. Mem. AAHPERD, Mich. Coun. for Phys. Fitness and Health, Assn. for Mil. Surgeons. Republican. Methodist. Avocations: walking, racquet sports, weight lifting, horses. Home: 942 Sierra Dr Benton Harbor MI 49022-3539

ALSBROOK, JAMES ELDRIDGE, journalist, educator; b. Kansas City, Mo., Nov. 28, 1913; s. Irving Adolphus and Elgeitha Dorothy (Stovall) A.; m. Brydie Rosetta Everett, June 6, 1942 (div. Dec. 1961); 1 child, James Eldridge Jr. BS, Kans. U., 1963, MS, 1964; PhD, U. Iowa, 1968. Reporter Kansas City (Kans.) Plaindealer, 1933-36; sports editor St. Louis Call, 1936-38; sports, theatricals editor Kansas City (Mo.) Call, 1938-40; copy editor, feature writer Afro-Am. Newspapers, Balt., 1940-42, 45-48; ghost writer Kansas City, Kans., 1948-61; reporter Courier-Jour., Louisville, 1963-65; dir. pub. rels. Cen. State U., Wilberforce, Ohio, 1968-71, prof., 1971-78, Ohio U., Athens, 1978-84, prof. emeritus, 1984—. Chain store owner, 1945-61; weekly columnist for 87 African-Am. newspapers, 1991—. Contbr. chpts. to books, and articles to profl. jours. With U.S. Army Signal Corps., Reserve, 1942-44. Mem. ASCAP, Assn. for Edn. in Journalism and Mass Comm., Nat. Assn. Black Journalists, Kappa Tau Alpha, Sigma Delta Chi. Avocations: study of history, contract bridge, hi-fi music, photography, grammar. Home: 902 Twining Ln Bosque NM 87006

ALSCHULER, ALBERT W. law educator; b. Aurora, Ill, Sept. 24, 1940; s. Sam and Winifred (King) Alschuler; m. Louise Evans Alschuler, Mar. 21, 1970 (div.); 1 child, Samuel Jonathan. BA, Harvard U, 1962, LLB, 1965. Bar: Ill. 1965. Prof. law U. Tex., Austin, Tex., 1969—76, U. Colo., Boulder, Colo., 1976—84, U Pa., Phila., 1984, U. Chgo., Chgo., 1985—88, Wilson-Dickinson, 1988—2002, Julius Kreeger, 2003. Office: U Chgo Sch Law 1111 E 60th St Chicago IL 60637-2776 Home: 1640 E 50th St Chicago IL 60615 E-mail: awaa@midway.uchicago.edu.

ALSOP, THOMAS WALTER, secondary education educator; b. Indpls., July 27, 1942; s. Russell and Carolyn (Alberti) A.; m. Jill E. DeShon, Aug. 24, 1968; children: Daniel, Nicole. BA in Spanish, Marian Coll., 1965; MA in Spanish Lit., Ind. U., 1968. Cert. secondary edn. tchr., Ind. Spanish tchr.-coach Scecina High Sch., Indpls., 1965-66, Brebeuf Prep. Sch., Indpls., 1968-69; instr. Spanish Kent (Ohio) State U., 1969-70; Spanish tchr., fgn. lang. chair Cathedral High Sch., Indpls., 1970-73, South Wayne Jr. High Sch., Indpls., 1973-82; Spanish tchr. Ben Davis High Sch., Indpls., 1982—. Coach state champion Spanish Acad. Competition Team, 1985-94, 10 consecutive State Acad. Competition Championships. Author: Mi Diario Español, 1990, Feliz Cumpleaños, 1992, Permiteme Hablar, 1992, Explorando España por Sus Matriculas, 1992, Mi Diario Español Intermedio, 1993, Alsop's Lesson Plan Enrichment Guide for Foreign Language Teachers, 1994, Spanish Conversation in Pairs, 1994, Telecocina Mexicana, 1995; author over 50 supplemental publs. for Spanish tchrs.; contbr. articles to profl. jours. Rockefeller fellow Rockefeller Found., 1986, Lilly Creative Tchr. fellow Lilly Found., 1988; finalist State Tchr. Yr., 1989; recipient Golden Apple award for Use of Tech. Indpls. Power and Light Co., 1993. Mem. Am. Assn. Tchrs. of Spanish (pres. Ind. chpt. 1988-92, mem. exec. bd. Ind. chpt. 1986—), Soc. Hon. Tchrs. of Spanish (regional dir. 1994—), Ctrl. States Conf. Fgn. Lang. Assn. (mem. adv. coun., bd. dirs.), Am. Coun. Tchrs. of Fgn. Lang. (Excellence in Tchg. of Culture Nelson Brooks award 1994), Ind. Fgn. Lang. Tchrs. Assn. (mem. exec. bd. 1985—, v.p., pres.-elect 1993—, bd. dirs. 1994—, internat. baccalaureate Spanish Oral Examiner, nominee AATSP Nat. Spanish Tchr. of Yr. 1994). Roman Catholic. Avocations: writing, softball, tennis, music, golf. Home: 6707 Yorkshire Pl Avon IN 46123-8812

ALSPAUGH, DALE WILLIAM, university administrator, aeronautics and astronautics educator; b. Dayton, Ohio, May 25, 1932; m. Marlowe Anne Alspaugh; 4 children. ME, U. Cin., 1955; MS in Engring. Scis., Purdue U., 1958, PhD in Engring. Scis., 1965. Profl. engr., Ohio. Project engr. GMC Frigidaire div., 1955-56, 59; instr. sch. aeronautics and astronautics & engring. Purdue U., West Lafayette, Ind., 1957-58, 59-64, asst. prof., 1964-68, assoc. prof., 1968-81; vice chancellor for acad. svcs., prof. Purdue U. North Cen. campus, Westville, Ind., 1981-82, acting chancellor, prof., 1982-84, chancellor, prof. aeronautics and astronautics, 1984-99, chancellor emeritus, prof. aeronautics and astronautics, 2000—. Mem. numerous coms. Purdue U.; cons. Midwest Applied Sci. Corp., West Lafayette, 1959-66, Roper Corp., West Lafayette, 1972-73, Switzer div. Wallace Murray Corp., Indpls., 1972-73, Los Alamos (N.Mex.) Scientific Lab., 1977, U.S. Army MICOM, Huntsville, Ala., 1978-82, Campbell & Pryor Cons. Corp., Michigan City, Ind., 1984-86, Colsa, Inc., Huntsville, 1988; reviewer Applied Mechs. Rev., J. Franklin Inst., ASME Jour. Heat

Transfer, Internat. Jour. Engring. Sci., also NSF rsch. proposals, various books; bd. dirs. Meml. Hosp. Michigan City, 1st Citizens Bank of Michigan City, Horizon Bancorp. Contbr. articles to profl. jours.; also numerous reports, papers, seminars. Mem. West Lafayette Bd. Sch. trustees, 1976-81, sec., 1976-77, v.p. 1977-78, pres. 1978-79; mem. West Lafayette Park & Recreation Bd., 1976-81, treas. 1979-80; mem. West Lafayette Sch. Bd. Negotiating Team, 1977-78, chief negotiator, 1978; mem. West Lafeyett Sch. Supt. screening Com., 1980-81; mem. West Lafayette Community Sch. Coun., 1970-73, pres., 1973; pres. Burtsfield PTA, 1970-71; supt. Covenant Presbyn. Ch. Sch., 1969-74; mem. West Lafayette Little League Bd., 1969-72; bd. dirs. N.W. Ind. Forum, 1983—, mem. subcom. on strategic planning, 1983-85, N.W. Ind. ednl. pub. TV consortium, 1984, subcom. on legis. affairs, 1985—, subcom. on hazardous materials, 1986-87, ednl. consortium, 1988—; mem. Barker Commn., 1986—; bd. dirs. Friends of Barker; mem. City of Valparaiso Ethics Commn., 1995—. Recipient grants NASA, Purdue Rsch. Found., Fund for Instructional Devel. & Innovative Teaching, Fund for Alternatives in Engring. Edn., U.S. Army MICOM. Mem. AIAA (coun. Cen. Ind. sect. 1969-71), Am. Soc. Engring. Edn. (space engring. com. 1970-78), Greater Valparaiso C. of C. (bd. dirs. 1985-90, chmn. div. on local & govtl. affairs 1987-88), Rotary. Office: Purdue U N Cen Campus Office of the Chancellor 1401 S Us Highway 421 Westville IN 46391-9542

ALSTAT, GEORGE ROGER, special education educator; b. Murphysboro, Ill., Aug. 20, 1941; s. George Lewis and Vernice C. Alstat; m. Carol Ann Sikora, Sept. 11, 1971 (div. Mar. 1982); children: Joseph Todd, George Ryan; m. Deborah Lynn Dame, June 19, 1986 (dec. June 1991); 1 child, Jessica Danielle. BS, So. Ill. U., Carbondale, 1971; MS, So. Ill. U., Edwardsville, 1974. Cert. tchr. and supervision in learning disabilities, emotional, social and educable mental handicapped, adminstrv. endorsement, Ill. Tchr. spl. edn. Centralia (Ill.) City Schs., 1974-78; supr. spl. edn. Franklin-Jefferson County Spl. Edn. Dist., Benton, Ill., 1978-83; direct salesman investment firm, Fairview Heights, Ill., 1983-86; owner So. Ill. Mktg., Benton, 1986-91; subsitute tchr. Murphysboro Sch. Dist., Ill., 1991-93; tchr. spl. edn. Nokomis (Ill.) Elem. Sch., 1993-94, East Richland Cmty. Unit Sch. Dist. 1, Olney, Ill., 1994-95; spl. edn. tchr. Chester Grade Sch., Ill., 1995-96. Avocations: bicycling, fishing, travel.

ALSTON, CHARLOTTE LENORA, college administrator; b. Greensboro, N.C., Oct. 14, 1933; d. Ernest William and Charlotte Franklyn (Taylor) A. BA, Bennett Coll., 1954; MMus, U. N.C., 1969, postgrad., 1996; PhD, U. Iowa, 1972; postgrad., Gallup Leadership Inst., 1996. Instr. music Hiroshima (Japan) Jogakuin Coll., 1955-58; instr., prof. music Bennett Coll., Greensboro, 1960-88, chairperson dept. music, 1973-88, dir. div. humanities, 1984-88, v.p. acad. affairs, provost, 1988—. Choral dir. Bennett Coll. Choir, Greensboro, 1974-88; min. music Trinity AME Zion Ch., Greensboro, 1975—; workshop dir., cons. Livingstone Coll., Salisbury, N.C., 1986-90; panelist N.C. Arts Coun., Charlotte, 1989; vis. prof. N.C. A&T State U., Greensboro, 1987; pres. So. Assn. Colls. for Women, 1999. Composer: (musical) HATT, 1976. Mem. City of Greensboro Sit-In 30th Anniversity Com., 1989; bd. dirs. Greensboro Symphony Orch., 1981-85, Eastern Music Festival, 1996—; mem. City of Greensboro Carolina Theatre Commn., 1990—; mem. A.M.E. Zion Bicentennial Hymnal Commn., 1996. Recipient Faculty Svc. award Bennett Coll. Nat. Alumnae Assn., 1986, Outstanding Svc. award Khalif Temple, 1981; named as African-Am. Woman of Distinction; listed among Greensboro 100; appeared in photography exhbn. and pub. documentary by African Am. Atelier, Inc., 1993; Ford Found. fellow, 1970-73. Mem. Alpha Kappa Mu, Delta Sigma Theta, Pi Kappa Lambda. Avocation: photography. Office: Bennett Coll Office of the Provost 900 E Washington St Greensboro NC 27401-3239

ALSTON, WILLIAM PAYNE, philosophy educator; b. Shreveport, La., Nov. 29, 1921; s. William Payne and Eunice (Schoolfield) A.; m. Mary Frances Collins, Aug. 15, 1943 (div.); 1 dau., Frances Ellen; m. Valerie Tibbetts Barnes, July 3, 1963. B.M., Centenary Coll., 1942; PhD, U. Chgo., 1951; LHD (honoris causa), Ch. Div. Sch. Pacific, 1988. Instr. philosophy U. Mich., 1949-52, asst. prof., then asso. prof., 1952-61, prof., 1961-71, acting chmn. dept., 1961-64; prof. philosophy Rutgers U., 1971-76, U. Ill., Champaign, 1976-80, chmn. dept., 1977-80; prof. philosophy Syracuse (N.Y.) U., 1980-99, prof. emeritus, 1999. Vis. asst. prof. UCLA, 1952-53; Austin Fagothey vis. prof. philosophy Santa Clara U., 1991; vis. lectr. Harvard U., 1955-56; fellow Ctr. for Advanced Study in the Behavioral Scis., 1965-66; dir. summer seminars for coll. tchrs. NEH, 1978-79, NEH Summer Inst. in Philosophy of Religion, 1986, NEH Fellowship for Univ. Tchrs., 1988-89, Vatican Obs. Project on Divine Action in the Light of Contemporary Sci., Symposium of Chinese-Am. Philosophy and Religious Studies, 1994; dir. Calvin Coll. Summer Seminar in Christian Scholarship, 1999. Author: Religious Belief and Philosophical Thought, 1963, (with G. Nakhnikian) Readings in Twentieth Century Philosophy, 1963, Philosophy of Language, 1964, (with R.B. Brandt) The Problems of Philosophy: Introductory Readings, 1967, 3d edit., 1978; Divine Nature and Human Language, 1989, Epistemic Justification, 1989, Perceiving God, 1991, The Reliability of Sense Perception, 1993, A Realist Conception of Truth, 1996, Illocutionary Acts and Sentence Meaning, 2000, A Sensible Metaphysical Realism, 2001, Realism and Antirealism, 2002; editor: Philos. Rsch. Archives, 1974-77, Faith and Philosophy, 1982-90, Cornell Studies in Philosophy of Religion, 1987—; contbr. articles to profl. jours., chpts. in books. Served with AUS, 1942-46. Recipient Chancellor's Exceptional Acad. Achievement award Syracuse U., 1990. Mem. Am. Acad. Arts and Scis., Am. Philos. Assn. (pres. Western divsn. 1978-79), Soc. Christian Philosophers (pres. 1978-81), Scholarly Engagement Anglican Doctrine, Am. Theol. Soc., Soc. for Philosophy Religion (pres. 2001-02). Home: 8 Bittersweet Ln Fayetteville NY 13066-1702 Office: Syracuse U Dept Philosophy Syracuse NY 13244-1170

ALT, BETTY L. sociology educator; b. Walsenburg, Colo., Nov. 12, 1931; d. Cecil R. and Mary M. (Giordano) Sowers; m. William E. Alt, June 19, 1960; 1 child, Eden Jeanette Alt Murrie. BA, Colo. Coll., 1960; MA, NE Mo. State U., 1968. Instr. sociology Indian Hills Community Coll., Centerville, Iowa, 1965-70; dept. chmn. Middlesex Community Coll., Bedford, Mass., 1971-75; instr. sociology Auburn U., Montgomery, 1975-76; div. chmn. Tidewater Community Coll., Virginia Beach, Va., 1976-80; program coord. Pikes Peak Community Coll., Woomera, Australia, 1980-83; instr. sociology Hawaii Pacific Coll., Honolulu, 1983-86, U. Md., Okinawa, Japan, 1987-88, Christopher Newport Coll., Newport News, Va., 1988-89, U. Colo., Colorado Springs, 1989-96, U. So. Colo., Pueblo, 1992—. Co-author: (nonfiction) Uncle Sam's Brides, 1990, Campfollowing: A History of the Military Wife, 1991, Weeping Violins: The Gypsy Tragedy in Europe, 1996, Slaughter in Cell House 3, 1997, Wicked Women, 2000, Black Soldiers-White Wars, 2002, Keeper of the Keys, 2003. Mem. League Women Voters. Mem. AAUW, Pen Women, N.E. Mo. State U. Alumni Assn. (bd. dirs. 1993-97). Home: 2460 N Interstate 25 Pueblo CO 81008-9614 Office: Colo State U - Pueblo 2200 Bonforte Blvd Pueblo CO 81001-4901

ALT, JAMES EDWARD, political science educator; b. N.Y.C., Aug. 16, 1946; s. Franz Leopold and Alice (Modern) A.; m. Elaine Fiore, June 26, 1968; children: Rachel, Adam. AB, Columbia U., 1968; MSc in Econs., London Sch. Econs., 1970; PhD, Essex U., Eng., 1978. Lectr. U. Essex, Wivenhoe Park, Eng., 1971-79; assoc. prof. Washington U., St. Louis, 1978-82, prof., 1982-86, Harvard U., Cambridge, Mass., 1986—; dir. Ctr. for Basic Rsch. in Social Sci., 1998—. Author: Politics of Economic Decline, 1979, (with K. Chrystal) Political Economics, 1983; editor: (with K. Shepsle) Perspectives on Positive Political Economy, 1990, (with M. Levi and E. Ostrom) Competition and Cooperation, 1999; contbr. articles to profl. jours. Rsch. grantee NSF, 1980, 85, 91, 93, 2001, 02; Guggenheim fellow, 1997-98. Mem. Brit. Politics Group (pres. 1983-85), Am. Polit. Sci. Assn. (coun. 1996-97), Midwest Polit. Sci. Assn. (exec. coun. 1985-88). Office: Harvard U Dept Govt Cambridge MA 02138 E-mail: james_alt@harvard.edu.

ALTAN, M(USTAFA) CENGIZ, mechanical engineering educator; b. Ankara, Turkey, Dec. 26, 1963; s. A. Rifki and Nursel Altan; m. Betul S. Marmara, July 4, 1992. BSME, Mid. East Tech. U., Ankara, 1985; PhD in Mech. Engring., U. Del., 1989. Tchg. asst. U. Del., Newark, 1985-86, rsch. asst., 1986-89; asst. prof. mech. engring. U. Okla., Norman, 1989-95, assoc. prof., 1995—. Editor: (conf. proc.) Developments in Non-Newtonian Fluid Mechanics, 1993, Intelligent Manufacturing and Material Processing, 1995, Processing and Design of Multicomponent Materials, 2000; contbr. articles to profl. jour. Recipient rsch. initiation award Soc. Mfg. Engr., 1990, Regents' award for superior tchg. U. Okla., 1998; rsch. grantee Okla. Ctr. for Advancement Sci. and Tech., 1991, NASA, 1996, Seagate Tech., 1996, Hawthorne York Internat., 1999, SIAC Corp., 2001, All Tech Inc., 2002, TMI Inc., 2003, USAF, 2003. Mem. ASME (assoc., chmn. materials processing com. materials div. 1994-97), Soc. R heology, Internat. Polymer Processing Soc., Am. Soc. Engring. Edn., Am. Phys. Soc., Am. Soc. for Composites, Pi Tau Sigma (hon., Most Outstanding Prof. award for U. Okla. 1997). Achievements include patents on computer-controlled curing of composite materials. Office: U Okla Sch Aero-Mech Eng 865 Asp Ave Rm 212 Norman OK 73019-1029 E-mail: altan@ou.edu.

ALTAN, TAYLAN, engineering educator, mechanical engineer, consultant; b. Trabzon, Turkey, Feb. 12, 1938; came to U.S., 1962; s. Seref and Sadife (Baysal) Kadioglu; m. Susan Borah, July 18, 1964; children: Peri Michele, Aylin Elisabeth Diploma in engring., Tech. U., Hannover, Fed. Republic Germany, 1962; MS in Mech. Engring., U. Calif.-Berkeley, 1964, PhD in Mech. Engring., 1966. Research engr. DuPont Co., Wilmington, Del., 1966-68; research scientist Battelle Columbus Labs, Ohio, 1968-72, research fellow, 1972-75, sr. research leader, 1975-86; prof. mech. engring., dir. engring. rsch. ctr. Ohio State U., Columbus, 1985—. Chmn. sci. com. N.Am. Mfg. Rsch. Inst. Soc. Mfg. Engrs., Detroit, 1982-86, pres., 1987; dir. Ctr. for Net Shape Mfg. Co-author: Forging Equipment, 1973, Metal Forming, 1983, Metal Forming and the Finite Element Method, 1989; assoc. editor Jour. Materials Processing Tech., Eng., 1978-99; contbr. over 400 tech. articles to profl. jours. Fellow Am. Soc. Metals (chmn. forging com. 1978-87), Soc. Mfg. Engrs. (Gold medal 1985), ASME. Avocations: languages, travel. Office: Ohio State U 210 Baker Bldg 1971 Neil Ave Columbus OH 43210-1210 E-mail: altan1@osu.edu.

ALTBACH, PHILIP, director, educator; b. Chgo., May 3, 1941; s. Milton and Josephine (Huebsch) A.; m. Edith Hoshino, June 16, 1962; children: Eric, Frederick Gabriel. BA, U. Chgo., 1962, MA, 1964, PhD, 1966. Lectr. Harvard U., Cambridge, Mass., 1967-68; from asst. prof. to assoc. prof. U. Wis., Madison, 1968-75; prof., chmn. dept. ednl. orgn., adminstrn. and policy SUNY, Buffalo, 1976-80, 86-92, dir. Comparative Edn. Ctr., 1978-94; prof. sch. edn. Boston Coll., 1994—, dir. Ctr. Internat. Higher Edn., 1995—, J. Donald Monan SJ prof. higher edn., 1996—. Fulbright rsch. prof. U. Bombay, 1968; cons. Regional Inst. Higher Edn., Singapore, 1979, 81, 82, Carnegie Found. Advancement Tchg., 1990-94, Rockefeller Found., 1991—; vis. prof. Moscow State U., 1981, Stanford U., 1989; Fulbright cons. U. Singapore, 1982; sr. assoc. Carnegie Found. Advancement Tchg., 1992-96; sec.-gen. Bellagio Publ. Network, 1992-98; guest prof. Peking U. Author: Student Politics in America, 1975, rev., 1997, Comparative Higher Education, 2000, Higher Education in Third World, 1982, Knowledge Context, 1987, International Higher Education: An Encyclopedia, 1991, Publishing and Development in the Third World, 1994, Higher Education in the 21st Century, 1999, Private Prometheus: Private Higher Education and Development, 2000, In Defense of American Higher Education, 2001, The Decline of the Guru, 2003, others; editor: Comparative Edn. Rev., 1979—89, Review of Higher Edn., 1996—, Ednl. Policy, 1989—, various newsletters and publs. Mem. capital budget rev. com. City of Buffalo, 1980. Grantee, NEH, 1976, Exxon Edn.. Found., 1982, 1984, NSF, 1987, Rockefeller Found., 1993, 1994, 1995, Ford Found., 1998, 2001, 2002, MacArthur Found., 2003, Toyota Found., 2003, Carnegie Corp. N.Y., 2003. Mem. Comparative Edn. Soc. (editor jour. 1980-89), Assn. Study Higher Edn. (editor jour. 1996—). Office: Boston Coll 207 Campion Hall Chestnut Hill MA 02467 E-mail: altbach@bc.edu.

ALTCHEK, EDWARD M. neurosurgeon, educator; b. N.Y.C., Mar. 9, 1931; s. Isaac David and Fanny (Horowitz) A.; m. Florence Zeleznik, 1960 (div. 1968); children: Leslie Rachel, Glenn David, Michael Geoffrey; m. Roberta Louise Walsh, June 7, 1968; 1 child, Alexandra. BA in Psychology, NYU, 1951; BS in Biomed. Engring., N.Y. Inst. Tech., 1984; MD, Chgo. Med. Sch., 1955. Diplomate Am. Bd. Neurologic Soc. Intern L.I. Jewish Hosp., New Hyde Park, N.Y., 1955-56; resident neurosurgery Montefiore & Bronx Mcpl. Hosps., 1956-61; neurologic surgeon pvt. practice N.Y.C., L.I., 1961-76; prof. neuroanatomy St. George's Coll. of Medicine, Grenada, W.I., 1979-80; prof. engring. technology N.Y. Inst. Technology, Old Westbury, N.Y., 1984-91; asst. dir. rsch. inst. N.Y. Chiropractic Coll., Old Brookville, N.Y., 1987-90; assoc. prof., asst. dean Touro Coll., Bay Shore, NY, 1992—. Patentee in field; contbr. articles to profl. jours. Mem. Soc. Automotive Engrs., Am. Assn. Med. Instrumentation. Republican. Jewish. Avocations: entomology, scuba diving, photography, woodworking. Office: Touro Coll 1700 Union Blvd Bay Shore NY 11706-7321

ALTER, MILTON, neurologist, educator; b. Buffalo, Nov. 11, 1929; s. Samuel and Rose (Schaffer) Alter; m. Reina Rolnick, Aug. 31, 1952; children: David S., Daniel M., Michael A., Naomi T., Joel A. BA, U. Buffalo, 1951, MD, 1955; PhD, U. Minn., 1966. Diplomate Am. Bd. Psychiatry and Neurology. Intern U. Minn., Mpls., 1955-56; sr. surgeon USPHS, Bethesda, Md., 1956-62; fellow Med. Coll. S.C., Charleston, 1956-57, Dalhousie U., Halifax, 1957, Columbia U. Coll. Physicians and Surgeons, N.Y.C., 1957-58, Hebrew U., Jerusalem, 1960-62; mem. faculty, chief neurology svc. U. Minn., Mpls., 1962—67, Mpls. VA Hosp., 1967-76; chmn. dept. neurology Temple U., Phila., 1976-87, prof. neurology, 1987—89; prof., dir. residency tng. Med. Coll. Pa., Phila., 1989-91; clin. prof. Allegheny U., 1995—. Mem. sci. adv. bd. Nat. Multiple Sclerosis Soc., N.Y.C., Dystonia Med. Rsch. Found., Alzheimer Disease Assn.; peer reviewer Epidemiology and Disease Control 1 and 2 NIH, Bethesda, Md.; adj. prof. Ctr. Clin. Epidemiology and Biostatistics U. Pa., 1995; adj. prof. Thomas Jefferson U., 1999. Guest editor: numerous profl. jours., editor-in-chief: Neuroepidemiology, 1989—96; editor emeritus Neuroepidemiology; contbr. articles to profl. jours., chapters to books. Capt. USPHS, 1962. Grantee, NIH, Multiple Sclerosis Soc. Mem.: AMA, World Fedn. Neurol. (chair rsch. group epidemiology 1998—2001), Am. Epidemiology Soc., Assn. Rsch. Nervous and Mental Diseases, Am. Neurol. Assn., Am. Acad. Neurology. Democrat. Jewish. Home: 236 Indian Creek Rd Wynnewood PA 19096-3404 also: Lankenau Med Rsch Ctr 100 E Lancaster Ave Wynnewood PA 19096-3404 E-mail: malter5280@aol.com.

ALTFEST, KAREN CAPLAN, diversified financial services company executive, director; b. Mont., Que., Can. d. Philip and Betty (Gamer) Caplan; m. Lewis Jay Altfest; children: Ellen Wendy, Andrew Gamer. Tchr.'s diploma, McGill U.; BA cum laude, Hunter Coll., 1970, MA, 1972; PhD, CUNY, 1979. CFP, N.Y. V.p. L. J. Altfest & Co., Inc., N.Y.C., 1985—; dir. fin. planning program New Sch. Univ., N.Y.C., 1989—. Dir. CFP program Pace U., White Plains, N.Y., 1988-90. Author: Robert Owen, 1978, Keeping Clients for Life, 2001; co-author: Lew Altfest Answers Almost All Your Questions about Money, 1992; contbr. articles to fin. jours. Founding chmn. Yorkville Common Pantry, N.Y.C., 1980-84; v.p. PS 6 PTA, N.Y.C., 1991-92; bd. dirs. Temple Shaaray Tefila, 1993—. Named Planner of Month, Mut. Funds Mag., 2000; named one of 200 Best Fin. Planners in U.S., Worth Mag., 1996, 1997, 1998, Best Fin. Advisors, Med. Econs. Mag., 1998, 100 Top Advisors, Mut. Funds Mgrs., 2002, Best 100 Planners, Mut. Funds Mag., 2002, Top Wealth Mgrs. (firm), Bloomberg, 2003; recipient Cmty. Svc. award, Temple Shaaray Tefila, 1985; profile on cover, Fin. Planning Mag., 2001. Mem.: Women's Econ. Round Table, Fin. Women's Assn., Nat. Assn. Personal Fin. Advisors (chair N.E.-Mid Atlantic Conf. 1995, bd. dirs. N.E. region 1996—2003, v.p. 1997—99, pres. N.E.-Mid Atlantic region 1999—2001, chmn. 2001—03), Achievement cert. N.E. Region 1995, award for outstanding svc. to NE region 2001, 2003), Fin. Planning Assn. (bd. dirs. N.Y. chpt. 1994—99, bd. dirs. 2000—, dir. for pub. rels., Dedicated Svc. cert. 1998, 1999, 2000, 2001, 2002, 2003), Assn. for Women's Econ. Devel., Assn. for Can. Studies in U.S., Nat. Assn. Women Bus. Owners (chmn. FOCUS 1993—95, bd. dirs.), CUNY PhD Alumni Assn. (v.p. 1982—84), Phi Alpha Theta. Achievements include featured on cover of Fin. Planning Mag., 2001. Office: LJ Altfest & Co Inc 116 John St Rm 1120 New York NY 10038-3305 E-mail: karen@altfest.com.

ALTIERI, CHARLES FRANCIS, English language educator; b. NYC, Nov. 11, 1942; s. Francis and Ida (Picciotti) A.; m. Joanne D. Smith (div. June 1991); children: Philip, Laura; m. Carolyn Jane Porter, Jan. 4, 1993. AB, LeMoyne Coll., 1964; PhD, U. N.C., 1968. Asst. prof., then assoc. prof. English Buffalo, 1968-76; assoc. prof., then prof. U. Washington, Seattle, 1976-92; prof. U. Calif., Berkeley, 1992—. Author: Act and Quality, 1981, Self and Sensibility in Contemporary American Poetry, 1985, Painterly Abstraction in Modernist American Poetry, 1989, Subjective Agency, 1994, Postmodernisms Now, 1999, Aesthetics of the Affects, 2003. Fellow, NEH, 1974, Guggenheim Found., 1980, Ctr. for Advanced Study in Behavioral Scis., Palo Alto, Calif., 1980. Mem.: MLA, Nat. Acad. Arts and Scis. Democrat. Avocations: tennis, golf. Office: Univ Calif Dept English Berkeley CA 94720-1030

ALTIERI ROSADO, JOSÉ ANIBAL, principal; b. July 13, 1954; B in Secondary Edn., Inter Am. U. P.R., 1978; M in Edn./Adminstrn. and Supervision, Cath. U. P.R., 1984. Lic. gen. supervisor sch. adminstrn., aux. supt. schs., secondary sch. prin., elem. sch. prin., biology tchr., sci. tchr., elem. sch. tchr., P.R. Sci. tchr. Dept. of Edn., P.R., 1980-88; sch. prin. Santa Isabel, Adjuntas Elem. Sch., P.R., 1988-90, José E. Lugo Ponce de León High Sch., Adjuntas, 1990-95. With Nat. Prin.'s Leadership Acad., U. Del., 1993; participant various edn. workshops, Dept. of Edn. P.R.; lectr. in field. Recipient Blue Ribbon Sch. award U.S. Dept. Edn., 1990-91, 1st Place award Environ. Quality Bd. P.R., 1993, awards and certificates Orgn. for Devel. of Thought, U. P.R., Senate and Legislature P.R., Lions Club Internat., Dept. of Edn. U.S.A. Mem. ASCD, Nat. Assn. Secondary Sch. Prins., Nat. Assn. Sci. Tchrs. of P.R., Nat. Assn. Biology Tchrs., P.R. Assn. Counseling and Devel., P.R. Assn. Math. Tchrs., Assn. Sch. Prins. P.R. Office: Jose Emilio Lugo Ponde De Leon High Sch Calle Francisco Pietri # 75 Los Cerros Adjuntas PR 00601-2252

ALTMAN, SALLY LUCILE, middle school educator; b. Berkeley, Calif., Mar. 28, 1934; d. E. Allen and Helen Lucile (Struthers) Phillips; m. Gerald C. Angove, Mar. 25, 1956 (div. 1985); children: Jay (dec.), Douglas, Bill; m. Arthur Lewis Altman, Dec. 27, 1987. BA, Stanford U., 1956, MA, 1957. Cert. tchr. Calif. Instr. Coll. of the Sequoias, Visalia, Calif., 1957-60; tchr. Divisadero Jr. High Sch., Visalia, Calif., 1960-61, Mt. Whitney High Sch., Visalia, Calif., 1962-68, Coll. of Sequois Evening Sch., Visalia, Calif., 1957-68, Modesto (Calif.) High Sch., 1968-75; coach Placer High Sch., Auburn, Calif., 1975-79, tchr. phys. edn., 1978-79; tchr.-coach Eureka Sch., Roseville, Calif., 1978-82, Cavitt Jr. High, Granite Bay, Calif., 1982-96; retired, 1996; substitute tchr., 1996—2001. Synchro. swim coach City of Roseville Recreation Dept., 1976-80; session presenter various workshops; cons. Nat. Evaluation Systems, 1996—. Instr./trainer ARC, Sacramento-Auburn, 1988-96, mem. health svcs. com., Auburn, 1989-96. active Valley Springs Presbyn. Ch. Mem. AARP, Calif. Assn. Health, Phys. Edn., Recreation and Dance (retiree sect. chair 1997-99, state v.p.-elect phys. edn. 1991-92, v.p. 1992-93, no. dist. pres. 1988-90, no. dist. rep. 1993-96, unit pres. 1986-88, No. Dist. Honor award 1991), Eureka Union Faculty Orgn., United Srs. Orgn., Sr.Coalition. Republican. Avocations: swimming, skiing, travel, reading, bridge. Home: 8240 Oak Knoll Dr Granite Bay CA 95746-9315 Fax: 916-791-4980.

ALTMAN, SIDNEY, biology educator; b. Montreal, Que., Can., May 7, 1939; BS, MIT, 1960; PhD in Biophys., U. Colo., 1967; DSc (hon.), McGill U., Montreal, 1991, York U., U. Colo., U. Montreal, U. B.C. Teaching asst. Columbia U., 1960—62; Damon Runyon Meml. Fund cancer rsch. fellow in molecular biology Harvard U., 1967—69; Anna Fuller Fund fellow, then Med. Rsch. Coun. fellow Med. Rsch. Coun. Lab. Molecular Biology, 1969—71; from asst. to assoc. prof. Yale U., New Haven, 1971—80, prof. molecular cellular and devel. biology, 1980—, Sterling prof. biology, 1990—, prof. biophysical chemistry, 1994—, chmn. dept., 1983—85; dean Yale Coll., 1985—90. Tutor Radcliffe Coll., 1968—69. Author: Transfer RNA, 1978. Recipient Nobel Prize in Chemistry, 1989. Fellow: AAAS; mem.: Am. Philos. Soc. (Rosenstiel award 1989), Nat. Acad. Scis., Genetics Soc. Am., Am. Soc. Biol. Chemists. Achievements include research in on effects of acridines on T4 DNA replication, mutants, precursors of tRNA processing by catalytic RNA and ribonuclease function. Office: Yale U Kline Biology Tower 402 New Haven CT 06520-8103*

ALTSHILLER, ARTHUR LEONARD, secondary education educator; b. N.Y.C., Aug. 12, 1942; s. Samuel Martin and Betty Rose (Lepson) A.; m. Carol Heiser, Aug. 16, 1980. BS in Physics, U. Okla., 1963; MS in Physics, Calif. State U., Northridge, 1971. Elec. engr. Garrett Corp., Torrance, Calif., 1963-64, Volt Tech. Corp., Phoenix, 1965; engr., physicist Aerojet Gen. Corp., Azusa, Calif., 1966-68; elec. engr. Magnavox Rsch. Labs., Torrance, 1968-69; sr. engr. Litton Guidance & Control, Canoga Park, Calif., 1969; physics tchr. L.A. Unified Sch. Dist./Van Nuys Math/Sci. Magnet High Sch., 1971—; math. instr. Valley Coll., Van Nuys, Calif., 1986—. Part-time physics and chemistry tchr. West Coast Talmudical Sem., L.A., 1978-88; foster tchr. Seti Inst. and NASA Ames Rsch. Ctr., 1994; coach Van Nuys (Calif.) H.S. Nat. Championship Sci. Bowl Team, 1995; tchr. mem. U.S. Olympic Physics Team, 1996; Chicos participant Calif. Inst. Tech., 2000—. Mesa Club sponsor Math.-Engring. Sci. Achievement L.A. High Sch. and U. So. Calif., 1984-87, Van Nuys H.S., 1997-98, Calif. State U. Northridge, 1997-98. Recipient Cert. of Honor Westinghouse Sci. Talent Search, 1990, Lucent Tech. Talent Search, 1998; Eisenhower fellow NSF, 2002—. Mem. AAAS, Am. Assn. Physics Tchrs., Am. Inst. Physics (ednl. advisor 1999), United Tchrs. L.A. Avocations: cycling, tennis, weight lifting, track and field. Home: 6776 Vickiview Dr Canoga Park CA 91307-2751 Office: Van Nuys High Sch 6535 Cedros Ave Van Nuys CA 91411-1599 E-mail: altshiller@aol.com.

ALTSHULER, ALAN ANTHONY, political scientist, educator; b. Bklyn., Mar. 9, 1936; s. Leonard M. and Janet A. (Sonnenstrahl) A.; m. Julie C. Maller, June 15, 1958; children: Jennifer, David. BA, Cornell U., 1957; MA, U. Chgo., 1959, PhD, 1961. Instr. Swarthmore Coll., 1960-61; Smith-Mundt vis. asst. prof. Makerere (Uganda) Coll., 1961-62; asst. prof. Cornell U., 1962-66; assoc. prof. MIT, 1966-69, prof. polit. sci. and urban studies and planning, 1969-71, 1975-83, head dept. polit. sci., 1977-82; dean Grad. Sch. Pub. Adminstrn. NYU, 1983-88, dir. Urban Research Ctr., 1986-87; prof. urban policy and planning Kennedy Sch. Govt. and Grad. Sch. Design Harvard U., 1988—; dir. Taubman Ctr. State and Local Govt. Harvard U., 1988—, acad. dean Kennedy Sch. Govt., 1993-95; dir. Rappaport Inst. for Greater Boston, 1999—. Sec. transp. and constrn. Commonwealth Mass., 1971-75; dir. Boston Transp. Planning Rev. (part-time), 1970-71. Author: The City Planning Process: A Political Analysis, 1965, Community Control: The Black Demand for Participation in Large American Cities, 1970, The Urban Transportation System: Politics and Policy Innovation, 1979; co-author: The Future of the Automobile, 1984, Regulation for Revenue: The Political Economy of Land Development

Exactions, 1993, Mega-Projects: The Changing Politics of Urban Public Investment, 2003; editor: Current Issues in Transportation Policy, 1979; co-editor: The Politics of the Federal Bureaucracy, 1977, Innovation in American Government, 1997, Governance and Opportunity in Metropolitan America, 1999; contbr. articles to profl. jours. Mem. Nat. Acad. Pub. Adminstrn., Am. Acad. Arts and Scis.

ALTURA, BELLA T. physiologist, educator; b. Solingen, Germany; came to U.S., 1948; d. Sol and Rosa (Brandstetter) Tabak; m. Burton M. Altura, Dec. 27, 1961; 1 child, Rachel Allison. BA, Hunter Coll., 1953, MA, 1962; PhD, CUNY, 1968. Instr. exptl. anesthesiology Albert Einstein Coll. Medicine, Bronx, 1970-74; asst. prof. physiology SUNY Health Sci Ctr., Bklyn., 1974-82, assoc. prof. physiology, 1982-97, rsch. prof. physiology, 1997—, rsch. prof. pharmacology, 1998—. Vis. prof. Beijing Coll. of Traditional Chinese Medicine, 1988, Jiangxi (China) Med. Coll., 1988, Tokyo U. Med. Sch., 1993, U. Brussels Esramé Hosp., 1995, Humboldt U.-Charité Hosp., 1995, Kagoshima U., Japan, 1995, U. Birmingham, England, 1996, Self Med. Def. Coll. Japan, 1996, Nat. Def. Med. Sch., Japan, 1996, Albert Szent Gyorgi Med. U., Szeged, Hungary, 1997; mem. Nat. Coun. on Magnesium and Cardiovascular Disease, 1991—; cons. NOVA Biomedical, 1989—; Niche pharm. cons. Protina GmbH, Munich, 1992—96, Otsuka Pharm. Co., Japan, 1995—97, Roberts Pharm. Co., 1999—2000; co-prin. investigator NIH, Nat. Heart, Lung and Blood Inst., NIMH, Nat. Inst. on Alcoholism and Alcohol Abuse. Contbr. over 700 articles to profl. jours. Fellowship NASA, 1966-67, CUNY, 1968; co-recipient Gold-Silver medal French Nat. Acad. Medicine, 1984, Silver medal Mayor of Paris, 1984, Seelig award for lifetime rsch. on magnesium, Am. Coll. Nutrition, 2002, Outstanding Inventor of Yr., SUNY, 2002. Mem. Am. Physiol. Soc., Am. Soc. Pharmacology and Exptl. Therapeutics, Am. Soc. for Magnesium Rsch. (founder, treas. 1984—), Hungarian Soc. Electrochemistry (hon. co-pres. 1995-96), Nat. Heart, Lung and Blood Inst., Nat. Inst. on Alcohol Abuse and Alcoholism, Phi Beta Kappa, Sigma Xi. Achievements include first measurement ionized magnesium with ion selective electrode in blood, serum and plasma in health and disease states; demonstration that substances of abuse can cause cerebrovasospasm and stroke. Office: SUNY Health Sci Ctr Box 31 450 Clarkson Ave Brooklyn NY 11203-2056 E-mail: baltura@downstate.edu.

ALTURA, BURTON MYRON, physiologist, educator; b. N.Y.C., Apr. 9, 1936; s. Barney and Frances (Dorfman) A.; m. Bella Tabak, Dec. 27, 1961; 1 child, Rachel Allison. BA, Hofstra U., 1957; MS, NYU, 1961, PhD (USPHS fellow), 1964. Diplomate Am. Bd. Forensic Med., Am. Coll. Forensic Medicine, Am. Bd. Forensic Examiners, Coll. Pharm. and Apothecary Scis., Am. Assn. Integrative Medicine. Tchg. fellow in biology NYU, N.Y.C., 1960-61, instr. exptl. anesthesiology Sch. Medicine, 1964-65, asst. prof. Sch. Medicine, 1965-66; rsch. fellow Bronx Mcpl. Hosp. Ctr., 1967-76; asst. prof. physiology and anesthesiology Albert Einstein Coll. Medicine, N.Y.C., 1967-70, assoc. prof., 1970-74, vis. prof., 1974-78; prof. physiology SUNY Health Sci Ctr., Bklyn., 1974—, prof. medicine, 1992—; mem. Ctr. Cardiovasc. and Muscle Rsch., 1995—; prof. pharmacology SUNY Health Sci. Ctr., Bklyn., 1998—; CEO Bio-Def. Sys., Inc. Mem. spl. study sect. on toxicology Nat. Inst. Environ. Health Scis., 1977—78; mem. Alcohol Biomed. Rsch. Rev. Com. Nat. Inst. Alcohol Abuse and Alcoholism, 1978—83; mem. spl. study sect. on toxicology Nat. Inst. Environ. Health Scis., 2001; mem. spl. study sect. medications Nat. Inst. Alcohol Abuse and Alcoholism, 2002; mem. panel CNF bd. Inst. Med., NAS, 1996—97; mem. A Food bd. FTC; adj. prof. biology Queens Coll., CUNY, 1983—84; pres. (hon.) Internat. Symposium on Interactions of Magnesium and Potassium on Cardiac and Vascular Muscle, Montbazon, France, 1984; pres. (hon.), lectr. (hon.) Hungarian Soc. Electrochemistry, Budapest, 1995; organizer, condr. symposia; organizer workshop Nat. Inst. Alcohol Abuse and Alcoholism, 1992; condr., chmn. Gordon Rsch. Conf. on Magnesium in Biochem. Processes and Medicine, 1984; chmn., organizer 1st Internat. Workshop Unique Magnesium Sensitive Ion Selective Electrodes, Orlando, Fla., 1993, 2nd Internat. Workshop Unique Magnesium Sensitive Ion Selective Electrodes, Crete, Greece; chmn. symposium Am. Soc. Nephrology, 1993, Crete, Greece, 97; v.p. 4th Internat. Symposium on Magnesium, Blacksburg, 1985; organizer 2nd Internat. Workshop Unique Magnesium Sensitive Ion Selective Electrodes, Crete, 1997; judge Am. Inst. Sci. and Tech., 1984, 85, 86, 1988—90, 1991, 93, Jr. Acad. N.Y. Acad. Scis., 1987, 89, 90; mem. adv. coun. Nat. Found. Addictive Drugs, 1986—; vis. prof. Yamaguchi U., Japan, 1988, 93, Beijing Coll. Traditional Chinese Medicine, China, 1988, Harvard U. Med. Sch., 1988, U. Tokyo, 1993, Kyoto U. Sch. Medicine, 1993, Kumamoto U., 1993, U. Copenhagen, 1994, U. Florence, 1994, Humboldt Univ., Berlin, 1995, U. Birmingham, England, 1996, Self Med. Def. Coll., Japan, 1996, U. Calif., Riverside, 1998, Fla. Atlantic U., 1998; vis. prof., lectr. (hon.) Inst. Water, Soil and Air Hygiene, Fed. Health Inst., Berlin, 1991, Max Planck Inst., Dortmund, Germany, 1992, 94, Yamanouchi Co. Ltd., Japan, 1995; mem. working group convened by Congressman Durbin III, 91; mem. Nat. Coun. Magnesium and Cardiovasc. Disease, 1991—; CEO Bio-Defense Sys., Inc.; spkr. in field; cons. NSF, Va. Grants Rev. Com., Nat. Heart, Lung, and Blood Inst., Nat. Inst. Drug Abuse, others. Author: Microcirculation, 3 vols., 1977—80, Vascular Endothelium and Basement Membranes, 1980, Pathophysiology of the Reticuloendothelial System, 1981, Ionic Regulation of the Microcirculation, 1982, Handbook of Shock and Trauma, Vol. 1: Basic Science, 1983, Magnesium and the Cardiovascular System, 1985, Cardiovascular Actions of Anesthetic Agents and Drugs Used in Anesthesia, vol. I, 1986, vol. II, 1987, Magnesium, Stress and the Cardiovascular System, 1986, Magnesium in Biochemical Processes and Medicine, 1987, Magnesium in Clinical Medicine and Therapeutics, 1992, Unique Magnesium-Sensitive Ion Selective Electrodes, 1994; editor-in-chief: Physiology and Pathophysiology Series, 1976—81, Microcirculation, 1980—84, Magnesium: Exptl. and Clin. Rsch., 1981—89, Microcirculation, Endothelium and Lymphatics, 1984—, Magnesium and Trace Elements, 1990—, mem. editl. bd.: Jour. Circulatory Shock, 1973—85, Advances in Microcirculation, 1976—92, Jour. Cardiovasc. Pharmacology, 1977—84, Prostaglandins, Leukotrienes and Fatty Acids, 1978—2001, Substance and Alcohol Actions/Misuse, 1979—84, Alcoholism: Clin. and Exptl. Rsch., 1982—87, assoc. editor: Jour. Artery, 1974—, Microvasc. Rsch., 1978—85, Agts. and Actions, 1981—88, Biogenic Amines, 1985—88, Jour. Am. Coll. Nutrition, 1982—94, Frontiers in Biosci., 1996—, Internat. Jour. Cardiovasc. Medicine, Surgery and Biomechanics, 1997—; contbr. over 900 articles to profl. jours. Recipient Rsch. Career Devel. award USPHS, 1968-72, Silver medal for furthering French-U.S. sci. rels. Mayor of Paris, 1984, Medaille Vermeille, French Nat. Acad. Medicine, 1984, Travel awards NIH, 1968, Am. Soc. Pharm. and Exptl. Therapeutics, 1969, Golden Hippocrates award, Haifa, Israel, 2002, Chancellor's Outstanding Inventor of Yr. award SUNY, 2002, Medal for Lifetime of Basic Med. Rsch. and Tchg., Haifa, Israel, 2002; grantee NIH, 1968-, NIMH, 1974-78, Nat. Heart Lung Blood Inst., 1974-86, Nat. Inst. Drug Abuse, 1979-83, Nat. Inst. Alcohol Abuse and Alcoholism, 1990-; named Eminent Fellow, Wisdom Hall of Fame, 1999, Winston Churchill Fellow, 2000. Fellow: AAAS, Nat. Acad. Clinical BioChemistry, Am. Physiol. Soc. (mem. circulation group 1971—, pub. info. com. 1980—84, symposium organizer), Am. Coll. Nutrition (Seelig award 2002), Am. Heart Assn. (coun. basic sci. 1969—, coun. on thrombosis 1971—, mem. coun. on stroke 1973—, cardiovasc. A study sect. 1978—81, coun. on circulation 1978—, coun. on high blood pressure 1978—, coun. on cardiopulmonary circulation 1987—, coun. on arteriosclerosis, thrombosis, and vascular biology 1997—, coun. on cardiovascular basic scis. 2001—, fellow coun. on high blood pressure rsch. 2002), Am. Bd. Forensic Examiners (life), Assn. Clin. Scientists (life; Wisdom Hall of Fame 1999—, Molecular Medicine Soc. 2000—), Am. Soc. Integrative Medicine (life), Am. Coll. Forensic Examiners (life), Internat. Coll. Angiology, Am. Coll. Angiology, Am. Inst. Chemists; mem.: APHA, AAUP, Aur. Physiological Soc. (organizer several symposia), Internat. Soc. Free Radical Rsch., Am. Soc. Biochemistry and Molecular Biology, Am. Inst. Biological Sci., Internat. Soc. Police Surgeons, Am. Med. Writers Assn., Nat. Coun. for Magnesium and Cardiovasc. Disease, Am. Assn. Pharm. Scis., Inter-Am. Soc. Hypertension, Am. Soc. Hypertension (founding mem.), Internat. Soc. for Hypertension, Internat. Anesthesia Soc., Coun. Biology Editors, N.Y. Soc. Electron Microscopy, N.Y. Heart Assn., N.Y. Acad. Scis. (symposium lectr.-spkr. com. mem.), Am. Soc. Magnesium Rsch. (exec. dir. 1984—, founder, pres., workshop lectr., symposium, lectr., organizer), Am. Soc. Bone and Mineral Rsch., Am. Soc. Cell Biology, The Oxygen Soc., Am. Soc. Zoologists, Am. Microscopical Soc., Am. Assn. Lab. Animal Sci., Soc. for Xenobiotics, Internat. Platform Assn., Soc. Scholarly Pub., Soc. Nutrition Edn., Soc. of Parenteral and Enteral Nutrition, Liposome Soc., Internat. Soc. Exposure Analysis, Reticuloendothelial Soc. (hon. lectr.), Soc. Cardiovasc. Pathology, Soc. Environ. Geochemistry and Health, Soc. Leukocyte Biology, Internat. Soc. Biorheology, Biomed. Optics Soc., Internat. Soc. Biomed. Rsch. on Alcoholism (founding mem.), Am. Soc. Microbiology, Am. Inst. Nutrition (organizer mini-symposium), Fedn. Am. Soc. Exptl. Biology (pub. info. com. 1981—86), Internat. Anesthesia Rsch. Soc., Neurotrauma Soc., European Conf. Microcirculation (symposium organizer, hon. lectr.), Microscopy Soc. Am., Am. Fedn. Clin. Rsch., Shock Soc. (founder, hon. lectr.), Soc. for Neurosci., Am. Thoracic Soc., Soc. for Critical Care Medicine, Rsch. Soc. on Alcoholism, Am. Soc. Pharm. and Exptl. Therapeutics, Am. Oil Chemists Soc., Rsch. Soc. on Alcoholism (organizer several symposia), Am. Coll. Toxicology, Harvey Soc., Endocrine Soc., Am. Soc. Nutritional Scis., Am. Soc. Pharm. and Exptl. Therapeutics (symposium organizer), Am. Chem. Soc. (divsn. medicinal chemistry, divsn. analytical chemistry), Am. Soc. Headache, Am. Assn. for Clin. Chemistry (hon. lectr. 1989, 1992, 1994), Soc. Exptl. Biology and Medicine (editl. bd. 1976—83), Microcirculatory Soc. (mem. nominating com. 1973—74, past mem. exec. coun.), Am. Soc. Investigative Pathology, Soc. for Magnetic Resonance, Sigma Xi. Office: 450 Clarkson Ave Brooklyn NY 11203-2056

ALUTTO, JOSEPH ANTHONY, university dean, management educator; b. Bronx, N.Y., June 3, 1941; s. Anthony and Concetta (Del Prete) Alutto; m. Carol Newcomb, Sept. 9, 1948; children: Patricia, Christina, Kerrie, Heather. BBA, Manhattan Coll., Riverdale, N.Y., 1962; MA, U. Ill., 1965; PhD, Cornell U., 1968. Asst. prof. orgnl. behavior SUNY, Buffalo, 1966-72, assoc. prof., 1972-75, prof., 1975-91, dean Sch. Mgmt., 1976-91, Clarence S. Marsh chair mgmt., 1991; dean Fisher Coll. of Bus. Ohio State U., Columbus, 1991—98, exec. dean for profl. coll., 1998—. Bd. dirs. United Retail Group, Inc., Nationwide Fin. Svcs., INROADS/Columbus, Barrister Global Systems; pres. Am. Assembly Collegiate Schs. of Bus., 1996—98. Author: (with others) Theory Testing in Organizational Behavior: The Varient Approach, 1983; contbr. 65 articles to profl. jours. United Way, Buffalo, 1982—91; pres. Amherst Cen. Sch. Bd., 1982—86. Mem. APA, AAAS, Acad. Mgmt. (pres. Ea. divsn. 1980-81), Am. Sociol. Assn., Capital Club, Athletic Club. Home: 810 Curleys Ct Columbus OH 43235-2161 Office: Ohio State U Main Campus Office Dean of Bus 201 Fisher Hall 2100 Neil Ave Columbus OH 43210-1309

ALVARADO, IVY ELIZABETH, special education educator; b. N.Y.C., Apr. 29, 1955; BS, So. Conn. Coll., 1979; MA, Fairfield U., 1984. Lic. profl. educator, comprehensive spl. edn. Resource tchr. Maple Ln. Sch., Claymont, Del., 1979-81; substitute tchr. Stamford, New Canaan and Greenwich (Conn.) schs., 1981-82; presch. tchr. Learning Ctr. at Piper's Hill, Stamford, 1982-84, kindergarten tchr., 1985-86; learning disabled tchr. Eagle Hill, Southport, Conn., 1984-85; math. tchr. Vitam Sch., Norwalk, Conn., 1986--87; remedial learning tchr. Davenport Ridge Elem. Sch., Stamford, 1987-88; remedial tchr. Julia A. Stark Elem. Sch., Stamford, 1988-90, socially/emotionally retarded tchr., 1990—. Mem. NEA, Coun. Exceptional Children, Conn. Edn. Assn. Home: 13584 N Placita Montanas De Or Oro Valley AZ 85737-8685

ALVARADO, REBECCA JANE, secondary education educator; b. LeMars, Iowa, Apr. 17, 1955; d. Robert Joseph and Beverly Anne (Smith) Meylor; m. John Frederick Clair, June 10, 1974 (div. June 24, 1987); 1 child, Christopher L. Clair; m. Hector Abel Alvarado, Sept. 5, 1987; children: David M. Strait, Randee M. Alvarado. BS in Edn., Ea. Mont. Coll., 1985. Cert. K-12 tchr., Mont. Pharmacy technician St. Anthony Hosp., Denver, Colo., 1972-78; sec. to pharmacy dir. Mercy Med. Ctr., Denver, 1980; with radio sales advt. Sta. KLYC, Laurel, Mont., 1981; realtor ERA Leuthold, Billings, Mont., 1981-84; art tchr. gifted and talented Lockwood (Mont.) Intermediate Sch., 1985-86; substitute tchr. Billings (Mont.) Pub. Schs., 1986-87; art tchr. Hardin (Mont.) Mid. Sch., 1987—, art-dist. curriculum coord., 1993—. Cons., judge Jailhouse Art Gallery, Hardin, 1991; postal stamp cancellation designer Little Big Horn Days, Hardin, 1993—. Watercolor, photography exhibited in Metrapark Art Gallery, 1985-94, Nothcutt Gallery, 1985, Jailhouse Art Gallery, 1994; Appeared in film: Son of the Morningstar, 1990. Tchr. Upward Bound Ea. Mont. Coll., Billings, 1991-94; acting cmty. theatre Der Schwartzwald Dinner Theatre, Billings Studio Theatre, Alberta Bair Theatre, Eastern Mont. Coll. Katoya Players, E.M.C. FIne Arts Festival; coach: Odyssey of the Mind, 1992-93, 95—; advisor photography and layout Hardin Mid. Sch. Yearbook, 1987-98; bd. dirs. Big Horn County Planning Bd., 1998—. Mem. NEA, Mont. Edn. Assn. (rep. 1996-97), Nat. Art Edn. Assn., Kappa Delta Epsilon (hon.), Alpha Psi Omega (hon.). Avocations: river rafting, horseback riding, quilting, art endeavors, remodeling, gardening. Home: RR 1 Box 1223C Hardin MT 59034-9721 Office: Hardin Mid Sch 611 5th St W Hardin MT 59034-1613

ALVAREZ, BLANCA MAGRASSI, educational director, psychotherapist; b. Tampico, Mex., Nov. 29, 1923; d. Camilo and Magdalena (Scagno) M.; m. Luis Hector Alvarez; children: Luis Jorge, Blanca Estela. BA, Incarnate Word Coll., San Antonio, 1944; MA, N.Mex. State U., Las Cruces, 1967; PhD, Union Grad. Sch., Cin., 1977. Sch. psychologist Inst. Femenino, Chihuahua, Mex., 1967-72; pvt. practice Chihuahua, Mex., 1967—; founder, dir. Inst. Psychology Studies, Chih, Mex., 1968-86; coord. Bilingual and Multiculture Divsn. Southwest Ednl. Lab., Austin, Tex., 1977; personal devel. dir. Women D.I.F. Mcpl., Chih, Mex., 1984-86; founder, dir. Instrn. Program, Chih, Mex., 1979-86, Edn. Cultural Arts, Chih, Mex., 1992—. Lectr. Social Work Sch., Chihuahua, Mex., 1967-71; sch. guidance Colegio Montessori, Chihuahua, Mex., 1968-70; founder Difusion Educativa y Cultural, Chihuahua, Mex., 1985, Escuela Miguel Ahumada, Chihuahua, Mex., 1981. Mem., 1956, mem. nat. coun., 1967—, candidate for mayor, 1968, candidate for senator, 1994, Partido Accion Nacional, Chihuahua, Mex. Named Disting. Contbn. Consejo Nacional de Ensenanza e Investigacion Psicologica, Mex., 1982, Inst. Superior de Ciencia y Tech. de La Laguna, Torreon, Coahuila, 1982, Woman of Yr., Profl. Womens Assn., Chihuahua, Mex., 1996. Mem. APA, Psychol. Mex. Assn., Internat. Sch. Psychology Assn. Avocations: travel, reading. Home: Dakota Del Norte 3213 31250 Chihuahua Mexico Office: Educacion Cultura Artes y Letras AC 1 de Mayo 1609D 31020 Chihuahua Mexico

ALVAREZ, OFELIA AMPARO, medical educator; b. Havana, Cuba, Mar. 29, 1958; BS, U. Puerto Rico, 1978, MD, 1982. Diplomate Nat. Bd. Med. Examiners, Am. Bd. Pediat., Sub-bd. Pediatric Hematology-Oncology. Pediatric residency Univ. Children's Hosp., San Juan, P.R., 1982-85; fellow pediatric hematology, oncology Children's Hosp. L.A., 1985-88; asst. prof. pediat. Loma Linda (Calif.) U., 1988-95, assoc. prof., 1995-2000; assoc. prof. clin. pediats. Univ. Miami, 2001—. Med. advisor Candlelighters, Inland Empire, 1988-2000. Contbr. articles to profl. jours. Bd. mem., med. advisor Make-A-Wish Found., Inland Empire, 1994-95. Clin. oncology fellow Am. Cancer Soc., 1985-86; pediatric rsch. fund Loma Linda U., 1993-95. Fellow: Am. Acad. Pediat.; mem.: AAUW, Histiocyte Soc., Am. Soc. Hematology, Am. Soc. Pediatric Hematology/Oncology, Am. Soc. Clin. Oncology, Beta Beta Beta. Roman Catholic. Office: Univ Miami Divsn Pediats Hematology Oncology Dept Pediats PO Box 016960 Miami FL 33101 E-mail: oalvarez2@med.miami.edu.

ALVAREZ, OLGA MENDOZA, elementary school educator; b. Mathis, Tex., Sept. 29, 1932; d. Fred Massiat and Mary (De Anda) Mendoza; m. John E. Epperson, Nov. 12, 1952 (div. May 1967); children: John E. Jr., Frederick Wayne, Mary Carmel, James Anthony; m. Jonas G. Alvarez, Nov. 1, 1968; children: Olga, Jonas F. BA, Trinity U., 1963; MA, U. Tex., San Antonio, 1981. Cert. elem. tchr., Tex., bilingual tchr., Tex. Clerk typist USAF, San Antonio, 1952-55; tchr. Saspamco (Tex.) Ind. Sch. Dist., 1955-56; tchr. bilingual and ESL Floresville (Tex.) Ind. Sch. Dist., 1956-95; ret. Bd. dirs. Wilson Meml. Hosp., 1984—, Oak Hills Water Bd., sec. treas. 1972-77; leader Brownie troop, 1977-79; mem. Floresville Deanery Coun. Cath. Women, pres. 1992—; sec. St. Anthony's Parish Coun., Elmendorf, Tex.; pres. Our Lady of Perpetual Help Coun. Catholic Women, coord. religious edn. Mem. Tex. Tchrs. Assn. (local chpt. sec.-treas. 1982-95). Home: RR 2 Box 192A Floresville TX 78114-9721

ALVES, ELIZABETH MARTHA HAGERTY, elementary education educator; b. Berea, Ky., May 23, 1946; d. Thomas and Dorothy F. (Van Winkle) Hagerty; m. James T. Alves, Apr. 23, 1990. BS in Edn., Bowling Green (Ohio) State U., 1968; MS in Edn., Lake Erie Coll., 1990. Tchr. grades 1-3 Euclid (Ohio) Bd. of Edn., 1968-96, retired, 1996. Mem. ASCD, NEA (bldg. rep.), Internat. Reading Assn., Ohio Edn. Assn., N.E. Ohio Edn. Assn., Euclid Tchrs. Assn. (tchr. liaison to PTA exec. bd., grade level lead tchr., advisor student coun., sch. newspaper and yearbook, Outstanding Euclid Tchr. award 1995). Avocations: gardening, reading, travel, sewing. Address: 8956 Ranch Dr Chesterland OH 44026-3138

ALWAN, ABEER, electrical engineering educator; b. Baghdad, Iraq, Feb. 26, 1959; came to U.S., 1981; d. Abdul-Hussain Alwan Shlash and Amina Wahab Mashta. BSEE, Northeastern U., 1983; SMEE, MIT, 1986, EE, 1987, PhD in Elec. Engring., 1992. Intern Concord Data Systems, Waltham, Mass., 1982-83; rsch. asst., teaching asst. dept. elec. engring. MIT, Cambridge, Mass., 1983-92; asst. prof. elec. engring. UCLA, 1992-96, assoc. prof., 1996-2000, vice chair biomed. engring., 1999-2001, prof., 2000—. Cons. Digital Equipment Corp., Waltham, 1990. Editor-in-chief Speech Comm., 2000—. Contbr. articles to profl. publs. Named one of Outstanding Young Women Am.; recipient Rsch. awards NSF, NIH and Okawa Found. Mem.: N.Y. Acad. Scis., Acoustical Soc. Am., IEEE, Tau Beta Pi, Sigma Xi. Office: UCLA Dept Electrical Engring 405 Hilgard Ave Los Angeles CA 90095-9000 E-mail: alwan@icsl.ucla.edu.

ALWOOD, EDWARD MCQUEEN, writer, journalist, media specialist; b. Macon, Ga., Sept. 12, 1949; s. Wiliam Edward A. and Mary Fisher. BA in Journalism and Polit. Sci., U of NC, 1972; MA in Pub. Comm., Am U, 1994; PhD, U of NC, 2000. Corr. WHSV-TV, Harrisonburg, Va., 1973-75, WWBT-TV, Richmond, 1975-77, WTTG-TV, Washington, 1977-81, Fin. News Network, NYC, 1981-82, WFTV-TV, Orlando, Fla., 1982-85, Cable News Network, Washington, 1985-87; mgr. pub. rels. Am. Bankers Assn., Washington, 1987-95; sr. media rels. specialist office of the comptr. of the currency U.S. Dept. Treasury, Washington, 1995-97; asst. prof. broadcast journalism Temple U., 2000—02; assoc. prof. journalism Quinnipiac U., Hamden, Conn., 2002—. Adj. prof. comm. No. Va. C.C., Alexandria. Author: Straight News: Gays, Lesbians and the News Media, 1996. Mem. nat. rsch. adv. bd. Gay and Lesbian Alliance Against Defamation. Fellow econs. Carnegie Mellon U., 1980; recipient Janus award Mortgage Bankers Assn. Am., 1981, Outstanding Achievement award Gay and Lesbian Alliance Against Defamation, 1997. Mem. Am. Journalism History Assn., Speech Comm. Assn., Nat. Lesbian and Gay Journalists Assn. (founding mem.), Assn. for Edn. in Journalism and Mass. Comm. (Nafaiger White Dissertation award 2001). Home: 96 Livingston St # 7 New Haven CT 06511

AL-ZUBAIDI, AMER AZIZ, physicist, educator; b. Najaf, Iraq, June 10, 1945; came to U.S., 1974; s. Aziz Allawi and Shahai Ali (Al Fartousi) A.; m. Haifa M. Al-Zubaidi, Aug. 24, 1972; children: Samer, Akrum. BS in Physics, U. Baghdad, Iraq, 1966; MS in Physics, Pa. State U., 1976, postgrad., 1977, 81, Va. Poly. Inst. and State U., 1977-82. bd. dirs. KCIK. High sch. tchr. Inst. for Tchrs., Riyadh, Suadi Arabia, 1966-68; high sch. tchr. physics, math., and related scis. Saudi Ministry of Edn., Riyadh, 1966-68; high sch. tchr. physics, math., mem. phys. lab. supplies and equipments com. Agrl. Vocat. Sch., Iraqi Ministry Edn., Baghdad, 1968-74; grad. teaching asst. Va. Poly. Inst. and State U., Blacksburg, 1976-82, rsch. sci. nuclear physics, 1982—; owner Al's Internat. Editor-in-chief Al-Kufa, 1994. Chmn. bd. dirs. Kufa Ctr. of Islamic Knowledge, editor-in-chief newsletter. Mem. Union of Concerned Scientists, Sigma Xi, Sigma Pi Sigma. Home: 2319 10th St NW Roanoke VA 24012-3929

AMADIO, BARI ANN, metal fabrication executive, former nurse; b. Phila., Mar. 26, 1949; d. Fred Deutscher and Celena (Lusky) Garber; m. Peter Colby Amadio, June 24, 1973; children: P. Grant, Jamie Blair. BA in Psychology, U. Miami, 1970; diploma in Nursing, Thomas Jefferson U., 1973, Johnston-Willis Sch. Nursing, 1974; BS in Nursing, Northeastern U., 1977; MS in Nursing, Boston U., 1978; JD, Quinnipiac Sch. Law, 1983. Faculty Johnston-Willis Sch. Nursing, Richmond, Va., 1974-75; staff, charge nurse Mass. Gen. Hosp., Boston, 1975-78; faculty New Eng. Deaconess, Boston, 1978-80, Lankenau Hosp. Sch. of Nursing, Phila., 1980-81; pres. Original Metals, Inc., Phila., 1985—, also bd. dirs. Owner Silver Carousel Antiques, Rochester, Minn. Treas. Women's Assn. Minn. Orch., Rochester, 1986-87, pres., 1987-89, life advisor, 1989—, editor newsnotes, 1985-87; mayor's coms. All Am. City Award Com., Rochester, 1984-88; bd. dirs. Rochester Civic League, 1988-94, pres.-elect, 1990-91, pres., 1991-92, Rochester Civic Theatre, 2003—; pres. Rochester Friends of Mpls. Inst. Arts, 1989-90, Folwell PTA, 1990-91; state liaison Gateway, 1990-91; bd. dirs. Rochester Civic Theatre, 1993-99, v.p., 1994-95, pres., 1995-96; Minn. site coord. Pew Charitable Trust's Project 540, 2002—. Recipient Joe Saidy award Rochester Civic Theatre, 1999. Mem.: NAFE, Nat. Assn. Food Equipment Mfrs., Zumbro Valley Med. Soc. Aux. (Rochester, fin. chmn. 1986—90, treas. 1988—90), Am. Soc. Law and Medicine, Rotary Club Rochester, Friends of Mayowood, Order of the Eastern Star (trustee), Sigma Theta Tau, Phi Alpha Delta. Avocations: fencing, painting, writing poetry, piano, squash.

AMADO, LISA, elementary education educator; b. N.Y.C., Aug. 28, 1955; d. Sam and Vera Ann (Capaci) Puccio; m. Manny Amado Jr., June 4, 1977; children: Christopher, Scott. BS, Bklyn. Coll., 1977; MS, SUNY, Albany, 1981. Cert. elem. edn. tchr. Reading tchr. Coxsackie (N.Y.)-Athens Cen. Sch., 1980—. Advisor/dir. Coxsackie Elem. Newspaper Club, Coxsackie Elem. Chess Club. Contbg. author: Coxsackie Elem. Newsletter. Cub scout den leader Rip Van Winkle Boy Scouts, Coxsackie, 1984-92. Mem. Internat. Reading Assn., Columbia-Greene Reading Assn. Avocations: reading, crafts. Office: Coxsackie Elem Sunset Blvd Coxsackie NY 12051

AMAN, MOHAMMED MOHAMMED, dean, library and information science educator; b. Alexandria, Egypt, Jan. 3, 1940; came to U.S., 1963, naturalized, 1975; s. Mohammed Aman and Fathia Ali (al-Maghrabi) Mohammed; m. Mary Jo Parker, Sept. 15, 1972; 1 son, David. BA, Cairo U., 1961; MS, Columbia U., 1965; PhD, U. Pitts., 1968. Librarian Egyptian Nat. Libr., 1961-63, Duquesne U., Pitts., 1966-68; asst. prof. libr. sci. Pratt Inst., N.Y.C., 1968-69; from asst. prof. to assoc. prof. St. John's U., Jamaica, N.Y., 1969-73, prof., dir. divsn. libr. and info. sci., 1973-76; prof. libr. sci., dean Palmer Grad. Libr. Sch., C.W. Post Ctr., L.I. U., 1976-79; prof., dean, interim dean Sch. Edn. U. Wis., Milw., 2000—, dean Sch. Info. Studies, 1979—. Cons. UNESCO, U.S., AID and UNIDO; USIA acad.

specialist, Germany, 1989; Fulbright lectr. Cairo U., 1990-91; USIA-sponsored lectr. Mohamed V. Univ., Rabat, Morocco, 1997. Author: Librarianship and the Third World, 1976, Cataloging and Classifications of Non-Western Library Material: Issues, Trends and Practices, 1980, Arab Serials and Periodicals: A Subject Bibliography, 1979, Online Access to Databases, 1983, On Developing Computer-Based Library Systems (Arabic), 1984, Information Services (Arabic), 1985, Trends in Urban Library Management, 1989, The Bibliotheca Alexandrina: A Link in the Chain of Cultural Continuity, 1991, Information Technology Use in Libraries (Arabic), 1998, Internet Use in Libraries, 2000, The Gulf War in World Literature, 2002; editor: Digest of Middle East Studies. Chmn. Black Faculty Coun., U. Wis., Milw.; mktg. com. Milw. Art Mus.; bd. dirs. Clara Mohammed Sch. Recipient Outstanding Achievement award Egyptian Libr. Assn., 1997. Mem. NAACP, ALA (chmn. internat. rels. com. 1984-86, standing com. on libr. edn., internat. subcom. 1990-91, chmn. 1991-93, internat. rels. Round Table 1993-94, John Ames Humphry/OCLC Outstanding Contbn. award 1989, Leadership award black caucus 1994, Excellence award black caucus 1995), Assn. Libr. and Sci. (Svc. award 1988), Am. Soc. for Info. Sci. (chmn. spl. interest group in internat. info. issues, internat. rels. com.), Egyptian Libr. Assn. (life, Outstanding Achievement award 1997), Arab/Jewish Dialogue, Egyptian-Am. Scholars Assn., Assn. for Libr. and Info. Sci. Edn. (chmn. internat. rels. com. 1983-85), Wis. Libr. Assn. (Svc. award 1992, P.N. Kaula Internat. award and medal 1996, Wis. Libr. of Yr. 1998), Libr. Svcs. and Constrn. Act. (adv. com. 1986-89), Internat. Archtl. Jury for Bibliotheca Alexandrina, Internat. Fedn. Libr. Assns. and Insts. (sec. on edn. and tng. 1983-92), Coun. on Egyptian Am. Rels., The Gamaliel Chair (bd. dirs. 1995-97), Leaders Forum (bd. dirs. 1995—), America's Black Holocaust Mus. (bd. dirs. 1999—), Islamic Social Family Svcs. (bd. dirs. 1999—), Milw. Tchr.'s Edn. Ctr. (bd. dirs.). Democrat. Moslem. Office: U Wis-Milw Sch Info Studies PO Box 413 Milwaukee WI 53201-0413 Business E-Mail: aman@uwn.edu.

AMAR, AKHIL REED, law educator; b. Ann Arbor, Mich., Sept. 6, 1958; s. Arjan D. and Kamla (Chabra) A.; m. Vinita Parkash, Sept. 3, 1989. BA summa cum laude, Yale U., 1980, JD, 1984; LLD (hon.), Suffolk U., 1997. From asst. prof. to assoc. prof. Yale Law Sch., New Haven, Conn., 1985-90, prof. law, 1990-93, Southmayd prof. law, 1993—. Samuel Rubin vis. prof. law Columbia Law Sch., N.Y.C., 1993. Author: The Constitution and Criminal Procedure, 1997, The Bill of Rights, 1998; co-author: For the People, 1998. Recipient Paul M. Bator award Federalist Soc., 1993; named 36th Ann. Coen lectr. U. Colo., 1992, Dillard lectr. U. Va., 1994, 7th ann. Barrett lectr. U. Calif., Davis, 1994, 57th Cleveland-Marshall lectr., 1994, Rutgers-Camden U., 1995, Suffolk U., 1996, Tuft lectr. U. Cin., 1998, Seegers lectr. Valparasio, 1998; DePaul Coll. Law Disting. scholar, 1991. Mem. United Ch. of Christ.*

AMARI, KATHRYN JANE, elementary education educator; b. Sopris, Colo. d. Thomas S. and Catherine (Ossola) Parker; m. Carl Leo Amari Sr., July 27, 1957; children: Jayne Amari, Carl Leo Amari Jr. AA, Trinidad State Jr. Coll., 1951; BA, Western State Coll., 1954. Cert. tchr., Colo. Tchr. Valdez (Colo.) Elem. Sch., 1951-54, Trinidad (Colo.) Pub. Sch. Dist. #1, 1954-95. Mem. lang. curriculum com., sch. improvement com. Contbr. articles to profl. mags. Mem. PTA, Trinidad, 1954-91. Mem. AAUW, Trinidad Edn. Assn. (sec. 1958-59), Colo. Edn. Assn. (rep. 1954-64), Trinidad State Jr. Coll. Alumni, Delta Kappa Gamma, Beta Sigma Phi. Democrat. Roman Catholic. Avocations: reading, crafts, hiking. Home: 307 S Spruce St Trinidad CO 81082-3536 Office: Park St Sch 612 Park St Trinidad CO 81082-2398

AMATANGELO, NICHOLAS S. retired financial printing and document management services exeutive; b. Monessen, Pa., Feb. 12, 1935; s. Sylvester and Lucy Amatangelo; m. Kathleen Driscoll, May 16, 1964; children: Amy Kathleen, Holly Megan. BA, Duquesne U., 1957; MBA, U. Pitts., 1958. Indsl. engr. U.S. Steel Co., Pitts., 1959-61; indsl. engr. mgr. Anaconda Co., N.Y.C., 1961-63; product mktg. mgr. Xerox Corp., N.Y.C., 1965-68; dir. mktg. Macmillan Co., N.Y.C., 1968-70; dir. product planning Philco-Ford Corp., Phila., 1970-72; pres., CEO Bowne San Francisco, Inc., 1972-79, Bowne Houston, Inc., Houston, 1979-87, Bowne Chgo., Inc., 1983-96, corp. cons., advisor, 1996-97; pres., CEO Bowne Detroit, Inc., 1987-96; ret., 1996. Instr. U. Pitts., Pitts., 1959—61; asst. prof. Westchester CC, N.Y.C., 1961—64, N.Y.C., 1970—72; ad. prof. grad. sch. bus. mgmt. and mktg. Roosevelt U. Grad Sch. Exec. MBA program, Chgo., 1996—. Contbr. articles to profl. jours. Bd. dirs. San Francisco Boys Club, 1974—79, Boys Town Italy, 1973—79, Alley Theatre, Houston, 1982—86; mem. pres.'s coun. Houston Grand Opera, 1980—86; mem. adv. bd. bus. sch. Roosevelt U., 1996—, vice chair, 1996—99. With U.S. Army, 1958—59, with U.S. Army, 1961—62. Mem.: Assn. Colls. Ill. (trustee 1993—), Pres. Assn., Am. Mgmt. Assn., Am. Soc. Corp. Secs., Printing Industries Am. (bd. dirs.), Duquesne U. Century Club (chmn. exec. com.), Union League Club Chgo., Econs. Club Chgo., Exec. Club Chgo. (bd. dirs.).

AMATO, ROSALIE, educator; b. Racalmuto, Agrigento, Sicily, June 3, 1920; came to U.S., 1923; d. Nicolo and Francesca (Macaluso) A. BS, Buffalo State U., 1964, MEd, 1968. Office supr. Wm. Hengerer Co. (Sibley's), Buffalo, N.Y., 1941-51; installation personnel Remington Rand, Dayton, Ohio, 1951-53; office supr., acctg. City of Buffalo, 1953-61; home econs. tchr. Buffalo Bd. Edn., 1964-70, supr. home econs. federally funded projects, 1971—. Vol. Civil Def., State of N.Y., 1953-58 (Cert. Pub. Service, 1958). Mem. Am. Home Econs. Assn. (area coord. 1973-75), Kappa Delta (treas. 1962-63), Phi Epsilon Omicron (pres. 1968-70). Roman Catholic. Avocations: art, design, concerts, opera, bowling. Home: 327 Colvin Ave Buffalo NY 14216-2338

AMAYA-THETFORD, PATRICIA, elementary education educator; b. Orange, Calif., Feb. 25, 1965; d. Guillermo Jimenez and Maria Angelina (Avalos) Mojarro; m. Elias Amaya, Oct. 22, 1988 (dec. Oct. 1993); children: Eliana Ashley, Hunter C.; m. Gary S. Thetford, June, 1999. BA in Spanish, U. Calif., Irvine, 1987; MS in Instrnl. Leadership Curr. & Instrn, Nat. U., 1998. Cert. elem. tchr., bilingual, cert. bilingual competence, Calif., 1989. Biliterate instrnl. asst. Franklin Elem. Sch., Santa Ana, Calif., 1986-89, bilingual tchr., 1989-91, Alcott Elem. Sch., Pomona, Calif., 1991-97, bilingual resource tchr., 1997—. Mem. ASCD, NEA, Calif. Tchrs. Assn., U. Calif.-Irvine Alumnae Assn., Calif. Assn. Bilingual Edn. Avocations: travel, reading, writing, collecting children's literature books. Home: 7415 Jola Drive Riverside CA 92506 Office: Alcott Elem Sch 1600 S Towne Ave Pomona CA 91766-5367

AMBACH, GORDON MAC KAY, educational association executive; b. Providence, Nov. 10, 1934; s. Russell W. and Ethel (Repass) A.; m. Lucy DeWitt Emory, Mar. 9, 1963; children: Kenneth Emory, Alison Repass, Douglas Mac Kay. BA, Yale U., 1956; MA, Harvard U. Grad. Sch. Edn., 1957, cert. advanced study, 1966. Tchr. social studies 7th and 8th grades East Williston Sch. Dist., L.I., N.Y., 1958-61; asst. program planning officer U.S. Office Edn., Washington, 1961-62, asst. legis. specialist, 1962-63, exec. sec. Higher Edn. Facilities Act Task Force, 1963-64; adminstrv. asst. to mem. Boston Sch. Com., 1964-65; staff seminar mgr., mem. staff Harvard U. Grad. Sch. Edn., Cambridge, Mass., 1966-67; spl. asst. to commr. for long range planning N.Y. State Edn. Dept., Albany, 1967-69, asst. commr. for long range planning, 1969-70, exec. dep. commr., 1970-77; commr. edn. and pres. U. State N.Y., Albany, 1977-87; exec. dir. Coun. Chief State Sch. Officers, Washington, 1987—2001. Del., chmn. resolutions com. The White House Conf. on Librs. and Info. Scis., 1991; mem. Nat. Coun. on Edn. Standards and Testing, 1993; mem. edn. com. Nat. Alliance for Bus., 1994-2001; mem. Nat. Bd. Internat. Comparative Studies in Edn., U.S. rep. to Internat. Assn. for Evaluation of Edn. Achievement, mem. standing com., 1990-2001; bd. dirs. Wallace-Reader's Digest Funds, Newspaper Assn. Am. Found., Ctr. for Naval Analysis Corp.; mem. edn. bd. NAS. With USAR, 1957-63. Mem. Acad. Polit. Scis., Am. Assn. Sch. Adminstrs., PEW Forum on Edn. Reform, Phi Delta Kappa. Home: PO Box 261 Bondville VT 05340

AMBRESTER, MARCUS LAROY, communication educator, program administrator; b. Scottsboro, Ala., Oct. 21, 1935; s. Marcus LaRoy and Mary (Howard) A.; m. Celia Beauchamp, June 23, 1956; children: Kim Ambrester McMillan, Marcus LaRoy III. BA, Samford U., 1956; MA, U. Ala., Tuscaloosa, 1959; PhD, Ohio U., 1972. Asst. prof. Samford U., Birmingham, Ala., 1961-65, U. South Ala., Mobile, 1966-67, Ouachita U., Arkadelphia, Ark., 1968-70; assoc. prof. Miss. State Coll. Women, Columbus, 1970-71; prof., dept. head Howard Payne U., Brownwood, Tex., 1971-78; assoc. prof. U. Tenn., Knoxville, 1978—, co-dir. conflict resolution program, 1992-94. Mediator/trainer Knoxville Bar Assn., 1992—. Author: Communicating Through Conflict, 1995; co-author: Speech Communication, 1983, A Rhetoric of Interpersonal Communication, 1984, G.A.M.E.S., 2d edit., 1988, Mediation Training Manual, 1993, A Rhetoric of Interpersonal Communication and Relationships, 1997; prodr.: (videotapes) Conflict Resolution, 1993, (tng. films) Sexual Harassment: Is Mediation the Solution?, 1994, Viva La Difference: Personality Types, Communication, and Conflict, 1995. Active Found. Community Encouragement, 1989—. Mem. Internat. Listening Assn., Acad. Family Mediators, Tex. Speech Comm. Assn., Mediation Assn. Tenn. (sec. 1992—), Speech Comm. Assn., Mediation Assn. Knoxville, So. Speech Comm. Assn. Avocations: tennis, reading, travel. Home: 7914 Gleason Rd Apt 1138 Knoxville TN 37919-3926 Office: U Tenn 104 Mcclung Tower Knoxville TN 37996-0001

AMBROS, ROBERT ANDREW, pathologist, educator, writer; b. Passaic, N.J., May 21, 1959; s. Henry and Adele (Ruta) A.; m. Maryla Warszawa, Aug. 22, 1981; children: Robert, Janek, Julia. MD, Copernicus Acad. Medicine, 1982. Resident in surgery Morristown (N.J.) Meml. Hosp., 1983-85; resident in pathology N.J. Med. Sch., Newark, 1985-89; fellow in gynecologic pathology Johns Hopkins Hosp., Balt., 1989-91; asst. prof. pathology Albany (N.Y.) Med. Coll., 1991-96, asst. prof. ob-gyn., 1993-96, assoc. prof. pathology, ob-gyn., 1996—. Cons. in gynecologic pathology Albany Med. Coll., 1991—. Author: (novels) The Brief Sun, 2002 (Best Genre Fiction award Writer's Digest, 2002); contbr. articles to profl. jours.; editor: Internat. Jour. Gynecol. Pathology, 1994—. Clin. oncology fellow Am. Cancer Soc., 1990; recipient Basic Oncology Rsch. award Am. Cancer Soc., 1988. Fellow Coll. Am. Pathologists; mem. AAAS, Internat. Soc. Gynecol. Pathologists, Internat. Acad. Pathology, N.Y. Acad. Scis., Johns Hopkins Med. and Surg. Assn. Achievements include research in the surgical and molecular pathology of gynecologic malignancies. Office: Albany Med Coll Dept Pathology 43 New Scotland Ave Albany NY 12208-3412 E-mail: ambrosr@mail.amc.edu.

AMBROSE, WILLIAM WRIGHT, JR., dean, educator, academic administrator; b. Norfolk, Va., Oct. 13, 1947; s. William Wright and Charlotte Gertrude (Williamson) Ambrose; m. Marcelia A. Conerly, Aug. 7, 1971 (div. Dec. 1986); children: William Wright III, Xandrea M., Mark S., Ariana R., LaConda G. Fanning; m. Jacqueline D. Woodard, Dec. 28, 1998. BSBA, Norfolk State U., 1974; MBA, postgrad. in EdD program, Pepperdine U. Enrolled agt. IRS; lic. ins. broker, notary pub., cmty. coll. teaching credential, Calif.; cert. tax profl. Quality assurance mgr. mfg. Corning (N.Y.) Glass Co., 1974-78; contr., plant mgr. Phillip Morris, Auburn, N.Y., 1978-79; sr. exec. mgr. Kerr Glass Corp., L.A., 1979-84; instr. Nat. Edn. Corp., Anaheim, Calif., 1985-87; assoc. prof., chmn. dept. acctg. and bus., dean, regional dean so. Calif. DeVry U., Calif., 1987—, prof. bus., 1994—, dean of bus., 1998—. CEO Global Bus. Agents, Inc., 2000; cons. Protrans, Santa Ana, Calif., 1985—, Castillo Electronics, Los Alamitos, Calif., 1986. Co-patentee polarized contaminate viewer. Sgt. Army Security Agy., U.S. Army, 1967-71, Vietnam. Mem.: Calif. Soc. CPA's, Nat. Soc. Tax Profls., Am. Prodn. and Inventory Control Soc., Am. Mgmt. Assn., Am. Acctg. Assn., Nat. Bus. Edn. Assn., Inst. Mgmt. Accts., Nat. Assn. Acad. Affairs Adminstrs., Am. Assn. Higher Edn., Sigma Beta Delta, Phi Delta Kappa. Avocations: computer programming, golf, writing, international consulting, ebusiness. Home: 795 S Pampas Ave Rialto CA 92376-2102 Office: DeVry U 901 Corporate Center Dr Pomona CA 91768-2642 E-mail: bambrose@socal.devry.edu

AMBROSI, SANDRA ELIZABETH, retired nurse, educator; b. Albany, N.Y., May 15, 1938; d. James Syme and Elizabeth Clare (Volwieder) Woodward; children: Lisa Marie Lawson, Ronald James Ambrosi. BS, Columbia U., 1962; MN, U. Wash., 1965; MPA, U. Hartford, Conn., 1983. RN, N.Y., Conn., Calif. Instr. Hartford Hosp. Sch. Nursing, 1965-66; dir. staff devel. Johnson Meml. Hosp., Stafford Springs, Conn., 1966-70, dir. utilization rev., 1970-75, dir. quality assurance, 1975-81; dir. delivery sys. AMI Health Advantage, San Diego, 1984-87; resource nurse Ask-A-Nurse, San Diego, 1988-91; sch. health specialist San Diego Unified Sch. Dist., 1991—2003; ret., 2003. Mem. Nat. Assn. Healthcare Quality (pres. 1978-80, cert. profl. healthcare quality), Nat. Assn. Sch. Nurses, S.D. Edn. Assn., Sigma Theta Tau.

AMELL, ROBERT EDWARD, educational facility administrator, business owner; b. S.I., Feb. 22, 1961; s. Woodrow E. and Lydia (Gorman) A.; m. Amy K. Spigelmyer, May 27, 1989. AST, Electronics Inst., 1983; ASB in Computer Programming, Thompson Inst.; BSBA, Phoenix U. Svc. mgr. Tandy Corp., Lancaster, Pa., 1983-84, Software Resources, Lancaster, 1984; dir. Nat. Edn. Ctr., Harrisburg, Pa., 1984-85. V.p. Greater Harrisburg Youth for Christ, 1990—. Pres. Greater Harrisburg Youth for Christ, 1985—. Mem. Electronics Technicians Assn. (super com., cert. adminstr. 1987—), Data Processing Mgmt. Assn. Republican. Avocations: youth service, music. Home: 2564 Tiffany Ln Harrisburg PA 17112-8627 Office: Nat Edn Ctr 5650 Derry St Harrisburg PA 17111-3571

AMEN, BETTY JEAN, special education educator; b. McCook, Nebr., Oct. 22, 1956; d. Robert Lee and Marilyn R. (Chapman) Shaffer; m. Alan K. Amen, Aug. 5, 1978; children: Andrew, Joshua, Emily. BA in Edn., Kearney State Coll., 1978. Resource tchr. Ednl. Svc. Unit II, Holdrege, Nebr., 1979—. Mem. Early Devel. Network, Kearney State Coll. Alumni Assn. Mem. Evangelical Free. Avocations: reading, sewing, skiing. Home: 1011 Grant St Holdrege NE 68949-1864

AMENDOLA, SAL JOHN, artist, educator, writer; b. Fiumefreddo, Calabria, Italy, Mar. 8, 1948; came to U.S., 1948; s. Joseph and Mary (Amendola) A. Grad., Erasmus Hall H.S., Bklyn.; 3-yr. cert., Sch. Visual Arts, N.Y.C., 1966-69. Illustator, writer DC Comics, Archie Comics, Marvel, N.Y.C., 1969-86; asst. editor, prodn. DC Comics, N.Y.C., 1970; talent coord., editor DC Comics, Warner Communications, N.Y.C., 1983-86; illustration instr. Sch. Visual Arts, Fashion Inst., N.Y.C., 1974—; founder SRV plus 1, 1990. Lectr., cons., instr. seminars at librs., mus., schs., U.S., Can., 1983-86; freelance illustrator, 1987—. Writer, illustrator: (comic book) Batman Night of the Stalker, 1972 (Best Story Nominee 1973); editor: (comic books) Elvira's House of Mystery, Talent Showcase, 1984-86; co-artist: (movie adaptation) Superman III, 1983, (comic book) Star Trek, 1984; author, artist: (book) Perspective for Artists, 1984, (book) Other Intelligences/A Sociopolitical View, 1990; artist: (comic book) Archie, 1987 (Best Artist nominee 1988); creator young adult books The Yoomee Adventures; designer toys and games; book illustrator, designer, illustrator book jackets; portrait painter. Mem. Nat. Cartoonist Soc. (profl. com. 1987), Soc. Illustrators. Liberal Democrat. Avocations: science, politics, foreign languages. Home: 1028 67th St Brooklyn NY 11219-5923 E-mail: srvplus1@aol.com.

AMENT, ARLENE SHUB, middle school educator; b. Chgo., Feb. 5, 1947; d. Seymour Victor and Estelle Mildred (Dreebin) Shub; m. Rickey J. Ament, June 21, 1970; 1 child, Maxine. BS, U. Ill., 1969; MEd, Northeastern Ill. U., 1971. Coord. sch. tech. West Northfield Sch. Dist. 31, Northbrook, Ill., 1969—. Mem. Internat. Soc. for Tech. in Edn., Ill. Computing Educators. Avocation: computers. Home: 1508 Rose Blvd Buffalo Grove IL 60089-3278 Office: Field Mid Sch 2055 Landwehr Rd Northbrook IL 60062-6411

AMES, IRA H. cell biologist, educator; b. Bklyn., Apr. 27, 1937; s. Lawrence and Blanche (Tannenbaum) A.; m. Joyce Toby Surnamer, June 26, 1958; children: Michael P., Sarah J. Ames Audi. BA, Bklyn. Coll., 1959; MS, NYU, 1962, PhD, 1966. Instr. biology Bklyn. Coll., 1960-63, lectr. in biology, 1963-64; rsch. assoc. Brookhaven Nat. Lab., Upton, N.Y., 1966-68; asst. prof. SUNY Upstate Med U., Syracuse, 1968-73, assoc. prof., 1973-89, prof. dept. cell devel. biology, 1989—. Mem. editl. bd. In Vivo, Athens, Greece, 1994-2002; contbr. over 30 articles to profl. publs., chpt. to book. NSF rsch. grantee, 1972. Mem. AAAS, Am. Assn. Anatomists, Am. Soc. Cell Biology, Phi Beta Kappa, Sigma Xi. Home: 105 Woodmancy Ln Fayetteville NY 13066-1534 Office: SUNY Upstate Med U Dept Cell Devel Biol Syracuse NY 13210

AMES, SANDRA CUTLER, secondary education educator; b. Putnam, Conn., Nov. 3, 1935; d. Loid C. and Sophie M. (Kowal) Cutler; m. David Crouse Ames, Oct. 28, 1955; children: Deborah Lee, Susan Lynn. BS, U. Conn., 1957, MS, 1959; postgrad., Ea. Conn. State U., 1965. Cert. elem. tchr., Conn. Tchr. elem. Killingly Ctrl. Sch., Dayville, Conn., 1959-88, tchr. K-4 resource math., testing coord., 1988—. Presenter math. workshops, Dayville, 1981—; co-chair Invention Conv., Dayville, 1987-90. Recipient Presdl. award in math. Fed. & State Bds. Edn., 1990, 93. Mem. Delta Kappa Gamma. Avocations: crafts, crocheting, knitting, decorating. Home: 235 Chase Rd Putnam CT 06260-2810 Office: Killingly Ctrl Sch 60 Soap St Dayville CT 06241-1622

AMEZCUA, CHARLIE ANTHONY, social science counselor, educator; b. Los Angeles, Sept. 1, 1928; s. Carlos and Inez (Nunez) A.; B.A., UCLA, 1958; M.S., Calif. State U., Los Angeles, 1961; m. Kathleen Joyce Greene, Mar. 7, 1964; children— Colleen Alvita, Charles Anthony. Student psychologist Rancho Los Amigos Hosp., Downey, Calif., 1959-60; instr. in psychology East Los Angeles Coll., 1962-72, asst. prof. counseling, 1972-74, assoc. prof. counseling, 1974—, prof. psychology, 1980—, spl. edn. counselor, 1981—, coordinator vet. affairs, 1972—; personnel asst. Los Angeles City Sch. Dist., 1963-64; counselor Youth Tng. and Employment Project, Los Angeles, 1965-66, counseling supr., 1966, project dir., 1966-67; counseling psychologist VA, Los Angeles, 1967-70; dir. Head Start, Los Angeles County Econ. and Youth Opportunities Agy., 1970-71; bd. dirs. Tng. and Research Found., Child and Family Resources Centers; lectr. counselor edn. Calif. State U., Los Angeles; guest lectr. John F. Kennedy U., 1987—. Mem. Calif. Gov.'s Adv. Com. on Children and Youth, 1966-67; judge blue ribbon panel Nat. Acad. TV Arts and Scis., 1966-76. Served with USN, 1948-52; Korea; cert. community coll. counselor, supr.-adminstrn., jr. coll. teaching in psychology. Mem. Am. Psychol. Assn., Calif. State Psychol. Assn., Calif. Assn. Post-Secondary Educators of the Disabled, Western Psychol. Assn. Democrat. Home: 8348 Fable Ave Canoga Park CA 91304-3036 Office: East Los Angeles Coll 1301 Brooklyn Ave Monterey Park CA 91754-6001

AMEZCUA, ESTHER HERNANDEZ, elementary education educator; b. Guadalajara, Jalisco, Mexico, Nov. 9, 1949; came to the U.S., 1961; d. Rodolfo (stepfather) and Guillermina (Hernandez) Sanchez; m. Juan Elizondo Amezcua, June 23, 1973; children: Juanguillermo Gabriel, Jaime Jose Vicente. BA, U. Calif., Davis, 1972. Life tchg. credential, Calif.; multicultural and bilingual credential. With Sacramento City Unified Sch., 1973—; intermediate tchr. William Land Elem., 1973-81, 83-93, primary tchr., 1981-83, 2002—; intermediate tchr., head tchr. Oak Ridge Elem., 1993-97, Caroline Wenzel Elem., 1997—2002. Head tchr. William Land Sch., Sacramento, 1976-83, 89-93, Oak Ridge Elem., Sacramento, 1993-94; mentor tchr. Sacramento Unified Sch. Dist., 1991-93. Vol. Short Term Emergency Assistance Ctr., Davis, Calif., 1990—; dance instr. ballet folklorico, Sacramento, 1990—; vol. tutor, Sacramento, 1993—. Named Educator of Yr. Yolo County, Mexican-Am. Concilio of Woodland, 1997. Mem. Hispanic Educators Sacramento, Calif. Tchrs. Assn., Sacramento City Tchrs. Assn. Democrat. Roman Catholic. Avocations: reading, crocheting, sightseeing, dancing, family activities. Home: 3207 Monte Vista Pl Davis CA 95616-4932 Office: William Land Sch 2120 12th St Sacramento CA 95818 E-mail: amezcua20@yahoo.com.

AMIE, BARBARA E. school system administrator; b. Dallas; d. Flemmie Lonzaro Jackson and Lillie James Burnley; m. Milton Amie, Dec. 13, 1982. BS, Bishop Coll., 1973; MEd, E. Tex. State U., 1985, postgrad., 1985—. Cert. elem. tchr.; mid.-mgmt. cert., Tex. Tchr. Dallas Ind. Sch. Dist., 1977-92, asst. prin., 1992—; reservations agent Am. Airlines, Arlington, Tex., 1986-88. Active Edwin Hawkins Music & Arts Mass Choir, Jr. Black Acad. Arts & Letters Concert Choir. Mem. Dallas Regional/Nat. Alliance Black Sch. Educators (fin. sec. 1991—, presdl. award 1992), Zeta Phi Beta. Church of Christ. Avocations: choir directing, song-writing, travel.

AMIN, MASSOUD, executive, systems science and mathematics educator; b. Tabriz, Iran, July 4, 1961; came to U.S., 1978; s. Mohammad Shafi and Nahid (Loghman-Adham) A.; m. Elizabeth Ambrose, May 28, 1994. BSEE, U. Mass., 1982, MS in Elec. and Computer Engrng., 1985; MSc, Washington U., 1986, DSc, 1990. Rsch. assoc. elec. and computer engrng. U. Mass., Amherst, 1982-84, tchg. assoc. elec. and computer engrng. dept. math, 1983-85; lectr., rsch. assoc. systems sci. and math. Washington U., St. Louis, 1987-92, sr. fellow Ctr. for Optimization and Semantic Control, 1990-94, asst. prof. systems sci. and math., 1992-97, assoc. prof., 1997-98, assoc. dir. Ctr. for Optimization and Semantic Control, 1994-98; mgr. math., info. sci. Electric Power Rsch. Inst., Palo Alto, Calif., 1998—. Co-chair conf. Internat. Fedn. Operational Rsch. Soc., St. Louis, 1995; advisor grad. theses and sr. projects Washington U., 1990-98; referee, reviewer jours. in field. Guest editor Math. and Computer Modelling, 1995, 98, Internat. Transactions in Operational Rsch., 1998; editl. bd. of four acad. jours.; contbr. numerous articles to profl. jours. Vol. Orgn. for Aged in St. Louis, 1988-91; vol. instr. Washington U. Kenpo Club, 1992-96. Mem. AIAA (Young Profl. award 1990), IEEE (liaison to neural network coun., assoc. editor Control Systems mag. 1998, Best Session Paper Presentation awards Am. Control Conf. 1997), AAAS, ASME, Inst. Ops. Rsch. & Mgmt. Scis., Soc. Indsl. and Applied Math., N.Y. Acad. Scis., Sigma Xi, Eta Kappa Nu, Tau Beta Pi (chief advisor Mo. Gamma chpt. 1994-98). Achievements include work as principal investigator or co-principal investigator on several collaborations with industry and government, original contributions to research and design of decision-aiding system for advanced tactical aircraft as well as cross-disciplinary contributions in intelligent control and optimization, research on development and application of the Semantic Control Paradigm; successful creation and launch of a 28-Univ. complex interactive networks research intiative. Office: EPRI 3412 Hillview Ave Palo Alto CA 94304-1395 E-mail: mamin@epri.com.

AMM, SOPHIA JADWIGA, artist, educator; b. Czestochowa, Poland, June 13, 1932; arrived in Can., 1948,arrived in U.S., 1987; d. Romuald Witold and Jadwiga Wactawa (Kotowska) Sulatycki; m. Bruce Campbell Amm, Aug. 5, 1961; children: Alicia, Alexander, Christopher, Bruce Jr., Gregory. Diploma in nursing, Ont. Hosp., 1953; cert. in pub. health nursing, U. Toronto, Ont., Can., 1960; BFA with honors, York U., 1980; MFA, Norwich U., 2000. RN. Pvt. duty nurse Allied Registry, Toronto, 1954-56; asst. head nurse Reddy Meml. Hosp., Montreal, Canada, 1957-59; pub. health nurse Dist. of Sudbury, Canada, 1960-62; pvt. duty nurse Gen. Hosp.,

Millinocket, Maine, 1962-66; counselor to new immigrants Ont. Welcome House, Toronto, 1982; vis. nurse St. Elizabeth Vis. Nurses Assn., Toronto, 1983-87; artist, tchr. YMCA, Appleton, Wis., 1994. Art rental and sales Art Gallery Hamilton, 1985—2003; condr. art workshops Very Spl. Arts Wis. festivals, 1989, 90, 92; artist resident Studios Midwest, Civic Art Ctr., Galesburg, Ill., 2003. One-woman shows include Bergstrom Mahler Mus., Neenah, Wis., 1991, Alfonse Gallery, Milw., 2001, exhibited in group shows at Harbourfront Exhbn. Gallery, Toronto, IDA Gallery, York U., 1980—81, 1986, Calumet Coll., York U., 1981, 1984, Simpson's Art Gallery, Toronto, 1984, Art Gallery Hamilton, Can., 1985—86, 2001, Pastel Soc. Can., Ottawa, 1985, Carnegie Gallery, Dundas, Can., 1986, Gallery 68, Burlington, Can., 1986, Del Bello Gallery, Toronto, 1986—93, Neville Pub. Mus., Green Bay, Wis., 1987—89, 1992, 1994—97, Consilium Pl., Scarborough, Can., 1987, 1989, 1992—93, Charles A. Wustum Mus. Fine Arts, Racine, Wis., 1990—91, 1994, Gallery Ten, Rockford, Ill., 1992 (3d pl. award, 1992), 1994—95, New Vision Gallery, Marshfield, Wis., 1992, 2001, U. Wis. Gallery, Madison, 1992, 1994, Butler Inst. Am. Art, Youngstown, Ohio, 1993, Lakeland Coll., Wis., 1994, Alverno Coll., Milw., 1994, 1997, Ariz. State U., 1995, Bergstrom Mahler Mus., 1995—96 (1st pl. award, 1995, 3d pl. award, 1996, 1997), Appleton Art Ctr., 1995, 1996, 2002, 2003, Ctr. Visual Arts, Wausau, Wis., 1996, Marian Coll. Art, Fond du Lac, Wis., 1996, Anderson Art Ctr., Kenosha, Wis., 1997, Stage Gallery, Merrick, N.Y., 1997, 1998, Norwich U. Vt. Coll. Gallery, Montpelier, 1998—2000, T. W. Wood Gallery, 2000, Hendrickson Art Ctr., Waupaca, Wis. (Hon. Mention, 2000, 2002), West Bend Gallery, 2000, Art Quest Nat. Juried Exhbn., Ft. Smith, 2001, N.E. Exposure, Priebe Gallery Exhbn. (Jurors award, 2001), Fulton St. Gallery, Troy, N.Y., 2002, Paine Art Ctr., Oshkosh, Wis., 2002, 2003, Galesburg (Ill.) Civic Art Ctr., 2003, Hothouse Ctr., Chgo., 2003, St. Norbert's Coll., De Pere, Wis., 2003. Vol. art tchr. children with disabilities, Appleton, 1988—89, disabled srs. Colony Oaks Nursing Home, Appleton, 1988—91. Recipient award of Excellence, North York (Can.) Arts Coun., 1982, 1986, Best in Show, Etobicoke (Can.) Arts Coun., 1982, 1987; Project grantee, Very Spl. Arts Wis., 1989. Mem.: Wis. Painters and Sculptors, Appleton Art Ctr., Nat. Mus. Women Arts. Roman Catholic. Avocations: golf, gardening. Home: 1109 N Briarcliff Dr Appleton WI 54915-2848

AMMAN, E(LIZABETH) JEAN, university official; b. Hoyleton, Ill., July 13, 1941; d. James Kerr and Marie Fern (Schnake) White; m. Douglas Dorrance Amman, Aug. 12, 1962; children: Mark, Kirk, Jill, Drew, Gwen, Joyce. BA in English, Ill. Wesleyan U., 1963; MA in English, U. Cin., 1975. Cert. tchr., Ill. Tchr. lang. arts John Greer Jr. High Sch., Hoopeston, Ill., 1963-64, Pleasant Hill Sch., East Peoria, Ill., 1966-67; tchr. English, chmn. Am. studies Anderson Sr. High Sch., Cin., 1967-69; instr. English, No. Mich. U., Marquette, 1976-82, Ball State U., Muncie, Ind., 1982-86, adminstrv. intern, 1983-84, asst. to chmn. dept., 1984-86, adminstrv. asst., 1986, asst. to provost, coord. provost's lecture series, 1986—, exec. sec. student and campus life coun., 1986—2002. Editor: Provost's Lecture Series: Perspectives on Culture and Society, Vol. I, 1988, Vol. II, 1991, The Associator, 1983-86. Mem. choir College Ave. Meth. Ch., Muncie, 1989—; fundraiser Delaware County Coalition for Literacy, 1989, 90; flutist Muncie Westminster Orch., 1989—, Am.'s Hometown Band, 1991—, Baroque Consort, 1998—. Recipient recognition Black Student Assn., Ball State U., 1988, cert. of svc. for minority student devel., 1990, 91, 92. Mem. AAUW (pres. Muncie br. 1997-98, Ind. dir. programs 1999-2003, Ind. pres. elect 2003-), Ind. Coll. English Assn. (editor 1983-85, exec. bd. 1983-86), P.E.O. (pres. Muncie 1985-87), Sigma Alpha Iota (v.p. 1994-97, pres. 1999-2000, Sword of Honor 1995), Kappa Delta (Ind. Kappa Delta of Yr. 1994, advisor 1992-95, collegiate province pres. 1995-98), Phi Kappa Phi. Democrat. Avocations: travel, reading, music. Home: 4305 Castleton Ct Muncie IN 47304-2476 Office: Ball State U 2000 W University Ave Muncie IN 47306-0002

AMNEUS, D. A. English language educator; b. Beverly, Mass., Oct. 15, 1919; d. Nils A. and Harriet S. (Anchersen) Amneus; divorced; children: Paul, Pamela. AB, U. Calif. Berkeley, 1941; MA, U. So. Calif., 1947, PhD, 1953. From asst. prof. to prof. Calif. State U., L.A., 1950-86, prof. emeritus, 1986—. Pub. Primrose Press, Alhambra, Calif. Author: Back to Patriarchy, 1979, The Mystery of Macbeth, 1983, The Three Othellos, 1986, The Garbage Generation, 1990, The Case for Father Custody, 1999; contbr. articles to profl. jours. Republican. Home: 2131 S Primrose Ave Alhambra CA 91803-3834 Office: Calif State U English Dept 5151 State University Dr Los Angeles CA 90032-4226

AMODIO, BARBARA ANN, philosophy educator, educational administrator; b. Middletown, N.Y., Feb. 14, 1948; d. Arthur West and Dorothy Elizabeth (Curran) Amodio. BA, Thomas More Coll., Fordham U., 1970; MA, Fordham U., 1972, PhD, 1979; student, U. Aix-Marseille, Aix-en-Provence, France, 1968; diploma in Bus. French & Euromkt. Instn., U. Strasbourg (France), 1992. Mediator, Chgo. Bar Assn. Ctr. for Conflict Resolution, Am. Acad. Family Mediators. Teaching fellow Fordham U., Bronx, N.Y., 1971-73; from lectr. to instr. philosophy Loyola U., Chgo., 1975-76, 79-83; contract monitor Pres.'s Office of Manpower Adminstrn., Chgo., 1976-78; acad. career advisor, vis. prof. U. Chgo., 1985-88; mediator Chgo. Bar Assn., 1985-87; pvt. mediation practice, 1985-89; coord. adminstrv. programs, adminstrv. intern to campus dir. U. Conn., Stamford, 1989-90, coord. student community svc. programs, lectr. French lang., 1990-93. Lectr. Oriental philosophies and philosophy Fairfield (Conn.) U., 1990—; lectr. Grad. Sch. Pub. Mgmt., U. New Haven, 1990; researcher China, 1994—; dir. Scarlet Bird Internat. Expeditions in Learning and Intelligent Travel, Asia, Europe, Mediterranean Basin, 1994—. Contbr. articles to profl. jours. Mem. Norwalk (Conn.) Human Rights and Rels. Commn., 1987—; mem. Conn. Gov.'s Adv. Com. on Am. and Francophone Affairs, 1992-96, adv. commr., 1996—. French Embassy Cultural Svcs. grantee, 1971, 92; invited Philosophy Edn. del. P.R. China, 1993; Fordham U. fellow, Woodrow Wilson fellow and finalist; Danforth Found. fellow and finalist, numerous other grants. Mem. Metaphys. Soc. Am., Internat. Soc. for Chinese Philosophy, Soc. for Study of Process Philosophies, Am. Maritain Soc., Yves Simon Inst., Am. Philos. Assn., Alliance Francaise, Am. Assn. Tchrs. French, Am. Acad. Divorce and Family Mediators. Avocations: archeology, comparative anthropology, aesthetics, oriental art. Home: PO Box 533 Westport CT 06881-0533

AMSTADT, NANCY HOLLIS, retired language educator; b. Chgo., Ill., Mar. 1, 1932; d. James George and Agnes Green Hollis; m. Ervin Carl Amstadt, Dec. 27, 1952; children: Elaine, Joan, Steven, Carolyn. BA, De Paul U., 1952; MA, San Diego State U., 1966. English & history tchr. Sweetwater H.S. Dist., Chula Vista, Calif., 1957—59; tchr., counselor Santa Clara City Schs., Santa Clara, Calif., 1959—63; secondary English tchr. San Diego City Schs., San Diego, 1966—91; English instr. San Diego C.C., San Diego, 1993—95; ret., 1995. Chmn. dept. English Kearny H.S., San Diego, 1985—91. Author: Confinement: Anne Frank's House, 1999; Confinement: Anne Frank's House, 1999, exhibitions include San Diego Art Inst., 1984—2003. Mem. U.N. Gender Equity, San Diego, 2001—03; docent art gallery U. Calif., San Diego, 1998—2003; program dir. San Diego Mus. Art, San Diego, 1968—2003. Democrat. Avocations: tennis, women refugees, art history, classical music, Chinese exercise. Home: 1097 Alexandria Drive San Diego CA 92107

AMSTER, JEANNE E. school director; b. Apr. 30, 1955; d. Richard and Barbara Levin A.; m. Kenneth Arnold; children: Alexandra Lillian Arnold, Arden Martin Arnold. AB, Mount Holyoke Coll., 1977; AM, Stanford (Calif.) U., 1979; EdM, Harvard U., 1987, EdD, 1990. Tchg. fellow history, social sci. Phillips Acad., Andover, Mass., 1977-78, dir. econs. project, 1979-84, instr. history, social sci., 1979-86, dean of studies, 1983-86; tchr. fellow 19th century soc. history Stanford U., 1979; tchg. fellow Harvard U., Cambridge, 1987-90, asst. to dean, grad sch. edn., 1987-89; dir. Ethical Culture Fieldston Schs., N.Y.C., 1991—. Vis. asst. prof. Brown U., Providence, R.I., 1990 Author; The Aspen Institute, 1990; contbr. articles to profl. jours. Larsen fellowship Harvard Grad. Sch./Edn., 1987-89; Class of 1905 fellowship Mount Holyoke Coll., 1987. Home: 314 Walnut St San Francisco CA 94118-2015 Office: Ethical Cultural Fieldston Schs 33 Central Park W New York NY 10023-6001

AMSTERDAM, ANTHONY GUY, law educator; b. Phila., Sept. 12, 1935; s. Gustave G. and Valla (Abel) A.; m. Lois P. Sheinfeld, Aug. 29, 1968. AB, Haverford Coll., 1957; LLB, U. Pa., 1960; LLD (hon.), John Jay Coll. Criminal Justice, 1987, Haverford Coll., 1993. Bar: D.C. 1960. Law clk. to U.S. Supreme Ct. Justice Felix Frankfurter, 1960-61; asst. U.S. atty., 1961-62; prof. law U. Pa., 1962-69, Stanford U., 1969-81, Montgomery prof. clin. legal edn., 1980-81; prof. law, dir. clin. programs and trial advocacy NYU, 1981—2001, univ. prof., 2001—. Cons. litigating atty. numerous civil rights groups; cons. govt. commns.; mem. Commn. to Study Disturbances at Columbia, 1968; trustee Death Penalty Info. Ctr., Lawyers Constl. Def. Com., NAACP Legal Def. Fund, Nat. Coalition to abolish the Death Penalty, So. Poverty Law Ctr., mem. Calif. Fed. Jud. Selection Com., 1976-80; mem. coord. coun. on lawyer competence Conf. of Chief Justices; gen. counsel N.Y. Civil Liberties Union; adv. counsel Civil Liberties Union No. Calif.; mem. ABA task force. Author: The Defensive Transfer of Civil Rights Litigation From State to Federal Courts, 1964, Trial Manual for Defense of Criminal Cases, 5th edit., 1989, (with Hertz and Guggenheim) Trial Manual for Defense Attorneys in Juvenile Court, 1991, (with Bruner) Minding the Law, 2000; editor-in-chief: U. Pa. Law Rev., 1959-60; contbr. articles to profl. jours. Named Outstanding Young Man of Year Phila. and Pa. Jaycees, 1967; recipient First Disting. Service award U. Pa. Law Sch., 1968; Haverford award Haverford Coll., 1970; Arthur V. Briesen award Nat. Legal Aid and Defender Assn., 1972, 76; named Lawyer of Year Calif. Trial Lawyers Assn., 1973; recipient 1st Earl Warren Civil Liberties award No. Calif. chpt. ACLU, 1973, Citizen of Merit award Sun Reporter, 1974, Walter J. Gores award Stanford U., 1977, William O. Douglas award Pub. Counsel, 1977, 2d ann. award Calif. Attys. Criminal Justice, 1978, award for enhancement human dignity Durfee Found., 1982, Francis Rawle award ALI-ABA, 1984, 3d ann. Civil Liberties award Pa. ACLU, 1985, clinical legal edn. award AALS Sect. on Clinical Legal Edn., 1986, August Vollmer award Am. Soc. Criminology, 1986, Disting. Tchr. award NYU, 1988, award N.Y. Criminal Bar Assn., 1989, Tchg. Achievement award Soc. Am. Law Tchrs., 1999, Kutak award ABA, 2002; named MacArthur fellow, 1989; hon. fellow for pub. interest svc. U. Pa. Law Sch., 2001. Fellow Am. Acad. Arts and Scis. Home: 68 Middle Line Hwy Southampton NY 11968-1645 Office: NYU Sch Law Clinical Ctr 161 Avenue of the Americas New York NY 10013

AMY, MICHAËL JACQUES, art historian, educator, art critic; b. Antwerp, Belgium, Sept. 26, 1964; s. Jean-Jacques Amy and Marie-Claire Nuyens. BA, Vrije U., Brussels, 1986; MA, NYU, 1989, PhD, 1997. Asst. to curator Mus. Contemporary Art, Ghent, Belgium, 1986-87; rsch. asst. Coe Kerr Gallery, N.Y.C., 1988-91; vis. specialist Montclair (N.J.) State U., 1996—97; adj. asst. prof. CUNY, 1997-99, Manhattanville Coll., Purchase, NY, 1997, NYU, 1997-99, The Cooper Union, 1999; vis. asst. prof. Oberlin (Ohio) Coll., 1999-2000; asst. prof. Rochester (N.Y.) Inst. Tech., 2000—. Sec. Mnemosyne, Antwerp, Belgium, 1995—; lectr. in field.; art critic Art et Culture, Brussels, 1997-99, Art in Am., N.Y.C., 1997—, Sculpture, Washington, 2001—, Tema Celeste, Milan, 2002-. Contbr. Santa Maria del Fiore: The Cathedral and its Sculpture, 2001. Recipient fellow Belgian Am. Ednl. Found., 1987-88, award Inst. Fine Arts fellow, 1988-89, 90-94, Bernard Berenson fellow, 1993-94, Samuel H. Kress Found. fellow, 1994-95; CIAS grantee, 2002. Mem. Internat. Assn. Art Critics, Renaissance Soc. Am., Coll. Art Assn., Italian Art Soc. Avocations: literature, music, politics, philosophy. Home: Apt 8 123 Holyoke St Rochester NY 14615-1927 Office: Rochester Inst Tech Coll Imaging Arts and Scis 73 Lomb Memorial Dr Rochester NY 14623-5603 E-mail: mjafaa@rit.edu.

AMY-MORENO DE TORO, ANGEL ALBERTO, social sciences educator, writer, oral historian; b. San Juan, P.R., Jan. 10, 1945; s. Alberto Sadí Amy-Ramírez and María de los Angeles Moreno Ledesma; m. Ana E. Cordero-Amy, May 30, 1973; children: Denise Yahara, Alberto Enrique, Juan Carlos. BA, U. P.R., Río Piedras, 1968; MA, SUNY, Fredonia, 1972; EdD, Boston U., 1982, PhD, 1998. Asst. librarian U. P.R., Río Piedras, 1968-69; tchr. social studies Juan José Osuna Mid. Sch., Hato Rey, P.R., 1969, Mother Cabrini Cath. Sch., Caparra Heights, P.R., 1969-70; instr. humanities U. P.R., Arecibo, 1970-74; lectr. in history Interam. U. P.R., San Juan, 1974-75; elem. tchr. Newton (Mass.) Pub. Schs., 1975—; prof., chair social scis. Roxbury Community Coll., Boston, 1975—. Photography curator Galería Labiosa, Boston and San Juan, 1984—; founder Taller Galería Borikén, Boston, 1994; bd. dirs. Boston Sch. for the Arts. Writer, photographer El Mundo Newspaper, Cambridge, Mass., 1980-90; corr., photographer El Carillón Newspaper, Andover, Mass., 1991-95, Galería Art Mag., San Juan, 1992—. Chairperson edn. com. State Adv. Bd. on Affirmative Action, Boston, 1988-91; chairperson Affirmative Action Ward 19 Dem. party, Boston, 1990-92; mem. history com. Commn. for Celebration of 500 Yr. Anniversary of Discovery of P.R., 1986—; bd. dirs. Boston ProArte Chamber Orch., 1993—; sec. bd. dirs. Jamaica Plain Arts Coun., 1986-87; clk., bd. dirs. Taller Galería Borikén. Recipient Puerto Rican art Excellence award Mass. P.R. Festival, Inc., 1987, Outstanding Recognition award Senate of Commonwealth of P.R., 1990; named Outstanding Citizen of San Juan, P.R., 1993; Summer fellow NEH, 1992, History fellow, 1994-95. Mem. New Eng. Spanish Inst., Oficina Hispana de la Comunidad (pres. bd. dirs. 1985-87), Jamaica Plain Arts Coun. (sec. bd. dirs. 1986-87), Oral History Assn. Am. (publs. com. 1987—), Hispanic Lions Club Boston (v.p. 1986-88), PanAm. Soc. New Eng. (bd. dirs., co-pres. 1999—), Taller Galería Borikén, Phi Delta Kappa, Phi Theta Kappa Internat., Phi Alpha Theta, Delta Mu. Avocations: music, pen and book collecting, antiques, travel, reading. Home: 12 Holbrook St Boston MA 02130-2756 Office: Roxbury Community Coll 1234 Columbus Ave Boston MA 02120-3423

ANANIAS, JOSÉ, retired school system administrator; b. N.Y.C., Aug. 17, 1929; s. Jose A. and Inez Beatrice Johnson; m. Mamie Seymour, Dec. 30, 1953 (div. Feb. 1978) children: Jose III, Antonio, Ersell; m. Wilhemina Wright, June 17, 1978 (dec. June 1992); m. Ivanete do Nascimento Pena Lins, May 24, 1994. BA, Morehouse Coll., 1951; postgrad., NYU, 1957-59; MEd, CUNY, 1968. Cert. sch. adminstr. and supr., attendance tchr., English tchr., phys. edn. and recreation tchr., subst. attendance tchr. Social investigator St. Nicholas Welfare Ctr. N.Y.C. Dept. Welfare, 1955-60; attendance tchr. N.Y.C. Bd. Edn., 1965-67; adminstrv. asst. to supr. recreation Cmty. Sch. Dist. # 7, Bronx, 1969-75; supr. Office of High Sch. SPARK program Drug Abuse Prevention Citywide, Bronx, 1971-77; borough supr., asst. coord. Office of High Sch. SPARK program, Bklyn., 1971-77; tchr. English High Sch. Redirection, Bklyn., 1977-78, asst. prin., 1978-79; dist. supervising attendance officer Chancellor's Task Force on Attendance, Bklyn., 1978-79; dist. supervising attendance officer Evander Childs High Sch Bronx High Sch. Attendance Dist., 1979; dist. supervising attendance officer office of dir. pupil personnel svcs., 1979-84; ret., 1984. Mem. Borough Pres. Sutton's Adopt a Child com., edn. com.; mem. bd. mgr. Harlem br. YMCA, 1974-96, mem. adv. com., editor, compiler brochure; founder Dist. 7 Scholarship Awards Fund, 1971-78; Dem. county committeeman 71st A.D.; edn. chmn. Com. to Rebuild Harlem, 1978; mem. parish coun. St. Charles Borromeo Cath. Ch., 1979; mem. PTA John F. Kennedy High Sch., DeWitt Clinton High Sch.; svc. officer VFW Post 1753, Las Vegas, 2000—; mem. Our Lady of Las Vegas Ch. Served with USN, 1951-55, Korea. Recipient Citation, Gov. Mario Cuomo, 1984, Citation, Mayor Edward I. Koch, 1984, Cert. Recognition Sec. of Def., Cert. Appreciation Harlem Bd. Mgrs., 1996; named Vol. of Yr., YMCA Greater N.Y., 1995; José Ananias Day proclaimed in his honor. Mem. VFW (Cmmdr.'s Spl. Merit award 2003), Assn. Black Educators N.Y., Am. Legion, USN Meml., Holy Name Soc. St. Charles Borromeo Cath. Ch., CCNY Alumni Assn. (Las Vegas chpt.), Kappa Alpha Psi. Democrat. Roman Catholic. Home: 11-1074 1600 S Valley View Blvd Las Vegas NV 89102-1869

ANARFI, ISAAC KWAME, economic educator, researcher; b. Kumasi, Ghana, June 25, 1945; came to U.S., 1986; s. James Kofi and Ama Beatrice (Pepraa) Asiamah-Anarfi; m. Serwaa Twum, Jan. 1, 1984 (div. Sept. 1992); children: Pepraa, Kwae, Oduraa; m. Afia Agyeman Duah, Dec. 15, 1993. BA in Econs., U. Cape Coast, Ghana, 1973; MA in Internat. Affairs, Ohio U., 1987, PhD in Econ. Edn., 1991. Budget rsch. officer Ministry of Fin. and Planning, Accra, Ghana, 1973-74; sr. supt. edn. Ministry of Edn., Accra, Ghana, 1974-79; lectr. social scis. Kaduna State Coll. Edn., Kafanchan, Nigeria, 1979-86; instr. Ohio U., Athens, 1989-90, adj. asst. prof. Ctr. for Econ. Edn., 1992-94; asst. prof. Rsch. in Edn. CUNY, 1995—. Cons. African issues U.S.-African Sister Cities Inc., Washington, 1994—; guest lectr. African Studies Curriculum Outreach Project, Yale U., New Haven, Conn., 1994—; guest speaker U.S.-African Sister Cities Conf., Mansfield, Ohio, 1994. Editor: The Living Classroom, 1986; contbr. articles to profl. jours. Recipient grants and fellowships Ohio U., 1987-91. Mem. ASCD, Assn. for Econ. Educators, African Studies Assn., Econ. Soc. Ghana. Avocations: lawn tennis, basketball, jogging. Home: 9 Fordham Hill Oval Apt 1H Bronx NY 10468-4851

ANASTASIO, THOMAS JOSEPH, neuroscientist, educator, researcher; b. Washington, Dec. 7, 1958; s. Albert Thomas and Giovanna Grace (Russo) A.; m. Anne E. McKusick, Sept. 2, 1990; children: Albert Thomas, Grace Elizabeth. BS, McGill U., Montreal, Que., Can., 1980; PhD, U. Tex. Med. Br., Galveston, 1986. NASA fellow Vestibular Rsch. Facility, Moffett Field, Calif., 1982; predoctoral rsch. fellow U. Tex. Med. Br., Galveston, 1980-86; postdoctoral fellow Johns Hopkins U. Sch. Medicine, Balt., 1986-88; rsch. asst. prof. dept. otolaryngology U. So. Calif., LA, 1988-91; asst. prof. dept. molecular and integrative physiology U. Ill., Urbana, 1991-97, assoc. prof., 1997—. Presenter seminars; reviewer jour. articles and grant proposals, others. Contbr. chpts. to books, numerous articles to peer-reviewed jours.; author abstracts. Mem. Internat. Brain Rsch. Orgn., Internat. Neural Network Soc., Soc. Neurosci. Achievements include development of computer models of various brain functions and teaching courses in this area. Home: 616 Bellerieve Dr Champaign IL 61822-7344 Office: U Ill Beckman Inst 405 N Mathews Ave Urbana IL 61801-2325

ANBAR, MICHAEL, biophysics educator; b. Danzig, June 29, 1927; came to U.S., 1967, naturalized, 1973; s. Joshua and Chava A.; m. Ada Komet, Aug. 11, 1953; children: Ran D., Ariel D. MSc, Hebrew U., Jerusalem, 1950, PhD, 1953. Instr. chemistry U. Chgo., 1953-55; sr. scientist Weizmann Inst. Sci., 1955-67; prof. Frienberg Grad. Sch., Rehovoth, Israel, 1960-67; sr. rsch. assoc. NASA Ames Rsch. Ctr., 1967-68; dir. phys. sci. SRI Internat., Menlo Park, Calif., 1968-72, dir. mass spectrometry research ctr., 1972-77; prof. biophysical sci., chmn. dept. Sch. Medicine, SUNY, Buffalo, 1977-90, rsch. prof. dental materials, rsch. prof. ophthalmology, 1990—, exec. dir. Health Instrument and Device Inst., 1983-85, assoc. dean applied research, 1983-85; v.p. R & D AMARA Inc, Amherst, N.Y., 1992—; rsch. prof. surgery Sch. Medicine, SUNY, 1998—. Author: The Hydrated Electron, 1970, The Machine of the Bedside: Strategies for Using Technology in Parient Care, 1984, Clinical Biophysics, 1985, Computers in Medicine, 1986, Quantitative Dynamic Telethermometry in Medical Diagnosis and Management, 1994; editor-in-chief: Thermology, 1993; contbr. articles to profl. jours. With Israeli Air Force, 1947-49. Fellow, AIMBE, 2001; grantee in field. Fellow Am. Inst. Biomed. Engrs.; mem. IEEE, AAAS, IEEE Computer Soc., IEEE Engring. in Biology and Medicine Soc., Assn. Am. Med. Colls., Am. Inst. Physics, Am. Chem. Soc., Am. Inst. Ultrasound in Medicine, Am. Assn. Clin. Chemistry, Am. Assn. Dental Rsch., Am. Assn. Mass Spectrometry, Am. Acad. Thermology, Am. Assn. Med. Systems Informatics, N.Y. Acad. Scis., Internat. Assn. Dental Rsch., Radiation Rsch. Soc., Internat. Med. Informatics Assn., Internat. Soc. Optical Engring., Radiol. Soc. N.Am., Am. Soc. Clin. Oncology. Office: SUNY 118 Cary Hall Buffalo NY 14214-3023

ANCES, I. G(EORGE), obstetrician, gynecologist, educator; b. Balt., July 3, 1935; s. Harry and Fanny A.; m. Marlene Roth, Oct. 23, 1966; 1 son, Beau Mark. BS, U. Md., 1956, MD, 1959. Diplomate Am. Bd. Ob-Gyn. Intern Ohio State U. Hosp., 1959-60; resident in ob-gyn. Univ. Hosp., Balt., 1960-61, 63-65; faculty U. Md. Med. Sch., Balt., 1966—, prof. ob-gyn., 1975-83, dir. labs. obstetrics and gynecol. rsch. and clin. labs., 1967-83, dir. divsn. adolescent ob-gyn. and family planning, 1981-83;; prof. ob-gyn., chmn. dept. Rutgers U. Sch. Medicine, Camden, N.J., 1983—. Contbr. chpts. to books, articles to profl. jours. Capt. sustaining fund drive Balt. Symphony Orch., Opera Co. Phila.; med. adv. com. Fire Dept. Balt. City. With USAF, 1961-63. Recipient of Outstanding Tchg. and Edn. award Robert-Wood Johnson Sch. of Medicine-Cooper Hosp., 1989, 92, 96, 2000, 01, 02, Appreciation Coverage award, 1999, 2000, 2002, Nat. Faculty award for excellence in resident edn., 1996. Fellow Am. Coll. Obstetrics and Gynecology; mem. Endocrine Soc., Soc. Gynecol. Investigation, Soc. Study Reprodn. (charter), Internat. Soc. Rsch. in Biology Reprodn. (charter), Md. Obstetrics and Gynecol. Soc. (sec. 1978-81, dir. 1979—), Med. and Chirurgical Soc. Md., Soc. Adolescent Medicine, Douglas Obstet. and Gynecol. Soc. (pres. 1984—), N.J. State Med. Soc. (chmn. neo-natal coop. So. Jersey 1986—), Phila. Ob-Gyn. Soc., English Speaking Union, Cooper Found., N.J. Conservation Coun., Harbour League Club, Md. Club, Towson Golf and Country Club, Sigma Xi. Clubs: Maryland, Towson Golf and Country. Home: 1 Lane Of Acres Haddonfield NJ 08033-3504 Office: Rutgers U Sch Medicine Dept Ob-Gyn 3 Cooper Plz Camden NJ 08103-1438

ANDELL, ERIC, school system administrator, judge; children: Bethany, John. BA, U. Ariz.; JD, U. Houston. Judge Juvenile Court System, Houston; justice Ct. Appeals for the State of Tex.; sr. adviser to Sec. of Edn. U.S. Dept. Edn., Washington, 2000—02, dep. under sec. Office of Safe and Drug Free Schs, 2002—. Chmn. Tex. Juvenile Probation Commn.; vice chmn. Bd. Mental Health and Mental Retardation Harris County, Tex.; chmn. At Risk Students; mem. Houston/Harris County Commn. on Children. Named Outstanding Tex. Jurist of Yr., Tex. Bar Found., Dist. Ct. Judge of Yr., Houston Police Officers Assn., Appellate Judge of the Year, 1997, 2000; recipient Judicial Excellence award, Houston Coun. on Alcoholism and Drugs, Mayor's award for Outstanding Vol. Svcs. to City of Houston. Office: Dept Edn 400 Maryland Ave SW Washington DC 20202

ANDERHALTER, OLIVER FRANK, educational organization executive; b. Trenton, Ill., Feb. 14, 1922; s. Oliver Valentine and Catherine (Vollet) A.; m. Elizabeth Fritz, Apr. 30, 1945; children: Sharon, Stephen, Dennis. B.Ed., Eastern Ill. State Tchrs. Coll., 1943, Ped.D. (hon.), 1956; A.M., St. Louis U., 1947, PhD, 1949. Mem. faculty St. Louis U., 1947—, prof. edn., 1957—; dir. Bur. Instl. Research, 1949-65, 1949-65, Univ. Computer Center, 1961-69, chmn. research methodology dept., 1968-76; v.p. Scholastic Testing Service, Chgo., 1951-89; pres. Scholastic Testing Svc., Chgo. and St. Louis, 1989—. Chmn. finance com. Greater St. Louis Campfire Girls Orgn., 1958-59 Author, editor standardized tests. Served as pilot USNR, 1943-46. Mem. Am. Edml. Research Assn., Nat. Council Measurement, Am. Statis. Assn., N.E.A. Home: 12756 Whispering Hills Ln Saint Louis MO 63146-4449 Office: Scholastic Testing Svc 4320 Green Ash Dr Earth City MO 63045-1208 E-mail: ststesting@email.com.

ANDERHUB, BETH MARIE, medical educator; b. St. Louis, Feb. 7, 1953; d. Anthony Pierre and Eleanor (Corich) A. A in Applied Sci., Forest Park C.C., St. Louis, 1974; BS in Radiologic Tech., U. Mo., 1975; MEd, St. Louis U., 1989, postgrad., 1989—. Cert. abdominal sonography, ob-gyn sonography. Nuclear medicine and ultrasound technician VA Hosp., St.

Louis, 1976-79; ultrasound technologist, sr. sonographer Deaconess Hosp., St. Louis, 1979-82, chief sonographer, 1982-83; assoc. prof., dir. ultrasound program St. Louis C.C., 1983—. Chmn. accreditation com. Ultrasound Program, Englewood, Colo., 1990-95; v.p. Commn. on Accreditation for Allied Health Program, 1994-1996; lectr., presenter programs in field confs., symposia, colls., univs. Author: Manual on Abdominal Sonography, 1983, General Sonography, 1994; contbr. articles to profl. jours. Fellow Soc. Diagnostic Med. Sonographers (chmn. edn. com. 1984-86, contbg. editor Jour. Diagnostic Med. Sonography 1984-89, bd. dirs. 1986-89, v.p. 1989-91, pres.-elect 1991-93, pres. 1993-95, treas. ednl. found. 1988-91, other coms.), Am. Soc. Radiologic Technologists (bd. dirs. 1982-85, task force modality del. roles 1988-89, rep. sonography summit 1988, chmn. ultrasound com. 1980, 82-85, others), Am. Inst. Ultrasound in Medicine, Mo. Soc. Radiologic Technologists (pres. 1979-80, pres. 4th dist. 1978-79). Avocation: singing. Home: 12449 Dawn Heights Dr Maryland Heights MO 63043-3636 Office: Saint Louis C C 5600 Oakland Ave Saint Louis MO 63110-1316

ANDERS, CLAUDIA DEE, occupational therapist; b. Buffalo, May 2, 1951; d. Walter Gregory and Helen (Cedizlo) A.; (div. 1983); 1 child, Andrew T. Kiko. BS in Occupational Therapy (high honors), Va. Commonwealth U., 1973; postgrad., Ashland (Ohio) Coll., 1984, Walsh (Ohio) Coll., 1985, Kent (Ohio) State U., 1988, 89, Colo. State U., 1991, 92; MS, Clayton Coll., 2002. Lic. occupational therapist, Ohio; bd. cert. pediatric occupational therapist. With Children's Rehab. Ctr., Warren, Ohio, 1974-76; mem. transdisciplinary team Goodwill Rehab. Ctr., Canton, Ohio, 1976-78; pvt. practice, 1978-83; with Timken Mercy Med. Ctr., Canton, 1978-83; occupational therapist adult tng. team Stark County Bd. Mental Retardation, Canton, 1983-85; developer occupational therapy svcs. Stark County Local Schs., 1985-87; pediat. occupational therapist home health care sch. and cmty. agys., 1985-91; owner Eagle Seminars and Therapy, 1998—. Presenter in field. Vol. Nat. Park Svc., Cleve. Metroparks; sec. Rocky River Trailsiders, 1993-95. A. D. Williams scholar Va. Commonwealth U., 1972, 73, rsch. scholar Deerfield Beach, Fla., 2000. Mem.: Ohio Occupl. Therapy Assn., Am. Occupl. Therapy Assn., Nature Conservancy. Avocations: gardening, bird watching, hiking, sewing, needlecraft. Office: Eagle Selminars and Therapy PO Box 81520 Cleveland OH 44181-0520

ANDERSEN, DEBORAH JEAN, elementary education educator; b. Glens Falls, NY, June 11, 1957; d. Ronald Roy and Carol Marie (Snyder) Alcan; m. Scott Peter Andersen, Oct. 5, 1985; children: Andrea Marie, Michael Gunther. BA, SUNY, Potsdam, 1979; MS, SUNY, Albany, 1985. Cert. tchr., reading tchr., N.Y. Elem. tchr. St. Peter's Sch., Rome, N.Y., 1979-84, Bolton Cen. Sch., Bolton Landing, N.Y., 1984—. Mem. Bolton Tchrs. Assn. (sec. 1990-92, shop steward 2000—), Bolton Parent/Tchr./Student Assn., NY State United Tchrs., Assn. Math. Tchrs. NY State. Republican. Roman Catholic. Avocations: reading, boating, snowmobiling, gardening, cooking. Home: Trout Lake Rd Bolton Landing NY 12814-0246 Office: Bolton Cen Sch Horicon Ave Bolton Landing NY 12814

ANDERSEN, FRANCES ELIZABETH GOLD, religious leadership educator; b. Hot Springs, Ark., Feb. 11, 1916; d. Benjamin Knox and Pearl Scott (Smith) Gold; m. Robert Thomas Andersen, June 27, 1942; children: Nancy Ruth (Mrs. Bernd Neumann), Robert Thomas. BA, UCLA, 1936, sec. teaching credential, 1937. Tchr. math. L.A. City Schs., 1937-42, 46-48; faculty Ariz. State Coll., Tempe, 1943-45; mem. nat. bd. missions United Meth. Ch., 1940-44; dir. Christian edn. 1st Presbyn. Ch., Phoenix, 1943-45, Trinity Meth. ch., L.A., 1953-55, 1st Bapt. Ch., Lakewood, Calif., 1955-57, Grace Bapt. Ch., Riverside, 1958-83, chmn. nursery sch. bd., 1969-83; mem. nat. bd. Bible sch. and youth Bapt. Gen. Conf., 1966-71; coord. leadership tng. insts. Greater L.A. Sunday Sch. Assn., 1956-80; exec. dir. San Bernardino-Riverside Sunday Sch. Assn., 1959—; prin. Riverside Christian Sch., 1985-87, bd. dirs., 1985—. Mem. Christian edn. bd. S.W. Bapt. Conf., 1956-59, 63-66, 72-75, 80-83; bd. dirs. GLASS, 1956—; dir. Women's guild, Calif. Bapt. Coll., Riverside, 1983-96. Author: How to Organize Area Leadership Training Institutes, 1964. Pres. Univ. Jr. H.S., PTA, Riverside, 1963-64, Poly. H.S., PTA, 1965-67; life mem. PTA; judge Nat. Sunday Sch. Tchrs. Awards, 1993-2003. Named Grace Bapt. Mother of Yr., 1981, People Who Make a Difference Press-Enterprise, 1984, One of Outstanding Women of Riverside, Calif. Bapt. Coll., 1985. Mem. Sons of Norway, Alpha Delta Chi (nat. pres. 1950-51, exec. sec. 1952-54), Pi Mu Epsilon. Avocations: travel, entertaining, music. Home: 1787 Prince Albert Dr Riverside CA 92507-5852

ANDERSEN, HANS CHRISTIAN, chemistry educator; b. Bklyn., Sept. 25, 1941; m. June Jenny, June 17, 1967; children: Hans Christian, Albert William. SB, MIT, 1962, PhD, 1966. Jr. fellow Soc. Fellows Harvard U., Cambridge, 1965-68; asst. prof. chemistry Stanford (Calif.) U., 1968—74; assoc. prof. Stanford U., 1974—80, prof., 1980—, assoc. dean Sch. Humanities and Scis., 1996—99, chmn. dept. chemistry, 2002—. Vis. prof. chemistry Columbia U., N.Y.C., 1981-82; co-dir. Stanford Ctr. for Materials Rsch., 1988-89, dep. dir., 1989-95; mem. allocation com. San Diego Supercomputer Ctr., 1986-89, chmn., 1988-89; vice-chmn. Gordon Rsch. Conf. on Physics and Chemistry of Liquids, 1989, chmn. 1991. Mem. editl. com.: Ann. Rev. Phys. Chemistry, 1983—87, mem. editl. bd.: Procs. of the NAS, 2002—, Jour. Chem. Physics, 1984—86, Chem. Physics, 1986—96, mem. adv. bd.: Jour. Phys. Chemistry, 1987—92. Sloan fellow, 1972-74, Guggenheim fellow, 1976-77. Fellow AAAS, Am. Acad. Arts and Scis., Am. Phys. Soc.; mem. NAS, Am. Chem. Soc. (chmn. phys. chemistry divsn. 1986, Joel Henry Hildebrand award 1988).

ANDERSEN, MARGO K. federal agency administrator; Bachelors Degree, Gettysburg Coll.; M in Mgmt., George Washington U. Program mgr. for arts programs Nat. Endowment for the Arts, Am. Correctional Assn.; dir. Office Fin. Mgmt. and Performance Measurement, Office Innovation and Improvement U.S. Dept. Edn., Washington. Office: US Dept Edn IES Rm 500F 555 New Jersey Ave NW Washington DC 20208*

ANDERSEN, MELVIN ERNEST, toxicologist, educator; b. Providence, Dec. 13, 1945; s. Magnus and Mildred Elaine (Petersen) A.; m. Christine Ann Jaeger, Aug. 3, 1968; children: Kathryn Louise, Heidi Lynn, Rebecca Arline. BSc in Chemistry, Brown U., 1967; PhD in Biochemistry, Cornell U., 1971. Diplomate Am. Bd. Indsl. Hygiene, Am. Bd. Toxicology. Civil svc. staff Dept. of Def., Dayton, Ohio, 1979-88; dept. head, sr. scientist Chem. Ind. Inst. Toxicology, Research Triangle Park, N.C., 1989-92; rsch. prof. Duke U., Durham, N.C., 1992-93; sr. scientist U.S. EPA, Research Triangle Park, 1993-94; v.p. The KS Crump Group, ICF Kaiser Internat., Research Triangle Park, N.C., 1994-98; prof. dept. environ. health Colo. State U., 1998—2002; divsn. dir. CIIT Ctrs. for Health Rsch., Morrisville, NC, 2002—. Mem. sci. adv. panel Chem. Industry Inst. Toxicology, Research Triangle Park, 1984-88; adj. prof. Wright State U., Dayton, 1979-89; adj. prof. medicine Duke U., 1994-95; adj. assoc. prof. U. N.C., Chapel Hill, 1993-97. Contbr. articles to profl. jours., chpts. to books. Lt. comdr. USN, 1971-78. Recipient Kenneth Morgareidge award Internat. Life Scis. Inst., 1989, George Scott award Toxicology Forum, 1993, Harry G. Armstrong award Aerospace Med. Rsch. Lab., 1982, Outstanding Profl. Achievement award Engring./Sci. Found. of Dayton, 1985. Mem. Soc. Toxicology (Frank Blood award 1982, Achievement award 1984), Soc. Risk Analysis, Am. Bd. Toxicology (bd. dirs. 1991-94), Am. Conf. Govtl. Indsl. Hygienists (Herbert Stokinger award 1988). Methodist. Avocations: birding, astronomy, blues harmonica. Home: 323 Bear Creek Path Bldg 300 Morrisville NC 27560- E-mail: manderson@ciit.org.

ANDERSEN, NIELS HJORTH, chemistry educator, biophysics researcher, consultant; b. Copenhagen, Oct. 9, 1943; came to U.S. 1949; s. Orla and Inger (Larsen) A.; m. Sidnee Lee (div. 1986); children: Marin Christine, Beth Arkady; m. Susan Howell, July 21, 1987. BA, U. Minn., 1963; PhD, Northwestern U., 1967. Rsch. assoc and fellow Harvard U., Cambridge, Mass., 1966-68; asst. prof. U. Wash., Seattle, 1968-72, assoc. prof., 1972-76, prof., 1976—; prin. scientist ALZA Corp., Palo Alto, Calif., 1970-75. Cons. Genetic Systems, Seattle, 1984-86, Bristol-Myer Squibb, Princeton, N.J., 1984-95, Amylin Pharmaceutics, San Diego, 1992-2001 Receptron Corp., Mountain View, Calif., 1995—2001, Chiron, Seattle, 1997—2003. Mem. adv. bd. Biopolymers; contbr. articles to profl. jours. Recipient Teacher-Scholar award Dreyfus Found., 1974-79, Career Devel. award NIH, 1975-80. Mem. AAAS, Am. Chem. Soc., Am. Peptide Soc., Protein Soc. Democrat. Avocations: contemporary folk music and swing, dulcimer playing. Office: U Wash Dept Chem PO Box 351700 Seattle WA 98195-1700 E-mail: andersen@chem.washington.edu.

ANDERSEN, SUSAN MARIE, educator, researcher, clinician, policy advisor; b. Santa Monica, California, June 6, 1955; BA in psychology(hon.), U. Calif., Santa Cruz, 1977; PhD in sychology, Stanford U., 1981. Lic. psychologist Calif., N.Y. Asst. prof. psychology Univ. Calif., Santa Barbara, 1981-87; assoc. prof. NYU, N.Y.C., 1987-94, prof., 1994—, dir. grad. studies in psychology, 1993—97, 2000—02. Cons. Edn. Commn. of the States; Grantmaker Forum for Cmty. and Nat. Svc., Common Cents N.Y.; grants panel, social and group processes rev. panel NIMH, 1992-94, 96, Integrative Grad. Edn. and Rsch. Tng. rev. panel NSF, 2003; other panels. Assoc. editor Jour. Social and Clin. Psychology, 1987-92; Social Cognition, 1993; Jour. Personality and Social Psychology: Attitudes and Social Cognition, 1994-95; Psychol. Rev., 1998-2000; mem. editl. bd. Jour. Personality and Social Psychology, 1990-93, 2000-01, Nouvelle Revue de Psychologie Sociale, 2002—; ad hoc reviewer Jour. Comm. Rsch., Jour. Exptl. Psychology: Learning, Memory & Cognition, Jour. Exptl. Social Psychology, Jour. Personality, Jour. Rsch. in Personality, Motivation and Emotion, Personality and Social Psychology Bull., Psychol. Sci., NSF, Australian Social Sci. Rsch. Coun., Social Sci. and Human Rsch. Coun. of Can., Brit. Jour. Clin. Psychology, Brit. Jour. Social Psychology, Jour. Abnormal Psychology; contbr. numerous articles to profl. jour. Chair svc. learning task force White House Congl. Conf. on Character Bldg.; mem. rsch. and evaluation com. Character Edn. Partnership; mem. rsch. adv. bd. Kellogg Found. Nat. Initiative on Cmty. Svc. in Edn.; Learning in Deed; mem. edn. policy task force Inst. for Comm. Policy Studies, George Washington U.; mem. Russell Sage Found.'s Social Identity Consortium. Recipient Golden Dozen Award N.Y.Univ., 1993; Harold J. Plous Award UCSB, 1985; NIMH grantee, 1985-86, 92-98; sr. fellow Inst. for Comm. Policy Studies, George Washington U. Fellow: APA, Soc. Personality and Social Psychology (mem. exec. com.), Am. Psychol. Soc.; mem.: Soc. Psychol. Study of Social Issues, Soc. Advancement of Socio Econ., Soc. Exptl. Social Psychology, Internat. Soc. Self and Identity. Office: Dept Psychology NY Univ 6 Washington Pl 4th Fl New York NY 10003-6603 E-mail: andersen@psych.nyu.edu.

ANDERSLAND, MARK STEVEN, electrical and computer engineering educator; b. Lansing, Mich., June 9, 1961; s. Orlando Baldwin and Phyllis Elaine (Burgess) A.; m. Mary Susan Pruzinsky, Oct. 7, 1995. BSEE, U. Mich., 1983, MSEE, 1984, PhD, 1989. Asst. prof. dept. elec. and computer engring. U. Iowa, Iowa City, 1989-95, assoc. prof., 1995—. Contbr. articles to IEEE Transactions on Automatic Control, SIAM Jour. on Control and Optimization, Automatica, Sys. & Control Letters, Jour. Optimization Theory & Applications, Jour. of the Operational Rsch. Soc; patentee in field. Hewlett Packard Faculty Devel. fellow, 1984-88. Mem. IEEE, Soc. Indsl. and Applied Math., Tau Beta Pi, Eta Kappa Nu. Office: U Iowa Dept Elec and Computer Engring Iowa City IA 52242

ANDERSON, ANITA A. secondary education educator; b. Winston-Salem, N.C., Sept. 13, 1938; d. Birden Dixon and Lovie Josephine McCoy; m. Clarence B. Crumpton (dec.); children: Clarence B., Victoria E.; m. William Webb (dec.); 1 child, William R.; m. William Wallace Parker, Sept. 8, 1992 (dec. June 1998); m. William G. Anderson, Mar. 27, 1999. BS in English and Social Studies, U. Detroit-Mercy, 1973; MEd, Marygrove Coll., Detroit, 1974, cert. secondary adminstrn., 1994; computerized office cert., Acock Computerized Ctr., Athens, Ga., 1986; postgrad., Oakland U., Rochester, Mich., 1996—. Tchr., dept. head Western H.S., Las Vegas, Nev., 1974-76; tchr. reading, dir. learning ctr. Ecorse (Mich.) H.S., 1976=81; tchr., coord. reading Winston-Salem-Forsyth County Schs., 1981-87; tchr. math. Holt (Ala.) H.S., 1987-88; tchr. algebra and sci. Pontiac (Mich.) Pub. Schs., 1988—, self-esteem, self-awareness and peer rels. grant writr, 1989—. Self-esteem facilitator, substance abuse specialist Washington Mid. Sch., Pontiac, 1991—. Author: (tng. manual) Surving Societal Stressors, 1990. Bd. dirs. Fedn. Youth Svcs., Detroit, 1991—. Recipient Tech. of Yr. award N.C. Bd. Edn., 1994; grantee 1st of Am. Bank, Inc., 1994-95. Mem. AAUW, Internat. Reading Assn., Am. Bus. Women Assn., NAACP (life, bd. dirs. Detroit 1990—), Lions (bd. dirs. Detroit 1992—, sec.-editor 1993-95, Melvin Jones fellow 1997), Order Ea. Star (worthy matron 1996—), Daus. of Isis (dir. team I 1996-97), Gamma Phi Delta (life, internat. Greek queen 1979). Avocations: horticulture, travel, reading, drama, surfing the internet. Office: Washington Middle Sch 701 Menominee Rd Pontiac MI 48341-1544

ANDERSON, ANN DAVIS, reading curriculum specialist; b. Washington, Mar. 24, 1946; d. George Perry and Irene Delores (Stewart) Davis; m. Ronald Clifford Anderson, Oct. 13, 1973; 1 child, Tahira Mali. BS in Edn., Bucknell U., Lewisburg, Pa., 1968; MA in Edn., George Washington U., 1972. Cert. reading specialist, Va. Tchr. grades 2-5 D.C. Pub. Schs., 1968-73; reading specialist Alexandria (Va.) City Pub. Schs., 1973-93, curriculum/staff devel. specialist, 1993-97, tchr. specialist for reading, 1998—. Cons. NEA, Washington, 1986-88; reviewer of grants Nat. Found. for Improvement of Edn., Washington, 1993—; mem. nat. rev. panel for blue ribbon schs. U.S. Dept. Edn., Washington, 1992—; staff devel. presenter Alexandria City Pub. Schs., 1989-94. Co-author: A Research Framework for the Middle Grades. Recipient Award of Excellence in Edn., Alexandria C. of C., 1986, Am. Tchr. award Walt Disney Corp., L.A., 1990; Washington Post grantee, 1987, Readers Choices 1000 Women for the Nineties, 1994, Reader's Choices 1000 Women for the Nineties, Mirabella mag., 1994. Mem. ASCD, NEA, Internat. Reading Assn., Nat. Coun. for Social Studies, Nat. Coun. Negro Women, Nat. Tots and Teens Inc. (v.p., youth coord. Prince Georges County chpt. 1991-93), Va. Edn. Assn., Edn. Assn. Alexandria, Phi Delta Kappa, Kappa Pi. Avocations: modern dancing, reading, walking, music. Home: 6305 Hard Bargain Circle Indian Head MD 20640 Office: Alexandria City Pub Schs 2000 N Beauregard St Alexandria VA 22311-1712

ANDERSON, ARTHUR G., JR., chemistry educator; b. Sioux City, Iowa, July 1, 1918; s. Arthur G. and Lois (Mueller) A.; m. Sue Rinker, Sept. 16, 1944; children— Lynn, Joyce, Beth. AB, U. Ill., 1940; M.Sc., U. Mich., 1942, PhD, 1944. Chemist Manhattan Project, Tenn. Eastman Corp., Oak Ridge, 1944-45; mem. faculty U. Wash., Seattle, 1946-88, assoc. prof. chemistry, 1952-57, prof., 1957-88, assoc. chmn., 1979-88, prof. emeritus, from 1988. Rsch. fellow U. Ill., 1946; NSF sr. postdoctoral fellow Heidelberg U., 1960-61; Vis. prof. Australian Nat. U., Canberra, 1966. Contbr. articles to profl. jours. Recipient Petroleum Research Fund Internat. award, 1966 Fellow N.Y. Acad. Scis., Am. Inst. Chemists, Chem. Soc. London; mem. Sigma Xi, Phi Beta Kappa, Phi Kappa Phi, Phi Lambda Upsilon. Achievements include research in synthesis and properties of nonbenzenoid aromatic, heterocyclic compounds. Home: Seattle, Wash. Died Oct. 10, 2000.

ANDERSON, AUSTIN GOTHARD, lawyer, consultant, academic administrator; b. Calumet, Minn., June 30, 1931; s. Hugo Gothard and Turna Marie (Johnson) A.; m. Catherine Antoinette Spellacy, Jan. 2. 1954; children: Todd, Susan, Timothy, Linda, Mark. BA, U. Minn., 1954, JD, 1958. Bar: Minn. 1958, Ill. 1962, Mich. 1974. Assoc. Spellacy, Spellacy, Lano & Anderson, Marble, Minn, 1958-62; dir. Ill. Inst. Continuing Legal Edn., Springfield, 1962-64; dir. dept. continuing legal edn. U. Minn., Mpls., 1964-70, assoc. dean gen. extension divsn., 1968-70; ptnr. Dorsey, Marquart, Windhorst, West & Halladay, Mpls., 1970-73; assoc. dir. Nat. Ctr. State Cts., St. Paul, 1973-74; dir. Inst. Continuing Legal Edn. U. Mich., Ann Arbor, 1973-92; dir. Inst. on Law Firm Mgmt., 1992-95; prin. Anderson-Boyer Group, Ann Arbor, 1995—; pres. Network of Leading Law Firms, 1995—. Adj. faculty U. Minn., 1974, Wayne State U., 1974-75; mem. adv. bd. Ctr. for Law Firm Mgmt. Nottingham Trent U., Eng.; draftsman ABA Guidelines for Approval of Legal Asst. Programs, 1973, Model Guidelines for Minimum Continuing Legal Edn., 1988; chair law practice mgmt. sect. State Bar Mich., 2000-2001; mem. Task Force on Court Filing, State Bar of Mich., 2000-2001; mem. Com. on Quality of Life, 2000-2001; cons. in field. Co-editor, contbg. author: Lawyer's Handbook, 1975, co-editor 3d edit., 1992; author: A Plan for Lawyer Development, 1986, Marketing Your Practice: A Practical Guide to Client Development, 1986; cons. editor, contbg. author: Webster's Legal Secretaries Handbook, 1981; cons. editor Merriam Webster's Legal Secretarial Handbook, 2d edit., 1996; co-author: The Effective Associate Training Program-Improving Firm Performance, Profits and Prospective Partners, 2000, Associate Retention: Keeping Our Best and Brightest, 2002; contbr. chpt. to book and articles to profl. jours. Chmn. City of Bloomington Park and Recreation Adv. Commn., Minn., 1970-72; chmn. Ann Arbor Citizens Recreation Adv. Com., 1981-89, Ann Arbor Parks Adv. Com., 1983-92, chair, 1991-92; rep. Class of '58 U. Minn. Law Sch., 1996-2002. Recipient Excellence award CLE sect. Assn. of Am. Law Schs., 1992. Fellow Am. Bar Found. (Mich. chmn. 2002-), State Bar Mich. Found.; mem. ABA (vice chmn. continuing legal edn. com. sect. legal edn. and admission to bar 1988-93, standing com. continuing edn. of bar 1984-90, 2000—, chmn. law practice mgmt. sect. 1981-82, Am. Law Inst.-ABA com. on continuing profl. edn. 1993-96, Am. Law Inst.-ABA com. on continuing profl. edn. 1999—2002, spl. com. on rsch. on future of legal profession 1998-2000, sec. Coll. of Law Practice Mgmt. 1993-97, house of dels. 1993-99, commn. on lawyer advt. 1994-97, futures com., chmn. econs. of torts and ins. practice 2002—, mem. task force Lawyer Ctr. on pers. legal svcs. and client devel. 200203, spl. advisor to standing com. on continuing edn. of the bar 2002—), Internat. Bar Assn., Mich. Bar Assn., Ill. Bar Assn., State Bar of Mich. (chair law practice mgmt. sect., 2000-2001), Minn. Bar Assn., Internat. Bar Assn., Assn. Continuing Legal Edn. Adminstrs.(pres. 1969-70), Ann Arbor Golf and Outing Club. Home: 4660 Bayberry Cir Ann Arbor MI 48105-9762 Office: AndersonBoyer Group 3840 Packard St # 110 Ann Arbor MI 48108-2280 E-mail: aga@andersonboyer.com.

ANDERSON, BRUCE JOHN, foundation administrator; b. Waterbury, Conn., Mar. 9, 1943; s. George E. and Mary M. (Taylor) A.; m. Ann Marie Heath, July 8, 1967; children: Christopher, Carrie, Mark. BS, Ctrl. Conn. State, 1965, MS, 1967; cert. advanced grad. study, Fairfield U., 1969; EdD, U. Va., 1971. Tchr. Southington (Conn.) Sch., 1965-68; instr. Ctrl. Conn. State U., New Britain, Conn., 1968-69; jr. instr. U. Va., Charlottesville, 1969-71; assoc. prof. Old Dominion U., Norfolk, Va., 1971-80, prof., chair dept., 1981-83; v.p. Danforth Found., St. Louis, 1983-91, pres., 1991—. Bd. dirs. St. Louis Regional Edn. Partnership; mem. adv. bd. Mo. Gov. Edn. Panel, Jefferson City, Mo. Co-editor: Democratic Leadership: Changing Context of Administrative Preparation, 1993. Bd. dirs. Met. Assn. Philanthropy, St. Louis, 1990—; mem. adv. bd. St. Louis Zoo, 1989—; mem. parish coun. St. Clares Roman Cath. Ch., St. Louis, 1991—. Office: Danforth Foundation 211 N Broadway # 2390 Saint Louis MO 63102-2733*

ANDERSON, CAROL ELAINE, primary and secondary school educator; b. Genoa, Colo., May 21, 1933; d. Owen Henderson and Ruth (Bruch) Self; m. Kenneth Lee Anderson, Mar. 21, 1959; children: Kelly Lea Anderson Salery (dec.), Charles Anthony. AA, Graceland Coll, Lamoni, Iowa, 1951-53; BA, No. Colo. U., 1957-60; MA, Calif. State U., Hayward, 1977; MA in Counseling, counseling credential, U. of Pacific, 1988. Cert. tchr., Calif.; ordained as seventy Cmty. of Christ, 1991. Jr. high tchr. Denair (Calif.) Unified Sch. Dist., 1962-64; elem. tchr. Modesto (Calif.) City Schs., 1967-76, resource specialist, spl. day class tchr., 1977-81; mentor tchr. at-risk students Hanshaw Mid. Sch., Modesto, Calif., 1981—93, chmn. dept. spl. edn., resource specialist, Chpt. I rep., 1991-93, coord. student study team, 1991-93; resource specialist Modesto (Calif.) City Schs., 1981—91; ret., 1991. Head tchr. Fairview Elem. Sch., Modesto, 1978-80. Mem. Modesto LWV, 1982-85; pastor Cmty. of Christ, 2001-03. Mem. AAUE (treas. 2000—), Council for Exceptional Children (sec. 1986-87), Stanislaus County Assn. Resource Specialists (v.p. 1986-87, pres. 1987-88), Modesto Tchrs. Assn. (state council rep. 1975-76, 2nd v.p. 1986-87, sabbatical com. 1977-89, mentor selection com. 1985-90, sch. improvement program com.). Avocations: sewing, downhill skiing, hiking and backpacking, reading, public speaking. Home: 1111 Wellesley Ave Modesto CA 95350-5043

ANDERSON, CAROL LYNN, counseling, career planning administrator; b. Cobleskill, NY, June 23, 1952; d. Edward Waldemar and Caroline (Burawa) A. BA in Psychology with honors, McGill U., 1974; MA in Psychology, SUNY, New Paltz, 1976. Social welfare examiner Dutchess County Dept. Social Svcs., Poughkeepsie, N.Y., 1977-78; employment interviewer N.Y. State Dept. Labor, Rego Park, 1978-83, employment counselor Jamaica, 1983-85; vocat. rehab. counselor N.Y. State Commn. for the Blind and Visually Handicapped, Harlem, 1985-92; supr., 1993—. Mem. Am. Assn. for Counseling and Devel., Assn. for Counselor Edn. and Supervision, Nat. Rehab. Counselors Assn., Am. Coll. Personnel Assn., Nat. Employment Counselors Assn., Greenpeace, Clearwater, People for the Ethical Treatment of Animals. Avocations: travel, environmental and animal rights issues. Office: NYS Commn for the Blind and Visually Handicapped 163 West 125 St New York NY 10027 E-mail: ax0350@dfa.state.ny.us., carolandersonl@aol.com.

ANDERSON, CATHIE KELLOGG, education educator; b. New Castle, Pa., Dec. 10, 1940; d. Glenn Franklin and Betty Jean (Stewart) Kellogg; m. Neale H. Anderson, Aug. 11, 1962; children: Erik Edward, Michael Neale. BS in Elem. Edn., Indiana U. Pa., 1962; MEd in Reading, Edinboro U. Pa., 1966, postgrad., 1978. Cert. tchr., reading specialist, Pa. Tchr. 1st grade Iroquois Sch. Dist., Erie, Pa., 1962-65, tchr. 5th and 6th grade math., 1966; tchr. 5th and 6th grade math., bldg. prin. Fairview Sch. Dist., Erie, 1967-70; reading instr. Behrend Coll. Pa. State U., Erie, 1970-78; dir., tchr. reading and study skills, lab, dir. coll. reading Mercyhurst Coll., Erie, 1978—. Cons., tchr. for learning differences, learning disabled program Mercyhurst Coll., 1988. Author: Streamlining College Reading, 1989. Mem. choir and Altar Guild, St. Mark's Episcopal Ch., Erie, 1986—. Mem. Coll. Reading Assn. (sec. 1982-86, chair idea exchange, divsn., 1986-90, divsn. chair 1992-94), Keystone State Reading Assn. (presenter). Republican. Episcopalian. Avocation: cross stitch designing for historical sites. Office: Mercyhurst Coll Reading Lab Glenwood Hls Erie PA 16504 Home: 709 Colonial Ave Williamsburg VA 23185-5360

ANDERSON, CHARLES DEAN, chemistry educator; b. Redwood Falls, Minn., Mar. 8, 1930; s. Carl Alfred and Dora Helena (Paulson) A.; m. Margaret Ann Tufte, Aug. 29, 1953; children: Kristen M. Kalbrener, Mark S.T., Peter C.O. BA, St. Olaf Coll., 1952; AM, Harvard U., 1954, PhD, 1959. Rsch. chemist Stanford Rsch. Inst., Menlo Park, Calif., 1956-59; assoc. prof. chemistry Pacific Luth. U., Tacoma, Wash., 1959-62, prof. chemistry, 1962-92, chair dept. chemistry, 1961-66, 78-80, 1986, dean, coll. of arts and scis., 1966-70, prof. chemistry emeritus, 1992—. Dir. PLU Sci. Faculty Devel. Program, Tacoma, 1966-69; dir., co-founder Chengdu-PLU Student and Faculty Exch. Program, Tacoma, Chengdu, PRC, 1985-89; vis. prof. Chengdu U. of Sci. and Tech., 1987; vis. scientist Pacific NW Labs.,

Battelle Meml. Inst., Richland, Wash., 1970-71, U. Wash., Seattle, 1981, 88-89; regency professorship Pacific Luth. U., 1974-75. Author: (with others) Methods in Lignin Chemistry, 1992; contbr. articles to profl. jours. Councilman Mt. Cross Luth. Ch., Tacoma, 1969-73, Peninsula Luth. Ch., Gig Harbor, Wash., 1995-98, Agnus Dei Luth. Ch., Gig Harbor, 2001—; bd. dirs., chmn. Sound Health Assn., Tacoma, 1972-80; co-founder Sixth Sense, Tacoma, 1980; bd. dirs. Hartstene Point Maintenance Assn., Shelton, Wash., 1985-86. NSF fellow, 1952-53, Sci. Faculty fellow, 1964-65. Mem. AAUP, Am. Chem. Soc., Royal Soc. of Chemistry, Phi Beta Kappa, Sigma Pi Sigma. Avocations: reading, woodworking, gardening. Home: 7402 Ford Dr NW Gig Harbor WA 98335-6479 Office: Dept Chemistry Pacific Lutheran Univ Tacoma WA 98447-0001 E-mail: anderscd@plu.edu.

ANDERSON, C(HARLES) HENRY, physical education educator; b. Stamford, Conn., Apr. 16, 1950; s. Walter James and Ethel Saltus (Ludington) A.; m. Christine Walsh, June 3, 1972; children: John-Henry, Erin Walsh, Corey Ellen. BS in Phys. Edn., U. Vt., 1972; MS in Phys. Edn., Mont. State U., 1975. Phys. edn. tchr. Mont. Abraham Union High Sch., Bristol, Vt., 1972-73; corral boss Lone Mont. Guest Ranch, Big Sky, Mont., 1973-74; teaching asst. Mont. State U., Bozeman, 1974-75; elem. phys. edn. Sch. Dist. # 1, Great Falls, Mont., 1975-92; phys. edn. tchr. Sch. Sist. # 1 Great Falls (Mont.) High Sch., 1992—. Conv. staff Mont. AAHPERD, Great Falls, 1988; curriculum com. chmn. Sch. Dist. # 1, Great Falls, 1989—. Founder Great Falls Youth Soccer Assn., 1976; vol. track official Mont., 1986-89; cons., vol. Great Falls (Mont.) Youth Volleyball, 1986—. Recipient Good Apple award Dist. # 1, Great Falls, Mont., 1987, Pepi award, Phys. edn. T.O.Y. for Mont. award, Mont. AAHPERD, 1989, 90. Mem. AAHPERD, Mont. AAHPERD, Am. Volleyball Coaches Assn., Mont. Coaches Assn. Avocations: reading, bike riding, playing guitar, fishing. Home: 2606 Lower River Rd Great Falls MT 59405-7201 Office: Great Falls High School 1900 2nd Ave S Great Falls MT 59405-2799

ANDERSON, CHRISTINA SUSANNE, speech and language therapist; b. Long Beach, Calif., Mar. 15, 1950; d. John Edwin and Mary Belle (Olson) Hockett; children: Michelle, Marc, Brian. BS, Ariz. State U., 1972, MS, 1976. Lic. speech pathologist, Ariz. Speech therapist Rio Linda Sch. Dist., Sacramento, 1973-76, Washington Elem. Sch. Dist., Phoenix, 1976—; pvt. practice speech therapy Phoenix, 1978—. Active St. Helen's Ch., Glendale, Ariz., 1980-86, St. Paul's Ch., 1986—. Elks Found. scholar, 1968-71. Mem. NEA, Am. Speech and Hearing Assn. (Clin. Compentency Cert.), Sigma Alpha Eta, Alpha Lambda Delta, Phi Kappa Phi. Democrat. Roman Catholic. Avocations: skiing, aerobics, needlecrafts. Home: 3136 W Zachary Dr Phoenix AZ 85027-6091

ANDERSON, CLAIRE W. computer gifted and talented educator; b. Albuquerque, May 22, 1930; d. Wentworth Henry and Clara Lea (Magruder) Corley; m. William James Young (div.); children: Gayle L. Mirkin, D. Young, Sherry B. Butler; m. Wallace L. Anderson. Student in Engring., U. Miss., 1946; BA, Rice U., 1951, postgrad., 1993; MEd, U. Houston, 1962, postgrad., 1963, Carnegie Mellon U., Tex. A&M, 1992. Cert. elem. and secondary tchr., early childhood, exceptional children tchr., Tex. Tchr. Golfcrest Elem. Shc., Houston, 1959-60, Montrose, Poe Elem. Sch., Houston, 1960-62, St. Mark's Private Sch., Houston, 1962-63; substitute teaching Spring Branch Ind. Sch. Dist., Houston, 1965-68; tchr. Meml. Hall, Houston, 1968-73; instr. English, math. Internat. Hispanic U., Houston, 1971-74; tchr. Dogan Elem. Sch., Houston, 1971-74, Lanier Mid. Sch., Houston, 1974-79, High Sch. Health Profl., Houston, 1979-90, Clifton Mid. Sch., Houston, 1990-91, Jesse H. Jones Sr. High Sch., Houston, 1992—. Adj. tutoring David Livingston and Assoc., Houston, 1960-65; instr. Internat. Hispanic U., Houston, 1971-74, Houston C.C., 1984—, Internat. Ednl. Comm. Ctr., High Point, N.C., 1990, Houston C.C. Sys., 1991; invited judge Kiev, Ukraine Math. and Sci. Competitions, 1989; facilitator Tex. Coun. of Women Sch. Execs. Summer Conf., 1994—; active The Rice/HISD Sch. Writing Project; acad. sponsor secondary edn. svc. and sci. clubs. Pres. bd. dirs. Women for Justice, 1990-94; active Houston Photography Ctr., Mus. Fine Arts, Houston Health Objectives 2000, Children's Mus.; coord. study and enrichment tutoring program, 1994. Recipient Tex. award for Excellence in Tchg. and Outstanding Svc. to the Cmty., 1994; scholar Precalculus Design Team, Dow Jones scholar Pa. State, Advance Placement scholar Tex. A&M, Woodrow Wilson; grantee NSF, Impact II. Mem. IEEE, Nat. Coun. Tchrs. Math., Nat. Coun. Tchrs. English, Am. Acoustic Soc., Assn. Calculating Machinery, Assn. for Early Childhood Edn. (internat. chairperson), Tex. Assn. Edn. Tech., Tex. Computers Educators Assn., N.Y. Acad. Sci., Internat. Coun. Computers in Edn., Phi Delta Kappa. Office: 7414 Saint Lo Rd Houston TX 77033-2732

ANDERSON, CRAIG ALLEN, art educator; b. Chgo., July 28, 1947; s. Elmer Albert and Rosanne Marie (Werner) A.; m. Mary Susan Scarnato, Apr. 23, 1971. BFA, Bradley U., 1970; MA in Art Edn., U. Ill., 1972; MFA, No. Ill. U., 1978. Cert. art specialist Ill. State Bd. Certification. Tchr., rsch. asst. U. Ill., Champaign, 1970-72; art tchr. Oliver W. Holmes Jr. H.S., Wheeling, Ill., 1972; art instr. Countryside Art Ctr., Arlington Heights, Ill., 1972-74, Harper Coll., Palatine, Ill., 1975-80; art tchr. Palatine H.S., 1972—2003, chmn. dept. art, 1996—; dist. art chair, 2000—03. Cons. Ill. Art Coun., Harvey, Ill., 1990; guest lectr. U. Ill. Commencement, Champaign, 1993, Temple U., 1985; mem. adv. bd. Masters program Sch. Art Inst. Chgo., 2000. One person shows include Gilman Galleries, Chgo., 1978, Heuser Art Ctr., 1989; exhibited in group shows at Abstract Chicago 1993. Co-dir. NAB Gallery, Chgo., 1977—; guest curator Gallery 400, Chgo., 1994, Wooden Gallery, Chgo., 1989; cultural exch. NAB Gallery Palais des Expo, Nice, France, 1987, NAB Gallery Diewand Gallery, Hamburg, Germany, 1983. Recipient Binney & Smith Inc. Tchrs. Portfolio award Nat. Scholastic Art awards, Washington, 1995, Art in Architecture award State of Ill., 1988, Outstanding Art Tchr. award Nat. Scholastic Art, 2003, Outstanding Tchr. award U. Chgo., 1996; Pougialis fellow Columbia Coll., 1990; named Ill. Painter, Ill. Arts Coun., 1980. Mem. Nat. Art Edn. Assn., Ill. Art Edn. Assn. (H.S. Art Tchr. of Yr. 1994, 2000), Chgo. Artists Coalition, Soc. Aesthetics, Soc. Rsch. in Art Edn., Internat. Assn. Emirical Aesthetics. Avocation: teaching creative thinking in a critical thinking gifted class. Home: 108 N Oak St Palatine IL 60067-5229 Office: 1111 N Rohlwing Rd Palatine IL 60074-3777 E-mail: canderson@d211.org.

ANDERSON, DAVID DANIEL, retired humanities educator, writer, editor; b. Lorain, Ohio, June 8, 1924; s. David and Nora Marie (Foster) A.; m. Patricia Ann Rittenhour, Feb. 1, 1953. BS, Bowling Green State U., 1951, MA, 1952; PhD, Mich. State U., 1960; D. Litt., Wittenberg U., 1986. From instr. to prof. dept. Am. thought and lang. to univ. disting. prof. Mich. State U., East Lansing, 1957-90; lectr. Am. Mus., Bath, Eng., 1980; editor U. Coll. Quar., 1971-80; Fulbright prof. U. Karachi, Pakistan, 1963-64. Am. del. to Internat. Fedn. Modern Langs. and Lit., 1969-93, Internat. Congress Orientalists, 1971-79, European Am. Studies Assn., 1994. Author: Louis Bromfield, 1964, Critical Studies in American Literature, 1964, Sherwood Anderson's Winesburg, Ohio, 1967, Sherwood Anderson, 1968 (Book Manuscript award, 1961), Brand Whitlock, 1968, Abraham Lincoln, 1970, Suggestions for the Instructor, 1970, Robert Ingersoll, 1972, Woodrow Wilison, 1978, Igantius Donnelly, 1980, William Jennings Bryan, 1981, Route Two, Titus, Ohio, 1993, The Path in the Shadow, 1998; editor: The Black Experience, 1969, Command Performances, 2003, The Literary Works of Abraham Lincoln, 1970, Sunshine and Smoke: American Writers and the American Environment, 1971; editor: (with others) The Dark and Tangled Path, 1971; editor: Mid America, 1974—, 27th edit., 2000, Sherwood Anderson: Dimensions of His Literary Art, 1976, Sherwood Anderson: The Writer at His Craft, 1979, Critical Essays on Sherwood Anderson, 1981, Michigan: A State Anthology, 1983, Myth, Memory and the American Earth: The Durability of Raintree County, 1998, Midwestern Miscellany, 1974—, numerous articles, essays, short stories, poems. Served with USN, 1942-45; with AUS, 1952-53. Decorated Silver Star, Purple Heart; recipient Disting. Alumnus award Bowling Green State U., 1976, Disting. Faculty award Mich. State U., 1974, Disting. Faculty award Mich. Assn. Governing Bds., 1988, Disting Research award Mich. State U., 1988. Mem. ASA, AAUP, MLA, Popular Culture Assn., Soc. Study Midwestern Lit. (founder, exec. sec., Disting. Service award 1982), Assn. Gen. and Liberal Edn. Am. Assn. Advancement Humanities, Internat. Assn. U. Profs. English, Univ. Club. Home: 6555 Lansdown Dr Dimondale MI 48821-9428 Office: Mich State U Dept Am Thought and Lang East Lansing MI 48824

ANDERSON, DAVID GASKILL, JR., Spanish language educator; b. Tarboro, N.C., Feb. 21, 1945; s. David G. Sr. and Lucile (Gammon) A.; m. Jonetta Gentemann, Jan. 29, 1968; children: Allene Q., David III, James H., John G. AB, U. N.C., 1967; MA, Vanderbilt U., 1974, PhD, 1985. Instr. of langs. Union U., Tenn., 1975-76; from instr. Spanish to asst. prof. Ouachita Bapt. U., Ark., 1976-85; asst. prof. fgn. langs. N.E. La. U., 1985-87; asst. prof. Spanish, John Carroll U., Cleve., 1987-93, assoc. prof., 1993—, acting chmn. dept. classical and modern langs., 1996, chmn., 1997—, George Grauel faculty fellow rsch. sabbatical, spring 1997. Tchg. fellow Vanderbilt U., 1983-84, NEH summer seminar on poetry, 1990; presenter in field. Author: On Elevating the Commonplace: A Structuralist Analysis of The Odas of Pablo Neruda, 1987; contbr. articles to profl. jours. Vol. ESL Peace Corps, Colombia, 1968-70. Named Outstanding Young Men of Am., 1979. Mem. Am. Assn. Tchrs. Spanish and Portuguese, Modern Lang. Assn., Cleve. Diocesan Fgn. Lang. Assn. (bd. mem. 1988-93), Cleve. Assn., Phi Beta Kappa. Democrat. Home: 2573 Dysart Rd Cleveland OH 44118-4446 Office: John Carroll Univ Classical & Modern Langs Cleveland OH 44118 E-mail: unc67@msn.com.

ANDERSON, DAVID WALTER, physics educator, consultant; b. Heron Lake, Minn., June 18, 1937; s. Walter Olaf and Martha Gladys (Bonnell) A.; m. Jane Louise Friedlund, Dec. 17, 1960; children: Bonnie Jean, Brian David. BS in Physics summa cum laude, Hamline U., 1959; PhD in Nuclear Physics, Iowa State U., 1965. Diplomate Am. Bd. Radiology, 1968. Postdoctoral fellow in physics Iowa State U., Ames, 1965-66; prof. U. Okla., Norman, 1966-82; prof. radiation physics U. Okla. Health Ctr., Oklahoma City, 1966-82; prof., dir. radiol. physics City of Faith Med. Ctr., Tulsa, 1982-88, Tulsa Regional Med. Ctr., 1988—. Presenter in field; advisor MS and/or PhD students, 1970-84. Author: Absorption of Ionizing Radiation, 1984; contbr. over 53 articles to profl. refereed jours. Chmn. coun. ministry McFarlin Meth. Ch., 1979, chmn. adminstrv. bd., 1978. Grantee Rsch. Corp., Am. Cancer Soc., Radiation Measurement Inc. Fellow Am. Coll. Radiology; mem. Am. Assn. Physicists in Medicine (physics com. on profl. activities 1986-90), Am. Bd. Radiology (physics examiner 1986-90), Am. Coll. Radiology, Soc. Nuclear Medicine, Phi Kappa Phi. Democrat. Achievements include responsiblity for shielding design, acceptance testing, primary data on 19 new or upgraded sites of clinical accelerators. Home: 3617 Guilford Ln Norman OK 73072-3037 Office: Tulsa Regional Med Ctr 744 W 9th St Tulsa OK 74127-9028 E-mail: dwajla@aol.com.

ANDERSON, DELLA JEAN, secondary school educator; b. Hardin, Mont., Aug. 11, 1956; d. Edward Frank and Lorraine M. (Bergquist) Pattyn; m. Michael Henry Anderson, June 5, 1982. BS in Bus. Edn., Mont. State U., 1979. Cert. vocat. tchr. Tchr. Poplar (Mont.) H.S., 1979-80, Campbell County H.S., Gillette, Wyo., 1980-81; tchr. bus. and computer sci. Lodge Grass (Mont.) H.S., 1985—. Adult edn. instr. Ft. Peck C.C., Poplar, 1979-80, Lodge Grass Pub. Schs., 1985—, Little Big Horn Coll., Crow Agency, Mont., 1987-88, Sheridan (Wyo.) Coll., 1994—. Carl Perkins Vocat. grantee, 1985—; recipient Mont. Bus. Edn. Glencoe 2000 award, 1996. Mem. Mont. Edn. Assn., Lodge Grass Tchrs. Assn. (treas. 1991—), Mont. Bus. Edn. Assn. (state historian 1979-80), Alpha Delta Kappa (Iota chpt. v.p. 1990-92, pres. 1992-94). Democrat. Roman Catholic. Avocations: antiques, biking, horseback riding, cooking, sewing. Home: Box 314646 Railway Ranchester WY 82839 Office: Lodge Grass High Sch Box 810 124 N George St Lodge Grass MT 59050

ANDERSON, DENNIS, computer scientist information technology educator; b. Korea, Nov. 5, 1969; s. Nam-Ki No and Woon-Ja Choi. BA, Fordham U., 1991; MS, NYU, 1993; EdM, Columbia U., 1998, MPhil, PhD, Columbia U., 1999. Cert. MIT profl. Mem. faculty CUNY, 1993, NYU, 1993; chmn. St. Francis Coll., Bklyn.; assoc. dean PACE U. Fulbrigh Sr. Specialist; editor Assn. Info. Sys. Newsletter, N.Y.C., 1996-98; reviewer N.Y. State Edn. Dept. Institutional Accreditation, 2003; Fulbright Sr. Specialist, 2001—.Chrm. Internat. Conf.on e-banking and Global Market Pl., 2003. Author: Introduction to Computers, 1996, Introduction to Programming, 1996; lectr., presenter in field. Tech. cons. Dem. Nat. Conv. Com., N.Y., 1992. Rsch. grantee St. Francis Coll., 1995, 96, faculty devel. grantee, 1995, 96, Microsoft Instrnl. Lab. grantee, NSF grantee; others. Mem. IEEE, Am. Soc. Engring. Edn., Assn. Info. Sys., Assn. Computer Machinery (chpt. chmn. 1995—, spl. interest group for computer sci. edn.), Nat. Coun. Tchrs. of Math., N.Y. Acad. Scis., Kappa Delta Pi. Achievements include becoming chmn. of computer info. sys. dept. at age 26. Home: 220 E 26th St Apt 4H New York NY 10010-2422 Office: Pace U 1 Pace Plz New York NY 10038

ANDERSON, DONALD KENNEDY, JR., English educator; b. Evanston, Ill., Mar. 18, 1922; s. Donald Kennedy and Kathryn Marie (Shields) A.; m. Kathleen Elizabeth Hughes, Sept. 11, 1949; children: David J., Lawrence W. AB, Yale U., 1943; MA, Northwestern U., 1947; PhD, Duke U., 1957. Instr. Geneva Coll., Beaver Falls, Pa., 1947-49; from instr. to asst. prof. Rose Poly. Inst., Terre Haute, Ind., 1952-58; asst. prof., assoc. prof. Butler U., Indpls., 1958-65; assoc. prof. U. Mo., Columbia, 1965-67, prof. dept. English, 1967-92, prof. emeritus, 1992—, assoc. dean Grad. Sch., 1970-74. Author: John Ford, 1972; editor: John Ford's Perkin Warbeck, 1965, John Ford's The Broken Heart, 1968, Concord in Discord, The Plays of John Ford, 1586-1986, 1987. Served to lt. (j.g.) USNR, 1943-46. Folger fellow, 1965; U. Mo. Summer Research fellow, 1966, 68, 76, 79, 84 Mem. MLA (midwest regional del. 1972-75), AAUP (sec.-treas. 1962-63) Democrat. Methodist. Home: 3700 S Lenoir St Apt 223 Columbia MO 65201

ANDERSON, DONNA ELAINE, elementary and secondary school educator; b. Lone Wolf, Okla., Mar. 26, 1935; d. William Herbert and Lois Alta (Montgomery) Tolleson; m. Frank D. Anderson, Sept. 3, 1955; 1 child, Valerie Elaine. BA cum laude, U. North Tex., 1957, MEd, 1960. Cert. edn. diagnostician, elem. tchr., bus. tchr.; registered profl. ednl. diagnostician. Tchr. White Deer (Tex.) Ind. Sch. Dist., 1957-62, Pampa (Tex.) Ind. Sch. Dist., 1962-70, ednl. diagnostician, 1973—2003. Missionette dir. First Assembly God Ch., Pampa, 1973—; mem. Pampa Fine Arts Assn., 1978—, Community Concert Assn., Pampa, 1965—. Mem. NEA (life), Tex. Ednl. Diagnosticians Assn., Tex. State Tchrs. Assn. (life), Ednl. Diagnosticians Golden Spread, Coun. Exceptional Children, Knife and Fork Club, Delta Kappa Gamma. Democrat. Mem. Assemby of God Ch. Avocations: photography, piano.

ANDERSON, DOUGLAS SANFORD, vocational supervisor; b. Mpls., Nov. 24, 1936; s. Raymond Melton and Naomi (Sanford) A.; children: Kevin Scott, Kelly Jo. AA in Gen. Edn., Butte (Calif.) C.C., 1960; BA in Social Welfare, U. Calif., Chico, 1962; MA in Vocat. Edn., U. Calif., Sacramento, 1968; PhD in Vocat. Edn., Columbia Pacific U., 1992. Counselor Dept. Youth Authority, Stockton, Calif., 1970-79, parole agt., 1979-81; vocat. instr. Dept. Corrections, Tracy, Calif., 1981-86, supr. vocat. inst. San Quentin, Calif., 1986—. Author: (workbook) Getting and Keeping a Job, 1984. Mem. Vocat. Edn. and Applied Tech. (com. mem. 1986-92, named supr. of yr. 1990, 91)_. Avocations: fishing, wood working. Home: 10217 Wren St NW Coon Rapids MN 55433-4550 Office: Dept Corrections San Quentin State Prison San Quentin CA 94964

ANDERSON, GLORIA LONG, chemistry educator; b. Altheimer, Ark., Nov. 5, 1938; d. Charley and Elsie Lee (Foggie) L.; 1 child, Gerald Leavell. BS, Ark. Agr. Mech. & Normal Coll., 1958; MS, Atlanta U., 1961; PhD, U. Chgo., 1968. Instr. S.C. State Coll., Orangeburg, 1961-62, Morehouse Coll., Altanta, 1962-64; teaching and rsch. asst. U. Chgo., 1964-68; assoc. prof., chmn. Morris Brown Coll., Atlanta, 1968-73, Callaway prof., chmn., 1973-84, acad. dean, 1984-89, United Negro Coll. Fund disting. scholar, 1989-90, Callaway prof. chemistry, 1990—, interim pres., 1992-93, Fuller E. Callaway prof. chemistry, 1993-99, 99—, dean sci. and tech., 1995-97, interim pres., 1998-99, Fuller E. Callaway prof. chemistry, 1999—. Contbr. articles to profl. jours. Bd. dirs. Corp. for Pub. Broadcasting, Washington, 1972-79, vice chmn. 1977-79; Pub. Broadcasting Atlanta, 1980—; mem. Pub. Telecommunications Task Force, Atlanta, 1980. Postdoctoral rsch. fellow NSF, 1969, faculty industry fellow, 1981, faculty rsch. fellow Southeastern Ctr. for Elec. Engring. Edn., 1984. Fellow Am. Inst. Chemists (cert. profl. chemist); mem. Nat. Sci. Tchrs. Assn., Am. Chem. Soc., Sigma Xi. Baptist. Home: 560 Lynn Valley Rd SW Atlanta GA 30311-2331 Office: Morris Brown Coll Dept Chemistry 643 ML King Jr Dr NW Atlanta GA 30314-4140

ANDERSON, GORDON LOUIS, foundation administrator; b. St. Croix Falls, Wis., Nov. 16, 1947; s. Erwin Louis and Eunice Arlene (Johnson) A.; m. Mary Jane Evenson, July 1, 1982; children: Tamara, Jayna, Greta, Evan. BME, U. Minn., 1975; MDiv in Ethics, Union Theol. Sem., N.Y.C., 1980; MA in Religion, Claremont Grad. Sch., 1985, PhD Philosophy Religion, 1986. Engr. Gull Engring. Inc., Mpls., 1974-80, also bd. dirs.; owner, mgr. Aerograph Aerial Photography, Claremont, Calif., 1981-84; sec. gen., bd. dirs. Profs. World Peace Acad., N.Y.C., 1984-93, sec. gen. St. Paul, 1993—; sec., gen., bd. dirs. Internat. Cultural Found., Washington, 1986—. Lectr. Unification Theol. Sem., Barrytown, N.Y., 1987-96, bd. dirs., 1988-96; lectr. 40 countries including Europe, Africa, Asia and South America. Assoc. editor Internat. Jour. World Peace, 1985—94; editor: Internat. Jour. World Peace, 1994—2000; pub. Internat. Jour. World Peace, 2000—, assoc. editor Morality and Religion in Liberal Democratic Societies, 1992, Worldwide State of the Family, 1995, The Family in Global Transition, 1997; contbr. articles, chapters to books; contbr. book revs. to profl. jours. Mem. Citizens for Better N.J., 1986-92; bd. dirs. Paragon House Pubs., 1993—, exec. dir., 1996—; trustee U. Bridgeport, Conn., 1994—. With U.S. Army, 1969-72, Vietnam. Mem. World Future Soc., Am. Acad. Religion, Am. Polit. Sci. Assn., Internat. Studies Assn., Consortium on Peace Rsch. Mem. Unification Ch. Office: Profs World Peace Acad 2285 University Ave W Saint Paul MN 55114-1635

ANDERSON, HOLLY GEIS, women's health facility administrator, commentator, educator; b. Waukesha, Wis., Oct. 23, 1946; d. Henry H. and Hulda S. Geis; m. Richard Kent Anderson, June 6, 1969. BA, Azusa Pacific U., 1970. CEO Oak Tree Antiques, San Gabriel, Calif., 1975-82; pres., founder, CEO Premenstrual Syndrome Med. Clinic, Arcadia, Calif., 1982—, Breast Healthcare Ctr., 1986-89, Hormonal Treatment Ctrs., Inc., Arcadia, 1992-94; with Thyroid Ctr., 2001—. Lectr. radio and TV shows, L.A.; on-air radio personality Women's Clinic with Holly Anderson, 1990—. Author: What Every Woman Needs to Know About PMS (audio cassette), 1987, The PMS Treatment Program (video cassette), 1989, PMS Talk (audio cassette), 1989. Mem. NAFE, The Dalton Soc., Am. Hist. Soc. of Germans from Russia. Republican. Avocations: writing, genealogy, travel, hiking, boating. Office: PMS Treatment Clinic 150 N Santa Anita Ave Ste 755 Arcadia CA 91006-3148

ANDERSON, IRIS ANITA, retired secondary education educator; b. Forks, Wash., Aug. 18, 1930; d. James Adolphus and Alma Elizabeth (Haase) Gilbreath; m. Donald Rene Anderson, 1951; children: Karen Christine, Susan Adele, Gayle Lynne, Brian Dale. BA in Teaching, U. Wash., 1969; MA in English, Seattle U., 1972. Cert. English teacher, adminr Calif. Tchr. Issaquah (Wash.) Sr. High Sch., 1969-77, L.A. Sr. High Sch., 1977-79. Nutrition vol Santa Monica Hosp Aux, Calif., Jules Stein Eye Inst, Los Angeles; mem Desert Beautiful, Palm Springs Panhellenic, Rancho Mirage Reps. Scholar W-Key Activities, Univ Wash. Mem.: LEV, AAUW (Anne Carpenter fellow 1998), NEA, DAR (1st vice regent Cahulla chpt), World Affairs Coun, Calif Ret Teachers Asn, Coachella Valley Hist Soc, Desert Music Guild, Palm Springs Press Women, Nat Thespians, Wash Speech Asn, Am League Pen Women, Living Desert Wildlife And Botanical Preserve, Desert Celebrities, Bob Hope Cultural Ctr, Skeptics Soc, Round Table West (3d pl. writing award 2003), Rancho Mirage Womens Club, CPA Wives Club, Palm Desert Womens Club.

ANDERSON, ISABEL, artist, educator; b. N.Y.C., Apr. 10, 1931; d. William and Mary Elizabeth Smith; m. Hugh Riddell Anderson, Feb. 4, 1955 (div. Jan. 1968); m. William Anthony Dietz, Apr. 29, 1978. Student, Art Students' League, 1951-52; BA, Antioch Coll., 1954; postgrad., UCLA, 1956; MFA, State U. of Iowa, 1956. Cert. h.s. tchr., Calif. C.C. standard teaching credential, instr. credential. Stained glass artist Paul L. Phillips Studio, Altadena, Calif., 1960-64, Roger Daricarrere Studio, L.A., 1965-66; h.s. art tchr. L.A. Unified Sch. Dist., 1967-76; instr. art Glendale (Calif.) C.C., 1979-80; asst. prof. screen printing Pasadena (Calif.) City Coll., 1980-90; artist, writer, 1990—. Invited spkr., panelist in field. Exhbns., prints, drawings, paintings, 1965—; represented in permanent collections Boston Coll. Art, Home Savs. and Loan, Antioch Coll., Pasadena City Coll., Kerala State U., India, Hanover Bank, L.A.; contbr. articles and art revs. to profl. jours. Recipient Award of Merit 11th All-City Art Exhbn., 1963, Purchase award State Coll. Art, 1963, Spl. award Inland XII Art Exhbn., 1981, James Jones Purchae award Ink & Clay Exhbn. Calif. Poly., 1982; grantee Screen Printing Assn. Internat., 1985-88. Mem. L.A. Printmaking Soc. (sec. 1978-79, newsletter editor 1978-79), Women's Caucus for Art. Avocations: hiking and camping, films, theater, musical events.

ANDERSON, JAMES ALFRED, psychology educator; b. Detroit, July 31, 1940; s. Courtney Alfred and Catherine (Bullock) A.; m. Diana De Vincenzi, Nov. 1, 1969; 1 child, Eric David. BS, MIT, 1962, PhD, 1967. Postdoctoral fellow UCLA, 1967-71; research assoc. Rockefeller U., N.Y.C., 1971-73; asst. prof. cognitive and neural scis. Brown U., Providence, 1973-78, assoc. prof., 1978-85, prof., 1985—, chmn. dept. cognitive and linguistic scis., 1993—2002. Chmn. cognitive functional neurosci. rev. panel NIMH, 1992-94; mem. adv. bd. Social, Behavioral and Econ. Scis. Directorate, NSF, 1996-99; co-founder QCD Associates Inc., 1997—; founder Artemis Assocs., Inc., 1989—. Editor: (with G. Hinton) Parallel Models of Associative Memory, 1981, (with S. Lehmkuhle and W. Levy) Synaptic Modification, Neuron Selectivity and Nervous System Organization, 1985, (with E. Rosenfeld) Neurocomputing: Some Important Papers, 1988, (with E. Rosenfeld and A. Pellionisz) Neurocomputing 2, 1990, An Introduction to Neural Networks, 1995; (with E. Rosenfeld) Talking Nets, 1998. Recipient Info. Sci. award, Joint Conf. on Info. Sci., 2002; grantee, NSF, 1979, 1985, 1991, 1997, Office Naval Rsch., 1986, 1991, 1996, Def. Advanced Rsch. Projects Agy., 2002. Mem. Cognitive Sci. Soc., Psychonomic Soc., Soc. for Neurosci., Soc. for Math. Psychology, Internat. Neural Network Soc. (governing bd. 1987-95), Sigma Xi. Avocation: amateur radio. Home: 1 Mathewson Rd Barrington RI 02806-4414 Office: Brown U Dept Cognitive & Linguistic Scis 190 Thayer St Providence RI 02912-9067

ANDERSON, JAMES ARTHUR, humanities educator, academic director; b. Providence, Aug. 9, 1955; s. Arthur Charles and Ruth M. (Marshall) A.; m. Patricia A. Braza, Aug. 27, 1977 (div. 1998); children: Erik James, Nicholas Perry; m. Lynn Toney, June 5, 1999. BA, R.I. Coll., 1977, MA in English, 1987; PhD, U. R.I., 1992. Cert. fundraising exec. Assoc. editor R.I. Rev., Providence, 1981-84; instr. Johnson & Wales U., Providence, 1984-88, adj. prof. humanities, 1988-93, devel. publs., rsch. coord., 1987-90, dir. rsch. and grants, 1990-93, asst. prof., 1993-95; prof., asst. dean Sch. of Arts and Scis., 1995—. Presenter in field. Author: The Illustrated Bradbury: A Structuralist Reading of Bradbury's "The Illustrated Man", 1990, Out of the Shadows: A Structuralist Approach to Understanding the Fiction of H.P. Lovecraft, 1993; columnist, writer East Side Monthly, Province, 1984—; contbr. articles, poems to profl. jours. Coach Warwick (R.I.) Firefighters Soccer Club, 1990, 94; fundraiser Friends of H.P. Lovecraft, Brown U., Providence, 1990. Mem. MLA, Nat. Soc. Fund Raising Execs., Horror Writers Am., N.E. Tchrs. English, Internat. Assn. for the Fantastic in the Arts, Small Press Writers and Artists Orgn. (Gene Day award 1982), Island Fencing Club. Avocations: science fiction, baseball, fishing, fencing. Home: 1467 Warwick Ave Apt 20 Warwick RI 02888-6924 Office: Johnson & Wales U 8 Abbott Park Pl Providence RI 02903-3775

ANDERSON, JANE ELLSWORTH, secondary school educator; b. Chillicothe, Ohio, Mar. 30, 1943; d. Henry Branch and Beatrice Clara (Trainer) Ellsworth: m. George Leonard Anderson, Jr., Sept. 9, 1964; children: Doug, Jeff, Michele. BS in Edn., Ohio State U., 1983, MS in Edn., 1994. Cert. tchr. grades 7-12, Ohio. Long distance operator Ohio Bell Telephone Co., Dayton, 1962-64; real estate agt. Donna Vaughn Realtors, Dayton, 1965-67; sales rep., mgr. Tupperware Dayton Party Sales, 1972-74; tchr. Westerville (Ohio) City Schs., 1984—. Advisor Westerville H.S. Yearbook, Golden Warrior, 1986 (1st pl. award), 1987 (1st pl. award). Various positions Englewood Hills Elem. Sch. PTA, Englewood, Ohio, 1971—76; phone counselor Bridge Counseling Ctr., Columbus, 1980—81; mem. Dem. Congl. Campaign Com., Dem. Senators Campaign Com.; youth dir. Unity Ch., Columbus, Ohio, 1978—80. Mem.: NEA, Westerville Edn. Assn., Ohio Edn. Assn., Emily's List, So. Poverty Law Ctr., U.S. Holocaust Meml. Mus. Avocations: writing, reading, biking. Office: Westerville City Schs 336 S Otterbein Ave Westerville OH 43081-2334

ANDERSON, JANE LOUISE BLAIR, librarian, horse breeder, poet; b. Wilkinsburg, Pa., Nov. 6, 1948; d. Francis Preston and Mary Louise (Maxwell) Blair; m. Russell Karl Anderson Jr., Apr. 20, 1973; children: Christina Lynn, Melissa Jane. BS in Edn., Clarion State Coll., 1971; MS in Library Sci., Duquesne U., 1974. Cert. pub. librarian, Pa. ; librarian Franklin Regional Schs., Murrysville, Pa., 1971-97; breeder quarter horses, Fenelton, Pa., 1978-97; owner, operator Fern Valley Farm Boarding Kennels. Contbr. poems to various anthologies. Vol. mem. Rescue 5 Ambulance, Murrysville, 1974-76, Medic I ambulance, 1976-78; first aid instr. ARC, Murrysville, 1975-80; instr. CPR, Am. Heart Assn., Westmoreland County, 1976-80; Mem. Westmoreland County Library Assn. (pres.), Pa. Sch. Libr. Assn. (presentor regional workshops 1989, 90, speaker 1989, adv. coun. 1992), internat. coord., pres., Owiti Ebenezer Found., Inc., 1997—;Butler County C. of C., Am. Boarding Kennel Assn. Home: Fern Valley Farm PO Box 12 Fenelton PA 16034-0012

ANDERSON, JANE TALLEY, artist, educator; b. Spur, Tex., Oct. 17, 1929; d. Marshall Herff and Louise (Winfield) Applewhite; m. Oran Kent Talley, Feb. 28, 1948 (dec. Mar. 1998); children: Carleen Dolan, Linda Oldham; m. Ken Anderson, Nov. 27, 1999. Attended, U. Tex., 1946-48. Gallery artist Top of the Line Gallery, Ft. Worth, 1980-89, Morales Gallery, Nags Head, N.C., 1985-91, Artenegies Gallery, Ft. Worth, 1988—, Tarbox Gallery, San Diego, 1990-92, Riuer Gallery, Reno, Nev., 1992-94; Castleberry Gallery, Arlington, Tex., 1992—; gallery artist Richelle Gallery, Bedford, Tex., 1993-94. Art tchr. Imagination Celebration, Ft. Worth, 1993; demonstrator various workshops.; tchr. water media and collaeg techniques to large and small groups in Ft. Worth and Arlington, Tex., 1999, 2000. Active Arlington Visual Artists, 1999—. Recipient Merit award Nat. Watercolor Okla., 1987, Citation award Tex. Fine Arts Assn., 1988. Mem. Soc. Watercolor Artists (bd. dirs., Pres. award 1994), Tex. Watercolor Soc. (Merit award 1982), Southwestern Watercolor Soc. Avocations: bird watching, beach combing, photography. Home: 6671 Townlake Cir Arlington TX 76016-2551

ANDERSON, JANET STETTBACHER, home economics educator; b. Somerville, N.J., Feb. 9, 1936; d. Norman Albert and Bessie Mildred (Woodruff) Stettbacher; m. David Lloyd Anderson, June 8, 1957; children: Heidi Ellen, Laurie Bette, Eric Woodruff, Douglas Scott. BS, Rutgers U., 1957; MA, San Diego State U., 1961. Cert. secondary tchr., Calif.; advanced profl. cert., Md. Tchr. San Diego Unified Sch. Dist., 1958-62; assoc. home economist McCalls's Corp., N.Y.C., 1963-65; tchr. adult edn. Palo Alto (Calif.) Unified Sch. Dist., 1970-74; substitute tchr. Montgomery County Pub. Schs., Rockville, Md., 1974-78, tchr. home econs., 1978—2002. Cons., mgr. dinner theatre Wootton High Sch., Rockville, 1981-90. Officer, pres. Greendell Sch. PTA, Palo Alto, 1972-74; safety chmn. Cold Spring Sch. PTA, Potomac, Md., 1974-76; sec. Cold Spring Civic Assn., 1976. Mem. NEA, Am. Assn. Family and Consumer Scis., AAUW (officer 1974—, pres. Bethesda-Chevy Chase br. 1984-86, honoree Ednl. Found. 1977), Smithsonian Assocs., Phi Delta Kappa. Avocations: collecting antiques, quilting. Home: RR 1 Box 6500 Sargentville ME 04673 E-mail: dander@bellatlantic.net.

ANDERSON, JANICE LEE ATOR, secondary education mathematics educator; b. LaSalle, Ill., Aug. 8, 1948; d. Glen Bertran and Josephine Mary (Urichko) Ator; m. Gene Vernon Hook, July 20, 1968 (dec. 1974); m. Robert John Anderson, May 11, 1979 (div. 1983); 1 child, Karen Lynn. AA, Ill. Valley Community Coll., 1968; BS in Edn., Minot State Coll., 1970; MS in Edn., Ill. State U., 1997. Cert. tchr., Ill. Tchr. reading Tonica (Ill.) Elem. Sch., 1970-71; tchr. math., sci. Tonica Jr. High Sch., 1971-80, Tonica High Sch., 1980; tchr. math. Bradley (Ill.)-Bourbonnais Community High Sch., 1983—. Coach math. team Bradley-Bourbonnais Community High Sch., 1983—. Mem. NEA, Ill. Edn. Assn., Bradley-Bourbonnais Edn. Assn. (sec. 1990-93, treas. 1993—), Women of Moose. Democrat. Roman Catholic. Avocations: coin collecting, stamp collecting, reading, tennis. Home: 904 Roosevelt Rd La Salle IL 61301-1405 Office: Bradley Bourbonnais Community High Sch 700 W North St Bradley IL 60915-1013 E-mail: jlander1@juno.com.

ANDERSON, JAY MARTIN, computer scientist educator; b. Paterson, N.J., Oct. 16, 1939; s. Carl Albert and Dorothy Hudson (Bradshaw) A.; m. Alison Ives Archbald, June 15, 1963 (div. Dec. 1991); 1 child, Carl Christopher; m. Patricia Ann Schaefer Jones, May 24, 1992. BA, Swarthmore Coll., 1960; AM, Harvard U., 1961, PhD, 1964. From asst. prof, to prof. chemistry, dir. academic computing Bryn Mawr (Pa.) Coll., 1963-86; designer software Tymlabs Corp., Austin, Tex., 1986-88; prof. computer sci. Franklin and Marshall Coll., Lancaster, Pa., 1988—, Richard S. and Ann B Barshinger prof. computer sci. Author: Mathematics for Quantum Chemistry, 1964, Introduction to Quantum Chemistry, 1968, Algorithmns for Computer Cartography, 1998. Mem. Assn. Computing Machinery, Sigma Xi, Phi Beta Kappa. Republican. Episcopalian. Office: Franklin & Marshall Coll Dept Math 501 Harrisburg Ave Lancaster PA 17603-2615 E-mail: jay.anderson@fandm.edu.

ANDERSON, JERRY WILLIAM, JR., technical and business consulting executive, educator; b. Stow, Mass., Jan. 14, 1926; s. Jerry William and Heda Charlotte (Petersen) A. ; m. Joan Hukill Balyeat, Sept. 13, 1947; children: Katheleen, Diane. BS in Physics, U. Cin., 1949, PhD in Econs., 1976; MBA, Xavier U., 1959. Rsch. and test project engr. Wright-Patterson AFB, Ohio, 1949-53; project engr., electronics div. AVCO Corp., Cin., 1953-70, program mgr., 1970-73; program dir. Cin. Electronics Corp., 1973-78; pres. Anderson Industries Unltd., 1978—. Chmn. dept. mgmt. and mgmt. info. svcs. Xavier U., 1980-89, prof. mgmt., 1989-94, prof. emeritus, 1994—; lectr. No. Ky. U., 1977-78; tech. adviser Cin. Tech. Coll., 1971-80; co-founder, exec. v.p. Loving God "Complete Bible" Christian Ministries, 1988—. Contbr. articles on radars, lasers, infrared detection equipment, air pollution to govt. pubs. and prof. jours.; author: 3 books in field; reviewer, referee: Internat. Jour. Energy Sys., 1985—86. Mem. Madeira (Ohio) City Planning Commn., 1962-80; founder, pres. Grassroots, Inc., 1964; active United Appeal, Heart Fund, Multiple Sclerosis Fund. With USNR, 1943-46 Named Man of Year, City of Madeira, 1964 Mem. MADD, VFW (life), Am. Mgmt. Assn., Assn. Energy Engrs. (charter), Internat. Acad. Mgmt. and Mktg., Nat. Right to Life, Assn. Cogeneration Engrs. (charter), Assn. Environ. Engrs. (charter), Am. Legion (past comdr.), Acad. Mgmt., Madeira Civic Assn. (past v.p.), Cin. Art Mus., Cin. Zoo, Colonial Williamsburg Found., Omicron Delta Epsilon. Republican. Home and Office: 7208 Sycamorehill Ln Cincinnati OH 45243-2101

ANDERSON, JEWELLE LUCILLE, musician, educator; b. Alexandria, La., Jan. 4, 1932; d. William Andrew and Ethel Dee (Hall) Anderson. Student, Springfield Coll., 1981-82; MusB, Boston U., 1984; postgrad., Harvard U., 1995-96. Cert. tchr. music and social studies Mass. Soloist Ch. of the Redeemer Episcopal Ch., Chestnut Hill, Mass., 1964-69, St. James Episcopal Ch., Cambridge, Mass., 1970-75; kindergarten tchr. and music dir. Trinity Episcopal Ch., Boston, 1984-86; chorus music dir. Spencer for Hire, Boston, 1986; music dir. Days in the Arts summer program Boston Symphony Orch., Tanglewood, Mass., summer 1991, 92; chorale dir. Boston Orch. Chorale, 1996-97; tchr. scholar Harvard Grad. Sch. of Edn., 1998-99. Founder Jewelle Anderson Found., Inc., Boston, 1996. Vol. ARC, Boston, 1994—; bd. dirs. Mattapan Cmty. Health Ctr., Boston, 1990—92; founder, pres. Dr. William and Ethel Hall Anderson Scholarship, 1989—. Recipient Am. Music award, Nat. Fedn. Music, 1970, Spl. Individual award, 1969, Outstanding Contbn. to Humanity award, Alexandria Civic Improvement Coun., 1967, Outstanding Achievement award, Boston Tchrs. Union, 2000, Cope Plaque for Outstanding Achievement, 2000, Action for Boston Cmty. Devel. award, 2003. Mem.: AAUW, Black Educators Alliance of Mass., Amnesty Internat., Women Svc. Club (head youth group 1989—, 1st v.p. 2002), Alpha Kappa Alpha. Democrat. Baptist. Avocations: walking, boating. Office: Jewelle Anderson Found Inc PO Box 1181 Boston MA 02103-1181

ANDERSON, JOAN BALYEAT, religion educator, minister; b. Cin., Apr. 14, 1926; d. Hal Donal and Myrtle (Skinner) Hukill Balyeat; m. Jerry William Anderson, Jr., Sept. 13, 1947: children: Katheleen, Diane. AA, Stephens Coll., 1946. Ordained Christian minister, Ohio, 1988. Christian ch. bible tchr., Cin., 1944—; Christian counselor, advisor, 1964—; founder, pres., dir., ruling elder, and pastor Loving God "Complete Bible" Christian Ministries and First Ch., Cin., 1988—. Christian Bible tchr., preacher, pastor daily and Sunday radio throughout the east and midwest, 1988—. Mem. Am. Conservative Cause, 1998—2001, Capitol His. Soc., 2000—; legacy leader supporter George Washington's Mt. Vernon, 2001—; coord., collector Heart Fund, T.B., 1948—90; civic assn. officer, rep. edn. com. to all Madeira Schs., 1960—62; co-founder, officer Grassroots, Inc., Cin., 1962—65; mem. Cin. Art Mus., 1972—, Cin. Zoo, 1974—, Colonial Williamsburg Found., 1979—, Nat. Right to Life, 1980—, MADD, 1985—, Heritage Found., 1996—, Am. Conservative Union, 1998, Ronald Reagan Presdl. Found., 1998—, Parents TV Coun., 1998—2001, Am. Policy Ctr., 1998—2001, U.S. Justice Found., 1998—, Nat. Right to Work Legal Def. Found., 1998—, Nat. Security Ctr., 1998—, U.S. Intelligence Ctr., 1998—, Jud. Watch, 1999—, Young Ams. Found., 2000—; supporter The Liberty Coun., 2001—; lifelong activist for preservation of U.S. Constn. and Bill of Rights; mem. U.S. Rep. Senatorial Adv. Com., Washington and Cin., 1987—88; mem. Rep. Senatorial Commn., Washington & Cin., 1996—2000; mem. Am. Prayer Network, 1998—. Mem. Blue Book of Cin. Avocation: touring america by car. Home: 7208 Sycamorehill Ln Cincinnati OH 45243-2101 Office: Loving God Complete Bible Christian Mins/1st Ch PO Box 43404 Cincinnati OH 45243-2101

ANDERSON, JOHN BAYARD, lawyer, educator, former congressman; b. Rockford, Ill., Feb. 15, 1922; s. E. Albin and Mabel Edna (Ring) A.; m. Keke Machakos, Jan. 4, 1953; children: Eleanora, John Bayard, Diane, Karen, Susan Kimberly. AB, U. Ill., 1942, JD, 1946; LLM, Harvard U., 1949; hon. doctorates, No. Ill. U., Wheaton Coll., Shimer Coll., Biola Coll., Geneva Coll., North Park Coll. and Theol. Sem., Houghton Coll., Trinity Coll., Rockford Coll. Bar: Ill. 1946. Practice law Rockford, 1946-52; with U.S. Fgn. Service, 1952-55; assigned West Berlin, 1952-55; mem. 87th-95th Congresses from 16th Dist. Ill., mem. rules com.; chmn. Ho. Republican Conf., 1969-79; ind. candidate for Pres. U.S., 1980. Vis. prof. Stanford U., 1981; vis. prof. Nova-Southeastern U. Ctr. for Study Law, 1987-2003, Washington Coll. Law Am. U., 1997—; vis. prof. polit. sci. Brandeis U., 1985, Oreg. State U., 1986, U. Mass., 1985—; lectr. polit. sci. Bryn Mawr Coll., 1985. Author: Between Two Worlds: A Congressman's Choice, 1970, Vision and Betrayal in America, 1976, The American Economy We Need, 1984, A Proper Institution: Guaranteeing Televised Presidential Debates, 1988; editor: Congress and Conscience, 1970. Ind. candidate for Pres. U.S., 1980. Mem. World Federalist Assn. (pres. 1992—), Ctr. for Voting and Democracy (chmn. bd. 1996—, co-chmn. nat. adv. bd. pub. campaign for campaign fin. reform 1997—), Coun. on Fgn. Rels., Phi Beta Kappa. Mem. Evang. Free Ch. (past trustee). E-mail: jbafed@aol.com.

ANDERSON, JOHN EDWARD, mechanical engineering educator; b. Chgo., May 15, 1927; s. Claus Oscar and Ruth Melvina (Engstrom) A.; m. Cynthia Louise Howard, May 24, 1975; children: Candice, James, Stanley. BME, Iowa State U., 1949; MSME, U. Minn., 1955; PhD, MIT, 1962. Registered profl. engr., Minn., Ill. Aero. research scientist Nat. Adv. Com. for Aeros., Langley Field, Va., 1949-51; devel. engr. Honeywell, Inc., Mpls., 1951-53, research engr., 1953-55, prin. research engr., 1955-58, research project engr., 1954-58, sr. staff engr., 1958-62, mgr. space systems, 1963; mem. faculty U. Minn., Mpls., 1963-86, prof. mech. engring., 1971-86, Boston U., 1986-94. Cons. Colo. Regional Transp. Dist., 1974-75, Raytheon Co., 1975-76, Mannesmann Demag, 1978-79, Arthr D. Little, Inc., 1981, Indpls. Transit Commn., 1979-81, Davy McKee Corp., 1984-85; founder, pres., CEO Taxi 2000 Corp. (formerly ATS Inc.), 1983—. Author: Magnetohydrodynamic Shock Waves, Magnetogasdynamics of Thermal Plasma, Transit Systems Theory; editor: Personal Rapid Transit II. With USN, 1945-46. Recipient Outstanding Inventor in Am. award Intellectual Property Owners Found., 1989; Convair fellow. NAS, 1967-68 Fellow AAAS; mem. ASME, Union Concerned Scientists, Mensa, World Federalists Assn., Sierra Club. Unitarian Universalist. Home: 5164 Ranier Pass NE Minneapolis MN 55421-1338

ANDERSON, JOHN HENDERSON, retired secondary education educator, retired army officer; b. Bklyn., Oct. 3, 1929; s. Alexander Paul and Elizabeth May (Henderson) A.; m. Mary Eleanor Kraus, Sept. 12, 1952; children: Virginia, John, Scott. B.Gen. Edn., U. Omaha, 1965; MS, Troy (Ala.) State U., 1973. Commd. 2d lt. U.S. Army, 1951, advanced through grades to lt. col.; exec. officer, chief evaluation br. Office of Dir. of Instr., U.S. Army Aviation Sch., Ft. Rucker, Ala., 1968-71; ret.; sr. army instr. Daleville (Ala.) High Sch., 1971-93. Coach rifle team; match dir. Ala. Jr. Olympic Rifle Championships, 1983-93; rifle tournament dir. Ala. Sports Festival, 1993-96; chief judge Ala. Jr. Olympic Rifle Championships, 1994-2002. Shooting sports info. supr. Olympic Centennial Games, Atlanta, 1996; mem., chmn. vol. com. Ft. Rucker Retiree Coun., 1980-86. Decorated Legion of Merit, Bronze Star with 3 oak leaf clusters and V, Purple Heart, Air medal (10), Army Commendation medal, Vietnamese Honor medal 1st class, Outstanding Civilian Svc. medal U.S. Army, Silver medal Internat. Shooting Union, 1996. Mem. VFW (life), Army Aviation Assn. Am. (charter life), Mil. Officers Assn. Am.(charter life, pres. Ft. Rucker chpt. 2000), Assn. U.S. Army (life, exec. coun. Ft. Rucker chpt. 1981-93), Ret. Mil. Instrs. U.S. (charter), USA Shooting (charter), Ozark Area C. of C. (retiree com. 1993-97). Home: 144 White Oak Cir Ozark AL 36360-8905

ANDERSON, KATHERYN LUCILLE, language arts educator and author; b. Aberdeen, Md., Aug. 17, 1949; d. Boyd Frederick and Lucy Charlotte Anderson. BS in Edn., U. Md., 1973; MA in Spl. Edn., Adams State Coll., Alamosa, Colo., 1977; MA in Ednl. Tech., U. Colo., 1986. Lic. profl. tchr., Colo. Mental health paraprofl. Prince George's County Mental Health, Landover, Md., 1970-73; spl. edn. tchr. Fountain/Ft. Carson (Colo.) Sch. Dist., 1973-75; instr. mil. program Pikes Peak Cmty. Coll., Colorado Springs, Colo., 1977-78; spl. edn. tchr. Harrison Sch. Dist., Colorado Springs, 1978-88, tchr. lang. arts, 1988—, team leader lang. arts, 1989—, dept. chair, 1992—. Lectr. in field. Author: English and American Culture, 1991, English and American Culture 6, 1993, English and American Culture 7, 1993, A Writing Companion, 1993; co-author: The Sound of the Apple IIe, 1986, The Shape of the Apple IIe, 1986. Chpt. II Ednl. Program Devel. grantee Harrison Sch. Dist., 1991, 92, 93; recipient 1996 Colo. State A World of Difference Educator of Yr. award. Mem. AAUW, ASCD, Colo. Assn. Middle Level Educators, Colo. Lang. Arts Soc., Nat. Coun. Tchrs. English, Nat. Women's History Project Network, Tenn. Walking Horse Assn. (rep., stock show and horse exposition 1993-94), Tenn. Walking Horse Breeders and Exhibitors Assn. Democrat. Avocations: riding, breeding and showing tennessee walking horses, reading, computers, authoring. Office: Carmel Middle Sch 1740 Pepperwood Dr Colorado Springs CO 80910-1599

ANDERSON, LEE, secondary school educator; b. Chgo., Jan. 26, 1938; d. Raymond A. and Adeline (Zabel) Girlock; children: Gail Elaine Tompkins, Donna Lee Nuger, Susan Lynn McCracken. BA, Northeastern Ill. U., 1979, MA in Reading, 1984; cert. advance studies, Nat. Louis U., 1992. Cert. K-9 tchr., K-12 reading tchr., mid. sch. curriculum and instrn., Ill. Tchr. Dist. 401, Elmwood Park, Ill., 1979-82, North Chgo. H.S., 1984-89, Dist. 60, Waukegan, Ill., 1989—. Adj. faculty Coll. of Lake County, Grayslake, Ill., 1985-98. Avocations: travel, reading. Home: 1228 N Streamwood Ln Vernon Hills IL 60061-1223

ANDERSON, LINDA KAY, elementary education educator; b. Winnsboro, Tex., June 16, 1952; d. Orsborne and Sammie K. (Fletcher) Hill; m. Rodney Wayne Anderson, Jan. 14, 1974; children: Christopher Terence, Christian Brice. AA, Tyler (Tex.) Jr. Coll., 1970; BS, E. Tex. State U., 1974, MS, 1976. Cert. tchr., kindergarten endorsement, instrnl. leadership, ednl. administr., Tex. Tchr. Rice (Tex.) Common Sch. Dist., 1975-76, Pine Tree Ind. Sch. Dist., Longview, Tex., 1976—. Mem. NEA, Tex. State Tchrs. Assn., Alpha Kappa Alpha, Sigma Tau Delta, Upsilon Beta. Democrat. Methodist. Avocations: sewing, cooking, arts and crafts, piano. Home: 812 Glencrest Ln Longview TX 75601-4421

ANDERSON, LORRAINE, secondary education educator; b. Beulah, Miss., May 23, 1954; d. Milton and Catherine Anderson. BA, U. Ill., 1977, MA, 1981. Cert. tchr., Ill.; diploma in computer programming Control Data, 1978. Tchr. spl. edn. Martin Luther King H.S., Chgo. Pub. Schs., 1984-88, tchr. English, Chgo. H.S. Agrl. Scis., 1988—, head dept. English, 2001—. Judge Chgo. Metro History Fair, 1983-84; pension judge Chgo. Tchrs., 1995—; reader judge Chgo. Sci. Fair Symposium, Chgo., 1997-98; cons. in field. Trustee, min.'s bd. dirs. Bethel House Prayer, United Holiness Ch. Am., Chgo., 1987—; bd. dirs. Youth Unshacled Ministries, 2000—, spkr., 2002—. Mem. Nat. Coun. Tchrs. English, Ill. Coun. Reading, Ill. Computing Educators, Secondary Reading League, Future Farmers Am. Alumni. Assn. Avocations: reading, singing in the community choir, writing poetry, travel. Office: Chgo HS Agrl Scis 3857 W 111th St Chicago IL 60655-4009

ANDERSON, MARCIA KAY, physical education educator; b. Waterloo, Iowa, Oct. 21, 1950; d. Amos Theodore and Barbara Louise (Gravatt) A. BS, Upper Iowa Coll., 1972; MS, Ind. U., 1980; PhD, U. Iowa, 1991. Lic. athletic trainer, Mass. Tchr. phys. edn., coach Jessup (Iowa) Community Schs., 1972-73, North Fayette Community Schs., West Union, Iowa, 1973-78; instr. sports emergency care Ind. U., Bloomington, 1979-80; prof. phys. edn., dir. athletic tng. program Bridgewater (Mass.) State Coll., 1981—, mem. president's coun. on women's issues, 1990—. Textbook cons., reviewer Times Mirror/Mosby Coll. Pub., St. Louis, 1984-91; women's athletic trainer U.S. Tennis Assn., N.Y.C., 1985-88. Author: Instructor's Manual for Modern Principles in Athletic Training, 1986, 7th edit., 1990, Sports Injury Management, 1995; contbg. author: Essentials in Athletic Training, 1991, Current Issues in Athletic Training, 1995. Mem. statewide comprehensive injury prevention program Mass. Dept. Health, 1985-88; chmn. affirmative action coun. Mass. State Coll., 1986-88. Recipient Disting. Svc. award in edn. Bridgewater State Coll., 1987, profl. devel. grantee, 1984, 85, 90. Mem. AAHPERD, Nat. Athletic Trainers Assn. (cert.), Mass. AAHPERD (exec. com. 1992—, sports medicine cons. 1992—, Honor award 1993), Ea. Athletic Trainers, Athletic Trainers Mass. (spkr.'s bur. 1983—, treas. 1985-86), Mass. State Coll. Assn. (v.p. and grievance officer 1993—), Women's Inst. Sport and Edn. Found. (chair exec. bd. 1993—). Democrat. Avocations: woodworking, hiking. Office: Bridgewater State Coll Park Ave Bridgewater MA 02325-0001

ANDERSON, MARILYN JUNE, retired secondary school educator; b. Aldrich, Mo., July 3, 1935; d. Lafayette and Helen Louise (Cheek) A. BS in Edn., S.W. Mo. State U., Springfield, 1958; MEd, U. Mo., 1966. Vocal, instrumental music Licking (Mo.) High Sch., 1958-62; vocal music, English I and English II Sullivan (Mo.) High Sch., 1962-65; vocal music Willard (Mo.) High Sch., 1965-67, Hillcrest High Sch., Springfield, Mo., 1967-92; substitute tchr. Springfield R-12 Schs., 1992-95. Sponsor Future Nurses Am., Licking, 1958-62; chpt. organizer and sponsor Hillcrest Tri-M, 1988-92; pvt. piano and voice tchr., music contest adjudicator; singer Mid. Am. Singers, Springfield, 1969-76. Chmn. of drive March of Dimes, Licking, Mo., 1961; edn. chmn. Am. Cancer Soc., Texas County, 1961-62; Bible sch. tchr. Ch. of Christ, Springfield, Mo., 1968-71, 80-2000; singer S.W. Mo. State U., Collegiate Chorale, 1992-99. Mem. NEA, Mo. Music Educators Assn. (dist. vocal v.p. 1986-87), Music Educators Nat. Conf., Am. Choral Dirs. Assn., Springfield Area Ret. Tchrs. Assn., Mo. Ret. Tchrs. Assn., Nat. Fedn. of State H.S. Assn., Delta Kappa Gamma (chpt. rec. sec. 1992—). Republican. Avocations: needlework, reading, walking, flower gardening, writing.

ANDERSON, MARILYN NELLE, elementary education educator, librarian, counselor; b. Las Animas, Colo., May 5, 1942; d. Mason Hadley Moore and Alice Carrie (Dwyer) Coates; m. George Robert Anderson, Sept. 4, 1974; children: Lisa Lynn, Edward Alan, Justin Patrick. BEd magna cum laude, Adams State Coll., 1962, postgrad., 1965; MEd, Ariz. State U., 1967; postgrad., Idaho State U., 1971, 86, Columbia Pacific U., 1991—. Cert. elem. tchr., K-12 sch. counselor. Tchr. Wendell (Idaho) Sch. Dist. 232, 1962-66, Union-Endicott (N.Y.) Sch. Dist., 1967-68; counselor, librarian West Yuma (Colo.) Sch. Dist., 1968-69; elem. sch. counselor Am. Falls (Idaho) Sch. Dist. 381, 1969-73; project dir. Gooding County (Idaho) Sr. Citizens Orgn., 1974-75; tchr. Castleford (Idaho) Sch. Dist. 417, 1982-92; placement specialist, referral counselor Idaho Child Care Program South Ctrl. Idaho Community Action Agy., Twin Falls, 1992—. Mem. Castleford Schs. Merit Pay Devel. program, 1983-84, Accreditation Evaluation com., 1984-85, Math. Curriculum Devel. com., 1985-86. Leader Brownie Scouts, Endicott, 1967-68; chmn. fundraising com. Am. Falls Kindergarten, 1971-73. Recipient Leader's award Nat. 4-H Conservation Natural Resources Program, 1984. Mem. NEA, ASCD, Nat. Assn. Edn. Young Children, Assn. Childhood Edn. Internat., Idaho Edn. Assn., So. Idaho Assn. for Childhood Edn. Internat. (pres.), Idaho Coun. Internat. Reading Assn., Magic Valley Reading Assn., Support Unltd. Providers and Parents. Republican. Baptist. Avocations: reading, painting, writing short stories, photography. Home: 1675 BBH Wendell ID 83355-9801

ANDERSON, MARILYN RUTH, retired multi-media specialist; b. Storm Lake, Iowa, Oct. 2, 1934; d. Ernest F. and Elvira (Getzmier) Otto; m. Leland A. Anderson, June 23, 1957; children: Pamela, Mitchell, Darren. BA, U. No. Iowa, 1975. Cert. tchr. Iowa. Tchr. 1st grade Holstein (Iowa) Comty. Sch., 1954-55, Humboldt (Iowa) Comty. Sch., 1955-57; substitute tchr.

Aurelia (Iowa) Comty. Sch., 1958-66, Kanawha (Iowa) Comty. Sch., 1966-74; libr. media specialist, reading tchr. Marcus-Meriden-Cleghorn Sch., Meriden, Iowa, 1974-2000; h.s. libr. media specialist Willow Comty. Sch., Quimby, Iowa, 1984-89. Mem. Cleghorn (Iowa) Pub. Libr. Trustees, 1976—86, chair, 1982—86. Mem. planning com., leader Meriden-Cleghorn New Libr.Bldg. Campaign, 1983—85, chair libr. design com., chmn. fed. grant-writing com.; spkr. dedication ceremony Meriden-Cleghorn Cmty. Libr., 1986. Mem.: Iowa Reading Assn., N.W. Iowa Reading Coun., Iowa Edn. Media Assn. (mem. Children's Choice award com. 1976—), Area Edn. Agy. 4 Media Specialists (sec. 1980—82, pres. 1984—86), Internat. Reading Assn. Republican. Lutheran. Avocations: travel, camping, touring state capitols, reading, investing. Home: 306 South Lewis Ave Cleghorn IA 51014 E-mail: lmand@mailstation.com.

ANDERSON, MARILYN WHEELER, English language educator; b. Tulsa, Mar. 18, 1946; d. Robert Leslie and Lola Madelene (Offutt) Wheeler; m. Austin Gilman Anderson, Mar. 17, 1968; children: Guy, Lisa, Michael, Emily. BA, Calif. State U., L.A., 1968; MA, UCLA, 1972, Calif. State U., Dominguez Hills, 1989. Actress and dir., L.A., 1977-83; cons. Redondo Beach (Calif.) Beach City Schs., 1981-83; prof. of English El Camino Coll., Torrance, Calif., 1986—. Fine arts com. mem. El Camino Coll., 1992—, affirmative action officer, 1995-96; presenter in field. Author: (textbook) Keys to Successful Writing, 1998, 2d edit., 2001; contbr. articles to profl. jours. Vol. 1736 House/Crisis Ctr., Hermosa Beach, Calif., 1985-86; bd. dirs. Brain Injury Rsch. Ctr., UCLA, 1998—, spkr. Calif. Coun. for Humanities, 2002, keynote spkr. Joint Symposium of Nat. and Internat. Neurotrauma Socs., 2002. Mem. MLA, Nat. Coun. Tchrs. of English, UCLA Alumni Assn. Democrat. Avocations: jogging, travel, hiking, book club membership. Office: El Camino Coll 16007 Crenshaw Blvd Torrance CA 90506-0001

ANDERSON, MARY JANE, music educator; b. St. Louis, Oct. 9, 1954; d. William Edward and Katherine Ruth Anderson. Student, The Juilliard Sch., 1967—72; BFA in Piano Performance, Stephens Coll., 1976; MM in Piano Performance, So. Ill. U., Edwardsville, 1991. Piano faculty St. Louis Conservatory and Schs. for the Arts, St. Louis, 1977—81, So. Ill. U., Edwardsville, 1984—; pvt. piano instr. St. Louis, 1975—. Adjudicator state and local piano competitions, Mo. and Ill.; soloist St. Louis Symphony, St. Louis Philharmonic; recitalist, orchestral soloist numerous performances throughout Midwest U.S., Pa, NY. Recipient 1st pl. Profl. Debut Recital, Artist Presentation Soc., 1975, 1st pl. Dimitri Mitropoulos Nat. Piano Competition, Stephens Coll., 1972, scholarship winner, Dimitri Mitropoulos Piano Competition; scholar Piano scholarship, Am. Acad. Arts in Europe, 1975. Mem.: St. Louis Area Music Tchrs. Assn. (pres. 2002—), Mo. Music Tchrs. Assn., Music Tchrs. Nat. Assn. Avocations: reading, fishing, crossword puzzles. Office: So Ill U Edwardsville Music Dept PO Box 1771 Edwardsville IL 62026-1771

ANDERSON, MICHAEL R. elementary school educator, writer; b. Washington, Ill., Jan. 2, 1952; s. Roy Robert and Mildred Louise Anderson; m. Martha Elizabeth Ward; children: Samuel Ward, Anna Louise. BA, Ill. Coll., 1974; MA, St. Xavier U., 2002. Cert. tchr. K-9 Ill. Educator Sch. Dist. 117, Jacksonville, Ill., 1974—. Cons. Ill. State Bd. Edn., Springfield, Ill., 1999—2001. Author: (children's book) Construction of the Classical Whanger, 1981, The Phantom Teacher, 2001; musician: (audio recording) Solo: Not Alone, 1990, Ice Out, 1998; author: The Great Sled Race, 2000 (Parents' Choice Silver Honor award, 2000). Dir. Lincoln's New Salem Storytelling Festival, Petersburg, 1986—2002; artist dir. Claville Music and Storytelling Festival, Pleasant Plains, 1981—86. Named Ten Outstanding Young Persons, Ill. Jaycees, 1989; recipient Outstanding Young Educator, Jacksonville Jaycees, 1987—88, Innovative Instrnl. Initiative award, West Ctrl. Ill. Assn. for Supervision and Curriculum, 1994, Disting. Alumni award, Ill. Coll., 2003. Mem.: Jacksonville Ednl. Assn. (mem. chmn. 1986—90), Riverwinds Storytelling Guild, Prairie Grapevine Folklore Soc. (pres. 1985—88), Nat. Storytelling Network, Kappa Delta Pi. Home: PO Box 35 Jacksonville IL 62651 Office: MW Prodn PO Box 35 Jacksonville IL 62651 Home Fax: 217-245-9752; Office Fax: 217-245-9752. E-mail: mike@dulcimerguy.com.

ANDERSON, MONICA LUFFMAN, school librarian, educator, real estate broker; b. Ramsgate, Kent, U.K., Sept. 28, 1914; arrived in U.S., 1952; d. Percy Victor Luffman and Rosalind Dismorr; m. Howard Richmond Anderson, Dec. 22, 1951 (dec.); children: Monica Jane, James Stewart. BA in English with honors, London U., 1936; MS in Libr. Sci., Simmons Coll., 1968; EdM in Ednl. Media, Boston U., 1970. Evacuation officer London Borough of Acton, 1940—41; dir. Coun. for Edn. in World Citizenship, London, 1941—47; from asst. to head of sect. with diplomatic status UNESCO, Paris, 1947—50; H.S. libr. Holliston, Mass., 1968—70; coord. libr. svcs. Lincoln-Sudbury (Mass.) Regional H.S., 1970—81; real estate broker Coldwell Banker Residential Brokerage, Wayland, Mass., 1982—. Author brochures. Troop leader Girl Scouts Am., Weston, Mass., 1963—65; tutor in English Laotian Refugees, Weston, Mass., 1981—82, Literacy Unltd., Framingham, Mass., 1998—. Democrat. Avocations: gardening, reading, Boston Annual Walk for Hunger. Home: 40 Arrowhead Rd Weston MA 02493 Office: Coldwell Banker Resdl Brokerage 311 Boston Post Rd Wayland MA 01778

ANDERSON, NANCY ELAINE, home economics educator; b. Chgo., Feb. 11, 1941; d. Ralph Daniel and Ruth Louise (Johanson) A. BS, So. Ill. U., 1963; postgrad., Mich. State U., 1966-67; Cert. of Advanced Grad. Studies, Am. Internat. Coll., 1994; MEd, Springfield Coll., 1980. Cert. tchr., Mass. Tchr. home econs. and spl. edn. Hennepin (Ill.) Sch., 1963-65; tchr. home econs. East Jordan (Mich.) Sch., 1965-67, Tech. High Sch., Springfield, Mass., 1967-68, Chicopee (Mass.) High Sch., 1968—. Tchr. adult edn. Bobbin Shop Fabric Store, South Hadley, Mass., 1982-94. Mem. nat. edn. bd. Covenant Ch. Women's Group, Chgo., 1986-89; mem. edn. bd. Springfield Covenant Ch., 1970-73, mem. mission bd., 1981-87, mem. fin. bd., 1987-90, trustee, 1995—. Mem. NEA, Mass. Edn. Assn., Chicopee Edn. Assn. Avocations: needlework, porcelain doll making. Home: 19 Pipit Dr Chicopee MA 01020-4894 Office: Chicopee High Sch 650 Front St Chicopee MA 01013-3198

ANDERSON, NANCY MARIE GREENWOOD, special education educator; b. Roanoke, Va., Aug. 19, 1944; d. John Reese and Alice T. (Powell) Greenwood; m. Samuel Edward Anderson, Apr. 30, 1960; children: Sheryl L. Anderson Wicklund, Samuel Edward Jr., Donna M. Anderson Schultz. BS, SUNY, Empire State Coll., Auburn, 1988; postgrad., SUNY, Oswego, 1989-90, SUNY, Geneseo, 1991-93; MS in Reading Edn., SUNY, Oswego, 1996. Cert. spl. edn., elem. tchr. K-6, reading tchr., N.Y. Libr., dir. Wolcott (N.Y.) Civic Free Libr., 1977-89; spl. edn. tchr. North Rose (N.Y.) Wolcott Mid. Sch., 1990-96, North Rose Elem. Sch., 1996—; head tchr. P.A.F. Summer Sch., 1998. Head tchr. PAF Summer Sch., 1998; summer reading tchr. Butler Correctional Facility, 1999, 2000. Mem. Nat. Fedn. Bus. and Profl. Women (chair issues mgmt. 1990), N.Y. State Assn. Tchrs. Handicapped, Rose Bus. and Profl. Womens Club (pres. 1993-95), Orton Dyslexia Soc., Coun. for Exceptional Children. Avocations: drawing, writing. Home: 14571 Lake St Sterling NY 13156-3229 Office: North Rose Elem Sch North Rose NY 14590 E-mail: nanderson2@nrwcs.org.

ANDERSON, PAUL MAURICE, electrical engineering educator, researcher, consultant; b. Des Moines, Jan. 22, 1926; s. Neil W. and Buena Vista (Thompson) A.; m. Virginia Ann Worswick, July 8, 1950; children: William, Mark, James, Thomas. BSEE, Iowa State U., 1949, MSEE, 1958, PhD in Elec. Engring., 1961. Registered profl. elec. engr., Ariz., Calif., Iowa, Guam; registered control sys. engr., Calif. Elec. engr. Iowa Pub. Service Co., Sioux City, 1949-55; prof. elec. engring. Iowa State U., Ames, 1955-75; program mgr. Electric Power Research Inst., Palo Alto, Calif., 1975-78; pres., prin. engr. Power Math Assocs. Inc., Palo Alto, Tempe, Del Mar and San Diego, 1978-99; prof. elec. engring. Ariz. State U., Tempe, 1980-84. Schweitzer vis. prof. elec. engring.97 Wash. State U., 1996. Author: Analysis of Faulted Power Systems, 1973; (with others) Power System Control and Stability, 1977, 3d edit., 2003, Subsynchronous Resonance in Power Systems, 1990, Series Compensation of Power Systems, 1996, Power System Protection, 1999; cons. editor: Ency. Sci. and Tech., 1979-92; contbr. articles to profl. jours. NSF faculty fellow, 1960-61; recipient Faculty citation Iowa State U. Alumni Assn., 1973, Profl. Achievement citation Iowa State U., 1981 Fellow IEEE (life mem., chmn. Iowa sect. 1959-60), Conf. Internat. des Grands Reseaux Electriques, Sigma Xi, Phi Kappa Phi, Eta Kappa Nu, Pi Mu Epsilon. Republican. Home: 13335 Roxton Cir San Diego CA 92130-1841 E-mail: p.anderson@ieee.org.

ANDERSON, PAUL NATHANIEL, oncologist, educator; b. Omaha, May 30, 1937; s. Nels Paul E. and Doris Marie (Chesnut) A.; m. Dee Ann Hipps, June 27, 1965; children: Mary Kathleen, Anne Christen. BA, U. Colo., 1959, MD, 1963. Diplomate Am. Bd. Internal Medicine, Am. Bd. Med. Mgmt., Am. Bd. Med. Oncology. Intern Johns Hopkins Hosp., Balt., 1963-64, resident in internal medicine, 1964-65, fellow in oncology, 1970-72; rsch. assoc., staff assoc. NIH, Bethesda, Md., 1965-70; asst. prof. medicine, oncology Johns Hopkins U. Sch. Medicine, 1972-76; attending physician Balt. City Hosps., Johns Hopkins Hosp., 1972-76; dir. dept. med. oncology Penrose Cancer Hosp., Colorado Springs, Colo., 1976-86; clin. asst. prof. dept. medicine Colo. Sch. Medicine, 1976-90, clin. assoc. prof., 1990—. Dir. Penrose Cancer Hosp., 1979-86, chief dept. medicine, 1985-86; founding dir. Cancer Ctr. of Colorado Springs, 1986-95, Pikes Peak Forum for Health Care Ethics, 1996—, Rocky Mountain Cancer Ctr., Colorado Springs, 1995—; med. dir. So. Colo. Cancer Program, 1979-86; pres., chmn. bd. dirs. Preferred Physicians, Inc., 1986-92; mem. Colo. Found. for Med. Care Health Stds. Com., 1985, sec., exec. com., 1990, bd. dirs., pres., 1992-93; mem., chmn. treatment com. Colo. Cancer Control and Rsch. Panel, 1980-83; prin. investigator Cancer Info. Svc. of Colo., 1981-87; pres., founder Timberline Med. Assocs., 1986-87, Oncology Mgmt. Network, Inc., 1985-95. Editor Advances in Cancer Control; editl. bd. Jour. Cancer Program Mgmt., 1987-92, Health Care Mgmt. Rev., 1988—; contbr. articles to med. jours. Mem. Colo. Gov.'s Rocky Flats Employee Health Assessment Group, 1983-84; mem. Gov.'s Breast Cancer Control Commn. Colo., 1984-89; founder, dir. So. Colo. AIDS project, 1986-91; mem. adv. bd. Colo. State Bd. Health Tumor Registry, 1984-87; chmn., bd. dirs. Preferred Physicians, Inc., 1986-92; bd. dirs. Share Devel. Co. of Colo. Share Health Plan of Colo., 1986-90, vice chmn., 1989-91; bd. dirs., chmn. Preferred Health Care, Inc., 1991-92; mem. health care stds. com., trustee colo. Found. for Med. Care (PRO); mem. nat. bd. med. dirs. Fox Chase Cancer Ctr. Network, Phila., 1987-89; mem. tech. expert panel Harvard Resource-Based Relative Value Scale Study for Hematology/Oncology, 1991-92. With USPHS, 1965-70. Mem. AMA (mem. practice parameters forum 1989-97, adv. com. to HCFA on uniform clin. data set), AAAS, Am. Coll. Forensic Examiners, Am. Soc. Clin. Oncology (chmn. subcom. on oncology clin. practice stds., mem. clin. practice com., rep. to AMA 1991—, mem. healthcare svcs. rsch. com., chmn. clin. guidelines subcom. 1993—), Am. Assn. Cancer Rsch., Am. Assn. Cancer Insts. (liaison mem. bd. trustees 1980-82), Am. Coll. Physician Execs., Am. Hospice Assn., Am. Soc. Internal Medicine, Nat. Cancer Inst. (com. for cmty. hosp. oncology program evaluation 1982-83), Colo. Soc. Internal Medicine, Assn. Cmty. Cancer Ctrs. (chmn. membership com. 1980, chmn. clin. rsch. com. 1983-85, sec. 1983-84, pres.-elect 1984-85, pres. 1986-87, trustee 1981-88), N.Y. Acad. Scis., Johns Hopkins Med. Soc., Colo. Med. Soc., Am. Mgmt. Assn., Am. Assn. Profl. Cons., Am. Soc. Quality, Am. Acad. Med. Dirs., Am. Coll. Physician Execs., El Paso County Med. Soc., Rocky Mountain Oncology Soc. (chmn. clin. practice com. 1989-94, pres.-elect 1990, pres. 1993-95), Acad. Hospice Physicians, Coalition for Cancer, Colorado Springs Clin. Club, Alpha Omega Alpha. Office: Rocky Mountain Cancer Ctr 3027 North Circle Dr Colorado Springs CO 80909 also: 32 Sanford Rd Colorado Springs CO 80906-4233

ANDERSON, PETER D. pharmacist, forensic scientist; b. Stoughton, Mass. BS in Pharmacy, U. R.I., 1989, PharmD, 1998. Diplomate Am. Bd. Forensic Examiners; cert. psychiat. pharmacist Bd. Pharm. Spltys. Lab. asst. U. R.I., Kingston, 1988—89; staff pharmacist Mass. Eye & Ear Infirmary, Boston, 1991—2000; clin. pharmacist pvt. practice, Boston, 1994—, forensic pharmacist, 1995—; criteria mgr., Drug Utilization Rev. Program, U. Mass. Med. Sch., 1999—2000; clin. pharmacist Mass. Eye & Ear Infirmary, 2000—01, McKesson Med. Mgmt., Inc., Taunton, Mass., 2001—. Clin. asst. prof. Northeastern U. Sch. Pharmacy, Boston, 2000—; adj. instr. med. imaging Bunker Hill C.C., 1999—; adj. assoc. prof. pharmacy U. R.I., 2001—; clin. instr. psychiatry Harvard Med. Sch., Boston, 2003—; acting chmn. pharmacy and therapeutics com. Taunton (Mass.) State Hosp., 2002. Biomed. comms. and informatics rev. sect. editor: Jour. Pharmacy Practice, 2000—; contbg. editor: The ADHD Challenge, 1997—2002. Chmn. rsch. steering com. Taunton State Hosp., Mass., 2001—. Grantee Am. Pharm. Assn. Found., Washington, 1994-95. Fellow: Am. Coll. Forensic Examiners (dir. divsn. of pharmacology 2003—), Am. Soc. Cons. Pharmacists; mem.: Mass. Tchrs. Assn., U. R.I. Emergency Med. Svcs. (vet. mem.), Nat. Space Soc., Mass. Pharmacists Assn., Coll. Psychiat. and Neurologic Pharmacists (founding mem.), Assn. Cert. Fraud Examiners (assoc.), Am. Coll. Clin. Pharmacology, Am. Acad. Clin. Toxicology, Am. Med. Writers Assn., Am. Coll. Clin. Pharmacy, Am. Soc. Health System Pharmacists, Am. Acad. Experts Traumatic Stress. Avocations: volleyball, space flight, jogging, computers. Home and Office: 1035 Southern Artery Apt 301 Quincy MA 02169-8304 Office: Taunton State Hosp PO Box 4007 Taunton MA 02780-0997 E-mail: PAnder7291@aol.com.

ANDERSON, RICHARD CHARLES, geology educator; b. Moline, Ill., Apr. 22, 1930; s. Edgar Oscar and Sarah Albertina (Olson) A.; m. Ethel Irene Cada, June 27, 1953; children: Eileen Ruth, Elizabeth Sarah, Penelope Cada. AB, Augustana Coll., Rock Island, Ill., 1952; SM, U. Chgo., 1953, PhD, 1955. Geologist Geophoto Svcs., Denver, 1955-57; from asst. prof. to prof. geology Augustana Coll., Rock Island, 1957-96; prof. emeritus, 1996—. Rsch. affiliate Ill. State Geol. Survey, Champaign, 1959—. Editor: Earth Interpreters, 1992; author reports. Recipient Neil Miner award Nat. Assn. Geology Tchrs., 1992. Fellow Geol. Soc. Am. (sect. co-chair 1990). Lutheran. Home: 2012 24th St Rock Island IL 61201-4533 Office: Augustana Coll Dept Geology 639 38th St Rock Island IL 61201-2210 E-mail: glanderson@augustana.edu.

ANDERSON, ROBERT HENRY, education educator, writer; b. Milw., July 28, 1918; s. Robert Dean and Eleanor (Weil) A.; m. Mary Jane Hopkins, July 19, 1941 (div. Jan. 1979); children: Dean Robert, Lynn Mary (Mrs. James Major), Scott William, Carol Jane (Mrs. Herbert Gilmore); m. Karolyn J. Snyder, Jan. 24, 1979. BA, U. Wis., 1939, MA, 1942; PhD, U. Chgo., 1949; AM (hon.), Harvard U., 1959. Tchr., Oconomowoc, Wis., 1940-43; research asst. ednl. field service U. Chgo., 1946-47; prin. Roosevelt Sch., River Forest, Ill., 1947-49; supt. schs. dist. 163, Park Forest, Ill., 1949-54; mem. faculty Grad. Sch. Edn., Harvard U., 1954-73, prof. edn., 1962-73; prof., dean Coll. of Edn. Tex. Tech U., Lubbock, 1973-83, prof. and dean emeritus, 1983—; prof. edn. U. South Fla., 1984—; pres. Pedamorphosis, Inc., 1977—. Lectr., cons. sch. orgn., adminstrn., staff devel. Author: Teaching in a World of Change, 1966, Education in Anticipation of Tomorrow, 1973, Opting for Openness, 1973; co-author: Managing Productive Schools, 1986, The Nongraded Elementary School, rev. edit., 1987, Clinical Supervision, 3d edit., 1993, Nongradedness, 1993; co-editor: As the Twig is Bent, 1971, Clinical Supervision Coaching, 1993; sr. editor: Current Trends in Education (pub. in Japanese), 1971; contbr. chpts. to books. With USNR, 1943-46. Mem. ASCD, Nat. Soc. Study Edn., Am. Assn. Sch. Adminstrs., Am. Ednl. Rsch. Assn., Phi Delta Kappa, Kappa Delta Pi (laureate chpt.). Episcopalian. Home: 13604 Waterfall Way Tampa FL 33624-6907 Office: PO Box 271669 Tampa FL 33688-1669

ANDERSON, ROGER CLARK, biology educator; b. Wausau, Wis., Oct. 30, 1941; s. Jerome Alfred and Virginia Stella (Hoffman) A.; m. Mary Rebecca Blocher, Aug. 5, 1967; children: John Allen, Nancy Lynn. BS magna cum laude, La Crosse State Coll., 1963; MS, U. Wis., 1965, PhD, 1968. Asst. prof. So. Ill. U., Carbondale, 1968-70; arboretum dir. U. Wis., Madison, 1970-73, assoc. prof., 1970-73, Cen. State U., Edmond, Okla., 1973-76; disting. prof. Ill. State U., Normal, 1976—. Mem. Ill. Nature Preserves Commn., 1985-90; mem., chmn. PARKNET adv. com. Fermilab, Batavia, Ill., 1986-93. Editl. bd. Jour. Restoration Ecology, 1992; author: Environmental Biology, 1970; author: (with others) Fire in North American Tallgrass Prairie, 1990, Grasses and Grasslands Systematics and Ecology, 1982, Phenology and Seasonality Modeling, 1974; editor: (with others) Savannas, Barrens, and Rock Outcrop Plant Communities of North America, 1999; contbr. 80 articles to profl. jours. Pres. Parkland Found. Bd., McLean County, Ill., 1987—. Named McMullen lectr. Monmouth Coll., 1983. Fellow Ill. Acad. Sci. (v.p. meetings); mem. Ecol. Soc. Am., Soc. for Ecol. Restoration, Am. Bot. Soc., Kappa Delta Pi. Achievements include research on the role of fire in native grassland and savannas, on the relationships between native prairie plants and mycorrhizae fungi. Home: 14 Mccormick Blvd Normal IL 61761 Office: Ill State U Biology Dept Normal IL 61790-4120 E-mail: rcander@ilstu.edu.

ANDERSON, RONALD TRENT, artist, educator; b. Madison, Wis., Oct. 10, 1938; s. Delmar LeRoy and Violet (Doering) A.; m. Barbara Groffman, June 9, 1962; 1 child, Brett Erland. BS in Art Edn., U. Wis., 1961, MS in Art, 1962, MFA in Art, 1963. Tchr. Waupun (Wis.) High Sch., 1961; tchg. asst. rural art program U. Wis., Madison, 1961-63; tchr. Bloom Twp. High Sch., Chgo. Heights, Ill., 1963-67; asst. prof. art edn. Nova Scotia Coll. of Art and Design, Halifax, Nova Scotia, 1967-69; tchr. Springfield (Mass.) Pub. Schs., 1969—2000. Represented in permanent collections U. Wis., Dalhousie U., Halifax, Westfield (Mass.) Coll., Walter J. Kohler, Jr., family, work reproduced in, Prize-Winning Watercolors Book I, 1963, Prize-Winning Watercolors Book II, 1964, The Art of Written Forms, 1969, one-man shows include Arts Unlimited Gallery, Milw., Wis., 1965, Bradley Gallery, 1967, exhibited in group shows at Smithsonian Instn., Washington, D.C., 1962, Ill. State Mus., Springfield, Ill., 1965, 1967, Nat. Design Ctr., Chgo., Ill., 1967, Dalhousie U., 1967, Montreal (Can.) Mus. Fine Arts, 1968, Colo. Coll., Colo. Springs, Colo., 1998, numerous others. Recipient Beacon award for excellence in edn., Springfield Sch. Com., 1992, 20 awards for painting and printmaking in juried art exhbns. U.S. and Can., Mass. Art Educator of Yr. award, Mass. Art Edn. Assn., 1999, Sch. Edn. Alumni Achievement Award, U. Wis. Madison, 2001; fellow Tchr.-Artist Program, The Marie Walsh Sharpe Art Found., 1998. Mem.: NEA, Internat. Platform Assn. (First Prize for Graphics Exhbn. 1995, Best of Show award 2001), Nat. Art Edn. Assn., Salmagundi Club (Rita Duis Meml. award 2003, Gene Magazzini Meml. award traditional oil 2003), Phi Delta Kappa. Lutheran. Avocations: studying the arts and humanities, foreign travel, bicycling, photography, fishing. Home: 9 Autumn Ln Amherst MA 01002-3316

ANDERSON, RUDOLPH VALENTINO, JR., principal; b. Chgo., Apr. 4, 1953; s. Rudolph Valentino and Norma (Milsap) A.; m. Cecile Angela Partee, Sept. 8, 1984; children: Carisa, Rudi. BS, Western Ill. U., 1976, MA, 1977; PhD, So. Ill. U., 1988. Tchr. Chgo. Pub. Sch. Dist. 299, 1977-79, audiologist, 1979-86; spl. asst. Chgo. Bd. Edn., 1986-89; adminstr. spl. edn. Chgo. Pubs. Schs., 1989-90, mgr. lang. and cultural edn., 1990-95; prin. Sayre Lang. Acad., Chgo., 1992—. Audiologist ONIT-Inc., Country Club Hills, Ill., 1980—. Chmn. adv. bd. spl. edn. dept. Northeastern Ill. U., 1990—. Recipient Meritorious Svc. in Edn. award Coppin Meml., 1984, Bell award Nat. Assn. Black Sch. Educators, 1991. Mem. Ill. Bd. Assitive Tech. (edn. com. 1990—), Coun. for Exceptional Children (adv. bd. publicity 1992—). Avocations: off road 4 wheeling, tennis. Office: Sayre Land Acad 1850 N Newland Ave Chicago IL 60707-3305

ANDERSON, RUTH LUCILLE, interior designer, educator, artist, librarian, archivist; b. Cyprus Hills, N.Y. d. Arthur Albert and Marie Rose (Weston) Buehler; m. Gunnar Bohlin Anderson; children: Anna Kristine Kornblatt, Deborah Val. Grad., N.Y. Sch. Applied Design Women; Cert., N.Y. Sch. Interior Design; BA, Adelphi U., 1979, MA, 1981; postgrad., NYU, Nat. Acad. Sch. Fine Arts, 1987. Cert. pub. libr. N.Y., pub. libr. profl. cert. SUNY Edn. Dept., 2001, archives, qualified interior designer Nat. Coun. Interior Design Qualification. Fabric cons. F. Schumacher & Co., N.Y.C., 1954-60; sr. interior designer W&J Sloane, N.Y.C., 1960-83; adj. assoc. prof. Nassau C.C., 1979—, Adelphi U., 1980; instr. Hofstra U., 1990—; asst. to rsch. libr. Cradle of Civilization, Mitchel Air Field, 1998—2000; libr. Planting Fields Libr., Oyster Bay, NY, 2001—. Mem. faculty Parson (New Sch.), 1980-81; lectr. in field. Paintings and sculptures exhibited at W&J Sloane, Cold Springs Harbor, Oyster Bay Cove, Adelphi U. and 75 Varick St., N.Y.C., Garden City and Cold Spring Harbor Gallery, 1993. Mem. Nat. Trust Historic Preservation. Recipient Spl. participation award Open Door Program, N.Y.C.; named Partner in Edn. N.Y.C. Pub. Schs., 1991-92. Mem. Am. Soc. Interior Designers (profl. mem. 1976), Early Flyers.

ANDERSON, RUTH YARNNELLE, real estate professional, educator; b. Celina, Ohio, Sept. 30, 1922; d. Dennis Sidney and Grace Yarnnelle (Reed) Springer; m. Orviel Willard Fallang, Sept. 2, 1944 (dec. 1970); children: Dennis Joseph, David James, Michelle Yarnnelle, Jennifer Leigh Fallang Bell; m. Nels Edward Anderson Sr., June 15, 1972 (dec.). BS, Miami U., Oxford, Ohio, 1950; MEd, Ohio State U., 1954. Cert. tchr., Ohio; lic. realtor, Ohio. Tchr. Franklin County Schs., Columbus, Ohio, 1951-55, Kettering (Ohio) City Schs., 1955-60; real estate professional Crestmark Realtors, Dayton, 1977—. Sec., treas. Luth. JOY Group, Oakwood, Ohio, 1989—; pres. Ohio Vet. Med. Assn. Aux., 1969-70. With USN, 1942-45. Named Honorary Ky. Col. Commonwealth of Ky., 1985. Mem. AAUW, Nat. Soc. Hist. Preservation, Nat. Assn. Realtors, Ohio Assn. Realtors, Dayton Area Bd. Realtors, Ohio Hist. Soc., Rails to Trails Conservancy, Order Amaranth (conductress 1990, royal matron 1993-94), Order Ea. Star, Dayton Woman's Club, Dayton Horse Show Assn. (sec. 1983-88, bd. dirs. 1983—, chmn. advt. 1981—). Republican. Avocations: photography, travel, bowling, bicycling, reading. Home: 939 Brittany Hills Dr Dayton OH 45459-1520 Office: Crestmark Realtors 310 Dellwood Ave Dayton OH 45419-3523

ANDERSON, SHARON RICE, special education educator; b. Nagoya, Japan, Aug. 6, 1948; d. Marvin E. and Oma (Brown) Rice; m. Michael Anderson, Nov. 19, 1990 (div. June 1993). AA, Ctrl. Tex. Coll.; BS in Social Scis., Mary Hardin Coll.; MS in Spl. Edn., Jacksonville State U. Tchr. U.S history & govt. Cobb Jr. H.S., Anniston, Ala., 1973-85; tchr. spl. edn. Talladega (Ala.) H.S., 1986—. Vol. Coosa Valley Juvenile Ctr., Anniston, 1973-74; tchr. CCD Cath. Ch., Anniston, 1984—; mem. Greater Talladega Multicultural Concerns com., 1994—. Mem. AAUW, NEA (conv. del. 1983), Ala. Edn. Assn. (conv. del. 1978-85, pres. Anniston chpt. 1983-84, v.p. 1982-83), Nat. Mus. Women in Arts. Republican. Roman Catholic. Avocations: reading, swimming, tennis, hiking, travel. Office: Talladega HS 1177 Mcmillan St E Talladega AL 35160-3128

ANDERSON, STANFORD OWEN, architect, architectural historian, educator; b. Redwood Falls, Minn., Nov. 13, 1934; s. Carl Alfred and Dora Helena (Paulson) A. BA, U. Minn., 1957; MA in Arch., U. Calif., Berkeley, 1958, postgrad., 1958-59; PhD, Columbia U., 1968. Registered arch., Mass. Tchr. Archtl. Assn., London, 1962-63, 74-78; co-dir. research project Inst. for Architecture and Urban Studies, N.Y.C., 1970-72, fellow, 1971-81; asst.

prof. history and architecture MIT, 1963-69, assoc. prof., 1969-72, prof., 1972—, head dept. architecture, 1991—. Co-dir. archtl. transl. project Am. Acad. Arts and Scis., 1977-80; mem. adv. council Mcpl. Art Soc., City N.Y., 1972-78. Author: Hermann Muthesius: Style-Architecture and Building-Art, 1994, Peter Behrens: A New Architecture for the Twentieth Century, 2000; editor: Planning for Diversity and Choice, 1969, On Streets, 1978. Mem. Boston Landmarks Commn., 1980—87, Massport Designer Selection Panel, 1993—97; bd. dirs. Boston Preservation Alliance, 1989—91, Batuz Found. USA, 1997—, pres., 2000—; bd. dirs. Fulbright Assn., 1998—, Boston Soc. Architects, 1992—; mem. Nat. Register Peer Profls., U.S. Gen. Svcs. Adminstrn., 2002—. Fulbright scholar, 1961-62; John Simon Guggenheim fellow, 1969-70; Graham Found. fellow, 1971; ACLS fellow, 1977-78; festschrift pub. in his honor, 1997. Mem. Assn. Collegiate Schs. Architecture, Brit. Soc. for Philosophy of Sci., Coll. Art Assn., Soc. Archtl. Historians (dir. 1969-72, 76-77). Home: 63 Commercial Wharf Boston MA 02110-3814 Office: MIT Dept Architecture 77 Massachusetts Ave Cambridge MA 02139-4307

ANDERSON, SUSAN ELAINE MOSSHAMER, education and organization consultant, musician; b. Detroit, Mar. 29, 1946; d. Edgar Lee and Reta (McDonough) Mosshamer; m. Thomas Scott Anderson Jr., Nov. 1, 1975; children: Elizabeth Erin, Kirk William. MusB with honors, Mich. State U., 1967; MEd with high honors, Wayne State U., 1982. Profl. singer (mezzo), pianist and organist, 1968—; sch. choral music dir. grades 7-12, 1968-77; instrnl. designer, orgnl. devel. cons. Myers-Briggs Adminstr., Ednl. Rschr., 1982—; pres. Orgl. Strategies Ltd., Bloomfield Hills, Mich., 1995—2002. Collaborating author: The Challenge of Living, 1983, Death and Dying, 1996; award-winning tng. programs for Ill. Dept. Employment Security and Ford Motor Co. Vol. Roeper Sch., Bloomfield Hills, 1988-95, Cranbrook Schs., Bloomfield Hills, 1993-2002. Mem. ASCD, Problem-Based Learning Network, Assn. Psychol. Type, Mortar Board, Phi Kappa Phi. Avocations: skiing, reading, music. Home and Office: 1825 Reis Ct Rochester Hills MI 48309

ANDERSON, URTON LIGGETT, accounting educator; b. Salem, Ohio, Dec. 10, 1951; s. Urton and Alice (Kenrich) A.; m. Deborah Mary Johnson, June 12, 1973; children: Bryony, Urton. BA in Greek and Philosophy magna cum laude, St. Olaf Coll., 1974; MA in Classics, U. Minn, 1977; PhD in Bus. Adminstrn., U. Minn., 1985. Cert. internal auditor Inst. Internal Auditors; cert. control self-assessment Inst. Internal Auditors. Instr. dept. acctg. U. Tex., Austin, 1984-85, asst. prof. dept. acctg., 1988-89, assoc. prof. dept. acctg., 1989-95, prof. dept. acctg., 1995—, assoc. dir. C. Aubrey Smith Ctr. for Auditing Edn. and Rsch., 1989-92, dir. C. Aubrey Smith Ctr. for Auditing Edn. and Rsch., 1992-93, acting dept. chair, 1996, assoc. dean ubdergrad. programs Coll. Bus., 1997—. Clark W. Thompson Jr. prof. in acctg. edn. U. Tex., Austin, 1997—. Author: Quality Asurance for Internal Auditing, 1983; co-editor: Internal Auditing, 1990—2001; contbr. articles to profl. jours.; : Implementing the Professional Practices Framework, 2002. Rsch. fellow KPMG Peat Marwick Found., 1988-89, faculty fellow, 1990-92, Rsch. Opportunities in Auditing grantee, 1991, 94, Ernst & Young faculty fellow, 1988-93, Atlantic Richfield Centennial fellow in acctg., 1993-97. Mem. Inst. Internal Auditors Rsch. Found. (bd. rsch. advisors 1985-94), Inst. Internal Auditors (bd. regents 1994-99, 2003—, chmn. 2003—, internal auditing standards bd. 1999-2003, chair 2002-03, cert. internal auditor, cert. control self-assessment, cert. govt. audit profl). Office: U Tex Austin Dept Acctg CBA 4M 202 Austin TX 78712-1172 E-mail: urton@mail.utexas.edu.

ANDERSON, VALERIE LEE, reading educator; b. Worcester, Mass., Dec. 9, 1955; d. John Willard and Shirley Anne (Enman) A. BS summa cum laude, Worcester State Coll., 1977, MEd summa cum laude, 1983, post-grad., 1987; EdD, Calif. Coast U., 1992. Cert. elem. tchr., prin., supt., spl. edn. tchr. and adminstr., Mass.; Wilson cert. reading tutor, 1996. Tchr. elem. grades Worcester Pub. Schs., 1977-80; resource tchr. high sch. Northbridge Pub. Schs., Whitinsville, Mass., 1980-81; supr. grade sch. programs Kindercare Learning Ctrs., Inc., Westboro, Mass., 1981-83; reading tchr. Millbury (Mass.) Pub. Schs., 1983-87, 89—, tchr. 3rd grade, 1987-88, tchr. 1st grade, 1988-89. Mem. Internat. Reading Assn., Mass. Reading Assn., Cen. Mass. Reading Coun. (rec. sec. 1985-87, 92-93, pres. 1993-96), Kappa delta Pi (treas.). Methodist. Avocations: restoring victorian house and antiques, classic cars, reading, aerobics, gourmet cooking. Home: 11 Ash St Spencer MA 01562-2246

ANDERSON, WILLIAM BANKS, JR., ophthalmology educator; b. Durham, NC, June 14, 1931; s. William Banks and Mildred Ursula (Everett) A.; m. Nancy Eldridge Walker, Sept. 17, 1960; children: Mary Banks, Mark Eldridge, Elizabeth Perry. AB, Princeton U., 1952; MD, Harvard U., 1956. Diplomate: Am. Bd. Ophthalmology (dir. 1986-92). Intern Duke U. Med. Ctr., Durham, N.C., 1956-57, resident, 1959-62, asst. prof. ophthalmology, 1962-67, assoc. prof. ophthalmology, 1967-76, prof. ophthalmology, 1976—, acting chmn., 1991-92. Mem. profl. adv. com. N.C. Div. Services to the Blind, Raleigh, 1972-84 Chmn. bd. trustees Durham Acad., 1975-77. Served to capt. M.C. U.S. Army, 1957-59. Fellow ACS; mem. Am. Ophthalmol. Soc. (sec.-treas. 1989-98, v.p. 1998-99, pres. 1999-2000), Am. Acad. Ophthalmology (bd. dirs. 1986-89), Am. Bd. Ophthalmology (bd. dirs. 1986-93). Episcopalian. Home: 2401 Cranford Rd Durham NC 27705-1011 Office: Duke U Eye Ctr Erwin Rd Durham NC 27710-7102

ANDERSON, WILLIAM ROBERT, pathologist, educator; b. Kittanning, Pa., Jan. 26, 1929; s. John Dickson and Amelia Caroline (Haferland) Anderson; m. Lorna McLeod, June 15, 1951 (div. 1974); children: Caroline Elizabeth Anderson Fraser, Frederick Charles; m. Carol Jane Gorder, Nov. 1975. BA, U. Rochester, 1951; MD, U. Pa., 1958. Asst. pathologist Mt. Sinai Hosp., Mpls., 1964-67; dir. anatomic pathology Hennepin County Med. Ctr., Mpls., 1967-84, chief pathology, 1984-95; prof. pathology U. Minn. Sch. Medicine, Mpls., 1975—. Pathology cons. Hennepin County Med. Ctr., Mpls., 1997—2002. Contbr. articles to profl. pubs. Writer Habitat for Humanity, Twin Cities, Minn., 1995—; ch. coun. mem. Mt. Calvary Luth. Ch., Excelsior, Minn., 1996—99. Lt. (j.g.) USN, 1951—54. Fellow: Coll. Am. Pathologists; mem.: Internat. Acad. Pathologists, Phi Beta Kappa, Sigma Xi. Avocations: history, travel, swimming, tennis. Home: 5725 Merry Ln Excelsior MN 55331-3310 E-mail: wranderson2002@aol.com.

ANDERSON, YASMIN LYNN MULLIS, educational consultant, small business owner; b. Roanoke, Va., Oct. 5, 1953; d. Lonnie Cecil Jr. and Sarah Frances (Cunningham) Mullis; m. Jerry Doyle Anderson, Mar. 1, 1991; 1 child from previous marriage, R. Allen. BS in Edn., U Tenn., 1975, postgrad., 1989-90, 93. Employment counselor State Dept. Employment Security, Knoxville, Tenn., 1975-79; GED instr. Loudon (Tenn.) County Schs., 1979-81; edn. specialist Tenn. Valley Authority, Knoxville, 1979-94; pvt. practice Knoxville, 1991—. Ednl. cons. Acad. Innovations, Santa Barbara, Calif., 1991—; edn. specialist Inclusion for All Children Task Force, Nashville, 1992—; advisor tech./Prep. Consortium, Tenn., 1993—; presenter in field; sr. cons. Mary Kay Cosmetics. Mem. ASCD, AAUW, Am. Vocat. Assn. (presenter). Baptist. Avocations: outdoor recreational activities, gardening, baseball. Home and Office: 1236 Lovell View Dr Knoxville TN 37932-2591

ANDERSON-CERMIN, CHERYL KAY, orthodontics, educator; b. Osceola, Wis., Aug. 28, 1956; d. Darrell Duane and Barbara Carolyn (Paulson) Peterson; m. Paul Bradley Anderson, Aug. 12, 1978 (div. June 1986); m. Jonathan A. Cermin, Dec. 31, 1995; children: Hayley Kristine, Jeremy Jonathan. AA, Normandale C.C., Bloomington, Minn., 1977; BS, U. Minn., 1985, DDS, 1986; cert. in advanced grad. studies, Boston U., 1990. Intern Sch. Dental Medicine Harvard U., Boston, 1986-87; pvt. practice, Boston, 1988-90; rsch. fellow U. Tex. S.W. Med. Sch., Dallas, 1990-91, asst. prof. orthodontics, dir. orthodontics, 1991—. Bd. dirs. Life Enhancement for People, Dallas, 1993-94; sec. ch. coun. Shepherd of Life Luth. Ch., Arlington, Tex., 1993-94. Mem. ADA, Am. Assn. Orthodontists, Am. Cleft Palate Assn. Avocations: skiing, rollerblading, camping, reading, needle-work. Office: U Tex SW Med Sch 5323 Harry Hines Blvd Dallas TX 75390-7208

ANDERSSON, BILLIE VENTURATOS, school learning specialist; b. Pitts., Jan. 16, 1947; d. George Steve and Aphrodite (Bon) Venturatos; m. Wolfgang Paul Andersson, July 12, 1969; children: Dita, Lise, Andrea. BA, Newcomb Coll., 1968; MEd in Counseling, La. State U., New Orleans, 1971; MEd in Spl. Edn., U. New Orleans, 1977, PhD in Curriculum and Instrn., 1981. Cert. Nat. Bd. Counselor, 1994; lic. profl. counselor, La., 1997. Biology and math tchr. Orleans Parish Sch. Bd., New Orleans, 1968-70; biology and gen. sci. tchr. Jefferson Parish Sch. Bd., Metairie, La., 1970-74, guidance counselor, 1974-78; reading specialist Trinity Episcopal Sch., New Orleans, 1978-96, admissions evaluator, ednl. evaluator, 1981-96, gifted and talented tchr., 1982-96, head student svcs., dir. curriculum. Gesell evaluator, 1985-96, learning specialist, 1994-96, lang. arts coord., 1994-96; learning specialist, head student svcs., dir. curriculum St. Martin's Epsicopal Sch., 1996—, curriculum dir., 2003—; instr. U. New Orleans, St. Mary's Dominican Coll., Holy Cross Coll., Loyola U., Xavier U.; lectr. and presenter in field. Author: Filo File for Filophiles, 1985, Simple and Classic: Greek Elegance for the Everyday Cook, 1991; editor: Greek Lagniappe, 1980, 2d edit., 1998, Greek Laginaippe, The Best of Best, 1998; dir. Author Fest, 1988-96; illustrator: The Greek Alphabet Coloring Book, 1993. Sunday sch. coord. Greek Orthodox Cathedral, New Orleans, 1984-87, chmn. gourmet booth, 1981—; developer, dir. La. Experience summer camp for girls, 1983-95. Mem. APA, ACA, Internat. Dyslexia Assn. (La. chpt. bd. mem., v.p.), Internat. Reading Assn., Nat. Assn. for Gifted Children, Assn. Supervision and Curriculum Devel., Phi Delta Kappa, Phi Kappa Phi, Kappa Delta Pi. Greek Orthodox. Avocations: batik, aerobics, pastry baking. Office: St Martins Episcopal Sch 5309 Airline Dr Metairie LA 70003-2401

ANDERSSON, HANS CHRISTOPH, human geneticist, educator; b. New Orleans, Dec. 23, 1956; s. Knud Dietrich A.; m. Whitney Stewart; 1 child, Christoph Reiner. BS in music and psychology, Tulane U., 1978, MD, 1984. Diplomate Am. Bd. Pediat., Am. Bd. Med. Genetics. Resident in pediat. Tulane Med. Sch., 1984-87; clin. genetics fellow Nat. Inst. Child Health & Human Devel. NIH, Bethesda, Md., 1987-91; Alexander von Humboldt Found. Rsch. fellow U. Göttingen, Germany, 1992-93; asst. prof. pediatrics, human genetics program Tulane U. Sch. Medicine, New Orleans, 1993—2000, assoc. prof., 2000—. Contbr. articles to profl. pubs. including Biochemistry Jour., N.Eng. Jour. Medicine, Jour. Pediat., others. Fellow Am. Coll. Med. Genetics (founding), Am. Acad. Pediat.; mem. AMA, Am. Soc. Human Genetics, Soc. Inherited Metabolic Diseases, Soc. Pediat. Rsch., Pediat. Acad. Soc. Achievements include research in lysosomal membrane transport; new screening methods for storage diseases, and characterization of inborn errors of metabolism. Office: Hayward Genetics Ctr 1430 Tulane Ave New Orleans LA 70112-2699

ANDERZON, NANCY JOY, special education educator; b. Des Plaines, Ill., Jan. 7, 1962; d. William T. and Gloria Pauline (Kuhn) Klemchen; m. David Lane Anderzon, June 22, 1985; children: Joseph, Hillary, Callan. BS in Edn., Ill. State U., 1984; MS in Edn., No. Ill. U., 1994. Tchr. of deaf Vandalia (Ill.) Cmty. Schs., 1984-85, Rockford (Ill.) Sch. Dist. 205, 1985—. Interpreter for the deaf RAMP (Regional Access and Mobilization Project, Rockford, 1992—. Vol. deaf youth baseball team Rockford Park Dist., summer 1993; mem. Rockford Deaf Awareness, 1992—. Recipient Cert. of Appreciation, Parents' Spl. Edn. Adv. Coun., Rockford Sch. Dist. 205, 1994. Mem. ASCD, Ill. Assn. for Supervision and Curriculum Devel., Ill. Tchrs. of Hearing Impaired, Childrenwith Attention Deficit Disorder, Quota Internat. Republican. Lutheran. Avocations: reading, aerobics, tennis, biking. Office: Lincoln Middle School 1500 Charles St Rockford IL 61104-2398

ANDRADE, CAROLYN L. foreign language educator; MA in Linguistics, MEd in Elem. Edn., Ohio U. Tchr. Instituto Guatemalteco-Americano, Am. Sch. Guatemala; sec. pub. edn. Dept. Técnico Pedagogico, Morelia, Mex.; spanish tchr. Cin. Public Schs., 1982-93. Recipient Florence Steiner Leadership in Foreign Lang. Edn. K-12 award, 1992; grantee Foreign Lang. Asst. Act, Sister Cities Internat. U.S.-USSR Youth Exchange Program. Mem. Ohio Foreign Lang. Assn., Nat. Network for Early Lang. Learning.*

ANDRADE, EDNA, artist, art educator; b. Portsmouth, Va. d. Thomas Judson and Ruth (Porter) Wright; m. C. Preston Andrade, Jr., July 12, 1941 (div. 1960). BFA, Pa. Acad. Fine Arts/U. Pa., 1937. Supr. art elem. schs., Norfolk, Va., 1938-39; instr. drawing and painting Newcomb Art Sch., Tulane U., 1939-41; lectr. U. N.Mex., 1971; prof. Phila. Coll. Art, 1959-72, 73-82, prof. emeritus, 1982—; prof. art Temple U., 1972-73. Adj. prof. art Ariz. State U., 1986—; critic Pa. Acad. Fine Arts, 1988—89. Artist, designer, OSS, 1942-44, free-lance designer, Washington, 1944-46, free-lance painter, designer, muralist, Phila. and, N.Y.C., 1946—, artist-in-residence, Hartford Sch. Art and Tamarind Inst., 1971, U. Sask., Can., 1977, U. Zulia, Maracaibo, Venezuela, 1980, Ariz. State U., Tempe, 1981, 83, Fabric Workshop, Phila., 1984, Hollins Coll., Va., 1985; vis. artist, Skidmore Coll., 1973, 74, one-woman shows, E. Hampton Gallery, N.Y.C., Peale Galleries Pa. Acad., Rutgers U., U. Hartford,Marian Locks Gallery, 1989, 1971,74, 77, 83, 1989, Phila., Hollins Coll., 1985; retrospective Pa. Acad. Fine Arts, 1993, Locks Gallery, Phila., 1993-94, 97, 99, 2002-03, Inst. Contemporary Art, Phila., 2003; group shows include AAAL, In This Acad., Pa. Acad. Fine Arts, Phila., William Penn Meml. Mus., Harrisburg, Three Centuries Am. Art, Phila. Collects Art Since 1940, Phila. Mus. Art, Bklyn. Mus., Ft. Worth Art Center, Des Moines Art Center, Philbrook Art Center, Tulsa, Contemporary Phila. Artists, 1990, Phila. Mus. Art, Artists Choose Artists, Inst. of Contemporary Art, Phila., 1991, Klein Gallery, Univ. City Sci. Ctr., Phila., 1998, Phila. Mus. Art, 2000, others; represented in permanent collections, Phila. Mus. Art, Pa. Acad. Fine Arts, Print Club, Balt. Mus. Art, Addison Gallery Am. Art, McNay Art Inst., San Antonio, Montclair (N.J.) Art Mus., Nat. Collection Fine Arts, Library of Congress, USIA, Albright-Knox Art Gallery, Buffalo, Tamarind Collection, U. N.Mex. Mus., Woodmere Art Mus., Phila., Yale Art Gallery, Am. Tel. & Tel. Co., Bell of Pa., Phila., Fed. Res. Bank, Phila., Price-Waterhouse, Phila., Edwin A. Ulrich Mus. Wichita State U., Pepsi-Cola, Leeway Found., Phila., Please Touch Mus., Phila., Va. Mus. Fine Arts, Richmond. Mem. Mayor's Cultural Adv. Council, Phila., 1984-85. Recipient 1st and 2d Cresson European Traveling scholarships Pa. Acad., 1936, 37, Eyre medal Phila. Water Color Club, 1968, Mary Smith prize Pa. Acad. Fine Arts, 1968, Childe Hassam Meml. purchases AAAL, 1967, 68, Hazlett Meml. award in arts, 1980, Honor award Women's Caucus for Art, 1983, Hunt award visual arts Phila. Women's Way, 1984, Roland Gallimore Meml. award Interior Design Coun., Phila. Mayor's Arts and Culture award, 1991, Founders award Samuel S. Fleisher Art Meml., 1993, Disting. Daughter Pa. award, 2002.. Mem. Fellowship of Pa. Acad. Fine Arts, Coll. Art Assn. (Disting. Tchr. of Art award 1996).

ANDRADE, JEFFREY R. government educational secretary; b. New Bedford, Mass. BA, Am. U. Dep. asst. sec. US Dept. Edn. Off. of Postsecondary Edn., Wash., DC, 2002—, spec. asst. to dep. sec.; dir.. regulatory admin. affairs private cons. firm, Wash., 1998—2000; staff mem. House Com. on Edn. and Workforce, Wash., 1997—98. Mem.: US Student Assn. Office: US Dept Edn Off of Postsecondary Edn Rm 8046 1990 K St NW Washington DC 20006 Office Fax: 202-401-3095. E-mail: jeff.andrade@ed.gov.*

ANDRAIN, CHARLES FRANKLIN, political science educator; b. Fortuna, Calif., Feb. 22, 1937; s. Milton D. and Alberta W. (Gatton) A. AB, Whittier Coll., 1959; MA, U. Calif., Berkeley, 1961, PhD, 1964. Asst. prof. dept. polit. sci. San Diego State U., 1964-67, assoc. prof., 1967-70, prof., 1970—98, chmn. dept., 1972—74, prof. emeritus, 1998—. Rsch. assoc. Inst. Internat. Studies, U. Calif.-Berkeley, 1975-76, 78-79, 80-81, 82, 86. Author: Children and Civic Awareness, 1971, Political Life and Social Change, 2d edit., 1975, Politics and Economic Policy in Western Democracies, 1980, Foundations of Comparative Politics: A Policy Perspective, 1983, Social Policies in Western Industrial Societies, 1985, Political Change in the Third World, 1988, Comparative Political Systems, 1994, (with David E. Apter) Political Protest and Social Change, 1995, Public Health Policies and Social Inequality, 1998. Woodrow Wilson Found. fellow, 1959-60; NDEA fellow, 1960-63; Ford Found. fellow, 1968-69; NIMH fellow, 1971-72. Mem. Am. Polit. Sci. Assn., Am. Sociol. Assn., Internat. Soc. Political Psychology, Internat. Studies Assn.

ANDREA, MARIO IACOBUCCI, engineer, scientist, gemologist, appraiser; b. Haverhill, Mass., May 21, 1917; s. Andrea and Lucia (Antolini) Iacobucci; m. Muriel Grace Litchfield, June 29, 1940 (div. Dec. 1947); children: Gail, Patricia; m. Elizabeth Dwight (Bowes) Bray, Dec. 31, 1949 (div. Jan. 1986); children: Marjorie, Lucia, Janet; m. Elma Williams, Nov. 29, 1986. BSc, Webb Inst., Glen Cove, N.Y., 1939; grad., Oak Ridge Sch. Reactor Tech., 1958; MSE, Cath. U. Am., 1967; PhD, Pacific Western U., 1984. Grad. gemologist Gemological Inst. Am.; registered profl. engr., Md. Application engr. GE Co., Schenectady, 1948-52; marine engr. Mil. Sea Transp. Svc., Washington, 1952-54; supervisory naval architect Yokosuka, Japan, 1954-56; nuc. and gen. engr. R&D Maritime Adminstrn., Washington, 1956-74; project engr. nuc. reactor merchant ship N.S. Savannah; grad. gemologist, appraiser The Gem Tree, Bethesda, Md., 1974—. Patentee helical ship hull form. Pres., treas. Maritime Recreation Assn., Washington, 1970. Lt. comdr. USNR, 1941-61. Decorated naval medals. Mem. Gemol. Inst. Am. Alumni Assn. (life), Naval Res. Assn. (life), Order Sons of Italy in Am., Montgomery County Lodge #2288 (treas. 1994-97, trustee 1998-2000), Consumers Union (life). Avocations: chess, bridge, gardening.

ANDREANO, RALPH LOUIS, economist, educator; b. Waterbury, Conn., Apr. 11, 1928; s. John and Loretta (Creasia) A.; m. Carol Jean Wessbecher, Sept. 5, 1955; children: Maria Carol, Nicholas George. AB, Drury Coll., 1952; MA, Washington U., St. Louis, 1955; MA Fulbright scholar, U. Oslo, Norway, 1952-53; PhD, Northwestern U., 1961. Instr. econs. Northwestern U., 1959-60; asst. prof. econs. Earlham Coll., 1961, asso. prof., chmn. dept., 1962-65; asst. prof. bus. adminstrn. Harvard Bus. Sch., 1961-62; Brookings Nat. Research prof., 1964-65; asso. prof. econs., dir. undergrad. program econs. U. Wis., 1965-67, prof., 1967—, dir. Health Econs. Research Ctr., 1969-87, chmn. dept. econs., 1980-83, dir. Ctr. for Devel.; emeritus prof. econs., 1994—. Ofcl. del. Am. Econ. Assn. to Am. Council Learned Socs., 1964-70; adminstr. Div. Health State of Wis., 1976-78; economist WHO, Geneva, 1973-74. Author: (with H.F. Williamson and others) A History of American Petroleum Industry, 2 vols., 1959, 63, No Joy in Mudville: The Dilemma of Major League Baseball, 1965, Student Economists Handbook, 1967, (with B.A. Weisbrod and others) Disease and Economic Development, 1973, (with B.A. Weisbrod) American Health Policy, 1973; editor, author: New Views on American Economic Development, 1965; editor: Economic Impact of the Civil War, 1963, rev., 1967, The New Economic History: Papers on Methodology, 1971, (with J. Siegfried) Economics of Crime, 1981, Essays on International Health, 2001, The International Health Policy Program: An Internal Assessment, 2001; editor, founder: Explorations in Entrepreneurial History, 2d series, 1963-71, Explorations in Economic History 1971-78; editor: Jour. Econ. History, 1974-75; sr. editor (econs.): Social Sci. and Medicine, 1983-87; contbr. articles to profl. jours. Ford Faculty Research fellow, 1968-69 Mem. Inst. Medicine of Nat. Acad. Scis. Home: 1815 Vilas Ave Madison WI 53711-2231 E-mail: rlandrea@wisc.edu.

ANDREAS, CYNTHIA BARBARA, art therapist; b. Mpls., Apr. 11, 1948; d. Perry Wilbur and Grace Ann (Hurd) Andreas; m. Michael Allen Broihahn, May 29, 1982 (div. Aug. 1993); children: David Michael, Matthew Allen. BA in Art Edn., Am. U., 1970; MA in Art Therapy, Coll. Notre Dame, Belmont, Calif., 1982. Cert. expressive therapist, elem. and secondary art tchr., Fla. Art tchr. Ledyard (Conn.) Pub. Schs., 1970-71; art therapy intern Youth Campus, San Francisco, 1981, Fairmont Hosp., San Leandro, Calif., 1981; spl. edn. tutor Tennyson High Sch., Hayward, Calif., 1983-85; art tchr. Castro Valley (Calif.) High Sch., 1984-85; art therapist pvt. practice Whitefish Bay, Wis., 1985-87; art therapist St. Mary's Ozaukee Hosp., Port Washington, Wis., 1987-88; art therapist pvt. practice Pembroke Pines, Fla., 1988—; art therapist Atlantis Acad., Miami, 1990—. Mem. Nat. Expressive Therapy Assn., Coun. Exceptional Children, Am. Art Therapy Assn., Nat. Art Edn. Assn., Children with Attention Deficit Disorders. Democrat. Presbyterian. Avocations: painting, stained glass work, rug hooking, reading, swimming. Home: 500 N Congress Ave Apt A105 Delray Beach FL 33445-3467 Office: Atlantis Acad 9600 SW 107th Ave Miami FL 33176-2759

ANDREEN, AVIVA LOUISE, dentist, researcher, academic administrator, educator; b. Frankfurt, Germany, Jan. 6, 1952; (parents Am. citizens); d. Robert Benjamin Andreen and Margie Corinne (LaPointe) Marshall; m. Merrill R. Penn, Nov. 8, 1987 (div.); 1 child from previous marriage, Robert Morton Salkin. BA, NYU, 1975; student, Westchester C.C., 1976; DDS, NYU Coll. Dentistry, 1996; postgrad., Laser Inst. Am., 1980. Cert. mobile laser operator, N.Y. Tchr. Kibbutz Regavim, D.N. Menasche, Israel, 1975-76; account rep. Traveler's Ins. Co., N.Y.C., 1976; spl. projects coord. Sapan Engring. Co., N.Y.C., 1976-78; sec., treas. founder J. Sapan Holographic Studios, N.Y.C., 1979; owner, pres. Universal Media Cons., White Plains, NY, 1980-84; dir. edn., owner Am. Ctr. for Laser Edn., Bronx, NY, 1984-96; pres. Penn Laser Systems Inc., 1994-96; chief dental resident St. Barnabas Hosp., Bronx, 1997—98; fellow in spl. patient care Helen Hayes Hosp., West Haverstraw, NY, 1998-99; clin. instr. spl. patient care, oral medicine and pathology NYU Coll. Dentistry, N.Y.C., 1999; dentist Marvin Family Dentistry, Nanuet, NY, 1999—2001; owner, ptnr. Dental Arts of Suffern, LLP, NY, 2001—02; assoc. Dr. Gerald B. Greitzer, Tarrytown, NY, 2002—. Attending dentist Bronx Park Dental; faculty practice St. Barnabas Hosp., 2003—. attending dentist Helen Hayes Hosp.; lectr. Hudson River Mus., Yonkers, N.Y., 1986-87; producer laser light show, Andrus Planetarium; taught 1st laser safety course in Am. high sch., 1980; designed laser safety course for Westchester C.C., 1992. Curator Holography A New Dimension White Plains Mus. Gallery, Hudson River Mus., Yonkers, Troster Hall Sci.; vol. forensic dentist for World Trade Ctr. attack N.Y.C. Med. Examiner's Office, 2001—02. Lt. comdr. Dental Corps USNR, 2001—03. Mem. ADA, Acad. Gen. Dentistry, Alpha Omega. Avocations: reading, dental laser research, crocheting, embroidery. Office: 200 S Broadway Tarrytown NY 10591

ANDREW, CATHERINE VIGE, elementary school educator; b. Lafayette, La., Mar. 10, 1938; m. David R. Andrew, Aug. 30, 1958; children: Robert Craig, Lisa Lenore, David Harold. BA in Edn., U. Southwestern La., 1969, MA in Edn., 1984. Lic. elem. and kindergarten tchr.; state cert. supr. student tchrs. Tchr. 1st grade Ascension Day Sch., Lafayette, La., 1970-78, tchr. 2nd grade, 1978-87, tchr. 3rd grade, 1987-93, tchr. 2nd grade, 1993—2003, ret., 2003; tchr. 1st grade Lafayette Parish Pub. Sch., 1969-70. Sch. bd. mem. St. Mary Cath. Ch. Early Learning Ctr., Lafayette, 1990-92; chmn. edn. commn. St. Mary Cath. Ch., Lafayette, 1985-88, dir. pre-sch., 1984-92; tchr. summer gifted and talented program U. Southwestern La., 1993-97; 1st chmn. Ascension Day Sch. Sci. Fair, 1999-2000, co-chmn., 2001-03. Sec., treas., v.p. City Pan Hellenic, Lafayette, pres., 1979-80.

Recipient Jane Hamlin Svc. award, 1997. Mem.La. Preservation Alliance (bd. dirs.), U. SW La. U. Women's Club (exec. bd.). Avocations: gardening, travel, reading, crafts. Home: 412 Kim Dr Lafayette LA 70503-4024

ANDREWS, BARBARA HARCOURT, retired elementary educator; b. Clintondale, N.Y., May 24, 1934; d. Ralph Palmer Harcourt and Lillian Sophia (Fowler) H.; m. Adolph Alexander Lanauskas, Sept. 21, 1957 (div. Sept. 1974); m. Louis Peter Andrews, July 9, 1976. BS in Acctg., Rider Coll., 1955; MA in Early Childhood Edn., Kean Coll., 1963. Cert. tchr., N.J. Asst. to treas. Rider Coll., Trenton, 1955-59; educator Manville (N.J.) Pub. Sch., 1959-94; ret., 1994; registrar FGC Gatherings, 1996—. Bd. dirs. Friends Pub. Corp. Trustee, house/fair clk., pers. clk. Yearly Meeting Friends Home, The McCutchen, North Plainfield, N.J., 1977—; active PTA, 1959-94, life mem.; asst. clk. long range conf. Friends Gen. Conf., 1990-96, mem. Gathering Planning Com., 1999—. Mem. AAUW, NEA-R, N.J. Ret. Educators Assn., Internat. Reading Assn., N.J. Reading Assn., Ctrl. N.J. Reading Coun. (pres. 1979-81), Somerset County Ret. Educators (membership chair 1995-97, pres. 1997—), Manville Edn. Assn. (sec. 1961-74, govt. rels. chair, membership chair 1976-94, treas. 1980-92), Women's History Network, Delta Kappa Gamma, Alpha Zeta, Lambda (world fellowship chair 1980-99, nominations chair 1984-2000, pres. 2000-2002, legis. chair 2002—, Rose award 1995, Key award 2000). Democrat. Avocations: walking, swimming, reading, volunteer work. Home: 23 Forest Hill Dr Flemington NJ 08822-7127 E-mail: loubari@aol.com.

ANDREWS, BETTY BAUSERMAN, retired secondary school educator, property manager; b. Luray, Va, Dec. 29, 1935; d. Raymond Edgar Bauserman and Elizabeth Elaine Houser; m. George Norman Andrews, July 26, 1964 (dec. Apr. 1996). BS, Madison Coll., 1958; postgrad., U. Va., 1964-68, George Mason U., 1969—. Cert. coll. profl. cert., Va. Classroom tchr. Clarke County HS, Berryville, Va., 1958-64, Loudoun Valley HS, Purcellville, Va., 1964-68; proofreader Missles and Rockets mag., Washington, 1964, Loudoun County HS, Leesburg, Va., 1968-69; head libr. media specialist Broad Run HS, Ashburn, Va., 1969-2000. Cons., libr. reorganizer Logetronics Corp., Springfield, Va., 1974; mem. sch. improvement team Broad Run HS, Ashburn, 1996-2000. Adv. bd. Sterling (Va.) Pub. Libr., 1998—. Mem. NEA, James Madison U. Alumni Assn., Va. Edn. Assn. (life), Loudoun Edn. Assn. (life), Loudoun Educators Media Assn. (life), Nat. Soc. DAR, Sparlandria Investment Club, Am. Assn. Univ. Women (AAUW), Alpha Gamma Delta. Democrat. Methodist. Avocations: antique collecting, gardening, investing, sailing, reading. Home: 821 Golden Arrow St Great Falls VA 22066-2517 E-mail: striperrtripes@aol.com.

ANDREWS, CAROL, primary education educator; b. Galveston, Tex., Apr. 21, 1945; d. Herbert and Amy Elsie (Johnson) Gumaer; m. Harlan Andrews, Dec. 30, 1968; children: Monique, Brad. BA in English with distinction, San Jose State U., 1970. Cert. multiple subject cred., Calif. Tchr. spl. edn. Moreland Sch. Dist., San Jose, Calif.; mid. sch. tchr. English, South Valley Carden Sch., San Jose, Calif., 1986—2002, Carden Day Sch. of San Jose, 2002—. History and K-8 ednl. cons. Carden Acad., Silicon Valley, 2002-. Docent Ainsley House Outreach Program. Recipient Francis Lanyon Meml. award. Mem. Campbell Hist. Soc.

ANDREWS, DEBORAH CREHAN, English studies educator; b. Hartford, Conn., Sept. 1, 1942; d. Mark J. and Gertrude (Parsons) Crehan; m. William D. Andrews, May 16, 1970; 1child, Christopher S. BA, Middlebury (Vt.) Coll., 1964; MA, U. Wyo., 1965, U. Pa., 1969. Instr. Utah State U., Logan, 1966-68; lectr., instr. Ohio State U., Columbus, 1970-77; asst. prof. Drexel U., Phila., 1977-82; asst. prof. English U. Del., Newark, 1982-85, assoc. prof., 1985-88, prof., 1988—. Cons. to various orgns. including Am. Chem. Soc., Sun Refining, Batelle Labs., NSF, Hercules Inc.; pres. Coun. for Programs in Tech. and Sci. Comm., 1998-2000. Co-author: Technical Writing: Principles and Forms, 1978, 2d edit. 1982, Write for Results, 1982, Business Communication, 1988, 3d edit., 1997; author: Technical Communication in the Global Community, 1998, 2d edit., 2001, Management Communication: A Guide; editor: (anthology) International Dimensions of Technical Communication, 1996; editor: Bus. Comm. Quar., 1997—. Unidel Found. grantee, 1986-89. Mem. Soc. for Tech. Comm. (assoc. fellow; pres. Ohio chpt.), Assn. Tchrs. Tech. Writing (exec. com. 1986-88). Office: U Del Dept English Newark DE 19716-2537 E-mail: dandrews@vdel.edu.

ANDREWS, GEORGE ARTHUR, school administrator; b. Chgo., June 2, 1941; s. George A. and Bernice V. (Brown) A.; m. Mary Lou Shuff, Aug. 17, 1968; children: Sandy Scott, Heather Brooke. BA, Bob Jones U., 1966; MA, Grace Theol. Sem., Winona Lake, Ind., 1981. Cert. supt. Instr. Bob Jones U., Greenville, S.C., 1966-74; athletic dir., chmn. dept. phys. edn. Temple Heights Christian Sch., Tampa, Fla., 1974-76; dean of students Shannon Forest Presbyn. Sch., Greenville, 1976-78; headmaster Faith Christian High Sch., Williams Bay, Wis., 1980-84; supt. Evansville (Ind.) Christian Sch., 1984-85; headmaster Covenant Christian Sch., Evansville, 1985-87; mid. sch. prin. Cypress (Tex.) Community Christian Sch., 1989-91, headmaster, 1991-94, First Bapt. Acad. of Katy, Tex., 1994-95; adminstr. Ctrl. Texas Christian Sch., Temple, Tex., 1995—. Ednl. cons., Evansville, 1986-88, Houston, 1988—; dist. rep. Assn. Christian Schs. Internat., 1993-95, chair Gulf States Christian Educators Conv., Houston, 1994—. Asst. editor S.C. Jour. Health, Phys. Edn. and Recreation, 1970-72, editor, 1973-74. Instr. water safety, Glenview, Ill., 1958-59, Columbus, Miss., 1959-62, Greenville, 1962-80; instr. first aid, Greenville, 1966-80; swimming ofcl. Amateur Athletic Union, 1968-80 Recipient Outstanding Svc. award Region III, Amateur Athletic Union, 1975, The Aquila award, 1985. Mem. Assn. Christian Schs. Internat. (dist. rep. 1993—, chmn. Christian Educators Conv. 1995—), Internat. Fellowship Christian Sch. Adminstrs., Phi Delta Kappa. Avocations: family activities, reading, white water rafting and canoeing, hiking. Home: 3205 Oakview Dr Temple TX 76502-2647 Office: Ctrl Texas Christian Sch 3205 Oakview Dr Temple TX 76502-2647

ANDREWS, GROVER JENE, adult education educator, administrator; b. Batesville, Ark., June 1, 1930; s. Grover Jones and Ruth Burlie (Ruble) A. BA, Vanderbilt U., 1963, MA, 1964; EdD, N.C. State U., 1972. Dir. univ. rels. Baylor U., Waco, Tex., 1955-61; asst. to pres. Peabody Coll. Vanderbilt U., Nashville, 1961-64; asst. prof. English, asst. acad. dean U. Ark., Little Rock, 1964-66; dir. of devel. Meredith Coll., Raleigh, N.C., 1966-67; asst. to dean of extension N.C. State U., Raleigh, 1967-68, assoc. vice chancellor for extension, assoc. prof. adult edn, 1979-89; assoc. exec. dir. commn. on colls. So. Assn. Colls. and Schs., Atlanta, 1968-79; assoc. dir. for instrn. U. Ga. Ctr. for Continuing Edn., 1989—, sr. pub. svc. assoc., chair sr. pub. svc. faculty, 1989—, adj. assoc. prof. adult edn., 1989—, asst. v.p. pub. svc. and outreach, 1998-99, interim dir., 1998—, assoc. v.p. pub. svc. and outreach, 1999—2001; ret., 2001. Bd. dirs. Am. Tech. Inst., Memphis, 1985-98; trustee Coun. for Adult and Exptl. Learning, Chgo., 1985-91; dir. rsch. Internat. Assn. for Continuing Edn. and Tng., Washington, 1987-92, pres., 1992-96. Member Raleigh Lions, 1967-68, 79-89; chair Christmas pageant Waco Jaycees, 1956-60; patron Atlanta Arts Ctr., 1968-79. With USN, 1948-50. Named Educator of the Yr., Fedn. of Women's Clubs, 1966; recipient Nat. Leadership award Assn. for Continuing Higher Edn., 1984, Gruman award N.C. Adult Edn. Assn., 1985, Pinnacle award for outstanding leadership Internat. Assn. for Continuing Edn. and Tng., 1996; named to Internat. Hall of Fame for Adult and Continuing Edn., 1996; Grover J. Andrews Rsch. Endowment established by Internat. Assn., for Continuing Edn. and Tng., 1996. Mem. Nat. Univ. Continuing Edn. Assn. (chair elect rsch. divsn. 1996-97, chair rsch. divsn. 1998-99, Julius M. Nolte award 1995, chair rsch. divsn. 1997-98), Ga. Adult Edn. Assn., So. Assn. Colls. and Schs. (chair accrediting coms. 1980—), Phi Delta Kappa, Sigma Tau Delta, Pi Kappa Alpha. Democrat. Baptist. Avocations: gardening, arts, antiques. Home: 243 Ashbrook Dr Athens GA 30605-3956 Fax: 706-369-9155.

ANDREWS, JOHN FRANK, editor, author, educator; b. Carlsbad, N.Mex., Nov. 2, 1942; s. Frank Randolph and Mary Lucille (Wimberley) A.; m. Vicky Roberta Anderson, Aug. 20, 1966 (div. 1983); children: Eric John, Lisa Gail; m. Janet Ann Denton, Oct. 15, 1994. AB, Princeton U., 1965; MAT, Harvard U., 1966; PhD, Vanderbilt U., 1971. Instr. English U. Tenn., Nashville, 1969-70; asst. prof. Fla. State U., Tallahassee, 1970-74, dir. grad. studies in English, 1973-74; dir. acad. programs Folger Shakespeare Library, Washington, 1974-84; chmn. Folger Inst., Washington, 1974-84; exec. editor Folger Books, Washington, 1974-84; dep. dir. div. edn. programs NEH, Washington, 1984-88; editor The Guild Shakespeare, 1988-92; pres. The Shakespeare Guild, 1992—; editor The Everyman Shakespeare, 1993—; exec. dir. Washington br. English-Speaking Union, 2001—. Cons. Time-Life TV, WNET/Thirteen, Corp. for Pub. Broadcasting, Pub. Broadcasting Svc., Nat. Pub. Radio, U.S. Dept. Edn., others; chmn. Nat. Adv. Panel for the Shakespeare Plays, 1979-85; core advisor The Shakespeare Hour, 1985-86; mem. adv. bd. Theatre for a New Audience, Humanities Coun. of Washington, Ctr. for Polit. and Strategic Studies, Ctr. for Renaissance and Baroque Studies, U. Md., others; cons. Shakespeare: The Globe and the World, touring exhbn., 1978-81; adminstr. program grants NEH, Andrew W. Mellon Found., Exxon Corp., Met. Life, Surdna Found., others; founder of the Guild's Gielgud Award for Excellence in the Dramatic Arts, 1994. Asst. editor: Shakespeare Studies, 1972-74; editor: Shakespeare Quar., 1974-85; editor-in-chief, contbr.: William Shakespeare: His World, His Work, His Influence, 1985; editor-in-chief: Shakespeare's World and Work, 2001; contbr. numerous articles to mags. and scholarly jours. Decorated officer Order Brit. Empire; recipient rsch. awards Folger Shakespeare Libr., Fla. State U., NEH. Fellow Royal Soc. Arts; mem. AAUP (sec. chpt. 1972-74), Modern Lang. Assn., Milton Soc. Am., Nat. Council of Tchrs. of English, Renaissance Soc. Am. (mem. council 1975-84), Internat. Shakespeare Conf., Shakespeare Assn. Am. (trustee 1979-82), The Lit. Soc., Cosmos Club. Home and Office: 2141 Wyoming Ave NW Apt 41 Washington DC 20008-3916

ANDREWS, M. DEWAYNE, dean, internist, educator; b. Enid, Okla., May 24, 1944; s. Mitchell S. and Truel Eva (Melton) A.; m. Rebecca Ellen Meltzer, Aug. 26, 1984. BS, Baylor U., 1966; MD, U. Okla., 1970. Diplomate Am. Bd. Internal Medicine. Resident internal medicine Johns Hopkins Hosp., Balt., 1970-71, U. Okla. Health Sci. Ctr., Oklahoma City, 1971-72, 74-76; asst. prof., assoc. prof., dir. residency program dept. medicine U. Okla., Oklahoma City, 1976-84, vice chmn., chief gen. internal medicine, prof. dept. medicine, 1986—, assoc. dean grad. med. edn. Coll. Medicine, 1994—2000, sr. assoc. dean, 1996—2002, v.p. health affairs, exec. dean, 2002—; chief of medicine regional med. ctr., vice chmn. dept. medicine U. Tenn. Coll. Medicine, Memphis, 1984-86; chief of staff U. Hosp., Oklahoma City, 1992-94, med. dir., 1994-96. Bd. dirs. Nat. Commn. Certification Physician Assts., 1995—. Editor: Jour. Okla. State Med. Assn., 1991—; contbr. numerous articles to profl. jours. Bd. dirs. Chamber Orch. Oklahoma City, 1982-84, Lyric Theatre, Oklahoma City, 1996-2000, Oklahoma City Philharm. Found., 2003—; del. Okla. State Leadership Initiative to Soviet Union, 1988. Surgeon CDC, USPHS, 1972-74. Surgeon U.S. Pub. Health Svc., 1972—74, Atlanta, GA and Hartford, CT. Recipient Stollermen Award U. Tenn., 1986, Aesculapian award U. Okla. Coll. Medicine, 1989; ACP tchg. and rsch. scholar, 1976-79. Fellow ACP (bd. govs. Okla. 1995-99); mem. AMA, Alpha Omega Alpha. Episcopalian. Avocation: piano. Office: U Okla Coll Medicine RM 357 BMSB PO Box 26901 Oklahoma City OK 73126-0901

ANDREWS, MARIE STAYLOR, special education educator; b. Farmville, Va., Oct. 29, 1959; d. Luther Presley and Betty Jean (Strum) Staylor; m. Gary Hilton Andrews, Dec. 22, 1990; children: Brian Edward, Forrest Presley. BM, Mars Hill Coll., 1982; postgrad., So. Bapt. Theol. Sem., 1982-89, Longwood Coll., 1989-90. Cert. music tchr., Va. Spl. edn. tchr. Bacon Dist. Elem. Sch., Charlotte County Pub. Schs., Charlotte Court House, Va., 1990—. Leader, receptionist Weight Watchers, Southside, Va., 1988-91; mem. choir, choir dir., pianist Crewe (Va.) Bapt. Ch., 1988-90. Republican. Home: RR 1 Box 424C Keysville VA 23947-9704 Office: Bacon Dist Sch RR 1 Box 134 Saxe VA 23967-9533

ANDREWS, MARY JUNE, elementary education educator; b. Odessa, Tex., June 6, 1946; d. Chester Floyd and Audie Mildred (Blevins) Somers; m. William Joe Andrews, May 27, 1967; children: Brent, Janna. BS in Edn., Abilene Christian U., 1967. Cert. tchr., Tex. Tchr. San Antonio Ind. Sch. Dist., 1967-68, N.E. Ind. Sch. Dist., 1968-70, Dallas Christian Sch., Mesquite, Tex., 1979-85, 90—. Mem. Ch. of Christ. Office: Dallas Christian Sch 4900 N Galloway Ave Mesquite TX 75150-1502

ANDREWS, RICHARD VINCENT, physiologist, educator; b. Arapahoe, Nebr., Jan. 9, 1932; s. Wilber Vincent and Fern (Clawson) A.; m. Elizabeth Williams, June 1, 1954 (dec. Dec. 1994); children: Thomas, William, Robert, Catherine, James, John; m. Wyoma Upward, Oct. 18, 1997. BS, Creighton U., 1958, MS, 1959; PhD, U. Iowa, 1963. Instr. biology Creighton U., Omaha, 1958-60; instr. physiology U. Iowa, 1960-63; asst. prof. Creighton U., Omaha, 1963-65, assoc. prof., 1965-68, prof. physiology, 1968-97, asst. med. dean, 1972-75, dean grad. studies, 1975-85, dean emeritus, 1995—, prof. emeritus, 1997—. Vis. prof. Naval Arctic Rsch. Lab., 1963-72, U. B.C., 1985-86, U. Tasmania, 1993-94; cons. VA, NSF, NRC, ARS; plenary speaker USSR Symposium on Environment, 1970, Internat. Soc. Biomet., 1972. Contbr. articles to profl. jours. Served with M.C. U.S. Army, 1951-54. NSF fellow, 1962-63; NSF-NIH-ONR-AINA grantee, 1963— Fellow Explorers Club, Arctic Inst. N.Am.; mem. Am. Physiol. Soc., Am. Mammal Soc., Endocrine Soc., Soc. Exptl. Biology and Medicine, Internat. Soc. for Biometeorology, Sigma Xi.

ANDREWS, WILLIAM DOREY, law educator, lawyer; b. NYC, Feb. 25, 1931; s. Sidney Warren and Margaret (Dorey) Andrews; m. Shirley May Herrman, Dec. 26, 1953; children: Helen Estelle (Noble), Roy Herrman, John Frederick, Margaret Dorey (Davenport), Susan Louise, Carol Mary (Reid). BA, Amherst Coll., 1952; LLD, 1977; LLB, Harvard U., 1955. Bar: Mass. 1959. Practice, Boston, 1959—63; assoc. Ropes & Gray, 1959—63; lectr. Harvard Law Sch., Cambridge, Mass., 1961—63; asst. prof., 1963—65; cons. Sullivan & Worcester, 1964—; prof., 1965—; cons., treasury dept., 1965—68; reporter subchapter C Am. Law Inst. Fed. Income Tax Project, 1974—82; Eli Goldston prof. law, 1986; assoc. reporter accession tax proposal Am Law Inst. Fed. Estate and Gift Tax Project; gen. reporter subchapter C Am. Law Inst. Fed. Income Tax Project, 1986—93. Lt. USNR, 1955—58. Mem.: Am. Bar Assn., Am. Law Inst. Office: Harvard U Law Sch 1545 Massachusetts Ave Cambridge MA 02138-2903

ANDRISANI, PAUL J. business educator, management consultant; b. Wilmington, Del., Oct. 19, 1946; s. Paul and Mary (Tavani) A.; m. Barbara Lee Frank, Nov. 23, 1968; children: Nathan, Damian, Danielle. BS, U. Del., 1968, MBA, 1970; PhD, Ohio State U., 1973, postgrad., 1973-74. Sr. rsch. assoc. Ctr. for Human Resource Rsch. Ohio State U., Columbus, 1973-74, vis. rsch. assoc., 1979; asst. prof. Sch. Bus., Temple U., Phila., 1974-76, assoc. prof., 1977-83, prof., 1983—; dir. Bur. Econ. Rsch., Phila., 1977-78, Ctr. for Labor and Human Resource Studies, 1987—; co-dir. Ctr. for Competitive Govt., Phila., 1997—2002, assoc. dean, 1989-91, chmn. dept. mgmt., 1993-95. Pres. Paul J. Andrisani Mgmt. Cons. Svcs., Wilmington, Del., 1974—, St. Anthony's Edn. Fund, 1986—; pres. West End Neighborhood House Social Svc. Agy., 1995-97; cons. Price Waterhouse, U.S. EEOC, UPS, U.S. Army Recruiting Command, Acme Markets, CBS, Coca-Cola, City of Tucson, City of Phila., Chevron, Chrysler, Olsten, La. Power and Light, La. Land and Exploration, PanAm, Smith Kline, Carpenter Tech., The Aerospace Corp. of Am., Boeing Co., Dynalectron Corp., Lukens Steel, Nordstrom, Phila. Police Dept., Shoney's Inc., Martin Marietta, CIGNA, Airline Pilots Assn., Prudential Ins., Traveler's Ins., Suffolk County Police Dept., Internat. Comms. Agy., N.Y. Times, U.S. Steel, Readers Digest, K-Mart, Wal-Mart, Russell Sage Found., United Food and Comml. Workers Union, Del. Econ. and Fin. Adv. Com., New Orleans Pub. Svc. Inc., Disability and Pension Rev. Com., Rockwell Internat., ARCO, Nationwide Ins., ICI Ams., DuPont, Witco Chem., Westinghouse, GTE, Inco, Gould Electronics, Chrysler, Dollar Bank, Rhone-Poulenc Rorer, Ohio Edison, Delmarva Power, LaSalle Univ., Carter Wallace, Nortel Networks, Enterprise Rent-a-Car, Gulfstream Aerospace Technologies, We. Digital, govt. agys., others; lectr. Internat. Comms. Agy., Japan, Portugal, Italy, Can., Brandeis U., Pa. State U., Columbia U., William and Mary Coll., U. So. Calif., U. Pa., Nat. Employment Law Inst., San Francisco and Washington; testimony before U.S. Congress, 1991; presentation on new economy to Pa. Legis., 2000. Author: Pre-Retirement Years, vol. III, 1973, vol. IV, 1974, Career Thresholds, 1975, Work Attitudes and Labor Market Experience, 1978, Making Government Work, 2000; mem. editl. bd. Jour. Econs. and Bus., 1979-83; reviewer U. Mich. Press, Ohio State U. Press, Temple U. Press and various scholarly jours.; contbr. over 40 papers to profl. jours. and socs. Temple U. Law Sch. Bd. Visitors, 1997—. With U.S. Army, 1972-73. Recipient Wilmington Man of Yr. award, 1995, West End Neighborhood House Leadership award, 1997, Prof. of Yr. award Temple U. Chpt. Soc. for Advancement of Mgmt., 1997, awards for vol. svc., Thomas J. Reese award for cmty. svc., 2000, U. Del. Alumni Hall of Fame award, 1999; Salzburg fellow, Roosevelt Youth Policy fellow; grantee U.S. Dept. Labor, 1974-77, Nat. Commn. for Employment Policy, 1979-83, Adminstrn. on Aging, 1981-82, Social Sci. Rsch. Coun., 1982, U.S. Dept. Army, 1986, 98, Human Resource Rsch. Orgn., 1989-90, PriceWaterhouse Coopers Endowment for the Bus. of Govt., 1998-2000. Mem. Am. Econs. Assn., Indsl. Rels. Rsch. Assn., Acad. of Mgmt., Soc. Labor Economists, Strategic Mgmt. Soc., U. Del. Alumni Assn. (bd. dirs. 2001—). Office: Temple U Fox Sch Bus & Mgmt Speakman Hall Rm 366 Philadelphia PA 19122

ANDROS, HAZEL LAVERNE (BRISSETTE ANDROS), speech professional, educator; b. St. Louis, Sept. 25, 1939; d. Louis Albert and Catherine Virginia (Gonzalas) Brissette; divorced; 1 child, Wendy Gay; m. Nicholas James Andros, Nov. 3, 1962; 1 child, James Nicholas II. AA, Rend Lake Coll., 1976; BS, So. Ill. U., 1979, MS, 1981, PhD, 1994. Office mgr. Tractor Supply Co., Bloomington, Ill., 1969-70; sec. Ill. State U., Normal, 1970-73; office mgr. Wit and Wisdom, Benton, Ill., 1978; intern So. Ill. U., Carbondale, 1978, instr., 1979-80, office mgr., 1980-83; tchr., coord. Benton High Sch., 1984-89; instr. J.A. Logan Coll., Carterville, Ill., 1989-91; rsch. asst. So. Ill. U., Carbondale, 1991-92; ext. instr. bus. edn., adult edn., violence prevention U. Ill., Vienna, 1993-95; motivational spkr., educator Benton, Ill., 1995—. Pres. Benton Youth Bd., 1984—, Benton Dist. Libr. Bd., 1987—, mayor's com. for celebration of 75th anniversary of 19th Amendment, Benton Airport Bd., 1991-93; cert. lay spkr. Mem.: Phi Kappa Phi (coord. 5E). Methodist. Avocations: golf, tennis, singing, biking, cross-stitching. Home: 532 E Main St Benton IL 62812-2521 Office: 532 E Main St Benton IL 62812-2521

ANDRUS, JOYCELON MARIE, art educator; b. Duluth, Minn., June 21, 1939; d. James W. and Rufina C. (Appert) A.; adopted children: Kimberly, Lisandra, Theresa, Tamara, Jacqueline, Cecilia, Michella, Antonya, Stephanie, Chandler, Michael, Kenneth, Austin, Halistin, Valerie, Kalanthe, Anton, Jamila, Lucas, Loveasha, Jasira; guardian to Kiana Andrus; Sponsored Young Soo Kim, John Weiwen Porter. BA in Art, Mont. State U., 1964; MA in Art, U. Mont., 1966. Cert. elem. and secondary tchr., Washington. Tchr. 7th grade St. Joseph's Sch., Mandan, N.D., 1960-61, tchr. 7th and 8th grades, 1964-65; tchr. elem. art sch. dist. 405, Bellevue, Wash., 1966-71; tchr. art Stevens Jr. High Sch., Port Angeles, Wash., 1971-76, Port Angeles High Sch., 1976-96. Nun Sisters for Christian Community, 1979-91. Chmn. Port Angeles art com., 1976-86. Mem. NEA, Wash. Edn. Assn., Port Angeles Edn. Assn. Republican. Mem. Baha'i Faith. Avocations: art, stained glass. Home: 3012 Porter St Port Angeles WA 98362-2749 E-mail: jandrus@olypen.com.

ANFINSON, DONNA MAE, elementary school educator, home economics educator; b. Williston, N.D., Nov. 24, 1944; m. Edward Anfinson, July 13, 1968; children: John, David. BS in Home Econs. Edn., N.D. State U., 1966; MA in Edn., Chapman Coll., 1970; BS in Elem. Edn., Minot State U., 1988. Cert. elem. tchr., N.D., Calif. Tchr. Dos Palos (Calif.) Joint Union High Sch., 1966-68, Grenora (N.D.) High Sch., 1968-69; substitute tchr. New Pub. Sch. Dist. 8, Williston, 1970-86, tchr. 1st and 2d grades, 1986—. Tutor ESL, Zahl, N.D., 1980. Sunday sch. tchr. Zahl Luth. Parish, 1975-80, lay catechist, 1980-90; local leader 4-H Club, Zahl, 1989-92; advisor Williams County Jr. Leaders, 4-H, Williston, 1985-92. Mem. NEA, Nat. Coun. Tchrs. of Maths., N.D. Edn. Assn. (local pres. 1990-91). Avocations: photography, travel, children's activities. Home: 8231 138th Ave NW Zahl ND 58856

ANGEL, ALLEN ROBERT, mathematics educator, author, consultant; b. NYC, Oct. 13, 1942; s. Isaac and Sylvia (Budnick) A.; m. Kathryn Mary Pollinger, Feb. 14, 1966; children: Robert Allen, Steven Scott. AAS in Electrical Tech., N.Y.C. Community Coll., 1962; BS in Physics, SUNY, New Paltz, 1965; MS in Math., SUNY, 1967; postgrad., Rutgers U., 1969. Tchr. physics Rhineback (N.Y.) Cen. Sch., 1965-66; instr. physics, math. Sullivan County Community Coll., Loch Sheldrake, N.Y., 1967-70; prof. math. Monroe Community Coll., Rochester, N.Y., 1970—, chmn. math./computer sci., 1988—. Asst. dir. nat. sci. found., math. summer insts. Rutgers U., New Brunswick, N.J., 1970-72; cons. reviewer various pub. cos. including Prentice-Hall Pub. Co., Englewood Cliffs, N.J., 1983—, Addison-Wesley Pub. Co., Reading, Mass., 1978—; bd. dirs. Am. Math. Assn. Two Yr. Colls. Found. Author: (textbooks) A Survey of Mathematics with Applications, 6th edit., 2001, Elementary Algebra-A Practical Approach, 1985, Intermediate Algebra-A Practical Approach, 1986, Elementary Algebra for College Students, 6th edit., 2003, Intermediate Algebra for College Students, 6th edit., 2003, Algebra for College Students, 2000, Elementary and Intermediate Algebra for College Students, 2000, 2d edit., 2003, Elementary Algebra for College Students, Early Graphing, 2000, 2d edit., 2003. Recipient Excellence in Tchg. award Nat. Inst. for Staff and Organizational Devel., 1991. Mem. Am. Math. Assn. of Two Yr. Colls. (v.p. 1985—, chmn. conv. 1984, bd. dirs., Pres.'s award), N.Y. State Math. Assn. of Two Yr. Colls. (pres. 1978-80, chmn. summer inst. 1976-78, Outstanding Contributions award), Math. Assn. of Am., Nat. Council of Tchrs. of Math., Assn. Math. Tchrs. of N.Y. State, New England Math. Assn. of Two Yr. Colls., Nat. Inst. Staff & Organizational Devel. (Excellence award 1991, 92). Avocations: camping, travel, investing. Home: 4036 Wellington Pkwy Palm Harbor FL 34685-1174 Office: Monroe Community Coll 1000 E Henrietta Rd Rochester NY 14623-5701

ANGELAKOS, EVANGELOS THEODOROU, physician, physiologist, pharmacologist, educator; b. Tripolis, Greece, July 15, 1929; came to U.S., 1948, naturalized, 1966; s. Theodore A. and Aglaia (Tsiverioti) A.; m. Eleanor Pell, Aug. 28, 1954 (div. 1984); 1 son, Theodore; m. Elizabeth Hegnauer, Jan. 2, 1993. Student, Athens (Greece) U., 1947-48, Fordham U., 1948-50, Cornell U., 1950-51; MA, Boston U., 1953, PhD, 1956; MD, Harvard, 1959. Mem. faculty sch. medicine Boston U., 1955-68, prof. physiology, 1963-68; prof. dept. physiology and biophysics Hahnemann U., Phila., 1968-83, chmn. dept., 1968-85, prof. dept. pharmacology and medicine, 1982-95, interim dean sch. medicine, 1982-83, dean Grad. Sch., 1983-92, dep. dean sch. medicine, 1985-86, dir. Med. Sci. Track Program, 1982-95, prof. emeritus physiology, pharmacology and medicine, 1995—; chmn. adv. com. Biomed. Rsch. Inst. Ctr. Rsch. and Advanced Studies, U.

Maine, Portland, 1971-80; dir., dept. chmn. physician asistance program Beaver Coll., 1995-96; provost, chief acad. officer Sch. Medicine Ross U., N.Y.C., 1996—. Rsch. assoc. biomath. MIT, 1959-60; vis. scientist Karolinska Inst., Stockholm, 1962-63; cons. U.S. Army Labs. Environ. Medicine, Natick, Mass., 1964-72, NASA Electronics Rsch. Ctr., Cambridge, Mass., 1966-68; Trustee, sec. bd. Hahnemann Med. Coll. and Hosp., Phila., 1977-81. Contbr. articles to sci. jours. and textbooks. Med. Found. Research fellow, 1959-60; USPHS Research and Career Devel. grantee, 1960-68 Home: 109 Wayside Dr Cherry Hill NJ 08034-3350 Office: Ross U Adminstrn 499 Thornall St Edison NJ 08837 Fax: 732-978-5309.

ANGERVILLE, EDWIN DUVANEL, accountant, educator; b. St. Marc, Haiti, May 22, 1961; came to U.S., 1974; s. Joseph Aniel and Marie Cecile (Phillip-August) A. BS, CUNY, 1984. CPA, N.Y. Coll. acct. CUNY, Jamaica, 1984-87; staff acct. F.S. Todman & Co., CPAs, N.Y.C., 1987; sr. acct. Zucker & Shernicoff, CPAs, N.Y.C., 1988-89; pvt. practice Jamaica, 1990—. Adj. lectr. CUNY, Jamaica, 1986—; co-founder, v.p. Precision Joint Venture, Inc., N.Y.C., 1992-95; co-founder, ptnr. The Success Trainers, N.Y.C., 1992—; bd. dirs. York Coll. Alumni. Contbr. articles to profl. jours. Mem. Carribean Am. C. of C. and Industry, Bklyn., 1992-95. Recipient Superior scholarships N.Y. State Soc. CPAs, 1984. Mem. Nat. Assn. Black Accts., York Coll. Alumni (bd. dirs. 1990-94), York Coll. Acctg. Soc. (hon.), Carribean Am. C. of C. and Industry. Avocations: reading, writing, public speaking, collecting, physical fitness. Home: 10745 142nd St Jamaica NY 11435-5219 Office: 10745 142nd St Jamaica NY 11435-5219

ANGINO, ERNEST EDWARD, retired geology and engineering educator; b. Winsted, Conn., Feb. 16, 1932; s. Alfred and Filomena Mabel (Serluco) A.; m. Margaret Mary Lachat, June 26, 1954; children— Cheryl Ann, Kimberly Ann. BS in Mining Engring., Lehigh U., Bethlehem, Pa., 1954; MS in Geology, U. Kans., 1958, PhD in Geology, 1961. Instr. geology U. Kans., Lawrence, 1961-62, prof. civil engring., 1971-99, prof. geology, 1972-99, prof. emeritus, 1999—, chmn. dept. geology, 1972-86, dir. water resources ctr., 1990-99; asst. prof. Tex. A&M U., College Station, 1962-65; chief geochemist Kans. Geol. Survey, Lawrence, 1965-70, assoc. state geologist, 1970-72. Cons. on water chemistry and pollution to various cos. and govt. agys. including Dow Chem. Co., Ocean Mining Inc., Envicon, Oak Ridge Lab., Fisheries Research Bd. Can., Midwest Research Inst., Coast and Geodetic Survey, U.S. Geol. Survey Author: (with G.K. Billings) Atomic Absorption Spectrometry in Geology, 1967; author, editor: (with D.T. Long) Geochemistry of Bismuth, 1979; editor: (with R.K. Hardy) Proc. 3d Forum Geol. Industrial Minerals, 1967, (with G.K. Billings) Geochemistry Subsurface Brines, 1969; contbr. more than 125 articles to sci. and profl. jours. Mem. Lawrence City Police Rels. Commn., 1970-76, Lawrence City Commn., 1983-87, mayor, 1984-85; mem. Lawrence 2020 Planning Commn., 1992-94, Police Adv. Coun., 1994—, Crimestoppers Bd., 1994-2003, Lawrence Tax Abatement Commn., 2001-02, Lawrence-Douglas County Planning Commn. 2002—, Health Care Access Bd., 1997-2002. With U.S. Army, 1955-57. NSF fellow Oak Ridge Lab., 1963; recipient Antarctic Service medal Dept. Def., 1969; Angino Buttress in Antarctica named in his honor, 1967 Mem. Geochem. Soc. (sec. 1970-76), Soc. Environ. Geochemistry and Health (pres. 1978-79), Internat. Assn. Geochemistry and Cosmochemistry (treas. 1980-94), Am. Polar Soc., Am. Philatelist Soc., Am. Soc. Polar Philatelists, Meter Stamp Soc., Forum Club (Factotum 1978-79), Rotary (pres. 1993-95). Republican. Roman Catholic. Avocations: philately, Western history, Indian lore. Home: 4605 Grove Dr Lawrence KS 66049-3777 Office: U Kans Dept Geology Lindley 120 Lawrence KS 66045-0001 E-mail: rockdoc@sunflower.com.

ANGIULI, ROSEMARIE, special education administrator; b. Highland Park, Ill., Apr. 20, 1947; d. Peter and Josephine (Dalto) A. BS, U. Wis., 1969; MA, U. Iowa, 1972; MEd, Ga. State U., 1975, EdS, 1981, PhD, 1985. Cert. spl. edn. tchr., adminstr., supr., Ga. Tchr. English Owatonna (Minn.) High Sch., 1969-71; spl. edn. tchr. educable mentally retarded Paulding County High Sch., Dallas, Ga., 1973; spl. edn. tchr. (learning disabled) Cobb County Schs., Marietta, Ga., 1973-75, itinerant tchr. learning disabled, 1975-77, spl. edn. program coord., 1977-84, 85-88; dir. spl. edn. Paulding County Sch. System, Dallas, Ga., 1989-93; assoc. dir. div. for exceptional students Ga. Dept. Edn., Atlanta, 1993—. Instr. edn. and English Kennesaw State Coll., Marietta, 1983-89, spl. edn. Ga. State U., Atlanta, 1987—; mem. State Adv. Panel for Spl. Edn., Ga., 1989-92, chairperson, 1990-91; presenter numerous confs. and workshops in Ga. and U.S., 1974—. Mem. Coun. for Exceptional Children (pres. local unit 1991-92, chair Ga. polit. action network 1984-92, Outstanding Mem. 1985), Ga. Coun for Adminstrs. in Spl. Edn. (gov. 1993—), Kappa Delta Pi, Phi Delta Kappa. Avocations: cats and dogs, reading, creative writing, dancing.

ANGLIN, LINDA MCCLUNEY, retired elementary school educator; b. Turrell, Ark., Apr. 20, 1929; d. Denton Sims and Helen Louise (Davis) McCluney; m. Joe Van Anglin, Aug. 30, 1952; children: Van, Cheryl, Dent, George. BA magna cum laude, Millsaps Coll., 1951; MEd, Miss. Coll., 1970; Edn. Specialist, Miss. State U., 1974. Cert. tchr., Miss. Tchr. St. Andrew's Episcopal. Sch., Jackson, Miss., 1952-53, Carthage Elem. Sch., 1956-57, Jackson Pub. Schs., 1957-94. Founder Miss. Profl. Educators, 1979, pres., 1979-82; dir. Pub. Edn. Forum Miss., Jackson, 1989-93; classroom cons. Scholastic Tchr.; bd. dirs. 1st Am. Bank, Jackson. Lobbyist for edn. and children's issues State of Miss., 1980—; charter mem. Jackson Assn. for Children with Learning Disabilities, bd. dirs., historian, mem. adv. bd. Miss. chpt.; active many civic groups. Recipient Book of Golden Deeds award Exch. Club North Jackson, 1989, Disting. Tchr. award White House Commn. Presdl. Scholars, 1996. Mem. Jackson Profl. Educators (pres. 1988-90), Jackson Area Reading Coun. (pres. 1975-76, Outstanding Svc. award 1987), Miss. Hist. Soc. (bd. dirs. 1998-2000), Jackson-Hinds Ret. Tchrs. Assn., Miss. Ret. Tchrs. Assn., Sigma Lambda, Kappa Delta Pi, Phi Kappa Phi, Delta Kappa Gamma (workshop presenter 1985, pres. Tau chpt. 1986-88, Woman of Distinction 1990, Disting. Svc. to Edn. award 1984). Methodist. Avocations: volunteer activities, church activities, reading. Home: 785 Cedarhurst Rd Jackson MS 39206-4954

ANGSTADT, FRANCES VIRGINIA, language arts and theatre arts educator; b. Dover, Del., Oct. 11, 1953; d. T. Richard Sr. and Frances Virginia (Kohout) A. BA, Del. State U., 1976; MFA, Cath. U. Am., 1982; postgrad. in PhD program, Tex. U. Tech. Lighting designer, assoc. dir. écarté dance Theatre, Dover, 1981-93; alternative tchr. Lake Forest H.S., Felton, Del., 1982-87; English tchr. Dover H.S., 1987-89; lang. arts and theater tchr. Ctrl. Mid. Sch., Dover, 1989—2003; lighting designer Harrisburg (Pa.) Ballet, 1991-93. Lighting designer, artistic advisor Act I Players, Dover, 1983-93, lighting designer Balt. Shakespeare Festival, 1994, Kimberly Mackin Dance Co., Balt., Axis Theatre, 1996-99, Women's Project at Theatre Project, Balt., 1997-2000; adj. faculty Del. State U., Dover, 1985-89, Wilmington Coll., Dover, 1996-2001; tech. advisor 2d St. Players, Milford, Del., 1994-2001; dance leadership Visual and Performing Arts Commn., Dover, 1994-2000; English devel. com. state (testing) assessment team Dover Dept. of Edn., 1997-2000, ESL assessment team, 2000-2001, intern visual and performing arts, 2002-2003. Mem. Vietnam Vets. Meml. Com., Dover, 1985-87; sec., founding mem. Dover Arts Coun., 1988-93, tech. advisor, 1988-94; sec. Capital Educators Assn., Dover, 1993-2001; tech. advisor City of Dover First Night, 1997-2001; mem. Balt. Theatre Alliance. All Am. Youth Honor Band scholar, 1972, Del. State U. scholar, Dover, 1974-76; Chancellor's guaranteed fellow 2001—; apptd. to adjudicator Del. Theatre Assn., 1986. Mem. ACLU, AAUW, HRC, NGLIF, Nat. Coun. Tchrs. English, U.S. Inst. Tech. Theatre, Assn. Theatre Higher Edn., Theatre Communicators Group. Avocations: swimming, biking, voice, visual art, dance lighting. Address: 3011 25th St Lubbock TX 79410

ANICH, KENNETH JAMES, priest, college administrator; b. Elkhorn, Wis., Feb. 15, 1947; s. Paul Peter and Audrey Kathern (Bronkalla) A. BA in Sociology, Divine Word Coll., Epworth, Iowa, 1969; MDiv Theology, Cath. Theol. Union, Chgo., 1974; MEd in Human Svcs./Counseling, DePaul U., Chgo., 1979; EdD in Ednl. Psychology, No. Ariz. U., 1994. Ordained priest Roman Cath. Ch., 1973; nat. cert. counselor. Dir. formation Divine Word H.S. Sem., East Troy, Mich., 1974-86; counselor/instr. Christ the King Coll., Quezon City, Philippines, 1987-89; grad. asst. No. Ariz. U., Flagstaff, 1989-92; acad. v.p. Divine Word Coll., Epworth, 1993—2003, assoc. prof. psychology, 2003—. Contbr. articles to profl. jours. Recipient Award of Distinction, Philippine Guidance and Pers. Assn. Intercontinental Hotel, Makati, Metro Manila, 1989. Mem. Am. Counseling Assn., Assn. for Spiritual, Ethical, Religious, Value Issues in Counseling (bd. dirs. 1981-83, pres. 1984-87, Outstanding Svc. award 1987), Wis. Assn. for Counseling and Devel. (pres. 1983-85, Disting. Svc. award 1986), Wis. Pers. and Guidance Assn. (bd. dirs. 1978-80, Outstanding Contbn. award 1981), Nat. Assn. for Acad. Affairs Adminstrs., Assn. of Governing Bds. of Univs. and Colls., Chi Sigma Iota. Republican. Roman Catholic. Avocations: back packing, volleyball, playing guitar/piano, cross country skiing. Office: Divine Word College PO Box 380 102 Jacoby Dr SW Epworth IA 53045-0380

ANKRUM, DOROTHY DARLENE, elementary education educator; b. Wessington Springs, SD, Feb. 23, 1933; d. Clifford Lee and Ella Martha (Crist) A. BA, Colo. State Coll., 1957; MEd, Black Hills State U., 1974. Cert. elem. tchr., SD. Tchr. Mitchell Ind. Sch. Dist., SD, 1953-56, Santa Ana Pub. Sch., Calif., 1957-58, Greybull Pub. Sch., 1958-62, Douglas Sch. Sys., Ellsworth AFB, SD, 1962-69, kindergarten coord., 1963-67; tchr. Rapid City Area Sch., SD, 1969-94; ret., 1994. Unit leader Individually Guided Edn., Rapid City, 1969-74. Author: Sit Up, Line Up, and Shut Up, 1987; contbr. articles to profl. jour.; artist oil painting (best of show 1987). Chair lit. divsn. Ctrl. States Fair, Rapid City, 1987-90; mem. choir, chair bd. edn. 1st Congl. Ch., 1962-92, chair bd. music, 1996-97. Mem. AAUW (life, sec., bd. dir. 1970-92, state corr. sec. 1992-94, br. pres. 1996-98, named Woman of Worth 1989, Gift fellow 1994), NEA, Greybull Classroom Tchr. Assn. (sec. 1960-62), Douglas Edn. Assn. (past sec.). Avocations: art, sewing, reading, writing. Home: 255 Texas St #F 333 Rapid City SD 57701

ANNULIS, JOHN THOMAS, mathematics educator; b. Cin., Nov. 13, 1945; s. John James and Vivian Marie (Jaeger) A.; m. Elizabeth Bruce, Jan. 25, 1969; children: Laura Elizabeth, Leah Catherine. BA, Grand Valley State Coll., 1966; MA, U. N.Mex., 1968, PhD, 1971. Asst. prof. math. U. Wis., Whitewater, 1971-72, U. Ark., Monticello, 1972-75, assoc. prof., 1975-81, prof., 1981—, head dept. math. and physics, 1979-82, dean, Coll. of Gen. Studies, 1993-97, dean Sch. Math. and Scis., 1997—. Contbr. articles to profl. jours. Named Disting. Alumnus, Grand Valley State Coll., 1985. Mem. Math. Assn. Avocations: gardening, reading. Home: 158 Glenwood Dr Monticello AR 71655-5544 Office: Univ Ark Sch Math & Natural Scis Monticello AR 71656-3480 E-mail: annulisj@UAMont.edu.

ANROMAN, GILDA MARIE, college program director, lecturer, educator; b. New Haven, Conn., July 19, 1959; d. Owen Francis Anroman and Edera (Vagnini) Felice. BA, Trinity Coll., Washington, 1983; M in Applied Anthropology, U. Md., 1994, grad. cert. in historic preservation, 1997, postgrad., 1994—. Cert. yoga instr. Clin. technologist Nat. Health Lab., Vienna, Va., 1983-85; dept. mgr., clin. technologist Anmed/Biosafe Inc., Rockville, Md., 1985-92; rsch. asst. U. Md., College Pk., 1992-94, instr. dept. anthropology, 1994-97, acad. advisor, 1996-99, asst. dir. College Park Scholars College Park, 1999—2000, asst. dir. undergrad. programs R.H. Smith Sch. Bus., 2000—03; program dir. Cath. U. of Am., Columbus Sch. Law, Washington, 2003—. Lectr. U. Md., 2003—. Rep. College Pk. Historic Dist. Commn., 1994-95. Scholar State of Conn., Hartford, 1977, Senatorial scholar, State of Md., Annpolis, 1995-99, Del. scholar, Annapolis, 1998-99; recipient Margaret Cook award for historic preservation Prince George's County, Md., 1997. Mem. AAUW, Am. Anthropol. Assn., Am. Hist. Assn., Am. Soc. Environ. History, Am. Studies Assn., Inst. of Early Am. History/Culture, Orgn. Am. Historians, Soc. for Hist. Archaeology, Nat. Trust for Historic Preservation, Nat. Coun. on Pub. History, Assn. for the History Medicine. Home: 34-D Ridge Rd Greenbelt MD 20770 Office: Cath Univ Am Columbus Sch Law Washington DC 20064 Business E-Mail: ganroman@eng.umd.edu.

ANSBRO, JOHN JOSEPH, philosopher, educator; b. N.Y.C., Nov. 16, 1932; s. Thomas and Katherine (Reilly) Ansbro. BA, St. Joseph's Sem., Yonkers, N.Y., 1954, postgrad., 1955; MA, Fordham U., 1957, PhD, 1964. Lectr. philosophy Manhattan Coll., Riverdale, NY, 1958-59, instr., 1959-63, asst. prof., 1963-68, assoc. prof., 1968-79, prof., 1979-96; ret., 1996; writer, 1996—. Curriculum guidance supr. faculty counselors Sch. Arts & Scis. Manhattan Coll., 1962—73, chmn. co-curricular interdisciplinary arts program, 1962—70, chmn. com. faculty rsch. projects and grants, 1976—78, 1989—92, chmn. dept. philosophy, 1977—81, chmn. sabbatical leave com., 1989—91, dir. rsch. peace studies program, 1990—91, com. faculty rsch. projects, mem. instnl. rev. bd. human subjects, task force acad. programs, liaison officer Danforth Found., others; adj. asst. prof. philos. resources contemporary problems program Grad. Sch. Arts & Scis., Fordham U., 1975; chmn. Met. Round Table Philosophy, 1972—75; project field coord. N.Y. State Dept. Edn., 1965—67; founder, pres. Manhattan Coll. Coun. World Hunger, 1977—85. Author: (book) Martin Luther King, Jr.: The Making of a Mind, 1982, Martin Luther King, Jr.: The Making of a Mind, Mex. trans., 1985, Martin Luther King, Jr.: Nonviolent Strategies and Tactics for Social Change, 2d edit., 2000; contbr. some 40 articles to publs. including N.Y. Times. Grantee Travel and Study, Ford Found., 1973, Summer, Am. Can. Co. Found., 1985, Samuel Rubin Found., 1985; scholar, Fordham U. Grad. Sch., 1956—57. Mem.: AAUP, Gandhi-King Soc., Soren Kierkegaard Soc., Soc. Ancient Greek Philosophy, Hegel Soc. Am., Am. Philos. Assn., Soc. Advancement Am. Philosophy.

ANSCHUTZ, MARY ANNA, special education educator; b. Minneapolis, Kans., Apr. 9, 1928; d. Henry Kinsey and Leona (Boucek) Ward; m. Willis Dean Anschutz, Feb. 14, 1954 (dec. Aug. 1981); 1 child, Lucy Ann. BA, U. Kans., 1951; MS, Ft. Hays State U., 1988. 3rd grade tchr. Simpson Grade Sch., Russell, Kans.; 1st/2nd combination tchr. Dorrance (Kans.) Grade Sch., chpt. 1 reading/math. tchr. K-8; tchr. learning disabilities/behavior disabilities Clyde (Kans.) Elem., Clifton (Kans.) Elem. and Jr. High Sch., 1988-90, Clifton Elem./Clifton-Clyde Jr. High Schs., 1990-91, Concordia (Kans.) Mid. Sch., 1991-92, tchr. learning disabilities/emotionally retarded, 1992-94. Supervising judge Receiving/Counting Bd. Elections, Russell, Kans.; treas. Russell County Extension Coun.; co-leader Smoline 4-H Club, Dorrance; supervising judge Russell County 4-H Fair. Mem. NEA (life), Coun. Exceptional Children (leadership com., del. conv. 1989, 94, leadership award 1988), Thunderbird Reading Assn. (v.p. 1992-93, pres. elect 1993-94), Internat. Reading Assn., Kans. Reading Assn., Kans. U. Alumni Assn. (life.), Ft. Hays State Alumni Assn. (life), Kans. Fedn. Coun. Exceptional Children (coun. mem. constn. 1991-92, sec. divsn. learning disabilities 1991-94, treas. 1994—, unit devel. chmn. 1992-94, pres. Wheat State chpt. 1993-94, citizen amb. program 1994), Thunderbird Reading Coun. (pres. 1994—), Delta Kappa Gamma. Avocations: travel, reading, crafts, sports. Home: PO Box 190 Russell KS 67665-0190

ANSLEY, JULIA ETTE, educator, poet, writer, consultant; b. Malvern, Ark., Nov. 10, 1940; d. William Harold and Dorothy Mae (Hamm) Smith; m. Miles Ansley, Nov. 8, 1964 (div. June 1976); children: Felicia Diane, Mark Damon. BA in Edn., Calif. State U., Long Beach, 1962; postgrad., UCLA Ext. Early childhood edn., life, gen. elem., kindergarten/primary, Miller-Unruh reading specialist credentials, Calif. Elem. tchr. L.A. Unified Sch. Dist., 1962—. Coord. Proficiency in English Program, L.A., 1991-93, 98-2001; mem., advisor P.E.P. Instrnl. Tchrs. Network, 1993-2001, workshop presenter, staff devel. leader, and classroom demonstration tchr. in field; also poetry presentations, L.A., 1989—; owner Poetry Expressions, L.A.; self-markets own poetry posters; creator, presenter KIDCHESS integrated lang. arts program, 1987—. Author: (poetry vols.) Out of Heat Comes Light, From Dreams to Reality. Bd. dirs. New Frontier Dem. Club, L.A., 1990-93; mem. exec. bd. L.A. Panhellenic Coun., rec. sec., 1993-95; vol., cmty. orgns. Greater South L.A. Affirmative Action Project, 1995-96; elected tchr. rep. Ten Schs. Leadership Team, 1992-93; active local sch. leadership 6 schs. L.A. Unified Sch. Dist., elected mem. sch. site coun., local sch. leadership coun., shared-decision-making coun. Honored by Teacher mag., 1990; recipient Spirit of Edn. award Sta. KNBC-TV, L.A., 1990, Shiny Apple award L.A. Tchr. Ctr., 1992, Dedicated Tchr. award Proficiency in English Program, 1994; grantee L.A. Ednl. Partnership, 1985, 87, 89, 93. Mem. L.A. Alliance African-Am. Educators (exec. bd. 1991-94, parliamentarian 1992-94), Black Women's Forum, Black Am. Polit. Assn. (edn. co-chair 1993-95), Sigma Gamma Rho. Mem. FAME Ch. Avocations: reading, listening to music, writing, playing chess (cert. chess instr. for grades K-3), political activist. Home: 3828 Sutro Ave Los Angeles CA 90008-1925

ANSORGE, HELEN J. retired elementary school educator; b. Clifton, N.J., Mar. 12, 1933; d. George and Helen V. (Jilek) Van Ness; m. Charles E. Ansorge, July 23, 1955; children: Valerie Jean, Cathy Marie. BS, Paterson State Coll., Wayne, N.J., 1954; MS in Edn., Kean Coll., Union, N.J., 1958; postgrad., Marywood Coll., Scranton, Pa., U. Calif. Kindergarten and elem. tchr. Clifton (N.J.) Bd. Edn., 1954-56; tchr. kindergarten, first grade, then reading Walnut Ridge Sch., Vernon (N.J.) Twp. Bd. Edn., 1966-92; now ret. Recipient Prin.'s Incentive award, 1988, Literacy award Northwest Jersey Reading Coun., 1992; grantee Vernon Twp., Gov.'s Tchr. Recognition grantee; Dr. George Iannacone scholar, 1990. Mem. NEA (rep.), N.J. Edn. Assn., Sussex County Edn. Assn. (del. assembly rep. 1989-92, Warren D. Cummings Disting. Svc. award 1992), Vernon Twp. Edn. Assn. (v.p. 1990-92), Assn. Kindergarten Educators (past v.p.). Home: 20 Meyers Rd Branchville NJ 07826-5110

ANSORGE, IONA MARIE, musician, educator; b. Nov. 3, 1927; d. Edgar B. and Marie Louise (Bleeke) Bohn; m. Edwin James Ansorge, Sept. 13, 1949; children: Richard, Michelle. BA, Valparaiso U., 1949; cert. teaching, Drake U., 1964; MA, U. Iowa, 1976. Min. of music Our Savior Luth. Ch., Des Moines, 1949-63; tchr. Johnston (Iowa) High Sch., 1964-75; instr. Iowa Meth. Sch. Nursing, Des Moines, 1978-87; owner, pres. Bed and Breakfast in Iowa, Ltd., 1982-86; realtor Better Homes and Gardens First Realty, Des Moines, 1986-92. Pres. Des Moines Jaycee-ettes; spearheaded drive Des Moines Zoo; founder Messiah Luth. Ch., Des Moines, 1978; started Iowa Bed and Breakfast Industry, 1982; owner, pres. Bed and Breakfast in Iowa, Ltd.; mem. First Luth. Ch.; permanent sec. Class of 1949, Valparaiso U. Mem. LWV, AAUW, Am. Choral Dirs. Assn., Des Moines Bd. Realtors, Women's Coun. Realtors, Realtor's Million Dollar Club, Jaycee-ettes (pres. Des Moines chpt. 1957-58), Valparaiso U. Guild (charter mem. Des Moines chpt.), Mortar Bd. Lutheran. Avocations: playing piano and organ, tennis, bridge, reading. Home: 8345 Twinberry Pt Colorado Springs CO 80920-5394

ANTHONY, KATHRYN HARRIET, architecture educator; b. NYC, Sept. 11, 1955; d. Harry Antoniades and Anne (Skoufis) Anthony; m. Barry Daniel Riccio, May 24, 1980 (dec. Jan. 2001). AB in Psychology, U. Calif., Berkeley, 1976, PhD in Architecture, 1981. Rsch. promotion Kaplan/McLaughlin/Diaz Architects and Planners, San Francisco, 1980-81; vis. lectr. U. Calif., Berkeley, Calif., 1980-81, 82-83, San Francisco State U., Calif., 1981; assoc. prof. Calif. State Poly. U., Pomona, Calif., 1981-84; asst. prof. U. Ill., Urbana-Champaign, Ill., 1984-89, assoc. prof., 1989-96, chair bldg. rsch. coun., 1994-97, prof. architecture, 1996—, chair design faculty, 2002—. Guest lectr. numerous orgns., coll. and univ.; mem. numerous comm. Coll. of Fine and Applied Arts, Sch. Architecture, Housing Rsch. and Devel. Program, Dept. Landscape Architecture. Author: Design Juries on Trial: The Renaissance of the Design Studio, 1991, Designing for Diversity: Gender, Race, and Ethnicity in the Architectural Profession, 2001; co-editor Jour. Archtl. Edn. 47:1, 1993; mem. editl. bd. Jour. Archtl. and Planning Rsch., 1989-92, Jour. Archtl. Edn., 1990-95, Environ. and Behavior Jour., 1991—; reviewer Landscape Jour., 1990; contbr. articles to profl. jours; co-designer, co-prodr. (exhibit) Shattering the Glass Ceiling: The Role of Gender and Race in the Archtl. Profession, Nat. Conv. AIA, 1996. Recipient Collaborative Achievement award AIA, 2003; Creative Achievement award Assn. Collegiate Sch. Architecture, 1992; grant US Army C.E.R.L., 1993, grant U. Ill., 1984, 87, 92, 93, 95, 96, grant Graham Found., 1989-91, 93-96, grant Decatur Housing Authority, 1988, grant Upgrade Cos., Peoria, Ill., 1987, grant Nat. Endowment for Arts, 1986-87, grant LA County Cmty. Devel. Commn., 1984, grant Calif. State U. and Coll., 1982, 83, summer grant U. Calif., Berkeley, 1980; fellow Acad. Leadership Program Com. Instnl. Coop., 1996-97. Mem. Environ. Design Rsch. Assn. (bd. dir. 1989-92, treas. 1990-92, co-editor Coming of Age: Proceedings of 21st Ann. Conf. 1990), Chgo. Women in Architecture. Home: 309 W Pennsylvania Ave Urbana IL 61801-4918 Office: U Ill Sch Architecture 611 Taft Dr Champaign IL 61820-6922 E-mail: kanthony@uiuc.edu.

ANTHONY, ROBERT ARMSTRONG, lawyer, educator; b. Washington, Dec. 28, 1931; s. Emile Peter and Martha Graham (Armstrong) Anthony; m. Ruth Grace Barrons, Feb. 7, 1959 (div.); 1 child, Graham Barrons; m. Joan Patricia Caton, Jan. 3, 1980; 1 child, Peter Christopher Caton. BA, Yale U., 1953; BA in Jurisprudence, Oxford U., 1955; JD, Stanford U., 1957. Bar: Calif. 1957, N.Y. 1971, DC 1972. Assoc. Pillsbury, Madison & Sutro, San Francisco, 1957-62, Kelso, Cotton & Ernst, San Francisco, 1962-64; assoc. prof. law Cornell U. Law Sch., 1964-68, prof., 1968-75, dir. internat. legal studies, 1964-74; chief counsel, later dir. Office Fgn. Direct Investments, Dept. Commerce, 1972-73; cons. Adminstrv. Conf. U.S., Washington, 1968-71, chmn., 1974-79; ptnr. McKenna, Conner & Cuneo, Washington, 1979-82; pvt. practice Washington, 1982-83; prof. law George Mason U., Arlington, Va., 1983—2002, prof. emeritus, 2002—. Fulbright lectr., Slovenia, 1994; lectr. Acad. Am. and Internat. Law, Southwestern Legal Found., Dallas, 1967—72; instr. Golden Gate U., 1961; cons., chmn. pubs. adv. bd. Internat. Law Inst., 1984—; cons. Inst. Pub. Adminstrn., Slovenia, 1994—. Mem. editl. adv. bd. Jour. Law and Tech., 1986—91; contbr. articles to profl. jours. Active Pres.'s Inflation Program Regulatory Coun., 1978—79; chmn. panel U.S. Dept. Edn. Appeal Bd., 1981—83; commr. Sausalito (Calif.) City Planning Commn., 1962—64; active Fairfax County (Va.) Rep. Com., 1984—86; bd. dirs. Nat. Ctr. Adminstrv. Justice, 1974—79, Marin Shakespeare Festival, San Rafael, Calif., 1961—64, Va. Assn. Scholars, 1990—98. Mem.: ABA (coun., sec. sect. adminstrv. law and regulatory practice 1988—94), Stanford U. Law Soc. Washington (pres. 1982), Am. Law Inst., Assn. Am. Rhodes Scholars, Cosmos Club. Home: 2011 Lorraine Ave Mc Lean VA 22101-5331 Office: George Mason U Law Sch 3301 N Fairfax Dr Arlington VA 22201-4426 E-mail: ranthony@gmu.edu.

ANTHONY, ROBERT NEWTON, management educator emeritus; b. Orange, Mass., Sept. 6, 1916; s. Charles H. and Grace (Newton) A.; m. Gretchen Lynch, Aug. 28, 1943; children: Robert N., Victoria Stewart; m. Katherine Worley, Aug. 4, 1973. AB, Colby Coll., 1938, MA (hon.), 1959, LHD (hon.), 1963; MBA, Harvard U., 1940, DCS, 1952. Mem. faculty Bus. Sch., Harvard U., 1940-42, 46-67, 68-83, Ross Graham Walker prof. mgmt. control, prof. emeritus, 1983—. Pres. Mgmt. Analysis Ctr., Inc., 1955-63; asst. sec., contr. Dept. Def., 1965-68; prof. Mgmt. Devel. Inst., Switzerland, 1957-58; with Stanford Exec. Devel. Program, 1962; mem. adv. com. IMEDE, Switzerland, 1961-65, 68-77; spl. asst. to chmn. Price Commn., 1971-73; mem. educators cons. com. GAO, 1973-87; dir., chmn. audit com. Carborundum Co., 1971-77; dir. Warnaco, Inc., 1971-86; mem. adv. com.

Kyoto Rsch. Inst., 1987-90, IPMI (Jakarta), 1983-90. Author: Management Controls in Industrial Research Organization, 1952, (with Dearborn and Kneznek) Shoe Machinery: Buy or Lease?, 1955, (with Reece) Accounting, Text and Cases, 1956, 11th edit. (with Hawkins and Merchant), 2004, Office Equipment, Buy or Rent?, 1957, Essentials of Accounting, 1964, 8th edit., 2003, Accounting Principles, 1965, 7th edit., 1995, Planning and Control Systems: A Framework for Analysis, 1965, (with Govindarajan) Management Control Systems, (With Vijay Govindarajan) 11th edit., 2004, (with Hekimian) Operations Cost Control, 1967, Plaid in Management Accounting, (with Welsch) Fundamentals of Financial Accounting, 1974, Fundamentals of Management Accounting, 1974, (with Young) Management Control in Nonprofit Organizations, 1975, 7th edit., 2003, Accounting for the Cost of Interest, 1976, Financial Accounting in Nonbusiness Organizations, 1978, Tell It Like It Was, 1983, Future Directions for Financial Accounting, 1984, Teach Yourself the Essentials of Accounting (computer software), 1999; (with Anderson) The New Corporate Director, 1986, The Management Control Function, 1988, Should Business and Nonbusiness Accounting Be Different?, 1989, Rethinking the Rules of Financial Accounting, 2003; editor Richard D. Irwin, Inc.; mem. bd. Harvard Bus. Rev., 1947-60; contbr. articles to profl. jours. Trustee Colby Coll., 1959-74, 75—, chmn., 1978-83; trustee Dartmouth Hitchcock Med. Ctr., 1983-93, treas., 1993; town auditor Town of Waterville Valley, N.H., 1976-92; mem. audit com. City of N.Y., 1977-85. Lt. comdr. USNR, 1941-46. Recipient Disting. Leadership award Fed. Govt. Accts. Assn., Disting. Pub. Svc. medal Dept. Def., Disting. Svc. award Harvard Bus. Sch., Marriner Disting. Svc. award Colby Coll., Meritorious Svc. award Exec. Office of Pres., CINPAC Letter of Commendation, Baker Scholar; named to Acctg. Hall of Fame. Fellow Acad. Mgmt.; mem. Am. Acctg. Assn. (v.p. 1959, pres. 1973-74, Outstanding Acctg. Educator of Yr. 1989, acctg. sect. Lifetime Achievement award 2003), Fin. Exec. Inst., Inst. Mgmt. Accts. (chmn. cost concepts subcom., mgmt. acctg. practices com.), Assn. Govt. Accts., Am. Soc. Mil. Compts., Cosmos Club, Phi Beta Kappa, Pi Gamma Mu, Beta Alpha Psi. Home: 80 Lyme Rd Apt 332 Hanover NH 03755-1233 E-mail: rnanthony@valley.net.

ANTHONY, SUSAN, secondary education educator; Tchr. secondary geography Anchorage Sch. Dist. Recipient Disting. Tchr. K-12 award Nat. Coun. for Geog. Edn., 1992. Office: Anchorage Sch District PO Box 196614 Anchorage AK 99519-6614

ANTHONY-PEREZ, BOBBIE COTTON MURPHY, psychology educator, researcher; b. Macon, Ga., Nov. 15, 1923; d. Solomon Richard and Maude Alice (Lockett) Cotton; m. William Anthony, Aug. 22, 1959 (dec.); 1 child, Freida; m. Andrew Silviano Perez, June 20, 1979. BS, DePaul U., 1953, MS, 1954, MA, 1975; MS, U. Ill., 1959; PhD, U. Chgo., 1967. Tchr. Chgo. Pub. Schs., 1954-68; math. coord. U. Chgo., 1965; prof. Chgo. State U., 1968-95, coord. Black Studies Program, 1982-83, 90-94; with psychol. svcs. Chgo. Pub. Schs., 1971-72; rsch. coord. Urban Affairs Inst. Howard U., Washington, 1978; coord. higher edn., careers counseling, campus ministry Ingleside Whitfield Parish, 1978-84, comm. chmn., 1991-92, 95. Contbr. numerous articles to profl. jours., chpts. to books. V.p. Cmty. Affairs Chatham Bus. Assn., 1981-85, asst. sec., 1985-86, sec., 1986-87, directory com., 1987, 88; bus. rels. chmn. Chatham Avalon Pk. Cmty. Coun., 1984—, newsletter editor, 1993—; bd. dirs. United Meth. Found. at U. Chgo., 1980-84, Cmty. Mental Health Coun. Inc., 1979-83; pub. edn. chairperson Chatham Avalon unit Am. Cancer Soc., 1977-88, 90-97, pub. info. chairperson, 1988-94; pres. Aux. Chgo. chpt. Tuskegee Airmen, Inc., 1994-95, rec. sec., 1998-99, parliamentarian, 1991-95, newsletter feature writer, 1999—. NSF fellow, 1957, 58, 59; recipient numerous awards religious, civic and ednl. instns. and assns. Mem. APA, Internat. Assn. Applied Psychology, Internat. Assn. Cross-Cultural Psychology, Internat. Assn. Ednl. and Vocat. Guidance, Assn. Black Psychologists (elder 1995—, pres. Chgo. chpt. 1995-96, past pres.), Chgo. Psychol. Assn., Nat. Coun. Tchrs. Math., Am. Ednl. Rsch. Assn., Midwest Ednl. Rsch. Assn., Am. Soc. Clin. Hypnosis, Midwestern Psychol. Assn., Chgo. Soc. Clin. Hypnosis. Methodist. Office: Chgo State U Dept Psychology 9501 S King Dr Chicago IL 60628-1501

ANTOINE, TERRY WAYNE, secondary school educator; b. Denton, Tex., Nov. 6, 1954; s. Hugh and Shirley Jean (Padgett) A.; m. Carmen Ann Griffin, May 22, 1976; children: Dylan Reeves, Megan Grace. BA, Tex. A&M U., 1977; MEd, Tarleton State U., 1981; postgrad., Tarrant County Jr. Coll., 1983-85; EdD, U. North Tex., 1997. Tchr. math. Nolan Mid. Sch., Killeen, 1978-81, Boswell HS, Saginaw, Tex., 1981-84, Bell HS, Bedford, Tex., 1984-86; prin. Lipan Ind. Sch. Dist., Tex., 1986-89, Alvord HS, Tex., 1989-93; adj. faculty U. North Tex., Tex., 1994; sci. tchr. TENET master trainer Decatur Mid. Sch., 1995-99. Instr. tech. applications Keller ISD, 2000-, FRHS Task Force, 2001-, FRHS Tech. Comm.,2001, FRHS PTSA, Keller ISD Admin. Cadre, gen. mgmt. tng. coun. Ednl. svc. Ctr. XI, Ft. Worth, 1989-91, h.s. prin. coun., 1990-93; mem. effective schs. project Tarleton State U., Stephenville, Tex., 1988-89; mem. Cycle 2 Tex. Sch. Improvement Initiative, Austin, 1989-93; mem. Prin's. Coun., 1990-93, Decatur Ind. Sch. Dist. Tech. Com., 1995-97; dir. sci. mentors project TENET. Mem. U. North Tex. Alumni Assn., Phi Delta Kappa. Mem. First Christian Ch. Avocations: photography, geneology, technology. Home: PO Box 532 Decatur TX 76234-0532 E-mail: tantoine@kellerisd.net.

ANTONIOU, ANDREAS, electrical engineering educator; b. Yerolakkos, Nicosia, Cyprus, 1938; immigrated to Can., 1969; s. Antonios and Eleni Hadjisavva; m. Rosemary C. Kennedy, 1964 (dec.); children: Anthony, David, Constantine, Helen BSc with honors, U. London, 1963, PhD, 1966; Dr honoris causa, Nat. Tech. U. Greece, 2002. Mem. sci staff GEC Ltd., London, 1966; sr. sci. officer P.O. Rsch. Dept., London, 1966-69; sci. staff in R & D No. Electric Co., Ottawa, Canada, 1969-70; from asst. prof. elec. engrng. to prof., dept. chmn. Concordia U., Montreal, Canada, 1970-83; founding chmn. elec. and computer engrng. dept. U. Victoria, Canada, 1983-90, prof., 1983—2003, prof. emeritus, 2003—. Author: Digital Filters: Analysis, Design, and Applications, 1979, 2d edit., 1993; co-author: Two-Dimensional Digital Filters, 1992; contbr. articles to profl. jours. Recipient Chmn.'s award for Career Achievement, B.C. Sci. Coun., 2000. Fellow: IEEE (assoc. editor Trans. on Cirs. and Sys. 1983—85, editor 1985—87, bd. govs. Cirs. Sys. Soc. 1995—97, Golden Jubilee award Cirs. Sys. Soc. 2000, Disting. Lectr. Sig. Proc. Soc. 2003); mem.: Assn. Profl. Engrs. and Geoscientists B.C. (councilor 1988—90), Instn. Elec. Engrs. (Ambrose Fleming premium 1969). Greek Orthodox. Home: 4058 Jason Pl Victoria BC Canada V8N 4T6 Office: U Victoria Dept Elec & Computer Engring PO Box 3055 STN CSC Victoria BC Canada V8W 3P6 E-mail: aantoniou@ece.uvic.ca.

ANTONIUK, VERDA JOANNE, secondary school educator; b. Moline, Ill., Sept. 10, 1936; d. Joe Oscar and Verda Mathilde (Oakberg) Butts; m. Vladimir Antoniuk, Sept. 1, 1972; children: Daniel Sean, Stephen Dwight. Diploma in missions, Moody Bible Inst., 1957; BS in Edn., Ea. Ill. U., 1960; MA in Internat. Rels., Calif. State U. Stanlslaus, Turlock, 1981, cert. in ESL, 1989. Cert. tchr., ESL tchr., bilingual, crosscultural, lang. and acad. devel. cert., Calif. Tchr. Wheatridge (Colo.) H.S., 1960-61, Modesto (Calif.) City Schs., 1971-73, Modesto Jr. Coll., 1979-80, 84-89, Turlock Christian H.S., 1980-83, Turlock H.S., 1989—; part-time faculty edn. dept. Chapman U., 1995; missionary Overseas Missionary Fellowship, Littleton, Colo., 1961-69. Tchr. Turlock Adult Sch., 1969-79, 84-89, program dir. ESL, 1976-79, amnesty coord., 1986-89; cons. Britannica-ARC Project, Oakland, Calif. and Boston, 1993-94; ednl. cons. Valley Fresh, Turlock, 1987-88. Translator multi-media U.S. Constitution, Britannica, 1993; cons. to book on amnesty, 1987; contbt. to book Intervarsity Christian Fellowship, 1965. Sunday sch. supt. Evang. Free Ch., Turlock, 1979-82; cons. Spanish work Turlock Covenant Ch., 1990—; mem. Malaysian Youth Coun., Kuala Lumpur, 1967-68. Mem. Calif. Tchrs. English to Spkrs. of Other Langs., Nat. Assn. Bilingual Educators, Tchrs. of English to Spkrs. of Other Langs. Republican. Avocations: reading, macintosh computers, writing, collecting stamps and coins. Home: 553 South Ave Turlock CA 95380-5606

ANTONOFF, STEVEN ROSS, educational consultant, author; b. Waukon, Iowa, Dec. 14, 1954; s. Ben H. and Florence R. A. BS, Colo. State U., 1967; MA, U. Denver, 1970, PhD, 1979. Spl. asst. to dean U. Denver, 1970-71, dean student life, 1971-74, dean Ctr. Prospective Students, 1974-75, exec. dir. admissions and students affairs, 1975-78, dean admissions and fin. aid, 1978-81. Adj. prof. speech communication, 1979-88; dir., now pres. Antonoff Assocs., Inc.; active Secondary Sch. Admission Testing Bd., Princeton, N.J. Author: College Match, The College Finder; contbr. articles to profl. jours., chpts. to books. Chmn. Mayor's Commn. arts, Denver, 1979-81; trustee Congregation Emanuel, 1977-82; chmn. bd. dirs. Hospice of Met. Denver, 1970-84; mem. Denver Commn. Cultural Affairs, 1984-86; mem. scholarship com. Mile High Cablevision, 1982-90; chmn. Cultural Affairs Task Force, City of Denver, 1988-89. Recipient Clara Barton award meritorious vol. leadership ARC, 1992. Mem. ACA, Rocky Mountain Assn. Coll. Admissions Counselors, Am. Ednl. Rsch. Assn., New Eng. Assn. Coll. Admission Officers, Ind. Ednl. Cons. Assn. (chmn. bd. 1992-94, chari nat. cert. commn. 1993—), Attention Deficit Disorder Advocacy Group, Rotary Internat., Zeta Beta Tau (found. bd. dirs. 1993-96). Office: 1181 S Parker Rd Ste 102 Denver CO 80231-2152

ANTONS, PAULINE MARIE, mathematics educator; b. Monticello, Iowa, Jan. 15, 1926; d. Henry and Eliza (Zimmerman) Tobiason; m. Richard William Antons, Aug. 13, 1950 (dec. 1999); children: Sharon Kay, Karen Lyn. BS, U. Dubuque, 1948. Cert. secondary tchr., Iowa. Tchr. math. Elkader (Iowa) Community Sch., 1948-50, Onslow (Iowa) Ind. Schs., 1950-60, Midland Community, Wyoming, 1960-90, Kirkwood Coll., Cedar Rapids, Iowa, 1982-90. Mem. scholarship adv. bd. Jones County Health Assn., Anamosa, Iowa, 1983—. Mem. adv. bd. Evang. Luth. Ch. Women; mem. Limestone Bluffs Resource Conservation and Devel.; co-treas. Jones County Soil and Water Commn., 1992-97 (Region 4 Commn. award 1997); sec. Iowa League, sec. Recipient Pres. award for excellencein math. edn., 1988, Friends of Math. award Iowa Tchrs. of Math., 1992, Jones County Conservation Outstanding Tchr. award, 1988, 93; Pres.'s scholar U. Dubuque, 1945-48, NSF scholar Drake U., 1967, Clarke Coll., 1968, U. Iowa, 1969. Mem. Delta Kappa Gamma (treas. Beta Nu chpt.). Lutheran. Avocations: gardening, reading, travel. Home and Office: 13481 105th Ave Center Junction IA 52212-7502 E-mail: pantons@netins.net.

ANTONY, ROSE MARY, physical education educator; b. Sparta, Wis., July 18, 1960; d. Aloysius Nicholas and AnnaMae Ruth (Leis) A. BS, U. Wis., La Crosse, 1982; MA, Tex. Woman's U., 1989. Cert. K-12 phys. edn. and physically handicapped edn. tchr., Tex. Tchr. adapted phys. edn. South Tex. Ind. Sch. Dist., Harlingen, 1982-85; tchr. phys. edn. Royse City (Tex.) Ind. Sch. Dist., 1986—, mem. curriculum devel. team, 1987—. Coach Tex. Spl. Olympics, Rockwall, 1983—; cons. Region XV Edn. Svc. Ctr., San Angelo, Tex., 1986—; mem. Dist. Improvement of Edn. Team, 1990-91, mem. Dist. Improvement Com., 1992. Bd. dirs. PTO, Royse City, 1988-91. Named Tchr. of Yr., South Tex. Ind. Sch. Dist., 1984, 85, Coach of Yr., Area 1 Spl. Olympics, Edinburg, Tex., 1984, 85, Campus Tchr. Yr. Royse City, Dallas, 2002, Area 10 Spl. Olympics Coach Yr., 1999. Mem. AAHPER and Dance, Tex. Assn. Health, Phys. Edn., Recreation and Dance, Assn. Tex. Profl. Educators, Phi Kappa Phi. Office: Royse City Ind Sch Dist PO Box 479 Royse City TX 75189-0479

ANTREASIAN, GARO ZAREH, artist, lithographer, art educator; b. Indpls., Feb. 16, 1922; s. Zareh Minas and Takouhie (Daniell) A.; m. Jeanne Glascock, May 2, 1947; children: David Garo, Thomas Berj. BFA, Herron Sch. Art, 1948; DFA (hon.), Ind. U.-Purdue U. at Indpls., 1972. Instr. Herron Sch. Art, 1948-64; tech. dir. Tamarind Lithography Workshop, Los Angeles, 1960-61; prof. art U. N.Mex., 1964-87, chmn. dept. art, 1981-84; tech. dir. Tamarind Inst., U. N.Mex., 1970-72; vis. lectr., artist numerous univs. Bd. dirs. Albuquerque Mus., 1980-90; printmaker emeritus Southern Graphics Coun., 1994; Fulbright vis. lectr U. São Paulo and Found. Armando Alvares Penteado, Brazil, 1985. Prin. author: The Tamarind Book of Lithography: Art and Techniques, 1970; one-man shows include Malvina Miller Gallery, San Francisco, 1971, Marjorie Kauffman Gallery, Houston, 1975-79, 84, 86, U. Colo., Boulder, 1972, Calif. Coll. Arts & Crafts, Oakland, 1973, Miami U., Oxford, Ohio, 1973, Kans. State U., 1973, Atlanta Coll. Art, 1974, U. Ga., Athens, 1974, Alice Simsar Gallery, Ann Arbor, 1977-79, Elaine Horwich Gallery, Santa Fe, 1977-79, Mus. of N.Mex., Santa Fe, 1979, Robischon Gallery, Denver, 1984, 86, 90, Moss-Chumley Gallery, Dallas, 1987, Rettig-Martinez Gallery, Santa Fe, 1988, 91, 92, U. N.Mex. Art Mus., 1988, Albuquerque Mus., 1988, Louis Newman Gallery, L.A., 1989, Expositum Gallery, Mexico City, 1989, State U. Coll., Cortland, N.Y., 1991, Mus. Art, U. Ariz., Tucson, 1991, Indpls. Mus. Art, 1994, Ruschmon Gallery, Indpls., 1994, Mitchell Mus. Art, Vernon, Ill., 1995, Cline-Lewallen Gallery, Santa Fe, 1997, 2002, Anderson Gallery, Albuquerque, 1997, Fenix Gallery, Taos, NM State U., Las Crucis, 1998, Lewallen Gallery, Santa Fe, 2002, Cline Gallery, Scottsdale, 2002, 03, Cline Fine Art, Scottsdale, Ariz., 2002, Santa Fe, 2003; exhibited group shows Phila. Print Club, 1960-63, Ind. Artists, 1947-63, White House, 1966, Nat. Lithographic Exhbn. Fla. State U., 1965, Library Congress, 1961-66, Bklyn. Mus., 1958-68, 76, U.S. Pavilion Venice Biennale, 1970, Internat. Biennial, Bradford, Eng., 1972-74, Internat. Biennial, Tokyo, 1972, City Mus. Hong Kong, 1972, Tamarind UCLA, 1985, Roswell Mus., 1989, Pace Gallery, 1990, Worcester (Mass.) Art Mus., 1990, Amon Carter Mus., Ft. Worth, 1990, Albuquerque Mus., 1991, 92, Art Mus. U. N.Mex., 1991, 92, 99, 2001, Norton Simon Mus., Pasadena, Calif., 1999, U. N.H., 1999, Cline Fine Art, Scottsdale, Ariz., 2002, 03, Fenix Gallery, Taos, 2003; represented in permanent collections: Albuquerque Mus., Bklyn. Mus., Guggenheim Mus., N.Y.C., Cin. Mus., Chgo. Art Inst., Ind. State Mus., Mus. Modern Art, N.Y.C., Library of Congress, Met. Mus., N.Y.C., N.Y. Pub. Libr., Mus. Fine Arts, Santa Fe, also, Boston, Indpls., Seattle, Phila., San Diego, Dallas, N.Mex., Worcester Art Museums, Los Angeles County Mus., Roswell Mus. and Art Ctr., Tucson Mus., murals, Ind. U., Butler U., Ind. State Office Bldg., Nat. Acad. Design, N.Y.C., N.Y., 2003. Combat artist with USCGR, World War II, PTO. Recipient Distinguished Alumni award Herron Sch. Art, 1972, N.Mex. Annual Gov.'s award, 1987; Grantee Nat. Endowment for Arts, 1983. Fellow NAD; mem. World Print Coun. (bd. dirs. 1980-87), Nat. Print Coun. Am. (co-pres. 1980-82), Coll. Art Assn. Am. (bd. dirs. 1977-80). Home: 5900 Canyon Vista Dr NE Albuquerque NM 87111-6621

ANUEBUNWA, CYNTHIA STATHAM, secondary education educator; b. Ft. Valley, Ga., June 1, 1954; d. Warren George and Evelyn (Mills) Statham; m. Frank David Anuebunwa, Dec. 30, 1978 (div.); children: El'Sharonika, Tiffany. BS in Edn., Ft. Valley State Coll., 1976, MA in Mid. Grades Edn., 1982; cert. in adminstrn. and supervision, U. Ga., 1991; cert. leadership devel. trainer, Fort Valley State Coll., 1994; student, 1996—. Cert. tchr., Ga., 1976. Sec. Robins Logistic Ctr., Warner Robins, Ga., 1972-74, Ft. Valley State Coll., 1975-76; tchr. Taylor County Bd. Edn., Butler, Ga., 1976-94; asst. prin. Peach County High Sch., Fort Valley, Ga., 1994-96. Instr. devel. studies Ft. Valley State Coll., 1984—; advisor broadcasting jr. high sch. newspaper Taylor County Bd. Edn., Butler, 1976—, sponsor cheerleader squad, 1977-78, sponsor oral interpretation, 1985-86, coord. GAE spelling bee, 1989—, sec. lang. arts dept., 1989—, coord. jr. high sch. Black history, 1990, chair student of month program, 1990—, advisor journalism club, 1990—, CVAE interlocking tchr., 1990—; advisor Jr. High Jour., 1976-92; co-writer, chair Black History Quiz, 1991. Coord. com. tutorial program Zellner's Chapel 1st Born Ch., Ft. Valley, 1987-90, coord. Edn. Day, 1989-90, Sunday sch. tchr., youth pres., 1977-80, chair anniversary appreciation, 1977—; active Peach County PTO, 1986—, Smithsonian Nat. Assocs. Recipient English award Young Women Coun., 1975, 76, Leadership Govt. award Taylor County Assn. Edn., 1983, Leadership award Toastmasters Dist. 14, 1992; named Choir Mem. of Month 1st Born Ch., 1989-90, Most Dedicated Tchr., Butler community, 1991; presenter South Eastern Reading Conf., 1983. Mem. ASCD, NEA, Ga. Assn. Educators (pres., sec. 1982—), Ft. Valley Toastmasters Club (ednl. v.p., pres. 1991-93, competent toastmasters award 1993), English Club, Delta Sigma Theta. Democrat. Pentecostal. Avocations: writing, public speaking, reading, drawing, singing.

APANASOV, BORIS N. mathematics educator; b. Sukhobuzimskoe, Russia, Oct. 24, 1950; s. Nikolay Aleksandrovich and Aleksandra Mikhailovna A.; children: Tatjana, Anton, Nikolay. Magister, Novosibirsk State U., Russia, 1973; PhD in Math., Inst. Math. USSR Acad. Sci., 1976. Spl. researcher Inst. Math. Acad. Sci. USSR, Novosibirsk, 1973, sci. researcher, 1974-80; asst. prof. math. Novosibirsk State U., 1975-80, assoc. prof., 1980-82, Novosibirsk Elektro-Tech. Inst., 1982-88; sr. researcher Inst. Math., Acad. Sci. USSR, Novosibirsk, 1981—; prof. Inst. Math. Kl. Ohridski U., Sofia, Bulgaria, 1986. Mem. Math Sci. Rsch. Inst., Berkeley, Calif., 1989, 96-97; prof. math. Ohio State U., Columbus, 1990, Mittag-Leffler Inst. of Sweden Royal Acad., 1989, U. Autonoma de Barcelona, 1990-91, U. Okla., Norman, 1991—, Tokyo U., 1997, Paris-Sud U. at Orsay, 1998. Co-author: Kleinian Groups and Uniformization in Examples and Problems, 1981; author: Discrete Transformation Groups and Manifold Structures, 1983, Discrete Groups in Space and Uniformization Problems, 1991, Geometry of Discrete Groups and Manifolds, 1991, Conformal Geometry of Discrete Groups and Manifolds, 2000; co-editor: Topology 90, 1992, Geometry, Topoloty and Physics, 1997. Mem. Am. Math. Soc., Siberian Math. Soc., Japanese Soc. Promotion of Sci. Office: Univ of Okla Dept Math Norman OK 73019-0001

APGAR, BARBARA SUE, physician, educator; b. Guthrie, Okla., Oct. 4, 1943; d. Wallace Duke and Gloria Jayne (Glover) McMillin; 1 child, Laria Ann. BA in Biology, Loretto Heights Coll., 1965; MS in Anatomy, U. Mich., 1968; MD, Tex. Tech. Med. Sch., 1976. Diplomate Am. Bd. Family Practice, Am. Bd. Med. Examiners; cert. instr. advanced life support sys. Rsch. asst. Parke Davis, Ann Arbor, Mich., 1965-66, Aerospace Med. Labs., Wright-Patterson AFB, Ohio, 1968-70; instr. anatomy dept. Tex. Tech. U., Lubbock, 1972-74, resident in family practice, 1976-79, clin. asst. prof., 1980-83; physician The Pavillion, Lubbock, 1981-83; sr. physician, dir. gynecology clinic U. Mich., 1983-86; instr. dept. family practice, 1984-89; asst. prof., 1989-93; assoc. prof., 1993—. Med. dir. Briawood Health Ctr., 1986—, also mem. steering com. for ambulatory care, dir. women's health, 1989—, asst. residency dir. dept. family practice, 1991—; dir. women;s health course Am. Acad. Family Practice; mem. staff Meth. Hosp., St. Mary of the Plains Hosp., U. Mich. Hosp.; mem. med. exec. com. dept. family practice U. Mich.; advanced life support in obstetrics instr., 1995—. Editl. reviewer Jour. Am. Bd. Family Practice, 1991—, Jour. Family Practice, 1994—, Primary Care Clinics North Am., Oncology Series; assoc. editor: Am. Family Physician, 1993, 1994-95, editor gynecologic care, 1996; editl. bd., co-editor: primary care series The Female Patient; cons. editor: Clinics in Family Practice. Mem. adv. bd. Lubbock chpt. March of Dimes, 1972-74. Recipient Upjohn Achievement award, 1976, Psychiatry Achievement award, 1976; Soroptimist Internat. grantee, 1978-79; fellow Mich. state U., 1989-90. Mem. Am. Acad. Family Practice (task force on clin. policy 1991, mem. faculty procedural skills), Am. Assn. Med. Writers, Lubbock County Med. Soc., Tex. Med. Assn., Mich. Acad. Family Practice (perinatal com. 1986&, sci. assembly program com.), Soc.. Tchrs. Family Medicine, Am. Soc. Colcoscopy and Cervical Pathology (task force on resident edn., mem. com. on colcoscopy recognition award, mem. multidisciplinary com., bd. dirs.), Alpha Omega Alpha. Democrat. Home: 883 Scio Meadows Dr Ann Arbor MI 48103-1586 Office: U Mich Chelsea Family Practice Dept 14700 E Old Us Highway 12 Chelsea MI 48118-1185

APOSTOLIDES, ANTHONY DEMETRIOS, economist, educator; b. Thessaloniki, Greece; s. Demos Demetrios and Kalliopi (Papadourakis) A.; m. Ipatia Koumoundouros, Feb. 20, 1996. BA in Econs., U. Cin., 1965; MA in Econs., U. Pitts., 1966; PhD in Econs., U. Oxford, Eng., 1970. Economist The Conf. Bd., N.Y.C., 1972-74; assoc. econ. affairs officer UN, Geneva, 1975-78; economist Inst. Internat. Law Econ. Devel., Washington, 1978-79, Jack Faucucett Assocs., Chevy Chase, Md., 1979-80; asst. prof. econs. Mary Washington Coll., Fredericksburg, Va., 1981-85; economist III Dept. Health Mental Hygiene, Balt., 1985-88; asst. prof. pub. and environ. affairs Ind. U., South Bend, 1988-95; prin. cons. ADA Assocs., Cin., 1995—. Summer faculty fellow Ind. U., 1989; adj. instr. U. Cin., 1996—; vis. asst. prof. econs. Miami U., Oxford, Ohio, 1997. Author: Energy Consumption in Manufacturing, 1974, Overseas R&D by U.S. Multinationals 1966-1975, 1976. Capt. U.S. Army, 1970-72. NuTone Inc. scholar, Cin., 1962-65; Whitney-Carnegie grantee ALA, Chgo., 1997. Greek Orthodox. Avocations: writing, tennis. Office: ADA Assocs 9217 Hunters Creek Dr Cincinnati OH 45242-6646

APPA, ANNA ANIKO, biology educator, Latin educator, writer, poet, editor; b. Budapest, Hungary, Oct. 25, 1948; d. Zoltan Akos and Elizabeth (Szilagyi) Kovacs; m. Anthony Michael Appa, June 9, 1976. BS in Culture Comms. cum laude, Nyack Coll., 1976; MREd, Gordon-Conwell Theol. Sem., 1983; tchr. diploma, Evangelical Tchr. Tng. Assn., 1983. Cert. tchr., profl. nutritionist. Rsch. asst. in biology/botany W.Va. U., Morgantown, 1969-74; histology lab. technician Morgantown Lab., 1973-75; office mgr., med./bus. asst. at pvt. dental practice Ipswich, Mass., 1978-79; faculty asst., manuscript editor, coord. Gordon-Conwell Theol. Seminary, So. Hamilton, Mass., 1979-81, instr., supr., counselor, resdl. adv., 1981-83; med. exec., clin. rsch. asst. Willowdale Med. Ctr., So. Hamilton, 1983-84, Pollen Rsch. Assocs., Inc., Wenham, Mass., 1985-86; program asst., proposal writer, researcher Gordon-Conwell Theol. Sem., 1986-89; sci. writer, editor, abstractor Acad. Editing, So. Hamilton, 1989-91; project mgr., asst. librarian Gordon Conwell Theol. Sem., So. Hamilton, 1991-92; instr. biology, Latin Essex Christian Acad., So. Hamilton, 1992-95; instr. botany Gordon Coll., Wenham, 1994, instr. biology lab., 1995; editor Ebsco Pub. Inc., 2002—. Author/poet: (anthology) Tomboy of the Tisza, 1994 (Best New Poems award Poets' Guild 1994), The Feeder and the Chicadee, 1994 (Iliad Lit. award 1994), Majestic Mystery Silent Orb, 1995 (Lit. award Nat. Libr. Poetry 1995), Spun Silver, Crystal, Frosty Forest, 1995 (award The Amherst Soc. 1995); author more than 200 poems. Newbern scholar Allliance Theol. Seminary, 1976, 77, Tele-Missions Acad. scholar, 1976, Eva P. Mosley scholar, 1975, Creative Writing scholar Hungarian Reformed Fedn. Am., 1970; Pa. Higher Edn. Assist. grantee, 1968-72. Mem. North Shore Poet's Forum, Mass. State Poetry Soc., Inc., North Shore Poets Forum, Nat. Fedn. State Poetry Socs., Inc., Phi Alpha Chi (scholar 1983). Avocations: health, adult education, family life enrichment, classical and operatic music. Home: 101 Colonial Dr Apt 133 Ipswich MA 01938

APPEL, NINA SCHICK, law educator, dean; b. Feb. 17, 1936; d. Leo and Nora Schick; m. Alfred Appel Jr.; children: Karen Oshman, Richard. Student, Cornell U.; JD, Columbia U., 1959. Instr. Columbia Law Sch., 1959-60; adminstr. Stanford U., mem. faculty, prof. law, 1973—, assoc. dean, 1976-83; dean Sch. Law Loyola U., 1983—. Mem. Am. Bar Found., Ill. Bar Found., Chgo. Bar Found., Chgo. Legal Club, Chgo. Network. Jewish. Office: Loyola U Sch Law 1 E Pearson St Chicago IL 60611-2055

APPEL, ROBERT EUGENE, lawyer, educator; b. Cleve., Oct. 18, 1958; s. Robert Donald and Jean Ann (Crites) Appel; m. Margaret Rose Curley, Aug. 24, 1985. BS, Cen. Conn. State U., 1980; JD, U. Bridgeport, Conn., 1982; MBA, U. Conn., 1984; LLM, Boston U., 1984. Bar: Conn. 1983. Asst. mgr. fin. services Lexington Ins. Co., Boston, 1984-85; tax. cons. Touche Ross and Co., Stamford, Conn., 1985-86; asst. dir. nat. design CIGNA Corp., Bloomfield, Conn., 1986—88, dir. nat. design, 1988—97; asst. v.p. Lincoln Nat. Life Ins. Co., Hartford, 1998—2002, 2d v.p., 2002—. Lectr. Real Estate Tng. and Ednl. Svcs., Bridgeport, 1985—88; lectr. real estate Dare Inst., Southbury, 1991—. Divsn. coord. United Way, 1988. Mem.: ABA, Conn. Bar Assn. Republican. Roman Catholic. Avocations: investing, running, weightlifting, motorcycling. Home: 80 Kingston Dr East Hartford CT 06118-2450 Office: Lincoln Fin Group 350 Church St Hartford CT 06103-1106

APPELBAUM, JUDITH PILPEL, editor, consultant, educator; b. N.Y.C., Sept. 26, 1939; d. Robert Cecil and Harriet Florence (Fleischl) Pilpel; m. Alan Appelbaum, Apr. 16, 1961; children: Lynn Stephanie, Alexander Eric. BA with honors, Vassar Coll., 1960. Editor Harper's Mag., N.Y.C., 1960-74; mng. editor Harper's Weekly, 1974-76; sr. cons. Atlas World Press Rev., 1977; mng. editor Pubs. Weekly, 1978-81, contbg. editor, 1981-82; columnist N.Y. Times Book Rev., 1982-84; founder Sensible Solutions, Inc., 1979, mng. dir., 1984—. Assoc. dir. Ctr. for Book Rsch., U. Scranton, 1985—88; book rev. editor Pub. Rsch. Quar., 1984—86; editor in chief, 1986—88; cons. editor, 1988—; chair book industry sys. adv. com. royalty subcom., 1996—98; chair Book Industry Standards and Comm. Rights Com., 1998—; mem. exec. com. BISAC, 1998—; vice chair, 1999—2002; contbg. editor Small Press mag., 1991—96; adv. bd. Foreward Mag., 1999—2001; mem. faculty Pub. Inst., U. Denver, 1981—; mem. CUNY Edn. in Publs. Program, 1982; chair Book Industry Study Group Publs., 1980—; adv. coun. mem. Small Press Ctr., 1998—; mem. rsch. com. Book Industry Study Group, 1984—, bd. dirs., 1997—, exec. com., 1998—; adv. bd. Coordinating Coun. Lit. Mags., 1980—84, PEN Ctr. USA West, 1988—90. Author: How to Get Happily Published, 1978, 5th edit., 1998, (with Fl. Janovic) The Writer's Workbook: A Full and Friendly Guide to Boosting Your Book's Sales, 1991; editor: (with T. Jones and G. Cravens) The Big Picture: A Wraparound Book, 1976, The Question of Size in the Book Industry Today, 1978, Getting a Line on Backlist, 1979, Paperback Primacy, 1981, Small Publisher Power, 1982; editor-at-large Publishers Mktg. Assn. Newsletter, 2001—. Mem.: PEN, Pubs. Mktg. Assn. (bd. dirs. 1990—92, Benjmain Franklin Lifetime Achievement award 1995), Women's Media Group (bull. editor 1990—92), Authors Guild. Office: Sensible Solutions Inc 500 Croton Lake Rd Mount Kisco NY 10549-4233 E-mail: verysensibly@aol.com.

APPENZELLER, HERB THOMAS, retired education administrator, coach; b. Newark, Sept. 28, 1925; s. Thomas Theodore and Helen Bertha (Hadley) A.; children: Thomas, Linda, Mary; m. Ann Terrill, Feb. 26, 1994. BA, Wake Forest U., 1948, MA, 1951; EdD, Duke U., 1966. Cert. tchr., N.C. Tchr. Rolesville (N.C.) H.S., 1948-50, Wakelon H.S., Zebulon, N.C., 1950-51, Chowan Coll., Murfreesboro, N.C., 1951-56, Guilford Coll., Greensboro, N.C., 1956-93, coach, 1956-62, athletic dir., 156-87, dean of students, 1964-65; retired, 1965. Cons. sport law. Author 10 books, including 7 in field of sports law; editor 17 books; co-editor Sport Law Newsletter. Recipient Disting. Svc. award Guildford Coll., 1993, Chowan Coll., 1993, Leadership award SSLASPA, 1999, Presdl. award SSLASPA, 2002, Guy M. Lewis Acad. Achievement award Internat. Sports Conf., 2002; named to Four Sports Halls of Fame, NAIA. Mem. AAHPERD, N.C. Assn. Health, Phys. Edn., Recreation and Dance, Nat. Assn. Collegiate Dirs. Athletics (Acad./Athletics award 1989). Presbyterian. Avocation: golf. Home and Office: 7503 Somersby Dr Summerfield NC 27358-8292

APPLE, MARTIN ALLEN, science executive, scientist, educator; b. Duluth, Minn., Sept. 17, 1938; m. M. Daina; children: Deborah Dawn, Pamela Ruth, Nathan, Rebeccah Lynn AB, ALA, U. Minn., 1959, MSc, 1962; PhD, U. Calif., 1968. Chmn. Multidisciplinary Drug Rsch. Group U. Calif., San Francisco, 1974-78; pres. IPRI, San Carlos, Calif., 1978-81; with EAN-Tech., Inc., Daly City, Calif., 1982-84, chmn. bd., 1983-84; with Adytum Internat., Mountain View, Calif., 1982-90, CEO, 1983-90, LEADERS, Washington, 1989—; pres., Coun. Sci. Soc. Presidents, Washington, 1993—; CEO Sci. Watch, Inc., 1996-98. With Hon. Doug Walgren co-chair Leadership Network, 1995-97; adj. prof. U. Calif., San Francisco, 1982-84; cons. SRI Internat. Dept. Edn., EPA, NIH, NSF, The Network, Hughes-GM, Nat. Cancer Inst., AAAS, Nat. Sci. Tchrs. Assn., others; adj. rsch. prof. George Mason U., Fairfax, Va., 1991-92; vis. scholar Nat. Humanities Ctr., 1990-91; nat. project mgr. NSTA Scope Sequence and Coordination Project, 1991-92; bd. dirs. Am. Med. Progress Ednl. Found.; bd. dirs. ACCTION, Inc., chmn. trustees, 1995-96; expert advisor Dept. of Edn., 1996-2001; mem. blue ribbon panel USDA, 2000-01; chmn. bd. trustees Ctr. Advanced Rsch. Behavioral Neurobiology U. Ill., Chgo., 2002-03; chmn. bd. visitors U. Md./U. Md. Biotech. Inst., 1999-2003. Author: (with F. Myers) Review Medical Pharmacology, 1976; (with M. Fink) Immune RNA in Neoplasia, 1976; (with F. Becker et al) Cancer: A Comprehensive Treatise, 1977; (with M. Keenberg et al) Investing in Biotechnology, 1981; (with F. Ahmad et al) From Genes to Proteins: Horizons in Biotechnology, 1983; (with J. Kureczka) Status of Biotechnology, 1987; (with M. Baum) Business Advantage, 1987 (winner Excellence award Software Pubs. Assn. 1987), (with R. Yager) Translating and Using Research for Improving Teacher Education in Science and Mathematics, 1998; mem. editl. bd. Computers in Medicine Mem. Calif. Coun. Indsl. Innovation, 1982. Recipient citation, East West Ctr. Bd. of Govs., 1988, Leadership citation, Coun. Sci. Soc. Pres., 1995, Support of Sci. award, 2002. Fellow Am. Coll. Clin. Pharmacology, Am. Inst. Chemists, Phi Beta Kappa Assocs. (Disting. Svc. award 1984, 85); mem. Assn. Venture Founders (bd. govs. 1982-83), East-West Ctr. Assn. (trustee 1982-88, vice chmn. 1983-85), Profl. Software Programmers Assn., Leaders of Tomorrow (chmn. 1987-88), Commonwealth Club Calif., Phi Beta Kappa, Sigma Xi (bd. dirs., chmn. long-range strategic planning com. 1988-92). Office: Coun Sci Soc Presidents PO Box 33999 Washington DC 20033-0999 also: PO Box 905 Benicia CA 94510-0905 E-mail: cssp@acs.org.

APPLEBAUM, EDWARD LEON, otolaryngologist, educator; b. Detroit, Jan. 14, 1940; s. M. Lawrence and Frieda (Millman) A.; m. Amelia J. Applebaum; children: Daniel Ira, Rachel Anne. AB, Wayne State U., 1961, MD, 1964. Diplomate: Am. Bd. Otolaryngology. Intern Univ. Hosp., Ann Arbor, Mich., 1964-65; resident Mass. Eye and Ear Infirmary Harvard Med. Sch., Boston, 1966-69; practice medicine specializing in otolaryngology Chgo., 1972—; assoc. prof. Northwestern U. Med. Sch., 1972-79; prof., head dept. otolaryngology, head and neck surgery Coll. Medicine, U. Ill., 1979-2000; acting chmn. dept. otolaryngolgoy Northwestern U. Med. Sch., Chgo., 2000—02, prof., 2000—, chmn. dept. otolaryngolgoy, 2002—. Mem. staff Northwestern Meml. Hosp. Author: Tracheal Intubation, 1976; mem. editorial bd. Am. Jour. Otolaryngology, Laryngoscope. Served as maj. U.S. Army, 1969-71. Recipient Anna Albert Keller Rsch. award Wayne State U. Coll. Medicine, 1964, Disting. Alumni award, 1989, William Beaumont Soc. Original Rsch. award, 1964. Fellow ACS, Am. Soc. for Head and Neck Surgery, Am. Acad. Facial Plastic and Reconstructive Surgery, Am. Acad. Otolaryngology, Head and Neck Surgery, Am. Laryngol., Rhinol. and Otol. Soc. (v.p. 1993, pres. 2000), Am. Laryngol. Assn., Am. Otol. Soc., Soc. Univ. Otolaryngologists, Head and Neck Surgeons (pres. 1988), Assn. Acad. Depts. Otolaryngology-Head and Neck Surgery (pres. 1995-96). E-mail: eapple@northwestern.edu.*

APPLEBERRY, JAMES BRUCE, higher education consultant; b. Waverly, Mo., Feb. 22, 1938; s. James Earnest and Bertha Viola (Lane) A.; m. Patricia Ann Trent, June 5, 1960; children: John Mark, Timothy David. BS, Central Mo. State Coll., 1960; MS, Cen. Mo. State Coll., 1963, EdS, 1967; postgrad., U. Kans., 1967; Ed.D., Okla. State U., 1969. Tchr. Knob Noster (Mo.) Pub. Sch., 1960-62; prin. Knob Noster Elem. Sch., 1962-63, Knob Noster Jr. High Sch., 1963-64; minister edn. Wornall Rd. Bapt. Ch., Kansas City, Mo., 1964-65; grad. fellow Cen. Mo. State Coll., Warrensburg, 1965-66, asst. dir. field service, 1966-67; grad. asst. Okla. State U., 1968-69, asst. prof. ednl. adminstrn., 1969-71, assoc. prof., 1971-73, prof., head dept. adminstrn. and higher edn., 1972-75; Am. Council on Edn. fellow acad. adminstrn. internship program U. Kans., Lawrence, 1973-74, dir. planning, prof. adminstrn., founds. and higher edn., 1975-76, asst. to chancellor, prof., 1976-77; pres. Pittsburg (Kans.) State U., 1977-83, No. Mich. U., Marquette, 1983-91, Am. Assn. of State Coll. and Univs., Washington, 1991-99, Appleberry Enterprises, 1999—; sr. cons. Acad. Search Consultation Svc., 2001—. Plenary rep. Univ. Council for Ednl. Adminstrn., 1968-72, mem. exec. com., 1973-76; ednl. adminstrn. rep. Council on Tchr. Edn., 1968-75; chmn. Am. Council Edn. Commn. Leadership Devel. and Acad. Adminstrn.; abstracter Univ. Council for Ednl. Adminstrn., Columbus, Ohio, 1969-75; asst. state liaison rep. to Am. Assn. Colls. for Tchr. Edn., 1971; coordinator Interested Profs. Ednl. Adminstrn.; cons. North Cen. Okla. Assn. Sch. Adminstrs.; vice chmn. adv. council Nat. Council Edn. Stats., 1980-83; Kans. rep. to Am. Assn. State Colls. and Univs., 1980-81; pres. Nat. Coll. Athletics Assn. Pres.'s Commn., 1988-89; chmn. bd. dirs. Thoroughbred Techs., 2000-02. Contbr. articles to ednl. jours. Trustee Marquette Gen. Hosp.; bd. dirs. Actor's Theatre, 2003—. Named Outstanding Alumnus Cen. Mo. State U., 1987, Disting. Alumnus Okla. State U., 1987. Mem. NEA, Am. Assn. for Higher Edn., Am. Assn. State Colls. and Univs. (chmn. policy and purposes com.), Am. Ednl. Rsch. Assn., Nat. Conf. Profs. Ednl. Adminstrn., Exec. Club Louisville, Mace and Torch, Rotary, Masons (33 deg.), Phi Delta Kappa, Phi Kappa Phi, Kappa Delta, Phi Sigma Phi, Kappa Mu Epsilon, Alpha Kappa Psy. Home: 504 Jarvis Ln Louisville KY 40207-1313

APPLEGATE, MINERVA IRONS, nursing educator, nurse; b. Lakewood, N.J., Mar. 8, 1939; d. Alfred Harold and Nancy Virgina (Webb) Irons. AAS, Ocean County Coll., Toms River, N.J., 1968; BSN, U. Miami, Fla., 1971; MEd, Columbia U., Fla., 1974; EdD, Columbia U., 1981. Nursing instr. U. Miami, Coral Gables, Fla., 1974; prof. of nursing U. South Fla., Tampa, 1976-89; dir., chair dept. nursing U. Tampa, 1990-92; pvt. practice cons., expert witness Brandon, Fla., 1992—. Project dir. W.K. Kellogg Found. Grant, U. South Fla., Tampa, 1984-88. Contbr. articles and rsch. to profl. jours. Mem. Fla. Nurses Assn., Sigma Theta Tau, Phi Kappa Phi, Pi Lambda Theta, EpsilonTau Lambda. Home and Office: 3020 Colonial Ridge Dr Brandon FL 33511-7643

APPLEMAN, PHILIP, poet, writer, educator; b. Feb. 8, 1926; m. Marjorie Haberkorn. BS in English, Northwestern U., 1950, PhD in English, 1955; AM in English, U. Mich., 1951; postgrad., U. Lyon, France, 1951-52. Teaching asst. Northwestern U., Evanston, Ill., 1953-55; instr. English Ind. U., Bloomington, 1955-58, asst. prof., 1958-62, assoc. prof., 1962-67, prof., 1967-82, disting. prof., 1982-86, disting. prof. emeritus, 1986—. Dir., instr. in world lit. and philosophy Internat. Sch. Am., 1960-63; vis. prof. lit. SUNY, Purchase, 1973; vis. prof. English Columbia U., 1974; panelist NEH, Washington, 1968, applications judge, 1978, 80; adv. panel Ind. Arts Commn., 1971; cons. NEH-sponsored Project on Ethics and Values in Health Care Columbia U. Coll. Physicians and Surgeons, 1979-81; lectr. in field, poetry reader. Author: The Silent Explosion, 1965, 2d edit., 1966, Portuguese transl., 1973, (poetry) Kites on a Windy Day, 1967, Summer Love and Surf, 1968, Open Doorways, 1976, Darwin's Ark, 1984, Darwin's Bestiary, 1986, Let There Be Light, 1991, New and Selected Poems, 1956-96, 1996, (novels) In the Twelfth Year of the War, 1970, Shame the Devil, 1981, Apes and Angels, 1989; founding co-editor Victorian Studies, 1957—63; co-editor: 1859: Entering an Age of Crisis, 1959; editor: The Origin of Species, 1975, 2d edit., 2002, An Essay on the Principle of Population, 1976, 2d edit., 2003, Darwin, 1970, 3d edit., 2001; contbr. articles to profl. jours., chpts. to books. Co-founder Bloomington Civil Liberties Union; faculty adviser Ind. U. Civil Liberties Union, Bloomington. Served with AC U.S. Army, 1944-45; served with U.S. Mcht. Marine, 1946, 48-49. Recipient Citation for In the Twelfth Year of the War Ind. Authors's Day, 1971, Humanist Arts award, 1994, Friends of Darwin award Nat. Ctr. for Sci. Edn., 2003; Fulbright scholar France, 1951-52; Huntington Hartford Found. fellow, 1964, Nat. Endowment for Arts fellow, 1975. Mem.: PEN, MLA (sec. English sect. II 1965, chmn. 1966, chmn. exec. com. 1972), AAUP (pres. Ind. U. chpt. 1968—69, nat. coun. 1969—72), Nat. Ctr. Sci. Edn. (Friends of Darwin award 2003), Authors Guild, Acad. Am. Poets, Poets Ho. (poets adv. com. 1987—), Poetry Soc. Am. (awards judge 1970, 1971, 1974, 1976, 1979, governing bd. 1981—83, Christopher Morley Meml. award 1970, Alice Fay di Castagnola award 1975), Nat. Coun. Tchrs. English, Phi Beta Kappa. Home: PO Box 39 Sagaponack NY 11962-0039

APPLETON, JAMES ROBERT, university president, educator; b. North Tonawanda, N.Y., Jan. 20, 1937; s. Robert Martin and Emma (Mollnow) A.; m. Carol Koelsch, Aug. 8, 1959; children: Steven, Jon, Jennifer. AB in Social Sci., Wheaton Coll., 1958; MA, PhD, Mich. State U., 1965. Lectr. Mich. State U., East Lansing, 1969-72; assoc. dean students Oakland U., Rochester, Mich., 1965-68, dean student life, 1968-72, assoc. prof. behavioral scis., 1969-72, v.p., 1969-72; v.p. student affairs U. So. Calif., L.A., 1972-82, v.p. devel., 1982-87; pres., Univ. prof. U. Redlands, Calif., 1987—. Author: Pieces of Eight: Rights, Roles & Styles of the Dean; guest editor Nat. Assn. Student Pers. Adminstrs. Jour., 1971; contbr. articles to profl. jours. Bd. dirs. So. Calif. Ind. Colls.; bd. dirs., treas., mem. exe. com. Nat. Assn. Ind. Colls. and Univs.; mem. exec. com. Inland Empire Econ. Partnership; mem. nat. exec. com. Tuition Exch.; trustee San Francisco Presbyn. Sem., 1985-95. 1st lt. U.S. Army, 1958-60. Named One of 100 Emerging Young Leaders in Higher Edn., Am. Council Edn./Change, 1978; recipient Fred Turner award Nat. Assn. Student Personnel Adminstrs., 1980. Mem. NCAA (pres.'s commn.), Assn. Ind. Calif. Colls. & Univs. (govtl. rels. com.), Am. Assn. Higher Edn., Western Coll. Assn. (past pres.). Avocations: music performance and appreciation, athletics. Home: 1861 Rossmont Dr Redlands CA 92373-7219 Office: U Redlands 1200 E Colton Ave PO Box 3080 Redlands CA 92373-0999

APPLIN, CATHERINE BALASH, primary school educator, consultant; b. Syracuse, N.Y., Aug. 7, 1943; d. Anthony George and Lois (Tucker) Balash; m. Frank Michael Applin, Nov. 21, 1965; children: Heidi Applin Flynn, John Applin. BA, Syracuse U., 1965; Edn. Cert., Ladycliff Coll., 1972-74; MS in Edn. with Spl. Edn. Concentration, Simmons Coll., Boston, 1996. Cert. tchr., N.Y., Kans., gen. edn., spl. edn., Mass. Early childhood educator, 1976-92; spl. edn. tchr. Arlington (Va.) Pub. Schs., 1996—. Adv. bd. mem. St. Bartholomew's Kindergarten, Bethesda, 1980-83; cons. St. Peter's Kindergarten, Olney, 1989-90, dir. early childhood assessment St. Bartholomew's Sch., Bethesda, 1981-83, St. Peter's Sch., Olney, 1990-92; curriculum devel. cons. Archdiocese of Washington, 1991-92. Bd. trustees St. John's Pre-Sch., Washington, 1998. Avocations: collecting american art and antiques, writing poetry and songs, travel.

APRISON, MORRIS HERMAN, biochemist, experimental and theoretical neurobiologist, emeritus educator; b. Milw., Oct. 6, 1923; s. Henry and Ethel Aprison; m. Shirley Reder, Aug. 21, 1949; children— Barry, Robert. BS in Chemistry, U. Wis., 1945, tchrs. cert., 1947, MS in Physics, 1949, PhD in Biochemistry, 1952. Grad. teaching asst. in physics U. Wis., Madison, 1947-49; grad. research asst. in pathology Sch. Medicine, 1950-51, grad. research asst. in biochemistry, 1951-52; tech. asst. in physics Inst. Paper Chemistry, Appleton, Wis., 1949-50; biochemist, prin. investigator, head biophysics sect. Galesburg (Ill.) State Research Hosp., 1952-56; prin. research investigator in biochemistry Inst. Psychiat. Research; asst. prof. depts. biochemistry and psychiatry Ind. U. Med. Sch., Indpls., 1956-60, asso. prof., 1960-64, prof. biochemistry, 1964-78, distinguished prof. neurobiology and biochemistry, 1978-93, disting. prof. emeritus, 1993—, chief neurobiology sect., 1969-74. Mem. exec. com. dept. psychiatry, exec. adminstr. Inst. Psychiat. Rsch., 1973-74, dir. inst., 1974-78, chief sect. applied and theoretical neurobiology, 1978-93; co-chmn. session on neurotransmitters 23d Internat. Physiol. Congress, 1965; chmn. session neurochemistry and neuropharmacology 25th Congress, 1971; ad hoc mem. study sect. psychopharmacology NIMH, 1967-71, mem. neuropsychology study sect., 1970-74; mem. molecular and cellular neurobiology program adv. panel NSF, 1984-86; mem. com. recommendations U.S. Army sci. rsch. Nat. Rsch. Coun. Bd. Physics and Astronomy, 1987-89; mem. gov. bd. Inst. for Advanced Study Ind. U., Bloomington, 1989-92; vis. prof. 4th ASPET Workshop, Vanderbilt U., 1972; guest scholar Grad. Sch., Kans. State U., 1973. Adv. editor Neurosci. Rsch., 1968-73, Jour. Biol. Psychiatry, 1968-83, Neuropharmacology, 1969-93, Jour. Neurochemistry, 1972-75, Pharmacology, Biochemistry and Behavior, 1973-89, Jour. Comparative and General Pharmacology, 1974-75, Jour. Gen. Pharmacology, 1975-93, Jour. Developmental Psychobiology, 1974-77; regional editor Life Scis., 1970-73; co-editor Advances in Neurochemistry, 1973-92; mem. editorial bd. Jour. Neurochemistry, 1975-79, dep. chief editor, 1980-83; mem. editorial bd. Neurochem. Rsch., 1975-82, Jour. Neurosci. Rsch., 1984-92; co-editor 10 books; contbr. more than 355 rsch. articles and abstracts to profl. jours., chpts. to books, including one in History of Neuroscience in Autobiography, vol. 3, 2001. Mem. Ind. regional adv. bd. Anti-Defamation League, 1973-76; bd. overseers St. Meinrad Sem., 1974-77. Served with USNR, 1944-46. Prof. M.H. Aprison awards for best rsch. toward PhD in med. neurobiology at dept. psychiatry Ind. U. Sch. Medicine created in his honor, 1999. Mem. Am. Physiol. Soc., Biophys. Soc., Soc. Biol. Psychiatry (program com. 1974-75, co-chmn. 1975-76, gold medal 1975), Internat. Brain Rsch. Orgn., Internat. Soc. Neurochemistry (co-chmn. session 1st internat. meeting Strasbourg, France 1967, 4th meeting Tokyo 1973, 7th meeting Jerusalem 1979, coun. 1973-75, sec. 1975-79, chmn. 1979-81, publicity com. 1975-83, nominating com. 1983-87, policy adv. com. 1985-98, ad hoc and founding rules com. 1998-2000, standing rules com., 2000—), Am. Soc. Neurochemistry (co-chmn. sci. program com. 1972, mem. 1973), Soc. for Neurosci. (pres. Indpls. chpt. 1970-71), Sigma Xi. Home: 9268 Spring Forest Dr Indianapolis IN 46260-1266 E-mail: maprison@iupui.edu.

APSELOFF, MARILYN FAIN, English educator; b. Attleboro, Mass. d. Arthur A. and Eva (Lubchansky) Fain; m. Stanford S. Apseloff, Nov. 21, 1956; children: Roy, Stan and Glen (twins), Lynn Susan. Student, Bryn Mawr Coll., 1952-54; BA, U. Cin., 1956, MA, 1957. From instr. to prof. English Kent (Ohio) State U., 1968—2003; ret., 2003. Adv. bd. mem. Parents' Choice, Waban, Mass., 1978—. Author: They Wrote for Children Too, 1989, Elizabeth George Speare, 1991; co-author: Nonsense Literature for Children, 1989 (award 1990); rev. editor Children's Literature Assn. Quarterly, 1984-87. Grad. fellow U. Cin., 1956-57. Mem. MLA (session chair 1977, 78), Children's Literature Assn. (pres. 1979-80, dir. Harvard conf. 1978). Avocations: bridge, swimming. Office: Kent State Univ English Dept Kent OH 44242-0001

APTEKAR, SHELDON I. speech, theatre, and performing art educator; b. Bklyn., Sept. 14, 1939; s. Al and Fanny (Horowitz) A. BA in Speech and Theatre, Bklyn. Coll., 1962; MA in Drama, Trinity U., 1964; postgrad. in Theatre, Northwestern U., 1966-68; PhD Equivalency in Theatre, CUNY, 1972. Mem. Repertory Co. Dallas Theater Ctr., 1962-64; asst. prof. speech and theatre L.I. U., Bklyn., 1964-66; lectr. in speech and theatre CUNY, Kingsborough C.C., Bklyn., 1969-70, asst. prof. speech and theatre, 1970-75, assoc. prof. speech and theatre, 1975-84, prof. speech and theatre, 1984-95, prof. speech, theatre, and performing arts, 1995—, dir. performing arts program, 2000—. Cons. theatre in edn. The Ednl. Alliance, N.Y.C., 1970-72; cons. staging spectacle Citibank's Bicentennial Spectacle, Bronx, N.Y., 1974-76; artistic advisor stand up comics No-Artificial Sweetner Co., N.Y.C., 1977-82; program developer performing arts Kingsborough C.C., 1994-98; lectr. in field. Co-prodr. Georgetown Prodns., Inc., N.Y.C., 1990-94; artistic dir. various play prodns.; awards dir. Kennedy Ctr. Am. Coll. Theatre Festival, region II, 1974, 84, 94; staged readings dir. Shakespeare's plays Genesis Repertory Ensemble, N.Y.C., 2003—. Mem., adjudicator Kennedy Ctr., Am. Coll. Theatre Festival, Region II; acting coach, 1994—, freelance dir. Recipient Cert. of Recognition, Centro Ecol. Akumal, 1998, citations in The Director as Artist, 1995, Theatre as the Essential Liberal Art in the American University, 2002; Study grant, Culture and the European Common Market in Belgium, 1985, Modern Drama and the Avant Garde, Mellon Found., 1986, Rsch. grantee, Kingsborough C., 2001—02, P.S./CUNY, 2002—. Mem. Am. Theatre Assn. (chair directing program 1981-83), Assn. for Theatre in Higher Edn., East Ctrl. Theatre Conf. (constl. com. 1985-89), Internat. Brecht Soc. Avocations: pen and ink drawing, photography, traveling, wood sculpturing. E-mail: saptekar@kbcc.cuny.edu.

AQEEL, SULAIMAN RAFEEQ SAADIQ (LAWRENCE EMEROLD BONNER), small business owner, minister, elementary school educator; b. Hot Springs Nat. Pk., Ark., Aug. 24, 1940; s. William Elrage Bonner Sr. and Myrtle Grady Bonner; m. Annette Jones (div.); m. Katie Williams-Lewis (div.); children: Charles Lewis Jr., Michael Lewis, Lauren Amanda. BS, Ark. AM&N (now U. Ark. at Pine Bluff), 1962. Notary, bookkeeper, Muslim minister, Hot Springs, 1977—; substitute tchr. Hot Springs Mid. Sch., 2000—. Author: Some Poems I Have Written, 1997. Mem. Garland County Interfaith Coun., Hot Springs, 1997—; bd. dirs. Webb Cmty. Ctr., Hot Springs, 1993—. With USAF, 1963—67. Decorated Purple Heart; named to Internat. Poetry Hall of Fame; recipient Mus of Fire Prometheus 200 award, Famous Poets Soc., 2001. Mem.: DAV (past. chmn., past sr. vice comdr. 1996—98), NAACP, Ga. Assn. Paralegals, Internat. Soc. Poets (named to Internat. Poetry Hall of Fame), Air Force Sgts. Assn., Am. Mil. Assn., Ark. Mil. Retirees Assn., Mil. Chaplin Assn., Shriners, Elks (sec. 1981—90), Am. Legion, Omega Psi Phi (keeper of record and seals 2001—02). Muslim. Avocations: reading, television, travel. Home: PO Box 956 338 Garden St Hot Springs National Park AR 71902-0956 E-mail: saqeel@hotmail.com.

ARAC, JONATHAN, English language educator; b. N.Y.C., Apr. 4, 1945; s. Benjamin and Evelyn (Charm) A. AB, Harvard U., 1967, MA, 1968, PhD, 1974. Jr. fellow Soc. Fellows Harvard U., Cambridge, Mass., 1970-73; asst. prof. English Princeton U., 1973-79; assoc. prof. U. Ill., Chgo., 1979-85, prof., 1985-86; prof. grad. program lit. Duke U., 1986-87; prof. English and comparative lit. Columbia U., 1987-90; prof. English U. Pitts., 1989-2000, Mellon prof. English, 2000-01; Harriman prof. English and comparative lit. Columbia U., 2001—. Assoc. dir. Inst. for Humanities, U. Ill., Chgo., 1983-84, dept. chair, 2001—; Drue Heinz vis. acad. Oxford U., 2000; Avalon disting. vis. prof. humanities Northwestern U., 2000. Author: Commissioned Spirits, 1979, Critical Genealogies, 1987, Huckleberry Finn as Idol and Target, 1997; editor: The Yale Critics: Deconstruction in America, 1983, Postmodernism and Politics, 1986, After Foucault, 1988, Consequences of Theory, 1990, Macropolitics of 19th Century Literature, 1991; contbr. to Cambridge History of American Literature, Vol. 2, 1995; mem. editl. bd. Comparative Lit., 1989—, Am. Lit., 2000—; asst. editor: Boundary 2: Jour. Postmodern Lit. and Culture, 1979—. Am. Coun. Learned Socs. fellow, 1978-79, NEH fellow, 1986-87, 94-95. Mem. MLA (mem. publs. com. 1997-2000), Soc. Critical Exch. (bd. dirs. 1983-90), English Inst. (mem. supervisory com. 1985-88, chmn. 1987-88), PMLA (mem. adv. com. 1990-94). Office: Columbia U Dept English & Comp Lit 602 Philosophy Hall New York NY 10027 E-mail: ja2007@columbia.edu.

ARAGONÉS-ENDA, LILLIAN ESTELLA, elementary educator; b. N.Y.C., June 8, 1954; d. Aragonés-Panis Fernando and Santa (Colon) Oyola; m. Robert Alan Enda, July 28, 1990; children: Damian Marcel Brown, Jeremy Isaiah. AA, Cumberland County Coll., 1974; BA in Elem. Edn., Glassboro State Coll., 1988; postgrad., Seton Hall U., 1995—. Resource lab. asst. Migrant/Bilingual Curriculum Resource, Vineland, N.J., 1981-82; bilingual/ESL tchr. Vineland Pub. Schs., 1983-87; bilingual tchr. Millville (N.J.) Pub. Schs., 1989-90; elem. tchr. Hillside (N.J.) Pub. Schs., 1990-97, Holocaust/tolerance presenter, 1997—. Outreach worker Casa Prac, Inc., Vineland, 1983-86; adult ESL instr. Cumberland County Coll., Vineland, 1986-87; adult ESL tchr. Atlantic City (N.J.) Casinos, 1986-87; reading tchr. Spark Summer Program, Vineland, 1989; dir. women's seminar N.J. Coun. of Humanities, Trenton, 1997. Editor: Lessons From the

Holocaust: Lesson Designs for Grades K-12, 1997. Participant ednl. seminar N.J. Holocaust Commn., Trenton, 1997; founding tchr. A.P. Morris Sr. Citizen Exch. Program, Hillside, 1996-97, A.P. Morris Homeless Collection Drive, Hillside, 1995-97; active pub. rels. Puerto Rican Festival N.J., Vineland, 1985-87. Recipient Axelrod award Anti-Defamation League, 1997, Technology in the Classroom award AT&T, 1995; grantee N.J. Coun. for Humanities, 1996. Mem. Puerto Rican Festival N.J. (pub. rels. com. 1985-87), ASCD. Avocations: art, writing, reading, storytelling. Office: AP Morris Sch 143 Coe Ave Hillside NJ 07205-2830

ARANDA, EVELYN BONNER, secondary educator; b. Dunn, N.C., July 24, 1953; d. Richard Foster and Louettie (Massengill) Bonner; m. Carlos Roberto Aranda, Aug. 9, 1986; children: Joshua Charles, Robert Caleb. BA in Arts Edn., Meth. Coll., Fayetteville, N.C., 1975; MA in Edn. and Sch. Adminstrn., Campbell U., Buies Creek, N.C., 1982. Cert. tchr., N.C. Tchr. visual arts Anne Chesnutt Jr. High Sch., Fayetteville, 1975-84, Cape Sr. High Sch., Fayetteville, 1984-88, Benson (N.C.) Elem. Sch., 1988-92, Benson Mid. Sch., 1992—. Bd. dirs. Benson Found. for Arts, 1989-91, Johnston County Arts Coun., Smithfield, N.C., 1989-91. Named Tchr. of Yr., Anne Chesnutt Jr. High Sch., 1980; Fulbright scholar Duke U., 1977. Mem. NEA, Nat. Art Edn. Assn., N.C. Art Edn. Assn., N.C. Edn. Assn., Johnston County Assn. Educators. Democrat. Methodist. Avocations: painting, crafts, reading. Home: 455 Turlington Dr Benson NC 27504-9709 Office: Benson Mid Sch 401 S Elm St Benson NC 27504-1717

ARANDA, JUAN M., JR., cardiologist, medical educator; b. San Juan, P.R., May 26, 1965; s. Juan M. and Carmen Aranda; m. Alysia L. Hines; children: Jennifer, Eva, Sarah. BS in Chemistry, U. P.R., 1987, MD, 1991; subsplty. degree in cardiology, U. South Fla., 1997; subsplty. degree in internal medicine, VA Med. Ctr., San Juan, 1994. Diplomate Am. Bd. Internal Medicine, Am. Bd. Cardiovascular Medicine. Resident VA Med. Ctr., San Juan, 1991—94; fellow in cardiology U. South Fla., Tampa, 1994—97; asst. prof. medicine divsn. cardiology U. Fla., Gainesville, 1997—. Chief cardiology fellow U. South Fla., 1996—97; cons. VA Med. Ctr., Gainesville, 1997—; assoc. dir. heart transplant program U. Fla., Gainesville, 2001—. Contbr. articles to profl. jours. Named one of Best Drs., 2001—02. Fellow: Am. Coll. Cardiology (Fla. chpt. govt. rels. com., 3d party reimbursement com.); mem.: Alachua County Med. Soc., Internat. Soc. Heart Lung Transplantation. Avocation: golf. Office: U Fla 1600 SW Archer Rd Box 100277 Gainesville FL 32610

ARANDIA, CARMELITA S. school administrator; b. Lemery, Batangas, The Philippines, Sept. 29, 1944; came to U.S., 1970; d. Vivencio and Eugenia (Serrano) A. MEd, Loyola U., Chgo., 1975. Cert. tchr., adminstr., Ill. Head tchr. Head Start program Evanston (Ill.)-Skokie Sch. Dist., 1985-89, asst. coord. Head Start and Cmty. Child Care, 1989-94, interim coord. Head Start and child care programs, 1994-96, dir. Head Start Program, 1996—. Mem. adv. bd. early childhood program Kendall Coll., Evanston, 1993—; mem. adv. bd. Early Start Local Interagy. Coun., Evanston, 1992—; mem. health adv. bd. Head Start Program, Evanston, 1989—. Democrat. Roman Catholic. Avocations: shopping, reading, health club. Office: Evanston/Skokie Sch Dist 3701 Davis St Skokie IL 60076-1744

ARANTES, JOSÉ CARLOS, industrial engineer, educator; b. Itamogi, Brazil, May 10, 1955; came to U.S., 1986; s. Antonio A. and Parizina (Marinzeck) A.; m. Nadia Maria Monti, July 26, 1986; children: Ellen Kay, Alex José, Isa Carolina. MSc in Indsl. Mgmt., Katholieke U. Leuven, Belgium, 1982; PhD in Indsl. Engring., U. Mich., 1991. Product engr. Kodak Co., Brazil, 1979-81; instr., cons. U. Campinas, Brazil, 1983-86; rsch. asst., tchg. asst. U. Mich., Ann Arbor, 1987-90; asst. prof. U. Cin., 1991-98; assoc. prof. EAESP-FGV, Brazil, 1997-98. Cons. Criminal Justice Task Force, Cin., 1992; co-founder, v.p. ImpEx Co.; cons. mgmt. sci., supply chain Anheuser-Busch, 1998—. Author: Degeneracy in Gereralized Networks, 1990; contbr. articles to profl. jours. 2d lt. Brazilian armed forces, 1973-75. Grantee Westinghouse Environ., Cin., 1992, County of Hamilton, Cin., 1992, Fernald Environ. Mng. Co., Cin., 1993-94, Revco, Inc., 1996-97, CVS, Inc., 1997. Mem. Sci. Rsch. Soc., Inst. Indsl. Engrs., Inst. Mgmt. Sci., Ops. Rsch. Soc. Am. Home: 361 Meadowbrook Dr Ballwin MO 63011-2414 E-mail: jarantes@aol.com., jose.arantes@anheuser-busch.com.

ARAOZ, DANIEL LEON, psychologist, educator; b. Buenos Aires, Apr. 23, 1930; came to U.S., 1951, naturalized, 1967; s. Jose Daniel and Maria Lia (Suarez) A.; m. Marie Carrese, July 27, 1991; m. Dorita Catherine Smyth, July 17, 1964 (div. 1984); children: Leon Daniel, Nadine Victoria. BA, Gonzaga U., 1953, MA, 1954; MST., U. Santa Clara, 1961; MA, Columbia U., 1964, EdD, 1969. Clin. psychologist, Ill., Pa. Diplomate in counseling psychology and family psychology Am. Bd. Profl. Psychology; diplomate in clin. hypnosis Am. Bd. Psychol. Hypnosis. Asst. chaplain Coll. Mt. St. Vincent, Bronx, N.Y., 1962-64; psychotherapist Cmty. Guidance Svc., N.Y.C., 1965-72, supr., 1972-82; faculty Am. Inst. Psychotherapy and Psychoanalysis, N.Y.C., 1972-82; assoc. prof. counseling L.I. U., 1973-82, prof., 1982—, chmn. dept. counseling and devel., 1995-97. Dir. L.I. Inst. Ericksonian Hypnosis, 1992-97. Editor-in-chief Am. Jour. Family Therapy, 1973-76, jour. adv., 1977—; author: Hypnosis and Sex Therapy, 1982, 98; Hypnosex, 1982; Self-Transformation Through the New Hypnosis, 1984; The New Hypnosis, 1985, 95, The New Hypnosis in Family Therapy, 1987; Selbst Hypnose: Kreative Imagination in Beruf und Alltag, 1992, Reengineering Yourself, 1994, Solution-Oriented Brief Therapy for Adjustment Disorders, 1996, Power Over Stress at Work, 1998; co-editor: Hypnosis Questions & Answers, 1986; contbr. articles to profl. jours. Named Hon. Prof. U. peruana Cayetano Heredia, Lima, Peru. Fellow APA, Am. Inst. Psychotherapy and Psychoanalysis, Am. Soc. Psychosomatic Dentistry and Medicine, Acad. Counseling Psychology, Acad. Family Psychology; mem. Am. Assn. Sex Educators (diplomate), Counselors and Therapists, Am. Assn. Marriage and Family Therapy (supr. 1973—), Pa. Psychol. Assn., Am. Mgmt. Assn. (unit trainer 1987-94). Home: 66 Gates Ave Malverne NY 11565-1912 Office: LI U CW Post Northern Blvd Greenvale NY 11548-1207

ARASTOOPOUR, HAMID, chemical engineering educator; b. Shirvan, Iran, Sept. 1, 1951; came to U.S., 1973; m. Sheila Norolouny, July 10, 1983; children: Golnaz, Nassim. BS, Abadan (Iran) Inst. Tech., 1973; MS, Ill. Inst. Tech., 1975, PhD, 1978. Adj. prof., rsch. engr. Inst. Gas Tech., Desplain, Ill., 1978-85; assoc. prof. Ill. Inst. Tech., Chgo., 1985-89, prof., chmn., 1989—, chmn. chem. and environ. engring. dept., 1995. Governing bd. Coun. Chem. Rsch. Author gas-solid flow sect. Ency. Fluid Mechanics, 1986; mem. editl. bd. Powder Tech. Jour., 1990—; contbr. over 50 articles to profl. jours. including AIChE Jour., Chem. Engring. Sci. and Power Tech. Jour. Recipient Univ. Excellence in Tchg. award Amoco Found., 1993. Mem. AIChE (chmn. area 3b 1995, Ernest W. Thiele award 1997, Fluor Danniel award 1999, Donald Q. Kim award 2001). Home: 7612 Florence Ave Downers Grove IL 60516-4445 Office: Ill Inst Tech 10 W 33rd St Chicago IL 60616-3730

ARBEITER, JOAN, artist, educator; b. N.Y.C., May 8, 1937; d. David and Winifred Arden (Lembke) Berman; m. Jay David Arbeiter, June 15, 1958 (div. May 1990); children: Lisa B. Arbeiter, Gail Arbeiter Goldstein. BA, CUNY, 1959; MFA, Pratt Inst., 1981. Lic. art tchr., N.Y., N.J. Tchr. N.Y.C. Sch. Sys. Bd. Edn., 1959-63; dir. Joan Arbeiter Studio Sch., Metuchen, N.J., 1976-90; instr. art, coord. founds. Ducret Sch. Art, Plainfield, N.J., 1978—, instr. color and design, 1978—, instr. art history, 1981—, instr. art appreciation, 1983—; workshop instr. N.J. Teen Arts Festival, 1998—. Juror various art orgns., N.J., 1981—; cons. Ednl. Testing Svc., Princeton, N.J., 1988; curator traveling art exhibit Age As a Work of Art,, Plainfield, Boston, N.Y.C., 1985-86, Lives and Works, N.Y.C., 2000; artist-in-residence Sch. Arts, N.J., 1995-2001; presenter paper, slides Coll. Art Assn. Conf., San Antonio, 1995, N.Y.C., N.Y., 2003; presenter, moderator Nat. Mus. Women in the Arts, Wash., 1997, Artists Talk on Art, N.Y.C., 2000; bd. dirs. Women's Studio Ctr. One-woman shows Ceres Gallery, N.Y.C., 1985, 87, 89, 93, 97, 2000, Columbia U., N.Y.C., 1986, Wagner Coll., S.I., N.Y., 1992, Douglass Coll. Ctr., New Brunswick, N.J., 1992, 96, Stony Brook-Millstone Watershead Assn. Gallery, Pennington, N.J., 1991 Union County Coll., Crawford, N.J., 1999; exhibited in group shows:Ramapo Coll., Mahwah, 1980, Brookdale Coll., Lincroft. N.J., 1980, Westbeth Gallery, N.Y.C., 1980. Ceres Gallery, 1983, N.Y. Feminist Art Inst., N.Y.C., 1985-88, Monmouth Mus., Lincroft, N.J., 1996, Kingsbourgh Comm. Coll., Brooklyn, N.Y., 1999, Soho 20 Gallery, N.Y.C., 1990, 98, Kunstler Forum, Bonn, Germany, 1999 Environ Protection Agency, Wash., D.C.,2001-02, Noyes Mus. Oceanville, N.J., 1995, 1998, Krasdale Corp. Gallery, Bronx, N.Y., 1995; represented in permanent collections at Noyes Mus., Oceanville, N.J., Fairmount Chem., Newark, CSR Group Architects and Builders-Leon Cohen, Nutley, N.J., JFK Med. Ctr., Edison, N.J., Muhlenberg Regional Med. Ctr., Plainfield, N.J., First Presbyterian church, Metuchen, N.J., MS Found., N.Y.C., 1995, also pvt. collections; co-author Lives and Works: Talks with Women Artists, Vol. 2, 1999. Recipient 1st place all media award Metuchen Cultural Arts Commn. Art Exhbn., 1988, best in show award Artists League Ctrl. N.J., 1989, AIA award Hunterdon Arts Ctr. N.J., 1996, excellence award Manhattan Arts Mag., 2000; grantee Vt. Studio Colony, 1987. Mem. Coll. Art Assn., Women's Caucus for Art, Art Table, Ceres Gallery, Varo Registry, Women's Studio Ctr. N.Y.C., (hon. mem. bd. dirs.) Alpha Beta Kappa. Studio: 41 Victory Ct Metuchen NJ 08840-1430

ARBITELLE, RONALD ALAN, elementary school educator; b. Danbury, Conn., Aug. 1, 1949; s. Roxy Joseph and Janet Helen (Otto) A.; m. Ruth Ann Young, Aug. 6, 1977. BS, Western Conn. State U., 1971, MS, 1973; postgrad. in adminstrn., supervision, So. Conn. State U., 1983. Tchr. Shelter Rock Sch. Danbury (Conn.) Bd. Edn., 1977—. Mem. text selection coms., Shelter Rock Sch., Danbury. Active Shelter Rock PTO. Mem. NEA, Conn. Edn. Assn., Danbury Edn. Assn. Avocations: bowling, swimming, coin, baseball card and Jim Beam car collecting. Home: 7 Belmont Cir Danbury CT 06810-6426 Office: Shelter Rock Sch Shelter Rock Rd Danbury CT 06810

ARBUCKLE-KEIL, GEORGIA ANN, chemistry educator; b. Phila., Sept. 29, 1961; d. Ralph Wesley and Marion Elizabeth (Wagner) A. BA in Chemistry, Rutgers U., Camden, N.J., 1983; PhD in Chemistry, U. Pa., 1987. Teaching fellow U. Pa., Phila., 1983-84, rsch. fellow, 1984-87; rsch. assoc. Princeton (N.J.) U., 1987-89; asst. prof. chemistry Rutgers U., Camden, 1989-95, assoc. prof. chemistry, 1995—2001, prof. chemistry, 2001—. Vis. scientist Princeton U., 2003—. Contbr. articles to Phys. Rev. B, Molecular Crystals Liquid Crystals, Chemistry of Materials, Macromolecules. Organist Calvary Assembly of God Ch., Pennsauken, N.J., 1978-83; pianist Lighthouse Tabernacle Ch., Lumberton, N.J., 1984-2000; faculty advisors Rutgers U. Christian Fellowship, 1989-95, Am. Chem. Soc. student affiliates, 1989-92. Recipient Young Investigator award NSF, 1992-97, Outstanding Faculty award Rutgers-Camden Alumni Assn., 1995, Provost award tchg. excellence, 2001; grantee Rsch. Corp., 1990-93, NSF, 1991-94, 96-99, 2000—, Petroleum Rsch. Fund, 1990; Douty fellow U. Pa., 1984-85, 86-87; Henry Rutgers rsch. fellow Rutgers U., 1989-91; Henry Dreyfus Tchr. scholar, 1995-2001; Alfred P. Sloan rsch. fellow, 1995-98. Mem. AAAS, Am. Chem. Soc. (local sect. tellers com. 1991-99, Nat. Chemistry Week com. 1991, 93, chair Phila. sect. 2001, nat. level councilor 2002—), Electrochem. Soc. Achievements include research on the role of defect units in polyacetylene leading to observation that defects which cluster have a minimal effect on conductivity, and on various polyacetylenes to show that the lower conductivity in Shirakawa polyacetylene can not be attributed to defect units; development of the spectroelectro-chemical quartz crystal microbalance to study electrode surfaces; synthesis and characterizational new poly(p-phenylene vinylene) derivatives. E-mail: arbuckle@camden.rutgers.edu.

ARBUTHNOT, JEANETTE JAUSSAUD, apparel executive, design educator, researcher; b. Walla Walla, Wash., Feb. 17, 1934; d. Andre P. and Lena Mae (Fox) Jaussaud; m. Alfred Harold Arbuthnot, Aug. 20, 1953 (div. July 1981); children: Kristi Noel Arbuthnot Bronkema, Lisa Gaye, Douglas Randal. BS, Fla. Internat. U., Miami, 1980; MS, Colo. State U., Ft. Collins, 1984; PhD, Okla. State U., 1990. Sect. mgr. The Treasury Dept. Store divsn. J.C. Penney, Miami, 1980-81; dept. mgr. The Denver, Boulder, Colo., 1981-82; lectr. U. Nev.-Reno, 1984-85; asst. prof. Utah State U., Logan, 1988-96, assoc. prof., 1996—, dir. grad. rsch., 1990—, coord. apparel merchandising and design program, 1990—. Reviewer for pubs. McMillan, Fairchild and Delmar, 1994, 95. Contbr. articles to profl. jours. Bd. dirs. Utah State U./Cmty. Assocs., Logan, 1995—; mem. exec. bd. Citizens Agains Phys. and Sexual Abuse, Logan, 1995—. Named Advisor of Yr., Coll. Family Life, Utah State U., 1990, 92; USDA rsch. grantee, 1993—. Mem. Internat. Textile and Apparel Assn. (strategic planning com. 1991-93), Costume Soc. Am. (membership adv. com. 1992-93), Am. Collegiate Retailing Assn., Am. Assn. Family and Consumer Scis., Internat. Fedn. Home Econs., Soroptimists Internat., Phi Upsilon Omicron, Kappa Omicron Nu. Episcopalian. Avocations: writing, fashion, silversmithing, travel, women's issues. Office: Utah State U 303A Coll Of Family Life Logan UT 84322-0001

ARCE, PEDRO EDGARDO, chemical engineering educator; b. Nogoya, Entre Rios, Argentina, Feb. 27, 1952; came to U.S., 1983; s. Pedro Ismael and Julia Celina (Traverso) A.; m. Maria Beatriz Trigatti, Feb. 9, 1978; children: Maria Paula, Andrea Lucia. Diploma in Chem. Engring., U. Nacional del Litoral, Santa Fe, Argentina, 1977; cert. of studies, Anglo-Continental Sch. of Eng., 1981; MSChemE, Purdue U., 1987, PhDChemE, 1990. Grad. fellow Coun. for Sci. Rsch. (CONICET), Argentina, 1978-84; lectr. Universidad Nacional de Litoral, Santa Fe, Argentina, 1980-87; instr. Purdue U., 1989; asst. prof. Fla. A&M U.-Fla. State U. Coll. Engring., Tallahassee, 1990-95, assoc. prof., 1995—, interim chair dept. chem. engring., 1995. Elected mem. Sci. and Technol. Career Coun. of Rsch., Argentina, 1984-90; Fulbright lectr. for Latin Am., 1994; vis. scientist Smith Herchel Lab., U. Cambridge, Eng., 1995; invited vis. prof. U. Nacional Mayor de San Marcos, Lima, Peru, 2000; assoc. faculty mem. Materials Rsch. Program, Fla. State U., 1991—, Geophys. Fluid Dynamics Inst., Fla. State U., 1997—; invited plenary lectr. Assn. Physics, Argentina, 1999, Latin Am. Congress Chem. Engring., Chile, 1998, Nat. Congress Chem. Engring., Santiago, Chile, 2000, others. Contbr. articles to profl. jours. including Chem. Engring. Sci., AIChE Jour., Comp. in Chem. Engring., I&E Chem. Rsch., Separations Tech., Hazardous Waste/Hazardous Materials, Internat. Comm. in Heat/Mass Transfer, Latin Am. Applied Rsch., Jour. Sci. Edn. and Tech., Jour. Chem. Engring. Edn. Argentina Coun. of Rsch. fellow, 1978, 80, 84, U. Queensland (Australia) fellow, 1982, Purdue U. fellow, 1988; recipient Excellence in Tchg. award Bd. Regents, U. Fla. Sys., 1994, Devel. Scholar award Fla. State U., 1996, Svc. award Fla. A&M U., 1996, 2001, award NSF-Coalition So. Engring. Colls. Univs., 1999, 2000. Mem. AIChE (student chpt. Prof. of Yr. 1990-91, Invited lectr. 1994, vice chair divsn. applied math. and numerical methods 1996-98, chmn. exec. com., 1998-99, program coord. 1998-99, chair session honoring Prof. D. Ramkrishna 1999, Nat. Student Competition award 1998), Am. Profs. Pharm. Scis., Am. Math. Soc., Am. Filt. Soc., Am. Assn. Aerosol Rsch., Am. Electrophoresis Soc. (councelor of bd. 1999—, co-chair annual meeting co-sponsored by Am. Inst. Chem. Engrs., Reno, 2001), Am. Soc. Engring. Edn. (Thomas C. Evans award 1994, 2001), Am. Chem. Soc., Am. Phys. Soc., N.Am. Membrane Soc., Soc. Rheology, Fla. Acad. Scis., Sigma Xi, Phi Lambda Upsilon. Achievements include research in (elec.) corona discharge in liquid phase for waste treatment; discovery of collaborative phenomena and pattern formation in catalytic reactors with implications for selectivity and yield improvement; of novel operator-theoretic structures in applied mathematics; development of the Integral-Spectral approach in computational methods, of the Colloquial Approach of coaching model of engineer instruction of team-based final exams teaching techniques; co-discoverer of pudlle formation flows in large drops with application to earth mantle convection and mixing in engring. operations. Office: Fla State U Chem Engring and GFDI Rm 18 Keen Bldg Tallahassee FL 32306-3017 Fax: 850-410-6150. E-mail: arce@eng.fsu.edu.

ARCH, GAIL THELMA, international business educator; b. Boston, July 16, 1952; d. Joseph Sherrard and Thelma Mathilde (Terkelsen) A.; m. George Nichols Vorys, July 31, 1977 (div. Feb. 1987); 1 child, George Christian. BA, Wheaton Coll., 1974; MA, Ohio State U., 1980, PhD, 1991. Grad. rsch. assoc. Ohio State U., Columbus, 1986-91; asst. prof. U. Houston, 1991-95, acad. fellow Inst. for Diversity and Cross-Cultural Mgmt., 1991; vis. asst. prof. Otterbein Coll., Westerville, Ohio, 1995-96, assoc. prof., 1996—, dir. MBA program, 1997—. Bd. gov. coun. Inst. for Bus. Ethics and Pub. Issues, Houston, 1991—. Contbr. articles to profl. jours. Recipient Greenwood award Houston City Coun., 1993; grantee Inst. Turkish Studies, 1991; bus. and econs. fellow Dept. Edn., 1992. Mem. Internat. Indsl. Rels. Rsch. Assn., Indsl. Rels. Rsch. Assn., Global Future Found. (treas. 1993), Internat. Design for Extreme Environments Assn. (treas. 1993), Acad. Internat. Bus., Acad. Mgmt., Phi Beta Kappa, Phi Kappa Phi. Home: 215 Academy Woods Dr Gahanna OH 43230-6201 Office: Otterbein Coll Business Dept Westervale Westerville OH 43081

ARCHER, CHALMERS, JR., retired education educator; b. Tchula, Miss., Apr. 21, 1938; s. Chalmers Sr. and Eva Alcola (Rutherford) A. AS, Saints Jr. Coll., 1969; BS, Tuskegee Inst., 1972, MEd, 1974; PhD, U. Ala., 1980; cert., MIT, 1980; PhD, Auburn U., 1979. Asst. to the pres. Saints Coll., Lexington, Miss., 1968-72; asst. v.p. Tuskegee (Ala.) Inst., 1972-83; prof. No. Va. C.C., Manassas, 1983-2001, prof. emeritus, 2001. Author: Growing Up Black in Rural Mississippi (recipient Miss. Inst. of Arts and Letters award for Nonfiction), Green Berets in the Vanguard: Inside Special Forces, 1953-1963; contbg. editor: The Jackson Advocate; contbr. articles to profl. jours. and newspapers. Mem. Dem. Spkr.'s Bur. for Clinton/Gore Re-election Campaign. Recipient Nat. Edn. Articulation Model, Conf. on Blacks in Higher Edn., Washington, 1986. Mem. Rotary (county transportation commnr.). Democrat. Baptist. Avocations: academic and community program development, motivational speaking, writing. Home: 7885 Flager Cir Manassas VA 20109-7435 E-mail: drarcher@aol.com.

ARCHEY, MARY FRANCES ELAINE (ONOFARO), academic administrator, educator; b. Elkins, W Va, Sept. 15, 1947; d. Ross and Carmela Gallo Onofaro; m. Rick Archey. BA in Social Sci. Edn., U. Pitts., 1968; MEd in Social Sci. Edn., Indiana U. of Pa., 1969; EdD in Higher Edn. Adminstrn. and Counseling, WVa. U., 1981; Profl. Cert. in Human Resource Devel., Pa. State U., 1996. Cert. nat. counselor 1984. Asst. prof. sociology West Liberty State Coll., Wheeling, W.Va., 1969—72; dean of students W. Va. Northern C.C., Wheeling, W.Va., 1972—85; asst. dean instrn. C.C. Allegheny County South Campus, West Mifflin, Pa., 1986—96; dean bus. and acctg. C.C. of Allegheny County, Pitts., 1996—99; dean arts and sci. C.C. of Allegheny County-South Campus, West Mifflin, Pa., 1999—, Adj. instr. bus., 1988. Adj. instr. bus. C.C. of Allegheny County-South Campus, West Mifflin, Pa., 1988—. Ctrl. Pa. regl. dir. U. Pitts. Alumni Assn., 2001—; past pres., current chair nominations com. U. Pitts. Alumnae Coun., 1998—; vol food packager Greater Pitts. Food Bank, Duquesne, 1995—; vol. tester, interviewer Greater Pitts. Literacy Coun., 1987—96. Fellow: The Ed. Policy and Leadership Ctr. (fellow 2002—03); mem.: ASTD, AAUW, Am. Coll. Personnel Assn., Am. Assn. Higher Edn. (life), Am. Counseling Assn., St. Elizabeth's Women's Club, Phi Lambda Theta, Phi Delta Gamma (v.p. 2000—), Beta Sigma Phi (svc. chairperson 1987—, Order of the Rose 1994), Delta Kappa Gamma-Alpha Phi Chpt. (past pres. 1996—, newsletter editor 1996—). Democrat. Roman Catholic. Avocations: reading, gardening. Home: 333 Old Clairton Rd Pittsburgh PA 15236 Office: CC of Allegheny -South Campus 1750 Clairton Rd West Mifflin PA 15122 Personal E-mail: marchey@ccac.edu.

ARCHIBALD, JANE MARTYN, secondary education educator; b. Springfield, Mass., May 30, 1943; d. Lyndon Sanford and Dorothy Loomis (Clapp) Martyn; m. Robert Alan Archibald, June 26, 1965; 1 child, Elizabeth. AB, Mount Holyoke Coll., 1965; MA, U. Oreg., 1968, postgrad., 1969. Tchr. English and Latin Agawam (Mass.) High Sch., 1965-66; Latin instr. U. Oreg., Eugene, 1966-68; tchr. Latin and English Miss Porter's Sch., Farmington, Conn., 1968-73, English tchr., 1982-87, Loomis Chaffee Sch., Windsor, Conn., 1973-76, 87—, Milton (Mass.) Acad., 1976-81. Speaker in field. Mem. Phi Beta Kappa. Home: 15 Mount Vernon Dr East Granby CT 06026-9553 Office: Loomis Chaffee Sch Batchelder Rd Windsor CT 06095

ARCHIBOLD, MILDRED HAYNES, bilingual education educator; b. Panama City, Panama, Nov. 21, 1923; came to U.S., 1950; d. James and Myra (Mandeville) Haynes; m. V. Rex Archibold, July 21, 1970; children: Lisa, Rex Jr., Alicia. BA in Edn., Bklyn. Coll., 1974, MS in Ednl. Guidance, 1976, cert. in advanced guidance-counseling, 1977; MS in Urban and Bilingual Edn., L.I. U., 1978. Cert. bilingual (Spanish) early childhood tchr., guidance counselor, N.Y. Cost acct., asst. supr. Clubs and Playgrounds Cristobal, Canal Zone, 1943-50; asst. supr. records mgmt. Esso Standard Oil Co. N.Y., 1951-58; Spanish and English translator Chem. Pharm. Co. N.Y., 1959-62; clk. to intake worker Dept. Social Svcs., N.Y.C., 1962-74; elem. bilingual tchr. N.Y.C. Bd. Edn., Bklyn., tchr. early childhood bilingual (Spanish), 1974-86, bilingual coord., 1987-90, ret., 1990. Part time tchr. lit. program Human Resource Adminstrn./Good Sheppard, 1990—. Mem. N.Y.C. Bd. Edn. Named Panamanian Mother of Yr., N.Y.C., 1987. Mem. Nat. Assn. Bilingual Educators, State Assn. Bilingual Edn., Nat. Assn. Panamenian Educators, Assn. Adminstrs. and Suprs., Guidance Counselors Assn., Orton Dyslexia Assn., United Fedn. Tchrs. N.Y. (facilitator), Bklyn. Coll. Alumni Assn., L.I. U. Alumni Assn.

ARCHIE, CAROL LOUISE, obstetrician and gynecologist, educator; b. Detroit, May 18, 1957; d. Frank and Mildred (Barmore) A.; m. Edward Louis Keenan III, Mar. 7, 1993. BA in History, U. Mich., 1979, postgrad. in Pub. Health Adminstrn., 1979-83; MD, Wayne State U., 1983. Diplomate Am. Bd. Ob-Gyn., Am. Bd. Maternal-Fetal Medicine. Resident ob-gyn. Wayne State U., Detroit, 1983-87; fellow in maternal fetal medicine UCLA, 1987-89, asst. prof. ob-gyn., 1989-97, asst. prof. dept of cmty. health scis., 1995-97, assoc. prof. ob-gyn. and cmty. health scis., 1997—; dir. maternal fetal medicine Northridge (Calif.) Med. Ctr., 2000—01. Cons. Office Substance Abuse Prevention, Washington, 1989—, NIH, Bethesda, Md., 1990—, RAND, 1995—; residency coord. UCLA Ctr. of Excellence, 2001—. Peer reviewer jours. Obstetrics and Gynecology, 1989—, Am. Jour. Pub. Health, 1994—, Am. Jour. Obstetrics and Gynecology, 1993—; contbr. chpts. to books. Internal rev. bd. Friends Med. Rsch., 1991—99; residency coord. UCLA Sch. Medicine Ctr. of Excellence; bd. dirs. Matrix Inst. on Addictions, L.A., 1993—; bd. dirs., vice chair Calif. Advs. for Pregnant Women, 1993—98; bd. dirs., asst. v.p. med. svcs. Venice (Calif.) Family Clin., 1994—98, v.p. svcs., 1998—2002, chair bd. dirs., 2002—. Clin. Tng. grantee UCLA, 1993-99; recipient Faculty Devel. award Berlex Found., 1992. Fellow ACOG; mem. AMA, APHA, Soc. Perinatal Obstetricians, Royal Soc. of Medicine (Eng.), Assn. Profs. of Gynecology and Obstetrics. Office: Dept Ob-gyn UCLA Sch Medicine Rm 22-132 10833 Le Conte Ave Los Angeles CA 90095-3075 E-mail: carchie@mednet.ucla.edu.

ARCHULETA, WALTER R. educational consultant, language educator; b. Embudo, N.Mex., Apr. 7, 1951; s. Luis M. and Josefina (Romero) A.; m. Carmel Bustos, Oct. 19, 1994. BS in Spanish and Social Sci., N.Mex. State U., 1974; MA in Spanish Linguistics, U. N.Mex., 1981, postgrad., 1991-93. Tchr. Spanish John F. Kennedy Jr. H.S., San Juan, N.Mex., 1974-76; oral history collector VISTA, Dixon, N.Mex., 1976-77; tchr. Spanish Santa Fe H.S., N.Mex., 1981-82, 85-88, Los Alamos (N.Mex.) H.S., 1982-85, Capital H.S., Santa Fe, 1988-91; edn. cons. N.Mex. State Dept. Edn., Santa Fe, 1995-99. Cons. Hispanic Culture Found., Albuquerque, 1991-93. U. N.Mex. Opportunity fellow, 1991-93, travel grantee, 1996. Mem. MLA, Am. Assn. Tchrs. Spanish and Portuguese, Am. Coun. on Tchg. of Fgn. Lang., Nat. Assn. Bilingual Edn., N.Mex. Assn. Bilingual Edn. Democrat. Roman Catholic. Avocations: collecting oral history, writing poetry.

ARCINIEGA, TOMAS ABEL, university president; b. El Paso, Tex., Aug. 5, 1937; s. Tomas Hilario and Judith G. (Zozaya) Arciniega; m. M. Concha Ochotorena, Aug. 10, 1957; children: Wendy H. Heredia, Lisa Gannon, Judy Shackleton, Laura. BS in Tchr. Edn., N. Mex. State U., 1960; MA, U. N. Mex., 1966, PhD, 1970; postdoc., Inst. for Ednl. Mgmt., Harvard U., 1989. Asst. dean Grad. Sch. U. Tex.-El Paso, 1972-73; co-dir. Southwestern Schs. Study, U. Tex.-El Paso, 1970-73; dean Coll. Edn. San Diego State U., 1973-80; v.p. acad. affairs. Calif. State U., Fresno, 1980-83, pres. Bakersfield, 1983—. Prof. ednl. adminstrn. and supervision U. N.Mex., U. Tex.-El Paso, San Diego State U., Calif. State U., Fresno, Calif. State U., Bakersfield; cons. in edn. to state and fed. agys., instns.; USAID advisor to Dominican Republic U.S. Dept. State., 1967-68; dir. applied rsch. project U. N.Mex., 1968-69, dep. chief party AID Project, Colombia, 1969-70; cons. in field. Author: Public Education's Response to the Mexican-American, 1971, Preparing Teachers of Mexican Americans: A Sociocultural and Political Issue, 1977; co-author: Chicanos and Native Americans: The Territorial Minorities, 1973; guest editor: Calif. Jour. Tchr. Edn., 1981; editor Commn. on Hispanic Underrepresentation Reports, Hispanic Underrepresentation: A Call for Reinvestment and Innovation, 1985, 88. Trustee emeritus Carnegie Corp. N.Y.; trustee Ednl. Testing Svc., Princeton, N.J., The Aspen Inst.; bd. dirs. Math., Engring., Sci. Achievement, Berkeley, Calif.; mem. bd. dirs. Air U., Hispanic Scholarship Fund; mem. Am. Coun. on Edn.; founding mem., trustee Tomas Rivera Policy Inst.; dir. Civic Kern Citizens Effective Local Govt.; mem. adv. bd. Beautiful Bakersfield; advisor Jr. League Bakersfield. Vis. scholar Leadership Enrichment Program, 1982; recipient Legis. commendation for higher edn. Calif. Legislature, 1975-78, Meritorious Svc. award Am. Assn. Colls. Tchr. Edn., 1977-78, Meritorious Svc. award League United L.Am. Citizens, 1983, Svc. award Hispanic and Bus. Alliance for Edn., 1991, Pioneer award Nat. Assn. Bilingual Edn., 1994; named to Top 100 Acad. Leaders in Higher Edn. Change Mag., 1978, Top 100 Hispanic Influentials Hispanic Bus. Mag., 1987, 97. Mem. Am. Ednl. Rsch. Assn. (editl. com. 1979-82), Am. Assn. State Colls. and Univs. (bd. dirs.), Hispanic Assn. Colls. and Univs. (bd. dirs.), Assn. Mexican Am. Educators (various commendations), Am. Assn. Higher Edn. (instl. rep.), Western Coll. Assn. (past pres.), Rotary, Stockdale Country Club, Bakersfield Petroleum Club. Democrat. Roman Catholic. Home: 2213 Sully Ct Bakersfield CA 93311-1560 Office: Calif State U 9001 Stockdale Hwy Bakersfield CA 93311-1022

ARCURI, LEONARD PHILIP, elementary education educator; b. Bklyn., Apr. 28, 1947; s. Leonard James And Elizabeth Eleanor (Jaeger) A.; m. Lillian Campo, Aug. 11, 1979. BA, St. John's U., Jamaica, N.Y., 1969; MS, St. John's U., 1974; profl. diploma, C.W. Post, Greenvale, N.Y., 1980. Sci. educator St. Agnes Parish Sch., Bklyn., 1969-73; narcotics coord. Dist. 32 Drug Prevention Program, Bklyn., 1973-74; common branches tchr. P.S. 86 K, Bklyn., 1974-75; narcotics coord. Dist. 32 Drug Prevention Program, Bklyn., 1975-77; sci. educator P.S. 123 K, Bklyn., 1977—. Tutor biology Empire State Coll., SUNY, N.Y.C., 1988-89; instr. sci. Coll. New Rochelle, N.Y., 1988-89; instr. camping St. John's U. Sch. Continuing Edn., Jamaica, 1989-91; del. to Assembly of United Fedn. Tchrs., 1996—. Pres. Greater Ridgewood (N.Y.) Hist. Soc., 1983-84; coun. commr. Boy Scouts Am., (Queens, N.Y.), N.Y.C. 1979-80; mem. nat. coun. Boy Scouts Am., Tex., 1979-80; scout master troop 154, Boy Scouts Am., Goldens Bridge, N.Y., 1994—. Recipient Energy Conservation Achievement award Dept. of Gen. Svcs. City of N.Y., 1983, Silver Beaver, 1980. Mem. Elem. Sch. Sci. Assn. N.Y., Planetary Soc., Astron. Soc. of the Pacific, Nat. Sci. Tchrs. Assn., Kiwanis. Democrat. Roman Catholic. Avocations: canoeing, hiking, camping, flyfishing. Office: PS 123 K 100 Irving Ave Brooklyn NY 11237-2952

ARDOLF, DEBORAH ANN, speech language pathologist; b. Mpls., Apr. 12, 1960; d. Bernard Joseph and Mary Ann (Snyder) A. BS cum laude, Moorhead State U., 1982; MA, U. Northern Colo., 1986. Cert. speech lang. pathologist, Minn., Hawaii. Speech pathologist Pelican Rapids (Minn.) Pub. Schs., 1982-84; speech pathologist intern Vet. Adminstrn. Medical Ctr., Seattle, Washington, 1985-86; speech pathologist Rehabilitation Hosp. Pacific, Honolulu, 1986-87, Dept. Edn., Honolulu, 1987-89, Queen's Med. Ctr., Honolulu, 1989-95; pvt. practice speech pathologist Honolulu, 1987—. Instr. U. Hawaii, 1993-94. Recipient Search for Excellence award U. Northern Colo., 1984-85. Mem. Hawaii Speech, Lang. Hearing Assn. (spkr. at conf. 1993, com. mem., pres.-elect 1995-96), Am. Hearing and Speech Assn., Austistic Soc. Hawaii, Hawaii Bicycle League, Mid-Pacific Road Runners Club (vol. 1991—), Hawaii Small Bus. Assn. Avocations: running, bike touring, hiking, triathalons, reading. Office: Ohana Speech Lang Cons 1201 Wilder Ave Ste 2005 Honolulu HI 96822

ARELLA, ANN MARIETTA, music educator, vocalist; b. Montclair, N.J., Jan. 29, 1951; d. Peter John and Evelyn Elizabeth (De Carlo) Arella; m. William John Wallace, Feb. 9, 1974 (dissolved May 1983); children: Ryan Wallace, Shannon Wallace. MusB, Ind. U., Bloomington, 1973; student, Manhattan Sch. Music, N.Y., 1975; grad. cert., William Patterson U., N., 1983; MA, New Jersey City Univ., N.J., 1991; postgrad., Shenanaoah Univ., Va., 2002—. Tchr. remedial reading & math Indep. Child Study Teams, Jersey City, 1983—86; tchr. choral music Lodi (N.J.) Bd. of Edn., 1986; singer Sacred Heart Ch., Suttern, NY, 1990—95, pianist, 1990—95; ch. music dir. Immaculate Conception, Mahwah, NJ, 1995—99; pvt. piano & voice tchr. Mahwah, NJ, 1998—2002. Ch. musician, 1974—99. Singer: Ridgewood Gilbert & Sullivan Opera Co., 1985—89; singer: (operatic soloist) Opera Festival di Roma, 2000; performer: Teotro Verdi, 1999. Fellow, Shenandoah Conservatory of Music, 2001. Mem.: NEA, Lodi Edn. Assn. (chmn. 1989—93, membership com. 1989—93, adj. rep. 1987—). Republican. Roman Catholic. Avocations: golf, weight training, decorating. Home: 1211 Sycamore Ln Mahwah NJ 07430 Office: Lodi Bd Edn S Main & Hunter Sts Lodi NJ 07644 E-mail: arella201@aol.com.

AREND, ANTHONY CLARK, international relations educator; b. Balt., Oct. 24, 1958; s. Paul Joseph and Cora Allen (Clark) A. BSFS magna cum laude, Georgetown U., 1980; MA, U. Va., 1982, PhD, 1985. Rsch. asst. U. Va. Sch. Law, Charlottesville, Va., 1981-84, sr. fellow, 1985-86; professorial lectr. dept. govt. Georgetown U., Washington, 1986, asst. prof., 1988-93, assoc. prof., 1993-2000, chair main campus exec. faculty, 1997-2001, prof., 2000—, v.p. main campus faculty senate, 2001—. Vis. asst. prof. Pa. State U., Harrisburg, 1987, Georgetown U., 1987—88; co-dir. Inst. for Internat. Law and Politics. Author: Pursuing a Just and Durable Peace: John Foster Dulles and International Organization, 1988, Legal Rules and International Society, 1999; co-author: International Law and the Use of Force: Beyond the United Nations Charter Paridigm, 1993; editor: The United States and the Compulsory Jurisdiction of the International Court of Justice, 1986; co-editor: The Falklands War: Lessons for Strategy, Diplomacy and International Law, 1985, International Rules: Approaches from International Law and International Relations, 1996; mem. bd. advisors Va. Jour. Internat. Law, 1992—; contbr. chpts. to books, articles to profl. jours. Chmn. adminstrv. coun. Severn United Meth. Ch., 1984-89, lay leader, 1990—; gov. bd. govs. Georgetown U. Alumni Assn., 2001—. Margaret Nils Butler Meml. DACOR fellow, 1980-81, Richard M. Weaver fellow, 1982-83, Lassen fellow, 1983-84, Philip Francis du Pont fellow, 1983-84. Mem. Am. Soc. Internat. Law, Georgetown U. Alumni Assn. (bd. govs. 2001—), Phi Beta Kappa. Democrat. Avocations: golf, squash. Home: 1301 33rd St NW Apt 1 Washington DC 20007-2850 Office: Georgetown U Dept Govt Washington DC 20057-0001 E-mail: arenda@georgetown.edu.

ARENS, KATHERINE MARIE, language educator, educator; b. Chgo., Nov. 25, 1953; d. Edward James and Eleanor (Baumgartner) A. BA, Northwestern U., 1975; AM, Stanford U., 1976, PhD, 1981. Tchg. fellow in German studies and humanities Stanford (Calif.) U., 1976-79; asst. prof. Germanic langs. U. Tex., Austin, 1980-86, assoc. prof. Germanic langs., 1986-93, prof. Germanic langs., 1993—. Author: Functionalism and Fin de Siècle, 1984, Structures of Knowing, 1989; co-author: (with Swaffar and Byrnes) Reading for Meaning, 1991, Austria and Other Margins, 1996, Empire in Decline, 2001. Fulbright Hays grantee, 1978-79, NEH grant, 1982; C.G. Whiting Found. fellow, 1979-80. Home: 4806 Red River St Austin TX 78751-3331 Office: Univ Tex Dept Germanic Studies Austin TX 78712-0304

ARETZ, BARBARA JANE, reading specialist, educator; b. Long Beach, Calif., Dec. 28, 1943; d. Raymond John and Violet Dorothy (Wurn) A. BA, U. San Diego, 1965; Cert. Elem. Tchr., Immaculate Heart Coll., 1968; MEd in Reading, Loyola U., 1975; postgrad. in Christian Spirituality, Creighton U., 1980-85. Cert. ESL tchr., reading specialist, lang. arts content specialist, alpha phonics tchr., lang. therapist. Tchr. 4th grade St. Laurence Sch., Amarillo, Tex., 1978-79; tchr. 6th grade, prin. St. Mary's Sch., Odessa, Tex., 1979-81; tchr. 6th grade Lamesa (Tex.) Mid. Sch., 1981-83; prin. St. Mary's Sch., 1983-85; tchr. reading Midland (Tex.) Ind. Sch. Dist., 1985—. Team leader Midland Ind. Sch. Dist., 1997—, mem. Reading Club, San Jacinto Jr. H.S., 1997—. Recipient grant Diocese of Amarillo, 1981, Linda Laird Meml. award Acad. Lang. Therapy, 1993. Mem. Internat. Reading Assn., Tex. Classroom Tchr. Assn., Midland Reading Assn. (sec. 1986). Roman Catholic. Avocations: house remodeling, gardening, animal lover, miniature house building.

ARGAST, ANNE SCOTT, geology educator; b. Long Branch, N.J., Sept. 19, 1956; d. James Fred and Charlotte Louise (Terry) A.; m. Deborah Hanson. BS, U. Rochester, 1978; MA, SUNY, Binghamton, 1981, PhD, 1986. Instr. geology Ind. U.-Purdue U., Ft. Wayne, 1985-86, asst. prof. geology, 1986-92, assoc. prof. geology, 1992—, dept. chair, 1993—. Contbr. articles to Jour. Sedimentary Petrology, Jour. Geology, etc. Mem. Clay Minerals Soc., Geol. Soc. Am., Sigma Xi (club pres. 1989-90, Res. of Yr. award 1988). Methodist. Home: 37 Cottonwood Dr Garrett IN 46738-9770 Office: Ind U-Purdue U 2101 E Coliseum Blvd Fort Wayne IN 46805-1445

ARIETI, JAMES ALEXANDER, classics educator, writer; b. N.Y.C., May 12, 1948; s. Silvano and Jane (Jaffe) A.; m. Barbara Ann Mapes, May 23, 1976; children: Samuel Abraham, Ruth Sophia. BA, Grinnell Coll., 1969; MA, PhD, Stanford U., 1972. Asst. prof. Stanford (Calif.) U., 1972-74, Pa. State U., University Park, 1974-75, Cornell Coll., Mt. Vernon, Iowa, 1975-77; prof. dept. classics Hampden-Sydney (Va.) Coll., 1978—. Author: Love Can Be Found, 1975, Longinus on the Sublime, 1985, Interpreting Plato: The Dialogues as Drama, 1991, Discourses on the First Book of Herodotus, 1995, The Scientific and the Divine: Conflict and Reconciliation from Ancient Greece to Today, 2003; editor: Hamartia, 1983; contbr. articles to profl. jours. Woodrow Wilson fellow, 1969; NEH fellow, 1977-78. Mem. Am. Philol. Assn., Classical Assn. Middle West and South, Classical Assn. Va., Phi Beta Kappa, Phi Alpha Theta, Eta Sigma Chi. Jewish. Home and Office: Hampden Sydney Coll PO Box 746 Hmpden Sydney VA 23943-0746

ARIOLA, MARIE J. school system administrator, principal; b. Syracuse, N.Y., Nov. 9, 1946; d. Anthony Joseph and Edith Marie (Trovato) Barnell; m. John James Ariola, June 18, 1986; children: Johnanthony, Courtney Marie. BS, Daemon Coll., 1968; MA, Calif. State U., 1972. With L.A. Unified Sch. Dist., 1968-86, counselor, adminstrv. dean, head counselor, sch. coord., asst. prin., acting prin.; with OCM BOCES, Syracuse, N.Y., 1990—. Co-pres. C.N.Y. Asst. Prin's. Orgn., Syracuse, 1990—; author curriculum devel. State of Calif., 1980. Vol. Red Cross, Syracuse, 1989, 93-95, Am. Cancer Soc., 1990, United Way, 1991. Recipient Outstanding Parent award No. Syracuse Schs., 1993. Mem. ASCD, Am. Vocat. Educators Assn. Avocations: reading, biking, swimming. Home: 7742 Bainbridge Dr Liverpool NY 13090-2574 Office: OCM Boces PO Box 4754 Syracuse NY 13221-4754

ARISMENDI-PARDI, EDUARDO J. mathematics educator; b. Caracas, Venezuela, May 28, 1960; s. Edward Jesse Arismendi and Cecilia Pardi-Valero; m. Cheryl Annette Knutson, Dec. 20, 1980; 1 child, Mikhail Andrej Arismendi-Knutson. AA, Cerritos Coll., 1981; BS, Calif. State U., Long Beach, 1984; MS summa cum laude, West Coast U., 1991; EdD, Nova Southeastern U., 1998. Cert. community coll. tchr. math., computers, bus. and mgmt., Calif. Asst. engr. Rockwell Internat., Downey, Calif., 1980-82; math. instr. Our Lady of Victory High Sch., Van Nuys, Calif., 1982-83; math. tchr. asst. Calif. State U., Long Beach, 1983-86; math. tchr. La Salle High Sch., Pasadena, Calif., 1986-87; statistics tchr. asst. U. Calif., L.A., 1987-88; mgmt. scientist McDonnell Douglas Corp., Long Beach, 1988-91; math. instr. Orange Coast Coll., Costa Mesa, Calif., 1989—, math. prof., v.p. acad. senate, 1991—. Mgmt. scientist Scandinavian Airline System, Oslo, Norway, 1989, Am. Airlines, Tulsa, 1989-91, Sorin Biomedical, Inc., Irvine, Calif., 1992—; lectr. quantitative methods West Coast U., L.A., 1992—, quantitative methods, statistics, ops. rsch. Keller Grad. Sch. Mgmt., 1998—. Contbr. articles to profl. jours. Recipient Nat. Inst. for Staff and Organizational Devel. award U. Tex. Austin, 1999, Rsch. Excellence award Nova Southea. U., 1999, Nat. Campus Faculty Diversity award Ctr. for Study of Diversity in Tchg. and Learning in Am. Higher Edn., 2000, chancellor's spl. individual award, Gov. Gray Davis and Bd. Govs. Calif. Cmty. Colls. Mem. Am. Math. Soc., Am. Statistical Soc., Math. Assn. Am., Am. Fedn. Tchrs., Ops. Rsch. Soc. Am., Faculty Assn. Calif. Community Colls. Democrat. Roman Catholic. Avocations: Spanish literature, writing, reading, travel. Home: Phillips Ranch 9 Wildflower Pl Pomona CA 91766-6601 Office: Orange Coast College PO Box 5005 2701 Fairview Rd Costa Mesa CA 92626-5561 E-mail: carismendi@aol.com., arismend@mail.occ.cccd.edu.

ARKILIC, GALIP MEHMET, mechanical engineer, educator; b. Sivas, Turkey, Mar. 10, 1920; came to U.S., 1943, naturalized, 1960; s. Sabir Mehmet and Zahra Fatima (Hocazade) A.; m. Ann A. Bryan, Mar. 31, 1956. BME, Cornell U., 1946; MS, Ill. Inst. Tech., 1948; PhD, Northwestern U., 1954. Registered profl. engr., Va. Mech. engr. Miehle Printing Press and Mfg. Co., Chgo., 1948-49, analyst, 1954-56; research and devel. engr. Mech. and Chem. Industries, Turkey, 1949-52; asst. prof. Pa. State U., University Park, 1956-58; assoc. prof. dept. civil engring. George Washington U., Washington, 1958-63, prof. engring. and applied sci., 1963—, prof. emeritus, 1990—, chmn. dept. engring. mechanics, 1966-69, asst. dean, 1969-74. Contbr. articles to sci. jours. Vice pres. Courtland Civic Assn., Arlington, Va., 1965-66; pres. Am. Turkish Assn., Washington, 1967-71. Served to 2d lt. Turkish Army, 1939-41 Recipient Disting. Leadership award Am. Turkish Assn., 1972; Recognition of Service award Sch. Engring. and Applied Sci., George Washington U., 1976, Spl. Appreciation award Engring. Alumni Assn., George Washington U., 1990; Air Force Office of Sci. Research grantee, 1963-69 Mem. ASME, AAUP, Am. Acad. Mechanics, Math. Assn. of Am., Am. Math. Soc., Wash. Soc. Engrs., Sigma Xi. Clubs: George Washington U. (Washington). Home: 8403 Camden St Alexandria VA 22308-2111 Office: George Washington Univ Sch Of Engringand Applied Sc Washington DC 20052-0001 E-mail: gmarkilic@aol.com.

ARKY, RONALD ALFRED, medical educator; b. New Brunswick, N.J., June 26, 1929; s. Eugene and Ida (Glick) A.; m. Marie Mahoney, Sept. 14, 1963. AB, Cornell U., Ithaca, N.Y., 1951; MD, Cornell U., N.Y.C., 1955. Intern Bellevue Hosp., N.Y.C., 1955-56; resident N.Y. VA Hosp., 1958-60; fellow Thorndike Meml. Lab., Boston City Hosp., 1961-63; dir. diabetes clinic Boston City Hosp., 1966-71; Charles S. Davidson prof. medicine Harvard U. Med. Sch., Cambridge, Mass., 1984—. Chmn. dept. medicine Mt. Auburn Hosp., 1971-93; pres. Assocs. Program for Dirs. Internal Medicine, 1990-91; chief diabetes sect. Brigham and Women's Hosp., Boston, 1996—. Fellow AAAS; Master ACP, Peabody Soc. Harvard Med. Sch.; mem. Am. Diabetes Assn. (pres. 1979-80), Am. Soc. Clin. Investigation, Endocrine Soc., Am. Clin. Climatol. Soc. Office: Francis W Peabody Soc Harvard Med Sch 260 Longwood Ave Boston MA 02115-5701

ARLEN, JENNIFER HALL, law educator; b. Berkeley, Calif., Jan. 7, 1959; d. Michael John and Ann (Warner) A.; m. Robert Lee Hotz, May 21, 1988; children: Michael Arlen Hotz, Robert Arlen Hotz. BA, Harvard U., 1982; JD, NYU, 1986, PhD in Econ., 1992. Bar: NY 1987, US Ct. Appeals (11th cir.) 1987. Summer clk. US Dist. Ct. (ea. dist.), Bklyn., 1984; summer assoc. Davis Polk & Wardwell, NYC, 1985; law clk. US Cir. Judge, 11th cir., Savannah, Ga., 1986-87; asst. prof. law Emory U., Atlanta, 1987-91, assoc. prof. law, 1991-93; prof. law U. So. Calif., LA, 1994—2002, Ivadelle and Theodore Johnson prof. law and bus., 1997—2002; prof. law NYU, 2002—, 2003—. Vis. prof. law U. So. Calif., 1993; dir. U. So. Calif. Ctr. Law, Econs. Orgn., 2000—02; vis. prof. law Calif. Inst. Tech., 2001, Yale U., 2001—02; mem. acad. bd. NYU Ctr. Law, Bus., 2003—. Olin fellow U. Calif. Sch. Law, Berkeley, 1991. Mem. ABA, Am. Assn. Law Schs. (chair remedies sect. 1994, chair elect 1993, mem. exec. com. 1990-91, 95, chair torts sect. 1995, chair-elect 1994, treas. 1991, sec. 1992-93, exec. com. bus. assns. sect. 1995-96, 2000—, chair law and econ., sect. 1996, chair-elect law and econs. sect. 1995, chair 1996), Am. Law and Econ. Assn. (bd. dirs. 1991-93, program com. 1999), Am. Econ. Assn., Order of Coif, Am. Law Inst. Democrat. Office: NYU Law Sch 40 Washington Square S New York NY 10012

ARLINGHAUS, SANDRA JUDITH LACH, mathematical geographer, educator; b. Elmira, N.Y., Apr. 18, 1943; d. Donald Frederick and Alma Elizabeth (Satorius) Lach; m. William Charles Arlinghaus, Sept. 3, 1966; 1 child, William Edward. AB in Math., Vassar Coll., 1964; postgrad., U. Chgo., 1964-66, U. Toronto, 1966-67, Wayne State U., 1968-70, MA in Geography, 1976; PhD in Geography, U. Mich., 1977. Vis. instr. math. U. Ill., Chgo., 1966; vis. asst. prof. geography Ohio State U., Columbus, 1977-78, lectr. math., 1978-79, Loyola U., Chgo., 1979-81, asst. prof. math., 1981-82; lectr. math. and geography U. Mich., Dearborn and Ann Arbor, 1982-83; founding dir. Inst. Math. Geography, Ann Arbor, 1985—; pres. Arlinghaus Enterprises, Ann Arbor, 1998—. Guest lectr. U. Chgo., 1979, 87, 2000-01, U. Calif., 1979, Syracuse U., 1991, U. No. Iowa, 1991; guest lectr. U. Mich., Ann Arbor, 1983, 90-93, adj. prof. math. geography, population-environ. dynamics Sch. Natural Resources and Environ., 1994—, adj. prof. Coll. Architecture and Urban Planning, 1997, 2001—; cons. Transp. Rsch. Inst., Coll. Architecture, 1985-86, Coll. Edn., 1992, Cmty. Sys. Found., 1993—; prodr. Ann Arbor Cmty. Access TV, 1988-90; dir. spatial analysis divsn. Cmty. Systems Found., 1996—, dir. fellowship tng. divsn., 1996—; co-founder Arlinghaus Enterprises, 1997, pres. 2000-02, mgr., 2003—. Author: Down the Mail Tubes: The Pressured Postal Era, 1853-1984, Essays on Mathematical Geography, 1986, Essays on Mathematical Geography-II, 1987, An Atlas of Steiner Networks, 1989, Essays on Mathematical Georgraphy-III, 1991; co-author: Population-Environment Dynamics, Sectors in Transition, 1992 and later editions through 1998, Mathematical Geography and Global Art, 1986, Environmental Effects on Bus Durability, 1990, Fractals in Geography, 1993, Graph Theory and Geography: An Interactive View, Ebook 2002, Wiley; founder, editor, co-author Solstice, 1990—, Image Interactive Atlases, Image Game Series, Image Discussion Papers, Internat. Soc. Spatial Scis., 1995—; author, editor-in-chief Practical Handbook of Curve Fitting, 1994; co-author, editor-in-chief Practical Handbook of Digital Mapping: Terms and Concepts, 1994; editor-in-chief Practical Handbook of Spatial Stats., 1995; editor internat. monograph series; reviewer Mathematical Reviews, 1992—; contbr. articles, book reviews to profl. jours. in field of geography, psychology, math., biology, history, philately. Mem. City of Ann Arbor Planning Commn., 1995-2003, sec., 1997-2002, chair, 2002-2003, vice-chmn., 2003; mem. City of Ann Arbor Environ. Commn., 2000-03; bd. dirs., chmn. Bromley Homeowners Assn., Ann Arbor, 1989-93, pres., 1990-93, 95-96; mem. ordinance revisions com. City of Ann Arbor, 1996-2003, mem. master planning com., 2002-03; bd. dirs. World Jr. Bridge Championships, Ann Arbor, 1990-91, Dolfins Inc., 1993-96; artist Math. Awareness Week, Lawrence Tech. U., 1988; trustee Cmty. Sys. Found., 1995-2001; co-vice chair citizens adv. com. NE Ann Arbor master plan revision, 1999-2000; adv. bd. City of Ann Arbor Police Dept. Neighborhood Watch, 2001—. Recipient Cmty. Svc. award, City of Ann Arbor, 1999. Fellow Am. Geog. Soc. (rep. search com. for curator of collection in Golda Meir Libr. U. Wis.-Milw. Libr. 1993-94); mem. AAAS, Am. Math. Soc., Math. Assn. Am., Assn. Am. Geographers, Internat. Soc. Spatial Scis. (founder), N.Y. Acad. Scis., Engring. Soc. Detroit, Regional Sci. Assn. Achievements include discovery of exact fractal characterization of the geometry of central place theory and its electronic interpretation; alignment of earth marking sculptures to solstices and equinoxes in Minnesota, Washington, Alaska, New Brunswick, Canada, and USSR; creator of one of world's first refereed electronic journals; creator of applications of chaos theory in geography and population environment dynamics, maps for major international projects for Syria and Pakistan. Office: U Mich Sch Natural Resources Ann Arbor MI 48109

ARLOFF, WILLIAM JOHN, elementary education educator; b. Kansas City, Mo. s. William Ernest and Barbara Ann Arloff; m. Brenda Jean Anderson, May 23, 1992. BA in English, U. Ill., 1984; MAT in Elem. Edn., Nat.-Louis U., 1989. Cert. tchr., K-9, Ill., 1-6, Ind. Pre-sch. tchrs. asst. Montessori Learning Ctr., Batavia, Ill., 1986-87; tchr. 5th grade Westgate Sch., Sch. Dist. 25, Arlington Heights, Ill., 1988-89, tchr. multi-age 4th and 5th grade, 1989-91; tchr. 5th grade Lincoln Trail Sch., Mahomet, Ill., 1991-92; substitute tchr. Monroe County Comty. Sch. Corp., Bloomington, Ind., 1992-93; profl. devel. coord. Nat. Ednl. Svc., Bloomington, 1992-93; tchr. 4th grade Binford Sch., Monroe County Comty. Sch. Corp., Bloomington, 1993-94; 5th grade tchr. Westside Sch., Cold Springs Harbor, N.Y., 1997—. Named Tchr. of Week, Sta. WRTV-6 Indpls. and John Dehaan Found., 1994; recipient All-Star Tchr. award SCOPE of L.I., 2000. Mem. Nat. Coun. Tchrs. English, Nat. Coun. Tchrs. Math., Tchrs. Applying Whole Lang. Home: 14 Media Ln Stony Brook NY 11790-2812

ARMACOST, MARY-LINDA SORBER MERRIAM, former academic administrator, consultant; b. Jeannette, Pa., May 31, 1943; d. Everett Sylvester Calvin and Madeleine (Case) Sorber; m. E. William Merriam, Dec. 13, 1969 (div. 1975); m. Peter H. Armacost, July 10, 1993. Student, Grove City Coll., 1961-63; BA, Pa. State U., 1963-65, MA, 1965-67, PhD, 1967-70; HHD (hon.), Carroll Coll., 1991; LLD (hon.), Wilson Coll., 1994. Rsch. assoc. Pa. State U., University Park, 1970-72; asst. prof. speech Emerson Coll., Boston, 1972-79, dir. continuing edn., 1974-77, spl. asst. to pres., 1977-78, v.p. adminstrn., 1978-79; asst. to pres. Boston U., 1979-81; pres. Wilson Coll., Chambersburg, Pa., 1981-91, Moore Coll. Art and Design, Phila., 1991-93; sr. fellow Office of Women in Higher Edn. Am. Coun. on Edn., 1994—; interim pres. Moore Coll. Art and Design, Phila., 1998-99; pres. emerita, 2000. Adj. prof. U. Pa. Grad. Sch. Edn., 2003; cons. Govt. Edn. and Secondary Edn. Act Title III, Alameda County, Calif., 1968. Bd. govs. New Eng. chpt. NATAS, 1980-81; bd. dirs. Sta. WITF, Inc., Harrisburg, Pa., 1982-91, chmn. bd., 1988-91; bd. dirs. Chambersburg Hosp., 1984-89, vice chmn. bd., 1987-89; bd. dirs. Elderhostel, 1997—; vice-chmn., 2000—; trustee Monmouth U., N.J., 1994-99, Sta. WHYY-FM-

TV, Phila., 1992-93, Boston Zool. Soc., 1980-81, Arts Boston, 1979-81, Scotland Sch. Vets. Children, Pa., 1984-90, Randolph-Macon Woman's Coll., Lynchburg, Va., 2001—; bd. dirs. Fla. Orch., 1993-97, co-chair edn. com., 1995-97, mem. exec. com., 1995-97; mem. exec. com. Found. for Ind. Colls., 1989-91, WEDU-TV, 1998—, chair planning com., mem. exec. com., 1998—; pres. Chambersburg Area Coun. Arts, 1988-90; chmn. higher edn. com. Gen. Assembly Presbyn. Ch., 1987-90; elder Falling Spring Presbyn. Ch., 1988-90; fellow Am. Coun. Edn., 1977-78, commn. on govtl. rels., 1985-89, commn. on women, 1992-93; mem. exec. com. Pa. Assn. Colls. and Univs., 1984-90, mem. exec. com. Assn. Presbyn. Colls. and Univs., 1983-88, pres., 1986-87; mem. edn. adv. com. John S. & James L. Knight Found., 1998-2000. Recipient Disting. Alumna award Pa. State U., 1984, Disting. Dau. of Pa., 1986, Athena award Chambersburg C. of C., 1988, Outstanding Alumnae award Sch. Dist. Jeannette, 1991. Mem.: Phi Kappa Phi. E-mail: mlsma@cs.com.

ARMACOST, PETER HAYDEN, academic administrator; b. N.Y.C., July 12, 1935; s. George Henry and Verda Gay (Hayden) A.; m. Suzanne Lee Sadosky, June 22, 1957 (dec. Feb. 1991); children: Martha Hayden, David Keys, Sarah Jane, Rebecca Ann; m. Mary-Linda Merriam, July 10, 1993. BA, Denison U., 1957; PhD, U. Minn., 1963. Dean students, chmn. dept. psychology Augsburg Coll., Mpls., 1959-65; program dir. Assn. Am. Colls., Washington, 1965-67; pres., prof. psychology Ottawa U., (Kans.), 1967-77; pres. Eckerd Coll., St. Petersburg, Fla., 1977—2000, pres. emeritus, 2000—; sr. adviser Coun. Ind. Colls., 2001—; pres., prin. Forman Christian Coll., 2002—. Author materials in field. Chmn. Kansas City (Mo.) Regional Coun. Higher Edn., 1972-74; pres. Am. Bapt. Chs. U.S., 1974-75, So. Univ. Conf., 1997; bd. dirs. United Way of Pinellas County, 1995—. Recipient Disting. Alumnus citation Denison U.; Woodrow Wilson fellow; Danforth fellow; named to Tampa Bay Bus. Hall of Fame, 1999. Mem. Assn. Am. Colls. (bd. dirs.), Am. Coun. Edn., Nat. Assn. Student Pers. Adminstrs. (bd. dirs. divsn. rsch., publs. and conf. chmn. Disting. Svc. award), Assn. Ind. Colls. Kans. (pres. 1970-72), Young Pres. Orgn. (chmn. Fla. chpt. 1983-84), So. Assn. of Colls. and Schs. (appeals com.), Am. Assn. Higher Edn., Soc. Values in Higher Edn., Nat. Assn. Ind. Coll. and U. Pres., Fla. Assn. Colls. and Univs. (pres. 1989-90), Ind. Colls. and Univs. Fla. (sec. 1984-86, treas. 1986-88, vice chmn. 1990-91, chmn. 1991-93), Coun. Ind. Colls. (bd. dirs. 1993—, sec. exec. com.), Nat. Assn. Ind. Colls. and Univs. (bd. dirs. 1995-98), Suncoast C. of C. (chmn. 1984-85), Pinellas Econ. Devel. Coun. (bd. dirs. 1989—), Fla. Coun. of 100, St. Petersburg C. of C. (bd. dirs. 1995—), St. Petersburg Yacht Club, Suncoasters Club, Rotary, SunTrust Bank of Tampa Bay (bd. dirs. 1983—), Blue Key, Phi Beta Kappa, Omicron Delta Kappa, Pi Gamma Mu, Psi Chi. Republican. Home: 555 5th Ave NE #914 Saint Petersburg FL 33701 Office: Eckerd Coll 4200 54th Ave S Saint Petersburg FL 33711-4744

ARMACOST, ROBERT LEO, management educator, former coast guard officer; b. Balt., July 17, 1942; s. Leo Mathias and Margaret Virginia (Ruth) A.; m. Susan Marie Danesi, Jan. 16, 1965 (div.); children: Robert Leo, Andrew Paul, Kathleen Erin; m. Julia Johanna Agricola Pet, Apr. 17, 1999. BS with honors, USCG Acad., 1964; MS, USN Postgrad. Sch., 1970; DSc in Ops. Rsch., George Washington U., 1976. Engring. officer USCG Cutter Mendota, Wilmington, N.C., 1964-66; ops. officer USCGC Cook Inlet, Portland, Maine, 1966-68; ops. rsch. analyst, ops. planning staff USCG Hdqrs., Washington, 1970-75, planning officer, aids to navigation divsn., 1976-78, comdr. Coast Guard Group Milw., 1978-81; comdg. officer USCG Marine Safety Office, Milw., 1981-84, capt. of port, 1981-84, officer in charge of marine inspection, 1981-84, ret., 1984. Instr. computer sci. Milw. Area Tech. Coll., 1982-83; asst. prof. mgmt. sci. Marquette U., Milw., 1984-91, assoc. prof. mgmt. sci., 1991; asst. prof. ops. rsch. U. Ctrl. Fla., 1991-96, assoc. prof. ops. rsch., 1996—, IE Grad. Program Coord., dir. office of univ. analysis and planning support, 2000—. Contbr. articles to profl. jours. First v.p. Md. Right to Life, 1976-78; active Milw. Pastoral Coun., 1984-89, vice chmn., 1986-87, chmn., 1987-88; bd. dirs. Nicholet H.S. Found., 1986-88. Named Outstanding Civic Vol., Bowie, Md., 1976, nat. finalist White House fellow, 1977—78; recipient USCG commendation award, 1972, 1974, 1978, 1981, 1984. Mem. Ops. Rsch. Soc. Am. (com. 1983-94, chmn. 1990-94, fin. com. 1993-94), Math. Programming Soc., Decision Scis. Inst., Inst. Ind. Engrs. (v.p. tech. networking), Inst. Ops. Rsch. and Mgmt. Scis. (chair membership com. 1995-96, fin. com. 1995-97, dir. at large 1995-97, bd. dirs. 1995-97). Roman Catholic. Home: 602 Shorewood Dr Unit 402 Cape Canaveral FL 32920-5082 Office: U Ctrl Fla Univ Analysis and Planning Support Orlando FL 32826-3207 E-mail: armacost@mail.ucf.edu.

ARMANIOS, ERIAN ABDELMESSIH, aerospace engineer, educator; b. Cairo, July 6, 1950; arrived in U.S., 1980; s. Abdelmessih Armanios; m. Mahera S. Philobos, May 2, 1980; children: Daniel, Laura. BS in Aero. Engring., Cairo U., 1974, MS in Aero. Engring., 1979; PhD in Aerospace Engring., Ga. Inst. Tech., 1985. Teaching asst. U. Cairo, 1974-79, asst. lectr., 1979-80; grad. rsch. asst. Ga. Inst. Tech., Atlanta, 1980-84, rsch. engr. I, 1985-86, asst. prof., 1986-91, assoc. prof., 1991-97, prof., 1997—. Cons. Bell Helicopter Textron Inc., Ft. Worth, 1984-85, Rolls-Royce Inc., Atlanta, 1989-95, Allison Engine Co., Indpls. 1995-96, Guided System Techs., 1991-92; judge Ga. Sci. and Engring. Fair, Atlanta, 1987; judge space sci. student program NASA, Atlanta, 1988-98, Internat. Sci. and Engring. Fair, 1998-2003; dir. Ga. Space Grant Consortium, 1991—; adv. bd. Ctr. Excellence in Sci., Engring. and Math., Morehouse Coll., 1997—. Editor: Interlaminar Fracture of Composites, 1989, Fracture of Composites, 1996, Composite Materials: Fatigue and Fracture, 6th vol., 1997; editl. bd. Jour. Composites Tech. and Rsch., 1992-99, editor-in-chief, 2000—; mem. editl bd. Jour. of Nat. Tech. Assn., 1995—; contbr. articles to profl. jours.; patentee in field. Recipient Tchg. Excellence award Ctr. for Enhancement of Tchg. and Learning, Amoco Found., 1990, Outstanding Paper award Jour. Aerospace Engring., 1990, Sigma Xi Outstanding PhD Thesis Advisor award, 1991, 98, Jr. Faculty award, 1991, Ga. Inst. Tech. Faculty Rsch. award 1996, Outstanding Tchr. award, 1999, Sci. Application Internat. Corp. cert. of award, 1990, 95, 97, Regents Tchg. Excellence award, 2000, Wayne W. Stinchcomb Meml. award, 2002. Fellow AIAA (assoc.); mem. ASTM (com. on high modulus fibers and composites 1988); Am. Soc. for Composites, Am. Helicopter Soc. (com. on structures and materials). Office: Ga Inst Tech Sch Aerospace Engring Atlanta GA 30332-0001

ARMENAKAS, ANTHONY EMMANUEL, aerospace educator; b. Mytilene, Greece, Aug. 23, 1924; came to U.S., 1946; s. Emmanuel Anthony and Efterpe (Sakis) A.; m. Stella Dimitri Petroutsa, Jan. 3, 1950 (dec. Jan. 1988); children: Alexandra Daphne, Noel Anthony, Melina Cybel. BSCE, Ga. Inst. Tech., 1950; MSCE, Ill. Inst. Tech., 1952; PhD in Applied Mechanics, Columbia U., 1959. Registered profl. engr., N.Y., N.J., Greece. Instr. Ill. Inst. Tech., Chgo., 1950-52; sr. structural engr. Edwards Kelcey and Beck Cons. Engrs., Newark, 1952-54; ptnr. Rynar Armenakas and McCann Cons. Engrs., Newark, 1954-59; lectr. civil engring. CUNY, N.Y.C., 1954-57; assoc. prof. civil engring. Cooper Union for the Advancement Sci. and Art, N.Y.C., 1958-65; prof. engring. sci. U. Fla., Gainesville, 1965-67; prof. aerospace Poly. U., Bklyn., 1967—; Fulbright lectr. to Greece, 1972-73, 73-74; prof., dir. Inst. Structural Analysis, Nat. Tech. U., Athens, Greece, 1977-84. Vis. prof. divsn. engring. Brown U., Providence, 1964-65; cons. Vector Engring., Springfield, N.J., 1954-59; rsch. cons. Poly. Inst., Bklyn., 1962-67, Northwestern U., Evanston, Ill., 1962-65; pres. Stress-Optics, Inc., Queens, N.Y., 1970-72; bd. dirs. Greek r.r.s, 1978-80; vice-chmn. bd. dirs. Greek agy. for design and rsch. earthquake protection, 1989-92. Author: Free Vibrations of Circular Cylindrical Shells, 1969, Tensor Analysis for Engineers, 1974, Classical Structure Analysis-A Modern Approach, 1988, Modern Structural Analysis-The Matrix Method Approach, 1991; patentee in field; contbr. articles to profl. jours. Chmn. bd. dirs. Poulos Philanthropic Found., Athens, Greece. Fellow ASCE, ASME. Avocation: photography. Home: 52 Clark St Brooklyn NY 11201-2402 also: Kifissou 3A Xalandri Attica 15234 Athens Greece Office: Polytechnic Univ 333 Jay St Brooklyn NY 11201-2990

ARMENAKAS, NOEL ANTHONY, medical educator; b. Orange, N.J., Sept. 29, 1958; s. Anthony E. and Stella P. (Petroutsa) A.; m. Macrene R. Alexiades, Oct. 26, 1996; children: Sophie Stella, Anthony Emmanuel. MD, U. Athens, Greece, 1985. Diplomate Am. Bd. Urology. Intern surgery Lenox Hill Hosp., N.Y.C., 1985-86; resident surgery Monmouth Med. Ctr., Long Branch, N.J., 1986-87; resident urology Lenox Hill Hosp., N.Y.C., 1987-91; fellow trauma and reconstructive surgery U. Calif., San Francisco, 1991-92, clin. instr. dept. urology, 1991-92; clin. instr. dept. surgery Cornell U. Med. Coll., N.Y.C., 1992-94; clin. asst. prof. dept. urology Cornell U. Med. Sch., N.Y.C., 1994—2002, clin. assoc. prof. dept. urology, 2002—. Mem. oper. rm. com. Lenox Hill Hosp., 1990, outpatient clinic com., 1993—; mem. ChubbHealth Physician Adv. Panel, 1994-2000; mem. scholarship com. Hellenic Med. Assn.; attending staff San Francisco (Calif.) Gen. Hosp., 1991-92; dir., physician-in-charge Outpatient Urologic Clinics Lenox Hill Hosp., 1992—; attending staff N.Y. Presbyn. Hosp., N.Y.C., 1992—, Lenox Hill Hosp., N.Y.C., 1992—; lectr. in field. Contbr. chpts. to books and articles to profl. jours. Fellow ACS; mem. Internat. Soc. Urology, Am. Assn. Clin. Urologists, Am. Urol. Assn., Hellenic Med. Assn., Soc. for Urology and Engring., Soc. Genitourinary and Reconstructive Surgeons, N.Y. Acad. Medicine. Avocations: skiing, tennis, traveling. Office: New York Urological Assocs 880 5th Ave New York NY 10021-4951 E-mail: drarmenakas@nyurological.com.

ARMES, WALTER SCOTT, vocational school administrator; b. Okmulgee, Okla., May 15, 1939; s. Ralph E. Armes; m. Jean Hopkins, June 5, 1965; children: Christina M., Rebecca J. BS in edn., Ohio No. U., 1960; MS, Ind. State U., Terre Haute, 1966; postgrad., Ohio State U. Cert. supt., prin., social studies tchr., Ohio. Tchr. social studies Holmes Liberty Sch. Dist., Bucyrus, Ohio, 1960-63, Painesville Twp. Schs., 1963-64, Weathersfield Twp. Sch. Dist., Mineral Ridge, Ohio, 1964-68, Eastland Career Ctr., Groveport, Ohio, 1968-97; dir. Eastland Vocat. Sch. Dist., Groveport, 1993—97; supr. Licking County Vocat. Sch., Newark, Ohio, 1998—2002; adj. faculty Ashland (Ohio) U., 2003—. Co-founder Franklin County Tchrs. Ctr.; adj. faculty Ashland U., 2003; exec. bd. Met. Edn. Coun. Chmn. Whitehall City Bd. Zoning and Bldg. Appeals; active C. Ray Williams Presch. Adv. Com.; pres. Whitehall City Bd. Edn.; adv. com. Ohio H.S. Athletic Assn. Track and Field; ofcl. USA Track and Field. Mem. Nat. Assn. Secondary Sch. Prins., Ohio Assn. Track and Field and Cross Country Ofcls., Track Registry Ctrl. Ohio, Ohio Sch. Bd. Assn., Am. Sch. Bds. Assn., Phi Delta Kappa. Home: 4010 Etna St Columbus OH 43213-2317

ARMINANA, RUBEN, academic administrator, educator; b. Santa Clara, Cuba, May 15, 1947; came to U.S., 1961; s. Aurelio Ruben and Olga Petrona (Nart) A.; m. Marne Olson, June 6, 1954; children: Cesar A. Martino, Tuly Arminana. AA, Hill Jr. Coll., 1966; BA, U. Tex., 1968, MA, 1970; PhD, U. New Orleans, 1983; postgrad. Inst. of Applied Behavioral Scis., Nat. Tng. Labs., 1971. Nat. assoc. dir. Phi Theta Kappa, Canton, Miss., 1968-69; dir. ops. and tng. Inter-Am. Ctr. Loyola U., New Orleans, 1969-71; adminstrv. analyst City of New Orleans, 1972, adminstrv. analyst and orgnl. devel. and tng. cons., 1972-78; anchor and reporter part time STA. WWL-TV, New Orleans, 1973-81; v.p. Commerce Internat. Corp., New Orleans, 1978-83; exec. asst. to sr. v.p. Tulane U., New Orleans, 1983-85, assoc. exec. v.p., 1985-87, v.p., asst. to pres., 1987-88; v.p. fin. and devel. Calif. State Poly U., Pomona, 1988-92; pres. Sonoma State U., 1992—. TV news cons., New Orleans, 1981-88; lectr. Internat. Trade Mart, New Orleans, 1983-89, U.S. Dept. Commerce, New Orleans. Co-author: Hemisphere West-El Futuro, 1968; co-editor: Colloquium on Central America-A Time for Understanding, Background Readings, 1985. Bd. dirs. Com. on Alcoholism and Substance Abuse, 1978-79, SER, Jobs for Progress, Inc., 1974-82, Citizens United for Responsive Broadcasting, Latin Am. Festival Com.; dir. bd. advisors Sta. WDSU-TV, 1974-77; mem. Bus. Govt. Rsch., 1987-88, Coun. Advancement of Support to Edn.; mem. League of United Latin Am. Citizens, Mayor's Latin Am. Adv. Com., Citizens to Preserve the Charter, Met. Area Com., Mayor's Com. on Crime. Kiwanis scholar, 1966, Books scholar, 1966. Mem. Assn. U. Related Rsch. Prks., L.A. Higher Edn. Roundtable, Soc. Coll. and U. Planning, Nat. Assn. Coll. and U. Bus. Officers Coun., Am. Econ. Assn., Assn. of Evolutionary Econs., Am. Polit. Sci. Assn., AAUP, Western Coll. Assn. (pres. 1994-95), Latin Am. C. of C. (founding dir. New Orleans and River Region 1976-83), Cuban Profl. Club, Phi Theta Kappa, Omicron Delta Epsilon, Sigma Delta Pi, Delta Sigma Pi. Democrat. Roman Catholic. Avocation: mask collecting. Office: Sonoma State U 1801 E Cotati Ave Rohnert Park CA 94928-3609 E-mail: ruben.arminana@sonoma.edu.

ARMSTEAD, TRESSA MADDUX, secondary school educator; b. Pecos, Tex., Apr. 23, 1949; d. Obie Eugene and Nell (Simpson) Maddux; m. Karl Frank Armstead, June 8, 1974; children: Stephen Kristopher, Tiffany Julene. BS, Sul Ross State U., 1970; MA, Eastern New Mex. U., 1977. Cert. secondary tchr., Tex. Educator Boyd (Tex.) Ind. Sch. Dist.; grad. asst. Eastern N.Mex. U., Portales; tchr. Pecos (Tex.)-Barstow-Toyah Ind. Sch. Dist., Midland (Tex.) Ind. Sch. Dist., Ector County Ind. Sch. Dist. Mem. Tex. Classroom Tchrs. Assn., Nat. Coun. Tchrs. English, Tex. Joint Coun. Tchrs. English, Delta Kappa Gamma.

ARMSTRONG, DARLENE L. elementary education educator; b. Skowhegan, Maine, June 20, 1949; d. Henry Bernard and Erma Lillian (Morrill) Dillingham; m. Robert W. Armstrong, June 5, 1971; 1 child, Jennifer Gail. BS cum laude, Eastern Nazarene Coll., 1971; MEd, U. Maine, Orono, 2001. Tchr. grades 2 and 3 St. Paul's Epsicopal. Parish Day Sch., Kansas City, Mo., 1971-73; tchr. grade 2 Ridgedale Local Sch. Dist., Marion, Ohio, 1973-76; tchr. grade 6 Sch. Dist. 54, Skowhegan, 1984-85; tchr. 1st grade Sch. Dist. 49, Fairfield, Maine, 1985—. Mem. Dist. Lang. Arts Com.; coord. Reading is Fundamental; mem. Student Assistance Team, Family Literacy Team, Local Assessment Devel. Pilot Project, No Child Left Behind Team. Co-host weekend radio program. Dir. Young Authors' Camp, 2000—; bd. dirs. Nat. Writing Project. Named Worker of Yr., Ch. of Nazarene, 1988; fellow, Nat. Writing Project, 1999. Mem. NEA, Maine Tchrs. Assn., Ohio Tchrs. Assn. (elem rep. exec. bd.), Ridgedale Tchrs. Assn., SAD #49 Tchr's. Assn. (rep. staff devel. team bldg.), Phi Delta Lambda, Pi Lambda Theta. Democrat. Avocations: reading, music, traveling, drama, poetry. also: 62 Old Benton Neck Rd Waterville ME 04901-3031

ARMSTRONG, EDWARD BRADFORD, JR., oral and maxillofacial surgeon, educator, naval officer; b. Teaneck, N.J., Sept. 24, 1928; s. Edward Bradford and Ruth Elizabeth (Fippinger) A.; AB, U. Pa., 1950; DDS, N.Y.U., 1954; m. Dusanka Vladimirovna Jakovljevic, Nov. 5, 1960; children: Edward Bradford, III, James B., Hugh B. Commd. lt. j.g. U.S. Navy, 1954, advanced through grades to capt. 1971; intern oral surgery Roosevelt Hosp., N.Y.C., 1958, assoc. attending oral surgery, 1959—, attending oral surgeon out-patient dept., 1959—, chmn., moderator Oral Surgery Staff Confs., 1963-70; resident Carle Hosp., Urbana, Ill., 1959; assoc. attending oral surgeon Flower and Fifth Ave. hosps., N.Y.C., 1960-78; asst. attending oral surgeon Hackensack (N.J.) Hosp., 1963-65; adminstrv. officer Naval Res. Dental Co. 3-2, 1965-68, exec. officer, 1968-71, comdg. officer, 1971-73; comdt.'s rep. 3d Naval Dist., Naval Acad., 1972-78, 3d Naval Dist for Dentistry, 1973-75, group staff officer for dentistry and medicine, 1973-75, Ready Res. Unit 502, 1975-77, VTU 0207, 1977-79, ret., 1979; assoc. clin. prof. oral surgery N.Y. Med. Coll., 1963-93; adj. assoc. clin. prof. oral surgery Columbia U. Sch. Dentistry, 1973-89; chmn. bd. E. & R. Armstrong, Inc., Albany, N.Y., 1966-77; pres. Edward B. Armstrong, P.C., N.Y.C., 1979-90; dir. Songtime, Inc., Boston; dir., mem. exec. com. PGP Internat. Corps, Inc. Bd. dirs., trustee Christian Mission Farms of Paraguay, Inc., 1974-84; pres., trustee Central Bible Chapel, Palisades Park, N.J.; area rep., ann. giving U. Pa., 1960-68; Blue and Gold officer Naval Acad. Admissions Com.; sec. bd. dirs., trustee Boys' Club of N.Y. Health Svcs., Inc. Diplomate Am. Bd. Oral Surgery. Fellow N.Y. Acad. Dentistry (sec., dir., pres. 1979-80), Am., Internat. Colls. Dentists (life), Am. Coll. Oral and Maxillofacial Surgeons (founding), Am. Dental Soc. Anesthesiology (hon. life); mem. ADA (life, 1st dist. life), Am. Assn. Oral and Maxillofacial Surgeons (life, N.J. rep. Ho. of Dels. 1963-65), N.Y. Soc. Oral Surgeons (life, chmn. audit and budget com. 1972-79), First Dist. Dental Soc. (life), N.Y. Dental Soc., Bklyn. Dental Soc., Yokosuka Dental Soc. (hon.), Assn. Mil. Surgeons U.S., Mil. Order World Wars, Naval Res. Assn. (life), Union League (chmn. art com. 1973-76, bd. govs. 1974-77, 82-84, v.p. 1977-80, 85-88), Met. Club (bd. gov. 1992-96, 98-2002), N.Y.C., U. Pa. Club, U. Pa. Club of Met. N.J. (dir. 1982—), Acacia, Xi Psi Phi, Psi Omega (hon.), Delta Sigma Delta. Mem. Plymouth Brethren Ch.

ARMSTRONG, (ARTHUR) JAMES (ARTHUR ARMSTRONG), minister, educator, consultant, writer; b. Marion, Ind., Sept. 17, 1924; s. Arthur J. and Frances (Green) A.; m. Sharon Owen, Apr. 8, 2000; children from previous marriages: Eve Stoughton, Allison, James, Teresa, John, Rebecca Putens, Leslye Armstrong Hope. AB, Fla. So. Coll., 1948; BD, Candler Sch. Theology, Emory U., 1952; DD, Fla. So. U., 1960, DePauw U., 1965; LHD, Ill. Wesleyan U., 1970, Dakota Wesleyan U., 1970, Westmar Coll., 1971, Ind. Ctrl. U., 1982, Emory U., 1982. Ordained to ministry Meth. Ch., 1948. Minister in Fla., 1945-58; sr. minister Broadway Meth. Ch., Indpls., 1958-68; bishop United Meth. Ch., Dakotas area, 1968-80, Ind. area, Indpls., 1980-83; exec. v.p. conflict resolution firm, Washington, 1984-87; vis. prof. preaching and social ministries Iliff Sch. Theology, Denver, 1985-91; sr. min. 1st Congl. Ch., Winter Park, Fla., 1991-99; exec. dir. Ctr. on Dialogue and Devel., Denver, 1984-96. Adj. prof. Rollins Col., 1992—, South Fla. Ctr. Theol. Studies, 1999—; instr. Christian Theol. Sem., Indpls., 1961-68; del. 4th Gen. Assembly, World Coun. Chs., 1968, 6th Gen. Assembly, 1983; pres. Nat. Coun. Chs., 1982-83; pres. bd. ch. and soc. United Meth. Ch., 1972-76, chmn. com. for peace and self devel. of peoples, 1972-76, pres. Commn. on Religion and Race, 1976-83; exec. v.p. Pagan Internat., 1982-87. Author: The Journey That Men Make, 1969, The Urgent Now, 1970, Mission: Middle America, 1971, The Pastor and the Public Servant, 1972, United Methodist Primer, 1973, 77, Wilderness Voices, 1974, The Nation Yet To Be, 1975, Telling Truth: The Foolishness of Preaching in a Real World, 1977, From the Underside, 1981, Feet of Clay, on Solid Ground, 2002; contbg. author: The Pulpit Speaks on Race, 1966, War Crimes and the American Conscience, 1970, Rethinking Evangelism, 1971, What's a Nice Church Like You Doing in a Place Like This?, 1972, The Miracle of Easter, 1980, Preaching on Peace, 1982, Ethics and the Multi-National Enterprise, 1986, The Best of the Circuit Rider, 1987, Prayerfully Pro-Choice, 1999. Vice-chmn. Hoosiers for Peace, 1968; mem. Ind. State Platform Com. Democratic Party, 1968, Nat. Coalition for a Responsible Congress, 1970. With USNR, 1942. Recipient Disting. Svc. award, Indpls. Jr. C. of C., 1959. Mem. Fla. Coun. Chs. (pres. 1996-97), Ctrl. Fla. Interfaith Alliance (co-chair 1994-96). Methodist.

ARMSTRONG, JOANNA, education educator; b. Vienna, Feb. 3, 1915; came to U.S., 1946; m. David B. Armstrong, Mar. 12, 1946 (dec. Feb. 1992). Diploma, Kindergarten Tchr. State Coll., Vienna, 1933; diploma French Lit., Sorbonne, Paris, 1935; MA, U. Utah, 1951; EdD, U. Houston, 1959. Caseworker, interpreter Czech Refugee Trust Fund, London, 1939-41; tchr. French Gt. Missenden, Bucks, Eng., 1941-43; sec., translator-interpreter U.S. Army, England and France, 1943-46; instr. Coll. William and Mary, Williamsburg, Va., 1951-55, U. St. Thomas, Houston, 1957-59; chmn. langs. sect. South Tex. Coll., Houston, 1961-62; assoc. prof. fgn. langs. Tex. So. U., Houston, 1962-68; dir. NDEA Inst. U. Tex. at Houston, Houston, summer 1964, 65; assoc. prof. sch. edn. tng. Headstart tchrs. U. Tex., El Paso, 1968-71; cons. office Child Devel. HEW, Kansas City, Mo., 1973-75; ret., 1975. Cons. Tex. Edn. Agy., Austin, 1965; sec. U.S. Forest Svc., Ely, Nev., 1948; dir. summer programs U. Bordeaux at Pau, U. Zaragoza at Jaca. Author: (book) A European Excursion-From the Mediterranean to the Alps, 1967, Surprising Encounters, 1994; contbr. articles to profl. publs. Vol. Long Beach (Calif.) Symphony, 1978-81, Long Beach Opera, 1982-88, Long Beach Cambodian Scs., 1983-85; mem. Normandy Found. (participant 50th D-Day anniversary 1994). Decorated chevalier Ordre des Palmes Academiques, 1969; recipient award Heart Start, 1971, Pres. plaque Alliance Francaise El Paso, 1971, Commemorative Medal of Freedom, Coun. of Normandy, France, 1994. Mem. Long Beach Women's Music Club (program chmn. 1986-88, mem. choral sect. 1989-96, 1st v.p. 1990-92, rec. sec., chmn. opera sect. 1993-94), U.S.-China Peoples Friendship Assn. (rec. sec. 1987—), W.A.C. (Queen City chpt. 57). Avocations: walking, swimming, travel, photography, opera. Home: 215 Long Beach Blvd Ste 206 Long Beach CA 90802-3136

ARMSTRONG, JOHN ALEXANDER, political scientist, educator; b. St. Augustine, Fla., May 4, 1922; s. John Alexander and Maria (Hernandez) A.; m. Annette Taylor, June 14, 1952; children: Janet Ann, Carol Louise, Kathryn Marie. Ph.B., U. Chgo., 1948, MA, 1949; student, U. Frankfurt, Germany, 1949-50; PhD, Columbia U., 1953. Research analyst War Documentation Project, Alexandria, Va., 1951, 53-54; asst. prof. internat. relations U. Denver, 1952; vis. asst. prof. internat. relations Columbia U., 1957; mem. faculty U. Wis., Madison, 1954-86, prof. polit. sci., 1960-78, Philippe de Commynes prof. polit. sci., 1978-86, emeritus prof., 1986—; exec. sec. Russian area studies program, 1959-63, 64-65; acting dir. Western European area studies program, 1966-67. Adv. panel European affairs State Dept., 1966-69, cons. bur. intelligence and rsch., 1972-81; mem. Cath. Commn. on Intellectual and Cultural Affairs, So. Conf. on Slavic Studies. Author: Ukrainian Nationalism, 3d edit, 1990, The Soviet Bureaucratic Elite, 2d edit, 1966, The Politics of Totalitarianism, 1961, Ideology, Politics and Government in the Soviet Union, 4th edit, 1978, The European Administrative Elite, 1973, Nations Before Nationalism, 1982; editor: Soviet Partisans in World War II, 1964. Served with AUS, 1942-46, ETO. Guggenheim fellow, 1967-68, 75-76 Mem. Am. Assn. Advancement Slavic Studies (pres. 1965-67), Council Fgn. Relations, Am. Hist. Assn., Am. Polit. Sci. Assn., Kennan Inst. Advanced Russian Studies (acad. council 1981-84), Phi Beta Kappa. Home: 40 Water St Saint Augustine FL 32084-2885

ARMSTRONG, KAREN LEE, special education educator; b. Schenectady, N.Y., Dec. 6, 1941; d. William James and Rita Mae (Peabody) Safford; m. John Edward Armstrong, July 14, 1962; 1 child, Lori Ellen. BA in English, SUNY, Albany, 1963, MS in Spl. Edn., 1986. Tchr. English Ballston Lake High Sch., Burnt Hills, N.Y., 1963-66; tchr. spl. edn. Oak Hill Sch., Scotia, N.Y., 1975-88, Schenectady City Schs., 1988—; mem. policy bd. Ctr. Profl. Edn., 2001—. Mem. curriculum coun., lead tng. sessions Schenectady Schs., 1988—; mem. Shared Decision Making Team, 1994—, spl. edn. del. to China, U.S. del. to South Africa, 1995; lectr. in field of behavior mgmt. V.p. bd. edn. Oak Hill Sch., mem. bd. edn., 2001—. Mem. Coun. for Exceptional Children, Coun. for Children with Behavioral Disorders., Amnesty Internat. (founding Schenectady br.), Adirondack Mountain Club. Sufi. Avocations: hiking, camping, gardening. E-mail: armstrongk@schenectady.k12.ny.us.

ARMSTRONG, LEONA MAY BOTTRELL, retired counselor, educator; b. Rochester, Ill., Aug. 14, 1930; d. Vernon Sampson Bottrell and Leonia Ruth (Meeks) Cooper; m. Bryce Glenn Armstrong, June 11, 1950 (div. 1975); children: Steven Lee, Rebecca Sue, Paul Bryce, (twins) Kevin John and Brian Mark. BS, U. Indpls., 1952; MS, U. Wis., 1967. Tchr., Dayton, Ohio, 1952-55; sch. counselor Oshkosh, Verona, West Allis, Wis., 1967-88; pvt. practice as counselor, astrologer, tchr. Milw., 1988-95; ret., 1995. Reiki master Reiki Healers Internat., 1992; guest spkr. in area of parapsychology and metaphysics U. Minn., U. Wis., Milw., other schs., 1980—; spkr. World

Peace Program, Milw., 1987. Ecumenical spkr. United Ch. Women, 1966. Named Outstanding Sr. Woman, Philalethea Lit. Soc., 1952, one of Outstanding Personalities in Midwest, AAUW and Profs. at U. Wis.-Oshkosh, 1968. Mem. Nat. Coun. for Geocosmic Rsch. Home and Office: 4514 67th St Kenosha WI 53142-1602 E-mail: leonaarmstrong@acronet.net.

ARMSTRONG, LESLIE ANN CRONKHITE, educational visual arts specialist, graphic artist; b. Pendleton, Oreg., Apr. 29, 1954; d. Jackson Edward and Ann Marie (Bogovich) Cronkhite; m. Robert John Armstrong, June 21, 1980; children: Lindsay, Cailey, Stacey. BA in Edn., BFA in Art, Ea. Wash. U., 1977; postgrad., Seattle U., 1983. Tour guide Ford Motor Co., Expo 74, Spokane, Wash., 1973-74; tchr. art, coach Kennedy High Sch., Seattle, 1977-84; art specialist Kent (Wash.) Sch. Dist., 1989—; co-owner Rosewood Farms Art Loft, Kent, Wash., 1993—. Freelance graphic artist; guest tchr. AG Petunia Art Works, Seattle, 1992. Exhibited in group show Bellevue (Wash.) Arts Festival, 1992, 93; illustrator: Our Best to Your, 1981, Kite Flight, 1986. Mem. U.S. Equestrian Campaign Team. Grantee King County Arts Commn., 1991. Mem. Nat. Art Edn. Assn., Kappa Alpha Theta. Roman Catholic. Avocations: horseback riding, drawing, gardening, cooking, travel. Home: 13836 SE 237th Pl Kent WA 98042-3232

ARMSTRONG, LLOYD, JR., university official, physics educator; b. Austin, Tex., May 19, 1940; s. Lloyd and Beatrice (Jackson) A.; m. Judith Glantz, July 9, 1965; 1 son, Wade Matthew. BS in Physics, MIT, 1962; PhD in Physics, U. Calif., Berkeley, 1966. Postdoctoral physicist Lawrence Berkeley (Calif.) Lab., 1965-66, cons., 1976; sr. physicist Westinghouse Research Labs., Pitts., 1967-68, cons., 1968-70; research asso. Johns Hopkins U., 1968-69, asst. prof. physics, 1969-73, assoc. prof., 1973-77, prof., 1977-93, chmn. dept. physics and astronomy, 1985-87, dean Sch. Arts and Scis., 1987-93; provost, sr. v.p. for acad. affairs U. So. Calif., L.A., 1993—, prof. physics, 1993—. Assoc. rsch. scientist Nat. Ctr. Sci. Rsch. (CNRS), Orsay, France, 1972—73; vis. fellow Joint Inst. Lab. Astrophysics, Boulder, Colo., 1978—79; program officer NSF, 1981—83, mem. adv. com. for physics, 1985—87, mem. visitors com. physics divsn., 1991; chmn. com. atomic and molecular scis. NAS/NRC, 1985—88, mem. bd. physics and astronomy, 1989—96; mem. adv. bd. Inst. for Theoretical Physics, Santa Barbara, 1992—96, chmn., 1994—95, Inst. Theoretical Atomic and Molecular Physics, Cambridge, Mass., 1994—97, Rochester Theory Ctr. for Optical Sci. and Engring., 1996—98; mem. Coun. on Fgn. Affairs, 2000—. Author: Theory of Hyperfine Structure of Free Atoms, 1971; contbr. articles to profl. jours. Bd. dirs. So. Calif. Econ. Partnership, 1994—2000, Calif. Coun. on Sci. and Tech., 1994—, Pacific Coun. on Internat. Policy, 1996—. NSF grantee, 1972-90; Dept. Energy grantee, 1975-82 Fellow Am. Phys. Soc. Office: U So Calif Office Provost University Park Los Angeles CA 90089-0001

ARMSTRONG, NEAL EARL, civil engineering educator; b. Dallas, Jan. 29, 1941; m. Nancy L. Weinerth; 5 children. BA, U. Tex., 1962, MA, 1965, PhD, 1968. Research engr. Engring. Sci., Inc., 1967-68; asst. office mgr., cons. san. engring., 1968-70; mgr. Washington Research and Devel. Lab., 1970-71; assoc. prof. civil engring. U. Tex., Austin, 1971-79, prof., 1979—, assoc. chmn. dept., 1989-96, assoc. dean acad. affairs Coll. Engring., 1996—. Mem. ASCE, Water Environ. Fedn. (Svc. award 1976, 84, 96, 2003), Am. Acad. Environ. Engrs. (diplomate), Internat. Water Assn., Estuarine Rsch. Fedn. (v.p. 1975-77), Am. Soc. Engring. Edn. Office: U Tex Dept Civil Engring Austin TX 78712

ARMSTRONG, ROBERT BEALL, physiologist, educator; b. Hastings, Nebr., Nov. 13, 1940; s. Edwin Ollis and Elena (Beall) A.; m. Ingrid Elizabeth Vaiciulenas, Apr. 9, 1966; children: Edwin John, Andrew Niel, Sarah Elizabeth. BA, Hastings Coll., 1962; MS, Wash. State U., 1970, PhD, 1973. Asst. prof. biology Boston U., 1973—78; assoc. prof. physiology Oral Roberts U., Tulsa, Okla., 1978—81, prof. physiology, 1981—85; prof. U. Ga., Athens, 1985—90, rsch. prof., 1990—92; Omar Smith prof. health and kinesiology Tex. A&M U., College Station, 1992—, Omar Smith chair, 1995—, disting. prof., 1995—, dept. head, 1992—97, 2000—02. Assoc. zoology Harvard U., Cambridge, Mass., 1977-87; external examiner Nat. U. Singapore, 1984-85; rsch. com. Am. Heart Assn., Athens, 1987-89. Assoc. editor Med. Sci. Sports Exercise, Indpls., 1985-87; contbr. articles to Jour. Applied Physiology, Am. Jour. Physiology. NSF fellow, 1970-73; grantee NIH, 1975-97, Am. Heart Assn., 1981-89, NASA, 1997-2000. Fellow Am. Coll. Sports Medicine (trustee 1986-88); mem. Am. Physiol. Soc. Office: Tex A & M U Dept Health & Kinesiology College Station TX 77843-0001 E-mail: rb-armstrong@hlkn.tamu.edu.

ARMSTRONG, THOMAS FIELD, history educator, college administrator; b. Kansas City, Mo., July 15, 1947; s. John David and Elizabeth Ann (Horine) A.; m. Katherine Findley (div. Jan. 1979); m. Janice Clinedinst Fennell; 1 child, Shannon. BA, U. Colo., 1969, MA, 1970; PhD, U. Va., 1974. Asst. prof. Ga. Coll., Milledgeville, 1974-79, assoc. prof., 1979-83, prof., 1983-93, asst. dean Arts and Scis. Sch., 1985-87, dean, 1987-93; v.p. for acad. affairs Francis Marion U., 1993-94; provost, sr. v.p. Tex. Wesleyan U., 1995—2001, prof. history, 2001—02; pres. Tenn. Wesleyan Coll., Athens, 2003—. Adv. bd. Hist. Westville Crafts, Lumpkin, Ga., 1987-91; bd. dirs. Ga. Coun. for Humanities, Atlanta, 1987-90, sec., 1990. Mem. adv. bd. Jour. Teaching History, 1985—; contbr. articles to profl. jours. Pres. Friends of Libr. Milledgeville, 1980-81, Old Capital Hist. Soc., Milledgeville, 1984-87; chmn. bd. dirs. Mary Vinson Libr., Milledgeville, 1989-93; vice chmn., chmn. Milledgeville Hist. Commn., 1988-91; bd. dirs. Milledgeville-Baldwin County C. of C., 1990-93, pres., 1992-93; bd. dirs. Florence C. of C., 1993-94, Longhorn Coun., BSA, 1996—, Shakespeare in the Park, 1997-2001, Allied Theatre Group, 1999-2001, Leadership Fort Worth, 2001-03, Friends of Ft. Worth Pub. Libr., 2001-03. Thomas Jefferson fellow U. Va., 1971-73; recipient Liberty Bell award Baldwin County Bar Assn., 1988. Mem. Am. Assn. for Higher Edn., Ga. Assn. Historians (pres. 1985-86), So. Hist. Assn., Ga. Hist. Soc. (bd. curators, 1991-94), Orgn. Am. Historians, Deans and Asst. Deans Univ. Systems of Ga. (chmn. 1988-90, bd. dirs. 1991-93), Rotary (bd. dirs. 1991-93), Phi Beta Kappa, Phi Kappa Phi. Avocations: philately, reading, walking. Home: 323 N Jackson Athens TN 37303 Office: Tenn Wesleyan Coll PO Box 40 Athens TN 37371

ARMSTRONG, WARREN BRUCE, former university president, historian, educator; b. Tidioute, Pa., Oct. 16, 1933; s. Mead C. and Mary (Griffin) A.; m. Elizabeth Ann Fowler, Aug. 7, 1954 (div. 1973); children: Linda Susan, Heidi Jo; m. Joan Elizabeth Gregory, Apr. 19, 1974; children: Susan Elizabeth, Pamela Anne. Th.B., Bapt. Coll. Pa., 1956; A.M., U. Mich., 1958, PhD, 1964. Instr. history Olivet Coll., 1961-63, asst. prof., 1963-65, chmn. dept., 1964-65; asst. prof. U. Wis., Whitewater, 1965-66, assoc. prof., 1966-69, prof., 1969-70, asst. dean Coll. Arts and Scis., 1966-69, assoc. dean, 1969-70; dean St. Cloud (Minn.) State U., 1970-75, prof. history, 1970-75; pres. Ea. N.Mex. U., Portales, 1975-83, Wichita (Kans.) State U., 1983-93, pres. emeritus, 1993, prof. history, 1993. Bd. dirs. Bank IV-Wichita, bd. dirs. The Coleman Co., 1985-89. Author: (with Dae Hong Chang) The Prison: Voices from the Inside, 1972, Populism Revisited: The Official Papers of Governor Joan Finney, 1997, For Courageous Fighting and Confident Dying: Union Chaplains in the Civil War, 1998; editor: Populsion Revived: The Selected Papers of Governor Joan Finnay (Kannas) 1991-95, 1998; contbr. articles to profl. jours. Councilman, Whitewater, 1968-70; bd. visitors Air U., Maxwell AFB, Montgomery, Ala., 1986-90. Mem. AAUP, Orgn. Am. Historians, Am. Conf. Acad. Deans., Am. Assn. Higher Edn., Am. Assn. State Colls. and Univs. (bd. dirs., chmn. 1992), Phi Kappa Phi. Democrat.*

ARMSTRONG-LAW, MARGARET, school administrator; b. Fargo, ND, Jan. 21, 1931; d. Theron L. and Besse Ross Armstrong; m. Robert Harold Law, Sept. 6, 1952 (div. Oct. 1964); children: William Robert, Anne Elizabeth Law Buckingham, Amy Catherine Law Burman. BS in English, N.D. State U., 1952, MS Secondary Sch. Adminstrn., 1974; postgrad., UCLA, Moorhead State U., 1984, Mich. State U., 1985; Cert., Harvard Prin.'s Sch., London, 1986. Cert. tchr., ednl. adminstr. Tchr. Agassiz Jr. High, 1963—66, Ben Franklin Jr. High, 1969—71, North HS, Fargo, ND, 1971—74, asst. prin., 1974—78; secondary head Taipei Am. Sch., Taiwan, 1978-87, Vienna Internat. Sch., Austria, 1987-90; dir. Internat. Sch. Amsterdam, The Netherlands, 1990-97; internat. ednl. cons., 1998—. Prof. devel. com. European Coun. Internat. Schs., London, chmn. bd., 1994-96; mem. No. European Coun. Internat. Schs., head coun., 1990-97; spkr. in field. Author: (booklet, film) Future: The Quality of Life, 1975; contbr. articles to profl. jours. Adv. bd. Coll. Arts, Humanities and Social Scis., N.D. State U., 1998—; pres. Fargo-Moorhead Opera Bd., 1999—2001; chmn. bd. Christian edn. Plymouth Congl. Ch., Fargo, 1998—99, mem. coun., 1988—99, vice chair women's fellowship bd., 1999; chair pres. adv. bd. Minn. State U., Moorhead, 2003; bd. dirs. Trollwood Performing Arts Sch., 2002. Recipient Bd. Dirs. award for Extraordinary Svcs. European Coun. Internat. Schs., Promotion of Internat. Edn. award, 1996; named hon. mem. for disting. svcs., European Coun. Internat. Schs., 1997; scholarship named in her honor by bd. govs. Internat. Sch. Amsterdam, 1997—. Mem. AAUW, LWV, ASCD, Assn. Advancement Internat. Edn., Am. Assn. Sch. Adminstrs., Am. Women's Club/Amsterdam, Am. C. of C., Rotary (bd. dirs. 1993-94, program chair 1993-94, v.p. 1994-96, pres. 1995-96/Amsterdam), World Future Soc., World Peace Com. (The Hague, Netherlands), De Amsterdamschekring Club, Phi Kappa Phi. Democrat. Congregationalist. Avocations: chinese brush painting, music, reading, tennis, interior decorating.

ARNDT, CYNTHIA, educational administrator; b. N.Y.C., Sept. 27, 1947; d. Charles Joseph and Pura Maria (Rios) A. BA, Hunter Coll., 1971, MA, 1975; profl. diploma in adminstrn., Fordham U., 1981. Adminstrv. asst. to asst. registrar Hunter Coll., N.Y.C., 1968-69; cataloguer asst. Finch. Coll. Libr., N.Y.C., 1974; tchr. N.Y. Bd. Edn., N.Y.C., 1974-82; bilingual coord. Jr. High. Sch. 143, 1982-89; asst. prin. IS 164, 1989-93; project dir. Elem. Schs. in Restructuring Bilingual Sci., 1993-96; supr.-in-charge IS 136, 1996-97; asst. prin. Mott Hall, 1997—. Reviewer Booklist, 1981. Mem. Am. Artist Soc., Hispanic Am. Hist. Soc., Nat. Council Social Studies, N.Y. State Assn. Curriculum Devel., Puerto Rican Edn. Assn., N.Y. State Assn. Bilingual Edn., Assn. Curriculum Devel., Kappa Delta Pi, Phi Delta Kappa. Democrat. Roman Catholic. Home: 110 W 90th St Apt 4C New York NY 10024-1209

ARNDT, JOAN MARIE, media specialist, educator; b. Stillwater, Minn., Sept. 7, 1945; d. Harriet Joan (Richert) A. BA, Coll. of St. Catherine, St. Paul, 1967; MA, U. Minn., 1970, degree in media specialty, 1973. Cert. librarian, elem. educator. Libr. media specialist Roseville Area Sch., Minn., 1967—. Prof. grad. and continuing studies dept. Hamline U., St. Paul, 1981—; guest lectr. U. Wis., Eau Claire, 1985, Coll. St. Thomas, St. Paul, Upper Mississippi Media Conf., 1988; book reviewer U. Minn., Mpls., 1988—, Five Owls, Mpls., 1988—; workshop cons. Columbia Hts. Sch., Mpls., Osseo Pub. Sch. Mem. ALA, NEA, Am. Assn. Sch. Libr., Minn. Edn. Media Orgn., Minn. Reading Assn., Minn. Edn. Assn., Friends of Ramsey County Libr. Kerlan Collection. Lutheran. Avocations: walking, reading, travel. Home: 5730 Donegal Dr Shoreview MN 55126-3701 Office: Cen Park Media Ctr 535 County Road B2 W Roseville MN 55113-3519

ARNEILL, B. PORTER, arts program educator; b. Denver, Jan. 31, 1961; s. Bruce Porter and Yvonne Blair (York) A. BFA, U. Colo., Boulder, 1988; MFA, Mass. Coll. Art, 1991. Artist, Boulder, 1991-93; curator of edn. Laumeier Sculpture Park, St. Louis, 1993—, mem. artist-educator-in-resident program, 1994. Adj. faculty St. Louis C.C., 1993—; dir. FUSE, Alt. Gallery Space, Boulder, 1992-93; tchr., lectr. St. Louis Art Mus. OASIS, St. Louis Gallery Assn. Fellow S.W. China Tchrs. U., Peoples Republic of China, 1993. Mem. Internat. Sculpture Ctr., Am. Assn. Mus., Coll. Art Assn., St. Louis Gallery Assn. (v.p. 1996). Avocations: hiking, biking, running. Office: Laumeier Sculpture Park 12580 Rott Rd Saint Louis MO 63127-1212

ARNETT, EDWARD MCCOLLIN, chemistry educator, researcher; b. Phila., Sept. 25, 1922; s. John Hancock and Katherine Williams (McCollin) A.; m. Sylvia Gettmann, Dec. 10, 1970; children: Eric, Brian; stepchildren: Elden, Byron, Colin Gatewood. BS, U. Pa., 1943, MS, 1946, PhD, 1949. Rsch. dir. Max Levy & Co., Phila., 1949-53; asst. prof. Western Md. Coll., Westminster, 1953-54, 1954-55; assoc. prof. chemistry U. Pitts., 1957-61, assoc. prof., 1961-64, prof., 1964-80; R.J. Reynolds prof. Duke U., Durham, N.C., 1980-92, prof. emeritus, 1992—. Vis. lectr. U. Ill., 1963; vis. prof. U. Kent, Canterbury, Eng., 1970; dir. Pitts Chem. Info. Ctr., 1967-70; mem. adv. bd. Petroleum Research Fund, 1968-71; mem. com. on chem. info. NRC, 1969-71. Contbr. 200 articles to sci. jours. DuPont fellow, 1948-49, rsch. fellow Harvard U., Cambridge, Mass., 1955-57, Guggenheim fellow, 1968-69, Mellon Inst. adj. sr. fellow, 1964-80, Inst. Hydrocarbon Chemistry sr. fellow, 1980. Fellow AAAS; mem. Am. Chem. Soc. (James Flack Norris award 1977, Pitts. award Pitts. chpt. 1976, Petroleum Chemistry award 1985), Nat. Acad. Scis., The Chem. Soc., Sigma Xi, Phi Lambda Upsilon. E-mail: narnett@chem.duke.edu.

ARNETT, JAMES EDWARD, retired insurance company executive, retired secondary school; b. Gullett, Ky., Oct. 3, 1912; s. Haden and Josephine (Risner) A.; m. Helen Mae Vallish, Mar. 23, 1943. AB, San Jose State Coll., 1947, MA, 1955; EdS, Stanford U., 1959. Tchr., prin. pub. schs., Salyersville, Ky., 1930-41; tchr., adminstr. pub. schs. Salinas, Calif., 1947-52; owner, mgr. Arnett Apts., Salinas, 1950-53; tchr. Innes H.S., Akron, Ohio, 1953-73; owner-mgr. Arnett Apts., Akron, 1953-72; dir. Educator & Exec. Co., 1962-73, Educator and Exec. Insurers, 1957-76, Educator and Exec. Life Ins. Co., 1962-76, Great Am. of Dallas Fire and Casualty Co., 1974-76, Great Am. of Dallas Ins. Co., 1974-76, J.C. Penney Casualty Ins. Co., 1976, cons., 1976-77. Mem. county, state ctrl. coms. Democratic party, 1952. Served with AUS, 1942-45. Mem. NEA (life mem., del. conv. 1957-65), Ohio (del. convs. 1957-73), Akron (1st v.p. 1964-65, parliamentarian 1965-72), edn. assns., San Jose State Coll., Stanford alumni assns., Phi Delta Kappa. Home: Rockynol Retirement Cmty 1150 W Market St Akron OH 44313-7129

ARNOLD, ALBERT JAMES, foreign language educator; b. Ballston Spa, N.Y., Nov. 8, 1939; s. Albert J. and Florence Emily (Cleveland) A.; m. Josephine Diane Valenza, June 8, 1963; 1 child, Elizabeth. AB, Hamilton Coll., 1961; MA, U Wis. Madison, 1964, PhD, 1968; cert French lang., lit., U. Paris, 1960. Instr. romance langs. Hamilton Coll., Clinton, N.Y., 1961-62; from asst. to prof. French U. Va., 1966—, chair com. comparative lit., 1974-79, 1986-89, co-chair comparative programs in literature and culture, 1989-95; dir. New World Studies, 1991-92. Vis. exch. prof. U. de Paris III, 1981; external examiner Queensland U., Australia, 1986, U. West Indies, 1991—, NYU, 1991, Yale U., 1994; external assessor French dept. U. West Indies, 1995, 2002-03; coord. com. on comp. lit. hist. Internat. Comp. Lit. Assoc., 1992-2001; mem. internat. adv. bd. New West Indian Guide, 1992—; mem. adv. bd. Review Lit. & Arts Americas, 2003-; spkr., cons. in field. Author: Paul Valéry, 1970, Sartre, 1973, Césaire, 1981, 90, Camus, 1983; gen. editor Caraf Books, 1987-93; editor New World Studies, 1992—, Plantation Soc. in the Ams., 1999—; contbr. articles to profl. jours. ACLS fellow, 1975-76; NEH fellow Nat. Humanities Ctr., 1989-90; Fulbright fellow, 1995-96; trans. grantee NEH, 1991-92; grantee U. Va., 1969, 70, 72, 75-76, 78, 80, 81-82, 86, 95-96, 2001-02, Camargo Found., 1981-82, 86, 2001, Va. Found. Humanities, 1992, 94; Queensland U. fellow, Australia, 1995. Mem. Phi Beta Kappa. Democrat. Avocations: gardening, photography, birding. Home: 310 E Beverley St Staunton VA 24401-4327 Office: U Va Dept French PO Box 400770 Charlottesville VA 22904-4770

ARNOLD, BARRY RAYNOR, philosophy educator, medical ethicist, clergyman, counselor; b. Mooresville, N.C., Sept. 29, 1951; s. Adrian Leicester and Cleo Agnes (Fisher) A.; m. Margaret Elizabeth Morelock, Aug. 15, 1984. AB cum laude, Davidson Coll., 1973; MDiv magna cum laude, Emory U., 1976, PhD, 1986. Ordained to ministry Presbyn. Ch.; cert. Christian clin. counselor Am. Counseling Assn.; lic. mental health counselor, Ind. Min. various parishes, Ga., Fla., 1976—; instr. religion, assoc. chaplain The Lovett Sch., 1980-82; prof. Andrew Coll., Cuthbert, Ga., 1983-84; asst. prof. to prof. and honors prof. U. West Fla., Pensacola, 1986—2002, acting chmn. dept. philosophy/religion, 1997—, chmn. dept. interdisciplinary humanities, philosophy, relig., 2000—, exec. dir. Univ. Office for Applied Ethics, 2000—, joint prof. biology and philosophy divsn. life and health scis., 2003—; prof. Bioethics and Philosophy, dir. Ctr. for Health Care Ethics U. West Fla./Sacred Heart Hosp., Pensacola, 2003—, dir. Ctr. for Health Care Ethics, 2003—; pvt. practice clin. counseling, Pace, Fla., 1996—. Counselor Pace Counseling Ctr., 1996-97; spkr. in field. Author: The Pursuit of Virtue, 1989; editor: Essays in American Ethics, 1992; gen. editor (11 vols.) The Reshaping of Psychoanalysis, 1992-2002; assoc. editor Explorations: Jour. Adventurous Thought, 1999—; contbr. articles to profl. jours. Bd. dirs. Sacred Heart Hosp., Pensacola, Bapt. Hosp.; pres., bd. dirs. Assn. for Retarded Citizens, Albany, Ga., 1978—79; bioethicist, bd. dirs. West Fla. Regional Med. Ctr., Pensacola, 1990—2003, Bapt. Hosp., 2003—, Sacred Heart Hosp., 2003—. Recipient Disting. Tchg. award UWF and Fla. State Legislature, 1988, 90, 95; Award for Disting. Contbn., Honors Program UWF, 2002; fellow Rice U., 1973-75, Emory U., 1975-76, 79-82, U. Glasgow, 1976. Fellow: Am. Coll. Counselors (cert. Christian clin. counselor, chair examiners for cert.), Am. Assn. Integrative Medicine (diplomate, nat. bd. dirs., chair nat. bd. 2002—03), Am. Bd. Child Mental Health Providers; mem.: ACA, Assn. for Cognitive Behavioral Therapists (cert. cognitive forensic therapist, cert. anxiety disorders specialist), So. Soc. Philosophy and Psychology, Am. Acad. Religion, Internat. Thomas Merton Soc., Rotary (sgt.-at-arms 1982—83), Phi Beta Kappa, A£D (hon.), Alpha Epsilon Delta, Phi Kappa Phi (sec. 1988). Democrat. Avocations: antique cards, antique cars, birdwatching. Home: 5820 Kirkland Dr Milton FL 32570-8251 Office: Univ West Fla 11000 University Pkwy Pensacola FL 32514-5750 E-mail: barnold@uwf.edu.

ARNOLD, DEBORAH LYNNE, elementary school educator; b. New Orleans, Mar. 8, 1953; d. Clinton M. and Betty E. (Lofton) Moore; m. Arthur Welsey Arnold, Mar. 23, 1974; children: Stephanie Ilene, Patricia Michelle, Jonathan Wesley. BS, La. State U., Baton Rouge, 1986; MEd Northwestern State U., Natchitoches, La., 2000. Tchr. St. John's Episcopal Presch., Ft. Worth, 1984-85; tchr. 1st grade Rapides Parish Sch. Bd., Alexandria, La., 1987—2001, Caddo Parish Sch. Bd., Shreveport, La., 2001—. Mem. Kappa Delta Epsilon, Phi Kappa Phi. Baptist. Home: 4025 Wisteria Ln Benton LA 71006

ARNOLD, GORDON B. social science educator; b. 1954; married; 2 children. BA, Clark U., 1976; MLS, U. R.I., 1982; PhD, Boston Coll., 1994. Libr. Goodnow Libr., Sudbury, Mass., 1980-87; libr. dir. Montserrat Coll. Art, Beverly, Mass., 1987-91, asst. dean, 1989-94, assoc. dean, 1994-97, assoc. prof. social sci., 1994—2002, prof. liberal arts, 2002—. Rsch. assoc. New England Resource Ctr. Higher Edn., U. Mass., Boston, 1991-96; adj. rsch. assoc. Ctr. Policy Analysis U. Mass., Dartmouth, 1995-2000; adj. lectr. Boston Coll., Chestnut Hill, 1999-2001, 2003. Author: Politics of Faculty Unionization, 2000; contbg. author: Revitalizing General Education in a Time of Scarcity, 1997; co-author: (chpt.) Handbook of the Undergraduate Curriculum, 1996. Mem. Am. Polit. Sci. Assn., Am. Soc. Assn., Boston Coll. Alumni (higher edn. coun. 1998-2002). Office: 23 Essex St # 26 Beverly MA 01915-4508

ARNOLD, JAMES AUSTIN, music educator, director of bands, administrator; b. Ruleville, Miss., July 15, 1952; s. James Lloyd and Dorothy Jewel (Mullen) A.; m. Betsy Jean Black, Dec. 24, 1990; children: Matthew L. Hopper, Daniel L. Hopper. B of Music Edn., U. Miss., 1974, M of Music Edn., 1977; EdD, U. Ala., 1993. Cert. tchr., Ga. Dir. of bands Lamar County, Vernon, Ala., 1974-90, Columbus (Ga.) H.S. Bands, 1990-96; asst. prin. Shaw H.S., 1996—2001; dir. Bob Barr/Columbus Cmty. Band, 1997-2000; prin. Shaw H.S., 2001. Presenter U. Ala. Rsch. Workshop, Tuscaloosa, 1992-93, Ga. Music Edn. Assn., Savannah, 1994, Music Educators Nat. Conf., Winston-Salem, N.C., 1994; mem. Leadership Acad., Columbus, Ga., 1994—. Contbr. articles to jours. in field. Named Disting. Bandmaster, First Chair of Am., 1981; recipient Classroom Rsch. award Phi Delta Kappa, 1992. Mem. Music Educators Nat. Conf., Ga. Music Educators Assn. (dist. v.p. 1994), Phi Kappa Phi, 1992. Avocations: reading, golfing. Home: 4824 Spring Ridge Ct Columbus GA 31909-2063 Office: Shaw HS 7601 Schomburg Rd Columbus GA 31909

ARNOLD, JAMES PHILLIP, religious studies educator, history educator; b. Greenville, S.C. s. David Lee and Vera Irene (Wilson) A. MA in Am. History, U. Houston, 1979; MA in Religious Studies, Rice U., 1984, PhD in Religious Studies, 1991. Instr. Am. History U. Houston, 1972-76; instr. religion Rice U., Houston, 1976-81; instr. ch. history, biblical studies, homiletics Houston Grad. Sch. Theology, 1984-86; instr. religion and history, exec. dir. The Reunion Inst., Houston, 1986—. Pres. Living History Studies, Inc., Houston, 1993—; counselor families divided by religious cult issues; advisor to FBI on Branch Davidian crisis, Waco, Tex., 1993, Freeman crisis, 1996. Dir. Fine Arts Found., Houston, 1987—; founder Religion-Crisis Task Force, 1994. Rice U. fellow, 1980-91, U. Houston fellow, 1972-76; Tex. Com. for Humanities grantee, 1979. Mem. Am. Acad. Religion, Soc. Biblical Lit. Avocations: air-hockey, archaeology. Office: Reunion Inst 5508 Chaucer Dr Houston TX 77005-2632 E-mail: reunion@blk.box.com.

ARNOLD, JEANNE ELOISE, anthropologist, educator; b. Cleve., 1955; d. Lawrence Fred and Marybelle Eloise Arnold. BA, U. Mich., 1976; MA, U. Calif., Santa Barbara, 1979, PhD, 1983. Prof. anthropology U. No. Iowa, Cedar Falls, 1984-88, UCLA, 1988—, assoc. dir. Inst. Archaeology, 1988-99. Vis. instr. anthropology Rice U., Houston, 1981; vis. prof. anthropology Oreg. State U., Corvallis, 1983-84; sr. archaeologist Infotec Rsch., Inc., Sonora, Calif., 1986-87; cons. in field. Author 4 books; contbr. more than 45 articles and revs. to profl. jours. and over 25 chpts. to books. Rsch. grantee NSF, 1988-91, 95-99, 98—; Rsch. and Ednl. grantee UCLA and Santa Barbara, 1977—. Mem. Soc. Am. Archaeology, Soc. Calif. Archaeology, Cotsen Inst. Archaeology (mem. editorial bd. 1988—), Sigma Xi, Phi Beta Kappa. Avocations: photography, cinema, collecting ethnographic arts. Office: UCLA Dept Anthropology Box 951553 Haines Hall Los Angeles CA 90095-1553

ARNOLD, KEVIN DAVID, psychologist, educational researcher; b. Massilon, Ohio, Jan. 7, 1957; s. Jack Olen and Arlene Adele (Harrold) A.; m. Melissa Wervey. BS, Grace Coll., 1979; MA, Ohio State U., 1981, PhD, 1983; advanced cert., Ctr. for Cognitive Therapy, N.Y., 1994, Atlanta Ctr. Cognitive Therapy, 1994. Fellow and diplomate Am. Bd. Med. Psychotherapists; diplomate in behavioral psychology Am. Bd. Profl. Psychology; lic. psychologist, Ohio, Wis.; listed divorce mediator Franklin County (Ohio) Ct. Common Pleas. Grad. rsch. assoc. Ohio State U., Columbus, 1980-83, rsch. assoc., 1983-84, prin. investigator deaf and blind project, 1984-92, asst. dir. Ctr. Spl. Needs Populations, 1988-93, asst. prof., 1988-92; psychologist Columbus, 1991—. Clin. asst. prof. dept. psychiatry Ohio State U., Columbus, 2003—; dir. Ctr. for Cognitive and Behavioral Therapy Greater Columbus, 1995—; founder, CEO, Ohio Proficiency Test Rev., Inc., 1990—95; v.p. Englefield & Arnold Pub., 1995—2001; bd. dirs. Am. Bd. Behavioral Psychology; v.p., work sample coord.; mem. Ohio State Bd. of Psychology, 2003—; sec.-treas., dir. wine tastings Tastings By the Glass, Inc. Co-author: Passing the Ohio Proficiency Test, 1993, Passing the Ohio Ninth Grade Proficiency Test, 1996, Passing with Honors on

Ohio's 12th Grade Proficiency Tests, 2000, Passing the Ohio Graduation Test, 2001, Show What You Know on the 7th Grade WASL, 2001, Show What You Know on the 10th Grade WASL, 2001, (test) Social Behavior Asessment Inventory, 1992; contbr. chapters to books, articles. Fundraiser Ohio Dem. gubernatorial campaign, 1989-90; twp. coord. Grass Roots campaign Tiberi Rep. U.S. Congl. Campaign, 2000; co-chair Franklin County (Ohio) Parenting Coord. Project, 2000—; mem. Ohio State Bd. of Pyschology; wine judge Columbus Food and Wine Festival, 2003. Deaf and Blind Ctr. grantee U.S. Dept. Edn., 1984-94, 99—, Sch. Psychology grantee, 1987-93, Evaluation Intervention Teams Ohio Dept. Edn. grantee, 1988-93, Drop-out Cost Study Ctr. Labor Rsch. grantee, 1990-91, Parent Satisfaction Study Ohio Devel. Disabilities Planning Coun. grantee, 1989-90, Tchr. Compentency Survey Study grantee, 1992-93. Fellow: Am. Bd. Med. Psychotherapists, Am. Acad. Behavioral Psychology (pres.); mem.: APA (former del. state leadership conf.), Ohio State Bd. Psychology, Acad. Family and Conciliatory Cts., Nat. Coun. Family Rels., Soc. Personality Assessment, Soc. Rsch. in Child Devel., Am. Psychology-Law Soc., Ohio Bar Assn. (assoc.), Ctrl. Ohio Psychol. Assn., Am. Assn. Mental Retardation, Ohio Psychol. Assn. (former mem. cont. edn. com., trustee, former chmn. publs. com., former co-editor Ohio Psychologist, past pres., mem. exec. com. cont. edn. com., mem. fin. com., publs. coun., former fin. officer), Acad. Family Mediators, Assn. for Advancement of Behavior Therapy, Am. Pscychol. Soc. Avocation: wine collecting. Office: CCBT 2121 Bethel Rd Ste D Columbus OH 43220-1804 E-mail: kda1757@earthlink.net.

ARNOLD, LESLIE ANN, special education educator; b. St. Louis, Mo., Oct. 20, 1953; d. Eugene L. and Louisa French (Gale) A. BS, Central State U., 1975, MEd, 1981. Cert. spl. edn., learning disabilities, mental retardation tchr., Kans. Tchr. level III educable mentally handicapped Unified Sch. Dist. 345, Topeka, 1976-82; tchr., specialist mentally retarded and occupationally handicapped Sch. Dist. 619, Wellington, Kans., 1982-87; coord. vocat. options level IV educable mentally handicapped Wellington Unified Sch. Dist. 353, Wellington, Kans., 1987—; area adminstr. Sangamon Area Spl. Edn. Dist., Springfield, Ill., 2002—. Coord. spl. edn. Wellington Unified Sch. Dist., 1995-98, dir. spl. edn., 1998, dir. spl. svcs., Poplar Bluff, Mo., 2000-02; cons. in field. Grantee Vocat. Rehab., 1992-95, Kansas Transition Network, 1994-98, Charter Sch., 1997; Access to Gen. Edn. grantee Positive Behavioral Intervention Strategies,(PBIS), 2001, Sangamon Area Spl. Edn. Dist. (SASED) Area Admin.

ARNOLD, MARGARET MORELOCK, music specialist, educator, performer; b. Craig AFB, Ala., May 12, 1959; d. William Daniel Morelock and Margaret Haynie Morelock Stapleton; m. Barry Raynor Arnold, Aug. 15, 1984. B of Music Edn., U. Montevallo, 1981; MEd in Music, U. South Ala., 1996. Cert. tchr. Fla., Ala. Tchr. music Staley Mid. Sch., Americus, Ga., 1981-82, Eastview Elem. Sch., Americus, Ga., 1982-84; tchr. music/mass prep. St. Thomas More Schs., Pensacola, Fla., 1984-85; tchr. music W.H. Rhodes Elem., Milton, Fla., 1985—; realtor Century 21, Richardson, Fla. Pvt. voice instr., Americus, 1981-84, Milton, 1989—; guest condr. Santa Rosa All-County Chorus, Milton, 1989, 95, Santa Rosa Celebrates the Arts, 1986—. Asst. dir.: arts festivals, 1993—; singer (soprano, soloist): Gulf Coast Chorale, Singfest, Inc., The Choral Soc. Pensacola; dir.: (band) Change of Command, 2003. Dir. elem. chorus performing for Santa Rosa Convalescent Ctr., Milton, 1985—, Whiting Field, 2003, Live at the Capital, Tallahassee, 1986, Santa Rosa Celebrates the Arts, 1986-, Ptnrs. in Edn.-K-Mart and City of Milton and WEAR-TV, 1990—. Recipient Young Artist Competition S.E. Regional award Nat. Assn. Tchrs. of Singing, S.E. region, 1993; winner State of Ala. Young Artist competition, 1993; Computer Software grant Santa Rosa Ednl. Found., 1994. Mem. NEA, Music Tchrs. Nat. Assn., Nat. Assn. Realtors, Fla. Assn. Realtors, Santa Rosa Profl. Educators, Music Educators Nat. Conf., Pensacola (Fla.) Music Tchrs. Assn., Delta Kappa Gamma (music chair 1988-94), Kappa Delta Pi, Phi Kappa Phi. Presbyterian. Avocations: walking, gardening, volunteer for nursing home. Home: 5820 Kirkland Dr Milton FL 32570-8251 Office: WH Rhodes Elem 5563 Byrom St Milton FL 32570-3822 Business E-Mail: arnoldm@santarosa.k12.fl.us.

ARNOLD, MARIE COLLETTE, elementary school educator; b. Dayton, Ohio, May 21, 1968; d. Clinton Anthony and Lula Theresa (Conner) A. BA cum laude, St. Edward's U., 1990; MS, Trinity Coll., 1996. Cert. bilingual tchr., Tex., Va., ESL tchr., Tex. Bilingual/gifted tchr. Beacon Hill Elem. Sch., San Antonio, Tex., 1990-93; bilingual tchr. Annunciation Sch., Washington, 1993-94; bilingual/inclusion tchr. Alexander Henderson Sch., Dumfries, Va., 1994-96; ednl. specialist Region 20 Edn. Svc. Ctr., San Antonio, 1996—. Tchr. trainer N.J. Writing Project in Tex., San Antonio, 1993; staff devel. facilitator San Antonio Ind. Sch. Dist., 1992-93. Mem. NEA, Internat. Platform Assn., Nat. Assn. Bilingual Edn., Tex. Assn. Bilingual Edn., Tex. TESOL, San Antonio Area Assn. for Bilingual Edn. (bilingual tchr. hall of fame 1991), Kappa Gamma Psi, Pi Lambda Theta. Avocations: reading, writing poetry, aerobics. Office: Region 20 Edn Svc Ctr Hines St San Antonio TX 78202

ARNOLD, NANCY ANN, special education educator, researcher; b. Joliet, Ill., Jan. 14, 1961; d. Edmund Earl and Betty Jane (Thompson) A. BS magna cum laude, Loyola U., Chgo., 1989. Cert. in elem. edn., spl. edn., Ill. Lifestyle instr. Jenny Craig, Cicero, Ill., 1989-90; tchr. behaviorally disordered Prove IV, Lyons, Ill., 1990-92; site supr. Abt Assocs., Chgo., 1993—. Sch. photographer Lifetouch, Des Plaines, Ill., 1993-94. Contbg. poet: New Voices in American Poetry, 1981; contbr. poetry to lit. mags. Mem. NAFE, Coun. for Exceptional Children (pres. 1987-88), Assn. for childhood Edn. Internat., Alpha Sigma Nu. Democrat. Jewish. Avocations: barbie doll collecting, art, writing, films. Address: 5321 Fairmont Ave Downers Grove IL 60515-5057

ARNOLD, P. A. special education educator; b. Toledo; d. Mattie Spear; m. Earl E. Arnold. BA, BS, David Lipscomb Coll., 1960; MA, Wayne State U., 1962; MS, Nova U., 1986. Cert. spl. edn., psychology, speech, mental retardation, emotional disturbance, Bible, Fla. Tchr. dactylology, interpreter for deaf, 1960—; tchr. Hobbs (N.Mex.) Mcpl. Schs., 1981-82; tchr. spl. edn. City Systems, Rockford and Warren, Mich., 1960-67; dir. Four-County Ctr. Handicapped, Ark., 1977-81. Dir. model project ACTION; Project TREE Tech. Resources in Exceptional Edn.; conf. presenter in fields. Author: Instructor, Light for Deaf, 1992, Ol' Time Preacher Man, 1995, Little Red Schoolhouse, 1998, Trapezoid of Children, 1999. Bd. dirs., deaf advisor Hearing Soc. Volusia County; mem. project TREE-Tech. Resources in Exceptional Edn.-Tech. Exceptional Edn.-SY 2000, Dept. Edn., Fla. State U. Ctr. Ednl. Tech. Grantee Pub. Welfare, Nat. Gardening Assn., FUTURES, Newspapers in Edn. Mem. NEA, ARC, ASCD, Volusia Ednl. Assn., Fla. Edn. Assn., Coun. for Exceptional Children, Am. Assn. on Mental Deficiency, Nat. Assn. Deaf.

ARNOLD, PERI ETHAN, political scientist; b. Chgo., Sept. 21, 1942; s. Joseph Evon and Eve (Jacobs) A.; m. Beverly Ann Kessler, Aug. 22, 1965; children: Emma, Rachel. BA, Roosevelt U., Chgo., 1964; MA, U. Chgo., 1967, PhD, 1972. Lectr. Roosevelt U., Chgo., 1966-68; instr. polit. sci. Western Mich. U., Kalamazoo, 1970-71; asst. prof. polit. sci. U. Notre Dame, Ind., 1971-76, assoc. prof. govt., 1976-86, prof. of govt. and internat. studies, 1986; chair dept. govt., 1986-92. Compton vis. prof. of world politics Miller Ctr., U. Va., 1993-94; dir. Hesburgh Program in Pub. Svc., 1995-2001; dir. Notre Dame Semester in Washington, 1997-2001. Author: Making the Managerial Presidency, 1986 (Louis Brownlow Book award 1987), 2nd rev. ed., 1998; mem. editl. bd. Am. Jour. Polit. Sci., 1991-94, Polity, 1995—, Presdl. Studies Quar., 1997—; co-editor Jour. of Policy History, 1987-88; mem. editl. adv. bd. Hughes Leadership Series, Tex. A&M U. Press, 1999—; contbr. articles to profl. jours. and edited vols. Bd. dirs. South Bend Hebrew Day Sch., Mishawaka, Ind., 1985—88; chair Cmty. Rels. Coun. of Jewish Fedn. of St. Joseph Valley, South Bend, Ind., 1990—94; mem. acquisitions com. Snite Mus. Art, Notre Dame, Ind., 1994—99; trustee Congregation Beth El, South Bend, 1994—2000, sec., exec. com., 2000—02; bd. dirs. Jewish Fedn. of St. Joseph Valley, 1999—2002, v.p., 2001—03. Recipient Spl. Presdl. award U. Notre Dame, 1993, Marshall Dimock award Am. Soc. Pub. Adminstrn., 1996; grantee Am. Coun. Learned Socs., 1974; rsch. grantee Herbert Hoover Libr. Assn., 1993-94; Ford Found. fellow, 1978-81. Mem. Am. Polit. Sci. Assn. (program chmn., exec. com. presidency sect.), Midwest Polit. Sci. Assn., The Cliff Dwellers Club (Chgo.). Democrat. Jewish. Avocations: literature, music, drama. Home: 1419 E Colfax Ave South Bend IN 46617-3307 Office: U Notre Dame Dept Polit Sci Notre Dame IN 46556 E-mail: peri.e.arnold.1@nd.edu.

ARNOLD, RUTH ANN, elementary education educator; b. Lebanon, Pa., June 3, 1955; d. Earl Edwin and Joan Marie (Meyer) Rittle; m. Elijah Joseph Arnold III, July 17, 1976; 1 child, Nathan Joseph. BS, Lebanon Valley Coll., 1977; MEd, Millersville U., 1982, MEd, 2002. Cert. reading recovery tchr. Elem. reading specialist, reading recovery tchr. Palmyra (Pa.) Area Sch. Dist., 1980—. Vol. Local 4-H Club, Lebanon, Pa., 1973-98; organist, choir dir. Tulpehocken United Ch. of Christ, Richland, Pa., 1982-95. Mem. Internat. Reading Assn., Keystone State Reading Assn., Lebanon-Lancaster Reading Coun., Reading Recovery Coun. North Am. Avocation: music.

ARNOLD-MASSEY, HELEN PHYLLIS, health education educator, motivational speaker; b. Chgo., Aug. 10, 1949; d. William Jesse and Alyce Mary (Hauck) Arnold; m. Rodney Glenn Massey; children: Jahmann Yendor Massey, Rashon Amiel Massey, Sharieff Carter Massey. BS in Phys. Edn., DePaul U., 1972; MS in Kinesiology, U. Ill., Chgo., 1993. Cert. phys. edn. tchr. K-12, Ill. Phys. edn. tchr. Chgo. Bd. Edn., 1972-81, tchr. health edn., 1989—; fitness cons. Affordable Fitness, Chgo., 1983-85; with corp. health svc. Hurley Med. Ctr., Flint, Mich., 1986-87; spl. projects coord. Jefferson & Williams Cmty. Schs., Flint, Mich., 1988-89. Recipient Kathy Osterman Superior Pub. Svc. award City Chgo., 1994, Those Who Excel award Ill. State Bd. Edn., 1995, Excellence in Teaching award Nat. Coun. Negro Women/Shell Oil, 1995, Milken Nat. Educator award Milken Family Found., 1995, City Ptnr. award U. Ill., Chgo., 1996. Mem. AAUW, Nat. Coun. Negro Women, Ill. Coalition Adapted Phys. Edn., Ill. Assn. Health, Phys. Edn., Recreation & Dance (Honor Fellow award 1993), Parents United Responsible Edn. Home: 637 E Woodland Park Ave Apt 612 Chicago IL 60616-4162 Office: Chgo Bd Edn 1819 W Pershing Rd Chicago IL 60609-2338

ARONSON, CARL EDWARD, pharmacology and toxicology educator; b. Providence, Mar. 14, 1936; s. Carl Ivar and Ruth (Workman) A.; m. Marjorie Peck Boutelle, Dec. 17, 1960; children— Linda J., Kristen L. AB, Brown U., Providence, 1958; PhD, U. Vt., Burlington, 1966; MA, U. Pa., Phila., 1973. Asst. prof. pharmacology U. Pa. Sch. Medicine, Phila., 1971-75, assoc. prof. pharmacology, 1975-92; asst. prof. pharmacology and toxicology dept. animal biology U. Pa. Sch. Vet. Medicine, Phila., 1971-73, head labs. of pharmacology and toxicology, 1972-86, assoc. prof. pharmacology and toxicology, 1973-96; retired to emeritus status, 1996; instrument specialist, dept. chemistry Haverford (Pa.) Coll., 1996—. Editor Veterinary Pharmaceuticals and Biologicals, 1978-79, 80-81, 82-83, 85-86; contbr. chpts. to books, articles to profl. jours. Active local sch. dist. coms. and other civic assns. Served to 1st lt. USAFR, 1958-65. Recipient Norden award for disting. tchg. U. Pa. Sch. Vet. Medicine, 1982, Legion of Honor, Chapel of the Four Chaplains, 1984. Fellow: Am. Acad. Vet. and Comparative Toxicology, Am. Acad. Vet. Pharmacology and Therapeutics (newsletter editor 1982—2001, pres. 1983—85, Svc. award 1994, L.E. Davis Career Achievement award 2001); mem.: AAUP, Am. Soc. Pharmacology and Exptl. Therapeutics, Bay Region Mariners Sailing Assn. (treas. 1981—83, vice commodore 1986, commodore 1987), The Haven Yacht Club (charter), Masons, Sigma Xi. Lutheran. Avocations: sailing, photography, woodworking. Office: Haverford Coll Dept Chemistry 370 Lancaster Ave Haverford PA 19041-1392

ARONSON, DAVID, artist, retired art educator; b. Shilova, Lithuania, Oct. 28, 1923; came to U.S., 1929, naturalized, 1931; s. Peisach Leib and Gertrude (Shapiro) A.; m. Georgianna B. Nyman, June 10, 1956; children: Judith, Benjamin, Abigail. Certificate, Boston Mus. Sch., 1946; LHD (hon.), Hebrew Coll., 1993. Instr. painting Boston Mus. Sch., 1943-54; prof. art Boston U., 1962-89, chmn. div., 1954-62, chmn. painting dept., 1962-89, prof. emeritus, 1989—. Contbr. articles to profl. jours.; one man shows include Niveau Gallery, N.Y.C., 1945, 56, Mus. Modern Art, N.Y.C., 1946, Boris Mirski Gallery, Boston, 1951, 59, 64, 69, Downtown Gallery, N.Y.C., 1953, Nordness Gallery, N.Y.C., 1960, 63, 69, Rex Evans Gallery, LA, 1961, Long Beach (Calif.) Mus., 1961, Westhampton (N.Y.) Gallery, 1961, J. Thomas Gallery, Provincetown, Mass., 1964, Zora Gallery, LA, 1965, Hunter Gallery, Chattanooga, 1965, Kovler Gallery, Chgo., 1966, Bernard Danenberg Galleries, N.Y.C., 1969, 72, Pucker Gallery, Boston, 1976, 78, 86, 90, 94, 99, Phila. Mus. Judaica, 1990, Louis Newman Gallery, LA, 1977, 81, 84, 86, 89, 92, Sadye Bronfman Art Ctr., Montreal, Que., Can., 1982, Horwitch Newman Gallery, Scottsdale, Ariz., 1995, 96, MB Modern Gallery, N.Y., 1997, Alter & Gil Gallery, L.A., 1999; Sp. Galerie Yoram GIL, LA, 2002. group shows include N.Y. World's Fair, 1964-65, Bridgestone Gallery, Tokyo, Royal Acad. London, Mus. Modern Art, Paris, Palazzo Venezia, Rome, Congresse Halle, Berlin, Charlottenborg, Copenhagen, Palais Des Beaux Arts, Brussels, Smithsonian Instn., 1965, retrospective exhbns. include Rose Mus., Brandeis U., Waltham, Mass., 1978, Jewish Mus., N.Y.C., 1979, Nat. Mus. Am. Jewish History, Phila., 1979, So. Middlesex U., South Dartmouth, Mass., 1983, Mickelson Gallery, Washington, 1985; represented in permanent collections Art Inst. Chgo., Va. Mus. Fine Arts, Richmond, Bryn Mawr Coll., Brandeis U., Tupperware Mus., Orlando, Fla., Decordova Mus., Lincoln, Mass., Mus. Modern Art, Atlanta U., Atlanta Art Assn., U. Nebr., Krannert Art Mus. U. Ill., Whitney Mus. Am. Art, Colby Coll., U. N.H., Portland Mus. Art, Maine, Corcoran Gallery Art, Washington, Munson Williams Proctor Art Inst., Ithaca, N.Y., Boston Mus. Fine Arts, Smithsonian Instn., Washington, Milw. Art Inst., Pa. Acad. Fine Arts, Johnson Found., Racine, Wis., Worcester (Mass.) Art Mus., Brockton (Mass.) Mus. Art, Longy Sch. Music, Cambridge, Mass., Boston U., Jewish Community Ctr., Boston, Nat. Acad. Design, N.Y., Joseph Hirschhorn Collection, Hebrew Coll., Newton, Mass., David and Alfred Smart Mus., U. Chgo., Two-Ten Found., Boston, Pa. State U. Mus. Art, Syracuse (N.Y.) U., Beth Israel Hosp., Boston Mass. Guilford Coll. U. N.C., Greensboro Campus, U. Judaism, LA, Fine Arts Ctr., Cheekville, Tenn., Skirball Mus., L.A., Herbert F. Johnson Mus. Art, Cornell U., others; sculpture commns. Container Corp. Am., 1963, 65, Reform Jewish Appeal, 1980, Combined Jewish Philanthropies, 1981, Temple Beth Elohim, Wellesley, Mass., 1982, Brandeis U. Library, Waltham, Mass., 1983, Brandeis U. Berlin Chapel, 1996. Recipient 1st Judges prize Inst. Modern Art, Boston, 1944, 1st Popular prize, 1944; Choice Friends of Art Art Inst. Chgo., 1946; Purchase prize Va. Mus. Fine Arts, 1946; Travelling fellow Boston Mus. Sch., 1946; Grand prize Boston Arts Festival, 1952, 54; 2d prize, 1953; 1st prize Tupperware Art Fund, 1954, cert. of merit for sculpture NAD, 1990; grantee in art Nat. Inst. Arts and Letters, 1958; Purchase prize, 1961, 62, 63; purchase prize Pa. Acad. Fine Arts, also other purchase prizes; Samuel F.B. Morse Gold medal NAD, 1973; Isaac N. Maynard prize NAD, 1975; Joseph S. Isidor gold medal NAD, 1976; Guggenheim fellow, 1960; Adolph and Clara Obrig prize NAD, 1968, Academician NAD, 1970. Home: 137 Brimstone Ln Sudbury MA 01776-3200

ARONSON, HOWARD ISAAC, linguist, educator; b. Chgo., Mar. 5, 1936; s. Abe and Jean A. BA, U. Ill., 1956; MA, Ind. U., 1958, PhD, 1961. Asst. prof. Slavic langs. and lit. U. Wis., Madison, 1961-62; asst. prof. Slavic linguistics U. Chgo., 1962-65, asso. prof. depts. slavic langs. and lit. and linguistics, 1965-73, prof., 1973—2002, chmn. dept. linguistics, 1972-80, prof. emeritus, 2002—, chmn. dept. Slavic langs. and lits., 1983-91, 2000-01. Editor: Annual of the Society for the Study of Caucasia, 1989—. Mem. Am. Assn. Advancement Slavic Studies, Am. Assn. Tchrs. Slavic and East European Langs. Jewish. Home: 415 W Aldine Ave Apt 7B Chicago IL 60657-3601 Office: U Chgo Dept Slavic Langs and Lit Chicago IL 60637 E-mail: hia5@mac.com.

ARONSON, JAY ELLIS, management information systems educator, consultant; b. Boston, July 19, 1953; s. Philip H. and Dorothea R. (Frankel) A.; m. Sharon Goldman, June 20, 1980; children: Marla Diane, Michael Lee, Stephanie Elisabeth. BSEE, Carnegie Mellon U., 1975, MSEE, 1976, MS in Ops. Rsch., 1978, PhD in Indsl. Adminstrn., 1980. Instr. Carnegie Mellon U., Pitts., 1975-80; asst. prof. ops. rsch. and engring. mgmt., asst. prof. MIS So. Meth. U., Dallas, 1980-87; assoc. prof. mgr. sci. and info. tech. U. Ga., Athens, 1987-92, assoc. prof. MIS, 1992-99, prof. MIS, 1999—. Cons. H.B. Maynard, Pitts., 1978-80, Ga. Kaolin, Dry Branch, 1988-89, UN and Peoples Republic of China, Beijing, 1991-92, English China Clay Internat. and Imerys, 1996—. Co-author: Decision Support Systems and Intelligent Systems, 6th edit., 2001; co-editor: Operations Research: Methods, Models and Applications, 1995; author articles. Terry fellow, 1991—; NSF grantee, 1983, RS/6000 Workstation grantee, 1993. Office: U Ga Dept MIS Terry Coll Bus Brooks Hall Athens GA 30602-6273 E-mail: jaronson@uga.edu.

ARONSON, JAY RICHARD, economics educator, researcher, academic administrator; b. N.Y.C., Aug. 26, 1937; s. Lester and Rose (Hacken) A.; m. Judith Libby Klein, Sept. 13, 1959; children: Sarah, Miriam, Anne. AB, Clark U., 1959, PhD, 1964; MA, Stanford U., 1961. Asst. prof. econs. Worcester Poly. Inst. (Mass.), 1961-65, Lehigh U., Bethlehem, Pa., 1965-68, assoc. prof., 1968-72, prof., 1972—, dir. Martindale Ctr. for Study Pvt. Enterprise, 1980—, William L. Clayton prof. bus. and econs., 1984—. Vis. scholar U. York (Eng.), 1973, hon. prof., 1996-; cons. Internat. City Mgmt. Assn.; commr. Pa. Pension Fund Study Commn. Author: books including (with J. Hilley) Financing State and Local Governments, Public Finance; editor: books including (with E. Schwartz) Management Policies in Local Government Finance, 1975, 3d edit., 1987; contbr. articles to profl. publs. Recipient Lindback award Lehigh U., 1968; recipient Stabler award Lindback award, 1974; Rockefeller fellow, 1959-61; named hon. fellow Clark U., 1962; grantee Ford Found., 1971-72, 76-77, HEW, 1978-79, Scaife Found., 1982; Fulbright research scholar, 1991, 96. Mem.: Roya Econ. Soc., Am. Fin. Assn., Nat. Tax Assn., Am. Econ. Assn. Democrat. Jewish. Home: 1804 Jennings St Bethlehem PA 18017-5235 Office: Lehigh U Dept Economy Bethlehem PA 18015

ARONSON, PETER SAMUEL, medical scientist, physiology educator; b. Bklyn., Feb. 3, 1947; s. Harry and Sydelle (Pincus) A.; m. Marie Louise Landry, Sept. 25, 1977; children: Paul L., William L. AB, U. Rochester, 1967; MD, NYU, 1970; MA (hon.), Yale U., 1987. Diplomate Nat. Bd. Med. Examiners, Am. Bd. Internal Medicine (subspeciality Nephrology). Intern and resident in internal medicine U. N.C. Sch. Medicine, Chapel Hill, 1970-72; clin. assoc. Gerontology Rsch. Ctr., NIH, Balt., 1972-74; fellow in nephrology Yale U. Sch. Medicine, New Haven, 1974-77, asst. prof. medicine and physiology, 1977-81, assoc. prof. medicine and physiology, 1981-87, prof. medicine and cellular and molecular physiology, 1987—, C.N.H. Long prof. internal medicine, 1995—. Chief sect. nephrology Yale U. Sch. Medicine, New Haven, 1987-2002; established investigator Am. Heart Assn., 1981-86. Mem. editl. bd. Am. Jour. Physiology, 1982-86, 87-90, 96-2000, Kidney Internat., 1990-94, Jour. Biol. Chemistry, 1995-2000; cons. editor Jour. Clin. Investigation, 1993-98; contbr. rsch. articles to profl. jours. With USPHS, 1972-74. Recipient Solomon Berson Med. Alumni Achievement award NYU, 1996. Fellow: AAAS; mem.: Soc. Gen. Physiologists, Internat. Soc. Nephrology, Am. Heart Assn. (exec. com. coun. on the kidney 1986—90), Am. Soc. Nephrology (Young Investigator award 1985, Homer Smith award 1994, councillor 2002—), Am. Soc. Clin. Investigation (councillor 1986—88, editl. com. 1993—98), Am. Physiol. Soc., Am. Fedn. Med. Rsch., Am. Assn. Physicians (editl. bd. procs. 1997—99), Salt and Water Club (sec. 1985—87), Alpha Omega Alpha, Phi Beta Kappa. Office: Yale School of Medicine Dept of Medicine/Nephrology PO Box 208029 New Haven CT 06520-8029

ARONSTEIN, MARTIN JOSEPH, law educator, lawyer; b. N.Y.C., Jan. 25, 1925; s. William and Mollie (Mintz) A.; m. Sally K. Rosenau, Sept. 18, 1948 (dec.); children: Katherine Aronstein Porter, David M., James K. BE, Yale U., 1944; MBA, Harvard U., 1948; LLB, U. Pa., 1965. Bar: Pa. 1965. Bus. exec., Phila., 1948-65; assoc. firm Obermayer, Rebmann, Maxwell & Hippel, Phila., 1965-67, partner, 1968-69; assoc. prof. law U. Pa., 1969-72, prof., 1972-78; counsel firm Ballard, Spahr, Andrews & Ingersoll, Phila., 1978-80, partner, 1980-81; prof. law U. Pa., 1981-86, prof. emeritus, 1986—; of counsel firm Morgan, Lewis & Bockius, Phila., 1986-95. Contbr. articles to law revs.; mem. Permanent Editorial Bd. Uniform Comml. Code, 1978-80, counsel, 1980-87, counsel emeritus, 1987—. Served with USN, 1943-46. Mem. Am. Law Inst., ABA (reporter com. on stock certs. 1973-77, chmn. subcom. on investment securities 1982-84), Phila. Bar Assn., Order of Coif, Sigma Xi, Tau Beta Pi. Home: The Fountains at Logan Sq E Two Franklin Town Blvd 2213 Philadelphia PA 19103

ARORA, SARDARI LAL, chemistry educator; b. Lahore, Pakistan, June 4, 1929; came to U.S., 1964; s. Uttam Chand and Kushal Devi Arora; m. Sunita Chawla, May 9, 1960; children: Nita, Nalini. MSc, Lucknow (India) U., 1953, PhD, 1959. Chief chemist, dir. R & D, Internat. Liquid Crystal Co., Cleve., 1971-74; rsch. assoc. Liquid Crystal Inst., Kent (Ohio) State U., 1966-71, researcher, 1983—, casual asst. prof. chemistry, 1975-77, vis. asst. prof., 1977-80, asst. prof., 1980-86, assoc. prof., 1986—. Cons. Crystaloid Electronic Corp., 1976-78, Timex Corp., 1976-78, Liquid Crystal Application, Inc., 1983; presenter in field. Contbr. articles to sci. jours.; inventor, patentee in field. Fellow Coun. Sci. Indsl. Rsch, Govt. of India, 1957; fellow Aerospace Med. Rsch Lab., 1966, NASA, 1968; grantee NSF, 1983, indsl. grantee, 1986. Fellow Am. Inst. Chemists; mem. AAAS, Am. Chem. Soc., Internat. Union Pure and Applied Chemistry, Sigma Xi. Achievements include patents for Field Effect Light Shutter Employing Low Temperature Nematic Liquid Crystals; for Liquid Crystal Materials; research in development of polymer and other new liquid crystal materials, their characterization and technical applications. Home: 162 Steeplechase Ln Munroe Falls OH 44262-1745 Office: Kent State U 6000 Frank Ave NW Canton OH 44720-7599

ARORA, VIJAY KUMAR, electrical engineering educator, researcher; b. Multan, Panjab, Pakistan, Nov. 13, 1945; came to U.S., 1968, naturalized, 1991. s. Hari C. and Chander (Bhagan) A.; m. Rashmi Indu-Bala, Dec. 2, 1976; children: Vineeta, Namita. BSc in Electronics with honors, Kurukshetra (India) U., 1965; MS in Solid State Electronics, U. Colo., 1970, PhD in Solid State Electronics, 1973; MS in Ops. Rsch. with honors, Western Mich. U., 1976. Rsch. asst. and assoc. U. Colo., Boulder, 1968-73, lectr. Denver, 1973-74; asst. prof., coord. rsch. and scholarly activities Western Mich. U., Kalamazoo, 1974-76; asst. prof., assoc. prof., prof., coord. engring. program King Saud U., Riyadh, Saudi Arabia, 1976-85; prof. dept. elec. engring. Wilkes U., Wilkes-Barre, Pa., 1985—, coord. Microelectronics and Device Fabrication Lab., 1985—. Vis. scientist quantum electronics div. Nat. Bur. Standards, Boulder, 1973; instr. Colo. Sch. Mines, Golden, 1971-73; vis. prof. Nat. U. Singapore, 1991-93, Nanyang Tech. U., Singapore, 1999-2000; Sir Gledden vis. prof. U. Western Australia, Perth, 2000-01; vis. assoc. prof. U. Ill., Urbana, 1981-82; vis. rsch. prof. Rsch. Ctr. for Advanced Sci. and Tech., U. Tokyo, 1989-91; participant numerous confs., seminars and workshops; professorial lectr. numerous nat. and internat. confs., profl. socs. and rsch. instns. worldwide; cons. in field.

Contbr. numerous articles to Applied Physics Letters, Microelectronics Jour., Internat. Jour. Applied Engring. Edn., Proc. Am. Soc. Engring. Edn., IEEE Trans. on Electron Devices, Surface Sci., Jour. Physics, Jour. Engring. Sci., Arabian Jour. Sci. and Engring., Elec. Letters, Japanese Jour. Applied Physics, Phys. Rev., numerous others; contbr. chpts. to books. Rsch. grantee Air Force Office Sci. Rsch., NSF, Office Naval Rsch., Nat. Bur. Standards, Dept. Energy, King Saud U. Rsch. Ctr., Western Mich. U., numerous others. Mem. IEEE (sr., disting. lectr.), AAAS, IEEE Electron Devices Soc., IEEE Profl. Communication Soc., IEEE Edn. Soc., IEEE Circuits and Systems Soc., Am. Soc. Engring. Edn., Am. Phys. Soc. (life), Am. Geog. Soc., Sigma Xi. Achievements include development of quantum theory for the study of modern nanoelectronic devices; research and development in high speed devices, microelectronics theory and processing, CAD-CAE of integrated circuits. Office: Wilkes Univ Dept Elec Engring Wilkes Barre PA 18766 Home: 29 Walden Dr Mountain Top PA 18707

AROSIO, CHARLYNE MARY, school librarian, educator; b. Gilroy, Calif., Jan. 6, 1938; d. Charles Joseph and Annie Rose (Olivieri) A. BA, San Francisco State, 1960; student in Libr./Media Studies, U. Ariz., Tempe, 1969, U. Nev., 1974; MA in Computer Edn., Fresno Pacific Coll., 1989; cert. in paralegal studies, U. Nev., 1992. Cert. media specialist. Tchr. Washoe County Sch. Dist., Reno, 1961—, media specialist, 1970—; tchr. Truckee Meadow Coll., Reno, 1989—. Libr. cons. Washoe County Sch. Dist., Reno, 1980—, insvc. tchr. Named Tchr. of Month Greater Reno C. of C., 1977; recipient Dedicated Performance award Washoe County Tchrs. Assn., 1980. Mem. AAUW (sec. parlimentarian 1989—), Am. Libr. Assn., Nev. Assn. Sch. Libr. (pres. 1980-81), No. Nev. Tchrs. English (bd. dirs.), Phi Kappa. Avocations: cooking, travel. Home: 3510 Yosemite Pl Reno NV 89503-3839

ARQUIT, NORA HARRIS, retired music educator, writer; b. Brushton, N.Y., June 30, 1923; d. Samuel Elton George and Esther Cecelia (Gillen) Harris; m. Gordon James Arquit, Nov. 12, 1948; children: Christine Elaine Arquit, Kevin James Arquit, Candace Susan Arquit-Martel. BS in Music Edn., Ithaca Coll., 1945, MS, 1962; postgrad., St. Lawrence U., 1964-47, 74, Cornell U., 1970-71, N.Y. State Coll., Potsdam, 1973. Cert. aerospace edn. with techicians rating. Music dir., band dir., tchr. N.Y. and N.J. State Schs., 1945—80. Guest conductor U.S. Air Force Band, Washington, Dutch and Am. band students, Schiedam, Holland, opening Am.-Can. Seaway, Massena, N.Y., 1975; U.S. Navy Band, Washington, various massed bands in U.S.A., Canada, Europe; dir. bands Worlds Fair, 1964, 65; 1st woman guest conductor Tri-State Honors Band Phillips U., Enid, Okla.; dir., coord. St. Lawrence County ann. H.S. Band Day, 1973-2002; past supvr. coll. student practice tchrs., N.Y.; mem. Mid-States Commn. Secondary Schs. and Colls. Evaluations. Author: Before My Own Time and Since, 1978, From Hamlet to Cold Harbor, 1989, Our Lyon Line, 1993, The History of the New York State, Society of the National Society of the Daughters of the American Colonists, 1994. Past adjudicator h.s. and coll. band contests; past dir., coord. ann. St. Lawrence County Band Day; past capt. aux. USAF Civil Air Patrol; past John Philip Sousa bd. dirs. rep. to Hall of Fame enshrinement of Sousa. Named Dist. Band Master Am., First Chair Am.; recipient Letter of Commendation for People to People Diplomacy for work with student band groups, Embassy at the Hague, Europe, honored for 39 yrs. of svc. on Band Day, St. Lawrence County, 2002. Mem.: AAUW (past divsn. meeting rep.), Women Band Dirs. Nat. Assn. (past nat. pres., Silver Baton), N.Y. State Ret. Tchrs. Assn., N.Am. Band Dirs. Coordinating Coun. (pres. 1978, past nat. v.p.), Am. School Band Dirs. Assn. (emeritus mem. 1980, N.Y. state chmn. 2003—, past chmn. internat. band com., past nat. and state ofcr., honored nat. covention 2003), Internat. Assn. U. Women, Colonial Daughters of the XVIIC (chpt. councillor 1988-91, past. mem. coms.), Soverign Colonial Soc., Soc. New England Women, De Schilpen Soc. (Holland), Kings County Hist. Soc. Nova Scotia, Daughters of Union Vets., N.Y. Ct. Assts. of Nat. Soc. Women Descendents of Ancient and Honorable Artillery Co. (past state officer, corr. sec., com. chmn.), Denison Soc., Daughters Am. Colonists (N.Y. state regent 1991—94, hon. state regent, life 1994), Soc. Colonial Dames of Seventeenth Century (past state officer, past state pres, registrar), Colonial Daughters Seventeenth Century (Atlantic Coast chmn. 2000—, nat. com. chmn. 2000—, past pres.), Daus. Colonial Wars, DAR (life; hon. regent Cayuga chpt., past state com. chmn., genealogical chmn.), Soc. Magna Charta Dames and Barons, Plantagenet Soc., Colonial Order of The Crown (Charlemagne), Soc. Sons and Daus. of the Pilgrims, Soc. U.S. Daughters 1812 (past pres., past Onondaga chpt. pres., past state ofcr.), Soc. Daughters of Founders & Patriots of Am. (past pres., past state pres., registrar), Soc. Sons and Daughters of Colonial Wars, Soc. New England Women, De Schilpen Mus. Soc. Netherlands, Daughters of Am. Colonists (nat. com chmn. 1994—97, atlantic sect.chmn genealogy 2003—), Summit N.J. Club (past mem. spl. panel), Nat. Fedn. Music Club (past mem. editl.com.), State Officers Club DAR, Ithaca Music Club (past pres.), Delta Omicron. Avocations: writing, photography, research. Home: 130 Christopher Cir Ithaca NY 14850-1702

ARRI, MICHELE RENEE, elementary school educator; b. Des Moines, Sept. 15, 1961; d. Kenneth Dee and Karalyn Sue (Maxwell) G. BS in Edn., U. Mo., 1984; MEd in Elem. Edn., U. Mo., St. Louis, 1992. Cert. tchr., Mo. Tchr. Fairview Elem., Columbia, Mo.; elem. tchr. Christian Fellowship Sch., Columbia; tchr. 4th grade Kennerly Elem. Sch., St. Louis. Home-school tchr., 1999—2003. Grantee Literacy Through Lit. and Writing. Mem. Mo. State Tchrs. Assn., Internat. Reading Assn.

ARRINGTON, CAROLYN RUTH, education consultant; b. May 20, 1942; d. Robert Ray and Grace Dotson; m. Wayne Vernon Arrington; children: Kevin Ray, Kemp Gray, Korey shay, Wayne, Kimberly. AA, Ohio Valley Coll., 1962; BA, Fairmont State Coll., 1964; MA, W.Va. U., 1966, EdD, 1994. Cert. pub. sch. adminstr., 1993. Tchr. Greenbrier Bd. Edn., Lewisburg, W.Va., 1964-68; supr. Mason County Bd. Edn., Point Pleasant, W.Va., 1968-70; media specialist Kanawha County Bd. Edn., Charleston, W.Va., 1970-71; asst. dir., dir., asst. divsn. chief W.Va. Dept. Edn., Charleston, 1971-89, asst. state supt. schs., 1989-98; v.p. Arrington Assocs., Inc., 1998—. Edn. and bus. cons.; inspirational motivational spkr. Author numerous poems and children's books; developer workshop materials. Bd. dirs. YWCA, Charleston, 1988-91. Recipient medal of merit Edn. Ohio Valley Coll.; SEA fellow U.S. Dept. Edn., 1984. Mem. Assn. Ednl. Comm. and Tech. (pres. 1979-80, Edgar Dale award 1975, Spl. Svc. award 1982), Wva. Ednl. Media Assn. (pres. 1975-76). Office: Arrington Assocs Inc PO Box 3912 Charleston WV 25339-3912 E-mail: Warrington@charter.net.

ARROW, KENNETH JOSEPH, economist, educator; b. N.Y.C., Aug. 23, 1921; s. Harry I. and Lillian (Greenberg) Arrow; m. Selma Schweitzer, Aug. 31, 1947; children: David Michael, Andrew. BS in Social Sci., CCNY, 1940; MA, Columbia U., 1941, PhD, 1951, DSc (hon.), 1973; LLD (hon.), U. Chgo., 1967, CUNY, 1972; LLD (hon.), Hebrew U. Jerusalem, 1975, U. Pa., 1976, Washington U., St. Louis, 1989, Harvard U., 1999; D. Social and Econ. Scis. (hon.), U. Vienna, Austria, 1971; LLD (hon.), Ben-Gurion U. of the Negev, 1992; D. Social Scis. (hon.), Yale, 1974; D (hon.), Université René Descartes, Paris, 1974, U. Aix-Marseille III, 1985, U. Cattolica del Sacro Cuore, Milan, Italy, 1994, U. Uppsala, 1995, U. Buenos Aires, 1999; D (hon.), U. Cyprus, 2000; Dr.Pol., U. Helsinki, 1976; MA (hon.), Harvard U., 1968; DLitt, Cambridge U., Eng., 1985; LLD (hon.), Harvard U., 1999; PhD (hon.), Tel Aviv U., 2001. Rsch. assoc. Cowles Commn. for Research in Econs., 1947—49; asst. prof. econs. U. Chgo., 1948—49; acting asst. prof. econs. and stats. Stanford, 1949—50, assoc. prof., 1950—53, prof. econs., stats. and ops. rsch., 1953—68; prof. econs. Harvard, 1968—74, James Bryant Conant univ. prof., 1974—79; exec. head dept. econs. Stanford U., 1954—56, acting exec. head dept., 1962—63, Joan Kenney prof. econs. and prof. ops. rsch., 1979—91, prof. emeritus, 1991—. Economist Coun. Econ. Advisers, U.S. Govt., 1962; cons. RAND Corp.; Fulbright prof. U. Siena, 1995; vis. fellow All Souls Coll., Oxford, 1996; overseas rsch. fellow Churchill Coll., Cambridge, 1963—64, Cambridge, 1970, Cambridge, 73, Cambridge, 86. Author: Social Choice and Individual Values, 1951, Essays in the Theory of Risk Bearing, 1971, The Limits of Organization, 1974, Collected Papers, Vols. I-VI, 1983—85; co-author: Mathematical Studies in Inventory and Production, 1958, Studies in Linear and Nonlinear Programming, 1958, Time Series Analysis of Inter-industry Demands, 1959, Public Investment, The Rate of Return and Optimal Fiscal Policy, 1971, General Competitive Analysis, 1971, Studies in Resource Allocation Processes, 1977, Social Choice and Multicriterion Decision Making, 1985. Capt. U.S. Army, 1942—46. Recipient Alfred Nobel Meml. prize in econ. scis., Swedish Acad. Scis., 1972, Kempé de Feriet medal, 1998, medal, U. Paris, 1998; fellow Social Sci. Rsch. fellow, 1952, Ctr. for Advanced Study in the Behavioral Scis., 1956—57, Churchill Coll., Cambridge, Eng., 1963—64, 1970, 1973, 1986, Guggenheim, 1972—73. Fellow: AAAS (chmn. sect. K 1983), Am. Fin. Assn. (mem. coun. 1990—93), Internat. Soc. Inventory Rsch. (pres. 1983—90), Am. Econ. Assn. (exec. com. 1967—69, pres. 1973, John Bates Clark medal 1957), Inst. Math. Stats., Am. Acad. Arts and Scis. (v.p. 1979—81, 1991—93), Econometric Soc. (v.p. 1955, pres. 1956), Am. Statis. Assn.; mem.: NAS/Inst. of Medicine, Game Theory Soc., Brit. Acad. (corr.), Pontifical Acad. Social Scis., Soc. Social Choice and Welfare (pres. 1991—93), Western Econ. Assn. (pres. 1980—81), Finnish Acad. Scis. (fgn. hon.), Inst. Ops. Rsch. and Mgmt. Sci. (pres. 1963, chmn. coun. 1964, Von Neumann prize 1986, Fellows' award), Am. Philos. Soc., Internat. Econs. Assn. (pres. 1983—86). Office: Stanford U Dept Econs Stanford CA 94305-6072 Fax: 650-725-5702. E-mail: arrow@stanford.edu.

ARROWSMITH, MARIAN CAMPBELL, secondary education educator; b. St. Louis, Nov. 12, 1943; d. William Rankin and Elizabeth (Mitchell) Arrowsmith; m. William Earl Schroyer, July 23, 1983; stepchildren: Carey Jo, Amy Lynn. BS, La. State U., 1961; MEd, Southeastern La. U., 1978. Lic. tchr., La.; cert. practicum supr. Inst. for Reality Therapy. Tchr. 1st grade McDonough #26, Jefferson Parish Sch. Bd., Gretna, La., 1966; 2nd grade tchr. Woodlawn High Sch., Baton Rouge, 1966-67; kindergarten tchr. Univ. Terrace Elem. Sch., Baton Rouge, summer 1967; 1st grade tchr. Westminster Elem. Sch., Baton Rouge, 1967-72, Elm Grove Elem. Sch., Harvey, La., 1972-73; kindergarden tchr. Westminster Elem. Sch., Baton Rouge, summers 1968, 69, 70, 71, Elm Grove Elem. Sch., summer 1973; 1st grade tchr. St. Andrews Episcopal Sch., New Orleans, 1973-74; kindergarten tchr. St. Tammany Parish Sch. Bd., Folsom, La., 1974-77; early childhood specialist St. Tammany Parish Sch. Bd., Covington, La., 1977-87; prin. Woodlake Elementary Sch., 1987—; off-campus coordinating asst. St. Tammany Parish for Dept. Continuing Edn., Southeastern La. U., 1985-87; condr. workshops in field; selected ofcl. pres. Sunbelt Region of Reality Therapists, 1983; regional dir. La. and Miss. Reality Therapists, Sunbelt Bd. of Reality Therapists, 1983. Author: Helping Your Child at Home, 1982-83; Handbook for Early Childhood Tutorial Program, 1983-84. Mem. AAUW, ASCD, La. Assn. Sch. Execs., Nat. Assn. Tchrs. Math., La. Assn. Tchrs. Math., Pontchartrain Yacht Club, Delta Kappa Gamma (v.p. 1986), Alpha Delta Kappa, Kappa Alpha Theta, Phi Delta Kappa. Democrat. Methodist. Avocations: horticulture, reading, fishing, dancing. Home: 1000 Montgomery St Mandeville LA 70448-5517

ARSHAM, GARY, medical educator; b. Cleve., 1941; s. Sanford Ronald and Florence A.; m. Diana Silver, 1971. AB cum laude, Harvard U., 1963; MD, Case-Western Res. U., 1967; PhD, U. Ill., 1971. Fellow in med. edn. U. Ill., Chgo., 1968-71; asst. then assoc. dean curriculum devel., asst. prof. medicine and health scis. communication SUNY, 1971-72; assoc. prof., prof. health professions edn. U. of Pacific, San Francisco, 1972-79; chmn. Council on Edn. Pacific Med. Ctr., San Francisco, 1976-81; v.p. Arsham Cons., Inc., San Francisco, 1981—. Adminstr. Pacific Vision Found., 1977-84, dir. edn., 1983-90; mem. nat. adv. bd. John Muir Hosp. Med. Film Festival, 1981—; mem. task force on interdisciplinary edn. Nat. Joint Practice Commn., 1973-74; bd. dirs. U.S.-China Ednl. Inst., 1980—, sec., 1986-88, treas., 1993-95; chair, CEO Nat. Accreditation Commn. for Schs. and Colls. of Acupuncture and Oriental Medicine, 1993-98. Co-author: Diabetes: A Guide To Living Well, 1989, 2d edit. 1992, 3d edit., 1997, 101 Tips for Coping With Diabetes, 2003; chief editor Family Medicine Reports, San Francisco, 1983. Office: Arsham Cons Inc PO Box 15608 San Francisco CA 94115-0608

ARSHAM, HOSSEIN, operations research analyst; b. Mashhad, Iran, Mar. 28, 1947; came to U.S., 1978; s. Gholam Reza and Habebeh (Babai) A.; m. Elaheh-Naaze Khoshghadam, Dec. 20, 1984; 1 child, Aryana. BSc in Physics, Arya-Mehr U. Tech., Tehran, Iran, 1971; MSc, Cranfield Inst., Eng., 1978; DSc, George Washington U., 1982. Cert. info. scientist, specialized in strategic decision making. Postdoctoral rschr. Internat. Water Resources Inst., Washington, 1982-83; prof. U. Balt., 1983—, Harry Wright disting. rsch. prof. mgmt. sci. and stats., chair dept. mgmt. scis., 1996—; rsch. prof. Info. Systems Rsch. Ctr., Balt., 1996—. Faculty advanced studies Calif. Nat. U., 1991—; faculty adv. bd. Western Govs. U., 1999; faculty cons. Kennedy-Western U., 1995—; mem. exec. adv. coun. Internat. Soc. for Theory and Application of Multi-Objective Decision Analysis; tech. lectr. Bethlehem Steel Co., Balt., 1983-84; sci. cons. in field. Editor InterStat: Stats. on the Internet, Ops. Rsch. category for the Netscape Open Directory, Jour. of Interdisciplinary Math.; sr. assoc. editor Computational Stats. and Data Analysis and Jour. Environ. Dynamics; mem. editl. bd. IEEE Ednl., Tech. and Soc. Jour., Jour. of End User Computing, Jour. Environ. Dynamics, Internat. Jour. Ops. and Quantitative Mgmt.; mem. editl. bd. Ednl. Tech. and Soc. Jour.; mem. internat. sci. com. Advances in Intelligent Data Analysis, 1997—. Internat. Symposium on Adaptive Systems, 1999—; contbr. articles to profl. jours. Commn. on Office Lab. Accreditation grantee, 1993, NSF grantee, 1995; recipient Black & Decker Corp. Rsch. award, 1987, 88, 98, Excellence in Rsch. award U. Sys. Md., 2000. Fellow Royal Statis. Soc., Operational Rsch. Soc., Inst. Combinatorics and Applications, World Innovation Found.; mem. AAAS, IEEE, Am. Math. Soc., Internat. Assn. Math. and Computer Modeling, Internat. Forecasting Soc., Am. Statis. Assn., Assn. for Computing Machinery, Digital Equipment Computer Users Soc., Info. Resources Mgmt. Assn., Math. Assn. Am., London Math. Soc., Inst. for Ops. Rsch. and Mgmt Scis., Soc. Indsl. and Applied Math., Soc. for Info. Mgmt., N.Y. Acad. Scis., Internat. Soc. for Theory and Application of Multi-Objective Decision Analysis (exec. adv. coun.), Beta Gamma Sigma, Omega Rho. Achievements include research in statistics, applied probability, discrete-event systems simulation, and mathematical programming and modeling. Office: U Balt 1420 N Charles St Baltimore MD 21201-5720 E-mail: harsham@ubmail.ubalth.edu.

ARTESANI, MARYANN, elementary education educator; b. Providence, Sept. 13, 1950; d. Frederick F. and Marrietta (DiSandro) Lanni; m. William A. Artesani III, Sept. 10, 1972; 1 child, Aubrie Anne. AA, R.I. Jr. Coll., 1970; BA, Mt. St. Joseph Coll., 1972; MA, R.I. Coll., 1974. Cert. tchr., R.I., paralegal. Tchr. Warwick (R.I.) Sch. Dept., 1972—. Pub. speaker N.Eng. Reading Conf., Newport, R.I., 1992. Editor, columnist Teaching Pre K-8 mag., 1991—; contbr. poetry to anthologies. Pres. Western Hills Elem. Sch. PTG, Cranston, R.I., 1991-92, 94-95; v.p. Western Hills Jr. High Sch. PTG, Cranston, 1992-93; bd. dirs. Robertson Sch. PRG, Warwick, 1992-93, 93-95. Recipient Key to the City, Mayor of Warwick, 1976, citation, Mayor of Warwick, 1976, 92, Citation for Excellence in Teaching, R.I. Ho. Reps., Providence, 1991, 93, Cert. Poetic Achievement, Amherst Soc., 1991, Key to City, Mayor of Cranston, 1995, Citation, Warwick Sch. Com., 1995, Share the Gold award Elfun Soc. G.E., 1995. Mem. RITAWL (guest pub. speaker 1991), Am. Fedn. Tchrs., Assn. Early Childhood Internat. (pub. speaker R.I. chpt. 1991), New Eng. Reading Assn., R.I. Fedn. Tchrs., Nat. Authors Registry, Warwick Tchrs. Union, Bus. and Profl. Womens Club, Providence Bus. and Profl. Womens Club (1st v.p.), Western Hills Jr. High Sch. PTG (pres. 1993-94), Assn. Supervision and Curriculum. Avocation: writing. Home: 67 Kimberly Ln Cranston RI 02921-2625 Office: Robertson Sch 70 Nausauket Rd Warwick RI 02886-7505

ARTHER, RICHARD OBERLIN, polygraphist, educator; b. Pitts., May 20, 1928; s. William Churchill Sr. and Florence Lind (Oberlin) A.; m. Mary-Esther Wuensch, Sept. 12, 1951; children: Catherine, Linda, William III. BS, Mich. State U., 1951; MA, Columbia U., 1960. Chief assoc. John E. Reid and Assocs., Chgo., 1951-53, dir. N.Y.C., 1953-58; pres. Sci. Lie Detection, Inc., N.Y.C., 1958—2003, chmn., 2003—; pres. Nat. Tng. Ctr. Polygraph Sci., N.Y.C., 1958—. Author: Interrogation for Investigators, 1958, The Scientific Investigator, 1964, 7th edit., Arther Polygraph Reference Guide, 1964—, 8th edit.; editor Jour. Polygraph Sci., 1966—. Fellow Acad. Cert. Polygraphists (exec. dir. 1962—), Am. Polygraph Assn. (founding mem.), Am. Assn. Police Polygraphists (founding mem., Polygraphist of Yr. 1980), N.Y. State Polygraphists (founder), N.J. Polygraphists (founder). Office: Sci Lie Detection Inc 200 W 57th St Ste 1400 New York NY 10019-3211

ARTINIAN, ARTINE, French literature scholar, collector; b. Pazardjick, Bulgaria, Dec. 8, 1907; came to U.S., 1920, naturalized, 1930; s. Peter and Akaby (Berberian) A.; m. Margaret Willard Woodbridge, June 27, 1936; children— Margaret, Robert Willard, Ellen. AB, Bowdoin Coll., Brunswick, Maine, 1931; diploma, U. Paris, 1932; A.M., Harvard U., 1933; PhD, Columbia U., 1941; Litt.D. (hon.), Bowdoin Coll., 1966; postgrad., U. Grenoble, France, 1931, U. Poitiers, 1932; LHD, Appalachian State U., 2001. Asst. French Bowdoin Coll., 1930-31; ednl. worker dept. correction organizing inmate sch. Welfare Island Penitentiary, N.Y.C., 1934-35; prof. French John Marshall Coll. Law, N.J., 1935-36; chmn. French dept. Bard Coll., Annandale-on-Hudson, N.Y., 1935-64, chmn. div. langs., lits., 1939-40, 44-45, 56-57, 58-59, 60-64, prof. emeritus French, 1964—; head instr. French Bard Coll. A.S.T.P. Unit, 1943-44. Prof.-in-charge Sweet Briar (Va.) Jr. Year in France, 1953-55; acting dir. U.S. house Cité Universitaire, Paris, summers 1955, 56, 58; mem. com. examiners (French sect.) Coll. Entrance Exam. Bd., 1962-64; trustee Am. Students Center, Paris, 1954-65; guest of French govt., summer 1946 Compiler extensive Guy de Maupassant collection, also French lit. manuscripts now at U. Tex., Austin; exhibited collection drawings and paintings by French writers, U.S. tour sponsored by French govt., 1968-70; Century and a Half of French Illustrators, Cornell U., Brandeis U., Harvard U., 1968, Tex., 1972, Auckland (N.Z.) Mus., 1977, U.S. Tour, 1980-85, The French Visage, A Century and a Half of French Portraits, Bowdoin Coll. Mus. Art, Hopkins Art Ctr., Dartmouth Coll., others, 1969; Music in Art Henry Morrison Flagler Mus., Palm Beach, Fla., Brandeis U., Wellesley Coll., 1971, Illustrated Letters, Seton Hall U., South Orange, N.J., 1978, French Illustrated Letters, Norton Gallery of Art, West Palm Beach, 1989; over 300 N.C. Self-Portraits donated to Appalachian State U., Boone, N.C.; over 300 Fla. self Portraits donated to Fla. Atlantic U., Boca Raton; also exhibited other collections numerous other univs. U.S. including Columbia, French Inst. N.Y.C., Vassar, U. Va.; Author: Maupassant Criticism in France, 1880-1940, With an Inquiry into His Present Fame and a Bibliography, 1941, 69; editor: La Correspondance inédite de Guy de Maupassant, 1951, Pour et Contre Maupassant, 1955, Complete Short Stories of Guy de Maupassant, 1955, La Queue de la Poire de la Boule de Monseigneur (Flaubert 1st edit.), 1958, Là-Haut (Huysmans 1st edit.), 1963, From Victor Hugo to Jean Cocteau, 1965; Maupassant biography (with Robert Artinian), 1982; contbr. to profl. jours., books. Mem. chancellor's coun. U. Tex.; philantrophist established scholarship funds, Attleboro, Mass., Sweet Briar Coll., Va., Appalachin State U., Boone, N.C, Bowdoin Coll., Brunswick, Me. Decorated officier d'Academie (France), 1948; Am. Council Learned Socs. fellow, 1943-44; Fulbright research scholar France, 1949-50; Am. Philos. Soc. research grantee Paris, 1960; named to Hon. Order Ky. Cols. Mem. Société des Amis de Guy de Maupassant (v.p. 1950-65), MLA (sec. 19th Century French sect. 1947, chmn. 1948), Am. Assn. Tchrs. French, AAUP (pres. Bard Coll. chpt. 1951-52), Société Littéraire des Amis d'Emile Zola (U.S. rep. bd. dirs. 1954-65), Expressions Paris (hon. pres. 1984—), Theta Delta Chi, Pi Delta Epsilon. Home: 100 Worth Ave Ph 6 Palm Beach FL 33480-4421

ARVESON, RAYMOND GERHARD, retired state official; b. Jamestown, N.D., May 11, 1921; m. Adelaide Arveson; children: Raymond, Susan Aden, John. BA, Mayville State U., 1942; MA, U. Minn., 1948; EdD, U. Calif., Berkeley, 1962. High sch. prin. Pub. Schs., Alamo and Langdon, N.D., 1942-44; supt. Langdon (N.D.) Pub. Schs., 1944-45, Leeds (N.D.) Pub. Schs., 1945-57; counselor, social sci. tchr. Hayward (Calif.) Union High Sch., 1957-58; dean of boys Tennyson High Sch. and Hayward Union High Sch., 1958-59, vice prin., 1958-59, prin., 1960-63; asst. supt. Hayward (Calif.) Union Sch. Dist., 1963-68; supt. Hayward (Calif.) Unified Sch. Dist., 1968-76, Mpls. Pub. Schs., 1976-80, East Baton Rouge (La.) Parish Pub. Schs., 1980-87, East Feliciana Parish Pub. Schs., 1989-90; asst. supt. acad. programs La. Dept. Edn., Baton Rouge, 1991, state supt. edn., 1991-96; ret., 1996. Bd. dirs. Operation Upgrade, S.W. Ednl. Devel. Lab., La. Edn. TV Authority, La. Sch. for Math., Sci. and Arts, La. Drug Policy, La. Children's Cabinet; co-chmn. bd. dirs. Satellite Ednl. Rsch. Consortium; co-project dir. La. Systemic Initiatives Program; bd. trustees La. Tchrs. Retirement System; mem. supts. adv. coun. State Bd. Elem. and Secondary Edn.; active Coun. Chief State Sch. Officers, Govs. Cabinet. Mem. joint adv. bd. Baton Rouge Gen. Hosp.; bd. dirs. Baton Rouge Symphony, La. Youth Orch., Playmakers, Crime Stoppers, Fairview Hosp., Tau Ctr.; trustee La. Arts and Scis. Coun., Our Lady of Lake Coll., pres. bd.; mem. visitation com. and bd. dirs. United Way, also ednl.hmn.; mem. standing com. for rsch. and analysis Am. Luth. Ch.; mem. tchr. edn. coun. La. State U.; and numerous others; mem. La. LEARN Commn. Recipient State Farmer award La. Assn. Future Farmers Am., Boss of Yr. award Am. Bus. Women's Assn. Mem. NEA (life), Am. Assn. Sch. Adminstrs. (emeritus), Nat. Sch. Bds. Assn. (mem. liaison com.), Nat. Speech Assn. (pres. debate and discussion divsn.), Nat. Soc. Study of Edn., Nat. PTA, La. Assn. Sch. Execs. (Outstanding Educator award), La. Assn. Sch. Supts. (bd. dirs.), Far West Lab. Ednl. Rsch. and Devel. (bd. dirs.), Assn. Supervision and Curriculum Devel. (bd. dirs.), Large City Schs. Supts. Assn. (pres.), PTA (hon. life), Baton Rouge C. of C. (mem. edn. com.) Horace Mann League, Phi Delta Kappa, Lambda Delta Lambda. Avocations: golf, tennis, camping, fishing, gardening.

ARVIZU, CHARLENE SUTTER, elementary education educator; b. San Jose, Calif., Mar. 1, 1947; d. Joseph Carl and Marjorie Loreen (Nylin) Sutter; m. Ambrose Emanuel Arvizu, Apr. 7, 1980; children: Joseph Todd Nottingham, Matthew Sutter. BA in Art, San Jose State U., 1964, lifetime tchg. credential grades K-9, lifetime spl. edn. grades K-14, specialist/learning handicapped, San Jose State U., 1969. Tchr. edn. mentally retarded class grades K-12 Berryessa Union Sch. Dist., 1969-71, resource ctr. dir. grades K-5, 1971-73, kindergarten tchr. Ruskin Sch., 1974—. Instr. Ohlone Coll., Fremont, Calif., 1980—89, chapman Coll., 1985—88, San Jose County Office Edn., 1985—94; cons., lectr. Bur. Edn. and Rsch., 1990—; nat. lectr., cons., presenter in field. Author: Whole Language Strategies in the Classroom, 2001, Strengthening Your Kindergarten Using Thrmatic, Integrate Literature Based Strategies, 2002, Kindergarten 5 Day Institute Book, 1994, Read It Again, 1998, Current Best Strategies to Help All Your Kindergartens to be Successful, 2002, Management for Kindergarten Success, 1999. Recipient Disting. Sch. award Office of Mayor of San Jose, Calif., 1987, Award Bur. of Edn. and Rsch., 1998. Mem. Internat. Reading Assn., Calif. Reading Assn., Internat. Book Assn. for Young Readers, Children's Book Coun. Inc., Calif. Sch. Age Consortium, Planetary Citizens-One World-One People, Soc. Children's Book Writers, Delta Kappa Gamma. Avocations: animals, horseback riding. Home: 3010 Daurine Ct Gilroy CA 95020-9552 Office: Ruskin Sch 1401 Turlock Ln San Jose CA 95132-2399

ARYA, SATYA PAL, meteorology educator; b. Mavi Kalan, Dist Meerut, India, Aug. 24, 1939; came to U.S., 1965. BE (Civil), U. Roorkee (India), 1961, ME (Civil), 1964; PhD, Colo. State U., 1968. Asst. engr. Irrigation Dept., Lucknow, India, 1961-62; lectr. U. Roorkee, 1963-65; rsch. asst. Colo. State U., Ft. Collins, 1965-68, rsch. assoc., 1968-69; rsch. asst., assoc. prof. U. Wash., Seattle, 1969-76; assoc. prof. N.C. State U., Raleigh, 1976-81, prof. meteorology, 1981—, acting head MEAS dept., 1982-83. Vis. prof. Indian Inst. Tech., Delhi, 1983-84. Author: Introduction to Micrometeorology, 1988, 2d edit., 2001, Air Pollution Meteorology and dispersion, 1999; contbr. sci. articles to jours. of atmospheric scis., applied meteorology, fluid mechanics, others. Fellow AAAS, Am. Meteorol. Soc.; mem. Am. Geophys. Union. Achievements include research in atmospheric sciences, applied meteorology, environmental fluid mechaincs, micrometeorology and air pollution. Office: NC State U Dept Marine Earth & Atmosphe Raleigh NC 27695-8208 E-mail: sparya@unity.ncsu.edu.

ARZOUMANIAN, LINDA LEE, early childhood educator; b. Madison, Wis., Apr. 29, 1942; d. James Arthur Luck and Rosemary M. (Peacock) Engstrom; children: Stephan, Aaron. BS, Stout State U., Menomonie, Wis., 1964; MEd, Ohio U., Athens, 1969; EdD, Nova U., 1994. Cert. tchr. vocat., secondary, cmty. coll., Ariz. Residence hall asst. Ohio U., Athens, 1965-67; quality control supr. Advalloy, Inc., Palo Alto, Calif., 1967; tchr. adult edn. Eau Claire (Wis.) Pub. Sch., 1964-65; patient svc. dietitian Camden Clark Meml. Hosp., Parkersburg, W.Va., 1970; adminstr. pre-sch. Fishkill (N.Y.) Meth. Nursery Sch., 1976-84; substitute tchr. Tucson Unified Sch. Dist., 1987; tchr. pre-sch. Tanque Verde Luth. Presch., Tucson, 1988-89; cons., early childhood ednl. curriculum specialist Tucson Unified Sch. Dist., 1988-93; instr. Ctrl. Ariz. Coll., 1990-98, Prescott Coll., 1991-92; dist. moderator Sch. Cmty. Partnership Coun., Tucson, 1988-90; dir. child and family svcs. in prevention, early intervention and treatment in sys. managed care CODAC Behavioral Health Svcs., Tucson, 1990-99, dir. mgmt. info. sys., 1999, dir. cmty. svcs., 1999-2000; supt. of schs. Pima County, 2000—. Mem. supts. adv. cabinet Tucson Unified Sch. Dist., 1988-89, mem. curriculum and instrn. coun., 1989-90, spl. edn. pre-sch. adv. com., 1989-91, info. tech. bond rev. com., 1989—, sex edn. curriculum adv. com., core curriculum com., 1988-90, 2000 com., 1988-89, and various others; nat. child devel. assoc. adv./field adv., nat. child devel. assoc. rep. Nat. Assn. for Edn. of Young Children; grantswriter Comstock Found.; validator early childhood programs for Nat. Acad. Early Childhood Programs; appt. Ariz. State Bd. Edn., 2002. Mem. Dutchess County Child Devel. Com., Poughkeepsie, N.Y., 1979-81; advancement chmn. troop 1968 Boy Scouts Am., Tucson, 1986, com. person troop 194, 1986-89; mem. joint com. on site based decision making Tucson Unified Sch. Dist./Tucson Edn. Assn., 1989-98; life mem. Ariz. PTA; mem. Early Childhood Edn. Coun. Consortium; mem. mgmt. com. Healthy Families of Pima County; commr. Met. Edn. Commn.; mem. Pima County Youth Coun., Greater Tucson Strategic Planning for Econ. Devel. Mem.: AAUW, Ariz. Sch. Bds. Assn., Am. Assn. Edn. Svc. Agys. (Fed. Relations Repr. (Ariz.)), Tucson Assn. Edn. Young Children (past pres.), Nat. Assn. Edn. Young Children, Tucson Rep. Women, Pima County Supt. and Governing Bd. Collaborative, Tucson Hispanic C. of C., Tucson Met. C. of C., So. Ariz. Forums on Children and Families, Cath. Cmty. Svc. (bd. dirs.). Avocations: basketmaking, quilting, hiking, gardening, cooking. Home: 8230 E Ridgebrook Dr Tucson AZ 85750-2442 Office: 3100 N 1st Ave Tucson AZ 85719-2513 : 130 W Congress Tucson AZ 85701

ASAAD, KOLLEEN JOYCE, special education educator; b. West Union, Iowa, July 13, 1941; d. Leonard Henry and Catherine Adelade (Bishop) Anfinson; children: Todd, Robin, Tara, Jason. BA in Elem. Edn., Upper Iowa U., 1961; MA in Spl. Edn. and Adminstrn., U. Cin., 1973. Elem. tchr. Fredericksburg (Iowa) Elem. Sch., 1961-62, Tyler Sch., Cedar Rapids, Iowa, 1962-64, Oasis Sch., 29 Palms, Calif., 1964-69, Longfellow Sch., Waterloo, Iowa, 1969-70; spl. edn. tchr. Fairview Sch., Cin., 1970-77; learning disabilities tchr. Lincoln Sch., Portsmouth, Ohio, 1977-78; dir. spl. edn. Vermilion Assn. for Spl. Edn., Danville, Ill., 1978-94; dir. edn. Swann Spl. Care Ctr., Champaign, Ill., 1994-97, ret., 1997. Mem. Govtl. Rels. Com., Ill. Coun. for Exceptional Children, Jacksonville, Ill., 1992. Bd. mem. Crosspoints, Danville, Catlin Music Boosters, pres. Named Best Adminstr., Regional Supt. of Schs., 1991. Mem. Coun. for Exceptional Children, Coun. for Adminstrs. of Spl. Edn., Ill. Adminstrs. of Spl. Edn., Assn. for Persons with Severe Handicaps, Exec. Club. Lutheran. Avocations: reading, art. Home: 122 Mapleleaf Dr Catlin IL 61817-9646

ASADI, ANITA MURLENE, business educator; b. Kirksville, Mo., Feb. 2, 1948; d. James Murl and Norma Waneva (Schillie) Wallace; m. Asad Asadi, Feb. 25, 1972; children: Soraya, Ali. BS in Bus. Edn., N.E. Mo. State U., 1970, MA, 1971. Grad. asst. N.E. Mo. State U., Kirksville, 1970-71; instr. bus. edn. Muscatine (Iowa) C.C., 1971-76; mem. faculty St. Ambrose U., Davenport, Iowa, 1977-83; instr. adminstrv. and office support programs Scott C.C., Davenport, 1977—. Adminstrv. asst. Stanley, Lande, Coulter & Pearce, Muscatine, 1971-74; cons. Rock Island (Ill.) Arsenal, 1983-85; writer Sci. Rsch. Assocs. a.k.a. SRA/Pergamon, Chgo., 1987-88, Paradigm Pub. Internat., Eden Prairie, Minn., 1989—. Author: (textbook) Stenoscript ABC Shorthand, 1989; mem. editorial bd. Answer Book, Illinois Legal Handbook; contbr. articles to profl. jours. Mem Pres. Club Rep. Nat. Com., 1990, Talent Identification Program Parent/Alumni Network, Duke U., Durham, N.C., 1989-90, Scott County Family YMCA, Davenport, 1984-90. Recipient Bus. Edn. award, 1990, Disting. Svc. and Scholarship award IBEA, 1990, Chancellor's award, 1991, Phebe Sudlow award Quad Cities Encouragement Bd., 1991; named Outstanding Postsecondary Bus. instr., IBEA, 1991. Mem. NAACP, NEA, Am. Careers and Tech. Edn., Iowa Am. Careers and Tech. Edn., Bus. Profl. Educators Iowa, Iowa Bus. Edn. Assn., Office Automation Network, Assn. Info. System Profl., Bus. Profl. Am., Iowa Women Ednl. Leadership, Internat. Soc. Bus. Educators, Iowa Bus. Edn. Assn. (pres. 1999-00), Delta Pi Epsilon. Avocations: Mideast artifacts, Am. antiques, music boxes, reading autobiographies. Home: 5075 Crestview Heights Dr Bettendorf IA 52722-5626 Office: Scott CC 326 W 3d St Davenport IA 52801-1201 E-mail: asadi4@aol.com.

ASADORIAN, DIANA C. electrical engineer, educator; b. Leninakan, Armenia, June 16, 1950; came to U.S., 1975; d. Eduard and Vartuhi (Seraidarian) Martirosyan; m. William R. Asadorian, July 22, 1978; 1 child, Ronald E. M in Electromech. Engring. Elec. Motors, Polytech. Inst., Odessa, USSR, 1972. Elect. engr. Odessa Cable Plant, 1972-75; draftsman Leviton Co., Bklyn., 1976-77; from engring. asst. to design engr. engring. and devel. CBS, N.Y.C., 1977-86, assoc. dir. engring. lab., 1986-89, dir. engring. lab. and drafting. engring. and devel., 1989-90, dir. tech. tng. and documentation engring., 1990—, assoc. dir. news engring. and document, 1994—. Mem. Soc. Motion Picture and TV Engring., Am. Soc. News Engring. and Documentation (assoc. dir.). Republican. Baptist. Avocation: concert pianist. Office: CBS 524 W 57th St New York NY 10019-2924

ASANI, ALI S. foreign language and religious studies educator; b. Nairobi, Kenya, Oct. 28, 1954; came to U.S., 1973; s. Sultaan Ali and Shirinkhanu (Velji) A. BA summa cum laude, Harvard Coll., 1977; MA, Harvard U., 1981, PhD, 1984. From instr. to assoc. prof. Indo-Muslim culture Harvard U., Cambridge, Mass., 1983-92, prof. practice of Indo-Muslim lang. and culture, 1992—. Vis. prof. Inst. Ismaili Studies, London, 1992—; dir., co-dir. Al-Ummah Summer Program for Muslim Youth, 1984—. Author: The Bujh Niranjan: An Ismaili Mystical Poem, 1991, The Harvard Collection of Ismaili Literature in Indic Literature, 1992, Celebrating Muhammad, 1995, Ecstasy and Enlightenment: Ismaili Devotional Literature of South Asia, 2002; editor Jour. Inst. Muslim Minority Affairs. Recipient Harvard Found. medal, 2002; rsch. fellow NEH, 1986; rsch. grantee Inst. Ismaili Studies, London, 1995, Consortium for Lang. Tchg. and Learning, 1993-94, 95-96, 99-2000; Aga Khan scholar Harvard U., 1973-84. Mem. Am. Acad. Religion, Assn. for Asian Studies, Phi Beta Kappa. Moslem. Avocation: travel. Home: 203 Pemberton St Apt 3 Cambridge MA 02140-2543 Office: Harvard Univ Study of Religion NELC Cambridge MA 02138

ASARE, KAREN MICHELLE GILLIAM, reading, math and English language educator; b. Bklyn., Jan. 21; d. James Henry and Frances (Walker) Gilliam; m. William Kofi, May 4, 1977; 1 child, Anton William Kwaku Asare Jr. BA, Hunter Coll., 1976, MS in Edn., 1979. Cert. tchr., N.Y. state. Tchr. Women's Prison Assn., N.Y., 1977-78, St. Augustine's Sch., Bronx, N.Y., 1978—, Ednl. Opportunity Ctr. of SUNY, 1989—. Mem. NAACP, Nat. Coun. Tchrs. English, Reading Reform Found., Nat. Cath. Edn. Assn., Profl. Staff Congress, Sigma Gamma Rho-Delta Nu Sigma. Avocations: reading, art, creative writing. Office: Saint Augustine's Sch 1176 Franklin Ave Bronx NY 10456-4306

ASATO, SUSAN PEARCE, business executive, educator; b. Dallas, Dec. 29, 1949; d. Joe Camp and Sue (Dickey) Pearce; m. Morris T. Asato, Apr. 1, 1973. Student, U. Internat., Saltillo, Mex., 1968; BE, U. Tex., 1973; MBA, Calif. State U., San Bernardino, 1981. Tchr. Austin (Tex.) Ind. Sch. Dist., 1972-73; rsch. assoc. U. Tex., Austin, 1973-77; dir. Tairyu (Japan) English Ctr., 1977-78; purchasing agt. U. Calif., Riverside, 1978-83; gen. mgr. corp. purchasing ABC-TV, Hollywood, Calif., 1983-90; dir. purchasing and material mgmt. Mira Costa Coll., Oceanside, Calif., 1990—. Instr., lectr. U. Calif., Riverside, 1981-83. Bd. dirs. Santa Margarita YCMA, 1996—, Theatre Found., 1993—. Mem. Nat. Assn. Purchasing Mgrs., Nat. Assn. Ednl. Buyers, Nat. Contract Mgmt. Assn., Calif. Assn. Sch. Bus. Ofcls., Calif. Assn. Pub. Purchasing Ofcls., Oceanside Rotary Internat. (bd. dirs., Paul Harris fellow 1998). Episcopalian. Home: Mira Costa Coll 1 Barnard Dr Oceanside CA 92056-3820

ASCHHEIM, EVE MICHELE, artist, educator; b. NYC, Aug. 30, 1958; d. Emil and Lydie Aschheim. BA, U. Calif., Berkeley, 1983; MFA, U. Calif., Davis, 1987. Asst. prof. Occidental Coll., L.A., 1990, Sarah Lawrence Coll., Bronxville, N.Y., 1994-97. Vis. critic Md. Inst. Coll. Art, Balt., 1998-2000; lectr. Princeton (N.J.) U., 1991, 93, 98, 2000, sr. lectr., 2001—, dir. visual arts program, 2003—. One-woman shows include Stefan Stux Gallery, 1997, Galerie Rainer Borgemeister, Berlin, 1999, 2001, Galleri Magnus Åklundh, Lund, Sweden, 1999, Galerie Benden and Klimczak, Cologne, Germany, 1999, U. Mass. Gallery, Amherst, 2003; group exhbns. include Sackler Mus., Cambridge, Mass., 1997, Kunstmuseum Winterthur, Switzerland, 1998, Akademie der Künste, Berlin, 1998, Fonds régional d'art contemporain de Picardie and Museé de Picardie Amiens, 1997, Parrish Mus., L.I., N.Y., 1999, Stark Gallery, N.Y.C., 1999, U. Calif., San Diego, 1999, Landesgalerie Oberosterreich, Linz, Austria, 1999, Pratt Gallery, N.Y.C., 1999, So. Meth. U., 2000, N.Y. Studio Sch., 2000, Hunter Coll. Leubsdorf Gallery, N.Y.C., 2000, Maier Mus., Lynchburg, Va., 2000, Tucson Art Mus., 2000, Mus. Contemporary Art, Miami, 2001, D.A.A.D. Galerie, Berlin, U. Art Mus. Calif. State U., Long Beach, 2001, Colby Coll., 2002, N.Y. Hist. Soc., 2002, O.S.P. Gallery, Boston, 2002, Black and White Gallery, Bklyn., 2003, U. Mass., Amherst, 2003; represented in permanent collections at Fogg Mus., Nat. Gallery, Washington, N.Y. Hist. Soc., Hamburger Bahnhof, Berlin, M.O.C.A., Miami; artist (catalog) Eve Aschheim Paintings and Drawings, 1999, Eve Aschheim Drawings, 2003. Recipient Rosenthal award AAAL, 1997; fellow NEA, 1989, Pollock-Krasner Found., 1990, 2001, NY Found. for Arts, 1991, 2001; grantee Elizabeth Found., 1997. Mem. Am. Abstract Artists. E-mail: easchh@aol.com.

ASCONE, TERESA PALMER, artist, educator; b. Cortland, N.Y., Nov. 1, 1945; d. Lawrence Henry and Bernice Rosella (Holcomb) Palmer; m. Michael Wayne Ascone, Oct. 15, 1965; 1 child, Michael Palmer. Student, Alaska Meth. U., Alaska Pacific U., U. Alaska. Painter/tchr. Alaska Pacific U., Anchorage, 1989-91, U. Alaska, 1992; pvt. tchr. watercolor Anchorage, 1992—; owner Alaskan Portfolio, 1981—; tchr. U. Alaska, Anchorage, 1992—, dir. Ultimate Watercolor Acad., 1998-2001. Juried shows include Alaska State Fair, 1979-80, Fur Rendezvous Juried Show, 1979, 80, All Alaska Juried Show, 1981, 84, 85, 90, Alaska Watercolor Soc. juried show, 1981, 83, 85, 86, 87, 88, 89, 90, 91, April in Paris juried exhibit at Capt. Cook Hotel, 1982, 83, 84, 87, Featured Artist, 1986, Watercolor Fairbanks, 1989, Women Artist of West 1st Ann. Internat. Show, 1990; one women shows include Anchorage Mcpl. Librs., 1980, 82, NBA Heritage Libr., 1986, Alaska Pacific U., 1989, Chitose City Hall, Chitose, Hokkaido, Japan, 1990; represented in permanent collection Alaska Pacific U., Raymond P. Atwood Collection, Lincoln, Nebr.; cover artist Arctic Horizons Mag., 1986, Alaska Horizons Mag., 1986, U. Alaska Anchorage Summer Sessions Catalog, 1997; subject of TV spl., 1988; developer, patentee original design, manufacture & mktg. The Ultimate Palette, 1993; author: We're All Artists: Watercolor for Everyone, 1994, Painting Pleasure: Adventures in Watercolor, 1999; editor, publisher Hot Press Mag., 1994; illustrator: Things in the Sky, 1995; contbr. articles to profl. publs. Mcpl. commr. Anchorage Sister Cities Commn., 1991-93. Recipient Vol. of Yr. Caverly Sr. Ctr., 1986, various art show awards to date; works chosen as ofcl. gifts to cities of Inchon, Korea and Magadan, Russia and Whitby, Eng. from city of Anchorage. Mem. Alaska Watercolor Soc. (v.p. 1983),Athena Soc. Avocations: writing, reading, skating, dancing.

ASCUENA, VIKKI PEPPER, secondary school educator; b. Jerome, Idaho, Oct. 13, 1953; d. Rex and Oneita P.; 1 child, Whitney. BA, Boise State U., 1975, MA, 1980. Tchr. Meridian (Idaho) Jr. H.S., 1975-87, Meridian (Idaho) H.S., 1987—, chairperson English dept., 1993—. Curriculum writer Meridian Schs., 1980—; mem. adj. faculty Boise State U., 1988-90; developer Micron project, 1994—; developer ISAT; presenter in field. Grantee NEH Victorian Seminar, 1987; named Meridian Jr. H.S. Tchr. of Yr., 1987, Meridian H.S. Tchr. of Yr., 1994, Meridian Dist. Tchr. of Yr., 1994; recipient Excellence in Edn. award Brigham Young U., 1997. Mem. NEA, Idaho Edn. Assn., Meridian Edn. Assn., Idaho Coun. Tchrs. English (treas. 1988-91, v.p. 1991-92, pres. 1992-93, past pres. 1993-94), Support for Learning and Tchg. English (newsletter editor 1993-94). Avocations: reading, golf, Basque dance. Office: Meridian HS 1900 W Pine Ave Meridian ID 83642-1961

ASH, MAJOR MCKINLEY, JR., dentist, educator; b. Bellaire, Mich., Apr. 7, 1921; s. Major McKinley Sr. and Helen Marguerite (Early) A.; m. Fayola Foltz, Sept. 2, 1947; children: George McKinley, Carolyn Marguerite, Jeffrey LeRoy, Thomas Edward. BS, Mich. State U., 1947; DDS, Emory U., 1951; MS, U. Mich., 1954; Doctoris Medicine Honoris Causa, U. Bern, 1975. Instr. sch. dentistry Emory U., Atlanta, 1952-53; instr. U. Mich., Ann Arbor, 1953-56, asst. prof., 1956-59, assoc. prof., 1959-62, prof., 1962—, chmn. dept. occlusion, sch. dentistry, 1962-89, dir. stomatognathic physiology lab., sch. dentistry, 1969-89, dir. TMJ/oral facial pain clinic, sch. dentistry, 1983-89, Marcus L. Ward prof. dentistry, 1984-89, prof. emeritus, rsch. scientist emeritus, 1989—; cons. N.E. Regional Dental Bd., 1988-92. Vis. prof. U. Bern, 1989, U. Tex., San Antonio, 1990-98; pres. Basic Sci. Bd., State of Mich., 1962-74; cons. over the counter drugs FDA, Washington, 1985-89. Author, co-author 70 textbooks, 1958—; editor 4 books; contbr. over 190 articles to profl. jours. Served to tech. sgt. Signal Corps, U.S. Army, 1942-45, ETO. Grantee, Nat. Inst. Dental Rsch., 1962—85. Fellow Am. Coll. Dentists, Internat. Coll. Dentists, European Soc. Craniomandibular Disorders, European Soc. Oral Physiology; mem. AAAS, Am. Dental Assn. (cons. coun. on dental therapeutics 1982—, cons. coun. sci. affairs 1995—), N.Y. Acad. Scis., Washtenaw Dist. Dental Soc. (pres. 1963-64), Phi Kappa Phi. Presbyterian. Avocations: photography, birdwatching. Office: U of Mich Sch of Dentistry Ann Arbor MI 48109 E-mail: mmash@umich.edu.

ASH, THOMAS PHILLIP, superintendent of schools; b. East Liverpool, Ohio, June 4, 1949; s. Bobby and Elizabeth Ann (Ludwig) A.; m. Nancy Elizabeth Gauron, June 8, 1951; children: Megan Elizabeth, John Gauron. BS in Edn., Bowling Green (Ohio) State U., 1971; MS in Edn., Youngstown (Ohio) State U., 1974. Tchr. East Liverpool City Schs., 1971-73, project coord., 1973-78, asst. supt., 1978-84, supt., 1984-99, Mid-Ohio Ednl. Svc. Ctr., 2000—. Bd. dirs. Ctrl. Fed. Savs. & Loan, Columbiana County Mental Health Assn.; chmn. Lincoln Way Spl. Edn. Resource Ctr., 1988-89, 93-94; treas. Richland County Youth and Family Coun., 2000—. Mem. exec. coun. Columbiana County Boy Scouts Am., 1989-91, Morrow County Workforce Investment Bd., 2000—; pres. East Liverpool Area United Way, 1990-92; mem. State Supt. Adv. Commn. for Spl. Edn., 1993-95. Recipient Disting. Alumni award East Liverpool High Sch. Alumni Assn., 1987, Ohio Adminstr. of Yr. award Ohio Ednl. Libr. and Media Assn., 1990. Mem. Am. Assn. Sch. Adminstrs., Buckeye Assn. Sch. Adminstrs. (pres. 1999-2000), East Liverpool Area C. of C. (bd. dirs. 1985-2000, Outstanding Educator award 1982, Disting. Svc. award 1982). Office: Mid-Ohio Educational Svs Center 1495 W Longview Ave Ste 202 Mansfield OH 44906

ASHBACHER, CHARLES DAVID, computer programmer, educator, mathematician; b. Fort Riley, Kans., Sept. 24, 1954; s. Rudolph Carl and Paula Louis (Enos) A.; m. Valencia Sue Ashbacher, Oct. 27, 1973 (div. May 1984); m. Mary L. Rhiner, Dec. 14, 1991 (div. Mar. 1994); 1 child, Katrina; m. Patti Lou Gregory, Nov. 4, 1998; stepchildren: Rachael, Steven, Rebecca. AS, Kirkwood Community Coll., Cedar Rapids, Iowa, 1978; BS, Mount Mercy Coll., 1980. Instr. math. and computer sci. Mount Mercy Coll., Cedar Rapids, 1983-89; instr. computers Kirkwood C.C., Cedar Rapids, 1990—; rsch. programmer U. Iowa, Iowa City, 1990-92; rsch. scientist Decisionmark, Cedar Rapids, Iowa, 1993-96; founder Charles Ashbacher Technologies, Hiawatha, Iowa, 1996—; computer instr. Hamilton Coll., Cedar Rapids, Iowa, 1997—, Kirkwood C.C., 1998—. Adj. instr., Mt. Mercy Coll., Cedar Rapids, Iowa, 2001-. Author: Collection of Problems on Smarandache Notions, 1996, Pluckings From the Tree of Smarandache Sequences and Functions, 1998, Sams Teach Yourself XML in 24 Hours, 2000, Introduction to Neutrosophic Logic, 2002; co-editor Jour. Recreational Math., 1991, Smarandache Notions, 1994—, An Introduction to the Smarandache Function, 1995; PC software revs. editor, review panelist videotape revs. editor Math. and Computer Edn.; mem. editl. bd. contests in math. series; IEEE Computer; contbr. articles to profl. jours. Basketball coach YMCA, 1990—; judge local sci. fair; active local PTA; soccer coach Am. Youth Soccer Orgn., 1998—. Mem. Am. Math. Assn. Two-Yr. Colls., Assn. Computing Machinery, Math. Assn. Am., Fibonacci Assn. Avocations: reading, languages, solving problems, travel. Home: 118 Chaffee Dr Hiawatha IA 52233-1406 E-mail: cashbacher@yahoo.com.

ASHBERY, JOHN LAWRENCE, language educator, poet, playwright, art critic; b. Rochester, N.Y., July 28, 1927; s. Chester Frederick and Helen Ashbery. Grad., Deerfield Acad., 1945; BA, Harvard U., 1949; MA, Columbia U., 1951; postgrad., NYU, 1957—58; DLitt (hon.), Southampton Coll. of L.I.U., 1979, U. Rochester, Harvard U. Copywriter Oxford U. Press, N.Y.C., 1951—54, McGraw Hill Book Co., N.Y.C., 1954—55; art critic European edit. N.Y. Herald Tribune, Paris, 1960—65; Paris corr. Art News, 1964—65, exec. editor, 1965—72; prof. English Bklyn. Coll., 1974—90, Disting. prof., 1980—90, Disting. emeritus prof., 1990; Charles P. Stevenson Jr. prof. langs. and lit. Bard Coll., 1990—; editor quar. rev. Art and Lit., Paris, 1964—67; art critic Art Internat., Lugano, Switzerland, 1961—62; editor Locus Solus, Lans-en-Vercors, France, 1960-62; poetry editor Partisan Rev., 1976—80; art critic New York Mag., 1978—80, Newsweek, 1980—85; Charles Eliot Norton prof. poetry Harvard U., 1989—90; conducted spl. rsch. on life and work of Raymond Roussel. Author: Turandot and Other Poems, 1953, Some Trees, 1956, The Poems, 1960, The Tennis Court Oath, 1962, Rivers and Mountains, 1966, Selected Poems, 1967, Three Madrigals, 1968, Sunrise in Suburbia, 1968, Fragment, 1969, The Double Dream of Spring, 1970, The New Spirit, 1970, Three Poems, 1972, The Vermont Notebook, 1975, Self-Portrait in a Convex Mirror, 1975, Houseboat Days, 1977, As We Know, 1979, Shadow Train, 1981, A Wave, 1984, Selected Poems, 1985, April Galleons, 1987, Flow Chart, 1991, Hotel Lautrèamont, 1992, And the Stars Were Shining, 1994, Can You Hear, Bird, 1995, Wakefulness, 1998, (plays) The Heroes, 1952, The Comprimise, 1955, The Philosopher, 1963, Three Plays, 1978, (poetry) Girls on the Run, 1999, Your Name Here, 2000, As Umbrellas Follow Rain, 2001, Chinese Whispers, 2002; author: (with James Schuyler) (novels) A Nest of Ninnies, 1969, represented in numerous anthologies; contbr. articles to periodicles;, author verse set to music. Named Lit. Lion, N.Y. Pub. Libr., 1984, Poet of Yr., Pasadena City Coll., 1984; recipient Yale Series of Younger Poets prize, 1955, Harriet Monroe Poetry award, Poetry Mag., 1963, Civic and Arts Found. prize, Union League, 1966, award, Nat. Inst. Arts and Letters, 1969, Shelley award, Poetry Soc. Am., 1973, Pulitzer prize, 1976, Nat. Book award, 1976, Nat. Book Critics Circle award, 1976, Jerome J. Shestack Poetry award, Am. Poetry Rev., 1983, Bollingen prize in poetry, Yale U. Libr., 1985, Lenore Marshall poetry prize, The Nation, 1985, Common Wealth award in lit., MLA, 1986, Creative Arts award, Brandeis U., 1989, Ruth Lilly Poetry prize, Poetry Mag. and Modern Poetry Assn. and Am. Coun. for Arts, 1992, Robert Frost medal, Poetry Soc. Am., 1995, Grand prize, Biennales Internat. Poetry, Belgium, 1996, Bingham Poetry prize, Boston Rev. Books, 1998, Walt Whitman Citation of Merit, State of N.Y., N.Y. State Writer's Inst., 2000, Medal for Achievement in the Arts, Signet Soc. Harvard U., 2001, Phi Beta Kappa Poet award, Harvard U., 1979; grantee, Poet's Found., 1960, 1964, Ingram Merrill Found., 1962, 1972; scholar Fulbright scholar, U. Montpellier, France, 1955—56, Rennes, France, 1956—57; Guggenheim fellow, 1967, 1973, Rockefeller Found. fellow, 1979—80, Wallace Stevens fellow, Yale U., 1985, McArthur Found. fellow, 1985—90. Fellow: Acad. Am. Poets (chancellor 1988—99, Wallace Stevens award 2001); mem.: Am. Acad. Arts and Scis., Am. Acad. Arts and Letters (Gold medal 1997). Office: c/o Georges Borchardt Inc 136 E 57th St New York NY 10022-2707 Address: Dept Langs and Lit Bard Coll PO Box 5000 Annandale On Hudson NY 12504-5000

ASHBROOK, ARTHUR GARWOOD, JR., economist, educator; b. Pitts., Jan. 30, 1921; s. Arthur Garwood and Theodora Arlene (Hoerle) A.; m. Cecilia Garcia Rodriguez, June 20, 1964; children: Marina-Yolanda, Alexandra. BS, Haverford Coll., 1941; PhD, MIT, 1947. Asst. prof. econs. Duke U., Durham, N.C., 1947-51; sr. economist Office of Price Stabilization, Charlotte, N.C., 1951-53; asst. prof. econs. Carnegie Inst. Tech., Pitts., 1953-54; sr. economist CIA, Washington, 1954-82, part-time contract economist, 1983—. Disting. vis. prof. econs. U.S. Naval Acad., Annapolis, 1976-77. Contbr. articles to profl. jours. Sgt. U.S. Army Air Corps, 1943-45. Mem. Am. Econs. Assn. Avocations: personal journal writing, Haverford alumni affairs. Home: 2925 39th St NW Washington DC 20016-5404

ASHBY, DENISE STEWART, speech educator, communication consultant; b. Charleston, W.Va., Aug. 15, 1941; d. Dennison Elmer and Marie Juanita (Queripel) Ellis; m. Rudolph Krutzner III, Dec. 6, 1958 (div. 1961); m. Garth Rodney Ashby, Feb. 15, 1976; children: Kevin Krutzner, Kevin Ashby, Lisa Ashby, Scott Ashby. AA with highest honors, Diablo Valley Coll., Pleasant Hill, Calif., 1981; BA in Speech summa cum laude, Calif. State U., Hayward, 1982; MA in Speech and Communication summa cum laude, Calif. State U., 1983. Lic. beautician NJ Bd. Cosmetology. Owner Salon 105, Somerville, NJ, 1964-66; pres. Second Hand Rose, New Providence, 1966-76, The Place Beauty Salon, 1966-76, The Place Boutique, 1966-76; mgr. LaTortuga Boutique, 1977-81; tenured instr. Diablo Valley Coll., Pleasant Hill, Calif., 1982—; instr. Los Positas Coll., Livermore, 1985—; pres. Ashby & Assocs., Danville. AAUW liaison Ctr. for Higher Edn., San Ramon, 1988-90. Vice pres. Danville United Presbyn. Women, 1978-79. Recipient Pres.'s award, Calif. State U., 1983. Mem.

AAUW (bd. dirs. 1988-90), NAFE, Speech Comm. Assn., Pi Lambda Theta, Pi Kappa Delta (pres. 1982). Home: 82 Cumberland Ct Danville CA 94526-1819 Office: Diablo Valley Coll Golf Club Rd Pleasant Hill CA 94523

ASHCRAFT, CHARLES OLIN, business educator; b. Kiowa, Kans., June 22, 1936; s. Olin N. and Esther Pauline (Young) A.; m. Letha May Bray, June 2, 1963; children: Farrah Elaine, Kyle Bray. BBA, Phillips U., 1958, MEd, 1965; postgrad., Air War Coll., 1977; diploma, Command & Gen. Staff Coll., 1975. Cert. tchr., Alaska, residential specialist. Tchr. Anchorage High Sch., 1958-61, East Anchorage (Alaska) High Sch., 1961-65; sch. adminstr. Ursa Maj. Elem. Sch., Ft. Richardson, Alaska, 1965-68, Arcturus Jr. High Sch., Ft. Richardson, 1965-73; instr. Anchorage Community Coll., 1959-73, Bartlett High Sch., Anchorage, 1973-90, rifle coach, 1980-90. Mem. adj. faculty Command & Gen. Staff Coll., Ft. Leavenworth, Kans., 1990—. Mem. Rep. Dist. 16, Anchorage, 1986-90; scoutmaster Western Alaska coun. Boy Scouts Am., 1976-80; post advisor Explorer Scout Post, Anchorage, 1980-91. Col. USAR, 1958-91. Recipient Silver Beaver award Western Alaska Boy Scouts Am., 1984; named to U.S. Army Inf. Officer Candidate Sch. Hall of Fame, 1991. Mem. NEA (life), NRA (life), Nat. Guard Assn. of U.S. (life), Res. Officers Assn. (life), Mil. Order of World Wars (life), F&AM Glacier Lodge (PM96), Pioneers for Ala. Igloo #15, Al Aska Shrine Temple, Royal Ct. Jesters Polarcourt, Scottish Rite, Orient of Alaska, Red Cross Constantine, Masons, Anchorage Yorkrite Coll. (past gov.), Prudential Jack White Real Estate. Republican. Methodist. Avocations: snow skiing, competition shooting and coaching. E-mail: cashcraft@alaskalife.net.

ASHDOWN, MARIE MATRANGA (MRS. CECIL SPANTON ASHDOWN JR.), writer, educator, lecturer, cultural organization administrator; b. Mobile, Ala. d. Dominic and Ave (Mallon) Matranga; m. Cecil Spanton Ashdown Jr., Feb. 8, 1958; children: Cecil Spanton III, Charles Coster; children by previous marriage: John Stephen Gartman, Vivian Marie Gartman. Degree, Maryville Coll. Sacred Heart, Springhill Coll. Feature artist, women's program dir. daily program Sta. WALA, WALA-TV, Mobile; v.p., dir. Met. Opera Guild, N.Y.C., opera instr. in-svc. program, 1970-80, Marymont Coll., N.Y.C., 1979-85; exec. dir. Musicians Emergency Fund, Inc., N.Y.C., 1985—. Internat. adv. coun. Van Cliburn Found., 1998—; cons. No. Ill. U. Coll. Visual and Performing Arts, 1985—; lectr. in field. Author: Opera Collectables, 1979, contbr. articles to profl. jours. Recipient Extraordinary Svc. award March of Dimes, Medal of Appreciation award Harvard Bus. Sch. Club NYC, Cert. Appreciation, Kiwanis Internat., Arts Excellence award NJ State Opera, Ciparo award, Albanese-Puccini award Lincoln Ctr., 2002. Mem. AAUW, Nat. Inst. Social Scis., Com. for U.S.-China Rels. Avocations: collecting art, antique ceramics and porcelains, bookbinding. Home: 25 Sutton Pl S New York NY 10022-2456 Office: Musicians Emergency Fund Inc PO Box 1256 New York NY 10150-1256

ASHDOWN, PAUL GEORGE, journalist, educator; b. N.Y.C., July 26, 1944; s. Cecil Spencer and Annabelle (Marrone) A.; m. Ellen Kay Abernethy, Apr. 24, 1966 (div. Feb. 1969); 1 child, Lance Spencer; m. Barbara Ann Green, Apr. 18, 1975; m. Joanne Wagstrom, Dec. 9, 1970 (div. Nov. 1973). BS, U. Fla., 1966, MA, 1969; PhD, Bowling Green State U., 1975. Reporter Gainesville (Fla.) Sun, 1966-67; pub. info. officer Fla. Dept. of Agr., Gainesville, 1967-68; corr. UPI, Miami, Fla., 1969-70; instr. U. So. Colo., Pueblo, 1970-71, U. Toledo, 1971-75; asst. prof. mass comm. Western Ky. U., Bowling Green, 1975-77; prof. journalism U. Tenn., Knoxville, 1977—. Vis. prof. journalism Dutch Sch. of Journalism, Utrecht, The Netherlands, 1993-94; vis. prof. N.Am. studies U. Bonn, Germany, 1994-95, 97. Editor: James Agee: Selected Journalism, 1985; co-author: The Mosby Myth, 2002; contbr. articles to books and profl. jours., columns to newspapers. Recipient Robert Foster Cherry Tchg. award Baylor U. Mem. Kappa Tau Alpha, Delta Tau Delta. Episcopalian. Avocation: international travel. Home: 9716 Franklin Hill Blvd Knoxville TN 37922-3331 Office: Univ Tenn 330 Communications Bldg Knoxville TN 37996-0001

ASHE, ARTHUR JAMES, III, chemistry educator; b. N.Y.C., Aug. 5, 1940; s. Arthur James and Helen Louise (Hawelka) A.; m. Penelope Guerard Vaughan, Aug. 25, 1962; children: Arthur J., Christopher V. BA, Yale U., 1962, MS, 1965, PhD, 1966; postgrad., Cambridge U., 1962-63. Asst. prof. chemistry U. Mich., Ann Arbor, 1966-71, assoc. prof., 1971-76, prof., 1976—, chmn. dept., 1983-86, prof. macromolecular sci. and engring., 2000—. Vis. scientist Phys. Chemistry Inst., U. Basle, Switzerland, 1974 Mem. editorial avd. bds. profl. jours, 1984—. Alfred P. Sloan fellow, 1972-76 Mem. Am. Chem. Soc. Office: U Mich Dept Chemistry Ann Arbor MI 48109 E-mail: ajashe@umich.edu.

ASHE, KATHY RAE, special education educator; b. Bismarck, N.D., Oct. 24, 1950; d. Raymond Charles and Virginia Ann (Mason) Lynch; m. Barth Eugene Olson, Aug. 11, 1973; 1 child, William Raymond; m. Fredrick A. Ashe, Aug. 5, 1994. BS, U. N.D., 1972, MS in Spl. Edn., 1987. Cert. elem. tchr. with spl. edn. credential, N.D. Instr. Grafton State Sch., N.D., 1972-74; tchr. spl. edn. Grand Forks Sch. Dist., N.D., 1974—. Bd. dirs. Agassiz Enterprises; mem. RAD com. Valley Jr. High; mem. transition governing bd., Region IV. Mem. spl. needs recreation program Grand Forks Park Bd., 1973—76; mem. Spl. Olympics Area Mgmt. Team, 1984—90; mem. region IV Low Incident Behavior Grant Com.; co-chair, vol. coord. Greater Grand Forks Soccer Club Tournament, 2000, 2001; bldg. rep. Grand Forks Edn. Assn., 2000—04; bd. dirs. Assn. Retarded Citizens, Devel. Homes, Inc., N.D. Sch. Blind Found., pres., 1997—. Named N.D. Tchr. of Yr., Coun. Chief State Sch. Officers, 1981. Mem. AAUW (pres. 1998-2000), Delta Kappa Gamma (sec. 1984-86, pres. 1990-94), Alpha Phi (alumni pres. 1984-86, 90-91, alumni treas. 1995—), Phi Delta Kappa. Republican. Roman Catholic. Avocations: sporting events, civic work, cross stitch, bowling, golf. Home: 3208 Walnut St Grand Forks ND 58201-7665 E-mail: ashekathy@hotmail.com.

ASHE, MAUDE LLEWELLYN, home economics educator; b. Bakersfield, Calif., Feb. 9, 1908; d. Richard Samuel and Marguerite J. (Loudon) A. AB, U. Calif., 1928; MS, Oreg. State U., Corvallis, 1944; postgrad., San Jose (Calif.) State Coll., 1936-38, Stanford U., 1948. Cert. tchr., Calif. Instr. in home econs. Oreg. State U., 1943; assoc. prof. home econs. San Jose State U., 1944-73, emeritus prof. home econs., 1973—. Author: Finding West Country Ancestors, 1989. Mem. Santa Clara County Fair Assn., San Jose, 1968; v.p. Kern Genealogy Soc., Bakersfield, Calif., 1986. Mem. AAUW (sec., chmn. San Jose chpt. 1978), Calif. Ret. Tchr.'s Assn., Calif. Ret. State Employees, Emeritus Faculty Assn., Nat. Trust for Hist. Preservation, Family Assn. of Austin, Geer Family Assn., Calif. Home Econs. Assn. (chmn. com. San Francisco chpt. 1965, state advisor to student clubs No. Calif. area 1966), Imperial Valley Gem and Mineral Soc. (charter), Phi Upsilon Omicron. Democrat. Avocations: gardening, california history, genealogy. Home: 9100 Park St # 509C Lenexa KS 66215-3328

ASHER, BETTY TURNER, academic administrator; b. Booneville, Ky., Oct. 19, 1944; BA, Ea. Ky. U.; MA, Western Ky. U.; EdD, U. Cin. Sr. assoc. vice provost U. Cin., 1978-80; assoc. vice chancellor acad. affairs Minn. State U. System, 1981-82; v.p. student affairs Ariz. State U., Tempe, 1982-89; pres. U. S.D., Vermillion, 1989-1996, Bus., Industry Tng., Destin, Fla., 1997—. Office: Bus and Industry Tng 898 Highway 98 E Destin FL 32541-2700 E-mail: bettyasher@cox.net.

ASHER, KATHLEEN MAY, communications educator; b. Vassar, Mich., Aug. 19, 1932; d. Thomas Henry and Jessie (Smith) Pierce; m. Donald William Asher, July 17, 1957; children: David Kevin, Diane Kerri. BS, Ctrl. Mich. U., 1956, MA, 1967. Cert. fundraiser Williamsburg Devel. Inst., cert. QTM trainer. Tchr. speech and theater Standish (Mich.) Pub. Schs., 1956-58, Vassar (Mich.) Pub. Schs., 1959-67; prof. speech, adminstr. Mott C.C., Flint, Mich., 1967-89; assoc. prof. speech Palm Beach C.C., Lake Worth, Fla., 1990—2001, fundraiser, 1991-95, faculty polit. action chairperson, 1996-97, faculty emeritus, 2001. Cons. in speech, Flint, Mich., 1973—89; cons. quality total mgmt.; cons. in comms. and mgmt., Lake Worth, Fla., 2001—. Pres. Homeowner Assn., Lake Worth, 1993—95, legal chair, 2003; mem. Vassar Zoning Bd.; officer City Coun.; chair Tuscola County Dem Com., 1975—85; del., whip Dem. Conv. and Rules Com., 1976; del. Fla. Dem. Conv., 1999. Mem. United Faculty Palm Beach C.C. (chpt. pres.), Fla. Tchg. Profession, NEA, Nat. Collegiate Hons. Coun. (collegiate 1991-95), Mich. Women's Studies Assn. (pres. 1974-75), C.C. Humanities Assn., Phi Theta Kappa (leadership prof.). Presbyterian. Avocations: percussion, reading, golf, bowling, biking. Home: 4713 Rainbow Dr Lake Worth FL 33463-3610 Office: Palm Beach CC 4200 Congress Ave Lake Worth FL 33461-4705 E-mail: profashl@directvinternet.com.

ASHFORTH, ALDEN, musician, educator; b. N.Y.C., May 13, 1933; m. Nancy Ann Regnier, June 12, 1956 (div. 1980); children— Robyn Richardson, Melissa Adams, Lauren Elizabeth AB, B.Mus., Oberlin Coll, 1958; M.F.A., Princeton U., 1960, PhD, 1971. Instr. Princeton U., N.J., 1961; instr. Oberlin Coll., Ohio, 1961-65, N.Y.U., N.Y.C., 1965-66, Manhattan Sch. Music, N.Y.C., 1965; lectr. CUNY, N.Y.C., 1966-67; asst. prof. music UCLA, 1967-72, assoc. prof. music, 1972-80, prof., 1980—. Coordinator electronic music studio, 1969-86. Composer numerous instrumental, vocal and electronic works including: Episodes (chamber concerto for 8 instruments), 1962, The Unquiet Heart (cycle for soprano and chamber orch.), 1968, Big Bang (piano-four hands) 1970, Byzantium (organ and electronic tape), 1971, Sailing to Byzantium (organ and electronic tape), 1973, Aspects of Love (song cycle), 1978, Christmas Motets (a cappella chorus), 1980, The Miraculous Bugle (flugelhorn and percussion), 1989, Palimpsests (organ), 1997; producer, recorder New Orleans Jazz including, New Orleans Parade: The Eureka Brass Band Plays Dirges and Stomps, 1952, Doc Paulins Marching Band, 1982, Last of the Line: The Eagle Brass Band, 1984; contbr. articles to profl. jours. and to New Grove Dictionary of Jazz. Office: UCLA Music Dept Los Angeles CA 90095-0001

ASHHURST, ANNA WAYNE, foreign language educator; b. Phila., Jan. 5, 1933; d. Astley Paston Cooper and Anne Pauline (Campbell) Ashhurst; m. Ronald G. Gerber, July 22, 1978. AB, Vassar Coll., 1954; MA, Middlebury Coll., 1956; PhD, U. Pitts., 1967. English tchr. Internat. Inst. Spain, Madrid, 1954-56; asst. prof. Juniata Coll., Huntingdon, Pa., 1961-63; asst. prof. Spanish dept. Franklin and Marshall Coll., Lancaster, Pa., 1968-74, acting chmn. Spanish dept., 1972, convenor, fgn. lang. council, 1972-74; assoc. prof. dept. modern fgn. langs. U. Mo., St. Louis, 1974-78. Author: La literatura hispano-americana en la crítica española, 1980. Mem. Welcome Wagon of Lancaster, Pa., 1968-70, 71-74 Fulbright-Hays grantee, Colombia, S.Am., summer 1963; Ford Humanities fellow, summer 1970; Mellon fellow, 1970-71 Mem. AAUW (pres. Ferguson-Florissant br. 1989-91, 95-98, chmn. St. Louis area interbranch coun. 1992-94, chair environ. task force Mo. 1992-95, local arrangements chair for Mo. state conv. 1997, Woman of Distiction award 1998), Internat. Inst. in Spain, Instituto Internacional de Literatura Iberoamericana, Am. Assn. Tchrs. Spanish and Portuguese. Home: 2105 Barcelona Dr Florissant MO 63033-2805

ASHLEY, HOLT, aerospace scientist, educator; b. San Francisco, Jan. 10, 1923; s. Harold Harrison and Anne (Oates) A.; m. Frances M. Day, Feb. 1, 1947 (wid.). Student, Calif. Inst. Tech., 1940-43; BS, U. Chgo., 1944; MS, MIT, 1948, ScD, 1951. Mem. faculty MIT, 1946-67, prof. aero., 1960-67; prof. aeros. and astronautics Stanford U., Palo Alto, Calif., 1967-89, prof. emeritus, 1989—. Spl. rsch. aeroelasticity, aerodynamics; cons. govt. agys., rsch. orgns., indsl. corps.; dir. office of exploratory rsch. and problem assessment and div. advanced tech. applications NSF, 1972-74; mem. sci. adv. bd. USAF, 1958-80, rsch. adv. com. structural dynamics NASA, 1952-60, rsch. adv. com. on aircraft structures, 1962-70, chmn. rsch. adv. com. on materials and structures, 1974-77; mem. Kanpur Indo-American program Indian Inst. Tech., 1964-65, governing bd. Nat. Rsch. Coun., 1988-91; AIAA Wright Bros. lectr., 1981; dir. Rann Inc. Co-author: Aeroelasticity, 1955, Principles of Aeroelasticity, 1962, Aerodynamics of Wings and Bodies, 1969, Engineering Analysis of Flight Vehicles, 1974. Recipient Goodwin medal M.I.T., 1952; Exceptional Civilian Service award U.S. Air Force, 1972, 80; Public Service award NASA, 1981; named one of 10 outstanding young men of year Boston Jr. C. of C., 1956; recipient Ludwig-Prandtl Ring, West German DGLR, 1987, Spirit of St. Louis Medal, ASME, 1992. Fellow AIAA (hon., assoc. editor jour., v.p. tech. 1971, pres. 1973, Structures, Structural Dynamics and Materials award 1969), Am. Acad. Arts and Scis., Royal Aero. Soc. (hon.); mem. AAAS, NAE (aeros. and space engring. bd. 1977-79, mem. coun. 1985-91), Am. Meterol. Soc. (profl., 50th Ann. medal 1971), Phi Beta Kappa, Sigma Xi, Tau Beta Pi. Home: 475 Woodside Dr Woodside CA 94062-2375

ASHLEY, LYNN, educator, consultant, administrator; b. Rock Island, Ill., Nov. 18, 1920; d. Francis Ford and Cleo Marguerite (Monahan) Haynes; m. Edward Messenger Ashley, Aug. 16, 1946; children: Edward Jr., Ann Rice, Rebecca Pocisk, William. BS in Social Psychology, Union Inst., Cin., 1978; MEd., U. Cin., 1979, EdD, 1985. Clk. Lumberman's Mutual Casualty Co., Chgo., 1940-41; account asst. Quaker Oats Co., Chgo., 1941-43; riveter Douglas Aircraft Co., Chgo., 1943-44; organizer, dir. Forest Park Youth Ctr., Forest Park, Ohio, 1967-73; staffing coord. Presbytery of Cin., 1973-78; grad. teaching asst. U. Cin., 1978-84; pres. Nat. Corrective Tng. Inst., Cin., 1979—. Adj. faculty, mem. undergrad. studies bd. Union Inst., 1986—; cons., trainer Hamilton County Probation Dept., Warren County Juvenile Ct., 1987—, Allen County Juvenile Ct., Worth Ctr., Allen County, field rep. Spkr., adv. women vets. to schs. and orgns.; mem. Cin.-Harare, Zimbabwe Sister Cities Assn., 1989—, Ohio Gov.'s Adv. Com. on Women Vets., 1993—99; with Women in Mil. Svc. for Am. Councilwoman City of Forest Park, 1981—85, organizer cmty. rels. coun., 1983. With WAC, 1944—46. Recipient in Recognition award Forest Park City Coun., 1985, In Appreciation award Union Inst., 1987, Recognition award AMVETS, U. Cin., 1993, award Commonwealth of Ky., 1989; inducted into Ohio Vets. Hall of Fame, 1999. Mem. Am. Corrections Assn., Nat. Assn. Corrective Tng. Affiliates (pres. 1987), Women's Army Corp Vet. Assn. (selected rep. to dedication of Dale Inst. of Politics), Assn. Family and Conciliatiion Cts., Am. Probation and Parole Assn. Avocations: photography, foreign travel, computers, camping, fishing. Office: Nat Corrective Tng Inst 811 Hanson Dr Cincinnati OH 45240-1921

ASHLEY, MARJORIE, retired secondary school educator; b. Schenectady, N.Y., Feb. 16, 1917; d. Richard J. and Margaret Middleton; m. John Edward Ashley, Aug. 20, 1940 (dec.); children: Richard M.(dec.), John E. Jr., Willard Bishop. BA cum laude, SUNY, Albany, 1955, MA, 1958; cert. in French, Goucher Coll., 1959. Tchr. Burnt Hills-Ballston Lake H.S., Burnt Hills, NY, 1956, Roger B. Taney Jr. High Sch., Camp Springs, Md., Oxon Hill (Md.) Sr. H.S. Contbr. commentaries Kerrville Times. Sec. AAUW, Kerrville, Tex., 1976—80, pres., 1980—82; chmn., patron Kerrville Performing Arts Soc., 1980—2001; active Point Theatre, Schreiner U. Recipient Lifetime Achievement award, Hill Country Arts Found., 2003. Mem.: LWV, Animal Welfare Soc. Kerr County, Hill Country Arts Found. Unitarian Universalist. Home: 8 Chaparral Dr Kerrville TX 78028

ASHLEY, SHEILA STARR, retired educator, translator; b. Wichita, Kans., May 29, 1941; d. Burton Edward and Virginia Lee (Capron) A. BA in Spanish, Wilson Coll., 1964; MS in Edn., U. Pa., 1967; translator cert., U. Madrid, 1979. Cert. secondary fng. lang. tchr., Pa. Fgn. lang. tchr. Radnor (Pa.) High Sch., 1967-98, chmn. of dept., 1990-97; ret., 1998—; sub. tchr., tutor, 1998—. Translator Johnson & Johnson, N.J., 1979—, Midas Muffler, Phila, 1979—. Mem. student assistance team, Students at Risk, 1987-98. Recipient grant, Coun. for the Humanities, 1983, Rockefeller Found., 1989. Mem. NEA, Pa. State Edn. Assn. (ret.), Radnor Tchrs. Edn. Assn., Pa. State MLA, Am. Coun. on Teaching Fgn. Langs., Assn. Am. Tchrs. Spanish and Portuguese, Phila. LaCrosse Assn. (dist. referee), Lang. and History Collaborative of Phila. and Delaware Valley. Office: Radnor High Sch 130 King Of Prussia Rd Wayne PA 19087-5298

ASHTON, DIANNE CHERYL, American studies educator; b. Buffalo, June 21, 1949; d. Irving and Miriam Ashton; m. Richard M. Drucker, Oct. 23, 1988. BA, Adelphi U., 1971; MA, Temple U., 1981, PhD, 1986. Lectr. Temple U., Phila., 1983-87, LaSalle U., Phila., 1985-88; program dir. Anne Frank Inst., Phila., 1986-88; prof. religion Rowan U., Glassboro, N.J., 1988—. Author: Rebecca Gratz: Women and Judaism in Antebellum America, 1997, Jewish Life in Pennsylvania, 1998; co-editor: Four Centuries of Jewish Women's Spirituality: A Sourcebook, 1992; editor: The Philadelphia Group: A Guide to Archival, Bibliographic, and Manuscript Collections, 1993; contbr. articles to profl. jours. Fellow, Gilder Lehrman Inst. fot Am. History; grantee, Nat. Endowment Humanities, 2003; Franklin fellow, Am. Jewish Archives, 1985, Rapoport fellow, 1989, Jacobs fellow, 1999, Rsch. grant, Rowan U., 1990—2003, Temple U., 1985, Hadassah Internat. Rsch. Inst. for Jewish Women. Democrat. Jewish. Office: Rowan U Bunce Hall Glassboro NJ 08028 E-mail: ashtond@rowan.edu.

ASHTON, PETER SHAW, tropical forest science educator; b. Boscombe, Hampshire, Eng., June 27, 1934; came to U.S., 1978; s. Dudley Shaw and Edna Marjorie (Knott) A.; m. Helen Mary Spence, June 14, 1958; children: Peter Mark, Mellard John, Rachel Mary. BA, U. Cambridge, 1956, MA, 1961, PhD, 1962; MA (hon.), Harvard U., 1979; LjDSc U. Peradeniya (hon.), 2001. Forest botanist Govt. of Brunei, 1957-62, Govt. of Sarawak, 1962-67; lectr. U. Aberdeen, Scotland, 1967-72, sr. lectr., 1972-78; dir. Arnold Arboretum Harvard U., Cambridge, Mass., 1978-87, Arnold prof. botany, 1978-87; prof. forestry Charles Bullard, 1991—99, rsch. prof., 1999—. Faculty Harvard Inst. for Internat. Devel., 1990-97, Ctr. for Internat. Devel., 1997-. Author 7 sci. books, 1958—; contbr. over 125 articles to sci. jours. Trustee Mount Auburn Cemetary, Cambridge, Mass., 1986—; bd. dirs. Falkener Hosp., Boston, 1981-86; corp. mem. Boston Mus. Sci., 1982-89. Recipient Environ. Merit award EPA, 1987, prize for Conservation Sci., UNESCO Sultan Qaboos. Fellow Royal Soc. Edinburgh, Linnean Soc. London; mem. Am. Acad. Arts and Scis., Assn. for Tropical Biology, Brit. Ecol. Soc., Internat. Assn. Botanic Gardens (pres. 1987-93), Ctr. for Plant Conservation (pres. 1988-91), Nature Conservancy (trustee 1989-95). Avocations: gardening, painting. Home: 22 Divinity Ave Cambridge MA 02138-2020 Office: Arnold Arboretum Harvard U 22 Divinity Ave Cambridge MA 02138-2020

ASHTON, TAMARAH M. special education educator, consultant; b. Toledo, Dec. 5, 1961; d. Harold Leroy and Patricia Marie (Casto) Ashton; m. John G. Coombs, Feb. 11, 1989; 1 child, Rebecca Marie. MusB, Western Mich. U., 1984; MS, San Diego State U., 1988, MA, 1990; PhD, Claremont Grad. U., 1997. Cert. tchr., Calif. Asst. project dir. San Diego State U., 1994-98; asst. prof. dept. of spl. edn. Calif. State U., Northridge, 1998—2003, assoc. prof. dept. of spl. edn., 2003—. Cons. in field. Mem. Coun. for Learning Disabilities. Mem. Coun. for Exceptional Children, Phi Kappa Phi, Pi Lambda Theta. Avocation: needlework. Home: 28721 W Highland C Castaic CA 91384-3080 E-mail: tamarah.ashton@csun.edu.

ASHWORTH, JULIE, elementary education educator; Tchr. Hawthorne Elem. Sch., Sioux Falls, S.D., 1990—. Participant Internat. Space Camp, Huntsville, Ala., 1993; S.D. tchr. participant Goals 2000 Forum, U.S. Dept. Edn., Washington, 1993; mem. S.D. Gov.'s Adv. Coun. on Cert. for Tchrs., 1994—; mem. exceptional needs standards com. Nat. Bd. for Profl. Tchg. Stds., Washington, 1994—; initiator, organizer S.D. Tchrs. Forum, 1994. Named S.D. Tchr. of Yr., Sioux Falls Sch. Dist., 1992, S.D. Elem. Tchr. of Yr., 1993. Home: 2015 Pendar Ln Sioux Falls SD 57105-3022 Office: Hawthorne Elem Sch 601 N Spring Ave Sioux Falls SD 57104-2721

ASHWORTH, KENNETH HAYDEN, public affairs specialist; b. Abilene, Tex., Feb. 24, 1932; s. Harold Laverne and Mae Beatrice (Grote) A.; m. Emily Yaung; children: Rodney Brian, Karen Grace. BA, U. Tex., 1958, PhD, 1969; M. Pub. Adminstrn., Syracuse U., 1959. Asst. commr. Tex. Higher Edn. Coordinating Bd., Austin, 1965-69, commr. higher edn., 1976-97; vice chancellor for acad. affairs U. Tex. System, Austin, 1969-73; exec. v.p. U. Tex. at San Antonio, 1973-76. Vis. prof. govt. and pub. affairs U. Tex., Austin, 1997—, Tex. A &M U., College Sta., 1997—. Author: Scholars and Statesmen, 1972, American Higher Education in Decline, 1979, (with Norman Hackerman) Conversations on the Uses of Science and Technology, 1996, Caught Between the Dog and the Fireplug or How to Survive Public Service, 2001. Served with USN, 1951-55. Mem. Philos. Soc. Tex., Phi Beta Kappa, Phi Delta Kappa, Phi Kappa Phi, Pi Sigma Alpha. Clubs: Town and Gown. Democrat. Unitarian Universalist. Home: 7616 Rustling Rd Austin TX 78731-1365 Office: U Tex LBJ Sch Pub Affairs PO Box Y Austin TX 78713-8925 also: Tex A&M U Bush Sch Govt And Pub Svc College Station TX 77843-0001

ASKANAS-ENGEL, VALERIE, neurologist, educator, researcher; b. Poland, May 28, 1937; came to U.S., 1969, naturalized, 1975; d. Marian and Leontyne Hornik; m. W. King Engel; 1 dau., Eve Monique Kerr. MD, Warsaw Med. Sch., Poland, 1960, PhD, 1967; Doctor honoris causa, U. d'Aix-Marseille, France, 1987. Rotating intern Univ. Hosp. Warsaw Med. Sch., 1960-61, resident in neurology, 1961-64, fellow in neuromuscular diseases, 1964-65; asst. prof. neurology Warsaw Med. Sch., 1965-69; assoc. mem. Inst. Muscle Diseases, N.Y.C., 1969-73; asst. prof. NYU Med. Sch., 1973-77; sr. investigator NIH, Bethesda, Md., 1977-81; prof. neurology and pathology U. So. Calif., L.A., 1981—; co-dir. Neuromuscular Ctr. at Hosp. Good Samaritan, 1981—, Muscular Dystrophy Assn. Clinic, 1981—, The Jerry Lewis ALS Clin. and Rsch. Ctr., 1988—. V.p. 6th Internat. Congress on Neuromuscular Diseases, 1986, 7th, 1990, 8th, 1994; vis. prof. internat. congresses, Europe, S.Am., Can., Far East; hon. lectr. Royal Coll. Physicians and Surgeons, 1999. Contbr. numerous articles, chpts., abstracts to med. publs.; sr. editor: (book) Inclusion-Body Myositis and Myopathies, 1998; assoc. editor Acta Neuromyologia, 2002—. Recipient Dean's prize for outstanding rsch., 1967, NIH Merit award, 1999—, Gaetano Conti Gold Medal for Basic Rsch., Napoli, 1999; Premio Associazione Stampa Medica Italiana Di Giurnal Italianalsmo Medico, 1980; grantee NIH, 1974-77, 83—, NIH Merit award, 1999—, Muscular Dystrophy Assn., 1969-77, 81—. Fellow Am. Acad. Neurology, L.A. Acad. Medicine; mem. Soc. for Neurosci., Am. Neurol. Assn., d'Honneur de la Soc. Francaise de Neurologie, Am. Soc. Cell Biology, Am. Assn. Neuropathology, Histochem. Soc., Uruguayan Neurological Assn. (hon. mem.), L.A. County Med. Assn., Polish Neurol. Assn. (hon.). Home: 527 S Arden Blvd Los Angeles CA 90020-4737 Office: U So Calif Neuromuscular Ctr Good Samaritan Hosp 637 Lucas Ave Los Angeles CA 90017-1912

ASKEW, THOMAS RENDALL, physics educator, researcher, consultant; b. Geneva, Ill., June 11, 1955; s. Thomas Addelbert and Jean Mary (Somerville) A.; m. Mary Louise Kazmaier, July 15, 1978; 1 child, Steven Thomas. MS, U. Ill., 1982, PhD, 1984. Mem. tech. staff DuPont Rsch., Wilmington, Del., 1984-91; assoc. prof. physics Kalamazoo (Mich.) Coll., 1991—. Vis. scientist Argonne (Ill.) Nat. Lab., 1992—; cons. to U.S. corps. Contbr. articles to profl. jours. Recipient Ball Meml. scholarship Gordon Coll., 1977, Mac Arthur scholarship John D. and Catherine T. Mac Arthur Found., 1991-93. Mem. Am. Phys. Soc., Material Rsch. Soc. Achievements include patents in superconductivity. Office: Kalamazoo Coll Physics Dept Kalamazoo MI 49006

ASKEW, WILLIAM EARL, chemist, educator; b. Maysville, N.C., Aug. 31, 1943; s. Carl Lee and Sally Chinese (Pope) A. BA in Chemistry, U. N.C., 1965; MA in Biology, East Carolina U., 1968; PhD in Biophys. Sci., U. Houston, 1973. Rsch. assoc. Baylor Coll. Medicine, Houston, 1973-77, Vets.' Hosp., Houston, 1973-77; instr. chemistry Houston C.C. Sys. N.W., 1977—, chair phys. scis. dept., 2000—. With U.S. Army, 1968-70. Mem. Am. Chem. Soc., Am. Acad. Sci., Tex. Jr. Coll. Tchrs. Assn., 2-Yr. Chemistry Soc. Office: Town and Country Ctr 1010 W Sam Houston N Houston TX 77043-5008

ASKINS, BILLY EARL, education educator, consultant; b. Burkburnett, Tex., Dec. 28, 1930; s. Sidney Earl and Nellie Alice (Johnson) A.; m. Sydney Loraine Gamblin, Feb. 21, 1954; 1 child, Dewayne Earl. BS, East Tex. State U., 1953; MEd, Midwestern U., 1959; EdD, U. North Tex., 1967. Instr., edn. specialist Sheppard Tech. Tng. Ctr., Wichita Falls, Tex., 1955-65; asst. dir. tchr. adminstrn. U. North Tex., Denton, 1965-66; tchr. Ft. Worth Pub. Schs., 1966-67; from asst prof. to prof. Tex. Tech. U., Lubbock, 1967-77, assoc. dean Coll. Edn., 1978-90, prof. edn., 1991—. Cons. to univs., fedn. edn. labs., state edn. svc. ctrs., pub. schs., state prisons schs., schs. of nursing, community colls., state bar assns., and pvt. agys., 1980—; presenter at profl. confs. Contbr. to profl. publs. 1st lt. USAF, 1953-55, lt. col. Res. to 1981. Mem. Am. Ednl. Rsch. Assn., Assn. Tchr. Educators (Disting. Maj. Prof. award 1982), Nat. Staff Devel. Coun., Tex. Staff Devel. Coun. (bd. dirs. 1989-92), Tex. Assn. Tchr. Educators (exec. bd. 1987-89), Internat. Rotary Club, Order Ky. Cols. Avocations: photography, fly fishing, travel. Home: 5214 28th St Lubbock TX 79407-3508 Office: Tex Tech U PO Box 41071 Lubbock TX 79409-1071

ASMUSSEN, J. DONNA, retired educational administrator, researcher, artist; b. Woonsocket, R.I., Aug. 22, 1951; d. John E. and Marion Annette (Fanning) A. BS in Edn., R.I. Coll., 1974, MEd, 1984; student in Elem. Edn. and Visual Arts, U. Maine; spl. student Visual Arts, Colby Coll. Spl. edn. tchr. Lincoln Sch. Dept., RI, 1971—78, diagnostician, 1978—85; tchr. spl. edn. Maine Sch. Adminstrv. Dist. 36, Livermore Falls, 1985—89, composite rm. tchr., cons., 1989—90; dir. spl. svcs. Maine Sch. Adminstrv. Dist. 34, Belfast, 1990—95; cons. State Dept. Edn., Augusta, 1995—2000; visual artist, 2000—. Author: Soon to Be Reality: High Standards for All, 1999, School Reform: Achieving Enduring Change, 1999; artist (paintings) numerous pvt. collections. Home: PO Box 426 Oakland ME 04963-0426 E-mail: artjourneys@aol.com.

ASMUSSEN, JES, JR., electrical engineer, educator, consultant; b. Milw., June 12, 1938; s. Jes and Anita (Weltzien) A.; m. Judith Adele Knopp, June 18, 1960 (div. Mar. 1980); m. Colleen Cooper, Jan. 4, 1987; children: Kirsten, Jes III, Stig; stepchildren: Scott Cooper, Jill Cooper. BSEE, U. Wis., 1960, MSEE, 1964, PhD in Elec. Engring., 1967. Design and devel. engr. Louis Allis Co., Milw., 1960-62; asst. prof. elec. engring. Mich. State U., East Lansing, 1967-71, assoc. prof. elec. engring., 1971-75, prof. elec. engring., 1975-96, Univ. Disting. prof. engring, 1997—, acting assoc. dir. div. engring. rsch., 1983-84, chairperson dept. elec. engring., 1990—. Cons. to industry. Mem. editorial bd. Plasma Sources Sci. and Tech., 1991-95, Jour. Physics D: Applied Physics, 1994-95; contbr. more than 200 articles to profl. jours. Recipient Disting. Faculty award Mich. State U., 1988, Disting. Svc. citation Coll. Engring. U. Wis.-Madison, 1993; grantee NSF, Dept. Energy, NASA, Def. Advanced Rsch. Projects Agy., 1971—; Withrow Disting. scholar, Mich. State U, 1997. Fellow IEEE (nuclear and plasma scis. adminstrv. com. 1997—); mem. AIAA, AAAS, Am. Vacuum Soc., Material Rsch. Soc., Sigma Xi, Eta Kappa Nu. Lutheran. Achievements include 18 patents in field for microwave, multipolar, electron cyclotron resonance plasma and ion source technology used in thin film deposition and submicron etching applications, microwave plasma assisted diamond thin film technology; research in microwave discharges (plasma) as applied to microchip technology and electric propulsion engines for spacecraft propulsion, microwave technology for materials processing, and wind power engineering. Home: 3811 Viceroy Dr Okemos MI 48864-3844 Office: Mich State U Dept Elec Engring East Lansing MI 48824

ASSAEL, HENRY, marketing educator; b. Sofia, Bulgaria, Sept. 12, 1935; s. Stanley Isaac and Anna (Behar) A.; m. Alyce Friedman, Aug. 19, 1961; children: Shaun Eric, Brenda Erica. BA cum laude, Harvard U., 1957; MBA, U. Pa., 1959; PhD, Columbia, 1965. Asst. prof. mktg. Sch. Bus. St. John's U., Jamaica, N.Y., 1962-65; asst. prof. mktg. Hofstra U., Hempstead, N.Y., 1965-66; prof. mktg. Stern Sch. Bus. NYU, 1966—, chmn. dept., 1979-91. Cons. AT&T, N.Y. Stock Exchange, Nestle Co., Inc., CBS. Author: Educational Preparations for Positions in Advertising Management, 1966, The Politics of Distributive Trade Associations: A Study in Conflict Resolution, 1967, Consumer Behavior and Marketing Action, 1981, 6th edit. 1998, Marketing Management: Strategy and Action, 1985, Marketing: Principles and Strategy, 1990, 2d edit., 1993, Marketing: Core Concepts, 1998, Consumer Behavior: A Strategic Approach, 2003; editor: A Century of Marketing, 33 vols., 1978, Early Development and Conceptualization of the Field of Marketing, 1978, History of Advertising, 40 vols., 1985; contbr. numerous articles to profl. jours. Mem. Am. Mktg. Assn., Assn. Consumer Research. Office: 44 W 4th St New York NY 10012-1106

ASSANIS, DENNIS N. (DIONISSIOS ASSANIS), mechanical engineering educator; b. Athens, Greece, Feb. 9, 1959; came to U.S., 1980; s. Nicholas and Kyriaki Assanis; m. Helen Stavrianos, Aug. 25, 1984; children: Nicholas, Dimitris. BSc in Marine Engring. with distinction, Newcastle U., U.K., 1980; SMME, SM in Naval Arch. Marine Engring., MIT, 1982, PhD in Power and Propulsion, 1985, SM in Mgmt., 1986. Asst. prof. mech. engring. U. Ill., Urbana-Champaign, 1985-90, assoc. prof. mech. engring., 1990-94; prof. mech. engring. U. Mich., Ann Arbor, 1994—, dir. program automotive engring., 1995—2002, Arthur F. Thurnau prof., 1999—2002, Jon R. and Beverly S. Holt prof. engring., 2000—, chair mech. engring., 2002—, dir. Automotive Rsch. Ctr., 2000—; co-dir. Gen. Motors Collaborative Rsch. Lab., 2002—. Part-time rsch. staff energy and environ. systems divsn. Argonne Nat. Lab., 1978—; cons. in field. Assoc. editor ASME Transactions, Jour. Engring. for Gas Turbines and Power, 1996—; contbr. over 100 articles to profl. jours.; presenter in field. Univ. scholar, 1991-94, Athens Coll. Acad. scholar, 1967-77; recipient IBM Rsch. award, 1991, NSF Presdl. Young Investigator award, 1988-93, NSF Engring. Initiation award, 1987, NASA Cert. of Recognition for Creative Devel. of a Tech. Innovation, 1987; Lilly Endowment Teaching fellow, 1988. Fellow Soc. Automotive Engrs. (faculty advisor U. Mich. student sect. 1997-2003, Ralph Teetor award 1987, Russell Springer Best Paper award 1991, award for rsch. on automotive lubricants 2002); mem. ASME (faculty advisor U. Ill. student sect. 1989-91, ASME/Pi Tau Sigma Gold Medal award 1990, Internal Combustion Engine Divsn. Speaker award 1993, 94, Meritorious Svc. award 1997), Am. Soc. for Engring. Edn., Combustion Inst., Sigma Xi. Achievements include development of comprehensive models of internal combustion engine processes. Office: U Mich Dept Mech Engring & Applied Mechanics 2045 WE Lay Automotive Lab Ann Arbor MI 48109-2121

ASSIE-LUMUMBA, N'DRI T. Africana studies educator; b. Potossou, Ivory Coast, 1952; d. Kouassi and Yaha (Kokora) Assie. Studnet, U. Abidjan, Ivory Coast, 1970-71; BA, U. Lyon, France, 1972; MA, U. Lyon, 1975; postgrad., U. Laval, Que., Can., 1976; PhD, U. Chgo., 1982. Rchr. U. Abidjan, 1975-76; postdoctoral fellow U. Houston, 1982-83; tchr., adminstr. U. Benin, CIRSSED, Lome, Togo, 1983-88; vis. Bard Coll., Annandale, N.Y., 1989, Vassar Coll., Poughkeepsie, N.Y., 1989-90; resident fellow Internat. Inst. for Ednl. Planning, Paris, 1990; dep. dir. Pan African Studies and Rsch. Ctr., Abidjan, 1996—; prof. Africana studies Cornell U., Ithaca, N.Y., 1991—. Cons. UNESCO, Paris, 1989, 94, UN Devel. Program, N.Y.C., 1997, 99, Forum for African Women, Nairobi, Kenya, 1997, Rockefeller Found., N.Y.C., 1999. Author: Les Africaine dans la politique, 1996; editor Jour. Comparative Edn., 1998—. Ford Found. fellow, 1991; Fulbright sr. rsch. felow, 1991-92; Rockefeller Found. grantee, 1996-97. Mem. AAUW, Assn. African Women for R&D (exec. com.), Comparative and Internat. Edn. Soc., Coun. for Devel. of Social Sci. Rsch. in Africa, Cornell Inst. for Social and Econ. Rsch., Pi Lambda Theta. Avocations: music (jazz, modern, african and classical), physical exercise, modern african dance, reading. Office: Cornell U Africana Studies 310 Triphammer Rd Ithaca NY 14850-2519

ASTAIRE, CAROL ANNE TAYLOR, artist, educator; b. Long Beach, Calif., Aug. 26, 1947; d. John Clinton and Carolyn Sophie (Wright) Taylor; m. Frederic Astaire, Jr., Feb. 14, 1971; children: John Carroll, Johanna Carolyn. BFA, UCLA, 1969; grad. summer studies, Salzburg Summer Sch., Klessheim, Austria, 1969; cert. secondary sch. tchr., Calif. State U., Long Beach, 1971; postgrad., Calif. Polytechnic State U., San Luis Obispo, 1986-87. Cert. secondary sch. tchr. Calif. Tchr., tutor, cons. art edn. San Luis Coastal Unified Sch. Dist., San Luis Obispo, 1980-89. Author: (book) Left Handed Poetry from the Heart, 1983; Represented in permanent collections Yergeau Musée Interant. Art, Montreal, Can., Travis AFB Mus., Calif., Huntington Libr. Founder, trustee San Luis Coastal Unified Sch. Dist./Found. Arts Art Core, 1988—92; mem. adv. coun. Coastal Cmty. Edn. and Svc., San Luis Obispo, 1989—92; screening com. UCLA Alumni Scholarship, 1993—95; mem. archtl. needs assessment com. Art Ctr., San Luis Obispo. Recipient Nat. finalist, Kodak Internat. Newspaper Snapshot award, 1993, 1st pl. black and white photo award, Ann. Visions 99 Photography Group, Visions 2001/Ctrl. Coast Photog. Soc., 2001, 1st pl., B/W Visions, 2001. Mem.: Ctrl. Coast Photog. Soc. (two 1st place black-and-white photo awards), Ctrl. Coast Watercolor Soc., Oil Pastel Acrylic Group Brushstrokes (hon. mention 1994), San Luis Obispo Art Coun., Fine Arts Coun., San Luis Obispo Art Ctr., Nat. Mus. Women in Arts. Republican. Episcopalian. Avocations: classical ballet, architectural design, swimming, ocean kayaking, reading.

ASTILL, KENNETH NORMAN, mechanical engineering educator; b. Westerly, R.I., July 16, 1923; s. John Henry and Mabel Nellie (Robotham) A.; m. Hazel Patricia Lamb, Apr. 10, 1948; children: Kenneth John, Robert Michael. BS, U. R.I., 1944; MA in Engring., Chrysler Inst. Engring., 1946; MS, Harvard U., 1953; PhD, MIT, 1961. Lab engr. Chrysler Corp., Detroit, 1944-47; prof. mech. engring. Tufts U., Medford, Mass., 1947-91, assoc. dean engring., 1980-88, prof. emeritus, 1991—. Mem. energy facilities siting coun. Commn. of Mass., 1989-92; mng. dir. U. Rsch. Engring. Assn., 1989—1997; cons. Sylvania Electric Co., Natick Labs., Kaye Instruments, C.S. Draper Labs.; vis. fellow U. Leeds, 1976, U. Sussex, 1983. Author: (with B. Arden) Numerical Algorithms, 1970, Elementary Experiments in Mechanical Engineering, 1971, (with others) Laboratory Demonstrations in Heat Transfer and Fluid Mechanics, 1968. Trustee Charles River Mus., 1992-2003. Recipient Ralph R. Teeter award Soc. Automotive Engrs., 1981; NSF fellow, 1968 Fellow ASME (life, chmn. Boston sect. 1981-82); mem. AAUP, Am. Soc. Engring. Edn., Engring. Soc. New Eng. (bd. dirs. 1982-87), Sigma Xi, Tau Beta Pi. Home: 72 Yale St Winchester MA 01890-2331 Office: Tufts U Anderson Hall Medford MA 02155

ASTIN, ALEXANDER WILLIAM, education educator; b. Washington, May 30, 1932; s. Allen Varley and Margaret L. (Mackenzie) A.; m. Helen Stavridou, Feb. 11, 1956; children: John Alexander, Paul Allen. AB, Gettysburg (Pa.) Coll., 1953, LittD (hon.), 1981; MA, U. Md., 1956, PhD, 1958; LLD (hon.), Alderson-Broaddus Coll., 1982, Whitman Coll., 1986; LHD, Chapman Coll., 1987, Am. Coll. Switzerland, 1989, SUNY, 1989; D of Pedagogy, R.I. Coll., 1987; DSc, Thomas Jefferson U., 1990; EdD (hon.), Merrimack Coll., 1993; LLD (hon.), Pepperdine U., 1993. Dep. chief psychology service USPHS Hosp., Lexington, Ky., 1957-59; dep. chief psychology research unit VA Hosp., Balt., 1959-60; research asso., dir. research Nat. Merit Scholar Corp., Evanston, Ill., 1960-64; dir. research Am. Council Edn., Washington, 1965-73; Allan M. Carter prof. edn. UCLA, 1973—; pres. Higher Edn. Research Inst., Los Angeles, 1973—. Author: The College Environment, 1968, The Educational and Vocational Development of College, 1971, The Power of Protest, 1975, Preventing Students from Dropping Out, 1975, Four Critical Years, 1977, Maximizing Leadership Effectiveness, 1980, Minorities in American Higher Education, 1982, Achieving Educational Excellence, 1985, Assessment for Excellence, 1991, What Matters in College?, 1993, others. Trustee St. Xavier Coll., Chgo., Marjorie Webster Jr. Coll., Washington, Gettysburg Coll., 1983-86, Eckerd Coll., Fla., 1986-91. Recipient Disting. Research award Am. Personnel and Guidance Assn., 1965, Disting. Research award Nat. Assn. Student Personnel Adminstrs., 1976, Outstanding Service award Am. Coll. Personnel Assn., 1978, Lindquist award for outstanding research on college students Am. Ednl. Research Assn., 1983, Excellence in Edn. award Nat. Assn. Coll. Admissions Counselors, 1985, Outstanding Research award Am. Coll. Personnel Assn., 1985, Outstanding Service award Council of Ind. Colls., 1986, Outstanding Research award Assn. for Study of Higher Edn., 1987, Roll of Svc. award Nat. Assn. Student Fin. Aid Adminstrs., 1991, Extended Rsch. award AACD, 1992, Sidney Suslow award Assn. for Instl. Rsch., 1992; fellow Center Advanced Study Behavioral Sci. Fellow Am. Psychol. Assn., AAAS; mem. Am. Assn. Higher Edn. (dir.) Office: UCLA Grad Sch Edn Higher Edn Rsch Inst 3005 Moore Hall Box 951521 Los Angeles CA 90095-9000

ASTUCCIO, SHEILA MARGARET, educational administrator; b. Biddeford, Maine, Apr. 24, 1943; d. James T. III and Margaret H. (Cameron) Rollinson; m. Joseph Kevin Astuccio, Aug. 22, 1976 (dec. Apr. 1992); children: James M., Sheila E. BS in Edn., Salem (Mass.) State Coll., 1968, MEd, 1975; cert. advanced grad. studies, Lesley Coll., Cambridge, Mass., 1983. Cert. elem. tchr. and prin., supr., dir., Mass.; cert. instrnl. tech. grades K-12. Elem. educator Hood Elem. Sch., Lynn, Mass., 1968-79; tchr. grades 3 and 4 Lynn (Mass.) Pub. Schs., comp. coord., facilitator, 1981-84, tchr. academically talented, 1979-81, 84-85, computer program specialist, 1986-87, computer implementation team leader, MIS dir., 1987-98; adminstr. IS/MIS, 1998—; owner operator Pilot Imaging Computer Imaging, Lynn, Mass., 1991-92. Tchr. adult edn. North Shore C.C., 1982-87; part-time real estate broker, 1979—; part-time mktg. cons. IDN, 1993-95; presenter Beijing Dist. Edn. Bur., 2001; presenter in field. Mem. Chpt. II adv. coun., 1979-83; nat. grad. alumni rep. Lesley Coll., 1984-85; chair Mayor's Computer Adv. Com., 1985-86; participant Educators in Industry GE/Salem State Coll., 1983; People to People Amb. to China, 2000, 2001; sec.-gen. United Cult. Convention, 2001—. Recipient Educators in Industry cert., 1983, Novell Netware Adminstr. and Sys. Installation/Configuration certs., 1994-95, Letters of Commendation Mass. Dept. Edn., 2000, 2001. Mem. ASCD, AAUW, NAFE, NSBA, DECUS, PEI Nat. Users Group, New Eng. Pentamation Users Group, Boston Computer Soc. Office: Data Center LVTI 80 Neptune Blvd Lynn MA 01902-4570 E-mail: astuccios@lynnschools.org., astuccio@comcast.net.

ATAIE, JUDITH GARRETT, middle school educator; b. San Francisco, July 24, 1941; m. A.J. Ataie Sr., Oct. 7, 1961; children: A.J. Jr., Andrew Jennati. BA, U. Calif., Berkeley, 1980; postgrad., U. Hawaii, Manoa, 1982—. Art instr., dean faculty The Athenian Sch., Danville, Calif., 1980—.

ATCITTY, FANNIE L. elementary school educator, education educator; b. Shiprock, NM, Dec. 4, 1952; d. John and Betty Martin Lowe; m. Eugene Ronald Atcitty, Apr. 22, 1972 (dec. May 10, 2000); children: Antoinette, Ronald. BEd, Ea. N.Mex. U., 1978; M in Curriculum and Instrn., Doane Coll., 1997; M in Ednl. Leadership, Doane Coll., 2002. Elem. tchr. Central Consolidated Sch. Dist. 22, Shiprock, N.Mex., 1979—. Adj. instr. early childhood edn. program N.Mex. Highland U., Las Vegas, 1997—2002; adj. instr. edn. and tchr. prep. program Diné Coll., Shiprock, N.Mex., 1997—2002; profl. standards commn. mem. N.Mex. State Dept. Edn., Santa Fe, 2000—, tchr. assessment rev. panel, 1993—99, nat. coun. for accreditation of tchr. edn., 1997—. Contbr. poetry to lit. publs. Edn. chairperson Shiprock (N.Mex.) Cmty. Planning Commn., 1994—96; vice chair San Juan County Dem. Party, Farmington, 1998—2001; chairperson Cmty. Gov. Planning Bd., Shiprock, N.Mex., 1995—98; U.S Presdl. elector N.Mex., 1996. Recipient Golden Apple Found. award, Golden Apple Found. N.Mex., 2001. Mem.: Internat. Reading Assn., Am. Assn. Sch. Adminstrs., Las Amigas Women's Club. Democrat. Avocations: reading, walker, community events, gardening. Home: PO Box 3320 Shiprock NM 87420 Office: Mesa Elementary Sch PO Box 1803 Shiprock NM 87420

ATENCIO, PEDRO LUIS, educational administrator; b. Espanola, N.Mex., Jan. 28, 1949; s. Luis L. and Frances (Torres) A.; m. Dinae Scheer, Aug. 4, 1975; children: Mario, Alicia, Javier. BA, U. N.Mex., 1971; student, Coll. Santa Fe, 1972; MA, N.Mex. Highlands U., 1973, postgrad., 1986. Cert. tchr., adminstr., N.Mex. Tchr. Universidad Autonoma de Guadalajara, Mex., 1972-73, Santa Fe Pub. Schs., 1973-75, No. N.Mex. C.C., Espanola, 1975-76, U. N.Mex., Santa Fe, 1976-78, Agua Fria Elem. Sch., Santa Fe, 1978-80; Title VII dir. Cuba (N.Mex.) Ind. Schs., 1980-82; tchr. Santa Fe Pub. Schs., 1982-85; prin. Sweeney Elem. Sch., Santa Fe, 1987-88; coord. Re:Learning N.Mex., Santa Fe, 1988—. Co-author curriculum guide, 1977. Mem. adv. group Nat. Govs.' Assn., State of N.Mex., 1991—. Recipient Juan Romero Jimenez award U. N.Mex., 1969, Excellence Quality award State of N.Mex. Edn. Rsch. and Coun., 1988. Mem. N.Mex. Elem. Prins. Assn. (v.p. 1988), N.Mex. Assn. for Bilingual Edn. (pres. 1976). Office: 1300 Camino Sierra Vis Santa Fe NM 87505-1091

ATIBA, JOSHUA OLAJIDE O. internist, pharmacologist, oncologist, educator, philanthropist; b. Enugu, Nigeria, July 6, 1956; s. Joseph Ojo and Abigail Olayo A.; m. Stella N. Mordi, June 26, 1981; children: April, Annamarie, Joseph. MD, U. Lagos, Nigeria, 1979; MHA, St. Mary's Coll., 1999. Diplomate Am. Bd. Internal Medicine, Am. Bd. Oncology. Rotating intern Ahmadu Bello U. Tchg. Hosp., Kaduna, Nigeria, 1979-80; resident in internal medicine Lagos U. Tchg. Hosp., 1981-83; fellow in med. oncology Cancer Control Agy., Vancouver, B.C., Can., 1988-90; fellow in clin. pharmacology Stanford U. Med. Ctr., Palo Alto, Calif., 1983-86; pvt. practice Irvine, Calif. Dir. clin. investigation U. Calif., Irvine, 1991-95; mem. U. Calif. Irvine Med. Ctr., Orange, North Bay Med. Ctr., Fairfield, Calif., Vaca Valley Hosp., Vacaville, Calif.; asst. prof. medicine, pharmacology U. Calif., Irvine; med. dir. N. Bay Hosp., 1997-99; pres. NOAH Med. Svc. Corp.; med. dir. NOAH, Inc.; rancher Med. dir. North Bay Hospice, Fairfield, Calif.; pres. Newport Oncology and Healthcare Found. Fellow Royal Coll. Physicians Can.; mem. ACP, AMA, Am. Fedn. for Clin. Rsch., Am. Soc. of Clin. Pharmacology and Therapeutics, Am. Soc. Clin. Oncology, Calif. Med. Assn., Solano County Med. Soc. (sec./treas., pres.-elect, pres.), Physician Peer Rev. Orgn. (dir.), KC (knight 1997). Republican. Roman Catholic. Office: PO Box 1631 Suisun City CA 94585-4631 E-mail: jatiba@pol.net.

ATIYEH, NAIM NICHOLAS, psychologist, educator; b. Amioun, Kura, Lebanon, May 26, 1930; came to U.S., 1992; s. Nicholas Hanna and Mary (Beshara) A.; m. Wafa Selim Mroueh, May 3, 1970; children: Leena, Ghassan. PhD, U. Chgo., 1956. Assoc. prof. dept. edn. Am. U., Beirut, Lebanon, 1956-67; tests and measurements expert UNESCO, 1967-69; sr. social officer UN, Beirut, 1969-70; chmn. div. edn. Beirut U. Coll., 1970-71; dean, prof. faculty of edn. Lebanese U., Beirut, 1971-75, prof. dept. psychology, 1977-85; pvt. practice Beirut, 1986-92. Vis prof. Am. U., Beirut, 1986-92; sch. psychologist, counselor Pinewood Coll., Beirut, 1961-67; vis. lectr. Sch. Edn., U. Jordan, 1968; cons. Ford Found., Beirut, 1962-65, World Bank, 1976-77, 94; cons. in field; cons., advisor UNESCO, 1971-92; sr. rsch. scientist Reading Ctr. George Washington U., 1992; ednl. cons., sr. cons. Internat. Coun. for Spl. Edn., 1993—; adviser Univ. Testing and Evaluation Ctr. King Fahd U. for Petroleum and Minerals, Dhahran, Saudi Arabia, 1995—. Author: A Scale of Mental Development for Children—Elementary Level, 1967, 72, 84, Purposive Education Evaluation, 1970, An Index of Social Stratification in Lebanon, 1979, An Expanded Scale of Intelligence Through a Draw-A-Man Test, 1984, Intelligence and Learning Disabilities, 1985, Test of Reasoning Ability for Children, 1985, Atiyeh Scale of Mental Development for Children, Pre-Elementary, 1992; co-author English Arabic Dictionary of Psychology and Education, 1961; contbr. numerous articles to profl. jours. Mem. APA, Am. Ednl. Rsch. Assn., Nat. Coun. Measurement in Edn. Avocations: reading, meditation, hiking, gardening, music appreciation. Home: 7910 Peyton Forest Trl Annandale VA 22003-1559

ATKIN, J MYRON, science educator; b. Bklyn., Apr. 6, 1927; s. Charles Z. and Esther (Jaffe) A.; m. Ann Spiegel, Dec. 25, 1947; children— David, Ruth, Jonathan. BS, CCNY, 1947; MA, NYU, 1948, PhD, 1956. Tchr. sci. Ramaz High Sch., N.Y.C., 1948-50; tchr. elem. sch. sci. Great Neck (N.Y.) pub. schs., 1950-55; prof. sci. edn. Coll. Edn., U. Ill., Urbana, 1955-79, assoc. dean, 1966-70, dean, 1970-79; prof. Sch. Edn., Stanford (Calif.) U., 1979—, dean, 1979-86. Cons. OECD, Paris, Nat. Inst. Edn.; mem. edn. adv. bd. NSF, 1973-76, 84-86, vice-chmn., 1984-85, sr. advisor, 1986-87; mem. Ill. Tchr. Certification Bd., 1973-76; Sir John Adams lectr. U. London Inst. Edn., 1980, vis. scholar com. scholarly commn. Nat. Acad. Scis., People's Republic China, 1987; math. sci. edn. bd. NRC, 1985-89, nat. com. sci. edn. standards and assessment, 1992-96, com. on sci. edn. K-12, 1996-2002, vice chair, 1998, chair, 1999-2002; invited lectr. Nat. Sci. Coun., Taiwan, 1989—; resident Rockefeller Found., Bellagio Ctr., 1999; nat. assoc., Nat. Acads. of Sci., 2001-. Author children's sci. textbooks. Served with USNR, 1945-46. Fellow: AAAS (v.p. sect. Q 73 1974); mem.: NAS (assoc.), Am. Ednl. Rsch. Assn. (exec. bd. 1972—75, chmn. govt. and profl. liaison com.), Coun. Elem. Sci. Internat. (pres. 1969—70), Sigma Xi (chmn. com. on sci., math. and engring. edn.). E-mail: atkin@stanford.edu.

ATKINS, CLAYTON H. family physician, epidemiologist, educator; b. Beech Grove, Ind., Nov. 12, 1944; s. Amos H. Atkins and Edythe E. (Dale) Heneghan; m. Carole A. Kirlin, Aug. 2, 1974; children: Brenda M. Spencer, Craig N., Angela C. AB in Chemistry, Ind. U., Bloomington, 1965, MAT in Chemistry, 1967; MD, Ind. U., Indpls., 1969; BS in Math. summa cum laude with highest honors, Butler U., 1980. Diplomate Am. Bd. Family Practice. Rotating intern Meth. Hosp. Ind. Inc., Indpls., 1969-70; pvt. practice Greenwood, Ind., 1970-94; mem. active staff family practice dept. St. Francis Hosp. and Health Ctrs., 1970—, hosp. epidemiologist, 1989—2002, with med. exec. com., 1993-96, pres. med. staff, 1995, mem. exec. mgmt. com., 1995-96; pvt. practice associated with St. Francis Med. Group, Indpls. and Beech Grove, Ind., 1995—. Mem. courtesy med. staff family practice dept. Cmty. Hosp. South, Indpls., 1970—; instr. NSF math. for high sch. tchrs. Ind. U., Bloomington, 1966-67; instr. microbiology Ind. Ctrl. Coll. (now U. Indpls.), 1968; adj. asst. prof. Butler U. Coll. Pharmacy, Indpls., 1991-95; mem. Ops. Coun. St. Francis Med. Group, 1998-99, Mgmt. Coun. 1999-2000. Lt. col. M.C., USAFR, 1971-77, 91—. Fellow Am. Acad. Family Physicians; mem. AMA, Ind. State Med. Assn., Inpls. Med. Soc., Assn. for Practitioners in Infection Control and Epidemiology, Soc. for Hosp. Epidemiology in Am., Math. Assn. Am., Sigma Xi, Phi Kappa Phi, Phi Delta Kappa, Alpha Epsilon Delta, Phi Lambda Upsilon, Phi Eta Sigma, Mu Alpha Theta. Avocations: astronomy, cosmology, mathematics, gardening, mountain hiking. Home: 7610 W Banta Woods Dr Bargersville IN 46106-8740 Office: 8778 Madison Ave Ste 200 Indianapolis IN 46227-7202

ATKINS, LEOLA MAE, special education educator; b. Belize City, Belize, Feb. 10, 1936; came to U.S., 2002; d. Wilfred Clinton and Grace Ethel (Sutherland) Reynolds; m. Manfred Denfield Atkins, Aug. 25, 1962; children: Karen, Carla, Kenric, Derek, Dianne, Davd, Vanessa. Tchrs. diploma, Belize Tchr.'s Coll., Belize City, 1970; diploma, Coll. of Preceptors, U.K., 1971; MS in Spl. Edn., L.I. U., 1986; MS in Early Childhood Edn., Herman Lehman Coll., 1988; postgrad., L.I. U.; Pub. Sch. Adminstrv.

Degree, SUNY, 1995. Cert. primary, elem., spl. edn. tchr., N.Y. Elem. tchr. Holy Redeemer Girl's Sch., Belize City, 1956-68; tchr. slow-learners class St. Ignatius Middle Sch., Belize City, 1971-78, St. Ignatius Upper Sch., Belize City, 1979-81; tchr. St. Catherine's Elem. Sch., Belize City, 1982, Grace Luth. Elem. Sch., Bronx, N.Y., 1982; substitute tchr. spl. edn. classes C.E.S., Bronx, 1983, spl. edn. tchr., 1983-86, Bronx Pub. Schs., 1986—. Co-developer tchr.'s manual Div. of Multicultural Edn. Unit, Div. Multilingual and Multicultural Edn., 1989—. Mem. Yonkers Interfaith Edn. and Leadership Devel., Inc. Mem. Phi Delta Kappa. Roman Catholic. Avocations: dance, reading, baseball, church activities, travel. Home: 18 Stanley Pl Yonkers NY 10705-1165

ATKINS, PATRICIA HOLLAR, primary school educator; b. Hickory, N.C., June 27, 1953; d. Harold Eugene and Millie Alphatine (Ball) Hollar; divorced; children: Harmony K., Cortney Lynn. BA in Psychology, elem. sch. certification, U. N.C., Asheville, 1975; MA in Elem. Edn., Western Carolina U., 1980. Tchr. kindergarten Marion (N.C.) Elem. Sch., 1975-79, Emma Elem. Sch., Asheville, 1984-89; tchr. 2d grade Weaverville (N.C.) Primary Sch., 1989-98, grade level chairperson for 2nd grades, 1992-93, 1st grade tchr., 1998—, 1st grade chairperson, 1999-2000, mem. report card com., 1993, 2002—03. Leader workshop Math. Their Way, Buncombe County Schs. and Asheville City Schs., 1988-89, 1st grade, 1999-2000; inst. leader K-1 Inst., Buncombe County and Asheville City Schs., 1988-89; mem. textbook adoption coms. for social studies and math. Tchr. Sunday sch. St. Marks Luth. Ch., Asheville, 1985-90, dir. bible sch., 1987-89; sec., mem. exec. bd. Asheville-Buncombe County Swim Team, 1986-89. Grantee Buncombe County Schs. Found., 1987-89. Mem. NEA, Internat. Reading Assn., Nat. Coun. for Tchrs. Math., Nat. Assn. for Edn. Young Children (conf. leader 1989), N.C. Assn. Educators, Asheville Area Assn. for Edn. Young Children (v.p. 1988-91). Democrat. Baptist. Avocations: flute, dancing, sewing, cooking. Office: Weaverville Primary Sch Main St Weaverville NC 28787-9205 Home: 46 North Lake Dr Weaverville NC 28787-1007

ATKINS, WILLIAM ALLEN, academic administrator; b. St. Louis, Sept. 19, 1934; s. William Allen and Nancy Lou (Hunter) A.; m. Joan Markmann, Feb. 6, 1954 (div. Feb. 25, 1977); children: Andrew Bennett, Stephen Hunter; m. Maxine Stegman, Apr. 6, 1977. BA, U. Denver, 1955; MA in Edn., Washington U., 1958; CAS, Harvard U., 1962, EdD, 1965. Cert. Supt., N.Y., Mass., Vt. Elem. tchr. Univ. (Mo.) City Pub. Schs., 1956-61; asst. supt. Williamstown (Mass.) Pub. Schs., 1963-65; supt. Rutland (Vt.) Pub. Schs., 1965-68; mgr. Gen. Learning Corp., Washington, 1968-71; assoc. dean Hofstra U. Sch. Edn., Hempstead, NY, 1971-77; exec. dir. Sexton Ednl. Ctr., Massapequa, NY, 1977-82; dir. Queensborough C.C., Bayside, NY, 1982-85; exec. dir. S.I. Continuum of Edn., Inc., 1985-90; asst. dean Nassau C.C., Garden City, NY, 1990-92, v.p., 1992-93, exec. asst. to pres., 1993-95, assoc. dean for acad. affairs, 1995—2001, acting dean of instrn., 2001—02, dean instrn., 2002—. Adj. prof. in field; edn. dir. Episcopal Diocese L.I., Garden City, 1973-77; pres. N.Y. State Coun. for Resource Devel., 1994-96; dir. region II Coun. Resource Devel., 1996-98, also bd. dirs. Co-author: Developing An Educationally Accountable Program, 1973. Chair United Way, Garden City, 1972—77; bd. dirs. St. Mary's and St. Paul Episcopal Schs., Garden City, 1973—77, Rutland (Vt.) Hosp., 1965—68, Urban League L.I., 1994—2002; v.p. fin. Northgate Homeowners Assn., 1993—2000; treas. Wantagh Jewish Ctr., v.p., 1995—97. Recipient Faculty Disting. Svc. award Hofstra U., 1977, Internat. Reading Assn., 1987, Presdl. award L.I. Univ., 1989, Disting. Kappan award, 1989. Mem. NEA, Am. Assn. Sch. Adminstrs., Coun. for Resource Devel., Kappa Delta Pi (faculty sponsor 1971-77), Phi Delta Kappa (pres. 1989-90). Democrat. Jewish. Avocations: reading, photography, travel, golf. Home: 8 Northgate Ct Melville NY 11747-3046 E-mail: atkinsw@ncc.edu.

ATKINSON, ALANNA BETH, music educator; b. Mobile, Ala., July 4, 1952; d. John Walter and Mildred Dalton Atkinson. BS in Music Edn., U. South Ala., 1974. Pvt. piano tchr., Mobile, 1973—; piano tchr. Indian Springs Elem. Sch., Mobile, 1975—, Morningside Elem. Sch., Mobile, 1987—2001. Organist Our Savior Luth., Mobile, 1973, Kingswood United Meth., Mobile, 1974—83, Forest Hill United Meth., Mobile, 1984—; vol. music leader Bible sch. Fulton Heights Meth., Mobile, 1998—; clarinetist Mobile Pops Band, 1995—; soprano Springhill Consort, 1992—97, Gloria Dei Chorale, 1999—; dulcimer player ch., cmty. and nursing home programs, Mobile, 1996—. Recipient United Meth. Women Mission Pin, Kingswood Meth., 1983, Forest Hill Meth., 1985. Mem.: Mobile Music Tchrs. Assn. (2d v.p. 1978, 1982, treas. 1988—89, honors recital and social coms.), Am. Organist Guild (bd. dirs. 1984, 1990). Democrat. Methodist. Avocations: sewing, cats. Home: 1500 S Shan Dr Mobile AL 36693 E-mail: melodycat@zebra.net.

ATKINSON, KENDALL EUGENE, mathematics educator; b. Centerville, Iowa, Mar. 23, 1940; s. Harold Eugene and Helen Jane (Fleming) Hart; m. Alice Jane Morse, Aug. 26, 1961; children: Elizabeth Jane, Kathryn Elaine. BS in Math., Iowa State U., 1961; MS in Math., U. Wis., 1963, PhD in Math., 1966. Vol. Peace Corps, Ethiopia, 1963-64; asst. prof., assoc. prof. Ind. U., Bloomington, 1966-72; rsch. fellow Australian Nat. U., Canberra, 1970-71; assoc. prof., prof. math. U. Iowa, Iowa City, 1972—, prof. computer sci., 1997—. Author: (book) A Survey of Numerical Methods for the Solution of Fredholm, 1976, An Introduction to Numerical Analysis, 1978, 1988, Elementary Numerical Analysis, 1984, 1993, The Numerical Solution of Integral Equations of the Second Kind, 1997; author: (with W. Han) Theoretical Numerical Analysis, 2001. Mem. Soc. Indsl. and Applied Math., Australian Math. Soc. Avocations: travel, photography, genealogy. Office: U Iowa Dept Math Iowa City IA 52242

ATKINSON, REGINA ELIZABETH, medical social worker; b. New Haven, May 13, 1952; d. Samuel and Virginia Louise Griffin. BA, U. Conn., Storrs, 1974; MSW, Atlanta U., 1978. Social work intern Atlanta Residential Manpower Center, 1976-77, Grady Meml. Hosp., Atlanta, 1977-78; med. social worker, hosp. coordinator USPHS, Atlanta, Palm Beach County (Fla.) Health Dept., West Palm Beach, 1978-81; dir. social services Glades Gen. Hosp., Belle Glade, Fla., 1981-95; case mgr. divsn. sr. svcs. Palm Beach County Cmty. Svcs., West Palm Beach, Fla., 1996—; instr. Palm Beach Jr. Coll.; participant various work shops, task forces. Vice pres. Community Action Council South Bay, 1978-79. Whitney Young fellow, 1977; USPHS scholar, 1977. Mem. NAFE, NAACP, Am. Hosp. Assn. (soc. for social work adminstrn. in health care), Soc. Hosp. Social Work Dirs., Assn. State and Territorial Pub. Health Social Workers, Nat. Assn. Black Social Workers, Nat. Assn. Social Workers, Fla. Soc. for Hosp. Social Work Dirs. (adminstrn. in health care), Glades Area Assn. for Retarded Citizens. Home: 525 1/2 SW 10th St Belle Glade FL 33430-3712 Office: 810 Datura St Ste 100 West Palm Beach FL 33401-5204

ATKINSON, RICHARD CHATHAM, university president; b. Oak Park, Ill., Mar. 19, 1929; s. Herbert and Margaret Atkinson; m. Rita Loyd, Aug. 20, 1952; 1 dau., Lynn Loyd. Ph.B., U. Chgo., 1948; PhD, Ind. U., 1955. Lectr. applied math. and stats. Stanford (Calif.) U., 1956—57, assoc. prof. psychology, 1961—64, prof. psychology, 1964—80; asst. prof. psychology UCLA, 1957—61; dep. dir. NSF, 1975—76, acting dir., 1976, dir., 1976—80; chancellor, prof. cognitive sci. U. Calif., San Diego, 1980—95; pres. U. Calif. Sys., 1995—2003, pres. emeritus, 2003—. Author: (with Atkinson, Smith and Bem) Introduction to Psychology, 13th edit., 2000, Computer Assisted Instruction, 1969, An Introduction to Mathematical Learning Theory, 1965, Contemporary Developments in Mathematical Psychology, 1974, Mind and Behavior, 1980, Stevens' Handbook of Experimental Psychology, 1988. Served with AUS, 1954—56. Guggenheim fellow, 1967; fellow Ctr. for Advanced Study in Behavioral Scis., 1963; recipient Distinguished Research award Social Sci. Research Council, 1962. Fellow APA (Disting. Sci. Contbn. award 1977, Thorndike award 1980), AAAS (pres. 1989-90), Am. Psychol. Soc. (William James fellow 1985), Am. Acad. Arts and Scis.; mem. NAS, Soc. Exptl. Psychologists, Am. Philos. Soc., Nat. Acad. Edn., Inst. of Medicine, Cosmos Club (Washington), Explorer's Club (N.Y.C.). Home: 6845 La Jolla Scenic Dr S La Jolla CA 92037 Office: U Calif San Diego Rm 5212 McGill Hall Oakland CA 92093-0109 E-mail: RCA@ucsd.edu.

ATLAS, DIANE ALLEN, Spanish language educator; b. Camden, Ark., Dec. 10, 1950; d. Edward Louis and Martha Virginia (Allen) Phythian; m. Jerry Lee Atlas, Nov. 5, 1972; children: Jeremy Kile, Amanda Allen. BS, Tarleton State U., 1972; M in Edn. Adminstrn., Prairie View (Tex.) A&M U., 1983. Tchr. social studies St. Mary Sch., West, Tex., 1976-78, prin., 1978-86; tchr. Spanish, history West High Sch., 1986—. Mem. West Ind. Sch. Dist. Adv. Coun., 1992-94; chmn. Land Acquisition Commn., West, 1993-94; dir. Trojan Dazzlers Dance Team, West, 1993—. Dir of youth, mem. adminstrv. coun., vision 2000 First United Meth. Ch., West, 1993-96; chair nurturing ministries Ctrl. United Meth. Ch., Waco, Tex. Nominee Tchr. of Year Tex. Excellence in Edn., U. Tex. and Hank Masur, 1990. Democrat. Methodist. Avocations: avid sports fan, dance, reading. Home: 519 S Harrison St West TX 76691-1706 Office: West High Sch 801 N Reagan St West TX 76691-1158

ATLAS, JAY DAVID, philosopher, consultant, linguist; b. Houston, Tex., Feb. 1, 1945; s. Jacob Henry and Babette Fancile (Friedman) A. AB summa cum laude, Amherst (Mass.) Coll., 1966; PhD, Princeton (N.J.) U., 1976. Mem. common rm. Wolfson Coll., Oxford, Eng., 1978, 80; vis. fellow Princeton U., 1979; rsch. assoc. Inst. for Advanced Study, Princeton, 1982-84; vis. lectr. U. Hong Kong, 1986; prof. Pomona Coll., Claremont, Calif., 1989—, chair dept. linguistics and cognitive sci., 2001—03, Peter W. Stanley Prof. linguistics and philosophy, 2003—. Sr. assoc. Jurecon, Inc., L.A.; lectr. 2d European Summer Sch. in Logic, Lang. and Info., 1990; examiner U. Edinburgh, Scotland, 1993, U. Groningen, The Netherlands, 1991, 93-97, vis. rsch. prof., 1995; vis. prof. UCLA, 1988-95, Max. Planck Inst. for Psycholinguistics, Nijmegen, The Netherlands, 1997. Author: Philosophy Without Ambiguity, 1989, Logic, Meaning, and Conversation, 2003; contbr. to PC Laptop Computer Mag., 1994, articles to profl. jours. Mem. Am. Philos. Assn., Linguistic Soc. Am. Office: Pomona Coll 550 N Harvard Ave Claremont CA 91711-4410 E-mail: jatlas@alumni.princeton.edu.

ATLEE, DEBBIE GAYLE, sales consultant, medical educator; b. Oklahoma City, Jan. 8, 1955; d. Harold Phillip and Ella Ruth (Birks) A. BS in Nursing, U. Okla., 1977. RN, Okla.; cert. diabetes educator. Team leader ob-gyn Bapt. Med. Ctr. of Okla., Oklahoma City, 1977-80, asst. clin. supr. urology, 1980-81, nursing educator, diabetes educator, 1981-84; sales specialist Boehringer Mannheim Diagnostics, Inc., Indpls., 1984-99; diabetes educator Dept. Endocrinology U. Okla. Coll. Medicine, 1999-2000; bus. sales mgr. NovoNordisk Pharms., Inc., Princeton, NJ, 2000—02; diabetes case mgr. Ediba Diabetes Ctr. Excellence Integris Bapt. Med. Ctr., Okla. City, 2002—. Mem. regional piloting adv. group Nat. Diabetes Adv. Bd., Oklahoma City, 1984-85. Named Outstanding Bus. Woman, Bus. and Profl. Women, Capitol Hill chpt., 1981, Salesperson of Yr. 1987; recipient Outstanding Sales Achievement award, 1985, 87, 90, 91. Mem. Am. Diabetes Assn. (exec. bd. Met. chpt. 1985—, pres. 1987), Am. Assn. Diabetes Educators, Western Okla. Diabetes Educators (pres. 1984, Outstanding Svc. and Dedication award 1984, chpt. svc. award 1985, chpt. edn. award 1984), Nat. Bd. Cert. Diabetes Educator, U.S. Power Squadron (bd. dirs. Oklahoma City 1984, 87), U. Okla. Alumni Assn. (life). Republican. Roman Catholic. Avocations: sailing, photography, gardening, music. Home: 2222 NW 49th Oklahoma City OK 73112 E-mail: debbie_atlee@integris_health.com.

ATREYA, SUSHIL KUMAR, planetary-space science educator, astrophysicist; b. Apr. 15, 1946; came to U.S., 1966, naturalized, 1975; s. Harvansh Lal and Kailash Vati (Sharma) A.; 1 child, Chloè E. ScB, U. Rajasthan, India, 1963, MSc, 1965; MS, Yale U., 1968; PhD, U. Mich., 1973. Rsch. assoc. physics U. Pitts., 1973-74; asst., then assoc. rsch. scientist U. Mich., Ann Arbor, 1974-78, ast. prof., 1978-81, assoc. prof. atmospheric sci., 1981-87, prof. atmospheric and space sci., 1987—, dir. planetary sci. lab. Assoc. prof. U. Paris, 1984-85, vis. prof., 2000, 01; vis. sr. rsch. scientist Imperial Coll., London, 1984; mem. sci. and exptl. team Cassini-Huygens Probe to Saturn-Titan, Galileo Jupiter Probe, Nozomi Japanese Mars Mission, Mars Express Mission, Russian Mars '96 and Soviet Phobos projects, Voyager spacecraft missions to the giant planets, Comet Rendezvous/Asteroid Flyby, 1986-92, and SpaceLab I; guest observer/investigator on Hubble Space Telescope, Internat. Ultraviolet Spectrometer and Copernicus Orbiting Astron. Obs.; mem. sci. working groups NASA, Jet Propulsion Lab., European Space Agy. Author: Atmospheres and Ionospheres of the Outer Planets and their Satellites, 1986; editor: Planetary Aeronomy and Astronomy, 1981, Outer Planets, 1989, Cometary Environments, 1989, Origin and Evolution of Planetary and Satellite Atmospheres, 1989; contbr. numerous articles to books and profl. jours. Recipient NASA award for exceptional sci. contbns. Voyager Project, 1981, NASA Group Achievement award for Voyager Ultraviolet Spectrometer Investigations, 1981, 86, 90, NASA Group Achievement awards for Galileo Probe Mass Spectrometer experiment, and for Significant Outstanding Contbns. to the Galileo Probe and Orbiter to Jupiter, Excellence in Rsch. award U. Mich. Coll. Engring., 1995. Mem. AAAS, Internat. Assn. Meteorology and Atmospheric Scis. (pres. commn. planetary atmospheres and their evolution 1987-95, sec. 1983-87), Am. Geophys. Union (assoc. editor Geophys. Rsch. Letters jour. 1986-89), Internat. Astron. Union, Am. Astron. Soc., Internat. Acad. Astronautics (academician 1993—). Office: Space Rsch Bldg Univ Mich Ann Arbor MI 48109-2143

ATTANASIO, JOHN BAPTIST, dean, law educator; b. Jersey City, N.J., Oct. 19, 1954; s. Gaetano and Madeline (Germinario) A.; m. Kathleen Mary Spartana, Aug. 20, 1977; children: Thomas, Michael. BA, U. Va., 1976; JD, NYU, 1979; diploma in law, Oxford U., 1982; LLM, Yale U., 1985. Bar: Md. 1979, U.S. Dist. Ct. Md. 1980, U.S. Ct. Appeals (4th cir.) 1980, U.S. Supreme Ct. 1983. Pvt. practice, Balt., 1979-81; vis. asst. prof. law U. Pitts., 1982-84; assoc. prof. law U. Notre Dame, Ind., 1985-88, prof. law, 1988-92; Regan dir. Kroc Inst. for Internat. Peace Studies, 1991-92; dean Sch. of Law St. Louis U., 1992-98; dean, William Hawley Atwell chair constnl. law So. Meth. U. Sch. Law, Dallas, 1998—. Co-author: Constitutional Law 1989. Chair adv. bd. Ctr. for Civil and Human Rights, 1990-92; mem. Fulbright awards area com., 1994-96; bd. dirs. Legal Svcs. Ea. Mo., 1996-98; bd. dirs. Ctr. for Internat. Understanding, 1993—. Recipient Legal Teaching award Sch. of Law, NYU, 1994. Mem. Ctrl. States Law Sch. Assn. (v.p. 1992-94), Phi Beta Kappa, Alpha Sigma Nu. Democrat. Roman Catholic. Office: So Meth U Dedman Sch Law PO Box 750116 3315 Daniel Ave Dallas TX 75275-0116*

ATTIG, JOHN CLARE, secondary education educator, consultant; b. Chgo., Apr. 2, 1936; s. Clare McKinley and Elsie Bertha (Nagel) A.; m. Harriet Jane Rinehart, June 13, 1959; children: Laura, Victoria. BA, DePauw U., 1958; MA, U. Chgo., 1961. Cert. tchr., Calif. Social studies tchr. Lyons Twp. H.S., LaGrange, Ill., 1961-65, Henry Gunn H.S., Palo Alto, Calif., 1965-72, 78-98; univ. faculty assoc. Simon Fraser U., Burnaby, Canada, 1972-73; social studies tchr. Jordan Jr. H.S., Palo Alto, 1973-75, Cubberley Sr. H.S., Palo Alto, 1975-78. Lectr., demonstrator, pub. simulation games for classes in history and govt. various univs. and sch. dists. in U.S. and Can. Author: College in Three Years: Stop Wasting Time and Money, 2002, numerous simulation games; contbr. numerous articles to profl. jours. With USAR, 1958-64. NEH fellow, 1983, 87, 89, Tchr. fellow St. Andrews U., Scotland, 1993. Mem. NEH (project dir. Masterworks Seminar 1991), Western History Assn. Methodist. Avocations: travel, reading, wine. E-mail: jnhattig@efn.org.

ATTOH, SAMUEL ARYEETEY, geographer, educator, planner; b. Accra, Ghana, June 26, 1956; came to U.S., 1980; s. Samuel Aryeetey and Cecilia (Taylor) A.; m. Antoinette Yawa Alipui, Sept. 6, 1980; children: Annette, Annabelle, Stefan, Sasha. BA with honors, U. Ghana, Legon, Accra, 1977; MA, Carleton U., 1980; PhD, Boston U., 1988. Rsch. asst. U. Ghana, 1975-77; teaching fellow, rsch. fellow Carleton U., Ottawa, Ont., Can., 1978-80; teaching asst. Boston U., 1980-85, lectr. Met. Coll., 1985-86, instr., 1986-87; asst. prof. U. Toledo, 1987-92, assoc. prof. geography and planning, 1992—, chair geography and planning dept., 1996—, prof. geography, 1998—. Author: Geography of Sub-Saharan Africa, 1997; contbr. articles to profl. jours. Mem. Com. of 100 Housing Task Force, Toledo, 1989-91. Fellow Am. Coun. Edn.; mem. Am. Inst. Cert. Planners, Assn. Am. Geographers (chair African splty. group 1994-96), Am. Planning Assn., Ohio Housing Rsch. Network, Ohio Geographic Alliance (exec. bd. 1997—), Mid-Continent Regional Sci. Assn. Roman Catholic. Avocations: reading, travel, sports. Office: Univ Toledo Geography and Planning 2801 W Bancroft St Toledo OH 43606-3390

ATWATER, MARY MONROE, science educator; b. Roswell, N.Mex., July 26, 1947; d. John C. and Helen (Wallace) Monroe; children: Helena A., Jonathen A. BS magna cum laude, Meth. Coll., 1969; MA, U. N.C., 1972; PhD, N.C. State U., 1980. Nat. sci. coord. Fayetteville (N.C.) State U., 1975-77; teaching asst. dept. maths. and sci. N.C. State U., Raleigh, 1977-79, rsch. asst., 1977-79; assoc. dir. N.Mex. State U., Las Cruces, 1980-83; asst. prof., program dir. sci., maths., tech. edn. Atlanta U., 1984-87, assoc. prof. and program dir. sci., math., tech. edn., 1987; asst. prof. dept. sci. edn. U. Ga., Athens, 1987-92, assoc. prof. dept. sci. edn., 1993-97, prof., 1997—. Vis. assoc. prof. Cornell U., 1993; adj. prof. Atlanta U., 1987-88; mem. rev. com. NSF, 1993, cons., 1994, Harvard-Smithsonian Ctr. Astrophysics, 1993, N.Y. Biology Network Workship, 1993, ABT Assocs., Inc., 1993, NSF, U.S. Dept. Edn.; mem. adv. com. World Book Publ., 1993; presenter at numerous convs., speaker in field. Co-editor Multicultural Edn.: Inclusion of All, 1994; contbr. chpts. to books; contbr. numerous articles to profl. jours. Cons. Sci. Edn. in Mich. Schs., 1990-91; elem. sci. curriculum guide project Ga. Dept. Edn., 1988-90; judge numerous internat., state, local sci. fairs, 1978-96. Recipient Herbert Lehman Edn. Fund award, 1965, NSTA OHAUS award for innovations in four-yr. coll. tchg., 1990, Coll. Edn. and Psychology Disting. Alumnus award N.C. State U., 1996, Top Minority Women in the Scis. award Nat. Tech. Assn., 1998, African-Am. Phenomenal Women award African-Am. Profl. Women of Athens Area, 1999; numerous rsch. grants; Lily Tchg. fellow, 1989; inducted into Acad. Top Women Sci. & Engring. Nat. Tech. Assn., 1998 Fellow AAAS; mem. ASCD, Am. Chem. Soc., Am. Edn. Rsch. Assn., Assn. Edn. Tchrs. in Sci., Assn. Tchr. Edn., Ga. Sci. Tchrs. Assn. (pres.), Nat. Assn. Multicultural Edn., Nat. Assn. Rsch. in Sci. Tchg., Southeastern Assn. Edn. Tchrs. in Sci., South African Assn. for Rsch. in Math. and Sci. Edn., Phi Beta Delta, Phi Delta Kappa (Warren Finley Rsch. award 1996). Office: U Ga 212 Alderhold Hall Athens GA 30602-7126

ATWATER, TONY, provost,dean, educator; b. Nashville, Mar. 11, 1952; s. Herman and Lonnie May A.; m. Beverly Laverne Roberts, Dec. 20, 1980. AAS in Radio and TV Prodn., Va. Western Cmty. Coll., 1972; BA in Mass Media Arts, Hampton U., 1973; PhD in Comm., Mich. State U., 1983. Prof. journalism Mich. State U., East Lansing, 1983-91; dept. chmn. Rutgers U., New Brunswick, N.J., 1991-95; assoc. v.p. Univ. Toledo, Ohio, 1995-99; dean profl. studies Northern Ky. U., Highland Heights, 1999-2001; provost Youngstown (Ohio) State U., 2001—. Asst. dir. Mich. State U. Honors Coll., East Lansing, 1988-91; bd. trustee Northwest Ohio Pub. TV Found., Toledo, 1997-99; bd. dirs. Covington (Ky.) Ednl. Found., 2000-01. Mem. editl. bd. Jour. of Broadcasting and Electronic Media, 1996-2000. Expert panel mem. Gov.'s Taskforce Youth and Substance Abuse, Lexington, Ky., 2000-01; mem. Leadership Cin., 2000-01. Mich. State U. doctoral fellow 1979, Tchg. fellow The Poynter Inst., 1990, Univ. Adminstrn. fellow Univ. Conn., Storrs, 1994, postdoctoral fellow Ford Found., U. Mich., 1988; rsch. grantee NSF, Toledo, 1988-89. Mem. Internatl Comm. Assn., Assn. Edn. Journalism and Mass Comm. (pres. 1992-93), Am. Assn. Higher Edn., Broadcast Edn. Assn., Soc. Profl. Journalists, Phi Kappa Phi. Avocations: international travel, theater, public speaking. Office: Youngstown State U Tod Hall One Univ Plz Youngstown OH 44555 E-mail: tatwater@ysu.edu.

ATWELL, ROBERT HERRON, higher education executive; b. Washington, Pa., Jan. 26, 1931; s. R. Boice and Elsie (Herron) A.; m. Suzanne Fogg, Apr. 22, 1989; children by previous marriages: Mary, Robert, John, Nancy, Carl, Catherine, Cynthia. BA, Coll. Wooster, 1953; MA in Pub. Adminstrn, U. Minn., 1957. Budget examiner U.S. Bur. Budget, Washington, 1957-60; fiscal economist, loan officer U.S. Devel. Loan Fund, Dept. State, 1960; budget examiner, program analyst for higher edn. and med. research programs U.S. Bur. Budget, 1961-62; program planning officer, asst. chief Cmty. Mental Health Ctrs. br. NIMH, HEW, 1962-65; vice chancellor for adminstrn. U. Wis., Madison, 1965-70; pres. Pitzer Coll., Claremont, Calif., 1970-78; v.p. Am. Coun. Edn., 1978-84, pres., 1984-96, pres. emeritus, 1996—. Chmn. coun. Claremont Coll., 1971—72; pres. Ind. Colls. So. Calif., 1974—75; trustee Eckerd Coll., Collegis Corp., Edn. Mgmt. Corp., Argosy U. With AUS, 1953-55. Home: 447 Bird Key Dr Sarasota FL 34236-1805

ATWOOD, GLENN ARTHUR, engineer, educator; b. Rock Rapids, Iowa, Oct. 24, 1935; s. Elmer Henry and Clara Marie (McCrory) A.; m. Mary Ellen Ensminger, Aug. 28, 1955; children: Ruth Marie, John Aaron, Robert Mark. BSChemE, Iowa State U., 1957, MS, 1959; PhD, U. Wash., 1963. Registered profl. engr., Ohio. Process engr. Exxon Rsch. and Engring., Flornam Park, N.J., 1962-65; asst. prof. U. Akron, Ohio, 1965-70, assoc. prof., 1970-77, prof., 1977-83, asst. dean, 1983-85, assoc. dean, 1985-88, acting dean coll. engr., 1988-89; R&D dir. Midwest Ore Processing Co., Inc., Plainville, Ind., 1990—95; prof. emeritus U. Akron, Ohio, 1990—. Cons. Knapp Foundry, Akron, Firestone Co. Patentee in field. Founder, officer Marriage Encounter United Meth. Ch., Ohio, 1977-89; pres., vice chmn. United Cerebral Palsy, 1966-77, trustee 1970-74. Mem. ASEE, NSPE, Am. Inst. Chem. Engrs., Sigma Xi, Tau Beta Phi. Home: 939 Devonwood Dr Wadsworth OH 44281-8859 Office: 939 Devonwood Dr Wadsworth OH 44281-8859

ATWOOD, JOYCE CHARLENE, curriculum and instruction administrator, consultant; b. Chillicothe, Ohio, Apr. 29, 1943; d. Pearl and Blanche (Martindill) Workman. BS in Edn., Ohio U., 1965, MEd, 1969; postgrad., Ohio State U., 1976-88, Ashland U., 1992-97. Cert. tchr., supr., adminstr. 4th-6th grade tchr. Chillicothe (Ohio) City Schs., 1965-73, K-3d grade reading tchr., 1973-86, tchr. leader reading recovery, 1986-88, asst. prin. mid. sch., 1988-89, adminstrv. asst., 1989—, asst. supt. for curriculum and instrn., 1993—. Cons. study skills for mgmt. in industry Pickaway-Ross Joint Vocat. Sch., Chillicothe, 1984-88; mem. Child Care Adv. Bd., Portsmouth (Ohio), 1993— Sec., v.p. Big Bros. and Sisters, Ross County, 1989-93; mem. Walnut St. Ch. Staff Parish, Chillicothe, 1991-94, 99—; coord. Area Artist Series, Ross County, 1989—; edn. chairperson Ross County Area Labor Mgmt., 1990—; mem. Interagy. Childcare Vocat. Choir; bd. dirs. YMCA, 2002—. Named to Ross County Women's Hall of Fame, Ross County C. of C., 1993; recipient North Ctrl. Accredition award, 2002; George Washington U. Partnership award, 2002. Mem. ASCD (Ohio Creative Staff Devel. award 1997), Internat. Reading Assn., Nat. Assn. Edn. Young Children, Buckeye Assn. Sch. Adminstrs., Ohio Assn. for Curriculum Devel. (Staff Devel. Creative award 1997), Bus. and Profl. Women Assn., Altrusa, Kiwanis, Phi Delta Kappa. Methodist. Avocations: reading, gardening. Home: 10 Overlook Dr Chillicothe OH 45601-1925 E-mail: jatwood@mailgsu.k12.oh.us.

ATZMON, MICHAEL, materials scientist, educator; b. Jerusalem, Oct. 15, 1956; came to U.S., 1980; s. David and Aliza (Weinstein) A.; m. Leslie Chandler, Aug. 1989; children: Amy Renee, Ethan Benjamin. BS, Hebrew U., Jerusalem, 1980; MS, Calif. Inst. Tech., 1982, PhD, 1986. Rsch. asst. Calif. Inst. Tech., Pasadena, 1981-85; rsch. fellow Harvard U., Cambridge, Mass., 1985-87; asst. prof. nuclear engring. U. Mich., Ann Arbor, 1987-93, assoc. prof. nuclear engring., 1993-94, assoc. prof. nuclear engring. and radiol. sci., materials sci. and engring., 1994—. EPSRC fellow U. Cambridge, Eng., 1996-97, By-fellow Churchill Coll., Cambridge, 1996-97. Contbr. articles to Acta Materialia, Jour. Applied Physics, Jour. Materials Rsch., Physical Rev. Letters. Grantee U.S. Dept. Energy, 1988, 99, NSF, 1989, 92, 95, 98. Mem. Am. Phys. Soc., Materials Rsch. Soc., Minerals, Metals, and Materials Soc., Internat. Mechanochemical Assn. (pres.) Achievements include patent for Metastable Alloy Materials Formed by Solid-State Reaction of Compacted Mechanically Deformed Mixtures; research interests include metastable metallic alloys, nanocrystalline metals, diffusion in solids, ion-solid interactions. Office: U Mich 2355 Bonisteel Blvd Ann Arbor MI 48109-2104

AU, KATHRYN HU-PEI, educational psychologist; b. Honolulu, May 8, 1947; d. Harold Kwock Ung and Mun Kyau (Hew) A. AB, Brown U., 1969; MA, U. Hawaii, 1976; PhD, U. Ill., 1980. Ednl. specialist Kamehameha Schs., Honolulu, 1971-80, ednl. psychologist, 1980-95; prof. U. Hawaii, Honolulu, 1995—. Author: Literacy Instruction in Multicultural Settings, 1993. Nat. scholar Nat. Assn. for Asian and Pacific Am. Edn., 1980; recipient Causey award for Reading Rsch., Nat. Reading Conf., 1998. Mem. Nat. Reading Conf. (pres. elect 1994-95, pres. 1996-97), Am. Ednl. Rsch. Assn. (v.p. 1992-94), Internat. Reading Assn. (dir. 1998-2001). Office: U Hawaii Coll Edn 1776 University Ave Honolulu HI 96822-2463

AU, MARY LEE, school system administrator; b. West Chester, Pa., June 17, 1931; d. James and Lau Shee (Fong) Lee; m. Markley Lee Au, June 24, 1956. BS in Elem. Edn., West Chester State U., 1953; MA in Elem. Edn., George Washington U., 1968; student, U. So. Calif., 1975-76. Cert. elem. and middle sch. adminstr., Md. Tchr. West Chester Sch. Dist., 1953-59, Marple Newton, Pa., 1959-62, Montgomery County Pub. Sch., Md., 1962-68; asst. prin. Roling Terr. Elem. Sch., Tacoma Park, Md., 1989-91; acting asst. prin. Wyngate Elem. Sch., Bethesda, Md., 1990-91; acting prin. Oakland Terr. Elem. Sch., Kensington, Md., 1991, asst. prin., 1991—2003, Thurgood Marshall Sch., 1994—99; cons. LA Assocs. Human Resources. Mem. undergrad. affairs com., mem. curriculum devel. Am. U., Washington, 1968-79; adv. multicultural curriculum devel. U. So. Calif., 1977; tchr. certification advisor to Md. state supt. Md. State Dept. Edn., 1979-85; pres., dir. L.A. Assocs. Cons. for Human Resources, 1977—, diversity trainer, 1999—; coord. tchr. tng. ctr. Am. U./Montgomery County (Md.) Pub. Schs.; pers. recruiter Montgomery County Pub. Schs. Author: Chronology of Asian Pacific American History, 1979-94. Deacon Bradley Hills Presbyn. Ch., 2003—. Named one of the Women of the 80's, Ms. Mag., Asian-Chinese Am. historian "Write Women Back Into History" project by Nat. Women's Project. Mem. ASCD, Nat. Assn. Elem. Sch. Prins., NAACP, Md. Assn. Elem. Sch. Adminstrs., Asian Pacific Am. Heritage Coun. (co-founder 1979—, nat. treas. 1990-91, nat. pres. 1998—), Orgn. Chinese Ams. (nat. pres. 1980, v.p. ednl., social, and cultural program 1975), Actors Guild. Avocations: golf, vocal music, interior decorating, jewelry designing. Home: 8800 Fox Hills Trl Potomac MD 20854-4211

AUBREY, SHERILYN SUE, elementary school educator; b. Louisville, Nov. 7, 1951; d. Sheridan and Alice (Rivera) A. BA in Edn., U. Ky., 1974; MA in Edn., Murray State U., 1979. Cert. elem. tchr., Ky. Primary tchr. Hopkins County Bd. Edn., Madisonville, Ky., 1975—; rank I early childhood edn. Murray State U., 1999. Mem. site-base coun. Grapevine Sch., Madisonville, 1991—. Mem. NEA, Ky. Edn. Assn., Hopkins County Edn. Assn. (rep. 1986-90), Alpha Delta Kappa (chair altruistic com. Omicron chpt. 1988-91). Baptist. Avocations: travel, reading, theater. Home: 501 E Morehead St Central City KY 42330-1238 Office: Grapevine Sch Hayes Ave Madisonville KY 42431-3296

AUCHTER, NORMA HOLMES, musician, educator; b. Rochester, N.Y., Jan. 3, 1922; d. Robert Edgar and Ruby (Lyon) Holmes; m. Ervin Frank Auchter, June 4, 1955; children: Robert Holmes Auchter, Ceci Ann Albecker, Allan Neil Auchter. BMus with distinction, U. Rochester, 1942, MMus Theory, 1944, DMus Arts Performance and Lit., 1977; studied with Carl Friedberg, N.Y.C., 1950-54. Instr. U. Conn., Storrs, 1943-45, U. Tex., Austin, 1945-46; faculty Eastman Sch. Music, Rochester, 1946-50; piano instr. Middlebury (Vt.) Coll., 1956-61; lectr., accompanist, mus. dir. St. Michael's Coll., Winnoski, Vt., 1967-72; assoc. prof. Tex. Tech. U., Lubbock, 1972-75; piano instr. SUNY, Geneseo, 1976-78; piano/theory prof. U. N.C., Pembroke, 1978-79; pvt. piano tchr. Houston, 1979—; mem. faculty Houston C.C. NW, 2003—. Adj. instr. Houston Cmty. Coll., 2003, piano instr. U. Vt., Burlington, 1960-72; co-owner Auchters House of Music, Burlington, 1956-72; debut recital, Town Hall, N.Y.C., 1952; concert tours U.S., Can., 1950-57; entertainer, lectr. adjudicator, workshops, master classes, TV sch., U.S., Can., 1950—; performing mem. Tuesday Mus. Club, Houston, 1980—. Collaborating artist with Paul Alvarez violin concerts; books and recordings for Mel Bay Pub. including Cabaret Treasures for Violin and Piano, 1995, Salon Gems for Violin and Piano, 1997. Mu Phi Epsilon Postgrad. grant, 1974. Mem. Nat. Guild of Piano Tchrs. (adjudicator), Music Tchrs. Nat. Assn. Home: 12431 Shepherds Ridge Dr Houston TX 77077-2919 E-mail: nauchter@juno.com.

AUERBACH, JEROLD S. university educator; b. Phila., May 7, 1936; s. Morry M. and Sophie (Soloff) A.; m. Susan H. Levin, May 16, 1982; children: Shira, Rebecca; children from previous marriage Jeffrey, Pamela. BA, Oberlin Coll., 1957; MA, Columbia U., 1959, PhD, 1965. Lectr. Queens Coll. CUNY, 1964-65; asst. prof. Brandeis U., Waltham, Mass., 1965-71, Wellesley (Mass.) Coll., 1971-72, assoc. prof., 1972-77, prof., 1977—. Vis. scholar Harvard Law Sch.; Fulbright lectr. Tel Aviv U., 1974-75. Author: Labor and Liberty, 1966, Unequal Justice, 1976, Justice Without Law?, 1983, Rabbis and Lawyers, 1990, Jacob's Voices, 1996, Are We One?, 2001. Guggenheim Meml. Found. fellow, 1974-75; fellow NSF, 1979-80, NEH, 1986-87, 91-92. Office: Wellesley Coll 106 Central St Wellesley MA 02481-8268 E-mail: jsauerbach@attbi.com.

AUERBACH, JOSEPH, lawyer, educator, retired; b. Franklin, N.H., Dec. 3, 1916; s. Jacob and Besse Mae (Reamer) A.; m. Judith Evans, Nov. 10, 1941; children: Jonathan L., Hope B. Pym. AB, Harvard U., 1938, LLB, 1941. Bar: N.H. 1941, Mass. 1952, U.S. Ct. Appeals (1st, 2d, 3d, 5th, 7th and D.C. cirs.), U.S. Supreme Ct. 1948. Atty. SEC, Washington and Phila., 1941-43, prin. atty., 1946-49; fgn. service staff officer U.S. Dept. State, Dusseldorf, W. Ger., 1950-52; ptnr. Sullivan & Worcester, Boston, 1952-82, counsel, 1982—; lectr. Boston U. Law Sch., 1975-76, Harvard Bus. Sch., Boston, 1980-82, prof., 1982-83, Class of 1957 prof., 1983-87, prof. emeritus, 1987—; prof. Harvard Extension Sch., 1988, 91-95. Bd. dirs. Nat. Benefit Life Ins. Co., N.Y.C. Author: (with S.L. Hayes, III), Investment Banking and Diligence, 1986, Underwriting Regulation and Shelf Registration Phenomenon in Wall Street and Regulation, 1987, also chpt. to book, papers and articles in field. Trustee Mass. Eye and Ear Infirmary, Boston, 1981—, chmn. devel. com., 1985-88, chmn. nominating com., 1993-94; mem. adv. bd., former chmn. devel. com. Am. Repertory Theatre, Cambridge, Mass., 1985—; bd. dirs., past pres. Friends of Boston U. Librs., 1972—; past v.p., bd. dirs. Shakespeare Globe Ctr., N.A., 1983-90; overseer New Eng. Conservatory of Music, 1992-98, mem. fin. com.; bd. dirs. English Speaking Union, Boston, 1995-98; chair 1938 Harvard Pres. Assn.; active Harvard Coll. Fund, Harvard Law Sch. Fund. Decorated Army Commendation medal; recipient Disting. Svc. award Harvard Bus. Sch., 1996, Disting. Teaching award 1993, Exemplary Svc. award Harvard Extension Sch., 1995. Mem. ABA, Mass. Bar Assn., Boston Bar Assn., Harvard Mus. Assn., St. Botolph Club, Harvard Club N.Y.C., Shop Club, Downtown Club. Home: 300 Boylston St Apt 512 Boston MA 02116-3923 Office: Sullivan & Worcester 1 Post Office Sq Ste 2300 Boston MA 02109-2129 also: Harvard Bus Sch Cumnock Hall Rm 300 Boston MA 02163

AUERBACH, KATHRYN ANN, architecture and preservation educator, consultant; b. Doylestown, Pa., Aug. 21, 1954; d. John Joseph and Elizabeth Rose Auerbach; m. John Michael Pivarnik, May 25, 1991 (dec. Nov. 6, 2000); 1 child, Anika Theresa Pivarnik. BA in History, Coll. William & Mary, 1976. Asst. commr. Va. Rsch. Ctr. for Archaeology, Williamsburg, 1976—77; dir. historic programs Bucks County Conservancy, Doylestown, Pa., 1977—86; cons. historic preservation Kathryn Ann Auerbach, Erwinna, Pa., 1986—; instr. historic preservation Bucks County C.C., Newton, Pa., 1991—. Mem. hist. preservation adv. bd. Bucks County C.C., Newtown, Pa., 1990—. Bd. dirs. Tinicum Conservancy, Erwinna, Pa., 1992—2002. Recipient 3d Place C.A. Peterson prize, Hist. Am. Bldgs. Survey, Washington, 2003. Mem.: Kappa Alpha Theta, Sigma Pi Kappa. Roman Catholic. Avocation: gardening. Home: PO Box 39 Erwinna PA 18920

AUG, ALBERTA J. educational administrator; b. Rochester, Minn., July 2, 1962; d. Donald Carl and Joanne Marcella Aug. BA, Central Coll., Pella, Iowa, 1984; MA, Monterey Inst. Internat. Study, Calif., 1993. Tchg. asst. Ministry Edn., Waidhafen, Ybbs, Austria, 1984-86; prof. U. Econs., Vienna, 1986-88; project mgr. Am. Joint Distbn. Com., Vienna, 1986-88; dir. devel. asst. Family Resource Ctr., Seaside, Calif., 1991-93; dir. recruiting and admissions Monterey Inst. Internat. Studies, 1993-2000, Twirlix Internet Techs., Santa Clara, Calif., 2000; with San Castle Techs. Inc., San Jose, Calif., 2000—02, World Fin. Group, 2003—. Cons. USIA, Vienna and Washington, 1984-86, 97, Internat. Rsch. and Exch. Bd., Washington, 1997, Am. Coun. Internat. Edn., Washington, 1998, Open Soc. Inst./Soros Found., N.Y.C., 1998-2000; Fulbright tchg. asst. Austrian Ministry Edn., Vienna, 1984. Author numerous poems. Bd. mem. World Affairs Coun., Monterey, 1994-95, Vol. Ctr. Monterey County, 1995-96; vol. Family Resource Ctr., Seaside, 1992-94. Recipient Delta Epsilon award Alpha Mu Gamma, Monterey, 1991. Mem. Nat. Assn. Fgn. Student Advisors, Nat. Assn. Grad. Admissions Profls. Avocations: writing, wine tasting, gourmet cooking, reading, volleyball.

AUGHENBAUGH, DEBORAH ANN, mayor, retired educator; b. Bklyn., Oct. 15, 1922; d. James R. and Alice Lillian (Walsh) Donecho; m. William Irving Hopwood, Mar. 31, 1946 (dec. July 1966); 1 child, William James; m. Kenneth Merle Aughenbaugh, Oct. 20, 1973 (dec. Sept. 1997). BS, Towson (Md.) State Coll., 1952; MS, Shippensburg (Pa.) U., 1967. Cert. elem. tchr., guidance counselor, Md. Tchr. Balt. City Pub. Schs., 1952-54, St. John's Cath. Ch., Frederick, Md., 1960-63, Frederick County Bd. Edn., Frederick, 1963-84; mem. city coun. City of Burkittsville, Md., 1971-74, 80-83, mayor, 1986-95; ret., 1995. Mem. Gov.'s Policy Com. on Edn., 1994-95, Frederick County Bd. Edn., 1995-2002, v.p., 2000-01; mem. Md. Assn. Bds. of Edn. legis. com., 1995-97, 98-99. Chmn. Burkittsville Planning and Zoning Commn., 1969-79; mem. Frederick Recycling Com., 1989-91; mem. Frederick Solid Waste Adv. Bd., 1991-93; mem. Frederick County Bd. of Edn., 1995-2002, v.p., 2000-01; mem. Frederick County Park and Recreation Com.; mem. legis. com. Md. Assn. Bd. Edn., Nat. Bd. Edn., 1998—; mem. Frederick County Future Growth and Sch. Schedule Adv. Com. Mem. Frederick County Ret. Sch. Personnel (pres.-elect), Md. Mcpl. League (pres. Frederick County chpt. 1992, state legis. com. 1985-95, chair 1992-93, bd. dirs. 1985-95), Nat. League Cities (human devel. com. 1991-95), pres. elect retired Frederick County Public Sch. Employees. Democrat. Avocations: reading, travel, crocheting. Home: PO Box 408 Burkittsville MD 21718-0408

AUGUST, DIANE L. independent education consultant, policy and reading researcher; b. N.Y.C., May 28, 1948; d. Burton and Flora A.; m. Michael Anthony Fainberg, Sept. 7, 1986; children: Nina Anne, Elisabeth Renee. BA, Wheaton Coll., 1970; MA, Stanford U., 1971, PhD, 1981, postgrad., 1982. Cert. tchr. administr., Calif. Tchr. Whisman Sch. Dist., Mountain View, Calif., 1972-79, program mgr., 1979-82; congl. sci. fellow AAAS, Washington, 1982-83; grants officer Carnegie Corp., N.Y.C., 1984-87; dir. edn. divsn. Children's Defense Fund, Washington, 1986-88; edn. cons. August & Assocs., Washington, 1988-95, 97—; sr. program officer Nat. Acad. Sci., Washington, 1995-97. Mem. social policy com. Soc. Rsch. in Child Devel., Washington, 1988-91. Author: Language Minority Education in the United States, 1988; editor: Improving Schooling for Language Minority Children: A Research Agenda. Mem. Internat. Reading Assn., Am. Ednl. Rsch. Assn. Office: 4500 Wetherill Rd Bethesda MD 20816-1813 E-mail: daugust@msn.com.

AUGUST-DEWILDE, KATHERINE, banker; b. Bridgeport, Conn., Feb. 13, 1948; d. Edward G. and Benita Ruth (Miller) Burstein; m. David deWilde, Dec. 30, 1984; children: Nicholas Alexander, Lucas Barrymere. AB, Goucher Coll., 1969; MBA, Stanford U., 1975. Cons. McKinsey & Co., San Francisco, 1975-78; dir. fin. Itel Corp., San Francisco, 1978-79; sr. v.p., CFO PMI Group, San Francisco, 1979-85, pres., CFO, 1988-91; CEO, pres. First Republic Thrift & Loan of San Diego, 1988-96; exec. v.p. First Republic Bank, San Francisco, 1987—, sr. v.p., chief fin. officer, 1985-87, COO, 1996—. Mem. policy adv. bd. Ctr. for Real Estate and Urban Econs., U. Calif., Berkeley, 1987—2000; bd. dirs. First Republic Bank, Trainer, Wortham & Co., Inc. Bd. dirs. San Francisco Zool. Soc., 1993-2001, vice-chair, 1995-2000; trustee Carnegie Found., 1999—, Town Sch. for Boys, San Francisco, 1999—; mem. adv. coun. Stanford U. Grad. Sch. Bus., 2003—. Mem. Women's Forum (bd. dirs.), Bankers Club, Belvedere Tennis Club, Villa Taverna. Home: 2650 Green St San Francisco CA 94123-4607 Office: First Republic Bank 111 Pine St San Francisco CA 94111-5602

AUGUSTINE, ROSEMARY, vocational counselor, writer; b. Millville, N.J., Sept. 2, 1950; d. Ernest and Rose (O'Brien) A. Adminstrv. Cert., Peirce Coll., Phila., 1969. Exec. sec. Wheaton Industries, Millville, N.J., 1969-71; sec. Sports Conf. USAF, Ramstein, Germany, 1973; vocat. rehab. sec. Leesburg (N.J.) State Prison, 1974-75; adminstrv. asst. 20th Century Fox Film Corp., L.A., 1976-79; asst. to CFO Minoco So. Corp., L.A., 1980-82; divsn. adminstrv. mgr. Integrated Resources, Denver, 1982-86; mgr. investor rels. Intercap Monitoring, Denver, 1987-90; writer, publisher, owner Blue Spruce Publ. Co., Denver, 1991—; career coach, author pvt. practice, Denver, 1990—. Trainer Career Transition Ctrs., Colo., 1994—; founder www.careeradvice.com., 1996—. Author: Facing Changes in Employment, 1995, How to Live and Work Your Passion (and still earn a living), 2000, (newsletter) Career StrateGems, 1991—. Assoc. mem. Colo. Women's Leadership Coalition, Denver, 1995—; weekly facilitator Career Connection Network, Denver, 1996—. Recipient 1st pl. writing and design Small Bus. Rev., Denver, 1993. Mem. Denver Bus. Women's Network (bd. dirs., newsletter editor, 1995-96), Colo. Ind. Publs. Assn. (bd. dirs., pub. rels. 1995-96), Internet C. of C., Am. Soc. Tng. and Devel. Avocations: walking, hiking, biking, fishing. Office: Blue Spruce Pub Co Inc PO Box 24938 Denver CO 80224-0938

AUH, YANG JOHN, librarian, educational administrator; b. Chulla Namdo, Korea, Mar. 18, 1934; came to U.S., 1962, naturalized, 1971; s. Sam Hyuck and So Yae (Suh) A.; m. Karen Kyung-ja Kim, Mar. 11, 1969; 1 child, Alice Kim. BA, Chung-ang U., 1957; MA in LS, Western Mich. U., 1964; Cert. in Libr. Adminstrn. Devel., U. Md., 1973; Cert. in Advanced Librarianship, Columbia U., 1975; Cert. in Mgmt., Clarkson U., 1978; MBA, St. John's U., 1979; postgrad., NYU, 1996, Oxford (Eng.) U., 1997. Asst. libr. Korean Nat. Libr., Seoul, 1957; tech. svcs. libr. Korean Mil. Acad. Libr., Seoul, 1958-61; asst. libr. Branch County Libr., Coldwater, Mich., 1964; head union catalog L.I. U. Librs., Greenvale, N.Y., 1965-68; head catalog dept., tech. svcs. coord. Wagner Coll. Libr., S.I., N.Y., 1968-71, libr. dir., 1972-84, dir. Libr. and Learning Resources Ctr., 1984-2000; dir. Internat. Exch. program Wagner Coll., S.I., N.Y., 2000—; vis. prof. Chung-Ang U., Seoul, 2000—; pres. Highland Realty Mgmt., 1984—; dean internat. study & program Daebul U., Mokpo, Republic of Korea, 2001—. Evaluator, Commn. Higher Edn., Middle States Assn. Colls. and Schs., 1984; trustee Am. Friends of Chung-ang U., 1979—, vis. prof., 2000—; dean internat. study and program Daebul U., Mokpo, Korea, 2001—; life dep. gov., bd. govs. Am. Biographical Inst., Inc., Raleigh, N.C., 1998—; adv. coun. Internat. Biographical Ctr., Cambridge, Eng., 1999—. Fellow, HEW, 1973, 1978. Mem. ALA, N.Y. State Libr. Assn., Korean Libr. Assn., N.Y. Librs. Club, Omicron Delta Kappa (chpt. admintrv. mem. 1995). Office: Wagner Coll Horrmann Libr One Campus Rd Staten Island NY 10301-4428

AUKLAND, ELVA DAYTON, retired biologist, educator; b. Arlington, Va., Apr. 25, 1922; d. William A. and Helen Gertrude (Rollins) Dayton; m. Merrill Forrest Aukland, June 18, 1949; children: Bruce Michael, Duncan Dayton, Rebecca Elizabeth. AB cum laude, Wheaton Coll., 1943; MS, U. Minn., 1946. Teaching asst. U. Minn., 1943-46; instr. botany Ohio Wesleyan U., Del., 1946-49; instr. zoology and microbiology Ohio U., Athens, 1949-50; bacteriologist E.R. Squibb & Sons, New Brunswick, N.J., 1951-53; tchr., chmn. sci. dept. Washington-Lee High Sch., Arlington, 1962-78; tchr. T.C. Williams High Sch., Alexandria, Va., 1978-87, biology coordinator, 1980-85; lectr. biology Marymount U., 1987—; dir. Insect Zoo, Smithsonian Instn., 1972, Va. Sci. Talent Search, 1980-82; ret., 1994. Editor sci. tchrs. sect. Va. Jour. Sci., 1971-76. Commr. Arlington Parks and Recreation Commn., 1971-77; mem. Environ. Improvement Commn. Arlington County, 1977-83; mem. Arlington Com. of 100, Com. for Housing in Arlington; bd. dirs. No. Va. Conservation Council. Named Outstanding Tchr. Sci. and Math., Washington Acad. Sci., 1966; exec. bd. Arlington United Way, 1989-92; mem. exec. com. Com. on Housing in Arlington. Mem. LWV, Nat. Assn. Biology Tchrs., Va. Jr. Acad. Sci. (bd. dirs., Outstanding Tchr. award 1975), Nat. Sci. Tchrs. Assn., NEA, Arlington Edn. Assn., Va. Edn. Assn. (task force on quality in edn. 1983-86), Audubon Soc., Delta Kappa Gamma, Phi Theta Kappa. Home: 69 S Dogwood Trl Southern Shores NC 27949

AULD, JAMES S. educational psychologist; Grad., U. Nebr. Cert. sch. counselor, profl. counselor. Dir. testing, asst. prof.; K-12 dir. guidance; kindergarten-12 dir. psychol. svcs. Author: Real Personality. Mem. APA, AACD, ASCD, Can. Psychol. Assn., Nebr. Profl. Counselors, Gold Key, Nat. Disting. Svc. Registry for Counselors, Phi Delta Kappa. Office: PO Box 6228 Lincoln NE 68506-0228

AULD, ROBERT HENRY, JR., biomedical engineer, educator, consultant, author; b. Akron, Ohio, Sept. 19, 1942; s. Robert Henry Sr. and Elsie Mae (Rollans) A.; children: Sheila Kay, Jason Craig; stepson: Christopher William Weiss. BSBA, Biomed. Engr., U. San Francisco, 1978. Registered profl. egnr., calif.; cert. clin. engr. Reg. svc. mgr. scientific products div. AHSC, Sunnyvale, Calif., 1963-68; founder, gen. mgr. Lab. Instrument Svc., Campbell, Calif., 1968-77; nat. mgr. Biomed. Svcs. Group Pilot Project Honeywell, Inc., Denver, 1977-79; internship Stanford U. Med. Ctr., 1976, UCSF, 1978; profl. engr. Robert Auld Enterprises, San Jose, Calif., 1979-86; dir. clin. engring. St. Louis Reg. Med. Ctr., 1987-89; engring. mgr. Robert Auld Engring.-West, Imperial, Mo., 1989—, biomedical engr. cons. Santee, Calif., 1989—; nat. svc. mgr. R.C. Network, Cleveland, OH, 1990-99; expert examiner State of Calif. Bd. Registration for Profl. Engrs., Sacramento, 1995-99. Seminar dir. ASMT, Phoenix AZ., 1968-79; instrument workshop seminar coordinator, Stanford U. Med. Ctr., 1980-84; engring. advisor St. Louis Reg. Career Access Ctr., 1987-89, U. Mo., Rolla and St. Louis. Author: The Clone Factory (A True Story About Police), 1992; contbr. articles to profl. jours. Del. at large Rep. Legion of Merit, Imperial, MO., 1990-93; apptd. hazardous waste com., State of Mo., 1988-90. With USN, 1959-61. Recipient Disting. Leadership award Am. Biographical Inst., Raleigh, N.C., 1988, 94, Golden Spike award, Calif., 1986. Mem. N.Y. Acad. Scis., IEEE, Am. Soc. Hosp. Engrs., NSPE, Mo. Soc. Profl. Engrs. (chmn. 1988-89, chmn. minority Math Counts pilot project 1987-89), Order Demolay (life). Republican. Achievements include development of device for equilibrating gases in a liquid or blood for measurement of gases in blood; patent pending for dual halogen colormetric light source; Innovator "Single Source Service", "Parts Banks" for Clinical Equipment for Health Care Facilities. Home: 3526 Fairmount Ave Apt 1006 San Diego CA 92105-3492 Office: Robert Auld Engring West 3526 Fairmount Ave Ste 1006 San Diego CA 92105-3492 E-mail: robertauld@juno.com., redwood2c2@aol.com.

AULT, ETHYL LORITA, special education educator, consultant; b. Bklyn., May 30, 1939; d. Albert Nichols Fadden and Marion Cecil (Corrigan) Snow; (div.); children: Debra Marie Ault Butenko, Milinda Lei Jones, Timothy Scott. BS, Ga. State U., MEd, 1976, cert. in spl. edn. 6th yr., 1984. Tchr. spl. edn. Butts County Sch. System, Jackson, Ga., 1972-73, Rockdale County Sch. System, Conyers, Ga., 1973-75, lead tchr., 1975-77; cons. spl. edn. Newton County Sch. System, Covington, Ga., 1977-79; curriculum specialist spl. edn. La Grange (Ga.) Sch. System, 1979-83, dir. spl. edn., 1983-94, dir. accredited studies curriculum, 1994—, dir. student svcs., 1995—; collaboration process trainer State of Ga., 1990—, dir. student svcs./spl. program, 1996-2000; fine arts cons. Troup County Schs., 2001—. Instr. La Grange Coll., 1984-97, assoc. prof., 1997—; mem. Tchr. Competency Testing Commn., Atlanta, 1988—, Task Force Documentation and Decision Making, Atlanta, 1988—. Contbg. editor: (manual) Mainstream Modification Handbook, 1989. Chairperson Jud. Adv. Panel, LaGrange, 1988; bd. dirs. Crawford Tng. Ctr. Adv. Panel, La Grange, 1985—; pres. West Ga. Youth Coun. Bd., La Grange, 1980—; mem. State Adv. Panel for Spl. Edn.; bd. dirs. Troup County Hist. Soc., 1999—; mem. State of Ga. Task Force on Alt. Edn., 1998—. Mem. Coun. Exceptional Children, Ga. Assn. Edn. Leaders, Ga. Assn. Curriculum and Instrn. Supervision, Ga. Coun. Adminstrs. Spl. Edn. (v.p. 1988—, pres.-elect 1989, pres. 1992—, Gifted State Task Force 1994—), La Grange Women's Club (v.p. 1989—), Profl. Assn. Ga. Spl. Educators (Adminstr. of Yr. 1993), Ga. Supporters of the Gifted, Nat. Assn. for Gifted Edn., Ga. Assn. for Gifted Students (pres.-elect 2000-2001), Kiwanis Club LaGrange (pres.-elect 1999-2000, pres. 2000-01), Phi Delta Kappa (pres. 2000-2001), Lafayette Soc. Arts (bd. dirs., v.p.). Democrat. Episcopalian. Avocations: swimming, fishing, walking, gardening. Home: 441 Gordon Cir Lagrange GA 30240-2621 Office: LaGrange Coll Board St Lagrange GA 30240

AURILIA, ANTONIO, physicist, educator; b. Napoli, Italy, May 14, 1942; came to U.S., 1967, naturalized, 1993; s. Clemente and Assunta (Ligesto) A.; m. Elizabeth Christine Adams, Dec. 1, 1972; children: Darius Matthew, Alexandra Rebecca. Laurea in Physics, U. Naples, Italy, 1966; PhD in Physics, U. Wis., Milw., 1970. Postdoctoral fellow dept. physics U. Alta., Edmonton, 1970-72; rsch. assoc. dept. physics Syracuse (N.Y.) U., 1972-74; rsch. scientist Internat. Ctr. Theoretical Physics, Trieste, Italy, 1974-75, Nat. Inst. Nuclear Physics, Trieste, 1975-86; prof. dept. physics Calif. State Poly. U., Pomona, 1986—. Mem. Am. Phys. Soc., Am. Assn. Physics Tchrs., N.Y. Acad. Sci., Sigma Xi. Democrat. Roman Catholic. Achievements include research in theoretical physics. Office: Calif State U Dept Physics 3801 W Temple Ave Pomona CA 91768-2557

AUSMAN, JAMES I. neurosurgeon, educator; b. Milw., Dec. 10, 1937; s. Donald C. and Mildred G. A.; m. Carolyn R. Ausman, June 30, 1960; children: Elizabeth, Susan. BS, Tufts U., 1955—59; MD, Johns Hopkins U., 1959—63; MA, SUNY-Buffalo, 1964; PAD, George Washington U., 1969. Cert. Bd. cert. neurosurgery 1974. Asst. prof. neurosurgery and pharmacology U. Minn., 1972—; chmn. dept. neurosurgery Henry Ford Hosp., Detroit, 1978—; prof. neurosurgery U. Mich., Ann Arbor, 1978—; prof., head dept. neurosurgery U. Ill., Chgo., 1991—2001, prof. neurosurgery,

2001—. Bd. dirs. Somanetics Corp., Detroit, 1993—. Editor: (jour.) Surg. Neurology, 1994—. Lt. col. USPHS. Mem.: Columbian Neurosurgery Soc. (hon.), Turkish Neurosurgery Soc. (hon.), French Speaking Neurosurgery Soc. (hon.), Argentine Neurosurgery Soc. (hon.), Brazil Neurosurg. Soc. (hon.), German Neurosurg. Soc. (hon.), Peru Neurosurg. Soc. (hon.), Japan Neurosurg. Soc. (hon.). Home: 70-950 Fairway Dr Rancho Mirage CA 92270

AUSTEN, K(ARL) FRANK, internist, educator; b. Akron, Ohio, Mar. 14, 1928; s. Karl and Bertle (Jehle) Austen; m. Joycelyn Chapman, Apr. 11, 1959; children: Leslie Marie, Karla Ann, Timothy Frank, Jonathan Arthur. AB, Amherst Coll., 1950; MD, Harvard U., 1954. Intern in medicine Mass. Gen. Hosp., 1954—55, asst. resident, 1955—56, sr. resident, 1958—59, chief resident, 1961, asst. in medicine, 1962—63, asst. physician, 1963—66, chief pulmonary unit, 1964—66, also cons. in medicine; practice medicine, specializing in internal medicine, allergy and immunology, 1962—66; USPHS postdoctoral research fellow Nat. Inst. Med. Research, Mill Hill, London, 1959—61; asst. in medicine Harvard Med. Sch., 1961, instr., 1961—62, asso. in medicine, 1962—64, asst. prof., 1965—66, assoc. prof., 1966—68, prof., 1969—72, Theodore B. Bayles prof., 1972—; physician-in-chief Robert B. Brigham Hosp., Boston, 1966—80; chmn. dept. rheumatology and immunology Brigham and Women's Hosp., Boston, 1980—95, dir. lab. inflammation and allergic disease rsch. sect., 1995—. Mem. fellowship subcom. Arthritis Found., 1968—71, chmn., 1971; mem. coun. Infectious Disease Soc. Am., 1969—71; mem. arthritis tng. grants com. Nat. Inst. Arthritis and Metabolic Diseases, NIH, 1970—73; NHLB adv. coun., 1994—; mem. directing group, task force on immunology and disease Nat. Inst. Allergy and Infectious Diseases, 1972—73; bd. dirs. Arthritis Found., 1972—75, chmn. manpower study com., 1972—73, chmn. rsch. com. Multipurpose Arth. Ctr., 1972—76; chmn. rsch. com. Med. Found., Inc., 1972—76; mem. Am. Bd. Allergy and Immunology, 1973—78, Nat. Commn. on Arthritis and Related Musculoskeletal Diseases, 1975—76, Allergy and Immunology Rsch. com., NIAID, 1975—79, chmn., 1976—79; chmn. nomenclature com. Internat. Union Immunol. Socs., 1983—; mem. adv. com. to the dir. NIH, 1986—90, mem. nat. heart, lung and blood adv. com., 1966—80. Mem. editl. bd.: Arthritis and Rheumatism, 1968—81, Proc. of Transplantation Soc., 1968—82, Jour. Infectious Diseases, 1969—79, Jour. Exptl. Medicine, 1971—, Immunol. Comm., 1972—85, Clin. Immunology and Immunopathology, 1972—89, Proc. of NAS, 1978—83, Clin. and Exptl. Immunology, 1978—88, Internat. Jour. Immunopharmacology, 1984, Advances in Immunology, 1985—, Advances in Pharmacology, 1989—; contbr. articles to profl. jours. Trustee Amherst Coll., 1981—. Capt. M.C. U.S. Army, 1956—58. Recipient Warren Alpert Found. prize, 1999. Mem.: ACP, NAS (chmn. sect. on med. microbiology and immunology 1983—86), Internat. Soc. Immunopharmacology (pres. 1994), Internat. Assn. Allergology and Clin. Immunology, Fedn. Am. Soc. Exptl. Biology, Am. Acad. Allergy and Immunology (exec. com. 1970—72, sec. 1977—80, pres. 1981), Assn. Am. Physicians (recorder 1978—84, pres. 1989—90), Am. Acad. Arts and Scis., Transplantation Soc., Am. Rheumatism Assn., Am. Soc. Clin. Investigation, Brit. Soc. Immunology, Am. Assn. Immunologists (pres. 1977—78), Am. Soc. Exptl. Pathology, Am. Soc. Pharm. and Exptl. Therapeutics, Inst. Medicine, Interurban Clin. Club. Office: BWH Dept Rhem & Allergy Smith Bldg 55 Francis St Boston MA 02115-6105

AUSTER, CAROL JEAN, sociology educator; b. Bloomington, Ind., Mar. 2, 1954; d. Donald and Nancy Eileen (Ross) Auster; m. Stanley A. Mertzman; children: Lauren Jean, Lisa Amy. AB in Social Rels., Colgate U., 1976; MA in Sociology, Princeton U., 1979, PhD in Sociology, 1984. Instr. sociology Franklin and Marshall Coll., Lancaster, Pa., 1981-84, asst. prof., 1984-88, assoc. prof., 1988-96, prof., 1996—, acting chair dept., 1982-83, chair dept., 1988—91, 1999—2004. NSF rsch. assoc. N.H. Coll., Manchester, 1974, Hampshire Coll., Amherst, Mass., 1975; cons. dept. planning Lancaster (Pa.) Gen. Hosp., 1984—. Author: The Sociology of Work: Concepts and Cases, 1996; contbr. articles, revs. to profl. jours. N.Y. State Regents scholar Colgate U., 1976; Princeton U. fellow, 1977-80; Rockefeller Found. grantee U. Ill., 1979-80, Alfred P. Sloan Found. grantee, 1993-96. Mem.: AAUP (dist. VII rep. to nat. coun. 1986—89, com. F. on confs. 1986—92, memberships grants com. 1987—89, 2d v.p. 1990—92, chair com. B. on ethics 1994—2000), So. Sociol. Soc., Ea. Sociol. Soc., Sociologists for Women in Soc., Soc. for Study Social Problems, Am. Sociol. Assn. (com. on employment 1994—96). Office: Franklin and Marshall Coll Dept Sociology Lancaster PA 17604

AUSTERMAN, DONNA LYNNE, Spanish language educator; b. Colorado Springs, Colo., Aug. 5, 1947; d. Herman Raymond Ogg and Shirley (Cooper) Price; m. Thomas Lanham Brown, Jan. 26, 1966 (div. Jan. 1972); 1 child, Thomas Roy; m. Randy Lynn Austerman, Nov. 25, 1972; 1 child, Michael Neil. Student, Washburn U., 1965-67; BS, Pittsburg State U., 1970, MS, 1971; postgrad., U. Kans., 1980, U. Okla., 1983, Okla. State U., 1990. Cert. tchr. (life), Mo., std. tchr., Okla. Tchr. Spanish, English Liberal (Mo.) R-2 Schs., 1970-72, Unified Sch. Dist. 346, Mound City, Kans., 1972-74, Nowata (Okla.) Pub. Schs., 1983-86; tchr. Spanish Bartlesville (Okla) Sch. Dist. # 30, 1986—2001. Steering com. mem. North Ctrl. Assn., 1993—2001. Mem. NEA, ASCD, Am. Assn. Tchrs. Spanish and Portuguese, Nat. Staff Devel. Coun., Okla. Edn. Assn., Okla. Fgn. Lang. Tchrs. Assn., Bartlesville Edn. Assn., Bartlesville Fgn. Lang. Coun., Bartlesville Profl. Improvement Com. (chmn. mid-h.s. staff devel. com.). Avocations: travel, swimming, country and western dancing, old movies, reading. Home: 170 Desert Inn Way Colorado Springs CO 80921

AUSTIN, ALVIN O. academic administrator; b. Tampa, Fla., Jan. 6, 1942; BA, Westmont Coll., 1964; MA, Calif. State U., 1967; PhD, U. Miss., 1971. V.p. Hardin-Simmons U., 1970-75; dean of student programs Calif. State U., Northridge, 1975-78; v.p. Seattle Pacific U., 1978-83, North Park Coll., 1983-86; pres. LeTourneau U., Longview, Tex., 1986—. Chmn. bd. dirs. Good Shepherd Health Sys., bd coun.Christian Colls. and Univs. Office: LeTourneau U Office of the President PO Box 7001 Longview TX 75607-7001

AUSTIN, ELIZABETH RUTH, retired elementary school educator; b. Glendale, Calif., June 28, 1928; d. Lloyd Lewis Austin and Mary Elizabeth Berryman. BA, Scripps Coll., 1950; postgrad., Occidental Coll., 1950—51, UCLA, 1959, U. S.C., 1961, Orange State Coll., 1964, U. Calif., Santa Barbara, 1975. Admitting office clk. Hosp. Good Samaritan, L.A., 1976—93; elem. tchr. Alhambra, Calif., 1951—55, L.A., 1957—62, Newport Beach, Calif., 1962—65, San Marino, Calif., 1974—76; ret. Home: 1428 S Marengo Ave Alhambra CA 91803

AUSTIN, JANE STEWART, educator; b. Hartford, Ky., July 24, 1935; d. Leslie Andrew and Zula Mae (Howard) Stewart; m. Franklin D. Austin, Dec. 28, 1957; children: Elizabeth, Ellen. BA in Music Edn., Western Ky. U., 1957, MA in Edn., 1971. Cert. tchr., Ill. Tchr. music Kalamazoo Pub. Sch., Mich., 1957-58, tchr. English, 1959-62, Rockford Pub. Sch., Ill., 1967-70, tchr. music, 1970-72, 75-77, music cons., 1972-75, tchr. elem. edn., 1978—2000, tchr. social English, 2000—; tchr. English and social studies Rockford Luth. H.S., 2000—. Cons., clinician Dist./State Music Edn. Confs., Ill., 1972-75; co-organizer student exch. Students Worlds Apart Project, Rockford, 1987—. Co-coord. Books for South Africa, Rockford, 1989—. Mem. NEA, Rockford Edn. Assn. Avocations: sewing, drawing, music, handbells. Home: 3603 Cardinal Ln Rockford IL 61107-4803 Office: Rockford Luth HS 3411 N Alpine Rd Rockford IL 61114 E-mail: weverdell@earthlink.net.

AUSTIN, JOHN RILEY, surgeon, educator; b. St. Louis, Feb. 19, 1960; s. Thomas L. and Barbara (Riley) A.; m. Sara Beth Goehringer, May 16, 1987; children: Claire Frances, Emily Grace, John Michael. BS with highest honors, U. Wyo., 1982; MD, U. Utah, 1986. Diplomate Am. Bd. Facial Plastic and Reconstructive Surgery, Am. Bd. Otolaryngolgy, Nat. Bd. Med. Examiners. Surg. intern U. So. Calif., L.A. County Med. Ctr., L.A., 1986-87, resident otolarynogology, head and neck surgery dept., 1987-91; fellow in head and neck surg. oncology M.D. Anderson Cancer Ctr. M.D. Anderson Cancer Ctr. U. Tex., Houston, 1991-92; asst. surgeon, clin. instr. U. Tex., Houston, 1992-93; asst. prof., asst. surgeon M.D. Anderson Cancer Ctr. U. Tex., Houston, 1993-95, clin. asst. prof., 1995—; adj. asst. prof. dept. otorhinolaryngology/comm. disorders Baylor Coll. Medicine, 1993-95. Otolaryngologic cons. dept. infectious diseases U. So. Calif., 1988-91; mem. utilization com. M.D. Anderson Cancer Ctr., U.Tex., 1993-95, mem. laser com., 1993-95; presenter in field. Cons. editor Head and Neck, Laryngoscope, Otolaryngology-Head and Neck Surgery, Cancer, 1993—, Archives of Otolaryngology; contbr. articles to profl. jours. Mem. Graduate Edn. com. U. Tex., 1994. Fellow ACS, Am. Acad. Otolaryngology (human resource com.), AMA, Am. Acad. Facial Plastic and Reconstructive Surgery (mem. publs. com.), Tex. Med. Assn. (mem. physician oncology edn. program 1993—, mem. com. cancer 1993—), M.D. Anderson Assocs., Soc. Univ. Otolaryngologists, N.Am. Skull Base Soc., Tex. Assn. Otolaryngology, Sir Charles Bell Soc. (founding), Travis County Med. Soc. (jour. com.), Salerni Colegium, Phi Kappa Phi, Phi Beta Kappa, Sigma Nu. Methodist. Avocations: photography, fishing, golfing, skiing, reading. Office: 3705 Medical Pkwy Ste 310 Austin TX 78705-1028

AUSTIN, LINDA R. COMPTON, elementary education educator; b. Mishawaka, Ind., July 11, 1948; d. Thomas F. and Dorothy Jane (Smith) Compton; m. Paul V. Austin, June 1973; children: Alisa Jayne, Jennifer Lynn. BS, U. Indpls., 1971, MA, 1975; master tchr. cert., Calif. State U., Sacramento. Cert. elem. tchr. Ind., Calif. Intermediate tchr. Mishawaka (Ind.) City Schs., Mooresville (Ind.) Consol. Schs.; primary and kindergarten tchr. Rio Linda (Calif.) Union Sch. Dist.; assoc. faculty, student tchr. supr. U. Indpls.; student tchr. supr. Purdue U. Facilitator sch. family math. program Rio Linda Union Sch. Dist., Calif. Mem.: INAEE, ATE, ASCD.

AUSTIN, MARGARET CULLY, school administrator; b. St. Louis, July 18, 1930; d. Ben Allen and Rosalie Ada (Mersman) Cully; m. June 19, 1954; children: Steven W., Katherine E., Andrea C. AA in Music, Motlow State C.C., Tullahoma, Tenn., 1973; BS in Elem. Edn., Mid. Tenn. State U., 1975, MEd in Reading, 1979; Cert. in Adminstrn., Trevecca Coll., Nashville, 1989. Elem. music tchr. St. Paul the Apostle Sch., Tullahoma, Tenn., 1969-73; teaching prin. Normandy Sch., Bedford County, Tenn., 1975-76; reading specialist Bedford County Schs., 1976-88, Chpt. I cons. tchr., 1989-94, supr. title I/fed. projects, 1994—, testing coord., 1994-97, reading cons. spl. edn., 1994—, supr. migrant edn./ESL programs, 1996—. Mem. NEA, Tenn. Edn. Assn., Bedford County Edn. Assn., Internat. Reading Assn., Tenn. Supr. of Edn. Assn. Avocations: reading, music, computers. Home: 601 Crestwood Dr Tullahoma TN 37388-2929 Office: Bedford County Bd of Edn 500 Madison St Shelbyville TN 37160-3341

AUSTIN, ROBERTA JONES, elementary school educator; b. Clearwater, Fla., July 28, 1930; d. Wallace Theodore and Eloise (Knight) Jones; m. Ned Payne Austin, Oct. 18, 1952; children: David, Robin, Samuel, Frances, Genevieve, Laura. BS in Pub. Sch. Music, Queens Coll., Charlotte, N.C., 1952; postgrad. Sch. Edn., U. Colo., 1962-64; MA in Adminstrn. and Supervision, Appalachian State U., 1981. Cert. elem. and music tchr., sch. adminstr., N.C. Tchr. music grades 7 and 8 Denver Pub. Schs., 1961-62, tchr. grade 6, 1970-71; tchr. music grades 1 through 6 Adams County Sch. Dist. 12, Northglenn, Colo., 1962-63, elem. tchr., 1963-70; tchr. Playhouse Presch., L.A., 1972; elem. tchr. Watauga County Schs., Boone, N.C., 1973-97; retired, 1997; home sch. dir., tchr., 1998-99. Chairperson curriculum com. Adams County Sch. Dist. 12, 1965-70; chairperson/liaison calendar com. Watauga County Schs., 1975-80, instr. writing workshop for tchrs., 1982, 86, 90, 92; dir. after-sch. program and cmty. sch. Hardin Pk. Sch., Boone, 1980-85. Editor: (compilation of children's writings) Out of Our Children's Minds, 1967, (compilation of tchr.'s writings) In the Shadow of Howard's Knob, 1990. Com. woman Dem. Precinct, Denver, 1968-71, pres., Boone, N.C., 1999—; vol. coord. Summer Youth Employment Program, Denver, 1969; active Boone chpt. N.C. Ctr. for Internat. Understanding, 1993—, Blue Ridge Cmty. Theatre, 1979—; tutor, coord. ESL program High Country Amigos, Boone, 2000—; treas. Boone Unitarian Universalist Fellowship, 2000-2002, v.p., 2002-2003, pres., 2003-2004, choir dir., 2000—; pres. Parents, Family, and Friends of Lesbians and Gays of Boone, 2001—03; pres. Boone Unitarian Universalist Fellowship, 2003—. Recipient trip to Russia, named N.C. Tchr. of the World, Children's Mus. About the World, Raleigh, N.C., 1993. Mem. NEA, N.C. Edn. Assn. (faculty rep. 1973—), Internat. Friendship Link. Avocations: music, drama, reading, writing. Home: 1561 Winklers Creek Rd Boone NC 28607-8904

AUSTIN, SAM M. physics educator; b. Columbus, Wis., June 6, 1933; s. A. Wright and Mildred G. (Reinhard) A.; m. Mary E. Herb, Aug. 15, 1959; children: Laura Gail, Sara Kay. BS in Physics, U. Wis., 1955, MS, 1957, PhD, 1960. Rsch. assoc. U. Wis., Madison, 1960; NSF postdoctoral fellow Oxford U., Eng., 1960-61; asst. prof. Stanford U., Calif., 1961-65; assoc. prof. physics Mich. State U., East Lansing, 1965-69, prof., 1969-90, univ. disting. prof., 1990-2000, univ. disting. prof. emeritus, 2000—, chmn. dept., 1980-83, acting dean Coll. Natural Sci., 1994, assoc. dir. Cyclotron Lab., 1976-79, rsch. dir., 1983-85, co-dir., 1985-89, dir., 1989-92. Guest Niels Bohr Inst., 1970; guest prof. U. Munich, 1972-73; sci. collaborator Saclay and Lab. Rene Bernas, 1979-80; vis. scientist Triumf-U. B.C., 1993-94; invited prof. U. Paris, Orsay, 1996; mem. grant selection com. for sub-atomic physics, NSERC (Can.), 1996-99; mem. com. on nuc. physics NRC, 1996-99; mem. steering com. Nuc. Physics Summer Sch.; mem. internat. adv. com. and exec. com. NSF Joint Inst. for Nuc. Astrophysics, 2003—. Author, editor: The Two Body Force in Nuclei, 1972, The (p,n) Reaction and Nucleon-Nucleon Force, 1980; editor Phys. Rev. C, 1988-2002, Virtual Jour. Nuclear Astrophysics; assoc. editor Atomic Data and Nuc. Data Tables, 1990—. Fellow NSF, 1960-61, Alfred P. Sloan Found., 1963-66; recipient Mich. Assn. of Governing Bds. Disting. Prof., 1992. Fellow AAAS (chair nominating com.), Am. Phys. Soc. (vice chmn. nuc. physics divsn. 1981-82, chmn. 1982-83, exec. com. 1983-84, 86-89, coun. 1986-89, coun. exec. com. 1987-88, panel on pub. affairs 1996-98); mem. APS, Sigma Xi (Sr. rsch. award 1977). Achievements include research in nuclear physics, nuclear astrophysics and nitrogen fixation. Home: 1201 Woodwind Trl Haslett MI 48840-8994 Office: Mich State U Nat Supercondr Cyclotron Lab East Lansing MI 48824 E-mail: austin@nscl.msu.edu.

AUSTIN, SANDRA IKENBERRY, nurse educator, consultant; b. Lexington, Va., Dec. 22, 1941; d. William Peters and June Virginia (Blackwell) Ikenberry; m. Joseph M. Austin, Apr. 10, 1965; children: Joseph M. Jr., Susan C., Christopher M. BSN, U. Va., 1963; MSN, U. Calif., L.A., 1967; EdD, U. Mass., 1997. RN, Mass. Pub. health nurse Dept. Health, Waynesboro, Va., 1963-64; instr. U. Va., Charlottesville, 1964-65; staff nurse Santa Monica (Calif.) Hosp., 1965-66; faculty nursing Boston U., 1968-69, Quinsigamond C.C., Worcester, Mass., 1969-70, Fitchburg (Mass.) State Coll., 1973-96; assoc. prof. nursing Framingham (Mass.) State Coll., 1997—; project dir., sr. health edn. cons. HealthCo Consulting Inc., Shrewsbury, Mass., 1996—. Mem. Shrewsbury Town Meeting, 1992—95; chair steering com. Framingham State Coll. Nursing Honor Soc., 1998, faculty counselor/advisor, 1999, pres., 1999—2002. HBO and Co. Nurse scholar, 1995. Mem.: Assn. Critical Care Nurses, Nat. League Nursing (awards com. 1999—2001), Assn. Women's Health, Obstet. and Neonatal Nurses, Am. Ednl. Rsch. ASsn., Sigma Theta Tau (Epsilon Beta edn. chair 1993—95, Rho Phi chpt. pres. 2002—, rsch. grant 1996), Pi Lambda Theta. Republican. Congregationalist. Avocations: computer multimedia production, reading, walking. Home: 100 Harrington Farms Way Shrewsbury MA 01545-4081 Office: Framingham State Coll Nursing Dept Framingham MA 01701

AUSTON, DAVID HENRY, former academic administrator, electrical engineer, educator; b. Toronto, Ont., Can., Nov. 14, 1940; arrived in U.S., 1963; BS, U. Toronto, 1962, MS, 1963; PhD, U. Calif., Berkeley, 1969. Rsch. physicist GM, Santa Barbara, Calif., 1963—66; tech. staff AT&T Bell Labs., Murray Hill, NJ, 1969—82, head dept., 1982—87; former prof. Columbia U., N.Y.C., 1987—90, chmn. elec. engring. dept., 1990, dean sch. engring. and applied sci., 1991—94; provost Rice U., Houston, 1994—99; pres. Case Western Res. U., Cleve., 1999—2002, Kavli Found. and The Kavli Inst., Oxnard, Calif. Author 1 book; contbr. scientific papers. Fellow: IEEE (Quantum Elecs. award 1990, Morris E. Leeds award 1991), Am. Phys. Soc., Am. Acad. Arts and Scis., Optical Soc. Am. (R.W. Wood prize 1985); mem.: NAE, Nat. Acad. Scis. Achievements include patents in field of 7. Office: The Kavli Inst 1801 Solar Dr Ste 250 Oxnard CA 93030

AUSTRIAN, ROBERT, physician, educator, department chairman; b. Balt., Apr. 12, 1916; s. Charles Robert and Florence (Hochschild) Austrian; m. Babette Friedmann Bernstein, Dec. 29, 1963; stepchildren: Jill Bernstein, Toni Bernstein. AB, Johns Hopkins U., 1937, MD, 1941; DSc (hon.), Hahnemann Med. Coll., 1980, Phila. Coll. Pharmacy and Sci., 1981, U. Pa., 1987; DSc (hon.), SUNY, 1996. Diplomate Am. Bd. Internal Medicine. House officer Johns Hopkins Hosp., 1941—50, asst. dir. med. out-patient dept., 1951—52; assoc. prof. medicine, then prof. medicine SUNY Coll. Medicine, 1952—62; John Herr Musser prof., chmn. rsch. medicine U. Pa. Sch. Medicine, 1962—86, prof. emeritus, chmn. emeritus, 1986—. Attending physician Hosp. U. Pa.; Tyndale vis. lectr. and prof. Coll. Medicine U. Utah, 1964; spl. rsch. on infectious diseases, bacterial genetics; mem. Meningococcal Infections Commn., 1964—72, Commn. on Acute Respiratory Disease, 1965—72, Commn. Streptococcal and Staphylococcal Diseases, 1970—72, Armed Forces Epidemiol. Bd.; cons. surg. gen. U.S. Army R&D Command, 1966—69; mem. subcom. streptococcus and pneumococcus Internat. Com. Bacteriol. Nomenclature; mem. allergy and immunology study sect. Nat. Inst. Allergy and Infectious Diseases, 1965—69, mem. bd. sci. counselors, 1967—70, chmn., 1969—70; mem. WHO Expert Adv. Panel Acute Bacterial Diseases, 1979—2001. Mem. editl. bd.: Jour. Bacteriology, 1964—69, Am. Rev. Respiratory Diseases, 1963—66, Bacteriol. Rev., 1967—71, Jour. Infectious Diseases, 1969—74, Antimicrobial Agents and Chemotherapy, 1972—86, Infection and Immunity, 1973—81, Revs. of Infectious Diseases, 1979—89, Vaccine, 1983—, guest editor: Drugs and Aging, 1999. Trustee Johns Hopkins U., 1963—69. Capt. M.C. U.S. Army, 1943—46. Recipient U.S. Typhus Commn. medal, 1947, Albert Lasker Clin. Med. Rsch. award, 1978, Phila. award, 1979, Willard O. Thompson award, Am. Geriatric Soc., 1981, Lifetime Sci. award, Inst. Advanced Studies in Immunology and Aging, 1997, Pasteur Merieux MSD award, 1st Internat. Symposium on Pneumococci and Pneumococcal Diseases, 1998, Maxwell Finland award for sci. achievement, Nat. Found. for Infectious Diseases, 2001. Master: ACP (James D. Bruce Meml. award 1979); fellow: AAAS (chmn. sect. on med. scis. 1975), Am. Acad. Microbiology, N.Y. Acad. Scis.; mem.: NAS, Johns Hopkins Soc. Scholars, Infectious Disease Soc. Am. (pres. 1971, Maxwell Finland lecture award 1974, Bristol award 1986), Coll. Physicians Phila. (pres.-elect 1986, pres. 1988—89, Meritorious Svc. award 1980, Disting. Svc. medal 1997), Phila. County Med. Soc. (Strittmatter award 1979), N.Y. Acad. Medicine (sec. sect. microbiology 1961—62), Am. Assn. Immunologists, Balt. Med. Soc., Inst. Medicine, Am. Fedn. Clin. Rsch., Harvey Soc., Soc. Exptl. Biology and Medicine, Am. Philos. Soc., Am. Soc. Microbiology (v.p. N.Y. br. 1961—62), Am. Clin. and Climatol. Assn. (pres. 1984), Am. Soc. Clin. Investigation, Assn. Am. Physicians, 14 W. Hamilton St. Club (Balt.) (Balt.), Interurban Clin. Club (pres. 1970), Omicron Delta Kappa, Alpha Omega Alpha, Sigma Xi, Phi Beta Kappa. Office: U Pa Sch Medicine Dept Rsch Medicine 522 Johnson Pavilion Philadelphia PA 19104-6088

AUTEN, ARTHUR HERBERT, history educator; b. Cleve., Dec. 25, 1936; s. Herbert and Gladys Perry (Sessions) A.; m. Patricia Ann Kichak, June 5, 1971; children: David Arthur, Daniel Joseph. AB magna cum laude, Case Western Res. U., 1959, MA, 1960, PhD, 1965; cert. ednl. mgmt., Harvard U., 1972, CAS, 1977. Instr., asst. prof. history Westminster Coll., New Wilmington, Pa., 1963-66; asst. prof. history Colo. State U., Ft. Collins, 1966—69; v.p. planning, devel. and evaluation, dean Arts & Scis., U. Guam, Agana, 1970—76; pres. Alliance Coll., Cambridge Springs, Pa., 1977-81; acad. dean Coll. Basic Studies, U. Hartford, West Hartford, Conn., 1981-87, prof. history, 1987—2002. Sec. Pa. region 9/10 HIgher Edn. Planning Coun., 1979—80; vis. scholar Grad. Sch. Edn., Harvard U., 1988, prof. emeritus, 2002. Author: Critical Thinking Exercises for Western Civilization Courses, 1993, Readings in the History of Western Civilization: From the Dawn of Civilization to Columbus, From Columbus to Napoleon, From Napoleon to the Space Age, 1996; adv. editor Ann. Edits.: Am. History, 12th edit., 1993, 13th edit., 1995, 14th edit., 1997, 15th edit., 1999, 16th edit., 2001, 17th edit., 2002, Ann. Edits.: Western Civilization, 6th edit., 1991, 7th edit., 1993, 8th edit., 1995, 9th edit., 1997, 10th edit., 1999, 11th edit., 2001, 12th edit., 2002, World Civilization: A Brief History, 2d edit., 1993, 3d edit., 1998, A History of Civilization, 9th edit., 1995, Discovering the Western Past, 3d edit., 1995, Sources of the West, 3d edit., 1996. Cmty. devel. assistance com. City/Colls./Bus. Partnership, Meadville, Pa., 1980; mem. ednl. svcs. for cmty. devel., Guam Terr., 1972-76; spkr., events planner Kiwanis, Cambridge Springs, Pa., 1978-81; mem. Nat. Trust for Hist. Preservation. Recipient Hon. Membership pin, Polish Nat. Alliance, 1980, Cmty. Svc. citation, Mayor of Meadville, 1980, Ann. Svc. award, Gov. of Guam, 1976, Hon. Jagiellonian U. pin, Internat. Student Exch., 1979, Outstanding Educators Am. award, 1972, Tchg. Excellence designation, 1969; scholar U. Hartford scholar in humanities, 1997. Fellow: Phi Beta Kappa; mem.: New Eng. Hist. Assn., Am. Hist. Assn., Nat. Coun. Social Studies, Nat. Assn. Devel. Edn. (presenter, chair nat. conf. 1987, 1989—91, chmn. profl. interest group 1989—94, presenter, chair nat. conf. 1993, 1997, Dean's Recognition award 1986, cert. appreciation 1990, 1991, 1992), Orgn. Am. Historians (life Recognition award 1992), Mystic Seaport Mus. Am. and the Sea, Colonial Williamsburg Found., Phi Delta Kappa, Chi Omicron Gamma. Avocations: travel, theater, chess, model railroading, reading. Home: 17 Peddler Dr Windsor CT 06095-1748

AUTIN, ERNEST ANTHONY, II, chemist, educator, consultant; b. Thibodaux, La., Sept. 18, 1957; s. Ernest Anthony Autin and Louella Theresa (Foret) Matherne; m. Debra Anne Breaux; children: Daniel Joseph, Theresa Renee, Beau-Thomas Bryan. BS, Nicholls State U., 1979; MS, U. So. Miss., 1982; postgrad., Tulane U., 1986-87. Cert. master practitioner neuro-linguistic programming. Sr. rsch. chemist DAP, Inc., Dayton, Ohio, 1982-83; head chemistry dept. South Coast Sugars, Raceland, La., 1983-84; asst. prof. chemistry Nicholls State U., Thibodaux, 1984-90; dir. tng., internal orgnl. planning and devel. cons. Fina Oil & Chem. Co., Port Arthur, Tex., 1990-92, process/quality engr. La Porte, Tex., 1992-93; internal Orgnl. Planning and Devel. cons. Entergy Svcs., Inc., Beaumont, Tex., 1993-95; mgr., performance improvement and change mgmt. Ernst & Young, Houston, 1995-96; exec.-in-residence info. svcs. and info. techs. Temple-Inland, Inc., Diboll, Tex., 1995—. Faculty advisor Nicholls State U. Scis. Soc., 1984-90; sci. coord. COGNIS program Upward Bound, Thibodaux, 1984-90; cons. La. sugar cane industry, 1984-90, heavy metal analysis, 1984-90; sr. lead project mgr. Engring. Tech. Support Fossil Energy Bus. Support, Beaumont, 1994-95; speaker on motivational topics, 1985—. Contbr. articles to various publs. Music min. St. Thomas Aquinas Cath. Student Ctr., Thibodaux, 1984-90; bd. dirs. fed. credit union Nicholls State U., 1984-86; bd. dirs. Port Arthur (Tex.) YMCA, 1990-92, sustaining campaign chairperson, 1991-92. Recipient T.K.E. Grand Prytanis award, 1995, Grand Prytanis Key Leader award, 1993-94. Mem. Am. Inst. Chemists, Soc. Plastic Engrs., Am. Soc. Sugar Cane Technologists, Am. Chem. Soc., Am. Soc. Tng. and Devel. (cert. HRD profl. U. Oklahoma

1992), Phi Kappa Phi (sec. 1985-86), Tau Kappa Epsilon (chpt. advisor 1981-82, grantee advisor 1980-90, named Top Alumni award 1982, 90), Tau Kappa Epsilon. Independent. Avocations: jogging, tennis, salt water fishing, weight lifting.

AUVENSHINE, ANNA LEE BANKS, school system administrator; b. Waco, Tex., Nov. 27, 1938; d. D.C. and Lois Elmore Banks; B.A., Baylor U., 1959, M.A., 1968, Ed.D., 1978, postgrad., 1989—, Colo. State U., 1970-71, U. No. Colo., 1972; m. William Robert Auvenshine, Dec. 21, 1963; children— Karen Lynn, William Lee. Tchr. math. and English, Lake Air Jr. High Sch., Waco Ind. Sch. Dist., 1959-63, Ranger (Tex.) Ind. Sch. Dist., Ranger High Sch., 1964, Canyon (Tex.) Ind. Sch. Dist., Canyon Jr. High Sch., 1964-66; instr. English, Baylor U., 1963; tchr. math. Canyon Ind. Sch. Dist., Canyon High Sch., 1968-70; tchr. math. and English, St. Vrain Sch. Dist., Erie (Colo.) High Sch., 1970-71; tchr. English and reading Thompson Sch. Dist., Loveland (Colo.) High Sch., 1971-72; instr., reading program dir. Ranger Jr. Coll., 1972-84, chmn. humanities div., 1978-82; tchr. math. Hillsboro High Sch., 1984-85, adminstr. Hillsboro Ind. Sch. Dist., 1985-92. Trustee, Ranger (Tex.) Ind. Sch. Dist., 1979-84, v.p. bd. trustees, 1980-82, pres., 1982-84; community chmn., publicity chmn., troop leader Ranger Girl Scout Assn., 1974-77; sec. Eastland County Heart Assn., 1975-77; ch. sch. supt. First United Meth. Ch., Ranger, 1979-81, organist, 1974-77, mem. adminstrv. bd., 1979-84; assoc. program dir. community and tech. colls. and fed. projects, equity dir. Tex. Higher Edn. Coordinating Bd., Austin, 1992—. Mem. Internat. Reading Assn., Assn. Supervision and Curriculum Devel., Western Coll. Reading Assn., Tex. Assn. Sch. Adminstrs., Tex. Assn. Gifted and Talented, Tex. Jr. Coll. Tchrs. Assn. (cert. of appreciation 1979, mem. profl. devel. com. 1974-79, vice chmn. 1976-77, mem. resolutions com. 1979-80), Ranger PTA (parliamentarian 1978-79), Ranger Jr. Coll. Faculty Orgn. (pres. 1980-81), Baylor Alumni Assn. (life, bd. dirs. 1988-94), director, Baylor Alum. Assn., 1988-92, Delta Kappa Gamma (pres. Beta Upsilon chpt. 1978-80, pres. Gamma Delta chpt. 1986—, achievement award 1980). Methodist. Clubs: 1947 (pres. 1977-78) (Ranger); Baylor Bear (Waco). Home: 1107 E Walnut St Hillsboro TX 76645-2637 Office: Texas Higher Edn Coordinating Bd PO Box 12788 7745 Chevy Chase Dr Bldg 5 Austin TX 78752-1508

AUVENSHINE, WILLIAM ROBERT, college president; b. Waco, Tex., June 21, 1937; s. E.H. and Corinne (Clark) A.; m. Anna Banks, Dec. 21, 1963; children: Karen, Lee. AA, Arlington State Jr. Coll., 1957; BS, Tex. Christian U., 1959; MS, West Tex. State U., 1967; EdD, U. No. Colo., 1973. Tchr. music Chico (Tex.) Pub. Schs., 1957-60, Ranger (Tex.) Pub. Schs., 1960-64; mgr., part-owner Megert Music Co., Amarillo, Tex., 1964-70; counselor Loveland (Colo.) Pub. Schs., 1970-72; dean Ranger Jr. Coll., 1972-84; pres. Hill Coll., Hillsboro, Tex., 1984—. Mem. Heritage League, Hillsboro, 1984—; chmn. State Task Force on C.C. Annexation, 1993; chmn. bd. dirs. Eastland County Tax Appraisal Dist., 1979-84; mem. Indsl. Com., Cleburne, 1984—, Hillsboro, 1984—; mem. First United Meth. Ch., Hillsboro; mem. gen. bd. discipleship com. that rewrote Book of Worship for Meth. Ch.; past lay leader Ctrl. Tex. Conf., leader del. to gen. conf.; bd. dirs. Nat. Jr. Coll. Atletic Assn., 1993—, Harris Meth. Hosp. Sys., 1997—, pres. Cleburne Christian Bus. Club, 2002— Recipient Disting. Alumni award West Tex. State U., Canyon, 1983, Jefferson Davis award United Daus. of Confederacy, 1991; named Man of Yr., Ranger C. of C., 1963. Mem. Tex. Jr. Coll. Assn. (pres. 1991-92), Tex. Pub. Community Jr. Coll. Assn. (sec., treas. 1985-90), Tex. Assn. for C.C. Chief Student Affairs Adminstrs. (pres. 1982-83), Tex. C.C. Ins. Consortium (pres. 1992—), Hillsboro C. of C., Lions (dist. gov. 1977-78, Internat. Press award 1983, Lion of Yr. award Ranger chpt. 1975, Citizen of Yr. award Hillsboro chpt. 1986), Sons of Confederate Vets. (past comdr. 1988-90), Sons of Union Vets. of Civil War (chaplain), Masons (32d degree), Shriners, Hillsboro Country Club (pres. 1993-95), Phi Delta Kappa. Avocations: golf, restoring antique cars, reading. Home: 1107 E Walnut St Hillsboro TX 76645-2637 Office: Hill Coll 111 Lamar Dr Hillsboro TX 76645-2712 E-mail: wra@hill-college.cc.tx.us.

AUWEN, JUDITH K. elementary education educator; BS, West Tex. State U., 1968, MEd, 1972. Tchr. Pampa (Tex.) Ind. Sch. Dist., 1977—. Home: 404 Louisiana Ave Pampa TX 79065-4748

AUXER, CATHY JOAN, elementary school educator; b. Chambersburg, Pa., May 16, 1951; d. Pat and Joan Irene Wedo; m. Jeffrey Lynn Auxer, Aug. 21, 1971 (dec. Aug. 23, 1996); 1 child, Jeffrey Lynn Auxer Jr. BS in Edn., Shippensburg State U., 1974; MEd, Shippensburg U., 1978. Cert. tchr. Pa., Md. 1st grade tchr. Mooreland Elem. Sch., Carlisle, Pa., 1975—2000, Worcester Prep. Sch., Berlin, Md., 2000—. Cons. Apple Learning Interchange, Berlin, 2001—. Co-author: (pamphlet) Whole Language, 1981; author: (lessons online) Computer Learning Found., 2000—01. Recipient 2d pl. award for lesson plan, Computer Learning Found. Tchrs., 2001. Mem.: Internat. Reading Assn., Eastern Shore Reading Coun. Home: 18 Carriage Ln Berlin MD 21811 E-mail: occookiemd@aol.com.

AVALLE-ARCE, JUAN BAUTISTA, Spanish language educator; b. Buenos Aires, May 13, 1927; came to U.S., 1948; s. Juan B. and Maria Martina Avalle-Arce; m. Constance Marginot, Aug. 20, 1953 (dec. 1969); children: Juan Bautista, Maria Martina, Alejandro Alcantara; m. Diane Janet Pamp, Aug. 30, 1969 (div.); children: Maria la Real Alejandra, Fadrique Martín Manuel. AB, Harvard U., 1951, MA, 1952, PhD, 1955; LittD (hon.), U. Castilla-La Mancha, Spain. Tutor, Harvard U., 1953-55; asst. prof., then assoc. prof. Spanish, Ohio State U., 1955-62; prof. Spanish, Smith Coll., Northampton, Mass., 1962-66, Sophia Smith prof. Hispanic studies, 1966-69; William Rand Kenan, Jr. prof. Spanish, U. N.C., Chapel Hill, 1969-85; prof. Spanish U. Calif., Santa Barbara, 1985—, chmn. dept. Spanish and Portuguese, 1991-95, dir. Summer Inst. Hispanic Langs. and Culture, 1991—, José Miguel de Barandiarán prof. Basque studies, 1993—. Vis. scholar Univ. Ctr. Ga., 1972, lectr., 1961—, Univ. Ctr. Va., 1976; vis. prof. U. Salamanca, 1982, 84, 86, 88, U. Málaga, 1987, 90, 91, U. della Tuscia (Italy), 1988, Sophia U. (Japan), 1988, Kyoto U. Fgn. Affairs, 1988, U. Cuyo, U. Buenos Aires, 1989, Alcalá de Henares, 1995; vis. Hillyer Prof. Humanities U. Nev., Reno, 1996; Eccles scholar State U. Utah, 2003, Garner vis. scholar, 2003; PhD program evaluator N.Y. State Bd. Regents; cons. Coun. Grad. Schs. in U.s.; reader Nat. Humanities Ctr., Govt. Found. for 5th Centennial of Discovery of Am., Spain; cultural corr. Radio Nacional de España; ofcl. guest Euskadiko Erradio, Spain, 1988-89. Author: Conocimiento y vida en Cervantes, 1959, La novela pastoril española, 1959, 2d enlarged edit., 1974, La Galatea de Cervantes, 2 vols., 1961, 2d rev. edit., 1987, Gonzalo Fernández de Oviedo, 1962, 2d edit., 1989, El Inca Garcilaso en sus Comentarios, 1961, Deslindes cervantinos, 1961, Three Exemplary Novels, 1964, Bernal Francès y su Romance, 1966, El Persiles de Cervantes, 1969, Los entremeses de Cervantes, 1969, Don Juan Valera y Morsamor, 1970, El cronista Pedro de Escavias Una vida del Siglo XV, 1972, Suma cervantina, 1973, Narradores hispanoamericanos de hoy, 1973, Las Memorias de Gonzalo Fernández de Oviedo, 2 vols., 1974, El Peregrino en su patria de Lope de Vega, 1973, Nuevos deslindes cervantinos, 1974, Temas hispánicos medievales, 1975, Don Quijote como forma de vida, 1976, Dintorno de una època dorada, 1978, Cervantes, Don Quixote, annotated critical edit., 2 vols., 1978, rev. and enlarged edit., 1995, Cervantes, Novelas ejemplares, annotated edit., 3 vols., 1982, Lope de Vega, Las hazañas del Segundo David, 1984; La Galatea de Cervantes: 400 Años Despuès, 1985, Garci Rodriguez de Montalvo: Amadís de Gaula, 2 vols., 1985, Amadís de Gaula: El primitivo y el de Montalvo, 1991, Lecturas, 1987, Gonzalo Fernández de Oviedo, Batallas y quinquagenas, 1989, Garci Rodriguez de Montalvo Amadis de Gaula, 2 vols., 1991, Cancionero del Almirante don Fadrique Euriquez, 1993, Enciclopedia Cervantina, 1995, Poesía completa de Jorge de Montemayor, 1996, La épica colonial, 2000, Una obra olviera de Gonzalo Fernandez de Ovideo, 2003. Trustee Teutonic Order of the Levant, Marqués de la Lealtad. Recipient Bonsoms medal Spain, 1961; Guggenheim fellow, 1961; grantee Am. Coun. Learned Socs., 1965, 68; grantee NEH, 1968, 1978-80; grantee Am. Philos. Soc., 1961, 67; recipient Susan Anthony Potter Lit. prize, 1951; Centro Gallego Lit. prize, 1947; Diploma of Merit, Universitá delle Arti, Italy; named Grand Companion, Societé Internationale de la Noblesse Hérédi-taire. Sr. fellow Southeastern Inst. Medieval and Renaissance Studies; hon. fellow Soc. Spanish and Spanish Am. Studies; fellow Colegio Mayor Arzobispo D. Alonso de Fonseca of U. Salamanca; mem. MLA, Acad. Lit. Studies, Am. Acad. Rsch. Historians Medieval Spain, Academia Argentina de Letras, Anglo Am. Basque Studies Soc., Cervantes Soc. Am. (pres. 1979—), Ctr. for Medieval and Renaissance Studies, UCLA (assoc.), Soc. de Bibliofilos Espanoles, Modern Humanities Rsch. Assn., South Atlantic MLA, Asociación de Cervantistas (bd. mem.), Assn. Internac. de Hispanistas, Renaissance Soc. Am. (nat. del. to exec. coun. 1971), Real Sociedad Vascongada de Amigos del Pais, Centro de Estudios Jacobeos, Inst. d'Etudes Medievales, Inst. de Lit. Iberoamericana, Hispanic Soc. Am., Acad. Lit. Studies (charter), Mediaeval Acad. Am., Real Academia de Buenas Letras de Barcelona, Instituto Internacional de Literatura Iberoamericana, Sovereign Mil. Teutonic Order of the Levant (bailiff, knight grand cross, Grand Prior, Grand Priory of the U.S.), Harvard Club. Clubs: Triangle Hunt (Durham) (gentleman Whipper-in); U. N.C. Polo, Combined Training Events Assn. Home: 4640 Oak View Rd Santa Ynez CA 93460-9331 Office: U Calif 4323 Phelps Hall Santa Barbara CA 93106

AVELLA, JOHN THOMAS, educational administrator; b. Passaic, N.J., June 23, 1957; s. John T. and Margaret Louise (Watson) Avella; m. Jane Marie Myers; children: Katelyn Mary, Shaylyn Clare. BS in Spl. Edn., Trenton State Coll., 1981; MA in Ednl. Adminstrn., Georgian Ct. Coll., 1986; EdD, Nova Southeastern U., 1999. Tchr. Lacey Twp. (N.J.) Bd. Edn., 1982-88; supr. Union City Edn. Svcs. Commn., Westfield, N.J., 1988-89; prin., asst. supt. Monmouth Ocean Edn. Svcs. Commn., Freehold, N.J., 1989—. Mem. Nat. Assn. Sch. Adminstrs. Avocations: sports, music. Office: 100 Tornillo Way Ste 1 Asbury Park NJ 07712-7520

AVERETT, ROBERT LEE, information system professional, educator; b. Richfield, Utah, Dec. 4, 1952; s. Robert Elmo and Patsy (Meyer) A.; m. Alice Greenhalgh, Mar. 23, 1972; children: Nathan Christopher, Rachel Leah, Christian Alexander, Jeduthan William. BA, Brigham Young U., 1975, MLS, 1976; MA, Ball State U., 1979; D of Pub. Adminstrn., George Mason U., 1991. Cert. computer profl.; cert. secondary tchr., counselor, Utah. Commd. 2d lt. U.S. Army, 1976, advanced through grades to lt. col., 1993, ret., 1996; info. systems project mgr. Orgn. of Joint Chiefs of Staff, The Pentagon, 1984-85; mgmt. info. systems officer Hqrs. Dept. of Army, The Pentagon, 1985-87; comdr. 201st Signal Co., Seoul, Republic of Korea, 1987-89, Mil. Entrance Process Sta., Amarillo, Tex., 1989-92; chair, prof. mil. sci. U. Utah, Salt Lake City, 1993—, 1993-96; counselor, asst. prin. Granite Sch. Dist., Salt Lake City, 1995-99; prin. Granger Elem., West Valley, 1999—2003, Kearns Jr. H.S., Salt Lake City, 2003—. Cons., adj. Amarillo Coll., 1989-92, Limestone Coll., 1979-82. Leader Nat.a Capitol coun. Boy Scouts Am., Alexandria, 1982-87, Golden Spread coun., Amarillo, 1987-89. Recipient Meritorious Svc. award N.G. Bur., 1987, Armed Forces Comm-Elec Assn., 1989. Mem. ASPA, Granite Assn. Sch. Adminstrs. (pres. 2003-04). Avocations: running, artistry. Home: 484 Rocky Mouth Ln Draper UT 84020-7665 E-mail: robert.averett@granite.k12.vt.us.

AVERETT-SHORT, GENEVA EVELYN, college administrator; b. Boston, Mar. 12, 1938; d. William Pinkney and Geneva Zepplyn (Stepp) A.; m. Roger Inman Blackwell, Dec. 19, 1959 (div. 1975); children: Thomas, LaVerne, Constance; m. Floyd J. Short Jr., July 3, 1984. BA in Social Sci., Bennett Coll., Greensboro, N.C., 1958; EdM, SUNY, Buffalo, 1972; paralegal cert., Prince George's C.C., Largo, Md., 1994. Social caseworker Erie County Dept. Pub. Welfare, Buffalo, 1958-59; substitute tchr. Buffalo Bd. Edn., 1959-60; employment inteviewer N.Y. Dept. Labor, Div. Employment, Buffalo, 1967-69; admissions counselor SUNY, Buffalo, 1969-72; assoc. dean students U. Utah, Salt Lake City, 1972-74; coordinator counseling svcs. Ednl. Devel. Prog., SUNY, Fredonia, 1974-77, acting dir., 1976-77; substitute tchr. Greensboro (N.C.) pub. schs., 1977-78; prog. asst. D.C. Dept. Human Svcs. Commn. on Pub. Health, 1978-89; assessment counselor, coord. Prince George's Community Coll., Largo, Md., 1989-94; tutor Title I programs neglected and delinquent children Palm Beach Sch. Sys., Boca Raton, Fla., 1996—99, ret., 2000. Substitute tchr. Guilford County Sch. System, 1999—; appears in commls. Actor: (advt.) Val-Pak, 2001, Palmetto Health, 2002. Sec. Christian Edn.-Episcopal Ch. Women, Diocese N.C., 2000-03; bd. mem. Parents as Tchrs., St. Andrew's Episcopal Ch., 2001—; active in past various charitable orgns. Mem. Nat. Alumnae Assn. Bennett Coll., S. Fla. Alumnae Assn. (sec. Bennett Coll. chpt., 1996—99), Bennett Coll. Nat. Alumni Assn., Pierians, Inc. (pres. D.C. chpt. 1992-94). Democrat. Episcopalian. Avocations: fine and performing arts, writing, swimming, travel. Address: 906 Avery Pl Greensboro NC 27408-7702

AVERILL, ELLEN CORBETT, secondary education science educator, administrator; b. Milledgeville, Ga. d. Felton Conrad and Vivian Iris (Brookins) Corbett; m. George Edmund Averill, July 31, 1971; 1 child, John Conrad. BS, U. Ga., 1966, MS, 1971; teaching cert., Columbus Coll., 1979, EdS, 1994. Grad. teaching asst. U. Ga., Athens, 1966-68; tchr. sci. Decatur (Ga.) City Schs., 1971-72; tchr. sci., chair dept. Kendrick High Sch., Columbus, Ga., 1980—. Rsch. asst. Caretta Rsch. Project, Savannah (Ga.) Sci. Mus., 1985, NEWMAST, Kennedy Space Ctr., 1986; rsch. assoc. Inhalation Toxicology Rsch. Inst., Albuquerque, summer, 1990; instr. sci. Gov.'s Honor Program Valdosta State Coll., summer, 1991, Woodrow Wilson Biotechnology Inst., Princeton, N.J., 1993. Contbr. articles to newspapers, jours.; inventor The Wrap-All, 1992. Mem. Nat. Sci. Tchrs. Assn. (program com., regional conf. 1993), Nat. Assn. Biology Tchrs. (Outstanding Biology Tchr. 1990-91), Ga. Sci. Tchrs. Assn. (dist. VI rep. 1988-90, secondary rep. 1990-91, pres.-elect 1991-92, pres. 1992-93, conf. coord. ann. conf. 1992, Dist. VI Sci. Tchr. of Yr. 1995), Coalition for Excellence in Sci. Edn. (orgnl. com. 1992-93), Ga. Sci. Tchrs. Edn. Found. (chair 1994-98), Valley Area Sch. Tchrs. (charter, pres.-elect 1996-97, pres. 1997-98), Muscogee Area Literacy Assn. (treas. 1992-93), Phi Delta Kappa (PDK Tchr. of Yr. 1992, v.p. 2002-), Delta Kappa Gamma Edn. Soc. Unitarian-Universalist. Avocations: procelain art, gardening, amateur radio operator. Home: 126 Waterway Dr Cataula GA 31804-4407 Office: Kendrick High Sch 6015 Georgetown Dr Columbus GA 31907-4698 E-mail: eaverill@ldl.net.

AVERILL, RONALD HENRY, dean; b. L.A., Jan. 9, 1938; s. Alexander Anthony Averill and Anita Marie (Moser) Mitchell; m. Janice Louise Vaughan, Apr. 4, 1961; 1 child, Ella Louise Averill Morales. BA in Fgn. Svc., U. So. Calif., 1959; MA, Am. U., 1974. Lt. U.S. Army, Darmstadt, Germany, 1959-62; asst. prof. Mil. Sci. Okla. St. U., Stillwater, 1963-66; staff officer U.S. Army, 1968-73, advanced to grade of col., 1974-89, ret., 1989; instr. Hawaii Pacific U., Honolulu, 1989-91, South Puget Sound C.C., Olympia, Wash., 1992—2000, dean social sci. divsn., 2000—. Soc. Sci. divsn. chair. Soccer coach Centralia H.S., 1969-97; chmn. St. Mary's Parish Coun., Centralia, 1993-96, Lewis County Nat. Resources Com., Chehalis, 1994-98, Lewis County Solid Waste Adv. Com., Chehalis, 1994—, Lewis County Rep. Cen. Com., 1997-2002. Mem. Am. Legion (post 17), Assn. U.S. Army, Mil. Officers Assn. Am., Lewis County Farm Bur. (legis. liaison 1994), Knights of Columbus (past grand knight, recorder, 1995—), VFW. Republican. Roman Catholic. Avocation: soccer coach. Home: 2523 Graf Rd Centralia WA 98531-9087 Office: S Puget Sound C C 2011 Mottman Rd SW Olympia WA 98512-6218

AVERSA, DOLORES SEJDA, educational administrator; b. Phila., Mar. 26, 1932; d. Martin Benjamin and Mary Elizabeth (Esposito) Sejda; m. Zefferino A. Aversa Jr., May 3, 1958; children: Dolores Elizabeth, Jeffrey Martin, Linda Maria. BA, Chestnut Hill Coll., 1953. Owner Personal Rep. & Pub. Rels., Phila., 1965-68; ednl. cons. Franklin Sch. Sci. and Arts, Phila., 1968-72; pres., owner, dir. Martin Sch. Bus., Inc., Phila., 1972—. File reader, cons. for ct. reporting and travel tng. Southwestern Pub. Co., 1990; mem. ednl. planning com. Ravenhill Acad., Phila., 1975-76. Active Phila. Mus. ARt, Phila. Drama Guild; mem. Met. Opera Guild, 2002, 8th Ward Rep. Exec. Com. Mem.: Lower Bucks County C. of C., Am. Soc. Travel Agts. (sch. divsn., nat. educators com., sec. Del. chpt., edn. chmn., PAC chmn. 1997—), Hist. Soc. Pa., World Affairs Coun. Phila., Phila. Hist. Soc., Pa. Sch. Counselors Assn., Am. Bus. Law Assn., Pa. Bus. Edn. Assn., Nat. Bus. Edn. Assn., Andrea Doria Survivor Assn., Chestnut Hill Coll. Alumnae Assn. (sec. class '53), Phila. Orch., Am.-Italy Soc., Met. Opera Guild, Stone Harbor Golf Club. Roman Catholic. Home: 2111 Locust St Philadelphia PA 19103-4802 Office: 2417 Welsh Rd Philadelphia PA 19114-2213 E-mail: msb-aversa@erols.com.

AVERY, PASCO BRUCE, secondary science educator; b. Groton, Conn., Nov. 27, 1954; s. Ralph Ely and Oma (Raybon) Avery; m. Cindy Lou Olien, July 1, 1990; 1 child, Josiah P. BS in Biol. Sci., Nebr. Wesleyan U., 1976; MS in Sci. Edn., U. Tenn., 1983; PhD in Microbiology/Insect Sci., U. London, 2002. Cert. secondary sci. tchr. in gen. phys. and biol. scis. Secondary sci. tchr. West End Acad., Knoxville, Tenn., 1983-88, Wilbraham (Mass.) & Monson Acad., 1988-91, Innsbruck Internat. H.S., Schönberg, Austria, 1991-92, Am. Comty. Sch., Hillingdon, Eng., 1992-98; insect technician USDA/ARS, Ithaca, N.Y., 1998-99, biol. sci. tech. (summers) Sidney, Mont., 2002, 2003; tchr. secondary sci. Lee (Maine) Acad., 2001—. Supr. Citrus Blackfly emergency eradication spray program Fla. Dept. Agr., 1976-77; lectr., instr. in entomology U. Tenn., Knoxville, 1978-80, rschr., organizer, participant insecticidal spray programs, 1980, condr. insecticidal efficacy studies, 1987; supr., participant lawn mgmt. Tom Coates Landscaping, 1981; rschr. Ijames Audubon Nature Ctr., 1982-83; monitor insect populations U. Mass., Amherst, 1989. Inventor: The Science Teacher, 1993. Merit badge counselor Boy Scouts Am., Hillingdon, 1994. Mem.: Soc. Invertebrate Pathology, Brit. Mycological Soc., London Internat. Schs. Assn. (subject oriented action com. 1993—98), Entomol. Soc. Am., Phi Delta Kappa. Home: 187 Winn Rd Lee ME 04455 E-mail: pavery@leeacademy.lee.me.us.

AVERY, RONALD DENNIS, school psychologist; b. Passaic, N.J., Oct. 24, 1940; s. George Anthony and Ethel (Nikovits) A.; children: George Anthony Jr., Ronald Dennis. BA in English, Calif. State U., 1970, MA in Secondary Edn., 1972; MS in Psychology, U.S. Internat. U., 1978, PhD in Profl. Psychology, 1977. Cert. psychologist, tchr., Calif. Tchr. reading Lynwood (Calif.) H.S., 1971-78, Lynwood Adult Sch., 1972-74; instr. bus. English and comm. L.A. C.C., 1973-84; tchr., reading specialist Hosler Jr. H.S., Lynwood, 1984-86, 88-94; tchr. Roosevelt Elem. Sch., Lynwood, 1986-87; sch. psychologist Lynwood Unified Sch. Dist., 1994—. Instr. psychology U.S. Internat. U., San Diego, 1975, Calif. Am. U., San Diego, 1976-77; pvt. practice clin. psychology, L.A., 1978—; clin. psychologist Claif. Youth Authority, Southern Reception Ctr., Norwalk, L.A., 1978, 94, Calif., 1980-82; sch. psychologist, Nellis, Whittier and Norwalk, 1993-94; expert witness Calif. Jud. Sys., L.A. and Orange Counties, 1978—. With USAF, 1960-61. Mem. Calif. Assn. Sch. Psychologists (Outstanding Sch. Psychologist Los Angeles County/Region V), Lynwood Tchrs. Assn. (chmn. grievance com. 1974, pres. 1975), KC, Phi Delta Kappa. Republican. Roman Catholic. Avocations: beach activities, fishing, hiking. Home: 1321 S Bromley Ave West Covina CA 91790-2453 Office: Lynwood Unified Sch Dist 11321 Bullis Rd Lynwood CA 90262-3666

AVILA, LIDIA D. school administrator; b. Phoenix; d. Pete A. and Elvira (Duarte) A. B.A. in Edn., M.A. in Edn., 1968; Ed.D., Ariz. State U., 1981. Cert. elem. tchr., counselor, adminstr. Successively tchr., counselor, coordinator, Phoenix, 1958-73, prin., 1973-75; adult edn. tchr., Tempe, Ariz., 1966-68; fed. project reader cons., Phoenix, 1968-72; prin. Glendale Elem. Sch. Dist. (Ariz.), 1976—88; prin. Tucson, 1988-91, Phoenix, 1991—; textbook cons. Active Robert A Taft Inst. Govt., 1981; del. Inter-Club Council Women's Orgn. Greater Phoenix area; bd. dirs. YWCA, 1968-70; mem. steering com. 1st US-China Ednl. Conf, Beijing, 1997. Baylor U. Leadership/Mgmt. Inst. grantee 1980; NDEA grantee, UCLA Inst. Linguistics, Manila, Philippines, 1968. Mem. AAUW (state pres., mem. edn. found. panel), Am. Bus. Women's Assn. (Woman of Yr. 1982), Assn. Supervision and Curriculum Devel., Nat. Assn. Elem. Sch. Prins. (participant nat. fellows program), Delta Kappa Gamma, Phi Delta Kappa. Office: 5810 N 49th Ave Glendale AZ 85301

AVILA, MARVIN ARTHUR, assistant principal student services; b. Belize, Cen. Am., Dec. 15, 1945; came to U.S., 1981; s. Peter Albert and Sotera (Nicholas) A.; m. Florita Lorraine Enriquez, Oct. 27, 1979; children: Marvin Arthur, Jr., Catherine Camille. Licentiate, Coll of Preceptors, London, 1976, Fellow, 1980; BS, U. San Francisco, 1983; MA, Calif. State U., L.A., 1991. Cert. multiple subjects, bilingual, adminstr., Calif. Tchr. St. Francis Xavier Cath. Sch., Belize, Cen. Am., 1966-74, tchr., vice prin., 1974-76; lectr. Belize Tchrs. Coll., 1977-81; tutor, lectr. extra mural dept. U. W. Indies, Belize, 1977-81; tchr. St. John Chrysostom Elem. Sch., Inglewood, Calif., 1981-84, San Miguel Jr. High Sch., L.A., 1984-85, tchr., vice prin., 1985-86, prin., 1986-88; bilingual tchr. (Spanish English) McKinley Elem. Sch. L.A. Unified Sch. Dist., 1988-91; advisor Bethune Sch. L.A. Unified Sch. Dist., 1991-94, bilingual/ESL coord., 1994-97; asst. prin. Lynwood H.S., 1997—; coord. bilingual, English as 2d lang. South Gate Cmty. Adult Sch., 1994-97. ESL tchr., L.A. Cmty. Adult Sch., 1989, South Gate Cmty. Adult Sch, summer 1994, Banning/Carson Adult Sch., 1992-93; ESL tchr. trainer Osage Tng. Ctr., L.A. Unified Sch. Dist., 1990-91; ESL coord. Banning site, 1993-94; tchr. citizenship, U.S. history and govt., South Gate Cmty. Adult Sch., 1994-97; organizer Advanced Tchr. Edn., No. Dist. Belize, 1975-76; cons. Garifuna Career Day, L.A., 1987—; tchr. summer and winter intersessions John C. Fremont H.S., L.A. Unified Sch. Dist., 1992—; mem. shared-decision making coun. Bethune Middle Sch., 1995—, chmn. discipline com.; adj. faculty Nat. U., 1997—. Advisor Emergency Immigrant Edn. Assistance Program. Recipient Commonwealth Fellowship scholarship, British Govt., London, 1976-77. Mem. NEA, ASCD, United Tchrs. L.A., Calif. Tchrs. Assn., Calif. Coun. for Adult Edn. Avocations: reading, music, rsch., travel, writing. Office: Bethune Middle Sch 155 W 69th St Los Angeles CA 90003-1823

AVIN, DOROTHY ELIZABETH CLARK, retired educator, artist; b. Gt. Barrington, Mass., Sept. 30, 1948; d. Frederick Holley and Catharine Annette (Lippincott) Clark; m. Brian Howard Avin, June 28, 1968 (div. Dec. 1986; children: Jacquelyn Estelle Avin Nicoll, Lori Catharine Avin Meringolo. Student, SUNY, Buffalo, 1966-68; BA in Art Edn., Roosevelt U., 1971. Cert. advanced 5-12 profl. math. tchr., 7-12 art tchr., Md. Substitute tchr. Chgo. Pub. Schs., 1971-72, Miami (Fla.) Jackson Sr. H.S., 1972-73, Montgomery County (Md.) Pub. Schs., 1977-79, Sherwood H.S., Sandy Spring, Md., 1985-86; office mgr. Brian H. Avin, M.D., P.A., 1980-84; tchr. math. Magruder H.S., Rockville, Md., 1986-87, Blair H.S., Silver Spring, Md., summer 1987, Bethesda (Md.)-Chevy Chase H.S., 1987-88, 90, tchr. art, 1987, 88-90; ret., 1990. Curriculum developer, textbook evaluator Montgomery County Pub. Schs., Rockville, 1985-89. Exhibited in group show Albright Knox Mus. Contemporary Art, Buffalo, 1966, Caraitas Soc. of St. John's Coll., Annapolis, Md., 1990-96, Agora Galalery, N.Y.C., 1992; represented in permanent collection Mus. Without Wall, Bemus Point, N.Y. Active various charitble orgns., Montgomery County, 1977-80, Anne Arundel County, Md., 1995-96; fundraiser Wolf Trap Ctr. for Performing Arts, Va., 1986, Sherwood H.S., 1985-86. Recipient achievement in arts award Washington Performing Arts, 1987, art award Nat. Renaissance Alive in Am., 1991, 92, letter of recognition Barker Found., Washington, 1993; named Soho Internat. Competition winner, 1992. Mem. NEA, Md. Fedn.

Art, Mus. in Arts Mus. (charter). Episcopalian. Avocations: photography, landscape and interior design, gardening, dogs. Home: Green River Valley Rd PO Box 442 South Egremont MA 01258-0442

AVIV, JONATHAN ENOCH, otolaryngologist, educator; b. NYC, Aug. 24, 1960; s. David Gordon and Rena (Rod) A.; m. Robin Kiam, Nov., 1998; children: Caleigh Kiam, Nikki Claire, Blake Victor. BA, Columbia U., 1981, MD, 1985. Diplomate Am. Bd. Otolaryngology, Nat. Bd. Med. Examiners. Resident dept. surgery Mount Sinai Med. Ctr., N.Y.C., 1985-87, resident dept. otolaryngology, 1987-90, fellow microvascular surgery, 1990-91; prof., dir. divsn. laryngology, med. dir. voice and swallowing ctr. Coll. Physicians and Surgeons, Columbia U., N.Y.C., 1991—. Co-founder AP Healthcare, L.L.C., Surgery 411. Contbr. articles to profl. jours., numerous book chpts. Fellow Am. Soc. Head and Neck Surgery; mem. AMA, ACS (faculty), Am. Acad. Otolaryngology, Am. Acad. Facial, Plastic and Reconstructive Surgery, Am. Broncho-Esophagological Assn. (v.p. 2001-03), Am. Laryngological Assn., N.Am. Skull Base Soc., N.Y. Head and Neck Soc., N.Y. Laryngological Soc. (pres. elect), Triological Soc. Achievements include development of and a patent for method and device to endoscopically measure sensory discrimination in throat and voice box. Office: Columbia-Presbyn Med Ctr Dept Otolaryngology 630 W 168th St New York NY 10032-3702 Business E-Mail: jea10@columbia.edu.

AVRAHAM, REGINA, retired secondary education educator; b. Ludenscheid, Germany, Aug. 15, 1935; Came to U.S., 1937. d. Joseph and Feiga (Press) Artman; m. Josef Esa Abraham, Mar. 12, 1962; children: Randi Beth, Jesse Richard. BS, City Coll., N.Y.C., 1955. Elem. tchr. N.Y. Bd. Edn., 1955-63, tchr., 1963-91; sci. cons., prin. writer N.Y.C. Bd. Edn. Sci. Curriculum, 1996—. Sci. and health magnet tchr. Bd. Edn., N.Y., 1987-91; presenter and cons. in field. Author: Our Founding Sisters, 1976, Readings in Life Science, 1986, Readings in Physical Science, 1986, The Downside of Drugs, 1988, Substance Abuse Treatment and Prevention, 1988, The Circulation System, 1989, The Digestive System, 1989, The Reproductive System, 1989; prin. writer Sci.-Lit. Connection, N.Y.C. Bd. Edn., 1996, contbg. writer, cons. A Study in Role Models, 1997, The Multiple Intelligences, 1998; contbg. editor: Celebrating the Century, 1999, Reading and Writing Connections, 2000, Celebrating Diversity, 2001; project coord., contbg. writer, editor, cons. Promoting Excellence through Best Practices, 2002. Woodrow Wilson fellow, 1989; named Tchr. of Yr., Bklyn. Sch. Bd., 1987. Mem. United Fed. Tchrs. Democratic. Avocations: theatre, opera, crossword puzzles, cats, N.Y. Mets. Home: 2218 Avenue P Brooklyn NY 11229-1508

AX, JOANNE E. special education educator; b. Chgo., Aug. 19, 1962; d. James W. and Pauline (Dolence) Conway; m. Michael D. Ax, Apr. 11, 1985; 1 child, Catherine. BS in Edn., Ind. State U., 1991. Cert. tchr. gen. edn. grades 1-6, 7-8 non-departmentalized, with endorsements in kindergarten and spl. edn. Tchr. for emotionally handicapped Vincennes (Ind.) Cmty. Schs., 1992—. Mem. Coun. for Exceptional Children, Phi Kappa Phi, Kappa Delta Pi, Psi Iota Xi (chpt. pres. 1990-91). Avocations: volunteering for children's organizations, nursing homes, outdoor recreational activities. Home: PO Box 1144 Vincennes IN 47591-7144 Office: Vincennes Cmty Schs Clark Middle Sch 500 Buntin St Vincennes IN 47591-2123

AXELSON, DONNA IRENE, elementary education educator; b. Bainbridge, Md., Feb. 21, 1946; d. Donald Ira Rigby and Jean Elizabeth (Trask) Mattia; m. Cordell Harry Axelson, June 12, 1965; children: Jeffrey Cordell, Matthew Gene. BA, San Francisco State U., 1967, degree in gen. elem. edn., 1968. Tchr. San Jose (Calif.) Unified Sch. Dist., 1968-73, Cupertino (Calif.) Union Sch. Dist., 1984—, site coord. Model Techs. Schs., 1992—. Conf. presenter Calif. Sch. Bds. Assn., 1989, ASCD, 1991, Calif. Reading Assn., 1992. Mem., officer Cupertino/Fremont PTA, Cupertino, 1979—; vol. youth dept. Los Altos (Calif.) 1st Bapt. Ch., 1980—; coach Cupertino Little League, 1982. Recipient Hon. Svc. award Faria PTA, 1985, Continuing Svc. award Garden State PTA, 1990. Mem. Computer Using Educators (conf. presenter 1989—), Santa Clara Reading Coun. Avocations: skiing, tennis, hiking, reading, sewing. Office: Cupertino Union Sch Dist 10301 Vista Dr Cupertino CA 95014-2040

AXFORD, ROGER WILLIAM, adult education educator, consultant; b. Grand Island, Nebr., July 22, 1920; married; 3 children. AB in Polit. Sci., Nebr. Wesleyan U.; MA in Sociology, PhD in Adult Edn., U. Chgo. Pres. Recareering Inst., Tempe, Ariz.; assoc. prof. adult ctr. Ctr. for Higher Adult Edn. Ariz. State U., Tempe, prof. emeritus. Adult edn. educator various U.S. instns.; condr. study tours in Norway, Gt. Britain, China and Japan; vis. prof. Inter Am. Univ., Calif., P.R., U. So. Calif., Fla. State U.; lectr.-cons. in adult edn. Ill. Migrant Coun., Commonwealth of Can., U. P.R., Universidad Nacional Exptl. Simon Rodrigues in Venezuela. Author: College Community Consultation, Adult Education: The Open Door, Black American Heroes, Native Americans: 23 Indian Biographies, Spanish Speaking Heroes: 23 Biographies, Too Long Silent: Japanese Americans SPEAK OUT!, Perspectives on Adult Education Administration, Speaking About Adults, Zany Jokes for Funny Folks, Successful Recareering: How to Shift Gears, The Best Fourth of Life, Mirror for Marriage, 2001, A Peace of My Mind: An Unrepentent Peacenick, Aging Graciously!, 2003. Died Aug. 1, 2003.

AXFORD, ROY ARTHUR, nuclear engineering educator; b. Detroit, Aug. 26, 1928; s. Morgan and Charlotte (Donaldson) A.; m. Anne-Sofie Langfeldt Rasmussen, Apr. 1, 1954; children: Roy Arthur, Elizabeth Carole, Trevor Craig Charles. BA, Williams Coll., 1952; BS, Mass. Inst. Tech., 1952, MS, 1955, Sc.D., 1958. Supr. theoretical physics group Atomics Internat., Canoga Park, Calif., 1958-60; assoc. prof. nuclear engring. Tex. A&M, 1960-62, prof., 1962-63; assoc. prof. nuclear engring. Northwestern U., 1963-66; assoc. prof. U. Ill., Urbana, 1966-68, prof., 1968—. Cons. Los Alamos Nat. Lab., 1963— Vice-chmn. Mass. Inst. Tech. Alumni Fund Drive, 1970-72, chmn., 1973-75; sustaining fellow MIT, 1984. Recipient cert. of recognition for excellence in undergrad. teaching U. Ill., 1979, 81; Everitt award for teaching excellence, 1985. Mem. ASME, Am. Nuclear Soc. (Excellence in Undergrad. Teaching award 1990, 95, 97, 99, 2002, Disting. faculty Alpha Nu Sigma 1991), SAR (sec.-treas. Piankeshaw chpt. 1975-81, v.p. chpt. 1982-3, pres. chpt. 1984-86), Kiwanis (charter life patron fellow 1992), Sigma Xi, Tau Beta Pi, Phi Kappa Phi. Home: 2017 S Cottage Grove Ave Urbana IL 61801-6353

AXLUND, MARY KATE, middle school education educator; b. Las Cruces, New Mexico, Sept. 9, 1962; d. John Wayne and Mary Elna (Weaver); m. Daniel P. Axlund, June 20, 1992. AS, Black Hills State Coll., Spearfish, S.D., 1986; BS, Black Hills State U., 1990. Nat. Bd. cert. tchr. middle childhood, 2001, cert. cirriculm dir. Prodn. dir. KSQY Raido, Deadwood, SD, 1990; tchr. fifth grade East Elem. Sch., Spearfish, SD, 1990-91; rural tchr. fourth through eighth grades Meade 46-I Sch., Sturgis, SD, 1991-92, tchr. fifth grade, 1192—2001, tchr sixth grade, 2001—. Contbr. articles to mag. Lutheran. Avocations: hunting, fishing, reading, sewing.

AXON, MICHAEL, education association field representative; b. Bradenton, Fla., Aug. 15, 1957; s. Gladys C. (Thomas) A. Student, Campbell U., 1975-77; BA in Social Sci. Edn., U. South Fla., 1979; MEd in Adminstrn. and Supervision, West Ga. Coll., 1995. Cert. paralegal Nat. Ctr. Paralegal Tng. Asst. mgr. Nat. Shirt Shop, Bradenton, 1979; account rep. Avco Fin. Svcs., Bradenton, 1979-80; tchr. Palm Beach County Sch. Bd., Palm Beach, Fla., 1980-86; customer svc. rep. Best Products Co., Inc., West Palm Beach, Fla., 1981-83; field rep. Atlanta Fedn. Tchrs., 1986—. V.p. Am. Fedn. Tchrs. of Palm Beach County, 1982-86; rep. Palm Beach County Cen. Labor Coun., West Palm Beach, 1982-86; commn. mem. Pres.'s Commn. on Excellence in Edn., Fla. Edn. Assn./United, Tallahassee, 1985; v.p. exec. coun. Fla. Edn. Assn./United, Tallahassee, 1985-86; staff coord. union newspaper Atlanta Fedn. Tchrs., 1988—. Membership chairperson Metro-Atlanta A. Philip Randolph Inst., 1987-89; editor vision newsletter Cathedral of Faith Ch. of God in Christ, Atlanta, 1989-95; counselor Juvenile Alt. Svc. Program, West Palm Beach, 1982-85; faculty sponsor key club Palm Beach Garden (Fla.) H.S., 1980-84. Avocations: poetry, cooking, walking, gardening. Office: Atlanta Fedn Tchrs Ste 439 2001 Martin Luther King Dr Atlanta GA 30310-5806

AYALA, JOHN, librarian, dean; b. Long Beach, Calif., Aug. 28, 1943; s. Francisco and Angelina (Rodriguez) Ayala; m. Patricia Marie Dozier, July 11, 1987 (dec. Jan. 19, 2001); children: Juan, Sara; m. Gloria Ann Aulwes, Dec. 28, 2003. BA in History, Calif. State U., Long Beach, 1970, MPA, 1981; MLS, Immaculate Heart Coll., L.A., 1971. Library paraprofl. Long Beach Pub. Library, 1963-70; librarian L.A. County Pub. Libr., 1971-72, Long Beach City Coll., 1972-90, assoc. prof., 1972-90, pres. acad. senate, 1985-87; dean, Learning Resources Fullerton (Calif.) Coll., 1990—, evening/weekend supr., 1997—99, adminstr. study abroad program, 2000—. Chmn. Los Angeles County Com. to Recruit Mexican-Am. Librs., 1971-74; mem. acad. senate Calif. Cmty. Colls., 1985-90; pres. Latino Faculty/Staff Assn., NOCCD, 1993-2000. Editor Calif. Librarian, 1971. Served with USAF, 1966-68, Vietnam. U.S. Office Edn. fellow for library sci., 1970-71. Mem. ALA (com. mem. 1971—, Melvil Dewey award com. 1998—), Calif. Libr. Assn., REFORMA Nat. Assn. to Promote Spanish Speaking Libr. Svc. (founding mem., v.p., pres. 1973-76), Arnul Fo Trejo Libr. of the Yr. Award 2001, from Reforma,CSULB, (Alumni Assn. (treas., 2003—). Democrat. Roman Catholic. Office: Fullerton College Library 321 E Chapman Ave Fullerton CA 92832-2011

AYALA, ROWENA WINIFRED, retired principal; b. Detroit; d. Reginald Peter Ayala, Sept. 17, 1955; children: Kevin, Terrence, Peter, Kathryn, Gail, Gladys. BS, Mich. State U., 1955; MEd, Marygrove Coll., 1972; EdD, Wayne State U., 1977. Tchr. Cass Tech. H.S., Detroit, 1967-75; jr. adminstrv. asst. Detroit Pub. Schs., 1975-80; prin. Crockett Adult Edn. & Career Ctr., Detroit, 1980-97; ret., 1997. Bd. dirs. Crockett Tech. H.S., Detroit Mem. Jack and Jill Am., Detroit, Great Lakes chpt. of the Links, Inc.; bd. dirs. Barat Human Svcs., Detroit. Recipient Disting. Svc. award Mich. Black Coll. Alumni Assn., 1987, Achievement award Booker T. Washington Assn., 1990. Mem. NAACP (life), Am. Vocat. Assn., Mich. Assn. Secondary Sch. Prins., Mich. Assn. Health Occupation (hon. life), Orgn. Sch. Adminstrs. and Suprs., Met. Area Svc. Orgn., Alpha Kappa Alpha, Phi Delta Kappa. Roman Catholic. Avocations: travel, reading. Home: 19444 Parkside St Detroit MI 48221-1834

AYDT, MARY I. secondary school educator; b. Lake Forest, Ill., Oct. 10, 1944; d. Stanley Adam Wrona and Sophie Steplyk; m. James C. Aydt, June 29, 1968; children: Michael, Stephen, Peter. BS in Edn., No. Ill. U., 1966; MA in Edn., St. Xavier U., Chgo., 1997. H.s. math. tchr. Mundelein (Ill.) Unit Dist., 1967—68, Sch. Dist. U-46, Elgin, Ill., 1968—74, 1985—; math. tchr. local CC, Elgin, 1980—87; ESL tchr. local YWCA, Elgin, 1980—87. Worker, local soup kitchen, Elgin, 1996—. Mem.: AAUW (corr. sec. 1998—), NEA, Elgin Tchr. Assn., Ill. Edn. Assn., Kappa Delta Pi. Roman Catholic. Avocations: sports, travel, needlecrafts. Home: 1500 Easy St Elgin IL 60123 Office: Elgin High Sch 1200 Maroon Dr Elgin IL 60120

AYERS, ANNE LOUISE, small business owner, consultant, counselor; b. Albuquerque, Oct. 22, 1948; d. F. Ernest and Gladys Marguerite (Miles) A. BA, Kans. U., 1970; MEd, Seattle Pacific U., 1971. Staff cons. in student devel. Cen. Wash. State U., Ellensburg, 1971-72; dir. Aerospace Def. Command Resident Edn. Ctrs. for N.D. and Mont. Chapman U., Orange, Calif., 1972-74; instr. psychology Hampton (Va.) U., 1973-75; edn. svc. specialist Gen. Ednl. Devel. Ctr., Fort Monroe, Va., 1975-77; edn. specialist U.S. Army Transp. Sch., Ft. Eustis, Va., 1977-79, Nat. Mine Health and Safety Acad., Beckley, W.Va., 1979-89; edn. svcs. specialist NASA Hdqrs., Washington, 1989-96; ret., 1996. Pres. Appalachian Love Arts, Martinsburg, W.Va., 1983—; tchr. undergrad. and grad. evening classes in psychology, 1972-74; program mgr. NASA Tchr. Resource Ctr. Network Program; sub. counselor Berkley County, W.Va.. Inventor decorative pen/thermometer holder/corsage, psychedelic jewelry process. Mem. Nat. Soc. Inventors, Nat. Assn. Women Deans Adminstrn. and Counselors, Internat. Soc. Photographers, Alumnus of Growing Vision (Century in Edn. award), Mayflower Soc. Methodist. Avocations: travel, collecting gems and shells, coin collecting, rock and fossil collecting, oboe and clarinet. Home and Office: 480 Tanbridge Dr Martinsburg WV 25401-4695

AYMAN, IRAJ, educational consultant; b. Tehran, Feb. 9, 1928; came to the U.S., 1978; s. Abbas and Lagha (Hamidi) A.; m. Lily Ahy; children: Roya, Saba, Rama. BA, Tehran U., 1949; EdD, Edinburgh U., 1952; PhD, U. So. Calif., 1957; postgrad., Harvard U., 1963. Cert. tchr. Assoc. prof. applied psychology, dir. Pers. Mgmt./Rsch. Ctr. U. Tehran, Iran, 1957-70; prof., chair psychology dept. Nat. U. Tchr. Edn., Tehran, 1963-70; dir. Inst. Ednl. Studies, Tehran, 1963-70; pres. Nat. Inst. Psychology, Tehran, 1970-80; rsch. assoc. U. Chgo., 1979-83; regional edn. advisor Asia and Pacific UNESCO, Bangkok, 1983-87, chief tng. ednl. pers. Paris, 1987-88; dir. internat. programs Human Resource Inst., Westport, Conn., 1979-83; founder, dir. Landegg Acad., Wienacht, Switzerland, 1988-94; dir. Inst. Internat. Edn., St. Gallen, Switzerland, 1988-94; internat. cons. Internat. Edn. Systems, L.A., 1994-96; dean Wilmette (Ill.) Inst., 1995—. Program evaluation cons. IIT, 1975—; vis. prof. grad. colls. edn. & mgmt. scis. UCLA, 1974-75; vis. prof., Ford Found.; cons. grad. colls. edn. and pub. adminstrn. U. Philippines, Mania, 1965-67; dir. inst. edn. Nat. Tchr. Edn. U., Tehran, 1960-63; mgmt. tng. advisor Pakistan Internat. Airline, Karachi, 1969-70; faculty Capella U., 1996—; acad. bd. Pacific Rim Inst. for Devel. and Edn., 1999; adv. coun. Ctr. for Global Integrated Edn., 2003. Author, co-editor: Personnel Administration, 1955; author: Merit Rating, 1958; gen. editor: Educational Psychology, 1960; author, editor: A New Framework for Moral Education, 1993; co-editor: Transition to Global Society, 1993. Cons. UN Devel. Program, N.Y.C., Sri Lanka, 1993; exec. sec., coord. Internat. Dialogue on Transition to Global Soc., Switzerland, 1989-94; cons. Activity Ctr. for Edn., Beijing, 1988—; commr. of audit Eastern Regional Orgn. for Pub. Adminstrn., Manila, 1962-82. Specialist grantee Govt. of U.S., 1963, U.K. Tech. Cooperation Dept., 1962, USAID, 1955-57. Fellow Chinese Assn. Local Edn. Annals (sr., advisor Coun. Edn.- Bus. Partnership 1995—); mem. Am. Ednl. Rsch. Assn., Religious Edn. Assn. (exec. bd. 1994-2000), Am. Psychol. Assn., Internat. Assn. Ednl. Assessment (v.p. 1975-82), Internat. Test Commn. (pres. 1978-82), Internat. Assn. Applied Psychology (pres. divsn. 1978-82), Internat. Union Sci. Psychology (adminstrv. coun. 1960-90). Avocations: mountaineering, swimming, stamp collecting, hiking, chess playing. Home: 5715 S Kenwood Ave Apt 3N Chicago IL 60637-1742 E-mail: iayman@usbnc.org.

AYOUB, AYOUB BARSOUM, mathematician, educator; b. Cairo, May 22, 1931; came to U.S., 1975, naturalized, 1997; s. Barsoum Ayoub and Linda (Naguib) Rizk; m. Germaine Hozayen Saad, Feb. 5, 1972; children: Sameh, Mariane. BSc in Math., Ain-Shams U., Cairo, 1951; MA in Math., Temple U., Phila., 1977, PhD in Math., 1980. Tchr. Tawfikia High Sch., Cairo, 1951-55; instr. Ain-Shams U., Cairo, 1955-75; teaching asst. Temple U., Phila., 1975-77, rsch. asst., 1977-80, vis. asst. prof., 1982-83; asst. prof. Ain-Shams U., Cairo, 1980-82; asst. prof. math. Pa. State U., Abington, 1983-90, assoc. prof., 1990-97, prof., 1997—, coord. math. dept., 1992-94. Referee Math. Mag., Coll. Math. Jour., Math & Computer Edn. Jour., Pi Mu Epsilon Jour.; reviewer Math. Tchr.; contbr. articles to profl. jours. Chmn. United Way Campaign, Pa. State, Ogontz Campus, 1990. Mem. Math. Assn. Am., Nat. Coun. Tchrs. Math., Am. Math. Assn. Two-Yr. Colls., Pa. State Math. Assn. Two-Yr. Colls., Pa. Coun. Tchrs. Math., Assn. Math. Tchrs. N.Y. State. Avocation: travel. Office: Pa State U Abington Coll Abington PA 19001 E-mail: aba2@psu.edu.

AYRES, MARY JO, professional speaker, writer, composer; b. Aberdeen, Miss., Jan. 27, 1953; d. Walter Stephen and Sarah Louise (Pearson) Peugh; m. William Stanley Ayres, June 28, 1975; children: Elizabeth, Will. BS, Miss. State U., Starkville, 1974; MEd, Delta State U., 1993. Tchr. Greenville (Miss.) Pub. Schs., 1974-75, Leland (Miss.) Acad., 1975-77, Leland United Meth. Child Devel. Ctr., Leland, 1984-91, chmn. bd. dirs., 1993—; profl. speaker Natural Learning, Leland, 1987—. Author: Happy Teaching and Natural Learning, 1992, Natural Learning from A-Z, 1997; prodr. cassette and CD 32 Natural Learning Songs from A-Z (Parent's Choice award), More Natural Learning Songs from A-Z (Parent's Choice award), Natural Learning Fun Songs (Parent's Choice award), Ms. Magnolia Puppet; contbr. articles to profl. jours. Mem. Assn. for Childhood Edn. Internat., Miss. Early Childhood Assn., So. Assn. for Children Under Six, So. Early Childhood Assn., Miss. Reading Assn., Internat. Reading Assn. Avocation: tennis. Home and Office: 103 Sycamore St Leland MS 38756-3136 E-mail: nlearn@naturallearning.com.

AZIZ, KHALID, petroleum engineering educator; b. Bahawalpur, Pakistan, Sept. 29, 1936; came to U.S., 1952; s. Aziz Ul and Rshida (Atamohammed) Hassan; m. Mussarrat Rizwani, Nov. 12, 1962; children: Natasha, Imraan. BS in Mech. Engring., U. Mich., 1955; BSc in Petroleum Engring., U. Alta., 1958, MSc in Petroleum Engring., 1961; PhD in Chem. Engring., Rice U., 1966. Jr. design engr. Massey-Ferguson, 1955-56; various position to asst. prof. petroleum engring. U. Alta., 1960-62; various positions, chmn. bd. Neotech. Cons. Ltd., 1972-85; mgr., dir. Computer Modelling Group, Calgary, Alta., 1977-82; various positions to chief engr. Karachi (Pakistan) Gas Co., 1958-59, 62-63; various positions to prof. chem. and petroleum engring. U. Calgary, 1965-82; hon. prof., 1994—2001; prof. petroleum engring. dept. Stanford (Calif.) U., 1982—, assoc. dean rsch. Sch. Earth Scis., 1983-86, chmn. petroleum engring. dept., 1986-91, 94-95, Otto N. Miller prof. in earth scis., 1989—. Co-author: Flow of Complex Mixtures in Pipes, 1972, Petroleum Reservoir Simulation, 1979; contbr. articles to profl. jours. Recipient Diploma of Honor, Pi Epsilon Tau, 1991; Chem. Inst. Can. fellow, 1974, Killam Resident fellow U. Calgary, 1977. Mem. AIME (hon.), European Assn. Geoscientists and Engrs., European Acad. Scis., Soc. Petroleum Engrs. (disting. mem., Ferguson award 1979, Reservoir Engring. award 1987, Lester C. Uren award 1988, Disting. Achievement award for Petroleum Engring. Faculty 1990, hon. mem. 1996), Nat. Acad. Engring., Russian Acad. Natural Scis. (fgn.), European Acad. of Sci.. Moslem. Achievements include rsch. in multiphase flow of oil/gas mixtures & steam in pipes & wells, multiphase flow in porous media, reservoir simulation (black-oil, compositional, thermal, geothermal), natural gas engring., hydrocarbon fluid phase behavior. Office: Stanford U Dept Petroleum Engring Stanford CA 94305-2220

AZIZKHAN, RICHARD GEORGE, pediatric surgeon, educator; b. London, Aug. 10, 1953; came to U.S., 1964; s. Reza George and Helga Marianne (Behnke) A.; m. Geralyn Brindisi; children: Richard Anthony, Kathryn Marie, Christine Elizabeth Ann, Aaron Brindisi. BS with honors, Dickinson Coll., Carlisle, Pa., 1972; MD, Pa. State U., 1975; PhD (hon.), Tuzla U., 2000. Diplomate in gen. surgery and pediat. surgery Am. Bd. Surgery. Resident in surgery U. Va., Charlottesville, 1976-78, 80-83; rsch. fellow in pediat. surgery Harvard Med. Sch. Boston Children's Hosp., 1978-80; fellow in pediat. surgery Johns Hopkins Univ., Balt., 1983-85; chief pediat. surgery U. N.C., Chapel Hill, 1985-93; surgeon-in-chief Child Hosp., Buffalo, 1993-98; prof. surgery and pediats. SUNY, Buffalo, 1993-98; surgeon-in-chief Children's Hosp. Med. Ctr., Cin., 1998—; prof. surgery and pediats., vice chair dept. surgery U. Cin., 1998—. Surg. adv. bd. Smith, Kline, Beecham, Phila., 1990-95; dir. pediat. surgery tng. program U. Cin., 1998—, founder hemangioma and vascular malformation treatment ctr. Cin. Childrens Hosp., 2001. Author: Congenital Malformations: Prenatal Diagnosis and Management, 1990, A Geneology of Pediatric Surgery of North America, 1997; co-author: Operative Pediatric Surgery, 2003; contbr. over 115 articles to profl. jours. Recipient Upjohn Achievement award U. Va. Sch. Medicine, 1981, Hugh J. Warren Tchg. award, 1983, Battle Disting. Excellence in Tchg. award U. N.C. Sch. Medicine, 1988, Disting. Alumnus award Pa. State U., 1995; Schering scholar ACS, 1982; SmithKline & French fellow ACS, 1986. Fellow ACS, Am. Acad. Pediats. (chair program com. 1995, surg. sect. exec. com. 1997—, chair surg. sect. 2001-02), Am. Pediat. Surgery Assn. (program com. 1990-93, bd. govs. 1998—), Pa. State U. Alumnae Assn. (life); mem. Assn. of Acad. Surgery (exec. coun. 1986-89), Alpha Omega Alpha. Roman Catholic. Achievements include research of heparin in the growth of new blood vessels (angiogenesis); development of novel technique utilizing fiberoptic laser to treat bronchial stenosis in infants. Office: Childrens Hosp Med Ctr 3333 Burnet Ave Cincinnati OH 45229-3026 E-mail: richard.azizkhan@cchmc.org.

AZODO, ADA UZOAMAKA, French language, African women's studies educator, writer; d. Bertram Enuma and Bessie Chineze; m. Michael Valentine Udennaka Azodo, Mar. 6, 1976; children: Uchendu I.C., Queen-Ijeoma A., Chijioke U., Okechukwu A. Dipl III degré, U. Dakar, Senegal, 1974; BA in French with honors, U. Ife, Nigeria, 1975; MA in French, U. Lagos, Nigeria, 1983, PhD in French/African Lit., 1990. French tutor Police Coll., Ikeja, Lagos, Nigeria, 1975-76; lectr. II Ministry of Edn., Lagos, 1976-77, 82-84; translator French/Portuguese French/Portuguese Festac (Black Festival of Art & Culture), Lagos, 1977; grad. asst. U. Lagos, 1984, 85, lectr., 1986; asst. mgr. pers. Nigerian Telecomm., Lagos, 1986-88; adj. asst. prof. St. John Fisher Coll., Rochester, N.Y., 1991-94, dir. internat. studies, 1993-94. Adj. asst. prof. SUNY, Geneseo, 1992-93, 95—. Author: L'Imaginaire Dans Les Romans de Camara Laye, 1993, Emerging Perspectives Ama Ata Aidoo, 1999, Emerging Perspectives on Mariama Bâ, 2003. Vol. Jewish Home of Rochester, 1988-92, Sunday Sch. Edn. Immaculate Conception Ch., Rochester, 1990—. Recipient Nat. award and Open scholarship U. Ife, 1972; rsch. grantee SUNY-Geneseo, 1992; named Disting. Dau. Ngene Village, Amawbia/Nigeria, 1992; recipient Friends of the Rochester Pub. Libr. recognition, 1994. Mem. MLA, Alliance Francaise Rochester, Assn. Depts. Fgn. Langs., African Lit. Assn., Rochester Assn. for UN (bd. dirs. 1994—), Upstate N.Y. African Assn. (exec. mem. 1994—). Roman Catholic. Avocations: walking, swimming, sewing.

BAAR, JOHN GREENFIELD, II, assistant principal; b. New Haven, Sept. 10, 1952; s. William Henry and Katherine Baar; m. Janet Gail Hansa, July 9, 1988. BA, U. of the South, 1975; MS, U. Ill., Chgo., 1980, MS in Tchg. Math., 1998; MEd, U. Ill., Urbana, 1991. Youth dir. Emmanuel Ch., La Grange, Ill., 1976—85; sci. instr. Evanston (Ill.) Twp. High Sch., 1981—82, Butler Sch., Oak Brook, Ill., 1982—, asst. prin., 1999—, cross country coach, 2003—. Varsity boys basketball coach, 1981-99, girls soccer coach, 1984-2002; cons. Dupage County Curriculum Com., Wheaton, Ill., 1990-91. Pres. Westchester (Ill.) Place Assn., 1988-91; advisor IMSA Leadership Conf., Aurora, Ill., 1990-91, Fermi Lab. Edn. Ctr., Batavia, Ill., 1990-92, DuPage Drug Edn. Com., Wheaton, Ill., 1988; v.p. Oak Brook Civic Assn., 1996-97, pres. 1997-2002; chmn. Oak Brook Police and Fire Commn., 2003—; mem. blue ribbon panel Family Recreation Ctr., Oak Brook Pak Dist., 1994; mem. Aquatic Ctr. Adv. Coun., 1997. Recipient Quest for Excellence in Chemistry award NSF, 1986, award of Excellence, Ill. Math. and Sci. Acad., 1991. Mem. NAESP, Ill. Sci. Tchrs. Assn., NSTA, Oak Brook Edn. Assn., Ill. Assn. Elem. Sch. Prins. Episcopalian. Avocations: golf, alpine skiing, canoeing. Home: 3 Brighton Ln Oak Brook IL 60523-2323 Office: Butler Sch 2801 York Rd Oak Brook IL 60523-2334 E-mail: jbaar@mail.butler53.com.

BAAS, ROBERT MILLER, school administrator; b. Cin., Oct. 2, 1935; s. Elmer and Clara (Miller) B.; m. Janet R. Fryburger, May 4, 1957; children: Jay Robert, Kevin, Robin, Bryan. BS in Edn., Miami U., Oxford, Ohio, 1957; MEd, Xavier U., 1963. Lic. sch. supt., Ohio. Tchr., prin. Madeira City Schs., Cin., 1957-69; prin. Indian Hill Sch. Dist., Cin., 1969—. Presenter Coun. Acad. Excellence, Columbus, Ohio, 1988-91, Nat. Mid. Sch. Conv., St. Louis, 1989. Co-founder Indian Hill Parent Networking, Cin., 1985-92. Mem. Nat. Mid. Sch. Assn., Nat. Assn. Secondary Prins., Ohio Assn. Secondary Sch. Adminstrs. Avocations: water skiing, golf, antiques, music. Home: 24 Rolling Green Ct Crossville TN 38558-8748

BABA, THOMAS FRANK, corporate economist, economics educator; b. Yonkers, N.Y., Mar. 10, 1957; s. Frank Thomas and Teresa Helen (Kratjeski) B.; 1 child, Frank Thomas. BA, Manhattan Coll., 1979; MA, Fordham U., 1982, postgrad., 1984—. Prof. Rose Hill campus Fordham U., N.Y.C., 1985-89; prof. Iona Coll., New Rochelle, N.Y., 1986-90; sr. U.S. economist, mgr. rsch. and planning group Toyota Motor Corp., N.Y.C., 1989-97; corp. economist, mkt. rsch, mgr. Mercedes-Benz USA, Montvale, NJ, 1998—. Mem. Nat. Assn. Bus. Economists, Am. Econ. Assn., N.Y. Assn. Bus. Economists, Am. Acad. Polit. Sci., World Assn. Former U.N. Interns and Fellows, Soc. Automotive Analysts. Home: 46 Linn Ave Yonkers NY 10705-2503 Office: Mercedes-Benz USA 1 Mercedes Dr Montvale NJ 07645-1833

BABARINDE-HALL, 'BUNMI, administrator educational cable station; b. Oshogbo, S.W., Nigeria, Oct. 4, 1948; came to U.S., 1977; d. Ezekiel Adekunle and Felicia Durowade (Fawumi) Babarinde; m. Larry Darnell Hall, Jan. 3, 1981. BS in Human Kinetics and Leisure Studies, George Washington U., 1979, MA in Edn. and Human Devel., 1981; MA in Mass Communication, Towson State U., 1989. Continuity announcer Radio Nigeria, Ibadan, 1968-71; producer, dir., sr. producer Nigerian Television Authority, Lagos, 1971-77; prof. theatre and dance edn. U. Ilorin, Nigeria, 1984-86; dir. Cable TV Cmty. Coll. Balt. County, Balt., 1989—. Adj. faculty phys. edn. No. Va. C.C., Annandale, 1983—; adj. faculty TV prodn. Morgan State U., Balt., 1991—, Essex Cmty. Coll., Balt., 1993—. Writer, producer, dir., editor: (TV feature series) A Salute to Women of Maryland, 1989, Another Kind of Hero, 1991, ...With Wings as Eagles, 1993; choreographer various works. Mem. Baltimorians United in Leadership Devel., 1988—; vol. Md. Correctional Institution, Jessup, 1990—. Mem. Internat. TV Assn. (treas. 1992—94), Women in Film & TV, Bus. Profl. Women, Inc. (Md. chpt.). Office: Community Coll Baltimore County Essex Campus 7201 Rossville Blvd Baltimore MD 21237-3855

BABB, MARGARET L. elementary school educator; b. Chgo., Ill., July 8, 1950; d. Charles Joseph and Marian Elaine (Andrews) Phelps; m. David Paul Babb, Jan. 5, 1985; children: Joseph Paul Ivacic, James Andrew Ivacic. BS in Edn., U. Ill., 1972; MS in Edn., No. Ill. U., 1976. Tchr. 1st, 2nd grade Clifford Carlson Sch., Rockford, Ill., 1972-77; primary cons. gifted program Martin Luther King Sch., Rockford, Ill., 1979-80, tchr. gifted edn. 2nd grade, 1980-81, tchr. gifted edn. 4th grade, 1983-86; tchr. gifted edn. 3rd grade John T. Haight Sch., Rockford, Ill., 1986-89, Martin Luther King Sch., Rockford, Ill., 1989-91; tchr. 3rd grade Marsh Sch., Rockford, Ill., 1991—. Instr. Level II tng. for gifted edn. cert., Edn. Svc. Ctr. #1 and Rockford (Ill.) Coll., 1990—; presenter in field. Co-author: Creative Wordcard Projects, 1974; author Blue Blazes and the Scientific Seven, 1998. Mem. steering com. Beattie Is., Rockford, Ill., 1983-84; bd. dirs. Rockford Woman's Club, 1977-94. Mem. Internat. Reading Assn. (presenter), Delta Kappa Gamma (officer, initiation chair 1981-94, ways and means com.), Phi Delta Kappa. Lutheran. Avocations: family activities, golf, reading, cooking. Home: 4390 Ruskin Rd Rockford IL 61101-9012 Office: Marsh Elem Sch 2021 Hawthorne Dr Rockford IL 61107-1383

BABB, ROBERTA JOAN, educational administrator; b. East Chicago, Ill., Jan. 5, 1944; d. Joseph A. and Katherine Phillips; m. Donald L. Babb, July 30, 1966; children: Sasha M., Holly S. BS in Edn., Ind. U., 1966; postgrad., De Paul U., 1972-73. Tchr. East Chicago Pub. Schs., 1969-70, Hammond (Ind.) Pub. Schs., 1966-68, 70-71; head tchr. The Lab Sch., Washington, 1968-69, 74-79; co-founder, dir. Creme de le Creme, Houston, 1982—. Scholar Ind. U., PTA. Mem. Nat. Child Care Assn., Tex. Lic. Child Care Assn; bd. dirs. Crem dela Creme Inc., Denver.

BABB, WYLIE SHERRILL, college president; b. Greenville, S.C., Aug. 20, 1940; s. J. Wylie and Sally P. B.; m. Linda Witmer, June 30, 1963; children: Corinne, Michelle, David. BA in History, Post Coll., 1963; Th.M., Dallas Theol. Sem., 1967; PhD in Edn1. Adminstrn, U. Pitts., 1979. Ordained to ministry Scottsdale, Ariz., 1967; pastor Bible Ch., 1967-71; dean acad. affairs Lancaster (Pa.) Bible Coll., 1971-76; dean faculty Moody Bible Inst., Chgo., 1976-79; pres. Phila. Coll. Bible, 1979—. Speaker, cons. in field. Mem. Am. Assn. Higher Edn., Doctoral Assn. Educators, Am. Assn. Bible Colls. (pres.), Lower Bucks County C. of C., Middle States Assn. Commn. for Higher Edn., Phi Delta Kappa. Home: 805 S Pine St Langhorne PA 19047-2924 Office: Phila Coll Bible Langhorne Manor 200 Manor Ave Langhorne PA 19047-2943

BABCOCK, JO, artist, educator; b. St. Louis, Feb. 24, 1954; s. Boyd Leon and Shirley Lynn (Hamm) B.; m. Kitty Costello, May 25, 2003. Student, UCLA, 1975; BFA, San Francisco Art Inst., 1976, MFA, 1979. Color printer Rolling Stone mag., San Francisco, 1976, Outside mag., San Francisco, 1977; cameraman 1st Calif. Press, San Francisco, 1977-80; electrician Bros. Electric, San Francisco, 1984-89; assoc. prof. San Francisco Art Inst., 1989-93; exhibit designer Levi Strauss & Co., 1989—. One-man shows include Zwinger Gallery, Berlin, 1987, Marcuse Pfeiffer Gallery, N.Y.C., 1988, Artspace, San Francisco, 1989, Visual Studies Workshop, Rochester, N.Y., 1990, Ctr. for the Arts, San Francisco, 1995, Oakland (Calif.) Mus., 1997, Kyle Roberts Gallery, San Francisco, 1992, Addison Gallery Am. Art, Andover, Mass., 1997, Chgo. Art Inst., 1982, CEPA, Buffalo, 1988, others; exhibited in group shows at Friends of Photography Gallery, Carmel, 1976, Sao Paulo (Brazil) Bienal, San Francisco Mus. of Modern Art, 1989, Rena Bransten Gallery, San Francisco, 1991, Oliver Art Ctr., CCAC, 1991, Lieberman & Saul, N.Y., 1991, Tampa Mus. Art, 1992, San Jose Mus. Art, 1992, Palm Springs Desert Mus., 1993, 100 Years of Landscape Art in the Bay Area, M.H. de Young Mus., San Francisco, 1995, Bay Area Landscapes, 1995, The Alternative Mus., N.Y., 1981, Wooster St. Gallery, N.Y., 1981, Living Mus., Rejkjavik, Iceland, 1983, 10 on 8, N.Y., 1983, Windows on White, N.Y., 1984, Public Image, N.Y., 1984, Otis Parsons Gallery, L.A., 1985, Hotel Project, Oakland, Calif., 1986, Roanoke (Va.) Mus. Fine Art, 1988, Ctr. for contemporary Arts, Santa Fe, 1988, Artists at the Rock, Alcatraz, Calif., 1988, others; represented in permanent collections at San Francisco Mus. Modern Art, Bklyn. Mus., Newport Harbor Art Mus., Lightwork, Syracuse, N.Y., La Biblioteque, Avignon, France, San Francisco Pub. Libr., San Francisco Arts Commn., George Eastman House, Rochester, N.Y., Nat. Collection, Smithsonian Instn., others. Grantee City of Oakland, 1985, N.Y. State Coun. on Arts, 1988, Nat. Endowment for Arts, 1990. Mem. Primitive Hunting Soc. Avocation: building pinhole cameras. Studio: 378 San Jose Ave Apt B San Francisco CA 94110-3700 E-mail: jobabcock@webtv.net.

BABCOCK, MARGUERITE LOCKWOOD, addictions treatment therapist, educator, writer; b. Jacksonville, Fla., Jan. 1, 1944; d. Allen Seaman and Emilie (Lockwood) B. BA in Art History, Am. U., 1965; M Counselor Edn., U. Pitts., 1982. Lic. profl. counselor, Pa.; cert. addictions counselor Pa., nat. cert. counselor, master's addiction counselor (nat.). Addictions therapist South Hills Health Sys., Pitts., 1978-81; addiction therapist, clin. supr., clin. dir. Alternatives- Turtle Creek Mental Health/Mental Retardation/D&A Ctr., Pitts., 1981-86; addictions therapist, coord. Ligonier Valley Treatment Ctr., Stahlstown, Pa., 1986—88; addictions clin. supr., unit dir. Ctr. for Substance Abuse Mon-Yough, McKeesport, Pa., 1988-96; quality assurance Mon-Yough, McKeesport, 1996-97; clin. supr. Sojourner House, Pitts., 1997-2000; co-founder, addictions cons. consortium Outcomes Builders, 2000—. Adj. instr. in addictions courses Seton Hill Coll., Greensburg, Pa., 1989-91, C.C. Allegheny County, West Mifflin, Pa., 1989-91, Pa. State U., McKeesport, 1993—; pvt. trainer, writer, Acme, Pa., 1985—; ind. info. profl. in addictions, 2003—. Co-author, co-editor: Challenging Codependency: Feminist Critiques, 1995; mem. editl. bd. Jour. Tchg. in Addictions, 2000—; contbr. articles to profl. jours. Fellow Andrew Mellon Found., 1966-68, NSF, 1967. Mem.: Alpha Lambda Delta, Phi Kappa Phi. Avocation: website designer. Home and Office: 3533 Rt 130 Acme PA 15610-9712 E-mail: allele@lhtc.net.

BABCOCK, MICHAEL WARD, economics educator; b. Bloomington, Ill., Dec. 10, 1944; s. Bruce W. and Virginia (Neeson) B.; m. Virginia Lee Brooks, Aug. 4, 1973; children: John, Karen. BSBA, Drake U., 1967; MA in Econs., U. Ill., 1971, PhD in Econs., 1973. Tchg. asst. U. Ill., Urbana, 1968, 71, rsch. asst., 1972; prof. econs. Kans. State U., Manhattan, 1972—. Cons. Santa Fe, Burlington No., and Union Pacific R.R., Brotherhood of Maintenece Way, United Transp. Union, Kans. Dept. Transp., Kans. Dept. Agr., U.S. Dept. Agr., Kans. Dept. Commerce. Gen. editor Jour. Transp. Rsch. Forum; contbr. articles to profl. jours., newspapers, mags. Apptd. to Kans. Govs. R.R. Working Group to Evaluate Class I R.R. Mergers, 1995, 96, 2000. With U.S. Army, 1969-71. Recipient A.T. Kearney award Transp. Rsch. Forum, 1987, 89, UPS Found. award, 1990, Edgar S. Bagley award Kans. State U., 1989, 93, 97, 03, Outstanding Rsch. in Agrl. Transp. award Burlington No. R.R., 1994, Rail-Tex. Corp. award Transp. Rsch. Forum, 1997, Sr. Faculty award for rsch. excellence in social sci. Kans. State U., 1998; grantee U.S. Army C.E., 1978-79, USDA, 1978-79. 80-82, 84-85, 96-97, 2000, Kans. Dept. Agr., 1987, Kans. Wheat Commn., 1989, 92, 93, Midwest Transp. Ctr., 1989, 92, 93, Kans. Dept. Transp., 1991—, Mid-Am. Transp. Ctr., 1995, 96. Mem. Am. Assn. Agrl. Economists, Missouri Valley Econ. Assn., Mid-Continent Regional Sci. Assn., So. Regional Sci. Assn., Transp. Rsch. Forum (gen. editor Jour.), Transp. Rsch. Bd., Coun. Logistics Mgmt., So. Econs. Assn., Western Econs. Assn., Beta Gamma Sigma, Omicron Delta Epsilon. Home: 720 Harris Ave Manhattan KS 66502-3614 Office: Kans State U Dept Econs Manhattan KS 66506

BABCOCK-NICE, MICHELE ELIZABETH, elementary school educator; b. Gowanda, N.Y., July 27, 1971; BA in Psychology, BA in Polit. Sci., SUNY, Buffalo, 1993, postgrad. in bus. mgmt., 1994; MS in Student Pers. Adminstrn., State U. Coll. N.Y., Buffalo, 1997. Cert. secondary social studies educator, N.Y., Ga., mid. sch. educator, Ga. Legal sec. First Investors Corp., Manhattan, 1993; investment acctg. sec. Tchr.'s Retirement System, Manhattan, 1993; sr. legal sec. Magner, Love & Morris, Buffalo, 1993-94; asst. tchr. Quality Day Care Svcs., Williamsville, N.Y., 1994; customer svc. rep. Key Corp., Amherst, N.Y., 1995-96; grad. intern Career Devel. Ctr. State U. Coll. N.Y., Buffalo, 1995-96; grad. intern career devel., student life Hilbert Coll., Hamburg, N.Y., 1996; legal asst. Davis, Augello, Matteliano & Gersten, Buffalo, 1996-97, Damon & Morey LLP, Buffalo, 1997-98; substitute tchr. Orchard Park (N.Y.) Ctrl. Sch., 1998—2000; substitute tchr. and home tutor Springville-Griffith Inst. Ctrl. Sch., NY, 1998—2000; tchr. history Freedom Mid. Sch., Stone Mountain, Ga., 2000—. Census enumerator U.S. Bur. Census, 2000; volleyball referee Ga. Ofcls. Assn., Atlanta, 2000—01; com. rep. Anti-drug and Alcohol Campaign SUNY Buffalo, 1999—2000, student govt. senator, 1999, jud. appeal bd. mem., 99; cons. writing Freedom Mid. Sch., Stone Mountain, 2001, advisor Nat. Jr. Honor Soc., 2001—. Author: Windows into My Soul, 1996; editor opinion sect. The Record newspaper, State Univ. Coll., Buffalo, 2000. Vol. educator Children's Mus. of Manhattan, 1993; campaign vol. Rep. Party, N.Y.C., 1993; intern N.Y. State Assemblyman Dem. Sam Hout, Buffalo, 2000; religious edn. tchr. St. Joseph's Ch., Gowanda, 1995-96. Recipient Sokolowski Meml History Scholarship award, 2000, Niagara Frontier Police Athletic Assn. scholarship, 1989, Erie County Agrl. Soc. scholarship, N.Y., 1989, Erie County Fair award in Photography, 1998. Mem. Profl. Assn. Ga. Educators, Nat. PTSA, Kappa Delta Pi, Phi Alpha Theta. Democrat. Roman Catholic. Avocations: photography, writing, theater, music, nature.

BABEL, RAYONIA ALLEEN, retired librarian, educator; b. Herrin, Ill., Sept. 5, 1935; d. Hubert Ray and Mabel Alleen (Manning) Vaughn; m. Jerald Lee Babel, Sept. 5, 1954 (div. 1973); children: Thomas, Carl, Penny, Heidi, Krista. Student, Milliken U., 1953-55; BA in Edn., No. Ill. U., 1970, MA in Libr. Sci., 1971. Cert. tchr., Ill. Head ref. svcs. Aurora (Ill.) U., 1971—2000; ret., 2000. Precinct committeeman Dems. of Kane County, 1973-78; treas. Charlemagne on the Fox Questers, 1991-93; sec. Restorations of Kane County. Mem. Libras, Inc. (v.p. 1991-92, pres. 1992-93). Methodist. Avocations: reading, miniatures, needlework. Home: 623 Katherine St Saint Charles IL 60174-3734

BABICH, HARVEY JEROME, biology educator; b. Bklyn., Mar. 19, 1947; s. Morris Lewis and Florence Esther (Silverman) B.; m. Marsha Friedman, June 12, 1969; children: Sara, Eric, Ariella. AA in Hebrew, BA in Biology, Yeshiva Coll., 1968; MS in Biology, L.I. U., 1971; PhD in Biology, NYU, 1976. Lab. asst. Lab. Histology Osborne Labs. Marine Scis., Coney Island Aquarium, Bklyn., 1969; teaching fellow dept. biology L.I. U., Bklyn., 1969-70; rsch. asst. Lab. Microbial Ecology NYU, N.Y.C., 1970-75, teaching fellow dept. biology, 1972-73, adj. instr., 1973-76, rsch. assoc. Lab. Microbial Ecology dept. biology, 1976-79, sr. rsch. scientist dept. biology Lab. Microbial Ecology, 1980-81; sr. staff scientist toxic substances program Environ. Law Inst., Washington, 1979-80; sr. rsch. assoc. Lab. In Vitro Toxicologic Assay Devel. Rockefeller U., N.Y.C., 1984-91; prof. dept. biology Stern Coll. for Women Yeshiva U., N.Y.C., 1987—. Presenter workshops and symposiums at various orgns., univs. and cos.; cons. Ctr. Sci. in Pub. Interest, Washington, Com. on Biol. Markers, NRC, Nat. Acad. Scis., Dept. Pharmacology, NYU Med. Ctr., Envirosphere, Ebasco Svcs., Inc., N.Y., Holt, Rinehard and Winston, N.Y., Inst. Risk Analysis Sch. Bus. Adminstrn., The Am. U., Washington, Intra/Dyne, N.Y., Middletown Twp., Levittown, Pa., Thompson Med. Co., N.Y., others. Author: (with others) Principles of Biology - I A Laboratory Manual, 1976, II, 1975, Principles of Biology A Laboratory Manual, 1979, revised, 1987; contbr. over 125 articles to profl. jours. Grantee U.S. EPA, Schering Plough Rsch. Inst., others; recipient award NYU Club, 1976; named Prof. of Year Stern Coll., Yeshiva U., 1990, 96, 2000, 02. Fellow Am. Acad. Microbiology; mem. AAAS, Am. Soc. Microbiology. Office: Stern Coll Women 245 Lexington Ave New York NY 10016-4605

BACA, JUDITH F. art educator; Founder, artistic dir. Social and Pub. Art Resource Ctr., Venice, Calif., 1976—; prof. fine arts UCLA, 1980—, prof. art for world arts and cultures, 1996—, vice chair Cesar Chavez Ctr., 1996—. Mural, The Great Wall of Los Angeles, Durango Mural Project: La Memoria De Nuestra Tierra, 15 Digital Tile Murals on the Venice Boardwalk, 2001, La Memoria de Nuestra Tierra: Colorado, La Memoria de Nuestra Tierra: California, Danzas Indigenas, World Wall: A Vision of the Future Without Fear, Represented in permanent collections Nat. Mus. Am. Art, Smithsonian, Wadsworth Antheneum, Hartford, Conn. Fellow, John Simon Guggenheim Meml. Found., 2003. Office: UCLA Bunche Hall 7349 Mailcode 155903 Los Angeles CA 90095-1559*

BACA, SHERRY ANN, secondary school educator; b. Huron, S.D., Jan. 11, 1950; d. Myron Marion Moberg and Emily Ann (Matkovich) Baxter; m. Ed R. Baca, Oct. 14, 1972; children: Jamie Marie, Jennifer Lea. BS in Edn., No. Ariz. U., 1971, MAT in Math., 1972. Cert. secondary sch. math. tchr., secondary sch. prin., supr. Math. tchr. Prescott (Ariz.) Jr. High, 1972-75; adj. math. tchr. Yavapai Coll., Prescott, 1975-84; math. tchr. grades 7-9 and dept. chmn. Granite Mt. Jr. High, Prescott, 1976-88; math. coord. Prescott Unified Schs., 1979—; math. tchr. grades 9-12 Prescott High Sch., 1988—. Adj. math. instr. Prescott Coll., 1980—, No. Ariz. U., 1988—; dir. math. sci. N. Ctrl. Ariz. Consortium, 1992—; presenter and lectr. at many ednl. workshops and confs.; mem. Math. Scis. Edn. Bd., Washington, 1997-2001. Editor (monthly sci./ math. newsletter) Prescott Unified Schs., 1979—; contbr. articles to profl. pubs. Recipient Quality Edn. Program award, Ariz. Dept. Edn., 1981, Gov.'s citation for excellence in math. teaching, 1984, Presidential award for excellence in math. teaching, 1984,, Disting. Alumni award No. Ariz. U., 1989, State Farm Good Neighbor award, 1992, Outstanding Women in Edn. award, Delta Kappa Gamma, 1992, 93, Toyota's Investment in Math. Excellence award, 1997; featured in mags. and on TV; named U.S. West Tchr. of Yr. for Ariz., 1993; recipient Tandy Tech. Scholar award for excellence in math. teaching, 1995. Mem. Nat. Coun. Tchrs. of Math., Nat. Coun. Suprs. of Math., Coun. Presdl. Awardees in Math. (co-historian 1989—), Ariz. Assn. Tchrs. of Math. (sec. 1984-87, v.p. 1989-91, newsletter editor 1991-95, 99—, pres. 1995-97), Ariz. Sci. Tchrs. Assn., Ariz. Alliance for Math. Sci. and Tech. Edn. (bd. dirs. 1986-88, adv. bd. 1988—, continued svc. award 1991), Ariz. Math. Coalition (adv. bd. 1990—), Ariz. Math. Network (regional dir. 1989-91), Sch. Sci. and Math. Assn., Phi Delta Kappa (many offices), Alpha Delta Kappa Avocations: clog dancing, piano. Office: Prescott High Sch 1050 Ruth St Prescott AZ 86301-1790

BACCALA, BEVERLY ANNE, adult education educator; b. Balt., Dec. 30, 1965; d. Julian Thomas and Mildred Florence (Preston) Brice m. Nicholas Herbert Baccala, May 13, 1995. BA in English, cert. in pub. policy, U. Md., Catonsville, 1987; MPA, Fla. State U., 1989. Ticket agt., sales clk. Md. Sci. Ctr., Balt., 1982-85, supr. visitor svcs., 1985-86; grad. rsch. asst. Fla. State U., Tallahassee, 1987-88; asst. planner Clark Roumelis & Assocs., Tallahassee, 1988; cmty. assistance cons. Fla. Dept. Cmty. Affairs, Tallahassee, 1989-90; coord. econ. devel. Washington County Econ. Devel. Commn., Hagerstown, Md., 1990-98; one-stop employment partnership coord. Frederick (Md.) C.C., 1998—2001; regional coord. for adult edn. and workforce devel. Regional Edn. Svc. Agy., 2001—. Mem. Commn. Adult Basic Edn. Editor: Alligators and Other Perceptions, 1997. Founder, pres. Discovery Sta. at Hagerstown, Inc., 1996-2001. Mem.: Coun. on Adult Basic Edn., Nat. Assn. Workforce Devel. Profls., W.Va. Adult Edn. Assn. Democrat. Episcopalian. Avocations: camping, hiking, gourmet cooking. Office: RESA VIII 109 S Coll St Martinsburg WV 25401

BACCARELLA, THERESA ANN, primary school educator; b. Bayonne, N.J., June 8, 1960; d. George Thomas and Antoinette (Barresi) Nolan; m. John Richard Baccarella, Oct. 27, 1984; children: Jaclyn Marie, Ryan Thomas. BA in Early Childhood Edn. summa cum laude, Jersey City State Coll., 1982, MBA, Reading Specialist, 1994. Cert. tchr. nursery, kindergarten, elem. Head tchr., asst. coord. Jersey City State Coll. Child Care Ctr., 1982-84; basic skills tchr. kindergarten, 1st grade Bayonne (N.J.) Pub. Sch. System, 1984-88; tchr. lst grade, kindergarten, 2nd grade Hazlet (N.J.) Twp. Sch. System, 1988—. Mem. curriculum coms. Hazlet Bd. Edn., 1988-90. Confraternity of Christian Doctrine tchr. Ch. of the Ascension, Bradley Beach, N.J., 1991—. Recipient Tchr. Recognition award, 1990-91. Mem. Monmouth Art Alliance, Hudson Reading Coun. (rec. sec. 1994-95, corr. sec. 1995-96), Hudson Reading Coun. (v.p. 1996-97), Alpha Upsilon Alpha (co-pres. 1993-94, v.p. 1994-96), Kappa Delta Pi. Roman Catholic. Avocations: drawing, painting, collage. Home: 53 Wyncrest Ln Neptune NJ 07753-7421

BACH, CYNTHIA, educational program director, writer; b. Oct. 28; BA in Art Edn., UCLA, 1955; MPA, U. So. Calif., 1978; LDS, Calif. Luth., 1993. Cert. gen. elem., spl. secondary art, and gen. jr. h.s. tchr. Staff asst. L.A. Unified Sch. Dist., 1976; rainbow tchr., gifted coord. Trinity Elem. Sch., L.A., 1978-81; field worker/in-svc. for parents and staff educator Hubbard Elem. Sch., Sylmar, Calif., 1981-90; student observer Liggett Elem. Sch., Panorama City, Calif., 1990-92; tng. tchr. Calif. State U. (Northridge)-Vena Sch., Arleta, Calif., 1992-93; pres. Comprehensive Learning Systems. Rsch. bd. advisors Am. Biograph. Inst., Inc. Author: Alternatives to Retail Marketing for Seniors (Bur. of Consumer Affairs); creator: (theological game) Might is the Wind. Lectr. Sr. Citizens Bur. Consumer Affairs, City Hall; past pres. local PTA; del. Children's Def. Fund Conf., 1998; sch. bd. mem. St. Martin-in-the-Fields Parish Sch.; mem. coun. bd. Amnesty Internat.; sponsor Christian Found. for Children and Aging; mem. Mus. of Tolerance, Alliance for Tolerance; co-founder scholarship fund for women ministers; ofcl. hostess rep. for vis. diplomats through the World Affairs Coun. City of Los Angeles; lay eucharistic min., 1998; established scholarship fund King's Sem. Ch. on the Way. Named 79 State Evaluation Mar Team-outstanding educator, Phi Alpha Alpha, Nat. Acad. Hon. Soc. Pub. Affairs Adminstrn., Order of Internat. Fellows Edn., Outstanding Woman of 20th Century, 2000, on Wall of Tolerance, Montgomery, Ala.; named to Nat. Divsn. Rsch. Bd. Advisors, Am. Biog. Inst.; recipient Spl. Recognition award, 21st Century Award for Achievement, Pres.'s Award of Merit as outstanding citizen in field of edn.; scholar, Nat. Art, Chouinard Art Inst. Mem. NAFE, AAUW, 1st Century Soc. UCLA, Nat. Mus. Women in Arts (assoc.), Phi Alpha Alpha. Avocations: reading, theology, old movies, writing, gardening. Home: 5140 White Oak Ave Apt 214 Encino CA 91316-2435

BACH, LINDA WALLINGA, special education educator; b. Rock Rapids, Iowa, Feb. 13, 1953; d. Warren Dale and Beverley (Gardner) Wallinga; m. Daniel Lee Beber, Nov. 2, 1974 (div. Nov. 1980); m. Daniel Louis Bach, June 10, 1981; children: Davin Lane, Thadeous Colin. BEd, U. Nebr., 1975; M Early Childhood Edn., U. S.C., 1989. Cert. tchr. Nat. Bd. Edn., 2002. Substitute tchr. Omaha Pub. Schs., 1975-76; drug mgr. Alan Eber Assocs., Denver, 1976-77; spl. edn. tchr. Winters (Tex.) Elem. Sch., 1978-81; substitute tchr. Dept. Def. Sch., Woodbridge, U.K., 1981-83; spl. edn. tchr. DeLaine Elem. Sch., Sumter, S.C., 1983-85; lead spl. edn. tchr. Oakland Elem. Sch., Sumter, 1985-94, tchr. spl. edn., 1994-96, Rafting Creek Elem. Sch., 1996—2000; spl. edn. tchr. Cherryvale Elem. Sch., Sumter, SC, 2001—. Mem. project team to write presch. and kindergarten inclusion program for handicapped children and regular children, 1994; mem. action team for site-based 5 yr. planning Oakland Spl. Olympics Team Coach Elem. Sch., 1994. Chair Oakland Elem. Sch. PTA Haloween Carnival, Sumter, 1989, 90, 92; delegation leader People to People student ambassador program, 1999; com. mem. Rafting Creek Behavior Alert Team/Healthy Schs., Boy Scout Troop 342, 1998-2001. Basic skills multi-sensory curriculum mini-grantee S.C. Coun. Exceptional Children and Upgrade Systems, 1990, Edn. Improvement Act grantee for improving math. and reading skills, 1995; named Tchr. of Yr. Rafting Creek Elementary, 1999-2000, Disting. Reading Tchr. Rafting Creek Elementary, 1999-2000, Delegation leader to Australia People to People Student Ambassadors, 2000. Mem. NEA, PTA, Coun. Exceptional Children (sec.-treas. 1988-90, membership chmn. 1990-93, pres. elect 1993-94, membership chmn. 1995—). Methodist. Avocations: sewing, boating, reading. Office: Cherryvale Elementary School 1480 Furman Drive Sumter SC 29151

BACH, MICHELE, education educator; b. Puyallup, Wa., Aug. 25, 1947; BA, U. Md.; MS, U. Utah, Kans. State U. Math. prof. Kansas City (Kans.) C.C., 1986—. Office: Kansas City Kans Cmty Coll 7250 State Ave Kansas City KS 66112

BACHICHA, JOSEPH ALFRED, physician, educator; b. Rock Springs, Wyo. s. Alfred and Helen B. BA, Stanford U., 1977; MD, Boston U., 1982. Diplomate Am. Bd. of Ob-Gyn. Intern St. Luke's-Roosevelt Hosp., N.Y.C., 1982-83; resident in ob-gyn. Stanford U. Hosp., Palo Alto, Calif., 1983-86; pvt. practice Chgo., 1986-95; asst. prof. ob-gyn. U. Calif., San Francisco, 1996-97, assoc. prof., 1997-99; med. dir. Pacific Occupl. Health Med. Assocs., South San Francisco, 1999—2003; assoc. physician Kaiser Permanente, 2000—. Cons. WHO, UN Family Planning Assn.; asst. prof. Northwestern U., Chgo., 1986-95; Gen. Hosp., 1996-99, dir. student edn. dept. ob-gyn., 1998-99, dir. obstetrics, 1995-98; dir. Excelsior Group Health

Care for Women and Children, San Francisco, 1995-98; dir. low-risk obstetrics, coord. undergrad. med. edn. Prentice Women's Hosp., Chgo., 1990-95; mem. Liaison Com. on Med. Edn.; physician, educator Carnegie Found., Ghana, 1989, Project Hope, Nicaragua, 1992. Contbr. articles to profl. jours. Mem. Chgo. Coun. Fgn. Rels. Grad. fellow Rotary Found., 1980; mem. Harvard Macy Scholars Inst., 1995. Fellow ACOG, Assn. Profs. Gynecology and Obstetrics, Internat. Coll. Surgeons, Royal Soc. Medicine; mem. AMA, APHA, Nat. Bd. Med. Examiners, Am. Assn. Maternal and Neonatal Health, Am. Fertility Soc., Chgo. Gynecol. Soc., San Mateo County Med. Soc., Stanford U. Alumni Assn., Boston U. Sch. Medicine Alumni Assn., Commonwealth Club Calif. Roman Catholic. Avocations: mystery books, cross country skiing, weight training, running, aerobics. Office: 27400 Hesperian Blvd Hayward CA 94545

BACHMAN, GEORGE, mathematics educator; b. N.Y.C., Jan. 17, 1933; s. Frederick Joseph and Ruth (Benson) B.; m. Joan Caggiano. B.E.E., N.Y. U., 1950, MS, 1952, PhD in Math, 1956. Asst. prof. math. Rutgers U., New Brunswick, N.J., 1957-60; mem. faculty Bklyn. Poly. Inst., 1960—, assoc. prof., 1962-66, prof., 1966—. Author: (with L. Narici and E. Beckenstein) Functional Analysis and Valuation Theory, 1971, (with L. Narici) Functional Analysis, 1966, Elements of Abstract Harmonic Analysis, 1964, Introduction to p-adic Numbers and Valuation Theory, 1964; Contbr. articles to profl. jours. Recipient Disting. Teaching award Bklyn. Poly. Inst., 1974, Disting. Research award Sigma Xi, 1982; NSF grantee, 1968— Mem. Am. Math. Soc., Math. Assn. Am. Home: 27 Summit Rd Riverside CT 06878-2104 Office: 333 Jay St Brooklyn NY 11201-2907

BACHMAN, NEAL KENYON, librarian; b. Iowa City, Aug. 10, 1950; s. Neal and Esther Elaine (Archer) B. B.Mus. in Edn., U. Nebr., 1972, MEd, 1978; cert. in distance edn., Ind. U., 2002. Tchr. instrumental and vocal music Osceola (Nebr.) Schs., 1972-73; band dir. Elkhorn (Nebr.) Pub. Schs., 1973-75; retail salesman Musicland, Lincoln, Nebr., 1975-76; media specialist Malcolm (Nebr.) Pub. Schs., 1978-83; libr. Clarinda (Iowa) H.S., 1983-85, Eisenhower Sch., Ft. Leavenworth (Kans.) Unified Schs., 1985-91; substitute tchr. Blue Valley (Kans.) Sch. Dist., 1991-92; substitute libr. Kansas City (Kans.) Pub. Libr., 1992-94; libr. asst. U. Kans. Med. Ctr., 1993-94; libr. Atchison Cath. Elem. Sch., Kans., 1994-95; substitute tchr. Olathe (Kans.) Dist. Schs., 1995-96; coord. elem. libr. media Liberal (Kans.) Unified Schs., 1996-2001; libr. Arkansas City (Kans.) Unified Schs., 2001—. Instr. Ft. Hays State U., 1997; vis. instr. U. Nebr.-Lincoln, 1982. Contbr. articles to profl. jours. Mem. Discovery Expedition of St. Charles, Mo., 1996—. Recipient Malcolm PTO Cert. of Recognition, 1981. Mem. Assn. for Ednl. Comm. and Tech. (Leader award, pres. sch. media tech. div. 2003—), Kans. Assn. for Ednl. Comm. and Tech. (bd. dirs. 1999-2001, pres.-elect 2001, pres. 2002-03), Kans. Sch. Libr. Media Dirs. (co-chair 2000-01), Kans. Assn. Sch. Librs., Malcolm Edn. Assn. (pres. 1980-81), Nebr. Alumni Band (charter), Nebr. Ednl. Media Assn. (dir. 1982-83), Phi Delta Kappa. Office: 1201 N 10th St Arkansas City KS 67005

BACHMEYER, STEVEN ALLAN, secondary education educator; b. Queens, N.Y., Feb. 8, 1945; s. Harold Frederick and Dorothy (Blackstone) B.; m. Mary Louise Bachmeyer, June 18, 1968; children: Steven Adam, Melanie Hope. AA, Miami Dade C.C., 1966; BEd in Indsl. Arts Edn., U. Miami, 1969; MS in Computer Edn. Tech., Barry U., 1995. Cert. tech. edn. Tchr. indsl. arts Miami Springs (Fla.) Jr. High Sch., 1969-73, dept. chmn., 1972-73; tchr. indsl. arts Hialeah-Miami Lakes Sr. High Sch., Hialeah, Fla., 1973-86, chmn. graphic arts, architecture and engring. drafting dept., 1986; instr. architecture and engring. drafting, tech. studies and aerospace tech. South Dade Sr. High Sch., Homestead, Fla., 1988-2000; part-time dir. Camp Adventure, Black Mountain, N.C., 1984-86, dir., 1986-88; chmn. tech. edn. dept. South Dade Sr. High Sch., Homestead, Fla., 1991—; vocat. dept. chmn. Felix Varela Jr. H.S., 2000—. Founder/exec. dir. Aerospace Edn. Alliance, 1997; dir. Tech. Concepts, Homestead, Fla., 1991—; instr. part-time dept. indsl. arts edn. U. Miami, Coral Gables, Fla., 1971-72; instr. part-time bldg. constrn. drawing and archtl. history dept. arch./bldg. constrn. Miami Dade C.C., 1980-84; writer curriculum framework aerospace tech. program Fla. State Dept. Edn., 1991; mem. equity com. South Dade Sr. H.S., 1989-90, mem. tchrs. as advisors steering com., 1989-91, mem. sch. based mgmt. team, 1990-91; mem. tech. com. for tech. edn. Fla. Dept. Edn., 1991, 92, 93, Fla. Tchr. Cert. Devel. Com., 1992-93; mem. state tech. com. Tech. Ed.; chmn. bd. Fla. Tech. Student Assn. and Found., Inc., 1993; demonstration tchr. Fla. Acad. Excellence in Teaching, Fla. Dept. Edn., 1993; part-time instr. Fla. Internat. Univ., 1996—; presenter blueprint workshop Fla. Dept. Edn., 1991, aerospace tech. curriculum project, Lakeland, Fla., 1993, aerospace tech. curriculum project Nat. Congress Aviation and Aerospace Edn., Orlando, Fla., 1993, Norfolk, Va., 1994, NASA Internat. Space Camp, Huntsville, Ala., 1993; workshop instr. Dade County Pub. Schs., 1993; adj. prof. dept. vocat./adult edn. U. South Fla., 1994, dept. vocat. edn., 1995; adj. prof. div. vocat. edn. Fla. Internat. U. Author: Aerospace Technology Curriculum Project--Principles of Aeronautics, 1991-93, Technology in Action Project Series, 1994, Parachutes Yesterday, Today, Tomorrow, 1993, Up From Clay A Beginners Guide to R/C, Space-Science and Technology Series, 1996; author The World of Comms. visual media, 1972, The World of Comms. audio visual media, 1973, An Introduction to Comms. Careers, 1974. Asst. supt. Dade County Youth Fair, 1990-95; supt. aerospace tech. divsn. Dade County Youth Fair, 1997; waterfront dir. McGregor-Smith Scout Reservation, Inverness, Fla., 1981, program dir., 1982-83; cert. camp dir. Boy Scouts Am., cubmaster, scoutmaster, explorer advisor troop 124, Hollywood, Fla., 1980-86, scoutmaster troop 811, Old Fort, N.C., 1987-88; mem. sch. bd. Prince of Peace Luth. Ch./Sch. 2d lt. U.S. Army. Recipient Graphic Arts Tchr. Excellence award Kiwanis Club Miami, 1981, Tchr. Excellence award Dade County DAVACCE, 1990, Newsmast Honor award NASA, 1990, scholarship Fla. Assn. Ednl. Data Systems, 1991, Tchr. Excellence award Internat. Tech. Edn. Assn., Fla., 1993, Excellence in Aviation Edn. award Gen. Aviation Mfrs. Assn., 1993, Best Practice award Fla. Vocat. Assn., 1993, 94, Ednl. Profl. Excellence award Kelvin Found. Tech., 1994, Tandy Tech. scholar, 1993-94/nat. hon. mention, 2 nat. awards, 1997, 1 regional award, Regional Tchr. of the Yr., Dade County Pub. Schs., Fla., 1997, Janice M. Dwyer Aviation Edn. award Aircraft Distbrs. and Mfrs. Assn., 1998, Christa McAuliffe award Air Force Assn./Nat. Aerospace Tchr. of the Yr., 1998, A. Scott Crossfield award Civil Air Patrol-Crown Cir., 1998, Glenn Curtis award Greater Miami Aviation Assn., 2002. Mem. Am. Vocat. Assn., Fla. Aerospace Edn. Assn. (mem. exec. bd. 1993), Fla. Vocat. Assn. (presenter conf. 1991-94), Fla. Tech. Edn. Assn. (conf. presenter 1989-94, pres. region V 1989-91, bd. dirs. 1989-91, pres.-elect 1992, pres. 1993, Tchr. of Yr. finalist 1990, 1, 92, Tchr. of Yr. award 1993), Fla. Assn. Computers Edn., Dade County Tech. Edn. Assn., Internat. Tech. Edn. Assn. (presenter nat. conf. 1992, 93, 94, 95, scholarship 1992, Program Excellence award Fla. chpt. 1992, Tchr. Excellence award 1993), Internat. Soc. Tech. Edn., Tech. Student Assn. (event chmn. aerospace tech. nat. conf. 1991-95, Outstanding Advisor award Fla. chpt. 1990, chmn. adv. coun. 1990-92, dir. adv. tng. conf. 1990, presenter nat. conf. 1990-92, instr. profl. workshop 1992, state advisor Vocat. Student Orgn., 1993, region tchr. year, 1997), Aerospace Edn. Found., Assn. Ednl. Comm. and Tech. (divsn. interactive systems and computers), Am. Camping Assn. (advanced campcraft, tripmaster and campcraft instr. certs.), Am. Canoe Assn. (whitewater canoe instr.), Epsilon Pi Tau (pres., Alpha Omega chpt.). Democrat. Avocations: sailing, photography. Office: Felix Varela Sr HS 15255 SW 96th St Miami FL 33196-1200 Home: 34845 SW 187th Ct Homestead FL 33034-4538 E-mail: bach1@earthlink.net., sbachmeyer@varela.dadeschools.net.

BACHTEL, ANN ELIZABETH, educational consultant, researcher, educator; b. Winnipeg, Man., Can., Dec. 12, 1928; d. John Wills. and Margaret Agnes (Gray) Macleod; m. Richard Earl Bachtel, Dec. 19, 1947 (dec.); children: Margaret Ann, John Macleod, Bradley Wills; m. Louis Philip Nash, June 30, 1978 (div. 1987). AB, Occidental Coll., 1947; MA, Calif. State U., L.A., 1976; PhD, U. So. Calif., 1988. Cert. life tchr., adminstr., Calif. Elem. tchr. various pub. and pvt. schs., Calif., 1947-50, 64-77; dir. emergency sch. aid act program, spl. projects, spl. art State of Calif., 1977-80; leader, mem. program rev. team Calif. State Dept. Edn., 1981-85; cons. Pasadena Unified Sch. Dist., 1981-85. Cons. Pasadena Unified Sch. Dist., 1981-86; tchg. asst., adj. prof. U. So. Calif.; cons., presenter in field. Editor: Arts for the Gifted and Talented, 1981; author Nat. Directory Programs for Artistically Gifted and Talented Students K-12; contbr. articles to profl. jours. Active legis. task forces; chair resource allocation com. City of Pasadena, 1982-90; mem. Pasadena-Mishima (Japan) Sister Cities Internat. Com., 1983—; asst. chair Pasadena-Jarvenpaa, Finland, 1990-92, chair, 1992-95; asst. chair Pasadena-Mishima, 1996-97; active L.A. World Affairs Coun., Bonita Unified Sch. Dist. Curriculum Coun., 1990-93, Dist. Task Force Fine Arts, 1990-93, Dist. Task Force Tech., 1990-93, Dist. Handwriting Task Force, 1993, Pasadena Hist. Soc., Pasadena Philharm. Com., Womens Com. Pasadena Symphony Assn.; deacon Pasadena Presbyn. Ch., 1989-92, elder, 1997-2000; vice-moderator Presbyn. Women, 2000—; bd. govs. Occidental Coll. Alumni Assn., 2000—. Emergency Sch. Aid Act grant, 1977-81; named to Bonita Unified Sch. Dist. Hall of Fame, 1990-91. Mem. World Coun. Gifted and Talented Children, Internat. Soc. Edn. Through Art, Nat. Art Educators Assn. (dels. assembly 1988-92), L.A. County Art Edn. Coun., Clan MacLeod Soc. (bd. dirs. So. Calif. chpt.), Phi Delta Kappa, Kappa Delta Pi, Pi Lambda Theta (pres. L.A. chpt. 1991-95, nat. rsch. awards com. 1989-91, chair 1991-95, co-pres. region V 1993-97, Ella Victoria Dobbs Nat. Rsch. award 1989, Outstanding Pi Lambda Thetan in region V 1993-95, Internat. by-laws com. 1999-2003), Assistance League Pasadena.

BACIGALUPE, GONZALO MANUEL, family therapist, educator; b. Santiago, Chile, Nov. 23, 1958; came to U.S., 1988; s. Pedro Raimundo and Flor Maria Bacigalupe; m. Antonieta María Bolomey, Oct. 13, 1959; 2 children: Bethania Constanza, Diego Andreas. BA in Psychology, Cath. U. Chile, Santiago, 1984, MA equivalent Psychologist, 1986; EdD in Marriage and Family Therapy, U. Mass., 1995. Lic. marriage and family therapist, Mass. Clin. dir. adolescent unit La Granja Cmty. Mental Health Ctr., Santiago, 1985-86; clin. staff mem. Family Therapy Inst. Santiago, 1985-87; psychologist, mental health supr. Protection for Youth Damaged by States of Emergency, Temuco and Valdivia, Chile, 1987-88; prof. U. Los Lagos, Osorno, Chile, 1987-88; teaching asst. U. Mass., Amherst, 1988-91; outreach family therapist Northampton (Mass.) Area Mental Health Svcs., 1989-90; clin. supr. Mass. Soc. for Prevention of Cruelty to Children, Holyoke, Mass., 1990-94; asst. prof. Sch. Social and Systemic Studies Nova Southeastern U., Ft. Lauderdale, Fla., 1994-96; asst. prof. Grad. Coll. of Edn. U. Mass., Boston, 1996—2002, dir. family therapy program, 2000—02, assoc. prof., 2002—; staff clinician trauma evaluation and intervention team Judge Baker Children's Ctr./Harvard Med. Sch., 1997-99. Adj. prof. La Araucania Coll., Temuco, 1987—88; cons. Roxbury Comprehensive Health Ctr., 1996—97; staff psychologist Judge Baker Children's Ctr. Harvard Med. Sch., 1997—99; assoc. con. L.Am. Consultancy Svcs., 1996—98; mem. faculty family therapy team Ctr. for Multicultural Tng. in Psychology, 1997—2000; Fulbright sr. rsch. scholar Autonomous U. Barcelona, Spain. Mem. editl. rev. bd.: Jour. Systemic Therapies, 1994—; co-editor, 2001—; mem. editl. bd.: Jour. Marital and Family Therapy, —, Jour. Trauma Practice, 1993—2001; mem. editl. bd. Jour. of Qualitative Rsch. in Psychology; overview book reviewer: Readings, 1993—2001; prodr.: (TV series) cable access ACTV, 1991—94; video prodn. coord. : MCTV, 1992. Bd. dirs. Coun. Contemporary Families, 2000—02. Fgn. student tuition scholar U. Mass., 1989-90; rsch. fellow Mauricio Gaston Inst. Latino Cmty. Devel. and Pub. Policy, 1998-99, Am. Assn. for Marriage and Family Therapy Coun. of Elections, 1999-2001, Fulbright Sr. scholar, 2004. Fellow: Chilean Soc. Clin. Psychology; mem.: APHA, APA, Acad. for Health Svcs. and Health Policy, Assn. for Family Therapy, Internat. Family Therapy Assn. (3d World Family Therapy Congress award 1991), Interam. Soc. Psychology, Chilean Psychol. Assn., Am. Soc. Cybernetics (Travel scholar 1990), Am. Assn. for Marriage and Family Therapy (chair elections coun. 2001, supr. and clin.), Latin Am. Studies Assn., Am. Family Therapy Acad. (bd. dirs. 2001—), Soc. for the Psychol. Study of Social Issues. Office: Univ Mass Boston Grad Coll Edn 100 Morrissey Blvd Boston MA 02125-3393 E-mail: gonzalo.bacigalupe@umb.edu.

BACKES, LORA STEPHENS, speech/language pathologist; b. Baton Rouge, Nov. 21, 1959; d. Preston M. and Geraldine (Ducote) Stephens; m. Charles E. Backes, Dec. 15, 1979; children: Michelle, Katherine, Emily. BS, La. State U., 1983; MEd, Southeastern La. U., Hammond, 1989. Cert. speech./lang./hearing specialist, supr. student teaching. Speech/lang. pathologist Ascension Parish Sch. Bd., Gonzales, La., 1983-93; asst. prof., clin. supr. Valdosta (Ga.) State U., 1993—. Mem. Am. Speech/Lang. Hearing Assn., Ga. Speech/Lang. Hearing Assn., Ga. Supervisory Network, Phi Delta Kappa. Roman Catholic. Avocations: camping, family outings, stitchery. Home: 5255 Cypress Dr Lake Park GA 31636-3143 Office: Valdosta State U Coll Edn Bldg Valdosta GA 31698-0001 E-mail: lsbackes@valdosta.edu.

BACKES, NANCY CONSTANCE, English educator; b. Petoskey, Mich., Apr. 25, 1949; d. Dale Meredith and Josephine Alvira (Pigeon) Switzer; m. Thomas John Backes, Apr. 19, 1969; 1 child, John-Thomas. BA, U. Wis., Eau Claire, 1971; MA, U. Wis., 1978, PhD, 1990. Cert. tchr. secondary edn., English, Wis. Asst. editor Country Beautiful, Waukesha, Wis., 1972-73; tchg. asst. U. Wis., Milw., 1977-78, 82-84; project asst. Ctr. for Improvement of Instrn., 1981-82; grants specialist U. Wis. Parkside, Kenosha, 1986-89; lectr. Marquette U., Milw., 1990-92, vis. asst. prof., 1992-97; asst. prof. Cardinal Stritch U., 1997—2001, assoc. prof., chair English, 2001—. Author: Great Fires of America, 1973; contbr. chpts. in books. Mem. Modern Lang. Assn., Midwest Modern Lang. Assn. Avocations: drawing, painting, bicycling. Home: 5943 N Berkeley Blvd Milwaukee WI 53217-4641

BACKHERMS, KATHRYN ANNE, parochial school educator; b. Cin., Aug. 19, 1955; d. Francis Walter and Mary Elizabeth (Healy) B. BA, Coll. Mount St. Joseph (Ohio), 1977; MusM, U. Cin., 1981. Cert. tchr., Ohio. Music specialist 1-8 St. Ursula Villa, Cin., 1977-79; choral music dir. McAuley High Sch., Cin., 1980-86; chairperson music dept. Coll. Mt. St. Joseph, 1986-89; music dir. St. Ursula Acad., Cin., 1989—. Mem. rev. teams area high schs. North Cent. Assn., Cin., 1987-89; presenter Archdiocesan In-Svc. Day, Cin., 1988; adjudicator Ohio Fedn. Music Clubs, Cin., Ohio Fedn. Music Clubs Collegiate Solo Auditions, Columbus, 1989. Composer: (musicals) Musical, 1973, Just Like Me, 1975, Take A Chance, 1976, Nothing Can Stop Us Now, 1979, Heaven Help Us, 1983, Some Things Never Change, 1984, The Real Me, 1985, Something Special, 1997, The Magic Touch, 2001. Recipient Tchr. award Greater Cin. Found., 1984; profl. devel. grantee St. Ursula Acad., 1997, 2000. Mem. Music Educators Nat. Conf., Mu Phi Epsilon (v.p. Cin. alumnae chpt. 1992-94), Kappa Gamma Pi (treas. Cin. alumnae chpt. 1988-89). Avocations: composing, playing instruments, pets, astronomy. Office: Saint Ursula Acad 1339 E McMillan St Cincinnati OH 45206-2180

BACKMAN, VADIM, biomedical engineer, educator; b. St. Petersburg, Russia, May 7, 1973; arrived in U.S., 1996, naturalized, 2002; s. Yuri and Galina Backman. MS, St. Petersburg Technical U., 1996, MIT, 1998; PhD, Harvard U., 2001. Rsch. asst. Ioffe Phys. Tech. Inst. Russian Acad. Sci., St. Petersburg, 1993—96; rsch. asst. MIT, Cambridge, Mass., 1996—2000, rsch. assoc., 2000—01; asst. prof., dir. biomed. optical imaging & spectroscopy lab. Northwestern U., Evanston, Ill., 2001—. Cons. MIT, Cambridge, 2001—. Author: Handbook of Optical Biomedical Diagnostics, 2002, Biomedical Optical Engineering, 2002; contbr. articles to profl. jours. Recipient Best Paper award in New Techs. in Biomedical Optics and Med. Imaging, Nat. Sci. Found., 2002, Nat. Sci. Found. Career award, 2003; fellow, George Soros Internat. Sci. Found., 1995, Lester Wolfe fellow, 1999, Poitras fellow, 2000; scholar, GM Cancer Rsch. Found., 2002. Mem.: Am. Physical Soc., Optical Soc. Am. Achievements include invention of light scattering spectroscopy; tri-modal spectroscopy of tissue. Office: BME Dept Northwestern University 2145 Sheridan Rd Evanston IL 60208 Office Fax: 847 491-4928. Personal E-mail: v-backman@northwestern.edu. Business E-Mail: v-backman@northwestern.edu.

BACKUS, ANN SWIFT NEWELL, education educator, consultant; b. Worcester, Mass., Sept. 23, 1941; d. C. Bradford and Elizabeth C. (Norlander) Newell; m. Robert A. Backus, June 28, 1964; children: Gillian, Bradford. AB, Mt. Holyoke Coll., 1963; MS, Antioch New Eng. Grad. Sch., 1994. Rsch. asst. Eaton-Peabody Lab., Boston, 1963-65; adminstrv. asst. Kakuri Hosp., Kaduna, Nigeria, 1965-66; biology tchr. Milford High Sch., Milford, N.H., 1967-69; organist, tchr. Manchester, N.H., 1969—; performing arts coord. N.H. State Commn. on Arts, Concord, N.H., 1980-83, acting exec. dir., 1982-83; dir. ops. Wolf Orgn., Cambridge, Mass., 1983-84; coord. collaborative programs N.H. Coll. and Univ. Coun., Manchester, 1984-93, coord. profl. devel., 1987-93; ednl. cons., 1993—; mem. faculty biology dept. Keene (N.H.) State Coll., 1994. Vis. scholar Harvard Sch. Pub. Health, 1993, vis. lectr. Occupl. Health Program, 1994; interim dir. Internat. Inst. Boston, Manchester, 1994-95; dir. Outreach Occupl. and Environ. Health, Harvard Sch. Pub. Health, 1994—, lectr. occupl. health program, 1995—. Author: Annotated Bibliography, 1988; contbr. articles to profl. jours. Founder Manchester Pro Musica, 1979; vol. coord. Nixon for Gov. N.H., 1974; bd. dirs. N.H. Symphony Orch., 1977-80, Manchester Hist. Soc.; project dir. Fund for Improvement Post-secondary Edn. Drug Prevention Grant, 1989-91; chmn. bd. dirs. N.H. Coun. for Humanities, Concord, 1976-77; pres. N.H. Coun. for Better Schs., 1979-81, Am. Lung Assn. N.H., 1987-89; mem. coms. Task Force on HIV/AIDS-N.H., 1990-92, chmn. edn. and prevention subcom., 1990-93; bd. dirs. Am. Lung Assn., N.H., 1996—; co-founder N.H. Coun. for HIV Edn. and Prevention, 1993; co-founder N.H. Higher Edn. Alcohol and Other Drug Com., 1995. Recipient grant Bean Found., 1985, grant Gov.'s Drug-Free Schs. and Communities Fund, N.H. Dept. Edn., 1993, grant Fund for Improvement Post-Secondary Edn. Drug Prevention, 1993-95, grant Health and Human Svcs. Strengthening Communities, 1994—, grant N.H. Office of Refugee Resettlement, 1994—. Mem. NSTA. Unitarian-Universalist. Office: Harvard Sch Pub Health Dept Environ Health Boston MA 02115

BACON, FRANK WILLIAM, finance educator, consultant; b. Richmond, Va., Sept. 14, 1950; s. Wellington and Ethel Prestley Bacon; m. Trudy Hite Bacon, July 12, 1975 (div. June 30, 1998); children: Frank William, Jr., Sally Ruth, Samuel Wellington, Christopher Hite; m. Dana Epley Bacon, Nov. 3, 2001; 1 child, Camille Ethel. BS, U. Richmond, 1972; MS, Va. Commonwealth U., 1974, phD, 1990. Adj. prof. Southside Va. C.C., Keysville, Va., 1975—78, assoc. prof., 1978—89; instr. fin. Va. Commonwealth U., Richmond, 1987—89; prof. fin. Longwood U., Farmville, Va., 1989—. Contbr. articles to profl. jours. Treas., bd. dirs. Southside Electric Coop., 1984—; chair fin. com. Lunenburg County Bd. Suprs., 1989—, vice chmn. 1st lt. U.S. Army Corps Engrs., 1972—73. Mem.: Nat. Assn. Counties, Va. Assn. Counties, Va.-Md.-Del. Assn. electric Coops., Nat. Rural Electric Coop. Assn., Ea. Fin. Assn., Midwestern Fin. Assn., Ea. Econ. Assn., Southwestern Fin. Assn., So. Fin. Assn., Fin. Mgmt. Assn., Am. Soc. Bus. and Behavioral Scis., Beta Gamma Sigma. Democrat. Methodist. Avocations: quail hunting, fishing, boating, running. Home: 2978 Bacon Fork Rd Kenbridge VA 23944 Office: Longwood U 201 High St Farmville VA 23909 E-mail: fbacon@longwood.edu.

BACON, LEONARD ANTHONY, accounting educator; b. Santa Fe, June 10, 1931; s. Manuel R. and Maria (Chavez) Baca; m. Patricia Balzaretti; children— Bernadine M., Jerry A., Tiffany A. B.E., U. Nebr.-Omaha, 1965; M.B.A., U. of the Americas, Mexico City, 1969; Ph.D., U. Miss., 1971. CPA; cert. mgmt. acct., internal auditor. Commd. 2d lt. U.S. Army, 1951, advanced through grades to maj., 1964, served fin. and acctg. officer mainly Korea, Vietnam; ret., 1966; asst. prof. Delta State U., Cleveland, Miss., 1971-76; assoc. prof. West Tex. State U., Canyon, 1976-79; prof. acctg. Calif. State U., Bakersfield, 1979—; cons. Kershen Co. (now Atlantic Richfield Oil Co.), Canyon, 1979-80. Contbr. articles to profl. jours. U.S., Mex., Can., papers to profl. confs. Leader Delta area Boy Scouts Am., Cleveland, 1971-76; dir. United Campus Ministry, Canyon, 1976-79; min. Kern Youth Facility, Bakersfield, 1983—, Christians in Commerce, 1990—. Paratrooper Brazilian Army, 1955. Mem. Am. Acctg. Assn., Am. Inst. CPA's, Am. Assn. Spanish Speaking CPA's, Inst. Mgmt. Accts. (pres. Bakersfield chpt. 1981-82, Most Valuable Mem. award 1981), Am. Mgmt. Assn., Inst. Mgmt. Acctg., Calif. Faculty Assn., Acad. Internat. Bus., Inst. Internal Auditors, Inst. Cost Estimators and Analysts, Alpha Kappa Psi (Dedicated Service award 1979), Omicron Delta Epsilon, Beta Gamma Sigma. Clubs: Jockey (Rio de Janeiro). Lodges: Lions (v.p. Cleveland 1971-73), Kiwanis (v.p. 1974-79, A Whale of a Guy award, Cleveland 1975, Plaque of Appreciation, 1992-93). Office: Calif State U 9001 Stockdale Hwy Bakersfield CA 93311-1022

BACON, ROGER LEE, English educator, consultant; b. Boise, Idaho, Oct. 23, 1939; s. Russell C. and Uvonna (Royle) B.; m. Christine Lee Wright, Dec. 18, 1965; children: Kim Bacon Stanger, Bryan Lee Bacon, Eric Lee Bacon, Melissa Lee Bacon Magelsen, Jill Leeann Bacon. BA in English, Bus., U. Oreg., 1964, MA in English, 1965; PhD in English, U. Utah, 1972, PhD in Cultural Founds. Edn., 1976. Asst. prof. So. Oreg. U., Ashland, 1965-69; tchg. fellow U. Utah, Salt Lake City, 1969-72; assoc. prof. English, coord. tech. writing program No. Ariz. U., Flagstaff, 1972-00, coop. edn. intern dir., 1975—. Vis. prof. U. Utah, Salt Lake City, 1973-77, U. Wash., Seattle, 1982; cons. Franklin Covey & Shipley Assocs., Salt Lake City, Utah, 1980—, Law Sch. Adminstrn. Test Board, 1980-2000. Cons. editor various textbooks Prentice Hall Publishers, Wadsworth Publishers, 1978—. Merit Badge Counselor Boy Scouts Am., Flagstaff, Ariz., 1973—; Bishop Ch. Latter Day Saints, Flagstaff, 1994-97. Col. USAFR, 1958-99, chaplain. Decorated USAF Meritorious Svc. medal (3). Mem. Assn. Tchrs. Tech. Writing, Soc. Tech. Comm., Reserve Officer Assn., Phi Kappa Phi. Avocations: christmas story collecting, environmental writing. Office: No Ariz U PO Box 6032 Flagstaff AZ 86011-0001

BACON, SHERRI LEAH, elementary education educator; b. Tipton, Mo., Jan. 24, 1968; d. Robert Lee and Sharon Regina (Schreck) Fulton. BS in Edn., Ctrl. Mo. State U., 1990; MS in Edn., Troy State U., 1996. 6-8th grade tchr. Moniteau R-V, Latham, Mo., 1990-92; 6th grade tchr. N.W. Middle Sch., Clarksville, Tenn., 1992-93; 1st grade tchr. Norman Smith Elem., 1993-94; early childhood ctr. tchr. Dawning Point, Enterprise, Ala., 1994-96; tchr. 3d grade Sacred Heart Sch., 1998-99, tchr. 1st grade, 1999-2000; tchr. 3d grade Columbia Cath. Sch., Mo., 2000—. Mem. Gamma Sigma Sigma (pres., 1st v.p., sec., Outstanding Mem. award 1990), Kappa Delta Pi. Avocations: reading, aerobics, computers. Home: 11298 Campbell Bridge Dr Prairie Home MO 65068

BACOW, LAWRENCE SELDON, academic administrator, environmental educator; b. Detroit, Aug. 24, 1951; s. Mitchell Leon and Ruth Wertheim Bacow; m. Adele Fleet, June 1, 1975; children: Jay, Kenneth. SB, MIT, 1972; JD, M in Pub. Policy, Harvard U., 1976, PhD, 1978. Bar: Mass. 1978. Asst. prof. law and environ. policy MIT, Cambridge, 1977-84, assoc. prof. law and environ. policy, 1984-90, dir. Ctr. for Real Estate, 1990-92, prof. law and environ. policy, 1992-97, Lee and Geraldine Martin prof. environ. studies, 1997—2001, chmn. faculty, 1995-97, chancellor, 1998—2001; pres. Tufts Univ., 2002—. Vis. assoc. prof. law Hebrew U., Jerusalem, 1981-82; rsch. assoc. Harvard Law Sch., Cambridge, 1982-88; vis. prof. Politecnico di Torino, Italy, 1990, U. Bari, Italy, 1991, Gabriela Mistral U., Santiago, Chile, 1992, 93, 94, 95, 97, Faculty Econs.-U. Amsterdam, The Netherlands, 1993-94; rsch. fellow The Tinbergen Inst., Amsterdam, 1993-

94. Author: Bargaining for Job Safety and Health, 1980; co-author: (with M. O'Hare and D. Sanderson) Facility Siting and Public Opposition, 1982, (with L. Susskind and M. Wheeler) Resolving Environmental Regulatory Disputes, 1983, (with M. Wheeler) Environmental Dispute Resolution, 1984. Mem. presdl. transition team Occupl. Safety and Health Adminstrn., 1977; mem. socio-econ. subcom. NAS Com. on Surface Mining and Reclamation, 1978-79; advisor Mass. Spl. Legis. Commn. on Hazardous Water, 1980; gubernatorial appointee Mass. Hazardous Waste Facility Site Safety Coun., 1980-83; Town Meeting mem., Arlington, Mass., 1981-83; advisor Israel Environ. Protection Svc., 1981-83; chair citizens adv. com. Mass. Water Resources Authority, 1989; exec. com. One Thousand Friends Mass., 1989-95; advisor Cross Israel Hwy. Commn., 1994-95; dir. MIT Hillel, Cambridge, 1995-98, Jewish Cmty. Housing for the Elderly, Brighton, Mass., 1995—; trustee Hebrew Coll., Brookline, Mass., 1999—, Wheaton Coll., Norton, Mass., 1999—, dir. Am. Coun. on Edn., 2003—. Recipient William S. Ballard award Am. Soc. Real Estate, 1991; adminstrn. fellow Harvard U., 1972-76, post-doctoral fellow Ford Found., 1977; Legal scholar Ctr. for Pub. Resources, 1985. Mem. Am. Acad. Arts and Scis., Mass. Bar Assn., Phi Beta Kappa. Jewish. Avocations: sailing, skiing, running. Office: Tufts University President's Office Ballou Hall Medford MA 02155 E-mail: bacow@tufts.edu.

BADALAMENTE, MARIE ANN, orthopedist, educator; b. Bronx, NY, July 17, 1949; d. John William and Elizabeth Ann (Castelluccio) B. BA, L.I. U., 1971, MS, 1973; PhD, Fordham U., 1977. Instr. of biology CUNY, Bronx, 1974-75; asst. prof. of biology C.W. Post Coll., L.I. U., Brookville, N.Y., 1975-78; asst. prof. of anatomy Sch. Medicine SUNY, Bklyn., 1978-79, asst. prof. of orthopaedics Stony Brook, 1979-86, assoc. prof., 1986-93; prof., 1993—. Author: Principles of Orthopaedic Practice, 1996, 2d edit., 1997, Surgery of the Hand and Upper Extremity, 1996; co-author: Dupuytren's Disease, 1990, 3d edit., 1999, Operative Nerve Repair and Reconstruction, 1991, Management of Peripheral Nerve Problems, 1998, Non-Operative Treatment of Dupuytren's Disease, 1999, Dupuytren's Disease, 2002-2002; contbr. articles to profl. jours. Grantee NIH, 1985-94, Orthopaedic Rsch. Found., 1982-87, Easter Seals Found., 1981-85, Muscular Dystrophy Assn., 1979-81, FDA, 1997—. Roman Catholic. Office: SUNY Sch Medicine Dept Orthopaedics Stony Brook NY 11794-0001 Business E-Mail: mbadalamente@notes.cc.sunysb.edu.

BADASH, LAWRENCE, science history educator; b. Bklyn., May 8, 1934; s. Joseph and Dorothy (Langa) B.; children: Lisa, Bruce. BS in Physics, Rensselaer Poly. Inst., 1956; PhD in History of Sci., Yale U., 1964. Instr. Yale. U., New Haven, 1964—65, research assoc., 1965-66; from asst. to assoc. prof. U. Calif., Santa Barbara, 1966-79, prof. history of sci., 1979—2002, prof. emeritus, 2002—. Dir. summer seminar on global security and arms control U. Calif., 1983, 86, energy rsch. group, 1992, pacific rim program mem., 1993-95; cons. Nuclear Age Peace Found., Santa Barbara, 1984-90. Author: Radioactivity in Am., 1979, Kapitza, Rutherford, and the Kremlin, 1985, Scientists and the Development of Nuclear Weapons, 1995; editor: Rutherford and Boltwood, Letters on Radioactivity, 1969; Reminiscences of Los Alamos, 1943-45, 1980. Bd. dirs. Santa Barbara chpt. ACLU, 1971-86, 96—, pres., 1982-84, 96-98; nat. bd. dirs. Com. for a Sane Nuclear Policy, Washington, 1972-81; mem. Los Padres Search and Rescue Team, Santa Barbara, 1981-94. Lt. (j.g.) USN, 1956-59. Grantee, NSF, Cambridge, Eng., 1965-66, 69-72, 90-92, Am. Philos. Soc., New Zealand, 1979-80, Inst. on Global Conflict and Cooperation, Univ. Calif., 1983-87; J.S. Guggenheim fellow, 1984-85. Fellow AAAS (sect. mem. at large 1988-92), Am. Phys. Soc. (chmn. divsn. of history of physics 1988-89, exec. com. forum on physics and society 1991-93); mem. History of Sci. Soc. (founder West Coast chpt., chpt. bd. dirs. 1971-73, nat. coun. 1975-78). Democrat. Jewish. Avocation: backpacking. Office: Univ Calif Dept History Santa Barbara CA 93106-9410

BADDERS, REBECCA SUSANNE, military officer, educator, writer; b. Knoxville, Tenn., Jan. 6, 1962; d. John Albert and Tamara Elizabeth Badders. BA in Edn., U. Fla., 1984; MA in Edn., U. South Fla., Tampa and St. Petersburg, 1997; MSM in Bus., Troy State U., 2002. Cert. profl. tchr., Fla. Commd. ensign USN, 1984, advanced through grades to lt. comdr., 1995; oceanographic watch officer Naval Facility Brawdy, Wales, 1984-86; oceanographic officer anti-submarine warfare Comdr. Undersea Surveillance, Norfolk, Va., 1986-90; dept. head Readiness Tng. Facility, Dam Neck, Va., 1990-93; tchr. Pinellas County Schs., Largo, Fla., 1994-97; commanding officer Naval Weapon Sta. res. det., Charleston, S.C., 1995-97; exec. officer Naval Res. Ctr., Kearny, N.J., 1997-99, Earle, N.J., 1999-2000, Naval Res. Profl. Devel. Ctr., New Orleans, 2000—03; commanding officer Naval Res. Ctr., Columbia, SC, 2003—. Faculty rep. Pinellas County Tchrs. Assn., Largo, 1994-97. Author: Maddy and the Peek-A-Boo Moon, 1995. V.p., bd. dirs. Pilot Club Internat., Mid-Pinellas, Fla., 1993-99. Recipient Navy Achievement medal, 1990, 93, 96, Navy Commendation medal, 2000, Meritorious Svc. medal, 2003. Mem. Naval Res. Assn., Res. Officers Assn., Navy League of U.S., Coun. for Exceptional Children, U. Fla. Alumni Assn., U. South Fla. Alumni Assn., Troy StateAlumni Assn., LHS Alumni Assn., Internat. Order of Rainbow (worthy advisor, pres. 1975-82), Scabbard and Blade, Kappa Delta Pi. Republican. Episcopalian. Avocations: travel, computers, reading, gourmet cooking, arts. Office: 513 Pickens St Columbia SC 29201 E-mail: rbadders@aol.com.

BADDOUR, RAYMOND FREDERICK, chemical engineer, educator, entrepreneur; b. Laurinburg, NC, Jan. 11, 1925; s. Frederick Joseph and Fannie (Rizk) B.; m. Anne M. Bridge, Sept. 25, 1954; children: Cynthia Anne, Frederick Raymond, Jean Bridge. BS, U. Notre Dame, 1945; MS, Mass. Inst. Tech., 1949; ScD, 1951; D (hon.), St. Andrew's Coll., 1999. Asst. dir. Engring Practice Sch., Oak Ridge, 1948-49; asst. prof. Mass. Inst. Tech., 1951-57, asso. prof., 1957-63, prof. chem. engring, 1963-89, Lammot du Pont prof. chem. engring., 1973-89, prof. emeritus, 1989—, also head dept., 1969-76; dir. Environ. Lab., 1970-76. Mem. Project Separation AEC, 1954; AIChE del. Mendeleev Conf. on Pure and Applied Chemistry, Moscow, 1959; lectr. Max Planck Insts., Germany, 1962; Shell lectr. Cambridge (Eng.) U., 1962; P.C. Reily lectr. Notre Dame U., 1964; Dr. Warren K. Lewis lectr., chmn. engring. MIT, 1998; mem. sci. adv. com. Gen. Motors Corp., 1971-82; co-founder, chmn. Abcor, Inc., Cambridge, Mass., 1963-72; dir. Raychem Corp., 1972-80; founder, chmn. Energy Resources Co., Inc. (ERCO), 1974-83; chmn. ERCO AG, 1980-83; co-founder dir. Amgen, Inc., 1980-97, Lam Rsch., 1980-82; co-founder BREH, Inc., 1983; co-founder, dir. SKB, Inc., 1984, MatTek Corp., 1985, BLW Corp., 1985, Enterprise Mgmt. Corp., 1985, Ascent Pediat., Inc., 1989-2001; cons. Mobil Chem. Co., NYC, 1963-84, U.S. Dept. Commerce, 1960-62, Freeport Minerals Co., NYC, 1976-83, Allied Chem. Co., 1980-81; bd. dirs. Scully Signal, 1996—; bd. dirs., chmn. Activ Biotics, Inc., 2001—; Warren K. Lewis lectr. chem. engring. MIT, 1998. Mem. corp. Boston Museum Sci.; mem. sci. and tech. adv. bd. Field Enterprises, Chgo. (World Book Ency.), 1966-68. United Engrs. and Constructors preceptorship, 1956; NSF sr. post-doctoral fellow, 1967-68; recipient honor award U. Notre Dame Coll. of Engring., 1976 Fellow Am. Inst. Chem. Engrs., Am. Inst. Chemists, Am. Acad. Arts and Scis., N.Y. Acad. Scis.; mem. AAAs, Am. Chem. Soc. Achievements include research publs. and patents in field.

BADEAU, CARLENE DIANNA, elementary education educator; b. Barre, Vt., Oct. 6, 1947; d. Wayne Sargent and Hazel Grace (Brown) Tillotson; m. Richard Jean-Louis B., May 11, 1968; children: Cara, R. Michael, Mark. Assoc., C.C. of Vt., 1990; BA, Norwich U., 1992. Cert. tchr., Vt. Weaver Walden Mills, Lawrence, Mass., Barre, 1976-90; student tchr. Barre Town Elem. Sch., 1991; Orton-Gillingham Instr. Washington Ctrl. Supervisory Union, Barre, 1992—. Author: It's Always Been Taboo for Me: An Exploration of Women and Art, 1992. Active parents, tchrs., neighbors assn. Barre Town Elem. Sch., 1991-92. Avocations: drawing, painting, reading, sewing. Home: 16 Carnes Rd East Barre VT 05649

BADEER, HENRY SARKIS, physiology educator; b. Mersine, Turkey, Jan. 31, 1915; came to U.S., 1965, naturalized, 1971; s. Sarkis and Persape Hagop (Koundakjian) B.; m. Mariam Mihran Kassarjian, July 12, 1948; children: Gilbert H., Daniel H. MD, Am. U., Beirut, Lebanon, 1938. Gen. practice medicine, Beirut, 1940-51; asst. instr. Am. U. Sch. Medicine, Beirut, 1938-45, adj. prof., 1945-51, asso. prof., 1951-62, prof. physiology, 1962-65, acting chmn. dept., 1951-56, chmn., 1956-65; research fellow Harvard U. Med. Sch., Boston, 1948-49; prof. physiology Creighton U. Med. Sch., Omaha, 1967-91, emeritus prof., 1991—, acting chmn. dept., 1971-72. Vis. prof. U. Iowa, Iowa City, 1957-58, Downstate Med. Center, Bklyn., 1965-67; mem. med. com. Azounieh Sanatorium, Beirut, 1961-65; mem. research com. Nebr. Heart Assn., 1967-70, 85-88. Author textbook Spanish translation; contbr. chpts. to books, articles to profl. jours. Recipient Golden Apple award Students of AMA, 1975, Disting. Prof. award, 1992; Rockefeller fellow., 1948-49; grantee med. research com. Am. U. Beirut, 1956-65 Mem. Internat. Soc. Heart Rsch., Am. Physiol. Soc., Internat. Soc. for Adaptive Medicine (founding mem.). Home: 2808 S 99th Ave Omaha NE 68124-2603 Office: Creighton U Med Sch 2500 California Plz Omaha NE 68178-0001

BADEN, MICHAEL M. pathologist, educator; b. N.Y.C., July 27, 1934; s. Harry and Fannie (Linn) B.; m. Judianne Densen-Gerber, June 14, 1958; children: Trissa, Judson, Lindsey, Sarah BS, CCNY, 1955; MD, NYU, 1959. Diplomate Am. Bd. Pathology. Intern, first med. div. Bellevue Hosp., N.Y.C., 1959-60, resident, 1960-61, resident in pathology, 1961-63, chief resident in pathology, 1963-64, fellow in pathology, 1964-65; pvt. practice in pathology N.Y.C., 1965—; asst. med. examiner City of N.Y., 1961-65, jr. med. examiner, 1965-66, assoc. med. examiner, 1966-70, dep. chief med. examiner, 1970-78, 79-81, 83-86, chief med. examiner, 1978-79; dep. chief med. examiner, dir. labs. Suffolk County, N.Y., 1981-83; dep. chief med. examiner N.Y.C., 1983-86; dir. forensic scis. unit N.Y. State Police, 1986—; instr. in pathology NYU, N.Y.C., 1964-65, asst. prof. pathology, 1966-70, assoc. prof. forensic medicine, 1970-89. Adj. prof. law N.Y. Law Sch., N.Y.C., 1975-88, John Jay Coll. Criminal Justice, N.Y.C., 1989-90, 93; vis. prof. pathology Albert Einstein Sch. Medicine, N.Y.C., 1975—; lectr. pathology Coll. Physicians and Surgeons, Columbia U., N.Y.C., 1975—, adj. prof. pathology and lab. medicine, 1993—; asst. vis. pathologist Bellevue Hosp., N.Y.C., 1965-75; adj. prof. pathology and lab. medicine Albany (N.Y.) Med. Sch.; lectr. Drug Enforcement Adminstrn., Dept. Justice, 1973—; vis. lectr. Fairleigh Dickinson Dentistry, Hackensack, N.J., 1968-70; spl. forensic pathology cons. N.Y. State Organized Crime Task Force, 1971-75; chmn. forensic pathology panel U.S. Ho. of Reps. select coms. on assassinations of Pres. John F. Kennedy and Dr. Martin Luther King, Jr., 1977-79; mem. med. adv. bd. Andrew Menchell Infant Survival Found., 1969-74; mem. cert. bd. Addiction Svcs. Agy., N.Y.C., 1966-69; preceptor health research tng. program N.Y.C. Dept. Health, 1968-79; v.p. Coun. for Interdisciplinary Communication in Medicine, 1967-69; forensic pathology cons. N.Y. State Police, 1985—. Author: Alcohol, Other Drugs and Violent Death, 1978, Unnatural Death, 1989; contbr. articles on forensic medicine to profl. jours.; mem. editorial bd. Am. Jour. Drug and Alcohol Abuse, 1973—, Internat. Microfilm Jour. Legal Medicine, 1969-73, Contemporary Drug Problems, 1971. Active N.Y. adv. bd. Odyssey House, Inc., 1966-76; bd. dirs. N.Y. Coun. on Alcoholism, sec., 1969-79; bd. dirs. Belco Scholarship Found., Inc., 1971-87. Recipient Great Tchr. award NYU, 1980 Fellow Coll. Am. Pathologists (chmn. toxicology subcom. 1972-74), Am. Soc. Clin. Pathologists (mem. drug abuse task force 1973—), Am. Acad. Forensic Scis. (program chmn. 1971-72, sec. sect. pathology and biology 1970-71, exec. com. 1971-74, v.p. 1982-83); mem. Med. Soc. County N.Y. (mem. pub. health com. 1966-76), Soc. Med. Jurisprudence (corr. sec. 1971-78, v.p. 1979-81, pres. 1981-85, chmn. bd. 1985—), Nat. Assn. Med. Examiners, N.Y. Path. Soc., N.Y. State Med. Soc., AMA, Internat. Royal Coll. Health Office: 142 E End Ave New York NY 10028-7503

BADER, CAROL HOPPER, dean; b. Navasota, Tex., Sept. 14, 1949; d. Hugh Leo and Virginia Frances (Sibley) Hopper; m. Lawrence Edward Bader, Aug. 4, 1973; 1 child, Joseph Scott. BA, La. Tech. U., 1971; MA, Purdue U., 1973; PhD, La. State U., 1978. Cert. tchr., Ind., La. Title I reading tchr. Ascension Parish Sch. Bd., Donaldsonville, La., 1973-74, reading tchr., dept. chair St. Amant, La., 1974-76; cons. Exxon Co., Baton Rouge, 1976-78; reading coord. La. State U., Baton Rouge, 1978-87; chair, prof. developmental studies Middle Tenn. State U., Murfreesboro, 1987—2002; asst. dean edn., prof. Ga. Coll. & State U., Milledgeville, 2002—. Cons. Bader Reading Cons., Baton Rouge, 1976-87; leader scholar Kellogg Inst., Boone, N.C., 1989. Author: Keys to Better College Reading, 1994, Improving Reading Comprehension, 1992; contbr. articles to profl. jours. Scout leader, asst. Cub Scouts, Baton Rouge, Murfreesboro, 1984-87. Mem. Nat. Assn. for Developmental Edn. (chair profl. devel. 1988-90, 95-96, chair election com. 1993-94, chair nat. conf. 1991-92, chair profl. liaison, 1990-91, co-chair membership 1996-99, treas. 2001-2003), Tenn. Assn. for Developmental Edn. (newsletter editor 1988-90, Outstanding Devel. Educator 1992), La. Assn. for Developmental Edn. (sec. 1985-87, sec. 1982-85, newsletter editor). Methodist. Avocations: reading, gardening, collegiate sports spectator, traveling. Home: 169 Lakecrest Dr Milledgeville GA 31061-9093 Office: Ga Coll & State U CBX 70 Milledgeville GA 31061

BADER, ROCHELLE LINDA (SHELLEY BADER), educational administrator; BA in Speech Arts, BA in Edn., Hofstra U., 1970; MLS, U. Md., 1973; EdD, George Washington U., 1993. Mgmt. intern Office Civil Pers., Dept. of the Army, Pentagon, Washington, 1971; circulation libr. George Washington U. Med. Libr., Washington, 1971-73; head reference libr. Himmelfarb Health Scis. Libr./George Washington U. Med. Ctr., Washington, 1973-75, head Audio Visual Study Ctr., 1975-78, chief Access and Facilities Svcs. Divsn., 1978-79, chief Reader Svcs. Divsn., 1979-80, assoc. dir., 1980, dir., 1980-90; dir. ednl. resources George Washington U. Med. Ctr., Washington, 1990—, assoc. v.p. ednl. resources, 1998—. Audio visual cons. Regional Med. Libr. Program, D.C. Metro area, 1977-79; mem. nat. adv. com. U. Iowa, 1984-85; mem. Med. Ctr. Faculty Senate Com. on Health Scis. Programs, George Washington U., Washington, 1989, chmn. Health Scis. Programs Ednl. Evaluation Com., 1993—, many other coms.; adv. com. Found. for Health Svcs. Rsch., 1992-93; presenter in field. Consulting editor: Biomedical Comms., 1983-84; mem. editorial rev. bd.: The Jour. of Biocommunication, 1988-92, Annual Statistics of Medical School Libraries in the United States and Canada, 12th, 13th and 14th edits., 1989-93; contbr. articles to profl. jours. Grantee Coun. on Libr. Resource, 1989-90, Nat. Libr. Medicine, 1991, NSF, 1993-94; recipient Disting. Svc. award Health Scis. Comms. Assn., 1986. Mem. Am. Med. Informatics Assn. (exec. com. edn. workshop group 1991—, MLA rep. to adv. coun. 1992—), Assn. Am. Med. Colls. (group on med. edn., coun. on acad. scos. 1991—), Assn. Acad. Health Scis. Libr. Dirs. (pres. 1986-87, chmn. fin. com. 1987-88), Assn. Biomedical Comms. Dirs. (membership com. 1989-91, program com. 1991), Health Scis. Comms. Assn. (coord. interactive media festival 1990-91, chmn. awards com. 1992, pres. 1984-85), Med. Libr. Assn. (bd. dirs. 1995—), Beta Phi Mu. Home: 12225 Seline Way Potomac MD 20854-2872 Office: George Washington U Med Ctr 2300 I St NW Washington DC 20037-2336

BADERTSCHER, DORIS RAE, elementary education educator; b. Akron, Ohio, May 10, 1935; d. Ray and Doris Ada (Lee) Shanaberger; m. James Lee Badertscher, Feb. 2, 1958; children: Leslie, Lynn. BS, Kent State U., 1957; MS, Calif. State U., Dominguez Hills, 1987. Tchr. Marion (Ohio) City Schs., 1968—. Supr. Saturday sch., 1989-90; coach Odyssey Mind, 1984-85; chmn. Marion City Schs. divsn. Marion Art Fair, 1970; drama coach for 54 programs, 1968—, dir. make up, 1975-79. Author: (children's books) The Prying Princess, 1990, The Dragon Dilemma, 1990. Vol. Marion Gen. Hosp., 1970; mem. Marion Little Theatre, 1975-79, com. Teach-In Day, 1980, com. ednl. fair, 1990, Marion Women's Roundtable, 1987; coord. Black History Month, 1990; participant sexual assault and abuse prevention workshop, 1990, Jennings Scholar Alumni workshop, 1986; mem. Christian edn. com., deacon 1st Presbyn. Ch., Marion, 1986-88; founding mem. Guild One Grady Meml. Hosp., past pres., sec., 1986—; founder Kids for Grady Christmas News Paper; chair Right-to-Read Week, 1989-90; wedding coord., stewardship com. Emanuel Luth. Ch., 1996, bd. edn., chmn. of day care bd., 1997. Martha Holden Jennings scholar, 1980-81, Ohio Theatre Alliance scholar, 1984, 86; Career Exploration grantee, 1987; recipient Disting. Alumni award Cuyahoga Falls (Ohio) High Sch., 1991, Golden Apple Achiever award Ashland Oil Co., 1990. Mem. AAUW (pres. 1986-87, pres. 1993-94), Phi Delta Kappa, Alpha Gamma Delta, Alpha Psi Omega. Avocations: theatre, travel, knitting, reading, interior decoratin. Home: 1660 Westminster Rd Marion OH 43302-5854

BADGER, SANDRA RAE, health and physical education educator; b. Pueblo, Colo., Nov. 2, 1946; d. William Harvey and Iva Alberta (Belveal) Allenbach; m. Graeme B. Badger, Oct. 9, 1972; 1 child, Jack Edward. BA in Phys. Edn., U. So. Colo., Pueblo, 1969; MA in Arts and Humanities, Colo. Coll., 1979; postgrad., Adams State U., Alamosa, Colo., 1980-91. Cert. tchr., secondary endorsement in health and phys. edn., Colo. Head women's swimming coach Mitchell High Sch., Doherty High Sch., Colorado Springs, Colo., 1969-90; head dept. health edn. Doherty High Sch., 1979-2000; asst. coach cross country and track, men and women, indoor and outdoor track men and women U. Colo., 1996—. Trainer student asst. program CARE, Colorado Springs, 1983—; trainer drug edn. U.S. Swim Olympic Tng. Ctr., Colorado Springs, 1988-89; coach in track and field, Colorado Springs, 1989, 91; cons. Assocs. in Recovery Therapy, 1989—; asst. instr. scuba diving, 1999; dir. Colo. Health, Fitness and Coaching Conf., 1999—; speaker in field. Author, editor: Student Assistant Training Manual, 1983-95. Bd. dirs. ARC, Colo. Springs, 1990-96, sec., 1991-92, mem. health and safety com., 1990-95; reviewer ARC/Olympic Com. Sports Safety Tng. Manual Handbook Textbooks; mem. comprehensive health adv. com. Dept. Edn., State of Colo., Denver, 1991. Recipient Svc. award ARC, 1985, Coach of Yr. award Gazette Telegraph, 1979, 84, CARE award State of Colo., 1988, others; Gamesfield grantee, 1985; Nat. Coun. on Alcoholism grantee, 1990; nominated Readers' Digest Tchr. of Yr., 1998-99. Mem. NEA, Colorado Springs Edn. Assn. Avocations: scuba diving, running, travel. Office: U Colo 1420 Austin Bluffs PO Box 7150 Colorado Springs CO 80933-7150

BADIAN, ERNST, history educator; b. Vienna, Aug. 8, 1925; arrived in U.S., 1968; m. Nathlie A. Wimsett, 1950; children: Hugh I., Rosemary J. BA, U.N.Z., 1945, MA, 1946; BA, Oxford U., Eng., 1950, MA, 1954, PhD, 1956; LittD, Victoria U., Wellington, N.Z., 1962; DLitt (hon.), Macquarie Univ., 1993, U. Canterbury, Eng., 1999. Jr. lectr. classics Victoria U., England, 1947-48; asst. lectr., classics and ancient history U. Sheffield, England, 1952-54; lectr. classics U. Durham, England, 1954-65; prof. ancient history U. Leeds, England, 1965-69; prof. classics and history SUNY, Buffalo, 1969-71; prof. history Harvard U., Cambridge, Mass., 1971-82, John Moors Cabot prof. history, 1982-98, John Moors Cabot prof. history emeritus, 1998—. Vis. prof. universities, Colo., Oreg., Wash., South Africa, Heidelberg, Tel-Aviv, Western Australia, UCLA; Sather prof., U. Calif., Berkeley, 1976; vis. mem. Inst. Advanced Study, Princeton, fall 1980, fall 1992, Nat. Humanities Ctr., fall 1988, Kommission für Alte Geschichte, Munich, May 1989. Author: Foreign Clientelae, 264-70 B.C., 1958 (Conington prize Oxford U.), Studies in Greek and Roman History, 1964, Roman Imperialism in the Late Republic, 1967, Publicans and Sinners, 1972, From Plataea to Potidaea: Studies in the History and Historiography of the Pentecontaetia, 1993, Zöllner und Sünder, 1997; editor: Polybius, 1966, Ancient Society and Institutions, 1966, Sir Ronald Syme, Roman Papers vols. 1-2, 1979, Am. Jour. Ancient History, 1976-2001. Fellow Am. Coun. Learned Soc., 1972-73, 82-83, Leverhulme fellow, Eng., 1973, Guggenheim fellow, 1984, hon. fellow Univ. Coll., Oxford, Eng.; decorated Austrian Cross of Honor for Sci. and Art, 1999. Fellow Brit. Acad., Am. Acad. Arts and Sci., Am. Numismatic Soc.; hon. mem. Soc. Promotion Roman Studies; corr. mem. Austrian Acad. Sci., German Archeol. Inst.; fgn. mem. Finnish Acad. Sci.; mem. Am. Philol. Assn., Assn. Ancient Historians, Classical Assn. Can., U.K. Classical Assn., adv. Australian Soc. Classical Studies, Soc. Promotion Hellenic Studies, Virgil Soc., Intrnat. Assn. for Greek and Latin Epigraphy, Australian Soc. for Classical Studies. Office: Harvard U Robinson Hall Cambridge MA 02138

BADLER, NORMAN IRA, computer and information science educator; b. L.A., May 3, 1948; s. Bernard and Lillian Lorraine Badler; m. Virginia Renke, June 14, 1968; children: Jeremy, David. BA in Creative Studies, U. Calif., Santa Barbara, 1970; MS in Computer Sci., U. Toronto, Toronto, 1971, PhD in Computer Sci., 1975. Lectr. U. Toronto, 1973-74; asst. prof. computer and info. sci. U. Pa., Phila., 1974-79, assoc. prof., 1979-86, prof., 1986—, Cecilia Fitler Moore prof., 1990-94, dir. Ctr. for Human Modeling and Simulation, 1994—, assoc. dean for acad. affairs Sch. Engring. and Applied Sci., 2001—. Mem., chmn. program coms. numerous confs. and workshops. Co-author: Simulating Humans, 1993; co-editor: Making Them Move, 1990; contbr. numerous articles to profl. jours. Grantee Advanced Rsch. Projects Agy., NSF, Nat. Libr. of Medicine, U.S. Army, USAF. Mem. IEEE Computer Soc., Assn. for Computing Machinery (vice chmn. spl. interest group on graphics 1979-81, mem. spl. interest group on artificial intelligence), Cognitive Sci. Soc., Am. Assn. for Artificial Intelligence, Phi Beta Kappa. Democrat. Jewish. Avocations: home renovation, cooking. Office: U Pa Computer & Info Sci Dept Philadelphia PA 19104-6389

BAEHR, CATHERINE MARIE, principal; b. Tulsa, Nov. 18, 1959; d. Richard and Gloria (Campos) Cohea; m. Karl J. Baehr, July 26, 1986; children: Evan J., Scott J. BBA Mgmt., Southwest Tex. State U., 1982; MA Ednl. Adminstrn., U. N.Mex., 1989. Tchr. Cypress-Fairbanks Ind. Sch. Dist., Houston, 1984-86, Albuquerque Pub. Schs., 1986-89, coord., cert. staff devel., 1989-94, acting asst. prin. La Mesa Elem., 1994—2000; asst. prin. Enchanted Hills Elem., Rio Rancho, 1994—99, prin., 2000—. Sec. Conroe (Tex.) Ind. Sch. Dist., 1982-83. Danforth fellow, U. N.Mex., 1988-89. Mem. ASCD, Nat. Staff Devel. Coun., Edn. Adminstrs. and Support Personnel Assn. (treas. 1992), Phi Delta Kappa. Office: 5400 Obregon Rd NE Rio Rancho NM 87124-1535

BAER, ALFRED, physician; b. Strasbourg, France, Mar. 15, 1917; came to U.S. 1939, naturalized, 1946; s. Arthur and Frances (Cohn) B.; m. Eva Hannah Rosenberg, Aug. 28, 1949; children: Barbary, Alan. BA, Ohio State U., 1942; MD, Johns Hopkins U., 1945. Diplomate Am. Bd. Internal Medicine, Am. Bd. Rheumatology. Intern, Lincoln Hosp., Bronx, N.Y., 1945-46, resident, 1948-50; intern in pathology Montefiore Hosp., Bronx, N.Y., 1946; practice medicine specializing in internal medicine and rheumatology, Washington, 1950-93; clin. prof. medicine George Washington U. Sch. Medicine, 1978-93, emeritus clin. prof., 1994—. Bd. dirs. Met. Washington chpt. Arthritis Found., 1973-85. Fellow ACP, Am. Coll. Rheumatology; mem. Am. Soc. Internal Medicine, AMA, N.Y. Acad. Scis., AAAS. Jewish. Home: 4400 Springdale St NW Washington DC 20016-2716

BAER, WERNER, economist, educator; b. Offenbach, Germany, Dec. 14, 1931; came to U.S., 1945, naturalized, 1952; s. Richard and Grete (Herz) B. 58776, CUNY, N.Y.C., 1953; MA, Harvard U., 1955, PhD, 1958; D honoris causa, Fed. U. Pernambuco, Brazil, 1988, New U. Lisbon, Portugal, 2000, Fed. U. Ceara, Brazil, 1993. Instr. Harvard U., 1958-61; asst. prof. Yale U., New Haven, 1961-65; asso. prof. Vanderbilt U., Nashville, 1965-69, prof., 1969-74; prof. econs. U. Ill., Urbana, 1974—. Vis. prof. U. São Paulo, Brazil, 1966-68, Vargas Found., Brazil, 1966-68; Rhodes fellow St. Antony's Coll., Oxford (Eng.) U., 1975 Author: The Brazilian Economy: Growth and Development, 5th edit., 2001, Privatization in Latin America, vol. 17, 1994, The Changing Role of International Capital in Latin America,

1998; co-author: (with P. Elosegui and A. Gallo) The Achievements and Failures of Argentina's Neo-Liberal Policies, 2002, (with J. Bang) Privatization and Equity in Brazil and Russia, 2002, (with E. Amann) Anchors Away: The Costs and Benefits of Brazil's Devaluation, 2003; co-editor: Latin America-Privatization, Property Rights and Deregulation, 1993, (with W. Maloney) Neo-Liberalism and Income Distribution in Latin America, 1997, (with W. Miles, A. Moran) The End of the Asian Myth, 1999, The State and Industry in the Development Process, 1999 (with E. Amann) Neoliberalism and it's Consequences in Brazil, 2002; contbr. articles to profl. jours. Decorated Order So. Cross (Brazil) Mem. Am. Econ. Assn., Latin Am. Studies Assn. Home: 1703 Devonshire Dr Champaign IL 61821-5901 Office: U Ill 1407 W Gregory Dr Urbana IL 61801-3606

BAGBY, GEORGE FRANKLIN, JR., English language educator; b. Washington, Dec. 10, 1943; s. George F. and J. Mildred (Ilgenfritz) B.; m. Susan M. Hrom, Nov. 20, 1971; children: Elizabeth S., Joseph L. BA in English with high honors, Haverford Coll., 1965; MA, Yale U., 1968, PhD, 1975. Asst. prof. English, Woodrow Wilson teaching intern LeMoyne-Owen Coll., Memphis, 1968-70; instr. U. Va., 1970-72; from asst. to assoc. prof. Hampden-Sydney (Va.) Coll., 1972-88, prof., 1988—, chair dept. English, 1981-82, 84-87. Vis. Lilly scholar program continuing edn. Coll. Faculty, Duke U., 1977-78; mem. NEH summer seminar U. Ariz., 1988; Fulbright lectr. U. Zulia, Maracaibo, U. Andes, Mérida, Venezuela, 1992-93; presenter in field. Author: (with others) American Literature, 1986, Twentieth Century Literature, 1992, Frost and the Book of Nature, 1993. Organizer, bd. dirs., chair, vol. Farmville (Va.) Area Community Emergency Svcs., 1988—; vol. Robert R. Moton Mus. project, 1997—. Woodrow Wilson fellow Yale U., 1965-66. Mem. AAUP, MLA (Am. lit. sect.), James Fenimore Cooper Soc., Robert Frost Soc., Assn. Study Afro-Am. Life and History, Phi Beta Kappa. Home: 304 1st Ave Farmville VA 23901-1902 Office: Hampden-Sydney Coll Dept English PO Box 26 Hampden Sydney VA 23943-0026

BAGGOTT, BRENDA JANE LAMB, elementary educator; b. Augusta, Ga., Nov. 10, 1948; d. Morgan Barrett Jr. and Ollie Virginia (Toole) Lamb; m. John Carl Baggott, July 8, 1967 (div. Jan. 1998); children: Carla Baggott Walczak, John Carl Jr. Student, Truett McConnel Jr. Coll., 1966-67; BS in spl. Edn., Augusta Coll., 1974; postgrad., Southeastern La. U., 1976-77, U. New Orleans, 1977-78, U. Ctrl. Fla., 1987, 97—; MEd, Nova Southeastern U., 1997. Cert. spl. edn. tchr. in varying exceptionalities and mental handicaps, elem. tchr. ESOL, coaching for Spl. Olympics, Fla. Spl. Olympics tchr. Copeland Elem. Sch., Augusta, Ga., 1973-74; spl. edn. tchr. Percy Julian Spl. Sch., Marrero, La., 1974-78; Spl. edn. resource tchr. Rosemary Mid. Sch., Andrews, S.C., 1978; spl. edn. tchr. Bynum Elem. Sch., Gerogetown, S.C., 1979, Ridgewood Park Elem. Sch., Orlando, Fla., 1979-97; reading recovery tchr. Rock Lake Elem. Sch., Orlando, 1997—2002, corrective reading tchr., 2003—; lab tchr. Read 180, 2002—. Curriculum coord. Percy Julian Spl. Sch., 1975-77; mem. state tchr. mentally handicapped exam validation team Inst. for Instnl. Rsch. and Practice, Fla. Dept. Edn., Tampa, 1990—. Coord. Orange County Spl. Olympics, Orlando, 1984-85, coach, 1974—. Mem. Coun. for Exceptional Children, Internat. Reading Assn., Orange County Reading Coun., Reading Recovery Coun. N.Am., Fla. Reading Assn. Democrat. Baptist. Avocations: directing children's choirs, coaching special olympics. Office: Rock Lake Elem Sch 408 N Tampa Ave Orlando FL 32805-1296

BAGGS, PATRICIA R. county educational administrator; b. Broken Bow, Okla. d. James W. and Mary J. (McCauley) Dagenhart; m. Clifford Baggs, May 24, 1951; children: Marilyn Baggs Tolbert, Richard, Gary. BS in Edn., Tex. Tech U., 1963; MEd, U. Cen. Okla., 1981. Asst. food svcs. dir. Midland (Tex.) Ind. Sch. Dist., 1962-74; dir. food svc. Deer Park (Tex.) Ind. Sch. Dist., 1974-75, McCurtain Meml. Hosp., Idabel, Okla., 1975-76; vocat. home econs. instr. Battiest (Okla.) Ind. Schs., 1976-81; coord. displaced homemaker program Kiamichi Area Vocat.-Tech. Sch., Idabel, 1981-93; agy. coord. McCurtain County Ednl. Coop., 1993—. Vice chair McCurtain F.E.M.A., Idabel, 1990—; mem. McCurtain County Econ. Devel. Team, 1994; bd. chair Little Dixie Cmty. Action Agy., 1994—. Pres. sch. bd. Battiest Ind. Sch. Dist., 1990—; bd. dirs. United Way of McCurtain County, Idabel, 1990—, Okla. Mental Health Region VI PAC, McAlester, Okla., 1989—; pres. bd. dirs. Southeastern Okls. Svcs. for Abused Women, Idabel, 1982—. Recipient Gov.'s Commendation award, 1993. Mem. LWV, Am. Vocat. Assn., Okla. Vocat. Assn., Okla. Displaced Homemakers Network (pres. 1986-88, Outstanding Program award), Idabel Bus. and Profl. Club (pres. 1986), Delta Kappa Gamma (vice chair 1989). Baptist. Avocations: travel, grandchildren. Home: HC 72 Box 799 Broken Bow OK 74728-9105

BAGHAEI-RAD, NANCY JANE BEBB, elementary educator; b. Amsterdam, N.Y., Apr. 8, 1963; d. Warren D. Bebb and Joan Pipito (Ruck) B. BS, SUNY, Oswego, 1986; MEd, Lesley Coll., 1989; AAS, Cazenovia Coll., 1983; post grad., Columbia U. Cert. tchr., N.Y., N.J. Program dir. Adirondack Camp for Boys and Girls, Glenburnie, N.Y.; tchr. kindergarten Perth Cen. Sch., Amsterdam, N.Y.; tchr. St. Mary's Inst., Amsterdam; literacy evaluator Boston Plan for Excellence/Trotter Sch., Roxbury, Mass.; 1st grade tchr. Doane Stuart Sch., Albany, N.Y.; tchr. Mildred E. Strang Mid. Sch., Yorktown Heights, N.Y.; coord. gifted and talented, primary computer tchr. Highland Avenue Sch., Midland Park, N.J. Coord. elem. gifted and talented Scotia (N.Y.)-Glenville Sch. Dist. Named Tchr. of Yr. Gov. of N.J., 1994. Mem. ASCD.

BAGLEY, DEMETRIUS H. urologist, educator, researcher; b. Whitefield, N.H., Aug. 21, 1945; s. Demetrius H. and Myrtle (Nolan) Bagley; m. Jacqueline L. Hickey, May 30, 1970; 1 child, D. Jacques. BA, Johns Hopkins U., 1966, MD, 1970. Diplomate Am. Bd. Urology. Intern Yale-New Haven Hosp., 1970—71, resident, 1971—72, 1975—79; instr. Sch. Medicine Yale U., New Haven, 1978—79; asst. prof., assoc. prof. U. Chgo., 1979—83; assoc. prof. urology Thomas Jefferson U., Phila., 1983—88, prof. urology, 1988—, prof. radiology, 1989—, Nathan Lewis Hatfield prof. urology, 2003—. Author: Endoscopic Urology: A Manual and Atlas, 1985; co-author: Ureteroscopy, 1988, Techniques in Flexible Ureteroscopy, 1991, Smith's Textbook of Endourology, 1996; editor: Endourology Jour., Surgical Endoscopy Jour., Ultrasound and Interventional Technology Jour., Diagnostic and Therapeutic Endoscopy Jour.; contbr. numerous articles to profl. jours. Asst. surgeon USPHS, 1972—75. Fellow: ACS, Coll. Physicians Phila.; mem.: Am. Assn. G.U. Surgery, Phila. Med. club, Phila. Urol. Soc. (pres. 1995—96), Soc. Internat. d'Urol., Am. Lithotripsy Soc., Soc. Univ. Urologists, Endourology Soc., Internat. Soc. Urologic Endoscopy, Am. Urol. Assn. Avocations: photography, antiques, hiking. Home: 506 Spruce St Philadelphia PA 19106-4112 Office: Thomas Jefferson U Dept Urology 1025 Walnut St Philadelphia PA 19107-5001 E-mail: demetrius.bagley@jefferson.edu.

BAGLEY, MARY CAROL, literature educator, writer, announcer; b. St. Louis, Mar. 11, 1958; d. Robert Emmet and Harriet Elaine (Hohreiter) B.; children: Jerry Joseph, Sarah Elizabeth. BA, U. Mo., St. Louis, 1980; MA, U. Mo., 1982; PhD, St. Louis U., 1993. Feature editor Current Newspaper, Normandy, Mo., 1977-82; mng. editor Watermark Lit. Mag., St. Louis, 1982-85; vis. lectr. So. Ill. U., Edwardsville, 1985—; instr., head. bus. writing St. Louis U., 1985—; news broadcaster Am. Cablevision, Florissant, Ferguson, Mo., 1986—; assoc. prof. Mo. Bapt. Coll. Guest speaker Sta. KMOX-TV, KSDK-TV, St. Louis Writing Festival, St. Louis Community Coll., and others, chancellor's com. Sta. KWMU Radio Adv. Bd., 1980, participant McKendree Writer's Conf., 1986. Author: The Front Row: Missouri's Grand Theaters, 1984, Professional Writing Types, 1990, Willa Cather's Myths, 1994, The Politics of Realism, 1995, Selected Readings in 19th and 20th Century Literature, 1994, (with others) The Fabulous Fox Theater, 1985; freelance writer, 1976—; editor: A Guide to St. Louis Theaters, 1984, Western World of Literature, 1994; bd. editors Business Writing Concepts, 1986, Handbook for Professional and Academic Writing, 1988 (recipient Cert. of Appreciation 1986); adv. bd. mem. Bus. Comm. Today, 1986; editor Cantos Lit. Mag., 1998—. Co-chmn, Theater Hist. Soc. Conclave, St. Louis, 1984; pres., Ambassador Theater Trust, 1986. Recipient William Barnaby Faherty award, 1992. Mem. Writer's Guild, Theater Hist. Soc. (bd. dirs. 1986), Am. Assn. Univ. Instrs., Nat. Coun. Tchrs. English, U. Mo. English Alumni Assn. (v.p. 1985, senator rep. 1979), Pi Alpha Delta (hon.), Sigma Tau Delta (sponsor), Phi Beta Kappa. Office: Mo Bapt U 337 Field Hall Saint Louis MO 63141 Home: 592 Wetherby Terrace Dr Ballwin MO 63021-4443

BAGLOS, ROBERT JOSEPH, secondary school educator; b. McKeesport, Pa., Apr. 26, 1957; s. Robert George and Rose Marie (Lame) B.; 1 child, Jaclyn Christine. BS, U. Fla., 1979; MS, Nova U., 1980; EdS, Barry U., 1985. Tchr. math., North Miami (Fla.) Sr. High Sch., 1979—; prof. computer sci. Barry U., Miami Shores, Fla., 1985-91; athletic bus. mgr., 1991—. Mem. United Tchrs. of Dade, Dade County Coun. Tchrs. Math., Nat. Coun. Tchrs. Math. Democrat. Roman Catholic. Avocations: song writing, guitar, recording music.

BAGNALL, ROGER SHALER, history educator; b. Seattle, Aug. 19, 1947; m. 1969; 2 children BA, Yale U., 1968; MA, U. Toronto, Ont., Can., 1969; PhD in Classical Studies, U. Toronto, 1972. Asst. prof. classics Fla. State U., 1972-74; asst. prof. Greek and Latin Columbia U., N.Y.C., 1974-79, assoc. prof. classics and history, 1979-83, prof., 1983—, dean Grad. Sch. Arts and Scis., 1989-93. Pres. Egyptological Sem. of N.Y., 1981-83; vis. prof. U. Florence, Italy, 1981, 89, Bar-Ilan U., Israel, 1986, U. Warsaw, Poland, 1989, U. Helsinki, Finland, 1994; Hamilton vis. rsch. fellow Christ Ch., Oxford, 1995-96. Author: The Administration of the Ptolemaic Possessions, 1976, Ostraka in Amsterdam Collections, 1976, The Florida Ostraka: Documents from the Roman Army in Upper Egypt, 1976, Bullion Purchases and Landholding in the 4th Century, 1977, Egypt in Late Antiquity, 1993, Reading Papyri, Writing Ancient History, 1995; co-author: Ostraka in the Royal Ontario Museum, 2 vols., 1971-76, The Chronological Systems of Byzantine Egypt, 1978, Columbia Papyri VII, VIII, 1978, 90, Consuls of the Later Roman Empire, 1987, Demography of Roman Egypt, 1994, Reading Papyri, Writing Ancient History, 1995. Am. Coun. Learned Soc. grantee, 1975, fellow, 1976-77; Am. Philos Soc. grantee, 1984, 84; NEH fellow, 1984-85, Guggenheim fellow, 1990-91, Fowler Hamilton Vis. Rsch. fellow Christ Church, Oxford, England, 1995—. Fellow Am. Numismatic Soc., Am. Acad. Arts and Scis.; mem. Am. Philol. Assn. (sec.-treas. 1979-85, bd. dirs. 1988-91), Am. Philos. Soc., Am. Soc. Papyrologists (pres. 1993—), Acad. Royale de Belgique. Office: Columbia U 606 Hamilton Hall New York NY 10027

BAGSHAW, MALCOLM A. radiation oncologist, educator; b. Adrian, Mich., 1925; BA, Wesleyan U., 1946; MD, Yale U., 1950. Diplomate Am. Bd. Radiology. Surg. intern Grace-New Haven Hosp., 1950-51, resident in surg. pathology, 1951-52; resident in radiology U. Mich., 1953-56, clin. instr. radiology, 1955-56; instr. Stanford U., Palo Alto, Calif., 1956-59, asst. prof., 1959-62, assoc. prof., 1962-69, prof., 1969-92, Henry S. Kaplan-Harry Lebeson prof. emeritus, 1992—, dir. div. radiation therapy, 1960-92, chmn. radiology dept., 1972-86, chmn. radiation oncology dept., 1986-92. Resident etranger Inst. Gustave-Roussy, France, 1962-63; cons. radiation therapy VA Hosp., Palo Alto, Calif., 1960-92. Recipient Medal of Honor, Am. Cancer Soc., 1984, Told medal Nihon U. Sch. Medicine, Japan, 1984,Gold Medal award Am. Soc. for Therapeutic Radiology and Oncology, 1985, Disting. Alumnus award Wesleyan U., 1996, Charles P. Kettering Gold medal Gen. Motors Co., 1996. Mem. AMA, Radiol. Soc. N.Am. (Gold medal 1999), Am. Coll. Radiology (Gold medal 2002). Office: 300 Pasteur Dr Palo Alto CA 94304-2203

BAHILL, A. TERRY, systems engineering educator; b. Washington, Pa., Jan. 31, 1946; m. Karen Bahill, July 31, 1971; children: Alex, Zach. BSEE, U. Ariz., 1967; MSEE, San Jose State U., 1970; PhD, U. Calif., Berkeley, 1975. Registered profl. elec. engr., Calif., Pa. Asst., then assoc. prof. biomed. engr. Carnegie Mellon U., Pitts., 1976-84; asst. prof., then assoc. prof. neurology Med. Sch. U. Pitts., 1977-84; prof. sys. engr. U. Ariz., Tucson, 1984—; pres. Bahill Intelligent Computer Systems, 1986—. Author: Bioengineering: Biomedical, Medical and Clinical Engineering, 1981, Keep Your Eye on the Ball: The Science and Folklore of Baseball, 1990, Verifying and Validating Personal Computer-Based Expert Systems, 1991, Linear Systems Theory, 1992, 2d edit., 1998, Engineering Modeling and Design, 1992, Metrics and Case Studies for Evaluating Engineering Designs, 1997, Keep Your Eye on the Ball: Curve Balls, Knuckle Balls and Baseball Falacies, 2000; contbr. articles to profl. jours. Patentee in field. Lt. USN, 1967-71. Named one of Baseball Hall of Fame traveling exhibit. Fellow: IEEE (v.p. 1980—87); mem.: Internat. Coun. Sys. Engrng. (chair Incose fellows com.). Roman Catholic. Office: Sys & Ind Engrng Univ Ariz Tucson AZ 85721-0020

BAHL, JANICE MIRIAM, director religious education; b. Allentown, Pa., Apr. 13, 1937; d. Franklin Clayton and Emma (Kosarek) B. BA, Newmann Coll., 1976; MA in religious studies, St. Charles Borromeo Sem., 1985; diploma religious studies, Sacred Congregation Clergy, Vatican City, Rome, 1985. Joined Sisters of St. Francis of Phila., 1962. Tchr. St. Mary of the Assumption, Phila., 1965-71, St. Mary Sch., Schwenksville, Pa., 1971-73; elem. tchr. St. Benedict Sch., Phila., 1973-76; jr. high tchr. Resurrection Sch., Chester, Pa., 1976-79, SS Coleman Neumann Sch., Bryn Mawr, Pa., 1979-80; elem. tchr. St. Stanislaus Sch., Lansdale, Pa., 1980-84; dir. religious edn. St. Stanislaus Parish, Lansdale, Pa., 1984-90, St. Andrew Roman Cath. Ch., Catasauqua, Pa., 1991-93, Assumption BVM, Northampton, Pa., 1991-93, St. Paul Parish, Norristown, Pa., 1993-99, St. Anastasia Parish, Newtown Square, Pa., 1999—2003; congl. records mgr. Our Lady of Angels Convent, Aston, Pa., 2003—. Religious cons. Silver Burdett Ginn, Morristown, N.J., 1987-99. Scout leader, coord. Gt. Valley coun. Girl Scouts U.S., Allentown, Pa., 1945-62, 89—, bus. mgr. Camp Woodhaven, Pine Grove, 1995—; mem. Catasauqua Ministerium, 1992-93; UN 50th anniversary com. Sister of St. Francis of Phila., 1994—; mem. Assn. Phila. PD/CARE Archdiocese Phila., 1984-90, 94-2003, coun. elem. sch. religion leaders, 1995-2003; mem. Allentown coord. religious edn. Diocese Allentown, 1991-93; mem. religious curriculum Archdiocesese Phila., 1973-90, planning com. Eastern Pa. DRE Gathering Planning CoCom., 1988-90, chair, 1990-94; pastoral coun., adult edn. com. St. Anastasia Parish, 1999-2003 Recipient Phila. Parish Dirs. award, Mother Katherine Drexel Assn., 1994—2003. Democrat. Roman Catholic. Avocations: photography, camping, wood carving, guitar, cooking. Home: St Anthony Convent 1715 S Sproul Rd Springfield PA 19064-1137 Office: Our Lady of Angels Convent 609 S Convent Rd Aston PA 19014 E-mail: jmbahl@osfphila.org.

BAHL, SAROJ MEHTA, nutritionist, educator; b. New Delhi, Apr. 4, 1946; came to U.S., 1972; d. L.D. and G.D. Mehta; m. Vishwa Mittar Bahl; children: Rahul, Ragini. BS in Home Sci., Delhi U., 1965, MS in Nutrition, 1967, PhD in Nutrition, 1973. Lectr. Lady Irwin Coll., New Delhi, 1970-71; instr. U. N.D., Grand Forks, 1972-74; from rsch. assoc. med. sch. to assoc. prof. dental sch. U. Tex., Houston, 1976—2002, assoc. prof. dental sch., 2002—. Program dir. Peace Corps, Houston, 1984. Author: Nutritional Management of the AIDS Patient; contbr. articles to profl. jours. Den leader Boy Scouts Am., Houston, 1983; mem. ednl. com. March of Dimes, Houston, 1986—; mem. exec. bd. Indo-Am. Charity Found. of Houston, 1995-98. Recipient several awards for tchg. excellence including John P. McGovern award, 1992, 95; named Outstanding Dietetic Educator Tex. Tex. Dietetic Assn., 1995; nominated for U.S. Prof. of Yr., 1993, 94. Mem. Am. Inst. Life Threatening Illness (assoc.), Soc. Nutrition Edn. (editor newsletter), Minority Faculty Assn. (pres. 1996-97), Vivekananda Vedanta Soc. (pres. 1993-1998). Avocations: painting, music, reading. Office: U Tex Dental Sch Rm B-37 6516 MD Anderson Blvd Houston TX 77025 E-mail: Saroj.M.Bahl@uth.tmc.edu.

BAHLS, STEVEN CARL, academic administrator, educator; b. Des Moines, Sept. 4, 1954; s. Carl Robert and Dorothy Rose (Jensen) B.; m. Jane Emily Easter, June 18, 1977; children: Daniel David, Timothy Carl, Angela Emily. BBA, U. Iowa, 1976; JD, Northwestern U., Chgo., 1979. Bar: Wis. 1979, Mont. 1989; CPA, Iowa. Assoc. Frisch, Dudek & Slattery, Milw., 1979-84, dir., 1985; assoc. dean and prof. U. Mont. Sch. of Law, Missoula, 1985-94; dean., prof. law sch. Capital U. Law Sch., Columbus, Ohio, 1994—2003; pres. Augustana Coll., Rock Island, Ill., 2003—. Coordinating exec. editor Northwestern U. Law Rev., 1979. Chair Columbus Works. Mem. ABA, Am. Agrl. Law Assn. (past pres.), Wis. Bar Assn., Mont. Bar Assn., Ohio Bar Assn., Ohio State Bar Found. (bd. govs.), Order of Coif. Avocations: photography, travel, hiking. Home: 2824 96th Ave Ct Milan IL 61264 Office: Augustana College 639 38th Street Rock Island IL 61201-2296

BAHORSKI, JUDY ANN WONG, computer specialist, learning strategist; b. Pueblo, Colo., Oct. 15, 1949; d. Yen Gim and Ngon (Mah) Wong. BA, So. Colo. State U., 1971; MEd, U. Nev., Las Vegas, 1976. Cert. tchr., Nev. 2d grade tchr. Sunrise Acres Elem. Sch., Las Vegas, 1971-77, Myrtle Tate Elem. Sch., Las Vegas, 1977-84, 3d grade tchr., 1984-85; reading specialist Martin Luther King Jr. Elem. Sch., Las Vegas, 1988-90, Charlotte Hill Elem. Sch., Las Vegas, 1990-91, computer specialist, 1991-93; learning specialist Mable Hoggard Math./Sci. Magnet Sch., Las Vegas, 1993—, mem. elem. tech. com., 1991-92, mem. supt. tech. study com., 1989-90. Computer tchr. trainer Clark County Sch. Dist., Las Vegas, 1984—. Life mem. PTA, 1986—. Mem. Internat. Reading Assn., Reading Improvement Coun., Clark County Classroom Tchrs. Assn., Nev. Edn. Assn., Computer Using Educators (pres. 1991-92), Phi Delta Kappa. Democrat. Roman Catholic. Avocations: boating, reading, computer activities. Office: Mabel Hoggard Math/Sci Magnet Sch 950 N Tonopah Dr Las Vegas NV 89106-1902

BAHRE, JEANNETTE, English language and literature educator, education educator, librarian, educational consultant and tutor; b. Darby, Pa., Dec. 28, 1948; d. Paul Florent and Jeanne (Shangraw) Gibson; m. Stephen Alan Bahre, May 14, 1974; children: Kimberly, Christian, Rachael. BA, Merrimack Coll., 1970; MEd, U. Ariz., 1979. Cert. experienced tchr., NH; English and social studies tchr., Mass. Tchr. Eng. and Social Studies, Mass., 1970—; libr. St. Augustine Sch., Andover, Mass., 1980-83, Beverly Sch. for Deaf, Mass., 1988-89; instr. No. Essex C.C., Haverhill, Mass., 1982-84, libr. evening svc., 1986-88; tchr., advisor Linton Hall Sch., Bristow, Va., 1985-86; lectr. George Mason U., Fairfax, Va., 1985-86; tchr., tutor Even Start: Family Lit. Project, Amesbury, Mass., 1990-93; Chpt. I tutor Seabrook Elem. Sch., NH, 1994-95; libr. So. Hampton Pub. Libr., NH, 1994—99. Summer seminar for tchr. Univ. N.H., N.H. Humanities Found., 1997; tchr. Family Scrapbooks program New England Found. Humanities, Lawrence, Mass., 1997; participantem. summer seminar for tchr. U. NH NHH Found., 1997, 2001. Editor Four Winds, adult student Lit. Jour., 1992-96. Grantee NEH, 1988. Home: PO Box 523 Amesbury MA 01913 Office: PO Box 523 Amesbury MA 01913

BAIER, JOHN LEONARD, university educator; b. Buffalo, Oct. 6, 1943; s. Harry Edward Baier and Florence (Manno) Militello; m. Nancy Jane, Aug. 28, 1965; children: John, Karen. BS in Indsl. Engrng., GMI Engring. and Mgmt. Inst., Flint, Mich., 1966; M Counselor Edn., SUNY, Buffalo, 1968; PhD in Higher Edn. Adminstrn., So. Ill. U., 1974; postgrad., Harvard U., 1986. Asst. labor rels. rep. Chevrolet Tonawanda (N.Y.) Forge Plant, 1965-66; asst. dir. student union SUNY, Buffalo, 1966-68; dir. student activities and student ctr. Temple U., Phila., 1969-71; asst. dean student devel. So. Ill. U., Carbondale, 1971-75; assoc. dean student devel. U. Nebr., Lincoln, 1975-76, acting dean student devel., 1976-77; asst. v.p. student affairs Tex. Tech. U., Lubbock, 1977-84, dean students, 1979-84; v.p. student affairs U. Ala., Tuscaloosa, 1984-90, prof. higher edn., 1990-92; prof., chair dept. higher edn. U. North Tex., Denton, 1992—. Vice-chmn. Tex. Tech. United Way Campaign, Lubbock, 1977-79. Mem. Am. Assn. Higher Edn., Am. Assn. Counseling and Devel., Nat. Assn. Student Personnel Adminstrs. (disting. svc. award region III 1988), So. Assn. Coll. Student Affairs, Tex. Assn. Coll. and Univ. Student Personnel Adminstrs. (pres. 1983-84, pres. award 1984), Sigma Chi (dir. House Corp. 1977-84, Grand Counsul's Citation award 1965, 80), Blue Key, Golden Key, Order of Omega. Roman Catholic. Office: U North Tex PO Box 311337 Denton TX 76203-1337

BAILEY, BETTE ANN PATRICIA, secondary school language arts educator; b. New Haven, Dec. 12, 1930; d. James Ward and Elizabeth Frances (Krausmann) Curtin; m. Wallace Edward Bailey, Nov. 22, 1952; children: Richard, Mary Patricia, Robert, Brian, Elizabeth Ann, Christopher. BA, Albertus Magnus Coll., 1952; MS, Ctrl. Conn. State U., 1971. Cert. prekindergarten-8th grade tchr., Conn. Substitute tchr. Southington (Conn.) Schs., 1968; kindergarten and 1st grade tchr. Holcomb and Ctrl. Elem. Schs., Southington, Conn., 1968-76; substitute tchr. Southington (Conn.) Schs., 1976—77; project uplift, tutor Kennedy Jr. HS, 1978—80, lang. arts tchr., 1980—2003, ret., 2003. Pres./sec. Cath. Coun., Southington, 1954—; sec. Mary Our Queen Parish Coun., Southington, 1986-90, Bradley Hosp. Aux., Southington, 1954—. Named Outstanding Young Woman Jr. Women's Club, 1966; recipient Svc. award Cath. Family Svcs., 1989, Humanitarian award Albertus Magnus Coll., 1992. Mem. NEA, Conn. Edn. Assn., Southington Edn. Assn., Nat. Coun. Tchrs. English, New Eng. Assn. Tchrs. English, Assembly on Literature for Adolescents, Albertus Magnus Coll. Alumni (sec. 1952—), Alpha Delta Kappa (publicity chmn., chaplain 1988—). Democrat. Roman Cath. Avocations: reading, travel. Home: 120 Forest Ln Southington CT 06489-3915 Office: 1071 S Main St Plantsville CT 06479-1672

BAILEY, CECIL DEWITT, aerospace engineer, educator; b. Zama, Miss., Oct. 25, 1921; s. James Dewitt and Matha Eugenia (Roberts) B.; m. Myrtis Irene Taylor, Sept. 8, 1942; children: Marilyn, Beverly. BS, Miss. State U., 1951; MS, Purdue U., 1954, PhD, 1962. Commd. 2d lt. USAF, 1944, advanced through grades to lt. col., 1965, pilot, 1944-56, sr. pilot, 1956-60, command pilot, 1960-67, asst. prof. Air Force Inst. Tech., 1954-58, assoc. prof., 1965-67, ret., 1967; assoc. prof. aero. and astronautical engring. Ohio State U., Columbus, 1967-69, prof., 1970-85, prof. emeritus, 1985—. Dir. USAF-Am. Soc. Engrng. Edn. summer faculty research program Wright-Patterson AFB, Ohio, 1976-78 Contbr. articles to profl. jours., scientific papers. Mem. Soc. Exptl. Stress Analysis, Am. Soc. Engrng. Edn., Am. Acad. Mechanics, Res. Officers (life), Ret. Officers Assn. (life), Am. Legion (life), Sigma Xi, Sigma Gamma Tau. Clubs: USAF Officers. Achievements include research in a unified theory of mechanics. The gen. energy law was first presented through NASA Grant NGR 36-008-197, April 1973, Application of the Gen. Energy Equation- A Unified Approach to Mechanics; proof that the gen. energy law is more gen. than Hamilton's "Law of Varying Action" is presented in Found. of Physics, vol. 32, Jan. 2002, pp. 159-176, The Unifying Laws of Classical Mechanics. Home and Office: 4176 Ashmore Rd Columbus OH 43220-4683 also: Dept Aerospace Engring Appl Mech Ohio State U Columbus OH 43210

BAILEY, EXINE MARGARET ANDERSON, soprano, educator; b. Cottonwood, Minn., Jan. 4, 1922; d. Joseph Leonard and Exine Pearl (Robertson) Anderson; m. Arthur Albert Bailey, May 5, 1956. BS, U. Minn., 1944; MA, Columbia U., 1945; profl. diploma, 1951. Instr. Columbia U., 1947-51; faculty U. Oreg., Eugene, 1951—, prof. voice, 1966-87, coordinator voice instrn., 1969-87, prof. emeritus, 1987—; faculty dir. Salzburg,

Austria, summer 1968, summer 1976. Vis. prof., head vocal instrn. Columbia U., summers 1952, 59; condr. master classes for singers, developer summer program study for h.s. solo singers, U. Oreg. Sch. Music, 1988—, mem. planning com. 1998-99 MTNA Nat. Convention. Profl. singer, N.Y.C.; appearances with NBC, ABC symphonies; solo artist appearing with Portland and Eugene (Oreg.) Symphonies, other groups in Wash., Calif., Mont., Idaho, also in concert; contbr. articles, book revs. to various mags. Del. fine arts program to Ea. Europe, People to People Internat. Mission to Russia for 1990. Recipient Young Artist award N.Y.C. Singing Tchrs., 1945, Music Fedn. Club (N.Y.C.) hon. award, 1951; Kathryn Long scholar Met. Opera, 1945 Mem. Nat. Assn. Tchrs. Singing (lt. gov. 1968-72), Oreg. Music Tchrs. Assn (pres. 1974-76), Music Tchrs. Nat. Assn. (nat. voice chmn. high sch. activities 1970-74, nat. chmn. voice 1973-75, 81-85, NW chmn. collegiate activities and artists competition 1978-80, editorial com. Am. Music Tchr. jour. 1987-89), AAUP, Internat. Platform Assn., Kappa Delta Pi, Sigma Alpha Iota, Pi Kappa Lambda. Home: 17 Westbrook Way Eugene OR 97405-2074 Office: U Oreg Sch Music Eugene OR 97403

BAILEY, HUGH COLEMAN, university president; b. Berry, Ala., July 2, 1929; s. Coleman Costello and Susie (Jenkins) B.; m. Ahleida Joan Seever, Nov. 17, 1962; children: Debra Jane, Laura Joan. AB with honors, Samford U., 1950; MA, U. Ala., 1951, PhD, 1954. Instr. history and polit. sci. Samford U., 1953-54, asst. prof., 1954-56, assoc. prof., 1956-59, prof., 1959-75, chmn. dept., head div. social scis., 1967-70; dean Howard Coll. Arts and Scis., 1970-75; v.p. for acad. affairs Francis Marion U., Florence, S.C., 1975-78; pres. Valdosta (Ga.) State Univ., 1978—2002, pres. emeritus, 2002—. Mem. commn. colls. So. Assn. Colls. and Schs., 1974-75; v.p. Ala. Acad. Sci., 1968-69; pres. Ala. Writers Conclave, 1971-73 Author: John Williams Walker, 1964, 2003, Hinton Rowan Helper: Abolitionist-Racist, 1965, 2003, Edgar Gardner Murphy: Gentle Progressive, 1968, 2003, Liberalism in the New South, Southern Social Reformers and the Progressive Movement, 1969, America: The Framing of a Nation, 2 vols, 1975; Editorial bd.: Social Sci. Vice pres. Homewood City Bd. Edn., 1972-75; pres. Valdosta chpt. ARC, 2001-03; bd. dirs. Salvation Army; chmn. Valdosta Habitat's Jimmy Carter Work Project, 2003. Guggenheim fellow, 1963-64; Am. Council Learned Socs. fellow, 1965-66; recipient award merit Am. Assn. State and Local History, 1967 Fellow Royal Soc. Arts; mem. Valdosta C. of C., Pi Gamma Mu (trustee, nat. trustee-at-large 1969-71, nat. 1st v.p. 1978-84, pres. 1984-90), Kiwanis. Episcopalian. Home: 3224 Wildwood Plantation Circle Valdosta GA 31605-1031 Office: Valdosta State Univ 1500 N Patterson St Valdosta GA 31698-0001

BAILEY, JAMES ANDREW, principal; b. Jackson, Tenn., Mar. 15, 1957; s. John Truman and Hazel (Cox) B.; m. Lisa McDaniel, June 13, 1992; children: Abby E., Amber N. AS, Jackson (Tenn.) State C.C., 1977; BS, Memphis State U., 1980; MA, Bethel Coll., 1989. Cert. tech. edn. instr. adminstrn. and supervision, Tenn. Indsl. arts instr. Kirby High Sch., Memphis, 1980-83; tech. edn. instr. Parkway Mid. Sch., Jackson, 1983-99; prin. South Elem. Sch., Pinson, Tenn., 1999—. Writing team mem. State Tenn. Tech. Edn. Curriculum Project, 1984-90; tech. edn. participant People to People/Citizen Amb. Program, People's Republic China, summer 1991. Co-author: Instructor's Guide to Metric 50, 1980; contbg. author: Production Technology, 1991. Chmn. Madison-Chester Assn. Bapt. Singles Coun., Jackson, 1990-91; mem. West Jackson (Tenn.) Bapt. Ch., dir., tchr. singles Sunday sch. Named Outstanding Young Man of Am., 1985, Indsl. Arts Advisor of Yr., Tenn. Indsl. Arts Students Assn., 1987, 2000 Notable Am. Men, 1994. Mem. NEA, Tenn. Edn. Assn. (Disting. Classroom Tchr. 1997), Am. Vocat. Assn., Jackson-Madison County Edn. Assn. (pres. 1998-99, exec. bd. 1995-99, 2002—, chmn. instruction and profl. devel. com. 1995-97, mem. legis. com. 1995-98), Tenn. Vocat. Assn. (Tech. Tchr. of Yr. 1989), Internat. Tech. Edn. Assn. (area rep. 1991-92), Tenn. Tech. Edn. Assn., West Tenn. Tech. Edn. Assn. (bd. mem. 1990-92). Avocations: tennis, spelunking, hunting, fishing. Home: 20 London Park Pl Jackson TN 38305-3547 Office: South Elem Sch 570 Stone Rd Pinson TN 38366-7914 E-mail: jabailey@jmcss.org.

BAILEY, JOHN P. director educational technology; b. Bethlehem, Pa. Mem. staff Clarke Ctr. for Interdisciplinary study of Contemporary Issues, Dickinson Coll., Carlisle, Pa.; dir. ednl. tech. State of Pa., Harrisburg, U.S. Dept. Edn., Wash., 2002—. Named one of Top 30 most influential people in ednl. technology, eSchool News, 1999. Achievements include design of with others of Link-to-Learn initiative internationally recognized; with others Pa. Commonwealth's award-winning portal PAPowerPort. Office: US Dept Edn 400 Maryland Ave SW Washington DC 20202

BAILEY, JOY HAFNER, counselor educator; b. Weehawkin, N.J., Aug. 15, 1928; d. Elmar William and Fern (Williams) Hafner; children: Kerry, Jan, Leslie, Liza, Annie Laurie, Kristin. BA, Austin Coll., 1974; MS, Tex. A&M U., 1975, EdD, 1977. Lic. marriage and family therapist, profl. counselor; nat. cert. counselor. Counselor, instr. Tex. A&M U., Commerce, 1976-80; dir. student support svcs. acad. and counseling program Ga. State U., Atlanta, 1980—, asst. prof. counseling and psychol. svcs., 1988—. Pvt. practice marriage and family therapy. Mem. APA, ACA, Am. Assn. Marriage and Family Therapists (approved supr.), Ga. Assn. Marriage and Family Therapists, Soc. Psychologists in Mgmt., Atlanta Mallet Club (v.p. 1989-92, pres. 1999-00), Psi Chi. Office: Ga State U 152 Sparks Atlanta GA 30303-2948 E-mail: oeojhb@langate.gsu.edu.

BAILEY, KATHLEEN ELLEN, reading educator; b. Everett, Mass., May 2, 1948; d. Wilfrid D. and Frances P. (Mullen) Sampson; m. John F. Bailey, Aug. 15, 1970; children: Timothy, Kenneth, Amy. BA in English, Bridgewater State Coll., 1970, MEd in Reading, 1994, cert. in Advanced Grad. Studies, 1999. Cert. tchr. in English, social studies, reading; cert. supr., dir. mid. sch. adminstrn. Coord. of vols. Abington (Mass.) Pub. Schs., 1986-90, history tchr. grade 8, 1986-88, history/English tchr., 1989, reading tchr. grade 7, 8, 1989-93; reading tchr. grade 8 Middleboro (Mass.) Pub. Schs., 1993-94; reading tchr. grade 7, 8 Silver Lake Regional Schs., Pembroke, Mass., 1994—. Devloper, co-chair Reading Olympics, Abington, 1988-93, Students to Assist Reading, Abington, 1993; mem. Abington Pub. Schs. Vision 2000 Com., Abington, 1993; steering com. mem. Cranberry Alliance of Mid. Schs., Southeastern, Mass., 1996-2000, chmn. 1998-2000; bldg. coord. Silver Lake Regional Jr. High-Title One program, Pembroke, 1997-98; lang. arts articulation com. Silver Lake Regional Schs., Kington, Mass., 1997-98. Publicity chmn. Abington Cultrual Coun., 1990-94; chmn. Concern Abington Residents for Edn., 1982-85; co-chmn. Abington Jr. H.S. Coun., 1993—. Recipient Disting. Svc. award Plymouth County Edn. Assn. Mem. ASCD, Internat. Reading Assn., Mass. Reading Assn., Mass. Tchrs. Assn. Democrat. Roman Catholic. Avocations: sewing, decorative painting. Home: 645 Washington St Abington MA 02351-2017 Office: Silver Lake Regional Jr HS 80 Learning Ln Pembroke MA 02359-3398

BAILEY, MARY JOLLEY, eucational administrator; b. Atlanta, July 23; d. Chester and Lila (Evans) Jolley; m. Angelo Bailey Jr., May 26, 1963; children: Sheri Bailey Render, Angela Fae. BA, Clark Coll., Atlanta, 1961; MEd, Ga. State U., 1971, Ednl. Specialist, 1976; EdD, Clark Atlanta U., 1989. Cert. ednl. leadership. Tchr. Atlanta Pub. Schs., 1969-71, reading specialist, 1971-78, instrnl. planner, 1978-83, curriculum coord., 1983-86, instrnl. tech. coord., 1986-95, instrnl. tech. dir., 1995—. Mem. task force Ga. Dept. Edn., Atlanta, 1984; cons. Ga. State Compensatory Group, Atlanta, 1979; presenter confs. ASCD, Internat. Reading Assn., NABSE, Tech. Vendors, 1979-94. Contbr.: Research Within Reach, 1984; editor Spotlight, 1979, Write Stuff, 1992-95, Instrnl. Tech., 1994. Vol. Local County Commrs. Campaign, Atlanta, 1994, Local City Coun. Mem. Campaign, Atlanta, 1994; vol. Children at Risk The Links Inc., Magnolia chpt., Altanta, 1992-94. Mem. ASCD (nat. nominating com. 1986), Internat. Reading Assn. (subcom. mem. 1985-86), Nat. Alliance Black Sch. Educators (v.p. local affiliate 1994-95, pres. 1995—), Links Inc. (local fin. sec. 1993-95, treas. 1995—). Democrat. Avocations: reading, dancing, water aerobics. Office: Atlanta Pub Schs 2930 Forrest Hills Dr SW Atlanta GA 30315-9027

BAILEY, NANCY JOYCE, elementary school educator; b. Detroit, May 9, 1942; d. Thomas Hill and Margaret (McGrath) Rainey; m. Carl John Bailey, June 12, 1963 (dec. 1996); 1 child, John; m. Thomas Barthelemy, 2000. BA, Vanderbilt U., 1960; internat. exchange student, Stuttgart, Germany, 1960; postgrad., U. Mex., 1957, U. Santa Clara, 1975, George Washington U., 1979-80. Cert. early childhood edn. tchr., early childhood specialist. Hostess Brentwood (Tenn.) Country Club, 1960; adminstrv. aide U.S. Senate, Washington, 1966; sec. U.S. Ho. of Reps., Washington, 1971-74; tchr. D.C. Pub. Schs., 1961—2001; prin., owner Historic Hilltop House Hotel, Harpers Ferry, W.Va., 2001—; pres., owner Hilltop House Hotel, Restaurant and Conf. Ctr., Harpers Ferry, W.Va. Bd. dirs Cabvin Internat. Corp., 1985—, Helms Passive Imaging, Inc., 2001--; rep. Washington Tchrs. union, 1982-94; founder David Lipscomb U., Nashville, 1988; participant Internat. Tchr. Exch. Program, Korea, 1994; mem. Ednl. Delegation to China, 1996; mem. postgrad. program NIH, Bethesda, Md., 1996. Keyperson United Way Campaign, Washington, 1974-93; docent The White House, Exec. Office of the Pres., Washington, 1987—; vol. First Lady's Corr., The White House, Washington, 1990—, Social Sec.'s Office, East Wing, 1993, 98—, Office of First Lady, 1993; coord. Presdl. Youth Vol. Day, 1993; mem. Nat. Trust for Historic Preservation, 1990—, Friendship Force of Nat. Capital Area, 1993—, People to People Internat. of Nat. Capital Area, 1993—; mem. adv. bd. New Visions for Child Care, Inc., 1993; chair Local Schs. Restructuring Team, 1992-93; participant Internat. Tchr. Exch. Program, Korea, 1994; mem. exec. com. YWCA Internat. Fair, Washington, 1994; del. Internat. Women's Friendship Conf. World Peace, Washington, 1995; mem. World Affairs Coun., Washington, 1995—; mem. Internat. Policy Inst., Washington, 1997-2000, v.p. edn., 1998-2000; tchr. adv. panel Nat. Capital Children's Mus., Japan, 1998; mem. ARK Found. Mission to Africa, RUVU Project, Tanzania, 1997; mem. adv. bd. ARK Found. to Africa, 1999—; supr. mcpl. elections Orgn. for Security and Coop. in Europe Mission in Bosnia/Herzegovina, 1997, supr. presdl. elections out of country voters, Croatia, 1998; supr. mcpl. elections, Kosovo, 2000; supr. Kosovo Assembly elections, out of country voters, Montenegro, 2001; mem. Coun. of European Election Observation Mission in Kosovo, 2002; pres. Hilltop House Hotel, Harpers Ferry, W. Va., 2003—. Recipient Internat. Cooperation award Am. Fgn. Study Program, Am. Study Program, 1984-86, Am. Student Ednl. Travel. Mem. Delta Group (mem. coun. 1989-92), Am. Fedn. Tchrs., Internat. Reading Assn., World Affairs Coun., Delta Kappa Gamma. Avocations: antiques, numismatics, flying, boating. Home: 6703 Lupine Ln Mc Lean VA 22101-1579 Office: Historic Hilltop House Hotel 400 E Ridge St PO Box 930 Harpers Ferry WV 25425

BAILEY, PHILIP SIGMON, JR., university official and dean, chemistry educator; b. Charlottesville, Va., Mar. 17, 1943; s. Philip Sigmon Bailey and Marie Jeanette (Schultz) Hatch; m. Christina Anne Wahl; children: Karl, Jennifer, Kristen, Michael. Student, Am. U., Cairo, 1961; BS in Chemistry, U. Tex., 1964; PhD, Purdue U., 1969. Asst. prof. chemistry Calif. Poly. State U., San Luis Obispo, 1969-73, prof., assoc. dean, 1973-83, prof. chemistry, dean Coll. Sci. and Math., 1983-89, v.p. acad. affairs, sr. v.p., 1989-90, dean, 1990—. Author: (lab texts) Experimental Chemistry for Contemporary Times, 1975, Organic Chemistry, 1978, (textbook) Organic Chemistry, 1978, 6th edit., 2000. Mem. Am. Chem. Soc., Alpha Chi Sigma. Home: 1628 Royal Way San Luis Obispo CA 93405-6334 E-mail: pbailey@calpoly.edu.

BAILEY, RANDALL CHARLES, religious studies educator, consultant; b. Lafayette, Ala., Feb. 15, 1951; s. Charlie Newton and Mary Florence (Head) B.; m. Peggy Lynn Waddell, June 27, 1971; children: Jonathan David, Hannah Lynn. AA, Ala. Christian Coll., 1971; BA, Ala. Christian Sch. Religion, 1973, MA, 1974, grad. spec. religious edn., 1976, M in Theology, 1979; MPhil, Drew U., 1985, PhD, 1987. Instr. Ala. Christian Sch. Religion, Montgomery, 1972-79; museum lectr. N.J. Mus. of Archaeology, Madison, 1985-86; assoc. prof. So. Christian U. (formerly Ala. Christian Sch. Religion), Montgomery, 1987—2000; dir. dr. of ministry So. Christian U., Montgomery, 1993—; tchr. Bible and Am. Hist. Ala. Christian Acad., Montgomery, Ala., 2000—02; assoc. prof. Faulkner U., Montgomery, 2003—. Adj. prof. Auburn U., Montgomery, 1987-89; cons. Russian dn ukrainian mission Chs. of Christ, 1991-94; dir. dr. of ministry So. Christian U., 1993—. Contbr. articles to profl. jours. Recipient Nat. Endowment for Humanities award Yale U., 1990, Internat. Ctr. fo rU. Teaching of Jewish Civilization award Jerusalem, 1992. Mem. Am. Oriental Soc., Am. Sch. oreintal Rsch., Am. Acad. Religion, Bibl. Archaeolog. Soc., Soc. Biblical Literature, Cah. Bibl. Assn., Evang. Theol. Soc. Avocations: golf, reading, travel, research, writing. Office: Faulkner U 339 Hillabee Dr Montgomery AL 36117

BAILEY, RICHARD WELD, English language educator; b. Pontiac, Mich, Oct. 26, 1939; s. Karl Deanor and Elisabeth Phelps (Weld) B.; m. Margaret Louise Bowman, 1960 (div. 1976); children— Eleanor Bowman (dec.), Charles Andrew Stuart; m. Julia Ruth Huttar, 1990; 1 child, Oceana Yi Huttar. Student, U. Edinburgh, Scotland, 1959-60; AB, Dartmouth Coll., 1961; MA, U. Conn., 1963, PhD, 1965. From asst. prof. English to assoc. prof. U. Mich., Ann Arbor, Mich., 1965-76, prof., 1976—, Fred Newton Scott Collegiate prof., 2002. Del. ACLS, 1996-2002. Author: Images of English, 1991, Nineteenth-Century English, 1996; Rogue Scholar: the Sinister Life and Celebrated Death of Edward H. Rulloff, 2003; editor: (with others) English Stylistics, 1968, Milestones in the History of English in America, 2002; Computing in the Humanities, 1982; Michigan Early Modern English Materials, 1975; English as a World Language, 1982, Literacy for Life, 1983, Dictionaries of English, 1987. Trustee Washtenaw C.C., Ann Arbor, 1974—, chair, 1985-95, 1999-2001; del. platform com. Nat. Dem. Conv., 1976; sr. warden St. Clare of Assisi Episcopal Ch., Ann Arbor, 1981-82, guild of scholars, NY, 1997—, pres., 2001—. Grantee NEH, 1971-75, 78, 85, 91-92, Ford Found., 1978-82; Inst. for Advanced Studies in the Humanities fellow, 1971 Mich. Linguistic Soc. (pres. 1975-76), Commn. on English Lang., Nat. Coun. Tchr. of English, Am. Dialect Soc. (exec. coun. 1980-84, v.p. 1985-87, pres. 1987-88), Dictionary Soc. N.Am. (exec. com. 1992-95, v.p. 1999-2001, pres. 2001-03), Assn. Computing in the Humanities (v.p. 1980-83), Am. Coun. Learned Soc. (del. 1996-2002), Flounders Club (Ann Arbor); The Athenaeum (London). Home: 1609 Cambridge Rd Ann Arbor MI 48104-3520 Office: U Mich Dept English Ann Arbor MI 48109-1003 E-mail: rwbailey@umich.edu.

BAILEY, RUTH JANET, retired home economics educator; b. Kinney County, Tex., Nov. 29, 1924; d. Frank Joseph and Elvira Hilda (Meyer) Zerr; m. Weldon Eugene Bailey, June 29, 1946 (div. 1971); children: Jan Thompson-Eve, Randall Bailey. BS, U. Mary Hardin-Baylor, 1945; MEd, U. Houston, 1956. Cert. secondary edn., home econs., Tex. Tchr. Goodrich H.S., Tex., 1945-47, Spring Branch Ind. Sch. Dist., Houston, 1952-85, dept. chmn., 1956—58, 1963—76; lectr., supr. U. Houston, 1986-95. Mem. AAUW (pres. chpt. 1997-99), N.W. Harris County Ret. Tchrs. (Spring Valley Parliamentarian 2000—), Alpha Delta Kappa. (sec., historian 1992-96, v.p. 1997-98). Avocations: reading, art, gardening, quilting, sewing, travel. Home: 2227 Mckean Dr Houston TX 77080-5509

BAILEY, SALLY DOROTHY, drama therapist, playwright; b. Pitts., Dec. 31, 1954; d. John Lemon and Sally Lee (Dietrich) B. Student, Allegheny Coll., 1972-73; BFA summa cum laude, U. Tex., 1976; MFA, Trinity U., 1981; MSW, U. Md., 1998. Apprentice Houston Stage Equipment, 1977-78; journeyman Dallas Theater Ctr., 1978-81; office mgr. NORCOSTCO/Tex. Costume, Dallas, 1981-83; asst. mng. dir. TheatreVa., Richmond, 1983-85; asst. to artistic dir. Shakespeare Theatre at the Folger, Washington, 1985-87; tchr. drama Fillmore Arts Ctr., Washington, 1988-94; drama specialist Hartwood Residencies, Alexandria, Va., 1988-91; drama therapist Second Genesis, Bethesda, Md., 1988—99; arts access dir. Bethesda Acad. Performing Arts, 1988—98; asst. prof. drama therapy Kans. State U., 1999—. Author: Wings To Fly: Bringing Theatre Arts to Students with Disabilities, 1993, Dreams to Sign, 2002; screenwriter, co-dir. ednl. video Making Connections, 1994. Mem. Nat. Assn. for Drama Therapy (registered drama therapist, cert. mentor and trainer, chmn. membership 1995-99, pres.-elect 1999-2001, pres. 2001-2003). Avocations: reading, gardening, sewing, writing, yoga. Home: 1626 Leavenworth St Manhattan KS 66502-4154 Office: Kans State U SCTD Dept 129 Nichols Hall Manhattan KS

BAILEY, TRACEY L. educational association administrator; Tchr. Satellite High Sch., Satellite Beach, Fla.; dir. office of charter schs. Fla. Dept. of Edn.; dir. nat. projects Assn. Am. Educators Found. Recipient State Teacher of the Yr. awd., Florida, Coun. of Chief State School Offices, 1993, Nat. Teacher of the Yr. awd., Coun. of Chief School Offices, 1993.*

BAILEY, VIRGINIA HURT, elementary education educator; b. Constantine, Mich., July 30, 1937; d. John Henry and Eunice Leona (Hufstedler) Hurt; m. Jerry Dee Skaggs, June 17, 1961 (dec. May 1969); 1 child, Susan Marie Skaggs; m. Elton Ray Bailey, Dec. 17, 1971; stepchildren: Michael, Marsha Smith, Ann Aviles. AB, William Jewell Coll., 1959; MA, N.Mex. State U., 1983; PhD, U. N.Mex., 1994; degree in elem. edn., y. Cert. elem. tchr., ESL endorsement, Ariz. Tchr. Window Rock (Ariz.) Dist. 8, 1959-61, 69-94, Liberty (Mo.) Pub. Schs., 1963-64, Kansas City (Mo.) Pub. Schs., 1964-67, Albuquerque Pub. Schs., 2001—03; civil svc. employee MECOM, St. Louis, 1967-69. Instr. Navajo Cmty. Coll., Window Rock, 1984-86; mem. career ladder steering com. Window Rock Dist. 8, Ft. Defiance, Ariz., 1984-85, 86-89; mem. child study team Window Rock Elem. Schs., 1985-94, test adminstr. Gessell Devel. Inst., 1986—; cons. in multicultural edn., 1994—. Author numerous poems (Golden Poet award 1985-92, Internat. Soc. Poets 1992-98), (books) Beyond the 4-D Perspective: (1) Changing Teacher Strategies, Approaches and Methods, 1996, (2) Changing Attitudes and Expectations, 1997, (3) Changing Teacher Education, 1997, (4) English for Navajos, 1997, The Pegasus Method, 1999; contbr. articles to profl. jours. Mem. choir Presbyn. Ch. Ft. Defiance, 1974-94, elder. lay reader, 1978—, clk. session, 1980-89; mem. choir Rio Grande Presbyn. Ch., liturgist, mem. worship com., stocker, vol., substitute food bank distributor, 1994—. Mem. NEA (local pres. 1978-79, state del. 1979-81, local sec. 1980-82), ASCD, Internat. Assn. Cognitive Edn., Tchrs. ESL, Alpha Delta Kappa. Republican. Avocations: philataly, dolls and doll houses, reading, painting, poetry. Home: 135 65th St SW Albuquerque NM 87121-2354

BAILEY, WILLIAM SCHERER, lawyer, educator; b. St. Charles, Ill., July 28, 1948; s. Robert Wilbank and Josephine Grant (Scherer) B.; m. Sylvia Lillian Sherry, July 15, 1977; children: Robert, Mimy Ann, Lillian. BS, U. Oreg., 1970; JD, Northwestern U., 1974. Bar: Ill. 1974, U.S. Dist. Ct. (no. dist.) Ill. 1976, Wash. 1977, U.S. Dist. Ct. (we. dist.) Wash. 1977; Diplomate Am. Bd. Trial Advocates. Legal counsel govt. com. Ill. Mental Health Code, 1974-76; asst. pub. defender State of Wash., Seattle, 1976-80, asst. atty. gen., 1980-82; ptnr. Levinson, Friedman, Vhugen, Duggan, Bland & Horowitz, Seattle, 1982-87, Schroeter, Goldmark & Bender, Seattle, 1987-90; litigation cons. Office Atty Gen. State Wash., Seattle, 1987-90; ptnr. Fury Bailey, Seattle, 1991—. Adj. prof. civil trial advocacy U. Puget Sound Sch. Law, Tacoma, 1981-85, U. Wash. Sch. Law, Seattle, 1993—; judge pro tem Seattle Mcpl. Ct., 1983-89, King County Superior Ct., 1988—; arbitrator, 1985—; faculty Nat. Inst. Trial Advocacy, 1986—, Nat. Coll. Advocacy Am. Trial Lawyers Assn., 1995—. Contbr. articles to profl. jours. Mem. jud. evaluation com. Mcpl. League, Seattle, 1980-82, Mayor's Jud. Merit Selection Com., Seattle, 1981-82; legal counsel Wash. Dems., Seattle, 1985-95; candidate primary and gen. election Seattle city atty., 1989. Named Top Super Lawyer, Washington Law and Politics, 2000—02, Litigator of the Month, Nat. Law Jour., 2002; named one of Top 30 Superlawyers, Wash. Law and Politics, 2001—03. Mem. ABA, Wash. State Bar Assn. (editor jour. 1985, spl. dist. counsel, 1984-92, instr. skills tng. program 1991—, vice-chmn. disciplinary bd. 1993-94, chmn. 1994-95), Seattle-King County Bar Assn., Wash. State Trial Lawyers Assn. (Trial Lawyer of Yr. 1991), Assn. Trial Lawyers Am. (Galaxy of Rising Stars 1991), Am. Inns of Ct. (co-founder, counselor William O. Douglas chpt. 1989-92, mem. William L. Dwyer chpt. 2002-, upper level 2001-2003). Democrat. Avocations: writing, music. Home: 6016 77th Ave SE Mercer Island WA 98040-4818 Office: Fury Bailey 710 Tenth Ave E Seattle WA 98102 E-mail: bill@furybailey.com.

BAILEY, WILLIAM HARRISON, artist, educator; b. Council Bluffs, Iowa, Nov. 17, 1930; s. Willard Kendall and Marjorie Esther (Cheyney) Bailey; m. Sandra Stone, May 28, 1958; children: Ford Hamilton, Alix Brook. Student, U. Kans., 1948-51; BFA, Yale U., 1955, MFA, 1957; HHD (hon.), U. Utah, 1987; DFA (hon.), Adelphi U. Instr. art Yale U., New Haven, 1957-61, asst. prof., 1961-62, adj. prof., 1969-73, prof., 1973-79, Kingman Brewster prof., 1979-95, Kingman Brewster prof. emeritus, 1995—, dean Sch. Art, 1974-75; from asst. prof. to assoc. prof. Ind. U., 1962—68, prof., 1968-69. Mem. Nat. Coun. Arts, 1992—97. Exhibitions include Robert Schoelkopf Gallery, N.Y.C., 1968, 1971, 1974, 1979, 1982, 1986, 1990, 1991, Glleriea Il Gabbiano, Rome, 1985, 1989, 1993, 1997, John Berggruen Gallery, San Francisco, 1988, Andre Emmerich Gallery, N.Y.C., 1992, 1994, 1995, Alpha Gallery, Boston, 1998, Robert Miller Gallery, N.Y.C., 1999, 2003, Represented in permanent collections Mus. Modern Art, Whitney Mus., Hirshorn Mus., St. Louis Art Mus., Neu Galerie Der Stadt Aachen, Germany, Pa. Acad., Yale Art Gallery. With U.S. Army, 1951—53. Alice Kimball English Travelling fellow, 1955, Guggenheim fellow, 1965, Ingram Merrill fellow, 1975. Mem.: Academia di Belli Arti, Perugia, Acad. San Luca, Rome, Am. Acad. Arts and Letters, Nat. Acad. Design, Smithsonian Archives Am. Art (trustee), Tiffany Found. (bd. dirs.), Yaddo (mem. corp.). Office: Yale U Sch Art Dept Painting Printmaking New Haven CT 06520

BAILIN, DAVID WILLIAM, artist, educator; b. Sioux Falls, S.D., July 3, 1954; s. Marvin Klein and Janet Helene (Gellman) B.; m. Amy Lee Stewart, Apr. 30, 1983; children: Patsy Campbell, Hannah Grady, Clara Livingston, Emma Stewart, Sarah Foster. BFA, U. Colo., Boulder, 1976; MA, Hunter Coll., 1983. Dir. Ark. Arts Ctr. Mus. Sch., Little Rock, 1986-96; adj. prof. art Hendrix Coll., Conway, Ark., 1996; lectr. U. Ctrl. Ark., 1996—, U. Ark., Little Rock, 1997—; faculty visual arts Gov.'s Sch., Hendrix Coll., Conway, Ark., 1998. Owner Bailin Studios, www.bailinstudio.com; panelist Ark. Arts Coun.; audition panelist Ark. Gov.'s Sch., Hendricks Coll., 1990—; arts programming chair Pulaski County Prevention Inst., 1992-96; mem. art frameworks com. Ark. State Edn. Dept.; grant reader Goals 2000 Ark. Dept. Edn., 1996; spkr. in field. Author: Art and Storytelling, 1990, Art & Interdisciplinary Studies, 1995; contbr. articles to arts publs.; solo exbn. at Ark. Art Ctr., 2000.Koplin Del Rio Gallery, 2002. Mem. adv. com. nat. and cmty. svc. art Ark. Dept. Human Svcs., 1991; mem. tutorial svcs. Little Rock Homeless Shelters, 1992; audition panelist, White House Regional Fellows Competition, 1993; mem. Ctrl. Ark. Cmty. AIDS Ptnrship.; mem. Kelogg Grant Site Selection Com. Pulaski County, 1995; mem. adv. bd. Baum Gallery of Art, U. Ctrl. Ark.; mem. devel. coun. Easter Seals, 1997. Named Ark. Mus. Educator of the Yr., 1994; painting fellow Mid-Am. Arts Alliance/Nat. Endowment for the Arts, 1988, Ark. Arts Coun., 1989, Nat. Endowment for the Arts, 1989. Mem. Coll. Art Assn.

BAILLIEUL, JOHN BROUARD, aerospace engineering and applied mathematics educator; b. Boise, Idaho, May 13, 1945; s. Paul Brouard and Geneva (Gillam) B.; m. Patricia Pfeiffer; children: Emily, Charlotte, John Paul. BA, U. Mass., Amherst, 1967; M in Math., U. Waterloo, Waterloo, Can., 1969; MS, Harvard U., 1973, PhD in Applied Math., 1975. Asst. prof. math. Georgetown U., Washington, 1975-79; sr. mathematician Sci. Systems, Inc., Cambridge, Mass., 1979-83; Vinton Hayes vis. scientist Harvard U., Cambridge, 1983-85; prof. aerospace and mech. engring. Boston U., 1985—, prof. mfg. engring., 1988—, prof. elec. and computer engring., 2001—, dir. div. engring. and applied sci., 1990-93, assoc. dean Coll. Engring., 1993—96, chmn. dept. mfg. engring., 1994-99, chmn. dept. aerospace/mech. engring., 1999—. Cons. Sci. Systems, Inc., Cambridge, 1985-87, AMD Corp., Stratford, Conn., 1986, Computational Engring., Inc., Laurel, Md., 1988-89; vis. sr. scientist Lab. for Info. and Decision Systems, MIT, 1991; chmn. dept aerospace/mech. engring., 1992-93. Author: Mathematical Control Theory, 1998; assoc. editor IEEE Transactions on Automatic Control, 1984—85, 1989—92, editor-in-chief, 1992—98; assoc. editor: IEEE Robotics and Automation Soc. newsletter, Bifurcation and Chaos in Applied Scis. and Engring.; mem. editl. bd. Procs. IEEE, Comm. in Info. and Systems, Robotics and Computer Integrated Mfg.; contbr. articles to profl. jours. U.S. Dept. Energy grantee, USAF Office Sci. Rsch. grantee Boston U., 1985—, NSF grantee; frequent grantee for study nonlinear control theory and mechanics Fellow IEEE (mem. publs. bd., 3D Millennium medal 2000). Home: 105 Longmeadow Rd Belmont MA 02478-1709 Office: Boston U Aero Mech Engring 110 Cummington St Boston MA 02215-2407

BAILYN, BERNARD, historian, educator; b. Hartford, Conn., Sept. 10, 1922; s. Charles Manuel and Esther (Schloss) Bailyn; m. Lotte Lazarsfeld, June 18, 1952; children: Charles David, John Frederick. AB, Williams Coll., 1945; MA, Harvard U., 1947, PhD, 1953; LHD (hon.), Lawrence U., Bard Coll., Clark U., Yale U., Grinnell Coll., Trinity Coll., Manhattanvill Coll., Dartmouth Coll., U. Chgo., Coll. of William and Mary, Pa. State U., Williams Coll.; LLD (hon.), Harvard U.; LittD (hon.), Rutgers U., Fordham U., La Trobe U., Australia, Washington U., St. Louis. Mem. faculty Harvard U., Cambridge, Mass., 1953—, editor in chief John Harvard Libr., 1962—70, Winthrop prof. history, 1966—81, Adams U. prof., 1981—93, dir. Charles Warren Ctr. for Studies in Am. History, 1983—94, prof. emeritus, 1993—. Vis. prof. Cambridge U., Montgomery; sr. fellow Soc. Fellows Harvard U.; Trevelyon lectr., 1971; mem. inst. advanced study Princeton U., 1980—81; postt. prof. am. history, 1986—87; Pitt prof. Cambridge U., 1986—87; trustee Princeton U., 1989—94; fellow Dartmouth Coll., 1991; dir. Internat. Seminar on History of Atlantic World, 1995—. Co-author (with Lotte Bailyn): Mass. Shipping 1697-1714, A Statis. Study, 1959; author: New Eng. Merchants in the 17th Century, 1955, Edn. in the Forming of Am. Society, 1960, The Ideological Origins of the Am. Revolution, 1967 (Pulitzer prize, 1968, Bancroft prize, 1968), The Origins of Am. Politics, 1968, The Ordeal of Thomas Hutchinson, 1974 (Nat. Book award, 1975), The Peopling of Br. North Am.: An Intro., 1986, Voyagers to the West, 1986 (Pulitzer prize, Saloutos award Immigration History soc., Triennial Book award Soc. of the Cin.), Faces of Revolution, 1990, On The Tchg. and Writing of History, 1994, To Begin the World Anew, 2003; co-author: The Gt. Republic, 1977; editor: Pamphlets of the Am. Revolution 1750-1776, 1965, The Apologia of Robert Keayne, 1965, The Debate on the Constn., 1993; co-editor: The Intellectual Migration, Europe and Am., 1930-1960, 1969, Law in Am. History, 1972, Perspectives in Am. History, 1967—77, 1984—86, The Press and The Am. Revolution, 1980, Strangers Within the Realm, 1990. With AUS, 1943—46. Recipient Robert H. Lord award, Emmanuel Coll., 1967, medal, Fgn. Policy Assn., 1998, Catton prize for lifetime achievement in writing of history, Soc. Am. Historians, 2000, Centennial medal, Harvard Grad. Sch. Arts and Scis., 2001; fellow Hon., Christ Coll., Cambridge U.; Jefferson lectr., NEH, 1998, First Millenium lectr., White House, 1998. Fellow: Royal Hist. Soc. (corr.); mem.: Academia Europaea, Russian Acad. Scis., Mex. Acad. History and Geography, Brit. Acad., Mass. Hist. Soc., Am. Philos. Soc. (Thomas Jefferson medal 1993, Henry Allen Moe prize 1994), Nat. Acad. Edn., Am. Acad. Arts and Scis., Am. Hist. Assn. (pres. 1981). Home: 170 Clifton St Belmont MA 02478-2604 Office: Harvard U History Dept Cambridge MA 02138

BAILYN, LOTTE, psychology and management educator; b. Vienna, July 17, 1930; came to U.S., 1937; d. Paul Felix Lazarsfeld and Marie (Jahoda) Albu; m. Bernard Bailyn, June 18, 1952; children: Charles, John. BA in Math. with high honors, Swarthmore Coll., 1951; MA in Social Psychology, Harvard U., 1953, PhD in Social Psychology, 1956; PhD (hon.), U. Piraeus, Greece, 2000. Rsch. assoc. Grad. Sch. Edn., Harvard U., Cambridge, Mass., 1956-57, rsch. assoc. dept. social rels., 1958-64, lectr., 1963-67; instr. dept. econs. and social sci. MIT, Cambridge, 1957-58, rsch. assoc. Sloan Sch. Mgmt., 1969-70, lectr., 1970-71, from sr. lectr. to prof., 1971-91, T Wilson prof. mgmt., 1991—, chair MIT faculty, 1997-99; acad. visitor Imperial Coll. Sci., Tech. and Medicine, London, 1991, 1995, 2000; disting. vis. prof. Radcliffe Coll., 1995-97. Trustee Cambridge Savs. Bank, 1975-98; mem. adv. coun. Suffolk U. Mgmt. Sch., Boston, 1983-86; mem. sr. coun. Leadership Devel. Inst., Rutgers U., 1986-89; panel mem. NAS, NRC, Washington, 1988-90; mem. task force in career devel. and maintenance IEEE, Washington, 1982-90; vis. scholar Imperial Coll. Sci. and Tech., London, 1982, New Hall, Cambridge (Eng.) U., 1986-87; scholar-in-residence Rockefeller Found. Study and Conf. Ctr., Bellagio, Italy, 1983; vis. fellow U. Auckland, N.Z., 1984. Author: Mass Media and Children, 1959, Living with Technology, 1980, Breaking the Mold: Women, Men, and Time in the New Corporate World, 1993; co-author: Working with Careers, 1984, Relinking Life and Work: Toward a Better Future, 1996, Beyond Work-Family Balance: Advancing Gender Equity and Workplace Performance, 2002; mem. editl. bd. Jour. Engring. and Tech. Mgmt., Cmty., Work and Family; contbr. chpts. to books and articles to profl. jours. Trustee Radcliffe Coll., 1974-79, Cambridge Fin. Group, Inc., 1998—; bd. dirs. Families and Work Inst., 1995—, Cambridge Savings Bank, 1998—. Recipient Grad. Soc. medal Radcliffe Coll., 1998, Everett Cherrington Hughes award for careers scholarship Acad. of Mgmt., 2003. Fellow APA; mem. Acad. Mgmt., Am. Sociol. Assn. Home: 170 Clifton St Belmont MA 02478-2604 Office: MIT Sloan Sch Mgmt 50 Memorial Dr Cambridge MA 02142-1347

BAIRD, DONALD ROBERT, retired secondary school educator; b. Boise, Idaho, June 26, 1941; s. Donald Whitney and Pauline June (Cox) B.; m. Donna Colleen Karnes, Sept. 18, 1970; children: Patricia Colleen Baird Duffey, Diane Marie Baird Henry. BS, Coll. Idaho, 1963; MS, Boise State U., 1980. Advanced secondary teaching cert. Instr. NESEP USN, San Diego, summers 1969-75; tchr. South Jr. H.S., Boise, 1969-80, Capital H.S., Boise, 1980-2000; instr. BOOST USN, San Diego, summers 1984-89. Tchr. Boise State U., 1981-82; computer cons. Capital H.S., Boise, 1990-2000; dept. chmn. South Jr. H.S., Boise, student body advisor, 1975-76. Info. officer U.S. Naval Acad., Annapolis, Md., 1991—. Comdr. USN, 1963-66, res., 1967-89. Recipient Outstanding Educator award Acad. of Am. Educators, 1973. Mem. Nat. Coun. Tchrs. Math., Idaho Coun. Tchrs. of Math. (sec.-treas. 1983-85), Naval Res. Assn. (chpt. pres. 1985-89), Boise Edn. Assn. (rep.), Order of Demolay (chevalier 1959), Masons (Master # 39). Republican. Presbyterian. Avocations: tennis, golf, computers, chess, model ship building.

BAIRD, DOUGLAS GORDON, law educator, dean; b. Phila., July 10, 1953; s. Henry Welles and Eleanora (Gordon) B. BA, Yale U., 1975; JD, Stanford U., 1979; LLD, U. Rochester, 1994. Law clk. U.S. Ct. Appeals (9th cir.), 1979, 80; asst. prof. law U. Chgo., 1980-83, prof. law, 1984—, assoc. dean, 1984-87, Bigelow prof. law, 1988—, dean, 1994-99. Author: (with others) Security Interests in Personal Property, 1984, 2d edit., 1987, Bankruptcy, 1985, 3d edit., 2000, Elements of Bankruptcy, 1992, 3d edit., 2001; (D. Baird, R. Gertner, R. Picker) Game Theory and the Law, 1994. Mem. AAAS, Order of Coif. Office: U Chgo Sch Law 1111 E 60th St Chicago IL 60637-2776 E-mail: Douglas_Baird@law.uchicago.edu.

BAIRD, SUSAN ELIZABETH, secondary education educator, writer; b. L.A., May 7, 1954; d. Thomas Alva Baird and Sarah Ann (Mott) Durand; m. David Patrick Hogan, Apr. 5, 1980; 1 child, Adam Michael Hogan. BA in Secondary Edn./English Media Endorsement, So. Oreg. State Coll., 1982, MA in Humanities, 1989. Cert. Oreg. std. tchr. secondary edn. media endorsement. Tchr. English Ashland (Oreg.) Mid. Sch., 1983—. Advisor Speech and Theatre Clubs, Ashland Mid. Sch., 1989—, Teen Poetry Readings, 1990—; lectr. human rights Ashland Sch. Dist., 1988—. Contbr. articles to mags. Spkr. Common Ground Conf., Ashland, 1991; adminstr. Rogue Valley Coalition Cultural Diversity Conf., Ashland, 1992, Nat. Coalition Bldg. Inst., Ashland, 1994; people to people citizen amb. del. to So. Africa, 1998. Miss. Project grantee So. Oreg. R&D, 1988, Mark Twain Prodn. grantee, 1989. Mem. NEA, NAACP, Nat. Coun. Tchrs. English, So. Poverty Law Ctr., N.W. Coalition Human Dignity. Avocations: theatre, travel, dogs, gardening. E-mail: susan.baird!ashland.k12.or.us. Office: Ashland Mid Sch 100 Walker Ave Ashland OR 97520-1399

BAIRD, WILLIAM MCKENZIE, chemical carcinogenesis researcher, biochemistry educator; b. Phila., Pa., Mar. 23, 1944; s. William Henry Jr. and Edna (McKenzie) Baird; m. Elizabeth A. Myers, June 21, 1969; children: Heather Jean, Elizabeth Joanne, Scott William. BS in Chem., Lehigh U., 1966; PhD in Oncology, U. Wis., 1971. Postdoctoral fellow Inst. Cancer Rsch., London, 1971—73; from asst. to assoc. prof. biochemistry Wistar Inst., Phila., 1973—80; assoc. prof. medicinal chem. Purdue U., West Lafayette, Ind., 1980—82, prof., 1982—97, Glenn L. Jenkins prof. medicinal chem., 1989—97; dir. Cancer Ctr., West Lafayette, Ind., 1986—97; faculty participant, biochemistry prog. Cancer Ctr., Purdue U., West Lafayette, Ind., 1980—97; dir. environ. Health Sci. Ctr., Oreg. State U., Corvallis, 1997—2000; prof., dept. environ. and molecular toxicology Oreg. State U., Corvallis, 1997—, prof. dept. biochemistry and biophysics, 1997—. Adv. com. on biochemistry and chem. carcinogenesis Am. Cancer Soc., 1983—86; mem. chem. pathology study sect. NIH, 1986—90; assoc. editor Cancer Rsch. Contbr. articles to profl. jours. Grantee NCI. Mem.: Soc. Toxicology, Environ. Mutagen Soc., Am. Soc. Biochemistry and Molecular Biology, Am. Chem. Soc., Am. Assn. Cancer Rsch., AAAS, ISSX. Office: Oreg State U Environ and Molecular Toxicology 1007 ALS Bldg Corvallis OR 97331-7301

BAIRSTOW, FRANCES KANEVSKY, arbitrator, mediator, educator; b. Racine, Wis., Feb. 19, 1920; d. William and Minnie (DuBow) Kanevsky; m. Irving P. Kaufman, Nov. 14, 1942 (div. 1949); m. David Steele Bairstow, Dec. 17, 1954; children: Dale Owen, David Anthony. Student, U. Wis., 1937-42; BS, U. Louisville, 1949; student, Oxford U., England, 1953-54; postgrad., McGill U., Montreal, Que., Can., 1958-59. Rsch. economist U.S. Senate Labor-Mgmt. Subcom., Washington, 1950-51; labor edn. specialist U. P.R., San Juan, 1951-52; chief wage data unit WSB, Washington, 1952-53; labor rsch. economist Can. Pacific Ry. Co., Montreal, Canada, 1956-58; asst. dir. indsl. rels. ctr. McGill U., 1960-66, assoc. dir., 1966-71, dir., 1971-85, lectr., indsl. rels. dept. econs., 1960-72, from asst. prof. to assoc. prof. faculty mgmt., 1972—83, prof., 1983-85; lectr. Stetson Law Sch., Fla.; spl. master Fla. Pub. Employees Rels. Commn., 1985-97. Cons. Nat. Film Bd. Can., 1965—69; arbitrator Que. Consultative Coun. Panel Arbitrators, 1968—83, Ministry Labour and Manpower, 1971—83, United Air Lines and Assn. Flight Attendants, 1990—95, Am. Airlines and Transport Workers Union, 1997—98, State U. Sys. Fla., 1990—2003, FDA, 1996—98, Social Security Adminstrn., 1996—2003, Am. Airlines, 1997—, Tampa Gen. Hosp., 1996—, Cargo Internat. Airlines, 2001, Govt. of Fla. and Fla. State Police, 2002—, Bell South and Comm. Workers Am., 2003—, USAF at Warner Robins and AFGE, 2003—; mediator Can. Pub. Svc. Staff Rels. Bd., 1973—85, So. Bell Tel., 1985—, AT&T and Comm. Workers Am., 1986—; cons. on collective bargaining arbitration OECD, Paris, 1979. Contbg. columnist: Montreal Star, 1971—85. Chmn. Nat. Inquiry Commn. Wider-Based Collective Bargaining, 1978; dep. commr. essential svcs. Province of Que., 1976—81. Fulbright fellow, 1953—54. Mem.: Ctrl. Fla. Indsl. Rels. Rsch. Assn. (pres. 1999), Nat. Acad. Arbitrators (bd. govs. 1977—80, program chmn. 1982—83, v.p. 1986—88, nat. coord. 1987—90), Indsl. Rels. Rsch. Assn. Am. (mem. exec. bd. 1965—68, chmn. nominating com. 1977), Can. Indsl. Rels. Rsch. Inst. (mem. exec. bd. 1965—68). Home and Office: 1430 Gulf Blvd Apt 507 Clearwater FL 33767-2856

BAISHANSKI, JACQUELINE MARIE, foreign language educator; b. Plouguernevel, France, Feb. 20, 1944; came to U.S., 1970; d. Jerome Marie and Marcelle Nicolas; m. Bogdan M. Baishanski, Sept. 23, 1972; childre: Yelena, Ana, Vanya, Tatyana. MS in Math., Sorbonne, Paris, 1964, DEA, 1966; PhD in French Lit., Ohio State U., 1998. Math., statis. Inst. Nat. Statis., Paris, 1966-67, French Coop., Libreville, 1967-68; asst. prof. U. Reims, France, 1969-70; teaching asst. Ohio State U., Columbus, 1970-73, lectr. math., 1978-80, 81-82, teaching asst. French, 1991-98, lectr. French, 1999—; prof. Denison U., Granville, Ohio, 2003—. Judge Ann. Lang. Olympics, Columbus, 1990; bd. dirs. early childhood edn. Ohio State U., 1985-86. Recipieent Fawcett award Ohio State U., 1987. Mem. Modern Lang. Assn. Am., Midwest Modern Lang. Assn. Avocations: reading, writing, classical music, travel. Home: 367 Blenheim Rd Columbus OH 43214-3219 Office: Denison U Modern Lang Dept Fellows Hall Granville OH 43023

BAISIER, MARIA DAVIS, English language educator, theater director; b. Louisville, Aug. 15, 1947; d. Alvin Joseph and Alice Josephine Davis; children: Bernard Paul Leon, Aimée Louise Davis. BA, St. Mary's Dominican Coll., 1969; secondary cert. in English, Tulane U., 1992. Asst. mng. editor So. Ins. Mag., New Orleans, 1979-85; tchr. St. Catherine of Siena Sch., Metairie, La., 1969-75, 85—, chair English dept., 1985—, dir. theatre, 1991—. Steering com. SACS evaluation team St. Catherine of Siena Sch., Metairie, La., 2000—01. Author: Pieces: Putting Life Back Together After Loss, 2003. Creator, dir. Camp Big Foot Summer Camp, Metairie, 1974, 75; v.p. Sacred Heart Sch. PTA, Anniston, Ala., 1977; vol. worker Sta. WYES-TV Auction, New Orleans, 1978-83; mem. women's com. New Orleans Opera Assn., 1979—, chair Opera Ball, 1984; various com. positions Women's Guild, 1980-84; chair ann. fundraiser fair St. Francis Xavier Ch., 1982-84; mem. hospitality com. Rep. Nat. Conv., 1988; mem. Les Amies Ensembles, 1996—, St. Patrick's Ch. Performing Choir, 1998—; presenter, events spkr. La. Middle Sch. Conv., 2000. Mem. La. Mid. Sch. Assn., Nat. Coun. Tchrs. English, Kappa Delta Pi, Phi Beta. Avocations: theatre, opera, museum, travel, reading. Home: 308 E Gatehouse Dr Apt B Metairie LA 70001-2128 Personal E-mail: mbaisier@aol.com.

BAITSELL, WILMA WILLIAMSON, artist, educator, lecturer; b. Palmyra, N.Y., July 5, 1918; d. Glen Hiram and Luetta (Newell) Williamson; m. Victor Harry Baitsell, Oct. 29, 1941; children: Corin Victor, Coby Allan, Corrine Luetta. BSE, SUNY, Oswego, 1957, MSE, 1964; postgrad., Iowa State Tchrs. Coll., Syracuse U., Ind. State U., Cooper Union, McGill U., Montreal, Western State U.; HHD, World U., 1982; PhD, U. Cambridge, Eng., 1981. Tchr. rural sch., 1939-41, Phoenix Central Sch., 1957-71, SUNY, Oswego, 1971-77; ret., 1977. Cons. area schs., Ford Found., 1965-68; art cons. N.Y. State Dept. Edn., summers 1968-70. Author: Creativity and Intelligence, 1965, Art for Campers, 1972, Crafts for Children, 1976, Christianity, Creativity and Democracy, 1978, Create or Destroy, Love or Hate, Peace or War, 1983; editor Summer Art mag., 1957-71. Chmn. Republican Twp. Com.; pres. Oswego County Women's Rep. Club; chmn. Sch. Bldg. and Orgn. Com., 1954; mem. ch. adminstrv. bd., 1948—, Ford Found. sci. and math. grantee, 1958-59; recipient 1st prize Mid-States Art Show, 1981, hon. mention for painting, Yamiguchi, Japan, 1981, 1st prize Am. Craftsman's Show, 1973. Mem. N.Y. State Ret. Tchrs. Assn. (life), Internat. Soc. Edn. Through Art, Oswego Art Guild (life), Nat. Ret. Tchrs. Assn., Oswego County and Scriba Hist. Soc. (life), SUNY Oswego Alumni Assn. (life), N.Y. State Grange, AAUW, DAR, Order Eastern Star (life). Methodist. Home and Office: 104 Whittemore Rd Oswego NY 13126-6613

BAKAC, ANDREJA, chemist, educator; b. Varazdin, Feb. 12, 1946; came to U.S., 1976; d. Zora (Bakac) Pekisic. BS in Chemistry, U. Zagreb, Croatia, 1968, MS in Chemistry, 1972, PhD in Chemistry, 1976. Asst. chemist Ames Lab., Iowa State U., 1979-82, assoc. chemist, 1982-84, chemist, 1984-00, sr. chemist, 2000—. Temp. assoc. prof. dept. chemistry Iowa State U., 1990; vis. scientist Tohoku Univ., Sendai, 1988, 90, MIT, 1993; acting program dir. Ames Lab., Iowa State U., 1994, 95. Reviewer jour. articles, grant proposals; contbr. chpts. to books, articles to profl. jours. Mem. AAAS, Am. Chem. Soc., Ia. Acad. Sci., Sigma Xi. Home: 1432 Breckinridge Ct Ames IA 50010-4224 Office: Iowa State U Ames Lab Ames IA 50011-0001 E-mail: bakac@ameslab.gov.

BAKANOWSKY, LOUIS JOSEPH, visual arts educator, architect, artist; b. Conn., Oct. 8, 1930; s. Louis Joseph Bakanowsky and Alice (Sullivan) Derda; m. Marie A. Golas, Jan. 27, 1951; 1 child, Louis J., III. BFA, Syracuse U., 1957; MArch, Harvard U., 1961. Registered architect. Asst. prof. architecture Cornell U., Ithaca, N.Y., 1961; assoc. prof. Harvard U., Cambridge, Mass., 1963-71, prof. architecture, 1972—, prof. visual arts., 1975-97, Osgood Hooker prof. visual studies emeritus, 1997—, chmn. dept. visual and environ. studies, 1976-86. Dir. Carpenter Ctr. for Visual Arts, 1984-90; prin. Cambridge Seven. Assocs., 1962—. Prin. works include U.S. Pavillion for Expo '67, Montreal, Can., Henry DuPont Libr., Pomfret Sch., Conn., Columbia Sch., Rochester, N.Y., Rostropovich residence; (sculpture) Carl Siembab Gallery, Boston, 1958; represented in various pub. an pvt. collection. With USAF, 1951-53. Grantee Nat. Endowment Arts, 1979, 83, Graham Found. for Advanced Studies in Fine Arts, 1983. Fellow AIA (design awards 1967, 70). Office: Harvard U Carpenter Ctr for Visual Arts 24 Quincy St Cambridge MA 02138-3804

BAKENHUS, AUGUST ANTHONY, mathematics educator, computer specialist; b. Houston, Feb. 22, 1958; s. August Frederick and Velia (Mancilla) B. AA, Deanza Jr. Coll., Cupertino, Calif., 1983; BA in Physical Scis., San Jose (Calif.) State U., 1985; MA in Ednl. Adminstrn., Calif. State U., L.A., 1994. cert. secondary school tchr. of physical scis., Calif. Tchr. San Jose Unified, 1987-89, L.A. Unified, Tarzana, Calif., 1989—. Mem. Nat. Coun. Tchrs. Math., L.A. City Tchrs. Math. Assn., Calif. Math. Coun., United Tchrs. L.A., Internat. Coun. Computers in Edn. Avocations: tennis, chess, sailing, reading, golf. Office: Portola Jr H S 18720 Linnet St Tarzana CA 91356-3313

BAKER, BETTY LOUISE, retired secondary education educator; b. Chgo., Oct. 17, 1937; d. Russell James and Lucille Juanita (Timmons) B. BE, Chgo. State U., 1961, MA, 1964; PhD, Northwestern U., 1971. Cert. tchr. secondary and elem. grades 3-8 math., Ill. Tchr. math. Harper H.S., Chgo., 1961-70, Hubbard H.S., Chgo., 1970-94, also chmn. dept.; ret., 1994. Part-time instr. Moraine Valley C.C., 1982-83, 84-86, 94—; reader AP calculus exams. Ednl. Testing Svc. Contbr. articles to profl. jours. Cultural arts chmn. Hubbard Parents-Tchrs.-Students Assn., 1974-76, 1st v.p., program chmn., 1977-79, 82-84, pres. 1979-81; organist Hope Luth Ch., 1964-95, accompanist S.W. Luth. Chorus, 1987—; organist and choir dir. Faith Luth. Ch., Oak Lawn, 1995—. Univ. fellow, 1969-70. Mem. Nat. Coun. Tchrs. Math., Ill. Coun. Tchrs. Math., Chgo. Tchrs. Union, Nat. Coun. Parents and Tchrs. (life), Sch. Sci. and Math. Assn., Am. Guild of Organists, Luth. Collegiate Assn., Walther League Hiking Club, Met. Math. Club Chgo., Kappa Mu Epsilon, Rho Sigma Tau, Mu Alpha Theta (sponsors), Kappa Delta Pi, Pi Lambda Theta, Phi Delta Kappa. Home: 6330 Pine Ridge Dr Apt 1D Tinley Park IL 60477-4928 E-mail: bakermus@aol.com.

BAKER, C. B. retired day care director, organizer, communicator; b. Ft. Wayne, Ind. d. James Edwin Doelling Sr. and Susie Mae Nutter; m. Gerald R. Baker, June, 1962 (div. 1966); 1 child, Erin Lee; m. Jeffrey E. Baker, June, 1967 (div. 1972); 1 child, Shannon Rae. Student, Internat. Bus. Coll., Ft. Wayne, 1961. Expeditor Wayne Fabricating, Ft. Wayne, 1971; county adminstr. Champaign (Ill.) County Bd., 1974-76; sec. WICD-TV, Champaign, 1976-77; dir. ops. 40 Plus of Colo., Inc., Denver, 1988, v.p., 1984-85, CEO, 1985-86; co-owner, CEO St. Anne's Extended Day Program and Day Care Program, Denver, 1986-89; self-employed organizer Denver, 1998—. CEO, editor The Village Voice newsletter, Savoy, Ill., 1974. Dir. Winfield Village Swimming Pool Com., Savoy, 1975; CEO, dir. Mich. Sugar Festival, Sebewaing, 1991. Mem. Am. Bus. Women's Assn., Colo. Women's C. of C. Avocations: reading, horseback riding, weights, walking.

BAKER, CAROL ANN, elementary school educator; b. Milw., Dec. 6, 1958; d. Alfred Walter and Gertrude Marian (Grabler) Krause; m. Donald Albert Baker, Aug. 11, 1984; 1 child, Caitlin Ann. BA in Psychology, Cardinal Strich Coll., 1982. Cert. tchr. grades kindergarten through 3rd, cert. tchr. spl. edn. grades kindergarten through 8th, Wis. Elem. tchr. St. Josaphat Sch., Milw., 1982-90; substitute tchr. Mukwonago Sch. Dist., 1997—. Mem. Psi Chi, Kappa Delta Pi (charter). Democrat. Roman Cath. Avocations: needle crafts, fishing, gardening.

BAKER, CHARLES STEPHEN, music educator; b. Cleve., July 25, 1942; s. LeRoy Williams and Nellie Angela (Burskey) B. BMus, Oberlin Coll. Conservatory, 1964; MA, Case Western Reserve U., 1967. Cert. music educator, Ohio. Tchr. music Madison Local Schs., Mansfield, Ohio, 1964-65, Wickliffe (Ohio) City Schs., 1967-96; pvt. clarinet instr., freelance clarinet performer Sch. of Fine Arts, Willoughby, Ohio, 1969—. Prin. clarinet, assoc. condr. Lakeland Civic Orch., Mentor, Ohio, 1972—. Recipient Disting. Svc. award Sch. of Fine Arts, 1992. Mem. NEA, Ohio Music Edn. Assn. (gen. music com. mem. 1972-99, 25 Yr. Svc. award 1991), Music Educators Nat. Conf. (N.E. region chair 1986-92, 94-98, all-state orch. chair 1990-92), Lake County Music Educators (sec. v.p., pres.), Ohio Edn. Assn., Am. Fedn. Musicians, U.S. Figure Skating Assn. Roman Catholic. Avocations: figure skating, photography, gardening, travel. Home: 5476 A Wildwood Ct Willoughby OH 44094-3261 E-mail: cbakermus@aol.com.

BAKER, CHRISTINE MARIE, secondary education educator; b. Tucson, Sept. 19, 1951; d. Howard Harold and Dorothy (Rice) B.; m. Steven Edward Willhoite, Aug. 24, 1968 (div. Dec. 1995); children: Stacey Leigh Rubalcava, Michael Edward Willhoite. BA, U. Calif., Berkeley, 1990; tchg. credential, San Francisco State U., 1991. Cert. tchr. secondary social sci., govt. and introductory English, Calif. Tchr. social sci. Franklin Jr. H.S., Vallejo, Calif., 1993—, mentor tchr., 1997—, dir. after sch. homework club, 1996—. Dept. chair social sci. Franklin Jr. H.S., Vallejo, 1994—; mem. newspapers in edn. adv. bd. San Francisco Newspaper Agy., 1995-96; mem. instrnl. improvement coun. Franklin Jr. H.S., Vallejo, 1995—, mem. leadership coun., 1994-95. Democrat. Office: Franklin Jr H S 501 Starr Ave Vallejo CA 94590-7154

BAKER, CLAUDE DOUGLAS, biology educator, researcher, environmental activist; b. El Dorado, Ark., Aug. 10, 1944; s. Claude Austin and Margaret Ester (Norman) B.; m. Karen Lee Sutterfield, Feb. 19, 1987; 1 child, Jessica Elizabeth. BS, U. Ark., 1966, MS, 1968; PhD, U. Louisville, 1972; postgrad., Fla. Atlantic U., 1985. Rsch. assoc. U. Ill., Champaign-Urbana, 1971-73; prof. biology Ind. U. S.E., New Albany, 1976—, preprofl. coord., 1994-98, coord. biology, 1996-97; mem. adj. faculty Fla. Atlantic U., 1997-99. Vis. scientist Ind. U., 1976—; selected spkr. Ind. Sci. Edn. Fund, Indpls., 1978-90; reviewer NSF, Washington, 1980-90; tchr. Ind. U./Aramco, Ras Tanura, Saudi Arabia, 1983. Contbr. chpts. to books, articles to profl. jours.; developer award winning field biology program,

Fla., Hawaii, Belize, Tahiti. Tchr. extracurricular program Ind. U., 1976-90; co-dir. S.E. Regional Sci. Fair, New Albany, 1976-83; bd. dirs. environ. adviser Save Our Rivers. Mem. Nat. Soc. SAR, Pi Kappa Alpha. Democrat. Avocations: scuba diving, photography, computers, travel, genealogy. Office: Ind U SE Dept Biology 4201 Grant Line Rd New Albany IN 47150-2158

BAKER, CYNTHIA JOAN, elementary education educator, historic site interpreter; b. Des Moines, Feb. 18, 1957; d. Lane Estil and Joan Arlene (Evenson) Goad; divorced; children: Wayne, Rachel, Nicholas. AA, Des Moines C.C., 1993; BA in Edn., Grandview Coll., Des Moines, 1996. Cert. elem. tchr., Iowa.. Mem. social svc. parent involvement prog. Head Start, Knoxville, Iowa, 1982-90, Knoxville (Iowa) Cmty. Sch., 1996; hist. interpreter Living History Farms, Urbandale, Iowa, 1994—; substitute tchr. various schs., Urbandale, Iowa, 1997—. Asst. leader Boy Scouts Am., Knoxville, Iowa, 1990-93; tchr., youth leader Pleasantville (Iowa) Bapt. Ch., 1993-97; mem. Candle of the Lord Ladies Group, 1994—, pres. 1996-97; dir. Vacation Bible Sch. Knoxville Christian Ch. Named to dean's list Grandview Coll., Des Moines, 1995, 96, 97; Eleanore J. Grube scholar Grandview Coll., 1995. Baptist. Avocations: reading, sewing, crafts. Home: 502 N 2nd St Knoxville IA 50138-1635

BAKER, D. JAMES, oceanographic and atmospheric administrator; b. Long Beach, Calif., Mar. 23, 1937; s. Donald James and Lillian Mae (Pund); m. Emily Lind Delman, Sept. 7, 1968. BS in Physics, Stanford U., 1958; PhD in Exptl. Physics, Cornell U., 1962; LHD (hon.), Nova U., 1993. Rsch. assoc. in phys. oceanography U. R.I., Kingston, 1962-63; NIH postdoctoral fellow in chem. biodynamics U. Calif., Berkeley, 1963-64, Harvard U., Cambridge, Mass., 1964-66, asst. prof. oceanography, 1966-70, assoc. prof., 1970-73; group leader deep-sea physics Pacific Marine Environ. Lab. Nat. Oceanog. and Atmospheric Adminstrn., Seattle, 1977-79; rsch. assoc. prof. dept. oceanography U. Wash., Seattle, 1973-75, rsch. prof. dept. oceanography, 1975-79, sr. oceanographer Applied Physics Lab., 1973-86, adj. prof. dept. atmospheric scis., prof. Sch. Oceanography, 1979-86, chmn. dept. oceanography, 1979-81, dean Coll. Ocean and Fishery Scis., 1981-83; disting. vis. scientist Jet Propulsion Lab., Calif. Inst. Tech., Pasadena, 1982-93; pres., bd. govs. Joint Oceanog. Instns. Inc., Washington, 1983-93; under sec. of commerce for oceans and atmosphere, adminstr. Nat. Oceanic and Atmospheric Adminstrn., Washington, 1993—. Guest investigator Woods Hole Oceanographic Instn., 1968-69, vis. scholar, 1970; mem. adv. com. NAS, Nat. Oceanic and Atmospheric Adminstrn. and other internat. bodies; co-chair environ. and natural resources com. Nat. Sci. and Tech. Coun., 1993—; ex-officio mem. Pres.'s Coun. on Sustainable Devel., 1993—; chair Fed. Com. for Meteorol. Svcs. and Supporting Rsch., 1993—; mem. Govt.-Univ.-Industry Rsch. Roundtable Coun., NAS/NRC, 1993—. Author: Planet Earth-The View from Space, 1990; co-editor-in-chief Geophys. Fluid Dynamics 1975-79; mem. editl. bd. Dynamics of Atmospheres and Oceans, 1979-88, Marine Tech. Soc. Journ., 1986-89, Oceanus Mag., 1992-93; contbr. articles to profl. jours.; patentee in field. Recipient COSPAR Vikram Sarabhai award, 1998. Recipient COSPAR Vikram Sarabhai award, 1998. Fellow AAAS, Am. Meteorol. Soc. (coun. 1982-88, pub. awareness com. 1991-93); mem. Am. Geophys. Union, The Oceanography Soc. (climate change com. 1977-80, cinterim pres. 1988-89, pres. 1989-92, past pres. 1992-93), Marine Tech. Soc., Challenger Soc. for Marine Sci., Can. Meteorol. and Oceanog. Soc., Am. Soc. Limnology and Oceanography, Sigma Xi. Office: US Dept Commerce Rm 5128 14th St & Constitution Ave Washington DC 20230-0001

BAKER, DON FORREST, secondary educator; b. Warren, Ohio, Apr. 30, 1947; s. Charles Forrest and Esther Lucille (Dilsaver) B.; m. Carol Marie Crosby, Aug. 20, 1977; children: Sarah Marie, Rachel Leigh. BS in Edn., Ohio U., 1969; MS in Edn., Youngstown State U., 1976. Tchr. Newton Falls (Ohio) Exempted Village Sch. Dist., 1969—, social studies dept. head, 1980—. Participant in field. Contbg. author: Ella A Woodward's History of Newton Falls Bicentennial, 1976. Mem. Newton Falls Bicentennial Commn., 1975-76; chmn. Newton Twp. Bd. Zoning Appeals, 1982-83, 84-86, vice chmn., 1986; mem. Selection Policy Rev. Com., Newton Falls Libr., 1988; mem. Future Goals Devel. Com., Newton Falls Pub. Libr., 1988 (long range planning com. 2003-),chair, Newton Falls Cemetary Assn. Ways and Means, 2003-; Rep. Precinct chmn., 1990—; fellow TAFT Inst. for Govt., 1978. Mem. Ohio Fed. Tchrs., Am. Fed. Tchrs., N.E. Ohio Edn. Assn., Newton Falls Classroom Tchrs. Assn. (v.p. 1978-80, pres. 1991—1996), Nat. Coun. for Social Studies, Friends of the Libr., Newton Falls Hist. Soc. (v.p. 1976-77). Methodist. Avocations: computers, reading. Office: Newton Falls High Sch 907 Milton Blvd Newton Falls OH 44444-1721

BAKER, FAITH MERO, retired elementary education educator; b. Pitts., May 9, 1941; d. Vincent G. and Georgetta (Rothwell) Mero; m. Gerald A. Baker, Dec. 22, 1968; children: Jeremy D., Kara L. BA, Carlow Coll., Pitts., 1963; MEd, U. Pitts., 1965, postgrad., 1966-68. Cert. elem. and spl. edn. tchr., Pa. Tchr. sci. Pitts. Pub. Schs., 1963-64, tchr. spl. edn., 1968-87, tchr., primary sci. specialist, 1987-98; ret. Leader instrnl. team Fulton Acad., Pitts., 1988—; facilitator, tchr. Project Wild and project Aquatic Wild, Project Learning Tree, Pitts., 1988—; mem. leadership team Fulton Acad. for New Am. Schs.-area Sch. to Career. Leader Girl Scouts U.S.A., Monroeville, Pa., 1979-86; mem. Supts. Roundtable Gateway Schs., Monroeville, Pa., 1987-89. Mem.: AAUW (chair scholarship com Monroeville br. 1996—), Pa. Bus. and Profl. Women's Assn. (mem. polit. action com., pres. Monroeville 1987—88, bd. dirs. dist.3 1991—, mem. polit. action com., pres. Monroeville 1992—93), Pitts. Fedn. Tchrs. (bldg. steward 1968—98), U. Pitts. Alumni Assn. (asst. v.p. 1987—88, sec. 1989—91, alumnae coun. recording sec. 1998—2000), Delta Kappa Gamma, Alpha Delta Kappa (treas. 1992—99), Phi Delta Gamma (pres. 1982—84, regional coord. 1984—86, sec. Kappa chpt. 1986—90, nat. v.p. 1992—94, nat. pres. 1994—96, nat. treas. 1998—2000, chpt. 2d v.p. 1999—2000, 1st v.p. 2000—02, pres. 2002—). Democrat. Roman Catholic. Avocations: sewing, gourmet cooking, writing, short stories and poetry. Home: 102 Penn Lear Dr Monroeville PA 15146-4734 E-mail: fayze@adelphia.net.

BAKER, GLORIA MARIE, visual artist, art educator; b. Petersburg, Ind. m. James Daniel Baker; children: David, Christopher. Pvt. practice, Evansville, Ind., 1976—. Artist (painting) Aztec Village, 1994 (Grumbacher Gold Medallion and The Excellence Gold award, 1994), The Dedicated, 1991 (Brown and Williamson Tobacco Corp. award, 1991, Dr. Martin Hydrus award Ga. Watercolor Soc., 03), The Domes, 1997 (2d pl.), Ascent to the Cathedral, 1998 (St. Cuthbert's Mill award, 1998, Grumbacner Bronze award), Double Ascent, 1999 (Winsor & Newton award, Document Framing Svc. award, 1999, 1st pl. Evansville Art Guild, Peabody Coal Co. award), Past, Present & Future, 1997, The Ascent (Houston B. Adams award, Evansville Mus. Arts & Sci.), Cathedral of Light, 2000 (2d pl., Dir.'s Choice award, 2000), The Dedicated, 1993, (included in books) Best of Watercolor, Best of Watercolor 2, Landscape Inspirations, The Complete Best of Watercolor, Vol.s 1 & 2, Chgo. Art Rev., 4th edit., Evansville Mus. of Arts and Sci. GiftShop, 2003. Chmn. Celia Sprue Assn., Evansville, 1995—2003. Mem.: Niagara Frontier Watercolor Soc. (chmn. 1995—2003), Watercolor Soc. Ala. (signature mem.), Ga. Watercolor Soc. (winner Nat. Exhibit 2003, Dr. Martin Hydrus award 2003), Pa. Watercolor Soc., Ky. Watercolor Soc., Petroleum Wives Club (v.p. 2003). Avocations: golf, gardening, reading, ballroom dancing. Home: 2711 Knob Hill Dr Evansville IN 47711

BAKER, JACK SHERMAN, architect, designer, educator; b. Champaign, Ill., Aug. 8, 1920; s. Clyde Lee and Jane Cecilia (Walker) B. BA with honors, U Ill., 1943, MS, 1949; cert., N.Y. Beaux Art Inst. Design, 1943. Aero engr., designer Boeing Aircraft, Seattle, 1943-44; assoc. Atkins, Barrow & Lasswith, Urbana, 1947-50; pvt. practice architecture Champaign, 1947—; mem. faculty U. Ill., Urbana, 1947—, prof. architecture, 1950-90, acting prof. emeritus, 1990—. Former mem. exec. com. Sch. Architecture, U. Ill.; hon. bd. dirs. Gerhart Music Festival, Guntersville, Ala., Stravinsky awards, Champaign, Conservatory of Cen. Ill.; hon. bd. dirs. Ruth Hindman Found., Huntsville, Ala.; dir., performer personal performance loft space for Interaction of the Arts and Architecture, 1960—; participant U. Ill. Exploring the Arts course (Act-NCEA award), 1970—, campus honors program, 1995—; former mem. Chancellor's com. on graphic design and art acquisition and installation, former mem. adv. bd., designer of exhbn., Krannert Mus., U. Ill., engr. basic, Ft. Leonard Wood, Mo., topog. engr., Ft. Blevoir, Va. Exhibitions include watercolors, archtl. drawings and photography, Monograph and Retrospective Arch. Exhibit: "I" Space Gallery, Chgo., 1997, U. Ill. Temple Buell Arch. Gallery, 1998, Temple Buell Hall Gallery, 2000, Japanese House Drawings Exhibit, Krannert Art Mus., U. Ill., 1998; contbr. articles to numerous jours. and confs. Mem. U. Ill. Pres.'s Coun., U. Ill. Bronze Cir., 1986; mem. mus. bd. and affiliate World Heritage Mus.; former mem. adv. bd. Krannert Ctr. for Performing Arts, Assembly Hall U. Ill.; exhbn. designer World Heritage Mus., U. Ill. Served with U.S. Army, AFH, 1945-46, Caserta, Italy, ETO. Recipient "prix d'Emulation Societe des Architectes Diplomes par le Gouvernment" Beaux-Arts medal, 1942, cert. for dedicated and disting. svc., Nat. AIA Com. on Environ. and Design, 1955, Decade of Achievement award, World Heritage Mus., 1992, Art and Humanities award medal, 1981, Art and Humanities award and medal, 1982, Honor award for advancing profession architecture, CIC/AIA, 1983, Excellence in Edn. award and medal, IC/AIA, 1989, Heritage award, PACA, 1997, numerous other honors and design excellence awards in field, Recognition award, U. Ill. Found., 2001. Fellow: AIA (medal 1977), Nat. Coun. Archtl. Registration Bds. (cert.); mem.: Soc. Archtl. Historians, Ill. Coun./AIA, The Nature Conservancy, Nat. Resources Def. Coun., Gargoyle, Scarab, Cliff Dwellers Club (Chgo.), Alpha Rho Chi. Home: 71 1/2 E Chester St Champaign IL 61820-4149 Office: U Ill 117 Temple Hoyne Buell Hall 611 Taft Dr MC-621 Champaign IL 61820-6922

BAKER, JOHN EDWARD, cardiac biochemist, educator; b. London, Eng., Dec. 12, 1954; arrived in U.S., 1984; s. Edward D. and Florence I. (Dobson) Baker; m. Mary E. Zurawski, Oct. 29, 1988; children: David J., Elizabeth A. BSc, Poly. Wolverhampton, Eng., 1977; PhD, St. Thomas' Med. Sch., London, 1984. Sr. biochemist Cen. Pathology Labs., London, 1977-78; rsch. asst. St. Thomas' Hosp. Med. Sch., London, 1978-84; rsch. fellow Med. Coll. Wis., Milw., 1984-86, vis. prof., 1986-87, asst. prof. cardiothoracic surgery, 1987-92, assoc. prof., 1992-99, assoc. prof. pediat. surgery, biochemistry, pharmacology, 1999-2001, prof., 2001—. Mem. peer rev. rsch. com. NIH, 2002—. Mem. editl. bd.: Am. Jour. Physiology, Heart and Circulatory Physiology; contbr. articles to profl. jours. Founder Heart Sci. Found., Ltd.; bd. dirs. Adelaide Banaszynski Sch. Piano Studies. Grantee, NIH, 1989, 1990, 1993, 1997, 2000, 2001, Culpeper Found., 1987, Ronald McDonald Children's Charities, 1989, 1991, Children's Hosp. Found., 1995. Mem.: Am. Heart Assn. (mem. peer rev. rsch. com. Wis. affiliate 1989—93, mem. peer rev. rsch. com. Northland affiliate 1999—2001, mem. coun. basic. sci., mem. Nat. Inst. of Health Study Sections 2002—). Methodist. Achievements include patents for method for sealing blood vessel puncture sites and method for coating intraluminal stents. Avocations: walking, music. Office: Med Coll Wis 8701 W Watertown Plank Rd Milwaukee WI 53226-3548 E-mail: jbaker@mcw.edu.

BAKER, KATHERINE JUNE, elementary school educator, minister, artist; b. Dallas, Feb. 3, 1932; d. Kirk Moses and Katherine Faye (Turner) Sherrill; m. George William Baker, Jan. 30, 1955; children: Kirk Garner, Kathleen Kay. BS, BA, Tex. Women's U., 1953, MEd, 1979; cert. in religious edn., Meadville Theol. U., 1970; postgrad., North Tex. State U., 1987—; DD (hon.), Am. Fellowship Ch., 1981. Cert. elem. and secondary tchr., adminstr., Tex.; lic. and ordained min. Kingsway Internat. Ministries, 1991. Mgr. prodn. Woolf Bros., Dallas, 1953-55; display mgr. J.M. Dyer and Co., Corsicana, Tex., 1954; advt. artist Fair Dept. Store, Ft. Worth, 1954-56; artist, instr. Dutch Art Gallery, Dallas, 1960-65; dir. religious edn. 1st Unitarian Ch., Dallas, 1967-69; edn. dir. day care, tchr. Richardson (Tex.) Unitarian Ch., 1971-73; dir. camp Tres Rios YWCA, Glen Rose, Tex., 1975-76; dir. program of extended sch. instrn. Hamilton Park Elem. Sch. Richardson Ind. Sch. Dist., 1975-78, tchr. Dover Elem. Sch., 1979—80, tchr. Jess Harben Elem. Sch., 1980—92; founder ednl., editorial and arts/evang. assn. Submitted Ministries, Richardson, 1992—. Dir. Flame Fellowship Internat., 1987-94, state rep., 1994-99—, asst. state overseer (Tex.), 1999-2001, chaplain, 2002--. Contbr. articles to ch. newspaper, 1967-69; exhibited in group show at Tex. Art Assn., 1966; one-woman show Dutch Art Gallery - Northlake Ctr., Dallas, 1965. Advocate day care Unitarian Unicersalist Women's Fedn., Boston, 1975—76, mem. nominating com., 1976—77; cert. instr. aquatics program Arthritis Found. YMCA AFYAP, Plano Rehab. Hosp., 1997—99, Aquatics Inst. Oak Point Ctr., Plano, 1999—, Aquatics Inst. Fun Fit Crew, 2001—. Mem. NEA, ASCD, Nat. Coun. Social Studies, Tex. State Tchrs. Assn. (treas. Richardson chpt. 1984-85), Tex. Ret. Tchrs. Assn., Richardson Ret. Tchrs. Assn., Women's Ctr. Dallas, Sokol Athletic Ctr., Smithsonian Assn., Dallas Mus. Assn., Alpha Chi, Delta Phi Delta (pres. 1952-53), Phi Delta Kappa. Avocations: gospel and folk singing, guitar, volleyball, camping. Fax: 972-312-9295.

BAKER, KEITH MICHAEL, history educator; b. Swindon, Eng., Aug. 7, 1938; came to U.S., 1964; s. Raymond Eric and Winifred Evelyn (Shepherd) B.; m. Therese Louise Elzas, Oct. 25, 1961 (div. 1999); children—Julian, Felix. BA, Cambridge U., 1960, MA, 1963; postgrad., Cornell U., 1960-61; PhD, U. London, 1964. Instr. history and humanities Reed Coll., 1964-65; asst. prof. European history U. Chgo., 1965-71, assoc. prof., 1971-76, prof., 1977-89, master collegiate div. social scis., 1975-78, assoc. dean coll., 1975-78, assoc. dean div. social scis., 1975-78, chmn. commn. grad. edn., 1980-82; chmn. Council Advanced Studies in Humanities and Social Scis., 1982-86; prof. European history Stanford U., 1989—, J.E. Wallace Sterling prof. in humanities, 1992—, chair dept. history, 1994-95; Anthony P. Meier family prof. humanities, dir. Stanford Humanities Ctr., 1995-2000, cognizant dean humanities, 2000—. Vis. assoc. prof. history Yale U., 1974; mem. Inst. Advanced Study, Princeton (N.J.), 1979-80; vis. prof., dir. studies Ecole des Hautes Etudes en Scis. Sociales, Paris, 1982, 84, 91; fellow Ctr. for Advanced Study in Behavioral Scis., Stanford (Calif.) U., 1986-87; vis. prof. UCLA, 1989; vis. fellow Clare Hall, Cambridge (Eng.) U., 1994; chair scholars com. Am. Com. on the French Revolution, 1989. Author: Condorcet: From Natural Philosophy to Social Mathematics, 1975, Inventing the French Revolution, 1990; prin. author: Report Commission on Graduate Education, U. Chgo., 1982; editor: Condorcet: Selected Writings, 1977, The Political Culture of the Old Regime: The Old Regime and the French Revolution, 1987, The Terror, 1994; co-editor Jour. Modern History, 1980-89, What's Left of Enlightenment?, 2001. Decorated chevalier Ordre des Palmes Académiques, 1988; NEH fellow, 1967-68, ACLS study fellow, 1972-73, Guggenheim fellow, 1979. Fellow AAAS; mem. Am. Hist. Assn. (com. on coms. 1991-94), Soc. French History Studies, Am. Soc. for 18th Century Studies (v.p. 1999, pres. 2000-01), Am. Philos. Soc. Office: Stanford U Dept History Stanford CA 94305 E-mail: kbaker@stanford.edu.

BAKER, KENDALL L. academic administrator; b. Clearwater, Fla., Nov. 1, 1942; s. Robert B. and Anne E. Baker; m. Tobin Ratliff McGough, Apr. 12, 1981; children: Kraig, Kris, John, Shannon, Brian. BA with honors, U. Md., 1963; MA, Georgetown U., 1967, PhD, 1969. Instr., Dept. Polit. Sci. U. Wyo., Laramie, 1967-69, asst. prof., 1969-73, assoc. prof., 1973-77, prof., 1977-82, chmn., 1979-82, asst. v.p. for Acad. Affairs, 1976-77; dean, Coll. Arts & Scis., Bowling Green State U., Ohio, 1982-87; v.p., provost No. Ill. U., DeKalb, 1987-92; pres. U. N. D., 1992-99, Ohio Northern U, 1999—. Cons. on survey research to various agys. and polit. candidates, 1967—; panel chmn. Rocky Mt. Social Sci. Conv. 1973, We. Social Sci. Conv., 1975, Council Colls. Arts and Scis., 1983, 86; guest participant study trip to Fed. Republic of Germany, 1977; election observer Fed. Republic of Germany, 1980. Author: The Wyoming Legislature: Lawmakers, the Public, and the Press, 1973; (with R. Dalton and K. Hildebrandt) Germany Transformed: Political Culture and the New Politics, 1981; contbr. articles on polit. sci. to profl. jours. Coach Laramie Soccer Assn., 1978-81. Mem. Am. Polit. Sci. Assn. (chmn. panel ann. conv. 1983), Midwest Polit. Sci. Assn. (chmn. panel ann. conv. 1985, 86), Conf. Group on German Politcs (exec. com. 1984-87, co-editor newsletter 1985-91), Phi Kappa Phi, Omicron Delta Kappa, Pi Sigma Alpha. Home: 920 West Lima Ada OH 45810 Office: President's Office 525 S Main St Ada OH 45810-1599 E-mail: k-baker@onu.edu.

BAKER, LEE EDWARD, biomedical engineering educator; b. Springfield, Mo., Aug. 31, 1924; s. Edward Fielding and Oneita Geneva (Patton) B.; m. Jeanne Carolyn Ferbrache, June 20, 1948; children: Carson Phillips, Carolyn Patton. BEE, U. Kans., 1945; MEE, Rice U., 1960; PhD in Physiology, Baylor U., 1965. Registered profl. engr., Tex. Asst. prof. electrical engring. Rice U., Houston, 1960-64; asst. prof. physiology Baylor U. Coll. Medicine, Houston, 1965-69, assoc. prof., 1969-75; prof. biomed. engring. U. Tex., 1975-82, Robert L. Parker Sr. Centennial Prof. Engring., 1982-2000, prof. emeritus, 2000—. Co-author: Principles of Applied Biomedical Engineering, 1968, 3d edit., 1989; author, co-author scientific papers. Served to lt. USN, 1943-46, PTO, 1951-53. Spl. research fellow NIH, 1964-65. Fellow Am. Inst. Med. and Biol. Engring., Royal Soc. Medicine; mem. IEEE (sr.), Biomed. Engring. Soc. (sr.), Am. Physiol. Soc. Avocation: gardening. Office: Univ Tex ENS 610 Biomed Engring Program Austin TX 78712

BAKER, LUCILLE STOEPPLER, sociology and anthropology educator; b. N.Y.C., Aug. 4, 1919; d. Charles W. and Henrietta (Krammer) Stoeppler; m. Walter Hewlett Baker Jr., June 29, 1946 (dec. 1981). BS, Coll. Mt. St. Vincent, 1941; MA in Econs., Fordham U., 1942; PhD, Cornell U., 1969; postgrad., U. Colo., 1967-68. Tchr. social sci. Unquowa Sch., Fairfield, Conn., 1942-46; high sch. adminstr. U.S. Dept. Def., Lajes AFB, Azores Island, 1951-54, vocat. ednl. counselor Ramey AFB, P.R., 1956-59; asst. prof. Fla. State U. Ctr., P.R.; lectr. East West Ctr. U. Hawaii, Honolulu, 1964-66; asst. prof., head sociology dept. Wilberforce (Ohio) U., 1966-69; prof. Tompkins-Cortland Community Coll. SUNY, Dryden, 1969—. Trustee Young-Morse Historic Site, Poughkeepsie, N.Y., 1986—, chairperson bicentennial, 1991. NSF fellow U. Boulder, 1966-67; Fordham U. scholar and fellow, 1941-42. Mem. AAUS (program chair 1983-85, pres. 1985-87), Am. Sociol. Assn., Am. Anthrop. Assn., Groton Hist. Assn. (pres. 1994—), Cornell Women's Club (pres. Cortland chpt. 1987-89), Zonta Internat., Delta Kappa Gamma. Avocation: historic preservation. Office: SUNY Tompkins Cortland CC Dryden NY 13053

BAKER, MARGERY LOUISE, elementary education educator; b. Leon, Iowa, July 10, 1922; d. William Elva and Minnie May (Hill) B. BA with honors, Simpson Coll., Indianola, Iowa, 1957; MA, Drake U., Des Moines, 1965. Classroom tchr. Rural Schs. of Decatur County, Iowa, 1940-53, Corydon (Iowa) Pub. Sch., 1953-56, Prescott (Iowa) Community Sch., 1957-61, Nevada (Iowa) Community Sch., 1962-72; learning disabilities tchr. Cardinal Community Sch., Eldon, Iowa, 1972-92. Cons. for home schooling, 1995. Writer of plays for learning disabled students to perform, 1975-83. Recipient Cert. of Appreciation Gov. of Iowa, 1992. Mem. NEA, Nat. Learning Disabilities Assn., Iowa State Edn. Assn., Learning Disabilities Assn. Iowa (Cert. of Appreciation 1994), Cardinal Edn. Assn. (chmn. govtl. affairs 1982-92). Lutheran. Avocations: photography, gardening, iowa hawkeye sports, reading, collecting books.

BAKER, MARY ALICE, communication educator, consultant; b. Stuart, Okla., Sept. 9, 1937; d. James Roy and Emma M. (Bird) B. BS, U. Okla., 1959, MA in Speech, 1966; PhD in Comm., Purdue U., 1983. Speech and debate tchr. SE High Sch., Oklahoma City, 1959-65; instr. Ea. Ill. U., Charleston, 1966-69; prof. Lamar U., Beaumont, Tex., 1966-75, 78—, dir. forensics, 1969-75, Regents' Merit prof., 1984, pres. faculty senate, 1986-88. Contbr. articles to profl. jours. Mem. R & D com. Nat. Coun. Tchr. Retirement Sys., 2003; trustee Tchrs. Retirement Sys. Tex., 1999—, chair ethcis com. David Ross fellow, 1977. Mem. Tex. Speech Comm. Assn. (regional rep. 1978-88), Nat. Comm. Assn. Am., Tex. Assn. Coll. Tchrs. (regional v.p. 1985-88, pres.-elect 1988-89, state pres. 1989-90, state bd. legis. liason 1997-99), Tex. Forensics Assn. (pres. 1974), Internat. Comm. Assn., Zeta Phi Eta, Alpha Delta Pi. Democrat. Episcopalian. Avocations: reading, politics, travel. Office: Lamar U Dept Communication Beaumont TX 77710

BAKER, PETER MITCHELL, laser scientist, educator, science administrator; b. London, July 18, 1939; s. George Edward and Clarice (Griffiths) Baker; m. Sunny Baker, Oct. 15, 1988; 1 child, Scott George. BSc in Physics with honors, London U., 1963. Sr. physicist Itek Corp., Lexington, Mass., 1966-69; sr. v.p. Micronetic Sys., Burlington, Mass., 1969-74; tchr. physics Hillcrest Sch., Nairobi, Kenya, 1975-77; pres. Quantrad Corp., Torrance, Calif., 1977-84, Ebtec Calif., Huntington Beach, 1985-88; exec. dir. Laser Inst. Am., Orlando, Fla., 1988—. Lectr. lasers UCLA Ext., 1986—88. Contbr. articles to profl. jours. Recipient CEO award for Outstanding Small Bus., 1982. Fellow: Laser Inst. Am. (pres. 1987); mem.: Engring. and Sci. Soc. Execs. (bd. dirs. 2000, v.p. 2003). Avocations: walking, tennis. Office: Laser Inst Am 13501 Ingenuity Dr Ste 128 Orlando FL 32826-3009

BAKER, REBECCA LOUISE, musician, music educator, consultant; b. Covina, Calif., Apr. 12, 1951; d. Allan Herman and Hazel Margaret (Maki) Flaten; m. Jerry Wayne Baker, Dec. 22, 1972; children: Jared Wesley, Rachelle LaDawn, Shannon Faith. Grad. high sch., Park River, N.D.; student, Trinity Bible Inst., 1968-69. Sec. Agrl. Stblzn. & Conservation Svc. Office, Park River, N.D., 1969; pianist, singer Paul Clark Singers & Vic Coburn Evangelistic Assn., Portland, Oreg., 1969-72; musician, singer Restoration Ministries Evangelistic Assn., Richland, Wash., 1972-80; musician, pvt. instr. Calvary Temple Ch., Shawnee, Okla., 1980-81; organist, choirmaster St. Francis Episcopal Ch., Tyler, 1984-87; co-founder, owner Psalmist Sch. of Music & Recording Studio, Whitehouse, 1983—; pianist/entertainer Willowbrook Country Club, Tyler, Tex., 1991—; pianist, vocalist Mario's Italian Restaurant, Tyler, 1994—. Pianist Garner Ted Armstrong, Tyler, 1986—; pianist, dir. Children's Choir, Calvary Bapt. Ch., Tyler, 1987—; pianist, entertainer Ramada Hotel, Tyler, 1988-90; pianist Whitehouse (Tex.) Sch. Dist. choirs, 1988—; accompanist Tyler Area Children's Chorale, 1988-90, Univ. Interscholastic League; pvt. instr. keyboard and vocal. Composer: Religious Songs (12 on albums), 1979; pianist, arranger, prodr., rec. artist 6 albums; editor, arranger: Texas Women's Aglow Songbook, 1987; editor Shekinah Glory mag., 1989—; developer improvisational piano course; star, prodr. weekly, nationally syndicated mus. religious programs for TV, 1995, 96, Proclaim His Glory, 1997—; played for receptions honoring Gov. George Bush, Tex. Senator Phil Gramm and Congressman John Bryant. Performer, spkr. many charitable, civic and religious orgns., Tex. and U.S. including AAUW, Kiwanis Clubs; co-founder Psalmist Mins. Internat., 1988—; founder, pres. Christian Music Tchr.'s Assn., 1991; worship leader Mayor's Prayer Breakfast, Tyler, 1994. Mem. Women's Aglow Fellowship (music dir., spkr., performer at retreats and tng. seminars). Republican. Full Gospel. Avocations: travel, reading, interior decorating, collecting. Home and Office: Psalmist Music & Recording PO Box 4126 Tyler TX 75712 E-mail: psalmistministries@netzero.com.

BAKER, RICHARD EARL, business management educator; b. Inglewood, California, Sept. 22, 1928; s. Glyn Maynard and Ruth Elizabeth (Norton) B.; m. Dorotha Jean (Mayo); children: Mary K. Walton, Thomas P., Kimberlee S. Tillman, Scott R. BS, U. So. Calif., 1951, MBA, 1956; post grad., U. Calif., Berkeley, 1958-60. Various mgmt. positions AT and T Co., Calif., 1952-76; cons. Graves and Campbell, L.A., 1974-79; prof. U. Calif., LaVerne, Calif., 1976-79, Calif. State Poly. U., Pomona, Calif., 1976-80; cons. Kingman, Ariz., 1980—; instr. Mohave Cmty. Coll., Kingman, Ariz., 1980—. Bd. dir. profl. sales Gen. Motors Dealership, Kingman, 1987; adj. prof., Prescott Coll., Ariz., 1982—; sr. cons. Roberts & Heck Assocs., L.A., 1974-78; cons. Svc. Corps of Retired Execs. SBA, 1980—. Editor: Stress/Assertiveness, 1981; contbg. articles to profl. jour. Foster parent, Foster Parent Assn., L.A., 1965-78; counselor Teenage Drug Rehab., L.A. 1970-78; coun. commr. Boy Scouts Am., L.A., 1975, scoutmaster, 1965-74; coord. Vocat. Adv. Coun., 1980-90. Lt. comdr. USN, 1945-48, PTO, 1950-52. Mem. Kingman C. of C., Kiwanis, Beta Gamma Sigma. Republican. Avocations: photography, marksmenship-gun collecting, landscaping, electronics. Home: 4909 Scotty Dr Kingman AZ 86401-1259 Office: Mohave Cmty Coll 1971 Jagerson Ave Kingman AZ 86401-1238

BAKER, RICHARD GRAVES, geology educator, palynologist; b. Merrill, Wis., June 12, 1938; s. Dillon James and Miriam Baker; m. Debby J.Z. Baker; children: Kristina Kae, James Dillon, Charity Ann. BA, U. Wis., 1960; MS, U. Minn., 1964; PhD, U. Colo., 1969. Asst. prof. geology U. Iowa, Iowa City, 1970-75, assoc. prof., 1975-81, prof., 1981—, chmn. dept., 1992-95, prof. botany, 1988-92, prof. biol. scis., 1992-2000, prof. emeritus, 2000—. Contbr. articles to profl. jours., chapters to books. Chmn. Iowa chpt. Nature Conservancy, Des Moines, 1981-82. Grantee NSF, 1984-86, 88-90, 94-97, NOAA, 1992-93; recipient Disting. Scientist award Iowa Acad. Sci., 2001. Fellow Geol. Soc. Am., Iowa Acad. Sci.; mem. AAAS, Am. Quaternary Assn., Ecol. Soc. Am. Office: Univ Iowa 121 Trowbridge Hall Dept Geosci Iowa City IA 52242-1319 Business E-Mail: dick-baker@uiowa.edu.

BAKER, ROBERT BERNARD, philosophy educator; b. N.Y.C., Dec. 5, 1937; s. Hal Murray and Freda (Ginsburg) B.; m. Arlene Shiela Bernstein Baker, Nov. 28, 1958; children: Nathanial Edward, Meredith Harrison. BA in History (hon.), CUNY, 1959; PhD, U. Minn., 1967. Instr. U. Minn., Mpls., 1964-65; asst. prof. U. Iowa, 1965-69, Wayne State U., Detroit, 1969-73, Union Coll., Schnectady, N.Y., 1973-80, assoc. prof., 1980-88, prof., 1989—, dir. Ctr. for Bioethics and clin. leadership, 2001—; vis. assoc. prof. NYU Med. Sch., 1981; vis. scholar Kennedy Inst. Ethics, Georgetown U., Washington, 1982, 94. Pres. Iowa Philos. Soc., 1968-69; mem. Gov.'s Taskforce on Victimless Crime, Mich., 1972-73; acad. coord. Study of Nat. Health Care Sys., Union Coll., 1979—; dir. Computers in Humanities Undergraduate Curriculum, Union Coll., 1984-88; vis. fellow Ctr. for Bioethics U. Pa., 1996—; assoc. Ctr. for Med. Ethics Albany Med. Coll., 1997—, co-dir. Masters of Bioethics program, 2000—. Editor: (with F. Elliston) Philosophy and Sex, 1975, 84, (with K. Wininger and F. Elliston) Philosophy and Sex, 1998, (with D. & R. Porter) Codification of Medical Morality, 1993, 95, (with M. Strosberg) Legislating Medical Ethics, 1995, (with A. Caplan, L. Emanuel, S. Latham) The American Medical Ethics Revolution, 1999; contbr. articles to profl. jours. Recipient Spl. Interest grant Digital Equipment Corp., Sloan Found., Union Coll., 1984-86, Travel grant Am. Philos. Soc., 1994, Wood Inst. fellow, 1996, NEH Collaborative rsch. grant, 1999-2002, Greenwall Found. grant, 2001. Mem. APA, Am. Assn. Historians of Medicine, Hastings Ctr., Am. Soc. Bioethics and Humanities (chair history of med. ethics group 1998—). Avocations: reading, travel, walking. Home: 1126 Waverly Pl Schenectady NY 12308-2612 Office: Ctr for Bioethics Union College Schenectady NY 12308 E-mail: bakerr@union.edu.

BAKER, ROBERT JAMES, elementary education educator; b. Tokyo, Oct. 31, 1963; s. Robert Charles and Lilliam (Aurora) B. BA, Rollins Coll., 1986; MS, Nova U., 1990, postgrad., 1990—. Cert. tchr., Fla. Tchr. social studies Glades Mid. Sch.-Dade County Pub. Schs., Miami, Fla., 1986—. Grantee Dade Pub. Edn. Fund, Miami, 1990. Mem. Nat. Coun. Social Studies, Fla. Coun. Social Studies, Dade County Coun. Social Studies, Phi Delta Kappa. Avocations: physical fitness, environmental education. Home: 20 Outlook Cir Pacifica CA 94044-2145 Office: Glades Mid Sch 9451 SW 64th St Miami FL 33173-2248

BAKER, ROBERT M. L., JR., academic administrator; b. L.A., Sept. 1, 1930; s. Robert M.L. and Martha (Harlan) B.; m. Bonnie Sue Vold, Nov. 14, 1964; children: Robert Randall, Robert M.L. III, Robin Michele Leslie. BA summa cum laude, UCLA, 1954, MA, 1956, Ph.D., 1958. Cons., Douglas Aircraft Co., Santa Monica, Calif., 1954-57; sr. scientist Aeronutronic, Newport Beach, Calif., 1957-60; head Lockheed Aircraft Rsch. Ctr., West Los Angeles, 1961-64; assoc. mgr. Math. analysis Computer Scis. Corp., El Segundo, Calif., 1964-80; pres. West Coast U., L.A., 1980— ; faculty UCLA, 1958-72; dir. Internat. Info. Systems Corp., Pasadena, Calif., Transp. Scis. Corp., L.A. Appointee Nat. Accreditation Adv. Com., U.S. Dept. Edn., 1987-90. Served to maj. USAF, 1960-61. Named Outstanding Young Man of Year, 1965; recipient Dirk Brouwer award, 1976. Fellow AAAS, Am. Astro. Soc., Meteoritical Soc., Brit. Astro. Soc., AIAA (assoc.); mem. Am. Phys. Soc., Phi Beta Kappa, Sigma Xi, Sigma Pi Sigma. Author: An Introduction to Astrodynamics, 1960; 2d edit., 1967; Astrodynamics-Advanced and Applied Topics, 1967, 87; editor: Jour. Astron. Scis., 1961-76, SCL; patentee in field. E-mail: bakerjr@attbi.com.

BAKER, ROLAND JERALD, educator; b. Pendleton, Oreg., Feb. 27, 1938; s. Roland E. and Theresa Helen (Forest) B.; m. Judy Lynn Murphy, Nov. 24, 1973; children: Kristen L., Kurt F., Brian H. BA, Western Wash. U., 1961; MBA, U. Mich., 1968. Cert. purchasing mgr., profl. contract mgr. Asst. dir. purchasing and stores U. Wash., Seattle, 1970-75; mgr. purchasing and material control Foss Launch & Tug Co., Seattle, 1975-79; faculty Shoreline C.C., 1972-79, 98—, Pacific Luth. U., 1977-79, Edmonds C.C., 1974-79; chmn. educators group Nat. Assn. Purchasing Mgmt., Tempe, Ariz., 1976-79, exec. v.p., 1979-98; pres. Nat. Assn. Purchasing Mgmt. Svcs., Tempe, Ariz., 1989-95. Faculty Ariz. State U., Tempe, 1988-91; world bus. adv. Coun. Am. Grad. Sch. of Internat. Mgmt., Glendale, Ariz., 1994-98; adv. bd. blockbuy.com, Inc., 1999-01, Perfect.com., Inc., 2000—; exec. v.p. MyGroupbuy Inc., 2000—, also bd. dirs.; mem. faculty Shoreline C.C., Seattle, Wash., 1998—. Author: Purchasing Factomatic, 1977, Inventory System Factomatic, 1978, Policies and Procedures for Purchasing and Material Control, 1980, rev. edit., 1992. With USN, 1961-70, comdr. Res., 1969-91. Recipient Disting. Achievement award Ariz. State U. Coll. Bus., 1997; U.S. Navy postgrad. fellow, 1967. Mem. Purchasing Mgmt. Assn. Wash. (pres. 1978-79), Nat. Minority Supplier Devel. Coun. (bd. dirs.), Am. Prodn. and Inventory Control Soc., Nat. Assn. Purchasing Mgmt. (exec. v.p. 1979-97), Nat. Contract Mgmt. Assn., Internat. Fedn. Purchasing and Materials Mgmt. (exec. com. 1984-87, exec. adv. com. 1991-98). Office: Shoreline CC 16101 Greenwood Ave N Seattle WA 98133-5667

BAKER, RUTH BAYTOP, music educator; b. Pittsfield, Mass., Nov. 6, 1908; d. Thomas Nelson and Lizzie (Baytop) B. BA, Oberlin (Ohio) Coll., 1933; BS in Music Edn., Oberlin Conservatory, 1934; MA, Columbia U., 1964, MEd, 1988. Cert. tchr., N.Y. Tchr. music Tillotson Coll., Austin, Tex., 1934-35, Winston-Salem (N.C.) Tchrs. Coll., 1935-37, Colonel Young Meml. Fedn., N.Y.C., 1937-38, Livingstone Coll., Salisbury, N.C., 1938-39, Colonel Young Meml. Fedn., N.Y.C., 1939—. Sec.-treas. Colonel Young Meml. Found., N.Y.C., 1950—. Recipient Contbr. as Voice Tchr. award Mary Cardwell Dawson Art Guild, 1993, Cert. of Achievement, Afro Arts Cultureal Ctr., Inc., 1993. Mem. Nat. Assn. Tchrs. Singing, N.Y. Singing Tchrs. Assn., Associated Music Tchrs. League N.Y., Inc. Congregationalist. Office: Colonel Young Meml Found PO Box 475 New York NY 10027-0475

BAKER, STANLEY BECKWITH, education educator; b. Mpls., Sept. 3, 1935; s. Stanley Forrest and Dorothy Ruth (Beckwith) B.; m. Barbara Ann Laufenburger, Aug. 17, 1957 (dec.); children: Susan Elizabeth, David Allen; m. Mary Esther Clark Martin, June 10, 2000. BA, Augsburg Coll., 1957; MA, U. Minn., 1963; PhD, SUNY, Buffalo, 1971. Lic. profl. counselor, N.C.; nat. cert. counselor. Tchr. social studies Spring Valley (Wis.) High Sch., 1957-63; tchr. history Janesville (Wis.) High Sch., 1963-66, sch. counselor, 1964-67, Parker High Sch., Janesville, 1967-69; asst. prof. edn. Pa. State U., University Park, 1971—74, assoc. prof. edn., 1974—84, prof. edn., 1984—94; prof., head dept. N.C. State U., Raleigh, 1994—2001, prof., 2001—. Office: NC State U PO Box 7801 Raleigh NC 27695-0001

BAKER, STEPHEN DENIO, physics educator; b. Durham, N.C., Nov. 30, 1936; s. Roger Denio and Eleanor Elizabeth (Ussher) B.; m. Paula Eisenstein, June 24, 1962; children: Hannah Hitzhusen, Sarah Topper. BS, Duke U., 1957; MS, Yale U., 1959, PhD, 1963. Lectr. physics Rice U., Houston, 1963-66, asst. prof., 1966-69, assoc. prof., 1969-73, prof., 1973—. Office: Rice Univ Dept Physics-MS 61 6100 Main St Houston TX 77005-1892

BAKER, STEPHEN MONROE, school system administrator; BA, Roanoke Coll., 1964; MS, Radford U., 1968; EdD, U. Va., 1976. Supt. Hanover County Pub. Schs., Ashland, Va., 1980-95; exec. dir. elem. and mid. sch. commn. So. Assn. Colls. and Schs., Decatur, Ga., 1995—. Chair Nat. Study Sch. Evaluation, 2000—; pres. Commn. on Internat. and Transregional Accreditation, 2002—. Named state finalist Nat. Supt. of Yr. award. Office: So Assn Colls & Schs 1866 Southern Ln Decatur GA 30033-4033 E-mail: sbimb@attglobal.net.

BAKER, TIMOTHY ALAN, healthcare administrator, educator, consultant; b. Myrtle Point, Oreg., July 30, 1954; s. Farris D. and Billie G. (Bradford) B.; 1 child, Amanda Susann. BS in Mgmt. with honors, Linfield Coll., McMinnville, Oreg., 1988; MPA in Health Adminstrn. with distinction, Portland State U., 1989, PhD in Pub. Adminstrn. and Policy, 1992; MPH in Epidemiology and biostatistics, Oreg. Health Scis. U., 2001. Gen. mgr. Pennington's, Inc., Coos Bay, Oreg., 1974-83; dep. dir. Internat. Airport Projects Med. Svcs., Riyadh, Saudi Arabia, 1983-87; adminstrv. intern Kaiser Sunnyside Hosp., Portland, Oreg., 1988-89; grant mgr. Oreg. Health Sci. U., Portland, 1989-90; dir. health sci. program Linfield Coll., Portland, Oreg., 1992—, assoc. prof. health scis. Rsch. assoc. Portland State U., 1990—; instr. S.W. Oreg. C.C., Coos Bay, 1980-83; pres. Intermed. Inc., Portland, 1987—; sr. rschr. small area analysis Oreg. Health Sci. U., 1990, The Oreg. Health Plan Project, 1990-91; developer, planner, prin. author trauma sys. devel. S.W. EMS and Trauma Sys., 1991-93, regional adminstr., Vancouver, 1990—; cons. ednl. def. Min. Civil Def., Riyadh, Saudi Arabia, 1992. Author: TQ:EMS: Total Quality Emergency Medical Services, 1996, TQ-EMS: The Tools of Total Quality, 1996, Health Sci. Rsch. Methods: From Pitfalls to Perfection, 1999; pub. Jour. Family Practice, Internat. Jour. Pub. Adminstrn., Internat. Jour. Emergency Med. Svcs., 1997. Planner mass disaster plan King Khaled Internat. Airport, 1983; EMS planner Emergency Med. Plan, Province of Cholburi, Thailand, 1985; bd. dirs. Coos County Kidney Assn., 1982, Coos Bay Kiwanis Club, 1979; regional adv. com. EMS and Trauma, State Wash. Dept. Health, 1990—. Recipient Pub. Svc. award Am. Radio and Relay League, 1969, Med. Excellence award KKIA Hosp., 1985; named Fireman of Yr. Eastside Fire Dept., 1982, Adminstr. of Yr., Wash. Dept. Health, 1993. Mem. Am. Mgmt. Assn., Am. Soc. Pub. Adminstrn. (doctoral rep. to faculty senate Portland State U. 1990), Am. Pub. Health Assn., Am. Coll. Healthcare Execs. Avocations: flying, scuba diving, travel, photography, racquetball, amateur radio. Home: 608 N Hayden Bay Dr Portland OR 97217-7964 Office: Linfield Coll Portland Campus 2255 NW Northrup St Portland OR 97210-2918 E-mail: tbaker@linfield.edu.

BAKER, WARREN J(OSEPH), university president; b. Fitchburg, Mass., Sept. 5, 1938; s. Preston A. and Grace F. (Jarvis) B.; m. Carol Ann Fitzsimons, Apr. 28, 1962; children: Carrie Ann, Kristin Robin, Christopher, Brian. BS, U. Notre Dame, 1960, MS, 1962; PhD, U. N.Mex., 1966. Research assoc., lectr. E. H. Wang Civil Engring. Research Facility, U. N.Mex., 1962-66; assoc. prof. civil engring. U. Detroit, 1966-71, prof., 1972-79, Chrysler prof., dean engring., 1973-78, acad. v.p., 1976-79; NSF faculty fellow M.I.T., 1971-72; pres. Calif. Poly. State U., San Luis Obispo, 1979—. Mem. Bd. Internat. Food and Agrl. Devel., USAID, 1983-85; mem. Nat. Sci. Bd., 1985-94, Calif. Bus. Higher Edn. Forum, 1993-98; founding mem. Calif. Coun. on Sci. and Tech., 1989—; trustee Amigos of E.A.R.T.H. Coll., 1991-96; bd. dirs. John Wiley & Sons, Inc., 1993—; bd. regents The Am. Archtl. Found., 1995-97; co-chair Joint Policy Coun. on Agr. and Higher Edn., 1995—; mem. Bus.-Higher Edn. Forum, 2001—; bd. dirs. Westport Innovations, Inc., 2002—, Soc. Manf. Engrs. Edn. Found., 2001—. Contbr. articles to profl. jours. Mem. Detroit Mayor's Mgmt. Adv. Com., 1975-76; mem. engring. adv. bd. U. Calif., Berkeley, 1984-96; bd. dirs. Calif. Coun. for Environ. and Econ. Balance, 1980-85, Soc. Mfg. Engrs. Edn. Found., 2001—; trustee Nat. Coop. Edn. Assn.; chmn. bd. dirs. Civil Engring. Rsch. Found., 1989-91, bd. dirs., 1991-94. Fellow Engring. Soc. Detroit; mem. ASCE (chmn. geotech. div. com. on reliability 1976-78, civil engring. edn. and rsch. policy com. 1985-89), NSPE (pres. Detroit chpt. 1976-77), Am. Soc. Engring. Edn., Am. Assn. State Colls. and Univs. (bd. dirs. 1982-84), Soc. Mfg. Engrs. Edn. (bd. dirs. 2002-). Office: Calif Poly State U Office of Pres 1 Grand Ave San Luis Obispo CA 93407 E-mail: presidentsoffice@calpoly.edu.

BAKER, WINSTON ALEXANDER, SR., academic administrator; b. Kingston, Jamaica, Nov. 2, 1955; came to the U.S., 1962; s. Issac Albert and Eucelin Monica (Reid) B.; m. Karen Parrish, June 22, 1983; children: Winston Alex Jr., Monika J. BS, Springfield Coll., 1978; MS, Hofstra U., 1980; grad. cert., Ind. U., 1989. Residence hall dir. Hofstra U., Hempstead, N.Y., 1978-79; counselor, fgn. student advisor SUNY, Old Westbury, 1979-80, counselor Ednl. Opportunity Program, 1980-81; counselor spl. svcs. program Ind. Univ. East, Richmond, Ind., 1981-83; coord. residence life Ind. U.-Purdue U., Indpls., 1983-85, dir. residence life, 1985-93; dir. residence svcs. Marshall U., Huntington, W.Va., 1993—. Bd. mem. Ind. chpt. Mid.-Am. Assn. of Ednl. Opportunity Program Personnel, 1982-83; cons. Learning Tree Tutorial/Counseling Cmty. Program, Indpls., 1988; cons., trainer Riverpointe Apts., Indpls., 1990-92. Bd. mem. Opportunities Indsl. Tech. Ctr., Richmond, Ind., 1982-83, Richmond (Ind.) Townsen Cmty. Ctr., 1982-83, A. Jordan YMCA Bd. Mgrs., Indpls., 1990-93, v.p. exec. bd., 1992-93; invited participant Leadership Tri-State, Ky., Ohio, W.Va., 1994.[ ]Named Vol. of Yr., Greater Indpls. (Ind.) YMCA, 1992. Mem. Nat. Assn. Coll./Univ. Food Svc., Nat. Assn. Student Pers. Assn., Am. Coll. Pers. Assn., Assn. Coll. and Univ. Housing Officers. Avocations: racquetball, chess, table tennis, travel, reading. Office: Marshall Univ 400 Hal Greer Blvd Huntington WV 25755-0003

BAKER-BRANTON, CAMILLE, counselor, educator; b. Greenwood, Miss., Aug. 30, 1950; d. Don Otho and Sarah (Goodpasture) Baker; children: Irene, Sarah. BS, MS, Miss. State U., 1972, PhD, 1989; MEd, MS, Delta State U., Cleveland, Miss., 1987. Lic. counselor, Miss.; cer. counselor; Diplomate Am. Bd. Med. Psychotherapists. Prof. curriculum instrn. Delta State U., Cleveland, Miss., 1989—. Mem. Job Tng. Placement Act Rev. Bd. Author: Coercive Sexual Behavior among College Students: A Causal Model, Coercive Sexual Behavior Rating Scale. Mem. AACD, DAR, Nat. Bd. Cert. Counselors, Coun. Exceptional Children, Assn. Children Learning Disabilities, Am. Mental Health Counselors Assn., Miss. Counseling Assn., Exch. Club, Phi Delta Kappa, Kappa Delta Pi, Delta Gamma. Home: 305 E Gresham St Indianola MS 38751-2426 Office: Delta State U PO Box 3112 Cleveland MS 38733-1300

BAKER DAILEY, ALICE ANN, exercise physiologist, exercise educator; b. Durant, Okla., Oct. 25, 1946; d. Finis Cortez and Alice Joyce (Hamilton) Baker; m. John Arthur Dailey, Nov. 23, 1985; 1 child, Megan Michelle. BA in Music, U. Okla., 1968; MS, North Tex. State U., 1985. Tchr. piano Dallas Ind. Sch. Dist., 1969-71; music tchr. Houston Ind. Sch. Dist., 1971-75; liquor license adminstr. Steak and Ale Restaurants Am., Inc., 1975-77; mail order adminstr. Neiman-Marcus, Dallas, 1978-81; exercise physiologist Tex. Instruments, Dallas, 1984-86, HealthCheck, 1985, Internat. Athletic Club Dallas, 1985-87, Verandah Club, 1986-89, Goodbody's, 1988-90; owner, pres. Alice Ann Baker Exercise: Therapeutic Conditioning, Dallas, 1980-90, Pilates, 1988—, Inner Body Workout (formerly PhysioSynthesis), 1991—; owner, pres. Oasis Mind-Body Conditioning Ctr., Inc., 1991—; cons. Region 10 Edn. Svc. Ctr., Dallas, 1985, RepublicBank, Dallas, 1985, Crescent Spa, Dallas, Landry Ctr., Dallas; exec. prodr., creator exercise video on therapeutic conditioning Warner Amex Community Svcs. Channel, Dallas, 1984-85; presenter in field; presenter AAHPERD Conf., Cin., 1986; writer, performer exercise program The Power of Posture, Dallas Cable TV; exec. prodr., creator (exercise video) The Inner Body Workout, 2000, Towel Work, 2001, (tv series) Your Dailey Inner Body Workout, 2003; mem. hon. adv. bd. Dance for Planet Festival, 1998.Contbr. articles to profl. jours. Provider continuing edn. credits, 1989—; founding mem. Physicalmind Inst. (formerly Inst. Pilates Method); active mem. Dallas Zoo, Dallas Mus. Art, Sci. Place; bd. dirs. Dallas Dance Coun., 1995-98; troop leader Girl Scouts U.S., 1998—. Mem. Am. Coun. on Exercise, Am. Coll. Sports Medicine (cert. fitness instr.), Internat. Dance Educators Assn., Dallas Dance Coun. (bd.), Kappa Alpha Theta, Phi Kappa Lambda. Home: 5839 Kenwood Ave Dallas TX 75206-5589

BAKHTIYAROV, SAYAVUR ISPANDIYAROGLU, rheologist, educator, researcher; b. Baku, Azerbaijan, May 18, 1952; came to U.S., 1995; s. Ispandiyar Bakhtiyaroglu and Zuleykha Gulmamedkizi (Huseynova) B.; m. Rasima Najafkulikizi Aliyeva, Nov. 9, 1980; children: Akshin, Ayten. Diploma in petroleum engring., Azerbijan Inst. Oil & Chem., Baku, 1974; PhD, Inst. Thermophysics, Novosibirsk, Russia, 1978; ScD, Azerbijan Inst. Math. & Mechs., Baku, 1992. Asst. prof. Azerbijan State Oil Acad., Baku, 1978-83, assoc. prof., 1983-92, prof., dept. head, 1992-94; sr. rsch. fellow Auburn (Ala.) U., 1995—. Vis. prof. Birmingham U., U.K., 1981-82, East China Tech. U., Shanghai, 1986-87, Auburn U., 1995; mem. adv. bd. Azerbijan State Oil Acad., 1985-92; expert com. Supreme Attestation Com., Baku, 1992-94. Contbr. articles to profl. jours. Recipient Outstanding Doctoral award Ministry Edn., Moscow, 1972; Nat. Economy Devel. award Nat. Econ. Exhbn., Moscow, 1987, Scientist Extraordinary Ability, U.S. Dept. Justice, Washington, 1996. Mem. ASME, Brit. Soc. Rheology, Vinigradov Soc. Rheology, Am. Soc. Rheology, Am. Inst. Physics. Achievements include patents for design and development of turbulent suppresion devices, drag reducing element in oil pipelines composite molds for metal casting, design and development of rheological systems in oil industry, rheology of fluidized beds, hydrodynamic processes in microgravity (NASA project). Home: 239 Cove Ct Auburn AL 36830-5578 Office: Auburn Univ Mech Engring Dept 202 Ross Hall Auburn University AL 36849-5341

BAKITA, SUE JO, secondary education educator; b. St. Johns, Mich., Oct. 23, 1941; d. Joseph Taylor and Blanche Ilene (Vaniman) Clark; m. Richard Walter Bakita, Aug. 3, 1963; children: Keary Thomas, Bret Joseph. BS in Edn., Ctrl. Mich. U., 1963; MA, Mich. State U., 1969. Cert. tchr., Mich. Tchr. Rockford (Mich.) Pub. Schs., 1963—, curriculum chmn., 1970-92, new tchr. induction coord., 2000—. Meml. chmn. Meth. Ch., Rockford, 1985-92; tchr., dir. mentor program Rockford Pub. Schs. Named Mid. Sch. Tchr. of Yr., Region 9 of State of Mich., 1992. Mem. NEA, Nat. Social Studies Coun., Mich. Assn. Mid. Sch. Educators, Mich. Edn. Assn., Rockford Edn. Assn. Republican. Avocations: reading, doll collecting, water skiing. Office: Rockford Mid Sch 397 E Division St Rockford MI 49341-1305

BAKKE, LUANNE KAYE, music educator; b. Rochester, Ind., Apr. 3, 1937; d. Lyman Dean and Anna Lorraine (Bull) Burkett; m. Ronald Roark (div. 1981); m. Jacques Roland Bakke, Feb. 24, 1988; 1 child, Kathleen Anne. BA, Calif. St. U., Northridge, 1977; MusM, Calif. State U., Fullerton, 1981. Instr. Calif. State U., Fullerton, 1979—81, City Coll. Chgo., Karlsruhe, Germany, 1985—86, Gadsden City Coll., Gadsden, Ala., 1986—87; pvt. practice piano & voice Lander, Wyo., 1995—. Music dir. Wood'N Ship Prodn., L.A., Calif., 1978—80; prodr. & dir. Off the Track Singers, L.A., 1975—77. Contbr. The Anniston Star Newspaper, 1982—91; composer: (plays) The Adventure of Doraleen, 1981. Pres. Pomona Valley Music Tchrs. Assn., 1969; music dir. Anniston Cmty. Theater, Anniston, Ala., 1987—89; cmty. choir dir. Harmonic Jam, Granite Falls, Minn., 1992—95; creator Performing Arts in Miniature, 1997—. Recipient Frank Jones award for leadership in the arts, City of Anniston, 1986. Mem.: Music Tchrs. Nat. Assn., Pi Kappa Lambda. Republican. Avocations: scuba diving, hiking, care of animals. Home and Office: PO Box 514 Lander WY 82520 E-mail: jbakke@wyoming.com.

BAKKEN, GORDON MORRIS, law educator; b. Madison, Wis., Jan. 10, 1943; s. Elwood S. and Evelyn A. H. (Anderson) B.; m. Erika Reinhardt, Mar. 24, 1943; children: Angela E., Jeffrey E. BS, U. Wis., 1966, MS, 1967, PhD, 1970, JD, 1973. From asst. to assoc. prof. history Calif. State U., Fullerton, 1969-74, prof. history, 1974—, dir. faculty affairs, 1974-86. Cons. Calif. Sch. Employees Assn., 1976-78, Calif. Bar Commn. Hist. Law., 1985—; mgmt. task force on acad. grievance procedures Calif. State Univ. and Colls. Systems, 1975; mem. Calif. Jud. Coun. Com. Trial Ct. Records Mgmt., 1992-97. Author 7 books on Am. legal history; contbr. articles to profl. jours. Placentia Jusa referee coord., 1983. Russell Sag resident fellow law, 1971-72, Am. Bar Found. fellow in legal history, 1979-80, 84-85; Am. Coun. Learned Socs. grantee-in-ai d, 1979-80. Mem. Orgn. Am. Historians, Am. Soc. Legal History, Law and Soc. Assn., Western History Assn., Calif. Supreme Ct. Hist. Soc. (v.p.), Phi Alpha Theta (v.p. 1994-95, pres. 1996-97). Democrat. Lutheran. E-mail: gbakken@fullerton.edu.

BAKO, PHYLLIS JEAN (PHYLLIS JEAN BLOTT), art educator, consultant; b. Warren, Ohio, May 14, 1949; d. Charles Edward and Anne Marie (Winovech) Blott; children: Lucas James, Jacob Edward, Zachary Charles. B in Art Edn., Ohio State U., 1972; MS in Edn., Youngstown State U., 1992. Cert. visual art tchr. Elem. art instr. Niles City (Ohio) Sch. Dist., 1972-82, jr. high art instr., 1982-92, high sch. visual art instr., 1992—. Art chair Niles City Sch. Dist., 1991—; art cons. Arts Excel Program, Trumbull County Schs., 1992. Author: Teaching Visual Art: An American Way, 1991. Mem. Northeast Scholastic Art Awards, Inc. (exec. adv. com. mem. 1987—), Ohio Art Edn. Assn., Steel Valley Art Tchrs. Assn. (treas. 1991—), Phi Kappa Phi, Kappa Delta Pi. Democrat. Lutheran. Avocations: visual art, handmade paper collages. Home: 2709 Niles Vienna Rd Niles OH 44446-4404

BALCERZAK, STANLEY PAUL, physician, educator; b. Pitts., Apr. 27, 1930; BS, U. Pitts., 1953; MD, U. Md., 1955. Diplomate Am. Bd. Internal Medicine, Am. Bd. Hematology, Am. Bd. Oncology. Instr. medicine U Chgo., 1959-60, U. Pitts., 1962-64, asst. prof., 1964-67; assoc. prof. medicine Ohio State U., Columbus, 1967-71, prof., 1971-99, prof. emeritus, 1999—, dir. div. hematology and oncology, 1969-94, dep. dir. Ohio State U. Comprehensive Cancer Ctr., 1984-97, assoc. chmn. dept. medicine, 1984-98, dir. Hemophilia Ctr., 1975-79, 1981-99. Mem. clin. rev. com. Am. Cancer Soc., N.Y.C., 1976-82 Contbr. chpts. to books, numerous articles to profl. jours. Served to capt. U.S. Army, 1960-62 Recipient numerous grants Fellow ACP; mem. Central Soc. for Clin. Research (chmn. subsplty. council in hematology 1980-81, councillor 1980-83), Am. Soc. for Clin. Oncology, Am. Assn. for Cancer Research, Am. Soc. Hematology, Phi Beta Kappa, Alpha Omega Alpha Home: 3113 N 3 Bs And K Rd Sunbury OH 43074-9582 Office: Ohio State U Divsn Hematology Oncology 320 W 10th Ave Columbus OH 43210-1240 E-mail: balcerzak.1@osu.edu.

BALDASSARE, LOUIS J. former school superintendent, educational consultant; b. Apr. 21, 1944; Supt. Highlands Sch. Dist., Natrona Heights, Pa., 1986—99; acting supt. North Gate Sch. Dist., 2000; cons. Comprehensive Ednl. Cons., 2001—. Designer early childhood/early intervention program. Recipient Leadership for Learning award Am. Assn. Sch. Adminstrs., 1995.*

BALDASSARRE, JOSEPH ANTHONY, musician, musicologist, music educator; b. Cleve., Oct. 16, 1950; s. Antonio Saverio and Mary Jane (Fondale) B.; m. Janeen Turner, Aug. 7, 1999; children: Genya Marie, Leyla Noelle, Stephen Joseph. B of Music Edn., Baldwin-Wallace Coll., 1972; MA, Kent State U., 1979; D of Mus. Arts, Cleve. Inst. Music, 1986. Cert. music tchr., Ohio. Freelance musician, rec. artist, Cleve., 1965-75; prof. music Boise (Idaho) State U., 1975—. Dir. Acad. St. Giles; classical guitar soloist; designer early string instruments; performer early music. Contbr. music revs. to Idaho Statesman, 1985-88, Soundboard mag., 1987. Founding mem. Idaho Camerata Baroque Music Ensemble, dir., Acad. of St. Giles Mem. Guitar Found. Am., Am. Lute Soc., Am. Musicol. Soc., Early Music Am., Boise Early Music Soc. (founder), Soc. for Am. Baseball Rsch., Phi Kappa Phi. Roman Catholic. Avocations: flintlock firearms, recording music, racquetball, baseball. Home: 1911 N Phillippi St Boise ID 83706-1160 Office: Boise State U Dept Music 1910 University Dr Boise ID 83725-1560

BALDERRAMA, SYLVIA RAMIREZ, psychologist, educator; b. Carlsbad, N.Mex., Jan. 12, 1952; d. Andres R. and Luz C. (Ramirez) B.; m. John F. Morley, Aug. 13, 1977; children: Laura de la Luz B. Morley, Lucas Macmillan B. Morley, Nicholas John B. Morley. AB, Harvard U./Radcliffe Coll., 1975; MEd, Boston U., 1977; EdD in Counseling Psychology, Columbia U., 1990. Lic. in psychology, N.Y. Dir. minority recruitment Yale U. Undergrad. Admissions, New Haven, 1977-81; house fellow Vassar Coll., Poughkeepsie, N.Y., 1982-85; psychotherapist Ctr. for Psychol. Svcs., N.Y.C., 1986-87; supr. Columbia U.-Tchrs. Coll., N.Y.C., 1986-87; counselor Cornell U./N.Y. State Sch. Indsl. and Labor Rels., N.Y.C., 1986-87; clin. intern Manhattan Psychiat. Ctr., Ward's Island, N.Y., 1987-88; staff psychologist SUNY, Purchase, 1990-92; dir. psychol. svcs. Vassar Coll., Poughkeepsie, 1992—. Instr. Columbia U.-Tchrs. Coll., 1988—90, adj. asst. prof., 1990—92. Charter mem. Arlington Mid. Sch. PTA, Poughkeepsie, 1993. Mem. APA, N.Y. State Psychol. Assn., Hudson Valley Psychol. Assn., Mental Health Assn. Office: Vassar Coll Box 706 124 Raymond Ave Poughkeepsie NY 12604-0001

BALDESCHWIELER, JOHN DICKSON, chemist, educator; b. Elizabeth, N.J., Nov. 14, 1933; s. Emile L. and Isobel (Dickson) B.; m. Marlene R. Konnar, Apr. 15, 1991; children from previous marriage: John Eric, Karen Anne, David Russell. B. Chem. Engring., Cornell U., 1956; PhD, U. Calif. at Berkeley, 1959. From instr. to asso. prof. chemistry Harvard U., 1960-65; faculty Stanford (Calif.) U., 1965-71, prof. chemistry, 1967-71; chmn. adv. bd. Synchrotron Radiation Project, 1972-75; vis. scientist Synchrotron Radiation Lab., 1977; dep. dir. Office Sci. and Tech., Exec. Office Pres., Washington, 1971-73; prof. chemistry Calif. Inst. Tech., Pasadena, 1973-99, chmn. div. chemistry and chem. engring., 1973-78, prof. emeritus. OAS vis. lectr. U. Chile, 1969; spl. lectr. in chemistry U. London, Queen Mary Coll., 1970; vis. scientist Bell Labs., 1978; mem. Pres.'s Sci. Adv. Com., 1969—, vice chmn., 1970-71; mem. Def. Sci. Bd., 1973-80, vice chmn., 1974-76; mem. carcinogenesis adv. panel Nat. Cancer Inst., 1973—; mem. com. planning and instl. affairs NSF, 1973-77; adv. com. Arms Control and Disarmament Agy., 1974-76; mem. NAS Bd. Sci. and Tech. for Internat. Devel., 1974-76, ad hoc com. on fed. sci. policy, 1979, task force on synfuels, 1979, Com. Internat. Security and Arms Control, 1992-95—; mem. Pres.'s Com. on Nat. Medal of Sci., 1974-76, pres., 1986-88, Pres.'s Adv. Group on Sci. and Tech., 1975-76; mem. governing bd. Reza Shah Kabir U., 1975-79; mem. Sloan Commn. on Govt. and Higher Edn., 1977-79, U.S.-USSR Joint Commn. on Sci. and Tech. Coop., 1977-79; vice chmn. del. on pure and applied chemistry to China, 1978; mem. com. on scholarly communication with China, 1978-84; chmn. com. on comml. aviation security NAS, 1988—, mem. def. sci. bd. task force on 'operation desert shield', 1990-91, mem. com. on internat. security and arms control, 1991-94—; mem. rsch. adv. coun. Ford Motor Co., 1979-94—, mem. chem. and engring. adv. bd., 1981-83; vis. lectr. Rand Afrikaans U., Johannesburg, South Africa, 1987, Found. Rsch. and Devel., Pretoria, South Africa, 1989. Mem. editorial adv. bd. Chem. Physics Letters, 1979-83, Jour. Liposome Rsch., 1986—. Served to 1st lt. AUS, 1959-60. Sloan Found. fellow, 1962-64, 64-65; recipient Fresenius award Phi Lambda Upsilon, 1968, Tolman award ACS, 1989. Mem. NAS, Am. Chem. Soc. (award in pure chemistry 1967, William H. Nichols medal 1990), Council on Sci. and Tech. for Devel., Am. Acad. Arts and Scis., Am. Philos. Soc. Office: Calif Inst Tech Divsn Chemistry & Chem Engring # 127-72 Pasadena CA 91125-0001

BALDWIN, C. ANDREW, JR., retired science educator; b. Chgo., May 18, 1927; s. C. Andrew Sr. and Lillian (Evans) B.; m. Claire Awkerman, July 10, 1954; children: Debbie, Judi. BA in Zoology, U. Tex., 1951; MA in Theology, Berkeley Bapt. Sem. of West, 1956, MDiv, 1961; postgrad., numerous colls., univs. Cert. elem. tchr., Calif., secondary tchr., Calif., Tex., Ill.; edn. adminstr., Calif., K-12 substitute and biology, Oreg. Sci. tchr. Brazosport Ind. Sch. Dist., Freeport, Tex., 1951-53; sustitute tchr. Chgo. Pub. Sch., 1953-54; child care and substitute tchr. Berkeley (Calif.) Pub. Sch., 1954-56; tchr. 7th and 8th grades Redwood City (Calif.) Elem. Sch., 1956-60; swimpool mgr. San Mateo County Parks/Recreation, 1957-64; 6th grade/jr. high biology/sr. high biology, geology tchr., coord. field biology Palo Alto (Calif.) Unified Sch. Dist., 1960-93; vice prin. Franklin-McKinley Sch. Dist., San Jose, Calif., 1970-71; Biology, 6-12th grade substitute Salem and Woodburn (Oreg.) Schs., 1993-2000; mem. faculty in ESL, Chemeketa C.C., 1997-2001. Founder, dir. pvt. summer ecology and field biology camp program-Summer Sci. Safaris, 1972-76; coord. sci. fairs Wilbur Jr. H.S. & Stanford Middle Sch. Contbr. articles to publs. Unit dir., counselor, mem. water safety staff YMCA, Chgo., Denver, Berkeley, Oakland, Calif.; counselor Chgo. Boys Club, 1945—56, Oakland Cath. Youth Orgn., 1945—56; pres. YMCA's Men's Club, Redwood City, 1967—69, Lorelei Homeowners Assn., Menlo Park, Calif., 1959—60; v.p. Hoover Elem. Sch. PTA, 1959—60; elected Sequoia United Sch. Dist. B.d; pres. Freeport Jr. High Sch. PTA, 1952—53, Senn High Sch. Crusaders Club, Chgo.; vol. YMCA, Chgo., Chgo. Boys' Clubs, Boy Scoouts Am., ARC; candidate U.S. Congress, 1967; elder, chair mission com. Trinity Presbyn. Ch., San Carlos, Calif.; elder, mem. choir, various coms. 1st Presbyn. United Mission Advance; staff assoc. Carlmont Meth. Ch.; vol. asst. min. Woodside Rd. Cmty. United Meth. Ch., Redwood City, People's Assembly of God Ch., Salem, Oreg., 1st Bapt. Ch., Salem; mem. Men's Bible Fellowship Internat., Salem; elected trustee Redwood City Sch. Dist. Bd. Edn., 1961—69, pres., 1968—69; active com. against racism, various others Sequoia High Sch. Dist. Sgt. USAAF, 1945—47. Decorated Brevet 2nd Lt. Commn. U.S. Army, 1945; named Outstanding Citizen, Redwood City YMCA, 1968, Realtors, South San Mateo County, 1967; recipient Oak Leaf and Life Membership award Calif. PTA, 1959, 5 and 10 yr. Vol. pin ARC, Vol. pin Chgo. Boys' Club; nominated for Presdl. award for excellence in tchg., 1992; Chevron Corp. grantee, 1985. Mem. AAAS, NEA, Calif. Tchrs. Assn., Palo Alto Edn. Assn. (sch. rep., salary com.), Christian Educators Assn. Internat., Astron. Soc. Pacific, Earth Sci. Tchrs. Assn., Calif. Sci. Tchrs. Assn., Nat. Sci. Tchrs. Assn. (12th dist. dir. 1984-86, local leader 1993-97), Oreg. Sci. Tchrs. Assn., Nat. Assn. Biology Tchrs. Avocations: hiking, swimming, reading (especially biographies and mysteries), sudying religion, history, Spanish, science and anthropology.

BALDWIN, DOROTHY LEILA, secondary school educator; b. Irvington, N.J., Feb. 28, 1948; d. Daniel Thomas and Lillian Frances (Wainright) B. BA, Kean Coll., Union, N.J., 1969, MA in Edn. and Humanities, 1971; EdD in Adminstrn. and Supervision, Seton Hall U., 1987, cert. reading specialist, 1979, cert. bus. adminstr., 1985. Tchr., reading coord. St. Paul Apostle Sch. Irvington, 1969-74; tchr. Summit (N.J.) Jr. High Sch., 1975-79; social studies coord. K-9, chmn. dept. 7-9 Summit Pub. schs., 1979-87; social studies supr. Livingston (N.J.) Pub. Schs., 1987; prin. Point Road Sch, Little Silver, N.J., 1987-89; dir. gifted edn. K-12 Clifton, N.J., 1989-90; prin. Sch. Two, Clifton, N.J., 1989-90, Deerfield Sch., Mountainside, 1990-92, Eisenhower Sch., Bridgewater-Raritan, NJ, 1992—2003; prof. Fairleigh Dickinson U., Teaneck, NJ, 2003—. Adj. prof. Montclair (N.J.) U., Passaic County C.C., Morris County C.C.; tchr. adult and cmty. schs.; workshop coord.; cons. in field. Author books; contbr. articles to profl. jours. PTA scholar, 1965. Mem. ASCD, Nat. Assn. Elem. Sch. Prins., Nat. Coun. Social Studies, Am. Assn. Sch. Adminstrs., N.J. Assn. Elem. Sch. Prins., N.J. Prins. Ctr., Somerset County Assn. Elem. Sch. Prins., Phi Delta Kappa, Kappa Delta Pi. Home: 737 River Rd Chatham NJ 07928-1136 Office: Fairleigh Dickinson U 1000 River Rd Teaneck NJ 07666

BALDWIN, JEFFREY KENTON, lawyer, educator; b. Palestine, Ill., Aug. 8, 1954; s. Howard Keith and Annabelle Lee (Kirts) B.; m. Patricia Ann Mathews, Aug. 23, 1975; children: Matthew, Katy, Timothy, Philip R. BS summa cum laude, Ball State U., 1976; JD cum laude, Ind. U., 1979. Bar: Ind. 1979, U.S. Dist. Ct. (so. dist.) Ind. 1979, U.S. Ct. Appeals (7th cir.) 1979, U.S. Dist. Ct. (no. dist.) Ind. 1984. Majority leader's staff Ind. Senate, Indpls., 1976; instr. Beer Sch. Real Estate, Indpls., 1977-78, Am. Inst. Paralegal Studies, Indpls., 1987—; dep. Office Atty. Gen., Indpls., 1979-81; mng. ptnr. Baldwin & Baldwin, Danville, Ind., 1979—. Agt. Nat. Attys. Title Assurance Fund, Vevay, Ind., 1983—; officer, bd. dirs. Baldwin Realty, Inc., Danville; conf. participant White House Conf. on Small Bus. (Ind. meeting 1994), congl. appointee, 1995; bd. dirs. Small Bus. Coun. Bd. dirs. Hendricks Civic Theatre, Inc.; organizer, Hendricks County Young Republicans, 1972; sec. Hendricks County Rep. Com., 1978-84; bd. dirs. Hendricks County Assn. for Retarded Citizens, Danville, 1982-86; cons. Hendricks County Right for Life, Brownsburg, Ind., 1984—; mem. philanthropy adv. com. Ball State U., Muncie, Ind., 1987—; judge Hendricks County unit Am. Cancer Soc., 1987; coordinator region 2 Young Leaders for Mutz, Indpls., 1987-88; cubmaster WaPaPh dist. Boy Scouts Am., 1988, S.M.E. chmn., 1988-89; steering com. Ind. Lawyers Bush/Quayle; founder, chmn. Christians for Positive Reform; candidate for Congress 7th Congl. Dist. of Ind.; del. to Annual Conf. South Ind. Conf. of United Meth. Ch., 1993, 95-98, 2000; host com. Midwest Rep. Leadership Conf., 1997; dist. coord. Hoosier Famiies for John Price for U.S. Senate; advisor John Price for Gov., 1999-2000; v.p. Danville Little League Baseball, 1998—. Recipient Presdl. award of honor Danville Jaycees, 1980; named hon. sec. State Ind., 1980. Mem. ABA, Ind. Bar Assn., Hendricks County Bar Assn., Indpls. Bar Assn., Internat. Platform Assn., Nat. Assn. Realtors, Ind. Assn. Realtors, Met. Indpls. Bd. Realtors (Hendricks County div.), Federalist Soc., Ind. Farm Bur., Nat. Fedn. Ind. Bus., Ind. C. of C., Danville C. of C. (sec. 1986), Moot Ct. Soc., Blue Key, Phi Soc. Methodist. Home: PO Box 63 Danville IN 46122-0063 E-mail: jbbfc@aol.com.

BALDWIN, JEFFREY NATHAN, pharmacy educator; b. Sidney, NY, Dec. 20, 1947; s. Reverdy Ernest and Helen Elizabeth (Humphrey) B.; m. Suzanne Marie Smith, Dec. 27, 1969; children: Paul Kevin, Gregory Michael. AS, Jamestown C.C., 1967; BS in Pharmacy summa cum laude, SUNY, Buffalo, 1970; DPharm, U. Ky., 1973. Lic. pharmacist Ky., Nebr. Resident in pharmacy U. Ky.-A.B. Chandler Med. Ctr., Lexington, 1970-73; pharmacy faculty U. Nebr. Med. Ctr., Coll. Pharmacy, Omaha, 1973—; med. faculty U. Nebr. Med. Ctr., Coll. Medicine, Omaha, 1977—. Pres., co-founder Nebr. Coun. for Continuing Pharm. Edn., Inc., Omaha, 1980-82. Author: (chpts.) Points of Light: A Guide for Assisting Chemically Dependent Health Professional Students, 1996; sect. editor: Applied Therapeutics: The Clinical Use of Drugs, 1995, 2001; contbr. 41 chpts. to books, 28 articles to profl. jours. Chmn. Nebr. Pharmacist Recovery Network, Lincoln, Nebr., 1988—; scout leader Mid Am. Coun., Boy Scouts, Omaha, 1983—, chair tng. com., 1997—98, trustee, 2000—, exec. com., 2001—; counselor Camp CoHoLo, Gretna, Nebr., 1985—98, 2000, 2002. Recipient Leadership award, McKesson, 1995. Fellow Am. Pharm. Assn. (Merit award 1995), Am. Soc. Health-Sys. Pharmacists (chair pediatric pharmacy spl. interest group 1977-78), Am. Assn. Colls. Pharmacy (chair substance abuse spl. interest group 1988-97, chair pharmacy practice sect. 1998-99), Nebr. Pharmacists Assn. (pres.-elect 1994-95, pres. 1995-96, chmn. bd. 1996-97, NARD Leadership award 1995) Avocations: travel, bicycling, backpacking, camping, whitewater rafting. Office: 982135 Nebr Med Ctr Omaha NE 68198-2135 E-mail: jbaldwin@unmc.edu.

BALDWIN, JOHN WESLEY, history educator; b. Chgo., July 13, 1929; s. Edward N. and H. Gladys (McDaniel) B.; m. Jenny Jochens, Dec. 24, 1954; children: Peter, Ian, Birgit (dec.), Christopher. BA, Wheaton Coll., 1950; MA, Pa. State U., 1951; PhD, Johns Hopkins, 1956. Instr., then asst. prof. U. Mich., Ann Arbor, 1956-61; mem. faculty Johns Hopkins U., Balt., 1961—, prof. history, 1966—, Charles Homer Haskins prof. history, 1986—, prof. emeritus, 2001—; prof. e'tranger Coll. de France, 1984, 95. Author: The Medieval Theories of the Just Price, 1959, Masters, Princes and Merchants, 2 vols, 1970, The Scholastic Culture of the Middle Ages, 1971, City on the Seine: Paris under Louis IX, 1226-1270, 1975, The Government of Philip Augustus, 1986 (French transl. 1991), Les Registres de Philippe Auguste, 1992, The Language of Sex: Five Voices from Northern France Around 1200, 1994, (French translation) Les Languages de l'amour, 1997, Aristocratic Life in Medieval France: The Romances of Jean Renart and Gerbert de Montreuil, 1190-1230, 2000, Le Livre de Terres et de Revenues de Pierre du Thillay, 2002; editor (with Richard Goldthwaite) Universities in Politics: Case Studies from the Late Middle Ages and Early Modern Period, 1972. Decorated Chevalier de la légion d'honneur (France), Chevalier Ordre des Arts et des Lettres (France); Prix Litteraire Etats-Unis-France, 1992; Guggenheim fellow, 1960-61, 83-84, Howard fellow, 1960-61, Fulbright fellow, 1953-55, 65-66, Sr. fellow NEH, 1972-73, 90-91; grantee Am. Coun. Learned Socs., 1965-66. Fellow Medieval Acad. Am. (v.p. 1994, pres. 1996-97, Charles Homer Haskins medal 1990), Am. Acad. Arts and Scis., Brit. Acad. (corr.); mem. Soc. for French Hist. Studies, Royal Danish Acad. Scis. and Letters (fgn.), Am. Hist. Assn., Commn. Internat. de Diplomatique (hon.), Acad. Inscriptions et Belles Lettres (France) (assoc. fgn.), Société Nationale des Antiquaires de France (assoc. corr. fgn.). Office: Johns Hopkins U Dept History Baltimore MD 21218

BALDWIN, LIONEL VERNON, retired university president; b. Beaumont, Tex., May 30, 1932; s. Eugene B. and Wanda (Wiley) B.; m. Kathleen Flanagan, Sept. 3, 1955; children: Brian, Michael, Diane, Daniel. BS, U. Notre Dame, 1954; SM, MIT, 1955; PhD, Case Inst. Tech., 1959. Rsch. engr. Nat. Adv. Com. Aeros., Ohio, 1957-59; unit head NASA, 1959-61; asso. prof. engring. Colo. State U., 1961-64; acting dean Coll. of Engring., 1964-65, dean and prof., 1966-84; pres. Nat. Tech. U., Fort Collins, 1984—2000; ret. Served to capt. USAF, 1955-57. Recipient award for plasma research NASA, 1964, Kenneth Andrew Roe award Am. ASsn. Engrin. Soc., 1996 Fellow Am. Soc. Engring. Edn. (chmn. engring. deans coun.); mem. ASME, IEEE, NSPE, Sigma Xi, Tau Beta Pi, Sigma Pi Sigma. Achievements include patentee apparatus for increasing ion engine beam density. Home: 1900 Sequoia St Fort Collins CO 80525-1540 E-mail: lionelvbld@attbi.com.

BALDWIN, MARIE HUNSUCKER, retired secondary school educator; b. Dallas, Dec. 22, 1923; d. Clyde Augustus and Charlotte (Moore) Hunsucker; m. Brewster Baldwin, Aug. 20, 1946 (dec. July 1992); children: Jean Baldwin McLevedge, David, Stephen, Christopher. BS in Edn., Tex. Tech. U., 1944; MFA in Writing, Norwich U., 1988. Tchr. Pub. Sch., Corpus Christi, Tex., 1944-45, Presbyn. Day Sch., Corpus Christi, 1945-46, Pub. Sch., Moriah, N.Y., 1964-66; field dir. Vt. Girl Scout Coun., Burlington, 1966-78; ret. Vice chair Vt. State Dem. Com., Montpelier, 1976-80; apptd. mem. Gov.'s Adult Edn. Coun., 1985-89; founder, pres. Vt. Caths. for Free Choice, 1989—; elected Justice of the Peace, Middlebury, Vt., 1989—. Mem. ACLU (bd. 1984-90), AAUW, LWV (founder, pres. 1952-56), Cath. Daus. Am., Bus. and Profl. Women. Avocations: creative writing, walking, reading.

BALÉE, WILLIAM L. anthropology educator; b. Ft. Lauderdale, Fla., Oct. 12, 1954; s. William Lockert Balée and Lorraine Kathryn Monahan; m. Pamela Van Rees, May 24, 1980 (div. Dec. 1986); m. Maria da Conceição Bezerra, Mar. 9, 1987; children: Nicholas, Isabel. BA with high honors, U. Fla., 1975; MA, Columbia U., 1979, MPhil, 1980, PhD, 1984. Assoc. rschr. ecology Museu Paraense Emílio Goeldi, Belém, Brazil, 1988-91, chair ecology, 1990-91; assoc. prof. anthropology Tulane U., New Orleans, 1991-98, prof., chair dept. anthropology, 1998-2001, prof. anthropology, 1998—. Adj. prof. anthropology CUNY, 1983-84, SUNY, Purchase, 1982; adj. prof. social scis. CUNY, 1983; adj. prof. sociology and anthropology Rutgers U., 1984; vis. assoc. prof. Ctr. for L.Am. Studies, U. Fla., 1990; fieldwork with forest peoples in Amazon of Brazil and Bolivia, 1980-97; acad. cons. Smithsonian Instn., 2000—. Author: Footprints of the Forest: Ka'apor Ethnobotany, 1994 (award Soc. Econ. Botany, 1996); editor: Advances in Historical Ecology, 1998, Jour. Ethnobiology, 1999—2002; mem. editl. bd., 2002—; co-editor: Resource Management in Amazonia: Indigenous and Folk Strategies, Advances in Economic Botany, vol. 7, 1989, Hist. Ecology Series, 1998—; contbr. articles to profl. jours., chapters to books. Decorated officer Order of the Golden Ark (Netherlands), 1993; NY Bot. Garden fellow, 1984-88, Fulbright-Hays fellow, 1980-81, Newcomb Coll. fellow, 1992-94, Conselho Nacional de Desenvolvimento Tecnológico e Científico fellow, 1988-91; grantee OAS, 1981-82, Ford Found., 1989-90, Jessie Smith Noyes Found., 1990-91, World Wildlife Fund, 1991-92, 2003, Tulane U., 1992, Wenner-Gren Found., 1993-94 ; apptd. to 60th and 61st Coll. Disting. Lectrs., Sigma Xi, 1997-99; recipient Outstanding Book of Yr. award Soc. Econ. Botany. Fellow Am. Anthrop. Assn.; mem. Soc. Ethnobotanists (India), Soc. Ethnobiology, Soc. Anthropology of Lowland S.Am. (pres. 2002—), Soc. Etnobiologia e Etnoecologia, Phi Beta Kappa (pres. Alpha of La. 1997-98), Phi Kappa Phi. Office: Tulane U Dept Anthropology 1021 Audubon St New Orleans LA 70118-5238 E-mail: wbalee@tulane.edu.

BALES, RUBY JONES, retired elementary school educator and principal; b. Fayetteville, Tenn., Aug. 17, 1933; d. Albin O. and Jenny Katharine (Pickett) Jones; m. Emory H. Bales, Nov. 25, 1954; children: N. Katharine (dec.), David Emory, Evelyn Ann, Patrick Lee. BS in Biology, Tenn. Technol. U., 1956; MA in Supervision, Human Rels., George Washington U., 1975; EdD in Curriculum Instrn. and Reading, U. Md., 1984. Cert. tchr. grades 1-6, prin., supr., elem., middle sch. reading tchr. K-12. Tchr. gen. sci., math. Niceville (Fla.) Elem. Sch., 1956-57, Ruckel Jr. H.S., Niceville, 1957-59; tchr. biology, physical sci. Leon H.S., Tallahassee, 1959-60; tchr. 5th grade Potomac Elem. Sch., Dahlgren, Va., 1960-61, Charles County Pub. Schs., La Plata, Md., 1965-73; acting adminstrv. asst. Charles County Middle Pub. Sch.s, La Plata, Md., 1973-74; program coord. Mitchell Elem. Sch., Charles County, La Plata, 1974-75, adminstrv. asst., 1975-77; prin. Dr. James Craik Elem. Sch., Pomfret, Md., 1977-84, Eva Turner Elem. Sch., Waldorf, Md., 1984-86; instrnl. supr. elem. schs. Charles County Sch. Dist., La Plata, 1986-94; retired. Supt. Charles County Fair Sch. Exhibit, County Fair Bd., 1986-94. NSF scholar Fla. State U., 1958. Republican. Avocations: music, gardening. Home: PO Box 373 Dahlgren VA 22448-0373

BALINT, DAVID LEE, engineering company executive; b. Cleve., June 27, 1946; s. Robert Stephen and Edna Mae (Alward) S. BBA, Cleve. State U., 1969; grad., U.S. Naval War Coll., 1982; MBA, Temple U., 1986. Cert. purchasing mgr., profl. contracts mgr. Commd. ensign USN, 1970, advanced through grades to lt. comdr., retired, 1990; dep. dir. contract adminstrn. Teledyne Brown Engring., Huntsville, Ala., 1990-96, mgr. compliance programs, 1996-2000; mgr. export compliance The Boeing Co., Huntsville, Ala., 2000—. Adj. faculty Temple U., Phila., 1986-90, Southeastern Inst. Tech., Huntsville, 1991-94, U. Ala., Huntsville, 1994-96. Del. mem. People-to-People Contract Mgmt.; del. People's Republic China, 1986, 1989; vol. Family Svcs. Ctr., 1999—2000, Family Svcs. Ctr. Found., 2003—; North Ala. Internat. Trade Assn. Ala., 1999—; bd. dirs. Vol. Ctr. Huntsville-Madison County, 1995—97; bd. trustees Employees Cmty. Fun, 2001; bd. govs. Sigma Phi Epsilon Ednl. Found., 2001. Fellow Nat. Contract Mgmt. Assn. (nat. v.p. N.E. region 1989-90, nat. v.p. membership 1990-91, nat. functional dir. 1991-98, 2001, Nat. Edn. award 1994, Disting. Svc. award 1995), Soc. Logistics Engrs., Am. Assn. Adult and Continuing Edn. Home: 107 Huntington Ridge Rd Madison AL 35757-8501 Office: The Boeing Co 499 Boeing Blvd Huntsville AL 35824

BALIS, JENNIFER LYNN, academic administrator, computer technology educator; b. Hamlin, W.Va., Nov. 23, 1946; 1 child, Theodore Berndt. AA, Del Mar Coll., 1987; BA, U. Tex., 1989; BS, So. Ill. U., 1992. Peer counselor U. Tex., Edinburg, 1989-90; tchr. Mission (Tex.) Ind. Sch. Dist., 1990; instr. San Diego Job Corps, 1992-95; instr. computer tech. Kaskaskia Coll., Centralia, Ill., 1997—2002. Coord. Kaskaskia Coll. Vandalia Ctr., Vandalia, 1999-2001. Chmn., sec. Mulberry Grove Zoning Bd. Appeals, 1999—2002; vol. advocate S.A.F.E., 2003—; asst. leader Living with Arthritis Support Group. With USNR, 1984—. Mem. Psi Chi (pres. 1989-90). Republican. Roman Catholic. Avocations: natural healing, folk medicine, mineral collector, archery.

BALK, MARY DALE, drug prevention specialist, elementary school educator; b. Nashville, July 30, 1939; d. Dale Ivan Knox and Mary Lucille (Clower) Cooke; children: Susan Lynne Kradel, Rebecca Lynne Demo, Melissa Lynne Balk. BS in Edn., Miami U., Oxford, Ohio, 1961, MEd, 1967. Cert. addictions prevention profl.; cert. elem. edn. English; cert. specific learning disabilities K-12; cert. guidance counselor. Tchr. Marion (Ind.) High Sch., 1971-73; guidance counselor Justice Jr. High Sch., Marion, 1973-74; tchr. of the emotionally handicapped Red Bug Elem. Sch., Maitland, Fla., 1974-76; English tchr. Teague Middle Sch., Altamonte Springs, Fla., 1976-78, Lake Brantley High Sch., 1988; guidance counselor Lake Mary (Fla.) Elem. Sch., 1978-88; drug prevention specialist Seminole Co. (Fla.) Schs., 1988—; county Red Ribbon chmn. Nat. Red Ribbon Campaign, Seminole County, 1989—. Adj. tchr. Seminole C.C.; guest speaker educators convs. Vice chmn. sch. bd. Sweetwater Episcopal Acad., 1985-88; active HRS Community Task Force for Residential Placement for Dep. Children, 1979-80; chmn. Seminole County Red Ribbon Campaign for a Drug-Free Am., 1989—; exec. com. Seminole County Am. Heart Assn. Mem. Winter Park Univ. Club, Fla. Alcohol and Drug Abuse Assn., Fla. Student Assistance Program Network (sec.). Home: 111 Valley Cir Longwood FL 32779-3460 Office: Drug Prevention Office 1401 S Magnolia Ave Sanford FL 32771-3400

BALL, ARDELLA PATRICIA, library media educator; b. Nashville, Dec. 15, 1932; d. Otis Hugh and Mary Ellen (Staples) Boatright; m. Wesley James Ball, June 15, 1931; children: Wesley James, Roderic Lynn, Weselyn Lynette, Patrick Wayne. AB, Fisk U., Nashville, 1953; MSLS, Atlanta U., 1956; ScD, Nova U., 1991. Tchr., libr. Fayetteville (Tenn.) H.S., 1954-57; children's libr. N.Y. Pub. Libr., summer 1957; cataloger Ala. A&M U., Huntsville, 1957-59; sr. cataloger St. Louis U., 1960-65; cataloger G.E.L. Regional Libr., Savannah, Ga., 1965-68, Armstrong Atlantic State U., Savannah, 1968-74, instrnl. devel. libr., 1974-77, libr. media educator, 1977—. Author course manuals for core media courses. Mem. Ga. Libr. Assn., Ga. Media Assn. Democrat. Mem. Ch. of Christ. Home: 67 Amanda Dr Savannah GA 31406 Office: Armstrong Atlantic State U 11935 Abercorn St Savannah GA 31419-1909

BALL, ARNETHA, education educator; BA in Edn., U. Mich., 1971, MA in Speech Pathology, 1972; PhD in Lang., Literacy and Culture, Stanford

U., 1991. Ethnic studies resource specialist, speech pathologist, classroom tchr. Richmond (Calif.) Unified Sch. Dist., 1972—73; adminstrv. dir., classroom tchr. Children's Creative Workshop, Richmond, 1974—80; classroom tchr. Aurora (Ill.) Elem. Sch., 1984—86; speech pathologist Audiology Assocs. of Dayton, Ohio, 1986—87; external program evaluator L.A. Unified Sch. Dist., 1991—92; postdoctoral fellow U. Mich., 1991—92, asst. prof. edn., 1992—98, assoc. prof. edn., coord. literacy, lang. and culture program, 1998—99; assoc. prof. edn. Stanford (Calif.) U., 1999—. Mem. exec. com. Conf. on Coll. Composition and Comm., 1996—; mem. Standing Com. on Rsch., 1995. Contbr. articles to profl. jours.; mem. editl. bd.: Urban Education, 1996—, Assessing WRiting, 1995. Mem.: Nat. Coun. Tchrs. of English Found. (trustee 1996—), Am. Ednl. Rsch. Assn. (chair divsn. G nominating com. 1998—). Achievements include research in linking sociocultural and linguistic theory with educational practices; linguistic resources; linguistic practices among culturally and linguistically diverse populations. Office: Stanford U Sch Edn 485 Lasuen Mall Stanford CA 94305-309*

BALL, BRENDA JOYCE SIVILS, secondary education educator; English tchr. Pine Bluff (Ark.) High Sch. Named Ark. State English Tchr. of Yr., 1992.*

BALL, DEBORAH LOEWENBERG, education educator; BA, Mich. State U., 1976, MA, 1982, postgrad., 1981—83, PhD, 1988. Arthur F. Thurnau prof. U. Mich. Sch. Edn., Ann Arbor, 2000—. Lead author Stds. for Tchg. sect. Profl. Stds. for Tchg. Math., Nat. Coun. Tchrs. Math., 1989—91; mem. adv. bd. Investigations in Number, Data, Space, 1991—96; mem. Commn. on Behavioral and Social Sci. Edn. Nat. Rsch. Coun., NAS, 1996—99, mem. math. learning study, 1999—2000; chair math. study panel RAND Project: Improving the Quality of Educational Research and Devel., 1999—2000; mem. commn. on undergrad. experience U. Mich., 2000—01; co-chair tchr. edn. study Internat. Commn. on Math. Instrn., 2002—; bd. trustees Math. Scis. Rsch. Inst. U. Calif., Berkeley, 2003—. Contbr. articles to profl. jours.; mem. editl. bd.: Am. Ednl. Rsch. Jour., 1999—, Jour. Ednl. Rsch., 1990—93, Elem. Sch. Jour., 1991—. Recipient Raymond B. Cattell Early Career award for programmatic rsch., Am. Ednl. Rsch. Assn., 1997, Award for outstanding Scholarship on Tchr. Edn., Assn. Colls. and Schs. of Edn. in State Univs. and Land Grant Colls. and Affiliated Pvt. Univs., 1990. Office: U Mich 4119 Sch Edn Bldg 610 E University Ann Arbor MI 48109-1259*

BALL, LINDA ANN, primary school educator; b. Des Moines, Aug. 10, 1942; d. Vern Ray and Orletha Ann Carmichael; m. Robert Ray Ball, Aug. 15, 1964; children: Lindsay, Ryan, Justin. BS in Edn., Drake U., 1964; MS in Edn., Ill. State U., 1981. Cert. reading specialist, early childhood specialist. Tchr., Marshalltown, Iowa, 1964-68; TV tchr. Sta. WAND-TV, Decatur, Ill., 1969-71; tchr. Des Moines Pub. Schs., 1973-79; adv. Ill. State U. Panhellenic, Normal, 1979-80; tchr., faculty assoc. Metcalf Lab. Sch. Ill. State U., Normal, 1980—. Presenter workshops and confs. Co-author: (books) Kaleidoscope, Language-Based Activities for Young Children, 1988, Look, Look I Wrote a Book, 1997, Home & Sch. Math, 2001. Past mem. Jr. Women's Club, Assn. Advocacy and Edn. Disabled Citizens, Mid-Central Planning Commn. for Handicapped, Friends of the Arts; past pres. JayceeEttes, Campfire Girls Council; bd. dirs. United Cerebral Palsy. Named finalist for Ill. Tchr. of Yr., 1997. Mem. Ill. Reading Council, Ill. State Kindergarten Conf. Commn. (chair), Early Childhood Edn. Assn., Ill. Edn. Assn., Ill. Assn. Supervision and Curriculum Devel. (Outstanding Early Childhood Educator 1992), Delta Zeta (collegiate province dir.), Delta Kappa Gamma. Democrat. Home: 3409 Windmill Rd Bloomington IL 61704-1224 Office: Metcalf Lab Sch Ill State U Normal IL 61761 E-mail: laball@ilstu.edu.

BALL, MARGIE BARBER, elementary school educator; b. San Antonio, Tex., June 28, 1943; d. Truman Joseph and Margaret Evelyn (Norman) Barber; m. Flamen Ball Jr., Aug. 20, 1966; children: Michael David, Matthew Joseph, Marissa Anne. BS, U. Houston, 1963; MS, Stephen F. Austin State U., 1985. Texas Tchr. Cert. Spanish tchr. Spring Branch Ind. Sch. Dist., Houston, 1964-66, tchr., 1966-68; dir. mother's day out Holy Spirit Episcopal, Tex., 1977-78; tchr. Nacogdoches (Tex.) Ind. Sch. Dist., 1979-82; kindergarten tchr. Christ Episc. Sch., 1982-87; early childhood tchr. Hudson Ind. Sch. Dist., Lufkin, Tex., 1987-94; tchr. pre-kindergarten/bilingual Lufkin Ind. Sch. Dist., 1994-95, tchr. pre-kindergarten/multi-age, 1995-96; tchr. kindergarten Hudson ISD, Lufkin, 1996-97; supr. student tchrs., adj. faculty Stephen F. Austin State U., Nacogdoches, 1997—2003. Mem. Tex. State Tchr. Assn., East Tex. Assn. Educators Young Children, Nacogdoches, Med. Wives Auxillary, Kiwanis, Phi Delta Kappa. Republican. Presbyterian. Avocations: gardening, reading, travel, volunteering, family.

BALL, M(ARY) ISABEL, chemistry educator, dean; b. Elmendorf, Tex., June 1, 1929; d. Raymond Xavier and Jane Elizabeth (Terrell) B. BA, Our Lady of the Lake U., San Antonio, 1950; MA, U. Tex., 1963, PhD, 1969. Cert. elem., secondary tchr., Tex. Tchr. Sacred Heart Sch., El Reno, Okla., 1952-54; head of chemistry Our Lady of the Lake U., 1969-80, prof. chemistry, 1974—, dir. sci./math. divsn., 1973-80, dean Coll. Arts and Scis., 1980—; assoc. grad. lectr. St. Mary's U., San Antonio, 1974-80. Contbr. articles to profl. publs.; author ednl. software; reviewer manuscript Jour. Chem. Edn. Tri-chair Biosci. Task Force-Target 90 Com., San Antonio, 1983-85; liaison Tex. Senate Commn. on Bus., Tech. and Edn., 1983, Sci.-Math.-Engr. Support Network-Tech. Hi-Sch., San Antonio, 1983-85. Named to San Antonio Women's Hall of Fame, 1984. Mem. Am. Chem. Soc. (chairperson local sect. 1981, mem. Project CHEMLAB, divsn. chem. edn.), Tex. Acad. Sci., Nat. Sci. Tchrs. Assn., Soc. Coll. Sci. Tchrs. Office: Our Lady of Lake U 411 SW 24th St San Antonio TX 78207-4666

BALL, RICHARD EVERETT, sociology educator; b. Pasadena, Calif., Oct. 31, 1937; s. Floyd Richard and Ruby Pauline (Wrest) B.; m. Charlotte Ann Wicks, Dec. 28, 1962; children: Jonathan, Graham. BA, Calif. State U., Long Beach, 1961; MA, U. Fla., 1975, PhD, 1980. Asst. prof. U. West Ala., 1978-79; asst. prof., assoc. prof. Ferris State U., Big Rapids, Mich., 1980-90, prof. sociology, 1990—. Vis. asst. prof. Erskine Coll., Due West, S.C., 1977-78; Fulbright lectr. Coun. Internat. Exch. Scholars, U. Tokyo, Keio U., Tsuda Coll., Japan, 1993-94, Hankuk U. Fgn. Studies, Yonsei U., Korea, 1998-99. Contbr. articles to profl. jours. Lt. (j.g.) USNR, 1961-64. Mem.: Mich. Sociol. Assn. (pres. 1987—87, v.p. 1985—86, treas. 1991—96, bd. dirs. 1982—), Japan Studies Assn. Avocations: travel, sailing, hiking, camping. Office: Ferris State U Dept Social Scis Big Rapids MI 49307-2225

BALL, TRAVIS, JR., educational consultant, editor; b. Newport, Tenn., July 13, 1942; s. Travis and Ruth Annette (Duyck) Ball. BA, Carson Newman Coll., 1964; MA, Purdue U., 1966. Instr., then asst. prof. English Ill. Wesleyan U., Bloomington, 1966—69; vis. prof. English Millikin U., 1969; asst. headmaster, chmn. English Brewster Acad., Wolfeboro, NH, 1969—72; dir. admissions, asst. to headmaster Park Tudor Sch., Indpls., 1972—88; cons. Selwyn Sch., Denton, Tex., 1988—89; pres. Travis Ball & Assocs., 1980—88; dir. comm. Verdey Valley Sch., Sedona, Ariz., 1988—91; editor Projects in Enrollment Mgmt., 1992—2000. Mem. commn. on curriculum and grad. requirements Ind. Dept. Pub. Instrn., 1974—76; mem. adv. coun. Ednl. Records Bur.; reviewer Nat. Stds. Project in Sci., Civics and Govt., 1994—95; ednl. cons., 1992—. Editor: Tchrs. Svc. Com. Newsletter for English Tchrs., 1977—82; dept. editor: English Jour., 1976—82, editor/pub.: Contact: Newsletter for Admissions Mgmt., 1980—88, contbg. editor: The Developing Leader, 2003—. Mem.: ASCD, Phi Delta Kappa, Pi Kappa Delta, Nat. Assn. Ind. Schs. (workshop faculty 1986, 1997), Coun. Advancement and Support Edn. (adv. com. on ind. schs.), Nat. Coun. Tchrs. English, Ind. Schs. Assn. Ctrl. States, Ind. Non-Pub. Edn. Assn. (treas., dir., vice chmn.), Sigma Tau Delta. Baptist. Office: 1739 Log Church Rd Newport TN 37821-5535 E-mail: ballt@juno.com.

BALL, WILLIAM PARKS, environmental engineer and educator; b. Newport News, Va., 1954; s. David Joseph and Elaine Taylor Ball; m. Mary Catherine Weigel, Oct. 25, 1980; children: Benjamin Parks, Kelly Elizabeth. BS in Civil Engring., U. Va., 1976; MS, Stanford U., 1977, PhD in Environ. Engring., 1990. Tchg. asst. Ecole Nationale Superieure des Arts et Industries, Strasbourg, France, 1977-78; assoc. engr. James M. Montgomery Cons. Engrs., Walnut Creek, Calif. and Williamsburg, Va., 1978-80, sr. engr., supervising engr. Reston, Va. and Washington, 1980—83; grad. rsch. asst. Stanford U., 1983-89; asst. prof. environ. engring. Duke U., Durham, N.C., 1989-92, Johns Hopkins U., Balt., 1992-98, assoc. prof. environ. engring., 1998—2001, full prof. environ. engring., 2001—. Contbr. articles to profl. jours. Recipient Achievement award for Coll. Scientists, ARCS Found., 1985, 86; Presdl. Young Investigator awardee NSF, 1991, Summer Faculty Rsch. awardee USAF, 1991. Mem. ASCE (Rudolph Hering medal, 1999), Assn. Environ. Engring. Profs., Am. Water Works Assn. (Acad. Achievement award 1991, Abel Wolman doctoral fellow 1986), Am. Geophys. Union, Sigma Xi. Office: Johns Hopkins U Geography and Environ Engrg Ames Hall/3400 N Charles St Baltimore MD 21218

BALLANTYNE, JOSEPH M. science educator, program administrator, researcher; b. Ariz. s. Alando and Annie Ballantyne; m. Martha Ballantyne; children: Joseph, Elizabeth, Catherine, Mary Joy, Annie, Richard, Merrill, Leonora. BS, BSEE, U. Utah, 1959; SM, MIT, 1960, PhD, 1964. Assoc. prof. Cornell U., Ithaca, N.Y., 1968-75, prof., 1975—, dir. elec. engring., 1980-84, v.p. rsch. adv. studies, 1984-89, dir. SRC ctr. of excellence in microscience and tech., 1992-98, L.B. Knight dir. nanofabrication facility, 1998-99, dir. Ctr. for Biochem. Optoelectronic Microsys., 2000—02. Bd. dirs. N.Y. Photonics Devel. Corp., Rome., vis. assoc. prof. Stanford U., Calif., 1970-71, vis. scientist IBM Watson Rsch. Ctr., Yorktown Heights, N.Y., 1978-79, vis. prof. U. Calif., Santa Barbara, 1990, Tech. U. Aachen, Germany, 1990, U. Calif., San Diego, 1997; mem. sci. adv. bd. Dimes, Delft U., The Netherlands, 1999-2001, Binoptics, Inc., 2000—; founding dir. Nat. Nanofabrication Facility, Ithaca, 1977-78; cons. in field. Contbr. articles to profl. jours. Bishop LDS Ch., Ithaca, 1972-77; v.p. bd. dirs. Tompkins County Area Devel. Corp., Ithaca, 1984-89, trustee Associated Univs. Inc., Washington, 1984-89, pres. Cornell Rsch. Found., Ithaca, 1984-89; high tech. adv. com. N.Y. State Urban Devel. Corp., N.Y.C., 1984-87; bd dirs. Coun. on Rsch. & Tech., Washington, 1987-89, Univ. Industry Partnership for Econ. Growth Waverly, N.Y., 1987-89; chmn. univ. adv. com. Semic Rsch. Corp., 1994-96. Recipient George Emery Fellows medal Phi Kappa Phi, 1959; Whitney fellow MIT, 1959-60, Schlumberger fellow MIT, 1961-62, sr. fellow NSF, 1970. Fellow IEEE. Achievements include patents for optoelectric devices. Office: Cornell U 313 Phillips Hall Ithaca NY 14853-5401

BALLARD, BRUCE LAINE, psychiatrist; b. Waverly Hills, Ky., Dec. 19, 1939; s. Orville Lee and Kathryn (Wise) B.; m. Eleanor Glynn Cross, Dec. 5, 1964; children: Tracy Ellen, Timothy Cross. BA, Yale U., 1960; MD, Columbia U., 1964; Cert. in Psychoanalytic Medicine, Columbia Psychoanalytic Ctr., 1974. Diplomate Am. Bd. Psychiatry and Neurology. Asst. dir., resident in psychiatry Harlem Hosp. Ctr., N.Y.C., 1970-72, assoc. dir., resident in psychiatry, 1972-76; assoc. dir. adult outpatient dept. N.Y. Hosp.-Westchester Divsn., White Plains, N.Y., 1976-81; assoc. dean equal opportunity Cornell U. Med. Coll., N.Y.C., 1981-87, assoc. dean student affairs and equal opportunity programs, 1987—. Bd. dirs. N.Y. Cmty. Trust, N.Y.C. Capt. USAF, 1968-70. Mem. AMA, Nat. Med. Assn., Am. Psychiat. Assn., N.Y. Acad. Medicine. Avocation: classical piano. Office: Weill Cornell Med Coll 445 E 69th St Rm 110 New York NY 10021-4805 E-mail: blballar@med.cornell.edu.

BALLARD, JACK STOKES, engineering educator; b. Gravette, Ark., July 23, 1928; s. Freeman Stokes and Chloe Katherine (Clarry) B.; m. Arleda Anne Greenwood, Feb. 21, 1954; children: Kenneth Stokes, Donald Steven, Cheryl Anne. BS in Edn., U. Ark., 1950; MA, U. So. Calif., 1953; PhD, UCLA, 1974. Cert. secondary tchr., Calif. Commd. 2nd lt. USAF, 1954, advanced through grades to lt. col., 1974, ret., 1980; tchr. Coalinga & Whittier (Calif.) High Schs., 1951-54; tng. and pers. officer USAF, Travis AFB, Calif., 1954—56, Elmendorf AFB, Alaska, 1956—59; asso. prof. air sci. Occidental Coll., L.A., 1959-64; asst. prof. history USAF Acad., Colorado Springs, Colo., 1964-69; sr. tng advisor Korean Air Force Tng. Wing, Taejon, Republic of Korea, 1969-70; air force historian Office of Air Force History, Washington, 1970-74; chief plans and requirement divsn. Lowry Tech. Tng. Ctr., Denver, 1974-80; chief strategic sys. tng. Martin Marietta Corp., Denver, 1980-92. Instr. history, U. Md., Alaska, 1958-59, U. Md., Taejon, Korea, 1969-70; adj. instr. history U. Colo., Colorado Springs, 1977-83, U. Colo., Denver, 1983-87. Author: Development and Employment of Fixed Wing Gunships, 1982, Shock of Peace, 1983; contbg. author USAF in S.E. Asia, 1977; contbr. articles to profl. jours. Pres. Occidental Coll. Faculty Club, 1962-63; chmn. Adv. Coun. Sch. Improvement, Littleton, Colo., 1984-89; sec. Large Sch. Dist. Accountability Coun., Denver, 1988-89; elected sch. bd. dirs. Littleton Pub. Schs., 1991; pres. Littleton Sch. Bd., 1995-99; recognized as Colo. All-State Sch. Bd. mem., 1996; bd. dirs. Friends of Fort Logan, 2000-03; mem. Arapahoe County Comprehensive Plan Adv. Com., 2000-01. Mem. Orgn. Am. Historians, Western History Assn., Air Force Hist. Found., Colo. Hist. Soc., Air Force Assn. (sec. Mile High chpt. 1988), Lions (pres. Littleton 1996-97). Republican. Methodist. Avocations: sports, tennis, racquetball, skiing. Home: 7820 S Franklin Way Centennial CO 80122-3116

BALLINGER, KATHRYN ANNETTE (PHELPS), mental health counseling executive, consultant; b. Creswell, Oreg., Aug. 1, 1940; d. Henry Wilbur and Lake Ilene (Wall) Monroe; children: David Bryan (dec.), Derek Alan, Darla Ailene; m. Ray Ballinger, June 27, 1998 (dec. Jan. 1, 2003). BS in edn., Western Oreg. State Coll., 1962; MSW, Columbia State U., 1992, PhD, 1993. Tchr., Germany, Thailand, U.S., 1962-88; acct. exec. ins. industry; weight-loss counselor; alchohol/drug abuse prevention/intervention counselor teens, 1990-93; counselor, 1989-94; sr. exec. v.p., edn. dir. Light Streams, Inc., Eugene, 1993; sr. exec. v.p., therapist Comprehensive Assessment Svcs./The Focus Inst., Inc., Eugene, 1994; mental health counselor in pvt. practice; ednl. cons. specializing in learning disability testing Comprehensive Assessment Svcs., Eugene, 1995-99; CEO Comprehensive Assessment Svcs., LLC, 1995-97; mental health coord. Geriatric Psychiat. Facility, Coos Bay, Oreg., 1999—2002, utilization and resources mgmt., 2002—. Cons. consumer edn.; mem. Am. Bd. Disability Analysts. Author: Easy Does It, books 1 & 2; hosted weekly TV cooking segment, Portland and U.S. Guardian Jobs Daughters, 1980-82; bd. dirs., den mother Cub Scouts, Boy Scouts, Kansas, Oreg., 1974-82; coach girls volleyball, 1974-80; vol. in orphanages, elderly nursing homes, Thailand, Germany, U.S., 1954-95; sunday sch. tchr., 1956-90; sponsored exchange student, 1984-88. Mem. Am. Bd. Disability Analysts, Eastern Star, Nat. Assn. Social Workers, Am. Counseling Assn., Columbia State U. Alumni Assn., Women's Internat. Bowling Conf. Avocations: cooking, gardening, reading, walking, car races, bowling. Home: 770 18th Ave Coos Bay OR 97420-7426

BALLINGTON, DON AVELL, medical educator; b. Batesburg, S.C., Oct. 20, 1946; s. James Ralph and Theo Madgeilee Ballington; m. Linda Barnett, Nov. 20, 1982; children: Kristin, Mark. BS, Clemson U., 1968, MS, 1969. Animal nutritionist Spartan Grain & Mill, Spartanburg, SC, 1970—71; microscopist S.C. Dept. Agr., Columbia, SC, 1971—72; instr. health sci. Midlands Tech. Coll., Columbia, 1972—79, dir. pharmacy tech. program, 1979—. Cons. in field; founder Pharmacy Technician Educator's Coun., Charleston, SC, 1991. Author: Pharmacology for Technicians, 1999, Pharmacy Math for Technicians, 1999, Pharmacy Practice for Technicians, 1999. Mem.: S.C. Pharmacy Assn., S.C. Soc. Health Sys. Pharmacists (Pub. award 1991), Am. Soc. Health-Sys. Pharmacists, Am. Assn. Pharmacy Technicians (Founder's award 1987). Avocations: gardening, woodworking, RC model planes. Home: 210 Horace Ct Lexington SC 29073 Office: Midlands Tech Dept Health Sci PO Box 2408 Columbia SC 29202-2408

BALLOU, JANICE DONELON, research director; b. New Brunswick, N.J., May 13, 1944; s. Peter and Kathryn (Koval) Donelon; m. Donald Thomas Ballou, Nov. 12, 1966 (div. 1984); children: Peter, David. BA, Douglas Coll., 1966; MA, Rutgers U., 1977. Tchr. Sayreville (N.J.) Jr. High Sch., 1966-71; dir. field ops. Eagleton Inst., Rutgers U., New Brunswick, N.J., 1977-80, assoc. dir., 1980-82, dir., 1989—; v.p. divsn. head Louis Harris & Assocs., N.Y.C., 1982-86; v.p. group head Response Analysis, Princeton, N.J., 1986-89; v.p. Mathematica Policy Rsch., Inc., Princeton, NJ, 2001—. Bd. dirs. Inst. Rsch. on Aging and Health Fin., Princeton, N.J., Essex C.C. Found. Co-founder Parents Drug and Alcohol Coun., Highland Park, N.J., 1991; bd. dirs. Rutgers Substance Abuse Task Force, New Brunswick, 1990-93, The Citizen's Com. on Biomed. Ethics, Summit, N.J., 1993-98; chair Pathways to Participation Civic Edn. Program com., New Brunswick, 1992; grad. bd. Leadership N.J., 1991-99; pres. Bd. Leadership N.J. Grad. Orgn., 1995; mayor Highland Park Econ. Devel. Com., 1999. Leadership N.J. fellow Partnership for N.J., 1990, Ford Found. fellow, 1990; named Alumnae of Yr. by Highland Park High Sch., 1992. Mem. Am. Assn. Pub. Opinion Rsch. (pubs. chair 1988-90, sec.-treas. 1991-93, standards chair 1999-2001, councillor-at-large 2002--), Nat. Network State Polls (mem. exec. coun. 1989—), Nat. Coun. Pub. Polls (mem. exec. coun. 1993—), N.J. Internat. Forum Women (sec.), Douglass Coll. Associate Alumnae Douglass Soc. Avocations: raising christmas trees, travelling, hiking, outdoor activities, reading. Office: Mathematica Policy Rsch PO Box 2393 Princeton NJ 08543-2392

BALLOWE, JAMES, English educator, author; b. Carbondale, Ill., Nov. 28, 1933; s. Frank Charles and Wilma Ruth (Maynard) B.; children: Jeffrey, Mary; m. Ruth Ganchiff. BA, Millikin U., 1954; MA, U. Ill., 1956, PhD, 1963. Tchr. pub. schs. Decatur, Ill., 1954-55; grad. asst. U. Ill., 1955-61; asst. prof. English Millikin U., 1961-63; mem. faculty dept. English Bradley U., Peoria, Ill., 1963-99, prof., chmn., 1971-74, dean Grad. Sch., 1974-86, assoc. provost, 1979-86, dean communications and fine arts, 1986-90, disting. univ. prof. emeritus, 1999—; chmn. Commn. Instns. Higher Edn., North Central Assn., 1985-86. Narrator Herrin Massacre, Nat. Pub. Radio, 1997. Author: (poetry) The Coal Miners, 1979, (history) The Story of the Morton Arboretum, 2003; editor: George Santayana's America, 1967, Anglo-Welsh Poetry, 1989. Mem. Ill. Arts Coun., 1975-83, Ill. State Mus. Bd., 1976—, Ill. Humanities Coun., 1997-2002. Recipient Poetry award Ill. Arts Coun., 1975, 78, Creative Non-fiction award Ill. Arts Coun., 1993. Mem. Ill. Assn. Grad. Schs. (pres. 1979-80), Midwestern Assn. Grad. Schs. (pres. 1978-79). Home: PO Box 302 Ottawa IL 61350-0302

BALOG, THERESA GALLAGHER, nursing educator; b. Pitts., Dec. 18, 1937; d. Bernard and Dorothy (Sherred) Gallagher; children: Megan Anne, Paul David. Diploma in nursing, Allegheny Valley Hosp., 1960; BSN, Duquesne U., 1963; M in Nursing, U. Pitts., 1968, PhD, 1984. RN, Pa. Nursing staff adminstr., educator Children's Hosp., Pitts., 1963-68; instr., asst. prof. nursing children and maternal nursing U. Pitts., 1968-72; tenured assoc. prof. nursing, coord. family nursing Duquesne U., Pitts., 1972-77; asst. prof. nursing, dir. pediatric affiliate program U. Pitts., 1977-81; asst. dean instrn., nursing Community Coll. Allegheny County, Pitts., 1981-88; dir. Sch. Nursing Uniontown (Pa.) Hosp., 1988-94; asst. prof., campus coord. nursing Pa. State U. Fayette campus, Uniontown, Pa., 1994-99, Elouise Ross Eberly prof. nursing, 1997-99; campus coord., program head nursing Commonwealth Coll., New Kensington, 1999—. Adj. asst. prof. grad. program in nursing adminstrn. U. Pitts., 1987-90, asst. prof. Helene Fuld grantee, Eberly Family Charitable Trustee grantee, Vocat. Edn. grantee. Mem. Nat. League Nursing, Pa. League Nursing (bd. dirs.), Nightingale Awards of Pa. (trustee), Carebreak (trustee 1982-97), Sigma Theta Tau (Rsch. award 1983, Leadership in Nursing. Excellence in Edn. award 1992). Home: 1564 Saint Andrews Dr Oakmont PA 15139-1035

BALON, RICHARD, psychiatrist, educator; b. Olomouc, Czechoslovakia, Oct. 11, 1951; s. Ota and Marie (Sindylek) B.; m. Helena Rachel Zador, July 24, 1976. MD, U. Karlova, Prague, Czechoslovakia, 1976. Diplomate Am. Bd. Psychiatry and Neurology; bd. cert. in psychiatry in Czechoslovakia, cert. clin. psychopharmacology Am. Soc. Clin. Psychopharmacology, 1998. Resident in psychiatry and clin. rsch. Psychiat. Rsch. Inst., Prague, 1978-81; resident in psychiatry Lafayette Clinic, Detroit, 1983-87; asst. prof. Wayne State U., Detroit, 1987-90, assoc. prof., 1990-96, prof., 1996—, assoc. dir. residency tng. in psychiatry, 2002—. Dir. jr. med. students program in psychiatry Wayne State U., Detroit, 1989-92, dir. med. student edn. psychiatry, 1993-97; staff psychiatrist Lafayette Clinic, Detroit, 1987-92, pres. med. staff, 1990-92; co-chair Mich. Tech. Adv. Rsch. com., 1991-99. Contbr. chpts to books and articles to profl. jours.; author, editor 4 books; co-author 1 book. Travel fellow Am. Coll. Neuropsychopharmacology, 1987. Fellow: Am. Coll. Psychiatrists, Am. Psychiat. Assn. (1st Nancy C.A. Roeske award 1991, George Tarjan award 1998); mem.: AMA, Mich. Psychiat. Soc. (pres. 2000—01), Assn. Dirs. Med. Student Edn. in Psychiatry, Collegium Internat. Neuro-Psychopharmacologicum, Soc. Biol. Psychiatry, Am. Assn. Suicidology, Internat. Soc. Psychoneuroendocrinology. Avocations: movies, books, politics, geography. Office: Univ Psychiat Ctr 2751 E Jefferson Ave Ste 200 Detroit MI 48207-4100 E-mail: rbalon@wayne.edu.

BALONEK, THOMAS JOSEPH, physics and astronomy educator; b. Rochester, N.Y., Dec. 15, 1951; s. John Joseph and Norma May (Meyer) B. BA, Cornell U., 1974; MS, U. Mass., 1977, PhD, 1982. Postdoctoral rsch. assoc., lectr. U. N.Mex., Albuquerque, 1982-83; vis. asst. prof. astronomy Williams Coll., Williamstown, Mass., 1983-85; asst. prof. physics and astronomy Colgate U., Hamilton, NY, 1985-91, assoc. prof., 1991—2002, prof., 2002—. Vis. rsch. scientist Nat. Radio Astronomy Obs., Tucson, 1992-93; vice chmn. N.Y. Astron. Corp., 1990-95, chmn., 1995-98; councillor Coun. on Undergrad. Rsch., 1990-93. Co-author instr.'s manual to accompany Introductory Astronomy and Astrophysics, 4th edit., 1998. Grantee coll. sci. instrumentation program NSF, 1987, grantee Rsch. Corp., 1987. Mem. Internat. Astron. Union, Am. Astron. Soc., Astron. Soc. N.Y. (instnl. rep. 1985—). Office: Colgate U Dept Physics and Astronomy 13 Oak Dr Hamilton NY 13346-1383

BALTHASER, GERDA HAAS, elementary school educator; b. Syracuse, N.Y., Apr. 3, 1936; d. Max Oskar and Luise (Emmert) Haas; m. Robert George Balthaser, June 13, 1959; children: Scott, Debbie Balthaser Ziegler. BS in Elem. Edn., Elizabethtown (Pa.) Coll., 1965; MS Elem. Edn., Kutztown U., 1968; Cert. in Early Childhood Edn., Millersville U., 1988. Tchr. kindergarten Hamburg Area Sch. Dist., Pa., 1963-68; tchr. 2nd grade Cornwall-Lebanon Sch. Dist., Pa., 1968-70, tchr. kindergarten, 1970—99; ret., 1999. Class agt. for devel. office Elizabeth Coll., 1989—; pres. Ch. Women United of Lebanon County, 1993-97; pres. Women of Evangelical Lutheran Ch. of Am.(WELCA), Hill Lutheran Ch., Cleona, Pa., 2001-; coord. World Day of Prayer, Ch. Women United Lebanon County, 1998-2002; vol. reader Reach Out and Read, Hyman Caplan Hosp., Lebanon, Pa., 2002-; elections clerk Lebanon County, Pa., 2001-. Mem. PASR (Pa. Assn. of Sch. Retirees), AAUW (Lebanon Valley br. sec. 1990-94, Lebanon Valley br. treas. 1999-2003, Woman of Yr. 1993), LebCoPASR (Lebanni County Pa. Assn. of Sch. Retirees),Lebanon County Ednl. Honor Soc. (corr. sec. 1979-80, rec. sec. 1990-92, treas. 1996-97), Elizabethtown Coll. Alumni Coun. (pres. 1985-86), Delta Kappa Gamma (chpt. pres. 1988-90, parliamentarian 1990-92, Alpha Alpha state hist. records chmn. 1991-93, state fin. com. 1993-96, Alpha Alpha State Conv. treas. 2002-, Alpha Alpha State scholarship com., 1996-99, Alpha Alpha State Founders' scholar 1987, Golden Gift leadership/mgmt. seminar scholarship 1993). Democrat. Lutheran. Avocations: reading, travel, swimming. Home: 2005 Kline St Lebanon PA 17042-5724

BALTHASER, LINDA IRENE, retired academic administrator; b. Kokomo, Ind., Feb. 25, 1939; d. Earl Isaac and Evelyn Pauline (Troyer) Showalter; m. Kenneth James Balthaser, June 1, 1963. BS magna cum laude, U. Ind., 1961; MS, Ind. U., 1962. Tchr. bus. edn. Southport H.S., Indpls., 1962-63; sec. administrv. sec. office of pres. Ind. U., Bloomington, 1963-66; with Ind. U.-Purdue U., Fort Wayne, 1969—, asst. to dean arts and letters, 1970—86, asst. dean arts and letters, 1986—87, asst. dean arts and scis., 1987—2002, asst. dean emerita, 2002—. Founding co-dir. Weekend Coll., 1979-80; bd. dirs. Associated Chs. Fort Wayne, 1980; mem. Ind. com. Nat. Mus. Women in Arts. Ind. Conf. N. Evang. United Brethren Ch. scholar, 1957-61. Trustee United Ch. of Christ, 1994-97, mem. exec. coun., 2000—. Recipient Women of Achievement award YWCA, 1990. Mem.: AAUW (trustee 1995—97, coll. & univ. rep. 2000—02, Nat. grantee Ft. Wayne br. 1995), Assn. IPFW Women (pres. 1967—68, steering com. co-chair 1998—99, steering com. sec. 1999—), Fort. Wayne Zool. Soc., Fort Wayne Mus. Art, Embassy Theatre Found., Fort Wayne-Allen County Hist. Assn., Mensa, Phi Kappa Phi, Alpha Chi, Phi Alpha Epsilon, Delta Pi Epsilon. Home: 2917 Hazelwood Ave Fort Wayne IN 46805-2403 Office: 2101 E Coliseum Blvd Fort Wayne IN 46805-1445 E-mail: balthase@ipfw.edu.

BALTHROP, CYNTHIA DIANE, elementary school educator; b. Munich, Apr. 20, 1967; d. Joe Lindsey and Carolyn Joanne (Cole) Self; m. David Charles Balthrop, July 25, 1987. Student, Tarleton U., 1985-86, Western Tex. Coll., 1986-87; BS, Cameron U., 1990. Student tchr. Sheridan Rd. Elem. Sch., Lawton, Okla., 1990; tchr. 1st grade Ft. Clayton (Panama) Elem. Sch., 1991-92; tchr. 6th grade Curundu Elem. Sch., Panama, 1992-93; tchr. 3d grade Throckmorton (Tex.) Elem. Sch., 1994—. Home: 1204 N Reynolds Throckmorton TX 76483

BALTIMORE, DAVID, academic administrator, microbiologist, educator; b. NYC, Mar. 7, 1938; s. Richard I. and Gertrude (Lipschitz) B.; m. Alice S. Huang, Oct. 5, 1968; 1 dau., Teak. BA with high honors in Chemistry, Swarthmore Coll., 1960; postgrad., MIT, 1960—61; PhD, Rockefeller U., 1964. Postdoctoral rschr. MIT, Cambridge, Mass., 1964—65; research assoc. Salk Inst. Biol. Studies, La Jolla, Calif., 1965—68; from assoc. prof. microbiology to dir. MIT, Cambridge, Mass., 1968—82, dir. Whitehead Inst. Biomed. Rsch., 1982—90; pres. Rockefeller U., N.Y.C., 1990—91, prof., 1990—94; pres. Calif. Inst. Tech., Pasadena, 1997—. Bd. govs. Weizmann Inst. Sci., Israel; co-chmn. Commn. on a Nat. Strategy of Aids; ad hoc program adv. com. on complex genome, AIDS rsch. adv. coun. NIH, chair vaccine adv. com., 1997—2002. Mem. editorial bd. Jour. Molecular Biology, 1971-73, Jour. Virology, 1969-90, Sci., 1986-98, New Eng. Jour. Medicine, 1989-94. Bd. govs. Weizmann Inst. Sci., Israel; bd. dirs. Life Sci. Rsch. Found. Recipient Gustav Stern award, 1970, Warren Triennial prize Mass. Gen. Hosp., 1971, Eli Lilly and Co. award, 1971, Nat. Acad. Scis. US Steel award, 1974, Gairdner Found. award, 1974, Nobel prize, 1975, Nat. medal of sci., 1999, Warren Alpert Found. prize, 2000, Sci. Achievement award AMA, 2002. Fellow AAAS, Am. Med. Writers Assn. (hon.), Am. Acad. Microbiology; mem. NAS, Am. Acad. Arts and Scis., Inst. Medicine, Am. Philos. Soc., Pontifical Acad. Scis., Royal Soc. (Eng., fgn.), French Acad. Scis. (fgn. assoc.). Office: Calif Inst Tech 1200 E California Blvd 204 Parsons Gate Pasadena CA 91125-0001

BALTZ, PATRICIA ANN (PANN BALTZ), elementary education educator; b. Dallas, June 20, 1949; d. Richard Parks and Ruth Eileen (Hartschuh) Langford; m. William Monroe Baltz, Sept. 6, 1969; 1 child Kenneth Chandler. Student, U. Redlands, 1967-68; BA in English Lit. cum laude, UCLA, 1971. Cert. tchr. K-8, Calif. Tchr. 4th grade Arcadia (Calif.) Unified Sch. Dist., 1972-74, 92—, substitute tchr., 1983-85, tchr. 3dr grade, 1985-87, tchr. 6th grade, 1987-90, tchr. 4th and 5th grade multiage, 1990—. Sci. mentor tchr. Arcadia Unified Sch. Dist., 1991-94; mentor Tech. Ctr. Silicon Valley, San Jose, Calif., 1991. Tchr. rep. PTA, Arcadia, 1980-93; mem. choir, children's sermon team, elder Arcadia Presbyn. Ch., 1980-93; chaperone, vol. Pasadena (Calif.) Youth Symphony Orch., 1988-90; vol. Am. Heart Assn., 1990-92. Recipient Outstanding Gen. Elem. Tchr. award, Outstanding Tchr. of the Yr. award Disney's Am. Tchr. Awards, 1993, Calif. Tchr. of Yr. award Calif. State Dept. Edn., 1993, Georgie award Girl Scouts of Am., 1993, The Self Esteem Task Force award L.A. County Task Force to Promote Self-Esteem & Personal & Social Responsibility, 1993, Profl. Achievement award UCLA Alumni Assn.; apptd. to Nat. Edn. Rsch. Policies & Priorities Bd., U.S. Sec. Edn. Richard Riley; Pann Baltz Mission Possible Scholar named in her honor. Mem. NEA, Nat. Sci. Tchrs. Assn., Calif. Tchr. Assn., Arcadia Tchrs. Assn. Avocations: reading, singing, calligraphy, book-making, computers. Home: 1215 S 3rd Ave Arcadia CA 91006-4205 Office: Arcadia Unified Sch Dist Camino Grove Elem Sch 700 Camino Grove Ave Arcadia CA 91006-4438

BALTZER, PATRICIA GERMAINE, elementary school educator; b. Johnstown, Pa., May 16, 1951; d. Harry and Doris Mae Findley; m. Dennis Duane Baltzer, Jan. 5, 1985; 1 child, Kourtney Noelle. BS, U. Pitts., Johnstown, 1973; cert. prin., Ind. U. Pa., 1994. Cert. prin., Pa. Tchr. Windber (Pa.) Area Sch. Dist., 1973—, chairperson sci. com. Coord. Project Hugs and Kisses, Windber, 1993-98. Mem. Assn. for Childhood Edn. Internat. (Successful Teaching award 1993), Keystone State Reading Assn., Laurel Highlands Math. Alliance, Pa. Assn. Elem. Sch. Prins. (student), Bus. and Profl. Women's Orgn. (Young Careerist chairperson). Avocations: reading, theater, writing, travel. Office: Windber Area Sch Dist Windber PA 15963

BALTZLEY, PATRICIA CREEL, secondary mathematics educator; b. Ft. Benning, Ga., Dec. 14, 1952; d. Buckner Miller and Mary Madeleine (O'Neill) Creel; m. Kevin Gerard Robinson, Nov. 15, 1975 (div. Dec. 21, 1981); children: Kevin G. Jr., Timothy Eugene; m. Jeffrey Lynn Baltzley, July 23, 1988 (dec. Dec. 1996). Student, St. Joseph's Coll., 1971-72; BA in Math., Coll. Notre Dame, 1975; MS in Math., Shippensburg State U., 1986. Cert. advanced profl., Md.; cert. in adminstn. and supervision. Acct. trainee Md. Nat. Bank, Balt., 1975-76; math. tchr. Notre Dame Preparatory Sch., Towson, Md., 1976-78, Carroll County Bd. Edn., Westminster, Md., 1978-91; math. program developer Ctr. for Social Orgn. of Schs. Johns Hopkins U., Balt., 1991—95; K-12 math. specialist Baltimore County Pub. Schs., 1995—98, 6-12 math. supr., 1998—. Adj. prof. Coll. Notre Dame, Balt., 1992--, Johns Hopkins U., 1995-97, Western Md. Coll., 1997--, Loyola Coll., 2000--; cons. Ctr. for Social Orgn., Johns Hopkins U., Learning Inst.; ind. cons. in field. Pres. Seton Ctr., Emmitsburg, Md., 1982-86; vol. Seton Shrine Ctr., Emmitsburg, 1986—. Recipient Presdl. Award for Excellence in Teaching Math. NSF, 1989; named Md. Math. Educator of Yr., 1977. Mem. ASCD, NEA, Md. Coun. Tchrs. Math. (pres. 1991-93), Nat. Coun. Tchrs. Math., Coun. Presdl. Awardees in Math., Md. Coun. Suprs. Math. (pres., 2000—), Coun. Adminstrs. and Suprs. in Edn. Democrat. Roman Catholic. Avocations: reading, basketball, walking. Home: 830 Glendale Rd York PA 17403-4130 Office: Baltiore County Pub Schs 6901 Charles St Towson MD 21204

BAMBAKIDIS, PETER, neurologist, educator; b. Akron, Ohio, Nov. 2, 1948; s. Nicholas and Zopigi (Dragoumanou) B.; m. Anna Savaris, Aug. 18, 1974; children: Athe, John A., Theodore. Student, U. Akron, 1966-67; BMus, Cleve. Inst. Mus., 1971, MMus, 1973; postgrad., U. Pitts., 1974-75, Ohio State U., 1978-80; MD, Case Western Res. U., 1984. Diplomate Am. Bd. Psychiatry and Neurology, Am. Bd. Clin. Neurophysiology. Resident in neurology Mayo Grad. Sch. Medicine, Rochester, Minn., 1984-88, fellow EEG, 1988-89; pvt. practice Cleve., 1989-92; asst. prof. neurology Case Western Res. U., Cleve., 1992—; neurologist Fairview Med. Group, 1994—2000, Cleve. Clinic Found., 2000—02, Premier Physicians, 2003—; vice chmn. Dept. Medicine Fairview Hosp., head Neurology Sect. Violinist Akron Symphony Orch., 1966-67, Richmond (Va.) Sinfonia, Richmond Symphony Orch., 1973-74, West Australian Symphony Orch., Perth, 1976-78, Columbus (Ohio) Symphony Orch., 1978-80; freelance musician, 1967-73; tchg. asst. Cleve. Inst. Music, 1971-73; tchg. fellow dept. music U. Pitts., 1974-75; follow-up asst. regional pediat. intensive care transport sys. Rainbow Babies and Children's Hosp., Cleve., 1981-82; hosp. affiliations Fairview Hosp., Cleve., St. John & Westshore Hosp., Westlake, Ohio, Luth. Med. Ctr., Cleve., S.W. Gen. Hosp., Middleburgh Hts., Ohio, Lakewood Hosp., Lakewood, Ohio. Tuesday Musical Club scholar, 1968, Ranney Found. scholar, 1968, Hellenic U. Club scholar, 1983. Mem. Am. Acad. Neurology, Am. Clin. Neurophysiology Soc., Phi Kappa Lambda. Avocations: weight lifting, near/middle eastern music and mysticism, writings of early church fathers. Office: 18099 Lorain Ave Ste 145 Cleveland OH 44111-5610

BAMBER, LINDA SMITH, accounting educator; b. Columbus, Ohio, Jan. 4, 1954; d. Charles Randall and Martha Jo (Wise) Smith; m. Edward Michael Bamber, Mar. 13, 1981. BS summa cum laude, Wake Forest U, 1976; MBA, Ariz. State U., 1980; PhD, Ohio State U., 1983. Cost acct. RJ Reynolds, Winston-Salem, N.C., 1975-76, gen. acct., 1976-77; tutor, rsch. asst. Ariz. State U., Tempe, 1977-78; teaching asst. Ohio State U., Columbus, 1978-82; asst. prof. U. Fla., Gainesville, 1983-88, assoc. prof., 1988-90, U. Ga., Athens, 1990-96, prof., 1996—. Vis. assoc. prof. Ind. U., Bloomington, 1989-90. Author: Annotated Instructor's Edition of Cost Accounting: A Managerial Emphasis, 1990, 93, 96, assoc. editor: Acctg. Horizon, 1993-97; mem. editl. bd. The Acctg. Rev., 1987-89, 93—, Advances in Acctg., 1992—; contbr. articles to profl. jours. Selig fellow U. Ga., 1991, Terry fellow U. Ga., 1994, 95, 96, 97; recipient Rsch. Devel. award U. Fla., 1985, Tchg. award Ohio State U., U. Fla., U. Ga., 1981-94. Mem. Am. Acctg. Assn. (S.E. dir. fin. reporting sect. 1993-94, group leader, panelist, chmn. New Faculty Consortium 1991-95, rsch. adv. com. 1996-98, mem. coun. 1995-97, mgmt. acctg. sect. chmn. membership outreach com. 1995-97, Wildman medal award com. 1996-97, nominations com. 1996-97, corp. acctg. policy seminar com. 1997-98), Phi Beta Kappa, Phi Kappa Phi, Beta Gamma Sigma Avocations: swimming, water skiing, travel. Office: U Ga JM Tull Sch Acctg Athens GA 30602

BAMBERGER, JOSEPH ALEXANDER, mechanical engineer, educator; b. Hamburg, Germany, Nov. 21, 1927; came to U.S., 1940; s. Seligman and Else (Buxbaum) B.; m. Dorothy Frank, Dec. 24, 1950; children: David, Michael. BME, CUNY, 1949; MME, NYU, 1954. R & D engr. Kramer Trenton Co., Trenton, N.J., 1949-59; mech. engr., scientific staff Brookhaven Nat. Lab., Upton, N.Y., 1959-82; prof. mech. tech. Suffolk Community Coll., Selden, N.Y., 1982-95; mem. staff R&D objects conservation Met. Mus. Art, N.Y.C., 1996—. Cons. Typhoon Air Conditioning, Div. Hupp Corp., Bklyn., 1952-59. Contbr. articles to ASHRAE Jour., Advances in Cryogenic Engring., Cryogenics, ASME Transactions, Jour. Vacuum Sci. and Tech., Nuclear Instruments and Methods, Studies in Conservation. Dir. Temple Beth El, Patchogue, N.Y., 1962-84; chmn. Cryogenic Safety Com., Brookhaven Lab., 1980-82. Mem. N.Y. Acad. Sci., AAAS, ASHRAE. Achievements include patent for Electrically Insulating Feedthrough for Cryogenic Applications; research in low temperature cooling systems for superconducting magnets, cryogenic pumping systems, liquid hydrogen bubble chamber design and operation.

BAME, JAMES EDWIN, English educator; b. Findlay, Ohio, Aug. 25, 1948; BS in Edn., Ashland (Ohio) U., 1970; MA in English, San Francisco State U., 1983. Vol. Peace Corps, Sana'a, Yemen, 1976-78; tchr., materials developer Ea. Mich. U./USAID, Sana'a, 1979-80; lang. instr. U. San Francisco, 1982-83, King Saud U., Riyadh, Saudi Arabia, 1983-84, N.Mex. State U./USAID, Las Cruces, 1984-86; internat. edn. specialist U. Ky./USAID, Lexington, 1987-90; prof. Intensive English Lang. Instrn./Utah State U., Logan, 1990—; personel dept. Utah State Univ., 2001—03. Presenter Tchrs. of English to Spkrs. of Other Langs., Washington, 1993—99, Washington, 2003; faculty senator Utah State U., 1995—99. Author, contbr.: New Ways Series/TESOL, 1993-99, Tasks in Independent Language Learning, 1996; mem. editl. adv. bd. Collegiate Press, Alta Loma, Calif., 1996-97; reviewer Fund for Improvement of Post-Secondary Edn., Washington, 1996, Cambridge (Eng.) U. Press, 1996, Houghton Mifflin Press, 2000-01. Mem. Am. Assn. for Adult and Continuing Edn., 2002, Ctr. for Internat. Bus. Edn. and Rsh., 2000—01. Mem. Intermountain Tchrs. of English to Spkrs. of Other Langs. (chair higher edn. interest sect. 1993-94, Prof. Devel. award 1994, sec. bd. dirs. 1998-2001, pres. 2002-03). Avocations: hiking, gardening, camping. Office: IELI 715 University Blvd Logan UT 84322-0715

BAMFORD, JOSEPH CHARLES, JR., gynecologist, obstetrician, educator, medical missionary, writer; b. Paterson, NJ, Oct. 23, 1930; s. Joseph Charles and Luise (Whitehead) Bamford; m. Susan Jane Hall, Apr. 13, 1951; children: Joseph Charles III, Elizabeth Ann. BS, Rutgers U., 1952; MD, NY Med. Coll., 1956. Diplomate Am. Bd. Ob-Gyn. Intern U. Vt., 1956—57; resident in ob-gyn NY Med. Coll., N.Y.C., 1957—60, asst. clin. instr. dept. ob-gyn, 1960—64, clin. instr., 1964—65, asst. prof., 1965—70, assoc. prof., 1970—72, asst. dean, 1966—68, assoc. dean, 1968—72, acting v.p. hosp. affairs, 1971—72; sect. chief psychosomatic ob-gyn Met. Hosp. Ctr., N.Y.C., 1963—72, chief svc., 1971—72; practice medicien specializing in ob-gyn Paterson, NJ, 1962—66, St. Johnsbury, Vt., 1972—76; asst. obstetrician and gynecologist Flower and Fifth Ave. hosps., N.Y.C., 1960—66, asst. attending, 1966—70, attending, 1970—72; asst. vis. obstetrician and gynecologist Met. Hosp. Ctr., N.Y.C., 1960—66, assoc., 1968—70, vis., 1970—72; vis. ob-gyn Indian Health Svc. Hosp., Ft. Defiance, Ariz., 1981; clin. asst. ob-gyn Paterson Gen. Hosp., 1962—64, assoc. attending, 1964—66, attending, 1966—67; cons., 1967; attending obstetrician and gynecologist Northeastern Vt. Regional Hosp., St. Johnsburg, 1972—76, cons., 1976—85. Vis. obstetrician and gynecologist St. Jude Missions Hosp., St. Lucia, 1986; med. officer Tumutumu Mission Hosp., Kenya, 1987—88; cons. Beatrice D. Weeks Meml. Hosp., Lancaster, NH, 1972—80; vol. program steering com. for retired physicians Vt. Med. Soc., 1996—2001; chmn. subcom. for fact finding Mayor's Com. for Hosp. Facilities Planning, Paterson, 1964—66. Contbr. articles to profl. jours. Chmn. med. adv. com. Passaic County (NJ) Com. for Planned Parenthood, 1965—67; mem. NJ Com. on Med. Edn., 1965—66; trustee Greater Paterson Gen. Hosp., 1966—2000, So. Vt. Art Ctr., 1997—2002; pres. Lyndon State Coll. Found., 1980—84. Lt. comdr. USNR, 1960—62. Fellow: ACOG (mem. com. on course coord. 1977—79); mem.: Caledonia County Med. Soc. (v.p. 1974—75), Vt. Med. Soc. (mem. jud. com. 1975—77), Ob-Gyn. Soc. NY Med. Coll. (mem. exec. com. 1963—66), No. New England Acad. Medicine. Home: Box 724 Myrickview Vlg Dorset VT 05251

BANAS, SUZANNE, middle school educator; b. Miami, Fla., Mar. 28, 1959; d. Frank and Norma (Eliscu) B. BA in Sci., U. Miami, 1981, MS, 1986; PhD, Union Inst., 1994. Cert. tchr. sci. gifted LD & EH, Fla.; Nat. Bd. Cert. Tchr. early adolescence generalist Nat. Bd. Profl. Tchg. Stds. Lead tchr. Dade County Pub. Schs., Miami, 1988—; curriculum writer Gender Equity Network, Miami, 1993—97, Arise Found., Miami, 1995—97; tchr., chairperson dept. sci., team leader Cutler Ridge Mid. Sch., Miami, 1990—; adj. prof. Fla. Internat. U., Miami, 1996—. Advisor Acad. for Instrnl. Leadership, Miami, 1994-96, Annenberg Challenge Grant, Miami, 1995-96; cons. Urban Sys. Initiative, 1995-98; Internet tchr. trainer/mentor, 1998—. Recipient Fla. Explores! award Fla. State U./TDRA, 1993, Tchr. of Yr. award Cutler Ridge Mid. Sch., 1996, Sharing success award dept. of environ. edn., 2000. Mem. Miami Dade County Sci. Tchrs. Assn. (pres. 1994—), Fla. Assn. Sci. Tchrs. (bd. dirs. 1998—), Nat. Sci. Tchrs. Assn. Office: Richmond Heights Mid Sch Sci Zoo Magnet 15015 SW103 Ave Miami FL 33176

BANATHY, BELA HENRICH, systems science educator, author, researcher; b. Gyula, Hungary, Dec. 1, 1919; came to U.S., 1951; s. Peter and Hilda (Becker) B.; m. Eva Balazs, Dec. 10, 1942; children: Bela, Laszlo, Tibor, Robert. BS, Hungarian Royal Ludovika Acad., Budapest, 1940; MA, San Jose State U., 1963; EdD, U. Calif., Berkeley, 1966. Instr. Hungarian Royal Ludovika Acad., 1943-44; pres. Collegium Hungaricum, Zell Amsee, Austria, 1948-50; prof., chmn. dept. Def. Lang. Inst., Monterey, Calif., 1951-59, dean lang. div., 1959-69; sr. program dir. Far West Lab. for R & D, San Francisco, 1969-80, assoc. lab. dir., 1980-86, sr. rsch. dir., 1987-90; prof. systems sci. Saybrook Grad. Sch., San Francisco, 1983—; pres. Internat. Systems Inst., Monterey, 1991—. Adj. prof. San Jose (Calif.) State U., 1966-80, U. Calif., Berkeley, 1972-77; mem. internat. adv. Jour. Systems Rsch., Jour. Systems Practice, Jour. World Futures. Author: Instructional Systems, 1966, The Design of Foreign Language Curriculum, 1972, A Systems Models Approach, 1972, Systems Design of Education: A Journey to Create the Future, 1991, A System View of Education, 1992; contbr. articles and rsch. reports to profl. publs. Nat. dir. youth leadership Hungarian Boy Scouts Assn., Budapest, 1943-46; coun. chair leadership devel. Boy Scouts Am., Monterey, Calif., 1956-68, mem. nat. com. leadership devel., New Brunswick, 1966-70; bd. dirs. ARC, Monterey, 1956-57. Capt. Royal Hungarian Army, 1940-44. Recipient Silver Beaver award Boy Scouts Am., 1960, Disting. Scholarship award Austrian Soc. for Cybernetics, 1986. Fellow Vienna Acad. for Study of Future; mem. Soc. for Gen. Systems (regional dir. 1970-76, v.p. 1980-84, pres. 1985-86), Internat. Soc. for Systems Scis. (chmn. bd. trustees 1987-89, Disting. Leadership award 1987), Internat. Fedn. Systems Rsch. (bd. dirs. 1981-93, pres. 1994—). Democrat. Presbyterian. Office: Internat Systems Inst 25781 Morse Dr Carmel CA 93923-8319

BANDER, CAROL JEAN, German and English language educator; b. NYC, Jan. 5, 1945; d. Frank Samuel and Susie Ruth Heimberg; m. Myron Bander, Aug. 20, 1967. BA, Queens Coll., 1966; MA, U. So. Calif., L.A., 1968, PhD, 1972. Cert. life commun. coll. credential, life standard secondary credential, ESL cert. Assoc. faculty Orange Coast Coll., Costa Mesa, Calif., 1974-77, North Orange Community Coll., Fullerton, Calif., 1974-77; prof. German and English as second lang. Saddleback Coll., Mission Viejo, Calif., 1977—, dept. chair English as a second lang., 1989-92, 96-98. NDEA Title IV fellowship U.S. Govt., 1966-70. Mem. Calif. Assn. Tchrs. of English to Speakers of Other Langs. (pre-conf. co-coord. 2001—, pres. 1999-2000, pres.-elect 1998-99, sec. 1992-93, bd. dirs. 1988-90, chpt. chair 1989-90, coord. Orange County chpt. 1988-90), Am. Assn. Tchrs. German, Tchrs. of English to Speakers of Their Langs., Phi Beta Kappa. Avocations: travel, music, theatre, movies, cooking. Home: 39 Northampton Ct Newport Beach CA 92660-4206 Office: Saddleback Coll 28000 Marguerite Pky Mission Viejo CA 92692-3635

BANDER, EDWARD JULIUS, law librarian emeritus, lawyer; b. Boston, Aug. 10, 1923; s. Abraham and Ida (Lendman) B. BA, Boston U., 1949, LLB, 1951; MLS, Simmons Coll., 1955. Bar: Mass. 1951. Asst. reference libr. Harvard U., Cambridge, Mass., 1954-55; libr. U.S. Ct. Appeals (1st cir.), Boston, 1955-60; asst. libr., asst. prof. NYU, N.Y.C., 1960-70, assoc. prof., curator, assoc. libr., 1970-78; prof., libr. Suffolk U. Law Sch., Boston, 1978-90, libr., prof. emeritus, 1991—. Author: Mr. Dooley and the Choice of Law, 1963, Mr. Dooley and Mr. Dunne, 1981, Justice Holmes Ex Cathedra, 1966, 91, Searching the Law, 1986, Shakespeare on Lawyers and the Law, 1998. Served with USN, 1942-46. Recipient Dean Frederick A. McDermott award, Suffolk U. Student Bar Ass, 1980. Mem. Assn. Am. Law Schs., New Eng. Law Libr. Democrat. Jewish. Office: 50 Church St Concord MA 01742-3050 E-mail: ebander@acad.suffolk.edu.

BANDLER, JOHN WILLIAM, electrical engineering educator, consultant; b. Jerusalem, Nov. 9, 1941; m. Beth; children: Lydia, Zoe. B.Sc., Imperial Coll. Sci. and Tech., London, 1963, PhD, 1967; D.Sc., U. London, 1976. With Mullard Research Labs., Eng., 1966-67; postdoctoral fellow, sessional lectr. U. Man., Can., 1967-69; asst. prof. McMaster U., Hamilton, Ont., Can., 1969-71, assoc. prof., 1971-74, prof. elec. engring., 1974-2000, prof. emeritus, 2000—, chmn. dept., 1978-79, dean faculty, 1979-81, coordinator group on simulation, optimization and control, 1973-83, dir. research in simulation optimization systems research lab., 1983—. Pres. Optimization Systems Assocs., Inc., 1983-97, Bandler Corp., Inc., 1997—. Author more than 355 tech. papers. Recipient Automated Measurements Career award Automatic Radio Frequency Techniques Group, 1994. Fellow IEEE, Inst. Elec. Engrs. U.K., Royal Soc. Can., Engring. Inst. of Can., Can. Acad. of Engring.; mem. Electromagnetics Acad., Assn. Profl. Engrs. Province of Ont. Office: McMaster U Dept Elec & Comp Engring Hamilton ON Canada L8S 4L7

BANDMAN, ELSIE LUCIER, mental health nurse, ethicist; b. Putnam, Conn., Sept. 16, 1920; d. Alfred J. Sr. and Lea (LeClair) Lucier; m. Bertram Bandman, Aug. 1951; 1 child, Nancy. Diploma, Hartford Hosp. Sch. Nursing, 1942; BS, Simmons Coll., 1949; MA, NYU, 1952; EdD, Columbia U., 1968. Sr. nurse Vis. Nurse Assn. Boston, 1949-51; staff nurse EENT Hartford (Conn.) Hosp., 1942-43; prof. Hunter Coll., N.Y.C., 1968-91. Adj. prof. Hunter Coll., N.Y.C., 1991-95. Author: Nursing Ethics Through the Life Span, 4th edit., 1995, Critical Thinking in Nursing, 2d edit., 1995, Bioethics and Human Rights; contbr. chpts. to books and articles to profl. jours. 1st lt. Nurse Corps, U.S. Army, 1943-46. Recipient award for geriatrics in nursing Pace Coll., Alumnae award for rsch. Columbia U., Pres.'s award Hunter Coll., 1983, award for edn. N.Y. State Nurse's Assn., 1991, Presdl. Citation, N.Y. Counties RN Assn., Dist. 13, 1992. Mem. ANA, Am. Acad. Nursing, Soc. for Rsch. and Edn. in Psychiat. Nursing. Home: 183 Linseed Rd West Hatfield MA 01088

BANDYOPADHYAY, SUPRIYO, electrical engineer, educator, researcher; b. Calcutta, India, July 9, 1958; came to U.S., 1980; s. Bimalendu and Bela (Mukherjee) B.; m. Anuradha Chakroborty, July 12, 1989. B Tech. in Electronics, Indian Inst. Tech., Kharagpur, India, 1980; MSEE, So. Ill. U., 1982; PhD in Elec. Engring., Purdue U., 1985. Asst. prof. U. Notre Dame, Ind., 1987-90, assoc. prof., 1990-96; prof. U. Nebr., 1996—. Vis. asst. prof. Purdue U., West Lafayette, Ind., 1986-87; cons. dept. environ. sci. So. Ill. U., Carbondale, Ill. Contbr. articles to Advances in Energy Tech., Jour. Applied Physics, Superlattices and Microstructures, Surface Sci., IEEE Transactions Elec. Devices, Jour. Vacuum Sci. Tech., Tech. Digest Internat. Electron Device Meeting, numerous others. Rsch. grantee USAF Office Scientific Rsch., 1988, 89, Jesse H. Jones Found., 1988, 91, IBM, 1988, 90-91, U.S. Office Naval Rsch., 1991, NSF. Mem. IEEE (sr.), Am. Phys. Soc., N.Y. Acad. Scis., Tau Beta Pi, Eta Kappa Nu, Sigma Pi Sigma. Hindu. Achievements include patent for quantum dots; research on ultra-high performance sub-micron semi-conductor devices, hot electron and quantum transport in quantum wells and superlattices, Aharonov-Bohm and related quantum interference effects in semiconductor nanostructures, ultrafast optical switching and wave function engineering, localization and wave propagation in disordered media, and experimental cryogenic electronics. Office: Va Commonwealth Univ Elec Engring Dept 601 W Main St Richmond VA 23284

BANERJEE, PRASHANT, industrial engineering educator; b. Calcutta, West Bengal, India, Apr. 15, 1962; came to U.S., 1986; s. Prabhat K. and Bani Banerjee; m. Madhumita Banerjee, Dec. 11, 1987; children: Jay, Ann. BSME, Indian Inst. Tech., Kanpur, India, 1984; MS in Indsl. Engring., Purdue U., 1987, PhD, 1990. Indsl. engr. Tata Steel Co., Jamshedpur, India, 1984-85; asst. prof. U. Ill., Chgo., 1990-96, assoc. prof., 1996—. Cons.

Caterpillar Inc., Peoria, Ill., 1992, Motorola Inc., 1994-97, Monsanto, Inc., 1996—. Author: Automation and Control of Manufacturing Systems, 1991, Object-oriented Technology in Manufacturing, 1992; contbr. articles to profl. jours. NSF rsch. grantee, 1992, 95, Nat. Inst. Standards and Tech. rsch. grantee, 1995. Mem. ASME, Inst. Indsl. Engrs., Inst. Mgmt. Scis., Soc. Mfg. Engrs. Avocations: sports, current events, religious discussions. Home: 708 Kirstin Ct Westmont IL 60559 Office: Univ Ill Engring Dept Chicago IL 60607-7022

BANEY, LORI A. education educator; b. Burke, S.D., Dec. 2, 1962; d. George E. and Lois L. Baney. AAS in Vet. Tech., Colby (Kans.) C.C., 1983; AAS in Histology, Presentation Coll., 1987; BS in Human Resources, Friends U., 1994. Histology technician St. Luke's Hosp., Aberdeen, SD, 1986—87; history/serology technician S.D. State U. Diagnostic Lab., Brookings, 1987—89; instr. Colby C.C., 1989—. Mem.: AAUW, Kans. Vet. Technicians Assn. (pres., NAVTA liaison 1989—), Nat. Vet. Technicians Assn.

BANFIELD, MARIAN D. federal agency administrator; BA in math, Transylvania U.; grad. classes in edn., U. Va, U. Colo., U. No. Colo., Grad. Sch. US Dept Agr. Mgmt. analyst US Dept Edn., Off. Under Sec. of Edn., Planning and Evaluation Svc., Wash., 2002—, US Dept Edn., Off. Intergovernmental and Interagency Affairs, 1997—2002; edn. program spec. US Dept Edn., Off. Vocat. and Adult Edn., 1993—97; project mgr. A.S.K. Assoc., Lawrence, Kans., 1988—90; math. instr. various jr. and sr. HS under contract with A.S. K. Assoc. Office: US Dept Edn 400 Maryland Ave SW Rm 6W223 Washington DC 20202 E-mail: marian.banfield@ed.gov.*

BANGERTER, VERN, secondary education educator; Physics tchr., chmn. dept. Timpview High Sch., Provo, Utah, 1998—. Recipient Gov.'s award, 1992, Pres.'s award, 1994, Huntsman Edn. award, 1995, Disting. Physics Tchr. from Utah award Am. Phys. Soc., 1999, Golden Apple award PTA, 2000; Tandy Tech. scholar, 1992; named Utah State Tchr. of Yr., US West, 1993. Office: Timpview High Sch 3570 N 650 E Provo UT 84604-4675

BANGS, SUSAN ELIZABETH, bilingual educator; b. Rockford, Ill., Sept. 14, 1952; d. Nesbitt Hoyt Bangs Jr. and Elizabeth (Van Wagner) Bangs; 1 child from previous marriage, Jonathan Michael DeJesus. Student, Merrimack Coll., 1970-72; BA, Pa. State U., 1973; MA, West Chester U., 1977; EdD, Boston U., 1986. Cert. tchr., Mass. Asst. prof. Cath. U. P.R., Ponce, 1978-83; bilingual tchr. 2d grade Frost Sch., Lowell, Mass., 1986-90; prof., coord. English as 2d lang. program Harrisburg (Pa.) Area Community Coll., 1990—. Adj. prof. U. Lowell, 1988-90. Author: Images of Puerto Rico, 1983. Lucretia Crocker fellow Mass. Dept. Edn., 1988-89. Fellow Lucretia Crocker Tchrs.' Acad.; mem. Serra (bd. dirs. 1988-89). Roman Catholic.

BANHAM, SANDRA RODGERS, language educator; b. Washington, June 3, 1947; d. Philip Ray Rodgers and Mildred Elizabeth (Rodgers) Nisonger; m. Richard LeRoy Banham; children: Kassaundra, Richard LeRoy Jr., Philip Rodgers, Jeffrey Edward. BA in English/French magna cum laude, U. Utah, 1969, MA, 1973; MA in English/Sociology, S.W. Tex. State U., 1986; MA in TESOL, U. Miss., 1994, PhD in English Edn., 1995. Tchr. Jordan Sch. Dist., Salt Lake City, 1972-74; instr. Austin (Tex.) C.C., 1974-87, So. Meth. U., Dallas, 1988-89; writing cons./instr. U. Memphis, 1989-91; instr. N.W. Miss. C.C., Senatobia, 1991—. Cons. in field. Author: Resource guide to Teaching Literature, 1980; co-author: Global business Trends Procedures, 1996; editor Acctg. Sys. Jour., 1989-91; contbr. articles to profl. jours. Named Woman of the Yr., Austin C.C., 1986, Tchr. of the Yr., 1981. Mem. MLA, Nat. Assn. Developmental English, Nat. Coun. Tchrs. English, Am. Coun. on Tchg. Fgn. Lang., Miss. Coun. Tchrs. English (presenter 1993, 99), Phi Kappa Phi, Phi Delta Kappa, Alpha Delta Pi. Avocation: reading. Office: Northwest Miss Cmty Coll 4975 Highway 51 N # 5504 Senatobia MS 38668-1714

BANIS, ROBERT JOSEPH, pharmaceutical company executive, educator, publisher; b. N.Y.C., Oct. 26, 1943; s. Vincent Nicholas and Roberta Irma (Shwedo) B.; m. Lois Elaine Polson, Jan. 25, 1970 (dec. Sept. 30, 2002); children: Andrea Berit, Lauren Nicole. BS in Sci. Edn., Cornell U., 1967; MS in Animal Nutrition, Purdue U., 1969; PhD in Biochemistry, N.C. State U., 1973; MBA in Mktg. and Fin. with honors, U. Chgo., 1982. Cert. mgmt. acct. NIH postdoctoral fellow Harvard U., Cambridge, Mass., 1973-75; sr. rsch. scientist Armour Pharm. Co., Kankakee, Ill., 1975-79, tech. mgr. biochems. and parenterals, 1979-81, mgr. biochem. and pharm. devel., 1981-83; rsch. group leader health care div. Monsanto Co., St. Louis, 1983-85, mgr. rsch. ops. and fin. planning, 1985-86, mgr. rsch. ops. and fin. planning, Searle R&D Div., 1986-88, dir. ops. and fin., 1988-94; pres. 21st Century Stewardship Inc., St. Louis, 1994-2000; prin. Banis & Assocs., St. Louis, from 1994; mem. adj. faculty Vincennes U., St. Louis, 1994, Webster U., St. Louis, 1995; instr. St. Louis C.C., St. Louis, from 1994. Adj. asst. bus. prof. U. Mo., St. Louis, 1987-92, adj. assoc. prof., full-time lectr., 1992—; founder Sci. & Humanities Press, St. Louis, 1995, prin., pub., CEO, 1995—. Contbg. author: COMPUTE!'s Second Book of VIC, 1983, The Science of Meat and Meat Products, 3d edit., 1987; editor: Copyright Issues for Teachers and Authors, 1997, Sexually Transmitted Diseases, A Practical Guide, 1997, 2d edit., 2003, Inaugural Addresses--Presidents of the U.S. from George Washington to 2004, 1998, Copyright Issues for Librarians, Tchrs. and Authors, 1998; : 2d edit., 2001. Co-chmn. Searle-St. Louis divsn. United Way campaign, 1988-89, chmn., 1989-90, allocations panel vol. Greater St. Louis area, 1991-95, loaned exec. fundraisers, 1993, torchlight spkr., 1993-94; vol. St. John's Mercy Med. Ctr., 1992-98; pres., chmn. bd. Burns Recovered Support Group, Inc., 1993-96; mgmt. cons. United Way Mgmt. Assistance Ctr., 1994—; regional coord. The Phoenix Soc., 1993; gen. chmn. World Burn Congress VII, 1995. Recipient Vol. of Yr. award Trinity Luth. Ch., 1991, United Way Star Communicator award, 1993, 94. Mem. AAAS, Am. Chem. Soc., Inst. Mgmt. Accts. (St. Louis chpt. dir. civic activities, assoc. dir. CMA rev. course 1993-95), Inst. for Ops. Rsch. and Mgmt. Scis. (sec. Gateway chpt. 1993-94, v.p./pres.-elect 1994-95, pres. 1995-96), Am. Burn Assn., St. Louis Pub. Assn. (v.p. 1999), Phi Lambda Upsilon, Beta Gamma Sigma. Home: Manchester, Mo. Deceased.

BANKERT, RICHARD BURTON, immunologist, educator; b. St. Louis, Apr. 22, 1940; children: Darin, Lauren, Katherine. BA, Gettysburg Coll., 1962; DVM, U. Pa., 1968, PhD, 1973. Postdoctoral rsch. fellow vet. medicine U. Pa., Phila., 1968-70, postdoctoral rsch. fellow pathobiology, 1970-73; cancer rsch. scientist II Roswell Pk. Cancer Inst., Buffalo, 1973-76, cancer rsch. scientist III, 1976-77, cancer rsch. scientist IV, V, 1977-83, assoc. chief cancer rsch. scientist VI, 1983—2001; prof. SUNY Med. Sch., Buffalo, 2001—. Achievements include the design and use of human-SCID mouse chimeric models for the evaluation of anti-cancer therapies. Office: Univ Buffalo Med Sch Dept Microbiology 3435 Main St Buffalo NY 14214

BANKOFF, SEYMOUR GEORGE, chemical engineer, educator; b. N.Y.C., Oct. 7, 1921; s. Jacob and Sarah (Rashkin) B.; m. Elaine K. Forgash; children: Joseph, Elizabeth, Laura, Jay. BS, Columbia U., 1940, MS, 1941; PhD in Chem. Engring., Purdue U., 1952. Research engr. Sinclair Refining Co., East Chicago, Ind., 1941-42; process engr. du Pont Manhattan project U. Chgo., Richland, Wash., Arlington, N.J., 1942-48; asst. prof. dept. chem. engring. Rose Poly. Inst., Terre Haute, Ind., 1948-52, assoc. prof., 1952-54, prof., chmn. dept. chem. engring., 1954-58; NSF sci. faculty fellow Calif. Inst. Tech., Pasadena, 1958-59; prof. chem. engring. Northwestern U., Evanston, Ill., 1959—, Walter P. Murphy prof. chem., mech. and nuclear engring., 1971-92; prof. emeritus, 1992—; chmn. energy engring. council Northwestern U., 1975-80, chmn. Ctr. for Multiphase Flow and Transport, 1988—. Vis. scientist Centre d'Etudes Nucléaires, Commissariat d'Energie Atomique, Grenoble, France, 1980; vis. prof. Imperial Coll. Sci. and Tech., London, 1985; cons. to U.S. Nuclear Regulatory Commn., 1974-87, Los Alamos Sci. Lab., 1974-89, Electric Power Research Inst., 1984-86, Westinghouse, 1984—, Savannah River Lab., duPont, 1987—, Korea Atomic Energy Research Inst., 1988; mem. adv. council Ams. for Energy Independence, Washington, 1978—; chmn. vis. com. Brookhaven Nat. Lab., 1984, engring. tech. div. Oak Ridge Nat. Lab., 1986; pres. SGB Assocs. Inc., 1986—. Mem. editl. adv. bd.: Internat. Jour. Multiphase Flow, 1975—, Nuc. Engring. and Design, 1984—; editor 6 vols. on heat transfer; contbr. 200 articles on rsch. in heat transfer and control theory to profl. jours. Recipient Max Jakob Meml. award AICE and ASME, 1987, Donald Q. Kern award AIChE, 1996, Outstanding Chem. Engr. award Purdue U., 1994; named Disting. Engring. Alumnus, 1971; Guggenheim fellow, 1966, Fulbright fellow, 1967, Internat. Ctr. Health and Mass Transfer, Yugoslavia. Fellow AICE (chmn. edn. com. 1968-71, chmn. heat transfer and energy conversion divsn. 1987, Robert E. Wilson Nuc. Chem. Engring. award 1994, Heat Transfer and Energy Conversion Divsn. award 1995), ASME; mem. Am. Nuclear Soc. (co-chmn. U.S. Sci. com., 9th Internat. Heat Transfer Conf., U.S. del. Internat. Heat Transfer Assembly), Nat. Acad. Engring. Achievements include co-invention of resistivity probe for void fraction measurement in gas-liquid flows; contbn. to theory of boiling heat transfer, vapor explosions, stratified condensing flows, stability of thin liquid films. Office: Northwestern Univ Chem Engring Dept Evanston IL 60208-0001

BANKS, CHERRY ANN MCGEE, education educator; b. Benton Harbor, Mich., Oct. 11, 1945; d. Kelly and Geneva (Smith) McGee; m. James A. Banks, Feb. 15, 1969; children: Angela Marie, Patricia Ann. BS, Mich. State U., 1968; MA, Seattle U., 1977, EdD, 1991. Tchr. Benton Harbor Pub. Sch., 1968; staff assoc. Citizens Edn. Ctr. N.W., Seattle, 1984-85; edn. specialist Seattle Pub. Schs., Seattle, 1985-87; pres. Edn. Material and Svcs. Ctr., Edmonds, Wash., 1987—; asst. prof. edn. U. Wash., Bothell, 1992-96, assoc. prof. edn., 1996-2000, prof. edn., 2001—. Cons. Jackson (Miss.) Pub. Schs., 1988, Seattle Pub. Schs., 1988-90, Little Rock Pub. Schs., 1989, Scott Foreman Pub. Co., Glenview, Ill., 1992—; vis. asst. prof. Seattle U., 1991-92. Co-author: March Toward Freedom, 1978, Teaching Strategies for the Social Studies, 1999; co-editor: Multicultural Education: Issues and Perspectives, 1989, rev. edits., 1993, 97; assoc. editor Handbook of Rsch. on Multicultural Edn.; contbr. chpts. to books. Mem. Jack and Jill Am., Seattle, 1978-94, First AME Headstart Bd., Seattle, 1981-83; trustee Shoreline C.C., Seattle, 1983-95; bd. dirs. King County Campfire, Seattle, 1985-88. Recipient Outstanding Commitment and Leadership of C.C. award Western Region Nat. Coun. on Black Am. Affairs, 1989. Mem. ASCD, Nat. Coun. for Social Studies Programs Com. (vice chairperson Carter G. Woodson Book award com. 1991-92, chair person 1992-93, mem. nominating com.), Am. Rsch. Assn., The Links, Inc. (pres. Greater Seattle chpt.), Phi Delta Kappa (founding, Seattle U. chpt.), Alpha Kappa Alpha. Avocations: tennis, swimming, reading, traveling. Office: U Wash Edn Program 22011 26th Ave SE Bothell WA 98021-4900

BANKS, EVELYN YVONNE, middle school educator; b. Houston, Sept. 7, 1951; d. Fred, Sr. and Mary Killings. BS, U. North Tex., 1974; M degree, Tex. So. U., 1993. Dean of instrn. North Forest Ind. Sch. Dist., Houston, 1976—. Counselor/coord. youth coun. N.W. Cmty. Bapt. Ch., 1989-96, dir. Sch. for Christian Living; bd. dirs. N.W. Cmty. Acad., 1996-99. Named Secondary Tchr. of Yr., North Forest Ind. Sch. Dist., Houston, 1992. Mem. Greater Houston Area Reading Coun., Tex. State Tchrs. of English, Delta Sigma Theta, Phi Delta Kappa (adv. 1992). Avocations: reading, participating in church activities, sewing. Home: 8530 Tilgham St Houston TX 77029-3246

BANKS, JAMES ALBERT, educational research director, educator; b. Marianna, Ark., Sept. 24, 1941; s. Matthew and Lula (Holt) Banks; m. Cherry Ann McGee, Feb. 15, 1969; children: Angela Marie, Patricia Ann. AA, Chgo. City Coll., 1963; BE, Chgo. State U., 1964; MA (NDEA fellow 1966-69), Mich. State U., 1967, PhD, 1969; LHD (hon.), Bank St. Coll. Edn., 1993, U. Alaska, Fairbanks, 2000, U. Wis., Parkside, 2001, DePaul U., 2003. Tchr. elementary sch. Joliet, Ill., 1965, Francis W. Parker Sch., Chgo., 1965-66; asst. prof. edn. U. Wash., Seattle, 1969-71, assoc. prof., 1971-73, prof., 1973—, Russell F. Stark univ. prof., 2001—, chmn. curriculum and instrn., 1982-87; dir. Ctr. for Multicultural Edn., Seattle, 1991—. Vis. prof. edn. U. Mich., 1975, Monash U., Australia, 1985, U. Warwick, Eng., 1988, U. Minn., 1991; vis. lectr. U. Southampton, Eng., 1989, Harry F. and Alva K. Ganders disting. lectr. Syracuse U., 1989; disting. scholar lectr. Kent State U., 1978, U. Ariz., 1979, Ind. U., 1983; vis. scholar Brit. Acad., 1983; Sachs lectr. Tchrs. Coll. Columbia U., 1996; Tyler eminent scholar chair Fla. State U., 1998; Carl and Alice Daeufer lectr. U. Hawaii, Manoa, 1999; com. examiners Ednl. Testing Svc., 1974-77; nat. adv. coun. on ethnic heritage studies, U.S. Office Edn., 1975-78; com. on fed. role in ednl. rsch. NAS, 1991-92, mem. com. on developing a rsch. agenda on edn. of ltd. proficient and bilingual students, 1995-97; mem. bd. on children, youth and families NRC and Inst. of Medicine/NAS. Author: Teaching Strategies for Ethnic Studies, 1975, 7th edit., 2003, Teaching Strategies for the Social Studies, 1973, 5th edit., 1999, Teaching the Black Experience, 1970, Multiethnic Education: Practices and Promises, 1977, An Introduction to Multicultural Education, 1994, 2d edit., 1999, Educating Citizens in A Multicultural Soc., 1997, (with Cherry Ann Banks) March Toward Freedom: A History of Black Americans, 1970, 2d edit., 1974, rev. 2nd edit., 1978, Multiethnic Education: Theory and Practice, 1981, 3rd edit., 1994, 4th edit., (new title) Cultural Diversity and Education: Foundations, Curriculum, and Teaching, 2001, (with others) Curriculum Guidlines for Multicultural Education, 1976, rev. edit., 1992, We Americans: Our History and People, 2 vols., 1982; contbg. author Internat. Ency. of Edn., 1985, Handbook of Research on Teacher Education, 1990, Handbook of Research on Social Studies Teaching and Learning, 1991, Encyclopedia of Ednl. Rsch., 1992, Handbook of Research on the Education of Young Children, 1993, Review of Research in Education, vol. 19, 1993; editor: Black Self Concept, 1972, Teaching Ethnic Studies: Concepts and Strategies, 1973, (with William W. Joyce) Teaching Social Studies to Culturally Different Children, 1971, Teaching the Language Arts to Culturally Different Children, 1971, Education in the 80's: Multiethnic Education, 1981, (with James Lynch) Multicultural Education in Western Societies, 1986, (with C. Banks) Multicultural Education: Issues and Perspectives, 1989, 3d edit., 1997, 4th edit., 2001, Handbook of Research on Multicultural Education, 1995, Multicultural Education, Transformative Knowledge, and Action, 1996; editorial bd. Jour. of Tch. Edn., 1985-89, Coun. Interracial Books for Children Bull., 1982-92, Urban Edn., 1991-96, Tchrs. Coll. Record, 1998—, Multicultural Perspectives, 2000—; contbr. articles to profl. jours. Recipient Disting. Career Rsch. award, Nat. Coun. for the Social Studies, 2001, Outstanding Young Man award Wash. State Jaycees, 1975, Outstanding Service in Edn. award Seattle U. Black Student Union, 1985, Pres.'s award TESOL, 1998; Spencer fellow Nat. Acad. Edn., 1973-76; Kellogg fellow, 1980-83; Rockefeller Found. fellow, 1980. Mem. ASCD (bd dirs. 1976-79, Disting. lectr. 1986, Disting. scholar, lectr. 1994, 97), Nat. Acad. Edn., Nat. Coun. Social Studies (bd. dirs. 1973-74, 80-85, pres. 1982, Disting. Career Rsch. in Social Studies award 2001), Internat. Assn. Intercultural Edn. (editl. bd.), Social Sci. Edn. Consortium (bd. dirs. 1976-79), Am. Ednl. Rsch. Assn. (com. on role and status of minorities in edn. rsch. 1992-94, publs. com. 1995-96, pres.-elect 1996-97, pres. 1997-98, exec. bd. 1998-99, Disting. scholar/rschr. on minority edn. 1986, Rsch. Review award 1994, Disting. Career Contbn. award 1996), Phi Delta Kappa, Phi Kappa Phi, Golden Key Nat. Honor Soc., Kappa Delta Pi. Office: U Wash 110 Miller Hall PO Box 353600 Seattle WA 98195-3600

BANKS, THERESA ANN, retired elementary education educator; b. Camden, N.J., Apr. 5, 1946; d. Frederick Douglas and Betty Mae (Norman) Clarke; m. James Donald Banks, Feb. 14, 1987; 1 child, Elizabeth Pearl Banks. BS, Cheyney U., 1968. Third grade tchr. Loudenslager Elem. Sch., Paulsboro, N.J., 1968-81, tchr. basic skills, 1981-86, Billingsport Elem. Sch., Paulsboro, 1986-98; ret., 1998. Tchr. art activities Enrichment Prog., Paulsboro, 1988-98. Chmn. youth program ARC for Paulsboro Sch. System, 1970-80, Sunshine Club/Billingsport Sch., 1990-98, Billingsport Sch. Store, 1992-95; active Aluminum Tab Program, Camden, 1991-98. Mem. NEA, N.J. Edn. Assn., Paulsboro Edn. Assn., Nat. Coun. Tchrs. Math., N.J. Ret. Edn. Assn. Baptist. Avocations: reading, cooking, sewing, art, horses. Home: 253 Deptford Ave Woodbury NJ 08096-3508

BANKS, VINA MICHELLE, primary education educator; b. Hazard, Ky., Dec. 1, 1960; d. William and Hattie (Stafford) B.; m. Jeffery Alan Roark, Aug. 16, 1980 (div. Oct. 1989); 1 child, William Andrew Roark Banks. BA in Elem. Edn. magna cum laude, Morehead State U., 1989, MA in Elem. Guidance and Counseling, 1994. Cert. elem. edn. guidance and counseling grades 1-8. Primary tchr. Letcher (Ky.) County Pub. Schs., 1989—. Emergency team mem. Letcher (Ky.) Elem. Sch., 1994—. Author: Dirty Gertie, 1988. Mem., elder Doermann Meml. Presbyn., Blackey, Ky., 1974—; active Letcher (Ky.) PTSA, 1994. Mem. NEA, Ky. Edn. Assn. (Carl Perkins Meml. scholarship 1988), Letcher County Tchrs. Orgn., Letcher Acad. Assn. (ofcl. 1991—), Kappa Delta Pi. Democrat. Avocations: travel, history. Office: Letcher Elem Sch School Rd Letcher KY 41832

BANNATYNE, MARK WILLIAM MCKENZIE, technical graphics educator; b. West Chester, Pa., May 22, 1952; s. Isobel Steel B.; m. Tatiana Yurievna Shcherbakova, Sept. 2, 1990; children: Yuri Markovich, Kirill Markovich, Anna Ylizaveta. AAS, B.C. Inst. Tech., Burnaby, Can., 1982; BS, Utah State U., 1988, MS, 1991; PhD, Purdue U., 1994. Staff tchr. indsl. tech. and edn. dept. Utah State U., Logan, 1986-89, lectr. indsl. tech. and edn. dept., 1990, grad. prof. indsl. tech. and edn. dept., 1990-92; grad. instr. Purdue U., West Lafayette, Ind., 1992-94; asst. prof. dept. instnl. and curricular studies Coll. Edn. U. Nev., Las Vegas, 1995-97, assoc. dept. head, 2002—03; assoc. prof. tech. graphics dept. Purdue U., West Lafayette, 1997—. Instr. Bridgerland Applied Tech. Ctr., Logan, 1988-92; mem. Engring. State Com., Logan, 1990-92, Gov.'s Coun. on Fgn. Exch., Salt Lake City, 1991-92; presenter Far West Popular Am. Culture Conf., 1996, 97, Rocky Mountain States Conf., Moscow, 1992, Tech. Edn. Assn., Kansas City, Mo., 1994, Jistec '96, Jerusalem, 1996, Far West Popular and Am. Culture Conf., 1996, 97, ASEE Conf., Seattle, 1998, IV'98 Conf. IV'2000, London, 1998, IV' 99 Conf., London, 1999, Siggraph, L.A., 1999; dir. Focus 1996, Moscow, 1996; presenter Winter Sch. Computer Graphics '99 Conf., Plzen, Czech Republic, 1999, 2000. Author: (book review) Tech. Tchr., 1989, ERIC Document, 1996, Popular Culture Rev., 1997; editl. bd. Jour. Tech. Studies; contbr. articles to profl. jours. Leader Boy Scouts of Am., Logan, 1984-86. Fulbright scholar Tula (Russia) State U., 1999-01, 2002. Mem. Internat. Tech. Edn. Assn. (conf. chair fgn. and internat. programs 1991), Am. Soc. Engring. Edn. (vice chmn. internat. divsn.), Assn. for Computing Machinery-Spl. Interest Group for Graphics, Am. Vocat. Assn. (presenter conf. 1991), Internat. Visualisation Soc. (com. mem.), Phi Kappa Phi, Epsilon Pi Tau. Mem. Lds Ch. Avocations: ice hockey, opera, art, foreign travel, history. Office: Purdue U Dept Computer Graphics Tech 1419 Knoy Hall Rm 363 West Lafayette IN 47907-1419 Fax: (765) 494-9267. E-mail: mwbannatyne@tech.purdue.edu.

BANNISTER, ROBERT CORWIN, JR., historian, educator; b. Bklyn., June 4, 1935; s. Robert C. and Ruth (Allen) B.; m. Joan Turner, June 8, 1958; children: Robert Stanley, Emily E., Paul Andrew, James Peter. BA, Yale U., 1955, Oxford U., Eng., 1957, MA, 1961; PhD, Yale U., 1961. Instr. history Yale U., New Haven, 1960-62; asst. to full prof. Swarthmore Coll., Pa., 1962-98, ret., 1998. Bicentennial prof. U. Helsinki, 1977-78; Fulbright prof. U. Rome, 1985, U. Leiden, Netherlands, 1992; mem. advanced placement program Ednl. Testing Service, Princeton, N.J., 1963-79; vis. prof. U. Queensland, Australia, 1988. Author: Ray Stannard Baker, 1966, Social Darwinism: Science and Myth, 1978, Sociology and Scientism, 1987, Jessie Bernard: The Making of a Feminist, 1991; editor: American Values in Transition, 1972, On Liberty, Society and Politics: The Essential Essays of William Graham Sumner, 1992. Mem. Am. Studies Assn., Orgn. Am. Historians Democrat. Office: Swarthmore College Ave Swarthmore PA 19081-1390 E-mail: rbannis1@swarthmore.edu.

BANSINATH, MYLARRAO, pharmacologist, educator; b. Mudigere, India, Sept. 4, 1950; came to U.S., 1985; s. Mylari G. and Nagarathnamma T. Rao; m. Sabitha M.K. Bansinath, Jan. 27, 1989; children: Bina B., Bindu B. BSc, U. Mysore, Karnataka, India, 1970; MSc, Kasturba Med. Coll., Manipal, India, 1974; PhD, Inst. Med. Edn. & Rsch., Chandigarh, India, 1984. Lectr. Kasturba Med. Coll., 1975-79, M.S.R. Med. Coll., Bangalore, India, 1983-84; rsch. assoc. U. Ill., Chgo., 1985-86; rsch. asst. prof. NYU Med. Ctr., N.Y.C., 1986—. External examiner for PhD, Gujarat U., Mangalore and Madras U. Contbr. articles to Jour. Pharmacology, Jour. Pharmacology Toxicology methods, Jour. Neurochemistry, Neurchem. Rsch., Neurosci., Gen. Pharmacology; contbr. chpts. to books. Inst. Med. Edn. and Rsch. scholar, 1979-83; fellow J.J. Hosp. Bombay, 1981, Indian Coun. Med. Rsch., 1981. Mem. Am. Soc. Pharmacology and Exptl. Therapeutics, Indian Pharmacol. Soc. (life), Assn. Physiologists and Pharmacologists India (life), N.Y. Acad. Scis. Achievements include research in defining the pharmacological and biochemical properties of opiate and excitatory amino acid receptor sytbypes, effect of nitric oxide and cocaine in regulation of glial and neuronal cell proliferation. Home: 26 Shawn Ct New Brunswick NJ 08902-5009 Office: NYU Med Ctr Anesthesia 550 1st Ave New York NY 10016-6402

BAO, JOSEPH YUE-SE, orthopedist, microsurgeon, educator; b. Shanghai, Feb. 20, 1937; s. George Zheng-En and Margaret Zhi-De (Wang) B.; m. Delia Way, Mar. 30, 1963; children: Alice, Angela. MD, Shanghai First Med. Coll., 1958. Intern affiliated hosps. Shanghai First. Med. Coll.; resident Shanghai Sixth People's Hosp., orthopaedist, 1958-78, orthopaedist-in-charge, 1978-79, vice chief orthopaedist, 1979-84; rsch. assoc. orthop. hosp. U. So. Calif., L.A., 1985-90, 94—, vis. clin. assoc. prof. dept. orthopedics, 1986-89; coord. microvascular svcs. Orthopaedic Hosp., L.A., 1989-91; clin. assoc. prof. dept. orthopedics U. So. Calif., L.A., 1989—, clin. assoc. prof. plastic surgery, 1997—; attending physician Los Angeles County and U. So. Calif. Med. Ctr., L.A., 1986, 90—, Orthopaedic Hosp., L.A., 1998—, Coast Plaza Doctors Hosp., Norwalk, Calif., 1999—. Cons. Rancho Los Amigos Med. Ctr., Downey, Calif., 1986. Contbr. articles to profl. jours., chpts. to books. Mem. Internat. Microsurg. Soc., Am. Soc. for Reconstructive Microsurgery, Am. Soc. for Peripheral Nerve, Orthop. Rsch. Soc., Societe Internationale de Chirurgie Orthopedique et de Traumatologie, Calif. Med. Assn., Calif. Orthopedic Assn., L.A. Med. Assn. Home: 17436 Terry Lyn Ln Cerritos CA 90703-8522 Office: 13132 Studebaker Rd Ste 7 A Norwalk CA 90650

BAR, ROBERT S. endocrinologist, educator; b. Gainesville, Tex., Dec. 2, 1943; s. Samuel and Emma (Kaplan) B.; m. Laurel Ellen Burns, June 23, 1970; children: Katharine June, Matthew Tomas. BS, Tufts Univ., 1964; MS in Biochemistry, MD, Ohio State U., 1970. Medicine intern Pa. Hosp., Phila., 1970-71; medicine resident Ohio State Univ., Columbus, 1971-72; asst. prof., dept. medicine Univ. Iowa, Iowa City, 1977-82, assoc. prof., dept. medicine, 1982-86, prof., dept. medicine, 1986—. Acting dir. divsn. of endocrinology and metabolism, U. Iowa, 1985-90; dir. diabetes-endocrinology rsch ctr., U. Iowa, 1986—, nat. rsch. svc. award in endocrinology, 1984—, endocrinology fellowship program, 1979—, divsn. of endocrinology and metabolism, 1990—; mem. ad hoc study sect. NIH, 1985, dir. diabetes-endocrinology rsch. ctr. 1986; mem. editorial bd. Jour. of Clin. Endocrinology and Metabolism, 1984-87; mem study sect. Nat.

Veterans Adminstrn., 1984-87; v.p. rsch. Nat. Am. Diabetes Assn., 1987-88; mem. orgn. com. Endothelium and Diabetes Symposium, Melbourne, 1988; dir. VA/JDF Diabetes Rsch. Ctr., 1997; mem. study sect. numerous assns. and coms.; guest reviewer numerous jours. Editor Endocrinology, 1987-89, Advances in Endocrinology and Metabolism, 1989—. Mem. Am. Diabetes Assn., Am. Soc. for Clin. Investigation, Assn. Am. Physicians, Endocrine Soc., Ctrl. Soc. for Clin. Rsch., Sigma Xi. Office: U Iowa Hwy 6 West 3E19 VA Iowa City IA 52246

BARABASH, CLAIRE, lawyer, special education administrator, psychologist; b. N.Y.C., Oct. 22, 1940; d. Maurice Isaac and Sarah (Libowsky) B. BA, Bklyn. Coll., 1960; MS, CUNY, 1962; PhD, NYU, 1979; JD, Bklyn. Law Sch., 1994. Bar: N.J. 1994, N.Y. 1995, Ala. 2000; Diplomate Am. Coll. Forensic Examiners; lic. psychologist, sch. psychologist; cert. sch. dist. adminstr. Psychology intern Bklyn. Coll. Edn. Clinic, 1962-63; sch. psychologist Yonkers (N.Y.) Bd. Edn., 1963-65, N.Y.C. Bd. Edn., 1965-78, regional coord., 1978-82, dept. asst. supt., 1982-95, asst. supt. for clin. svcs., 1991-92; pvt. practice Margaretville, NY, 1996—; forensic cons., 1999—. Adj. assoc. prof. NYU, 1979-80, L.I. U., Bklyn., 1988-93. Named Outstanding Spl. Educator of Yr. Orthodox Jewish Tchrs., 1990, Brian E. Tomlinson award for disting. contbns. in psychology, 1991. Mem. APA, ABA, N.Y. State Bar Assn., N.Y.C. Assn. Sch. Psychologists (pres. 1979-80), Adminstrv. Women in Edn. (Woman of Yr. 1989, chair mentoring com. 1989-90), Acad. for Pub. Edn. Home: 101 Clark St Brooklyn NY 11201-2746

BARAL, LILLIAN, artist, retired educator; b. Perehinsko, Poland; d. Leon and Esther (Ludmer) B. BA, Hunter Coll., 1939, MA in Art, 1969. Cert. fine arts, secondary English, elem. tchr., N.Y. Sec., publicity asst. Coun. for Democracy, N.Y.C.; translator, radio script writer, announcer U.S. Office of War Info., Voice of Am., N.Y.C.; writer, publicity specialist Citizens Com. on Displaced Persons, N.Y.C., Consulate Gen. of Israel, N.Y.C.; publicity specialist Madison Books, Pub. House, N.Y.C., Brandeis U., Waltham, Mass.; pub. rels. dir. Israel Govt. Tourist Office, N.Y.C.; publicity asst. Huntington Hartford Gallery of Modern Art, N.Y.C.; fine arts tchr. Parsons Jr. H.S., Queens, N.Y., 1962-82; painter, sculptor, 1956—. Art tour leader 92d St YMHA, 1985, 86. Exhbns. include N.Y. Pub. Libr., Little Gallery, 1966, Whitehouse Gallery, N.Y.C., 1967, Am. House, N.Y.C., 1968, Lord & Taylor, N.Y.C., 1970, Center Art Gallery, N.Y.C., 1971, Marie Pellicone Gallery, N.Y.C., 1979, Womanart Gallery, N.Y.C., 1979, BFM Gallery, N.Y.C., 1980, Bennet Gallery, Fairfield, Conn., 1981, Queens Mus., 1981, New Sch. for Social Rsch., N.Y.C., 1982, Lever House, N.Y.C., 1983, W.C. Post Coll., L.I., N.Y., 1984, Southhampton Coll., L.I., 1984, Queensborough C.C. Art Gallery, N.Y.C., 1985, 86, UAHC Gallery, N.Y.C., 1988, Mari Galleries, Mamaroneck, N.Y., 1989; represented in permanent collections Yad Vashem Mus., Jerusalem, Hebrew U., Jerusalem; shows at B'nai B'rith Klutznick Nat., Jewish Mus., Washington, Libr. Gallery, U. Maine, Augusta, Chaffee Ctr. Visual Arts, Rutland, Vt., Holocaust Mus. and Resource Ctr. Jewish Fedn., Scranton, Pa., 1995, Davidson and Daughters Gallery, Portland, Maine, 1998; also numerous pvt. collections; subject newspaper, mag. articles, TV interview. Mem. N.Y. Artists Equity (exec. bd. 1985-86), United Fedn. Tchrs., Mus. Modern Art (N.Y.C.). Home: 98-50 67th Ave Forest Hills NY 11374-4965 E-mail: bobblat@worldnet.att.net.

BARAL, WANDA, elementary school educator; b. Phila., Feb. 23, 1949; d. Jerome and Gloria Baral. BA, Calif. State U., Long Beach, 1971; MA, U. San Francisco, 1974. Tchr. Ocean View Sch. Dist., Huntington Beach, Calif., 1973—. Cons. in field; mem. Calif. History Project, 1989—, Calif. Lit. Project, 1988—, Calif. Dept. Edn., Calif. Learning Assessment System History/Social Studies Devel. Team Calif. State Dept. Edn., CDE/CTC Accreditation Rev. Team, Nes Bias Rev. Team; tchr., researcher UCLA; author Interact, Inc. Mem. Calif. Coun. for Social Studies (bd. dirs. 1992—, pres. 2000-01), Orange County Assn. for Social Studies (bd. dirs. 1988—, pres.), Phi Delta Kappa. Avocations: guitar, art, travel, cooking, intellectual exploration.

BARANOVICH, DIANA LEA, music educator; b. New Orleans, Nov. 1, 1961; d. Walter Horace and Margaret (Rothman) B.; m. Robert Charles Shoup, June 12, 1982; children: Nadia Lea, Raymond Christopher., Tammy Tran MusB, Loyola U., 1983, MEd, 1986; Dalcroze cert., Carnegie-Mellon U., 1993; postgrad., U. Houston, 1990-93. Cert. tchr. music, dance, drama, English, h.s. counselor, Tex. Tchr. music St. Tammany Schs., Slidell, La., 1983-84, Lynn Oaks Sch., Braithwaite, La., 1984-86; choir dir. Fort Bend Pub. Sch., Houston, 1990-93; tchr., cons. music and dance New Orleans, 1996—. Prof. music edn. Normal U. Beijing, China, 1995-97; cons., trainer tchrs. music and dance Kinderland Learning Ctr., Singapore, 1996—; vol. tchr. dance, movement and Chinese studies Alice Harte Elem. Sch., New Orleans, 1996-99; pvt. tchr. piano and movement, 1996—; tchr. tap dancing and choreography New Orleans Dance Acad., 1997-99; fine arts coord. Malaysian Ministry Edn., Kuala Lumpur, 2002—. Contbr. articles to profl. jours. Sponsor St. Joseph's Indian Sch., Childreach, Food for the Poor. Mem. Music Tchrs. Nat. Assn., Music for People, Dalcroze Soc. Am. (patron). Avocations: theater, ethnic dancing, creative writing, composing children's music, piano. Home: 2531 Binz St Houston TX 77004-7565

BARANSKI, LOIS MAE, special education educator; b. Chgo., Nov. 22, 1947; d. Kenneth Everett and Luella Marjorie (Gunderson) Nelson; m. Richard Baranski, Sept. 13, 1969; 1 child, Adam Jon. BS in Elem. Edn., So. Ill. U., 1970; MA in Edn. and Reading, Calif. State Coll., 1978. Cert. tchr., Calif., Ill. Tchr. Steeleville (Ill.) Community Unit Dist., 1970-71; substitute tchr., then tchr. 3d grade San Felipe Del Rio (Tex.) Consol. Sch. Dist., 1972-73; substitute tchr. San Bernardino (Calif.) Unified Dist., 1974-76; tchr. reading 8th grade Colton Unified Sch. Dist., Bloomington, Calif., 1978-79, tchr. high sch. spl. edn. Colton, Calif., 1979-80; tchr. spl. edn., jr. high reading Cypress (Ill.) Elem. Sch. Dist., 1980—. Presenter at profl. confs. Co-author: Reading Resource Book for Reading Teachers, 1978, L.D./B.D. Curriculum Guide for Special Education Teachers, 1988. Chmn., sec. bd. dirs. Sunrise Pre-Sch., Anna, Ill., 1980-83; chmn., treas., troop leader Anna area Boy Scouts Am., 1984-90. Mem. NEA, Ill. Edn. Assn., Cypress Edn. Assn. (pres. 1990-92, v.p. 1992—). Avocations: reading, crewel stitching, crafts, travel, collecting stamps. Home: 9768 Bitten Dr Brighton MI 48114-9699

BARANY, JAMES WALTER, industrial engineering educator; b. South Bend, Ind., Aug. 24, 1930; s. Emery Peter and Rose Anne Barany; m. Judith Ann Flanigan, Aug. 6, 1960 (div. 1982); 1 child, Cynthia Getty. BSME, Notre Dame U., 1953; MS in Indsl. Engring., Purdue U., 1958, PhD, 1961. Prodn. worker Studebaker Corp., 1949-52; prodn. liaison engr. Bendix Aviation Corp., 1955-56; mem. faculty Sch. Indsl. Engring. Purdue U., West Lafayette, Ind., 1958—, now prof., assoc. head indsl. engring. Sch. Indsl. Engring. Cons. Taiwan Productivity Ctr., Western Electric, Gleason Gear Works, Am. Oil Co., Timken Co. Served with U.S. Army, 1954—55. Recipient Best Counselor award Purdue U., 1978, Best Engring. Tchr. award, 1983, 89, Outstanding Indsl. Engring. Tchr. award, 1983, 87, 89, Outstanding Tchr. award Purdue U., 1989, Marion Scott Faculty Exemplary Character award Purdue U., 1993, 2000, NSF and Easter Seal Found. rsch. grantee, 1961, 63, 64, 65; Purdue Tchg. Acad. founding fellow, 1997, Indiana Gov.'s Sagamore of the Wabash award, 1998; named Purdue Book Great Tchrs., 1999. Mem. Inst. Indsl. Engring. (life, Fellows award 1982, Disting. Educator award 1989, Disting. Svc. award 1992, Cert. of Svc. Appreciation 1994, Work Measurement award 2000, Young Engr. Mentoring award 2001), Soc. Mfg. Engr., Am. Soc. Engring. Edn., Methods Time Measurement Rsch. Assn., Human Factors and Ergonomics Soc., Order of Engr., Sigma Xi, Alpha Pi Mu, Tau Beta Pi (Eminent Engr. award 1982). Home: 1120 Northwestern Ave W West Lafayette IN 47906-2503 Office: Purdue U IE GRIS 315 N Grant St West Lafayette IN 47907-2023 E-mail: jwb@ecn.purdue.edu.

BARAT, CHRISTOPHER EUGENE, mathematician, educator; b. N.Y.C., Oct. 18, 1962; s. G. Steven and Rosemary (Lee) B. BS in Math. with highest honors, U. Notre Dame, 1984; MS in Applied Math., Brown U., 1986, PhD in Applied Math., 1989. Asst. prof. math. Randolph-Macon Coll., Ashland, Va., 1989-93; adj. faculty Va. State U. and J. Sargeant Reynolds C.C., 1993; assoc. prof. math. Va. State U., 1994—. Mem. Am. Stats. Assn., Math. Assn. Am., Phi Beta Kappa. Republican. Roman Catholic.

BARBA, HARRY, author, educator, publisher; b. Bristol, Conn., June 17, 1922; s. Michael Hovanessian and Sultone (Mnatsignanian) B.; m. Roberta Ashburn Riley, 1955 (div. 1963); 1 child, Gregory Robert; m. Marian Andrea Homelson, Oct. 29, 1965. AB, Bates Coll., 1944; MA, Harvard U., 1951; MFA, U. Iowa, 1960, PhD with honors, 1963; postgrad., NYU, 1955-56, Boston U., 1950-51, NYU, 1955-56, CCNY, 1956-57, Columbia U., 1957-58, U. Middlebury, 1945. Stringer, feature writer Bristol (Conn.) Press, 1944-45; file clk. supr. new departure GM Corp., 1944-45; instr. English and writing Wilkes Coll., 1947, U. Conn., Hartford, 1947-49; tchr. English Seward Park H.S., N.Y.C., 1955-59; instr. U. Iowa, 1959-63; asst. prof. Skidmore Coll., 1963-68; prof. English, dir. writing Marshall U., Huntington, W.Va., 1968-70, title I writing arts dir., 1969-70; comml. and pub. svcs. radio-TV interviewee, reader, lectr., 1961—; prof. English, dir. writing Marshall U., Huntington, W.Va., 1968-70; Title I Writing Arts dir. W.Va., 1969-70. Vis. prof., Fulbright grantee, vis. Am. specialist Damascus U., 1963-64; disting. vis. lectr. contemporary lit., cons. SUNY, Albany, 1977-78; reader, lectr. USIS Libr., Damascus, Syria, 1963-64; innovator, dir., devel. writers confs. for creative growth in several nat., regional and urban contexts, 1964—; dir. The Workshop Under the Sky, 1968—; pres., pub., exec. dir. Harian Creative Books, Ballston Spa, N.Y., 1967—; cons. Bantam Books, Random House, 1967, 69-70, Nat. Found. for Arts, Nat. Found. for Humanities, U.S. Dept. Edn., N.Y. State Coun. Arts, N.Y. State Edn. Dept., Poets & Writers, Inc., Harvard U., others; pres. several instns. (acad. and civic), 1963—, founding pres. and socially functional writer; founder, dir. Skidmore's Writers and Educator's Conf., 1967, The Workshop Under the Sky, 1970—. Author: For the Grape Season, 1960, 3 By Harry Barba, 1967, 3 X 3, 1969, The Case for Socially Functional Education, Art and Culture, 1970—74, One of A Kind (The Many Faces and Voices of America), 1976, The Day the World Went Sane, 1979; author: (compiled and co-edited with Marian Barba) (series) What's Cooking in Congress? A Congressional Smorgasbord of Recipes, 1979, 1983; author: Gospel According to Everyman, 1981, Round Trip to Byzantium, 1985 (Pulitzer prize nominee, 1985), When the Deep Purple Falls, a Story (PEN Syndicated Fiction award, 1985); author: (co-published with Princeton U. Press) Mona Lisa Smiles, 1993; reviewer: plays Three Plays by William Saroyan; author: The Nightingale Sings. Founder, dir. Skidmore Coll. Writers and Educators Conf., 1967, Adirondack-Metroland Writers and Educators Conf., 1967—. Recipient cert. of merit Dictionary Internat. Biography Ctr., 1974, Internat. Man of Yr. award Cambridge (Eng.) Internat. Biographical Ctr., 1995-96, Internat. Biog. Inst.; grad. fellow U. Iowa, 1961-62, Yaddo residence fellow, 1950, Macdowell Colony residence fellow, 1970, World's Hall of Fame in Lit., 1997—, Guggenheim fellow, 1989-90; Skidmore rsch. grantee, 1965-68, N.Y. State coun. Arts grantee, 1971, U. Benedeum grantee, 1969; established Harian Creative awards for fiction, poetry, essays, mus. compositions, photography and graphic arts, 1973. Mem. MLA, Coll. English Assn., Authors Guild, Writers Union PEN, Com. Small Press Editors and Pubs., Harvard Grad. Soc. Advanced Study and Rsch., Harvard Alumni Assn., Harvard Club Ea. N.Y. (dir. 1975-79). Achievements include writing and educating for the mainstreaming of Am.'s multiple ethnic, religious, and racial groups, and for increasing the authority of the UN for the benefit of world's peoples. Home and Office: 47 Hyde Blvd Ballston Spa NY 12020-1607

BARBER, CHARLES TURNER, political science educator; b. Washington, Aug. 30, 1941; s. Charles Turner and Vera Hess (Nolt) B.; m. Billie Kathleen Jaco, June 16, 1968 (div. 1976); children: Gretchen, Katrina; m. Sandra Powell Anderson, Apr. 18, 1978 (div. 1987); m. Carolyn Louise Roth, Aug. 4, 1991. BA cum laude, W.Va. Wesleyan Coll., 1963; MA, Am. U., 1965; PhD, The Am. U., 1967. Asst. prof. polit. sci. East Tenn. State U., Johnson City, 1967-71, Ind. State U., Evansville, 1971-75, assoc. prof., 1975-83; prof. U. So. Ind., Evansville, 1983—, chmn. dept. polit. sci., 1986—. Rep. Truman Scholarship Found., Washington, 1975-90; editl. cons. Prentice Hall, 1987, West Pub., 1990, 94, 95, Houghton-Mifflin, 1991, Harcourt, Brace, Jovanovich, 1992, Wadsworth, 1993; faculty sponsor Polit. Sci. Club U. So. Ind., 1988—; bd. dirs. Ind. Cons. Internat. programs, 1987—; dep. dir. Ind. Com. for U.S.-Arab Rels., 1989—, U. Mich. Inst. on Islam, 1989, Internat. Faculty Devel. Seminar, Maastricht, The Netherlands, 1994. Contbr. articles to profl. jours. Chmn. UN Day Evansville, 1980; moderator deacons 1st Presbyn. Ch., Evansville, 1982-85; judge coord. oratorical contest Am. Legion, Evansville, 1987-93; active All-Star Conv. and Visitors Bur., Evansville, 1987; candidate sch. bd. Evanville-Vanderburgh Sch. Corp., 1990. Recipient Group Study Exchange award Rotary Found., India, 1975-76, Faculty Enrichment award Can. Embassy, 1987, Summer Seminar award NEH, 1977; Malone fellow, 1987, 92. Mem. Am. Coun. Québec Studies, Internat. Polit. Sci. Assn., Acad. Coun. on the UN Sys., Internat. Studies Assn., Ind. Acad. Social Scis., Am. Polit. Sci. Assn., Western Polit. Sci. Assn., Soc. for Utopian Studies, Communal Studies Assn. Friends of Mesker Park Zoo. Democrat. Presbyterian. Home: 10801 S Woodside Dr Evansville IN 47712-8422 Office: U So Ind 8600 University Blvd Evansville IN 47712-3534

BARBER, MICHELE A. special education educator; b. Titusville, Pa., Jan. 18, 1964; d. Robert R. Averill and Carol A. (Fish) Covell; m. Timothy M. Barber, July 12, 1986. BS in Elem. Edn., U. of Pa., Clarion, 1985; MEd in Reading, U. of Pa., Slippery Rock, 1990; reading recovery cert., Edinboro U. Pa., 2000; postgrad., Nova Southeastern U., 2001. Substitute tchr. Warren County Sch. Dist., 1985-86; head tchr. Happy Hours Children's Ctr., Vienna, Va., 1986; substitute tchr. Fairfax County Sch. Dist., Springfield, Va., 1987, various suburban schs., New Castle, Pa., 1987-90, Pitts., 1990-91; ESL tchr. Allegheny Intermediate Unit, Pitts., 1991, 92-93; reading specialist Woodland Hills Sch. Dist., Pitts., 1991-92, 93-94, New Brighton (Pa.) Sch. Dist., 1993; reading recovery tchr. Oil City (Pa.) Sch. Dist., 1994-95, Erie City (Pa.) Sch. Dist., 1994—. Fed. programs monitor Pa. Dept. Edn., Harrisburg, 1993-94; early childhood task force Woodland Hills Sch. Dist., 1994. Mem. Sch. Improvement Coun.; asst. troop leader Girl Scouts U.S.; Ophelia Project leader. Dr. Barbara Barnes scholar, Titusville, Pa., 1981; Title I Parent Involvement grant. Mem. NEA, ASCD, Three Rivers Reading Coun., Internat. Reading Assn., Reading Recovery Coun. N.Am., Nat. Coun. Tchrs. Math., Pa. Assn. Fed. Programs Coords., Erie Reading Coun. Avocations: reading, travel, volleyball, golfing, swimming. Home: 3810 Blossom Terr Erie PA 16506 E-mail: barbers@erie.net.

BARBER, MURIEL P. retired special education educator; b. St. Louis, Oct. 30, 1946; d. Conway C. and Rose M. (Blow) Pinkston. BS, So. Ill. U., 1969, MS, 1997. Spl. edn. tchr. Vandalia (Ill.) Unit Dist., 1969-72, Carlyle (Ill.) Community Unit Dist. # 1, 1972-91, CC tchr., 1991-94, inclusion facilitator, 1994-95. Sec. Bond Co. Parent Group, Greenville, Ill., 1970-74; head coach Area 12 Spl. Olympics, Carlyle, 1973-91, vol., 1992-93. Fellow Ill. State U., Bloomington, 1969. Mem. Carlye Photography Club, Coun. Exceptional Children (sec. 1989-93), Phi Kappa Phi. Avocations: photography, travel.

BARBER, NORMA ANN, secondary education educator; b. Emmett, Idaho, June 22, 1953; d. Willard Andrus and Theo Elaine (Garner) Jensen; m. Clinton Earl Barber, Mar. 17, 1979; children: Laura Ann, Janet Marie, Susan Elaine. AA, Treasure Valley C.C., 1973; BS in Edn., Ea. Oreg. State Coll., 1975; MEd, Ea. Oreg. U., 1998. Cert. secondary tchr., Oreg. Owner, mgr. Gen. Store, Ukiah, Oreg., 1988—; tchr. Ukiah Sch. Dist., 1991—. Tchr., rschr. Oreg. Writing Project at Eastern, LaGrande, 1997—, co-dir., 1999—; instr. student writers workshop, Ukiah, 1992-98; mem. crisis interventin flight team Umatilla-Morrow Schs., 1999—. Vol. EMT Ukiah Quick Response Team, 1984—; adv. com. Umatilla County Health Dept., Pendelton, Oreg., 1986-88; sch. bd. mem. Ukiah Sch. Dist., 1981-83. Named Homemaker of Yr., Umatilla County, 1986, Oreg. Tchr. of Yr., 2001. Mem. ASCD, Assn. Rural Tchrs. English, Oreg. Tchrs. English. Avocations: quilting, cooking, reading, writing, gardening.

BARBER, ROBERT CHARLES, physics educator; b. Sarnia, Ont., Can., Apr. 20, 1936; s. Alexander Sinclair and Emma Violet (Jackson) B.; m. Carole Holland, Sept. 15, 1962; children: Anne Margaret Barber-Somers, Ruth Elizabeth Barber-Dueck, Keith Robert Watson-Barber. BSc, McMaster U., 1958, PhD, 1962. Postdoctoral fellow McMaster U., Hamilton, 1962-65; asst. prof. physics U. Man., Winnipeg, 1965-68, assoc. prof., 1968-75, prof., 1975—, acting head dept., 1984, head dept., 1987—96. Vis. prof. U. Minn., Mpls., 1971-72; chmn. grad. and postdoctoral fellowships com. 3, Nat. Scis. and Engring. Rsch. Coun., 1988, 89, mem. postdoctoral fellowship grant selection com., 1987, mem. adv. com. tenure abroad, 1988; mem. Internat. Postdoctoral Com., 1991-93, chmn., 1993. Bd. dirs. Alcohol and Drug Edn. Svcs., Inc., Man., 1976-79; asst. leader 135th Winnipeg Cub Pack, Boy Scouts Can., 1977-80; mem. Winnipeg S. Foster Parents Assn., foster parent, 1983-84, 85, 87, 88; bd. deacons Broadway-First Bapt. Ch., 1966-68, 73-74, chmn. bd. 1968, 1986-88, chmn. Christian edn. com., 1969-71, 82-83, 85-86; bd. dirs. Bapt. Union of Western Can., 1981-84, chmn. task force on Bapt. Leadership Tng. Sch., Calgary, 1982-83, mem. Man. exec. bd., 1981-84. Nat. Scis. Engring. Rsch. Coun. grantee. Mem. Internat. Union Pure and Applied Physics (assoc. sec.-gen. 1993-99, sec. commn. symbols, units, nomenclature atomic masses and fundamental constants 1978-81, 81-84, chmn. commn. 1984-87, 87-91, head Can. del. to gen. assembly 1981, 84, active other coms.), Internat. Union Pure and Applied Chemistry (titular 1979-98, assoc. 1987-91, mem. commn. atomic weights and isotope abundances), Can. Assn. Physicists (chair profl. cert. com. 1999—, dir. full mems. 1988-2000, councillor Man. sect. 1974-76), Can. Assn. Univ. Tchrs. Office: U Manitoba Dept Phys & Astronomy 301 Allen Bldg Winnipeg MB Canada R3T 2N2 Office Fax: 204-474-7622.

BARBER, SHANNON MICHELLE, secondary school educator; b. Aurora, Ill., Sept. 30, 1974; d. Joseph Howard Barber and Cynthia Jane (Stanke) Grossman. BS in Biology with honors, Eckerd Coll., 1996; postgrad. student U. Minn. Tchg.-lab. asst. for vertebrate and cell biology Eckerd Coll., St. Petersburg, Fla., 1993-96, Howard Hughes med. grant-rsch. asst., 1995-96; mid. sch. and h.s. sci. tchr. Makua Lani Christian Sch., Holualoa, Hawaii, 1996-98, tchg., adminstrn., parents, and students (TAPS) voting mem., 1996-97; sec. Luth. Bible Translators, Aurora, Ill., 1998—. Voting mem. Eckerd Coll. Natural Sci. Senate, St. Petersburg, 1995-96. Vol. disaster relief svcs. ARC, St. Petersburg, 1995. Mem. Sigma Xi, Omicron Delta Kappa. Independent. Achievements include first to determine nucleotide and protein encoding sequencing for grey wolf and polar bear interluekin-2. Home: YCR Officers' Row Bldg 27 Yellowstone National Park WY 82190 Mailing: PO Box 644 Gardiner MT 59030

BARBER, SUSAN CARROL, biology educator; b. Anson, Tex., Oct. 2, 1952; d. Raymond Reginald and Loreta (Judkins) Barber; m. Robert Joseph Mulholland Jr., Oct. 17, 1981 (dec. 1989); m. David P. Nagle Jr., Oct. 11, 1991. BS, Howard Payne U., 1974; MS, Okla. State U., 1975; PhD, U. Okla., 1980. Asst. prof. biology Sam Houston State U., Huntsville, Tex., 1979-82; from asst. to assoc. prof., chair dept. biology Okla. City U., 1983—92, prof., chair dept. biology, 1992—2003, asst. v.p. acad. affairs, prof. biology, 2003—. Adj. prof. U. Okla., Norman, 1982—; cons. Okla. Biol. Survey, Norman, others; presenter in field. Recipient Sears Teaching 2d pl. award Oklahoma City U., 1991, United Meth.-related Instn. Exemplary Teaching award, 1992. Mem. Bot. Soc. Am., Am. Soc. Plant Taxonomists, Beta Beta Beta (advisor 1985—). Home: 1313 Brookside Dr Norman OK 73072-6348 Office: Oklahoma City Univ Dept Biology 2501 N Blackwelder Ave Oklahoma City OK 73106-1493

BARBERA, ANTHONY THOMAS, accountant, educator; b. Bklyn., Oct. 5, 1955; s. Thomas Anthony and Rachelle Regina (Crocitto) Barbera. BS summa cum laude, St. John's U., N.Y., 1977; MBA, 1987. CPA N.Y. Staff acct. Price Waterhouse, N.Y.C., 1977-80, sr. acct., 1980-83, audit mgr., 1983-84; grad. asst. St. John's U., Jamaica, NY, 1985-87, asst. prof., 1987-96; vis. asst. prof. SUNY, Old Westbury, 1996—, dir. internships, placement and adminstrn., 1998—. Mem. com. fin. acctg. Savs. Banks Assn. N.Y. State, N.Y.C., 1983—84. Contbr. articles to profl. jours. Recipient William R. Donaldson award, Cath. Accts. Guild, Diocese of Bklyn., 1977; N.Y. State Regents scholar, 1973—77, Robert E. Gillece fellow, CUNY Grad. Sch., 1989—93, AICPA doctoral fellow, 1989—92. Mem.: AICPA, Decision Scis. Inst., Securities Industry Assn., Am. Acctg. Assn., N.Y. State Soc. CPAs (prof. conduct com., mem. recruitment com. CPA careers, mem. cooperation com. with ednl. instns.), KC, Omicron Delta Epsilon, Beta Gamma Sigma, Beta Alpha Psi. Republican. Roman Catholic. Home: 32 Northcote Rd Westbury NY 11590-1504 Office: SUNY-Old Westbury Sch Bus Old Westbury NY 11568

BARBERI, LYNN CLAIRE FENELLI, principal; b. Trenton, N.J., Feb. 25, 1955; d. Joseph and Claire Fenelli; m. John Robert Barberi, Nov. 18, 1978; children: Michelle, David. BS, Trenton State Coll., 1977; MA in Ednl. Adminstrn. with distinction, Rider U., 2000. Cert. in elem. edn. K-8, N.J. Elem. sch. tchr. St. Joseph's Sch., Trenton, 1977-80, Constable Sch., South Brunswick, NJ, 1987-92, Indian Fields Sch., South Brunswick, NJ, 1992—2000, asst. prin., 2000—02; prin. Mill Lake Sch., Monroe Twp., NJ, 2002—. Recipient Gov.'s Tchr. Recognition award State of N.J., 1989, 99. Mem. NEA, ASCD, Internat. Reading Assn., Nat. Coun. Tchrs. Math., N.J. Prins. and Suprs. Assn. Democrat. Roman Catholic. Home: 16 Pinehurst Dr Cranbury NJ 08512-3028 Office: Mill Lake Sch 115 Monmouth Rd Monroe Township NJ 08831 E-mail: LBarberi@monroe.k12.nj.us.

BARBERI, MATTHEW, physical education and health educator; b. New Haven, Nov. 12, 1916; m. Maryhannah Slingerland, Sept. 22, 1941; children: Robert, Richard, Susan, Marnie, Tom. BS, Arnold Coll., 1938; MS, NYU, 1949; postgrad., Yale U., 1953. Recreation dir. Children's Ctr., Hamden, Conn., 1938-40; tchr. phys. edn. New Haven Pub. Schs., 1940-41, tchr. health and phys. edn., 1945-46; asst. supr. phys. edn. dept. Hamden (Conn.) Pub. Schs., 1947-54, dir. health and phys. edn., 1955-81; adj. prof. So. Conn. State U., New Haven, 1956-98. Mem. Conn. Gov.'s Fitness Com., Hartford, 1968-75. Contbr. articles to profl. jours. Instr. water safety and first aid ARC, New Haven, 1945-81. Lt. USNR, 1941-45, PTO. Recipient cert. of achievement ARC, 1960; named Adminstr. of Yr. City Dirs. Coun. of AAHPERD. Mem. Conn. Assn. Health, Phys. Edn. and Recreation (pres. 1958-59, Profl. Honor award), Hamden Edn. Assn. (pres. 1952-53). Roman Catholic. Avocations: farming, fishing. Home: 42 Thornton St Hamden CT 06517-1320

BARBIE, CATHY THERESE, middle school educator; b. Ottumwa, Iowa, Apr. 29, 1955; d. Willard Eugene and Andree Marie (Joseph) Watts; m. Billy Joe Barbie, July 26, 1986; children: Bryan Michael Joseph (dec.), Joshua Ryan. BA, U. No. Iowa, Cedar Falls, 1977. Cert. tchr. English, speech, theatre, social studies, U.S. history. Tchr. Alburnett (Iowa) H.S., 1978-79, Salmon (Idaho) H.S., 1980-82, Shishmaref (AK) H.S., 1982-84, Emmonak (AK) H.S., 1984-86, Rocky Boy (Mont.) Tribal Sch., 1986-87; instr. English Big Sandy (Mont.) Schs., 1987-89; mid. sch. instr. social studies Eagle Valley Mid. Sch., Carson City, Nev., 1989—, head dept. social studies. Avocation: professional crafter/designer. Home: 5300 Goni Rd Carson City NV 89706-0352

BARBOUR, ALTON BRADFORD, human communication studies educator; b. San Diego, Oct. 13, 1933; s. Ancel Baxter and Mary Jane (Fay) B.; m. Betty Sue Burch, Aug. 19, 1961 (div. 1991); children: Elizabeth, Christopher, Damon, Meagan; m. Jacqueline Moorhead, Feb. 29, 1996. BA, U. No. Colo., 1956; MA, U. Denver, 1961, PhD, 1968; postdoctoral, Moreno Inst., 1976. Diplomate Am. Bd. Psychotherapy. Lectr. Colo. Sch. Mines, Golden, 1964-65; instr. U. Denver, 1965-68, asst. prof. human comm. studies, 1968-71, assoc. prof., 1971-77, prof., 1977—, chairperson dept. human comm. studies, 1980—98. Vis. lectr. Swiss Inst. for Group Psychotherapy, Switzerland, 1992, Remin U., China, 1999, Chinese U. of Hong Kong. Co-author: Interpersonal Communication: Teaching Resources, 1972, Louder Than Words: Nonverbal Communication, 1974, Assessing Functional Communication, 1978; editor: Free Speech Yearbook, 1974-76; contbg. editor Internat. Jour. Action Methods, Psychodrama, Skill Tng., and Role Playing, Psychodrama Network News; contbr. articles to profl. jours. With USN, 1956-58. Recipient Intellectual Freedom award Nat. Coun. Tchrs. English, 1997, William McBride Writing award Colo. Lang. Arts Soc., 1998. Fellow Am. Soc. for Group Psychotherapy and Psychodrama (Disting. Profl. Svc. award 1998, Outstanding Scholar award 2002), Am. Bd. of Med. Psychotherapists, Internat. Acad. of Behavioral Medicine, Counseling and Psychotherapy; mem. Am. Bd. Examiners in Group Psychotherapy (sec. 1983-93, chair 1997-98). Avocation: trapeze catcher and flier. Home: 1195 S Vine St Denver CO 80210-1830 Office: Univ Denver Human Comm Studies Denver CO 80208-0001

BARBOUR, CLAUDE MARIE, minister, educator; b. Brussels, Oct. 2, 1935; came to U.S., 1969; Diploma d'État d'Infirmières, École d'Infirmières, Paris, 1956; diploma d'Études Religieuses, Faculté Libre de Théolog, Paris, 1958; MST, N.Y. Theol. Sem., 1970; DST, Garrett Evang. Theol. Sem., 1973. Ordained to ministry Presbyn. Ch., 1974. Youth counselor Young Women's Christian Assn., Geneva, 1959-61, Edinburgh, 1965-67; missionary Paris Evang. Missionary Soc., So. Africa, 1962-64; deaconess Ch. of Scotland, Edinburgh, 1967-69; from asst. to assoc. pastor First United Presbyn. Ch., Gary, Ind., 1974-80; from asst. to assoc. prof. Cath. Theol. Union, Chgo., 1976-86, prof., 1986—, McCormick Theol. Sem., Chgo., 1990-96. Founder, dir. Shalom Ministries and Community, Chgo., 1975—; parish assoc. First Presbyn. Ch., Evanston, Ill., 1983—. World Coun. Chs. scholar, Geneva, 1969, United Presbyn. Ch. Commn. on Ecumenical Mission and Rels., N.Y., 1972; recipient Laskey award United Meth. Ch. Womens Div. the Bd. Global Ministries, N.Y., 1972, Civic award Ind. Women's Coun., 1976, Challenge of Peace award Chgo. Ctr. for Peace Studies, 1991, Martin P. Wolf O.F.M. award Justice, Peace and Integrity of Creation Coun. of the English-Speaking Conf. of the Order of Friars Minor, 1996. Mem. AAUW, Internat. Assn. for Mission Studies, Nat. Assn. Presbyn. Clergywomen, Am. Soc. Missiology, Assn. Prof. Mission, Midwest Fellowship Prof. Mission, Assn. Presbyn. in Cross-Cultural Mission. Home: 1649 E 50th St Apt 21A Chicago IL 60615-6110 Office: Catholic Theological Union 5401 S Cornell Ave Chicago IL 60615-5664

BARCELO, JOHN JAMES, III, law educator; b. New Orleans, Sept. 23, 1940; s. John James Jr. and Elfrida Margaret (Bisso) B.; m. Lucy L. Wood, July 14, 1974; children— Lisa, Amy, Steven. BA, Tulane U., 1962, JD, 1966; SJD, Harvard U., 1977. Bar: La. 1967, D.C. 1974, U.S. Supreme Ct. 1974, N.Y. 1975. Fulbright scholar U. Bonn, Fed. Republic Germany, 1966-67; prof. law Cornell U. Law Sch., Ithaca, N.Y., 1969—, A. Robert Noll. prof. of law, 1984-96, William Nelson Cromwell prof. internat. and comprative law, 1996—, dir internat. legal studies, 1972-88, 90—. Cons. Import Trade Adminstrn., Dept. Commerce Author: (with others) Law: Its Nature, Functions and Limits, 3rd edit., 1986, International Commercial Arbitration, 1999, 2d edit., 2003; co-editor: Lawyers' Practice and Ideals: A Comparative View, 1999, A Global Law of Jurisdiction and Judgments: Lessons from the Hague, 2002; contbr. articles to profl. jours. Mem. Am. Assn. for Comparative Study of Law (bd. dirs.), Am. Soc. Internat. Law, Am. Soc. Comparative Law, Maritime Law Assn. U.S. Office: Cornell U Law Sch Myron Taylor Hall Ithaca NY 14853

BARCENAS, CAMILO GUSTAVO, physician; b. Managua, Nicaragua, Sept. 18, 1944; came to U.S., 1969; s. Camilo and Margarita (Levy) B.; M.D., U. Nicaragua, 1968; m. Aurora Cardenas, Dec. 22, 1969; children: Margarita, Marcela, Camilo. Diplomate Am. Bd. Internal Medicine. Intern, Managua (Nicaragua) Gen. Hosp., 1967-68, Mt. Sinai Hosp., U. Conn., 1969; resident internal medicine Baylor Coll. Medicine, Houston, 1970-72; chief resident St. Luke's Episcopal Hosp., Houston, 1971; chief resident VA Hosp., Houston, 1972; fellow nephrology U. Tex. Health Sci. Ctr., Dallas, 1972-74; practice medicine specializing in nephrology, Dallas, 1974-76, Houston, 1976— ; chief home dialysis unit VA Hosp., Dallas, 1974-75, chief hemodialysis unit, 1975; chief nephrology sect. St. Luke's Episcopal Hosp., Houston, 1976— ; chief nephrology Tex. Heart Inst., dir. renal transplant svc.; asst. prof. medicine U. Tex. Health Sci. Ctr., Dallas, 1974-75; clin. asst. prof. medicine Baylor Coll. Medicine, Houston, 1976-79, clin. asso. prof., 1979-85, clin. prof., 1985— . Gen. sec. Juventud Social Christiana, 1968. Fellow A.C.P.; mem. Internat. Soc. Nephrology, Houston Soc. Internal Medicine, Am. Soc. Nephrology, Harris County Med. Soc., Tex. Med. Assn., Colegio Medico Nicaraguense. Roman Catholic. Contbr. articles on nephrology to med. jours. Office: 6624 Fannin St Ste 2510 Houston TX 77030-2337 also: 9197 Winkler Dr Ste D Houston TX 77017-5970

BARCHI, ROBERT LAWRENCE, clinical neurologist, neuroscientist, educator; b. Phila., Nov. 23, 1946; s. Henry John and Elizabeth (Pesci) B.; children: Jonathan Robert, Jennifer Elizabeth. BS, Georgetown U., 1968, MS, 1969; PhD, U. Pa., 1972, MD, 1973. Diplomate Am. Bd. Neurology and Psychiatry, Am. Bd. Med. Examiners. Resident in neurology U. Pa. Hosp., 1973-75; asst. prof. biochemistry U. Pa. Med. Sch., Phila., 1974-75, asst. prof. neurology and biochemistry, 1975-78, assoc. prof., 1978-81, prof., 1981—, David Mahoney prof. neurol. scis., 1985—, chmn. neurosci. grad. program, 1983-89, dir. Mahoney Inst. Neurol. Scis., 1983-96, vice-dean rsch. sch. medicine, 1989-91, chmn. dept. neurosci., 1992-95, chmn. depts. neurology and neurosci., 1995-99; provost and chief acad. officer U. Pa., 1999—. Mem. med. adv. bd. Muscular Dystrophy Assn., 1982—94, Soc. To Prevent Blindness, 1999—2001, Cephalon Inc., 1992—, chmn., 1996—; mem. sci. adv. bd. Phila. Ventures Inc., 1992—95, TransMolecular, Inc., 1996—; bd. mgrs. The Wistar Inst., 2000—; bd. dirs., vice chair Pa. BioAdvance, Inc., 2002—; bd. dirs. Internat. House, Inc., The Lauder Inst., Benjamin Franklin Partnership, Covalent, Inc. Author: (with Rosenberg, Prusiner, DiMauro) Molecular and Genetic Basis of Neurological Disease, 3 edits.; mem. editorial bd. Muscle and Nerve Jour., 1981-82, 95—, Jour. Neurochemistry, 1981-90, Jour. Neurosci., 1988-91, Ion Channels, 1988—, Current Opinion Neurology and Neurosurgery, 1992—, The Neuroscientist, 1993—, Neurobiology of Disease, 1994—; contbr. chpts. to textbooks, numerous articles to profl. jours. Recipient Lindback award U. Pa., 1979, Javits award NIH, 1985, Sci. Achievement award Am. Heart Assn., 1997, Disting. Grad. award U. Pa. Med. Sch., 2000. Fellow AAAS, Am. Acad. Neurology, Am. Neurol. Assn. (bd. councillors 1992-94); mem. Inst. Medicine of the NAS, Biophys. Soc., Soc. for Neurosci. (pub. lectr. 1985), Am. Soc. Clin. Investigation, Assn. Am. Physicians, Phila. Coll. Physicians, Phi Beta Kappa, Alpha Omega Alpha. Avocation: antiquarian horology. Office: U Pa Office of Provost 122 College Hall Philadelphia PA 19104 E-mail: barchi@mail.med.upenn.edu.

BARCHILON, JACQUES, foreign language educator, researcher, writer; b. Casablanca, Morocco, Apr. 8, 1923; came to U.S., 1947; s. Jaime and Perla (Bendavid) B.; m. Judith S. Merrill, 1999; children from previous marriage: Nicole Andrée, Paul Émile. BA in History, U. Rochester, 1950; MA in Comparative Lit., Harvard U., 1951, PhD in Romance Langs., 1956. Tchg. fellow Harvard U., Cambridge, Mass., 1953-55; instr. Smith Coll., Northampton, Mass., 1955-56, Brown U., Providence, 1956-59; asst. prof. U. Colo., Boulder, 1959-65, assoc. prof., 1965-71, prof., 1971-91, prof. emeritus, 1991—. Dir. study abroad program, U. Bordeaux, France, 1966-67; exch. prof. French and comparative lit. Ctr. Univ. de Savoie, Chambéry, France, 1978-79; dir. internat. colloquium on Conte merveilleux Ctr. Culturel Internat., Cerisy-La-Salle, France, 1983; lectr. in field. Author: Perrault's Tales of Mother Goose, The Dedication Manuscript of 1695, 1956, The Authentic Mother Goose Fairy Tales and Nursery Rhymes, 1960, Le Conte merveilleux français de 1690 à 1790, cent ans de féerie et de poésie ignorées de l'histoire littéraire, 1975, Le Nouveau Cabinet des Fées, 18 vols., 1978, Contes de Perrault, 1980, Charles Perrault, 1981; co-editor: (with E.E. Flinders and J. Anne Foreman) A Concordance to Charles Perrault's Tales, Vol. I Contes de Ma mère l'Oye, 1977, Vol. II, The Verse Tales, Griselidis, Peau d'Ane and Les Souhaits ridicules, 1979, Charles Perrault, a Critical Biography, 1981, (with Catherine Velay-Vallantin and J. Anne Foreman) Pensées chrétiennes, 1987, (with R. Holman) Concordance to La Rochefoucauld's Maximes, 1995, (with P. Hourcade) Contes de Madame d'Aulnoy, vol. I and vol. II, 1998; editor Cermeil, 1984-86, Marvels and Tales, 1987—; contbr. numerous articles to profl. jours. With Free French Forces, 1943-45. Grantee Am. Philos. Soc., 1962, 63, 71, 79, 93; travel Am. Coun. Learned Socs., 1983, Coun. Internat. Exch. Scholars, 1978-79, Fulbright Found., 1978-79. Mem. MLA, Am. Assn. Tchrs. of French, Soc. d'Études du 17ème Siècle, N.Am. Soc. 17th Century French Lit. Democrat. Mem. Soc. Of Friends. Avocations: skiing, hiking, camping, travel, writing. Office: U Colo Dept French & Italian Box 238 Boulder CO 80309-0238

BARCLAY, ELLEN S. not-for-profit developer; b. Rochester, N.Y., Aug. 30, 1957; d. Harley J. and Virginia J. Barclay. BA, Coll. Wooster, 1979; MA, U. Fla., 1982. Coord. Conf. Coun. for Advancement and Support of Edn., Washington, 1983—86; dir. Profl. Edn. Svcs. Coun. Advancement and Support of Edn., Washington, 1988—94; dir. Conf. Svcs. and Procurement Coun. for Advancement and Support of Edn., Washington, 1994—98; coord. Conference and Spl. Events Nat. Parks and Conservation Assn., Washington, 1986—88; exec. dir. Am. String Tchrs. Assn., Fairfax, Va., 1998—2001; dep. exec. dir. Coun. Internat. Exch. of Scholars, Washington, 2001—. Grantee Grant, Fund for the Improvement of Postsecondary Edn., 2000. Mem.: Am. Soc. Assn. Execs. Avocations: travel, gardening. Office: Coun Internat Exch Scholars Inst Internat Edn 3007 Tilden St NW Ste 5L Washington DC 20008-3009

BARCOME, MARIGAIL, special education educator; b. Green Bay, Wis., July 7, 1945; d. Elvin and Helen (Pecor) B.; m. Peter J. Serlemitsos, Mar. 27, 1978. BS, U. Wis., Oshkosh, 1969; MEd, U. Md., 1976; profl. devel. cert. level VII, Kennedy Ctr. Performing Arts. Spl. edn. tchr. Eisenhower Jr. H.S., Laurel, Md., 1969-83; learning disabilities mainstreaming support tchr. Laurel H.S., 1983—. Recipient Exceptional Tchrs. award St. Mary's Coll., 1985. Mem. Coun. Exceptional Children, Md. Student Asst. Program, Learning Disability Assn. of Am., Learning Disability Assn. of Montgomery County, Women Chefs and Restauranteurs. Avocations: pastry arts, culinary arts, ikebana, pottery, fiber and textile arts. Office: Laurel High Sch 8000 Cherry Ln Laurel MD 20707-9264

BARCUS, GILBERT MARTIN, medical products executive, business educator; b. N.Y.C., Sept. 20, 1937; s. Leon A. and Dorothy (Brownstein) B.; m. Sondra Ettin, May 6, 1961; children: David A., Ruth A. Barcus Feinberg. BS, NYU, 1959; MBA, L.I. U., 1969. Stock broker Ernst & Co., N.Y.C., 1962-65, Johnson & Johnson, 1965-80; sales mgr. McNeil Labs., Ft. Washington, Pa., 1965-75; mktg. mgr. USA Devices Ltd., New Brunswick, N.J., 1976-77; dir. product mgmt. TENS div. Stimtech, Inc., Mpls., 1977-78; products dir. Critikon, Inc., Raritan, N.J., 1979-80; v.p. mktg. Electro Biology, Inc., Fairfield, N.J., 1980-82; dir. sales, mktg. Medtronic/Med. Data Systems, Ann Arbor, Mich., 1982-85; v.p. corp. devel. Am. Biomaterials Corp., Princeton, N.J., 1985-86, sr. v.p., 1986-88; pres. Sandar Assocs. L.L.C., North Brunswick, N.J., 1980-00, Rsch. Resources Internat. L.L.C., North Brunswick, 1998-00. Gen. mgr. Creative Care Sys., Maplewood, N.J., 1986-88; sales and mktg. staff Life Scis., Inc., Lebanon, N.H., 1988-90, Healthwatch, Inc., Vista, Calif., 1990-95, Lunar Corp., Madison, Wis., 1992-95, Norland Med. Systems, Ft. Atkinson, Wis., 1995-97, Norland Med. Sys.; exec. dir. Clinsites, Charlotte, N.C., 1997; pres., CEO Rsch. Resources Internat., North Brunswick, N.J., 1998-00; exec. dir. Clinsites, Charlotte, N.C., 1997; pres. Rsch. Resources Internat., North Brunswick, N.J., 1998-00; lectr. Bus. Week Mktg. Seminars, 1988, UN Soviet Econs. Mission, 1992; prof. mktg. Coll. S.I., CUNY, 1990—, chmn. bus. dept. curriculum adv. bd., 1995—, dir. internship program, 1994—; vis. prof. mktg. Montclair (N.J.) State U., 1992-94; vis. prof. Kingsborough Coll., 1995—, Touro Coll., N.Y.C., 1999—; adj. prof. Middlesex Coll., Edison, N.J., 1987-99; lectr. dept. bus. Brookdale C.C. Author books; contbr. articles to profl. jours. Chmn. Marlboro (N.J.) Fire Commn., 1970-76; dir. Small Bus. Devel. Ctr. Middlesex County, 1988-91. Students in Free Enterprise fellow Walmart Found., 1992-95. Fellow Assn. Advancement Med. Instrumentation, Internat. Assn. Study of Pain; mem. Ann Arbor C. of C. (legis. com. 1981-84), NYU Alumni Assn. (dir. 1987-92), Accts. for Pub. Interest N.J. (chmn. golf com. 1995-97), Travis Pointe County Club (Mich.), Princeton Club of N.Y. (program com. 1993-96), NYU Club, Forsgate Country Club (v.p. 1986-91, house com. 1993-99), Pi Lambda Phi. Home: 421A Andover Dr Jamesburg NJ 08831-4307 E-mail: profbar@aol.com.

BARCUS, MARY EVELYN, primary school educator; b. Peru, Ind., Apr. 3, 1938; d. Arthur Gibson and Mildred (Neher) Shull; m. Robert Gene Barcus, Aug. 9, 1959; children: Jennifer Sue, Debra Lynn. BS, Manchester Coll., 1960; MA, Ball State U., 1964. Kindergarten tchr. Miami Elem. Sch., Wabash, Ind., 1960-64; elem. tchr. Crooked Creek Sch., Indpls., 1964-72; preschool tchr. Second Presbyn. Preschool, Indpls., 1980-85, Speedway Coop., Indpls., 1985-86; tchr. asst. St. Monica Cath. Sch., Indpls., 1990; preschool tchr., fun club tchr. Arthur Jordan YMCA, Indpls.; preschool tchr. Indpls. (Ind.) Children's Mus., 1979—. Docent sch. tours Children's Mus., Indpls., 1987—; interpreter at Indpls. children's mus.; facilitator Systematic Tng. Effective Parenting, Indpls. Writer: (children's songs) Piggyback Songs for Infants and Toddlers, 1985, Piggyback Songs in Praise of God, 1986; editor elem. sch. newspaper; producer (with others) weekly show for cable TV. Profl. vol., libr. helper in local sch. systems; office helper North Cen. High Sch.; served on PTOs in various capacities; mem. Crossroads Guild, Parents Day Out of St. Luke's Meth. Ch., past mem. ch. bd., Two's Tchr. Early Childhood Ctr.; Sun. sch./vacation ch. sch. tchr.; bd. dirs. Manchester Coll. Parents Assn. Mem. AAUW (charter, sec.), NEA (life), Ind. Assn. Edn. Young Children (state conf. com.), Pi Lambda Theta. Democrat. Mem. Church of Brethren. Home: 2230 Brewster Rd Indianapolis IN 46260-1521

BARCUS, NANCY B. education educator, writer; b. Cleve., Nov. 9, 1937; d. Paul and Doris (Garvin) Bidwell; m. James E. Barcus, May 28, 1961; children: Heidi Anne, J. Hans, Jeff Thomas. AB, U. Ky., 1961; MA in English Lit., SUNY, Geneseo, 1970; postgrad., Temple U. Cert. tchr., Tex., Ky. Tchr. Suzuki method violin Waco (Tex.) Ind. Sch. Dist., fine arts specialist at magnet sch.; past asst. dir. pub. rels., writer Baylor U., Waco; asst. prof. English and writing Houghton (N.Y.) Coll.; co-dir. Ctrl. Tex. Writing Project. Spkr. at workshops and seminars; script writer for media presentations; mag. editor and writer. Author ten books, including The Family Takes a Child, Central Texas Souvenirs; columnist The Wacoan; also feature articles, poems, brochures, newsletters. Named Outstanding Educator Danforth Found. Assn. Mem. Nat. Coun. Tchrs. English, Suzuki Assn. Am., Nat. Writing Project, Ctrl. Tex. Watercolor Soc., Phi Beta Kappa.

BARCUS, ROBERT GENE, retired educational association administrator; b. Oct. 22, 1937; s. Harold Eugene and Marjorie Irene (Dilling) B.; m. Mary Evelyn Shull, Aug. 9, 1959; children: Jennifer Sue, Debra Lynn. BPE, Purdue U., 1959; MA, Ball State U., 1963; postgrad., Ind. U., summer 1966; supts. lic., Butler U., 1967. Tchr., coach Wabash (Ind.) Jr. H.S., 1959-63; tchr. Wabash H.S., 1963-64; tchr., coach North Cen. H.S., Indpls., 1964-65; salary cons. Ind. State Tchrs. Assn., Indpls., 1965-67, asst. dir. rsch., 1967-68, dir. spl. svcs., 1968-70, exec. asst., 1971-72, adminstrv. asst., 1972-73, asst. exec. dir. spl. svcs. and tchr. rights, 1973-82, asst. exec. dir. adminstrn., pers. and governance, 1982-85, asst. exec. dir. labor rels. and adminstrn., 1985-93, assoc. exec. dir. labor rels. and adminstrn., 1993—2002, ret., 2003. Clk. Ch. of the Brethren, 1966-74, chmn., 1979-83, 87, 92-96, 97-98, 98-99, fin. sec., 2000; mem. Ind State Libr. and Hist. Bd., 2000. Alumni scholar Purdue U., 1959. Mem. NEA, Wabash City Tchr. Assn. (past pres.), Washington Twp. Tchr. Assn. (past pres.), Indpls. Press Club. Home: 2230 Brewster Rd Indianapolis IN 46260-1521 Office: 150 W Market St Indianapolis IN 46204-2806 E-mail: rbarcus@ista-in.org.

BARDOS, KAROLY, television and film educator, writer, director; b. Budapest, Pest, Hungary, Dec. 31, 1942; came to U.S., 1970; s. Laszlo and Klara (Weisz) B.; m. Eva Beres, 1964 (div. 1967); m. Gizella Viczko, 1970 (div. 1987); 1 child, Melinda. BA, U. Budapest, 1963, MA, 1966, postgrad., 1969, NYU, 1970; postgrad., dir. fellow, Am. Film Inst. Ctr. Advanced Film Studies, 1972-75. Lectr. film adult audiences Hungarian Film Inst., 1966-69; asst. dir., writer Hungarian TV, Budapest, 1966-69; prodr., dir. Am.-Hungarian TV Channel 68-60, NJ, 1978-80, Am.-Hungarian TV Channel 25, NY, 1992—, Am.-Hungarian TV Channel 17, Miami, 1992—, Ctr. for the Media Arts, N.Y.C., 1980-85; asst. prof. St. John's U., Jamaica, N.Y., 1985-93; master tchr. Dept. Film & TV NYU, 1998—; dir., editor The World of Films PBS, 1990-91. Cons., lectr. Am. Film Inst. Ctr. for Advanced Film Studies, 1972-73; tech. cons. N.Y. Ctr. For Visual History, N.Y.C., 1983; sr. lectr. CMA, 1980-85; blue ribbon panel judge Nat. Emmy TV awards, 1981—. Author: (screenplays) Father of the Moving Picture, 1975, The Crown, 1980, Forced March, 1987, The Containment, 1989-90; dir. Backstage at the Tony Awards, 1997, (live webcasting) Tony Awards Online; co-prodr. Fallen Nest, 1998-99; exec. prodr. Static, 1998-99, Millenium Gala TV Show. Recipient 1st prize Internat. Ednl. Film Festival, Tokyo, 1968, Best Am. Short Feature award U.S. Am. Film Festival, 1977, 1st prize Internat. Rehab. Film Festival, N.Y.C., 1981, Blue Ribbon award, 1st prize Am. Film Festival, N.Y.C., 1985, 2d prize Nat. Coll. Advt. awards, 1991. Mem. AAUP, Univ. Film and TV Assn., Nat. Acad. TV Arts and Scis., Am. Film Inst. Alumni Assn., Writers Guild of Am. Jewish. Office: NYU Dept Film & TV 721 Broadway Fl 9 New York NY 10003-6862

BARDSLEY, KAY, historian, archivist, dance professional; b. Port Said, Egypt, Apr. 17, 1921; came to U.S., 1928; d. Chris and Helen (Jones) Lanitis; m. James Calvert Bardsley, May 30, 1947 (wid. Sept. 1978); children: Wendy Jane, Amy Kim; m. Donald Marshall Kuhn, Feb. 25, 1990. Student, Duncan Dance Tng./Carnegie Hall, Steinway Hall Studios, N.Y.C., 1931—35; BA in Journalism cum laude, Hunter Coll., 1942. Dance debut Maria-Theresa Duncan Heliconiades, N.Y.C., 1934; prin. dancer Maria-Theresa Heliconiades, N.Y.C., 1935-42; Duncan tchr. Maria-Theresa Sch., N.Y.C., 1937-46; tchr. Creative Dance for Children, N.Y.C., 1960-66, Isadora Duncan-Maria-Theresa Heritage Group, N.Y.C., 1977-81; fashion editor Woman's Day, N.Y.C., 1943-46; TV Script WPIX Gloria Swanson Hour, 1948-49; writer TV Guide, 1949; writer/prodr. culture news and fashion ABC Network/Don Ameche-Langford Show, 1949-50. Syndicated film series prodr., Your Beauty Clin., 1950-60; prodr. video documentation of Duncan Repertory, 1976-80. Writer, lectr. in field: ; prodr.: (documentaries) The Last Isadorable, 1988, re-issued, 1997; contbr. to profl. dance jours. and pubs. including Dance Scope, 1977, Ballet Rev., 1991, 1994, staging of ReAnimations of Duncan Masterworks, A Four-year Project, presented at Dance ReConstructed Conf., Rutgers U., 1992; author: numerous conf. presentations and earliest documentation of Isadora Duncan's 1st sch.; resident dancer scholar U. Oreg., Eugene, 1997—98, staging of Duncan solos for Colo. Ballet Dancelab, 1999, Duncan's masterwork to seventh Symphony of Beethoven, 2000; owner, curator Legacy of Isadora Duncan: The Kay Bardsley Collection. Trustee Coun. for the Arts in Westchester, N.Y., 1973-76; bd. dirs. Bicentennial Com., Chappaqua, N.Y., 1973-76; co-chmn. Community Day, 1973, 75. Grantee NEA, N.Y.C., 1980; pioneer NYU/Master Tchr. Dance Tng. Inst., 1987; recipient 1997-98 Creativity award in Dance U. Oreg. Mem.: Isadora Duncan Internat. Inst. (dir., founder 1978—), Dance Critics Assn. (bd. dirs. 1997—2000), World Dance Alliance, Am. Dance Guild, Soc. Dance History Scholars. Office: Isadora Duncan Internat Inst 6305 S Geneva Cir Englewood CO 80111-5437 E-mail: kaybardsley@earthlink.net.

BARDWELL, ROSEMARY ANN, elementary school educator; b. California, Mo., Nov. 4, 1958; d. Willard C. and Hanorah Josephine (Leonard) Wingate; m. Mark Steven Bardwell, July 25, 1981. BS in Edn., Lincoln U., Jefferson City, Mo., 1981; postgrad., U. Mo., 1988; MAT, St. Mary's Coll., Leavenworth, Kans., 2001. Cert. elem. tchr., secondary English and social studies tchr., Mo. Tchr. St. Francis Xavier Sch., Taos, Mo., 1981-82, Annunciation Sch., California, 1982-83, St. Martins Sch., Jefferson City, 1983—. Campaigner Rohrbach for Senate Campaign, Jefferson City, 1990. Mem. Nat. Coun. Tchrs. English, Mo. Tchrs. English. Roman Catholic. Avocations: reading, crocheting, knitting, sewing, crafts. Home: 32042 Jacket Factory Rd California MO 65018-3526 Office: St Martins Sch 7206 Saint Martins Blvd Jefferson City MO 65109-3035

BAREFOOT, ANNE FARLEY, secondary education educator, consultant; b. Hallsboro, N.C., Mar. 9, 1934; d. Chester Arthur and Mildred Collier (Norment) Farley; m. Joe Blake Barefoot, Aug. 29, 1952; children: Jo Anne Barefoot Biser, Fredrick Arthur. BSS, East Carolina U., 1956, MA, 1960; EdS, U. S.C., 1985. Tchr. sci. Columbus County Schs., Delco, N.C., 1955-64, Whiteville (N.C.) H.S., 1964-93; nat. sci. and math. cons. Glencoe Publs., 1993—. Author: Science Connections, 1989, Science Interactions, 1991. Recipient Presdl. award NSF, 1983, N.C. Bus. Sci. Teaching award Region IV, 1983, 87, Austin Bond award East Carolina U., 1984, Outstanding Alumni award, 1986. Mem. NSTA (life, bd. dirs. dist. IV), NEA, Am. Assn. Physics Tchrs., Am. Chem. Soc., N.C. Sci. Tchrs. Assn., Assn. Presdl. Awardees in Sci. Teaching (past pres.), Sigma Xi. Democrat. Methodist. Avocations: reading, new experiments with household articles. Office: 1221 Dismal Rd Hallsboro NC 28442-9407

BAREFOOT, CONSTANCE MAUREEN, special education educator; b. Phila., June 11, 1950; d. Harold John and Berniece Catherine (Quirin) Kaufmann; m. Richard O'Malley, Aug. 17, 1974 (div. 1991); m. Robert Barefoot, July 10, 1993; stepchildren: Sharon, Douglas. BS, Pa. State U., University Park, 1971; Masters equivalency, Pa. State U., King of Prussia, 1974; MEd, U. Houston, 1986. Cert. tchr., Tex., Pa., N.Y.; cert. ednl. diagnostician, Tex. Tchr. spl. edn. George Crothers Meml. Sch., Wallingford, Pa., 1973-78, Chemung County ARC, Elmira, N.Y., 1979-80; resource rm. tchr. Horseheads (N.Y.) Cen. Sch. Dist., 1980-81; tchr. spl. edn. Ft. Bend Ind. Sch. Dist., Sugar Land, Tex., 1981-87; learning support tchr. Sch. Dist. of York, Pa., 1987-96, Lancaster Lebanon Intermediate Unit 13, East Petersburg, Pa., 1997—. Mem. Lincoln Intermediate Unit #12 In-Svc. Coun., New Oxford, Pa., 1989-96. Mem. NEA, Pa. State Edn. Assn., Coun. Exceptional Children Avocation: travel.

BAREFOOT, HYRAN EUVENE, academic administrator, educator, minister; b. Mantee, Miss., Jan. 14, 1928; s. James Lee and Martha Caroline (Martin) B.; m. Joyce Lynn Camp, Nov. 24, 1949; children— Judy Barefoot Thomas, June Barefoot Dark, Jane Barefoot Hunter. B.A., Miss. Coll., 1949; B.D., New Orleans Bapt. Theol. Sem., 1952, Th.D., 1955; postdoctoral U. N.Mex., 1965-66, Bapt. Theol. Sem., 1971. Asst. prof. religion Union U., Jackson, Tenn., 1957-60; asst. prof. N.T., So. Bapt. Theol. Sem., Louisville, 1960-62; prof. religion Union U., 1962—, chmn. dept. religion, 1966-75, chmn. div. humanities, 1972-75, v.p. acad. affairs, 1975-87, acad. dean; pres. 1987-96, chancellor, 1996—; pastor Liberty Bapt. Ch., Calhoun,

La., 1946-49, Goss Bapt. Ch., Miss., 1949-52, Hebron Bapt. Ch., New Hebron, Miss., 1952-55, First Bapt. Ch., Crowley, La., 1955-57, Woodland Bapt. Ch., Brownsville, Tenn., 1957-60, 66-75. Recipient Tchr. of Yr. award Union U., 1967, Disting. Faculty award, 1973; named Jackson Tenn. Man of the Yr., 1993. Mem. Assn. So. Bapt. Colls. (sec. 1984-85). Club: Jackson Rotary. Avocations: antique furniture refinishing, hunting, fishing. Home: 120 Redfield Dr Jackson TN 38305-8526 Office: Union U Office of Chancellor Jackson TN 38305

BARENT, BARBARA ANN, elementary education educator; b. Benkelman, Nebr., Dec. 28, 1946; d. Guy Royal and Nellie Melba (Ham) Fries; m. Wayne L. Barent, Apr. 4, 1980; children: DeWayne, Dean, Dan. BA, U. Nebr., 1969; M in Elem. Edn., U. Nebr., Kearney, 1993. Cert. elem., gifted/talented tchr., Nebr. Adult basic edn. tchr. Mid Plains Community Coll., North Platte, Nebr.; tchr. grade 4 Ogallala (Nebr.) pub. schs. Mem. curriculum coord. coun., com. tech. Mem. PTA, Sandhill Reading Coun. Mem. NEA, ASCD, Internat. Reading Assn., Nebr. State Edn. Assn., Ogallala Edn. Assn., Nat. Coun. Social Studies, Nebr. Assn. Gifted. Home: RR 1 Box 257 Ogallala NE 69153-9801

BARENZ, JOHN RICHARD, secondary education educator; b. Livingston, Mont., Sept. 18, 1951; s. Norman John and Gena Ruth (Schuman) B.; m. Christine Ann Schupperhauer, July 24, 1974; children: Amy, Rebecca, Paul, Andrew. B of Sci. Edn., DMLC, 1974. Prin., tchr. Grace Luth. Sch., Geneva, Nebr., 1974-78, Zion Luth. Sch., Denver, 1978-90; instr. social studies Minn. Valley Luth. High Sch., New Ulm, 1990—2000; prin. Rocky Mountain Luth. H.S., Denver, 2000—. Sch. counselor Wis. Luth. Synod Schs., Milw., 1976-90. Conv. del. Rep. State Conv., Mankato, Minn., 1994; mem. Nat. Right to Life Com., Washington, 1992—. Mem. ASCD, Minn. State High Sch. Coaches Assn., Minn. Coun. Social Studies. Avocations: sports, woodcarving, drawing, choir. Home: 9614 S Cordova Dr Highlands Ranch CO 80130-3788 Office: Rocky Mountain Luth High Sch 9614 S Cordova Dr Highlands Ranch CO 80130-3788 E-mail: jbarenz@attbi.com.

BARETSKI, CHARLES ALLAN, political scientist, librarian, educator, historian, municipal official; b. Mt. Carmel, Pa., Nov. 21, 1918; s. Charles Stanley and Mary Ann (Gorzelnik) B.; m. Gladys Edith von Nyitrai Yartin, Aug. 19, 1950 (dec. Oct. 1989). BA cum laude (scholar), Rutgers U., 1945; BSLS, Columbia, 1946, MSLS, 1951; Diploma, Inst. Bibliog. Orgn. of Knowledge U. Chgo., 1950; diplomas in archival adminstrn., Am. U., 1951, 55; MA in Polit. Sci., U. Notre Dame, 1957, PhD, 1958; MA in Govt. and Internat. Rels., NYU, 1965, PhD in Politics, 1969. From reference libr. to sr. libr. Newark Pub. Libr., 1938-54, profl. book reviewer, from 1938; rsch. intern Am. State Dept. Archives, Nat. Archives, 1951, br. libr. Van Buren br., 1954-56, br. dir., 1957-88, dir. fgn. lang. book collection, 1954-88; nat. archivist, historian Am. Coun. For Polish Culture, 1954-91; commr. Mcpl. Commn. on the Elderly, Richmond, 1991-95, sec., 1992-94. Dir., chief lectr., rev. seminars on liberal arts courses and libr. sci., mem. staff groups for N.J. state civil svc. libr. exams., 1950-77, elected to N.J. State Gallery of Disting. Citizens, 1962; cons. doctoral candidates in grad. studies, 1957-88, Richmond Mcpl. Coun.; election campaign, 1990; Richmond del. 4th & 5th Nat. Cath. Golden Age Assn. confs., 1990, 91; Va. state rep. Nat. Legis. Advocacy Commn., Nat. Catholic Golden Age Assn., 1991-92; judge Richmond Mcpl. Spelling Bee in conjunction with Richmond Pub. Sch. System & Sr. Citizen Orgns., 1991, 92; rep. and spokesman for Sr. Citizen Population Greater Richmond Area Anti-Violent Crime Crusade, 1992, chmn. Richmond Mcpl. Com. to revise the criteria of selection for honorees, Richmond's Sr. Citizen Hall of Fame, 1991-92, Richmond Mcpl. Transp. Task Force, 1991-94; dir., program chmn. Richmond's Forum on Nat. Comprehensive Health Care System for Am., 1992-93; chmn. Cosco's Com on Med. Rsch. Devel. of Concern to Va. State's Elderly Population, 1994—; mem. Richmond Mcpl. Needs and Assessment Com., Richmond Mcpl. Dept. Human Resources and Employee Rels., 1992-93, Richmond Mcpl. com. compilation svs. directory for Richmond's Sr. Citizens, 1993-94; chief judge award com. Joseph Conrad Lit. Contest, 1968; mem. faculty Univ. Coll., Rutgers U., Newark, 1965-66; coord. Slavic-Am. hist. studies Sr. Citizens' Inst., Essex County Coll., Newark, 1977-78; dir. Baretski Tutoring Svc., 1935-68; Ednl. Cons. Adv. Bd. Essex County, (N.J.) Office on Aging, founder, dir. Ethnic Rsch. Archives, 1971-91, dir. Rsch. Libr.; mcpl. budget analyst cmty watchdog orgns., Newark, 1954-88, Richmond, 1988—; pres. Associated Community Couns. Newark, 1969-88; mcpl. budget analyst Cmty. Watchdog Orgn., Newark, 1954-88, Richmond, 1988—; pres. Ironbound (Newark) Cmty. Coun., 1961-88; lectr., cons. Am. Ethnic Polit. History, 1968—; ednl. cons. adv. bd. Essex County (N.J.) Office on Aging; vol. tutor, South Bend, Ind.; cons. Doctoral Candidates, U. Notre Dame, 1957-58, genealogical rsch., 1987—; mem. adv. coun. North Essex Ednl. Center, Essex County Coll., Belleville, N.J., 1973-88; treas., chmn. N.J. Coalition for Safe Cmtys., Anti-Crime N.J. State-wide Fedn., 1978-80; cons., speaker problems of elderly Va. State Coun. Sr. Citizens, 1993. Author: Our Quarter Century: History of the American Council of Polish Cultural Clubs 1948-1973, 1973, Fond Memories of Ann Street School Newark, N.J.: 1920's to 1950's, 1986, A Decade of Caring and Sharing: The History of Our Lady of Peace Chapter, Catholic Golden Age Association, Richmond, Virginia: 1981-91, 1991, Ten Commandments for Senior Citizens Prescription Use: Informational Outreach Service for Richmond's Elderly, 1993; co-author: The Polish University Club of New Jersey; A Concise History: 1928-88, 1988, Shearings from the Flock, 1995; author taped narrative The Legend of America's Santa Claus, 1987; author (radio play) The Life and Times of Samuel F.B. Morse: The Inventor of the Telegraph, 1936; editor: Higher Horizons Ednl. Program N.Y.C., 1961; editor and pub. Ironbound (N.J.) Counselor, Newark, 1965; profl. book reviewer, 1938—; contbr. Letters-to-the-Editor columns in newspapers and periodicals including N.Y. Times, Newark Star-Ledger, Richmond News Leader, The Christian Science Monitor, Life mag., ALA Bull., Shearings From the Flock by Seasoned Citizens, articles to numerous profl. jours., also chpts. to books, compiler. Rsch. on contbns. Polish and other immigrants to Am. culture and history; contbg. poet, cons. Richmond Publ. Group; editorial advisor After-Glow: Anthology of Poetry, 3d. edit., 1994. Rep. Clean Govt. candidate for U.S. Congress, 10th Dist. N.J., 1962; N.J. chmn. Polish-Am. Citizens for Goldwater, 1964; N.J. liaison dir. Polish Am. Rep. Nat. Coun., 1971-88; rsch. dir., pub. rels. dir. Polish-Am. Rep. Club N.J. Vol., tutor Mt. Carmel, Pa. and Newark Elem. Schs., 1927-32, Newark Pub. High Schs., 1932-35; reporter Newark Sunday Ledger, 1935; mem. Va. Mus. Fine Arts, Richmond, The Poe Found., Inc.; founder, dir. Inst. Polish Culture, Seton Hall U., South Orange, N.J., 1953-54; rsch. historian of inst., 1953-88; nat. gen. sec. Am. Polish Civil War Centennial com., 1961-65; founder, dir., libr. Ctr. Advancement Slavic Studies, 1970-91; chmn. internat. com. 300th Ann. of Founding of Newark, 1965-66; founder, pres. Ind. Polish-Am. Voters of N.J., 1953-88; state del. Polish Hungarian World Fedn., 1977-83; founder, pres. Newark Pub. Libr. Employees Union Local 2298, Am. Fedn. State, County and Municipal Employees, AFL-CIO, 1971-77, del. internat. convs., 1974, 76, 78, 80, 82, trustee N.J. Pub. Employees Council 52, No. N.J. Pub. Employee Unions, 1978-84; mem. exec. bd. Newark Labor Coalition, 1972-77; ofcl. historian N.J. State Polish-Am. Ethnic Group, 1976-78; bd. dirs. N.J. chpt. Confedn. Am. Ethnic Groups; organizer, cons. Newark Ironbound Sr. Citizen's Multi-Purpose Ctr. Satellite Libr., 1986-88; resource scholar N.J. Gov.'s Commn. on Eastern European and Captive Nation History, 1985-88; historian Newark Multi-Ethnic Coun., 1986-88; trustee Cath. Golden Age Sr. Citizens Club Richmond, 1990-91, historian and v.p., 1991-93; v.p., program chmn. Coun. Sr. Citizens Orgn. Richmond, 1991-93, pres. 1993-94; commr., bd. dirs. Richmond Mcpl. Commn. on Elderly, 1991-95; sec. 1992-94; judge 4th, 5th Ann. Mcpl. Intergenerational Spelling Bee, 1991, 92; chmn. for revising criteria for selection of honoree's for Richmond Municipal Com. for Richmond Sr. Citizen Hall of Fame, 1992; mem. Richmond Mcpl. Com. Real Estate Tax Relief program for Richmond's Elderly, 1993-94; v.p., program chmn. Cosco Coun. 95 Federated Sr. Citizen Orgns. Richmond, 1991-93, pres. 1993-94; chmn. comm. com. Richmond Story League, 1991-92; ethnic rsch. Historian N.J. State Am. Revolution Celebration commn., 1976-77, Richmond COSCO fedns.; chmn. com. med. and health care rsch. for elderly Cosco Fedn., Richmond, 1994—; mem. Richmond Neighborhood Cmty. Devel. task force, 1994-95. Rutgers U. Scholar, 1939-45; Edna Sanderson fellow, Columbia U., 1946, Newark Pub. Libr. Scholar, 1951; rsch. fellow U. Notre Dame, 1956-57; elected to N.J. State Gallery of Dist. Citizens, 1962; recipient Brotherhood award City of Newark, 1962, Presdl. Leadership and Disting. Svc. award Am. Fedn. State, County and Mcpl. Employees, 1972, Founder's Day award N.Y. U., 1970, Svc. awards Newark Pub. Libr., 1972, 74, 76, 85, 88, Nat. Am. Heritage award J.F. Kennedy Library for Minorities, 1972, Outstanding State Labor Leader award N.J. Pub. Employees, AFL-CIO, 1978; Disting. Educator Am. award, 1979; Nat. Founder's award Am. Coun. Polish Culture, 1980; New Internat. award Polish Govt. in exile, London, 30 years Profl. Svc. award Newark's Ironbound Community, 1984, Sixty Five Yrs Dedicated Vol. Tutoring citation, 1927-92, Humanitarian award for Vol. Tutoring recognizing 65 yrs., 1993; named for the outstanding contbns. to the greater Newark community and devoted svcs. to the growth of the Newark Pub. Libr. system, 1988; grantee N.J. League of Women Voters Ednl. Fund seminar for Newark Inter-Group leaders; elected Nat. Role Model for Am. Youth to Hall of Fame U.S. Acad. Achievement, Lexington, Ky., 1983, Disting. Presdl. Svc. award Coun. Sr. Citizen Orgns. Greater Richmond, Va. & Adjoining Counties, 1996, numerous others; decorated Knight's cross Polonia Restituta Mem. ALA, Polish-Am. Soc. Va., Italian-Am. Cultural Assn. Va., Polish-Am. Unity League, Polish-Am. Hist. Assn. (asst. editor monthly bull. 1959-61, nat. editor-in-chief 1961-65), Nat. Coun. Sr. Citizens, Nat. Polish Coun. (Am. divsn., del. rep. Polish-Ams. of N.J., pub. rels. counselor), Writers Soc. N.J. (exec. dir. 1947-56), Am. Polit. Sci. Assn., Am. Soc. Internat. Law, Am. Sociol. Assn., Soc. Historians Am. Fgn. Rels., Am. Hist. Assn., N.Y. Libr. Club, Polish-Hungarian World Fedn., Immigration History Soc. N.J., Mid. Atlantic States Coun. Social Studies, Am. Coun. for Polish Culture, Newark Pub. Libr. Guild (founder, pres. 1970), Va. State Coun. Sr. Citizens, Libr. Pub. Rels. Coun., N.J. Libr. Assn., Essex County Librs. Assn., Coll. Art Assn., Assn. Historians of Am. Art, Polish U. Club N.J. (pres. 1953-54), Polish Arts Club Newark (pres. 1980-88, historian 1975-91), Nat. Coun. Sr. Citizens, Nat. Assn. Sr. Travel Planners, Va. State Coun. Sr. Citizens, Nat. Assn. of Sr. Travel Planners. Roman Catholic. Died July 5, 2000.

BARFIELD, CYNTHIA MARIE, secondary school educator; b. Pt. Gibson, Mississippi, June 29, 1956; d. Viola (Barber) Reynolds; m. Aaron Patten Sr.(div. 1986); children: Aaron Jr., Sharon Alicia, Travis; m. Michael Barfield, 1997. BS, Alcorn State Univ., 1978, MS, 1982. Tchr. Claibome County Sch., Pt. Gibson, Miss., 1977—, computer sci. cons., 1985-89; tchr. Natchez Adams County Sch., 1997—99; prof. Copiah Lincoln CC, 1999—. Mem. Miss. Math. Teachers. Assn. Home: 103 Oriole Terr Natchez MS 39120

BARFIELD, KENNY DALE, religious school administrator; b. Florence, Ala., Nov. 17, 1947; s. Henry Perry and Bernice Elizabeth (Olive) B.; m. Nancy Ann Cordray, Aug.7, l970; children: Amber Eiizabeth, Lora Allyn. BA in Speech Communication, David Lipscomb Coll., l969; MA in Speech Communication, U. Ala., Tuscaloosa, l972; EdS in Ednl. Adminstrn., U. North Ala., l986; EdD in Ednl. Adminstrn., U. Ala., Tuscaloosa, 1989. Dir. debate, instr. Mars Hill Bible Sch., Florence, l969—, acad. dean, l986-2000, prin., 1990-95, v.p., 1999-2000, pres., 2001—; minister Highland Park Ch. of Christ, Muscle Shoals, Ala., 1970-74, Jackson Heights Ch. of Christ, Florence, 1974-78, Sherrod Ave Ch. of Christ, Florence, 1978—. Instr. speech communication Internat. Bible Coll., l972-75, U. North Ala., Florence, l98l-83. Author: 50 Golden Years: The N.F.L. Nationals, l980, Why The Bible Is Number One, 1988, The Prophet Motive, 1995; editor Pacesetter; contbr. articles to profl. jours. Recipient Outstanding Young Religious Leader award Ala. Jaycees, l976, Ala. Speech Tchr. of Yr. award l977, Outstanding Speech and Debate Coach award Comml. Appeal, 1977, Key Coach award Barkley Forum for High Schs., Emory U., l98l, High Sch. Debate Coach of Yr. award Bishop's Guild, Samford U., l983, Disting. Svc. award Nat. Forensic League, 1981, 86, Gregg Phifer svc. award Fla. State U., 1997; named Four Diamond Coach Nat. Forensic League, 1999, H.S. Debate Coach of Yr. Carson Newman U., 1992, 2000; Faulkner fellow U. Miss., 1987. Mem. Am. Forensic Assn. (ednl. practices com. 1984-86, high sch. affairs com. 1988-90, pub. rels. com. 1990-93, v.p. high sch. affairs 1998-00), Ala. Forensic Educators Assn. (pres. 1976-77, 82-83, 85-86), Nat. Assn. Secondary Sch. Prins., So. Assn. Colls. and Schs. (cen. rev. com. 1991-95), Deep South Nat. Forensic League (chmn. 1977-79, 81-85), Nat. Debate Coaches Assn. Office: Mars Hill Bible Sch 698 Cox Creek Pky Florence AL 35630-6624

BARFIELD, ROBERT F. retired mechanical engineer, educator, dean; b. Thomaston, Ga., Feb. 8, 1933; s. Jason Malcome and Nettie Lee Barfield; m. Marion Janelle Neill, June 25, 1953 (div. Jan. 1980); children: Kimberly Faith, Robert Frederick Jr.; m. Sara de Saussure Davis, Nov. 27, 1981 (div. Jan. 1984); m. Leonette Walker, May 1990 (div. June 1994). B.M.E., Ga. Inst. Tech., 1956, MSM.E., 1958, PhD, 1965. Diplomate: registered profl. engr. Preliminary design engr. AiResearch Corp., Los Angeles, 1957-59; asst. prof. mech. engring. Ga. Inst. Tech., Atlanta, 1959-65; corp. mech. engr. Thomaston Mills Corp., Ga., 1965-67; prof. mech. engring. U. Ala., Tuscaloosa, 1967-94, prof. emeritus, 1994, dean of engring., 1982-94, dean emeritus, 1994. Dir., sr. adv. Shiraz Tech. Int., Iran, 1975-77; gen. bd. Assn. Internt. practical Tng., 1980-85; dir. Capstone Engring. Soc., 1982-94; head mech. engring. program, dir. Oil Testing Ctr., U. Petroleum and Minerals, Dhahran, Saudi Arabia, 1971-73; advisor King Saud U., Riyhad, Saudi Arabia, 1982-89, U. Jordan, 1984, Yarmouk U., Jordan, 1986, Birzeit U., Israel, 1985, Kabul U., Afghanistan, 1963; mem. Accreditation Bd. for Engring. and Tech., visitor in Mech. engring., 1982-94; mem. Ala. Commn. High Tech. Bd. dirs. Salvation Army Ala., 1996—, Turning Point, Inc., 1995—. Recipient Disting. Service award Imperial Orgn. for Social Services, Tehran, Iran, 1977, U. Ala. Faculty Senate, 1980, Engr. of Yr. award Ala. Soc. Profl. Engrs., 1987, Liberty Bell award Ala. Law Assn., 1987; inductee Engring. Hall of Fame, 1998. Fellow ASME; mem. Am. Soc. Engring. Edn., Nat. Soc. Profl. Engrs., Ala. Acad. Sci., Tuscaloosa C. of C., Sigma Xi, Tau Beta Pi, Pi Tau Sigma, Phi Kappa Phi, Upsilon Pi Epsilon, Tau Alpha Pi. Presbyterian. Home: 703 Shallow Creek Rd Tuscaloosa AL 35406-2085 Office: Univ Ala PO Box 870200 Tuscaloosa AL 35487-0200

BARGER, VERNON DUANE, physicist, educator; b. Curllsville, Pa., June 5, 1938; s. Joseph F. and Olive (McCall) Barger; m. M. Annetta McLeod, 1967; children: Victor A., Amy J., Andrew V. BS, Pa. State U., 1960, PhD, 1963. Rsch. assoc. U. Wis., Madison, 1963-65, from asst. prof. to assoc. prof., 1965-68, prof. physics, 1968—, J.H. Van Vleck prof., 1983—, dir. Inst. Elem. Particle Physics Rsch., 1984—, Hilldale prof., 1987-91, Vilas prof., 1991—. Vis. prof. U. Hawaii, 1970, 79, 82, U. Durham, 1983, 84; vis. scientist CERN, 1972, Rutherford Lab., 1972, SLAC, 1975, Kavli Inst. for Theoretical Physics, U. Calif., Santa Barbara, 2003. Co-author: (book) Phenomenological Theories of High Energy Scattering, Classical Mechanics, Classical Electricity and Magnetism, Collider Physics. Recipient Alumni Fellow award, Pa. State U., 1974; Guggenheim fellow, 1972, Fermilab Frontier fellow, 1999. Fellow: Am. Phys. Soc. Methodist. Achievements include research in in elementary particle theory and phenomenology; classification of hadrons as Regge recurrences; analyses of neutrino scattering and oscillations; research in weak boson, Higgs boson and heavy quark production; electroweak models; supersymmetry and grand unification; future collider physics; cosmology. Office: U Wis Dept Physics 1150 University Ave Madison WI 53706-1302

BARIK, SAILEN, biomedical scientist, educator; b. Midnapur, India, June 15, 1954; came to U.S., 1982; s. Narayan C. and Promila (Maiti) B.; m. Kumkum Maiti, June 26, 1981; children: Titus, Tiasha. BSc with honors, R.K.M.R. Coll., Calcutta, India, 1972; MSc, Calcutta U., 1975; PhD, Bose Inst., Calcutta, 1982. Rsch. fellow dept. sci. and tech. Govt. India, Calcutta, 1976-81; postdoctoral assoc. U. Conn. Health Ctr., Farmington, 1982-88; project scientist Cleve. Clinic Found., 1989-91, asst. staff, 1992-93; asst. prof. dept. biochemistry and molecular biology U. South Ala., Mobile, 1994-99, assoc. prof., 1999—. Spl. reviewer NIH, Bethesda, Md., 1994. Contbr. articles to profl. jours.; radio host John Carroll U., Cleve., 1992. Soccer coach South Euclid-Lyndhurst Recreation Club, Cleve., 1991-93. Mem. Am. Soc. Virology. Achievements include determination of the mechanism of transcription antitermination; discovery of the role of actin and profilin in respiratory syncytial viral transcription; discovery of bacteriophage protein phosphatase. Home: 7771 Mallard Dr Mobile AL 36695-4239 Office: U South Ala Dept Biochem & Mol Biology 307 University Blvd N Mobile AL 36688-0002 E-mail: sbarik@jaguar1.usouthal.edu.

BARKER, CLYDE FREDERICK, surgeon, educator; b. Salt Lake City, Aug. 16, 1932; s. Frederick George and Jennetta Elizabeth (Stephens) B.; m. Dorothy Joan Bieler, Aug. 11, 1956; children: Frederick George II, John Randolph, William Stephens, Elizabeth Dell. BA, Cornell U., 1954, MD, 1958. Diplomate Am. Bd. Surgery. Intern Hosp. U. Pa., Phila., 1958-59, resident in surgery, 1959-64, fellow in vascular surgery, 1964-65; fellow in med. genetics U. Pa. Sch. Medicine, Phila., 1965-66, assoc. in surgery, 1964-68, assoc. in med. genetics, 1966-72; attending surgeon Hosp. U. Pa., Phila., 1966—; chief div. transplantation U. Pa. Sch. Medicine, Phila., 1966—2001, asst. prof. surgery, 1968-69, assoc. prof. surgery, 1969-73, prof. surgery, 1973—, J. William White prof. surg. research, 1978-82, chief div. vascular surgery, 1982—2001, Guthrie prof. surgery, 1982—, John Rhea Barton prof. surgery, 1983—2001, chmn. dept. surgery, 1983—2001; chief surgery Hosp. U. Pa., Phila., 1983—2001. Dir. Harrison Dept. Surgery Rsch. U. Pa., Phila., 1983-2001; mem. immunobiology study sect. NIH; chmn. clin. practices U. Pa., 1987-89; v.p. United Network for Organ Sharing, 2001-02, pres., 2002--. Mem. editl. bd. Jour. Transplantation, 1977-2001, Clin. Transplantation, 1988—, Jour. Surg. Rsch., 1979-85, Jour. Diabetes, 1981-86, Archives of Surgery, 1987-96, Transplantation Procs., 1990-2001, Surgery, 1991-95, Cell Transplantation, 1991—, Postgrad. Gen. Surgery, 1991-95, Jour. ACS, 1994—, Annals of Surgery, 1995—; contbr. articles to profl. jours. and textbooks. Markle Found. Scholar, 1968-74; NIH grantee, 1974—; recipient Merit award NIH, 1987-95. Fellow AOA, NAS (Inst. Medicine), ACS (com. Forum on Fundamental Surg. Problems 1983-88, vice chmn. 1987-88, bd. govs. 1994-2001, pres. Phila. chpt. 1991-92), Coll. Physicians Phila., Royal Coll. Surgeons Eng. (hon.), Royal Coll. Surgeons Ireland (hon.); mem. AMA, Royal Coll. Surgeons of Ireland (hon.), Assn. Acad. Surgery, Am. Diabetes Assn., Am. Soc. Artificial Internal Organs, Am. Fedn. Clin. Rsch., Juvenile Diabetes Found., Soc. Univ. Surgeons, Am. Surg. Assn. (recorder 1991-96, pres. 1996-97), Soc. Clin. Surgery (chmn. membership 1984-85), Halsted Soc. (chmn. membership 1984-85, v.p. 1985-86, pres. 1986-87), Surg. Biology Club II, Soc. Vascular Surgery, Internat. Cardiovascular Soc., Internat. Surg. Group (treas. 1988-94, pres. 1994-95), Internat. Soc. Surgery (v.p. U.S. chpt. 1995-97, pres. 1997-99), Transplantation Soc. (councilman 1978-84, 94—), Am. Soc. Transplant Surgeons (chmn. membership 1980-81, treas. 1988-91, pres. 1992-93), Unitd Network for Organ Sharing (v.p. 2001-02), (pres.2002-03), Am. Acad. Arts and Scis., Assn. Am. Physicians, Phila. Acad. Surgery (program chmn. 1984-86, v.p. 1986-88, pres. 1988-89), Greater Delaware Valley Soc. Transplant Surgeons (pres. 1978-80), Am. Philos. Soc. (coun. 2003—). Home: 3 Coopertown Rd Haverford PA 19041-1012 Office: Hosp Univ Pa Dept Surgery 3400 Spruce St Philadelphia PA 19104-4206

BARKER, COLIN GEORGE, education educator; b. Devon, United Kingdom, Aug. 3, 1939; came to U.S., 1965; s. George Henry and Hilda M. (Finch) B.; m. Yvonne I. Meredith, Apr. 28, 1965; 1 child, Conan N. BA, Oxford (England) U., 1962, DPhil, 1965. Post-doctoral U. Tex., Austin, 1965-67; sr. rsch. chemist Exxon Prodn. Rsch. Co., Houston, 1967-69; prof. U. Tulsa, 1969—, prof., chmn., 1987—2002, McMan chair in geoscis., 1998—. Cons. Oil & Gas Consultants Internat., Tulsa, 1978—. Author: Organic Geochemistry in Petroleum Exploration, 1979, Thermal Modeling of Petroleum Generation: Theory and Applications, 1996. Named Disting. Lectr. Am. Assn. Petroleum Geologists, 1980-81, Esso Disting. Lectr. U. Sydney, 1985, Outstanding Educator Am., 1973; recipient Matson award Am. Assn. Petroleum Geologists, 1978, 92. Mem. Am. Assn. Petroleum Geologists (bulletin editor 1980-86, chair vis. geologist program 1996-2000), Geochemical Soc. (chmn. organic geochemistry divsn. 1978-79, assoc. editor 1978-85), Sierra Club. Office: U Tulsa Dept Geoscis Tulsa OK 74104 E-mail: colin-barker@utulsa.edu.

BARKER, RALPH MERTON, JR., special education and gifted education educator; b. Glenolden, Pa., Dec. 02; s. Ralph Merton and Pauline Kaufman (Isenberg) B.; m. Diana Dawn Kline, June 22, 1963; 1 child, Timothy Jon. BS in Edn., Kutztown U., 1963; MEd, Temple U., 1969. Cert. tchr., Pa. Tchr. Muhlenberg Twp. Sch. Dist., Laureldale, Pa., 1963-70; tchr. gifted students Berks Intermediate Unit # 14, Reading, Pa., 1970—. Tchr.-mentor Pa. Gov.'s Sch. of Excellence for Teaching, Millersville U., 1990-92; mem. com. to develop gifted curriculum Brandywine Sch. Dist., Topton, Pa., 1990; com. mem. state conv. Pa. Coun. Social Studies; presenter program to Pa. Dept. Edn. Contbr. articles to profl. publs. Com. chmn. for Troop 150, dist. commr. Hawk Mountain coun. Boy Scouts Am., 1983-84. Named Outstanding Tchr. Reading chpt. Coun. Exceptional Children, 1972. Mem. NEA, Pa. State Edn. Assn., Nat. Coun. Social Studies, Pa. Assn. Gifted Edn. Republican. Methodist. Avocations: writing poetry, travel, fishing, cartooning. Home: 1778 Ocean Dr Avalon NJ 08202-2225

BARKER, ROBERT OSBORNE (BOB BARKER), educator, mediator; b. Cleve., June 13, 1932; m. Sharon Ann (div.); children: Debra, Stephen, Dawn, Michael, Colleen. Student, Henry Ford C.C., 1950; BA in Comm. Arts and Sci., Mich. State U., 1954; LLB, LaSalle U., 1969; postgrad., U. Wis., 1989, U. Fla., 1996, postgrad., 2000—03. Lic. cmty. assn. mgr. 1993—, real estate agent; registered lobbyist Nat. Assn. Mfrs. 1972-87; cert. ct./pvt. mediator Alternative Dispute Resolution, 1995—. With pub. rels. dept. Ford Motor Co., Dearborn, Mich., 1953; mgr. Kaiser Aluminum Co., Chgo., 1956-58; advt. mgr. Bastian Blessing Co., Chgo., 1958-59; mgr., regional mgr. Sun Oil Co., Ohio and Detroit, 1959-71; mgr. Goodyear Tire & Rubber Co., Detroit, 1971-72; mgr., v.p. Nat. Assn. Mfrs., Washington, Boston and Detroit, 1972-87; pres., CEO Barker Cons. Inc., 1987-96; mgr., v.p. seminars and materials dept. Am. Supplier Inst. (div. of FoMoCo), 1987-90; nat. mdse./mktg. mgr. Costa del Mar Sunglasses, Ormond Beach, Fla., 1990-91; resort mgr. Oceanside 99 Condo, Ormond Beach, Fla., 1992-93, Outrigger Beach Club, Ormond Beach, Fla., 1994-95. Adj. prof. pub. rels., advt., retailing, sales fundamentals, global and internat. mktg., quality svc. mgmt. Daytona Beach C.C., 1994—; owner Dolphin Beach Club Condo, 1981-2001, bd. dirs., 1991-99. Twp. trustee, Findlay, Ohio, 1962; lay min. Episcopal ch., 1960-85, vestry, 1981-2001; mem. exec. bd. dirs. Volusia County Rep., 1991-2000; bd. dirs. Am. Cancer Soc., 1991—; bd. dirs. Dearborn Civic Theatre, 1980-84, Volusia Presdl. forum, 1991-99, Dearborn City Beautiful commr. emeritus, 1970-90; commr. Ormond Beach Quality of Life, Beautification and Planning bds., 1990-99; mem. adv. coun. bd. Habitat Humanity, 1995-99; res. police officer, Dearborn, 1968-88; pres. Dearborn High and Lindbergh Elem. PTA; bd. dirs. Bldg. Assn. Mgrs., 1991-95, Cmty. assoc. Inst., 1993-97, Volusia County Pers. Bd., 1991-93; mem. adv. coun. bd. Coun. of Aging, 1991-2000; mem. Fla. Police Benevolent Assn., Fla. Sheriffs Assn.; bd. dirs. Daytona and Ormond Beach Rep. Club, 1991-99, heritage mem. Ormond

Meml. Art Mus., 1991-2001; amb. Daytona Internat. Airport, 1996-2002; team selection scout Fla. Citrus Sports for New Year's Bowl football game, Orlando, Fla., 1997—; mem. elder voice focus group Genesis Elder Care, 2001; asst. publicity dir. bd. dirs. Ormond Sr. Games, 1994-96. Served with USNR, 1949-58, AFROTC, 1951-54. Recipient Vol. of Yr. award Am. Cancer Soc., 1998. Mem. Advt. Fedn., Assn. Execs., Am. Heart Assn. (bd. dirs. Volusia/Flagler 2002-), Fla. Pub. Rels. Soc. (Volusia chpt., former v.p. bd. dirs. 1996-98), Am. Legion (life), Mich. State U. Alumni (life, past. pres. 4 alumni clubs), Mich. State Varsity Alumni Club (life), U. Fla. Alumni Assn. (bd. dir. 1997- Gator Club Volusia County, v.p. edn. 1999-2002), Ormond Beach C. of C. (former amb., chmn. pub. rels. Beautification, JazzMatazz, social com. 1990-2002), Nat. Assn. Sr. Friends of Volusia/Flagler Counties (pres. 2000—), Ormond Shrine Club (pres. 1994-95), Elks, Exch. Club, Rotary (pres. 1987-88), Masons, Moose-Legion, Shriners (dir. pub. rels. 1984, provost unit, Fez on Wheels and Vets. unit), Delta Tau Delta. Home: Unit 613 229 S Ridgewood Ave Daytona Beach FL 32114-4334 E-mail: bobbarker13_99@yahoo.com., robert_barker42@falconmail.dbcc.edu.

BARKER, VERLYN LLOYD, retired minister, educator; b. Auburn, Nebr., July 25, 1931; s. Jack Lloyd and Olive Clara (Bollman) B. AB, Doane Coll., 1952, DD, 1977; BD, Yale U., 1956, STM, 1960; postgrad., U. Chgo., 1960-61; PhD, St. Louis U., 1970. Ordained to ministry United Ch. of Christ, 1956. Instr. history, chaplain Doane Coll., Crete, Nebr., 1954-55; pastor U. Nebr., 1956-59; sec. ministry higher edn. United Ch. Bd. Homeland Ministries, N.Y.C., 1961-96, ret. Cleve., 1996. Author: Premises about Education, 1981, Creationism, the Church and Public Education, 1981, Health and Human Values: A Ministry of Theological Inquiry and Moral Discourse, 1987; editor: The Church and the Public School, 1980, Science, Technology and the Christian Faith, 1990; contbg. author: Campus Ministry, 1964, Religious Colleges in America: A Selected Bibliography, 1988, The New Faith-Science Debate, 1989; mem. editorial adv. com. Jour. Current Social Issues; contbr. articles to various publs. Pres. United Ministries in Higher Edn., N.Y.C., 1971-77. Mem.: ACLU, AAAS, Nat. Assn. for Sci., Tech. and Society, Soc. Health and Human Values, Am. Acad. Polit. and Social Sci., Acad. Polit. Sci., Am. Studies Assn., Am. Assn. Higher Edn., Doane Coll Alumni Assn. (pres. 1957—58), Yale Club N.Y.C.

BARKER, VIRGINIA LEE, nursing educator; Diploma, Ind. U. Sch. Nursing, 1952, BS, 1955, MS, 1961, EdD, 1969. Dean sch. nursing, prof. Alfred (N.Y.) U., 1969-78; prof., dean nursing U. Louisville, 1978-81; dean Mary Black Sch. Nursing, prof. U. S.C., Spartanburg, 1981-90; dean profl. studies, prof. nursing SUNY, Plattsburg, 1990-98, prof. nursing Plattsburgh, 1990—, dir. virtual reality devel. Cons. N.Y. Regents Coll. Nursing Program, 1972—91; project dir. federally funded telenursing project rural upstate N.Y., 1993—98; dir. project to develop virtual reality simulations edn. physicians, nurses, allied health pers., 1995—. Contbr. articles to profl. jours., papers nat. and internat. confs. Mem. ARC. Grantee Disting. Practitioners, N.Y. State Nurses Assn. Mem.: AAUW, ANA, Internat. Coun. of Nurses, S.C. Deans and Dirs. Nursing Fedn. (chair), Am. Assn. Higher Edn., S.C. League Nursing, Nat. League Nurses (com. mem.), N.Y. Nurses Assn. (pres.), Ind. U. Sch. Nursing Alumni Assn. (pres.), Kappa Delta Pi, Phi Kappa Phi, Sigma Theta Tau. E-mail: virginia.barker@plattsburgh.edu.

BARKER-LASHLEY, ANNE ELIZABETH, elementary education educator; b. Port of Spain, Trinidad and Tobago, Aug. 12, 1953; came to U.S., 1972; d. Ethelbert and Ajoolan (Latiff) Barker; children: Natasha, Leroy. BA, U. Md., 1983; MS, Fla. Internat. U., 1992. Lic. tchr., Fla. Adminstrv. asst. Price Waterhouse, N.Y.C., Washington, Miami, Fla., 1978-86; tchr. art Rockway Elem., Miami, 1986-87, Royal Green Elem., Miami, 1987-96. Supervising tchr. Fla. Internat. U., Miami, 1992. Recipient Outstanding Dedication to Art Edn. Plaque Royal Green Elem. PTA, 1990-91. Democrat. Episcopalian. Avocations: reading, painting, cooking, listening to music, theatre. Home: 14816 SW 166th St Miami FL 33187-1422 Office: Zora Neale Hurston Elem 13137 SW 26th St Miami FL 33175-1817

BARKLEY, ANDREW PAUL, economics educator; b. Manhattan, Kans., Feb. 5, 1962; s. Paul Weston and Lela Mel (Kelly) B.; m. Mary Ellen Cates, July 14, 1984; children: Katherine Ann, Charles Kelly. BA in Econs., Whitman Coll., 1984; MA in Econs., U. Chgo., 1986, PhD in Econs., 1988. Asst. prof. Kans. State U., Manhattan, 1988-93, assoc. prof., 1993—. Coffman chair for outstanding tchg. scholars Kans. State U., 2003—; vis. prof. Quaid-I-Azam U., Islamabad, Pakistan, 1990, U. Ariz., Tucson, 1994—95, U. Cambridge, England, 2002; faculty advisor Pakistan Student Assn., Kans. State U., Agrl. Econs. Club, 1989—94. Assoc. editor Review of Agrl. Econs., 1993—. Recipient Agrl. and Rural Transp. Rsch. Paper award, 1994; named CASE Kans. Prof. of Yr., 1993. Mem.: Western Agrl. Econs. Assn. (Outstanding Undergrad. Tchg. award 1994), Nat. Agrl. Coll. Tchrs. Assn. (Knight Outstanding Jour. Article award 1992, Ctrl. Region Outstanding Tchr. 1994, Tchr. fellow 1994), Am. Agrl. Econs. Assn. (nat. advisor student sect. 1993—95, Outstanding Undergrad. Tchg. award 1995). Avocations: running, reading, travel. Home: 925 Wildcat Rdg Manhattan KS 66502-2927 Office: Kans State U Dept Agrl Econs Waters Hall Manhattan KS 66506

BARLIS, BETTYE MONTGOMERY, medical center administrator, elementary educator; b. Jackson, Miss., Aug. 5, 1940; d. William Franklin and Minnie Love (Greer) Montgomery; m. Jerry Donald Moore, Jan. 29, 1959; children: Jerry Donald Jr., David Montgomery, Elizabeth Ann Singleton; m. Arthur A. Barlis, Sept. 9, 1985. BS, Miss. Coll., 1960. Cert. elem. tchr., Miss. Elem. tchr. Jackson (Miss.) Pub. Schs., 1962-63; adminstr., v.p. Barlis Cataract & Eye Care Ctr., Dunedin, Fla., 1987—. Mem. NAFE, AAUW. Republican. Avocation: tennis. Home: 2080 Muirfield Way Oldsmar FL 34677-1937 Office: Barlis Cataract Eyecare Ctr 601 Main St Dunedin FL 34698-5848

BARLOW, JEAN, art educator, painter; b. L.A., Dec. 13, 1940; d. Sydney R. and Rose (Ballen) Barlow; m. Gordon M. Nunes, Sept. 21, 1973 (dec. Dec. 1991). BA cum laude, UCLA, 1963, MA, 1965, MFA, 1968. Tchg. assoc. UCLA, 1964-68; instr. Univ. Adult Sch., L.A., 1966-70; lectr. Calif. State U., Long beach, 1967-69; instr. Beverly Hills (Calif.) Adult Edn., 1969, East L.A. Jr. Coll., 1969-70; lectr. UCLA, 1986, instr. ext. divsn., 1969-96; instr. Santa Monica (Calif.) City Coll., 1969—. Mentor program mem. Santa Monica City Coll., 1989-90; pvt. art tchr., L.A., 1970-96; cons. in field. One woman shows include Jenet Gallery, L.A., 1965, Santa Monica City Coll., 1974; new works on view at home, invitation only, 2001—03; exhibited in group shows at So. Calif., 1965, Orlando Gallery, L.A., 1967, 68, Santa Monica City Coll., 1974, 78, 80, 87, 88, 91, 94, 95, Living Room Gallery, 1997, Bergemot Station T2, 1999, Brentwood Park Group Art Exhibit; invitational pastel drawing Scripps Coll., So. Calif., 1965. Avocations: drawing and painting, photography, home landscape and decoration, creative cooking, writing.

BARMORE, FRANK EDWARD, physics educator; b. Manhattan, Kans., June 20, 1938; s. Mark Alfred and Elizabeth (Jenkins) B.; m. Irene Elizabeth Wilcox, Jan. 21, 1967; children: Nathaniel, Christopher. BS with honors, Wash. State U., 1960; MS, U. Wis., Madison, 1963, PhD, 1973. Asst. prof. natural sci. Milton Coll., Wis., 1970-73; asst. prof. physics Mid. East Tech. U., Ankara, Turkey, 1974-76; rsch. assoc. physics U. Calgary, Alta., Can., 1976-77; project scientist Ctr. for Rsch. in Exptl. Space Sci. York U., Toronto, Ont., Can., 1977-78; lectr. physics U. Wis., LaCrosse, 1978-83, asst. prof., 1983-86, assoc. prof., 1986—. Contbr. articles to profl. publs. Mem. AAAS, Am. Geophys. Union, Am. Assn. Physics Tchrs., Optical Soc. Am., Soc. Archtl. Historians, Sigma Xi, Phi Beta Kappa. Home: 2025 State St La Crosse WI 54601-3735 Office: U Wis-LaCrosse Dept Physics Cowley Hall La Crosse WI 54601-3788 E-mail: barmore.fran@uwlax.edu.

BARNARD, ANN WATSON, retired academic administrator, educator, writer; b. Kansas City, Mo., Feb. 17, 1930; d. Howard Dale and Gladys (Conklin) Watson; (div. 1959); children: Faith, John. BA in English, U. Kansas City, 1950, MA in English, 1952; PhD in Humanities, U. Mo., Kansas City, 1963. Tchr. English Blackburn Coll., Carlinville, Ill., 1960-93, chair dept. English, 1964-93, prof. emerita, 1993—. Chair humanities div. Blackburn Coll., 1979-85, coll. marshal, 1989-93. Author poetry; contbr. articles to profl. jours. Mem. Common Cause, Defenders of Wildlife; co-chair Mary Hunter Austin Soc., 1996—; tutor Project Read, 1996—. Blackburn Coll. grantee, 1987-90. Mem. Assn. for Can. Studies in the U.S., Am. Studies Assn., Modern Lang. Assn., Nat. Coun. Tchrs. of English, AAUW, NOW, Western Lit. Assn. Democrat. Episcopalian. Avocations: gardening, hiking, nature study, environmental issues. E-mail: abcarl@earthlink.net.

BARNARD, ANNETTE WILLIAMSON, elementary school principal; b. Phoenix, Nov. 29, 1948; d. Water Albert and Geraldine Williamson; m. Richard W. Heinrich, Sept. 1969 (div.); 1 child, Jennifer Anne; m. Charles Jay Barnard, June 6, 1981. AA, Mesa C.C., 1979; BA in Spl. Edn., Elem. Edn., Ariz. State U., 1981, postgrad., 1989; M in Edn. Leadership, 1996, No. Ariz. U., 1996. Cert. tchr., prin., Ariz. Tchr. spl. edn. Tempe (Ariz.) Sch. Dist., 1981-83, tchr. Indian community, 1983-84; tchr. elem. sch. Kyrene Sch. Dist., Tempe, 1984-97; sch. dist. mentor coord., 1994-96; tchr. Chandler (Ariz.) Sch. Dist., 1986-89; v.p. Pendergast Elem. Sch., Phoenix, 1997-98; prin. Arredondo Elem. Sch., Tempe Sch. Dist., 1999—. Chair profl. stds. and cert. com. Ariz. Bd. Edn., Phoenix, 1990-94; chair facilitator Kyrene Legis. Action Community, 1991-94; mentor Kyrene Sch. dist., 1990—; commencement spkr. Ariz. State U., 1981; design. team. mem. Quality Cert. Employee Appraisal System; speaker in field. Contbg. author: Environmental Education Compendium for Energy Resources, 1991, System of Personnel Development, 1989; contbr. articles to profl. jours. Bd. dirs. Ariz. State Rep. Caucus, Phoenix, 1990-93, precinct committeewoman, Tempe, 1990-92. Recipient Profl. Leadership award Kiwanis Club Am., Tempe, 1984; nominee to talent bank Coun. on Women's Edn. Programs U.S. Dept. Edn., 1982; named Tchr. of Yr., local newspaper, 1993. Mem. ASCD, Kyrene Edn. Assn. (chair legis. com. 1990-94), Kappa Delta Pi, Phi Kappa Phi, Phi Theta Kappa, Pi Lambda Theta. Achievements include being featured in PBS Cornerstones video, 1994. Home: 3080 S Greythorne Way Chandler AZ 85248-2149

BARNARD, JOHN PHILLIP, technology educator; b. Watertown, NY, Jan. 30, 1950; s. Lewis Addison and Emma (Halsey) B.; m. Che du Puich, Aug. 26, 1977. BS, USNY Regents Coll., Albany, 1989; MEd, Ariz. State U., 1990, PhD, 2000. Cert. C.C. instr. Photographer Ariz. State U., Tempe, 1971-81, media specialist, 1981-90, instrnl. specialist, 1990-91, acad. profl., 1991—2002; asst. prof. instl. tech. Gordon Coll., Barnesville, Ga., 2002—. Contbr. articles to profl. jours. Mem. Am. Ednl. Rsch. Assn., Assn. for Ednl. Comm. and Tech., Ariz. Ednl. Media Assn. (pres. 1994-95), Phi Kappa Phi. Democrat. Office: Gordon Coll Barnesville GA 30204

BARNARD, WALTHER M. geosciences educator; b. Hartford, Conn., May 30, 1937; s. Walter Monroe and Florence Elzada (Wheeler) B. BS, Trinity Coll., 1959; AM, Dartmouth Coll., 1961; PhD, Pa. State U., 1965. Asst. prof. dept. geology/geosciences SUNY, Fredonia, 1964-70, assoc. prof., 1970-77, prof., 1977—, acting chairperson, 1986-87, chairperson, 1987-97. Mem. affiliate faculty U. Hawaii, Hilo, 1995—; dir. NSF undergrad. rsch. programs, summers, 1975-80. Recipient grant-in-aid Research Found. of SUNY, 1964, 66, 69, 72, faculty research fellowship, summers, 1966, 70, 73; research grantee Research Corp., 1965, U.S. Dept. Energy, 1975-77; Lake Erie Environ. Studies Research fellowship SUNY, Fredonia, summers, 1972-75, 78. Mem. AAAS, AAUP, Am. Geophys. Union, Am. Inst. Chemists, ASTM, Geochem. Soc., Geochem. Soc. Japan, Geol. Assn. Can., Geol. Soc. Am., Internat. Assn. Geochemistry and Cosmochemistry, Am. Meteorol. Soc., Nat. Earth Sci. Tchrs. Assn., Internat. Assn. Theoretical and Applied Limnology, mineral socs. Gt. Brit., Can., Am., Nat. Assn. Geology Tchrs., Internat. Assn. Gt. Lakes Research, N.Y. Acad. Scis., Soc. Applied Spectroscopy, Soc. Environ. Geochemistry and Health, Am. Chem. Soc., Am. Soc. Agronomy, Crop Sci. Soc. Am., Internat., Am., Can. socs. soil sci., Fedn. Am. Scientists, Nat. Sci. Tchrs. Assn., Soc. Coll. Sci. Tchrs., Nat. Ground Water Assn., Explorers Club, N.Y. State Geol. Assn. (pres. 1990), Sigma Xi. Author: Kaho'olawe, 1996; editor: Mauna Loa—A Source Book: Historical Eruptions and Exploration, From 1778-1907, Vol. 1, 1990, The Early HVO and Jaggar Yrs. (1912-40), Vol. 2, 1991, The Post-Jaggar Yrs. (1940-91), Vol. 3, 1992, Mauna Loa—A Potpourri of Anecdotes, 1996. Home: 2950 Straight Rd Fredonia NY 14063-9400 Office: Dept of Geoscis SUNY Coll Fredonia NY 14063 E-mail: barnard@fredonia.edu.

BARNES, A. KEITH, management educator; b. Peterborough, Eng., July 5, 1934; came to U.S., 1975; s. Archibald and Constance Louise (Snart) B.; m. Judith Anne Lamplugh, Dec. 26, 1955; children: Warren, Douglas, Lisa. BSc in Engring., Nene Univ., 1955; MBA in Mgmt., Pepperdine U., 1980, EdD in Adminstrn., 1984. Engr., designer Perkins Diesel, Eng. and Can., 1954-57; various positions Blackwood Hodge, Toronto, Can., 1957-70; various mgmt. positions J.I. Case Co. (Tenneco), Toronto, Can., 1970-81; from asst. to assoc. prof. U. La Verne, Calif., 1981-84; from assoc. prof. to Hunsaker prof. mgmt. U. Redlands, Calif., 1984—. Spkr. numerous orgns., 1974—. Author: Management Maturity: Prerequisite to Total Quality, 1994; editor Jour. Applied Bus. Rsch., 1988-93; mem. editl. bd. Jour. Mgmt. Sys., 1986—. Bd. dirs. San Gorgonio Meml. Hosp., 1993-94. Republican. Avocations: carpentry, tennis, chess, computer programming, writing fiction. Office: U Redlands Box 3080 1200 E Colton Ave Redlands CA 92374-3755

BARNES, ALETA WILLIS, communication and drama educator; b. Lake Charles, La., Aug. 6, 1950; d. Earl William and Iva Eloise (Hatsfelt) Willis; divorced; 1 child, Jason Andrew. BA, McNeese U., 1972, MEd, 1978. Cert. educator. Tchr. St. Louis H.S., Lake Charles, 1977-78, Sulphur H.S., Lake Charles, 1984—. Tchr. Upward Bound, McNeese U., Lake Charles, Sowela Tech. Inst., Lake Charles Am. Banking Inst.; motivational/mgmt. spkr., workshop dir. Author curriculum guides and dramatic prodns. Pres., organizer Youth Soccer League, Lake Charles, 1980—; dir., author, organizer Spring Drama Prodn., Sulphur; coach, dir. Dance Line/soccer/speech team, Sulphur. Recipient Class Act award Sta. KPLC-TV, Lake Charles, 1993. Mem. NEA, La. Assn. Educators, Calcasieu Educators Assn. Democrat. Avocations: music, water activities, theater, writing, reading. Office: Sulphur H S 100 Sycamore St Sulphur LA 70663-4550 Home: 4170 Iberville St New Orleans LA 70119-5139

BARNES, BETTY JEAN, educational administrator; b. Aug. 11, 1948; BS, Miss. State U., Starkville, 1971, MEd, 1978; postgrad., U. Miss., Oxford, 1987. Tchr. Burnsville (Miss.) Sch., 1972-84; dir. exceptional children Tishomingo County Schs., Iuka, Miss., 1984—. Vol. Am. Cancer Soc., 8 yrs., Tishomingo Manor Nursing Home, 9 yrs. Mem.: Miss. Profl. Educators, Coun. Adminstrs. in Spl. Edn., Miss. Spl. Edn. Coop, Delta Kappa Gamma. Office: Tishomingo County Schs 1620 Paul Edmondson Dr Iuka MS 38852-1212

BARNES, CHARLES ANDREW, physicist, educator; b. Toronto, Ont., Can., Dec. 12, 1921; came to U.S., 1953, naturalized, 1961; m. Phyllis Malcolm, Sept., 1950. BA, McMaster U., 1943; MA, U. Toronto, 1944; PhD, Cambridge U., 1950. Physicist Joint Brit.-Canadian Atomic Energy Project, 1944-46; instr. physics U. B.C., 1950-53, 55-56; mem. faculty Calif. Inst. Tech., 1953-55, 56—, prof. physics, 1962-92; prof. emeritus physics, 1992—. Guest prof. Niels Bohr Inst., Copenhagen, 1973-74. Editor, contbr. to profl. books and jours. Recipient medal Inst. d'Astrophysique de Paris, 1986, Alexander von Humboldt U.S. Sr. Scientist award, Fed. Republic of Germany, 1986; NSF sr. fellow Denmark, 1962-63. Fellow AAAS, Am. Phys. Soc. Office: Calif Inst Tech 1201 E California Blvd Pasadena CA 91125-0001

BARNES, CYNTHIA LOU, retired gifted and talented educator; b. Yale, Okla., Jan. 14, 1934; d. Ira and Billie (Reed) Canfield; m. Edward M. Barnes, Jr., June 1, 1954; children: Edis, Barbara, Warren, Adrienne. BS, U. Tulsa, 1970; MS, Okla. State U., 1981. Substitute tchr. Tulsa Pub. Schs., 1970-73, kindergarten tchr., 1981-94, gifted edn. tchr., 1994-97, cons. Guide for Tchg. Gifted in the Regular Classroom, 1996, substitute tchr., 1997—2002, 2nd semester gifted edn. tchr. Carver Mid. Sch., 1998; pre-sch. tchr. Meml. Drive Meth., Tulsa, 1976-81; ret., 1997. Curriculum coord. Barnard Elem. Sch., Tulsa, 1992—97, site-base co-chmn., 1992—93; bd. dirs. Gt. Expectations Educators, Inc., Tulsa; cons. kindergarten guide Tulsa Pub. Schs., 1985; presenter Elem. Educators Conf., 1994, 97. Author: (curriculum guide) Special Connections, 1996. Confirmation class coord. 1st Meth. Ch., Broken Arrow, Okla., 1999—2002, Collinsville (Okla.) Story Hour Reader, 2001—02. Grantee, Tulsa Edn. Fund, 1994, 1996. Mem.: Okla. Assn. Gifted, Creative, Talented, Tulsa Classroom Tchrs. Math. (conf. presider 1994), Tulsa County Reading Coun. Home: 7824 E 22nd Pl Tulsa OK 74129-2416

BARNES, JACQUELINE C. LINSCOTT, education consultant, retired educator; b. Franklin, N.C., Feb. 26, 1941; d. Clyde W. and Katherine (Ray) Clark; m. Leonard Lee Linscott, Aug. 16, 1964; 1 child, Laura Leigh Linscott Bledsoe; m. Graham B. Barnes, Sept. 2, 2001. BS in Edn., U. N.C., 1964; M in Elem. Edn., Adminstrn. Supr., Stetson U., 1980. Edn. Cert., Fla. Tchr. Riverview Elem. Sch., Titusville, Fla., 1964-66, Jackson Middle Sch., Titusville, Fla., 1966-67, Coquina Elem. Sch., Titusville, Fla., 1967-86, Challenger 7 Elem. Sch., Cocoa, Fla., 1986-89, PRIME specialist, 1989-91, YRE coord., 1991-96. Cons. on yr.-round edn. Dept. Edn., Tallahassee, 1990—. Author: Blue Bell Paper Weights and Other Bells, 1990, rev. edit., 1992, addendum, 1995, rev. edit., 2003. Grantee PAC-MAN Reading Program Brevard Pub. Schs., Melbourne, Fla., 1982, Caring Adults Reading with Elem. Students, Brevard Pub. Schs., 1990. Mem. ASCD, Nat. Assn. Yr.-Round Edn. (presenter confs. 1993—), Fla. Assn. Yr.-Round Edn. (presenter conf. 1991—, pres.), Alpha Delta Kappa. Avocations: antiques, reading, crafts. Home: 3557 Nicklaus Dr Titusville FL 32780-5356 E-mail: bluebellwt@aol.com.

BARNES, JAMES JOHN, history educator; b. St. Paul, Nov. 16, 1931; s. Harry George and Bertha (Blaul) B.; m. Patience Rogers Plummer, July 9, 1955; children— Jennifer Chase, Geoffrey Prescott BA, Amherst Coll., 1954, New Coll., Oxford, 1956, MA, 1961; PhD, Harvard U., 1960; DHL, Coll. of Wooster, 1976, Amherst Coll., 1999. Instr. history Amherst Coll., 1959-62; asst. prof. history Wabash Coll., Crawfordsville, Ind., 1962-67, assoc. prof. history, 1967-76, prof. history, 1976—, chmn. dept. history, Hadley prof., 1979-97. Author: Free Trade in Books: A Study of the London Book Trade since 1800, 1964, Authors, Publishers and Politicians: The Quest for an Anglo-American Copyright Agreement 1815-54, 1974, (with Patience P. Barnes) Hitler's Mein Kampf in Britain and America 1930-39, 1980, (with Patience P. Barnes) James Vincent Murphy: Translator and Interpreter of Fascist Europe, 1880-1946, 1987, (with Patience P. Barnes) Private and Confidential Letters from British Ministers in Washington to the Foreign Secretaries in London, 1849-67, 1993, (with Patience P. Barnes) Nazi Refugee turned Gestapo Spy: The Life of Hans Wesemann, 1895-1971, 2001, (with Patience P. Barnes) The American Civil War through British Eyes: Dispatches from British Diplomats, Vol. 1: Nov. 1860-Apr. 1862, 2003; contbr. articles to profl. jours. Mem. Rhodes Scholar Selection Com. for Ind., 1965-89, Crawfordsville Community Action Coun., 1966-69, Crawfordsville Community Day Care Com., 1966-67; mem. vestry St. John's Episcopal Ch., 1966-69; mem. Ind. Adv. Com. State Rehab. Svcs. for Blind, 1979-81; trustee Ind. Hist. Soc., 1982—. Recipient Disting. Alumni award St. Paul Acad. and Summit Sch., 1989; Rhodes scholar, 1954-56, Fulbright scholar, 1978; Woodrow Wilson fellow, 1956-57, Kent fellow, 1958, Great Lakes Colls. Assn. Teaching fellow, 1958, Great Lakes Colls. Assn. Teaching fellow, 1975; rsch. grantee Amherst Coll., 1960-61, Social Sci. Rsch. Coun., 1962, 70, Wabash Coll., 1962—, Am. Coun. Learned Socs., 1964-65, 80, Am. Philos. Soc., 1964, 68, 76, 91; named Hon. Alumnus, Wabash Coll., 1994. Mem. Am. Hist. Assn., Ouiatenon Literary Soc., Conf. Brit. Studies, Rsch. Soc. Victorian Periodicals, Am. Rhodes Scholars, Soc. Historians Am. Fgn. Rels., Ind. Hist. Soc., Montgomery County Hist. Soc., Midwest Victorian Studies Assn. (pres. 1989-91), Ind. Assn. Historians, N.E. Victorian Studies Assn., Soc. for History of Authorship, Reading and Pub., Am. Coun. of Blind, United Oxford and Cambridge Club of London, Phi Beta Kappa. Home: 7 Locust Hl Crawfordsville IN 47933-3347 Office: Wabash Coll History Dept Crawfordsville IN 47933 E-mail: barnesj@wabash.edu.

BARNES, LARRY GLEN, journalist, editor, educator; b. Louisville, July 10, 1947; s. Roy Glen and Phyllis Jane (Dunn) B.; m. Susan Gayle Morrow, Dec. 27, 1969 (dec. July, 1973); 1 child, Brian; m. Mary Frances Meiman, July 14, 1979. Student, Murray State U., 1965-68, 71-73, Def. Info. Sch., 1968. Journalist, editor various locations Dept. of the Army, 1968-71; staff writer Louisville Courier-Jour., 1972-75, Lexington (Ky.) Herald-Leader, 1975; mng. editor Corydon (Ind.) Harrison County Press, 1976-77; assoc. editor Ky. Sports World, Louisville, 1977-81; editor Publs. Divsn., Ft. Knox, Ky., 1981-82, Inside the Turret, Ft. Knox, 1982—. Editor Army's Best Newspaper, 1984, 86, 91, 93, 96, 98, (named Army's Dean of Newspaper editors 2000), DOD Newspaper, 1986. With U.S. Army, 1968-71. Recipient Naismith citation Atlanta Tipoff Club, 1981, Journalist award Dept. Army, Washington, 1986, Master Craftsman award, 2002, 1st pl. commentary writing Tng. & Doctrine Command. Ft. Monroe, Va., 1985, 87-90, Thomas Jefferson award Dept. Def., Washington, 1982, 86; named Editor of Yr., Army Tng. & Doctrine Command, 1982. Mem. Soc. Profl. Journalists, Am. Fedn. Govt. Employees. Democrat. Baptist. Avocations: photography, watching movies, collecting, 45 r.p.m. records, reading. Home: 2220 Manchester Rd Louisville KY 40205-3044 Office: Pub Affairs Office PO Box 995 Fort Knox KY 40121-0995 E-mail: turret@ftknox-emh3.army.mil.

BARNES, PATRICIA ANN, art educator; b. San Antonio, Sept. 26, 1942; d. John Homer and Dorothy Bernice (Foster) Sanders; m. Henry Franklin Snodgrass, Oct. 31, 1960 (div. 1966); children: William Franklin, George Huston II, John Charles Joseph; m. Joseph LeRoy Barnes Jr., Aug. 18, 1969; children: Shana Lynn, Janna Lee, Joseph Leroy III. AAS, Bee County Coll., 1986; BFA, Corpus Christi State U., 1988; MA, Tex. A&M U., 1990. Art tchr. J.T.P.A. Summer Youth Program, Beeville, Tex., 1990; adj. art tchr. St. Philips Coll., San Antonio, 1991-93; art tchr. Runge (Tex.) Ind. Sch. Dist., 1993-96; art tchr., chmn. fine arts Skidmore (Tex.)-Tynan Ind. Sch. Dist., 1996—2001, chmn. fine arts, 2000—01; ret., 2001. Owner Patty's Pyrographics, Three Rivers, Tex., 1995—; Upward Bound art tchr. Coastal Bend Coll., Beeville, Tex., 1999; rep. Polyform Products, 1999—, Jacquard Products, 2001—; polymer clay instr. Michaels Arts and Crafts; tchr. JoAnn's, 2001—. Contr. art in book: Transfering Designs., 2002. Mem.: Victoria Polymer Clay Guild (founding), San Antonio Polymer Clay Guild (founding mem., parliamentarian), South Tex. Polymer Clay Guild (pres. 1999—, charter, founder), Coastal Bend Art Edn. Assn., Tex. Art Edn. Assn. (presenter convs. 1997—99, Region 5 rep. 2000—01), Nat. Polymer Clay Guild, Nat. Art Edn. Assn., Skidmore-Tynan Nat. Art Honor Soc. (sponsor 2001—), Skidmore-Tynan Fine Arts Booster Club (founder 2000—01, sponsor). Avocations: glass fusing, polymer clay art, reading, fishing, sewing. Home: RR 1 Box 497 Three Rivers TX 78071-9711 E-mail: pbarnes@the-i.net.

BARNES, PAULETTE WHETSTONE, school system administrator; b. Depew, Okla., Oct. 7, 1942; d. Paul Raymond and Dorothy (Pitts) Whetstone; m. Fredrick Joseph Barnes, Feb. 22, 1964; children: Bradley Mark, Amy Michelle Barnes Harnish. BA, Okla. Coll. for Women, 1964; MS, Emporia State U., 1971; postgrad., Okla. State U., 1982-84. Cert. sch. psychologist, psychometrist, speech pathologist, hearing clinician, elem. and secondary prin., supt., dist. sch. adminstr., Okla., Kans. Speech pathologist Topeka Pub. Schs., 1963-67; tchr. educably mentally handicapped Hutchinson, Kans., 1967-68; speech pathologist Lyons (Kans.) Unified Sch. Dist., 1968-69, Seamon Pub. Schs., Topeka, 1969-70; sch. psychologist Topeka Pub. Schs., 1970-74; coord. spl. edn. Kansas State Dept. Edn., Topeka, 1974-77; coord. 5 County Spl. Edn. Coop., Ardmore, Okla., 1977-78; dir. spl. svcs. Bixby (Okla.) Pub. Schs., 1978-82, 1982-87; asst. supt./prin. Children's Devel. Program, Tulsa County, 1987-88; coord. sec. spl. edn. Tulsa Pub. Schs., 1987-88; dir. edn. Shadow Mountain Inst., Tulsa, 1988-93; supt. Pretty Water Sch. CO-34, Sapulpa, Okla., 1993—. Mem. Regional Adv. Bd. for Spl. Needs Children, Tulsa, 1990-93; cons. Child Identification Project of Kans., Topeka, 1977, Okla. State Dept. of Edn., Oklahoma City, 1977-78. Co-author handbook for Okla. State Dept. Edn., 1977-78; contbr. articles to profl. publs. Mem. Coun. for Exceptional Children (pres. Kans. Fedn. 1976), Okla. Dirs. of Spl. Svcs. (pres. 1981-82, charter mem., Spl. Edn. Adminstr. of Yr. 1986-87), Tulsa Area Dirs. of Spl. Svcs. (pres. 1980-81, sec. 1987-88, area rep. 1990-92), Midwest Regional Dirs. of Spl. Svcs. (chair 1984-85), Coop. Coun. Sch. Adminstrs., Assn. Supervision and Curriculum Devel. Avocations: writing, sewing, clothing design, public speaking, history. Home: 8535 Westway Rd Tulsa OK 74131-3865 Office: Pretty Water Sch CO-34 15223 W 81st St Sapulpa OK 74066-2984

BARNES, RAMON MURRAY, chemistry educator; b. Pitts., Apr. 24, 1940; s. Jack N. and Sally L. (Silver) B.; m. Dorothy M. Soja, May 17, 1969. BS, Oreg. State U., 1962; MA, Columbia U., 1963; PhD, U. Ill., Champaign-Urbana, 1966. Lectr. Baldwin Wallace Coll., Bera, Ohio, 1967-68; materials engr. NASA Lewis Research Ctr., Cleve., 1968-69; postdoctoral fellow Iowa State U., Ames, 1969; asst. to prof. chemistry U. Mass., Amherst, 1969-2000, dir. Univ. Rsch. Inst. for Analytical Chemistry, 2000—, prof. emeritus chemistry, 2000—. Chmn. Winter Conf. on Plasma Spectrochemistry, 1980—. Mem. editorial bd. Jour. Analytical Atomic Spectrometry, Canadian Jour. Analytical Scis. and Spectroscopy, Spectroscopy (Eugene), Spectroscopy Europe, Analytical Abstracts, Guangpuxue Yu (Spectroscopy and Spectral Analysis), Spectrochimica Acta Revs., Spectrochimica Acta Electronica; editor, pub., treas. (newsletter) ICP Info. Newsletter, 1975—; editor six books; inventor in field; contbr. articles to profl. jours. Capt. USAR, 1966-68. Fellow AAAS; mem. Am. Chem. Soc., Royal Soc. of Chemistry, Soc. for Applied Spectroscopy, Optical Soc. Am., Spectroscopy Soc. of Can., Soc. Toxicology, Sigma Xi. Avocation: gardening. Office: U Mass Chem Dept Lederle GRC Tower 710 N Pleasant St Amherst MA 01003-9336 E-mail: icpnews@chem.umass.edu., rmbarnes@chem.umass.edu.

BARNES, REBECCA MARIE, assistant principal; b. Jackson, Tenn., Nov. 5, 1942; d. Hewitt C. and Willette (Atwater) Johnson; m. Timothy Barnes; children: Mark, Michael, Matthew. BA in Edn., Harris Tchrs. Coll., 1965; MA, Webster U., 1983. Cert. tchr. mid. sch., reading specialist, gifted/talented edn. Tchr. St. Louis Pub. Schs., 1965-95; asst. prin. Compton-Drew ILC Middle Sch. at the Sci. Ctr., 1996—. Vol. Black Repertory Theater. Recipient Outstanding Svc. award United Negro Coll. Fund. Mem. ASCD, Internat. Reading Assn., Nat. Mid. Schs. Assn., Gifted Assn. Mo., Mo. Botanical Gardens, St. Louis Sci. Ctr., Delta Sigma Theta, Phi Delta Kappa. Avocations: reading, gardening, computers, the arts. Home: 2655 Wedgwood Dr Florissant MO 63033-1429

BARNES, RICHARD GEORGE, physicist, educator; b. Milw., Dec. 19, 1922; s. George Richard and Irma (Ott) B.; m. Mildred A. Jachens, Sept. 9, 1950; children: Jeffrey R., David G., Christina E., Douglas A. BA, U. Wis., 1948; MA, Dartmouth Coll., 1949; PhD, Harvard U., 1952. Teaching fellow Harvard, 1950-52; asst. prof. U. Del., 1952-55, asso. prof., 1955-56, Iowa State U., 1956-60, prof., 1960-88, chmn. dept. physics, 1971-75, prof. emeritus, 1988—; sr. physicist Ames Lab., U.S. Dept. Energy, 1960-88; assoc. Ames lab. US Dept. Energy, 1988—; chief physics divsn. Ames lab. AEC, 1971-75. Vis. rsch. prof. Calif. Inst. Tech., 1962-63; guest profl. Tech. U. Darmstadt, Germany, 1975-76; vis. prof. Cornell U., 1982-83; program dir. solid state physics NSF, 1988-89, condensed matter physics NSF, 1995; chmn. Metal Hydrides Gordon Rsch. Conf., 1987. Served with USAAF, 1942-43; C.E. AUS, 1944-46 (Manhattan Project). Recipient U.S. Sr. Scientist award Alexander von Humboldt Found., 1975-76 Fellow Am. Phys. Soc. Home: 3238 Aspen Rd Ames IA 50014 Office: Iowa State U Physics Dept Ames IA 50011-0001

BARNES, RICHARD NEARN, biology educator emeritus; b. Washington, Dec. 10, 1928; s. Wilbur Brents and Helen Fronica (Hottenfeller) B.; m. Mary Elizabeth DeLauter, Jan. 19, 1957; children: Kathryn Ann, Marcia Louise. AB, U. Calif., Berkeley, 1952; MA, U. Calif., Davis, 1957, PhD, 1962. Instr. Calif. State U., Sacramento, 1957-62; from asst. prof. to prof. biology Berea (Ky.) Coll., 1962-72, full prof., 1972-94, prof. emeritus, 1994. Cpl. U.S. Army, 1952-54, Korea. Office: Berea Coll Dept Biology Berea KY 40404-0001

BARNES, ROBERT VINCENT, retired elementary and secondary school art educator; b. Flint, Mich., May 27, 1948; s. Albert J. and Mary Elizabeth (Morey) B.; m. Sandra E. Mathews-Barnes, Dec. 20, 1986; 1 child, Kathryn R. BA, Adrian Coll., 1970; postgrad., U. Mich., 1973-75, Ctrl. Mich. U., 1976-80, Getty Ctr. Edn. Arts, Cin. Art Mus., Cranbrook Acad. Art, Marygrove Coll., Cranbrook Acad. Art, 1995—; MA, Marygrove Coll., 1997. Cert. tchr. art grades kindergarten through 12, Mich. Tchr. art Flushing (Mich.) Cmty. Schs., 1971—2002; instr. Flint Inst. Arts, 1975-76; tchr. genealogy adult edn. program Mott C.C., Flushing, Fenton and Grand Blanc, Mich., 1976-84; pvt. art tchr., 2002—. Tchr. pvt. art lessons. Author: Flushing Area Families, 1981, Fenton Area Families, 1984; editor Flint Geneal. Quar., 1981. Past pres. Flint Geneal. Soc., Fenton Hist. Soc.; bd. dirs., past pres. Flushing Area Hist. Soc.; pres. Fenton Mus. Bd., 1984-86; chmn. Fenton 150th Com., 1984; co-chmn. Fenton Civic Com. for New Mus., 1985-86; com. mem. Genesee County Sesquicentennial, Flint, 1986; mentor for jr. h.s. youth Logas program Fenton United Meth. Ch., mem. edn. commn., 2000—. Recipient 1st prize Flushing Art Fair, Flushing Jr. Women's League, 1975, 78, Orren Hart award Flushing Area Hist. Soc., 1983. Mem. NEA, Mich. Edn. Assn., Nat. Art Edn. Assn., Mich. Art Edn. Assn., Ohio Geneal. Soc., Ohio Hist. Soc. Methodist. Avocations: pottery, painting, family history research.

BARNES, SARA LYNN, school system administrator; b. Lampasas, Tex., Jan. 9, 1940; d. Wesley Homer and Wilma Chlotide (Robertson) Scott; m. Rodney Roy Barnes, Jan. 26, 1980; children: Rodney Roy Jr., Cathie Darlene Jackson Elder, Nikki Marie Jackson Seimears, Robin Lou Barnes Groskurth. BS, U. Mary Hardin-Baylor, 1960; MEd, Tarleton State U., 1985. Cert. tchr., vocat. tchr., supt., adminstr., Tex. Tchr., chmn. bus. dept. Copperas Cove (Tex.) H.S., 1969-70, vocat. tchr., 1970-74; adminstrv. asst. for bus. Copperas Cove Sch. Dist., 1974-81; dir. bus. svcs. Copperas Cove Ind. Sch. Dist., 1981-88, bus. mgr., 1988-90, exec. dir. bus. svcs., 1990-92, asst. supt. ops., 1992—, interim supt., 1994. Instr. evening coll. Ctrl. Tex. Coll., Killeen, Tex., 1973-80, mem. budget task force, 1989; mem. First Vocat. Office Edn. Adv. Bd., 1971-72. Bd. dirs. Copperas Cove United Way, 1984-87, Copperas Cove Econ. Devel. Corp., 1990, Greater Ft. Hood United Way, Copperas Cove, 1992-95. Fannie Breedlove Davis scholar, 1958-60; recipient cert. of achievement in excellence Govt. Fin. Officers Assn., 1991-95. Mem. Tex. Assn. Sch. Bus. Ofcls., Am. Assn. Sch. Bus. Ofcls. (internat. panel rev. mem. 1991—, cert. of excellence 1991-94), Copperas Cove Exch. Club (treas. 1996, bd. dirs. 1991-93, Exchangite of Yr. 1992), Delta Kappa Gamma (v.p. 1988-90, State scholar 1995). Avocations: reading, computer games, photography, bird-watching, crafts. Home: 2960 Grimes Crossing Rd Copperas Cove TX 76522-7431 Office: Copperas Cove Ind Sch Dist PO Box 580 Copperas Cove TX 76522-0580

BARNES, WENDELL WRIGHT, JR., education educator; b. Macon, Ga., July 15, 1950; s. Wendell Wright and Elizabeth (Johnson) B.; m. Reba Hall, Sept. 17, 1977; 1 child, Wendell Wright III. BFA, U. Ga., 1973, MEd, 1981; MS, U. Tenn., 1998. Court reporter Atlanta Reporting Co., Inc., 1973-74; high sch. tchr. Muscogee County Sch. Dist., Columbus, Ga., 1974-76; spl. edn. tchr. Ga. Dept. Offender Rehab., Columbus, 1976-77; rehab. counselor Ga. Dept. Human Resources, Columbus, 1977-84, Athens, 1984-87; rsch. instr., asst. dir. Orientation to Deafness Programs U. Tenn., Knoxville, 1987-95; dir., assoc. prof. Am. Sign Lang. Immersion Tng. Program for Interpreters Floyd Coll., Rome, Ga., 1995—; coord. Stagehands and Sightlines Programs VSA Arts of Ga., 1997—2001. Chmn. Mayor's Com. for Employment of Handicapped, Columbus, 1983-84; regional rep. Miss Ga. Pageant, 1984-87; pres. Parables Sunday Sch. Class, Ch. St. United Meth. Ch. Mem. Am. Deafness and Rehab. Assn., Nat. Assn. of the Deaf, Am. Sign Lang. Tchrs. Assn., Coalition for Inclusive Performing Arts (sec.), Accessibility Mgrs. in the Performing Arts, Phi Kappa Theta (rec. sec. 1971-72). Avocations: theatre, church activities, reading. Home: 1014 Cave Spring Rd SW Rome GA 30161-4701 Office: Floyd Coll PO Box 1864 Rome GA 30162-1864 E-mail: wbarnes@darlingtonschool.org., wbarnes@floyd.edu.

BAR-NESS, YEHESKEL, electrical engineer, educator; b. Baghdad, Iraq, Apr. 28, 1932; arrived in Israel, 1950; came to U.S., 1978; m. Varda Bar-Ness, Aug. 21, 1952; children: Yael, Yaron, Yegal. BEE, Technion U., Haifa, Israel, 1958, MEE, 1963; PhD, Brown U., 1969. Chief engr. Elscint Inc., Haifa, 1971-75; assoc. prof. Tel-Aviv U., 1973-78; vis. prof. Brown U., 1978-79, U. Pa., Phila., 1979-81; prof. elec. engring. Drexel U., Phila., 1981-83; tech. staff mem. AT&T Bell Lab., Holmdel, N.J., 1983-85; disting. prof. elec. and computer engring. N.J. Inst. Tech., Newark, 1985—, dir. ctr. communication and signal processing rsch., 1985—, found. chair comm. and signal processing, 2000—. Vis. prof. elec. engring. Tech. U. Delft, The Netherlands, 1993-94, Stanford U., 2000-01. Recipient Kaplan Price award Gov. of Israel, 1974. Fellow IEEE; mem. Communication Soc. of IEEE (sec. communications systems engring. com. 1985-87, vice chmn., 1987-89, chmn. 1990-91, editor IEEE transaction on comm., founder and editor-in-chief IEEE Comm. Letters). Home: 2 Etna Ct Marlboro NJ 07746-1307 Office: NJ Inst of Tech 323 King Blvd Newark NJ 07102-1824

BARNETT, BENJAMIN LEWIS, JR., retired physician, educator; b. Woodruff, S.C., July 22, 1926; s. Benjamin Lewis and Mattie Bernice (Skinner) B.; m. Annalyne Louise Hall, Oct. 25, 1958; children: Benjamin Lewis III, Jane Kristen. BS, Furman U., 1946, LLD, 1978; MD, Med. U. S.C., 1949. Diplomate Am. Bd. Family Practice. Intern Protestant Episcopal Hosp., Phila., 1949-50; pvt. practice Woodruff, 1950-70; from assoc. prof. family practice to asst. dean Med. U. S.C., Charleston, 1970—75, asst. dean for student affairs, 1975—77; clin. staff Med. U. Hosp., Charleston County Hosp., 1970-77; from prof. to prof. emeritus U. Va. Med. Sch., 1977—2000, prof. emeritus, 2000—; family medicine physician-in-chief U. Va. Med. Ctr. Hosp., 1977-96. Admissions com. U. Va. Med. Sch., 1997-99; Stoneburner lectr. Med. Coll. Va., 1975; Daniel Drake lectr. U. Cin., 1976; Robert P. Walton lectr. Med. U. S.C., 1978; Goodlark prof. U. Tenn., 1979; Roy J. Gerard lectr. Mich. State U., 1992; vis. scholar U. Mich. Med. Sch., 1984; vis. lectr. Med. Coll. of Ga., 1982; vis. prof. Case Western Res. Sch. Medicine, 1984, U. Vt., 1988, U. N.Mex., 1991, U. S.C. Sch. Medicine, 1999; spkr. baccalaureate address U. Va., 1986, 2000; Mack Lipkin vis. prof. U. Oreg., 1987, U. Utah, 1989; Donald J. Welter Meml. lectr. Med. Coll. Wis., 1989; Frederick Lytel Meml. lectr., Abington, Pa., 1989; Bradford Strock lectr. Harrisburg (Pa.) Gen. Hosp., 1989; 7th Leland Blanchard Meml. lectr. Soc. Tchrs. Family Medicine ann. meeting, Nashville, 1985; health officer, Town of Woodruff, 1950-54; keynote speaker Assn. Depts. Family Medicine, Clearwater, Fla., 1991; commencement speaker U. Va. Med. Sch., 1992, 97; Grand Prof. Rounds St. Margaret's Hosp., Pitts., 1993; Julian Keith lectr. Bowman Gray Sch. Medicine, 1993; keynote speaker leadership conf. Fla. Med. Assn., Ponta Vedra, 1994, AHEC conf. S.C. Family Practice, Myrtle Beach, 1994; B. Leslie Huffman lectr. Med. Coll. of Ohio, Toledo, 1994; lectr. Atlanta Med. Ctr., 2000—; grad. speaker McLennan County Med. Edn. and Rsch. Found., Waco, Tex., 1995; Inaugural Buck Crockett lectr., Roanoke, Va., 2000; founder's prof. U. Okla. Health Scis. Ctr., Tulsa, 2000; Harlan Thomas Meml. lectr.; Hiram B. Curry Meml. lectr. MUSC, 1990, 2001; lectr. and cons. in field. Author: Between the Lines (Reflections of a Physician), 1989, Pebbles in the Water, 2003; editor: S.C. Family Physician, 1973—74; contbr. articles to med. jours. and chpts. to textbooks. Mem. Spartanburg County Bd. Edn., 1968-70, sec. 1969-70; trustee Bethea Bapt. Home for Aged, Darlington, S.C., 1972-73; mem. bd. trustees Furman U., 1994-99; dir. Marietta-Lost Mtn. Kiwanis, 2003—; mentor character curriculum Kennesaw Mountain HS, 2002—. Named Citizen of Year Woodmen of World, 1968; recipient Golden Apple award for clin. teaching Student AMA, 1973; Thomas W. Johnson award Am. Acad. Family Physicians, 1976, Disting. Alumnus award Med. U. S.C., 1993; endowed Barnett Professorship in Family Medicine established U. Va. Bd. Visitors, 1997; Thomas Jefferson award U. Va., 1997. Mem. AMA (mem. residency rev. com. for family practice 1974-79), Am. Bd. Family Practice (exam. bd. 1975-81, dir. 1976-81, exec. com. 1979-81, pres. 1980-81), Va. Med. Soc., Albemarle County Med. Soc., Soc. Tchrs. Family Medicine (v.p. 1974, sec.-treas. 1975, dir. 1981-85, Cert. of Excellence 1983, F. Marian Bishop award 1996), Am. Acad. Family Physicians, S.C. Acad. Family Physicians (v.p. 1973, pres. 1975-76), Spartanburg County Med. Soc. (v.p. 1968), Am. Philatelic Soc., Coun. Acad. Socs., Furman U. Alumni Assn. (dir. 1972-77), U. Va. Raven Soc., Kiwanis, Alpha Omega Alpha (faculty councilor, vis. prof. U. S.C. Sch. Medicine 1999), Alpha Kappa Kappa (pres. 1948), Kappa Alpha (v.p. 1944) Baptist (deacon, chmn. bd.). Home: 4734 Talleybrook Dr NW Kennesaw GA 30152-5484

BARNETT, CHERYL LEE, sculptor, educator; b. Calif., Feb. 24, 1956; d. Charles A. and Neville Rae Barnett. BA in Art, U. Calif., Santa Cruz, 1977, postgrad., 1983; MA in Art, Calif. State U., Fresno, 1985. Art therapist Merced (Calif.) Manor Psychiat. Hosp., also others, 1979-81, 83; dir. art gallery Merced Coll., 1981-83, instr. art Summer Coll. for Kids, 1983-84, instr. art, 1981-86, 88—. Instr. Fresno Art Ctr., 1985; patina specialist Artworks Foundry & Gallery, Berkeley, Calif., 1986-88; lectr. AAUW, Merced, 1979, U. Calif., 1979. One-woman shows include Merced Coll. Art Gallery, 1982, 84, 89, 94, Fresno Art Mus., 1984, Phebe Conley Art Gallery, Calif. State U., Fresno, 1985, The Art Ctr., Visalia, Calif., 1986, Erika Meyerovich Gallery, San Francisco, 1986-87, Banaker Gallery, Walnut Creek, Calif., 1988, Eleonore Austerer Gallery, San Francisco, 1990-; group exhbns. include Kamaehameha Libr., Honolulu, 1981, Sparkasse Bank, Innsbruck, Austria, 1982, Merced Coll. Art Gallery, 1982-83, Calif. State U., Stanislaus Art Gallery, Turlock, Calif, 1984, Fig Tree Gallery, Fresno, 1985, Coll. of the Sequoias, Visalia, Calif., 1986, Fresno City Coll., 1986, Artworks Gallery, Berkeley, Calif., 1986-87, Civic Arts Gallery, Walnut Creek, Calif., 1988, 3 COM Corp., Santa Clara, Calif., 1988, Berkeley Art Ctr., 1988, Artworks Foundry Gallery, Berkeley, 1986-93, Carnegie Ctr. for the Arts, Turlock, 1989, Pro Arts Gallery, Oakland, Calif., 1989, The Arts Commn. of San Francisco, 1989, Merced Civic Ctr., 1989, Humboldt Cultural Ctr., Eureka, Calif., 1989, Herbert Palmer Gallery, L.A., 1990, One Market Plz., San Francisco, 1990, Austerer Gallery, San Francisco, 1990-2003, Hitachi Corp., Santa Clara, 1991, Napa Art Ctr., 1991, Artifacts, San Francisco, 1991-92, A Garden Gallery, Berkeley, 1992, Merced County Arts Ctr., 1992, Ops Art, San Francisco, 1993, Cadence Design Ctr., San Jose, 1993, Network Gen., Menlo Park, 1994, Synopsys Inc., Mountain View, 1994, Contract Design Ctr., San Francisco, 1995, 96, Mendocino Art Ctr., 1995, 97, Eleonore Austerer Gallery, 1990-, Bradford Gallery, 1996, The Vault, 1996, Sonora & Murphy, Calif., 1996, Stephen Wirtz Gallery, San Francisco, 1998, Hayward City Hall Galleria, Calif., 1998, 99, Merced Civic Ctr., 1998-99, Gallery Ocean Ave, Carmel, Calif., 2002, Austerer Gallery, Palm Springs, Calif., 2002-03, Brumley Art Gallery, Bass Lake, 2002-2003. Recipient Achievement award Bank Am., 1974, award for tchg. Nat. Inst. for Staff and Orgnl. Devel., 1996, Frances DeB. Henderson Sculpture prize, Cambridge Art Assn. Nat. Prize Show, Cambridge, Mass., 1998. Mem. AAUW, Internat. Sculpture Ctr., Pacific Rim Scupture Group, Nat. Mus. of Women in the Arts (charter). Office: Merced Coll Art Dept 3600 M St Merced CA 95348-2806

BARNETT, CRAWFORD FANNIN, JR., internist, educator, cardiologist, travel medicine specialist; b. Atlanta, May 11, 1938; s. Crawford Fannin and Penelope Hollinshead (Brown) B.; m. Elizabeth McCarthy Hale, June 6, 1964; children: Crawford Fannin III, Robert Hale. Student, Taft Sch., 1953-56, U. Minn., 1957; AB magna cum laude, Yale U., 1960; postgrad. (Davison scholar), Oxford (Eng.) U., 1963; MD (Trent scholar), Duke U., 1964. Intern internal medicine Duke U. Med. Ctr., Durham, N.C., 1964-65, resident, 1965; resident internal medicine Wilmington (Del.) Med. Ctr., 1965-66; dir. Tenn. Heart Disease Control Program, Nashville, 1966-68; pvt. practice medicine in internal/travel medicine Atlanta, 1968—. Dir. Travel Immunization Ctr., Atlanta; mem. staff Crawford Long, Northside, Grady Meml., West Paces, Piedmont, North Fulton hosps. (all Atlanta); mem. tchg. staff Vanderbilt Med. Ctr., Nashville, 1966-68, Crawford Long Meml. Hosp., 1969—; clin. instr. internal medicine, dept. medicine Emory U. Med. Sch., Atlanta, 1969—. Contbr. articles to profl. publs. Bd. govs. Doctors Meml. Hosp., 1971-80; bd. dirs. Atlanta Speech Sch., 1976-80, 92—, Historic Oakland Cemetery, 1976-86, So. Turf Nurseries, 1977-92, Tech Industries, 1978-92; bd. dirs. Am. Chestnut Found., 1990, bd. trustees Mary Brown Found. of Atlanta, 1998—, Woodward Found., 2001—. Surgeon USPHS, 1966-68. Fellow Am. Geog. Soc., Royal Soc. of Tropical Medicine and Hygiene, Royal Geog. Soc., Royal Soc. Medicine, Explorers Club (life, N.Y.C.); mem. Am. Soc. Tropical Medicine and Hygiene, Am. Fedn. Clin. Rsch., Coun. Clin. Cardiology, AMA, Ga. Med. Assn., Atlanta Med. Assn., Am. Heart Assn., Ga. Heart Assn., Am. Soc. Internal Medicine, Am. Assn. History, Medicine, Ga. Hist. Soc., Atlanta Hist. Soc. (bd. govs. 1976-84), Ga. Trust for Hist. Preservation, Nat. Trust Hist. Preservation, Internat. Hippocratic Found. Soc. (Greece), Faculty of History of Medicine and Pharmacy Worshipful Soc. Apothecaries of London, Atlanta Com. on Fgn. Rels. (chmn. exec. com. 1972-88), So. Coun. Internat. and Pub. Affairs, Newcomen Soc., Atlanta Clin. Soc., Wilderness Med. Soc., Internat. Soc. Travel Medicine (founding), Travelers Century Club, Circumnavigators Club, South Am. Explorers Club, Victorian Soc. Am. (bd. advisers Atlanta chpt. 1971-86), Mensa, Gridiron, Piedmont Driving Club, Yale Club (dir. 1970-74), Nine O'Clocks Club, Pan Am. Doctors Club, Phi Beta Kappa. Episcopalian. Home: 2739 Ramsgate Ct NW Atlanta GA 30305-2817 Office: Ste 302 3193 Howell Mill Rd NW Atlanta GA 30327-2100

BARNETT, DOROTHY PRINCE, retired university dean; b. Charlotte, N.C., Aug. 18, 1931; d. Abraham Hamilton and Susan (Peacock) Prince; m. Isaac Barnett, Dec. 27, 1977. AB, Oberlin Coll., 1953; MA, Syracuse U., 1954; EdD, Ind. U., 1962. Instr. Alcorn Coll., Lorman, Miss., summer 1954, So. U., Baton Rouge, 1954-55; asst. prof. N.C. Agrl. and Tech. State U., Greensboro, 1955-62, prof., 1962-94, chairperson dept. edn., 1966-77, chairperson dept. secondary edn. and curriculum, 1977-89, asst. dean, dir. tchr. edn. Sch. Edn., 1983-90, dean Sch. Edn., 1991-94, ret., 1994. Educator, reader U.S. Dept. Edn., Washington, 1968-94; mem. multicultural com. Met. project Am. Assn. Colls. for Tchr. Edn., Washington, 1990-92; cons. initiative conf. Phelps State Consortium, N.Y.C., 1971-73, Norfolk State U., Washington, 1981-89; reader Corp. for Pub. Broadcast, Washington, 1982; mem. bd. examiners Nat. Coun. for Accreditation of Tchr. Edn.; presenter state, nat. and local tchr. edn. confs., 1970-94; bd. dirs. Holmes Group. Contbr. articles to ednl. publs. Bd. dirs. Charlotte Hawkins Brown Hist. Found., Sedalia, N.C., Holmes Group, 1991-94. Recipient Honored Alumnus award Sch. Edn. Syracuse (N.Y.) U., 1992; John Hay Whitney Found. fellow, N.Y., 1961-62; Ellis L. Phillips Found. intern, N.Y., 1964-65. Mem. Phi Delta Kappa, Pi Lambda Theta, Kappa Delta Pi. Democrat. Presbyterian. Avocations: reading, music, walking, bridge. Home: 4702 Royalshire Rd Greensboro NC 27406-8705

BARNETT, HAROLD THOMAS, school system superintendent; b. Pasadena, Tex., Dec. 8, 1948; s. Herbert G. and Nettie Mae (Sanders) B.; m. Erin Lynn McCommon, Dec. 28, 1971; children: Erin Averyl, Benjamin T. MusB in Edn., Baylor U., 1971; MEd, U. Ga., 1974, EdD, 1983. Cert. tchr., adminstr., Ga. Tchr. St. Albans Episc. Elem. Sch., Waco, Tex., 1972-73, North Clayton Jr. High Sch., College Park, Ga., 1973-75, asst. prin., 1975-82; prin. Griffin (Ga.) High Sch., 1982-90; supt. of schs. Cartersville (Ga.) City Sch. System, 1990—. Trustee Etowah Found., Cartersville; bd. dirs. Cartersville-Bartow County United Way, Christian Counseling Svc., ARC of Bartow County; bd. control Northwest Ga. Regional Edn. Svcs. Agy. Mem. Ga. Sch. Bd. Assn., Ga. Assn. Ednl. Leaders, Profl. Assn. Ga. Educators, Am. Assn. Sch. Adminstrs., Ga. Sch. Supts. Assn., Cartersville-Bartow County C. of C., Cartersville Rotary Club. Baptist. Avocations: fishing, hunting, reading. Office: Cartersville City Schs 310 Old Mill Rd Cartersville GA 30120-4027

BARNETT, LINDA KAY SMITH, vocational guidance counselor; b. Booneville, Miss., Nov. 20, 1955; d. John Thomas and Clara Vernell (Brown) Smith; m. William Wayne Barnett, June 26, 1982; 1 child, John William. AA, N.E. Miss. C.C., Booneville, 1975; BS, Miss. State U., 1977, MEd, 1978, EdS, 1982. Vocat. guidance counselor, dist. test coord. Iuka (Miss.) City Schs., 1979-91; vocat. guidance counselor Tishomingo County Schs., Iuka, from 1991. Treas. Iuka H.S. PTA, 1984-85. Mem. Miss. Sch. Counselors Assn. (state v.p. secondary divsn. 1992-94), N.E. Counseling Assn. (pres. 1989-90, pres.-elect 1987-88, 88-89, sec.-treas. 1982-83, 96-99), Nat. Bd. for Cert. Counselors (nat. cert. counselor, nat. cert. sch. counselor). Ch. of Christ. Avocations: travel, sports, meeting people. Home: Booneville, Miss. Died Nov. 11, 2000.

BARNETT, MARILYN DOAN, secondary education business educator; b. Trafalgar, Ind., Jan. 14, 1934; d. Roscoe James and Nellie Margaret (Betts) Doan; m. Joe A. Barnett, Mar. 23, 1952; 1 child, Michael Shayne. BS, Ball State U., 1965, MA, 1972. Cert. bus. tchr., Ind. Vocat. bus. tchr. John H. Hinds Area Vocat. Sch., Elwood, Ind., 1966-72; bus. tchr. Elwood Community High Sch., 1973-91, chair bus. dept., 1979-89. Sponsor Future Bus. Leaders Am., Elwood, 1973-91. Mem. YMCA; vol. Meals on Wheels, Elwood. Mem. NEA, Ind. State Tchrs. Assn., Ind. Bus. Edn. Assn., Elwood Classroom Tchrs. Assn., Delta Kappa Gamma, Pi Omega Pi, Delta Pi Epsilon, Epsilon Sigma Alpha. Mem. Christian Ch. (Disciples Of Christ). Avocations: travel, piano. Home: 9416 N Meadowlark Ln Elwood IN 46036-8844

BARNETT, MARY LOUISE, elementary education educator; b. Exeter, Calif., May 1, 1941; d. Raymond Edgar Noble and Nena Lavere (Huckaby) Hope; m. Gary Allen Barnett, Aug. 9, 1969; children: Alice Marie, Virginia Lynn. BA, U. of Pacific, 1963; postgrad., U. Mont., 1979-82, U. Idaho, 1984—. Cert. life elem. tchr., Calif.; standard elem. credential, Idaho; elem. tchr., Mont. Tchr. Colegio Americano de Torrean, Torreon, Coahuila, Mexico, 1962-63, Summer Sch. Primary Grades South San Francisco, 1963-66, Visalia (Calif.) Unified Sch. Dist., 1966-69, Sch. Dist. # 1, Missoula, Mont., 1969-73, Fort Shaw-Simms Sch. Dist., Fort Shaw, Mont., 1976-83, Sch. Dist. #25, Pocatello, Idaho, 1983-93, Greenacres Elem., Pocatello, 1993-94; tchr. 2d grade Bonneville Elem., Pocatello, 1994-95; tchr. Windsong Presch., Missoula, Mont., 1995-98, Headstart of Missoula,

1998-99; dir. Mary's Munchkins Presch., Missoula, 1999—. Beauty cons. Mary Kay. Foster mom Ednl. Found. Fgn. Students, Pocatello, Idaho, 1986-89; vol. Am. Heart Assn., Am. Cancer Soc., Pocatello, 1986-88, Bannock March of Dimes, Pocatello, 1988, Pocatello Laubach Lit. Tutoring, 1989; state v.p. membership, del. to P.W. Australian Mission Study; vice moderator Kendall Presbyn. Women, moderator, 1991—; moderator Kendall P.W. 1990-92; dean, treas. Presbyn. Ch., 1997—. Recipient scholarship Mont. Delta Kappa Gamma Edn. Soc., Great Falls, Mont., 1976, Great Falls AAUW, 1980, Great Falls Scottish Rite, 1981, Five Valleys Reading Assn., Missoula, Mont., 1982. Mem. AAUW (v.p. 2002—, mem. com. Idaho divsn. 1990-92, book chair 1995—, pres. Missoula chpt. 1998—), ASCD, NEA, Nat. Coun. Tchrs. English, Internat. Reading Assn., Assn. Childhood Edn. Internat., Laubach Literacy Tutors (sec. 1993—), Bus. and Profl. Women Pocatello (sec. 1993—, contact advisor Missoula After 5 1999—), Mortar Bd., Alpha Lambda Delta, Delta Kappa Gamma (state fellowship chmn., corr. sec. Pocatello chpt. 1986-88, 2d v.p. 1994-96, chmn. Western expansion, 200-03), Moose (musician 1981-82), Order Eastern Star (musician 1984-85), Gamma Phi Beta (sec. Laubach Tutors 1993-95), Delta Kappa Gamma (2d v.p. Phi chpt. 1996—, pres. 2000-02, 2002—). Democrat. Presbyterian. Avocations: music, aquacise, aerobics, crafts, cross stitch. Home: 103 E Crestline Dr Missoula MT 59803-2412 Office: Clark Fork School 2525 Rattlesnake Drive Missoula MT 59803-2412 E-mail: Gabmarybarnett@aol.com.

BARNETT, PHILIP, science librarian, educator; b. N.Y.C., May 26, 1946; s. Paul and Beatrice (Blume) G.; m. Sarah Ellen Friend; children: David, Reena. BS in Chemistry, Bklyn. Coll., 1967; MS in Libr. Svc., Columbia U., 1981; PhD in Biochemistry, Rutgers U., 1973. USPHS postdoctoral fellow NYU, Tuxedo, 1972-74; postdoctoral staff assoc. Columbia U., N.Y.C., 1974-81; indexer H. W. Wilson Co., Bronx, N.Y., 1981-82; info. scientist Ayerst Labs., N.Y.C., 1982-87; corp. libr. Becton Dickinson Inc., Franklin Lakes, N.J., 1987-88; sr. info. scientist Warner-Lambert Co., Morris Plains, N.J., 1988-90; assoc. prof. CUNY, 1990—. Author: (with others) Methods Enzymol., 1982; contbr. articles to sci. jours. Mem. AASA, Am. Chem. Soc. Democrat. Jewish. Office: CUNY Convent Ave # 138 New York NY 10031-9127

BARNETT, R(ALPH) MICHAEL, theoretical physicist, educational agency administrator; b. Gulfport, Miss., Jan. 25, 1944; s. Herbert Chester and Lisa Margaret (Kielley) B.; children: Leilani Pinho, Julia Alexandra, Russell Alan. BS, Antioch Coll., 1966; PhD, U. Chgo., 1971. Postdoctoral fellow U. Calif., Irvine, 1972-74; rsch. fellow Harvard U., Cambridge, Mass., 1974-76; rsch. assoc. Stanford (Calif.) Linear Accelerator Ctr., 1976-83; vis. physicist Inst. Theoretical Physics U. Calif., Santa Barbara, 1983-84; staff scientist Lawrence Berkeley Nat. Lab., 1984-89, sr. scientist and head particle data group, 1990—; co-dir. QuarkNet Ednl. Project, 1999—. V.p. Contemporary Physics Edn. Project, 1987-98, pub. info. coor. Am. Phys. Soc. Dvsn. of Particles and Fields, 1994-97; edn. coord. ATLAS experiment at CERN, Geneva; prodr. film: The Atlas Experiment, 2000. Author: Teachers' Resource Book on Fundamental Particles and Interactions, 1988, Review of Particle Physics, 1990, 6th edit., 2002, Particle Physics—One Hundred Years of Discoveries, 1996, Guide to Experimental Particle Physics Literature, 1993, 2d edit., 1996, The Charm of Strange Quarks, Mysteries and Revolutions of Particle Physics, 2000, (chart) Fundamental Particles and Interactions, 1987, 4th edit., 1999, World-Wide Web feature, The Particle Adventure, 1995, rev. edit. 2000, (CD ROM) The Quark Adventure, 2000. Fellow Am. Phys. Soc. (pub. info. coord. divsn. particles and fields 1994-97, taskforce on informing the public, chair-elect Calif. sect.), Am. Assn. Physics Tchrs. (v.p., sect. North Calif.). Achievements include research on the Standard Model and its extensions, including studies of nature and validity of quantum chromodynamics; analyses of neutral current couplings; calculations of the production of heavy quarks; predictions of properties and decays of supersymmetric particles and higgs bosons. Office: Lawrence Berkeley Nat Lab MS-50-308 1 Cyclotron Rd Berkeley CA 94720-0001

BARNETTE, CANDICE LEWIS, speech/language pathologist; b. Huntington, W.Va., Sept. 4, 1950; d. Angelo Ted and Amelda Lucille Lewis; m. John Emile Barnette II, June 13, 1987; stepchildren: Jennifer, Jeffrey, Jason. BA, U. Ala., 1972, MA, 1973; cert. evaluation, Ctr. for ESE Speech Enhancer, 1998. Cert. speech pathologist. Speech pathologist Partlow State Sch. and Hosp., Tuscaloosa, Ala., 1973-75; speech/lang. pathologist Children's Hosp., New Orleans, 1975-77; asst. prof. St. Mary's Dominican Coll., New Orleans, 1977-84; pvt. practice speech/lang. pathologist New Orleans, 1977-87; speech pathologist Novacare, Savannah, Ga., 1988-89; pvt. practice speech/lang. pathologist, owner Barnette Speech & Lang. Ctr., Savannah, 1989—. Mem. profl. adv. bd. Staff Builders, New Orleans, 1983-84, Healthmasters Home Health Agy., Savannah, 1984-94, Olsten Kimberly Quality Care, Savannah, 1994-97; bd. dirs. Rehab. Interest Group, Savannah, 1992-96. Bd. dirs. New Orleans Contemporary Dance Ctr., 1978-80; vol. fundraiser Children's Hosp., New Orleans, 1977-82; vol. sailing venue Atlanta Centennial Olympic Games, Savannah, 1996. Mem. Am. Speech, Lang. and Hearing Assn., Ga. Speech and Hearing Assn. Avocations: collecting antiques, reading, travel, boating, gardening. Office: Barnette Speech & Lang Ctr 6815 Forest Park Dr Ste 124 Savannah GA 31406-1511

BARNEY, LINDA SUSAN, manufacturing specialist; b. Latrobe, Pa., Mar. 31, 1948; d. William Kramer and Kathryn (Voytilla) B. BS in Edn., Ind. U. of Pa., 1970; BBA, Tampa (Fla.) Coll., 1983; MBA, Fla. Met. U., Tampa, 1996. Tchr. Greater Latrobe (Pa.) Sch. Dist., 1970-81; from staff acct. to acctg. supr. Systems and Simulation, Tampa, Fla., 1986-89; project acct. Olin Ordnance, St. Petersburg, Fla., 1989-96; mfg. specialist BIC Spl. Mkts. Divsn., Clearwater, Fla., 1997-98; cost acctg. mgr. HIT Promotional Products, Largo, Fla., 1998—. Recipient Small Bus. award, 1993. Mem. NAFE, AAUW, Internat. Platform Assn., Women's Inner Cir. of Achievement, Am. Biographical Inst. (dep. gov.). Democrat. Lutheran. Avocations: travel, golf, hiking, studies. Home: 9100 9th St N Apt 1604 Saint Petersburg FL 33702-3081

BARNHART, CHARLES ELMER, animal sciences educator; b. Windsor, Ill., Jan. 25, 1923; s. Elmer and Irma (Smysor) B.; m. Norma McCarty, Dec. 28, 1946 (dec. Dec. 25, 1970); children: John D., Charles E., Norman R.; m. Jean M. Hutton, Jan. 12, 1973; stepchildren: Mark, David, Bonnie, Beth Hutton. BS in Agr., Purdue U., 1945; MS, Ia. State U., 1948, PhD, 1954. Mem. faculty U. Ky., Lexington, from 1948, assoc. prof. animal sci., 1955-57, prof., 1957-88, prof. emeritus, 1988—, dean, dir. exptl. sta. and coop. extension service, 1969-88, dean emeritus, 1988—. Pres. So. Assn. Agrl. Scientist, 1982-83 Patentee in field. Bd. dirs. Ky. Bd. Agr., 1966-88, Ky. State Fair and Expn. Ctr., 1969-88, Ky. Tobacco Rsch. Bd., Farm Credit Svcs. Mid Am., 1988-93, Ky. Farm Bur., 1969-76; mem. Gov.'s Coun. on Agrl., 1971-80. Named Man of Yr. in Ky. Agr. Progressive Farmer, 1962, Man of Yr. for Ky. Agr. Ky. Agrl. Communicators, 1979; elected to Saddle and Sirloin Portrait Gallery, 1987. Mem. Am. Soc. Animal Sci., Ky. Hist. Soc., Farmhouse Fraternity, Masons (32 deg.), Shriners, Epsilon Sigma Phi, Gamma Sigma Delta., Omicron Delta Kappa, Sigma Xi. Methodist. Home: 1017 Turkey Foot Rd Lexington KY 40502-2712 Address: 5013 Southern Pine Cir Venice FL 34293-4245

BARNHILL, JOHN WARREN, psychiatrist, educator; b. Oklahoma City, Mar. 4, 1959; s. John Willis and Patricia Beth (Dale) B. AB magna cum laude, Duke U., 1981; MD, Baylor Coll. Medicine, 1985; grad. Ctr. Psychoanalytic Tng. and Rsch., Columbia U., 1996. Diplomate Am. Bd. Psychiatry and Neurology. Resident in pediatrics Baylor Coll. Medicine, Houston, 1985-86; resident in psychiatry The N.Y. Hosp.-Cornell Med. Ctr., N.Y.C., 1986-89, instr., 1989, asst. prof., 2000—, assoc. prof. clin. psychiatry, 2003—; pvt. practice, staff psychiatrist Cornell Med. Ctr., 1989—. Lectr. in psychoanalysis Columbia U. Coll. Physicians and Surgeons, 1996—; student co-chmn. Baylor Med. Admissions Com., 1983-85; co-chmn. N.Y.C. Residents Com., 1987-89. Author: If You Think You Have An Eating Disorder, Why Am I Still So Afraid - Understanding PTSD; contbr. articles to med. jours. Rock Sleyster scholar AMA, 1984-85. Fellow Am. Psychiat. Assn. (rep. exec. coun. 1987-89); mem. Am. Psychoanalytic Assn. Office: NY Presbyn Hosp 525 E 68th St New York NY 10021-

BARNICLE, STEPHAN PATRICK, secondary school educator; b. Worcester, Mass., Jan. 23, 1948; s. John Francis and Catherine Mabel (Kilgore) B.; m. Mary Anne Petrovick, Aug. 23, 1969; children: Michael Edward, Patricia Ann, Daniel John, Kevin Patrick. MusB cum laude, U. Hartford, 1970, M of Music Edn., 1974, postgrad., 1987, 88. Tchr. music Farmington (Conn.) High Sch., 1970-74, Simsbury (Conn.) High Sch., 1974—. Singer-bass soloist Concora Conn. Choral, New Britain, 1974—; exec. dir. Simsbury Music and Arts Ctr., 1988-94; music dir., prin. condr. Visit Can. Internat. Polychoral Festivals, Montreal and Quebec City, 1994—; project chmn. HS music panel Preparing Tomorrow's Tchrs. to Use Tech., 2002—. Author: Teaching Examples: Ideas for Music Education, 1994, Music at the Middle Level, 1994, Teacher's Guide to Classical Music For Dummies, 1997; pub. choral compositions & arrangements; contbr. articles to profl. jours.; author of poetry. Goodwill amb. Simsbury-Wittmund (Germany) Sister Town Com., 1990, 98, 99; music dir. Sacred Heart Ch., Bloomfield, Conn., 1990—; mem. Simsbury Bd. Assessment Appeals, 1999—, Simsbury Dem. Town Com., 2000—, Simsbury Hist. Dist. Commn., 2000—. Recipient Excellence in H.S. Tchg. award U. Conn., 1995, Disney Channel and McDonald's Am. Tchrs. Awards honoree, 1996; named Winning Composer, Am. Choral Dirs. Assn. Choral Composition Contest, 1995; Travel grantee Ptnrs. of Ams., Washington, 1984. Mem. Music Edn. Technologists Assn. (past pres., co-founder, grantee 1995), Conn. Music Educators Assn. (chair music tech. com. 1993-95, chair music composition com. 2000, Music Tchr. of Yr. 1994-95), Music Educators Nat. Conf. (tchg. music adv. com. 2000-02), Assn. Ednl. Comms. and Tech. (H.S. music chmn. project 2002—). Democrat. Roman Catholic. Avocations: sports, family, travel, swimming, flying. Home: 91 E Weatogue St Simsbury CT 06070-2503 Office: Simsbury High Sch 34 Farms Village Rd Simsbury CT 06070-2399 E-mail: stephanB2@attbi.com.

BARNUM, BARBARA STEVENS, writer, retired nursing educator; b. Johnstown, Pa., Sept. 2, 1937; d. William C. and Freda Inzes (Claycomb) Burkett; m. H. James Barnum (dec.); children: Lauren, Elizabeth, Catherine, Anne (dec.), Shauna, Sallee, David. AA in Nursing, St. Petersburg Jr. Coll., 1958; BPh, Northwestern U., 1967; MA, DePaul U., 1971; PhD, U. Chgo., 1976. RN, Ill., N.Y. Dir. nursing svcs. Augustana Hosp. and Health Care Ctr., Chgo., 1970-71; dir. staff edn. U. Chgo. Hosps. and Clinics, 1971-73; prof. U. Ill., Chgo., 1973-79; dir. div. health svcs., sci. and edn. Columbia U. Tchrs. Coll., N.Y.C., 1979-87; editor Nursing & Health Care Nat. League for Nursing, N.Y.C., 1989-91; editor div. nursing Columbia-Presbyn. Med. Ctr., Columbia U., N.Y.C., 1991-95; prof. Sch. Nursing Columbia U., N.Y.C., 1995-98; ret., 1998. Chmn. bd. Barnum & Souza, N.Y.C., 1989-92; civilian cons. to surgeon gen. USAF, 1980-87. Author: Nursing Theory, Analysis, Application and Evaluation, 4th edit., 1994, Writing for Publication: A Primer for Nurses, 1995; author: (with K. Kerfoot) The Nurse as Executive, 4th edit., 1995; author: Spirituality and Nursing: From Traditional to New Age, 1996, 2d edit., 2003, Teaching Nursing in the Era of Managed Care, 1999, The New Healers: Minds and Hands in Complementary Medicine, 2002, (fiction) The Haunting of Lisa Tilden, 1999; editor: Nursing Leadership Forum, 1994—98. Mem. governing bd. Nurses House, 1979-86, Nat. Health Coun., 1981-90, others. Fellow Am. Acad. Nursing (governing bd. 1982-84); mem. Sigma Theta Tau (Founders' award 1979). Home: 80 Park Ave Apt 15G New York NY 10016-2547

BARNWELL, FRANKLIN HERSHEL, zoology educator; b. Chattanooga, Oct. 4, 1937; s. Columbus Hershel and Esther Bernice (Ireland) B.; m. Adrienne Kay Knox, June 13, 1959; 1 child, Elizabeth Brooks. BA, Northwestern U., 1959, PhD, 1965. Instr. biol. sci. Northwestern U., Evanston, Ill., 1964, research assoc., 1965-67; asst. prof. U. Chgo., 1967-70; from asst. prof. to prof. zoology, ecology and behavioral biology U. Minn., Mpls., 1970—, head dept. ecology, evolution and behavior, 1986-93. Mem. adv. panel NASA, 1963-67, NSF, Washington, 1980; faculty Orgn. for Tropical Studies, San Jose, Costa Rica, 1966-85, bd. dirs.; Nat. Confs. on Underground Rsch., bd. dirs., treas., 1990-96; investigator rsch. R/V Alpha Helix, various locations, 1979, vis. scientist. Contbr. articles on zoology to profl. jours. NSF fellow, 1965; named Minn. Coll. Sci. Tchr. of Yr., Minn. Acad. Sci. and Minn. Sci. Tchrs. Assn., 1997, dist. tchg. prof. of ecolgoy, U. Minn., 1997. Fellow Linnean Soc. London, AAAS; mem. Soc. Intergrative and Comparative Biology, Internat. Soc. for Chronobiology, Assocs. Orgn. for Tropical Studies, Crustacean Soc. (founding and sustaining mem., bd. dirs., sec. 1991-98), Phi Beta Kappa, Sigma Xi. Office: U Minn Dept Ecology Evol & Behav 1987 Upper Buford Cir Saint Paul MN 55108-1051 E-mail: fhb@umn.edu.

BAROLINI, HELEN, writer, translator, educator; b. Syracuse, N.Y., Nov. 18, 1925; m. Antonio Barolini, Nov. 8, 1950 (dec.); children: Teodolinda, Susanna, Nicoletta. AB magna cum laude, Syracuse U., 1947; MLS, Columbia U., 1959. Lectr. Pace U., Pleasantville, N.Y., 1990—. Lectr. Padua, Italy and Westchester C.C., Valhalla, N.Y., 1988; writer-in-residence Quarry Farm, Elmira Coll., 1989; resident scholar Rockefeller Found.'s Bellagio Study Ctr., Lake Como, Italy, 1991; vis. artist Am. Acad. Rome, 2001. Creative works include Umbertina, 1979, 1999, The Dream Book, 1985, 2000, Love in the Middle Ages, 1986, Festa, 1988, 2002, Aldus and His Dream Book, 1991, Chiaroscuro, 1999, More Italian Hours, and Other Stories, 2001, stories in Literary Olympian II, Love Stories by New Women, An Inn Near Kyoto, and numerous jours.; cited in The Best American Essays, 1991, 93, 98, 99, 2000; scholar-cons., advisor to film Tarantella. Recipient MELUS 2000 Lifetime Achievement award, Soc. for Study of Multi-Ethnic Lit. of U.S., 2000, Susan Koppelman award, Am. Culture Asn., 1987, Am. Book award, 1986, Marina-Velca Journalism prize, Italy, 1970, Sons of Italy Lit. Award, 2003; fellow, MacDowell Colony, 1974; grantee, Nat. Enwodment for Arts, 1976. Mem. PEN Am. Ctr., Authors Guild, Hudson Valley River Writers Assn., Phi Beta Kappa. Home and Office: 86 Maple Ave Hastings On Hudson NY 10706 E-mail: helenbarolini@juno.com.

BAROLINI, TEODOLINDA, literary critic; b. Syracuse, N.Y., Dec. 19, 1951; d. Antonio and Helen (Mollica) B.; m. Douglas Gardner Caverly, June 21, 1980 (dec. Nov. 1993); 1 child: William Douglas; m. James J. Valentini, Feb. 10, 2001. BA, Sarah Lawrence Coll., 1972; MA, Columbia U., 1973, PhD, 1978. Asst. prof. Italian U. Calif., Berkeley, 1978-83; assoc. prof. Italian NYU, 1983-89; prof., 1989-92; prof. Italian, chmn. dept. Italian Columbia U., N.Y.C., 1992—, Lorenzo Da Ponte prof. Italian, 1999—. Author: Dante's Poets, 1984 (Howard R. Marraro prize MLA 1986, John Nicholas Brown prize Medieval Acad. Am. 1988, transl. into Italian as Il miglior fabbro 1993), The Undivine Comedy, 1992, transl. into Italian as La Commedia Senza Dio, 2003; contbr. articles to profl. jours. AAUW fellow, 1977, ACLS fellow, 1981, NEH fellow, 1986, Guggenheim fellow, 1998. Fellow Medieval Acad. Am., Am. Acad. Arts and Scis., Am. Philos. Soc.; mem. MLA, Dante Soc. Am. (v.p. 1983-86, 91-94, 95-97, pres. 1997-2003), Renaissance Soc. Am. Office: Columbia U Dept Italian 510 Hamilton Hall New York NY 10027

BARON, DENNIS E. English language educator; b. NYC, May 9, 1944; s. R.C. Roy and Sylvia (Mayer) Baron; m. Iryce White, Oct. 21, 1979; children: Cordelia, Rachel, Jonathan. AB, Brandeis U., 1965; MA, Columbia U., 1968; PhD, U. Mich., 1971. Cert. tchr. English, N.Y., Mass. Tchr. English Francis Lewis High Sch., N.Y.C., 1966-68, Wayland (Mass.) High Sch., 1968-69; asst. prof. English Ea. Ill. U., Charleston, Ill., 1971-73, CCNY, N.Y.C., 1973-74; asst. prof. English/linguistics U. Ill., Urbana, 1975-81, assoc. prof. English/linguistics, 1981-84, prof. English/linguistics, 1984—, head English dept., 1997—2003. Author: Grammar and Good Taste, 1982, Grammar and Gender, 1986, Declining Grammar, 1989, The English-Only Question, 1990, Guide to Home Language Repair, 1994. Fulbright fellow CIES, France, 1978-79, fellow Ctr. for Advanced Study, U. Ill., 1984-85, program for study of cultural values and ethics, U. Ill., 1992, NEH, 1989. Mem. MLA, Am. Dialect Soc. (editor monograph series 1984-93), Nat. Coun. Tchrs. English (commn. on lang. 1984-87, chmn. commn. on pub. policy 2003—), Linguistic Soc. Am. (com. on lang. and the schs. 1992-95), Coun. Writing Program Adminstrs., Conf. on Coll. Composition and Comm. Avocations: reading, writing, art. Office: Univ Ill Dept English 608 S Wright St Urbana IL 61801-3630 Business E-Mail: debaron@uiuc.edu.

BARON, JAMES NEAL, organizational behavior and human resources educator, researcher; b. L.A., June 24, 1955; s. Robert Filger and Lila Jean (Lederer) B.; m. Mary Therese Dumont, Dec. 20, 1980; children: Isaac, Nina. BA in Sociology, Reed Coll., 1976; MS in Sociology, U. Wis., 1977; PhD in Sociology, U. Calif., Santa Barbara, 1982. Instr. dept. sociology U. Calif., Santa Barbara, 1981-82; from asst. prof. to prof. orgnl. behavior Stanford (Calif.) U., 1982-92, Walter Kenneth Kilpatrick prof. orgnl. behavior and human resources, 1992—, assoc. dean acad. affairs, 1994-97. Asst. prof. sociology Stanford U., 1982-86, assoc. prof., 1986-90, prof., 1990-94; co-dir. Human Resources Rsch. Initiative, 1992-94; affiliate faculty mem. Stanford Ctr. Orgns. Rsch., Pub. Mgmt. Program, Inst. Rsch. on Women and Gender, Orgns. and Mental Health Rsch. Tng. Program, 1982-89, Orgns. and Aging Rsch. Tng. Program, 1985-88; mem. adv. bd. freefor.com; researcher and presenter in field. Mem. editorial bd. Rsch. in Social Stratification and Mobility, 1983-89, Adminstrv. Sci. Quar., 1984-90, Indsl. Rels., 1993—; contbr. articles to profl. jours. Mem. policy bd. Ctr. Rsch. on Women, Stanford U., 1983-85, steering com. Stanford Ctr. Orgns. Rsch., 1989-90, 92-94, com. on performance appraisal for merit pay Nat. Rsch. Coun., 1989-91, adv. com. Grad. Mgmt. Admissions Coun. Rsch. Program on Test Registrants and Minority Students, 1989-96, com. acad. policy, planning and mgmt., bd. trustees, Stanford U., 1990-93; bd. dirs. Las Lomitas Found., Found. Ednl. Excellence, Menlo Park, 1993-95; educator various nat. and internat. orgns; adv. bd. Citigroup Behavioral Scis. Rsch. Coun., 1994—; adv. com. Indsl. Rels. Ctr., Carlson Sch. Mgmt., U. Minn., 1997—. Bus. Sch. Trust Faculty fellow Stanford U., 1990-92, Bass Faculty fellow, 1989-90, fellow Ctr. Advanced Study in Behavioral Scis., 1988-89, Marvin Bower fellow Harvard Bus. Sch., 1997-98, Jacdicke faculty fellow Stanford, 1998-99; Disting. Rsch. vis. Nat. U. Singapore, 1991. Mem. Am. Sociol. Assn. (coun. sect. orgns. and occupations 1988-91, chair nominations com. sect. on orgns. and occupations 1993-94, EGOS prize 1985), Acad. Mgmt.

BARON, MELVIN FARRELL, pharmacy educator; b. L.A., July 29, 1932; s. Leo Ben and Sadie (Bauchman) B.; m. Lorraine Ross, Dec. 20, 1953; children: Lynn Baron Friedman, Ross David. PharmD, U. So. Calif., 1957, MPA, 1973. Lic. pharmacist, Calif. Pres. Shield Health Care Ctrs., Van Nuys, Calif., 1957-83; dir. externship program U. So. Calif., L.A., 1991—; v.p. Shield Health Care Ctrs., Inc. (C.R. Bard, Inc. subsidiary), 1983-86; pres. Merit Coll., 1988-92, PharmaCom., L.A., 1990—; assoc. prof. clin. pharmacy U. So. Calif., L.A., 1991—, asst. dean pharm. care programs, 1995—97, dir. PharmD/MBA program, asst. dean programmatic advancement, 1998—; prin. New Horizon Pharmacy Cons. Adj. asst. prof. U. without Walls, Shaw U., Raleigh, NC, 1973; project dir. Haynes Found. Drug Rsch. Ctr., U. So. Calif., L.A., 1973; assoc. dir. Calif. Alcoholism Found., 1973—75; adj. asst. prof. clin. pharmacy Sch. Pharmacy, U. So. Calif., 1981—91; cons. Topanga Terr. Convalescent Hosp., 1970—80, Calif. Labor Mgmt. Plan of alcoholism programs and coords., 1974, Office of Alcoholism, State of Calif., Nat. In-Home Health Svc., 1975, Continuity of Life Team, 1975, Triad Med., Longs Drug Stores, HealthTek, others; vis. prof. Tokyo Coll. Pharmacy, 1994, Sandoz Pharm. Co., 1995, Clin Oscar Romero, 2000; lectr. Meijo U., Nagoya U., Japan, 1994; presenter Nat. Pharmacy Dir. Conf., 1995; cons., mem. sci. adv. bd. Leiner Health Products, 1998—; cons. Prime Care Pharmacy, 1998—, Jackson Meml. Hosp., 1998, New Horizon Pharmacy, Avalon Hosp., Queenscare Family Clinics; cons., mem. adv. bd. Medpin, 2001; chair nominating com. CPHA, 1998; co-developer Trends in Healthcare Svcs.; presenter in field. Adv. bd. Pharmacist Newsletter, 1980—. Chmn. Friends of Operation Bootstrap, 1967-77; svc. chmn. tng. coord. Am. Cancer Soc., San Fernando Valley, Calif., 1980; mem. adv. bd. L.A. VNA, 1982; bd. dirs. pres. QSAD, 1987-88; pres. bd. Everywoman's Village, 1988-89; bd. dirs. Life Svcs., 1988-94; pres. bd. counselors, U. So. Calif., 1988-92, co-chmn. good neighborhood campaign Sch. Pharmacy, 1998; mem. Calif. Bd. Pharmacy Com. on Student/Preceptor Manual, 1991-92. Named Disting. Alumnus of Yr., U. So. Calif., Sch. of Pharmacy Alumni Assn.. 1983, U. So. Calif. Torchbearer, 1990-91, Hon. Tchr. of Yr. U. So. Calif. Sch. Pharmacy, 1997. Fellow Am. Coll. Apothecaries; mem. Am. Pharm. Assn., Am. Soc. Health Sys. Pharmacists, Calif. Pharmacist Assn. (chair edn. com.), Am. Soc. Pub. Adminstrn., Am. Assn. Colls. of Pharmacy (spkr. ann. meeting 2000), Phi Kappa Phi, Phi Lambda Sigma (hon., faculty advisor), Rho Chi. Home: 1245 Wellesley Ave Apt 201 Los Angeles CA 90025-1170 Office: 1985 Zonal Ave Los Angeles CA 90089-0105 E-mail: mbaron@usc.edu.

BARON, ROBERT ALAN, psychology and business educator, author; b. N.Y.C., June 7, 1943; s. Bernard Paul and Ruth (Schlossberg) B.; child, Jessica Lynn BS, CUNY, 1964; MS, U. Iowa, 1967, PhD, 1968. Asst. prof. U. S.C., 1968-71; assoc. prof. psychology Purdue U., West Lafayette, Ind., 1971-75, prof., 1975-87; prof. and chair dept. mgmt. Rensselaer Poly. Inst., 1991-93, Wellington prof. mgmt., 2000. Vis. assoc. prof. U. Minn., 1972, U. Tex., 1974-75; vis. prof. Princeton U., 1977-78; vis. prof. mgmt. U. Wash., 1985; program dir. NSF, 1979-81; vis. fellow U. Oxford, Eng., 1982 Author: (with D. Richardson) Human Aggression, 2d edit., 1994, (with D. Byrne) Social Psychology, 1974, 10th edit., 2002, (with J. Greenberg) Behavior in Organizations, 1983, 8th edit., 2003, Psychology, 5th edit., 2000; contbr. numerous articles to profl. jours.; patentee apparatus for enhancing the environ. quality of work spaces. NSF grantee Fellow APA, Am. Psychol. Soc.; mem. Acad. Mgmt. Home: 27 Sunnyside Rd Scotia NY 12302-2408 Office: Rensselaer Poly Inst Dept Mgmt Troy NY 12180-3590 E-mail: baronr@rpi.edu.

BARONE, DONALD ANTHONY, neurologist, educator; b. Bklyn., Dec. 18, 1948; s. John Dominick and Nancy Anne (Salzano) B.; m. Kathleen Ann Kelley, May 22, 1976; children— Steven, Matthew, Daniel. AB, Rutgers U., 1970; DO, Phila. Coll. Osteo. Medicine, 1974. Diplomate Am. Bd. Psychiatry and Neurology, Am. Bd. Electro Diagnostic Medicine. Intern Kennedy Meml. Hosp., Stratford, N.J., 1974-75; resident in neurology U. Vt. Med. Ctr., Burlington, 1975-78; fellow in neuromuscular diseases Columbia-Presbyn. Med. Ctr., N.Y.C., 1978-79; practice medicine specializing in neurology Voorhees and Stratford, N.J., 1979—. Clin. asst. prof. U. Medicine and Dentistry of N.J. Sch. Osteo. Medicine, Camden, 1979-88, clin. assoc. prof., 1988—; sect. head neurology Kennedy Meml. Hosp., Stratford, 1979-99, cons. neurologist, 1999—; dir. Muscular Dystrophy Assn. Clinic, 1984—; cons. Nat. Bd. Examiners for Osteo. Physicians and Surgeons, 1980—; med. adv. bd. Garden State chpt. Myasthenia Gravis Found.; profl. adv. com. Greater Delaware Valley chpt. Multiple Sclerosis Soc.; mem. adv. com. Delaware Valley Transplant Assn., 1987-92; examiner Am. Bd. Psychiatry and Neurology, 1981—. Editorial reviewer Jour. of the Am. Osteopathic Assn., 1988—; contbr. articles to med. jours. Bd. dirs. Kennedy Health Sys., 1992—, sec., 2000, treas., 2001—; trustee Kennedy Meml. Hosps., Univ. Med. Ctr., 1995—; chmn. bd. trustees Kennedy Surg. Ctr., 1995—. Recipient Golden Apple award for teaching N.J. Sch.

Ostoepathic Med., 1987, 88, 89, 90, Excellence in Teaching award U. Medicine and Dentistry of N.J. Found., 1980. Mem. Am. Acad. Neurology, Am. Assn. Electrodiagnostic Medicine (membership com., mem. hist. com.), Am. Osteo. Assn., N.J. Assn. Osteo. Physicians and Surgeons, Camden County Assn. Osteo. Physicians and Surgeons, Sigma Sigma Phi, Sigma Alpha Omicron. Roman Catholic. Office: Voorhees Profl Bldg Ste 101 102 W White Horse Rd Kirkwood Voorhees NJ 08043-0330

BAROWSKY, HARRIS WHITE, physician, educator; b. Holyoke, Mass., Mar. 6, 1949; s. Maurice and Rosalie Lenore (White) B.; m. Diane Mariann Turajlich, June 10, 1979; children by previous marriage: Robert Jr., Randall. AB, Clark U., 1971; MD, U. Chgo., 1975. Diplomate Am. Bd. Internal Medicine, Am. Bd. Endocrinology. Intern, then resident U. Pitts., 1975-78, clin. instr., 1978-79; fellow in endocrinology Michael Reese Hosp., Chgo., 1979-81; instr. medicine Rush Med. Coll., Chgo., 1981-82; affiliate dir. internal medicine resident program South Chgo. Cmty. Hosp., 1982-89, dir. med. edn., 1982-90; assoc. med. dir. Healthcare Compare Corp., Downers Grove, Ill., 1990-91; active med. staff Chgo. Osteo. Hosps. & Med. Ctr., 1991-96; clin. regular asst. prof. internal medicine Chgo. Coll. Osteo. Medicine, 1991-96. Adj. asst. prof. internal medicine and pathology Midwestern U., Downers Grove, Ill.; ptnr. Ind. Endocrinology specialists, Inc., Munster, 1996—; clin. asst. prof. medicine Ind. U. Sch. Medicine, Gary. Republican. Jewish. Avocation: golf. Home: PO Box 68 Beverly Shores IN 46301-0068

BARR, DAVID JOHN, retired art educator; b. Detroit, Oct. 10, 1939; s. John A. and Phyllis E. (Prince) B.; m. Elizabeth Margaret Dwaihy, June 19, 1982; children: Heather, Gillian. BFA, Wayne State U., 1962, MFA, 1965. Prof. art Macomb C.C., Warren, Mich., 1965—2002, ret., 2002. Founder, artistic dir. Mich. Legacy Art Park, Thompsonville, Mich., 1995—. One-man shows include Hanamura Gallery, Detroit, 1965, Kazimir Gallery, Chgo., 1968-69, 71-72, Evanston (Ill.) Art Ctr., 1969, Donald Morris Gallery, Detroit, 1973, Art Rsch. Ctr., Kansas City, Mo., 1974, Marianne Friedland Gallery, Toronto, Ont., Can., 1975, Richard Gray Gallery, Chgo., 1975, 86, U. Pitts., 1975, Donald Morris Gallery, Birmingham, Mich., 1976, 79, 81, 84, 87, 89, 92, San Jose Mus. Art, 1978, Kent (Ohio) State U., 1979, Meadowbrook Art Gallery, Oakland U., Rochester, Minn., 1982, Mot Coll., Flint, Mich., 1985, Momentum Gallery, Mpls., 1986, Swords into Plowshares Gallery, Detroit, 1990, Dennos Mus., Traverse City, Mich., 2000, Krasl. Mus., St. Joseph, Mich., 2002, Midland (Mich.) Art Ctr., 2002, Washtenaw Coll., Ann Arbor, Mich., 1993; exhibited in group shows at Flint Inst. Art, 1990, Pontiac (Mich.) Art Ctr., 1992; commns. include Fairlane Town Ctr., Dearborn, Mich., 1976, Macomb C.C., 1976, Meadowbrook Festival Ground, Oakland U., 1981, Lakeview Sq., Battle Creek, Mich., 1983, Mich. Hist. Mus., Lansing, 1988, Hoffman Corp., Appleton, Wis., 1989, Bishop Internat. Airport, Flint, 1994, Detroit Zoo Wildlife Interpretive Ctr. Butterfly-Hummingbird Garden, 1995, Chrysler World Hdqrs., Auburn Hills, Mich., 1996, Revolution II, Brussels, Belgium, 1998, Dennos Mus., Traverse City, 1999-2000, Mich. Legacy Art Pk., 2002, Thompsonville, Mich., 2002, Pfizer, Ann Arbor, Mich., 2002, Pisa Town Hall, Pisa, Italy, 2002, Hart Plaza, Detroit, 2003, others; represented in permanent collections Dennos Mus. Ctr., Northwestern Mich. Coll., Traverse City, Detroit Inst. Arts, Flint Inst. Arts, Ft. Lauderdale Mus., Oakland U., Portland (Oreg.) Art Recipient Mich. Arts award Arts Found. Mich., 1977, Disting. Alumni award Wayne State U., 1983, Gov. of Mich.'s artist award Concerned Citizens for Arts in Mich., 1988, Humanity in the Arts award Wayne State U., 1998. Mem. AIA (hon.). Home: 22600 Napier Rd Novi MI 48374-3202

BARR, MARY JEANETTE, art educator; b. Chgo., Dec. 30, 1928; d. George Leonard and Leonore Loretto (Marsicano) Tompkins; m. David Harper Barr, Aug. 28, 1954; children: Michael, Nadine, Thomas, Ellen. BS, Ill. State U., 1971, MS, 1981, EdD, 1988. Art specialist teaching cert. K-12, Ill. Art specialist K-8 Chester-East Lincoln Sch. Dist. #61, Lincoln, Ill., 1971-74, Lincoln Elem. Sch. Dist. #27, 1974-80; instr. art edn. Ill. State U., Normal, 1980-85; prin. Carroll Elem. Sch., Lincoln, 1985-87; prof. art edn. Wichita (Kans.) State U., 1988-90, U. of West Ga., Carrollton, 1990—. Art tchr. Lincoln Recreation Dept., summers, 1975-79, Carrollton Cultural Arts Ctr., summers, 2000-03; writer grant Arts in Gen. Edn. program Lincoln Elem. Sch. Dist. 27, 1979-80; presenter tchr. inst. workshops Ill. State Bd. Edn., 1980-83; mem. Ill. Curriculum Coun., Ill. State Bd. Edn., 1982-88, sec., 1987; panelist gen. meeting Ill. Assn. Art Educators State Conf., Peoria, 1984; workshop participant Getty Ctr. Edn. in the Arts, Cin., 1993; judge numerous profl. and amateur art shows. Author: (with Michael Youngblood) Illinois Art Education Association Position Paper on Art Education, 1987; The Illinois Curriculum Council: Visions and Directions, 1988; contbr.: Art Activities for the Handicapped, 1982. Float designer/parade Jr. Women's Club, Lincoln, 1974-80; chmn. mural C. of C., Lincoln, 1980; festival presenter Carrollton Elem. Schs., 1993, 94; judge H.S. art show U.S. Rep. Darden, Carrollton, 1993, Dallas, Ga., 1994, Gov.'s Honors Art Show, Carrollton, 2002. Recipient Ada Bell Clark Welsh Scholarship Ill. State U., 1984, Exemplary Svc. award Ill. State U. Student Elem. Edn. Bd., Ill. State U., 1985. Mem. ASCD, AAUP, Nat. Art Edn. Assn. (Tchr. of Yr. 1984), Assn. Tchr. Educators, Found. Internat. Cooperation (chpt. chair 1963—), Ga. Art Edn. Assn. (bd. mem. ret. tchrs. 1998—, Higher Edn. Tchr. of Yr. 1994). Roman Catholic. Avocations: watercolor painting, walking, travel. Home: 110 Frances Pl Carrollton GA 30117-4332 Office: State Univ West Ga 1600 Maple St Carrollton GA 30118-0002

BARRAGĀN, CELIA SILGUERO, elementary school educator; b. Corcoran, Calif., Feb. 4, 1955; d. Frutoso Silguero and Olinda Gonzalez S.; m. Mario Barragān Jr., Nov. 12, 1977; children: Maricela Aimē, Mario Armando. BS, S.W. Tex. State U., 1976, MA, 1977. 3rd grade tchr. Crockett Elem. Sch., San Marcos, Tex., 1977—78, Bowie Elem. Sch., San Marcos, 1978—84; 5th grade tchr. Travis Elem. Sch., San Marcos, 1984—94, Hernandez Intermediate Sch., San Marcos, 1994—99; asst. prin., bilingual coord. Bonham Elem. Sch., San Marcos, 1985—86, title I reading tchr., trainer, cons., 1995—99; coord., tchr. AVID Miller Jr. H.S., San Marcos, Tex., 1999—2000; ESL/Dyslexia tchr. Miller Jr. High, 2000—01; ESL/dyslexia tchr. Goodnight Jr. H.S., 2001—. Winter High ability program tchr. S.W. Tex. State U.; project math trainer, migrant tchr., Princeville, Ill.; cons., nat. trainer Lang. Cir. Project Read, Minn. Recipient Latino award for cmty. recognition S.W. Tex. State U. Mem. Internat. Reading Assn., Tex. Reading Assn., Tex. State Tchrs. Assn., Tex. Assn. Bilingual Edn., Tex. Classroom Tchrs. Assn., San Marcos (Tex.) Assn. Bilingual Edn. (v.p. 1990-91, 94—, pres. 1995—, Bilingual Tchr. of Yr. 1991, Travis Elem. Tchr. of Yr. 1993, Hernandez Intermediate Tchr. of Yr. 1995, Secondary Tchr. of Yr. 1995), Orton Dyslexia Soc., Nat. Coun. Tchrs. Math., Tex. Assn. Bilingual Educators, Ill. Migrant Edn. Assn., Tex. Assn. Gifted and Talented, N.J. Writing Project, Assn. Comprehensive Edn. in Tex. Roman Catholic. Home: 1763 Loma Verde Dr New Braunfels TX 78130-1297 Office: Goodnight Jr H S 1805 Peter Garza Dr San Marcos TX 78666-5062 E-mail: celia.barragan@san-marcos.isd.tenet.edu.

BARREN, MICHAEL JOSEPH, secondary education educator, coach; b. Atlanta, Sept. 15, 1957; s. Ralph George and Jane (Smith) T. BA, U. Ky., 1979, MA, 1985. Tchr. Paul L. Dunbar High Sch., Fayette County Pub. Schs., Lexington, Ky., 1980—. Youth leader Southland Christian Ch., Lexington, 1990—; huddle coach Fellowship of Christian Athletics, 1990—. Recipient Outstanding Alumni award Theta Chi, 1988; named Coach of Yr., Ky. Track and Cross Country Coaches Assn., 1988; named Outstanding Tchr. of Yr., Sta. WTVQ, 1991; named Ky. Col., 1983. Mem. Ky. Assn. Tchrs. History, Nat. Coun. for Social Studies, Ky. Coun. for Social Studies, Fayette County Coun. for Social Studies, U. Ky. Alumni Assn., Ky. Softball Coaches Assn. (pres. 1992—), Ky. Football Coaches Assn. Avocation: softball. Home: 905 Quarter Horse Ct Lexington KY 40503-5456

BARRERA, EDUARDO, Spanish language and literature educator; b. Rio Grande City, Tex., May 29, 1921; s. Bonifacio and Antonia (Rodrígues) B.; m. Maria Ninfa Cárdenas, Aug. 13, 1944; children: Maria Elena, Eduardo Ubil, David. BS, Tex. A&I Coll., 1952, MS, 1953; PhD, U. Tex., 1976. Cert. elem. and secondary sch. tchr., Tex. Tchr. grade 5 Ringgold Annex, Rio Grande City, 1952-53; tchr. Spanish Rio Grande H.S., Rio Grande City, 1956-63; cons. Tex. Edn. Agy., Austin, 1964, 65; tchr. Spanish Pan Am. U., Edinburgh, Tex., 1966-83, chmn. dept. fgn. langs., 1983-86; lectr. U. Tex. Pan Am., Edinburgh, 1987—. Evaluator in bilingual proficiency Tex. Edn. Agy., Austin and Edinburgh, 1978-86. With U.S. Signal Corps, 1941-45. Mem. Tex. Assn. Coll. Tchrs. (life, pres. local chpt. 1966—), KC (grand knight 1988-89). Roman Catholic. Avocations: violin, church choir, fishing. Home: 1007 W Samano St Edinburg TX 78539-4052 Office: Univ Tex Pan Am 1201 University Dr Edinburg TX 78539

BARRERA, ELVIRA PUIG, counselor, therapist, educator; b. Alice, Tex., Dec. 11, 1943; d. Carlos Rogers and Delia Rebecca (Puig) B.; 1 child, Dennis Lee Jr. BA, Incarnate Word Coll., 1971; M of Counseling and Guidance, St. Mary's U., San Antonio, 1978; specialist degree in marriage and family therapy, St. Mary's U., 1989. Lic. profl. counselor; lic. marriage & family therapist; lic. chem. dependency counselor. Tchr. Edgewood Ind. Sch. Dist., San Antonio, 1965-74, Dallas Ind. Sch. Dist., 1971-72, Northside Ind. Sch. Dist., San Antonio, 1974; ednl. cons. Region 20-Edn. Service Ctr., San Antonio, 1974-79; career edn. coordinator San Antonio Ind. Sch. Dist., 1979-84, counselor, 1984-91; family coord. C.A.T.C.H. Project, U. Tex. Health Sci. Ctr., Houston and Austin, 1991-94; counselor Austin Ind. Sch. Dist., 1994-97, dist. transition counselor, 1997-98; vice prin. San Antonio Ind. Sch. Dist., 1998—. Cons. SBA, 1981, U.S. Office Edn., Washington, 1981-82, Tex. Edn. Agy., Austin, 1979-80; cons., writer San Antonio Ind. Sch. Dist. and Tex. Edn. Agy., 1985; cons. to various edn. pubis. Chairperson career awareness exploring div. Boy Scouts Am., 1982-87. Named Disting. Alumna, Incarnate Word Coll., 1983; recipient Spurgeon award Boy Scouts Am., 1985, Merit award, 1986, Growth award, 1986, Internat. Profl. and Bus. Women's Hall of Fame, 1995. Mem. Am. Assn. Marriage and Family Therapy, San Antonio Hash House Harriers (treas. 1990-91), San Antonio Assn. Women Admistrs. Counselors, Incarnate Word Coll. Alumni Assn. (mem. adv. bd. 1990—), St. Mary's U. Alumni Assn. (v.p. Austin alumni chpt. 2003—), The Harp and Shamrock Soc. of Tex., Delta Kappa Gamma (2d v.p. 1982-84, 1st v.p. 1986-88), Chi Sigma Iota. Roman Catholic. Avocation: running. Home: 907 Aurora Cir Austin TX 78757-3415 Office: San Antonio Ind Sch Dist 515 Willow San Antonio TX 78202-1255

BARRETT, BERNARD MORRIS, JR., plastic and reconstructive surgeon; b. Pensacola, Fla., May 3, 1944; s. Bernard Morris and Blanche (Lischkoff) B.; children: Beverly Frances, Julie Blaine, Audrey Blake, Bernard Joseph. BS, Tulane U., 1965; MD, U. Miami, 1969. Diplomate Am. Bd. Plastic Surgery. Surg. intern Meth. Hosp. and Ben Taub Hosp., Houston, 1969-70; resident in gen. surgery Baylor Coll. Medicine, Houston, 1970-71, UCLA, 1971-73; resident in plastic surgery U. Miami (Fla.) Affilated Hosps., 1973-75, chief resident in plastic surgery, 1975; fellow in plastic surgery Clinica Ivo Pitanguy, Rio de Janeiro, 1973; instr. surgery Baylor Coll. Medicine, 1970-71, clin. instr. plastic surgery, 1977-80, clin. asst. prof., 1980-90, clin. assoc. prof., 1991-97, clin. prof. surgery, 1997—; instr. surg. emergeicies L.A. County Paramedics, 1972-73; plastic surgery coord. for jr. med. students Sch. Medicine U. Miami, 1975; practice medicine specializing in plastic and reconstructive surgery Houston, 1976—. Pres., chmn. bd. dirs. Plastic and Reconstructive Surgeons, P.A., 1978—; chmn. Tex. Inst. Plastic Surgery, Houston; assoc. chief plastic surgery St. Luke's Episcopal Hosp., Houston, 1991—; attending physician Jr. League Clinic, Tex. Children's Hosp., Houston, 1977—; active staff St. Luke's Hosp., Houston, Meth. Hosp., Houston; clin. assoc. in plastic surgery U. Tex. Med. Sch., Houston, 1976—; instr. surg. emergencies Harris County C.C.; dir. Am. Physicians Ins. Exch., Austin, 1976—, vice chmn., bd. dirs., 1995—; past chief of staff, chief plastic surgery Travis Centre Hosp., Houston, 1985—; dir. Physicians for Peace, Norfolk, Va., 1991—; cons. physician Houston Oilers, 1978-97; attending physician Ontario Motor Speedway, Calif., 1972-73. Author: Patient Care in Plastic Surgery, 1982, 2d edit., 1996, Manuel de Ciudados en Cirugia Plastica, 1985, Atencion al Paciente de Cirugia Plastica, 1998; contbr. articles to med. publs., presentations to profl. confs.; inventor Barrett sterling surgigrip. Bd. dirs. Plastic Surgery Ednl. Found., Chgo.; mem. Fed. Coun. on Aging, Washington, 1991-93, Pres.'s Coun. U. Miami, 1997—; adv. bd. Johnson & Johnson, New Brunswick, N.J. Lt. comdr. M.C., USNR, 1969-74. Surg. exch. scholar to Royal Coll. Surgeons, London, 1968; hon. dep. sheriff Harris County, Tex. (Houston). Fellow ACS; mem. Am. Assn. Plastic Surgery, Am. Soc. Plastic Surgeons, Royal Soc. Medicine, Michael E. DeBakey Internat. Cardiovascular Surg. Soc., Am. Soc. for Aesthetic Plastic Surgery, Denton A. Cooley Cardiovascular Surg. Soc., Tex. Med. Assn., Tex. Soc. Plastic Surgery, Harris County Med. Soc., Houston Soc. Plastic Surgery, D. Ralph Millard Plastic Surg. Soc. (pres. 1993-94, v.p. 1977-79, sec., treas. 1975-77, historian 1980—), U. Miami Sch. Medicine Nat. Alumni Assn. (bd. dirs. 1975-77, pres. coun. 1997—), Houston City Club, Houstonian Club, Royal Biscayne Racquet Club, Commodore Club, Coral Beach and Tennis Club, Sweetwater Country Club, Alpha Kappa Kappa (pres. 1968-69). Office: 6624 Fannin St Ste 2200 Houston TX 77030-2334 E-mail: txips@swbell.net.

BARRETT, EVELYN CAROL, retired secondary education educator; b. Ocean Springs, Miss., Feb. 6, 1928; d. Charles Edward and Irene Effie (Hopkins) Engbarth; m. Arthur James Barrett, June 10, 1951; children: George Stanley, Ruth Anne, James Sidney, Carolyn Jean. Diploma with honors, Jr. Coll. (now Miss. Coast Coll.), Perkinston, Miss., 1945; BS in Commerce with high honors, Miss. So. Coll. (now U. So. Miss.), 1947; MBA in Acctg., La. State U., 1950; also numerous continuing edn. courses, 1950-82. Bookkeeper-sec. Non-Commn. Officers Club, Kessler AFB, Miss., summer 1947; asst., secretarial practice office and divsn. rsch.; instr. in typing Coll. Commerce, La. State U., 1947-50; instr. Miss. So. Coll., summer 1950; clk.-stenographer dept. physics U. Ill., Urbana, 1951-52; instr. in shorthand Ill. Comml. Coll., 1951-52; tchr. Milford (N.H.) H.S., 1957-58; tchr. bus. edn. Merrimack (N.H.) H.S., 1958-90, head dept. bus. edn., 1971-81; ret., 1990. Grad. asst. La. State U., 1947-50; instr. auditing Rivier Coll., 1982; registered rep. R. Danais Investment Co., Manchester, N.H.; account exec. John, Edward & Co., Lebanon, N.H.; ind. beauty cons. Mary Kay Cosmetics, Merrimack; tutor in shorthand, acctg.; cons. acctg. sys. Organizer, 1st pres. Merrimack Group Hillsborough County Ext. Svc., 1957-58; active Girl Scouts U.S.A., including Cadette leader, 1959-63, sr. troop leader Switwater coun., 1970-72, adult vol. trainer, 1964-66, troop program cons., 1963-64. Mem. AAUW, NEA, N.H. Edn. Assn., N.H. Bus. Educators Assn. (v.p. 1964-65, pres. 1965-67, rep. to N.H. Vocat. Assn. 1986-87, sec. 1967-68, treas. 1973-75, historian 1986-87), N.H. Supervisory Union 27 (sec.-treas. 1961-62), Merrimack Tchrs. Assn. (sec. 1984-85, Disting. Educator award 1980, Excellence in Edn. award 1985), New Eng. Bus. Educators Assn., Assn. Career Tech. Edn., N.H. Assn. Computer Edn. Statewide, Ea. Bus. Edn. Assn., Nat. Bus. Edn. Assn., Manchester User's Group of Apple Computers (treas. 2000), Delta Zeta, Phi Theta Kappa, Pi Omega Pi, Delta Pi Epsilon, Alpha Delta Kappa (chpt. award of appreciation 1980, historian N.E. region 1981-83, sec. N.E. region 1995-97, v.p. N.H. Alpha chpt. 1978-79, pres. N.H. Alpha chpt. 1979-82, N.H. state sgt.-at-arms 1982-84, N.H. state treas. 1984-88, N.H. state membership chmn. 1988-92, N.H. state chaplain 1992-94, N.H. state pres. elect 1994-96, N.H. state pres. 1996-98, N.H. state immediate past pres. 1998-2000), Audubon Soc. N.H., Delta Sigma Epsilon (chpt. corr. sec.), Gen. Electric Women's Club, Reeds Ferry Women's Club, Manchester Coll. Women's Club, Our Lady of Mercy Ladies Guild (v.p. 1999, pres. 2000), Merrimack Sr. Citizen Club, Manchester Area Ret. Educators Assn., Nashua Area Ret. Educators Assn., N.H. Ret. Educators Assn. Roman Catholic.

BARRETT, JAMES THOMAS, immunologist, educator; b. Centerville, Iowa, May 20, 1927; s. Alfred Wesley and Mary Marjorie (Taylor) B.; m. Barbro Anna-Lill Nilsson, July 31, 1967; children— Sara, Robert, Annika, Nina BA, State U. Iowa, 1950, MS, 1951, PhD, 1953. Asst. prof. bacteriology and parasitology U. Ark. Sch. Medicine, Little Rock, 1953-57; asst. prof. microbiology U. Mo. Sch. Medicine, Columbia, 1957-59, assoc. prof., 1959-67, prof., 1967-94, St. George's (Grenada, W.I.) U. Sch. Medicine, 1994—2002; prof. emeritus U. Mo. Sch. Medicine, 1994—, ret., 2003. Exchange prof. U.S. and Romanian Acads. Sci., 1971; vis. scientist Spanish Ministry Edn. and Sci., 1986, Sch. Vet. Medicine, 2000 Author: Textbook of Immunology, 5th edit., 1988, Basic Immunology and Its Medical Application 2d edit., 1980, Medical Immunology, 1991, Microbiology and Immunology Casebook, 1995, Microbiology and Immunology Concepts, 1998; editor: Contemporary Classics in the Life Scienes, 1986, Contemporary Classics in Clinical Medicine, 1986, Contemporary Classics in Plant, Animal and Environmental Sciences, 1986. Served with USN, 1944-45 NIH Fogarty sr. fellow, 1977-78; Fulbright scholar, 1984 Mem. Am. Assn. Immunology, Am. Soc. Microbiology. Home: 901 Westport Dr Columbia MO 65203-0741 E-mail: niann@aol.com.

BARRETT, KATHLEEN ANNE, assistant principal; b. Jersey City, Aug. 16, 1954; d. Judson Bernard and Patricia Mary Ann (Conlon) B. BA, Iowa Wesleyan Coll., 1976; MA, Jersey City State Coll., 1993. Tchr. elem. Jersey City Pub. Schs., 1976-90, tchr. spl. edn., 1990-97, asst. prin., 1997—. Vol. oper. rm. Riverview Hosp., Red Bank, N.J. Mem. ASCD, NEA, Caucus for Educators Exceptional Children, Jersey City Edn. Assn., Phi Delta Kappa. Roman Catholic. Avocations: reading, needlework, arts and crafts. Office: PS 28 167 Hancock Ave Jersey City NJ 07307-2098

BARRETT, LEVERNE A. agricultural studies educator; Prof. Pa. State U.; prof. Agriculture U. Nebr., Lincoln, 1980—. Fellow Nat. Assn. Colls. Tchrs. Agriculture, 1992. Mem.: U. Nebr. Acad. Disting. Tchrs. Office: U Nebraska Dept Agriculture E Campus # 300 Ag H Lincoln NE 68583*

BARRETT, LIDA KITTRELL, mathematics educator; b. Houston, May 21, 1927; d. Pleasant Williams and Maidel (Baker) Kittrell; m. John Herbert Barrett, June 2, 1950 (dec. Jan. 1969); children: John Kittrell, Maidel Horn, Mary Louise. BA, Rice U., 1946; MA, U. Tex., Austin, 1949; PhD, U. Pa., 1954. Instr. math. U. Conn., Waterbury, 1955-56; vis. appointment U. Wis., Madison, 1959-60; lectr. U. Utah, Salt Lake City, 1956-61; assoc. prof. U. Tenn., Knoxville, 1961-70, prof., 1970-80, head math. dept., 1973-80; assoc. provost No. Ill. U., DeKalb, 1980-87; dean, arts and scis. Miss. State U., Mississippi State, 1987-91; sr. assoc. Edn. and Human Resources Directorate NSF, Washington, 1991-95; prof. math. U.S. Mil. Acad., West Point, N.Y., 1995-98; adj. prof. U. Tenn., 1998—. Ind. math. cons., Knoxville, Tenn., 1964-80, 98—. Contbr. articles on topology, applied math. and math. edn. to profl. jours. Mem. Math. Assn. Am. (pres. 1989, 90), Am. Math. Soc., Soc. Indsl. and Applied Math., Nat. Coun. Tchrs. Math., Am. Assn. Higher Edn., Phi Kappa Phi, Sigma Xi. Episcopalian. E-mail: barrett@math.utk.edu.

BARRETT, NANCY SMITH, university administrator; b. Balt., Sept. 12, 1942; d. James Brady and Katherine (Pollard) Smith; children: Clark, Christopher. BA, Goucher Coll., 1963; MA, Harvard U., 1965, PhD, PhD, Harvard U., 1968. Dep. asst. dir. Congl. Budget Office, Washington, 1975-76; sr. staff Council of Econ. Advisors, Washington, 1977; prin. research assoc. The Urban Inst., Washington, 1977-79; dep. asst. sec. U.S. Dept. Labor, Washington, 1979-81; instr. Am. U., Washington, 1966-67, asst. prof. econs., 1967-70, assoc. prof., 1970-74, prof., 1974-89; dean Coll. of Bus. Adminstrn. Fairleigh Dickinson U., Teaneck, N.J., 1989-91; provost, v.p. acad. affairs Western Mich. U., Kalamazoo, 1991-96, U. Ala., Tuscaloosa, 1996—2003, Wayne State U., Detroit, 2003—. Author: Theory of Macroeconomic Policy, 1972, 2d rev. edit., 1975, Theory of Microeconomic Policy, 1974, (with G. Gerardi and T. Hart) Prices and Wages in U.S., 1974; contbr. articles on econs. to profl. jours. Woodrow Wilson fellow, 1963-64; Fulbright scholar, 1973. Mem. Am. Econs. Assn., Phi Beta Kappa. Office: Wayne State Univ 4092 Faculty Adminstrn Bldg Detroit MI 48202 Home: 2033 Shorepointe Grosse Pointe Woods MI 48236 E-mail: nancy.barrett@wayne.edu.

BARRETT, PATRICIA LOUISE, mathematician, educator; b. Pitts., July 11, 1947; d. Walter James and Helen Louise (Booty) White; m. Jan F. Segovis, Aug. 2, 1970 (dec. Aug. 1984); m. Telford H. Barrett, Jr., Nov. 15, 1985; stepchildren: Joseph Keith and Telford Lee (twins). BS, Valdosta State Coll., 1969, MEd, 1970; EdS, Ga. So. Coll., 1985. Tchr. math. Lowndes High Sch., Valdosta, 1970-83, 86—; math. coord. Lowndes County Schs., Valdosta, 1983-86. Instr. math. Valdosta State Coll., 1975—; registrar Ga. Math. Conf., Eatonton, Ga., 1985-89, chmn., 1990. Mem. adult choir lst Bapt. Ch., 1966—, dir. children III Sunday sch., 1972—, pianist presch. choir, 1988-92, dir., 1992—. Recipient Star Tchr. award Valdosta C. of C., 1976, 82. Mem. NEA, Nat. Coun. Tchrs. Math., Ga. Coun. Tchrs. Math. (dist. chmn. 1981-83, Gladys M. Thompson dist. award 1986, state treas. 1992-94, sec. 1999-2003), Ga. Assn. Educators, Lowndes Assn. Educators (treas. 1979-80, pres. 1981-82), AAUW. Avocations: reading, teaching, travel. Home: 114 Fairway Dr Valdosta GA 31605-6431 Office: Lowndes High Sch 1112 N St Augustine Rd Valdosta GA 31601-3545

BARRETT, REGINALD HAUGHTON, biology educator, wildlife management educator; b. San Francisco, June 11, 1942; s. Paul Hutchison and Mary Lambert (Hodgkin) B.; m. Katharine Lawrence Ditmars, July 15, 1967; children: Wade Lawrence, Heather Elizabeth. BS in Game Mgmt., Humboldt State U., 1965; MS in Wildlife Mgmt., U. Mich., 1966; PhD in Zoology, U. Calif., Berkeley, 1971. Rsch. biologist U. Calif., Berkeley, 1970—71, acting asst. prof., 1971—72; rsch. scientist divsn. wildlife rsch. Commonwealth Scientific and Indsl. Rsch. Orgn., Darwin, Australia, 1972—75; from asst. prof. to prof. U. Calif., Berkeley, 1975—, George and Wilhelmina Goertz disting. prof. wildlife mgmt., 2002—. Author: (with others) Report on the Use of Fire in National Parks and Reserves, 1977, Research and Management of Wild Hog Populations, Proceedings of a Symposium, 1977, Sitka Deer Symposium, 1979, Symposium on Ecology and Management of Barbary Sheep, 1980, Handbook of Census Methods for Birds and Mammals, 1981, Wildlife 2000: Modeling Habitat Relationships of Terrestrial Vertebrates, 1986, Translocation of Wild Animals, 1988, Wildlife 2001: Populations, 1992; contbr. articles, abstracts, reports to profl. jours. Recipient Outstanding Profl. Achievement award Humboldt State U. Alumni Assn., 1986, Bruce R. Dodd award, 1965, Howard M. Wight award, 1966; Undergrad. scholar Nat. Wildlife Fedn., 1964, NSF grad. fellow, 1965-70; Union found. Wildlife Rsch. grantee, 1968-70. Mem. The Wildlife Soc. (pres. Bay Area chpt. 1978-79, pres. western sect. 1997-98, cert. wildlife biologist, R.F. Dasmann Profl. of Yr. award western sect. 1989), Am. Soc. Mammalogists (life), Soc. for Range Mgmt. (life), Ecol. Soc. Am. (cert. sr. ecologist), Soc. Am. Foresters, Australian Mammal Soc., Am. Inst. Biol. Scis., AAAS, Calif. Acad. Scis., Internat. Union for the Conservation of Nature (life), Calif. Bot. Soc., Orgn. Wildlife Planners, Sigma Xi, Xi Sigma Pi. Episcopalian. Avocations: hunting, fishing, photography, camping, backpacking. Office: U Calif 151 Hilgard Hall Berkeley CA 94720-3110

BARRETT, ROBERT MATTHEW, law educator, lawyer; b. Bronx, N.Y., Mar. 18, 1948; s. Harry and Rosalind B. AB summa cum laude, Georgetown U., 1976, MS in Fgn. Service, JD, 1980. Bar: Calif. 1981. Assoc. Latham & Watkins, L.A., 1980-82, Morgan, Lewis & Bockius, L.A., 1982-84, Skadden, Arps, Slate, Meagher & Flom, L.A., 1984-86, Shea & Gould, L.A., 1986-87, Donovan, Leisure, Newton & Irvine, L.A., 1988-90; ptnr. Barrett & Zipser, L.A., Calif., 1991-93; prof. law U West L.A. Law Sch., Woodland Hills, Calif., 1993—. Civilian vol. L.A. Sheriff's Dept., 1997-99. Mem. State Bar Calif. (standing com. on profl. responsibility and conduct 1995-99, chair 1997-98, spl. advisor 1998-99), L.A. Bar Assn. (bd. advisors vols. in parole com. 1981—). Address: 21300 Oxnard St Woodland Hills CA 91367-5058 Fax: 818-883-8142. E-mail: robertbarrett@charter.net.

BARRETT-HAYES, DEBRA PAIGE, art educator; b. Newport News, Va., Mar. 12, 1957; d. Edgar Camp and Sarah (Turner) Barrett; m. John Martin Hayes, June 12, 1988; 1 child, Cosby Martin. BS in Studio Art, Randolph-Macon Women's Coll., 1979; MS in Art Edn., Radford U., 1980; postgrad., Fla. State U., 1981—. Cert. tchr., Fla. Dir. art edn. program Alumni Village Housing Dept. Fla. State U., Tallahassee, 1981-85, instr. art. edn. Devel. Rsch. Sch., 1981-83, 84-88, asst. prof., 1988-91, assoc. prof., 1991-94, prof., 1994—. Adj. prof. art edn. Fla. State U., Tallahassee, 1991, Fla. A&M U., Tallahassee, 1991, 92; cons. improving visual arts edn. Getty Ctr. for Arts, 1980-82, Fla. Inst. for Art Edn., 1990—, mem. writing team comprehensive holistic assessemnt task, 1992—. Exhibited in group shows including Artworks Mixed Media, 1982. Sponsor Young Dems., vol. various charities. Grantee Nat. Endowment for the Arts, Arts for Complete Edn., Coun. for Basic Edn., Getty Ctr. for Edn. in Arts, 1992, Nat. Assn. Lab. Schs., 1992; dean's grantee Fla. State U., 1991; named Fla. Art Educator of the Year, 1995-96. Mem. Nat. Art Edn. Assn., Nat. Assn. Lab. Schs., Fla. Art Edn. Assn. (div. chmn. mid. sch.), League Artists, Thomasville Artists Guild, Tallahassee Jr. Woman's Club (bd. dirs.), Phi Delta Kappa. Democrat. Avocations: saltwater fishing, photography, creative vegetarian cooking. Office: Fla State U Sch 1023 FSU W Call St Tallahassee FL 32306

BARRIE, JOAN PARKER, elementary school educator; b. L.A., Aug. 25, 1932; d. Joseph Alexander and Madeline Agnes (Smith) Parker. EdB, Seattle U., 1959; MEd, Loyola Marymount, 1973. Cert. elem., secondary tchr., Calif.; cert. reading specialist, lang. devel. specialist. 6th grade tchr. Sisters of Immaculate Heart, Hollywood, Calif., 1953-56; reading specialist Lakewood (Wash.) Schs., 1959-60, Beverly Hills (Calif.) Sch. Dist., 1960-62; 2nd grade tchr., 6th grade reading specialist Inglewood (Calif.) Unified Sch. Dist., 1962-76; owner Everest Cultural Enrichments, L.A., from 1975; various positions Torrance and Redondo, Calif., 1979-82; office mgr. Starbecca Records, Redondo Beach, Calif., 1982-83; 5th and 6th grades tchr. St. Anthonys, El Segundo, Calif., 1984-85; 2nd grade bilingual tchr. Hawthorne (Calif.) Sch. Dist., from 1985. Author, illustrator: Did You See It, Too?, 1982, Tiggy, Primary Academies, 1989, Reading English, 1994, Reading Spanish, 1995; composer, lyricist Valentine, 1986, (screenplay) Castles of Dreams, 1995. Active United We Stand, 1994, Concern America, Redondo Beach, 1994. Mem. NEA, Calif. Tchrs. Assn., Nat. Coun. Social Studies, S.W. Manuscripters, Dramatist Guild, Smithsonian, Ednl. Dealer. Roman Catholic. Avocations: computers, reading, beach walking, gardening. Home: Los Angeles, Calif. Died Oct. 10, 2001.

BARRINGTON, LEONARD BARRY, chemist, educator, writer; b. Hutchinson, Kans., Jan. 21, 1924; s. August Leroy and Alice Amanda (Goodenough) B.; m. Katharine Lucy Cibes, Dec. 26, 1945 (div. 1975); 1 child, Belinda; m. Sharyn Marie Carlson, Oct. 3, 1975. BSc, DePaul U., Chgo., 1951; PhD in Biochemistry, U. Chgo., 1955. Exec. sec. Congl. Office of Tech. Assessment, Washington, 1976-79; exec. study dir. NRC, Washington, 1979-81; mgr. tech. planning Atlantic Richfield/Arco Metals, Rolling Meadows, Ill., 1981-84; prin. Cue Systems, Chgo., 1980—; sr. assoc. Pugh Roberts Assocs., Cambridge, Mass., 1983-86; dir. tech. ctr. U. Ill., Chgo., 1986-87, dir. tech. devel., 1987-93; mem. tchg. staff Prairie Crossing Charter Sch. Author/editor: Strategies/Applied Research Management, 1978; author: (novel) Feasting With the Deacon, 1988; columnist Arlington Heights (Ill.) Post; contbr. articles to profl. jours. Panelist World Conf./Rsch. Pks., Chgo., 1990. AEC fellow, 1951-54. Fellow Am. Inst. Chemists; mem. ASTM (acad. mem.), Japan Soc. Chgo., Futurist Soc., Ind. Writers of Chgo., Irish Inst. Chemistry, Nat. Silver-Haired Congress, Sigma Xi, Beta Beta Beta. Achievements include development of production process for polyurethane foam structural panels; patents on cultivation of micro-organisms, food safe inhibitors of polymerization. Home: 1525 Portia Rd Grayslake IL 60030-3544

BARRON, BRIGID, education educator; BS in Psychology, U. Calif., Santa Cruz, 1984; MA in Psychology, Vanderbilt U., 1989, PhD in Clin. Developmental Psychology, 1992. Intern in child clin. psychology U. Wash., 1991—92; instr. Peabody Coll., Vanderbilt U., 1992—93; sr. rsch. assoc. Learning Tech. Ctr., Vanderbilt U., 1992—95; asst. prof. edn. Stanford (Calif.) U., 1996—. Mem. adv. bd. tech. task force SPEAK-UP! Leadership Program for Girls; cons. Plugged-In Tech. Access Ctr., Comty. Kids Children's Program. Office: Stanford U Sch Edn 485 Lasuen Mall Stanford CA 94305-3096*

BARRON, SANDRA MCWHIRTER, library media specialist; b. Ft. Myers, Fla., Jan. 6, 1945; d. Charles Earl and Mary Belle (Aldridge) McWhirter; m. Charles Hunter Barron, June 4, 1968; children: Lynn Ann, Steven Andrew. BS in Edn., U. Ala., 1968; MEd, Loyola U., New Orleans, 1972; MLS, Sam Houston State U., 1982. Cert. tchr., libr. media specialist, Tex. Tchr. Pascagoula (Miss.) High Sch., 1968-69; tchr. reading Jefferson Parish Sch. Dist, Metairie, La., 1969-73, Tomball (Tex.) Ind. Sch. Dist., 1978-82; libr. media specialist Tomball High Sch., 1982—. Treas. Cripple Creek Homeowners Assn., Pinehurst, Tex.,1978-80. Mem. ALA, Tex. Libr. Assn., Tex. State Edn. Assn., Tex. Assn. Edn. Tech., Tex. Assn. Sch. Librs. (sec. 1994), Tomball Edn. Assn. (pres. 1986-88), Sirsi Internat. Users Group (chair-elect 1994). Avocations: reading, computer, gardening. Office: Tomball High Sch Libr 30330 Quinn Rd Tomball TX 77375-4300 Home: 2815 Pine Arbor Dr Montgomery TX 77356-5426

BARROW, CLYDE WAYNE, political scientist, educator; b. Alice, Tex., Feb. 15, 1956; s. Floyd Smith and Wanda Ruth (Conner) B. BA in Polit. Sci., Tex. A&I U., 1977; MA in Polit. Sci., UCLA, 1979, PhD in Polit. Sci., 1984. Teaching fellow UCLA, 1978-82, dir. instrnl. devel., 1982-84; vis. asst. prof. U. Tex., San Antonio, 1984-85, Tex. A&M U., College Station, 1985-87; from asst. prof. to prof. polit. sci. U. Mass. at Dartmouth, North Dartmouth, 1987-96, prof., 1996—, acting chmn. dept., 1992-93, 95, sr. rsch. assoc. Ctr. for Policy Analysis, 1993-94, dir. Ctr. for Policy Analysis, 1994—. Mem. adv. bd. Arnold Dubin Labor Edn. Ctr., North Dartmouth, 1988—; policy cons. Office of Mayor, City of Fall River, Mass., 1993—, New Bedford CEO Club, 1994—99, Fall River Sch. Dept., 1995—, Sandwich Sch. Dept., 1996—, Fall River Housing Authority, 1997—, New Bedford Housing Authority, 1999—; exec. staff analyst Gov.'s Commn. on Commonwealth Port Devel., Mass., 1994, Gov.'s Regional Econ. Devel. Strategies Project, 1996, 2000—01; regional analyst Mass. Benchmark Project, 1997—; pub. mem. Cranberry Mktg. Com., 2003—. Author: Universities and the Capitalist State, 1990, Critical Theories of the State, 1993, More Than a Historian: The Political and Economic Thought of Charles A. Beard, 2000, Economic Impacts of the Textile and Apparel Industries in Massachusetts, 2000, Portuguese-Americans and Contemporary Civic Culture in Massachusetts, 2002; co-author: Globalisation Trade Liberalisation and Higher Education in North America, 2003; mem. bd. editors Acad. Labor, 2003-, Sociol. Inquiry, 1992-95, Jour. Politics, 1993-97, Acad. Labor, 2003-; mng. editor New England Jour. Pub. Policy, 1994-97; also articles. Recipient Fontera Meml. award Arnold Dubin Labor Edn. Ctr., 1991, Disting. Svc. award Mass. Fedn. Tchrs., 2001. Mem. Am. Polit. Sci. Assn., Western Polit. Sci. Assn., Caucus for a New Polit. Sci., Policy Studies Orgn., U. Mass. Faculty Fedn. (treas. 1991-96, 2002-03, pres. 1998-2000). Office: U Mass Ctr Policy Analysis 285 Old Westport Rd North Dartmouth MA 02747-2356

BARROW, JOSEPH CARLTON, elementary school principal; b. Cheyenne, Wyo., Mar. 12, 1958; s. Joseph C. and Alberta Dee (Bethel) B. BS in Edn., Ga. So. U., 1980, MEd, 1987; postgrad., Nova U., Ft. Lauderdale, Fla., 1990—. Cert. education adminstr., supr., Ga. Tchr. Appling County Jr. High Sch., Baxley, Ga., 1980-81, Appling County High Sch., Baxley, 1981-87; asst. prin. Appling County Primary Sch., Baxley, 1987-88; prin. Bethlehem (Ga.) Elem. Sch., 1989-93, Sally D. Meadows Elem. Sch., Vidalia, Ga., 1993—. Mem. steering com. Ga. Leadership Acad., 1988, cons., 1992; cons. Jeff Davis High Sch., Hazelhurst, Ga., 1992. Mem. Leadership Appling County, 1985, bd. dirs., 1986; bd. dirs. Community Leadership Barrow County, Winder, Ga., 1991. Named to Edn. Leadership Ga., Ga. Leadership Acad., Atlanta, 1988, Gov.'s Sch. Leadership Inst., State Dept. Edn., Atlanta, 1992; grantee Ga. PTA, 1991, Phi Delta Kappa, 1992. Mem. ASCD, Nat. Assn. Elem. Sch. Prins., Ga. Assn. Elem. Sch. Prins. (Disting. Elem. Sch. Bell award), Ga. Assn. Ednl. Leaders, Ga. Coun. Against Child Abuse, Phi Delta Kappa. Methodist. Avocations: reading, bike riding, music.

BARROW, MARIE ANTONETTE, elementary school educator; b. Jamaica, Nov. 2, 1952; d. Edward Emmanuel and Mildred Pancheta (Brown) Rerrie; children: Melissa Alicia, Matthew Andre. BA, Coll. of New Rochelle, 1976; MA, Bank St. Coll. Edn., 1982. Tchr. spl. edn. Ossining (N.Y.) Pub. Schs., 1978-91, tchr. 2d grade, 1991—. Presenter Brookside Sch., Ossining, 1994, Staff Devel. Ctr., White Plains, N.Y., 1992; mem. study group to examine elem. sch. gifted/talented programs, Ossining Union Free Sch. Dist., 1993-94. Nominee N.Y. State Tchr. Yr., 1997. Mem. Assn. for Supervision and Curriculum Devel., Tchr.s for Child Centered Learning, Brookside Sch. Behavior Com. (chmn. 1990-92). Avocations: reading, writing, dancing, singing, tennis. Home: PO Box 24 White Plains NY 10603-0024

BARROWS, FRANCINE ELEANOR, early childhood educator; b. Bridgeport, Conn., Nov. 16, 1948; d. Joseph John and Eleanor Sylvia (Torok) Csonka; m. Robert Lynn Barrows, Oct. 8, 1983; children: Joshua Lyn, Craig Scott (twins). BA, Sacred Heart U., 1970; postgrad., Fairfield U., 1978. Cert. profl. tchr., Conn. Sales head, asst. office head Howland-Steinbach, Fairfield, Conn., 1967-86; tchr. elem. grades Wheeler Sch., Bridgeport, Conn., 1970-71, Garfield Sch., Bridgeport, 1971—; sec. RC Hobbies of Conn., Inc., Milford, Conn., 1983-92. Assoc. Regional Lab. Grantee Bridgeport Pub. Edn. Fund, 1985, 89. Mem. NEA, Conn. Edn. Assn., Bridgeport Edn. Assn., Pi Sigma Phi. Roman Catholic. Avocation: collecting dinosaur memorabilia. Office: Garfield Sch 655 Stillman St Bridgeport CT 06608-1331

BARRY, LOUISE MCCANTS, retired college official; b. Appleton, Ark., Apr. 22, 1924; d. Jesse Blaine and Piety Ethel (Griffin) Spears; m. Robert Orville McCants, Aug. 22, 1947 (div. 1982); children: Blaine, Janice, Robert; m. William Burnett Barry, Feb. 16, 1993. BS, Okla. State U., 1944, MS, 1948; PhD, Ohio State U., 1974. Statistician Stanolind Oil & Gas Co., Tulsa, 1944-46; instr. Okla. State U., Stillwater, 1946-49; analytical statistician U.S. Air Force, Wright-Patterson AFB, Ohio, 1949-52; prof. math. Sinclair Community Coll., Dayton, Ohio, 1966-78; dir. rsch. U. Mid-Am., Lincoln, Nebr., 1978-79; acad. dean Kirkwood Community Coll., Cedar Rapids, Iowa, 1979-83; dir. instrn. Met. Community Colls., Kansas City, Mo., 1983-88. Cons. numerous colls. in U.S. and Gt. Britain, 1974-. Author: Womanchange!, 1986, Retire to Fun and Freedom, 1988, A Price Beyond Rubies, 1996, Cinderella Doesn't Work Here Anymore, 1992; contbr. articles to profl. jours. Mem. Iowa Humanities Bd., 1980-83; bd. dirs. Cedar Rapids Symphony, 1980-83, United Way Fund Drive, Cedar Rapids, 1982, Mo. Humanities Coun., 1984—, Mo. Bio-Ethics Coun., 1987—; del. Iowa Rep. Conv., 1982. Mem. Am. Assn. Cmty. Jr. Colls., Nat. Speakers Assn., Kansas City Women's C. of C. (edn. com. 1986—), Friends of Art, AAUW, Civil War Roundtable, Western Posse, Phi Mu Epsilon, Kappa Delta Pi. Roman Catholic. Home and Office: 121 W 48th St Apt 2105 Kansas City MO 64112-3923

BARRY, MARILYN WHITE, retired special education educator, dean; b. Weymouth, Mass., Sept. 12, 1936; d. Harland Russell and Alice Louise (Dwyer) White; m. Dennis Edward Barry, July 11, 1959; children: Dennis Edward, Christopher Gerard. BS in Edn., Bridgewater State Coll., 1958; EdM in Spl. Edn., Boston U., 1969, EdD in Spl. Edn., 1974. Tchr. Weymouth (Mass.) pub. schs., 1958-60; spl. edn. instr. Boston U., 1972-74; ast. prof. in spl. edn. Bridgewater (Mass.) State Coll., 1974-79, assoc. prof., 1979-83, prof., 1983-87, chmn. spl. edn. dept., 1979-87, coord. dept. grad. programs, 1979-87, adminstr. bilingual spl. edn., 1983-86, dean Grad. Sch., 1987-98; ret., 1998. Co-author human svc. workers curriculum materials. Recipient 3 Disting. Svc. awards Bridgewater State Coll., 1980, 82, 85; Bilingual Spl. Edn. grantee, 1980, 83; Boston U. fellow, 1967-74 Mem. CEC (Mass. chpt. founder, past pres., learning disabilities chpt.), Mass. Assn. Children with Learning Disabilties (past v.p.), Phi Delta Kappa, Pi Lambda Theta. Democrat. Roman Catholic. Home: 138 Bedford St Lakeville MA 02347-1351

BARSAMIAN, J(OHN) ALBERT, lawyer, judge, educator, criminologist, arbitrator; b. Troy, N.Y., May 1, 1934; s. John and Virginia Barsamian; m. Alice Missirilan, Apr. 21, 1963; children: Bonnie, Tamara. BS in Psychology with honors, Union Coll., 1956; JD, 1968; LLB, Albany Law Sch., 1959; postgrad., SUNY, Albany, 1964, Nat. Jud. Coll., 1997. Bar: N.Y. 1961, U.S. Dist. Ct. (no. dist.) N.Y. 1961, U.S. Supreme Ct. 1967; fire tng. cert. N.Y. State Exec. Dept. Pvt. practice, 1961—; dir. criminal sci., chmn. dept. Russell Sage Coll., 1970-88, assoc. prof. criminal sci., 1977-82, prof., 1982-87, prof. emeritus, 1987—. Lectr. office local govt. divsn. criminal justice svcs. State N.Y., 1964—72, N.Y. State Police Acad., 1970; judge adminstrv. law N.Y. State Pub. Employment Rels. Bd., 1996—2001, supervising judge, asst. dir. pub. employment practice and representation, 2001—; faculty pub. affairs and policy pub. svc. tng. program Nelson A. Rockefeller Coll., 1986—91, Sch. Labor Rels. Ext. divsn. Cornell U., 1986; gaming cons. Gov's Office Indian Rels., NY, 1991—92; spl. counsel Office of Police Chief, Cohoes, NY, 1986—92, to city mgr., Troy, NY, 1993; counsel Watervliet Police Assn., 1967—74, Cohoes Police Assn., 1967—74, Colonie Police Assn., 1977—80, Troy Police Command Officers Assn., 1981—85, North Greenbush Police Assn., 1985—90, Office of the Police Chief, Syracuse, NY, 1985—90, Fire Dept. Union, Albany, NY, 1986, Shenectady Fire Fighters Union, 1992—95; gen. counsel Internat. Narcotic Enforcement Officers Assn., 1982—84, Troy Uniformed Firefighters Assn., 1977—97; spl. investigator Rensselaer County Dist. Atty., 1959—61; mem. law guardian panel N.Y. State Family Ct., 1967—77; mem. mediation panel N.Y. State Pub. Employment Rels. Bd., 1968—73; supervising judge, asst. dir. Pub. Employment Practices and Representation, 2001—; lectr. Inst. Legal Studies Albany (N.Y.) Law Sch., 2003. Founder, chmn. dept. police sci. Hudson Valley C.C., 1961-69; mem. adv. bd. History Ctr. Skidmore Coll., 1993—; bd. dirs. Rensselaer County ARC, 1966-70; mem. alumni coun. Union Coll., 1981-86; mem. parish coun. St. Peter Armenian Ch., Watervliet, N.Y., 1979-83, chmn., 1981-83, vice chmn., 1984; evaluator office of non-collegiate programs N.Y. State Dept. Edn., 1985—; hon. dep. sheriff St. Mary Parish (La.); mem. Rensselaer County Criminal Justice Coordinating Coun., 1976-78. Decorated chevalier, knight comdr. Sovereign Order of Cyprus; recipient Lawyers Coop. Pub. Co. prize in criminal law, 1957, Police Sci. Students award, Hudson Valley C.C., 1968, meritorious svc. to law enforcement award, Law Enforcement Officers Soc., 1969, Archbishop's cert. merit, Armenian Ch. Am., 1973, Gabrielli Meml. award, Albany Law Sch., 2003; scholar Tarzian, Union Coll., 1952—56, Porter, Albany Law Sch., 1954—56, Saxton, 1956—59. Mem.: Internat. Coll. Master Advocates, N.Y. State Assn. Adminstrv. Law Judges (bd. dirs. 1999, 2001), Am. Coll. Barristers, N.Y. State Trial Lawyers Assn., Union Coll. Alumni Assn. (Silver medal 1956), Am. Assn. Criminology, Acad. Criminal Justice Scis., Am. Arbitration Assn. (svc. award 1983), Nat. Assn. Adminstrv. Law Judges, N.Y. Bar Assn. (chmn. com. on police 1970—72, trial lawyers sect. com. contg. legal edn. 1977—97, subcom. on adminstrv. law judges 2000—), ABA (com. on police selection and tng. 1967—69), ATLA, N.Y. Vet. Police Assn. (life), Rose Croix (most wise master Delta chpt. 1986), Masonic Vet. Assn. Troy (life), Les Amis d'Escoffier Soc., Lambda Epsilon Chi, Alpha Phi Sigma, Phi Delta Theta. Home and Office: 5 Sage Hill Ln Albany NY 12204-1315

BARSANO, CHARLES PAUL, medical educator, dean; BS in Biology, Loyola U., Chgo., 1969; PhD in Pathology, U. Chgo., 1974, MD, 1975. Diplomate Am. Bd. Internal Medicine. Resident internal medicine Barnes Hosp./Washington U., St. Louis, 1975-77; fellow endocrinology U. Chgo. Sch. Medicine, 1977-79, rsch. assoc. endocrinology, 1979-80; asst. prof. medicine Northwestern U. and Lakeside VA Med. Ctr., 1980-85, U. Health Scis./Chgo. Med. Sch. and North Chgo. VA Med. Ctr., 1985-87, assoc. prof., 1987-92, prof. medicine, 1992-98, assoc. prof. pharmacology and molecular biology, 1992-94, prof. pharmacology and molecular biology, 1994-98, acting dean Med. Sch., 1998—99, assoc. dean for clin. affairs, vice-chmn. dept. medicine, 1999—2001, interim dean, 2001—; staff physician med. svc./endocrinology sect. North Chgo. VA Med. Ctr. Mem. editl. bd. Thyroid, 1990-95; mem. adv. bd. Toxic Substance Mechanisms, 1993-99. Recipient Bausch and Lomb Nat. Sci. award, 1965, Individual Nat. Rsch. Svc. award, 1979-80. Mem. Internat. Coun. for Control of Iodine Deficiency Disorders, Assn. Am. Med. Colls. (group on ednl. affairs sect. on resident edn.), Am. Assn. Clin. Endocrinologists, Am. Thyroid Assn. (fiscal com. 1982-85, pub. health com. 1986-88, membership com. 1990-93, chmn. membership com. 1993, local organizing com. 1994, bylaws com. 1995—), Endocrine Soc., Chgo. Endocrine Club (pres. 1984-85), Sigma Xi, Alpha Omega Alpha. Office: Office Clin Affairs Finch Univ Health Scis Chgo Med Sch North Chicago IL 60064 Fax: 847-578-3320. E-mail: barsanoc@finchcms.edu.

BARSNESS, RICHARD WEBSTER, management educator, administrator; b. Elbow Lake, Minn., Apr. 26, 1935; s. Russel E. and Joanna (Warga) B.; m. Dorothea L. Gother, Aug. 22, 1964; children: Karen Louise, Erik Richard. BS, U. Minn., 1957, MA, 1958, MAP.A., 1960, PhD, 1963. Budget analyst U.S. Bur. Budget, Washington, 1960-61; instr., asst. prof. Northwestern U., Evanston, Ill., 1962-69, assoc. prof., 1969-78, assoc. dean, 1972-78; dean, prof. Lehigh U., Bethlehem, Pa., 1978-92, prof., 1978—, Iacocca prof. bus., 1992-93, exec. dir. Iacocca Inst., 1992-95, Univ. disting. svc. prof., 1995—; pres. Lexington Group, Inc., 1997—. Exec. sec. Lexington Group in Transport History, 1969-89; pres. Bus. History Conf., 1981-82; lectr. Transp. Ctr., Evanston, Ill., 1964-84; editl. cons. Various pubs. Contbr.: articles to profl. jours.; editor: Lexington Newsletter. Mem. Gov.'s Adv. Coun. State of Ill., 1969—72; gen. chmn. United Way Lehigh U., 1981; v.p., bd. dirs. Episcopal Ho., Allentown, Pa., 1999—, pres., 2003. Recipient R.R. and E.C. Hillman award Lehigh U., 1991. Mem.: Acad. Internat. Bus., Internat. Assn. for Bus. and Soc., Bus. History Conf. (trustee 1978—81, pres. 1981—82), Transp. Rsch. Forum, Acad. Mgmt., Phi Beta Kappa, Beta Gamma Sigma. Republican. Episcopalian. Home: 769 Apollo Dr Bethlehem PA 18017-2556 Office: Lehigh U Coll Bus 621 Taylor St Bethlehem PA 18015-3117 E-mail: rwb0@lehigh.edu.

BARTELL, ERNEST, economist, educator, priest; b. Chgo., Jan. 22, 1932; PhB, U. Notre Dame, 1953; AM, U. Chgo., 1954; MA, Coll. Holy Cross, 1961; PhD, Princeton U., 1966; LLD (hon.), China Acad., Taipei, Taiwan, 1975, St. Joseph's Coll., 1983, King's Coll., 1984, Stonehill Coll., 1992. Ordained priest Roman Cath. Ch., 1961. Instr. econs. Princeton (N.J.) U., 1965-66; asst. prof. econs. U. Notre Dame, Ind., 1966-68, assoc. prof., 1968-71, chmn. dept. econs., 1968-71, dir. Ctr. Study of Man in Contemporary Soc., 1969-71, prof. econs., 1981—2003, prof. emeritus, 2003—; exec. dir. Helen Kellogg Inst. Internat. Studies, Ind., 1981—97, fellow, 1997—; pres. Stonehill Coll., North Easton, Mass., 1971-77; dir. Fund for Improvement Post Secondary Edn. U.S. Dept. Health, Edn. and Welfare, Washington, 1977-79; dir. Project 80 Assn. Cath. Colls. and Univs., Washington, 1979-80; overseas mission coord. Priests of Holy Cross, Ind. Province, 1980-84, assoc. dir. Holy Cross Mission Ctr., 1984-95; asst. to pastor St. Anthony Ch., Ft. Lauderdale, Fla., 1993—2003. Active Inst. East-West Securities Studies Working Group on Sources in Instability, 1989-90, Internat. Ctr. Devel. Policy Commn. on U.S.-Soviet Rels., 1988-89, Overseas Devel. Coun., 1988-2000, The Bretton Woods Com., 1992-2002; mem. policy planning commn. Nat. Inst. Ind. Colls. and Univs., 1982-85; bd. dirs. Ctr. for Health Promotion, Internat. Life Scis. Inst.; hon. trustee Stonehill Coll., 2002—. Author; Costs and Benefits of Catholic Elementary and Secondary schools, 1969; co-editor: Business and Democracy in Latin America, 1995, The Child in Latin America, 2000; contbr. articles to profl. jours. Bd. regents U. Portland, Oreg., 1984—; bd. dirs. Missionary Vehicle Assn. Am., 1981-88, Big Bros. and Big Sisters Am., 1978-80, Brockton Community Housing Corp., 1974-77, The Brighter Day, 1974-77, Brockton Hosp., 1973-77, King's Coll., Wilkes-Barre, Pa., 1969-82; bd. trustees Emmanuel Coll., 1977-78, U. Notre Dame, 1974-2002, bd. fellows, 1974-2002; bd. trustees Regis Coll., 2002--; adv. bd. Brockton Art Ctr., 1974-77; exec. com. Opera New Eng., 1977. Recipient Fenwick Alumni Recognition award, 1974; named to Fenwick Hall of Fame, 1990; faculty fellow Kellogg Inst., 1997—. Fellow Soc. Values in Higher Edn.; mem. Am. Econ. Assn., Am. Assn. Higher Edn., Nat. Cath. Ednl. Assn. (chmn. govtl. rels. com. 1976-77, vice chmn. exec. com. 1976-77, chmn. mgmt. and planning com. 1974-76), Assn. Soc. Econs., Latin Am. Studies Assn., Young Pres. Orgn. (sec. 1974-77), Delta Mu Delta (hon.). Home: 227 Corby Hall Notre Dame IN 46556-5680 Office: U Notre Dame Kellogg Inst 211 Hesburgh Ctr Notre Dame IN 46556-5677 E-mail: ebartell@nd.edu.

BARTELS, JEAN ELLEN, nursing educator; b. Two Rivers, Wis., July 15, 1949; m. Terry D. Bartels, Aug. 14, 1971; children: Justin Dean, Ashlee Jill. Diploma, Columbia Hosp. Sch. Nursing, 1970; BSN with honors, Alverno Coll., 1981; MSN, Marquette U., 1983; PhD in Nursing, U. Wis., 1990. Staff nurse ICU Columbia Hosp., Milw., 1970-76; prof. nursing Alverno Coll., Milw., 1983-99, dean nursing, 1990-99; chair Sch. Nursing Ga. So. U., Statesboro, 1999—. Asst. edn. editor Jour. Profl. Nursing; contbr. articles to profl. jours. Mem. ANA, AACN (pres.-elect), Internat. Soc. for Sci. Study Subjectivity, Midwest Nursing Rsch. Soc., Am. Assn. Collegiate Schs. Nursing, Am. Ednl. Rsch. Assn., Am. Assn. Higher Edn., Sigma Theta Tau, Phi Kappa Phi. Home: 912 Brittany Ln Statesboro GA 30461-4499 Office: Ga So U PO Box 8158 Statesboro GA 30460-1000

BARTELS, PATRICIA RHODEN, masters fine art educator; b. Toledo, July 29, 1950; d. Alfred Edward and Virginia June (Bramwell) Rhoden; m. Gary L. Bartels, Nov. 17, 1973; children: Lance R., Christopher L. BA, Toledo U., 1971; MA, Bowling Green U., 1976, MFA, 1977. Tchr. art Liberty Ctr. (Ohio) Pub. Sch., 1974-81, Brown County Pub. Schs., Nashville, Ind., 1983—. One-woman shows include Ft. Wayne Mus., Tweed Mus., Toledo Mus. Art Collectors Corner, group shows include San Guiseppi Coll. St. Joseph, Craftsman Gallery, Emerging Artist Show Sothebys.com, Mayer's Fine Arts Book, 2003; represented in permanent collection Ft. Wayne Mus; exhbn. Ind. State Mus., Fort Wayne Mus. of Art, Birmingham, Ala., Civil Rights Mus, Emerging Artist, Sotheby's.com. Wallbridge Sinclair grantee Toledo Mus. Art, 1972, Art Interest grantee, 1973; Kent Blossom Summer Arts scholar, 1973; Eli Lily Creative fellow, 1992, 2002; NEH grantee, 1994, Hoosier Salon, Ind. Artist Club. Mem. Psi Iota Xi. Avocation: painting. Home: 2510 S State Road 135 Nashville IN 47448-9089 Office: Brown County Jr High Sch School House Ln Nashville IN 47448

BARTELT, JOHN ERIC, physics researcher and educator; b. Milw.aukee, Aug. 11, 1955; s. Robert Louis and Lois Marie (Wallschlaeger) B.; m. Lucy Mary (Huntzinger), Oct. 21, 1989. BS, U. Wis., 1977; PhD, U. Minn., 1984. Rsch. assoc. Stanford Linear Accelerator Ctr., Calif., 1983-88; exptl. physicist Stanford Linear Accelerator Ctr., Calif., 1988-89; asst. prof. Vanderbilt Univ., Nashville, 1990-97; scientist, programmer Stanford Linear Accelerator Ctr., Calif., 1997—. Conducted seminars and lectr. in field. Contbrg. articles to profl. jour. Mem.: Am. Physic Soc. Avocations: genealogy, photography. E-mail: bartelt@slac.stanford.edu.

BARTER, MARY F. academic administrator; BA, U. Minn., 1964; MS, U. Wis., Milw., 1969, PhD, 1975. Supt. Three Village Cen. Sch. Dist., L.I., NY, 1992—99, Durango (Colo.) Sch. Dist. 9-R, 1999—. Recipient Disting. Supt. and Outstanding Supt. awards, Suffolk County and N.Y. Coun. Sch. Supts. Mem.: Horace Mann League, N.Y. Assn. for Women in Adminstrn. (bd. dirs.), Wis. Elem. Kindergarten Nursery Educators (pres.), N.Y. Coun. Sch. Supts. (pres.), Am. Assn. Sch. Adminstrs. (exec. com., women adminstrs. adv. com., fed. policy and legis. com., exec. dir.'s adv. com., del. assembly). Office: Durango Sch Dist 9-R 201 E 12th St Durango CO 81301

BARTH, JOHN ROBERT, English educator, priest; b. Buffalo, Feb. 23, 1931; s. Philip C. and Mary K. (Eustace) B. AB, Bellarmine Coll., 1954, PhL, 1955; MA, Fordham U., 1956; STB, Woodstock Coll., 1961, STL, 1962; PhD, Harvard U., 1967. Joined Society of Jesus, Roman Catholic Ch., 1948; tchr. English, French, Latin (Canisius High Sch.), Buffalo, 1955-58; asst. prof. English Canisius Coll., Buffalo, 1967-70, Harvard U., Cambridge, Mass., 1970-74; assoc. prof. English U. Mo.-Columbia, 1974-77, prof., 1977-79, Catherine Paine Middlebush prof. English, 1979-82, prof. English, chmn. dept., 1980-83, prof. English, 1983-85; Thomas I. Gasson prof. English Boston Coll., 1985-86; prof. English U. Mo.-Columbia, 1986-88; dean Coll. Arts and Scis. Boston Coll, 1988-99; James P. McIntyre prof. English Boston Coll., 1999—. Author: Coleridge and Christian Doctrine, 1969, 2d edit., 1987, The Symbolic Imagination: Coleridge and the Romantic Tradition, 1977, 2d edit., 2000 (Book of Yr. award, Conf. on Christianity and Lit. 1977), Coleridge and the Power of Love, 1988 (U. Mo. Curators Publ. award 1989), Romanticism and Transcendence: Wordsworth, Coleridge, and the Religious Imagination, 2003; editor: Religious Perspectives in Faulkner's Fiction, 1972, The Fountain Light: Studies in Romanticism and Religion, 2002; co-editor: Marginalia in Collected Works of Samuel Taylor Coleridge, 1984—, Coleridge, Keats and the Imagination: Romanticism and Adam's Dream, 1990; mem. bd. advisors Wordsworth Circle, Phila., 1976—; mem. editl. bd. cons. Thought, 1980-93, mem. adv. bd. Studies in Romanticism, 1981—, European Romantic Rev., 1990—, Renascence, 1993—; mem. editl. adv. bd. Christianity and Literature, 1989—; mem. editl. planning bd. Religion and the Arts, 1996—. Trustee St. Louis U., 1974-79, St. Peter's Coll., 1985-91, Coll. of the Holy Cross, 1989-93, Canisius Coll., 1992-98. Recipient Howard Mumford Jones prize Harvard U., 1967; Dexter fellow, 1967; NEH summer grantee, 1969; Am. Council Learned Socs. grantee, 1970; Harvard U. research grantee, 1973. Mem. AAUP, Conf. on Christianity and Lit. (dir. 1980-83), MLA (del. assembly 1979-83, exec. com. romantic divsn. 1975-79, exec. com. religious approaches 1983-87), N.Am. Soc. Study Romanticism, Wordsworth-Coleridge Assn. (v.p. 1978, pres. 1979), Keats-Shelley Assn., Friends of Coleridge. Address: St Mary's Hall Boston College Chestnut Hill MA 02467 Office: Boston Coll Dept English 24 Quincy Rd Chestnut Hill MA 02467-3937 E-mail: robert.barth@bc.edu.

BARTHOLET, ELIZABETH, law educator; b. N.Y.C., Sept. 9, 1940; d. Paul and Elizabeth (Ives) B.; divorced; children: Derek DuBois, Christopher, Michael. BA in English, Radcliffe Coll., 1962; LLB, Harvard U., 1965. Bar: Mass., U.S. Supreme Ct. Staff atty. legal def. fund NAACP, N.Y.C., 1968-72; counsel VERA Inst. of Justice, N.Y.C., 1972-73; pres., dir. Legal Action Ctr., N.Y.C., 1973-77; asst. prof. law Harvard U., Cambridge, Mass., 1977-83, prof. law, 1983—. Bd. dirs. Legal Action Ctr., N.Y.C. Author: Family Bonds: Adoption and the Politics of Parenting, 1993; contbr. articles to profl. jours. Mem. overseers com. to visit Harvard Law Sch., 1971-77; bd. overseers Harvard U., 1973-77, Civil Rights Rev. Authority U.S. Dept. Edn., 1979-81; mem. ethics adv. coms. Brigham and Women's Hosp., 1990—, Boston Fertility and Gynecology Assn., 1991—; bd. dirs. Legal Action Ctr., 1977—. Mem. Assn. Bar City of N.Y. (exec. com. 1973-77), Am. Arbitration Assn. (labor and comml. panels), Soc. Am. Law Tchrs. (bd. govs. 1977-88), Fed. Mediation and Conciliation Svc. Roster Arbitrators, Harvard Club. Democrat. Office: Harvard U Sch Law 1575 Massachusetts Ave Cambridge MA 02138-2801

BARTHOLOMEW, GORDON WESLEY, health and physical education educator; b. Bath, Pa., May 6, 1940; s. Wesley S. and Elizabeth R. (Davis) B.; m. Ann G. Michalgyk, June 24, 1961; children: Kim L. Bartholomew Meyers, Bart G., Michael W. BS, U. Md., 1962; MS, Temple U., 1971; postgrad., East Stroudsburg U., 1971, Kutztown U., 1971, Marywood Univ. Scranton, 1974-76. Cert. tchr., Pa. Tchr. North Hunterdon Regional High Sch., Clinton, N.J., 1962-63; tchr. phys. edn. Northampton (Pa.) Area Sch. Dist., 1963—, chmn. dept. safety edn., driver tng. and health/phys. edn., 1970—, coop. tchr. for student tchrs., 1982-88. Chmn. Community Halloween Parade, Bath, 1969, 70; mem. Bath Borough Coun., 1984-90, v.p., 1986-88, pres., 1988-90, Zoning Hearing Bd., 1990—. State of Pa. grantee, 1989. Mem. NEA, AAHPERD, Pa. Edn. Assn., Northampton Area Edn. Assn. (v.p. 1969-70). Republican. Avocations: fly-tying, fishing, archery, antiques, farming. Home: 2555 Fox Rd Bath PA 18014-1444 Office: Northampton Area Sch Dist 1619 Laubach Ave Northampton PA 18067-1517

BARTLETT, DOLORES BRE VEGLIERI (DOE BARTLETT), artist, educator; b. Springfield, Mass., July 1, 1927; d. Armand and Emma (Clo) Bre Veglieri; m. Edward Pierre Bartlett, Jr., Oct. 12, 1950; children: Edward P. III, David Jonathan, Dale Dolores Bartlett MacDonald, Daniel Clo. BS in Art Edn., Mass. Coll. Art, 1949, BFA (hon.), 1993. Instr. elem. sch. art Dept. Edn., Meriden, Conn., 1949—52; instr. arts/crafts Adult Edn., Meriden, 1949-53, instr. painting Wallingford, Conn., 1965-94; instr. art Horace C. Wilcox Tech. Sch., Meriden, 1974, Mercy High Sch., Middletown, Conn., 1976-77; instr. drawing and painting Plainville (Conn.) Art League, 1970-90, Meriden Arts-Crafts Assn., 1992—2003; supr. arts program Park and Recreation Dept., Wallingford, 1974—94; represented by Gallery 53, Meriden, Conn. Judge arts exhibits Plainville Art League, 1989-92, Conn. Pastel Soc. (founding mem.), Meriden, 1986, Kensington (Conn.) Art League, 1990-93, Mum Show, Bristol, Conn., 1980-82 Artist: (watercolor) Marche Militare (Best in Show Hamden, Conn. 1993), (mixed media) Italia (1st place Meriden, Conn. 1994), (pastel) Abutments (Best in Show Pastel Soc. 1989), (graphic) Byways (1st place ACAM 1991); one-woman shows include So. Conn. State U., 2002, Meridian Pub. Libr., 2002; group shows include Slater Meml. Mus., Norwich, Conn., 1993, 95, Burritt Libr., New Britain, Conn., 1990-95, Willoughby Wallace Libr., Stony Creek, Conn., 1981-90, Meriden Pub. Libr., 1985-89, 95, John Slade Ely House, New Haven, Conn., 1980. Active partial hosp. crafts, Meriden's Woman's Club, 1977-79; leader Girl Scouts U.S., Meriden, 1969-77, Boy Scouts Am., Meriden, 1963-75; active YWCA, PTA, PTO, others, Meriden, 1959-73. Named to Outstanding Women of Am. Mem. Conn. Pastel Soc. (founding mem.), Meriden Arts Crafts Assn. (pres. 1977-79, 94, bd. dirs. 1980-94), Brownstone Group (charter mem., pres. 1977-79), Mt. Carmel Art Assn. (v.p. 1975-78), Cheshire Art League (pres.), Paint in Clay Club (recording sec., bd. dirs. 1980-92), Friends of the New Brit. Mus. Roman Catholic. Avocations: world travel, antiques, working with fabrics, fibers and soft sculpture.

BARTLETT, NEIL, chemist, emeritus educator; b. Newcastle-upon-Tyne, Eng., Sept. 15, 1932; s. Norman and Ann Willins (Vock) B.; m. Christina Isabel Cross, Dec. 26, 1957; children: Jeremy John, Jane Ann, Christopher, Robin. B.Sc., Kings Coll., U. Durham, Eng., 1954; PhD in Inorganic Chemistry, Kings Coll., U. Durham, 1957; D.Sc. (hon.), U. Waterloo, Can., 1968, Colby Coll., 1972, U. Newcastle-upon-Tyne, 1981, McMaster U., Can., 1992; D.Univ. (hon.), U. Bordeaux, France, 1976, U. Ljubljana, Slovenia, 1989, U. Nantes, France, 1990; LLD, Simon Fraser U., Can., 1993; Dr. rer. nat. (hon.), Freie U., Berlin, 1998. Lectr. chemistry U. B.C., Vancouver, Canada, 1958—63, prof., 1963—66; prof. chemistry Princeton U., NJ, 1966—69, U. Calif., Berkeley, 1969—99; guest sr. scientist chem. sci. divsn. LBNL, Berkeley, 1999—. Mem. adv. bd. on inorganic reactions and methods Verlag Chemie, 1978—; mem. adv. panel Nat. Measurement Lab., Nat. Bur. Stds., 1974-80; E.W.R. Steacie Meml. fellow NRC, Can., 1964-66; Miller vis. prof. U. Calif., Berkeley, 1967-68; 20th G.N. Lewis Meml. lectr., 1973; William Lloyd Evans Meml. lectr. Ohio State U., 1966; A.D. Little lectr. Northeastern U., 1969; Phi Beta Upsilon lectr. U. Nebr., 1975; Henry Werner lectr. U. Kans., 1977; Jeremy Musher Meml. lectr., Israel, 1980, Randolph T. Major Meml. lectr. U. Conn., 1985, J.C. Karcher lectr. U. Okla., 1988; Brotherton vis. prof. U. Leeds, Eng., 1981; Erskine vis. lectr. U. Canterbury, New Zealand, 1983; Wilsmore fellow Melbourne U., Australia, 1983; vis. fellow All Souls Coll., Oxford U., 1984; Miller prof. U. Calif.-Berkeley, 1986-87; George H. Cady lectr. U. Wash., Seattle, 1994; Leermakers lectr. Wesleyan U., 1995; Davis Meml. lectr. U. New Orleans, 1997, Pierre Duhem seminaires, U. Bordeaux, 1998. Bd. editors Inorganic Chemistry, 1967-79, Jour. Fluorine Chemistry, 1971-80, Synthetic Metals, Revue Chimie Minerale; mem. adv. bd. McGraw-Hill Ency. Sci. and Tech. Recipient Rsch. Corp. prize; E.W.R. Steacie prize, 1965; Elliott Cresson medal Franklin Inst., 1968; Kirkwood medal Yale U. and Am. Chem. Soc. (New Haven sect.), 1969; Dannie-Heinemann prize The Gottingen acad. 1971; Robert A. Welch award in chemistry, 1976; Alexander von Humboldt Found. award, 1977; medal Jozef Stefan Inst., Slovenia, 1980; Moissan medal, 1986; Prix Moissan, Paris, 1988; fellow Alfred P. Sloan Found., 1964-66; Bonner Chemiepries, Bonn, 1991; Berkeley citation, 1993. Fellow Royal Soc. (Davy medal, 2002), Royal Soc. Chemistry (U.K., hon.), Am. Acad. Arts and Scis., Chem. Inst. Can. (1st Noranda lectr. 1963), Royal Soc. Can.; mem. NAS (fgn. assoc.), Leopoldina Acad. (Halle, Salle), Akademie der Wissenschaften in Gottingen, Associé Etranger, Academia Europaea, Académie des Sciences, Institut de France, Am. Chem. Soc. (chmn. divs. fluorine chemistry 1972, inorganic chemistry 1977, award in inorganic chemistry 1970, W.H. Nichols award N.Y. sect. 1983, Pauling medal of Pacific N.W. sects. 1989, Disting. Svc. award 1989, award for Creative Work in Fluorine Chemistry 1992), Phi Lambda Upsilon (hon.) Home: 6 Oak Dr Orinda CA 94563-3912 Office: Bldg 70A c/o Rm 3307 LBNL Berkeley CA 94720 Office Fax: 510-486-6033. E-mail: nbartlett@lbl.gov.

BARTLETT, ROBERT JAMES, principal; Prin. Robinwood Elem. sch., Florissant, Mo., 1985-98; dir. staff devel. Furguson Florissant (Mo.) Sch. Dist., 1998—. Recipient Elem. Sch. Recognition award U.S. Dept. Edn., 1989-90, St. Louis Prin. of Yr., 1994. Mem. St. Louis Suburban Prins. Assn. Office: Furguson Florissant Sch Dist 1005 Waterford Dr Florissant MO 63033-3649

BARTLETT, ROBERT WATKINS, educator, consultant, metallurgist; b. Salt Lake City, Jan. 8, 1933; s. Charles E. and Phyllis (Watkins) B.; m. Betty Cameron, Dec. 3, 1954; children: John C., Robin Parmley, Bruce R., Susanne. BS, U. Utah, 1953, PhD, 1961. Registered profl. engr., Calif. Group leader ceramics SRI Internat., Menlo Park, Calif., 1964-67; assoc. prof. metallurgy Stanford U., Palo Alto, Calif., 1967-74; mgr. hydrometallurgy Kennecott Minerals Co., Salt Lake City, 1974-77; dir. materials lab. SRI Internat., Menlo Park, Calif., 1977-80; v.p. rsch. Anaconda Minerals Co., Tucson, 1980-85; mgr. materials tech. Idaho Sci. and Tech. Dept., Idaho Falls, 1985-87; dean Coll. Mines and Earth Resources, U. Idaho, Moscow, 1987-97. Dir. Idaho Geol. Survey, Moscow. Author approximately 100 rsch. publs. in metallurgy; 12 patents in field; 1 textbook. Served to lt. (j.g.) USN, 1953-56. Recipient Turner award Electrochem. Soc., 1965, McConnell award AIME, 1985. Mem. Nat. Acad. Engring., Metall. Soc. (pres. 1989, EPD lecturer 1997), Soc. Mining Engrs. (disting. mem., Wadsworth award 1996), Sigma Xi, Tau Beta Pi. Office: 2505 Loch Way El Dorado Hills CA 95762 E-mail: bobbartlett@cs.com.

BARTLEY, MARY LOU RUF, school administrator; b. Orange, N.J., Feb. 10, 1940; d. Julius and Florence (Holland) Ruf; 1 child, Marcia Lyn (dec.). AB, Upsala Coll., 1961; MA, Seton Hall U., 1965; EdD, Rutgers U., 1976. Dir. testing, lang. arts coordinator East Orange (N.J.) Sch. Dist., 1968-72; prin. Deane-Porter Sch., Rumson, N.J., 1972-73; supt. Rumson (N.J.) Sch. Dist., 1973-78, River Dell Regional Sch. Dist., Oradell, N.J., 1978-94; dep. supt. Sachem Sch. Dist., Holbrook, N.Y., 1994—. Instr. Upsala Coll., 1967-72, Georgian Ct. Coll., Lakewood, N.J., 1977-78. Fellow Rutgers U., 1971-72; Fulbright Found. grantee, 1966-67. Mem. Am. Assn. Sch. Adminstrs., N.Y. Assn. Sch. Adminstrs., N.J. Council Edn. (com. chmn. 1982-86), N.J. Tchr. Edn. Roundtable (state pres. 1985-86), Northeast Coalition Ednl. Leaders, River Edge Rotary, Gamma Sigma Sigma, Phi Delta Kappa. Roman Catholic. Home: 118 Meadowbrook Rd Spring Lake NJ 07762-1951 Office: Sachem Ctrl Sch Dist 245 Union Ave Holbrook NY 11741-1800

BARTO, BRADLEY EDWARD, small business owner, educator; b. N.Y.C., N.Y., Nov. 25, 1956; s. Kenneth William and Edna Ruth (Dalton) B.; m. Cheryl Annette Pray, Nov. 28, 1987; 1 child, David Bradley. B in Engring., N.Y. Maritime Coll., 1982; M in Gen. Adminstrn., U. Md., 1989; postgrad., U. Sarasota. Sr. engr. Advanced Tech., Inc., McLean, Va., 1982-85, Arinc Rsch., Inc., Annapolis, Md., 1985-87; pres., owner B Square Computing, Inc., Riva, Md., 1987—; pres. BCD Enterprises, Riva, Md., 1995—. Prof. U. Md., College Park, 1990—, portfolio reviewer Prior Learning program, 1995—. Inventor Chocks, 1995. Republican. Lutheran. Avocations: golf, writing children's books, gofl, baseball, tennis, writing children's books. Home: 905 Malvern Hill Dr Davidsonville MD 21035-1242 Office: B Square Computing PO Box 606 Riva MD 21140-0606 Personal E-mail: bbarto@mindspring.com.

BARTOLOTTI, JOSSIF PETER See CARRINGTON, J.P.

BARTON, BETTY LOUISE, school system administrator; b. Shawnee Mission, Kans., Jan. 12, 1931; d. David and Dora Elizabeth (Grother) Schulteis; m. William Clayton Barton, Aug. 11, 1951; children: Linda Ann, Sharon Elaine. BA, Washburn U., 1951; MS in Curriculum and Instrn., Kans. U., 1976, EdD, 1983. Cert. ednl. adminstrn., curriculum and instrn., Kans. Classroom tchr. Topeka Pub. Schs., 1951-52; music tchr. Shawnee Mission Schs., 1959-62, classroom tchr., 1962-65, 69-72, asst. prin., 1976-83, prin., 1983—96; elem. adminstr. DeSoto (Kans.) Schs., 2001—. Bd. dirs. Headstart, Shawnee Mission, 1991—, Child Abuse Coalition, Shawnee Mission, 1984-94, Parents as Tchrs., Shawnee Mission, 1989-93, Srs. Serving Schs., Shawnee Mission. Bd. dirs. Multidisciplinary Team, Johnson County, Kans., 1992-94; mem. early childhood adv. com. Johnson County C.C., 1988-93. Named Adminstr. of Yr., Shawnee Mission Schs., 1996; recipient award for outstanding dissertation, Internat. Reading Assn., 1984. Mem. ASCD, Shawnee Mission Adminstrs. Assn. (pres., Adminstr. of Yr. 1990), Phi Delta Kappa. Lutheran. Avocations: music, writing, gardening, reading. Home: 9301 High Dr Leawood KS 66206-1918 Office: Cherokee Elem Sch 8714 Antioch Rd Shawnee Mission KS 66212-3698

BARTON, CHARLES DAVID, religious studies educator, writer, historian, researcher; b. Austin, Tex., Jan. 28, 1954; s. Charles Grady and Hilda Rose (Seely) B.; m. Cheryl Edith Little, Mar. 18, 1978; children: Damaris Ann, Timothy David, Stephen Daniel. Degree in religious edn., Oral Roberts U., 1976; D.Litt (hon.), Pensacola Christian Coll., 1997. Dir. youth Aledo (Tex.) Christian Ctr., 1974-75, dir. Christian edn., dir. youth, 1977-87, dir. Christian edn., elder, 1987—; dir. youth Jenks (Okla.) 1st Assembly, 1975-76; dir. Christian edn., dir. youth Sheridan Christian Ctr., Tulsa, Okla., 1976-77. Pres. Splty. Rsch. Assocs., Inc./WallBuilders, Aledo, 1987—. Author: America: To Pray or Not to Pray, 1987, What Happened in Education?, 1989, The Bulletproof George Washington, 1990, Original Intent, 1995; prodr.: (video) America's Godly Heritage, Keys to Good Government, Education and the Founding Fathers, Spirit of the American Revolution, Foundations of American Government. Bd. dirs. Youth Leadership Coun., Cin., 1990, Tex. Christian Coalition, 1993—; mem. bd. advisors Released Time, Sacramento, 1987, Nat. Prayer Embassy, Washington, 1988; mem. coun. Nat. Policy Forum, 1994. Recipient Writing award Amy Found., 1989, 2 Angel awards Excellence in Media, 1995, George Washington medal Freedoms Found. at Valley Forge, Medal of Honor, DAR, 1998. Republican. Office: WallBuilders PO Box 397 Aledo TX 76008-0397

BARTON, JANICE SWEENY, chemistry educator; b. Trenton, N.J., Mar. 22, 1939; d. Laurence U. and Lillian Mae (Fletcher) S.; m. Keith M. Barton, Dec. 20, 1967. BS, Butler U., 1962; PhD, Fla. State U., 1970. Postdoctoral fellow Johns Hopkins U., Balt., 1970-72; asst. prof. chemistry East Tex. State U., Commerce, 1972-78, Tex. Woman's U., Denton, 1978-81; assoc. prof. Washburn U., Topeka, 1982-88, prof., 1988—, chair chemistry dept., 1992—. Mem. undergrad. faculty enhancement panel NSF, Washington, 1990; mem. NSF instr. lab. improvement panel, 1992, 96, 99; mem. NSF-AIRE site visit team, 2000; WUKBRIN (NIH grant) coord., 2001—. Contbr. articles to profl. jours. Active Household Hazardous Waste Collection, Topeka, 1991, Solid Waste Task Force, Shawnee County, Kans., 1990; mem. vol. com. YWCA, Topeka, 1984-87; bd. dir. Helping Hand Humane Soc., 2002—; grant coord. Kans. Biomedical Rsch Infrastructure Network, 2002—. Rsch. grantee Petroleum Rsch. Fund, Topeka, 1984-86, NIH, Topeka, 1985-88; instrument grantee NSF, Topeka, 1986, 95. Mem. Am. Chem. Soc. (sec. Dallas-Ft. Worth sect. 1981-82), Kans. Acad. Sci. (pres.-elect 1991, pres. 1992, treas. 1995—), Biophys. Soc., Sigma Xi (pres. TWU club 1980-81), Iota Sigma Pi (mem.-at-large coord. 1987-93). Home: 3401 SW Oak Pky Topeka KS 66614-3218 Office: Washburn U Dept Chemistry Topeka KS 66621 E-mail: janice.barton@washburn.edu.

BARTON, LAURALEE GRIFFIN, secondary school educator; b. Three Rivers, Mich., Nov. 25, 1937; d. Francis William Barton and Lenore Irene (Griffin) Shaft; m. William Terry Jones, June 13, 1959 (div. Oct. 1981); children: Meredith Shawn, Gregory Sherwood, Robyn Stacey. BA, Alma (Mich.) Coll., 1959; MS, Calif. State U., San Bernardino, 1989, Rensellear Poly. Inst., 2001. Tchr. chemistry Detroit Pub. Schs., 1959-62; tchr. biology, life and phys. sci. Riverside (Calif.) Unified Schs., 1965-71, tchr. biology and chemistry, 1971—94, tchr. ind. study, 1994—95; tchr. biology, chemistry, anatomy and physiology Notre Dame H.S., Riverside, 1996—2003, self-study coord., 2003—. Mem. writing com. integrated sci. curriculum devel., 1992-93; rsch. technician U. Calif., Riverside, 1981-84; sci. lit. writing com. Calif. State Dept. Edn., Sacramento, 1990-91; WASC accreditation com. Diocese of San Bernardino, 2000—; mentor Notre Dame HS, 2001—. Youth vocal and music history tchr. Calvary Presbyn. Ch., Riverside, 1971-79; mem. adv. com. Whittier Diabetes Assn.; mem. accreditation vis. com. WASC, 2000-01. Relm scholar Alma Coll., 1958-59, Ella B. Baccus scholar U. Mich., 1960-61; grantee NSF, 1969, 85, 87, Sci. Tchr. Inst. grantee Rutgers U., 1990, Sunsystems scholarship, 1999, RPI scholarship, 2000-01. Mem.: CSTA, NSTA, Nat. Assn. Biology Tchrs. (mem. interdisciplinary com.). Avocations: reading, sewing, gardening, travel, creative writing. Office: Notre Dame HS 7085 Brockton Ave Riverside CA 92506

BARTON, RAYBURN, educational administrator; m. Kathy Barton; children: Kathryn, James. BA, MS, PhD, U. Ala. Cmty. rels. specialist U.S. Dept. Justice, 1972—78; instr. U. North Ala., 1978—81, Boise (Idaho) State U., 1981—84, acting dean Sch. Social Scis. and Pub. Affairs, 1984—86; assoc. academic officer to chief academic officer Idaho State Bd. Edn., 1986—88, exec.dir., 1988—97, S.C. Commn. Higher Edn., 1997—; exec. vice chancellor Academic Affairs U. S.C., Beaufort, SC, 2003—. Office: Univ South Carolina 801 Carteret Street Beaufort SC 29902-3201*

BARTON, RUSSELL RICHARD, business and engineering educator, academic administrator; b. Buffalo, Aug. 11, 1951; s. Harvey Russell Jr. and Doris Beatrice B.; m. Robin Adele Holliday, June 29, 1975. BSE, Princeton U., 1973; MS, Cornell U., 1976, PhD, 1978. Electric car test engr. ESB Inc., Yardley, Pa., 1971-72; tchg. asst. Cornell U., Ithaca, 1973-75; ops. rsch. analyst Econ Inc., Princeton, N.J., 1975-76, The Mentoris Co., Princeton, 1977-78, Mathematica, Princeton, 1977-78; mem. tech. staff RCA David Sarnoff Rsch. Ctr., Princeton, 1978-87; cons. State Coll., Pa., 1987—; assoc. prof. Pa. State U., Univ. Park, 1990—98, prof., 1998—, assoc. dean rsch. and grad. programs coll. bus., 2002—. Vis. assoc. prof. Cornell U., 1987-90; exec. bd. Leonhard Ctr. Engring. Edn., State Coll., 1994—; vis. prof. Ecole Centrale Paris, 1998-99. Assoc. editor: Mgmt. Sci. Jour., 1993-97, IIE Transactions Jour., 1994-97, Naval Rsch. Log, 1999—, Internat. Jour. Man Maths., 1999—; contbr. articles to profl. jours. Asst. treas. Washington Twp. Mcpl. Utilities Auth., Robbinsville, N.J. Nat. Merit scholar Nat. Merit Scholarship Corp., 1969. Mem. IEEE (sr.), Am. Soc. Engring. Edn. (DEED program chair), Inst. Indsl. Engrs. (sr.), Ops. Rsch. Soc. Am. (v.p. coll. simulation) Achievements include U.S. patent for optical vehicle tracking system; development of algorithm for dynamic adjustment of finite difference interval size, graphical methods for design of experiments, reliability qualification of first commercial application of microwave transistors in space. Home: 2522 Tara Cir State College PA 16803-2274 Office: Pa State U 801 Bus Adminstrn Bldg State College PA 16802-1401

BARTOO, EUGENE CHESTER, academic administrator, educator; b. Wellsboro, Pa., Jan. 31, 1940; s. Eldred Llewellyn and Viola May (Mudge) Bartoo; m. Ruth Grace Walker, June 27, 1961 (div. May 1986); children: Steven, James, Thomas, Jennifer. BS, Pa. State U., 1961; MEd, SUNY, Buffalo, 1967, EdD, 1972. Tchr. Onondaga Ctrl. Sch., Syracuse, NY, 1961-63, Hamburg (N.Y.) Sr. HS, 1963-65; tchr., dept. head Newfane (N.Y.) Ctrl. Sch., 1965-69; asst. supt. Griffith Inst., Springville, NY, 1970-71; asst. prof. Case Western Res. U., Cleve., 1971-78; assoc. prof. U. Tenn., Chattanooga, 1978-84, prof., 1984—. Cons. State Edn. Dept. Ohio, Columbus, 1974—77, Lillian Ratnor Montessori Sch., Cleve., 1975—78, State Edn. Dept. Tenn., Nashville, 1983—86. Contbr.: book Curriculum: An Introduction to the Field, 1978. Bd. dirs., past pres. ACLU Tenn., 1985—90. Named Best Supporting Actor, Chattanooga Little Theatre, 1992, Mildred Routt Disting. Tchg. Prof., 2000. Mem.: Soc. Advancement Am. Philosophy, Am. Ednl. Rsch. Assn. Avocation: amateur acting. Office: U Tenn 615 Mccallie Ave Chattanooga TN 37403-2504 E-mail: Eugene-Bartoo@utc.edu.

BARTUNEK, JEAN MARIE, management educator; b. Cleve., Oct. 25, 1944; d. Robert Richard Bartunek and Clare Elizabeth Lonsway. PhD, U. Ill., Chgo., 1976. Vis. asst. prof. orgnl. behavior U. Ill., Urbana, 1976—77; asst. prof., assoc. prof., prof. orgn. studies Boston Coll., Chestnut Hill, Mass., 1977—. Author: (book) Organizational and educational change: The life and role of a change agent group, 2003, Insider-Outsider team research, 1996; editor: Hidden conflict in organizations: Uncovering behind the scenes disputes, 1992; author: Creating alternative realities at work: The quality of worklife experiment at FoodCom, 1990; mem. editl. bd.: Adminstrv. Sci. Quar., 1997—, Jour. Applied Behavioral Sci., 1986—, Jour. Orgnl. Behavior, 1999—, Qualitative Orgnl. Rsch., 2001—; co-editor: Jour. Mgmt. Inquiry, 1994—97. Recipient Best Manuscript award, Mass. Soc. CPAs, 1980; grantee, Marion and Jasper Whiting Found., 1997—99, Soc. for Orgnl. Learning, 1998—99. Fellow: Acad. Mgmt. (exec. com., chmn. orgn. and devel. change divsn. 1986—91, exec. com. women in mgmt. divsn. 1993—96, editl. bd. Acad. Mgmt. jour. 1997—2001, officer

1998—2003, pres. 2001—02, coord. external rels. 2002—03, Best Practice-Related Paper orgn. devel. and change divsn. 1996); mem.: Ea. Acad. Mgmt. (bd. dirs. 1993—96), Soc. for Orgnl. Learning, Am. Ednl. Rsch. Assn. Roman Catholic. Office: Boston Coll 140 Commonwealth Ave Chestnut Hill MA 02467-3808

BAS, JUAN REINERIO RADER, physical education educator; b. Manila, Jan. 31, 1969; s. Reinerio Quijano and Jeanne Dolores (Rader) B. BS, Rutgers U., 1991. Cert. tchr. phys. edn., K-12. Counselor South Mountain YMCA, Maplewood, N.J., 1988-89; instr. Universal Martial Arts Inst., Bloomfield, N.J., 1991-93; owner, instr. Bamboo Inst. Martial Arts, 1993; instr. Eagle Martial Arts, 1993—. Soccer coach Hanover Park H.S., N.J., 1994; fitness trainer Tiger Racquet Club, 1991-94, N.J. Pub. martial arts author, 1992—. Leader Livingston Coll. Orientation Com., Rutgers U., New Brunswick, N.J., 1988-90. Recipient award of Appreciation South Mountain YMCA, 1988-89, Presdl. Sports award Pres. Coun. in Sports, 1991, 93, 94, 95, Recognition/Leadership award Livingston Coll., 1991, Black Belt World Taekwondo Fedn., 1989, 92, 95, also several martial arts awards, 1986—. Mem. N.J. Assn. Health, Phys. Edn., Recreation and Dance, U.S. Taekwondo Union, N.J. Edn. Assn., N.Y. Road Runners Club, N.J.-USA Track and Field. Roman Catholic. Avocations: sports, writing, musicals, philosophy, computers, photography. Home: 400 Highland Ter Apt 4U Orange NJ 07050-2283

BASCH, PAUL FREDERICK, international health educator, parasitologist; b. Vienna, Nov. 10, 1933; came to U.S, 1939; s. Richard and Anne Herta Basch; m. Maria Natalicia Mourão, Aug. 16, 1966; children: Richard Joseph, Daniel David. BS, CCNY, 1954; MS, U. Mich., 1956, PhD, 1958; M in Pub. Health, U. Calif., Berkeley, 1967. Asst. prof. biology Kans. State Tchrs. Coll., Emporia, 1959-62; from asst. to assoc. research zoologist U. Calif., San Francisco, 1962-70; assoc. prof. internat. health Stanford (Calif.) U., 1970-83, prof., 1983-97, prof. emeritus, from 1997. Cons. WHO, Pan Am. Health Orgn., UN Indsl. Devel. Orgn., NIH, U.S. Agy. for Internat. Devel. Author: Textbook of International Health, 1990, 2d edit., 1999, Schistosome Biology, 1991, Vaccines and World Health, 1994, also numerous articles. Grantee USPHS, WHO, others. Fellow Royal Soc. Tropical Medicine and Hygiene; mem. APHA, Am. Soc. Parasitologists, Am. Soc. Tropical Medicine and Hygiene, Global Health Coun. Democrat. Died June 14, 2001.

BASH, FRANK NESS, astronomer, educator; b. Medford, Oreg., May 3, 1937; s. Frank Cozad and Kathleen Jane (Ness) B.; m. Susan Martin Fay, Sept. 10, 1960; children: Kathryn Fay, Francis Lee BA, Willamette U., 1959; MA in Astronomy, Harvard U., 1962; PhD, U. Va., 1967; DSc (hon.), Willamette U., 2000. Staff scientist Lincoln Lab. MIT, 1962; assoc. astronomer Nat. Radio Astronomy Obs., Green Bank, W.Va., 1962-64; rsch. asst. U. Va., 1965-67; postdoctoral faculty assoc. U. Tex., Austin, 1967-69, asst. prof. astronomy, 1969-73, assoc. prof., 1973-81, prof., 1981—, Frank N. Edmonds Regents prof., 1985—, chmn. dept. astronomy, 1983-86, dir. W.J. McDonald Obs., 1989—. Mem. astronomy adv. panel NSF, 1988-91; chmn. vis. com. Nat. Radio Astronomy Obs., 1990, mem., 1990-93; mem. vis. com. Arecibo Obs., 1990-95, chmn., 1994; mem. planning com. NASA Astrophys. Data Systems, 1991-95; bd. dirs., mem. rep. Assoc. Univs. for Rsch. in Astronomy, 1995-2000; chmn. bd. dirs. Hobby-Eberly Telescope, So. African Large Telescope. Author: (with Daniel Schiller and Dilip Balamore) Astronomy, 1977; contbr. articles to profl. jours. Grantee NSF, 1967—, The Netherlands NSF, 1979, W.M. Keck Found., 1988. Mem. Am. Astron. Soc. (councillor 1996-98), Astron. Soc. Pacific (bd. dirs. 1995-97, v.p. 1997-99, pres. 1999-2000), Internat. Astron. Union, Internat. Sci. Radio Union, Tex. Assn. Coll. Tchrs. (pres. U. Tex. chpt. 1980-82), Tex. Philos. Soc., Town and Gown Club (Austin). Office: U Tex McDonald Obs Mail Code C1402 Austin TX 78712 E-mail: FNB@astro.as.utexas.edu.

BASHKOW, THEODORE ROBERT, electrical engineering consultant, former educator; b. St. Louis, Nov. 16, 1921; s. Maurice Louis and Caroline (Davidson) B.; m. Delphina Brownlee, Sept. 12, 1960; 1 stepdau., Lynn Michele. BS, Washington U., St. Louis, 1943; MS, Stanford U., 1947, PhD, 1950. Mem. tech. staff David Sarnoff Research Labs., RCA, 1950-52, Bell Telephone Labs., 1952-58; mem. faculty Columbia U., 1958-91, prof. elec. engring., 1967-79, prof. computer sci., 1979-91, chmn. dept. elec. engring., 1968-71, mgr. Sch. Engring. Computing Center, 1961-64. Cons. to industry, 1959—; dir. MSI Inc., Woodside, N.Y., 1961— ; chmn. tech. program 1968 Spring Joint Computer Conf.; chmn. sci. sect. Internat. Fedn. Info. Processing Congress, 1965 Author articles, chpts. in books. Served to 1st lt. USAAF, 1943-45. Mem. Assn. Computing Machinery, IEEE, Profl. Group Circuit Theory and Electronic Computers. Home: 92 Jay St Katonah NY 10536-3729

BASHORE, IRENE SARAS, art association administrator; b. San Jose, Calif. d. John and Eva (Lionudakis) Saras; m. Vincent Bashore (div.); 1 child, Juliet Ann. BA, Pepperdine U., 1950; MA in Theatre Arts, Calif. State U., Fullerton, 1977. Founder, exec. dir. Inst. for Dramatic Rsch., Fullerton, Calif., 1967—.

BASHORE, THOMAS MICHAEL, cardiologist, educator; b. Paulding, Ohio, Apr. 9, 1946; s. Raymond Earl and Bertha Gladys (Smith) B.; m. Jill Eickhoff; children: Todd Thomas, Tiffany Lynn, Blake William. AB in Zoology, Miami U., 1968; MD, Ohio State U., 1972. Intern, resident U. N.C., Chapel Hill, 1972-75; fellow in cardiology Duke Med. Ctr., Durham, N.C., 1975-77, from asst. prof. to prof., dir. cardiac cath. lab., dir. fellowship tng., prof., 1980-85; asst. prof., dir. nuc. cardiology Ohio State U., Columbus, 1980-85; prof. Duke Med. Ctr., Durham, N.C., 1985—. Assoc. editor Am. Heart Jour., 1996—; mem. editl. bd. Am. Jour. Cardiology, 1987—, Catheterization and Cardiovasc. Diagnosis, 1990—, Emergency Medicine, 1992-2002, Circulation, 1995-2001, Duke Med. Update, 1996, Cardiology Today, 1998—; contbr. articles to profl. jours., chpts. to books. Fellow Am. Coll. Cardiology. (mem. coms. cardiac catheterization 1996-2001, cardiac imaging 1997-2000, congenital heart disease 2003—, mem. bd. rev. CD ROM 1996-2002, chmn. ACC/AHA com. on cardiac cath. lab. guidelines 1998-2000), Alpha Omega Alpha. Avocations: medical antiques, fishing, basketball, computers, spirituality issues. Home: 3825 Westchester Rd Durham NC 27707-5072 Office: Duke Med Ctr PO Box 3012 Durham NC 27715-3012

BASHOUR, FOUAD ANIS, cardiology educator; b. Tripoli, Lebanon, Jan. 3, 1924; s. Anis E. and Mariana (Yazigi) B.; m. Val Imm, Sept. 28, 1978. BA, Am. U. of Beirut, Lebanon, 1944, MD, 1949; PhD, U. Minn., 1957. Intern Am. U. of Beirut Hosp., Beirut, 1949-50; med. officer UNRWA, 1950-51; resident in internal medicine U. Minn. Hosps., 1951-54; rsch. fellow U. Minn. Med. Schs., 1954-55; instr. in medicine U. Minn., 1955-57; rsch. assoc. Am. U. Med. Sch., Beirut, 1957, asst. prof. medicine cardiopulmonary lab. sect., 1957-59; instr. internal medicine U. Tex. Southwestern Med. Ctr., Dallas, 1959-60, assoc. prof. internal medicine, 1963-71, dir. Cardiovascular Inst., 1967-78, prof. medicine, 1971-85, prof. medicine and physiology, 1985-95; mem. staff Parkland Meml. Hosp., Dallas; prof. emeritus of physiology and internal medicine, 1995-99; mem. staff Zale-Lipshy Univ. Hosp., Dallas, Ashbel Smith prof. medicine and physiology, 1999—. Founder, pres. Cardiology Fund, Inc., 1972-93; program dir. consultation agreement lectrs. Univ. Kuwait, U. Tex., 1977-85; mem. chancellor adv. coun. U. Tex., 1982—; mem. bd trustees of coms. on promotions and med. sch. Am. U. Beirut, 1996—; cons. in field. Mem. editorial bd. Chest, 1963-69, Lebanese Med. Jour., 1957-59, cited in the Warren Commn. Pub., 1963; contbr. more than 200 articles to profl. publs. Elder Christ Luth. Ch., Dallas. Recipient Americanism award DAR, 1970; named Knight Order of Holy Cross Jerusalem; Fouad Bashour ann. lectr. disting. physiologist in their honor, 1974—, Fouad A. and Val Imm Bashour distinguished chair in physiology in his honor, 1990, eminent scholar, Tex., 1985, Wisdom Hall of Fame, eminent Wisdom fellow, 1998. Fellow Am. Coll. Chest Physicians (emeritus), Am. Physiol. Soc. (circulation group), Am. Heart Assn. (coun. on basic sci., coun. on circulation); mem. Am. Fedn. Clin. Rsch. (emeritus), Ctrl. Soc. Clin. Rsch. (emeritus), So. Soc. Clin. Investigation (emeritus), Tex. Med. Assn., Dallas County Med. Assn., Am. Soc. Internal Medicine, Tex. Med. Found., Order of Cedars of Lebanon (officer 1971), cons. Tex. Bd. of Med. Examiners. Office: U Tex Southwestern Med Ctr 5323 Harry Hines Blvd Dallas TX 75390-9040 Fax: 214-648-9376.

BASIL, BRAD L. technology education educator; Middle sch. tchr. Mt. Logan Middle Sch., Chillicothe, Ohio, asst. prin.; middle sch. tchr. Smith Middle Sch., Chillicothe, 1988—. Recipient Tchr. Excellence for Ohio award Internat. Tech. Edn. Assn., 1992. Office: Smith Middle Sch 345 Arch St Chillicothe OH 45601-1519 also: Mt Logan Middle Sch 841 E Main St Chillicothe OH 45601-3509

BASKARAN, MAHALINGAM, marine science educator; b. Watrap, India, May 31, 1956; came to U.S., 1987; s. Solaiappan Mahalingam and Mahalingam Seeniammal; m. Inthumathi Balasubramoniam, Apr. 23, 1983; children: Angelin R., Gracelin C., Justin P. BS, Virudhunagar Hindu Nadars', Senthikumara Nadar Coll., Tamilnadu, 1977; MS, M.K. U., Madurai, Tamilnadu, 1979; PhD, Phys. Rsch. Lab., Ahmedabad, Gujarat, 1985. Postdoctoral fellow Phys. Rsch. Lab., Ahmedabad, Gujarat, 1985-87, U. Alaska, Fairbanks, 1987-88; lectr. Tex. A&M U., Galveston, 1988-92, sr. lectr., 1992—; rsch. scientist, 1995—. Contbr. articles to profl. jours; pub. over 120 peer-reviewed papers, abstracts and reports. Rsch. grantee NSF, 1990-93, 1997—, Tex. Higher Edn. Coordinating Bd., Austin, 1992, Dept. of Energy, Washington, 1992-95, Office Naval Rsch., Washington, 1993-95. Mem. Am. Geophys. Union, Sigma Xi. Evangelical Christian. Achievements include devel. of a new method to date recently growing speleothems using excess Pb-210 subsequent to this, it was shown that speleothems can be used as a proxy to retrieve C-13/C-12 variations in atmospheric CO2. Office: Tex A&M U 5007 Avenue U Galveston TX 77551-5926

BASKERVILLE, CHARLES ALEXANDER, geologist, educator; b. Jamaica, N.Y., Aug. 19, 1928; s. Charles H. and Annie M. (Allen) Baskerville; children: Mark Dana, Shawn Allison, Charles Morris, Thomas Marshall. BS, CCNY, 1953; MS, NYU, 1958, PhD, 1965. Cert. profl. geologist Maine. Asst. civil engr. N.Y. State Dept. Transp., Babylon, 1953-66; prof. engring. geology CUNY, N.Y.C., 1966-79, dean sch. of gen. studies, 1970-79, prof. emeritus, 1979—; project rsch. geologist U.S. Geol. Survey, 1979-90; prof. geology Ctrl. Conn. State U., New Britain, 1990—, dept. chmn., 1992-94. Commonwealth vis. prof. George Mason U., Fairfax, Va., 1987-89; mem. U.S. Nat. Com. on Tunnelling Tech., NRC, chmn. subcom. on edn. and tng.; mem. Am. del Internat. Tunnelling Assn. to Internat. Colloquim of Tunnelling and Underground Works, Beijing, People's Republic of China, 1984; geol. cons. N.Y.C. Dept. Environ. Protection Water Tunnel #3; guest lectr. various colls., 1964—; geol. program evaluator for colls. seeking continued mid. states accreditation. Author numerous sci. papers. Mem. com. for minority participation in the geoscis. U.S. Dept. Interior, 1972-75; panelist Grad. Fellowship Program NRC; chmn. Minority Grad. Fellowship Program, 1979-80; mem. com. of visitors for edn. and human resources program divsn. earth scis. NSF, 1991; mem. N.Y. State Low Level Radioactive Waste Com. NAS, 1994-96. Recipient Founders Day award N.Y. U., 1966, 125th Anniversary medal The City Coll., 1973, award for excellence in engring. geology Nat. Consortium Black Profl. Devel., 1978, Recognition award Nat. Assn. Black Geologists and Geophysicists, 1998. Fellow Geol. Soc. Am. (sr., com. on minorities in geoscis., chmn. com. on coms. 1989), N.Y. Acad. Scis., Geol. Soc. Washington, Am. Inst. Profl. Geologists, Assn. Engring. Geologists (rep. to nat. bd. dirs. 1973-74, chmn. N.Y.-Phila. sect. 1973-74), Internat. Assn. Engring. Geology, Yellowstone-Bighorn Rsch. Assn., Sigma Xi. Office: Ctrl Conn State Univ 1615 Stanley St New Britain CT 06050-4010 E-mail: baskerville@ccsu.edu.

BASKIN, OTIS WAYNE, business educator; b. Houston, Oct. 26, 1945; s. Samuel and Ollie Estell (Key) B.; m. Maryan Kay Patrick, Dec. 26, 1970. BA, Okla. Christian Coll., 1968; MA, U. Houston, 1970; PhD, U. Tex., 1975. Asst. prof. Tex. Luth. Coll., Seguin, 1970-75; prof. U. Houston, 1975-87; prof., acad. dir. Ariz. State U., Phoenix, 1987-91; prof., dean Memphis State U., 1991-92, prof., dir. family bus., 1992-95; dean George L. Graziadio Sch. Bus. and Mgmt. Pepperdine U., Malibu, Calif., 1995-2001, prof. mgmt., 1995—. Vis. faculty U. Md., London, 1979, Oxford U., 1994; ons. Ministry Trade, Sophia, Bulgaria, 1990, Utara U., Malaysia, 1992; spl. advisor to the pres. AACSB Internat. Author: Guidelines for Research in Business Communication, 1977, (With Craig Aronoff) Interpersonal Communication in Organizations, 1980, Getting Your Message Across, 1981, Public Relations: The Profession and the practice, 1983, (with Grover Starling) Issues in Business and Society: Capitalism and Public Purpose, 1985; contbr. articles to profl. jours. Bd. dirs. Jr. Achievement Memphis, 1991-92, Econ. Club Memphis, 1991-94, Margurite Piazza Gala for St. Jude's Hosp., Memphis, 1992-95, Durham Found., Memphis, 1992-95, World Affairs Coun. Ventura County, 2001, L.A. Econ. Devel. Corp., 2000-02. Recipient Advancing Pub. Rels. Through Rsch. award Tex. Pub. Rels. Soc., Houston, 1983. Mem. Acad. Mgmt. (divsn. chair 1985), Rotary, Sigma Iota Epsilon (bd. dirs. 1986—), Beta Gamma Sigma. Mem. Ch. of Christ. Avocations: reading, travel. Office: George L Graziadio Sch Bus & Mgmt Pepperdine Univ Malibu CA 90263 E-mail: Otis.Baskin@pepperdine.edu.

BASKIN, VLASTA JANA MARIE, language educator; b. Klatovy, Czechoslovakia, Jan. 20, 1929; came to U.S., 1948, naturalized, 1953; d. Josef Kolena and Marie (Hoskova) Kolenova; m. Wade Jacob Baskin, Jan. 1, 1949 (dec.); children— Wade Jacob Jr., Daniel Gregory, Michael Kenmar; m. Dewey T. Goad, Mar. 21, 1994. Ed. Gymnasium for Women, Cheb, Czechoslovakia. Instr. Russian, S.E.Okla. State U., Durant, 1960—, adviser to internat. students, 1960-74, instr. German and Russian, research analyst, 1983—; instr. German and French summer Upward Bound program, S.E. Okla. State U., 1985-94; pvt. tutor of Russian and German, 1994—. Translator: Hysteria, Reflex, and Instinct (Ernst Kretschmer), 1960, also children's story. Official interpreter Okla. Tourism and Recreation Dept. Bicentennial Com., 1976; contbr. ethnic history project Okla. Image, 1978; mem. steering com. City Council of Durant, 1981, citizen amb. program People to People Internat., New Zealand, Australia, 1992. Mem. Okla. Edn. Assn., Okla. Fgn. Tchrs. Assn., Internat. Platform Assn., Alpha Mu Gamma. Democrat. Presbyterian. Address: 1620 Radio Rd Durant OK 74701-2040 Office: Southeastern Okla State U Durant OK 74701

BASKINS, TAMARA ANNE, secondary school educator; b. Fort Collins, Colo., Jan. 16, 1944; d. Donald William and Helen June (Stroh) Lynch; m. Gary Lee Powers (div. 1981); children: Michelle Powers Burkhart, Melissa Powers Coombs; m. Donald Ray Baskins, Oct. 23, 1981. BS in Elem. Edn., Worcester State Coll., 1984; MS in Spl. Edn., Cen. Mo. State U., 1991. Cert. tchr. spl. edn., Mass., Mo. Substitute tchr. K-12 Ayer (Mass.) Pub. Schs., 1984-86; spl. edn. tchr. Page Sch., Ayer, 1985; adj. lectr. City Colls. of Chgo. Europe, Helmstedt, Germany, 1986-88; tchr. K-5 Dept. Def. Dependents' Schs., Helmstedt, Germany, 1989; substitute tchr. K-12 Leeton R-X, Leeton, Mo., 1990-91; learning disabilities tchr. Lakeland R-III, Deepwater, Mo., 1991-92, tchr. educable mentally handicapped 7-12, 1992—95; tchr. 7-9 social studies, 1996—; tchr. 7-9 german, 1996—. Regents Grad. scholar Cen. Mo. State U., 1991. Mem.: Foreign Lang. Assn. of Mo., Am. Assn. of Tchrs of German, Lakeland R-III Classroom Tchrs. Assn. (pres. 1994—95), Mo. State Tchrs. Assn., Nat. Coun. for Social Studies, Coun. for Learning Disabilities, Coun. for Exceptional Children, Rebekah Lodge of Internat. Order Odd Fellows (dist. pres. 1992), Alpha Gamma Delta, Phi Kappa Phi, Kappa Delta Pi, Beta Sigma Phi (v.p. 1992). Home: 10700 SE Hwy Osceola MO 64776-9431 Office: Lakeland R-III 12530 Lakeland School Dr Deepwater MO 64740-8122

BASLER, THOMAS G. librarian, administrator, educator; b. Cleve., Mar. 8, 1940; s. Gordon Fred and Bertha Elizabeth (Gerspacher) B.; m. Samille Jones, Nov. 25, 1986; children from previous marriage: William T., Elizabeth E., Charles G. BEd, U. Miami, Coral Gables, Fla., 1962; MS, Fla. State U., 1964; PhD, Laurence U., Santa Barbara, Calif., 1977. Intern Emory U., Atlanta, 1965; asst. prof., librarian Insts. Marine Scis., Miami, Fla., 1966-68; librarian Am. Mus. Natural History, N.Y.C., 1968-70, N.Y. Acad. Medicine, N.Y.C., 1970-72; prof., dir. library Med. Coll. Ga., Augusta, 1972-91; dir. libr. and learning resources ctrs. Med. U. S.C., Charleston, 1991—, dir. environ. hazards assessment program info. sys., 1994—, chair dept. of libr. sci. and informatics. Cons. Abbott Pharm. Co., North Chicago, Ill., 1973-83; chmn. Regents Acad. Com. on Libraries, Univ. System Ga., 1984-85; mem. adv. council SE Atlantic Regional Med. Library, 1984— Author: Health Science Librarianship, 1977, Medical School Library Directorship, 1977, also articles Mem. Consortium So. Biomed. Libraries, Inc. (sec.-treas. 1983—) Home: 1205 Manor Ln Mount Pleasant SC 29464-5188 Office: Med U SC 171 Ashley Ave Charleston SC 29425-0001

BASOLO, FRED, chemistry educator; b. Coello, Ill., Feb. 11, 1920; s. John and Catherine (Marino) Basolo; m. Mary P. Nutley, June 14, 1947; children: Mary Catherine, Freddie, Margaret-Ann, Elizabeth Rose. BE, So. Ill. U., 1940, DSc (hon.), 1984; MS, U. Ill., 1942, PhD in Inorganic Chemistry, 1943; LLD (hon.), U. Turin, 1988; Laurea Honoris Causa (hon.), U. Palermo, Italy, 1997. Rsch. chemist Rohm & Haas Chem. Co., Phila., 1943—46; mem. faculty Northwestern U., Evanston, Ill., 1946—, prof. chemistry, 1958—, Morrison prof. chemistry, 1980—90, chmn. dept. chemistry, 1969—72; Charles E. and Emma H. Morrison prof. emeritus Nortwestern U., Evanston, Ill., 1990—. Guest lectr. NSF summer insts.; chmn. bd. trustees Gordon Rsch. Conf., 1976; pres. Inorganic Syntheses, Inc., 1977—81; mem. bd. chem. scis. and tech. NRC-NAS; adv. bd. Who's Who in Am., 1983; cons. in field. Recipient Ballar medal, 1972, So. Ill. U. Alumni Achievement award, 1974, Dwyer medal, 1976, James Flack Norris award for Outstanding Achievement in Tchg. of Chemistry, 1981, Oesper Meml. award, 1983, IX Century medal, Bologna U., 1988, Mosher award, 1990, Padova U. medal, 1991, Chinese Chem. Soc. medal, 1991, G.C. Pimental award, 1992, Chem. Pioneer award, 1992, Gold medal, Am. Inst. Chemists, 1993, Joseph Chatt medal, Royal Soc. Chemistry, 1996, Inauguration mem. Hall of Fame, Chem. Dept. So. Ill. U., 1996; fellow Guggenheim, 1954—55, NSF, 1961—62, NATO sr. scientist, Italy, 1981, Sr. Humboldt, 1992. Fellow: AAAS (chmn. chemistry sect. 1979), NAS, Am. Acad. Arts and Scis.; mem.: Nat. Acad. Lincei (Italy), Royal Soc. Chemistry (Joseph Chatt medal 1996), Italian Chem. Soc. (hon.), Am. Chem. Soc. (assoc. editor jour. 1961—64, chmn. divsn. inorganic chemistry 1970, pres. 1983, bd. dirs. 1982—84, award for rsch. in inorganic chemistry 1964, Disting. Svc. award in inorganic chemistry 1975, N.E. regional award 1971, award in chem. edn. 1992, Chem. Pioneer award 1992, Gold medal 1993, Willard Gibbs medal 1996), Sigma Xi (Monie A. Ferst medal 1992), Kappa Delta Phi, Phi Kappa Phi, Alpha Chi Sigma, Phi Lambda Upsilon, Phi Lambda Theta (hon.). Office: Northwestern U Chemistry Dept Rm GG40 2145 Sheridan Rd Evanston IL 60208-0834

BASS, GLORIA BAILEY, mathematician, educator; b. Macon, Ga., June 17, 1947; d. Donald Oswald and Edna Mozelle (Terry) Bailey; m. Jerry Wayne Bass, July 21, 1968; 1 child, Dwayne Carlton. BA, Mercer U., 1969; MEd, Ga. Coll., 1974. Tchr. math. Jones County High Sch., Gray, Ga., 1969-73, NE High Sch., Macon, 1973-78; tchr. math., chmn. dept. 1st Presbyn. Day Sch., Macon, 1978—99; instr. Mercer U., Macon, Ga., 2000—. Adj. prof. math. Mercer U., Macon, Ga., 1993-99, vis. instr. Mercer U., 1999-2000. Chmn. nominating com. 1st Bapt. Ch., Macon, 1986-89, chmn. orgnl. manual com., 1992—; mem. Macon Jr. Woman's Club, 1974. Recipient Family of Yr. award Macon Jr. Woman's Club, 1988, 92. Mem. Nat. Coun. Tchrs. Math., Ga. Coun. Tchrs. Mem. (regional chmn. 1979-81), Delta Kappa Gamma (chmn. fin. com. Macon 1984-86, budget com. 1986-88). Avocations: cross-stitching, aerobics, walking, reading. Home: 3021 Clairmont Ave Macon GA 31204-1003 Office: Mercer U 1400 Coleman Ave Macon GA 31207

BASS, LYNDA D. retired medical/surgical nurse, retired nursing educator; b. Suffolk, Va. d. H.M. and Katie Lea Bass. BSN, N.C. Agrl. and Tech. State U., Greensboro, 1968; MS in Nursing, Cath. U. Am., 1974; Gen. Surgery Clin. Specialist, George Washington U. Hosp., Washington. Cert. BCLS instr., CPR instr.-trainer. Med. surg. nurse Walter Reed Army Hosp., Washington; clin. instr. Suburban Hosp., Bethesda, Md.; edn./tng. quality assurance coord. Howard U. Hosp., Washington; clin. educator Providence Hosp., Washington; edn. specialist Vets. Affairs Md. Healthcare Sys., Balt.; ret., 2003. Coord. clin. staff Devel. Mount Vernon Hosp., Alexandria, Va. Capt. USAR, 1967—71, Vietnam. Mem. Nat. Nursing Staff Devel. Assn., Vietnam Vets. Am., Chi Eta Phi.

BASS, MARTHA POSTLETHWAITE, high school principal; b. Wichita, Kans., Dec. 6, 1942; d. John Emmett and Norma Louise (Lanning) Postlethwaite; m. Elmer Lee Bass, July 22, 1981; step children: Sheryl, Terry. BA in Edn., U. N.Mex., 1964, MA, 1966. Endl. lic. adminstr., supt., English tchr., drama speech tchr., counselor. Asst. dean women, instr. Hanover (Ind.) Coll., 1966-68; asst. dean women U. N.Mex., Albuquerque, 1968-69; elem. counselor Alburquerque Pub. Schs., 1969-74, guidance coord., 1974-77, high sch. asst. prin., 1977-87; high sch. prin. Del Norte High Sch. Alburquerque Pub. Schs., 1987-97; ret., 1997. Bd. dirs. Albuquerque Child Guidance Ctr.; pres., cons. Acad. Endl. Leadership, Albuquerque, 1986-90. Title VII Fed. grantee Child Encouragement Project, Alburquerque, 1977; named Woman on the Move YWCA, Albuquerque, 1990. Mem. Nat. Assn. Secondary Sch. Prins., Albuquerque Assn. Secondary Sch. Prins. (past bd. dirs., treas. 1986-87), Rotary Club of Albuquerque (RYLA chair 1990-93). Avocations: rv traveling, silk flower arranging, photography. Office: Del Norte High Sch 5323 Montgomery Blvd NE Albuquerque NM 87109-1300

BASS, MARY LEE, education educator, administrator; b. Phila., Jan. 1, 1947; d. Leon Jr. and Mary Katherine (Magarian) Attarian; m. Harris Merrill Bass, July 1, 1973; 1 child, Mandy Michelle. BS, Millersville U. Pa., 1969; MS in Edn., Monmouth U., 1992; EdD., Rutgers U. Cert. tchr., N.J., Pa.; cert. reading specialist, N.J. Pers. clk. Jefferson Med. Ctr., Phila., 1965-67; elem. tchr. Lancaster (Pa.) City Schs., 1969-71; transition elem. tchr. Springfield (Pa.) Sch. Dist., 1971-77; lang. arts tchr. Benchmark Sch., Media, Pa., 1987-90; reading lab. instr. Brookdale C.C., Lincroft, N.J., 1990-92; adj. instr., dir. Reading Ctr. Monmouth U., West Long Branch, N.J., 1992—. Mem. steering com. N.J. Consortium for Placement Testing, 1994—. Contbr. articles to profl. jours. Exec. bd. dirs. Adult Edn., Marple Newtown, Pa., 1987; vol. program coord. Neighborhood Model Cities, Lancaster, 1971; vol. tchr.'s asst. Headstart, Lancaster, 1969. Mem. Internat. Reading Assn., N.J. Reading Assn., Coll. Reading Assn., Phi Delta Kappa, Alpha Upsilon Alpha, Kappa Delta Pi. Avocations: reading, writing, concerts, piano, crossword puzzles. Office: Monmouth U Coll Skills Ctr Cedar Ave West Long Branch NJ 07764 E-mail: mbass@monmouth.edu.

BASSETT, DEBRA LYN, lawyer, educator; b. Pleasanton, Calif., Oct. 28, 1956; d. James Arthur and Shirley Ann (Russell) Bassett. BA, U. Vt., 1977; MS, San Diego State U., 1982; JD, U. Calif., Davis, 1987. Bar: Calif. 1987, DC 1990, U.S. Dist. Ct. (no. and ea. dists.) Calif. 1988, U.S. Ct. Appeals (9th cir.) 1988, U.S. Supreme Ct. 1991. Guidance counselor Addison Cen. Supr. Union, Middlebury, Vt., 1982-83, Milton (Vt.) Elem. Sch., 1983-84;

assoc. Morrison & Foerster, San Francisco, 1986; jud. clk. U.S. Ct. Appeals (9th cir.), Phoenix, 1987-88; assoc. Morrison & Foerster, San Francisco and Walnut Creek, Calif., 1988-92; sr. atty. Calif. Ct. Appeal (3d appellate dist.), Sacramento, 1992-99; assoc. prof. Mich. State U., East Lansing, 2002—. Tutor civil procedure, rsch. asst. U. Calif., Davis, 1985—87, instr., 1995—2002, lectr., 1997—2002; adj. prof. McGeorge Sch. Law, 1998—99, dir. legal process, 1999—2000, vis. prof., 2000—01. Editor: U. Calif. Law Rev., 1985—86; sr. articles editor:, 1986—87. Mem. Steiner Chorale, 2002—. Mem.: ABA (vice chmn. ethics com. young lawyers divsn. 1989—91, exec. com. labor and employment law com. 1989—90), AAUW, APA (assoc.), Scribes. Democrat. Avocations: music, tennis, travel, hiking. Home: 915 Snyder Rd East Lansing MI 48823 Office: Mich State U DCL Coll Law 417 Law Coll Bldg East Lansing MI 48824 E-mail: debbie.bassett@law.msu.edu.

BASSETT, WILLIAM AKERS, geologist, educator, retired; b. Bklyn., Aug. 3, 1931; s. Preston Rogers and Jeanne Reed (Mordorf) B.; m. Jane Ann Kermes, Sept. 8, 1962; children: Kari Nicalo, Jeffrey Kermes, Penelope North. BA, Amherst Coll., 1954; MA, Columbia U., 1956, PhD, 1959. Research assoc. Brookhaven Nat. Lab., 1960-61; Asst. prof. U. Rochester, NY, 1961-65, asso. prof., 1965-69, prof. geology, 1969-77, Cornell U., Ithaca, NY, 1978—99, ret., 1999. Vis. prof. Brigham Young U., 1967-68; Crosby vis. prof. MIT, 1974 Research, publs. on the devel. of techniques for investigation of properties of minerals at pressures and temperatures within the earth's interior Recipient Bridgman award Internat. Assn. for Rsch. at High Pressure and Temperature, 1997; NSF grantee; Guggenheim fellow, 1985. Fellow Geol. Soc. Am., Mineral. Soc. Am. (Roebling medal 1994, Bridgman award 1997), Am. Geophys. Union, AAAS; mem. Sigma Xi (pres. Rochester chpt. 1977-78). Home: 765 Bostwick Rd Ithaca NY 14850-9310 E-mail: bassett@geology.cornell.edu.

BASSIS, MICHAEL STEVEN, academic administrator; b. N.Y.C., Sept. 8, 1944; s. Lewis and Barbara (Fay) B.; m. Mary Suzanne Wilson, Dec. 27, 1977; children: Anne Elizabeth, Christina, Jessica, Nicholas. BA with honors, Brown U., 1967; MA, U. Chgo., 1968, PhD, 1974. Asst. dir. acad. potential project Brown U., 1966-67; rsch. assoc. Ctr. for the Study of the Acts of Man U. Pa., 1968; instr., asst. prof.-assoc. prof. dept. sociology and anthropology U. R.I., 1971-81, acting asst. dean Coll. Arts and Scis., 1977-78; assoc. Harvard U. Grad. Sch. Edn., 1980-81; assoc. dean faculty U. Wis., Parkside, 1981-85, assoc. prof. sociology, 1981-86, interim asst. chancellor ednl. svcs., 1985-86; v.p. acad. affairs Ea. Conn. State U., 1986-89; exec. v.p., univ. provost Antioch U., Yellow Springs, Ohio, 1989-93; pres. Olivet (Mich.) Coll., 1993-98; dean, warden New Coll., U. South Fla., Sarasota, 1998—2001; president Westminster Coll. of Salt Lake City, 2002—. Presenter in field. Author (with W.R. Rosengren) The Social Organization of Nautical Education: The U.S., Great Britain and Spain, 1976, (with R.J. Gelles and A. Levine) Sociology: An Introduction, 4th edit., 1991, Social Problems, 1982; editor Teaching Sociology, 1982-85; contbr. articles to profl. jours. NIMH grantee, 1967-71, Exxon Edn. Found. grantee, N.Y.C., 1975, Fund for Improvement of Post-Secondary Edn. grantee, Washington, 1978. Mem. Am. Sociol. Assn. (undergrad. edn. sect., membership com. 1979-81, com. 1980, 82, 86-89, teaching resources group 1984-86, publs. com. 1985, chair 1987-88), Am. Assn. Higher Edn., Nat. Soc. Experiential Edn. Home: 4055 East Adonis Circle Salt Lake City UT 84124 Office: Office of the President Westminster College 1840 South 1300 East Salt Lake City UT 84105 E-mail: mbassis@westminstercollege.edu.

BASSIST, DONALD HERBERT, retired academic administrator; b. Dallas, Oct. 28, 1923; s. Ellis and Adele (Gutz) B.; m. Norma Dale Andersen, Oct. 14, 1950; children: Matthew Perry, Bradford Beaumont. AB, Harvard U., 1948; MBA, Portland State U., 1975; grad., U.S. Army Command and Gen. Staff Coll., 1967. Pres. Bassist Coll., Portland, Oreg., 1963-98; ret. Chmn. ednl. adv. bd. pvt. vocat. schs., Salem, Oreg., 1972-78; active Oreg. Ednl. Coordinating Coun., 1970-73. Writer, dir. (film) Fashion: The Career of Challenge, 1969 (N.Y. Internat. Bronze award). Lt. A.C., U.S. Army, 1943-46; 14th AF, 1944, lt. col. Corps of Engrs., ret., 1972. Mem. Nat. Assn. Scholars, Japanese Garden Soc. (bd. dirs. 1988-93), Portland Advt. Fedn. (bd. dirs. 1969-72). Avocations: japanese gardening, travel.

BASSO, KEITH HAMILTON, cultural anthropologist, linguist, educator; b. Asheville, N.C., Mar. 15, 1940; s. Joseph Hamilton and Etolia (Simmons) B.; div. BA, Harvard U., 1962; MA, Stanford U., 1965, PhD, 1967. Asst. prof. anthropology U. Ariz.-Tucson, 1967-71, assoc. prof., 1972-76, prof., 1977-81; prof. anthropology Yale U., 1982-88, U. N.Mex., Albuquerque, 1988—. Fellow Inst. Advanced Study, Princeton, N.J., 1975-76; Weatherhead fellow Sch. Am. Research, Santa Fe, N.M., 1977-78; cons. cultural and historical topics White Mountain and San Carlos Apache Tribes, Alfonso Ortiz Ctr. for Intercultural Studies, 2000—, Native Nations Inst., 2000—; mem. steering com. Nat. Coalition for Am. Indian Religious Freedom; bd. trustees Nat. Mus. of the Am. Indian, 1991-96. Author: Wisdom Sits in Places: Landscape and Language Among the Western Apache, 1996 (Western States Book award 1996, Victor Turner prize for ethnographic writing 1997, J.I. Staley award 2001), Western Apache Language and Culture: Essays in Linguistic Anthropology, 1991, Portraits of the White Man, 1979, The Cibecue Apache, 1970; editor: Senses of Place, 1996, Meaning in Anthropology, 1976, Western Apache Witchcraft, 1969. Mem. AAAS, Assn. Am. Indian Affairs (bd. dirs. 1978-86), Am. Anthropol. Assn., Am. Ethnol. Soc. (pres. 1983-84), Linguistic Soc. Am. Democrat. Home: 12 Pool St NW Albuquerque NM 87120-1809

BAST, ROBERT CLINTON, JR., medical researcher, medical educator; b. Washington, Dec. 8, 1943; s. Robert Clinton and Ann Christine (Borland) B.; m. Blanche Amy Simpson, Oct. 21, 1972; 1 child, Elizabeth Simpson Bast. BA cum laude, Wesleyan U., Middletown, Conn., 1965; MD magna cum laude, Harvard U., 1971. Diplomate Am. Bd. Internal Medicine, Am. Bd. Med. Oncology, Am. Bd. Hematology. Predoctoral fellow dept. pathology Mass. Gen. Hosp., Boston, 1967-69; intern Johns Hopkins Hosp., Balt., 1971-72; rsch. assoc. biology br. Nat. Cancer Inst., NIH, Bethesda, Md., 1972-75; asst. resident Peter Bent Brigham Hosp., Boston, 1975-76; fellow med. oncology Sidney Farber Cancer Inst., Boston, 1976-77; asst. prof. medicine Harvard U. Med. Sch., Boston, 1977-83, assoc. prof., 1983-84; prof. Duke U. Med. Ctr., Durham, N.C., 1984-92, Wellcome clin. prof. medicine in honor of R. Wayne Rundles, 1992-94, co-dir. div. hematology-oncology, 1984-94; dir. clin. research programs Duke U. Comprehensive Cancer Ctr., Durham, 1984-87; dir., 1987-94; Harry Carothers Wiess chair cancer rsch. U. Tex. M.D. Anderson Cancer Ctr., 1994—, head divsn. med., 1994-2000, v.p. translational rsch., 2000—; dir. divsn. med. oncology dept. medicine U. Tex. Health Sci. Ctr., Houston, 1994-2000. Hosp. appointments include asst. in medicine Peter Bent Brigham Hosp., 1976-77; jr. assoc. in medicine Brigham and Women's Hosp., 1977-82; cons. oncologist Boston Hosp. Women, 1978-80; physician Duke U. Med. Ctr., 1984-94; internist M.D. Anderson Cancer Ctr., 1994—; mem. biol. response modifiers decision network com. Nat. Cancer Inst., 1984-87, exptl. immunology study sect., 1983-84, 90-92; mem. grant rev. com. Leukemia Soc. Am., 1985-87, adv. com. oncologic drugs FDA, 1985-89, chmn. 1988-89; bd. dirs. Cancer and Leukemia Group B., 1986-88, Am. Council Transplantation, 1985-87; mem. grant rev. com. Am. Cancer Soc., 1987; numerous other coms.; Edward G. Waters Meml. lectr., 1987; John Ohtani Meml. lectr., 1991; D. Nelson Henderson lectr., 1991; Stolte Meml. lectr., 1992; Arnold O. Beckman Disting. Lectureship, 1993; Robert C. Knapp lectr., 1996; Alan Dembo Meml. Keynote lectr., 1997, George Willbanks lectr., 2000. Contbr. numerous articles on tumor immunology, immunodiagnosis and immunotherapy of cancer and cellular immunology to profl. jours. Served as surgeon USPHS, 1972-75. Named Disting. Spkr., Chas Family Comprehensive Cancer Ctr., 2002; recipient Dominus award, 1984, Robert C. Knapp award, 1990, Recognition Outstanding Leadership and Advocacy award, Nat. Coalition for Cancer Rsch., 1995, Smith Kline Beecham Clin. Labs. award, Clin. Ligand Soc., 1996, award of Achievement, Ptnrs. in Courage, ACS, 1998, Abbott award, Internat. Soc. Oncodevelopmental Biology and Markers, 2001, 150 BM Abbott award, 2001, 151 Higher Cited Investigator award, 2003; grantee, Nat. Cancer Inst., NIH, HHS, 1978—; scholar, Leukemia Soc. Am., 1978—83. Fellow: AAAS, ACP; mem.: Am. Clin. and Climatological Assn., Am. Soc. Hematology, Soc. Biol. Therapy (bd. dirs. 1984—86), Internat. Soc. Immunopharmacology, Am. Soc. Clin. Investigation, Am. Fedn. Clin. Rsch., Am. Soc. Clin. Oncology, Assn. Am. Physicians, Am. Assn. Immunologists, Am. Assn. Cancer Rsch., Am. Soc. Microbiology, The Reticuloendothelial Soc., Internat. Gynecol. Cancer Soc. (coun. 1997—), Soc. Gynecol. Oncology (assoc.). Achievements include development of monoclonal antibodies to react with human ovarian cancer, leading to CA125 blood test; techniques for selective elimination of tumor cells from human bone marrow; identification of molecular changes associated with malignant transformation of ovarian epithelium. Office: U Tex MD Anderson Cancer Ctr 1515 Holcombe Blvd # 355 Houston TX 77030-4009

BASTIEN, JANE SMISOR, music educator; b. Hutchinson, Kans., Jan. 15, 1936; d. Herbert D. and Gladys I. (Haston) Smisor; m. James W. Bastien; children: Lisa Bastien Hanss, Lori Bastien Vickers. AA, Stephens Coll., 1955; BA, Barnard Coll., 1957; MA, Columbia U., 1958. Asst. prof. Tulane U., New Orleans, 1958-75; pvt. piano tchr., La Jolla, Calif., 1975—. Author/composer: Bastien Piano Books/Ednl. Piano Books for Children and Adults. Recipient Alumnae award Stephens Coll., 1960. Mem. Nat. Assn. Music Tchrs. (Lifetime Achievement award 1999), Music Tchrs. Assn. of Calif. (State Tchg. award 1996). Republican. Presbyterian. Avocations: gardening, collecting antiques. Home: 2431 Vallecitos Ct La Jolla CA 92037-3146 E-mail: jsbastien@aol.com.

BASTOW, RICHARD FREDERICK, civil engineer, educator, surveyor; b. Waterville, Maine, Apr. 20, 1934; s. Frank W. and Susan (Strong) B.; m. Nancy Dodge, Sept. 13, 1958; children: Susan Weimer, Bonnie Jean Kuykendall. BS in Civil Engring., U. Maine, Orono, 1961; MS, U. So. Maine, Gorham, 1975. Site planner, engr. Harriman Assocs., Architects and Engrs., Auburn, Maine, 1957-65, Taylor Engring., C.E., Auburn, 1966-68; chmn. archtl. and civil engring. tech. Ctrl. Maine Tech. Coll., Auburn, 1968—. Pres. Maine Planning & Engring. Assocs., Auburn, 1969—; mem., chmn. Maine Bd. Land Surveyors, 1978-87. Contbr. articles to profl. jours. Fellow ASCE; mem. Maine Soc. Land Surveyors (charter; bd.dirs., sec., pres., Appreciation award 1987), Am. Congress Surveying and Mapping (chmn. New Eng. sect. 1992). Home: 10 Weaver St Auburn ME 04210-4627 Office: Ctrl Maine Tech Coll 1250 Turner St Auburn ME 04210-6436 E-mail: RFBastow@cmtc.net.

BASTRESS, ROBERT LEWIS, principal; b. Balt., Sept. 18, 1944; s. Arthur Milton and Frances Elizabeth (Sellman) B.; m. Diane Marie Smith, Aug. 26, 1967; children: Elizabeth, Robert, Jennifer, James, Mark. BA, Loyola Coll., 1966, MEd, 1969; PhD, U. Md., 1980. Cert. tchr. sci., adminstr., Md. Tchr. sci. Mt. St. Joseph's High Sch., Balt., 1966-69, Mt. Hebron High Sch., Ellicott City, Md., 1969-70, adminstrv. asst., 1970-73; asst. prin. Glenelg (Md.) High Sch., 1973-76, Centennial High Sch., Ellicott City, 1977-79; prin. Liberty High Sch., Eldersburg, Md., 1979—. Instr. Western Md. Coll., Westminster, 1985; assessor Md. Assessment Program, Balt., 1986—; mem. State Task Force on Outcomes-Based Edn., Balt., 1991-93. Eucharistic minister St. Joseph's Cath. Ch., Sykesville, Md., 1974—. Named Man of Yr. Freedom Jaycees, 1980. Mem. ASCD, Nat. Assn. Secondary Sch. Prins., Md. Assn. Secondary Sch. Prins. (treas. 1989-91, pres.-elect 1991-92, pres. 1992-93). Democrat. Avocations: coaching sports, reading world war ii history, playing chess. Office: Liberty High Sch 5855 Bartholow Rd Eldersburg MD 21784-8499

BATAMACK, PATRICE THEODORE DESIRE, chemistry educator, researcher; b. Douala, Littoral, Cameroon, Nov. 1, 1962; s. Joseph Etote Robert and Philomene Claire (Ngo Batadjam) B.; m. Ndjee Aurélie, Apr. 25, 1998. Grad. in chem. engring., Poly. Inst. Loraine, Nancy, France, 1988; cert. in computer sci., Indsl. Computer Sci. Inst., Brest, France, 1989; PhD in Chemistry, U. Pierre et Marie Curie, Paris, 1991; MBA, Nat. Conservatory Arts & Craft, 2000; diploma for directing postgrad. works, U. Pierre et Marie Curie, 1999. Postdoctoral fellow Loker Hydrocarbon Inst. U. So. Calif., L.A., 1992-94; lectr. chemistry U. Pierre et Marie Curie, 1994—. Vis. scholar Loker Hydrocarbon Inst., U. So. Calif., L.A., 2002—03, rsch. assoc., 2003. Contbr. articles to profl. jours. Mem. French Chem. Soc. (prize catalysis divsn. 1995), Am. Chem. Soc. Avocations: reading, meditation, sports. Office: U Pierre et Marie Curie 4 Pl Jussieu 75252 Paris France E-mail: pba@ccr.jussieu.fr.

BATCH, MARY LOU, guidance counselor, educator; b. McKeesport, Pa. BS in Edn., Cen. State U., Wilberforce, Ohio, 1970; MS in Spl. Edn., Syracuse U., 1971; PhD in Counselor Edn., U. Pitts., 1982. Cert. in spl. and elem. edn., Ohio; cert. in elem. and mid. sch. edn., secondary guidance, Va.; cert. in NK-8 edn., edn. of mentally retarded, Va. Various edn. and counseling positions Va. schs., military and other insts., 1965-72; tchr. adult edn. Big Bend C.C., Germany. Am. Coll. System Overseas, 1973-75; counselor, coord. U. Pitts., 1976-79; asst. prof. spl. edn. Ind. U. of Pa., 1979-85; testing specialist C.C. of Allegheny County, Braddock Ctr., Pa., 1985-86; guidance counselor Henrico H.S., Henrico County Schs., Richmond, Va., 1987—, John Rolfe Middle Sch., Richmod, 1991-96, Maude Trevett Elem. Sch., 1996—. Edn. specialist U.S. Govt. in Germany, 1974-75; cons., workshop conductor, in Pa., N.J., Va. at ednl. facilities, civic orgns. and with parent groups, 1978—; mem. So. States Evaluation Team, Manassas Va., 1988; mem. peer advisor steering com. and student peer advisor supr. Henrico High Sch., 1987-90; extended del. position Citizen Ambassador Program of People to People Internat. to Soviet Union and Hungary, Am. Sch. Counselor Assn., 1991, U.S./China Joint Conf. on Edn., 1992. Bd. dirs. Richmond Residential Svcs., 1989—, sec., 1990-91, chmn. program and planning com., 1991-92, vice chmn., 1992—; group facilitator Henrico County Ct. Alternative; mem. Henrico County Edn. 2000 Commn., mem. action team; active in Head Start movement and teen parenting counseling; mem. Statewide Mid. Sch. Coun., 1994—; mem. tech. pres. steering com. Henrico County Pub. Schs., 1994—; active Nat. Multiple Sclerosis Soc., inductee leadership cir., 1995; mem. steering com. Tech Prep Henrico County, Richmond, Va., 1994-95; mid. sch. state rep. coun. mem., 1995. Inductee, Nat. Leadership Circle. Mem. LWV, ASCD, Am. Fedn. Tchrs., Nat. Coun. of Negro Women, Va. Personnel and Guidance Assn., Va. Sch. Counselors Assn., Richmond Personnel and Guidance Assn., Henrico County Guidance Assn. (pres. 1989-91), Va. Assn. Multicultural Devel., Greater Richomnd Involved Parents, Nat. Coun. for Self Esteem, Nat. Coun. Sr. Citizens, Alpha Kappa Mu, Zeta Phi Beta. Home: 8223 Brookfield Rd Richmond VA 23227-1501 Office: John Rolfe Mid Sch 6901 Messer Rd Richmond VA 23231-5507

BATCHELOR, KAREN LEE, English language educator; b. Oregon City, Oreg., June 17, 1948; d. Jewel Elaine Durham; m. Luis Moncado, Mar. 17, 1978 (div. Aug. 1988); children: Virginia, Travis. BA in English, San Fransicso State U., 1971, MA in English, 1980. Vol. U.S. Peace Corps, Andong, South Korea, 1972-74; tchr. English as second lang. City Coll. San Francisco, 1975—; tchr. trainer U. Calif., Berkeley, 1986—; acad. specialist USIA, 1991—; lectr. English Sonoma State U., 1999—. Speaker in field. Co-author: (textbooks) Discovering English, 1981, In Plain English, 1985, More Plain English, 1986, The Writing Challenge, 1990, The English Zone, Books 1-4, 1998; contbr. articles to profl. jorus. Mem. Tchrs. English to Speakers of Other Langs., Calif. Tchrs. English to Speakers of Other Langs. Office: City Coll San Francisco 50 Phelan Ave San Francisco CA 94112-1821

BATCHMAN, THEODORE EARL, electrical engineering educator, researcher; b. Gt. Bend, Kans., Mar. 29, 1940; s. Jake T. and Dorothy E. (Bardwell) B.; m. Nancy L. Leatherman, Dec. 23, 1961; children: Teddie Suzanne, Timothy Brent, Tracey Nanette. BSEE, U. Kans., 1962, MSEE, 1963, PhD, 1966. Engr., sci. specialist LTV, Dallas, 1966-70; sr. lectr. U. Queensland, Brisbane, Australia, 1970-75; from asst. prof. to prof. elec. engring. U. Va., Charlottesville, 1975-88; prof., dir. Sch. Elec. Engring. and Computer Sci. U. Okla., Norman, 1988-95; dean Coll. Engring. U. Nev., Reno, 1995—. Cons. Commonwealth of Va., Richmond, 1982-83, U.S. Army FSTC, Charlottesville, 1986-90; mem. adv. bd. Chromachron Technology Corp., Columbia, Md., 1988-90. Rsch. grantee NASA, 1978-84, NSF, 1979-84, HHS, 1984-85, Naval Rsch. Labs., 1987-88, U.S. Army, 1989-90, NSF EPSCOR, 1991-94. Fellow IEEE (mem. edn. activities bd. 2003—, Achievement award 1998), Am. Soc. Engring. Edn., Optical Soc. Am. Republican. Methodist. Avocations: woodworking, model railroading, photography. Home: 12500 Fieldcreek Ln Reno NV 89511-6659 Office: U Nev Coll Engring Office Of Dean Reno NV 89557-0001

BATES, BARRY LEON, biology educator; b. Gainesville, Tex., Oct. 15, 1944; s. Diviger Leon and Irene Hazel (Williams) B.; m. Cheryl Ann Pederson, Sept. 9, 1990; children: Brandy, Crystal. BS, Stephen F. Austin U., Nacogdoches, Tex., 1967, MS, 1969; postgrad., East Tex. U., Commerce, 1974-90; cert., Rsch. Inst. Environ. Medicine, Boston, 1972. Cert. hazardous waste regulations, Tex. Owner, cons. Environ. Lab., Pottsboro, Tex., 1978-90; biology prof. Grayson County Coll., Denison, Tex., 1969-87; lab. coord. El Centro Coll., Dallas, 1990-92, dean phys./social scis., 1994-95, biology coord., 1994—, prof. biology, 1990—; lectr. biology So. Meth. U., Dallas, 1992-93; course dir. physiology Parker Coll., Dallas, 1992-93, asst. prof. basic sci, 1992-93. Owner, mgr., cons. Environ. Lab., Pottsboro, Tex., 1978-90; appraiser Am. Soc. Equine, Pottsboro, 1986-92; legal assisting adv. bd. mem. El Centro Coll., Dallas, 1994-95, tchr. edn. adv. bd. mem., 1994-98, guest tchr., 1995. Author: Fundamentals/Concepts of Physical Science, 1974 (excellence award 1975), Factors and Elements in General Biology, 1975 (excellence award 1976). Mem. Tex. State Steering Com., 1996; coord. Tex. Alliance for Minorities, 1997; assoc. Baylor Med. Found.; hon. chmn. Bus. Adv. Coun., Nat. Rep. Congl. Com.. Recipient Rsch. Excellence award Rsch. Inst. Enviro-Med., Boston, 1972; named to Tex. State Employment Charitable Campaign Leadership Cir., 1998; mem. Leadership Acad. Dallas County Dist., 1995-96. With U.S. Army, 1970-72. Mem. Phi Delta Kappa (chmn. membership 1980-86, excellence award 1986), Beta Biol. Honor Soc. (pres. 1968-69, Spirit award 1969), Phi Theta Kappa (Spirit award 1995). Republican. Mem. Ch. of Christ. Achievements include first to identify and publish fishes, amphibians, reptiles and mammals of Hagerman National Wildlife Refuge, 1974. Office: El Centro Coll Main and Lamar Dallas TX 75020

BATES, GEORGE WILLIAM, obstetrician, gynecologist, educator, medical products executive; b. Durham, N.C., Feb. 15, 1940; s. George W. and Lillian M. (Streete) B.; m. Susanne Rayburn, Oct. 18, 1969; children: Jonathan Rayburn, Jeffrey William, Robert Wiser. BS, U. N.C., 1962, MD, 1965; SM, MIT, 1984. Diplomate Am. Bd. Ob-Gyn. (examiner 1984-93). Intern U. Ala., Birmingham, 1965-66; resident ob-gyn U. N.C., Chapel Hill, 1966-70; prof., chmn. ob-gyn U. Tenn., Knoxville, 1972-76; fellow reproductive endocrinology U. Tex., Dallas, 1976-78; prof., dir. reproductive endocrinology U. Miss. Med. Ctr., Jackson, 1978-86; prof. ob.-gyn. Coll. Medicine, Med. U. S.C., Charleston, 1986-90, dean, 1986-89; v.p. med. edn. Greenville (S.C.) Hosp. System, 1990-96; exec. v.p., chief med. officer Prin.Care, Inc., Brentwood, Tenn., 1996-98; v.p. devel. Vanderbilt U. Med. Ctr., Nashville, 1998—. CEO digiChart, Inc. Co-author: Obstetrics and Gynecology for Medical Students, 1992, 95; editor: Manual of Clinical Problems in Obstetrics and Gynecology, 1982, 86, 90; contbr. numerous articles to profl. publs. Commr. coun. Boy Scouts Am., 1989-90, v.p. adminstrn., 1992, pres., 1993-94, bd. dirs. Mid. Tenn. Coun., 2002--; elder Mt. Pleasant Presbyn. Ch., Westminster Presbyn. Ch.; mem. pres.'s adv. coun. Mars Hill Coll., Presbyn. Coll., Nat. Devel. Coun., U. N.C. Maj. USAF, 1970-72. Morehead scholar, 1958; NIH rsch. trainee, 1976-78; Sloan fellow, 1983; recipient Eagle Scout award, 1955, Henry Fordham award, 1966, Golden Apple award, 1987, Silver Beaver award, 1989, Hon. Alumnus award Med. U. S.C., 1990, Disting. Eagle Scout award, 1991; named Prof. of Yr., U. Miss., 1980, Top 100 Healthcare Exec., 2002. Mem. ACOG (chmn. fin. com. 1990-94, health care commn. 1994-97, Jr. Fellow Profl. of Y. award dist. IV 1991), AMA, AAAS, Assn. Profs. Ob-Gyn. Found. (bd. dirs. 1993), Am. Gyn.-Ob. Soc., Nat. Bd. Med. Examiners, Gynecol. Investigation, Am. Fertility Soc. (bd. dirs. 1991-94, treas. 1994-96), Soc. Gynecol. Surgeons, Accreditation Coun. Grad. Med. Edn., So. Atlantic Assn. Obstetricians and Gynecologists, Ctrl. Assn. Obstetricians and Gynecologists, Endocrine Soc., Rotary, Alpha Omega Alpha. Office: digiChart Inc 102 Woodmont Blvd Ste 500 Nashville TN 37205-5254

BATES, JAMES EARL, academic administrator; b. Ligonier, Pa., Aug. 10, 1923; s. Earl Barrington and Margaret (Kinsey) B.; m. Lauralou Courtney, Apr. 15, 1950; children: Susan Bates Jaren, Sara Bates Hudson, James Barrington, Willa Bates Leitten. DSc, Temple U., 1946; DPM, Pa. Coll. Podiatric Medicine, 1970, LHD (hon.), 1996; EdD (hon.), Franklin Pierce Coll., 1972; DSc (hon.), Calif. Coll. Podiatric Med., 1995; LLD, Barry U., 1995; LHD (hon.), Pa. Coll. Podiatric Medicine, 1996. Practice podiatric medicine, Phila., 1946-71; assoc. prof. roentgenology Temple U., Phila., 1948-60; prof., pres. Pa. Coll. Podiatric Medicine, Phila., 1962-95, chancellor, 1995-96, chancellor, CEO, 1997-98; cons. to dean Sch. Podiatric Medicine Temple U., 1998—; chancellor Temple Sch. Podiatric Medicine. Cons. BHRD Region IX, HEW, San Francisco, 1973-74, Region V, Chgo., 1974-75; del. Nat. Commn. on Certifying Health Manpower; mem. health adv. com. HEW, 1972-73; adv. panel for podiatry Inst. Medicine, Nat. Acad. Scis., 1972-74; adv. council for comprehensive health planning Pa. Dept. Health, 1972-75, health manpower task force edn. com., 1976; task force on health manpower distbn. Nat. Health Council, 1973, com. on manpower, 1976-83; mem. Nat. Adv. Council on Health Professions Edn., 1983-87; cons. team So. Regional Ednl. Bd. Feasibility Study for So. Podiatry Sch., 1975-76; mem. Statewide Profl. Standards Rev. Council, 1976-82, Greater Phila. Com. for Med.-Pharm. Scis. Contbr. articles to profl. jours. Trustee First United Meth. Ch. of Germantown, 1965-72, past chmn. fin. com.; v.p. bd. Germantown Businessmen's Assn., Disting. Service award, 1964; chmn. 277th and 278th Ann. Germantown Week, 1958-59; dep. service dir. Phila. CD Council, 1966-73; mem. Health Adv. Commn., Phila., 1976; past pres., bd. mgrs. Germantown YMCA; v.p. Phila. Boosters Assn.; trustee Univ. City Sci. Center, Phila. Served with M.C. AUS, WWII. Recipient citation Pa. Coll. Podiatric Medicine, 1970, citation Gov. Pa., 1973, Lifetime Achievement award Podiatric Mgmt. Mag., 1993. Fellow Internat. Acad. Preventive Medicine (dir. 1973-78), Brit. Soc. Podiatric Medicine (hon.), Royal Soc. Health (Eng.), Am. Coll. Foot Roentgenologists (pres. 1958-59), Coll. Physicians Phila.; mem. Am. Podiatry Assn. (Merit award 1962, gen. chmn. Region Three Ann. Conv. 1975—), Pa. Podiatry Assn. (pres. 1959-60, Man of Yr. award 1961, Spl. citation 1973), Greater Phila. Podiatry Soc. (pres. 1955-56), Fedn. Assns. Schs. of Health Professions (pres. 1975-76), Am. Assn. Colls. Podiatric Medicine (pres. 1969-72), Pi Epsilon Delta, Pi Delta. Clubs: Greate Bay Country, Union League, Pyramid Club. Republican. Office: Pa Coll Podiatric Medicine 810 N Race St Philadelphia PA 19107-2496

BATES, MABLE JOHNSON, retired business technology educator; b. Carthage, Miss., July 13, 1930; d. Horace Lawrence and Mable Barnette Johnson; children: Lisa Susan Stone, Rayburn Holmes Bates Jr. BS in Commerce, U. Miss., 1952; MEd, Miss. State U., 1976. Cert. tchr. bus. edn., mktg. Bus. tchr. Clinton (Miss.) Pub. Schs., 1952-53; sec. Jackson (Miss.) Pub. Schs., 1954-64, tchr. bus., 1964-69, tchr., coord. mktg., 1971-78; instr. bus. Jones County Jr. Coll., Ellisvile, Miss., 1978-84; instr. bus. tech. Miss.

Gulf Coast C.C., Gautier, 1984-92. Mem. Am. Vocational Assn., Delta Kappa Gamma, Phi Beta Lambda (adviser, Outstanding Adviser 1991). Episcopalian. Avocations: gardening, volunteer work. Home: 3715 Cabildo Pl Ocean Springs MS 39564-8585

BATES, MARGARET HABECKER, secondary education educator; b. Seattle, June 23, 1951; d. Jack Norman and Catherine Lenard (Hamilton) Bigford; m. Thomas Benjamin Habecker, Mar. 30, 1985 (div.); m. Jerry L. Bates, Apr. 1, 1992. BA in Anthropology, Ctrl. Wash. U., 1973; MA in Anthropology and Demography, U. Ill., 1977. Cert. tchr., Wash.; nat. cert. in early adolescent English/lang. arts Nat. Bd. Profl. Tchg. Stds. Teaching fellow U. Ill., Urbana, 1975-76; with theme reader program Kent (Wash.) Sch. Dist., 1977-81; tchr. Ridgefield (Wash.) Sch. Dist., 1981-92, Vancouver (Wash.) Sch. Dist., 1992—; asst. supt. Hockinson (Wash.) Sch. Dist., 2001—. Curriculum cons., Vancouver, 1991—2001; mem. sci. cadre Vancouver Sch. Dist., 1992—; field test candidate Nat. Bd. for Profl. Teaching Standards, Detroit, 1993—; student tchr. mentor E.S.D. # 112, Vancouver, 1988-91; mem. renewal devel. team Nat. Bd. for PRofl. Tchg. Std., 2000—. Mem. steering com. Sci. Math. Advancement Reachout for Tchr., Vancouver, 1992—, Leadership and Assistance for Sci. Edn. Reform State Steering Com., 2001—; active Citizens for Sch., Ridgefield, 1985-91, Shumway Site Coun., co-chair, 1992—; active Shumway Bldg. Leadership Team, 1992-93, Middle Sch. Vision Task Force, 1993-97; site co-chair Discovery Mid. Sch., 1994-97; commr. Wash. State Acad. Achievement and Accountability Comm., 1999—2002. Rsch. fellow NSF, 1993, Harvard Sch. Edn., 1992, Nat. Endowment for Humanities, 1990-91, 84; Memory Project fellow Libr. Congress, 1998, grantee NSF, 1999. Mem. Ridgefield Edn. Assn. (pres.-elect, pres.), Wash. Edn. Assn. (chair PAC), S.W. Wash. FOund. (Clark County Tchr. of Yr. 1990). Episcopalian. Avocations: gardening, reading, birding, writing. Office: 17912 NE 159th St Brush Prairie WA 98606 E-mail: maggie.bates@hock.k12.wa.us.

BATES, MARGARET HELENA, special education educator; b. Irvington, N.J., Jan. 27, 1943; d. Marcel Bogstahl and Helena Christina (Yaroszynsky) Bogstahl; divorced; children: Robert Crew, Diane Carlyle. BA, Coll. Steubenville, 1966; MS, St. Cloud State U., 1982. Cert. tchr. English, spl. edn., emotionally/behaviorally disorders and learning disabilities, Minn. Tchr. Ind. Sch. Dist. # 742, St. Cloud, 1976—. Adv. bd. Minn. Acad. Excellence Found., St. Paul., 1993-94; state coun. chair Minn. Edn. Assn., 1993-97; co-chair. St. Cloud Edn. Assn., 1979-84; sec. Audubon Soc., 1992-97; historian Stearns County Theatrical Co., 1992, 93, 94; bd. dirs. The New Tradition Theatre Co., 1988-89. Grantee Bremer Found., 1991, incentive grantee Ind. Sch. Dist. 742. Mem. Coun. Exceptional Children, Minn. Coun. with Behavior Disorders, Minn. Educators of Children with Emotional Disorders, Delta Kappa Gamma Internat. (1st vp. 1994-96, pres. 1998—, internat. legis. state chair, state chmn. 1998—). Avocations: theatre, canoeing, travel, environment. Home: 825 17th Ave S Saint Cloud MN 56301-5234 Office: Area Learning Ctr 20 32nd Ave N # D Saint Cloud MN 56303-4138

BATES, RICHARD DOANE, JR., chemistry educator, researcher; b. Elizabeth, N.J., July 24, 1944; s. Richard Doane and Sarah Newbold (Deacon) B.; m. Ruthann Iovanni, Mar. 13, 1971; children: Spencer Deacon, Dunlea Ristine. BA, Cornell U., 1966; MA, Columbia U., 1967, PhD, 1971. Asst. prof. chemistry Georgetown U., Washington, 1973-80, assoc. prof., 1980—95, prof., 1995—, chair dept. chemistry, 2002—. Contbr. articles to sci. jours. V.p. C.Z. Study Group, Schaumburg, Ill., 1980-86, pres., 1987-96; v.p. Montgomery Youth Hockey Assn., Silver Spring, Md., 1993-2002. 1st lt. U.S. Army, 1971-73. Predoctoral fellow NIH, 1967-70, Hammett travel fellow Columbia U., 1970, SONY Tchr. scholar, 1993—. Mem. Am. Chem. Soc., Am. Phys. Soc., Royal Soc. Chemistry, Sigma Xi. Office: Georgetown U Dept Chemistry 606 Reiss Sci Bldg Washington DC 20057-1227

BATES STOKLOSA, EVELYNNE (EVE BATES STOKLOSA), educational consultant, educator; b. Camden, N.J., Mar. 13, 1946; d. Linwood T. and Eve Mary (Widzenas) Bates; m. Leslie E. Stoklosa, Apr. 15, 1968; children: Phillip J., Kristine L. BS in Home Econs. Edn., Buffalo State U. Coll., 1968, MS in Home Econs. Edn., 1971, Cert. Advanced Studies, 1994. Cert. sch. dist. adminstr. Tchr. Parkside Elem. Sch., Kenmore, N.Y., 1968-69, Kenmore West High Sch., 1968-71, 73-75, Kenmore Jr. High Sch., 1977-80, Ken-Ton Continuing Edn., Kenmore, 1980-87, Kenmore Mid. Sch., 1981—2001. Owner, pres. EBS Decors, Tonawanda, N.Y.; edn. cons. Villa Maria Coll., Buffalo, 1980-2000; adv. bd. interior design dept.; facilitator student of the month award program Kenmore Mid. Sch., 1982—, active mem. sch. planning team, 1984—, facilitator design team, 1990—; participant Buffalo Summits, 1994; ind. fashion cons. Editor parent informational pamphlet, 1992, faculty informational newsletter, 1992-94. Vol., Frankl Loyd Wright Found. of the Martin House Restoration Corp., 1999—; vol. various charitable functions and events in and around Buffalo; mem. Amateur Chamber Music Players, 2000—, Buffalo Philharmonic Orch. Women's Com. Found., 2000—. Erie County Nutrition Assn. grantee. Mem. AAUW (bd. dirs. 1992-94), ASCD, DAR (life), Family and Consumer Scientists Am. (life), Am. Vocat. Assn., Am. Fedn. Tchrs., N.Y. State Home Econs. Tchrs. Assn. (Tchr. of Yr. 1992-93, Most Outstanding Leadership and Creativity award 1987), N.Y. State Assn. Family and Consumer Sci. Educators (life), N.Y. State United Tchrs., Western N.Y. Women in Adminstrn., Kenmore Tchrs. Assn. (bldg. rep.), Amatuer Chamber Mus Soc., Chautaqua Lit. and Sci. Cir. (life), Phi Delta Kappa, Phi Upsilon Omicron. Avocations: travel, singing, swimming, golf, piano.

BATISTONI, RONALD, educational association administrator; b. Plainfield, N.J., Oct. 22, 1938; s. Atillio Raymond and Ann Agnes (Paznick) B.; children: Raymond, Jeanine, Melissa. BS in Secondary Edn., Seton Hall U., 1960, EdD in Ednl. Adminstrn., 1991; MA in English/Am. Lit., Montclair (N.J.) U., 1968. Tchr. English/Latin Bergenfield (N.J.) Pub. Schs., 1960-64; tchr. English West Morris Regional H.S. Dist., Chester, N.J., 1964-69, chmn. dept. English, 1969-70, supt., 1991-92, asst. supt., 1992-94; dir. nat. assessment programs N.J. Prins. and Suprs. Assn., Chester, 1995—; prin. West Morris Ctrl. Sch., Chester, 1979-91. Pres. Iron Hills Conf., Morris County, N.J., 1988-89; exec. sec. Washington Twp. Outreach, N.J., 1979-84. Recipient Presdl. Citation for Vol. Svc., Pres. Reagan, 1981. Mem. Am. Ednl. Rsch. Assn., Nat. Assn. Secondary Sch. Prins., N.J. Prins. and Suprs. Assn. Avocations: reading, computers travel, outdoors. Home: Unit 38 24375 Widgeon Pl Saint Michaels MD 21663-2263

BATLIVALA, ROBERT BOMI D. oil company executive, economics educator; b. Bombay, Feb. 17, 1940; came to U.S., 1962, naturalized, 1968; s. Dean Shaw and Rose (Engineer) B.; m. Carole Gretchen Feustel, May 9, 1964; children: Amy, Dina. BS in Geology, Chemistry, St. Xavier Coll., Bombay, Ind., 1960; MBA in Bus., Econs., Loyola U., Chgo., 1970; PHD in Bus., Econs., Ill. Inst. Tech., 1971; postgrad., U. Chgo., 1972-73. Rsch. chemist Reynolds Metals Co., McCook, Ill., 1962-64; from sales engr. to staff dir. econs. Amoco Corp., Chgo., 1964-1988, dir. antitrust econs., 1988-93, dir. regulatory econs., 1993-99. Adj. prof. bus. and econs. Rosary Coll., Dominican U., River Forest, Ill., 1976—, Graduate Sch. Bus., 1980-99; bd. dirs. Vesta Ins. Group, Inc., Ill. Ins. Exch. (INEX), Parsee Internat. Ltd. Contbr. articles to profl. jours. Bd. dirs. Ctr. for Conflict Resolution, 1991-96. Stuart Tuition scholar Ill. Inst. Tech., 1970-71; recipient Recognition award Rosary Coll. Grad. Sch. Bus. Alumni Assn., River Forest, 1986. Mem. ABA (assoc.), Nat. Assn. Mfrs. (corp. fin., mgmt. & competition com., regulation, transp. com. 1980-99), Am. Econ. Assn., Assn. of Energy Economists, Loyola U. Grad. Bus. Alumni Assn. (pres., sr. v.p. 1971-73, Disting. Alumni award 1975), Oak Park Country Club. Avocations: ancient history, reading, writing, travel, languages. Home: 1106 Keystone Ave River Forest IL 60305-1326

BATRA, ROMESH CHANDER, engineering mechanics educator, researcher; b. Dherowal, Panjab, India, Aug. 16, 1947; came to U.S., 1969; s. Amir Chand and Dewki Bai (Dhamija) B.; m. Manju Dhamija, June 26, 1972; children: Monica, Meenakshi. BSME, Panjabi U., Patiala, India, 1968; MASc, U. Waterloo, Ont., Can., 1969; PhD, Johns Hopkins U., 1972. Postdoctoral rsch. assoc. Johns Hopkins U., Balt., 1972-73; rsch. assoc. McMaster U., Hamilton, Ont., 1973-74; asst. prof. U. Ala., Tuscaloosa, 1976-77; asst. prof. engrng. mechanics U. Mo., Rolla, 1974-76, assoc. prof., 1977-81, prof., 1981-94; Clifton C. Garvin prof. Va. Polytech. Inst. & State U., Blacksburg, 1994—. Mem. NRC Panel on Armaments, 1996—99, NRC Panel on Survivability and Lethality, 2001—; S.W. Mechanics Series lectr., 2000; Michael L. Sadowski mechanics lectr. Rensselaer Poly. Inst., 2000. Editor: Contemporary Research in Engineering Science, Springer Verlag, 1995; co-editor: Contemporary Research in the Mechanics and Mathematics of Materials, Internat. Ctr. for Numerical Methods in Engrng., 1996, Constitutive Laws, Experiments and Numerical Implementation, Internat. Ctr. for Numerical Methods in Engrng., 1995, Material Instabilities, Theory and Applications, 1994, Impact, Waves and Fracture, 1994, Contemporary Research in Mechanics, 2002; mem. editl. bd. Internat. Jour. Plasticity, 1989-2003, Internat. Jour. Engrng. Design and Analysis, 1992—, Continuum Mechanics and Thermodynamics, 1993—, Computational Mechanics, 1994—, Jour. Engrng. Materials and Tech., 1996-2001, Polish Jour. Theoretical and Applied Mechanics, 2000—, Computer Modeling in Engrng. and Sci., 2003—; editor: Mathematics and Mechanics of Solids, 1995—; reviewer for various jours. in field; contbr. articles to profl. jours. Grantee NSF, 1980-83, 87—, Army Rsch. Office, 1985—, Office of Naval Rsch., 1994—; recipient Alexander von Humboldt award for sr. scientists, 1992, Jai Krishna award Indian Geotech. Soc., 1994, Eric Reissner medal Internat. Congress in Computational Engrg. Sci., 2000; inducted into Hopkins Soc. Scholars, 1993. Fellow ASME (chair elasticity com. 1995-2000, co-editor symposium procs. 1991, 94-95, co-editor meeting procs. 1999, awards nominating com. 1997—), Am. Acad. Mechanics (awards nominating com. 2002—, sec. 2003—), Am. Soc. Engrng. Edn. (Centennial award 1993), Soc. Engrng. Sci. (bd. dirs. 1991-96, editor meeting procs. 1982, v.p. 1995, pres. 1996); mem. Midwestern Mechanics Conf. (editor procs. 1991, bd. dirs. 1989-93), Soc. Natural Philosophy (treas. 1987-89, editor meeting procs. 1981), Mechs. and Materials Conf. (organizer, cochair 1999), U.S. Nat. Congress Theoret. and Applied Mechs. (organizer, co-chmn. 2002). Office: Va Polytech Inst & State U Dept Engrng Sci & Mechanics 220 Norris Hall Blacksburg VA 24061-0219 E-mail: rbatra@vt.edu.

BATSHAW, MARILYN SEIDNER, education administrator; b. East Orange, N.J., Aug. 19, 1946; d. Gerald and Sylvia (Weinstein) Seidner; 1 child, Andrew Curt. BA, Newark State Coll., Union, N.J., 1968; MA, Kean Coll., Union, 1972, prin. cert., 1984. Cert. hearing aid dispenser, audiologist, elem. and deaf and hearing impaired tchr., supr., prin., N.J. Tchr. of deaf N.J. Dept. Edn., Trenton, 1972-74, audiologist, 1974-82, cons. in spl. edn., 1982-86; prin., dir. edn. Lakeview Sch., Cerebral Palsy Assn. Middlesex County, Edison, NJ, 1986-94; prin. ARC Essex Sch., Livingston, NJ, 1994-96; billing and eligibility case mgr. Prudential Health Care Group, Cranbury, NJ, 1997-99; dir. ESC Sch. West Amwell Campus Hunterdon County Ednl. Scvs. Commn., Lambertville, NJ, 1999; supr. Bright Beginnings Learning Ctr. Middlesex County Ednl. Svcs. Commn., Piscataway, NJ, 1999—2001; supr. special edn. North Arlington Bd. Edn., NJ, 2001—. Officer Parents for Deaf Awareness. Mem. ASCD, N.J. ASCD, Ednl. Audiology Assn., Am. Speech-Lang. and Hearing Assn. (cert. clin. competence in audiology), N.J. Speech-Lang. and Hearing Assn., A.G. Bell Assn., Am. Auditory Soc., Am. Acad. Audiology, N.J. Acad. Audiology, Coun. Exceptional Children, N.J. Coun. Exceptional Children, Nat. Assn. Edn. Young Children. Home: 166 Westgate Dr Edison NJ 08820-1158 Office: North Arlington HS Child Study Team 222 Ridge Rd North Arlington NJ 07031 E-mail: mbatshaw@optonline.net.

BATSON, STEPHEN WESLEY, university administrator, consultant; b. Wilmington, NC, Aug. 20, 1946; s. John Thomas and Mildred (Pritchard) B.; m. Kathleen Lawless, Apr. 11, 1985. BA, Mercer U.; MEd, EdS, Ga. Coll.; EdD, U. Ga. H.S. tchr., adminstr. various, Ga., 1970-79; asst. v.p. for acad. affairs, dir. instnl. rsch. Ga. So. U., Statesboro, 1979-82; asst. to pres., dir. planning Tex. A&M, Commerce, 1982-86; v.p. planning and advancement W.Va. State Coll., 1986-97; v.p. univ. rels. Ga. Southwestern State U., Americus, 1997—. Contbr. articles to profl. jours. Co-chmn. United Way campaign, Commerce, 1984; bd. dirs. Ctrl. W.Va. chpt. ARC, 1993-97, The Friends of W.Va. Pub. Radio, 1996-97, Americus/Sumter County Arts Coun., 1999-2003. Named Bulloch County Leader, Ga. Power Leaders of Tomorrow Program, 1980, Outstanding Young Alumnus, Ga. Coll., 1981; recipient Disting. Svc. award for ednl. fundraising Ga. Edn. Advancement Coun. Mem. Am. Assn. Higher Edn., Am. Coun. Edn., Assn. Fundraising Profls. (cert., W.Va. chpt. sec. 1991-92, pres. 1993-94, nat. bd. dirs. 1995—, vice-chmn. profl. advancement, 1996-98, chmn.-elect 1999-2000, chair 2001-02, immediate past chmn. 2003-), Soc. for Coll. and Univ. Planning, Coun. for Advancement and Support of Edn. (Gold award 1993, 95), Commerce C. of C. (Disting. Cmty. Svc. award 1984), Charleston C. of C., So. Assn. for Inst. Rsch. (pres. 1986-87), Leadership Charleston Alumni Assn. (bd. dirs., pres. 1995-96), Edn. Law Assn. (bd. dirs. 1985-91, pres. 1992-93), Kiwanis (bd. dirs., disting. pres., disting. lt. gov.), USCG Aux. (Flotilla 10-10), Americus C. of C., Rotary. Office: Ga Southwestern State U Office Univ Rels 800 Wheatley St Americus GA 31709-4376 E-mail: sbatson@canes.gsw.edu.

BATTENFELD, JOHN LEONARD, secondary school educator, journalist, editor, education educator; b. Norwalk, Conn., Aug. 25, 1943; s. John Leonard and Mary Florence Fay B.; m. Yasuyo Aso, Apr. 23, 1977; children: John O., Sachiko C. BA, NYU, 1969; MFA, New Sch. Social Rsch., 1998. Journalist UPI, N.Y.C., 1969-76; asst. press sec. Mayor's Office, N.Y.C., 1976-81; editor UPI, N.Y.C., 1981-83, fgn. corr. Tokyo, 1983-85, Reuters Ltd., Hong Kong, New Delhi, & Seoul, 1985-95; lectr. NYU, N.Y.C., 1999—, Boston U., 1998—99, Purchase Coll., SUNY, 1999—; tchr. English and social studies Truman H.S., Bronx, NY, 2000—01, Chestnut Ridge Mid. Sch., NY, 2001—02, Warren Harding H.S., Bridgeport, Conn., 2002—. With USNR, 1965-67. Mem. MLA, Soc. Profl. Journalists, Nat. Coun. for the Social Studies, Vietnam Vets. Am., Nat. Coun. Tchrs. English. Democrat. Roman Catholic.

BATTERMAN, BORIS WILLIAM, physicist, educator, academic director; b. N.Y.C., Aug. 25, 1930; children: Robert W., William E., Thomas A. Student, Cooper Union Coll., 1949-50, Technische Hochschule, Stuttgart, Germany; SB, MIT, 1952, PhD, 1956. Mem. tech. staff Bell Tel. Labs., Murray Hill, N.J., 1956-65; assoc. prof. Cornell U., Ithaca, N.Y., 1965-67, prof. applied and engring. physics, 1967—, dir. Sch. Applied and Engring. Physics, 1974-78, dir. Synchrotron Radiation Lab. (CHESS), 1978-97, Walter S. Carpenter Jr. prof. engring., 1985—2001, Walter S. Carpenter Jr. prof. emeritus, 2002—. Mem. U.S.A. Nat. Com. Crystallography, NAS, 1969-72. Assoc. editor Jour. Crystal Growth, 1964-74. Fulbright scholar, 1953-54; Guggenheim fellow, 1971, Fulbright Hayes fellow, 1971, Alexander von Humboldt fellow, 1983. Fellow AAAS, Am. Phys. Soc. Office: 150 Lombard St #603 San Francisco CA 94111 E-mail: bwb1@cornell.edu.

BATTERSBY, JAMES LYONS, JR., English language educator; b. Pawtucket, RI, Aug. 24, 1936; s. James Lyons and Hazel Irene (Deuel) B.; m. Lisa J. Kiser, Aug. 6, 1990; 1 child, Julie Ann. BS magna cum laude, U. Vt., 1961; MA, Cornell U., 1962, PhD, 1965. Asst. prof. U. Calif., Berkeley, 1965-70; assoc. prof. English Ohio State U., Columbus, 1970-82, prof., 1982—. Cons. Ohio State U. Press, U. Ky. Press, U. Calif. Press, Prentice-Hall, McGraw Hill, Fairleigh Dickinson U. Press, U. Mich. Press, U. Ala. Press. Author: Typical Folly: Evaluating Student Performance in Higher Education, 1973, Rational Praise and Natural Lamentation: Johnson, Lycidas and Principles of Criticism, 1980, Elder Olson: An Annotated Bibliography, 1983, Paradigms Regained: Pluralism and the Practice of Criticism, 1991, Reason and the Nature of Texts, 1996, Unorthodox Views: Reflections on Reality, Truth, and Meaning in Current Social, Cultural, and Critical Discourse, 2002; contbg. author: Domestick Privacies: Samuel Johnson and the Art of Biography, 1987, Fresh Reflections on Samuel Johnson: Essays in Criticism, 1987, Criticism, History and Intertextuality, 1988, Beyond Poststructuralism: The Speculations of Theory and the Experience of Reading, 1996; contbr. articles to profl. jours. With U.S. Army, 1954—57. Woodrow Wilson fellow, 1961-62, 64-65, Samuel S. Fels fellow, 1964-65, U. Calif. Summer Faculty fellow, 1966, Humanities Research fellow, 1969; recipient Kidder Medal U. Vt., 1961. Mem. MLA, Am. Soc. 18th Century Studies, Midwest Soc. 18th Century Studies, Royal Oak Found., Phi Beta Kappa, Phi Kappa Phi, Kappa Delta Pi. Home: 472 Clinton Heights Ave Columbus OH 43202-1277 E-mail: batterjay@msn.com.

BATTERSBY, KATHERINE SUE, elementary school educator; b. Middletown, N.Y., Nov. 17, 1960; d. George William and Joanne Marie (Endrich) Blaha; m. Jeffery Aaron Battersby, Sept. 18, 1988; children: Kristin Sierra, Joanna Reye, Colon Muir. BS cum laude, SUNY, Potsdam, 1983; MEd, SUNY, New Paltz, 1992. Coord. internat. sch., Spanish instr. Christian Min., Reynosa, Mexico, 1983—85; receptionist Chase NBW Bank, White Plains, N.Y., 1985-86; adminstr. NYNEX Bus. Ctr., White Plains, N.Y., 1986-87; admin. asst. Rsch. Inst. Am., N.Y., 1987-88; tchr. Haldane Elem. Sch., Cold Spring, N.Y., 1989—. Singer: Crane Chorus, 1978—82, Lake Placid Winter Olympics, 1980. Mem. Crane Chorus SUNY, Potsdam, 1978—82. Mem. PTA, Am. Fedn. Tchrs., N.Y. State United Tchrs., N.Y. State Tchrs. Retirement System, Kappa Delta Phi, Sigma Tau Delta. Avocations: reading, hiking, photography, travel, spanish. Office: Haldane Elem Sch Craigside Dr Cold Spring NY 10516

BATTESTIN, MARTIN CAREY, retired English language educator; b. N.Y.C., Mar. 25, 1930; s. Martin Augustus and Marion (Kirkland) B.; m. Ruthe Rootes, June 14, 1963; children: David (dec. 1999), Catherine. BA summa cum laude, Princeton U., 1952, PhD, 1958. English master Westminster Sch., Simsbury, Conn., 1952-53; instr. Wesleyan U., Middletown, Conn., 1956-58, asst. prof., 1958-61, U. Va., Charlottesville, 1961-63, assoc. prof., 1963-67, prof., 1967-75, William R. Kenan, Jr. prof. English, 1975-98, emeritus prof., 1998—, chmn. dept. English, 1983-86. Vis. prof. Rice U., Houston, 1967-68; assoc. Clare Hall, Cambridge (Eng.) U., 1972. Author: The Moral Basis of Fielding's Art, 1959, 1975, The Providence of Wit, 1974, 1989, Henry Fielding: A Life, 1989, 2d edit., 1993, New Essays by Henry Fielding, 1989, 1993, A Henry Fielding Companion, 2000; editor: Joseph Andrews (Henry Fielding), 1961, 1967, Shamela (Henry Fielding), 1961, Tom Jones (Henry Fielding), 1974, 2d edit., 1975, Amelia (Henry Fielding), 1983, Tom Jones: A Collection of Critical Essays, 1968, British Novelists, 1660-1800, 1985, Tobias Smollett, translator Cervantes' Don Quixote, 2003; co-editor: The Correspondence of Henry and Sarah Fielding, 1993. Am. Coun. Learned Socs. fellow, 1960-61, 72; Guggenheim fellow, 1964-65; Sr. fellow Coun. Humanities, Princeton U., 1971; Ctr. for Advanced Studies fellow U. Va., 1974-75; NEH Bicentennial Rsch. fellow, 1975-76. Mem. MLA (chmn. sec. VII 1967, adv. editor publs. 1982-86), South Atlantic Modern Lang. Assn., Internat. Assn. Univ. Profs. English (chmn. sect. V 1990-92), Assn. of Lit. Scholars and Critics, Nat. Assn. Scholars, The Johnsonians. Mem. Ch. of England. Home: 1832 Westview Rd Charlottesville VA 22903-1648 E-mail: mcb9g@virginia.edu.

BATTISTA, LEON JOSEPH, JR., economics educator; b. NYC, Oct. 12, 1962; s. Leon Joseph and Clara (Gigli) B.; m. Kimberly Jeanne Romano, June 14, 1986; children: Matthew, Mollie, Patrick. BA, SUNY, Cortland, 1984; MA, New Sch. for Social Rsch., 1991, postgrad., 1992—. Billing clk. Pubs. Clearing House, Port Washington, N.Y., 1984-86; mgmt. info. systems coord. Citicorp Mortgage, Inc., Westport, Conn., 1986-87, customer svc. rep., 1987-88; fin. account coord. Homequity, Inc., Wilton, Conn., 1988; rsch. asst. New Sch. for Social Rsch., N.Y.C., 1988-92; coord., lectr. econs. CUNY, Bronx Cmty. Coll., Bronx, N.Y., 1994—. Adj. lectr. in econs. Quinnipiac U., 1992—94. Author: MIS Manual, 1986, Property Directory, 1987, also articles. Baseball coach Cath. Youth Orgn., Port Washington, 1977-84, Black Rock Litte League, Bridgeport, Conn., 1996-99. Recipient Excellence in Econs. award, 1984, Lions Club award, 1980; Presdl. Fac. Devel. grant, 1996-2003. Mem. Am. Econ. Assn., Indsl. Rels. Rsch. Assn., Ea. Econ. Assn., Soc. for Am. Baseball Rsch., Ea. C.C. Social Scis. Assn. (sec. 1996—), Omicron Delta Epsilon, Phi Alpha Theta. Avocations: collecting autographs, reading, baseball. Home: 281 Lake Ave Bridgeport CT 06605-3538 Office: CUNY Bronx CC Dept Social Scis University Ave & W 181st St Bronx NY 10453-3102 E-mail: proflbattista@hotmail.com.

BATTLE, LUCY TROXELL (MRS. J. A. BATTLE), retired middle school administrator; b. Bridgeport, Ala., June 28, 1916; d. John Price and Emily Florence (Williams) Troxell; m. Jean Allen Battle, Aug. 25, 1940; 1 child, Helen Carol. Student. U. Ala., Montevallo, 1934-35; BS, Fla. So. Coll., 1951; postgrad., U/ Fla., 1954, Fla. State U., 1963, Oxford (Eng.) U., 1979, 80, 81; MA, U. South Fla., 1970. Asst. postmaster, Bridgeport, 1936-40; dir. pers. office Sebring (Fla.) AFB, 1942-44; tchr. Cleveland Court Sch., Lakeland, Fla.; also Forest Hill Sch., Carrollwood Sch., Tampa, Fla., 1949-64; dean girls Greco Jr. H.S., Tampa, 1964-68. Author: (with J.A. Battle) The New Idea in Education, 1968. Bd. dirs. Tampa Oral Sch. for Deaf. Recipient Outstanding Svc. award Fla. So. Coll. Woman's Club, 1942. Mem. NEA, Am. Childhood Edn. Internat., AAUW, Carrollwood Village Golf and Tennis Club, Delta Kappa Gamma, Kappa Delta Pi, Phi Mu. Methodist. Home and Office: 11011 Carrollwood Dr Tampa FL 33618-3905

BATTLE, ROMONA ANITA, educational administrator, consultant; b. N.Y.C., Dec. 31, 1950; d. Conley Napoleon and Annie Laurie (Simmons) B.; 1 child, Dinah Cianci Washington. BA in History and Secondary Edn., Morris Brown Coll., 1973; MEd in Elem. Edn., Ala. State U., 1976, cert. edn. specialist in elem. edn., 1985. Cert. in adminstrn. and supervision, Ga. History tchr. Waycross (Ga.) H.S., 1974-75; 4th grade tchr. Crawford St. Elem. Sch., Waycross, 1976-80, 5th grade tchr., 1981-84; k-5 lead tchr. McDonald St. Elem. Sch., Waycross, 1984-88; 7th grade lang. arts tchr. Charles T. Walker Magnet Sch., Augusta, Ga., 1989; asst. prin. Willis Foreman Elem. Sch., Augusta, 1989-92; lead tchr., counselor Mcdonald Street Elem. Sch., Waycross, 1992-93; child serve coord., cons. GLR5/Okefenokee RESA, Waycross, 1993—. Participant Gov.'s Sch. Leadership Inst., Ga. Edn. Leadership Acad., Atlanta, 1993-94. Developer instnl. game, 1981. Mem. Family & Children Svcs. Adoption Adv. Bd., Waycross, 1987. Mem. Phi Delta Kappa, Inc. (Delta Zeta chpt., chair Teach-A-Rama 1984-86, chair human rights and edn. com. 1988-89, chair asst.-youth guidance program 1986-87, Achievement in Edn. award 1983-84, 85-86, 88-89, Nat. Citation 1984-85). Avocations: reading, arts and crafts, decorating. Home: 1204 Riverside Ave Waycross GA 31501-6349

BATTLE, TURNER CHARLES, III, art educator, educational association administrator; b. Oberlin, Ohio; s. Turner and Annie (McClellan) B.; m. Carmen Helena Gonzalez Castellanos; children: Anne E. McAndrew, Turner C. IV, Conchita Yvonne, Carmen Rosario. Student, Andrews U.; BA, Oakwood Coll.; postgrad., Wagner Inst. Sci., Cheyney State Coll., Temple U., Columbia U., NYU; MFA, Temple U.; HHD, Wiley Coll. Instr. art Oakwood Coll., Huntsville, Ala.; auditor, acct. Navy Regional Acct. Office; instr. art Phila.; dir. Art League Sch. Gifted Children, Phila.; asst. prof. art Elmira Coll., NY; assoc. prof. art Moore Coll. Art, Phila.; vis. assoc. prof. NYU, NY; tchg. fellow. Vis. assoc. prof., dir. program Westminster Choir Coll.; art cons., lectr. pvt. and pub. orgns.; edn. cons. cmty. planners group U.S. Office Edn.; cons. E. Africa, Mid. E. Exhibited in group shows ea. U.S., including Bucknell U., Phila. Art Alliance, Newport (R.I.) Art Assn., Phila. Mus. Art, Susquehanna U., Atlantic City Boardwalk Show, Greenwich Village, N.Y.C., numerous others; represented in pvt. collections throughout U.S., India, Eng., Africa, Japan. Exec. dir. Higher Edn. Coalition Southeastern Pa.; dir. Open Door Program, LaSalle U.; asst. exec. dir., sec. corp. United Negro Coll. Fund, N.Y.C., pres. ednl. devel. svc., 1994—. Mem. Am. Assn. Higher Edn., Tyler Sch. Temple U. Alumni Assn. (pres. 1965-66), Am. Mus. Natural History, Smithsonian Inst., Sierra Club, Phi Delta Kappa. Home: 1519 W Turner St Allentown PA 18102-3634 also: 175 Adams St Apt 7G Brooklyn NY 11201-1815 E-mail: turnercbattle3@cs.com.

BATTLE, WILLA LEE GRANT, clergywoman, educational administrator; b. Webb, Miss., Sept. 30, 1924; d. James Carlton and Aslean (Young) Grant; m. Walter Leroy Battle, July 4, 1941. Diploma, Northwestern Coll., Mpls., 1956; B.A. cum laude, U. Minn., 1975, M.A., 1979; Ph.D. summa cum laude, Trinity Sem., 1982. Ordained to ministry, 1959. Founder, pastor Grace Temple Del. Ctr., Mpls., 1958— ; founder, pres., Willa Grant Battle Ctr., Mpls., 1980— ; founder House of Refuge Mission, Haiti, W.I., 1957— ; adminstr., dir. Kiddie Haven Pre-Sch., Mpls., 1982— . Mem. Interdenominational Ministerial Alliance (sec. 1986—), Mpls. Ministerial Assn., AAUW, AAUP, U. Minn. Alumni Assn. (life), NAACP, Nat. Council Negro Women, Christian Educators, Nat. Assn. Female Execs. Home: 620 E 42nd St Minneapolis MN 55409-1634 Office: Willa Grant Battle Ctr 1816 4th Ave S Minneapolis MN 55404-1844

BATTLES, ROXY EDITH, novelist, consultant, educator; b. Spokane, Wash., Mar. 29, 1921; d. Rosco Jirah and Lucile Zilpha (Jacques) Baker; m. Willis Ralph Dawe Battles, May 2, 1941 (dec. 2000); children: Margaret Battles Holmes, Ralph, Lara. AA, Bakersfield (Calif.) Coll., 1940; BA, Calif. State U., Long Beach, 1959; MA, Pepperdine U., 1976. Cert. tchr. English, adult basic edn. and elem. edn., Calif. Free-lance writer 50 nat. and regional mags., 1940—; tchr. elem. Torrance (Calif.) Unified Schs., 1959-85; tchr. adult edn. Pepperdine U., Torrance, 1969-79, 88-89; free-lance children's author, 1966—; mystery novelist Pinnacle Publs., N.Y.C., 1980; with Tex. A&M U., 1988. Instr. Mary Mount Coll., Harbor Coll., 1995; author-in-residence Young Authors Festival, Am. Sch. Madrid, 1991; lectr. in field. Author: Over the Rickety Fence, 1967, The Terrible Trick or Treat, 1970, 501 Balloons Sail East, 1971, The Terrible Terrier, 1972, One to Teeter-Totter, 1973, 2d edit., 1975, Eddie Couldn't Find the Elephants, 1974, reprints, 1982, 84, 88, What Does the Rooster Say, Yoshio?, 1978, reprinted in Swedish, German, French, 1980, The Secret of Castle Drai, 1980, The Witch in Room 6, 1987, 3d edit., 1989 (nominee Garden State, Nene, and Hoosier awards), The Chemistry of Whispering Caves, 1988, rev. edit., 1997, Computer Encryptions in Whispering Caves, 1997; playwright: Roxy, 1995, The Lavender Castle, 1996, mus. version, 1997, Sacred Submarine, 2000, Embarking on Rebellion, 2001. Active So. Calif. Coun. on Lit. for Children and Young People, 1973-80, 87—. Recipient Commendation UN, 1979; Hoosier award nominee, 1990; Garden State award nominee, 1990, Nene award nominee, 1992, 93. Mem. S.W. Manuscripters (founder), Surfwriters. Home: 560 S Helberta Ave Redondo Beach CA 90277-4353 E-mail: groxy@aol.com.

BAU, HAIM HENRICH, mechanical engineering educator; b. Cracow, Poland, Jan. 2, 1947; m. Sheryl L. Jones, Jan. 2, 1982; children: Benjamin, Natalie. BS, Technion, Israel Inst. Tech., Israel, 1969, MS, 1972; PhD, Cornell U., 1980. Staff R&D IDF, Israel, 1970-77; prof. U. Pa., Phila., 1980—. Cons. Panametrics, Waltham, Mass., 1985-95, Hewlett Packard, Wilmington, Del., 1991-95, Scitefair Internat., Phila., 1996-97. Editor books and procs.; contbr. over 130 articles to profl. jours. and conf. procs.; patentee in field. Recipient Presdl. Young Investigator award, Ralph Teetor award Soc. Automotive Engrs., 1985. Fellow ASME (Best Paper award 1982); Am. Phys. Soc. Office: Univ Pa Dept Mech Engring Philadelphia PA 19104-6315

BAUDOIN, ANTONIUS B. A. M. plant pathologist, educator; b. Vught, The Netherlands; MSc in Plant Protection, Agrl. U., Wageningen; PhD in Plant Pathology, U. Calif., Riverside, 1980. With Statewide Air Pollution Rsch. Ctr. U. Calif., Riverside; with dept. plant pathology, physiology and weed sci. Va. Polytechnic Inst. and State U., Blacksburg, 1981—, mem. teaching com., 1981—, chair teaching com., 1985-91, assoc. prof. Recipient Excellence in Teaching award APS Coun., 1994. Office: Va Polytech Inst & State U dept Plant Path Physiol Weed Sci 417 Price Hall Blacksburg VA 24061-0331 Office Fax: 540-231-7477. E-mail: abaudoin@vt.edu.*

BAUER, A(UGUST) ROBERT, JR., surgeon, medical educator; b. Dec. 23, 1928; s. A(ugust) Robert and Jessie Martha-Maynard (Monie) Bauer; m. Charmaine Louise Studer, June 28, 1957; children: Robert, John, William, Anne, Charles, James. BS, U. Mich., 1949, MS, 1950, MD, 1954; M in Med. Sci.-Surgery, Ohio State U., 1960. Diplomate Am. Bd. Surgery. Intern Walter Reed Army Med. Ctr., 1954—55; resident in surgery Univ. Hosp., Ohio State U., Columbus, also instr., 1957—61; pvt. practice medicine, specializing in surgery Mt. Pleasant, Mich., 1962—74; chief surgery Ctrl. Mich. Cmty. Hosp., Mt. Pleasant, 1964—65, vice chief of staff, 1967, chief of staff, 1968; clin. faculty Mich. State Med. Sch., East Lansing, 1974; mem. staff St. Mark's Hosp., Salt Lake City, 1974—91; pvt. practice surgery Salt Lake City, 1974—91. Clin. instr. surgery U. Utah, 1975—91; rschr. surg. immunology. Contbr. articles to profl. publs. Trustee Rowland Hall, St. Mark's Sch., Salt Lake City, 1978—84; mem. Utah Health Planning Coun., 1979—81. With M.C. U.S. Army, 1954—57. Fellow: ACS, Southwestern Surg. Congress; mem.: AAAS (affiliate), AMA, Pan Am. Med. Assn. (affiliate), Salt Lake Surg. Soc., Utah Soc. Certified Surgeons, Utah Med. Assn. (various coms.), Salt Lake County Med. Soc., Zollinger Club, Phi Rho Sigma, Sigma Phi Epsilon. Episcopalian. Office: PO Box 17533 Salt Lake City UT 84117-0533 Address: 1366 Murray Holladay Rd Salt Lake City UT 84117-5050

BAUER, LAURIE KOENIG, educational administrator; b. Mohall, N.D., Feb. 5, 1953; d. Raymond Doyle and Patricia JoAnn (Crank) Koenig; married Cary M. Bauer, May 17, 1975; children: J.D., Matthew. BS, Tex. A&M U., 1975; MS, U. So. Miss., 1989; EdD, U. Ala., 1993. Cert. tchr., Miss., Tex. Tchr earth sci. Fairway Jr. High Sch., Killeen, Tex., 1975-78; tchr. chemistry and earth scis. C.E. Ellison High Sch., Killeen, 1978-70; sales rep., pharmaceuticals Procter & Gamble, Cin., 1980-82; tchr. chemistry and physics Crosby (Tex.) High Sch., 1982-84; tchr., head dept. physics and chemistry Stroman High Sch., Victoria, Tex., 1984-88; tchr. chemistry and biology Oak Grove High Sch., Hattiesburg, Miss., 1988-90; tchr., head dept. chemistry and physics Brookwood High Sch., Tuscaloosa, Ala., 1990-92; asst. prin. Schulenberg (Tex.) Ind. Sch. Dist., 1992-93, prin. high sch., 1993—; with Royal Ind. Sch. Dist., Brookshire, Tex. Mem. adv. coun. Internat. Sci. and Engring. Fair, 1989-92, sec. adv. bd., 1990-91, mem. computer adv. bd.; mem., sec. ednl. adv. bd. U.Ala., 1990-92; presenter in field. Contbr. articles to profl. jours. Recipient Presdl. award Excellence in Sci. Teaching, Tex., 1988, Miss., 1990, grants in field; named to Ala. Tchr. Hall of Fame, Tchr. of Yr. Mem. ASCD, AAAS, NEA, Miss. Educators Assn. (pres. elect 1990), Nat. Assn. Secondary Sch. Prins., Tex. Assn. Secondary Sch. Prins., Miss. Acad. Sci., Nat. Sci. Tchrs. Assn., Am. Assn. Physics Tchrs., Am. Bus. Women's Assn., Lions Club, Rotary Club. Avocations: stained glass, painting, sewing, crafts, reading. Home: 615 Westview Terrace Cir Sealy TX 77474-3116 Office: Royal Ind Sch Dist 2520 Durkin Rd Brookshire TX 77423-9418 E-mail: ikb@fbtc.net.

BAUER-SANDERS, KATHERINE ANN, primary school educator; b. Yankton, S.D., Mar. 6, 1953; d. James M. and Jean E. (Kennedy) Bauer; m. Steven L. Sanders, July 10, 1971; children: David L., William J., James B. BS in Elem. Edn., U. S.D., 1990, MA, 1996. Cert. K-12 tchr. Houseparent St. Anthony's Boys Home, Sioux City, Iowa, 1985-89; kindergarten tchr. Winnebago (Nebr.) Pub. Sch., 1991—; substitute tchr. Sioux City (Iowa) Pub. Schs., 1991; presch. dir. Rhymes and Rainbows Presch., North Sioux City, S.D.; Title VII project dir. Little Priest Tribal Coll., Winnebago, 1998—99; tchr. St. Augustine Mission Sch., Winnebago, Nebr., 1999—. Adj. ECE faculty Little Priest Tribal Coll., Winnebago, 1996—; soccer coach Sioux City YMCA; softball coach Siouxland Youth Athletics, coach, bd. dirs., t-ball dir.; t-ball coach Youth Devel. Ctr., Winnebago, Nebr.; participant Jr. Class Learning, Auckland, New Zealand, 1995. Author: NEA Pub., 2000. Puppeteer, Kids on the Block, Jr. League, Sioux City, 1988-92; camp dir., troop leader Boy Scouts Am., Sioux City, 1976-80; steering com. McCook Lake United Meth. Ch. Ringley Arts and Sci. scholar, U. S.D., 1984-85. Mem. NEA, Nebr. Indian Edn. Assn., Internat. Reading Coun., Nat. Assn. for the Edn. of Young Children. United Methodist. Avocations: coaching, writing, puppeteering, music. Home: PO Box 320 152 Suncoast Dr North Sioux City SD 57049-4016 Office: St Augustine Mission Sch PO Box GG #1 Mission Rd Winnebago NE 68071

BAUGH, CHARLES MILTON, biochemistry educator, college dean; b. Fayetteville, N.C., June 20, 1931; s. John Yewell and Dorothy Ann (Shaw) B.; m. Ebby O. Jonsdottir, Oct. 24, 1953; children: Dorothy Baugh Ledbetter, Barbara Baugh Baumer, Charis Baugh Spyridon, Lisa Baugh Eckert. BS in Biochemistry, U. Chgo., 1958; PhD in Biochemistry, Tulane U., 1962. Instr. Tulane U., New Orleans, 1963-64, asst. prof. biochemistry, 1964-65; asst. prof. medicine and pharmacology Washington U., St. Louis, 1965-66; assoc. prof. medicine and biochemistry U. Ala., Birmingham, 1966-70, prof. pediatrics, medicine and biochemistry, 1970-73; prof. biochemistry U. South Ala., Mobile, 1973—, chmn. dept., 1973-81, assoc. dean basic sci., 1976-87, dean Coll. Medicine to dean and v.p. med. affairs, 1987-92, 99—. Extensive rsch. cons. Australian Nat. Health and Med. Rsch. Coun., 1975—, Med. Rsch. Coun. Can., 1976—; pres. South Ala. Med. Sci. Found., Mobile, 1982-92. Contbr. numerous articles, book chpts. to profl. publs. With USN, 1951-55. Predoctoral fellow NIH, Walter Libby Rsch. fellow Am. Heart Assn., La. chpt.; scholastic scholar U. Chgo.; recipient numerous grants NIH, Am. Cancer Soc., others. Fellow Royal Soc. Medicine (Eng.); mem. Soc. Exptl. Biology and Medicine, Am. Inst. Nutrition, Am. Soc. Biochemistry and Molecular Biology, Ala. Acad. Sci. (pres. 1982), So. Med. Assn. (hon.), Alpha Omega Alpha (hon.). Home and Office: 105 Deer Ct Daphne AL 36526-4012

BAUGH, IVAN WESLEY, retired educator, computer consultant; b. Louisville, Ky., Dec. 8, 1933; s. Paul Franklin and Anne Elizabeth (Gagel) B.; m. Jean Greer, Aug. 1, 1954; children: Grace Lenelle Baugh-Bennett, David Wayne. BA, Miss. Coll., 1954; MSM, So. Bapt. Theol. Sem., Louisville, 1958; post-grad. study, U. Tex., 1963-69; Rank I, U. Louisville, 1974; EdS in Computer Sci., Spalding U., 1988. Minister of music and religious edn. Southside Estates Bapt. Ch., Jacksonville, Fla., 1954-56, Winter Park Bapt. Ch., Wilmington, N.C., 1958-59, Poplar Springs Bapt. Ch., Meridian, Miss., 1959-61; assoc. prof. Howard Payne U., Brownwood, Tex., 1961-67; tchg. assoc. U. Tex., Austin, 1967-69; asst. prof. Delta State U., Cleveland, Miss., 1969-71; adjunct prof. Bellarmine U., Louisville, 1989—2002; music and computer resource tchr. Jefferson County Pub. Schs., Louisville, 1971—96. Choral clinician schs., regions, chs., Fla., Miss., Tex., Ky., 1958-86; adjudicator choral festivals, Schs. and Chs., Miss., Tex., Ky., 1958-86; soloist Greenville (Miss.) Symphony Orch., 1970; ednl. tech. cons., Ky. State Dept. Edn., Internat. Cons., Barbados, Jamaica and state schs., 1988-2002; participant Vision Tech. Enriched Schs. of Tomorrow, 1990, Nat. Info. Infrastructure Edn. Forum, U.S. Dept. Energy, 1993; webmaster MC-ctrl. region, Nat. Model Railroad Assn., 2001-. Contbr. articles to profl. jours; presenter at numerous ednl. confs. and convs., 1982—; editor The Pie Card, Divsn. 8, Nat. Model R.R. Assn., Louisville, 1990-97, 2002—; co-author: Making Math Magic Happen Using the Best of Learning and Leading with Teachnology, 2003. Mem. NEA, Ky. Edn. Assn., Music Educators Nat. Conf., Ky. Music Educators Assn. (middle sch. chmn. 1982-84), Am. Choral Dirs. Assn., Internat. Soc. for Tech. in Edn., Phi Mu Alpha. Avocations: model railroading, genealogy, reading, bridge. Home: 9910 Shelbyville Rd Louisville KY 40223-2908

BAUGHMAN, GEORGE WASHINGTON, III, retired university official, financial consultant; b. Pitts., July 7, 1937; s. George W. and Cecile M. (Lytel) B.; m. Sandra Anne Johnson, June 21, 1987; 1 child, Lynn. BS in Psychology, Ohio State U., 1959, MBA, 1961, postgrad., 1961-63. Pres. Advanced Rsch. Assocs., Worthington, Ohio, 1960—; asst. instr. fin. Ohio State U., Columbus, 1961-63, rsch. assoc., office of contr., 1964-66, dir. data processing, 1966-68, 70-72, dir. adminstrv. rsch., 1966-72, assoc. to acad. v.p., 1968-70, exec. dir. univ. budget, 1970-72, dir. spl. projects, office of pres., 1972-88, ret., 1988. Chmn. bd. Hosp. Audiences Inc., 1974-80; spl. advisor Ohio Super Computer Ctr., 1989—; bd. dirs. Consortium for Higher Software Support Inc., La Marquise Inc., Halliday Techs. Inc., Sleep Medicine Internat. Inc., Sleep Medicine Rsch. Found., Duramed. Pharm. Inc., Forerunner Corp., Implementation Assocs. Inc., Greek Island Ltd., Take a Break Inc., Parkfield Insulation Svcs. Inc., CIRA Techs., Inc. Author: (with D. H. Baker) Writing to People, 1963; (with R.W. Brady) University Program Budgeting, 1968, Administrative Data Processing, 1975; contbr. articles to profl. publs. Founding bd. dirs. Coll. and U. Machine Records Conf., 1971-73; bd. dirs. Uniplan Environ. Groups Inc., 1970-73, chmn., 1971-73, Eagle Exhibit Systms Inc., 1993—; chmn. Franklin County (Ohio) Rep. Demographics and Voter Analysis Com., 1975-80; active Ohio State Dental Bd., 1980-85, Gov.'s Export Coun., 1982-83, Gov.'s Tech. Task Force, 1982-83. Grantee Am. Coun. on Edn., 1976-77, Nat. Assn. Coll. and Univ. Bus. Officers, 1977-79, NSF, 1980-86; Reisman fellow, 1962. Mem. AAAS, Press Club Ohio, Coll. and Univ. Sys. Exch., World Future Soc., Ohio State Univ. Alumni Assn., Ohio State Univ. Faculty Club, Ohio State U. President's Club, Phi Alpha Kappa, Delta Tau Delta. Republican. Presbyterian. Home and Office: 833 Lake Shore Dr Columbus OH 43235-1289

BAUGHMAN, PAMELA ANN, secondary school counselor; b. Topeka, Nov. 6, 1948; d. Virgil D. and Harriett Ellen Crow; m. John Marshall Baughman, June 14, 1970; children: John Austin Marshall, James Michael Andrew, Jed Alan Matthew. BA, Kans. U., 1970, BS in Edn., 1972, MEd, 1985. Cert. tchr., Kans. Sec. Regents Press Kans., Lawrence, 1978-81; tchr. Unified Sch. Dist. 232, DeSoto, Kans., 1981-2000. Staff devel. coun. Unified Sch. Dist. 232, DeSoto, 1990-96; steering com. DeSoto Days 5K Run; coach Math Counts program DeSoto Jr. H.S., 1990-93. Past pres., past treas. Douglas County Assn. Retarded Citizens, Lawrence, 1970s; bd. dirs. Trinity Cmty. Svcs., Lawrence, 1970s-88; badge counselor, mem. troop com. Boy Scouts Am., Lawrence, 1986-92. Mem. Nat. Coun. Tchrs. of English, Kans. Assn. Tchrs. of English, River Valley English Alliance, Alpha Delta Kappa. Office: 8800 W 85th St Shawnee Mission KS 66201-0509 E-mail: pamelabaughman@smsd.org.

BAUGHMAN, PAUL EARL, agriculture educator; b. Lima, Ohio, Mar. 11, 1947; s. Earl F. and Gertrude (Knierman) B.; m. Kristine Decker, July 28, 1979; children: David, Brittany, Brenna. Student, Ft. Belvor Coll., 1968. Cert. mechanic, truck tech. Polisher Excello Corp., Lima, Ohio, 1968; warehouse supr. Wilson Sporting Goods, Ada, Ohio, 1968-72; shop supr. McDaniel Equipment, Lima, 1972-74; mgr. Vent Implement, Upper Sandusky, Ohio, 1974; mechanic Bowen Implement Co., Findlay, Ohio, 1974-77, Village of Ada, 1977; small engine tchr. Lawrence County JVS, Get A Way, Ohio, 1977-78; agrl. indsl. equipment tchr. Columbus N.W. Career Ctr., Dublin, Ohio, 1978—. Mem. adv. bd. small engines class, Columbus, Ohio, 1978-83; mem. adv. com. Diesel Truck, Columbus, 1989—; chmn. FFA State Tractor Troubleshooting, Columbus, 1986—; 8th grade girls basketball coach Highland Jr. High Sch., Sparta, Ohio, 1989—. Author: Job Stations, 1987. Asst. scoutmaster Boy Scouts Am., Ada, 1968-77; RA advisor So. Bapt. Ch., Mt. Gilead, Ohio, 1987-89; dir. Breakaway Teen Ctr., 1994—. With U.S. Army, 1966-68, Vietnam. Mem. NEA, Nat. Vocat. Assn., Ohio Vocat. Agrl. Edn. Assn. (county chair 1990—, agr. mechanics chmn. 1991), Ohio Edn. Assn. Avocations: steam engines, fishing, camping, woodworking, railroading. Office: NW Career Ctr 2960 Cranston Dr Dublin OH 43017-1710

BAUKNECHT, BARBARA BELLE, retired pre-school educator; b. Gleason, Wis, Apr. 21, 1933; d. William John and Jessie Marie (Fox) Beyer; m. Ross Eugene Bauknecht, Aug. 11, 1956; children: JoDee Ann Moran, Shelley Marie Courter, Wanda Jean Pace, Todd Randall. Tchr. cert., Lincoln County Normal, Merrill, Wis., 1953; BS, U. Wis., Stevens Point, 1964, M, 1974. Lic. tchr. grades 1-8, reading tchr. K-12, reading specialist K-12. Tchr. grades 5 and 6, Crandon, Wis., 1953-57; tchr. grades 7 and 8 Elcho, Wis., 1957-59; pub. libr. Three Lakes, Wis., 1963-66; tchr. Title 1, reading tchr., 1966-74; tchr., reading specialist, 1974—95; retired, 1995; tchr. Caregiver classes, 2002—. Tchr., founder Story Hour - Presch. Program, Three Lakes and Sugar Camp, Wis., 1964—; reading coord. Three Lakes Sch. Dist., Three Lakes and Sugar Camp, 1978—95; mem., chmn. read com. Three Lakes Dist., 1978—. Chmn. bd. Ed U. Demmer Meml. Libr., Three Lakes, 1989—96; local organizaer, leader Campfire Girls, 1970—75; leadership coun. Alzheimers, 2000—; mem. com. Memory Walk com., 2001—03, Motorcycle Rally, 2002—03, Golf Tournament, 2002, Support Group Facilitator, 2002—03; co-founder Ecumenical Vacation Bible Sch., 1978—; Sunday sch. supt. Union Congl. Ch., Three Lakes, 1977—95, moderator, 1988—93, 2001—. Recipient Ind. Celebrate Lit. award Headwaters Reading Coun., Rhinelander, Wis., 1990; Kohl Scholarship/Fellowship CESA Dist. Winner, 1992. Mem.: Delta Kappa Gamma (treas., pres. Alpha Eta chpt). Mem. Ch. of Christ. Avocations: collecting bells, collecting hallmark ornaments, crocheting, reading, grandchildren. Home: 6653 Schoenfeldt Rd Three Lakes WI 54562-9703 Office: Sch Dist Three Lakes PO Box 280 Three Lakes WI 54562-0280

BAULE, STEVEN MICHAEL, principal; b. Southfield, Mich., Sept. 2, 1966; s. Charles L. and Betty Ann (Lange) B.; m. Kathy Ann Schilling, June 13, 1992; children: Sydney Elizabeth, Samuel Michael. BA, Loras Coll., Dubuque, Iowa, 1988; MALS, U. Iowa, 1991; EdD, No. Ill. U., 1997; PhD, Loyola U., 2002. Cert. tchr. Ill., Iowa, adminstr. Ill. Tchr. Aquin Sch., Cascade, Iowa, 1989-90; libr. media specialist Haines Mid. Sch., St. Charles, Ill., 1991-94; coord. info. svcs. Glenbrook South H.S., Glenview, Ill., 1994-97; dir. info. tech. New Trier H.S. Dist., Winnetka, Ill., 1997-2001, asst. supt., 2001—03; prin. Zion (Ill.) Benton HS Dist., 2003—. Editl. cons. Linworth Pub., Worthington, Ohio, 1995—; affiliate prof. No. Ill. U., DeKalb, 1994—. Author: Technology Planning, 1997, Facilities Planning for School Libraries and Technology Centers, 1999, Technology Planning for Effective Teaching and Learning, 2001, Case Studies in Educational Technology Management, 2003; contbr. articles to profl. jours.; author: British Army Officers Who Served in the American Revolution 1775-1783, 2003. Firefighter, St. Charles Fire Dept., 1992-96. Recipient Iowa Gov.'s Cup for Outstanding ROTC Grad., Gov. of Iowa, 1987; named Sch. Libr. of Yr., North Suburban Libr. Sys., Wheeling, Ill., 1997. Mem. Am. Assn. Sch. Adminstrs., Ill. Sch. Libr. Media Assn. (bd. dirs. 1997-2000, Highsmith Innovation award 1996), Am. Assn. Sch. Librs. (awards com. 1999-2000, chair 2000-01, conf. planning com. 2000-2001), Ill. Assn. Ednl. and Comms. Tech., Ill. Libr. Assn. (mem. technology task force 1997). Home: 3918 Carousel Dr Northbrook IL 60062-7535 Office: Zion-Benton Twp HS 21st & Kenosha Rd Zion IL 60099 E-mail: baules@zbths.org.

BAUM, WILLIAM ALVIN, astronomer, educator; b. Toledo, Jan. 18, 1924; s. Earle Fayette and Mable (Teachout) B.; m. Ester Bru, June 27, 1961. BA summa cum laude, U. Rochester, 1943; PhD magna cum laude, Calif. Inst. Tech., 1950. Physicist U.S. Naval Research Lab., Washington, 1946-49; astronomer Mt. Wilson and Palomar observatories, Pasadena, Calif., 1950-65; dir. Planetary Research Center, Lowell Obs., Flagstaff, Ariz., 1965-90; with astronomy dept. U. Wash., Seattle, 1990—. Adj. prof. astronomy Ohio State U., 1969-91; adj. prof. physics No. Ariz. U., 1973-91; rsch. prof. astronomy U. Wash., Seattle, 1990-97, prof. emeritus, 1997—; cons. physics, astronomy, optics; cons. U.S. Army Research Office, Durham, N.C., 1967-74; vis. prof. Am. Astronomy Soc., 1961-98; adv. com. Nat. Acad. Sci., 19 58-67; mem. optical instrumentation panel adv. Air Force, 1967-76; coms. and panels NSF and NASA Office Space Scis., 1967-91; mem. NASA Viking Orbiter Imaging Team, 1970-79, Hubble Space Telescope Camera Team, 1977-96. Contbr. articles to tech. publs. Served to lt., jr. grade USNR, 1943-46. Guggenheim fellow, 1960-61; Asteroid 4174 named Billbaum, 1990. Mem. Am. Astron. Soc. (chmn. div. planetary scis. 1976-77), Royal Astron. Soc., Astron. Soc. Pacific, Internat. Astron. Union, Phi Beta Kappa, Sigma Xi, Theta Delta Chi. Achievements include asteroid 4175 named "Billbaum" in his honor, 1990. Home: 2124 NE Park Rd Seattle WA 98105-2422 Office: U Wash Dept Astronomy Seattle WA 98195-0001 E-mail: baum@astro.washington.edu.

BAUMAN, SANDRA SPIEGEL, nurse practitioner, mental health counselor; b. N.Y.C., June 30, 1949; d. Siegmund and Ruth (Josias) S.; m. H. Lee Bauman, Nov. 3, 1978 (div.); 1 child, Brandon Spiegel; m. P. McGrath, 1991. Student, Boston U., 1967-70; BSN, Adelphi U., 1971, postgrad., 1973-74; MS in Cmty. Counseling, Barry Coll., 1981; postgrad., Fla. Atlantic U./Fla. Internat, 1982—, Gestalt Inst., Miami, 1982—; PhD, Kennedy-Western U., 2000. Staff nurse educator obstetrics Albert Einstein Hosp., N.Y.C., 1971-72, head nurse newborn nurseries, 1973-74; asst. instr. maternity nursing St. Johns Riverside Hosp., 1972-73; head nurse obstetrics and nurseries, high risk nursery Mt. Sinai Hosp., Miami Beach, Fla., 1974-78; clin. nursing supr., divsn. pediatrics Jackson Meml. Hosp., Miami, 1978, coord. divsn. clin. edn., 1978-81; quality assurance coord. Maternal-Child Hosp. Ctr., 1979-81, perinatal coord., 1980-81, also core nursing mem. child protection team, 1979-81, asst. adminstr. ob-gyn., 1981-82; adminstr. Meadowbrook Med. Ctr., Inc., Danta, Fla., 1982—; pvt. practice psychotherapy, 1983—; asst. adminstr. nursing Miami Gen. Hosp., 1985, assoc. adminstr. pvt. care svcs., 1985—; contract nursing supr. Griswold Spl. Care, Miami, 2001—. Asst. prof. Sch. Nursing, Fla. Internat. U., North Miami, 1982-84; coord. child bearing and child rearing courses, 1982-84; mem. Fla. Bd. Nursing, 1979-85, vice chmn. 1981-82, chmn. 1982-85; CPR instr., 1978; dir. nursing HCA Grant Ctr. Hosp., Miami, 1986-89, asst. adminstr. Dr.'s Hosp., 1990-91, pvt. practice 19991—; cons. State Fla., 1992-95; interim dir. nursing Charter Hosp., Miami, 1995-96; surveyor Fla. Correctional Med. Authority, 1996; cons. State of Fla. Children's and Family Svcs., 2000; nursing patient care supr. Griswold Spl. Care, 2002—. Contbr. articles to RN mag., Fla. Nursing News, Fla. Nurses Assn. Newsletter and Nursing Mgmt. Mem. mental health disaster team ARC, 2001—, vol. disaster mental health team, 2000—. Mem. ANA (regional editor 1980—), Fla. Nurses Assn., Fla. Soc. Nurse Execs., Fla. Nursing Adminstn. Assn., Fla. Hosp. Assn., Fla. Nursing Adminstrn. Soc., Sigma Theta Tau, Victim Advocate Com., bd., 2001. Office: 7800 SW 57th Ave Ste 203 South Miami FL 33143-5523

BAUMANN, MATTHEW LOUIS, business education educator, elementary school educator; b. Phila., Apr. 2, 1968; s. John Louis and Emma Marie (Mellinger) B.; m. Kathy Louise Flurie, Dec. 3, 1993; children: Justin Zachariah, Jesse Ian. BSBA, West Chester U., 1990; MEd, Widener U., 1993. Cert. tchr. acct., data processing, mktg., elem. edn. Tng. rm. supervisor UPS, Tinicum, Pa., 1990-91; corrosion inspection advisor Sun Oil Refinery, Marcus Hook, Pa., 1990-91; freshman boys soccer coach Interboro Sch. Dist., Prospect Park, Pa., 1991; bus. edn. tchr., elem. edn. tchr. East Pennsboro Sch. Dist., Enola, Pa., 1992—, jr. varsity, asst. varsity boys soccer coach, 1992-93, jr. varsity, asst. varsity boys baseball coach, 1993. Mem. NEA, ASCD, Pa. State Edn. Assn., Ea. Pennsboro Area Edn. Assn. (bldg. rep., treas.). Avocations: church activities, outdoor sports, reading, music. Office: E Pennsboro High Sch 425 W Shady Ln Enola PA 17025-2242

BAUMANN, SARA MARGARET CULBRETH, retired elementary school educator; b. Camilla, Ga., Oct. 20, 1949; d. Max Ronald and Sara Emily (Rivers) Culbreth; m. Curtis Darrah Baumann; children: Ford Pearce, Brad Pearce. BS in Edn., U. Ga., 1971; MEd, Ga. State U., Atlanta, 1974. Tchr. 5th and 6th grades Carver Elem. Sch., Columbus, Ga., 1971-78; tchr. 5th grade Gould Elem. Sch., Savannah, Ga., 1979; tchr. 7th grade Edwards Mid. Sch., Conyers, Ga., 1981-91; tchr. Salem H.S., Conyers, 1991-93, Meml. Mid. Sch., Conyers, 1993-2001, Woodstock (Ga.) Mid. Sch., 2001—03; ret., 2003. Tchr. of gifted, 1999-2003. Recreation, all-star, premier and classic coach Rockdale Youth Soccer Assn., Conyers, 1984-94, dir., 1990; youth, H.S. and coll. soccer referee. Named Rockdale County Tchr. of the Yr. 1991, Edwards Middle Sch. Tchr. of the Yr. 1990, Math./Sci. Outstanding Tchr. in Ga., 1990, Female Referee of Yr., Ga. State Soccer Assn., 1998. Mem.: Ga. Ret. Educators Assn. Methodist. Avocations: tennis, photography, soccer, bridge. Home: 906 Audrey Dr Woodstock GA 30188-4209 Personal E-mail: scbaumann@hotmail.com.

BAUMERT, PAUL WILLARD, JR., physician, educator; b. Washington, Iowa, July 16, 1960; s. Paul Willard Sr. and Elsie Marie (Aldridge) B.; m. Julie Ann Bussell, Aug. 31, 1991; children: Paul Willard III, Brock Lawrence, Keiffer Jacob, Kylie Ann. BS in Gen. Sci., U. Iowa, 1983, MD, 1987. Diplomate in family practice and in sports medicine Am. Bd. Family Practice. Rsch. asst. dept. orthop. surgery U. Iowa, Iowa City, 1978-83, grad. rsch. asst. dept. preventive medicine, 1983-85, resident in family practice, 1987-90; faculty physician Baptist Med. Ctr., Kansas City, 1990-91; fellow in primary care sports medicine Hughston Sports Medicine, Columbus, Ga., 1991-92; staff physician Kaiser Permanente, Overland Park, Kans., 1992-98, College Park Family Care Ctr., P.A., Olathe, Kans., 1998-2000; physician U. Iowa Student Health Svc., Iowa City, 2000—. Clin. assoc. prof. family medicine U. Mo.-Kansas City Sch. Medicine, 1996-2000. Contbr. articles to profl. jours., chpts. to books, monographs. Vol. team physician Johnson County C.C., Overland Park, 1992-2000, Baker U., 1993-2000; vol. physician U.S. Olympic Com., Colorado Springs, 1997, U. Iowa, 2000— Fellow Am. Acad. Family Physicians; mem. Am. Med. Soc. Sports Medicine (charter mem.), Am. Coll. Sports Medicine, Nat. Athletic Trainers' Assn. (assoc.), Hughston Soc. Christian. Avocations: genealogy, choral music, community theatre. Office: U Iowa Student Health Svc 4189 Westlawn Bldg Iowa City IA 52242-1100 E-mail: paul-baumert@uiowa.edu.

BAUMGARDT, BILLY RAY, professional society administrator, agriculturist; b. Lafayette, Ind., Jan. 17, 1933; s. Raymond P. and Mildred L. (Cordray) Baumgardt; m. D. Elaine Blain, June 8, 1952; children: Pamela K. Baumgardt Farley, Teresa Jo Baumgardt Adolfsen, Donald Ray. BS in Agr., Purdue U., 1955, MS, 1956; PhD, Rutgers U., 1959. From asst. to assoc. prof. U. Wis., Madison, 1959-67; prof. animal nutrition Pa. State U., University Park, 1967-70, head dept. dairy and animal sci., 1970-79, assoc. dir. agrl. expt. sta., 1979-80; dir. agrl. research, assoc. dean Purdue U., West Lafayette, Ind., 1980-98; exec. v.p. Am. Registry Profl. Animal Scientists, Savoy, Ill., 1998—2003. Contbr. chapters to books, articles to profl. sci. jours. Recipient Wilkinson award, Pa. State U., 1979. Fellow: AAAS, Am. Dairy Sci. Assn. (pres. 1984—85, Nutrition Rsch. award 1966, award of Honor 1993, Disting. Svc. award 2003); mem.: Nat. Agrl. Biotech. Coun. (chair 1993—94), Am. Soc. Animal Sci., Am. Inst. Nutrition, Rotary, Sigma Xi. Home and Office: 2741 N Salisbury St West Lafayette IN 47906-1431

BAUMGARTNER, DONALD LAWRENCE, entomologist, educator; b. Chgo., June 4, 1954; s. Lawrence and Gloria Ann (Winkler) B.; m. Claudia Jeanne Zaloudek, Aug. 21, 1982; 1 child, Kenneth. BS, U. Ill., 1979, MS, 1984. Apiary rsch. asst. U. Ill., Chgo., 1977, 78, 81, teaching asst., 1979-84; mgr. Ill. Lyme Disease Project Coll. of Medicine, U. Ill., Rockford, 1990-91; mus. specialist Field Mus. Natural History, Chgo., 1978-80, adult edn. instr., 1981-85; field supr., rsch. coord. N.W. Mosquito Abatement Dist., Wheeling, Ill., 1985-90; life scientist U.S. EPA, Chgo., 1991—. Adj. faculty William Rainey Harper Coll., Palatine, Ill., 1987—; entomol. cons. Kane County Health Dept., Aurora, Ill., 1990. Contbr. articles to Jour. Med. Entomology, Jour. Am. Mosquito Control Assn., Gt. Lakes Entomologist, Proceed, Ill. Mosquito and Vector Control Assn. Newsletter; state editor: Vector Control Bull. North Cen. States. Grantee Biosystematic Rsch. Inst., 1981, U. Ill. Rsch. Bd., 1990, Ill. Vector Control, 1991-92. Mem. Entomol. Soc. Am., Am. Mosquito Control Assn., Soc. for Vector Ecologists, Mich. Entomol. Soc., Ill. Mosquito and Vector Control Assn. Democrat. Home: 120 S Walnut St Palatine IL 60067-6042 Office: US EPA DT-8J 77 W Jackson Blvd Chicago IL 60604-3511 Fax: 312-353-4788. E-mail: baumgartner.donald@epa.gov.

BAUMGARTNER, FREDERIC JOSEPH, history educator; b. Medford, Wis., Sept. 26, 1945; s. Michael and Theresa Mary (Stauner) B.; m. Lois Ann Hoffman, Jan 31, 1970; children: Eric Michael, Nathan Robert. BA, Mt. St. Paul Coll., 1967; MA, U. Wis., 1969, PhD, 1972. Asst. prof. history Ga. Coll., Milledgeville, 1972-76; assoc. prof. Va. Poly. Inst. and State U., 1976-85, prof., 1985—. Author: Radical Reactionaries, 1976, Change and Continuity, 1986, Henry II King of France, 1988 (Charles Smith prize 1989), From Spear to Flintlock, 1991, Louis XII, 1995, France in the Sixteenth Century, 1996, Longing for the End, 1999, Behind Locked Doors, 2003; contbr. articles to profl. jours. Mem. Am. Cath. Hist. Assn. Office: Va Poly Inst Blacksburg VA 24061-0117

BAUMGARTNER, INGEBORG, foreign language educator; b. Horna Stubna, Czechoslovakia, Jan. 29, 1936; came to U.S., 1949; m. Jörg Baumgartner, Nov. 25, 1967; 1 child, Nicholas. BA, U. Mich., 1958, PhD, 1970; MA, U. Wis., 1959. Prof. dept. fgn. langs. Albion (Mich.) Coll., 1966—2001, assoc. provost, 1982-85, prof. emeritus, 2001—. Editor: There You Are, 1982; contbr.articles to profl. jours. Home: 411 Darrow St Albion MI 49224-2226

BAUMGARTNER, MARY ANNE SGARLAT, academic administrator, entrepreneur; b. Boston, Apr. 5, 1958; d. Francis Abbott and Elizabeth Maria (Paragallo) Sgarlat; m. Michael von Arx Baumgartner, Nov. 18, 2000. Grad., Milton Acad.; student, Roedean Sch., Brighton, Eng.; BA, Bennington Coll., 1979. Adminstr. Harvard U., Cambridge, Mass., 1979-86; pub. rels. dir. Graham Gund Architects, Cambridge, 1986-89; mktg. and comms. mgr. Elkus/Manfredi Architects, Boston, 1989-90; comms. mgr. Turan Corp., Boston, 1990-92; mktg. dir. The Design Partnership of Cambridge, 1992-97; mng. dir. The Bounty Group, 1997—; mktg. mgr. Yolles Ptnrship. Ltd., 1998-99, Bishoff Solomon Comms., 1999-2000; adminstr. Kennedy Sch. Govt., Cambridge, 2000—. Mem.: LWV, Mus. Fine Arts, Harvard U. Art Museums, Focus Internat., Bennington Coll. Alumni Assn. (regional dir. 1993—97, exec. com. 1986—93). Avocations: politics, music, dancing, antiques, sailing. Office: Kennedy Sch Govt 79 JFK St Cambridge MA 02138

BAUMHART, RAYMOND CHARLES, Roman Catholic church administrator; b. Chgo., Dec. 22, 1923; s. Emil and Florence (Weidner) B. BS, Northwestern U., 1945; PhL, Loyola U., 1952, STL, 1958; MBA, Harvard U., 1953; DBA, Harvard, 1963; LLD (hon.), Ill. Coll., 1977; DHL (hon.), Scholl Coll. Podiatric Medicine, 1983, Rush U., Chgo., 1987, Northwestern U., 1993, Xavier U., Cin., 1994, Ill. Benedictine Coll., 1994. Joined Jesuit Order, 1946; ordained priest Roman Cath. Ch., 1957. Asst. prof. mgmt. Loyola U., Chgo., 1962-64, dean Sch. Bus. Adminstrn., 1964-66, exec. v.p., acting v.p. Med. Ctr., 1968-70, pres., 1970-93; cons. to Cardinal George, Cath. Archdiocese of Chgo., 2000—. Alfred Ring lectr. U. Fla., 1988; John and Mildred Wright lectr. Fairfield U., 1992; D. B. Reinhart lectr. Viterbo Coll., 2000; bd. dirs. Ceres Food Group, Inc. Author: An Honest Profit, 1968, (with Thomas Garrett) Cases in Business Ethics, 1968, (with Thomas McMahon) The Brewer-Wholesaler Relationship, 1969; corr. editor: America, 1965-70. Trustee St. Louis U., 1967-72, Boston Coll., 1968-71; bd. dirs. Coun. Better Bus. Burs., 1971-77, Cath. Health Alliance Met. Chgo., 1986-93; mem. U.S. Bishops and Pres.'s Com. on Higher Edn., 1980-84, Jobs for Met. Chgo., 1984-85, Chgo. Health Care Industry, 1990-94. Decorated cavalier Order of Merit, Italy, 1971, commendatore, 1994; recipient Rale medallion Boston Coll., 1976, Daniel Lord S.J. award Loyola Acad., Wilmette, Ill., 1992, Mary Potter Humanitarian award Little Company of Mary Hosp., Ill., 1993, Sword of Loyola Loyola U., Chgo., 1993, Theodore Hesburgh award Assn. Cath. Colls. and Univs., 1995; John W. Hill fellow Harvard U., 1961-62, Cambridge Ctr. for Social Studies Rsch. fellow, 1966-68. Mem. Comml. Club, Mid-Am. Club, Tavern Club. Roman Catholic. Home: 6525 N Sheridan Rd Chicago IL 60626-5344 E-mail: rbaumhart@archdiocese-chgo.org.

BAUMOL, WILLIAM JACK, economist, educator; b. N.Y.C., Feb. 26, 1922; s. Solomon and Lillian (Itzkowitz) B.; m. Hilda Missel, Dec. 27, 1941; children: Ellen Frances, Daniel Aaron. B Soc. Sci., CCNY, 1942; PhD, London U., 1949; LLD (hon.), Rider Coll., 1965; fellow (hon.), London Sch. Econs., 1970; fellow hon. doctorate (hon.), Stockholm Sch. Econs., Sweden, 1971, U. Basel, Switzerland, 1973; D (hon.), U. Limburg, The Netherlands, 1996, U. Belgrano, Buenos Aires, 1996, U. Lille, France, 1997; LHD (hon.), Knox Coll., 1973; PhD (hon.), Hebrew U., 1999; LHD (hon.), Princeton U., 1999; D (hon.), U. Paris, 2001. With USDA, 1942-43, 46; asst. lectr. London Sch. Econs., 1947-49; asst. prof. Princeton (N.J.) U., 1949-52, assoc. prof., 1952-54, prof., 1954-92, NYU, 1971—; joint appointment Princeton U. and NYU, 1971—; prof. emeritus Princeton U., 1992—, sr. rsch. economist, 1992—. Dir. C.V. Starr Ctr. for Applied Econs., NYU, 1984—; mem. Fishman-Davidson Ctr. for Study Svc. Sector, U. Pa., bd. dirs. Theatre Devel. Fund; cons. for govt. and industry. Author: Economic Dynamics: An Introduction, 1951, 3d edit., 1970, Welfare Economics and the Theory of the State, 1952, 2d edit., 1965, Business Behavior, Value and Growth, 1959, 2d edit., 1966, Economic Theory and Operations Analysis, 1960, 4th edit., 1976; author: (with L.V. Chandler) Economic Processes and Policies, 1954; author: (with Klaus Knorr) What Price Economic Growth?, 1961; author: The Stock Market and Economic Efficiency, 1965; author: (with W.G. Bowen) Performing Arts: The Economic Dilemma, 1966; author: (with S.M. Goldfeld) Precursors in Mathematical Economics, 1969; author: (with W.E. Oates) The Theory of Environmental Policy, 1975, 2d edit., 1988; author: Selected Economic Writings of William Jack Baumol, 1976; author: (with W.E. Oates and S.B. Blackman) Economics, Environmental Policy and the Quality of Life, 1979; author: (with A.S. Blinder) Economics: Principles and Policy, 1979, 6th edit., 1994; author: (with J.C. Panzar and R.D. Willig) Contestable Markets and the Theory of Industry Structure, 1982, rev. edit., 1987; author: (with H. Baumol) Inflation and the Performing Arts, 1984; author: (with K. McLennan) Productivity Growth and U.S. Competetiveness, 1985; author: Superfairness: Applications and Theory, 1986 (Best Book in Mgmt. and Econs. award Assn. Am. Pubs., 1986); author: (with Sue Anne Batey Blackman and Edward N. Wolff) Productivity and American Leadership: The Long View, 1989 (hon. mention Soc. Sci., Assn. Am. Pub., 1989); author: (with Stephen M. Goldfeld, Lilli A. Gordon, Michael F. Koehn) The Ecomomics of Mutual Fund Markets: Competition Versus Regulation, 1990; author: (with Sue Anne Batey Blackman) Perfect Markets and Easy Virtue: Business Ethics and the Invisible Hand, 1991; author: (with Gregory Sidak) Toward Competition in Local Telephony, 1994; author: Entrepreneurship, Management and the Structure of Payoffs, 1993; author: (with Richard R. Nelson and Edward N. Wolff) Convergence of Productivity: Cross-National Studies and Historical Evidence, 1994; author: (with J.G. Sidak) Transmission Pricing and Stranded Costs in the Electric Power Industry, 1995; author: (with Ralph E. Gomory) Global Trade and Conflicting National Interests, 2000; author: The Free-Market Innovation Machine: Analyzing the Growth Miracle of Capitalism, 2002; author: (with A.S. Blinder and E.N.Wolff) Downsizing in America: Reality, Causes and Consequences, 2003; author: (compendium of articles) Growth, Industrial Organization and Economic Generalities, 2003; editor: Public and Private Enterprise in a Mixed Economy, 1980; editor: (with W.G. Becker) Assessing Educational Practices: The Contribution of Economics, 1995; editor: (with J.G. Sidak) Transmission Pricing and Stranded Costs in the Electric Power Industry, 1995; editor: (with Ruth Towse) Baumol's Cost Disease: The Arts and Other Victims, 1997; editor: (with C.A. Wilson) Welfare Economics, Vol. I, II, III, 2001; periodic mem. bd. editors jours. Am. Econ. Rev., Jour. Econ. Lit., Jour. Econ. Perspectives, Mgmt. Sci., Kyklos; contbr. numerous articles to profl. jours. Past pres. Am. Friends of London Sch. Econs.; trustee Rider Coll., Lawrenceville, 1960-70, Joint Coun. Econ. Edn.; past chmn., mem. State of N.J. Econ. Policy Coun., 1967-75. Recipient Townsend Harris medal CCNY, 1975, John Commons award Omicron Delta Epsilon, 1975, F.E. Seidman Disting. award in Polit. Economy, 1987, Best Book in Econs. and Bus. award Assn. Am. Pubs., 1986, First Sr. scholar in Arts & Scis. award NYU, 1992; Guggenheim fellow, 1957-58; Ford faculty fellow, 1965-66; named Joseph Douglas Green '95 Prof. Econs. Princeton U., 1988. Fellow Econometric Soc., Am. Econ. Assn. (disting. fellow, mem. exec. com., v.p. 1966-67, pres. 1981); mem. Nat. Acad. Scis., AAUP (v.p., chmn. com. on econ. status of the profession 1968-70, mem. com. on hon. mems.), Am. Acad. Arts and Scis., Am. Philos. Soc., Eastern Econ. Assn. (pres. 1978-79), Assn. Environ. and Resource Economists (pres. 1979), Atlantic Econ. Soc. (pres. 1986), Econ. Assn. P.R. (disting. mem.) Home: PO Box 3514 Princeton NJ 08543-3514 Office: Princeton U Dept Econs 104 Fisher Pl Princeton NJ 08540-6432

BAUSELL, R. BARKER, JR., research methodology educator; s. Rufus B. and Nellie (Bowman) B.; m. Carole R. Vinograd, Jan. 6, 1978; children: Jesse T., Rebecca B. BS in Edn., U. Del., 1968, PhD in Ednl. Rsch. and Evaluation, 1975. Rsch. methodologist Med. Coll. Pa., 1975-76; prof., coord. faculty rsch. U. Md., Balt., 1976-91, dir. office rsch. methodology, 1991-94, prof. rsch., 1994-98, dir. rsch. complementary medicine program, 1998—. Sr. scientist Demarna Found. for Med. Care, 1994-98; cons., part-time dir. prevention rsch. ctr. Rodale Press, Inc.; presenter numberous seminars and confs. Author: (with C.R. Bausell and N.B. Bausell) The Bausell Home Learning Guide: Teach Your Child to Read, 1980, (with C.R. Bausell and N.B. Bausell) The Bausell Home Learning Guide: Teach Your Child to Write, 1980, (with C.F. Waltz) Nursing Research: Design, Statistics and Computer Analysis, 1981, (with C.R. Bausell and N.B. Bausell) The Bausell Home Learning Guide: Teach Your Child Math, A Practical Guide to Conducting Empirical Research, 1986, An Instructor's Manual for a Practical Guide to Conducting Empirical Research, 1986, (with C. Inlander and M. Rooney) How to Evaluate and Select a Nursing Home, 1988, Advanced Research Methodology: An Annotated Guide to Sources, 1991, Conducting Meaningful Experiments, 1994, (with Yu-Fang Li) Power Analysis for Experimental Research, 2002; editor: Evaluation and the Health Professions; author numerous monographs; contbr. numerous articles to profl. jours. Recipient Outstanding Rsch. award Nat. Wellness Conf., 1986, 87, Gov.'s award Meritorious Svc., 1992, award for Disting. Assessment Project Md. Assessment Resource Ctr., 1993. Achievements include research on documented effects of class size on student learning, effects of teacher experience on student learning, and determinants of health seeking (preventative) behavior. Home: 1311 Doves Cove Rd Baltimore MD 21286-1426 Office: U Md Complementary Med Program 2200 Kernan Dr Baltimore MD 21207-6665

BAUTISTA, KIMBERLY RAE, elementary school educator; b. Fayetteville, N.C., Nov. 24, 1965; d. William R. and Laura M. (Mahaffey) Daugherty; m. Robert Bautista Jr., Oct. 24, 1983. AA, Okaloosa-Walton Jr. Coll., 1987; BA, U. W. Fla., 1989, MEd in Leadership, 1990. Cert. elem. tchr., Fla. 5th grade tchr. Okaloosa County Sch. Bd., Ft. Walton Beach, Fla., 1989-90, elem. alternative edn. tchr., 1990—. Voter registrar Okaloosa County, 1990—; pres. U. W. Fla. Eglin/Ft. Walton Beach Student Govt. Assn., Eglin AFB, 1988-89, v.p., 1988. Fellow Phi Delta Kappa (v.p. membership 1992-93, 93-94), Alpha Sigma Lambda, Kappa Delta Pi, Phi Theta Kappa; mem. Am. Bus. Women's Assn., Tchr. Edn. Coun. (chmn.). Republican. Mem. Charismatic Ch. Avocations: cooking, crafts. Office: Wright Elem Sch 305 Lang Rd Fort Walton Beach FL 32547-3122 Home: 8982 W Parkview Terrace Loop Eagle River AK 99577-8541

BAUTISTA, MICHAEL PHILLIP, school system administrator; b. Merced, Calif., June 15, 1952; s. Ynacio and Frances (Garcia) B.; m. Nancy Ruth End, Aug. 4, 2000; children: Michael P., Lisa M., Rachel, Sam. B Music Edn., Emporia State U., 1974, MA, 1975; PhD, Tex. Tech U., 1981; adminstrv. cert., Okla. State U., 1986. Cert. adminstr., Colo., Supt., secondary prin., Okla., bldg. adminstr., Kans. Instr. U. Nebr., Lincoln, 1977-79; asst. prof. U. Tulsa, 1979-82; dir., adminstr. Jenks Pub. Schs., Tulsa, 1983-92; coord., adminstr. Denver Sch. of the Arts, Denver Pub. Schs., 1991-97, adminstrv. dir., 1997-99; divsn. dir. Kenneth King Acad. and Performing Arts Ctr., 1999—. Part-time instr. Tex. Tech U., Lubbock, 1975-77, Tulsa Jr. Coll., 1982-83; theatrical cons. MPB Assocs., Tulsa, 1983-91; v.p. internat. Network for Performing and Visual Arts Schs. Author: Ten Years of Stage Design at the Met (1966-1976); theatrical designer for various stage prodns. Bd. dirs. Carson-Brierly Dance Libr., Denver, 1992-99, Friends of Chamber Music, Denver, 1992-99, Rocky Mountain Coll. of Art and Design, 1997—; mem. steering com. Harwelden Inst., Tulsa, 1983-91; inactive Boy Scouts Am.; mem. Mayor's subcom. Arts Edn.; mem. exec. bd. Colo. Arts Assn. for Edn.; cantor Holy Family Cath. Ch. Recipient Svc. award St. Bernhards Parish, 1990, Amoco award for set design Am. Coll. Theatre Festival, 1989, Documentary citation Kansas City, Mo. Star, 1970. Mem. ASCD, U.S. Inst. Theatre Tech. Roman Catholic. Avocations: hiking, photography, music, design, painting, videography. Home: 5980 Dunraven Ct Golden CO 80403 Office: Kenneth King Acad and Perf Arts Ctr Auraria Higher Edn Ctr BoxR PO Box 173361 Denver CO 80217-3361

BAUTISTA, RENATO GO, chemical engineer, educator; b. Manila, Mar. 27, 1934; s. Teodulo Herera and Felicidad (Tiongko-Go) B.; m. Elaine Tveng, July 1, 1978; 1 child, Derek Kevin BS in Chem. Engring., U. Santo Tomas, 1955; S.M. in Metallurgy, MIT, 1957; PhD in Metall. Engring., U. Wis., 1961. Registered profl. engr., Iowa, Nev., The Philippines. Research metallurgist Allis Chalmers Corp., Milw., 1957-58; research assoc. chemistry dept. U. Wis., Madison, 1961-63; staff metallurgist A. Soriano Corp., Manila, 1963-67; research assoc. dept. chemistry Rice U., Houston, 1967-69; asst. prof. chem. engring Iowa State U., Ames, 1969-73, assoc. prof., 1973-78, prof., 1978-84; prof. dept. chem. and metall. engring Mackay Sch. Mines U. Nev., Reno, 1984—99, prof. metall. and materials engring. Mackay Sch. Mines, 1999—. Vis. prof. Imperial Coll., London, 1976; vis. scientist Warren Spring Lab., Stevenage, Britain, 1975-76; cons. NASA, Asahi Chem. Co., Olin Corp., W.R. Grace, Gen. Motors, Behre-Dolbear-Riverside, Inc., Jamaica Bauxite Inst. Editor: Hydrometallurgical Process Fundamentals, 1984; (with Rolf Wesely) Energy Reduction Techniques in Metal Electrochemical Processes, 1985; (with Rolf Wesely, Gary W. Warren) Hydrometallurgical Reactor Design and Kinetics, 1986; (with J.E. Hoffman, V.A. Ettel, V. Kudryk, R.J. Wesely) The Electrorefining and Winning of Copper, 1986; (with M.M. Wong) Rare Earths, Extraction, Preparations and Applications, 1988; (with Knona C. Liddell, Donald R. Sadoway) Refractory Metals, Extraction, Processing and Applications, 1990; (with Norton Jackson) Rare Earths: Resources, Science, Technology and Applications, 1991; (with V.I. Lakshmanan and S. Somasundaran) Emerging Separation Technologies for Metals and Fuels, 1993; (with Knona C. Liddell and Rick J. Orth) Metals and Materials Waste Reduction, Recovery, and Remediation, 1994; Emerging Separation Technologies for Metals II, 1996; (with Timothy W. Ellis, Charles O. Bounds and Barry Kilbourn) Rare Earths, Science, Technology, and Applications III, 1997, (with B. Mishra) Rare Earths and Actinides: Science, Technology, and Applications IV ; (with Brajendra Mishra) Rare Earths and Actinides: Science, Technology and Applications IV, 2000, (with P. Taylor and D. Chandra) EPD Congress and Fundamentals of Advanced Materials for Energy Conversion, 2002; contbr. articles to profl. jours. Mem. AICE, AIME, Soc. Mining Engrs., Metall. Soc. AIME, Am. Chem. Soc., U. Nev.-Reno Alumni Assn. (Faculty Mentor award 1995), Sigma Xi, Phi Lambda Upsilon. Roman Catholic. Achievements include patents in field. Home: 3622 Big Bend Ln Reno NV 89509-7427 Office: U Nev Material Sci & Engring MS 388 Reno NV 89557-0001 E-mail: bautista@unr.edu.

BAUZA, CHRISTINE DIANE, special education educator; b. Santa Monica, Calif., Sept. 16, 1961; d. William Gene and Dorothy Louise (Evans) Lough; m. Joseph Henry Bauza, July 26, 1986; 1 child, Crystal Marie. AA in Liberal Arts, Crafton Hills Coll., Yucaipa, Calif., 1981; BA in Liberal Studies, Calif. State U., Northridge, 1983, MA in Deaf Edn., multiple subjects-spl. edn. credentials, Calif. State U., Northridge, 1986. Tchr. comm. handicapped edn. San Bernardino County Supt. Schs., Rialto, Calif., 1986-98, Rialto Unified Sch. Dist., 1998—. Tchr., cons. Cmty. Adv. Com., San Bernardino, Calif., 1990-91. Avocations: bowling, reading, crafts. Home: 1031 Cimarron Dr Redlands CA 92374-6335 Office: Bemis Elem Sch 774 E Etiwanda Ave Rialto CA 92376-4508

BAXTER, BARBARA MORGAN, Internet service provider executive, educator; b. Cleve., Apr. 14, 1939; d. James Clifford and Mildred Elizabeth (Button) Baxter; m. David S. Unkefer, Dec. 28, 1956 (div.); children: Rachel, Clifford David, Elizabeth, Monica, Todd James. BSBA in MIS, Bowling Green State U., 1977, MBA, 1979, postgrad. in psychology, 1984, Wright State U., 1984-85. Clk. J.C. Baxter Co., Minerva, Ohio, 1962-66; v.p., co-founder Sherwood Plastics, Inc., Fostoria, Ohio, 1966-75, pres., CEO, 1975-89, Compututor Inc/Internet of Sandhills, Southern Pines, N.C. Mem. adj. faculty Tiffin (Ohio) U., 1984-90; MIS cons. to small bus., 1984-90; adj. continuing edn. faculty Sandhills C.C., Pinehurst, N.C., 1992-93; adj. faculty St. Andrews Coll., Lauringburg, N.C., 1993; CEO, co-founder CompuTutor, Inc., Southern Pines, N.C., 1994—, Internet of the Sandhills ISP, 1996—. V.p. Carroll County Young Reps., 1960-61; mem. Carroll County Rep. Cen. and Exec. Com., 1961-65, Wood County Rep. Com., 1967-70; troop leader, troop organizer, badge cons. Girl Scouts U.S., 1967-81; vestrywoman, sr. warden Trinity Episcopal Ch., Fostoria,, 1972-75; therapist Community Hospice Care Seneca County, Tiffin, 1987-89, also Carroll, Wood, Fostoria Counties; del. U.S.-China Trade Talks People to People, Spokane, Wash., 1988; adv. bd. Tiffin U. Students in Free Enterprise, 1986-87; tchr. applied econs. Jr. Achievement, 1988-89. Mem. Ladies Oriental Shrine N.Am., DAR, Alpha Lambda Delta. Avocation: classical music.

BAXTER, BETTY CARPENTER, educational administrator; b. Sherman, Tex., Oct. 10, 1937; d. Granville e. and Elizabeth (Caston) Carpenter; m. Cash Baxter; children: Stephen Barrington, Catherine Elaine. AA in Music, Christian Coll., Columbia, Mo., 1957; MusB in Voice and Piano, So. Meth. U., Dallas, 1959; MA in Early Childhood Edn., Tchrs. Coll., Columbia, 1972, MEd, 1979, EdD, 1988. Tchr. Riverside Ch. Day Sch., N.Y.C., 1966-71; headmistress Episcopal Sch., N.Y.C., 1972-87, headmistress emeritus, 1987—. Founding head Presbyn. Sch., Houston, 1988-94; dir. Chadwick Village Sch., Palos Verdes Peninsula, Calif., 1995—; head of sch. St. Margaret's Episcopal Sch., Palm Desert, Calif., 2001-02. Author: The Relationship of Early Tested Intelligence on the WPPSI to Later Tested Aptitude on the SAT. Mem. ASCD, Nat. Assn. Episcopal Chs. (former gov. bd., editor Network publ.), Nat. Assn. Elem. Sch. Prins., Ind. Schs. Assn. Admissions Greater N.Y. (former exec. bd.), Nat. Assn. for Edn. of Young Children, L.A. Assn. Sch. Heads, Nat. Assn. Elem. Sch. Prins., Assn. Supervision and Curriculum Devel., Kappa Delta Pi, Delta Kappa Gamma. Republican. Presbyterian. Office: 72-828 Joshua Tree St Palm Desert CA 92260 E-mail: baxterbuty@jps.net.

BAXTER, RUTH HOWELL, educational administrator, psychologist; b. Washington; d. Robert R. and Georgie (Murray) Lassiter; m. Edward A. Howell; children: Robert, Astrid, Mova, Mava, Josephine. BS, D.C. Tchrs. Coll.; MA, cert. in Edn., George Washington U.; cert. (N.Am. Com. of Oslo scholar), Oslo U.; grad. Adminstr.'s Acad. Class, D.C. Public Schs. Founder, dir., propr. Jewels of Ann. Pvt. Day Sch., Washington, 1970—; tchr. Newlands Infant, Southampton, Eng.; instr. math. demonstration lessons dept. edn. Howard U. Dir. early childhood edn. workshop Brent Elem. Sch., Washington; tchr. adult edn. Bel Air Sch., Woodbridge, Va.; founder, cons. Ask Dr. Ruth Rdnl. Cons. Group; state treas. D.C. PTA; mem. Ednl. Instn. Licensure Commn. Task Forces; mem. Mayor's Pre-White House Conf. on Libraries and Info. Services; exec. high sch. internship program D.C. Public Schs. Author: A Norwegian Birthday Party; contbr. children's stories to various publs. Mem. planning com. Eastern region Jr. Red Cross, Washington; cons. coll. youth motivation task force program Nat. Alliance for Bus.; chair edn. com. Dale City Civic Assn.; bd. dirs. Ctr. Ednl. Change D.C. Pub. Schs. Fulbright scholar; North Atlantic scholar; named Outstanding Tchr. of Yr., Future Tchrs. Am.; recipient Outstanding Contbn. award Nat. Assn. Negro Women, Commemorative Medal of Honor. Mem. Bus. and Profl. Women, English Speaking Union, Columbia Women (sec.), Jaycees, Zeta Phi Beta (life), Phi Delta Kappa. Presbyterian. Home: 13349 Delaney Rd Dale City Woodbridge VA 22193 Office: 2011 Bunker Hill Rd NE Washington DC 20018-3223

BAXTER, SHARON A. special education educator; b. Tacoma, Aug. 23, 1957; d. Acil Lamon Baxter and Fern A. Nichols. BA, Weber State Coll., 1986. Cert. secondary edn. tchr., Utah, special edn., Utah. Resource educator Salt Lake City Sch. Dist., 1988-90, tchr. emotionally handicapped, 1990—. Tchr. Failure Free Program, Bryant Internat., Salt Lake City, 1990—; mem. student svc. com., placement com. Salt Lake City Sch. Dist., 1992—. Avocations: northwest indian art, training and showing dogs, hiking, travel. Home: 614 E 3065 S Salt Lake City UT 84106-1351

BAY, MARJORIE SEAMAN, secondary school educator; b. Phila., Sept. 2, 1937; d. Charles A. and Esther (Hammond) Seaman; m. Park E. Bay, June 20, 1959; children: Charles, Janet, Catherine. BA, U. Pa., 1959; MS in Edn., U. Mo., 1990. Cert. tchr. chemistry, biology, English, Mo. Rsch. technician U. Mo. Hosp., Columbia, 1959-60; tchr. biology Jefferson Jr. H.S., Columbia, 1960-67; honors biology tchr. Rockbridge H.S., Columbia, 1974-80, chemistry/biology tchr., 1984—, biology/human anatomy and physiology tchr., 1976-80, 95—. Coach/advisor Sci. Olympiad Team, Columbia, 1990—; lectr./presenter in field. Soprano in choir First Bapt. Ch., Columbia, 1960—, Sunday sch. tchr., 1960—, deacon, 1984-87. Recipient Yearbook award Josen's Pubs., Topeka, Kans., 1990, CCTA Outstanding Tchr. of Yr., 1995. Mem. ASCD, Nat. Sci. Tchrs. Assn., Sci. Tchrs. Mo. (presenter/del., rep.), Mo. State Tchrs. Assn., Columbia Comty. Tchrs. Assn., PEO Internat. (sec., v.p., pres. 1964—), Delta Kappa Gamma (pres. 1972-74, 82-84), Phi Delta Kappa. Avocations: needlework, swimming, traveling, cooking. Home: 416 Parkade Blvd Columbia MO 65202-1454 Office: Rock Bridge Sr High School 4303 S Providence Rd Columbia MO 65203-7159

BAYARD, SUSAN SHAPIRO, adult education educator, small business owner; b. Boston, Dec. 26, 1942; d. Morris Arnold and Hester Muriel (Blatt) Shapiro; m. Edward Quint Bayard, Jan. 4, 1969; children: Jeffrey David, Lucy Quint. BA, Syracuse U., 1964; MA, U. Calif., Berkeley, 1966; cert. in advanced grad. study, Boston U., 1984. Rsch. chemist Harvard Med. Sch., Boston, 1966; asst. scientist Polaroid Corp., Cambridge, Mass., 1966-67; instr. Boston U., 1968-70, Wheelock Coll., Boston, 1978-81; chmn. sci. dept. Tower Sch., Marblehead, Mass., 1981-85; dir., owner Bayard Learning Ctr., Marblehead, 1985—94; vis. lectr. Salem (Mass.) State Coll., 1994—2000, coord. Instrnl. Design Lab., 1995—2000, coord. PALMS presvc. program, 1998—2000; dir. Ctr. Tchg., Learning and Assessment N. Shore CC, Danvers, Mass., 2003—. Ednl. cons., workshop facilitator Swampscott (Mass.) Pub. Schs., Lynn (Mass.) Pub. Schs., Marblehead, Mass., 1986—96; instr., cons. N.E. Consortium, North Andover, Mass., 1986—94. Mem. Curriculum Evaluation Com., Swampscott, 1978—80, Mass. Ednl. TV Program Selection Com., 1979—87, Supt. Screening Com., Swampscott, 1987, Town Meeting, Swampscott, 1988—, Sch. Improvement Coun., Swampscott, 1988—89. Named Outstanding Woman Grad. Student, Boston U. Women's Guild, 1977; grantee, NSF, Syracuse U., 1962, 1964. Mem.: Nat. Sci. Tchrs. Assn., Pi Lambda Theta. Jewish. Avocations: tennis, reading, computers, piano.

BAYER, ADA-HELEN, industrial organizational psychologist, educator; b. Hamburg, Germany, Sept. 26, 1961; came to U.S., 1962; d. Manfred E. and Margret H. (Janssen) B.; m. Steven L. Patrick, Aug. 20, 1994. BA, BS summa cum laude, Brock U., Ont., Can., 1984; MS, Rensselaer Polytech. Inst., 1987; MA, PhD, George Mason U., 1992. Asst. prof. Johns Hopkins U., Balt., Va., 1992-97; divsn. dir. behavioral scis. group EISI, Alexandria, Va., 1991-93; sr. rsch. psychologist HADRON/EISI, Balt., Va., 1993-97; adj. asst. prof. Va. Tech., Falls Church, 1994—, Johns Hopkins U., Balt., 1994—; dir. behavioral scis. divsn. Dougherty & Assocs., Inc., Balt., Va., 1996—; pres. Performance Devel. Inc., Burke, Va., 1996—. Bd. dirs. PMO, Alexandria, Va.; bd. dirs., v.p. The Coe Group, Burke, Va., 1992—; rsch. scientist AARP Rsch. Group, 1996—; pres. Performance Devel. Inc., 1996—. Contbr. articles to profl. jours. Recipient merit fellowship Rensselaer Polytech. Inst., Troy, N.Y., 1984-86, George Mason U., Fairfax, Va., 1989-92. Mem. APA, NAFE, Soc. for Indsl./Orgnl. Psychology. Avocations: skiing, whitewater rafting, swimming, scuba diving. Home and Office: 10864 Burr Oak Way Burke VA 22015-2400

BAYER, KAREN ELAINE, special education educator; b. Tulsa, Sept. 24, 1950; d. Kenneth Charles and Vivian (Smith) B. B.S. in Edn. and Psychology, James Madison U., 1975; M.Ed. in Edn., George Mason U., 1985. Cert. tchr. emotional disturbed, mentally retarded and learning disabled, Va. Tchr. mentally retarded Fairfax County Pub. Schs., Va., 1976-81, tchr. learning disabled, 1981—, mem. spl. edn. curriculum team for computer applications, 1985, condr. inservices for classroom mgmt. and new tchr. tng., sch. team leader, sci. fair coordinator, middle sch. sci. fair judge, sci. lead tchr. Fairfax County; mem. adv. council Fairfax County Supts., 1987; co-sponsor Young Astronauts Program, 1986-88, invited guest 2 NASA confs. Decorated U.S. Army Commendation medal; recipient commendation Fairfax County Sch Bd., 1984; named one of Outstanding Young Women Am., 1985. Mem. NEA, Va. Edn. Assn. (del. state convs.), Fairfax Edn. Assn., Council Exceptional Children, Nat. Sci. Tchrs Assn. (presenter paper conv. 1987), Va. Psychol. Assn., Kappa Delta Pi. Avocations: U.S. Army. Office: Crestwood Elementary Sch 6010 Hanover Ave Springfield VA 22150-3837

BAYES, PAUL EUGENE, accounting educator; b. Balt., Oct. 5, 1944; s. Virgil and Oda (Bowling) B.; m. Emily Jean Starkey, Aug. 12, 1967; 1 child, Kenneth (dec.). BS, U. Ky., 1965; MS, Ind. State U., 1968; DBA, U. Ky., 1983. Acctg. clk. Western Electric, Indpls., 1965-66; instr. Morehead (Ky.) State U., 1968-69; asst. prof. Clinch Valley Coll., U. Va., Wise, 1969-73, Berea (Ky.) Coll., 1973-75, Ea. Ky. U., Richmond, 1975-84; assoc. prof. East Tenn. State U., Johnson City, 1984—. Assoc. Associated Cons. Group, Johnson City, 1987—. Contbr. articles to profl. jours. Prochnow Found. grantee, 1987; East Tenn. State U. grantee, 1986, 89. Mem. Am. Acctg. Assn. (membership chmn. internat. sect. 1988-90), Nat. Assn. Accts., S.W. Decision Scis. Inst. Republican. Avocations: fishing, hunting, travel. Office: East Tenn State U PO Box 70710 Johnson City TN 37614-1710

BAYES, RONALD HOMER, English language educator, author; b. Freewater, Oreg., July 19, 1932; s. Floyd Edgar and Mildred Florence (Cochran) B. BS, East Oreg. State Coll., 1955, MS, 1956; postgrad., U. Pa., 1959-60; DDM, U. Delle Arti, Termi, Italy, 1982. Asst. prof. English Ea. Oreg. State Coll., LaGrande, 1955-56, assoc. prof. English, 1960-68; lectr. English U. Md., College Park, 1958-59, 66-67; disting. prof. creative writing St. Andrews Presbyn. Coll., Laurinburg, 1968—. Founder, exec. bd. St. Andrews Rev. & Press, Laurinburg, 1970-95; mem. N.C. State Arts Coun., Raleigh, 1987-89; master poet Atlantic Ctr. for Arts, New Smyrna Beach, Fla., 1988; cons. Nat. Coun. for Arts, Washington, 1969-71. Author: (poetry) Dust & Desire, 1961, Cages & Journeys, 1964, Child Outside My Window, 1965, History of the Turtle, 1970, The Casketmaker, 1972, Porpoise, 1974, Tokyo Annex, 1977, King of August, 1979, Fram, 1979, Beast in View, 1985, Guises, 1992, Greatest Hits 1969-2002, 2003; (fiction) Sister City, 1971. Chmn. Rep. Ctrl. Com., Union County, Oreg., 1967-68, Scotland County, N.C., 1980-81; bd. dirs. Scotland County Humane Soc., Laurinburg, 1993—. With U.S. Army, 1956-58. Named one of Outstanding Young Men of Am., 1960, master poet Atlantic Ctr. for the Arts, 1988, Disting. Prof. Creative Writing Chair named in his honor, 1999, Emeritus, 2002, Lifetime Achievement award in writing named in his honor, N.C. Writers' Network, 2001; recipient Outstanding Alumni award Ea. Oreg. State Coll., 1973, Roanoke-Chowan prize for poetry, 1973, N.C. Writers' Conf. award, 1987, N.C. award for Literature, 1989, cert. honor Poetry Coun. N.C., 1994, Honor for contr. to N.C. Writers, N.C. State Senate, 2002; fellow Woodrow Wilson Nat. fellow, 1959—60; grantee N.C. arts grantee, 1988. Mem. Danforth Found. (assoc.), Internat. House Japan, Japan Soc., N.C. Poetry Soc. (life), Oregon Poetry Assn. (life), Mason. Episcopalian. Avocations: gardening, reading, jogging, travel. Home: PO Box 206 Laurinburg NC 28353-0206

BAYLY, PATRICIA ANNE, psychologist, educator; b. Troy, N.Y., Dec. 4, 1952; d. Richard Yeilding and Martha (Coffey) Bayly. BA in Psychology cum laude, Russell Sage Coll., 1974; MS in Ednl. Psychology and States., SUNY, Albany, 1975; CAS in Sch. Psychology, 1976, postgrad., 1986—98. Nat. cert. sch. psychologist; cert. sch. psychologist, N.Y. Psychologist North Colonic Ctrl. Schs., Loudonville, N.Y., 1976-77, Enlarged City Sch. Dist. of Troy, 1977—. Psychologist, ednl. cons. St. Colman's Home, Watervliet, N.Y., 1985—; adj. instr. psychology Russell Sage Coll., Troy, 1978—. Bd. dirs. Drug Abuse and Prevention Coun., Troy, 1979-80, sec., 1980-83; bd. dirs., edn. chmn. Jr. League Troy, 1978-79, adv. planning chmn., 1980-81, tng. chmn., 1982-83, adv. mem., 1983—; bd. dirs. Am. Cancer Soc., 1982-84; bd. dirs. Pahl House, 1983-85, adv. mem., 1988-93. Parsons Child and Family Ctr. doctoral fellow, 1987-89. Mem. APA, N.Y. State Psychol. Assn., Psychol. Assn. Northeastern N.Y. (sec. 1984-86), Nat. Assn. Sch. Psychologists, N.Y. Assn. Sch. Psychologists, Russell Sage Coll. Alumnae Assn. (exec. bd. 1974-78, sec. 1978-82, 1st v.p. 1982-86, alumnae rep. faculty affairs trustee com. 1986-91), Athenian Honor Soc., Russell Sage Troy Alumnae (pres. 1976-83), Psi Chi. Roman Catholic. Home: 19 Brentwood Ave Troy NY 12180-8301 Office: 1950 Burdett Ave Troy NY 12180-3741

BAYNES, ROY DENNIS, hematologist, educator; b. Johannesburg, Mar. 1, 1955; came to U.S., 1989; s. Roy Dennis and Theresa Mary (Chellew) B.; children: Terry Louise, Richard Dennis. MB, BChir, U. Witwatersrand, Johannesburg, 1978, M of Medicine, 1986, PhD, 1987. Diplomate Am. Bd. Internal Medicine and Hematology, Am. Bd. Internal Medicine. Intern Johannesburg Hosp., 1979; medicine resident U. Witwatersrand Med. Sch., 1980-83, rsch. fellow Med. Rsch. Coun., 1984-85, lectr., cons. physician, 1986-89; rsch. prof. U. Kans. Med. Ctr., Kansas City, 1989-90, prof. medicine, 1990-97; prof. medicine & oncology, dir. bone marrow transplantation Wayne State U., Detroit, 1997—2002, pres. Ctr. for Cell Therapy, 2001—02; sr. dir. med. affairs Amgen Inc., Thousand Oaks, Calif., 2002—. Cons. South African Inst. Med. Rsch., Johannesburg, 1986-89, Nat. Livestock Bd., Chgo., 1993-94; pres. Med. Grads. Assn., Johannesburg, 1988, Univ. Rsch. Network Inc.; dir. J.P. McCarthy Umbilical Cord Stem Cell Bank, 1999-2002. Author: Iron Metabolism in Health and Disease, 1994; contbr. articles to profl. jours. Capt. S. African Def. Fource Med. Svcs., 1980, 85-86, Namibia. Recipient Suzman Gold Medal award Coll. Medicine, 1983, Blignault award Med. Assn., South Africa, 1990; Zoutendyk fellow Med. Rsch Coun., South Africa, 1985. Fellow ACP (diplomate); mem. Am. Soc. Hematology, Am. Soc. Clin. Oncology, Ctrl. Soc. Clin. Investigation, South African Soc. Med. Oncology (founding mem.), Sigma Xi (treas. 1992-95). Achievements include biochemical characterization of the serum form of transferrin receptor; definition of the mechanism of production of the serum form of transferrin receptor; discovery of a serum form of erythropoietin receptor; description of an enhancing effect of IL-II on iron absorption; defining the role of bone marrow transplantation in solid malignancies; evaluating the use of immunotheraphy in elimination of minimal residual malignancy after transplantation; establishment of major bone marrow transplant problem; establishment of a minority focused umbilical cord stem banking facility; establishment of a GMP grade cell processing facility and cell therapy center; establishment of a community based oncology network; conceptualization and incorporation of a university based CRO. Office: Amgen Inc One Amgen Ctr Dr Mailstop 27-5-4 Thousand Oaks CA 91320-1799

BAYNES, THOMAS EDWARD, JR., judge, lawyer, educator; b. N.Y.C., Mar. 19, 1940; s. Thomas Edward and Ann Jane (Burke) B.; m. Maija Eva Kokko, Dec. 30, 1963; children: Cynthia Lynn, Barbara Ann. BBA, U. Ga., 1962; JD, Emory U., 1967, LLM, 1972, Yale U., 1973. Bar: Ga. 1968, U.S. Supreme Ct. 1971, Ct. of Mil. Appeals 1978, Fla. 1981. Dir. Legal Assistance to Inmates Program, Emory U., 1968-69; asst. dean, asst. prof. bus. law Ga. State U., 1969-72; acting regional dir. Nat. Ctr. for State Cts., Atlanta, 1973-74; prof. law and public adminstrn. Nova U. Law Ctr., Ft. Lauderdale, Fla., 1974-76, 77-81; jud. fellow U.S. Supreme Ct., 1976-77; speedy trial reporter U.S. Dist. Ct., So. Dist. Fla., 1977-81; ptnr. Peterson, Myers, Craig, Crews, Brandon & Mann, Lake Wales, Fla., 1981-87; U.S. bankruptcy judge for mid. dist. Fla. U.S. Bankruptcy Ct., Tampa, 1987—, chief bankruptcy judge, 2000—03. State chmn., Ga., Nat. Council on Crime and Delinquency, 1971-72; legal counsel Reorgn. Study Commn. Ga., 1971-72 Author: (with W. Scott) Legal Aspects of Laboratory Medicine in Quality Assurance in Laboratory Management, 1978, Eminent Domain in Florida, 1979, Florida Mortgage Law, 1999, (with others) Supreme Court Justices, Illustrated Biographies, 1993; supplement editor Fla. Real Estate Law and Procedure, 1976; contbg. editor Norton Bankruptcy Law and Practice, 1995. Bd. dirs. F. Lee Moffitt Cancer Rsch Hosp., Tampa, 1989-94, 97—. Comdr. JAGC, USNR, 1960-80, ret. Sterling fellow Yale U. Law Sch., 1972-73; Harry J. Loman Found. rsch. fellow, 1979. Mem. Ga. Bar Assn., Fla. Bar Assn. (cert. cir. ct. mediator and arbitrator), Am. Law Inst., Hillsborough Assn. Women Lawyers (bd. dirs. 2001--), Fla. Acad. Profl. Mediators Inc., Supreme Ct. Hist. Soc., Am. Arbitration Assn., Nat. Adv. Com. for Bankruptcy, Ferguson-White Inn (pres. 1992-93, master), Omicron Delta Kappa. Office: US Bankruptcy Ct 801 N Florida Ave Tampa FL 33602-3849

BAYSINGER, JANE ANN, elementary school music educator; b. Tell City, Ind., Oct. 16, 1951; d. James William and Alice Ellen (Connor) B. BS, Ind. State U., 1973, MS, 1978. Cert. K-12 music tchr., Ind. Music tchr. Pine Village Elem. and Williamsport Elem. Met. Sch. Dist. Warren County, Williamsport, Ind., 1973—. Organist St. Patrick Cath. Ch., 1973—; mem., substitute accompanist Benton County Ext. Homemakers Chorus, 1984—, dir., 1999—; vol. for Pan Am Games, Indpls. Mem. Ind. Gen. Music Edn. Assn. (adv. bd. 1989-99), Warren County Edn. Assn. (treas. 1970's, scholarship com. 1980's), Music Educator's Nat. Conf., Ind. State Tchrs.' Assn. Avocations: reading, early american folksongs, travel, counted cross-stitch. Home: 307 E Lafayette St # 223 Pine Village IN 47975-8000 Office: Williamsport Elem Sch 206 E Monroe St Williamsport IN 47993-1242

BAYTOPS, JOY L. gifted education administrator, consultant; b. Richmond, Va., Oct. 22, 1953; d. James R., Sr. and Mildred (Smith) Lawson; m. Larry A. Baytops, July 26, 1975; children: Alexis, Adrienne, Brandon. BFA, Va. Commonwealth U., 1975; MEd, Coll. William and Mary, 1992. Cert. elem. and secondary art, gifted program adminstr., Va. Art tchr. King and Queen County Schs., Va., 1975-85, gifted resource coord., 1985-87; gifted coord. Lancaster County Schs., Lancaster, Va., 1987-90; project coord. Javits grant program Coll. William and Mary, Williamsburg, Va., 1990-93. Dir. No. Neck Gov.'s Sch. for Gifted, Warsaw, Va., 1988, 89; mem. adv. bd. Jacob's Ladder/Christchurch (Va.) Sch. Pres. King and Queen Ctrl. High PTA, King and Queen NAACP, 1992—; chairperson King and Queen County Sch. Bd., 1989-92; assoc. pastor Wayland Bapt. Ch., Stevensville, Va. Mem. Coun. Expectional Children, Nat. Assn. for Gifted Children, Kappa Delta Pi. Baptist. Avocations: reading, writing, drawing, community work with children. Home: RR 14 Box 32 Stevensville VA 23161

BAZALDUA, CHRISTINA JO, secondary education educator; b. Yakima, Wash., Jan. 31, 1969; d. Edward Loren Shinn and Marita Faye (Harris) Larson. BA in Human Environ. Scis. cum laude, Seattle Pacific U., 1991. Cert. tchr. Wash. Educator Mabton (Wash.) Sch. Dist., 1991—. Mem. Seattle Pacific U. Falconettes, 1989-91; vol. asst. ch. youth group Ch. of Nazarene, Grandview, Wash., 1989-92, mem. choir, 1991—. Mem. NEA, Am. Home Econs. Assn., Am. Vocat. Assn., Wash. Edn. Assn., Wash. Home Econs. Assn., Wash. Vocat. Assn., Alpha Kappa Sigma. Republican. Avocations: aerobics, bicycling, water sports, piano, vocal music. Office: Mabton Sch Dist PO Box 38 Mabton WA 98935-0038

BAZERMAN, CHARLES, English language educator, writing researcher; b. Bklyn., June 30, 1945; s. Solomon and Miriam (Kirschenberg) B.; m. Shirley Geok-lin Lim, Nov. 24, 1972; 1 child, Gershom Kean. BA, Cornell U., 1967; MA, Brandeis U., 1968, PhD, 1971. Asst. prof. English Baruch Coll., CUNY, 1971-78, assoc. prof., 1979-84, prof., 1985-90; prof. lit., communication and culture Ga. Inst. Tech., Atlanta, 1990-94; prof. U. Calif., Santa Barbara, 1994—, chair, dept. edn., 2000—. Vis. prof. Nat. U. Singapore, 1985—86; Watson disting. vis. prof. composition U. Louisville, 1997; John S. Knight vis. scholar Cornell Univ., 1999. Co-author: Reading Skills Handbook, 1978; Co-author: Writing Selves, Writing Societies, 2003, What Texts Do and How They Do It, 2003; author: Informed Writer, 1981, Shaping Written Knowledge, 1988, Constructing Experience, 1994, Textual Dynamics of the Professions, 1991, Landmark Essays in Writing across the Curriculum, 1995, Involved, 1997, Languages of Edison Light, 1999, Recipient McGovern medal Am. Writers' Assn., 1990, NCTE Award of Excellence, 1990, Best Book in History of Sci. and Tech., Am. Publ. Assn., 2000; grantee NEH, 1989. Mem. AERA, Soc. for Lit. and Sci., Conf. Coll. Composition and Comm., Soc. for Social Studies Sci. (coun. 1989-92), CUNY Assn. Writing Suprs. (chmn. 1978-80). Democrat. Home: 574 Calle Anzuelo Santa Barbara CA 93111-1721 Office: U Calif Santa Barbara Dept Edn Santa Barbara CA 93106

BAZIK, EDNA FRANCES, mathematician, educator; b. Streator, Ill., Dec. 26, 1946; d. Andrew and Anna Frances (Vagasky) B.; BSEd, Ill. State U, 1969; postgrad. Hamilton Coll., summer 1971, Ill. State U., 1972, Augustana Coll., summer 1973; MEd, U. Ill., 1972; PhD, So. Ill. U., 1976, gen. adminstrv. cert., 1980. Tchr. math. Northlawn Jr. High Sch., Streator, 1969-74; instr. math. edn. So. Ill. U., 1974-76; asst. prof. math. Concordia U., 1976-78; asst. prof. math. Ill. State U., Normal, 1978-85; assoc. prof. math. Eastern Ill. U., 1985-88; math. specialist, coord. Oak Park (Ill.) Pub. Schs., 1988-89; math coord. Hinsdale Sch. Dist. 181, 1989—; coord. inservice presentations, workshops for tchrs.; cons. to sch. dists. NSF grantee, 1980—. Presdl. award NSF, 1990. Mem. AAUP, Ill. State Bd. Edn. (mem. assessment team math. 1998—), Assn. Tchr. Educators, Ill. Assn. Tchr. Educators, Nat. Coun. Tchrs. Math. (chair elections com. 1990-91, Ill. Coun. Tchrs. Math. (governing bd., dir. coll. and univ. level), Math. Assn. Am., Nat. Coun. Suprs. Math., NEA, Ill. Edn. Assn., Sch. Sci. and Math. Assn., U.S. Metric Assn., Am. Ednl. Rsch. Assn., Assn. Supervision and Curriculum Devel., Ill. Assn. Supervision and Curriculum Devel., Ill. Standards Achievement Test Math Validation Com., Ill. State Bd. Edn. Math. Assessment Com., Assn. Childhood Edn. Internat., Coun. Exceptional Children, Ill. Curriculum Coun., Rsch. Coun. Diagnostic and Prescriptive Math., Kappa Delta Pi, Phi Delta Kappa (pres. Ill. State U. chpt. 1982-83), Pi Mu Epsilon, Delta Kappa Gamma, Phi Kappa Phi. Republican. Lutheran. Co-author: Elementary Mathematical Methods, 1978, Mind Over Math, 1980, Teaching Mathematics to Children with Special Needs, 1983, Step-by-Step: Addition, 1984, Step-by-Step: Subtraction, 1984, Step-by-Step: Multiplication, 1984, Step-by-Step: Division, 1984, Problem-Solving Sourcebook, 1985, Step-by-Step: Fractions, 1987, Step-by-Step: Decimals, 1988. Home: 1501 Darien Lake Dr Darien IL 60561-5069 Office: Hinsdale Sch Dist 181 100 S Garfield Ave Hinsdale IL 60521-4252 E-mail: ebazik@d181.dupage.k12.il.us.

BAZIN, NANCY TOPPING, retired English language educator; b. Pitts., Nov. 5, 1934; d. Frank Williamson Topping and Helen Luther Arnold Wilson; m. Maurice Jacques Bazin, Dec. 21, 1958 (div. 1978); children: Michel Francois, Christine Nicole; m. Robert Eliot Reardon, Jan. 4, 1992. BA, Ohio Wesleyan U., 1956; MA, Middlebury Grad. Sch. French, 1958; PhD, Stanford U., 1969; postgrad., Inst. Higher Edn. Adminstrn., 1977. Asst. prof. English Rutgers U., New Brunswick, N.J., 1970-77; dir. women's studies U. Pitts., 1977-78; assoc. prof. English and women's studies Old Dominion U., Norfolk, Va., 1978-84, dir. women's studies, 1978-85, chair dept. English, 1985-89, prof. English and women's studies, 1984-2000, eminent scholar, 1996—, prof. emeritus, 2000—. Manuscript reader for various publs.; exch. faculty lectr. U. Rabat, Morocco, 1988; vis. scholar Inst. for Advanced Studies, Ind. U., Bloomington, 1994; Coun. on Internat. Ednl. Exch. faculty devel. seminar in South Africa, 1998, Turkey, 2000; presenter in field. Author: Virginia Woolf and the Androgynous Vision, 1973; co-editor: Conversations with Nadine Gordimer, 1990; contbr. over 40 articles to profl. jours. Recipient Outstanding Faculty award State Coun. for Higher Edn. in Va., 1994, Burgess Faculty Rsch. and Creativity award, 1996; Ball Bros. Rsch. Found. fellow, 1994, Resident fellow Va. Ctr. for the Humanities, 1995; Nancy Topping Bazin Graduate Scholarship in Womens Studies created in her honor, 2000—. Mem. MLA (v.p. women's caucus 1978-81), South Atlantic MLA, Nat. Women Studies Assn., African Lit. Assn., Phi Beta Kappa, Phi Kappa Phi, Sigma Tau Delta, Kappa Delta Pi (mortar bd.). Democrat. Avocation: artist. Home: 4005 Gosnold Ave Norfolk VA 23508-2917

BEACH, BETH, elementary educator; b. Binghamton, N.Y., June 5, 1951; d. Martin Patrick and Mildred (Neary) Regan; 1 child, Martin Robert. BA in Elem. Edn., SUNY, Cortland, 1973; MS in Elem. Edn., Binghamton U., 1976. Cert. tchr., N.Y. Kindergarten tchr. Christ the King Sch., Endwell, N.Y., 1973-74, Blessed Sacrament Sch., Johnson City, N.Y., 1974-85, Chenago Forks Schs., Binghamton, 1985-90, 2d grade tchr., 1990-96, 5th grade tchr., 1996-98, 4th grade tchr., 1998—. Lectr. grad. edn. Binghamton U., 1988; mem. adv. bd. Hearts and Hands, Inc., Binghamton; leader workshops in field. Author: (with Muriel Rossie) Discipline and Self-Esteem, 1987. Tchr. safety town program Jr. League of Binghamton, 1982-90. Mem. N.Y. State United Tchrs., Binghamton Area Reading Coun., Binghamton Assn. for Edn. of Young Children (local bd. dirs., publs. com. 1984-86, historian 1986-88, nominating com. 1992). Avocations: sewing, reading. Home: 56 Lathrop Ave Binghamton NY 13905-4224 Office: Chenango Forks Cen Schs 1 Gordon Dr Binghamton NY 13901-5614

BEACH, DAVID WILLIAMS, music educator, dean; b. Hartford, Conn., Sept. 5, 1938; s. Raymond Schwarz and Avis (Sugden) B.; m. Marcia Francesca Salemme, June 20, 1964; children: Juliana Williams, Matthew David. BA, Brown U., 1961; MMus, Yale U., 1964, PhD, 1974. Instr. Yale U., New Haven, 1964-67, asst. prof., 1967-71, Bklyn. Coll., CUNY,

1971-72; assoc. prof. Eastman Sch. Music U. Rochester, 1974-85, chair dept. music theory Eastman Sch. Music, 1981-90, 95-96, prof. Eastman Sch. Music, 1985-96, univ. dean grad. studies, 1991-95; dean faculty music U Toronto, 1996—. Translator: The Art of Strict Musical Composition (by J.P. Kirnberger), 1982; editor: Aspects of Schenkerian Theory, 1983, Music Theory in Concept and Practice, 1997; contbr. numerous articles to profl. jours. Mem. Soc. for Music Theory (chair publs. 1979-84, exec. bd. 1984-87), Am. Musicol. Soc., Music Theory Soc. N.Y. State. Democrat. Avocations: golf, hiking.

BEACH, JOHN DOUGLAS, education educator; b. N.Y.C., Nov. 10, 1948; s. Herbert Clason and Lillian June (Loehmann) B.; m. Carol Louise Geisler, Aug. 29, 1968; children: Stephanie Lillian, Margaret Cordelia, Peter Gregory. BA in French, SUNY, Oswego, 1970; MA in French, SUNY, Binghamton, 1974; MS in Elem. Sch., L.I. U., 1975; PhD in Reading, SUNY, Albany, 1988. Cert. K-12 reading tchr., 7-12 French and Russian tchr., nursery sch. and kindergarten tchr., elem. tchr., N.Y. Adj. asst. prof. C.W. Post Ctr., L.I. U., Greenvale, N.Y., 1975-82; 1st grade tchr. William Floyd Unified Sch. Dist., Shirley, N.Y., 1976-77; reading tchr. Walton (N.Y.) Ctrl. Schs., 1978-79; reading specialist Cairo (N.Y.)-Durham Schs., 1979-86; asst. prof. edn. U. Wis., Kenosha, 1986-88, U. Maine, Orono, 1988-90, U. Nev., Reno, 1990-94, SUNY, Cortland, 1994—97; assoc. prof. edn. U. Nebr., Omaha, 1997—2000, Boise (Idaho) State U., 2001—. Editl. cons. Allyn and Bacon Pubs., Needham Heights, Mass., 1988—; freelance storyteller, Cortland, 1975—; sr. assoc. for assessment N.W. Regional Ednl. Lab., Portland, Oreg., 2000. Contbr. articles to profl. publs. Cubmaster Boy Scouts Am., Cairo, 1983-86, cubmaster, leader trainer, Reno, Nev., 1990-94, summer camp dir., Dryden, N.Y., 1995. Bird and Bird Fund grantee U. Maine, 1989; NDEA Title IV fellow, 1970-72; recipient Ednl. Rsch. award Assn. Am. Pubs., 1986. Mem. Internat. Reading Assn. (mem. pubs. rev. bd., 1997—), N.Y. State Reading Assn., Nat. Coun. Tchrs. English (chair com. on storytelling 1994—). Avocations: classical piano, gardening, art, cooking, history. Home: # L103 3344 N Lakeharbor Ln Boise ID 83703-6260 Office: Boise State Univ 1910 University Drive Boise ID 83725

BEACH, NANCY ANN HELEN, special education educator, educator; b. Kansas City, Kans., Nov. 10, 1944; d. Charles Andrew and Victoria Virginia (Handzel) Nugent; divorced; children: Cathe, Denise, Michelle. AA, East Los Angeles Coll., 1964; BS, Calif. State U., L.A., 1966; postgrad., UCLA, 1966-70. Cert. English teaching credential (life). Tchr. Calif. Pub. Schs., San Gabriel Valley, 1966-77; recreation therapist State of Calif., Pomona, 1966-67; recreation supr. City of Baldwin Park (Calif.), 1967-70; restaurant owner Baldwin Park, 1977; instr. English So. Bay Coll., Baldwin Park, 1984-89; instr. English and success skills Eldorado Coll., West Covina, Calif., 1989-90; tchr. blind and retarded spl. edn. Los Angeles County Schs., 1990—. Author: Reading Skills, 1971. Bd. dirs. pub. rels. com. CAP, El Monte, Calif., 1960-64. Democrat. Avocation: race car driving.

BEAGLE, CHARLOTTE ANN, secondary school educator; b. Watertown, N.Y., Apr. 16, 1947; d. Addison Leo and Gertrude Agnes (Hodkinson) McDonald; m. Joseph Gerrard Beagle, May 23, 1970; children: Benjamin, Michael. BA, D'Youville Coll., 1969; MA Tchg. in History, SUNY, Binghamton, 1972. Cert. tchr., N.Y. Intern Union-Endicott (N.Y.) H.S., 1969-70; social studies tchr. Lowville (N.Y.) Acad., 1970-87, social studies chair, 1987—, bd. dirs. sch. house com. Adj. faculty Jefferson C.C., Watertown, N.Y., 1985-94; exam item writer N.Y. State Dept. Edn., Albany, 1990; mentor Jeff-Lewis Tchr. Ctr., Watertown, N.Y., 1986-87; presenter North Country Computer Conf., 1989. Rschr. Lewis County Hist. Soc., Lyons Falls, N.Y., 1990; mem. Lewis County Local and State Parole Program, Lowville, 1989—; bd. dirs. Thousand Islands Girl Scout Coun., 1995-97. Mem. Nat. Coun. for the Social Studies (articles rsch. reviewer), Ctrl. N.Y. State Social Studies Coun., Orgn. for Am. Historians. Avocations: travel, reading, geneaology research. Office: Lowville Acad and Ctrl Sch 7668 State St Lowville NY 13367

BEAHM, JOHN METZ, middle school educator; b. Carlsbad, N.Mex., Mar. 7, 1953; s. Ernest Metz and Elizabeth Marie (Vallentgoed) B. BA, Hope Coll., 1975. Gen. mgr. WTAS, Holland, Mich., 1973-75; tchr. Zuni Secondary Sch., Zuni Pueblo, N.Mex., 1976-79, Zuni Alternative Sch., Zuni Pueblo, N.Mex., 1976-79, Kennedy Middle Sch., Albuquerque, 1979—, math chair, 1990—. Computer graphics coord. People Link Computer BBs, Chgo., 1986-90; workshop leader Albuquerque Pub. Schs., 1984—. Author: Shareware for Computers, 1984—. Treas., pres. Albuquerque Friendship Force, 1981-83, 1983-84. Named Outstanding Tchr. N.Mex. NW Regional Sci. Fair., Albuquerque, 1992. Mem. Phi Delta Kappa. Avocations: photography, travel, computers. Home: 1423 Roma Ave NE Albuquerque NM 87106-4617 Office: Kennedy Middle School 721 Tomasita St NE Albuquerque NM 87123-1251

BEAHRS, OLIVER HOWARD, surgeon, educator; b. Eufaula, Ala., Sept. 19, 1914; s. Elmer Charles and Elsa Katherine (Smith) B.; 1 child, Gean Beahrs Landy; m. Helen Edith Taylor, July 27, 1947; children: John Randolf, David Howard, Nancy Ann Beahrs Oster. BA, U. Calif., Berkeley, 1937; MD, Northwestern U., 1942; MS in Surgery, Mayo Grad. Sch. Medicine, 1949; D of Mil. Medicine honoris causa, Uniform Svcs. U. Health Sci., 1999. Diplomate Am. Bd. Surgery. Fellow surgery Mayo Grad. Sch. Medicine, Rochester, Minn., 1942, 46-49, prof. surgery, 1966-79; Joel and Ruth Roberts prof. surgery Mayo Med. Sch., 1978-79; prof. emeritus Mayo Grad. Sch. Medicine, Rochester, Minn., 1979—; asst. surgeon Mayo Clinic, 1949-50, head sect. gen. surgery, 1950-79, vice-chmn. bd. govs., 1964-75. Bd. dirs. Rochester Meth. Hosp.; trustee Mayo Found.; mem. cancer control and rehab. adv. com. Nat. Cancer Inst., 1975-84; mem. Am. Joint Com. on Cancer, 1975-78, exec. dir., 1980-92. Editor: Surgical Consultations; editorial bd.: Surgery, Surg. Techniques Illustrated; contbr. over 400 articles to profl. jours. Hon. life, bd. dirs. Am. Cancer Soc., 1975—; trustee Rochester Meth. Hosp.; adv. bd. Uniform Svcs. Univ. Health Scis.; med. cons. Pres. and Mrs. Reagan. Capt. USNR, 1942-64, ret. Recipient Leadership and Humanitarian awards Am. Cancer Soc. Fellow Royal Coll. Surgery in Ireland (hon.), Royal Australasian Coll. Surgery (hon.); mem. AMA, ACS (mem. exec. com., bd. govs., chmn. cen. jud. com., long-range planning com., chmn. bd. govs., chmn. bd. regents, pres. 1988-89), Am. Group Practice Assn. (sec.-treas. 1974-75), Minn. Surg. Soc. (pres. 1960-61), Am. Thyroid Assn., James IV Assn. Surgeons, Am. Surg. Assn. (pres. 1979-80, chmn. com. on issues 1980-83), So. Surg. Assn., Cen. Surg. Assn., Western Surg. Assn., Soc. Head and Neck Surgeons (pres. 1966-67), Am. Assn. Endocrine Surgeons (pres. 1986-87), Am. Assn. Clin. Anatomists (pres. 1986-87), Soc. Surgery Alimentary Tract, Soc. Pelvic Surgeons (pres. 1983-84), Soc. Surg. Oncology, Am. Assn. Clin. Anatomists (pres.), Philippine Coll. Surgeons (hon.), Hellenic Coll. Surgery (hon.), Assn. Française de Chirurgie Française, Northwestern U. Alumni Assn. (Merit award), Sigma Xi, Phi Kappa Epsilon, Phi Beta Pi, Theta Delta Chi. Republican. Methodist. Home: 2253 Baihly Ln SW Rochester MN 55902-1023 Office: 200 1st St SW Rochester MN 55905-0001 E-mail: beahrs.oliver@mayo.edu.

BEAL, MARY FRANCES, adult education educator; b. Long Beach, Calif., Jan. 31, 1931; d. Charles Emery Willard and Margaret Blanche Tyhurst-Willard; m. Robert Lafayette Beal, May 5, 1951; children: Michael, Rebecca, Rock, Mark, Jon. BS, Tex. A&M U., 1973. Cert. tchr. Tex., 1973. Elem. sch. tchr. Del Rio (Tex.) Ind. Sch. Dist., 1966—81; instr. English Yonsei U., Seoul, Republic of Korea, 1981—88, Region VI Tex. Edn. Svcs., Bryan, 1988—. Columnist Del Rio News Herald, 1972—73. Spkr. for Christian orgns., including Stonecroft ministries, on coping with tragedy Tex., La., Calif., N.Mex., Republic of Korea. Recipient Family of Month award, Ladies' Home Jour., 1973. Mem.: Tex. Adult Literacy and Edn. Assn. Home: PO Box 332 Wellborn TX 77881 Office: Bryan Adult Learning Ctr 1700 Palasota Bryan TX 77803

BEALE, GEORGIA ROBISON, historian, educator; b. Chgo., Mar. 14, 1905; d. Henry Barton and Dora Belle (Sledd) Robison; m. Howard Kennedy Beale, Jan. 2, 1942; children: Howard Kennedy, Henry Barton Robison, Thomas Wight. AB, U. Chgo., 1926, AM, 1928; PhD, Columbia U., 1938; postgrad., Sorbonne and Coll. de France, 1930-34. Reader in history U. Chgo., 1927-29; lectr. Barnard Coll., 1937-38; instr. Bklyn. Coll., 1937-39; asst. prof. Hollins (Va.) Coll., 1939-41, Wellesley Coll., 1941-42, Castleton (Vt.) State Coll., 1968-70; vis. assoc. prof. U. Ky., Lexington, 1970-72; professorial lectr. George Washington U., 1983-84. Author: Révellère-lépeaux, Citizen Director, 1938, 72, Academies to Institut, 1973, Bosc and the Exequatur, 1978, The Botanophiles of Angers, 1996; contbg. author Historical Dictionary of the French Revolution, 1985; also articles. Mem. Madison (Wis.) Civic Music Assn. and Madison Symphony Orch. League, 1958—; hon. trustee Culver-Stockton Coll., 1974—. Univ. fellow Columbia U., 1929-30. Mem. AAUW (European fellow 1930-31), Am. Hist. Assn., So. Hist. Assn., Soc. French Hist. Studies, Western Soc. French History (hon. mem. exec. coun.), Am. Soc. 18th Century Studies, Brit. Soc. 18th Century Studies, Reid Hall Club (Paris), Brit. Univ. Women's Club (London), Phi Beta Kappa, Pi Lambda Theta, Phi Alpha Theta, Pi Kappa Delta. Office: The Ridge Orford NH 03777

BEALE, MARK DOUGLAS, psychiatrist, educator; b. Richmond, Va., May 11, 1962; BA, U. Va., 1984; MD, Ea. Va. Med. Sch., 1989. Diplomate Am. Bd. Psychiatry and Neurology; lic. S.C. State Bd. Med. Examiners. Intern Med. U. S.C., Charleston, 1989-90, resident in psychiatry, 1989-93, fellow in electroconvulsive therapy, 1992-93, instr. dept. psychiatry and behavioral scis., 1993-94, asst. prof. dept. psychiatry and behavioral scis., 1994—, assoc. prof., 1999—; pvt. practice Charleston Psychiatric Assocs., 2000—. Cons. electroconvulsive therapy, attending psychiatrist Inst. Psychiatry, Med. U. S.C., Charleston, 1993—2000, Ralph Johnson VA, Charleston, 1996—; cons. electroconvulsive therapy Charleston Meml. Hosp., 1993-96; lectr. in field. Author: (with others) Handbook of ECT, 1996, (book chpts.) Handbook of Child and Adolescent Psychiatry, 1996, Textbook of Consultation-Liaison Psychiatry, 1996, (jours.) Convulsive Therapy, Psychosomatics, Neuropsychiatry/Neuropsychology & Behavioral Neurology; book reviewer: Clinical Gerontologist; editl. bd. Jour. of ECT. Recipient Young Investigator award Nat. Alliance Rsch. on Schizophrenia and Depression, 1998. Mem. Am. Psychiat. Assn., Assn. Convulsive Therapy, S.C. Psychiat. Assn. Avocations: guitarist in the psychodymanics band, saltwater fly fishing, motorcycling. Office: Charleston Psyciatric Associates 669 St Andrews Blvd Charleston SC 29407

BEALEY, LAURA ANN, artist, educator; b. Spencer, W.Va., Dec. 19, 1934; d. William Howard and Virginia Stone (Smith) Miller; m. Mike Bealey, Aug. 18, 1956; children: Virginia, Michael, Julie. BS, Mary Washington Coll., U. Va., Fredericksburg, 1956; AA in Fine Arts with honors, No. Va. Community Coll., Annandale, 1981; MA in Studio Art, Art Edn., Art History, George Mason U., 1990. Chemist Univ. Hosp. Western Res., Cleve., 1956-57; spl. art instr. Fairfax County (Va.) Sch. System, 1986-87. Pvt. tchr. drawing and painting in oil and watercolor; juror Claymount Ct. Art Show, Charlestown, W.Va., 1997; tutor Burren Painting Ctr., Lisdoonvarna, Ireland, 1996-97, 2001; lectr. in field; condr. workshops in field. One-woman shows at George Mason U., 1988, 1993, Fishscale Mousetooth, 1996, Broadway Gallery, Fairfax, Va., 2000, 2001, Bobbies Van's Gallery, Bridge Hamptons, N.Y., 2003; exhibited in group shows at George Mason U., 1988, Springfield Art Guild, 1977, 80, 84, 86, 87, Vienna Art Soc., 1979, 80, 81, 83, 85, Seventh Ann. Manassas Exhbn. of Fine Art, 1983, No. Va. C.C., 1978, 81, Art League of Alexandria, Va., 1980, Claymont Ct., Charles Town, W.Va., 1998, Broadway Gallery, Fairfax, Va., 1998, 99, 2001, Broadway Gallery, Old Towne, Alexandria, 1999, 2000, 2002-03, Fairfax Arts Coun., 1999, Twentieth Century Gallery, Williamsburg, Va., Island Inn Gallery, Ocracoke, N.C., Hayloft Theater Art Gallery, Manassas, Va., Fairfax Hosp. Galleries; represented in permanent collections Wire Reinforcement Inst., McLean, Va., Craftsman Press, Cheverly, Md., NCI, McLean, Va., No. Va. C.C., Nat. Com. Creative Nonviolence. Methodist. Home: 12010 Wayland St Oakton VA 22124-2236 Gallery: Extra Touch of Class 5641B Gen Washington Dr Alexandria VA 22312-2403 E-mail: artistlaura@juno.com.

BEALL, CHARLES DONALD, former special education educator; b. Lumpkin, Ga., Oct. 7, 1932; s. Charlie Will and Margaret Louise (Williams) B.; m. Donna C. Ross, June 12, 1960 (div.). BS, Tougaloo Coll., 1953; MA, U. Mich., 1957, sch. diagnostician and reading clinician, 1959; spl. edn. cert., Wayne State U., 1961. Substitute tchr. Detroit Pub. Schs., 1959; reading clinician Oakland County Reading Clinic, Pontiac, Mich., 1959; spl. edn. tchr. Pontiac State Hosp., 1959-62; tchr. children's svc. Lafayette Clinic, Detroit, 1962-68, head spl. edn. dept., 1968-92. Assoc. prof. spl. edn. dept. Va. State Coll., Petersburg, 1968; lectr. U. Detroit, Marygrove Coll.; instr. Wayne State U., 1968; cons. Mich. Edn. Assn. Conf. for Tchrs./Counselors for Physically Handicapped, Tustin, 1967, Detroit Pub. Schs., 1972, St. Joseph Mercy Hosp., Pontiac, 1982. Contbr. articles to profl. jours. Mem. Coun. Exceptional Children, Am. Orthopsychiatric Assn., Mich. Assn. for Tchrs. of Emotionally Disturbed Children (pres. 1963-64, 66-67), Mich. State Employee's Spl. Edn. Com., Tougaloo Coll. Alumni Assn. (Detroit pres. 1960-92, nat. treas. 1988-91), U. Mich. Alumni Assn. (chmn. Martin Luther King Scholarship com. 1990-91), United Negro Coll. Fund, Inc. (treas., chmn. publicity 1984-90), Plymouth Congregational Ch. (treas. scholarship com., bd. trustees), Alpha Phi Alpha. Home: 4811 Yosemite Dr Columbus GA 31907-1753

BEALL, DENNIS RAY, artist, educator; b. Chickasha, Okla., Mar. 13, 1929; s. Roy A. and Lois O. (Phillips) B.; 1 son, Garm. Student, Okla. City U., 1950-52; BA, San Francisco State U., 1956, MA, 1958. Registrar Oakland (Calif.) Art Mus., 1958; curator Achenbach Found. for Graphic Arts, Calif. Palace of the Legion of Honor, San Francisco, 1958-1965; asst. prof. art San Francisco State U., 1965-69, assoc. prof., 1969-76, prof. art, 1976-92; prof. emeritus, 1992—. Numerous one-man shows of prints, 1957—, including: Award Exhbn. of San Francisco Art Commn., Calif. Coll. Arts and Crafts, 1978, San Francisco U. Art Gallery, 1978, Los Robles Galleries, Palo Alto, Calif.; numerous group shows 1960— including Mills Coll. Art Gallery, Oakland, Calif., Univ. Gallery of Calif. State U., Hayward, 1979, Marshall-Meyers Gallery, 1979, 80, Marin Civic Ctr. Art Galleries, San Rafael, Calif., 1980, San Francisco Mus. Modern Art, 1985; touring exhibit U. Mont., 1987-91, An Inner Vision, Oysterponds Hist. Soc., Orient, N.Y., 1998, Modernism in Calif. Printmaking, Annex Gallery, Santa Rosa, Calif., 1998, The Stamp of Impulse, Worcester (Mass.) Art Mus., 2001, Palm Springs (Calif.) Desert Mus., 2003; represented in numerous permanent collections including Libr. of Congress, Washington, Mus. Modern Art, N.Y.C., Nat. Libr. of Medicine, Washington, Cleve. Mus., Whitney Mus., Phila. Mus., U.S. embassy collections, Tokyo, London and other major cities, Victoria and Albert Mus., London, Achenbach Found. for graphic Arts, Calif. Palace of Legion of Honor, San Francisco, Oakland Art Mus., Phila. Free Libr., Roanoke (Va.) Art Ctr., Worcester (Mass.) Art Mus., Whitney Mus. Am. Art, Cleve. Mus., various colls. and univs. in U.S. Served with USN, 1947-50, PTO. Office: San Francisco State Univ Art Dept 1600 Holloway Ave San Francisco CA 94132-1722 E-mail: chukar@thegrid.net.

BEALL, GRACE CARTER, business educator; b. Birmingham, Ala., Sept. 12, 1928; d. Edgar T. and Kate (Eubank) Carter; m. Vernon D. Beall, Aug. 27, 1948; children: Robert, Timothy. BS, La. Coll., 1949; MEd, La. State U., 1955; postgrad., U. Wis., East Tex. State U., Temple U., Southwestern Bapt. Theol. Sem., U. Ga. Tchr., asst. prin. Franklin Parish Sch. Bd., Crowville, La., 1949-54; tchr. Grant Parish Sch. Bd., Dry Prong, La., 1954-55; tchr., coord. Rapides Parish Sch. Bd., Pineville, La., 1955-73; assoc. prof. La. Coll., Pineville, 1974-93, past vice chair of faculty, prof. emeritus, 1993—. Cons. in field; sec.-treas. Gulf Coast Athletic Conf., 1983—, Nat. Assn. Intercollegiate Athletics Dist. 30, 1983—. Vice chair Civil Svc. Bd., Pineville, Ala., 1975—; vol. chaplain assoc. Rapides Regional Med. Ctr. Recipient Outstanding Svc. award La. Vocat. Assn., 1971, Outstanding Secondary Educators Am., 1973. Mem. AAUP (past sec.), La. Bapt. Hist. Assn. (pres., bd. dirs.), La. Coll. Ret. Faculty Assn. (pres. 1998—), Phi Delta Kappa (historian), Delta Kappa Gamma (past pres.), Kappa Kappa Iota. Republican. Baptist. Avocations: reading, traveling, volunteer work. Home: 3232 Crestview Dr Pineville LA 71360-5804

BEALS, PAUL ARCHER, religious studies educator; b. Russell, Iowa, Feb. 18, 1924; s. Archer Edwin and Myrtle Mae (Kelsey) B.; m. Vivian Brown, Sept. 29, 1945; children: Lois Ruth, Stephen Paul, Samuel Archer, Timothy Joel. AB, Wheaton (Ill.) Coll., 1945; diploma, Moody Bible Inst., Chgo., 1948; ThM with high honors, Dallas Theol. Seminary, 1952, ThD, 1964. Missionary in Cen. African Republic Bapt. Mid-Missions, Cleve., 1952-64; prof. of missiology Grand Rapids (Mich.) Bapt. Seminary, 1964-97, prof. emeritus missiology, 1998—, dir. continuing edn., 1977-90. Theol. cons. Bapt. Mid-Missions, 1969-72, missionary emeritus, 2002--; conf. speaker. Author: A People for His Name, 1985, rev. edit., 1995; contbr. articles to profl. jours. Mem. Evang. Theol. Soc., Evang. Missiological Soc. (pres. 1990-93), Am. Soc. Missiology, Pi Gamma Mu. Home: 2111 Audley Dr NE Grand Rapids MI 49525-1517

BEAN, SANDRA G. special education educator; b. Birmingham, Ala., Dec. 5, 1954; d. Arnold M. and Doris (B.) Bean. BS, U. Montevallo, 1977, MEd, 1979; MEd in Spl. Edn., U. Ala., Birmingham, 1989, postgrad., 1990—. Cert. spl. edn. tchr., Ala. Tchr. maths. Berney Points Bapt. Ch., Birmingham, Ala., 1977-80, Ctrl. Park Christian Schs., Birmingham, 1983-88; tchr. spl. edn. Jefferson County Bd. Edn., Birmingham, 1988-90; tchr. learning disabled Birmingham Pub. Schs., 1990—. Mem. Internat. Reading Assn., Ala. Reading Assn., Birmingham Area Reading Coun., Tchrs. Applying Whole Lang., Coun. for Exceptional Children, Coun. for Learning Disabilities, Ala. Dachshund Club, Dachshund Club Am. Baptist. Home: 1216 Rutledge Dr Birmingham AL 35228-2933

BEAR, LARRY ALAN, lawyer, educator; b. Melrose, Mass., Feb. 28, 1928; s. Joseph E. and Pearl Florence B.; m. Rita Maldonado, Mar. 29, 1975; children: Peter, Jonathan, Steven. BA, Duke U., 1949; JD, Harvard U., 1953; LLM, (James Kent fellow), Columbia U., 1966. Bar: Mass. 1953, PR 1963, NY 1967. Trial lawyer Bear & Bear, Boston, 1953-60; cons. legal medicine P.R. Dept. Justice, 1960-65; prof. law sch. U. P.R., 1960-65; legal counsel, then commr. addiction svcs. City of NY, 1967-70; dir. Nat. Action Com. Drug Edn. U. Rochester, NY, 1970-77; pvt. practice NYC, 1970-82; pub. affairs radio broadcaster Sta. WABC, NYC, 1970-82; US legal counsel Master Enterprises of P.R., 1982-90. Vis. prof. legal medicine Rutgers U. Law Sch., 1969; mem. alcohol and drug com. Nat. Safety Coun., 1972—82; cons. in field of substance abuse prevention, edn. programming, 1980—; adj. prof. markets, ethics and law Stern Sch. Bus. NYU, 1986—99; pres. Found. for a Drug Free Pa., 1991—92; mem. Atty. Gen.'s Med./Legal Adv. Bd. on Drug Abuse, Pa., 1992; lectr. in legislation and ethics Wharton Sch. exec. program U. Pa., 1996—2000; vis. prof. legal, social and ethical context of bus. Athens Lab. Bus. Adminstrn., 1996; vis. prof. bus. ethics NYU, 2000—. Author: Law, Medicine, Science and Justice, 1964, The Glass House Revolution: Inner City War for Interdependence, 1990, Free Markets, Finance, Ethics, and Law, 1994; contbr. articles to profl. jour. Adv. com. on pub. issues Advt. Coun., 1972-95; mem.-at-large Nat. coun. Boy Scouts Am., 1972-85; chmn. Bd. Ethics, Twp. of Mahwah (NJ), 1990-91; alumni admissions adv. com. Duke U., 1987—. Mem. ABA, NY State Bar Assn., Forensic Sci. Soc. Great Britain, Acad. Colombiana de Ciencias Medico-Forenses, Harvard Club (N.Y.C.). Home: 95 Tam Oshanter Dr Mahwah NJ 07430-1526 Office: Markets Ethics and Law Program NYU Stern Sch Bus 40 W 4th St Ste 3-305 New York NY 10012-1106 E-mail: lbear@stern.nyu.edu.

BEAR, ROBERT EMERSON, secondary school educator; b. Artesia, Calif., Oct. 6, 1953; s. Samuel Ronald and Erlene Mable (Wobick) B.; m. Katherine Luella Culp, Aug. 14, 1976; children: Nathaniel Emerson, Benjamin Robert, Aaron Anthony. BS in Art Edn., Bemidji (Minn.) State U., 1978; MS in Art, Tex. A&I U., 1987; postgrad., Tex. A&M U., 1997—. Cert. K-12 art tchr., Minn.; cert. 7-12 spl. edn., K-12 art tchr., Tex.; cert. supr. Tex. Tchr. art Ind. Sch. Dist. 710, Virginia, Minn., 1978-79, Ind. Sch. Dist. 363, Northome, Minn., 1979-81; exhibit specialist John E. Conner Mus., Kingville, Tex., 1985-87; tchr. spl. edn., art Webb Consol. Ind. Sch. Dist., Bruni, Tex., 1987-89; tchr. spl. edn. Cotulla (Tex.) Ind. Sch. Dist., 1989-90; edn. svc. specialist USAR, Indpls., 1989; tchr., art specialist Bryan (Tex.) Acad. Visual and Performing Arts, 1990-96; tchr. art Somerville (Tex.) Ind. Sch. Dist., 1998—2000, Fremont (Tex.) County Sch. Dist., 2000, Lampasis (Tex.) Ind. Sch. Dist., 2001—. Art dir. print shop Trinity Ch., Lubbock, Tex., 1984; tchr. photography Eveleth (Minn.) Area Vocat. Tech. Sch., 1989; judge Odessy of the Mind, 1999; guest lectr. art dept. Tex. A&I U., Kingsville, 1987; condr. workshops in field; guest artist Bee Frame Shop, Alexandria, Minn., 1983, Ducks Unltd. and Landmark Gallery, Redwood Falls, Minn., 1984; tchr. spl. edn. Big Horn (Wyo.) Sheridan County Sch. Dist. #1, 1997-98. Exhibited in group shows at Nat. Audobon Soc., 1979, Wildlife Heritage Found., 1984, Nat. Wildlife Art Collectors Soc., 1985, Okla. Wildlife Festival, 1983, No. Minn. Wildlife Art Show, 1983, Thief River Falls Art Coun., 1983, Okla. Wildlife Art Festival, 1984-85 (2 1st pl. awards 1984, Best of Show 1985), Nat. Wildlife Art Collectors Soc., 1985; one man shows include Bemidji State U., 1978, Ducks Unltd., 1984, Tex. A&I U., 1987; author: Oh Ho Ho game, 1993, Bear Classroom Management Portfolio, 1995, Curriculum and Instructional Unit Appraisal and Rating Instrument, 1998, Bearball, Sport, 2002. Asst. scoutmaster Boy Scouts Am., Indpls., 1989, Cotulla, 1990-91, Webelos leader, Bryan, 1990-91; pres., founder "Cool"ality Kid Found., 1995. With U.S. Army, 1972-74. Recipient People's Choice award, Lewis & Clark Ctr. for Art & History, 2003; scholar, Leigh Yawkey Woodson Art Mus., Wausau, Wis., 1986. Mem. Nat. Art Edn. Assn., Tex. Art Edn. Assn., Braxos Valley Art Educators Assn. (pres. 1991-93), Brazos Valley Art League, Kappa Delta Pi. Avocations: building houses, carpentry, ornithology. Home: 704 S Spring St Lampasas TX 76550-2667

BEARD, CAROL ELAINE, art educator; b. Boston, May 26, 1945; d. William John and Madolyn Ruth (Johnson) Beard; children from previous marriage: John C. Zajac, Matthew D. Zajac. BSE, Mass. Coll. Art, 1967; student, U. Mass., Dartmouth, 1986, Stonehill Coll., Stoughton, Mass., 1989. Cert. art tchr. Mass., art supr. Mass. Art tchr. Framingham (Mass.) Sch. Dept., 1967—71; art dir. Norfolk (Mass.) Recreation Dept., 1974—83; instr. art Franklin (Mass.) HS Adult Edn., 1986—87; dir. art Norfolk Sch. Dept., 1980—, student coun. advisor, 1993—. Freelance artist graphic designs for various town bds. and orgns., 1967—; collaborator Step-Outside: Cmty.-Based Art Edn., 1994; invited exch. tchr. Wash. Ambassadorship Program, 1994. Author: (poetry) Fallen Requiem, 1964; soft sculptures. Mem. Norfolk Ins. Com., 1989—97, Norfolk Sch. Com., 1990—97; chair Collective Bargaining Com., Norfolk, 1988—96. Mem.: NEA, ASCD, Norfolk County Tchrs. Assn., Mass. Art Edn. Assn., Nat. Art Edn. Assn., Norfolk Tchrs. Assn. (pres. 1988—97, Tchr. of the Yr. 1992), Mass. Tchrs. Assn. Avocations: creative writing, clothes design, golf, photography, toy design. Home: 9 Lincoln St Franklin MA 02038 Office: Centennial Sch 70 Boardman St Norfolk MA 02056-1099 E-mail: beard@norfolk.k12.us.ma.

BEARD, RICHARD BURNHAM, engineering educator emeritus, researcher; b. Boston, Dec. 17, 1922; s. Daniel and Anne (Curran) B.; m. Marilyn D. W. Beard, Sept. 18, 1948; children: Beverly, Amy, Adrienne. BSChemE, Northeastern U., 1947; SM in Elec. Engring., Harvard U., 1950; PhD in Elec. Engring., U. Pa., 1965. Chemist Weymouth Artificial Leather, South Braintree, Mass., 1947-48; rsch. engr. Honeywell, Phila., 1950-58;

instr. Drexel U., Phila., 1958-60; rsch. assoc. U. Pa., Phila., 1960-65; assoc. prof. elec. engring. Drexel U., Phila., 1965-73, prof. elec. engring., 1973-93, prof. emeritus, 1993—. Dir. biomed. engring. and sci. inst. Drexel U., Phila., 1974-76. Contbr. articles to profl. jours. and procs. including Jour. Applied Polymer Sci., Polymer Bull., Procs. Soc. Photo-Optical Instrument Engrs. Vol. 2309, Vol. 2678. Cpl. U.S. Army, 1943-46. Mem. IEEE (sr.), AAAS, Acoustical Soc. Am., Am. Chem. Soc. Achievements include patents in field. Home: 880 Willow Way Atco NJ 08004-1339

BEARMAN, TONI CARBO See CARBO, TONI

BEASLEY, DIANA LEE, educational administrator; b. Akron, Ohio, Aug. 9, 1952; d. Walter and Margaret (Webb) Sims; 1 child, Leon. BS, Cent. State U., 1973; MA, Howard U., 1983; doctoral student, U. Md., 1991--. Cert. tchr. Md. Classroom tchr. Prince Georges (Md.) County Pub. Schs., 1975-88; coord. social studies Largo (Md.) High Sch., 1989-91; coord. program Potomac H.S. Acad. of Law and Pub. Policy and Acad. Fin., Oxon Hill, Md., 1991--; instructional specialist (K-12) Oxon Hill Staff Devel. Ctr., 1995—. Tchr. cons. Houghton Mifflen Pub. Co., 1989; chair Potomac High Sch. Multicultural Com., 1993-94; instr. African Am. history and culture staff devel. course Prince Georges County Pub. Schs., 1994. Co-author: Study Guide for Anthony Browder's Nile Valley Contribution to Civilization; contbr. articles to profl. publs. Active Potomac H.S. PTSA. Nat. Endowment for the Humanities fellow, 1988, 89. Mem. Nat. Coun. Social Studies (chair 1989—), Minority Involvement Com., Nat. Alliance Black Sch. Educators (sec. 1991-92), Largo High Parent Tchr. Assn., Phi Alpha Theta. Democrat. Methodist. Avocations: reading, roller skating, horseback riding. Home: PO Box 364 Mahwah NJ 07430-0364

BEASLEY, MARY CATHERINE, home economics educator, administrator, researcher; b. Portersville, Ala., Nov. 29, 1922; d. Albert Otis and Beulah Green (Killian) Reed; m. Percy Wells Beasley, Dec. 15, 1956 (dec. Dec. 1958). BS in Home Econs., Bob Jones U., 1944; MS, Pa. State U., State College, 1954, EdD, 1968. Tchr. Geraldine and Collinsville (Ala.) High Sch., 1944-45; vocat. home econs. tchr. Glencoe (Ala.) High Sch., 1945-48, Washington County High Sch., Chatom, Ala., 1948-51; home econs. tchr. Homewood Jr. High Sch., Birmingham, Ala., 1958-60; asst. supr. and subject matter specialist Ala. Dept. Edn., Montgomery, 1951-57; asst. prof. Samford U., Birmingham, 1960-62; instr. U. Ala., Tuscaloosa, 1951, asst. prof. then assoc. prof., 1962-68, dir. continuing edn. in home econs., 1968-84, prof., 1984-88, prof. emeritus consumer sci. Coll. Human Environ. Sci., 1988—. Author: (with others) Human Ecological Studies, 1986. Pres. Joint Legis. Coun. of Ala., 1973-75; dir. On Your Own Program, 1970-80; v.p. bd. dirs. Collinsville Cemetery Assn., 2000-02, pres., 2002—. Recipient Creative Programming award Nat. U. Extension Assn., 1979, Women of Achievement award, 2000; named N.E. Ala Woman of Distinction, Girl Scouts North Ala., Inc., 2002. Mem. Am. Home Econs. Assn. (chmn. rehab. com. 1973, 75, leader 1986), Southeastern Coun. on Family Rels. (pres. 1982-84, Disting. Svc. award 1988), Ala. Home Econs. Assn. (pres. 1961-63, leader 1985), Ala. Coun. on Family Rels. (pres. 1981-83, Disting. Svc. award 1987), Altrusa Club of Tuscaloosa (pres. 1988-89, exec. bd. Ft. Payne/DeKalb 1989-93, corr. sec. 1995-96), Collinsville Study Club (v.p. 1992-94, pres. 1996-98, 2002--, reporter 1998-2000, parliamentarian 2000-2002), Ala. Federated Womens Clubs (dir. dist. II 1999-00), Alpha Delta Kappa (treas. Tuscaloosa chpt. 1973-75), Phi Upsilon Omicron, Kappa Omicron Nu. Republican. Baptist. Home: 12860 US Highway 11 Collinsville AL 35961-4321

BEASLEY, MAURINE HOFFMAN, journalism educator, historian; b. Jan. 28, 1936; d. Dimmitt Heard and Maurine (Hieronymus) Hoffman; m. William C. McLaughlin, May 20, 1966 (div. 1969); m. Henry R. Beasley, Dec. 24, 1970; 1 child, Susan Sook. BA in History, U. Mo., 1958; MS in Journalism, Columbia U., 1963; PhD in Am. Civilization, George Washington U., 1974. Edn. editor Kansas City (Mo.) Star, 1959—62; staff writer Washington Post, 1963—73; from asst. prof journalism to prof. U. Md., College Park, 1975—87, prof., 1987—, grad. dir. Coll. Journalism, 2000—02; sr. lectr. Fulbright Jinan U., Guangzhou, China, 2000. Author: Eleanor Roosevelt and the Media: A Public Quest for Self-Fulfillment, 1987; author: (with others) Women in Media, 1977, The New Majority, 1988, Taking Their Place! Documentary History of Women and Journalism, rev., 2002 (Outstanding Acad. Books Choice, 1994); editor: White House Press Conferences of Eleanor Roosevelt, 1983; co-editor: Voices of Change: Southern Pulitzer Winners, 1978, One Third of a Nation, 1981 (hon. mention Washington Monthly Book award, 1982), Eleanor Roosevelt Encyclopedia, 2000 (Editor's Choice award Booklist, 2001); mem. adv. bd. Am. Journalism, 1983—, Jour. Mass Media Ethics, —, Mass Com. Rev., —; corr. editor: Journalism History, 1995—; contbr. articles to profl. jours. Violinist Montgomery County Symphony Orch., 1975—; pres. Little Falls Swimming Club, Inc. 1988-89; bd. dirs. Sino-Am. Ctr. for Media Tech. and Tng., 2000—. Gannett Tchg. Fellowships Program fellow, 1977, Pulitzer Travelling fellow Columbia U., 1963; Eleanor Roosevelt studies grantee Eleanor Roosevelt Inst., 1979-80, Arthur Schlesinger rsch. fellow and grantee Roosevelt Inst., 1998; named one of nation's outstanding tchrs. of writing and editing Modern Media Inst. and Am. Soc. Newspaper Editors, 1981, most outstanding woman U. Md. Coll. Park Pres. Commn. on Women's Affairs, 1993; recipient Haiman award Speech Comm. Assn., 1995, Founders Disting. Sr. Scholar award AAUW Ednl. Found., 1999, Columbia U. Sch. Journalism Alumni award, 2000, Smith-Cotton H.S. Hall Fame award, Sedalia, Mo., 2000. Mem.: AAUW (v.p. Coll. Pk. br. 2002—), Am. Journalism Historians Assn. (pres.-elect 1988—89, pres. 1989—90, Kobre award for lifetime achievement 1997, Rsch. Paper award named in her honor 1998), Internat. Assn. Mass. Comms. Rsch., Soc. Profl. Journalists (chair nat. hist. site com. 1986—87, bd. dirs. Washington chpt. 1988—90, pres. 1990—91, dir. region 2, nat. bd. dirs. 1991—92, Disting. Local Svc. award 1994, First Amendment award with others 1998), Assn. Edn. in Journalism and Mass Comms. (sec. history divsn. 1986—87, vice-head 1987—88, head history divsn. 1988—89, chair profl. freedom and responsibility 1990—91, exec. com. 1990—91, nat. pres. elect 1992, pres. 1993—94, leader People-to-People delegation to China and Hong Kong 1994, exec. com. 1994—95, Outstanding Contbn. to Journalism Edn. award 1994, Disting. Leadership award 2001), Am. Hist. Assn., Am. News Women's Club (bd. govs. 2001—03), Women in Comms., Orgn. Am. Historians, Omicron Delta Kappa, Phi Beta Kappa. Democrat. Unitarian Universalist. Home: 4920 Flint Dr Bethesda MD 20816-1746 Office: U Md Coll Journalism College Park MD 20742 E-mail: mbeasley@jmail.umd.edu.

BEATH, PAULA MARIE RUARK, education educator, consultant; b. Cambridge, Md., Dec. 1, 1950; d. Paul Kenneth and Ellen Marie (Parks) Ruark; 1 child, Ernest Ballard Beath. BS in Elem. Edn., Salisbury State Coll., 1972, MS in Elem. Edn., 1975; PhD in Reading and Early Childhood Edn., U. Md., 1979. Cert. elem./mid. sch. supr., prin., reading specialist grades K-12, elem. grades 1-6 and mid. sch. supt. Elem. tchr. Dorchester County Bd. Edn., Cambridge, Md., 1972-78, sch. prin., 1979-94, reading specialist, 1995—; specialist Md. State Dept. Edn., Balt., 1994-95. Vis. prof., coord. Reading Ctr., and liaison with Montgomery and Prince George's Counties, U. Md., College Park, 1978-79; adj. prof. Salisbury (Md.) State U., 1994—. Author: Survival Reading Task Cards, 1976, Teacher's Survival Guide-Dimensions of Learning and Its Role in Maryland's Educational Initiatives, 1996. Choir dir. Hoopers Meml. Ch., Hoopersville, Md., 1970-80, cert. lay leader, 1975-80, mem. adminstrv. bd., 1979-84, Sunday sch. tchr., 1972-81; collaborate with YMCA to implement programs for county youths; designer vol. program in collaboration with Dorchester County Commn. on Aging; mem. Dorchester County Mus. Com. Named Md. Tchr. of Yr., 1978; recipient award Dorchester Ret. Tchrs. Assn., 1978; named to Outstanding Young Women of Am., 1980. Mem. ASCD, Md. Assn. Elem. Sch. Prins., Nat. Staff Devel. Coun., Delta Kappa Gamma, Phi Delta Kappa. Home: 2216 Horn Point Rd Cambridge MD 21613-3379

BEATTIE, EDWARD JAMES, surgeon, educator; b. Phila., June 30, 1918; m. Nicole Mary; 1 son, Bruce Stewart. BA, Princeton U., 1939; MD, Harvard U., 1943. Diplomate Am. Bd. Surgery, Am. Bd. Thoracic Surgery (mem. bd. 1960-69, chmn. bd. 1967-69). Intern, surg. resident Peter Bent Brigham Hosp., Boston, 1942-46; Mosely traveling fellow (Harvard) to U. London, Eng., 1946-47; surg. fellow, Markle scholar George Washington U., 1947-52; chief thoracic surgery Presbyn. Hosp., 1952-54; chmn. dept. surgery Presbyn.-St. Luke's Hosp., 1954-65; cons. thoracic surgery Hines VA Hosp., Ill., 1953-65, Chgo. Tb San., 1954-65, Ill. Research and Edn. Hosp., 1956-65, Rockefeller U. Hosp., 1978-83; prof. surgery U. Ill., 1955-65, Cornell U., 1965-83, emeritus, 1983—; prof. surgery, prof. oncology U. Miami, Fla., 1983-85; prof. surgery Mt. Sinai Sch. Medicine, N.Y.C., 1988-94, Albert Einstein Coll. Medicine, 1994—. Chief thoracic surgery Meml. Hosp., N.Y.C., 1965-75, chmn. dept. surgery, 1966-78, chief med. officer, 1966-83, gen. dir., chief oper. officer, 1975-83; chief thoracic surgery, dir. Kriser Lung Cancer Ctr., dir. clin. cancer programs Beth Israel Med. Ctr., N.Y.C., 1985-95, dir. emeritus Kriser Lung Cancer Ctr., 1995, med. dir. Cancer Ctr., 1994—. Mem. editl. bd. Jour. Thoracic and Cardiovascular Surgery, 1962-83, Pediat. Digest, 1962-85, Cancer Clin. Trials, 1977-85, Internat. Advances in Surg. Oncology, 1977. Fellow A.C.S.; mem. Am. Assn. Thoracic Surgery, Am. Surg. Assn., Soc. Vascular Surgery, AMA, Central, Western surg. assns., Internat. Soc. Surgery, Soc. Clin. Surgery, Am. Radium Soc., Soc. Thoracic Surgeons, Transplantation Soc., Am. Assn. Med. Colls., Pan Am. Med. Assn., Am. Cancer Soc., Am. Fedn. Clin. Research, Soc. Surg. Oncology.

BEATTY, BETTY JOY, library educator; b. Columbus, Ohio, Mar. 25, 1926; d. Lee E. and Gladys (Heffner) Howard; m. James Auerhan Hecht, May 6, 1950 (dec. July 9, 1974); children: James Auerhan (dec.), Timothy Lee, David Arthur; m. Benjamin M. Beatty, Dec. 19, 1975 (dec. Oct. 1997). BFA, Ohio State U., Columbus, 1947, MA, 1948. Branch librarian Warder Public Library (now Clark County Library), Springfield, Ohio, 1957-59; librarian, teacher Shawnee H.S., Springfield, 1959-66; acquisition librarian Wittenberg U., Springfield, 1966-72, head, technical svcs., 1972-84, acting dir. univ. libraries, 1983-84, assoc. prof. emerita, 1992—. Mem. bd. dirs. Faculty Devel. Orgn., Springfield, 1975-78 pres. Wittenberg U. Fed. Credit Union, Springfield, 1979-81, sec. 1984-87; pres. AAUP, Springfield, 1980. Treas. Springfield Symphony Women's Assn., 1974-76; sec. bd. dirs. Touch of Love AIDS Support, Springfield, 1988-95. Mem. Alpha Chi Omega Sorority (pres. 1964-66, sec. 1985-87, 94-96). Democrat. Roman Catholic. Avocations: painting, reading. Home: 615 Piney Branch Dr Springfield OH 45503-2315

BEATTY, JUDY IOLA SPENCER, educational specialist; b. McAllen, Tex., Oct. 12, 1954; d. Wayne Ellsworth and Vivian Ruth (Comer) S.; m. Terry L. Beatty, Mar. 21, 1976; children: Amanda Marie, Emily Renee, Matthew Spencer. Student, Iowa Ctrl. C.C., 1973-75, LaSalle U. Libr. dir. Gentry County Libr., Stanberry, Mo. Bd. dirs. United Meth. Ch., Parnell, Mo. Mem. ALA, AAUW, NAFE, Mo. Libr. Assn., Grand River Libr. Assn. (pres.), Am. Legion Aux. Avocations: music, reading, gardening. Office: Gentry County Libr 2d and Park Sts Stanberry MO 64489

BEATTY, MARILYN BARTON, special education educator; b. Cin., June 7, 1952; d. Robert Scott and Evelyn (Barton) B. BS, Ball State U., 1974; MEd, Xavier U., Cin., 1977. Cert. elem. tchr., spl. edn. tchr., Ohio. Spl. edn. tchr. Columbus (Ohio) Pub. Schs., 1974-75, Western Brown Local Schs., Mt. Orab, Ohio, 1975—. Mem. NEA, Oho Edn. Assn., Western Brown Edn. Assn.

BEATTY, ROBERT ALFRED (R. ALFRED), surgeon, educator; b. Colchester, Vt., May 7, 1936; s. George Lewis and Leila Margaret (Ebright) B.; m. Frances Calomeni, Aug. 24, 1963; children: Bradford, Roxanna. BA, U. Oreg., 1959, BS, 1960, MD, 1961. Diplomate Am. Bd. Neurol. Surgery. Intern U. Ill. Rsch. and Edn. Hosp., Chgo., 1961-62; resident neurosurgery U. Ill., Chgo., 1962-66; practice neurosurgery Hinsdale, Ill., 1967—; mem. staff Hinsdale Hosp., 1967—, Cmty. Meml. Hosp., LaGrange, Ill., 1967—, U. Ill. Hosp., Chgo., 1967—, Good Samaritan Hosp., Downers Grove, Ill., Elmhurst (Ill.) Hosp.; clin. assoc. prof. neurosurgery U. Ill., 1967—. Founding adviser Marion Joy Rehab. Center, Wheaton, Ill., 1969-7; mem. State Ill. Spinal Cord Injury Adv. Coun., 1995, vice-chmn. 1997. Contbr. articles to profl. jours. Mem. founder's coun. Field Mus. Capt. USMC, AUS, 1968. Rsch. fellow St. George's Med. Sch., London, 1966-67. Mem. AMA, ACS, SAR, Ill. Med. Soc., Dupage County Med. Soc., Am. Assn. Neurol. Surgeons, N.Am. Spine Soc., Congress Neurol. Surgeons, Soc. Brit. Neurol. Surgeons, Internat. Microsurg. Soc., Nat. Assn. Spine Specialists, English Speaking Union, John Evans Club (N.W. U.), Theodore Thomas Soc., Chgo. Symphony Orch. (governing mem.), Hinsdale Golf Club, Phi Beta Kappa, Phi Beta Pi, Phi Kappa Psi. Republican. Achievements include research on intracranial aneurysms, lumbar discs; inventor medical instruments; profl. sculptor (under name R. Alfred). Office: 333 Chestnut St Hinsdale IL 60521-3247

BEATTY, ROBERT CLINTON, religious studies educator; b. Needham, Mass., May 19, 1935; s. Henry Russell and Alice Cornelia (van Schagen) B.; m. Carolyn Phyllis Caton, Oct. 5, 1957; children: Robert Russell, Daniel Clinton, Melissa Lynn, Alicia Felicity. AB in Econs., Northeastern U., 1957; MBA in Mgmt., Fairleigh Dickinson U., 1973; MDiv, Columbia Biblical Sem., 1983, MA in Bible, 1985; DMin in Orgn. Devel., Fuller Theol. Sem., 1993. Ordained to ministry Harmony Ch., 1984. Commd. 2d lt. U.S. Army, 1957, advanced through grades to lt. col., ret., 1980; dir. U.S. extension ctrs. Columbia (S.C.) Internat. U., 1983-89; assoc. prof., chmn. bus. mgmt. Miami Christian Coll., 1989-92, Trinity Internat. U., Miami, 1992-2001, undergrad. program coord., 2001—02; MAR program coord. South Fla. ext. Trinity Evang. Div. Sch., 1994—; prof. Calvary Chapel Bible Inst., 2000—. Lectr. Christian Leadership Tng. Inst., Chisinau, Moldova, 2001—; adj. prof. Embry Riddle Aero. U., Mannheim, Germany, 1976—77, City Colls. of Chgo., Mannheim, 1976—77; bible study tchr. Prison Fellowship, Columbia, 1981—89, Calvary Chapel, Ft. Lauderdale, 1996—2000; ch./ministry bd. cons., 1987—. Author: Extension Coordinator's Handbook, 1984, 1985, 1987, 1989, (student manual) Practical Applications of Biblical Hermeneutics, 1992—94, 2000, 2003, Human Resource Management, 1992, (manual) Business Ethics, 1991, Organization Behavior, 1991, Acts: A Sociological and Cross Cultural Communications Perspective, 1991; editor: Adjunct-Extension Faculty Handbook, 1984, 1985, 1989. Decorated Legion of Merit, Bronze Star with oak leaf cluster, Air medal, Meritorious Svc. medal, Gallantry Cross with Silver Star; recipient Vol. of Yr. award Goodman Correctional Instn., 1985, Broad River Correctional Instn., 1989, Prof. of Yr. award Trinity Internat. U., 2001. Mem.: DAV, Mil. Officers Assn. of Am., AARP. Republican. Avocation: travel. Home: 10500 NW 21st Ct Sunrise FL 33322-3509 Office: Calvary Chapel Bible Inst 2401 W Cypress Creek Rd Fort Lauderdale FL 33309 E-mail: bibleprof@msn.com.

BEAUDIN, KIMBERLY ANN, special education educator; b. Dixon, Ill., Dec. 12, 1959; d. Wayne Arlen and Patricia Ann (Coursey) Pierce; children: Dawn Marie, Christopher M., Alexandra F. Student, Sauk Valley Coll., 1977; BS in Edn., Mt. Vernon (Ohio) Coll., 1979; postgrad., Des Moines Area C.C., 1988-95, Grandview Coll., 2002—. LPN. Clk. Ohio Sec. of State, Mt. Vernon, 1977—79; office mgr. BDM Corps., Amboy, Ill., 1977—80; asst. mgr. SBM Bus., Dixon, 1980—90; prin. Happy House Day Care and Presch., Des Moines, 1981—91; spl. advocate juvenile ct. system Des Moines, 1986—96; pres. Animal House Day Care and Presch. Inc., Des Moines, 1991—96; v.p. GB Constrn., 1996—98; exec. leader Avon, 1997—2000; ind. cons. Longaberger, 1998—2000; bank supr. Praurie Meadows, 1999—2000; spl. edn. tchr. Des Moines Pub. Schs., 2001—. County coordinator Ams. for Robertson, Des Moines, 1987-88. Recipient Gov.'s award State of Iowa, 1988. Mem. NAFE, ASCD, BBB, Nat. Fedn. Ind. Bus., Nat. Assn. Young Children, Iowa Assn. Young Children (sec., treas. 1986-87, pres. 1987-88), Child Care Coun. (bd. dirs. 1985—), U.S. C. of C., AIB Inst. Republican.

BEAUFAIT, FREDERICK W(ILLIAM), civil engineering educator; b. Vicksburg, Miss., Nov. 28, 1936; s. Frank W. and Eleanor Chambliss (Haynes) B.; m. Lois Mary Erdman, Nov. 27, 1964; children: Paul Frederick, Nicole. BSc, Miss. State U., 1958; MSc, U. Ky., 1961; PhD, Va. Poly. Inst., 1965. Structural engr. U.S. Army C.E., Vicksburg, 1958-59; engr. L. E. Gregg & Assocs., Lexington, Ky., 1959-60; vis. lectr. civil engring. U. Liverpool, Eng., 1960-61; prof. civil engring. Vanderbilt U., Nashville, 1965-79; prof., chmn. dept. civil engring. W.Va. U., Morgantown, 1979-83, assoc. dean Coll. Engring., 1983-86; dean Coll. Engring. Wayne State U., Detroit, 1986-95; dir. NSF Greenfield Engring. Edn. Coalition, 1996-98; pres. N.Y.C. Coll. Tech. of the CUNY, 1999—. Vis. prof. civil and structural engring. U. Wales, Cardiff, 1975-76; cons. in field; mem. Engring. Accreditation Commn. Accreditation Bd. for Engring. and Tech., 1988-93, Engring. Manpower Commn., 1988-92; bd. dirs. Ford (Motor) Design Inst., 1991-96. Co-author: Computer Methods of Structural Analysis, 1970; author: Basic Concepts in Structural Analysis, 1977; also over 40 articles to profl. jours. Vice chmn. stewardship com. 1st Presbyn. Ch., Morgantown, 1982, elder, 1983-85, mem. long-range planning com., 1985-86; deacon Southminster Presbyn. Ch., Nashville, 1968-69, elder, 1971-73, 78-79, clk. of session, 1971-73; bd. dirs. Presbyn. Campus Ministry, Nashville, 1972-78, treas., 1972-75, pres., 1976-78; mem. citizens adv. com. Met. Sch. System, Nashville, 1978-79; bd. dirs. Independence Cmty. Found., 2001—. Named Outstanding Vol. of Yr. Mich. Ctr. for High Tech., 1991. Mem. ASCE, NSPE, Mich. Soc. Profl. Engrs. (bd. dirs. Detroit metro chpt. 1987-90, vice chmn. 1991, chmn.-elect 1992, chmn. 1993, pres. profls. in engring. edn. divsn. 1990-93, state bd. dirs., treas. 1995-97, v.p. 1997-98, Outstanding Engr. in Edn. 1994), Am. Soc. Engring. Edn. (chmn. civil engring. divsn. 1992-93, Centennial medallion 1993, George K. Wadlin award of Civil Engring. Divsn. 1994), Engring. Soc. Detroit (Coll. of Fellows 1994, gold award 1997), Order of Engrs. (bd. governance 1989-97), Chevalier dans l'Ordre des Palmes Academiques (France), Chi Epsilon, Tau Alpha Pi, Tau Beta Pi. Home: One Main St Apt 4D Brooklyn NY 11201 Office: NYC Coll Tech CUNY 300 Jay St Brooklyn NY 11201-1909 E-mail: fbeaufait@citytech.cuny.edu.

BEAULIEU, CAROL MARIE, special education educator; b. Highland Park, Mich., June 8, 1963; d. Alfred Robert and Shirley Ann (McLarney) Beaulieu. BS, Ea. Mich. U., 1994. Cert. in elem. edn. K-8, edn. of mentally impaired K-8, Fla., Mich. Program specialist Mich. Human Svcs., Ann Arbor, 1980-84; program mgr. Washtenaw County Cmty. Mental Health, Ypsilanti, Mich., 1984-86; program specialist Adminstrv. Specialists, Belleville, Mich., 1990-92; spl. edn. tchr. Lee County Pub. Schs., Ft. Myers, Fla., 1992—. Served to sgt. USAF, 1986-90. Phi Delta Kappa scholar, 1993, Disabled Vets. scholar, 1993. Mem. ASCD, Coun. for Exceptional Children, Phi Delta Kappa. Avocations: golf, gardening, computers. Home: 1987 Washington St Algonac MI 48001-1060 Office: 9822 Foxway Ct Dexter MI 48130-9533

BEAULIEU, RODNEY JOSEPH, academic administrator, education educator; b. Van Buren, Maine, Sept. 24, 1957; s. O'Neil and Theresa (Grivois) B. BA in Psychology, U. Mass., 1980; MA in Ednl. Psychology, U. Calif., Santa Barbara, 1991, PhD in Ednl. Psychology, 1995. Ind. computer cons., Santa Barbara, 1983-90; instr. U. Calif., Santa Barbara, 1989-93, rsch. assoc., 1992—; adminstr. Fielding Inst., Santa Barbara, 1990—; prof., co-founder ednl. leadership and change program, 1998—. Adj. prof. Ventura (Calif.) Coll., 1998-2000, Calif. State U., San Marcos, 2001—. Asst. editor Phenomenology and Human Scis. Jour., 1994—97; contbr. articles to profl. jours. Vol. Women's Resource Ctr., Oceanside, Calif., 2000—. Mem. Am. Ednl. Rsch. Assn., Am. Sociol. Assn. (com. on tchg. 1994—), Pacific Sociol Assn. Avocations: painting, gardening. Home: 421 S Barnwell St Oceanside CA 92054-4510 E-mail: rjbeaulieu@earthlink.net.

BEAUMONTE, PHYLLIS ILENE, retired secondary school educator; b. Seattle, Dec. 15; d. Albert Hendrix and Bessie Dorothy (Buford) Ratcliff; m. Pierre Marshall Beaumonte, Mar. 12, 1962 (div. Aug. 1974). BA in Polit. Sci., U. Wash., 1973, BA in Editl. Journalism, 1973, MPA, 1975; postgrad., N.W. Theol. Union, Seattle, 1990-92; M in Pastoral Studies/Theology, Seattle U., 2001. Cert. tchr. K-12 Wash. Adminstrv. intern Office of the City Coun., Seattle, 1974; guest lectr. Pacific Luth. U., Tacoma, 1975; tchr. Hebrew Acad., Seattle, 1979; instr./tchr. Seattle Ctrl. C.C., 1988; tchr. Seattle Pub. Schs., 1980—2000; coord. hs Bus. Ptnrs. in Pub. Edn., Seattle, 1989-92; social studies chairperson Rainier Beach HS, Seattle, 1992—2000; ret., 2000. Cons. RA Beau Enterprises, Seattle, 1987—; participant Ctr. R&D in Law-Related Edn. Wake Forest U., Winston-Salem, NC, 1994; adv. com. Wash. State Commn. Student Learning, Social Studies Acad. Learning Requirements, 1994—; part-time faculty South C.C., Seattle, 1998—99. Author: (poetry) Satyagraha; author, editor: Roses and Thorns, 1994, writer, pub.: Parent Guardian Handbook: A Guide to Understanding Public Education and Standardized Testing, 2002. Mem. King County Women's Polit. Caucus, Seattle, 1993—; v.p. Ch. Women United, Wash. and Idaho, 1976—78, pres., 2002—, Seattle Ch. Women United, 2001—02; mem. candidate evaluation com. Seattle Mcpl. League, 1972—74; Seattle edn. sch. rep. Seattle Tchrs. Union, 1983—85; alumni advisor Grad. Sch. Pub. Affairs U. Wash., 1994—; pres. Black Heritage Soc. Wash. Scholar Minority Journalism, U. Wash., 1972. Mem.: NAACP (mem. exec. bd., v.p. state conf. Wash., v.p. state conf. Oreg., v.p. state conf. Alaska, state chair edn., Daisy Bates Adv. award), Edn. Social and Pub. Svcs. Assn. (pres.), Nat. Coun. Social Studies, Nat. Coun. History Edn. (cert. of appreciation 1993), Internat. Soc. Poets (life Internat. Poet of Merit award 1993), Mus. History and Industry, Sigma Gamma Rho. Baptist. Avocations: singing, writing, reading, teaching. Home: 10012 61st Ave S Seattle WA 98178-2333

BEAVER, BONNIE VERYLE, veterinarian, educator; b. Mpls., Oct. 26, 1944; d. Crawford F. and Gladys I. Gustafson; m. Larry J. Beaver, Nov. 25, 1972 (dec. Nov. 1995). BS, U. Minn., 1966, D.V.M., 1968; MS, Tex. A&M U., 1972. Instr. vet. surgery and radiology U. Minn., 1968-69; instr. vet. anatomy Tex. A&M U., College Station, 1969-72, asst. prof., 1972-76, assoc. prof., 1976-82; prof. Tex A&M U., College Station, 1982-86, prof. vet. small animal medicine and surgery, 1986—, chief medicine, 1990-99. Mem. vet. medicine adv. com. HEW, 1972-74, nat. adv. food and drug com., HEW, 1975, com. on animal models and genetic stocks NAS, 1984-86, 87-89, panel on microlivestock NRC, 1986-87, task force on animal use study Inst. Lab. Animal Resources, 1986, adv. com. for Pew Nat. Vet. Edn. Program, Pew Charitable Trusts, 1987-92, 10th symposium on Vet. Med. Edn. Com., 1988-89. Mem. editl. bd. Applied Animal Ethology, 1981-82, 83-84, VM/SAC, 1982-85, Applied Animal Behavior Sci., 1982-84, 84-86, 86-88, 88-2000, Bull. on Vet. Clin. Ethology, 1994-1999, Jour. Am. Animal Hosp. Assn., 1995—; contbr. articles to profl. jours. Vice pres. Brazos Valley Regional Sci. and Engring. Fair, 1974— 83, dir., 1983-85; bd. dirs. Brazos Valley unit Am. Cancer Soc., 1976-83, v.p., 1976-83. Named Citizen of Week, The Press, 1981, Outstanding Woman Veterinarian of 1982, Disting. Practitioner, Nat. Acads. Practice; Recipient Friskies PetCare award Am. Animal Hosp. Assn., 2001, Bustad Human-Animal Bond award, 2001, Elanco Disting. Lectr. award, 2002. Mem.: AVMA (exec. bd. 1997—2003, chair exec. bd. 2001—02, pres.-elect 2003—04, Animal Welfare award 1996), AAAS, Am. Horse Coun., Am. Quarter Horse Assn., Tex. Palomino Exhibitors Assn., Palomino Horse Breeders Am. (v.p.

1983—88, treas. 1984—85, pres.-elect 1988—89, pres. 1989—90), Nat. Acad. Practice, Am. Coll. Vet. Behaviorists (chair organizing com. 1976—91, pres. 1991—96, charter diplomat 1993—, exec. dir. 1996—), Animal Behavior Soc., Am. Assn. Bovine Practitioners, Am. Assn. Equine Practitioners, Am. Assn. Vet Clinicians, Am. Vet. Soc. Animal Behavior (pres. 1975—80), Am. Animal Hosp. Assn., Brazos Valley Vet. Med. Assn., Tex. Vet. Med. Assn. (3d v.p. 1990, 2d v.p. 1991, 1st v.p. 1992, pres.-elect 1993, pres. 1994), Phi Delta Gamma (pres. 1974—75), Phi Zeta (nat. pres. 1979—81), Sigma Epsilon Sigma, Phi Sigma, Delta Soc. Office: Tex A&M Univ Coll Vet Medicine Vet Small Animal Medicine & College Station TX 77843-4474

BEAVER, FRANK EUGENE, communication educator, film critic and historian; b. Cleve., N.C., July 26, 1938; s. John Whitfield and Mary Louise (Shell) B.; m. Gail Frances Place, June 30, 1962; children: Julia Clare, John Francis, Johanna Louise. BA, U. N.C., 1960, MA, 1966; PhD, U. Mich., 1970. Instr. speech Memphis State U., 1965-66; instr. radio-TV-motion pictures U. N.C., Chapel Hill, 1966-68; asst. prof. speech comm. U. Mich., Ann Arbor, 1969-74, assoc. prof., 1974-79, assoc. prof. comm., 1979-84, prof., chmn. dept. comm., 1987-91, Arthur F. Thurnau prof., 1989-92, dir. grad. program in telecom. arts and film, 1991-96. Advisor Muskegon (Mich.) Film Festival, 2001. Film critic radio Stas. WUOM, WVGR, WFUM, Ann Arbor, Grand Rapids, Mich., 1975-97; author: Bosley Crowther, 1974, On Film, 1983, Dictionary of Film Terms, 1983, 94 (Mandarin-Chinese translation 1993), Oliver Stone: Wakeup Cinema, 1994, 100 Years of American Film, 2001; writer, dir. documentary film Under One Roof, 1967; editor (book series) Framing Film, 98-, gen. editor Twayne Pubs., N.Y., 1987—. Bd. dirs. Mich. Theater Found., Ann Arbor, 1977-79, 86—; alumni adv. bd. Lambda Chi Alpha, Ann Arbor, 1989-94; advisor Ann Arbor Film Festival, 1975—. With M.I. Corps, U.S. Army, 1962-65, Vietnam. Recipient Playwriting award Carolina Playmakers, 1962, Major Hopwood writing awards for drama and essays U. Mich., 1969, Outstanding Teaching award Amoco Found., Ann Arbor, 1985; fellow NEH, 1975. Mem.: Speech Comm. Assn., Soc. Cinema Scholars, Racquet Club, Azazels Club, Phi Kappa Phi, Kappa Tau Alpha. Democrat. Roman Catholic. Home: 1835 Vinewood Blvd Ann Arbor MI 48104-3609 Office: U Mich Film and Video Studios 2512 Frieze Bldg Ann Arbor MI 48109-1285 E-mail: fbeaver@umich.edu.

BEAVERS, PATSY ANN, elementary teacher; b. Omaha, Nov. 15, 1937; d. William and Ethelyn Esther (Rowan) Murphy; m. Thomas E. Beavers, June 19, 1959; children: Brian Lee, Amy Lyn. BA Elem. Edn., NW Mo. State U., 1966, postgrad. Tchr. schs., Iowa, 1958—99; ret., 1999. Asst. chmn. Am. Cancer Crusade, Shenandoah, Iowa, 1964-66; bd. dirs. Meals on Wheels, Shenandoah, Iowa; mem. meml. com. First Christian Ch., also elder and bd. trustees. Recipient Am. Citizenship awd., Iowa State Bar Assn., 1956; named Outstanding Young Woman Am., 1966, Young Mother of Year, Young Mother's Club, Shenandoah, Iowa, 1972. Mem. NEA (life), AAUW (treas. 1987-90), Iowa State Edn. Assn. (life), Iowa Reading Assn., SW Iowa Reading Assn., Page-Taylor County Ret. Sch. Pers., Order Eastern Star (chaplain, Esther, electa), PEO, Athenaeum (pres. 2002—), Study Club, Delta Kappa Gamma, Beta Sigma Phi (pres., sec., treas.) Mem. First Christian Ch. Avocations: reading, aerobics, walking. Home: 1304 Mitchell St Shenandoah IA 51601-2349

BEBO, JOSEPH ANTHONY, counselor, educator; b. Boston, Dec. 31, 1954; s. John Thomas and Leah B.; m. Frances Gail Coker, Oct. 10, 1978 (dec. Aug. 1988); children: Joseph Anthony Jr., John James; m. Patricia Ann Bebo. BA, U. Mass., 1976, MA in Sociology, 1996, postgrad. in edn., 1999—. Cert. substance abuse counselor Mass. Bd. Counselor Certification. Substance abuse counselor Sullivan House Middlesex Human Svcs., Jamaica Plain, Mass., 1993—99; program coord. alcohol and substance abuse studies cert. and grad. cert. forensci svcs. Coll. Arts and Sci. criminal justice program U. Mass., Boston, 1997—99; lectr. U. Mass, 1999—, Rivier Coll., 1999—2000, Fitchburg State Coll., 1999—; vis. lectr. Bridgewater State Coll., 2001—. Treas. Internat. Coalition Addictions Studies Educators, 2000—, convention coord., 2000; alcohol and drug counselor Divsn. Youth Svcs., Phoenix Ctr., Brockton YMCA, Plymouth County Correctional Facility. Contbr. articles to profl. jours. Recipient Cert. Appreciation, Higher Edn. Ctr. Mem.: Acad. Criminal Justice Scis., Nat. Assn. Alcohol and Drug Abuse Counselors, Northeastern Assn. Criminal Justice Scis. (contbr. criminal justice edn. task force), Am. Soc. Criminology, Alpha Kappa Delta. Office: U Mass 100 Morrissey Blvd Boston MA 02125

BECERRA-FERNANDEZ, IRMA, electrical engineer, researcher, educator; b. Havana, Cuba, Mar. 28, 1960; came to U.S., 1960; d. Daniel Ivan Becerra and Irma Maria Peiteado; m. Vicente L. Fernandez, June 29, 1985; children: Anthony John, Nicole Marie. BSEE, U. Miami, Coral Gables, Fla., 1982, MSEE, 1986; PhDEE, Fla. Internat. U., Miami, 1994. Cert. engr. in tng., Fla., 1982. Engr., corp. instr. Fla. Power and Light, Miami, 1983-90; rsch. assoc. Fla. Internat. U., Miami, 1990—94, dir., vis. prof. Coll. Engring., 1994—98, asst. prof. Coll. Bus. Adminstrn., 1998—. Scholar Nat. Hispanic Scholarship Fund, Miami, 1982, Unico Nat. Soc., Miami, 1978; Women's History Month honoree Coalition Hispanic Am. Women, 1997. Mem. IEEE, Assn. Cuban Engrs. (v.p. 1994-96, pres. 1996, Student of Yr. 1993, faculty advisor), Soc. Women Engrs. (faculty advisor), Eta Kappa Nu (v.p. 1981-82, Most Valuable Mem. 1982), Tau Beta Pi, Phi Kappa Phi. Roman Catholic.

BECHERER, RICHARD JOHN, architecture educator; b. East St. Louis, Ill., Nov. 8, 1951; s. Adam Jacob and Agnes Evelyn (Baker) B.; m. Charlene Castellano, Aug. 13, 1982. Student Courtauld Inst., U. London, 1973; BA, BArch, Rice U., 1974; MA, Cornell U., 1977, PhD, 1981. Archtl. asst. Colin St. John Wilson and Ptnr., London, England, 1972-73; designer The Brooks Assn., Houston, 1973-74; grad. asst. Cornell U., Ithaca, N.Y., 1974-80, asst. prof. architecture, 1981; asst. prof. Auburn (Ala.) U., 1980-82, U. Va., Charlottesville, 1982-86; head grad. architecture program Carnegie Mellon U., Pitts., 1986-90, assoc. prof. architecture, 1987-96; assoc. prof. Cornell U., 1996, Am. U. Beirut, 1999—2001, Iowa State U., 2001—. Presenter seminars NEH, 1982, 88, 89, Am. Collegiate Schs. Architecture, 1988, 93, 97, 2002; lectr. Centre Canadien d'Architecture, Montreal, Carnegie Mus., Pitts., and various colls., univs. and nat. confs.; vis. assoc. prof. U. Pitts., 1997-99; assoc. prof. Am. U. Beirut, 1999—, Iowa State U.; mem. Fulbright Fellowship selection com. Author: Science Plus Sentiment; César Daly's Formula for Modern Architecture, 1984, (mus. catalogue and display) Urban Theory and Transformation, 1976, (tourist guidebook) Canandaigua: A Walking Tour, 1977; contbr. articles to profl. jours.; prin. works include interiors Michael P. Keeley House, Belleville, Ill., 1978, Robert Becherer House, Stonybrook, 1990; selected exhibitor Venice Biennale, Prato della Valle, Padua, 1985; exhibitor Heart of the Park, Houston, 1992. Recipient Design Arts award Nat. Endowment for Arts, 1989-90, Graham Found. award, 1993; grad. fellow Cornell U., 1975-79, Eidlitz fellow, 1978, Soc. for Humanities and Mellon Found. fellow, 1984-85, NEH fellow, 1986, Paul Mellon vis. sr. fellow Ctr. for Advanced Study in Visual Arts, Nat. Gallery of Art; Travel to Collections grantee NEH, 1985. Mem. AAUP, Soc. Archtl. Historians (session chmn. ann. meeting 1989), Coll. Art Assn., Rice U. Alumni Assn. Democrat. Roman Catholic. Avocations: free-hand drawing, ballroom dancing, film. Home and Office: 119 Race St Pittsburgh PA 15218-1337 E-mail: agnes@iastate.edu.

BECHTOL, DENNIS L. education educator, sport and business management consultant; b. Lima, Ohio, Oct. 27, 1947; s. Marque F. and Margaret S. B.; m. Janie G. Fuller, June 8, 1988. AA in Edn., Miami-Dade C.C., 1970; BS in Edn., Fla. State U., 1973; MA in Edn., U. South Fla., 1981; PhD in Edn., U. N.Mex., 1994. Cert. tchr., Fla., Md. Tchr. Pinellas County Schs., Clearwater-St. Petersburg, Fla., 1973-76; pharm. ter. mgr. Ayerst Labs., Inc., N.Y.C., 1976-78; coll. textbook ter. mgr. Holt, Rinehart and Winston Pubs., Inc., N.Y.C., 1978-81; Southeastern regional ter. mgr. Person & Covey, Inc., Glendale, Calif., 1981-88; regional ter. mgr. Hermal Pharm. Labs., Inc., Oak Hill, N.Y., 1988-90, Neutrogena Dermatologics, Inc., L.A., 1990-91, Hill Dermaceuticals, Inc., Orlando, Fla., 1991-92. Adj. prof. edn. U. N.MEx., No. Va. C.C., 1995—. Sgt. USAF, 1968-71. Mem. AAHPERD, Assn. Ednl. and Sport Adminstrs. (v.p.), Am. Mgmt. Assn. Avocations: running, tennis, fly fishing, reading. Home: PO Box 223383 West Palm Beach FL 33422-3383

BECK, BARBARA NELL, elementary school educator; b. Corpus Christi, Tex., Oct. 25, 1940; d. Marshall Joseph and Madie Ann (Spence) Robertson; m. Joel J. Beck, June 23, 1973. BA, Baylor U., 1964. Tchr. Killeen (Tex.) Ind. Sch. Dist., 1964-2001. Sunday sch. tchr., 1967—, co-treas., 2000—, ch. clk. First Bapt. Ch. of Nolanville. Mem. NEA, Tex. State Tchrs. Assn. (life), Tex. Assn. for the Gifted and Talented, Killeen Edn. Assn. (treas., past pres., bd. dirs.), Clifton Park PTA (past treas.). E-mail: jbeck1@hot.rr.com.

BECK, CURT WERNER, chemist, educator; b. Halle/Saale, Germany, Sept. 10, 1927; came to U.S., 1950, naturalized, 1955; s. Curt Paul and Clara (Fischer) B.; m. Lily Yallourakis, Feb. 10, 1953; children— Curt Peter, Christopher Paul. Student, U. Munich, 1946-48; BS, Tufts U., 1951; PhD, Mass. Inst. Tech., 1955. Instr. Franklin Tech. Inst., Boston, 1955-56; asst. prof. Roberts Coll., Istanbul, Turkey, 1956-57; lectr. Vassar Coll., Poughkeepsie, N.Y., 1957-59, asst. prof., 1959-62, asso. prof., 1962-66, prof. chemistry, 1966-93, Matthew Vassar Jr. prof., 1970-93, rsch. prof., 1993—. Co-editor Art and Archaeology Tech. Abstracts, 1966—; sect. editor Chem. Abstracts, 1967-95; editor: Archaeological Chemistry, 1974; mem. editl. bd. Jour. Field Archaeology, 1975-93, Jour. Archaeol. Sci., 1979-87. Mem. Zoning Bd. Appeals, La Grange, N.Y., 1965-91, chmn., 1974-91; mem. Dutchess County council Boy Scouts Am., 1965-67, Candidate supr., La Grange, 1967. Recipient Rsch. award Mid-Hudson sect. Am. Chem. Soc., 1965, Pomerance award Archaeol. Inst. Am., 2001. Fellow Royal Soc. Arts, Internat. Inst. for Conservation Historic and Artistic Works (London); mem. Am. Chem. Soc. (past sect. chmn.), Royal Soc. Chemistry (London), Gesellschaft Deutscher Chemiker, Archeol. Inst. Am., Internat. Union Prehistoric and Protohistoric Scis. (chmn. com. study of amber, mem. permanent coun., mem. exec. com.), Assn. for Field Archaeology, Sigma Xi. Home: La Grange 149 Skidmore Rd Pleasant Valley NY 12569-5001 Office: Vassar Coll Poughkeepsie NY 12604-0001 E-mail: beck@vassar.edu.

BECK, DONALD JAMES, veterinarian, educator; b. N.Y.C., Aug. 17, 1957; s. Donald Spence and Margaret Eugene (Moan) B.; m. Julie Anne Hayes, June 14, 1986 (div. Aug. 1995); m. Maria Patricia Marmolejo, June 28, 1997. BS in Animal Sci., U. Fla., 1980, DVM, 1986. Pvt. practice, Largo, Fla., 1986-88, 90—; instr. St. Petersburg (Fla.) Jr. Coll., 1988-90. Track veterinarian Derby Lanes, St. Petersburg, 1988-89; show veterinarian Cen. Fla. Hunter & Jumper Assn., St. Petersburg, 1987; veterinarian surgeon Pinellas County Animal Control, Clearwater, Fla., 1990—. Dir., v.p., pres. Somerset Village Condominium Assn., Gainesville, Fla., 1983-86; events judge 4-H, Largo, 1989. Mem. AVMA, Fla. Vet. Med. Assn., Sigma Phi Epsilon. Democrat. Roman Catholic. Avocations: computer program, chess, investing, horses. Home and Office: 9374 117th Ave Largo FL 33773-4343

BECK, GEORGE PRESTON, anesthesiologist, educator; b. Wichita Falls, Tex., Oct. 21, 1930; s. George P. and Amanda (Wilbanks) Beck; m. Constance Carolyn Krog, Dec. 22, 1953; children: Carla Elizabeth, George P., Howard W. BS, Midwestern U., 1951; MD, U. Tex., 1955. Diplomate Am. Bd. Anesthesiology. Intern John Sealy Hosp., 1955—56; resident in anesthesiology Parkland Meml. Hosp., Dallas, 1959—62, vis. staff, 1964—; pvt. practice Lubbock, Tex., 1964—. Asst. prof. anesthesiology U. Tex. Southwestern Med. Sch., Dallas, 1962—64, asst. clin. prof., 1964—71, prof., 1996—; assoc. clin. prof. anesthesiology U. Tex. Med. Br., Galveston, 1971—; pres. Gt. Plains Ballistics Corp., 1967—; clin. prof. Tex. Tech U. Sch. Medicine, Lubbock, 1986—. Pres. coun. Luth. Ch., 1965—66. With USAF, 1956—59. Fellow: Am. Coll. Anesthesiologists; mem.: Lubbock Surg. Soc., Lubbock County Med. Soc., Tex. Soc. Anesthesiologists (pres. 1974), Tex. Med. Soc., Am. Soc. Anesthesiologists. Achievements include invention of Beck Airway Airflow Monitor. Home: 4601 18th St Lubbock TX 79416-5713 Office: PO Box 16385 Lubbock TX 79490-6385

BECK, J. GAYLE, psychologist, educator; b. Richmond, Ind., Dec. 12, 1956; d. Robert Warren and Sallie Gayle Beck. AB, Brown U., 1979; PhD, SUNY, Albany, 1984. Lic. psychologist, N.Y., Tex. Asst. prof. psychology U. Houston, 1984-90, assoc. prof. psychology, 1990-93, SUNY, Buffalo, 1993—, assoc. chair, 2002—. Cons. in field. Author: (with others) Patterns of Sexual Arousal: Psychophysiological Processes and Clinical Applications, 1988, Handbook of Clinical Behavior Therapy, 2d. edit., 1992, Handbook of Sexual Dysfunctions, 1993, Innovations in Clinical Practice, vol. 12, 1993, Adult Behavior Therapy Casebook, 1994, others; mem. editorial bd. Jour. Anxiety Disorders, Archives Sexual Behavior, Behavior Therapy; cons. editor Annals of Behavioral Medicine; reviewer jours.; contbr. articles to profl. jours. Presdl. fellow SUNY, 1979-82; grantee U. Houston, 1984-86, NIH, 1985-86, Am. Heart Assn., 1986-90, Tex. Higher Edn. Coordinating Bd., 1989-94, NIMH, 1996-2001, 2002-05. Fellow APA (sec. divsn. 38, 1990-93 program reviewer 1989—); mem. AAAS, Tex. Psychol. Assn. (chair behavior therapy com. 1987-89), Houston Psychol. Assn. (continuing edn. com. 1987), Houston Behavior Therapy Assn. (treas. 1985-86), Assn. for Advancement Behavior Therapy (publs. com. 1988-91, coord. workshop 1991-94), Internat. Acad. Sex. Rsch., Soc. Psychophysiol. Rsch., Soc. Sex Therapy and Rsch. Home: 155 Burroughs Dr Buffalo NY 14226-3968

BECK, JANICE MCKLOSKEY, government affairs educator; b. Green Bay, Wis., June 16, 1937; d. Theodore Andrew and Ruth Eleanor (Huybrecht) McKloskey; m. James Donald Beck, Oct. 8, 1971 (dec. 1986); children: Jennifer Jaye. BA in English, Coll. St. Scholastica, 1962; MA in English, U. Wis., 1973. Cert. secondary tchr. Elem. tchr., Minn., 1959-62; secondary tchr., 1962-68; instructional aids specialist Extension Course Inst., Gunter AFB, Ala., 1969-70, edn. specialist, 1970-80; mem. faculty Air War Coll., Maxwell AFB, Ala., 1980-84; mng. editor Air Univ. Rev., Maxwell AFB, 1984-86; mem. faculty dept. nat. security affairs Air War Coll., Maxwell AFB, 1986-88; supr. course devel. br. Extension Course Inst., Gunter AFB, Ala., 1988—95; 20th century history tchr. LIR program, Univ. Wis., Green Bay, 2002—. Mem. Call to Action, Phi Delta Kappa, Lambda Iota Tau. Clubs: Toastmasters. Roman Catholic. Avocations: gardening, swimming, canoeing, writing, painting.

BECK, JEAN MARIE See **WIK, JEAN MARIE**

BECK, JOHN CHRISTEN, sociologist, educator; b. Provo, Utah, Dec. 7, 1959; s. Jay Vern and Allida Faye (Ellison) B.; m. Martha (Nibley), June 21, 1983; children: Katherine, Adam, Elizabeth. BA, Harvard U., Cambridge, Mass., 1983, MA, 1988, PhD, 1989. Pub. The Asian Century Bus. Report, Provo, Utah, 1991-97; prof. Am. Grad. Sch. of Internat. Mgmt., Glendale, Ariz., 1994-98; sr. strategic advisor Royal Govt. of Cambodia, 1994—; ptnr. Anderson Cons., Phoenix, 1997—; prof. UCLA Anderson Sch., L.A., 1998; dir. Internat. Rsch. Accentive, 1997—2003; bd. of trustees Monterey Inst. of Internat. Studies, 2002—; sr. rsch fellow UCLA, Ctr. for Comm. Policy, Calif., 2002—. Author: Breaking the Cycle of Compulsive Behavior, 1990, The Change of a Lifetime, 1994; The Attention Economy, 2001; Docomo: The Wireless Tsunami, 2002; contbr. articles to profl. jour. Harvard Bus. Sch. grantee, 1988, fellow, 1984-89; recipient: Hoopes Rsch. prize Harvard U., 1983; Rotary scholar, 1983-84. Office: PO Box 55870 Phoenix AZ 85078-5870

BECK, JOHN HERMAN, retired business education educator; b. Aberdeen, S.D., Nov. 2, 1933; s. Herman O. and Ferdina M. (Petersen) B. BS, No. State U., 1955, MS, 1964. Tchr. bus. edn. Sch. Dist., Rapid City, S.D., 1960-61, Sch. Dist. Jefferson County, Evergreen, Colo., 1961-63, San Bernardino Sch. Dist., 1963-67, Sch. Dist. 271, Bloomington, Minn., 1967-95. Dept. chmn. Kennedy H.S., Bloomington, 1984-95. With USNR, 1956-58. Mem. Bloomington Edn. Assn. (treas. 1992-95), Elks, Moose. Home: 319 S Sunset Dr Mina SD 57451 E-mail: bgbdjohn@nvc.net.

BECK, JOHN MATTHEW, education educator; b. Rogoznig, Austria, Apr. 10, 1913; s. Matthias and Antoinette (Bukowski) B.; came to U.S., 1914, naturalized, 1942; BS, Ind. State Coll. (Pa.), 1936; MA, U. Chgo., 1947, PhD, 1953; JD, Concordia U., 1990; m. Frances Josephine Mottey, Aug. 23, 1941. Tchr., Clymer (Pa.) High Sch., 1937-41; instr. history and philosophy of edn. De Paul U., 1948-53; instr. Chgo. State College, 1953-56, chmn. dept. edn., 1959-60, asst. dean, prof. edn., 1960-66, dean coll., 1966-67; dir. Chgo. Tchr. Corps, 1967—; exec. dir. Chgo. Consortium Colls. and Univs., 1968—; prof. urban tchr. edn. Govs. State U., 1972—; cons. U.S. Office of Edn., 1968—. Mem. Ill. State Advisory Com. on Guidance, 1963—, Citizens Schs. Com., Chgo., 1953—; chmn. curriculum adv. com. Ednl. Facilities Center, Chgo., 1971—; exec. bd. Cook County OEO, 1971—; adv. com. interstate interinstnl. cooperation Ill. Bd. Higher Edn., 1972—; mem. Chgo. Mayor's Adv. Commn. Sch. Bd. Nominations, 1975, Mayor's Adv. Coun. on Aging, 1976—, Exec. Svc. Corps. of Chgo., 1983—, Mayor Washington's Task Force on Edn., 1983. Bd. govs. Chgo. City Club, 1961—, v.p., 1962-63, 64-65; mem. Exec. Service Corps of Chgo., 1983— . Served with AUS, 1941-46. Decorated Bronze Star. Recipient W. Germany grant, 1972. Fellow AAAS, Philosophy of Edn. Soc.; mem. Am. Hist. Assn., Am. Edn. Research Assn., Ill. Edn. Assn. (pres. Chgo. div. 1960-62). Co-author: Extending Reading Skills, 1976. Editor: Chgo. Sch. Jour., 1964-65; co-editor: Teaching the Culturally Disadvantaged Child, 1966; contbr. articles to profl. jours. and encys. Home: Chicago, Ill. Died Aug. 6, 2000.

BECK, PAUL ALLEN, political science educator; b. Logansport, Ind., Mar. 15, 1944; s. Frank Paul and Mary Elizabeth (Flanegin) B.; m. Maria Teresa Marcano, June 10, 1967; children: Daniel Lee, David Andrew. AB, Ind. U., 1966; MA, U. Mich., 1968, PhD, 1971. Asst. prof. U. Pitts., 1970-75, assoc. prof., 1976-79; prof. Fla. State U., Tallahassee, 1979-87, chmn. dept., 1981-87; prof. Ohio State U., Columbus, 1987—, chmn. dept., 1991—. Co-author: Political Socialization Across the Generations, 1975, Individual Energy Conservation Behaviors, 1980, Electoral Change in Advanced Industrial Democracies, 1984, Party Politics in America, 10th edit., 2003. Chmn. coun. Inter-Univ. Consortium for Polit. and Social Research, 1982-83, mem., 1980-83; mem. NSF polit. sci. panel, 1988-89. Recipient Disting. Svc. award Ohio State U., 2000. Mem. Am. Polit. Sci. Assn. (exec. coun. 1981-82, 93-94, book rev. editor 1976-79, program chair 1994, chair strategic planning com. 1999-2000), Midwest Polit. Sci. Assn. (exec. coun. 1987-90, mem. editl. bd. 1988-90, program chair 1991, v.p. 1996-98), So. Polit. Sci. Assn. (mem. editl. bd. 1982-87), Pi Sigma Alpha (exec. coun.). Democrat. Home: 7003 Perry Dr Columbus OH 43085-2815 Office: Ohio State U Dept Polit Sci Columbus OH 43210-1373 E-mail: beck.9@osu.edu.

BECK, RHONDA JOANN, paramedic, educator, writer; b. Hawkinsville, Ga., Apr. 20, 1965; d. Franklin Lamar and Ida (Scarborough) Woodard; m. Gary Wendell Bramlett, Apr. 9, 1983 (div. May 1995); 1 child, Gary Michael Bramlett; m. Kenneth Steve Beck, June 8, 1997. Gen. Banking Degree, Am. Inst. Banking. Cert. BTLS, CPR, PHTLS, ACLS, BLS instr. trainer, emergency med. technician-paramedic, instr. Collateral clk. Bank South, N.A., Perry, Ga., 1986-94; emergency med. technician Taylor Regional Hosp., Hawkinsville, 1993-94; paramedic Med. Ctr. Ctrl. Ga., Macon, 1994-99; emergency med. technician instr., paramedic instr. Ctrl. Ga. Tech. Coll., Macon, 1997—; paramedic Houston Med. Ctr., Warner Robins, Ga., 1997—. Instr. ACLS, Pediat. Life Support, PreHosp. Trauma Life Support, Basic Trauma Life Support, Am. Heart Assn.; reviewer Delmar Thomson, 1999—, Jones & Bartlett, 2000-, GEMS Faculty, 2003-present, Am. Geriatric Soc.; Brady, 2001—. Author: Emergency Care and Transportation of the Sick and Injured, student workbook, AAOS, 8th edit., 2001; pub. author, reviewer: Jones & Bartlett. Vol. firefighter Houston County Vol. Fire Dept., Hayneville, Ga., 1986-95. Recipient Heartsaver award Laerdal Med. Corp., 1994, Vol. Svc. award Am. Lung Assn. Ga., 1995. Democrat. Baptist. Avocations: reading, swimming, exercise, writing, coin collecting. Office: Houston County EMS Warner Robins GA 31093 E-mail: takai_sensei@yahoo.com.

BECK, ROBERT EDWARD, computer scientist, educator; b. Denver, June 7, 1941; s. Arthur Walter and Caroline Adelheid (Petrie) B.; m. Barbara Ruth Pennell, Aug. 21, 1965; children: Philip Arthur, Christopher William, Jennifer Grove. BS in Math., Harvey Mudd Coll., Claremont, Calif., 1963; PhD in Math., U. Pa., 1969. Instr. Villanova (Pa.) U., 1966-69, asst. prof., 1969-74, assoc. prof., 1974-78, prof. computer sci., 1978—, dept. chair, 1992—. Team chair computing accreditation commn. ABET, 1986—. Author: Elementary Linear Programming, 2d edit., 1995; editor: Computers in Nonassociative Rings and Algebras, 1978. Fulbright Exchange fellow, 1981-82. Mem. AAUP, ACM (chair computer sci. conf. 1995, 96, chair preparing future faculty program 1998-2002), Am. Math. Soc., Sigma Xi. Office: Villanova U Dept Computing Sci Villanova PA 19085 E-mail: robert.beck@villanova.edu.

BECK, RONALD DUDLEY, university administrator; b. Louisville, Feb. 3, 1946; s. Carl D. and Suzanne (Weeks) B.; m. Bonnie Lee Basham, Aug. 26, 1967; children: Matthew, Lori. BS, Western Ky. U., 1968; MA, So. Bapt. Theol. Sem., 1970. Staff asst. student affairs Western Ky. U., Bowling Green, 1970-74, asst. dean student affairs, 1974-76, asst. dean, dir. univ. ctrs., 1976-85, acting dean of students, 1985-86, assoc. dir. alumni affairs, 1986-93; dir. planned giving, 1993—. Contbr. articles to profl. jours. Mem. exec. bd. Nat. Edn. Alumni Trust, Chgo., 1987—, chmn., 1991-93; deacon Eastwood Bapt. Ch., 1989—; bd. dirs. Ky. Planned Giving Coun., 1996—, v.p. 1998. Mem. Nat. Com. on Planned Giving, Coun. for Advancement & Support of Edn., Bowling Green-Warren County C. of C. (com. vice chair 1990-91, chmn. met. govt. com. 1991, Leadership Bowling Green 1989). Avocations: tennis, college and professional sports, boating. Home: 595 Elrod Rd Bowling Green KY 42104-7559

BECK, SHARON ELLEN, nursing educator, nursing administrator; b. Phila., Nov. 2, 1943; d. Albert and Ruth (Reiff) Bralow; m. Morton S. Beck, July 11, 1965; children: Paul, Lisa. BS, Adelphi U., 1965; EdM, Temple U., 1976; MSN, Villanova U., 1985; DNSc in Nursing, Widener U., 1992. RN. Nurse Abington Meml. Hosp., Pa., 1970-73; nursing instr. Abington Meml. Hosp. Sch. Nursing, Pa., 1973-82; psychiat. liaison nurse Abington Mem. Hosp., Pa., 1981-82, nurse mgr. psychiat. unit, 1982-85; asst. DON Fairmount Inst., Phila., 1985-86; nursing instr. psychiat. nursing Frankford Hosp. Sch. Nursing, Phila., 1986-89; asst. prof. La Salle U., Phila., 1989-95; asst. hosp. dir. nursing edn.-quality improvement Temple U., Phila., 1995—2001; adj. faculty Temple Univ. Sch. of Nursing, Phila., 2003, Holy Family Univ. Sch. of Nursing, Phila., 2003; cons. Thomas Edison Coll., Trenton, NJ, 2003, Fitzerald Meml. Hosp., Darby, Pa., 2003. Teaching asst. Pa. State U., Abington, 1977-83; adj. faculty La Salle U., Phila., 1988, Pa. State U. Sch. Nursing, Abington, 1989, Temple U., 1996—, Holy Family U., 2001—; cons., lectr. in field; faculty mem., cons. Thomas Edison Coll., 2003—. Bd. dirs. Benjamin Rush Mental Health Ctr., 1972-79, pres., 1977-79; bd. dirs. Bldg. Blocks, 1990-91. Named Outstanding Young Woman, 1975. Mem. ANA (cert. nursing adminstrn.), Pa. Nurses Assn., Montgomery County Nurses Assn. (v.p. 1991-95, pres. 1995-97), Nat. League for Nursing, Pa. League for Nursing (bd. dirs., co-membership chair, Hadassah Nurses Couns. pres.), Southeastern League Nursing, Sigma Theta Tau (jr. advisor 1991-93, sr. advisor 1993-94), Phi Kappa Phi. Home: 7819 Clyde Stone Dr Elkins Park PA 19027-1111 Office: Temple U Broad 2 Ontario Philadelphia PA 19140

BECKER, BRUCE CARL, II, physician, educator, health facility administrator; b. Chgo., Sept. 8, 1948; s. Carl Max and Lillian (Podzamski) B.; m. Irene Stepien-Thibault, 1991; 1 child, Joseph. BS in Aero. and Astron. Engring., U. Ill., 1970; MSME, Colo. State U., 1972; postgrad., Wright State U., 1973-74; MD, Chgo. Med. Sch., 1978; MS in Health Svcs. Adminstrn., Coll. of St. Francis, Joliet, Ill., 1984; Diploma in Spanish, U. Chgo., 1988; Diploma in Polish, Coll. of Du Page, 1989. Diplomate Am. Bd. Med. Mgmt., cert. physician exec. Resident in surgery U. N.C., Chapel Hill, 1978-79; resident in family practice St. Mary of Nazareth Hosp. Ctr., Chgo., 1979-81, chmn., program dir. dept. family practice, 1985-90, asst. dir. med. edn., 1981-82, dir. family practice residency, 1983-90, chief Family Practice Ctr., 1983-85, chmn. dept. family practice, 1985-90, med. dir. home health svc., 1985-2001, med. dir. HMO-Ill., 1985-2001, mem. planning and devel. com. governing bd., 1987-91, v.p. med. affairs, 1989-2001; clin. instr. Chgo. Med. Sch., 1982, affiliate instr., 1982-83, asst. prof., 1983, vice chmn. dept. family medicine, 1983-91; chief med. officer Med. Ctr. Hosp., Odessa, Tex., 2002—. Mem. family practice residency act Adv. Com. Ill. Dept. Pub. Health, 1991-2002; mem. VHA S.W. Physician Coun., 2003—. Mem. editl. rev. bd. Postgrad. Medicine, 1987-89; contbr. articles to med. jours. Mem. pub. health adv. network HHS, 1990-91; bd. dirs. Midwest region Inn Care Am., 1991—; mem. dinner com. Ill. chpt. Lupus Found. Am., 1991. Capt. USAF, 1970-75. Fellow Am. Acad. Family Physicians (rep. to accrediation rev. com. for physician assts. 1989-94, chmn., 1991-93), Am. Coll. Physician Execs., Am. Coll. Health Care Execs. (regents adv. coun. 1996-2000), Inst. of Medicine Chgo.; mem. AMA, Ill. Acad. Family Physicians (commn. on internal affairs 1986, commn. pub. and govt. policy 1987-89, chmn. 1989-90, bd. dirs. 1988-92, chmn. pub. rels. and info. com. 1988-92, state rep. family practice res. act com. 1990-92, vice spkr. 1991-92), Tex. Acad. Family Physicians (commn. on pub. health clin. affairs 2003—), Tex. Med. Assn. (processess com.), Soc. Tchrs. Family Medicine, Assn. Am. Med. Colls., Alliance Continuing Med. Edn., Am. Coll. Occupl. Medicine, Am. Acad. Med. Adminstrn., Chgo. Med. Soc. (councilor for Chgo. Med. Sch. 1986-91, alt. councilor 1991-95, mem. physicians stress ad hoc com. 1989-90, vice chmn. 1990-91, adv. com. on pub. health policy 1990-2001, presdl. adv. com. 1991-2001), Ill. Med. Soc. (coun. on edn. and manpower 1986-96, chmn. com. on CME activities 1991-96, chmn. subcom. physician placement and practice issues 1986-90, third party payment and processes com., Ill. Acad. Family Physicians rep. 1990-92), Phi Delta Epsilon. Roman Catholic. E-mail: bbecker@echd.org.

BECKER, CHARLES MCVEY, economics and finance educator; b. Cleve., Nov. 13, 1937; s. William Nevison and Helen (McVey) B.; m. Natalie Sage Slaughter, July 25, 1964; children: William Nevison II, James Pahl. BA cum laude, U. Ariz., 1960, MA, 1962, PhD, 1966. Chartered fin. analyst. Asst. prof. fin., econs. Nev. So. U., Las Vegas, 1965-67; asst. prof. Tex. Christian U., Ft. Worth, 1967-70, assoc. prof., 1970—2002, assoc. prof. emeritus, 2003—. Asst. dir. Am. Free Enterprise Inst. Contbr. articles to 50 profl. jours. Mem. Southwestern Econs. Assn. (pres. 1990-91), Southwestern Soc. Economists (pres. 1992-93), N.Am. Econs. and Fin. Assn. (adv. bd.), Assn. for Investment Mgmt. and Rsch., Am. Econ. Assn. (life), Alpha Kappa Psi, Beta Gamma Sigma, Phi Alpha Theta, Alpha Sigma Phi, Omicron Delta Epsilon, Order of Omega. Avocations: tennis, golf.

BECKER, DOROTHY LORETTA, education educator, librarian; b. Long Beach, Calif., May 27, 1933; d. Francis Ryan and Constance Marie Wolff; m. Paul Hermann Karl Heinz Peter Becker, Feb. 14, 1964 (div. Nov. 1971). BS, U. Calif., L.A., 1954; MLS, San Jose State U., 1981. Tchr. Monterey (Calif.) Peninsula Unified Sch. Dist., 1956-66, 81-91, reading specialist, cons., 1966-78, sch. libr., 1978-81; supr. student tchrs. Chapman U., Monterey, 1991-99; reference libr. Monterey County Free Librs., Seaside, Calif., 1996—2003. Elder, Stephen min. First Presbyn. Ch., Monterey. Mem. Calif. Ret. Tchrs. Assn., Total Reading Assn. (cons. 1966—), Delta Kappa Gamma Soc. Internat. (Calif. corr. sec. 1993-95, Calif. state exec. sec. 1995-97, Chi state strategic plan ad hoc com. 1995-99, chmn. Chi state bylaws 1999—2001), Chi State Learning Is For Everyone Found. (pres. bd. dirs. 1999-2002, bd. dirs. 1999—). Democrat. Avocations: travel, reading, literacy advocate, flower arranging.

BECKER, ELEEN MARIE, secondary education educator; b. Seattle, Aug. 23, 1949; d. Glenn O.N. and Marjorie Eleen (Hays) Riedasch; m. Richard Lee Northcutt, Aug. 12, 1972 (dec. Jan. 1984); children: Brian Lee, Sara Eleen; m. Larry Lee Becker, May 19, 1990. BA in History, Wash. State U., 1972; MA in Teaching, Whitworth Coll., 1985. Cert. tchr. Wash. Substitute tchr. Spokane (Wash.) Sch. Dist. 81, 1979-84; tchr. talented and gifted in history and English Mead Sch. Dist. 354, Spokane, Wash., 1984—. Chmn. Mead Vocabulary Com., 1989-91, co-adv. Northwood Jr. High Sch. Writing Club, Spokane, 1988-90, mem. Secondary Lang. Arts Curriculum, Spokane, 1985-92, edn. svc. dist. 101 mini-grant com., 1986-94, Mead essential learnings com., 1991-92, Mead writing assessment com., 1991—, mem. exec. com. Learning Across Curriculum, Spokane, 1987-90, co-adv. State History Day Northwood Jr. High Sch., 1987-91; presenter Nat. Sci. Conf., 1989, student-tchr. seminar Washington State U., 1991-93; varsity coach girls golf team Mead High Sch., 1993—. Mem. Parent Adv. Coun. Woodridge Elem. Sch., Spokane, 1987-88, asst. dir. Wash. Jr. Golf Assn., Spokane, 1988—, v.p. Ascension Luth. Ch. Women, Spokane, 1981-82, asst. supt. Sunday Sch., 1982-84. Mem. Nat. Coun. Tchrs. English, Nat. Coun. Social Studies, Internat. Order Rainbow Girls (adv. bd. pres. 1978-80), Secondary Social Studies Com., Order Ea. Star. Avocations: golf, travel.

BECKER, ELIZABETH ANNE, secondary education educator; b. Winston-Salem, N.C., Aug. 27, 1959; d. Byron Gustav Becker and Shirley Anne Howard; m. Duane Allen Johnson, June 27, 1981 (div. 1991); children: Christopher, Matthew; m. Thomas Everett Edmonds, Aug. 17, 1991; stepchildren: Jacob, Sarah. AAS, Sauk Valley Coll., Dixon, Ill., 1979; BS in Biology summa cum laude, Radford U., 1998; postgrad. in neurobiology and anatomy, Wake Forest U., 1998-99; MS in Edn., Radford U., 2000. Registered clin. lab. scientist; lic. collegiate profl., Va. Med. lab. technician St. Joseph Hosp., Belvedere, Ill., 1980-88, Pulaski (Va.) Hosp., 1988-90; clin. lab. scientist Giles Meml. Hosp., Pearesburg, Va., 1990-95; biology tchr. Carroll County H.S., Hillsville, Va., 2000—; sci. rschr. Radford U., 1996—99. Vol., Spl. Olympics, Radford, Va., 1998; cub scout leader, Cub Scouts A., 1990, 91; coord. infant and child support group, SHARE, Belvedere, 1986, 87, 88; ednl. advisor Nat. Youth Leadership Forum Medicine, 2002. Mem. AAAS, Nat. Sci. Tchrs. Assn., Nat. Cert. Agy. for Clin. Scientists, Beta Beta Beta (pres. Sigma Rho chpt. 1997-98, Excellence in Rsch. award 1998), Omicron Delta Kappa (life). Achievements include research in desert funnel-web spiders courtship behavior; discovery of male pheromone transmission. Avocations: sculpting, pen and ink, hiking, remodeling, behavior research. Home: 286 Huddle Rd Wytheville VA 24382 Office: Carroll County High Sch Rt 58 Hillsville VA 24343

BECKER, GARY STANLEY, economist, educator; b. Pottsville, Pa., Dec. 2, 1930; s. Louis William and Anna (Siskind) Becker; m. Doria Slote, Sept. 19, 1954 (dec.); children: Judith Sarah, Catherine Jean; m. Guity Nashat, Oct. 31, 1979; children: Michael Claffey, Cyrus Claffey. AB summa cum laude, Princeton U., 1951, PhD (hon.), 1991; AM, U. Chgo., 1953, PhD, 1955, Hebrew U., Jerusalem, 1985, Knox Coll., 1985, U. Ill., Chgo., 1988, SUNY, 1990, U. Palermo, Buenos Aires, 1993, Columbia U., 1993, Warsaw (Poland) Sch. Econs., 1995, U. Econs., Prague, Czech Republic, 1995, U. Miami, 1995, U. Rochester, 1995, Hofstra U., 1997, U. d'Aix-Marselles, 1999, U. Athens, 2002, Harvard U., 2003. Asst. prof. U. Chgo., 1954—57; from asst. prof. to assoc. prof. Columbia U., N.Y.C., 1957—60, prof. econs., 1960—68, Arthur Lehman prof. econs., 1968—70; prof. econs. U. Chgo., 1970—83, Univ. prof. econs. and sociology, 1983—2002, chmn. dept. econs., 1984—85, Univ. prof. econs., sociology, and Grad. Sch. Bus., 2002—. Ford Found. vis. prof. econs. U. Chgo., 1969—70; assoc. Econs. Rsch. Ctr. Nat. Opinion Rsch. Ctr., Chgo., 1980—; mem. domestiv adv. bd. Hoover Instn., Stanford, Calif., 1973—91, sr. fellow, 1990—; mem. acad. adv. bd. Am. Enterprise Inst., 1987—91; rsch. policy advisor Ctr. for Econ. Analysis Human Behavior Nat. Bur. Econ. Rsch., 1972—78; mem. and sr. rsch. assoc. Monetary Policy, Min. Fin., Japan, 1988—; bd. dirs. Unext-.com, 1999—2003; affiliate Lexecon Corp., 1990—2002. Author: The Economics of Discrimination, 1957, (2d edit.) 1971, Human Capital, 1964, (3d edit.), 1993, (Japanese transl.), 1975, (Spanish transl.), 1984, (Chinese transl.), 1987, (Romanian transl.), 1997, Human Capital and the Personal Distribution of Income: An Analytical Approach, 1967, Economic Theory, 1971, (Japanese transl.), 1976; author: (with Gilbert Ghez) The Allocation of Time and Goods Over the Life Cycle, 1975; author: The Economic Approach to Human Behavior, 1976, (German transl.), 1982, (Polish transl.), 1990, (Chinese transl.), 1993, (Romanian transl.), 1994, (Italian transl.), 1998, A Treatise on the Family, 1981, (expanded edit.), 1991, (Spanish transl.), 1987, (Chinese transl.), 1988, 2000, Accounting for Tastes, 1996, (Czech transl.), 1998, (Chinese transl.), 1999, (Italian transl.), 2000; author: (with Guity Nashat Becker) The Economics of Life, 1996, (Chinese transl.), 1997, with Guity Nashat Becker: The Economics of Life, 1998, (Spanish transl.), 2002; author: (in German) Family, Society and State, 1996; author: (in Italian) L'approccio Economico al Comportamento Umano, 1998; author: (with Kevin M. Murphy) Social Economics, 2000; editor: Essays in Labor Economics in Honor of H. Gregg Lewis, 1976; co-editor (with William M. Landes): Essays in the Economics of Crime and Punishment, 1974; columnist: Bus. Week, 1985—; contbr. articles to profl. jours. Recipient W.S. Woytinsky award, U. Mich., 1964, Profl. Achievement award, U. Chgo. Alumni Assn., 1968, Frank E. Seidman Disting. award in Polit. Economy, 1985, merit award, NIH, 1986, John R. Commons award, Omicron Delta Epsilon, 1987, Nobel prize in Econ. Sci., 1992, award, Lord Found., 1995, Irene Taueber award, 1997, Nat. medal Sci., 2000, Phoenix award, U. Chgo., 2000, award, Am. Acad. Achievement, 2001, Heartland prize, 2002. Fellow: Am. Econ. Assn. (Disting., v.p. 1974, pres. 1987, John Bates Clark medal 1967), Am. Acad. Arts and Scis., Nat. Assn. Bus. Economists, Econometic Soc., Am. Statis. Assn.; mem.: NAE, NAS, Nat. Assn. Bus. Economists, Econ. History Assn., Pontifical Acad. Scis., Western Econ. Assn. (v.p. 1995—96, pres. 1996—97), Mont Pelerin Soc. (exec. bd. dirs. 1985—96, v.p. 1989—90, pres. 1990—92), Internat. Union for Sci. Study Population, Am. Philos. Soc., Nat. Assn. Bus. Economists, Phi Beta Kappa. Office: U Chgo Dept Econs 1126 E 59th St Chicago IL 60637-1580

BECKER, GERALDINE ANN, psychology educator; b. Chgo., Oct. 14, 1945; d. Frank Joseph and Pauline Rose (Pichman) Fiefer; divorced; children: Rhonda Lynn, Patrick Richard. AA, Waubonsee C.C., 1987; BA, No. Ill. U., 1989, MA, 1992, PhD, 1995. Advanced teaching asst. No. Ill. U., DeKalb, 1992-94; asst. prof. Nat.-Louis U., Chgo., 1994—. Adj. faculty Waubonsee C.C., Sugar Grove, Ill., 1993-94; grad. coord. psychology program Nat.-Louis U., 1996—, social sci. rsch., 1992—, student advisor, 1994—; presenter in field. Cons. editor: Jour. Psychology, 1997—. Commr. Planning Commn., Aurora, Ill., 1983-94; bd. dirs. Unit Sch. Dist. #131, Aurora, 1981-85. Mem. Soc. Indsl./Organizational Psychologists, Phi Kappa Phi, Sigma Xi. Democrat. Avocations: reading, computers, friends. Home: 2859 Alandale Cir Naperville IL 60564-8917 Office: Nat-Louis U 18 S Michigan Ave Chicago IL 60603-3200

BECKER, JULIA MARGARET, artist, educator; b. Cin., July 12, 1957; d. Flavian Thomas Becker and Peggy Becker Jackson; m. Daniel Shaw Biehl; 1 child, Eula Viva Becker Biehl. Student, Edgecliff Coll., 1976, U. Mont., 1977-79, Art Acad. Cin., 1975, 80; BA, Evergreen State Coll., 1985; MFA, Mont. State U., 1993. Tchr. Art for Kids Cin. Art Mus., 1987-90, Beall Park Art Ctr., Bozeman, Mont., 1994-96; facilitator, instr. Very Spl. Arts Mont., Bozeman, 1995-97, Great Falls, 1998—; adj. prof. Mont. State U., Bozeman, 1994-99, Great Falls, 1997—; artist-in-residence Great Falls Sch. Dist., 1996-98; asst. prof. art, dept. head U. Great Falls, 1998—2003, assoc. prof. art, dept. head, 2003—. Vis. lectr. Mont. State U., Bozeman, 1993-97; featured artist Festival of the Dead, Missoula, Mont., 1997; juror Sweet Pea Festival of the Arts, Bozeman, 1994; participant, artist The Caravan Project, Mont., 1995—. Artist numerous exhbns.; contbr. articles to profl. jours. Grantee Beall Park Art Ctr. and Mont. Arts Coun., 1994, P.E.O. Sisterhood, 1993, Mont. State U., 1994, Helena Presents and Colo. Dance Festival, 1995; Travel scholar grantee to South India, 2002, Svc. Learning Faculty fellow, 2002-03. Mem. Coll. Art Assn., Internat. Film and Video Assn., Rural Inst. on Disabilities. Democrat. Avocations: education, health, world ecology, disability studies, cultural studies, creative arts, world travel, endurance swimming. Office: U Great Falls Dept Art 1301 20th St S Great Falls MT 59405-4934 E-mail: jbecker@ugf.edu.

BECKER, KAREN ANN, university program administrator; b. Willoughby, Ohio, Apr. 9, 1963; d. William Herbert and Janet Mae (Wilkins) B. BA in English and Speech, Allegheny Coll., 1985, MEd, 1986; postgrad., Baldwin-Wallace Coll., 1987-88; PhD, Ohio State U., 1993. Cert. tchr. English and speech provisional, Ohio. Student asst. Allegheny Coll., Meadville, Pa., 1981-85; high sch. tchr. North Royalton (Ohio) City Schs., 1985-87, substitute tchr., 1987-88; instr., researcher Townsend Learning Ctr., Chagrin Falls, Ohio, 1987-90; cognitive interventionist Excellence in Learning, Upper Arlington, Ohio, 1990; rsch. asst. Nat. Assn. Secondary Sch. Prins., Va., 1990; grad. teaching assoc. Ohio State U., Columbus, 1988-93; upper sch. tchr., dir. Learning Unltd. Internat. Schs. Inc.-Village Acad., Powell, Ohio, 1994-96; coord. reading and study skills program Youngstown (Ohio) State U., 1996—. Adj. faculty Columbus State C.C., 1989-94, Capital U., 1994-96, Franklin U., 1995-96, Otterbein U., 1996; instr. and cons. Learning 20/20 and Kids in Coll., 1993-94. Rsch. author: Word Atlas, 1988. Mem. ASCD, Phi Kappa Phi. Avocations: pets, gardening, running, biking. Home: 267 E Main St Cortland OH 44410-1260 Office: Youngstown State U One Univ Plz Youngstown OH 44555

BECKER, KATHARINE ELIZABETH, special education educator; b. Madison, Wis., Nov. 30, 1952; d. Robert Mettler Becker and Katharine Jane (Morris) Bruère; m. Lyle Franklin Strehlow, Mar. 29, 1986. BS in Elem. Edn., U. Wis., 1976; MS in Speech and Hearing, Washington U., St. Louis, 1978; EdD, Nova Southeastern U., 1995. Cert. elem. tchr., hearing handicapped tchr., Ariz. Tchr., evaluator, cons. hearing impaired program Cartwright Sch. Dist., Phoenix, 1979—, mem. spl. edn. adv. com., 1992—. Mem. hearing impaired stds. working com. Dept. Edn., Phoenix, 1992-93. State chmn. Better Hearing and Speech Month, Ariz., 1991. Mem. Alexander Graham Bell Assn. for the Deaf (co-founder Ariz. chpt. 1986, bd. dirs., sec. 1986-87, pres. 1987-88), Phi Delta Kappa. Avocations: walking, gardening, reading. Home: 2528 Commonwealth Ave Madison WI 53711-1913

BECKER, LAWRENCE CARLYLE, philosopher, educator, writer; b. Lincoln, Nebr., Apr. 26, 1939; s. Albert Carlyle and Harriette (Toren) B.; m. Charlotte Ann Burner, June 10, 1967. BA in History, Midland Coll., 1961; MA in Philosophy, U Chgo., 1963, PhD in Philosophy, 1965; LHD (hon.), Midland Luth. Coll., 1994. Instr. philosophy Hollins Coll., Roanoke, Va., 1965-67, asst. prof. philosophy, 1967-71, assoc. prof., 1971-78, prof., 1978-89, fellow of coll., 1989—, dir. summer inst. for ethics and pub. policy, 1990-92; prof. philosophy, William R, Kenan, Jr. prof. humanities Coll. William and Mary, Williamsburg, Va., 1989-2001, acting chair, 1992-93; pres. Bookwork, L.L.C., 2000—. Mem. summer conf. in metaphysics Coun. for Philos. Studies, 1968, mem. summer conf. on moral problems in medicine, 1974; vis. fellow in philosophy Harvard U., Cambridge, Mass., 1975-76; invited lectr. in field. Author: On Justifying Moral Judgments, 1973, Property Rights: Philosophic Foundations, 1977, Reciprocity, 1986, A New Stoicism, 1998; editor: (with Kenneth Kipnis) Property: Cases, Concepts and Critiques, 1984 (with Charlotte B. Becker) A History of Western Ethics, 1992, Encyclopedia of Ethics, 2 vols., 1992, 2d edit., 3 vols., 2001; mem. editl. bd. Ethics, 1979-85, 2000, assoc. editor, 1985-2000, acting editor, 1994-95, book rev. editor, 1998-2000; contbr. over 70 articles and book revs. to profl. jours. Woodrow Wilson grad. fellow, 1961-62, Danforth grad. fellow, 1961-65, Woodrow Wilson dissertation fellow (hon.), 1964-65, fellow NEH, 1971-72, 93-94, Oxford (Eng.) U., 1971-72, Harvard U., 1975-76, Am. Coun. Learned Socs., 1975-76, humanities fellow Rockefeller Found., 1982-83, Ctr. for Advanced Study in Behavioral Scis., 1983-84. Mem. Am. Philos. Assn. (com. on philosophy and law 1984-87, adv. com. to program com. ethics divsn. 1989-92, com. on status and future of profession 1993-96), Am. Soc. for Legal and Polit. Philosophy, Va. Philos. Assn. (sec. 1978-79, v.p. 1979-80, pres. 1980-81).

BECKER, NETTIE, preschool administrator; b. Bklyn., Aug. 29, 1930; d. Harry and Molly (Small) Shames; m. Paul Becker, Dec. 26, 1954; children: Lynn, Lesley. BS in Health and Phys. Edn., Bklyn. Coll., 1953; M in Profl. Studies, Adelphi U., 1988. Cert. tchr., N.Y. Phys. edn. and dance tchr. Wash. Irving H.S., N.Y.C., 1953-56, Abraham Lincoln H.S., Bklyn., 1956-59, Springfield Gardens H.S., Queens, N.Y., 1967-87; interactive movement specialist early intervention program Kennedy Child Study Ctr., N.Y.C., 1988-94; child devel. therapist for presch. children, N.Y.C. and Rockville Ctr., 1994—. Author: A Special Kind of Love: A Guide for Parents and Teachers of Children with Disabilities, 1994, A Comprehensive Guide for Caregivers in Day-Care Settings, 1999. Vol. Cmty. Dance Programs, Queens, 1967-87. Mem. AAHPERD, Acad. Dance Therapy (registered), Laban Movement Inst., United Fedn. Tchrs. (sec. Springfield Gardens chpt. 1986-87). Democrat. Avocations: dance, mountain climbing, theatre, travel. Home and Office: PO Box 504 Rockville Centre NY 11571-0504

BECKER, RICHARD CHARLES, retired college president; b. Chgo., Mar. 1, 1931; s. Charles Beno and Rose Mildred (Zak) B.; m. Magdalene Marie Kypry, June 19, 1954; children: Richard J., Daniel P., Douglas F., Steven G., Pamela J. BS in Elec. Engring, Fournier Inst. Tech., 1953; MS in Elec. Engring, U. Ill., 1954, MS in Math., 1956, PhD in Elec. Engring, 1959; postgrad., Harvard Inst. Ednl. Mgmt., 1976. Engr. Ill. Bell Tel. Co., Chgo., 1952, Andrew Corp., Chgo., 1953; rsch. asst. U. Ill., Urbana, 1954-58, asst. prof., 1959; sr. staff engr. Amphenol Corp., Chgo., 1959-60, sr. rsch. scientist, 1961-64, dir. program mgmt., 1965-67; dir. Amphenol Corp. (Far Eastern ops.), 1968; group v.p., corporate dir. adminstrn. Bunker Ramo Corp., Oak Brook, Ill., 1968-73; chief exec. officer and chmn. bd. Fortune Internat. Enterprises, Inc., Oak Brook, 1973-76; pres. Benedictine Univ. (formerly Ill. Benedictine Coll.), Lisle, 1976-95, pres. emeritus, 1995—. Trustee, prof. Midwest Coll. Engring., Lombard, Ill., 1968—86; trustee Ill. Benedictine Coll., Lisle, 1973—76; bd. dirs. Amphenol Tyree Proprietary, Ltd., Australia, Amphetronix, Ltd., India, Oxbow Resources, Ltd., Canada; v.p. Bonita Springs Incorporation Com., Inc., 1998—99, pres., 1999—2000; bd. dirs. Arthur J. Schmitt Found., 1970—, pres., 1995—; mem. exec. adv. bd. Internat. Engring. Consortium. Contbr. articles and chpts. to profl. jours. and books. Gov. Brook Forest Community Assn., 1971-74; del. Oak Brook Caucus, 1970; trustee, pres. Arthur J. Schmitt Found., Ill. Benedictine Coll.; chmn. Coun. West Suburban Colls., Chgo. Met. Higher Edn. Coun., officer Fedn. Ind. Ill. Colls. and Univs.; chmn. Associated Colls. of Ill., West Suburban Regional Acad. Consortium. Named Disting. Eagle Scout, 1989, Regent Nat. Eagles Scout Assn.; Arthur J. Schmitt fellow U. Ill., 1953-56. Mem. Am. Phys. Soc., Nat. Assn. Ind. Colls. and Univs. (bd. dirs.), Albertus Magnus Guild, Rotary (Paul Harris fellow), Equestrian Order of the Holy Sepulchre of Jerusalem (knight commdr.), KC (4th deg), Sigma Xi, Eta Kappa Nu, Tau Beta Pi. Home: 25761 Creek Bend Dr Bonita Springs FL 34135-9523 E-mail: rpapinani@aol.com.

BECKER, ROBERT DEAN, retired education educator, retired academic administrator; b. Sutton, Nebr., Dec. 15, 1936; s. E. A. McNulty and Leona (Peters) Becker; m. Darlene Carroll, Dec. 18, 2002. BA, U. Colo., Colorado Springs, 1967; MA, U. Colo., 1969, PhD, 1972. Internal auditor Calif. Fed. Savs. and Loan, L.A., 1960-61; comptr. Security Savs. and Loan, Colorado Springs, 1961-65; from instr. to assoc. prof. Midwestern State U., Wichita Falls, Tex., 1970-85; prof. gen. studies, history Western State Coll., Gunnison, Colo., 1988-95, coord. core II and gen. studies, 1988-91, dean core and gen. studies, 1991-94, dean acad. programs, 1994-95; dean Sch. Arts and Scis., prof. history Clayton Coll. and State U., Morrow, Ga., 1995-98; v.p. for acad. affairs, prof. history Ga. Perimeter Coll., 1998—2000; dir. St. Paul Acad., Daegu, Republic of Korea, 2001—02; ret., 2002. Contbr. articles to profl. jours. Named Hardin Prof., Hardin Found., 1980; fellow NDEA Title IV, 1969—70; grantee NEH, 1983. Avocations: computers, reading, travel, writing, gardening.

BECKER, ROBERT STEPHEN, digital multimedia producer; b. Yonkers, N.Y., June 12, 1950; s. Alfred and Maria B.; m. Jody Rae Schwartz, June 1, 1985; children: Samuel Harrison, Elayne Audrey. BA, NYU, 1972, MA, 1975; PhD, U. Reading, Eng., 1980. A.W. Mellon postdoctoral fellow U. Pitts., 1981-82; asst. prof. English Emory U., Atlanta, 1982-85; mgr. multimedia Crawford Comm. Inc., Atlanta, 1987-92; dir. multimedia TW Design, Atlanta, 1992-94; pres. Becker Multimedia, 1994—. Designer and producer bus. and ednl. programs, CD-ROM titles, interactive TV programming. Grantee numerous orgns. Democrat. Jewish. Avocation: ireland. Office: 2353 Massey Ln Decatur GA 30033-1210

BECKER, SANDRA LOUISE, education technical specialist; b. Reading, Pa., July 14, 1949; d. James H. and Stella (Rosol) Marshman; m. Robert Howard Becker, Dec. 23, 1972. BS in Edn., Kutztown U., 1971, MEd, 1973; EdD, Lehigh U., 1994. Cert. math. tchr., instnl. tech. specialist, Pa. Math. tchr. Gov. Mifflin Schs., Shillington, Pa., 1971-94, dir. tech., 1994—; rsch. assoc. Lehigh U., Bethlehem, Pa., 1992-93; mgmt. info. scientist Hoffmann-LaRoche, Nutley, N.J., 1993. Tech. cons. Bethlehem Area Sch. Dist., 1993; test writer in field, 1988—. Pres. consistory Immanuel United C. of Christ, Shillington, 1992-93. Recipient Apple Disting. Educator award. Mem. ASCD, Am. Ednl. Rsch. Assn., Internat. Soc. for Tech. in Edn., Assn. for Ednl. and Comms. Techs., Assn. for Advancement of Computing in Edn., Nat. Coun. Tchrs. Math., Reading C. of C. (mem. subcom. on tech. 1994). Home: 526 Harding Ave Shillington PA 19607-2802 Office: Gov Mifflin Sch Dist 10 S Waverly St # C750 Shillington PA 19607-2642 E-mail: beckersl@ptdprolog.net., sbecker@gmsd.k12.pa.us.

BECKER, SUSAN KAPLAN, management and marketing communication consultant, educator; b. Newark, Jan. 4, 1948; d. Charles and Janet Kaplan; m. William Paul Becker, 1969 (div. 1977). BA in English cum laude, with distinction, U. Pa., 1968, MA, 1969, PhD, 1973, MBA in Fin., 1979. Instr. English Bryn Mawr (Pa.) Coll., 1972-74; assoc. editor U. Pa., Phila., 1975, asst. dir., lectr. urban studies, 1975-77; fin. analyst Phila. Nat. Bank, 1979-82; asst. v.p. Chem. Bank, N.Y.C., 1982-84; v.p. Bankers Trust Co., N.Y.C., 1984-85; prin. Becker Cons. Svcs., N.Y.C., 1985—; adj. assoc. prof. mgmt. comm. Stern Sch. Bus. N.Y.U., 1990—. Cons./evaluator Pa. Humanities Council, Phila., 1977-78; mem. editorial bd. Mgmt. Comm. Quar., 1993-97. Author: How to Develop Profitable Financial Products for the Institutional Marketplace, 1988; contbr. articles and revs. to profl. jours. Vol. N.Y. Cares, 1989-92, N.Y.C. affiliate Am. Heart Assn., 1995-97. U. Pa. fellow, 1968-72; E.I. DuPont de Nemours fellow, 1979, N.Y. Regents Coll. Teaching fellow, 1968-70. Mem. Internat. Comm. Assn. (reviewer tech. and comm. divsn. 1991), Fin. Women's Assn. N.Y. (profl. devel. com. 1995—),

Profl. Assn. Investment Comm. Resources. Democrat. Avocations: painting and drawing, swimming. Office: 155 E 29th St New York NY 10016-8173 E-mail: susan.kaplan.becker.wg79@wharton.upenn.edu.

BECKER, ULRICH J. physics educator, particle physics researcher; b. Dortmund, Germany, Dec. 17, 1938; came to U.S., 1968; s. Georg Ludwig and Auguste (Buehner) B.; m. Gerda Katharina Barthel, Apr. 29, 1966; children: Katharina, Peter, Robert. Grad., Leibniz Gymnasium, Dortmund, Germany, 1958; BS, Philipps U., Marburg, Germany, 1960; diplom, U. Hamburg, Germany, 1964; PhD, U. Hamburg, 1968, Dr.habil., 1976. Rsch. scientist Deutsches Elektronen Synchrotron, Hamburg, 1964-68; asst. prof. MIT, Cambridge, 1968-74, assoc. prof., 1974-77, prof., 1978—. Staff scientist CERN, European Orgn. for Rsch., Geneva, 1970-72, 86-88, mem. LEP physics com., 1986-89; vis. prof. ETH, Zürich, Switzerland, 1991-92; mem. rsch. coun. DESY, Hamburg, 1970-74. Originator Particle Chambers, permanent exhibit Smithsonian Instn., Washington. Mem. Am. Phys. Soc., AAS (high energy physics sect.). Achievements include co-discovery of the J/4 particle, most precise, large detector for muon particles. Office: MIT 51 Vassar St Cambridge MA 02139-4308

BECKER, WALTER HEINRICH, vocational educator, planner; b. St. Louis, Mar. 20, 1939; s. Anthon and Maria (Fleischman) B.; m. Ayse Nur Alpyoruk, Aug. 3, 1971; children: Volkan P., Kristal S. BS, S.E. Mo. State U., 1963; MS, U. Mo., Columbia, 1969; PhD, St. Louis U., 1978; MS, Fontbonne Coll., 1989. Cert. tchr. Secondary tchr. Sch. Dist. of Hancock Pl., Lemay, Mo., 1963-64, Mascoutah (Ill.) Sch. Dist., 1964-65, U.S. Dept. of Def., Japan, Turkey, Philippines, 1965-70; vocat. edn. supr. Mo. Divsn. of Mental Health, Farmington, Mo., 1971-79; program analyst Arabian Am. Oil Co., Dhahran, Saudi Arabia, 1979-80, planning and programs analyst, 1981-85; vocat. edn. supr. Mo. Dept. of Corrections, Jefferson City, 1990-93.

BECKER, WAYNE MARVIN, biologist, educator, retired biologist; b. Waukesha, Wis., May 29, 1940; s. Marvin E. and Adela H. B.; m. Patricia M., June 20, 1963; children: Lisa, Heather. BS, U. Wis., 1963, MS, 1965, PhD, 1967. Postdoctoral fellow Beatson Inst. Cancer Rsch., Glasgow, Scotland, 1967-69; from asst. prof. to prof. botany U. Wis., Madison, 1969—2002; ret., 2002. Cons. U. Indonesia, Jakarta, 1986; vis. prof. Canterbury U., Christchurch, New Zealand, 1995, 98, U. Puerto Rico, Mayaguez, 1995; external examiner biology Chinese U., Hong Kong, 1997-2000. Author: Energy and the Living Cell, 1977, The World of the Cell, 1985, 5th edit., 2002; contbr. articles to profl. jours. Guggenheim fellow, 1975-76, Fulbright fellow Charles U., Prague, Czech Republic. Mem. Internat. Soc. Plant Molecular Biologists, Am. Scientific Assn., Am. Soc. Plant Physiologist, Am. Assn. of Bioethics. Avocations: writing, camping, traveling. Office: U Wis Dept Botany B115 Birge Hall Madison WI 53706 E-mail: wbecker@wisc.edu.

BECKET, JOHANNA NINA, special education educator; b. Bronx, N.Y., Dec. 14, 1949; d. Vincent Angelo and Jenny (Filippino) Vecchione; children from previous marriage: Jenny, Victoria; m. Lee Hatton, Nov. 8, 1991. BA, Adelphi U., 1964, MA, 1968; MS, Barry U., 1981. Art tchr. Syosset (N.Y.) Pub. Schs., 1964-74; art therapist Jackson Meml. Hosp., Miami, 1978-81; brain mapping technician St. Francis Hosp., Miami, 1981-83, head nuerometrics dept., 1981-83; tchr. severely emotionally disturbed Dade County Pub. Schs./Miami Sunset Sr. High, 1983—, dept. head, spl. edn., 1988—; psychotherapist Christian Counseling Ctr, Meml. Med. Ctr. East Tex., 1992-93, Four Corners Mental Health-Green River High Sch., 1992-93. Editor Counselor Assn. newspaper, 1980-81. Co-chmn. Very Spl. Arts, 1988. Recipient Found. for Excellence grant, Miami, 1988, Citicorp Success Fund grant, 1988; named region VI finalist, Tchr. of the Yr., Dade County Pub. Schs., 1991-92. Mem. Coun. Exceptional Edn., United Tchrs. Dade. Democrat. Roman Catholic. Avocations: art, music, cooking, dancing. Home: 455 W Ferron Creek Dr Ferron UT 84523 Address: 25826 Hunter Ln Katy TX 77494-5570

BECKINGHAM, KATHLEEN MARY, education educator, researcher; b. Sheffield, Yorkshire, Eng., May 8, 1946; came to U.S., 1976; d. Philip and Mary Ellen (Flint) B.; m. Alan Edward Smith, Oct. 7, 1967 (div. Oct. 1978); m. Robert Bruce Weisman, July 25, 1986; 1 child, Caroline Mary Weisman. BA, U. Cambridge, Eng., 1967, MA, 1968, PhD, 1972. Grad. student Strangeways Rsch. Lab., Cambridge, 1967-70; postdoctoral Inst. Molecular Biology, Aarhus, Denmark, 1970-72; rsch. assoc. Nat. Inst. Med. Rsch., London, 1972-76; rsch. assoc., instr. U. Mass. Med. Sch., Worcester, 1976-80; asst. prof. Rice U., Houston, 1980-85, assoc. prof. biochemistry, cell biology, molecular biology, 1985-92, prof., 1992—. Recipient award Camille and Henry Dreyfus Found., 1979. Office: Rice U Dept Biochemistry and Cell Biology PO Box 1892 Ms-140 Houston TX 77251-1892

BECKLEY, ROBERT MARK, architect, educator; b. Cleve., Dec. 24, 1934; s. Mark Ezra and Marie Elizabeth (Kuhl) Beckley; m. Jean Dorothy Love, Feb. 26, 1956 (div. May 1988); children: Jeffery, Thomas, James; m. Jytte Dinesen, Oct. 24, 1990. BArch, U. Cin., 1959; MArch, Harvard U., 1961. Registered architect, Mich., Ohio, Ill., Wis. From asst. to assoc. prof. U. Mich., Ann Arbor, 1963—69, dean, prof., 1987—97, prof., 1997—2002, prof., dean emeritus, 2002—; from assoc. prof. to prof. U. Wis., Milw., 1969—86. Prin. Beckley-Myers, Architects, Milw., 1980—91; mem. Nat. Archtl. Accrediting Bd., 2000—03. Prin. works include Theater Facilities, 1980—81 (award, 1983), Theater Dist., 1981—82 (award, 1984), Bellevue Downtown Park, 1985 (1st place award, 1985). Recipient Distinction award, Milw. Art Mus., 1986. Fellow: AIA (Mich. Pres.'s award 1994), Graham Found., Inst. Urban Design; mem.: Assn. Collegiate Schs. Architecture (bd. dirs. 1987—90, pres. 1988—89). Home: 1016 Scott Pl Ann Arbor MI 48105-2585 Office: U Mich Coll Arch 2000 Bonisteel Dr Ann Arbor MI 48109-2069

BECKMAN, JUDITH KALB, financial counselor and planner, educator, writer; b. Bklyn., June 27, 1940; d. Harry and Frances (Cohen) Kalb; m. Richard Martin Beckman, Dec. 16, 1961; children: Barry Andrew, David Mark. BA, Hofstra U., 1962; MA, Adelphi U., 1973, cert., 1984. CFP; registered investment adviser, stockbroker. English tchr. Long Beach H.S., 1962-65; Promotion coordination pub. rels. Mandel Sch. for Med. Assts., Hempstead, N.Y., 1973-74; exec. dir. Nassau Easter Seals, Albertson, N.Y., 1974-76; dir. pub. info. Long Beach (N.Y.) Meml. Hosp., Long Beach, 1976-77; account rep. First Investors, Hicksville, N.Y., 1977-78; from sales asst. to acct. exec. Josephthal & Co. Inc., Great Neck, N.Y., 1978-81; v.p., fin. planner Arthur Gould Inc., Great Neck, N.Y., 1981-88; pres. Fin. Solutions (affiliated with Seco West Ltd., Goldner Siegfried Assocs. Inc.), Westbury, NY, 1988—2002; with Am. Portfolio Fin. Svcs., 2002—. Adj. instr. Adelphi U., Garden City N.Y., 1981-83, Molloy Coll., Rockville Ctr., N.Y., 1982-84; lectr. SUNY, Farmingdale, 1984-85; creater, presenter seminars, workshops on fin., investing, 1981—; adv. bd. L.I. Devel. Corp., 1993—; advisor investment clubs, 1996—. Fin. columnist The Women's Record, 1985-93; writer quar. newspaper The Reporter, 1987. Coord. meat boycott, L.I., 1973; mentor SUNY Old Westbury, 1989-93; co-founder, chair L.I. del. High Profile Men and Women, Colonie Hill, Hauppauque, N.Y., 1985; treas. L.I. Alzheimer's Found., 1989-93, trustee, 1993-95; apptd. to Nassau County Women's Adv. Coun. by County Exec., 1990; chief adv. coun. Ctr. for Family Resources, 1996-98; bd. dirs. L.I. Small Bus. Assistance Corp., (sec. 2003—), For Our Children (FOCUS), 20012—adviser to 4 investment clubs. Recipient citation for leadership Town of Hempstead, N.Y., 1986, 89, L.I. Press Club award, 1987, 92, Mentor award SBA, 1989, Fin. Svcs. award SBA, 1991, L.I. Assn. Fin. Svc. Advocate award, 1991, Woman of Distinction in Bus. award Women on the Job, 1989, Bus. Leadership citation Nassau County, N.Y., 1989, Supr. award Town of Hempstead, 1989, Pathfinder Bus. award, 1997, Bus. Adv. of Yr. N.Y. Dist. award U.S. SBA, 1998, Women's Bus. Advocate award, 1998, NAWBO LI Small Bus. Entrepreneur of the Yr. award, 1998; named one of 50 Leading Bus. Women, L.I. Bus. News, 2002, 2003, one of 90 Women in 90 Yrs. Making a Difference, Girls Scouts Nassau County, 2002. Mem. Nat. Assn. Women Bus. Owners L.I. (bd. dirs. 1987-89, membership chair 1996, v.p. membership 1996-98, v.p. edn. 1998-99, v.p. R&D 2002-03), Women's Econ. Developers of L.I. (bd. dirs. 1985-92), Internat. Assn. Fin. Planners, Inst. Cert. Fin. Planners, Fin. Planning Assn. L.I., L.I. Ctr. Bus. and Profl. Women (adv. coun. 1996-98, pres. 1984-86, Pres.' award 1992, Hall of Fame Achiever inductee 2001, steering com., co-founder L.I. Women's Agenda 1998, exec. v.p. Women's Agenda 1998-2000), Art League L.I. (bd. dirs. 2002—), Kiwanis (bd. dirs. 1994-97, chair fund raising 1994, chair cmty. svcs. 1995-97, v.p. membership 1996). Republican. Jewish. Avocations: theater, classical music, opera, reading. Home: 2084 Beverly Way Merrick NY 11566-5418 Office: Fin Solutions Fin Planning Office 2084 Beverly Way Merrick NY 11566-5418 also: 400 Post Ave Ste 200 Westbury NY 11590-2226 E-mail: jbeck0627@aol.com.

BECKMAN, L. DAVID, university chancellor; b. Denver, Aug. 21, 1926; BA, Wheaton Coll., 1947; MTh, Dallas Theol. Sem., 1952, ThD, 1956; MA, Columbia U., 1962; DD, Colo. Christian Coll., 1987. Instr. Dallas Bible Inst., 1952-55, London (Ont., Can.) Bible Inst. and Theol. Sem., 1955-61; chmn. Bible dept. The King's Coll., Briarcliff Manor, N.Y., 1961-63; pres. Rockmont Coll., Longmont/Denver, Colo., 1963-81, pres. emeritus Lakewood, Colo., 1981-83, 1983-85; pres. Colo. Christian Coll./Colo. Christian U., Lakewood, 1985-91, Colo. Christian U., Lakewood, 1991-93, chancellor, 1993-95, pres. emeritus, 1995—. Home: Heritage Eagle Bend 7775 S Biloxi Way Aurora CO 80016

BECKMEYER, HENRY ERNEST, anesthesiologist, medical educator, pain management specialist; b. Cape Girardeau, Mo., Apr. 13, 1939; s. Henry Ernest Jr. and Margaret Gertrude (Link) B. BA, Mich. State U., 1961; DO, Des Moines U., 1965. Diplomate Am. Bd. Med. Examiners, Am. Acad. Pain Mgmt.; cert. Am. Osteo. Bd. Anesthesiology. Chief physician migrant worker program and op. head start Sheridan (Mich.) Community Hosp., 1967-69; resident in anesthesia Bi-County Community Hosp./DOH Corp., Detroit, 1969-71, chief resident, 1968-69; staff anesthesiologist Detroit Osteo. Hosp./BCCH, 1971-75; founding chmn. dept. anesthesia Humana Hosp. of the Palm Beaches, West Palm Beach, Fla., 1975-79; assoc. prof. Mich. State U., East Lansing, 1979-88, prof. anesthesia, 1988—, chmn. dept. osteo. medicine, 1985-96; chmn. dept. osteo. surg. specialities, 1996-97; chief staff Mich. State U. Health Facilities, 1988-90, chmn. med. staff exec. and steering coms., 1988-90; chmn. of anesthesia St. Lawrence Hosp., Lansing, Mich., 1984-90, adminstrv. dir. dept. anesthesia and pain mgmt., 1994-98. Chief of staff Sheridan Cmty. Hosp., 1968-69; adminstrv. coun. Mich. State U., 1988-97, acad. coun., 1992-96, faculty coun., 1992-96, U. hearing bd., 2000-, bylaws com., 2000-, clin. practice bd., bd. dirs. sports medicine, athletic coun., 2003–; internal mgmt. com. Mich. Ctr. for Rural Health; cons. Ministry Health, Belize C.A., 1993-97; amb. Midwestern U. Consortium Internat. Activities, 1993; chmn. com. student performance, 2002-03, com. on acad. policy, 2000—, admissions com., 2000-2002, chmn. admissions com., 2003—; adv. com. on pain mgmt. State of Mich., 1999-2001; program chmn. Am. Russian Med. Exch., 1993-97; bd. dirs. Belize Med. Partnership. Spkr. Sta. WKAR, Mich. State U.; bd. dirs. Boy Scouts Am., W. Bloomfield, Mich., 1973-74, Palm Beach Mental Health, 1977-79, Care Choices HMO, Lansing, 1987-88; mem. adv. com. pain and symptom mgmt. State of Mich., 1999-2002; mem. athletic coun. Mich. State U., 2003–. Fellow Am. Coll. Osteo. Anesthesiologists; mem. AMA, Am. Osteo. Coll. Anesthesiology (chmn. commn. on colls. 1988-89), Soc. Critical Care Medicine, Internat. Anesthesiology Rsch. Soc., Am. Coll. Physician Execs., Am. Osteo. Assn. (spkr., mem. evaluators registry), Am. Acad. Pain Mgmt., Am. Arbitration Assn., Mich. State Med. Soc., Mich. Pain Soc., Mich. Peer Rev. Orgn., Mich. Osteo. Assn. (chmn. edn. com. 2002—), Ingham County Med. Soc. (edn. com.), Am. Soc. Regional Anesthesia, Soc. Security Disability Evaluation, Soc. Internat. Scholars, Phi Beta Delta. Office: Mich State U West Fee Hall East Lansing MI 48824

BECKWITH, CHRISTOPHER IRVING, social sciences educator, writer, composer; b. Stambaugh, Mich., Oct. 23, 1945; s. Irving Eugene and Florence Mary (Howd) B.; m. Connie Huei-Jen Yang, May 11, 1974 (div. 1993); children: Ming, Lee; m. Inna Y. Murataeva, Nov. 28, 1999. BA in Chinese, Ohio State U., 1968; MA in Tibetan Studies, Ind. U., 1974, PhD in Inner Asian Studies, 1977, postgrad., 1989—. Part-time lectr. Dept. Uralic and Altaic Studies Ind. U., Bloomington, 1976-77, asst. prof., 1978-87, assoc. prof., 1987—, assoc. prof., chmn. dept. Central Eurasian Studies (formerly Uralic & Altaic Studies), 1991-94, prof., 1994—. Author: The Tibetan Empire in Central Asia, 1987; composer: Barbara, 1993; editor: Silver on Lapis, 1987, Jour. of the Tibet Soc., 1981-84, Medieval Tibeto-Burman Languages, 2002; contbr. articles to profl. jours. Recipient Outstanding Young Faculty award Ind. U., 1986; MacArthur Found. fellow, 1986-91. Mem. T'ang Studies Soc. (organizer, treas., 1981-86), S.E. Asian Linguistics Soc., Linguistic Soc. Am. Office: Ind U Dept Central Eurasian Studies 157 Goodbody Hall Bloomington IN 47405

BECNEL, ALBERT THOMAS, retired educational administrator; b. Taft, La., June 24, 1916; B.S. in Vocat. Edn., La. State U., Baton Rouge, 1939; grad. Command and Gen. Staff Sch.; M.Ed. in Guidance, Adminstrn. and Supervision, Nicholls State U., Thibodaux, La., 1968; married, 2 children. Tchr., supr. St. John Parish Schs., Reserve, La., 1939-64, supt. schs., 1964-85, ret., 1985; mem. supt.'s adv. council La. State Bd. Edn. Chmn. Reserve Charity to Birth Defects March Dimes Fund, 1964-84; sch. bd. St. John's Parish, 1990-91. Served to maj. AUS, 1942-46. Mem. La. Assn. Sch. Supts., South Central La. Supts. Assn. La. Assn. Sch. Execs., La. Tchr. Assn., NEA, La. Edn. Assn., Nat. Assn. Ret. Persons, La. Ret. Tchrs. Assn. (pres. St. John's Chpt.), Phi Delta Kappa. Lodge: KC. Home: PO Box 191 182 W 1st St Reserve LA 70084-6012

BECTON, AMY EARLE, elementary school educator; b. Oklahoma City, Oct. 10, 1945; d. Oren Kenneth and Hattie Loucelle (Edmison) Epperson; m. Tom Pinkerton Becton, June 1, 1968; children: Thad Ledghett, Braye Belinda. BS Mid. Tenn. State U., 1967; MEd, Mid. Tenn. State U., 1968. Former tchr. jr. high Shady Grove H.S.; former kindergarten tchr. Silas (Ala.) Elem., former spl. edn. tchr.; tchr. fourth grade Millry (Ala.) H.S., 1977—2003.

BEDAU, HUGO ADAM, philosophy educator; b. Portland, Oreg., Sept. 23, 1926; s. Hugo Adam and Laura (Romeis) B.; m. Jan Lisbeth Peterson Mastin, 1952 (div. 1988); children— Lauren, Mark Adam, Paul Hugo, Guy Antony; m. Constance Elizabeth Putnam, 1990. Student, U. So. Calif., 1944-45; BA summa cum laude, U. Redlands, 1949; MA, Boston U., 1951, Harvard, 1953, PhD, 1961. Instr. Dartmouth, 1953-54; instr. Princeton, 1954-57, lectr., 1958-61; assoc. prof. Reed Coll., 1962-66; prof. philosophy Tufts U., 1966-72, Austin Fletcher prof. philosophy, 1972—97, Romanell-Phi Beta Kappa prof. philosophy, 1994-95, prof. emeritus, 1997—. Vis. prof. law faculty U. Natal, South Africa, 1981, U. Westminster, London, 1994; vis. life fellow Clare Hall, Cambridge U., 1980; vis. fellow Wolfson Coll., Oxford, 1988; hon. rsch. fellow Bentham Project, U. London, 1997-99, 2003—. Author: The Courts, The Constitution and Capital Punishment, 1977, Death is Different, 1987, Thinking and Writing About Philosophy, 2d edit., 2002; co-author: Victimless Crimes, 1974, Current Issues and Enduring Questions, 1987, 6th edit., 2002, In Spite of Innocence, 1992, Critical Thinking, Reading, and Writing, 4th edit., 2002; editor: Death Penalty in America, 1964, 4th edit., 1997, Civil Disobedience, 1969, Justice and Equality, 1971, Civil Disobedience in Focus, 1991; co-editor: Capital Punishment in the US, 1976; contbr. articles and essays on social, polit., and legal philosophy to books and profl. jours. Bd. dirs. Am. League Abolish Capital Punishment, 1959—72, pres., 1969—72; bd. dirs. ACLU, Mass., 1984—87, 1988—93, 1995—98, v.p., 1987; chmn. Nat. Coalition Against Death Penalty, 1990—93. Danforth fellow, 1957-58, Liberal Arts fellow in law and philosophy Harvard U. Law Sch., 1961-62. Mem. Am. Philos. Assn., AAUP, Am. Soc. Polit. and Legal Philosophy (v.p. 1981), Phi Beta Kappa. Office: Tufts U Dept Of Philosophy Medford MA 02155

BEDENBAUGH, ANGELA LEA OWEN, chemistry educator, researcher; b. Seguin, Tex., Oct. 6, 1939; d. Wintford Henry and Nelia Melanie (Fischer) Owen; m. John Holcombe Bedenbaugh, Dec. 27, 1961; 1 child, Melanie Celeste. BS cum laude, U. Tex., 1961; PhD in Organic Chemistry, U. S.C., 1967. Geol. mapping asst. Roland Blumberg Assocs., Seguin, summer 1958, 59; chemistry lab. instr. U. Tex., Austin, 1960-61; rsch. assoc. chemistry U. So. Miss., Hattiesburg, 1966-80, rsch. assoc. prof. chemistry, 1980—, bd. mem. women's studies program, 1996-97. Co-prin. investigator Bell South Found. grant, 1998; dir. website NASA grant, 1999-00. Author: Nomenplayture, 1998; co-author: (with John H. Bedenbaugh) Handbook for High School Chemistry Teachers, 1985, (with John H. Bedenbaugh) Teaching First Year Chemistry, 4th edit., 1993; patentee in field. Adminstrv. bd. Parkway Heights United Meth. Ch., 1974-75, women's unit leader, 1973-75, women's unit treas., 1977, Wesleyan Svc. Guild v.p., 1970, Sunday Sch. tchr., 1973-74; bd. dirs. Forrest Stone Area Opportunity Inc., 1970-72, bd. dirs. exec. com., 1972, mem. com. to rewrite pers. policies and procedures, 1971, mem. Headstart monitoring com., 1971-72, mem. pers. screening com., 1971; mem. nat. Women's Polit. Caucus, 1976—; mem. Toastmasters Internat., 1986—, club. pres., 1993, area gov., 1994; adminstr., dir. Tchr. Mentoring Initiative through Bell South Found. Grant, 1998-2000; Miss. state coord. Bldg. a Presence for Sci. Recipient John and Angela Bedenbaugh award Coastal Miss. Assn. H.S. Chemistry Tchrs., 1996—; Rsch. grantee U.S. Dept. Energy, U. So. Miss., 1980, NSF, U. So. Miss., 1985, Adminstrv. Dir. Rsch. grant, 1988-91, 1993-96, 2001-04, NSF, 2000—, others. Mem. NSTA (nat. resource rev. panel for rev. of instrnl. materials), LWV, AAUW, Am. Chem. Soc. (chmn. 1984-85, program chmn. 1983-84, exec. bd. 1983—, Chemist of Yr. award 1991), Miss. Sci. Tchrs. Assn. (exec. bd. 1994—, pres.-elect 1998-2000, pres. 2000-02, state bldg. a presence for sci. coord. 2002—, Disting. Sci. Tchr. award 1994), Delta Kappa Gamma (pres. Miss. br. 1989-91, chmn. internat. rsch. com. 1980-82, chmn. internat. computer share fair at internat. conv. 1994, editor U.S. Forum Connection 2000-), Sigma Xi (charter, sec.-treas. 1967-69, treas. 1970, pres. 1973-74, program chmn. 1972-73). Democrat. Methodist. Home: 63 Suggs Rd Hattiesburg MS 39402-3639 Office: Univ So Miss PO Box 8466 Hattiesburg MS 39406-1000

BEDIKIAN, AGOP Y. internist, oncologist, educator; b. Lebanon; arrived in U.S., 1972, naturalized, 1978; BS, Am .U. Beirut, 1967; MD, Am. U. Beirut, 1971. Diplomate Am. Bd. Internal Medicine, Am. Bd. Med. Oncology. Intern St. Louis City Hosp., 1972—73; resident Barnes Hosp., St. Louis, 1973—75; fellow U. Tex. M.D. Anderson Hosp. and Tumor Inst., Houston, 1975—77, clin. instr., faculty assoc. dept. devel. therapeutics, 1977—78; asst. prof. medicine, assoc. internist U. Tex. M.D. Anderson Hosp. Cancer Ctr., Houston, 1978—82; cons. oncologist, dep. chmn. oncology dept. King Faisal Specialist Hosp. and Rsch. Ctr., Riyadh, Saudi Arabia, 1981—91; assoc. prof. medicine dept. melanoma/sarcoma med. oncology U. Tex. M.D. Anderson Cancer Ctr., Houston, 1991—97, internist dept. melanoma/sarcoma med. oncology, 1991—2000, prof., 1997—2000, dep. dir. Melanoma and Skin Ctr., 1997—, prof. dept. melanoma med. oncology, 2000—, ad interim chmn. dept. melanoma med. oncology, 2000—. Presenter numerous papers at profl. conf.s. Contbr. over 95 articles to profl. jours., 13 chpts. to books; reviewer (jours.) Cancer, Jour. Clin. Oncology, Annals Saudi Medicine, Melanoma Rsch., MedImmune, 2003—, Astra Zeneca, 2003—. Grantee, Rhone-Poulenc Rorer Pharms. Inc., 1992—93, UpJohn, 1993—94, Sanofi Winthrop, 1994—95, 1996—97, Schering Plough, 1996—, Ligand Pharms., 1997—98, NaPro Biotherapeutics, 1998—2000, Supergen, 1999—2000, Agouron Pharms. Inc., 2000—02, Bristol-Myers Squibb Co., 2000—, Genta, Inc., 2000—, Vical Inc., 2001, Cell Therapeutics, 2002—, Protarga, Inc., 2002—, INEX, 2002—, Celgenes, 2003—, Med Immune, 2003—, Astrazeneca, 2003—. Mem.: AAAS, ACP, Harris County Med. Soc., Tex. Med. Assn., N.Y. Acad. Scis., Am. Soc. Clin. Oncology, Am. Assn. Cancer Rsch. Home: 5661 Piping Rock Houston TX 77056 Office: U Tex MD Anderson Cancer Ctr 1515 Holcombe Blvd Box 430 Houston TX 77030 Fax: 713-745-1046. E-mail: abedikia@mdanderson.org.

BEDNAREK, ALEXANDER ROBERT, mathematician, educator; b. Buffalo, July 15, 1933; s. Alexander G. and Bertha (Wlodarz) B.; m. Rosemary Anderson, Aug. 29, 1954 (dec.); children: Robert A., Andrew R., Thomas C., Eugene P. BS, SUNY, Albany, 1957; MA, SUNY, Buffalo, 1959, PhD, 1961. Sr. mathematician Goodyear Aerospace Corp., Akron, Ohio, 1961-62, cons. info. scis. dept., 1963-65; asst. prof. math. U. Akron, 1962-63, U. Fla., Gainesville, 1963-66, assoc. prof., 1967-69, prof., 1969—, chmn. dept. math., 1969-86, interim chmn., winter 1988, co-dir. Center Applied Math., 1974-92, prof. dept. math., 1993—96, prof. emeritus, 1996—. Vis. staff mem. Los Alamos Sci. Lab., 1976-85; mem. adv. bd. CRC Handbook Math. Tables; NAS exchange prof., Warsaw, Poland, 1972 Editor (with L. Cesari) Dynamical Systems, Vol. I, 1977, Vol. II, 1982; contbr. to Ency. of Libr. and Info. Sci., Vol. 3, 1970; editor (with F. Ulam) Analogies Between Analogies, 1990; contbr. articles to profl. jours. Served with U.S. Army, 1952-54. Mem. Math. Assn. Am. (past chmn. Fla. sect.). Home: 530 NE 7th Ave Gainesville FL 32601-4387 Office: U Fla Dept Math 358 Little Hall Gainesville FL 32611-2082

BEDNARK, JAMES DAVID, company executive; b. Detroit, Feb. 22, 1950; s. Vernon G. and Mildred Helen (Wilkie) B.; m. Terri L. Smith, Apr. 8, 1974; children: Jesse Aaron, Jeffery Garreth. BA, Harvard U., 1972; MEd, Chapman U., 1992. Cert. tchr., Nev. Tchr. Lyon County Sch. Dist., Yerington, Nev., 1973-75; rschr. State Dept. Edn., Carson City, Nev., 1975-76; exec. dir. edn. Inter-Tribal Coun. of Nev., Reno, 1976-78; tribal mgr. Yerington (Nev.) Paiute Tribe, 1978-86; v.p. ops. Rite of Passage, Inc., Minden, Nev., 1987-92, pres., 1992—. Pres. American Human Svcs., Minden, 1989-92; exec. dir. ROP Schs., Minden, 1988—. Sch. bd. pres. Lyon County Sch. Dist., Yerington, 1985-89; mem. ctrl. com. Rep. Party, Lyon County, Nev., 1985-89; mem. Nev. Pro Family Coalition, Reno, 1986—, Nat. Right to Life, Washington, 1987—. Mem. ASCD, Nat. Assn. Sch. Bds., Aircraft Owners and Pilots Assn. Office: Rite of Passage Inc 1561 Us Highway 395 N Minden NV 89423-4100

BEDWORTH, DAVID ALBERT, health educator; b. Cortland, N.Y., Mar. 31, 1949; s. Albert Ernest and Agnes Sheldon (Franklin) B.; children: Jodi Michele, Michael David. BS, Butler U., 1971; MS, U. Ill., 1972, PhD, 1976. Instr. Russell Sage Coll., Troy, N.Y., 1973-75; asst. prof. SUNY, Brockport, 1976-78; program coord. Heart Health Edn. R.I., Pawtucket, 1978-79; prof. SUNY, Plattsburgh, 1979—. Cmty. edn. cons. STOP Ctr. for Domestic Violence, Plattsburgh, 1982; drug edn. cons. Federal Correction Instn., Ray Brook, N.Y., 1982, Ticonderoga (N.Y.) Ctrl. Sch. Dist., 1985. Author: (with Albert E. Bedworth) Health Education: A Process for Human Effectiveness, 1978, Health for Human Effectiveness, 1982, The Profession and Practice of Health Education, 1992; contbr. articles to profl. jours., chpts. to books. Task force on youthful alcohol abuse N.Y. State Dept. Mental Hygiene, 1977; profl. edn. com. Am. Lung Assn., 1980-84, exec. com., 1981-82. Mem. APHA, ASCD, N.Y. State Fedn. Profl. Health Educators (pres. 1977). Democrat. Avocations: antiques, travel. Office: SUNY Plattsburgh NY 12901

BEE, ANNA COWDEN, dance educator; b. Feb. 17, 1922; d. Porter Guthrie and Marion Irene (McCurry) Cowden; m. Alon Wilton Bee, Oct. 21, 1942; children: Anna Margaret Bee Foote, Alon Wilton. AB, Samford U., 1944; student, Chalif Sch. Dance, N.Y.C., 1950-54. Mem. faculty Byram H.S., JAckson, 1945-52, Hinds Jr. Coll., Raymond, Miss., 1952—. Dir. Hi-Steppers, girls' precision dance group; chaperone Miss Mississippi to Miss Am. Pageant; condr. charm clinics for teenagers; judge beauty pageants. Prodr. half-time shows for Gator Bowl, 1958, 64, 81, Sugar Bowl, 1960, Hall of Fame Bowl, 1977-79, Mid-Am. Bowl, 1988, Sr. Bowl, 1988. Bd. dirs. Multiple Sclerosis Soc., Jackson, 1966-72; state chmn. Miss. Easter Seals Soc. campaign, 1966, 79; chmn. women's divsn. United Way, Jackson, 1973; commencement spkr. Hinds C.C., 1999. Recipient Hinds C.C. Svc. award, 1993, Miss Miss. Vol. of Yr. award, 1995, Miss Am. Vol. of Yr. award, 1995, Dance Tchrs. Unlimited Lifetime Achievement award, 1996, Dance Tchrs. United Achievement award in dance, 1996; named Woman of Achievement, Jackson Bus. and Profl. Women's Club, 1967-78, Outstanding Vol. Goodwill Industry Miss., 1997, Golden Isles Bowl Classic, 1997; Miss. Legislature commendation for contbn. to youth, 1981; Anna Cowden Bee Hall named in her honor Hinds C of C., bd. trustees, 1993; named Ageless Hero, Blue Cross/Blue Shield, 2001, Hometown Hero, WJTV, 2000; honored Legis., 2003. Mem. Nat. Faculty Dance Educators Am., Dance Masters Am., Miss. Edn. Assn., Miss. Assn. Health and Phys. Edn., Beta Sigma Omicron. Baptist. Home: 256 Azalea Ct Brandon MS 39047-7264 Office: Hinds Cmty Coll Box 10415 Raymond MS 39154

BEEBE, GRACE ANN, retired special education educator; b. Wyandotte, Mich., Feb. 16, 1945; d. Cecil Vern and Elizabeth Lucille (Tamblyn) B. BA, Ea. Mich. U., 1967; MEd, Wayne State U., 1970; postgrad., U. Mich., 1973-78; student, Meth. Theol. Sch., Ecumenical Theol. Sem. Cert. spl. edn. tchr., Mich. Tchr. POHI 1st grade Grand Rapids (Mich.) Pub. Schs., 1967-69; tchr. title VI Taylor (Mich.) Pub. Schs., 1970-73, tchr. Physically or Otherwise Health Impaired pre-kindergarten, 1973-79, tchr. POHI 1st-3rd grades, 1979-81, tchr. POHI pre-kindergarten, 1981-84, tchr., cons. POHI, 1984-2000; ret., 2000. Sem. student Ecumenical Theol. Sch., Detroit, 2000—01, Meth. Theol. Sch., Delaware, Ohio, 2001—. Area coord. Indian Trails Camp, Grand Rapids, 1979-97; Brownie troop leader Girl Scouts U.S., 1997-98. Recipient Recognition award 4-H Wayne County Handicapped Riding, 1986, Indian Trails Camp, 1990; Ronald McDonald Children's Charities grantee, 1990; State of Mich. Spl. Edn. scholar, 1966-67, Vocat. Rehab. scholar, 1969-70. Mem. SCADS (alt. rep.), N.Am. Riding for the Handicapped Assn., Mich. Fedn. Tchrs., Physically Impaired Assn. Mich., Taylor Fedn. Tchrs. (ancillary v.p. 1990-92), Taylor Handicapped Assn., Allen Park Assn. for Handicapped, Trenton Hist. Soc. (exec. bd. 1988-97), Coun. for Exceptional Children, Phi Delta Kappa, Alpha Delta Kappa. Democrat. United Methodist. Avocations: horseback riding, gardening, walking. Home: 2225 Emeline St Trenton MI 48183-3653 E-mail: Beebega@aol.com.

BEEBE, JANE GERTRUDE ALBRIGHT, headmaster; b. Bklyn. d. James David Sr. and Gertrude Angeline (Whipp) Albright; m. Harvey Beebe Jr., July 25, 1954; children: Steven Harvey, Eric James. BS in Edn., N.J. State Coll., 1954; M, Oxford U., Dayton, Tenn., 1992, Doctoral Candidate, 1994. Tchr. kindergarten Monroe Twp. Bd. Edn., Jamesburg, N.J., 1955; tchr. 1st grade Riverside (N.J.) Twp. Bd. Edn., 1955; tchr. 3rd grade East Brunswick (N.J.) Sch. Sys., 1956-59; bonds/debenture dept. AT&T, N.Y.C., summers 1950-53; tchr. kindergarten Crossroads Christian Acad., Clinton, N.J., 1977-91, adminstr., headmaster, 1991—2001. Cons. Sch. Edn. Subject, Clinton, 1977—, advisor mission trips, 1977—; presenter seminars edn. convs. nationally; remedial reading tutor. Author children's lit., stories and poems, children's songs, devotionals; creator nearly 100 learning aids; contbr. articles to profl. jours. Den coord. Boy Scout Group, Milford, N.J., 1975—; children's choir dir. Milford Presbyn. Ch., 1969-76, pianist, organist Clinton Bapt. Ch., 1977-2000; mem. coun. Ramabai Mukti Mission to India.. Oxford U. grantee, 1989. Fellow Internat. Fellowship Christian Sch. Adminstrs.; mem. Assn. Christian Schs. Internat., Mid. Atlantic Christian Sch. Assn., N.J. Christian Sch. Assn., N.J. Coun. Learning Disabilities, N.J. Gifted and Talented Assn. Avocations: travel, languages, traditions and customs other nations, arts/crafts, piano. Office: Crossroads Christian Acad 9 Pittstown Rd Clinton NJ 08809-1208

BEEBE, JOHN DREW, SR., secondary education educator; b. Patterson, N.J., July 18, 1950; s. John E. and June R. (Hultberg) B.; m. Marie Busch, July 24, 1971; children: John Drew Jr., Rebecca Elizabeth, Meredith Marie. AA in Humanities, Brookdale C.C., Lincroft, N.J., 1972; BA in Geosci., Jersey City State Coll., 1976; MA in Edn., Georgian Ct. Coll., 1994. Cert. supr./curriculum, tchr. of sci., earth sci. and English. Sci. tchr. Monsignor Donovan H.S., Toms River, N.J., 1977-88; tchr., sci. dept. chair St. Rose H.S., Belmar, NJ, 1988—2001; tchr. sci. Brick Twp. H.S., 2001—. Advisor Environ. Explorers, Toms River, 1985-88. Named Conservation Tchr. of Yr., Ocean County Soil Conservation, Toms River, 1985, 87, Outstanding Conservation Educator, N.J. Soil Conservation Dists., 1985, 87. Mem. Fossil Riders Classic Motorcycle Assn. Home: 57 Frost Cir Middletown NJ 07748-2305 Office: Brick Twp HS 346 Chambers Bridge Rd Brick NJ 08723 Personal E-mail: b2thedinonerd@aol.com. Business E-Mail: dbeebe@brickmail.k12.nj.us.

BEEBE, LARRY EUGENE, quality engineering educator, management consultant; b. Zanesville, Ohio, Feb. 9, 1947; s. George Franklin and Pauline Betty (White) B.; m. Donna Kaye Miles, Apr. 20, 1964 (div.); children: Troy William, Todd Eugene; m. Danna Darlene Smith, Dec. 12, 1986. Diploma in gen. indsl. engring., Granton Inst. Tech., 1987; MBA, City U., Bellevue, Wash., 1989; postgrad., U. Pa., 1990; PhD in Computer Info. Sys., Nova Southeastern U., 1994. Buyer, quality analyst, mgmt. trainee Continental Can Co., Columbus, Ohio, 1966-70; gen. foreman Ohio Malleable Iron, Columbus, Ohio, 1970-74; foreman Ford Motor Co., L.A., 1974-76; ops. mgr. Vallee Machine Works, Houston, 1976-79, Gt. Lakes Engring., Houston, 1979-84; v.p. info. tech. human resources Atlantic Computer Tech., Melbourne, Fla., 1984—, dir. info. tech. Cons. info. sys., Melbourne, 1985—; mem. adj. faculty Webster U., 1992—; asst. prof. Barry U. Contbr. articles to profl. jours. Mem. Weson Park Townhome Assn., Melbourne, 1985-89; sponsor Spl. Olympics, 1991-92. Fellow Am. Soc. Quality Control, Am. Soc. Non Destructive Test; mem. Am. Welding Soc., Am. Purchasing Assn., Am. Mgmt. Assn., Assn. Info. Profls., Assn. Computer Machinery.

BEEBE, SANDRA E. retired English language educator, artist, writer; b. March AFB, Calif., Nov. 10, 1934; d. Eugene H. and Margaret (Fox) B.; m. Donald C. Thompson. AB in English and Speech, UCLA, 1956; MA in Secondary Edn., Calif. State U., Long Beach, 1957. Tchr. English, Garden Grove (Calif.) High Sch., 1957-93, attendance supr., 1976-83, ret., 1993. Tchr. watercolor courses, Asilomar, Calif., 1997; jury chmn. N.W.S., 1997. Contbr. articles to English Jour., chpts. to books; watercolor artist; exhbns. include AWS, NWS, Okla. Watercolor Soc., Watercolor West, Midwest Watercolor Soc., Butler Inst. Am. Art, Youngstown, Ohio, Kings Art Ctr., Audubon Artists N.Y.; cover artist Exploring Painting, 1990, title page Understanding Watercolor, American Artist, 1991. Mem. faculty Asilomar, 1997; chmn. of jurors N.W.S. Open, 1997. Named one of the Top Ten Watercolorists The Artists Mag., 1994; recipient Best Watercolors award Rockport Press, 1995; chosen for Design Poster selection, 1995, 97. Mem. Am. Watercolor Soc. (dir. 1999—), Nat. Watercolor Soc., Midwest Watercolor Soc., Watercolor West, Allied Artists N.Y., Knickerbocker Artists N.Y., Audubon Artists N.Y., West Coast Watercolor Soc., Rocky Mountain Nat. Watermedia Honor Soc., Jr. League Long Beach, Kappa Kappa Gamma. Republican. Home: 239 Mira Mar Ave Long Beach CA 90803-3899 Address: 239 Mira Mar Ave Long Beach CA 90803-6153 E-mail: sebeebeaws@aol.

BEEBE, STEVEN ARNOLD, communication educator, author; b. Independence, Mo., Sept. 19, 1950; s. David Russell and Muriel Jeanett (Hughes) B.; m. Susan Jane Dye, May 25, 1974; children: Mark, Matthew. BS in Edn. in Speech Comm., Cen. Mo. State U., 1972, MA in Speech Comm., 1973; PhD in Speech Comm., U. Mo., Columbia, 1976; postgrad., U. Oxford, Eng., 1993, postgrad., 2002. Assoc. prof. U. Miami, Fla., 1981-86; prof., chmn. dept. speech comm. S.W. Tex. State U., San Marcos, 1986—, assoc. dean Sch. Fine Arts and Comm., 1989—. Comms. cons. IBM, 3M, Amoco, Motorola, Am. Express, Prentice Hall, Knight Ridder Pub.; guest lectr. Moscow State U., Russia, 1994, Jissen Women's U., Japan, 1998, Pyitigorsk State Linguistic U., Russia, U. Silesia, Poland; vis. scholar Cambridge U., Eng., 1997; mem. U.S. Dept. Def. Tex. Govs. Exec. Devel. Program; vis. scholar Cambridge (Eng.) U., 1997. Author: Family Communication, 1983; co-author: Speech Communication, 1983, Family Talk, 1986, Effective Speech Communication, 1989, 2d edit., 2002, Communication in Small Groups, 1994, 7th edit., 2003, Public Speaking, 1994, 5th edit., 2003, Interpersonal Communication, 2000; contbr. articles to profl. jours. Named Outstanding Comm. prof., Nat. Spkrs. Assn.; fellow, ACE, 2002—03. Mem. Speech Comm. Assn. (chmn. instrnl. devel. com. 1991, chmn. applied comm. sect. 1988), Internat. Comm. Assn., Internat. Performance Rsch. Assn., So. States Comm. Assn., Tex. Nat. Comm. Assn., Russian Comm. Assn. Mem. Cmty. Of Christ Ch. Avocations: music, walking, swimming. Home: 110 W Mimosa Cir San Marcos TX 78666-3710 Office: Tex State U Dept Comm Studies San Marcos TX 78666

BEEBE, SUSAN JANE, English language educator; b. Sacramento, Calif., Nov. 20, 1952; d. William Herbert and Janie Lou (Jennings) Dye; m. Steven A. Beebe, May 25, 1974; children: Mark, Matthew. BSE in Comm., Ctrl. Mo. State U., 1973; MA in English Lit., U. Miami, Coral Gables, Fla., 1979. Cert. secondary edn. tchr., Mo. Tchr. English, debate coach Moberly (Mo.) H.S., 1974-76; tchr. English Deerborne Sch., Coral Gables, 1977; lectr. Sch. Comm., U. Miami, 1980-86; coord. of vols. San Marcos (Tex.) Consol. Ind. Sch. Dist., 1989-93, mem. ednl. improvement coun., 1995-2001, trustee, 2000-01; lectr., assoc. dir. first-year English, dept. English, S.W. Tex. State U., San Marcos, 1988—. Co-author: (textbook) Interpersonal Communication: Relating to Others, 1996, 3d edit., 2002, Public Speaking: An Audience-Centered Approach, 5th edit., 2003, Communication: Principles for a Lifetime, 2001, 2d edit., 2004; (manual) Instructor's Manual for Communicating in Small Groups: Principles and Practices, 2d edit., 1986. Bd. dirs. Tex. Assn. Ptnrs. in Edn., 1992-93; founding coord. Volunteers in Pub. Schs., San Marcos, 1987—; mem. San Marcos Sch. Bd., 2000-2001; active Cmty. of Christ Ch. Recipient Gov.'s Ednl. Excellence award, Tex., 1991, pvt. citizen award Tex. Classroom Tchrs. Assn., 1993. Mem. Conf. of Coll. Tchrs. of English, Tex. Coun. Tchrs. of English, Nat. Coun. Tchrs. of English. Democrat. Avocations: reading, music. Office: SW Tex State U Dept English San Marcos TX 78666

BEEKMAN, ERIC M. language educator; b. Amsterdam, The Netherlands, 1939; arrived in U.S., 1957; BA in English and Comparative Lit., U. Calif., Berkeley, 1963; PhD in Comparative Lit., Harvard U., 1968. Prof. Germanic langs. U. Mass., Amherst, 1968—. Translator, editor, annotator: The Ambonese Curiosity Cabinet, 1999. With U.S. Army. Named Knight of the Order of the Netherlands Lion, 1997; fellow, John Simon Guggenheim Meml. Found., 2003. Office: U Mass Dept Germanic Langs and Lit 161 Presidents Dr Amherst MA 01003-9312*

BEEKS, CHERYL ELAINE, elementary school educator; b. Concord, NC, Aug. 28, 1946; d. Ray Edward and Maxine (Peterson) Barringer; m. Raymond Neil Beeks, July 12, 1971; 1 child, Alison Elaine Rios. B in Music Edn., So. Meth. U., Dallas, 1968. Tchr. Lamesa (Tex.) Ind. Sch. Dist., 1968—69, 1970—73, Loraine (Tex.) Ind. Sch. Dist., 1976—77, Highland Ind. Sch. Dist., Roscoe, Tex., 1980—. Coach 5th grade events Univ. Interscholastic League, Roscoe, 1980—, elem. poetry judge, 1995—. Pianist, organist Hermleigh (Tex.) United Meth. Ch., 1990—, treas., 1995—98; lay delegate United Meth. Northwest Conf., Lubbock, Tex., 1999—. Mem.: Tex. Assn. Cmty. Schs., Tex. Music Edn. Assn., Nat. Assn. Music Edn. Home: 206 Lowe Hermleigh TX 79526 Office: Highland Ind Sch Dist 6625 FM608 Roscoe TX 79545 Business E-Mail: cbeeks@highland.esc14.net.

BEEM, JOHN KELLY, retired mathematician, educator; b. Detroit, Jan. 24, 1942; s. William Richard and June Ellen (Kelly) B.; m. Eloise Masako Yamamoto, Mar. 24, 1964; 1 child, Thomas Kelly AB in Math., U. So. Calif., 1963, MA in Math., 1965, PhD in Math., 1968. Asst. prof. math. U. Mo., Columbia, 1968-71, assoc. prof., 1971-79, prof., 1979—2002; ret., 2002. Author: (with P. Y. Woo) Doubly Timelike Surfaces, 1969, (with P. E. Ehrlich) Global Lorentzian Geometry, 1981, (with P.E. Ehrlich and K.L. Easley), 2d edit., 96; condr. research in differential geometry and gen. relativity. Recipient Kemper Tchg. award, 1996; NSF fellow, 1965, 68. Mem. Math. Assn. Am., Am. Math. Soc., Phi Beta Kappa Home: 5204 E Tayside Cir Columbia MO 65203-5191

BEEMAN, RICHARD ROY, historian, educator; b. Seattle, May 16, 1942; m. Pamela Jane Butler, Dec. 26, 1964; children: Kristin Dowds, Joshua Douglas. AB in History, U. Calif., Berkeley, 1964; MA in History, Coll. of William and Mary, 1965; PhD in History, U. Chgo., 1968. Asst. prof. history U. Pa., 1968-73, assoc. prof., 1973-82, prof., 1982—, acting chmn. dept., 1986-87, chmn., 1987-91, assoc. dean, 1991-96; vis. prof. Am. studies U. Hull, Eng., 1976-77; dean Coll. Arts and Scis. U. Pa., 1998—2003; William R. Kenan prof. history, chmn. Colby Coll., 1979-80; Vyvian Harmsworth prof. Am. history Oxford U., 2003—. Dir. Phila. Ctr. for Early Am. Studies, 1980-85. Author: The Old Dominion and the New Nation, 1788-1801, 1972, Patrick Henry: A Biography, 1974, The Evolution of the Southern Backcountry, 1984; editor: Beyond Confederation: The Origins of the American Constituion and National Identity, 1987, The Varieties of Political Experience in Eighteenth Century America, 2003; also articles and book revs. Dept. of History fellow Coll. William and Mary, 1964, Univ. fellow U. Chgo., 1966-67, Newberry Library jr. fellow, Chgo., 1967-68, U. Pa. summer research grants, 1969, 71, Am. Philos. Soc. research grants, 1971, 76, 80, 89, Social Sci. Research Council post-doctoral fellowship, 1972-73, Nat. Book Award nominee, 1974, Fulbright sr. lectr., U.K., 1976-77, NEH basic research grant, 1983-84, summer seminar grant, 1986, sr. fellow, 1989—; fellow Inst. Advanced Study, 1989-90, Huntington Libr., 1997. Home: 301 Glenwood Ave Media PA 19063-4131 Office: U Pa 120 Logan Hall Philadelphia PA 19104 E-mail: rbeeman@sas.upenn.edu.

BEER, MICHAEL, biophysicist, educator, environmentalist; b. Budapest, Hungary, Feb. 20, 1926; came to U.S., 1958, naturalized, 1965; s. Paul and Lidia (Pap-Kovacs) B.; m. Margaret Terry Peters, Jan. 22, 1954; children: Nicholas, Suzanne, Wendy. MA, U. Toronto, 1950; PhD, U. Manchester, Eng., 1953. Rsch. assoc. U. Mich., Ann Arbor, 1953-56; rsch. fellow Nat. Rsch. Coun. Can., 1956-58; mem. faculty Johns Hopkins U., Balt., 1958—, prof. biophysics, 1964-96, prof. emeritus, 1996—, chmn. dept. biophysics, 1974-80, assoc. dean arts and scis., 1989-92. Mem. Biophys. Soc. (pres. 1975-76), Electron Microscopy Soc. Am. (pres. 1980), Chesapeake Bay Trust (Ellen Fraites Wagner award, 1999). Home: 4623 Wilmslow Rd Baltimore MD 21210-2549

BEER, PAMELA JILL PORR, writer, retired vocational school educator; b. Denver, Sept. 23, 1941; d. Wyeth Wittwer and Mary Porr (DuReece) Beer; m. Calvin George Beer, Dec. 25, 1968. BS, Pittsburg State U., Kans., 1963; MBE, 1979. Clk. Bookkeeper Hubbard Auto Supply, Pitts., 1960—63; tchr. bus. edn. Sabetha HS, Kans., 1963—65, Nevada HS, Mo., 1965—71; head bus. dept. Nev. Vocat. Area Sch., 1971—93; ret., 1993; freelance writer, 1993; instr. continuing edn. Mo. Southern State Coll., Joplin, 1987—. Instr. 4-H, 1987. Contbr. articles profl. jour. Named Nev. R-5 Tchr. of Yr., 1992, Bus. Edn. Tchr. of Yr., Mo. Southwest Dist., 1993, Tchr. of Yr., Mo. Bus. Edn. Assn. SW Dist. Mem.: Alpha Gamma Delta, Nev. C. of C. (Area Educator of Yr. 1987), Am. Vocat. Assn., Nat. Bus. Edn. Assn., Roxburg Pub. Co. (mem. editorial adv. bd. 1984), articulation com., Delta Kappa Gamma. Meth. Avocations: bowling, swimming, bridge, tennis. Home: 1827 F Kennedy Pittsburg KS 66762

BEERING, STEVEN CLAUS, academic administrator, medical educator; b. Berlin, Aug. 20, 1932; arrived in U.S., 1948, naturalized, 1953; s. Steven and Alice (Friedrichs) Beering; m. Catherine Jane Pickering, Dec. 27, 1956; children: Peter, David, John. BS summa cum laude, U. Pitts., 1954; DSc (hon.), Ind. Cen. U., 1983; MD, U. Pitts., 1958; DSc (hon.), U. Evansville (Ind.), 1984; ScD (hon.), U. Pitts., 1998; DSc (hon.), Ramapo Coll., 1986, Anderson Coll., 1987; ScD (hon.), Ind. U., 1988; LLD (hon.), Hanover Coll., 1986; DsC (hon.), Purdue U., 2000; LLD (hon.), Tex. Wesleyan, 2001. Intern Walter Reed Gen. Hosp., Washington, 1958—59; resident Wilford Hall Med. Center, San Antonio, 1959—62, chief internal medicine, edn. coordinator, 1967—69; prof. medicine Ind. U. Sch. Medicine, Indpls., 1969—, asst. dean, 1969—70, assoc. dean, dir. postgrad. edn., 1970—74, dir. statewide med. edn. system, 1970-83, dean, 1974—83; chief exec. officer Ind. U. Med. Center, Indpls., 1974—83; pres. Purdue U. and Purdue U. Rsch. Found., West Lafayette, Ind., 1983—2000, pres. emeritus, 2000—; chmn. Purdue Rsch. Found., West Lafayette, 2000—. Prof. pharmacology and toxicology Purdue U.; bd. dirs. Eli Lilly Co., NISource, Inc., Am. United Life; cons. Indpls. VA Hosp., St. Vincent Hosp.; chmn. Med. Edn. Bd. Ind., 1974—83, Liaison Com. Med. Edn., 1976—81, Ind. Commn. Med. Edn., 1978—83. Contbr. articles to sci. jours. Sec. Ind. Atty. Gen.'s Trust, 1974—83; regent Nat. Libr. Medicine, 1987—91; trustee U. Pitts. Lt. col. M.C. USAF, 1957—69. Fellow: ACP, Royal Soc. Medicine; mem.: Nat. Sci. Bd., Ind. Acad., Nat. Acad. Sci. Inst. of Medicine, Assn. Am. Univs. (chair 1995—96), Coun. Med. Deans (chmn. 1980—81), Assn. Am. Med. Colls. (chmn. 1982—83), Endocrine Soc., Am. Diabetes Assn., Am. Fedn. Med. Rsch., Meridian Hills Club, Skyline Club, Phi Rho Sigma (U.S. v.p. 1976—85), Alpha Omega Alpha, Sigma Xi, Phi Beta Kappa. Presbyterian. Home: 10487 Windemere Dr Carmel IN 46032 Office: Purdue U Office of Pres Emeritus Rm 218 Memorial Union West Lafayette IN 47906-3584 Fax: 765-496-7561. E-mail: scb@purdue.edu.

BEERMAN, JOSEPH, health educator; b. N.Y.C., Aug. 31, 1937; s. Herbert and Frances B.; m. Andrea Ellenhorn, Aug. 15, 1987; 1 child, Eric Hunter. BA, Hunter Coll., 1959; MA, NYU, 1963; diploma Tchr.'s Coll., Columbia U., 1970. Cert. in health and phys. edn., N.Y. Tchg. asst., track coach NYU, 1959-61; tchr. health edn. Herman Ridder Jr. H.S., N.Y.C., 1961-65; prof. health and phys. edn. Manhattan C.C.-CUNY, N.Y.C., 1965-96, assoc. dean faculty, 1978-79, prof. emeritus, 1996—, adj. prof., 1996—. Cons. Nat. Coun. Jr. Colls., NEA, Washington, 1965—; rep. Coun. Health Educators, CUNY, 1965—. Author: Chemical Dependency and the Minorities, 1993, Basic Tennis: Skills and Strategies, 1995. Guest speaker YMCA and sr. citizen orgns., N.Y.C., 1965—; presenter tennis clins. Ea. Tennis Patrons, N.Y.C., 1965-75; presenter seminars N.Y.C. Bd. Edn., 1961-70. Sgt. U.S. Army, 1959-61. Nat. Humanities Faculty grantee, 1978; recipient McGovern award U.S. Tennis Assn., 1987; inducted into Hunter Coll. Athletic Hall of Fame, 1993. Fellow Internat. Inst. Cmty. Svc., Friends of Penn Relay's; mem. Am. Alliance Phys. Edn., Health, Recreation and Dance (mem. various coms. 1960—), Democrat. Jewish. Avocations: philately, numismatics, antiques, tennis. Home: 16-70 Bell Blvd Apt 113 Bayside NY 11360 Office: CUNY 199 Chambers St New York NY 10007-1044

BEERS, SUSAN ALICE, dean; b. Tucson, July 21, 1946; d. Laverne G. and Claire M. (Liles) B. BA, Chapman U., 1968; MA, Calif. State U., Long Beach, 1972; EdD, Pepperdine U., 1997. Cert. tchr., Calif. Tchr. Norwalk (Calif.) H.S., 1969-74; realtor assoc. Nolan Real Estate, Laguna Beach, Calif., 1988-90; prof. Fullerton (Calif.) Coll., 1974-89, athletic dir., dept. chair, 1989-92, dean phys. edn./athletics, 1992—, interim dean counseling/student devel., 1995—. Mem. dist. mgmt. negotiation team Fullerton Coll., 1994-95, pres. Orange Empire Conf. Com., 1995—, Title IX officer, 1994—; presenter in field. Editor Scope newsletter, 1992-96. Mem. Dept. Social Svc., Orange, Calif., 1992; Scope rep./presenter State Legis. Conf., 1994; prsenter Calif. Assn. Health, Sacramento, 1995. Mem. AAHPERD, State Commn. on Athletics, State Cmty. Coll. Orgn. of Phys. Educators (pres. 1993-95, spkr. 1995). Democrat. Avocations: snow skiing, swimming, travel. Office: Fullerton Coll 321 E Chapman Ave Fullerton CA 92832-2011 Home: 37 Channel Pl Newport Beach CA 92663-4423

BEERY, BARBARA FAYE, secondary school educator; b. Flint, MI, Nov. 6, 1937; d. Ralph Lester and Anne Louise Rose; m. Carl Leonard Beery, Jan. 10, 1966 (dec. Sept. 1987); stepchildren: Julieanne, Elizabeth, Mary June, Deborah, John. BA in History, MA in Spl. Edn., Ariz. State U., 1971, DEd, 1992. Cert. paralegal Ariz., 1994. Tchr., coach Glendale (Ariz.) Union Sch. Dist., 1974—84, human resources adminstr., 1984—94. Adj. prof. No. Ariz. U., Flagstaff, Ottawa U., Phoenix.

BEERY, PAMELA ELAYNE, intermediate school educator; b. San Marcos, Tex., July 3, 1956; d. Dwight Edward Beery and Nancy Louise (Snyder) Collert; m. Paul David Billiat, Aug. 18, 1975 (div. May 1982); 1 child, Korinne Elayne; m. Donald Jay Hartsock, Oct. 31, 1993 (div. Apr. 2002). BA in Music Edn., Ohio Wesleyan U., 1978; MA in Edn., Ohio State U., 1988. Cert. tchr. Tchr. music Westover Elem. Sch., Stamford, Conn., 1978-80, Oak Ridge Elem. Sch., Darien, Conn., 1980-81; tchr. lang. arts, music, drama Willis Intermediate Sch., Delaware, Ohio, 1983—. Instr. Ashland U., Columbus, Ohio, 1990—. Bd. dirs. Ctrl. Ohio Symphony, Deleware, 1994—, prin. flutist, 1982—. Grantee, NEH, 1992, Fulbright Meml. Fund grant, 2003. Mem. Nat. Coun. Tchrs. English, Ohio Coun. Tchrs. English Lang. Arts, Internat. Reading Assn. Avocations: flute, reading, writing, poetry. Office: 78 W William St Delaware OH 43015-2339

BEETS, HUGHLA FAE, retired secondary school educator; b. Eustace, Tex., Aug. 1, 1929; d. Hubert Edgar and Beatrice (Roark) Bonsal; m. Anneel Randolph Beets, Sept. 14, 1946. BA, North Tex. State U., 1958, MA, 1960; postgrad., U. Mass., 1967. Cert. tchr., Tex. Tchr. Seagoville (Tex.) Ind. Sch. Dist., 1958-65, Dallas Ind. Sch. Dist., 1965-70; owner, mgr. Mabank (Tex.) Ins. Agy., 1970-77, Beets Interiors, Mabank, 1970—; ptnr., mgr. Cedar Creek Title Co., Mabank, 1977-80; tchr. govt. and econs. Athens (Tex.) Ind. Sch. Dist., 1981-91. Cons. U.S. Office Edn., Washington, 1968-69; mem. devel. com. Edn. Profl. Devel. Act Tex. Edn. Agy., 1969. Cons. edn. com. Goals for Dallas, 1969; vice chairperson Kaufman (Tex.) County Improvement Council, 1975. Chmn. beautification com. Keep Tex. Beautiful, Mabank, 1990-91; grant adminstr. Avanti Comty. Theater, 1993-95, bd. dirs., 1993-98, 99, v.p., 1995-98, treas., 1999—; co-chair United Way Campaign, 1991-92, dir. Henderson County, 1992-96; mem. Planning and Zoning Commn., City of Mabank, 1992—; sec. Indsl. Found., 1971-75; mem. Mabank Centennial Com., 1999-2000; bd. dirs. First United Meth. Ch. Found., Mabank, Tex., 1999—. Recipient Outstanding Ex-Student award Trinity Valley C.C., Athens, 1974; Cert. of Recognition, Internat. Thespian Soc., 1994, Lifetime Achievement award Cedar Creek C. of C., 1996. Mem. NEA, Athens Edn. Assn. (pres. 1982-83), Tex. State Tchrs. Assn. (pres.-elect dist. X 1970), Tex. Classroom Tchrs. Assn. (state bd. dirs. 1969-70), Classroom Tchrs. Dallas (pres. 1968-69), Mabank C. of C. (bd. dirs. 1978-80, 91-92, Citizen of Yr. 1977). Democrat. Methodist. Avocations: sewing, interior design. Home: 112 N Canton St Mabank TX 75147-9712

BEGIN, JACQUELINE SUE, environmental education specialist; b. Urbana, Ohio, Oct. 20, 1951; d. Gerald L. Sr. and Norma M. (Bezold) B. AA, Clark State c.C., 1991; BA, Antioch Coll., 1993, MA, 1996. Rschr., organizer Holywell Trust, Derry, No. Ireland, 1992; rsch. asst. peace studies dept. Antioch Coll., Yellow Springs, Ohio, 1993; adminstrv. asst. Comty. Action Commn. Fayette County, Washington Court House, Ohio, 1994-95; asst. dir. admissions office Antioch Coll., Yellow Springs, 1995—; environ. edn. specialist Fayette County, Ohio. Student presenter Boulding Libr. dedication Antioch Coll. and McGregor Sch. of Antioch U., Yellow Springs, 1995; rschr. on women in No. Ireland, McGregor Sch., Yellow Springs, 1996; chair, organizer Beyond Hate: Living with Our Deepest Difference

Conf., Holywell Trust, Derry, 1992; environ. edn. specialist for Fayette County, 1997—. Founder, activist for environment Students Against Violation of Earth (S.A.V.E.), Springfield, Ohio, 1989-91; activist for animal rights People for Ethical Treatment of Animals (PETA), Springfield, 1987-93; peace activist Clark State and Antioch Coll., Yellow Springs, 1991—; activist for women specific issues The McGregor Sch. of Antioch U., Yellow Springs, 1994—. Comty. scholar Clark State C.C., 1990, News-Sun scholar, 1991, Chatterjee scholar Antioch Coll., 1992. Avocations: reading, aerobics, camping, hiking, bicycling.

BEGLEY, NAN ELIZABETH, psychotherapist, psychology educator; b. Springfield, Mass., Oct. 20, 1951; d. Howard George and Marguerite Rosalie (Christodolou) Gauthier; children: James, Taryn. AA, Springfield Tech. Community Coll., 1981; BA, Westfield State Coll., 1983, MA, 1985. Lic. marriage and family therapist, Mass.; lic. mental health counselor, Mass. Dir. parent empowerment project United Cerebral Palsy Inc., Springfield, 1983-84, dir., 1984-85, staff psychotherapist, 1985-87, Osborn Clinic, Agawam, Mass., 1985-92; pvt. practice Springfield, 1985—; prof. psychology Springfield Tech. Community Coll., 1985—, Springfield Coll., 1987—; staff psychotherapist Child Guidance Clinic, Springfield, Mass., 1991-97, Clinician Psychotherapy Resource Network, Springfield, 1997—2000. Cons. spl. edn. area schs., Springfield, Agawam, Chicopee, Hampden and Wilbraham, Mass., 1985—. Active in pub. rels. and fundraising Springfield Tech. Community Coll., 1981-88; producer DGR Prodns. Theatre Co., Springfield, 1981—. Mem. APA (assoc.), Am. Counseling Assn., Am. Assn. for Marriage and Family Therapy, Am. Assn. Mental Health Counselors, Mass. Assn. Mental Health Counselors. Avocations: theatre, travel, walking, bridge, reading.

BEGOVICH, MICHAEL, public defender, law educator; b. Burnaby, B.C., Can., Nov. 20, 1959; came to U.S., 1963; m. Samantha L. Rijken; 2 children. BA summa cum laude, U. Calif., Davis, 1981; JD, U. Calif., San Francisco, 1985. Bar: Ind. 1987, Calif. 1988, U.S. Dist. Ct. (so. and no. dists.) Ind. 1987, U.S. Dist. Ct. (so., ea. and no. dists.) Calif., U.S. Ct. Appeals (7th cir.) 1987, U.S. Supreme Ct. 1993. Assoc. Law Offices Ramon D. Asedo, Oceanside, Calif., 1987-88; dep. pub. defender San Diego County, 1988—; prof. law Palomar Coll., San Marcos, Calif., 1990—, U. San Diego, 1991—, Grossmont Coll., El Cajon, Calif., 1991—. Prof. U. San Diego Sch. Law, 1997—; adj. prof. Thomas Jefferson Sch. Law, San Diego, 1998—; mem. exec. com. criminal law sect. State Bar Calif.; spkr. in field. Contbr. articles to profl. jours. 1st tenor San Diego Master Chorale. Mem. Ind. Bar Assn., Am. Inns of Ct. (barrister Enright chpt.), San Diego County Bar Assn., San Diego Criminal Defense Bar Assn., Serbian Bar Assn., Calif. Pub. Defender's Assn., Serbian Nat. Fedn. (bd. dirs. 1987-95), San Diego Zool. Soc., Phi Beta Kappa, Phi Delta Phi, Phi Kappa Phi, Pi Sigma Alpha, Phi Kappa Psi. Serbian Orthodox. Avocations: singing, snow skiing. Office: San Diego County Pub Defender 233 A St Ste 500 San Diego CA 92101-4097 Fax: 619-338-4811. E-mail: michael.begovich@sdcounty.ca.gov.

BEHAR, LISA DENISE, elementary and secondary educator; b. Little Neck, N.Y., Nov. 1, 1963; BA in Comm., SUNY, Albany, 1985; MS in Edn., English, Long Island U., 1993. Clk. Avis Rent-a-Car, Garden City, N.Y., 1983-84; pub. rels. coord. N.Y. State Dept. Tax & Fin., Albany, 1985; account exec., pub. rels. coord. Harriett Ruderman, Bertin Design, Port Washington, N.Y., 1985-87; mktg. and advt. specialist, editor Computer Assocs., Islandia, N.Y., 1988-92; tchr. Nassau County Pub. Schs., Long Island, NY, 1992—95; elem. and secondary English tchr.; mktg. specialist Sulzer Metco, 1997—2002. Home: 3359 Ocean Harbor Dr Oceanside NY 11572

BEHLER, PHILIP KEIFER, secondary education educator; b. Dayton, Ohio, May 31, 1954; s. William Keifer and Bernice Marie (McElfresh) B. BS in Edn., Ohio U., 1977; MS in Edn., U. Dayton, 1992. Cert. tchr., supr., principal Ohio. Tchr. Wayne High Sch., Huber Heights (Ohio) City Schs., 1978—, also attendance dean, 1985-91; coord. disadvantaged pupil program, 1985—. Dep. registrar Montgomery County (Ohio) Bd. Elections, 1985—. Mem. Ohio Edn. Assn., Nat. Edn. Assn. Avocations: golf, tennis, skiing, going to the beach. Office: Wayne High Sch 5400 Chambersburg Rd Huber Heights OH 45424-3798

BEHM, MARK EDWARD, university administrator, consultant; b. Balt., Apr. 21, 1945; s. Carl and Margaret Anderson (Weichman) B.; m. Linda Ann Walker, Oct. 9, 1976; children: Scott Anderson, Craig Redgwick. BS, U. Md., 1967; MBA, Loyola Coll., Balt., 1980. Co-owner Applied Light Tech. Co., Silver Spring, Md., 1968-69; product area adminstr. Singer Co., Link Div., Silver Spring, Md., 1969-73; asst. comptroller U. Md. Balt. County (UMBC), 1973-75, dir. fin. planning, 1976-85, dir. planning and budget, 1986-88, v.p. for adminstrv. affairs, 1988—, also mem. adv. bd. Tech. Enterprise Ctr. Founding mem., bd. dirs. Grant-a-Wish Found., Balt., 1979-87, Baltimore County Govt. Econ. Devel. Commn., BWI Partnership Bd.; steering com. Md. Ctr. for Indsl. Energy Efficiency; econ. devel. subcom. Md. Info. tech. Bd.; chmn. Troop 880 com. Boy Scouts Am. Mem. Assn. Univ. Rsch. Parks, Ea. Assn. Coll. and Univ. Bus. Officers (bd. dirs.). Home: 13809 Princess Anne Way Phoenix MD 21131-1521 Office: U Md Baltimore County (UMBC) 1000 Hilltop Cir Baltimore MD 21250-0001

BEHMER, KEVIN SHEA, mathematics educator; b. Detroit, Oct. 26, 1966; s. Kenneth Royden and Mary Eileen (MacMichael) B. BS, Ea. Mich. U., 1988, MA, 1996. Cert. tchr., Mich. Tchr., asst. football coach, head women's track coach Ovid-Elsie (Mich.) High Sch., 1988-91; tchr. math., head freshman football coach Huron H.S., Ann Arbor, Mich., 1991—, head women's track coach, 1996—. Head girls track coach, asst. varsity football coach Ovid Elsie High Sch., 1989-91. Mem. Nat. Coun. Tchrs. Math., Mich. Coun. Tchrs. Math., Mich. Interscholastic Track Coaches Assn., Mich. High Sch. Football Coaches Assn. Avocations: music, reading, travel, biking, sports. Office: Huron High Sch 2727 Fuller Rd Ann Arbor MI 48105-2499

BEHREND, DONALD FRASER, environmental educator, university administrator; b. Manchester, Conn., Aug. 30, 1931; s. Sherwood Martin and Margaret (Fraser) B.; m. Joan Belcher, Nov. 9, 1957; children: Andrew Fraser, Eric Hemingway, David William. BS with honors and distinction, U. Conn., 1958, MS, 1960; PhD in Forest Zoology, SUNY, Syracuse, 1966. Forest game mgmt. specialist Ohio Dept. Natural Resources, Athens, 1960; res. asst. Coll. Forestry, SUNY, Newcomb, 1960-63, res. assoc., 1963-67; dir. Adirondack ecol. ctr. Coll. Environ. Science and Forestry, SUNY, Newcomb, 1968-73; acting dean grad. studies Syracuse, 1973-74; asst. v.p. research programs, exec. dir. Inst. Environ. Program Affairs, 1974-79; v.p. acad. affairs, prof., 1979-85; prof. emeritus, 1987—; asst. prof. wildlife mgmt. U. Maine, Orono, 1967-68; provost, v.p. acad. affairs U. Alaska Statewide System, Fairbanks, 1985-87, exec. v.p., provost, 1988; chancellor U. Alaska, Anchorage, 1988-94, chancellor emeritus, 1994—. Mem. patent policy bd. SUNY, 1983-85, chmn. Res. Found. com. acad. res. devel., 1984-85; chmn. 6-Yr. planning com. U. Alaska, 1985-86; bd. dirs. Commonwealth North, 1991-92, Alaska Internat. Ednl. Found., 1997; mem. selection com. Harry S. Truman Scholarship Found.; mem. Pres.'s Commn., NCAA, 1992-95; chmn. spl. com. on student athlete welfare access and equity, 1993-95; chmn. 20th Great Alaska Shootout, 1997. Contbr. numerous articles and papers to profl. jours. Mem. Newcomb Planning Bd., 1967-69; mem., pres. Bd. Edn. Newcomb Cent. Sch., 1967-73; chmn. governing bd. N.Y. Sea Grant Inst., 1984-85; trustee U. Ala. Found., 1990-94. Served with USN, 1950-54. Mem. Alaska Internat. Edn. Found. (bd. dirs. 1997—), Wildlife Soc., Soc. Am. Foresters, AAAS, Phi Kappa Phi (hon.), Sigma Xi, Gamma Sigma Delta, Sigma Lambda Alpha (hon.). Lodges: Rotary (bd. dirs. Fairbanks club 1985-86), Lions (bd. dirs. Newcomb club 1966-67). Avocations: reading, writing, photography, fly fishing, bagpiping. Home: 333 M St Apt #403 Anchorage AK 99501-1902

BEHRENS, BEREL LYN, physician, academic and healthcare administrator; b. New South Wales, Australia, 1940; MB, BS, Sydney (Australia) U., 1964. Cert. pediatrics, allergy and immunology. Intern Royal Prince Alfred Hosp., Australia, 1964; resident Loma Linda (Calif.) U. Med. Ctr., 1966-68; with Henrietta Egleston Hosp. for Children, Atlanta, 1968-69, T.C. Thompson Children's Hosp., Chattanooga, 1969-70; instr. pediatrics Loma Linda U., 1970-72, with dept. pediatrics, 1972—, dean Sch. Medicine, 1986-91, pres., 1990—; pres., CEO Loma Linda U. Med. Ctr., 1999—. Office: 11175 Campus St Loma Linda CA 92354 E-mail: myhanna@ahs.llumc.edu.

BEHRING, DANIEL WILLIAM, educational and business professional, consultant; b. Sheboygan, Wis., Jan. 9, 1940; s. Melvin William and Frieda (Ostwald) B.; m. Nancy Jean Steeno, July 28, 1962; children: Deanna, Shelley, Tanya, Jonathan. BA, Ripon Coll., 1962; MA, Ohio U., 1964, PhD, 1969. Tchg. fellow Ohio U., Athens, 1965-66, acting instr., 1966; asst. prof. So. Ill. U., Edwardsville, 1968-71; dean students, asst. prof. Monmouth Coll., Ill., 1971-76; assoc. prof., v.p. Alma Coll., Mich., 1976-86; v.p. acad. affairs Adrian (Mich.) Coll., 1986-91, interim pres., 1988-89; v.p., dir. schs. Cranbrook Edn. Cmty., 1991-95; pres. SQT Sys., 1995—. Assoc. prof. DeVos Grad. Sch. Mgmt., 1998-2000, prof., 2000-; cons. colls., high schs., mental health orgns., businesses, mfrs. and C. of C. Contbr. articles to profl. jours. Bd. dirs. Hoogerland Meml. Workshop, St. Louis, Mich., 1977-86, Lenawee Tomorrow Econ. Devel. Assn., 1989-91, Lenawee Symphony, 1986-91, Farm Credit Svcs., 1990-94; reviewer United Way, Alma, 1983, 84; bd. dirs. Prodn. Credit Assn., 1990-94. Capt. U.S. Army, 1966-68. Grantee Kellogg Found., 1976-80, U.S. Office Edn., 1977, 78, 79, Lilly, 1988, Towsely Found., 1989, State of Mich., 1989, 91. Mem. APA, Am. Assn. Higher Edn., Rotary (pres. 1983-84, bd. dirs. Adrian chpt.), Oakland County Bus. Roundtable, Sigma Xi, Sigma Chi (Grand Consul Merit award 1984). Avocations: numismatics, studebaker automobiles, model trains, science, sailing. Home and Office: 3695 Lakeshore Dr Manistee MI 49660-9760

BEHRMAN, ELIZABETH COLDEN, physics educator; b. Boston, Jan. 29, 1958; d. Edward Joseph and Cynthia (Fansler) B.; 1 child, Joanna Francesca. ScB, Brown U., 1979; MS, U. Ill., 1981, PhD, 1985. Postdoctoral fellow SUNY, Stony Brook, 1985-86; asst. prof. N.Y. State Coll. Ceramics, Alfred (N.Y.) U., 1986-90, Wichita State U., Kans., 1990-94, assoc. prof., 1994—2002, prof., 2002—. Contbr. articles to profl. jours. NSF undergrad. rsch. fellow, 1978, U. Ill. grad. fellow, 1979, Rsch. Corp. grantee, 1992, 93, NSF grantee, 1993, 99, 2002, ONR grantee, 1995. Mem. Am. Phys. Soc., Materials Rsch. Soc., Am. Assn. Physics Tchrs., Assn. Women in Sci., Sigma Xi. Office: Wichita State U Physics Dept Wichita KS 67260-0001

BEHUNIAK, PETER, psychometrician, educational psychologist, educational consultant; b. Derby, Conn., Feb. 11, 1950; s. Peter and Stella (Spak) Behuniak; m. Gail Ann Tomala, Mar. 8, 1986; 1 child, Alexander T. BS with high honors, U. Conn., 1971, MA, 1973, PhD in Ednl. Psychology, 1981; postgrad., U. Mass., 1975-77. Cert. tchr. Conn. Tchr. Glastonbury (Conn.) Pub. Schs., 1971-78; rsch. asst. U. Conn. Bur. Ednl. Rsch., Storrs, 1979-80; pres. Edn. Resource Assocs., Glastonbury, 1980-83; edn. cons. Conn. Dept. Edn., Hartford, 1983-89, coord. student assessment, 1989-91, chief Bur. Evaluation and Student Assessment, 1991-92, dir. student assessment and testing, 1992—2002, chief bur. cert. and profl. devel., 2002—03; pres. Criterion Consulting, LLC, 2001—; prof. in residence, dept. ednl. psychology U. Conn., Storrs, 2002—. Lectr. U. Conn., Storrs, 1980—85, U. Bridgeport, Conn., 1982—83, Ea. Conn. State U., 1987—89; adj. faculty U. Hartford, dir. student assessment, 1988—2001; mem. validity panel Nat. Assessment Ednl. Progress, 2000—; prof. ednl. psychology U. Conn., 2003—. Contbr. articles to profl. jours. Mem. evaluation com. Cmty. Coun. Capital Region, Hartford, 1984—87; bd. overseers N.E. Regional Labs.; pres. Edn. Adminstrs. Union, Conn. State Dept. Edn.; chmn. tech. guidelines for performance assessment Coun. Chief State Sch. Officers; Nat. Coun. Measurement Edn. rep. Joint Com. Testing Practices; bd. dirs. S.E. Conn. Civil Liberties Union, Windham, 1977—80. Mem.: Am. Evaluation Assn. (presenter), Nat. Coun. Measurement Edn. (presenter), Am. Ednl. Rsch. Assn. (presenter), Phi Delta Kappa. Avocation: photography. Office: Conn State Dept Edn PO Box 2219 Hartford CT 06145-2219 E-mail: PeterBehuniak@cox.net.

BEIERWALTES, WILLIAM HENRY, physician, educator; b. Saginaw, Mich., Nov. 23, 1916; s. John Andrew and Fanny (Aris) B.; m. Mary Martha Nichols, Jan. 1, 1942; children: Andrew George, William Howard, Martha Louise. AB, U. Mich., 1938, MD, 1941. Diplomate: Am. Bd. Internal Medicine and Nuclear Medicine. Intern, then asst. resident medicine Cleve. City Hosp., 1941-43; mem. faculty U. Mich. Med. Center, 1944-87, prof. medicine, 1959-87, prof. emeritus, 1987—; dir. nuclear medicine, also dir. Thyroid Research Lab., 1952-86, cons., 1987-95. Cons. nuclear medicine depts. St. John Hosp., Detroit, Wm. Beaumont Hosp., Royal Oak and Troy, Mich., 1987-95, The UpJohn Co. Rsch. div., 1952-65, The Abbott Labs. Rsch. div., 1960-67; sr. med. cons. MD (Med. Fedn.), Bagdad, Iraq, 1963; mem. exec. com. Inst. Sci. and Tech., 1963; lectr. Nat. Naval Med. Ctr., 1964-88, Ctr. for Environ. Health Mich. State Dept. Health, 1988-89; Peter Heimann lectr. 34th meeting Internat. Congress Surgery, Stockholm, Sweden, 1991; adv. panel on radionuclide labeled compounds for tumor diagnosis Internat. AEC, 1974-75; mem. Mich. State Radiation Bd., 1980-84; co-chmn. Nat. Coop., Thyroid Cancer Therapy Group, 1978-81 Author: Clinical Use of Radioisotopes, 1957, Manual of Nuclear Medicine Procedures, 1971, Love of Life Autobiog. Sketches, 1996; contbr. numerous articles to profl. jours.; assoc. editor Jour. Lab. and Clin. Medicine, 1954-60; editl. bd. Jour. Nuclear Medicine, 1964-69, assoc. editor, 1975-81; editl. bd. Jour. Clin. Endocrinology and Metabolism, 1963; adv. bd. Annals of Saudi Medicine, 1986-90; patentee for monoclonal antibodies to HCG, and radionuclide in vivo biochem. imaging of endocrine glands, 1951; first to treat a patient for cancer with radio labeled antibodies, 1951; co-inventor radiopharms, 1971; originator of radioimmunodetection of human cancer; first description of cytogenetic evolution of thyroid cancer; first description of fall of serum antithyroid antibodies during pregnancy with rise after delivery, other med. techniques. Guggenheim fellow, 1966-67; Commonwealth Fund fellow, 1967; recipient Hevesy Nuc. Medicine Pioneer award, 1982, Disting. Faculty award U. Mich., 1982, Johann-Geor-Zimmerman Trust for Cancer Rsch. Sci. prize for greatest contbn. to treatment of thyroid cancer, 1983, WWJ 950 Detroit Citizen of Week award, 1994; named Internat. Man of Yr. Internat. Biog. Ctr., Cambridge, Eng., 1992-93. Mem. AMA (Outstanding Scientific Achievement award 1994), ACP, Am. Fedn. Clin. Rsch. (pres. 1954-55), Soc. Nuclear Medicine (pres. 1965-66, Disting. Educator's award 1989, The Best Doctors in Am. award 1993-95), Ctrl. Clin. Rsch. Club (pres. 1958-59), Am. Thyroid Assn. (v.p. 1964-65, 66-67, Disting. Svc. award 1972), Ctrl. Soc. Clin. Rsch. (councillor 1964-67, 67-71), Galens Med. Soc., Assn. Am. Physicians, Mich. Med. Soc., Am. Endocrine Soc., Am. Soc. Clin. Oncology. Home: Independence Village 965 Hager Dr Apt 327 Petoskey MI 49770-8748

BEIN, FREDERICK L. geography educator; BA in geography, U. Colo., 1969; MA in geography, U. Fla., Gainesville, 1971, PhD in geography, 1974. Instr. regional geography U. Catolica do Mato Grosso, Camp Grande, Brazil, 1972; asst. prof. of geography U. N.D., Grand Forks, 1977-78; asst. prof., acting coord. of geography program Ind. U., Purdue U., 1981-93, prof., 1978—2003, dept. chair geography, 1979—96. Coord. State Geography Alliance, 1988—96; dir. Environmental Rsch. and Mgmt. Ctr. Papua New Guinea Univ., 1996—99; Rotary Internat. Acad. Ambassador Dept. Surveying PNG Univ. Tech., 2000. Contbr. articles of profl. jours. Office: Indiana Univ Purdue Dept of Geography 425 University Blvd Dept Of Indianapolis IN 46202-5148

BEINEKE, LOWELL WAYNE, mathematics educator; b. Decatur, Ind., Nov. 20, 1939; s. Elmer Henry and Lillie Agnes (Snell) B.; m. Judith Rowena Wooldridge, Dec. 23, 1967; children: Jennifer Elaine, Philip Lennox. BS, Purdue U., 1961; MA, U. Mich., 1962, PhD, 1965. Asst. prof. Purdue U., Ft. Wayne, Ind., 1965-68, assoc. prof., 1968-71, prof., 1971-86, Jack W. Schrey prof., 1986—. Tutor Oxford (Eng.) U., 1974, The Open U., Milton Keynes, England, 1974, 75; vis. lectr. Poly. North London, 1980—81; vis. scholar Wolfson Coll., Oxford U., 1993—94, 2000—01; mem. SCR Keble Coll., 2000—01. Co-author, co-editor Selected Topics in Graph Theory, 3 vols., 1978, 1983, 1988, Applications of Graph Theory, 1979, Graph Connections, 1997, mem. editl. bd., assoc. editor Jour. Graph Theory, 1977—80, editl. bd., 1977—, mem. editl. bd. Internat. Jour. Graph Theory, 1991—95; co-editor: Congressus Numerantium, Vols., 1963—64, 1988; editor-elect The Coll. Math. Jour.; contbr. numerous articles to profl. jours. Corp. mem. Bd. for Homeland Ministries, United Ch. of Christ, N.Y., 1988-91, del. Gen. Synod, 1989, 91. Recipient Outstanding Tchr. award AMOCO Found., 1978, Friends of the Univ., 1992, Outstanding Rsch. award Ind. U.-Purdue U. Ft. Wayne, 1999; Fulbright Found. grantee London, 1980-81, rsch. grantee Office Naval Rsch., Washington, 1986-89; fellow Inst. Combinatorics and its Applications, 1990—. Mem. AAUP, Math. Assn. Am. (chairperson Ind. sect. 1987-88, bd. govs. 1990-93, Disting. Tchg. award Ind. Sect. 1997, Disting. Svc. award Ind. sect. 1998), Am. Math. Soc., London Math. Soc., Common Cause, Amnesty Internat., Summit Book Club, Internat. Affairs Forum, Sigma Xi (club pres. 1984-86, chpt. pres. 1997-98), Phi Kappa Phi (chpt. pres. 1993), Pi Mu Epsilon. Achievements include characterization of line graphs and thickness of complete graphs; enumeration of multidimensional trees. Home: 4529 Bradwood Ter Fort Wayne IN 46815-6028 Office: Ind U-Purdue U Dept of Math Scis 2101 E Coliseum Blvd Fort Wayne IN 46805-1445 E-mail: beineke@ipfw.edu.

BEISCH, JUNE, freelance/self-employed writer, literature educator, poet; b. Ashland, Wis., Nov. 23, 1939; d. Theodore and Josephine Robertson; m. Charles Beisch, Sept. 5, 1964; children: Brooks, Leigh. BA, Harvard U., 1987, MA, 1991. Freelance writer, Boston, 1976—2001; journalist Boston Globe, 1976—90; interviewer Sta. WGBH, Boston, 1977—78; dir. Bus. Writing Program, Boston, 1984—87; instr. lit. Mass. Bay Coll., Wellesley, 1985—96, Emerson Coll., Boston, 1990—2000, Fisher Coll., Boston, 1992. Actress French Libr., 1992—97; poet-in-the-schs. Boston Schs., 1995—, Stonehan, Somerville. Author: (poetry book) Take Notes, 1990; contbr. essays and fiction to mags. and jours. Recipient 1st pl. poetry, Middlesex CC, Boston, 1990; fellow, VA Ctr. for the Arts, 2002.

BEISSER, SALLY RAPP, education educator; b. Ft. Dodge, Iowa, Nov. 11, 1949; d. Alvin LeRoy Rapp and Betty (Williams) Tuttle; m. Kim David Beisser, July 19, 1975; children: Andrea Lynn, Sarah Ann. BS, Iowa State U., 1971, MS, 1977, PhD, 1999. Cert. tchr., Iowa. Tchr. Maquoketa (Iowa) Community Schs., 1971-73; tchr., gifted and talented facilitator Ames (Iowa) Community Schs., 1974-90, West Des Moines (Iowa) Community Schs., 1992; supr. student tchrs. U. Iowa, Iowa City, 1991-92; instr. Coll. Edn. Iowa State U., Ames, 1992-99; prof. effective teaching Drake U., Des Moines, 1999—. Ednl. cons. Crayola Kids mag., 1994; ind. edn. cons., cen. Iowa. Contbr. to profl. publs. Bd.dirs. Friends of the Libr., West Des Moines, 1992; mem. literacy com. Greater Des Moines Literacy Coalition. Mem. NEA, ASCD, AAUW, Iowa State Edn. Assn., Nat. Assn. Gifted Children, Iowa Talented-Gifted Assn. (bd. dirs. 1994—, co-chair, conf. coord., speakers bur. 1988—), Nat. Assn. Soc. Studies, Soc. Info. Tech. in Tchr. Edn., State Historical Soc. Iowa, Am Ednl. Rsch. Assn., Assn. Tchrs. Educators, Phi Delta Kappa, Delta Kappa Gamma, Phi Kappa Phi. Avocations: classical music, creative writing, church activities. Home: 3126 Sycamore Rd Ames IA 50014-4510 Office: Drake U Sch Edn 3206 University Ave Des Moines IA 50311-3820

BEITZ, CHARLES R. political science educator, researcher; b. Buffalo, July 20, 1949. B.A. in History summa cum laude, Colgate U., 1970; M.A. in Philosophy, U. Mich., 1974; M.A. in Politics, Princeton U., 1976, Ph.D. in Politics, Polit. Philosophy Program, 1978. Preceptor in philosophy and politics Princeton U., 1974-76; asst. prof. polit. sci. Swarthmore Coll., Pa., 1976-82, assoc. prof., 1982— ; vis. lectr. Bryn Mawr Coll., fall 1982, spring 1987; invited lectr. various univs.; guest lectr. Author: (with Michael Washburn) Creating the Future: A Guide to Living and Working for Social Change, 1974; Political Theory and International Relations, 1979, Korean transl., 1982; also articles, revs. Co-editor: Peace and War: Introductory Readings, 1973; Law, Economics, and Philosophy, 1983; International Ethics (A Philosophy and Public Affairs Reader), 1985; editorial bd. Ethics, 1980—, World Politics, 1983-86; rev. editor Philosophy and Pub. Affairs, 1982— . Vis. scholar John F. Kennedy Sch. Govt., Harvard U., Cambridge, Mass., fall 1979; fellow Rockefeller Found., 1979-80, Am. Council Learned Socs., 1983-84, MacArthur Found., 1987-88; research fellow Ctr. for Sci. and Internat. Affairs, Harvard U., 1987-88. Mem. Phi Beta Kappa. Office: Bowdoin College Academic Affairs Brunswick ME 04011

BEJA, MORRIS, English literature educator; b. N.Y.C., July 18, 1935; s. Joseph and Eleanor (Cohen) B.; children: Andrew Lloyd, Eleni Rachel; m. Ellen Carol Jones, 1990. BA, CCNY, 1957; MA, Columbia U., 1958; PhD, Cornell U., 1963. From instr. to prof. English Ohio State U., Columbus, 1961-2000, prof. emeritus, 2001—. Vis. prof. U. Thessaloniki, Greece, 1965-66, Univ. Coll. Dublin, 1972-73. Author: Epiphany in the Modern Novel, 1971, Film and Literature, 1979, Joyce the Artist Manqué and Indeterminacy, 1989, James Joyce: A Literary Life, 1992; editor: Virginia Woolf's Mrs. Dalloway, 1996, Joyce in the Hibernian Metropolis, 1996, Perspectives on Orson Welles, 1995, Samuel Beckett: Humanistic Perspectives, 1983, James Joyce Newestlatter, 1977—, James Joyce's Dubliners and Portrait of the Artist, 1973, 5 other books. Pres. Internat. James Joyce Found., 1982-90, sec. 1990—; dir. Internat. James Joyce Symposia, 1982, 86, 92. With USAR, 1958-63. Guggenheim fellow, 1972-73; Fulbright lectr., 1965-66, 72-73. Mem. MLA, Internat. Virginia Woolf Soc. (trustee 1976-84), Am. Conf. Irish Studies. Jewish. Avocations: photography, travel, cycling. Home: 1135 Middleport Dr Columbus OH 43235-4060 Office: Ohio State U Dept of English 164 W 17th Ave Columbus OH 43210-1326 E-mail: beja.1@osu.edu.

BEKAVAC, NANCY YAVOR, academic administrator, lawyer; b. Pitts., Aug. 28, 1947; d. Anthony Joseph and ELvira (Yavor) Bekavac. BA, Swarthmore Coll., 1969; JD, Yale U., 1973. Bar: Calif. 1974, U.S. Dist. Ct. (cen. dist.) Calif. 1974, U.S. Dist. Ct. (no. dist.) Calif. 1975, U.S. Ct. Appeals (9th cir.) 1975, U.S. Dist. Ct. (so. dist.) Calif. 1976, U.S. Surpeme Ct. 1979, U.S. Ct. Appeals (8th cir.) 1981. Law clk. at large U.S. Ct. Appeals (D.C. cir.), Washington, 1973-74; assoc. Munger, Tolles & Rickershauser, L.A., 1974-79, ptnr., 1980-85; exec. dir. Thomas J. Watson Found., Providence, 1985-87, cons., 1987-88; counselor to pres. Dartmouth Coll., Hanover, N.H., 1988-90; pres. Scripps Coll., Claremont, Calif., 1990—. Adj. prof. law UCLA Law Sch., 1982—83; mem. Calif. Higher Edn. Roundtable, 1996—; trustee Am. Coun. Edn., 1994—97. Bd. mgrs. Swathmore Coll., 1984—; trustee Wenner-Gren Found. Anthrop. Rsch., 1987—94; bd. trustees Am. Coun. Edn., 1994—97; chair Assn. Ind. Colls. and Univs., 1996—97. Recipient Human Rights award, L.A. County Commn. Civil Rights, 1984; fellow Woodrow Wilson fellow, Thomas J. Watson fellow, 1969. Mem.: Am. Assn. Ind. Calif. Colls. and Univs. (chair 1996), Sierra Club. Avocations: hiking, reading, travel. Office: Scripps Coll Office of Pres 1030 Columbia Ave Claremont CA 91711-3986*

BELANGER, CHERRY CHURCHILL, elementary school educator; b. Berea, Ky., May 14, 1923; d. David Carroll and Anna Eleanor (Franzen) Churchill; m. Paul Adrien Belanger, Oct. 15, 1950 (dec. Feb. 1987); children: Peter Carroll, Karen Michelle Belanger-Magon. BA, Pomona Coll., Claremont, Calif., 1944; MA in Elem. Edn., Calif. State U.,

Northridge, 1983. Cert. tchr. early childhood edn. Actress Actor's Equity Assn., 1944-49; retail promotion asst. Bloomingdale's, N.Y.C., 1948-52; editor Living for Young Homemakers, N.Y.C., 1953-54, Bride-To-Be Mag., N.Y.C., 1955; off-camera editor NBC Home Show, N.Y.C., 1955-56; publicist home furnishing Alfred Auerbach, Bell & Stanton, N.Y.C., 1956-61; retail rep. Betsy Ross Martin Assocs., L.A., 1961-66; exec. sec. So. Calif. Assn. Bedding Mfrs., L.A., 1966-70; retail rep. Hercules Corp., L.A., 1971; tchr. early childhood edn. Carthay Nursery, Beverly Hills, Calif., 1971-78, L.A. Unified Sch. Dist., 1976-79, tchr. kindergarten and 1st grade, 1979-99. Den mother, treas., chmn., inst. rep. Boy Scouts Am., Beverly Hills, 1961-85; troop leader Brownies, Girl Scouts U.S., 1968-83. Recipient Silver Fawn award Boy Scouts Am., L.A., 1972, Elizabeth H. Brady Tchr. award So. Calif. Kindergarten Assn., 1997; honored Cherry Belanger Day in Beverly Hills, City Coun., 1976. Mem. DAR, AAUW, United Tchrs. of L.A. Avocations: drama, music, camping.

BELANGER, MADELINE, principal; b. Ft. Kent, Maine, July 26, 1940; d. Helaier and Jeannette (Morin) Saucier; widowed; children: Renee Ann, Shelley Rae. BA in Edn., Rivier Coll., 1967; MEd, U. Maine, 1981. Cert. tchr. French & English K-12, adminstr. K-12, supt. K-12, literacy specialist, early childhood, curriculum coord., supr. K-12. Tchr. Head Start Program, Ft. Kent, summer 1966; tchr. 3d grade SAD 27 Sch. Dept., Ft. Kent, 1967; tchr. French/English jr. and sr. h.s. SAD 32 Sch. Dept., Ashland, Maine, 1967-69, tchr. 2d, 3d, 4th and 5th grade Portage, Maine, 1969-73, tchr. 4th grade Ashland, 1973-82, curriculum coord., asst., 1982-84; prin. h.s. Hilltop Sch. Caribou (Maine) Sch. Dept., 1984-90, prin. Teague Park Sch., 1990—. Dir. curriculum SAD 32 Ashland Sch. Bd., 1989-90, adminstr., 1982-84, alt. sch. dir.; curriculum coord. K-6 Caribou Sch. Dept., 1983-84, grant writing coord., 1994—; speaker, contbr. Pine Tree Burn Found. Conf., 1994; adminstr. State Dept. of Edn. Recipient Cert. of Appreciation Pine Tree Burn Found. Conf., Cert. of Appreciation, State Dept. of Edn., 1990; grantee Maine State Dept. of Edn., 1985, 91, 94, innovative edn. grantee State Dept. Edn., 1990. Mem. ASCD, Maine Edn. Assn., Aroostock Prins. Assn. (pres. 1993-94, Recognition plaque). Avocations: reading, listening to music, cooking. Office: Teague Park Sch 59 Glenn St Caribou ME 04736-1908

BELARBI, ABDELDJELIL, civil engineering educator, researcher; b. Tlemcen, Algeria, Apr. 21, 1959; came to US, 1983; s. Sid-Ahmed and Rabia (Benchouk) B.; m. Samira Bereksi, Aug. 14, 1986; children: Sihem L., Hishem I., Yasmine E. BSc, U. Oran, Algeria, 1983; MSc, U. Houston, 1986, PhD, 1991. Rsch. asst. U. Houston, 1984-90, tchg. fellow, 1990-91; asst. prof. civil engring. U. Mo., Rolla, 1991-97, assoc. prof., 1997—2003, prof., 2003—. Rsch. investigator Grad. Ctr. for Materials Rsch., Intelligent-Systems Ctr.; proposal and jour. reviewer. Contbr. articles to profl. jours. Recipient Outstanding Tchr. award U. Houston, 1991, U. Mo.-Rolla., 1995, 96, 97, 98, 99, 2000, 02, 03; Faculty Excellence award 1995-2003; Algerian Govt. scholar, 1984-90; NSF rsch. grantee, 1992, 98-2001, Outstanding Paper award Earthquake Spectra Jour., 1995, Disting. Young Alumnus award U. Houstn, 1999. Fellow Am. Concrete Inst.(bd. dir., pres. Mo. chpt.); mem. ASCE, Am. Soc. Engring. Edn., Earthquake Engring. Rsch. Inst., Masonry Soc., Transp. Rsch. Bd.Sigma Xi (scholar 1986), Tau Beta Pi, Chi Epsilon (Excellence in Tchg. award ctrl. dist. 2001). Islamic. Achievements include rsch. on shear, torsion and in-plane forces on reinforced concrete, nonlinear modelling of reinforced concrete, performance and durability of archtl. glazing systems under wind and earthquake effects, smart structures and smart sensors as applied to civil infrastructures. Home: 11110 Breeden Dr Rolla MO 65401-9313 Office: Univ Mo - Rolla Dept Civil Engring Rolla MO 65401

BELCHER, REBECCA NEWCOM, special education educator; b. Cameron, Mo., Nov. 21, 1948; d. Daryl Cypert and Parolee Elaine (Beers) Newcom; m. Charles William Belcher, May 10, 1985. BA in Elem. Edn., Graceland Coll., 1970; MA in Spl. Edn., U. N.Mex., 1976; MA in Counseling, U. Mo., Kansas City, 1984; MA in Edn. Adminstrn., N.Mex. State U., 1989, PhD, 1997. Cert. tchr., Tex., tchr., spl. edn. tchr., counselor, Mo., adminstr., spl. edn., elem. tchr., Colo., N.Mex. Elem. tchr. Brownsville (Tex.) Pub. Schs., 1970-73; elem. resource rm. spl. edn. tchr. Mescalero (N.Mex.) Apache Reservation, 1976-79; dist. elem.-secondary learning disabled tchr. Grain Valley (Mo.) Pub. Schs., 1979-81; secondary spl. edn. tchr. N.W. Regional Youth Ctr., Kansas City, Mo., 1984-85, Independence (Mo.) Pub. Schs., Ind, 1985-86; elem. spl. edn. tchr. Bloomfield (N.Mex.) Pub. Schs., 1986-91, Gadsden Ind. Schs., Anthony, N.Mex., 1991—99, master tchr., 1993—; divsn. chair, dept. head, asst. prof. Lincoln Univ., Jefferson City, Mo., 1999—2003; asst. prof. Northwest Mo. State U., 2003—; dir. Horace Mann Lab Sch. NW Mo. State U., 2003—. Adj. prof. Park Coll., Parkville, Mo., summer 1986; adminstr. Women's Seminars, summer 1987-summer 1990; sci. tchr. Kid's Kollege, Dona Ana Br. N.Mex. State U., Las Cruces, summer 1992; instr. extended sch. year program Gadsden Ind. Schs., summer 1992; dist. coord. Reading is Fundamental program Bloomfield, 1990-91, adminstrv. intern, 1988-89; corp. bus. adminstr. Saints' Alive, Inc., Creative Educators, Inc., 1980-82, 88-93, sch. adminstr., 1981-82; cons. Mescalero Apache Tribe, 1978; mem. Bent-Mescalero's Elem. Reading Curriculum Com., 1977-78, chair, 1978-79, NAABA ANI Elem. Schs. Core Com., Bloomfield, 1988-89, 90-91, Multidisciplinary Forum Evaluation Spl. Edn. Students, 1989-90, state adv. forum I.D.E.A., 1991-94, chair adminstrv. task force, 1992; presenter in field. Mem. PL94-142 parent adv. com. Bloomfield Sch. Dist., 1986-87, chair 1987-88, 88-89, spl. edn. curriculum com., 1987-88, Anthony Elem. and Berino Elem. Ednl. Tech. Coms., 1992-93. Mem. Coun. for Exceptional Children, Phi Kappa Phi, Phi Delta Kappa. Avocations: reading, writing. Office: NW Mo State U 1234 Parkdale Rd Maryville MO 64468

BELCHER RANDALL, MARY SUE, remedial reading educator; b. Carthage, Ark., Apr. 15, 1938; BS in Elem. Edn., U. Ark., Pine Bluff, 1959; MS, Ala. A&M Coll., 1966; postgrad., Trenton State Coll., 1967-68; EdD, U. Houston, 1977; postgrad., U. Utah, 1980-85. 3d grade tchr. Mo. and Ark. schs., 1960-61; 2d grade tchr. Huntsville (Ala.) schs., 1963-66; 1st grade tchr. Trenton (N.J.) schs., 1966-67; 1st-6th grade tchr. Houston Ind. Sch. Dist., 1968-93; elem. tchr. Cath. schs., Houston, 1967; tchr. Tex. State U., Houston, 1977; remedial reading tchr. Houston C.C., 1983-85, 86. Contbr. numerous articles on reading and edn. to profl. publs. Home: 4305 Fernwood Dr Houston TX 77021-1640

BELCHEVA, ANNA BERONOVA, pharmacology educator; b. Dresden, Germany, Oct. 2, 1937; d. Belcho Ivanov and Elsa Ernst (Kilian) B.; m. Nedelcho Krumov Beronov, Apr. 22, 1962; 1 child, Kamen Nedelchev Beronov. MD, Higher Med. Sch., Sofia, Bulgaria, 1961; PhD, Higher Med. Sch., Varna, Bulgaria, 1969, DSci, 1999. Med. diplomate. Physician City Hosp., Stara Zagora, 1961-65; asst. prof. Higher Med. Sch., Varna, 1970-85, assoc. prof., 1986; prof., 2000—; head dept. Med. U. Varna, 1991—, vice rector, 1994-99. Author: Pharmacology, 1991; editor, author: Pharmacology, 1995, 98, 2003; contbr. articles to profl. jours. Mem. Union Bulgarian Scientists, European Histamine Rsch. Soc., European Biomed. Rsch. Assn. Mem. Orthodox Ch. Avocations: swimming, classical music, literature. Home: bl 11 G app 56 Quartal Tchayka 9005 Varna Bulgaria Office: Med U Varna 55 Marin Drinov St 9002 Varna Bulgaria

BELFORT, GEORGES, chemical engineering educator, consultant; b. Johannesburg, Transvaal, Republic of South Africa, May 8, 1940; came to U.S., 1964; s. Nathan Leveen and Sophie (Konviser) Belfort; m. Marlene Bertha Stern, Dec. 28, 1967; children: David, Gabriel, Jonathan. BSc-ChemE, U. Capetown, 1963; MS in Engring., U. Calif., Irvine, 1969, PhD in Engring., 1972. Rsch. engr. Astropower Labs., McDonnel Douglas Corp., Newport Beach, Calif., 1964-70; acting instr. U. Calif., Irvine, 1971-72; sr. lectr. Hebrew U., Jerusalem, 1973-77; vis. assoc. prof. Northwestern U., Evanston, Ill., 1977-78; assoc. prof. Rensselaer Poly. Inst., Troy, NY, 1978-82, prof., 1982—, Russell Sage prof. chem. engring, 2003—. Chair Gordon Rsch. Conf. on Membranes, Materials and Processes, 1977; cons. in field. Co-editor (author (with others): Fundamentals of Adsorption, 1984, Advanced Biochemical Engineering, 1987; contbr. articles over 140 articles to profl. jours. Fellow Japanese Soc. for Promotion Sci., 1981, 96; rsch. grantee U.S. Dept. Energy, 1994—, USN, 1990-94, NSF, 1995—; elected Nat. Acad. Engring., 2003; apptd. to Russel Sage Endowed chair chem. engring., 2003. Mem. NAE, AIChE (Sci. and Tech. award 2000), Am. Chem. Soc. (Award in Separations Science and Technology 1995), N.Am. Membrane Soc. (pres. 1995, bd. of dirs. 1993—), European Membrane Soc. Office: Rensselaer Poly Inst Chem Engring Dept Troy NY 12180-3590 E-mail: belfog@tpi.edu.

BELFORT-CHALAT, JACQUELINE, art educator, sculptor; b. Mt. Vernon, NY, Feb. 23, 1930; d. Jacob Samuel and Mildred (Belfort) Chalat; m. Warren Leigh Ziegler, Sept. 17, 1950 (div. 1979); children: David Matthew, Catherine Amalia. Student, Frederick V. Guinzburg, 1943, Ruth Nickerson, 1944, Oronzio Maldarelli, Ettore Salvatore, Columbia U., 1947, Stuart Klonis, Art Students League, 1948, Fashion Inst. Tech., 1948-50, Royal Acad. Fine Arts, Copenhagen, 1960-62; BA, U. Chgo., 1948. Prof., chair fine arts Moyne Coll., Syracuse, NY, 1969—2003; artist-in-residence, dir. visual arts U. Pa., 2003—. Lectr. Cath. U., Howard U., Lorton Prison, Smithsonian Instn., Syracuse U., Govt. of Nigeria, artist-in-residence, 2003—, others. One-woman shows include Le Moyne Coll., 1969, 73, 83, St. Peter's Gallery, Soc. Art, Religion and Culture, N.Y.C., 1975, Everson Mus., Syracuse, 1979, City Hall, Syracuse, 1981, Schweinfurth Meml. Art Ctr., Auburn, N.Y., 1983, Yager Art Mus., Oneonta, 1985; exhibited in group shows at Charlottenborg Slot, Copenhagen, 1962, Nat. Collection Fine Arts, Washington, 1963, Washington Gallery Art, Washington, 1966, Everson Mus., Syracuse, 1972-74, Munson-Williams-Procter Mus., Utica, N.Y., 1974, Boston Coll., Chestnut Hill, 1974, St. Joseph's Coll., Phila., 1976, Internat. Art Fair, Boston, 1980, Festival of Arts, St. David's Ch., Syracuse, 1969—; prin. works include statue of Mary monument, Life-size Christ, sports paintings; appeared in videos; writer in field. Bd. dirs. Cultural Resources Coun. Mem. Am. Aesthetic Soc., Coll. Art Assn. Am., Nat. Soc. Am. Pen Women, Internat. Sculpture Ctr., Internat. Women's Writing Guild, Syracuse Ceramic Guild, Soc. for Art, Religion and Culture, Theta Chi Beta. Republican. Roman Catholic. Home: 321 Hurlburt Rd Syracuse NY 13224-1822 Office: Le Moyne Coll Dept Fine Arts Syracuse NY 13214-1399

BELJAN, JOHN RICHARD, university administrator, medical educator; b. Detroit, May 26, 1930; s. Joseph and Margaret Anne (Brozovich) B.; m. Bernadette Marie Marenda, Feb. 2, 1952; children: Ann Marie, John Richard, Paul Eric. BS, U. Mich., 1951, MD, 1954. Diplomate: Am. Bd. Surgery. Intern U. Mich., Ann Arbor, 1954-55, resident in gen. surgery, 1955-59; dir. med. services Stuart div. Atlas Chem. Industries, Pasadena, Calif., 1965-66; from asst. prof. to assoc. prof. surgery U. Calif. Med. Sch., Davis, 1966-74, from asst. prof. to assoc. prof. engring., 1968-74, from asst. dean to assoc. dean, 1971-74; prof. surgery, prof. biol. engring. Wright State U., Dayton, Ohio, 1974-83, dean Sch. Medicine, 1974-81, vice provost, 1974-78, v.p. health affairs, 1978-81, provost, sr. v.p., 1981-83; prof. arts and scis., assoc. v.p. med. affairs Cen. State U., Wilberforce, Ohio, 1976-83; provost, v.p. acad. affairs, dean Sch. Medicine Hahnemann U., Phila., 1983-85, prof. surgery and biomed. engring., 1983-86, spl. adviser to pres., 1985-86; v.p. acad. affairs Calif. State U., Long Beach, 1986-89, prof. anat., physiology and biomed. engring., 1986-91, provost, 1989-91; pres. Northrop U., L.A., 1989-93, pres. emeritus, 1993—. Trustee Cox Heart Inst., 1975-77, Drew Health Ctr., 1977-78, Wright State U. Found., 1975-83, CSULB Found., 1986-89, 49er Athletic Found., 1986-89; trustee, regional v.p. Engring. and Sci. Inst. Hall of Fame, 1983—; bd. dirs. Miami Valley Health Sys. Agy., 1975-82, UCI Ctr. for Health Edn., 1987-90, Long Beach Rsch. Found., 1989-94; cons. in field. Author articles, revs., chpts. in books. Served with M.C. USAF, 1955-65. Decorated Commendation medal; Braun fellow, 1949; grantee USPHS, NASA, 1968—. Fellow A.C.S.; mem. Los Angeles County Med. Assn., Mich. Alumni Club (Dayton, Outstanding Alumnus award 1976), Oakwood Fur Club, Fin and Feather Club, Phi Beta Delta, Phi Beta Kappa, Alpha Omega Alpha, Phi Eta Sigma, Phi Kappa Phi, Alpha Kappa Kappa. Home and Office: 1671 Mission Hills Rd Apt 501 Northbrook IL 60062-5735

BELK, JOAN PARDUE, English educator; b. Lancaster, SC, Oct. 4, 1933; d. William Hazel and Alfleda Steele Pardue; m. Joe Harvey Belk, Sr.; children: Joe Harvey Jr., Jennifer Elizabeth. Degree, Winthrop U., 1954; BA summa cum laude, U. Houston, 1957. Cert. tchr. Tex. Asst. to dir. librs. U. Houston, Houston, 1957—61; tchr. English Galena Park HS, Galena Park, Tex., 1961—62; tchr. English (advanced placement) Meml. HS, Houston, 1962—96; instr. English Houston C.C., Houston, 1996—2003. Musician, piano accompanist, piano tchr. Editor articles for profl. pubs. Mem. chancel choir Spring Branch Presbyn. Ch., Houston, accompanist children's choir, elder; mem. Royal Spring Civic Assn., Houston, 1989—, newsletter editor, 2002—; mem. Happy Hide-a-Way Civic Assn., Crosby, 1972—, Cancer Fighters Houston, Inc., Houston, 1998—, bd. dirs., 2003—; chmn. evaluations com. Expanding Your Horizons (conf. jr. HS girls), Houston, 1997—. Recipient Friedheim Found. award, Winthrop U., 1954, Mrs. James P. Houstoun Found. award, U. Houston, 1957, Excellence in Tchg. award, So. Meth. U., 1992. Mem.: AAUW (com. chair 1997—), NEA, Spring Branch Ind. Sch. Dist. Minority Lit. Reading and Discussion Group (discussion leader 1990—96), U. Houston Reading and Discussion Group (sec. 1990—), Tex. Coun. Tchrs. English, Nat. Coun. Tchrs. English, Outstanding Lit. Book Club, Les Belles Lettres Club (pres. 1967—68), Shadow Oaks Garden Club (v.p. 1958—60, pres. 1960—61), En Amie Book Rev. Club, Phi Mu (award 1957), Kappa Delta Pi (award 1957), Phi Kappa Phi (treas. 1958—60, award 1957), Delta Kappa Gamma (rsch. com. chair 1998—2002). Presbyterian. Avocations: piano, bridge, travel, crocheting. Home: 2014 Southwick Dr Houston TX 77080 Office: Houston CC 1010 West Sam Houston Parkway North Houston TX 77043 Home Fax: 713-465-9535. Personal E-mail: joebelksr@aol.com.

BELKNAP, ROBERT LAMONT, Russian and comparative literature educator; b. N.Y.C., Dec. 23, 1929; s. Chauncey and Dorothy (Lamont) B.; m. Josephine E. Hornor, Aug. 20, 1955 (separated 1992); children: Lydia Duff, Ellen Belknap, Abigail Krueger; m. Cynthia H. Whittaker, Aug. 24, 1997. AB, Princeton U., 1951; postgrad., U. Paris, 1951-52; MA, Columbia U., 1954; cert., Russian Inst., 1957, PhD, 1960; postgrad., Leningrad U., 1963-64. Instr. Russian, Columbia U., 1957-60, asst. prof., 1960-63, chmn. freshman humanities, 1963, 67-68, 88-91, assoc. prof., 1963-68, assoc. dean student affairs, 1968-69, prof., 1968—2001, acting dean of Coll., 1976-77; dir. Russian Inst., 1977-80; prof. emeritus Columbia U., 2001—. Vis. assoc. prof. Russian Ind. U., 1966, 67; adj. prof. Russian Yale U., 1967; vis. foreign scholar, Hokkaido U., 1999-2000; dir. Columbia U. Seminars, 2001—. Author: The Structure of the Brothers Karamazov, 1967, reprint, 1989, Russian translation, 1997, The Genesis of The Brothers Karamazov, 1990, Russian translation, 2003; co-author: General Education and the Reintegration of the University, 1977; editor, Russianness, 1990. Pres. bd. trustees Brearley Sch., N.Y.C., 1981-87; trustee Whiting Found., 1985—, pres. 2001—; with U.S. Army, 1953-55. Fellow Kennan Inst., 1987-88, Guggenheim, 1994-95. Office: Univ Seminars Columbia Univ New York NY 10027

BELL, CAROLYN WILKERSON, English educator; b. El Paso, Tex., Nov. 16, 1943; d. Jack and Dorothy (Davenport) Wilkerson; m. Alexander Wayne Bell, June 11, 1966; 1 child, Stephen. AB, Randolph-Macon Woman's Coll., 1965; AM, U. Pa., 1966; PhD, U. Tex., 1972. Prof. English Randolph-Macon Woman's Coll., Lynchburg, Va., 1971—, Susan Duval Adams prof. English, 1992—. Usage panelist Am. Heritage Dictionary, 1987—; panelist NEH, 1980, 81; cons. Legacy Project, Inc., Lynchburg, 1995—. Author: Learning the Contradictions: A History of Randolph-Macon Woman's College 1950-93, 1998; contbr. articles to profl. jours. Precinct worker Dem. Party, Tex., Va., 1968—. Mem. Nat. Coun. Tchrs. English, Phi Beta Kappa, Omicron Delta Kappa. Democrat. Methodist. Avocation: gardening. Home: 42 N Princeton Cir Lynchburg VA 24503-1547 Office: Randolph Macon Woman's Coll 2500 Rivermont Ave Lynchburg VA 24503-1555

BELL, CHRISTINE MARIE, secondary educator; b. Bluefield, W.Va., Nov. 5, 1961; d. Robert Warren and Therese (Wolinski) Stroh; m. Harlin Lindel Bell, Aug. 3, 1991; children: Shelby Katherine. BA, Mary Washington Coll., Fredericksburg, Va., 1983; MEd, U. Va., 1986. Cert. history and social studies tchr., Va. Adminstrv. asst. U. Va. Hosp., Charlottesville, 1984-85; tchr., counselor Oakland (Va.) Residential Sch., 1986-87; tchr. social studies Hopewell (Va.) High Sch., 1987—, coord. computers for edn. program, 1991-93. (workshops) Va. Gov. Best Practice Ctr., 2001; (documentaries) Dept. of Edn. Hour, 2001. Advisor model exec. br. YMCA, Richmond, Va., 1991-92, advisor model gen. assembly, 1991—. Recipient YMCA service to youth award, YMCA, 1996, Resolution of Appreciation, Va. Dept. of Edn. Sch. Bd., 2001, Tchr. of the Yr., Hopewell City Sch., 2001. Mem. APA (affiliate), ASCD, Nat. Coun. for Social Studies, Va. Geog. Soc., New Va. Dept. of Edn. Database ofexemplary educators, Avocations: politics, reading, travel, swimming, jogging. Home: 96 Sand Hill Rd Williamsburg VA 23188-6600 Office: Lafayette High Sch Williamsburg VA 23188

BELL, DERRICK ALBERT, law educator, author, lecturer; b. Pitts., Nov. 6, 1930; s. Derrick Albert and Ada Elizabeth (Childress) B.; m. Jewel Allison Hairston, June 26, 1960 (dec. Aug. 1990); m. Janet Dewart, June 28, 1992; children: Derrick Albert III, Douglass Dubois, Carter Robeson. AB, Duquesne U., 1952; LLB, U. Pitts., 1957; hon. degree in law, Toogaloo Coll., 1983, Northeastern U., 1985, Mercy Coll., 1988, Allegheny Coll., 1989, Howard U., 1995, Bates Coll., 1997, Medgar Evers Coll., 1998; degree in law (hon.), Metro. Coll. N.Y., 2003. Bar: DC 1957, Pa. 1959, NY State 1966, Calif. 1969. Atty. civil rights div. Dept. Justice, Washington, 1957-59; 1st asst. counsel NAACP Legal Def. Edn. Fund, NYC, 1960-66; dep. dir. Office Civil Rights, HEW, Washington, 1966-68; exec. dir. Western Ctr. on Law and Poverty, 1968-69; lectr. law Harvard U., Cambridge, Mass., 1969-71, prof. law, 1971-80, 86-92; dean U. Oreg. Law Sch., 1981-85;, 1991-93. Vis. prof. NYU Sch. Law, 1991—. Author: Race, Racism and American Law, 1973, 4th edit., 2000, Constitutional Conflicts, 1992, Shades of Brown: New Perspectives on School Desegregation, 1980, And We Are Not Saved: The Elusive Quest for Racial Justice, 1987, Faces at the Bottom of the Well: The Permanence of American Racism, 1992, Confronting Authority: Reflections of an Ardent Protester, 1994, Ethical Ambition: Living a Life of Meaning and Worth, 2002. Gospel Choirs Psalms of Survival in an Alien Land Called Home, 1996, Afro/antica Legacies (1998), Ethical Ambition: Living a Life of Meaning and Worth, 2002; 1st lt. USAF, 1952-54. Grantee Ford Found., 1972, 75, 91, 93, 94-96, NEH, 1980-81. Home: 444 Central Park W Apt 14B New York NY 10025-4358 Office: NYU Sch Law 40 Washington Sq S New York NY 10012-1005

BELL, ELVA GLENN, retired secondary school educator, retired counseling administrator, interpreter; b. Phila., Sept. 3, 1922; d. Arthur Edward Glenn, Ruth Ann Marie Demby Glenn; m. Howard Wesley Bell, Sr.; children: Howard Bell, Jr., Linda Bell-Powell. BS in Edn., Cheyney State Coll., 1945; MS in Edn., Temple U., 1970. Case worker Dept. Pub. Assistance, Phila., 1945—51; tchr., guidance counselor Phila. Sch. Dist., 1956—71; guidance counselor Abington (Pa.) Sch. Dist., Pa., 1971—82; interpreter at Clivden - Hist. Mansion Nat. Trust Property, Germantown, Pa., 1987—. Sch./cmty. rep. human rels. adv. coun. Abington Sch. Dist., 1974—. Mem., chairperson ways and means com. United Neighbors, Willow Grove, 1975—; mem. Abington Coalition of Civics - Abington Township, 1996—; bd. mem., Unity Day chairperson, life mem. NAACP - Willow Grove, 1939—; Congl. sr. intern CLOSE-UP, Washington, 1997—. Recipient Cmty. Svc. and Leadership award, Citizens for Progress, 1976, Trailblazer award, Willow Grove NAACP, 1985, Cmty. Svc. and Leadership award, Optimist Club Lower Montgomery County, 1986, Ho. of Reps. citation, Pa., 1987, 1999, Martin Luther King award, Abington Twp., 1988, Svc. award, Willow Grove NAACP, 2001. Mem.: AAUW, Black Women's Ednl. Alliance (treas., fin. sec. 1980—86, newsletter editor, Svc. award 1986, Cmty. Svc. and Leadership award 1986), Zeta Phi Beta Sorority - Beta Delta Zeta Chpt. (vol.). Lutheran. Avocations: travel, church activities, community activist.

BELL, GLORIA JEAN, academic administrator, literature educator, dean; b. Greensboro, N.C., Oct. 10, 1939; d. John T. and Mary Ellen (Gray) Bell. BA, So. Wesleyan U., 1961; MA, U. N.C., 1963; PhD, U. Colo., 1982. English tchr. N.W. Guilford HS, Greensboro, 1962-63; tchr. Partlow State Sch., Tuscaloosa, Ala., 1963-64; English and reading tchr. Tuscaloosa HS, 1964-65; English instr. U. Ala., Birmingham, 1965-70; asst. prof. English Presbyn. Coll., Clinton, SC, 1974-77; faculty mem. So. Wesleyan U., Central, SC, 1977—, English prof., 1981—, chair divsn. humanities, 1981-93, acad. v.p., dean, 1993—. Mem. transfer adv. bd. Tri-County Coll., Pendleton, SC, 1993—98, chair, 1996—97. Contbr. articles to profl. jours. Ad hoc com. mem. Wesleyan Ch., 1997—; S.E. regional steering com. Conf. Christianity and Lit., 1985—88, 1994—96; mem. Clemson Area Leadership Program, 1995; judge Lt. Gov.'s Award for Composition, Pickens County, 1981. Recipient Govs. Disting. prof., Susan B. McWhorter Outstanding Woman Profl., 1998. Fellow: Coun. Christian Colls. & Univs. (exec. leadership inst.); mem.: S.C. Women Higher Edn. (conf. steering com. 1983—84, 1996—97), Phi Delta Kappa. Avocations: travel, needlepoint, gardening, reading. Office: Southern Wesleyan U PO Box 1020 907 Wesleyan Dr Central SC 29630-9748

BELL, JOYCE ANNE, elementary school educator; b. Uniontown, Pa., Nov. 23, 1947; d. Sanford Emory and Helen Elizabeth (Pryor) S; m. George Alonso Bell, July 17, 1971 (div. 1979); 1 child, Tiffany Rae. AA, U. Minn., 1967, BS, 1970, M of Elem. Edn., 1985. Elem. educator Roseville (Minn.) Area Schs., 1970—; multicultural coord. Roseville (Ninn.) Area Schs., 1986—. Staff office of minority and spl. affairs counselor, U. Minn. Summer Inst., Mpls., 1986; adj. faculty mem. Hamline U., St. Paul, 1991-92; leader Seeking Edn. Equity Diversity (SEED), 1991—; panel mem. Minn. Dept. Edn., Brainerd, 1992; chosen for Minn. Inst. for the Advancement of Teaching Seminar, Sept., 1992. Mem. NAACP; panel mem. Roseville LWV, 1990; Sunday sch. tchr. Pilgrim Bapt. Ch., 1991-92; v.p. INROADS, St. Paul, 1991-92. Recipient Outstanding Tchr. award Roseville Area Schs. #623, 1990, Tchr. Achievement award Ashland Oil, Minn., 1992; grantee Edn. Ventures Inc., Mn., 1991. Mem. NEA, Minn. Edn. Assn. (state coun. 1992, minority affairs com. 1992), Roseville Edn. Asssn. Avocations: reading, collecting bells, sports, music. Office: Edgerton Elem Sch 1929 Edgerton St Saint Paul MN 55117-2198

BELL, JUDITH CAROLYN OTT, interdisciplinary educator; b. Cin., Feb. 15, 1948; d. William Requarth and Lillian Inez (Dowling) Ott; 1 child, Raven Dylan Bell. BFA, Miami U., Oxford, Ohio, 1970, MA in Art Edn., 1982. Cert. tchr., Wash., N.C. Program developer, art educator Cherokee Indian Reservation, N.C., 1969; freelance artist, art educator, 1971-76; ops. monitor Santa Fe Model Cities Program, 1975; visual art edn. cons. Yakima Indian Reservation, Toppenish, Wash., 1979, sci. curriculum devel. specialist Tribal Kindergarten, 1980; grad. asst. Miami U., 1981-82; visual art educator Grady Brown Elem. Sch., Hillsborough, N.C., 1982-87; arts edn. coord. Wilson County Schs., Wilson, N.C., 1987-91; art survey instr. Wilson Tech. C.C., 1990; interdisciplinary educator (6th grade art, lang. arts, social studies) Carrington Mid. Sch., Durham, N.C., 1991-94; tchr. 7th grade lang. arts Coitheus Mid. Sch., Durham, 1994-95; tchr. 9th grade civics, English, reading & math competency Durham Magnet Ctr. of Visual & Performing

Arts, 1995—. Trainer Learning to Read Through the Arts, 1990—. Author poetry, slide program, newspaper feature articles, TV script. Bd. dirs. Hearth Found., Chapel Hill, N.C., 1992—; interim exec. dir. Creative Learning Ctr. Hearth Found. Inst., 1993; student advisor Students Against Violence Everywhere, 1994-97, coord. ann. peace festivals. Grantee Nat. Diffusion Network, 1989, 90, N.C. Arts Coun., 1988-91, Durham Public Edn. Network, 1993, Orange County Edn. Found., 1986. Mem. ASCD, Nat. Coun. of Tchrs. of English, N.C. Art Edn. Assn. (bd. dirs. 1989-91, editor newsletter, program chair 1989-91), N.C. Alliance for Arts Edn. (editor newsletter, bd. dirs. 1989-93, awards chair 1990), Arts Advocates of N.C., Orange County (N.C.) Arts Commn. Democrat. Avocations: visual art, video production, creative writing, dancing, swimming. Office: Durham Magnet Ctr Visual Performing Arts 401 N Duke St Durham NC 27701-2001

BELL, KIM A. educational program administrator, consultant; b. Seoul, Korea, June 13, 1953; arrived in U.S., 1959; d. Romeo Joseph and Mary Herring Aussant; m. Walter Dennis Bell, July 26, 1975 (div. Dec. 18, 1988); children: Phillip Stuart, Christine Nicole, Stephanie Lauren; m. Jerry Wayne Cox, Nov. 26, 1999; 1 child, Jason W. Cox. BSP, Ea. Carolina U., Greenville, 1975. Registered health info. adminstr. Health info. mgmt. cons. Bell & Assocs., Greenville, NC, 1978—95, 2000—; dir. med. records and admissions State of N.C. Walter B. Jone Alcohol Rehab. Ctr., Greenville, 1975—88; dir. quality improvement and staff devel. alcohol and drug abuse treatment ctr., divsn. mental health/devel. disability/substance abuse svcs. State of N.C., Greenville, 1988—96; dept. chair, program dir. Edgecombe C.C., Rocky Mount, 1996—; online educator, 1999—. Part-time faculty Pitt C.C., Greenville, NC, 1985—87. Pitt County Fair Bd. cons. Pitt County Am. Legion Agrl., Greenville, NC, 1997—; course chmn. Michael Jordan Celebrity Classic, Greenville, 1994—2000; vol. Greenville Host Lions, Greenville, 1988—99; adv. bd. mem. NCCCS PAC, Raleigh, 2000—02; moderator Bd. Deacons; chmn. fin. and edn. com.; SS supt., assoc. supt., asst. supt.; SS tchr.; advisor Youth Group. Recipient Mini Grant award, Instr. of the Yr., ECC Found., 1999, Mini Grant award, 2000, Academic Excellence Award Nominee, NCCCS, NISOD, 1999. Mem.: Am. Health Info. Mgmt. Assn., Edgecombe Cmty. Coll. Found. (bd. mem. 2000—02), N.C. Health Info. Mgmt. Assn. (com. chief publicity, fin., pub. rels., legal affairs 1970—, bd. mem., v.p., treas. 1978—81, mental health section coord., Coastal Carolina Region coord.-elect 2003—), Greenville Host Lions Club (hon.; vol. 1988—99). Presbyterian. Achievements include being one of the earliest educators to have entire curriculum online in Health Information Technology pairing a pathway for many students who otherwise could not further their career. Avocations: music, art, health scis.. Office: Edgecombe C C 225 Tarboro St Rocky Mount NC 27801

BELL, LORETTA MAE, elementary education educator; b. Chana, Ill., Dec. 13, 1936; d. Floyd R. and Ida Ruth (Hepfer) Long; m. Donald Lee Bell, Aug. 18, 1962; children: Robert, John, Linda. BS in Edn., No. Ill. U., 1960, MEd, 1967. Cert. tchr., Ill. Tchr. Rochelle (Ill.) Twp. High Sch., 1960-64, Steward (Ill.) Elem. Sch., 1967-69, Eswood Elem. Sch., Lindenwood, Ill., 1976—2000; ret., 2000—. Recipient Outstanding Tchr. award Ill. Math. and Sci. Acad., Aurora, Ill., 1992.

BELL, NANCY LEE HOYT, real estate investor, middle school educator, volunteer; b. L.A., Oct. 25, 1929; d. James and Mabel Ruth (Lockard) Hoyt; m. Ralph Rogers Bell, July 3, 1953; children: Linda Lee, John Curtis, James Hoyt, Martha Chambers, Ralph Rogers II, Nancy Lee II. Student, Whittier Coll., 1948, San Jose State Coll., 1949; BA in Edn., U. Calif., Santa Barbara, 1950; postgrad., San Francisco State Coll., 1952, UCLA, 1953; MS in Edn., U. So. Calif., 1955. Tchr. John Adams Jr. H.S., Santa Monica, Calif., 1950-54; real estate investor. Pres. Santa Clarita Cmty. Concerts, Saugus, Calif., 1968-69; vol. worker USO, YWCA, 1944-45, Cancer Crusade, Calif. and Wash., 1960-90. Mem. AAUW (charter life; pres.), Big Bear Valley Hist. Soc. (life; sec.), DAR (charter life; treas.), Gen. Soc. Mayflower Descs. (life; bd. dirs.), Alpha Delta Pi. Republican. Methodist. Avocations: world travel, collecting antiques, genealogy researcher, music. Home: 615 Main St Apt B Edmonds WA 98020-3804

BELL, NANCY SUTTON, finance educator; b. Toledo, Ohio, Dec. 16, 1948; d. Robert Coveney and Donna Kenower Sutton; m. Ray Douglas Bell; 1 child, Robert Simon. BEd in Sociology and Anthropology, U. Toledo, 1972, MA in History, 1974; PhD in Bus., U. Ga., 1985. CLU. Mgr. State Farm Life Ins. Co., Newark, Ohio, 1974-79; grad. tchg. asst. U. Ga., Athens, 1979-83; prof. Fla. State U., Tallahassee, 1983-93; Disting. Prof. Risk Mgmt. and Ins. Washington State U., Pullman, 1993-99; chair dept. fin. ins., real estate/Coll. Bus. Econs. Wash. State U., Pullman, 1995-99. Prof., dean of Coll. of Bus. at Univ. of Montevallo, AL, 1999-2002, prof. bus., 2002—. Author: (book) Small Business Managers' Guide to Employee Benefits, 1988; contbr. numerous articles to profl. jours. Mem. Am. Risk and Ins. Assn., We. Risk and Ins. Assn., So. Risk and Ins. Assn., Am. Soc. CLUs, Acad. Fin. Svcs. Avocations: swimming, bicycling, camping, hiking. Home: 1112 Indian Crest Dr Pelham AL 35124-3008 E-mail: belln@montevallo.edu.

BELL, RONALD MACK, university foundation administrator, consultant; b. Atlanta, Mar. 4, 1937; m. Deborah Jean Slaton, Dec. 28, 1989. BS in Indsl. Mgmt., Ga. Inst. Tech., 1959; MBA, U. Mich., 1965; attended, Cornell U., 1980. Commd. USN, 1959, advanced through grades to capt., 1979, ret., 1985; assoc. dir. rsch. contracts Ga. Inst. Tech., Atlanta, 1985-88; v.p., gen. mgr. Ga. Tech. Rsch. Corp., Atlanta, 1988-97; exec. dir. S.C. Rsch. Inst., Columbia, 1997-2001; v.p., bd. dirs. Pisgah Astrol. Rsch. Inst., 1999—; pres., CEO UCRF Support Assoc., St. Simons Island, Ga., 1998—. Bd. dirs., past pres., now dir. emeritus Nat. Supply Corps. Assn.; cons. Wesvaco/Post, Buckley, Coastal Cons., Inc., also others, 1985—; expert witness ELSCO, U. Tenn., others, 1987-90; nat. chmn. Univ. Connected Rsch. Found., 1990-91. Past chmn., dir. emeritus Naval Supply Corps. Sch. Mus. Com., Athens, mem., 1983—; mem. Exec. Roundtable, Atlanta, 1985-97; resource staff Gov.'s Com. Tech. & Devel., Atlanta, 1992-97; bd. dirs. Ga. Tech. Sch. Mgmt., 1995-98. Decorated Legion of Merit (2), Meritorious Svc. medal (2), Navy Commendation medal (2). Mem. Soc. Rsch. Adminstrs. (nat. coms., chair regional com. 1985-2002), Licensing Execs. Soc., Nat. Coun. Univ. Rsch. Adminstrs. (chair regional com., nat. panelist 1985-2001), Coun. Rsch. and Tech. (dir. workshop, tax com. 1986-92), Ga. Tech. Nat. Alumni Assn. (various coms.), Nat. Conf. on the Advancement of Rsch. (conf. com. 2000), Assn. Univ. Tech. Mgrs., Theta Chi (past chpt. pres.), Phi Kappa Phi, Beta Gamma Sigma. Avocations: golf, woodworking. Home: 113 Thompson Cv Saint Simons Island GA 31522-3768 Office: UCRF Support Assoc PO Box 20272 Saint Simons Island GA 31522 E-mail: bellssi@earthlink.net.

BELL, RUBY AYCOCK, educational administrator; b. Clinton, N.C., Feb. 16, 1954; d. Robert Lee and Hilda Ruth (Oates) Aycock; m. Lacy Wendell Bell, Jr., June 17, 1978; children: Lacy Antrell, Brandon Lemár. BS in edn. dean's list, Fayetteville State U., 1976, EdD in Ednl. Leadership; MEd, N.C. Ctrl. U., 1980. Cert. tchr., curriculum specialist, ednl. adminstr., N.C. Tchr. Clinton City Schs., 1977-89; home-sch. coord. Goldsboro (N.C.) City Schs., 1900-91; tchr. Sampson County Schs., Clinton, 1976-77; asst. prin. Midway Elem. Sch., Clinton, 1991-95, Hargrove Elem. Sch., Faison, N.C., 1995-96; prin. Ctrl. Primary Sch., Laurinburg, N.C., 1996-97; asst. prin. Eastern Wayne H.S., Goldsboro, N.C., 1997-2000; prin. Dillard Edison Jr. Acad., Goldsboro, 2000—01, Dillard Mid. Sch., Goldsboro, 2001—02, Goldsboro (N.C.) Mid. Sch., 2002—. Author: (booklet) Legacy of the Past, 1986, Seeking New Horizons, 1985, Black History Activity Booklet, 1984. Mem. Tri-County Cmty. Health Bd., Newton Grove, N.C., 1988-89; co-chair Clinton/Sampson United Negro Coll. Fund; Christian edn. coord. Poplar Grove Missionary Bapt. Ch.; mem. Sampson County Dem. Women. Named Tchr. of Yr., Butler Avenue Sch., Clinton, 1986, Butler Avenue Sch. Outstanding Young Educator, Clinton Jaycees. Mem. NEA, N.C. Assn. Educators, Clinton City Assn. for Educators (pres. 1986-87, 88-89), N.C. Prins. and Asst. Prins. Assn., Sampson County Voters League, Delta Sigma Theta. Democrat. Baptist. Home: 2812 E Darden Rd Faison NC 28341-5982 E-mail: ruby.bell@wcps.org.

BELL, SCOTT WILLIAM, private school educator, principal; b. Aurora, Ill., Aug. 7, 1961; s. William Laurence and Violet Annabelle (Miller) B.; m. Jill Robin Burton, July 26, 1986; 1 child, Seth Andrew Thomas. BA in Edn., Concordia Coll., River Forest, Ill., 1985; MA in Ednl. Leadership, Marian Coll., Fond du Lac, Wis., 1999. Cert. tchr., Ill. Min. of music, tchr. Peace Luth. Sch., Ft. Lauderdale, Fla., 1985-86; music tchr. St. Paul Luth. Sch., Boca Raton, Fla., 1986-88; min. of music, tchr. Immanuel Luth. Ch., Houston, 1988-92; prin. St. Peter Luth. Sch., Hilbert, Wis., 1992-96, St. John Luth. Sch., Mayville, Wis., 1996—2001, Trinity Luth. Sch., Mequon, Wis., 2000—. Firefighter Hilbert Vol. Fire Dept., 1992-96, Mayville Vol. Fire Dept., 1997-2000; mem. South Wis. Dist. Supts. Cabinet, 1994-97, 2000—; bd. dirs. Wis. Non-pub. Schs. Accreditation Assn., 2001—; commr. Nat. Luth. Sch. Accreditation Dist., 2002—. Mem. ASCD, NAESP, Luth. Edn. Assn. Office: Trinity Luth Sch 10729 W Freistadt Rd Mequon WI 53092 Home: 11915 N Ridgeway Ave Mequon WI 53097-3022 E-mail: sbell@trinityfreistadt.com.

BELL, SHARON TERESA ECHERD, elementary physical education specialist; b. Gastonia, NC, June 23, 1950; d. Lyman Joe and Ruby Colleen (Hicks) Echerd; m. Rufus Joseph Jr., Oct. 19, 1974 (dec.); children: Emily Brooke, Lauren Nicole. BS, Mars Hill Coll., 1972. Tchr. Grier Jr. High, Gastonia, NC, 1972—, Sherwood Elem. & Forest Heights Elem. Republican. Methodist. Avocations: piano, reading. Home: 1208 Mccorkle Rd Charlotte NC 28214-9442 Office: Sherwood Elem 1744 Dixon Rd Gastonia NC 28054-5176

BELLENGER, GEORGE COLLIER, JR., physics educator; b. Gadsden, Ala., Oct. 15, 1926; s. George Collier Sr. and Corrie Anna (Sitz) B.; m. Anna Conwell Hubbard, July 4, 1959; children: Baily, George III, James Thomas. B in Indsl. Engring., Ga. Inst. of Tech., 1952. Constrn./indsl. engring. E.I. DuPont Co., Augusta, Ga., 1952-54, Richmond, Va., 1955-58, ops. rsch. Wilmington, Del., 1958-63, group supr.-engring. Chattanooga, 1963-65, sr. supr. systems Wilmington, 1965-67, chief supr. Deep Water, N.J., 1967-70, systems mgr. Wilmington, 1970-78, mgr. project devel., 1978-87; math/physics educator Wilmington Coll., New Castle, Del., 1987-91, chair gen. studies divsn., 1991—, chair faculty senate, 1998-2000. PTA pres. Mt. Pleasant Sch. Dist., Wilmington, 1972-76; commr. North Brandywine Youth Baseball, Wilmington, 1974-77; head coach Mt. Pleasant Youth Football, Wilmington, 1977-79. Lt. U.S. Army, 1944-47. Named Disting. ROTC Mil. Grad.; recipient Disting. Mil. Student award, Ga. Inst. of Tech., 1952. Mem. Rotary Internat. (pres. 1983-84, Paul Harris fellow 1987), Nat. Norwich/Norfolk Terrier Assn. (pres. 1993-96), Army and Navy Club, Phi Delta Theta. Achievements include research on a micro/macro production and inventory system based on a stochastic deterministic, partial differential set of equations, a manufacturing capacity expansion plan based on combining a unique LP model and computer simulation methods. Home: PO Box 449 Unionville PA 19375-0449 Office: Wilmington Coll 320 Dupont New Castle DE 19720

BELLFLOWER, DEBORAH K. gifted and talented education educator, special education educator; b. Lakeland, Fla. d. Millard and Janet Marie (Follet) B.; 1 child, William. BA in Psychology, U. South Fla., 1975, MA, 1977; postgrad., U. Ga. Cert. administr., supr., gifted edn. secondary social studies tchr., psychology and learning and behavior disabilities counselor. Rsch. asst. dept. spl. edn. U. South Fla., Tampa, 1976-77, U. So. Miss., Hattiesburg, 1979-80; dir. evaluation Miss. Future Problem Solving Program, statewide, 1981-82; asst. prof. spl. edn. Delta State U., Cleveland, Miss., 1980-82, dir. Saturday scholars program for gifted children, 1981-82; state cons. gifted edn. Fla. Dept. Edn., Tallahassee, 1982-85; supr. programs for gifted Va. Dept. Edn., Richmond, 1985-88; supr. gifted edn. and chpt. I programs Williamsburg (Va.) James City County Schs., 1988-90; dir. acad. talent program U. Calif., Irvine, 1990-93; dir. West Coast office Agere Found., 1993-95; sect. chief for student achievement Md. State Dept. Edn., Balt., 1995—. Adj. prof. Maryville (Tenn.) Coll., 1978, U. So. Miss., Hattiesburg, 1979, U. West Fla., Pensacola, 1983, Fla. State U., Tallahasee, 1984, U. Va., Charlottesville, 1985-90, Va. Commonwealth U., Richmond, 1986-90, Hampton (va.) U., 1987-90, Coll. William and Mary, Va., 1986-90, mem. adv. com. gifted edn. ctr., 1988-90; instr. Maryville (Tenn.) Coll., 1978; coord. talent devel. project, Maryville, 1977-78; facilitator lab sch. and practicum, U. S. Fla., Tampa, 1975-77; mem. numerous rev. coms. for grants, 1989—; cons. Tex. Dept. Edn., 1985, Allegheny County Pub. Schs., 1989-90; sec., dir. at large Coun. State Dirs. of Programs for Gifted, 1982-88, assoc.; regional dir. Odyssey of the Mind, 1988-89; mem. adv. com. for gifted Va. Dept. Edn., 1985-88; chair State Adv. Coun. for Gifted and Talented Program Study, 1984-85, Gov.'s Summer Program Rev. Com., 1983-85, state steering com. for gifted edn., Fla. Dept. Edn., 1982-85; state bd. dirs. Calif. Future Problem Solving Program; mem. various coms. for gifted edn.; speaker in field, presenter in field. Author: Senior Mentors for Creative Students-Program Manual, 1984, The Gifted and Talented Program Study, 1984, Statewide Study of Gifted and Talented, Florida, 1985, Gifted Students and the Technical Arts, 1988, (with R. Demond) Parent Guide for the Career Orientation and Planning Profile, 1993; contbr. articles to profl. jours. Rsch. grantee Delta State U. Mem. ASCD, Nat. Assn. Gifted Children (publs. com.), Calif. Assn. For Gifted, Coun. Exceptional Children (student advisor, tchr. edn. divsn.), Zonta Internat., Delta Kappa Gamma.

BELLIS, CARROLL JOSEPH, surgeon, educator; b. Shreveport, La. s. Joseph and Rose (Bloome) B.; m. Mildred Darmody, Dec. 26, 1939; children: Joseph, David. BS summa cum laude, U. Minn., 1930, MS in Physiology, 1932, PhD in Physiology, 1934, MD, 1936, PhD in Surgery, 1941. Diplomate Am. Bd. Surgery, cert. Internat. Bd. Proctology, Internat. Bd. Surgery. Fellow in physiology U. Minn., Mpls., 1930-34; resident in surgery U. Minn. Hosps., Mpls., 1937-41; pvt. practice surgery Long Beach, Calif., 1945-95. Prof., chmn. dept. surgery Calif. Coll. Medicine, 1962—; surg. cons. to surgeon gen. U.S. Army; adj. prof. surgery U. Calif. Author: Fundamentals of Human Physiology, A Critique of Reason, Lectures in Medical Physiology; contbr. numerous articles on surgery and physiology to profl. jours. Served to col. M.C. AUS, 1941-46. Recipient Charles Lyman Green prize in physiology, 1934, prize Mpls. Surg. Soc., 1938, ann. award Mississippi Valley Med. Soc., 1955; Alice Shevlin fellow U. Minn., 1932-34. Fellow: ACS, Peripheral Vascular Soc. Am. (founding), Internat. Acad. Proctology, Nat. Cancer Inst., Phlebology Soc. Am., Gerontol. Soc., Am. Med. Writers Assn., Internat. Coll. Surgeons, Royal Soc. Medicine, Am. Coll. Gastroenterology, Internat. Coll. Angiology (sci. coun.), Am. Soc. Abdominal Surgeons; mem.: AAAS, Pan Am. Med. Assn. (diplomate), Indsl. Med. Assn., Pan Pacific Surg. Assn., Am. Assn. History Medicine, Irish Med. Assn., Am. Geriatrics Soc., Hollywood Acad. Medicine, N.Y. Acad. Scis., Miss. Valley Med. Soc., Am. Assn. Study Neoplastic Diseases, Alpha Omega Alpha, Sigma Xi, Phi Beta Kappa. Home: PMB 808 904 Silver Spur Rd Rolling Hills Estates CA 90274

BELLIZZI, JOHN J. law enforcement association administrator, educator, pharmacist; b. N.Y.C., July 26, 1919; s. Francis X. and Carmela (Bruno) B.; m. Celeste Morga, Sept. 1, 1942; children: John J. Jr., Robert F. PhG, St. John's U., N.Y.C., 1939; LLB, Albany Law Sch., 1960; JD, Union U., 1968; LLD, St. John's U., 1981. Pharmacist St. Luke's Hosp., N.Y.C., 1939-44; police officer N.Y.C. Police Dept., 1944-53; narcotics agt. N.Y. Bur. Narcotics Enforcement, N.Y.C., 1953-59, dir. Albany, 1959-81; exec. dir. N.Y. State Drug Abuse Commn., Albany, 1981-84, Internat. Narcotics Enforcement Assn., Albany, 1984—. Prof. pharmacy law St. John's U., N.Y.C., 1962-76; lectr. in field. Contbr. articles to profl. jours. Recipient Papal medal Vatican, 1965. Mem. Internat. Narcotics Enforcement Officers Assn. (pres. 1960-62, Anslinger medal 1979, chmn. law enforcement com. Paramount Pictures, 1972-75, Svc. award 1975), Ft. Orange Club, Albany Country Club, Univ. Club (Albany), Am. Friends of Law Enforcement Found. (bd. dirs., sec. Japanese), Phi Alpha Delta, Phi Sigma Chi (pres. 1939), Sigma Chi (fellow). Office: Internat Narcotics Enforcement Officers Assn 112 State St Albany NY 12207-2005

BELLO, ZAKRI YAU, academic administrator; b. Daura, Katsina, Nigeria, Feb. 2, 1956; s. Jibril B. and Tababa S. Fulani. BS, Va. Commonwealth U., 1976-79, MBA, 1979-80; PhD, Va. Poly. Inst. and State U., 1981-83. Bank clk. Barclays Bank Internat., various locations, 1971-72, instr. Lagos, Nigeria, 1972-74, acct. Sokoto, Nigeria, 1974-75; sr. mgr. United Bank for Africa, Lagos, 1985-86; instr. Va. Tech., Blacksburg, 1986-87; assoc. prof. fin. Salisbury (Md.) State U., 1987—. Presenter in field. Contbr. articles to profl. jours. Mem. Am. Statis. Assn., Chartered Inst. of Bankers (Eng. and Wales assoc. 1972—), Fin. Mgmt. Assn., Ea. Fin. Assn. (session chairperson Charleston, S.C. 1990), Am. Fin. Assn., So. Fin. Assn., Assn. of Third World Studies (session chairperson Phila. 1991—). Home: 17 Jill Hall Newark DE 19711-5928 Office: Salisbury State U Perdue Sch Camden Ave Salisbury MD 21801

BELLOHUSEN, RONALD MICHAEL, orthodontist, educator; b. McKeesport, Pa., July 25, 1947; s. Michael and Ann (Montrenes) B.; m. Gail Jean Davies, Nov. 22, 1969; children: Michael, Beth. BS, U. Pitts., 1968, MS in Organic Chemistry, 1974, DMD, 1978. Cert. in splty. of orthodontics. Rschr. NIH/Nat. Cancer Inst., Bethesda, Md., 1971-72; clin. instr. Eastman Dental Ctr., Rochester, N.Y., 1994—; orthodontist Orthodontic Assocs. of So. Tier, Elmira, N.Y., 1994—. Lt. USN, 1969-72. Recipient Pierre Fauchard Acad. award, 1992; NESO rsch. grantee on asymmetry in cleft palate, 1993. Fellow Internat. Coll. Dentists; mem. ADA, Am. Assn. Orthodontists, Am. Bd. Orthodontists (bd. eligible). Avocations: flying, sailing, kayaking, skiing. Office: Orthodontic Assoc So Tier 440 E Water St Elmira NY 14901-3411 E-mail: ortho1@infoblvd.net.

BELLOW, ALEXANDRA, mathematician, educator; b. Bucharest, Romania, Aug. 30, 1935; d. Dumitru and Florica Bagdasar; m. Cassius Ionescu Tulcea, Apr. 1956 (div. 1969); m. Saul G. Bellow, Oct. 1974 (div. 1986); m. Alberto P. Calderon, Sept., 1989 (dec. 1998). MS in Math, U. Bucharest, 1957; PhD in Math., Yale U., 1959. Research assoc. Yale U., New Haven, Conn., 1959-61, U. Pa., Phila., 1961-62, asst. prof., 1962-64; assoc. prof. U. Ill., 1964-67; prof. Northwestern U., Evanston, Ill., 1967-96, prof. emeritus, 1996—. Emmy Noether lectr., 1991. Author: (with C. Ionescu Tulcea) Topics in the Theory of Lifting, 1969; assoc. editor: Annals of Probability, 1979-83, Advances in Math., 1979— . Recipient Sr. Disting. Scientist award Alexander von Humboldt Found., 1987; Fairchild Disting. scholar Calif. Inst. Tech., 1980; NSF grantee Mem. Sigma Xi. Office: Northwestern U Dept of Math 2033 Sheridan Rd Evanston IL 60208-2730 E-mail: a_bellow@math.northwestern.edu.

BELLOWS, THOMAS JOHN, political scientist, educator; b. Chgo., Aug. 15, 1935; s. Charles Everett and Dorothy (Morrison) B.; m. Marilyn Denise Corbell; children: Scott Anthony, Justin Thomas, Trevor Cullen, Ethan Forrest; children by previous marriage: Roderick Alan, Adrienne Marie, Jeannine Louise, Derek John, Marshall Everett. Student, Am. U., 1956, UCLA, 1956-57; BA, Augustana Coll., 1957; MA, U. Fla., 1958, Yale U., 1960, PhD, 1968. Asst. prof. polit. sci. West Ga. Coll., Carrollton, 1962-64, 66; from asst. prof. to prof. polit. sci. U. Ark., Fayetteville, 1967-81, chmn. dept., 1971-78; dir. divsn. social policy scis. U. Tex., San Antonio, 1981-88, prof. polit. sci., 1981—. Vis. lectr. depts. history, polit. sci. Nanyang U., Singapore, 1965; vis. prof. Nat. Chengchi U., Taiwan, 1979. Author: The People's Action Party of Singapore: Emergence of a Dominant Party System, 1970, (with S. Erikson and H. Winter) Political Science: Introductory Essays and Readings, 1971, Taiwan's Foreign Policy in the 1970's, 1976, (with H. Winter) People and Politics: An Introduction to Political Science, 1985, Bridging Tradition and Modernization: The Singapore Bureaucracy, 1989, (with H. Winter) Conflict and Compromise, 1992; Taiwan and Mainland China, 2000, (with Felix Almaraz) Modern Texas, 2003; editor: Am. Jour. Chinese Studies, 1999—. Mem.: Am. Assn. for Chinese Studies (pres. 1998—2000), Assn. Asian Studies, S.W. Conf. Asian Studies (pres. 1995), Phi Beta Kappa, Phi Kappa Phi. Methodist. Office: U Tex Dept Polit Sci San Antonio TX 78249 E-mail: TBellows@Lonestar.UTSA.edu.

BELLUM, FRED LEWIS, school system administrator, retired; b. Timber Lake, S.D., May 3, 1932; s. Fred L. and Olive Fern (Forney) B.; m. Renee Ann Olson, Dec. 19, 1954; children: Michelle Bellum Goedeken, Mark, Jon. BS, Sioux Falls Coll., 1955; MEd, No. State U., Aberdeen, S.D., 1961; EdD, U. S.D., 1973. Tchr., coach Timber Lake Pub. Schs., 1955-62, athletic dir., coach, guidance counselor, 1962-65; prin. Lemmon (S.D.) High Sch., 1965-66; supt. Lemmon Ind. Sch. Dist., 1966-72; grad. asst. U. S.D., Vermillion, 1972-73; supt. schs. Columbus (Nebr.) Pub. Schs., 1973-95; ret., 1995. Recipient Nebr. Supt. of Yr. award Am. Assn. Sch. Adminstrs. and Servicemaster Co., 1993, David Hutchison Disting. Svc. award Tchrs. Coll. U. Nebr., Lincoln, 1994. Mem. Am. Assn. Sch. Adminstrs., Nebr. Assn. Sch. Adminstrs. (pres. 1981), Nebr. Coun. Sch. Adminstrs (bd. dirs. 1980-83, Disting. Svc. award 1985), Rotary (pres. 1989), Columbus Area C. of C. (bd. dirs. 1990-93, pres.-elect 1993-94, pres. 1994-95).

BELL-VILLADA, GENE H. literature educator, writer; b. Port-au-Prince, Haiti, Dec. 5, 1941; came to U.S. 1959; s. Gene H. Bell and Carmen (Villada) Romero; m. Audrey M. Dobek, Aug. 9, 1975. BA, U. Ariz., 1963; diploma, U. Paris, 1966; MA, U. Calif., Berkeley, 1967; PhD, Harvard U., 1974. Instr. SUNY, Binghamton, 1971-73; lectr. Yale U., New Haven, 1973-74; from asst. to prof. dept. romance langs. Williams Coll., Williamstown, Mass., 1975—, chair dept., 1993-95, 1997—2000. Instr. Middlebury (Vt.) Coll., summer 1971-72; reader, grader Advance Placement Readings, Ednl. Testing Svc., 1978-85, 94—; vis. prof. Wellesley (Mass.) Coll., 1984-85, 89-90; resident dir. Acad. Yr. in Spain program Hamilton Coll., Madrid, 1986-87, 95-96; freelance editl. cons., 1987—. Author: Borges and His Fiction, 1981, Garcia Marquez, 1990 (Best Book award New England L.Am. Studies 1991), The Carlos Chadwick Mystery, 1990, Art for Art's Sake and Literary Life, 1996 (finalist Nat. Book Critics Cir. award 1997), The Pianist Who Liked Ayn Rand: A Novella & 13 Stories, 1998; editor: Gabriel Garcia Marquez's One Hundred Years of Solitude: A Casebook; contbr. articles to profl. jours. and gen. interest mags. Nat. Endowment for Humanities fellow, 1979; Am. Philos. Soc. grantee, 1982. Mem. MLA, Latin Am. Studies Assn., Am. Assn. Tchrs. Spanish and Portuguese. Avocations: music, travel, films, swimming. Office: Williams Coll Dept Romance Langs Williamstown MA 01267

BELMONTÉ, KATHRYN (KIKI BELMONTÉ), writer, small business owner; b. Tallahassee. MEd, Fla. Atlantic U.; owner KiKi's Creative Assembly for Native Am. Arts & Crafts; developer, mgr. Helping Hands Classroom Sheltered Workshop for Mentally Handicapped Adults, 1988-97. Author: Black, Brown and Amber, 1979, Comes a Riderless Horse, 1983, reading home tutoring system Tutor Your Child, 1983; compiler, editor Where to Find Thrift Treasures, 1988, Where to Buy Antiques in Palm Beach County, 1989; author: American Heroes and Heroines, 1998. Dir. Kambi Youth Theatre, West Palm Beach, 1979-82, Creative Arts Workshop, Cities in Schs., 1985; organizer, dir. SRO Players Dramatics Club for Handicapped Adults; tech. dir. Performing Arts Summer Sch., Palm Beach Gardens, Fla., 1983-84, 85; workshop originator lecturer Seminole Indian History 1992, Mobile Art Craft Show 1993; active Palm Beach County Cultural Coun., Lake Worth Art League, Palm Beach County Art in Pub. Places Com., 1991-92, Nat. Mus. Am. Indian. Recipient 1st place award Cleveland Creative Arts, Tenn., 1981, Walter Bogle award Creative Arts Guild, 1983, Colored Pencil Painting Best in Show award Lake Worth Art

League, 1993; grantee Palm Beach County Edn. Found., 1987, Community Found. Palm Beach and Martin Counties. Mem. NEA, Nat. Writers Club (hon. mention 1983), Fla. Freelance Writers Assn. (1st pl. awards 1984, 85, 3rd pl. 1990, honorable mention 1991), North Palm Beach C. of C., Norton Gallery Art, Armory Sch. Arts, Fla. Humanities Coun., St. Labre Indian Sch., Arrow Club. Avocations: drawing, painting, collecting Native Am. art, photography. Home: 7820 Canterbury Ln Plantation FL 33324-1934

BELOFF, ZOE, artist, educator; Student, Edingburgh (Scotland) U.; MFA in Film, Columbia U. Tchr. digital media Pratt Inst., City Coll. N.Y. Prodr. (CD-ROM) Beyond (First prize QuickTime VR Competition), Where There There Where, (film) Life Underwater, Lost. Found. Contemporary Arts grantee, 1997.

BELSKY, MARTIN HENRY, law educator, lawyer; b. May 29, 1944; s. Abraham and Fannie (Turnoff) Belsky; m. Kathleen Waits, Mar. 9, 1985; children: Allen Frederick, Marcia Elizabeth. BA cum laude, Temple U., 1965; JD cum laude, Columbia U., 1968; cert. of study, Hague Acad. Internat. Law, The Netherlands, 1968; diploma in Criminology, Cambridge U., England, 1969. Bar: Pa. 1969, Fla. 1983, N.Y. 1987, U.S. Dist. Ct. (ea. dist.) Pa. 1969, U.S. Ct. Appeals (3d cir.) 1970, U.S. Supreme Ct. 1973. Chief asst. dist. atty. Phila. Dist. Atty.'s Office, Pa., 1969—74; assoc. Blank, Rome, Klaus & Comisky, Phila., 1975; chief counsel U.S. Ho. of Reps., Washington, 1975—78; asst. adminstr. NOAA, Washington, 1979—82; dir. ctr. for govtl. responsibility, assoc. prof. law U. Fla. Holand Law Ctr., 1982—86; dean Albany Law Sch., 1986—91, dean emeritus, prof. law, 1991—95; dean U. Tulsa Coll. of Law, Okla., 1995—. Chmn. Select Commn. on Disabilities, NY, Spl. Commn. on Fire Svcs.; bd. advs. Ctr. Oceans Law and Policy; mem. corrections task force Pa. Gov.'s Justice Commn., 1971—75; adv. task force on cts. Nat. Adv. Commn. on Criminal Justice Standards and Goals, 1972—74; mem. com. on proposed standard jury instrns. Pa. Supreme Ct., 1974—81; lectr. in law Temple U., 1971—75; mem. faculty Pa. Coll. Judiciary, 1975—77; adj. prof. law Georgetown U., 1977—81. Author (with Steven H. Goldblatt): (non-fiction) Analysis and Commentary to the Pennsylvania Crimes Codes, 1973; author: Handbook for Trial Judges, 1976, Law and Theology, 2003, (non-fiction) Rehnquist Court: A Retrospective, 2002; editor (in chief): (jour.) Jour. Transnat. Law, Columbia Law Sch., 1968; editor: The Rehnquist Court: Farewell to the Old Order in the Court, 2002; contbr. articles to legal pubs. Chmn. N.Y. region, mem. D.C. bd. Anti-Defamation League, 1977—78, chmn. N.Y. region, mem. nat. leadership coun.; exec. v.p. Urban League Northeastern N.Y. and Tulsa Urgan League; state chair exec. com. Okla. Anti-Defamation League; pres.-elect Tulsa (Okla.) Metro. Ministry; bd. dir. Coun. on Aging & Disability; pres. Jewish Fedn.; mem. exec. com. NCCJ, Okla. Ethics Commn. Fellow Intenat., Columbia U. Law Sch.; scholar Stone. Mem.: ABA (del. young lawyers sect. exec. bd. 1973—75), Fund for Modern Cts. (bd. dirs.), Am. Law Inst., Am. Arbitration Assn. (referee N.Y. State Commn. on Jud. Discipline), Am. Soc. Internat. Law, Nat. Dist. Attys. Assn., Am. Judicature Soc., Fed. Bar Assn., Fla. Bar Assn., Pa. Bar Assn. (exec. com. young lawyers sect. 1973—75), Phila. Bar Assn. (chmn. young lawyers sect. 1974—75), Albany County Bar Assn., N.Y. State Bar Assn., United Jewish Fedn. Northeastern N.Y. (v.p., pres. elect), Cardoto Soc., B'nai B'rith (v.p. lodge 1973—75), Sword Soc., Hudson-Mohawk Assn. Coll. and Univs. (v.p.), Temple U. Liberal Arts Alumni Assn. (v.p. 1971—75). Office: U Tulsa Coll Law 3120 E 4th Pl Tulsa OK 74104-2418

BELSON, CAROLYN BARWICK, elementary education educator; b. Altavista, Va., Jan. 6, 1950; d. Arnold Francis and Evelyn Clare (Kilpatrick) Barwick; m. Stanley Belson, Aug. 26, 1978. BS in Edn., Longwood Coll., 1972; MS in Edn., Old Dominion U., 1985. Cert. tchr., Va. Elem. tchr. Chesapeake (Va.) City Sch., 1972—; lead tchr. Chesapeake (Va.) City Schs., 1992. Grade chmn. Sparrow Road Inst., Chesapeake, 1983—; co-owner BelMarc Advt. & Pub. Rels. Coord. concessions hdqs. Virginia Beach Events Unltd. Neptune Festival, 1988—; coord. Mayor's Homecoming Parade Com. from Desert Storm, 1991; co-chmn. Keep Homelights Burning for Desert Storm, 1991; parade chmn. Holidays at Beach, Virginia Beach, 1990; coord. relief effort for Hurricane Andrew victims Chesapeake Sch. System, 1992. Mem. NEA, Va. Edn. Assn., Chesapeake Edn. Assn., Kappa Delta Pi, Phi Kappa Phi. Home: 500 Pacific Ave Apt 1108 Virginia Beach VA 23451-3544 Office: Sparrow Rd Intermediate Sch 1605 Sparrow Rd Chesapeake VA 23325-4027

BELTON, BETTY KEPKA, retired art educator, artist; b. Wilson, Kans., Mar. 11, 1934; d. Frank and Rose Betty (Kepka) Hochman; m. Glen S. Belton, 1969 (div. 1974); 1 child, Risa-Marie. BS in Art Edn., Emporia State U., 1956; MS in Art Edn., Ft. Hays State U., 1966. Cert. art tchr., Kans. Jewelry apprentice Ursula Letovsky, Omaha, 1957-60; designer Hallmark Cards, Kansas City, Mo., 1960-62; art tchr. Linn (Kans.) Unified Sch. Dist. 223, 1966-69; murals, design Parsons (Kans.) Jr. High Sch., 1974-75; freelance writer, designer, artist Better Homes and Gardens, Creative Crafts, Woman's Day, Popular Crafts, Eng., 1975-77; inspector El Kan, Ellsworth, Kans., 1977-79; dist. coord., art tchr. Unified Sch. Dist. 328, Wilson, Kans., 1979-98, ret., 1998. Adv. bd. Wilson C. of C., 1980-84, Kans. Scholastic Art Awards, 1991-94; mem. Inst. for Improving Visual Arts in Edn., The Getty Ctr., Cin. Art Mus.; participant, cultural contbr. Smithsonian Instn., Nat. Park Svc., Washington, 1976; workshop leader Kans. State U., Manhattan, 1983; nat. folk art contbr. Kans. Future Homemakers, Reston, Va., 1988; panelist Southwest Regional Rural Arts Conf., Garden City, Kans., 1989, Arts in Edn., Kans. Arts Commn., Salina, 1991; cons. DeCordova Mus. Art, Lincoln, Mass., 1990. Author: Egg Lap Studio and Batiking Method for Making Czechoslovakian Kraslice, 1984; contbr. Crafts in America, 1988, American Folk Masters, 1992; prepresented in collection Internat. Mus. Folk Arts, Santa Fe; atentee lap studio for Czech Kraslice, 1984. Recipient Nat. Heritage fellowship Nat. Endowment Arts, Washington, 1988, Gov.'s award Kans. Gov. Joan Finney, Topeka, 1992, Master Folk Artist Apprenticeship Program, Kans. State Hist. Soc., 1985-86, 87-88, 91-92, Disting. Alumni award Emporia State U., 2002 Mem. NEA, Kans. Art Edn. Assn. (Art Enhancer award 1985), Czech Soc. Arts and Scis., Ellsworth Area Arts Coun. (v.p. 1992-94, adv. bd.). Avocations: czech folklore, history, giving workshops, public speaking, prairie grasses. Home: PO Box 1214 Midland MI 48641

BELTZNER, GAIL ANN, music educator; b. Palmerton, Pa., July 20, 1950; d. Conon Nelson and Lorraine Ann (Carey) Beltzner. BS in Music Edn. summa cum laude, West Chester State U., 1972; postgrad., Kean State Coll., 1972, Temple U., 1972, Westminster Choir Coll., 1972, Lehigh U., 1972. Tchr. music Drexel Hill Jr. H.S., 1972-73; music specialist Allentown (Pa.) Sch. Dist., 1973—; tchr. Corps Sch. and Cmty. Devel. Lab., 1978-80, Corps Cmty. Resource Festival, 1979-81, Corps Cultural Fair, 1980, 81. Mem. bd. assocs. Lehigh Valley Hosp. and Health Network. Mem. Mus. Fine Arts, Boston, aux. Allentown Art Mus., aux. Allentown Hosp.; mem. woman's com. Allentown Symphony, The Lyric Soc. of the Allentown Orch.; mem. Allentown 2nd and 9th Civilian Police Acads.; bd. dirs. Allentown Area Ecumenical Food Bank, Allentown Arts Commn; mem. Growing with Sci. partnership—Air Products and Chems., Inc. and Allentown Sch. Dist., Good Shepherd Home Aux.; bd. assocs. Lehigh Valley Hosp. and Health Network. Decorated Dame Comdr., Ordre Souverain et Militaire de la Milice du St. Sepulcre; recipient Cert. of Appreciation, Lehigh Valley Sertoma Club; Excellence in the Classroom grantee Rider-Pool Found., 1988, 91-92. Mem. AAUW, NAFE, ASCD, Am. String Tchrs. Assn., Am. Viola Soc., Internat. Reading Assn., Internat. Platform Assn., Allentown Edn. Assn., Music Educators Nat. Conf., Pa. Music Educators Assn., Am. Orff-Schulwerk Assn., Orgn. Am. Kodaly Educators, Am. Recorder Soc., Phila. Area Orff-Schulwerk Assn., Soc. Gen. Music, Am. Assn. Music Therapy, Internat. Soc. Music Edn., Internat. Tech. Edn. Assn., Assn. for Tech. in Music Instrn., Civil War Roundtable Ea. Pa., Choristers Guild, Lenni Lenape Hist. Soc., Lehigh Valley Arts Coun., Allentown Symphony Assn., Midi Users Group, Pa.-Del. String Tchrs. Assn., Nat. Sch. Orch. Assn., Lehigh County Hist. Soc., Confedn. Chivalry (life mem. of merit, grand coun.), Maison Internat. des Intellectuels Akademie, Order White Cross Internat. (apptd. dist. comdr. for Pa./U.S.A. dist., nobless of humanity), Airedale Terrier Club of Greater Phila., Kappa Delta Pi, Phi Delta Kappa, Alpha Lambda. Republican. Lutheran. Home: PO Box 4427 Allentown PA 18105-4427

BELVAL, JOSEPHINE ANTANETTE, retired elementary school educator; b. Newton, Mass., Dec. 1, 1937; d. Natale and Geraldine (Rizzo) Scarcella; m. Peter C. Belval, July 8, 1961; children: Linda, Peter, Scott. BS in Bus. Adminstrn., Boston U., 1959, MEd, 1960. Cert. elem. tchr., Mass. Tchr. Natick (Mass.) Sch. System, 1959-61, Needham (Mass.) Sch. System, 1973—96; ret., 1996. Mem. various coms. Needham Sch. System, 1974—. Bd. dirs. St. Bartholomew Guild, Needham, 1975—; mem. Broadmeadow PTC, Needham, 1973—, Greater Boston Coun. of Reading, 1991—. Recipient Supt.'s Svc. award for Disting. Achievement, Needham Sch. System, 1990-91. Fellow Mass. Tchrs. Assn., Needham Edn. Assn.; mem. Boston U. Women's Grad. Club (sec.), Needham Jr. Women's Club (chmn. activities 1978-83).

BELYTSCHKO, TED, civil and mechanical engineering educator; b. Proskurov, Ukraine, Jan. 13, 1943; came to U.S., 1950; s. Stephan and Maria (Harpinak) B.; m. Gail Eisenhart, Aug. 1967; children: Peter, Nicole, Justine. BS in Engring. Sci., Ill. Inst. Tech., 1965, PhD in Mechanics, 1968; PhD (hon.), U. Liege, 1997. Asst. prof. structural mechanics U. Ill., Chgo., 1968-73, assoc. prof., 1973-76, prof., 1976-77; Walter P. Murphy prof. civil and mech. engring. Northwestern U., Evanston, Ill., 1977—, chair mech. engring., 1998—2002. Editor (assoc.): (journals) Computer Methods in Applied Mech. and Engring., 1977—, Jour. Applied Mechanics, 1979—85; editor: Nuclear Engring. and Design, 1980—88, Engring. with Computers, 1984—98, Internat. Jour. Numerical Methods in Engring., 1998—. NDEA fellow, 1965-68; recipient Thomas Jaeger prize Internat. Assn. Structural Mechanics in Reactor Tech., 1983, Japanese Soc. Mech. Engrs. Computational Mechanics award, 1993, Gold medal Internat. Conf. on Computational Engring. and Scis., 1996, Computational Mechanics award Internat. Assn. for Computational Mechanics, 1998, Gauss-Newton medal, 2002. Fellow: ASME (chmn. applied mechanics divsn. 1991, Pi Tau Sigma Gold medal 1975, Timoshenko medal 2001), Am. Acad. Arts and Scis.; mem.: NAE, ASCE (chmn. engring. mechanics divsn. 1982, Walter Huber Rsch. prize 1977, Structural Dynamics and Materials award 1990, Theodore von Karman medal 1999), Shock and Vibration Inst. (Baron medal 1999), U.S. Assn. for Computational Mechanics (pres. 1992—94, von Neumann medal 2001, Computational Structural Mechanics award 1997). Office: Northwestern Univ Mech Engring Dept 2145 Sheridan Rd Evanston IL 60208-3111 E-mail: t_belytschko@northwestern.edu.

BENABOU, ROLAND JEAN-MARC, economist, educator; Degree in Engring., Ecole Poly., 1980, Ecole Nat. des Ponts et Chaussées, 1982; PhD, MIT, 1986. Prof. econs. and pub. affairs Princeton (N.J.) U., 1999—; chargé de rsch. Ctr. Nat. de la Rsch. Sci., CEPREMAP, Paris, 1986—88; asst. prof. econs. MIT, Mass., 1988—92, assoc. prof. econs., 1992—94, NYU, NY, 1994—96, prof. econs., 1996—99; prof. econs. and pub. affairs dept. econs., Woodrow Wilson Sch. Pub. and Internat. Affairs Princeton (N.J.) U., 1999—. Vis. prof. U. Paris X-Nanterre, France, 1995, IDEI, Toulouse, France, 1997—99, CERAS, Paris, 1997—99; mem. Sch. Social Sci., Inst. for Advanced Studies Princeton U., NJ, 2002—03; lectr. in field. Assoc. editor: Jour. Econ. Growth, 1995—, Macroeconomic Dynamics, 1997—, Quarterly Jour. Econs., 1997—2001, QR Jour. Macroeconomics, 2000—, Jour. Pub. Econs., 2000—, Jour. European Econ. Assn., 2003—, fgn. editor: Rev. Econ. Studies, 1993—2001, overseas assoc. editor: European Econ. Rev., 1994—2000, mem. editl. bd.: Annals d'Economie et de Statistique, 1993—. Fellow, Guggenheim Found., 2003; grantee, NSF, 1990—92, 1992—94, 1996—99, 2001—; sr. fellow, Bur. for Rsch. and Econ. Analysis of Devel., 2002—. Fellow: Econometric Soc.; mem.: Inst. for Rsch. on Poverty (assoc.). Office: Woodrow Wilson Sch Pub and Internat Affairs Princeton Univ Princeton NJ 08544*

BEN-AKIVA, MOSHE EMANUEL, civil engineering educator; b. Tel Aviv, June 11, 1944; came to U.S., 1968; s. Eliezer and Rivka (Reiner) B.A.; children: Ori, Lea, Danna, Elana, Erez. BSCE, Technion-Israel Inst. Tech., Haifa, 1968; MSCE, MIT, 1971, PhD in Transp. Systems, 1973; docteur honoris causa, U. Lumiere Lyon, France, 1992; Docterate (hon.), U. of the Aegean, 2000. Registered profl. engr., Israel. Edmund K. Turner prof. civil engring. MIT, Cambridge, Mass., 1973-96. Vis. prof. Technion-Israel Inst. Tech., Haifa, 1978—79, Haifa, 1981—82, Tel Aviv, 1981—82; vis. scholar NTT Rsch. Labs., 1988; cons. Am. Airlines, 1987; Atty. Gen. Mass., Boston, 1985—88, The Hague Cons. Group, 1985—2000, Cambridge Systematics, Inc., 1972—, RAND, 2001—. Editor-in-chief: Transport Policy; assoc. editor: Intelligent Transportation Systems Jour. and Transp. Sci.; mem. editl. bd. Jour. Transp. and Statistics. Lady Davis fellow Technion-Israel Inst. Tech., 1978. Mem. Transp. Rsch. Bd., Transp. Rsch. Forum, Regional Sci. Assn., Ops. Rsch. Soc. Am. (award 1973), World Conf. on Transp. Rsch. Soc. Office: MIT 77 Massachusetts Ave Rm 1-181 Cambridge MA 02139-4307 E-mail: mba@mit.edu.

BENANTI, NERINA SPOTTI, secondary school educator; b. N.Y.C., June 24, 1930; d. Louis Spotti and Angela (Delnevo) Spagnoli; m. Jerome Charles Benanti, Dec. 20, 1952 (dec. 1973); children: Marc, Lynn. BA in Econs., Hunter Coll., 1952, MA in Edn., 1954. Tchr. Dutch Broadway Sch., Elmont, N.Y., 1952-58, Westport Pub. Schs., Conn., 1974—99; ret., 1999. Author lit. pamphlets and texts for computer programs. Regional chpt. Westport-Weston United Fund, 1968. Mem. NEA, Conn. Edn. Assn., Westport Edn. Assn., AAUW. Roman Catholic.

BENAROYA, HAYM, aerospace engineer, educator, researcher; b. May 12, 1954; BE in Civil Engring., The Cooper Union, 1976; MS, U. Pa., 1977, PhD in Probabilistic Structural Dynamics, 1981. Sr. rsch. engr. Weidlinger Assoc., N.Y.C., 1981-89; prof. dept. mech. and aerospace engring. Rutgers U., Piscataway, N.J., 1989—. Rsch. on lunar structures, vortex-induced oscillations, probabilistic mechanics, and offshore structural dynamics; founder, dir. Lab. for Extraterrestrial Structures Rsch., Rutgers U., 1990—. Founder, mng. editor (2 e-jours.on space and engring.). Avocations: mathematics, science, history and policy. Office: Rutgers U Sch Engring 98 Brett Rd Piscataway NJ 08854-8058 E-mail: benaroya@rci.rutgers.edu.

BENAVIDES, MARIAN TERRY, secondary education educator; b. Batesville, Ind., Sept. 25, 1952; d. Robert Ward and Edith Mary (Huber) Terry; m. Fernando Benavides, Sept. 8, 1990. BA in Edn., Morehead (Ky.) State U., 1974; cert. for tchrs. ESL, Brit. Royal Soc. Arts, Madrid, 1986; postgrad., U. Cin., 1992-96; MA in edn., curriculum instrn., U. Cinn., 1996; MA in edn., ednl. adminstrn., No. Ky. U., 2002. Cert. secondary Spanish and geography tchr., Ohio. Tchr. English as fgn. lang. Briam Inst., Madrid, 1974-76; tchr. Spanish, Middletown (Ohio) City Schs., 1979-81; tchr., head English studies Mangold Eurocentres, Madrid, 1981-90; tchr. lang., adminstrv. asst. Inlingua Language Inst., Cin., 1990-91; tchr. Spanish, Covington (Ky.) Ind. Schs., 1991—. Pvt. tutor Internat. House Lang. and Linguasec Lang. Sch., Madrid, 1984-89; cons. Inst. Mangold, S.A., Madrid, 1990-91; supervising tchr. for Spanish practicum students No. Ky. U. and Holmes Sr. H.S., Covington, 1992-97; vol. Spanish tutor IRS, Covington, 1992-1994 Co-author: Modern English Workbook, 1986. Active Sch. Based Decision Making Coun., Covington, Ky., 1998—2003. Mem. ASCD, NEA, Ky. Edn. Assn., No. Ky. Edn. Assn., Kappa Delta Pi, Pi Gamma Mu. Avocations: travel, piano, Spain and Hispanic studies, color-typing, cultural interchange programs. Home: 3691 Coral Gables Rd Cincinnati OH 45248-3132

BENCLOSKI, JOSEPH W. geography educator; BS in Edn., Indiana (Pa.) U., 1964, MA, 1970; PhD, Pa. State U., 1976. Grad. teaching asst. dept. geography Pa. State U., University Park, 1970-72; vis. asst. prof.dept. geography Ohio State U., Columbus, 1976-77; temp. asst. prof. dept. geography U. Ga., 1978-83, asst. prof. dept. geography, 1983-85; asst. prof. dept. geography and regional planning Indiana (Pa.) U., 1988—. Vis. prof. dept. geoscis. Pa. State U., 1988; vis. assoc. prof. U. N.C., Greensboro, 1985-87; researcher in field. Contbr. articles to profl. jours. Recipient Teaching Excellence award Teaching Excellence Ctr., 1993. Mem. AAAS, Nat. Coun. Geographic Edn. (dep. exec. dir. 1988—, editor Perspective, 1988—, coord. svc. coords. program 1988-91, ad hoc mem. long range planning com. 1989-91, awards com. 1983-86, chair awards com. 1985-86, Disting. Teaching Achievement award 1990), Assn. Am. Geographers (population geography specialty group, climatology specialty group), Nat. Collegiate Honors Coun., Pa. Geographic Soc. (Devel. Exemplary Teaching Materials award 1993), Kappa Delta Pi, Sigma Xi, Phi Delta Kappa, Pi Gamma Mu, Gamma Theta Upsilon. Office: Indiana U Pa Dept Geography & Regional Planning 1011 S Drive 1C Leonard Hall Indiana PA 15705-0001*

BENDER, CARL MARTIN, physics educator, consultant; b. Bklyn., Jan. 18, 1943; s. Alfred and Rose (Suberman) B.; m. Jessica Dee Waldbaum, June 18, 1966; children— Michael Anthony, Daniel Eric AB summa cum laude with distinction, Cornell U., 1964; AM, Harvard U., 1965, PhD, 1969. Mem. Inst. for Advanced Study, Princeton, N.J., 1969-70; asst. prof. math. MIT, Cambridge, 1970-73, assoc. prof., 1973-77; prof. physics Washington U., St. Louis, 1977—; research assoc. Imperial Coll., London, 1974. Cons. Los Alamos Nat. Lab., 1979—; vis. prof. Imperial Coll., London, 1986-87, 95-96, Technion Israel Inst. of Technology, Haifa, Israel, 1995; fellow Engring. and Phys. Scis. Rsch. Coun., U.K., 2003—. Author: Advanced Mathematical Methods for Scientists and Engineers, 1978; editor: Am. Inst. Physic series on math. and computational physics; mem. editl. bds. Jour Math. Physics, 1980-83, Advances in Applied Math., 1980-85, Jour. Physics A, 1999-2003; editor-in-chief, Jour. Physics A, 2004—; contbr. more than 200 articles to sci. jours. Trustee Ctr. for Theoretical Study of Phys. Sys., Clark Atlanta U. Recipient Burlington No. Found. Faculty Achievement award, 1985, Fellows award Acad. Sci. St. Louis, 2002; Telluride scholar, 1960-63, NSF fellow, 1964-69, Woodrow Wilson fellow, 1964-65, Sloan Found. fellow, 1973-77, Fulbright fellowship to U.K., 1995-96, Lady Davis fellowship to Israel, 1995, Rockefeller Found. grantee to visit Bellagio Study and Conf. Ctr., 1999; Guggenheim Fellow, 2003—, fellow Engring. and Physical Scis. Rsch. Coun., London, 2003—. Fellow: St. Louis Acad. Sci., Am. Phys. Soc. (vice chmn. Danny Heineman prize selection com., chmn. Danny Heineman prize selection com.); mem.: Phi Kappa Phi, Phi Beta Kappa. Home: 509 Warren Ave Saint Louis MO 63130-4155 Office: Washington U Dept Physics Saint Louis MO 63130

BENDER, EDWARD ERIK, geology educator, researcher; b. Bronxville, N.Y., Dec. 9, 1962; s. Edward Joseph and Mae Virgina (Camera) B.; m. Linda Dee Young, June 8, 1964; 1 child, Alexandra Dominique. BS in Geology, Rider U., 1985; MS, Vanderbilt U., 1990; PhD, U. So. Calif., 1994. Instr. Calif. State U., Fullerton, 1991-92; asst. prof. Orange Coast Coll., Costa Mesa, Calif., 1994—. Adj. prof. Chaffey Coll., Alta Loma, Calif., 1991—, Mt. San Antonio Coll., Walnut, Calif., 1992-93, Pasadena (Calif.) City Coll., 1992-94; adv. com-edn. So. Calif. Earthquake Ctr., L.A., 1995—; spkr. Earthquake Awareness Orange Coast Coll., 1996, Costa Mesa Mineral Soc., 1995. Contbr. articles to profl. jours. Mem. Seismological Soc. Am., Geol. Soc. Am. (Penrose grant 1986), Am. Geophys. Union, Mineralog. Soc. Am. Achievements include examination of growth of North American continent, mechanisms and timing; discovery that many terranes of California have not travelled as previously believed. Office: Orange Coast Coll 2701 Fairview Rd Costa Mesa CA 92626-5563

BENDER, LARRY WAYNE, vocational educator; b. Indpls., May 23, 1942; s. Wayne Crawford and Margaret Dell (Ramer) B.; m. Barbara Agnes Kroll, Aug. 26, 1967; children: Anissa Gayle, Timothy Alan. BS in Indsl. Edn., Purdue U., 1967, MS in Indsl. Edn., 1972. Tchr. South Newton Sch. Corp., Kentland, Ind., 1967-81; tchr. tech. edn. Franklin (Ind.) Community Schs., 1981—. Recipient IPALCO Golden Apple award 1997, Newmast award 1997; Eli Lilly Found. grantee, 1999. Mem. Internat. Tech. Edn. Assn. (Outstanding Program of Yr. award 1987), Tech. Educators of Ind. (Meritorious Tchr. award 1987). Episcopalian. Avocations: photography, computers, bowling, golf, woodworking. Home: 4215 North Graham Rd Whiteland IN 46184-9326 Office: Custer Baker Middle Sch 101 W State Road 44 Franklin IN 46131-8936 E-mail: lbender@netdirect.net., benderl@fcsc.k12.in.us.

BENDER, MAURICE, health science administrator, consultant; b. N.Y.C., July 22, 1918; s. Max and Leah (Levitin) B.; m. Rosine Winokur, Dec. 23, 1941; children: Laurie Ann, David Max. BA, Johns Hopkins U., 1938; BS in Pharmacy, Temple U., 1944, MS in Pharmacy, 1945; PhD, Georgetown U., 1950. Registered pharmacist, Pa., Md., Alaska. Bioassayist, Munch Lab., Upper Darby, Pa., 1943-45; pharmacologist Fish Tech. Lab., College Park, Md., 1945-48; toxicologist, Army Med. Ctr., 1951-52; chemist Eastern Regional Research Lab., U.S. Dept. Agr., Phila., 1948-51; asst. prof. biochemistry Rutgers U., Newark, 1952-55; biochemist div. Indsl. Research and Services, Bur. Comml. Fisheries, U.S. Dept. Interior, Washington, 1955-58; pub. health research program analyst div. gen. med. services NIH, Bethesda, 1958-59, exec. sec. cancer chemotherapy study sect., 1959-60; chief research and tng. grants br. div. air pollution USPHS, Bethesda, 1960-65, asst. to adminstr. Health Services and Mental Health Adminstrn., Rockville, Md., 1970-72; asst. dir. Statewide Air Pollution Research Ctr., U. Calif.-Riverside, 1965-67; spl. asst. to commr. Nat. Air Pollution Control Adminstrn., HEW, Washington, 1967-68, dir. extramural research and devel. Consumer Protection and Environ. Health Service, 1968-70, team chmn. Fed. Assistance Streamlining Task Force, Office of Sec., 1970, dir. Arctic Health Research Ctr., Fairbanks, Alaska, 1972-73; exec. dir. Comprehensive Health Planning Council Spokane County, Inc., Spokane, Wash., 1973-76; exec. dir. Rock Island Health Council, Inc. (Ill.), 1976-77; health programs mgmt. and planning cons., Bellevue, Wash., 1977— ; mem. King County Health Planning Council, Seattle, 1978-81; vice chair King County Bd. for Devel. Disabilities, 1979-85. Contbr. articles to profl. publs. Bd. dirs. Residence East, Bellevue, 1984; mem. service com. RSVP, Seattle, 1984. Served to cpl. AUS, 1942-43. Recipient Cert. of Honor, Temple U., 1969; spl. award USPHS, 1971. Fellow Am. Pub. Health Assn., Am. Inst. Chemists, Royal Soc. Health; mem. AMA (affiliate), Inst. Food Technologists (profl. emeritus), Am. Pharm. Assn., Am. Soc. Pub. Adminstrn., Am. Chem. Soc. (emeritus), AAAS, Wash. Acad. Sci. (emeritus), Am. Inst. Nutrition (emeritus), Delta Sigma Theta, Rho Pi Phi. Unitarian. Home: 1684-152d Ave NE Apt 103 Bellevue WA 98007-4278

BENDER, SUSAN ARLYCE, secondary school educator, educational consultant; b. Seattle, Apr. 12, 1962; d. Alvin F. and Betty H. B. BS in Edn., Jackson State U., 1984; postgrad., Miss. Coll., 1986—. Cert. tchr., Miss. Tchr. Northwest Rankin Sch., Brandon, Miss., 1984-92, Jim Hill High Sch., Jackson, Miss., 1992—. Co-author: Mississippi State Science Curriculum, 1994. Nominee Presdl. award for Math. and Sci., 1994. Mem. NSTA, Miss. Acad. Sci., Nat. Sci. Tchrs. Assn., Miss. Mus. Natural Sci., Miss. Sci. Tchrs. Assn. (legis. rep. 1989-91, sec. 1991, pres. 1993—), Ctrl. Miss. H.S. Chemistry Tchrs. Assn. (pres. 1994—). Avocations: arts and crafts, travel, photography, animals, gardening. Home: PO Box 855 Brandon MS 39043-0855 Office: Jim Hill High Sch 2185 Fortune St Jackson MS 39204-2387

BENDER, VICTOR M. educational administrator; b. Pitts., Apr. 18, 1946; m. Patricia Ann Pike, Jan. 27, 1968; children:Trisha Ann Bender-Labbe, John Scott Bender, Michael Ray Bender. BS, Northeast La. U., 1969; MEd,

Southeastern La. U., 1973. Football coach Northeast La. U., Monroe, 1974, Miss. State U., Starkville, 1974-76; exec. asst. Tangipahoa Parish Sheriff's Office, Amite, La., 1976-78; supr. Davill Petroleum, Natalbany, La., 1978; pogram dir. City of Hammond (La.) Recreation Dept., Hammond, La., 1978; acct., bookkeeper Triangle Timber, Hammond, 1978-79; tchr., coach Kentwood (La.) H.S., 1979-80; prin. Ponchatoula (La.) Jr. H.S., 1990—. Emergency mgmt. coord. Tangipahoa Parish Police Jury, Amite, 1982. Capt. U.S. Army Inf., 1969-71. Recipient award for contbrn. to amateur athletics Nat. Football Found. and Coll. Hall of Fame, 1996. Mem. Nat. Assn. Secondary Prins., La. Assn. Prins., La. Assn. Sch. Execs., Am. Legion (vice-comdr. 1989), K.C. (patriotic chair 1980—, Knight of Yr. 1980), Phi Delta Kappa (pres. 1995-97). Avocations: camping, hiking, golf, fishing. Home: 47191 Bender Rd Hammond LA 70401-6829

BENDER, VIRGINIA BEST, computer scientist, educator; b. Rockford, Ill., Feb. 10, 1945; d. Oscar Sheldon and Genevieve Best; m. Robert Keith Bender, July 19, 1969; children: Victoria Ruth, Christopher Keith. BS in Chemistry, Math., No. Ill. U., 1967; postgrad., U. Ill., 1967-69; MBA, Loyola U., Chgo., 1973. Cert. computer profl. Sr. sys. rep. Burroughs Corp., Chgo., 1969-73; sys. analyst Marshall Field & Co., Chgo., 1973-74; project leader Fed. Home Loan Bank, Chgo., 1974-76; sr. sys. analyst United Air Lines, Elk Grove Village, Ill., 1976-78; supr. Kemper Group, Long Grove, Ill., 1978-82; prof. computer info. sys., coord. computer info. sys. William Rainey Harper Coll., Palatine, Ill., 1982—2002, prof. emeritus, 2002—. Spkr. Midwest Computer Conf., DeKalb, Ill., 1988, moderator, 91; exch. prof. Maricopa CC, Mesa, Ariz., 1990, rsch. sabbatical, 93, 98; spkr. conf. info. tech. League for Innovation, Kansas City, Mo., 1995; steering com. Midwest Computer Conf., 1995—99; facilitator ToolBook User's Conf., Colorado Springs, Colo., 2000, presenter, 2001—03; adj. prof. SUNY/Westchester C.C., Valhalla, 2003—. Nat. chief mother-dau. group Indian Maidens YMCA, Des Plaines, 1982—83; mem. Vols. Pks. Environ. Edn. Westchester County Dept. Pks., Recreation and Conservation, NY, 2002—; mem. choir Kingswood United Meth. Ch., Buffalo Grove, Ill., 1982—2002, asst. organist, 1982—89; mem. choir 1st Congl. Ch., Chappaqua, NY, 2002—, mem. bell choir, 2003—. Named Tchr. of the Month, Burroughs Corp., Chgo., 1972. Mem.: No. Ill. Computer Soc., Ill. Assn. Data Processing Instrs., Inst. Cert. Computer Profls. (life), No. Ill. Alumni Assn. (life), Mortar Bd., Sigma Zeta, Phi Theta Kappa. Avocations: swimming, sewing, needlecrafts, reading, playing piano. Office: William Rainey Harper Coll 1200 W Algonquin Rd Palatine IL 60067-7373 E-mail: vbender@hotmail.com.

BENDO, AUDRÉE ARGIRO, anesthesiologist, educator; b. N.Y.C., Jan. 24, 1953; BS, Cornell U., 1974; MS, Columbia U., 1977; MD, U. Health Scis./Chgo. Med. Sch., 1981. Bd. cert. in anesthesiology. Rotating intern St. Lukes Hosp., N.Y.C., 1981-82; resident in anesthesiology SUNY Health Sci. Ctr., Bklyn., 1982-84, fellow in neurosurg. anesthesiology, 1984-85. Assoc. prof., vice chair edn. SUNY, Bklyn. Mem. Am. Soc. Anesthesiologists, Internat. Anesthesia Rsch. Soc., N.Y. Acad. Medicine, N.Y. State Soc. Anesthesiologists, Soc. Neurosurg. Anesthesia and Critical Care. Office: SUNY Dept Anesthesiology Box 6 450 Clarkson Ave Dept Brooklyn NY 11203-2056

BENEDICT, GAIL CLEVELAND, music educator; b. Rockville Ctr., N.Y., Dec. 15, 1942; d. Walter Charles and Louise Cleveland; m. Donald Alexander Davis, July 4, 1967 (div. Apr. 14, 1980); 1 child, Scott Paul Davis; m. Robert Lorin Benedict, July 6, 1983. BS in Music Edn., SUNY, Fredonia, 1964; MS in Adminstrn. and Supervision, Nova U., 1980; EdD, U. Sarasota, Fla., 1982. Cert. tchr. Fla., N.Y. Music tchr., dept. chair North Country Elem. Sch., Stony Brook, NY, 1964—66; music tchr., chorus dir. Narimasu Elem. Sch., Tokyo, 1966—67; vocal music tchr. Mineral Wells (Tex.) H.S., 1967—68; music tchr., chorus dir. Park Ave. Elem. Sch., Amityville, NY, 1968—70; music tchr., resource tchr. Magruder Elem. Sch., Newport News, Va., 1970—72; music specialist Skyview Elem. Sch., Pinellas Park, Fla., 1979—; adj. instr. Nova Southea. U., Tampa, Fla., 1991—. Gen. mgr. V.I. Properties, St. Petersburg, Fla., 1989—. Author: (book) Cruzan Child, 2002. Grantee, Pinellas County Arts Coun., 2001. Mem.: Pinellas Co. Music Educators Assn. (vocal chair 1980—83), Fla. Elem. Music Educators Assn. (chair Dist. III 1979—84), Music Educators Nat. Conf. Avocations: travel, reading, history, writing. Home: 6712 Cardinal Dr S Saint Petersburg FL 33707 Office: Skyview Elem Sch 8601 60th St N Pinellas Park FL 33782 E-mail: drmommusic@aol.com.

BENEDICT, GARY CLARENCE, school system administrator, psychotherapist, educator; b. Valley City, ND, Oct. 22, 1938; s. Clarence Augustus and Mary Rae (Spink) Benedict; m. Carmen Jean Schreiner, May 29, 1965; children: Andrew Scott, Anne Kathleen. BEdn, Wis. State U., 1964; MS, U. Wis., 1968; EdD, Marquette U., 1978; postgrad., Webster U., 1994—95. Tchr. New Berlin (Wis.) Pub. Schs., 1960—67; supt. Merton (Wis.) Joint Sch. Dist. 9, 1967—75; dir. curriculum and instrn. Mukwonago (Wis.) Sch. Dist., 1975—84; adminstrv. asst. curriculum Shorewood Sch. Dist., 1984—87; supt. Affton Sch. Dist., St. Louis, 1987—95; psychotherapist Family Psychol. Svcs., Chesterfield, Mo., 1995—2000; adj. asst. prof. U. Fla., 2000—. Contbg. author Invitational Learning for Counseling and Development, 1990; contbr. articles to profl. jours. Charles F. Kettering Found. fellow, 1981—92. Mem.: ASCD, Am. Assn. Sch. Adminstrs., Phi Delta Kappa. Home: 7711 SW 43rd Pl Gainesville FL 32608-4219 E-mail: drgcb@bellsouth.net.

BENEDICT, MARY-ANNE, nursing educator, consultant; b. Cambridge, Mass., Apr. 14, 1944; d. Preston E. and Mary Rose (Murphy) Woodward; m. Charles A. Benedict, Sept. 20, 1969; children: Annmarie, Helene, Laura. BS in Nursing, Boston Coll. Sch. Nursing, 1967; MSN, Salem State Coll., 1995. Cert. orthopedic nurse. Instr. Sch. Nursing New Eng. Bapt. Hosp., Boston, 1969-79, edn. specialist, 1979-96; coord. edn. and tng. Emerson Hosp., Concord, Mass., 1997-99; ednl. accreditation cons., 1999—. Lt. (j.g.) USN, 1966-69. Mem. Nat. Assn. Orthopedic Nurses, Sigma Theta Tau (Alpha Chi chpt.), Am. Nurses Credentialling Ctr. Com. on Accrediatation, 2003. Home: 84 Rockland Pl Newton MA 02464-1234 E-mail: maryannebenedict@aol.com.

BENEDICT, THERESA MARIE, retired secondary education mathematics educator; b. East Rutherford, N.J., Feb. 6, 1939; d. Michael and Rosaria Trivigno; m. Willliam F. Benedict, Oct. 3, 1964' children: Gerard Michael, Willliam Francis. BS in Edn., Seton Hall U., 1978; MA in Adminstrn., Jersey City State Coll., 1989. Math tchr. Wayne (N.J.) Hills High Sch., 1978-79, Ramsey (N.J.) High Sch., 1980, Lakeland Regional High Sch., Wanaque, NJ, 1980—2000, ret., 2000. Advisor Vol. in Edn., Passaic County, N.J., 1986-89, Student Asst. Team, Lakeland High Sch., Wanaque, N.J., 1990-2000; coord. student/tchr. lunch program for at-risk students, 1991-2000. Leader 4-H Clubs, Wayne, N.J., 1975-88, 95, 2001—; advisor Parish Ch. Coun., Wayne, n.J., 1989—; church eucharistic minister, 1986—; vol. Ch. Outreach Program. Roman Catholic. Avocations: horticulture, cooking, hiking. Home: 45 Brandywine Rd Wayne NJ 07470-3201

BENEFIEL, DIANE MARIE, home health nurse supervisor; b. Albuquerque, June 15, 1957; d. Bryant Michael and Barbara (Thomason) Curry; m. Randy Benefiel, June 1, 1979; children: Darin Michelle, Bryant Randal. BSN, Point Loma Coll., 1979; MSN, Calif. State U. Dominguez Hill, Carson, 1993. RN, Calif.; cert. pub. health nurse; cert. BCLS instr. Am. Heart Assn.; cert. neonatal resuscitation hosp. based instr. Am. Heart Assn. Charge and staff RN St. Francis Hosp., Tulsa, 1979-80; staff RN Boswell Meml. Hosp., Sun City, Ariz., 1980-82, Sharp Meml. Hosp., San Diego, 1982-83; charge RN diabetic edn. Coll. Pk. Hosp., San Diego, 1982-84; edn. dir., staff RN Santa Paula (Calif.) Meml. Hosp., 1984-89; staff RN Antelope Valley Hosp. Meml. Ctr., Lancaster, Calif., 1989-90; clin. instr. Antelope Valley Community Coll., Lancaster, 1990—; staff RN Visiting Nurse's Assn., Lancaster, 1990-94; supr. Antelope Valley Home Care, 1994-95, Vis. Nurses Assn., Clovis, Calif., 1996—. Coord. Nursing Resource Ctr., Calif. State U., Fresno, 1996—. Mem. NAACOG, Phi Kappa Phi. Nazarene. Avocations: crafts, bowling, softball, gardening, music. Home: 2299 Houston Ave Clovis CA 93611-8141

BENEKOHAL, RAHIM FARAHNAK, civil engineering educator, researcher, consultant; b. Tabriz, Iran;, naturalized, U.S. s. Mohammed and Batol (Farahnak) Benekohal. BS in Agrl. Engring., U. Rezaieh, 1977; BSCE, MSCE, Ohio State U., 1981, PhD in Civil Engring., 1986. Tchg. asst. Ohio State U., Columbus, 1981-86, instr., 1986; traffic engr. RKA, Inc., Tarrytown, N.Y., 1986-87; asst. prof. civil engring. U. Ill., Urbana, 1987—92, assoc. prof., 1993—2000, prof., 2001—. Transp. cons.; dir. Ill. Traffic and Safety Conf., Champaign, 1987—; chmn. Traffic Congestion and Traffic Safety in 21st Century Conf., 1997. Editor: Traffic Congestion and Traffic Safety in the 21st Century, 1997; contbr. articles to profl. jours. Mem. ASCE (Arthur M. Wellington prize, chair traffic ops. com.), Tranp. Rsch. Bd., Inst. Transp. Engrs. (Past Pres. award Ill. sect.), Phi Kappa Phi (hon., faculty), Chi Epsilon (hon., faculty). Home: 2719 Lakeview Dr Champaign IL 61822-7532 Office: U Ill 205 N Mathews Ave Urbana IL 61801-2350

BENENSON, CLAIRE BERGER, investment and financial planning educator; b. NYC; d. Nathan H. and Alice E. (Zeisler) B.; m. Lawrence A. Benenson: children: Harold, Gary. BA, Wellesley Coll.; postgrad., N.Y. Inst. Fin., New Sch. Social Rsch., 1965-69. Security analyst Merrill Lynch, N.Y.C., 1940-43; rsch. assoc. Conn. Coll., 1943-45; lectr. NYU Mgmt. Inst., N.Y.C., 1960-68, New Sch. for Social Rsch., N.Y.C., 1963-86, dir. ann. conf. Wall St. and Economy, 1967-87, dir. ann. conf. Futures and Options, 1979-86, chmn. dept. investment and fin. planning, 1974-86. Adv. bd. The First Women's Bank, N.Y.C., 1984-86; bd. trustees Burnham Investors Trust, Phoenix Trust; trustee Simms Global Fund, 1987-89, Phoenix-Euclid Mkt. Neutral Fund, 1998—; pres. Money Marketeers, NYU, N.Y.C., 1979-80; cons. in field. Contbg. editor Exec. Jeweler, 1981-83; creator, moderator NBC-TV series, Wall St. for Everyone, 1967-78. Bd. overseers Parsons Sch. Design, N.Y.C., 1974-93; coun. conservaters N.Y. Pub. Libr., 1990—, chair SIBL com., 1994—; bus. leadership coun. Wellesley Coll., 1991—, bd. dirs. Ctrs. for Women, 1998-2002; v.p. 92d St. YMHA & YWHA, N.Y.C., lectr. com., co-chair planned giving com. Named Disting. Alumna Wellesley Coll., 1968, Durant Scholar, Wellesley Coll.; Alt. fellow in econs. Columbia U., 1938-39. Mem. Fin. Women's Assn. (bd. dirs., chair dirs. resource adv. com., co-chair program com. 1988-89), Nat. Assn. Bus. Econs., Women's Econ. Roundtable, Econ. Club N.Y., N.Y. Assn. Bus. Economists, Money Marketeers NYU, Durant Soc. Wellesley Coll., Women's Bond Club, Harmonie Club (bd. mem., chair forum com.), Cosmopolitan Club (investment and fin. com.), Phi Beta Kappa. Jewish.

BENET, CAROL ANN LEVIN, journalist, teacher; b. Albany, N.Y., Mar. 21, 1939; d. Morton Harold and Ethel Leona (Maitland) Levin; m. Leslie Z. Benet, Sept. 8, 1960; children: Reed Michael, Gillian Vivia. AB, U. Mich., 1961, MA, 1964; PhD, U. Calif., Berkeley, 1987. Freelancejournalist, arts critic Ark newspaper, Belvedere, Calif., 1975—; book seminar tchr. U. Calif. Extension, Berkeley, in San Francisco, 1991-98; book group leader Marin County, San Francisco, 1987—; PhD career advisor/counselor U. Calif., Berkeley, 1993-97; journalist, arts critic Bay City News Svc., San Francisco, 1993—2000, Ind. Jour. newspaper, Marin, Calif., 1993—2002; theater critic ARTSF.com, San Francisco, 2000—. Adj. prof. Antioch Coll., Yellow Springs, Ohio, 1995-96, lectr. grad. humanities program, Dominican Coll, San Rafael, Calif., 1996-97; instr. lit. seminars San Franciso and Marin Counties. Author: The German Reception of Sam Shephard, 1990. Docent Asian Art Mus., San Francisco, 1987, De Young Mus., San Francisco, 1984. Jewish. Avocations: swimming, travel, gardening, hiking/walking, reading. Home: 53 Beach Rd Belvedere CA 94920-2364

BENEZET, LOUIS TOMLINSON, retired psychology educator, former college president; b. La Crosse, Wis., June 29, 1915; s. Louis Paul and Genevieve (Tomlinson) B.; m. Mildred Twohy, 1940 (dec. 1977); children: Joel (dec.), Laura, Julia, Barbara, Martha; m. Virginia Iglehart Clifford, 1988 (dec. 1999). AB, Dartmouth, 1936, LL.D., 1966; A.M., Reed Coll., 1939; PhD, Columbia, 1942; LL.D., Mt. Union Coll., U. Pitts., U. Denver, Knox Coll., Loyola U., Chgo., Colo. Coll., U. Colo., U. Calif.; L.H.D., Westminister (Utah) Coll., Hebrew Union Coll. Instr. The Hill Sch., 1936-38; assoc. in psychology Reed Coll., 1938-40; assoc. prof. psychology, asst. dir. admissions Knox Coll., 1942-43; asst. dean Univ. Coll., Syracuse U., 1946-47, asst. to chancellor, 1947-48; pres. Allegheny Coll., 1948-55, Colo. Coll., 1955-63; pres. emeritus, from 1995; pres. Claremont Grad. U., 1963-70, SUNY, Albany, 1970-75, rsch. prof. human devel. Stony Brook, 1975-85, cons. on coll. adminstrn., 1987-90. Pres. Pa. Assn. Colls. and Univs., 1951-52; chmn. Ind. Coll. Funds of Am., 1961-62; chmn. Rhodes scholar selection com., Colo., Calif., N.Y., 1958-74; mem. instl. rels. com. NSF, 1967-70, chmn., 1969-70; mem. Calif. Gov.'s Commn. on Tax Reform, 1969, N.Y. Gov.'s Task Force on Financing Higher Edn., 1972-73. Author: General Education in the Progressive College, 1943, Private Higher Education and Public Funding, 1976, Style and Substance: Leadership in the College Presidency, 1981, People Versus Pyramids, 1999, Restoring America's Failed Democracy, 2000; contbr. articles to profl. jours. Trustee Aspen Inst., 1956-68, moderator Exec. Seminar, 1958-79. Served with USNR, 1943-46, PTO. Named Disting. Alumnus Columbia Tchrs. Coll., 1984. Mem. Western Coll. Assn. (pres. 1969-70), Assn. Am. Colls. (chmn. commn. on acad. freedom and tenure 1955-58), Am. Coun. on Edn. (exec. com. 1955-58, bd. dirs. 1961-64, chmn. 1965-66), Phi Beta Kappa. Home: Seattle, Wash. Died Jan. 23, 2002.

BENGE, RAYMOND DOYLE, JR., astronomy educator; b. Houston, Oct. 10, 1961; s. Raymond Doyle and Gladys Jean (Patrick) B. BS, Duke U., 1983; MS, Tex. A&M U., 1988. Tchg. asst. Tex. A&M U., College Station, 1984-88; tchg. fellow U. N. Tex., Denton, 1988-94; part-time faculty mem. Tarrant County Jr. Coll., Ft. Worth, 1994-97; assoc. faculty Collin County C.C., Plano, Tex., 1994-97; assoc. prof. physics Tarrant County Coll., Hurst, Tex., 1997—. Adj. faculty Richland Coll., Dallas, 1994-98, Tex. Christian U., Ft. Worth, 2002; astronomy lab. coord. Tex. A&M U., College Station, 1986-88; observatory dir. U. N. Tex., Denton, 1991-94; SPICA agt. Harvard-Smithsonian Ctr. for Astrophysics, Cambridge, 1993-95. Author, editor: (lab. manual) Experiments on Stars and the Universe, 1994, asst. publ. Star Watch Nights, Tex. Dept. Pks. and Wildlife; contbr. articles to profl. jours. Dorm rep. Baldwin Fedn., Duke U., 1985; organizer pub. observation nights U. N. Tex., Denton, 1991-94; asst. pub. planetarium shows Richland Coll. Mem. Am. Astron. Soc., Astron. Soc. Pacific, Royal Astron. Soc. Can., Am. Assn. Variable Star Observers., Tex. Astron. Soc. Republican. Achievements include measurement of period changes in the eclipsing binary star GK Cephei; establishment of undergrad. rsch. program in astronomy at the U. N. Tex.; development of several astronomy workshops for pre-college tchrs. Office: Tarrant County Coll Dept Natural Scis 828 W Harwood Rd Hurst TX 76054-3219

BEN-GHIAT, RUTH, historian, educator; b. May 17, 1960; D. Raphael and Margaret (Spence) Ben-Ghiat. BA, UCLA, 1981; PhD, Brandeis U., 1991. Asst. prof. U. N.C., Charlotte, 1991-95; asst. prof. history Fordham U., N.Y.C., 1995-98, assoc. prof. history, 1998—. Author: Fascist Modernities: Italy, 1922-45, 1999; contbr. articles to profl. jours. Fellow Fulbright Found., 1993-94, Am. Philos. Soc., 1993-94, Getty Ctr. for History of Art, 1992-93. Mem. Am. Hist. Assn., Soc. for Italian Hist. Studies, Assn. for Studies in Modern Italy (U.K.), Am. Assn. Italian Studies, Phi Beta Kappa, Phi Alpha Theta.

BENHAM, PHILIP OWEN, JR., business marketing educator, consultant; b. Gloucester, Mass., July 8, 1944; s. Philip Owen and Elizabeth S. (Crowell) B.; m. Elizabeth Ann McCormack, June 18, 1966; children: Rebecca Ann, Rachel Marie, Philip Owen III, Emily Jessica. BS, U.S. Mil. Acad., 1966; MBA, U. Colo., 1974, PhD, 1980. Commd 2d lt. U.S. Army, 1966, advanced through grades to capt., 1968, resigned, 1977; instr. U. Colo., Boulder, 1977-80; asst. prof. Bucknell U., Lewisburg, Pa., 1980-85; mgr. Newport News (Va.) Shipbuilding, 1985-91; v.p. Mfrs. Nat. Corp., Detroit, 1991-92; cons. Benham Consultancy, Southfield, Mich., 1992-94, Hollidaysburg, Pa., 1994—; dean grad. sch. human resource mgmt. and indsl. rels. St. Francis U., Loretto, Pa., 1994—. Co-author: Managing Human Resources, 1988; contbr. articles to profl. jours. Mmem. Leadership Blair County, 1997-98. Decorated Bronze Star "V" medal, Purple Heart medal; scholar Eisenhower Meml. Found., Indpls., 1977; named Outstanding Human Resources Profl., Blair County Human Resource Mgmt. Assn., 2001. Mem. Soc. for Human Resource Mgmt. (sr. profl. cert., mem. rsch. com., chmn. nat. book award 2003), Soc. for Advancement Mgmt. (editl. bd. 1987—), Pa. Bankers Assn. (advisor), Human Resource Cert. Inst. (mem. cert. exam. rev. panel), Beta Gamma Sigma; mem. bd. dir.,Family Svc. of Blair County, Pa., 2003— . Republican. Roman Catholic. Office: St Francis Univ Dean Grad Sch Hum Resource Mgmt Loretto PA 15940 E-mail: pbenham@francis.edu.

BEN-HARARI, RUBEN ROBERT, research scientist, medical writer, medical communications consultant; b. London, Mar. 17, 1954; came to U.S., 1981; s. Jacob and Marga (Levy) Ben-H.; m. Liora Nissanian, Dec. 9, 1979; children: Yaakov, Vered, Inbal, Hadar, Maskit. BS in Pharmacology with honors, U. London, 1976, PhD in Pharmacology, 1979. From instr. to asst. prof. Mt. Sinai Sch. Medicine, N.Y.C., 1982-90, dir. rsch. dept. anesthesiology, 1986-90; asst. prof., dir. rsch. dept. anesthesiology NYU Sch. Medicine, N.Y.C., 1990-94; pres., creative dir. RBH Assocs., Inc., N.Y.C., 1994—. Legal cons. Medquest Inc., N.Y.C., 1993, Bower & Gardner, N.Y.C., 1993; writer, med. cons. various orgns. 1993— including Alliance Meeting Planners, N.J., AM Medica Commn., N.Y.C., Phase V Comm., N.Y.C., Copyright Coun. Am., N.Y.C., Health Edn. Techs., N.Y.C., Ruder Finn, N.Y.C., Medicus Intercon PR, N.Y.C., Makovsky and Co., N.Y.C., Dudnyk Healthcare Commn., NYU Med. Ctr., N.Y.C., SynerMed, N.J., Brown and Powers, N.Y.C., Spectral Resources, N.Y., BBK, Mass., C&M Advt., N.J., Ketchum Pub. Rels., N.Y.C., Triclinica Comms., N.Y.C., Applied Clin. Comms., N.Y.C., Dorland Sweeney Jones, Pa., Performance Tng. & Consulting, N.J., Davids Prodns., N.J., GEM Comm., Conn., Exeter Group, N.Y.C., Klemtner Advt., N.Y.C., Physicians World Comm., N.J., Sci. and Medicine, N.Y.C., Lehman Millet, Mass., IntraMed, N.Y.C., Med. Forum, N.J., Sudler & Hennessey, N.Y.C., Healthways, N.J., Gonocom, N.Y.C., Healthways, N.J., HSL Corp., N.J., Med. Forum, N.J. Bd. dirs. NYU Med. Ctr. (mem. med. bd.), N.Y.C., 1990-93, Sephardic Jewish Congregation Queens, N.Y.C., 1990-93; vice-chmn. Yeshivat Ohr Haiim, N.Y.C., 1992—. Rsch. fellow Wellcome Trust, London, 1979-81, Parker B. Francis Found., 1981-82; Rsch. grant Am. Lung Assn., 1982-84. Mem. AAAS, N.Y. Acad. Sci., Brit. Pharmacol. Soc., Nat. Assn. Sci. Writers, Am. Med. Writers Assn., Pharm. Advt. Coun., Healthcare Pub. Rels. and Mktg. Soc., Pub. Rels. Soc. Am., Med. Mktg. Assn. Jewish. Avocations: squash, reading. Home: 14429 76th Rd Flushing NY 11367-3119

BENIRSCHKE, KURT, pathologist, educator; b. Glueckstadt, Germany, May 26, 1924; came to U.S., 1949, naturalized, 1955; s. Fritz Franz and Marie (Luebcke) B.; m. Marion Elizabeth Waldhausen, May 17, 1952; children: Stephen Kurt, Rolf Joachim, Ingrid Marie. Student, U. Hamburg, Germany, 1942, 45-48, U. Berlin, 1943, U. Wuerzburg, 1943-44; MD, U. Hamburg, 1948. Resident, Teaneck, N.J., 1950-51, Peter Bent Brigham Hosp., Boston, 1951-52, Boston Lying-in-Hosp., 1952-53, Free Hosp. for Women, Boston, 1953, Children's Hosp., Boston, 1953; pathologist Boston Lying-in-Hosp., 1955-60; teaching fellow, assoc. Med. Sch. Harvard, 1954-60; prof. pathology, chmn. dept. pathology Med. Sch. Dartmouth, Hanover, N.H., 1960-70; prof. reproductive medicine and pathology U. Calif., San Diego, 1970-94; chmn. dept. pathology U. Calif. at San Diego Sch. Med., La Jolla, 1976-79; ret. U. Calif., San Diego, 1994. Dir. research San Diego Zoo, 1975-86, trustee, 1986—, pres., 1998-2000; cons. NIH, 1957-70. Served with German Army, 1942-45. Mem. Am. Soc. Pathology, Internat. Acad. Pathology, Am. Coll. Pathology, Am. Acad. Arts and Scis., Teratol. Soc., Am. Soc. Zool. Vets. Home: 8457 Prestwick Dr La Jolla CA 92037-2023 Office: Univ Calif San Diego Med Ctr 200 W Arbor Dr San Diego CA 92103-8321 E-mail: kbenirsc@ucsd.edu.

BENITZ, WILLIAM EDWIN, medical educator; b. Juneau, Alaska, Feb. 20, 1952; s. Earl and H. Ruth Benitz; m. Andrea Layne Andrews, May 21, 1973; children: Lindsey, Maija, Annika. BS in Math., U. Alaska, 1973; MD, Stanford U., 1978. Diplomate Nat. Bd. Med. Examiners, Am. Bd. Pediatrics sub bd. neonatal-perinatal medicine. Asst. prof. pediatrics Stanford U., Palo Alto, Calif., 1985-93, assoc. prof. pediatrics, 1993-99, prof. pediats., 1999—. Assoc. dir. nurseries Stanford U. Hosp., Palo Alto, 1985-91; assoc. dir. nurseries Packard Children's Hosp., Palo Alto, 1991-92, dir., 2000, clin. dir. neonatal ICU, 1992-2000, assoc. chief divsn. neonatology, dir. nurseries, 2000—; clin. scientist Am. Heart Assn., Dallas, 1984, established investigator, 1989. Author: Pediatric Drug Handbook, 1981, 3d edit., 1995; contbr. numerous articles to profl. jours. Fellow Am. Acad. Pediatrics; mem. Western Soc. for Pediatric Rsch., Soc. Pediatric Rsch. Office: Stanford U Divsn Neonatology 750 Welch Rd Ste 315 Palo Alto CA 94304-1510 E-mail: benitzwe@stanford.edu.

BENJAMIN, BARBARA BLOCH, writer, editor; b. May 26, 1925; d. Emil William and Dorothy (Lowengrund) B.; m. Joseph B. Sanders, Aug. 3, 1944 (div. 1961); children: Elizabeth Sanders, Ellen Janice Benjamin; m. Theodore S. Benjamin, Sept. 20, 1964 (dec.). Student, NYU, 1943-45, New Sch. Social Rsch., 1966. Office mgr. Writers War Bd., N.Y.C., 1943-45, Westchester Dem. Com., White Plains, N.Y., 1955-56; mgr. Westchester Symphony Orch., 1957-62; mng. editor, Cooking Ency. Rutledge Books, N.Y.C., 1970-71; pres. Internat. Cookbook Svcs., White Plains, 1978—. Columnist House Beautiful, 1984-87; cookbook editor Benjamin Co., 1990-97; cons. in field; tchr. cooking classes White Plains, 1975-80; lectr. in field. Author: Anyone Can Quilt, 1975; Meat Board Meat Book, 1977; If It Doesn't Pan Out, 1981; Garnishing Made Easy, 1983, Microwave Party Cooking, 1988, A Little Jewish Cookbook, 1989, A Little New England Cookbook, 1990, A Little Southern Cookbook, 1990, A Little New York Cookbook, 1990, The Little Book of Chocolate, 2003; editor/author: All Beef Cookbook, 1973; In Glass Naturally, 1974; Fresh Ideas with Mushrooms, 1977; Holly Farms Complete Chicken Cookbook, 1984; Gulden's Cookbook, 1985, A Centennial Celebration of Recipes from Solo, 1988, Salute to the Great American Chefs, 1988, TCBY and More, 1989, GoldStar Micro-Convection Cookbook, 1991, Healthy Cooking with Amway Queen Cookware, 1993, McCormick/Schilling's New Spice Cookbook, 1994, Simply the Best Chicken, 1997, Fabulous Things To Do With Chocolate, 1998, The Pasta Pack, 1998; Am. adapter The Cuisine of Olympe, 1983, Baking Easy and Elegant, 1984, series of 3 English cookbook mags., 1984-87, Best of Cold Foods, 1985, Cakes and Pastries, 1985, series of 12 Creative Cuisine books, 1985, The Art of Cooking, 1986, The Art of Baking, 1987, Perfect Pasta, 1992, Rocky Food, 1994; columnist Westfair Comm., 2000—; editor, contbr. various books; contbr. articles to profl. jours. Nat. bd. dirs. Encampment for Citizenship, N.Y.C., 1966-72; bd. dirs. YWCA Ctrl. Westchester, 1965-71, Westchester Ethical Humanist Soc., 1968—; exec. com., pres. Internat. Student Exch. of White Plains, 1955-70; bd. dirs. Westchester Chamber Music Soc., 1986—: chmn. Concerned Citizens for Open Space, 1997—. Jewish. Home and Office: Internat Cookbook Svcs 21 Dupont Ave White Plains NY 10605-3537 Fax: 914-997-7214. E-mail: bbenj2626@aol.com.

BENJAMIN, KARL STANLEY, artist, art educator; b. Chgo., Dec. 29, 1925; s. Eustace Lincoln and Marie (Klamsteiner) B.; m. Beverly Jean Paschke, Jan. 29, 1949; children: Beth Marie, Kris Ellen, Bruce Lincoln.

Student, Northwestern U., 1943, 46; BA, U. Redlands, 1949; MA, Claremont Grad. Sch., 1960. With dept. arts Pomona Coll., Claremont, Calif., 1979-97, Loren Barton Babcock Miller prof., artist-in residence, 1978-94, prof. emeritus, 1997—; prof. art Claremont Grad. Sch. Traveling exhbns. include New Talent, Am. Fedn. Arts, 1959, 4 Abstract Classicists, Los Angeles and San Francisco museums, 1959-61, West Coast Hard Edge, Inst. Contemporary Arts, London, Eng., 1960, Purist Painting, Am. Fedn. Arts, 1960-61, Geometric Abstractions in Am, Whitney Mus., 1962, Paintings of the Pacific, U.S., Japan and Australia, 1961-63, Artists Environment, West Coast, Amon Carter Mus., Houston, 1962-63, Denver annual, 1965, Survey of Contemporary Art, Speed Mus., Louisville, 1965, The Colorists, San Francisco Mus., 1965, Art Across Am, Mead Corp., 1965-67, The Responsive Eye, Mus. Modern Art, 1965-66, 30th Biennial Exhbn. Am. Painting, Corcoran Gallery, 1967, 35th Biennial Exhbn. Am. Painting, 1977, Painting and Sculpture in California: The Modern Era, San Francisco Mus. Modern Art, 1976-77, Smithsonian Nat. Collection Fine Arts, Washington, 1976-77, Los Angeles Hard Edge: The Fifties and Seventies, Los Angeles County Mus. Art, 1977, Corcoran Gallery, Washington, Cheney Cowles Mus., Spokane, 1980, Calif. State U., Bakersfield, 1982, Henry Gallery, U. Wash., 1982, U. Calif., Santa Barbara, 1984, L.A. Mcpl. Art Galleries, Barnsdall Park, 1986, Turning the Tide: Early Los Angeles Modernists, Santa Barbara Mus. Art, Oakland Mus., others, 1989-91, L.A. County Mus. Art, 1996; rep. permanent collections, Whitney Mus., L.A. County Mus. Art, San Francisco Mus. Art, Santa Barbara (Calif.) Mus. Art, Pasadena (Calif.) Art Mus., Long Beach (Calif.) Mus. Art, La Jolla (Calif.) Mus. Art, Fine Arts Gallery San Diego, U. Redlands, Mus. Modern Art, Israel, Pomona Coll., Scripps Coll., Univ. Mus., Berkeley, Calif., Wadsworth Atheneum, Nat. Collection Fine Arts, Seattle Mus. Modern Art, Newport Harbor Mus., U. N.Mex. Mus. Art, Wash. State U., L.A. Mus. Contemporary Art; retrospective exhbn. covering yrs. 1955-87 Calif State U. at Northridge, 1989, retrospective exhbn. 1979-94, Pomona Coll., 1994, 450 year survey Calif. art Orange County Mus. Art, Newport Beach, 1998-99. Served with USNR, 1943-46. Visual Arts grantee NEA, 1983, 89. Office: Pomona Coll Dept Arts 333 N College Way Dept Arts Claremont CA 91711-4429 also: Claremont Grad U Art Dept 251 E 10th St Claremont CA 91711-3913

BENJAMIN, LENI BERNICE, elementary education educator; b. Durham, N.C., Aug. 15, 1945; d. Irving Jack and Svea Elisabeth (Wohlers) Kruger; m. Stuart Dychtwald, Sept. 21, 1968 (div. May 1985); children: Dana Kyle, Scott Eric, Rachel Ann; m. Wellington Leon Benjamin, Nov. 30, 1985. BA, Newark (N.J.) State Coll., 1967; MA, NYU, 1969; postgrad., Drake U., 1980-81, Kean Coll., 1984-85. Cert. reading tchr., N.J., Iowa, elem. tchr., N.J., Iowa, Mass., prin./supr., N.J. Tchr. Elizabeth (N.J.) Bd. Edn., 1967-69, 84-85, Diocese of Green Bay, Wis., 1977-79, Diocese of Des Moines, 1979-81; acting dept. mgr., sales assoc. Lord & Taylor, Northbrook, Ill., 1981-82; tchr. Diocese of Metuchen-St. Helena's, Edison, N.J., 1982-83; instr. Edison Job Corps Ctr., 1983-84; tchr. Plainfield (N.J.) Bd. Edn., 1985-87, Pleasantville (N.J.) Bd. Edn., 1987—; team leader mid. level, tchr. 8th grade; coord. PRISM math. project Pleasantville (N.J.) Bd. Edn., career awareness specialist elem. sch., 1995—2000, HSPA math. prep. tchr., 2000—; adminstr. Night H.S., 2002—. Chair Reading Curriculum Com., Green Bay, 1978-79; mem. English Curriculum Com., Des Moines, 1979-81, Family Life Edn. Curriculum Com., Plainfield, 1985-86, Dist. Test Com., Pleasantville, 1987—. Treas. Boy Scouts Am., Green Bay, 1977. Elizabeth Edn. Assn. scholar, 1963. Mem. NEA, ASCD, N.J. Edn. Assn., Nat. Reading Assn., Nat. Coun. Tchrs. Math., N.J. Tchrs. Math., Nat. Reading Assn., Kean Coll. Alumni Assn., NYU Alumni Assn. Democrat. Jewish-Christian. Avocations: reading, needlework. Home: 39 Masters Cir Marlton NJ 08053-3745

BENJAMIN, SHEILA PAULETTA, secondary education educator; b. Sept. 28, 1948; AA, Montreat-Anderson Coll., 1966; BA in History, Belhaven Coll., 1968; MEd in History, U. Tampa, 1979. Cert. gifted, social studies and bible tchr. Tchr. Hillsboro County, Fla., 1970-98, Bloomingdale H.S., Valrico, Fla., 1998—. Clinician tchr. Suncoast Area Tchr. Tng. Honors Program; supervising tchr. Fla. Beginning Tchr. Program; dir. workshops in field. Aviation educator USAF-CAP; vol. Nat. Pks. Svc. 99s-Internat. Women's Pilot Assn. Recipient Photography awards Fla. Strawberry Festival and Hillsborough County Fair; Latin Am. Studies grantee NEH, 1983, African Studies, 1985; Fulbright-Hays scholar in Egypt, 1986, Honduras, 1993. Mem. ASCD, DAR, Nat. Space Soc., Nat. Coun. Social Studies, World Aerospace Edn. Orgn. (U.S. del., Amman, Jordan), Internat. World Aerospace Edn. Assn., Women in Aviation, Gulf Coast Archeol. Soc., Fla. Alliance for Geography, Fla. Aerospace Edn. Assn. (founding pres.), Fla. Anthrop. Soc. (bd. dirs., Appreciation award, Preservation award), Men of Menendez (Historic Fla. Militia Inc.), Mid. East Educators Network, Hillsborough Classroom Tchr. Assn. (NEA), Hillsborough County/Fla. Social Studies Coun., Challenger Ctr. Found. (founding sponsor), Fulbright Alumni Asns., Sun-N-Fun EAA, Phi Delta Kappa. Avocations: flying and soaring, scuba diving and snorkeling, archaeology. Home: 605 Fieldstone Dr Brandon FL 33511-7936 Office: Bloomingdale High Sch 1700 Bloomingdale Ave Valrico FL 33594-6220

BENJAMIN, SUSAN SELTON, elementary school educator; b. N.Y.C., June 3, 1946; m. Robert F. Benjamin, Nov. 30, 1968; children: Joshua, Alana. BS, Cornell U., 1968; MEd, Tufts U., 1969. Tchr. Wakefield (Mass.) Schs., 1969-73, Los Alamos (N.Mex.) Schs., 1973—. Resource tchr. Montessori Sch. House, San Diego, 1986; tchr. U. N.Mex., Los Alamos, 1989, 90; cons. Activities Integrating Math. and Sci. (AIMS) Nat. Leadership, Fresno, Calif., 1992—. Chair leadership Hadassah, Los Alamos, 1991—. Named Outstanding Women of N.Mex., 1980, N.Mex. State Tchr. of Yr., 2002; recipient Presdl. award for excellence in math. tchg. N.Mex. State, 1990, 92, Leadership award Hadassah, 1996. Mem. Nat. Coun. Math. Tchrs. Avocations: hiking, travel, tennis, aerobics. Home: 315 Rover Blvd Los Alamos NM 87544-3559

BENJOSEPH, DAN C. travel company executive, educator; b. Haifa, Israel, June 9, 1962; came to U.S., 1985; s. Andre A. and Kathy K. (Tuschak) B.; m. Jill L. Spiegler, Sept. 2, 1991; children: Moriah, Sara, Oliver-Eran. Assoc. degree, Tadmore Hotel Sch., Herzlia, Israel, 1985; BS, Johnson & Wales U., 1987, MS, 1989. Dir. resource ctr. Johnson & Wales U., Providence, 1985-90; instr. Mt. Aloysius Coll., Creson, Pa., 1990-91; pres. TravelTalk Tourism Edn., Providence, 1991—; mem. faculty, dir. travel internship Johnson & Wales U., Providence, 1996—. Mgr. Galilee Tours, Needham, Mass., 1991-96. With Israel Def. Forces, 1980-83. Avocations: teaching, travel research.

BENKE, PAUL ARTHUR, academic administrator; b. Michigan City, Ind., May 27, 1921; s. Paul Rol and Virginia (Peterson) B.; m. Beverly Anne Benke, Mar. 14, 1982; children: Janet, Eric. Student, Ind. U., 1941-42; AB, Ind. State U., Terre Haute, 1948; MA, U. Chgo., 1951, MBA, 1954. Gen. mgr. war prodn. div. Cline Electric Mfg. Co., Chgo., 1951-55; gen. mgr. Paasche Airbrush Co., Chgo., 1955-58; asst. to pres. H.K. Porter Co., 1956-57; gen. mgr. div. Coldform, 1957-58, Coldform (Thermoid div.), 1958-63; pres. (Colt's Firearms Div.), Hartford, Conn., 1963-73; v.p. Colt Industries Inc., 1969-73; group exec., marine products group, v.p. AMF Inc., White Plains, N.Y., 1973-81; pres. Jamestown (N.Y.) Community Coll., 1981-91; pres./CEO Metacomet, Ltd. Cons., 1996—. Bd. dirs. Bush Industries, Inc.; mem. regional adv. bd. HSBC Bank (USA). Pres., CEO Roger Tory Peterson Inst. Natural History, 1982-96. 1st lt. Ordnance Corps U.S. Army, 1942-45, CBI. Pres., exec. dir. Roger Tory Peterson Inst. Natural History, 1982-96. Served to 1st lt. Ordnance Corps. U.S. Army, 1942-45, CBI. Mem. Blue Key, Beta Gamma Sigma, Alpha Phi Gamma, Pi Gamma Mu. Office: Metacomet Ltd 3270 Gerry Levant Rd Falconer NY 14733-9639 E-mail: pab5279@netsync.net.

BENN, DOUGLAS FRANK, information technology and computer science executive; b. Detroit, May 8, 1936; s. Frank E. and Madeline (Pond) B.; m. Shirley M. Flanery, July 16, 1955; children: Christopher, Susan, Kathy. BS in Math., Mich. State U., 1960, MA, 1962; cert. data processing (NSF scholar), Milw. Inst. Tech., 1965; postgrad., U. Wis., 1965-66; Ed.Adminstrn., Washington U., 1972; MS in Computer Sci., So. Meth. U., 1982, D of Engring. in Computer Sci., 1990. Tchr. math. and sci. Lansing (Mich.) Public Schs., 1960-64; chmn. computer sci. dept. Kenosha (Wis.) Area Tech. Inst., 1964-67, mgr. data processing, 1965-67; sr. project leader Abbott Labs., North Chicago, Ill., 1967-68, world-wide sr. IT cons. (67 countries), 1968-69; dir. data processing div. St. Louis Public Schs., 1969-74; dir. info. systems div. mental health State of Ill., Springfield, 1974-78; v.p., chief info. officer Med. Computer Systems, Inc., Dallas, 1978; dir. bus. adminstrn. Dallas County Mental Health Center, 1979-80; prof. computer sci. So. Meth. U., Dallas, 1979-82, 89-96; sr. dir. corp. research and devel. Blue Cross & Blue Shield of Tex., Dallas, 1980-83; v.p., chief info. officer svcs. Western States Adminstrs., Fresno, Calif., 1984—88; chmn., pres. D.F. Benn & Assocs. Inc., 1989—; prof. Info. Tech. U. Tex., Dallas, 1990-92, 2000—; exec. U. Tex. Digital Forensics and Emergency Preparedness Inst., Dallas, 2002—; chief info. officer Tex. Natural Resource Conservation Commn., 1996-98. Exec. dir. for tech. Corpus Christi Ind. Sch. Dist., 1998-99; lectr. and adv. coun. Great Cities Pub. Sch. Sys., 1969-74; chief info. officer Ill. Dept. Mental Health and Developmental Disabilities, 1974-78, Wis. Bd. Vocat. Tech. and Adult Edn., 1964-67; co-dir. mgmt. adv. group Ill. Dept. Mental Health, 1974-78; mem. adv. group Tex. Gov.'s Task Force on Mental Health, 1980; adj. prof. computer info. sys. Wash. U., 1972-74; expert witness/software appraisal svcs. U.S. Tax Ct., 1995; chief info. officer State of Tex., 1997-99, Strategic Planning Coun., 1997, Geog. Info. Sys. Coun., 1997—, Nat. Gov.'s Assn./EPA Joint Task Force Electronic Commerce, 1997-99; project mgr. EPA E-Plan, 2000-; faculty sen. U. Tex., 2002—. Contbr. articles on info. techs., engring. mgmt., and software valuation to profl. jours. Arbitrator computer and bus. contract cases, 1976—. Mem. Data Processing Mgmt. Assn., Assn. for Sys. Mgmt. (Disting. Svc. award 1980, Merit award 1976, Achievement award 1978, chpt. pres. 1976-77, dist. dir. 1976-78), Am. Arbitration Assn., Data Processing Mgmt. Assn. (bd. dirs. 1987-89), Am. Soc. Engring. Mgmt., Telecom Corridor Tech. Club (founder, bd. dirs., officer 2002—), Sigma Xi (chpt. officer 2002—). Presbyterian. Home and Office: 3417 Mount Vernon Way Plano TX 75025-3611 E-mail: dfbenn@attbi.com.

BENNET, DOUGLAS JOSEPH, JR., university president; b. Orange, N.J., June 23, 1938; s. Douglas Joseph and Phoebe (Benedict) B.; m. Susanne Klejman, June 27, 1959 (div. 1995); children: Michael, James, Holly; m. Midge Bowen Ramsey, July 27, 1996. BA, Wesleyan U., Middletown, Conn., 1959; MA, U. Calif., Berkeley, 1960; PhD, Harvard, 1968. Asst. to econ. adv. AID, New Delhi, 1963—64; spl. asst. to Am. ambassador to India, 1964—66; asst. to Vice Pres. Hubert H. Humphrey, 1967—69; adminstrv. asst. to U.S. Senator Thomas Eagleton, 1969—73, to U.S. Senator Abraham Ribicoff, 1973—73; staff dir. com. budget U.S. Senate, 1974—77; asst. sec. state congressional relations, 1977—79; adminstr. AID, Washington, 1979—81; pres. Roosevelt Ctr. for Am. Policy Studies, 1981—83; pres., CEO Nat. Pub. Radio, Washington, 1983—93; asst. sec. state Internat. Orgnl. Affairs Dept. State, Washington, 1993—95; pres. Wesleyan U., Middletown, Conn., 1995—. Mem. Coun. Fgn. Rels., Cosmos Club. Democrat. Home: 269 High St Middletown CT 06457-3208 Office: Office of Pres Wesleyan U 229 High St Middletown CT 06459-3208

BENNETT, BETTY T. English literature educator, university dean, writer; b. N.J. children: Peter, Matthew. BA, Bklyn. Coll., 1962; MA, NYU, 1963, PhD, 1970. Adj. asst. prof. dept. English and comparative lit. SUNY, Stony Brook, 1970-75, asst. chmn. comparative lit., 1971-72, asst. to dean Grad. Sch., 1970-79, adj. assoc. prof., 1975-79; assoc. prof. English and humanities Pratt Inst., Bklyn., 1979-81, prof., 1981-85, dean Sch. Liberal Arts and Scis., 1979-85; dean Coll. Arts and Scis. Am. U., Washington, 1985-97, disting. prof. lit., 1997—. Fellowship reader Danforth Found., 1978-79; edn. liaison officer N.Y. State, 1977-80; co-dir. NEH Inst., 1989-90. Author: British War Poetry in the Age of Romanticism: 1793-1815, 1976, The Letters of Mary Wollstonecraft Shelley, Vol. I, 1980, The Letters of Mary Wollstonecraft Shelley, Vol. II, 1983, The Letters of Mary Wollstonecraft Shelley, Vol. III, 1988, Mary Diana Dods: A Gentleman and a Scholar, 1991, Mary Diana Dods: A Gentleman and a Scholar, paperback edit., 1994, Mary Wollstonecraft Shelley: An Introduction, 1998; editor (with Donald H. Reiman and Michael Jaye): The Evidence of the Imagination, 1978; editor: (with Charles Robinson) The Mary Shelley Reader, 1990; editor: Proserpine and Midas and Relation of the Cenci, 1992, The Selected Letters of Mary Wollstonecraft Shelley, 1995, Lives of the Great Romantics III: Mary Shelley, 1999; editor: (with Stuart Curran) Mary Shelley in Her Times, 2000; cons. editor and author gen. intro.: The Novels and Selected Works of Mary Wollstonecraft Shelley, 1996, book rev. editor: Keats-Shelley Jour., 1976—94. Keats-Shelley Assn. Am. Disting. scholar, 1992; NEH fellow, 1974-75, Henry E. Huntington Libr. fellow, 1976, Am. Coun. Learned Socs. fellow, 1977-78; Am. Philos. Soc. grant, 1980-81, NEH grant, 1984-87. Mem. MLA, Byron Assn., Keats-Shelley Assn. Am. (bd. dirs.), Soc. for Textual Scholarship (exec. com. 1993—), NYU Alumni Assn., Phi Beta Kappa (founding pres. Zeta chpt. of D.C.). Office: Am U Dept Lit Coll Arts and Scis 4400 Massachusetts Ave NW Washington DC 20016-8001 E-mail: bbennet@american.edu.

BENNETT, CATHERINE JUNE, information technology executive, educator, consultant; b. Augusta, Ga., June 19, 1950; d. Robert Stogner and Catherine Sue (Jordan) Robinson; m. Danny Marvin Bennett, Sept. 5, 1971; children: Timothy Jordan, Robert Daniel. BS in Stats., U. Ga., 1971, MA in Bus., 1973. Cert. project mgmt. profl. Project Mgmt. Inst., rational cert. cons., fellow Life Mgmt. Inst. Programmer William M. Shenkel & Assocs., Athens, Ga., 1971-73; sys. analyst U. Ga., Athens, 1973-76; product cons. ISA/SUNGUARD, Atlanta, 1976-78, mgr. product support, 1980-85, hotline mgr., sr. fin. specialist, 1986-88, mem. edn. staff Investment Client Support, 1988-90, mgr. investment reporting, 1991-93, mgr. devel., 1993-95; dir. Fin. Reporting Solutions, 1998-99; project mgr. CGI, Atlanta, 1999, dir. cons. svcs., 1999—2002, dir. outsourcing svcs., 2002—. Presenter in field. Den leader Cub Scouts, 1989-90, treas., 1990-95; head ofcl. Duluth Thunderbolts, 1994; mem. Gwinnett Swim League (sec. 1995-2003). Avocations: bridge, swimming, travel. Office: CGI 3740 Davinci Ct # 400 Norcross GA 30092-2670 E-mail: cathieben@worldnet.att.net., cathie.bennett@cgi.com.

BENNETT, CHARLES LEON, vocational and graphic arts educator; b. Salem, Oreg., Feb. 5, 1951; s. Theodore John and Cora Larena (Rowland) B.; m. Cynthia Alice Hostman, June 12, 1976 (div.); m. Lynn Marie Toland, Aug. 12, 1977 (div.); children: Mizzy Marie, Charles David.; m. Christina M. Crawford, Dec. 19, 1987 (div.); m. Iris J. Perrigo, Mar. 17, 2001. AS in Vocat. Tchr. Edn., Clackamas C.C., 1977; AS in Gen. Studies, Linn Benton C.C., 1979; BS in Gen. Studies, Ea. Oreg. State Coll., 1994. Tchr. printing Tongue Point Job Corps, Astorial, Oreg., 1979-80; tchr., chmn. dept. Portland (Oreg.) Pub. Schs., 1980—; owner, mgr. printing and pub. co. Portland, 1981-87. With AUS, 1970-72. Mem. NRA, Oreg. Vocat. Trade-Tech. Assn. (sept. chmn., pres. graphic arts divsn., Indsl. Educator of Yr. 1981-82), Oreg. Vocat. Assn. (Vocat. Tchr. of Yr. 1982-83), Graphic Arts Tech. Found., In-Plant Printing Mgmt. Assn., Internat. Graphic Arts Edn. Assn. (v.p. N.W. region VI), Oreg. Assn. Manpower Spl. Needs Pers., Oreg. Indsl. Arts Assn., Internat. Platform Assn., Nat. Assn. Quick Printers, Am. Vocat. Assn., Pacific Printing and Imaging Assn., Inplant Printing Mgmt. Assn., Portland Club Lithographers and Printing House Craftsmen. Republican. Home: 20295 S Unger Rd Beavercreek OR 97004-8884 Office: 546 NE 12th Ave Portland OR 97232-2719 E-mail: cbennett@aracnet.com., cbennett@pps.k12.or.us.

BENNETT, DELORES ELAINE (DEE BENNETT), elementary education educator; b. Talihina, Okla., Sept. 8, 1950; d. Delbert Raymond and Ona Irene (Harjochee) Logan; m. Calvin Loyd Bennett, July 24, 1970; 1 child, Jonathan Loyd. AS, Seminole (Okla.) Jr. Coll., 1975; BS, East Ctrl. U., 1981, MEd, 1985. Cert. elem. tchr., Okla., sch. counselor, Okla.; endorsed lang. arts, math, social studies, Okla. Tchr. 3d grade Seminole (Okla.) Pub. Schs., 1981-91, tchr. 1st grade, 1991—. Cons., pilot Growing Up Strong program U. Okla., Norman, 1988-89. Coord. Campaign State Rep. Danny Williams, Seminole, 1990. Mem. Okla. Edn. Assn. (zone 6, pres. elect 1992-93, pres. 1993-94, lobbying co-chair 1992—), Seminole Assn. Tchrs. (pub. rels. chair 1988-90, Dem. contact 1990-92, legis. chair 1990-92, treas. 1991, legis. chair 1993-94, pres. elect 1993-94, pres. 1994—), Phi Delta Kappa, Delta Kappa Gamma (com. chair 1988-90, music chair 1992—), C. of C. (edn. com. 1993—), Seminole Arts Coun. Democrat. Avocations: music, fishing, golfing, travel and politics. Home: 1215 Carson Dr Seminole OK 74868-2224 Office: Seminole Pub Schs PO Box 1031 Seminole OK 74818-1031

BENNETT, DOROTHY JEAN, art educator; b. Detroit, June 10, 1950; d. George Leonard and Shirley Isabell (Heston) Dunkirk; m. James Morgan Bennett, Nov. 6, 1976; children: Alex James, Brett Dunkirk, Kelly Anne. BA, Ea. Ill. U., 1974, MA, 1980, Tchr. Cert., 1988. Draftsperson Moore Bus. Forms, Charleston, Ill., 1973-86; art tchr. Lakeland Coll., Mattoon, Ill., 1989, Crestwood Sch., Paris, Ill., 1989-94, Jefferson Sch., Charleston, Ill., 1994—, Ea. Ill. U., Charleston, 1998—. Visual arts dir. Coles County Arts Coun., Charleston, 1988—; regional inst. com. Regional Supt. of Schs., Charleston, 1991-94; tchr. Ill. Art Edn. Conf. Workshops, Charleston, 1988, 91, 93, 95, 96, 99, 2003; lectr. Nat. Art Edn. Conf., Phoenix, 1992, Houston, 1995, San Francisco, 1996, Chgo., 1998, Washington, 1999, L.A., 2000, Mpls., 2003; tchr. sculpture summer art sch. Ea. Ill. U., 1994—, dir. summer art sch., 1997—, tchr. adult art sch., 1996, tchr. minority sch., 1995-98; tchr. Tarble Art Ctr. Workshop, 1988—. Mem.: NEA, Ill. Edn. Assn., Nat. Art Edn. Assn., Ill. Art Edn. Assn. (multicultural specialist for ctrl. region 1996—, Ill. Art Tchr. award in conjunction with Ea. Ill. U. 1994, Ill. Elem. Art Educator of Yr. 2002). Methodist. Avocations: art, aerobics, sewing, biking, knitting.

BENNETT, EDWARD MOORE, historian, educator; b. Dixon, Ill., Sept. 28, 1927; s. J. Frank and Marguerite Marion (Moore) B.; m. Margery Mae Harder, Sept. 3, 1950; 1 son, Michael Dana. BA, Butler U., 1952; MA, U. Ill., 1956, PhD, 1961. Teaching asst. U. Ill., 1956-60; instr. Tex. A. and M. U., 1960-61, Wash. State U., Pullman, 1961-62, asst. prof., 1962-66, assoc. prof., 1967-71, prof. history, 1971-94, prof. emeritus, 1994—, chmn. faculty exec. com., 1970-71. Ford Found. Community Seminar lectr., 1965; Peace Corps lectr. on U.S.-Indian fgn. policy, U. Wis., Milw. summer 1967; adviser on Democratic Party platform planks on fgn. policy for Whitman County and State of Wash., 1964-68; mem. adv. council Wash. Council on Higher Edn., 1970-74; pres. Pacific 8 Athletic Conf., 1973, Pacific 10 Athletic Conf., 1980, Pacific-10 Athletic Conf., 1990; mem. Theodore Roosevelt award jury Nat. Collegiate Athletic Assn., 1973-76; participant U.S.-Soviet Symposium on origins World War II and Am.-Soviet relations, Moscow, 1986, Franklin D. Roosevelt Library, 1987. Author: Recognition of Russia: An American Foreign Policy Dilemma, 1970, (with Howard C. Payne and Raymond Callahan) As The Storm Clouds Gathered: European Perceptions of American Foreign Policy in the 1930's, 1979, Franklin D. Roosevelt and the Search for Security: American-Soviet Relations, 1933-1939, 1985, Franklin D. Roosevelt and the Search for Victory: American-Soviet Relations, 1939-45, 1990, Separated By a Common Language: Franklin Delano Roosevelt and Anglo-American Relations, 1933-1939: The Roosevelt-Chamberlain Rivalry, 2002; editor: Polycentrism: Growing Dissidence in the Community Bloc?, 1967; co-editor co-author: Diplomats in Crisis: U.S.-Chinese-Japanese Relations, 1919-1941, 1974; contbg. editor: Annotated Bibliography American Foreign Relations, 1983—; contbr. to Ency. Am. Fgn. Policy, 1978, Notable U.S. Ambassadors Since 1775, 1997. Served with AUS, 1946-47; Served with USAF, 1952-54. Recipient Faculty of Yr. award Wash. State U., 1979 Mem. Am. Hist. Assn. (mem. exec. council Pacific Coast br. 1975-78), Orgn. Am. Historians, AAUP, Soc. for Historians of Am. Fgn. Relations, (Graebner Prize com. 1985-87, chmn. 1986-87), Tau Kappa Epsilon, Phi Alpha Theta. Home: 1240 SE Harvest Dr Pullman WA 99163-2443

BENNETT, ELSIE MARGARET, music school administrator; b. Detroit, Mar. 30, 1919; d. Sy and Ida (Carp) Blum; m. Morton Bennett, June 20, 1937 (dec.); children: Ronald, Kenneth. Cert., Ganapal Conservatory Detroit, 1941; B.Mus. in Theory, Wayne State U., 1945; M.A. in Music Edn., Columbia U., 1946; postgrad. Columbia U., Manhattan Sch. Music. Music studio mgr., tchr. Bennett Music Sch., Bklyn., 1946—, dir. 1946—; music arranger, 1946—; tchr. Schiff Sch. Music, 1972-80, owner, 1972—; tchr. Robotti Accordion Acad. and Pkwy. Music Sch., 1945-46; owner Margolies Sch. Music, Acad. of Music Sch.; editor Accordion World Mag., 1945-56; works include: Easy Solos for Accordion, 1946; Bass Solo Primer, 1948; Hebrew and Jewish Songs and Dances for Accordion, 1959, Vol. 1, 1951, Vol. 2, 1953; Hanon for Accordion, 1953; Accordion Music in the Home, 1953; Folk Melodies for Accordion, 1954; Five Finger Melodies for Accordion, 1954; First Steps in Scaleland for Accordion, 1956; First Steps in Chordland for Accordion, Vol. 1, 1961, Vol. II, 1961. Mem. Bklyn. Community Council. Mem. Am. Accordionists Assn. (governing bd., pres. 1973-74, plaque, 1962, service to governing bd. award 1942-60, Silver Cup 1974-75, Dedicated Svc. award 1997), Bklyn. Music Tchrs. Guild (dir., past sec.), Accordion Tchrs. Guild, L.I. Music Tchrs. Assn.

BENNETT, GEORGE NELSON, biochemistry educator; b. St. Edward, Nebr., Oct. 26, 1946; s. Glenn Nelson and Esther Adelaide (McBride) B.; m. Lolin T. Wang, Dec. 11, 1983; children: Alan N., Neal K. BS, U. Nebr., 1968; PhD, Purdue U., 1974. Postdoctoral fellow Stanford U., Palo Alto, Calif., 1975-78; asst. prof. Rice U., Houston, 1978-84, assoc. prof., 1984-92, prof., 1992—. Grantee NIH, NSF, USDA, Dept. of Energy, Army Rsch. OFfice, R.A. Welch Found. Mem. Am. Chem. Soc., Am. Soc. for Microbiology, Fedn. Soc. Exptl. Biology. Office: Rice Univ Biochemistry & Cell Biology 6100 Main St Houston TX 77005-1892

BENNETT, JANICE LYNN, publisher, educator; b. Chgo., Jan. 31, 1951; d. Harry Albert and Dorothy Marie Goodman; m. James Stephen Bennett, Oct. 6, 1973; children: Scott James, Anne Christine. BA in Graphic Design, No. Ill. U., 1973; BA in Spanish, Met. State Coll. of Denver, 1993; MA in Spanish Lit., U. Colo., 1997. Graphic artist Montgomery Ward, Chgo., 1973-74; asst. prodn. mgr., art dir. Crow Publs., Denver, 1977-80; owner, graphic artist, typographer Charter Graphics, Classic Typography, Denver, 1980-89; Spanish instr. Met. State Coll. of Denver, 1995—2000; pub., editor, author Libri de Hispania, Littleton, Colo., 2000—. Translator Denver Pub. Schs., Greenlee Elem., Denver, 1993-94; translator, interpreter World Youth Day, Denver, 1993; bilingual tchg. asst. Knapp Elem., Denver, 1990-91; freelance writer Denver Cath. Register. Author: Guía práctica a la literatura, el análisis y la redacción, 1998; author, pub., editor: Sacred Blood, Sacred Image: The Sudarium of Oviedo, New Evidence for the Authenticity of the Shroud of Turin, 2001, St. Laurence and the Holy Grail: The Story of the Holy Chalice of Valencia, 2002. Mem. MLA, Altar and Rosary Soc. (pres. 2000-01, 2002-03), Am. Assn. of Tchrs. of Spanish and Portuguese, Pub. Mktg. Assn., Cath. Book Pub. Assn., Spanish Ctr. for Sindonology, Sigma Delta Pi, Phi Sigma Iota. Avocations: traveling, photography, piano, biblical studies, drawing and painting. Office: Libri de Hispania PO Box 270262 Littleton CO 80127-0005 Fax: 303-973-3014. E-mail: acbc@sprintmail.com.

BENNETT, KATHLEEN MAROURNEEN, elementary school educator; b. Harlingen, Tex., Jan. 26, 1943; d. Owen James Bennett and Betty Margaret Bell. BS, No. Mich. U., 1966. Cert. elem. edn. Mich. Tchr. Head

Start, Iron Mountain, Mich., 1966, Iron Mountain Pub. Schs., 1966, Gladstone (Mich.) Area Schs., 1967. Chair Sch. Improvement Team, Gladstone, Mich., 1988—90; dir. musicals various elem. schs. Actor: Area Children's Theatre. Active Recreation Adv. Bd., Escanaba, Mich., 1980—82; dir. children's musicals; actor children's theater. Named Disting. Alumni, No. Mich. U., 1988. Mem.: AAUW (pres., Outstanding Educator Escanaba br. 1980), Mich. Edn. Assn. (sec. 1977—79, Outstanding Person in Edn. award 2003). Democrat. Episcopalian. Avocations: reading, walking, movies, interior decorating, travel. Home: 321 S 6th St Escanaba MI 49829

BENNETT, MARY ELLEN, tax consultant, accounting consultant, business consultant; b. Artesia, N.Mex., Aug. 11, 1953; d. George E. and Alice V. (Youngman) B. BA with honors, Rutgers U., Camden, N.J., 1975, MEd with honors, 1978; JD in Tax Law magna cum laude, LaSalle U., 1996. Cert. secondary social studies tchr., supr., prin., N.J.; cert. tax profl., practitioner in taxation. Tchr. history honors program Camden Cath. High Sch., Cherry Hill, N.J., 1987-89; tchr. history Camden County Vocat.-Tech. High Sch., Pennsauken, N.J., 1975-87; owner Aligeb Tax & Acctg. Cons. Mem. Bradley Commn. on History in Schs. Mem. ABA-LSD (taxation sect.), Am. Hist. Assn., Nat. Soc. for History Edn., Orgn. History Tchrs., N.J. Coun. for Social Studies, Nat. Soc. Tax Profls., Inst. Cert. Practitioners, Nat. Notary Assn. (notary signing agt.), Athenaeum, Kappa Delta Pi, Phi Alpha Delta, Tau Alpha Chi. Home: 214 Belle Arbor Dr Cherry Hill NJ 08034-1803

BENNETT, MAX DIAL, internal medicine educator; b. Clovis, N.Mex., June 30, 1944; s. Reece L. and Lila M. (Boss) B.; m. Pamela Ann Montgomery, Aug. 4, 1965; children: Nolan Keene, Meredith Kirsten. BA in Chemistry, Eastern N.Mex. U., 1966; MHA, U. Mich., 1969; MA in Econs., Johns Hopkins U., 1971, PhD in Econs., 1973. Adminstrv. resident Johns Hopkins Hosp., Balt., 1967-69; asst. prof. Purdue U., West Lafayette, Ind., 1973-74; asst. v.p. health svcs. U. N.Mex., Albuquerque, 1974-77, assoc. dir. med. ctr., 1978-93, assoc. prof. econs., prof. family medicine, 1993—. V.p. Interstudy, Mpls., 1974; cons. Nat. U. Mex., 1982-88; cons. Dept. HEW, Washington, 1972-76, Gov.'s Office, Santa Fe, 1979-94. Author: New Mexico Statistical Summary 1977-1992; contbr. articles to profl. jours. Co-chmn. Gov.'s Task Force on Rural Med. Practice, 1979-82; chmn. Gov.'s Health Policy Adv. Com., 1987-90; dir. N.Mex. Health Resources Registry, 1976-90. Recipient Outstanding Alumni award Eastern N.Mex. U., 1983. Mem. APHA, Am. Econ. Assn., Assn. Am. Med. Colls. (chair we. region Group on Instnl. Planning 1981-82). Democrat. Avocations: water, snow skiing. Home: 13206 Manitoba Dr NE Albuquerque NM 87111-2955 Office: Sch of Medicine Family Practice Ctr Albuquerque NM 87131-0001

BENNETT, MILDRED LORLINE, elementary school educator; b. Pierce, W.Va., Jan. 17, 1931; d. Pete L. and Lectie Lorline (Lipscomb) Bava; m. William Von Bennett, 1951; 1 child, William Albert. BS, Davis & Elkins Coll., 1978; MA, W.Va. U., 1983, postgrad. Cert. elem. edn. tchr. Title I reading aide Tucker County Bd. Edn., Parsons, W.Va., 1963-78, elem. tchr., 1978-96. Mem. book com. Tucker County Bd. Edn., Blue Ribbon Math. com.; mem. curriculum com. Parsons Elem./Mid. Sch., 1991-95. V.p. Tucker County chpt. Am. Cancer Soc., Parsons, 1982-90, PTO, Parsons; primary tchr. Sunday Sch., 1987-95; mem. Tucker County Chorus, 1990-92. Mem. AAUW, Nat. Presveta, W.Va. Edn. Assn., Slovene Lodge, Foresters. Democrat. Avocations: music, piano, travel, reading. Home: 302 Pennsylvania Ave Parsons WV 26287-1151 Office: WVa U PO Box 6009 Morgantown WV 26506-6009

BENNETT, PAUL EDMOND, engineering educator; b. Somerville, Mass., June 27, 1924; s. William Francis and Ellen Elizabeth (Cotter) B.; m. Carolyn Stevens Gove, June 16, 1956; children: Cynthia, David P., Steven W. BSEE, U. Mass., 1950; MSEE, Pa. State U., 1974. Registered profl. engr., Pa. Electronic engr. USN Underwater Sound Lab., New London, Conn., 1950-51, Woods Hole (Mass.) Oceanographic Inst., 1951-55; sr. engr., staff engr., sect. mgr. HRB-Singer, State College, Pa., 1956-67; rsch. assoc. Ordnance Rsch. Lab., State College, 1967-72; rsch. asst. Ionosphere Rsch. Lab., University Park, Pa., 1972-74; staff engr. Locus, State College, 1974-76; prof. engring. tech. U. So. Ind., Evansville, 1976-92, prof. emeritus, 1992—, adj. prof., 1992-95. Mem. Ind. Vocat. Tech. Coll. Joint Adv. Com., 1987-92. Author: Advanced Electrical Circuit Analysis, 1991; contbr. articles to profl. jours. Coord. vols. Peregrine Hacking Project Ind. Dept. Natural Resources, 1994; steering com. Friends Ayrshire, 1997—, Audubon-Ind., 2000-01; Hoosier Audubon Coun. del., 1997—, Ind. IBA tech. com., 1999; mem. citizen adv. com. Evansville Urban Transp., 1999; mem. Evansville Philharm. Chorus. Mem. IEEE (faculty sponsor U. So. Ind. student br. 1978-85, 91, mem. regional student affairs com. 1978-85, chair sect. ednl. activities com. 1978-79, sect. chair 1979-80, chair sect. membership com. and nominations com. 1980-81, exec. bd. 1978-84, bd. govs. 1980-84), ACM (reviewer computing revs.), Am. Soc. for Engring. Edn. (reviewer Jour. Engring. Tech. 1986-97, sect. moderator internat. divsn. ann. conf. 1987, vice chair programs-elect internat. divsn. 1989-90, program internat. divsn. 1990-91, chair 1991-93, past chair 1993-95), Nat. Audubon Soc. (steering com. Ind. State office), Evansville Audubon Soc. (bd. dirs.), Hoosier Audubon Coun. (del.), Tau Beta Pi, Tau Alpha Pi (chpt. sponsor 1980-92). Avocation: birdwatching. Home: 7321 Washington Ave Evansville IN 47715-4440 E-mail: pcbennett1@mindspring.com.

BENNETT, PETER BRIAN, researcher, hyperbaric medicine; b. Portsmouth, Hampshire, Eng., June 12, 1931; s. Charles Risby and Doris Isobel (Peckham) B.; m. Margaret Camellia Rose, July 7, 1956; children: Caroline Susan, Christopher Charles BSc, U. London, 1951; PhD, U. Southampton, 1964, DSc, 1984; Dr. honoris causa, U. de la Mediterranean, France, 2001. Asst. head surg. sect. Royal Navy Physiol. Lab., Alverstoke, Eng., 1953-56, head inert gas narcosis sect., 1953-66; dep. dir., prin. sci. officer, head pressure physiology sect. Royal Naval Physiol. Lab., Alverstoke, 1968-72; head pressure physiology group Can. Def. and Civil Inst. for Environ. Rsch., Toronto, Ont., 1966-68; prof. biomed. engring. Duke U., Durham, N.C., 1972-75, assoc. prof. physiology, 1975—, prof. anesthesiology, 1972—, dir. rsch. dept. anesthesiology Med. Ctr., 1973-84, dir. Nat. Divers Alert Network, 1980—; dep. dir. F.G. Hall Lab. Environ. Rsch., 1973-74; co-dir. F.G. Hall Lab. Environ. Research, 1974-77, dir., 1977-88; sr. dir. Hyperbaric Ctr., 1988—. Cons. in field Author: The Aetiology of Compressed Air Intoxication and Inert Gas Narcosis, 1966; author, editor: The Physiology and Medicine of Diving and Compressed Air Work, 1969, Russian edit., 1987, 4th edit., 1993; contbr. over 200 articles to profl. jours. With RAF, 1951-53. Recipient Letter of Commendation, Pres. Ronald Reagan, 1981, Sci. award Underwater Soc. Am., 1980, Leonard Greenstone Safety award Nat. Assn. Underwater Instrs., 1985, 1st Prince Tomohito of Mikasa Japan prize, 1990, Craig Hoffman Meml. award, 1992, Dan Seap Mentor award, 1998, Ernst & Young Entrepreneur of Yr. in Life Scis. award, NC and SC, 2002, Reaching Out award Diving Equipment Mfrs., 2002. Fellow Nat. Underwater Explorers Club; mem. Undersea Med. Soc. (pres. 1975-76, mem. exec. com. 1972-75, editor jour. 1976-79, 1st Oceaneering Internat. award 1975, Albert R. Behnke award 1983), Am. Physiol. Soc., European Undersea Biomed. Soc., Russian Acad. Sci. (fgn. mem., Pavlov medal 2001), Aerospace Med. Soc., Marine Tech. Soc., Croatian Undersea and Hyperbaric Med. Soc. (hon.), Nat. Acad. Scuba Educators (Meritorious Svc. award 1997). Avocations: gardening, swimming, boating. Home: 213 Lancaster Dr Chapel Hill NC 27517-3430 Office: Duke U Med Ctr Divers Alert Network 6 W Colony Pl Durham NC 27705

BENNETT, ROBERT M. educational association administrator; m. Audrey Bennett; children: Maurine, Andrew. BA in English, U. Notre Dame, 1962; MS in Interdisciplinary Studies, SUNY, Buffalo, 1977; grad. CEO Inst., Harvard U., 1984; grad. CEO Leadership, U. Mich., 1987. Mgr. dept. urban planning Buffalo Area C. of C., 1965—69; sec.'s liaison to pvt. sector U.S. Dept. Health, Edn. and Welfare, 1969—70; dir. Fed./State Aid-County Execs. Office Erie County Govt., 1970—71; dir. employment and tng. svcs. Mayor's Office City of Buffalo, 1971—73; dir. grant devel. United Way Buffalo and Erie County, 1973—77, adminstrv. v.p., 1977—85, pres., 1985—2000; sr. policy advisor Grad. Sch. Edn. SUNY, Buffalo, 2001—. Disting. lectr. Niagara U., 2001—; instr. English Erie C.C., 1970; instr. cmty. planning Sch. Mgmt. SUNY, Buffalo, 1974—78, instr. grantsmanship Sch. Urban Affairs, 1979—80, instr. adminstrn. and mgmt. in social svcs. Grad. Sch. Edn./Social Work, 2000; instr. human svc. mgmt. Medaille Coll., 1980—82; instr. ednl. policy Buffalo State Coll.-Grad. Sch. Edn., 1999; instr. policy and politics in edn. Grad. Sch. Edn. Niagara U., 2001. Co-chair Domestic Violence Coalition, 1979—81; adv. coun./city and county chair CETA, 1979—81; coord. Econ. Action Task Force/Erie County, 1982—83; chair Emergency Food and Shelter Program, 1982—2000; dir. Study on Hunger, 1984; co-chair News Neediest Bd., 1984—2000; exec. dir. Goodfellows Found., 1985—2000; coord. Comprehensive Needs Assessment/Erie County, 1992—93; trustee Statler Found., 1992—; chair program com. Pvt. Industry Coun., 1992—95; strategic planning advisor St. Christopher Sch., 1993; founder Success by Six, 1993; founder, coord. Family Support Ctrs. in Schs., 1994—2000; participant Leadership Buffalo, 1994; mem. pres. adv. coun. SUNY, Buffalo, 1995—; profl. adv. com. chair United Way N.Y. State, 1996; chair Kids Voting, 1996—2000; chair human svcs. com. State of the Region, 1998; founder, bd. mem. Edn. Fund Greater Buffalo, 1998—; mem. Joint Schs. Constrn. Bd., 1999—; co-chair Erie County Task Force on the Performance Gap, 1999—; chair Erie County Pub. Benefits Task Force, 2000—; Eucharistic min. Home Vis. Program St. Christopher Parish, 1980—, strategic planning advisor, 1995, 2001—; bd. mem. Erie C.C., 1992—95; dir. Robert J. Donough Fund, 1992—; mem. higher edn. com. N.Y. State Bd. Regents, 1995—, mem. VESID com., 1995—, co-chair task force on the performance gap, 1995—, chair quality com., 1995—, chancellor, 2002—; bd. mem. Shea's Performing Arts Ctr., 2000—, Oishei Found., 2000—, EPIC, 2000—, Goodfellows, 2001—; cons. for strategic planning, grant writing, and fund devel. for pub. and not-for-profit orgns. Home: 201 Millwood Ln Tonawanda NY 14150*

BENNETT, RODNEY DEE, music educator; b. Wichita Falls, Tex., Mar. 7, 1958; s. Vernon Clifton and Beulah Lee (Johnson) B.; m. Marilyn K. Spencer, Aug. 15, 1980; 1 child, Ronald David. MusB, B of Music Edn., Midwestern State U., 1982; MusM, Ea. N.Mex. U., 1998. All-level music cert., Tex. Field musician USMC, Camp Pendleton, Calif., 1976-78; equipment mgr. Midwestern State Univ. Band, Wichita Falls, Tex., 1978-82; dir. bands Munday (Tex.) Ind. Sch. Dist., 1983—. Pvt. music tchr., Wichita Falls, 1980—; music adjudicator Tex. Music Adjudication Assn., Pleasanton, Tex., 1991—. Named Citizen of Yr., Munday C. of C., 1993. Mem. Assn. Tex. Small Sch. Bands, Tex. Music Educators Assn. (region II band chmn. 1994—, Leadership and Achievement award 1994, 2000, Honor Condr.-Honor Band 1994, 2000), Nat. Band Assn. (Citation of Excellence 1993, 2000), Am. Sch. Band Dirs. Assn., Phi Beta Mu. Baptist. Avocations: photography, model trains, railroad history. Home: PO Box 776 Munday TX 76371-0776 Office: Munday Ind Sch Dist PO Box 300 Munday TX 76371-0300

BENNETT, SHARON KAY, music educator; b. West Jefferson, Ohio; BMus, Eastman Sch. Music, 1960, MMus, 1962. Asst. prof. U. Iowa, Iowa City, 1980-84; from asst. prof. to prof. Capital U., Columbus, Ohio, 1992—. Adj. lectr. Otterbein Coll., Westerville, Ohio, 1986-87, Capital U., 1985-92; resident coloratura Nurnberg (Germany) Opera, 1970-73, Hamburg (Germany) State Opera, 1973-76; resident guest artist Scottish Opera, Glasgow, 1976-77; presenter symposium. Author: 40 Vocalises, 1993, Class Voice Simplified, 1994. Recipient 1st place Iowa Symphony competition, 1981; named to Women of Achievement, YWCA, 1986; Rockefeller Found. grantee, N.Y.C., 1966-68; Old Gold fellow U. Iowa, Iowa City, N.Y. and Paris; Capital U. faculty devel. grantee, 1995. Mem.: Music Tchrs. Nat. Assn. (nat. cert.), Coll. Music Soc., Nat. Assn. Tchrs. of Singing, LWV of Met. Columbus (v.p. for voter svc.), Sigma Alpha Iota (sec. 1985—87). Avocations: gardening, painting.

BENNETT, SHIRLEY ANN, maintenance executive, business technologist educator; b. Buffalo, Nov. 5, 1952; d. Edward Stoklosa and Florence (Ulanowski) Valin; m. Jeffrey Michael Bennett, July 3, 1975; children: Tara, Shauna, Shira, Brett, Eric. BS in Edn., SUNY Coll. at Buffalo, Buffalo, 1974; MBA, SUNY, Buffalo, 1982. Cert. tchr., N.Y. Tchr. Niagara Falls (N.Y.) Bd. Edn., 1974-75, Kensington Bus. Inst., Buffalo, 1976-80; asst. prof. SUNY, Buffalo, 1980—. Mem. Epsilon Delta Epsilon, Iota Lambda Sigma (Alpha Lambda chpt.). Home: 76 Alran Dr Williamsville NY 14221-1409 Office: SUNY at Buffalo EOC 465 Washington St Buffalo NY 14203-1707

BENNETT, WILLIAM RALPH, JR., physicist, educator; b. Jersey City, Jan. 30, 1930; s. William Ralph and Viola (Schreiber) B.; m. Frances Commins, Dec. 11, 1952; children: Jean, William Robert, Nancy. AB, Princeton U., 1951; MA, PhD, Columbia U., 1957; MA (hon.), Yale U., 1965; D.Sc. (hon.), U. New Haven, 1975. Rsch. asst. physics Columbia Radiation Lab., 1952-54; mem. Pupin Cyclotron Group, 1954-57; mem. faculty Yale U., New Haven, 1957-59, 62—, prof. physics and applied sci., 1965-72, Charles Baldwin Sawyer prof. engring. and applied sci., prof. physics, 1972-98, prof. emeritus, 1998—, fellow Berkeley Coll., 1963-81, master Silliman Coll., 1981-87, life fellow Silliman Coll., 1981—. Tech. staff Bell Telephone Labs., Murray Hill, NJ, 1959—62; cons. Tech. Rsch. Group, Melville, NY, 1962—67, Inst. Def. Analysis, Washington, 1963—70; vis. scientist Am. Inst. Physics Vis. Scientist Program, 1963—64; vis. prof. Brandels Summer Inst. Theoretical Physics, 1969; cons. mem. bd. dirs. Laser Scis. Corp., Bethel, Conn., 1968—71; mem. adv. panels atomic physics and astrophysics Nat. Bur. Stds., 1964—69; cons. CBS Labs., Stamford, Conn., 1967—68, AVCO Corp., 1978—81, Reeves Sci. Co., New Haven, 1989—91, Oak Ridge Assn. Univs., Washington, 1991—92, MCG Internat., New Haven, 1992—93, Kahn Electronics, NY, 1998—2000, Premier Heart, 1999, U. Cin., 2000; mem. lab. adv. bd. for rsch. Naval Rsch. Adv. Com., 1968—78; guest Soviet Acad. Scis., 1967, 69, 79; rschr. gas lasers and atomic physics, gravitational physics, applications of computers to med. diagnostics. Author: Introduction to Computer Applications, 1976, Scientific and Engineering Problem Solving With the Computer, 1976, The Physics of Gas Lasers, 1977, Atomic Gas Laser Transition Data: A Critical Evaluation, 1979, Health and Low Frequency Electromagnetic Fields, 1994; editl. adv. bd. Jour. Quantum Electronics, 1965-69; guest editor Applied Optics, 1965. Recipient Western Electric Fund award for outstanding tchg. Am. Assn. Engring. Educators, 1977, Outstanding Patent award R & D Coun. N.J., 1977, Eli Whitney Patent award Conn. Patent Lawyers Assn., 1994, DeVane medal Phi Beta Kappa, 2000; fellow Alfred P. Sloan Found., 1967, Guggenheim Found., 1967, John Fenders fellow, 1987. Fellow IEEE (life, Morris Liebmann award 1965), Am. Phys. Soc., Optical Soc. Am.; mem. Sigma Xi.

BENNIN, HOPE ELIZABETH, communication educator; b. Columbus, Wis., Jan. 23, 1959; d. Eugene Donald and Sally Ann (Virchow) B. BS in English, BS in Communication, U. Wis., Stevens Point, 1982, MA in Communication, 1987. Adminstrv. asst. C.Y. Allen/Profl. Comm. Svcs., Stevens Point, 1982-84; LTE office asst. U. Wis., Stevens Point, 1984-87, lectr. divsn. comms., 1984-86; tchr. summer sch. Stevens Point Sch. Dist., 1984-87; tchr. lang. arts St. Paul Luth. Sch., Stevens Point, 1983-87; instr. Prestonsburg (Ky.) C.C., 1987-90, asst. prof., 1990-92, assoc. prof. comm., 1992-99, prof. comm., 1999—. Tchr. summer sch. Stevens Point Sch. Dist., 1984-87; coord. acad. grants and assessment, 1996-98. Author poetry pub. in N.Y. Poetry Anthology, Disting. Poets of Am., Whispers in the Wind, Best Poets of 1995. Corr. sec. Jenny Wiley Festival Bd., Prestonsburg, 1992-95; judge KCTE Writing Competition, Ky., 1987—, Young Authors Competition, Prestonsburg, 1987—; presenter Candlelight Vigil/Desert Storm, Prestonsburg, 1991. Recipient Excellence Award for Tchg. Nat. Inst. Staff and Orgnl. Devel., 1993, 99; U. Ky. C.C. Sys. grantee, 1990, 91, 95, Great Tchr. grantee, 1988, AACC Svc. Learning grantee, 1995. Mem. ASCD, Nat. Coun. Instrnl. Adminstrs., Nat. Comm. Assn., S. St. Comm. Assn., Ky. Comm. Assn., Nat. Coun. Tchrs. English, Ky. Coun. Tchrs. English, Ky. ASCD. Avocations: reading, writing, ceramics, sewing, playing cards. Office: Prestonsburg Cmty College One Bert T Combs Dr Prestonsburg KY 41653 E-mail: Hope.Bennin@kctcs.edu.

BENNING, JOSEPH RAYMOND, principal; b. Streator, Ill., May 23, 1956; s. Joseph Charles and Shirley Ann (Smith) B.; m. Katherine Marie Turner, Apr. 24, 1976; children: Jennifer Nichole, Joseph Donald. BA, Augustana Coll, 1978; MS in Edn., No. Ill. U., 1988. Cert. state supr., teaching, Ill. Tchr., coach Fulton (Ill.) High Sch., 1978-79; recreation dir. Fulton Recreation Corp., 1979; tchr., coach Streator (Ill.) High Sch., 1979-80, Woodland High Sch., Streator, 1980-83; program dir. Ill. State Bd. Edn., Ottawa, 1983-85; prin. St. Mary Grade Sch., Streator, 1985-89; assoc. supt. schs. Cath. Diocese Peoria, Ill., 1989-91, supt. schs., 1991-94; prin. St. Bede Acad., Peru, Ill., 1994-99, St. Columba Sch., Ottawa, Ill., 1999—. Pres. Streator Youth Football League, 1984-90; adv. bd. Streator High Sch., 1985-89; prins. adv. bd. Cath. Diocese Peoria, 1987-89. Recipient CJ McDonald award Streator Youth Football League, 1989. Mem. ASCD, Nat. Cath. Edn. Assn., Nat. Assn. Secondary Sch. Prin., Nat. Assn. Elem. Sch. Prin., Ill. Elem. Sch. Assn., Cath. Conf. Ill., KC. Roman Catholic. Avocations: sports, music. Office: St Columba Sch 1110 Lasalle Ottawa IL 61350 E-mail: benningjr@hotmail.com.

BENNINGFIELD, TROY LEE, language arts educator; b. Lebanon, Ky., Sept. 3, 1969; s. Leroy and Betty Lou (Adams) B. BA, U. Ky., 1992. Cert. tchr. Ky. Facilitator, scorer Advanced Systems in Measurement and Evaluation, Inc., Louisville, 1992-93; program presenter The Sci. Ctr., Louisville, 1992-93; English, journalism tchr. Newport (Ky.) Ind. Schs., 1993-97, Washington County Schs., Springfield, Ky., 1997—2001, Taylor County Schs., Campbellsville, Ky., 2001—. Mem. Nat. coun. of Tchrs. of English, U. Ky. Alumni Assn., Ky. H.S. Journalism Assn. (steering com. 1997). Democrat. Baptist. Home: 1425 Bradfordsville Rd Lebanon KY 40033-9718 Office: Taylor County HS 300 Ingram Ave Campbellsville KY 42718

BENNION, JOHN STRADLING, engineering educator, consultant; b. Salt Lake City, Sept. 19, 1954; s. Mervyn S. Jr. and LaRee (Stradling) B. BS in Chemistry, BSChemE, U. Utah, 1987, MS in Nuclear Engring., 1990, PhD in Nuclear Engring., 1996. Lic. profl. engr., Utah, Idaho; registered radiation protection technologist Nat. Registry of Radiation Protection Technologists; lic. sr. reactor operator U.S. Nuclear Regulatory Commn.; cert. health physicist; diplomate environ. engr. Carpenter various cos., Utah, 1974-86; sr. reactor engr. U. Utah Nuclear Engring. Lab., Salt Lake City, 1987-93; instr. mech. engring. dept. U. Utah, Salt Lake City, 1992-98; asst. prof. Coll. Engring. Idaho State U., Pocatello, 1995-2000; reactor adminstr. Idaho State U. Coll. Engring., 1996—2001, reactor mgr., 2001—; assoc. prof. coll. engring. Idaho State U., Pocatello, 2000—. Author tech. papers and reports. Mem. AAAS, ASME, NSPE, AAUP, Am. Soc. Engring. Edn., Am. Nuclear Soc., Am. Soc. Quality, Am. Acad. Health Physics, Am. Acad. Environ. Engrs., Idaho Acad. Sci., Health Physics Soc., Internat. Soc. Radiation Physics, Phi Kappa Phi, Alpha Nu Sigma, Pi Tau Sigma, Tau Beta Pi, Sigma Xi. Republican. Mem. LDS Church. Office: Idaho State U Coll of Engring PO Box 8060 Pocatello ID 83209-0001

BENNION, JOHN WARREN, urban education educator; b. Salt Lake City, Nov. 25; s. M. Lynn and Katherine Bennion; m. Sylvia Lustig; children: Philip, Stanford, David, Bryan, Grant, Andrew. BS in Philosophy, English, U. Utah, 1961, MA in Edn. Adminstrn., 1962; PhD in Edn. Adminstrn., Ohio State U., 1966. Tchr. Granite High Sch., Salt Lake City, 1961-63; asst. instr. Ohio State U., Columbus, 1963-64, adminstrv. asst., 1965-66; adminstrv. intern Parma (Ohio) Sch. Dist., 1964-65; asst. supt. Elgin (Ill.) Pub. Schs., 1966-68; asst. prof. edn. adminstrn. Ind. U., Bloomington, 1968-69; supt. Brighton Cen. Schs., Rochester, N.Y., 1969-79, Bloomington (Minn.) Pub. Schs., 1979-80, Provo (Utah) Sch. Dist., 1980-85, Salt Lake City Schs., 1985-94; prof. urban edn., dir. Utah Edn. Consortium U. Utah, Salt Lake City, 1994—. Dir. Utah Urban Sch. Alliance, Salt Lake City; ednl. cons. Comprehensive Sch. Reform, Salt Lake City. Mem. ASCD, Assn. Early Childhood Edn., Am. Assn. Sch. Adminstrs. (Nat. Superintendent of Yr. award 1992, Disting. Svc. award 2002), Phi Delta Kappa, Rotary. Home: 1837 Harvard Ave Salt Lake City UT 84108-1804 Office: Utah Urban Sch Alliance 1865 S Main St Ste 22 Salt Lake City UT 84115-2045

BENOIT, PHILIP GROSVENOR, communications executive, educator, writer; b. Syracuse, N.Y., June 11, 1944; s. Paul Grosvenor and Doris Louise (Pond) B.; m. Candace Gail Blohm, Sept. 11, 1971; children: Kimberly Whitney, Marie Suzanne. BA, St. Lawrence U., 1966; MA, SUNY-Oswego, 1973. Asst. prof. communications SUNY-Oswego, 1971-79; dir. pub. rels. Hartwick Coll., Oneonta, N.Y., 1979-84; dir. comms. Dickinson Coll., Carlisle, Pa., 1984-96; dir. pub. affairs Middlebury Coll., Vt., 1996—. Chmn. bd. dirs. Ctr. Media Pub. Interest, New Canaan, Conn., 1993—. Author: (with Carl Hausman) Do Your Own Public Relations, 1983, Radio Station Operations, 1989, Positive Public Relations, 1990, (with O'Donnell and Hausman) Announcing: Broadcast Communicating Today, 5th edit., 2003, Modern Radio Production, 6th edit., 2003. Served to capt. U.S. Army, 1966-69. Decorated Bronze Star. Avocations: photography, music. Home: 517 High St Bridport VT 05734-9500 Office: Middlebury Coll Munford Hse Office Pub Affairs 139 S Main St Middlebury VT 05753-1442 E-mail: benoit@middlebury.edu.

BENOVITZ, MADGE KLEIN, civic volunteer; b. Wilkes-Barre, Pa., Nov. 26, 1934; d. Nathan and Esther (Miller) Klein; m. Burton S. Benovitz, Sept. 5, 1954; 1 child, Jane. Student, Cornell U., 1952-54, U. Pa., 1955; AB, Wilkes U., 1956. Bd. dirs. King's Coll., Wilkes-Barre, Pa., exec. com. mem., acad. and profl. affairs com. mem., chmn. phys. plant com., 1980-86, chmn. acad. affairs com., 1995-98; bd. dirs. Leadership Wilkes-Barre, 1981-83, organizing com. mem., 1981, mentor, 1984, 86, 87; mem. exec. com. Econ. Devel. Coun. Northeastern Pa., 1971-78, tax task force mem., 1978-79; state bd. mem. Pa. Crime Stoppers, 1986-88; mem. organizing bd. Pa. Women's Campaign Fund, 1982. Various coms., dir. Nat. Assn. State Bds. Edn., 1984-89, Pa. State Bd. Edn., 1974-94; site rev. team mem. So. Regional Edn. Bd., 1993; nat. orgn. com. mem. LWV, 1971-73, Pa. pres., 1971-73, 1st v.p. and bd. dirs., 1967-71, chair, bd. trustees edn. fund, 1971-73; bd. trustees United Way Pa., 1983, Gold award, 1980; pres. bd. United Way Wyoming Valley, 1980-82, bd. dirs., 1976-83, chmn. planning, allocations, and resources devel. com., 1977-80, chmn. needs assessment com., 1977, chmn. recreation com., 1976; sec. Kingston Borough Civil Svc. Commn., 1997—; trustee Temple Israel, 1986-92, chair endowment allocations com., 1992—. Recipient Disting. Svc. award Wyoming Sem., 1992, Pathfinder award Wyoming Valley Women's Network, 1986, Cmty. Svc. award S.J. Strauss Lodge B'nai B'rith, 1983, Disting. Pennsylvanian award William Penn Com., 1982, Recognition award Penn's Woods Girl Scout Coun., 1977; named Disting. Dau. Pa., 1989, Hon. Order Ky. Cols., 1987. Mem. Hadassah, Jr. League Wilkes-Barre, Women's Aux. Wyoming Valley Health Care Sys., Wilkes-Barre Gen., Women's Aux. Luzerne County Med. Soc., Disting. Daus. of Pa. (area dir. 1995-97, v.p. 1997-99, pres., 1999-2001), Columbine Codominium Assn. (bd. dirs. 2000—), Health and Tennis Club (bd. dirs. 2002—), Huntsville Golf Club, Women's Golf Assn. (co-chair 2003—). Home: 840 Nandy Dr Kingston PA 18704-5608

BENSELER, DAVID PRICE, foreign language educator; b. Balt., Jan. 10, 1940; s. Ernest Parr and Ellen Hood Escar (Turnbaugh) B.; m. Suzanne Shelton, May 25, 1985; children: James Declan, Derek Justin. BA, West

Wash. U., 1964; MA, U. Oreg., 1966, PhD, 1971. Prof. german, dept. chair Ohio State U., 1977—91; chair dept. modern langs and lits. Case Western Reserve U., 1991-98, Louis D. Beaumont U. Prof. Humanities, 1991-98, Emile B. de Sauzé prof. modern lang. and lit., 1998—. Disting. vis. prof. fgn. langs. U.S. Mil. Acad., West Point, N.Y., 1987-88, N.Mex. State U., Las Cruces, 1989; founding dir. German Studies program Case Western Reserve U. and Max Kade Ctr. for German Studies; mem. numerous coms. Case Western Res. U., U.S. Military Acad., U.S. Naval Acad., U. Akron, Ohio State U., Wash. State U., Ind. U., Emory U., U. Md., U. Cin., U. Wis., Pa. State U., U. Va., U. Mich., various others; lectr., panel mem., workshop condr., cons. in field. Compiler, editor: (with Suzanne S. Moore) Comprehensive Index to the Modern Language Journal, 1916-1996, MLJ Electronic Index, 1997—; author/editor 50 books, bibliographies, jours.; contbr. chpts. to books and articles to profl. jours. With USN, 1957—63. Decorated Bundesverdienstkreuz I. Klasse (Germany); recipient Army Commendation medal for disting. civilian svc. U.S. Mil. Acad., 1988; Lilly Found. Faculty Renewal fellow Stanford U., 1975, Fulbright grad. fellow, 1967-68, NDEA fellow, U. Oreg., 1964-67; various other grants, fellowships, scholarships. Mem. MLA, TESOL, Am. Assn. Applied Linguistics, Am. Assn. Tchrs. of German, Am. Assn. Univ. Profs., Am. Goethe Soc., Am. Soc. for 18th Century Studies, German Studies Assn., Lessing Soc., Soc. German-Am. Studies, Phi Sigma Iota, Sigma Kappa Phi, Delta Phi Alpha. Office: Case Western Res U Dept Modern Langs and Lits Cleveland OH 44106-7118 E-mail: dpb5@cwru.edu.

BENSMAIA, REDA, French studies educator, researcher; b. Kouba, Algeria, Oct. 15, 1944; arrived in U.S., 1979; s. Kaddour and Saleha (Benouniche) Bensmaia; m. Joelle Proust, Feb. 2, 1947 (div. June 1989); children: Sliman, Djamel; m. Maurizia Natali, Oct. 22, 1995. Licence es-lettres, Facultes des lettres, Aix-En-provence, France, 1969, MPhil, 1971; BA, Ecole Pratique, Paris, France, 1977, PhD, 1981. Asst. prof. Institut d' Etudes Politiques, Algiers, Algeria, 1973-74, U. Algiers, Algeria, 1974-76; prof. philosophy Lycée Français, San Francisco, 1979-81; assoc. prof. U. Minn., Mpls., 1981-85; dir. Paris Ctr. for Critical Studies, 1985-88; assoc. prof. U. Minn., Mpls., 1988-89; prof. U. Va., Charlottsville, Va., 1989-91, Brown U., Providence, 1991—. Author: The Barthes Effect, 1987, The Year of Passages, 1995, Alge ou la maladie de la mémoire, 1997, Experimental Nations of the invention of the Maghreb, 2003; editor: On Gilles Deleuze, 1989; contbr. articles to profl. jours. Recipient award, Am. Inst. for Maghrebi Studies, 1995; grantee, NEH, 1983, Chevalier des Palmes Academiques, French Min. of Culture, 2001; EDP grant, U. Minn., 1989. Mem.: MLA, Coun. for Internat. Ednl. Exch. (steering com., adv. bd. curriculum), Sites (adv. bd.), Lendemains (adv. bd.), Continuum (adv. bd.). Avocations: writing poetry and fiction, music, hiking. Office: Brown U Dept French Studies PO Box 1961 Providence RI 02912-1961

BENSMAN, STEPHEN J. school librarian, researcher; b. Sheboygan, Wis., Aug. 26, 1938; s. Solomon and Leah Z. Bensman; m. Miriam Roza, July 9, 1936. MLS, U. Wis., 1975, PhD in History, 1977. Fgn. law libr. U. Wis., Madison, 1975—78; libr. La. State U., Baton Rouge, 1978—. Contbr. articles to profl. jours. Specialist 6 U.S. Army, 1963. Mem.: ALA, Am .Soc. Info. Sci. and Tech., Beta Phi Mu, Phi Beta Kappa, Phi Eta Sigma. Home: 724 Shady Lake Pky Baton Rouge LA 70810-4328 Office: LSU Librs La State Univ Baton Rouge LA 70803-3300 Office Fax: 225-578-6535. Personal E-mail: bensmans@bellsouth.net. Business E-Mail: notsjb@lsu.edu.

BENSON, ALLEN B. chemist, educator, consultant; b. Sioux Rapids, Iowa, Oct. 1, 1936; s. Bennett and Freda (Smith) B.; m. Marian Richter, Aug. 24, 1959; children: Bradley Gerard, Jill Germaine. BS in Secondary Edn. magna cum laude, Western Mont. U., 1960; postgrad., U. Mont., Missoula, 1960-61, Seattle U., 1962-63; M in Natural Sci., Highlands U., 1965; postgrad., Ill. Inst. Tech., 1969; PhD in Chemistry, U. Idaho, 1970. Chemistry instr. U. Wis., Whitewater, 1968-69, Spokane (Wash.) Falls Community Coll., 1969—. Mem. steering com. Hanford Edn. Action League, Spokane, 1984-86; energy and nuclear cons., 1970—; mem. Hanford Health Effects Panel, Richland, Wash., 1986; numerous speeches, interviews and pub. articles on energy and nuclear issues, including speaker nat. conv. Physicians for Social Responsibility, Denver, 1990; lead sci. cons. Hanford Radiation Litigation Lawsuit for Hanford Downwinders against GE, DuPont and Rockwell, Wash., 1991, 93; sci. conf. leader UNLV on radiation and health effects, 1992; advisor internat. team of experts of contamination and health affects Simultec Ltd., Zurich, 1996-97. Author: Hanford radioactive Fallout: Are There Observable Health Effects?, 1989; co-author: Benson-Nguyen Proposal on Kazakhstan's Nuclear Test Site and the Human Health Effects, 1994, On Practical Application of the Yakima Holistic Concept to Environmental Restoration, 1995. Active Spokane County Dem. Platform Com., 1980, 84; prepared and gave testimony for Yakama Nation to U.S. Pres.'s Risk assessment Com., Seattle, 1995. With U.S. Army, 1955-57. Roman Catholic. Achievements include designed, invented and experimentally verified a holistic fertilizer being commercialized in Nevada and California, 1999. Home: 2011 Island Dreams Ave North Las Vegas NV 89031-0994 Office: Spokane Falls Community Coll Spokane WA 99204

BENSON, ALVIN K. physicist, geophysicist, consultant, educator; b. Payson, Utah, Jan. 25, 1944; s. Carl William and Josephine Katherine (Wirthlin) B.; m. Connie Lynn Perry, June 17, 1966; children: Alauna Marie, Alisa Michelle, Alaura Dawn. BS, Brigham Young U., 1966, PhD in Physics, 1972. Cert. environmentalist; registered profl. engr., Utah. Nuclear group physicist Phillips Petroleum Co., Arco, Idaho, 1966; assoc. prof. physics Ind. U., New Albany, 1972-78, head physics dept., 1976-78; sr. rsch. geophysicist Conoco, Inc., Ponca City, Okla., 1978-81, supr. geophysical rsch., 1981-85; geophysics rsch. assoc. DuPont, Ponca City, 1985-86; prof. geophysics Brigham Young U., Provo, Utah, 1986—2001, prof. emeritus, 2001—; prof. physics Utah Valley State Coll., 2001—. Cons. Dames and Moore Engring., Salt Lake City, 1987-88, 98-99, DuPont, Ponca City, 1989-91, Kuwait U., 1991-92, Coleman Rsch., Laurel, Md., 1991, Centennial Mine, Boise, 1990-91, Certified Environ., Salt Lake City, 1991-92, EPA, Washington, 1992, Digital Exploration Ltd., East Grinstead, Eng., 1993-94, Paterson, Grant & Watson Ltd., Toronto, 1994, Ground Water Tech., Norwood, Mass., 1995, Inst. for Geology and Geotech. Engring., Lyngby, Denmark, 1995-96, Conoco, Inc., Houston, 1997, Centurion Mines, Salt Lake City, 1997, ThermoRetec, Billings, Mont., 1999, Environ. Contractors, Inc., Provo, 2000, Anadarko, Houston, 2000, Kleinfelder, Salt Lake City, 2001, Monsanto, Soda Springs, Idaho, 2002; developer vis. geoscientist program Brigham Young U., Utah Valley State Coll.; rsch. bd. Am. Biog. Inst., 1995; developer vis. physicist program Utah Valley State Coll. Author: Seismic Migration, 1986, Theory and Practice of Seismic Imaging, 1988, The Birth and Growth of Planet Earth, 1996; (CD-ROM) Seismic Migration, 1997; mem. editl. bd. Jour. Applied Geophysics, 2000—; contbr. over 450 articles to profl. jours. Bishop LDS Ch., New Albany, 1976-78, Stake High Coun., Tulsa, 1979-81; active polit. adv. com. Rep. Party, Provo, 1990; polit. cons. Guatemala, 1991-92. Recipient Hon. Sci. award Bausch and Lomb, Rochester, N.Y., 1966, Disting. Leadership award Am. Biog. Inst., 1994, Citation of Meritorious Achievement in Geophysics, Soc. Exploration Geophysicists, 1994, Alcuin award Brigham Young U., 1994, Best Tchg. award, 1999, Excellence in Tchg. award, 2001; named Geosci. Prof. of Yr. Brigham Young U., 1994-95; Geophysics grantee Rotary, Provo, 1987, Am. Assn. Petroleum Geologists, Tulsa, 1988, Geol. Soc. Am., Boulder, Colo., 1988, Bur. of Reclamation, Washington, 1994, Nat. Pk. Svc., Washington, 1995, NSF, 1997, Dyn Corp., Boston, 1998, ThermoRetec, 1999, Dames and Moore, 1999, NSF, 2002. Mem. Am. Phys. Soc., Am. Geophys. Union, Soc. Exploration Geophysicists (referee 1980-99), Environ. and Engring. Geophys. Soc., Utah Geol. Assn., Utah Acad. Scis., Arts and Letters. Achievements include development of a stable, explicit seismic depth imaging algorithm, a residual depth imaging algorithm for seismic data, phase-shift plus variable-length transform imaging algorithm, linearized elastic wave decomposition and inversion process for seismic data, an aperture compensated migration-inversion process for seismic data, a modified self-consistent quantum field theory, algorithm to estimate dry-rock compressibility, compressional and shear wave velocities for porous fluid-filled rocks in situ, 3-D, prestack seismic imaging algorithm; research in ground penetrating radar and very low frequency electromagnet and electrical resisistivity methods, delineating hazardous materials and faulting in the subsurface, solution to the Heisenberg magnetic exchange model and to the BCS model of superconductivity and to the model of superfluidity. Home: 249 W 1100 S Orem UT 84058-6709 Office: Utah Valley State Coll Dept Physics Orem UT 84058

BENSON, BERNICE LAVINA, elementary education educator; b. Wolford, N.D., Sept. 30; d. Therman George and Annie Catherine (Hittle) Ritzman; m. Benjamin Melvin Benson, June 11, 1941 (dec.); 1 child, Beverly Ann. Student, Jamestown Coll.; BS in Edn., No. State Coll., 1964, MA equivalent. Cert. elem. tchr., S.D.; commd. Stephen's min., 1995. Tchr. 1st-6th grade Southam (N.D.) Sch. System, 1935-41; tchr. 1st grade Pierre (S.D.) Sch. System, 1953-84; tchr. Title I Fed. Devel. Reading Program, Pierre, 1984-87. Tchr.-tutor Title IV Fed. Tutorials for Native Americans, Pierre; supr. student tchrs. No. State Coll., Pierre. Past officer, past mem. various state coms. Delta Kappa Gamma; charter mem. Capital U., Pierre; sponsor Discovery Ctr., Pierre; mem. YMCA, Pierre; spl. events worker VFW Aux., Pierre; mem. Fine ARts Coun., Pierre; actress Never Too Late, Pierre Players Drama Assn.; mem. planning com. for new bldg., mem. meml. com. Luth. Meml. Ch. Mem. NEA (state exec. uni-serve com.), Pierre Edn. Assn., S.D. Edn. Assn., Pierre Tchrs. Assn. (pres.), Internat. Reading Assn., Assn. for Childhood Edn., AAUW, DAR (past offices), PEO (past pres., all offices), Annie D. Tallent Club. Avocations: bridge, reading, traveling, gardening. Home: PO Box 998 Pierre SD 57501-0998

BENSON, BRUCE LOWELL, economics educator; b. Havre, Mont., Mar. 18, 1949; s. Russell Lowell and Cora Mae (Emerson) B.; m. Terrie LaVerne Johnson, Aug. 25, 1973; children: Lacey Jean, Kaitlin Bree. BA in Econs., U. Mont., 1973, MA in Econs., 1975; PhD in Econs., Tex. A&M U., 1978. Vis. asst. prof. Pa. State U., University Park, 1978-79, asst. prof., 1979-82; assoc. prof. Mont. State U., Bozeman, 1982-85; prof. Fla. State U., Tallahassee, 1987—93, disting. rsch. prof., 1993—, DeVoe Moore prof., 1997—; Fulbright sr. specialist in Econ. to the Czech Republic, 2003—04. Assoc. Polit. Economy Rsch. Ctr., Bozeman, 1982—; rsch. fellow Pacific Rsch. Inst., San Francisco, 1982—90; mem. adv. bd. James Madison Inst., Tallahassee, 1987—; grant reviewer Fla. State U., Earhart Found., Social Sci. and Humanities Rsch. Coun. Can., NSF; fellowships reviewer Inst. for Humane Studies, Fairfax, Va., 1989—; fellow Ind. Inst., Oakland, 1990—97, sr. fellow, 1997—; co-editor Econ. Jour. Watch, 2001—; mem. sci. com. Jour. Economistes et des Etudes Humaine, 2002—; adj. scholar Ludwig von Mises Inst., 1995—; adv. coun. Friedrich A. Von Hayek Found., Buenos Aires, 2001—; adj. fellow Enterprise Prison Inst., 1998—; assoc. Inst. Econ. Affairs, London, 1999—. Co-author: (books) Am. Antitrust Laws, 1989, The Econ. Anatomy of a Drug War, 1994; author: The Enterprise of Law, 1990, To Serve and Protect, 1998 (Sir Antony Fisher Internat. Meml. award, 2000); assoc. editor: Jour. Reg. Sc., assoc. editor: Rev. Austrian Econs., contbg. editor The Ind. Rev.; editl. bd.: Quar. Jour. Austrian Econ., editl. bd.: Jour. Libertarian St.; contbr. articles to profl. jours., chapts. to books; mem. editl. bd.: Jour. Libertarian St., —. Sgt. U.S. Army, 1969-70, Vietnam. Recipient Ludwig von Mises prize, 1992, F. Leroy Hill faculty fellow, Inst. for Humane Studies, 1985—86, Earhart fellow, 1991—92, 1995, 2002, Salvatori fellow, Heritage Found., 1992—94, Best Paper award, Jour. Pvt. Enterprise, 1999—. Mem.: Soc. for Legal and Econ. Studies (bd. cons. 1999—), Franz Oppenheimer Soc., Soc. for Devel. of Austrian Econ., European Soc. for Social Drug Rsch., Assn. Pvt. Enterprise Edn. (exec. com. 1999—2001, v.p. 2001—02, pres. 2002—03, exec. com. 2003—04, Disting. Scholar award 2001), Am. Law and Econ. Assn., Inst. for Humane Studies (charter), Free Nation Found., Pub. Choice Soc., Western Econ. Assn., So. Econ. Assn. (trustee 1995—97, Georgescu-Roegen prize 1989), Am. Econ. Assn. Home: 2007 Chimney Swift Holw Tallahassee FL 32312-3501 Office: Fla State U Dept Econs Tallahassee FL 32306

BENSON, CHARLES EVERETT, microbiology educator; b. Dayton, Ohio, Dec. 15, 1937; s. Charles Prue Jr. and Virginia Elizabeth (Zindorf) B.; m. Gail Elizabeth Smith, June 5, 1960; children: Deborah Elizabeth, Charles Nathaniel. AB, Franklin Coll., 1960; MS, Miami U., Oxford, Ohio, 1963; PhD, Wake Forest U., 1969; MS (hon.), U. Pa., 1985. Tchr. Dayton Pub. Schs., 1960-61; rsch. asst. Miami Valley Hosp., Dayton, 1963-65; asst. prof. U. Pa. Sch. Allied Med. Professions, Phila., 1975-80; assoc. prof. U. Pa. Sch. Vet. Medicine, Phila., 1980-88, prof., 1988—, chmn. dept. clin. studies Kennett Square, Pa., 1989-94, chief Clin. Vet. Microbiology, 1997—. Author/co-author rsch. papers in field. Pres. Haddonfield (N.J.) Rep. Party, 1982-85, pres. Haddonfield Friends of the Libr., 1986-90; chmn. Haddonfield United Meth. Ch. Nursery Sch. Com., 1980-88; scout master Cub Scouts, Boy Scouts Am., Haddonfield, 1985-89. Scholar U. Pa. Sch. Medicine, 1972-75. Mem. AAAS, Am. Soc. for Microbiology (fellowship 1969), Soc. for Gen. Microbiology, N.Y. Acad. Scis., U.S. Animal Health Assn., Am. Assn. of Vet. Lab. Diagnosticians, Lions Club, Sigma Chi Alpha. Avocations: phys. fitness, reading, carpentry and home repair, creative writing. Home: 123 Hawthorne Ave Haddonfield NJ 08033-1401 Office: Univ Pa Sch Vet Medicine 382 W Street Rd Kennett Square PA 19348-1691

BENSON, JOAN DOROTHY, secondary school educator; b. Paterson, N.J., Aug. 23, 1948; d. Arnold A. and Dorothy M. (Fischer) Benson; children: Kristina, Julie. BA, Rowan Coll., 1975; cert., William Paterson Coll., 1984; postgrad., Jersey City State Coll., 1987-88; student, Katrinebergs Folkhogskolan, 1989; MS in Computer Sci., Iona Coll., 2000. Cert. elem. tchr., secondary tchr., N.J. Asst. to spl. edn. tchr. Pequannock Twp. Schs., Pompton Plains, NJ, 1981—84; instr. computers Pequannock Adult Sch., Pompton Plains, NJ, 1983—97; media specialist, computer tchr., math. tchr. DePaul Cath. H.S., Wayne, NJ, 1984—98; math. tchr. Livingston (NJ) Pub. Sch., 2001—02; computer tchr., math. tchr. Mahwah (NJ) HS, 2002—. Part-time tchr. computers Pequannock Adult Sch., Pompton Plains, N.J., 1987-97; guest tchr. Katrinebergs Folkhögskola, Vessigebro, Sweden, 1989—; delegate Internat. Tchr. Exch., Australia, 2001. Elder, deacon 1st Ref. Ch., Pompton Plains, NJ. Mem. NEA, NJ Edn. Assn., Mahwah Edn. Assn., Nat. Coun. Tchrs. Math., Kappa Delta Pi. Avocations: handbell choir, reading, computers, travel. E-mail: jbenson@mahwah.k12.nj.us.

BENSON, KAREN A. nursing educator; b. Havre, Mont., Sept. 10, 1946; d. William Duncan and Norma Evelyn (Erickson) Ross; children: Alice, Evan, David, Marc. BSN, Mont. State U., 1968; MS in Biology, Wash. State U., 1978, PhD in Vet. Sci., 1983; MS in Nursing, Oreg. Health Scis. U., 1986. Lectr. Seattle U. Contbr. articles to profl. publs. Dr. Lynn A. George scholar; Sigma Xi rsch. grantee. Mem. ANA, Wash. State Nurses Assn., Am. Holistic Nurses Assn., Sigma Theta Tau, Phi Kappa Phi. Home: 17103 25th Ave NE Seattle WA 98155-6124

BENSON, RICHARD CARTER, mechanical engineering educator; b. Newport News, Va., July 29, 1951; s. Willard Raymond and Helene Antonia (Kraus) B.; m. Leslie Ellen Brault; children: Stephanie A., James P., Kenneth C. BSE with hons., Princeton U., 1973; MS, U. Va., 1974; PhD, U. Calif., Berkeley, 1977. Registered profl. engr., N.Y. Tech. specialist Xerox Corp., Rochester, N.Y., 1977-80; asst. prof. mech. engring. U. Rochester, N.Y., 1980-83, assoc. prof. mech. engring., 1983-89; sabbatical vis. U. Calif., San Diego, 1986-87; prof. mech. engring. U. Rochester, 1989-95, assoc. dean grad. studies, 1989-92, chmn. dept. mechanical engring., 1992-95; prof. mech. engring. Pa. State U., University Park, 1995—, head dept. mech. engring., 1995-98, head dept. mech. and nuclear engring., 1998—. Founder, dir. Mechanics of Flexible Structures, 1982—. Contbr. more than 60 articles to profl. jours. concerning mechanics of flexible structures. Fellow ASME (press oversight com. 1990—, Henry Hess award 1984); mem. Soc. Tribologists and Lubrication Engrs., Am. Soc. Engring. Edn. Avocations: squash, game of go. Office: Pa State U Dept Mech & Nuclear Engring State College PA 16802

BENSON, SHARON JOAN, mathematics educator; b. Glendale, Calif., Aug. 23, 1964; d. Paul John and Arleen Camille (Green) B. BS in Math., Calif. Poly. State U., 1987; MST in Math., U. N.H., 1992; postgrad., N.Mex. State U., 1998—. Cert. single subject clear math., Calif. Tchr. math. Victor Valley Union High Sch. Dist., Victorville, Calif., 1988-98; grad. asst. dept. curriculum and instrn. N.Mex. State U. Part-time instr. Victor Valley C.C., Victorville, 1993-98. Mem. Nat. Coun. Tchrs. Math., Calif. Math. Coun., Oreg. Coun. Tchrs. of Math., Assn. Women in Math. Republican. Roman Catholic. Avocations: cross-stitch, reading, collecting carousel horses and cherished teddies.

BENSON, SHARON STOVALL, primary school educator; b. Clovis, N.Mex., Apr. 18, 1946; d. Travis and Anna Gene (Crump) Stovall; m. Merle John Benson, Aug. 21, 1966; children: Brenda Kay, Linda Carol. BS, U. N.Mex., 1968, MA, 1980. Cert. tchr., N.Mex. Kindergarten aide Albuquerque Pub. Schs., 1976-78; tchr. LaMesa Little Sch., Albuquerque, 1987-88, Congl. Presch., Albuquerque, 1991—. Parent rep. South Atlantic Regional Resource Ctr., Plantation, Fla., 1986-87; sec. bd. Albuquerque Spl. Presch., 1975. Trained evaluator Assn. Retarded Citizens, Albuquerque, 1988—. Mem. Parents Reaching Out, Assn. Retarded Citizens, N.Mex. Assn. Edn. Young Children, Pi Lambda Theta. Methodist. Avocations: bell choir, programs for handicapped. Home: 7409 Carriveau Ave NE Albuquerque NM 87110-1490 E-mail: mbenson54@comcast.net.

BENSON, THOMAS WALTER, rhetoric educator, writer; b. Abington, Pa., Jan. 25, 1937; s. Walter Adelbert and Beatrice (Newton) B.; m. Margaret Sandelin, Sept. 3, 1960; children: Margaret, Sarah Beverly. AB, Hamilton Coll., 1958; MA, Cornell U., 1961, PhD, 1966. From asst. to assoc. prof. SUNY, Buffalo, 1963-71; assoc. prof. Pa. State U., University Park, 1971-75, prof., 1975—, Sparks prof. rhetoric, 1990—. Vis. asst. prof. U. Calif., Berkeley, 1969-70; Shorenstein fellow Harvard U., 1999. Editor: (books) Am. Rhetoric, 1989, Rhetoric and Polit. Culture, 1997; co-author: Reality Fictions, 1989, 2002, Documentary Dilemmas, 1991; editor: (jours.) Comm. Quar., 1976—78, Quar. Jour. of Speech, 1987—89, CRTNET, 1985—97, Rev. of Comm., 1999—2003. Shorenstein fellow Harvard U., 1999. Mem. Internat. Soc. for History of Rhetoric, Nat. Comm. Assn. (Kibler award 1983, Presdl. citation 1997, Disting. Scholar 1997, Disting. Rhetorical Scholar 1997), Ea. Comm. Assn. (Distng. Rsch. fellow), Soc. for Cinema Studies, Univ. Film and Video Assn. Home: 327 Mcbath St State College PA 16801-2744 Office: Pa State U 227 Sparks Bldg University Park PA 16802-5201

BENSUR, BARBARA JEAN, art educator, researcher; b. Erie, Pa., Feb. 11, 1950; d. Jean Elizabeth and Durker William Braggins; children: Adele, Rebecca. BA, Mercyhurst Coll., 1972; MA, U. Md., 1992, PhD, 1995. Cert. art tchr. grades K-12, adminstrv. endorsement. Art tchr. St. Mary's County Pub. Schs., Leonardtown, Md., 1989—98; instr. Frostburg (Md.) State U., 1996—98; asst. prof. Millersville (Pa.) U., 1998—. Exhibitions include Delaware County C.C., 2001 (Purchase award, 2001), 30th Ann. Spring Arts Festival, 2001, Lancaster Open Award Exhibit, 2001, Millersville Faculty Art Show, 2001; contbr. articles to profl. jours. Cons. Demuth Found., Lancaster, 2000—01. Mem.: Am. Edn. Rsch. Assn., Pa. Art Edn. Assn., Nat. Art Edn. Assn. Roman Catholic. Avocation: jogging. Home: 743 Steeplechase Rd Landisville PA 17538 Office: Millersville Univ Art Dept PO Box 1002 Millersville PA 17551 Home Fax: (717) 871-2004; Office Fax: (717) 871-2004. Personal E-mail: barbara.bensur@millersville.edu. Business E-Mail: barbara.bensur@millersville.edu.

BENTLEY, CHARLES RAYMOND, geophysics educator; b. Rochester, N.Y., Dec. 23, 1929; s. Raymond and Janet Cornelia (Everest) B.; m. Marybelle Goode, July 3, 1964; children: Molly Clare, Raymond Alexander. BS, Yale U., 1950; PhD, Columbia U., 1959. Rsch. geophysicist Columbia U., 1952-56; Antarctic traverse leader and seismologist Arctic Inst. N.Am., 1956-59; project assoc. U. Wis., 1959-61, asst. prof., 1961-63, assoc. prof., 1963-68, prof. geophysics, 1968-98, A.P. Crary prof. geophysics, 1987-98, prof. emeritus, 1998—. Recipient Bellingshausen-Lazarev medal for Antarctic rsch. Acad. Scis. USSR, 1971; NSF sr. postdoctoral fellow, 1968-69; NAS-USSR Acad. Sci. exch. fellow, 1977, 90 Fellow AAAS, Am. Geophys. Union, Arctic Inst. N.Am., Am. Polar Soc. (hon., bd. dirs.); mem. AAUP, Soc. Exploration Geophysicists, Internat. Glaciological Soc. (Seligman Crystal award 1990), Am. Quarternary Assn., Oceanography Soc., Am. Geol. Inst., Geol. Soc. Am., Phi Beta Kappa, Sigma Xi. Achievements include research on Antarctic glaciology and geophysics, satellite studies of geomagnetic anomalies, magnetotelluric exploration of Earth structure, satellite radar and laser altimetry, ice coring and drilling services. Home: 5618 Lake Mendota Dr Madison WI 53705-1036 Office: U Wis Geophys & Polar Rsch Ctr Weeks Hall 1215 Dayton St Madison WI 53706 E-mail: bentley@geology.wisc.edu.

BENTLEY, DONALD LYON, mathematics and statistics educator, minister; b. Los Angeles, Cal., Apr. 25, 1935; s. Byron R. and Clara Viola (Lyon) B.; m. Anne P. Alexander, Aug. 28, 1957; children: James, Jillene, Janet. BS, Stanford U., 1956, MS, 1958, PhD, 1961; MDiv, Claremont Sch. Theology, 1998. Ordained Congregationalist minister, 1998. Asst. prof. math. stats. Colo. State U., Ft. Collins, 1961-64; asst. prof. math. Pomona Coll., Claremont, Calif., 1964-67, assoc. prof., 1967-74, Burkhead prof. maths., 1974—2001, ret., 2001. Cons. Allergen Pharm., Irvine, Calif., 1968-80, Intermedics IntraOcular, Pasadena, Calif., 1981-86, Tokos Med. Corp., 1986-90, Cardio Genisis Corp., 1995-2000; cons. min. Pilgrim Congl. Ch., Pomona, Calif., 1998—. Co-author: Linear Algebra with Differential Equations, 1973. Fellow Royal Statis. Soc., Am. Statis. Assn.; mem. Inst. Math. Stats., Nat. Assn. Congrl. Christian Chs. (chair exec. com. 1994-95, moderator-elect 1992-93, moderator 1993-94). Avocations: music, woodworking, genealogy.

BENTLEY, KIA JEAN, social worker, educator; b. Mineola, NY, June 17, 1956; d. William Gerald and Zilpha Ann (Draper) B. BA, Auburn U., 1978; MSSW, U. Tenn., 1979; PhD, Fla. State U., 1987. Diplomate in Clin. Social Work; lic. clin. social worker. Social worker East Ala. Med. Ctr., Opelika, 1979-84; asst. prof. La. State U. Sch. Social Work, Baton Rouge, 1987-89; prof., dir. PhD program Va. Commonwealth U. Sch. Social Work, Richmond, 1989—. Chair human rights com. Ctrl. State Hosp.; mem. commn. on accreditation Coun. on Social Work Edn., 2003—. Co-author: The Social Worker and Psychotropic Medication, 2d edit., 2001; editor: Social Work Practice in Mental Health, 2002; cons. editor: Jour. Social Work Edn., 2003—. Active St. Paul's Episcopal Ch. Mem. NASW, Coun. on Social Work Edn. (mem. commn. on accreditation), Nat. Alliance for the Mentally Ill. Democrat. Avocations: wine, movies, cooking, golf. Office: Va Commonwealth U Sch Social Work 1001 W Franklin St Richmond VA 23284-2027

BENTLEY, MARJI, music educator; b. Louisville, Feb. 9, 1925; d. Frank Loyd and Sara Elizabeth (Hazlewood) Tullis; m. Richard Raymond Bentley, June 14, 1947; children: Richard R. Jr., Beth Ann, Martha Jane. B of Music Edn., Cornell Coll., 1946; MA, Tex. Woman's U., 1972. Supr. music Arlington Heights (Ill.) Pub. Schs., 1946-47; orch. dir. Redfield (S.D.) Pub. Schs., 1947-50; pvt. tchr. violin, viola Winfield, Kans., 1955-56, Napa,

Calif., Denton, Tex., 1965—, Ardmore, Okla., 1973-88. Dir. children's and adult choirs, L.A., 1950-55; performed with U. So. Calif. Opera Orch., L.A., 1950-55, Southwestern Coll. Orch. and Faculty String Quartet, 1955-56, Napa Cmty. Symphony Orch. and Faculty String Quartet. Contbr. articles to profl. jours. Vol. Cross Timbers Coun., Girl Scouts Am. Mem. Music Educators Nat. Conf., Am. String Tchrs. Assn., Music Tchrs. Nat. Assn., Nat. Fedn. Music Clubs (founder Napa chpt.), Am. State Tchrs. Assn. (S.D. pres. 1948-49), Tex. Music Educators Assn., Tex. Music Educators Conf., Tex. Am. String Tchrs., Dallas Music Tchrs. Assn. Methodist. Avocations: reading, biking. Home: 2907 Foxcroft Cir Denton TX 76209-7809

BENTON, ANDREW KEITH, university administrator, lawyer; b. Hawthrone, Nev., Feb. 4, 1952; s. Darwin Keith and Nelda Lou Benton; m. Deborah Sue Strickland, June 22, 1974; children: Hailey Michelle, Christopher Andrew. BS in Am. Studies, Okla. Christian Coll., 1974; JD, Oklahoma City U., 1979. Bar: Okla. 1979, U.S. Dist. Ct. (we. dist.) Okla. (admitted to) 1982. Sole practice, Edmond, Okla., 1979-81, 83-84; ptnr. Benton & Thomason, Edmond, 1981—83; asst. v.p. Pepperdine U., Malibu, Calif., 1984—85, v.p., 1985—87, v.p. adminstrn., 1987—89, v.p. univ. affairs, 1989—91, exec. v.p., 1991—2000, pres., 2000—. Chmn. precinct, state conv. del. Okla. Reps., 1980. Mem.: Okla. Bar Assn. (contbr. articles to ednl. community), ABA (chmn. subcom. emerging land use trends 1987—88, chmn. subcom. decisional trends 1988—90). Republican. Mem. Ch. Of Christ. Office: Pepperdine U 24255 Pacific Coast Hwy Malibu CA 90263-0002

BENTON, GERALDINE ANN, preschool owner, director; b. Plymouth, N.H., Apr. 25, 1960; d. Alton G. and Geraldine (Holecek) B. BS, Plymouth State Coll., 1984. Cert. bus driver, N.H. Tutor, Math., reading; bus driver Robertson Transit, Campton, N.H., 1986-96; owner, dir. Mad River Learning Ctr. and Daycare, Thornton, N.H., 1996—; sub. tchr., 1982-96. Mem. Interested Citizens in Town Govt. Mem. Nat. Head Injury Found., Nat. Arbor Day Found., Nat. Audubon Soc., Nat. Wildlife Found. Home: PO Box 25 Campton NH 03223-0025

BENTON, GLADYS GAY, educator, musician; b. Fayette, Mo., Nov. 17, 1906; d. Benjamin Franklin and Celoa Alice (Perry) Hill; m. Robert Withrow, 1929; m. Charles B. Howell, July 12, 1939; children: Frances, Alice; m. Chester Roland Benton, July 7, 1951 (dec. 1989). BA in Edn., San Francisco State U., 1937; MA in Reading, U. Calif.-Northridge, 1979. Cert. Ryan reading specialist; Laubach tutor trainer; life cert. kindergarten, primary and elem. tchr., Calif. Tchr. Malen Burnett Sch. Music, San Francisco, 1925-29, Mendocino County, Solano, Santa Maria, Imperial, Ventura County Pub. Schs., Calif., 1929-91; owner, tchr. Gladys Benton Music Studio and Reading Clinic, Ojai, Calif. Organizer, dir. Laubach Literacy Ctr., Ojai, Santa Paula, Calif. Piano accompanist for ch. svc. Victorian Retirement Home, 1992-93. Vol. ESL tchr., Ojai, Calif.; helper Little House, Ojai, 1978; docent Ojai Mus., 1984-85; tutor Topa Topa-Meiners Oaks Sch., Ojai, 1988-89; dir., organist, choir dir. Meth. Ch., Oak View, Calif., 1952; founder, organizer, trainer literacy ctrs., Ventura and Saticoy, Calif.; asst. leader Girl Scouts U.S.A.; vol. Boy Scout Camp, Meals on Wheels; accompanist various chs. Mem. Calif. Retired Tchrs. Assn., Am. Assn. Retired Persons, Legion Aux. (past pres.), Rural Carriers Aux., Music Tchrs. Assn. Woman's Club, Shakespeare Club, Bus. and Profl. Club (v.p.), Order Eastern Star (organist, sec.). Office: 225 N Lomita Ave # 10 Ojai CA 93023-1541

BENTON-BORGHI, BEATRICE HOPE, secondary education educator, author, publisher; b. San Antonio; d. Donald Francis and Beatrice Hope Benton; m. Peter T. Borghi; children: Kathryn Benton Borghi, Sarah Benton Borghi. BA in Chemistry, North Adams State Coll. (now known as Mass. Coll. Liberal Arts); MEd, Boston U. Tchr. chemistry Cathedral H.S., Springfield, Mass.; tchr. chemistry and history Munich (W.Ger.) Am. H.S.; tchr. English Tokyo; tchr. chemistry and sci. Marlborough (Mass.) H.S.; project dir., adminstr. ESEA, Marlborough Pub. Schs.; CEO, pres., chmn. bd. dirs. Open Minds, Inc. Project dir., proposal writer Title III, Title IX, U.S. Dept. Edn.; evaluation teams New Engl. Assn. Schs. and Colls.; mem. regional dept. edn. com.; ednl. cons., lectr. Author: Project ABC (Access By Computer), Kathryn Borghi Digital Libr., Alternative Funding/Recycling Project, Down the Aisle, Best Friends, A Thousand Lights, Whoa, Nellie!, Best Friend Jour., Down the Aisle Jour., Whoa, Nellie! Jour., A Thousand Lights Jour., Best Friend: Teacher and Parent Guide, Whoa Nellie! Teacher and Parent Guide, Down the Aisle: Teacher and Parent Guide, Subtle Inclusion Through Literature, Kathryn Borghi Digital Library with Accessible Technology Center Model, 2001, others; contbr. articles to profl. jours. Energy conservation rep. Marlborough's Overall Econ. Devel. Com., 1976; mem. strategic planning com. Upper Arlington Sch., Ohio, 1994, 1999, tech., 1999; chmn. Marlborough's Energy Conservation Task Force, 1975; dir. Walk for Mankind, 1972; sec. Group Action for Marlborough Environment, 1975—76; pres. Sisters, Inc., dba Open Minds; with Project Digital Jones Mid. Sch., Upper Arlington, Ohio, 2001—03; bd. dirs. Girls Club, Marlborough, 1979. Mem. AAUW, Coun. for Exceptional Children, Nat. Women's Health Network. Home: 2449 Edington Rd Columbus OH 43221-3047 Office: Open Minds Inc PO Box 21325 Columbus OH 43221-0325

BENTZ, PENNY LENNEA, special education educator; b. Fremont, Nebr., Nov. 29, 1949; d. Edward Earl and June Lorraine (Larson) B.; 1 child, Nikole Lorraine. BA in Edn., Wayne State Coll., 1972. Cert. tchr., Wash., Nebr. Tchr. grades K-2 Sch. Dist. 23, Valley, Nebr., 1972-74; tchr. Sch. Dist. 90, Scribner, Nebr., 1976-77; substitute tchr. Westside Sch. Dist., Millard Pub. Schs., Omaha, 1974-88; spl. edn. tchr. Lake Washington Sch. Dist., Kirkland, 1988-89, 91-96, Renton (Wash.) Schs., 1989-90, CHILD Inst., Bellevue, Wash., 1990-91. Mem. adv. com. Comprehensive Sys. of Pers. Devel., Olympia, Wash., 1993-95; mem. Lake Washington Sch. Dist. Leadership Com. Severe Behavior Disabled Edn. grantee Seattle U., 1993. Mem. NEA, Wash. Edn. Assn. spl. edn. commn. 1992-95, spl. edn. cert. prarprofl. task force), Lake Washington Edn. Assn. (bldg. rep. 1991-95), Delta Kappa Gamma (pres. 1994-96). Methodist. Avocations: spectator sports, reading. Address: PO Box 1786 Woodinville WA 98072-1786

BENZ, EDWARD JOHN, JR., physician, educator; b. Pitts., May 22, 1946; s. Edward John and Verna Marie (Cuddyre) B.; m. Margaret A. Vettese; children: Timothy Edward, Jennifer Kirsten. AB in Biology cum laude, Princeton U., 1968; MD magna cum laude, Harvard U., 1973. Diplomate Am. Bd. Internal Medicine, Am. Bd. Hematology. Resident Peter Bent Brigham Hosp., Boston, 1973-75; fellow pediatric hematology Children's Hosp. Med. Ctr., Boston, 1974-75; fellow adult hematology Yale U. Sch. of Medicine, New Haven, 1978-79, asst. prof. internal medicine, 1979-82, assoc. prof. internal medicine, human genetics, 1982-87, prof. internal medicine, human genetics, 1987-92, chief sect. hematology, 1987-92, chmn. dean's curriculum task force, 1987-88, assoc. chmn. dept. internal medicine, 1988-92; Jack D. Myers prof., chmn. dept. medicine U. Pitts. Sch. Medicine, 1993-95; Sir William Osler prof., dir. dept. medicine Johns Hopkins U. Sch. Medicine., Balt., 1995-2000; physician-in-chief Johns Hopkins Hosp., Balt., 1995-2000; prof. molecular biology and genetics Johns Hopkins U. Sch. of Medicine, 1995-2000; pres., CEO Dana Farber Cancer Inst., Boston, 2000—; Richard & Susan Smith prof. medicine, prof. pediat. and path Harvard Med. Sch., Boston, 2000—. CEO Dana Farber Ptnrs. Cancer Care, Boston, 2000—; dir. Dana Farber Harvard Cancer Care, Boston, 2000—; rsch. assoc. molecular hematology Nat. Heart, Lung, Blood Inst., Bethesda, Md., 1975—78; chmn. curriculum com. Yale Sch. of Medicine, New Haven, 1985—88; prof. pro-tem, hon. vis. chief of svc. Brigham & Women's Hosp., 1997; surgeon USPHS, 1975—78; adj. prof. biol. scis. Carnegie Mellon U., 1993—95; Howard Hiatt vis. prof. Harvard Med. Sch., 1998; Clement Finch prof. U. Wash., 1998; Bulfinch vis. prof. medicine Mass. Gen. Hosp., Harvard Med. Sch., Boston, 2000; Haynes disting. vis. prof. medicine Duke U., 2000; Franz Inglefinger vis. prof. Boston U., 2001; Litchfield lectr. Oxford U., 1999; lectr. in field. Author: Molecular Genetics Methods, 1987; co-editor: Hermatology, Principles and Practice, 1990, Hermatology, Principles and Practice, 3d edit., 1999; mem. editl. bd. Blood, 1988—94, New Eng. Jour. Medicine, 2002—; assoc. editor: New Eng. Jour. Medicine, —; contbr. articles to profl. jours. Recipient Career Devel. award nat. Inst. Health, 1982, Edward Paradiso Research award Cooley's Anemia Found., N.Y.C., 1985, Basil O'Connor award March of Dimes, 1980. Fellow: Molecular Med. Soc., ACP; mem.: Inst Medicine, Assn. Profs. Medicine, Am. Soc. Human Genetics, Am. Clin. and Climatological Soc., Am. Soc. Hematology (exec. coun. 1994, v.p. 1998, pres.-elect 1999, pres. 2000), Am. Fedn. Clin. Rsch., NIH (study sect. 1984—, chmn. 1993—95), Assn. Am. Physicians, Am. Soc. Clin. Investigation (nat. coun. 1987—91, pres. 1991—92), Md. Club, Johns Hopkins Club, Princeton Elm Club, Interurban Clin. Club, St. Botoph's Club, Alpha Omega Alpha, Sigma Xi, Phi Beta Kappa. E-mail: Edward_Benz@dfci.harvard.edu.

BENZ, MARILYN CHRISTINE, elementary education educator; b. Stamford, Conn., Sept. 13, 1948; d. Laurence Paul and Marjorie Helen (Scribner) Benz; m. James Sloan Nelson, June 4, 1971 (dec. Apr. 1975); 1 child, Becky. BA in Sociology, Notre Dame Coll., 1970. Social worker N.H. Divsn. Welfare, Concord, 1970-71; tutor remedial reading Title I BASK Program, Manchester, N.H., 1976-80; tchr. 4th grade Raymond (N.H.) Sch. Dist., 1980-89, tchr. 3d grade, 1989—. V.p. Lamprey River Elem. PTO, Raymond, 1983-85; mentor writing process Lamprey River Elem. Sch., 1983—. Named N.H. Tchr. of Yr., 2003. Mem. N.H. Nat. Edn. Assn. (negotiator 1992-2002), Raymond Edn. Assn. (v.p. 2001-02). Avocations: travel, quilting, reading. Home: 49A Dale Rd Hooksett NH 03106 Office: Lamprey River Elem Sch 33 Old Manchester Rd Raymond NH 03077-2345

BENZLE, CURTIS MUNHALL, artist, art educator; b. Lakewood, Ohio, Apr. 20, 1949; s. Arthur George and Martha (Munhall) B; m. Suzan Scianamblo, Feb. 6, 1972 (div. 1995); children: Elliott, Kyle, Marisa; m. Sally Jo Havas, Aug. 28, 1996 (div. 1999). Student, Hillsdale Coll., 1967-69; BFA, Ohio State U., 1972; postgrad., Rochester Inst. Tech., 1973; MA, No. Ill. U., 1978. Owner, mgr. Oz Crafts, Hilton Head, S.C., 1973-76, Benzle Porcelain Co., Columbus, Ohio, 1980—, Benzle Applied Arts, Hilliard, Ohio, 1988—. Owner Creative Spirit Workshop; exec. dir. Ohio Designer Craftsmen, 1996—99; instr. U. S.C., Beaufort, 1978—79; prof., chair dept. dimensional studies Columbus Coll. Art and Design, 1982—, dir. com. art project; pres. Japan-USA Exch. Exhbn., 1988—92; bd. overseers Am. Crafts Assn., 1991—96; trustee Am. Crafts Coun., 1992—96. One-man show U. S.C., 1979, Indpls. Mus. Art, 1984, Lawrence Gallery, Portland, Oreg., 1986, Running Ridge Gallery, Santa Fe, 1986, Akasaka/Green Gallery, Tokyo, 1987, 90, Zanesville Art Ctr., 1988, Swidler Gallery, 1990, Tsukushi Gallery, Kitakyushu, Japan, 1991, del Mano Gallery, 1998, also others; exhibited in numerous group shows, 1971—, including Smithsonian Instn., 1980, 83, Suntory Art Mus., Tokyo, 1984, Cermaic Nat. Everson Mus., Syracuse, 1988, Internat. Competition of Ceramics, Mino, Japan, 1989, Seto (Japan) Ceramic and Glass Ctr., 2001 21st Century Ceramics, Canzani Gallery, Columbus, Ohio; represented in numerous permanent collections, including Smithsonian Instn., Everson Mus. Art, Los Angeles County Mus. Art, Cleve. Mus. Art., White House Collection Contemporary Craft. Mem. Ohio Citizens Com. for Arts, 1986—. Nat. Endowment for Arts fellow, 1980, Ohio Arts Coun. fellow, 1981, 83, 84, 86, 88, Greater Columbus Arts Coun. fellow, 1987. Mem. Am. Crafts Coun. (bd. overseers 1991-96, trustee 1992-96), Nat. Coun. on Edn. in Ceramic Art, Ohio Designer Craftsmen (bd. dirs. 1984-88, pres. 1985-87). Avocation: gardening. E-mail: cbenzle@ccad.edu.

BEN-ZVI, JEFFREY STUART, gastroenterologist, internist; b. Bklyn., Aug. 19, 1957; s. Seymour and Doris (Salzman) B.-Z.; m. Julie Genuth, May 11, 1982; children: Chana, Adina, Ilana, Aviva, Samuel, Sara, Jonathan David. BSc, CUNY, Bklyn., 1979; MD, Columbia U., 1983. Diplomate Am. Bd. Internal Medicine, Am. Bd. Gastroenterology, Am. Bd. Geriatrics. Intern St. Luke's-Roosevelt Hosp., N.Y.C., 1983-84, resident in internal medicine, 1984-86, fellow in gastroenterology, 1986-88; asst. prof. clin. med. Columbia U., N.Y.C., 1988—. Attending physician Columbia-Presbyn. Med. Ctr., Lenox Hill Hosp., Beth Israel Med. Ctr., N.Y.C., St. Luke's Roosevelt Hosp. Ctr. Contbr. articles to profl. jours. Med. dir./advisor Hatzolah Vol. Ambulance Corp., N.Y.C., 1985—; bd. dir. Coun. Jewish Organ. of Flatbush, Ave. N. Jewish Cmty. Ctr. Fellow ACP, Am. Coll. Gastroenterology; mem. AMA, Am. Gastroent. Assn., Am. Soc. Gastrointestinal Endoscopy, Am. Radio Relay League (life), Agudath Israel Am. (life), Am. Geriatric Soc., Am. Soc. for Parental and Enteral Nutrition, Bklyn. Coll. Alumni Assn. (bd. dirs., pres.), Assn. Alumni Coll. P&S Columbia U. (alumni coun.). Avocations: philately, photography, amateur radio, personal computers, aquaria. Home: 2414 Avenue R Brooklyn NY 11229-2430 Office: 911 Park Ave New York NY 10021-0337 also: 2907 Kings Hwy Brooklyn NY 11229-1805

BEPKO, GERALD LEWIS, university administrator, law educator, lecturer, consultant, lawyer; b. Chgo., Apr. 21, 1940; s. Lewis V. and Geraldine S. (Bernath) B.; m. Jean B. Cougnenc, Feb. 24, 1968; children: Gerald Lewis Jr., Arminda B. BS, No. Ill. U., 1962; JD, Ill. Inst. Tech.-Chgo. Kent Coll. Law, 1965; LLM, Yale U., 1972. Bar: Ill. 1965, U.S. Supreme Ct. 1968, Ind. 1973. Assoc. Ehrlich, Bundesen, Friedman & Ross, Chgo., 1965; spl. agt. FBI, 1965-69; asst. prof. law Ill. Inst. Tech.-Chgo. Kent Coll. Law, 1969-71; prof. Ind. U., Indpls., 1972-86, assoc. dean acad. affairs, 1979-81, dean, 1981-86, v.p., 1986—2002, interim pres., 2003. Vis. prof. Ind. U.-Bloomington, summers, 1976, 77, 78, 80, U. Ill., 1976—77, Ohio State U., 1978—79; cons. and reporter Fed. Jud. Ctr.; bd. dirs. First Ind. Bank/Corp., Ind. Energy Inc. & Ind. Gas Co., Inc., 1989—97, Lumina Found. for Edn., Indpls. Life Ins. Co.; mem. Conf. Commrs. on Uniform State Laws, 1982, Permanent Editl. Bd. for the Uniform Comml. Code, 1993—; mem. Ind. Lobby Registration Commn., 1992—, vice chair, 1992—96, chair, 1996—2000. Author: (with Boshkoff) Sum and Substance of Secured Transactions, 1981; contbr. articles on comml. law to profl. jours. Indpls. Chgo. Title and Trust Co. Found. scholar 1962-65; Ford Urban law fellow, 1971-72. Fellow Am. Bar Found., Ind. State Bar, Indpls. Bar Found.; mem. ABA, Ind. State Bar Assn., Indpls. Bar Assn., Country Club Indpls., Rotary. Methodist. Office: Ind U 355 Lansing St Indianapolis IN 46202-2815

BERDAHL, ROBERT MAX, academic administrator, historian, educator; b. Sioux Falls, S.D., Mar. 15, 1937; s. Melvin Oliver and Mildred Alberta (Maynard) B.; m. Margaret Lucille Ogle, Aug. 30, 1958; children— Daphne Jean, Jennifer Lynne, Barbara Elizabeth. BA, Augustana Coll., 1959; MA, U. Ill., 1961; PhD, U. Minn., 1965. Asst. prof. history U. Mass., Boston, 1965—67; asst. prof. history U. Oreg., Eugene, 1967—72, assoc. prof., 1972—81, prof., 1981—86; dean U. Oreg. (Coll. Arts and Scis.), 1981—86; prof. U. Ill., 1986—93, vice chancellor academic affairs, 1986—93; pres. U. Tex., Austin, 1993—97; chancellor U. Calif., Berkeley, 1997—. Research asso. Inst. for Advanced Study, Princeton, 1972-73 Author: The Politics of Prussian Nobility, 1988; (with others) Klassen und Kultur, 1982; contbr. articles to profl. jours. Fulbright fellow, 1975-76; Nat. Endowment Humanities fellow, 1976-77 Office: U Calif at Berkeley 200 California Hall Spc 1500 Berkeley CA 94720-1500*

BEREITER, CARL, academic administrator, educator; BA in Comparative Lit., U. Wis., 1951, MA in Comparative Lit., 1952, PhD in Edn., 1959; LLD (hon.), Queen's U., 1993. From asst. prof. to prof. U. Ill., 1961—67; prof. Ont. Inst. for Studies in Edn., U. Toronto, Canada, 1967—, co-dir. programs and rsch. Edn. Commons, 1996—. Fellow Ctr. for Advanced Study in the Behavioral Scis., 1973—74, 1992—93; George A. Miller vis. prof. U. Ill., 1986. Recipient Guggenheim fellowship, 1968, Whitworth award, Can. Edn. Assn., 1989, Contbn. to Knowledge award, Ont. Psychol. Found., 1989. Mem.: NAE (bd. dirs.). Office: U Toronto Ont Inst for Studies in Edn 252 Bloor St W Toronto M5S 1V6 Canada*

BEREKI, DEBRA LYNN, secondary education educator; b. Riverside, Calif., Oct. 5, 1954; d. Donald Leon and Marthena Maude (Morris) Stemwedel; m. Michael Andrew Bereki, June 24, 1972 (div. Dec. 1977); m. Eric Jon Hellweg, Apr. 1, 1989 (div. Nov. 1998). AS, Barstow C.C., 1977; BS in Nutrition, U. Calif., Davis, 1980. Cert. secondary tchr., Calif. Tutor Barstow (Calif.) C.C., 1974-77, instr., 1983-85; mgr. Bray's Investments, Barstow, 1977-81; substitute tchr. Barstow Unified Sch. Dist., 1981-86; instr. Barstow Cmty. Coll., 1985-86; instr. sci. Fillmore (Calif.) Unified Sch. Dist., 1988—2000, sci. mentor, 1993-94, chair dept. sci., 1993—2000. Participant Calif. Earth Sci. Acad. Fellow Calif. Sci. Project; mem. Calif. Sci. Tchrs. Assn. (presenter at comfs., Nat. Assn. Geology Tchrs. (treas. Gold Coast Sci. Network 1993-95), Nat. Earth Sci. Tchr. Assn., Nat. Assn. Biology Tchrs., NSci. Tchrs. Assn., Gold Coast Sci. Network (pres. 1995—), Tchrs. Soc. (v.p. 1987-88), Alpha Gamma Sigma (pres. 1976-77). Avocations: camping, snorkeling, skiing, travel, dry flower arranging. Home: PO Box 390 Fillmore CA 93016-0390 Office: Fillmore High Sch 555 Central Ave Fillmore CA 93015-1392

BERENATO, PATRICE SIMON, special education educator; b. Bklyn., Dec. 7, 1956; d. Maurice and Susan (Bendekovitz) Simon; m. Anthony J. Berenato, Nov. 24, 1984; children: Anthony Jr., Susana Rose, Nicholas, Daniel. BA in Spl. Edn./Early Childhood, Glassboro (N.J.) State Coll., 1978. Resource rm. instr. Deerfield Twp. Bd. Edn., Rosenhayn, N.J., 1978-79, Hammonton (N.J.) Bd. Edn., 1979-82, tchr. perceptually impaired, 1982-88, tchr. neurologically impaired, 1988-94; tchr. multiply handicapped Warren Sooy Jr. Elem. Sch., Hammonton, N.J., 1994—. Coach N.J. Tournament of Champions, 1983—. Mem. Coun. Exceptional Children, N.J. Coun. Exceptional Children, N.J. Edn. Assn., Atlantic County Edn. Assn., Hammonton Edn. Assn. (sec. 1983-85), Glassboro State Alumni Assn. (spl. affairs com.). Home: 555 S 1st Rd Hammonton NJ 08037-8405 Office: Warren Sooy Jr Elem Sch 601 N 4th St Hammonton NJ 08037-9720

BERENDSEN, SALLYANN LAWRENCE, secondary education educator; b. Greensburg, Pa., May 10, 1939; d. Malcolm and Margaret (Grant) Lawrence; m. Peter B. Berendsen, Oct. 27, 1962; children: Thomas, Margaret, Raymond. BS in Edn., Madison Coll., 1961; MA in Math., Montclair State Coll., 1976. Cert. tchr., Va., Md., N.J., Mich. Tchr. math. Walter Johnson High Sch., Bethesda, Md., 1961-63, Slauson Jr. High Sch., Ann Arbor, Mich., 1965-67; tchr. math., dept. chair Stone Ridge Country Day Sch. of Sacred Heart, Bethesda, 1968-72; tchr. math. Hanover Park High Sch., East Hanover, N.J., 1976 spring; tchr. Newark Acad., Livingston, N.J., 1983-85; summer sch. tchr. Seton Hall Acad., South Orange, N.J., 1988-90; dept. chair, math. tchr., dir. computer sci. Far Hills (N.J.) Country Day Sch., 1976—2002. Mem. Internat. Soc. for Tech. in Edn., Nat. Coun. Tchrs. Math. E-mail: sallyannber@yahoo.com.

BERENTSEN, KURTIS GEORGE, music educator, choral conductor; b. North Hollywood, Calif., Apr. 22, 1953; s. George O. and Eleanor J. (Johnson) B.; m. Jeanette M. Sacco, Aug., 1975 (div. 1977); m. Floy I. Griffiths, March 17, 1984; 1 child, Kendra Irene. MusB, Utah State U., 1975; MA in Music, U. Calif., Santa Barbara, 1986; cert. colloguy, Concordia Coll., 1996. Cert. cmty. coll. tchr., Calif., pub. tchr., Calif.; commd. minister Luth. Ch., Mo. Synod, 1996. Dir. music Hope Luth. Ch., Daly City, Calif., 1975-81; gen. mgr. Ostara Press, Inc., Daly City, Calif., 1975-78; condr. U. Calif., Santa Barbara, 1981-86; dir., condr. Santa Barbara oratorio Chorale, 1983-85; dir. music 1st Presbyn. Ch., Santa Barbara, 1983-84, Goleta (Calif.) Presbyn. Ch., 1984-85; minister music Trinity Luth. Ch., Ventura, 1985-92, Christ Luth. Ch. & Sch., Little Rock, Ark., 1992-98; dir. choral music Concordia U., Portland, Oreg., 1998—; instr. Ventura Coll., 1987-88; music dir., condr. Gold Coast Community Chorus, Ventura, 1988-92. Choir dir. Temple Beth Torah Jewish Community, Ventura, 1982-87; adj. prof. Pepperdine U., Malibu, Calif., 1988; chorus master Ventura Symphony Orch., 1987. Condr. oratorios Christus Am Oelberg, 1983, Elijah, 1984, Hymn of Praise, 1988, cantata Seven Last Words, 1979, 84, Paukenmesse, 1989, Mozart's Requiem, 1990, Requiem-Fauré, 1991, 2002, Judas Maccabaeus-Handel, 1992; soloist 15 major oratorio and opera roles, 1971-92, Nat. Anthem, L.A. Dodgers, 1989; dir. (with John Rutter) Gold Coast Community Chorus, Carnegie Hall, N.Y.C., 1991, Tribute to America, Lincoln Ctr. Concert, N.Y.C., 1991. Min. music, tchr. Christ Luth. Ch. and Sch., Little Rock, 1992—. First place winner baritone vocalist Idaho Fedn. Music Clubs, 1971, recital winner Utah Fedn. Music Clubs, 1974. Mem. Choral Condrs. Guild, Assn. Luth. Ch. Musicians, Am. Guild of English Handbell Ringers, Am. Choral Dirs. Assn., Music Educators Nat. Conf., Sigma Nu (sec., song leader 1973-75). Home and Office: 2811 NE Holman St Portland OR 97211-6067 E-mail: Kberentsen@cu-portland.edu.

BERES, MARY ELIZABETH, management educator, organizational consultant; b. Birmingham, Ala., Jan. 19, 1942; d. John Charles and Ethel (Belenyesi) Beres. BS, Siena Heights Coll., Adrian, Mich., 1969; PhD, Northwestern U., 1976. Joined Dominican Sisters, 1960. Tchr. St. Francis Xavier Sch., Medina, Ohio, 1962-64, St. Edward Sch., Medina, Ohio, 1964-67, Our Lady of Mt. Carmel Sch., Temperance, Mich., 1967-69, asst. prin., 1968-69; tchr. math. St. Ambrose H.S., Detroit, 1969-70; vis. instr. Cornell U., 1973-74; assoc. prof. orgn. behavior Temple U., Phila., 1974-84; assoc. prof. mgmt. Mercer U., Atlanta, 1984-91; founder, sr. assoc. Leadership Sys., Atlanta, 1988—. Mem. World Pilgrims, 2002—; bd. dirs. Aquinas Ctr. Theology, 2001—. Contbr. chpts. to books; organizer of symposia in areas of corp. leadership, orgn. change and cross-cultural comm. Bd. dir. Ctr. for Ethics and Social Policy, Phila., 1980—84, Assn. Global Bus., 1989—91; mem. program planning com. of interdepartmental group in bus. adminstrn. U. Ctr. in Ga., 1987—91, chair, 1988—90; trustee Adrian Dominican Ind. Sch. Sys., Adrian, Mich., 1971—79; pres. bd. dirs. New Ventures Network, 1998—2001; mem. Atlanta Clergy and Laity Concerned, 1986—95; econ. pastoral imlementation com. Archdiocese of Atlanta, 1988—89, Atlanta Archdiocesan Planning and Devel. Coun., 1991—93; episcopal moderator women Religious Archdiocese of Atlanta, 1993—97, Atlanta Conf. Sisters, 1984—, pres., 1993—97, 2001—; vicar Religious Archdiocese of Atlanta, 2001—. Recipient Legion of Honor membership Chapel of the Four Chaplains, Phila., 1982, Disting. Tchg. award Lindback Found., 1982, Cert. for Humanity Mercer U, 1985. Mem. NAFE, Acad. of Mgmt., Dominican Sisters of Adrian, Mich. (strategic planning com. 2000-01). Democrat. Roman Catholic. Office: Leadership Sys PO Box 76475 Atlanta GA 30358-1475 E-mail: LeadSys@aol.com.

BERESFORD, THOMAS PATRICK, psychiatry educator, alcoholism researcher; b. Danville, Ill., Mar. 16, 1946; s. Thomas Edmund and Susan Elizabeth Beresford; m. Carol Ahmann, Aug. 22, 1970; children: Thomas Edward, Henry Francis, Charles Edmund. BA, Stanford U., 1969; MD, U. Colo., 1973; MA, Boston Coll., 1978. Diplomate Am. Bd. Psychiatry and Neurology. Resident, chief resident Cambridge Hosp.-Harvard Med. Sch., Cambridge, Mass., 1973-76; jr. assoc. in medicine Peter B. Brigham Hosp., Boston, 1976-78; clin. instr. Stanford (Ca.) U. Sch. Medicine, 1978-80; asst. prof. psychiatry Med. Coll. Wis., Milw., 1980-82; assoc. prof. psychiatry U. Tenn. Sch. Medicine, Memphis, 1982-86; assoc. prof., prof. psychiatry U. Mich. Med. Sch., Ann Arbor, 1986-92; prof. psychiatry U. Colo. Sch. Medicine, Denver, 1992—. Chief psychiatry VA Med. Ctr., Memphis, 1982-86; assoc. chair psychiatry U. Mich., 1986-88, sci. dir., Alcohol Rsch. Ctr., 1988-91; mem. numerous profl. coms.; presenter, cons. in field. Author: (poetry) The Pharos, 1979, Annals of Internal Medicine, 1981, (poetry) A Father's Handbook, 1982, Front Range, 1984, Handbook of Psychiatric Diagnostics Procedures, vol. I, 1984, editor vol. II, 1985;

author: Liver Transplantation and the Alcoholic Patient, 1994, Neuropsychiatry: An Introductory Approach, 2001; editor: Alcohol and Aging, 1995; assoc. editor Psychiat. Medicine, 1981-92, Psychosomatics, 1982—; asst. editor, co-author numerous titles, contbr. numerous articles to profl. jours. Recipient Emanuel Friedman award U. Colo., 1972, Henry Russel award U. Mich., 1988; Stegner fellow Stanford U., 1978-79; rsch. grantee Nat. Inst. Alcohol Abuse and Alcoholism, 1986, ctr. grantee, 1988, tng. grantee, 1990, Dept. Vets. Affairs Tng. grantee, 1995. Fellow Acad. Psychosomatic Medicine, Am. Psychiat. Assn., Acad. Psychosomatic Medicine (Best Poster award 1991, Disting. Svc. award 1994, Ann. Rsch. award 2000), Rsch. Soc. on Alcoholism. Home: 6410 S Olathe St Aurora CO 80016-1034 Office: U Colo VA Med Ctr 116 1055 Clermont St Denver CO 80220-3808 E-mail: thomas.beresford@uchsc.edu.

BERESFORD, WILMA, retired elementary and gifted education educator; b. Kensett, Ark., Nov. 3, 1931; d. Newton A. and Anna Lucille Murray (Bedair) Graham; m. Robert B. Beresford, Aug. 5, 1949; children: Anna C. Walker, Angela D. Thomas, Robert L. BS, Lamar State Coll., 1963; MEd, McNeese State U., 1971; postgrad., Lamar U. Cert. tchr., Tex. Tchr. Groves (Tex.) Pub. Schs.; spl. assignment tchr. Port Neches Ind. Sch. Dist., Groves, 1963—; Chpt. I tchr., tchr. ESL and computer literacy Port Neches Groves Ind. Sch. Dist.; now ret. Cons., presenter workshops in field. Mem. ASCD, Tex. Tchrs. Assn., Tex. Gifted and Talented Assn. (cert.), Tex. Computer Edn. Ass., Future Problem Solvers Tex. (cert. evaluator), Tex. States Tchr. Assn., Am. Bus. Women's Assn., Tex. Classroom Tchrs. Assn., Phi Delta Kappa.

BERG, BARBARA KIRSNER, health education specialist; b. Cin., Dec. 6, 1954; d. Robert and Mildred Dorothy (Warshofsky) Kirsner; m. Howard Keith Berg, Apr. 8, 1984; children: Arielle, Allison, Stacy. BA, Brandeis U., 1976; MEd, U. Cin., 1977. Cert. health edn. specialist Nat. Commn. for Health Edn. Credentialing, Inc., Mass. Health educator S.W. Ohio Lung Assn., Cin., 1977-79; coord. adminstrv. edn. N.E. Regional Med. Edn. Ctr., Northport, N.Y., 1979-81; patient health edn. coord. VA Med. Ctr., Buffalo, 1981-87; clin. asst. prof. SUNY, Buffalo, 1982-87; dir. comty. health edn. N.W. Hosp. Ctr., Balt., 1987-89; coord. law and health care program U. Md. Sch. Law, Balt., 1989-90; med. mgmt. cons. Dr. Howard K. Berg, Owings Mills, Md., 1990—. Cons. health edn. Edward Bartlett, Assoc., Rockville, Md., 1987-88; mem. adult edn. com. Chizuk Amuno Congregation, Balt., 1993-99, mem. bd. dirs., 1996-98, chair cultural arts com., 1996-98. Bd. dirs., mem. Am. Lung Assn. Western N.Y., Buffalo, 1983-86, Pumpkin Theater, Balt., 1990-91; chair domestic concerns com. Balt. Jewish Coun., 1994-96, chair govt. rels. com., 1996-98, sec., bd. dirs., 1996-98, 2d v.p. 1998-2000; sec. women's dept. Associated Jewish Charities, Balt., 1994-97; mem. sch. bd. nominating conv. Baltimore County, 1995—; pres. Pikesville Mid. Sch. PTA, 1998-2001. Mem. APHA, Soc. for Pub. Health Edn., Am. Jewish Com., Balt. Brandeis Alumni Assn. (pres.), Phi Delta Kappa. Jewish. Avocations: reading, travel, advocacy. Home and Office: 12116 Heneson Garth Owings Mills MD 21117-1629

BERG, BERND ALBERT, physics educator; b. Delmenhorst, Germany, Aug. 23, 1949; came to U.S., 1985; s. Max and Irmgard (Tetzlaff) B.; m. Ursula A. Schroder, Mar. 26, 1975; 1 child, Felix. Dr rer Nat., Free U., Berlin, 1977. Postdoctoral fellow Free U., Berlin, 1977-78, Univ. Hamburg, Germany, 1978-80, asst. prof., 1982-85; fellow CERN, Geneva, 1980-82; assoc. prof. Fla. State U., Tallahassee, 1985-88, prof., 1988—. Fellow Inst. for Advanced Study, Berlin, 1992-93. Contbr. articles to profl. jours. Achievements include work in quantum field theory and computational physics. Office: Fla State U Physics Tallahassee FL 32306

BERG, DANIEL, science and technology educator; b. N.Y.C., June 1, 1929; s. Jack and Hattie (Tannenbaum) B.; m. Frances Helena Ely, Aug. 18, 1956; children: Brian, Laura, Meredith. BS, CCNY, 1950; MS, Yale U., 1951, PhD, 1953; grad. execs. program, Carnegie-Mellon U., 1972. With Westinghouse Electric Corp., Pitts., 1953-77, research div. mgr., then tech. dir., 1976-77; prof. sci. and tech. Carnegie-Mellon U., 1977-83, dean Mellon Coll. Sci., 1977-81, univ. provost, 1981-83; v.p. acad. affairs, provost, Inst. prof. sci. and tech. Rensselaer Poly. Inst., Troy, N.Y., 1983-85, pres., 1985-87, Inst. prof., 1987—. Bd. dirs. Hy-Tech. Machine Co., Inc.; chmn. bd. Crystek Inc.; mem. Pa. Sci. and Engring. Found., 1975-76; mem. vis. coun. sci. and engring. CCNY, 1980-84; mem. vis. coun. Sch. Computer Sci., Carnegie-Mellon U., 1992—; mem. Yale U. Coun., 1981-85; assoc. fellow Jonathan Edwards Coll., 1982—; cons. to industry and govt. Author, editor, patentee in field. Fellow IEEE, AAAS, INFORMS, Am. Inst. Chemists, N.Y. Acad. Scis.; mem. Nat. Acad. Engring. (coun. 1985-88), Am. Chem. Soc., Am. Phys. Soc., Cosmos Club of Washington, Rivers Club of Pitts., Century Club N.Y.C., Phi Beta Kappa, Sigma Xi, Alpha Chi Sigma, Tau Beta Pi. Home: 12 The Crossways Troy NY 12180-7263 Office: Rensselaer Poly Inst 5015 CII Troy NY 12180-3522

BERG, EVELYNNE MARIE, geography educator; b. Chgo. d. Clarence Martin and Mildred Berg. BS with honors, U. Ill., 1954; MA, Northwestern U., 1959. Geography editor Am. Peoples Ency., Chgo., 1955-57; social studies tchr. Hammond (Ind.) Tech.-Vocat. H.S., 1958-59; geography tchr. Carl Schurz H.S., Chgo., 1960-66; faculty geography Morton Coll., Cicero, Ill., 1966-95. Contbr to profl. jours. Asst. leader Cicero coun. Girl Scouts U.S.A., 1951-53. Fulbright scholar, Brazil, 1964, NSF scholar, 1963, 65, 71-72; NDEA fellow, 1968-69; fellow Faculty Inst. S. and S.E. Asia, 1980; NEH scholar Depaul U., 1984; recipient award Ill. Geog. Soc., 1977. Fellow Nat. Coun. Geog. Edn. (state coord. 1973-74, exec. bd. 1973-77); mem. AAUW (Chgo. br. rec. sec. 1963-65, Hot Springs Ark. br. 1995-2001, northwest suburban br. 2001—), Nat. Ill. Geog. Socs. (sec.-treas. 1968-69, sec. 1969-70, v.p. 1970-71, pres. 1971-72), Am. Overseas Educators (sec. Ill. chpt. 1974-76, v.p. chpt. 1977-78), Assn. Am. Geographers, Ill. Acad. Sci., Ill. Coun. Social Studies, Geol. Soc. Am. (membership chair Morton Coll. chpt.), Ill. C.C. Faulty Assn. (v.p. membership and del. affairs 1982-84), Des Plaines Valley Geol. Soc., Fulbright Assn., Sierra Club, Sigma Xi, Gamma Theta Upsilon, Delta Kappa Gamma (pres. Gamma Omicron chpt. 1988-90, parliamentarian 1990-94, membership chair 1992-94, noninations chair 1994-95), Oak Park Bus. Club, Women's Club (acting pres. 1980-81, parliamentarian 1989-90), The Nineteenth Century Club. Home: Apt 201 6950 W Forest Preserve Ave Norridge IL 60706-1371

BERG, HOWARD C. biology educator; b. Iowa City, Iowa, Mar. 16, 1934; s. Clarence P. and Esther M. (Carlson) B.; m. Mary E. Guyer, Dec. 19, 1964; children— Henry G., Alexander H., Elena C. BS in Chemistry, Calif. Inst. Tech., Pasadena, 1956; AM in Physics, Harvard U., 1960, PhD in Chem. Physics, 1964. Jr. fellow Harvard Soc. Fellows, Cambridge, Mass., 1963-66; asst. prof. dept. biology Harvard U., Cambridge, 1966-69, assoc. prof. dept. biochemistry and molecular biology, 1969-70, prof. dept. molecular and cellular biology, 1986—; prof. physics, 1997—; assoc. prof. to prof. dept. molecular, cellular and developmental biology U. Colo., Boulder, 1970-79; prof. div. biology Calif. Inst. Tech., Pasadena, 1979-86. Mem. Rowland Inst., Cambridge, 1986—. Author: Random Walks in Biology, 1983, revised edit., 1993, E. coli in Motion, 2003; contbr. articles to profl. jours. Fulbright fellow, 1956-57, Guggenheim fellow, 2000-01; NSF Sci. Faculty Devel. awardee, 1978-79. Mem. AAAS, Am. Phys. Soc. (Biol. Physics prize 1984), Biophys. Soc., Am. Soc. Microbiology, Nat. Acad. Sci., Am. Acad. Arts and Sci., Am. Philos. Soc. Office: Harvard U Biology Labs 16 Divinity Ave Cambridge MA 02138-2020 also: Rowland Inst 100 Edwin H Land Blvd Cambridge MA 02142

BERG, KAREN LYNN ANDERSON, educator; b. Oak Park, Ill., Oct. 29, 1956; d. Ralph Lewis and Barbara Ann (Caspers) Brown; m. Timothy William Anderson, June 7, 1980 (dec. Nov. 1990); m. Terence Michael Berg, June 23, 2001. BA, U. No. Colo., 1978, MA, 1985; adminstrn. cert., Denver U., 2001. Intern Cherry Creek Schs., Walnut Hills Elem. Sch., Englewood, Colo., 1978-79; customer svc. rep. United Bank Am., Denver, 1979-80; substitute tchr. Cherry Creek Schs., Aurora (Colo.) Pub. Schs., 1980-82; advisor of Master's prog. in Whole Learning Regis U., Denver, 1991—98; tchr. Independence Elem. Sch., Aurora, 1982—85, Indian Ridge Elem. Sch., Aurora, Colo., 1985—. Dir. steering com. Regis U. Literacy Inst., 1985-94; steering com., Regis U. Early Childhood Inst., 1990-93; staff devel. liaison Cherry Creek Schs., 1991—; mem. Literacy Planning for Cherry Creek Schs., 1995—. Deacon Cherry Creek Presbyn. Ch., 1997—2000. Recipient Cherry Creek Schools Tchr. of Yr., 1988, Tchr. Who Makes a Difference award Channel 4, 1989. Mem. ASCD, Internat. Reading Assn., Young Life (com. chair 1990-96, vol. leader 1990-96, com. mem. 1998—). Republican. Presbyterian. Avocations: skiing, hiking, reading, tennis, entertaining. Home: 5558 S Telluride St Centennial CO 80015-2643 Office: Indian Ridge Elem 16501 E Progress Dr Aurora CO 80015-4135

BERG, LILLIAN DOUGLAS, chemistry educator; b. Birmingham, Ala., July 9, 1925; d. Gilbert Franklin and Mary Rachel (Griffin) Douglas; m. Joseph Wilbur Berg, June 26, 1950; children: Anne Berg Jenkins, Joseph Wilbur III, Frederick Douglas. BS in Chemistry, Birmingham So. Coll., 1946; MS in Chemistry, Emory U., 1948. Instr. chemistry Armstrong Jr. Coll., Savannah, Ga., 1948-50; rsch. asst. chemistry Pa. State U., University Park, 1950-54; instr. chemistry U. Utah, Salt Lake City, 1955-56; prof. chemistry No. Va. C.C., Annandale, 1974-96, 98—, adj. prof., 1998—. Mem. Am. Chem. Soc., Am. Women in Sci., Am. Guild Organists, Mortar Bd. Soc., Iota Sigma Pi, Sigma Delta Epsilon, Phi Beta Kappa. Avocation: music. Home: 3319 Dauphine Dr Falls Church VA 22042-3724

BERG, LORINE MCCOMIS, retired guidance counselor; b. Ashland, Ky., Mar. 28, 1919; d. Oliver Botner and Emma Elizabeth (Eastham) McComis; m. Leslie Thomas Berg, Apr. 27, 1946; children: James Michael, Leslie Jane. BA in Edn., U. Ky., 1965; MA, Xavier U., 1969. Tchr. A.D. Owens Elem. Sch., Newport, Ky., 1963-64, 6th dist. Elementary Schs., Covington, Ky., 1965-69; guidance counselor Twenhofel Jr. H.S., Independence, Ky., 1969-78, Scott H.S., Taylor Mill, Ky., 1978-84. Bd. dirs. Mental Health Assn., Covington, Ky, 1970-76, v.p., 1973 (valuable svc. award 1973); mem. Lakeside Christian Ch., Ft. Mitchell, Ky. Named to Honorable Order of Ky. Colonels, Hon. Admissions Counselor U.S. Naval Acad.; cited by USN Recruiting Command for Valuable Assistance to USN, 1981. Mem. Am. Assn. of Univ. Women, Covington Art Club, Retired Tchrs. Assn., Kappa Delta Pi, Delta Kappa Gamma, Phi Delta Kappa. Democrat. Avocations: oil painting, dancing, reading, arts and crafts. Home: 11 Idaho Ave Covington KY 41017-2925

BERG, SISTER MARIE MAJELLA, retired academic administrator; b. Bklyn., July 7, 1916; d. Gustav Peter and Mary Josephine (McAuliff) B. BA, Marymount Coll., 1938; MA, Fordham U., 1948; DHL (hon.), Georgetown U., 1970, Marymount Manhattan Coll., 1983. Registrar Marymount Sch., N.Y.C., 1943-48; prof. classics, registrar Marymount Coll., N.Y.C., 1948—57; registrar Marymount Coll. of Va., Arlington, 1957-58, Marymount Coll., Tarrytown, N.Y., 1958-60; pres. Marymount U., Arlington, Va., 1960-93, chancellor, 1993—2001, pres. emerita, 2001—03. Pres. Consortium for Continuing Higher Edn. in Va., 1987-88; mem. com. Consortium of Univs. in Washington Met. Area, 1987-93, chmn., 1992-93. Contbr. five biographies to One Hundred Great Thinkers, 1965; editor Otherwords column of N.Va. Sun newspaper, Arlington, College to University: A Memoir, 1999. Bd. dirs. Internat. Hospice, 1984-96, Ballston Partnership, 1992—, Hope, SOAR, 10th Dist. Congl. Award Coun., No. Va.; vice chmn. bd. Va. Found. Ind. Colls., 1992-93; cmty. advisor Jr. League No. Va., 1992—; mem. Friends of TACT, 1994—. Recipient commendation Va. Gen. Assembly, Richmond, 1990, 93, Elizabeth Ann Seton award, 1991, Arlington Notable Women award Arlington Commn. on Status of Women, 1992, Voice and Vision award Arlington Cmty. TV Channel 33, 1993, Pro Ecclesia et Pontifice medal Holy See, 1993; elected to Va. Women's Hall of Fame, 1992; named Washingtonian of Yr., Washingtonian mag., 1990, Arlington Cmty. Hero award, 1999; named to Washington Bus. Hall of Fame, Washingtonian mag. 1998, Jr. Achievement, 1998. Roman Catholic. Avocations: sewing, crocheting, reading. Home: Marymount Convent 32 Warren Ave Tarrytown NY 10591

BERG, MARY JAYLENE, pharmacy educator, researcher; b. Fargo, N.D., Nov. 7, 1950; d. Ordean Kenneth and Anna Margaret (Skramstad) B. BS in Pharmacy, N.D. State U., 1974; PharmD, U. Ky., 1978. Lic. pharmacist, N.D., Ky., Iowa. Fellow in pharmacokinetics Millard Fillmore Hosp./SUNY, Buffalo, 1978-79; asst. prof. U. Iowa, Iowa City, 1980-85, assoc. prof., 1985-95, prof., 1995—; with dept. clin. rsch., clin. pharmacology/pharmacokinetics F. Hoffmann-La Roche, Ltd., Basel, Switzerland, 1992; with Office of Rsch. on Women's Health NIH, 1999. Bd. dirs. Soc. for Women's Health Rsch., 1998—; mem. adv. com. rsch. on women's health NIH, 1995-99, mem. task force rsch. on women's health NIH, 1997-99; mem. adv. bd. Pfizer Women's Health, 1998—; mem. adv. com. on pharm. scis. FDA, 1999-2002. Reviewer Cin. Pharmacy, 1984—, Epilepsia, 1987—, Annals of Pharmacotherapy, 1997—; editor: (med. symposia) Internat. Leadership Symposium, The Role of Women in Pharmacy, 1990, Women-A Force in Pharmacy Symposium, 1992, Gender Related Health Issues: An International Perspective, 1996, Global Visions of Women Pharmacists, 1998; mem. editl. adv. bd.: The Internat. Jour. of Applied and Basic Nutritional Scis., 1998, Jour. Gender Specific Medicine, 1998—2001; mem. editl. bd. Jour. Women's Health, 2003—, XXvsYY: The Internat. Jour. of Sex Differences in the Study of Health, Disease and Aging, 2003; contbr. articles to numerous med., pharmacy and nutrition jours., 1998. Advisor Kappa Epislon, Iowa City, 1980-94; pres. Mortar Bd. Alumnae, Iowa City, 1986-88. NIH grantee, 1984, Nat. Insts. on Drug Abuse grantee, 1986; recipient Career Achievement award Kappa Epsilon, 1985, Vanguard award Kappa Epsilon Merck, 1999, Master award N.D. State U., 2000; named to Iowa Women's Hall of Fame, 1999. Mem.: Leadership Internat-Women for Pharmacy (bd. dirs. 1991—), Fedn. Internat. Pharmaceutique (del. World Health Assembly 1992, pres. acad. sect. 2000—02), Internat. Forum of Women for Pharmacy (U.S. contact) (U.S. contact 1988—), Am. Pharm. Assn., Am. Epilepsy Soc., Am. Soc. Hosp. Pharmacists (chair spl. interest group clin. pharmokinetics 1987—89), Am. Assn. Pharm. Scientists, Phi Beta Delta, Kappa Epsilon, Rho Chi, Sigma Xi. Lutheran. Achievements include research in multiple doses of oral activated charcoal to clear totally absorbed drug, pharmacokinetics of drug-nutrient interaction between phenytoin and folic acid, also on both national and international levels, pharmacological differences between men and women (gender analysis of medications) and among ethnic groups for prescription medicines, over-the-counter medications and alternative natural drugs, research on the interrelations among folic acid, vitamin B6, vitamin B12 and zinc in diet and vitamin supplementation in pregnant and non-pregnant women with and without epilepsy; initiating graduate program in clinical pharmaceutical sciences at the U. Iowa College of Pharmacy. Office: U Iowa Coll of Pharmacy Iowa City IA 52242

BERGEMAN, CLARISSA HELLMAN, special education educator, retired; b. Davenport, Iowa, Feb. 28, 1947; d. Karl Herman and Virginia Clara (Morgan) Hellman; m. George William Bergeman, Oct. 24, 1968; 1 child, Jessica Ann. BA, U. Iowa, 1970. Cert. spl. edn. kindergarten-12th grade, mentally retarded, Va. Spl. edn. tchr. Iowa City Schs., 1970-72; elem. tchr. Peace Corps, Liberia, West Africa, 1972-75; English as second lang. tchr. Loudoun County Pub. Schs., Lessburg, Va., 1975-76; spl. edn. tchr. Loudoun County Pub. Shs., Leesburg, Va., 1976-97; ret., 1997. Curriculum developer in field, 1970-92. Cmty. organizer Vols. in Svc. to Am., Ctrl. Fla., 1968-69; bd. dirs. Every Citizen Has Opportunities Sheltered Workshop, Purcellville, Va., 1987-90. Named Spl. Educ. Tchr. of Yr., Assn. Retarded Citizens Va., 1990. Mem. NEA, Va. Edn. Assn., Alpha Delta Kappa (chaplain 1991-94, sgt. at arms 1994—). Home: 35441 Williams Gap Rd Round Hill VA 20141-2231

BERGEMAN, GEORGE WILLIAM, mathematics educator, software author; b. Ft. Dodge, Iowa, July 16, 1946; s. Harold Levi and Hilda Carolyn (Nuhn) B.; m. Clarissa Elaine Hellman, Oct. 24, 1968; 1 child, Jessica Ann. BA, U. Iowa, 1970, MS, 1972; postgrad., Va. Inst. Tech., 1978-83. Teaching asst. U. Iowa, Iowa City, 1970-72; coll. instr. Peace Corps, Liberia, 1972-75; asst. prof. math. No. Va. C.C., Sterling, 1975—; software author George W. Bergeman Software, Round Hill, Va., 1984—. Cons. Excel Corp., Reston, Va., 1983-84; developer software including graphics and expert systems. Author: (software, book) 20/20 Statistics, 1985, 2nd edit., 1988 (software) MathCue, 1987, 2nd edit., 1991, Graph 2D/3D, 1990, 93, MathCue Solution Finder, 1991, 2nd edit., 1992, F/C Graph, 1993, F/C.P Graph, 1995-96, MathCue Practice, 1994, 95-96, MathCue Business, 1997, 2000, 02, MathCue, 1998, 2000, MathCue Course Management, 1999, 2000, MathCue Express, 2001, IVSB/MathCue, 2003. Cmty. worker VISTA, Ctrl. Fla., 1968-69. Named Outstanding Educator Phi Theta Kappa, 1987. Mem. Math. Assn. Am., Am. Math. Soc., Am. Math. Assn. Two-Yr. Colls., Phi Kappa Phi. Home: 35441 Williams Gap Rd Round Hill VA 20141-2231

BERGEN, STANLEY SILVERS, JR., retired university president, physician; b. Princeton, N.J., May 2, 1929; s. Stanley Silvers and Leah (Johnson) B.; m. Suzanne E. Miller, Nov. 16, 1965; children: Steven Richard, Victoria Elizabeth, Stuart Vaughn; children by previous marriage: Stanley Silvers III, Amy Dorle. AB, Princeton U., 1951; MD, Columbia U., 1955; hon. degrees, Bloomfield Coll., 1972, Stevens Inst., 1985; LLD (hon.), Princeton U., 1995; DSc Patterson (N.J.) State U. (hon.), 1997; DSc (hon.), Ramapo Coll. N.J., 1997, N.J. Inst. Tech., 1998; DHL (hon.), Univ. Medicine Dentistry N.J., 2002. Resident St. Luke's Hosp., N.Y.C., 1955-58, chief resident, Francis Zabriskie fellow, 1958-59, asst. chief dept. medicine, 1959-60, asst. attending physician, 1962-64; med. dir. Convalescent and Research Unit, Greenwich, Conn., 1962-64; chief medicine Cumberland Hosp., Bklyn., 1964-68; asst. dir. dept. medicine Bklyn.-Cumberland Med. Center, 1964-68, chief community medicine, 1968-70; sr. v.p. N.Y.C. Health & Hosps. Corp., 1970-71; instr. medicine Columbia, 1959-64; asso. prof. medicine Downstate Med. Sch., Bklyn., 1964-71; pres. U. Medicine and Dentistry N.J., Newark, 1971-98, founding pres. emeritus, 1998—. Prof. medicine N.J. Med. Sch., Robert Wood Johnson Med. Sch., Sch. Osteo. Medicine; prof. cmty. dentistry N.J. Dental Sch.; attending med. staff Univ. Hosp., Newark, 1971—, VA Hosp., East Orange, 1972-98, Robert Wood Johnson U. Hosp., 1981-98; trustee Univ. HealthCare Corp., 1993-99; chair bd. trustees Univ. Health Plans N.J., 1994-99; trustee University Heights Sci. Park, 1995—, chmn. bd., 1996—. Author articles in field. Mem. Mayor's Commn. Health and Hosps., N.Y.C., 1969-70; mem. N.J. Comprehensive Health Planning Coun., 1971-91; chmn. N.J. Commn. to Study Structure and Function N.J. Dept. Health, 1973, N.J. Abortion Commn., 1975, Adv. Coun. Grad. Edn. N.J., 1978-98; adv. com. mcpl. health svc. program R.W. Johnson, also, Nat. Conf. Mayors, 1980-85; mem. Bd. Comprehensive Health, Newark, 1976-81, treas., 1972-80; bd. dirs. Cancer Inst. N.J., 1974-98; bd. dirs. Ednl. Commn. Fgn. Med. Grads., 1982-91, vice chmn., 1985-86, chmn., 1986-91; bd. dirs., mem. exec. com. Hastings Ctr. on Biomed. Ethics, 1976-, chmn. devel. com., 1980-95, mem. governance com., 1995-, chmn. elect, 1997, chmn., 1998-; bd. dirs., mem. exec. com. Art Center No. N.J., 1978-82; chmn. N.J. Blood Banks Task Force, 1980-90; trustee Robert Wood Johnson U. Hosp., 1985-98, exec. com. 1987-98; trustee Hackensack Med. Ctr., 1990-99, exec. com., 1992-99; bd. joint mgrs. Cancer Inst. N.J., 1991-98, trustee 1998-2002; trustee Bergen Pines County Hosp., 1994-98, exec. com. 1994-98, trustee Univ. Healthcare Corp. of N.J., 1993-97, Gilda's Club No. N.J., 1997-2000, treas., mem. exec. com., 1998-2000, Kessler Med. Rehab. Rsch. Edn. Corp., 1998-2003, Matheny Sch. and Hosp., 1998-2000, Internat. Ctr. Pub. Health Inc., 1999-; treas. Pres.'s Coun. N.J. Commn. Higher Edn., 1996-98; chmn. bd. trustees U. Health Plan N.J., 1997-99; chair bd. mgrs. N.J. Ctr. Biomaterials, 1997-02; bd. trustees University Heights Sci. Park, 1989-, chair, 1995-; bd. dirs. Blue Hill Meml. Hosp., 2000-, vice chmn. bd., 2001-, Eastern Maine Healthcare Sys., 2002-; bd. dirs. Blue Hill Meml. Hosp. Found., 2000-, vice chmn. bd., 2001-; chair bd. dirs. MedTower, 2000-; trustee Ea. Maine Health Sys., 2002-. First recipient Woodrow Wilson medal for pub. svc. leadership Gov. of N.J., 1987, Univ. medal UMDNJ, 1995. Fellow ACP, Assn. Am. Med. Colls., Am. Fedn. Clin. Rsch., Endocrine Soc., Clin. Soc. N.Y., Diabetes Assn. (v.p. 1969-70, chmn. clin. soc. 1968-69), N.Y. Acad. Scis., Am. Inst. Nutrition; mem. AMA (ho. dels. sect. on med. schs. 1978-98), Assn. Acad. Health Ctrs., Am. Diabetes Assn. (bd. dirs. N.J. affiliate), Am. Soc. Clin. Nutrition, Am. Coll. Healthcare Execs. (hon. fellow), Essex County Med. Soc., Med. Soc. N.J., Am. Hosp. Assn. (trustee 1992-94, chmn. com. grad. med. edn. 1974-76, mem. coun. profl. svcs. 1973-76, mem. governing coun. sect. met. hosps. 1984-87, com. med. edn. 1984-91, ad hoc com. on AIDS 1987-91, chmn. tech. com. biomed. ethics 1986-91, alt. del. Ho. Dels., 1991, mem. AHA regional policy bd., 1988-94, mem. internat. med. scholars program 1987-92, mem. com. to study single pathway to nat. med. licensure 1987-90, mem. com. to study clin. med. skills assessement 1988-92, trustee 1991-94, trustee regional plan commn. 1995-98), Greater Newark C. of C. (dir. 1978-84), Nat. Assn. Pub. Hosps. (trustee 1982-88), State N.J. Health Coord. Coun., Univ. Health System N.J. (trustee, exec. com. 1987-98), Univ. Hosp. Consortium (trustee 1988-92, exec. com. 1990-92), N.Y. Acad. Scis., Opera House Arts (mem. bd. advisors, 2002-, chair facilities com., 2003-). Home: 164 Glenwood Rd Englewood NJ 07631-1951 Office: U Medicine & Dentistry NJ 100 Bergen St Newark NJ 07103-2407 E-mail: sasbergen@aol.com.

BERGEN, VIRGINIA LOUISE, principal, language arts educator; b. St. Louis, Apr. 5, 1945; d. Roland Daniel Paton and Gladys (Crawford) Gibson; m. Robert Elwood Bergen, July 11, 1964; children: Robert Brandon, Jennifer Lynn. BA, So. Ill. U., 1971, MS, 1973, EdS, 1975; Ednl. Adminstrn. Cert., U. Oreg., 1981. Cert. K-12 Ed. Ad., K-9 tchr., K-12 spl. edn., speech corr., reading specialist, Colo., Oreg., Ill, Mo., N.Mex. Speech therapist Dist. #175, Belleville, Ill., 1971-73; K-12 clin. tchr. Collinsville (Ill.) Unit #10, 1973-74, jr. high sch. LD tchr., 1974-78; edn. resource cons. Douglas Edn. Svc. Dist., Roseburg, Oreg., 1978-80; child devel. specialist Roseburg Dist. #4, 1980-82; asst. prin. Mesa County Valley Dist. #51, Grand Junction, Colo., 1982-85, prin., 1985—. Vis. lectr. So. Ill. U., 1976-78; instr. Met. State Coll., Denver, 1989-91; lectr. Mesa State Coll., Grand Junction, 1991-92; in-svc. provider Mesa County Valley Sch. Dist. #51, 1982—, mem. standards and assessment steering com.; founding mem. governance bd. Basil T. Knight Staff Devel. Ctr., Dist. #51, Grand Junction, 1986-89. Mem. Colo. Assn. Sch. Execs., Phi Delta Kappa. Avocations: reading, alpine skiing, travel, nordic skiing. Office: Fruitvale Elem Sch 585 30 Rd Grand Junction CO 81504-5602

BERGER, BENNETT MAURICE, sociology educator; b. N.Y.C., May 1, 1926; s. Julius and Ethel (King) B.; m. Jean Kirkham, Dec. 9, 1956 (div. 1971); children: Jane, Nora.; m. Chandra Mukerji, Jan. 1981 (div. 1999); children— Kenneth, Stephanie. AB, Hunter Coll., 1950; PhD, U. Calif.-Berkeley, 1958. Asst. prof., then assoc. prof. sociology U. Ill., 1959-63; mem. faculty U. Calif.-Davis, 1963-73, prof. sociology, 1965-73, chmn. dept., 1963-66, 67-69; prof. sociology U. Calif.-San Diego, 1973-91, prof. emeritus, 1991—, chmn. dept., 1979-81. Author: Working-Class Suburb, 1960, Looking for America, 1971, The Survival of a Counterculture, 1981, 2d edit., 2003, Authors of Their Own Lives, 1990, An Essay on Culture, 1995; assoc. editor: Sociometry, 1966-69, Social Problems, 1969-72; editor: Contemporary Sociology, 1974-77; sr. editor: Society, 1983-87. Served with USMCR, 1944-46. Fellow Am. Sociol. Assn.; mem. AAUP. Home: PO Box 872 Albion CA 95410-0872 Office: U Calif Dept Sociology San Diego CA 92093

BERGER, BONNIE G. sport psychologist, educator; b. Champaign, Ill., May 20, 1941; d. Bernard G. and Mildred W. Berger; 1 child, Stephen Casher. BS, Wittenberg U., 1962; MA, Columbia U., 1965, EdD, 1972. Tchr. George Rogers Clark Jr. H.S., Springfield, Ohio, 1962-64; supr. phys. edn. Agnes Russell Elem. Sch., N.Y.C., 1964-65; asst. prof. SUNY, Geneseo, 1965-66, Dalhousie U., Halifax, N.S., Can., 1969-71, Bklyn. Coll., 1971-77, assoc. prof., 1978-82, prof., 1982-93, dir. Sport Psychology Lab., dep. chair dept. phys. edn., 1989-93; prof., assoc. dean Sch. Phys. and Health Edn. U. Wyo., Laramie, 1993-96, prof., assoc. dean Coll. Health Scis., 1996-99; prof., dir. Sch. Human Movement, Sport and Leisure Studies, Bowling Green (Ohio) State U., 1999—. Cons. in field. Author: Free Weights for Women, 1984, Foundations of Exercise Psychology, 2002; contbr. chpts. to books, articles to profl. jours. Fellow Assn. for Advancement of Applied Sport Psychology (exec. bd.) Am. Acad. Kinesiology and Phys. Edn.; mem. APA, AAHPERD, Internat. Soc. Sports Psychology, N.Am. Soc. Psychology and Phy. Activity. Home: 640 Pine Valley Dr Bowling Green OH 43402

BERGER, BRUCE SUTTON, mechanical engineering educator; b. Phila., May 23, 1932; m. Fredericka Jane Nolde, Mar. 14, 1958; children: Eric, Conrad. BSc, U. Pa., 1954, MSc, 1959, PhD, 1962. Math. analyst GE Co., Phila., 1956-57; asst. instr. U. Pa., Phila., 1957-59, rsch. asst., 1960-61; asst. prof. mech. engring. Vanderbilt U., Nashville, 1962-63, U. Md., College Park, 1964-65, assoc. prof., 1965-68, prof., 1969—. Activity dir. Harvard Internat. Seminar, Cambridge, Mass., 1959-62. Contbr. over 100 articles to profl. jour. Mem. ASME (dir. Washington sect. 1980—, Devel. award 1989), Soc. Engring. Sci., Pi Tau Sigma. Achievements include develop. of math. methods in nonlinear dynamical sys., time series analysis and metal cutting. Office: Dept of Mech Eng Univ of Md Hyattsville MD 20782 E-mail: berger@eng.umd.edu

BERGER, DIANNE GWYNNE, family life educator, consultant; b. N.Y.C., Mar. 10, 1950; d. Harold and Mary Bell (Mott) Gwynne; m. Robert Milton Berger, Aug. 25, 1974; children: Matthew Robert Gwynne, Daniel Alan Gwynne BS, Cornell U., 1971; MS, Drexel U., 1974; PhD, U. Pa., 1992. Cert. home econs. tchr., sexuality educator, family and consumer sci. educator and family life educator, Pa.; cert. supervision, curriculum and instrn. Tchr. family and consumer scis., sexuality edn. Wallingford-Swarthmore Sch. Dist., 1972—. Cons., Swarthmore, 1986—, Swarthmore Presbyn. Ch., 1995, Elwyn Insts., Media, Pa., 1989-91, Phila. Task Force on Sex Edn., 1991-93. Cons. Trinity Coop. Day Nursery, Swarthmore, 1980-93, Renaissance Edn. Assn., Valley Forge, Pa., 1987-94, A Better Chance, Inc., Swarthmore, 1990-91; mem. sci. bd. Adolescent Wellness and Reproductive Edn. Found. Grantee Impact, Inc., 1990. Mem. NEA, Am. Assn. Family and Consumer Scis. (presenter), Soc. for Sci. Study of Sex (sec. ea. region presenter), Nat. Coun. on Famly Rels., Am. Assn. Sex Educators, Counselors and Therapists (chmn. Delaware Valley sect. 1996-98). Home: 304 Dickinson Ave Swarthmore PA 19081-2001

BERGER, FRANK RAYMOND, secondary education educator, county legislator; b. Rochester, N.Y., June 8, 1934; s. Raymond George and Caroline Betsy (Ferguson) B.; m. Nancy Jane Wilson, Aug. 25, 1956; children: Gary Raymond, Bryan Louis. BS in Indsl. Arts Edn., SUNY, Oswego, 1959; MS in Indsl. Arts Edn., SUNY, Buffalo, 1963. Lic. tchr. indsl. arts, supervision indsl. arts, drivers edn. Secondary tchr. Medina (N.Y.) Ctrl. Sch., 1959—89; county legislator Orleans County, Albion, NY, 1980—94. Mem. exec. bd. Lewiston Trail coun. Boy Scouts Am., mem. N.E. region com., nat. coun. com., lodge advisor Order of Arrow, sect. advisor N.E. region; Presbyn. Scouters; deacon, elder Medina Presbyn. Ch., past pres. men's group; head Medina Meml. Day Parade, 1971—, Medina Canal Festival Parade, 1982—, Orleans County Legislator, 1980, vice-chmn., chmn., 1992-93; treas. Orleans County Soil & Water Conservation Dist., 1987-93; mem. exec. bd. Iroquois Trail Coun., Boy Scouts Am., 1993—, chmn. Orleans dist., 1998—. Recipient various awards Boy Scouts Am.,Disting. Svc. award Nat. Order of the Arrow, Silver Beaver, Dan Beard Mason Scouting award; George Meany award AFL-CIO, award Medina C. of C., 1986; named Regional Tchr. of Yr., N.Y. State Indsl. Arts Tchrs. Assn., 1973-74, 88-89, Medina Citizen of Yr., Jour.-Register, 1972, Am. Legion Dept. N.Y. Scouter of the Yr., 2001. Mem. Am. Legion (life, comdr. post 204 1986-87, 93-94, Orleans County comdr. 1993-94, chef de gare Orleans County 40 et 8 Voiture 971 1993—, Post 204 Legionnaire of Yr. 1988, Orleans County Legionnaire of Yr. 1989), N.Y. State Indsl. Arts Assn. (life), N.Y. State Ret. Tchrs. Assn. (life, pres. Orleans chpt. 1992-96, pres. Ctrl. We. Zone 1997-2000), Medina Hist. Soc. (past pres.), Orleans County Hist. Assn. (past pres.), Vets. Assn., Intercounty of Western N.Y. (pres. 1993), Nat. Eagle Scout Assn., Presbyn. Scouters Assn., Scottish Heritage Soc. Rochester, Masons, Scottish Rite. Republican. Presbyterian. Avocations: camping, scouts, historical societies. Home: 3626 N Gravel Rd Medina NY 14103-9402

BERGER, FREDERICK JEROME, electrical engineer, educator; b. Szatmar, Hungary, Nov. 26, 1916; came to U.S. 1929; s. Joseph and Goldie (Weiss) B. BS, CCNY, 1959, BEE, 1961; MEE, NYU, 1964; LLD, Frank Ross Stuart U., 1981; DSc, Capitol Coll., Laurel, Md., 1986. Tool and die maker Brewster Aero. Co., 1935-39, chief tool, gauge and plant engr., 1939-45; process engr. Arma Co., 1946-51; entrepreneur Elec. Electronic Communication Systems and Machine Shop Equipments, 1952-61; prof., dep. chmn., chmn. and engring. sci. coord. CUNY, 1962-82. Evaluator Accrediting Bd. Engring., 1962-81; cons. NSF, 1969-80. Editor Jour. of Tau Alpha Pi, 1975-95. With U.S. Army, WWII. Recipient Letter of Recognition for Outstanding Contbn. to Edn. Pres. Ronald Regan, 1987, Pres. William Clinton, 1993. Fellow Am. Soc. Engring. Edn. (Frederick J. Berger ann. scholarship award 1990—, James H. McGraw award in Engring. Tech. Edn. 1992, Centennial cert. and medallion 1993); mem. IEEE (life, Engring. Svc. award 1964-81), Am. Nuclear Engring. Soc., Instrument Soc. Am. (life), Masons, Tau Alpha Pi (founding exec. dir. 1973-98), Tau Beta Pi.*

BERGER, HARRIS MERLE, ethnomusicologist, educator; s. Charles and Judith B.; m. Giovanna Patrizia Del Negro, Feb. 1, 1993. BA, Wesleyan U., Middletown, Conn., 1988; MA, Ind. U., 1991, PhD, 1995. Instr. Ind. U., Bloomington, 1994; auditory cognition rschr. Sound/Video Analysis and Instrn. Lab., Ind. U., Bloomington, 1995; asst. prof. music Tex. A&M U., 1996—2002, assoc. prof. music, 2002—. Author: Metal, Rock, and Jazz, 1999; co-editor: Global Pop, Local Language, 2003— composer, performer jazz composition Flying: A Evening of Contemporary Jazz, 1984; contbr. articles to Ethnomusicology, Jour. Folklore Rsch., Popular Music, Jour. Am. Folklore. Jacob K. Javitz fellow U.S. Dept. Edn., 1989-92. Mem. Soc. for Ethnomusicology (founder, chair popular music sect. 1996—), Am. Folklore Soc., Internat. Assn. Study of Popular Music. Office: Music Program Tex A&m Univ College Station TX 77843-0001

BERGER, JANE MAULDIN, psychologist, educator; b. Atlanta, July 28, 1945; d. John Frank and Lilly Bell (Casey) Mauldin; B.A., U. Ga., 1966; M.S. (NDEA fellow), U. Ga., 1967; Ph.D. in Psychology, U. Miami, 1971; M.B.A., Nova U., 1984; m. Michael L. Berger, Jan. 8, 1966; children—Louis Jefferson Mauldin, James Ivan Mauldin, Sarah Elizabeth Mauldin. Instr. psychology Miami-Dade Community Coll., 1968-71, asst. prof., 1971-73, assoc. prof., 1976-79, prof., 1979— ; pvt. practice psychology, Miami, 1971— ; guest lectr. U. Miami; cons. Dade County Rape Treatment Center; guest speaker civic groups. Cert. psychologist, Fla. Mem. Am. Psychol. Assn., Fla. Psychol. Assn., Dade County Psychol. Assn., Mental Health Assn. Dade County, S. Fla. Forum Death Edn. and Counseling, Phi Beta Kappa, Phi Kappa Phi, Psi Chi. Address: 2500 W Broad St Ste 413 Athens GA 30606-3440

BERGER, MIRIAM ROSKIN, creative arts therapy director, educator, therapist; b. N.Y.C., Dec. 9, 1934; d. Israel and Florence Roskin; m. Meir Berger, July 16, 1967; 1 child, Jonathan Israel. Student, Barnard Coll., 1952-53; BA, Bard Coll., 1956; postgrad., CCNY, 1956-58; Dr. Arts, NYU, 1998. Alumni dir. Bard Coll., Annandale-on-Hudson, N.Y., 1958-59; dance therapist Manhattan Psychiatric Ctr., N.Y.C., 1959-60; performer, educator Jean Erdman Theater of Dance, N.Y.C., 1959-62; dir. adult program Hebrew Arts Sch., N.Y.C., 1981; faculty Dance Notation Bur., N.Y.C., 1974-75, 77; asst. prof. dance therapy program NYU, 1975—, acting dir. dance therapy program, 1991, dir. dance edn. program, 1993—2002; dir. creative arts therapies Bronx Psychiatric Ctr., N.Y.C., 1970-90. Workshop leader in field. Prodr. off-Broadway The Coach with the Six Insides, 1962-63; author, prodr. Non-Verbal Group Process, 1978; co-editor Am. Jour. Dance Therapy, 1991-94; led dance therapy session Senate hearing on Aging, 1992; contbr. articles to profl. jours.; editl. bd. Arts in Psychotherapy, Jour. Dance Edn. Chair Nat. Coalition of Creative Arts Therapies Assns., 2002—; bd. dirs. Theater Open Eye, 1978—82, v.p. bd. trustees, 1982—89, pres., 1989—94. Recipient NYU scholarship, 1981, Best Paper award Med Art World congress on Arts and Medicine, 1992. Mem.: Acad. Registered Dance Therapists, Am. Dance Therapy Assn. (founder, bd. dirs. 1967—76, v.p. 1974—76, 1992, credential com. 1976, 1982, keynote speaker at nat. conf. 1991, pres. 1994—98), Dance Libr. Israel (v.p.). E-mail: miriam.berger@nyu.edu.

BERGER, STANLEY ALLAN, mechanical and biomechanical engineering educator; b. Bklyn., Aug. 9, 1934; s. Jack and Esther B.; m. Anna Ofman, Jan. 30, 1966 (div. Aug. 1984); children: Shoshana, Maya. BS, Bklyn. Coll., 1955; PhD, Brown U., 1959. Rsch. assoc. Princeton U., N.J., 1959-60; from lectr. to prof. U. Calif., Berkeley, 1961—. Cons. IBM, The Rand Corp., Lockheed Missiles and Space Co., Sci. Applications, Inc., Aluminum Co. Am. Author: Laminar Wakes, 1971; editor: Introduction to Bioengineering, 1996; contbr. articles to profl. jours. Fellow: AIAA, ASME (chair applied mechanics divsn. 1997—98), AAAS, Am. Inst. Med. and Biol. Engring., Am. Phys. Soc. (chair divsn. fluid dynamics 2001—02). Home: 899 Arlington Ave Berkeley CA 94707-1926 Office: U Calif Dept Mech Engring Berkeley CA 94720-1740 E-mail: saberger@me.berkeley.edu.

BERGER, SUE ANNE, secondary education educator, chemist; b. Wichita, Kans., Oct. 8, 1941; d. Oscar Henry and Josephine Mildred (Stucky) B. BE, Kans. State Tchrs. Coll., 1963; MS in Chemistry, U. Miss., 1968; MS in Mineral Econs., Colo. Sch. Mines, 1982. Cert. chemistry and math. tchr., Colo. Tchr. Davy Crockett Jr. High Sch., Amarillo, Tex., 1963-67, Bear Creek Sr. High Sch., Denver, 1968-94. Dept. chmn. Bear Creek Sr. High Sch., 1980-85; adj. prof., Physics, (Golden) Colo. Schl. of Mines, 1994—. Author: (with others) Element of the Week, 1986, CHEM-PACS, 1989. Named Disting. Tchr., White House Commn. on Presdl. Scholars, 1987, 88; recipient Exemplary H.S. Sci. Tchg. award CIBA-Geigy, 1992, A Plus for Breaking the Mold award Mobile Sci. Show, 1993, Disting. Svc. to Sci. Edn. award Colo. Assn. Sci. Tchrs., 1994. Mem. Am. Chem. Soc. (named Tchr. of Yr. Colo. chpt. 1988), Nat. Sci. Tchrs. Assn., Colo. Assn. Sci. Tchrs., Colo. Chem. Tchr. Assn., Phi Delta Kappa. Democrat. Mennonite. Avocations: cross country skiing, golf, bridge. Home: 6372 S Annapurna Dr Evergreen CO 80439-5334

BERGERON, SHEILA DIANE, retired science educator, educational consultant; b. Decatur, Ill., Aug. 17, 1940; d. Lewis F. and Elizabeth A. (Hoff) Brown; m. Richard A. Bergeron, Sept. 25, 1965; 1 child, Cynthia Diane. BS in Spl. Edn., Ill. State U., 1962; MA in Counseling, U. Colo., 1980. Tchr. Villa Park (Ill.) Dist. # 45, 1962-68, Jefferson County Schs. R-1, Golden, Colo., 1968-98; ret., 1998. Cons. in field; adj. instr. U. No. Colo., Greeley, 1980-86, Met. State U., 1986-88, 2000-2002, U. Colo., Denver, 1986-88, Colo. Christian U., 1998-2002, Colo. Mtn. Coll., 2000-01; staff devel. cons. Denver Pub. Schs., Summit County Schs., Dillon, Colo., Dallas Pub. Schs., Lake City Schs., Colo., Mpls. Pub. Schs., 1982-93; team mem. North Ctrl. Accreditation Assn., 1978, 90. Steering com. mem., pres. Leadership Golden, 1986-2002; emergency communicator ARC, Denver, 1990-98; vol. Pub. TV, KRMA-TV, Denver, 1991-2002, Golden Civic Found., 1986-94; commr. Golden Urban Renewal Authority, 1999-2002. Named A-Plus Tchr. Rocky Mountain News and KCNC-TV, 1992; recipient Presdl. Excellence in Sci. Teaching award, 1995. Mem. ASCD, NSTA (Nat. Sci. Tchrs. Assn.), Nat. Staff Devel. Coun. Avocation: amateur radio operator. Home: 606 Alaska St Golden CO 80403-1308 E-mail: dianebergeron@attbi.com.

BERGESON, TERESA, school system administrator; b. Mass. BA in English, Emmanuel Coll., Boston, 1964; M in Counseling and Guidance, Western Mich. U., 1969; PhD in Edn., U. Wash. Tchr., j.h. sch. guidance counselor, Mass., Alaska, Wash.; exec. dir. Ctrl. Kitsap Sch. Dist., 1989-92, Wash. State Commn. on Learning, 1993-95; state supt. pub. instrn. Olympia, Wash., 1997—. V.p. Wash. Edn. Assn., 1981, pres., 1985—89. Mem.: Wash. Edn. Assn. (v.p. 1981—85, pres. 1985—89). Office: PO Box 47200 Olympia WA 98504-7200 Fax: 360-753-6712.*

BERGEY, GREGORY KENT, neurology educator, neuroscientist; b. Bryn Mawr, Pa., Nov. 9, 1949; s. Robert Harr and Kathryn (Schmidt) B.; m. Stefanie Friday Antonakos, Aug. 27, 1972; children: Alyssa Noelle, Alexander Christian. AB, Princeton U., 1971; MD, U. Pa., 1975. Diplomate Am. Bd. Psychiatry and Neurology, diplomate internal medicine. Intern internal medicine Yale U., New Haven, 1975-76, resident internal medicine, 1975-77; fellow neurophysiology Lab. Devel. Neurobiology Nat. Inst. Child Health and Human Devel., NIH, Bethesda, Md., 1977-79, 82; resident neurology Johns Hopkins, Balt., 1979-83; assoc. prof. U. Md. Sch. Medicine, Balt., 1989-96, prof. neurology and physiology, 1996-99; dir. Md. Epilepsy Ctr. Md. Epilepsy Ctr., Balt., 1988-99; prof. neurology Johns Hopkins Sch. Medicine, Balt., 1999—; dir. Johns Hopkins Epilepsy Ctr., Balt., 1999—, vice chmn. for neurol. labs., 2002—. Contbr. articles to med. jours. Lt. cmdr. USPHS, 1977-79, 81-82. Mem. Soc. for Neurosci., Am. Acad. Neurology, Am. Epilepsy Soc. (bd. dirs. 1999-2002). Office: 5207 Springlake Way Baltimore MD 21212-3421 also: Johns Hopkins Hosp Dept Neurology Meyer 2-147ogy 600 N Wolfe St Baltimore MD 21287-0005

BERGFIELD, GENE RAYMOND, engineering educator; b. Granite City, Ill., July 11, 1951; s. Walter Irvin Bergfield and Venie Edith (Sanders) Bennett; m. Juanita Pauline Kapp, Sept. 19, 1970; children: Gene Raymond Jr., Timothy Shawn. BA in Applied Behavioral Scis., Nat. Coll. Edn., Chgo., 1988. Field engr. Westinghouse PGSD, St. Louis, 1979-81, instr. Phila., 1982-84, asst. resource mgr. Chgo., 1984-89; power plant instr. Westinghouse PGPD, Orlando, Fla., 1989-93; ops. and maintenance supr. Edison Mission O&M Inc., Auburndale, Fla., 1993-97; power plant cons. Pen-Power, Auburndale, Fla., 1997-99; ind. power plant cons., 1999—. With USN, 1971-79.

BERGFORS, CONSTANCE MARIE, artist, educator; b. Quincy, Mass., Feb. 8, 1931; d. Fred Eric Bergfors and H. Margaret Sandberg; m. Andrew E. Rice, Dec. 2, 1972; children: Stefan Andrej, Brandt Eric. BA, Smith Coll., 1952; postgrad., Concoran Coll. Art, Washington, D.C., 1956, postgrad., 1957, postgrad., 1981, postgrad., 1982, Acad. di Belle Arte, Palermo, Naples, and Rome, Italy, 1957—60. Dir. Cabin John Visual Studies Workshop, Cabin John, Md., 1970—75; founding mem. Gallery 10, Washington, 1974—78; tchr. sculpture dept. Corcoran Sch. Art, Washington, 1991—95. Judge art scholarships for h.s. srs., 1981—2001. One-woman shows include Peabody, Rivlin, Gore, Caldouhos and Lambert Law Firm, Washington, 1970, Gallery Modern Art, Fredericksburg, Va., 1974, Gallery 10, Washington, 1974, 1976, U.S. Govt., 1978, Langley, Va., 1985, Galleria Editalia, Rome, 1980, Strathmore Hall Arts Ctr., Rockville, Md., 1984, Capital Ctr. Gallery, Landover, Md., 1984, Plum Gallery, Kensington, Md., 1986, 1988, 1991, Cmty. Gallery Lancaster, Pa., 1988, South Shore Art Ctr., Cohasset, Mass., 1988, Urban Inst., Washington, 1996, Workshop Gallery, Cabin John, Md., 1997, Temple Sinai Commn., Washington, 1998, Renwick Alliance visits the Workshop Gallery, 2000, Arts Coun. of Montgomery County, 2000, exhibited in group shows at 14 Sculptors Gallery, N.Y.C., 1977, Art Barn, Washington, 1983, Georgetown Ct. Artists' Space, 1984, Arlington Arts Ctr., Va., 1984, 1985, Three Rivers Arts Festival, Pitts., 1984, Sculpture 84 Washington Square, Washington, 1984, Washington Women's Art Ctr., 1985, Audubon Naturalist Soc. Sculpture Show, Washington, 1985, Brandeis Coll. Art Exhibit, Rockville, Md., 1986, D.C. Sculpture Now Show Summer Sch. Mus., Washington, 1989, Bldg. Mus., 1989—90, Montgomery County Art Exhibit, Rockville, Md., 1990, Internat. Sculpture 90 Montgomery Coll., 1990, Washington Sculpture Group Show Summer Sch., Washington, 1990, Mus. Nat. de Belas Artes, Rio de Janeiro, 1991—92, Oxon Hill Manor Found., Oxon Hill, Md., 1992, Fairfax County Coun. Arts Northern Va. C.C., Annandale, Va., 1992, Washington Sculptors Group Exhbn., Bethesda, Md., 1992, Fairfax County Coun. Arts Northern Va. C.C., 1993, The Cutting Edge: 20 Years at Gallery 10, Washington, 1994, Corcoran Sch. Art Washington Square, 1994, Washington Sculptors Group Show Washington Square, 1995, Arts 901, 1996, Bldg. Mus., 1999—2000, Represented in permanent collections. Recipient Mary Lay Thom award for Outstanding Achievement in Sculpture, Washington, 1983, Montgomery County Purchase prize, Exec. Office Bldg, Rockville, Md., 1987, 3rd prize, Montgomery County Art Exhibit, Strathmore Hall, Rockville, Md., 1990. Avocations: travel, architecture, archaeology. Home: 6517 80th St Cabin John MD 20818-1208 Home Fax: 301-229-4293.

BERGGREN, WILLIAM ALFRED, geologist, research micropaleontologist, educator; b. N.Y.C., Jan. 15, 1931; s. Wilhelm Fritjof and Lilly Maria (Skog) B.; m. Lois Albee, June 19, 1954 (div. July 1981); children: Erik, Anna Lisa, Anders, Sara Maria; m. Marie Pierre Aubry, June 19, 1982 BS, Dickinson Coll., 1952; M.Sc., U. Houston, 1957; PhD, U. Stockholm, 1960, D.Sc., 1962; doctorate (hon.), U. Utrecht, 2001. Research micropaleontologist Oasis Oil Co., Tripoli, Libya, 1962-65; asst. scientist Woods Hole Oceanographic Inst., Mass., 1965-68, assoc. scientist, 1968-71, sr. scientist, 1971-98, sr. scientist emeritus, 1998—; Disting. vis. prof. Rutgers U., New Brunswick, N.J., 2001—. Adj. prof. Brown U., Providence, 1968-93. Editor: Catastrophes and Earth History, 1984, Late Eocene-Early Oligocene Climatic and Biotic Change, 1992, Geochronology Time-Scales and Global Stratigraphic Correlation, 1995, Late Paleocene-Early Eocene Climate and Biotic Events, 1998; contbr. articles to sci. jours. Recipient Cushman Found. award for foraminiferal rsch., 1995, Raymond C. Moore medal in paleontology Soc. of Sedimentary Geology, 1997. Fellow Geol. Soc. Am., Geol. Soc. London (hon.); mem. NAS (Mary Clark Thompson medal 1982), Am. Assn. Petroleum Geologists, Soc. Econ. Paleontologists and Mineralogists (hon.), Paleontol. Soc. Am. (co-editor jour. 1980-84), Am. Geophys. Union, Geol. Soc. Switzerland. Avocation: skiing. Office: Woods Hole Oceanographic Inst 22 Water St Woods Hole MA 02543-1024

BERGGREN-MOILANEN, BONNIE LEE, education educator; b. L'Anse, Mich., June 2, 1940; d. Alvin Carl and Emma Leola (Wandell) Lydman; m. Grant Lorns Berggren, Jr., Aug. 22, 1959; children: Grant Victor Berggren, Rex Alvin Berggren, Konnie Kay Berggren; m. Glenn Moilanen, 2003. BA, U. Hawaii, 1961; MA, Ea. Mich. U., 1988; MA in Ednl. Adminstrn., No. Mich. U., 1991. Tchr. home econs. Baraga (Mich.) Twp. Schs., 1960-61, L'Anse Twp. Schs., 1963-65, Spencerport (N.Y.) Cen. Schs., 1979-84; presch. tchr. NCA Sch., Cmty. Action Agy., Hermansville, Mich., 1971-73; circulation supr. Spring Arbor (Mich.) Coll. Libr., 1985-87; adj. prof., supr. student tchrs. No. Mich. U., Marquette, 1989—96; co-owner, co-mgr. Menominee (Mich.) Floral, 1993-96; curriculum and tng. coord./spl. project coord. Campus Crusade for Christ, Children of The World Dept., San Clemente, Calif., 1997-2000; sr. staff Internat. Student Resources Campus Crusade for Christ, Madison, Wis., 2000—. Tchr. trainer Negaunee Pub. Schs., Negaunee, Mich., 1988—90; leader workshop Republic-Michigamme Schs., Republic, Mich., 1989—90; mem. evaluation team Marquette Pub. Schs., 1991; mem. tchr. edn. adv. coun. No. Mich. U., Marquette, 1991—96, mem. Hoppes award com., 1990—92, mem. pers. com., 1992. Libr. bd. Republic-Michigamme Schs., 1988—91; spkr. Christian Women's Club, 1989—90; bd. regents Liberty U., 1990—91; active Operation Carelift to Russia, 1997, Operation Sunrise to Africa, 2002. Fellow: Roberts Wesleyan Coll.; mem.: AAUW, DAV Aux. (life; Mich. historian 1975), AAUP, Concerned Women Am., U. Hawaii Alumni Assn., Ea. Mich U. Alumni Assn., Univ. Women No. Mich. U., Phi Delta Kappa, Phi Kappa Phi. Baptist. Avocations: reading, travel, writing, crafts. Home: 10 Oakbridge Ct Madison WI 53717 E-mail: bonnielb@chorus.net.

BERGHAHN, VOLKER ROLF, history educator; b. Berlin, Feb. 15, 1938; came to U.S., 1988; s. Alfred and Gisela (Henke) B.; m. Marion Ilse Koop, Dec. 29, 1969; children: Sascha, Vivian, Melvin. MA, U. N.C. Chapel Hill, 1961; PhD, U. London, 1964; Habil., U. Mannheim, 1966-69. Sr. scholar St. Anthony's Coll., Oxford, Eng., 1964-66; rsch. fellow U. Mannheim, 1966-69; lectr. U. East Anglia, Norwich, 1969-71; reader U. E. Anglia, Norwich, 1971-75; prof. U. Warwick, Coventry, 1975-88, Brown U., Providence, 1988-97, Columbia U., N.Y.C., 1998—. Author: Der Stahlhelm, 1966, Der Tirpitz Plan, 1970, Germany and the Approach of War, 1973, Modern Germany, 1982, The Americanization of West German Industry, 1945-1973, 1986, Otto A. Friedrich, 1902-1975, 1992, Imperial Germany, 19871-1914, 1995, America and the Intellectual Cold Wars in Europe, 2001, Europa im Zeitalter der Weltkriege, 2002. Various grants and fellowships. Fellow Royal Hist. Soc.; mem. German History Soc. (pres. 1986-88), Am. Hist. Assn., German Studies Assn. Avocations: tennis, walking. Office: Columbia U Dept History New York NY 10027 E-mail: vrb7@columbia.edu.

BERGHAUS, NONA ROSE, business education educator; b. Ashland, Kans., Oct. 2, 1931; d. John Bernard and Rose L. (Bohn) B. BA, Marymount Coll., 1953; MS, Kans. State Tchrs. Coll., Emporia, 1956; EdD, U. Okla., 1966. Tchr. bus. Beverly (Kans.) H.S., 1953-55, Wellington (Kans.) H.S., 1956-63; grad. asst. U. Okla., Norman, 1963-66; prof. Emporia State U., 1966—. State advisor Future Bus. Leaders Am., Kans., 1967—. Author: WordPerfect 6 First Run, 1993, Star Series: Lotus 1-2-3, Rel 5, 1994; editor Kans. Bus. Tchrs., 1979—. Mem. Mountain-Plains Bus. Edn. Assn. (treas. 1980-84, pres. 1985-86, Outstanding Leadership award 1987, Collegiate Tchr. of Yr. 1990), Kans. Bus. Edn. Assn. (pres. 1978-79), Kappa Kappa Iota. Roman Catholic. Avocation: microcomputers. Home: 2074 Fanestil Dr Emporia KS 66801-5420 Office: Emporia State U Sch Bus Emporia KS 66801

BERGHEL, HAL L. computer science educator, columnist, author, consultant; b. Mpls., May 10, 1946; s. Oscar H. and Edna M. (Muller) B.; m. Margi Millard, May 7, 1983; children: David, Steven, Kevin. BA, U. Nebr., 1971, MA, 1973, MA, 1976, PhD, 1977. Asst. prof. mgmt. U. Nebr., Lincoln, 1979-80, asst. prof. computer sci., 1981-86; prof. computer sci. U. Ark., Fayetteville, 1986-99; prof., dir. Sch. Computer Sci. U. Nev., Las Vegas, 1999—, dir. Cybermedia Rsch. Ctr., 2003—. Bd. dirs. The Rosebush Co., N.Y.C.; pres. Fourth Generation Cons., Lincoln, Nebr., 1980-84. Contbr. numerous articles to profl. jours. Fellow IEEE (Disting. visitor 1994-97, 98-2000); Assn. for Computing Machinery (dist. lectr. 1991-93, 96—, vice chair membership bd. 1996—, publs. bd. 1992-98, 2000—, local activities bd. 1993-95, Disting. Svc. award 1996, Outstanding Contbn. award 2000); mem. Ark. Soc. for Computer and Info. Tech. (chair, bd. dirs. 1988-96). Office: U Nev Las Vegas Sch Computer Sci Las Vegas NV 89154-4019

BERGIA, ROGER MERLE, school system administrator; b. Peoria, Ill, Nov. 26, 1937; s. Merle Frederick and Doris Ann (Markham) B.; m. Valerie Jean Lane, Oct. 16, 1960; children: Lori, Amy, Beth. BA, Eureka Coll., 1960; MA, Bradley U., 1967, postgrad., 1968—. Tchr., coach jr. h.s. Peoria

Hts. (Ill.) Sch., 1960-65; prin. Kelly Ave Grade Sch., Peoria Hts., 1965-74; supt. Peoria Hts. Schs., 1974—. Adminstrv. agt. Ill. State Bd. Early Childhood Edn. Early Childhood Exemplary Program. Named Sch. Adminstr. of Yr., Ill. Bd. Edn., 1981-82; recipient Exemplary Practices award, 1992. Mem. Phi Delta Kappa, Lambda Chi Alpha. Republican. Presbyterian. Home: 6723 N Gem Ct Peoria IL 61614-2901 Office: 500 E Glen Ave Peoria Heights IL 61616

BERGIN, BARBARA DAWN, adult education educator; b. Elmira, N.Y., May 29, 1935; d. Leon Bert and Leah M. (Kniffin) Corey; m. Jack Henry Lindquist, Apr. 5, 1957 (wid. Mar. 1959); 1 child, Kai Lindquist Enenbach; m. John Joseph Bergin, June 29, 1968; 1 child, Amy Louise. Student, SUNY, Fredonia, 1954-57; BS TV/Radio, Ithaca Coll., 1961; MA Reading, Ea. Mich. U., 1986. Cert. tchr. K-8, Mich., reading K-12. Pub. rels. prodn. asst. WGBH-TV Pub. Broadcasting, Boston, 1961-63; promotions asst. WKBD-TV, Southfield, Mich., 1965-67; tchr. Detroit Pub. Schs., 1967-69, 83-84; lang. arts/computer instr. Dearborn (Mich.) Adult and Community Edn., 1987-92, faculty, coord., 1992—. Part-time faculty schoolcraft Coll.; cons. Brooks Correctinal Facility, Muskegon, Mich., 1991; steering com. Livonia Sch. Bd. Adv. Coun., Mich., 1975-78. Co-editor: Lines: An Autoworkers' Anthology, 1990; presenter in field. Vol. Livonia Pub. Schs., 1971-83. Mini-grantee Mich. Dept. Edn., Lansing, 1988; named Mich. Region 1 Adult Edn. Tchr. of Yr., Mich. Coun. on Learning for Adults/Mich. Dept. Edn., Owosso, 1994. Mem. Internat. Reading Assn. (newsletter co-editor adult literacy spl. interest group 1990-96, Mich. Coun. on Learning for Adults (mem. chmn. 1991—), Adult Lit. and Tech., Mich. Reading Assn., Mich. Assn. for Computer Users for Learning. Avocations: reading, travel, genealogy. Home: 35310 W Chicago St Livonia MI 48150-2588 Office: UAW/Ford Rouge Acad Dearborn Assembly Plant 3001 Miller Rd Dearborn MI 48120-1458

BERGMAN, RICHARD LEE, secondary school educator, band director; b. Bronx, N.Y., June 9, 1945; s. Allen H. and Gertrude Trudy (Dingenthal) B.; m. Judy Beth Merlin, June 22, 1975; children: Shayne Ellen, Jordanna Lynne. BS, U. Md., 1967, MS, 1975. Tchr. Benjamin Foulois Jr. H.S., Forestville, Md., 1967-69, Suitland (Md.) H.S., 1969-72, Crossland H.S., Camp Springs, Md., 1972-77, Herndon (Va.) H.S., 1977—. Guest performer in N.Y., Pa., Va., Md., Chgo., Fla., La., Toronto, St. Louis, and others. Recipient 3 citations, Nat. Bands Assn. Mem. Am. Bandmasters Assn., Am. Fedn. Assn., Musicians Union, Nat. Band Assn., Percussive Arts Soc., Music Educators Nat. Conf., Va. Band and Orchestra Assn., Nat. Assn. for Suprs. Home: 1291 Browns Mill Ct Herndon VA 20170-2078 Office: Herndon HS 700 Bennett St Herndon VA 20170-3104 E-mail: rlbergman@fcps.edu.

BERGMANN, BARBARA ROSE, economics educator; b. N.Y.C., July 20, 1927; d. Martin and Nellie Berman; m. Fred H. Bergmann, July 16, 1965; children: Sarah Nellie, David Martin. BA, Cornell U., 1948; MA, Harvard U., 1955, PhD, 1959; PhD (hon.), De Montford U., 1996, Muhlenberg Coll., 2000. Economist U.S. Bur. Labor Stats., N.Y.C., 1949-53; sr. staff ecomomist, cons. Council Econ. Advisors, Washington, 1961-62; sr. staff Brookings Inst., Washington, 1963-65; sr. econ. advisor AID, Washington, 1966-67; assoc. prof. U. Md., College Park, 1965-71, prof. econs., 1971-88; disting. prof. econs. Am. U., Washington, 1988-97, prof. emeritus, 1997—. Author: (with Chinitz and Hoover) Projection of a Metropolis, 1961; (with George W. Wilson) Impact of Highway Investment on Development, 1966; (with David E. Kaun) Structural Unemployment in the U.S., 1967; (with Robert Bennett) A Microsimulated Transactions Model of the United States Economy, 1985, The Economic Emergence of Women, 1986, Saving Our Children from Poverty: What the United States Can Learn from France, 1996, In Defense of Affirmative Action, 1996, Is Social Security Broke? A Cartoon Guide to the Issues, 1999, (with Suzanne W. Helburn) America's Child Care Problem: The Way Out, 2002; mem. editl. bd. Am. Econ. Rev., 1970-73, Challenge, 1978—, Signs, 1978-85; columnist econ. affairs N.Y. Times, 1981-82. Mem. Economists for McGovern, 1977; mem. panel econ. advisors Congl. Budget Office, Washington, 1977-87; mem. price adv. com. U.S. council on Wage and Price Stability, 1979-80. Mem. AAUP (coun. 1980-83, pres. 1990-92), Am. Econ. Assn. (v.p. 1976, adv. com. to U.S. Census Bur. 1977-82), Ea. Econ. Assn. (pres. 1974), Internat. Assn. for Feminist Econs. (pres. 1999), Soc. for Advancement of Socio-Econs. (pres. 1995-96). Democrat. Home: 5430 41st Pl NW Washington DC 20015-2911 E-mail: bbergman@wam.umd.edu.

BERGO, CONRAD HUNTER, chemistry educator; b. Evanston, Ill., Jan. 5, 1943; s. Arthur Conrad and Mary Margret (Hunter) B.; m. Nancy Wallace, Mar. 12, 1977; children: Stacey Lynn, Fred Monteabaro. BA, St. Olaf Coll., 1965; PhD, U. Minn., 1972. Asst. prof. Chieng Mai (Thailand) U., 1972-75; rsch. assoc. dept. pharmacology U. Ky., Lexington, 1975-77; asst. prof. Alliance Coll., Cambridge Springs, Pa., 1977-80; prof. East Stroudsburg (Pa.) U., 1980—. Exec. dir. Pa. State Coll. Chemistry Consortium, 1991-99; book reviewer McGraw-Hill, Freeman, Houghton Mifflin, John Wiley and West Pub. Pres. bd. dirs. Burnley Workshop, Stroudsburg, 1993-96, 99—. Recipient Cert. of Citizen Svc., Commonwealth of Pa., 1989, award Beyond War, 1990. Mem. Am. Chem. Soc., Sigma Xi. Office: East Stroudsburg Univ Chemistry Dept East Stroudsburg PA 18301

BERGQUIST, JAMES MANNING, history educator; b. Council Bluffs, Iowa, Feb. 1, 1934; s. Reuben Neil and Irene Mary (Norton) B.; m. Joan Marie Solon, May 17, 1969; children: John Norton, Charles James. BA, U. Notre Dame, 1955; MA in History, Northwestern U., 1956, PhD in History, 1966. Instr. history Coe Coll., Cedar Rapids, Iowa, 1961-63, Villanova (Pa.) U., 1963-66, asst. prof., 1966-69, assoc. prof., 1969-86, prof., 1986—2002, prof. emeritus, 2002. Contbr. articles on Am. social history and immigration to profl. jours., chpts. to books. Trustee Balch Inst. for Ethnic Studies, Phila., 1988—92, 1994—2001; mem. Pa. Task Force on Diversity in Higher Edn., 1991—94. Fellow, NEH, 1967, 1977, 1980. Mem.: AAUP (pres. Pa. divsn. 1988—90, nat. coun. 1995—2001), Ethnic Studies Assn. Phila. (pres. 1980—82), Hist. Soc. Pa., Am. Assn. State and Local History, Immigration and Ethnic History Soc. (bd. dirs. 1995—), Am. Studies Assn., Orgn. Am. Historians, Am. Hist. Assn. Democrat. Roman Catholic. Avocations: swimming, travel. Home: 217 Devon Blvd Devon PA 19333-1616 Office: Villanova U History Dept Villanova PA 19085

BERGQUIST, PETER, music educator emeritus; b. Sacramento, Aug. 5, 1930; s. Ed Peter and Margaret (Rogers) B.; m. Dorothy Catherine Clark, June 16, 1956; children: Carolyn, Emily (dec.). Student, Eastman Sch. Music, Rochester, N.Y., 1948-51; BS, Mannes Coll. Music, N.Y.C., 1958; MA, Columbia U., 1960, PhD, 1964. Asst. prof. Sch. Music, U. Oreg., Eugene, 1964-69, assoc. prof., 1969-73, prof., 1973-95, prof. emeritus, 1995—. Editor: Orlando di Lasso, Samtliche Werke neue Reihe, vol. 22-25, 1992—93, Orlando di Lasso: The Complete Motets, 18 vols., 1995—, Orlando di Lasso Studies, 1999; music reviewer Eugene Register Guard; contbr. articles to profl. jours. Sr. warden, jr. warden, vestryman St. Mary's Episcopal Ch., Eugene. With USAF, 1951-55. Recipient Ersted award for disting. teaching U. Oreg., 1973; Fulbright sr. rsch. awardee, 1985; Nat. Endowment for Humanities grantee, 1994-98; rsch. and travel awardee DAAD, ACLS. Mem. AAUP, Am. Musicol. Soc., Internat. Musicol. Soc., Soc. for Music Theory, Music Libr. Assn., Coll. Music Soc. Democrat. Home: 3195 Portland St Eugene OR 97405-5140 Office: Sch Music 1225 U Oreg Eugene OR 97403-1225 E-mail: pbergq@darkwing.uoregon.edu.

BERGSTRAND, LAURA JOYCE, elementary education educator; b. South Bend, Ind., May 2, 1940; d. Paul and Ruth Fay (Dillinger) Goins; m. Jay L. Bergstrand, June 12, 1962; children: Kristina, James. BA in Edn., So. Ill. U., 1961; MA in Edn., U. Alaska, 1968. Tchr. Streator (Ill.) Sch. Dist., 1961-62, Anchorage Sch. Dist., 1962-68, 73—. Alpine race official U.S. Ski Assn., Anchorage, 1989-92; tax aide, instr., county coord. AARP/IRS, Polk County, Wis., 1994. Recipient Excellence in Aviation Edn. award Alaska Region Fed. Aviation Agy., 1987, Maj. Achievmeent in Edn. award Expt. Aircraft Agy., 1989. Mem. NEA, ASCD, Nat. Coun. Tchr. Math., Phi Delta Kappa. Home: 750 S White Ash Ct Balsam Lake WI 54810-2407

BERGSTROM, MARIANNE ELISABETH, program coordinator, special education educator; b. Sodertalje, Sweden, Aug. 18, 1941; came to U.S., 1967; d. Uno G. Bergstrom and Agnes (L.B.) Gustafsson. BA, Linkopings Tchrs. Coll., Sodertalje, 1964, Pacific Luth. U., 1973, MA, 1979; EdD, Seattle U., 1988; profl. mediation cert., U. Wash. Cert. tchr., prin., program adminstr., Wash.; cert. in profl. meditation skills tng. Tchr. spl. edn. Jarna and Botkyrka Sch. Dists., Sweden, 1964-67, Bellevue (Wash.) Sch. Dist., 1969-80, head tchr., 1980-91, program coord., 1991—. Ednl. advisor Swedish Sch., Bellevue, 1991-92, pres. bd. dirs., 1993-94. Recipient Outstanding Guardian Ad Litem for abused and neglected children King County Superior Ct., Seattle, 1967-91, Outstanding Tchrs. in Exceptional Edn. award Acad. Therapy Publs., 1975. Mem. ASCD, Coun. for Exceptional Children. Lutheran. Avocations: hiking, skiing, dancing, tennis, traveling. Office: Bellevue Sch Dist Bellevue WA 98009-9010

BERGSTROM, STIG MAGNUS, geology educator; b. Skovde, Sweden, June 12, 1935; s. Axel Magnus and Karin Margareta (Engberg) B.; m. Disa Birgitta Kullgren Fil. lic., Lund U., Sweden, 1961, hon. doctorate, 1987. Amanuensis Lund U., 1958-62, asst. lectr., 1962-68; asst. prof. geology Ohio State U., Columbus, 1968-70, assoc. prof., 1970-72, prof., 1972—2002; dir. Orton Geol. Mus., 1968—2002. Contbr. numerous articles to profl. jours. Served with Swedish Army, 1955—56. Recipient Assar Hadding prize 1995, Raymond C. Moore medal, 1999, Golden medal Faculty of Sci., Charles U., Czech Rep., 1999, Pander Soc. medal, 2001; Am.-Scandinavian Found. fellow, 1964; Fulbright scholar, 1960; grantee numerous orgns., 1958—. Fellow Geol. Soc. Am., Ohio Acad. Sci.; mem. Royal Physiographic Soc. Office: Ohio State U Orton Geol Mus 155 S Oval Mall Columbus OH 43210-1308

BERIO, BLANCA, editor; b. San Juan, P.R., Aug. 26, 1950; d. Gaspar and Blanca (Morales) B.; m. Martin Martino, Nov. 11, 1972; children: Blanca Iris, Martin, Bibiana. BA, U. P.R., 1968, MA, 1985, EdD, 1997. Prof. Guadalajara (Mex.) Autonomus U., 1973-76; tchr. Spanish Colegio de La Salle, Bayamón, P.R., 1980-88; prof. edn. U. Sacred Heart, Santurce, P.R., 1984-91; ednl. editor Editorial Norma, Cataño, 1991-92; chief editor Editorial Rio Ingenio, 1987—2003; dir. grad. program U. Cen. Bayamon, 1998—2000. Cons. Learn Aid, Rio Piedras, P.R., 1990-98, dean U. Central Bayamon, 2000-03. Author: De 13 a 19, 1969, El Paso, 1971, Tapatea, 1987, 2nd edit., 1994, Bibliografia de Literatura Puertorriqueña Para Niños, 1994; editor bull. Algo Nuevo, 1990, (software) Nos Comunicamos: K-3, 1992, Lectoescritura, 20 modulos, 2002; contbr. articles to profl. jours. Recipient Excelsa Benjamina Assn. Autores Puertorriqueños San Juan, 1971. Mem. Internat. Reading Assn., Assn. Grads. U. P.R., Alpha Delta Kappa. Roman Catholic. Avocations: reading, stamp collecting, swimming, writing. Home: Rio Hondo 2 Ah14 Calle Rio Ingenio Bayamon PR 00961-3234 Office: Rio Ingenio Bayamon PR 00961

BERK, LEE ELIOT, academic administrator; m. Susan Berk. BA, Brown U., 1964; JD, Boston U., 1967. Pres. Berklee Coll. Mus., Boston, 1979—. Author: Legal Protection for the Creative Musician (ASCAP/Deems Taylor award, 1971). Recipient Am. Eagle award, Nat. Music Coun., 1995. Office: Berklee Coll Music Office of the President 1140 Boylston St Boston MA 02215-3631*

BERK, PAUL DAVID, physician, scientist, educator; b. Bklyn., Apr. 3, 1938; s. Charles and Helen (Goell) B.; m. Aviva Ancona, July 4, 1965 (div. Aug. 1990); children: Claire, Philip, Edward; m. Nicole Polak, 1991. BA, Swarthmore Coll., 1959; cert., U. St. Andrews, Scotland, 1960; MD, Columbia U., 1964. Diplomate Am. Bd. Internal Medicine, Am. Bd. Hematology. Intern Columbia-Presbyn. Med. Ctr., N.Y.C., 1964-65, resident, 1965-66, fellow in hematology, 1969-70; clin. assoc. metabolism br. Nat. Cancer Inst., Bethesda, Md., 1966-69, sr. investigator, 1970-73; clin. asst. prof. medicine Georgetown U., Washington, 1971-75, clin. assoc. prof., 1975-77; chief sect. on diseases of the liver Nat. Inst. Arthritis, Metabolism and Digestive Diseases, NIH, Bethesda, 1973-77; prof. medicine Mt. Sinai Sch. Medicine, N.Y.C., 1977—, Albert and Vera List prof. medicine, 1980-89, prof. biochemistry, 1987-99, Henry and Lillian Stratton prof. molecular medicine, 1989—, chief divsn. hematology, 1977-89, acting chief, 1989-90, chief divsn. liver disease, 1989-01. Prof. biochemistry and molecular biology Mt. Sinai Sch. Medicine, 1999—; adj. prof. Rockefeller U., 1987-89; cons. in liver disease NIH, 1977-80, mem. adv. coun. Nat. Inst. Diabetes and Digestive and Kidney Diseases, 1990-94. Editor: (with others) Chemistry and Physiology of the Bile Pigments, 1977, Frontiers in Liver Disease, 1981, Myelofibrosis and the Biology of Connective Tissue, 1984, Hans Popper: A Tribute, 1992, Hepatic Transport and Bile Secretion, 1993, Polythemia Vera, 1994; editor-in-chief Seminars in Liver Disease, 1981-90, 96—, Hepatology, 1991-96; mem. editorial bd. Artificial Organs, 1979-92, Liver, 1980-93; contbr. articles to profl. jours. Served as sr. surgeon USPHS, 1966-69, 75-77. Recipient Merck award Columbia U., 1964; Fulbright scholar, 1959 Fellow ACP, Am. Coll. Gastroenterology; chmn., bd. dirs. Am. Liver Found., 2000—; mem. Am. Soc. Clin. Investigation, Assn. Am. Physicians, Am. Assn. Study of Liver Disease (councillor 1985-93, v.p. 1988, pres. 1989), Internat. Assn. Study of Liver (councillor 1988-91), Am. Soc. for Hematology, Am. Clin. and Climatological Assn., Nat. Polycthemia Vera Study Group (vice chmn. 1978-95), Soc. Exptl. Biol. Medicine (councillor 1993-96), N.Y. Soc. Study of Blood (pres. 1982-83), Sigma Xi, Phi Beta Kappa, Alpha Omega Alpha. Office: Mt Sinai Sch Medicine Box 1039 1 Gustave L Levy Pl New York NY 10029-6500 E-mail: paul.berk@mssm.edu.

BERKA, MARIANNE GUTHRIE, health and physical education educator; b. Queens, N.Y., Dec. 25, 1944; d. Frank Joseph and Mary (DePaul) Guthrie; m. Jerry George Berka, June 1, 1968; children: Katie, Keri. BS, Ithaca Coll., 1966, MS, 1968; EdD, NYU, 1990. Tchr. Northport H.S., 1966—67; prof. Health, Phys. Edn. and Recreation Nassau C.C., Garden City, NY, 1968—. Adj. assoc. prof. Hofstra U., Hempstead, NY, 1998—. Mem.: AAHPER, AAHPERD, Am. Coll. Sports Medicine (cert. health/fitness instr.), Am. Assn. Sex Educators, Counselors and Therapists (cert. sex educator), N.Y. State Assn. Health, Phys. Edn., Recreation and Dance (J.B. Nash scholarship com. 1983—2000, Nassau Zone Disting. Svc. award 1988, Disting. Svc. award, Nassau zone 1988, Higher Edn. Tchr. of Yr. (Nassau Zone) 2003), Assn. Women Phys. Educators N.Y. State (chpt. chmn. 1973—74, chpt. treas. 1980—84). Roman Catholic. Home: 90 Bay Way Ave Brightwaters NY 11718-2012 Office: P226 HPER Nassau Community Coll Garden City NY 11530

BERKEBILE, MARY LOU, librarian; b. Stonycreek Twp., Pa., May 19, 1950; d. Merle Jay and Elnora Catherine (Deeter) Snyder; m. Lionel Robert Berkebile, May 27, 1972; 1 child, Michael Lee. BS in Elem. Edn. and L.S., Shippensburg (Pa.) State Coll., 1972, MSLS, 1975. Elem. sch. libr. Conemaugh Twp. Area Sch. Dist., Davidsville, Pa., 1972—. Mem. NEA, Pa. Edn. Assn., Conemaugh Twp. Area Edn. Assn. (sec. 1987-89). Republican. Mem. Ch. of Brethren. Avocations: reading, sewing. Home: 3145 Dark Shade Dr Windber PA 15963-6025 Office: Conemaugh Twp Area Sch Dist RR 4 Box 49 Johnstown PA 15905-9804

BERKEIHISER, VIRGINIA MARIE, elementary education educator; b. Coatesville, Pa., June 16, 1949; d. Robert William and Dorothy (Covington) Clifton; m. Elmer Wesley Berkeihiser III, Mar. 25, 1972. BS in Edn., Lock Haven (Pa.) State Coll., 1971; MA in Ednl. Leadership/Adminstrn., Immaculata (Pa.) Coll., 1990. Cert. tchr., sch. adminstr., Pa. Tchr. Coatesville (Pa.) Area Sch. Dist., 1971—. Recipient Cert. of Achievement, Pa. Dept. Edn., 1992; Coatesville Area Sch. Dist. profl. growth grantee, 1989. Mem. NEA, Pa. State Tchr. Assn. Democrat. Lutheran. Avocation: travel. Office: Reeceville Elem Sch 100 Reeceville Rd Coatesville PA 19320-1527 Home: 20 Rolling Hills Est Columbia PA 17512-9626

BERKELEY, BETTY LIFE, gerontology educator; b. St Louis, May 25, 1924; d. James Alfred and Anna Laura (Voltmer) Life; m. Marvin Harold Berkeley, Feb. 7, 1947; children: Kathryn Elizabeth, Barbara Ellen, Brian Harrison, Janet Lynn. AB, Harris Tchrs. Coll., 1947; MA in Ednl. Adminstrn., Washington U., 1951; PhD, U. North Tex., 1980. Tchr. St. Louis Pub. Schs., 1946-48, Clayton Pub. Schs., Mo., 1948-49, Lamplighter Pvt. Sch., Dallas, 1964-67; program devel. specialist Richland Coll., Dallas, 1980-84, instr., 1981. Adj. prof. U. North Tex., Denton, 1981, cons. Sch. Cmty. Svcs. Ctr. for Studies on Aging, 1981; pres. Retirement Planning Svcs., Dallas, 1984. Contbr. articles to profl. jours. Mem. Dallas Commn. on Status of Women, 1975-79; bd. dirs. Dallas Mcpl. Libr., 1979-83, Sr. Citizen Greater Dallas, 1986-92, Coun. on Adult Ministry Lovers Lane United Meth. Ch., 1982, trustee, 1997, dir. found., 1997, mem. bldg. com., 1999; charter mem., bd. dirs., life. mem. Friends U. North Tex. Libr.; mem. Pres.'s Coun. U. North Tex., mem. vol. mgmt. edn. task force, 1978-82. Named Outstanding Alumna Coll. Edn. U. North Tex., 1992. Mem. AAUW (pres. 1973-75, Outstanding Woman of Tex. 1981), Women's Coun. Dallas County (v.p. 1977-79). Avocations: travel, cooking, needlework. Home and Office: 13958 Hughes Ln Dallas TX 75240-3510

BERKELL, DORIS AUDREY, elementary education educator; b. N.Y.C., Aug. 25, 1934; d. Samuel and Hannah (Appel) Cohen; m. Gerald S. Berkell, July 17, 1954; children: Fran, Susan. B of Edn., U. Miami, 1956, M of Edn., 1983. Cert. tchr., Fla. Tchr. Dade County Schs., Miami, Fla., 1967—. Dir. Student Coun., Miami Beach, Fla., 1984-86; directing tchr. Bay Harbor Elem., Miami Beach, 1990—. Liaison Bay Harbor PTA, Miami Beach, 1989—, hon. life mem., 1990; leader Girl Scouts Am., Miami, 1963-68. Mem. Assn. for Childhood Edn. Internat., Fla. Reading Assn., Delta Kappa Gamma (chair scholarship 1982-84, historian 1984-86, 2d v.p. 1992), Phi Delta Kappa (program chair 1990). Avocations: theater, set design and painting. Office: Bay Harbor Elem 1165 94th St Miami FL 33154-2306

BERKELMAN, KARL, physics educator; b. Lewiston, Maine, June 7, 1933; s. Robert George and Yvonne (Langlois) B.; m. Mary Bowen Hobbie, Oct. 10, 1959; children: Thomas, James, Peter. BS, U. Rochester, N.Y., 1955; PhD, Cornell U., 1959. From asst. prof. to prof. physics Cornell U., Ithaca, N.Y., 1961—, dir. lab. nuclear studies, 1985-2000; sci. assoc. DESY, Hamburg, Fed. Republic of Germany, 1974-75, CERN, Geneva, 1967-68, 81-82, 91-92, 2000-2001. Office: Cornell U Newman Lab Ithaca NY 14853

BERKEY, DOUGLAS BRYAN, dental educator, researcher, gerontologist, clinician; b. L.A., Apr. 24, 1949; s. Harvey Garfield and Sytha Jean (Roberts) B.; m. Gail Jo Harmon, Aug. 4, 1972; children: Bryan, Lori, Kristen, Tyler. DMD, U. Louisville, 1977; MPH in Dental Pub. Health, U. Minn., 1981, MS in Oral Health Svcs. for Older Adults, 1983. Dir. postdoctoral geriat. fellowship programs VA Med. Ctr., Denver, 1985-87, Rocky Mountain coord. geriat. dental programs, 1985-87; dental dir. HHS geriat. tng. grant U. Colo. Health Scis. Ctr., Denver, 1988-95, assoc. dir. for dental area health edn. ctr., 1990-93, 96—, assoc. dir. for dental geriat. edn. ctr., 1991-2000. Dir. advanced edn. in gen. dentistry programs U. Colo. Sch. Dentistry, Denver, 1991-93, chair dept. applied dentistry, 1992-2000; Carolyn G. Knuemann disting. prof. of geriatric/special care dentistry, U. N.C., 2000—. Mem. internat. editl. bd. (manuscripts) Gerodontology, 1997; author of monographs and manuscripts. Various leadership positions Boy Scout Am., Minn., Idaho and Colo., 1977—; cons. Ariz. Dept. Health Svcs., 1986—; reviewer, referee Am. Fund for Dental Health, Ill., 1990-95; mem. external adv. bd. Cmty. Oriented Dental Edn. (CODE), N.J., 1995-96. USPHS scholar, Mpls., 1980-81; Pew Nat. Dental Leadership fellow Pew Charitable Trusts, Phila., 1991-92, finalist for W.J. Fulbright Scholar, 1995. Mem. ADA (spkrs. bur. 1990-93, del. JCAHO, 1995—, 98, Prof. of Yr. Rocky Mtn. Study Club 1998), Internat. Assn. for Dental Rsch. (pres. geriat. oral rsch. group 1990), Gerontol. Soc. Am., Am. Soc. for Geriat. Dentistry (bd. dirs. 1985-91), Am. Assn. Dental Schs. (del. coun. faculties 1996-2000), Am. Assn. Pub. Health Dentistry, Internat. Dental Fedn. (chair-elect gerondontology sect. 1997-99), Phi Kappa Phi. Mem. Lds Ch. Avocations: bicycling, running, mountain sports. Office: UNC Chapel Hill Dept Dental Ecol Sch Dentistry Cb 7450 Brauer Hl Chapel Hill NC 27599-0001

BERKEY, JULIE MARIE, school psychologist; b. Beaver Falls, Pa., Aug. 21, 1957; d. William and Amalia (Lauer) B. BA, Westminster Coll., New Wilmington, Pa., 1979; MS, California U. of Pa., 1984; EdD, Indiana U. of Pa., 1994. Cert. sch. psychologist, Pa. Sch. psychologist Dept. Spl. Edn., Intermediate Unit 8, Somerset, Pa., 1984-91, Allegeny Neuropsychiat. Inst./Allegeny Gen. Hosp., Pitts., from 1991. Tutor Adult Literacy, Beaver, Pa., 1992. Named to Outstanding Young Women of Am., 1984; California U. of Pa. Presdl. scholar, 1984. Mem. ASCD, Assn. of Sch. Psychologists of Pa., Nat. Assn. Sch. Psychologists, Phi Delta Kappa (Outstanding Grad. Honor award 1984). Avocations: white water rafting, piano, gardening, antiques. Home: Beaver Falls, Pa. Died May 15, 2002.

BERKOVITS, ANNETTE ROCHELLE, educational association administrator, biologist, educator; b. Kizyl-Kija, Kirgiz Republic, Russia, Sept. 13, 1943; came to U.S., 1959; naturalized, 1964; d. Nachman and Dora (Blaustein) Libeskind; m. David Berkovits; children: Jessica Dawn, Jeremy Haskell. BS in Biology, CUNY, 1965; MS in Ednl. Adminstrn. and Supervision, Manhattan Coll., 1977. Cert. sch. adminstr., N.Y. Research asst. Sloan Kettering Cancer Research Inst., N.Y.C., 1965-66; sci. tchr. N.Y.C. Bd. Edn., 1966-72; zoology instr. N.Y. Zool. Soc., N.Y.C., 1972-75, coordinator curricula and programs, 1975-77, asst. curator of edn., 1978-80, assoc. curator edn., 1980-82, curator of edn., 1983-88. dir. edn., 1988—93, v.p., 1993—99, sr. v.p., 1999—. Project dir. Wildlife Inquiry through Zoo Edn. program N.Y. Zool. Soc., 1981—; dir. Animal Kingdom Zoo Camp, N.Y.Zool. Soc., 1977—; project dir., prin. investigator grants program NSF, 1980—; panelist N.Y. State Coun. on Arts, 1986—; cons., panelist NSF; Chauncey Stillman chair in wildlife edn. Wildlife Conservation Soc. Author: (with others) Science for the Fun of It, 1988; editor numerous ednl. publs.; speaker in field. Chairperson Pan-Am. Congress on Conservation of Wildlife Through Edn., Caracas, Venezuela, 1989-91; mem. nat. diffusion network adv. coun. U.S. Dept. Edn., 1991—; mem. chancellor's adv. coun. Arts Edn. and Task Force on Environ. Edn., Bd. Edn., N.Y.C., 1991—; mem. tech. and sci. com. European Environ. Studies. Fellow Am. Assn. Zool. Parks and Aquariums (profl.), Consortium of Aquariums, Univs. and Zoos (bd. dirs.), Wildlife Conservation Soc. (v.p. edn. 1993—), N.Y.C. Mus. Educators Roundtable (chmn. 1982, nat. sci. bd. adv. panel 2002—); mem. Internat. Zoo Educators Assn. (pres. 2000—). Office: Wildlife Conservatin Soc 185th St & Southern Blvd New York NY 10460

BERKOWITZ, ALICE ORLANDER, management consultant, hearing and speech educator; b. N.Y.C. BA, MA, PhD, NYU, 1970; MBA, CUNY, 1986. Lic. in audiology and speech pathology, N.Y. Dir. audiological and speech svcs. Manhattan Eye, Ear and Throat Hosp., N.Y.C., 1966-77; regional dir. profl. and ednl. svcs. Audiotone, Inc., N.Y.C. and Phoenix, Ariz., 1977-88; regional mgr. Frye Electronics, Inc., N.Y.C. and Tigard, Oreg., 1987-92; N.E. regional mgr. hearing instruments group Telex Comms., Inc., N.Y.C. and Mpls., 1988-90; exec. dir. Practice Mgmt. Cons. Co., LLC, N.Y.C., 1986—. Adj. prof. hearing and speech St. John's U., N.Y.C., 1993-94; lectr., panel participant various profl. meetings, univs. and hosps. Contbr. to numerous profl. publs. Mem. Am. Speech-Lang.-Hearing Assn. (dual cert. in audiology and speech pathology), Am. Auditory Soc.,

Alliance for Healthcare Strategy and Mktg., Acoustical Soc. Am., Am. Acad. Audiology, N.Y. State Speech Lang. Hearing Assn., N.Y. Soc. Health Planning. Office: Practice Mgmt Cons Co LLC 39 Gramercy Park N New York NY 10010-6302

BERKOWITZ, ERIC NEAL, school administrator, consultant; b. Brookline, Mass., Aug. 19, 1949; s. Carl and Laura (Stearn) B.; m. Sandra Jean Brouck, July 21, 1975; children: Anne Brouck, Julia Brouck. BA in Classics, U. Mass., 1971, MBA, 1973; PhD in Bus., Ohio State U., 1976. From asst. to assoc. prof. sch. mgmt. U. Minn., Mpls., 1976-84; prof., head of mktg. sch. mgmt. U. Mass., Amherst, 1984-96, dir. grad. programs Isenberg Sch. Mgmt., 1996—2002, assoc. dean for profl. programs, 2003—. Cons. and lectr. field. Author: (with R. Kerin, S. Hartley and W. Rudelius) Marketing, 1986, 6th edit., 2000, (with S. Hillestad) Health Care Mktg. Plans: From Strategy to Action, 1984, 2d edit., 1991, (with Flexner and Brown) Strategic Planning in Health Care Management: Marketing and Finance Perspectives, 1981; editor Jour. Health Care Mktg., 1988-93; editor Trendwatch, 1996-99; mem. editl. bds. Jour. Retailing, 1982-87, Jour. Health Care Mktg., 1982-97, Jour. Personal Selling and Sales Mgmt., 1983-87, Am. Jour. Med. Practice Mgmt., 1984-92, Physicians Mktg., 1984-86, health Care Planning and Mktg., 1981-82, others. Bd. trustees Cooky Dickinson Hosp.; mem. adv. bd. Ctr. Health Svcs. Rsch., Case Western Res. U. Named Tchr. of Yr., Coll. Bus. Adminstrn. U. Minn., 1979, 84; fellow Ohio State U., 1975, AMA Doctoral Consortium, 1975; recipient Frank J. Weaver award for contbns. to field of health care mktg., 1998. Fellow Am. Acad. Med. Dirs. (hon.); mem. Assn. Consumer Research, Am. Mktg. Assn., Am. Assn. Advances in Health Care Research (bd. dirs. 1985-87), Acad. for Health Svcs. Mktg. (pres.-elect 1992-93, pres.). E-mail: enb@mktg.umass.edu.

BERLIN, FRED SAUL, psychiatrist, educator; b. Pitts., July 27, 1941; s. Sidney Danial and Pauline (Ritt) B.; m. Mary Ann Pazics, Oct. 3, 1969; children: Debra, Alison, Samantha, Ryan. BS, U. Pitts., 1964; MA, Fordham U., 1966; PhD, Dalhousie U., Halifax, N.S., Can., 1970, MD, 1974. Intern McGill U. Sch. Medicine, Jewish Gen. Hosp., Childrens Hosp., Montreal, Can., 1974-75; psychiat. resident Johns Hopkins Hosp., Balt., 1975-76; Johns Hopkins exch. resident Maudsley Hosp., London, 1977; chief resident dept. psychiatry and behavioral sci. Johns Hopkins Hosp., Balt., 1977-78; assoc. prof. dept. psychiatry and behavioral sci. Johns Hopkins U. Sch. Medicine; dir. Sexual Disorders Clinic Johns Hopkins Hosp. Attending physician Johns Hopkins Hosp., mem. house staff coun., 1976-77, mem. adv. com. house staff coun., 1977-78, mem. utilization rev. com., 1977-78, gender identity com., 1980-81; mem. Johns Hopkins U. Med. Sch. Coun., 1982-84; mem. bd. student advisors Johns Hopkins U. Sch. Medicine, 1980—; bd. dir. Nat. Inst. for Study Prevention and Treatment Sexual Trauma. Contbr. numerous articles to profl. pubs. Recipient cert. appreciation Balt. County Police, 1989, 93. Fellow Am. Psychiat. Assn.; mem. AMA, Am. Acad. Psychiatry and Law (pres. Chesapeake Bay chpt.), Md. Psychiat. Assn. (legis. com. 1989—). Avocations: amateur radio, ponds and gardens.

BERLIN, IRA, historian, educator; b. N.Y.C., May 27, 1941; s. Louis and Sylvia Toby (Lebwohl) B.; m. Martha L. Chait, Aug. 31, 1963; children—Lisa Jill, Richard Aaron. PhD, U. Wis., 1970. Vice pres. I.B. Alan, Inc., 1967-69; book rev. editor Wis. Mag. History, 1969; instr. U. Ill.-Chgo., 1970-72; asst. prof. history Fed. City Coll., Washington, 1972-74. Prof. history U. Md., 1976—; mem. Columbia U. Seminar, Columbia U. Econ. History Program; dir. Freedmen and So. Soc. project Nat. Archives, also mem. adv. council Author: Slaves Without Masters: Free Negros in the Antebellum South, 1975 (Book prize Nat. Hist. Soc. 1975), Freedom: Documentary History of Emancipation, Slavery and Freedom in the Era of the American Revolution (J.F. Jameson award, Am. Hist. Assn., Founders award Confederate Meml. Literary Soc., Thomas Jefferson award Soc. Historians of Fed. Govt.); Power and Culture: H.G. Gutman and the American Working Class, 1988; also articles. Recipient Distinguished Teaching award U. Wis., 1969; Younger Humanist fellow Nat. Endowment Humanities, 1971; Bi-Centennial prof. Centre de Recherche sur l'histoire des Etats-Unis, Paris, 1987; fellow Davis Ctr. Hist. Studies, Princeton U., 1975, Ctr. for Advanced Studies in the Behavioral Scis., 1989-90. Mem. Am. Hist. Assn., So. Hist. Assn., Orgn. Am. Historians, Internat. Sociol. Assn. (com. on race and ethnicity) Jewish. Office: Univ Md Dept History College Park MD 20742-0001

BERLIN, KENNETH DARRELL DARRELL, chemistry educator, consultant, researcher; b. Quincy, Ill., June 12, 1933; s. Kenneth Marion Fischer and Mary Esther (Beckley) B.; m. Grace Frances Smith, Apr. 3, 1937; children: Grace Esther, James Darrell. BA cum laude, North Cen. Coll., Naperville, Ill., 1955; PhD, U. Ill., 1958. Postdoctoral fellow U. Fla., Gainesville, 1958-60; asst. prof. chemistry Okla. State U., Stillwater, 1960-63, assoc. prof., 1963-66, prof., 1966-71, Regents prof., 1971—. Spl. cons. Nat. Cancer Inst., Bethesda, Md., 1969—; cons. E.I. DuPont Co., Wilmington, Del., 1969-70, Am. Heart Assn., Oklahoma City, 1983-86, Ariz. Disease Control Commn., 1989—. Co-author: Organic Chemistry, 1972, Phosphorous Stereochem, 1977; contbr. rsch. Jour. Organic Chemistry, 1960, articles to profl. jours. Recipient Regents Disting. Tchg. award, 1998, Sigma Xi rsch. award Okla. State U., Stillwater, 1969, Okla. Chemist of Yr. award, 1977, Okla. Medallion Found. for Excellence in Coll./Univ. Tchg., 2003. Fellow Okla. Acad. Sci. (scientist of yr. 1976), Burlington No. Faculty Achievement award 1988, Eminent Faculty award 1998, Okla. medallion Excellence in Tchg. at Coll./Univ. Regents Disting. Rsch. award 2003); mem. Am. Chem. Soc. (sr.), Internat. Soc. Hetercyclic Chemists, Alpha Chi Sigma. Assembly of God. Office: Okla State Univ Dept Chemistry Ps I Stillwater OK 74078-0001 E-mail: kdberlin@bmb-fs1.biochem.okstate.edu.

BERLINER, DAVID CHARLES, educational psychology educator, researcher; b. N.Y.C., Mar. 15, 1938; s. Emanuel Joseph and Nettie (Pekelner) B.; children— Bethann, Brett Alan. B.A., UCLA, 1961; M.A., Calif. State U.-Los Angeles, 1962; Ph.D., Stanford U., 1968. Asst. prof. U. Mass., Amherst, 1968-70; assoc. lab. dir. Far West Lab., San Francisco, 1970-77; prof. ednl. psychology U. Ariz., Tucson, 1977— . Editor: Review of Research in Education, 1979-81. Author: (with N.L. Gage) Educational Psychology, 3d edit., 1984; (with C.W. Fisher) Perspectives on Instructional Time, 1984. Mem. Am. Ednl. Research Assn. (pres. 1984-85), Am. Psychol. Assn. Democrat. Jewish. Home: 14040 S 24th Way Phoenix AZ 85048-9002 Office: Dept Ednl Psychology Coll Ed Tucson AZ 85721-0001

BERLINER, HERMAN ALBERT, university provost and officer, economics educator; BA, CCNY, 1965; PhD, CUNY, 1970. Assoc. prof. econs. Hofstra U., Hempstead, N.Y., 1970-85, assoc. dean advisement, 1975-76, assoc. provost, 1976-83, dean Sch. Bus., 1980-82, 83-90, prof. econs., 1985—, provost, dean faculties, 1989-2001, Lawrence Herbert disting. prof., 1996—, provost, sr. v.p., 2001—. Mem. External Periodic External Review Evaluator, Mid. States, 2003, Health and Welfare Coun., LI, NY, 1997—, Nassau County Assessments Improvement Commn., NY, 1999-2000. Assoc. editor Am. Economist, 1975-80, 83—. Periodic rev. report external reviewer Middle States Commn., 2003—. Home: 93 Plymouth Dr N Glen Head NY 11545-1126 Office: Hofstra U Office of Provost Hempstead NY 11550 E-mail: herman.berliner@hofstra.edu.

BERMAN, BARBARA, educational consultant; b. N.Y.C., Oct. 15, 1938; d. Nathan and Regina (Pasternak) Kopp; children: Adrienne, David. BS, Bklyn. Coll., 1959, MS, 1961; adminstrv./supervision cert., Coll. S.I., 1971; EdD, Rutgers U., 1981. Tchr. N.Y.C. Pub. Schs., 1959-70; project coord., dir. fed. projects Rutgers U., New Brunswick, N.J., 1976-80; math. cons. B&F Cons., S.I., NY, 1978—2003, BB Consulting, S.I., NY, 2003—; dir. fed. math. project Ednl. Support Systems, Inc., S.I., 1981-94; dir. Foresight Sch., S.I., 1985—, Great Beginnings Infant and Toddler Ctr., 1989—; cons. B&F, 1985—2003. Cons. to sch. dists. for restructuring/sch. reform and math. staff devel. Co-author of many books and articles on teaching mathematics for elem. and jr. h.s. tchrs. Mem. Nat. Coun. Tchrs. Math., Nat. Staff Devel. Coun., N.Y. Acad. Scis., Nat. Coun. Suprs. Math. Avocations: reading, travel, theatre. Office: BB Consulting 446 Travis Ave Staten Island NY 10314-6149 E-mail: BarbBerman@aol.com.

BERMAN, DANIEL K(ATZEL), educational consultant, university official; b. Detroit, Nov. 17, 1954; s. Louis Arthur and Irene (Katzel) B. BS, Northwestern U., 1976, MS, 1977; AM, Harvard U., 1983; MA, U. Calif., Berkeley, 1984, PhD, 1991; cert. study, U. Paris, 1973, Peking (China) Normal U., 1981, Nat. Taiwan U., 1982. Subscription mgr. The N.Y. Times, 1983-84; editorial and rsch. asst. Inst. for Contemporary Studies, San Francisco, 1984-85; lang. cons. Berlitz Translation Svcs., San Francisco, 1986-89; v.p. Golden Gate Investment, San Francisco, 1985-87; lectr. St. Mary's Coll., Moraga, Calif., 1987; instr. U. Calif., Berkeley, 1984-90; chief exec. officer Pacific Fin. Svcs., San Francisco, 1987-92; editor Credit Report Newsletter for Consumer Edn., San Francisco, 1989-92; sales and mktg. cons. The Deerwood Corp./MRI, San Ramon, Calif., 1989-91; lectr. dept. mass comm. Calif. State U., Hayward, 1993-94; lectr. dept. elec. engring. San Jose State U., 1997-98; founder/dir. Acad. Cons. Internat., San Francisco, 1993—; assoc. provost Summit U. La., New Orleans, 1995—. Author: The Hottest Summer in Peking, 1982, The Credit Power Handbook for American Consumers, 1988, 89, Words Like Colored Glass: The Role of the Press in Taiwan's Democratization Process, 1992; co-author: Proverb Wit & Wisdom, 1997; editor, translator: The Butterfly's Revenge and Other Chinese Mystery Stories, found. CyberTip4theDay.com, 1998—. Edn. scholar Rep. of China Ministry of Edn., 1979-82; rsch. grantee Pacific Cultural Found., 1981; fgn. lang. and area studies fellow in Chinese U. Calif., 1983-84. Fellow John F. Kennedy Libr. Found.; mem. The Harvard Club of San Francisco, Soc. of Profl. Journalists, Acad. of Polit. Sci., Nat. Ctr. for Fin. Edn. (profl. sponsor), Kappa Tau Alpha (grantee). Jewish. Avocations: computers, foreign languages, piano, t'ai-chi-ch'uan, tennis. Office: Acad Cons Internat PO Box 4489 Foster City CA 94404-0489

BERMAN, MURIEL MALLIN, optometrist, humanities lecturer; b. Pitts. d. Samuel and Dora (Cooperman) Mallin; m. Philip I. Berman, Oct. 23, 1942; children: Nancy, Nina, Steven. Student, U. Pitts., 1943, Carnegie Tech. U., 1944-45; BS, Pa. State Coll. Optometry, 1948; postgrad., U. Pitts., 1950, Muhlenberg Coll., 1954, Cedar Crest Coll., 1953, DFA (hon.), 1972; hon. degree, Hebrew U., Israel, 1982; DHL (hon.), Ursinus Coll., 1987, Lehigh U., 1991. Lic. Pa., N.J. Practice optometry, Pitts.; sec.-treas., dir. Philip and Muriel Berman Found.; underwriting mem. Lloyd's of London, 1974—94. Lectr. on travels, art, UN activities, women's status and affairs. Producer: (TV) College Speakout, 1967-77; producer, moderator: (TV) Guest Spot. Active in UNICEF, 1959—, ofcl. non-govtl. orgns., 1964, 74; U.S. State Dept. del. UN Internat. Women's Yr. Conf., Mexico City, 1975; mem. State Dept. Arts and Humanities Com. Nat. Commn. on Observance of Women's Yr., 1975; adv. com. U.S. Ctr. for Internat. Womens Yr., Washington; founder, donor Carnegie-Berman Coll. Art Slide Library Exchange; mem. Aspen (Colo.) Inst. Humanistic Studies, 1965, Tokyo, 1966; chmn. exhibits Great Valley council Girl Scouts U.S.A., 1966; adminstrv. head, chmn. various events Allentown Bicentennial, 1962; vice-chmn. Women for Pa. Bicentennial, 1976; co-chmn. Lehigh County Bicentennial Bell-Trek, 1976; patron Art in Embassies Program, Washington, 1965—; chmn. Lehigh Valley Ednl. TV, 1966— ; program chmn. Fgn. Policy Assn. Lehigh County, 1965-67; treas. ann. ball Allentown Symphony, 1955— ; mem. art adv. com. Dieruff High Sch., Allentown, 1966— ; co-chmn. art. com. Episcopal Diocese Centennial Celebration, 1971; mem. Pa. Council on Status of Women, 1968-73; reappointed Pa. Gov.'s Commn. on Women, 1984; chmn. numerous art shows; mem. Art Collectors Club Am., Am. Fedn. Art, Friends of Whitney Mus., Mus. Modern Art, Mus. Primitive Art, Jewish Mus., Kemmerer Mus., Bethlehem, Pa., Univ. Mus., Phila., Archives of Am. Art, Met. Opera Guild, others; ofcl. del. Dem. Nat. Conv., 1972, 76, mem. Democratic Platform Com., 1972; mem. Pa. Humanities Coun., 1979—; bd. dirs. Heart Assn. Pa., Allentown Art Mus. Aux., Phila. Chamber Symphony, Baum Art Sch., Lehigh County Cultural Ctr., Heart Assn. Pa., Baum Art Sch., Young Audiences, Israel Mus., Hadassah Womens Orgn.; bd. govs. Pa. State System of Higher Edn., 1986—; trustee Kutztown State Coll., 1960-66, vice-chmn. bd., 1965; trustee, sec. bd. Lehigh Community Coll.; mem. nat. bd. UN-U.S.A., 1977— ; trustee Pa. Council on Arts, Pa. Ballet, Smithsonian Art Council, Bonds for Israel, Hadassah (nat. bd. with portfolio), Am. Friends Hebrew U., 1984; bd. regents Internat. Ctr. for Univ. Teaching of Jewish Civilization, Israel, 1982—; fine arts chmn. Women's Club; mem. com. on Prints, Drawings, & Photography Pa. Mus. Art, 1984; hon. chmn. Bucks County Coillectors Art Show; hon. bd. dirs., trustee Phila. Mus. Art, 1997—. Named Woman of Valor State of Israel, 1965; recipient Centennial citation Wilson Coll., 1969, Henrietta Szold award Allentown chpt. Hadassah, Outstanding Woman award Allentown YWCA, 1973, George Washington Honor medal Freedoms Found. at Valley Forge, 1985, Hazlett award Outstanding Svc. to Arts Pa., Outstanding Citizen award Boy Scouts Am., 1982, Myrtle Wreath award Pa. Region Hadassah, Mt. Scopus award State of Israel Bonds, 1984, Woman of Yr. award Am. Friends Hebrew U., Phila., 1984, Arts Ovation award, 1989, Cmty. Spirit award City of Allentown, 1990, Pres.' Medallion award West Chester U., 2002, Eberly award Pa. State Sys. Higher Edn., 2002, Am. Coun. Jewish Mus. award, 2003, others; hon. fellow Hebrew U., 1975. Mem. LWV, NOW, Am. Fedn. of Art., Pa. Hist. Soc. (life), Jewish Publ. Soc. Am. (former pres., chmn. bd. 1984), Disting. Daus. Pa., Art Collector's Club Am., Wellesley Club. Jewish. Avocation: american and english sculpture art. Address: 2000 Nottingham Rd Allentown PA 18103

BERMANN, SANDRA LEKAS, English language educator; b. Chgo., Mar. 30, 1947; d. Clarence and Theria Belle (Pollard) Lekas; m. George Alan Bermann, Dec. 28, 1969; children: Sloan Douglas, Suzanne Evelyne, Grant Alexander. AB, Smith Coll., 1969; MA, Columbia U., 1971, PhD, 1976. Asst. prof. Princeton (N.J.) U., 1976-83, assoc. prof., 1983-94, prof., 1994—, chmn. comparative lit. dept., 1998—. Dir. undergrad. studies dept. comparative literature Princeton U., 1978-82, 83-84, master of Stevenson Hall, 1984-92, dir. grad. studies dept. comparative literature, 1993-95; visitor Inst. for Advanced Study, Princeton, fall 2001; fellow Columbia U. Inst. for Scholars at Reidl Hall, Paris, 2002. Author: The Sonnet Over Time, 1988; translator, introducer: Manzoni's On the Historical Novel, 1984; contbr. articles to profl. jours. Fellow Fulbright Commn., Italy, 1969-70, Mrs. Giles Whiting Found., Columbia U. and Paris, 1974-75. Mem. MLA, Internat. Comparative Literature Assn., Am. Comparative Literature Assn. (chair undergrad. com. 1987-90, adv. bd. 1989-92, chair constitution 1991-93). Avocations: dance, music. Office: Princeton Univ Dept Comparative Literature 325 E Pyne Princeton NJ 08544-0001 E-mail: sandralb@princeton.edu.

BERMINGHAM, JOHN SCOTT, business executive, educator; b. Jackson, Wyo., Nov. 1, 1951; s. George Carpenter and Harriet (McVaugh) B. BA in English, U. N.C., 1974; MA in Edn. Psychology, Northwestern U., Evanston, Ill., 1977, MA in Counseling Psychology, 1979. Cert. clin. mental health counselor. Tchr. Tabor Acad., Marion, Mass., 1974-76, Lake Forest (Ill.) Country Day Sch., 1977-78; counselor, coord. crisis Lake County Youth Svc. Bur., Lake Villa, Ill., 1978-79; clin. dir., co-founder Greenhouse Youth Svcs., Inc., Mundelein, Ill., 1979-86; assoc. dean Lake Forest Grad. Sch. Mgmt., 1987-96; chmn. NewCo Internat., Inc., 1996—; prin. Process Solutions, Inc., 1997—. Instr. Northwestern U., Evanston, summer 1977; exec. v.p., sec.-treas., bd. dirs. Chpt. Ho., Ltd., Lake Forest, 1981-85; mng. dir. Mgmt. Resource Cons., Lake Bluff, Ill., 1986—. Bd. dirs. Cen. Lake County United Way, Libertyville, Ill., 1985, Condell Meml. Hosp. Found., Libertyville, 1989—; chmn. bd. Lake County Youth Svc. Network, Waukegan, Ill., 1983-85, CROYA-Lake Forest Youth Commn., 1985—. Recipient Cert. of Recognition, Kiwanis Libertyville, 1985, Cert. of Honor, Village Bd. Libertyville, 1986, City Coun. Lake Forest, 1989. Mem. APA (assoc.), AACD, Ill. Psychol. Assn., Nat. Acad. Cert. Clin. Mental Health Counselors. Republican. Episcopalian. Avocations: racquet sports, dancing, piano, art collecting, wood working. Home: 36 Sunset Pl Lake Bluff IL 60044-2738 Office: 1000 Oak Spring Ln Libertyville IL 60048-1614

BERNADETTA, SISTER MARIA, special education educator; b. Chgo., Apr. 25, 1925; d. Anthony and Maria Grace (Rizzo) Beninato. Student, Pestolozzi Frobel Coll., 1967-70; cert. tchr., DePaul U., 1985; degree in spl. edn., Nat.-Louis U., 1990. Joined Queen of Peace Order, Roman Cath. Ch., 1945. Sec. bishop Sacred Heart Ch., Chgo., 1965-89, catechism tchr., 1967; founder, tchr., adminstr. Little Sisters Sch., Chgo., 1970-90; founder, spl. edn. tchr., adminstr. St. Bernadette's Sch., Chgo., 1991—. Mistress of novices Queen of Peace Order, 1972-82, rev. mother superior, 1985—; pres. St. Bernadette's Corp.; mem. Case Rsch. Com. Organist Sacred Heart Ch., 1955. Mem. ASCD, Nat. Assn. Pvt. Sch. for Exceptional Children, Ill. Coun. for Exceptional Children, Ill. Affiliation of Pvt. Sch. for Exceptional Children, Ill. Coun. for Behavioral Disorders. Avocations: skating, work outs, softball, volleyball, bicycling, piano. Office: Saint Bernadette's Sch 3550 W Peterson Ave Chicago IL 60659-3270

BERNARD, APRIL, poet, literature educator; BA, Harvard U. Former sr. editor Premiere, GQ, Vanity Fair; instr. Amherst Coll., Yale U.; prof. lit., MFA core faculty Bennington (Vt.) Coll., 1998—. Author: (novels) Pirate Jenny, (poetry) Blackbird Bye Bye, Psalms: Poems, 1993, Swan Electric: Poems, 2002; contbr. poems, literary essays, and articles to various publs. Guggenheim fellow, 2003. Office: Bennington Coll One College Dr Bennington VT 05201*

BERNARD, DONALD RAY, law educator, international business counselor; b. San Antonio, June 5, 1932; s. Horatio J. and Amber (McDonald) B.; children: Doren, Kevin, Koby; m. Elizabeth Priscilla Gilpin, 1986. Student, U. Mich., 1950-52; JD, U. Tex., 1958, BA, 1954, JD, 1958, LLM, 1964. Bar: Tex. 1958, U.S. Ct. Mil. Appeals, 1959, U.S. Supreme Ct. 1959; lic. comml. pilot. Commd. ensign U.S. Navy, 1954, advanced through grades to commdr., 1956-75, retired, 1975; briefing atty. Supreme Ct. Tex., Austin, 1958-59; asst. atty. gen. State of Tex., Austin, 1959-60; ptnr. Bernard & Bernard, Houston, 1960-80; pvt. practice law Houston, 1980-94; prof. internat. law U. St. Thomas, Houston, 1991-94; guest lectr. Sch. Bus. Mont. State U., 1995-96. Mem. faculty S.W. Sch. Real Estate, 1968-77. Author: Origin of the Special Verdict As Now Practiced in Texas, 1964; co-author: (novel) Bullion, 1982. Bd. dirs. Nat. Kidney Found., Houston, 1960-63; chmn. Bd. Adjustment, Hedwig Village, Houston, 1972-76; bd. regents Angeles U. Found., The Philippines; chmn. of the bd. Metro Verde Devel. Corp., The Philippines;; bd. dirs. Gloria Dei Luth. Ch., Endowment Found. Comdr. USN, 1950-92; ret., air show pilot Confederate Air Force, 1970-80. Mem. Lawyers Soc. Houston (pres. 1973-74), Houston Bd. Realtors, ABA, Inter-Am. Bar Assn., Tex. Bar Assn. (com. liaison Mex. legal profession), Houston Bar Assn. (chairperson emeritus internat. law sect.), Internat. Bar Assn. (del. to 1st seminar with Assn. Soviet Lawyers, Moscow, 1988), Assn. Soviet Lawyers, Lawyer-Pilot Bar Assn., Sons of the Republic of Tex., Lic. Execs. Soc., St. James's Club, Masons, Shriners, Alpha Tau Omega, Phi Delta Phi. Lutheran. Home: 14 Scenic Dr Whitehall MT 59759-9789 E-mail: donbernard@msn.com.

BERNARD, JOHN MARLEY, lawyer, educator; b. Phila., Feb. 6, 1941; s. Edward and Opal (Marley) B.; children: John Marley Jr., Kendall M., Katherine M., James M.; m. Esther L. von Laue, May 31, 1986. BA, Swarthmore Coll., 1963; LLB, Harvard U., 1967. Bar: Pa. 1967. Assoc. Montgomery McCracken Walker & Rhoads, Phila., 1967-73, ptnr., 1973-86, Ballard Spahr Andrews & Ingersoll, LLP, Phila., 1986—. Lectr. Temple U. Law Sch., Phila., 1975-95; instr. Phila. Acad. for Employee Benefits Tng., 1996-99; guest instr. U.S. Dept. Labor, Washington, 1984-96; instr. U. Pa. Wharton Sch., Phila., 1989-90; bd. dirs. PENJERDEL Employee Benefits Assn., Phila. Contbg. author: Handbook of Employee Benefits, 1989. Mem. ABA, Pa. Bar Assn. Office: Ballard Spahr Andrews & Ingersoll LLP 1735 Market St Fl 51 Philadelphia PA 19103-7599 E-mail: bernard@ballardspahr.com.

BERNARD, RICHARD LAWSON, retired geneticist, educator; b. Detroit, Aug. 12, 1926; s. Clarence Rolla and Ilda Gentry (Lawson) B.; m. Ruth V. Thorne, June 14, 1952 (div. 1975); children: Betty Ruth Marnell, Richard Thorne Bernard, Alice Jean Woodley, Daniel Lawson Bernard. Student, U. Mich., 1943—45, Okla. State U., 1947—48; BS, Ohio State U., 1949, MS, 1950; PhD, NC State U., 1960. Research geneticist USDA, Urbana, Ill., 1954-88; prof. plant genetics U. Ill., Champaign, 1966-92, prof. emeritus, 1992—. Served with USAF, 1945-47. Baptist.

BERNARDS, PAMELA J. school system administrator; b. Panama City, Fla., July 11, 1958; d. James Perdie and Patricia Ann (Campbell) Raines; m. Timothy J. Bernards, May 6, 1986. Coaching cert., BS magna cum laude in Phys. Edn., U. Dayton, 1980; elem. edn. cert., U. Tenn., 1981; postgrad., Xavier U., 1985; MS in Ednl. Adminstrn. & Supervision, U. Tenn., 1994. Coach, dir. day care program, athletic dir., phys. edn. tchr. Sacred Heart Cathedral Sch., Knoxville, Tenn., 1981-92, prin., 1992—. Co-chair tchr. phase Annual Fund Campaign Sacred Heart Cathedral Sch., 1991-92, mem. planning/devel. com. 1989—, computer com. 1992. Sacred Heart Cathedral School rep. Knoxville Ind. Sch. League Bd., 1982-92 (treas. 1986-90, pres. 1990-91, v.p. 1991-92).; active edn. ad hoc com. St. John Neumann Catholic Ch., 1992. Recipient James M. Landis Memorial award of Excellence, John L. MacBeth award of Excellence, Health & Phys. Edn. Dept. The Univ. Dayton, 1980. Mem. AAHPERD, ASCD, Nat. Assn. Elem. Sch. Principals, Nat. Assn. Secondary Sch. Principals, Nat. Middle Sch. Assn., Nat. Assn. Edn. Young Children, Nat. Catholic Edn. Assn., Tenn. Assn. Health, Phys. Edn., Recreation and Dance, Tenn. Assn. Young Children (co-chair exhibits conf. 1991-93), Knoxville Area Assn. on Young Children (co-chairperson 1991 Week of Young Child, 1990-91, chairperson 1992, chairperson phys. edn. curriculum devel. 1981-92). Office: Sacred Heart Cathedral Sch 711 Northshore Dr Knoxville TN 37919

BERNDT, CLARENCE FREDRICK, JR., social studies educator; b. Chgo., Feb. 2, 1939; s. Clarence F. and Thekla O. (Buerger) B.; m. Mary Rosalie Salmon, July 31, 1971; children: Jonathan, Sara. MA, Mich. State U., 1966, MEd, 1978. Tchr. Trinity Luth. Ch., Lansing, Mich., 1961-63, Our Savior Luth. Ch., Lansing, 1963-99; editor sch. and weekday materials Concordia Publ. House, St. Louis, 1999—. Bd. dirs. Mich. Dist. Luth Ch. Mo. Synod, Ann Arbor, 1978-82, 94-99, Luth. Child and Family Svc., Bay City, Mich. Author: (devotional materials) My Devotions. Mem. adv. coun. Regional Ednl. Media, Mason, Mich., 1978-91. Mem. ASCD, Nat. Coun. Social Studies, Luth. Edn. Assn. Home: 1042 Winter Park Dr Fenton MO 63026-5689 Office: 3558 S Jefferson Saint Louis MO 63118 E-mail: crberndt@earthlink.net.

BERNDT, JANE ANN, writer, poet, researcher, educator; b. Portsmouth, Ohio, 1954; BS in Edn., Ohio U., 1977; grad. degree, George Washington U., 1993. Cert. secondary sch. biology, middle sch. sci. educator. Curriculum specialist, rschr., tchr., supr. of tchrs. Washington D.C.; grad. tchg. asst. W. Va. U. Part-time tchr. W. Va. U., Scioto County Sch., Montgomery City Sch.; sci. fair judge W. Va. State Sci. Fairs; presenter Nat. Assn. Sci. Tech. Curriculum writer, cons.: A Science Based History Curriculum Walking Through time; book reviewer Presdl. Studies Quar. Vol. reading tutor Ken. Horse Park, 1997. Fellow: Internat. Biog. Inst. (bd. gov.); mem.: Ctr. Study Presidency, Am. Biog. Assn. (life bd. govs.), Phi Kappa Phi. Avocations: outdoor activites, political science, nature.

BERNHAGEN, DEBBIE ANNE, middle school educator; b. Agusta, Ga., Aug. 23, 1958; d. August T. and Maria C. (Obidienté) B. BS in Phys. Edn., U. S.C., 1981, Interdisciplinary MA in Phys. Edn., 1990. Cert. tchr., S.C.; nat. bd. cert. tchr. in phys. edn.; cert. water safety instr. and trainer, lifeguard tng. instr. ARC. Student trainer women's athletic dept. U. S.C., Columbia, 1979-81, grad. asst., 1981-82; fitness dir. Nautilus, Columbia, 1982-83; water safety instr. trainer phys. edn.-health, athletic dir., dept. chmn., coach Richland County Sch. Dist. 2, Columbia, 1983—; cashier, asst. bookkeeper Piggly Wiggly, Columbia, S.C., 1976-79. Pool mgr. Columbia Parks and Recreation Dept., summers 1985—, Recreation vol. Midlands Ctr., Columbia, summers 1973-74. Named Outstanding Mid. Sch. Phys. Edn. Tchr. of Yr., State of S.C., 1991, 99, Tchr. of Yr., Summit Pky., 1991, Red Cross Vol. of Yr., 1998. Mem. AAHPER and Dance, NEA, S.C. Assn. Phys. Edn., Health, Recreation and Dance, Nat. Athletic Trainers Assn., S.C. Edn. Assn. Avocations: swimming, softball, physical fitness, camping, guitar. Home: 710 Westover Rd Columbia SC 24210 E-mail: dbernhag@spm.richland2.org.

BERNHARD, JEFFREY DAVID, dermatologist, editor, educator; b. Buffalo, Oct. 31, 1951; AB, Harvard Coll., 1973; MD, Harvard Med. Sch., 1978. Diplomate Am. Bd. Dermatology. Knox fellow St. John's Coll. Cambridge U., England, 1973—74; chief resident dermatology Harvard Med. Sch., Boston, 1982; fellow photomedicine Mass. Gen. Hosp., 1983; mem. faculty Med. Sch. U. Mass., Worcester, 1983—, chief dermatology, assoc. prof. Sch. Medicine, 1986—, assoc. dean for admissions Med. Sch., 1989-95, prof. Med. Sch., 1992—. Author: Itch: Mechanisms and Management of Pruritus, 1994; asst. editor Jour. Am. Acad. Dermatology, 1993-98, editor, 1998—; mem. editl. bd. Jour. European Acad. Dermatology and Venereology, Yearbook of Cancer, 1981-88, Yearbook of Dermatology, 1988-97, Internat. Jour. Dermatology, Jour. Geriat. Dermatology, 1993-97. Named J. Graham Smith, Jr., hon. lectr., 2000, Narins Meml. Lectr., 2001, Novy lectr., U. Calif., Davis, 2002, Lorincz lectr., Chgo. Derm. Soc., 2002, Luscombe lectr., Jefferson Med. Coll., 2003; named an hon. mem., Czech. Soc. Dermatol, 2002. Mem.: Coun. Sci. Editors, European Soc. for History of Dermatology, History of Dermatology Soc., Quinsigamond Dermatol. Soc., New Eng. Dermatol. Soc. (pres. 1990—91), Assn. Profs. Dermatology, Sir James Saunders Soc., Royal Soc. Medicine, Am. Dermatol. Assn., European Acad. Dermatology and Venereology, Soc. for Investigative Dermatology (bd. dirs. 1981—83), Am. Acad. Dermatology (Presdl. citation 2000), Czech Soc. Dermatology (hon.), James C. White Club, Aesculapian Club Boston, Sigma Xi, Alpha Omega Alpha, Phi Beta Kappa. Office: U Mass Meml Med Ctr 55 Lake Ave N Worcester MA 01655-0002

BERNHARD, ROBERT JAMES, mechanical engineer, educator; b. Algona, Iowa, July 28, 1952; s. David Louis and Darlene Justine (Kohlhaas) B.; m. Deborah S. Kell; children: Jay David, Jacqueline Elizabeth, Jonathan Christian, Justin Brian. BS in Mech. Engring., Iowa State U., 1973, PhD, 1982; MS, U. Md., 1976. Engr. Westinghouse Electric, Inc., Balt., 1973-77; asst. prof. Iowa State U., Ames, 1977-82; asst. prof. dept. mech. engring. Purdue U., West Lafayette, Ind., 1982-87, assoc. prof., 1987-91, prof., 1991—. Dir. Ray W. Herrick Labs Purdue U., 1994—, Inst. for Safe, Quiet, and Durable Hwys, 1998—; cons. to GM, Electricite de France, Automated Analysis; prin. investigator many firms; lectr. CETIM, U. Wis., U. Mich. Assoc. editor: Noise Control Engring. Jour., 1984-85, 90—. Fellow ASME (co-editor procs. 1989), Acoustical Soc. Am.; mem. AIAA, Soc. Automotive Engrs., Inst. Noise Control Engrs. (bd. dirs. 1988-97, pres. 1994), Am. Soc. Engring. Educators. Office: Purdue U 1077 Ray W Herrick Labs Lafayette IN 47907

BERNHARDT, WILLIAM WOLF, English language educator; b. Washington, Dec. 15, 1937; s. Joshua and Hanna (Gichner) B.; m. Elizabeth Farber, Nov. 21, 1973; children: Doris, Sophia. BA, Reed Coll., 1960; MA, Cornell U., 1961. Lectr. U. Keele, Eng., 1964-67; instr. Fisk U., Nashville, 1967-68; asst. prof. Reed Coll., Portland, Oreg., 1968-71; assoc. prof. English Coll. of S.I., N.Y., 1971—. Vis. prof. Hebei Tchrs. U., Shijiazhuang, China, 1981-82; cons. Hebei Province, 1986-89, N.Y.C. Schs., 1986—. Author: Just Writing, 1977; co-author: Becoming a Writer, 1986; editor: Journal of Basic Writing, 1988-94; contbr. articles to scholarly publs. Trustee Bronx chpt. Sch. for Better Learning, 2003. Mem. Assn. for Sci. of Edn. (pres. 1994—), Phi Beta Kappa. Home: 924 W End Ave New York NY 10025-3534 Office: Coll of S I 2800 Victory Blvd Staten Island NY 10314-6609 E-mail: bernhardt@postbox.csi.cuny.edu.

BERNICK, ROBERT LLOYD, engineering educator; b. St. Paul, May 7, 1938; s. Leslie Leo and Zena (Cofman) B.; m. Joan Merle Glick, Jan. 30, 1966; children: Elizabeth Charlotte, Elena Patrice, Andrew Stuart. BA in Math., U. Minn., 1959; MA in Physics, U. Calif., Berkeley, 1962; PhD, U. So. Calif., 1970. Jr. engr. GM Corp., El Segundo, Calif., 1959-60; engr. N.Am. Aviation, Canoga Park, Calif., 1962-65; mem. tech. staff, sect. head Hughes Aircraft Co., Torrance, Calif., 1969-79; prof. elec. and computer engring. Calif. State Polytech. U., Pomona, 1979—. Contbr. tech. papers to profl. publs. NSF fellow, 1960. Mem. IEEE, Am. Soc. Engring. Edn., Phi Beta Kappa, Tau Beta Pi, Eta Kappa Nu. Avocations: amateur radio, camping. Office: Calif State Polytech U 3801 W Temple Ave Pomona CA 91768-2557 E-mail: rlbernick@csupomona.edu.

BERNIERI, FRANK JOHN, social psychology educator; b. Bklyn., May 2, 1961; s. Gene J. and Rose (Autunnale) B.; divorced; 1 child, Jennifer. BA, U. Rochester, 1983; PhD, Harvard U., 1988. Asst. prof. social psychology Oreg. State U., Corvallis, 1988—93, assoc. prof., 1993—94, 2003—, chmn. psychology dept., 2003—; assoc. prof. U. Toledo, 1994—2003. Author: (with others) Coordinated Movement in Human Interaction, 1991, Interpersonal Sensitivity, 2001; mem. editorial bd. Jour. Nonverbal Behavior, 1990—; contbr. articles to profl. jours. Fellow Harvard U., 1987; grantee NIH, 1988, Oreg. State U. Coll. Liberal Arts, 1990; NSF Young Investigator awardee, 1992. Mem. AAAS, APA, Am. Psychol. Soc., Soc. for Personality and Social Psychology, Soc. for Exptl. Social Psychology. Democrat. Office: Oreg State Univ Dept Psychology Corvallis OR 97331

BERNINGER, VIRGINIA WISE, psychologist, educator; b. Phila., Oct. 4, 1946; d. Oscar Sharpless and Lucille (Fike) Wise; m. Ronald William Berninger, Aug. 3, 1968. BA in Psychology, Elizabethtown (Pa.) Coll., 1967; MEd in Reading and Lang., U. Pitts., 1970; PhD in Psychology, Johns Hopkins U., 1981. Lic. psychologist, Wash. Educator Phila. Pub. Schs., 1967-68, Pitts. Pub. Schs., 1968, Baldwin-White Hall Pub. Schs., Pitts., 1969-72, Frederick (Md.) Pub. Schs., 1972-75, Balt. Pub. Schs., 1975-76; instr. Med. Sch. Harvard U., Boston, 1981-83; asst. prof. Sch. of Medicine Tufts U., Boston, 1983-86; asst. prof. Coll. Edn. U. Wash., Seattle, 1986-89, assoc. prof., 1989-93, prof., 1993—, co-dir. U. Brain, Edn. and Tech. Ctr., 2003—. Mem. Ctr. for Study of Capable Youth, U. Wash., Seattle, 1989—; cons. grant rev. NICHD, 1990—, NIH, 1990—, others; rsch. affiliate Ctr. for Human Devel. and Disability, U. Wash., 1994—; coord. for learning disabilities Ctr. for Human Devel. and Disability, 2002—. Author: Reading and Writing Acquisition: A Developmental Neuropsychological Perspective, 1994, Process Assessment of the Learner: Guides for Intervention, 1998, PAL Test Battery for Reading and Writing, 2001, (with T. Richards) Brain Literacy for Educators and Psychologists, 2002, PAL Research-Supported Reading and Writing Lessons, 2003; contbr. articles to profl. publs.; editor vols.; mem. various editorial bds. NIMH fellow 1978-80; rsch. grantee: U. Wash. 1987-88, Inst. for Ethnic Studies in the U.S., 1989-90, NIH, 1989—, Dept. Edn., 1993-95. Mem. AAAS, Am. Psychol. Assn., Soc. Scientific Studies Reading, Soc. for Rsch. on Child Devel., N.Y. Acad. Sci., Internat. Dyslexia Assn. Office: U Wash 322 Miller Box 353600 Seattle WA 98195-3600

BERNSTEIN, EVA GOULD, retired elementary education educator, reading specialist; b. Milw., Nov. 25, 1918; d. Nathan and Lena Fried Gould; m. E. Ace Bernstein (dec.); children: Marcy B. Lichtig, Lynn C. Arriale. BS in Elem. Edn., State Tchrs. Coll., Milw., 1940; MS in Reading, U. Wis., Milw., 1970. Tchr. S.S. Jr. High, Sheboygan, Wis., 1940-42, Greendale (Wis.) Pub. Sch., 1947-49; reading specialist Milw. Pub. Schs., 1970-79; with Lake Worth (Fla.) Schs., 1989—, picture lady, 1996—. Docent Milw. Art Mus., 1987—. Mem. AAUW (coll. women's club, leader, mem. book group 1989—), Nat. Coun. Jewish Women (v.p. pub. affairs 1950-54), Hadassah (v.p. Am. affairs 1951-53), Pi Lambda Theta (v.p. conv. tours chair, v.p. U. Wis.-Milw. chpt. 1976-78). Jewish. Avocations: gardening, swimming, walking, politics, art appreciation.

BERNSTEIN, I. MELVIN, university official and dean, materials scientist; b. N.Y.C., N.Y., Oct. 14, 1938; s. Emanuel and Helen (Wolitzer) B.; m. Katherine Sarah Russo, June 7, 1964; 1 child, Elana BS, Columbia U., 1960, MS, 1962, PhD, 1965. Postdoctoral assoc. Central Electricity Generating Bd., Berkeley, Eng., 1966-67; scientist U.S. Steel Research Lab., Monroeville, Pa., 1967-72; from asst. prof. to prof. Carnegie-Mellon U., Pitts., 1972-87, assoc. dean engring., 1978-82, prof., head dept. metall. engring and materials sci., 1982-87; provost, acad. v.p. Ill. Inst. Tech., Chgo., 1987-90, chancellor, 1990-91; v.p. arts, scis. and engring., dean faculty Tufts U., Medford, Mass., 1991-2001; provost, sr. v.p. Brandeis U., 2001—03; dir. univ. programs Dept. of Homeland Security, Washington, 2003—. Chief cons. MCL, Monroeville, 1972-82; liaison scientist Office Naval Research, London, 1977-78; mem. Nat. Materials adv. bd., 1990-96. Co-editor: Handbook of Stainless Steel, 1977, Hydrogen Effects in Metals, 1973, 76, 1981; assoc. editor Metall. Trans., 1977-82. Mem. Pitts. Dem. Com., 1971-75; bd. govs. Ben Gurion U., Israel, 1993—. Jewish. E-mail: mel.bernstein4@verizon.net.

BERNSTEIN, IRA HARVEY, psychology educator; b. N.Y.C., Aug. 10, 1938; s. Louis and Sally (Cantor) B.; m. Linda Jean Greif, June 4, 1961; children: Cari Gaye, Dina Louise. BA, U. Mich., 1959; MA, Vanderbilt U., 1961, PhD, 1963. Instr. U. Ill., Urbana, 1963-64; clin. prof. U. Tex. S.W. Med. Sch., Dallas, 1976-78, 80-89; asst. prof. to prof. U. Tex., Arlington, 1965—. Vis. prof. North Tex. State U., Denton, 1972. Author: Applied Multivariate Analysis, 1988, (with J.C. Nunnally) Psychometric Theory, (WITH J.C. Nunnally) 3d edit., 1994, Computer Literacy: Getting the Most From Your PC, 1998,(P.Havig), Statistical Data Analysis for the Personal Computer, 2001(N.Rowe); contbr. over 70 articles to profl. jours. Mem. Dallas Police Review Bd., 1983-87. Recipient award Am. Med. Assn., 1969, Am. Acad. Ophthalnology-Otolaryngology, 1969. Democrat. Jewish. Avocation: jazz. Office: Univ Tex Dept Psychology PO Box 19528 Arlington TX 76019-0001

BERNSTEIN, JANNA S. BERNHEIM, art educator; b. Memphis, July 21, 1951; d. Berthol Moise and Aline Joy (Kahn) Bernheim; m. Eugene Bernstein Jr., Aug. 12, 1978 (div. Apr. 1992); children: Rachel, Claire, Ruth. BFA, Washington U., 1973; MFA, Memphis State U., 1979, MAT, 1991. Graphic artist Cleo Wrap, Inc., Memphis, 1978-80, Memphis Bd. of Edn., 1980-81; art instr. Memphis Arts Coun., 1983-86, Memphis Brooks Mus., 1985-88; art tchr. St. Agnes Acad./St. Dominic Sch. for Boys, Memphis, 1991—. Chmn. cultural arts Richland Elem. Sch., Memphis, 1988-90. Co-author: (lesson packets) Ancient Egypt: An Educator's Guide, 1991, Imprint on the World, 1993; exhibited in group shows at Memphis Brooks Mus., 1976, Memphis May Banner Competition, 1981. Curator docent edn. Temple Israel Judaica Mus., Memphis, 1994; mem. gifts and arts com. Temple Israel, Memphis, 1994—; docent Wonders Internat. Cultural Svcs., Memphis, 1986, 92, 93; worker Temple Israel Habitat for Humanity, Memphis. Shakespeare Festival grantee Tenn. Arts Commn., 1994. Mem. Tenn. Art Edn. Assn., West Tenn. Art Edn. Assn. (exhbn. coord. 1993-95), Memphis Artists Crafts Mem. Assn. (bd. dirs. 1993-95). Avocations: gardening, water sports. Home: 319 Fernway Cv Memphis TN 38117-2012 Office: St Dominic Sch for Boys 30 Avon Rd Memphis TN 38117-2596

BERNSTEIN, JUDI ELLEN, elementary school educator; b. Bronx, N.Y., Apr. 03; d. Julius Weber and Pauline Shein; m. Al B. Bernstein, Nov. 29, 1959; children: Mildred, Jacalyn, Helaine, Louis. AA in Liberal Arts, Suffolk C.C., Brentwood, N.Y., 1987; BS in Elem. Edn., SUNY, Old Westbury, 1990; MS, L.I. U./C.W. Post U., Brentwood, 1994. Cert. elem. tchr., N.Y.; cert. tchr. elem. and secondary reading, N.Y. Student tchr. 3rd grade Burr Intermediate Sch., Commack, N.Y., 1989; student tchr. 1st grade Wood Pk. Sch., Commack, 1989; with Kumon Sch., 1993-94; substitute elem. and secondary tchr. Commack Sch. Dist., 1990-95. Active, hon. life. mem. Commack PTA Coun., 1984—; treas. Commack Youth Devel. Assn., 1976-84; active Dan Beard dist. Cub Scouts, Boy Scouts Am., Suffolk coun. Girl Scouts U.S., Huntington Substance Abuse Coalition, 1985-87, Youth Bur., Town of Huntington, 1976-84. Recipient certs. of svc. Girl Scouts U.S., Commack, 1970-76, North Ridge PTA, 1987, cert. of appreciation Dan Beard dist. Cub Scouts, Boy Scouts Am., 1987, Commack PTA, 1994, Cmty. Svc. award Town of Huntington, 1987, Disting. Svc. award N.Y. State PTA, 1984. Mem. ASCD, Nat. Coun. Tchrs. of English, Internat. Reading Assn. Home: 26 Bethal Ln Commack NY 11725-1004

BERNSTEIN, SOL, cardiologist, educator; b. West New York, N.J., Feb. 3, 1927; s. Morris Irving and Rose (Leibowitz) B.; m. Suzi Maris Sommer, Sept. 15, 1963; 1 son, Paul. AB in Bacteriology, U. Southern Calif., 1952, MD, 1956. Diplomate Am. Bd. Internal Medicine. Intern Los Angeles County Hosp., 1956-57, resident, 1957-60; practice medicine specializing in cardiology L.A., 1960—; staff physician dept. medicine Los Angeles County Hosp. U. So. Calif. Med. Center, L.A., 1960—, chief cardiology clinics, 1964, asst. dir. dept. medicine, 1965-72; chief profl. services Gen. Hosp., 1972-74; med. dir. Los Angeles County-U So. Calif. Med. Center, L.A., 1974-94; med. dir. central region Los Angeles County, 1974-78; dir. Dept. Health Services, Los Angeles County, 1978; assoc. dean Sch. Medicine, U. So. Calif., L.A., 1986-94, assoc. prof., 1968—; med. dir. Health Rsch. Assn., L.A., 1995—. Cons. Crippled Childrens Svc. Calif., 1965—. Contbr. articles on cardiac surgery, cardiology, diabetes and health care planning to med. jours. Served with AUS, 1946-47, 52-53. Fellow A.C.P., Am. Coll. Cardiology; mem. Am. Acad. Phys. Execs., Am. Fedn. Clin. Research, N.Y. Acad. Sci., Los Angeles, Am. heart assns., Los Angeles Soc. Internal Medicine, Los Angeles Acad. Medicine, Sigma Xi, Phi Beta Phi, Phi Eta Sigma, Alpha Omega Alpha. Home: 4966 Ambrose Ave Los Angeles CA 90027-1756 Office: 1640 Marengo St Los Angeles CA 90033-1036

BERNSTEIN, VIVIAN D. special education author, educational consultant; b. Bklyn., Mar. 14, 1948; d. Irving J. and Nettie (Tambor) Bernstein; m. Neil H. Bernstein, June 23, 1974; children: Aliza, Rachel. BA cum laude, Bklyn. Coll., 1969; MA in Ednl. Psychology, NYU, 1970. Cert. tchr. spl. edn., deaf edn., common brs., N.Y. Tchr. hearing and lang. impaired N.Y.C. Pub. Schs., Bklyn. and Queens, 1970-80; spl. edn. author Steck Vaughn Pub. Co., Austin, Tex., 1978—; edn. cons., workshop leader Schs. in N.Y. State, 1990—. Author: American Government: Freedom, Rights, Responsibilities, 1992, Decisions for Health, 1993, Life Skills for Today's World, 1994, World History and You, 1997, America's History: Land of Liberty, 1997, World Geography and You, 1998, America's Story, 2001, 02. Avocations: swimming, reading, gardening, aerobics. E-mail: viv31448@aol.com.

BERON, KURT JAMES, economics educator; b. N.Y.C., Sept. 12, 1956; s. Peter K. and Ilene (Israel) B.; m. Laurie L. LeFebvre, May 23, 1987; children: Jenna, Celia. BSBA, U. N.C., Greensboro, 1977; MSW, U. N.C., Chapel Hill, 1980, PhD in Econs., 1985. Assoc. prof. U. Tex., Richardson, 1985—; assoc. dean, dir. undergrad. studies, Sch. of Social Scis. Univ. Tex., Dallas, 1993—96, assoc. dir. Ctr. Edn. and Social Policy, 1994—98; faculty rep. Nat. Collegiate Athletic Assn., 2000—. Reviewer TCMP grants IRS, Washington, 1990—; coord. undergrad. econ. prog., 1992-94; chair, computing in the Social Scis. com., 1992-2001. Assoc. editor Structural Equation Modeling: A Multidisciplinary Jour., 1993-96, Evaluation Rev., 1989-92; contbr. articles to profl. jours. Rsch. grantee State of Tex., 1988-90. Mem. Am. Econ. Assn., So. Econ. Assn., Law and Soc. Assn. Avocations: soccer, computers, chess. Office: U Tex at Dallas PO Box 830688 Richardson TX 75083-0688

BERRY, BRIAN JOE LOBLEY, geographer, political economist, urban planner; b. Sedgley, Stafford, Eng., Feb. 16, 1934; came to U.S., 1955, naturalized, 1965; s. Joe and Gwendoline Alice (Lobley) B.; m. Janet Elizabeth Shapley, Sept. 6, 1958; children: Duncan Jeffrey, Carol Anne (dec.), Diane Leigh, Karen. BSc with honors, Univ. Coll., London, 1955; MA, U. Wash., 1956, PhD, 1958; AM (hon.), Harvard U., 1976. Instr. geography, civil engring. U. Wash., Seattle, 1957-58; asst. prof. geography U. Chgo., 1958-62, assoc. prof., 1962-65, prof., 1965-72, Irving B. Harris prof. urban geography, 1972-76, dir. Ctr. Urban Studies, chmn. dept. geography, 1974-76; Frank Backus Williams prof. urban and regional planning Harvard U., 1976-81, chmn. Ph.D. Program in Urban Planning, dir. Lab. for Computer Graphics and Spatial Analysis, fellow Inst. Internat. Devel., 1976-81, prof. sociology, 1978-81; dean H. John Heinz III Sch. of Pub. Mgmt. Carnegie-Mellon U., 1981-86, Univ. prof. urban studies and pub. policy, 1981-86; founders prof. U. Tex., Dallas, 1986-91, prof. polit. econ., 1986—; Lloyd Viel Berkner Regental prof., 1991—; chmn. Bruton Ctr. for Devel. Studies U. Tex., Dallas, 1988-95. Author numerous books; contbr. articles to profl. jours. Fellow Univ. Coll., U. London, 1983; recipient Victoria medal Royal Geog. Soc., 1988, Rockefeller prize Dartmouth U., 1992; named Lord of Hastingleigh, County Kent, 2000. Fellow AAAS, Am. Acad. Arts and Scis., Urban Land Inst., Brit. Acad. (corr.), Weimer Inst. Real Estate and Land Econs., Royal Geog. Soc., So. Regional Sci. Assn.; mem. NAS (coun. 1999-2002), Assn. Am. Geographers (hon. award 1968, pres. 1978-79, Anderson medal 1987), Am. Inst. Cert. Planners, Regional Sci. Assn., Inst. Brit. Geographers, Sigma Xi. Office: U Tex-Dallas Sch Social Sci Richardson TX 75083-0688 E-mail: heja@utdallas.edu., bjlb@comcast.net.

BERRY, GUY CURTIS, polymer science educator, researcher; b. Greene County, Ill., May 11, 1935; s. Charles Curtis and Wilma Francis (Wickes) B.; m. Marilyn Jane Montooth, Jan. 26, 1957; children: Susan Jane, Sandra Jean, Scott Curtis. BSCh.E., U. Mich., 1957, MS in Polymer Sci., 1958, PhD, 1960. Fellow Mellon Inst., Pitts., 1960-65, sr. fellow, 1965—90; assoc. prof. chemistry Carnegie-Mellon U., Pitts., 1966-73, prof., 1973—2002, acting dean, 1981-82, acting head dept. chemistry, 1983-84, head dept. chemistry, 1990-95, Univ. prof., 2002—. Vis. prof. U. Tokyo, 1973, Colo. State U., Ft. Collins, 1979, U. Kyoto, Japan, 1983 Editor Jour. Polymer Sci., 1988-93, Progress in Polymer Sci., 2002--; mem. editl. bd. Jour. Rheology, 1990—, Chemtracts-Macromolecular Chemistry, 1990-94; contbr. over 200 articles to sci. jour. Recipient Bingham medal Soc. of Rheology, 1990; Polymeric Materials: Sci. and Engring. fellow. Fellow Am. Phys. Soc., Polymeric Materials: Sci. and Engring.; mem. AAAS, Am. Chem. Soc. (Pitts. Chemistry prize 1994), Soc. Rheology. Office: Carnegie Mellon U Dept Chem 4400 5th Ave Pittsburgh PA 15213-2617 E-mail: gcberry@andrew.cmu.edu.

BERRY, JAMES DECLOIS, special education and history educator; b. Alto, Tex., Dec. 1, 1929; s. David Jonathan Berry and Albradle (Tidwell) Dearman; m. Marie Wickware, Aug., 1958 (div. 1961); children: Catrina Bass, Renee Berry; m. Shirly Davis, Aug. 12, 1962; children: Vera, Delnoir Hubbard. BS, Butler Coll., 1954; MEd, Tex. So. U., 1973, postgrad. in education, 1990—; postgrad. in pastoral counseling and care, So. Meth. U., 1981; ThM, So. Meth. U., Dallas, 1986; postgrad., Houston Sch. Theology, 1987-88. Cert. tchr. elem., secondary, spl. edn., Tex. Tchr. history U. So. Calif., 1954-55; pvt. detective WMN Internat. Detective Agy., Dallas, 1957-58; agt. Universal Life Ins. Co., Houston, 1959-64; tchr. Houston Ind. Sch. Dist., 1964—. Supervising tchr. for teaching corp. Univ. of Houston, Tex. So. U. at Lantrip Elem. Sch., Houston, 1973-79; supervising tchr. for student tchr. Lantrip Elem. Sch., Houston, 1973-79, vice prin. Lantrip Elem. Sch., 1976-77. Co-author, researcher Hagg Found. Group Project, 1984-85. Chmn. Houston Legal Found., 1954-56, pres.; v.p. Scenic Wood Plaza Civic Club, Houston, 1971-72; del. Houston Tchrs. Assn., Houston, 1966—; vol. worker Food and Clothing for the Poor of Houston, United Meth. Ch., 1987—; active Nat. Dem. Com., 1993, Pres.'s Com. for Change; pastor of various chs. and chapels throughoutTex., 1979-91. Decorated Slama Rhee Medal of Honor, Korean Govt., Korea, 1955. Mem. Am. Fedn. Tchrs. (bd. dirs., tchr. rep.), Houston Fedn. Tchrs. (cabine, 1978-79, faculty rep.), A. Phillip Randolph Soc. (cabinet mem., rep.). Democrat. Avocations: reading, checkers, dominoes. Home: 5406 Yorkwood St Houston TX 77016-2644

BERRY, JAY ROBERT, JR., English educator; b. Cleve., Oct. 12, 1957; s. Jay Robert and Nettie Marie (Stanish) B.; m. Regenia Dee Bailey, Nov. 25, 1989. PhB, Miami U., 1979; MA, U. Iowa, 1983. Instr. U. Iowa, Iowa City, 1980-87, 88-93, Iowa State U., Ames, 1994-97, adj. asst. prof., 1997—2002; instr. Kirkwood Cmty Coll., 2002—. Vis. instr. Carleton Coll., Northfield, Minn., 1987-88, Mt. Mercy Coll., Cedar Rapids, Iowa, 1991-93. Mem.: Coll. Lang. Assn. Office: Kirkwood Cmty Coll Dept English Cedar Rapids IA 52406 E-mail: jrb@avalon.net.

BERRY, JOHN JOSEPH, educational administrator; b. Chgo., Mar. 6, 1953; s. Richard Martin and Dorothy Mae (Lyke) B. BA, Marquette U., Milw., 1975; MA, U. San Francisco, 1985. Cert. tchr. spl. edn., sch. adminstrn. Tchr. Kelseyville (Calif.) Unified Sch. Dist., 1980-88, adminstr., 1988—. Golf columnist On the Links, 1993—. Commr., Lake County Athletic League, Lakeport, Calif., 1990—; exec. dir. Lake County Jr. Golf Coun., Loch Lomand, Calif., 1989—. Mem. Assn. Calif. Sch. Adminstrs., Calif. Golf Writers Assn. Democrat. Roman Catholic. Avocations: golf, coaching basketball, audiophile. Home: 2844 Buckingham Dr Kelseyville CA 95451-7004 Office: Mount Vista Mid Sch PO Box 308 Kelseyville CA 95451-0308

BERRY, JONI INGRAM, hospice pharmacist, educator; b. Charlotte, N.C., June 6, 1953; d. James Clifford and Patricia Ann (Ebener) Ingram; div.; children: Erin Blair, Rachel Anne, James Rosser. BS in Pharmacy, U. N.C., 1976, MS in Pharmacy, 1979, postgrad., 1999. Lic. pharmacist, N.C. Resident in pharmacy Sch. Pharmacy, U. N.C., Chapel Hill, 1977-79, adj. asst. prof., 1985—; pharmacist Durham County Gen. Hosp., Durham, N.C., 1977-79; coord. clin. pharm. Wake Med. Ctr., Raleigh, N.C., 1979-80; co-dir. pharmacy edn. Wake Area Health Edn. Ctr., Raleigh, 1980-85; pharmacist cons. Hospice of Wake County, Raleigh, 1980—; co-owner Integrated Pharm. Care Systems, Inc., 1995—. Mem. editorial adv. bd. Hospice Jour., 1985-91, 94—, Jour. Pharm. Care in Pain and Symptom Mgmt., 1992—; reviewer Am. Jour. Hospice Care, 1996-98; editor pharmacy sect. notes NHO Coun. Hospice Profls.; contbr. articles to profl. jours. Troop leader Girl Scouts U.S.A., Raleigh, 1987—, trainer, 1989-91, mgr. svc. unit, 1990-94; Sunday sch. tchr. St. Phillips Luth. Ch., Raleigh, 1990-92, 94-95, asst. min., 1995—, choir mem. 1998—. Recipient Silver Pinecone award Girl Scouts U.S., 1991, Golden Rule award J.C. Penney Co., 1991. Mem.: Wake County Pharm. Assn. (sec. 1982—85), N.C. Hosp. Pharmacists (bd. dirs. 1984—86, program com. 1988—91), N.C. Pharm. Assn. (mem. continuing edn. com. 1986—87, chair com. 1981—84, Don Blanton award 1985), Am. Pain Soc., Nat. Hospice Orgn., Am. Soc. Hosp. Pharmacists, Acad. Pharmacy Practice and Mgmt. (mem.-at-large 1996, chair specialized sect. 1999—2002), Am. Pharm. Assn. (hospice pharmacist steering com. 1990—), Nat. Coun. Hospice Profls. (pharmacy sect. leader 1998—), Rho Chi. Democrat. Avocations: gardening, weight lifting, aerobics. Office: Hospice Wake County 1300 Saint Marys St Raleigh NC 27605-1276 E-mail: momsberry@aol.com.

BERRY, MICHAEL CODY, educational administrator; b. Covington, Ky., July 10, 1951; s. Harvey Wells and Dorothy Helen (Cody) B.; m. Melanie Ann Klotter Garner, July 6, 1985; stepchildren: Erin K. Garner, Shannon C. Garner, Sean B. Garner. AA, BA, No. Ky. U., Highland Heights, 1973; MA, U. Cin., 1978. Cert. secondary tchr., Ky. Tchr. 7th and 8th grade English Ockerman Jr. H.S., Florence, Ky., 1973-76; adj. instr. English U. Cin., 1978-81, No. Ky. U., Highland Heights, 1979-81, spl. lectr. English, 1981-84, cooperating lectr. English, 1984—, admissions counselor, 1984-87, acting dir. student support svcs., 1995, distance learning adv. bd., dir. ednl. talent search, 1987—, dental hygiene adv. bd., 1991-95, acting dir. Upward Bound, 1996, rsch. grants and contracts adv. bd., 1996—. Mem. futures adv. bd. Ky. Coun. on Higher Edn., Frankfort, 1994-95; mem. No. Ky. Local Labor Market's Sch.-to-Work Commn., 1995-97. Author short stories. Mem. No. Ky. Youth Collaborative in Edn., No. Ky. U., 1988-89, mem. alumni coun., 1988-94; vol. mentor Project Continued Success, Aiken H.S., Cin., 1985-87; bd. dirs. Greater Cincinnati Coll. Access Network, 2002—; liaison Am. Coun. on Edn., 2001—. Recipient Award for Outstanding Leadership, Coca Cola, 1995, Disting. Svc. award No. Ky. U. Alumni Assn., 1995; named to Outstanding Young Men of Am.; U.S. Dept. Edn. grantee, 1987—. Mem. No. Ky. Counseling Assn., Southeastern Assn. Ednl. Opportunity Program Pers. (Pres.'s award 1996, bd. dirs. 1994-95, editor regional newsletter The Sentinel 1995-96, 1999-2001, conf. co-chair 1997, sec. 1997-99), Ky. Assn. Ednl. Opportunity Program Pers. (v.p. 1992-93, pres. 1994-95), No. Ky. C. of C. (participant No. Ky. Edn. alliance 1992—, Paul Luxmore Lifetime Achievement award for Profl. Excellence 1996). Home: 3727 Middlebrook Ave Cincinnati OH 45208-1118 E-mail: berrym@nku.edu.

BERRY, NANCY JUNE, elementary school educator; b. Logansport, Ind., June 26, 1943; d. Oliver A. and Pauline (Scott) Wade; m. E. Jon Berry, Oct. 29, 1961; children: Samuel G., Christopher W. BS with distinction, Ind. U., Kokomo, 1974, MS, 1977, student, 1990. Adj. prof. Ind. U., 1987—; tchr. grade 1 Franklin Elem. Logansport (Ind.) Com. Schs., 1974—; cons. Ind. Bur. of Edn. and Rsch., 1989—93; prin. Columbia Elem. Sch., Logansport, Ind., 1995—2000; 1st grade tchr. Liza Jackson Prep. Sch., Ft. Walton Beach, Fla., 2000—. Cons. Fla. Dept. Edn., 2003—; mem. selection com. Disney's Am. Tchrs. award, 1999—; presenter papers, workshops and seminars. Author: Teaching Total Child, 1990. V.p. Big Brother, Big Sister of Cass County, 1988-93; trustee Nat. Tchrs. Hall of Fame, 2002—. Named Outstanding Young Educator JayCees, Cass County 1978, Ind. 1979; recipient Ind.'s Shining Star award WTHR-TV, Tchr. of Week award WRTV, 1993, Disting. Alumna award Ind. U. at Kokomo, 1993, Tchr. of Yr. award State of Ind. Cass County Environment and Conservation, 1992, 93, Ind. Wildlife Tchr. of Yr. Ind. Wildlife Assn., 1993, Am. Tchr. award, Disney, 1995-96; inducted into Nat. Tchr. Hall of Fame, 2000. Mem. Greater Logansport Reading Council (pres., v.p., sec.), Hoosier Assn. Sci., Ind. State Reading, Delta Kappa Gamma. Home: 279 Echo Cir Fort Walton Beach FL 32548

BERRY, NANCY WESTPHAL, art educator; b. San Angelo, Tex., Aug. 22, 1935; d. William H. and Lillian (Womble) Westphal; m. Thomas R. Berry, Sept. 12, 1957; children: Ann-Leslie Berry, Blair Bardwell. BS in Interior Design, U. Tex., 1957; MFA in Art Edn., So. Meth. U., 1976, MA in Art History, 1983. Art specialist The Trinity Sch., Midland, Tex., 1965-71; art educator Dallas Mus. Art, 1974-78; cons. art The Winston Sch., Dallas, 1974-75; instr. art edn. So. Meth. U., Dallas, 1976-81; curator of edn. Meadows Mus., Dallas, 1976-85; asst. prof. art So. Meth. U., Dallas, 1981-86; dir. edn. Dallas Mus. Art, 1989-91; prof. emeritus art U. N. Tex., Denton, 1991—; mem. faculty North Tex. Inst. for Educators in the Arts, Dallas, 1992—; program dir. Nat. Ctr. for Art Mus./Sch. Collaborations, Dallas, 1994—. Cons. Amon Carter mus., Ft. Worth, 1983-91, Museo Del Prado, Madrid, 1983. Editor: Museum Education: History, Theory, Practice, 1990; author, editor: Art Links, 1993; author: Experience Art, 1998. Fellow Nat. Art Edn. Assn. (dir. mus. divsn., 1987-89, mem. devel. com.); mem. Tex. Art Edn. Assn. (dir. mus. divsn. 1979-81), Am. Assn. Mus. (mem. edn. com.), Tex. Assn. Mus. Episcopalian. E-mail: nberry@untedu.

BERRY, ROBERT WORTH, lawyer, retired law educator, retired military officer; b. Ryderwood, Wash., Mar. 2, 1926; s. John Franklin and Anita Louise (Worth) Berry. BA in Polit. Sci., Wash. State U., 1950; JD, Harvard U., 1955; MA, John Jay Coll. Criminal Justice, 1981. Bar: D.C. 1956, U.S. Dist. Ct. (D.C.) 1956, U.S. Ct. of Appeals (D.C. cir.) 1957, U.S. Ct. Mil. Appeals 1957, Pa. 1961, U.S. Dist. Ct. (ea. dist.) Pa. 1961, U.S. Dist. Ct. (ctrl. dist.) Calif. 1967, U.S. Supreme Ct. 1961, Calif. 1967, U.S. Ct. Claims 1975, Colo. 1997, U.S. Dist. Ct. Colo. 1997, U.S. Ct. Appeals (10th cir.) 1997, U.S. Tax Ct. 1959. Research assoc. Harvard U., 1955-56; atty. Office Gen. Counsel U.S. Dept. Def., Washington, 1956-60; staff counsel Philco Ford Co., Phila., 1960-63; dir. Washington office Litton Industries, 1967-71; gen. counsel U.S. Dept. Army, Washington, 1971-74, civilian aide to sec. army, 1975-77; col. U.S. Army, 1978-87; prof., head dept. law U.S. Mil. Acad., West Point, N.Y., 1978-86; ret. as brig. gen. U.S. Army, 1987; mil. asst. to asst. sec. of army, Manpower and Res. Affairs Dept. of Army, 1986-87; asst. gen. counsel pub. affairs Litton Industries, Beverly Hills, Calif., 1963-67; chair Coun. of Def. Space Industries Assns., 1966; resident ptnr. Quarles and Brady, Washington, 1971-74; dir., corp. sec., treas., gen. counsel G.A. Wright, Inc., Denver, 1987-92, dir., 1987-2000; pvt. practice law Fort Bragg, Calif., 1993-96; spl. counsel Messner & Reeves LLC, Denver, 1997—. Bd. dirs. G.A. Wright Mktg., Inc., v.p./gen. counsel, 2001-; bd. dirs. Denver Mgmt. Svcs. Inc., v.p., gen. counsel, 2001—; foreman Mendocino County Grand Jury, 1995-96. Served with U.S. Army, 1944-46, 51-53, Korea. Decorated Bronze Star, Legion of Merit, Disting. Service Medal; recipient Disting. Civilian Service medal U.S. Dept. Army, 1973, 74, Outstanding Civilian Service medal, 1977. Mem. FBA, Bar Assn. D.C., Calif. Bar Assn., Pa. Bar Assn., Colo. State Bar Assn., Denver Bar Assn., Army-Navy Club, Army-Navy Country Club, Phi Beta Kappa, Phi Kappa Phi, Sigma Delta Chi, Lambda Chi Alpha. Protestant. E-mail: rberry@messner.reeves.com.

BERRY, WILLIAM BENJAMIN NEWELL, geologist, educator, former museum administrator; b. Boston, Sept. 1, 1931; s. John King and Margaret Elizabeth (Newell) B.; m. Suzanne Foster Spaulding, June 10, 1961; 1 child, Bradford Brown. AB, Harvard U., 1953, A.M., 1955; PhD, Yale U., 1957. Asst. prof. geology U. Houston, 1957-58; asst. prof. to prof. paleontology U. Calif., Berkeley, 1958—; prof. geology, 1991—; curator Mus. of Paleontology U. Calif., Berkeley, 1960-75, 87—, dir., 1975-87, chmn. dept. paleontology, 1975-87; marine scientist Lawrence Berkeley Lab., 1989—. Cons. U.S. Geol. Survey., Environ. Edn. to Ministry for Environ., Catalonia, Spain. Author: Growth of a Prehistoric Time Scale, 1968, revised edit., 1987, Principles of Stratigraphic Analysis, 1991; assoc. editor Paleoceanography; contbr. numerous articles on stratigraphic, paleontol. and environ. subjects to profl. jours.; editor publs. in geol. scis. Guggenheim Found. fellow, 1966-67 Fellow Calif. Acad. Scis.; mem. AAAS (pres. Pacific divsn. 2003—), Paleontol. Soc., Geol. Soc. Norway, Internat. Platform Assn., Explorers Club, Commonwealth Club Calif. Home: 1366 Summit Rd Berkeley CA 94708-2139 Office: U Calif Dept Earth/Planetary Scis McCone Hall Berkeley CA 94720 E-mail: bnberry@uclink4berkeley.edu.

BERS, ABRAHAM, electrical engineering and physics educator; b. Cernauti, Bukovina, Romania, May 28, 1930; came to U.S., 1949; s. Isaias and Berta (Lechter) B.; m. Anita Alden Burrage, June 17, 1966; children: Rachel, Joshua. BS, U. Calif. with highest honors, Berkeley, 1953; SM, MIT, 1955, ScD, 1959. Rsch. asst. Rsch. Lab. Electronics MIT, Cambridge, Mass., 1953-58, instr. dept. elec. engring. and computer sci., 1958-59, asst. prof., 1959-63, assoc. prof., 1963-71, prof., 1971—. Dir. rsch. Ecole Polytechnique, Paris, 1979-80; vis. prof. U. Paris-Orsay, 1981-92; vis. scientist CEA-Euratom, Cadarache, France, 1995, Limeil-Valenton, France, 1995. Co-author: Waves in Anisotropic Plasmas, 1963, Physique des Plasmas, Vols. 1-2, 1994; contbr. chpts. to books, articles to profl. jours. Faculty Exch. fellow Ford Found., Tech. U. Berlin, 1966, fellow J.S. Guggenheim Meml. Found., U. Paris, 1968-69. Fellow: Am. Phys. Soc. (chmn. divsn. plasma physics 1991—92); mem.: AAAS, Univ. Fusion Assn. (pres. 1988—89), N.Y. Acad. Sci., St. Botolph Club Boston. Avocations: tennis, skiing.

BERSCH, MARTHA RATLEDGE, secondary education educator; b. Elizabeth City, N.C., Nov. 29, 1951; d. John H. and Marian (Doherty) Ratledge; m. Robert S. Bersch, June 30, 1989. BA, Carson-Newman Coll., Jefferson City, Tenn., 1974. Cert. collegiate profl. tchr., Va. Tchr. Roanoke (Va.) Valley Christian Schs., 1975-78, Franklin County High Schs., Rocky Mount, 1979-84; adminstrv. asst. Physicians to Women, Roanoke, 1978-79; tchr. social studies Roanoke City Schs., 1984—, chmn. dept., 1992—. Named to Roanoke City Hall of Fame, 1994. Mem. Naat. Coun. for Social Studies, Roanoke Profl. Educators Assn., Delta Kappa Gamma. Republican. Baptist. Avocations: cross-stitching, knitting, reading. Office: Patrick Henry HS 2102 Grandin Rd SW Roanoke VA 24015-3599

BERSH, PHILIP JOSEPH, psychologist, educator; b. Phila., Sept. 9, 1921; s. Michael and Sophie (Faggen) B.; m. Jacqueline Edith Fratkin, June 8, 1952; children: Lauren Helene, Marilyn Ellen. AB, Temple U., 1944; AM, Columbia U., 1947, PhD, 1949. Lectr. Columbia U., 1948-54, research assoc., 1951-54; lectr. U. Wis., 1951; chief intelligence and electronic warfare br. Rome Air Devel. Ctr., N.Y., 1954-62; lectr. Utica Coll., Syracuse U., N.Y., 1958-60, Hamilton Coll., 1961-62; chief combat systems lab. U.S. Army Behavioral Sci. Rsch. Inst., Washington, 1962—67, assoc. dir. human performance experimentation, 1966—67; lectr. George Washington U., 1966-67; prof. psychology Temple U., Phila., 1967—. Vis. prof. dept. psychology Inst. Psychiatry U. London, 1979; cons. U.S. Army Research Inst. for Behavioral and Social Scis. Cons. editor: JSAS; Catalog Selected Documents in Psychology, 1976-79; mem. editorial bd. Jour. Exptl. Analysis of Behavior, 1980-83, 85-87; contbr. articles on psychology to profl. jours. Served with AUS, 1942-46, ETO. NRC postdoctoral fellow, 1950 Fellow APA, AAAS, Am. Psychol. Soc., Assn. Behavior Analysis; mem. Psychonomic Soc., Ctr. for Behavioral Studies, Ea. Psychol. Assn., Sigma Xi. Home: The Fairmont # 413 41 Conshohocken State Rd Bala Cynwyd PA 19004-2438 E-mail: pbersh@astro.temple.edu.

BERSON, JEROME ABRAHAM, chemistry educator; b. Sanford, Fla., May 10, 1924; s. Joseph and Rebecca (Bernicker) B.; m. Bella Zevitovsky, June 30, 1946; children: Ruth, David, Jonathan. BS cum laude, CCNY, 1944; MA, Columbia U., 1947; PhD, 1949. NRC postdoctoral fellow Harvard U., 1949-50; asst. chemist Hoffmann-LaRoche, Inc., Nutley, N.J., 1944; asst. prof. U. So. Calif., 1950-53, assoc. prof., 1953-58, prof., 1958-63, U. Wis., 1963-69, Yale U., 1969-79, Irénée du Pont prof., 1979-92, Sterling prof., 1992-94; Sterling prof. emeritus, 1994—; dir. div. phys. sci. and engring. Yale U., 1983-90. Vis. prof. U. Calif., U. Cologne, U. Western Ont., U. Karlsruhe, U. Lausanne; Fairchild Disting. scholar Calif. Inst. Tech.; cons. Riker Labs., Goodyear Tire & Rubber Co., am. Cyanamid Co., IBM, Cord Labs., SMC Corp., B.F. Goodrich Corp., Lubrizol Corp.; mem. medicinal chemistry study sect. NIH, 1969-73; mem. adv. panel chemistry NSF, 1964-70. Author: Chemical Creativity, 1999, Chemical Discovery and the Logistician's Program, 2003; mem. editorial adv. bd.: Jour. Organic Chemistry, 1961-65, Accounts of Chemical Rsch., 1971-77, 94-96, Nouveau Journal de Chimie, 1977-85, Chem. Revs., 1980-83, Jour. Am. Chem. Soc., 1988-93; contbr. articles to profl. jours. Served with AUS, 1944-46, CBI. Recipient Alexander von Humboldt award, 1980, Townsend Harris medal Alumni Assn. CCNY, 1984, Merit award NIH, 1989, Lit. award German Chem. Industry Assn., 2000; John Simon Guggenheim fellow, 1980 Fellow Am. Acad. Arts and Scis.; mem. NAS, Am. Chem. Soc. (Calif. sect. award 1963, James Flack Norris award 1978, Nichols medal 1985, Roger Adams award 1987, Arthur C. Cope scholar 1992, Oesper award 1998, chmn. div. organic chemistry 1971), Chem. Soc. London, Phi Beta Kappa, Sigma Xi, Phi Lambda Upsilon. Home: 45 Bayberry Rd Hamden CT 06517-3401 Office: Yale U Dept Chemistry PO Box 208107 New Haven CT 06520-8107 E-mail: jerome.berson@yale.edu.

BERSON, MICHAEL JAY, secondary education educator; b. Huntsville, Ala., June 2, 1965; s. Harvey and Roberta Berson; m. Ilene Ruth Zaritsky, July 31, 1988; 1 child, Elisa Rachel. BA, U. Buffalo, 1987; MEd, U. Toledo, 1989, PhD, 1990—. Cert. tchr., Ohio. Educator social studies Ottawa Hills Local Schs., Toledo, 1989—, chairperson social studies dept., 1992—. Asst. dir. Inst. on Improving Urban Edn. U. Toledo, 1989, 90; prsenter confs. Ednl. cons. Congresswoman Marcy Kaptur's Office, Toledo, 1989—; curriculum cons. Toledo Jewish Bd. Edn., 1993. Mem. NEA, ASCD, Ohio Edn. Assn., Ohio Coun. Social Studies, Nat. Coun. Social Studies. Avocations: swimming, weight training, philately. Office: Ottawa Hills High Sch 2532 Evergreen Rd Toledo OH 43606-2399 Address: Berson % The Citadel Dept Of Education Charleston SC 29409-0001

BERT, CAROL LOIS, retired educational assistant; b. Bakersfield, Calif., Oct. 15, 1938; d. Edwin Vernon and Shirely Helen (Craig) Phelps; m. John Davison Bert, Sept. 26, 1964; children: Mary Ellen, John Edwin, Craig Eric, Douglas Ethan. BSN, U. Colo., 1960. Med. surg. nurse U.S. Army, Washington, 1960-62, Ascom City, Korea, 1962-63, San Antonio, 1963, Albuquerque, 1964-65; ednl. asst. Jefferson County Schs., Arvada, Colo., 1979-2000, ret. Sec. Parent Tchr. Student Assn. Arvada West H.S., 1987-88. Mem. Colo. Quilting Coun. (1st v.p. 1988, 89, Hall of Fame 1992). Avocations: quilting, reading, camping, fishing, tennis. Home: 5844 Oak St Arvada CO 80004-4739

BERT, CHARLES WESLEY, mechanical and aerospace engineer, educator; b. Chambersburg, Pa., Nov. 11, 1929; s. Charles Wesley and Gladys Adelle (Raff) B.; m. Charlotte Elizabeth Davis (June 29, 1957); children: Charles Wesley IV, David Raff. BSME, Pa. State U., 1951, MS, 1956; PhD in Engring. Mechanics, Ohio State U., 1961. Registered profl. engr., Pa., Okla. Jr. design engr. Am. Flexible Coupling Co., State Coll., Pa., 1951-52; aero. design engr. Fairchild Aircraft div. Fairchild Engine and Airplane Corp., Hagerstown, Md., 1954-56; prin. M.E. Battelle Inst., Columbus, Ohio, 1956-61; sr. research engr., 1961-62; program dir., solid and structural mechanics research, 1962-63; cons., 1964-65; assoc. prof. U. Okla., 1963-66, prof., 1966—; dir. Sch. Aerospace and Mech. Engring., 1972-77, 90-95, Benjamin H. Perkinson Chair prof. engring., 1978—. Instr. engring. mechanics Ohio State U., Columbus, 1959-61; vis. scholar U. Calif., San Diego, 1996; cons. in field; chmn. Midwestern Mechanics Conf., 1973-75; Honor lectr. Mid-Am. State Univs. Assn., 1983-84; seminar lectr. Midwest Mechanics, 1983-84; Plenary lectr. Internat. Conf. on Composite Structures, Paisley, Scotland, 1987. Mem. editl. bd. Composite Structures Jour., 1982—, Jour. Sound & Vibration, 1988—, Composites Engring., 1991-95, Mechanics of Composite Materials and Structures, 1993-2001, Applied Mechanics Revs., 1993—, Composites, 1996-98, Internat. Jour. Structural Stability and Dynamics, 2000—, Jour. of Sandwich Structures and Materials, 1997—, Mechanics of Advanced Materials and Structures, 2002-; assoc. editor: Exptl. Mechanics, 1982-87, Applied Mechanics Revs., 1984-87; contbr. chpts. to books and articles to profl. jours. 1st lt. USAF, 1952-54. Sr. Rsch. scholar U. Calif., San Diego, 1996; recipient Disting. Alumnus award Ohio State U. Coll. engring., 1985. Fellow AAAS, AIAA (nat. tech. com. structures 1969-72, chmn. Ctrl. Okla. sect. 1966-67), ASME (Cen. Okla. sect. exec. com. 1973-78, 90-95, 99-01, sec. 1990-91, region X mech. engring. dept. heads com. 1972-77, 90-95, chmn. 1975-77, 10-session symposium named in his honor 1999), Am. Soc. Composites (bd. dirs. 1996-98, Disting. Rsch. award 1999), Am. Acad. Mechs. (bd. dirs. 1978-82, pres.-elect 2001-02, pres. 2002-03), Soc. Exptl. Mechanics (monograph com. 1978-82, chmn. 1980-82, sec. Mid-Ohio sect. 1958-59, chmn. 1959-60, adv. bd. 1960-63), Soc. Engring. Sci. (bd. dirs. 1982-88); mem. NSPE, Okla. Acad. Sci., Okla. Soc. Profl. Engrs., Scabbard and Blade, Pa. State Alumni Assn. (Outstanding Engring. Alumnus award 1992), Sigma Xi, Sigma Tau, Pi Tau Sigma, Sigma Gamma Tau (Disting. Engr. award), Tau Beta Pi (Disting. Engr. award). Achievements include co-development of world's smallest pressure transducer capable of measuring both steady and fluctuating pressures; first general solution of cylindrically orthotropic plates of radially varying thickness under arbitrary body forces; origination of several minimum-weight optimal designs for multicell cylindrical pressure vessels, experimental techniques and associated data reduction equations for determining residual stresses in both flat-sheet and thick-walled cylindrical specimens of composite materials; first successful application of Kennedy-Pancu system identification method to shell structures, noninteger polynomial version of Rayleigh's method to heat conduction; first application of differential quadrature method to static structural problems, structural vibration problems and non-linear structural problems; first application of noninteger polynomial method to finite element analysis; first dynamic stability analysis of unicycles and monocycles; origination of concept of stress gages for composite materials; research on sandwich structures with bimodular facings, prediction of ply steer behavior of automobile tires, non-linear flutter of laminated composite panels; many others. Home: 2516 Butler Dr Norman OK 73069-5059 Office: U Okla Sch Aerospace and Mech Engring 865 Asp Ave Norman OK 73019-1052

BERT, CLARA VIRGINIA, retired home economics educator, school system administrator; b. Quincy, Fla., Jan. 29, 1929; d. Harold C. and Ella J. (McDavid) B. BS, Fla. State U., 1950, MS, 1963, PhD, 1967. Cert. tchr., Fla.; cert. home economist; cert. pub. mgr. Tchr. Union County High Sch., Lake Butler, Fla., 1950-53, Havana High Sch., Fla., 1953-65; cons. rsch. and devel. Fla. Dept. Edn., Tallahassee, 1967-75, sect. dir. rsch. and devel., 1975-85, program dir. home econs. edn., 1985-92, program specialist resource devel., 1992-96, program specialist, spl. projects, 1996-99, program dir. grants mgmt., 1999-2000; ret., 2000. Cons. Nat. Ctr. Rsch. in Vocat. Edn., Ohio State U., 1978; field reader U.S. Dept. Edn., 1974-75. Author, editor booklets. Mem. devel. bd., mem. adv. bd. Fla. State U. Coll. Human Scis. Family Inst., 1994—; mem. nat. com. for the capital campaign Fla. State U. Found., 2002—. U.S. Office Edn. grantee, 1976, 77, 78; recipient Dean's award Coll. Human Scis., Fla. State U., 1995; named Disting Alumna Coll. Human Scis., Fla. State U., 1994. Mem. Am. Home Econs. Assn. (state treas. 1969-71), Am. Vocat. Assn., Fla. Vocat. Assn., Fla. Vocat. Home Econs. Assn., Am. Vocat. Edn. Rsch. Assn. (nat. treas. 1970-71), Nat. Coun. Family Rels., Am. Ednl. Rsch. Assn., Fla. State U. Alumni Assn. (bd. dirs. home econs. sect. 1976-81, pres.-elect 1978-79, 79-80), Havana Golf and Country Club, Fla. State U. Ctr. Club, Kappa Delta Pi, Kappa Omicron Nu (chpt. pres. 1965-66), Delta Kappa Gamma (pres. 1974-76), Sigma Kappa (pres. corp. bd. 1985-91), Phi Delta Kappa.

BERTH, DONALD FRANK, university official, consultant; b. Ludlow, Mass., Mar. 2, 1935; s. Frank and Wilma (Duffus) B. BSChemE, Worcester Poly. Inst., 1957, MSChemE, 1959; postgrad., Cornell U., 1959-65. Instr. chemistry and physics, dir. admissions Corning (N.Y.) Community Coll., N.Y., 1960-62; adminstrv. asst., asst. dean and assoc. dean engring. Cornell U., Ithaca, N.Y., 1962-83, dir. engring. coop. program, 1975-80; v.p. univ. rels. (devel., pub. rels.) Worcester (Mass.) Poly. Inst., 1983-93, dir. entrepreneurs collaborative, 1993—; prin. cons. Nat. Plastics Ctr. and Mus., Leominster, Mass., 1993-97. Prin. cons. New England Sci. Ctr., Worcester, 1994—; engring., ednl. and devel. cons. colls. and univs. Founding editor Engring.: Cornell Quar., 1965-71; contbr. numerous articles to profl. jours. Trustee Rockwell Found., Denver, 1965-80; trustee Worcester Hist. Mus., chmn. trustee nominating com., 1985-93; active Montshire Mus., Vt., Mus. Fine Arts, Boston, Worcester Art Mus., Smithsonian Instn.; corporator Found. U. Mass. Med. Ctr., 1991-94; trustee, mem. devel. program and nominating coms. New Eng. Sci. Ctr., 1992—. NSF summer fellow U. Colo., 1962. Mem. Am. Soc. for Engring. Edn. (editl. bd. 1985-90), Soc. for History Tech., Coun. for Advancement and Support Edn. (grand award for univ. mag. 1966, 69), Nature Conservancy, Cornell Lab. Ornithology, Mass. Audubon Soc., Trustees of Reservations, Quechee Club Vt., Cornell Club N.Y., Sigma Xi, Phi Delta Kapp. Avocations: fine arts, history, photography, architecture, outdoor activities. Office: Worcester Poly Inst Provosts Office 100 Institute Rd Worcester MA 01609-2247

BERTI, MARGARET ANN, early childhood education educator; b. Jersey City, Oct. 1, 1961; d. John Albert and Jane Matilda (McNair) Condon; m. Douglas Anthony Berti, Aug. 4, 1990; children: Matthew Douglas, Allison Nicole. BA, William Paterson Coll., Wayne, N.J., 1983, MEd, 1985. Tchr. 1st grade Paterson (N.J.) Pub. Schs., 1984-85; tchr pre-kindergarten and ESL Dallas Ind. Sch. Dist., 1985-92; tchr. kindergarten Pearland (Tex.) Ind. Sch. Dist., 1992-95; pre-sch. tchr. Early Childhood Program St. Paul's Cath. Ch., Nassau Bay, Tex., 1997—, St. Paul's Cath. Ch., Nassuaby, Tex., 1997—2000; ednl. cons., 2000—. Named Tchr. of Yr., George W. Truett Elem. Sch., 1988, Rustic Oak Elem. Sch., Pearland, 1994; named to Outstanding Young Women of Am., 1991; Title VII grantee Tex. Woman's U., 1987. Mem. Nat. Assn. Edn. Young Children, Classroom Tchrs. Dallas (bldg. rep. 1991), Dallas-Internat. Reading Assn. (corr. sec. 1992), Pearland Edn. Assn. (bldg. rep. 1993-95), Delta Kappa Gamma (Delta Rho chpt.). Roman Catholic. Avocations: reading, power walking, cycling, cooking. Home: 1526 Saxony Ln Houston TX 77058-3442

BERTIN, JOHN JOSEPH, aeronautical engineer, educator, researcher; b. Milw., Oct. 13, 1938; s. Andrea and Yolanda G. (Pasquali) B.; m. Ruth Easterbrook; children: Thomas Alexander, Randolph Scott, Elizabeth Anne, Michael Robert. BA, Rice Inst., Houston, 1960; MS, Rice U., 1962, PhD, 1966. Aerospace technologist NASA Johnson Space Ctr., Houston, 1962-66; prof. U. Tex., Austin, 1966-89; program mgr. for space initiative MTS, Sandia Nat. Labs., Albuquerque, 1989-94; vis. prof. USAF Acad., Colorado Springs, Colo., 1988-89, prof. aero. engring., 1994—. Cons. McGinnis, Lochridge & Kilgore, Austin, 1978-83, Sandia Nat. Labs., Albuquerque, 1980-89, BPD Difesa e Spazio, Rome, 1980-82, NASA, 1994-96, Sci. Applications Internat. Corp., 1996; detailed to Office of Space, U.S. Dept. Energy Hdqs., 1991-92; dir. Ctr. Excellence for Hypersonic Tng. and Rsch., 1985-89; mem. sci. adv. bd. USAF, 1989-93, mem. adv. group Flight Dynamics Labs., 1989-93; tech. chmn. Space 2000 Conf., 1998-99; aerothermodynamics cons. Columbia Accident Investigation Bd., 2003. Author: Engineering Fluid Mechanics, 1987, Hypersonic Aerothermodynamics, 1994, Aerodynamics for Engineers, 2002; contbg. author Letter-winner, 1999—; editor: Hypersonics, 1989, Advances in Hypersonics, 1992; assoc. editor Jour. Spacecraft and Rockets, 2000-01. Pres. Western Hills Little League, Austin, 1975; mem. arts subcom. NASA, 1987-91; mem. Aerospace Engring. Bd. Panel NRC, 1996-97, USAF hypersonics program rev. com., 1997-98; mem. attendance com. Rice Athletic Dept., 2002--; mem. adv. bd. Rice Owl Club, 2002--. Recipient Gen. Dynamics tchg. award U. Tex. Coll. Engring., 1978, Tex. Exec. tchg. award Ex-Students Assn. U. Tex., 1982, faculty award Tau Beta Pi, 1986, award for meritorious civilian svc. Dept. Air Force, 1993, Gen. Daley award USAFA, 1996, Exemplary Civilian Svc. Award medal, 1996, F.J. Seiler Rsch. award, USAFA, 1997. Fellow AIAA (dir. region IV 1983-86, Disting. Lectr., Thermophysics award 1997, publs. bd. 1998-2000, aerothermodynamic cons. Columbia accident investigation bd. 2003).

BERTRAM, JOAN M. school system administrator; Supt. Gardner Cmty. Consol. Sch. Dist. 72C, Gardner, Ill.

BERTRAM, MICHAEL WAYNE, secondary education educator; b. Princeton, Ind., Jan. 24, 1945; s. Leroy Victor and Lela Mae (Redman) B.; m. Bonnie Lee Holmes, Aug. 21, 1985; 1 child, John. BS, U. Indpls., 1967; MS, U. Wyo., 1972; MA, U. Evansville, 1975. Cert. secondary math. and physics tchr., Ind. Tchr. math. and physics South Gibson Sch. Corp., Ft. Branch, Ind., 1967—, chmn. math. dept., 1974—. Athletic dir. Gibson So.

High Sch., 1977-79. Recipient cert. of merit Ind. Acad. Competitions for Excellence, 1988, 95, 96; grantee NSF, 1971. Mem. Nat. Coun. Tchrs. Math., Math. Assn. Am., Am. Assn. Physics Tchrs. Methodist. Avocation: farming. Home: RR 1 Box 197 Fort Branch IN 47648-9717 Office: Gibson So High Sch RR 1 Box 496 Fort Branch IN 47648-9776

BERTRAND, ANNETTE MARIA, elementary education educator; b. L.A., June 24, 1955; d. Wendell Oliver and Marjorie Marie Henderson; m. Jerry Pierre Bertrand, Feb. 14, 1976 (dec. May, 1982); children: Jerrold, Keith. BA in Liberal Studies, Pepperdine U., 1977; MA in Edn., U. San Francisco, 1982. Tchr. L.A. Unified Sch. Dist., 1980-87, mentor tchr., 1987-88, 89-93, program coord., acting adminstr., 1988-89. Mem. Polit. Action Coun. of Educators, L.A., 1987. Named Outstanding Vol. Head Start Project, U.S. Dept. Health and Human Svcs., L.A., 1981-82. Mem. ASCD. Democrat. Roman Catholic. Avocations: hiking, swimming, sewing, reading, cooking.

BERTUCELLI, ROBERT EDWARD, accountant, educator; b. Bklyn., Mar. 23, 1948; s. Leo and Gertrude Augusta (Roggenkamp) B.; m. Maryann Marchese, June 13, 1970; children: Nikole, Gina. AAS, Suffolk C.C., 1968; BS, C.W. Post Coll., 1970; MS, L.I. U., 1974. CPA, N.Y.; cert. fin. planner; chartered life underwriter. Acct. Arthur Young & Co., Westbury, N.Y., 1970-72; sr. tax. mgr. Peat Marwick Mitchell & Co., Jericho, N.Y., 1972-77; prof. acctg. and taxation C.W. Post Coll., 1977—; pvt. practice Smithtown, N.Y., 1977-83, Hauppauge, N.Y., 1989-94; ptnr. Bertucelli Barragato & Co., Smithtown, 1983-89, Bertucelli & Malaga L.L.P., Ronkonkoma, NY, 1994—. Lectr. Person Wolinsky Assocs., 1977—. Mem. St. Patrick's Sch. Bd., Smithtown, N.Y., 1982-92, pres., 1985-88, 90-92; bd. trustees, St. Charles Hosp. and Rehab. Ctr., Port Jefferson, NY, 2003—. Mem.: AICPA, Estate Planning Coun. (pres. 1996—97), Nat. Assn. Accts., N.Y. Soc. CPAs (author, lectr. 1989—, Haskins Silver medal 1972), Smithtown C. of C. (treas. 1988—90). Roman Catholic.

BERWALD, HELEN DOROTHY, education educator; b. Lac Qui Parle County, Minn., Mar. 15, 1925; BA, U. Minn., 1948, BS, MA, 1951, PhD, 1962. Tchr. Robbinsdale (Minn.) High Sch., 1951-52; mem. faculty Carleton Coll., Northfield, Minn., 1952—, prof. Emeritus edn., 1987—; prof. edn. Mem. Minn. State Adv. Com., 1962-89; dir. programs in tchr. edn. Asso. Colls. Midwest; dir. Chgo. Urban Semester, Video Tape Project; mem. African Edn. Survey Team; mem. accreditation task force Am. Assn. Colls. Tchr. Edn., formerly mem. exec. com., bd. dirs.; mem. standards and process com., mem. exec. com., also chmn. appeals bd. Nat. Council Accreditation Tchr. Edn., formerly mem. coordinating bd. Pres. Minn. Assn. Colls. Tchr. Edn.; mem. Phi Beta Kappa, Pi Lambda Theta. Home: 4963 S Prairie Hill Dr Green Valley AZ 85614

BERWICK, ROBERT CREGAR, computer science educator; b. Phila., July 25, 1951; s. Leonard and Mary (Cregar) B.; m. Marilyn Matz, Sept. 7, 1984; children: Elissa Matz, Shana Alexandra. BA, Harvard U., 1976; MS, MIT, 1980, PhD, 1982. Asst. prof. computer sci. MIT, Cambridge, 1982-87, assoc. prof., 1987-89, prof., 1989—, co-dir. Ctr. for Biol. and Computational Learning, 1993—. Bd. dirs. Ctr. for Biological and Computational Learning. Author: The Grammatical Basis of Linguistic Performance, 1984, The Acquistion of Syntactic Knowledge, 1985, Computational Linguistics, 1986, Computational Complexity and Natural Language, 1987, Principle-based Parsing, 1992, Cartesian Computation, 1995, Principal-based Parsing: From Theory to Practice, 1998; editor: Computational Models of Discourse, 1982. Recipient Edgerton Faculty award MIT, 1985; Guggenheim fellow, 1987. Mem. AAAS, Assn. Computational Linguistics, Sigma Xi. Avocation: astronomy. Home: 19 Brenton Rd Weston MA 02493-1003

BESCH, LORRAINE W. special education educator; b. Orange, N.J., June 27, 1948; d. Robert Woodruff and Minnie (Wrightson) B.; m. William Lee Gibson, July 10, 1982. AA in Liberal Arts, Mt. Vernon Coll., 1968; BA in Sociology, U. Colo., 1970; MA in Spl. Edn., U. Denver, 1973. Cert. handicapped thcr., N.J. Elem. resource rm. tchr. Beeville (Tex.) Ind. Sch. Dist., 1973-75; trainable mentally retarded tchr. Kings County Supt. Schs., Hanford, Calif., 1975-78; h.s. resource rm. tchr. Summit (N.J.) Bd. Edn., 1980-81, Westfield (N.J.) Bd. Edn., 1981-99, head coach field hockey, 1981-83, mem. crisis mgmt. team, 1982-87, in class support tchr. English, 1993-99. Named to Women's Inner Circle Achievement, 1996; recipient Internat. Sash of Academia, ABI, 1997. Mem. AAUW, Smithsonian Nat. Mus. Am. Indian (charter), Sky Meadows Cir. Nat. Mus. Women in Arts, CEC (learning disabilities divsn.), Westfield Edn. Assn. (del. 1983-90, tech. com. 1993-94, conf. funds com. 1994-99), Hartford Family Found. (v.p., sec. 1991-97, trustee 1997—), Wrighston-Besch Found. (sec.-treas. 1994-99, pres. 1999—), Archaeology Conservancy (life), 1892 Founders Soc., Morristown Meml. Health Found., Col. Williamsburg Burgesses, Nat. Trust Historic Preservation, N.J. Hist. Society. Avocations: traveling, reading, gardening, cooking, tennis. Home: 8 Lone Oak Rd Basking Ridge NJ 07920-1613

BESHUR, JACQUELINE E. special needs educator; b. Portland, Oreg., May 8, 1948; d. Charles Daniel and Mildred (Domreis) Beshears. BA, UCLA, 1970; MBA, Claremont Grad. Sch., 1980; postgrad., City U., Seattle, 1989-90. Dir. and founder L.A. Ctr. for Photog. Studies, 1972-76; precious gem distbr. Douglas Group Holdings, Australia, 1976-78; small bus. owner BeSure Cleaning, 1981-90; animal trainer, exotic livestock farmer, writer, 1990-2000; activities and disadvantaged children's tutor, 2000—. Author: Good Intentions Are Not Good Enough, 1992. Dir. County Citizens Against Incineration, 1987—, Ames Lake Protection Com., 1989—. Mem. Bridges for Peace, Nature Conservancy, Wash. Wilderness Coalition, Issaquah Alps Club. Republican. Office: BeSure Tng PO Box 225 Carnation WA 98014-0225

BEST, CAROLYN ANNE HILL, elementary school educator; b. Columbia, S.C., Apr. 27, 1951; d. Sidney Sutcliffe Hill and Elizabeth Anne Boylston Hill Matney; m. Ralph Leslie Best, June 29, 1974; 1 child, Leslie Anne. BA in Edn., U. S.C., 1973; MEd, Francis Marion U., Florence, S.C., 1976; postgrad., Francis Marion U., 1996. Tchr. 2d grade Blenheim (S.C.) Pub. Sch., 1973-84; tchr. pre-sch. 1st United Meth. Ch., Bennettsville, S.C., 1985-86; tchr. Bennettsville Mid. Sch., 1988—2001, Bennettsville Elem. Sch., 2001—. Contbr. poetry to River of Dreams, 1994, Best Poems of 1995, Best Poems of 1996, Whispers in the Garden, 1997, Best Poems of the 90's, 1997, Wales, 1997. Recipient Editor's Choice award Nat. Libr. of Poetry, 1994, 95, 96, Good News award Marlboro County Sch. Sys., Bennettsville, 1996, 97. Mem. NEA, S.C. Edn. Assn., Internat. Reading Assn., Internat. Soc. Poets, Nat. Soc. Poets, Famous Poets Soc. (Diamond Homer Trophy 1995), Marlboro County Edn. Assn. Republican. Methodist. Office: Bennettsville Elem Sch 801 Country Club Dr Bennettsville SC 29512

BEST, FREDERICK NAPIER, artist, designer, educator; b. Macon, Ga., Jan. 17, 1943; s. John Frederick and Sara (Napier) B.; m. Rebecca Alice Freeman, Apr. 6, 1974; children: Eric Jonathan, Emily Anne. Student, Auburn U., 1961-64; BA, Birmingham So. Coll., 1969; MA, U. Ala., Birmingham, 1994. Artist Birmingham News, 1969; design dept. mgr. Dampier-Harris, Alabaster, Ala., 1976—78; model designer Rust Engring., Birmingham, 1978—81; owner, mgr. Best Finesse Studio, Trussville, Ala., 1981—94; design instr. Jefferson State Coll., Birmingham, 1981—98; instr. Erwin H.S., Birmingham, 1994—95; edn. supr. ITT Tech. Inst., Birmingham, 1996—97; freelance artist, educator, 1997—2001. Artist in residence Moody Mid. Sch., 1998; art tchr. Smiths Station H.S., 2001-2002; freelance artist educator, 2002—. Contbr. articles to profl. jours. Recipient award of honor Birmingham Advt. Club, 1982, Purchase award, 2000; Artist Fellowship grantee Ala. State Coun. on the Arts, 1993, 94. Home: 209 Wildwood Dr Trussville AL 35173-2391

BEST, MARY LANI, university program coordinator; b. Hilo, Hawaii, June 3, 1944; d. Stanley Clark and Emma Holokahiki (Martinson) Brooks; m. Leningrad Elarionoff, Aug. 14, 1965 (div. 1981); children: Kimberly Kehaunani, Grad. Ikaika; m. Gary Dean Best, Dec. 7, 1984 (div. 1996). BA, U. Hawaii, Hilo, 1988; MS, Creighton U., 1991. Substitute tchr. Hilo High Sch., 1990; counselor secondary alternative program Westside High Sch., Omaha, 1991; coord. Ctr. for Gifted & Talented Native Hawaiian Children U. Hawaii, Hilo, 1991—. Contbr.: (book) Sociology of Hawaii, 1992; co-editor: Glimpses of Hawaiian Daily Life and Culture, 1994. Active Hale O Na Alii, Hilo, 1988—. Mem. AACD. Republican. Avocations: writing, oil painting, reading, collecting colored liquer crystal. Home: 84 Pukihae St Apt 1104 Hilo HI 96720-2409 Office: U Hawaii 200 W Kawili St Hilo HI 96720-4075

BEST, PAUL ALLEN, education executive; b. Erie, Pa., Aug. 27, 1939; m. Veronica Richards, Dec. 2, 1964; 1 child, Gwen. Executive dir. Meriks Education Inc., Newton Centre, Mass., 1979—. Catholic. Office: Meriks Education Inc. 831 Beacon St #195 Newton Centre MA 02459-1840

BEST, SUSAN MARIE, artist, educator; b. Peoria, Ill., July 4, 1949; d. Robert H. and Shirley (Critchlow) Coyle; m. David G. Best, Sept. 12, 1970 (div. May 1987); children: Timothy, Molly, Abby, George; m. Richard J. Gualandi, Dec. 20, 1996. BPhar, U. Ill., Chgo., 1972; MA in Fine Arts, Ill. State U., Normal, 1988, MFA, 1991. Grad. pharmacist S&C Drugs, Peoria, 1972, Indian Hosp., Pine Ridge, S.D., 1974-76; instr. art Ill. State U., Normal, 1988-91, Bradley U., Peoria, 1992-93, Ill. Ctrl. Coll., Peoria, 1991-93; artist, 1970—. Gallery artist Struve Gallery, Chgo., 1991-93; active Longue Vue Mus. Art Program. Exhbn. Contemporary Art Ctr., Oleczyn, Poland. Bd. dirs. St. Thomas Sch., Peoria, 1980-83, Amateur Mus. Club, Peoria, 1982-84; bd. dirs. Peoria Art Guild, 1994—. Recipient Percent for Art award City of New Orleans, 1997, also various awards for art including 2 grants from Ill. Arts Coun. Access Program, 1995; Ill. State U. fellow, 1988-91. Mem. AAUP, AAUW, NOW, Contemporary Arts Ctr. of New Orleans, New Orleans Mus. Art, Chgo. Artists Coalition, Lakeview Art Mus., Sun Found., Planned Parenthood Assn. Democrat. Avocations: skiing, jogging, piano. Studio: 811 1/2 Opelousas Ave New Orleans LA 70114-2429

BESTEHORN, UTE WILTRUD, retired librarian; b. Cologne, Germany, Nov. 6, 1930; came to U.S., 1930; d. Henry Hugo and Wiltrud Lucie (Vincentz) B. BA, U. Cin., 1954, BEd, 1955, MEd, 1958; MS in Library Sci., Western Res. U. (now Case-Western Res. U.), 1961. Tchr. Cutter Jr. High Sch., Cin., 1955-57; tchr., supr. libr. Felicity (Ohio) Franklin Sr. High Sch., 1959-60; with libr. sci. dept. Pub. Libr. Cin. and Hamilton County, 1961-78, with libr. info. desk, 1978-91; ret., 1991. Textbook selection com., Felicity-Franklin Sr. High Sch., 1959-60; supr. Health Alcove Sci. Dept. and annual health lectures, Cin. Pub. Library, 1972-77. Book reviewer Library Jour., 1972-77; author and inventor Rainbow 40 marble game, 1971, Condominium game, 1976; patentee indexed packaging and stacking device, 1973, mobile packaging and stacking device, 1974. Mem. Clifton Town Meeting, 1988—; mem. Bookfest 90 com. Pub. Libr. Cin. and Hamilton County. Recipient Cert. of Merit and Appreciation Pub. Library of Cin., 1986. Mem. Cin. Chpt. Spl. Libraries Assn. (archivist 1963-64, 65-70, editor Queen City Gazette bull. 1964-69), Pub. Library Staff Assn. (exec. bd., activities com. 1965, welfare com. 1966, recipient Golden Book 25 yr. service pin, 1986), Friends of the Library, Greater Cin. Calligraphers Guild (reviewer New Letters pub. 1986-88), Delta Phi Alpha (nat. German hon. 1951). Republican. Mem. United Ch. of Christ. Avocations: calligraphy, painting and sketching, writing, photography, violin. Home: 3330 Morrison Ave Cincinnati OH 45220-1440

BESTOR, THEODORE CHARLES, anthropologist, educator; b. Urbana, Ill., Aug. 7, 1951; s. Arthur and Dorothy Alden (Koch) B.; m. Victoria Lyon, Aug. 16, 1975; 1 child, Nicholas. BA in Anthropology magna cum laude, Fairhaven Coll., Bellingham, Wash., 1973; MA in East Asian Studies, Stanford U., 1976, MA in Anthropology, 1977, PhD in Anthropology, 1983. Dir. Japanese and Korean studies Social Sci. Rsch. Coun., N.Y.C., 1983-86; asst. prof. anthropology Columbia U., N.Y.C., 1986-89, assoc. prof., 1990-93; assoc. prof. anthropology Cornell U., Ithaca, N.Y., 1993—. Curriculum cons. Asia Soc., 1984-85, 93—, Japan Soc., 1986-88, Matsushita Found., 1986-91, NEH project on Asia in the Core Curriculum, Columbia U., 1988-93; mem. human subjects instl. rev. bd. Columbia U., 1991-93; USIS del. Korea-Am. Cultural Exch. Commn., 1984; lectr. in field. Author: Neighborhood Tokyo, 1989; contbr. numerous articles to profl. jours., chpts. to books; book and film reviewer; video documentary filmmaker. Recipient Robert E. Park award for urban and community studies Am. Sociol. Assn. for Neighborhood Tokyo, 1990, Hiromi Arisawa Meml. award for Japanese Studies, Am. Assn. Univ., Presses for Neighborhood Tokyo, 1990; grantee NSF, 1979-81, 90-94, Sigma Xi, 1983, Wenner-Gren Found., 1984, N.E. Asia Coun. Assn. Asian Studies, 1986, Suntory Found., 1987, Social Sci. Rsch. Coun., 1988-89, N.Y. Sea Grant Inst., 1994—; Abe Fellow Ctr. Global Partnership, 1994—, Japan Found. fellow, 1984, 88-89, others. Mem. Am. Anthropol. Assn. (program com. for ann. meetings 1993, 94), N.Y. Acad. Sci. (chair Anthropology sect. 1990-92), Social Sci. Rsch. Coun. (joint com. on Japanese studies 1993—), Assn. for Asian Studies (bd. dirs. 1995—, chair northeast Asia coun. 1995—), Soc. for Urban Anthropology (pres. 1994—), Am. Ethnol. Soc., Japan Soc., Internat. House Japan, Royal Anthropol. Inst., Soc. Econ. Anthropology. Office: Cornell Univ Dept Anthropology Ithaca NY 14853

BETANCOURT, HECTOR MAINHARD, psychology scientist, educator; b. Chile, Sept. 1, 1949; came to U.S. 1979; s. Hector and Eleonora (Mainhard) B.; m. Bernardita Sahli; children: Paul, Daniel. BA, Cath. U., Santiago, Chile, 1976; MA, UCLA, 1981, PhD in Psychology, 1983. From asst. prof. to assoc. prof. psychology Cath. U., Santiago, Chile, 1977-79, 83-85; from assoc. prof. to prof. psychology Loma Linda U., Riverside, Calif., 1985-93, chmn., 1990-93; prof. psychology Grad. Sch. Loma Linda U., Calif., 1993—, founding chmn., 1993-98, sr. rschr., 2001—. Internat. cons. in higher edn./tng. in psychology, 1997—. Editor: Interam. Psychologist, 1982—86; mem. editl. bd.: Jour. Cmty. Psychology, 1986—89, Spanish Jour. Social Psychology, 1986—, Conflict and Peace, 1993—99, 2001—, Jour. Personality and Social Psychology, 1997—98; contbr. articles to profl. jours. and books. Recipient Rotary Found. award for Internat. Understanding, Rotary Internat., 1976-77; Fulbright fellow, UCLA, 1979-80. Fellow: APA (pres.divsn. 48 1997—98, exec. com. and chmn. task force on ethnicity); mem.: Psychologists for Soc. Responsibility (nat. steering com. 1999—), Soc. Personality and Social Psychology, Soc. for Psychol. Study Social Issues, Interam. Soc. Psychology (sec.-gen. 1983—87, v.p. U.S. and Can. 1999—2001, 2001—03), Internat. Soc. Cross-Cultural Psychology (exec. com. 1984—86), Internat. Soc. Polit. Psychology. Avocations: social issues, international politics, literature, philosophy. Office: Loma Linda U Dept Psychology Grad S Loma Linda CA 92350-0001

BETHE, HANS ALBRECHT, physicist, educator; b. Strassburg, Alsace-Lorraine, Germany, July 2, 1906; arrived in U.S., 1935; s. Albrecht Theodore and Anna (Kuhn) Bethe; m. Rose Ewald, 1939; 1 child, Henry;1 child, Monica. Ed. Goethe Gymnasium, Frankfurt on Main, U. Frankfort; PhD, U. Munich, 1928; DSc (hon.), Bklyn. Poly. Inst., 1950, U. Denver, 1952, U. Chgo., 1953, U. Birmingham, 1956, Harvard U., 1958. Instr. in theoretical physics univs. of Frankfort, Stuttgart, Munich and Tubingen, 1928—33; lectr. univs. of Manchester and Bristol, England, 1933—35; asst. prof. Cornell U., 1935, prof., 1937—75, prof. emeritus, 1975—. Dir. theoretical physics divsn. Los Alamos Sci. Lab., 1943—46; mem. Presdl. Study Disarmament, 1958. Author: Mesons and Fields, 1953, Elementary Nuclear Theory, 1957, Quantum Mechanics of One- and Two-Electron Atoms, 1957, Intermediate Quantum Mechanics, 1964; contbr. Handbuch der Physik, 1933, Revs. Modern Physics, 1936—37, Phys. Rev., Astrophys. Jour. Recipient A. Cressy Morrison prize, N.Y. Acad. Scis., 1938—40, Presdl. medal of Merit, 1946, Max Planck medal, 1955, Benjamin Franklin medal, 1959, Enrico Fermi award, AEC, 1961, Eddington Medal, 1961, Rumford prize, 1963, Nobel prize in Physics, 1967, Nat. medal of Sci., 1976, Order Pour le Merite for Arts & Sciences, Govt. of Germany, 1984, Vannevar Bush award, NSF, 1985, Albert Einstein Peace Prize Found., 1993, Oersted prize, Am. Assn. Physics Tchrs., Los Alamos Nat. Lab. Medal, 2001, Bruce Medal, 2001. Mem.: NAS (Henry Draper medal 1947), Am. Astron. Soc., Am. Phys. Soc. (pres. 1954), Am. Philos. Soc., Royal Soc. London (fgn. mem.). Office: Cornell U 320 Newman Lab Ithaca NY 14853*

BETHIN, CHRISTINA Y. linguist, language educator; b. Rochester, N.Y., Aug. 12, 1950; BA in Russian and Spanish, U. Rochester, 1972; MA in Slavic Langs. and Lit., U. Ill., 1974, PhD in Slavic Linguistics, 1978. Cert. secondary lang. tchr., N.Y. Lectr. U. Va., Charlottesville, 1978-79; asst. prof. SUNY, Stony Brook, 1979-85, assoc. prof., 1985-95, prof., 1995—, dir. Dr. Arts program in fgn. langs., 1992-94, dept. chair, 1994-98. Author: Polish Syllables: The Role of Prosody in Phonology and Morphology, 1992, Slavic Prosody, 1998; assoc. editor Slavic and East European Jour., 1995-99; mem. editl. bd. Jour. Slavic Linguistics, 1993—. NEH fellow, 1988-89, 93-94; IREX grantee for summer exch. of lang. tchrs., Moscow, 1990. Fellow Ukrainian Acad. Arts and Scis. in U.S.; mem. Am. Assn. Tchrs. of Slavic and East European Langs., Am. Assn. for Advancement of Slavic Studies, Am. Assn. for Ukrainian Studies, Linguistic Soc. Am., Phi Beta Kappa (v.p. Stony Brook chpt. 1987-88). Office: SUNY Dept Linguistics Stony Brook NY 11794-4376

BETHLEN, ILONA R. designer, educator; b. Budapest, Hungary, Apr. 10, 1921; came to U.S., 1952; d. Dezso and Vilma Gizella (Laszlo) Szentimrey; m. Francis R. Bethlen, Oct. 7, 1948; children: Anna Maria Bethlen LaFontaine, Mihaly Antal. MS, U. Econ. Sci., Budapest, Hungary, 1945; MA, Liszt Acad. Music, Budapest, Hungary, 1947; BA, SUNY, Plattsburgh, 1982. Tchg. asst. Econ. Faculty Jozsef Nador U., Budapest, Hungary, 1943-46; lady driver, trainer Hungarian Horse Racing Assn., Budapest, 1946-48; supplier, artist Gath & Chaves Dept. Stores, Buenos Aires, 1949-52; trainer of standardbreds A. Miller Stables, E. Aurora, N.Y., 1952-56; decorator, art adv. Am. Wallpaper Co., Buffalo, 1956-61; art instr. St. Mary Acad., Champlain, 1962-68; prof. art Coll. Cont. Edn. SUNY, Plattsburgh, 1970-81; gallery mgr. Four Winds Gallery, Burlington, Vt., 1970-77; artist, exhibitor Holt & Renfrew Co., Lupton DuVal Co., others, Toronto and Montreal, 1982—. Chairperson disasters ARC, N.Y., 1965-75; bd. dirs., chair edn. progress Joint Coun. Econ. Opportunities, Plattsburgh, N.Y., 1980-88. Named Outstanding Lady-Horse Trainer Buffalo Courier Express, 1952. Mem. AAUW, Rotary (mem. bd. world cmty. svcs. 1985-97, del. Rotary Internat. 91st annual conv. Buenos Aires, 2000). Avocations: travel, painting, small gardening.

BETINIS, EMANUEL JAMES, physics and mathematics educator; b. Oak Park, Ill., Oct. 31, 1927; s. James Emanuel and Ioanna Helen (Kallas) B.; children: Demetrios, Joanna, Markos. BS in Chemistry and Math., Northwestern U., 1950; MS in Applied Math., U. Ill., 1952; MS in Physics, U. Chgo., 1979. Aerodynamicist Northrop Aviation, Hawthorne, Calif., 1953-54; theoretical reactor physicist Atomics Internat., Canoga Park, Calif., 1954-57; applied sci. rep. IBM, Chgo., 1957-61; math. cons. Math. Cons. Svc., Chgo., 1961-81; adj. prof. math. and physics IIT, Roosevelt U., Chgo., 1981-88; mathematician Batelle Meml. Labs., Willowbrook, Ill., 1988-89; asst. prof. physics Elmhurst (Ill.) Coll., 1990—. Contbr. articles to Jour. Geophys. Rsch., Jour. Brit. Interplanetary Soc., Hadronic Jour., Matrix, Lensor Soc. Great Britain; composer, prodr. (CD) Candia Suite. Mem. PTO. With U.S. Army, 1946-47. Fellow Brit. Interplanetary Soc.; mem. Am. Nuclear Soc., Sigma Pi Sigma, Pi Mu Epsilon. Republican. Orthodox. Achievements include patent in golf ball trajectory with lift and drag; research in analytic solution of boundary-value problems in arbitrary geometry, special relativity, quantum mechanical proof of speed of light limitation, analytic solution of 3 dimensional heat conduction equation in arbitrary geometry, nuclear potential and prediction of 470MeV elementary particles, analytic solution of non-linear hydrodynamics equations; development and manufacture of devices for entropy and Biot-Savart physics experiments, calculation of velocity of nucleons in the deuteron, EM theory relativistic time dilation and removal of velocity of light speed limit, EM theory relativistic Schroedinger equations, scattering cross-section for superluminal particles, faster than light quantum mechanics; quantum field theory derivation of the superluminal Schroedinger equation. Office: Elmhurst Coll Dept Physics 190 Prospect Ave Elmhurst IL 60126-3271

BETLACH, MARY CAROLYN, biochemist, molecular biologist; b. Madison, Wis., June 12, 1945; d. William Thompson Stafford and Carolyn Jesse Gillette McCormick; m. Charles J. Betlach, Nov. 14, 1970 (div. 1978); children: John F., Melanie Carolyn. Student, U. Wis., 1963-68; PhD, U. Calif., San Francisco, 1992. Staff rsch. assoc. dept. pediatrics U. Calif., San Francisco, 1970-72, staff rsch. assoc. dept. microbiology/biochemistry, 1972-83, rsch. specialist dept. biochemistry, 1983-93; sr. scientist Parnassus Pharms., Alameda, Calif., 1993-94; dir. molecular biology Kosan Bioscis., Hayward, Calif., 1995-98, dir. scientific ops., 1999—; dir. grant rsch. collaborations Sunesis Pharms., South San Francisco, 2001—. Adj. assoc. prof. dept. pharm. chemistry, U. Calif., San Francisco, 1993—; mem. various grant rev. panels. Contbr. chpts. to books, articles to Gene, Microbiology, Nucleic Acids Rsch., Biochemistry, Jour. Bacteriology, others. Mem. AAAS, Am. Soc. for Microbiology. Achievements include development of recombinant DNA technology and early cloning vectors. E-mail: mbetlach@sunesis.com.

BETTENCOURT, DON, educator; b. Long Beach, Calif., Feb. 2, 1948; s. Joseph and Helena (Penning) B.; m. Sara Jean Wood, June 26, 1971; children: April Iulani, Donald Charles. BA in Speech, Calif. State U., Long Beach, 1970; MA in Edn., Pepperdine U., 1976, MA in Bus. Adminstrn., 1977, PhD in Speech Comm., 1979. Cert. tchr., Calif., Hawaii. Tchr., chair dept. U.S. history Bonita Unified Sch. Dist., San Dimas, Calif., 1976—; master tchr. of tchr. tng. Calif. Poly. U., 1979—. Corp. treas. Micocellar Tech. Corp; v.p., treas., sec. Waipouli Ranches Ltd., Kauai, Hawaii, 1976—; owner, operator Piliohana Project, 1981—. Sr. officer CAP So. Calif., 1987—; mem. Gang Task Force Cities of San Dimas, La Verne, Ontario, 1990—. Named Tchr. of Yr. Bonita Unified Sch. Dist., 1987-88. Mem. Walnut Valley Riders, UCLA Alumni Assn. (life). Republican. Roman Catholic. Office: Bonita Unified Sch Dist 115 W Allen Ave San Dimas CA 91773-1437

BETTERIDGE, ELIZABETH ANN, elementary education educator; b. Pilot Grove, Mo., Aug. 25, 1932; d. Claude Cecil and Arrena Elizabeth (Woods) Beckner; m. Robert Verne Betteridge, May 31, 1953; children: William Dan, Karen Sue Betteridge Plaster. A in Commerce, Southwest Bapt. Coll., 1952; BS in Edn., U. Mo., 1974, M in Edn., 1978, EdS, 1986. Life cert. tchr. K-8, remedial reading K-12, psychol. sch. examiner, Mo. Kindergarten tchr., Pilot Grove, Mo., 1964-68, Pilot Grove Pub. Sch., 1968-78; remedial reading tchr. Moniteau County R-6 Pub. Sch., Tipton, Mo., 1978—, sch. psychol. examiner, 1984—. Head start tchr. Pilot Grove Pub. Sch., summers 1967-68; leader Internat. Reading Assn. Reading Conf. on the Prairie, Kansas City, 1994; tchr. "Parents as Tchrs.", Otterville Sch. Dist., 1995-97; accelerated reading tchr. Otterville Pub. Sch., 1997—; spkr. in field. Author: (books) History of Cooper County, 1992, (award Am. Assn.

State and LocalHistory 1996), Discover Cooper County, 1995; (grant) Big Book Libr., 1990. Bd. dirs., chmn. women's com. Mo. County Farm Bur. Fedn., 1980-90; leader 4-H, Univ. Extension Coun.; Sunday Sch. tchr. Mt. Nebo Ch., Pilot Grove, 1955—, ch. libr., 1975—, ch. pianist, 1965—, chmn. hist. com. (ch. named to Nat. Register of Hist. Places 1986, home named 1982), dir. Vacation Bible Sch., 1988—. Recipient Leadership award U. Mo. Extension Program, Columbia, 1971. Mem. AAUW (Woman of Yr. award Booneville, Mo. chpt. 1996), Mo. State Tchrs. Assn. (Outstanding Tchr. cen. dist. 1986), Moniteau County Tchrs. Assn. (chmn. prof. sec. devel., Outstanding Tchr. award 1986), Mo. Shorthorn Assn., Mo. Lassie Assn., Cooper County Hist. Assn. (project chmn., pres. 1998, award 1997), Phi Delta Kappa, Pi Lambda Theta, Delta Kappa Gamma. Baptist. Avocations: restoration of personal hist. home, showing registered Shorthorn cattle, tour guide. Home and Office: 7400 A Hwy Pilot Grove MO 65276-3027

BETTIS, ELMER ARTHUR, III, physical science educator; b. Sioux City, Iowa, Feb. 14, 1953; BS in Anthropology, Iowa State U., 1975, MS in Agronomy, 1979; PhD in Geology, U. Iowa, 1995. Rsch. geologist Iowa Dept. Natural Resources, Iowa City, 1982-96, supr., 1996-98; asst. prof. dept. geoscience U. Iowa, Iowa City, 1998—2003, assoc. prof. dept. geoscience, 2003—. Fellow: Geol. Soc. Am.; mem.: Soc. Am. Archaeology, Am. Quarternary Assn., Geol. Soc. Am. Office: U Iowa Dept Geoscience 121 Trowbridge Hall Iowa City IA 52242-1319 E-mail: art-bettis@uiowa.edu.

BETTMAN, JAMES ROSS, management educator; b. Laurinburg, N.C., Sept. 15, 1943; s. Roland David and Virginia Gertrude (Hare) B.; m. Joan Carol Scribner, Dec. 16, 1967; 1 child, David James. BA, Yale U., 1965, MPhil, PhD, Yale U., 1969. Prof. mgmt. Grad. Sch. Mgmt., UCLA, 1969-82; IBM rsch. prof. Fuqua Sch. Bus., Duke U., Durham, N.C., 1982-83, Burlington Industries prof., 1983—. Author: An Information Processing Theory of Consumer Choice, 1979, The Adaptive Decision Maker, 1993, Emotional Decisions: Tradeoff Difficulty and Coping in Consumer Choice, 2001; co-editor Jour. of Consumer Rsch., 1981-87, editor monographs, 2002--; contbr. chpts. to books, articles to profl. jours. Recipient Melamed prize for bus. rsch., 2000; named ISI HIghly Cited Rschr., Econs./Bus., 2003. Fellow APA, Am. Psychol. Soc.; mem. Assn. Consumer Rsch. (bd. dirs. 1976-79, pres. 1987, fellow in consumer behavior 1992), Inst. Ops. Rsch. and Mgmt. Sci., Am. Mktg. Assn. (Harold M. Maynard award 1979, Paul D. Converse award 1992, Irwin/McGraw-Hill Disting. Mktg. Educator award 2000). Democrat. Episcopalian. Home: 213 Huntington Dr Chapel Hill NC 27514-2419 Office: Duke U Fuqua Sch of Bus Durham NC 27708-0120 E-mail: jrb12@mail.duke.edu.

BETTS, BARBARA STOKE, artist, educator; b. Arlington, Mass., Apr. 19, 1924; d. Stuart and Barbara Lillian (Johnstone) Stoke; m. James William Betts, July 28, 1951; 1 child, Barbara Susan (dec.). BA, Mt. Holyoke Coll., 1946; MA, Columbia U., 1948. Cert. tchr., N.Y., Calif., Hawaii. Art tchr. Walton (N.Y.) Union Schs., 1947-48, Presidio Hill Sch., San Francisco, 1949-51; freelance artist San Francisco, 1951; art tchr. Honolulu Acad. Arts, summer 1952, 59, 63, 85, spring 61, 64; libr. aide art rm. Libr. of Hawaii, Honolulu, 1959; art tchr. Hanahauoli Sch., Honolulu, 1961-62, Hawaii State Dept. Edn., Honolulu, 1958-59, 64-84; owner Ho'olaule'a Designs, Honolulu, 1973—; art editor Scrapbook Press, 2002—, Portfolio Cons. of Hawaii, 1990—. Staff artist: The Arcadian newsletter, 2000—; illustrator: Cathedral Cooks, 1964, In Due Season, 1986, From Nowhere To Somewhere On A Round Trip Ticket, 2003; exhibited in Hawaii Pavilion Expo '90, Osaka, Japan, State Found. Culture and Arts, group shows since 1964, one woman shows 1991, 96, 99; represented in Arts of Paradise Gallery, Waikiki, 1990-2001, Hale Ku'ai, a Hawaiian Coop., 1998-2001; traveling exhbns. include Pacific Prints, 1991, Printmaking East/West, 1993-95, Hawaii/Wis. Watercolor Show, 1993-94. Mem. Hawaii Watercolor Soc. (newsletter editor 1986-90), Nat. League Am. Pen Women (art chmn. 1990-92, sec. 1992-94, 2000-02, nat. miniature art shows 1991, 92, 93, 95), Honolulu Printmakers (dir. 1986, 87), Assn. Hawaii Artists, scholarship aid programs, Mount Holyoke Coll., Mary Lyon Soc., Rutgers Univ., Col. Henry Rutgers Soc. Republican. Episcopalian. Avocations: art, travel, writing, photography. Home: 1434 Punahou St Apt 1028 Honolulu HI 96822-4740

BETTS, DIANNE CONNALLY, economist, educator; b. Tyler, Tex., Sept. 23, 1948; d. William Isaac and Martine (Underwood) Connally; m. Floyd Galloway Betts Jr., Feb. 14, 1973. BA in History, So. Meth. U., 1976, MA in History, 1980; MA in Econ., U. Chgo., 1986; PhD in Econ., U. Tex., 1991. Affiliated scholar Inst. for Rsch. on Women and Gender/Stanford U., 1993—; economist, tech. analyst, fin. cons. Smith Barney, Dallas, 1994—2000; economist, fin. cons. Morgan Keegan, Dallas, 2000—. Mem. women studies coun. So. Meth. U., 1993-94, Fulbright campus interviewing com. mem. 1992-93, pub. rels. and devel. liaison dept. econ., 1990-92, faculty mentor U. honors first year mentoring program, adj. asst. prof. dept. econ. and history, 1992—, vis. asst. prof. 1990-92; faculty, Oxford, summer 1991-93, adj. instr. dept. history, 1989-90, adj. instr. dept. econ., 1985-89, tchg. asst. dept. history, spring 1980; lectr. dept. polit. economy U. Tex., Dallas, summer 1988. Author: Crisis on the Rio Grande: Poverty, Unemployment, and Economic Development on the Texas-Mexico Border, 1994, Historical Perspectives on the American Economy: Selected Reading, 1995; contbr. articles to profl. jours. Rsch. Planning grant NSF, 1992; recipient Marguereta Deschner Teaching award, 1991; Humanities and Scis. Merit scholar, 1978. Mem. Am. Econ. Assn., Am. History Assn., Econ. History Assn., Cliometric Soc., Social Sci. History Assn., N.Am. Conf. on British Studies, Nat. Coun. for Rsch. on Women (affiliate), Omicron Delta Epsilon, Phi Alpha Theta. Home: 6267 Revere Pl Dallas TX 75214-3099 Office: Morgan Keegan 5956 Sherry Ln # 2002 Dallas TX 75225-6531 E-mail: dcbetts@airmail.net.

BETTS, DOROTHY ANNE, elementary school educator; b. Washington, Nov. 3, 1946; d. Thomas Joseph and Elizabeth Anne (McGee) Salb; m. Jerold LeRoy Betts, July 14, 1975; 1 child, Ellen Marie. BS in Elem. Edn., U. N.Mex., 1968, MA in Edn., 1976. Cert. tchr. N.Mex. Tchr. Newman (Calif.)-Gustine Dist., 1968—69, Albuquerque Pub. Schs., 1969—79, 1980—84, 1999—, ednl. asst., 1993—99; co-owner Stork News N.Mex. Zuni Elem. Sch. coord. Pennies for Patients Leukemia and Lymphoma Soc., Albuquerque, 2001. Mem.: Delta Kappa Gamma (1st v.p. 1982—84, pres. 1984—86, 2d v.p. 2000—02). Roman Catholic. Avocations: travel, family outings, crafts. Home: 10118 4th St NW Albuquerque NM 87114

BETTS, ELAINE WISWALL, retired headmistress; b. Albany, N.Y., Aug. 24, 1925; d. Frank Lawrence and Clara Elizabeth (Chapman) Wiswall; m. Darby Wood Betts, June 2, 1951; children: Victoria, Catherine, Darby Wood Jr. BA, Smith Coll., 1947; MA, Holy Names Coll., Oakland, Calif., 1975. Head upper sch. Anna Head Sch., Oakland, 1971-78, Head-Royce Sch., Oakland, 1978-80; headmistress Albany Acad. for Girls, 1980-84, Dana Hall Sch., Wellesley, Mass., 1984-95; ret., 1995. Mem. Nat. Assn. Prins. Schs. for Girls, Headmistresses of East.

BETTS, RICHARD KEVIN, political science educator; b. Easton, Pa., Aug. 15, 1947; s. John Rickards and Cecelia Agnes (Fitzpatrick) B.; m. Adela Maria Bolet, July 25, 1987; children: Elena, Michael, Diego. BA, Harvard U., 1969, MA, 1971, PhD, 1975. Lectr. in government Harvard U., Cambridge, Mass., 1975-76, vis. prof., 1985-88; rsch. assoc. Brookings Instn., Washington, 1976-81, sr. fellow, 1981-90; dir. Inst. War and Peace Studies, Columbia U., N.Y.C., 1990—, Shifrin prof. polit. sci., 1998—2002, Saltzman prof., 2002—; dir. nat. securities studies Coun. on Fgn. Rels., 1996-2000. Mem. staff Senate Select Com. on Intelligence, Washington, 1975-76, NSC, Washington, 1977; adj. prof. Johns Hopkins U., Washington, 1978-85, 88-90; cons. CIA, 1980-91, 93-99, 2003—; dir. ctrl. intelligence Nat. Security Adv. Panel, 1993-99; mem. Nat. Commn. on Terrorism, 1999-2000; occasion lectr. Nat. War Coll., Fgn. Svcs. Inst., U.S. Mil. Acad. Author: Soldiers, Statesmen and Cold War Crises, 1977 (2d edit. 1991, Lasswell award 1979), Surprise Attack, 1982, Nuclear Blackmail and Nuclear Balance, 1987, Military Readiness, 1995; co-author: The Irony of Vietnam, 1979 (Woodrow Wilson award 1980), Nonproliferation and U.S. Foreign Policy, 1980; editor: Cruise Missiles, 1981, Conflict After the Cold War, 1994, 2d edit., 2001. Mem. foreign policy staff Mondale Presidential Campaign, Washington, 1984; mem. Assn. for Retarded Citizens, Bergen County, N.J., 1990—. Recipient Sumner prize Harvard U., 1976, Article award Nat. Intelligence Study Ctr., Washington, 1979, '81. Mem. Internat. Inst. for Strategic Studies, Am. Polit. Sci. Assn., Internat. Studies Assn., Soc. for Historians Am. Fgn. Rels., Consortium for Study Intelligence. Democrat. Avocation: cinema history. Home: 1199 The Strand Teaneck NJ 07666-2020 Office: Columbia U Saltzman Inst War & Peace Studies 420 W 118th St New York NY 10027-7213

BEUTLER, SUZANNE A. retired middle school educator, artist; b. Cin., Oct. 23, 1930; d. Robert and Marguerite (Pierson) Armstrong; m. Frederick J. Beutler, Jan. 5, 1969; children: Richard and Mark Ireland. BA, U. Wis., 1954; MA, U. Mich., 1966, PhD, 1974, BFA, 2000. Cert. tchr. Middle sch. tchr. Ann Arbor (Mich.) Pub. Schs. Vis. lectr. U. Mich., Ann Arbor; adj. lectr. Eastern Mich. U., Ypsilanti. Author 3 manuals with Lang. Art Projects; contbr. articles to profl. jours.; developed writing program using personal classroom experiences. Recipient Tchr. Recognition award, 1986; grantee in field. Mem. Phi Delta Kappa (Svc. Key award 1992). Home: 1717 Shadford Rd Ann Arbor MI 48104-4543

BEVERLY, LAURA ELIZABETH, special education educator; b. Glen Jean, W.Va., Nov. 26; d. Sidney and Alma Logan. BA in Elem. Edn., W.Va. State Coll., 1960; MS in Spl. Edn., Bklyn. Coll., 1969; postgrad., Oxford (Eng.) U., 1974, N.Y.U., 1982. Cert. elem./spl. edn. tchr., N.Y. Tchr. Bd. Coop. Ednl. Svcs., Westbury, N.Y., 1966—. Mem. adv. bd. Am. Biographical Inst. Inc., Raliegh, N.C., 1985—. Mem. ASCD, Am. Inst. of Parliamentarians, Royal Soc. Health, Phi Delta Kappa. Avocations: reading, traveling. Home: PO Box 346 Glen Jean WV 25846-0346

BEVERS, THERESE BARTHOLOMEW, physician, medical educator; b. Amarillo, Tex., Apr. 5, 1960; d. James Oliver Bartholomew and Ruth Ann Berg. BS, Tex. Woman's U., 1981; MD, U. Tex. Health Scis. Ctr., San Antonio, 1987. Intern, then resident U. Tex. Health Sci. Ctr., San Antonio/Bexar County Hosp., 1987-90; physician pvt. practice, Wichita Falls, Tex., 1990-91, Dallas, 1991-94; chief med.dir. Medi Clinic, Houston, 1994-96; asst. prof. clin. cancer prevention, med. dir. cancer prevention ctr. U. Tex., M.D. Anderson Cancer Ctr., Houston, 1996—. Mem. expert panel Nat. Comprehensive Cancer Network Breast Screening and Diagnosis Com., Nat. Comprehensive Cancer Network Breast Cancer Prevention Com. Mem. editl. bd. Oncolog, Breast Diseases: A Year Book Quarterly. Mem. AMA (task force on prevention), Am. Cancer Soc. Tex. div. (mem. breast cancer detection com., colorectal cancer detection com.), Am. Acad. Family Physicians, Tex. Acad. Family Physicians (mem. com. health care svcs. 1992-96, mem. com. clin. preventive medicine 1996-98, commr. pub. health and clin. affairs 1998—). Avocations: skiing, hiking, antiques, decorating, reading. Office: U Tex M D Anderson Cancer Ctr 1515 Holcombe Blvd # 336 Houston TX 77030-4009

BE VIER, WILLIAM A. religious studies educator; b. Springfield, Mo., July 31, 1927; s. Charles and Erma G. (Ritter) Be V.; m Jo Ann King, Aug. 11, 1949; children: Cynthia, Shirley. BA, Drury Coll., 1950; ThM, Dallas Theol. Sem., 1955, ThD, 1958; MA, So. Meth. U., 1960; EdD, ABD, Wayne State U., 1968. With Frisco Rlwy., 1943-45, 46-51, John E. Mitchell Co., Dallas, 1952-60; instr. Dallas Theol. Sem., 1958-59; prof. Detroit Bible Coll., 1960-74, registrar, 1962-66, dean, 1964-73, exec. v.p., 1967-74, acting pres., 1967-68; prof., dean edn., v.p. for acad. affairs Northwestern Coll., Roseville, Minn., 1974-81, prof., 1981-95, prof. emeritus, 1995—. Editor The Discerner. Bd. dirs. Religion Analysis Svc., Mpls., 1979—, pres., 1989—. With USMC, 1945-46, 50-51; ret. col. Army Res. Mem. Res. Officers Assn., Ind. Fund Chs. of Am. (nat. exec. com. 1991-94, v.p. 1993-94), Huguenot Hist. Soc., Bevier-Elting Family Assn., Phi Alpha Theta. Office: Religion Analysis Svc 5693 Geneva Ave N Oakdale MN 55128-1018 E-mail: wabjab41@juno.com.

BEVINGTON, DAVID MARTIN, English literature educator; b. N.Y.C., May 13, 1931; s. Merle Mowbray and Helen (Smith) B.; m. Margaret Bronson Brown, June 4, 1953; children: Stephen, Philip, Katharine, Sarah. BA, Harvard U., 1952, MA, 1957, PhD, 1959. Instr. English Harvard U., 1959-61; asst. prof. U. Va., 1961-65, asso. prof., 1965-66, prof., 1966-67; vis. prof. U. Chgo., 1967-68, prof., 1968—, Phyllis Fay Horton disting. svc. prof. in the humanities, 1985—. Vis. prof. N.Y. U. Summer Sch., 1963, Harvard U. Summer Sch., 1967, U. Hawaii Summer Sch., 1970, Northwestern U., 1974 Author: From Mankind to Marlowe, 1962, Tudor Drama and Politics, 1968, Action is Eloquence, Shakespeare's Language of Gesture, 1984, Shakespeare, 2002; editor: Medieval Drama, 1975, The Complete Works of Shakespeare, 5th edit., 2003, The Bantam Shakespeare, 1988, English Renaissance Drama: A Norton Anthology, 2002. Served with USN, 1952-55. Guggenheim fellow, 1964-65, 81-82; sr. fellow Southeastern Inst. Medieval and Renaissance Studies, summer 1975; sr. cons. and seminar leader Folger Inst. Renaissance and Eighteenth-Century Studies, 1976-77 Mem. MLA, AAUP, Renaissance Soc. Am., Shakespeare Assn. Am. (pres. 1976-77, 95-96), Am. Acad. Arts and Scis., Am. Philos. Soc. Home: 5747 S Blackstone Ave Chicago IL 60637-1823 Office: Univ Chgo English Dept 5801 S Ellis Ave Chicago IL 60637-5418

BEYER, LA VONNE ANN, special education educator; b. Estherville, Iowa, Mar. 24, 1925; d. (George) Harold and Florence Catherine (Mulvey) Schafer; m. Gerald P. Beyer, June 7, 1943; children: Gregg Allan Beyer, Douglas Lee Beijer, Jodie Lu Beyer, Michael E. Beyer, Stefan A. Beyer. BA, Calif. State U., Northridge, 1959, MA, 1974; EdD, U. So. Calif., 1985. Cert. spl. edn. tchr., Calif. Tchr., regular and spl. edn. L.A. Unified Sch. Dist., 1959-88; cadre mem. Beginning Tchr. Assistance Program Calif. State U., Northridge, 1992—. Faculty U. So. Calif. reading clinic, 1974-75, Valley C.C., Burbank, 1974-75, L.A. C.C. (ESL), 1976-78. Contbr. articles to profl. jours. Literacy tutor Laubach Literacy Internat. (Van Nuys, Calif. chpt.), 1967—; mem. steering com. Roosevelt Commn., 1988. Recipient Mayor's Cert. of Appreciation, L.A., 1970, Dir. of Vols. in Agencies award, Van Nuys, 1989, Community award L.A. Times, 1990. Mem. DAR, Coun. for Exceptional Children,Laubach Literacy Internat., Pi Lambda Theta (v.p., pres. 1985-91), Phi Delta Kappa. Avocations: volunteering, gourmet cooking, travel, genealogy.

BEYER, NORMA WARREN, secondary education educator; b. Bklyn., Dec. 1, 1926; d. Norman Hayden and Catherine Mary Warren; m. Daniel Joseph Beyer, July 10, 1954; children: Catherine Norma, Daniel Joseph Jr., Peter Norman, Maureen Bernadette. BS, CUNY, Bklyn., 1949; MA in Edn., NYU, 1953. Tchr. home econs. N.Y.C. Bd. Edn., Bklyn., 1950—. Bd. dirs. Clearmeadow Civic Assn., East Meadow, 1985—; pres. St. Brigid's Rosary Soc., Westbury, N.Y., 1987-94, 99-02; vol. spl. edn. tchr. religious edn., St. Raphael's; del. U. Fedn. Tchrs., 1989-90. Recipient St. Pius award Diocese of Rockville Ctr., 1975, Leader's Gold medal Nassau County 4H, 1978, Outstanding Community Svc. award Salisbury Rep. Club, 1993, Sr. Elizabeth Ann Seton medal, 1997. Mem. NAFE, Am. Home Econs. Assn., N.Y.C. Home Econs. Assn. (historian 1978-79), Cath. Tchrs. Assn., Bklyn. Coll., NYU Alumni Assn., Salisbury Rep. Club. Republican. Roman Catholic. Avocations: quilting, clothing design and construction, gardening. Home: 251 Clearmeadow Dr East Meadow NY 11554-1211

BEYER, TERESA LYNN, elementary counselor; b. Balt., Dec. 19, 1953; d. Don E. and Betty Denisar; m. Verlyn D. Beyer, July 2, 1983. BA in Elem. Edn., Cen. Coll., Pella, Iowa, 1976; postgrad., Drake U., 1979-86, Marycrest Coll., 1986, Lincoln U., 1989-91. Cert. counselor, elem. tchr., reading, Mo., Iowa, Wash. Beverage mgr., officer mgr. Strawtown Inn, Pella, 1976-79; 5th grade tchr. North Mahaska Community Sch., 1979-80; 5th and 6th grade tchr. Oskaloosa Community Sch., 1980-86; 6th grade tchr. Morgan County R-II Schs., Versailles, Mo., 1987-88, elem. group guidance counselor, 1990—, 5th grade tchr., 1988-90. Aerobics tchr. Lodge of the Four Seasons Racquet Club, summers 1986—; dir. cheer and drill team camps So. Mo. State U., 1988-92; aerobics instr. BlueCross BlueShield, 1985-87; flexibility coach Oskaloosa Community Sch.; summer work supr. U.S. Youth Conservation Corp., 1979-80; camp head counselor, St. Charles, Iowa, 1975; peer counselor Upward Bound and Spl. Svcs. Program, 1973-76; ballet tchr. N.Y. Youth and Recreation Commn., 1968-72. Named D.A.R.E. Educator of the Year State of Missouri, 1993. Mem. NEA, Mo. State Tchrs. for At-Risk, Nat. Cheerleaders Assn., Mo. State Tchr. Assn., Mo. Counselor Assn., Reading Assn. Elem. Tchrs., Iowa Student Edn. Assn. Avocations: swimming, aerobics, water skiing, weightlifting, reading. Home: RR 2 Box 188D Eldon MO 65026-9525 Office: Morgan County R-2 Sch Dist 309 S Monroe St Versailles MO 65084-1387

BEYERLEIN, SUSAN CAROL, educational administrator; b. Royal Oak, Mich., Apr. 23, 1948; d. Jack Frederick and Eleanore Jean Schaper; m. Kerry Norman Beyerlein, July 18, 1970 (div. May 1990); children: Kraig Kerry, Reid Ryan. BS in Elem. Edn., Valparaiso U., 1970; MPA in Ednl. Adminstrn., U. Mich., 1999. Elem. tchr. Warren (Mich.) Consol. Schs., 1970-75; tchr. Adult Edn., Royal Oak, 1979-97; coord. Teen Parent Program, Royal Oak, 1991-98; program supr. Royal Oak Continuing Edn., 1996-99; adminstr. Lincoln Early Childhood Ctr., Royal Oak, 1998—2000; supr. Jefferson Adult Edn. Ctr., Ferndale, Mich., 2000—. Owner, dir. Sue's Summer Swimming, Royal Oak, 1972-99; adj. prof. U. Mich., 2000—; chair com. Royal Oak Adv. Coun., 1994—; mem. Royal Oak Continuing Edn. Adv. Coun., 1994—. Chair Royal Oak Youth Assistance, 1997—; mem. Royal Oak Prevention Coalition, 1992—; chair Royal Oak Family Adv. Com., 1993—. Recipient Cmty. Spirit award Youth Assistance, 1998. Mem. ASCD, Am. Soc. for Pub. Adminstrn., Mich. Assn. for Edn. of Young Children, Mich. Assn. Adult and Cmty. Educators, Pi Lambda Theta. Lutheran. Avocations: reading, swimming, cross country skiing, dining out. Home: 4209 Manor Ave Royal Oak MI 48073-1905 Office: Jefferson Ctr 22001 Republic Oak Park MI 48237 E-mail: b1bunch@aol.com.

BEYERSDORF, MARGUERITE MULLOY, retired secondary school educator; b. Terry, Mont., Apr. 20, 1922; d. John William and Laura Agnes (Mahar) Mulloy; m. Curtis Alexander Beyersdorf, 1946; 1 child, Mary Jo Wright. Kindergarten-Primary Cert., Coll. St. Catherine, St. Paul, 1942; PhB, Marquette U., 1945; postgrad., Gonzaga U., Spokane, Wash., 1957-62, Ea. Wash. State U., 1977-79. Tchr. grade 3 Sacred Heart Sch., Oelwein, Iowa, 1942-43; tchr. grades 1 and 2 Jr. Mil. Acad., Chgo., 1943-44; tchr. history, English Fairfield (Wash.) High Sch., 1945-46; substitute tchr. Riverside High Sch., 1957; tchr. Mead (Wash.) Sch. Dist., 1958-75; owner/mgr. First Ave. Parking Lot, Spokane, Wash., 1977—. Vol. Spokane N.W. Communities Found., 1982—; active United Way Spokane, 1950—95, ARC, Am. Cancer Soc., Multiple Sclerosis Soc., others; vol. coord. Dominican Outreach Found. to Domicile Single Parent Families; canteen vol. Spokane Blood Bank, 1981—; vol. Miryam's House of Transition, 1989—. Recipient Vol. of Yr. Golden Rule award J.C. Penney Co., 1993; grantee NSF, Whitworth Coll., 1967. Mem. NEA, APGA, AAUW (bd. dirs. Spokane br., chmn. scholarship com.), Wash. Edn. Assn.-Retired (del. rep. assembly, mem. comm. com 1993—, chmn. comm. commn. 1993—), Mead Edn. Assn. (sec., exec. bd., former bldg. rep., mem. curriculum com.). Avocations: golf, travel, reading, needlepoint, walking, bridge, crossword puzzles.

BEYTAGH, FRANCIS XAVIER, JR., law educator; b. Savannah, Georgia, July 11, 1935; BA magna cum laude(hon.), U. Notre Dame, 1956; JD, U. Mich., 1963. Bar: Ohio, 1964, U.S. Supreme Ct., 1967, Ind., 1972. Clk. Fuller, Seney, Henry, and Hodge, Toledo, 1961; sr. law clk. to Chief Justice Earl Warren U.S. Supreme Ct., Washington, 1963-64; assoc. Jones, Day, Cockley, and Reavis, Cleve., 1964-66; asst. to solicitor gen. U.S. Dept. Justice, Washington, 1966-70; prof. law U. Notre Dame, 1970-74, 75-76; prof., dean U. Toledo, 1976-83; Cullen prof. law U. Houston, 1984-85; prof., dean Ohio State U. Coll. Law, 1985-93, prof., 1993-97; spl. counsel Jones, Day, Reavis, and Pogue, Columbus, Ohio, 1993-96; pres., prof. Fla. Coastal Sch. Law, Jacksonville, 1997-98, prof., 1998—, founders' chair, 2000—. Vis. prof. law, U. Va., Charlottesville, 1974-75; U. Mich., 1983-84; So. Meth. U., Dallas, 1997. Editor in chief Mich. Law Rev., 1962-63; author: Supplement to Kauper's Constitutional Law: Cases and Materials, 1977; Constitutional Law: Cases and Materials, 5th edit., 1980,; supplements, 1981, 82, 84; Constitutionalism in Contemporary Ireland, 1997; contbg. articles to profl. jour. Capt. USNR; ret. Fulbright Fellow, 1994. Fellow Am. Bar Found.; mem. ABA; Fla. Bar, Jacksonville Bar Assn., Order of Coif. Home: 49 Marsh Creek Rd Amelia Island FL 32034-6414 Office: Fla Coastal Sch Law 7555 Beach Blvd Jacksonville FL 32216-3000

BÉZARD, JEAN ALPHONSE, science educator; b. Saint Eugéne, Aisne, France, June 11, 1930; s. Léon and Aline (Ruc) B.; m. Arlette Renaux, July 18, 1953; children: Bruno, Thierry, Hervé. BS, U. Paris, 1956, MS, 1957; DSc, U. Dijon, France, 1965. Asst. U. Paris, 1956-60, U. Dijon, 1960-66, asst. prof., 1966-71, prof., 1971-96, prof. emeritus, 1996—. Scientific cons. UNESCO, 1980-82. Author: (with others) Fat Absorption, 1986, New Trends in Lipid and Lipoprotein Analysis, 1995, Lipid Analysis in Handbook of Food Analysis, 1996. Mem. Am. Oil Chemists Soc. (pres. European sect. 1995), Biochem. Soc., Acad. Agr. Roman Catholic. Avocations: painting, music, jogging. Home: 154 Rue Claude Martin 21850 St Apollinaire France Office: Univ Bourgogne Nutrition Fac Mirande BP400 21004 Dijon France

BEZDEK, DONNA ANNE, secondary school educator; b. Houston, Jan. 11, 1953; c. Clollan O. and Avale Lavern (Preston) Cross; m. Charles L. Bezdek, Feb. 22, 1975; children: Christopher M., Casey M. Student, San Jacinto Jr. Coll., Pasadena, Tex., 1971-72; BS summa cum laude, Houston Bapt. U., 1975; MEd, U. Houston, 1980. Cert. tchr., Tex. Tchr. Deer Park (Tex.) Ind. Sch. Dist., 1975—, mem. ednl. productivity coun., 1994. Rsch. participant Third Internat. Math. and Sci. Study. Active South Main Bapt. Ch., Pasadena, 1994—, Teague Elem. PTA, Pasadena, 1994—, Sam Rayburn HS PTA, Pasadena, 1994—, pres. boys baseball team booster club, 2000-03. Fellow Assn. Tex. Profl. Educators; mem. Parkgate Civic Club. Avocations: walking, water skiing, bicycling. Home: 4506 Seneca St Pasadena TX 77504-3568

BHALLA, DEEPAK KUMAR, cell biologist, toxicologist, educator; b. Kasauli, India, Aug. 31, 1946; s. Khazan Chand and Shyama Bhalla; 1 child, Neel. BS, Punjab U., India, 1968, MS, 1969; PhD, Howard U., Washington, 1976. Postdoctoral fellow Harvard U., Boston, 1976-79; asst. rsch. cell biologist U. Calif., San Francisco, 1979-82, asst. prof. Irvine, 1982-86, assoc. prof., 1986-95, Wayne State U., Detroit, 1995-98, prof., 1998—. Cons. USEPA, NIH; spkr. in field. Guest editor, mem. editl. bds. profl. jours.; contbr. articles and revs. to profl. jours. NIH grantee, 1985-99, Calif. Air Resources Bd. grantee, 1990-95. Mem. AAAS, Am. Thoracic Soc., Am. Soc. Cell Biology, Soc. Toxicology. Office: OEHS 5134 Eugene Applebaum Coll Pharmacy & Health Sci Wayne State U Detroit MI 48202

BHANU, BIR, computer information scientist, educator, director university program; b. Etah, India, Jan. 8, 1951; came to U.S., 1975; naturalized, 1987. s. Rameshwar Dayal and Omwati Devi; m. Archana Bhanu Bhatnagar, Dec. 21, 1982; children: Shiv Bir, Ish Bir. BS with honors, Inst. Tech., Banaras

Hindu U., Varanasi, India, 1972; M in Engring. with distinction, Birla Inst. Tech. and Sci., Pilani, India, 1974; SM and EE, MIT, 1977; PhD Image Processing Inst., U. So. Calif., 1981; MBA, U. Calif., Irvine, 1984; diploma in German, B.H.U., India, 1971. Lectr. in elec. engring. Birla Inst. Tech. and Sci., Pilani, 1974-75; acad. assoc. IBM Research Lab., San Jose, Calif., 1978; research fellow INRIA, Rocquencourt, France, 1980-81; engring. specialist Ford Aerospace and Communications Corp., Newport Beach, Calif., 1981-84; asst./assoc. prof. and dir. grad. admissions, dept. computer sci. U. Utah, Salt Lake City, 1984-87; staff scientist, Honeywell fellow, sr. Honeywell fellow Honeywell Systems and Rsch. Ctr., Mpls., 1986-91; prof. electrical engring., computer sci., program leader electrical engring. U. Calif., Riverside, 1991-94; dir. Visualization and Intelligent Systems Lab, U. Calif., Riverside, 1991—. Cons. U. Calif., Irvine, 1983-84, Evolving Tech. Inst., San Diego, 1983-85, Bonneville Sci. Co., Salt Lake City, 1985-86, TRW, L.A., 1991—; pres. Internat. Student Assn. U. So. Calif., 1978-79; prin. investigator grants from DARPA, NSF, NASA, AFOSR, ARO, Rockwell, Ford, others. Co-author: Qualitative Motion Understanding, Kluwer, 1992, Genetic Learning for Adaptive Image Segmentation, Kluwer, 1994, Computational Learning for Adaptive Computer Vision, 1998; assoc. editor Jour. Math. Imaging and Vision, Pattern Recognition Jour., Internat. Jour. Machine Vision Applications; guest editor, co-editor IEEE Computer, 1987, Jour. Robotic Systems, 1992, Internat. Jour. Machine Vision and Applications, 1994, IEEE Transactions on Pattern Analysis and Machine Intelligence, 1994, IEEE Transactions on Robotics and Automation, 1994, IEEE Transactions on Image Processing, 1997; 10 patents in field; contbr. numerous reviewed publs. on subject of image processing, computer vision, artificial intelligence, machine learning and robotics. Recipient Outstanding Paper award Pattern Recognition Soc., 1990, Honeywell Motec and Alpha team awards, 1989, Project award Outstanding contbn. IBM Corp., 1978. Fellow IEEE (gen. chair IEEE workshop applications computer vision 1992, chair DARPA Image Understanding Workshop 1994, gen. chmn. IEEE conf. on computer vision and pattern recognition 1996), AAAS; mem. Assn. Computing Machinery, Soc. Photo-Optical and Instrumentation Engrs., Pattern Recognition Soc., Sigma Xi. Avocations: swimming, skiing, tennis, table tennis, writing. Home: 6733 Canyon Hill Dr Riverside CA 92506-5672 Office: U Calif Coll Engring Riverside CA 92521-0001

BHARADWAJ, PREM DATTA, physics educator; b. Gorakhpur, India, May 20, 1931; arrived in U.S., 1960; s. Ganga Dhar and Bhagwati Devi (Sharma) B.; m. Vidya Wati Sharma, Feb. 14, 1949; children: Rakesh Kumar, Rajnesh Kumar, Vidhu Rani Eranki, Sudha Kar. BS 1st class with merit, NREC Coll. Khurja, India, 1950; MS 1st class 1st, Agra (India) Univ., 1952; PhD, SUNY, Buffalo, 1964. Asst. prof. physics B.R. Coll. Agra, 1952-54; lectr. physics GPIC Tehri, Tehri Garhwal, India, 1954-56, Govt. Coll. Meerut, India, 1956-59; asst. prof. physics B.R. Coll. Agra, 1959-60; grad. asst. physics SUNY, Buffalo, 1960-62; from asst. prof. physics to assoc. prof. physics Niagara U., Niagara Falls, N.Y., 1962-66, prof. physics, 1966—, chmn. dept. physics, 1976-86. Cons. NSF, 1966-71; reviewer N.Y. State Regents Exams. in Medicine and Dentistry, 1976; co-founder India Assn. Buffalo, 1961, Hindi Samaj Greater Buffalo, 1986; summer rsch. participant NSF, La. State U., Baton Rouge, 1965; vis. prof. dept. crystallography Rosewell Park Cancer Inst., Buffalo, N.Y., 1970-71. Co-author: Intermediate Agriculture Physics and Climatology, 1954; contbr. articles to profl. jours. Pres. Sathya Sai Ctr. Buffalo, Amherst, N.Y., 1990-93, Hindi Samaj of Greater Buffalo, Amherst, 1996-97; mem. trust com. Hindu Cultural Soc. Western N.Y., 1999-2001. Recipient Rajiv Gandhi Nat. Unity award for excellence Govt. India, 1995, Hind Rattan (Jewel of India) award Govt. of India, 1995; named Internat. Man of Yr. Internat. Biog. Ctr., Cambridge, Eng., 1999. Mem. India Assn. of Buffalo (award for outstanding work in edn. and cmty. 1997), Hindi Samaj of Greater Buffalo, Am. Phys. Soc. Democrat. Hindu. Home: 100 N Parrish Dr Amherst NY 14228-1477 Office: Niagara U Physics Dept Lewiston Rd Niagara Falls NY 14109 E-mail: pdb@niagara.edu.

BI, SHUWEI, management information systems educator; b. Dalian, China, Mar. 24, 1937; s. Xufeng Bi and Jingzhen Zhai; m. Zongxian Gao, Jan. 22, 1965 (dec. Aug. 1992); children: Keduan, Keshu; m. Shirley Ann Dennis Kvitle, Oct. 15, 1994. Grad., Jilin U. Tech., Changchun, China, 1961. Asst. instr. Jilin U. Tech., 1961-70, asst. prof., 1978-85, assoc. prof., 1985-92, prof., 1992—; chief engr. Yushu Tractor Factory, Yushu, China, 1971-78. Management information sys. dir. #201 Factory, Jilin, 1987-88, Iron Alloy Factory, Jilin, 1988-89, Chem. Fertilizer Factory, Jilin, 1989-90. Co-author: (textbook) Introduction to Management Information Systems, 1986 (nat. 2d rank prize 1992), Management Information Systems Assignment and Solution, 1989 (ministry 2d rank prize 1993); author: Management Information Systems Analysis and Design, 1992; encyclopedist: China Enterprises Management Encyclopedia, 1984. Mem. Nat. Higher Edn. Mgmt. Info. Sys. Splty. Directing Group, Beijing, 1987-95; com. mem. Nat. Mgmt. Info. Sys. Com., Beijing, 1989-97. Recipient Excellent Rsch. award Mech. Indsl. Ministry, Beijing, 1989. Mem. Nat. Computer Simulation Soc. (dir. 1988-97). Home: 306 10th St Lincoln IL 62656-1564 Office: Coll Mgmt 142 People Ave Changchun Jilin 130025 China

BIANCA, JOANNE MARIE, elementary and early childhood educator; b. Scranton, Pa., Apr. 28, 1950; d. Joseph Frank and Frances Anne (Parise) B. BA in Elem. Edn., Marywood Coll., 1972, MS in Early Childhood Edn., 1991. Permanent cert. elem. and early childhood tchr., Pa. Tchr. kindergarten Charles Sumner, 1972-73, Thomas Longfellow, 1974-75, Neil Armstrong, 1975-76; tchr. grade 3 Charles Webster, Scranton, Pa., 1977-78; tchr. kindergarten James Monroe A.M. and Kindergarten Woodrow Wilson P.M., Scranton, Pa., 1978-79, St. Ann's Monastery Sch., 1980-81; tchr. grade 4 St. Mary's, Avoca, Pa., 1983-84. Per diem and permanent substitute tchr. Scranton Pub. and Parochial Sch. Dists.; coord., condr. workshops for parents of kindergarten children. Part-time vol. Lackawanna Day Care Ctr., Scranton, 1983; membership, coord. newsletter mail list Pa. Humanlife, Scranton, 1974-77. Mem. Nat. Assn. for Edn. of Young Children, Assn. Childhood Edn. Internat. (early childhood divsn.), Obsessive Compulsive Found., Kappa Delta Pi. Roman Catholic. Avocations: art, walking, obsessive compulsive support groups, educational research, resources and developmentally appropriate curiculum practices. Home: 323 Green St Scranton PA 18508-2715

BICE, SCOTT HAAS, dean, lawyer, educator; b. Los Angeles, Mar. 19, 1943; s. Fred Haas and Virginia M. (Scott) B.; m. Barbara Franks, Dec. 21, 1968. BS, U. So. Calif., 1965, JD, 1968. Bar: Calif. bar 1971. Law clk. to Chief Justice Earl Warren, 1968-69; asst. prof., assoc. prof., prof. law U. So. Calif., Los Angeles, 1969—, assoc. dean, 1971-74, dean Law Sch., 1980-2000, Carl Mason Franklin prof., 1983-2000, Robert C. Packard prof. law, 2000—; CEO Five B Investment Co., 1995—. Vis. prof. polit. sci. Calif. Inst. Tech., 1977; vis. prof. U. Va., 1978-79; bd.dirs. Western Mut. Ins. Co., Residence Mut. Ins. Co., Imagine Films Entertainment Co., Jenny Craig, Inc. Mem. editl. adv. bd. Calif. Lawyer, 1989-93; contbr. articles to law jours. Bd. dirs. L.A. Family Housing Corp., 1989-93, Stone Soup Child Care Programs, 1988—, L.A. Child Guidance Clinic, 2003-; trustee Bice Passavant Found., 2000—. Affiliated scholar Am. Bar Found., 1972-74 Fellow Am. Bar Found. (life); mem. Am. Law Inst. (life), Calif. Bar, Los Angeles County Bar Assn., Am. Law Deans Assn. (pres. 1997-99), Am. Judicature Soc., Calif. Club, Chancery Club (treas. 2001-02, sec. 2002-03, v.p. 2003-), Long Beach Yacht Club, Catalina Island Yacht Club (judge adv. 2002—). Home: 787 S San Rafael Ave Pasadena CA 91105-2326 Office: U So Calif Sch Law Los Angeles CA 90089-0071 E-mail: sbice@law.usc.edu.

BICK, RODGER LEE, hematologist, oncologist, researcher, educator; b. San Francisco, May 21, 1942; s. Jack Arthur and Pauline (Jensen) B.; m. Marcella Bick, Mar. 3, 1980 (dec. Feb. 1995); children: Shauna Nicole, Michelle Leanne. MD, U. Calif., Irvine, 1970; PhD, Acad. Medicine, Bialystok, Poland, 1995. Diplomate Am. Bd. Quality Assessment, Am. Bd. Forensic Medicine in Oncology, Hematology, Thrombosis, Hemostasis and Product Liability, Internat. Bd. Thrombosis, Hemostasis & Vascular Medicine, Am. Bd. Pain Mgmt. Med. intern Kern County Gen. Hosp., UCLA, Bakersfield, Calif., 1970-71, internal medicine resident, 1971-72; fellow in hematology-med. oncology Bay Area Hematology Oncology Med. Group, West Los Angeles, Calif., 1974-76; med. staff various hosps., Calif., 1974-77, med. staff, extensive adminstrv. and com. work, 1977-92; med. dir. oncology hematology Presbyn. Comprehensive Cancer Ctr., Presbyn. Hosp., Dallas, 1992-95. Staff hematologist/oncologist Bay Area Hematology Oncology Med. Group, Santa Monica, Calif., 1976-77, med. dir. Calif. Coagulation Labs., Inc., Bakersfield, 1977-92, San Joaquin Hematology Oncology Med. Group, 1977-92, Regional Cancer and Blood Disease Ctr. Kern, Bakersfield, 1986-92; asst. clin. prof. to clin. prof. medicine UCLA Ctr. Health Scis., 1976-94, assoc. prof. to prof. allied health profns. Calif. State U., Bakersfield, 1980-92, clin. prof. nursing and health scis., 1982-92; adj. assoc. prof. medicine/physiology, Wayne State U., Detroit; adj. clin. faculty Wesley Med. Ctr. and U. Kans. Med. Sch., Wichita, 1984-86; clin. prof. medicine U. Tex. Southwestern Med. Ctr., 1993—, clin. prof. pathology, 1993—; prof. haematology U. Tasmania Sch. Medicine, 1996; hematology cons. NASA; med. dir. UCLA/Kern Cancer Program, 1991-92, Ctrl. Calif. Heart Inst., 1990-92; invited spkr. and presenter in field, numerous internat. symposia and confs.; dir. numerous workshops in field. Author: Disseminated Intravascular Coagulation and Related Syndromes, 1983, Disorders of Hemostasis and Thrombosis: Principles of Clinical Practice, 1985, 2d. edit., 1992, 3d edit., 1997; guest editor, contbr.: Thrombohemorrhagic Disorders Perplexing to the Hematologist Oncologist, 1992; guest editor: Laboratory Diagnosis of Hemostasis Problems, I, 1994, II, 1995, (monograph) Seminars in Thrombosis and Hemostasis, 1994, Common Bleeding and Clotting Problems for the Internist, 1994; editor-in-chief: Hematology: Princples of Clinical and Laboratory Practice, 2 vols., 1993, Paraneoplastic Syndromes, Hematology Oncology Clinics of North America, 1996; editor: Current Concepts of Thrombosis, 1998; contbr. numerous chpts. to books; author monographs and lab. manuals; contbr. over 250 articles and papers and numerous revs. to profl. jours. and conf. procs.; patentee in field; editor-in-chief Jour. Clin. and Applied Thrombosis/Hemostasis & Vascular Medicine; mem. editl. bd. Am. Jour. Clin. Pathology, Internat. Jour. Haematology. Bd. dirs., exec. com. Bakersfield Symphony Orch., 1988-92. Fellow ACP, Am. Soc. Clin. Pathologists, Assn. Clin. Scientists, Am. Soc. Coagulationists, Internat. Soc. Hematology, Am. Coll. Angiology, Internat. Coll. Angiology, Nat. Acad. Clin. Biochemistry, Am. Heart Assn. (coun. on thrombosis, circulation and atherosclerosis; rsch. and grnat peer rev. com. 1980-86), Am. Geriat. Soc. (founding fellow); mem. AMA, AAAS, Am. Assn. Blood Banks, Am. Soc. Internal Medicine, Am. Soc. Hematology, Internat. Soc. Thrombosis and Haemostasis, Am. Assn. Study of Neoplastic Disease, Am. Assn. Clin. Rsch., Am. Cancer Soc., Internat. Assn. Study of Lung Cancer (founding mem.), Fedn. Am. Scientists, N.Y. Acad. Scis., Calif. Soc. Internal Medicine, Calif. Med. Assn., Calif. Thoracic Soc., Haematology Soc. Australia, Internat. Consensus Com. on Autithrombotic Therapy, numerous others. Lutheran. Avocations: ocean sailing, classical piano, brass musical instruments, photography, target archery, astronomy and astrophotography. Office: 10455 N Central Expy Ste 109 Dallas TX 75231-2215

BICKART, THEODORE ALBERT, university president emeritus; b. N.Y.C., Aug. 25, 1935; s. Theodore Roosevelt and Edna Catherine (Pink) B.; m. Carol Florence Nichols, June 14, 1958 (div. Dec. 1973); children: Karl Jeffrey, Lauren Spencer; m. Frani W. Rudolph, Aug. 14, 1982; 1 stepchild, Jennifer Anne Cumming. B Engring. Sci., Johns Hopkins U., 1957, MS, 1958, DEng, 1960; D Univ. (hon.), Dneprodzerzhinst State Tech. U, Ukraine, 1996. Asst. prof. elec. and computer engring. Syracuse (N.Y.) U., 1963-65, assoc. prof., 1965-70, prof., 1970-89, assoc. to vice chancellor for acad. affairs for computer resources devel., 1983-85, dean L.C. Smith Coll. Engring., 1984-89; prof. elec. engring., dean engring. Mich. State U., East Lansing, 1989-98; pres. Colo. Sch. Mines, Golden, 1998-2000. Vis. scholar U. Calif., Berkeley, 1977; Fulbright lectr. Kiev Poly Inst., USSR, 1981; vis. lectr. Nanjing Inst. Tech., China, 1981; hon. disting. prof. Taganrog Radio Engring. Inst., Russia, 1992—; mem. Accreditation Bd. for Engring. and Tch., Engring. Accreditation Commn., exec. com., 1998-2000; chmn. Engring. Workforce Commn., 1996-98; elected-mem. Johns Hopkins U. Soc. Scholars, 2001. Co-author: Electrical Network Theory, 1969, Linear Network Theory, 1981; contbr. numerous articles to profl. jours. Served to 1st lt. U.S. Army, 1961-63 Recipient numerous rsch. grants; Disting. Alumni award, Johns Hopkins U. Fellow IEEE (best paper awards Syracuse sect. 1969, 70, 73, 74, 77, chmn. com. on engring. accreditation activities 1996-98, chmn. accreditation policy coun. 2001—), Am. Soc. Engring. Edn. (v.p. 1997-99); mem. Am. Math. Soc., Assn. for Computing Machinery, Soc. for Indsl. and Applied Math., N.Y. Acad. Scis., Ukrainian Acad. Engring. Scis.), Internat. Higher Edn. Acad. Scis. (Russia), Internat. Acad. Informatics (Russia), Johns Hopkins U. Soc. Scholars., Johns Hopkins U. Alumni Assn. (Disting. Alumnus award). Avocations: bicycling, hiking, gardening. Home: 541 Wyoming Cir Golden CO 80403-0900 E-mail: tbickart@mines.edu.

BICKEL, PETER JOHN, statistician, educator; b. Bucharest, Romania, Sept. 21, 1940; arrived in U.S., 1957, naturalized, 1964; s. Eliezer and P. Madeleine (Moscovici) B.; m. Nancy Kramer, Mar. 2, 1964; children: Amanda, Stephen. AB, U. Calif., Berkeley, 1960, MA, 1961, PhD, 1963; PhD (hon.), Hebrew U. Jerusalem, 1988. Asst. prof. stats. U. Calif., Berkeley, 1964-67, assoc. prof., 1967-70, prof., 1970—, chmn. dept. stats., 1976-79, dean phys. scis., 1980-86, chmn. dept. stats., 1993-97. Vis. lectr. math. Imperial Coll., London, 1965-66; fellow J.S. Guggenheim Meml. Found., 1970-71, J.D. and Catherine T. MacArthur Found., 1984-89; NATO sr. sci. fellow, 1974; chmn.com. on applied and theoretical stats. NRC, 1998-2000, chmn. bd. on math. scis., 2000—; chmn. sci. adv. coun. Stats. and Applied Math. Inst., NSF. Author: (with K. Doksum) Mathematical Statistics, 1976, 2d edit., 2000, (with C. Klaassen, Y. Ritov and J. Wellner) Efficient and Adaptive Estimation in Semiparametric Models, 1993; assoc. editor Annals of Math. Stats., 1968-76, 86-93, PNAS, 1996—2000, Bernouilli, 1996—, Statistics Sinica, 1996—2003; contbr. articles to profl. jours. Fellow J.D. and Catherine T. MacArthur Found., 1984-89. Fellow AAAS (chair sect. U 1996-97), Inst. Math. Stats. (pres. 1980), Am. Stats. Assn.; mem. NAS, Royal Statis. Soc., Internat. Statis. Inst., Am. Acad. Arts and Scis., Royal Netherlands Acad. Arts and Scis., Bernoulli Soc. (pres. 1990). Office: U Calif Dept Stats Evans Hall Berkeley CA 94720 E-mail: bickel@stat.berkeley.edu.

BICKERSTAFF, MINA MARCH CLARK, university administrator; b. Crowley, Tex., Sept. 27, 1936; d. Winifred Perry and Clara Mae (Jarrett) Clark; m. Billy Frank Bickerstaff, June 12, 1954 (div. 1960); children: Billy Mark, Mina Gayle Bickerstaff Basaldu. AA, Tarrant County Jr. Coll., 1982; BBA, Dallas Bapt. U., 1991. Dir. pers. svcs. Southwestern Bapt. Theol. Sem., Ft. Worth, 1976—. Mem. Coll. and Univ. Pers. Assn., Seminary Woman's Club (past treas.), Alpha Chi. Baptist. Avocations: reading, music, genealogy. Office: Southwestern Bapt Theol Sem PO Box 22000 Fort Worth TX 76122-0001

BICKERTON, JANE ELIZABETH, university research coordinator; b. Shrewsbury, Shropshire, Eng., Apr. 16, 1949; came to U.S., 1978; d. Donald Samuel George and Lucy Mary (Hill) B.; m. Anthony Andrew Hudgins, Mar. 18, 1978 (div. Feb. 1995); children: Alexis Kathryn, Samantha Lucy. Grad. health visitor, North London U., 1977; BA, Oglethorpe U., 1980; MA, Ga. State U., 1991; women's health nurse practitioner, Emory U., 1997. RN, Ga., U.K.; cert. family planning nurse, U.K., RNC cert., 1997. Nurse St. Bartholomews Hosp., London, 1967-72; housing advisor Shelter Housing Aid Ctr., London, 1973-76; owner, dir. Jane Bickerton Fine Arts, Atlanta, 1978-85; co-curator Arts Festival of Atlanta, 1995; coord. rsch. study Emory U., Atlanta, 1995—2002. Co-presenter More Prodns., Ga. State U. Gallery; chair Art Papers Inc., 1983-85,, acting chair, 1987, art reviewer, 1980-1993—; co-curator bathhouse, billboards, art-in transit Arts Festival Ga., 1995; guest co-curator Ga. State U. Gallery, 1985; co-prodr. grant Ga. Humanities Coun., 1989; adj. instr. Atlanta Coll. Art, 1993-2002; lectr. City Univ, London; panelist NEA, 1993; nurse Feminist Women's Health Ctr., 1980-90; pers. mgr., asst. mgr. Brit. Pavilion Shop, Expo '92, Spain; visual arts panelist Bur. Cultural Affairs, 1987; juror Arts Festival, Atlanta, 1989. Author: (with John Fletcher) Guide to First-Time House Buyers, 1975; contbg. editor Art Papers, 1981-85; writer: Suns, 1996; exhibited in group shows at Atlanta Coll. Art, 1996=97. Vol. cmty. worker, Guatemala, 1976; mem. adv. com. Arts Festival Atlanta, 1991-93; com. mem. Grady H.S. Parents, Tchrs. and Students Assn.; chmn. com. fine arts Inman Mid. Sch. PTA, 1990-92, Morningside Elem. Sch. PTA, 1986-88; bd. dirs. Pub. Domain, 1992-98; ex-officio bd. dirs. The High Mus. Art, 1996-98. Mem. 20th Century Art Soc. at High Mus. (programming com. mem. 1993, bd. dirs. 1993-98, v.p. 1994-95, pres. 1996-98), Illien Adoptions Internat., Inc., (bd. dirs.), 1998—. Home: 1036 High Point Dr NE Atlanta GA 30306-3235 E-mail: jbicker@emory.edu.

BICKFORD, DAVID LAWRENCE, librarian, educator; b. Bronxville, N.Y., Sept. 16, 1965; s. Lawrence Clark and Ann Elizabeth Bickford; m. Bonnie Mai Carr, June 14, 1998. BA, Brown U., 1987; MS in LS, U. N.C., 1989. Libr. Phoenix Pub. Libr., 1989-93; mgr. acad. info. svcs. U. Phoenix, 1993-96, asst. to dir. for acad. devel., 1996-99, univ. libr., 1999—2003, instr., 1996—, dir. univ. libr., 2003—. Mem. ALA, Spl. Librs. Assn. (pres. Ariz. chpt. 1995-96), Assn. Coll. and Rsch. Librs. Office: U Phoenix 4615 E Elwood St MS 10-0068 Phoenix AZ 85040 Fax: 480-557-1436. E-mail: dlbickfo@email.uophx.edu.

BICKLEY-GREEN, CYNTHIA ANN, art educator, artist; b. Marshall, Mich., Oct. 3, 1942; d. James Irving and Donietta Ann (Scarcia) Bickley; div.; 1 child, Ethan Allen Bickley. MA in Art, U. Md., 1967; MA in Edn., George Washington U., 1985; PhD, U. Ga., 1990. Cert. art tchr., N.C. Asst. prof. art U. Md., College Park, 1967-78; lectr. Montgomery Coll., Germantown, Md., 1978-83; tchr. Lord Baltimore Jr. H.S., Oxon Hill, Md., 1980-81, Job Corps, Laurel, Md., 1983, Ctrl. H.S., Pleasant, Md., 1983-84; asst. prof. U. No. Iowa, Cedar Falls, 1990-93; prof. art edn. Sch. of Art East Carolina U., Greenville, N.C., 1994—. Art reviewer Banner Herald/Daily News, Athens, Ga., 1986-89; tech. asst. edn. Lyndon House Art Ctr., Athens, 1985-87. Contbr. to art jours.; contbg. editor: Interdisciplinary Art: Lessons and Resources, 1998. Recipient Premio di Cortona award U. Ga. Studies Abroad, 1987, Edn. mini grant Iowa Arts Coun., 1991, Seminar grant NEH, 1992. Mem. Nat. Art Edn. Assn., NC Art Edn. Assn. (pres. 2003—). Episcopalian. Avocation: fitness.

BIDDLE, BRUCE JESSE, social psychologist, educator; b. Ossining, N.Y., Dec. 30, 1928; s. William Wishart and Loureide Jeanette (Cobb) B.; m. Ellen Catherine Horgan; children: David Charles, William Jesse, Jennifer Loureide; m. Barbara Julianne Bank, June 19, 1976. AB in Math., Antioch Coll., Yellow Springs, Ohio, 1950; postgrad., U. N.C., 1950-51; PhD in Social Psychology, U. Mich., 1957. Asst. prof. sociology U. Ky., 1957-58; assoc. prof. edn. U. Kansas City, 1958-60; assoc. prof. psychology and sociology U. Mo., Columbia, 1960-66, prof., 1966-2000, prof. emeritus, 2000—, dir. Ctr. Rsch. in Social Behavior, 1966-96. Vis. assoc. prof. U. Queensland, Australia, 1965; vis. prof. Monash U., Australia, 1969, vis. fellow Australian Nat. U., 1977, 85, 93. Author: (with R.S. Adams) Realities of Teaching: Explorations with Videotape, 1970, (with M.J. Dunkin) The Study of Teaching, 1974, (with T.L. Good and J. Brophy) Teachers Make a Difference, 1975, Role Theory: Expectations, Identities and Behaviors, 1979, (with D.C. Berliner) The Manufactured Crisis: Myths, Fraud, and the Attack on America's Public Schools, 1995, (with L.J. Saha) The Untested Accusation: Principals, Research Knowledge, and Policy Making in Schools, 2002; editor: (with W.J. Ellena) contemporary Research on Teacher Effectiveness, 1964, (with E.J. Thomas) Role Theory: Concepts and Research, 1966, (with P.H. Rossi) The New Media: Their Impact on Education, 1966, (with D.S. Anderson) Knowledge for Policy: Improving Education Through Research, 1991, (with T.L. Good and I.F. Goodson) International Handbook of Teachers and Teaching, 1997, Social Class, Poverty, and Education, 2001. Served with U.S. Army, 1954-56. Fellow APA, Am. Psychol. Soc., Australian Psychol. Soc.; mem. Am. Ednl. Research Assn., Australian Assn. Rsch. Edn., Am. Sociol. Assn., Midwest Sociol. Soc. Home: 924 Yale Columbia MO 65203-1874 Office: U Mo Dept Psychology McAlester Hall Rm 210 Columbia MO 65211-0001 E-mail: BiddleB@missouri.edu.

BIDWELL, CHARLES EDWARD, sociologist, educator; b. Chgo., Jan. 24, 1932; s. Charles Leslie and Eugenia (Campbell) B.; m. Helen Claxton Lewis, Jan. 24, 1959; 1 son, Charles Lewis. AB, U. Chgo., 1950, AM, 1953, PhD, 1956. Lectr. on sociology Harvard U., 1959-61; asst. prof. edn. U. Chgo., 1961-65, assoc. prof., 1965-70, prof. edn. and sociology, 1970-85, Reavis prof. edn. and sociology, 1985-2001, Reavis prof. emeritus edn. and sociology, 2001—, chmn. dept. edn., 1978-88, chmn. dept. sociology, 1988-94, dir. Ogburn-Stouffer Ctr., 1988-94. Author books in field; contbr. numerous articles to profl. jours.; editor Sociology of Edn., 1969-72, Am. Jour. Sociology, 1973-78, Am. Jour. Edn., 1983-88. With U.S. Army, 1957-59. Guggenheim fellow, 1971-72 Fellow AAAS; mem. Sociol. Rsch. Assn., Nat. Acad. Edn. (sec.), Phi Beta Kappa. Office: Dept Sociology 5848 S University Ave Chicago IL 60637-1515 E-mail: cbidwell@uchicago.edu.

BIEBL, PATRICIA ANN, secondary education educator; b. Milw., Nov. 13, 1940; d. Edwin and Esther (Liniewski) Skowron; m. Joseph Frank Biebl, June 23, 1962; children: Colleen, Jeanne, Roger, Russell, Sandra, Susan. BA, Alverno Coll., 1962. Tchr. Spanish and English North Crawford High Sch., Gays Mills, Wis., 1962-65; tchr. Spanish Viroqua (Wis.) High Sch., 1979—2001. Teacher CCD St. Mary's Altar Soc., Viroqua.

BIEGEL, DAVID ELI, social worker, educator; b. N.Y.C., July 3, 1946; s. Jack and Estelle (Lentin) B.; m. Margaret S. Smoot, Jan. 31, 1976 (div.); 1 child, Geoffrey S. BA, CCNY, 1967; MSW, U. Md., 1970, PhD, 1982. Field coord. United Farm Workers, AFL-CIO, Balt., 1971; exec. dir. Junction, Inc., Westminster, Md., 1971—72; dir. office planning and program devel. Cath. Charities, Balt., 1973—76; ctr. assoc., dir. neighborhood and family svcs. project U. So. Calif., Washington Pub. Affairs Ctr., 1976—80; asst. prof. social work U. Pitts., 1980—85, assoc. prof., 1985—86; Henry L. Zucker prof. social work practice Mandel Sch. Applied Social Scis., Case Western Res. U., 1987—, prof. psychiatry and sociology, 1987—, co-dir. Ctr. for Practice Innovations, 1991—97, chair doctoral program, 1998—2001. Co-dir. Cuyahoga County Cmty. Mental Health Rsch. Inst., 1994—2002; pres. Inst. for the Advancement of Social Work Rsch., 1999—2002; dir. rsch. and evaluation Ohio Substance Abuse and Mental Illness Coord. Ctr. of Excellence, 2000—; co-dir. Ctr. Substance Abuse & Mental Illness, 2002—. Co-editor: Innovations in Practice and Service Delivery with Vulnerable Populations Series, Family Caregiving Applications Series; editor Practice Concepts sect., The Gerontologist; contbr. articles to profl. jours., books; co-author: Neighborhood Networks for Humane Mental Health Care, 1982, Community Support Systems and Mental Health: Practice, Policy and Research, 1982, Building Support Networks for the Elderly: Theory and Applications, 1984, Social Networks and Mental Health: An Annotated Bibliography, 1985, Social Support Networks: A Bibliography 1983-1987, 1989, Aging and Caregiving: Theory, Research and Policy, 1990, Family Preservation Programs: Research and Evaluation, 1991, Family Caregiving in Chronic Illness: Alzheimer's Dsiease, Cancer, Heart Disease, Mental Illness, and Stroke, 1991, Family Caregiving: A Lifespan Perspective, 1994, The Jewish Aged in the U.S. and Israel: Diversity, Programs and Services, 1994, Innovations in Practice and Service Delivery with Vulnerable Populations Across the

Lifespan, 1999. Cons. Vol. VISTA, Raton, N.Mex., and Balt., 1967-70; active Big Bros. Am., Balt., 1974-77. N.Y. State Incentive scholar, 1963-64; VISTA Fellows Program fellow, 1968-70. Fellow Gerontol. Soc. Am.; mem. NASW, Acad. Cert. Social Workers, Soc. Social Work Rsch. Democrat. Jewish. E-mail: deb@po.cwru.edu.

BIEGEL, JOHN EDWARD, retired industrial engineering educator; b. Eau Claire, Wis., Nov. 19, 1925; s. Otto Robert and Charlotte Mary (McGough) B.; m. Geraldine Elizabeth Lawrence, July 22, 1955 (div. Feb. 1978), remarried Nov. 22, 1986; children: Steven, N. Dale, Kurt. BS in Indsl. Engring., Mont. State U., 1948; MS in Engring. Sci., Stanford U., 1950; PhD in Solid State Sci., Syracuse U., 1972. Registered profl. engr., Fla. Instr. math. Mont. State U., Bozeman, 1948-49; instr., asst. prof. U. Ark., Fayetteville, 1950-52; engr. Ford Motor Co., Claycomo, Mo., 1952-53, Sandia Corp., Albuquerque, 1953-58; prof. Syracuse (N.Y.) U., 1958-78, Kans. State U., Manhattan, 1978-82; prof. indsl. engring. U. Ctrl. Fla., Orlando, 1982-98; ret., 1998. Rschr. in intelligent tchg. sys.; cons. IBM, Endicott, N.Y., 1980-81. Author: Production Control, 1963, 2d edit., 1971; inventor high strain rate tensile test device. With USNR, 1944-46, PTO. NSF sci. faculty fellow U. Calif., Berkeley, 1964-65. Mem. Inst. Indsl. Engrs. Avocation: woodworking. Office: U Ctrl Fla Alafaya Trl Orlando FL 32816-0001 E-mail: johnbiegel@juno.com.

BIEKER, RICHARD FRANCIS, economics educator, consultant, program director; b. St. Anthony, Ind., July 2, 1944; s. Oscar Edward and Viola Eva (Lubbers) B.; m. Kathleen Ann Keusch, June 10, 1967; 1 child, Daniel Michael. BA with honors, Murray (Ky.) State U., 1965; PhD, U. Ky., 1970. Tchr. St. Ferdinand (Ind.) High Sch., 1966; rsch. assoc. U. Ky., Lexington, 1969-70; asst. prof. U. Del., Newark, 1970-72; assoc. prof. Del. State Coll., Dover, 1972-75, prof., 1975—, dir. MBA program, 1985—. Pvt. practice econ. and fin. cons., Dover, 1972—. Contbr. articles to profl. jours. NDEA fellow, 1966-69, UCLA fellow, 1989. Mem. Am. Econ. Assn., Assn. for Fin. Planning and Counseling Edn., Am. Agrl. Econs. Assn., N.E. Resource Econs. Assn., Inst. Cert. Fin. Planners, Delta Mu Delta, Alpha Chi. Roman Catholic. Avocations: hiking, camping, personal computers, reading history. Home: 482 S Old Mill Rd Dover DE 19901-6202

BIEN, PETER ADOLPH, English language educator, author; b. N.Y.C., May 28, 1930; s. Adolph F. and Harriet (Honigsberg) B.; m. Chrysanthi Yiannakou, July 17, 1955; children: Leander, Alec, Daphne. Student, Harvard U., 1948-50; BA, Haverford Coll., 1952; MA, Columbia U., 1957, PhD, 1961; postgrad., Bristol (Eng.) U., 1958-59, Woodbrooke Coll., Eng., 1970-71. Lectr. Columbia U., N.Y.C., 1957-58, 59-61; instr. dept. English Dartmouth Coll., Hanover, N.H., 1961-62, asst. prof., 1963-65, assoc. prof., 1965-68, prof., 1969-97, Geisel prof., 1974-79, Frederick Sessions Beebe '35 prof. in art of writing, 1989-97, prof. emeritus, 1997—; vis. prof. Harvard U., 1983, U. Melbourne, 1983, Woodbooke Coll., 1995, U. Thessaloniki, 1996, 2000, Princeton U., 2001. Author: L.P. Hartley, 1963, Constantine Cavafy, 1964, Kazantzakis and the Linguistic Revolution in Greek Literature, 1972, (with others) Demotic Greek I, 1972, Demotic Greek II, 1982, Nikos Kazantzakis, 1972, Antithesis and Synthesis in the Poetry of Yannis Ritsos, 1980, Three Generations of Greek Writers, 1983, Tempted by Happiness: Kazantzakis' Post-Christian Christ, 1984, Kazantzakis: Politics of the Spirit, Nikos Kazantzakis-Novelist, 1989, Words, Wordlessness, and the Word: Quaker Silence Reconsidered, 1992, (with Darren J.N. Middleton) God's Struggler: Religion in the Works of Nikos Kazantzakis, 1996, (with Chuck Fager) In Stillness There Is Fullness: A Peacemaker's Harvest, 2000, On Retiring to Kendal, 2003, Beyond: A Literary Excursion, 2003; translator: The Last Temptation, 1960, Saint Francis, 1962, Report to Greco, 1965 (all by Nikos Kazantzakis), Life in the Tomb (Stratis Myrivilis), 1977, 87, 2003; co-editor: Modern Greek Writers, 1972; assoc. editor Byzantine and Modern Greek Studies, 1975-82; assoc. editor Jour. Modern Greek Studies, 1983-89, editor, 1990-99. Trustee Kinhaven Music Sch., Weston, Vt., 1972-78, 81-84, 86-92, pres., 1988-90; trustee Pendle Hill, Wallingford, Pa., 1977-92, 94—, presiding clk., 1983-84, 86, Quaker in Residence, 1998; mem. corp. Haverford Coll., 1974-2001; pres. bd. trustees Hanover Monthly Meeting, Soc. of Friends, 1977-84; chair bd. overseers Kendal at Hanover, 1989-95, chair bd. dirs., 1995-96; trustee Am. Farm Sch., 1998—. Recipient E. Harris Harbison award for disting. teaching Danforth Found., 1968, Golden Cross St. Andrew Greek Orthodox Archdiocese Australia, 2000; Fulbright fellow, 1958, 83, 87. Mem. Modern Greek Studies Assn. (pres. 1982-84, 99-2002, mem. exec. com. 1968-85, 99—), Yale Club (N.Y.C.). Democrat. Home: 80 Lyme Rd # 171 Hanover NH 03755 Home (Summer): Terpni 207 Waddell Rd Riparius NY 12862 E-mail: peter.bien@dartmouth.edu.

BIENEN, HENRY SAMUEL, political science educator, university executive; b. N.Y.C., May 5, 1939; s. Mitchell Richard and Pearl (Witty) Bienen; m. Leigh Buchanan, Apr. 28, 1961; children: Laura, Claire, Leslie. BA with honors, Cornell U., 1960; MA, U. Chgo., 1961, PhD, 1966. Asst. prof. politics U. Chgo., 1965—66; asst. prof. politics & internat. affairs Princeton U., NJ, 1966—69, assoc. prof., 1969—72, prof., 1972—95, William Stewart Tod prof. politics and internat. affairs, 1981—85, James S. McDonnell Disting. Univ. prof., 1985, dir. Ctr. Internat. Studies, 1985—92, chair dept. politics, 1973—76, dir. African studies progrm, 1977—78, 1983—84, dir. rsch. Woodrow Wilson Sch. Pub. & Internat. Affairs, 1979—82, dean, 1992—94; pres. Northwestern U., Evanston, Ill., 1995—. Mem. exec. com. Inter-Univ. Seminar on Armed Forces and Soc., 1968—78; cons. U.S. State Dept., 1972—88, Nat. Security Coun., 1978—79, World Bank, 1981—89; mem. sr. review panel CIA, 1982—88; cons. Hambrecht & Quist Investment Co., Boeing Corp., Econ Corp., Enserch Corp., Ford Found., Rockefeller Found., John D. and Catherine T. MacArthur Found.; nat. co. dir. Movement for A New Congress, 1970—71; mem. Inst. Advanced Study, 1984—85, Ctr. Advanced Study in the Behavioral Scis., 1976—77; vis. prof. Makerere Coll., Kampala, Uganda, 1963—65, U. Coll., Nairobi, Kenya, 1968—69, U. Ibadan, 1972—73; bd. dirs. Univ. Corp. for Advanced Internet Devel.; mem. Coun. on Fgn. Rels., Matthews Internat. Capital Mgmt., LLC, Consortium on Financing Higher Edn., John G. Shedd Aquarium, Steppenwolf Theatre, Alain Locke Charter Sch., Com. on Roles of Acad. Health Ctrs. in the 21st Century at Nat. Acad.'s Inst. of Medicine; Acad. fellow Carnegie Corp. on Internat. Devel. Program. Editor: World Politics, 1970—74, 1978—, Vices of Power: World Leaders Speak, 1995—; author: Tanzania: Party Transformatin and Economic Development, 1967, The Military Intervenes: Case Studies in Political Change, 1968, Violence and Social Change, 1968, Tanzania: Party Transformatin and Economic Development, 1970, The Military and Modernization, 1970, Kenya: The Politics of Participation and Control, 1974, Armies and Parties in Africa, 1978, The Politcal Economy of Income Distribution in Nigeria, 1981, Political Conflict and Economic Change in Nigeria, 1985, Arms and the African Military Influence in Africa's International Relations, 1985, Of Time and Power: Leadership Duration in the Modern World, 1991, Power, Economics, and Security: The U.S.-Japanese Relationship, 1992. Grantee, Rockefeller Found., 1968—69, 1972—73; Seeger fellow, 1989. Mem.: Am. Acad., Coun. Fgn. Rels., Am. Polit. Sci. Assn. Office: Northwestern U z- 130 Crown, Evanston Campus Evanston IL 60208-0001

BIENENSTOCK, ARTHUR IRWIN, physicist, educator, federal official; b. N.Y.C., Mar. 20, 1935; s. Leo and Lena (Senator) Bienenstock; m. Roslyn Amy Goldberg, Apr. 14, 1957; children: Eric Lawrence, Amy Elizabeth (dec.), Adam Paul. BS, Poly. Inst. Bklyn., 1955, MS, 1957; PhD, Harvard U., 1962, Poly. U., 1998. Asst. prof. Harvard U., Cambridge, Mass., 1963—67; mem. faculty Stanford (Calif.) U., 1967—, prof. applied physics, 1972—, vice provost faculty affairs, 1972—77, dir. synchrotron radiation lab., 1978—97, dir. Lab. for Advanced Materials, 2002—03, vice provost, dean rsch. and grad. policy, 2003—; assoc. dir. sci. Office of Sci. and Tech. Policy, Washington, 1997—2001. Mem. U.S. Nat. Com. Crystallography, 1983—88; mem. sci. adv. com. European Synchrotron Radiation Facility, 1988—90, 1993—96; mem. com. condensed matter and materials physics NRC, 1996—97, mem. bd. chem. scis. and techs., 2001—03. Contbr. scientific papers to profl. jours. Bd. dirs. Calif. chpt. Cystic Fibrosis Rsch. Found., 1970—73, mem. pres.'s adv. coun., 1980—82; trustee Cystic Fibrosis Found., 1982—88. Recipient Sidhu award, Pitts. diffraction Soc., 1968, Disting. Alumnus award, Poly. Inst. N.Y., 1977; NSF fellow, 1962—63. Fellow: AAAS, Am. Phys. Soc. (gen. councilor 1993—96); mem.: Materials Rsch. Soc., Am. Crystallographic Assn. Jewish. Home: 967 Mears Ct Stanford CA 94305 Office: Geballe Lab Advanced Materials 476 Lomita Mall Stanford CA 94305 E-mail: a@slac.stanford.edu.

BIENIAWSKI, ZDZISLAW TADEUSZ RICHARD, engineering educator emeritus, writer, consultant; b. Cracow, Poland, Oct. 1, 1936; came to U.S., 1978, naturalized; m. Elizabeth Hyslop, 1964; 3 children. Student, Gdansk (Poland) Tech. U., 1954-58; BS in Mech. Engring., U. Witwatersrand, Johannesburg, South Africa, 1961, MS in Engring. Mechanics, 1963; PhD in Rock Engring., U. Pretoria, South Africa, 1968; D in Engring. (hon.), U. Madrid, 2001. Prof. mineral engring. Pa. State U., Univ. Park, 1978-96, prof. sci., tech. & society, 1994-96, prof. emeritus, 1996—; pres. Bieniawski Design Enterprises, Prescott, Ariz., 1996—; Disting. prof. geol. engring. U. Madrid, Spain, 2001—. Vis. prof. U. Karlsruhe, Germany, 1972, Stanford U., 1985, Harvard U., 1990, Cambridge (Eng.) U., 1997; chmn. U.S. Nat. Com. on Tunneling Tech., 1984-85; U.S. rep. to Internat. Tunnel Assn., 1984-85. Author: Rock Mechanics Design in Mining and Tunneling, 1984, Strata Control in Mineral Engineering, 1987, Aiming High-A Collection of Essays, 1988, Engineering Rock Mass Classifications, 1989, A Tale of Three Continents, 1991, Design Methodology in Rock Engineering, 1992, Gaudeamus Igitur Poems, 1997, Alec's Journey, 1999; editor: Tunneling in Rock, 1974, Exploration for Rock Engineering, 1976, Milestones in Rock Engring., 1996; contbr. over 170 articles to profl. jours. Recipient Mayor's Proclamation of City of State College Bieniawski Day, 1983, Rock Mechanics Rsch. award, 1984, disting. toastmaster internat. award, 1974 Avocations: genealogy, cosmology, foreign policy, financial planning. Home: The Ranch 3023 Sunnybrae Cir Prescott AZ 86303-5770 Business E-Mail: z1b@psu.edu.

BIENSKI, PETE JOSEPH, JR., school superintendent; b. Bryan, Tex., July 26, 1946; m. Carol; children: Jason, Pete III, Wade, Joseph. BS, Tex. A&M U., 1968; MEd, Sam Houston State U., 1973. Adminstrv. cert., Tex.; registered tax assessor-collector, asbestos inspector. Tchr. Cleveland (Tex.) Ind. Sch. Dist., 1968-69; prin. St. Joseph Sch., Bryan, Tex., 1971-77; supt. Mumford (Tex.) Ind. Sch. Dist., 1977—. Chmn. exec. com. Region VI, ESC, Huntsville, Tex., 1993-94, adv. com. Region VI, ESC, Huntsville, 1993-94, ednl. leadership com., Huntsville, 1993-94. Mem. KC, Ch. Usher Club, Crime Stoppers. Mem. Tex. Sch. Assessors Assn., Tex. Assn. Sch. Adminstrs., Tex. Assn. Assessing Officers, Tex. Coun. Tchrs. English, Tex. Cmty Sch. Assn., Tex. Assn. Rural Schs. Roman Catholic. Office: Mumford Ind Sch Dist PO Box 268 Mumford TX 77867-0268 E-mail: pbienski@mumford.k12.tx.us.

BIESELE, JOHN JULIUS, biologist, educator; b. Waco, Tex., Mar. 24, 1918; s. Rudolph Leopold and Anna Emma (Jahn) B.; m. Marguerite Calfee McAfee, July 29, 1943 (dec. 1991); children: Marguerite Anne, Diana Terry, Elizabeth Jane; m. Esther Aline Eakin, Mar. 9, 1992. BA with highest honors, U. Tex., 1939, PhD, 1942. Fellow Internat. Cancer Research Found., U. Tex., 1942-43, Barnard Skin and Cancer Hosp., St. Louis, also, U. Pa., 1943-44, instr. zoology, 1943-44; temporary research assoc. dept. genetics Carnegie Instn. of Washington, Cold Spring Harbor, 1944-46; research assoc. biology dept. Mass. Inst. Tech., 1946-47; asst. Sloan-Kettering Inst. Cancer Research, 1946-47, research fellow, 1947, assoc., 1947-55, head cell growth sect., div. exptl. chemotherapy, 1947-58, mem., 1955-58, assoc. scientist div., 1959-78; asst. prof. anatomy Cornell U. Med. Sch., 1950-52; assoc. prof. biology Sloan-Kettering div. Cornell U. Grad. Sch. Med. Scis., 1952-55, prof. biology, 1955-58; prof. zoology, mem. grad. faculty U. Tex., Austin, 1958-78; also mem. faculty U. Tex. (Coll. Pharmacy), 1969-71, prof. edn., 1973-78; prof. emeritus zoology U. Tex., Austin, 1978-99; prof. emeritus sect. molecular cell and developmental biol. U. Tex. Sch. Biol. Scis., Austin, 1999—. Cons. cell biology M.D. Anderson Hosp. and Tumor Inst., U. Tex., Houston, 1958-72; dir. Genetics Found., 1959-78; mem. cell biology study sect. NIH, 1958-63; Sigma Xi lectr. NYU Grad. Sch. Arts and Scis., 1957; Mendel lectr. St. Peter's Coll., Jersey City, 1958; featured spkr. on first Earth Day, Old Westbury Campus of N.Y. Inst. Tech., 1970; Mendel Club lectr. Canisius Coll., Buffalo, 1971; adv. com. rsch. etiology of cancer Am. Cancer Soc., 1961-64, pres. Travis County unit, 1966, adv. com. on personnel for rsch., 1969-73; counsellor Cancer Internat. Rsch. Coop., Inc., 1962-90; cancer rsch. tng. com. Nat. Cancer Inst., 1969-72; gen. chmn. Conf. Advancement Sci. and Math. Teaching, 1966. Author: Mitotic Poisons and the Cancer Problem, 1958; mem. editorial bd. Year Book Cancer, 1959-72; mem. editorial adv. bd. Cancer Rsch., 1960-64, assoc. editor, 1969-72; cons. editor: Am. Jour. Mental Deficiency, 1963-68; mem. editorial bd. The Jour. of Applied Nutrition, 1987-91; contbr. articles to profl. jours. Research Career award NIH, 1962, 67, 72, 77 Fellow N.Y., Tex. acads. scis., AAAS; mem. Am. Assn. Cancer Research (dir. 1960-63), Am. Soc. Cell Biology, Am. Inst. Biol. Scis., Phi Beta Kappa, Sigma Xi (pres. Tex. chpt. 1963-64), Phi Eta Sigma, Phi Kappa Phi. Achievements include rsch. in provision of early evidence for abnormal chromosome numbers in cancer cells, for occasional excessively multiple-stranded state of cancer chromosomes; demonstration of a direct relation of chromosomal size in mammalian tissues and organs to the local metabolic activity, as evidenced by the local content of B vitamins, of differential toxicity in certain antimetabolites to cancer cells in culture. Home: 2500 Great Oaks Pky Austin TX 78756-2908

BIGELOW, SHARON LEE, elementary school educator; b. Chgo., Ill., Oct. 13, 1942; d. Clarence Ellsworth and Frances Lorraine Bigelow. BA in Edn., SUNY, 1964; MA in Ednl. Psychology, N.Y.U., 1965. Tchr. Union Free Sch. Dist., Pleasantville, NY, 1966—. Art dir. Chappaqua Recreation, Chappaqua, NY, 1961—64. Named a Sharon Lee Bigelow Day, Town Bd. & Mayor, 2001. Mem.: N.Y. State Tchrs. Assn., Pleasantville Tchrs. Assn. (pres., deleg.). Avocations: reading, calligraphy, travel .

BIGGS, ROBERT DALE, Near Eastern studies educator; b. Pasco, Wash., June 13, 1934; s. Robert Lee and Eleonora Christina (Jensen) B. BA in Edn, Eastern Wash. Coll. Edn., 1956; PhD, Johns Hopkins U., 1962. Research asso. Oriental Inst., Univ. Chgo., 1963-64; asst. prof. Assyriology, 1964-67, asso. prof., 1967-72, prof., 1972—. Author: ŠÀ.ZI.GA: Ancient Mesopotamian Potency Incantations, 1967, Inscriptions from Tell Abu Salabikh, 1974, Inscriptions from al-Hiba-Lagash: The First and Second Seasons, 1976; co-author: Cuneiform Texts from Nippur, 1969, Nippur II: The North Temple and Sounding E, 1978; editor: Discoveries from Kurdish Looms, 1983; assoc. editor: Assyrian Dictionary, 1964-87; editor Jour. Near Ea. Studies, 1972—; mem. editorial bd. Assyrian Dictionary, 1995—. Fulbright scholar Univ. Toulouse, France, 1956-57; fellow Baghdad Sch., Am. Schs. Oriental Rsch., 1962-63, Am. Rsch. Inst. in Turkey, 1972, Danforth fellow, 1956-62. Mem. Am. Oriental Soc. (pres. Mid. Western br. 1978-79), Archaeol. Inst. Am. (pres. Chgo. soc. 1985-92), Brit. Sch. Archaeology Iraq. Office: U Chgo 1155 E 58th St Chicago IL 60637-1540

BIGHAM, DARREL E. history educator; b. Harrisburg, Pa., Aug. 12, 1942; s. Paul D. and Ethel Bigham; m. Mary Elizabeth Hitchcock, Sept. 23, 1965; children: Matthew, Elizabeth. BA, Messiah Coll., 1964; postgrad., Harvard Div. Sch., 1964-65; PhD, U. Kans., 1970. Asst. prof. history U. So. Ind., Evansville, 1970-75, assoc. prof., 1975-81, prof., 1981—. Author: We Ask Only a Fair Trial, 1987, An Evansville Album, 1988, Towns and Villages of the Lower Ohio, 1998, Images of America: Evansville, 1998; contbr. articles to scholarly jours. and anthologies. Dir. Hist. So. Ind. 1986—; exec. dir. Leadership Evansville, 1976-79; chmn. Evansville Bicentennial Coun., 1974-76; bd. dirs. Evansville Mus., 1972—, treas., 1977-78, pres., 1979-81; bd. dirs. Met. Evansville Progress Commn., 1981-85, chmn., 1983-85; bd. dirs. Conrad Baker Found., 1971-85, Planned Parenthood S.W. Ind., 1978-79; trustee Evansville Vanderburgh County Pub. Libr., 1971-81; chmn. 175th Anniversary Com. City of Evansville, 1985-87; Presdl. appointee Abraham Lincoln Bicentennial Commn., 2000—. Rockefeller Bros. Theol. fellow, 1964-65, NDEA fellow, 1965-68. Mem. Soc. Ind. Archivists (dir. 1972-75, pres. 1977-79), Am. Hist. Assn., Orgn. Am. Historians (newsletter editl. bd. 2001—), Ind. Assn., Historians (chair hist. edn. com. 1994—, pres. 1999-2000), Ind. Hist. Soc., Vanderburg County Hist. Soc. (pres. 1981-84, 93-96). Mem. United Ch. of Christ. Home: 8215 Kuebler Rd Evansville IN 47720-7427 Office: U So Ind Dept History Evansville IN 47712

BILANIUK, OLEKSA MYRON, physicist, educator; b. Ukraine, Dec. 15, 1926; came to U.S., 1951, naturalized, 1957; s. Petro and Maria B.; m. Larissa T. Zubal, Nov. 14, 1964; children: Larissa, Laada. Student, U. Louvain, 1947-51; MS, U. Mich., 1953, MA, 1954, PhD, 1957; Dr. honoris causa (hon.), Nat. Univ. Lviv, Ukraine, 2002. Postdoctoral fellow U. Mich., 1957-58; rsch. assoc., asst. prof. U. Rochester, 1958-64; assoc. prof. physics Swarthmore Coll., 1964-70, prof., 1970-82, Swarthmore Centennial prof., 1982—. Vis. scientist Argentine Atomic Energy Commn., Buenos Aires, 1961-62, Institut de Physique Nucléaire, Orsay, France, spring 1980, Laboratori Nazionali di Frascati, Italy, spring 1984, U. Munich, Germany, fall 1988; vis. prof., cons. Delhi U., summer 1966, Shivaji U., Kolhapur, India, summer 1969, Faculté des Scis., Rabat, Morocco, spring 1978, Kiev U. Ukraine, spring 1994, Inst. Med. Radiology, Kharkiv, Ukraine, summer 1996; Fulbright prof. Lima, Peru, summer 1971, Kinshasa, Zaïre, fall 1975. NSF fellow Max Planck Inst., Heidelberg, Germany, 1967-68, Inst. Physique Nucléaire, Orsay, 1972; NAS exch. scientist Kiev, Ukrainian SSR, 1976. Mem. Am. Phys. Soc., Nat. Acad. Scis. Ukraine, Ukrainian Acad. Arts and Scis. in U.S. (pres. 1998—), Schevchenko Sci. Soc. in U.S., European Phys. Soc., Société Française de Physique, Phi Beta Kappa, Sigma Xi. Achievements include research on nuclear structure; with Deshpande and Sudarshan challenged the view that Einstein's relativity precludes the possibility of existence of particles that travel faster than light, 1962. Office: Swarthmore Coll Dept Physics Swarthmore PA 19081 E-mail: obilani1@swarthmore.edu.

BILENAS, JONAS, mechanical engineer, educator; b. Kaunas, Lithuania, Dec. 2, 1928; came to U.S., 1949; s. Pranas and Jadvyga (Ambraziejus) B.; m. Dana Melynis, Apr. 17, 1955; children: Jonas V., Andrius R., Laura R. B in Mech. Engring., CCNY, 1955; diploma, Oak Ridge (Tenn.) Sch. Reactor Tech., 1957; PhD, CUNY, 1969. Registered profl. engr., N.Y. Engr. Babcock & Wilcox Co., N.Y.C., 1955-56, Oak Ridge (Tenn.) Nat. Lab., 1956-57; group head Am. Machine & Foundry Co., Greenwich, Conn., 1957-64, Grumman Aerospace Corp., Bethpage, N.Y., 1964-72, specialist infrared countermeasures (IRCM) tech., 1972-83, projects mgr. IRCM, 1983-93; retired, 1993; prof. CCNY and CUNY Grad. Ctr., N.Y.C., 1969—. Part-time prof. mech. engring. SUNY, Stony Brook, 1988—; mem. program com. Nat. Infrared Countermeasures Symposia, 1990-93. Assoc. editor feature sect. The Engring. Word Jour., 1971—; reviewer of various publs. in field; contbr. articles to profl. jours. Chmn. bd. dirs. Lithuanian Cultural Ctr., Inc., Bklyn., 1995—; mem. platform planning com., del.-at-large Nat. Rep. Senatorial Com., Washington, 1993—. Nuc. scholar U.S. Atomic Energy Commn., 1956-57; recipient citation for infrared suppression advancement Army Sci. Adv. Panel, Carlisle Barracks, Pa., 1972, citation for OV-1 aircraft infrared program, Army Aviation Sys. Command, St. Louis, 1978; recipient best paper award 25th Ann. Infrared Countermeasures Conf., 1987. Mem. ASME (tech. com. on aero. and aerospace heat transfer 1974-80), NSPE, AIAA, Tau Beta Pi, Pi Tau Sigma. Achievements include patents and pioneering work in and devel. of infrared (IR) suppressors and IR countersurveillance equipment for U.S. Army OV-1D Mohawk aircraft, M1 Abrams battle tank, M2 Bradley fighting vehicle, mil. ground installations, and for the USAF Joint-STARS aircraft. Home: 75 Beaumont Dr Melville NY 11747-3431

BILLETER, MARIANNE, pharmacy educator; b. Durham, N.C., Feb. 28, 1963; d. Ralph Leonard and Nancy Jane (Chambers) B. BS in Pharmacy, Purdue U., 1986, PharmD, 1987. Cert. pharmacotherapy specialist. Pharmacy extern Commd. Officer Student Tng. and Extern Program, USPHS-FDA, Rockville, Md., 1983; radiopharmacy extern Commd. Officer Student Tng. and Extern Program, USPHS-NIH, Bethesda, Md., 1984; pharmacy extern Indian Health Svc. Commd. Officer Student Tng. and Extern Program, USPHS, Tahlequah, Okla., 1985; pharmacist Beaumont Hosp., Royal Oak, Mich., 1986; pharmacy resident U. Ky., Lexington, 1987-89, fellow in infectious diseases, 1989-90; asst. prof. Xavier Univ. of L.A., New Orleans, 1990-97; relief pharmacist Ochsner Med. Instns., New Orleans, 1991-96; assoc. prof. Sch. Pharmacy Shenandoah U., Winchester, Va., 1997—. Cons. Abbott Labs., Abbott Park, Ill., 1991—, Rhone Poulenc Rorer, 1996—. Contbr. chpts. to books and articles to profl. jours. Mem. Am. Assn. Colls. Pharmacy, Am. Coll. Clin. Pharmacy, Am. Soc. Health-Sys. Pharmacists, Soc. Infectious Diseases Pharmacists, Am. Soc. Microbiology. Office: Shenandoah U Sch Pharmacy 1460 University Dr Winchester VA 22601-5100

BILLIG, SHELLEY HIRSCHL, educational research and training consultant; b. Canton, Ohio, June 23, 1951; d. Alex T. and Flora H. Hirschl; m. Stephen M. Billig, Aug. 7, 1977; children: Lisa, Joshua. BA, Boston U., 1973; MA, Tufts U., 1975, PhD, 1978. Prof. U. R.I., Kingston, 1977-78, Northeastern Coll., Boston, 1978-80, Regis Coll., Weston, Mass., 1980-82, Merrimack Coll., N. Andover, Mass., 1982-86; rsch. assoc. N.W. Region Ednl. Lab., Denver, Colo., 1987-88; v.p. RMC Rsch. Corp., Denver, 1988—. Mem. editl. bd. JESPAR, Johns Hopkins, Balt., 1995—; mem. adv. bd. Colo. Parent Involvment Ctr., 1995—, Circle, Pew Charitable Trusts, other adv. bds.; bd. mem. Character Edn. Partnership, 2002—; prin. investigator Region VIII Comprehensive Ctr. and svc.-learning project lead to establishing Rsch. Network, 1998—, Kellogg Found. Svc.-Learning Initiative, Nat. Study of Civic Engagement, Carnegie Found., Nat. Study of Higher Edn. Tech. Integration, 1998-2000. Lead author: Federal Programs and Service-Learning, 1999; book series editor: Advances in Service-Learning Research; editor: Service-Learning: Essence of the Pedagogy, 2002, Studying Service-Learning, 2003; contbg. author, co-editor: Parent Involvment in the Middle Grades, Service-Learning Through a Multi-Disciplinary Lens, 2002; co-editor and contbg. author: Deconstructing Service-Learning: Research Exploring Context, Participation, and Impacts, 2003; contbr. articles to profl. jours. Office: RMC Rsch Corp 1512 Larimer St Ste 540 Denver CO 80202-1620 E-mail: billig@rmcdenver.com.

BILLINGS, JUDITH A. state education official; Supt. public instrn. State of Washington, 1988-97. Chairwoman Gov.'s Adv. Coun. on HIV/AIDS, Washington, 1998—.*

BILLINGS, NANCY CARTER, secondary education educator; b. Springfield, Mo., July 29, 1943; d. Frank Robinett and Elizabeth Elvada (Thomas) Carter; m. Clarence David Billings, Dec. 14, 1963; children: John David, Amanda Gayle. BS in Edn., S.W. Mo. State U., 1965; MS in Edn., U. Mo., 1970; postgrad., U. Ga., 1970-81, U. Ala., 1982-84. Cert. elem. tchr., cert. tchr. vocat. home econs., Ala. Tchr. vocat. home econs. Pilot Grove (Mo.) H.S., 1965-68; instr. edn. U. Mo., Columbia, 1968-69; tchr. vocat. home econs. Ft. Hunt H.S., Fairfax County (Va.) Pub. Schs., 1969-70; tchr. reading Clarke County Pub. Schs., Athens, Ga., 1970-71; instr. clothing Clarke County Vocat. Tech., Athens, 1971-73; ind. instr. clothing Athens, 1973-77; instr. clothing Singer Co., Athens, 1978-79; tchr. Elbert County Pub. Schs., Elberton, Ga., 1979-81; instr. microwave use Amana Corp., Birmington, Ala., 1982-84; tchr. vocat. home econs. Huntsville (Ala.) City

Schs., 1984—. Mem. adv. bd. in edn. U. North Ala., Florence, 1990-92; mem. Univ. Women, U. Ga., Athens, 1970-81, U. Ala., Huntsville, 1981-2003, v.p., 1982. Tchg. docent Huntsville Mus. Art, 1982-84, chairperson vols., 1983-84, mem. guild, 1983-98. Recipient Tchr. of Yr. award Ala. Assn. Family and Consumer Scis., 1996. Mem. Am. Assn. Family and Consumer Scis. (del. 1978, 94, 95, 96, 2001-02, v.p. fin. and properties, 2002-03, Top Ten Tchr. award 1997), Ga. Home Econs. Assn. (chairperson 1976, state treas. 1977-79), Ala. Home Econs. Assn. (dist. pres. 1986-87, 95—, state chairperson dels. 1989-92, state treas. 1993-97, Dist. B Tchr. of Yr. 1995), Am. Vocat. Assn. (state v.p. 1986-87, Tchr. of Yr. 1994, A1 vocat. home econ. sect.), Internat. Fedn. Home Econs. (del. world congress 1992, 96, 2002), DAR, Rotary, Delta Kappa Gamma. Methodist. Avocations: travel, reading, needlework, quilting. Home: 706 Corlett Dr SE Huntsville AL 35802-1906

BILLITER, FREDA DELOROUS, retired elementary education educator; b. McAndrews, Ky., Oct. 15, 1937; d. David Wilson and Evalyn May (Puckett) Kendrick; m. William Jefferson Billiter, Sept. 12, 1954; 1 child, Cynthia Delourous Newman. BS in Edn., Ohio U., 1969, MEd, 1987. Cert. elem. tchr., media specialist, reading specialist. Departmental tchr. Ironton (Ohio) City Schs., 1965-66, 3d grade tchr., 1966-67; 2d grade tchr. Portsmouth (Ohio) City Schs., 1969-96. Coord. sec. Scioto County Hist. Soc., Portsmouth, 1980-82; choir mem. Shawnee State U. and Cmty. Choir, Portsmouth, 1973—, Wesley United Meth. Ch. Chancel Choir, Portsmouth, 1985—, Portsmouth Cmty. Chorale, 1993—; mem. Scioto County Hist. Soc. and Nat. Trust. Martha Holden Jennings scholar Ohio U., 1988-89; recipient Cert. of Participation, Portsmouth Area Arts Coun., 1990. Mem.: AAUW, NEA, Ret. Tchrs. Assn. (v.p. 2003—), S.E. Ohio Coun. Tchrs. English, Internat. Reading Assn., Ohio Edn. Assn., Portsmouth Bus. and Profl. Women (v.p. 1990—92, pres. 2000—02, Portsmouth Bus. and Profl. Woman of Yr. 2001), Scioto County Mus. and Cultural Ctr., Ohio Hist. Soc., Portsmouth Rep. Women, Order Ea. Star, Kappa Delta Pi (svc. award 1986), Delta Kappa Gamma (1st v.p. 1990—92, pres. 1992—94), Phi Delta Kappa (awards chmn. 1990—91, 1994—95). Republican. Avocations: reading, singing, piano, sewing. Home: 2890 Circle Dr Portsmouth OH 45662-2445

BILLUPS, NELDA JOYCE, elementary educator; b. Kirksville, Mo., Sept. 23, 1939; d. Parley Bennett and Grace June (Cunningham) Rudy; m. Kenneth Lee Ebling, June 16, 1963 (div. 1976); 1 child, Vinton Eric; m. Donald Paul Billups, June 5, 1981; stepchildren: Donna Gonzalez, Debbie Banuche. BS in Elem. Edn., N.E. Mo. State Tchrs. Coll., 1960; MEd, Northeast Mo. State Coll., 1963. Cert. elem. tchr. 1st grade tchr. Bloomfield (Iowa) Elem. Sch., 1960-63; 2d grade tchr. Cherokee Elem. Sch., Overland Park, Kans., 1963-67, 3d grade tchr., 1968—97; ret. Mem. NEA, NEA Shawnee Mission, PEO, Alpha Delta Kappa. Avocations: gardening, music, flowers, church work.

BILLY, GEORGE JOHN, library director; b. Rahway, N.J., Apr. 10, 1940; s. George and Marie (Zeleznik) B.; m. Valerie Jean McGreevy, July 19, 1969; children: Margaret, Christine. BA in History, Rutgers U., 1962; MLS, Pratt Inst., 1968; MA in HIstory, Adelphi U., 1973; PhD in History, CUNY, 1982. Ref. libr. Buffalo and Erie County Pub. Libr., 1968-70; acquisitions and ref. libr. Queensborough Community Coll., Bayside, N.Y., 1970-76; reader svcs. libr. U.S. Mcht. Marine Acad. Libr., Kings Point, N.Y., 1977-84, chief libr., 1984—. Adj. prof. Palmer Sch. Libr. Info. Sci., C.W. Post/Long Island U., Greenvale, N.Y., 1983—. Author: Palmerston's Foreign Policy: 1848, 1993; compiler booklets in field. Mem. Selection com. Sch. Bd., Manhasset, 1992-94. Charles Freeman Meml. scholar, 1958-62, Buffalo and Erie County Pub. Libr. scholar, 1967-68. Mem. ALA, Assn. Coll. and Rsch. Librs., Spl. Librs. Assn. (transp. divsn.), L.I. Coun. Acad. Libr. Dirs., Nassau County Libr. Assn., Beta Phi Mu. Office: US Mcht Marine Acad 300 Steamboat Rd Kings Point NY 11024-1699

BILOTTA, JAMES DOMINIC, history educator; b. North Tonawanda, N.Y., Jan. 11, 1942; s. Louis and Lena (Apollo) Cambria; m. Sharon Ann Stenzel, Jan. 19, 1963; children: James Lee, Carolyn Marie. AAS in Bus. Adminstrn., U. Buffalo, 1963; BSBA, SUNY, Buffalo, 1966, BA in History, 1970, MA in Am. History, 1972, PhD in Am. History, 1985. Instr. Trocaire Coll., Buffalo, fall 1980; mem. faculty SUNY, Buffalo, 1976-84; instr. Medaille Coll., Buffalo, fall 1982; mem. faculty Niagara U., Niagara Falls, N.Y., 1984-86, instr.; mem. faculty Brock U., St. Catharines, Ont., Can., 1987-99. Panelist, guest lectr. off-campus coll. divsn. CUNY, spring 1979, Brock U., winter 1994, spring 1994; Medaille Coll., Buffalo, 1982, SUNY, Geneseo, 1989, SUNY, Oswego, 1989-92, asst. prof. Author: Race and the Rise of the Republican Party, 1848-1865, 1992, 2002; also articles; guest John Otto Show, Sta. WGR radio, Buffalo, 1978. Head coach ice hockey Northea. Jr. Hockey League. Mem. Orgn. Am. Historians, Am. Hist. Assn., So. Hist. Assn., Am. Indian Hist. Soc., United Ostomy Assn. Avocations: hunting, fishing, hiking, golf. Home: 399 Fredericka St North Tonawanda NY 14120-2649

BINA, CYRUS, economist, poet; b. Mar. 21, 1946; came to U.S., 1971; naturalized citizen; children: Babak, Roxanna. BS, U. Tehran, 1968; MBA, Ball State U., 1972, MA in Econs., 1976; PhD in Econs., Am. U., 1983. Internat. fin. analyst The Plan Orgn. Tehran Treasury Dept., 1966-68; chief auditor Tehran Div. Social Ins., Gen. Gendarmerie, 1969-71; mem. faculty dept. econs. Am. U., Washington, 1977-79, summer 1982, Towson (Md.) State U., 1979-80; sr. economist Emay Corp., McLean, Va., 1980-81; mem. faculty Washington Internat. Coll., 1981-82; prof. econs., dir. econs. program Olivet (Mich.) Coll., 1982-87; prof. Providence Coll., 1987-90; rsch. assoc. Ctr. Middle Eastern Studies Harvard U., Cambridge, Mass., 1991—95; lead faculty, dir. Ctr. Unified Global and Applied Rsch., U. of Redland, Calif. (COUGAR), 1996—98; prof. U. Minn., Morris, 2000—. Cons. reviewer CHOICE jour., ALA, 1987—. Author: The Economics of the Oil Crisis by St. Martin's, 1985, The Sun and the Earth (Persian poetry), 1998; editor Jour. Econ. Democracy, 1989-94, Rev. Radical Polit. Econs., 1981-90, 2001—; assoc. editor Center for Iranian Research & Analysis, 2000; freelance referee econ. jours. and pubs.; co-editor Modern Capitalism and Islamic Ideology in Iran by St. Martin's, 1991, Beyond Survival: Wage Labor in The Late Twentieth Century, 1996. Nominee Grawemeyer World Order award, 1991; recipient Gorton Riethmiller Rsch. Award, Mich., 1983, Faculty Enrichment award, Ctr. for Near Ea. and North African Studies, U. Mich., Ann Arbor, 1985, Disting. Faculty Rsch. award, U. of Redlands, 1998. Mem. Mid. East Econ. Assn., Am. Econ. Assn., Union for Radical Polit. Econs. Avocations: chess, reading poetry, jogging. Office: U Minn Divsn Social Scis Camden Hall Morris MN 56267-2134 E-mail: bina@mrs.umn.edu.

BINFORD, JESSE STONE, JR., chemistry educator; b. Freeport, Tex., Nov. 1, 1928; s. Jesse Stone and Eglan Lee (Bracewell) B.; m. Lolita Ramona Fritz, June 8, 1955; children: Lincoln Bracewell, Jason Jolly. BA in Chemistry, Rice U., 1950, MA in Chemistry, 1952; PhD in Phys. Chemistry, U. Utah, 1955. Instr. chemistry U. Tex., Austin, 1955-58; asst. prof. U. of the Pacific, Stockton, Calif., 1958-60, assoc. prof., 1960-61; Fulbright prof., chmn. dept. chemistry Univ. Nacional Autonoma de Honduras, Tegucigalpa, 1968-69; vis. rsch. prof. Thermochemistry Lab., U. Lund, Sweden, 1971, researcher, 1982-83; rsch. fellow Chelsea Coll., U. London, 1983; assoc. prof. U. South Fla., Tampa, 1961-72, prof., 1972—. Cons. Fla. consortium AID, Honduras, 1969, Exxon Prodn. Rsch. Co., Houston, 1974; chmn. State Univ. Faculty Senate Coun., Fla., 1975-76; dir. gen. chemistry program U. South Fla., 1978-82, 98-2003; vis. prof. dept. chem. engring. Rice U., 1993-94, rschr. Cox Lab. for Biomed. Engring., Inst. Bioscis. and Bioengring., 1993-94; mem. Inst. for Biomolecular Sci., U. South Fla., pres. faculty senate, 1999-2000. Author: (textbook) Foundations of Chemistry, 1977, 2nd edit., 1985; contbr. articles to profl. jours., 1956—. Active bicycle adv. com. Hillsborough County, Tampa, 1975-93, chairperson bicycle adv. com., 1990-93; faculty advisor U. South Fla. Bicycle Club, 1972—; coord. spl. tutoring program Danforth Found., Tampa, 1968. Grantee Petroleum Rsch. Fun, 1960-62, USPHS (NIH), 1966-68, Rsch. Corp., 1986. Mem. AAUP, AAAS, Am. Chem. Soc. (nat. and Fla. sect.), Calorimetry Conf., League of Am. Bicyclists, Golden Key, Sigma Xi, Phi Beta Kappa, Phi Lambda Upsilon, Sigma Pi Sigma, Omicron Delta Kappa. Avocations: bicycling, travel, reading. Home: 1905 E 111th Ave Tampa FL 33612-6150 Office: U South Fla Dept Chemistry 4202 E Fowler Ave Tampa FL 33620-8000

BING, SARAH ANN, educational psychologist; b. Rutland, Vt., Aug. 10, 1943; d. Byron M. and Mildred G. (Marks) Blanchard; m. John R. Bing, June 14, 1967; 1 child, David M. BA, U. Vt., 1965; MEd, U. Ga., 1973, PhD, 1976. Cert. tchr. elem. edn. and spl. edn., N.Y. Tchr. pub. schs., Middletown, N.Y., 1968-71, Jackson County, Ga., 1971-72; teaching asst., rsch. asst. U. Ga., 1973-76; assoc. prof. ednl. psychology U. Md. Ea. Shore, Princess Anne, 1976—. Contbr. articles to ednl. jours. Rsch. grantee U. Md. Ea. Shore, 1982, 85. Mem. ASCD, Coun. for Exceptional Children, Ea. Ednl. Rsch. Assn., Am. Edn. Rsch. Assn., Phi Delta Kappa (rsch. rep., found. rep.), Kappa Delta Pi. Office: U of Md Ea Shore Princess Anne MD 21853 E-mail: sabing@mail.umes.edu.

BINGHAM, CHRISTOPHER, statistics educator; b. N.Y.C., Apr. 16, 1937; s. Alfred Mitchell and Sylvia (Knox) B.; m. Carolyn Higinbotham, Sept. 23, 1967 AB, Yale U., 1958, MA, 1960, PhD, 1964. Research fellow Conn. Agrl. Expt. Sta., New Haven, 1958-64; research assoc. in math. and biology Princeton U., N.J., 1964-66; asst. prof. stats. U. Chgo., 1967-72; assoc. prof. applied stats. U. Minn., Mpls., 1972-79, prof., 1979—. Contbr. articles to profl. jours. Fellow Am. Statis. Assn., Inst. Math. Stats.; mem. Royal Statis. Soc., Biometric Soc., Soc. Indsl. and Applied Math. Unitarian Universalist. Home: 605 Winston Ct Mendota Heights MN 55118-1039 Office: U Minn Sch Stats 313 Ford Hall 224 Church St SE Minneapolis MN 55455-0493 E-mail: kb@umn.edu.

BINGHAM, JAMES FREDERICK, healthcare educator; b. Clinton, Iowa, July 5, 1950; s. George and Joyce Lorraine (Swanson) B.; m. Donna Jean Petersen, Aug. 16, 1969; children: Lynn C. Bingham Downey, Benjamin James. Student, Eastern Iowa C.C., 1968-70, N.E. Mo. State U., 1970-71. Cert. fin. mgr. Merrill Lynch Coll. Fin. Planning. Realtor Americana Group, Las Vegas, 1979-81; owner, pub. Pubs. Svc. Co., Clinton, Iowa, 1971-73; sales mgr. Sta. KCLN Radio, Clinton, Iowa, 1973-75; realtor Howes & Jefferies Realtors, Clinton, Iowa, 1975-78; loan rep. Nev. Savs. and Loan, Las Vegas, 1978; investment broker Paine Webber, Las Vegas, 1981-85; v.p. Merrill Lynch, Las Vegas, 1985-2000, 1st v.p. investments, 2000—. Mem. N.Y. Stock Exch., 1982—. Author: (newspaper jour.) The Country Life, 1971-73. Hon. chmn. Jaycees-Muscular Dystrophy Assn., Clinton, 1975; mem. membership com. Spanish Trail, Las Vegas, 1996-97. Named one of Most Influential Men of So. Neb., In Bus. of Las Vegas, 2001. Mem. Nat. Assn. Securities Dealers, Nat. Assn. Realtors, Spanish Trail Golf and Country Club (com. 1985—). Avocations: golf, travel. Office: Merrill Lynch 2300 W Sahara Ave Ste 1200 Las Vegas NV 89102-4354 E-mail: jbingham@pclient.ml.com.

BINKLEY, JONATHAN ANDREW, secondary education educator, government educator; b. Princeton, Ill., Dec. 18, 1940; s. Carl Victor and Catherine Madie (Willson) B.; m. Barbara Ann Meyers, June 6, 1964; children: Tregg Jonathan, Trent Stephen. AB, U. Findlay, Ohio, 1963; MA, U. Toledo, 1966; EdS, Eastern Mich. U., 1970. Film mounter Eastman Kodak Co., Findlay, 1960-61; stock processor Kroger's, Scheck's and Joseph's Super Markets, Findlay, Toledo, 1961-65; tchr. Donnell Jr. High Findlay Pub. Schs., 1963-64, Romulus (Mich.) Jr. High Sch., 1965-66, Romulus High Sch., 1966-67; instr. in govt. Whitmer High Sch., Washington Local Schs., Toledo, 1967-96; sales assoc. Apple Creek Realty, Toledo, 1979-84, Dew Realty Co., 1987-89; instr. in polit. processes Cmty. and Tech. Coll., U. Toledo, 1983, 93-94. Faculty advisor Whitmer High Sch. Pub. Forum Club, 1981-96; bd. dirs. NWOEA (Northwest Ohio Education Association), 1977-82, 93-96. Author: (with others) A History of the Ohio Conference, 1986; contbr. articles to profl. jours.; patentee lawn furniture weights. Pres. State of Ohio Conf. Chs. of God, Findlay, 1984—86, 1990—91, v.p., 1982—84, 1991—92; chmn. bd. dirs. Home Acres Cmty. Ch., 1982—85, 1994—98; chair hist. soc. com. Chs. of God Gen. Conf., 1997—; del. nat. gen. conf. sessions Chs. of God, 1986, 1992, 1998, 2001. Recipient Disting. Alumnus award, U. Findlay, 2001. Mem.: NEA (del. to nat. convs. 1979—80, 1983—84, 1988—96, nat. chair NEA Rep. Educators' Caucus 1995—97, nat. treas. 1993—95), Am. Polit. Items Collectors (dir. Region 3 1999—2003), Rep. Polit. Items Collectors (nat. pres. 1998—). Republican. Avocations: travel, writing, organizational work, collecting political memorbilia, golf. Home and Office: 1786 Bucklew Dr Toledo OH 43613-2310

BINKLEY, MARILYN ROTHMAN, educational research administrator; b. N.Y.C., Jan. 27, 1948; d. Edgar and Mollie (Rothenberg) Rothman. BA, Bklyn. Coll., 1968; MA, Columbia U., 1971; EdD, George Washington U., 1983. Tchr. N.Y.C. Pub. Schs., 1972-77; reading splst. Internat. Sch., Geneva, 1975-77; instr. Marymount Coll. Va., Arlington, 1978-80; edn. cons. Washington, 1980-85; sr. assoc. Office Ednl. Rsch. and Improvement U.S. Dept. Edn.; edn. policy fellow Inst. Ednl. Leadership, 1987-88; sr. assoc. Nat. Ctr. Edn. Statistics, 1988—. Nat. rsch. coord. Internat. Assn. for the Evaluation of Edn. Adv., reading literacy study, 1988—95; U.S. coord. Internat. Adult Literacy Study, 1994—99; cons. Severn Sch., 1980—83, Dept. Def. Dependent Schs., 1979, Dover Sch. Singapore, 1978; dep. dir. Internat. Life Skills Study, 1998—2001; nat. project dir. OECD Program for Indicators of Student Achievement, 1998—2001; internat. co-dir. Adult Literacy and Life Skills Survey, 1998—2000; dir. item devel. Nat. Assessment of Edn. Progress, 2001—. Mem. Am. Ednl. Rsch. Assn., Am. Statistical Assn., Nat. Assn. Ind. Schs., Nat. Coun. Tchrs. English, Nat. Assn. Measurement and Evaln., Nat. Reading Conf., Internat. Asn. Evaln. of Ednl. Achievement, Internat Reading Assn., Coll. Reading Assn., Orton Soc., Assn. Supervision and Curriculum Devel., Va. Reading Assn., Md. Reading Assn., Greater Washington Reading Assn., Delta Phi Epsilon, Phi Delta Kappa. Home: 12024 Gatewater Dr Potomac MD 20854-2875 Office: US Dept Edn 1990 K St NW Washington DC 20001-2029

BINSTOCK, LINDA GROSSMANN, educational administrator; b. Chgo., Feb. 15, 1939; d. Marcus Aurelius and Miriam Helen (Berkson) Grossmann; m. Morton Harvey Binstock, June 27, 1958; 1 child, Cliff. BS, U. Pitts., 1960, MEd, 1963, PhD, 1975; JD, Duquesne U., 1992. Demonstration tchr. Falk Lab. Sch., U. Pitts., Pa., 1966-73; sr. rsch. asst. Learning Rsch. Ctr., Pitts., 1974-75; sr. staff scientist Innovatrix Consulting, Pitts., 1976; assoc. dir. aging programs Mon Valley Health and Welfare Coun., Monessen, Pa., 1977-79; prin. Hamilton-Martin Sch., North Hills Sch. Dist., Pitts., 1979-80; analyst fed. compliance Carnegie Mellon U., Pitts., 1980-81, mgr. fed. compliance, 1981-83, dir. fed. compliance, 1983-87, dir. legal affairs, 1987-92. Chair environ. health and safety Nat. Safety Coun., Chgo., 1985-87; chair long range planning Alumni Coun. U. Pitts., 1986-87; bd. Exec. Women's Coun., Pitts., 1987, Soc. for Profs. in Dispute Resolution, Pitts., 1988. Bd. chair Ret. Sr. Vol. Program, 1990-92. Recipient Ford Found. scholarship U. Pitts., 1960-63. Avocations: decorating, gardening, cooking, reading, animals. Home: 1150 Windermere Dr Pittsburgh PA 15218-1144

BIRAM, GERALDINE LOUISE, elementary education educator; b. Bosler, Wyo., May 10, 1923; d. Frank Walther and Jeanette Caroline (Gluesing) Berner; m. George Emery Biram, Nov. 29, 1946; children: Beverly Kay Biram Burban, Barbara Lynn Biram Eldridge. BA, U. Wyo., 1944; postgrad., Western Wash. Coll. Edn., Bellingham, 1946, Coll. Puget Sound, Tacoma, Wash., 1956, Johns Hopkins U., Balt., 1958-59. Instr. Superior (Wyo.) Pub. Schs., 1944-45, Yakima (Wash.) Pub. Schs., 1945-47, Am. Sch. System, Baumholder, Fed. Republic Germany, 1952-53, Sch. Dist. 400 Pierce County, Lakewood, Wash., 1949-50, 55-57, Balt. County Pub. Schs., Towsen, Md., 1958-60, Albany County Sch. Dist. 1, Laramie, Wyo., 1960-82; vol. tchr. Cherry Creek Schs., Denver, 1989-90. Contbr. articles to profl. jours. and mags. Troop leader Girl Scouts U.S., San Antonio, 1957, Balt., 1958-60, Laramie, 1960-71. Mem. Assn. Vols. Children's Hosp. (pres. 1986—), Ladies Aux. fot VFW (pres. 1969-70, Dist. 6 pres. 1972-73), Order Eastern Star (chaplain 1965, 67, 69, 73-75), Women's Club Windsor Gardens (Denver) treas. 1986, 90-92), Wyoming Club of Windsor Gardens (pres. 1991—), Psi Chi, Kappa Delta Pi, Phi Kappa Phi, Delta Kappa Gamma. Avocations: writing, reading, travel. Home: Apt 4A 9335 E Center Ave Denver CO 80247-1216

BIRBAHADUR, DINDIAL, secondary educator; b. Albion Estate, Guyana, Oct. 28, 1944; came to the U.S., 1980; s. Pandit and Mangree Birbahadur; m. Rabby Devi Jaikaran, Feb. 23, 1969; 1 child, Devendra. BA, U. Guyana, 1971, diploma in edn., 1972; advanced diploma in ednl. studies, U. Leeds, 1976; MEd, U. V.I., 1984. Elem. tchr. Dept. Edn., Guyana, 1963-71, secondary tchr., 1971-74; math. lectr. Lilian Dewar Coll. Edn., Guyana, 1974-80; secondary math. tchr. V.I. Dept. Edn., 1980-89, master tchr., 1989—, chmn. math. dept., 1986—99, registrar/sys. analyst, 1999—. Math. lectr. U. Guyana, 1975-80; instr. U. V.I., 1981-89; math. examiner Caribbean Examination Coun., Barbados, 1978-80; statis. advisor U. V.I., 1982—; mem. Territorial Tech. Com., V.I., 1994—; state coord. for Presdl. award in elem. and secondary math. Author: Use of Objective Testing in Mathematics, 1976. Fellow Govt. of U.K., 1975; recipient Presdl. award for excellence in math. teaching Pres. of U.S., 1995. Mem. Nat. Coun. Tchrs. Math., Math. Assn. Am., V.I. Math. Tchrs. Assn., St. Croix Fedn. Tchrs., Coun. Presdl. Awardees in Math., Lions. Avocations: reading, playing chess, swimming, fishing, touring. Home: PO Box 2811 Frederiksted VI 00841-2811 Office: Arthur A Richards Jr High 20 & 21 Stoney Ground Frederiksted VI 00840

BIRCH, GRACE MORGAN, library administrator, educator; b. N.Y.C., June 3, 1925; d. Milton Melville and Adeline Ellsdale (Springer) Morgan; m. Kenneth Francis Birch, Oct. 26, 1947; children: Shari R., Timothy F. BA, U. Bridgeport, 1963; MLS, Pratt Inst., 1968. With Bridgeport (Conn.) Pub. Libr., 1949-66; asst. town libr. Fairfield (Conn.) Pub. Libr., 1966-69; dir. Trumbull (Conn.) Libr. Sys., 1969—. Lectr. Housatonic Community Coll., Bridgeport, 1970—; lectr. self-motivation, 1989—. Judge Barnum Festival Soc., Bridgeport, 1971-73; mem. Trumbull Multi-Arts Com., Trumbull Prevention Coun.; Fairfield County bd. Literacy Vols. Am., 1990-92. Mem. ALA, New Eng. Libr. Assn., Conn. Libr. Assn. (pres. 1972), Southwestern Conn. Libr. Coun. (pres. 1975-77), Fairfield Libr. Adminstrs. Group (pres. 1976-77), Kiwanis (v.p. 1999-2000). Democrat. Episcopalian. Avocations: sketching, dancing, traveling. Home: 175 Brooklawn Ave Bridgeport CT 06604-2011 Office: The Trumbull Libr 33 Quality St Trumbull CT 06611-3140 E-mail: gbirch@optonline.net.

BIRCHEM, REGINA, cell biologist, environment consultant, educator, writer; b. Sisseton, S.D., Dec. 20, 1938; d. Victor John and Hazel Mary (O'Brien) Birchem; m. Dan I. Bolef, Aug. 29, 1981. BS in Edn., U. N.D., 1964; MEd, U. Ga., 1970, PhD, 1977. Rsch. assoc. U. Ga., Athens, 1977-79, U. Colo., Boulder, 1979-80, Washington U., St. Louis, 1980-81; asst. prof. Fontbonne Coll., St. Louis, 1981-84; vis. asst. prof. U. South, Sewanee, Tenn., 1984; asst. rsch. prof. St. Louis U. Sch. Medicine, 1985-88; assoc. prof. Pa. State U., McKeesport, Pa., 1988-90; assoc. prof. Florence Scott chair in devel. biology Seton Hill Coll., Greensburg, Pa., 1990-94. Coord. Pitts. Beijing '95 and Beyond Coalition, 1995-96; biology cons. Pa. Environ. Network, Yukon; cons. in edn.; cons. on plant tissue culture and plant micropropagation. Contbr. numerous articles to profl. jours. in biology and electron microscopy, environment and peace; editl. bd. Haversack: A Franciscan Rev., 1987-94. Internat. cons., v.p. Women's Internat. League for Peace and Freedom, Geneva, 1989—; credentialed NGO del. to UN Earth Summit, Rio de Janeiro, 1992, UN Conf. in Copenhagen, 1995, UN Conf. on Women, Beijing, 1995, UN Conf. on Human Settlements, Istanbul, Turkey, 1996, World Summit on Sustainable Devel., Johannesburg, 2002, World Social Forum, Porto Alegre, Brazil, 2003. Grantee NSF, 1969-70, 82, 84, 91, NIH, 1979-80; fellow NDEA, 1971-74. Mem. Internat. Assn. for Plant Tissue Culture. Roman Catholic. Avocations: classical music, writing, hiking, local history.

BIRCHER, ANDREA URSULA, psychiatric nurse practitioner; b. Bern, Switzerland, Mar. 6, 1928; arrived in U.S., 1947; d. Franklin E. Bircher and Hedy E. Bircher-Rey. Diploma, Knapp Coll. Nursing, Santa Barbara, Calif., 1957; BS, U. Calif., San Francisco, 1961, MS, 1962; PhD, U. Calif., Berkeley, 1966. RN. Staff nurse, head nurse Cottage Hosp., Santa Barbara, 1957—58; psychiat. nurse, jr., sr. Langley-Porter Neuropsychiatric Inst., San Francisco, 1958—66; asst. prof. U. Ill. Coll. Nursing, Chgo., 1966-72; prof. U. Okla. Coll. Nursing, Oklahoma City, 1972-93, prof. emeritus, 1993—. Contbr. articles to profl. jours. Mem.: NAFE, ANA, AAUP, Calif. Assn. Psychiat. Nurses in Advanced Practice, N.Am. Nursing Diagnosis Assn., Internat. Soc. Psychiat.-Mental Health Nursing, Am. Psychotherapy Assn. (diplomate), ANA Calif., Ventura County Writers Club, Phi Kappa Phi, Sigma Theta Tau. Republican. Avocations: indoor gardening, cooking, reading, yoga, writing. Home: 1161 Cypress Point Ln Apt 201 Ventura CA 93003-6074

BIRD, MARY FRANCIS, secondary education educator; b. Mesilla, N.Mex., July 19, 1941; d. A.D. and Mary Theresa (Veitch) Alexander; m. Willis Monroe Bird Jr., May 3, 1962; children: William Michael, Keith Alexander, Steven Wayne. AA, N.Mex. State U., Farmington, 1977; BS, N.Mex. State U., Las Cruces, 1988. Med. transcriptionist Ctr. for Phys. Therapy and Sports Rehab., Las Cruces, 1988-92; family and consumer scis. tchr. Zia Middle Sch., Las Cruces, 1992—. Bd. sec. Farmington Amateur Baseball Congress, 1977-80; pres. Jr. Women's Club, Farmington, 1979-80; charter sec. Burley (Idaho) Amateur Baseball Assn., 1982-84; chairperson Monument for San Albino Ch., Mesilla, N.Mex., 1992. Recipient Outstanding Svc. award City Coun. and Mayor, Burley, Idaho, 1984; named N.Mex. Outstanding Young Home Economist, N.Mex. Home Econs. Assn., Las Cruces, 1987. Mem. AAUW, Am. Vocat. Assn., Family and Consumer Scis. (N.Mex. pres. 2002-03, N.Mex. counselor 2003—). Avocations: singing, theatre performances, volunteering. Office: Zia Middle Sch 1300 W University Las Cruces NM 88005

BIRDSALL, CHARLES KENNEDY, electrical engineer; b. N.Y.C., Nov. 19, 1925; s. Charles and Irene Birdsall; m. Betty Jean Hansen, 1949 (div. 1977); children: Elizabeth(dec.), Anne(dec.), Barbara, Thomas, John; m. Virginia Anderson, Aug. 21, 1981. BS, U. Mich., 1946, MS, 1948; PhD, Stanford U., 1951. Various projects Hughes Aircraft Co., Culver City, Calif., 1951—55; leader electron physics group GE Microwave Lab., Palo Alto, Calif., 1955-59; prof. elec. engring. U. Calif., Berkeley, 1959-91, prof. Grad. Sch., 1994—. Founder Plasma Theory and Simulation Group, 1967; founder, 1st chmn. Energy and Resources Com., 1972—74; cons. to industry, Lawrence Livermore Lab. of U. Calif., 1960—86; prof. Miller Inst. Basic Rsch. in Sci., 1963—64; sr. vis. fellow U. Reading, England, 1976; rsch. assoc. Inst. Plasma Physics Nagoya (Japan) U., 1981, co-founder computational engring. sci. undergrad. program, 2000; Chevron vis. prof. energy Calif. Inst. Tech., 1982; area coord. phys. electronics/bioelectronics, 1984—86; lectr. Plasma Sch. Internat. Ctr. for Theoretical Physics, Trieste, Italy, 1985—99; joint U.S.-Japan Inst. Fusion Theory vis. prof. Inst. Plasma Physics, Nagoya U., fall 1988, spring 2002; vis. prof. Gunma U., Kirya, Japan, 2003; IPA Airforce Rsch. Lab., Albuquerque, 2002—. Author: (with W.B. Bridges) Electron Dynamics of Diode Regions, 1966, (with A.B. Langdon) Plasma Physics via Computer Simulation, 1985, 91, 93, 2002, (with S. Kuhn) Bounded Plasmas, 1994; patentee in field. Served with USNR, 1944-46. U.S.-Japan Coop. Sci.

Program grantee, 1966-67; Fulbright grantee U. Innsbruck, 1991; recipient Berkeley Citation, 1991. Fellow IEEE (1st recipient Plasma Sci. and Applications award June 1988), AAAS, Am. Phys. Soc.; mem. Sigma Xi, Tau Beta Pi, Eta Kappa Nu. Achievements include being the co-originator many-particle plasma simulations in two and three dimensions using cloud-in-cell methods, 1966. Home: 4050 Valente Ct Lafayette CA 94549-3412 Office: U Calif EECS Dept Cory Hall Berkeley CA 94720-1770 E-mail: birdsall@eecs.berkeley.edu.

BIRGE, ESTHER BONITA, elementary school educator; b. Greenville, S.C., Nov. 29, 1961; d. Robert Wayne and Ruth Evelyn (Bush) Koenig; m. Hubert Lamar Birge, Aug. 2, 1985; children: Travis Lamar, Robert Collin Birge. BS in Elem. Edn., Bob Jones U., 1983; MEd in Early Childhood Edn., Mercer U. Atlanta, 1990. Cert. tchr. Ga. Tchr. 2d grade Cornerstone Bapt. Sch., Stone Mountain, Ga., 1983-90, tchr. 7th and 8th grades, 1992—98; tchr. 2d grade Hebron Christian Acad., Dacula, Ga., 1998—2000, elem. prin., 2000—. Recipient Tchr. of the Year Dekalb (Ga.) County Private Sch., 1994-95. Mem. Ga. Assn. Christian Schs. (cert.), Chrisitian Schs. Internat. Republican. Avocations: sewing, reading, cross stitch, bike riding. Home: 3803 Palisade Ct Snellville GA 30039-6128 Office: Hebron Christian Acad PO Box 1028 Dacula GA 30019 E-mail: letbirge@juno.com.

BIRGE, ROBERT RICHARDS, chemistry educator; b. Washington, Aug. 10, 1946; s. Robert Bowen and Dorothy (Richards) B.; m. Constance A. Reed, Aug. 3, 1993; children: Jonathan Richards, David Porter; stepchildren: David R. Salvetti, Bryan J. Salvetti. BS in Chemistry, Yale U., 1968; PhD in Chem. Physics, Wesleyan U., Middletown, Conn., 1972. NIH postdoctoral fellow Harvard U., Cambridge, Mass., 1973-75; asst. prof. dept. chemistry U. Calif.-Riverside, 1975-81, chmn. com. on research, 1981-82, assoc. prof. dept. chemistry, 1981-84; Weingart sabbatical fellow Calif. Inst. Tech., Pasadena, 1982-83; prof., head dept. chemistry Carnegie-Mellon U., Pitts., 1984-87, dir. Ctr. Molecular Electronics, 1984-87; prof. chemistry, dir. W.M. Keck Ctr. Molecular Electronics W.M. Keck Ctr. Molecular Electronics Syracuse (N.Y.) U., 1988—; dir. grad. biophysics program Syracuse (N.Y.) U., 1989-93; rsch. dir. N.Y. State Ctr. for Advanced Tech. in Computer Applications and Software Engrng., 1992—; disting. prof. chemistry Syracuse U., 1995—, Harold S. Schwenk disting. prof. biol. chemistry, 2000—, prof., 2001—. NATO prof. Advanced Study Inst., Maratea, Italy, 1983; permanent mem. molecular and cellular biophysics study sect. NIH, Bethesda, Md., 1984-89; bd. dirs. West Penn Hosp. Rsch. Found., 1987-88; co-chmn. adv. com. molecular electronics NAS, 1987. Mem. editl. bd. Jour. Nanotech., Brit. Inst. Physics, 1990-2000, Supramolecular Sci., 1993-98, Biocomputing, 1995—; assoc. editor Biospectroscopy, 1993—; regional editor Biosensors and Bioelectronics, 1995-98; editl. adv. bd. The Jour. Phys. Chemistry, 1996—; contbr. chpts. to books, more than 200 articles to profl. jours. Treas. council Carnegie Inst. Natural History, Pitts., 1985-87. Served to 1st lt. USAF, 1972-73 Recipient Chancellor's Citation for Exceptional Acad. Achievement, 1996, Nat. Sci. award Am. Cyanamid Corp., 1964, 3M Sci. award of Can., 2002; named to Time Digital Top 50 Cyber Elite, Time Inc., 1997; Regents fellow U. Calif., 1976. Mem. Am. Chem. Soc. (Rsch. award 1992), Am. Phys. Soc., Biophys. Soc. Home: 137 Forest Rd Storrs Mansfield CT 06268-1126 Office: Syracuse U Dept Chemistry Wm Keck Ctr Molecular Elec Syracuse NY 13244-0001 also: U Conn Dept Chemistry 55 N Eagleville Rd Storrs Mansfield CT 06269-3060

BIRKBY, PAUL DONALD, library media specialist, consultant; b. Camden, N.J., Dec. 6, 1953; s. Fred Charles and Estella Kathryn (Senor) B.; children: Kathryn Elizabeth, Michael Thomas. BA, Hobart Coll., 1976; JD, Rutgers U., 1979; MLS, U. Buffalo, 1992. Bar: N.J. 1980; cert. sch. media specialist, N.Y., 1992. Jud. clk. Superior Ct. of N.J., Camden, 1980-81; pvt. practice Camden, 1981-88; spl. mcpl. pros. City of Camden, 1981-82; freelance legal writer, editor Rochester, N.Y., 1992-93; libr. media specialist Penfield (N.Y.) Ctrl. Schs., 1989—, mem. shared decision making team Scribner Rd. Sch., 1992-96, 2001—. Bd. trustees Penfield Pub. Libr., 1989—, pres., 1994-95. Mem. ASCD, N.Y. Libr. Assn., Rochester Area Sch. Libs. Office: Scribner Rd Elem Sch 1750 Scribner Rd Penfield NY 14526-9785 E-mail: Paul_Birkby@penfield.monroe.edu.

BIRKES, MARILYN, guidance resource teacher, behavior specialist, special education educator; b. N.Y.C., Oct. 26, 1947; d. George and Pearl (Sandel) Weinstein; m. Jerry Alan Birkes, Dec. 29, 1979; 1 child, Beth Elana Fabinsky. BA in Elem. Edn., Bklyn. Coll., 1968, MS in Spl. Edn., 1974; Cert. in Psychotherapy, Alfred Adler Inst., N.Y.C., 1981. Cert. tchr. emotionally handicapped, N.Y., Fla.; cert. psychotherapist, N.Y.; cert. instr. non-violent crisis prevention interventions, Fla.; cert. trauma and loss sch. specialist. Tchr. 1st grade Bd. Edn., N.Y.C., 1968-71, tchr. emotionally handicapped, 1969-90; psychotherapist in pvt. practice Staten Island, N.Y., 1981-88; tchr. emotionally handicapped Orange County Schs., Orlando, Fla., 1990-91, behavior specialist, guidance resource tchr., sch. coord. mental health svcs., 1991—, tchr. workshop presenter and trainer, staffing coord., 1991—. Coord. Ptnrs. In. Edn., Orange County, 1993—; coord. Student Assistance Family Empowerment Com., 1991—. Mem. Coun. for Exceptional Children, Nat. At-Risk Edn. Assn., Fla. Tchg. Profession/NEA. Avocations: reading, collecting art, travel. Office: Rolling Hills Elem Sch 4903 Donovan St Orlando FL 32808-2699

BIRMAN, LINDA LEE, retired elementary school educator; b. Bellingham, Wash., Sept. 2, 1950; d. Ronald L. and Shirley Lee (Smith) Kindlund; m. Steven D. Birman, May 28, 1988; children: Stacy, Michele, Cameron, Colin. BA in Edn., We. Wash. State Coll., 1973; MA in Edn., We. Wash. U., 1978. Cert. elem. and secondary tchr., Wash. Tchr. 2d grade, Bellingham, Wash., 1973—2003; ret., 2003. Affiliated teaching faculty We. Wash. U.; Bellingham, 1992; subject advisory com. Washington State Student Learning Commn. Author Stewart the Skyscraper Falcon, 1997. Mem. NEA.

BIRMAN, VICTOR MARK, mechanical and aerospace engineering educator, academic administrator; b. Leningrad, Russia, Jan. 13, 1950; came to U.S., 1984; s. Mark Samuel and Sima (Pesenson) B.; m. Anna Irene Rabkin, Apr. 9, 1977; children: Michael, Shirley. MS, Shipbuilding Inst., Leningrad, 1973; PhD, Technion, Haifa, Israel, 1983. Engr. Steel Structures Design Inst., Leningrad, 1973-78; grad. teaching asst. Technion, Haifa, 1979-82, rsch. fellow, 1983; engr. Israel Aircraft Industries, Lod, 1984; asst. prof. U. New Orleans, 1984-87, assoc. prof., 1987-89, U. Mo.-Rolla, St. Louis, 1989-96, prof., 1996—, dir. Engring. Edn. Ctr., 2000—. Mem. summer faculty Air Force Office of Sci. Rsch., Wright-Patterson AFB, 1992, 97, NASA Lewis Ctr., 1993-94; vis. scientist Air Force Inst. Tech., 1993, U. Natal (South Africa), 1993. Assoc. editor Composites Part B: Engring., 1991—, Applied Mechs. Revs., 2000—; translator; reviewer profl. jours., 1989—; contbr. rsch. papers to profl. jours., papers to profl confs. Recipient McDonnell Douglas Faculty Excellence award, 1993-94, 94-95, 95-96, 97-98, Award for Excellence in Rsch., U. New Orleans Alumni Assn., 1987; summer scholar U. New Orleans, 1986. Fellow AIAA (assoc.), ASME (composite materials com., structures and materials com.) Achievements include research in mechanics of composite and smart structures, sandwich structures, imperfection-sensitivity, thermoelasticity and buckling of stiffened composite shells, mechanics of ceramic matrix composites; research for Army Research Office, Office Naval Research, Air Force, Air Force Office of Sci. Rsch., NASA, and industry. Office: U Mo-Rolla Engring Edn Ctr 8001 Natural Bridge Rd Saint Louis MO 63121-4401

BIRMINGHAM, KATHLEEN CHRISTINA, secondary school educator; b. Newark, July 29, 1950; d. Charles J. and Mary D. (DiZio) B. BA in History, Montclair State Coll., 1972; postgrad., Syracuse U., 1978-80. Cert. tchr., N.Y., N.J. Social studies tchr. Cath. Diocese of Syracuse (N.Y.), 1977-88, Sherburne-Earlville Mid. Sch., Sherburne, N.Y., 1989—. Coord. standardized testing Blessed Sacrament Sch., Syracuse, 1978-86; mem. policy bd. Cen. N.Y. Teaching Ctr., Syracuse, 1987-88. Tutor Literacy Vols., Syracuse, 1977-78; vol. Everson Mus., Syracuse, 1988-89. Mem. Nat. Coun. of the Social Studies, N.Y. State Coun. of the Social Studies, Ctrl. N.Y. Coun. of the Social Studies, Pi Gamma Mu. Avocations: movies, reading. Home: 108 Wheeler Ave Norwich NY 13815-3574

BIRN, RAYMOND FRANCIS, historian, educator; b. N.Y.C., May 10, 1935; s. Saul Albert and Celia (Markman) B.; children— Eric Stephen, Laila Marie. BA, NYU, 1956; MA, U. Ill., 1957, PhD, 1961. Mem. faculty U. Oreg., Eugene, 1961—, assoc. prof., 1966—72, prof. history, 1972—2001, prof. emeritus, 2001—, head dept., 1971—78. Vis. prof. École des Hautes Études en Sciences sociales, Paris, 1992, Coll. de France, Paris, 2001. Author: Pierre Rousseau and the Philosophes of Bouillon, 1964, Crisis, Absolutism, Revolution: Europe, 1648-1789/91, 1977, revised edit., 1992, Forging Rousseau, 2001; adv. editor Eighteenth-Century Studies, 1974-85; mem. editl. bd. French Hist. Studies, 1977-80, Eighteenth Century Studies, 1999-2002; editor: The Printed Word in the Eighteenth Century, 1984; contbr. articles to profl. jours. Mem. adv. screening com. Council for Internat. Exchange of Persons (Fulbright program), 1974-76. Served with AUS, 1959-60. Fulbright rsch. fellow to France, 1968-69; Nat. Endowment for Humanities sr. fellow, 1976-77, 87-88; Ctr. for History of Freedom fellow, 1992. Mem. Am. Hist. Assn., Soc. French Hist. Studies, Am. Soc. 18th Century Studies. Office: U Oreg Dept History Eugene OR 97403

BIRNBAUM, NORMAN, author, humanities educator; b. N.Y.C., July 21, 1926; s. Silas Jacob and Jean (Bermen) B.; children: Anna, Antonia. BA, Williams Coll., 1947; MA, Harvard, 1951, PhD, 1958. Editor OWI, 1943-45; teaching fellow Harvard, 1948-52; tutor Adams House, 1949- 52; asst. lectr. London Sch. Econs. and Polit. Sci., U. London, 1953-55, lectr., 1955-59; fellow Nuffield Coll., Oxford (Eng.) U., 1959-66; vis. prof. faculty letters and human scis. U. Strasbourg, France, 1964-66; prof. grad. faculty New Sch. Social Research, 1966-68; prof. Amherst Coll., 1968—. Mem. Inst. Advanced Study, 1975-76; guest fellow Wissenschaftskolleg, Berlin, 1986; Mellon vis. prof. humanities Georgetown U. Law Ctr., 1979-81; prof. Georgetown U., 1981-2001, prof. emeritus, 2001—; cons. NSC, Exec. Office Pres., 1978; vis. prof. Ecole des Hautes Etudes en Scis. Sociales, Paris, 1991; chair scholarly adv. bd. Internat. Inst. Peace, Vienna, 1991—. Author: Sociological Study of Ideology (1940-60), 1962; (with others) Sociology and Religion, 1968, Crisis of Industrial Society, 1969, Towards a Critical Sociology, 1971, Beyond the Crisis, 1977, Social Structure and the German Reformation, 1980, The Radical Renewal, 1988, Searching for the Light, 1993, After Progress, 2001; contbg. editor Change mag. of Higher Edn., 1970-74; mem. editl. bd. Praxis, 1986-92, The Nation, 1978—; editl. cons. Patisan Rev., 1971-83. Cons. Giovanni Agnelli Found., 1972-75; mem. Wellfleet Psychohistory Conf., 1970— ; adviser United Automobile Workers, Congrl. Progressive Caucus, 1996—; mem. exec. com. New Democratic Coalition, 1978—, chmn. policy adv. council, 1980-82; mem. nat. exec. com. Dem. Socialist Organizing Com., 1973-77, nat. adv. bd., 1980-82; Mem. founding editorial bd. New Left Rev., London, 1959; sec. com. sociology religion Internat. Sociol. Assn., 1959—, chmn., 1970-74; adviser Democratic Nat. Campaign, 1976, Edward M. Kennedy campaign, 1979, Cranston campaign, 1980, Jackson campaigns, 1980, 1988; adviser, Euro. Socialist parties, 1979—; founding com. Campaign for Am. Future, 1996; Fulbright chair, Univ. Bologna, 1998; Visitor, London School of Economics, 1998; Nuffield College, 2001. Guggenheim fellow, 1971 Fellow: Inst. Policy Studies (sr.); mem.: Am. Sociol. Assn. (coun. 1979—82). Office: Georgetown U Law Ctr 600 New Jersey Ave NW Washington DC 20001-2075 E-mail: birnbaum@law.georgetown.edu.

BIRON, CHRISTINE ANNE, medical science educator, researcher; b. Woonsocket, R.I., Aug. 8, 1951; d. R. Bernard and Theresa Priscilla (Sauvageau) B. BS, U. Mass., 1973; PhD, U. N.C., 1980. Rsch. technician U. Mass., Amherst, 1973-75; grad. researcher U. N.C., Chapel Hill, 1975-80; postdoctoral fellow Scripps Clinic and Rsch., La Jolla, Calif., 1980; fellow U. Mass. Med. Sch., Worcester, 1981-82, instr., 1983, asst. prof., 1984-87; vis. scientist Karolinska Inst., Stockholm, 1984; asst. prof. Sch. Medicine Brown U., Providence, 1988-90, assoc. prof., 1990-96, prof., 1996—, Esther Elizabeth Brintzenhoff prof., 1996—, chair Dept. Molecular Microbiology & Immunology, 1999—, dir. grad. program in pathobiology, 1995-99. Mem. AIDS and related rsch. study sect. 3 NIH, 1991-93; mem. exptl. immunology study sect. NIH, 1993-97, immunology working group sci. rev. Assoc. editor: Jour. Immunology, 1990—94, 2000, bd. editors: Procs. of Soc. for Exptl. Biology and Medicine, 1993—99, sect. editor: Jour. Immunology, 1995—99; editor: Jour. Nat. Immunity, 1994—98, Jour. Leukocyte Biology, 1999—2000; mem. editl. bd.: Virology, 2001—; contbr. articles, revs. to sci. jours.; mem. adv. bd. editors: Jour. Exptl. Medicine, 2002—. Leukemia Soc. Am. fellow, 1981, Spl. fellow, 1983, scholar, 1987; grantee NIH, 1985—; rsch. grantee MacArthur Found., 1991-96. Mem. AAAS (scholar 2002--), Am. Assn. Immunologists (co-chmn. symposium 1990, 94, 95, 96, 98, 99), Am. Soc. Virology, Am. Assn. Immunology (block co-chair nat. meetings 1996-99, program com. 1998-2000), Soc. Natural Immunity (co-chair program for 2001 meeting), Sigma Xi. Office: Brown U PO Box G-B618 Providence RI 02912-0001

BIRRENKOTT, GLENN P., JR., poultry science educator; BS, U. Wis., 1973, MS, 1975, PhD, 1978. Prof. animal and vet. sci. Clemson (S.C.) U. Recipient Purina Mills Teaching award Poultry Sci. Assn., 1992, award Gamma Sigma Delta, 1992, N.Am. Colls. and Tchrs. Agr., 1994. Office: Clemson U Dept Animal And Vet Sci Clemson SC 29634-0001 E-mail: gbrrnkt@clemson.edu.*

BIRRER, MICHAEL FLOYD, school system administrator; b. Kalispell, Mont., Dec. 11, 1945; s. Joseph George and Mabel Priscilla (Poe) B.; m. Carolyn Jean Richmond, June 9, 1972; children: Michael Joseph, Sunny Jane. BS in Edn., Ea. Mont. Coll., 1972; MEd, Mont. State U., 1988. Cert. secondary adminstr., English 9-12, music K-12. Tchr. English 9-12, music 5-12 Fromberg (Mont.) Pub. Schs., 1968-70; tchr. English 11, music K-12 Custer (Mont.) Pub. Schs., 1970-77; tchr. music K-12 Rudyard & Hingham Pub. Schs., Mont., 1977-79; tchr. English 9, music 5-12 Harlowton (Mont.) Pub. Schs., 1979-87; tchr. music K-12 Opheim (Mont.) Pub. Schs., 1988-89; prin., tchr. English 8-12 Froid (Mont.) Pub. Schs., 1989-92; curriculum coord. Poplar (Mont.) Pub. Schs., 1992—. Mem. Mont. Eisenhower Adv. Team, 1997—2002; curriculum cons. Ft. Peck C.C., 2002—. Sec. Vol. Fire Dept., Custer, 1975-77; scoutmaster Cub Scouts, Harlowton, 1985-87; dir. Comty. Orch., Harlowton, 1979-87, Kiwanis Club Choir, Harlowton, 1986-87. Mem. ASCD, Mont. Assn. for Supervision and Curriculum Devel. (dir. 1993-2000, pres. 1997-98). Avocations: hunting, fishing. Home: PO Box 437 Poplar MT 59255-0437

BIRSTEIN, ANN, writer, educator; b. N.Y.C., May 27, 1927; d. Bernard and Clara (Gordon) B.; m. Alfred Kazin, June 26, 1952 (div. 1982); 1 child, Cathrael. BA, Queens Coll., 1948. Lectr. The New Sch. Queens Coll., N.Y.C., 1953-54; writer-in-residence CCNY, 1960; lectr. The Writers Workshop, Iowa City, 1966, 72; lectr. Sch. Gen. Studies Columbia U., N.Y.C., 1985-87; dir., founder Writers on Writing Barnard Coll., N.Y.C., 1988—. Adj. prof. English Hofstra U., L.I., 1980, Barnard Coll., N.Y.C., 1981-93; film critic Vogue mag. Author: Star of Glass, 1950, The Troublemaker, 1955, The Sweet Birds of Gorham, 1966, Summer Situations, 1972, Dickie's List, 1973, American Children, 1980, The Rabbi on Forty-Seventh Street, 1982, The Last of the True Believers, 1988, What I Saw at the Fair, 2003; co-editor: The Works of Anne Frank; contbr. articles to numerous mags. Nat. Endowment of Arts grantee, 1983; Fulbright fellow, 1951-52. Mem. PEN (former mem. exec. bd., former chair admissions com.), Authors Guild (former mem. coun.), Phi Beta Kappa (hon.). Democrat. Jewish. Home: 1623 3rd Ave # 27jw New York NY 10128-3638 E-mail: abirstein@aol.com.

BIRTS, KIMBERLY EDWARDS, elementary educator; b. Norristown, Pa., Apr. 11, 1961; d. Freeman Lee and Bette Mae (Young) E.; m. David Darwin Birts, Nov. 8, 1997; 1 child, David Darwin Jr. BA, Eastern Coll., 1984. Residential supr. Devereux Found., Devon, Pa., 1981-84, North East Mental Health Ctr., Phila., 1984-86; instr. for tellers Penn Savings Bank, Reading, Pa., 1986-88; 5th grade tchr. Reading Sch. Dist., 1988—; 4th grade tchr. Prince George County Sch. Dist., Waldorf, Md., 1999—. Mem. Reading Edn. Assn. (recipient We Honor Our Own award 1991). Democrat. Avocations: reading, writing, working with children, cooking, listening to music. Office: Prince George County Pub Schs Apple Grove Elem 7400 Bellefield Ave Fort Washington MD 20744-3301

BISCHOF, GÜNTER JOSEF, history educator; b. Mellau, Austria, Oct. 6, 1953; came to U.S., 1982; s. Josef and Leopoldine (Feurstein) B.; m. Melanie Boulet, May 11, 1990; children: Andrea Julia, Marcus Christopher, Alexander Carroll. MA, U. New Orleans, 1980; MPhil, U. Innsbruck, 1982; MA, Harvard U., 1983, PhD, 1989. Tchr. Gymnasium Bregenz, Austria, 1982; tchg. fellow Harvard U., Cambridge, Mass., 1984-89; asst. prof. U. New Orleans, 1989-94, assoc. prof., 1994-99, prof., 1999—, assoc. dir. Eisenhower Ctr., 1989-97, assoc. dir. Ctr. Austria, 1997—2000, exec. dir., 2001—02, dir., 2002—, Marshall Plan Professor of Austrian Studies, 2003—. Vis. prof. U. Munich, 1992-94, U. Innsbruck, 1993, 94, U. Salzburg, Austria, 1998, U. Vienna, 1998; founding chmn. bd. Austrian Marshall Plan Anniversary Found., 2000-02, vice-chair, 2002—; v.p., program chair World Affairs Coun. New Orleans, 2002-03. Mem. editl. bd. H-German, Internet Prof. Group, 1997—; co-editor: Eisenhower and the German POWs, 1992, Eisenhower: A Centenary Assessment, 1995, The Pacific War Revisited, 1997, Germany and the Marshall Plan, 1992, Contemporary Austrian Studies (11 vols.) 1993-2003, Die Invasion in der Normandie 1944, 2001, Austria in the Twentieth Century, 2002, Österreich in der EU - Bilanz einer Mitgliedschaft 1995-2000, 2003; author: Austria in the First Cold War 1945-55, 1999; co-editor: 80 Dollar: 50 Jahre ERP-Fonds und Marshall-Plan in Österreich, 1999, Kriegsgefangenschaft im Zweiten Weltkrieg, 1999, Cold War Respite: The Geneva Summit of 1955, 2000. Pvt. in Austrian Army, 1973-74. Recipient Harry Truman Libr. Inst. Dissertation award Truman Libr., Independence, Mo., 1988-89, Jedlicka Dissertation award Austrian Ministry of Sci., Vienna, 1990, Gross Dissertation award Harvard History Dept., Cambridge, 1990, Early Career Achievement award U. New Orleans, 1990, Rsch. prize Haslauer Found., Salzburg, Austria, 2003; Krupp Found. fellow Ctr. for European Studies Harvard U., 1985, 86, Mem. Am. Hist. Assn., Orgn. of Am. Historians, Soc. of Historians of Am. Fgn. Rels., Austrian Assn. for Am. Studies, Harvard Club of La. (sec./treas. 1997-98). Roman Catholic. Avocations: running, crabbing. Home: PO Box 1335 Larose LA 70373-1335 Office: Dept History U New Orleans New Orleans LA 70148-0001

BISH, L. ANN, retired secondary school educator; b. Schenectady, Apr. 1, 1929; d. Howard P. and Vivian (Townsend) B. BS in Edn., Ohio State U., 1951; MA in Edn., Syracuse (N.Y.) U., 1956. Cert. secondary tchr. Tchr. 6th grade Shaker Hts. (Ohio) Pub. Schs., 1952-54; head resident Syracuse U., 1954-56; dean of women Wilmington (Ohio) Coll., 1956-58; dir. women's housing SUNY, Buffalo, 1958-62; tchr. English, Ken-Ton Pub. Schs., Kenmore, N.Y., 1962-91; tchr. devel. studies Schenectady (N.Y.) County C.C., 1993-95. Mem. cmty. adv. coun. SUNY, Buffalo, 1992-97. Mem. AAUW (pres. Buffalo br. 1989-90, N.Y. State pub. policy dir. 1998-2001, state bd. dirs. 1998-2001), Mortar Bd., Pi Lambda Theta, Kappa Alpha Theta. Home: 2280 Cayuga Rd Niskayuna NY 12309

BISHARA, MONICA STEWART, art educator; b. San Antonio, Apr. 6, 1949; d. Donald B. and Mary Louise (Hoch) Stewart; m. James J. Bishara, July 28, 1975; children: James Andrew, Elizabeth Anne. BA, Our Lady of Lake U., San Antonio, 1972; MA, Tulane U., 1974. Cert. tchr., La. Tchr. Ursuline Acad., New Orleans, 1975-95, ret., 1995. Mem. Nat. Art Edn. Assn., La. Watercolor Soc. (pres. 1999-2001), New Orleans Art Assn. Roman Catholic. Avocations: painting, calligraphy, travel, bicycling. Home: 1327 Notting Hill Dr Baton Rouge LA 70810-3631 E-mail: artbyMB@yahoo.com.

BISHOP, BONNIE, principal; b. Cin., June 3, 1947; d. Bedford John and Gertrude (Steinwart) B.; divorced; children: Cary Brandon, Annja-leis Nicole. BS in Edn., U. Ky., 1972; M in Reading, Xavier U., 1980, cert. in supervision, 1992, cert. in adminstrn., 1993. Cert. tchr., Ohio; cert. prin., Ohio. Tchr. St. Bernard (Ohio) Sch., 1972-74, Goshen (Ohio) Sch. Dist., 1985-93; prin. Greenfield (Ohio) Exempted Dist., 1993—. Presenter Cin. Schs., 1991, Clermont Tchr. Rep. for Regional Tchr. Contbr. (newspaper series) Cin. Post, 1980. Bd. dirs. Highland County (Ohio) Domestic Violence Task Force, 1995—; dist. coord. Odyssey of Mind Gifted Program, Greenfield, 1993-95; founder Parent Ctr. for Goshen Schs., 1991. Grantee Highland County Bd. Edn., 1993-94, Excellence in Edn. award. Mem. Phi Delta Kappa. Avocations: reading, exercising, travel, church activities. Home: 329 South St Greenfield OH 45123-1429

BISHOP, C. DIANE, state agency administrator, educator; b. Elmhurst, Ill., Nov. 23, 1943; d. Louis William and Constance Oleta (Mears) B. BS in Maths., U. Ariz., 1965, MS in Maths., MEd in Secondary Edn., 1972. Lic. secondary educator. Tchr. math. Tucson Unified Sch. Dist., 1966-86, mem. curriculum council, 1985-86, mem. maths. curriculum task teams, 1983-86; state supt. of pub. instrn. State of Ariz., 1987-95, gov.'s policy advisor for edn., 1995-97, dir. gov.'s office workforce devel. policy, 1996-2000; asst. dep. dir. Ariz. Dept. Commerce, 1997-2000; exec. dir. Gov.'s Strategic Partnership for Econ. Devel., 1997—2002; pres. The Vandegrift Inst., 2000—; exec. dir. Maricopa Health Found., 2002—. Mem. assoc. faculty Pima C.C., Tucson, 1974-84; adj. lectr. U. Ariz., 1983, 85; mem. math. scis. edn. bd. NRC, 1987-90, mem. new standards project governing bd., 1991; dir. adv. bd. sci. and engring. edn. panel, NSF; mem. adv. bd. for arts edn. Nat. Endowment for Arts. Active Ariz. State Bd. Edn., 1984-95, chmn. quality edn. commn., 1986-87, chmn. tchr. crt. subcom., 1984-95, mem. outcomes based edn. adv. com., 1986-87, liaison bd. dirs. essential skills subcom., 1985-87, gifted edn. com. liaison, 1985-87; mem. Ariz. State Bd. Regents, 1987-95, mem. com. on preparing for U. Ariz., 1983, mem. high sch. task force, 1984-85; mem. bd. Ariz. State Community Coll., 1987-95; mem. Ariz. Joint Legis. Com. on Revenues and Expenditures, 1989, Ariz. Joint Legis. Com. on Goals for Ednl. Excellence, 1987-89, Gov.'s Task Force on Ednl. Reform, 1991, Ariz. Bd. Regents Commn. on Higher Edn., 1992. Woodrow Wilson fellow Princeton U., summer 1984; recipient Presdl. Award for Excellence in Teaching of Maths., 1983, Ariz. Citation of Merit, 1984, Maths. Teaching award Nat. Sci. Research Soc., 1984, Distinction in Edn. award Flinn Found., 1986; named Maths. Tchr. of Yr. Ariz. Council of Engring. and Sci. Assns., 1984, named One of Top Ten Most Influential Persons in Ariz. in Field of Tech., 1998. Mem. AAUW, NEA, Nat. Coun. Tchrs. Math., Coun. Chief State Sch. Officers, Women Execs. in State Govt. (bd. dirs. 1993), Ariz. Assn. Tchrs. Math., Women Maths. Edn., Math. Assn. Am., Ednl. Commn. of the States (steering com.), Nat. Endowment Arts (adv. bd. for arts edn.), Nat. Forum Excellence Edn., Nat. Honors Workshop, Phi Delta Kappa. Republican.

BISHOP, DELORES ANN, artist, educator; b. Balt., May 27, 1946; d. Edward James Boyle, Sr. and Norma Delores Boyle; m. John James Bishop, Jr.; children: Denise Anderson, Christine. Grad. h.s., Balt. Elite, one stroke cert. instr., cert. William Alexander instr. Fgn. lang. lab. asst. Baltimore County Md. Pub. Schs., Balt., 1964—71; asst. mgr. Ben Franklin Crafts, Cockeysville, Md., 1982—99; freelance decorative artist Balt., 1999—2001. Program mgr. Premises Providers, Inc (Arundel Mills Mall), Hanover, Md., 2000. Painted sculpture, The Shopper, 2000, Bushel of Crabs, 2000, Bass, 2000. Holiday vol. Cowenton Vol. Fire Dept. Sta. 200,

Balt., 2000—01; Vol., asst. leader Girl Scouts Am., Balt., 1960—80. Mem.: Md. Art League, Inc., Balt. (Md.) Watercolor Soc., Decorative Painters Soc. Personal E-mail: dabishop@dabitup.com.

BISHOP, JOYCE ANN, director; b. West Mansfield, Ohio, June 16, 1935; d. Frederick J. and Marjorie Vere (Stephens) Armentrout; m. Belinda Lee, Thomas James. AB, Albion Coll., 1956; MA, Western Mich. U., 1969, postgrad., 1972-87. Cert. social worker; lic. profl. counselor. Tchr. phys. edn., health and cheerleading Walled Lake (Mich.) Jr. High Sch., 1956-58; instr. slimnastics adult edn. Milw. Pub. Schs., 1959-65; demonstrator, co. rep. Polaroid Corp., Cambridge, Mass., 1960-81; rsch. asst. fetal electro-cardiography Marquette U., Milw., 1962-64; tchr. phys. edn., health and cheerleading Brown Deer (Wis.) High Sch., 1963-65; instr. slimnastics adult edn., instr. volleyball Lakeview High Sch., Battle Creek, Mich., 1966—. Dir. student activities, asst. prof. Olivet (Mich.) Coll., 1969-71; transfer counselor spl. programs Kellogg C.C., Battle Creek, 1971—; fin. planner Richard M. Groff Assocs., Inc., 1987. Sec. adult bd. Teens, Inc., 1965-68; bd. dirs. Battle Creek Day Care Ctrs., sec., 1984, pres., 1984-86; founder Battle Creek Breast Cancer Support Group, 1996-2000; pres.-elect Susan G. Komen Breast Cancer Found. (S.W. Mich. affiliate), 1999-2000; team capt. United Way Awareness Week, 1984, allocations com. 1985-92; chmn. allocations com. United Way, 1990, 91, 92, 93, United Arts Fund Drive, 1985, chmn., 1986; chair Battle Creek Race for the Cure Survivors, 1996-2000 (You Can Make a Difference award 1999); v.p. S.W. Mich. affiliate Susan G. Komen Breast Cancer Found., 1998-99, pres., 2000—; mem. Battle Creek Leadership Acad. Recipient Master Tchg. award Lakeview Schs., 1969, 87, You Can Make a Difference award Kellogg Corp., 1999, Kellogg C.C. Starfish award, 2003. Mem. AAUW, Mich. Assn. Collegiate Registrars and Admissions Officers (pres. 1979-80, historian 1984-87, hon. mem. 1992), Am. Assn. Coolegiate Registrars and Admissions Officers (mem. com. 1984-87), Am. Pers. and Guidance Assn., Am. Coll. Pers. Assn., Mich. Pers. and Guidance Assn., Mich. Coll. Pers. Assn., Mich. Assn. Women Deans, Adminstrs. and Counselors, Mich. Assn. Coll. Admissions Counselors, Mich. Occupl. Edn. Assn. (Outstanding Svc. award 1991), Mich. Occupl. Needs Assn. (Spl. Needs Profl. of Yr. 1991), Alpha Chi Omega (selected Outstanding Spl. Needs Profl. in Mich. 1991), Beta Beta Beta, Battle Creek Road Runners Club (v.p. 1983-85), Battle Creek Altrusa Club, Battle Creek Host Lions Club (asst. sec. 1994-96). Home: 721 Eastfield Dr Battle Creek MI 49015-3823 Office: Kellog Community Coll 450 North Ave Battle Creek MI 49017-3306 E-mail: porsche_lady@hotmail.com.

BISHOP, LORAINE KELLY, middle school educator; b. Pocahontas, Miss., Jan. 16, 1945; d. Eddie and Elee (Cooper) Kelley; children: Stephanie, Thomas. BA in History, Jackson State U., 1966, MS, 1967, MS in Guidance, 1968, AA in Social Studies Edn., 1972. Tchr. Hinds County Schs., Utica, Miss., 1966-68, Jackson (Miss.) Pub. Schs., 1968—, chair dept. social studies, 1980-94, ednl. specialist social studies. Sponsor student coun. N.W. Mid. Sch., Jackson, 1989, sponsor hist. soc., 1990, sponsor active citizenship, 1990, team acad. arts, 1989; student counselor 1985—. Contbr. to book: Africa and Its People, 1971. Mem. AAUP, NEA, Nat. Assn. of Student Activity Advisors, Hist. Soc., Alpha Kappa Alpha. Democrat. Baptist. Avocations: piano, reading, walking, crossword puzzles. Home: 820 Rutherford Dr Jackson MS 39206-2138 Office: NW Jackson Mid Sch 7020 Hwy 49N Jackson MS 39213

BISHOP, ROY LOVITT, physics and astronomy educator; b. Wolfville, N.S., Can., Sept. 22, 1939; s. Lovett Grant and Florence May (Jodrey) B.; m. Gertrude Orinda Wellwood, June 3, 1961. BS, Acadia U., Wolfville, 1961; MS, McMaster U., 1963; PhD, U. Man., 1969. Asst. prof. physics Acadia U., Wolfville, N.S., Can., 1963-72, assoc. prof., 1972-80, prof., 1980-94. Head physics dept. Acadia U., 1976-83, 86-92, hon. rsch. assoc., 1994—. Contbr. articles to profl. jours. Recipient Gov. Gen.'s medal Acadia U., 1961; asteroid (6901) Roybishop named in his honor, 1997. Mem. Royal Astron. Soc. Can. (pres. 1984-86, editor Observer's Handbook 1982—2000, hon. pres. Halifax Ctr. 1998—), hon. pres. nat. 2001—), Internat. Astron. Union, Can. Astron. Soc., Am. Assn. Physics Tchrs., Blomidon Naturalists Soc. (pres. 1994-97). Avocation: sailing. Home: Avonport Avonport NS Canada B0P 1B0 Office: Acadia U Dept Physics Wolfville NS Canada B0P 1X0

BISHOP, RUTH ANN, coloratura soprano, voice educator; b. Homewood, Ill., Feb. 21, 1942; d. George Bernard and Grace Mildred (Hoke) Riddle; m. John Allen Reinhardt, June 9, 1962 (div. 1975); children: Laura, Jonathon; m. Merrill Edward Bishop, Aug. 16, 1975; stepchildren: Mark, Lynn. BS in Music Edn., U. Ill., 1962; M of Music in Voice, Cath. U. Am., 1972; postgrad., U. Md., 1975. Music tchr. Prince Georges County (Md.) Schs., 1963-71, Yamaha Music Co., College Park, Md., 1971-73; voice tchr. Prince Georges Community Coll., Largo, Md., 1972-75, U. Md., College Park, 1975; profl. lectr. voice Chgo. Mus. Coll. Roosevelt U., 1977-82; tchr. voice McHenry County Coll., Crystal Lake, Ill., 1978-97; instr. voice Elgin (Ill.) C.C., 1981-97; pvt. voice tchr. Crystal Lake, 1975-97, Charlottesville, Va., 1997—; tchr. chorus, music and drama Burley Mid. Sch., Charlottesville, Va., 1997; asst. prof. music Piedmont Va. C.C., 1998—. Dir. music Epworth United Meth. Ch., Elgin, 1984-86, Cherub choir 1st Congl. Ch., Crystal Lake, 1986-88; mem. Camerata Singers, Lake Forest, 1988, Arts Chorale of Elgin Choral Union; performer, vocal dir. Woodstock (Ill.) Mus. Theatre Co., 1983-97; soprano soloist Internat. Band Festival, Besana Brianza, Italy, 1993; pvt. voice tchr., Charlottesville, Va., 1997—. Soprano soloist, Oratorio- The Psalms of David, 1986, opera, The Light of the Eye, 1985-86, Children's Day at the Opera, Washington, 1972, U.S. Navy Band, The White House, 1969; soloist with Crystal Lake Cmty. Choir and Band, 1987-97, 1st Congl. Ch., 1975-97, also others; performer Heritage Repertory Theatre, Charlottesville, Va., 1998, 99. Bd. mem. Opera Soc. Charlottesville, 1998-2000. Ill. State scholar, 1959. Mem. Nat. Assn. Tchrs. Singing (chpt. rec. sec. 1984-86, bd. mem. Chgo. chpt. 1995-97), Music Tchrs. Nat. Assn., Sigma Alpha Iota, Pi Kappa Lambda, Kappa Delta. Methodist. Avocations: travel, camping, hiking, bicycling, wildlife. Home: 1363 Wimbledon Way Charlottesville VA 22901-0635 E-mail: rambishop@aol.com.

BISHOP, VIRGINIA WAKEMAN, retired librarian and humanities educator, small business owner; b. Portland, Oreg., Dec. 28, 1927; d. Andrew Virgil and Letha Evangeline (Ward) Wakeman; m. Clarence Edmund Bishop, Aug. 23, 1953; children: Jean Marie Bishop Johnson, Marilyn Joyce. BA, Bapt. Missionary Tng. Sch., Chgo., 1949, Linfield Coll., McMinnville, Oreg., 1952, MEd, 1953; MA in Librarianship, U. Wash., 1968. Ch. worker Univ. Bapt. Ch., Seattle, 1954-56, 59-61, pre-sch. tchr. parent coop presch., 1965-66; libr. N.W. Coll., Kirkland, Wash., 1968-69; undergrad. libr. U. Wash., Seattle, 1970; libr., instr. Seattle Cen. Community Coll., 1970-91; co-owner small bus. Seaside, Oreg., 1972—. Leader Totem coun. Girl Scouts U.S., 1962-65; pres. Wedgwood Sch. PTA, Seattle, 1964-65; chair 46th Dist. Dem. Orgn., Seattle, 1972-73; precinct com. officer Dem. Party, 1968-88, 96-2000; candidate Wash. State Legislature, Seattle, 1974, 80; bd. dirs. Univ. Bapt. Children's Ctr., 1989-95, chair, 1990-95; vol. Ptnrs. in Pub. Edn., 1992-96. Recipient Golden Acorn award Wedgwood Elem. Sch., 1966. Mem. AAUW of Seaside, LWV of Seattle (2d v.p. 1994-96), U. Wash. Grad. Sch. Libr. and Info. Sci. Alumni Assn. (1st v.p. 1986-87, pres. 1987-88). Baptist. Avocations: swimming, walking, reading. Home: 3032 NE 87th St Seattle WA 98115-3529 Office: 300 5th Ave Seaside OR 97138

BISHOP, WILSIE SUE, dean, nursing educator; b. Lynchburg, Va., Sept. 9, 1948; d. William Curtis and Arye (Holmes) Paulette; m. Paul A. Bishop; 1 child, Joseph. BSN, Va. Commonwealth U., 1970; MS in Edn., U. So. Calif., 1976, MPA, 1987, DPA, 1989. RN, Tenn. Staff nurse in cardiac surgery ICU Med. Coll. Va., Richmond, 1970-71; assoc. instr. Western Ky. U., Bowling Green, 1971-74; clin. nurse 97th Army Gen. Hosp., Frankfurt, Germany, 1974-76; from asst. to assoc. prof. East Tenn. State U., Johnson City, 1978-83, asst. v.p. for acad. affairs, 1983-89, assoc. v.p. for health affairs, 1989-94, dean, prof., 1994—. Contbr. articles to profl. jours. including Pediat. Nursing, Am. Jour. Maternal-Child Nursing; prodr. (videotape) Factors which Promote Successful Breastfeeding, 1978. Bd. dirs. Tenn. Women's Econ. Coun., Nashville, 1998-2002; mem. Gateway Commn., Kingsport, 1996-2001; 2d v.p., fin. com. chair Appalachian Girl Scouts Coun., Johnson City, 1992-94; chairperson Appalachian chpt. Nat. Found. March of Dimes, Johnson City, 1991-92. Recipient Outstanding Nurse Alumna awrad Med. Coll. Va., 1980, Altrusa Hon. for Women and Industry Kingsport Altrusa Club, 1990, A.D. Williams scholarship award for Outstanding Grad. Student Med. Coll. Va., 1978. Mem. So. Assn. Colls. and Schs. (accreditation site vis. 1982—), Assn. Schs. Allied Health Professions (chair edn. com. 2000-01), So. Assn. Allied Health Deans Acad. Health Ctrs. (sec. 1998-2001, 2001-2004), Tenn. Pub. Health Assn., Rotary (Paul Harris fellow 1992). Presbyterian. Avocations: reading, tennis, travel, gardening. Home: 1421 Linville St Kingsport TN 37664 Office: East Tenn State U PO Bxo 70623 Johnson City TN 37614 Fax: (423) 439-5238. E-mail: bishopws@mail.etsu.edu.

BISSADA, NABIL KADDIS, urologist, educator, researcher, author; b. Cairo, Sept. 2, 1938; s. Kaddis B. and Negma Bissada; m. Samia; children: Sally, Nancy, Mary, Amy, Andrew. MD, Cairo U., 1963. Diplomate Am. Bd. Urology. Intern Cairo Univ. Hosp., 1964-65; resident in surgery Babelsharia Gen. Hosp., 1965-69; resident in urology U. N.C. Hosp., 1970-72, chief resident, 1972-73; asst. prof. urology U. Ark. for Med. Scis., 1973-77, assoc. prof., 1977-79; cons. urologist King Faisal Specialist Hosp. and Rsch. Ctr., Riyadh, Saudi Arabia, 1979-87; prof., chief urologic oncology Med. U. S.C., 1987—; chief urologic surgery Ralph H. Johnson Med. Ctr., 1987—2003; vice-chmn. dept. urology Med. U. S.C., 1999—2003; prof. urology U. Ark. for Med. Scis., Little Rock, 2003—, exec. vice chmn. dept. urology, 2003—; chief urology Ark. Children's Hosp., 2003—, dir. rsch., 2003—. Frequent spkr. to regional, nat. and internat. med. groups. Author: Lower Urinary Tract Function and Dysfunction: Diagnosis and Management, 1978; Pharmacology of the Urinary Tract and the Male Reproductive System, 1982; cons., guest editor several med. jours. and periodicals; sect. editor Archives of Andrology; bd. dirs. Internat. Edl. Bd., Arab J. Urol.; contbr. to hundreds of articles and book chpts.; pioneered several significant surgical and med. urologic treatment methods, developed the Charleston Pouch Technique for continent urinary diversion; conducted numerous local, nat., and internat. tchg. courses on urologic reconstructive techniques. Fellow ACS, Internat. Coll. Surgeons (co-chmn. divsn. urology U.S. sect. 1989-91, chmn. 1991-93); mem. Am. Urol. Assn.,, Egyptian-Am. Urol. Assn. (pres. 1990-92), Arab-Am. Urol. Assn. (pres. 1993-96), Carolina Urol. Assn. (pres. 1997-99), Soc. Internat. D'Urologie, Soc. Urologic Oncology, Urodynamic Soc., Soc. Urology and Engring., Sigma Xi. Office: Ark Children's Hosp Mail Slot 840 800 Marshall St Little Rock AR 72202

BISSON, ROGER, middle school educator; b. Biddeford, Maine, Oct. 16, 1944; s. Napoleon and Simonne (Desrochers) B.; m. Janet Elizabeth Gerace, Aug. 9, 1969. BA in Biology, St. Michael's Coll., Winooski, Vt., 1969; MEd in Adminstrn. and Planning, U. Vt., 1991; tech. edn. cert., Lyndon State Coll., 1991. Cert. sci. tchr. grades 7-12, tech. edn. tchr. grades 7-12, prin. grades K-12, sci. and tech. edn. middle grades 5-8, mid. level endorsement Vt. Dept. Edn., 2001. 5th and 7th grade tchr. Sacred Heart Sch., Sharon, Mass., 1964-66; algebra I, French I and II and Latin I tchr. Notre Dame H.S., Fitchburg, Mass., 1966-68; 7th and 9th grade sci. tchr. Meml. Jr. and Sr. H.S., Bellingham, Mass., 1968-79; sci. and tech. edn. instr. grades 6, 7, 8 Folsom Sch., South Hero, Vt., 1979—2002, 8th grade sch.-to-work instr., 1992—2002; 8th grade sci. tchr. Albert D. Lawton Sch., Essex Junction, Vt., 2002—. Mem. info. tech. com. Grand Isle Supervisory Dist., North Hero, Vt., 1985-2002; tech. edn. cons. Alburg (Vt.) Elem. Sch., 1992-2002; sch.-to-work lead tchr. New Am. Sch.-Folsom, South Hero, 1992-2002, sci. lead tchr., 1994-2002; mem. tchr./bus. internship program Vt. Math. Coalition, Montpelier, summer 1994; initiator Electronic Portfolio Project 6, 7, 8, 1994-2002, Student/Bus. Internship Program, 1994—2002; tech. cons. Burlington Sch. Sys., 1996; presenter Nat. Ednl. Computing Conf., Boston, spring 1994, Vt. Fest '94, Fairlee, Vt., fall 1994, Sch.-to-Work Initiative Conf., Burlington, summer 1996, Regional Edn. Television Network Conf., Burlington, fall 1997, Vt. Fest '98 Info. Tech. Conf.; presenter in field. Contbr. articles to profl. jours. Initiator Grand Isle County Networking Initiative, Grand Isle County, Vt., 1991, Grand Isle County Peer Coaching Program, Grand Isle County, 1991. Recipient Sch.-to-Work Initiative Gov.'s Office, 1995, award Lake Champlain Regional C. of C., 1996, Vocat. Edn. award Grand Isle Rotary Club, 1998; co-recipient IBM Test Flight 1991 award, Essex Junction, Vt., 1992. Mem. ASCD, NEA, NSTA, Vt. Edn. Assn., Vt. Sci. Tchrs. Assn., Vt. Tech. Edn. Assn., Grand Isle Supervisory Union (bldg rep., negotiator, grievance com., past pres.), Vt. State Tech. Coun., Vt. Inst. Sci., Math. and Tech., Vt. Info. Tech. Assn. for Avancement of Learning. Roman Catholic. Avocations: woodworking, furniture refinishing, carpentry, computer technology, fine dining. Office: Folsom Sch 75 South St South Hero VT 05486-4913 E-mail: rbisson@ejhs.k12.vt.us.

BISSONNETTE, JEAN MARIE, retired elementary school educator, polarity therapist; b. May 4, 1942; d. Frederick Joseph and Ella Lucia (Michaud) B. B Diploma, Scolasticat Notre Dame, Rimouski, Que. Can., 11961; tchg. diploma, St. Joseph Coll., Cross Point, Que., 1962; BS, Gorham State Coll., 1967; MS, U. So. Maine, 1976. Joined Sisters of Holy Rosary, Roman Cath. Ch., 1957-64. Elem. tchr. Rowe Sch., Yarmouth, 1967-92, Yarmouth Elem. Sch., 1992-95; ret. Edn. coordinator parish ch., Yarmouth, Maine, 1969-71; Cath. Youth Orgn. adviser Sacred Heart Parish, Yarmouth, 1972-73, parish coun., 1991-94, 98-01, vice-chair, 1994-95, 99-2001, chmn., 2001—, mem. parish coun. by-laws com., 1994-95, worship/spirituality chair, 1990-95; cons. Holistic Ctr., Lewiston, Maine, 1982-85; mem. Spiritual Direction, Concordia, Kans., 1985. Author: Oceanography, 1969; Death/Dying for Children, 1985; contbr. articles to profl. jours. Trustee Yarmouth Hist. Soc., 1976; instr. adult phys. fitness Town of Yarmouth., 1979-90; mem. Yarmouth Chem. Free Teenagers, 1985. Recipient Brevet du CJN award Naturaliste du Can., 1963, leadership award Maine Wellness Conf., 1986-90; grantee Maine Oceanography Com., 1970; fellow Maine Coun. Econ. Edn., 1972. Mem. Yarmouth Profl. Com. (chmn. 1973-76), Volksmarch Club (So. Maine). Avocations: canoeing, camping. Home: 54 Anderson Ave Yarmouth ME 04096-8300 E-mail: Bissyland@aol.com.

BITTNER, BARBARA NEWMAN, educational administrator; b. Pitts., May 4, 1931; d. Daniel Stephen and Hallie Harper (Wager) Newman; BA, U. Pitts., 1953; MEd, Fla. Atlantic U., 1966; 1 child, Benjamin J. Lectr. dept. speech U. Pitts., 1953-55; sec. to v.p. Farmers Bank of Pompano, Pompano Beach, Fla., 1956-57; tchr. Hillsboro Country Day Sch., Pompano Beach, 1957-68; tchr., div. chmn. A.D. Henderson U. Sch., 1968-73, dir., 1973—. Mem. Am. Assn. Sch. Adminstrs., Assn. Supervision and Curriculum Devel., Nat. Assn. Lab. Schs. (dir. 1983-84, rec. sec. 1984-85, pres. 1987-88), Fla. Assn. for Gifted, Fla. Assn. Supervision and Curriculum Devel., Phi Delta Kappa, Delta Kappa Gamma. Clubs: Pilot (Ft. Lauderdale, Fla.); Torch (Boca Raton, Fla.). Home: 4420 W Tradewinds Ave Fort Lauderdale FL 33308-4423 Office: 500 NW 20th St Boca Raton FL 33431-6415

BIVENS, CONSTANCE ANN, retired elementary education educator; b. Madison, Ind., June 26, 1938; d. Nelson and Virginia (Cole) B. BS, George Peabody Coll. for Tchrs., now Vanderbilt U., 1960, MA, 1966; EdD, Nova Southeastern U., Ft. Lauderdale, Fla., 1982. Cert. educator. Tchr. Broward County Schs., Ft. Lauderdale, Fla., 1960-61, 65-97, Jefferson County Schs., Louisville, Ky., 1961-62, Ft. Knox (Ky.) Schs., 1962-64, Madison (Ind.) Consol. Schs., 1964-65; ret., 1997. Chmn. K-Adult Coun., Nova Schs., Ft. Lauderdale, 1976-78; cons. 1978-80. Author: Boots, Butterflies, and Dragons, 1982. Mem. Hollywood Hills United Meth. Ch., 1966—, mem. Sing in Chancel Choir, pres. Sunday Sch. class, 1991-94, Walk to Emmaus, 1990, 91-92; active Children's Cancer Caring Ctr. Inc., Broward County chpt., 1986—, Hollywood Hist. Soc., Zool. Soc. Fla. Mem. AAUW, NEA (life), Hist. Madison, Inc., Jefferson County Hist. Soc., Internat. Order King's Daus. and Sons, Irish Cultural Inst., Ft. Lauderdale Lawn Bowling Club, Delta Kappa Gamma Soc. Internat. (internat. expansion com. 1986-88, chmn. internat. program of work com. 1988-90, internat. rep. World Confedn. Orgns. of Tchg. Profession 1989, chmn. S.E. regional conf. 1991, internat. nominations com. 1992-96, chmn. 1994-96, state hdqrs. adminstrv. com. 1997—; 1st v.p. Mu State 1993-95, Mu State pres. 1995-97, Sara Ferguson Achievement award 1990, internat. convention credentials com. 1998). Republican. Methodist. Avocation: travel. Home: 5516 Arthur St Hollywood FL 33021-4608

BIVENS, LYNETTE KUPKA, director; b. Chgo., June 1, 1950; d. Walter Edward and Agnes (Berry) Kupka; m. William Joseph Bivens, Sept. 29, 1973; 1 child, Tia Lyn. BE, Govs. State U., 1990, MA in Math. Edn., 1994; grad., Nat. Staff Devel. Coun. Acad., 1998. Cert. elem. tchr., Ill. Tchr. math. Brooks Jr. High, Harvey, Ill., 1990-97; tchr. gifted OW Huth Mid. Sch., Matteson, Ill., 1997—2000; dir. tech. South Cook Intermediate Svc. Ctr., Chicago Hts., Ill., 2000—. Adj. prof. math edn., Governor's State U., 1998—. Mem.: ASCD, Nat. Staff Devel. Coun., Ill. Computing Educators (webmaster Ill. chpt.), Phi Delta Kappa. Democrat. Avocations: fine needlework, reading, photography, computers and technology. E-mail: lbivens@s-cook.org.

BIZUB, BARBARA L. elementary school educator; b. Newark, Jan. 14, 1947; d. Anthony Edward and Mary Travers Petti; m. William Joseph Bizub, Aug. 27, 1966; children: William Anthony, Melissa Catherine Bizub. BA in Elem. Edn., Kean Coll., 1975, MA in Early Childhood Edn., 1985. Cert. tchr. N-8. Tchr. grade one Roselle (N.J.) Bd. Edn., 1975-76, Title VII reading specialist, grades 1-4, 1976-78, tchr. second grade, 1978-79, kindergarten tchr., 1979—. Cons. whole lang. Roselle Bd. Edn., 1993—94; guest spkr. 31st Ann. Reading Conf./Kean Coll., Union, NJ, 1994; guest lectr. Kean Coll., 1996, 98, 99, 2000, 01; materials presenter 28th Ann. Reading Conf./Rutgers U., 1996; workshop presenter N.J. Assn. Edn. Young Children, 1997, 98, Nat. Coun. Tchrs. English, N.Y.C., 1998, N.J. Assn. Kindergarten Educators, 2003; presenter in field. Co-author: Family Life Curriculum, K-7, 1985-89; pilot tchr. Whole Lang. Initiative, Roselle, 1993. Recipient A-Plus for Kids Grant, A-Plus for Kids, 1994, 96. Mem. Nat. Coun. Tchrs. English (guest spkr. 1994), Internat. Reading Assn., Ctrl. Jersey Tchrs. of Whole Lang., N.J. Assn. Kindergarten Educators (workshop presenter 2003), Ctrl. Jersey Tchrs. Whole Lang., Phi Kappa Phi. Roman Catholic. Avocations: reading, fly fishing, aerobics, cooking, antiquing. Office: Roselle Bd Edn 710 Locust St Roselle NJ 07203-1919

BIZZELL YARBROUGH, CINDY LEE, school counselor; b. Griffin, Ga., June 20, 1951; d. William Emerson and Senora Elizabeth (Henderson) B.; m. Randy Yarbrough (dec. July 1999); m. Cary W. Martin, July 9, 2001; 1 child, Delana Michelle. Student, North Ga. Coll., 1969-70; BA in Elem. Edn., MS in Behavior Disorders, West Ga. Coll., 1993; MS in Learning Disabilities, MS in Counseling and Ednl. Psychology,, 1993. K-12 reading, math., sci. and elem. edn. tchr. Pike County Schs., Zebulon, Ga., 1972—; tchr., counselor of emotionally disturbed Pike County Elem. Sch., 1973—; tchr. of emotionally disturbed and behavior disorders Pike County H.S., 1993—; crisis counselor McIntosh Trail Mental Health Mental Retardation, 1994; counselor Pike County Primary Sch., 1999, Morningstar Family Svcs., 2001. Cons. Alcoholics Anonymous, Griffin, 1982—. Pike County Coun. on Child Abuse, 1990—; lectr., presenter in field. Author: Hippotherapy for the Emotionally Disturbed, 1988; contbr. articles to profl. pubs. Leader, instr. Girl Scouts U.S., Meansville, Ga., 1969-90; co-coord. Ga. Spl. Olympics, Pike County, 1980—; pres. Internat. Reading Assn., Griffin, 1978; asst. leader 4H, 1992-93; substitute Sunday sch. tchr. local Meth. Ch. Recipient Sci. award Ford Found., 1966; named Res. Champion Open Jumper, Dixieland Show Cir., 1989. Mem. N.Am. Handicapped Riders Assn. (presenter), Profl. Assn. Ga. Educators. Democrat. Avocations: horseback riding, showing hunter jumpers. Home: 250 Silver Dollar Rd Barnesville GA 30204 Office: Pike County Schs Hwy 19 Zebulon GA 30295

BJERKAAS, CARLTON LEE, technology services company executive; b. Fergus Falls, Minn., Apr. 17, 1948; s. Jay Oscar and Anna Marie (Bangert) B.; children: Kristopher Scott, Eric Stefan, Todd Philip. BS, U. N.D., 1970; MS, MIT, 1977; MPA, Auburn U., Montgomery, Ala., 1983. Commd. 2d lt. USAF, 1970, advanced through grades to col., 1992; weather forecaster Weather Detachment, Homestead AFB, Fla., 1971-73; flight examiner Weather Reconnaissance Squadron, Andersen AFB, Guam, 1973-75; radar rsch. meteorologist A.F. Geophysics Lab., Hanscom AFB, Mass., 1976-82; chief support br. operational requirements & testing Hdqrs. Mil. Airlift Command, Scott AFB, Ill., 1983-85; chief aerospace environ. requirements Hdqrs. A.F. Systems Command, Andrews AFB, Md., 1985-87; comdr. Weather Detachment, Lajes Field, Azores, Portugal, 1987-89; asst. chief of staff Hdqrs. Air Weather Svc., Scott AFB, 1989-91, dir. resource mgmt., 1991-92, dir. program mgmt., integration, 1992-94; dir. sys. and comm., 1994-95; dir. tech., plans and programs, 1995—; sr. scientist Hdqrs. Air Weather Svc., Scott AFB, Ill., 1995-96; divsn. mgr. Sci. Applications Internat. Corp., O'Fallon, Ill., 1996—2001, ops. mgr., 2001—. Contbr. articles to profl. jours. Com. chmn. Boy Scouts Am., O'Fallon, Ill., 1991-92; coach, referee youth sports, O'Fallon, 1989—; chmn. Sch. Bd., Lajes Field Azores, 1988-89; mem. Sch. Dist. Com., Lajes Field Azores, 1987. Fellow Am. Meteorol. Soc.; mem. AAAS, ASPA, N.Y. Acad. Scis., Acad. Polit. Sci., Air Weather Assn., Air Lift and Tanker Assn., Phi Beta Kappa, Sigma Xi, Phi Eta Sigma, Pi Alpha Alpha, Rotary. Methodist. Avocations: computers, soccer coaching, boy scouts. Office: Science Applications Intl Corp 731 Lakepointe Centre Dr O Fallon IL 62269-3073

BJORKLUND, NANCY MARGARETTE WATTS, music educator; b. Maryville, Tenn., Aug. 14, 1942; d. Charles Burdett and Alma Pauline (Calhoun) Watts; m. Ralph Edward Bjorklund, June 14, 1963; children: James Andrew, Deborah Elisabeth, John Carl. AA, Manatee C.C., Bradenton, Fla., 1964; BA, Stetson U., Deland, Fla., 1964; MusB, Stetson Univ., 1964. Founder, dir. music, pianist First Bapt. Ch., Freeport, Grand Bahama Is., 1964—70; dir. Cmty. Chorus Show Choir, Freeport, Grand Bahama Island, 1964—70. Recipient Crystal Heart award, Girl Scouts Am., 1995. Mem.: Music Spectacular, Pianorama, Fla. State Music Tchr. Assn. (exec. bd. 1993—95, 1993—, pres. dist. 7 2001—), Manatee County Music Tchr. Assn. (exec. bd. 1978—, chmn. Pianorama 1980, pres. 1993—95, chmn. music spectacular 2001, exec. bd. 1983—), Nat. Assn. Music Clubs (chmn. Fedn. Festival Manatee County 1980—), Manatee County Assn. Retarded Citizens, Fla. State Assn. Retarded Citizens. Republican. So. Bapt. Avocations: reading, crewel, swimming, cooking. Office: MCMTA 1912 48th St W Bradenton FL 34209

BJORNCRANTZ, LESLIE BENTON, librarian; b. Jersey City, Mar. 1, 1945; d. David and Jeanne (Proctor) Benton; m. Carl Eduard Bjorncrantz, Aug. 31, 1968; 1 child, William. BA, Wellesley Coll., 1967; MLS, Columbia U., 1968. Rsch. libr. Alderman Libr. U. Va., Charlottesville, 1968-70; reference libr. Northwestern U. Libr., Evanston, Ill., 1974-78, curriculum libr., 1970—, edn. bibliographer, 1974—, psychology bibliographer, 1989—, core libr., 1989-97, mgmt. bibliographer, 1997—. Co-editor: (book) Curriculum Material Center Collection Policy, 1984, Guide for the Development & Management of Test Collections, 1985. Bd. dirs. Internat. Visitors Ctr., Chgo., 1973-76; class rep., fund raiser class of 1967, Wellesley (Mass.) Coll., 1987-92. Scholar Wellesley Coll., 1967. Mem.

ALA, Assn. Coll. & Rsch. Librs. (sec. 1977-79, 85-87, chair curriculum materials com. 1984-85), Am. Ednl. Rsch. Assn., Am. Bus. Libr. Dirs., Spl. Libr. Assn., Phi Delta Kappa (historian NU chpt. 1982—). Avocations: reading, travel, food and wine. Home: 2146 Forestview Rd Evanston IL 60201-2057 Office: Northwestern U Libr 1970 Campus Dr Evanston IL 60208-0821 E-mail: l-bjorncrantz@northwestern.edu.

BLACH, AMANDA CAROLYN W. special education educator; b. Huntsville, Ala., Dec. 5, 1963; d. Harry A. and Margaret Elizabeth (Sims) White. BS cum laude, U. Ala., 1985, MA, 1988. Program specialist Sparks Ctr. for Devel. Learning Disorders, Birmingham, Ala., 1986—; tchr. emotional conflict Birmingham City Bd. of Edn., Birmingham, 1986-87; tchr. mild learning handicaps Jefferson County Bd. of Edn., Birmingham, 1988-89; tchr. emotional conflict Tarrant (Ala.) City Schs., 1989—98; tchr. mild learning handicaps Jefferson County Bd. Edn., Birmingham, 1998—2000; tchr. learning disabilities Hoover (Ala.) City Schs., 2000—. Tchr. Reading and Math Ctr., Homewood, Ala., 1988-90. Mem. Coun. for Exceptional Children, Christian Edn. Assn. Internat.

BLACK, B. R. retired educational administrator, consultant; b. Tampa, Fla., Apr. 6, 1942; s. R.C. and Gladys (Gaines) B.; m. Katy Black, Apr. 2, 1987; children: Amy Christine, Dale Rainer. AA, Marion (Ala.) Inst., 1962; BA, Fla. State U., 1964; MEd, Rollins Coll., 1974; EdD, Nova U., Ft. Lauderdale, Fla., 1988. Tchr. biology, chmn. sci. dept., asst. prin. high sch., 1970-85; supr. MIS, Sch. Bd. Polk County, Bartow, Fla., 1985-86, supr. instrnl. computing, 1986-93, dir. instrnl. tech., 1993-97; ret., 1997; ednl. cons. Instrnl. Tech. Rsch., Crawfordville, Fla., 1997—. Presenter numerous workshops and confs. Author: Trouble Shooting Microcomputers; mem. nat. editl. adv. bd. Electronic Learning, 1989-92. Bd. dirs. Keep Wakulla County Beautiful, 2000—. Capt. U.S. Army, 1964-70. Mem.: ASCD (ednl. futurists network 1989—95), Internat. Soc. Tech. in Edn., Fla. Assn. Ednl. Data Systems, Fla. Assn. Computers in Edn., Fla. Instnl. Computing Suprs. (bd. dirs. 1988—90, state chmn. 1989), Fla. Coun. Instnl. Tech. Leaders (sec. 1995—97, newsletter editor 2000—03), Rotary (pres. 2003), Phi Delta Kappa. Home: 343 River Plantation Rd Crawfordville FL 32327-1517 Office: Instrnl Tech Rsch 343 River Plantation Rd Crawfordville FL 32327-1517 E-mail: blackbr@comcast.net.

BLACK, BARBARA ARONSTEIN, legal history educator; b. Bklyn., May 6, 1933; d. Robert and Minnie (Polenberg) A.; m. Charles L. Black, Jr., Apr. 11, 1954; children— Gavin B., David A., Robin E. BA, Bklyn. Coll., 1953; LLB, Columbia U., 1955; MPhil, Yale U., 1970, PhD, 1975; LLD (hon.), N.Y. Law Sch., 1986, Marymount Manhattan Coll., 1986, Vt. Law Sch., 1987, Coll. of New Rochelle, 1987, Smith Coll., 1988, Bklyn. Coll., 1988, York U., Toronto, Can., 1990, Georgetown U., 1991. Assoc. in law Columbia U. Law Sch., N.Y.C., 1955-56; lectr. history Yale U., New Haven, 1974-76, asst. prof. history, 1976-79, assoc. prof. law, 1979-84; George Welwood Murray prof. legal history Columbia U. Law Sch., N.Y.C., 1984—, dean faculty of law, 1986-91. Editor Columbia Law Rev., 1953-55. Active N.Y. State Ethics Commn., 1992-95. Recipient Fed. Bar Assn. prize Columbia Law Sch., 1955 Mem. Am. Soc. Legal History (pres. 1986-90), Am. Acad. Arts and Scis., Am. Philos. Soc., Mass. Hist. Soc., Supreme Ct. Hist. Soc., Selden Soc., Century Assn. Office: Columbia U Sch Law 435 W 116th St New York NY 10027-7201

BLACK, BARRY MAITLAND, music educator, educator; b. Washington, Dec. 3, 1945; s. Kenneth Henry and Lillian (Winfree) B.; m. Cathy Coffin, Nov. 26, 1977. B.Mus., No. Ariz. U., 1971, M.Mus., 1974. Grad. asst. No. Ariz. U. Band, Flagstaff, 1971-73; band dir. Phoenix Union High Sch., 1973-78, Trevor G. Browne High Sch., Phoenix, 1978-84; founding dir. Young Sounds of Ariz. Jazz Orch., Phoenix, 1975-85; jazz instr./counselor No. Ariz. U. Summer Music Camp, Flagstaff, 1971—; dir. bands Camelback High Sch., Phoenix, 1984—. Music coord. Phoenix Union High Sch. Dist., 1993—. Producer, dir. music albums: Tribute to Poltergeist, 1978, Round Midnight, 1979, Live at the Doubletree, 1980, Soul Collector, 1981; editor: Jazz Arizona, 1990-93. Bd. dirs. Jazz in Ariz., Inc., Phoenix, 1986. Mem. NEA, Music Edn. Nat. Conf., Ariz. Music Educators, Ariz. Band/Orch. Dirs. Assn., Coll. Band Dirs. Nat. Assn., Internat. Assn. Jazz Educators. Republican. Presbyterian. Avocation: golf. Office: Camelback High Sch 4612 N 28th St Phoenix AZ 85016-4999

BLACK, CAROLYN MORRIS, microbiologist, educator, science administrator; b. L.A., July 23, 1957; d. Dock Felton Black and Diane Morris DeBlock; m. Efrain Maldonado Ribot; children: Elise Ribot, Denis Ribot. BS, Iowa State U., 1979; PhD, U. Calif., Davis, 1985. Rsch. assoc. NRC, Atlanta, 1988—90; rsch. microbiologist Immunology Lab. divsn. bacterial and mycotic diseases Nat. Ctr. Infectious Diseases, Ctrs. Disease Control and Prevention, Atlanta, 1989—93; chief Molecular Diagnostic Lab. Nat. Ctr. Infectious Diseases, Ctr. Disease Control and Prevention, Atlanta, 1992—93; chief chlamydia sect., divsn. AIDS/STDs and tuberculosis lab. rsch. Nat. Ctr. Infectious Diseases, Ctrs. Disease Control and Prevention, Atlanta, 1993—99, acting assoc. dir. minority and women's health, 1998—99, dir. sci. resources program, 1999—. Ad hoc mem. NIH subcom. vaccine devel. for chlamydial diseases Nat. Inst. Allergy and Infectious Diseases, NIH, Bethesda, Md.; advisor subcom. on immunologic testing for infectious diseases Nat. Com. Clin. Lab. Stds., Wayne, Pa., 1994—95; mem. organizing com. Internat. Conf. Emerging Infectious Diseases, Atlanta, 1999—; organizer, moderator Forum on STDs, U.S. Medicine Inst./Dept. of Def., Washington, 2001; adj. asst. prof. dept. medicine Emory U. Sch. Medicine, Atlanta, 1991—. Contbr. articles to numerous med. jours., also chpts. to books; reviewer: over 15 sci. jours. Fellow Regent's Grad. fellow, U. Calif., 1982, Earl C. Anthony fellow in microbiology, 1982, Dean's Postdoctoral fellow, Stanford U. Sch. Medicine, 1985—87. Mem.: AAAS, Am. Social Health Assn. (reviewer funding proposals 1997—), Assn. Pub. Health Labs. (mem. nat. chlamydia lab. com. 1998—2000), Am. STD Assn., Am. Soc. Microbiology (chair pub. health divsn. 2001—), Sigma Xi (pres. CDC chpt. 1996—97). Office: Centers for Disease Control and Preventi MS C17 1600 Clifton Rd NE Atlanta GA 30333 Office Fax: 404-639-3199. Business E-Mail: cblack@cdc.gov.

BLACK, CHERYL ANN, special education educator; b. Reno, Nev., Sept. 16, 1964; d. Gale Wolf and Charlene Joy (Holden) Hyde; m. Jess Gregory Black, May 31, 1985; children: Whitney Elizabeth, Lindsay Ann, Heidi Lynne. BA in Spl. Edn., U. Wyo., 1987. Cert. tchr., Wyo. Elem. spl. edn. tchr. Big Horn County Sch. Dist. #3, Greybull, Wyo., 1987—. Primary pres. Greybull ward LDS Ch., 1990-92. Mem. NEA, Coun. Exceptional Children (Outstanding Tchr. Wyo. chpt. 1992), Wyo. Edn. Assn. Avocations: rafting, snowmobiling, bicycling, piano.

BLACK, CLIFFORD MERWYN, academic administrator, sociologist, educator; b. Lafayette, Ohio, Mar. 6, 1942; s. Richard Allen and Ivaloo Mae (Mosher) B.; m. Angelica Hernandez; children: Jonathan Andrew, Marisela, Jose Angel, Carlos Alberto. BA, Adrian Coll., 1963; MDiv, Meth. Theol. Sch., 1966; PhD, Northwestern U., 1972. Cert. clin. sociologist; lic. profl. counselor. Asst. prof. Wilberforce (Ohio) U., 1973-74, The Ohio State U., Mansfield, 1974-78; instr. U. North Tex., Denton, 1978-79, asst. prof., 1979-83, sociology program dir., 1982-83, assoc. prof., 1983-89, chair Ctr. for Pub. Svc., 1984-86, chair dept. sociology, 1986-87, assoc. dean Sch. Cmty. Svc., 1986-88, 91-92, acting dean Sch. Cmty. Svc., 1988-90, prof., 1989-92, Tex. A&M Internat. U., Laredo, 1989-92, dean Sch. Edn. and Arts and Scis., 1992-94, dean Coll. of Arts and Humanities, 1994-96, 96-2001, Webb Co. Tex. Planning Coun., 1996-2001, Webb Co. Tex. Drug Planning Com., 1996-2001, Webb Co. Tex. Jail Case Mgmt. Supervision, 1998-2001, Webb Co. Drug Ct. Supervising Com., 1998-2001; prin. investigator US Dept. Justice/Webb Co. Tex., Laredo, Tex., 1996—2001, 3d Party Payment Com.; dir. Internat. Justice Ctr., 1996—2002; pres. CJUS Rsch. and Program Cons. Internat. Inc., 2002—. Cons. Denton County Sheriff's Dept., Denton, 1984-89; mem. state coordinating bd. com. on Two Yr. Coll. Curriculum, 1986-89. Author: (book) Alternative Sentencing: Electronically Monitored Correction Supervision, 1992; contbg. editor for Clin. Sociology Newsletter, 1983-84; mem. editorial bd. Sociol. Practice, 1984-89; contbr. numerous articles to profl. jours. Pres. Sam Houston Elem. PTA, Denton, 1985-86; trustee Denton Ind. Sch. Dist., 1986-89; mem. United Way Bd., Laredo, 1994-95; active St. Martin de Porres Cath. Ch. Recipient U.S. Dept. Justice award for Rsch. Prgms. for Elimination of Illegal Drugs. Mem. Nat. Clin. Sociology Assn. (v.p. 1984-86, certification bd. mem. 1984-90, nat. certifier 1985-92, nat. program chair for ann. meeting 1984-85), Clin. Sociology Assn. Tex. (pres. 1982-84), Nat. Sociol. Practice Assn. (exec. bd. 1990-91), Nat. Sociol. Practice Assn. (certification bd. 1990-91), Am. Sociol. Assn. (sect bd. 1981-84, sociol. practice sect. sec./treas. 1981-84), Southwestern Sociol. Assn. (chair com. on professions 1983-86), Am. Criminology Soc., Acad. Criminal Justice Scis. Avocations: field archaeology, walking, reading, writing, drawing. Home and Office: 8506 Callow Ct Laredo TX 78045-1983

BLACK, DAVID, writer, educator, producer; b. Boston, Apr. 21, 1945; s. Henry Arnold and Zelda Edith (Hodosh) B.; m. Deborah Hughes Keehn, June 22, 1968 (div. 1994); children: Susannah Haden, Tobiah Samuel McKee; m. Barbara Weisberg, June 20, 1996. BA cum laude, Amherst Coll., 1967; MFA, Columbia U., 1971. Free-lance writer, 1971—; writer-in-residence Mt. Holyoke Coll., South Hadley, Mass., 1982-86. Author: Like Father, 1978 (Notable Book of Yr. N.Y. Times, 1978, One of 7 Best Novels of Yr. Washington Post), Minds, 1982, Peep Show, 1986, An Impossible Life, 1998; (non-fiction) Ekstasy, 1975, The King of Fifth Avenue (Notable Book of Yr. N.Y. Times AP, N.Y. Mag. 1981), Murder at the Met, 1984, Medicine Man, 1985, The Plague Years, 1986 (Nat. Mag. award reporting, Nat. Assn. Sci. Writers award); (play) An Impossible Life, 1998; (screenplay) The Confession, 1999 (Winner Writers Guild Best TV Movie of Yr., Adaptation 1999), (teleplay) Final Jeopardy; contbr. articles and stories to Harper's, The Atlantic, N.Y. Times Mag., others; story editor Hill Street Blues; prodr. Miami Vice; supervising prodr. H.E.L.P., Gidgon Oliver, Law and Order (Golden Globe nominee 1992, Edgar nominee 1992, 99, Emmy nominee 1992, 98, ABA Certificate of Merit 1998); co-creator, supervising prodr.: The Nasty Boys; co-creator, exec. prodr.: Under Fire, The Good Policeman, The Cosby Mysteries, co-exec. prodr.: Sidney Lumet's 100 Centre Street, 1999-2002; exec. prodr.: CSI-Miami, 2003; cons. prodr. Richard Dreyfuss, The Education of Max Bickford, 2002, Monk, 2002; contbg. editor Rolling Stone, 1986-89. Recipient Atlantic Firsts award Atlantic Monthly, 1973, Playboy's Best Article of Yr. award Playboy Mag., 1979, Nat. Assn. Sci. Writers award, 1985, hon. mention for Best Essay of Yr., 1986, Giorgi award, Cert. Merit for excellence in writing, 1998; grantee Nat. Endowment Arts, 1979. Mem. SAG, Mystery Writers Am. (bd. dirs.), PEN, Internat. Assn. Mystery Writers, Authors Guild, Writers Guild East, Williams Club, Century Assn., Players, Explorer's Club, Columbia Club. Jewish/Unitarian.

BLACK, DAVID R. superintendent; b. Albuquerque, Apr. 19, 1950; s. Robert E. and Ethyl M. (Nutt) B.; m. Trudy Rae Letts, June 12, 1971; children: Kasey Ellin, Joanna Kate. BS in Edn., No. Ariz. U., 1972, MA in Edn., 1975; EdD, Nova Southeastern U., 1994. Tchr./coach Ajo (Ariz.) Schs., 1972-75; coach/tchr./counselor Show Low (Ariz.) Schs., 1976-82; prin. Blue Ridge Schs., Pinetop, Ariz., 1983-85; vice-prin. Show Low Schs., 1985-88, prin., 1988-93; asst. supt. schs. Winslow (Ariz.) Unified Sch. Dist. # 1, 1993-96, supt. schs., 1996—. Mem. state curriculum task force Ariz. Dept. Edn., Phoenix, 1991-92; chmn. Winslow Personnel Bd.; mem. state bd. dirs., v.p. Ariz. Schs. Svc. through Educating Tech. Mem. Gov.'s Alliance Against Drugs, Phoenix, 1988-92, Gov.'s Alliance Against Gangs, Phoenix, 1992—; chmn. Parks/Recreation Commn., Show Low, 1982-92, Winslow Parks/recreation chmn., 1995; mem. Ch. Fin. Planning, Roman Cath. Ch., Show Low, 1987; bd. dirs. Am. Heart Assn., 1992; mem. Native Am. adv. com. Johnson OMalley; active La Posada Gardening Angel, 1993-94, La Posada Found., 1995. Named Ariz. Regional Coach of the Yr. Ariz. Interscholastic Assn., 1980, Ariz. Coach-All Stars Ariz. Coaches Assn., 1980. Mem. Ariz. Sch. Adminstrs., Boy Scouts of Am. Eagle Scout Assn., Kiwanis, Phi Delta Kappa. Republican. Avocations: fishing, yard work, golf, educational research.

BLACK, DENISE LOUISE, secondary school educator; b. Ft. Sill, Apr. 16, 1950; d. Nelson Arthur and Virginia Mary (Smith) Taber; m. Robert Paul Black, Aug. 12, 1972; children: Paula Ann, Jennifer Lea. AA, C.C. of Allegheny County, Boyce campus, 1970; BS, Slippery Rock State Coll., 1972; MA, Ea. Mich. U., 1978; postgrad., Wayne State U. Cert. guidance and counselor. Adult edn. tchr. ecology and physiology Huron Valley Schs., Milford, Mich., 1973-74; tchr. gen. biology and earth sci. Howell (Mich.) Pub. Schs., 1974-75; adult edn. tchr. life sci. Holly (Mich.) Area Schs., 1978-80, Hartland (Mich.) Consol. Schs., 1978-86; tchr. biology Walled Lake (Mich.) Consol. Schs., 1988—, Hartland Consol. Schs., 1990-99. Coach, Milford Youth Athletic Assn., 1973-85; leader 4-H Club; Huron Valley Horse Com.; youth advisor Mich. State Rabbit Breeders Assn., 1990-92. Mem. ASCD, Nat. Sci. Tchrs. Assn., Beta Beta Beta, Phi Kappa Phi, Phi Theta Kappa. Methodist. Home: 2576 Shady Ln Milford MI 48381-1438

BLACK, EILEEN MARY, retired elementary school educator; b. Bklyn., Sept. 20, 1944; d. Marvin Mize and Anne Joan (Salvia) B. Student, Grossmont Coll., El Cajon, Calif., 1964; BA, San Diego State U., 1967; postgrad., U. Calif., San Diego, Syracuse U. Cert. tchr., Calif. Tchr. La Mesa (Calif.)-Spring Valley Sch. Dist., 1967-2001, ret., 2001. NDEA grant Syracuse U., 1968. Mem.: AARP, Calif. Ret. Tchrs. Assn., Wilderness Soc., Greenpeace, San Diego Zool. Soc., Sierra Club. Roman Catholic. Avocations: reading, baseball, walking. Home: 9320 Earl St Apt 15 La Mesa CA 91942-3846 E-mail: eblack44@aol.com.

BLACK, GEORGIA ANN, educational administrator; b. DeSoto, Mo., Feb. 3, 1945; d. Walter Vernon and Mabel (Luebbers) Hardin; m. Gary R. Black Sr., Jan. 9, 1965; children: Gary Jr., Nancy, Walter, Kelly. AS, Mineral Area Coll., 1966; BS in Elem. Edn., U. Mo., 1969; M.Adminstrn. and Supervision, Southeast Mo. State U., 1979. Cert. elem. tchr., prin., Mo., supervision and mid-mgmt., tchr. math., Tex. Tchr. 4th grade Sacred Heart Sch., Festus, Mo., 1964-65; tchr. math. 7-8th grades Athena Sch., DeSoto, Mo., 1969-71, Spring Br. Ind. Sch. Dist., Houston, 1971-74; tchr. math. 7-9th grades Cen. R-111 Sch. Dist., Flat river, Mo., 1974-84; tchr. math. 6-8th grades El Paso (Tex.) Ind. Sch. Dist., 1984-91, curriculum and instrn. facilitator, 1993—2000; asst. prin. Clardy Sch., 1991-93; tchr. 7th grade DeSoto Jr. High, 2001—. Sponsor Math. Club, 1990; campaign coord. U.S. Senate Race, St. Francois County, Mo., 1976. Named Tchr. of Yr. MacArthur Faculty, 1989-90. Mem. Greater El Paso Coun. Tchrs. Math. (treas. 1986-90). Avocation: reading.

BLACK, KATHIE M. science educator; b. Albuquerque, Oct. 3, 1956; d. Donald Blaine and Phyllis Ann (Cross) U.; m. Lenny E. Black, May 19, 1979; children: Jeremy J., Joseph L., Kyle E. BSED in Secondary Sci. Edn., U. N. Mex., 1990, MA in Tech. Edn., 1993; PhD in Sci. Edn., U. N.Mex., 1993. Cert. secondary tchr., N.Mex., B.C. Tchrs. Fedn. Tchr., instr. Profl. Ski Instrs. Am.-Rocky Mountain Dvsn., Albuquerque, 1975-95; instr. U. N.Mex., Albuquerque, 1991-93, asst. prof. dept. social and natural scis.; asst. prof. dept. curriculum and instrn. U. Victoria, B.C., Can., 1993—. Instr. Albuquerque Child Birth Assn., Albuquerque, 1980-84; tchr. Albuquerque Pub. Schs., 1988-91. Am. Bus. Women's Assn. scholar, 1988. Mem. AAAS, ASCD, Nat. Assn. Rsch. in Sci. Tchg. (rschr.'s com.), Nat. Sci. Tchrs. Assn., Assn. Tchg. Scis., Can. Sci. Tchrs. Assn., Can. Soc. Study Edn., Phi Kappa Delta. Avocations: alpine skiing, snowboarding, biking, hiking, sports, writing.

BLACK, LORI ANNETTE, academic administrator; b. Tiffin, Ohio, Feb. 11, 1967; d. Marlin Jacob and Mary Jane (Gosche) B. BS, Ohio State U., 1989; MA, Calif. State U., Bakersfield, 2000. Tchr. English and speech Calvert H.S., Tiffin, 1989-96; tchr. English and speech, volleyball coach Lakota H.S., Kansas, Ohio, 1996-98; tng. coord. AFSA Data Corp., 1998-2000; regional program coord. U. Calif., Merced, 2000—. Advisor Sr. Class Calvert H.S., Tiffin, 1989-90, cheerleaders, 1989-91, Nat. Honor Soc., 1994-96; volleyball coach, 1989-98, musical and play dir. 1990-94. Named Tchr. of Month, Student Coun., Calvert H.S., 1992, 94. Mem. Ohio State U. Alumni Assn. Roman Catholic. Avocations: sports, music, reading. Home: 4309 Appleton Way Bakersfield CA 93311-1807 Office: Univ Calif Merced Ctr 2000 K St 3rd Flr Ste 300 Bakersfield CA 93301 E-mail: lablack11@yahoo.com.

BLACK, MAUREEN MCWEENY, special education educator; b. Boston, Feb. 10, 1942; d. Philip Paul and Emma Mary (Dostal) McW.; children from previous marriage: Adam J. McLean, Scott T. McLean; m. Glenn Arthur Black, June 25, 1985. Student, U. Colo., 1962; BA in French, Edn., U. Mass., 1963, postgrad., 1982-84; MEd in Moderate Spl. Needs., Am. Internat. Coll., 1979, EdD, 1993. Cert. tchr. spl. edn., elem. edn., Conn., cert. tchr. secondary French, secondary English, elem. edn., moderate spl. needs, Mass. Tchr. French various sch. dists., Conn., Md., St. Thomas Jr. High Sch., 1967-68; subs. tchr. Dag Hammarskjold Jr. High Sch., Wallingford, Conn., 1970-74; libr. South Hadley, Mass., 1976; instrl. aide spl. needs Northampton (Mass.) Jr. High Sch., 1976; subs. tchr. spl. needs. Chicopee, Mass., 1977-78; tchr. spl. needs Northampton, 1978-87, Bloomfield, Conn., 1987-89, Suffield, 1989-90, Noah Webster Sch., Hartford, Conn., 1990—. Adj. prof. Edn. and Psychology Dept. Am. Internat. Coll. Springfield, Mass. 1989—; intern Shriner's Hosp. for Crippled Children, Springfield, Mass., 1977, Western Mass. Devel. Sch., Westfield, 1977, Goodwill Industries, Springfield, 1977, Substantially Separate Spl. Needs Jr. High Sch., Northampton, 1978, Curtis Blake Child Devel. Ctr., 1989-90; ind. agt. in life skills and personal care, Northampton, 1980-82; tutor life skills for adult population Mass. Rehab. Commn., Greenfield, 1981-82; spl. needs head tchr. Hampshire Ednl. Collaborative, South Hadley, 1980, 81, 82. Vol. Slosson Ednl. Publs., East Aurora, Boy Scouts Am., Chicopee, scout leader, 77; mem. Handicapped Svcs. Adv. Com., Northampton, 1982. Recipient Kennedy Libr. Teaching award, 1989, Profl. Best Tchr. Excellence award Learning Mag., 1990; Carmen Arace grantee, 1988; Phipps Meml. scholar Gen. Fedn. Women's Clubs of Conn., Inc., 1989, Big Y Foods schoar, 1989. Mem. APA, Coun. for Exceptional Children, Orton Dyslexia Soc., Phi Delta Kappa. Congregationalist. Avocations: bicycling, swimming, skiing, racquetball, rollerblading. Home: 994 Overhill Dr Suffield CT 06078-1940

BLACK, PATRICIA ANNE, special education educator; b. Detroit, Mar. 21, 1959; d. William C. and Eileen A. (Droste) B. BS, Wayne State U., 1982; MEd, Ariz. State U., 1989. Cert. in spl. edn. K-12, elem. edn. K-8, Ariz., Mich. Tchr. spl. edn./severely handicapped Chandler (Ariz.) Sch. Dist., 1983-88, tchr. 2d grade, 1988-91, tchr. 3d grade, 1991-92; tchr. trainable mentally impaired Lake Shore Sch. Dist., St. Clair Shores, Mich., 1993—. Avocations: reading, basketball (watching nba), travel. Office: Rodgers Elem Sch 21601 Lanse St Saint Clair Shores MI 48081-1282

BLACK, REBECCA LEREE, special education educator; b. Pasadena, Calif., Sept. 15, 1954; d. James and Mary Black; m. Mario Isabella, Aug. 10, 1996. BA, San Diego State U., 1977, MA, 1987. Multiple subject tchg. credential Calif., cert. specialist credential-learning handicapped Calif., resource specialist. Substitute tchr. San Diego Unified Dist., 1978—80, Poway (Calif.) Unified Sch. Dist., 1978—79; resource specialist Coronado (Calif.) H.S., 1980—. Support provider Beginning Tchr. Support Assessment, Coronado, 2000—02; focus group leader Coronado H.S. Accreditation Com., Coronado, 2001—02. Club advisor Coronado H.S. Friday Night Live Club, Coronado, 1991—2001, Girls' Svc. Club, Coronado, 1980—83, Youth to Youth, Coronado, 1986—89. Scholar Anita Snow Meml., San Diego South County Selpa and Bonita Optimist Found., 2001. Mem.: Calif. Assn. Resource Specialists and Spl. Edn. Tchrs. Avocations: martial arts, golf, softball.

BLACK, RECCA MARCELE, educator; b. Marion, Ind., Feb. 4, 1964; d. Charles Lee and Jerry Ann Barbour. BA in Elem. Edn., Marion Coll., 1987, MEd; postgrad., Ind. Wesleyan U. Tchr. Marion (Ind.) Community Schs.; food svc. worker Marion Coll. Baldwin Food Svc.; casual clerk, cashier, sec. U.S. Post Office; audio-visual asst. VA Med. Ctr. Reporter Marion Newspaper. Contbr. numerous articles to profl. jours. Bd. dirs. YWCA. Recipient Freshman scholar, Shugar scholar. Mem.: NEA, AAUW (bd. dirs.).

BLACK, RHONDA STOUT, special education educator; b. Salt Lake City, Feb. 5, 1960; d. Doyle and Afton Glenna (Nebeker) Stout; m. Richard Terrell Black, Mar. 25, 1989. BS in Child-Family Devel. magna cum laude, BS in Psychology magna cum laude, U. Utah, 1982, MS in Spl. Edn., 1991, EdD in Occupl. Studies, 1996. Behavior specialist, instr. Columbus Community Ctr., Salt Lake City, 1984-85, program mgr. occupational skill tng., 1985-93; rsch. asst. U. Ga., Athens, 1993-96; asst. prof. U. Hawaii, Honolulu, 1996—. Faculty scholar U. Utah, 1980-81; recipient postdoctoral scholarship COMRISE, 1999. Mem. Am. Vocat. Assn., Am. Ednl. Rsch. Assn., Nat. Assn. Vocat. Spl. Needs Pers., Coun. for Exceptional Children (tchr. edn., career devel. divsn. and mental retardation), Phi Beta Kappa, Phi Eta Sigma, Phi Kappa Phi, Phi Delta Kappa, Omicron Theta Tau. Democrat.

BLACK, SARAH JOANNA BRYAN, secondary school educator; b. Port Arthur, Tex., Sept. 30, 1948; d. Foster Paul and Evelyn June (Whetsel) Bryan; m. David Lee Black, Nov. 26, 1971; children: Bryan Joseph, Kelley Allison, David Neal. BA, U. Tex., 1971. Tchr. math. Robert E. Lee H.S., Baytown, Tex., 1971-87, Lee Coll., Baytown, 1987—; tchr. math., chair dept. math. Ross S. Sterling H.S., Baytown, 1987—. Pres. Svc. League, Baytown, 1980; pres. Peter McKenney Soc. C.A.R., Baytown, 1984; treas. PTA of Stephen F. Austin Elem., Baytown, 1984; mem. John Lewis chpt. DAR, Baytown, 1980—, Colonial Dames, Tex., 1980—; treas. East League Little League, Baytown, 1986; treas. Grace Meth. Ch. Women, Baytown, 1985; mem. Cedar Bayou Meth. Ch., 1988-90; pres. Cedar Bayou PTO, 1988; historian Sterling PTSO, 1989. Named Secondary Tchr. of Yr., GCC Ind. Sch. Dist., 1991, 2003, Unsung Hero, Baytown Sun Newspaper, 2003, Ross. S. Sterling Tchr. of Yr., Southwest Bank, 2003; recipient Tex. Excellences award Outstanding H.S. Tchr., U. Tex. Ex-Student Assn., 1993, Seminole Pipeline Tchg. Achievement award, 1995, Unsung Hero award Baytown, 2003, Tchr. Achievement award Southwest Bank, 2003. Mem. Baytown Classroom Tchrs. (treas.), Baytown Edn. Assn., San Jacinto Coun. Math. Tchrs., Nat. Coun. Tchrs. of Math., Tex. Execs. (bd. dirs.), Welfare League, Bay Area Panhellenic (rush chmn.), Alpha Xi Delta (area rush chmn.), Alpha Delta Kappa, Delta Kappa Gamma. Republican. Methodist. Home: 3702 Autumn Ln Baytown TX 77521-2707 Office: 300 W Baker Rd Baytown TX 77521-2301

BLACK, SUZANNE WATKINS DUPUY, psychology educator; b. Farmville, Va., Aug. 25, 1939; d. Edward Laurence and Mary Catherine (Little) DuPuy; m. George Donald Black, June 29, 1963; children: Matthew DuPuy, Edward Purnell. BA, U. Richmond, 1961; MS, Ind. U., 1963; postgrad., Va. Tech., 1985, U. Iowa, 1999. Tchr. social studies Norfolk (Va.) City Schs., 1963-65; tchr. sacred studies St. Michael's Episcopal Sch., Richmond, Va., 1969-78; asst. registrar's office Va. Tech., Blacksburg, 1979-81; eligibility worker Montgomery County Social Svcs., Christiansburg, Va., 1981-85; rsch. assoc. "Va. View" Va. Tech., 1985-86; curriculum cons. Job Tng. and Placement Act Floyd Coll., Rome, Ga., 1987-88; coord., instr. Health Svc. Technician program Floyd Coll., Rome, Ga., 1988-93, asst. prof. psychology, 1993—2003, adj. prof. psychology, 2003—. Workshop leader Shelter for Abused Children, Cartersville, Ga., 1994—; organizer local support group for Adults with Attention Deficit Disorder. Organizer, group leader Disciples of Christ in Cmty., St. Peter's Episcopal Ch., Rome, 1993-95; vol. Good Neighbors, Rome, 1990—; mem. Wednesday Book Club, Rome, 1987—. Mem. AAUP, APA, Psi Beta. Avocations: antique dolls, flower garden, books. Home: 215 N Edenfield Ridge Dr SE Rome GA 30161-8711 Office: Floyd Coll PO Box 1864 Rome GA 30162-1864

BLACKBOURN, DAVID GORDON, history educator; b. Spilsby, England, Nov. 1, 1949; s. Harry and Pamela Jean (Youngman) B.; m. Deborah Frances Langton; 2 children. BA with honors, Cambridge U., England, 1970, PhD, 1976. Lectr. Queen Mary Coll., U. London, 1976-79, Birkbeck Coll., U. London, 1985-89, prof. history, 1989-92, Harvard U., Cambridge, Mass., 1992-97, Coolidge prof., 1997—. Vis. Kratter prof. history Stanford (Calif.) U., 1989-90; guest lectr. U.S., England, Italy, Yugoslavia, Germany, 1976—; ann. lectr. German Hist. Inst., London, 1998; Malcolm Wynn lectr. Stetson U., Fla., 2002; hist. cons. Channel 4 TV (U.K.), History Channel (U.S.). Author: Class, Religion and Local Politics in Wilhelmine Germany, 1980, (with G. Eley) The Peculiarities of German history, 1984, Populists and Patricians: Esssays in Modern German History, 1987; co-editor: (with R.J. Evans) The German Bourgeoisie, 1991, Marpingen: Apparitions of the Virgin Mary in Bismarckian Germany, 1993 (Am. Hist. Assn. prize best book), The Long Nineteenth Century: A History of Germany, 1780-1918, 1998, 2d edit., 2003; mem. editl. bd. Past and Present, 1988—; numerous appearances on Brit. Broadcasting Sys., 1977—; contbr. articles to profl. jours. Gov. Goodrich Sch., London, 1983—86. Rsch. fellow Jesus Coll., Cambridge, 1973-76, Inst. European History, Mainz, Germany, 1974-75, Alexander von Humboldt Found. fellow, 1984-85, John Simon Guggenheim Meml. Found. fellow, 1994-95; German Acad. Exch. grantee, 1977. Fellow: Royal Hist. Soc.; mem.: Am. Hist. Assn. (com. on honorary foreign membership 2001—, pres. conf. group on ctrl. European history 2003), German History Soc. (sec. 1979—81, com. 1981—86), Inst. European History Mainz (adv. bd. 1995—), German Hist. Inst. (acad. adv. bd. 1983—92). Avocations: writing, reading, jazz, politics, classical music. E-mail: dgblackb@fas.harvard.edu.

BLACKBURN, JOHN D(AVID), legal educator, lawyer; b. Connersville, Ind., Dec. 19, 1949; s. James Edwin and Julia Jane (Hubbard) B.; m. Vitalia Berezina, Oct. 29, 1999; children— Jennifer Anne, Melissa Christine. B.S., Ind. State U., 1971; J.D., U. Cin., 1974. Bar: Ohio 1974. Instr. bus. adminstrn. U. Cin., 1974-75; asst. prof. bus. Ohio State U., Columbus, 1975-80, assoc. prof., 1981— ; vis. asst. prof. U. Pa., Phila., 1980-81, Ind. U., Bloomington, summer 1980; vis. assoc. prof. U. Fla., Gainesville, 2002. Author (with Elliot I. Klayman and Martin H. Malin): Legal Environment of Business, 8th edit. 2003; (with Julius Getman) Labor Relations: Law, Practice, and Policy, 1983; author (with others): Modern Business Law, 3d edit., 1990, Law and Business, 1987; (with Jack Steiber) Protecting Unorganized Employees Against Unjust Discharge, 1984; editor-in-chief: Jour. Legal Studies Edn., 1990-92, Am. Bus. Law Jour., 1986-89. Mem. Am. Bus. Law Assn. (best article award 1980). E-mail: blackburn.3@osu.edu. Home: 382 E Sycamore St Columbus OH 43206-2278 Office: Ohio State Univ 2100 Neil Ave Columbus OH 43210

BLACKBURN, LOU JEAN, elementary school educator; b. Roy, Utah, Mar. 20, 1928; d. Lionel Earl and Mavis Fern (Johnston) Gibby; m. Oriel Dale Blackburn, June 10, 1949 (div. June 1964); children: Michael Dale, Diane Taylor, Terry Kent, Kirk Lee. Student, Weber State Coll., 1946-48, Utah State U., 1948-49, BS, 1964. Cert. elem. tchr. Tchr. Taylor Sch., Ogden, Utah, 1964-67, Grandview Sch., Ogden, 1967-84, Wasatch Sch., Ogden, 1984—. Asst. prin. Wasatch Sch., Ogden, 1990-91; cons. Houghton Mifflin Math., 1983, Tchr. Acad. Weber State U., 1989-90. Del. Rep. State Conv., Ogden, 1969. Mem. NEA, Utah Edn. Assn., Utah Coun. Internat. Reading Assn. (treas. 1989-91, pres., named Reading Tchr. of Yr. 1990), Delta Kappa Gamma (state treas. 1985-87,Ogden treas. 1988-91, Ogden v.p. 1974-76, 78-80, 82-84, Ogden sec. 1972-73). Mem. Lds Ch. Avocations: reading, sewing, crafts, making reading and math games.

BLACKBURN, MICHAEL LYNN, athletic administrator; b. Kokomo, Ind., Jan. 19, 1950; s. Everett Leroy and Virginia Blanche (Cagle) B.; m. Brenda Lou Overman, Aug. 22, 1970; children: Ryan Everett, Michael Scott, Amy Lynn. BS, Ind. State U., 1972, EdS, 2002; MS, St. Francis Coll., 1975. Cert. tchr. U.S. history, sociology, geography, phys. edn., health, driver edn. Tchr. U.S. history, coach Caston Jr.-Sr. H.S., Fulton, Ind., 1972-74; tchr. U.S. history, health, phys. edn., driver edn., coach Cen. Noble Jr.-Sr. H.S., Albion, Ind., 1974-77; dir. athletics Northwestern Sr. H.S., Kokomo, Ind., 1977—. Presenter Nat. Conf. workshop, 1992, 96, 97, 2000. Contbr. articles to profl. jours. Recipient Charles F. Maus award Ind. H.S. Ofcls. Assn., 1987, Nat. Fedn. citation award, 1998; named Ind. Adminstr. of Yr., Ind. Assn. of Ednl. Office Pers., 1992-93. Mem. Nat. Interscholastic Athletic Adminstrs. Assn. (cert. master athletic adminstr., publs. com. 1993—, cert. instr. leadership tng. program, Disting. Svc. award 2000, State Merit award 1997), Nat. Fedn. Interscholastic Coaches Edn. Program (cert. instr.), Ind. H.S. Athletic Assn. (bd. dirs. 1995—, exec. com. v.p. bd. dirs. 1999-2000, vice chmn. exec. com. 2000—), Ind. Interscholastic Athletic Adminstrs. Assn. (1st and 2d v.p., membership chmn. 1991-94, pres. 1994-95, Outstanding Membership Chmn. 1990-91), Nat. Coun. Secondary Sch. Athletic Dirs. (Midwest Athletic Dir. Yr. 1997), Nat. Assn. Sports and Phys. Edn., Phi Delta Kappa, Phi Alpha Phi. Republican. Mem. Society Of Friends. Avocations: woodworking, boating. Office: Northwestern Sr HS 3431 N 400 W Kokomo IN 46901-9107

BLACKLEDGE, DAVID WILLIAM, retired academic administrator; b. Cin., Mar. 10, 1930; s. William Clinton and Helen Louise (Van Curen) B.; m. Diana Marjorie Wiley, June 5, 1953; children: David Noel, William Dean, Alan Keith, Naomi Karen. BS, Purdue U., 1953; MA, Rutgers U., 1965; grad., Nat. War Coll., 1975. Commd. 2d lt. U.S. Army, 1953, advanced through grades to col., 1974; asst. prof. mil. sci. Rutgers U., New Brunswick, N.J., 1961-64; instr. Am. history U. Md.-Far East Divsn., Bangkok, 1967-68; dir. nat. security studies U.S. Army War Coll., Carlisle, Pa., 1978-83; dir. fin. aid Pa. State U. Dickinson Sch. Law, Carlisle, 1983-94, dir. admissions and fin. aid, 1984-94, exec. asst. to the dean, 1994-2000; ret., 2000. Co-compiler: Blackledges in America: A Genealogy of Blackledge/Blacklidge Descendants with Roots in the USA, 2002. Bd. dirs. Carlisle area United Way, 1983-86, Sarah Todd Retirement Home, Carlisle, 1989-95. Decorated Legion of Merit with oak leaf cluster. Mem. Rotary. E-mail: dvb4@psu.edu.

BLACKMON, RONALD H. biologist, science educator; b. Phila., Sept. 26, 1953; s. Henry L. and Lillian Rayford Blackmon. BS, Del. State U., 1980; MS, Howard U., 1985, PhD, 1988. Postdoctoral rsch. assoc. USDA-Insect Attractants, Behavior/Basic Biology Rsch. Lab., Gainesville, Fla., 1988-89; asst. prof. Elizabeth City State U., 1989-94, assoc. prof., 1994-96, prof., 1996—, chmn., 1995—2002, interim dean sch. math sci. tech., 2002—. Mem. acad. ops. com. Program for Minority Advancement in Biomolecular Scis., Chapel Hill, N.C., 1991—; mem. Historically Minority Univs. program adv. bd. N.C. Biotech. Ctr., Research Triangle Park, N.C., 1997—. Mem. adv. bd. State Employees' Credit Union, Elizabeth City, 1999. Recipient Biotech. Leadership award N.C. Inst. for Minority Econ. Devel., Durham, N.C., 1993. Mem. AAAS, Soc. for In Vitro Biology, N.C. Acad. Sci., Sigma Xi. Avocations: reading science fiction, piano. Office: Elizabeth City State Univ ECSU Campus Box 970 Elizabeth City NC 27909 Fax: 252-335-3697. E-mail: blackmrh@hotmail.com.

BLACKSHEAR, HELEN FRIEDMAN, retired educator; b. Tuscaloosa, Ala., June 5, 1911; d. Samuel and Annie Laurie (Longshore) Friedman; m. William Mitchell Blackshear, Apr. 21, 1934 (dec. Sept. 1986); children: Anne Spragins-Harmuth, Sue Blackshear-Bowen, Helen M. Stevenson. BA, Agnes Scott Coll., 1931; MA, U. Ala., Tuscaloosa, 1932. Visitor social work Child Welfare Dept., Ala., 1937-39; English tchr. Montgomery County, Ala., 1942-73. Author: Robert Loveman, Belated Romanticist, 1932, Mother Was A Rebel, 1973, Southern Smorgasbord, 1974, Creek Captives and Other Alabama Stories, 1975 (poems) Along Alabama Roads, 1982, (poems) And Time Remembered, 1987, Alabama Album, 2000, These I Will Keep, 2001, From Peddler to Philanthropist, The Friedman Story, 2002, Silver Songs, 2002, Sidney Lanier, 2003. Named Poet of Yr. Ala. State Poetry Soc., 1985. Mem. Ala. Writers Conclave (pres. 1985-87), Ala. State Poetry Soc. (treas. 1980-82), Nat. League Am. Penwomen (pres. Montgomery br. 1982-84), Creative Writers Montgomery (v.p. 1978-80), Art Coun. Montgomery (sec. 1983-88, poet laureate, Ala., 1995-98) Avocations: swimming, golf, reading, research, writing. Home: 9570 Bee Branch Rd Cottondale AL 35453

BLACKSTON, BARBARA JEAN, dean; b. Camden, N.J., Jan. 11, 1944; d. Allen Maxie and Phyllis Irene (Armstrong) Kee; m. Claude Anthony Kellam, Feb. 2, 1963 (div. June 1972); children: Claude Anthony Jr., Derrick Laeon, Debra Lynn Kellam Elshaikh; m. Harry Henry Blackston, Aug. 23, 1986. BA in Theology, United Christian Coll., Wilmington, Del., 1987; AA in Christian Ministry, Geneva Coll., Beaver Falls, Pa., 1992, BS in Urban Ministry Mgmt., 1994. Ordained to ministry, 1994. Clerk-typist II New Castle County Prothonotary's Office, Wilmington, Del., 1969-80; dep. sheriff New Castle County Sheriffs Dept., Wilmington, Del., 1980-90; substitute tchr. Smyrna (Del.) Sch. Dist., 1994—, Appoquinimink Sch. Dist., Middletown, 1994—. Bible class tchr. Faith Unity Fellowship Ministries, Millington, Md., 1994—, ministerial and adminstrv. bd., 1994—. Author: (book) Developing A Bible Institute, 1992. Mem. cmty. group Say No To Drugs, Middletown, 1988; coord. seminars Neighborhood House, Middletown, 1993-94. Recipient award for outstanding achievements with Sunday sch. Trinity A.M.E. Ch., 1993. Avocations: reading, bowling, singing, attending seminars, piano. Home: PO Box 386 Middletown DE 19709-0386 Office: Fellowship Bibl Theol Inst Box 31850 Millington MD 21651

BLACKWELL, CAMELLIA ANN, art educator; b. Balt., Feb. 21, 1949; BS, Morgan State U., Balt.; MFA, MEd, Md. Inst. Coll. Art, Balt.; U. Md., U. Maryland. Art dir., asst. art dir. McKeldin Ctr., lectr. art dept. Morgan State U., 1971-76, art dir. McKeldin Ctr., 1976-81; assoc. prof. Bowie (Md.) State Coll., 1981-83; mus. specialist Smithsonian Instn., Washington, 1984, dir. mus. publs., 1984-88; asst. prof. Howard U., Washington, 1988-89; assoc. prof. Prince George's C.C., Largo, Md., 1989-91; artist-in-residence Montpelier Cultural Arts Ctr., Laurel, Md., 1991-97; prof. U. D.C., Washington, 1991-95; exec. dir. Internat. Ctr. for Artistic Devel. Inc., 1991—; art specialist Montgomery County Pub. Schs., 1993—. Panelist individual artists' grants Indpls. Arts Commn., 1991; del. U.S./USSR Emerging Leaders Summit-Russia, Kazakhstan, 1990; art cons. to Cultural Ctr. of Nagyatad, Hungary, 1994, 95; owner art studio, gallery and gift shop, Historic Savage Mill, Savage, Md., 1997—. One-women shows include Blackwell Home Gallery, Balt., 1974-77, U. Ife, Ile-Ife, Nigeria, 1979, McCrillis Gardens Gallery, Bethesda, Md., 1991, Johns Hopkins Space Sci. Telescope Inst., 1992, State Fine Arts Mus. of Almaty, Kazakhstan, 1993, Howard C.C., 1996, Montpelier Cultural Art Ctr., 1996; exhibited in group shows The Finnish Sch. Design, Finland, 1977, Chgo. Southside Community Art Ctr., 1991, Museu Da Gravura Cidade De Curitiba, Brazil, 1991, McCrillis Gardens Gallery, Bethesda, 1991, Katzenstein Gallery, Balt., 1991, The Print Club, Phila., 1991, James E. Lewis Mus. Art, Balt, 1992, Montpelier Cultural Arts Ctr., Morgan State U., Balt., 1992; executed mural Howard County Rehab. Ctr., Columbia, Md., 1996. Recipient Jurors' Choice award Md. Fedn. Art, Annapolis, 1977, NEA Grant to African Am. Mus. Assn. Conf., 1984, Merit award-design Printing Industries of Commonwealth of Va., 1985, First Pl. in Design, Printing Industries of Met. Washington, 1986, Best in Category Printing Industries of Md. Ann. Competition, 1987, Robert Rauschenberg's Learning Disabilities Workshop award, 1995; print selected to travel to the Belgium Congo Embassy, 1996; named Outstanding Advisor to Art League, Prince George's C.C., 1990; grantee to direct students to design and produce a mural for the Md. Sci. Ctr., Balt., Montgomery County Pub. Schs., 1996. Mem. Nat. Art Edn. Assn., The Smithsonian, Md. Printmakers, So. Graphics Coun., Nat. Mus. Native Americans, Assn. Am. Museums, African Am. Museums Assn., Balt. Mus. Art, Walters Art Gallery, U. Md. Alumni Assn., Md. Inst. Coll. Art Alumni Assn., Morgan State U. Alumni Assn., Lake Clifton/Ea. High Sch. Alumni Assn. Home and Office: 6001 Jamina Downs Columbia MD 21045-3819

BLACKWELL, CAROL DIANE, special education educator; b. Sulpher Springs, Tex., Feb. 2, 1948; d. Luther Curtis and Era Immogene (Cave) Canaday; m. Robert Duncan Blackwell, Mar. 23, 1968; 1 child, Christopher. BS, East Tex. State U., 1970, MEd, 1976. Cert. tchr. elem. mentally retarded, lang. and/or learning disabled and physically handicapped, Tex.; cert. profl. ednl. diagnostician, Tex. Tchr. Richardson (Tex.) Sch. Dist., 1971-73, tchr. spl. edn., 1973—. Chairperson Spl. Edn. Team, Richardson, 1976—; contact person Learner Support Program, Richardson, 1990-92; mem. core team Site-Based Mgmt., Richardson, 1987—. Block chairperson Am. Heart Assn., Dallas, 1989; vol. Meals on Wheels program Presbyn Ch., Plano, Tex., 1985, dir. Christmas Toys for Itasca Children's Home program, 1986; life mem. Tex. PTA, Richardson PTA. Scholarship recipient Assn. for Retarded Citizens, 1974, City Coun. of Richardson PTA, 1992. Mem. Assn. for Children with Learning Disabilities (Award of Recognition 1985), Assn. Tex. Profl. Educators, Richardson Edn. Assn., Alpha Delta Kappa. Democrat. Avocation: collecting antiques. Home: 608 Horton St Quitman TX 75783-2514

BLACKWELL, JACQUELINE PFLUGHOEFT, school district administrator; b. Milw., Oct. 31, 1936; d. Arthur Karl and Lucille Henrietta (Kraft) Pflughoeft; m. Clifton Blackwell, Aug. 6, 1955; children: Arthur, Clifton, Jeanne, Corwyn. Student, Mount Senario Coll., Ladysmith, Wis., 1966; BA, San Jose State U., 1969, MA, 1972, MS, 1989; postgrad., Pacific Grad. Sch. Psychology, Palo Alto, Calif., 1986—. Lic. sch. psychologist, Calif., U.S. Tchr. San Jose Unified Sch. Dist., 1970-83, psychologist, 1983-86, dir. spl. edn. and psychol. schs., 1986-90, prin., 1990-94, dir. student svcs., 1994—. Author: District Student Behavior Handbook, District Special Education Guidebook. With WAC-U.S. Army, 1954-55. Mem. Am. Psychol. Assn., Calif. Psychol. Assn., San Jose Tchrs. Assn. (bd. dirs. 1979-83).

BLACKWELL, THOMAS T. leadership educator, consultant; b. Jackson, Mich., Aug. 8, 1948; s. Thomas and Maria (Joyner) B. BA, Spring Arbor Coll., 1973; MA, Ea. Mich. U., 1976, MA, 1978; PhD, Golden State U., 1986. Dept. chair Willow Community, Ypsilanti, Mich., 1973—; instr. Washtenaw C.C., Ypsilanti, 1984—, Wayne County C.C., Taylor, Mich., 1988-89; cons. basketball team Ea. Mich. U., Ypsilanti, 1986—. Pres. IMPEL, Ypsilanti, 1978—, chmn. bd. dirs., 1992. Author: Hierarchy of Achievement, 1990, Junior High-Good Grief, 1991, Grow By Thinking Successfully, 1992, The Quest for Certainty, 1992, Increasing your OE, 1993, Restructuring: Methods and Models, 1995. Fundraising chair Meals on Wheels, Ypsilanti, 1990. Mem. Profl. Speakers Assn. Mich. (exec. bd. 1984-88), Mich. Coun. Social Studies (awards chair 1980), Ypsilanti Area Jaycees (leadership chair 1980), Ypsilanti Minority Bus. Owners (human resources com. 1988). Home and Office: IMPEL 1122 Lori St Ypsilanti MI 48198-6294

BLACKWOOD, LOIS ANNE, elementary education educator; b. Denver, Sept. 18, 1949; d. Randolph William and Eloise Anne (Green) Burchett; m. Clark Burnett Blackwood, June 26, 1971; children: Anna Colleen, Courtney Brooke. BA, Pacific U., 1971; MA, U. Colo., 1997. Tchr. Forest Grove (Oreg.) Pub. Schs., 1971-72, Clarksville (Tenn.) Pub. Schs., 1972-73, Dept. of Defense Schs., Frankfurt, Germany, 1973-76, St. Vrain Valley Schs., Longmont, Colo., 1977—, presenter insvcs. and symposia, 1977-97, also tchr. of tchrs. Cons. Brush Pub. Schs., 1985; presenter U. No. Colo. Symposium, 1987, Greater San Diego Math. Conf., 1992-99, rural math. connections project U. Colo., 1992-94, So. sect. Calif. Coun. Math. Tchrs., 1992-98; cons. Brighton Pub. Schs., 2000-01. Recipient sustained superior svc. award U.S. Army, Frankfurt, 1975, outstanding performance award, 1976; Presdl. award for excellence in math. tchg. State of Colo., 1991, 94, Outstanding Elem. Math. Tchr. award Colo. Coun. Tchrs. Math., 1993; named Outstanding Tchr. of Yr., Longmont Area C. of C., 1992. Mem. NEA, Colo. Edn. Assn., St. Vrain Valley Tchrs. Assn., Phi Delta Kappa. Republican. Avocations: water and snow skiing, camping, tennis, family activities. Home: 1175 Winslow Cir Longmont CO 80501-5225 Office: Cen Elem Sch 1020 4th Ave Longmont CO 80501-5356 E-mail: clblackwood@hotmail.com.

BLADE, MELINDA KIM, archaeologist, educator, researcher; b. Jan. 12, 1952; d. George A. and Arline A. M. (MacLeod) B. BA, U. San Diego, 1974, MA in Tchg., MA, 1975, EdD, 1986. Cert. secondary tchr., Calif.; cert. C.C. instr., Calif.; registered profl. historian, Calif. Instr. Coronado Unified Sch. Dist., Calif., 1975-76; head coach women's basketball U. San Diego, 1976-78; instr. Acad. of Our Lady of Peace, San Diego, 1976—, chmn. social studies dept., 1983—, counselor, 1984-92, co-dir. student activities, 1984-87, coord. advanced placement program, 1986-95, dir. athletics, 1990. Mem. archaeol. excavation team U. San Diego, 1975—, hist. researcher, 1975—; lectr., 1981—. Author hist. reports and rsch. papers; editor U. San Diego publs. Vol. Am. Diabetes Assn., San Diego, 1975—; coord. McDonald's Diabetes Bike-a-thon, San Diego, 1977-78; bd. dirs. U. San Diego Sch. Edn. Mem. ASCD, Nat. Coun. Social Studies, Calif. Coun. Social Studies, Soc. Bibl. Archeology, Assn. Scientists and Scholars, Internat. for Shroud of Turin, Medieval Acad. Am., Medieval Assn. Pacific, Am. Hist. Assn., Register of Profl. Archaeologists, San Diego Hist. Soc., Phi Alpha Theta (sec.-treas. 1975-77), Phi Delta Kappa. Office: Acad Our Lady of Peace 4860 Oregon St San Diego CA 92116-1340

BLADEL, RITA CATHERINE, mathematics educator; b. Bronx, N.Y., Feb. 8, 1949; d. John Vincent and Anna Elizabeth (Rapp) Donaldson; m. John Thomas Bladel, July 3, 1976; children: John F., Elizabeth K., Kristen N. BS in Math. and BS in Elem. Edn., St. Thomas Aquinas Coll., 1971; MSEd, Fordham U., 1973. Cert. tchr. N-6, math. 7-12, N.Y. Math. tchr. seventh and eighth grade Felix Festa Jr. High Sch., West Nyack, N.Y., 1971-84; math. tchr. 9-12 Clarkstown South High Sch., West Nyack, 1984—. Tuition grantee NSF, CUNY, 1982, Impact II grantee, 2000-2002. Mem. Nat. Coun. Tchrs. of Math. Roman Catholic. Avocations: reading, tutoring, phys. fitness, sports, embroidering. Office: Clarkstown South High Sch Demarest Mill Rd West Nyack NY 10994

BLADES, JANE M. special education educator; b. Jersey City, Dec. 1, 1953; d. Nunzio Thomas and Evelyn Rose (Spizzirro) Savino; m. Brian Hilton Blades, Sept. 20, 1980; children: Adam Hilton, Erik Thomas. BA, Kean Coll., 1983. Cert. handicapped tchr., N.J. Staff asst. AT&T, Parsippany, N.J., 1979-81; spl. edn. tchr. Perth Amboy Pub. Schs., N.J., 1984; mgmt. cons. J. Anthony and Assocs., Inc., Hillsborough, N.J., 1986, project mgr., 1987; cons. Datanomics, Inc., Piscataway, N.J., 1987-88; tchr. of the handicapped Edison (N.J.) Twp. Bd. Edn., 1988—. Cons. in field. Mem. NEA, N.J. Edn. Assn., Edison Tchrs. Assn. Republican. Presbyterian. Home: 52 Stirrup Ln Flemington NJ 08822-3438

BLAGG, JAMES DOUGLAS, JR., university administrator; b. Pontotoc, Miss., Dec. 26, 1946; s. James D. and Amanda Lavenia (Andrews) B.; children: JaemiRae C., Kaelas S. BS in Biology, Memphis State U., 1968; MEd in Cultural Founds. of Edn., U. Utah, 1976; PhD in Higher Edn., U. Wash., 1981. Registered radiologic technologist. Instr., dir. Sch. of Radiologic Tech. USAF Acad. Hosp., Colo. Springs, Colo., 1972-74, U. Utah Med. Ctr., Salt Lake City, 1974-77; grad. tchg. asst. Grad. Sch. of Edn. U. Wash., Seattle, 1978-79; instr. dept. of vocat.-tech. edn. Grad. Sch. Edn. Rutgers U., New Brunswick, N.J., 1979-81, asst. prof. dept of vocat.-tech. edn. Grad. Sch. Edn., 1981-83; asst. prof. dept. radiologic tech. Coll. Health Related Professions U. Ark. for Med. Scis., Little Rock, 1989-92, assoc. prof., 1989-93, acting chmn. dept. emergency med. scis., 1984, asst. dean for acad. and student affairs, 1984-86, assoc. dean for acad. and student affairs, 1986-92; assoc. prof. radiologic tech. and dean coll. nursing and health professions Ark. State U., Jonesboro, 1992-95; founding dean Coll. Health Professions Fla. Gulf Coast U., 1995-98; dean No. Ariz. U., 1998—. Dir. grad. program in allied health edn. Grad. Sch. Edn., Rutgers U., New Brunswick, 1979-83, U. Medicine and Dentistry of N.J., Newark; mem. editl. bd. Jour. of Allied Health, 1984-92, 94-97. Contbr. articles to profl. jours.; presenter at confs. and meetings. Mem. adv. com. for Radiologic Tech., N.Y.C. Tech. Coll., 1980-83, adv. com. phys. therapy, Sch. of Health Related Professions, U. Medicine and Dentistry N.J., Newark, 1981-82, adv. com for N.E. Allied Health Leadership Project, Sch. of Health Related Professions, SUNY, Buffalo, 1982-83, Health Care Edn. adv. com Cook Coll., New Brunswick, 1982-83, adv. com. Montclair (N.J.) State Coll., 1983, others. Staff sgt. USAF, 1970-74. Memphis State U. scholar, 1965-68; Kellogg Allied Health fellow U. Wash., 1977. Fellow Assn. Schs. of Allied Health Professions; mem. Am. Soc. Radiologic Technologists (editl. rev. bd. 1982-85), N.J. Soc. Allied Health Profls., other state radiologic tech. socs., Pi Tau, Omicron Tau Theta, Chi Beta Phi. E-mail: james.blagg@nau.edu.

BLAINE, HENRI REMI, cosmetology school administrator; b. Blackston, Mass., Mar. 31, 1938; s. Donat Alfred and Fortunate Adriane (Hebert) B. Hairdressing cert., Mansfield Acad. Mgr. Palace Barber Shop, Woonsocket, R.I., 1956-57; founder, pres. Henri's-Blaine Salon Chain, So. Mass., 1959-73; pres. Blaine Hir Sch. Chain, various cities, Mass., 1973—. Mem. task force Coun. Beauty Exec., Washington, 1991—. Active numerous civic orgns. Recipient Pioneer award Creative Nail Co., 1992; named Best of Boston, 1986, Merit of Excellence award Internat. Art Fashion Group, 1992. Mem. Mass. Sch. Owners Assn. (pres. 1982-86), Assn. Accredited Cosmetology Schs. (vice chmn. 1981—). Avocations: boating, fishing. Office: Blaine Hair and Beauty Schs 510 Commonwealth Ave Boston MA 02215-2602

BLAIR, CHARLIE LEWIS, elementary school educator; b. Troy, Ala., Dec. 22, 1940; s. James Horace and Dollie Rosa (Cannon) B.; m. Doshia Mae Anderson, mar. 31, 1962; children: Duane Alan, Mark Lewis. AAS, C.C. of Air Force, 1980; AS, U. S.C. Sumter, 1988; BA in Edn., Coastal Carolina Coll., 1989; MEd, U. So. Miss., 1995. Cert. elem. edn. educator, K-12 adminstr. Sgt. USAF, 1958-86; tchr. Lemira Elem. Sch., Sumter, S.C., 1989-90, High Hills Mid. Sch., Sumter, 1990-96; asst. prin. Lakewood H.S., Sumter, S.C., 1996-99; prin. Mayewood Mid. Sch., Sumter, 1999—2001, St. John Elem. Sch., Lynchburg, SC, 2001—02, Ebenezer Mid. Sch., Sumter, 2002. Mem. Disabled Am. Vets., 1989—, Am. Legion, Columbia, S.C., 1989—. Named Dean's Honor Student U. S.C. Sumter, 1988, Pres.'s Honor Student U. S.C. Sumter, 1989, to Nat. Dean's List U. S.C. Sumter, 1987-89. Mem. NEA, ASCD, Nat. Assn. of Secondary Sch. Prinicpals, Palmetto State Tchrs. Assn., S.C. Edn. Assn., U. S.C. Sumter Edn. Assn. (pres. 1988-89), Kappa Delta Pi, Phi Delta Kappa. Baptist. Avocations: woodworking, auto repair, upholstery, reading, music. Office: Ebenezer Mid Sch 3440 Ebenezer Rd Sumter SC 29153

BLAIR, HARRY WALLACE, political science educator, consultant; b. Washington, Mar. 25, 1938; s. James Newell and Greta (Flintermann) B.; m. Barbara Ann Shailor, Dec. 26, 1981; 1 child, Emily Rebecca. AB in History, Cornell U., 1960; MA in Polit. Sci., Duke U., 1966, PhD in Polit. Sci., 1970. Instr. polit. sci. Colgate U., 1968-70; asst. prof. polit. sci. Bucknell U., Lewisburg, Pa., 1970-77, assoc. prof., 1977-83, prof., 1983—2000, chair dept., 1982—85, 1988—90, prof. emeritus, 2000—, chair dept., 1997—98. Vis. fellow Ctr. for Internat. Studies, Cornell U., 1972-73, vis. assoc. prof. rural sociology and rsch. assoc., spring-summer 1979, vis. assoc. prof.,

1980-81, vis. prof. rural sociology, fall 1987; rsch. assoc. So. Asian Inst., Sch. Internat. Affairs, Columbia U., spring-summer 1974; social analyst Bur. Sci. and Tech., Office of Rural Devel., U.S. Agy. for Internat. Devel., 1981-82, sr. social sci. analyst Ctr. for Devel. Info. and Evaluation, 1992-94, sr. democracy advisor Bur. for Policy and Program Coord., Ctr. for Devel. Info. and Evaluation, 1995, 96-97; vis. fellow Sch. Forestry and Environ. Studies, Yale U., spring-summer 1986, sr. rsch. scholar, lectr. polit. sci., 2001—; sr. democracy advisor global bur. Ctr. Democracy and Governance, 1998-2001. Contbr. articles to books and profl. jours. Lt. U.S. Army, 1961-63. Home: 58 Quarry Dock Rd Branford CT 06405-4654

BLAIR, REBECCA SUE, English educator, lay minister; b. Terre Haute, Ind., Mar. 26, 1958; d. Albert Eldon and Genevieve Virginia (Smith) B.; m. Richard Volle Van Rheeden, May 27, 1989. BA in English magna cum laud, U. Indpls., 1980; MA in Medieval Lit. with honors, U. Ill., Springfield, 1982; MA, Ind. U., 1986, PhD, 1988. Grad. asst. U. Ill., Springfield, 1980—82; dir. English language tng. Ind. U., Bloomington, 1982-83, assoc. instr., 1982-88; assoc. prof., chmn. dept. English Westminster Coll., Fulton, Mo., 1989-99, dir. writing assessment, 1989-99; assoc. prof. U. Indpls., 1999—2003, Wartburg Coll., Waverly, Iowa, 2003—. Vis. prof. Webster U., St. Louis, Mo., 1988-89; writing assessment cons. Pepperdine U., Malibu, Calif., 1995, others; exec. com. of the faculty Westminster Coll.; mem. Assessment Com., College-Wide Budget Com., Profl. Stds. Com., Pers. Com., Dean's Cabinet Coun. of Chairs and Dirs., Edn. Task Force, Task Force to Reorganize the Acad. Area, Enrollment Svcs. Task Force; women's studies rep. Mid-Mo. Am. Coun. of Univs.; faculty sponsor Alpha Chi Scholastic Hon. Soc.; faculty organizer awareness of rape/domestic violence Take Back the Night Rally; presenter, spkr. in field. Author: The Other Woman: Women Authors and Cultural Stereotypes in American Literature, 1988; contbr. articles to profl. jours. Bd. dirs. Am. Cancer Soc., Callaway County, Mo., 1989-92; mem. pastor nominating com. First Presbyterian Ch., Fulton, Mo., 1990-91, elder, 1990—, session mem., elected mem., 1990-93, 97-2000, chmn. nominating com., 1993-94, chmn. music search com., 1994-95; pulpit supply Mo. Union Presbytery, 1995—, com. on ministry, 1997-2000, stated clk., 1997—; mem. Greater Mo. Focus on Leadership, 1992; vol. Habitat for Humanity, Fulton, 1993—; bd. dirs., founding mem. Coalition Against Rape and Domestic Violence, Fulton, 1995-97; bd. dirs. Friends of the Libr., Fulton, 1995-98, pres., 1997-98; sec. Fulton Art League, 1996—. Named Outstanding Faculty Mem., Westminster Coll., Fulton, 1991-92, Panhellenic Faculty Mem. of Year, Westminster Coll., 1996-97. Mem. Nat. Coun. for Rsch. on Women, Nat. Coun. Tchrs. of English, Am. Studies Assn., Midwest Modern Lang. Assn., Modern Lang. Assn., Writing Prog. Adminstrs., Coll. Composition and Comm., Fulton C. of C. (vol. 1992-96), Kiwanis (bd. dirs. 1990—, founder Circle K Club 1994, v.p. 1995-96, pres.-elect 1996-97, pres. 1997-98). Presbyterian. Avocations: gourmet cooking, reading, trains, writing. Home: 1916 Rainbow Dr Cedar Falls IA 50613 Office: Wartburg Coll 100 Wartburg Blvd Waverly IA 50677 Business E-Mail: rebecca.blair@wartburg.edu.

BLAIR, ROSEMARY KASUL, social work educator; b. Chgo., Oct. 19, 1941; d. Vincent J. Therese (DeKreon) Kasul; m. Neal Edward McKinney, Nov. 11, 1962 (div. Jan. 1992); children: Michael, Kevin; m. Robert A. Blair, Dec. 17, 2002. B in Social Work, George Williams Coll., 1978, MSW, 1980. Lic. clin. social worker, Ill.; cert. sr. addiction counselor, eating disorders counselor, gerontol. counselor. Coord. inpatient program The Abbey, Winfield, Ill., 1980-82; counselor Parkside Med. Svcs., Winfield, 1982-83, coord. tng. Park Ridge, Ill., 1983-86; clin. social worker Pape & Assocs., Wheaton, Ill., 1986-88; prof. Coll. of Du Page, Glen Ellyn, Ill., 1988—2003, prof. emeritus, 2003—; counseling and cons. McKinney, Blair and Assocs., Wheaton, 1995—. Co-tchr. nat. symposium Internat. Assn. Eating Disorder Profls., 1994, 95, 96, 97; presenter Midwest NOHSE conf. 1995; presenter in field. Mem. NASW, Am. Soc. on Aging, Addiction Counselor Tng. Program Dirs. Home: 1240 Reading Ct Wheaton IL 60187-7710 E-mail: rmck1240@aol.com.

BLAIS, ROGER NATHANIEL, physics educator; b. Duluth, Minn., Oct. 3, 1944; s. Eusebe Joseph and Edith Seldina (Anderson) B.; m. Mary Louise Leclerc, Aug. 2, 1971; children: Christopher Edward, Laura Louise. BA in Physics and French Lit., U. Minn., 1966; PhD in Physics, U. Okla., 1971; cert. in computer programming, Tulsa Jr. Coll., 1981; cert. in bus., UCLA, 1986. Registered profl. engr., Okla. Instr. physics Westark C.C., Ft. Smith, Ark., 1971-72; asst. prof. physics and geophys. scis Old Dominion U., Norfolk, Va., 1972-77; asst. prof. engring. physics U. Tulsa, 1977-81, assoc. prof., 1981-98, prof., 1998—; assoc. dir. Tulsa U. Artificial Lift Projects, 1983—98, chmn. physics, 1986-88, vice-provost, 1989-92, provost, v.p. acad. affairs, 1998—. Contbr. articles to profl. jours. Active Leadership Okla., 2002—03; mem. Leadership Pkla. XVI; bd. dirs. Light Opera Okla., 2003—, Hillcrest Splty. Hosps., 2003—. Recipient Great Leadership Okla. XVI, 2003. Fellow Instrumentation Sys. and Automation Soc. (dir. test measurement divsn. 1995-97, v.p. automation and tech. dept. 2003-), Leadersship Okla. XVI; mem. AAAS, AAUP, NSPE, Am. Phys. Soc., Am. Geophys. Union, Soc. Petroleum Engrs., Am. Assn. Physics Tchrs., Am. Soc. Engring. Edn., N.Y. Acad. Scis., Iron Wedge Soc., Phi Beta Kappa, Sigma Xi, Sigma Pi Sigma, Tau Beta Pi, Phi Kappa Phi. Home: 5348 E 30th Pl Tulsa OK 74114-6314 Office: U Tulsa Office of Provost 600 S College Ave Tulsa OK 74104-3139 E-mail: roger-blais@utulsa.edu., rblais71@cox.net.

BLAKE, DARLENE EVELYN, political worker, consultant, educator, author; b. Rockford, Iowa, Feb. 26, 1947; d. Forest Kenneth and Violet Evelyn (Fisher) Kuhlemeier; m. Joel Franklin Blake, May 1, 1975 (dec. Jan. 1989); 1 child, Alexander Joel. AA, North Iowa Area Community Coll., Mason City, 1967; BS, Mankato (Minn.) State Coll., 1969; MS, Mankato (Minn.) State U., 1975. Cert. profl. tchr., Iowa; registered art therapist. Tchr. Bishop Whipple Sch., Faribault, Minn., 1970-72; art therapist C.B. Wilson Ctr., Faribault, 1972-76, Sedgwick County Dept. Mental Health, Wichita, Kans., 1976-79; cons. Batten, Batten, Hudson & Swab, Des Moines, 1979-81; pres. J.F. Blake Co., Inc., Des Moines, 1990—. Nat. adv. bd., polit. cons. to Alexander Haig for Pres., 1987-88; mgmt. tng. specialist Comms. Data Svcs., Inc., Des Moines, 1988-90, exec. mgr. customer svc. spl. interest fulfillment divsn., 1990-92; cert. cons. assoc. Drake, Beam, Morin, Inc., Mpls., 1993—; coord. staff devel. U. Iowa Hosps. and Clinics, Iowa City, 1998-01. Exhibited in one-woman show at local libr., 1970. Mem. U.S. Selective Svc. Bd. 26 and 27, Polk County, Iowa, 1981-98; sustaining mem. Rep. Nat. Com.; Rep. cand. Polk County Treas., Des Moines, 1982; chmn. Polk County Rep. Party, 1985-88; commr. Des Moines Commn. Human Rights and Job Discrimination, 1984-89; mem. Martin Luther King Scholarship Com., 1986-88; mem. Iowa State Bd. Psychology Examiners, 1983-90; active 5th Dist. Jud. Nominating Commn., 1990-96, Iowa Supreme Ct. Jud. Nominating Commn., 1996—, State Jud. Nominating Commn, 1996—, Des Moines Sister Cities Commn., 1997-98, Am. in Bloom Judge, 2003—. Mem. Am. Art Therapy Assn., Iowa Art Therapy Assn. (pres. elect 1984-85, founder), Des Moines Garden Club (pres. 1984-85), Polk County Rep. Women (pres. elect 1983-85, Am. in bloom judge). Lutheran. Avocations: sewing, gardening, fine arts, music, reading. Home and Office: Unit 32 6001 Creston Ave Des Moines IA 50321-1255

BLAKE, SALLY STEINSIEK, education educator, researcher; b. Jonesboro, Ark. d. Ruth (Allison) Steinsiek; m. Ron Blake, July 2, 1980 (div. 1983); 1 child, Candice Blake. BSE in Early Childhood and Elem. Edn., Ark. State U., Jonesboro, 1971, MSE in Early Childhood Edn., 1978; PhD in Curriculum and Instrn., U. Miss., 1991. Tchr. Newport (Ark.) Pub. Schs., 1973-79, Highland Sch. Dist., Hardy, Ark., 1979-85; dance instr. Verome Sch. Dance, Hardy, 1980-83; owner Blake Sch. Dance, Hardy, 1983-85; tchr. Spring Br. Ind. Sch. Dist., Houston, 1985-87, Forrest City (Ark.) Sch. Dist., 1987-88; instr. U. Miss., Oxford, 1988-91; asst. prof. Ky. Wesleyan Coll., Owensboro, 1991—. Cons. ARVAC, Russelville, Ark., 1975-85, Childhood Svcs., Jonesboro, 1986—; lectr. numerous schs., 1979—. Author: Multilevel Thematic Mathematic Instruction, 1992; contbr. articles to profl. jours. Active Parent Tchr. Community Assn. Rockefeller Found. grantee, 1988. Mem. ASCD, NEA, NSTA, Nat. Coun. Tchrs. Math., Nat. Assn. for Edn. of Young Children, Nat. Dance Tchrs. Assn., Ky. Coun. Tchrs. Math., Mid-South Ednl. Rsch. Assn., Ky. Assn. on Children Under Six, So. Assn. on Children Under Six, Phi Delta Kappa, Gamma Beta Phi, Kappa Delta Pi. Home: 2400 E Johnson Ave Jonesboro AR 72401-2403

BLAKLEY, EARNESTINE, elementary education educator; b. Steele, Mo., June 6, 1952; d. Thomas Bob and Mary Anna (Jones) R.; m. Charles Vernon Blakley, July 31, 1976; children: Charles Vernon Jr., Andrew Harvey. BS Elem. Edn., Lincoln U., 1974; writing diploma, Inst. Children's Lit., 1981; MS Elem. Teaching, Northwest Mo. State U., 1986. Tchr. 2d grade Humboldt Elem. Sch., St. Joseph, Mo., 1974-78; tchr. 5th grade Edison Elem. Sch., St. Joseph, Mo., 1984-85, tchr. 2d grade, 1985-89, tchr. 3d grade, 1989-90, Bessie Elem. Sch., St. Joseph, Mo., 1990-93. Team writer Environ. Protection, Washington, 1992; edn. panel Energizer Battery, Washington, 1992; com. mem. America 2000, Kansas City, 1991-93; spkr. Scholarship Banquet Alton, Ill., 1993; creator at-risk program Ptnrs. in Edn., 1989-90, Parent involvement Children & Parents, 1989-93. Supt. St. Francis Bapt. Temple, St. Joseph, Mo., 1987-92; bd. dirs. Girl Scout Coun., 1992-93, Family Guidance Ctr., 1980; founder, dir. HOPE Outreach Ministries. Recipient Excellence in Edn. award East Side Human Resource Ctr., 1990; Apple Seed Mini grantee project Aware, 1991; nomine Walt Disney Am. Tchr. awards, 1992; named Mo. State Tchr. of Yr., 1991-92, St. Joseph Tchr. of Yr., 1991-92. Mem. St. Joseph Community Tchrs. Assn. (sec. 1986-88), Mo. State Tchrs. Assn., Student Mo. State Tchrs. Assn. (pres. 1973-74), Delta Kappa Gamma, Phi Delta Kappa, Kappa Omicron Phi (v.p. 1973-74). Avocations: writing, reading, fishing, sewing, biking.

BLAKNEY, WILLIAM GILBERT GROVER, engineer, educator; b. Moncton, N.B., Canada, Apr. 4, 1926; came to U.S., 1958; s. Donald Mariner and Ruth M. (Keans) B.; m. L. Marie Woodman, Oct. 20, 1951; children: Dawn Marie, Carol Lynn. Diploma in engring., Dalhousie U., Halifax, Nova Scotia, Canada, 1947; BS in Mining, Nova Scotia Tech. Coll., 1949; MS, Ohio State U., 1965. Topographic engr. Mines and Tech. Surveys, Ottawa, Ont., Canada, 1950-58; assoc. prof. civil engring. Auburn (Ala.) U., 1958-81, assoc. prof. tech. svcs., 1981-83, assoc. prof. indsl. engring., 1983-90, assoc. prof. emeritus, 1990—. Fellow Am. Congress Surveying and Mapping; mem. Am. Soc. Photogrammetry and Remote Sensing (life), Canadian Inst. Surveying (life), Ala. Soc. Profl. Land Surveyors (pres. 1980, life), Am. Soc. Engring. Educators, Danforth Assocs. (sec. 1990—). Democrat. Home: 603 Cary Dr Auburn AL 36830-2503

BLANCHARD, GLENN ROBERT, principal; b. Raymond, N.H., Oct. 17, 1943; s. Theodore Maxwell and Ruth (Hoyt) B.; m. Sandra Ann Malette, May 14, 1971; 1 child, Amy Ruth. BA, Notre Dame Coll., 1975; MEd, U. N.H., 1985. Cert. tchr. elem. edn., sch. adminstr., N.H. Tchr. 6th grade Derry (N.H.) Village Sch., 1975-88, asst. prin., 1977-88, prin., 1988—. Chair bd. Extended Day Care, Derry, 1988—; adminstrv. chair Crisis Intervention Program, Derry, 1991—; adminstrv. liaison Derry Village PTA, 1980—. With USAF, 1962-66. Mem. Nat. Assn. Sch. Prins., N.H. Assn. Sch. Prins., Phi Delta Kappa (v.p. 1987-88). Avocations: reading, golf. Home: 6 Nevens St Hudson NH 03051-4639

BLANCHARD, PAMELA SNYDER, special education educator; b. Winston-Salem, N.C., Feb. 5, 1951; d. Roger Alexander and Marie Gobble Snyder; m. George Winborne Blanchard, July 26, 1975; children: Andrew Micah, Justin Warren, Nathan Winborne. BA in Elem. Edn., St. Andrews Presbyn. Coll., 1973; Cert. in Spl. Edn., U. Tenn., 1990; MA in Ednl. Tech., Bible, Johnson Bible Coll., 2000. Cert. tchr. N.C., edn. and spl. edn., and Career Ladder I tchr. Tenn. Title I math. tchr. Durham (N.C.) City Schs., 1973—75; algebra tchr. Davidson County Schs., Welcome, NC, 1976; Chpt. I reading and math. tchr. Knoxville (Tenn.) City Schs., 1976—79, 1980—85; ednl. cons. Discovery Toys, Knoxville, 1989—90; spl. edn. extended resource tchr. Sevier County Schs., Sevierville, Tenn., 1990—91; spl. edn. resource specialist Knox County Schs., Strawberry Plains, Tenn., 1992—. Mem. leadership com., sch. improvement team, tech. com., webmistress Carter Elem. Sch., 1999—. Vol. counselor Sexual Assault Crisis Ctr., Knoxville, 1991—92; chairperson missions bd. Seymour (Tenn.) United Meth. Ch., 1988—90, chairperson assimilation com., 1990—92, sec. adminstrv. coun., 2000, 2001—02; missionary Charleston, SC, 2001—02, Damascus, Va., 2001—03; missionary to Zimbabwe, 2003. Grantee Multicultural Cooking Unit, Knoxville Jr. League, 1994, Accelerated Reader Books, East Tenn. Edn. Found., 1995. Mem.: ASCD, NEA, Internat. Reading Assn., Knox County Edn. Assn., Tenn. Edn. Assn., Children with Attention Deficit Disorder, Learning Disabilities Assn., Divsn. Learning Disabilities, Coun. for Exceptional Children, Nat. Honor Soc. Democrat. Methodist. Avocations: reading, hiking, computers, travel. Home: 705 Forest View Ct Seymour TN 37865 Office: Carter Elem Sch 9304 College Ln Strawberry Plains TN 37871

BLANCHARD, ROSEMARY ANN, university program administrator, consultant, educator; b. Hartford, Conn., Oct. 15, 1946; d. Bernard Richard and Ann Rosemary (Kelly) B.; m. James W. Zion, Dec. 26, 1967 (div. June 1983); 1 child, Jeannette Blanchard Zion; m. Dimitsri Mihalas, June 20, 1995. BA in History cum laude, Trinity Coll., Washington, 1967; MA in Sociology, Johns Hopkins U., 1972; JD cum laude, U. Conn., 1972; postgrad., U. Ill., 1996—. Bar: Conn. 1972, Mont. 1973, Navajo Nation 1983, N.Mex. 1985. Staff atty. Mont. Legislature, Helena, 1973-74; asst. prof. sociology Coll. of Great Falls, Mont., 1974-76; gen. counsel Mont. Human Rights Commn., Helena, 1976-78; atty.-advocate Devel. Disabilities Mont. Advocacy Program, Helena, 1978-79; atty. Zion, Reynolds & Taylor, Helena, 1978-81; ednl. policy analyst divsn. edn. Navajo Nation, Window Rock, Ariz., 1982-88; assoc. prof. social scis. U. N.Mex., Gallup, 1988-95; spl. asst. for disability issues office of affirmative actio U. Ill., Champaign, 1996—. Cons. Tech. Rsch. Svcs., Gallup and Albuquerque, 1988—, Navajo Area Sch. Bd. Assn., Window Rock, 1989-97; chair Dept. Human Svcs., Sociology and Tribal Studies, U. N.Mex., Gallup, 1988-95; mem. adv. coun. U. Ill. Champaign-Urbana Divsn. Rehab. Edn. Svcs., 1996—. Author: Legal Status of Homemakers in Montana, 1975; contbr. articles to profl. jours. Exec. dir. ACLU of Mont., Great Falls, 1974-76; mem. Young Dems., Helena, 1977-80; clk. Helena Friends Meeting, 1977-80; convenor Gallup Friends Worship Group, 1983-90; mem. Fighting Back Core Com., Gallup, 1992-93, Gov.'s Com. on Concerns of the Handicapped, Santa Fe, 1994—; recording clk. Intermountain Yearly Meeting, Durango, Colo., 1994; clk. peace and svc. com. Urbana/Champaign Friends Meeting, Champaign, 1996-97. TIIAP grantee U.S. Dept. Commerce, 1994. Mem. Assn. on Higher Edn. and Disability, Nat. Indian Edn. Assn. (non-Indian assoc.), Western Social Sci. Assn., Navajo Bar Assn., N.Mex. Bar Assn. Mem. Soc. Of Friends. Avocations: hiking, swimming, theater, music, creative writing. Office: U Ill Office Affirmative Action 601 E John St Champaign IL 61820-5711

BLANCHARD, SHIRLEY LYNN, primary school educator, consultant; b. Medford, Oreg., Sept. 5, 1954; d. Richard L. Grigsby, Helen L. Grigsby; m. John T. Blanchard, Sept. 6, 1975; children: Andrew Blanchard children: Martin Blanchard, Richelle Blanchard. BA in Edn., So. Oreg. State Coll., 1975, BS, 1978; MA in Edn., So. Oreg. U., 1985. Nat. bd. cert. tchr. Nat. Bd. Profl. Tchg. Stds., 2000. Music tchr. Jackson County Sch. Dist. #6, Central Point, Oreg., 1975—81, kindergarten tchr. Eagle Point, Oreg., 1983—99; primary tchr. Jackson County Sch. Dist. #9, Eagle Point, Oreg., 1999—. Home schooling parent educator RIGGS Inst., So. Oreg., 1987—91, reading cons. for home schooling parents, 1987—91; continuing edn. presenter early childhood literacy So. Oreg. U./Medford Sch. Dist. 549C, Medford, 1995—96; site based mgmt. team chmn., mem. Glenn D. Hale Elem. Scho., Eagle Point, 1996—98; contract bargaining team mem. Eagle Point Edn. Assn., Eagle Point, 1997—98. Leader Wynema Girl Scout Counsel, Medford, 1972—75; 4H leader Oreg. State Ext. Svc., Central Point, Oreg., 1997—98. Recipient Slice of Life award, Williams Bread & McKenzie Farms Bakery and KOBI-TV, 2002. Fellow: Nat. Kindergarten Alliance Network; mem.: NEA, Internat. Soc. for Tech. in Edn., Oreg. Edn. Assn., Nat. Assn. Edn. Young Children. Avocations: internet mentoring, horses, technology, writing music, birds. Home: PO Box 1511 Eagle Point OR 97524 Office: Jackson County Sch Dist #9 PO Box 197 215 E Main Eagle Point OR 97524 Home Fax: (541) 826-3221; Office Fax: (541) 826-3221. Business E-Mail: blanchards@eaglepnt.k12.or.us.

BLANCHET, JEANNE ELLENE MAXANT, artist, educator, performer; b. Chgo., Sept. 25, 1944; d. William H. and L. Barbara (Martin) Maxant; m. Yasuo Shimizu, Apr. 28, 1969 (div. 1973); m. William B. Blanchet, Aug. 21, 1981 (dec. May 1993). BA summa cum laude, Northwestern U., 1966; MFA, Tokyo U., 1971; MA, Ariz. State U., 1978; postgrad., Ill. State U., 1979-80; PhD, Greenwich U., 1991. Instr. Tsuda U., Kodaira, Japan, 1970-71; free-lance visual, performing artist various cities, U.S., 1973—; artist in residence YMCA of the Rockies, Estes Park, Colo., 1976-81 summers; prof. fine arts Rio Salado Coll., Surprise, Ariz., 1976-91. Lectr. Ariz. State U. West, Sun City, 1985-93; evaluator several arts couns. including Ariz. Humanities Coun., 1993, Ariz. Humanities Coun. Scholar's SPkrs. Bur., 1998—; Prescott Melodrama ragtime pianist, 1993, 94; artist with Performing Arts for Youth, 1994—. Selected for regional, state, nat. juried art shows, 1975—, mus. and gallery one-woman shows of computer art, 1988—; author: Original Songs and Verse of the Old (And New) West, 1987, A Song in My Heart, 1988, Reflections, 1989, The Mummy Story, 1990; contbr. articles to newspapers, profl. jours. Founding mem. Del Webb Hosp. Woodrow Wilson fellow, 1966; ADA B.C. Welsh scholar, 1980; recipient numerous art, music awards, 1970—, major computer art awards in regional, nat., and internat. shows, 1990—. Mem. Nat. League Am. Pen Women (sec. chpt. 1987, v.p. 1988, pres. 1990-92, pres. Colo. chpt. 1996-97), Ariz. Press Women (numerous awards in original graphics and writing 1980s, 90s), Nat. Fedn. Press Women, Northwestern U.'s John Evans Club, Henry W. Rogers Soc., P.E.O. (rec. sec. chpt. BV 1998—), Phi Beta Kappa. Avocations: computers, ragtime piano, hiking, parapsychology, duplicate bridge (life master). Home and Office: 10330 W Thunderbird Blvd # C-311 Sun City AZ 85351

BLANCHET-SADRI, FRANCINE, mathematician, educator; b. Trois-Rivieres, Quebec, Can., July 25, 1953; came to U.S., 1990; d. Jean and Rolande (Delage) B.; m. Fereidoon Sadri, July 28, 1979; children: Ahmad, Hamid, Mariamme. BSc in Math., U. Quebec a Trois-Rivieres, Can., 1976; MS, Princeton U., 1979; PhD, McGill U., 1989. Rsch., tchg. asst. U. Quebec, Trois-Rivieres, Quebec, Can., 1974-76, lectr., 1976; rsch. asst. Princeton (N.J.) U., 1978; lectr. U. Tech. Isfahan, Iran, 1982-84, McGill U., Montreal, Quebec, 1988-89; prof. U. N.C., Greensboro, 1990—. Contbr. articles to profl. jours. Recipient Rsch. Excellence award 1991; Natural Scis. and Engring. Coun. Can. postgrad. fellow, 1976-80, Fonds pour la Formation de Chercheurs et L'aide a la Rsch. fellow, 1985-87, Natural Scis. and Engring. Rsch. Coun. Can. fellow, 1990; New Faculty grantee U. N.C., Greensboro, 1990-91, NSF grantee, 1991—. Mem. Am. Math. Soc., Assn. for Computing Machinery. Achievements include discovery that the dot-depth of a generating class of aperiodic monoids is computable. Office: U NC Dept Math Scis PO Box 26170 Greensboro NC 27402-6170 E-mail: blanchet@uncg.edu.

BLAND, ANNIE RUTH (ANN BLAND), nursing educator; b. Bennett, N.C., Oct. 14, 1949; d. John Wesley and Mary Ida (Caviness) Brown; m. Chester Wayne Bland; 1 child, John Wayne; stepchildren: Jason Tyler, Adam Mathew. BSN, East Carolina U., Greenville, N.C., 1971; MSN, U. N.C., 1978; postgrad., U. S.C., 1996—2003. RN, N.C.; cert. clin. specialist in adult psychiat./mental health nursing. Staff nurse VA Med. Ctr., Durham, N.C., 1974-75, 77-80; psychiat. clin. instr. Duke U. Med. Ctr., Durham, 1980-82, asst. head nurse, 1982-90, staff nurse, 1993—99; psychiat. clin. nurse specialist John Umstead Hosp., Butner, N.C., 1990-93; psychiat. lead nursing instr. Alamance C.C., Graham, N.C., 1994-96; asst. prof. Sch. Nursing, U. N.C., Greensboro. Asst. Sunday sch. tchr. Mt. Hermon Bapt. Ch., Durham, 1994, 96, 99-2000. Capt. USN, 1971-74, USNR, 1974-97, ret. 1997. Recipient award for nursing excellence Great 100 Orgn., Raleigh, N.C., 1991, Letter of Appreciation Am. Heart Assn., Chapel Hill, 1992. Mem. ANA, N.C. Nurses Assn. (sec. dist. 11, 1981), Assn. Mil Surgeons U.S., U. N.C. Chapel Hill Alumni Assn. and Sch. Nursing, East Carolina U. Alumni Assn. and Sch. Nursing, Res. Officers Assn. U.S. Baptist. Avocations: tennis, swimming, water skiing, snow skiing. Home: 2534 New Hope Church Rd Chapel Hill NC 27514-8218 Office: U NC Greensboro Sch of Nursing CPG PO Box 26170 Greensboro NC 27402-6170

BLAND, SARAH BELL, retired elementary school educator; b. Gaffney, S.C., July 16, 1934; d. N. H. and Maxine (Lee) Bell; m. Charles Bland, June 5, 1955; children: Barry, Wayne, Helen, Barbara, Ann, Donnie, Jimmy. BA, Columbia Coll., 1955. Cert. tchr., S.C. 4th grade tchr. Cherokee County Sch., Gaffney, 1955; 1st to 5th grade tchr. Volusia County Sch., Ormond Beach, Fla., 1957-78; 2d, 5th and 6th grade tchr. Spartanburg Sch. Dist., Glendale, SC, 1978—98, ret., 1999. Mem. Chesnee Wesleyan Ch. Mem. NEA, Spartanburg County Edn. Assn., Cowpens Garden Club (v.p.). United Methodist. Avocations: cheerleading sponsor, family activities.

BLANE, HOWARD THOMAS, research institute administrator; b. De Land, Fla., May 10, 1926; s. Chesley Thomas and Olive Henrietta (Van Heest) B.; children: Benjamin, Eva. BA cum laude, Harvard U., 1950; MA, Clark U., 1951, PhD, 1957. Instr. Harvard Med. Sch., Cambridge, Mass., 1957-66, asst. clin. prof., 1966-70; assoc. prof. U. Pitts., 1970-72, prof., 1972-86; rsch. prof. SUNY, Buffalo, 1986—; dir. Rsch. Inst. Addictions, Buffalo, 1986-96. Cons. Nat. Inst. on Alcohol Abuse and Alcoholism, Washington, 1970—; v.p. Health Edn. Found., Washington, 1975—; bd. dirs. Rsch. Found. for Mental Hygiene, Albany, N.Y., 1986-96; principal investigator numerous grants. Author: The Personality of the Alcoholic, 1968; editor: Frontiers of Alcoholism, 1970, Youth, Alcoholism and Social Policy, 1979, Psychological Theories of Drinking and Alcoholism, 1987, 2nd edit., 1999. Bd. dirs. Jellinek Meml. Fund, Toronto, 1995—. Clark U. scholar, Worcester, Mass., 1950-51. Fellow APA, Am. Psychol. Soc.; mem. APHA, AAAS, Rsch. Soc. on Alcoholism. Office: Rsch Inst on Addictions 1021 Main St Buffalo NY 14203-1014 E-mail: blaneonfmb@msn.com.

BLANEY, M. KATHLEEN, elementary education educator; b. Pitts., Nov. 26, 1941; d. William Charles and Margaret (Rogan) B. BA, Seton Hill Coll., Greensburg, Pa., 1964; postgrad., Duquesne U., Pitts. Cert. in lang. arts, elem. tchr., instructional tchr. leader. Intermediate lang. arts, math. and social studies tchr. Pitts. Bd. Edn., 1964—. Mem. Am. Fedn. Tchrs. (tchr. rsch. linker, conv. steering com.), Pitts. Fedn. Tchrs. (bldg. rep., polit. action com., elem. grass roots com., nominations and election com., social com.). Home: 141 Pony Dr Freedom PA 15042-2829

BLANK, FLORENCE WEISS, literacy educator, editor; b. Bridgeport, Conn. d. Maurice Herbert and Henrietta Helen (Shapiro) Weiss; m. Bernard Blank, Apr. 10, 1965 (dec. Aug., 1989). Student Journalism, English, Psychology, Richmond Profl. Inst.; student, U. Richmond, Northwestern U., Va. Union U., 1967, 73, 74, U. Wis., Milw., 1971, Va. Commonwealth U., 1973, D.C. Tchrs. Coll., 1975. Tchr. adult edn. dept. Richmond (Va.) Pub. Sch. System, 1952-77; project dir., tchr. tng. and edn. dir., tchr. Right to Read Fed. Grant, D.C., 1976-79; in-svc. tchr. tng. U. D.C., Washington, 1975-87; cons.-tchr. in-svc. tchr. tng. program Durham (N.C.) City Schs., 1983-87; tchr. adult edn. dept. Henrico County (Va.) Pub. Schs., 1987—. Dir., condr. numerous in-svc. tng. seminars, classes for elem. and secondary sch. and adult edn. tchrs. in Va., D.C., Md.; tchr. of ESL classes in evening sch.; tchr., spl. com. tng. program for Chesapeake and Ohio Ry., Richmond, 1955-59; tchr. spl. class for postal and fed. employees at Phyllis Wheatley YWCA, Richmond, 1968; dir., tchr. Weiss Reading Inst., Richmond, 1960-76. Co-author: (with Carolyn W. Guertin) Sound Skill Builder, 1976; editor-in-chief: Sure Steps to Reading and Spelling, 1976, The Science of Reading and Spelling. Mem. Am. Assn. for Adult and Continuing Edn., Learning Disabilities Assn., The Learning Disabilites Coun. of Richmond, Altrusa Internat. Inc. of Capital City of Va. Avocations: creative writing, English lang. rsch., composer, lyricist. Home: 5309 W Grace St Richmond VA 23226-1113

BLANK, WILLIAM RUSSELL, mathematics educator; b. Utica, N.Y., Aug. 7, 1916; s. William Nicholas and Marguerite Dorothy (Pugh) B.; m. Elizabeth Jeanette Roman, Sept. 12, 1942; children: William Keith, Marvin Darryl, Ronald Paul. BA, Union Coll., Nebr., 1939; postgrad., U. Mich., 1939-40, Syracuse U., 1952-56; MA, U. Nebr., 1953. Cert. tchr. math., phys. sci., N.Y. Tchr. math., sci. Staatsburg (N.Y.) Union Sch., 1941-42, Fresno (Calif.) Union Acad., 1946-48; instr. math. Union Coll., Lincoln, Nebr., 1948-50; tchr., dept. head Whitesboro (N.Y.) Cen. Sch., 1950-78. Adj. faculty Mohawk Valley C.C., Utica, 1956-2003; pvt. tutor in math., 1950—. Sgt. U.S. Army, 1942-45. Recipient awards NSF, 1957, 58, 59, 60. Mem. Ret. Tchrs. Assn., VFW, Am. Legion, IBM Magicians Club, SAM Magician Club, Pi Mu Epsilon, Phi Delta Kappa, Nat. Coun. Tchrs. Math. Avocations: travel, reading, music, church functions. Home: 34 Burr Ave New York Mills NY 13417-1305

BLANKENSHIP, DOLORES MOOREFIELD, principal, music educator, retired; b. Atlanta, June 4, 1929; d. Albert Talmadge and Willie Mae (Cole) Moorefield; divorced; 1 child, Diane Lee. BME, Northwestern U., 1951; MA, Ohio State U., Columbus, 1958. Cert. music tchr., secondary principal, Ohio. Vocal music tchr. Hoke Smith High Sch., Atlanta, 1951-52; vocal instr., tchr. Reynoldsburg (Ohio) Sch., 1952-53; substitute music tchr. various public schs., El Paso, Tex., 1953; vocal music tchr. Columbus (Ohio) Public Schs., 1956-73, asst. prin., 1973-86, prin., 1986-94. Adv. bd. Capital Area Humane Soc., Columbus, 1987-94; pres. Altrusa, Columbus, 1973, 87; mem. Columbus Mus. of Arts; docent Wexner Ctr. for Arts, 1994-2001; mem. planning com. Columbus Arts Festival, 1994-2001; vol. FACTLIVE Columbus Pub. Sch.; docent Columbus Symphony Orch., 1995; AARP coord. Capital City Task Force, 1997-2000. Mem. Nat. Middle Sch. Adminstr. Assn. (Ohio chpt., Columbus chpt. pres. 1990-91), Columbus Adminstr. Assn. (exec. bd. 1989-91), Ohio Assn. Deans, Adminstr., Counselors (treas. 1988-90). Avocations: reading, jazz music, movies, plays, travel. Home: 1291 Hanford Sq Columbus OH 43206-3668

BLANKENSHIP, ROBERT EUGENE, biochemistry educator; b. Auburn, Nebr., Aug. 25, 1948; s. George Robert and Jane (Kehoe) Leech; m. Elizabeth Marie Dorland, June 26, 1971; children: Larissa Dorland, Samuel Robert. BS, Wesleyan U., Nebr., 1970; PhD, U. Calif., Berkeley, 1975. Postdoctoral fellow Lawrence Berkeley Lab., Berkeley, 1975-76, U. Washington, Seattle, 1976-79; asst. prof. Amherst (Mass.) Coll., 1979-85; assoc. prof. Ariz. State U., Tempe, 1985-88, prof., 1988—, chair, dept. chem. and biochem., 2002—, dir. Ctr. Study of Early Events in Photosynthesis, 1988-91. Author: Molecular Mechanisms of Photosynthesis, 2002; editor Anoxygenic Photosynthetic Bacteria, 1995; editor-in-chief Photosynthesis Rsch., 1988-99; cons. editor Advances in Photosynthesis, 1991-98; mem. editl. bd. Biophys. Jour., 2000-03, Biochemistry, 2001—, Internat. Jour. Astrobiology, 2001—; contbr. 190 articles to sci. jours. Recipient Alumni award Nebr. Wesleyan U., 1991, Disting. Rsch. award Ariz. State U., 1992, Mentoring award Ariz. State U., 1998. Mem. AAAS, Am. Chem. Soc., Biophys. Soc., Union of Concerned Scientists, Internat. Soc. of Photosynthesis Rsch. (pres. 2001-), Internat. Soc. for Study of Origin of Life. Democrat. Avocations: hiking, cooking, travel, fossil collecting. Home: 13824 S Canyon Dr Phoenix AZ 85048-9085 Office: Ariz State U Dept Chemistry And Bio Tempe AZ 85287-1604

BLANKENSHIP, TRENT, state official, educator; married; 3 children. BS in Sci. Edn., U. Wyo., 1986, MA in Ednl. Adminstrn., 1991, PhD in Leadership and Human Devel., 1995. Chemistry tchr. Riverton H.S., Wyo.; chemistry and physics tchr. Heidelburg H.S. Dept. of Defense, Germany; asst. prin. Sheridan Jr. H.S., Sheridan County, Wyo.; prin. DuBois H.S. and Middle Sch., Wyo.; supt. Fremont Sch. District, DuBois, Wyo., Carbon County Sch. Dist., Rawlins; state supt. pub. instrn. State of Wyo., Cheyenne, 2003—. Mem. Wyo. CAS Policy Com. Mem. adv. bd. U. Wyo. Coll. Edn.; mem. Gov.'s Substance Abuse Com. Home: 1317 W Walnut Rawlins WY 82301-6548 Office: Wyo Dept Edn Hathaway Bldg 2300 Capitol Ave 2d Fl Cheyenne WY 82002-0050 E-mail: champion4children@yahoo.com.

BLASCHKE, ROBERT CARVEL, education coordinator; b. Elizabeth, N.J., May 3, 1928; s. Albert Charles and Beulah Katherine (Stone) B.; m. Carol Lee Stoker, June 2, 1960; children: Robert, Elizabeth, Stephen, Philip, Joel. BA in Anthropology, Wheaton Coll., 1949; BD in Theology, Gordon Conwell Sem., Wenham, Mass., 1952; MA in Linguistics and Literacy, Hartford (Conn.) Theol. Sem., 1969. Missionary linguist Soc. Internat. Ministries, Rep. of Benin, Africa, 1954-79, interim dist. supt., 1979-80, dir. hosp., 1980-81; instr. Le Tourneau U., Longview, Tex., 1981-85; coord. missionary children's ednl. care Soc. Internat. Ministries, Charlotte, N.C., 1985-95. Mem. sch. bd. Kent Acad., Jos, Nigeria, 1972-81; mem. steering com. Internat. Conf. Missionary Kids, 1985—; mem. MK CART/CORE, 1987—; mem. Mu Kappa Internat., 1987-95. Recipient Century Club award Wheaton Coll., 1972, Disting. Svc. award Wheaton Coll. Alumni Assn., 1983. Baptist. Avocations: photography, refinishing furniture. Office: SIM Internat 14830 Choate Cir Charlotte NC 28273-9105

BLASING, MUTLU KONUK, English language educator; b. Istanbul, Turkey, June 27, 1944; came to U.S., 1963; d. Mustafa Celal Konuk and Muzeyyen (Uzun) Dursunoglu; m. Randolph Charles Blasing, Aug. 21, 1965; 1 child, John Konuk. Student, Carleton Coll., 1963-65; BA, Coll. William and Mary, 1969; PhD, Brown U., 1974. Lectr. English U. Mass., Mass., 1974-76; asst. prof. Pomona Coll., Claremont, Calif., 1977-79, Brown U., 1979-83, assoc. prof., 1983-88, prof., 1988—. Dir. Copper Beech Press, Providence. Author: The Art of Life, 1977, American Poetry: The Rhetoric of Its Forms, 1987, Politics and Form in Postmodern Poetry, 1995; translator: Human Landscapes (N. Hikmet), 1982, Epic of Sheik Bedreddin (N. Hikmet), 1975, Things I Didn't Know I Loved, (N. Hikmet), 1975, Rubaiyat (N.Hikmet), 1985, Selected Poetry (N. Hikmet), 1986, Poems of Nazim Hikmet, 1994, Human Landscapes from my Country (N. Hikmet), 2002, Poems of Nazim Hikmet, 2002. Fellow U. Mass., 1974-76. Office: Brown U English Dept PO Box 1852 Providence RI 02912-1852

BLASS, JOHN PAUL, medical educator, physician; b. Vienna, Feb. 21, 1937; s. Gustaf and Jolan (Wirth) B.; m. Birgit Annelise Knudsen, Dec. 20, 1960; children: Charles, Lisa. AB summa cum laude, Harvard U., 1958; PhD, U. London, 1960; MD, Columbia U., 1965. Postdoctoral fellow Am. Cancer Soc., Columbia U., 1962-63; intern Mass. Gen. Hosp., Boston, 1965-66, resident in medicine, 1966-67; research assoc. Nat. Heart and Lung Inst., Bethesda, Md., 1967-70; asst. prof. psychiatry and biol. chemistry UCLA, 1970-76, assoc. prof., 1976-78; mem. staff UCLA Hosps. Clinics, 1970-78; Winifred Masterson Burke prof. neurology, prof. medicine Cornell U. Med. Center, 1978—. Attending neurologist N.Y. Hosp.; mem. NBS-1 rev. com. NIH, 1981-84; councilor Nat. Inst. Aging, 1986-89; chmn. Nat. Adv. Panel on Alzheimers's Disease U.S. Congress, 1987-91, mem., 1993-96. Jour. Neurochemistry, 1981—86, Neurochem. Rsch., 1984—86, Neurochem. Pathology, Neurobiol. Aging, Jour. Neurol. Sci., 1990—2000, Jour. Molecular Neurosci., 1999—, assoc. editor Jour. Am. Geriatric Soc., 1982—87, Age, 1993—95, Yearbook of Neurology and Neurosurgery, 1992—; co-editor: Caring for Alzheimer's Patients, 1990—, Familial Alzheimer's Disease, 1989—, Treatment of Alzheimer's Disease, 1989—, Principles of Geriatrics and Gerontology, 2d edit., 1990—, Principles of Geriatrics and Gerontology, 3d edit., 1994—, Principles of Geriatrics and Gerontology, 4th edit., 1998—; contbr. articles to profl. jours. Mem. sci. adv. bd. Will Rogers Inst., 1981-97, Allied Signal Aging Award Com., 1993-95. Served as asst. surgeon USPHS, 1967-70. Marshall scholar, 1958-60. Mem. Soc. Neurosci. (chmn. social issues com.), Biochem. Soc., Am. Soc. Biol. Chemists, Am. Soc. Neurochemistry (council, chmn. public policy com.), Internat. Soc. Neurochemistry (council, chmn. clin. com.), Am. Soc. Clin. Investigation, Am. Geriatrics Soc., Am. Fedn. Aging Rsch. (v.p., chmn. research com. 1982-87, pres. 1994-96), Assn. Alzheimers and Related Disease (sci. adv. bd. 1982-86), Am. Chem. Soc., Phi Beta Kappa, Sigma Xi, Alpha Omega Alpha. Jewish. Home: 1 Orchard Pl Bronxville NY 10708-2509 Office: Burke Med Rsch Inst 785 Mamaroneck Ave White Plains NY 10605-2523 E-mail: jpblass@mail.med.cornell.edu.

BLASS, WALTER PAUL, consultant, management educator; b. Dinslaken, Germany, Mar. 31, 1930; s. Richard B. and Malvi (Rosenblatt) B.; m. Janice L. Minott, Apr. 2, 1954; children: Kathryn, Christopher, Gregory. BA, Swarthmore Coll., 1951; postgrad., Princeton U., 1951-52; MA, Columbia U., 1953. Asst. Laos and Cambodia desk offoicer ICA, Wash., 1957-58; gen. mgr. R.B. Blass Co., Deal, NJ, 1958-61; economist AT&T, N.Y.C., 1961-65; country dir. Peace Corps., Afghanistan, 1966-68; asst. v.p. revenue requirement studies NY Telephone Co., N.Y.C., 1968-70; dir. corp. planning AT&T, 1970-82, dir. strategic planning, 1982-85; ret., 1985—. Pres., Strategic Plans, Unltd., Warren, N.J., 1985—. Exec. Fellow-in-Residence Martino Grad. Sch. Bus. Adminstrn., Fordham U., N.Y.C., 1986-90; cons. McKinsey & Co., Telecom. Authority Ireland, McDonnell Douglas, Heller Fin., Inc.; lectr. in field; vis. prof. U. Grenoble, France, 1988, Ecole Superieure de Commerce, Chambery and Grenoble, France, 1989—. Trustee Guilford Coll., 1975—, chmn. planning com., 1992-99, vice chmn. tchrs. and officers com., 1999—. Co-author: The Strategic Planning Handbook, 1982, Handbook of Strategic Planning, 1986. Lt., j.g., USNR, 1953-56, Woodrow Wilson Found., sr. fell., 1974-85. Mem., N.Y. Acad. Scis., Soc. Values in Higher Edn. (dir. 1983-86), Am. Econ.Assn., Nat. Assn. Bus. Economists, The Planning Forum (dir. 1972), Royal Econ. Soc. Home and Office: 6 Casale Dr Warren NJ 07059-6703

BLATTEIS, CLARK MARTIN, physiology educator, researcher; b. Berlin, June 25, 1932; s. Ernest E. and Gerda S. (Lewinski) B.; m. Yolanda (Fuentes), Mar. 16, 1958; children: Beatrice, Elisa, Charles. BS, Rutgers Univ., 1954; MS, U. Iowa, 1955, PhD, 1957. Rsch. physiologist USA Inst. Environ. Medicine, Natick, Mass., 1963-66; assoc. prof. U. Tenn., Memphis, 1966-74, prof., 1974—. Vis. prof. in physiology. Editor: Thermoregulation, 1997, 98; assoc. editor Am. Jour. Physiology, News in Physiological Sci.; mem. editl. bd.; co-editor: APS Handbook on Environmental Physiology, 1996; contbg. papers and reviews to profl. journals. Leader Boy Scouts Am., Memphis, 1972-79; chmn. Chs. and Social Svc. Fund, Memphis, 1974-76; mem. State Bd. Med. Examiners, Nashville, 1975-76. 1st lt. USA, 1957-60. Postdoctoral fellow NIH, 1960-63, grantee, 1967—; Fulbright-Hays Sr. Fellow, 1975, 94. Mem. Am. Physiol. Soc., Internat. Union Physiol. Scis. Commn. on thermal Physiology (chmn. 1989-96), others. Office: U Tenn 894 Union Ave Memphis TN 38163-0001

BLATTNER, FLORENCE ANNE, retired music educator; b. Rockford, Ill., Nov. 27, 1935; d. Keith F. and Grace L. (Turney) Perkins; m. Lewis Olof Blattner, Mar. 28, 1959; children: Gloria Grace Blattner Mundt, Gayle Mary Blattner Ludwig. BA, Carroll Coll., 1958; studied with, Vladimir Levitski, 1984—95, Weekly and Arganbright, U. Ind, 1993, 98, 2000, Joanne Tierney, 1995—2002. Elem. and jr. high sch. libr. Racine (Wis.) Pub. Schs., 1958—60, elem. substitute tchr., 1961—62, elem. and jr. high tchr., 1962; pvt. practice piano instr. Indpls., 1970—78; data processor OMS Internat., Greenwood, Ind., 1978; pvt. practice piano and theory instr. Des Moines, 1980—83; piano and theory instr. Prelude Piano Studio, Apple Valley, Minn., 1983—2003; ret., 2003. Duettist concerts duet lit., Racine, Wis., 1996, 1999, Apple Valley, Minn., 1996, 1998—2002, White Bear Lake, 1996, Dodge City, Kans., 2001, Bloomington, Minn., 1996—97, 2001, Godfrey, Ill., 1998, 2000, Alton, Ill., 1998, 2000. Ch. pianist, accompianist, 1970—; vol. Rep. Party-Minn., Apple Valley, 1992, 94, 96, 98. Mem. Music Tchrs. Nat. Assn., Minn. Music Tchrs. (assoc. cert., state ensemble festival chair 1994-97, cert. com. 1997-2001), South Suburban Music Tchrs. Assn. (1st v.p. 1995-97, pres. 1998-2000, newsletter editor 1995-2001, yearbook editor 2001-2002), Nat. Guild Piano Tchrs., Am. Fedn. Music Clubs. Avocations: canoeing, hiking, traveling, reading, piano. E-mail: flblattner@usfamily.net.

BLATTNER, MEERA MCCUAIG, computer science educator; b. Chgo., Aug. 14, 1930; d. William D. McCuaig and Nina (Spertus) Klevs; m. Minao Kamegai, June 22, 1985; children: Douglas, Robert, William. BA, U. Chgo., 1952; MS, U. So. Calif., 1966; PhD, UCLA, 1973. Rsch. fellow in computer sci. Harvard U., 1973-74; asst. prof. Rice U., 1974-80; assoc. prof. applied sci. U. Calif.-Davis, Livermore, 1980-91, prof. applied sci., 1991-99, prof. emeritus, 2000—; pres. Color Wheel Creations, 2001—. Adj. prof. U. Tex., Houston, 1977—99; vis. prof. U. Paris, 1980; program dir. theoretical computer sci. NSF, Washington, 1979—80. Co-editor: (with R. Dannenberg) Multimedia Interface Design, 1992; contbr. articles to profl. jours. NSF grantee, 1977-81, 93-99. Mem. Assn. Computing Machinery, Computer Soc. of IEEE. Office: Color Wheel Creations 850 S Durango Rd Ste 107 Las Vegas NV 89145 E-mail: meera.blattner@cvi.net.

BLAU, HELEN MARGARET, molecular pharmacology educator; b. London, May 8, 1948; (parents Am. citizens); d. George E. and Gertrude Blau; m. David Spiegel, July 25, 1976; children: Daniel Spiegel, Julia Spiegel. BA in Biology, U. York (Eng.), 1969; MA in Biology, Harvard U., 1970, PhD in Biology, 1975. Predoctoral fellow dept. biology Harvard U., Cambridge, Mass., 1969-75; postdoctoral fellow div. med. genetics, dept. biochemistry and biophysics U. Calif., San Francisco, 1975-78; asst. prof. dept. pharmacology Stanford (Calif.) U., 1978-86, assoc. prof. dept. pharmacology, 1986-91, prof. dept. molecular pharmacology, 1991—, prof. dept. microbiology and immunology, 2002—, chair dept. molecular pharmacology, 1997—2001, Donald E. and Delia B. Baxter prof., 1999—, dir. Baxter Lab. in Genetic Pharmacology, 2002—. Co-chmn. various profl. meetings. Mem. editorial bd. 14 jours. including Jour. Cell Biology, Somatic Cell Molecular Genetics and Exptl. Cell Rsch., Molecular and Cellular Biology, Genes to Cells, Molecular Therapy; contbr. articles to profl. jours. Mem. ad hoc molecular cytology study sect. NIH, 1987-88; mem. five-yr. planning com genetics and teratology br. NICHHD/NIH, 1989. Recipient Rsch. Career Devel. award NIH, 1984-89, SmithKline & Beecham award, 1989-91, Women in Cell Biology Career Recognition award, 1992, Excellence in Sci. award FASEB, 1999, McKnight Endowment Fund for Neurosci. award, 2001; Mellon Found. faculty fellow, 1979-80, William H. Hume faculty scholar, 1981-84; grantee NIH, NSF, Ellison Med. Found., Muscular Dystrophy Assn., March of Dimes, 1978—; Yvette Mayent-Rothschild fellow for vis. profs. Inst. Curie, Paris, 1995. Fellow AAAS; mem. NAS (del. to China 1991), Internat. Soc. Differentiation (pres. 2002—), Am. Soc. for Cell Biology (nominating com. 1985-86, program com. 1990), Soc. for Devel. Biology (pres. 1994-95). Avocations: skiing, swimming, hiking, music, theatre.

BLAUNSTEIN, PHYLLIS REID, communications and marketing executive; b. N.Y.C., July 4, 1940; d. Alex and Elsie (Rothstein) Lepler; m. Robert Philip Blaunstein, June 17, 1962; children: Eric Reid, Marc Reid. BA in English, SUNY, Albany, 1962; MA in Speech Pathology and Audiology, U. Tenn., 1967. English tchr. Knox County Bd. Edn., East Cleveland Bd. Edn., Cleve., 1962-66; instr. speech pathology and audiology U. Tenn., Knoxville, 1968-73; dir. Hearing and Speech Clinic U. Tenn. Meml. Rsch. Hosp., Knoxville, 1972-73; program mgr., coord. for ethical practice affairs Am. Speech, Hearing and Lang. Assn., Washington, 1973-75; spl. asst. to dep. commr. Bur. Edn. for the Handicapped U.S. Dept. Edn., Washington, 1976-77; dir. spl. projects Nat. Assn. State Bds. Edn., Washington, 1977-78, assoc. exec. dir., 1978-79, dep. exec. dir., 1979-80, exec. dir., 1981-87; sr. counsel Widmeyer Comms., Washington, 1988—; pres. Phyllis Blaunstein and Assocs., Inc., Chevy Chase, Md., 1989—. Cons. Ford Found., U.S. Edn. Dept., USPHS, Md. State Dept. Edn., Ednl. Comm., Inc., Nat. Assn. State Dirs. Spl. Edn. Bd. dirs.nat. capital area NCCJ. Office: Phyllis Blaunstein and Assoc 2703 Daniel Rd Chevy Chase MD 20815-3150

BLAZEY, JUDITH LEISTON, school district administrator; b. Rochester, N.Y., Mar. 6, 1941; d. Emanuel R. and Julia (Nicoletti) Leiston; m. John T. Blazey, May 11, 1963; children: John T. II, James R., Jeffrey S. BS, SUNY, Brockport, 1962, MS, 1987, CAS, 1988. Cert. sch. dist. adminstr., sch. adminstr. and supr. English dept. coord. Palmyra (N.Y.)-Macedon High Sch., 1979-82, 84-88, 89-91, tchr., 1962-63, 64-66, 1972-95, ret., 1995; dist. English/lang. arts coord. Palmyra Macedon Cen. Sch., 1988-89. Adj. instr. SUNY Finger Lakes Cmty. Coll., Canandaigua, N.Y., 1982-86. Mem. Nat. Coun. Tchrs. English, N.Y. State English Coun., Delta Kappa Gamma.

BLECHMAN, WILBUR JORDAN, medical educator; b. Washington, May 7, 1932; s. Charles and Florence (Goodman) B.; m. Sidell Ray Cohen, June 26, 1955 (dec. Mar. 1983); children: Michele, Michael, Ivy; m. Rachel Simonhoff Rudin, May 26, 1985. BS, Yale U., 1954; MD, Med. Coll. of Va., 1957. Diplomate Am. Bd. Internal Medicine and Rheumatology. Pvt. practice, North Miami Beach, Fla., 1961-94; clin. prof. of medicine U. Miami Sch. Medicine, 1980-95; dir. Resources for Children, Inc., Miami, 1994-95; state health officer Fla., 1995-96; courtesy prof. pub. health U. South Fla., 1996—2000; sr. cons. Fla. Dept. Health, Dept. Children and Families, 1996-98; program officer Lawton & Rhea Chiles Ctr. for Healthy Mothers & Babies, 1997-98, cons., 1998. Co-dir. Miami Arthritis Ctr., 1985-93; cons. Bertha Abess Children's Ctr., Miami, 1999—; co-chair child health and well-being task force Miami-Dade County Early Childhood Initiative, 1999—. Contbr. articles to profl. jours. Chmn. Fla. Kids Count Adv. Coun., 1992-94; mem. U.S. Kids Count Adv. Group, 1991-94; vice-chmn. Children's Trust, Miami-Dade County, 2003—; bd. dirs. Fla. Children's Forum, 1991—. Recipient Disting. Svc. award The Arthritis Found., 1971, Physician's award for Outstanding Cmty. Svc. Fla. Med. Assn., Wyeth-Ayerst Labs., 1990, Hannah G. Solomon award Nat. Coun. Jewish Women, 1992, State Health Office Cmty. Friend award, 1993, Help and Hope award for Excellence in Rheumatology Arthritis Found. S.E. Fla., 1994, Recognition letter Sec. U.S. Dept. Health and Human Svcs., 1995; named 1993 Champion for Children Miami-Dade C.C., Friend of Coop. Extension, 1993. Mem. ACP, Am. Coll. Rheumatology, Fla. Soc. of Rheumatology (pres. 1970-71), Internat. Coun. for the Control of Iodine Deficiency Disorders (bd. dirs. 1994-96), Kiwanis (pres. Internat. 1990-91, Citizen of Yr. Biscayne club 1992), Fla. Assn. for Infant Mental Health (charter pres. 2001-03). Home and Office: 5250 SW 84th St Miami FL 33143-8434 E-mail: wilblechman@aol.com.

BLECKE, ARTHUR EDWARD, retired principal; b. Oak Park, Ill., Sept. 21, 1926; s. Paul Gerard and Mathilda (Ziebell); m. June Audrey Eckholm, Jan. 22, 1949; children: William, Robert, Carol. BS in Phys. Edn., U. Ill., 1950; M.Edn., Loyola U., 1967. Tchr., coach Buckley High Sch., Ill., 1951-52, Paxton High Sch., Ill., 1952-53; tchr., coach, dept. chmn. Luther High Sch. North, Chgo., Ill., 1953-65; asst. coach football and basketball Elmhurst Coll., Ill., 1965-66; dean, prin. Antioch Community High Sch., Ill., 1966-91. Cons. in field; lectr. Contbr. articles to profl. jours. Mem. sanitary dist. Village of Lindenhurst, Ill., 1968-92, chmn., 1972-92; planning commn., 1967-77; chmn. long range planning com. and bldg. com. Bella Vista Luth. Ch. Served with U.S. Army, 1945. Recipient Hon. Mention Those Who Excel, Ill. State Bd. Edn., 1980; named Prin. of Yr. for Ill. Nat. Assn. of Secondary Sch. Prins., The Coun. of Chief State Sch. Officer, and The Burger King Corp., 1987. Mem. Ill. Prins. Assn. (dir. 1980-81, 83-84, Herman Graves award, 1991), Nat. Assn. Secondary Sch. Prins. Lutheran. Avocations: golf, model building, model ralroading.

BLEES, JOAN MARGARET, music educator; b. St. Paul, Apr. 12, 1948; d. James Spotts and Margaret Elizabeth (Laufenberg) Travis; m. James Edward Blees. BA, U. Minn., St. Paul, 1970; MPS, Loyola U., New Orleans, 1991. Nationally cert. tchr. music, kindermusik cert. Owner, instr. Blees Music Instrn., Anchorage, 1973—, Blees Kindermusik, Anchorage, 1994—; organist, choir dir. Cath. Ch., Anchorage, 1973—; liturgical music cons. Archdiocese of Anchorage, 1987-94; music tchr. Anchorage Montessori Sch., 1996—. Choir dir. Archdiocese of Anchorage; adjudicator Am. Keyboard Tchrs. Assn., Am. Music Tchrs. Assn., 1985—. Named master cantor Nat. Pastoral Musicians, 1987. Mem. Anchorage Keyboard Tchrs. Assn. (mem. bd., 1974-77, 80-83, 93-95.

BLETHEN, HAROLD TYLER, III, history educator; AB, Bowdoin Coll., 1967; MA, U. N.C., 1969, PhD, 1972. Asst. prof. history Western Carolina U., Cullowhee, N.C., 1972-78, assoc. prof. history, 1978-87, prof. history, 1987—; dir. Mountain Heritage Ctr., Western Carolina U., Cullowhee, 1985—. Bd. dirs. Western N.C. Tomorrow. Co-author: From Ulster to Carolina, 1983, revised edit., 1998, A Mountain Heritage, 1989, Ulster and North America, 1997; editor: Irons in the Fire, 1992, Diversity in Appalachia: Images and Realities, 1993. Mem. N.C. Humanities Coun., 1989-93. Mem. Hist. Soc. N.C., Western N.C. Hist. Assn. (trustee 1990-97), N.Am. Conf. on Brit. Studies, Appalachian Studies Assn., Appalachian Consortium (vice-chmn. 1995-97, chair 1997-99), So. Hist. Assn. Avocations: sailing, hiking. Office: Western Carolina U Dept History Cullowhee NC 28723

BLEVINS, ANDREA ELIZABETH, secondary education educator; b. Colorado Springs, Dec. 22, 1944; d. Sydney Stewart and Olive Elizabeth (Reed) McLean; m. Bobby Eldon Blevins, Nov. 15, 1969. BA in Polit. Sci. with Distinction, Wash. State U., 1966, MA, 1969; profl. cert., West Ga. Coll., 1982. Cert. polit. sci. tchr., middle grades tchr., Ga. Tchr. social studies, lang. arts, math., computer tech. Clayton County Bd. Edn., Jonesboro, Ga., 1979—. Swim team coach Pointe South Middle Sch., Jonesboro, 1982-94, mem. multicultural edn. com., 1990—, supr. sch. publs., 1982—. Recipient Hon. life membership for outstanding svc. to our children and youth Ga. PTA. Mem. AAUW, ASCD, Profl. Assn. Ga. Educators, Pi Sigma Alpha. Methodist. Avocations: recreational reading, golf, bowling, computer science, german. Home: 8282 Winston Way Jonesboro GA 30236-4057 Office: Pointe South Middle Sch 626 Flint River Rd Jonesboro GA 30238-3407

BLEVINS, DALE GLENN, agronomy educator; b. Ozark, Mo., Aug. 29, 1943; s. Vernon Henry and Edna Gertrude Blevins; 1 child, Jeremy. BS in Chemistry, S.W. Mo. State U., 1965; MS in Soils, U. Mo., 1967; PhD in Plant Physiology, U. Ky., 1972. Postdoctoral fellow botany dept. Oreg. State U., Corvallis, Oreg., 1972-74; asst. prof. botany U. Md., College Park, 1974-78; assoc. prof. agronomy dept. U. Mo., Columbia, 1978-86, prof., 1986—. Mem. Am. Soc. Plant Physiology, Am. Soc. Agronomy, Crop Sci. Soc. Am. Office: Univ Mo Dept Agronomy 1-87 Agriculture Building Columbia MO 65211-7140

BLIZNAKOV, MILKA TCHERNEVA, architect, educator; b. Varna, Bulgaria, Sept. 20, 1927; came to U.S., 1961, naturalized, 1966; d. Ivan Dimitrov and Maria Kesarova (Khorozova) Tchernev; m. Emile G. Bliznakov, Oct. 23, 1954 (div. Apr. 1974). Architect-engr. diploma, State Tech. U., Sofia, 1951; PhD, Engring.-Structural Inst., Sofia, 1959; PhD in Architecture, Columbia U., 1971. Sr. researcher Ministry Heavy Industry, Sofia, 1950-53; pvt. practice architecture Sofia, 1954-59; assoc. architect Noel Combrisson, Paris, 1959-61; designer Perkins & Will Partnership, White

Plains, N.Y., 1963-67; project architect Lathrop Douglass, N.Y.C., 1967-71; assoc. prof. architecture and planning Sch. Architecture, U. Tex., Austin, 1972-74; prof. Coll. Architecture, Va. Poly. Inst. and State U., Blacksburg, 1974-98, prof. emerita, 1998—; prin. Blacksburg, 1975—. Bd. dirs. founder Internat. Archives Women in Architecture, Va. Poly. Inst. and State U., The Parthena award, 1994. Prin. works include Speedwell Ave. Urban Renewal, Morristown, N.J., 1967—69, Wilmington (Del.) Urban Renewal, 1968—70, Springfield (Ill.) Ctrl. Area Devel., 1969—71, Arlington County (Va.) Redevel., 1975—77; author (with others): Utopia e Modernitá, 1989, Reshaping Russian Archtecture, 1990, Russian Housing in the Modern Age, 1993, Nietzsche and Soviet Culture, 1994, New Perspectives on Russian and Soviet Artistic Culture, 1994, The Eastern Dada Orbit: Russia, Georgia, Ukraine, Central Europe, 1996, Signs of Times, Culture and the Emblems of Apocalypse, 1998, Women Architects in Eastern Europe: The Contributions of the Bulgarians, 1997, International Archive of Women in Architecture, 1997, 1999, 2001, 2002, Encyclopedia of Eastern Europe, 2000, Centropa, 2001; author: (with others), 2003; author: (with others) Women Architects in Japan, 2002, Housing in Russia: 20th Century, 2002; author: (with others) Encyclopedia of Twentieth Century Architecture, 2003. William Kinne scholar, 1970, vis. scholar Inst. Advanced Russian Studies, The Wilson Ctr. of Smithsonian Instn., 1988; NEA grantee, 1973-74, Am. Beautiful Found. grantee, 1973, Internat. Rsch. and Exch. Bd. grantee, 1984-93; Fulbright Hays rsch. fellow, 1983-84, 91; recipient Parthena award, 1994. Mem. Internat. Archive Women in Architecture (founder, chair bd. dirs.), Am. Assn. Tchrs. Slavic and East European Langs., Soc. Archtl. Historians, Nat. Trust Hist. Preservation, Am. Assn. Advancement of Slavic Studies, Assn. Collegiate Schs. of Planning, Inst. Modern Russian Culture (chairperson architecture, co-founder, dir.), Bulgarian Studies Assn., Assn. Collegiate Schs. of Architecture. Home: 2813 Tall Oaks Dr Blacksburg VA 24060-8109 Office: Va Poly Inst and State U Coll Architecture Blacksburg VA 24061 E-mail: mbliznak@vt.edu.

BLOCH, ERICH, retired electrical engineer, former science foundation administrator; b. Sulzburg, Germany, Jan. 9, 1925; arrived in U.S., 1948, naturalized, 1952; s. Joseph and Tony Bloch; m. Renee Stern, Mar. 4, 1948; 1 child, Rebecca Bloch Rosen. Student, Fed. Poly. Inst., Zurich, Switzerland, 1945—48; BSEE, U. Buffalo, 1952; hon. degrees, U. Mass., George Washington U., Colo. Sch. Mines, SUNY Buffalo, U. Rochester, Oberlin Coll., U. Notre Dame, Ohio State U.; hon. degree, Rensselaer Poly. Inst., 1989, Washington Coll., 1989, CUNY, N.Y.C., 1991, Poly. U., Bklyn., N.Y., 1993. With IBM, 1952—75, v.p. gen. mgr., 1975—80, v.p. tech. personnel devel. Armonk, NY, 1980—84; mem. com. computers in automated mfg. NRC, 1980—84; dir. NSF, Washington, 1984—90; fellow Coun. on Competitiveness, 1990—; prin. Washington Adv. Group, 1998—; mem. Pres.'s Coun. of Advisors for Sci. and Tech., 2001—. Past vis. disting. prof. George Mason U. Patentee in field. Recipient U.S. medal of tech., 1985, Computer World/Smithsonian award for innovation, 1991, Swedish Royal Order of the Polar Star, Robert Noyce award, Semiconductor Industry Assn., 1999, Eugene Merchant Mfg. medal, ASME and Soc. Mfg. Engrs., Vanevar Bush award, Nat. Sci. Bd., 2002. Fellow: AAAS, IEEE (Founder's award 1990, Computer Pioneer award 1993, 1994); mem.: NAE (Arthur M. Bueche award 1997), Japan Acad. Engring., Royal Swedish Acad. Engring. Scis., Am. Soc. Engring. Edn., Am. Soc. Mfg. Engrs. (hon.). E-mail: ebloch@theadvisorygroup.com.

BLOCH, SUSAN LOW, law educator; b. N.Y.C. d. Ernest and Ruth (Frankel) Low; m. Richard I. Bloch; children: Rebecca, Michael. BA in Math., Smith Coll., 1966; MA in Math., U. Mich., MA in Computer Sci., PhC, 1972, JD, 1975. Bar: D.C. 1975. Law clk. to chief judge U.S. Ct. Appeals, Washington, 1975-76; law clk. to assoc. justice Marshall U.S. Supreme Ct., Washington, 1976-77; assoc. Wilmer, Cutler & Pickering, Washington, 1978-82; prof. Georgetown U. Law Ctr., Washington, 1983—. Legal analyst for impeachment procs. CBS, 1998; impeachment expert U.S. Ho. of Reps. Jud. Com., 1998. Author: Supreme Court Politics: The Institution and Its Procedures, 1994; contbr. Constl. Commentary, Duke Law Jour., Mich. Law Rev., Wis. Law Rev., Law and Contemporary Problems, Georgetown Law Rev., St. Louis U. Law Jour., ABA Jour., Supreme Ct. Preview, Voice of Am., Supreme Ct. Hist. Soc. Yearbook, 1987, Supreme Ct. Hist. Soc. Yearbook, 1992, Oxford Companion to the Supreme Ct. of the United States, 1992, Biology, Culture and Law, 1993. Active Common Cause, Women's Legal Def. Fund. Mem. ABA, Am. Bar Found., Am. Law Inst., D.C. Bar (Bicentennial of Constn., mem. ethics com., jud. evaluation com.), D.C. Cir. Judicial Conf. (prog. chair 1993, 96), U. Mich. Com. Visitors, 1982—, Inst. Pub. Representation (bd. dirs.), Order of Coif, Phi Beta Kappa, Sigma Xi. Home: 4335 Cathedral Ave NW Washington DC 20016-3560 Office: Georgetown U Law Ctr 600 New Jersey Ave NW Washington DC 20001-2075

BLOCHER, PAUL THOMAS, secondary education educator; b. Burbank, Calif., Sept. 20, 1948; s. Howard Dwain and Shirley Irene (Dammson) B.; m. Dianne Lynn Borchardt, Apr. 11, 1992; children: Jennifer Irene, Jeanette Rose, Ross Dwain. BA, San Jose State Coll., 1970; MA, San Jose State U., 1977. Calif. standard secondary teaching credential, Calif. community colls. instr. credential. Math. tchr. Terrace Sch., Lakeport, Calif., 1972-75, Baymonte Christian High Sch., Scotts Valley, Calif., 1975-85, Bethany Bible Coll., Santa Cruz, Calif., 1981-85, Watsonville (Calif.) High Sch., 1985-86, Santa Paula (Calif.) High Sch., 1986-87, Ventura (Calif.) Coll., 1987, Cabrillo Coll., Aptos, Calif., 1986—, San Lorenzo Valley High Sch., Felton, Calif., 1987—, computer mentor, 1989-93, site coun. mem., 1988-90. Guest speaker Bethany Bible Coll., Santa Cruz, 1989; conv. speaker Assn. Christian Schs. Internat., Sacramento, 1978-82. Material coord. Christian Life Ctr., Santa Cruz, 1988-92; mem. children's ch. Christian Life Ctr., Santa Cruz, 1985; crew leader Youth Conservaiton Corps, Niscene Marks Forest, 1978. Cpl. USMC, 1970-74. Mem. NEA, Nat. Coun. Tchrs. Math., Calif. Math. Coun., Calif. Tchrs. Assn., Gideons Internat. (treas. 1982-85). Democrat. Methodist. Avocations: spelunking, stamp collecting, hiking, auto repairs, computers. Office: San Lorenzo Valley High Sch 7105 Hwy 9 Felton CA 95018-9718

BLOCK, NED, philosopher, educator; b. Chgo., Aug. 22, 1942; s. Eli William and Blanche (Rabinowitz) Block; m. Susan Carey, May 17, 1970; 1 child, Eliza. SB in Physics and Philosophy, MIT, 1964; postgrad., Oxford (Eng.) U., 1964-66; PhD, Harvard U., 1971. Asst. prof. philosophy MIT, Cambridge, Mass., 1971-77, assoc. prof., 1977-83, prof., 1983-96, chair dept. philosophy, 1989-95, chair press cognitive rev. bd., 1992—95; prof. NYU, N.Y.C., 1996—. Mem. faculty NEH Inst., 1981, 93; grant reviewer NSF, Can. Coun.; vis. rschr. Ecole Poly., Paris, 1995—96; vis. prof. Harvard U., 2002—03. Adv. editor: Contemporary Psychology; mem. editl. bd. Cognition, Cognition and Brain Theory, Cognitive Sci., mem. adv. editl. bd. Lang. and Cognitive Processes, Mind and Lang. Philos. Studies, mem. bd. editl. advisors Behavioral and Brain Scis.; contbr. articles to profl. jours. Named one of 10 Best, Philosphers' Ann., 1983, 1990, 1995, 2002; fellow, Old Dominion Found., 1973—74, Sloan Found., 1980—81; grantee, U.S. Nat. Com. Internat. Union History and Philosophy Sci., 1979, 1983, NEH, 1979—82, NSF, 1985—86, 1988—90, Am. Coun. Learned Socs., 1988—89; Postdoctoral fellow, NIH, 1970—71, Sr. fellow, Ctr. Study Lang. and Info., Stanford U., 1984—85. Mem.: Assn. Sci. Study Consciousness (pres.-elect 2002—). Home: 37 Washington Sq W New York NY 10011-9181 Office: NYU Dept Philosophy Main Bldg 100 Washington Sq E New York NY 10003-6688 E-mail: ned.block@nyu.edu.

BLOCK, RICHARD ATTEN, psychology educator; b. Evanston, Illinois; BA, U. Mich., 1968; PhD, U. Oreg., 1973. Vis. asst. prof. State U. of N.Y., Plattsburgh, NY, 1973-74; asst. prof. Mont. State U., 1974-79, assoc. prof., 1979-85, prof. psychology, 1985—, head dept. psychology, 1986-94. Editor: Cognitive Models of Psychological Time, 1990; cons., editor Memory and Cognition, 1994-97; contbg. chapters to books. Mem. Am. Psychol. Soc.; Psychonomic Soc.; Internat. Soc. for Study of Time,(treas. 1989-95). Office: Mont State U Dept Psychology Bozeman MT 59717-3440

BLOCK, ROBERT CHARLES, nuclear engineering and engineering physics educator; b. Newark, Feb. 11, 1929; s. George and Sue (Ehrenkranz) B.; m. Rita Adler, June 28, 1952; children: Keith, Robin. BSEE, Newark Coll. Engring., 1950; MA in Physics, Columbia U., 1953; PhD in Nuclear Physics, Duke U., 1956. Elec. engr. Nat. Union Radio Corp., W. Orange, N.J., 1950-51, Bendix Aviation Co., Teterboro, N.J., 1951; physicist Oak Ridge Nat. Lab., 1955-66; prof. nuclear engring. and sci. Rensselaer Poly. Inst., 1966-96, head dept. nuclear engring. and engring. physics, 1987-93, 1987-93, assoc. dean engring. for acad. & student affairs, 1993-96; prof. emeritus, 1997—; founder, v.p., treas. Becker, Block & Harris Inc., 1981-92. Vis. scientist Atomic Energy Rsch. Establishment, Harwell, Eng., 1962-63, Am. Inst. Physics, 1961-67; vis. prof. Kyoto (Japan) U., 1973-74; vis. physicist Brookhaven Nat. Lab., 1975, mem. vis. com. nuclear energy dept., 1982-86; cons. Gen. Electric Co., 1968-79; cons., mem. nuclear cross sect. adv. com. AEC, 1969-72; mem. U.S. Nuclear Data Com., 1972-74, NRC panel on low and medium energy neutrons, 1977; dir. Gaerttner Linac Lab., 1974—; vis. faculty Sandia Nat. Lab., 1986. Co-author chpt. in books. Recipient Glenn Murphy award Am. Soc. Engring. Edn., 1991, William H. Wiley Disting. Faculty award Rensselaer Poly. Inst., 1995; Japanese Ministry Edn. rsch. grantee, 1973-74. Fellow Am. Nuclear Soc.; mem. AAAS, AAUP, IEEE, Am. Phys. Soc., Sigma Xi, Sigma Pi Sigma, Phi Beta Tau, Tau Beta Pi. Achievements include research on neutron physics, radiation effects in electronics, and radiation applications. Home: 114 3rd St Troy NY 12180 Office: Rensselaer Poly Inst Gaerttner LINAC Lab 110 8th St Troy NY 12180-3590 E-mail: blockr@rpi.edu.

BLOCK, ROBERT I. psychologist, researcher, educator; b. Newark, N.J., Jan. 30, 1951; s. Milton and Harriet (Safier) B. BA with honors, Shimer Coll., 1969; MS, Harvard U., 1972, Rutgers U., 1977, PhD, 1981. Teaching asst. psychology dept. Rutgers U., New Brunswick, N.J., 1975-76; psychologist Lafayette Clinic, Detroit, 1982-84; rsch. assoc. psychiatry dept. Wayne State U., Detroit, 1982, instr., 1982-84; assoc. rsch. scientist dept. anesthesia U. Iowa, Iowa City, 1984-88, asst. prof. dept. anesthesia, 1988-94, assoc. prof. dept. anesthesia, 1994—. Cons. State of Mich., Lafayette Clinic, Detroit, Hoffmann La-Roche, Inc.; reviewer Psychopharmacology and Anesthesiology, NIH; mem. faculty senate Sch. of Medicine, Wayne State U., Detroit, 1982-84. Contbr. articles to Anesthesiology, Brit. Jour. Anaesthesia, Psychopharmacology, Pharmacol. Biochem. Behavior, Neuro Report. Fellow Rutgers U.; grantee Nat. Inst. on Drug Abuse, 1987-91, 93-2000. Mem. AAAS, Collegium Internat. Neuro-Psychopharmacologicum, Am. Psychol. Assn., Soc. Neurosci. Achievements include research on effects of nitrous oxide, benzodiazepines, marijuana, and other drugs on human associative processes, memory, cognition, brain structure and function. Home: 2029 Waterford Dr Coralville IA 52241-2734 Office: U Iowa Dept Anesthesia Westlawn Bldg Iowa City IA 52242

BLOCK, ROBERT MICHAEL, endodontist, educator, researcher; b. Ann Arbor, Mich., Oct. 15, 1947; s. Walter David and Thelma Violet (Levine) B.; m. Anne Powell Marshall, Sept. 4, 1977. BA, DePauw U., 1969; DDS, U. Mich.-Ann Arbor, 1974; cert. in endodontics, Va. Commonwealth U., 1977; MS in Pathology, Va. Commonwealth U., 1978. Diplomate Am. Bd. Endodontics. Clin. instr. Va. Commonwealth U., 1975-77, instr. pathology, 1977-78; rsch. assoc. endodontics U. Conn.-Farmington, 1975—; vis. sr. scientist Nat. Med. Rsch. Inst., Bethesda, Md., 1976-78; rsch. assoc. McGuire Vets. Hosp., Richmond, Va., 1975-78; vis. rsch. scientist U. Conn.-Farmington, 1978—; lectr. endodontics Flint Community Schs.; bd. dirs. Republic Bancorp, S.E., Republic Bank-S.E. div. Republic Bancorp. Contbr. articles profl. jours., chpt. in book. Exec. mem. campaign com. candidate for U. Mich. Bd. Regents, 1980; candidate for Mich. State Bd. Edn., 1982. HEW and NIH summer research fellow, 1970-71; research grantee McGuire Vets. Hosp., 1976-78. Fellow Am. Coll. of Endodontics; mem. Internat. Assn. Dental Rsch. (Edward P. Hatton award 1977), Am. Assn. Dental Rsch., Am. Assn. Endodontists (Meml. Research award 1977), Va. Dental Assn. (VAPAC com., state com. on infection control), Lapeer Dental Study Club (treas. 1978-82), ADA (Preventive Dentistry award 1973), Loudoun County Dental Soc. (v.p.). Office: Loudoun Tech Ctr 21525 Ridgetop Cir # 220 Sterling VA 20166-6510 E-mail: Blcokendo@aol.com.

BLODGETT, FORREST CLINTON, economics educator; b. Oregon City, Oreg., Oct. 6, 1927; s. Clinton Alexander and Mabel (Wells) B.; m. Beverley Janice Buchholz, Dec. 21, 1946 (dec. Dec. 2000); children: Cherine Eiline Klein, Candis Melis, Clinton George; m. Ilene E. Jensen Anderson, Jan. 12, 2002. BS, U. Omaha, 1961; MA, U. Mo., 1969; PhD, Portland State U., 1979. Joined C.E. U.S. Army, 1946, commd. 2d lt., 1946, advanced through grades to lt. col., 1965, ret., 1968, engring. assignments, 1947-49, 1950-53, 1955-56, 1958-60, 1963, staff engr. 2d Army Air Def. Region, 1964-66; base engr. Def. Atomic Support Agy., Sandia Base, N.Mex., 1966-68; bus. mgr., trustee, asst. prof. econs. Linfield Coll., McMinnville, Oreg., 1968-73, assoc. prof., 1973-83, prof., 1983-90, emeritus prof. econs., 1990—; pres. Blodgett Enterprises, Inc., 1983-85; founder, dir. Valley Community Bank, 1980-86, vice chmn. bd. dirs., 1985-86. Commr., Housing Authority of Yamhill County (Oreg.), chmn., 1980-83; mem. Yamhill County Econ. Devel. Com., 1978-83; bd. dirs. Yamhill County Found., 1983-91, Oreg. Internat. Coun., 1995—. Decorated Army Commendation medal with oak leaf cluster; recipient Joint Service Commendation medal Dept. of Def. Mem. Soc. Am. Mil. Engrs. (pres. Albuquerque post 1968), Am. Econ. Assn., Western Econ. Assn. Internat., Nat. Ret. Officers Assn., Res. Officers Assn. (pres. Marion chpt. 1976), SAR (pres. Oreg. soc. 1985-86, v.p. gen. Nat. Soc. 1991-93), Urban Affairs Assn., Soc. for The History of Tech., Am. Law and Econs. Assn., Pi Sigma Epsilon, Pi Gamma Mu, Omicron Delta Epsilon (Pacific NW regional dir. 1978-88), Rotary (pres. McMinnville 1983-84). Republican. Episcopalian. Office: 1153 NE Multnomah Drive Fairview OR 97024-3783

BLODGETT, HARRIET, English educator; b. N.Y.C., Sept. 4, 1932; d. Morris and Fannie (Cohen) Horowitz; m. William Edward Blodgett, Sept. 4, 1955; 1 child, Bruce. BA, Queens Coll., 1954; MA, U. Chgo., 1956; PhD, U. Calif., Davis, 1968. Lectr. in English and comparative lit. U. Calif., Davis, 1973-85, 86-87, lectr. in English Irvine, 1985-86; lectr. in English, humanities and women's studies Calif. State U., Sacramento, 1982-87; lectr. Calif. State U. Stanislaus, Turlock, 1989-92, asst. prof., then assoc. prof., 1992-98, prof., 1998—. Lectr. Stanford U., U. Calif. Santa Cruz, 1988; vis. scholar Inst. for Rsch. on Women and Gender, Stanford U., 1983, affil., 1984-92. Author: Patterns of Reality: Elizabeth Bowen's Novels, 1975, Centuries of Female Days: Englishwomen's Private Diaries, 1988; editor, compiler Capacious Hold-All: An Anthology, 1991; essayist, article writer, contbr. South-Atlantic Quar., Critique, N.Y. Times Book Rev., Internat. Fiction Rev., 19th-Century Prose, James Joyce Quar., others. Mem. Assn. Lit. Scholars and Critics, Phi Beta Kappa, Phi Kappa Phi. Avocations: painting, gardening, reading. Home: 781 Mulberry Ln Davis CA 95616-3430 Office: Calif State U Stanislaus English Dept 801 W Monte Vista Ave Turlock CA 95382-0256

BLODGETT, JUANITA RICE, retired elementary school educator; b. Collista, Ky., Dec. 8, 1936; d. Elbert and Sibyl (Picklesimer) Rice; m. William Warren Blodgett, Nov. 26, 1959 (div. 1983); children: Bruce, Douglas. BS, Berea Coll., 1958; MA, Mich. State U., 1973. Homemaking tchr. Centreville (Mich.) Pub. Schs., 1958-59, Three Oaks (Mich.) Pub. Schs., 1959-61; kindergarten tchr. Cassopolis (Mich.) Pub. Schs., 1961-62; 1st grade tchr. Vandercook Lake (Mich.) Pub. Schs., 1962-63; 2nd grade tchr. Holt/Dimondale (Mich.) Pub. Schs., 1967, Charlotte (Mich.) Pub. Schs., 1970—92; part-time pub. libr. asst. Charlotte Cmty. Libr., Charlotte, Mich., 1992—. Mem. AARP, Am. Bus. Women's Assn. (corres. sec. 1989, rec. sec. 1990, Woman of Yr. 1988), Mich. Assn. Ret. Sch. Personnel, Eaton County Assn. Ret. Sch. Personnel, Delta Kappa Gamma. Avocations: crafts, sewing, reading. Home: 130 S Sheldon St Apt 4 Charlotte MI 48813-1480 Office: Charlotte Cmty Libr 226 S Bostwick Ave Charlotte MI 48813-1801

BLOEDE, VICTOR CARL, lawyer, academic executive; b. Woodwardville, Md., July 17, 1917; s. Carl Schon and Eleanor (Eck) B.; m. Ellen Louise Miller, May 9, 1947; children— Karl Abbott, Pamela Elena AB, Dartmouth Coll., 1940; JD cum laude, U. Md., Balt., 1950; LLM in Pub. Law, Georgetown U., 1967. Bar: Md. 1950, Fed. Hawaii 1958, U.S. Supreme Ct. 1971. Pvt. practice, Balt., 1950-64; mem. Goldman & Bloede, Balt., 1959-64; counsel Seven-Up Bottling Co., Balt., 1958-64; dep. atty. gen. Pacific Trust Ter., Honolulu, 1952-53; asst. solicitor for ters. Office of Solicitor, U.S. Dept. Interior, Washington, 1953-54; atty. U.S. Justice, Honolulu, 1955-58; assoc. gen. counsel Dept. Navy, Washington, 1960-61, 63-64; spl. legal cons. Md. Legislature, Legis. Council, 1963-64, 66-67; assoc. prof. U. Hawaii, 1961-63, dir. property mgmt., 1964-67; house counsel, dir. contracts and grants U. Hawaii System, 1967-82; house counsel U. Hawaii Research Corp., 1970-82; legal counsel Law of Sea Inst., 1978-82; legal cons. Rsch. Corp. and grad. rsch. divsn. U. Hawaii, 1982-92. Spl. counsel to Holifield Congl. Commn. on Govt. Procurement, 1970-73. Author: Hawaii Legislative Manual, 1962, Maori Affairs, New Zealand, 1964, Oceanographic Research Vessel Operations, and Liabilities, 1972, Hawaiian Archipelago, Legal Effects of a 200 Mile Territorial Sea, 1973, Copyright-Guidelines to the 1976 Act, 1977, Forms Manual, Inventions: Policy, Law and Procedure, 1982; writer, contbr. Coll. Law Digest and other publs. on legislation and pub. law. Mem. Gov.'s Task Force Hawaii and The Sea, 1969, Citizens Housing Com. Balt., 1952-64; bd. govs. Balt. Cmty. YMCA, 1954-64; bd. dirs. U. Hawaii Press, 1964-66, Coll. Housing Found., 1968-80; appointed to internat. rev. commn. Canada-France Hawaii Telescope Corp., 1973-82, chmn., 1973, 82; co-founder, incorporator First Unitarian Ch. Honolulu. Served to lt. comdr. USNR, 1942-45, PTO. Grantee ocean law studies NSF and NOAA, 1970-80. Mem. ABA, Balt. Bar Assn., Fed. Bar Assn., Am. Soc. Internat. Law, Nat. Assn. Univ. Attys. (founder & 1st chmn. patents & copyrights sect. 1974-76). Home: 635 Onaha St Honolulu HI 96816-4918

BLOEMER, GARY FRED, orthopedic surgeon, educator; b. Cin., Aug. 18, 1954; s. Raymond Charles and Mildred (Hudephol) B.; children: David Edward, Klye Raymond, Elizabeth Rose. BS, U. Louisville, 1976, MD, 1982. Diplomate Am. Bd. Orthopedic Surgeons. Intern gen. surgery U. Lousiville, 1982-83, asst. clin. prof. orthopedics, 1988—; orthopedic surgery resident Med. Coll. of Ga., Augusta, 1984-87; sports medicine fellow Hughston Sports Medicine Clinic, Columbus, Ga., 1987; pvt. practice, Louisville, 1988—. Med. advisor St. Anthony Sports Medicine Ctr., Louisville, 1989-95; orthopedic cons. Campbellsville (Ky.) Coll., 1990—; exec. com. Frazier Rehab. Ctr., Louisville, 1992; vice chmn. emergency rm. com. Jewish Hosp., Louisville, 1994-96. Contbr. articles to profl. jours. Med. cons. Ky. Commn. for Handicapped Children, Louisville, 1988—; team physician Moore H.S., Louisville, 1988—. Fellow Am. Acad. of Orthopedic Surgeons; mem. AMA, Ky. Orthopedic Assn., Hughston Soc., Floyd E. Bliven Soc., Nat. Athletic Trainers Assn., Alpha Omega Alpha. Roman Catholic. Avocations: snow skiing, bicycling, boating, racquetball. Office: 3 Audubon Plaza Dr Ste 220 Louisville KY 40217-1319

BLOESCH, DONALD GEORGE, theologian, writer, educator; b. Bremen, Ind., May 3, 1928; s. Herbert Paul and Adele Josephine (Silberman) B.; m. Brenda Mary Jackson, Nov. 23, 1962. BA, Elmhurst coll., 1950; BD, Chgo. Theol. Sem., 1953; PhD, U. Chgo., 1956; DDiv, Doane Coll., 1983. Ordained to ministry Evang. & Reformed Ch., 1953. Prof. theology U. Dubuque Theol. Sem., 1957-93, emeritus prof. theology, 1993—. Vis. prof. religion U. Iowa, Iowa City, 1982, Ont. Theol. Sem., Toronto, Can., 1984, 92. Author: Essentials of Evangelical Theology, 2 Vols., 1978, 79, The Ground of Certainty, 1971, Freedom for Obedience, 1987, A Theology of Word and Spirit, 1992, Holy Scripture, 1994, God the Almighty, 1995, The Church, 2002, others; contbr. numerous articles to profl. jours. Fellow Am. Assn. Theol. Schs., 1963-64, 90, World Coun. Chs., 1956-57, Inst. for Advanced Christian Studies, 1978. Mem. Am. Theol. Soc. (pres. Midwest divsn. 1974-75), Karl Barth Soc. N.Am. Republican. United Ch. of Christ. Avocations: gospel and country music, swimming, piano playing. Home: 2185 St John Dr Dubuque IA 52002-2751 Office: U Dubuque 2000 University Ave Dubuque IA 52001-5050

BLOMBERG, DOUGLAS GORDON, education educator; b. Sydney, Australia, June 30, 1951; m. Heather Anne Goldsworthy, Aug. 18, 1984; children: Rebecca, Marijke, Jessica. BA with honors, U. Sydney, 1974, PhD, 1980; grad. diploma in edn., Gippsland Coll. Edn., Churchill, Australia, 1980; MEd, Monash U., Melbourne, Australia, 1995. Cert. tchr., Victoria. Coord. sr. sch. Mt. Evelyn Christian Sch., Melbourne, 1978-82, curriculum cons., 1983, vice-prin. curriculum, 1987-91; prin. Inst. Christian Edn., Melbourne, 1978-91, Nat. Inst. Christian Edn., Melbourne and Sydney, 1992-98, acad. dean, 1999—2000; sr. mem. in philosophy of edn. Inst. for Christian Studies, Toronto, 1998—2000, 2003—. Trustee Assn. Christian Scholarship, 1985—; hon. dir. Christian Parent Controlled Schs., Ltd., Sydney, 1989-91; vis. fellow Calvin Coll., Grand Rapids, Mich., 1991-92. Co-author, editor: A Vision with a Task, 1993, Humans Being, 1996, Reminding, 1998; editor Radix jour., 1974-78; contbr. to profl. publs. Fellow Australian Coll. Edn.; mem. ASCD, Assn. for Reformational Philosophy, Philosophy of Edn. Soc., Philosophy Edn. Soc. Australasia, Internat. Assn. Promotion Christian Higher Edn., Nat. Soc. Study of Edn., Am. Ednl. Rsch. Assn. Office: Inst Christian Studies 229 College St Toronto ON M5T 1R4 Canada

BLOMBERG, SUSAN RUTH, training executive, consultant, author; b. Troy, N.Y., Apr. 23, 1941; d. Philip J. and Marion (Burke) Beckman; m. Harvey Blomberg; children— Michael, Jonathan. B.S. in Edn., SUNY-Plattsburg, 1963. Cert. tchr., N.Y.; cert. tng. instr. Author, educator Nat. Textbook Co., Skokie, Ill., Stamford Bd. Edn. (Conn.), 1970-78; sales and mktg. dir., v.p., ptnr. B/D Assocs., Stamford, 1978-81; dir. mktg., v.p., owner Self Paced Learning Ctr., Stamford, 1981-84; pres., owner the Tng. Connection, Stamford, 1986—; tchr. Bayshore/Brook Ave. Sch., Bayshore, N.Y., 1963-65; dir. and creator Creative Playtime ednl. sch., Stamford, 1969-70; writing cons. Stillmeadow Sch., Stamford, 1972-74; cons., inservice instr. seminars and workshops, Stamford Bd. Edn., 1974-77. Author ednl. series: Let's Create: Think and Write, 1978; lectr., author program Basic Skills in English and Creative Writing for Teachers, 1977; author Creative Writing Activity Cards, 1975. Recipient Excellence award New Eng. Tng. and Employment Coun. and Nat. Alliance of Bus., Exemplary award U.S. Dept. Labor. Mem. Internat. Reading Assn., Southwestern Area Commerce and Industry Assn., Am. Soc. Tng. and Devel. (So. Conn. br.).

BLOMGREN, DAVID KENNETH, dean, pastor; b. Rochelle, Ill., June 1, 1940; s. Darwin Wayne and Roslyn (Castle) B.; m. Susan Marie Blomgren, Nov. 3, 1961; children: Brenda Lynn, Bradley Wayne, Bryan Robert. BA, Tenn. Temple U., 1963; MA, U. Portland, 1969; MDiv, Western Cons. Bapt. Sem., 1967, ThM, 1968, DMin, 1976; ThD, Logos Grad. Sch., 1986; MACE, Luther Rice Sem., 1989. V.p. Portland (Oreg.) Bible Coll., 1967-71; pres. Logos Bible Coll. and Grad. Sch., Tampa, Fla., 1987-89; grad. dean Fla. Beacon Bible Coll., Largo, Fla., 1989—; sr. pastor Tampa Bay Christian Ctr., Brandon, Fla., 1983—. Asst. mgr. Sta. KPAZ-TV Christian TV, Phoenix, 1971-73; advisor Victory Christian Univ., San Diego, 1990—. Author: The Song of the Lord, 1978, Prophetic Gatherings, 1979, Restoring God's Glory, 1985 (Bestseller 1987), Restoring Praise and Worship, 1989;

exec. editor: The Trumpet Call Mag., 1989—. Chmn. Montavilla Community Assn., Portland, 1977-78. Mem. Mins. Fellowship Internat. (apostolic team Portland chpt. 1985—). Office: Tampa Bay Christian Ctr 3920 S Kings Ave Brandon FL 33511-7749

BLOOD, PEGGY A. academic administrator; b. Pine Bluff, Ark., Feb. 8, 1947; m. Lawrence A. Davis, May 31, 1975; children: Lauren A., Pawnee A., Zelana P. BS, U. Ark., Pine Bluff, 1969; MFA, U. Ark., 1971; PhD, Union Inst., Cin., 1986; MA, Holy Names Coll., 1987. Art dir. Office Econ. Opportunity, Altheimer, Ark., 1969; acting. dept. chair, asst. prof. art Univ. Ark., Pine Bluff, 1971-74; activity coord. Good Samaritan Home, Oakland, Calif., 1978-80; art instr. Chabot Community Coll., Hayward, Calif., 1980-81, Solano Community Coll., Suisun, Calif., 1980-90; prin. Palma Ceia Christian Elem. Sch., Hayward, Calif., 1983-84; curriculum chmn., instr. Calif. IMPACT, Oakland, 1985-87; ctr. dir. Chapman U., Fairfield, Calif., 1988-97; head fine arts divsn. Savannah (Ga.) State U., 1998—. Cons. in field;; presenter workshop Savannah (Ga.) Art Assn., The SCAGA Comparative Design Study, Augusta, Ga.; presenter workshop (oils) Savannah Art Assn.; presenter paper Holy Names Coll. The Impact of Cuts in Aid to Calif., Oakland, 1975, Holy Names Coll. The Elementary School Teacher, Oakland, Coll. Assn. Inc. Transformation Vision from H.S. to Coll.; cons. universal web based courses, South Africa, St. Petersburg, Russia; presenter, cons. on curriculum devel., web-based courses on art and culture. One-woman shows include Chapman Univi, Fairfield, Calif., AAUW, Oakland, Calif., Fort Mason, San Francisco, Calif., Hospic Savannah, Ga., CinQue Gallery, N.Y.C., and otherss, exhibitions include Univ. of Mobile, Ala., Horizon Art Festival, Martinex, Ga. (Selected Best of Show and First Prize), 2001—02, No. Calif. Women Art Festival, exhibitions include Seattle Ann. State Exhbn., Univ. Wash. Festival Show, Seattle, and many more; contbr. articles to profl. jour.; author: Apples are Blue, Fostering Creativity in the Challenged Student, Color Transformation, Knowledge Based Curriculum. Sch. bd. trustee Benicia (Calif.) Unified Sch. Dist., 1989-93; bd. mem. Nat. Inst. Art & Disabilities, Richmond, Calif., 1988-90, Girl Scouts Am., Solano County, Calif., 1995-96; legis. dist. action com. mem. Omega Boys and Girls Club, Oakland, Calif. Recipient Ledalle Morehead scholarship, U. Ark., Pine Bluff, 1968; scholar Fulbright Sr. Splt. Candidate award, 2002—; named first Afro-Am. grad. MFA in Art, U. Ark., Fayetteville, 1971, Outstanding Bay Area Artist, Oakland (Calif.) Arts, 1985; numerous grants Mem.: LWV (bd. dirs. 1980—82), AAUW, Willie B. Adkins Coll. Bound Program, Southeastern Art Assn., Nat. Art Edn. Assn., Coll. Arts Assn. Am., Artist Alliance of Assorted Black Colls. and Univs., Ga. Art Assn., Rotary, Alpha Kappa Alpha (1st Prize art award 1982—83). Roman Catholic. Achievements include traveled extensively thoughout Europe, Asia, and Africa.

BLOODWORTH, GLADYS LEON, elementary school educator; b. Natchitoches, La., July 9, 1946; d. Rudolph and Mary (LeRoy) Leon; m. John Edward Bloodworth, Aug. 14, 1971; children: John, Jeremy. BA, Southern U., Baton Rouge, 1968; MA, Calif. State U., Dominguez Hills, 1989. Nat. bd. cert. tchr. mid. childhood generalist NBCT/MC, 2001. Lang. arts tchr. grades 6-10 Natchitoches Parish Schs.; categorical program adviser L.A. Unified Schs., mentor tchr., 1999—, coord. gifted coord., 1988. Named Outstanding Math Tchr., 1987-88. Mem. NEA, United Tchrs. L.A., Calif. Tchrs. Assn., Women in Ednl. Leadership, Kappa Kappa Iota. Methodist.

BLOOM, ALFRED HOWARD, academic administrator, educator; b. N.Y.C., Feb. 27, 1946; s. Alfred H. and Martha (Berrol) Bloom; m. Margaret Hennigan, Aug. 22, 1971. BA, Princeton U., 1967; PhD, Harvard U., 1974. Asst., assoc. prof. Swarthmore Coll., Pa., 1974—86, assoc. provost, 1985—86, pres., 1991—; dean of faculty, v.p. acad. affairs Pitzer Coll., Claremont, Calif., 1986—90, exec. v.p., 1990—91. Author: The Linguistic Shaping of Thought, 1981; contbr. articles to profl. jours. Fellow, Fulbright-Hays, 1968; grantee, SSRC, 1978, 1981, NEH, 1975, 1986. Mem.: Assn. Asian Studies. Avocations: study of languages and cultures, intercultural gastronomy. Office: Swarthmore Coll Office of Pres 500 College Ave Swarthmore PA 19081-1306 E-mail: abloom1@swarthmore.edu.*

BLOOM, DAVID ALAN, pediatric urology educator; b. Buffalo, July 26, 1945; m. Martha Lichty, June 8, 1980. BS, Rensselaer Poly. Inst., 1967; MD, SUNY, Buffalo, 1971. Diplomate Am. Bd. Surgery, Am. Bd. Urology (exam. com. 1992-1996, Trustee, 2003), Nat. Bd. Med. Examiners. Intern UCLA, 1971-72, resident in surgery, 1972-75, chief resident, 1975-76, resident in urology, 1976-77, sr. resident, 1978-79, chief resident, lectr., 1979-80; vis. fellow, registrar Inst. Urology and St. Peter's Hosp., U. London, 1977-78; asst. prof. surgery U. Mich., Ann Arbor, 1984-86, assoc. prof., 1986-93, prof., 1993—, chief pediatric urology, 1984—, assoc. dean faculty affairs Sch. Medicine, 2000—. Cons. urology surgery br. Nat. Cancer Inst., NIH, Bethesda, Md., 1982, Naval Regional Med. Ctr., Portsmouth, Va., 1983, Walter Reed Army Med. Ctr., Washington, 1985, VA Hosp., Ann Arbor, 1985; locum in urology Gt. Ormond Street Hosp. for Sick Children and Inst. Urology, Shaftesbury Hosp., London, 1986; asst. prof. surgery, then assoc. prof. Uniformed Svcs. U. Health Scis. Sch. Medicine, Bethesda, 1980-84, clin. assoc. prof., 1985, assoc. prof. pediat., 1984; mem. exam com. Am. Bd. Urology, 1992-96, trustee, 2003—; presenter and cons. in field. Author: (with McGuire, Catalona and Lipshultz) Advances in Urology, 1995-97; mem. editl. bd. Urology, 1992—, Jour. Endourology, 1997-2003, Contemporary Urology, 1997—, British Jour. Urology, 1999-2002. Lt. col. M.C., U.S. Army, 1980-84. Mem. USAR 1984-1986, Fellow ACS (motion picture com. 1996-2002); mem. AMA, Am. Acad. Pediat. (exec. com. sect. on urology 1989-93, historian 1993-2000, chmn. 2001-02); Am. Assn. Clin. Urologists, Halsted Soc. (photographer, dir. 1999-2001), Longmire Surg. Soc., Reed M. Nesbit Soc., Soc. for Pediatric Urology, Soc. Genitourinary Reconstructive Surgeons, Soc. Univ. Urologists, Am. Assn. Genito-uniary Surgeons, Uniformed Svcs. U. Surg. Assocs., Nat. Urologic Forum (sec.-treas. 1995-2002), European Assn. Urology, Soc. Internat. Urology. Office: U Mich 1500 E Medical Center Dr Ann Arbor MI 48109-0330

BLOOM, EUGENE CHARLES, gastroenterologist, educator; b. Tupelo, Miss., June 3, 1933; s. Robert Harold and Anna Esther (Kronick) B.; m. Joan Ellen Margoles, July 22, 1956; children: Marjorie Wynne Bloom Albert, Stacey Bloom Schlafstein, Robin Bloom Wolf. Student, Emory U., 1951-55, U. Fla., 1955-56; MD, U. Miami, 1960. Diplomate Am. Bd. Internal Medicine. Intern Cook County Hosp., Chgo., 1960-61; resident in internal medicine Jackson Meml. Hosp., Miami, 1961-63; resident in gastroent. Coral Gables VA Hosp., 1963-64; rsch. fellow dept. medicine, divsn. gastroent. U. Miami (Fla.) Sch. Medicine, 1964-65, rsch. scientist, 1964-66, instr. medicine, 1964-74, clin. asst. prof. medicine, 1974—; gen. practice medicine Miami, 1966—96. Mem. staff Bapt. Hosp. Miami, sec.-treas. med. staff, 1979-80, chief of staff, 1980-82; acting chief of staff Oakland Park VA Med. Ctr., 1998-99; med. cons. Social Security Adminstrn., 1996—. Contbr. articles to profl. jours. Bd. dirs. Jewish Vocat. Svc.; active Greater Miami Jewish Fedn., chmn. physicians divsn., 1979-80. Capt. M.C., U.S. Army, 1963-67, Vietnam. Recipient Disting. Alumnus award, U. Miami Sch. Medicine, 1998, Cmty. Tchr. award, Fla. chpt. ACP, 1999. Mem. AMA, AAAS, Am. Acad. Sci., Am. Coll. Gastroenterology, Am. Soc. Gastroent. Endoscopy, U. Miami Med. Alumni Assn. (chmn. Dade County chpt. 1972-75, nat. pres. 1975-77, v.p. pub. rels. 1987-89, v.p. 1987-90), Gen. Alumni U. Miami (bd. dirs. 1973-77, v.p. 1988-95, bd. overseers 1988—, sec. 1990, v.p. 1991), Fla. Gastroent. Soc., Greater Miami Jewish Fedn., Woodfield Country Club, Alpha Omega Alpha, Omicron Delta Kappa. Democrat.

BLOOM, MICHELLE, foreign language educator; b. Bklyn., Feb. 28, 1947; d. Seymour and Zena (Bayuk) M.; m. Michael Robert Bloom, Aug. 20, 1967; children: Marc, Deborah. BA, SUNY, Albany, 1967, MA, 1982. Cert. tchr., adminstr., N.Y. Tchr. Guilderland Jr. H.S., Guilderland Ctr., N.Y., 1967-70, Acad. of the Holy Names, Albany, 1979-81, Ravena (N.Y.)-Coeymans-Selkirk Ctrl. Sch. Dist., 1981-85; dept. chair Ravena (N.Y.)-Coeymans-Selkirk Ctrl. Sch. Dist., 1985-87; supr. fgn. langs. Shenendehowa Ctrl. Sch. Dist., Clifton Park, NY, 1987-93; supr. fgn. langs. and ESL Guilderland Ctrl. Sch. Dist., 1993—2003; faculty, field time clin. supr. Univ. Albany, 1999—. Mem. curriculum assessment com. (langs. other than English) N.Y. State Edn. Dept., Albany, 1992—; mem. fgn. lang. implementation com. State Edn. Dept., 1997-98, fgn. lang. assessment com., 1999-2000. Mem. Am. Coun. Teaching Fgn. Langs., N.Y. State Assn. Fgn. Lang. Tchrs. (bd. dirs. 1989-91, sec. 1993-94, v.p. 1995, exec. com. 1993-98, Service award 1991, Anthony Papalia award 1991, pres.-elect 1996, pres. 1997, Ferdinand DiBartolo award 1997). Office: Guilderland H S School Rd Guilderland Center NY 12085

BLOOMBERG, TERRY, early childhood education administrator; b. St. Louis, July 18, 1938; d. Herbert Valentine Goldwasser and Ruth (Ferer) Kopman; m. Gordon Richard Bloomberg, June 29, 1958; children: Jayne Bloomberg Langsam, Judy, Jill, Jacqui. BS in Edn. (with highest honors), Northwestern U., 1959; MA in Teaching, Webster Coll., St. Louis, 1978; A.G.C., Webster Coll., 1979. Cert. elem. educator, Mo. Tchr. elem. Washington Sch., Elmhurst, Ill., 1959-60, Dielman Sch., Ladue, Mo., 1960-61; early childhood tchr. Lucky Lane Nursery Sch., St. Louis, 1969-77; tchr. in parent-toddler and parent-infant program Clayton (Mo.) Early Childhood Program, 1977-80; early childhood specialist Child Day Care Assn., St. Louis, 1982-85; exec. dir. Developmental Child Care, Inc., St. Louis, 1983—. Regional cons. Project Construct-Mo. Early Childhood Curriculum and Assessment Project, 1988. Pres. Am. Jewish Com., 1989-91, sec. 1986-89, v.p. 1982-86, bd. dirs. 1979-82; bd. dirs. Govt. Rels. Office for Mo. Jewish Fedns., 1990; St. Louis contact Action for Children's TV, 1975—; bd. dirs. Metro Theater Circus, 1975-89, Jewish Fedn. of St. Louis, 1983-88, 90-97, v.p. planning, 1993-96, v.p. allocations, 1996-97, v.p. agency rels., 1997—; bd. mem., study group leader Brandeis Univ. Nat. Women's Com., St. Louis, 1968-74; mem. Congregation Temple Israel, 1961—; dir. consumer affairs Nat. Coun. Jewish Women, 1978-79; v.p. St. Louis Jewish Light, 1995—. Recipient Outstanding Svc. award Midwest Assn. Edn. Young Children, 1989, The Love of Children award St. Louis Assn. for Edn. Young Children, 1991, Woman of Valor award Bus. and Profl. Women of Jewish Fedn. St. Louis, 1993, Netzach award Am. Jewish Com., 1993, Early Childhood and Parent Edn. Disting. Svc. award Mo. Dept. Elem. and Secondary Edn., 1995. Mem. Assn. for Edn. Young Children (Outstanding Svc. award 1986). Democrat. Jewish. Home: 47 Frontenac Estates Dr Saint Louis MO 63131-2615

BLOOME, DAVID MICHAEL, education educator; BA, U. Conn., 1972; postgrad., SUNY, Albany, 1973—74, MA, 1975; PhD, Kent State U., 1981. Intern Tchr. Corps Program Schenectady (N.Y.) Pub. Schs., 1974—75; English and reading tchr. Cleve. Pub. Schs., 1975—78, 1979—80; elem. sch. tchr. Kent (Ohio) State U. Sch., 1978—79; vis. asst. prof. specialized instrnl. programs Coll. Edn. Cleve. State U., 1980—81; asst. prof. edn. Sch. Edn. U. Mich., Ann Arbor, 1981—86, assoc. prof. edn., 1986—87; assoc. prof. edn., reading and writing program Sch. Edn. U. Mass., Amherst, 1987—92, prof. edn., reading and writing program, 1992—95; prof. edn. Peabody Coll. Edn. Vanderbilt U., Nashville, 1995—. Mem. com. on early childhood and literacy devel. Internat. Reading Assn., 1981—84, mem. com. on spl. projects and insts., 1983—85; chair spl. interest group on lang. devel. AERA, 1984—86; pres.-elect Nat. Conf. on Rsch. in English, 1991—92, pres., 1992—93, past pres., 1993—94; vis. Fulbright scholar Ctr. for Internat. Edn., Inst. for Continuing and Profl. Edn. U. Sussex, Brighton, England, 1992—93; vis. summer faculty U. Alaska, Fairbanks, 1995; co-organizer Impact II Insts. on Understanding Lang. as a Found. for Curriculum and Instrn., 1994—96; mem. U. Mass. exec. bd. Mass. Soc. Profs., 1994—95; co-chair Jewish faculty and staff group U. Mass., 1994—95; chair affirmative action and diversity com. Peabody Coll. Faculty Coun., 1996—98, rep. at-large, 1996—99; co-chair Martin Luther King Jr. Commemorative Series Vanderbilt U., 1998—99. Mem. editl. rev. bd.: Reading Rsch. Quarterly, 1991—, Jour. Literacy Rsch., 1995—99, mem. editl. com.: Revista de Investigacion Educativa, 1992—, mem. editl. adv. bd.: Jour. Reading Behavior, 1994—, The Reading Tchr., 1995—97, mem. adv. bd.: English Edn., 1994—97, mem. editl. bd.: Qualitative Rsch., Mass-Observation Occasional Paper Series; contbr. articles to profl. jours. Mem.: Nat. Coun. Tchrs. English (mem. commn. on reading 1985—88, mem. commn. on lang. 1990—93, mem. promising rsch. award com. 1999—2000, mem. standing com. of rsch. 1999—2000, pres. 2003—, com. on alt. ways assessing children's oral and written lang. devel. 1983—87). Office: Vanderbilt Univ Peabody Coll Edn Box 330 Nashville TN 37203*

BLOOM-FESHBACH, SALLY, psychologist, educator; b. Balt., Feb. 11, 1953; d. Jordan and Carol (Wallerstein) Bloom; m. Jonathan Feshbach, Aug. 29, 1976 (dec. June 1999); children: Alison, Kimberly; m. Donald Evans, July 2002. AB, Brown U., 1975; MS, Yale U., 1977, MPhil, 1979, PhD, 1980. Lic. clin. psychologist, Washington. Staff psychologist Am. U. Ctr. for Psychol. and Learning Svcs., Washington, 1980-84, dir. postgrad. tng., 1982-84; pvt. practice psychotherapy, Washington, 1982—; rsch. cons. com. on child devel. NAS-NRC, Washington, 1980-83. Assoc. clin. prof. dept. psychiatry and behavioral sci. George Washington U., Washington, 1985—; mem. faculty Inst. for Contemporary Psychotherapy and Psychoanalysis, 1996—, Washington Sch. Psychiatry, 2001—; cons. in field. Co-editor: Psychology of Separation and Loss, 1987; contbr. articles to profl. jours., chpts. to books. Fellow Yale U., 1975-77, NIMH, 1977-80; travel grantee NATO, APA, 1981, 82, rsch. grantee Sigma Xi, 1978. Mem. APA (bd. dirs. sect. on women and psychoanalysis), Brown U. Club, Yale U. Club, Phi Beta Kappa, Sigma Xi. Home: 2919 Garfield St NW Washington DC 20008-3504 Office: 1301 20th St NW Ste 608 Washington DC 20036-6016

BLOOMFIELD, DENNIS, physician, educator, dean; b. Perth, Australia, May 4, 1933; arrived in U.S., 1962; s. Gordon and Ruby Violet Bloomfield; m. Elaine R. Bloomfield, June 21, 1964; children: Lisa Feinman, Leslie Gerstenfeld, Nanette Herman. MBBS, U. Adelaide, Australia, 1956. Cert. Am. Bd. Internal Medicine, Am. Bd. Cardiology. Intern Royal Perth Hosp., 1957—59; resident Royal Prince Alfred Hosp., Sydney, Australia, 1960—61; instr. Vanderbilt U., Nashville, 1962—65; dir. cardiac catheterization lab. Maimonides Med. Ctr., Bklyn., 1967—75; assoc. prof. medicine SUNY, Downstate, 1967—75; chmn. medicine, dir. cardiac catheterization lab. St. Vincent Cath. Med. Ctrs., S.I., 1975—2002; prof. clin. medicine, assoc. dean N.Y. Med. Coll., Valhalla, 1975—. Author, editor: book Dye Curves, 1974; author: Cardioactive Drugs, 1982; columnist: newspaper S.I. Advance, 1990—. Recipient Prominent Immigrant award, Borough Pres. S.I., 1986. Fellow: ACP, Am. Coll. Cardiology, Royal Australian Coll. Physicians; mem.: Royal Coll. Physician Edinburgh, Royal Coll. Physician London. Avocations: painting, flying, sailing, tennis, golf. Office: 1102 Victory Blvd Staten Island NY 10301 Business E-Mail: dabloomfieldmd@aol.com.

BLOOMFIELD, LOUIS AUB, physicist, educator; b. Boston, Oct. 11, 1956; s. Daniel Kermit and Frances (Aub) B.; m. Karen Shatkin, Aug. 28, 1983; children: Elana, Aaron. BA in Physics, Amherst Coll., 1979; PhD in Physics, Stanford U., 1983. Postdoctoral physicist AT&T Bell Labs., Murray Hill, NJ, 1983-85; asst. prof. U. Va., Charlottesville, Va., 1985-91, assoc. prof., 1991-96, prof, 1996—. Author: (Book) How Things Work: The Physics of Everyday Life. Recipient Alumni Tchr. award U. Va., 1992, Pres.'s Rsch. prize, 1994; named Presdl. Young Investigator NSF, 1986, Young Investigator Office of Naval Rsch., 1988, Va. Outstanding Faculty award, 1998; Alfred P. Sloan fellow, 1989. Fellow Am. Phys. Soc. (Apker award 1980, Pegram medal 2001). Jewish. Office: Univ of Va Dept Physics PO Box 400714 Charlottesville VA 22904-4714 E-mail: bloomfield@virginia.edu.

BLOTT, PHYLLIS JEAN See BAKO, PHYLLIS JEAN

BLOTTNER, MYRA ANN, retired elementary school educator; b. Albuquerque, Dec. 31, 1935; d. John Edgar and Hazel Christine (Bloomgren) Manton; m. Frederick Gwynn Blottner, Dec. 28, 1957; children: Laura Christine, Cheryl Ann. BS, U. N.Mex., 1957, MA, 1992. Cert. elem. tchr., spl. edn. tchr., tchr. of gifted. Tchr. 6th grade Redwood City (Calif.) Pub. Schs., 1959—61, Albuquerque Pub. Schs., 1957—58, tchr. 5th grade, 1986—98, tchr. gifted, 1976—86, 1991—2000, sci. cons., 1990—2000; ret., 2000. Tchg. cons. sr. block U. N.Mex. students . Albuquerque Pub. Schs., 1988—91; lectr. Albuquerque Mus. Art and History, 2000, lectr. coord., 2002—03, dir. Sculpture Garden docents, 2002—; tutor in field; pvt. piano tchr., 1958—. Lectr., tour guide, v.p. vol. assn. N.Mex. Mus. Natural History, 1989; mem. coun. Diocese of Rio Grande, 1986-90; active Assistance League, Albuquerque. Named N.Mex. Sci. Tchr. of the Yr., N.Mex. Mus. Natural History, 1990; Tchr. Enhancement Program fellow U. N.Mex., 1991. Mem. AAUW (pres. Albuquerque br. 1973-75), P.E.O. (chpt. recording sec. 2003-), Alpha Delta Pi (pres. 1968, v.p. 1990-91), Phi Delta Kappa. Republican. Episcopalian. Avocations: aerobics, handbell choir, bridge, gardening (master). Home: 12601 Trillium Trl NE Albuquerque NM 87111-8080

BLOUIN, FRANCIS XAVIER, JR., history educator; b. Belmont, Mass., July 29, 1946; s. Francis X. and Margaret (Cronin) B.; m. Joy Alexander; children: Benjamin, Tiffany. AB, U. Notre Dame, 1967; MA, U. Minn., 1969, PhD, 1978. Asst. dir. Bentley Library U. Mich., Ann Arbor, 1974-75, assoc. archivist Bentley Library, 1975-81, dir. Bentley Library, 1981—, asst. prof. history and library sci., 1979-83, assoc. prof., 1983-89, prof., 1989—. Author: The Boston Region..., 1980, Vatican Archives: An Inventory and Guide to Historical Documentation of the Holy See, 1998; editor Intellectual Life on Michigan Frontier, 1985, Archival Implications Machine..., 1980. Trustee Much. Student Found., 1986-91; dir. Am. Friends of Vatican Libr., 1981—, Coun. on Libr. and Info. Resources, 2001—. Fellow Soc. Am. Archivist (mem. governing council 1985-88); mem. Am. Hist. Assn., Hist. Soc. Mich. (trustee 1982-88, pres. 1987-88), Assn. Records Mgrs. and Adminstrs., Internat. Council on Archives. Office: U Mich Bentley Hist Libr 1150 Beal Ave Ann Arbor MI 48109-2113

BLOUNT, PETER ALLEN, educational administrator, educator, researcher; b. Melbourne, Fla., Dec. 18, 1962; s. John Henry and Lillie Alberta (Mumphry) B.; m. Shervin Regina Gambles, Dec. 31, 1994; 1 child, Kiana Danielle. AA in Bus., Brevard C.C., Melbourne, 1982; student, U. Fla., 1983-85; BS in Edn., U. Ctrl. Fla., 1989, postgrad., 1990-91, 94—. Cert. master tchr., Fla. Recreation supr. City of Melbourne, 1988-89; K-12 tchr. phys. edn. Orange County Pub. Schs., Orlando, Fla., 1989—, dept. chmn., wellness rep., 1992—; founder, pres., cons. Nat. Athlete Career Ctr., Orlando, 1988—. Head coach Fla. Gold, Orlando, 1989-94; athlete's rep. 1991 Olympic team trials U.S. Bobsled and Skeleton Fedn., mem. U.S. World Cup Team, 1990-91, 92-93. Mem. So. Christian Leadership Coun., Orlando, 1991—, Better Bus. Bur., Orlando, 1995. Recipient Disting. Alumnus award Brevard C.C., 1994; grad. fellow U. Ctrl. Fla., 1990. Mem. ASCD, NEA, Fla. Tchg. Profession, Epsilon Phi Epsilon (historian 1984—). Avocations: public speaking, running and jogging, reading, watching sporting events.

BLOVITS, LARRY JOHN, retired art educator; b. Detroit, Oct. 19, 1936; s. George Edward and Audrey (Codde) B.; m. Jean Curtis; children: Laurie, Lisa, Jay, Jack, Greg; m. Joyce Elaine Dreyer, Nov. 17, 1978 (div. 1992); m. Linda Jeanne Felde, Feb. 14, 1997. BFA, Wayne State U., Detroit, 1964, MFA, 1966. Clk. U.S. P.O., Royal Oak, Mich., 1958-64; grad. teaching asst. Wayne State U., Detroit, 1964-66, adj. instr., 1966-67, U. Detroit, 1966-67, Macomb County Community Coll., Warren, Mich., 1966-67; instr. Europe program Providence Coll., 1971, 73, 75,77; instr. No. Mich. U., Marquette, 1966-67; prof. art Aquinas Coll., Grand Rapids, Mich., 1967-93, retired, 1993. Visual arts advisor Mich. Coun. Arts, 1976-81, mem. in artist-in-schs. pool, 1977-81, artist in residence, 1977-78; vis. artist Henry Ford Community Coll., Dearborn, Mich., 1972, Montcalm Community Coll., Sidney, Mich., 1982, 83, Mich. Tech. U., Houghton, 1989; artist in residence Lowell (Mich.) Middle Schs., 1984, Forest Hills Middle Schs., Grand Rapids, 1987, St. Jude Elem., Grand Rapids, 1989. One-man shows include Aquinas Coll., Grand Rapids, 1993; solo exhbns. include Grand Rapids Art Mus., 1977, City Art Gallery, Grand Rapids, 1984, Farmhouse Gallery, Montcalm C.C., Sidney, 1985, Arnold Klein Gallery, Royal Oak, Mich., 1985, 88, Aquinas Coll., 1986, Muskegon (Mich.) Mus. Art, 1988; group shows include Krasl Art Ctr., St. Joseph, Mich., 1987, Canyon Gallery, Riudoso, N.Mex., 1987, Soc. Pastellistes de France Internat. Exhbn. Pastells, Lille, 1987, 33d Knickerbocker Artists NMat., N.Y.C., 1983; author: Pastel for the Serious Beginner, 1996; cover artist, featured Pastel Interpretations, North Light Books, 1993; featured artist in several books. With U.S. Army, 1954-57. Grantee Mich. Coun. Arts, 1980, 83, Nat. Endowment for Arts, 1983, Aquinas Coll., 1988; recipient art awards Kans. Pastel Soc., Met. Portrait Soc., Internat. Exhbns. Pastels, Pen and Brush Gallery, 1989, 90, Am. Artist mag., 1990, Nat. Portrait Seminar, Atlanta, 1991, 93, others; named Master Pastelist, 1993. Mem. Pastel Soc. Am., Am. Portrait Soc. (co-chmn. edn. com.), Kans. Pastel Soc., Oil Pastel Assn., Midwest Pastel Soc., Am. Soc. Portrait Artists, Salmagundi Club, Knickerbocker Artists. Avocations: golf, tennis. Home: 1835 Luce St SW Grand Rapids MI 49544-8916

BLOWER, JOHN GREGORY, special education educator; b. Orange, Calif., Mar. 18, 1952; s. James Girard and Juanita Mae (Pierce) B.; 1 child, Becky Renee. BS in Psychology, Pacific Christian, 1975; MEd in Spl. Edn., Idaho State U., 1982. Assoc. minister edn. 1st Christian Ch., Santa Ana, Calif., 1972-75; spl. edn. tchr. Fremont County Schs., St. Anthony, Idaho, 1977—. Vice chmn., con. People for Spl. People, St. Anthony, 1986—. Program coord. Idaho Spl. Olympics, St. Anthony, 1978—, bd. dirs., Boise, 1982-88, chmn. bd. dirs., Boise, 1987-88. Mem. Coun. for Exceptional Children, Nat. Edn. Assn. Office: South Fremont High Sch 855 S Bridge St Saint Anthony ID 83445-2034

BLOYD, RUTHANNE, gifted and talented mathematics educator; b. Houston, Sept. 22, 1952; d. Ted and C. Ruth (Carson) Bloyd. BA, Stephen F. Austin State U., 1974; MA in Math. Edn., U. Houston, Clear Lake, 1980; doctoral studies, U. North Tex., Denton, 1993-97. Cert. secondary edn. educator in English, math., sociology, Tex. Tchr. math. Friendswood (Tex.) Ind. Sch. Dist., 1977-78, Columbia-Brazoria Ind. Sch. Dist., West Columbia, Tex., 1978-84, Cypress Fairbanks Ind. Sch. Dist., Houston, 1984-85, Birdville Ind. Sch. Dist., N. Richland Hills, Tex., 1985-89, Jasper (Tex.) Ind. Sch. Dist., 1989-90; tchr. gifted and talented math. Grapevine (Tex.)-Colleyville Ind. Sch. Dist., 1990-96. Advisor Colleyville Mid. Sch. Nat. Jr. Honor Soc., Colleyville, Tex., 1991-96, coord. Acad. Pentathlon, 1992-96, coach CMS Math./Sci. Club, 1990-96, mentor tchr., 1991-96, tchr. Cross Timbers Mid. Sch. gifted/talented math, Math Sci. club advisor, Nat. Jr. Hon. Soc. advisor, coordinator mentor tchr. Les Dix. Colleyville mid. sch. liaison to Colleyville C. of C., 1994-96. Recipient Colleyville Mid. Sch. Tchr. of Yr. award, 1994, Grapevine-Colleyville Ind. Sch. Dist. Tchr. of Yr., Grapevine C. of C., 1994. Mem. ASCD, Nat. Coun. Tchrs. Math., Phi Delta Kappa, Delta Kappa Pi. Baptist. Avocations: painting, music, sports. Home: 98 Regents Park St Bedford TX 76022-6558 Office: Cross Timbers Mid Sch 2301 Pool Rd Grapevine TX 76051-4273

BLUE, KATHY JO, elementary school educator; b. Martinsburg, W.Va., Nov. 13, 1955; d. Daniel Walker and Agnes Rosalie (Hull) Tabler; m. John Kyner Blue, July 12, 1981; 1 child, Sarah Virginia. AS in Nursing, Shepherd Coll., Shepherdstown, W.Va., 1976; BA in Elem. Edn., Shepherd Coll., Sheperdstown, W.Va., 1979; MA, W.Va. U., 1988; reading authorization, 1988. Cert. profl. elem. tchr., tchr. gifted edn. 1-6, reading, W.Va. Nurse City Hosp., Inc., Martinsburg, 1976-78; substitute tchr. Jefferson and Berkeley counties, Charles Town, Martinsburg, 1979-80; elem. tchr. Morgan County Schs., Berkeley Springs, W.Va., 1980-81; substitute tchr. Jefferson County Schs., Charles Town, 1981-86, Title I tchr. reading, 1986-97, 1st grade tchr., 1997—. Tutor, Shenandoah Junction, W.Va., 1989—. Recipient Regional Edn. Svc. Agy. Exemplary Teaching Technique in Lang. award, 1994, Blue Ridge Elem. Sch. Tchr. of Yr., 1996; grantee W.Va. Edn. Fund, 1988, 89, 95. Mem. NEA, Internat. Reading Coun., W.Va. Reading Coun., Jefferson County Reading Assn., W.Va. Edn. Assn., Jefferson County Edn. Assn., W.Va. Reading Assn., Jefferson County Reading Coun., Blue Ridge Elem. PTO, T.A. Lowery PTO, Order Ea. Star (worthy matron Shepherdstown 1983-84, 88-89), Alpha Delta Kappa. Republican. Methodist. Avocations: reading, sewing, counted cross-stitch, stamping. Home: PO Box 112 Shenandoah Junction WV 25442-0112 Office: Blue Ridge Elem Sch RR 2 Box 362 Harpers Ferry WV 25425-9802

BLUE, MONTE LYNN, college president; b. Ft. Worth, Feb. 25, 1945; s. Bert Leonard and Mary Lee (Cooper) B.; m. Sheryl Doris O'Connor, July 1, 1966; children: Michelle Denea, Laura Lynn. BA, North Tex. State U., 1967, MA, 1972; EdD, U. Houston, 1979. Illustrator Gen. Dynamics, Ft. Worth, 1967-71; instr. advt. art, Cen. Campus San Jacinto Jr. Coll., Pasadena, Tex., 1971-74, dist. dir., instr. media, 1975-79, dean student services, South Campus, 1979-81, dean student services, Cen. Campus, 1981-83, pres., 1983—. Bd. dirs. Deer Park Ednl. Found., 1996—; bd. dirs. Southeast Econ. Devel. Coun., 1995—, chmn. bd., 1997-98; moderator Bd. of Southmore Med. Ctr.; consumer credit counselor svc. bd. dirs., 1999-2000; spkr. numerous presentations to various comty., civic and profl. groups. Contbr. articles to profl. jours.; speaker numerous presentations to various community, civic and profl. groups. Vice chmn. bd. dirs. San Jacinto YMCA, Pasadena, 1986-87, chmn., 1987-88. Named Outstanding Alumni, Ft. Worth Ind. Sch. Dist., 1984. Mem.: Tex. Pub. Cmty. Jr. Coll. Assn., Assn. Tex. Colls. and Univs., Nat. Orgn. on Legal Problems in Edn., Am. Assn. Higher Edn., Am. Assn. Cmty. Jr. Colls., LaPorte/Bayshore C. of C. (bd. dirs. 1987—89, pres. 1989), Rotary (local pres. 1986—87), Phi Theta Kappa (hon. mem. Mu Omicron Chpt., Hall of Honor 1985). Republican. Baptist. Avocation: painting. Office: San Jacinto Coll Cen 8060 Spencer Hwy Pasadena TX 77501-2007

BLUE, NANCY ANN, retired home economics educator; b. Huron, SD, Aug. 18, 1934; d. Edward Martin and Gladys (Erickson) Rudloff; m. Vernon Wilford Blue, June 3, 1954; children: Debra, David, Diana, Paul, Mark, Ruth. Student, Augustana Coll., Sioux Falls, S.D., 1952-53, Huron Coll., 1953-54, U. Ill., Chgo., 1966-67; BA in Home Econ. Edn., Western Wash. U., 1970. Cert. vocat. home economist. Home econs. tchr. Mt. Vernon (Wash.) HS, 1970—94; ret., 1994. Docent Valley Mus. Art, La Conner, Wash., 1984-85; bd. dirs. Youth Encouragement Svc., 1985-94; sec. to council Immaculate Conception Ch., 1980-83. Mem. AAUW (2d v.p. 1984-86), NEA, Am. Vocat. Assn., Wash. Vocat. Assn., Am. Home Econs. Assn., Wash. Home Econs. Assn. (mktg. chmn. 1984-85, recognition chmn. 1986-87), Wash. Assn. Edn. Young Child. Roman Catholic. Avocations: bridge, golf, travel, gourmet cooking. Home: 521 Shoshone Dr Mount Vernon WA 98273-3747

BLUE, RHONDA HOLMES, kindergarten educator; b. High Point, N.C., July 15, 1954; d. Robert Lee and Alice (Carter) Holmes; m. David Reginald Blue, Oct. 20, 1984 (div.); 1 child, Darius Rashad. BA in Early Childhood Edn., U. N.C., Greensboro, 1976, M in Elem. Edn., 1994. Kindergarten tchr. High Point (N.C.) Pub. Schs., 1976-84, 85-93, tchr. 2d grade, 1984-85; kindergarten tchr. Guilford County Schs., Greensboro, N.C., 1993—. Co-chair Differentiated Pay for High Point Pub. Schs., 1990-93. Pres. St. Luke Luth. Ch., 1989—, Coalition of Luth. in Black Ministry, 1995-2000; mem. Citizens Adv. Com., High Point, 1993-99. Recipient of Woman of Achievement award, YWCA (High Point), 1994. Mem.: NEA, NAACP, ASCD, Am. Bus. Womens Assn. (Nathaniel Greene Sunshiners chpt. v.p. 1998—99), Guilford Assn. Educators, N.C. Assn. Educators (past pres. High Point chpt. 1986), Internat. Reading Assn. (membership chmn. 1994—96, v.p. 1997—99, pres. 2001—), Order Ea. Star, Eta Phi Beta (chaplain 1999—2000, sec. 2001—), Beta Xi. Home: 1711 Stoneybrook Dr High Point NC 27265-2450 E-mail: RHDBRB@aol.com., bluer@guilford.k12.nc.us.

BLUE, ROBERT LEE, secondary education educator; b. Columbiaville, Mich., Apr. 23, 1920; s. Arthur Floyd and Elma (Ellis) B.; BA, Mich. State U., 1941; MA, U. Mich., 1952; m. Dorothy L. Seward, July 15, 1961. Tchr., Chesaning (Mich.) H.S., 1941-42, 45-57; prin. Ricker Jr. H.S., Saginaw, Mich., 1957-59, Buena Vista H.S., Saginaw, 1960-69; asst. prof. secondary edn. Central Mich. U., Mt. Pleasant, 1969—. Bd. dirs. Hartley Edn. Nature Camp, 1957-69; pres. Saginaw County Assn. Ret. Sch. Pers., Mich. Assn. Ret. Sch. Pers. (chmn. awards com., Disting. Svc. award 1995). With U.S. Army, 1942-45. Decorated Bronze Star. Mem. NEA (life), Mich. Edn. Assn., Assn. Tchr. Educators, Mich. Assn. Tchr. Educators, Nat. Assn. Secondary Sch. Prins., Mich. Assn. Secondary Sch. Prins., Mich. PTA (hon. life), Am. Legion, Mich. Hist. Soc., Saginaw County Hist. Soc., Lapeer County Hist. Soc., Optomist, Pit and Balcony, Masons, Phi Delta Kappa. Republican. Methodist. Author: Footsteps Into The Past, A History of Columbiaville, 1979, also articles. Home: 1437 Lathrup Ave Saginaw MI 48603-4787 Office: 3037 Davenport Ave Saginaw MI 48602-3652

BLUM, ELEANOR GOODFRIEND, social sciences educator; b. Detroit, July 16, 1940; d. William Henry and Dorothy Elaine (Oslander) Goodrriend; children: Beth Goodfriend, Sara Caroline. BS in Edn., Wayne State U., 1962, MEd, 1983. Kindergarten tchr., Livonia, Mich., 1962-63, Montgomery County, Md., 1963-64; tchr. Detroit Pub. Sch., 1977—. Reading coord. King HS; mem. edm. com. New Detroit Inc., 1981—; mem. adv. coun. State Bd. Edn., 1996—; mem. state spl. edn. adv. com., 1996-2000. Vol. Detroit Office of Sen. Robert Griffin, 1972-74, asst. to appointments sec. to Pres. Nixon, Washington, 1972-74; chmn. March of Dimes Drive, Farmington, Mich., 1975; pres. Potomac Village Homeowners Assn., 1975; mem. 19th dist. Rep. Com., 1975—, precinct del. 20th precinct, West Bloomfield, Mich.; alt. del. to Nat. Rep. Conv., 1976; mem. exec. com. Oakland County Rep. Com., 1977-78; mem. Bloomfield Women's Rep. Club, West Bloomfield Rep. Women's Club; chmn. health com. Doherty Elem. Sch., 1975—; social studies tchr. Longfellow Mid. Sch., 1983-91; tchr. continuing edn. for girls Teen-Age Parent Edn. Ctr., Detroit, 1991—; mem. libr. com. Temple Beth El, Birmingham, Mich., 1976, mem. libr. & arts coms., 1977-78, worship com., 1989-96; mem. urban affairs com. Jewish Cmty. Coun., 1977-78, cmty. rels. com., 1978-80, chmn. met. concerns com., 1979; mem. adv. bd. Oakland County March of Dimes, 1977-78, mem. bd., 1979; bd. dir. Oakland Citizens League, 1983—; mem. Friends of West Bloomfield Libr., 1975—, NAACP, 1979—; mem. com. on sheltered workshops, dept. mgmt. and bidget State of Mich., 1978-80, cmty. rels. com. Jewish Cmty. Coun., 1986-91; social worker Mich. Bd. Social Work, 2002-; appointed by Governor John Engler to the State Bd. of Social Work, 2002-. Chmn. March of Dimes Drive, Farmington, Mich., 1975; pres. Potomac Village Homeowners Assn., 1975; mem. 19th dist. Rep. Com., 1975—, precinct del. 20th precinct, West Bloomfield, Mich.; alt. del. to Nat. Rep. Conv., 1976; mem. exec. com. Oakland County Rep. Com., 1977-78; mem. Bloomfield Women's Rep. Club, West Bloomfield Rep. Women's Club; chmn. health com. Doherty Elem. Sch., 1975—; social studies tchr. Longfellow Mid. Sch., 1983-91; tchr. continuing edn. for girls Teen-Age Parent Edn. Ctr., Detroit, 1991—; mem. libr. com. Temple Beth El, Birmingham, Mich., 1976, mem. libr. & arts coms., 1977-78, worship com., 1989-96; mem. urban affairs com. Jewish Cmty. Coun., 1977-78, cmty. rels. com., 1978-80, chmn. met. concerns com., 1979; mem. adv. bd. Oakland County March of Dimes, 1977-78, mem. bd., 1979; bd. dir. Oakland Citizens League, 1983—; mem. Friends of West Bloomfield Libr., 1975—, NAACP, 1979—; mem. com. on sheltered workshops, dept. mgmt. and bidget State of Mich., 1978-80, cmty. rels. com. Jewish Cmty. Coun., 1986-91; social worker Mich. Bd., 2002-; education Com., 2002-present, Jewish Cmty. Coun. State Spl. Ed. Com., 1996-2000; Mich. Bd. of Soc. Work, 2002-. Address: 31755 Ridgeside Dr Apt 21 Farmington MI 48334-1276

BLUM, GERALD SAUL, psychologist, educator; b. Newark, Mar. 8, 1922; s. Benjamin Paul and Augusta (Cohen) B.; m. Myrtle Wolf, Mar. 3, 1946; children— Jeffrey, Nancy. BS, Rutgers U., 1941; MA, Clark U., 1942; PhD, Stanford, 1948. Clin. psychology intern Palo Alto (Calif.) VA Hosp., 1946-48; mem. faculty U. Mich., 1948-68, prof. psychology, 1959-68; prof. U. Calif. at Santa Barbara, 1968-88, chmn. dept., 1969-72, 86-88; emeritus prof., 1988—. Cons. clin. psychology VA, 1949-59 Author: Psychoanalytic Theories of Personality, 1953, A Model of the Mind, 1961, Psychodynamics: The Science of Unconscious Mental Forces, 1966; Cons. editor: Bobbs-Merrill reprint series in psychology. Served with USAAF, 1942-46. Fulbright research scholar, 1954-55; fellow Center Advanced Study Behavioral Scis., 1959-60; fellow Social Sci. Research Council, 1962-63 Fellow Am. Psychol. Assn., AAAS; mem. Phi Beta Kappa, Sigma Xi. Inventor of Blacky Pictures, 1950. Home: 300 Hot Springs Rd # L-221 Santa Barbara CA 93108-2038

BLUM, LAWRENCE ALAN, moral philosophy educator; b. Balt., Apr. 16, 1943; m. Judith Ellen Smith, June 22, 1975; children: Benjamin, Sarah, Laura. BA, Princeton U., 1964; PhD, Harvard U., 1974. Prof. philosophy and disting. Prof. of Lib. Arts and Ed. U. Mass., Boston, 1973—. Vis. assoc. prof. philosophy UCLA, 1984; vis. prof. edn. Stanford (Calif.) U., 1990; vis. prof. ednl. philosophy Tchrs. Coll., 1997. Author: Friendship, Altruism, and Morality, 1980, Moral Perception and Particularity, 1994, I'm Not a Racist, But... The Moral Quandary of Race, 2002. NEH fellow, 1986-87, 95-96. Mem. Am. Philos. Assn., Assn. for Moral Edn. E-mail: lawrence.blum@umb.edu.

BLUM, LESTER, educator; b. June 25, 1919; s. Morris and Rae (Altman) Blum; m. Harriet Schlesinger, Apr. 11, 1943; children: Dilys Ellen, Sydney Laura, Galen Elizabeth. BS cum laude, Mich. State U., 1942; MS, Iowa State U., 1944, PhD, 1949. Economist OPA, 1942—43; instr., rsch. and extension assoc. Iowa State U., 1943—47; mem. faculty Colgate U., Hamilton, NY, prof. econs., 1959—84, chmn. dept., 1962—70, prof. emeritus, 1984—, dir. econs. study groups in Norway, Eng., Israel. Cons. OPS, 1951—52; pub. mem. NY State Minimum Wage Bd. for Cleaning and Dyeing Industry, 1956—57. Recipient Creative Tchg. in Econs. Nat. award, Joint Coun. on Econs. Edn., 1982; fellow, Fund for Advancement Edn., Stanford, 1950—51, Asian Study Israel, 1967—68. Mem.: AAUP (pres. Colgate chpt. 1952—53), Am. Econ. Assn. Home: 2353 Brookview Dr Hamilton NY 13346-0057

BLUMBERG, AVROM AARON, physical chemistry educator; b. Albany, N.Y., Mar. 3, 1928; s. Samuel and Lillian Ann (Smith) B.; m. Eleanor Leah Simon, Aug. 5, 1955 (dec. Sept. 1967); 1 child, David Martin; m. Judith Anne Kohlhagen, Mar. 9, 1969; children: Susan Margaret, Jonathan Samuel. BS in Chemistry, Rensselaer Poly. Inst., 1949; PhD in Phys. Chemistry, Yale U., 1953. Fellow glass sci. Mellon Inst., Pitts., 1953-59, fellow polymer sci., 1959-63; from asst. to assoc. prof. phys. chemistry DePaul U., Chgo., 1963-75, prof., 1975—, head div. natural scis. and math., 1966-82, chmn. dept. chemistry, 1986-92. Vis. lectr. chemistry dept. U. Pitts., 1957-58; cons. in field. Author: Form and Function, 1972; contbr. articles to profl. jours. Participant scientists and speakers program Mus. Sci. and Industry, Chgo., 1985—; Dem. precinct capt., Evanston, Ill., 1970-78. Mem. Am. Chem. Soc. (speakers program Chgo. sect. 1983—), Royal Soc. Chem. London, Arms Control Assn., Sigma Xi. Jewish. Avocations: music, reading, art, travel, cooking. Home: 1240 S State St Chicago IL 60605-2405 Office: DePaul U Dept Chemistry 2320 N Kenmore Ave Chicago IL 60614-3210

BLUMBERG, NAOMI, symphony musician, educator; b. Chgo. married. Student, Northwestern U., Juilliard Sch. Music; B in Mus. Edn., Roosevelt U., Chgo.; studied with Karl Fruh, Dudley Powers, Bernard Greenhouse, Frank Miller, Claus Adam. Cellist Oregon Symphony, Portland, 1965—; prin. cellist West Coast Chamber Orchestra, 1980-90, North Coast Chamber Orchestra, 1972-77; cellist Portland Opera Orchestra, 1973-84, prin. cellist, 1979-80; private instr. Community Mus. Ctr., Portland, 1965—, dir., coach chamber mus. program, 1985—; founder and cellist Trio Encore, Portland, 1992—. Instr. U. Portland, Pacific U., Portland State U., George Fox College; adjudicator OMTA Syllabus, and others. Recipient Gruber award Chamber Mus. Am., 1992. Mem. MNTA, Am. String Tchrs. Assn., Oregon Cello Soc. (co-founder, pres. 1984-96), Bd. Mem. Friends of Chamber Music 1998—. Office: Community Music Ctr 3350 SE Francis St Portland OR 97202-3066*

BLUMBERG, PHILLIP IRVIN, law educator; b. Balt., Sept. 6, 1919; s. Hyman and Bess (Simons) B.; m. Janet Helen Mitchell, Nov. 17, 1945 (dec. 1976); children: William A.M., Peter M., Elizabeth B., Bruce M.; m. Ellen Ash Peters, Sept. 16, 1979. AB, Harvard U., 1939, JD, 1942; LLD (hon.), U. Conn., 1994. Bar: N.Y. 1942, Mass. 1970. Assoc. Willkie, Owen, Otis, Farr & Gallagher, N.Y.C., 1942-43, Szold, Brandwen, Meyers and Blumberg, N.Y.C., 1946-66; pres., CEO United Ventures Inc., 1962-67; pres., CEO, trustee Federated Devel. Co., N.Y.C., 1966-68, chmn. fin. com., 1968-73; prof. law Boston U., 1966-74; dean U. Conn. Sch. Law, Hartford, 1974-84, prof. law, 1984-89, dean, prof. law emeritus, 1989—. Bd. dirs. Verde Exploration Ltd.; mem. legal adv. com. to bd. dirs. N.Y. Stock Exch., 1989-93; mem. adv. com. on transnat. corps. U.S. Dept. State, 1976-79; advisor corp. governance project, restatement of suretyship and restatement of agy. Am. Law Inst.; vis. lectr. U. Brabant, Tilburg, Netherlands, 1985, U. Internat. Bus. and Econs., Beijing, 1989, U. Sydney, 1992, Jagiellonian U., Cracow, Poland, 1992. Author: Corporate Responsibility in a Changing Society, 1972, The Megacorporation in American Society, 1975, The Law of Corporate Groups: Procedure, 1983, The Law of Corporate Groups: Bankruptcy, 1985, The Law of Corporate Groups: Substantive Common Law, 1987, The Law of Corporate Groups: General Statutory Law, 1989, The Law of Corporate Groups: Specific Statutory Law, 1992, The Multinational Challenge to Corporation Law, 1993, The Law of Corporate Groups: State Statutory Law, 1995, The Law of Corporate Groups: Enterprise Liability, 1998; mem. editl. bd. Harvard Law Rev., 1940-42, treas., 1941-42; contbr. articles to profl. jours. Trustee Black Rock Forest Preserve, Inc.; trustee emeritus Conn. Bar Found. Capt. USAAF, 1943-46, ETO, maj. Res. 1946-55. Decorated Bronze Star Mem. ABA, Conn. Bar Assn., Am. Law Inst., Hartford Club, Harvard Club (Boston), Army & Navy Club (Washington), Phi Beta Kappa, Delta Upsilon. Home: 791 Prospect Ave Apt B-5 Hartford CT 06105-4224 Office: U Conn Sch Law 65 Elizabeth St Hartford CT 06105-2290 E-mail: pblumber@law.uconn.edu.

BLUME, MARSHALL EDWARD, finance educator; b. Chgo., Mar. 31, 1941; s. Marshall Edward Blume and Helen Corliss (Frank) Gilbert; m. Loretta Ryan, June 25, 1966; children: Christopher, Caroline, Catherine. SB, Trinity Coll., Hartford, Conn., 1963; MBA, U. Chgo., 1965, PhD, 1968; MA (hon.), U. Pa., 1970. Lectr. applied math. Grad. Sch. Bus., U. Chgo., 1966, instr. bus. fin. and applied math., 1967; lectr. fin. U. Pa., Phila., 1967, asst. prof., 1968-70, assoc. prof., 1970-74, prof., 1974-78, Howard Butcher prof., 1978—, chmn. dept., 1982-86, assoc. dir. Rodney White Ctr., 1978-86; prin. Prudent Mgmt. Assocs., 1982—; dir. Rodney White Ctr., 1986—. Mem. U.S. Compt. Gen. adv. bd. on Oct. 1987 stock market crash, 1987-88; prof. fin. European Inst., Brussels, 1975-76, New U. Lisbon, Portugal, 1982; vis. prof. Stockholm Sch., spring 1976, U. Brussels, 1975. Author: Mutual Funds and Other Institutional Investors, 1970, The Changing Role of the Individual Investor, 1978, The Structure and Reform of the U.S. Tax System, 1985, Revolution on Wall Street: The Rise and Fall of the New York Stock Exchange, 1993; editor: Encyclopedia of Investments, 1982, The Complete Guide to Investment Opportunities, 1984; assoc. editor Jour. Fin. and Quantitative Analysis, 1967-76, Jour. Fin. Econs., 1976-81, Jour. of Portfolio Mgmt., 1985—; mng. editor Jour. Fin., 1977-80, assoc. editor, 1985-88, Jour. of Fin. Income, 1990—. Contbr. articles to profl. publs. Trustee Trinity Coll., Hartford, Conn., 1980-86, Rosemont (Pa.) Sch., 1991—; commr. Bi-Partisan Commn. on Pa. Pension Fund Investments, 1989-93. Mem. Am. Fin. Assn. (officer 1977-80), Am. Econs. Assn., Fin. Economist Roundtable, Corinthian Yacht Club Phila., New Castle (Del.) Sailing Club, NASD (chmn. econ. adv. bd. 1998), NASDAQ Ednl. Found. (dir. 2000-2001), Measey Found. (mgr. 1997—), Shadow Regulatory Commn. Home: 204 Woodstock Rd Villanova PA 19085-1419 Office: U Penn Rodney L White Ctr Fin Rsch 3250 Steinberg Hall Philadelphia PA 19104

BLUMENFELD, JEFFREY, lawyer, educator; b. N.Y.C., May 13, 1948; s. Martin and Helen Kay (Smith) B.; m. Laura Madeline Ross, June 11, 1970; children: Jennifer Ross Blumenfeld, Joshua Ross Blumenfeld. AB in Religious Thought cum laude, Brown U., 1969; JD, U. Pa., 1973. Bar: D.C. 1973. Asst. U.S. atty. U.S. Atty. for D.C., Washington, 1975-79; trial atty. Antitrust div. U.S. Dept. of Justice, Washington, 1973-75, sr. trial atty. U.S. versus AT&T staff, 1979-82, asst. chief spl. regulated industries, 1982-84, chief U.S. versus AT&T staff, 1984, spl. counsel, 1995-97; ptnr. Blumenfeld & Cohen, Washington, 1984—2002; sr. trial counsel, antitrust divsn. U.S. Dept. Justice, 1996-97; gen. counsel, chief legal officer Rhythms Net Connections, 1997-2001; ptnr. Gray, Cary, Ware & Freidenrich, LLP, Washington, 2002—. Adj. prof. Georgetown U. Law Ctr., Washington, 1983—; spl. counsel antitrust divsn. U.S. Dept. Justice, 1995-97. Bd. dirs. Charles E. Smith Jewish Day Sch., Washington, 1991-93. Democrat. Jewish. Office: Gray Cary Ware & Freidenrich LLP Ste 300 1625 Massachusetts Ave NW Washington DC 20036-2247

BLUMENTHAL, ANNA CATHERINE, English educator; b. Providence, R.I., Feb. 7, 1952; d. Andrew J. and Marion Sabol; m. Robert A. Blumenthal, Aug. 22, 1973 (div. Mar. 2000); 1 child, Rachel A. BA, Univ. Rochester, 1974; M in Eng., Washington Univ., 1976, PhD, 1986. Asst. prof. Eng. Morris Brown Coll., Atlanta, 1989-93, Morehouse Coll., Atlanta, 1993-97, assoc. prof. Eng., 1997—. Invited spkr. confs., 1992, 93, 97, 98; referee for articles, 94; Faculty Resource Scholar (summer participant at NYU), 1999—2002. Contbr. articles to profl. jours. Named Activity Dir. (with Joan Hildenbrand), U.S. Dept. Edn., 1991-93. Mem. MLA, South Atlantic MLA. Office: Morehouse Coll Dept Eng 830 Westview Dr SW Atlanta GA 30314-3773

BLUMENTHAL, CARLENE MARGARET, vocational-technical school and language arts educator; d. Carl and Helen (Chervenak). BA, U. Ill., 1959; MA, Chgo. State U., 1969; student, No. Ill. U., Oxford, Eng., Nat. Louis U. Cert. in secondary lang. arts, social studies. Tutor Triton Coll., River Grove, Ill.; tchr. bus. English Robert Morris Coll., Chgo.; developer vocat. and bus. English curriculum Chgo. Pub. Schs. Participant Nat. Louis U. Right-o-Soar Project, YMCA Coll., 1990; curriculum cons. Pyramid Tech., Rassias Inst.; columnist Substance newspaper, 1999—; student tchr. supr. DePaul U., 2003—; presenter in field. Contbr. articles to profl. jours. Del. Dem. Nat. Conv., 1996; vol. Field Mus., 1999-2000. Tchr.-Sponsor of Yr., VFW, Ill., 1993; grantee U. Chgo., 1990, 91, 93; Mellon fellow, 1992-94, Annenberg fellow, 1995. Mem. NAFE, ACTE (VIM-secretary 2001-02, AIM sec. 2002-03), Nat. Coun. Tchrs. English (panel chair conv. 1996), Ill. Assn. Tchrs. English (workshop presenter 1995, 99), IACTE (affiliate mem. bd. dirs. 1997, del. Nat. Women's Rights Conv., workshop presenter 1999, 2000-01), Ill. Fedn. Tchrs., Chgo. Tchrs. Union (3 coms., workshop presenter 1994, 30 yr. award 2003), Coalition Labor Union Women (chair membership com. 2003—), Phi Delta Kappa (tchr. task force 1996). Home: 5649 W Leland Ave Chicago IL 60630-3221

BLUMENTHAL, RALPH HERBERT, natural science educator; b. N.Y.C., Feb. 24, 1925; s. Max and Celia (Sametsky) B.; m. Renee Cohen, Jan. 31, 1948; children: David S., Robert I., Meryl A. Orlando. BA, Bklyn. Coll., 1945, MA, 1949; PhD, NYU, 1956. Jr. engr. Hamilton Radio Corp., N.Y.C., 1945; lectr. physics Bklyn. Coll., 1946-48; physicist, project leader Naval Supply Activities, Bklyn., 1948-52; physicist, supr. test group Picatinny Arsenal, Dover, N.J., 1952; lectr. physics Bklyn. and Queens Colls., 1952-54; instr. physics CCNY, N.Y.C., 1954-61; assoc. mem. tech. and mgmt. staff Sperry Gyroscope Co., New Hyde Park, N.Y., 1958-63; sr. staff physicist Grumman Aerospace Corp., Bethpage, N.Y., 1963-70; adj. assoc. prof. physics Queensborough C.C., Queens, 1970-81; physics tchr. Sewanhaka H.S., Elmont, N.Y., 1970-88; adj. assoc. prof. physics Adelphi U. H.S. Program, 1976-87; adj. assoc. prof. natural sci. Hofstra U., Hempstead, N.Y., 1988—. Co-author: College Physics: A Programmed Aid, 4 vols., 1967, Spanish edit. (Fisica Basica), 1973; contbr. articles to profl. jours. Fellow AAAS; mem. Am. Phys. Soc. Avocations: history of science, bicycling, travel. Home: 5105 Pelican Cove Dr Boynton Beach FL 33437-1691 Office: Hofstra U Chemistry Dept Hempstead NY 11549-0001

BLUMRICK, CAROL SUSAN, elementary school educator; b. Warsaw, NY, Dec. 17, 1958; d. Richard and Alice (Saunderson) Pease; m. Anthony William Bochniarz, June 10, 1978 (div. Aug. 19, 1988); children: Stephen Richard Bochniarz, Michael Christopher Bochniarz; m. Wayne Bruce Blumrick, June 28, 1991; 1 child, David Wayne. BS in Edn. cum laude, Buffalo State Coll., 1980, MS in Reading, 1986. Tchr. Happy Times Day Care, Lockport, N.Y., 1981, Lockport Cath. Sch., 1982-84; owner/tchr. The Learning Home-Pre-Sch., Lockport, 1984-85; remedial reading/math. specialist Gasport (N.Y.) Elem. Sch., 1986-98; 3d grade tchr. Gasport (NY) Elem. Sch., 1998—2003, 2d grade tchr., 2003—. Computer coord. Gasport Elem., 1986-97, child study team, 1986—; policy bd. Tchr. Ctr., Lockport, 1987—97; dir., prodr. annual musical Royalton-Hartland Ctrl. Sch., 1991—. Active Lake Plains Players, Cmty. Theatre, 1980—; mem. Middleport Cmty. Choir, 1999—. Mem.: Delta Kappa Gamma, Kappa Delta Pi. Republican. Methodist. Avocations: singing, acting with community theatre, church choir. Home: 31 State St Middleport NY 14105-1123 E-mail: cblumrick@aol.com.

BLUMSTEIN, JAMES FRANKLIN, law educator, lawyer, consultant; b. Bklyn., Apr. 24, 1945; s. David and Rita (Sondheim) B.; m. Andree Kahn, June 25, 1971 BA in Econs., Yale U., 1966, MA in Econs., LLB, 1970. Bar: Tenn. 1970, U.S. Ct. Appeals (6th cir.) 1970, U.S. Dist. Ct. (mid. dist.) Tenn. 1971, U.S. Supreme Ct. 1974, N.Y. 1985. Instr. econs. New Haven Coll., 1967-68; pre-law adviser office of dean Yale U., New Haven, 1968-69, sr. pre-law adviser office of dean, 1969-70, asst. in instrn. law shc., 1969-70; asst. prof. law Vanderbilt U., Nashville, 1970-73, assoc. prof., 1973-76, prof., 1976-99, spl. advisor to chancellor for acad. affairs, 1984-85, Centennial prof., 1999—, Univ. prof. law and medicine, 2003—, chair faculty senate, 2001—02, univ. prof., 2003—. Assoc. dir. Vanderbilt Urban and Regional Devel. Ctr., 1970-72, dir. ctr., 1972-74; sr. rsch. assoc. Vanderbilt Inst. for Pub. Policy Studies, 1976-85, sr. fellow, 1985—, dir. health policy ctr., 1995—; Commonwealth Fund fellow, vis. assoc. prof. law and policy scis. law sch. Duke U. and Inst. of Policy Scis. and Pub. Affairs, 1974-75; adj. prof. health law med. sch. Dartmouth U., scholar-in-residence intermittently, 1976-78; John M. Olin vis. prof. Sch. Law, U. Pa., 1989; elected mem. Inst. Medicine NAS, 1990—; cons. law, health policy, civil and voting rights, land use, state taxation, torts; lectr. in field. Editor: (with Eddie J. Martin) The Urban Scene in the Seventies, 1974, (with

Benjamin Walter) Growing Metropolis: Aspects of Development in Nashville, 1975, (with Lester Salamon) Growth Policy in the Eighties (Law and Contemporary Problems Symposium), 1979; (with Frank A. Sloan and James M. Perrin) Uncompensated Hospital Care: Rights and Responsibilities, 1986, (with Frank A. Sloan and James M. Perrin) Cost, Quality, and Access in Health Care: New Roles for Health Planning in a Competitive Environment, 1988; (with Frank A. Sloan) Organ Transplantation Policy: Issues and Prospects, 1989, (with Frank A. Sloan) Antitrust and Health Care Policy (Law and Contemporary Problems Symposium), 1989, (with Clark C. Havighurst and Troyen A. Brennan) Health Care Law and Policy, 1998, bd. Jour. Health Politics, Policy and Law, 1981-01; mem. adv. bd. NF IB Legal Found., 2003-; mem. pub.'s adv. bd. Nashville Banner, 1982-98; contbr. articles to profl. jours., op-ed articles to newspapers. Mem. Health Econs. Task Force, Middle Tenn. Health Sys. Agy., 1979; mem. adv. bd. LWV, 1979-80; mem. Nashville Mayor's Commn. on Crime, 1981; cons. Leadership Nashville, 1977—, Tenn. Motor Vehicle Commn., 1986-87, Leadership Music, 1989-02; panelist Am. Arbitration Assn., 1977-02; chmn. Tenn. adv. com. U.S. Commn. on Civil Rights, 1985-91, mem., 1991-97; sec. Martin Luther King Jr. Holiday Com., State of Tenn., 1985-87; bd. dirs. Jewish Fedn. Nashville and Middle Tenn., 1981-90, mem. exec. com., 1988-90, chmn. cmty. rels. com., 1980-82, chmn. campus com., 1987-89; chmn. Yale Alumni Schs. Com. Middle Tenn., 1983—; mem Tenn. Gov.'s Task Force Medicaid, 1992-94; mem. adv. panel Office Tech. Assessment study of defensive medicine and use of med. tech., 1991-94; chmn. task force cost containment and med. malpractice Rand Corp., 1991-92; active Inst. Medicine Com. on Adequacy of Nursing Staffing, 1994-96; mem. adv. com. on The Records of Congress, 1997-99. Bates Jr. fellow, 1968-69; grantee Ford Found./Rockefeller Found. Population Program, 1970-73, Health Policy grantee HCA Found., 1986-90; grantee State Justice Inst., 1991—, Robert Wood Johnson Found., 1994—; nominated Adminstr., Office Info. and Regulatory Affairs, Office Mgmt. and Budget, 1990; named One of Outstanding Young Men in Am. U.S. Jaycees, 1971; recipient award Univ. Rsch. Coun., 1971-72, 73-74, 79-80, 94-95, Earl Sutherland prize achievement in rsch. Vanderbilt U., 1992, Paul J. Hartman award Outstanding Prof., 1982. Mem. ABA (sec. sect. legal edn. and admissions to bar 1982-83, chmn. subcom. on state and local taxation com. on corp. law and taxation sect. on corp., banking and bus. law 1983—, mem. accreditation com. sect. legal edn. and admissions to bar 1983-89, mem. com. on state and local taxation sect. on taxation 1983—), NAS (inst. of medicine), Assn. Am. Law Schs. (chmn. law, medicine and health care sect. 1987-88, mem. exec. com. 1988-92, 2d vice chmn. sect. local govt. law 1976-78, mem. sect. coun. 1980-86), Tenn. Bar Assn., N.Y. State Bar Assn., Nashville Bar Assn. (Liberty Bell award 1987), Hastings Ctr., Assn. for Pub. Policy Analysis and Mgmt., Assn. Yale Alumni (del.), Yale U. Law Sch. Alumni Assn. (exec. com. 1985-88), Univ. Club (Nashville). Home: 2113 Hampton Ave Nashville TN 37215-1401 Office: Vanderbilt U Sch Law 21st Ave S Nashville TN 37240-0001

BLUMSTEIN, SHEILA ELLEN, former academic administrator, linguistics educator; b. N.Y.C., Mar. 10, 1944; d. Edgar and Bernice Marjorie (Heineman) B. BA, U. Rochester, 1965; PhD, Harvard U., 1970. Asst. prof. linguistics Brown U., Providence, 1970—76, assoc. prof., 1976—81, prof., 1981—91, Albert D. Mead prof. cognitive and linguistic scis., 1991—, dean of coll., 1987—95, interim pres., 2000—01, interim provost, 1998; research assoc. Aphasia Research Ctr., VA Med. Ctr., Boston, 1970—. Vis. scientist MIT, Cambridge, 1974, 77-78; mem. study sect. NIH, 1976-80, exec. com. Com. on Hearing, Bioacoustics, Biomechanics, NRC, 1980-82, sci. program adv. com. Nat. Inst. Neurol. and Comm. Diseases and Strokes, 1982-84; Henry R. Luce vis. prof. Wellesley Coll., Mass., 1982-83; mem. adv. coun. Nat. Inst. Deafness and Other Comm. Disorders, 1989-93; mem. sci. adv. bd. McDonnell-Pew Program in Neuroscis., 1989-2000. Author: A Phonological Investigation of Aphasic Speech, 1973, (with P. Lieberman) Speech Physiology Acoustics and Speech Perception, 1987; editor: (with H. Goodglass) Psycholinguistics and Aphasia, 1973; mem. editorial bd. Brain and Lang., 1978-83, Cognition, 1982-90, Applied Psycholinguistics, 1984-89; adv. editor Contemporary Psychology, 1981-83; contbr. articles to profl. jours., chpts. to books Recipient Javits neurosci. investigator award, 1985-92; Guggenheim fellow, 1977-78, Radcliffe Inst. fellow, 1977-78 Fellow Acoustical Soc. Am., Am. Acad. Arts and Scis.; mem. Linguistics Soc. Am., Acad. Aphasia, Am. Philos. Soc., Phi Beta Kappa, Phi Sigma Iota. Jewish. Avocations: tennis, piano, music, gardening. Home: 14 Broadview Dr Barrington RI 02806-4012 Office: Brown Univ PO Box 1978 Providence RI 02912-1978

BLY, JAMES LEE, secondary education educator; b. Elmira, N.Y., Aug. 23, 1948; s. Lee Irvin and Helen Irene (Piasecki) B.; m. MaryLou Starry, Mar. 22, 1969; children: Michael, Joseph, James. AAS in Avionics Systems, C.C. of Air Foce, 1980; AAS, Inst. Tech. C.C. of Air Force, 1985; AAS in Health Adminstrn., C.C. of Air Foce, 1986; BS in Human Resource Mgmt., New Sch. Social Rsch., N.Y.C., 1980, MPS in Health Svcs. Adminstrn., 1986. Cert. secondary tchr., N.Y. Enlisted USAF, 1966, profl. mil. instr., 1982-86, mgmt. instr. Rome, N.Y., 1984-86; resource mgmt. supr. USAF Hosp., Griffiss AFB, N.Y., 1986; retired master sergeant USAF, 1986; program dir. New Sch. for Social Rsch., Rome, 1987-89; tchr. social studies Vernon-Verona-Sherrill Mid. Sch., Verona, N.Y., 1990—. Owner Orzel Enterprises, Rome, 1980—; adj. instr. Embry-Riddle Aeronautical U., Rome, 1982—. Vol. fireman Vol. Fire Dept., Box Elder, S.D. and Waterloo, N.Y., 1972-79; leader Boys Scouts Am., Rome, 1979—; asst. coach soccer YMCA, Rome, 1989, 90; treas. PTO, Rome, 1992-93. Decorated 3 Air medals, Conspicuious Svc. medal, Meritorious Svc. medal, 3 Commendation Medals. Mem. N.Y. Tchrs. Assn., N.Y. Guard (battalion comdr.), Orgn. Am. Historians, N.Y. Coun. for Social Studies, Nat. Coun. for Social Studies, VFW, DAV, Elks (leading knight 1974), Knights of Columbus, V.V.A., Sons of Union Veterans of the Civil War. Republican. Roman Catholic. Avocations: historical research, photography, model building, scuba diving. Home: 736 Camp St Rome NY 13440-3950 Office: Vernon Verona Sherrill Mid Sch RR 31 Verona NY 13478

BLYSTONE, ROBERT VERNON, cell biologist, educator; b. El Paso, Tex., July 4, 1943; s. Edward Vernon and Cecilia (Mueller) Blystone; m. Donna Joan Moore, Mar. 26, 1964; 1 child, Daniel Vernon. BS in Biol. Sci., U. Tex., El Paso, 1965; MA in Zoology, U. Tex., Austin, 1968, PhD in Zoology, 1971. Instr. U. Tex., El Paso, 1965, tchg. asst. Austin, 1965-68, NIH predoctoral fellow, 1968-70; from asst. prof. to assoc. prof. biology Trinity U., San Antonio, 1971—84, prof., 1984—, chmn. dept., 1984-86. Cons. Ednl. Testing Svc., Princeton, NJ, others; text and trade book cons. McGraw-Hill, 1987, Harper-Collins, 1991—93, Oxford U. Press, 1988, Addison-Wesley, 1987—91, others. Contbr. articles to profl. jours., chapters to books. Asst. dir., dir., sec., v.p., historian Alamo Regional Sci. Fair, 1973—85; bd. dirs. Sci. Collaborative, San Antonio, 1987—95. Named Piper Prof., Tex. Piper Found., 1986; Scott fellow for tchg., 1991, Rsch. grantee, USAF Office Sci. Rsch., 1990—91, 2000—, NSF, 1991, 1995. Fellow: AAAS (film/book reviewer 1982—95), Tex. Acad. Sci. (life; exec. bd. 1976—79); mem.: AAUP (treas. chpt. 1984—86), Assn. Computing Machinery (mem. SIGGRAPH edn. com. 1994—97), Tex. Soc. Electron Microscopy (program chmn., assoc. jour. editor 1982—83), Nat. Assn. Biology Tchrs., Am. Soc. Cell Biology (mem. edn. com. 1985—89, 1991—), Microscopy Soc. Am., Am. Inst. Biol. Scis. (assoc. editor BioScience 1995—2002), Sigma Xi (pres. chpt. 1990—91). Avocation: computer graphics. Office: Trinity U Dept Biology 715 Stadium Dr San Antonio TX 78212-3104

BLYTH, ANN MARIE, secondary education educator; b. Sharon, Pa., June 18, 1949; d. Chester Stanley and Mary Clara (Roman) Kacerski; m. Lynn Allan Blyth, June 26, 1976 (dec. June 1983); 1 stepchild, Breton Alan Blyth; 1 child, Amanda Lynn. BS in Edn., Kent (Ohio) State U., 1971; postgrad., Loyola U., New Orleans, 1973-74; MS in Teaching, John Carroll U., 1978. Cert. comprehensive sci., maths. and physics tchr., Ohio. Jr. high math. tchr. New Philadelphia (Ohio) Bd. of Edn., 1971-72; high sch. sci. and math. tchr. Hubbard (Ohio) Exempted Village Bd. of Edn., 1972-76, Painesville (Ohio) City Local Bd. Edn., 1976—; head dept. sci. Harvey H.S., 2001—. Instr. math. Morton Salt, Painesville, 1979-80; part-time faculty Lake Erie Coll., 1992. Mem. Adv. Bd. Western Res. br. Am. Lung Assn. of Ohio, Painesville, 1986-89, sec. 1988-89, Northeastern br., Youngstown, Ohio, 1989-99; judge state level Nat. Pre-teen and Pre-Teen Petite Pageants, 1990. Martha Holden Jennings Found. scholar, 1984-85; named Tchr. of the Yr., Harvey High Sch. Key Club, 1981-82. Mem. NEA, Ohio Edn. Assn., Northeastern Ohio Edn. Assn., Painesville City Tchrs. Assn., Am. Assn. Physics Tchrs. (Ohio sect.), Nat. Sci. Tchrs. Assn., Cleve. Regional Coun. of Sci. Tchrs. Democrat. Episcopalian. Avocations: travel, gourmet cooking, baking, gardening, music. Home: 7243 Scottsdale Cir Mentor OH 44060-6408 Office: Thomas W Harvey High Sch 167 W Washington St Painesville OH 44077-3328

BOAL, BERNARD HARVEY, cardiologist, educator, author; b. Winnipeg, Man., Can., May 14, 1937; came to U.S., 1964; s. Charles and Bessie (Carr) B.; m. Pamela Sures Brownstone, Oct. 28, 1962; children: Steven, Jeremy, Hilary. BS in Medicine, MD, U. Man., 1962. Licentiate Med. Coun. Can.; diplomate Nat. Bd. Med. Examiners, Am. Bd. Internal Medicine in medicine and cardiology. Intern Winnipeg Gen. Hosp., 1962-63, resident in medicine, 1963-64, U. Utah Hosps., Salt Lake City, 1964-66; USPHS trainee in cardiology NYU Med. Ctr., N.Y.C., 1966-68; practice medicine specializing in cardiology Queens, N.Y., 1969—; chief sect. cardiology Booth Meml. Med. Ctr., 1969-87; chief cardiology Cath. Med. Ctr. Bklyn. and Queens, 1987—2002; cons. L.I. Jewish Hosp.; mem. staff NYU Hosp., Bellevue Hosp., 1968-81; clin. assoc. prof. medicine N.Y. Med. Coll., 1981-89, Cornell U. Med. Coll., 1989-95; assoc. prof. medicine Albert Einstein Coll. Medicine, 1995-2000, N.Y. Med. Coll., 2000—03; chief cardiology Bklyn.-Queens region St. Vincents Cath. Med. Ctrs. N.Y., Jamaica, 2000—02; physician, electrophysiology sect. North Shore Univ. Hosp., Manhasset, NY, 2003—. Lectr. worldwide on cardiac pacing. Guest editor several major cardiology jours.; asst. editor: HeartNet; contbr. chpts. to books, articles to med. jours. Co-inventor Kolker-Boal Cardiac Pacemaker Electrode. Chmn. physicians divsn. Queens County Cabinet United Jewish Appeals of Greater N.Y., 1978-80; charter mem., founding treas. B'nai B'rith UN unit, 1984—; U.S. physician rep. pacemaker working group of the Internat. Standards Orgn., Geneva, 1988—, chmn., 1990—. Capt. M.C., USAR, 1970-73. Fellow N.Y. Cardiol. Soc., Am. Coll. Cardiology (chmn. med. devices com. Heart House campaign 1976-78, chmn. bequests and endowments com. 1980-85, pacemaker com. 1987-95, trustee 1985-90, mem. electrocardiology com. 1995-2001, mem. budget/fin./investment com. 1996-2002, devel. com. 1997-2003), ACP (treas. Queens chpt. 1976-78, sec. 1978-79, v.p. 1979-81, pres. 1981-85; govs. adv. coun. N.Y. State 1982-85); mem. AMA, Assn. Advancement of Med. Instrumentation (pacemaker com. 1976—, chmn. pacemaker com. 1988—, bd. dirs. 1983-86, co-chmn. strategic planning com. 1983-85), Am. Heart Assn. (fellow coun. clin. cardiology), N.Y. Heart Assn., Am. Soc. Internal Medicine, Queens Soc. Internal Medicine, N.Am. Soc. Pacing and Electrophysiology (founding mem., mem. nat. adv. coun. 1984-85, mem. exec. com. 1985-88, chmn. fin. com. 1985-88, trustee 1987-91), U.S. divsn. Israeli Med. Assn. (founding mem.). Office: North Shore Univ HOsp Manhasset NY E-mail: bboal@boal.com.

BOALER, JO, education educator; BSc in Psychology, U. Liverpool, Eng., 1985; MA in Math. Edn., London U., 1991, PhD in Math. Edn., 1996. Tchr. secondary sch. math., Camden, London, 1986—89; dep. dir. math. assessment project King's Coll., London U., 1989—93, lectr., rschr. on math. edn., 1993—98; assoc. prof. Stanford (Calif.) U., 2000—. Mem. Math. Edn. Study Panel; bd. dirs. Gender and Edn. jour. Mem.: Internat. Orgn. for Women in Math. Edn. Office: Stanford U Sch Edn 485 Lasuen Mall Stanford CA 94305-3096*

BOARD, JOHN ARNOLD, JR., electrical engineer educator, computer engineer; b. Atlanta, Jan. 13, 1960; s. John Arnold and Anne Johnson (Woodrum) B.; m. Rebecca Ruth Batchelor, Mar. 9, 1991. BS in Engring., MS, Duke U., 1982; DPhil, Oxford (Eng.) U., 1987. Asst. prof. elec. engring. Duke U., Durham, N.C., 1987-94, assoc. prof. elec. engring., 1994-97, Bass assoc. prof. elec. engring., 1997—, assoc. chair dept. elec. and computer engring., 1998—2001. Rhodes scholar, 1981. Mem. IEEE, Assn. for Computer Machinery, Am. Phys. Soc. Home: 10 Winslow Pl Chapel Hill NC 27517-9408 Office: Duke Univ Dept Elec/Computer Engring PO Box 90291 Durham NC 27708-0291

BOARDMAN, EUNICE, retired music educator; b. Cordova, Ill., Jan. 27, 1926; d. George Hollister and Anna Bryson (Feaster) Boardman. B. Mus. Edn., Cornell Coll., 1947; M. Mus. Edn., Columbia U., 1951; Ed.D., U. Ill., 1963; DFA (hon.), Cornell Coll., 1995. Tchr. music pub. schs., Iowa, 1947-55; prof. music edn. Wichita State U., Kans., 1955-72; vis. prof. mus. edn. Normal State U., Ill., 1972-74, Roosevelt U., Chgo., 1974-75; prof. mus. edn. U. Wis., Madison, 1975-89, dir. Sch. Music, 1980-89; prof. music, dir. grad. program in music edn. U. Ill., Urbana, 1989-98; ret. Author: Musical Growth in Elementary School, 1963, 6th rev. edit., 1996, Exploring Music, 1966, 3d rev. edit., 1975, The Music Book, 1980, 2d rev. edit., 1984, Holt Music, 1987; editor: Dimensions of Musical Thinking, 1989, Dimensions of Musical Thinking: A Different Kind of Music, 2002, Up the Mississippi: A Journey of the Blues, 2002. Mem. Soc. Music Tchr. Edn. (chmn. 1984-86), Music Educators Nat. Conf. Avocations: reading, antiques. E-mail: EunBoardman@aol.com.

BOARDMAN, MAUREEN BELL, community health nurse, educator; b. Hartford, Conn., June 11, 1966; d. Jack Russell and Mary Elizabeth (Brumm) Bell; m. Byron Earl Boardman, June 4, 1988; 1 child, Meghan Elizabeth. BSN, U. Maine, Orono, 1988; MSN, U. Tenn., 1991. RN, Tenn.; ACLS; cert. family nurse practitioner. Charge nurse med.- surg. divsn. Scott County Hosp., Oneida, Tenn., 1988-89, employee health nurse, 1989-92; nurse team leader Oneida Home Health, 1989, Quality Home Health, Oneida, 1989-90; FNP, Straightfork Family Care Clinic, Pioneer, Tenn., 1992-96, Huntsville (Tenn.) Family Care Clinic, 1996-98, Oak Grove Primary Care Clin., 1998-2001, Cmty. Health Ctr., Hanover, NH, 2001—; instr. cmty. and family medicine Dartmouth Med. Sch., Hanover, 2001—. Mem. child abuse rev. team Dept. Human Svcs., Huntsville, Tenn., 1993-2001; adj. prof. Coll. Nursing U. Tenn., 1997-2001. Med. advisor, liaison Scott County (Tenn.) Sch. Systems Sci. Fair Com., 1992-2001; bd. dirs., editor newsletter Appalachian Arts Coun., Oneida, 1993-2001, v.p., 1996-98, del., 1997; com. on health policy TNA, 1998-2000. Mem. Sigma Theta Tau (sec. Gamma Chi chpt. 1996-2000). Roman Catholic. Avocations: reading, biking, swimming, dancing. Home: 72 Anderson Hill Rd Enfield NH 03748-3152 Office: Cmty Health Ctr 1 Medical Center Dr Lebanon NH 03756 Personal E-mail: maureen.b.boardman@hitchcock.org. Business E-Mail: maureen.b.boardman@dartmouth.edu.

BOATMAN, HELEN ADELL, school district administrator; b. Karnes City, Tex. BS in Edn., S.W. Tex. U., 1961; MEd, U. Houston, Victoria, 1989. Cert. tchr., Tex. Tchr. Taft (Tex.) Ind. Sch. Dist., 1961, North East Ind. Sch. Dist., San Antonio, 1961-65, McAllen (Tex.) Ind. Sch. Dist., 1965-67, Karnes City (Tex.) Ind. Sch. Dist., 1975-76, Victoria (Tex.) Ind. Sch. Dist., 1977-90, gifted and talented program, magnet schs. coord., 1990—. Project wild facilitator Tex. Parks and Wildlife, Austin, 1988—. Named Outstanding Tchr., Victoria Soil and Water Conservation Dist., 1987. Mem. ASCD, Tex. Elem. Prins. and Suprs., Delta Kappa Gamma, Phi Delta Kappa (1st v.p. 1992-93, 93-94). Office: Victoria Ind Sch Dist 102 Profit Dr Victoria TX 77901-7346

BOATRIGHT, GREGORY BRUCE, school system administrator, educator; b. Newcastle, Ind., Mar. 13, 1947; s. Meredith Jefferson and Gladys Louise (Ealy) B.; m. Connie Joan Gross, Oct. 9, 1971 (div. 1979); children: Rebecca Boatright Adsit, Jason Gregory. BS, Anderson U., 1970; MS, Ind. U., 1974, cert. in spl. edn., 1979. Social worker Anderson (Ind.) Urban League, 1969-70; tchr. spl. edn. Newcastle Pub. Sch., 1970-72; tchr. Indpls. Tchr. Corp.-Indpls. Pub. Schs., 1972-74; tch. spl. edn. Indpls. Pub. Sch., 1974-75; with dept. vocat. edn. Ind. Dept. Pub. Instrn., Indpls., 1975-80; mem. state bd. vocat. edn. State of Ind., Indpls., 1980-88; tchr. spl. edn. Indpls. Pub. Schs., 1988-89, vice-prin., 1989-90, dean of students, 1990—. Tchr. learning disabilities Anderson U., 1982-83; cons. Ft. Wayne Latin Ctr., 1987. Team leader Combined State campaign United Way Ind., 1985, 86, mem. exec. com., 1987. Home: 3431 Seaway Dr Indianapolis IN 46214-4106 Office: Indpls Pub Sch 401 E Walnut St Indianapolis IN 46202-3365

BOATWRIGHT, JANICE ELLEN WILLIS, school system administrator; b. Bremen, Ga., Apr. 15, 1939; d. Wilson Matthew and Sue Winifred (Pope) Willis; m. James Bolden Boatwright, Sr., Feb. 11, 1961; children: James B. Jr., Jamee Ellen. BS in Edn., West Ga. Coll., 1960, MEd, 1974; EdD, Nova Southeastern U., 1991. Tchr. Haralson County Bd. of Edn., Buchanan, Ga., 1961-63, media specialist, 1970-71, tchr., asst. prin., 1974-76, curriculum dir., 1977-96, supt., 1996—; media specialist Tallapoosa (Ga.) Bd. of Edn., 1963-67. Adv. bd. Haralson Edn. Collaborative, Buchanan, 1992—. Editor: Haralson County Georgia A Resource Guide for the Teaching of Social Studies, 1991. Dir. Haralson County Adult Edn., Tallapoosa, 1991—; active Buchanan Women's Club, 1993—; bd. dirs. Ga. Youth Sci. and Tech. Ctr., Inc., 1992—. Recipient Mother of Yr. award Buchanan Women's Club, 1993, Disting. Svc. award Ga. Assn. Curriculum and Instructional Supervision, 1994. Mem. ASCD, Nat. Assn. Edn. Young Children, Ga. Assn. Supervision and Curriculum Devel., Nat. Assn. for Supervision and Curriculum Devel., Ga. Assn. Ednl. Leaders, Ga. Assn. Sch. Superintendents, Am. Sch. Supts. Assn. (bd. dirs. RESA 1996—), Haralson County C. of C. (bd. dirs. 1996—), Haralson County Health Bd. (bd. dirs. 1996—). Methodist. Avocations: reading, fishing, traveling. Home: 735 Seabreeze Lake Rd Buchanan GA 30113-4474 Office: Haralson County Bd Edn 10 Van Wert St Buchanan GA 30113-4879

BOBBITT, HELEN DAVIS, secondary school educator; b. Kansas City, Mo., Dec. 2, 1913; d. Robert and Georgia Helen (Lucas) Davis; m. George Presley Bobbitt, Apr. 9, 1938; 1 child, Charles Robert. BS in Edn., Cen. Mo. State U., Warrensburg, 1941; MS, Emporia (Kans.) State U., 1964. Cert. tchr., Mo., Kans. Tchr. Camden County, Mo., 1933-35, Stoutland (Mo.) Schs., 1936-39, Clinton (Mo.) Schs., 1942-44, Hutchinson (Kans.) Schs., 1945-48, El Dorado (Kans.) Schs., 1960-83, ret., 1983. Mem. AAUW, (sec. 1953-54, pres. 1958-61), Ret. Tchrs. Butler County (courtesy chmn. 1984—, treas. 1989—), Book Lovers Club, Delta Kappa Gamma Internat. (chmn. 1979-89, Phi State Scholar, Helen D. Bobbitt Hostelship award 1989). Avocation: travel. Home: 940 E Paradise Ln Phoenix AZ 85022-3128

BOBBITT, PHILIP CHASE, writer, educator, public official; b. Temple, Tex., July 22, 1948; s. Oscar Price and Rebekah Luruth (Johnson) B.; m. Selden Anne Wallace (div. 1990). AB, Princeton U., 1971; JD, Yale U., 1975; PhD, Oxford U., 1983, MA, 1984. Bar: Tex. 1977, U.S. Supreme Ct. 1989. Law clk. to Judge Henry Friendly U.S. Ct. Appeals (2d cir.), 1975-76; asst. prof. law U. Tex., Austin, 1976-79, prof., 1979—, A.W. Walker chair in law, 1996—. Assoc. counsel to Pres. U.S. for intelligence and internat. security, 1980-81; legal counsel U.S. Senate Select Com. on Secret Mil. Assistance to Iran and Nicaraguan Opposition, 1987-88; counselor on internat. law U.S. Dept. of State, 1990-93; dir. for intelligence NSC, 1997-98, sr. dir. critical infrastructure, 1998-99, sr. dir. strategic planning, 1999; mem. faculty Salzburg Seminar, 1987; vis. fellow Internat. Inst. Strategic Studies, 1981-82; jr. rsch. fellow Nuffield Coll., Oxford U., 1982-84, rsch. fellow, 1984-85, Anderson sr. rsch. fellow, 1985-91, mem. modern history faculty, 1984-91; guest scholar Woodrow Wilson Ctr. for Internat. Scholars, 1994; sr. rsch. fellow war studies King's Coll./U. London, 1994-97. Author: Democracy and Deterrence, 1988; (with Guido Calabresi) Tragic Choices, 1979, Constitutional Fate, 1982; (with Lawrence Freedman and Gregory Treverton) Nuclear Strategy, 1988, Constitutional Interpretation., 1991, The Shield of Achilles: War, Peace and the Course of History, 2002. Trustee Princeton U. Mem. Am. Law Inst., Internat. Inst. Strategic Studies (London), Austin Coun. Fgn. Affairs (pres. 1983—), Coun. Fgn. Rels. (N.Y.C.), Adminstrv. Conf. U.S. (spl. com. on ethics in govt.), Pacific Coun. on Internat. Policy, Nat. Infrastructure Assurance Coun., State Infrastructure Protection Adv. Com. (editl. bd. biosecurity and bioterrorism), Tex. Philos. Soc., Met. Club (Washington), Yale Club, Century Assn., The Brook, Knickerbocker Club (NYC). Democrat. Baptist. Office: U Tex Law Sch 727 E 26th St Austin TX 78705-3224

BOBINSKI, GEORGE SYLVAN, librarian, educator; b. Cleve., Oct. 24, 1929; s. Sylvan and Eugenia (Sarbiewski) B.; m. Mary Lillian Form, Feb. 20, 1953; children-George Sylvan, Mary Anne. BA, Case Western Res. U., 1951, MS in Libr. Sci., 1952; MA, U. Mich., 1961, PhD, 1966. Rsch. asst. Bus Info. Bur., Cleve. Pub. Libr., 1954-55; asst. dir. Royal Oak (Mich.) Pub. Libr., 1955-59; dir. librs. State U. Coll. at Cortland, N.Y., 1960-67; prof., asst. dean Sch. Libr. Sci. U. Ky., 1967-70; prof. SUNY, Buffalo, 1970—2001, dean Sch. Info. and Libr. Studies, 1970-99, prof. emeritus, 2002—. Fulbright-Hays lectr. in libr. sci. U. Warsaw, Poland, 1977; trustee Western N.Y. Libr. Rsch. Coun., 1971-87, pres., 1972, 82; vis. scholar Jagiellonian U., Krakow, Poland, 1992, 97. Author: A Brief History of the Libraries of Western Reserve University, 1826-1952, 1955, Carnegie Libraries, Their History and Impact on American Public Library Development, 1969, Dictionary of American Library Biography, 1978, also articles. Mem. N.Y. Gov.'s Commn. on Librs., 1990—. With AUS, 1952-54. Recipient Meritorious Svc. medal Jagellonian U., Krakow, Poland, 1997. Mem. ALA (mem. pub. com., mem. coun.), N.Y. Libr. Assn., Assn. Am. Libr. Schs. (chmn. coun. of deans 1985-86) Home: 69 Little Robin Rd Buffalo NY 14228-1125 Office: SUNY Buffalo Sch Informatics Baldy Hall Buffalo NY 14260 E-mail: bobinski@acsu.buffalo.edu.

BOCKWITZ, CYNTHIA LEE, psychologist, psychology and women's studies educator; b. Hallock, Minn., Apr. 11, 1954; d. Rodney Lee and Jeanette Yvonne (Vilen) B. AA in Arts and Scis., Richland Coll., 1983; BA in Devel. Psychology, U. Tex., Dallas, 1985; MA in Counseling Psychology, Tex. Woman's U., 1992. Lic. profl. counselor, Ga.; registered play therapist and supr. Pers. adminstr. Automatic Data Processing, Miami, Fla., 1974-77; office mgr. G.A. Dexter Co., Atlanta, 1977-79; regional human resources mgr. No. Telecom, Atlanta and Dallas, 1979-84; mental health asst. Timberlawn Psychiat. Hosp., Dallas, 1984-85; acct. NEC Am., Dallas, 1986-87; asst. program dir. Arbor Creek Hosp., Sherman, Tex., 1989; lic. profl. counselor Trinity Counseling Ctr., Carrollton, Tex., 1989-93; pvt. practice Atlanta, 1993—. Adj. instr. psychology Tex. Woman's U., Denton, 1988—92, Ga. Perimeter Coll., Atlanta, 1993—; adj. faculty Argosy U., Atlanta; cons. The Resource Ctr., Atlanta, 1993—94; clin. team leader Laurel Hts. Hosp., 1994—2000; mem. exec. com. Women Clinicians Network, Atlanta, 1994—95; psychiat. assessments Emory Pkwy. Med. Ctr., 2001. Mem.: Lic. Profl. Counselors Assn., Ga. Assn. for Play Therapy (bd. dirs. 2000—), Internat. Assn. for Play Therapy, Ga. Marriage and Family Therapy Assn. (legis. com. 1993—94, mem. metro Atlanta chpt. bd. officers 1999—2000), Am. Assn. for Marriage and Family Therapy (affiliate), Am. Psychotherapy Assn. (diplomate). Democrat. Avocations: wilderness camping, photography. Home: 711 Tuxworth Cir Decatur GA 30033-5620 E-mail: clbockwitz@aol.com.

BOCOBO, CHRISTIAN REYES, rehabilitation medicine educator; b. Manila, May 28, 1954; s. Israel de Castro and Teresita Reyes B. BS, U. Philippines, Manila, 1975, MD, 1979. Diplomate Am. Bd. Phys. Medicine and Rehab., Fed. Licensure Exams. Philippine Med. Bds. Intern Makati Med. Ctr., Manila, 1979-80; resident in family practice U. Mass. Med. Ctr., Worcester, 1982-83; chief resident in phys. medicine and rehab. Nassau County Med. Ctr., SUNY, Stony Brook, 1985—86; clin. instr. phys. medicine and rehab. U. Medicine and Dentistry N.J.-N.J. Med. Sch., Newark, 1986-89, assoc. dir. residency tng. program, 1987-89; clin. instr. rehab. medicine Stanford Med. Sch., Palo Alto, Calif., 1989-91, clin. asst. prof., 1991—. Dir. phys. medicine and rehab. Elizabeth (N.J.) Gen. Med. Ctr., 1986-89; cons. Kessler Inst. for Rehab., West Orange, N.J., 1986-89; dir. outpatient clinics Rehab. Medicine Svc., Palo Alto, 1990-92. Contbr. articles to med. jours. Physician Zonta Internat., Manila, 198l. Fellow Am. Acad. Phys. Medicine and Rehab.; mem. Calif. Med. Assn., San Mateo County Med. Assn. Avocation: painting. Office: 101 S San Mateo Dr Ste 302 San Mateo CA 94401-3844

BODANSKY, DAVID, physicist, educator; b. N.Y.C., Mar. 10, 1924; s. Aaron and Marie (Syrkin) B.; m. Beverly Ferne Bronstein, Sept. 7, 1952; children: Joel N., Daniel M. BS, Harvard U., 1943, MA, 1948, PhD, 1950. Instr. physics Columbia U., N.Y.C., 1950-52, assoc., 1952-54; mem. faculty U. Wash., Seattle, 1954—, assoc. prof. physics, 1958-63, prof., 1963-93, prof. emeritus, 1993—, chmn. dept., 1976-84. Co-author: (with Fred H. Schmidt) The Energy Controversy: The Fight over Nuclear Power, 1976, (with others) Indoor Radon and Its Hazards, 1987, Nuclear Energy: Principles, Practices, and Prospects, 1996; editl. bd.: Rev. Sci. Instruments, 1967-69. With AUS, 1943-46. Sloan Research fellow, 1959-63; Guggenheim fellow, 1966-67, 74-75 Fellow Am. Phys. Soc. (chair Panel on Pub. Affairs 1995), AAAS; mem. Am. Assn. Physics Tchrs., Am. Nuc. Soc., Health Physics Soc., Phi Beta Kappa. Achievements include research in nuclear physics, nuclear astrophysics and energy policy. Office: U Wash Dept Physics Seattle WA 98195-0001

BODDE, DAVID LEO, technology educator; b. Kansas City, Mo., Jan. 27, 1943; s. Leo Antony and Frances (Henkes) B.; m. Priscilla Anne Dick, Aug. 5, 1967; children: Mark David, Douglas Somers, Daniel Philip, Katherine Elizabeth. BS, U.S. Mil. Acad., 1965; MS, MIT, 1972, MS, 1973; DBA, Harvard U., 1976. Mgr. engring. analysis office, energy sys. planning divsn. TRW, Inc., 1976-78; dep. asst. sec. for coal, nuc. and synthetic fuels U.S. Dept. Energy, 1978-81; asst. dir. Congl. Budget Office, Washington, 1981-86; exec. dir. Commn. Engring. and Tech. Sys., NAS, Washington, 1986-91; v.p. Midwest Rsch. Inst., 1991-96; Charles N. Kimball chair tech. and innovation U. Mo., 1996—. Bd. dirs. Great Plains Energy, 1994—, The Commerce Funds, 1995—, AION Photonics, 2000-, chmn. Environ. Mgmt. Adv. Bd. U.S. Dept. Energy, 1995—; mem adv. coun. Electric Power Rsch. Inst., 1995—. Contbr. articles to profl. jours. Capt. U.S. Army, 1965-70. Decorated Bronze star, Army Commemdation medal; AEC fellow, 1970-73, Harding Found. fellow, 1974-75. Mem. AAAS. Episcopalian. Office: U Mo Bloch Sch of Bus 5110 Cherry St Kansas City MO 64110-2426 E-mail: bodded@umkc.edu.

BODEK, RUTH NAOMI, art educator; b. St. John, N.B., Can., Jan. 27, 1948; d. Henry Lewis and Bernice C. (Castelbaum) Kaplan. BFA, Fairleigh Dickinson U., 1969; teaching cert., Kean Coll., 1974; ML, Drew U., 1984; MA in Adminstrn., Supervision, Jersey City State Coll., 1988. Tchr. art Jefferson Twp. High Sch., Oak Ridge, N.J., 1973—. Mem. core course proficiences panel N.J. Dept. Edn., 1992; mem. Jefferson Twp. Drug Coun.; presenter at profl. confs. Recipient Gov.'s Tchr. Recognition award, 1990. Mem. ASCD, Nat. Art Edn. Assn., Art Pride N.J., Alliance for Arte Edn. N.J., Art Educators N.J., Phi Delta Kappa. Avocations: art, classic cars, reading, painting. Home: PO Box 367 Oak Ridge NJ 07438-0367 Office: Jefferson Twp High Sch Weldon Rd Oak Ridge NJ 07438

BODENHAUSEN, JUDITH ANNE, school system administrator; Phd with honors, U. Calif., Berkeley, 1993. Head math. dept. Berkeley (Calif.) HS, 2001—. Mem.: Nat. Bd. Profl. Tchg. Standards. Office: Berkeley HS Math Dept 2223 Martin Luther King Jr Way Berkeley CA 94704

BODENHEIMER, SALLY NELSON, reading educator, retired; b. Bedford, Ind., Aug. 31, 1939; d. Paul Edwin Sr. and Sarah Kathryn (Scott) Nelson; m. Robert Edward Bodenheimer, June 24, 1961; children: Robert Edward, Marc Alan, Bryan Lee. BS, U. Tenn., Knoxville, 1961, postgrad., Northwestern U., Carson Newman Coll., Johnson Bible Coll. Cert. tchr. K-3, 1-9, K-12, music. Interni Crow Island Elem., Winnetka, Ill., 1961-62; tchr. 1st grade Wilmot Elem Sch., Deerfield, Ill., 1962-63, Vestal Elem. Sch., Knoxville, 1981-82; 7th grade math. tchr. Knox County Schs., Doyle Middle Sch., Knoxville, 1982-83; kindergarten tchr. Mt. Olive Sch., Knoxville, 1983-93, chpt. I lang, reading, reading recovery tchr., 1993—95, tchr. kindergarten, 1995—2001. Recipient Knoxville Arts Coun. Art in Edn. award, Golden Apple award Knoxville News Sentinel, Outstanding Environ. Edn. award. 21st Century Classroom. Mem. NEA, ASCD, Tenn. Edn. Assn., Knox County Edn. Assn., Smoky Mountain Reading Assn., Internat. Reading Assn., Nat. Coun. Tchrs. Math., Smoky Mountain Math. Educators Assn., Nat. Sci. Tchrs. Assn., Music Educators Nat. Conf., East Tenn. Foxfire Tchrs. Network (steering com.), Greater Knoxville C. of C. (Leadership Edn., Best Tchr. award 1989, 1996), Delta Kappa Gamma, Pi Lambda Theta, Sigma Alpha Iota. Home: 3335 Tipton Station Rd Knoxville TN 37920-9565

BODEY, GERALD PAUL, medical educator, physician; b. Hazelton, Pa, May 22, 1934; s. Allen Zartman and Marie Frances (Smith) B.; m. Nancy Louise Wiegner, Aug. 25, 1956; children: Robin Gayle Sparwasser, Gerald Paul Jr., Sharon Dawn Brantley. AB magna cum laude, Lafayette Coll., 1956; MD, Johns Hopkins U., 1960. Diplomate Nat. Bd. Med. Examiners, Am. Bd. Internal Medicine, Am. Bd. Infectious Diseases, Am. Bd. Oncology. Intern Johns Hopkins U., Balt., 1960-61, resident, 1961-62; clin. assoc. Nat. Cancer Inst., Bethesda, Md., 1962-65; resident U. Wash., Seattle, 1965-66; internist, prof. U. Tex./M.D. Anderson Cancer Ctr., Houston, 1975-95, chmn. dept. med. specialities, 1987-95, chief sect. infectious diseases, 1981-95, chief chemotherapy, 1975-83, med. dir. Cancer Clin. Rsch. Ctr., 1977-81, emeritus prof. medicine, 1995—2001, prof. medicine, 2001—. Prof. internal medicine and pharmacology Univ. Tex. Health Sci. Ctr. Med. Sch., 1976—; clin. prof. Univ. Tex. Health Sci. Ctr. Dental Sch., 1977—95; adj. prof. microbiology, immunology and medicine Baylor Coll. of Medicine, Houston, 1975—99; mem. lunar quartine ops. team Apollo 11-14, Manned Spacecraft Ctr., NASA, joint commn. accreditation health-care orgns. Hospitalwide Indicators Task Force, 1987—89. Mem. editl. bd. Acad. Internat. Jour. of Oncology; contbr. over 1000 articles to profl. jour. Dir. Korean Collaborative Program, 1985-95; past trustee Med. Benevolence Found. Nat. AIDS Prevention Inst.; past bd. dir. Christian Coalition Reconciliation; scholar Leukemia Soc. of Am., 1969-74. Recipient Am. Chem. Soc. prize, 1956, Merck award, 1956, Robert B. Youngman Greek prize Lafayette Coll., 1956, Eugene Yourassowsky award U. Libre de Bruxelles, Belgium, 1995; Henry Strong Denison fellow Johns Hopkins Sch. Medicine, Balt., 1958-60; scholar Leukemia Soc. Am., 1969-74. Fellow ACP, Am. Coll. Chest Physicians, Am. Coll. Clin. Pharmacology, Royal Coll. Medicine, Royal Soc. Promotion Health; mem. AMA, Am. Soc. Clin. Oncology, Infectious Diseases Soc. Am., Am. Soc. Clin. Pharmacology and Therapeutics, Am. Soc. Hematology, Am. Soc. Microbiol., Am. Sci. Affiliation, Internat. Soc. Complexity, Info. and Design, Christian Med. Soc., Tex. Med. Assn., Houston Acad. Medicine, Academia Peruana de Cirugia (hon.), Mediterranean Med. Soc. (hon.), Le Soc. Peruana Cancerologia (hon.), La Costarricensa Oncologie (hon.), Soc. Brasileira Cancerologia (hon.), Phi Beta Kappa, Sigma Xi. Methodist. Office: U Tex MDACC Box 402 1515 Holcombe Blvd Houston TX 77030-4009 E-mail: gbodey@mdanderson.org.

BODI, SONIA ELLEN, library director, educator; b. Chgo., June 24, 1940; d. Franz Frithiof and Elsa (Noren) Bergquist; m. Peter Phillip Bodi, July 30, 1966; 1 child, Eric Christopher; stepchildren: Glenn Peter, John Jeffrey. Student, U. Edinburgh (Scotland), 1960-61; BA, Augustana Coll., Rock Island, Ill., 1962; MA Libr. Sci., Rosary Coll., 1977; MA, Northwestern U., 1986. Tchr. English and history Gemini Jr. H.S., Niles, Ill., 1962-64, Nagoya (Japan) Internat. Sch., 1964-65; tchr. English, Old Orchard Jr. H.S., Skokie, Ill., 1965-67; reference libr. Wilmette (Ill.) Pub. Libr., 1977-79, Kendall Coll., Evanston, Ill., 1979-81; head reference and instructional libr. North Park U., Chgo., 1981—, asst. prof. bibliography, 1985-87, assoc. prof., 1988-92, prof., 1992—, chmn. divsn. humanities, 1988-99, interim libr. dir., 1996-98, libr. dir., 1998—. Contbr. articles to profl. jours. Pres. PTA, Lincolnwood, Ill., 1977—79; mem. Bd. Edn., Lincolnwood, 1980—91, sec., 1981—84, pres., 1984—87, LIBRAS, 2001—02; chair Ill. Coop. Collection Mgmt. Program, 2002—03; elder First Presbyn. Ch. of Evanston, 1989—, Stephen ministry leader, 1992—98; bd. dirs. Chgo. Libr. Sys., 1999—, ILCSO, 2003—. Mem. Ill. Libr. Assn., ALA, Am. Assn. Coll. and Rsch. Librs., Beta Phi Mu. Democrat. Avocations: reading, bicycling, opera, music, piano. Home: 6710 N Trumbull Ave Lincolnwood IL 60712-3740 Office: North Park U 3225 W Foster Ave Chicago IL 60625-4895 E-mail: sbodi@northpark.edu.

BODINE, WILLIS RAMSEY, JR., music educator, organist; b. Austin, Tex., Nov. 15, 1935; s. Willis Ramsey and Freda Serena (Buchan) B.; m. Anna Schoff Hartung, Mar. 9, 1957; children: Elizabeth Ramsey, Catherine Lynn. MusB, U. Tex., 1957, MusM, 1960; postgrad., Nortwestdeutsche Musikakademie, Lippe-Detmold, Germany, 1957-59. Instr. in music and univ. organist U. Fla., Gainesville, 1959, asst. prof., 1962, assoc. prof., 1967, prof., 1976—2003, grad. program advisor for performance, 1993-99, prof. emeritus, 2003—. Cons. in organ design chs. in Fla., N.C. and Tex., 1962—; mus. dir. The Willis Bodine Chorale, 1987—; mem faculty Montreat and Westminster Confs. on Worship and Music, 1985—; recitals throughout Southeast, Europe, N.Y.C., 1958—. Composer: Sixth Communion Service, The Hymnal 1940 Supplement, 1960, 76. Chmn. Gainesville Cultural Commn., 1980-82. Named Fulbright Scholar, Nordwestdeutsche Musikakadamie, Fed. Republic of Germany, 1957-59, Musician of Yr., Found. for the Promotion of Music, Gainesville, 1988; recipient Disting. Faculty award Fla. Blue Key, 2002. Mem. Am. Guild of Organists (regional coord. for edn.). Democrat. Episcopalian. Avocations: architecture, genealogy. Home: 3838 SW 4th Pl Gainesville FL 32607-2713

BODINSON, NANCY SUE, art educator; b. Kansas City, Mo., May 5, 1948; d. Herbert Van Dyke and Julia Antonette (Omerzu) Davis; children: Scott Gordon, Carrie Anne Moore; m. Larry Joseph Bodinson, Dec. 24, 1989. BA, Baker U., Baldwin, Kans., 1970; MEd, Lesley Coll., 1990. Cert. art tchr. grades K-12, Mo. Art instr. grades K-6 Mary Harmon Weeks Sch., Kansas City, Mo., 1970-73, 74-75, Doty Elem. Sch., Detroit, 1973-74, Notre Dame de Sion, Kansas City, Mo., 1975-87; Montessori pre-sch. art instr. grades K-8 Mt. Washington German Magnet, Kansas City, 1987-95; art instr. Harold Holliday Montessori, Kansas City, 1995—. Curriculum writer Kansas City Sch. Dist., 1992-94; presenter in field. Mentor Baker U. Alumni Profl., 1995—; mem. visual & perf. arts curriculum and assesment devel. Kansas City, Mo. Sch. Dist., 1995—; selected to participate in the Mo. Assessment Project (MAP 2000). Named Elem. Art Tchr. of Yr. for State of Mo., Mo. Art Edn. Assn., 1991; recipient Dorothy 60 Award for excellence in tchg. the visual arts Kansas City Artists Coalition, 1996. Mem. Am. Fedn. of Tchrs., Nat. Art Edn. Assn., Mo. State Tchrs. Assn., Delta Delta Delta Alumni. Avocations: camping, rafting, hiking, creating with natural objects, teaching art. Home: 4921 Parish Dr Roeland Park KS 66205-1371 Office: Harold Holiday Montessori Sch 7227 Jackson Ave Kansas City MO 64132-3955

BODKIN, RUBY PATE, corporate executive, real estate broker, educator; b. Frostproof, Fla., Mar. 11, 1926; d. James Henry and Lucy Beatrice (Latham) P.; m. Lawrence Edward Bodkin Sr., Jan. 15, 1949; children: Karen Bodkin Snead, Cinda, Lawrence Jr. BA, Fla. State U., 1948; MA, U. Fla., 1972. Lic. real estate broker Fla. Banker Barnett Bank, Avon Park, Fla., 1943-44, Lewis State Bank, Tallahassee, 1944-49; ins. underwriter Hunt Ins. Agy., Tallahassee, 1949-51; tchr. Duval County Sch. Bd., Jacksonville, Fla., 1952-77; pvt. practice realty Jacksonville, 1976—; tchr. Nassau County Sch. Bd., Jacksonville, 1978-83; sec., treas., v.p. Bodkin Corp., R&D/Inventions, Jacksonville, 1983—; assoc. Brooke Shields Innovative Designer Products, Inc., Kendall Park, N.J., 1988-92. Author: 100 Teacher Chosen Recipes, 1976, Bodkin Bridge Course for Beginners, 1996, Class Conscious, 1999, (autobiography) Grandma Bodkin, 2000, Essay on Death, 2003; author numerous poems. Mem. Jacksonville Symphony Guild, 1985—; mem. Southside Bapt. Ch. Recipient 25 Yr. Svc. award Duval County Sch. Bd., 1976, Tchr. of Yr. award Bryceville Sch., 1981. Mem. Am. Contract Bridge League, Nat. Realtors Assn., Southside Jr. Woman's Club, Garden Club Sweetbriar (bd. dirs.), Riverside Woman's Club Jacksonville (fin. dir. 1991-92, 3rd v.p. social dir. WCOJ, 1992-99), UDC (Martha Reid chpt. #19), Fla. Edn. Assn. (pers. problems com. 1958), Duval County Classrooms Tchrs. (v.p. membership 1957), Woman's Club Jacksonville Bridge Group, Fla. Ret. Tchrs. Assn., Fla. Realtors Assn., N.E. Fla. Realtors Assn., Jacksonville Geneal. Soc. (practicing genealogist, family historian 1986—), Friday Musicale of Jacksonville, San Jose Golf Country Club, Jacksonville Sch. Bridge. Baptist. Avocations: reading, writing, genealogy, photography, club bridge. Home: 1149 Molokai Rd Jacksonville FL 32216-3273 Office: Bodkin Jewelers & Appraisers PO Box 16482 Jacksonville FL 32245-6482 Fax: 904-725-6692.

BODNAR, RICHARD, psychology educator; b. N.Y.C., Feb. 21, 1946; s. Julius J. and Irene A. (Monette) B.; m. Carol B. Greenman, July 4, 1981; children: Benjamin, Nicholas. BA, Manhattan Coll., 1967; MA, CCNY, 1973; PhD, CUNY, 1976. Postdoctoral fellow N.Y. State Psychiat. Inst., N.Y.C., 1976-78, rsch. scientist, 1978-79; asst. prof. Queens Coll., CUNY, N.Y.C., 1979-82, assoc. prof., 1982-85, prof., 1986—; dept. chmn., 1998—. Adj. prof. pharmacology Mt. Sinai Sch. Medicine, N.Y.C., 1991—. Contbr. more than 220 sci. articles and abstracts to profl. jours. Capt. USAF, 1967-71, Vietnam. Recipient NSF grant, 1999—. Mem. Soc. for Neurosci., Am. Psychol. Soc. (charter), AAAS. Achievements include research on role of opioid systems in ingestive behavior and analgesia, role of stress in analgesic processes, roles of gender and aging in opioid function. Office: CUNY Queens Coll Dept Psychology Flushing NY 11367

BODONYI, RICHARD JAMES, engineering educator, researcher; b. Cleve., Nov. 26, 1943; s. Peter and Rose (Baczay) Bodonyi; m. Josette Hovance, Jan. 15, 1966; children: Jami Lisa, Rebecca. BS in Math., Ohio State U., 1966, PhD in Aerospace Engring., 1973; MS in Engring., Case Western Res., 1970. Aerospace technologist NASA Lewis Rsch. Ctr., Cleve., 1967-68; asst. prof. Va. Poly. Inst., Blacksburg, 1974—82; from asst. prof. to assoc. prof. Ind. U. Purdue U. at Indpls., 1976-79, prof., 1982-86, Ohio State U., Columbus, 1986—, sect. head aerospace engring. program, 1994—. Rsch. assoc. Indpls. Ctr. Advanced Rsch., 1976; cons. Inst. Computational Mechanics Propulsion, Cleve., 1987, Cleve., 89, Inst. Computer Applications Sci. and Engring., Hampton, Va., 1989, Hampton, 93. Contbr. articles to profl. jours. Fellow, NSF, 1969—73, Sci. Engring. Rsch. Coun., 1983. Mem.: AIAA, Am. Acad. Mechanics, Am. Phys. Soc., Sigma Xi, Phi Beta Kappa. Democrat. Home: 1350 Stoneygate Ln Columbus OH 43221-1553 Office: Aerospace Engring and Aviation 2036 Neil Ave Columbus OH 43210-1226

BODY-LAWSON, VICTOR F. architect, educator; b. Lagos, Nigeria, Sept. 1, 1955; came to U.S., 1973; s. Isaac Larte and Aimeé (Tychus) B.-L.; m. Elizabeth Adetokunbo Adewumi, June 18, 1991; 1 child, Angelica Latre. AA in Architecture, Montgomery Coll., Rockville, Md., 1978; BS, Cath. U. Am., 1980; MArch, Columbia U., 1984. Architect Bond Ryder James Assocs., N.Y.C., 1983-84; ptnr. Tong & Body-Lawson, Ft. Lee, N.J., 1984-85; prin. Body-Lawson Assocs., N.Y.C., 1987—; prof. design, dept. architecture City Coll., N.Y.C., 1985—; architect Davis Brody & Assocs., N.Y.C., 1990-93. Mem. editorial bd. The Point, 1983-84. Mem. Archtl. League of N.Y., N.Y.C., 1985. Recipient cert. for superior design work AIA, 1984, Eleanor Allwork award N.Y. chpt. AIA Women's Archtl. Aux., 1983; William Kinne Fellows Meml. traveling fellow, 1983, 84; Nat. Endowment for Arts fellow, 1981. Avocations: chess, tennis, swimming, bicycling, special areas of architecture in developing countries and in africa. Home: 515 W 151st St Apt 5E New York NY 10031-2255

BOEDEKER, BEN HAROLD, anesthesiologist, educator; b. Jackson, Wyo., Mar. 17, 1953; s. Harold Steven and Eva Andra (Andrews) B.; m. Lisa Carol Mau, June 26, 1988; children: Kirsten, David. BS, Colo. State U., 1976, DVM, 1979; PhD, Georgetown U., 1988; MD, John Byrns Sch. Med., 1987. Diplomate Am. Bd. Anesthesiology, Specialty Qualifications in Pain Mgmt., Am. Bd. Clin. Pharmacology, Nat. Bd. Med. Examiners. Advanced through ranks to col. USAF, 1979-96; resident in internal medicine Georgetown U., Washington, 1987-88; chief gen. med. Kirk Army Health Clin., Aberdeen Proving Ground, Md., 1988-90; resident in anesthesiology Walter Reed Army Med. Ctr., Washington, 1990-93, chief combat anesthesia, 1993-94, staff anesthesiologist, 1993-96; dir. pain mgmt. and rehab. svcs. VAMC, Columbia, Mo., 1996—. Adj. faculty Acad. Health Scis. Ft. Sam Houston, Tex., 1995—; adj. asst. prof. anesthesiology Uniformed Svc. U., Bethesda, Md., 1994-96; pres. Intellimed Biorsch., Wheatland, Wyo., 1992—; assoc. prof. anesthesia and perioperative medicine U. Mo. Student editor Med. Student, 1982-86; contbr. articles to profl. jours., chpts. to books. Pres. Casper (Wyo.) Coll. Young Reps., 1971-73; vol. fireman Dubois (Wyo.) Fire Dept., 1971-76; vol. ambulance attendent Dubois Vol. Ambulance, 1971-76; treas. students for Reagan, Honolulu, 1984. Mem. Am. Coll. Clin. Pharmacology, Am. Soc. Anesthesiology (cert. appreciation 1993, 94, Burroughs Welcome scholar 1992), Am. Pain Soc., Soc. Ambulatory Anesthesia, Am. Soc. Regional Anesthesiology, Wyo. Soc. Roman Catholic. Avocations: fishing, hunting. Home: 4499 Ridge Pine Dr Evans GA 30809 Office: VAMC Anesthesia Dept 124 500 Hospital Dr Dept 124 Columbia MO 65212-0001 also: 1 Freedom Way Augusta GA 30904-6258

BOEGEHOLD, ALAN LINDLEY, classics educator; b. Detroit, Mar. 21, 1927; s. Alfred Lindley and Katherine Eleanore (Yager) B.; m. Julie Elizabeth Marshall, Apr. 3, 1954; children: Lindley, Alan M. Jones, David, Alison. AB in Latin, U. Mich., 1950; AM in Classical Philology, Harvard U., 1954; student, Am. Sch. Classical Studies, Athens, Greece, 1955-57; PhD in Classical Philology, Harvard U., 1958. From instr. to asst. prof. dept. classics U. Ill., Champaign-Urbana, 1957-60; from asst. prof. to prof. dept. classics Brown U., Providence, R.I., 1960-2001. Dir. summer session Am. Sch. Classical Studies, Athens, 1963-64, 74, 80, vis. prof., 1968-69; dir. Ancient studies program Brown U., 1985-91, chmn. dept. classics, 1966-71, acting chmn., 1973-74; vis. lectr. history Harvard U., 1967; vis. prof. classics Yale U., 1971, U. Calif., Berkeley, 1978; disting. vis. prof. Amherst Coll., 2001-03; vice-chmn. mng. com. Am. Sch. Classical Studies, 1985-90, chmn., 1990-98. Editor: (with A.C. Scafuro) Athenian Identity and Civic Ideology, 1993; author, editor: Agora XXVIII, Law Courts at Athens, 1995; author: When A Gesture was Expected. A Selection of Examples from Archaic and Classical Greek Literature, Princeton, 1999; translator: In Simple Clothes (by Constantine Cavafy), 1992. Active ACLU. Amnesty Internat., Providence Athenaeum, Mass. Audubon Soc., Common Cause; trustee Gennadius Libr., Am. Sch. Classical Studies, Athens. Cpl. U.S. Army. Thomas Day Seymour fellow Am. Sch. Classical Studies Athens, 1955-56, Rsch. fellow, 1974-75, Rsch. fellow Agora Excavations, 1980-81, Charles Eliot Norton fellow Am. Sch. Classical Studies Athens (Harvard U.), 1956-57, Howard fellow Brown U., 1964-65, Sr. fellow NEH, 1980-81; grantee Am. Coun. Learned Socs., 1964-65. Fellow Explorers Club; mem. Am. Assn. Ancient Historians, Am. Philol. Assn., Archaeol. Inst. Am. (various coms.), Classical Assn. New Eng., Aegean Inst. (bd. advisors 1976-95), Inst. Nautical Archaeology (bd. dirs. 1973-82). Office: Brown Univ 48 College St Providence RI 02912-9021

BOEHM, EDWARD GORDON, JR., college administrator, educator; b. Washington, Jan. 30, 1942; s. Edward and Catherine (Murray) B.; m. Regina Ellen Evans, June 25, 1966; children: Evan Arnold, Andrew Edward. BS in Edn., Frostburg State U., 1964; MEd, The Am. U., 1970, D of Higher Edn., 1977. Dir. univ. devel., dean for student devel., assoc. dean/dir. admissions, instr. Coll. Arts & Scis. The Am. U., Washington, 1968-79; assoc. vice chancellor acad. affairs, asst. prof. edn., dean admissions Tex. Christian U., Ft. Worth, 1979-89; sr. v.p., asst. prof. Coll. Edn., exec. dir. Found. Marshall U., Huntington, W.Va., 1989-95; pres. Keystone Coll., La Plume, Pa., 1995—. Mem. adv. coun. Tandy Tech. Scholars, Ft. Worth, 1989-99; trustee, mem. com. The Coll. Bd., N.Y.C., 1987-91. Contbr. book chpt.: Student Services and the Law, 1988; contbr. articles to profl. jours. Bd. dirs., v.p. Boys & Girls Club, Huntington, 1989-95, Tri-State coun. Boy Scouts Am., Huntington, 1989-95; bd. dirs., pres. United Way River Cities, Huntington, 1989-95; bd. dirs. Leadership W. Va., Charleston, 1992-95, Leadership Tri-State, Ironton, Ohio, 1991-95; mem. scholastic evaluation panel Am.'s Jr. Miss, 1995—; bd. dirs. Tyler Hosp., 1995-2001, Waverly Cmty. House, 1996-2000; mem. Leadership Wilkes-Barre Exec. Program, Class of '96, Leadership Lackawanna Exec. Program, Class of '96, N.E. Regional Cancer Inst. Adv. Bd.; pres. bd. dirs. Pa. Assn. of Nonprofit Orgns., 1998; mem. nonprofit adv. bd. Nonprofit Resource Ctr., U. Scranton, 1998—; bd. mem. Tyler Meml. Hosp. Cmty. Health Care Vision Task Force, 1999—; mem. Pa. Soc., 1997—, Team Pa. Amb., 1999—; life mem. Lackawanna Indsl. Fund Enterprises, 1999—; mem. task force Healthy N.E. Pa. Intiative, 1999-2001; bd. govs. Scranton Area Found., 2002—; bd. dir. PACU, 2003—, Pa. Campus Compact, 2003—. Named W.Va. Outstanding Fundraising Exec., Nat. Soc. Fundraising Execs., 1993, Citizen of Yr., Herald Dispatch, 1993, Disting. West Virginian, 1995; recipient Cir. of Excellence in Fundraising award Coun. for Advancement and Support of Edn., 1993, Nat. Tchr.'s award Radio Shack Adv. Coun., 2000; John Deaver Drinko Acad. fellow Marshall U. Mem. Huntington C. of C., Lawrence County C. of C., Greenup County C. of C., Engrs. Club Huntington, Huntington Rotary Club (bd. dirs. 1989-95). Avocations: tennis, soccer, history, golf, hiking. Home: 29 College Ave La Plume PA 18440 Office: Keystone Coll One College Green La Plume PA 18440-0200 E-mail: edward.boehm@keystone.edu.

BOEHM, P. DIANN, elementary education educator; b. Tulsa, Apr. 13, 1954; d. George Mural and Mabel Adella (Harris) Floyd; m. John Charles Boehm, Jr., June 2, 1979; children: Rachel Rebbecca, John Patrick, Katherine Louise. BS in Edn., George Mason U., 1981. Cert. elem. tchr., Tex. Tchr. 4th grade Internat. Sch., Manila, Philippines, 1981-82; tchr. pre-kindergarten Resurrection Episc. Ch., Austin, Tex., 1982-83; tchr. 9th grade St. Louis Cath. Sch., Austin, 1983-84; tchr. 4th grade St. John's Sch., Houston, 1984-85; tchr. kindergarten St. Thomas Cath. Sch., Austin, 1986-87; tchr., tech. coord. St. Andrew's Episc. Sch., Austin, 1989—; prin., coord. High Tech Schoolhouse, Tex. Tchr. HHC, Austin, 1991—; keynote speaker Fla. State Computer Conf.,1991—; cons. Scholastic pubs. Author: (book) The Internet Schoolhouse, A Teacher's Best Friend; contbr. articles on tech. in edn. to various pubs. Chair person bd, Episc. Ch. Women, St. David's Episc. Ch., 1989—, chair person United Thank Offering, 1991—. Named Tex. Tchr. of Yr. in Tech., Tex. Dept. Edn., 1992, Apple Disting. Educator. Mem. Tex. Ctr. Edn. Technology (hon. mention 1991, '92), VITAL (Leadership in Tech. award 1992). Republican. Avocations: singing, crocheting, biking. Office: Internet Schoolhouse 58 Saint Stephens School Rd Austin TX 78746-3231

BOEHM, TONI GEORGENE, seminary dean, nurse, minister; b. New Kensington, Pa., Dec. 28, 1946; d. Sylvio Chipoletti and Eula Gene (Smittle) Fox; m. Raymond Stawinski, Dec. 11, 1965 (div. Sept. 1978); 1 child, Michelle Stawinski Ivy; m. Jay Thomas Boehm, Apr. 28, 1983;

children: Jonathon, Kimberly, Allison Cole, Amanda. Diploma, Allegheny Valley Sch. Nursing, Natrona Heights, Pa., 1967; family nurse practitioner cert., U. Kans., 1976; BA in Edn., Ottawa (Kans.) U., 1978; MSN, U. Mo., Kansas City, 1981; grad., Unity Sch. of Christianity, Unity Village, Mo., 1989; PhD in Religious Studies, Am. World U., 1997. Ordained to ministry Assn. of Unity Chs.; cert. occupl. health nurse. Nurse Allegheny Valley Hosp., Natrona Heights, 1967-74; head nurse, dir. nursing Truman Med. Ctr., Kansas City, Mo., 1974-78; mgr. med. Hallmark Card Inc., Kansas City, Mo., 1978-85; sr. staff specialist ANA, Kansas City, Mo., 1985-87; dean of adminstrn. Unity Sch. Christianity, 1987—2001, dir. strategic initiatives, 2001—02, dir. retreats and outreach and spl. events, 2003, interim dir. ministerial sch., 2003—, dir. retreats, 2004. Nat. spkr. and freelance writer for ministry and self-unfoldment. Author: The Spiritual Entrepreneur, 2003, One Day My Mouth Just Opened: Reverie, Reflections and Rapturous Musings on the Cycles of a Woman's Life, 2001, Embracing the Feminine Nature of the Divine, 2002. Mem. nat. steering com. for fundraising Unity Sch. of Christianity; mem. women's coun. U. Mo. Recipient scholarships. Mem.: NCCJ, ANA, Assn. Unity Chs. (urban curriculum com. 1987—2001, ministerial edn. com. 1987—2001, field licensing com. 1990—2001), Mo. Nurses Assn. (bd. dirs. 1975—85), U. Mo. Sch. Nursing Alumni Assn. Republican. Avocations: travel, reading, music, writing. Home: 430 N Winnebago Dr Greenwood MO 64034-9321 Office: Unity Sch Christianity Unity Village MO 64065-0001

BOEKHOUDT-CANNON, GLORIA LYDIA, business education educator; b. Portsmouth, Va., Jan. 18, 1939; d. William and Clara (Virgil) Boekhoudt; m. George Edward Cannon, Dec. 27, 1959. AB in Sociology/Psychology, Calif. State U., San Diego, 1977; MA in Spl. Edn./Learning Disabilities, Calif. State U., Sacramento, 1981; EdD in Orgn. and Leadership of Higher Edn. and Curriculum and Instrn., U. San Francisco, 1989. Instr. bus. edn. Midway Adult Sch. extension San Diego City Coll., San Diego, 1974-78, San Diego City Coll., 1974-78; prof. bus. edn. Sacramento City Coll., 1979—. Author: Fundamentals of Business English, 1986. Mem. Women in Community Colls., Phi Delta Kappa. Democrat. Jewish. Avocations: golf, needlepoint. Office: Sacramento City Coll Dept Bus 3835 Freeport Blvd Sacramento CA 95822-1318

BOERSMA, P. DEE, marine biologist, educator; b. Mt. Pleasant, Mich., Nov. 1, 1946; d. Henry W. and Vivian (Anspach) B. BS, Ctrl. Mich. U., 1969; PhD, Ohio State U., 1974; DSc (hon.), Ctrl. Mich. U., 2003. Asst. prof. Inst. Environ. Studies U. Wash., Seattle, 1974-80, assoc. prof., 1980-88, prof. environ. studies, 1988-93, prof. zoology, 1988—, adj. prof. women's studies, 1993—2003, assoc. dir., 1987-93, acting dir., 1990-91, prof. biology, prof. womens studies, 2003—; mem. sci. adv. com. for outer continental shelf Environ. Studies Program, Dept. Interior, 1980-83; prin. investigator Magellanic Penguin Project Wildlife Cons. Soc., 1982—. Evans vis. fellow U. Otago, New Zealand, 1995, Pew fellow in marine conservation, 1997-2000. Assoc. editor Ecological Applications, 1998-2001; exec. editor Conservation in Practice, 2000—; contbr. articles to profl. jours. Mem. adv. U.S. del. to UN Status Women Commn., N.Y.C., 1973, UN World Status Women Commn., N.Y.C., 1973, UN World Population Conf., Romania, 1974; mem. Gov. Lowry's Task Force on Wildlife, 1993; sci. adv. EcoBios, 1985-95; bd. dirs. Zero Population Growth, 1975-82, Washington Nature Conservancy, 1995-98; adv. bd. Walt Disney World Animal Kingdom, 1993—, Island press, 1999—, Compass, 2000—, ; bd. dirs. Peregine Fund, 1995—, Bullitt Found., 1996-2000, Islandwood, 2001—; mem. scholar diplomatic program Dept. State, 1977. Recipient Outstanding Alumni award Ctrl. Mich. U., 1978, Matrix award Women in Comm., 1983; named to Kellogg Nat. Leadership Program, 1982-85; recipient Top 100 Outsiders of Yr. award Outside Mag., 1987, Outstanding Centennial Alumni award Ctrl. Mich. U., 1993; sci. fellow The Wildlife Conservation Soc., 1982—, Aldo Leopold Leadership fellow, 2000-01. Fellow AAAS, Am Ornithol. Union (regional rep. Pacific seabird group 1981-85); mem. AAAS, Ecol. Soc. Am., Wilson Ornithol. Soc., Cooper Ornithol. Soc., Soc. Am. Naturalists, Soc. for Conservation Biology (bd. govs. 1991-94, pres-elect 1995-97, pres. 1997-99, past pres. 1999-2001), Gopher Brokers Club (pres. Seattle chpt. 1982-83). Office: U Wash Dept Biology PO Box 351800 Seattle WA 98195-1800 E-mail: boersma@u.washington.edu.

BOESCH, DEBORAH ANN, elementary school educator; b. Wenatchee, Wash., Aug. 13, 1948; d. Lloyd Wilbur and Julia Marie (Cernickey) B. BS, No. Ill. U., 1970, MS in Edn., 1977. Cert. elem. tchr., Ill. Tchr. Edgar Allan Poe Sch., Arlington Heights, Ill., 1971-85, Henry Wadsworth Longfellow Sch., Buffalo Grove, Ill., 1985—. Mem. ASCD, NEA, Ill. Edn.Assn., Assn. for Childhood Edn. Internat. Home: 1937 N Coldspring Rd Arlington Heights IL 60004-7242 Office: Longfellow Sch 501 N Arlington Heights Rd Buffalo Grove IL 60089-1607

BOESCH, DIANE HARRIET, retired elementary education educator; b. Erie, Pa., July 3, 1942; d. William Jacob and Dorothy Gertrude (Call) B. BS, Edinboro (Pa.) State U., 1964; MA, Kent (Ohio) State U., 1968; postgrad., So. Ill. U., Carbondale, 1969, CUNY, 1972, Norwalk State Tech. Coll., 1979, Northeastern U., Boston, 1982, Fla. State U., 1988. Tchr. math. Iroquois Area Sch. Dist., Erie, 1964-67; grad. asst. Kent State U., 1967-68; tchr., writer Comprehensive Sch. Math. Project, Carbondale, Ill., 1968-70; tchr. math. Weston (Conn.) Pub. Schs., 1970-2000, dept. chmn. math., 1989-2000; math edn. cons., 2000—. Dir. Weston Tchr. Ctr., 1983-84; condr. workshops on math. and writing, Conn., 1970—. Contbr. articles to profl. publs. Vol. nat. elections, Erie, 1960, West Haven, Conn., 1972. Recipient Celebration of Excellence award Conn. State Dept. Edn., 1988, Presdl. award NSF, 1990. Fellow Conn. Acad. for Edn. in Math. and Sci.; mem. NEA, Nat. Coun. Tchrs. Math., Conn. Educator Talent Pool, Conn. Edn. Assn., Weston Tchr. Assn., Coun. Presdl. Awardees in Math., Pi Mu Epsilon, Kappa Delta Pi. Republican. Lutheran. Avocations: genealogy, writing, music, reading, atlanta braves baseball. E-mail: dhb703@aol.com.

BOGAN ALLEN, JOYCE, special education educator, consultant; b. Byhalia, Miss., Nov. 28, 1953; d. Connie B. and Bertha (Withers) Bogan; m. Zegary J. Allen, June 27, 1992; 1 child, Jameson Prescott. BS, Jackson State U., 1975, MS, 1976; MA, Ea. Mich. U., 1983. Cert. tchr., Miss., Ohio, Mich. Tchr. Cleve. Pub. Schs., 1976-77, Beecher Schs., Flint, Mich., 1977-79, Bentley Sch. Dist., Burton, Mich., 1981; work-experience coord. Genesee Intermediate Sch. Dist., Flint, 1978-84; tchr., cons. Flint Community Schs., 1981—. Active NAACP. Mini-grantee Dept. Edn., Lansing, Mich., 1991. Mem. ASCD, Coun. Exceptional Children, Jackson State Alumni. Methodist. Avocations: gardening, golf, reading. Home: 1264 Arrowwood Ln Grand Blanc MI 48439-4893

BOGART, LOUISE BERRY, education educator; b. N.Y.C., July 15, 1942; d. Herbert George and Flora Louise (Porcelli) Berry; m. Burton Stanley Bogart, Aug. 29, 1965; children: Samuel Isaac, Jonathan Douglas. BA, Kans. State U., 1964; MEd, Coll. Notre Dame, Belmont, Calif., 1973; PhD, U. Hawaii-Manoa, 2000. Cert. Montessori tchr.; cert. pvt. tchr., Hawaii; cert. tchr., prin., Ohio; cert. neurolinguistic profl., neurolinguistic master. Field advisor, sr. program dir., day camp dir. Kaw Valley Girl Scout Coun., Topeka, 1964-65; field advisor Seal of Ohio Girl Scout Coun., Columbus, 1966-67; elem. tchr. St. Joseph Montessori Sch., Columbus, 1970-78; pre-kindergarten tchr. Maryknoll Grade Sch., Honolulu, 1978-80; head tchr. elem. classes Montessori Cmty. Sch., Honolulu, 1980-83; asst. prof. edn. Chaminade U. of Honolulu, 1982-92, assoc. prof. edn., 1993—, acting chair dept. edn., 1988-90, dept. chair, 1994-96, Montessori Program dir., 1986-92. Active Girl Scouts U.S., Honolulu, 1978—. Eisenhower grantee U.S. Dept. Edn., 1989-90, 90-91, 91-92, 93-94, 95-96, others. Mem. ASCD, Am. Montessori Soc. (vice chair 1987-91; mem. tchr. edn. com.), Montessori Assn. Hawaii (v.p. 1980-81), Nat. Assn. Edn. of Young children, Hawaii Coun. Tchrs. Math., Internat. Inst. Peace Educators, World Coun. for Curriculum and Instrn., Am. Assn. of Univ. Women, Am. Edn. Rsch. Assn., Pi Lambda Theta. Home: 1035A Alewa Dr Honolulu HI 96817-1506 Office: Chaminade U Honolulu 3140 Waialae Ave Honolulu HI 96816-1510 E-mail: lbogart@chaminade.edu.

BOGDANOFF, STEWART RONALD, physical education educator, coach; b. London, Aug. 16, 1940; came to U.S., 1945; s. David and Muriel (Kirby) B.; m. Eileen Dolan, Aug. 27, 1993; children: Suelyn, Jennifer, Andrew. BS, King's Coll., Briarcliff Manor, N.Y., 1963; MA, NYU, 1965, profl. degree, 1970; postgrad., Harvard U., 1988-91. Cert. in health and phys. edn., sch. adminstrn./supervision, N.Y. Tchr. health and phys. edn. Lakeland Ctrl. Sch. Dist., Shrub Oak, N.Y., 1965-96, head tchr. Thomas Jefferson Elem. Sch., 1984-96, acting prin. Thomas Jefferson Elem. Sch., 1985-86, basketball, cross country and gymnastics coach, 1964-96; ednl. cons., spkr. in field, 1996—. Writer syllabi; developer programs; author handbooks; presenter in field. Mem. N.Y. State PTA. Recipient N.Y. State Tchr. of Yr. award State Edn. Dept., 1983, Disting. Cmty. Svc. award Yorktown Jaycees, 1983, Disting. Cmty. Svc. award Am. Heart Assn., 1983, Disting. Cmty. Svc. award Muscular Dystrophy Assn., 1983, Point of Light award, 1992, Westchester Vol. of Yr. and J.C. Penney Golden Rule award United Way, 1995, Spl. Olympics Worldwide Games Commemorative Coin, 1996, Am. Medal of Hon. award Am. Biographical Inst., 2003; inducted into Nat. Tchrs. Hall of Fame, 1993, inducted into the Briarcliff HS Hall of Disting. Alumni, 1995; named one of 50 Most Influential People in Westchester County in 20th Century, Gannett Jour. News, 2000. Mem. AAHPERD (Founders 2000 award 1995), ASCD, Nat. Assn. for Sport and Phys. Edn. (Project Inspiration award 1992), Internat. Platform Assn., N.Y. State Assn. for Health, Phys. Edn., Recreation and Dance,, Phi Delta Kappa, Kappa Delta Pi (Outstanding Svc. to Society award 1983). Democrat. Avocations: N.Y. Yankees games, beach at Cape Cod, golf, tennis, baseball memorabilia. Home: 588A Heritage Hls Somers NY 10589-1908 Office: 3636 Gomer St Yorktown Heights NY 10598-2000

BOGEN, NANCY, writer, English educator; b. Bklyn., Apr. 24, 1932; d. George Meyer and Rose (Zwaifler) Warshaw; m. Hyman Bogen, May 1965 (div. 1969); m. Arnold Greissle-Schönberg, Jan. 13, 1989. BA, NYU, 1952; MA in English Lit., Columbia U., 1962, PhD in English Lit., 1968. Asst. prof. English Richmond Coll., CUNY, S.I., N.Y., 1967-76; prof. English Coll. of S.I., 1976—. Artistic dir. The Lark Ascending, N.Y.C., 1997. Author: A Critical Edition of William Blake's book of Thel, 1971; (novels) Klytaimnestra Who Stayed at Home, 1980, Bobe Mayse, A Tale of Washington Square, 1993, Bagatelle.Guinevere, 1995, (textbook) How to Write Poetry, 1990, 3d edit., 1998. Fellow Va. Ctr. Creative Arts, 1987; grantee Poets and Writers, 1995—. Mem. PEN. Home: 31 Jane St Apt 17B New York NY 10014-1982 E-mail: eminancyrbogen@cs.com.

BOGER, DAN CALVIN, statistical and economic consultant, educator; b. Salisbury, N.C., July 9, 1946; s. Brady Cashwell and Gertrude Virginia (Hamilton) B.; m. Gail Lorraine Zivna, June 23, 1973; children: Gretchen Zivna, Gregory Zivna. BS in Mgmt. Sci., U. Rochester, 1968; MS in Mgmt. Sci., Naval Postgrad. Sch., Monterey, Calif., 1969; MA in Stats., U. Calif., Berkeley, 1977, PhD in Econs., 1979. Cert. cost analyst, profl. estimator. Rsch. asst. U. Calif., Berkeley, 1975-79; asst. prof. econs. Naval Postgrad. Sch., Monterey, 1979-85, assoc. prof., 1985-92, prof., 1992—, chmn. dept. command, control and comm., 1995—2001, chmn. dept. computer sci., 1997—2001, chmn. dept. info. warfare, 1997—2001, dean divsn. computer and info. scis. and ops., 1997—2001, founding chmn. dept. info. scis., 2002—. Bd. dirs. Evan-Moor Corp.; cons. econs. and statis. legal matters CSX Corp, others, 1977—. Assoc. editor The Logistics and Transp. Rev., 1981-85, Jour. Cost Analysis, 1989-92; mem. editl. rev. bd. Jour. Transp. Rsch. Forum, 1987-91; contbr. articles to profl. jours. Lt. USN, 1968-75. Flood fellow Dept. Econs. U. Calif., Berkeley, 1975-76; dissertation rsch. grantee A.P. Sloan Found., 1978-79. Mem.: IEEE, Inst. for Ops. Rsch. and Mgmt. Sci. (sec.-treas. mil. aplications soc. 1987—91), Econometric Soc., Am. Statis. Assn., Am. Econ. Assn., Internat. Coun. on Sys. Engring., Sigma Xi. Home: 27 Cramden Dr Monterey CA 93940-4145 Office: Naval Postgrad Sch Code IS Monterey CA 93943

BOGER, GAIL LORRAINE ZIVNA, reading specialist; b. Portland, Oreg., Sept. 15, 1946; d. Stephen Edward and Harriet Lucille (Laws) Zivna; m. Dan Calvin Boger, June 23, 1973; children: Gretchen, Gregory. BS in Edn., Oreg. State U., 1968; MA in Edn., Stanford U., 1973; MA in Reading, U. LaVerne, 1982. Cert. reading and lang. arts specialist, Calif. Elem. tchr. Monterey (Calif.) Peninsula Unified Sch. Dist., 1968-72, 73-75, lang. arts tchr., 1979-81; elem. tchr. San Ramon (Calif.) Unified Sch. Dist., 1976-79; Miller-Unruh reading specialist Monterey (Calif.) Peninsula Unified Sch. Dist., 1983—. Mem.: Reading is Fundamental Program, Monterey County Reading Assn., Calif. Reading Assn., Internat. Reading Assn., Delta Kappa Gamma (rec. sec. 1992—94, 2002—). Avocations: ballet, music, piano, reading, golf. Home: 27 Cramden Dr Monterey CA 93940-4145 E-mail: bogers@mbay.net.

BOGGS, BARBARA JEAN, secondary education educator; b. Beaumont, Tex., Oct. 13, 1940; d. Dennis M. and Helen Grace (Ferrell) B. B.S., Tex. Woman's U., 1962; Cert. in Elem. Edn., U. Houston, 1970; Cert. in Learning Disabled, Lamar U., 1974; M.Ed., Stephen F. Austin U., 1980; Ed. Diagnosticians Cert., U. Houston, 1984. Statistician, Humble Oil & Refining Co., Houston, 1963-67; tchr. Sheldon Ind. Sch. Dist., Houston, 1967-93, ednl. diagnostician, 1984-91, dir. spl. svcs., 1991-93. Mem. Sheldon Edn. Assn. (pres. 1982-84) Tex. Tchrs. Assn., Tex. Ednl. Diagnosticians Assn., Tex. Profl. Ednl. Diagnosticians, Tex. Coun. Adminstrs. Spl. Edn., Gulfcoast Adminstrs. Spl. Edn. Republican. Roman Catholic. Home: 3230 Elmridge St Houston TX 77025-4312 Office: Sheldon Ind Sch Dist 8450 C E King Pky Houston TX 77044-2211

BOGGS, GEORGE ROBERT, academic administrator; b. Conneaut, Ohio, Sept. 4, 1944; s. George Robert and Mary (Mullen) B.; m. Ann Holladay, Aug. 8, 1969; children: Kevin Dale, Ian Asher, Micah Benjamin. BS in Chemistry, Ohio State U., 1966; MA in Chemistry, U. Calif., Santa Barbara, 1968; postgrad. in ednl. adminstrn., natural scis., and edn., Calif. State U., 1969-72; PhD in Ednl. Adminstrn., U. Tex., 1984. Cert. std. tchg. specialization in jr. coll., C.C. supr., C.C. chief adminstrv. officer. Instr. chemistry Butte Coll., Oroville, Calif., 1968-85, divsn. chmn. nat. sci. and allied health, 1972-81, assoc. dean of instrn., 1981-85; pres., supt. Palomar C.C. Dist., San Marcos, Calif., 1985-2000; pres. Am. Assn. C.C.s, Washington, 2000—. Spkr. SCCCIRA, Calif., 1985; adj. instr. Austin (Tex.) C.C., 1982; guest lectr. Calif. State U., Chico, 1970, 83, 84, panelist, 1975; tchg. asst. U. Calif., Santa Barbara, 1966-68, Ohio State U., 1965-66; mem. numerous coms. for colls. and univs., Calif., 1968—; cons. U. Calif., Berkeley, 1995-2000, U. Wis., Madison, 1997-2000, Pellissippi State Tech. Coll., 1995, El Camino Coll., 1994, U. Hawaii C.C., 1994, Dept. Nat. Edn., Rep. South Africa, 1993, San Joaquin Delta C.C. Dist., 1986, Marin C.C. Dist., 1985. Contbr. articles to profl. jours.; cons. editl. adv. bd. Jour. Applied Rsch. in the C.C., 1993-2000; mem. editl. bd. C.C. Rev., 1997-2000. Presenter Nat. Conf. Teaching Excellence and Conf. of Pres.'s, 1983, 93, 95, presenter, mem. coordinating com., 1984, chmn. steering com., 1985; presenter Profl. and Orgl. Devel. Network, 1984; ad hoc com. CPEC/FIPSE/Chancellor's Office, 1984; mem. steering com. Learning Assessment Retention Com., 1983-85, pres.-elect 1985-86; mem. instl. research design team No. Calif. Higher Edn. Council, 1984, mission charrette writing team, 1985. Named a scholar Gen., Ohio State U., 1963; named hon. elder, Nat. Coun. on Black Am. Affairs, 1993; named to Stadium Dormitory, 1962—65, San Diego Hall of Success, 1988; recipient Scholastic R, 1962, Nat. Honor Soc., 1962, Stanley A. Mahr Cmty. Svc. award, San Marcos Coun. C. of C., 1994, Cert. Achievement, Leadership Excellence and Cmty. Svc., Congress of U.S. Ho. Reps., 1994, Pacific Region CEO award, Assn. C. C. Trustees, Victoria, B.C., Can., 1993, Recognition award, Nat. Coun. for Rsch. and Planning Mgmt., 1997, Harry Buttimer Disting. Adminstr. award, Assn. Calif. C.C. Trustees, 1994, Dr. George R. Boggs Day proclaimed Jan. 14, in Vista, Calif., 1994, PBS O'Banion prize for tchg. and learning, 2001; fellow Richardson fellow, 1982—83. Mem. NSF (adv. com. to directorate for edn. and human resources 1995-97, evaluator 1992, 93, 98), Nat. Rsch. Coun. (undergrad. sci. edn. com. 1993-95, chmn. subcom. tchg. and learning 1993-95), Assn. Calif. Coll. Tutorial and Learning Assistance (presenter 1984), Calif. Assn. C.C. (conf. presenter 1984, com. on rsch. 1985—), Assn. Calif. C.C. Adminstrs. (commn. membership devel. 1985), C.C. League Calif. (bd. dirs. 1990-92, presenter confs. 1990-98), Faculty Assn. Calif. C.C., Calif. C.C. Chief Exec. Officers' Assn, San Diego and Imperial Counties C.C. Assn., Am. Assn. Cmty. and Jr. Colls. (presenter 1989, 90, 91, 94, 95, bd. dirs. 1990-95, fed. rels. com. 1990-91, 94-95, chair elect 1993—, chair bd. dirs. 1993-94, exec. com. 1993-95, chair bd. nominating com. 1994-95), So. Calif. C.C. Chief Exec. Officers Assn. (sec., treas. 1990-2000), Phi Kappa Phi, Upsilon Pi Upsilon (pres. 1965-66), Phi Rho Pi, Rotary (pres. Durham club 1980-81, dist. sec. Calif., 1983-84, various other offices and comm. positions held locally and nationally). Home: 2301 N St NW Apt 616 Washington DC 20037-1138 Office: Am Assn CCs 1 Dupont Cir NW Ste 410 Washington DC 20036 E-mail: gboggs@aacc.nche.edu.

BOGGS, JAMES ERNEST, chemistry educator; b. Cleve., June 9, 1921; s. Ernest Beckett and Emily (Reid) B.; m. Ruth Ann Rogers, June 22, 1948 (dec. 2002); children: Carol, Ann, Lynne. AB, Oberlin Coll., 1943; MS in Chemistry, U. Mich., 1944, PhD, 1953. Rsch. chemist Manhattan Dist. Project, Linde Air Products, Tonawanda, N.Y., 1944-46; asst. prof. dept. chemistry Eastern Mich. U., Ypsilanti, 1949-52; instr. U. Mich. at Ann Arbor, 1952-53; mem. faculty dept. chemistry U. Tex., Austin, 1953—, assoc. prof., 1958-66, prof., 1966-98; emeritus prof., 1998—; asst. dean Grad. Sch. U. Tex., Austin, 1958-67, dir. Center for Structural Studies, 1969-79, acting dir. Inst. Theoretical Chemistry, 1979-81. Program officer for theoretical and computational chemistry NSF, 1991-94; founder, organizer series Austin Symposia on Molecular Structure, 1966—; chmn. subcom. on theoretical chemistry Internat. Union Pure and Applied Chemistry, 1995-01; internat. lectr. in field. Mem. editl. bd. Jour. Molecular Structure; contbr. over 280 articles to profl. jours. Mem. Am. Chem. Soc., Am. Phys. Soc., Nat. Acad. Scis. (India), Phi Beta Kappa, Sigma Xi, Phi Lambda Upsilon, Gamma Alpha. Achievements include research in structural chemistry, microwave spectroscopy, quantum chemistry. Office: U Tex Dept Chemistry Austin TX 78712 E-mail: james.boggs@mail.utexas.edu.

BOGGS, JOSEPH DODRIDGE, pediatric pathologist, educator; b. Bellefontaine, Ohio, Dec. 31, 1921; s. Walter C. and Birdella Z. (Coons) B.; m. Donna Lee Shoemaker, June 12, 1964; 1 son, Joseph Dodridge. AB, Ohio U., 1941, Litt.D., 1966; MD, Jefferson Med. Coll., 1945. Intern Jefferson Med. Coll. Hosp., Phila., 1945-46; resident Peter Bent Brigham Hosp., Boston, 1946-48, asso. pathologist, 1947-51; instr. pathology Harvard Med. Sch., Boston, 1948-51; with Children's Meml. Hosp., Chgo., 1951—, dir. labs., 1951—; prof. pathology Northwestern U., Chgo., 1952-92, prof. emeritus, 1992—; dir. BSP Ins. Co., Phoenix. Contbr. articles to profl. jours. Mem. med. adv. bd. Ill. Dept. Corrections, Springfield, 1971-77; bd. dirs. Blood Systems Inc., Phoenix, 1972-94, Community Hosp., Evanston, Ill., 1958-61, Lorretto Hosp., Chgo., 1971-72; chmn. Chgo. Regional Blood Program, 1978-80; bd. dirs. Ben Venue Labs., 1985—. Capt. M.C., U.S. Army, 1948-51. Mem. Am. Soc. Study of Liver Disease, N.Y. Acad. Scis., Midwest Soc. Pediatric Research, Inst. Medicine, Ill. Soc. Pathologists (pres. 1965), Ill. Assn. Blood Banks (pres. 1969-70) Office: 1448 N Lake Shore Dr Chicago IL 60610-6655

BOGLE, JANICE L. elementary and special education educator; b. Bloomington, Ill., June 30, 1949; d. Richard L. and Mary Kathryn (Frerich) Van Seyoc; m. Robert M. Bogle, Dec. 21, 1969; children: Tiffany, Stacy. BS, Murray State U., 1971; MA, U. Ill., 1991. Cert. elem. educator, pre-vocat. coord., learning disabilities tchr. Tchr. emotionally disturbed Stanton Elem. Sch., El Paso, Tex., 1971-73; tchr. educable mentally handicapped, gifted Nashville (Ill.) Middle Sch., 1978-82; tchr. English Carlyle (Ill.) Jr. High Sch., 1984-85; spl. educator Mt. Vernon (Ill.) High Sch., 1985-91; pres. Diversivied Ednl. Svcs. and Tech., Inc., Centralia, Ill., 1991—. Participant Dept. Rehab. Statewide Focus Group, Springfield, 1990; mem. State Bd. of Ill. Coop. Vocat. Edn. Coords. Assn., 1991. Asst. Spl. Olympics; mem. Ill. Assn. Spl. Needs, 1989-90, 91. Mem. NEA, Mt. Vernon Edn. Assn. (sec. 1990-91), Am. Vocat. Assn., Ill. Assn. Vocat. Spl. Needs, Ill. Coop. Vocat. Coord. Assn. Home: 1811 Oakwood Dr Pekin IL 61554-6330

BOGOS, FRANCES LEE, secondary school educator; b. Pitts., Oct. 26, 1950; d. Francis Leo and Hilda (Richard) Pegher; m. Richard K. Bogos, Aug. 23, 1975; children: Nathan, Andrea. BS, Edinboro U., 1972; MEd, U. Pitts., 1977. Cert. secondary reading tchr., Pa. 4th-6th grade tchr. St. Alphonsus Sch., Wexford, Pa., 1973-75; 6th grade tchr. St. Louise de Marilac, Pitts., 1975-76; reading specialist McKeesport (Pa.) Area Schs., 1976-79, North Allegheny H.S., Wexford, 1979—. Pres. Parent Tchrs. Guild, Wexford, 1989-90, 90-91; dist. chair Pa. H.S. Speech League, 1998-99, 99-2000, speech and debate coach, 1992-2002. Recipient Diamond Key award, Nat. Forensics League. Mem. North Allegeny Fedn. Tchrs. (union rep. 1991—). Roman Catholic. Avocations: rock climbing, rappelling, swimming, reading, refinishing antique furniture. Office: North Allegheny HS 10375 Perry Hwy Wexford PA 15090-9209

BOGREN, HUGO GUNNAR, radiology educator; b. Jönköping, Sweden, Jan. 9, 1933; came to U.S., 1970; s. Gunnar Hugo and Signe Victoria (Holmström) B.; m. Elisabeth Faxén, Nov. 1, 1956 (div. 1976); children: Cecilia, Niclas, Joakim; m. Gunilla Lady Whitmore, July 2, 1988. MD, U. Göteborg, Sweden, 1958, PhD, 1964. Diplomate Swedish Bd. Radiology. Resident, fellow U. Göteborg, 1958-64, asst. to assoc. prof. radiology, 1964-69; from assoc. prof. to prof. radiology and internal medicine U. Calif. Davis, Sacramento, 1972—. Vis. assoc. prof. U. San Francisco, 1970-71; vis. prof. U. Kiel, Fed. Republic Germany, 1980, cardiac magnetic resonance unit Royal Brompton Hosp. and Imperial Coll., London, 1986-87, 93-94, 2002-03; participant in med. aid fact finding mission, Bangladesh, 1992. Contbr. numerous articles to profl. jours., chpts. to books. Sr. Internat. Fogarty fellow NIH, London, 1986-87. Fellow Am. Heart Assn., Radiol. Soc., N.Am. Soc. Cardiac Imaging, Assn. Univ. Radiologists, Soc. Thoracic Radiology, Internat. Soc. Magnetic Resonance, Soc. Cardiovasc. Magnetic Resonance, Swedish Assn. Med. Radiology; mem. Royal Gothenburg Sailing Club Sweden (hon.), Swedish Cruising Club, Rotary (del.). Lutheran. Avocations: ocean sailing, skiing, classical music. Office: U Calif Davis Med Ctr Div Diagnostic Radiology 4860 Y St Ste 3100 Sacramento CA 95817-2307 E-mail: hugo.bogren@ucdmc.ucdavis.edu.

BOGUS, CARL THOMAS, law educator; b. Fall River, Mass., May 14, 1948; s. Isidore E. and Carolyn (Dashoff) B.; m. Dale Shepard, Sept. 5, 1970 (div. 1987); children: Elizabeth Carol, Ian Troy; m. Cynthia J. Giles, Nov. 5, 1988; 1 child, Zoe Churchill. AB, Syracuse U., 1970, JD, 1972. Bar: Pa. 1973, U.S. Dist. Ct. (ea. dist.) Pa. 1973, U.S. Dist. Ct. Appeals (3d cir.) 1976, U.S. Supreme Ct. 1977. Assoc. Steinberg, Greenstein, Gorelick & Price, Phila., 1973-79, ptnr., 1979-83; assoc. Mesirov, Gelman, Jaffe, Cramer & Jamieson, Phila., 1983-84, ptnr., 1985-91; assoc. prof. Roger Williams U. Sch. Law, Bristol, RI, 1996—2002, prof., 2002—. Vis. prof. Rutgers U. Sch. Law, Camden, 1992—96; mem. bd. visitors Coll. Law, Syracuse (N.Y.) U., 1976—2001; mem. Nat. adv. panel Violence Policy Ctr., 1993—. Author: Why Lawsuits Are Good for America: Disciplined Democracy, Big Business and the Common Law, 2001; editor: The Second Amendment in Law and History, 2001; contbr. articles to profl. jours. Bd. dirs. Handgun Control, Inc., 1987-89, bd. govs., 1992-93; bd. dirs. Ctr. to Prevent Handgun Violence, 1989-92, Lawyers Alliance for Nuclear Arms

Control, 1987-89; mem. state governing bd. Common Cause R.I., 1999-2001. Recipient Common Cause Pub. Svc. award, RI, 2002. Mem. ABA (Ross Essay award 1991), Syracuse Law Coll. Assn. (exec. sec. 1979-83, 2d v.p. 1983-85). Democrat. Mem. Soc. Of Friends. Office: Roger William U Sch Law 10 Metacom Ave Bristol RI 02809-5103 E-mail: cbogus@law.rwu.edu.

BOGUSLAVSKY, GEORGE WILLIAM, psychologist, educator; b. Razdolnoye, Maritime, Russia, Oct. 17, 1911; came to U.S., 1930. s. Vasilii P. and Anna (Lysenko) B.; m. Geneva K. Bowers, Jan. 8, 1943. BA, U. Wash., 1939, MS, 1941; PhD, Cornell U., 1953. Lic. psychologist, N.Y. Instr. U. Conn., Storrs, 1947-51; asst. prof. Cornell U., Ithaca, N.Y., 1953-57; prof., chmn. dept. psychology Rensselaer Poly. Inst., Troy, N.Y., 1957-77. Cons. Am. Inst. Rsch., Pitts., 1952-77, Pergamon Inst., London, 1959-62; adv. N.Y. State Edn. Dept., Albany, 1957-59, Rensselaer Family Court, Troy, 1958-60. Contbg. author: Group Processes, 1957, Physiological Bases Psychiatry, 1958; also articles. Capt. Adjutant Gen.'s Dept., 1942-46, PTO. Rsch. grantee HEW, 1962-65. Mem. AAAS, APA, Assn. N.Y. Acad. Scis., Pavlovian Soc., Archives of History of Am. Psychology, Sigma Xi. Home: 71 Forest At Duke Dr Durham NC 27705-5639

BOHACHEF, JANET MAE, medical educator; b. Glendale, Calif., Aug. 24, 1957; d. William George and Lois Elizabeth Bohachef; 1 child, Andrew William Sauer. BA, Calif. State U., 1982; AAS, Shoreline Coll., 1985; student, Wayland Baptist U., 1999—. Cert. Clin. Lab. Tech., Med Lab. Tech. Nat. Certification Agy. Med. Lab. Pathologists, Med. Technologist Am. Soc. Clin. Pathologists. Med. technologist VA Med. Ctr., Seattle, Va., 1985—86, Amarillo, Tex., 1987—90, High Plains Baptist Hosp., Amarillo, 1990—93; med. lab. instr. Amarillo Coll., Amarillo, 1993—94, med. lab. program dir., 1994—. Mem. adv. bd. Amarillo Coll., 1994—, faculty senator, 1994—96; paper rev. Nat. Accrediting Agy. Clin. Lab. Sci., Chgo., 1995—, med. lab. accred. site visitor, 1995, 2000—02. Author: (poetry) www.Poetry.com, 2001. With USN, 1975—79. Grantee, Tech. Prep. Sch. to Careers, 2000. Mem.: Tex. C.C. Tchrs. Assn., Tex. Soc. Clin. Lab. Sci., Am. Soc. Clin. Lab. Sci., Am. Soc. Clin. Pathologists. Avocation: web design. Office: Amarillo College PO Box 447 Amarillo TX 79178 Home: 8101 Prosper Dr Amarillo TX 79119

BOHAN, WANDA M. secondary school educator; b. Faribault, Minn., July 27, 1940; d. Wayne A. and Evelyn A. (Goben) B.; m. Kenneth M. Schmidt, July 3, 1988; 1 child, Regina Lee Strand. BS, Mankato (Minn.) State U., 1962, postgrad., St. Thomas U., St. Paul. Cert. tchr., Minn. Tchr. English and social studies Dist. 739 Kimball (Minn.) Schs., 1962-63, Kickapoo Area Schs., Viola, Wis., 1963-64; tchr. social studies New Richmond (Wis.) Jr. High Sch., 1964-66; tchr. English, social studies and geography Dist. 196 Rosemount/Apple Valley/Eagan, Rosemount, Minn., 1966-92. Mem. site coun. Rosemount Mid. Sch., 1989-92. Editor newsletters. Recipient Quest for Excellence award Rosemount Mid. Sch., 1990. Mem. Rosemount Edn. Assn. (past. pres.), Minn. Coun. Tchrs. English, Assn. for Supervision and Curriculum Devel., Metro South UNISERV Bd. Home: PO Box 510 Kimball MN 55353-0510 Office: RMS 3135 143rd St W Rosemount MN 55068-4016

BOHM, SUSAN MARY, special education educator; b. Chgo., June 2, 1956; d. Martin and Esther Leah (LaPine) B. BS, Ill. State U., 1979. Cert. tchr., Ill.; cert. tchr. deaf edn., Ill.; cert. cognitive disabilities. Resource aide Ctr. Deafness, Des Plaines, Ill., 1978-79; adminstrv. asst. Job Resource Disabled, Chgo., 1980-82; resource tchr. Chgo. Bd. Edn., 1982—. Mem. round table com. Hearing Impaired Programs, Chgo., 1990-91. Author: Community Resource Manual for the Disabled, 1982. Vol. Congregation Bene Shalom of the Deaf, Skokie, Ill., 1978—, mem. choir, 1978—. Scholar Ill. Dept. Edn., 1974-79. Mem. Coun. Exceptional Children, Kappa Delta Epsilon. Avocations: needle crafts, reading. Office: Northside Learning Ctr 3730 W Bryn Mawr Chicago IL 60659 E-mail: suebesure@cs.com.

BOHMS, PATRICIA ANNE, elementary education educator; b. Toledo, Jan. 15, 1950; d. Shirley Erwin and Lenna Belle (Kidder) Joy; m. Richard Dennis Bohms, Dec. 21, 1974; children: Paul, Jacque, Katelyn. BA, Spring Arbor Coll., 1972; MA, Oakland U., 1983. Cert. elem. tchr., social sci., elem. edn., Mich. Tchr. Mt. Morris (Mich.) Consol. Schs., 1972—. Coach Future Problem Solving, Mt. Morris, 1986-89. Handchime dir. Free Meth. Ch., Davison, Mich., 1990-92. Mem. Mich. Edn. Assn. Avocations: ceramics, basket weaving, cross stitch. Office: Mt Morris Ctrl Elem 1000 Genesee St Mount Morris MI 48458-2058

BOHN, JAMES FRANCIS, physical education educator; b. Pitts., July 14, 1950; s. William L. and Rita (Graham) B.; children: J. Matthew (dec.), Stephanie. BS, Slippery Rock State U., 1972, postgrad., 1979. Cert. tchr., Pa. Tchr. South Fayette Twp., McDonald, Pa., 1972—; instr. Community Coll. of Allegheny County, Pitts., 1975. Evaluator Middle States Assn. of Secondary Schs. and Colls., 1980-81. Dir. Bethel Park (Pa.) Girls Softball Assn., 1991-93; mem. Pa. State Stds. for HSPE Task Force, 1999. Recipient Gift of Time Tribute, Am. Family Inst., 1992. Mem. AAHPERD, NEA, Nat. Assn. Sport and Phys. Edn., Pa. Edn. Assn., South Fayette Edn. Assn. Home: 5600 Libr Rd 17A Bethel Park PA 15102-3722

BOHN, MONICA J. multi-media specialist, educator; b. Sheboygan, Wis., Feb. 2, 1957; d. Eugene J. Bohn, Marilyn J. Bohn. BS, U. Wis., Oshkosh, 1980. Cert. edn. libr. Substitute tchr. Kewaskum (Wis.) Pub. Schs., 1980—81; elem. & mid. sch. media dir. Horicon Pub. Schs., 1981—. Bd. dirs. Horicon Pub. Libr., 1981—99. Recipient Mem. of the Yr., Winnebagoland Uniserv, 1998, Svc. award, Horicon Pub. Libr., 1999. Mem.: Wis. Ednl. Media Assn., Kiwanis (pres. elect 1999—2001). Lutheran. Avocations: travel, precious moments collector, football, basketball. Home: 721 Minerva St Horicon WI 53032 Office: Van Brunt Elem/Mid Sch 611 Mill St Horicon WI 53032 Business E-Mail: mbohn@horicon.k12.wi.us.

BOHN, RALPH CARL, educational consultant, retired educator; b. Detroit, Feb. 19, 1930; s. Carl and Bertha (Abrams) B.; m. Adella Stanul, Sept. 2, 1950 (dec.); children: Cheryl Ann, Jeffrey Ralph; m. JoAnn Olvera Butler, Feb. 19, 1977 (div. 1990); stepchildren: Kathryn J., Kimberly J., Gregory E.; m. Mariko Tajima, Jan. 27, 1991; 1 child, Thomas Carl; 1 stepchild, Daichi Tajima. BS, Wayne State U., 1951, EdM, 1954, EdD, 1957. Instr. part-time Wayne State U., 1954-55, summer 1956; faculty San Jose (Calif.) State U., 1955-92, prof. div. tech., 1961-92, chmn. dept. indsl. studies, 1960-69, assoc. dean ednl. svc., 1968-70, dean continuing edn., 1970-92, prof. emeritus, 1992—; cons. Calif. State U. Sys., 1992—; cons. quality edn. sys. USAF, 1992-2000; dir. nat. program on non-collegiate sponsored instrn. Calif. State Univ. Sys., 1995—2000, Calif. State U. Inst., 1997—99; pres. Univ. Cons., 1994—. Guest faculty Colo. State Coll., 1963, Ariz. State U., 1966, U. P.R., 1967, 74, So. Ill. U., 1970, Oreg. State U., 1971, Utah State U., 1973, Va. Poly. Inst. & State U., 1973, U. Idaho, 1978; cons. U.S. Office Edn., 1965-70, Calif. Pub. Schs., 1960, Nat. Assessment Ednl. Progress, 1968-79, ednl. div. Philco-Ford Corp., 1970-73, Am. Inst. Rsch., 1969-83, Far West Labs for Ednl. Rsch. Devel., 1971-86; adv. bd. Ctr. for Vocat. and Tech. Edn., Ohio State U., 1968-74; dir. project Vocat. Edn. Act, 1965-67, NDEA, 1967, 68; co-dir. Project Edn. Profession Devel. Act, 1969, 70; mem. commn. coll. and univ. contracts Western Assn. Schs. and Colls, 1976-78, chmn. spl. com. on off-campus instrn. and continuing edn., 1978-88; chmn. continuing edn. accreditation visit U. Santa Clara, 1976; chmn. accreditation team Nellis AFB, Nev., 1992, 2002, U. Nev., Las Vegas, 2000, Nat. U., 2000, Oreg. State U., 2001, Golden Gate U., 2001; chmn. accreditation team to Yokusaka Naval Sta., Japan, 2000, Atsugi Naval Air Facility, Japan, 2000, Yokota Air Base, Japan, 2000, Camp Pendleton Marine Corps Base, 2001, Naval Air Sta., Lamoore, 2002, Dyess AFB, 2003, Twentynine Palms Marine Corps. Base, Calif., 2003, eArmyU web-based degree programs U.S. Army, Washington; sr. cons. Global Partnership Devel. Calif. State U. Sys., 2000-03. Author: (with G.H. Silvius) Organizing Course Materials for Industrial Education, 1961, Planning and Organizing Instruction, 1976; (with A. MacDonald) Power-Mechanics of Energy Control, 1970, 2d edit., 1983, The McKnight Power Experimenter, 1970, Power and Energy Technology, 1989, Energy Technology: Power and Transportation, 1992; (with others) Basic Industrial Arts and Power Mechanics, 1978, Technology and Society: Interfaces with Industrial Arts, 1980, Fundamentals of Safety Education, 3d edit., 1981, Energy, Power and Transportation Technology, 1986; (with A. MacDonald) Energy Technology, Power and Transportation, 1991; editor (with Ralph Norman) Graduate Study in Industrial Arts, 1961; indsl. arts editor Am. Vocat. Jour., 1963-66; editor Jour. Indsl. Tchr. Edn., 1962-64. Lt. (j.g.) USCGR, 1951-53, capt. Res. ret. Recipient award Am. Legion, 1945; Wayne State U. scholar, 1953. Mem. NEA, Nat. Assn. Indsl. Tech. (bd. accreditation), Am. Indsl. Arts. Assn. (pres. 1967-68, Ship's citation 1971), Am. Coun. Indsl. Art Tchrs. Edn. (pres. 1964-66, Man of Yr. award 1967), Nat. Univ. Continuing Edn. Assn. (chair accreditation com. 1988-91), Nat. Assn. Indsl. Tchr. Educators (past v.p.), Calif. Indsl. Edn. Assn. (State Ship's citation 1971), Am. Drive Edn. Assn., Nat. Fluid Power Soc., Am. Vocat. Assn. (svc. awards 1966, 67), N.Am. Assn. for Summer Sessions (v.p. western region 1976-78), Luth. Acad. Scholarship, Calif. Employees Assn. (pres. San Jose State Coll. chpt. 1966-67), Western Assn. Summer Session Adminstrs. (newsletter editor 1970-73, pres. 1974-75), Calif. C. of C. (edn. com 1969-77), Industry-Edn. Coun. Calif. (bd. dirs. 1974-80), Sci. and Human Values, Inc. (bd. dirs. 1974-2003, chmn. bd. 1976-2002), Tahoe Tavern (bd. dirs. 1987-91, chmn. bd. 1988-90), Seascape Lagoon Homeowners Assn. (bd. dirs. 1988-95, chmn. 1989-95), Nat. Gold Key Honors Soc. (hon. life). Home and Office: 713 Clubhouse Dr Aptos CA 95003-5431 E-mail: rmbohn@cruzio.com.

BOHNE, JEANETTE KATHRYN, retired mathematics and science educator; b. Quincy, Ill., June 7, 1936; d. Anton Henry and Hilda Wilhelminia (Ohnemus) B. BA, Ursuline Coll., Louisville, 1961; MA, St. Louis U., 1962. Cert. math. and chemistry tchr., N.D., Ill., Mo. Math. tchr. Ryan High Sch., Minot, N.D., 1962-66, Althoff Cath. High Sch., Belleville, Ill., 1966-72, St. Francis Borgia High Sch., Washington, Mo., 1974-77, St. Louis Pub. Schs., 1977-98, head dept. math., 1977-85, 1998. Speaker in field. Treas. Welcome Wagon Club, Washington, 1974-76; pres. Bus. and Profl. Women's Club, Washington, 1978-79; active Animal Protective Assn., Zoo Friends of St. Louis Zoo, S.W. Garden Neighborhood Assn., S.W. Garden Neighborhood Assn. Mobile Patrol.; elected mem. profl. devel. com. St. Louis Pub. Schs., chmn. Math. Fair, 1998. Mem. AAUW, NEA, Mo. State Tchrs. Assn., St. Louis Tchrs. Union, Nat. Coun. Tchrs. Math., Math. Educators Group St. Louis, Mo. Coun. Tchrs. Math., St. Louis Sci. Ctr., Urban Math. Collaborative St. Louis, Math. Assn. Am. (gen. chmn. St. Louis Pub. Schs. math. fair 1998). Avocations: collecting thimbles, raising plants. Home: PO Box 3771 Quincy IL 62305-3771 E-mail: jeanettebohne@webtv.net.

BOHNENKAMPER, KATHERINE ELIZABETH, library science educator; b. Wichita, July 20, 1955; d. William Eugene and Emily Jane (Yount) Miller; m. David Allen Bohnenkamper, May 29, 1994; 1 child, Daniel William. BS in Edn., Emporia State U., 1977; MEd, Wichita State U., 1981; MA, Kans. State U., 1988; MLS, Emporia State U., 1990. Tchr. high sch. Brown County Pub. Schs., Horton, Kans., 1978-79; substitute tchr. Wichita Pub. Schs., 1979-81, 86-90, tchr. jr. high sch., 1981-86; libr. Kans State Hist. Soc., Topeka, 1990-91; asst. prof. libr. sci. Drury U., Springfield, Mo., 1991—. Instr. 1st aid & CPR ARC, Wichita and Springfield, 1976—. Recipient Arnie H. Richards Meml. scholar Sch. Libr. and Info. Mgmt. Emporia State U., 1990. Mem. Mo. Libr. Assn. (officer-reference coun. 1995-98), Springfield Area Libr. Assn. (v.p. 1995-97), DAR (chpt. historian 1982-84, 94-98), Order Eastern Star. Presbyterian. Avocations: church choir, travel, reading, photography. Home: 1022 E Greenwood St Springfield MO 65807-3713 Office: FW Olin Libr Drury U 900 N Benton Ave Springfield MO 65802-3712

BOILLAT, GUY MAURICE GEORGES, mathematical physicist; b. Pontarlier, France, May 18, 1937; s. Georges Paul Charles and Lucie Marguerite Charlotte (Jubin) B. Licence scis., U. Besançon, France, 1959; postgrad., Inst. Henri-Poincaré, Paris, 1959-60, Inst. Theoretical Physics, Copenhagen, 1960-62, Norwegian Tech. U., Trondheim; DSc, Sorbonne U., Paris, 1964. Assoc. prof. dept. math. U. Clermont, Aubière, France, 1966-69, prof., 1969—. Lectr., Italy, 1970—; researcher U. Messina, U. Catania, U. Bologna, Italy, 1970—. Co-author: Recent Mathematical Methods in Nonlinear Wave Propagation, 1996; contbr. 100 rsch. articles on nonlinear waves and fields to profl. jours. Dep. mem. Internat. Parliament for Safety and Peace. Recipient Commemorative Millennium Meml. award Albert Einstein Internat. Acad. Found. Mem.: Internat. Soc. for the Interaction of Mechanics and Math., Internat. Assn. Math. Physics, Am. Math. Soc., Unione Matematica Italiana, French Horological Assn. (bd. dirs. 1983—, sec. gen. 1998—), Acad. M.I.D.I., Maison Internat. Intellectuels (senator), Acad. Peloritana dei Pericolanti (corr.; Messina). Roman Catholic. Home: 16 rue Ronchaux 25000 Besancon France E-mail: boillat@ciram.unibo.it.

BOISE, AUDREY LORRAINE, retired special education educator; b. Hackensack, N.J., Feb. 12, 1933; d. Paul George and Lillian Rose (Goedecker) B. BA, Wellesley (Mass.) Coll., 1955; MA, Fairleigh Dickinson U., 1977. Cert. tchr. K-8, learning disabilities, supervision. Tchr. Township of Berkeley Heights, N.J., 1958-67; learning cons. Borough of New Providence, N.J., 1978-82, 86-00, ret., 2000; learning cons. Scotch Plains/Fanwood, N.J., 1984-86; instr. Fairleigh Dickinson U., Madison, N.J., 1975-78. Several other short-term tchg. positions; supr. student tchrs., 1968, 1975-78, 2000-02; lectr. on fgn. countries in areas of U.S.; part-time travel agt. Mem. Rep. Nat. Com.(life)(pres. club 2003), Nat. Rep. Senatorial Com., Washington, Rep. Presdl. Task Force, Washington, Rep. Congl. Com., Washington, N.J. State Rep. Com., Trenton, Nat. Fedn. Rep. Women, Washington. Recipient Rep. of Yr. Gold medal, Nat. Rep. Congress, 2002, 2003. Mem. NEA, AAUW, N.J. Assn. Learning Cons., Assn. for Children with Learning Disabilities, N.J. Edn. Assn., Internat. Platform Assn., Fortnightly Club, Hist. Soc. Summit, Canoe Brook Country Club, The Pres.'s Club (Washington). Methodist. Avocations: travel, photography.

BOISVERT, DOROTHY LOZOWSKI, science educator; b. Lowell, Mass., July 30, 1950; d. Edward S. and Mildred E. (Leary) Lozowski; m. Alfred N. Boisvert, Aug. 1, 1971; 1 child, Stephen J. BS in Med. Tech., Merrimack Coll., 1973; MEd, U. Lowell, 1982; EdD, U. Mass., 1992. Chemistry tech. Salem (Mass.) Hosp., 1972-73; blood bank tech. Symmes Hosp., Arlington, Mass., 1973-74, Bon Secours Hosp., Methuen, Mass., 1974-77; prof. tech., instr. U. Lowell (Mass.), 1977-83; prof., chmn. Fitchburg (Mass.) State Coll., 1983—2000, dean graduated continuing edn., 2000—. Cons. in field. Contbr. articles to profl. jours. Active Sacred HEart Ch., Lowell, 1994—. Recipient Bd. Dirs. award Mass. Assn. Med. Tech., 1990. Mem. Am. Soc. Clin. Lab. Scis., Am. Assn. Blood Banks, Mass. Assn. Blood Banks, Clin. Lab. Soc. Ctrl. New England. Avocations: gardening, golf, skiing. Office: Fitchburg State Coll 160 Pearl St Fitchburg MA 01420-2631

BOK, DEREK, law educator, former university president; b. Bryn Mawr, Pa., Mar. 22, 1930; s. Curtis and Margaret (Plummer) B.; m. Sissela Ann Myrdal, May 7, 1955; children: Hilary Margaret, Victoria, Tomas Jeremy. BA, Stanford U., 1951; JD, Harvard U., 1954; MA, George Washington U., 1958. Fulbright scholar, Paris, 1954-55; faculty Harvard U. Law Sch., Cambridge, Mass., 1958—, prof., 1961—, dean, 1968-71; pres. Harvard U., Cambridge, 1971-91, 300th anniversary univ. prof., 1991—. Editor: (with Archibald Cox) Cases and Materials on Labor Law, 1962; author: (with John T. Dunlop) Labor and the American Community, 1970, Beyond the Ivory Tower: Social Responsibilities of the Modern University, 1982, Higher Learning, 1986, Universities and the Future of America, 1990, The Cost of Talent, 1993, (with William G. Bowen) The Shape of the River, 1998, The Trouble with Government, 2001; contbr.: In the Public Interest, 1980, The State of the Nation, 1997. Bd. dirs., nat. chmn. Common Cause, 1999—; chmn. bd. overseers Cts. Inst. Music, 1997-2002; chmn. bd. Spencer Found., 2002-; facility chmn. Haupen Ctr. for Non-Profit Orgs., 2002-. Fellow Ctr. for Advanced Studies in the Behavioral Scis., 1991-92. Fellow Am. Acad. Arts and Scis., mem. Nat. Acad. Edn., Phi Beta Kappa. Office: Harvard U JFK Sch of Govt Cambridge MA 02138

BOLAND, FELICIA CAROL, principal; b. Fort Payne, Ala., Apr. 23, 1959; d. Donald Clayton and Randell (Hosch) Colvard; m. Stephen Michael Boland, Dec. 29, 1984. BS, U. Ala., 1981; MS, Jacksonville State U., 1987; masters cert. in edn. adminstrn., U. Ala., 1991; EdS in Mild Learning Handicaps, Jacksonville State U., 1992, EdS in Ednl. Adminstrn., 1994. Dept. sec. Tarrant County Jr. Coll., Fort Worth, 1981-83; mail supr. ALABAMA Band Fan Club, Fort Payne, Ala., 1983-85; learning disabilites tchr. DeKalb County Schs., Fort Payne, 1985—94; asst. prin. Plainview Sch., Rainsville, Ala., 1994—98; prin. Plainview H.S., 1998—. Group recorder DeKalb Spl. Educators, DeKalb City, Ala., 1985-87, group leader, 1992-93; advisor Plainview Sch., Rainsville, Ala., 1986-91. Security and pass info. ALABAMA June Jam, Ft. Payne, 1985—89; mem. com. DeKalb County Young Woman of Yr. Scholarship Program, Rainsville, 1991—92; sec. bd. Mark Herndon Speech and Hearing Found., Chattanooga, 1991—95; host parent Fgn. Exchange Student, 1990—91; foster parent, 1997—; area and regional chmn. Bryant-Jordan Scholarship, 1998—. Mem.: NEA, ASCD, Ala. Cheerleader Coaches and Advisors Assn. (state bd. dirs. 1990—99), Coun. for Exceptional Children, DeKalb Edn. Assn. (assn. rep. 1986—88, 1992—93), Ala. Edn. Assn., Bapt. Young Women, U. Ala. Nat. Alumni Assn., Civitan (bd. dirs.), Delta Kappa Gamma, Kappa Delta Pi. Office: Plainview Sch PO Box 469 Rainsville AL 35986

BOLAND, MARGARET FRANCES, secondary education educator; b. Yonkers, N.Y., Mar. 27, 1942; d. Hugh and Mary (Trainor) Marren; m. Joseph E. Boland, Apr. 20, 1968; 1 child, Joseph Francis. BA in History, Notre Dame Coll., 1964; MA in Edn. and Guidance, Kean Coll., 1967; postgrad., Seton Hall U. Tchr. pub. schs., S.I., 1964-71; substitute tchr. pub. schs., 1972-74, St. Joseph Pvt. Sch., Toms River, N.J., 1983-85, tchr. 8th grade, 1985-93; prin. St. Benedict Sch., Holmdel, N.J., 1993—. Evaluator mid. states, 1989; chairpersonMiddle States Assoc. and Commn. Elem. Edn. Mem. exec. bd. elem. and pvt. schs., 1977-85; mem. exec. bd. pvt. high schs., 1985-89; treas. PTA, 1988-89. Mem. ASCD, Nat. Cath. Tchr.'s Assn., Nat. Coun. Tchrs. of Math., Nat. Geographic Soc. Avocations: gardening, reading, sewing, travel.

BOLASH, SUSAN ROBERTS, special education and corrections education program director; b. Northampton, Pa., Aug. 30, 1950; d. Robert H. and Mary (Glomb) Roberts; 1 child, Robert Benjamin. BS, Coll. Misericordia, Dallas, Pa., 1972; MEd, Lehigh U., 1976. Cert. tchr., Pa. Program dir. spl. edn. Colonial Northampton Intermediate Unit, Easton, Pa., 1972-76; spl. edn. ednl. cons. Colonial Northampton Intermediate Unit #20, Nazareth, Pa., 1976-91; program dir. Easton (Pa.) Sch. Dist., 1991—. Cons. curriculum devel., 1972—, Pa. State Edn. Assn., 1972-84, Coun. Adminstrs. Suprs. Spl. Edn., 1994—, Coun. Exceptional Children, 1994—; spl. Olympics ski coach, 1986-92. Fundraiser ARC, Bethlehem, 1975. Named Olympic Ski Coach of Yr., Northampton County, 1989, Tchr. of Yr. in Dist. 20, 1976. Avocations: music, skiing. Home: 1535 Thompson Ave Bethlehem PA 18017-2670 Office: Easton Area Sch Dist 811 Northampton St Easton PA 18042-4229

BOLDRA, SUE ELLEN, social studies educator, business owner; b. McPherson, Kans., Sept. 9, 1949; d. Herman Glenn and Betty Rose (Krehbiel) Holloway; m. Carl Sterling Boldra, Dec. 19, 1970; children: Jeremy, Brandon, Amber, Chelsea. BA in History and English, McPherson Coll., 1971; MS in Polit. Sci., Ft. Hays State U., 1977. Cert. tchr. Nat. Bd. Profl. Tchg. Standards. Tchr. English Canton (Kans.)-Galva Mid. Sch., 1971-72; tchr. English and social studies Felten Mid. Sch., Hays, Kans., 1972-90; tchr. social studies Hays H.S., 1990—; edn. instr. Ft. Hays State U., summer 1995—. Adj. prof. ednl. adminstrn. and counseling Ft. Hays State U., Hays, 1995—. Mem. Hays City-Ellis County Planning Commn., Hays, 1995, sec., 1996-97, vice-chmn., 1997-98. Recipient Kans. Tchr. of Yr. award, 2001. Home: 2405 General Custer Rd Hays KS 67601-2321 Office: Hays HS 2300 E 13th St Hays KS 67601-2646

BOLDT, ELIHU, astrophysicist, educator; b. New Brunswick, N.J., July 15, 1931; s. Joel and Yetta (Miller) B.; m. Yvette Benharroch, Nov. 25, 1971; children: Adam, Abigail, Jessica. SB, MIT, 1953, PhD, 1958. Rsch. asst. MIT, Cambridge, 1954-58; asst. prof. Rutgers U., New Brunswick, 1958-64; NAS assoc. NASA Goddard Space Flight Ctr., Greenbelt, Md., 1964-65, sr. scientist in x-ray astrophysics, 1966—. Vis. assoc. Ecole Poly., Paris, 1960-62; mem. adv. bd. planning and evaluation panels NASA, Washington, 1974—; adj. prof. physics U. Md., College Park, 1981—; cons. rev. panel NSF, Washington, 1988; mem. Astron. Task Group, Nat. Rsch. Coun., 1996-97. Author: (monograph) The Cosmic X-ray Background, 1987; co-editor: X-ray Binaries, 1975; contbr. over 100 articles to Astrophys. Jour., Reference Ency. Astronomy and Astrophysics. Chmn. Greenbelt Peace Com., 1967-70. Recipient Lindsay Meml. award Goddard Space Flight Ctr., 1977, Outstanding Sci. Achievement award NASA, 1978, Goddard award of Merit, 1995; fellow Waksman Found., Paris, 1960; sr. Goddard fellow, 1992—. Fellow Am. Phys. Soc. (exec. com. cosmic physics divsn. 1978-80); mem. Am. Astron. Soc. (high energy astrophysics divsn. exec. 1987-88), Internat. Astron. Union. Achievements include principal investigator for cosmic x-ray experiment on High Energy Astronomy Observatory 1 mission which determined principal properties of the extragalactic flux of background radiation that dominates the x-ray sky. Office: NASA Goddard Space Flight Ctr Code 660 Greenbelt MD 20771-0001

BOLDYREV, PETER MATVEEVICH, Russian language and culture educator, writer; b. Leningrad/St. Petersburg, USSR, Dec. 12, 1936; came to U.S., 1977; MA equivalent in History of Philosophy, Leningrad State U., 1975. Tchr. Russian lang. and culture Def. Lang. Inst., Monterey, Calif., 1981—. Author: Introduction to Soviet Period of Russian History, 1992, Russia's Lessons, 1993; mem. editorial bd. quar. mag. Contemporary, Toronto, 1979-80; author articles and essays. Founding mem. exec. bd. Russia Without Colonies, N.Y.C., 1977-80. Mem. Internat. PEN Club, Am. Philos. Assn. Home: PO Box 1362 Marina CA 93933-1362

BOLEJACK, SHELLY BESS, secondary education educator; b. Topeka, Mar. 22, 1967; d. Gary Robert and Shirley Sue (Goodwin) Evans; m. Richard Jay Bolejack, Dec. 21, 1991. BA, Washburn U., 1989. English tchr. Robinson Middle Sch., Topeka, 1989—. Drug and alcohol intervention specialist Unified Sch. Dist. #501, Topeka, 1990-91; drug and alcohol group leader Robinson Middle Sch., Topeka, 1990-91. Recipient Women Educator Hon. Sorority award Alpha Delta Kappa, Topeka, 1994. Mem. Alpha Phi Sorority (alumni). Republican. Baptist. Avocations: jet-skiing, crafts, cooking, reading. Bus. Office: Robinson Middle Sch 1125 SW 14th St Topeka KS 66604-2996 E-mail: sbolejac@topeka.k12.ks.us., cash21mac@aol.com.

BOLEK, CATHERINE, university research director; b. Pitts., Feb. 14, 1945; d. Paul and Catherine Schwabedissen; m. Frank Bolek, Nov. 26, 1985; children: John Errico, Katrina, Sarah. BA, U. North Fla., 1978, MS, 1979. Project officer Nat. Cancer Inst., Bethesda, Md., 1980-83; dir. spl. populations rsch. and tng. Nat. Insts. on Drug Abuse, Rockville, Md.,

1983-91; dir. office of sponsored rsch. and programs U. Md. Ea. Shore, Princess Anne, 1991—. Author: Substance Abuse Among Ethnic Minorities in America, 1992; editor: Ethnic and Multicultural Drug Abuse, 1992. Biomed. capacity bldg. grant USPHS, 1992-95; grantee EPA, 1995—, U.S. Dept. Def., 1998—.

BOLEN, BRENDA WINDHAM, elementary education educator; b. Booneville, Miss., Feb. 22, 1947; d. Percy W. and Arleen (Spence) Windham; m. John David Bolen, Dec. 23, 1967; children: Lori Bolen Horn, John C. A, N.E. C.C., 1966; BS, Miss. U. for Women, 1968; MEd, U. Miss., 1977. Cert. tchr., Miss. Tchr. 2d grade Booneville (Miss.) Mcp. Sch. Dist., 1968-86; tchr. 1st grade Marietta (Miss.) Elem. Sch., 1986—. Tchr. Sunday sch., nursery dir. 1st Bapt. Ch., Booneville. Mem. ASCD, PTO, Miss. Assn. Educators (Mem. of Yr. award 1988), Prentiss County Assn. Educators (pres., v.p., sec.) Booneville Assn. Educators (faculty rep. 1975-90), Bus. and Profl. Women's Club, Booneville Jr. Aux. Club, Kappa Delta Pi. Democrat. Baptist. Avocations: shopping, talking with children. Home: 100 Parkwood Grove Rd Booneville MS 38829-1531 Office: Mareitta Elem Sch PO Box 70 Marietta MS 38856-0070

BOLES, LENORE UTAL, nurse psychotherapist, educator; b. N.Y.C., July 3, 1929; d. Joseph Leo and Dorothy (Grosby) Utal; m. Morton Schloss, Dec. 17, 1955 (div. May 1961); 1 child, Howard Alan Schloss; m. Sam Boles, May 24, 1962; children: Anne Leslie, Laurence Utal; stepchildren: Harlan Arnold, Robert Gerald. Diploma in nursing, Beth Israel Hosp. Sch. Nursing, 1951; BSN, Columbia U., 1964; MSN, U. Conn., 1977. Lic. clin. specialist in adult psychiatry/ mental health nursing, advanced practice registered nurse. Staff nurse Beth Israel Hosp., N.Y.C., 1951, Kingsbridge VA Hosp., Bronx, N.Y., 1951-55; night supr. Gracie Square Hosp., N.Y.C., 1959-60; head nurse Elmhurst City Hosp., Queens, N.Y., 1960-62; nursing instr. Norwalk (Conn.) Hosp., 1966-74; asst. prof. U. Bridgeport, Conn., 1976-78; nurse psychotherapist Nurse Counseling Group, Ltd., Norwalk, 1979—; nursing faculty Western Conn. State U., Danbury, 1978-80. Adj. asst. prof. Sacred Heart U., Bridgeport, Conn., 1983-89; adj. faculty Western Conn. State U., Danbury, 1994, 96-2000; lectr. Yale U. Sch. Nursing, 2000-02; nurse cons. Bradley Meml. Hosp., Southington, Conn., 1982, Lea Manor Nursing Home, Norwalk, 1982, St. Vincent's Hosp., Bridgeport, 1982-92; staff devel. nurse Silver Hill Hosp., New Canaan, Conn., 1980-86, 94; cons. in field, 1980—. Author: (book chpt.) Nursing Diagnoses for Psychiatric Nursing Practice, 1994. V.p. Sisterhood Beth El, Norwalk, 1969-71; bd. dirs. religious sch. Congregation Beth El, Norwalk, 1971-75, 79-80, rec. sec. bd. trustees, 1975-77, v.p. congregation, 1977-80, bd. trustees, 1980-83. Named Speaker of Yr., So. Fairfield County chpt. Am. Cancer Soc., 1976. Mem. ANA, Northeastern Nursing Diagnosis Assn. (chair N.E. region conf. 1985, chair planning com. 1984-85, chair nominating com. 1989-91), N.Am. Nursing Diagnosis Assn., Coun. Psychiat./Mental Health Clin. Specialists, Conn. Nurses Assn. (Del. to convs. 1975-2000, legis. com. dist. 3 1984-86, nominating com. 1988-90, Florence Wald award 1984, Conn. Nursing Diagnosis Conf. Group 1980-87), Conn. Soc. Nurse Psychotherapists (founding mem.). Democrat. Jewish. Avocations: travel, reading, gardening, spending time with grandchildren. Home: 173 E Rocks Rd Norwalk CT 06851-1715 Office: Nurse Counseling Group Ltd 71 East Ave Ste F Norwalk CT 06851-4903 E-mail: ncgshrinks@aol.com.

BOLGER, MARY PHYLLIS JUDGE, special education educator; b. Newark, Aug. 19, 1926; d. Michael Francis and Loretta Margaret (Reinhardt) Judge; m. William Patrick Bolger, Nov. 27, 1948 (dec. May 1973); children: Loretta, Francis, Christopher, Michael. BA, Montclair State U., 1946; MA, Reading Specialist, Seton Hall U., 1973. Cert. reading specialist, tchr. English, social studies, Spanish, and reading, learning disabilities tchr., cons. Tchr. English Bd. Edn., Irvington, NJ, 1946-49; tchr. West Side HS, Newark, 1963-69; reading specialist Roosevelt Jr. HS, West Orange, NJ, 1969-77; learning disability tchr., cons. West Orange HS and Hazel Ave., 1977-91. Tchr. ESL South Orange (N.J.) Maplewood Adult Schs., 1949—64; adj. prof. edn. Seton Hall U., South Orange, 1974—96; cons. dept. curriculum and spl. svcs. West Orange Bd. Edn., 1987—2002, cons., workshop presenter, 2000—01; mem. adv. bd. Prospect Ho., East Orange, NJ, 1994—97; cons. to therapeutic friendship groups for retarded adults, 1999—; cons., workshop presenter Lifelong Learning Inst., Caldwell (N.J.) Coll., 2000—01; freelance lectr., workshop presenter. Editor: (book) Beyond Common Sense: The Art of Intelligent Living, 1992, doctoral dissertations Seton Hall U., 1993—97. Eucharistic min. St. Barnabas Hosp., Livingston, NJ, 1991—2001, Ward Homestead, Maplewood, NJ, 1992—2000; coord. eucharistic ministry to the homebound Our Lady of Sorrows, South Orange, NJ, 1989—2000, Homebound Ministry, 1989—2002. Mem.: Seton-Essex Reading Coun. (pres., v.p.), N.J. Reading Assn. (co-chairperson Reading/Learning Disabilities com.), South Orange Sr. Circle (rec. sec. 2001—), Rosary Altar Soc. Roman Catholic. Avocations: writing, travel, reading, watercolors. Home and Office: 34 Mitchell Ave Roseland NJ 07068-1306 E-mail: ga-ga@prodigy.com.

BOLING, ROBERT BRUCE, physical education educator; b. Hammond, Ind., July 28, 1939; s. Kermit W. and Linda E. (Swan) B.; m. Nancy Carol Adams, Dec. 4, 1965. BS, Murray State U., 1964, MS, 1965; PhD, U. So. Miss., 1972. Tchr., coach Casey (Ill.) High Sch., 1965-66, Trigg County High Sch., Cadiz, Ky., 1966-67, Christian County High Sch., Hopkinsville, Ky., 1967-69; tchr. Miss. State U., Mississippi State, 1975—. Author: KINES: Kinesiology in an Interactive New Educational Strategy, 1992. Mem. AAHPERD, Miss. AAHPERD, Am. Coll. Sports Medicine. Baptist.

BOLLEN, SHARON KESTERSON, artist, educator; b. Cin., Apr. 27, 1946; d. Marc J. and Regina (Mills) Kesterson; m. Jerry H. Bollen, June 22, 1968; children: Heather, Christopher. BA in Art, Coll. of Mt. St. Joseph, Cin., 1968; MA in Art Edn., U. Cin., 1970, EdD in Art Edn., 1980. Tchr. art Marian H.S., Cin., 1968-77; prof. art Coll. of Mount St. Joseph, Cin., 1977—. Fabric surface design art works in juried and invitational regional and nat. exhbns.; book reviewer Nat. Art Edn. Assn. Women's Caucus newsletter, 1985—. Recipient Alumni Appreciation award Coll. of Mount St. Joseph, 1993, Disting. Teaching award, 1981. Mem. Nat. Art Edn. Assn. (Student Chpt. Sponsor award 1994, Outstanding Ohio Art Educator of Yr. 1990, Western Region Higher Edn. Art Educator of Yr. 2001), Ohio Art Edn. Assn. (Outstanding Art Educator 1988, Higher Edn. Art Educator of Yr. 2000), Nat. Surface Design Assn., Am. Crafts Coun., Nat. Mus. for Women in the Arts (charter), Georgia O'Keeffe Mus. Roman Catholic. Home: 1138 Cryer Ave Cincinnati OH 45208-2803 Office: Coll of Mount St Joseph Art Dept 5701 Delhi Rd Cincinnati OH 45233-1670

BOLLINGER, LEE CARROLL, academic administrator, law educator; b. 1946; BS, U. Oreg., 1968; JD, Columbia U., 1971. Law clk. to Judge Wilfred Feinberg U.S. Ct. Appeals (2nd cir.), 1971—72; law clk. to Chief Justice Warren Burger U.S. Supreme Ct., 1972—73; asst. prof. law U. Mich., 1973—76, assoc. prof., 1976—78, prof., 1978—94, dean, 1987—94, pres., prof. law, 1997—; provost, prof. govt. Dartmouth Coll., 1994—96; pres. Columbia Univ., 2002—. Rsch. assoc. Clare Hall, Cambridge U., 1983. Co-author (with Jackson): (novels) Contract Law in Modern Society, 1980, The Tolerant Soc., 1986, Images of a Free Press, 1991. Bd. dirs. Gerald R. Ford Found., Royal Shakespeare Co. Fellow Am. Rockefeller Humanities. Fellow: Am. Acad. Arts and Scis. Office: Columbia University 2960 Broadway New York NY 10027-6902 also: 535 W 116th St 202 Low Library Mail Code 4309 New York NY 10027

BOLNICK, HOWARD JEFFREY, insurance company executive, educator, investor; b. Detroit, Oct. 27, 1945; s. Arnold J. and Rebecca (Schuff) B.; m. Kay Zimring, Nov. 29, 1970; children: Lori Ann, Lee Scott. AB with distinction, U. Mich., 1966; MBA, U. Chgo., 1970. Actuary CNA Ins. Cos., Chgo., 1967-76; prin. Coopers & Lybrand, Chgo., 1976-80; pres., bd. dirs. Celtic Life Ins. Co., Chgo., 1980-94, vice chmn. bd. dirs., 1995; pres. Celtic Health Plans, Chgo., 1994; bd. dirs. PM Squared, Inc., San Francisco, 1996-98, Third Coast Ins. Co., Chgo., 1996—; pres., CEO Radix Health Connection, 1997—2001; chmn., CEO InFocus Fin. Group, 2001—. Adj. prof. Kellogg Grad. Sch., Northwestern U., 1996—; fellow Inst. for Health Svcs. Rsch. and Policy Studies, Northwestern U., 1996—. Contbr. articles to profl. and trade publs. Bd. dirs. Schwab Rehab. Ctr., Chgo., 1982-85, Mt. Sinai Med. Ctr., Chgo., 1985-87, Grant Hosp., Chgo., 1991-93, Fla. Small Employer Health Reins. Program, 1992-93; mem. Ill. Comprehensive Health Inst. Plan Bd., Chgo., 1987—, chmn. fin. com., 1989-2002. Fellow Soc. Actuaries (bd. dirs. 1990-92, 94-96, 97-2001, v.p. 1994-96, pres. elect 1997-98, pres. 1998-99); mem. Internat. Actuarial Assn. (chmn. health sect. 2003—), Am. Acad. Actuaries (bd. dirs. 1990-94, 97—, v.p. 1992-94), Health Ins. Assn. Am. (bd. dirs. 1988-90). Jewish. Avocations: scuba diving, travel. Office: InFocus Fin Group Inc 30 N LaSalle St Ste 3440 Chicago IL 60602

BOLOGNIA, JEAN LYNN, academic dermatologist; b. Hammond, Ind., July 1, 1954; d. John Paul and Jo Ann (Dill) B.; m. Dennis Lawrence Cooper, Aug. 25, 1985. BA summa cum laude, Rutgers U., 1976; MD cum laude, Yale U., 1980. Diplomate Nat. Bd. Med. Examiners. Intern, resident in internal medicine Yale-New Haven Hosp., 1980-82, resident in dermatology, 1982-85; rsch. fellow dermatology Yale U. Sch. Medicine, New Haven, 1985-87, asst. prof. dermatology, 1987-93, assoc. prof. dermatology, 1993-97, prof. dermatology, 1997—, dir. residency tng. program, 1994-2000. Mem. coalition for dermatol. care women Am. Acad. Dermatology/Soc. Investigative Dermatology/Women's Dermatol. Soc., Schaumburg, Ill., 1994-98, chair 1997-98; med. coun. Skin Cancer Found., N.Y.C., 1995—; mem. grad. med. edn. com. Yale New Haven Hosp., 1996-2000; lectr. at over 80 univs. and internat. meetings. Author: Harrison's Principles of Internal Medicine, 1990, 1994, 1997, 2000; Jour. Am. Acad. Dermatology. Recipient Individual Nat. Rsch. award Nat. Inst. Cancer, 1987-89; rsch. fellow Dermatology Found., 1985. Mem.: Med. Dermatology Soc. (pres.-elect 1999, pres. 2000), Pan Am. Soc. for Pigment Cell Rsch. (coun. 1998—2000), Dermatology Found., Assn. Profs. Dermatology (med. and sci. com. 1997—2000), Soc. for Investigative Dermatology (resident/fellow program com. 1996—2000, membership com. 2001—, v.p. 2002—), Women's Dermatol. Soc. (chair 1996—98, networking com. 1996—99, audit com. 1998—2000, newsletter editor 1999—2001, chair internat. affairs 1999—2001, bd. dirs. 1999—), Am. Dermatol. Assn. (membership com. 2000), Am. Acad. Dermatology (regulatory guidelines 1994—96, melanoma/skin cancer com. 1995—99, interdisciplinary edn. com. 1996—2000, intersoc. liaison coun. 1997—98, environment coun. 1997—2001, manpower com. 1998—2002, bd. dirs. Sulzberger Inst. 1998—, audit com. 1999—, nominating com. 2000—, ethics cente 2002—). Achievements include patent for enhancing depigmentation therapy; research in depigmentation therapy, characteristics of nevi and melanoma, disorders of pigmentation. Office: Yale U Sch Medicine 500 LCI 333 Cedar St New Haven CT 06510-3289

BOLONESI, NAOMI GRANT, principal; b. San Diego, Mar. 3, 1955; d. Floyd Marshall and Winona Naomii (Richards) Grant; m. Bruce Albert Bolonesi, May 12, 1979; children: Ryan Marshal, Alexander Grant. AA, Southwestern Coll., 1975; BA, San Diego State U., 1977; MEd, U. Wash., 1981; adminstr. certification, U. Puget Sound, 1992. Cert. tchr., prin., Wash., Utah. Community edn. leader State of Calif., El Cajon, 1977; substitute tchr. Cajon Valley Union Sch. Dist., El Cajon, Calif., 1977, tchr., 1977-79, Enumclaw (Wash.) Sch. Dist., 1979-92; prin. intern Enumclaw Sch. Dist. U. Puget Sound, 1991-92; cons., substitute prin. Salt Lake City Sch. Dist., 1992-93; asst. prin. Granger Elem. Sch. and Woodrow Wilson Elem. Sch. Granite Sch. Dist., Salt Lake City, 1993—. Co-author: Learning Centers that Teach, 1977. Bd. dirs. Byron Kibler PTA, Enumclaw, 1991-92; polit. action chair Puget Sound Uniserv Dist., Auburn, Wash., 1983; mem. Sch. Community Group of Canyon View Elem. Sch., Jordan Sch. Dist., Sandy, Utah, 1992-93. Named Young Career Woman of Yr. Bus. and Profl. Women Wash., 1982. Mem. ASCD, AAUW, Nat. Assn. Elem. Prins., Nat. Coun. Social Studies, Wash. Edn. Assn. (state del. 1983-84), Pi Lambda Theta, Alpha Gamma Delta Alumni. Democrat. Avocations: walking, jogging, reading, theater, hiking. Home: 18022 SE 280th Pl Kent WA 98042-5347 Address: 18022 SE 280th Pl Kent WA 98042-5347

BOLZ, SARAH JANE, mathematics educator; b. Milw., June 6, 1955; d. Robert Arthur and Carol Esther (Gruetzmacher) B. BS, U. Wis., Milw., 1977, MS, 1983. Cert. secondary tchr., Wis. Math. tchr. Hamilton High Sch., Milw., 1978, Washington High Sch., Milw., 1978-80; math., computer tchr., head math. dept. Milw. Luth. High Sch., 1980—. Volleyball ofcl. Wis. Ind. Athletic Assn., 1975-88; asst. basketball coach Milw. Luth. High Sch., 1980-87, asst. softball coach, 1981-2003, asst. volleyball coach, 1995-98, varsity head volleyball coach, 1999—. Mem. Nat. Council Tchrs. of Math., Wis. Math Council, Wis. Volleyball Coaches Assn., Nat. Fedn. Interscholastic Coaches, Nat. Fedn. Interscholastic Ofcls. Lutheran. Avocations: softball, tennis, golf, jogging, bicycling. Office: Milw Luth High Sch 9700 W Grantosa Dr Milwaukee WI 53222-1497

BOMBA, ANNE KILLINGSWORTH, family relations and child development educator; b. Port Lavaca, Tex., Sept. 12, 1959; d. John Gilbert and Jane (Killingsworth) B. BS, Okla. State U., Stillwater, 1981, MS, 1987, PhD, 1989. Cert. in family and consumer scis. Tchr. kindergarten Tulsa Okla. Pub. Schs., 1981-85; asst. to editor Home Econs. Rsch. Jour., Stillwater, 1986; grad. asst., grad. assoc. in family rels. and child devel. Okla. State U., 1987-89; asst. prof. home econs. U. Miss., Oxford, 1989-95, assoc. prof. family and consumer scis., 1995—. Contbr. articles to profl. jours. Mem. AAUP, AAUW, Am. Assn. Family and Consumer Scis., Soc. for Rsch. in Child Devel., Nat. Assn. for Edn. of Young Children, Nat. Coun. on Family Rels., So. Early Childhood Assn., Kappa Omicron Nu. Home: PO Box 1345 University MS 38677-1345 Office: U Miss Dept Family and Consumer Scis PO Box 1848 University MS 38677-1848 E-mail: abomba@olemiss.edu.

BOMBA, CHERYL LYNNE, educational researcher; b. Bayonne, N.J., July 21, 1965; d. Harold Edward and Carol Lynne (Teqtmeyer) Cummings; m. Paul Stanley Bomba, Oct. 11, 1987. BA in Psychology, Rutgers U., 1987; MAT, Trenton State Coll., Ewing, N.J., 1991. Teaching asst. Douglass Devel. Disability Ctr., New Brunswick, N.J., 1986-87; respite worker Eden Inst., Princeton, N.J., 1987-88, teaching asst., 1988-90, head tchr., 1990-91, tech. support specialist, 1991-94; asst. dir. for tech. support, 1995—. Cons. Wawa House, Princeton, 1991—, E. Brunswick (N.J.) Pub. Schs., 1993, Old Bridge (N.J.) Pub. Schs., 1993—. Contbg. author curriculum series: Eden Inst. Curriculum Series, 1991; series editor curriculum series: Eden Svcs. Employment and Residential Curricula, 1994. Mem. Kappa Delta Pi, Phi Beta Kappa. Office: Eden Family of Svcs One Logan Dr Princeton NJ 08540

BOMBOY, JOHN DAVID, mathematics educator; b. Somerset, Pa., May 22, 1953; s. David E. and Betty (Smith) B.; m. Nancy L. Dutrow, Apr. 22, 1978; children: Amanda Joy (dec.), Amy Lynn (dec.). BS, Clarion State Coll., 1975, MS, 1980. Cert. secondary tchr., Ohio, Pa.; registered athletic dir., Pa. Math. tchr. East Palestine (Ohio) City Schs., 1975-77, Marion Center (Pa.) Area Schs., 1977—, dir. athletics, 1982—, dir. cmty. svcs., 1998-99. Mem. Pa. State Athletic Dir.'s Assn. (mem. exec. coun., chmn. awards com.), Nat. Interscholastic Athletic Adminstrs. Assn. (cert. master athletic adminstr.), Pa. Interscholastic Athletic Assn., Wrestling Ofcls., Am. Sport Edn. Program Instrs., Dist. 6 Athletic Dirs. Assn. (treas. 1994—), Appalachian Conf. (sec.-treas. 1987-2000), Heritage Conf. (sec.-treas. 2000—), Therapy Dog Internat. (assoc. vol. cert. handler). Republican. Lutheran. Avocations: jogging, collecting license plates, wrestling referee. Home: 306 Highland Dr Home PA 15747-9608 Office: Marion Ctr Area High Sch 22800 Rte 403 Hwy N PO Box 209 Marion Center PA 15759 E-mail: jbomboy@mcasd.net.

BONA, JERRY LLOYD, mathematician, educator; b. Little Rock, Feb. 5, 1945; s. Louis Eugene and Mary Eva (Kane) B.; m. Pamela Anne Ross, Dec. 23, 1966; children: Rachael Elizabeth, Jennifer Dani'el. BS in Applied Math. and Computer Sci., Washington U., St. Louis, 1966; PhD in Math., Harvard U., 1971. Rsch. fellow U. Essex, Colchester, Eng., 1970-72; L. E. Dickson instr. U. Chgo., 1972-73, from asst. prof. to assoc. prof. to prof., 1973-86; prof. Pa. State U., University Park, 1986-90, Raymond Shibley prof., 1990-95, acting chmn., 1990-91, chmn., 1991-95; CAM prof. math. and physics U. Tex., Austin, 1995—2002; prof., chmn. U. Ill., Chgo., 2002—. Rsch. fellow Harvard U. dept. math., 1970, 73; U.K. Sci. and Engrng. Rsch. Coun. sr. vis. fellow Fluid Mechanics Rsch. Inst., U. Essex, 1973, 74, 75, 77, 78; vis. rsch. assoc. Brookhaven Nat. Lab., 1976, 77; NAS exch. visitor to Poland, 1977; vis. prof. Centro Brasileiro Pesquisas Fisicas, Rio de Janeiro, 1980, Math. Rsch. Ctr., 1980-81, U. Brasilia, 1982, Lab. Anvendt Matematisk Fysik, Danish Tech. Sch., 1982, Inst. Math. and its Applications, U. Minn., 1985, 88, 90, 91, 2001; rsch. prof. Applied Rsch. Lab., Pa. State U., 1986-95; prof. invité U. Paris-Sud, Ctr. d'Orsay, 1982, 86-87, 88, 89, 92, 2001, 03, l'Inst. Nat. Sci. Rsch.-Oceanology, U. Que., 1982-87, Ecole Normale Superieure de Cachan, 1990-91, dir. rsch. CNRS, 1995, U. Bordeaux, 1995, 2001, 03; invited prof. Inst. Pure and Applied Math., Rio de Janeiro, 1991, 92, 93, 99, 2000, 02, Acad. Sinica, Beijing, 1991, 96, 99, Math. Scis. Rsch. Inst., Berkeley, Calif., 1994, U. de Paris Nord, Math. Lab. Villetaneuse, 1993, 95, 99, U. Oxford, 1995, TATA Inst., Bangalore, 1999, 2001, 03, Inst. Sci. de la Mer, U. Que., 1999—; invited spkr. ann. meeting Am. Phys. Soc., Notre Dame, 1979; invited spkr. Am. Math. Soc. meeting, Mpls., 1984, San Francisco, 1995; invited spkr. Internat. Biennial Fluid Mechanics Meeting, Blazjewko, Poland, 1979, Internat. Congress of Mathematicians, Helsinki, 1978; Britton lectr., McMaster U., 1986, SIAM ann. meeting, San Diego, 1989, Porcelli lectr. LSU, 1993, Taft lectr. U. Cin., 1996, Industl. Math Inst. Disting. Lctr., Univ. S. C., 2002; chmn. Com. Applied Math. U. Chgo., 1981-86; mem. coll. coun.U. Chgo., 1981-84; mem. Pa. State U. task force on undergrad. edn., 1989-91, hon. degree recipient recommendation com., 1994-95 ; mem. sci. adv. com. basic rsch. math. scis. U.S. Army Rsch. Office, 1979-82, review com. divsn. math. and computer sci. Argonne Nat. Lab., 1984-90, chmn., 1985-89; mem. rev. panel, site visit team NSF Sci. and Tech. Ctrs., 1988; mem. NATO postdoctoral fellowships rev. panel, 1991; mem. ABET evaluating team, 1992; chmn. proposal rev. panel Dept. Energy, 1993; co-dir. Math. Edn. Reform Network, 1993—; mem. vis. com. dept. math. U. Ill., Chgo., 1993, MIT, 1993-97, CUNY Bklyn. Coll., 1994, U. N.C., 1996, Howard U., 1999; mem. forum post secondary edn. Math. Scis. Edn. Bd., 1994—; chmn. nat. vis. com. N.Y. Collab. for Excellence in Tchr. Prep. in Math., Sci., Tech., 1996-2000. Mem. editl. bd. SIAM J. Math. Anal., 1979—, editor-in-chief, 1987-92; mem. editl. bd. 25 profl. jours.; contbr. more than 150 papers to profl. jours. Grantee W. M. Keck Found., 1989, NSF, 1972—; NSF grad. fellow Harvard U., 1966-70; Woodrow Wilson fellow Harvard U., 1966-67. Fellow AAAS (nat. com. chair 1994-97, nat. elected office 2001—); mem. Soc. for Indsl. and Applied Math. (com. mng. editors 1987-92, com. on coms. and appts. 1988-95, vis. lectr. 1992—, rep. to AAAS sect. com. on math. 1994-97, nat. com. chair 1987-92, Am. Math. Soc. (nat. com. chair 1989-96, 99—, mem. com. to select Steele prize winner 1984-87, adv. com. on newsletter on collegiate math. edn. 1987-88, bd. judges for Nat. Sci. and Engrng. Fair 1990, 1991, chmn. liaison com. AAAS 1990-92, com. on edn. 1992-96, chmn. subcom. grad. and postdoctoral edn. 1993-95, univ. lectr. series com. 1994—, chmn., 1999—, nomination com. 1995-97, chmn. nomination com. 1995-96, com. on coms. 1998-2002, chmn. 1998-2002), Math. Assn. Am. (com. on undergrad. program in math. 1987-91, subcom. on major in math. scis. 1989-90, subcom. on calculus reform and 1st 2 yrs. 1989-91, rep. to AAAS sect. com. on math. 1993-96, program of cons. 1994—), Tau Beta Pi. Achievements include setting up a fluid mechanics lab in math. depts.; helping to organize interdisciplinary programs in science, engineering, economics, finance, computer science and mathematics. Home: 360 E Randolph St Apt 3903 Chicago IL 60601 Office: U Ill Chgo Math, Stat and Computer Sci Dept Chicago IL 60607

BONACORSI, LARRY JOSEPH, mathematics educator; b. Christopher, Ill., Feb. 10, 1948; s. Alfred Joseph and Anna (Guidazzio) B.; m. Karen Marie Donini, Aug. 19, 1972; children: Gina Ann, Mary Theresa. BA, So. Ill. U., 1970, MS, 1974. Instr. math. Henry (Ill.) Grade Sch., 1970-96, Henry-Senachwine H.S., Henry, 1996—. Mem. St. Mary's Parish Bd., Henry, 1976-78, sec. Henry Pub. Library Bd. Trustees, 1977-79, treas., 1980-97; alderman City of Henry, 1997—. Mem. NEA, Ill. Coun. Tchrs. of Math., Ill. Edn. Assn., Nat. Coun. Tchrs. of Math., Henry Elem. Tchrs. Assn. (treas. 1975-89), Henry-Senachwine Edn. Assn. (treas. 1989—), Heart of Ill. Tchrs. Math, Optimist Club (sec. 1980-85), KC (dep. grand knight 1992-94, treas. 1994—). Roman Catholic. Home: 205 Conrad St Henry IL 61537-1669 Office: Henry Senachwine HS 1023 College St Henry IL 61537-1074 E-mail: lkbona@yahoo.com.

BONAFFINI, LUIGI, language and literature educator, translator; b. Isernia, Italy, Apr. 26, 1947; came to U.S., 1961; s. Gioacchino and Adelina (Antenucci) B. BA, U. Conn., 1969, PhD, 1976. Instr. U. Tex., Austin, 1973-74, SUNY, Albany, 1974-76; asst. prof. Bklyn. Coll., 1976-88, assoc. prof., 1989-91, prof. Italian lang. and lit., 1991—. Author: La Poesia Visionaria Di Dino Campana, 1980; translator: For the Baptism of Our Fragments, 1992; editor, translator: Moliseide, 1992, Anthology of Molisan Poetry, 1993, Orphic Songs, 1992, The Peacock/The Scraper, 1994, The Crevice, 1994, Alien Cantica, 1995, Dialect Poetry of Southern Italy, 1997, Moliseide and Other Poems, 1998, Vi America, 1999, Phrases and Passages of a Salutary Song, 1999, Variable Star, 1999, Jazzymood, 1999, Cantalesia, Poems in the Neapolitan Dialect, 1999, Via Terra - An Anthology of Contemporary Italian Dialect Poetry, 1999, Molisan Poems, 2000, Orphic Songs, 2003, Selected Poems of Carlo Emilio Colucci, 2003, Italian Vocabulary, 2003; translator: Earthy and Heavenly Journey of Simone Martini, 2003, Selected Poems of Albino Pierro, 2002, Dialect Poetry of Northern and Central Italy, 2001. Mem. Am. Translators Assn. (chmn. Italian div. 1990—), Am. Assn. Tchrs. of Italian, Dante Soc. Am., Am. Assn. Italian Studies, Am. Lit. Translators Assn. Home: 259 Garfield Pl Apt 3R Brooklyn NY 11215-2209 Office: Bklyn Coll 2900 Bedford Ave Brooklyn NY 11210-2814 E-mail: l.bonaffini@worldnet.att.net.

BONAIUTO, JOHN A. state education official; Sec. edn. and cultural affairs South Dakota; exec. dir. Nebraska Assoc. School Boards, Lincoln. Office: Nebraska Assoc of School boards 140 S 16th St Lincoln NE 68508-1805*

BONANNO, A. RICHARD, weed management scientist, educator; b. Lawrence, Mass., Apr. 3, 1958; s. Angelo F. and Rose S. (Alicata) Bonanno; m. Bonanno Luanne, June 21, 1980; children: Cara Anne, Alison Rose, Heather Marie. BS, Cornell U., 1979, MS, 1980; PhD, Oreg. State U., 1982. Asst. prof. N.C. State U., Raleigh, 1983-88, assoc. prof., 1988-89; owner Pleasant Valley Garden, Metheun, Mass., 1989—; sr. extension specialist U. Mass., Amherst, 1990—. Adj. prof. U. Mass., Amherst, 1990—; pub. mem. Mass. Pesticide Bd., Boston, 1990—; lectr. in field. Contbr. articles to profl. jours. Recipient Homer C. Thompson award, Am. Soc. Horticulture Sci., 1984, Extension Blue Ribbon award, Am. Soc. Agrl. Engrs., 1985, So. Region Horticulture Soc., 1986, 1987, 1990, 1991. Mem.: Mass. Farm Bur. Fedn. (mem. exec. com. 1997—, v.p. 2001—), Coun. Agrl. Sci. and Tech., Weed Sci. Soc. Am. (chiar Washington liaison com. 1994—, Oustanding Young Weed Scientist 1999), Northeastern Weed Sci. Soc. (chair legis. com. 1990—97, mem. exec. com. 1990—2001, v.p. 1997—98, pres.-elect

1998—99, pres. 1999—2000), New Eng. Coun. Plant Protection (pres. 1994—96), New Eng. Vegetalbe and Berry Growers Assn. (mem. exec. com. 1989—, pres. 1995—98), Sigma Xi. Home and Office: Univ of Mass 255 Merrimack St Methuen MA 01844-6433

BONAWITZ, MARY FEENEY, accountant, educator; b. NYC, June 13, 1951; d. John Michael and Mary Rosalind (Fitzgerald) Feeney; m. Irving M. Bonawitz, Dec. 7, 1991. BS, SUNY, 1981, MS, 1984; PhD, Fla. Internat. U., 2002. CPA Fla., N.Y., Pa., V.I. Adminstrv. asst. Chase Manhattan Bank, NYC, 1970-77; credit card supr. Vt. Nat. Bank, Brattleboro, 1977—78; sr. acct. Urbach, Kahn & Werlin P.C. CPA's, Albany, NY, 1981-83; tchg. asst., lectr. SUNY, 1983-85; self-employed Albany, 1983-85; firm mgr. Brammer, Chasen & O'Connell CPA's, St. Thomas, Vt., 1985-88; asst. prof. Wilkes U., Wilkes-Barre, Pa., 1988-90. Asst. prof. Capital Coll. Pa. State U., 1998—. Scholar Sayles-Pierce, SUNY Alumni Assn., 1979—81. Mem.: AICPA (subcom. profl. ethics 1988—90), V.I. Soc. CPAs, Pa. Inst. CPAs, Fla. Inst. CPAs (mem. sole practitioners com. 1991—92), Am. Acctg. Assn., Am. Soc. Women Accts. (nat. treas. 1998—99, nat. v.p. 1999—2000, pres.-elect 2001—02, nat. pres. 2002—03), Am. Women's Soc. CPA. Roman Catholic. Avocations: reading, music, needlework, gardening. Home: 3102 Village Rd Orwigsburg PA 17961 Office: Pa State U Capitall Coll 200 University Dr Schuylkill Haven PA 17972 E-mail: Busmfb5@psu.edu.

BONCHEV, DANAIL GEORGIEV, chemist, educator; b. Burgas, Bulgaria, Feb. 20, 1937;, naturalized, 2001; s. Georgi Nikolov and Penka Danailova Bonchev; m. Pravdolyuba Vladimirova, Oct. 31, 1960 (div. 1983); 1 child, Adelina Boncheva; m. Dimitrina Kostova, June 10, 1984; 1 child, Elina. MSChemE, High Inst. Chem. Tech., Sofia, Bulgaria, 1960; PhD in Quantum Chemistry, Acad. Scis., Sofia, Bulgaria, 1970; DSc in Math. Chemistry, State U., Moscow, 1984. Process engr. Chem. Kombinat, Dimitrovgrad, Bulgaria, 1960-63; asst. prof. chemistry High Inst. Chem. Tech. (name now Assen Zlatarov U.), Burgas, Bulgaria, 1963-72, assoc. prof., head dept phys. chemistry, 1973-91, prof. chemistry, 1987—, dean inorganic chemistry faculty, 1987-91. Head lab. math. chemistry Bulgarian Acad. Scis., Sofia, 1986-91; rector, founder Free Univ., Burgas, Bulgaria, 1991-94; rsch. cons., Houston, 1995—; adj. prof. Tex. A&M U., Galveston, 1999—; referee internat. jours. in theoretical chemistry; vis. scientist U. Tex., Houston, 1992-94; tchr. chemistry and physics Texas A&M U., 1994-96. Author: Information-Theoretical Characterization of Chemical Structures, 1983, (textbook) Structure of Matter, 1979, Physical Chemistry, 1994, Chemical Reaction Networks, 1996; editor: (series) Mathematical Chemistry, Graph Theoretical Approach to Chemical Reactivity; mem. editl. bd. Jour. Math. Chemistry, 1987-93, MATCH, 1989—, SAR and QSAR in Environ. Rsch., 1994—, Asian Jour. Spectroscopy, 1997—, ARKIVOC, 2000—, Chemistry and Biodiversity, 2003—; contbr. over 190 articles to internat. sci. jours., 2 monographs, 3 textbooks. Decorated Cyril and Methodius order II, State Coun. Bulgaria, Sofia, 1987. Mem. AAAS, . Soc. Math. Chemistry (officer), Am. Chem. Soc., N.Y. Acad. Scis., Bulgarian Acad. Scis. (corr.). Achievements include contbns. to characterization of molecular topology, molecular branching, cyclicity, centrality; in deriving the properties of chem. elements (transactinids), compounds, polymers and crystals from their structure; in the classification, coding, and complexity of chemical compounds and mechanisms of chemical reactions, in developing chemical information theory in quantifying biocomplexity, in characterising biological and ecological networks, etc. Office: Tex A&M U 5007 Ave U Galveston TX 77551 also: Assen Zlatarov U 8010 Burgas Bulgaria E-mail: bonchevd@tamug.tamu.edu., bonchevd@sbcglobal.net.

BOND, EVELYN ROBERTA, elementary education educator; b. Charlotte, N.C., Mar. 11, 1946; d. James and Jessie (McCaw) Young; m. William Edward Bond, Apr. 3, 1975; 1 child, Karyn.. Winston-Salem State U., 1968; MA in Teaching Reading, Oakland U., 1972; EdS, Wayne State U., 1992—. Cert. tchr., Mich. Tchr. McConnell Elem. Sch., 1968-71, Mark Twain Elem. Sch., 1971-72; tchr. remedial reading chpt. 1 McCarroll Elem. Sch., 1972-81; tchr. remedial reading Walt Whitman Elem. Sch., 1981-82; tchr. English/lit. Lincoln Jr. High Sch., 1982-89; tchr. chpt. 1 remedial reading Jefferson/Whittier Sch., 1989—. Mem. NAACP, Mich. Named Tchr. of Month, Pontiac (Mich.) Schs., 1984, Outstanding Grad. Advisor, Alpha Kappa Alpha, 1986. Mem. NEA, Mich. Edn., Assn., Pontiac Edns. Assn., Alpha Kappa Alpha Sorority (grad. advisor 1983-86), Phi Delta Kappa. Home: 131 E Iroquois Rd Pontiac MI 48341-1610

BOND, GEORGE CLEMENT, anthropologist, educator; b. Knoxville, Tenn., Nov. 16, 1936; s. J. Max and Ruth Elizabeth (Clement) B.; m. Alison Murray, Sept. 21, 1940; children: Matthew, Rebecca, Jonathan, Sarah. BA, Boston U., 1959; MA, London Sch. Econs., 1962, PhD, 1968. Lectr. U. East Anglia, Norwich, Eng., 1966-68; asst. prof. Columbia U., N.Y.C., 1968-74, assoc. prof. Tchrs. Coll., 1974-80, prof., 1980—, dir. Inst. African Studies, 1989—. Author: Politics of Change in a Zambia Community, 1976; editor: African Christianity, 1979, Social Stratification and Education, 1981, The Social Construction of the Past, 1994, AIDS in Africa and the Caribbean, 1997; contbr. articles to scholarly publs. Home: 229 Larch Ave Teaneck NJ 07666-2345 Office: Columbia U Inst of African Studies 420 W 118th St New York NY 10027-7213

BOND, JOAN, retired elementary school educator; b. Americus, Ga., Dec. 24, 1945; d. Doyle Holden and Frances (Brown) B. BS in Elem. Edn., U. Ga., 1975, MEd, 1979, EdS, 1982. Clk. emergency room St. Mary's Hosp., Athens, Ga., 1963-64; receptionist, asst. Office Dr. Shu-Yun T. Tsao, Athens, 1964-66; tchr. remedial reading Danielsville (Ga.) Elem. Sch., 1975-76, primary tchr., 1975-2000; substitute tchr. Madison County Bd. Edn., Danielsville, 2000—. Tchr., dir. presch. Hull (Ga.) Bapt. Ch., 1970-84, asst. tchr. adult class, 1985—; mem. honor roll com. Danielsville Elem. Sch. PTO, 1990-92. Mem. Madison County Ret. Educators Assn., Ga. Ret. Educators Assn. Democrat. Avocations: beach activities, U. Ga. football, basketball and gymnastics fan. Home: 999 Glenn Carrie Rd Hull GA 30646-4210 Office: Danielsville Elem Sch PO Box 67 Danielsville GA 30633-0067

BOND, KARLA JO, educator; b. Abilene, Tex., Oct. 11, 1951; d. David Lipscomb and Elizabeth Rosalie (Henthorn) Kennamer; m. Dennis Earl Bond, July 28, 1979; children: Ryan Jeffrey, Blake Justin. BS in Edn., Abilene Christian U., 1972; MA, Maryville U., 1994. Tchr. Abilene (Tex.) Christian Campus Sch., 1972-73, LaMarque (Tex.) Pub. Schs., 1973-78, Kansas City (Kans.) Unified Sch. Dist. 500, 1979-90, Ft. Zumwalt Pub. Schs., O'Fallon, Mo., 1990—, coord. elem. sch. math., 1993—. Instr. math. Math. Learning Ctr., Portland, 1990-92; leader math. insvc. Ft. Zumwalt Pub. Schs., 1990-94. Mem. NEA, Nat. Coun. Tchrs. Math., Mo. Coun. Tchrs. Math., Math. Educators Greater St. Louis. Republican. Mem. Ch. of Christ. Avocations: water skiing, reading, piano, children's sports. Office: Mid Rivers Elem 7479 Mexico Rd Saint Peters MO 63376

BOND, RICHARD RANDOLPH, foundation administrator, legislator; b. Lost Creek, W.Va., Dec. 1, 1927; s. Harley Donovan and Marcella Randolph B.; m. Reva Stearns, Apr. 20, 1946; children: David, Philip, Josette, Michael. BS, Salem Coll., 1948, LHD (hon.), 1979; LHD (hon.), U. No. Colo.; MS, W.Va. U., 1949; PhD, U. Wis., 1955; postdoctoral studies, U. Mich., 1958-59. Various teaching and fellowship positions, 1949-59; dean of faculty Elmira (N.Y.) Coll., 1959-63; dean coll. of Liberal Arts U. Liberia, Monrovia, 1963-64; chief of party Cornell U. Project in Liberia, Monrovia, 1964-66; v.p. acad. affairs Ill. State U., Normal, 1966-71; pres. U. No. Colo., Greeley, 1971-81, pres. emeritus, prof. zoology, 1981-89; state rep. Colo. Gen. Assembly, Denver, 1984-90; interim pres. Front Range Community Coll., Westminster, Colo., 1991; pres. Morgan Community Coll., Ft. Morgan, Colo., 1991-96, Cmty. Found., Greeley and Weld County, 1996—2000, Bond Family Found., 1995—. Founder Nat. Student Exch., 1st No. Savs. and Loan; cons., examiner North Ctrl. Accrediting Assn., 1969-82. Author: Colorado Postsecondary Options Act., 1988; contbr. articles to profl. jours. Bd. dirs., chmn. Sunrise Community Health Ctr.; founding mem. Dream Team on Dropout Prevention; Dem. candidate for Col. 4th Congl. Dist., 1990; founder Colo. chpt. Dem. Leadership Coun., 1991—; co-chmn. Clinton Campaign, Colo., 1992; bd. dirs. Colo. chpt. Nat. Multiple Sclerosis Soc.; chmn. bd. dirs. Univ. Schs. Found., 2002—; bd. govs. Univ. Schs., 2003—; bd. of trustee Aims C.C., 2001—. With U.S. Army, 1945-47. Recipient Legislator of Yr. award DAV, 1988, Colo. Acad. Pediatrics, 1989; Mental Health award, 1990, Polit. Educator of Yr. award, Colo. Edn. Assn., 1991; fellow NSF, 1953-54, Am. Physiol. Soc., 1958, Carnegie Found., 1958-59. Mem. Am. Ornithologists Union, Am. Assn. Colls. and Univs. (bd. dirs. 1979-81), Colo. Assn. Colls. and Univs. (chmn. 1979-81), Rotary (bd. dirs. local chpt.), Sigma Xi. Independent. Mem. United Ch. Of Christ. Avocations: gardening, stamp collecting, camping, genealogy. Home and Office: 5601 18th St #51 Greeley CO 80634-2925 E-mail: rrbond@comcast.net.

BOND, SHIRLEY, legislator, educator; m. William Bond; 2 children. Diploma in Arts and Sci., Coll. of New Caledonia; student, U. Northern B.C. Bus. mgr. continuing edn, divsn. Prince George Sch. Dist.; elected rep. B.C. Legis. Assembly, Victoria, 2001, appointed minister of advanced edn., 2001—. Protocol dir. Spl. Olympics Summer Games; bd. dirs. Carey Theol. Coll., Personal Living Choices Soc., Trinity Opportunity Fund Grants Com., City of Prince George Standing Com. on Youth. Office: Stn Provincial Govt PO Box 9059 Victoria BC V8W 9E2 Canada

BOND-BROWN, BARBARA ANN, musician, educator; b. Kansas City, Mo., July 1, 1955; d. John Bartley, Jr. and Tressie Laverne (Nichols) Bond; m. Lance Elliott Brown, Mar. 11, 1979. Student, Ctrl. Mo. State U., 1973-74, 75-77, U. Mo., 1974, William Jewell Coll., 1975; studies with Karen Halverhout, Prarie Village, Kans., 1995—. Dist. accompanist Kansas City Pub. Schs., 1979-82; ind. music tchr. Independence, Mo., 1982-84; ind. music tchr., accompanist San Francisco, 1984-92; ind. music tchr. Barbara Bond-Brown Music Studio, Lee's Summit, Mo., 1992—. Developer method for young music beginners; spkr. at workshops and confs.; active adjudicator for competitions and auditions. Mem.: Federated Music Tchrs., Las Vegas Music Tchrs. Assn., Nev. Music Tchrs. Assn., Music Tchrs. Nat. Assn., Mo. Music Tchrs. Assn. (chmn. honors auditions 1993—, officer 1995—), Kans. City Music Tchrs. Assn. (v.p. achievement auditions 1994—, v.p. fall festival 1994—, chmn. pre-coll. honors auditions 1995—). Avocations: reading, writing, cooking, traveling. Home: Ste 2-249 9811 W Charleston Blvd Las Vegas NV 89117 E-mail: fridaybrown@yahoo.com.

BONDINELL, STEPHANIE, counselor, academic administrator; b. Passaic, NJ, Nov. 22, 1948; d. Peter Jr. and Gloria Lucille (Burden) Honcharuk; m. Paul Swanstrom Bondinell, July 31, 1971; 1 child, Paul Emil. BA, William Paterson U., 1970; MEd, Stetson U., 1983. Cert. elem. educator Fla., guidance counselor grades K-12 Fla. Tchr. Bloomingdale (N.J.) Bd. Edn., 1971-80; edn. dir. Fla. United Meth. Children's Home, Enterprise, 1982-89; guidance counselor Volusia County Sch. Bd., Deltona, Fla., 1988—. Coord. sch. improvement svcs., Deltona Lakes, 1996—98, Deltona Lakes, 2002—03. Sec. adv. com. Deltona Jr. HS, 1996—98, sec. PTA, 1982; vice-chmn. adv. com. Deltona Mid. Sch., 1988, chmn., 1991—92, 1991—92; mem. adv. com. Deltona HS, 1995—96; secondary sch. task force Volusia County Sch. Bd., 1986—; mem. exec. com. Volusia County Reps.; mem. Rep. Presdl. Task Force; mem. state adv. bd. Fla. Future Educators Am., 1990—92. Named Girls State Rep., Am. Legion, 1966, Deltona Lakes Tchr. of Yr., 1991; recipient Outstanding Ednl. Partnership award, S.W. Volusia C. of C., 1998, Sunshine State Medallion award, Fla. Pub. Rels. Assn., 1998, award, Volusia/Flagler Alcohol and Drug Abuse Prevention Coun., 1998—2003, Fla. Lottery Creative Tchg. award, 2002, Deltona Lakes Tchr. of Yr., 1996; Acad. scholar, Becton, Dickinson & Co., 1966, N.J. State scholar, 1966—70. Mem.: AAUW, ASCD, Internat. Platform Assn., Volusia Tchrs. Orgn., N.J. Edn. Assn., Fla. Assn. Counseling and Devel., Disvn. Learning Disabilities, Coun. Exceptional Children, Stetson U. Alumni Assn., Deltona Civic Assn., 4 Townes Federated Rep. Women's Club (sec., v.p.), Deltona Rep. Club (v.p. 1991—93). Avocations: painting, creative writing, dancing. Home: 1810 W Cooper Dr Deltona FL 32725-3623 Office: Volusia County Sch Bd 2022 Adelia Blvd Deltona FL 32725-3976 E-mail: sbondine@mail.volusia.k12.fl.us.

BONDURANT, STUART, physician, educational administrator; b. Winston-Salem, N.C., Sept. 9, 1929; s. Stuart Osborne Bondurant; m. Susan Haughton Ehringhaus, May 5, 1991; children from previous marriage: Stuart, Margaret Lynn, Nancy Vance. BS, Duke U., 1952, MD, 1953; DSc (hon.), Ind. U., 1980. Intern Duke Hosp., Durham, NC, 1953—54, resident in internal medicine, 1954—55; resident Peter Bent Brigham Hosp., Boston, 1958—59; asst. prof. medicine Ind. U. Sch. Medicine, Indpls., 1959—61, assoc. prof., 1961—66, prof., 1966—67; assoc. dir. Ind. U. Cardiovascular Research Ctr., 1961—67; chief med. br. artificial heart-myocardial infarction program NIH, Bethesda, Md., 1966—67; prof. medicine, chmn. dept., physician in chief Albany Med. Ctr. Hosp., NY, 1967—74; pres., dean Albany Med. Coll., 1974—79; prof. medicine U. N.C., Chapel Hill, 1979—, dean Sch. Medicine, 1979—94, interim dean, 1996—97; dir. Ctr. for Urban Epidemiology Studies N.Y. Acad. Medicine, N.Y.C., 1994—96. Contbr. articles to med. jours. Named Citizen Laureate, Univ. Found., Albany, 1979; recipient Disting. Alumnus award, Duke U. Sch. Medicine, 1974, Merit award, Am. Heart Assn., 1975, Thomas Jefferson award, U. N.C.-Chapel Hill, 1998. Fellow: ACP (regent, pres. 1980), Royal Coll. Physicians London, Royal Coll. Physicians Edinburgh; mem.: Am. Clin. and Climatological Assn. (pres. 1996), Assn. Am. Med. Colls. (exec. com. 1977, chmn. coun. deans 1979—82, chmn. 1993—94), Inst. of Medicine (interim pres. 1992, David Rall award 2000), Assn. Am. Physicians (pres. 1985—86), Am. Soc. Clin. Investigatio (v.p. 1974). Office: U NC Sch Medicine CB # 7000 Office of Dean Chapel Hill NC 27599-7000 E-mail: sbondurant@med.unc.edu.

BONE, ROSEMARY COOK, elementary education educator; b. Columbia, Tenn., Apr. 26, 1944; m. Thomas D. Bone Jr., Mar. 4, 1983; 1 child, Bryan D. BS, Mid. Tenn. State U., 1971. Tchr. 4th grade Mt. Pleasant (Tenn.) Elem. Sch., 1971-90, J.E. Woodard Elem. Sch., Columbia, 1990—. Mem. Nat. Tchrs. Assn., Tenn. Edn. Assn., Maury County Edn. Assn. (ednl. mini-grantee 1992-93). Baptist. Home: 3005 Mcintire Dr Columbia TN 38401-5016 Office: J E Woodard Elem Sch 207 Rutherford Ln Columbia TN 38401-5084

BONEMERY, ANNE M. language educator; b. Springfield, Mass., Nov. 1, 1950; d. Alley and Radie Bonemery. BA, Am. Internat. Coll., 1972, MAT, 1974; AS, Springfield Tech. C.C., 1993. Cert. tchr. in English and Bilingual English Mass., tchr. French and Bilingual French Mass., tchr. Spanish and Bilingual Spanish Mass. Tchr. Northampton Pub. Schs., Mass., 1972—85; prof. Springfield Tech. C.C., 1985—; acct., office mgr. Emery Devel., Ltd., Mass., 1985—. English lang. cons. Springfield Instn. Savings (now First Mass. Bank), 1996—97; treas. Emery Devel., Ltd., 1985—, bd. dirs. Vol. U.S. citizenship studies and English lang. studies Springfield Literacy Network, 1987—; bd. dirs. Am. Internat. Coll. Alumni Bd., Mass., 1997—2000, bd. dirs. Springfield chpt., 2000—. Recipient Nat. Inst. Staff and Orgnl. Devel. Excellence award, U. Tex. Austin, 1997, 2000, Ptnr. in Philanthropy award, We. Mass. chpt. Assn. Fundraising Profls., 2001. Mem.: TESOL, MLA, NEA, Springfield Tech. C.C. Profl. Assn. (bldg. rep.), We. Mass. Fgn. Lang. Assn., Mass. Fgn. Lang. Assn., Mass. Assn. TESOL, Mass. Tchrs. Assn., Am. Coun. Tchg. Fgn. Langs., Am. Assn. Tchrs. French, Springfield Libr. and Mus. Assn., Sigma Lambda Kappa (sec. 1985—2000). Avocations: travel, reading, photography, hiking. Office: Springfield Tech CC One Armory Sq Springfield MA 01105

BONEY, NORMA MARIE DAVIS, elementary school educator; b. San Antonio, Aug. 13, 1950; d. Odie E. Jr. and Nadine (Jefferson) Davis; m. Marcus Boney, Sept. 26; 1 child, Marcus Boney II. BS, Prairie View A&M U., 1972, MEd, 1974. Cert. tchr. home econs., elem. edn., guidance and counseling, phys. edn.; cert. mid-mgmt. adminstr., Tex. Tchr. various subjects, including phys. edn. Shadydale Elem., Houston, 1973—, counselor, 1994—. Elem. phys. edn. cons. North Forest Ind. Sch. Dist., Houston, 1990-91. Author: (dist. curriculum guides) Science, 1988, Physical Education, 1985—, Art, 1987-91, APEX, 1989-90, Health 1990—. Prog. chmn. Shadydale PTA, Houston; site coord. Mayor's Summer Fun Youth Prog., Houston, 1977; sr. counselor Young Men's Christian Assn., San Antonio, 1985, 87. Named Tchr. of Yr., Shadydale Elem., Houston, 1986-87, 89-90, Elem. Tchr. of Yr., North Forest Ind. Sch. Dist., 1989-90, Outstanding Educator, 1990-91, Outstanding Coach, Shadydale Elem. and PTA, 1990-91. Mem. AAHPERD, NEA, Am. Fedn. Tchrs., Tex. State Tchrs. Assn., Greater Houston Reading Coun., Tex. Counseling Assn., Tex. Assn. Health, Phys. Edn., Recreation and Dance, Houston Area Alliance Black Sch. Educators, Tex. Edn. Agy. (mem. Tex. state book com., mem. site-based decision-making com. 1992—, mem. prin.'s adv. bd. 1992—, Meritorious award 1986), Am. Softball Assn. Methodist. Avocations: coaching, bowling, softball, drill team, swimming. Home: 6315 Westover St Houston TX 77087-6545

BONFIELD, ARTHUR EARL, lawyer, educator; b. New York City, May 12, 1936; s. Louis and Rose (Lesser) B.; m. Doris (Harfenist), June 10, 1958 (dec. 1995); 1 child, Lauren; m. Eva (Tsalikian), Apr. 8, 2000. BA, Bklyn. Coll., 1956; JD, Yale Univ., 1960, LLM, 1961, post grad. (sr. fellow), 1961-62; DHL (hon.), Cornell Coll., 1999. Bar: Conn., 1961; Iowa, 1966. Asst. prof. U. Iowa Law Sch., 1962-65, assoc. prof., 1965-66, prof., 1966-69, Law Sch. Found. disting. prof., 1969-72, John Murray disting. prof., 1972—2003, assoc. dean for rsch., 1985—, Alan D. Vestal disting. chair, 2003—; summer vis. prof. law U. Mich., 1970; summer vis. prof. U. Tenn., 1972, U. N.C., 1974, Hofstra U., 1977, Lewis and Clark U., 1984. Vis. prof. law U. Mich., 1970, U. Tenn, 1972, U. N.C., 1974, Hofstra U., 1977, Lewis and Clark U., 1984; gen. counsel spl. joint com. state adminstrv. procedure act Iowa Gen. Assembly, 1974-75; spl. counsel adminstrv. procedure exec. br. State of Iowa, 1975; chmn. com. constl. law Nat. Conf. Bar Examiners Multi-State Bar Exam, 1977-2003; reporter 1981 Model State Adminstrv. Procedure Act, Nat. Conf. Commn. Uniform State Laws, 1979-81; cons. Ark. State Constl. Conv., 1980; chmn. Iowa Governor's Com. State Pub. Records Law, 1983; Iowa Commn. Nat. Conf. Commn. on Uniform State Laws, 1984-2000; chmn. Iowa Governor's Task Force on Uniform Adminstrv. Rules, 1985-92; chmn. Iowa Governor's Task Force Team on Regulatory Process, Rule Making, and Rules Rev., 1999-2000. Prin. draftsman Iowa Civil Rights Act, 1965; Iowa Fair Housing Act, 1967; Iowa Adminstrv. Procedure Act, 1974,; Iowa Open Meetings Act, 1978; Iowa Civil Rights Act, 1978; Amendments to Iowa Pub. Records Law, 1984; Amendments to Iowa Adminstrv. Procedure Act, 1998; author: State Adminstrv. Rule Making, 1986; State and Federal Adminstrv. Law, 1989; contbg. numerous articles to law jour. Recipient Outstanding Svc. to Civil Liberties Award, Iowa Civil Liberties Union, 1974; Hancher Finkbine Outstanding Faculty Mem. Award, U. Iowa, 1980; Faculty Excellence Award, Iowa Bd. Regents, 1995; Outstanding Law Sch. Tchg. Award, U. Iowa, 1996; Frederick Klocksiem fellow Aspen Inst. Humanistic Studies, summer 1978. Mem. ABA (chmn. divsn. state adminstrv. law 1976-80, coun. 1980-84, chmn. sect. 1987-88, sect. adminstrv. law and regulatory practice); Am. Law Inst. (life mem.); Iowa State Bar Assn. (chmn. com. adminstrv. law 1971-85, coun. sect. adminstr. law 1990-93, 94-97, 98-99, 2000-03, reporter and mem., task force on state adminstrv. law reform 1994-96; Pres. Award Outstanding Svc. to Bar and Public 1996); Am. Coun. Learned Soc. (del. from Assn. Am. Law Sch. 1984-94). Home: 206 Mahaska Dr Iowa City IA 52246-1606 Office: U Iowa Sch Law Iowa City IA 52242

BONHAM, MARTHA DIANNE, elementary art educator, watercolorist; b. Columbus, Ga., June 6, 1953; d. William Wallace and Martha Louise (Lumpkin) Ward; m. John Andrew Bonham, May 6, 1989; 1 child, Jessie Ann. BA in Art Edn., Columbus Coll., 1976. Cert. in elem. and secondary art edn., Ga. Paraprofl. Blanchard Elem. Pub. Sch., Columbus, 1989; asst. tchr. spl. edn. Columbus Specialized Presch., 1988-89; art tchr. Rigdon Rd. Elem. Pub. Sch., Columbus, 1989-90, Rose Hill Elem. Pub. Sch., Columbus, 1989-90, Waverly Terrace Pub. Elem. Sch., Columbus, 1989-90, Eastway Elem. Pub. Sch., Columbus, 1990-92, Britt David Elem. Pub. Sch., Columbus, 1990-92; spl. edn. asst. tchr. Bristol (Vt.) Elem. Pub. Sch., 1993-94. Swift Textiles Inc. scholar, 1971. Christian. Avocations: watercolor, crafts, cooking, camping, gardening. Home: 8025 Waterview Ct Midland GA 31820-3456

BONHAM-HONTZ, NANCY LYNNE, art educator; b. Nanticoke, Pa., May 15, 1939; d. Russel George and Mildred Elizabeth (Symons) B.; m. Arthur Dean Hontz, Aug. 19, 1961. BS in Art Edn., Wilkes Coll., 1961; postgrad., Bloomsburg (Pa.) State Coll., 1962, Kutztown (Pa.) State Coll., 1963, Coll. Misericordia, 1973-75. Cert. art instr., supr., Pa. Art supr. Hanover (Pa.) Area Schs., 1961-62; jr. high sch.-mid. sch., art educator Dallas (Pa.) Area Schs., 1962-91, retired, 1991—. Illustrator (book) Verses & Visions, 1984. Mem. State PASR, Luzerne/Wyo. PASR, Cider Painters of Am., Sordoni Art Gallery, MacDonald Art Gallery (life). Avocations: crafts, clay, plaster, wood. Home: RR 2 Box 2117 Shickshinny PA 18655-9657

BONILLA, DAISY ROSE, parochial school English language educator; b. N.Y.C., May 9, 1964; d. Frank J. and Aurea (Rivera) B. A in Computer Sci. cum laude, Bayamon U., 1984; BA in Edn. summa cum laude, Caribbean U., 1991, MA in TESOL. Cert. tchr. secondary English. Data entry clk. Dept. Health, San Juan, 1987-91; tchr. English Colegio Santa Rosa, Bayamon, P.R., 1991-92, Disciples of Christ Acad., Bayamon, 1992-95, Colegio Marista, Guaynabo, 1995—. Recipient Hostos medal Tchr.'s Assn., 1991, Outstanding Internship award Phi Delta Kappa, 1991. Mem. ASCD, Nat. Coun. Tchrs. English. Home: 17 Calle 12 Bayamon Gardens Bayamon PR 00957-1719

BONINA, SALLY ANNE, secondary school educator; b. Stamford, Conn., Jan. 30, 1951; d. Salvatore Edward and Mary Dolores (Giancola) Bonina; children: Vincent Salvatore, Michael Christopher. BA in Spanish with honors, Coll. New Rochelle, 1972; MS in Reading Cons., Bridgeport U., 1975; 6th yr. degree adminstrn., So. Conn. State U., 1994. Spanish tchr. Westhill H.S., Stamford, 1973-78; pvt. tutor John Jay Middle and High Schs., Katonah, N.Y., 1978-89; substitute tchr. Katonah (N.Y.)/Lewisboro Schs., 1990-91; Spanish tchr. Cloonan Middle Sch., Stamford, 1991-2001, Shelton (Conn.) H.S., 2001—. Scheduling com. mem. Cloonan Sch., Stamford, 1992-95, student-of-the-month com., 1993-94, character counts com., 1998—; active middle sch. confs., Champion Internat., Stamford, 1991-94; mem. fgn. lang. curriculum writing team Stamford Pub. Schs., 1997-99, character counts com., 1998-2001, prof. devel. com., 1999—2001; ednl. adv. Nat. Young Leaders Conf., Washington, D.C. Religious edn. tchr. St. Aloysius Ch., New Canaan, Conn., 1984-91; pub. ctr. coord. Meadow Pond Sch., Katonah, 1988-90, book fair co-chairperson, 1989-90; schedule co-coord. Westchester (N.Y.) Putnam Baseball Assn., 1992-94; mem. Cloonan Site Based Com., 1997-98; mentor Connecticut BEST program, 2000—. Mem.: ASCD, Stamford Edn. Assn. (negotiations team 1999—2000), Shelton Edn. Assn. (negotiations team 2002), Am. Coun. Tchg. Fgn. Langs., N.E. League Mid. Schs., Adminstrn. and Supervision Assn. So. Conn. State U. Roman Catholic. Avocations: swimming, reading, walking, cooking, theatre. Office: Shelton H S 120 Meadow St Shelton CT 06484

BONJEAN, CHARLES MICHAEL, foundation executive, sociologist, educator; b. Pekin, Ill., Sept. 7, 1936; s. Bruno and Catherine Ann (Dancey) B. BA, Drake U., 1957; MA, U. N.C., 1959, PhD in Sociology, 1963. Mem. faculty U. Tex., Austin, 1963—2003, Hogg prof. sociology, 1974—2003, chmn. dept., 1972-74; exec. assoc. Hogg Found., 1974-79; v.p., 1979-93; exec. dir. Hogg Found., 1993—2003. Sociology editor Chandler Pub. Co., 1967-73, Crowell Pub. Co., 1973-77, Dorsey Press, 1979-88, Wadsworth Pub. Co., 1988-93; mem. coun. Intern-Univ. Consortium Polit. and Social Rsch., 1972-76; mem. steering com. Coun. Social Sci. Jour. Editors, 1975-81; 2d v.p. Conf. S.W. Found., 1984-85, 1st v.p., 1985-86, pres., 1986-87; exec. com. Grantmakers Evaluation Network, 1994-98; mem. exec. com. Grantmakers in Health, 1995-98, bd. dirs., 1993-2000; chmn. rsch. com. Coun. Founds., 1991-94, bd. dirs., 1998-2003; mem. adv. com. Am. Sociol. Found., 1992-97, chmn., 1995-97. Co-author: Sociological Measurement, 1967, Sociology: A Core Text with Adapted Readings, 1990; co-editor: Blacks in the United States, 1969, Planned Social Intervention, 1969, Community Politics, 1971, Political Attitudes and Public Opinion, 1972, The Idea of Culture in the Social Sciences, 1973, Social Science in America, 1976, The Mexican Origin People in the United States, 1985, Community Care of the Chronically Mentally Ill, 1989, Mental Health Research in Texas, 1990; editor Social Sci. Quar., 1966-94; cons. editor Am. Jour. Sociology, 1974-76, The Am. Sociologist, 1990-96; contbr. to profl. jours. Bd. dirs. Lake Travis Ednl. Found., 1986-91. Recipient tchg. excellence award U. Tex. Students Assn., 1965, Alumni Disting. Svc. award Drake U., 1979, Disting. Svc. award Southwestern Social Sci. Assn., 2001; Sigma Delta Chi scholar, 1957. Mem. Am. Sociol. Assn. (chmn. cmty. sect. 1976-78, publs. com. 1978-81, chmn. 1979-81, pres. sect. on orgns. 1983-84, chmn. dist. scholarship com. 1992-84, coun. 1985-88, exec. office and budget com. 1994-97), Southwestern Sociol. Assn. (pres. 1972-73), Southwestern Social Sci. Assn. (exec. com. 1966-97, v.p. 1992-93, pres.-elect 1993-94, pres. 1994-95, Disting. Svc. award 2001), Philos. Soc. Tex. Home: 16310 Clara Van St Austin TX 78734-3928 E-mail: bonjean@mail.utexas.edu.

BONKOVSKY, HERBERT LLOYD, gastroenterologist, educator; b. Cleve., Dec. 29, 1941; s. Otto Rudolph and Hanna (Ludwig) B.; m. Marilyn Louise Cahoon, June 3, 1967; children: Laura, Sarah, Erik. AB, Earlham Coll., 1963; MD, Case Western Res. U., 1967. Diplomate Am. Bd. Internal Medicine, Am. Bd. Gastroenterology, Nat. Bd. Med. Examiners. Intern Duke U. Med. Ctr., 1967-68; rsch. fellow, chief resident Dartmouth Med. Sch., Hanover, NH, 1971-73, asst. prof., then assoc. prof., 1974-83, prof., 1983-85; rsch., clin. fellow Yale U. Sch. Medicine, New Haven, 1973-74; dir. digestive disease and liver rsch. lab. VA Med. Ctr., White River Junction, Vt., 1976-85; prof. medicine and biochem., dir. liver study unit Emory U., Atlanta, 1985-90, dir. hemochromatosis unit, dir. porphyria unit, 1985-90; dir. digestive disease lab. Emory Clinic, 1988-90; dir. divsn. digestive disease and nutrition U. Mass. Med. Ctr., 1990—2000, prof. medicine biochemistry and molecular biology, 1990—2002; dir. Liver-Biliary-Pancreatic Ctr., Ctr.Study Disorders Iron and Porphyrin Metabolism Liver-Biliary-Pancreatic Ctr. U. Conn. Health Ctr., 2002—, dir. clin. rsch. Liver-Biliary-Pancreatic Ctr., Ctr.Study Disorders Iron and Porphyrin Metabolism, 2002—. Chmn. sci. adv. bd. Iron Disorders Inst. Author, editor ednl. materials, articles, papers, book chpts. Bd. deacons Evang. Congl. Ch., Harvard, Mass., 1994-2000; mem. adminstrv. bd. Oak Grove Meth. Ch., Decatur, Ga., 1989-90; trustee, chmn. bd. Norwich (Vt.) Congl. Ch., 1975-78, moderator, 1978-85, deacon, 1978-79; mem. Harvard Pro-Musica, 1990-93. Lt. comdr. USPHS, 1969—. Earlham merit scholar, 1959-63, Binz Meml. scholar, 1963-67. Fellow ACP, Am. Coll. Gastroenterology, Alpha Omega Alpha; mem. Am. Fedn. Clin. Rsch., Am. Soc. Clin. Investigation, Am. Gastroenterol. Assn., Assn. Am. Physicians, Am. Porphyria Found. (chair profl. edn. com.), Am. Assn. for Study Liver Diseases (editorial bd., nominating com., assoc. editor Hepatology), AMA, Am. Soc. Biochemistry and Molecular Biology, European and Internat. Assn. Study Liver. Avocations: tennis, basketball, cycling, swimming, skiing. Office: U Conn Health Ctr Farmington CT 06030

BONNER, BESTER DAVIS, school system administrator; b. Mobile, Ala., June 9, 1938; d. Samuel Matthew and Alma (Davis) Davis; m. Wardell Bonner, Nov. 28, 1964; children: Shawn Patrick, Matthew Wardell. BS, Ala. State Coll., 1959; MS in Library Sci., Syracuse U., 1966; PhD, U. Ala., 1982. Cert. tchr. Librarian Westside High Sch., Talladega, Ala., 1959-64; librarian, tchr. lit. Lane Elem. Sch., Birmingham, Ala., 1964-65; head librarian Jacksonville (Ala.) Elem. Lab. Sch., 1965-70; asst. prof. library media Ala. A&M U., Huntsville, 1970-74; adminstv. asst. to pres. Miles Coll., Birmingham, 1974-78, chmn. div. edn., 1978-85; specialist media Montgomery County Pub. Schs., Md., 1987-88; dir. libr. and media svcs. div. curriculum and ednl. tech. Dist. of Columbia Pub. Schs., 1988—. Forum leader Nat. Issues Forum, Domestic Policy Assn. U. Ala., Birmingham, 1983-84; mem. Libr. Svcs. Construction Act Adv. Com. Contbr. writer The Developing Black Family, 1975. Chmn. ethics commn. St. Ala., Montgomery 1977-81; radiothorn site coordinator United Negro Coll. Fund, Birmingham 1981. Mem. ALA, Ala. Instructional Media Assn. (pres. dist. II 1971-72), Assn. Women Deans and Adminstrs., Com. 100, D.C. Assn. Sch. Librs., D.C. Libr. Com., Am. Assn. Sch. Librs., Nat. Assn. State Ednl. Profls. Democrat. Methodist. Avocations: writing, speaking, consulting, piano. Home: 9601 Burgess Ln Silver Spring MD 20901-4701

BONNER, BRENDA CAROL, secondary school English educator; b. Whitesboro, Tex., Nov. 8, 1948; d. John Wesley, Jr. and Wanda Lee (Shirey) Bullard Sikes; stepfather: Walter Marvin Sikes; m. Richard Donald Bonner, June 30, 1979. BA in English, North Tex. State U., 1971, MEd, 1982. Cert. tchr., Tex. High sch. English and Spanish tchr. Springlake-Earth (Tex.) Ind. Sch. Dist., 1972-74, Van Alstyne (Tex.) Ind. Sch. Dist., 1974-90; 10th grade English tchr. Pleasant Grove Ind. Sch. Dist., Texarkana, Tex., 1992—2003; high sch. English tchr. Leonard (Tex.) Ind. Sch. Dist., 2003—. Mem. Nat. Coun. Tchrs. English. Tex. Coun. Tchrs. English, Tex. State Tchrs. Assn. Democrat. Baptist. Avocations: crafts, calligraphy, reading, movies, music. Office: Leonard Ind Sch Dist 1 Tiger Alley Leonard TX 75452

BONNER, JACK WILBUR, III, psychiatrist, educator, administrator; b. Corpus Christi, Tex., July 30, 1940; s. Jack Wilbur and Irldene (Turner) B.; m. Myra Lynn Taylor; children: Jack Wilbur, IV, Katherine Lynn, Shelley Bliss. AA, Del Mar Coll., Corpus Christi, 1960; BA with honors, U. Tex., Austin, 1961; MD, S.W. Med. Sch., U. Tex., Dallas, 1965. Diplomate Am. Bd. Psychiatry and Neurology. Intern U. Ark. Med. Center, 1965-66; resident Duke U. Med. Center, 1966-69; assoc. in psychiatry Highland Hosp. divsn. Duke U. Med. Center, Asheville, N.C., 1971, asst. prof. psychiatry, 1972-80, dir. outpatient services, 1972-75, med. dir., 1975-81; chmn. bd. dirs., CEO, med. dir. Highland Hosp., Asheville, N.C., 1981-92; med. dir. The Oaks Psychiat. Health Sys., Austin, Tex., 1992-93, exec. med. dir., 1993-94; med. dir. Behavioral Health Svcs. Greenville (S.C.) Hosp. Sys., 1994—, adminstr. Behavioral Health Svcs., 1996-2000, acad. chair, 1999—. Asst. clin. prof. Duke U. Med. Ctr., Durham, N.C., 1982-87, asst. cons. prof. psychiatry, 1987—; clin. assoc. prof. U. N.C. Sch. Medicine, Chapel Hill, 1986-92, Quillen-Dishner Coll. Medicine, Johnson City, Tenn., 1989-92, U. Tex. Health Sci. Ctr., San Antonio, 1993-94, U. S.C. Sch. Medicine, Columbia, 1995—. Author: (with others) The Psychology of Discipline, 1983, Unmasking the Psychopath: Antisocial Personality and Related Syndromes, 1986; contbr. articles to profl. jours. Chmn. bd. dirs. The Highland Found., 1980-93; bd. dirs. Western N.C. Med. Peer Rev. Found., 1975-78; trustee La Amistad Found., Maitland, Fla., 1985-95, N.C. Symphony, 1987-92, Cooper Riis Found., Mill Spring, N.C., 2000—. Fellow Am. Psychiat. Assn. (Disting. Life Fellow; trustee 1999—, Warren Williams award 2002), So. Psychiat. Assn. (v.p. 1984-85, chmn. bd. regents 1988-89, pres.-elect 1991-92, pres. 1992-93), Am. Coll. Psychiatrists (treas. 1992-95, 2d v.p. 1999-2000, 1st v.p. 2000-01, pres.-elect 2001-02, pres. 2002-03, E.B. Bowis award 2000); mem. AMA, Nat. Assn. Psychiat. Health Sys. (trustee 1989-94, 1st v.p. 1990-91, pres.-elect 1991-92, pres. 1992-93), Am. Group Psychotherapy Assn., Nat. Acads. Practice, Buncombe County (NC) Med. Soc. (pres.-elect 1982, pres. 1983), NC Psychiat. Assn. (pres.-elect 1981-82, pres. 1982-83), Nat. Anorexic Aid Soc. (nat. anorexia adv. coun. 1979-86), So. Med. Assn. (sec. sect. on neurology, neurosurgery and psychiatry 1977-80, chmn.-elect 1980-81, chmn. 1981-82), Ctrl. Neuropsychiat. Hosp. Assn. (councillor 1981-85, pres.-elect 1982-83, pres. 1983-84), Group Advancement Psychiatry (treas. 1991-99, pres.-elect 1999-2001, pres. 2001-03), U. Tex. Southwestern Med. Sch. Alumni Assn. (bd. dir. 1988-95, pres. 1989-91), Benjamin Rush Soc., Phi Theta Kappa. Home: Four Brookside Way Greenville SC 29605-1212 Office: Greenville Hosp Sys Behavioral Health Svcs 701 Grove Rd Greenville SC 29605-5601 E-mail: jbonner@ghs.org.

BONNER, KATHRYN ESTHER, nursing administrator, nursing educator; b. Pensacola, Fla., Jan. 27, 1943; d. Minor Jimmie and Mary Leona (Fagerstrom) B. Diploma, Providence Hosp. Sch. Nursing, Mobile, Ala., 1967; AA, Pensacola Jr. Coll., 1974; BS, U. West Fla., 1988, MS, 1991. RN, Fla., Ala. Asst. chief aeromed. nursing 37 Air EVAC group, Tampa, Fla.; dir. nurses Walton County Convalescent Ctr., De Funiak Springs, Fla.; dir. home health Choctaw Valley Home Health, De Funiak Springs; dir. nursing svcs. Naval Reserve Fleet Hosp. 14, Jacksonville, Fla. Oper. rm. educator Flowers Hosp., Dothan, Ala. Commanding officer USN, 1967-73, Vietnam, flight nurse USAF, 1979-88; capt. USNR. Mem. ANA, VFW (life), Assn. Mil. Surgeons of U.S. (life), Res. Officers Assn. (life). Home: PO Box 415 Defuniak Springs FL 32435-0415 E-mail: aflying06@gdsys.net.

BONNER, LAWRENCE EMEROLD See AQEEL, SULAIMAN

BONNER, MARY CHRISTINE, secondary education educator, school system administrator; b. Phila., Dec. 12, 1934; d. Joseph Fanelli and Christine Mary (Ferri) Gabage; m. John Joseph Bonner, Sept. 11, 1954; children: Lynne M. Appino, Brian Patrick. BA in English, Gwynedd-Mercy Coll., 1973; MA in English, Villanova U., 1976. Cert. English tchr., Pa., Hawaii. Instr. evening divsn. Gwynedd Mercy Coll.; elem. sch. tchr. St. Cath., St. John B., Bucks County, 1956-59, 68-73; English tchr. St. Hubert High Sch., Phila., 1973-74, A.B. Wood Girls High Sch., Warminster, Pa., 1974-81; chmn. English dept. Bishop Egan High Sch., Fairless Hills, Pa., 1981-88; dean of activities A.B. Wood High Sch., Warminster, 1988—, asst. prin. for student affairs, 1994—. Mem. English curriculum com. for diocese of Phila. (Pa.), Secondary Sch. System, Archdiocese of Phila., 1980-88; lectr. in English sch. cont. studies La Salle U., 1981—; presenter in field. Mem. Lambda Iota Tau Internat. (v.p. 1973-74, pres. 1980-81), Delta Kappa Gamma Internat. Avocations: piano, painting, reading, astronomy. Office: AB Wood High Sch 655 York Rd Warminster PA 18974-2098

BONNER, SHIRLEY HARROLD, business communications educator; b. Pitts., July 22, 1929; d. William DeWitt Jr. and Erma Dorothy (Ruppert) Harrold; m. Joseph A. Bonner, Apr. 21, 1956; children: Margaret Leslie, Joseph Edward. BS in Edn., U. Pitts., 1951, MEd, 1971, PhD, 1981. With Gulf Oil Corp., Pitts.; tchr. Three Rivers Bus. Sch., Pitts., Antwerp (Belgium) Internat. Sch., Duff's Bus. Sch., Pitts., C.C. of Allegheny County, Pitts., Learning Ctr. Chatham Coll., 1994—. Pres. Chatham Coll. literacy bd., 1997—. Author: Margaret of Austria, Governess of the Low Countries, 1507-1530, 2 vols.; contbr. articles to The Balance Sheet. Mem. Baltzer Meyer Hist. Soc.; past bd. dirs. Am. Protestant Ch. of Antwerp. Mem.: AAUW (pres. DuBois area br. 1967—69), Assn. for Bus. Comm., World Affairs Coun. Pitts. (consul), Delta Zeta. Republican. Avocations: travel, mysteries, biographies. Home: 403 Denniston Ave Pittsburgh PA 15206-4411

BONNER, THOMAS, JR., English language educator; b. New Orleans, Sept. 19, 1942; s. Thomas and Mercedes Mary (Vulliet) B.; m. Judith Ann Hopkins, Aug. 27, 1966; children: Ashley Elizabeth, Laura Vulliet. BA, Southeastern La. U., 1965; MA, Tulane U., 1968, PhD, 1975. English instr. U. Southwestern La., Lafayette, 1966-68; prof. Xavier U. La., New Orleans, 1971—, Kellogg prof. English, 2001—, chair dept. English, 1976—82, 2003—. Disting. vis. prof. English USAF Acad., 1991-92, 2000-02; reader-evaluator Ednl. Testing Svc., Princeton, N.J.; writer-judge Varsity Quiz Bowl, WYES-TV, New Orleans, 1982-92; book reviewer Times-Picayune, New Orleans, 1980-89; editor Xavier Rev. Press, 1988—. Author: William Faulkner, 1980, The Kate Chopin Companion, 1988, The Epistolary Poe, 2001; editor Xavier Rev., 1982—, Above Ground, 1993; editor and contbr. John Faulkner Issue of Miss. Quarterly, 2001; author numerous poems; contbr. articles to profl. jours. Dir. lit. series, New Orleans Pub. Libr. and NEH, 1979. Recipient Bush Found. award, 1990; United Negro Coll. Fund-Mellon fellow, 1982. Mem. MLA, South Ctrl. MLA (pres. 1996, exec. com. 1990-92), South Atlantic MLA, Soc. Study So. Lit. (exec. com. 1983-85, 93—), Conf. on Christianity and Lit., South Ctrl. Conf. on Christianity and Lit. (exec. com. 1979—), So. Am. Studies Assn. (pres. 2002—). Roman Catholic. Avocations: tennis, hiking, fishing, travel.

BONNER, THOMAS PERRY, academic administrator; b. Meridian, Miss., Dec. 15, 1958; s. Martin Columbus and Edith Howard (Grayson) B.; m. Deborah Ann Kenyon, Nov. 26, 1982; children: Hannah Clare, Sarah Anne. BSBA, U. So. Miss., 1980. Buyer Sunbeam Appliance Co., Oakbrook, Ill., 1980-81, product mgr., 1981-83; field rep. U. So. Miss., Hattiesburg, 1983-87, dir. ann. fund, 1987-89, dir. planned giving, 1989-91; assoc. dir. planned giving U. of the South, 1991-94, exec. dir. of devel., 1994-97, v.p. for univ. rels., 1998—. Pres. Miss. Com. on Planned Giving, 1991, Chattanooga Area Planned Giving Coun., 1995. Bd. dirs. U. So. Miss. Wesley Found. (treas., fin. chair 1988-89), United Way Forrest-Lamar, Hattiesburg, 1985; mem. adminstrv. bd. Parkway Heights United Meth. Ch., 1987, coun. on ministries, 1987. Named one of Outstanding Young Man in Am., 1982. Mem. Coun. for Advancement and Support Edn., Am. Mktg. Assn., Beta Gamma Sigma, Omicron Delta Epsilon. Republican. Avocations: reading, woodworking, hunting, gardening. Office: U of South Office Univ Relations 735 University Ave Sewanee TN 37383-0001

BONNIE, RICHARD JEFFREY, law educator, lawyer; b. Richmond, Va., Aug. 22, 1945; s. Herbert Herman and Helene Selma (Berz) B.; m. Kathleen Ford, June 15, 1967; children: Joshua Ford, Zachary Andrew, Jessica Katherine. BA, Johns Hopkins U., 1966; LLB, U. Va., 1969. Var: Va. 1969, U.S. Dist. Ct. (ea. dist.) Va. 1969; U.S. Ct. Appeals (4th cir.) 1969, U.S. Supreme Ct. 1986. Asst. prof. law U. Va., Charlottesville, 1969-70, assoc. prof., 1973-77, prof., 1977-87, John S. Battle prof., 1987—; dir. Inst. Law, psychiatry, and Pub. Policy, 1979—. Vis. prof. Cornell Law Sch., 1993-94; assoc. dir. nat. Commn. Marijuana and Drug Abuse, 1971-73; reporter Nat. Conf. Commrs. on Uniform State Laws, 1972-74; cons. Spl. Action Office for Drug Abuse Prevention Exec. Office of the Pres., 1973-75; spl. asst. to U.S. Atty. Gen., 1975; mem. and sec. Nat. Adv. Coun. on Drug Abuse, 1975-80; mem. Com. on Problem of Drug Dependence, Inc., 1979-84; charter fellow Coll. Problems of Drug Dependence, 1992—; cons. Am. Psychiat. Assn., Coun. Psychiatry and Law, 1979—; mem. U.S. State Dept. Del. to investigate psychiat. practices in the Soviet Union, 1989; mem. World Psychiat. Assn. rev. team to investigate Soviet psychiatry, 1991; mem. adv. bd. permanent coordination office Reforms in psychiatry in Ctrl. and Ea. Europe, former Soviet Union, 1993—; bd. dirs. Geneva Initiative on Psychiatry, 1996—; pres. Am. Friends of Geneva Initiatives on Psychiatry, 1997—, mem. MacArthur Found. Network on Mental Health and the Law, 1988-96; bd. dirs. Va. Capital Representation Resource Ctr., 1994-97, 2002—; mem. MacArthur Found. Network on Mandated Treatment, 2000—. Author: The Marijuana Conviction: The History of Marijuana Prohibition in the United States, 1974, 2d edit. 1999, Legal Aspects of Drug Dependence, 1975, Psychiatrists and the Legal Process: Diagnosis and Debate, 1977, Marijuana Use and Criminal Sanctions: Essays in the Theory and Practice of Decriminalization, 1980, Criminal Law: Cases and Materials, 1982, 2d edit., 1986, The Trial of John W. Hinckley, Jr.: A Case Study in the Insanity Defense, 1986, rev. edit. 2000, Criminal Law, 1997, Growing Up Tobacco Free, 1994, Mental Disorder, Work Disability and the Law, 1997, Reducing the Burden of Injury, 1999, The Evolution of Mental Health Law, 2001, Elder Mistreatment, 2002, Adjudicative Competence, 2002. Chmn. Va. Human Rights Com., Dept. mental health and Mental Retardation, 1979-85; bd. dirs. Coll. on Problem of Drug Dependence, 1996-2000. Served to capt. USAF, 1970-73. Inst. Criminology fellow Cambridge U., 1977. Fellow: Va. Law Found.; mem.: NAS (nat. assoc.), ABA (criminal justice-mental health stds. project adv. bd. 1981—87), Inst. Medicine (Yarmolinsky medal 2002), Am. Acad. Psychiat. Law (Amicus award 1994), World Psychiat. Assn. (rev. team to investigate Soviet psychiatry 1991), Va. Bar Assn. (chmn. com. mentally disabled 1981—90, criminal law sect. coun. 1992—96), Am. Psychiat. Assn. (Isaac Ray award 1998, Spl. Presdl. Commendation 2003), Nat. Rsch. Coun. (com. on data and rsch. for policy on illicit drugs 1998—2000, chair com. elder abuse and neglect 2001—02, common law and justcie com. 2002—, chair com. underage drinking 2002—, divsn. com. behavioral and social scis. and edn. 2003—), Inst. Medicine of NAS (bd. neurosci. and behavioral health 1992—2001, vice chair com. preventing nicotine dependence in children and youth 1993—94, membership com. 1995—98, chair com. on opportunities in drug abuse rsch. 1995—96, chair com. injury prevention control 1997—98, com. to assess sci. base for tobacco harm reduction 1999—2001, com. to assess sys. for protection of human rsch. subjects 2000—02, chair com. to propose strategy to prevent/reduce underage drinking 2002—03). Office: U Va Sch Law 580 Massie Rd Charlottesville VA 22903

BONO, CHARLENE CECILIA, elementary school educator; b. New Orleans, Mar. 19, 1949; d. Charles Eugene and Cecilia Hattie (Poche') B. BA in Elem. Edn., Nicholls State U., 1967-71; summer student, Nicholls State/La. Tech., Rome, 1971, U. N.O., Austria, 1976, St. Mary's Dominican, Europe, 1983. Tchr. Jefferson Parish Sch. Bd., Metairie, La., 1972—. Chairperson Instl. Cm. Sch. Effectiveness Team, Metairie, 1988-90; coop. tchr. U. New Orleans, 1993-94. Career Edn. grantee Jefferson Parish, Metairie, 1986; named Tchr. of Yr. Bridgedale Elem., Metairie, 1989, Supr. Tchr. U. New Orleans, 1993-94. Mem. Internat. Reading Assn. Democrat. Roman Catholic. Avocations: reading, counted cross stitch.

BONONI, ROBERT ANDREW, music educator; b. Uniontown, Pa., Sept. 21, 1950; s. Charles and Ann Bononi. BS in Music Edn., Duquesne U., 1972, MS in Music Edn., 1981; postgrad., Northwestern U., 1990; D Music Edn., U. Cin., 2000. Grad. asst. Duquesne U., Pitts.; instrumental music tchr. grades 6-8 Uniontown (Pa.) Area Schs., 1972-74; profl. clarinetist Monterey (Calif.) Symphony, 1974-78; asst. to the dean, founding dir. Bene-Duq Cmty. Sch. of Music Duquesne U., Pitts., 1979-81; instrumental music tchr. grades 4-8 Keystone Oaks Schs., Pitts., 1980—, gen. music tchr. grades 1-8, 1985—; doctoral tchg. asst. Coll.-Conservatory of Music, U. Cin., Ohio, 1990-92. Clarinet instr., chamber music coach Hartnell Coll., Salinas, Calif., 1977-78; del. Cross Disciplinary Collequium, The Coll. Bd.; presenter in field. Mem. educators com. Pitts. Symphony Orch. Recipient A Gift of Time award Am. Family Inst.; summer fellow Northwestern U.; scholar The Aspen Music Festival, Vera Heinz scholar Pitts. Youth Symphony. Mem. ASCD, NEA, Am. Sch. Band Dirs. Assn., Music Educators Nat. Conf., Pa. Music Educators Assn. Home: 109 Lakeview Dr Mc Murray PA 15317-2732 Office: Keystone Oaks Sch Dist Keystone Oaks HS 1000 Kelton Ave Pittsburgh PA 15216 E-mail: rbononi@aol.com., bononi@kosd.org.

BOODHOOSINGH, YASMIN SHANTA, secondary education educator; b. Washington, May 6, 1950; d. Lazina Ali BoodhooSingh. BS in Spl. Edn., U. Md., 1972; MS in Spl. Edn., Coppin State Coll., Balt., 1974; postgrad., Loyola Coll., Balt., 1974—. Tchr. Balt. City Pub. Schs., 1973, Catonsville Middle Sch., 1973-75, Lansdowne High Sch., 1975-86; with WEBCO, 1987-88; field counselor Balt. County Occupational Tng. Adminstrn., 1989; tchr. social studies and English Ea. Voc-Tech High Sch., 1986—, spl. edn. tchr.-in-charge, 1983-84, spl. edn. dept. chmn., 1984-86; adj. faculty mem. Catonsville C.C., 1988-91; tchr., coord. coop. edn. Lansdowne High Sch., 1991-93; tech. prep./spl. edn. support svcs. specialist Milford Mill Acad. Magnet Sch., 1993—. Chair staff devel. com. Lansdowne H.S., sponsor Balt.-Kiev Exch. Initiative, 1992; resource coord. Tech. Edn. Support Svc. Program Milford Mill Acad., 1993—; participant Leadership Devel. Project for Women & Minorities Md. State Dept. Edn., 1994—; coord. sexual harassment workshops for colleagues and students, 1994-95; transition facilitator h.s. spl. edn. students, 1996—; chair pub. rels. for Magnet Sch. Internat. Baccalaureate and Tech. Prep. Programs; conductor workshops in field; lectr. in field. Contbg. writer Essex Times, 1986-89, Teacher-to-Teacher, 1986-89. Mem. NEA, Am. Vocat. Assn., Coun. Exceptional Children, Md. Tchrs. Assn., Md. Vocat. Assn., Md. Assn. Coop. Edn., Tchrs. Assn. of Baltimore County, Profls. Serving Adult Learning Disabled. Avocations: camping, tennis, sewing, ethnic cooking. Home: 6025 Hanover Rd Hanover MD 21076-1037

BOOGHREY, LAWANDA, elementary school educator; b. Shreveport, La., Aug. 02; d. Albert and Elizabeth (Ford) Booghrey. BA, Grambling State U. Cert. tchr., Tex. Tchr. Mitchell Blvd. Elem., Ft. Worth, 1990—; mem. dist. textbook adv. com. Ft. Worth Ind. Sch. Dist., 1993-94, mem. math. cadre, 1992—, tech. coord., 1994, dist. tech. trainer. Mem. Pathways to Excellence (curriculum writing for math grades 3-5). Mem. Rainbow Coalition, Dallas, 1994, Allied Cmtys. of Tarrant, 1991—. Named Carroll Peak Tchr. of Yr., 1992-93, 95-96, 98-99, Mitchell Blvd. Tchr. of Yr., 2002-03. Mem. United Educators Assn. (bldg. rep. 1993-99, exec. bd. dirs. 1997-2002), Nat. Coun. Tchrs. Math., Gamma Theta Upsilon (sec. Grambling chpt. 1977-79), Delta Sigma Theta (scholarship Shreveport chpt. 1975). Democrat. Baptist. Avocations: reading, playing tennis, listening to music. Home: 109 Nonesuch Pl Irving TX 75061 Office: Mitchell Blvd Elem 3601 Mitchell Blvd Fort Worth TX 76105-5799

BOOR, MYRON VERNON, psychologist, educator; b. Wadena, Minn., Dec. 21, 1942; s. Vernon LeRoy and Rosella Katharine (Eckhoff) B. BS, U. Iowa, 1965; MA, So. Ill. U., 1967, PhD, 1970; MS, U. Pitts., 1981. Lic. psychologist, Mo. Research psychologist Milw. County Mental Health Ctr., 1970-72; asst. prof. clin. psychologist Ft. Hays State U., Hays, Kans., 1972-76, assoc. prof., 1976-79; NIMH postdoctoral fellow in psychiat. epidemiology U. Pitts., Western Psychiat. Inst. and Clinic, 1979-81; research psychologist R.I. Hosp. and Butler Hosp., Providence, 1981-84; clin. psychologist Newman Meml. County Hosp., Emporia, Kans., 1985-93, Heartland Health Sys., St. Joseph, Mo., 1994—. Clin. psychologist Ft. Hays State U., 1972-79; asst. prof. psychiatry and human behavior Brown U., Providence, 1981-84; adj. faculty Emporia State U., 1985-94. Contbr. articles to profl. jours. U.S. Pub. Health Service fellow, 1965-67, NIMH fellow 1979-81. Home: 3018 Cambridge St Saint Joseph MO 64506-1164 E-mail: mboor@ccp.com.

BOOTH, DIRIE MURPHY DEE, music educator, church musician; b. Altavista, Va., May 12, 1947; d. Prentis Allen and Margaret Delilah (Swain) Murphy; m. Raymond Addison Booth, Feb. 9, 1969; children: Sheryl Lynn Booth Gray, Vickie Marie Booth Lagos, Kevin Addison. BS in Elem. Edn., Radford U., 1969; cert. of major in music, Randolph-Macon Women's Coll., 1995. Organist-music dir. Randolph Meml. Bapt. Ch., Madison Heights, Va., 1971-78, White's United Meth. Ch., Rustburg, Va., 1986-88; piano and organ tchr. Lynchburg, Va., 1986—; organist First Ch. Christ Scientist, Lynchburg, Va., 1988-89; music dir. Madison Heights Christian Ch., Lynchburg, Va., 1989-90; music edn. tchr. James River Day Sch., Lynchburg, Va., 1992-93; organist, pianist Keystone Bapt. Ch., Lynchburg, Va., 1992-94; organist Beulah Bapt. Ch., Lynchburg, Va., 1995—. Vol. musician Lynchburg Christian Women's Club, 1986—. Mem. Nat. Fedn. Music Clubs, Am. Guild Organists, Nat. Guild Piano Tchrs. (dist. ch.

1992-97, pres. 1998—), Music Tchrs. Nat. Assn., Ctrl. Va. Music Tchrs. Assn. (v.p. 1985—), Va. Music Tchrs. Assn. Avocations: aerobics, reading, cross-stitch. Home and Office: 206 Dean St Lynchburg VA 24502-2414

BOOTH, DONALD RICHARD, economist, educator; b. Marble, Minn., June 1, 1931; s. Floyd James and Maude (Marquart) B.; m. Louise Hitt, Aug. 22, 1953; 1 child, David. BA, Whittier Coll., 1955; MA, Claremont Coll., 1956; PhD, UCLA, 1970. Grad. dean Chapman Coll., Orange, Calif., 1973-77, acad. dean, 1977-78, exec. v.p., 1978-79, dean, sch. of bus., 1979-81, prof. econs., 1959—, v.p. fin., 1988-89; sr. economist Claremont (Calif.) Inst., 1989—. Bd. dirs. United Am. Bank, Westminster, Calif., Consumer Credit Counseling of Orange County, Calif. Recipient Eliot Jones award, We. Econs. Assn., 1958; Danforth Teaching fellow, Danforth Found., 1962, NSF fellow, 1970. Avocations: chess, stamp collecting, swimming. Office: Chapman U One University Dr Orange CA 92866-1011

BOOTH, HILDA EARL FERGUSON, clinical counselor, Spanish language educator; b. Pinehurst, N.C., Aug. 14, 1943; d. Arthur C. and Edna Estelle (Henry) Ferguson; m. Thomas Gilbert Booth, Oct. 25, 1966 (dec. Apr. 1990). AA, Montreat-Anderson Coll., 1963; BA, Pembroke State U., 1965; MS, Valdosta State U., 1985; postgrad., U. S.C., 1991. Lic. profl. counselor, S.C., cert. counselor, hypnotherapist. Spanish instr. C.C., Lake City, Fla., 1983-86; clin. counselor Columbia Counseling, Lake City, 1985-87; children's psychologist I Coastal Empire Mental Health Ctr., Allendale, S.C., 1987, psychologist II, 1988, office mgr., 1987-91; pvt. practice Allendale, 1989-91; aquatics instr. Harbison Recration Ctr., 1993-97; mem. mobile assessment team Richland Meml. Hosp., Rischland Springs, 1994, Palmetto Health Richland, 2001, chilel gi gong tchr., 2003. Mem. assessment team, mental health cons. Richland Meml. Hosp., Richland Springs; spl. svcs. coord., area coord. Allendale office, 1989; dir. women FORSPRO (Spain), Coral Gables, Fla., 1984-88; aquatics leader Nat. Arthritis Found., 1994; emergency svcs. staff Mental Health, Lake City, 1985-87; mem. Children at Risk team, Children's Advocacy team, 1987-91; instr. Chilel Qigong, 2001. Mem. extension cmty. planning com. City of Allendale, 1989-91, Shandon Presbyn. Ch.; pres. Protestant Women of Chapel, Nfld., Can., 1969, Ch. Women United, Lake City, 1976; deacon First Presbyn. Ch., Lake City, 1976-86, chmn. bd. deacons, 1982, elder 1985, elder Allendale Presbyn. Ch., 1988—, clk. of session, 1989—, tchr. Sunday sch., 1994; mem. mission com. to Nicaragua Shandon Presbyn. Ch., 1996, 98; vol. Spanish transl. Palmetto Richland Meml. Hosp., 1994—, Palmetto Health Alliance. Lt. (j.g.) USN, 1965-67. Fellow Internat. Biog. Assn.; mem. SEICUS, LWV, Inter-Am. Soc. of Psychology, Am. Legion (life), Nat. Beta Club, Robert Burns Soc. Republican. Avocations: painting, swimming, traveling, reading, spanish. Home and Office: 3134 Prentice Ave Columbia SC 29205-3940

BOOTH, LINDA LEIGH, vocational school educator; b. Dallas, May 12, 1953; d. Federico Rose and Gladys Ruth (Petty) Buenrostro; m. Joe Henry Booth Jr., May 24, 1985; children: Kathryn Leigh, Elizabeth Rose. BS in Home Econs., Abilene Christian U., 1985. Instr. Abilene (Tex.) Ind. Sch. Dist., 1988-99; instr. in family and consumer sci. Memphis City Schs., 2001—02. Mem. edn. vocat. adv. bd. Abilene Ind. Sch. Dist., Abilene, 1991-99, mem. textbook selection com., 1990-91. Judge Future Homemakers Am., Abilene, 1987—88; mem. citizens rev. panel child care United Way Abilene, 1997, 1998; trainer Girl Scout Coun. Mid-South, 1999—; troop leader Girl Scouts USA, 1997—; mem. children's ministries com. U. Ch. Christ, 1993—99, co-dir. children's worship; co-dir. Children's Worship and Presch. Bible Hour, 1998—99; share time leader Sycamore View Ch. Christ Children's Ministries, 2001—, tchr. bible camp jr. week, 2001—. Mem. Am. Vocat. Assn., Tex. Vocat. Spl. Needs Assn., Vocat. Home Econs. Tchrs. Assn. of Tex. (alt. dir. 1996-98), Tex. Restaurant Assn., Abilene Restaurant Assn., Tex. Classroom Tchrs. Assn., Assn. Tex. Profl. Educators (faculty campus rep. 1997-99, state conf. del.), Memphis Area Home Edn. Assn., Hospitality Educators Assn. Tex., Future Homemakers Am. Avocations: reading, gardening, sewing, home improvements, counted cross-stitch. Home: 2237 Goldbrier Ln Memphis TN 38134-5953

BOOTH, PATRICIA VOGT (TRISH BOOTH), education consultant; b. Bklyn., Jan. 10, 1947; d. Frank C. and Evelyn (Peterson) Vogt; m. Jon V.C. Booth, Aug. 26, 1967; children: Katherine, Tyler. BA, Denison U., 1968; MA, St. Mary's U. Minn., 1991. Lamaze cert. Childbirth Educator; fellow Am. Coll. Childbirth Educators. Pvt. practice, Brattleboro, Vt., 1972-74, Lamaze Childbirth Preparation Assn., Ann Arbor, Mich., 1975-79, Childbirth Edn. Assn. of Greater Mpls., 1979-82; cons. Family Tree Clinic, St. Paul, 1982-87, perinatal edn. coord., 1982-87; co-developer and presenter basic tchr. edn. workshop Seminar Svcs., 1985-87; basic tchr. edn. workshop faculty Internat. Childbirth Edn. Assn., Mpls., 1987-92; perinatal edn. cons. pvt. practice Mpls., 1988-94; edn. cons., 1994—. Mem. Internat. Childbirth Edn. Assn. Profls. Tng. Workshop faculty, 1998—; founding mem. and editor Preterm Birth Prevention Consortium St. Paul, 1987-90, perinatal guidelines work group Minn. Dept. Health, 1988-89, Prenatal Care Initatives Task Force Minn., 1986-88, edn. cons. Community Clinic Consortiums Mothers-to-Mothers project, 1985-90; adv. edn. cons. Pediat. Residency Program SUNY, Syracuse, 1998—. Editor: LCPA Childbirth and Parenting Handbook, 1976, Perinatal Connection Quar., 1992-94; author (booklet) Before You Get Pregnant, 1986, Preparation for Pregnancy, Birth, and Early Parenting, 1992, 93, (pamphlet) Relaxation, 1986, rev. edit., 1992, 98, Breathing Awareness, 1993, rev. edit., 1998, International Childbirth Education Association Educator Certification Program Study Modules and Examination, 1994, 00, Family Centered Education: The Process of Teaching Birth, 1995, Teaching Parenting Within the Childbirth Class Curriculum: a Teacher's Guide, 1999, Pampers Childbirth Edn. Program Teacher's Companion, 2001, rev. edit., 2003. Com. mem. Healthy Mothers, Healthy Babies Minn. 1985-94. Mem. Lamaze Internat., Childbirth Edn. Assn., Phi Beta Kappa. Home: 7507 Northfield Ln Manlius NY 13104-2374 E-mail: TrishBooth@aol.com.

BOOTH, ROBERT ALAN, artist, educator; b. Mt. Kisco, N.Y., Apr. 22, 1952; s. George Warren and Ellen (Cooley) B. BFA, Mass. Coll. Art, 1976; MFA, Syracuse U., 1978. Prof. visual arts SUNY, Fredonia, 1978—, dept. chmn., 1988-96. Lectr. coll. and univ. art programs. Numerous exhbns. Faculty Rsch. Fellow SUNY 1982, 83; grantee Ford Found. Syracuse U., 1977, 78. Mem.: Mid. Am. Coll. Art Assn. (bd. dirs. 1999—2003), Internat. Sculpture Ctr. Democrat. Home: 3197 Route 83 Fredonia NY 14063-9784 E-mail: booth@fredonia.edu.

BOOTH, STEPHANE ELISE, history and women's studies educator, assistant dean; b. Springfield, Ill., July 13, 1952; d Joseph and Mary Lorraine (Sandretto) Davies; m. David Eugene Booth, June 19, 1971. BA in Edn., U. N.C., 1973; MS in History, Ill. State U., Normal, 1979, DA in History, 1983. Cert. in early childhood edn. and K-9 edn., N.C. Tchr. St. Thomas More Sch., Chapel Hill, N.C., 1974-74, Blessed Sacrament Sch., Morton, Ill., 1976-80; teaching asst. Ill. State U., Normal, 1980-82, instr., 1982-85; assoc. prof. history and women's studies Kent (Ohio) State U., 1986—, asst. dean Salem campus, 2000—02, 2003—, interim dean acad. and student svcs. regional campuses, 2002—03. Rsch. cons. Ill. State Hist Soc., Springfield, 1985-87; editor, reviewer Issues in Inquiry in Coll. Learning and Teaching, Ypsilanti, Mich., 1992-93; mem. editorial adv. bd. Roxbury Pub. Co., L.A., 1992-93. Contbr. articles to profl. jours. Fellow Ill. Hist. Soc., 1981-82. Mem. AAUP (pres. 1995-2000), NOW, Am. Hist. Assn., Orgn. Am. Historians, Nat. Coun. for Social Studies, Phi Beta Kappa, Phi Alpha Theta. Office: Kent State U-Salem Campus 2491 State Rte 45 South Salem OH 44460 E-mail: sbooth@kent.edu.

BOOTH, WAYNE CLAYSON, English literature and rhetoric educator, author; b. American Fork, Utah, Feb. 22, 1921; s. Wayne Chipman and Lillian (Clayson) B.; m. Phyllis Barnes, June 19, 1946; children: Katherine, John Richard (dec.), Alison. AB, Brigham Young U., 1944; MA, U. Chgo., 1947, PhD, 1950; DLitt (hon.), Rockford Coll., 1965, St. Ambrose Coll., 1971, U. N.H., 1977; DHL (hon.), Butler U., 1984, Lycoming Coll., 1985, SUNY, 1987, Wabash Coll., 1990; DHL (hon.), Kalamazoo Coll., 1991; DHL (hon.), Ball State U., 1992; DHL (hon.), DePaul U., 1994; DHL (hon.), Earlham Coll., 1995, Carleton Coll., 1995, Villanova U., 2002. Instr. U. Chgo., 1947-50; asst. prof. Haverford Coll., 1950-53; prof. English, chmn. dept. Earlham Coll., 1953-62; George M. Pullman prof. English U. Chgo., 1962-91, dean Coll., 1964-69, prof. emeritus, 1992—, chmn. com. on ideas and methods, 1972-75. Vis. cons. (with wife) South African schs. and univs., 1963; Amnesty Internat. lectr. Oxford U., 1992. Author: The Rhetoric of Fiction, 1961 (Christian Gauss prize Phi Beta Kappa, 1962, David H. Russell award Nat. Coun. Tchrs. English, 1966), Now Don't Try To Reason With Me: Essays and Ironies for a Credulous Age, 1970, A Rhetoric of Irony, 1974, Modern Dogma and the Rhetoric of Assent, 1974, Critical Understanding: The Powers and Limits of Pluralism, 1979 (Laing prize, 1981), The Company We Keep: An Ethics of Fiction, 1988; author: (with M. Gregory) Harper & Row Reader, 1984; author: The Vocation of a Teacher: Rhetorical Occasions, 1967-88, 1988, The Art of Growing Older, 1992; author: (with J. Williams and Gregory Colomb) The Craft of Research, 1997, 2003; author: For the Love of It: Amateuring and Its Rivals, 1999, The Rhetoric of Rhetoric, 2004; editor: The Knowledge Most Worth Having, 1967; co-editor: Critical Inquiry, 1974—85. Trustee Earlham Coll., 1965-75. Served with inf. AUS, 1944-46. Recipient Disting. Alumni award Brigham Young U., 1975, Lifetime Achievement award Assn. for Mormon Letters, 1995, Lifetime Achievement award Conf. on Christianity and Literature, 1995, Quantrell prize for undergrad. tchg. U. Chgo., 1971, lifetime tchg. award, 1997, award for contbns. to edn. Am. Assn. Higher Edn., 1986; Ford Faculty fellow, 1952-53, Guggenheim fellow, 1956-57, 69-70, NEH fellow, 1975-76, Rockefeller Found. fellow, 1981-82; Phi Beta Kappa vis. scholar, 1977-78. Fellow Am. Acad. Arts and Scis., Am. Philos. Soc.; mem. MLA (exec. coun. 1973-76, pres. 1981-92, Francis Andrew March award for Disting. Svc. of Profession of English 1991), Coll. Conf. on Composition and Comm., Nat. Commn. on Educating Undergrads. in Rsch. Univs. Democrat. Mem. Lds Ch. Home: 5411 S Greenwood Ave Chicago IL 60615-5103

BOOTHE, LEON ESTEL, academic administrator emeritus, consultant; b. Carthage, Mo., Feb. 1, 1938; s. Harold Estel and Merle Jane (Hood) B.; m. Nancy Janes, Aug. 20, 1960 (dec. Jan. 1997); children: Cynthia, Diana and Cheri (twins); m. Karen Ball, Nov. 11, 2000. BS (Curators' scholar), U. Mo., 1960, MA, 1962; PhD in History, U. Ill., 1966; LLD, Kyung Hee U., Korea, St. Thomas Inst. Advanced Study, 1985, Hebrew Union Coll., 1994. Tchr. history Valparaiso (Ind.) H.S., 1960-61; asst. prof. history U. Miss., Oxford, 1965-68, assoc. prof., 1968-70; assoc. prof. history George Mason Coll., U. Va. (now George Mason U.), Fairfax, 1970-73, prof. history, 1973-80, assoc. dean, 1970-71, dean, 1971-72, dean coll. arts and scis., 1972-80; provost, v.p. acad. affairs Ill. State U., Normal, 1980-83; pres. No. Ky. U., Highland Heights, 1983-96, pres. emeritus, 1996—; sr. advisor Nat. Underground R.R. Freedom Ctr., 1997-2000; prof. history No. Ky. U., 1983—. Bd. dirs. Fifth Third Bank No. Ky.; chmn. Am. Assn. of State Colls. and Univs., 1993; bd. dirs. Commn. on Internat. Edn. of Am. Coun. Edn., Nat. Underground Railroad Free Ctr., exec. com., 2001. Former mem. adv. bd. Cin. Coun. World Affairs; trustee Cin.-Kharkiv Project, hon. mem., 1995-96; bd. dirs. Met. YMCA, Cinn., 1984—, Met. Cin. chpt. ARC, former mem., McLean County Heart Assn., McLean County United Way, INROADS/Cin., Inc., NCCJ, 1983—, Cin.'s Enjoy the Arts, 1988-90, Cin. Music Festival, Cin. Nat. Classical Music Hall Fame, Cin. Ballet, 1999—, No. Ky. U. Found., Sr. Citizens No. Ky., 1996—, May Festival, 1998—; vice chmn. No. Ky. United Way, chmn., 1988; Greater Cin. YMCA; mem. steering com. Cin. Bicentennial; chmn. Multiple Sclerosis Soc. Gifts Campaign; mem. steering and exec. coms. Cin. Youth Collaborative; co-chair blue ribbon econ. devel. study No. Ky. Area Devel. Dist.; mem. Leukemia Soc.; bd. dirs. Greater Cin. Conv. and Visitors Bur., 1989—, Kids Helping Kids, 1998—, Merc. Libr., 1998—, Festival of Arts, 1998—; bd. dirs., mem. exec. com., vice-chair cmty. edn. svcs., 1989-90, Cin. chpt. ARC, Wood Hudson Cancer Rsch. Lab. Inc., 1987-92; chmn. Ky. Bicentennial Com., 1990, chmn. steering com., 1992; chmn. Leadership Ky. Class; trustee Greater Cin. United Way and Cmty. Chest, 1991; steering com. greater Cin. summit on racism, 1994; sr. advisor Nat. Underground Railroad freedom Ctr., 1997; mem. Underground R.R. Freedom Ctr. Bd., 2000—; former bd. dirs. Am. Music Scholarship Assn., Cin. Scholarship Found., Leadership Ky. Found.; lifetime advisor to pres. Nat. Coun. for Cmty. and Justice; advisor Cin. Hispanic C. of C.; bd. dirs. Sr. Svcs. of No. Ky., 1996. NEH fellow, 1967-68; scholar Diplomat Seminars Dept. State; recipient Coll. Liberal Arts and Scis. award U. Ill., 1988, Alumni Coun. Pres.'s Spl. Recognition award No. Ky. U., 1989, Alumni award U. Mo., 1989, Walter R. Dunlevey Frontiersman award, 1994, Disting. Citizens Citation award NCCJ, Disting. Pub. Svc. award No. Ky. U. Found., 1995, Character award YMCA, 1997, Kinsman award Urban Appalachian Coun., 1998, Pres. award Pub. Rels. Soc., 2000, Lighthouse Beacon Light award, 2001. Mem. Soc. Historians for Am. Fgn. Rels., McLean County Assn. for Commerce and Industry, Am. Assn. State Colls. and Univs. (internat. programs com. 1986-94), No. Ky. C. of C. (Walter R. Dunlevey-Frontierman award 1994), Greater Cin. C. of C. (asst. sec.-treas. 1989-93), Rotary, Masons, Leon Boothe Soc. (svc. award No. Ky. 2002), Sigma Rho Sigma, Omicron Delta Kappa, Phi Alpha Theta, Phi Delta Kappa. Home: 1378 Collinsdale Ave Cincinnati OH 45230-2308 E-mail: boothel@nku.edu.

BORCHARDT, KENNETH ANDREW, microbiology consultant, educator; b. Chgo., Sept. 20, 1928; s. Leo Arthur and Edith R. (Peterson) B.; m. C. Joyce Truitt, Feb. 6, 1954; children: Gregory David, Kimberly Jo, Jeffrey Andrew. BS, Loyola U., Chgo., 1950; MS, Miami U., Oxford, Ohio, 1951; PhD, Tulane U., 1961. Chief clin. microbiologist Fitzsimmons Army Hosp., Denver, 1957-58, Letterman Army Hosp., San Francisco, 1961-65; commd. USPHS, 1965, advanced through grades to capt., 1983, ret., 1982; prof., cons. microbiology San Francisco State U., 1982—; chief rsch. Biomed Diagnostics, San Jose, Calif., 1990—. Contbr. articles to med. jours. Fellow in Tropical Medicine, La. State U., 1970. Fellow Am. Acad. Microbiology, Royal Acad. Tropical Medicine and Hygiene (London); mem. N.Y. Acad. Scis., Sigma Xi. Republican. Lutheran. Avocation: organ. Home: 15 Capilano Dr Novato CA 94949-5824 Office: San Francisco State U 1600 Holloway Ave San Francisco CA 94132-1722

BORCHERS, KAY ELIZABETH, school counselor; b. Sidney, Ohio, Jan. 15, 1955; d. Frank Jr. and Carol Sue (Martin) Pellman; m. Ted Borchers, July 14, 1979; children: Ryan, Maria. BS, Miami U., Oxford, Ohio, 1976; MS, U. Dayton, 1979; postgrad., Wright State U., Ohio State U. Cert. tchr., counselor, Ohio. Tchr. bus. Hardin-Houston (Ohio) Schs., 1976-85, counselor, 1985—. Sec. Shelby County Schs., Sidney, 1973-76, Shelby County Children's Svcs., 1975; membership chmn. Achievement Cmty. for Excellence, Ft. Loramie, Ohio, 1994; Ft. Loramie band parent officer, 1999-2001; organist, pianist St. Michael Ensemble, 1998—. Recipient Golden Apple award Houston Faculty, 1993-94. Mem. NEA, Ohio Edn. Assn. Office: Houston High School 5300 Houston Rd Houston OH 45333 E-mail: hh_kay@woco-k12.org.

BORCHERS, MARY AMELIA, middle school educator; b. Miles City, Mont., July 6, 1935; d. Earl Gordon and Lulu Irene (Ankerman) Forgaard; m. Justus Charles Borchers, Nov. 25, 1960; 1 child, James Gordon. AA, Lassen Jr. Coll., 1955; BA, Chico State Coll., 1960. Cert. tchr., Calif. Tchr. Loyalton (Calif.) High Sch., 1957-60, Point Arena (Calif.) High Sch., 1960-64, Nelson Ave Sch., Oroville, Calif., 1965-81; math. tchr. Weaver Elem. Sch., Merced, Calif., 1986—. Mem. math. educators del. People to People, Russia and Estonia; AIMS trainer Fresno (Calif.) Pacific Coll., 1988-90. Mem. Calif. Tchrs.' Assn., Weaver Tchrs.' Assn., Phi Delta Kappa.

BORCHERT, WARREN FRANK, elementary education educator; b. Faribault, Minn., Mar. 5, 1948; s. Harold C. and Beata J. (Hoffmann) B.; m. Mari L. Runquist, Aug. 7, 1971 (div. Oct. 1985); children: Nicholas, Kyle, Megan. BA, Gustavus Adolphus Coll., 1971; postgrad., Boise State U., 1975—, U. Idaho, 1979—; MEd, Coll. Idaho, 1983; cert. instr. leader level, Nat. Fedn. Interscholastic Coaches Edn. Program-Am. Coaching Effectiveness Program, 1991. Cert. advanced elem. and phys. edn. tchr. Phys. edn. tchr. Hopkins (Minn.) Sch. Dist., 1972-73; elem. tchr., phys. edn. tchr. Mountain Home (Idaho) Sch. Dist. 193, 1974-84, phys. edn. tchr., 1984—; coach boys basketball Mountain Home Jr. High Sch., 1986—, coach girls basketball, 1998—2001; coach girls softball Mountain Home High Sch., 1993-97. Instr. Intermountain Environ. Edn. Tng. Team, Salt Lake City, 1979—. Instr., mgr. ARC-pool, Mountain Home, 1975-83; pres. Men's Slo Pitch Softball Assn., Mountain Home, 1975-79; bd. dirs., coach Elmore County Youth Baseball Assn., Mountain Home, 1989-92; treas., bd. dirs. Grace Luth. Ch., Mountain Home, 1991-95. Mem. AAHPERD, Idaho Assn. Health, Phys. Edn, Recreation and Dance, Idaho ASCD, Idaho Soc. for Energy and Environ. Edn. (treas. 1985-87). Democrat. Avocations: reading, racquetball, fishing, hunting, horseback tour guide. Office: Base Primary Sch 100 Gunfighter Ave Mountain Home A F B ID 83648

BORDAGE, GEORGES, physician, medical education educator; b. St.-Louis-De-Kent, N.B., Can., May 30, 1947; came to U.S., 1992; s. Edmond and Rita (Gionet) B.; m. Joanne R. Fisher, Dec. 9, 1978; children: Anna, Daniel. BA, Coll. Bathurst, N.B., 1969; MD, U. Laval, Quebec City, Que., Can., 1973; MSc in Biometry, Case Western Res. U., 1976; PhD in Ednl. Psychology, Mich. State U., 1982; PhD (hon.), U. Sherbrooke, Can., 1999; DSc (hon.), U. Moncton, Can., 2002. Intern Hotel Dieu de Que. Hosp., Quebec City, 1973-74; rsch. fellow dept. biometry Case Western Res. U., Cleve., 1974-76; rsch. fellow office med. edn. R&D Mich. State U., East Lansing, 1976-78; prof. U. Laval, 1978-92, founding dir. MA degree, 1984; prof., dir. grad. studies U. Ill., Chgo., 1992—. Hon. cons. Greenwich Dist. Hosp., London, 1987-88; cons. WHO, Brussels, Karachi, 1982-83, 93, Eli Lilly, Awashima, Hakone, Tokyo and Kobe, 1994-97. Recipient John P. Hubbard award Nat. Bd. Med. Examiners, 1994, Disting. Career award in health professions edn. Am. Edn. Rsch. Assn., 2002. Mem. Assn. Am. Med. Colls. (chmn. rsch. in med. edn. 1991, chmn. group on ednl. affairs 1995-96, Merrel Flair award 1999), Assn. for Surg. Edn., Assn. for Study Med. Edn., Soc. Tchrs. in Family Medicine, Friends of Osler Libr., Club Pedagogie Med. Que. (chmn., exec. sec. 1989-92). Avocations: reading, music, cooking. Office: U Ill Chgo Dept Med Edn 808 S Wood St Dept Med Chicago IL 60612-7300

BORDELON, CAROLYN THEW, elementary school educator; b. Shelby, Ohio, Dec. 28, 1942; d. Burton Carl and Opal Mae (Harris) VanAsdale; m. Clifford Charles Spohn, Aug. 28, 1965 (div. Feb. 1982); m. Al Ramon Bordelon, Oct. 26, 1985. BA in History and Polit. Sci., Otterbein Coll., 1966; MA in Edn., Bowling Green State U., 1972; postgrad., Ohio State U., 1986—. Cert. tchr. grades 1-8, Ohio. Elem. tchr. Allen East Schs., Harrod, Ohio, 1966-68, Marion (Ohio) City Schs., 1968-78, chpt. I reading tchr., 1978-86, reading recovery tchr., 1986-88, Dublin (Ohio) City Schs., 1988—. Adj. instr. reading dept.grad. studies Ashland (Ohio) U., 1996. Author: The Parent Workshop, 1992, Octopus Goes to School, 1995. Vol. Am. Heart Assn., Worthington, Ohio, 1991; mem. Rep. Nat. Com., Washington, 1994-95; mem. Royal Scots Highlanders, Mansfield, Ohio, 1976—. Recipient Excellence in Edn. award Dublin City C. of C., 1991-93, 96, 97; Dublin City Schs./Ohio Dept. Edn. Tchr. Award grantee, 1993; Martha Holden Jennings Found. scholar, 1978. Mem. Archaeol. Inst. Am., Ohio Edn. Assn., Reading Recovery Coun. N.Am., Opera/Columbus, Mus. of Art, Columbus, Phi Delta Kappa, Phi Alpha Theta. Presbyterian. Avocations: bagpiping and scottish activities, archaeology, interior design, harpsichord. Home: 3958 Fairlington Dr Columbus OH 43220-4531 Office: Griffith Thomas Elem Sch 4671 Tuttle Crossing Blvd Dublin OH 43017-3575 E-mail: cbordelonread@aol.com.

BORDELON, DENA COX YARBROUGH, retired special education educator, director; b. Gorman, Tex., June 20, 1933; d. William Thomas and Imogene (Dunlap) Cox; m. James Edgar Yarbrough, June 20, 1950 (dec.); m. Cecil J. Bordelon, Sept. 24, 1999. BA, Nicholls State U., 1964, MEd, 1971, postgrad., 1978. Supr. profl. pers., prin. schs., elem. tchr. Terrebonne Parish Sch. Bd., Houma, La., 1964-79, dir. spl. edn. svcs., 1980-91; ret., 1991. Mem. La. Ret. Tchrs. Assn. Democrat. Methodist. Avocations: reading, theatre. Home: 202 White St Houma LA 70364-2934 E-mail: terrebonne@msn.com.

BORDEN, DIANE LYNN, communications educator; b. Chgo., Jan. 25, 1947; d. H. Frederick and Vera L. Borden; m. Robert Easley (div. 1970). BA, Colo. State U., 1972; MA, Stanford U., 1989; PhD, U. Wash., 1993. Mng. editor Bellingham (Wash.) Herald, 1977-80; dep. mng. editor Tribune, Oakland, Calif., 1981-85; pres. Santa Fe (N.Mex.) New Mexican, 1986-87; assoc. prof. Temple U., Phila., 1993-95; project dir. Am. Soc. Newspaper Editors, Reston, Va., 1995-96; asst. prof. George Mason U., Fairfax, Va., 1996-98; prof. San Diego State U., 1998—. Gannett profl. in residence U. Kans., Lawrence, 1985-86; cons. and expert witness in communication law and ethics. Co-editor: The Electronic Grapevine, 1997; co-author: Creative Editing, 4th edit., 2003; contbr. articles to scholarly and profl. jours.; editor: (book) Women and Language, 1997-99. Active NOW, Habitat for Humanity, World Wildlife Fund, Washington. Profl. journalism fellow Stanford U., 1980-81, fellow in telecomm. policy Annenberg Washington Program, 1995; rsch. grantee Temple U., 1994, San Diego State U., 1999, 2000. Mem. Assn. for Edn. in Journalism and Mass Communication, AAUW, Am. Journalism Historians Assn. Avocations: hiking, golf, reading biographies of women. Office: San Diego State U Office of Pres 5500 Campanile Dr San Diego CA 92182-8000

BORDER, GLADYS LOUISE, piano educator; b. Cleve., Feb. 11, 1926; d. Frederick August and Edith Elliot (Spellman) Schnell; m. Tondra Harrison Border, Nov. 16, 1946; children: David, Thomas, Calvin. Diploma, Wilcox Coll. Commerce, Cleve., 1944; student, Baptist Bible Inst., Cleve., 1944-46. Sales clk. part time F.W. Woolworth Co., Cleveland Heights, Ohio, 1942-44; office sec. part time Wilcox Coll. Commerce, Cleve., 1944; sec. Standard Oil Co., Cleve., 1944-47; temporary office work Ballou Svcs., Cleve., 1954; piano tchr. pvt. practice, Cleve., 1955-59, Hollywood, Fla., 1959—; sec. indsl. and pub. rels. Food Fair Offices, Miami, 1961-62; piano tchr. pvt. practice, Hollywood, Fla., 1997—. Ch. pianist First Brethren Ch., Cleveland Heights, Ohio, 1941-46; regular pianist Phi Gamma Fishing Club, Cleve., 1944-46; asst. pianist Youth For Christ, Cleve., 1945; 2nd v.p., corr. sec., awards chmn. Broward County Music Tchrs., Ft. Lauderdale, Fla., 1970-90; pianist in churches Nazarene, Bapt. Hollywood Christian Sch., Cleve., 1947-58; accompanist for band solos McArthur H.S., Driftwood Jr. H.S., Hollywood, Fla., 1961-69; regular pianist 1st Bapt. Choir and Ch., W. Hollywood, Fla., 1971-89, part time 1993—. Author: (life story) On the Life of Gladys Louise (Schnell) Border. Den mother Boy Scouts Am. Cub Scouts, Cleve., 1958-59; Sunday sch. tchr. Ch. of Nazarene, Cleve., 1947-48, 57-58; treas. Band Parents Driftwood Jr. H.S., Hollywood, Fla., 1962, 63; recording sec. Women;s Soc. 1st Meth., Hollywood, Fla., 1962, 64; Sunday Sch. tchr. 1st Meth., Epworth Meth., Hollywood, Fla., 1960, 71. Recipient Electronic Metronome McArthur High Band Soloists, Hollywood, Fla., 1967, Bowling trophies Bapt. Fellowship League, Hollywood, Fla., 1973-86, music min. plaques (2) 1st Bapt. W. Hollywood, Fla., 1980, 89; named Fairest of the Island Mother's Banquet 1st Bapt. W. Hollywood, Fla., 1994. Mem. Nat. Guild of Piano Tchrs., Jolly Srs., Fla. Fedn. Music Clubs, Broward County Music Tchrs. Assn. Republican. Baptist. Avocations: piano playing, reading, sewing, bowling, writing letters. Home: 7091 Scott St Hollywood FL 33024-3849

BORDERS, CAROL LEE, primary school educator; b. Peoria, Ill. d. Boyce Bradshaw and Alice Edna Victoria (Peterson) B. BS, Bradley U., 1958; MS, Ill. State U., 1967. Tchr. Lee Sch., Peoria, 1958-68, Kellar West, Peoria, 1968-80, Lindbergh Sch., Peoria, 1980-86, Kellar Cen. Primary Sch., Peoria, 1986—. Bd. dirs. Peoria County Extension Svc.-Youth Coun., 1991—; steward Nature Conservancy, 1992. Bd. dirs., pres. botany sect. Peoria Acad. Scis., 1983—. Grantee Ill. Math and Sci. Acad., Kellar Sch., 1991, First of Am. Bank, 1994, Ill. Math & Sci. Acad.; scholar Alpha Delta Kappa. Mem. AAUW (1st v.p., sec.), Ill. Native Plant Soc. (treas. 1988-90), Lincoln Soc., Peoria County Old Settlers (bd. dirs. 1966-91), Phi Delta Kappa, Alpha Delta Kappa (pres., altruistic chmn. 1988—, scholar 1992), Sigma Kappa (2d v.p. alumni 1987-88). Presbyterian. Avocations: reading, botany, entomology. Home: 2328 W Sherman Ave Peoria IL 61604-5458

BORDOGNA, JOSEPH, engineer, educator; b. Scranton, Pa., Mar. 22, 1933; s. Raymond and Rose (Yesu) B. BSEE, U. Pa., 1955, PhD, 1964; SM, MIT, 1960. With RCA Corp., 1958-64; asst. prof. U. Pa., Phila., 1964-68, assoc. prof., 1968-72, prof., 1972—, assoc. dean engring. and applied sci., 1973-80, acting dean, 1980-81, dean, 1981-90, dir. Moore Sch. Elec. Engring., 1976-90, Alfred Fitler Moore chair, 1979—; dir. engring. Nat. Sci. Foundation, Washington, 1991-96; COO, acting deputy dir. Nat. Sci. Found., Washington, 1996-99, dep. dir., COO, 1999—. Bd. dirs. Indsl. Imaging Corp., Weston Inc. (chmn. 1996-97), Univ. City Sci. Ctr.; master Stoufer Coll. House, 1972-76; cons. industry, govt., founds.; mem. Nat. Medal of Sci. com., 1989-91; chair adv. com. for engring. NSF, 1989-91. Author: (with H. Ruston) Electric Networks, 1966, (with others) The Man-Made World, 1971; chmn. editorial bd. Engring. Edn., 1987-90 With USN, 1955-58. Recipient commendation for first space capsule recovery, 1957, Lindback award for disting. teaching U. Pa., 1967, Centennial medal Phila. Coll. Textiles and Sci., 1988, Am. Indsl. Modernization Leadership award Nat. Coalition for Advanced Mfg., 1993, Chmn.'s award Am. Assn. Engring. Socs., 1994, Engr. of Yr. award NSPE Phila., 1984, George Washington medal Engrs. Club. Phila., 1997, Gold medal Soc. Mfg. Engrs., 2001, Leadership in Tech. Mgmt. award Portland Internat. Conf. on Mgmt. of Engring. and Tech., 2003; inducted into Engring. Educators Hall of Fame, 1993. Fellow AAAS (chair engring. sect. 1998-99), IEEE (chmn. Phila. sect. 1987-88, Centennial medal 1984, pres. 1998), Am. Soc. Engring. Edn. (George Westinghouse award 1974), Internat. Engring. Consortium; mem. Sigma Xi, Eta Kappa Nu, Tau Beta Pi, Phi Beta Delta. Office: Nat Sci Found Office Dir 4201 Wilson Blvd Ste 1205 Arlington VA 22230-1859

BORDONARO, JOSEPHINE FRANCES, retired secondary school educator; b. Solvay, N.Y., Oct. 24, 1920; d. Angelo and Angela (Pontillo) B. BS magna cum laude, Syracuse (N.Y.) U., 1944, MS summa cum laude, 1946. Cert. tchr., N.Y. Tchr. elem. Syracuse City Sch. Dist., 1941-45, tchr. jr. high sch., 1945-56, tchr. h.s. biology, 1956-79, ret., 1979. Elected alt. del. to bd. N.Y. State Ret. Tchrs. Sys., 1994. Mem. Citizen's Adv. Coun., 1978—; appointed commr. Met. Commn. on Aging, Onondaga County, 1990. Fulbright-Hayes scholar Cambridge, Eng., 1948-49. Mem. Sci. Tchrs. Assn. N.Y. State (pres.), N.Y. State Ret. Tchrs. Assn. (pres. Ctrl. Zone 1993-95), Syracuse Tchrs. Assn. (del. to NEA), Women High Sch. Tchrs. Assn. (pres. Syracuse chpt.), Am. Assn. Ret. Persons (legis com. N.Y. chpt. 1990-94), Bus. and Profl. Women's Club (pres. Camillus, N.Y. chpt. 1966-68), N.Y. State Bus. and Profl. Women's Club (chmn. legis. conf. Syracuse chpt. 1973), Pi Lambda Phi. Republican. Roman Catholic.

BOREL, LUDMILA IVANOVNA, ballerina, educator; b. Saratov, Russia, Aug. 4, 1928; came to U.S., 1993; d. Ivan and Taisia (Yulpatova) Borel; m. Vladimir Levinovsky, July 29, 1956; 1 child, Konstantin. Grad., Nat. Choreographic Sch., Saratov, 1946; M Degree, Russian Acad. of Theater Art, Moscow, 1961. Prin. dancer Nat. Opera and Ballet Theater, Saratov, 1946-66, M. Gorky's Mus. Theater, Magadan, USSR, 1966-74; ballet mistress in chief Nat. Light Music Theater, Saratov, 1976-80; artistic dir. Children's Ballet Studio, Moscow, 1980-92; prin. tchr. Russian Sch. Classical Dance, N.Y.C., 1994—. Contbr. articles to Soviet Ballet Mag., Internat. Ballet Ency. Mem. All-Russian Theater Socs., 1954-93. Home: 9 Nixon Ct Apt C4 Brooklyn NY 11223-6506

BOREN, LYNDA SUE, gifted education educator; b. Leesville, La., Apr. 1, 1941; d. Leonard and Doris (Ford) Schoenberger; m. James Lewis Boren, Sept. 1, 1961; 1 child, Lynda Carolyn. BA, U. New Orleans, 1971, MA, 1973; PhD, Tulane U., 1979. Prof. Northwestern State U., Natchitoches, La., 1987-89; propr. Colony Country House, New Llano, La., 1992-94; tchr. of gifted Leesville (La.) H.S., 1992—. Vis. prof. Newcomb Coll., Tulane U., New Orleans, 1979-83, U. Erlangen-Nuremburg, Germany, 1981-82, Middlebury (Vt.) Coll., 1983-84, Ga. Inst. Tech., Atlanta, 1985-87, Srinakharinwirot U., Bangkok, 1989-90; mem. planning com. 1st Kate Chopin Internat. Conf., Natchitoches, La., 1987-89; Fulbright lectr. USIA and Bd. Fgn. Scholars, 1981-82, 89-90. Author: Eurydice Reclaimed: Language, Gender and Voice in Henry James, 1989; co-editor, author: Kate Chopin Reconsidered, 1992; contbg. author: Encyclopedia of American Poetry, 1998; contbr. numerous articles to profl. jours. Founding mem. John F. Kennedy libr. Recipient awards for watercolors; Mellon fellow Tulane U., 1977-78; NEH seminar fellow Princeton U., 1986. Mem. MLA, AAUW, DAR, AFT, Fulbright Alumni Assn. Avocations: painting, video film documentaries, photography. Home: 1492 Fords Dairy Rd Newllano LA 71461-4530 E-mail: alborn@peoplepc.com.

BORESI, ARTHUR PETER, writer, educator; b. Toluca, Ill. s. John Peter and Eva B.; m. Clara Jean Gordon, Dec. 28, 1946; children: Jennifer Ann Boresi Hill, Annette Boresi Pueschel, Nancy Jean Boresi Broderick. Student, Kenyon Coll., 1943-44; BSEE, U. Ill., 1948, MS in Mechanics, 1949, PhD in Mechanics, 1953. Research engr. N. Am. Aviation, 1950; materials engr. Nat. Bur. Standards, 1951; mem. faculty U. Ill., Urbana, 1953—, prof. theoretical and applied mechanics and nuclear engring., 1959-79; prof. emeritus U. Ill. at Urbana, Urbana, 1979; Disting. vis. prof. Clarkson Coll. Tech., Potsdam, N.Y., 1968-69; NAVSEA research prof. Naval Postgrad. Sch., Monterey, Calif., 1978-79; prof. civil engring. U. Wyo., Laramie, 1979-95, head, 1980-94, prof. emeritus, 1995—. Vis. prof. Naval Postgrad. Sch., Monterey, Calif., 1986-87.; cons. in field. Author: Engineering Mechanics: Statics, 2001, Engineering Mechanics: Dynamics, 2001; Elasticity in Engineering Mechanics, 4th edit., 2000, Advanced Mechanics of Materials, 6th edit., 2002, Approximate Solution Methods in Engineering Mechanics, 1991, 2d edit., 2002; also articles. Served with USAAF, 1943-44; Served with AUS, 1944-46. Fellow ASME, ASCE, Am. Acad. Mechanics (founding, treas.); mem. Am. Soc. Engring. Edn. (Archie Higdon Disting. Educator award 1993). Office: U Wyo Box 3295 Univ Station Laramie WY 82071 E-mail: boresi@uwyo.edu.

BORETZ, NAOMI MESSINGER, artist, educator; b. Bklyn. BA, Bklyn. Coll.; MA in Fine Arts, CUNY; MA in Art History, Rutgers U.; postgrad., Art Students League N.Y. Exhibitions include Westminster Arts Coun. Arts Ctr., London, 1971, Hudson River Mus., N.Y., 1975, Katonah Gallery, 1976, Condeso-Lawler Gallery, N.Y.C., 1987, Carnegie-Mellon Art Gallery, Pitts., 1989, The Nelson Atkins Mus. of Art, St. Louis, 1994, Westbeth Gallery, N.Y., 1996, Mishkin Gallery, Baruch Coll., 1997, Rutgers (N.J.) U. Art Gallery, 1998, Hillwood Art Mus., N.Y., 2000, Muhlenburg Coll. Art Gallery, 2002, others, Represented in permanent collections Met. Mus. Art, N.Y.C., Solomon R. Guggenheim Mus., DeLand Art Mus., Fla., Brit. Mus., London, Nat. Mus. Am. Art, Washington, Yale U. Art Gallery, Joslyn Art Mus., Omaha, Walker Art Ctr., Mpls., Miami U. Art Mus., Oxford, Ohio, Fogg Art Mus. Harvard U., Cambridge, Mass., Glasgow (Scotland) Mus., San Jose (Calif.) Art Mus., Asheville (N.C.) Art Mus., Whitney Mus. Am. Art, N.Y., Mus. Modern Art, Princeton U. Graphic Arts Collection, N.J., Mus. S.W., Midland, Tex., Swope Art Mus., Terre Haute, Ind., others; contbr. to arts publs. Artist-fellow Va. Ctr. Creative Arts, 1973, 86, Ossabaw Found., 1975, Tyrone Guthrie Arts Ctr., Ireland, 1987, Writers-Artists Guild Can., 1988; grantee N.J. State Coun. on Arts, 1985-86. Studio: Princeton NJ

BORGEN, IRMA R. music educator; b. McPherson, Kans., Jan. 15, 1911; d. Nels J.W. Nelson and Ida Elizabeth Shallene; m. Clifford E. Borgen, July 6, 1942 (dec. Oct. 1967); children: David John, Elizabeth Marie. BA, Gustavus Adolphus Coll., St. Peter, Minn., 1932; postgrad., U. Colo., 1964—65. Tchr. Am. Sch. for Dependents, Essen, Germany, 1950—51; pvt. music tchr. Colorado Springs, Colo., 1969—. Mem.: Mil. Widows, Fountain Valley Sr. Orgn. Democrat. Lutheran. Avocations: music, fitness classes. Home: 114 Harvard St Colorado Springs CO 80911

BORGER, MICHAEL HINTON IVERS, osteopathic physician, educator; b. Kirksville, Mo., Nov. 10, 1951; s. Donald L. Borger and Dorothy M. Hinton. BA in Sociology, U. Akron, 1974; DO, Coll. Osteo. Medicine and Surgery, Des Moines, 1977. Diplomate Nat. Bd. Examiners in Osteo. Medicine and Surgery, Am. Coll. Osteopathic Family Physicians; ordained elder Presbyn. Ch., 1969. Rotating extern Youngstown (Ohio) Osteo. Hosp., 1976; extern in family medicine Dietz Diagnostic Clinic, Des Moines, 1977; rotating intern South Bend (Ind.) Osteo. Hosp. (now St. Mary's Cmty. Med. Ctr.), 1977-78, active staff, 1978-79, assoc. staff, 1979-82; pvt. practice Nappanee, Ind., 1978—; mem. staff Elkhart (Ind.) Gen. Hosp., 1978—, Goshen Gen. Hosp., 1981—; clin. asst. prof. gen. practice Kirksville (Mo.) Coll. Osteo. Medicine, 1990-93; apptd. clin. preceptor Kansas City U. of Health Scis. Coll. of Osteo. Medicine, 1993—, asst. clin. prof. family practice, 1995—; pres. Northwood Physicians, Inc., 1992—; asst. prof. clin. medicine Pikeville (Ky.) Coll. Sch. Osteo. Medicine, 2000—, asst. prof. osteo. manipulative medicine, 2000—. Assoc. manuscript reviewer Jour. Respiratory Diseases, 1986-88, Jour. Musculoskeletal Medicine, 1989—; pres. Northwood Profl. Assocs., Inc., 1995—; mem. quality improvement com. Ptnrs. Health Plan, 1996-99, mem. physician credentialling com., 2002-2003; founder Circle of Care Healthcare Sys., 1996, manuscript reviewer, Jour. of Musculoskeletal Medicine, 1981-. Bd. dirs. Nappanee C. of C., 2001—, Nappanee chpt. Families in Action, 1980-82; bd. dirs., chmn. Mission and Svcs. Commn., 1st Mennonite Ch., Nappanee, 1984-90, chmn. pastoral search com., 1989-90; mem. screening com. for elem. prin. Wa-Nee Sch. Dist., 1988; med. advisor United Presbyn. Ch. Nursery Sch., Nappanee, 1995—. Recipient Physician of Yr. award Ind. Assn. Emergency Med. Technicians, 1981, Good Citizens award Tower Savs., 1982, 1st degree black belt Tae Kwon Do, 1988, Tae Kwon Do Student of Yr. award, Hong's USA Tae Kwon Do, 1988; Burroughs-Wellcome Osteo rsch. fellow, 1980-81. Mem. Am. Osteo. Assn., Ind. Assn. Osteo. Physicians and Surgeons, Am. Acad. Applied Osteopathy, Nat. Honor Soc. Home: 353 N Hartman St Nappanee IN 46550-1417 E-mail: northwood@fourway.net.

BORGES, INGRID, industrial psychologist, trainer; b. N.Y.C., Dec. 5, 1946; d. Jose Diego and Herminia (Martinez) Borges; m. Rolando Antonio de la Maza, June 11, 1966 (dec. Oct. 1966); 1 child, Rolando Jose de la Maza. BS, Inter-Am. U., Hato Rey, P.R., 1972; MEd, U. Houston, 1978. Lic. psychologist, P.R. Ednl. coord. Harris County Community Action, Houston, 1972-74; case worker Harris County Psychiat. Hosp., Houston, 1974-75; pers. specialist Civil Svc. Dept., Houston, 1975-78; coll. instr. Inter Am. U., Hato Rey, 1978-82; tng. developer Citibank, Hato Rey, 1982-85; tng. mgr. Citibank-Spain, Madrid, 1985-87; tng. and orgnl. devel. mgr. ICI Pharms., Carolina, P.R., 1987-88; tng. mgr. Latin Am. and Caribbean Avis Rent A Car, Carolina, 1988-95, also mem. adv. bd. and coms., 1988-95; instr. Inter-Am. U., 1995-96; tng. and devel. mgr. Citibank, Puerto Rico, Ctrl. Am., Caribbean, 1996—. Cons. Borges, Fitzpatrick & Assocs. Inc., Santurce, P.R., 1981-82. Author seminars. Mem. ASTD, Assn. of Indsls. Roman Catholic. Avocations: opera, theatre, classical and popular music, spanish dancing. Office: Citibank 1 Citibank Dr San Juan PR 00926-9631

BORGESON, EARL CHARLES, law librarian, educator; b. Boyd, Minn., Dec. 2, 1922; s. Hjalmer Nicarner and Doris (Danielson) B.; m. Barbara Ann Jones, Sept. 21, 1944; children— Barbara Gale, Geoffrey Charles, Steven Earl. BS in Law, U. Minn., 1947, LLB, 1949; BA in Law Librarianship, U. Wash., 1950. Libr. Harvard U. Law Sch. Libr., 1952-70; assoc. dir. Stanford U. Librs., 1970-75; assoc. law libr. Los Angeles County (Calif.) Law Libr., 1975-78; prof. and law libr. So. Meth. U., Dallas, 1978-88, prof. emeritus of law, 1988; lectr. UCLA Grad. Sch. Libr. Sci., 1975-78; adj. prof. Tex. Women's U., 1979-80; adj. prof. U. North Tex., Denton, 1988-90; librarian AccuFile, Inc., 1992-2001; cons. in field. With USNR, 1943-46. Mem. Am. Assn. Law Librs. Home: 867 Tangle Oaks Ct Bellville TX 77418-2861

BORGMAN, LOIS MARIE, biology educator, college science administrator; b. Rochester, N.Y., Apr. 2, 1932; d. Charles and Marie Groet; m. Kenneth Eugene Borgman, June 5, 1954; children: Cheryl Ann, William Charles, James Kenneth. BS cum laude, Syracuse U., 1954; MEd, Mass. State Coll., Framingham, 1967; PhD, Northeastern U., Boston, 1982. Lab. technician U. Rochester, 1954; rsch. asst. kidney rsch. lab. Peter Bent Brigham Hosp. Harvard U., Boston, 1956; prof. biol. scis. Mt. Ida Coll., Newton Ctr., Mass., 1962-97; faculty emeritus, ret., 1997. Program dir. sci. Mt. Ida Coll., 1976-83, sci. curriculum coord., 1982-97, dir. sch. sci. and allied health, 1995-97. Mem. Wetlands Protection Com., Town of Wellesley, Mass., 1988-96; vol. lake assn. monitor Dept. Environ. Svcs. State of N.H., Concord, 1987-97; boardwalk naturalist vol. Corkscrew Swamp, Naples, Fla., 1998—. Mem. Nat. Sci. Tchrs. Assn., Nat. Audubon Soc., N.Am. Lake Mgmt. Soc., Soc. Coll. Sci. Tchrs., Phi Kappa Phi, Phi Sigma, Pi Sigma. Avocations: watercolor painting, horticulture, swimming, skiing.

BORGMANN, NORMA LEE, school superintendent; b. Belleville, Ill., Sept. 9, 1948; d. William Henry and Loraine Anna (Wolff) B. BA, Greenville Coll., 1970, BS, 1973; MS in Edn., So. Ill. U., 1979, EdS in Adminstrn., 1994. Cert. adminstr., tchr., Ill. Tchr. elem. edn. Patoka (Ill.) Community Unit # 100, 1971-90, tchr. jr. high sch., adminstrv. asst., 1990-91, tchr. jr. high sch., prin., 1991-92, prin. K-12, 1992-94, supt., 1994—. Author: (cookbook) Our Family Favorites, 1987; compiler: (cookbook) Cookin' with DuBois Center Auxiliary, 1983. Recipient Human Svcs. award Ill. Edn. Assn., 1984. Mem. Ill. Assn. Sch. Adminstrs., Am. Camping Assn., Ill. Women Adminstrs., Pakota Cmty. Edn. Assn. (sec.-treas. 1977-79, v.p. 1979-81, pres. 1981-83), Beta Sigma Phi (pres. Delta chpt. 1993-94, 4 Mem. of Yr. awards). Mem. United Ch. of Christ. Avocations: playing piano and organ, baking, cooking. Home: 502 E Bond Ave Patoka IL 62875-1193 Office: Patoka Cmty Unit 1220 Kinoka Rd # 100 Patoka IL 62875-1300

BORIE, RENEE DEBRA, English language educator; b. Phila., Feb. 2, 1961; d. E. Jack and Fannie (Silverberg) Sherman. AA, Harrisburg Area C.C., 1981; BS in Secondary English, Millersville U., 1983; postgrad., Pa. State U., 1991—. English tchr. Caesar Rodney H.S., Dover, Del., 1983-88; subs. tchr. Cen. Dauphin Sch. Dist., Harrisburg, Pa., 1988-90; English tchr. Linglestown Jr. H.S., Harrisburg, 1990—. Adv. bd. Capitol Area Writing Project, Middletown, Pa., 1993-94; ednl. advisor Planned Parenthood of Ctrl. Pa., Harrisburg, 1992-93; tchr. liason PTA Exec. Bd., Linglestown Jr. H.S.; class act tchr. WHTM-TV-27, Harrisburg, 1996; cheerleading coach, 1996-97, literary mag. advisor, 1996-2002, play dir., 1995—; team leader Making Strides Against Breast Cancer, Linglestown Jr. H.S., 2000—, field hockey coach, 1990, newspaper advisor, 1990-96. Mem. NEA, Nat. Coun. Tchrs. of English, Pa. State Edn. Assn., Cen. Dauphin Edn. Assn. (bldg. rep. 2002—). Office: Linglestown Jr HS 1200 N Mountain Rd Harrisburg PA 17112-1754

BORKO, HILDA, education educator; BA in Psychology, UCLA, 1971, MA in Philosophy of Edn., 1973, PhD in Ednl. Psychology, 1978. Elem. tchg. credential Calif., specialization in mental retardation U. So. Calif. Asst. and assoc. prof. Coll. Edn., Va. Poly. Inst. and State U., 1980—85; assoc. prof. Coll. Edn., U. Md., College Park, 1985—91, Sch. Edn., U. Colo., Boulder, 1991—94; prof. Sch. Edn. U. Colo., Boulder, 1994—. Co-author (with M. Eisenhart): (book) Designing Classroom Research: Themes, Issues, and Struggles, 1993 (Outstanding article award, 1992); contbr. articles to profl. jours. and chpts. to books. Recipient grants in field. Mem.: APA, Nat. Coun. for Tchrs. of Math., Invisible Coll. for Rsch. on Tchg., Am. Assn. Colls. of Tchr. Edn., Am. Ednl. Rsch. Assn. (pres. 2003—), Pi Gamma Mu, Phi Beta Kappa, Phi Delta Kappa. Office: U Colo Sch Edn CB249 Boulder CO 80309*

BORKON, DORIS, educational administrator, entrepreneur; b. Pitts., Nov. 23, 1936; d. Louis and Ruth (Ashinsky) B.; m. Joseph S. Tekula, June 6, 1957 (dec. 1980); children: Nadine, Juliana, Joan Michel. BA magna cum laude, Hunter Coll., 1954; MS, Bank St. Coll., 1973, EdM, 1982. Cert. ednl. adminstr. Tchr. N.Y.C. Bd. Edn., Spanish bilingual guidance counselor, 1968-77, bilingual ednl. evaluator, 1977-84, chair com. on spl. edn., 1984-85, ednl. adminstr., 1985—; pres. EduVal Ednl. Cons., N.Y.C., 1980—. Charter mem. Adult Literacy Initiative, U.S. Dept. Edn.; cons. in field. Mem. youth com. Community Bd., N.Y.C., 1988—; mem. exec. bd. Ansonia Ind. Dems., N.Y.C., 1988—. Mem. Nat. Coun. on Assistance to Classroom Tchrs. (bd. dirs., founder), Chinese Lang. Study Inst., Am. Orthopsychiat. Assn., N.Y. C. of C., Orton Soc., Nat. Puzzlers' League, Women Entrepreneurs Bus. Assn. (co-founder, mem. exec. bd. 1994—), World Assn. for Psychosocial Rehab. Avocation: ballroom dancing. Office: EduVal PO Box 231139 New York NY 10023-0019 E-mail: president@eduval.org., val-u@eduval.org.

BORN, FRANCES EMMARY HOLLICK, middle school art educator; b. The Philippines, Philippine, July 24, 1948; d. Francis Haas and Wanda Mae (Kirch) Hollick; m. Philip L. Born, Dec. 22, 1973; 1 child, Frank Edward. BS in Edn., No. State Coll., 1970; MEd, U. Tex., El Paso, 1982. Cert. art and lang. arts edn., curriculum and instruction. Art and lang. arts tchr. Grand Junction (Colo.) H.S., 1970-82, East Middle Sch., Grand Junction, 1982—. Judge Asst. Art Exhibits, Grand Junction, 1970-82; art curriculum com. Sch. Dist. #51, Grand Junction, 1988-93. Choir First United Meth. Ch., 1973—. Mem. NEA, Mesa Valley Edn. Assn. (bldg. rep. 1974-92, area dir. 1991, 92, 94, 95), Colo. Edn. Assn. (del. assembly 1991, 92, 95), Nat. Art Edn. Assn., Colo. Art Edn. Assn., Parent Tchr. Student Assn. (sec. 1994, 95), Delta Kappa Gamma (1st v.p., 2d v.p., pres., scholarship 1982, 83). Democrat. Methodist. Avocations: art, music, writing, reading. Home: 2215 N 13th St Grand Junction CO 81501-4204 Office: East Middle Sch 830 Gunnison Ave Grand Junction CO 81501-3295

BORNINO-GLUSAC, ANNA MARIA, mathematics educator; b. Naples, Italy, Apr. 2, 1946; came to U.S., 1946; d. Bruno and Anna Maria (De Simone) B.; m. Howard Keith Wolff, July 29, 1966 (div. 1971); 1 child, Francesca Yvonne Wolff Hatzakis; m. Ronald G. Glusac, Sept. 4, 1993. BA in Chemistry, Calif. State U., Dominguez Hills, 1968, MA in Edn. Adminstrv. Svcs., 1986. Cert. standard secondary tchr., Calif., preliminary adminstrv., Calif., TFAS instr.; Calif. BCLAD credential. Tchr. math. L.A. Unified Sch. Dist., 1968—, dept. chair, 1982-84, 90-92, sch. improvement coord., 1998—2002; math. coach Dist. K., Wilmington, Calif., 2002—. Editor: Accreditation Report, 1983. Mem. United Tchrs. L.A., Nat. Coun. Tchrs. Math., Calif. Math. Coun. Democrat. Roman Catholic. Avocations: needlework, travel, reading, music. Office: 1527 Lakme Ave Wilmington CA 90744-1526

BORNSTEIN, GEORGE JAY, literary educator; b. St. Louis, Aug. 25, 1941; s. Harry and Celia (Price) B.; m. Jane Elizabeth York, June 22, 1982; children— Benjamin, Rebecca, Joshua. AB, Harvard U., 1963; PhD, Princeton U., 1966. Asst. prof. MIT, Cambridge, 1966-69, Rutgers U., 1969-70; assoc. prof. U. Mich., Ann Arbor, 1970-75, prof. English, 1975—, C.A. Patrides prof. lit., 1995—. Cons. various univ. presses, scholastic jours., funding agys., 1970—; mem. adv. bd. Yeats: An Annual, 1982—, South Atlantic Rev., 1985-88, Rev., 1991—, Text, 1993—, Paideuma, 2003—. Author: Yeats and Shelley, 1970, Transformations of Romanticism, 1976, Postromantic Consciousness of Ezra Pound, 1977, Poetic Remaking, 1988, Material Modernism: The Politics of the Page, 2001; editor: Romantic and Modern, 1977, Ezra Pound Among the Poets, 1985, W.B. Yeats: The Early Poetry, vol. 1, 1987, vol. 2, 1994, W.B. Yeats: Letters to the New Island, 1990, Representing Modernist Texts, 1991, Palimpsest: Editorial Theory in the Humanities, 1993, W.B. Yeats: Under the Moon, the Unpublished Early Poetry, 1995, Contemporary German Editorial Theory, 1995, The Iconic Page in Manuscript, Print, and Digital Culture, 1998. Cubmaster Wolverine council Boy Scouts Am., 1977-79. Recipient good teaching award Amoco Found., 1983, Warner Rice prize for rsch. in humanities, 1988, Rosenthal award for Yeats studies W.B. Yeats Soc., 2000; fellow Am. Coun. Learned Soc., 1972-73, NEH fellow, 1982-83, fellow Old Dominion Found., 1968, fellow Guggenheim Found., 1986-87. Mem. MLA (exec. com. Anglo-Irish 1976-80, exec. com. 20th Century English 1980-85, exec. com. Poetry 1987-92, exec. com. bibliography and textual studies 1993-98, exec. com. methods of rsch. 1998-2003), Soc. Textual Scholarship (program chair 1997, exec. com. 1998-), Am. Conf. on Irish Studies (book prize judge 1991), Racquet Club, Princeton Club (N.Y.C.), Phi Beta Kappa. Home: 2020 Vinewood Blvd Ann Arbor MI 48104-3614 Office: U Mich Dept English Ann Arbor MI 48109-1003 E-mail: georgeb@umich.edu.

BORNTRAGER, JOHN SHERWOOD, principal; b. Oak Harbor, Wash., July 3, 1953; s. George H. and Norma E. Borntrager; m. Linda Diane, Aug. 30, 1975; children: Melissa, Shanna. BA, San Diego State U., 1975; MA, U. Ctrl. Ark., 1984. Cert. elem. educator, Ariz., Mo., Ark.; cert. prin., Mo., Ark. Tchr. Alhambra Pub. Schs., Phoenix, 1976-79; tchr., prin. Norfork Pub. Schs., Ark., 1979-87; prin. Cedarville Pub. Schs., 1987—2003. Mem. ASCD, Ark. Edn. Assn., Ark. Christian Educators Assn., Ark. Assn. Elem. Sch. Prins., Phi Delta Kappa.

BOROWICK, BERNADINE ANN, school system administrator; b. Perth Amboy, N.J., July 16, 1942; d. Alexander and Bernice (Zawilinski) Jankowski; m. John Borowick, June 13, 1964; children: Matthew, Daniel, Cheryl. BA, Kean Coll., 1964; MA, Georgian Ct. Coll., 1984. Cert. tchr., reading specialist, prin., supr., N.J. Tchr. handicapped Perth Amboy (N.J.) Pub. Schs., 1964-66; tchr. grades 3 and 5 Howell Twp. (N.J.) Pub. Schs., 1976-89, supr. instrn., 1989—. Workshop presenter in field. Mem. ASCD, Internat. Reading Assn., N.J. Prins. and Suprs. Assn., Nat. Coun. Tchrs. of English, Monmouth County Reading Assn., Profl. Devel. Inst., Monmouth County Literacy Awareness Consortium. Roman Catholic. Avocations: piano, reading, exercise, walking. Office: Howell Twp Pub Schs Rt 524 Adelphia Farmingdale Rd Howell NJ 07731

BORROFF, MARIE, English language educator; b. N.Y.C., Sept. 10, 1923; d. Albert Ramon and Marie (Bergersen) B. Ph.B., U. Chgo., 1943, MA, 1946; PhD, Yale U., 1956. Teaching asst. U. Chgo., 1946-47; instr. dept. English Smith Coll., 1948-51, asst. prof., 1956-59, asso. prof., 1959; vis. asst. prof. English Yale U., 1957-58, vis. asso. prof., 1959-6O, asso. prof. English, 1960-65, prof., 1965-71, William Lampson prof., 1971-92, Sterling prof. English, 1992-94; Sterling prof. English emeritus, 1994—; Phi Beta Kappa vis. scholar, 1973-74. Fellow Ezra Stiles Coll., Yale. Author: Sir Gawain and the Green Knight: A Stylistic and Metrical Study, 1962, (with J. B. Bessinger, Jr.); recorded dialogues read in Middle English, 1965, Sir Gawain and the Green Knight: A New Verse Translation, 1967, Pearl: A New Verse Translation, 1977, Language and the Poet: Verbal Artistry in Frost, Stevens, and Moore, 1979, Sir Gawain and the Green Knight, Patience and Pearl: Verse Translations, 2000, Stars and Other Signs:

Poems, 2002; essay collection: Traditions and Rewewals Chaucer, the Gawain-Poet, and Beyond, 2003; editor: Wallace Stevens, A Collection of Critical Essays, 1963; videotaped lectures: To Hear Their Voices, Chaucer, Shakespeare and Frost, Assn. of Yale Alumni Great Tchrs. Series, Chapter Headings: Remarks Made at the Annual Initiation Ceremonies of Phi Beta Kappa, Alpha Chapter of Connecticut, 1989-1994, 1996. Bd. Govs. Yale U. Press, 1988-98. Recipient James Billings Fiske poetry prize U. Chgo., 1943; Eunice Tietjens Meml. prize Poetry mag., 1945; Margaret Lee Wiley fellow AAUW, 1955-56; Guggenheim fellow, 1969-70 Fellow Am. Acad. Arts and Scis.; mem. MLA, Acad. Am. Poets, Medieval Acad. Am., Phi Beta Kappa. Home: 311 St Ronan St New Haven CT 06511-2328 E-mail: marie.borroff@yale.edu.

BORROMEO, ANNABELLE R, critical care nurse, educator, consultant; b. La Union, Philippines, June 10, 1955; came to U.S., 1979; d. Mauricio F. and Delfina M. Reyes; m. Andres D. Borromeo, Oct. 5, 1983; 1 child, James Andrew. GN, U. Philippines, Manila, 1976; BSN, St. Louis U., Baguio, 1978; MSN, U. Tex., Houston, 1988. CCRN. Staff nurse Hendrick Med. Ctr., Abilene, Tex., 1979-81, St. Luke's Episcopal Hosp., Houston, 1981-83, head nurse, unit tchr., 1983-86, nurse mgr., 1987-88, nurse liason cons., 1988-91, staff nurse, 1991—. Accustomation course instr. St. Lukes Episcopal Hosp., Houston, 1989—; prin. cons. Borromeo & Assoc., Houston, 1990—. Author: Nursing Care of the Adult, Adolescent, and Aged, 1989, Clin. Component Handbook for Accustomation Course, 1991; contbr. articles to jours. Grantee AACN Houston Gulf Coast Chpt., 1987. Mem. Philippine Nurses Assn. of Met. Houston (bd. mem. 1992—, sec.), Sigma Theta Tau. Home: 2626 Holly Hall St Apt 311 Houston TX 77054-4173 Office: 2626 Holly Hall St Apt 311 Houston TX 77054-4173

BORTZ, ALFRED BENJAMIN, science and technology educator, writer; b. Pitts., Nov. 20, 1944; s. Harry A. and Rose (Taksa) B.; m. Susan G. Grossberger, June 17, 1967; children: Brian S., Rosalie E. BS in Physics, Carnegie-Mellon U., 1966, MS in Physics, 1967, PhD in Physics, 1971. Asst. prof. physics Bowling Green State U., Huron, Ohio, 1970-73; rsch. assoc. Yeshiva U., N.Y.C., 1973-74; sr. engr. Westinghouse Electric Co., Pitts., 1974-77; staff scientist Essex Group Inc., Pitts., 1977-79; scientist computer engring. ctr. Carnegie Mellon U., Pitts., 1979-83, asst. dir. magnetics tech. ctr., 1983-90, dir. special projects engring. edn., 1990-92, sr. fellow sci. and tech. edn., 1992-94; sr. rsch. fellow Duquesne U. Sch. Edn., Pitts., 1994-96; instr. Chatham Coll., 2000—; ind. writer, cons., instr. Inst. Children's Lit., West Redding, Conn., 1996—. Cons. various children's book pubs., 1984—; cons., rapporteur rsch. briefing panel NAS, 1986. Author: (children's books) Superstuff! Materials That Have Changed Our Lives, 1990, Mind Tools the Science of Artificial Intelligence, 1992, Catastrophe! Great Engineering Failure-and Success, 1995, To the Young Scientist, 1997, Martian Fossils on Earth?, 1997, Dr. Fred's Weather Watch, 2000, Collision Course, 2001, Techno Matter, 2001 (Am. Inst. Physics Sci. Writing award 2002), The Library of Subatomic Particles (6 books), 2004; book reviewer many met. newspapers; sci. book columnist: Dallas Morning News; contbr. articles to profl. jours. Mem. AAAS (cons. panel on tech. Project 2061, 1985), Am. Phys. Soc., Soc. Children's Book Writers and Illustrators, Nat. Book Critics Cir., Sigma Xi. Home: 1312 Foxboro Dr Monroeville PA 15146-4441 Office: 1312 Foxboro Dr Monroeville PA 15146-4441

BOSAH, FRANCIS N. molecular biochemist, educator; b. Onitsha, Anambra, Nigeria, Sept. 13, 1959; s. Michael and Comfort (Odiari) Bosah. BS, Shaw U., 1985; MS, N.C. Ctrl. U., 1988; PhD, Clark Atlanta U., 1995. Rsch. asst. N.C. Ctrl. U., Durham, 1985-88, instr., 1988-90; rsch. assoc. Rsch. Triangle Inst., Research Triangle Park, NC, 1989-90; rsch. assoc. dept. biochemistry Morehouse Sch. Medicine, Atlanta, 1990-95, NASA postdoctoral rsch. fellow dept. medicine, 1995-98, rsch. instr. dept. biochemistry, 1998—. Coord. health career Atlanta Met. Coll., 1993—94, instr., 1993—, DeKalb Coll., Clarkston, Ga., 1998—; presenter in field. Contbr. abstracts and articles to profl. jours. Recipient Minority Biochemical Rsch. Support award, 1990—93. Mem.: AAAS, Soc. Exptl. Biology and Medicine, Minority Biomedical Rsch. Soc., N.Y. Acad. Scis., Am. Chem. Soc., Am. Physiol. Soc. (predoctoral fellow 1993—95), Am. Soc. Cell Biology, Beta Kappa Chi. Roman Catholic. Avocations: photography, table and lawn tennis, handball, racquetball, basketball. Home: 5056 Rails Way Norcross GA 30071-4514 Office: Morehouse Sch Medicine Dept Medicine 720 Westview Dr SW Atlanta GA 30310-1458 E-mail: BosahF@msm.edu.

BOSCHINI, VICTOR JOHN, JR., academic administrator; b. Cleve. m. Megan Boschini; children: Elizabeth, Mary Catherine, Edward Mark, Margaret. B in Sociology and Psychology, Union Coll.; M in Coll. Student Pers., Bowling Green State U.; D in Higher Edn. Adminstrn., Ind. U. Asst. to the dir. of residence life Bowling Green (Ohio) State U., 1978—79; student adviser Western Ill. U., Macomb, 1979—82; asst. dean of students DePauw U., Greencastle, Ind., 1982—84; asst. dean studies Ind. U., Bloomington, 1984—90; assoc. provost Butler U., Indpls., 1990—97; v.p., dean student affairs, edn. prof. Ill. State U., Normal, 1997—99, pres., 1999—2003; chancellor, prof. edn. Tex. Christian U., Ft. Worth, 2003—. Office: Tex Christian Univ Box 297080 3861 Bellaire Cir Fort Worth TX 76109

BOSHES, LOUIS D. physician, scientist, educator, historian, author; b. Chgo. s. Jacob and Ethel (London) B.; children: Arlene Phyllis Boshes Hirschfelder, Judi Myrl; m. Natalie A. Boshes. BS, Northwestern U., 1931, MD, 1936, postgrad., 1947-51; HHD (hon.), 1976. Diplomate neurology, psychiatry, and child neurology Am. Bd. Psychiatry and Neurology. Intern Michael Reese Hosp., Chgo., 1935-36, Cook County Hosp., 1936-37; fellow psychiatry Ill. Neuro-psychiat. Inst., Chgo., 1941-42, 46-47; sr. attending neurologist and psychiatrist, chief neurology clinic Michael Reese Med. Center, 1940—; sr. attending neurologist, psychiatrist emeritus Michael Reese Hosp. Med. Ctr.; prof. neurology and psychiatry Northwestern U., 1955-63; prof. neurology U. Ill. Coll. Medicine, Chgo., 1970-78, prof. emeritus, 1978—, historian and archivist in neurology; emeritus Cook County Hosp.; attending neurologist Ill. Research and Ednl. Hosps., 1963—, dir. consultation clinic for epilepsy, 1963-78; assoc. and attending neurologist, cons. neurology Cook County Hosp., 1947—; sr. cons. neurology Downey VA Hosp., 1952-60; prof. neurology Cook County Grad. Sch. Medicine, 1970—; practice medicine specializing in neurology and psychiatry, 1975—. Med. adv. com. Cook County chpt. Nat Found., 1947-55, March of Dimes, 1956—; med. adv. com. Epilepsy Assn. Am., 1964— ; bd. dirs., med. adv. com. Epilepsy Found. Am., 1964— ; ambassador Internat. Bur. Epilepsy, 1969— ; profl. adv. com. Nat. Parkinson Found., 1960—, Nat. Myasthenia Gravis Found., 1972— ; profl. adv. bd. United Cerebral Palsy; adv. bd. Cognitive Neurology and Alzheimer's Disease Ctr. Northwestern U., 2002--. Author, contbr. to books, med. jours.; assoc. editor Diseases of the Nervous System, 1962—; editor Chgo. Neurol. Soc. Bull., Behavioral Neuropsychiatry; mem. editorial bd. Excerpta Medica, Internat. Jour. Neurology and Neurosurgery. Historian, curator, archivist neurology U. Ill. Coll. Medicine at Chgo., 1990—, historian to Central Neuropsychiatric Assn, 1975—, Lt. comdr. M.C., USNR, 1941-46. Fellow ACP, Am. Acad. Neurology, Am. Psychiat. Assn. (disting. life); mem. AMA (cons. JAMA, bd. govs. 1991—), Inst. Medicine Chgo., Pan Am. Med. Assn. (pres. sect. neurology 1973—, hon. D.Hum. 1976), Ctrl. Neuropsychiat. Assn. (pres. 1973-74, historian, curator), Ill. Psychiat. Soc. (life, sec.-treas., acting pres. 1949-50), Chgo. Neurol. Soc. (pres. 1965-66, historian 1965—, curator), Michael Reese Hosp. and Med. Ctr. Alumni Assn. (pres. 1961-62), Assn. for Rsch. in Nervous and Mental Diseases, Internat. League Against Epilepsy, Am. League Against Epilepsy, Ill. League Against Epilepsy (med. adv. com.), Ill. Med. Soc. (chmn. sect. neurology and psychiatry 1961—), Chgo. Med. Soc., World Fedn. Neurology, AAAS, Am. Med. Soc. Vienna (life), Ctrl. Assn. Electroencephalographers, Sigma Xi, Phi Delta Epsilon, Alpha Omega Alpha. Home: 3150 N Lake Shore Dr Chicago IL 60657-4829 E-mail: l.boshes@uic.edu.

BOSLEY, KAREN LEE, English and journalism educator; b. Beech Grove, Ind., Sept. 23, 1942; d. Lowell Holmes and Kathryn Gertrude (Drake) Foley; m. Norman Keith Bosley, Dec. 21, 1964; children: Mark Harold, Rachael Kathryn, Keith Lowell, Sidney Clark. AB in Lang. Arts summa cum laude, U. Indpls., 1965; MA in English, Northwestern U., 1967; MA in Journalism, Ball State U., 1984; postgrad. (Newspaper Fund fellow), U. Mo., 1973; postgrad., Ohio U., 1977. Copy editor, reporter Indpls. News, 1963-65; English tchr., yearbook adviser Beech Grove (Ind.) Jr. H.S., 1965-66; English tchr. So. Regional H.S., Manahawkin, N.J., 1967-68; prof. humanities, journalism, and English Ocean County Coll., Toms River, N.J., 1971—, student newspaper adviser, 1971—, yearbook adviser, 1999—. Part-time reporter Daily Times-Observer, Toms River, 1972-77, part-time copy editor, 1993. Contbr. articles to publs. in field. Trustee Long Beach Island Hist. Assn., Friends of Island Libr., 1975-79; pres. Long Beach I PTA; chmn. Long Beach Twp. Dem. Mcpl. Com., 1971-78; Dem. committeeman Long Beach Twp. Dist. 2, 1971-78, 85—; mem. Long Beach Twp. Recreation Commn., 1972-75; bd. dirs. Ocean County Red Cross, 1972-78, Ocean County Family Planning, Inc., 1972-78, Student Press Law Ctr., 1987-2002, sec., 1998-2000, mem. adv. coun., 2002—; chmn. Cub Scout pack 32, Ocean County Coun. Boy Scouts Am.; founder, bd. dirs. Long Beach I Hist. Assn., Island Dems., Inc.; mem. adminstrv. bd. First United Meth. Ch. Beach Haven Terrace (N.J.); So. Regional H.S. Band Parent Orgn., 1995-96, pres., 1996-97, corr. sec; So. Regional Jazz Band Parents Assn., charter mem., 2001—. Mem. AAUW (pres., dir. Barnegat Light Area br.), NEA, N.J. Edn. Assn., Ocean County Edn. Assn., Faculty Assn. Ocean County Coll. (v.p. 1984-85), Coll. Media Advisers, Inc. (disting. newspaper adviser for U.S. 2-yr. colls. 1978, dir., sec.), Assn. Edn. in Journalism and Mass Comms., C.C. Journalism Assn. (dir., v.p.), Soc. Profl. Journalists, Internat. Platform Assn., Sigma Delta Chi. Home: 9 E Old Whaling Ln Long Beach Township NJ 08008-2930 Office: Ocean CC PO Box 2001 College Dr Toms River NJ 08754-2001 E-mail: kbosley@mac.com.

BOSMA, BETTE DEBRUYN, education educator; b. Ogilvie, Minn., Dec. 18, 1927; d. Jacob C. and Alice (Bajema) DeBruyn; m. John J. Bosma, Aug. 4, 1949; children: Susan, Timothy, Jane, Paul. BA, Calvin Coll., 1948; MA, Mich. State U., 1975, PhD, 1981. Tchr. Oakdale Sch., Grand Rapids, Mich., 1949-51; reading cons. Northview Mid. Sch., Grand Rapids, Mich., 1968-76; instr. Calvin Coll., Grand Rapids, Mich., 1976-77, asst. prof. edn., 1977-79, assoc. prof. edn., 1979-84, prof. edn., 1984-92, prof. emeritus, 1992—. Mem. adv. bd. Potters House Sch., Grand Rapids, 1981—; cons. in field. Author: Fairytales, Fables, Myths, Legends, 1987, 2d edit. 1992; author/editor: Children's Literature in Integrated Classrooms, 1995; contbr. articles to profl. jours. Com. mem. Park Commn., Grand Haven Twp., Mich., 1990-2002. Mem. Nat. Coun. Tchrs. English (com. mem. 1976-93), Internat. Reading Assn., Internat. Bd. Books for Young People, Children'sLit. Assembly (com. mem. 1984-90). Avocations: travel, hiking, reading, knitting. Office: Calvin Coll Edn Dept Grand Rapids MI 49546

BOSTER, JUDY LANDEN, primary school educator; b. Foster, Ky., Aug. 20, 1941; d. George Stanton and Cora Helen (Egnew) Landen; m. Kenneth Barry Boster, Sr., Dec. 26, 1964; children: Kenda Kaye Rabe, Kenneth Barry Boster, Jr. AB, U. Ky., 1965; MA, No. Ky. U., 1981, Rank I, 1991. Tchr. Woodford County Bd. Edn., Versailles, Ky., 1965-66, Erlanger-Elsmere Bd. Edn., Erlanger, Ky., 1966-69, Kenton County (Ky.) Bd. Edn., Independence, 1972—. Mem. Alpha Delta Kappa (pres. 1988-90), Phi Delta Kappa. Avocations: reading, sewing. Office: Beechgrove Elem 1029 Bristow Rd Independence KY 41051-9600

BOSTICK, CHARLES DENT, retired lawyer, educator; b. Gainesville, Ga., Dec. 28, 1931; s. Jared Sullivan and Charlotte Catherine (Dent) B.; m. Susan Oliver, Sept. 8, 1956; children: Susan, Alan. Student, Emory-at-Oxford U., 1948-49; BA, Mercer U., 1952, JD, 1958. Bar: Ga. 1957, Tenn. 1974, U.S. Dist. Ct. (no. dist.) Ga. 1958, U.S. Ct. Appeals (5th cir.) 1959. Pvt. practice, Gainesville, Ga., 1958-66; asst. prof. law U. Fla., Gainesville, 1966-68, assoc. prof., 1968, Vanderbilt U., Nashville, 1968-71, prof., 1971-92, assoc. dean, dir. admissions, 1975-79, acting dean, 1979-80, dean, 1980-85; ret., 1992. Vis. prof. law U. Leeds, Eng., 1985-86, prof. law emeritus, dean emeritus Sch. Law, 1992. Served to lt. USNR, 1952-55. Mem. Tenn. Bar. Assn. Episcopalian. Office: Vanderbilt U Sch Law 21st Ave S Nashville TN 37240-0001

BOSTON, BILLIE, costume designer, costume history educator; b. Oklahoma City, Sept. 22, 1939; d. William Barrett and Margaret Emeline (Townsend) Long; m. William Clayton Boston, Jr., Jan. 20, 1962; children: Kathryn Gray, William Clayton III. BFA, U. Okla., 1961, MFA, 1962. Asst. to designer Karinski of N.Y., N.Y.C., 1966-67; prof. costume history Oklahoma City U., 1987—. Rep. Arts Coun., Oklahoma City, 1987-90, Arts Festival, Oklahoma City, 1972-80; dir. ETC Theater, Oklahoma City SW Coll., 1979-83; actress Lyric Theatre, Oklahoma City, 1979-81; designer Casa Mahara Theatre, Ft. Worth, 1998. Exhibited in group shows at Taos, N.Mex., Santa Fe; represented in permanent collections in Dallas, Taos, Santa Fe, Tulsa, N.Y.C., La Jolla; costume designer Ballet Okla., Oklahoma City, 1979-84, Agnes DeMillie's Rodeo Ballet Okla., 1982, Royal Ballet Flanders, 1983, Pitts. Ballet, 1983, BBC's Childrens Prodn., 1984, 86, Lyric Theatre, Oklahoma City, 1987-95, Red Oak Music Theatre, Lakewood, N.J., 1988, Winter Olympics, 1988, Miss Am. Pageant, 1988, for JoAnne Worley in Hello Dolly, San Francisco Opera Circus, 1991, Jupiter (Fla.) Theatre, 1991-92, Mobile (Ala.) Light Opera, 1992, The Boy Friend, Temple U., Japan, 1995, The Sound of Music, Lyric Stage, Dallas, 1995, Annie Get Your Gun, Guys and Dolls with Vic Damone, 1995, Westbury Flash Valley Forge Music Fair, Oklahoma and Sound of Music, Casa Manana, Theatre, Ft. Worth, 1997, Singing in the Rain, Lone Star Theatre, Galveston, Tex., 1997, Most Happy Fellow, Lyric Stage Dallas, 1997, To Gillian on her 37th Birthday, Watertower Theatre, Dallas, 1998, Carousel, Annie Get Your Gun, Cinderella, Casa Manana, 1998; designer Titanic, Irving, Tex., 2003, Specture Bridegroom, Irving, 2003, Opal, Lyric Stage, Irving, 2003. Rep. Speakers Bur. Oklahoma City for Ballet, 1979-85; judge State Hist. Speech Tournament, Oklahoma City, 1985-87; chmn. State of Okla. Conf. on Tchr./Student Relationships, Oklahoma City, 1981. Recipient Gov.'s Achievement award, 1988, Lady in the News award, 1987; Excellence in Costume Design award Kennedy Ctr. Am. Coll. Theatre Festival XXXIV, 2001; nom. Outstanding Costume Designer Southwest, Dallas Theatre League, 2003. Mem. Alpha Chi Omega (house corp. bd. 1986-90). Methodist. Avocation: watercolorist. Home: 1701 Camden Way Oklahoma City OK 73116-5121

BOSTON, MARTHA BIBEE, psychologist, educator; b. L.A., Sept. 16, 1948; d. Ernest Arnold Bibee and Elsie (Fryling) Vincent; m. Daniel G. Coston, Aug. 17, 1968 (div. 1982); 1 child, Seth Bibee Coston; m. Christopher McKenney, Aug. 29, 1987; 1 child, Amy Jo. BS, Harding U., 1970; MS, U. Del., 1982, PhD, 1984. Lic. clin. psychologist, N.J., Del., Pa. High sch. tchr. Indian River Sch. Dist., Georgetown, Del., 1970-79; rsch. asst. U. Del., Newark, Del., 1980-84, instr., 1982-84; asst. prof. Allentown Coll., Center Valley, Pa., 1984-87, Neumann Coll., Aston, Pa., 1987-90, assoc. prof., 1990-93; pvt. practice part-time psychologist, 1992-94; adj. prof., 1993-95; staff psychologist med. dept. nuclear Pub. Svc. Electric and Gas, Hancocks Bridge, N.J., 1993-96; state dir. mental health Correctional Med. Svcs., Delaware Dept. Corrections, 1996; lead psychologist Correctional Behavioral Solutions, N.J. Dept. Corrections, 1996-97; state dir. mental health N.J. Correctional Behavioral Solutions Dept. Corrections, 1997-98; psychologist young criminal offender program Correctional Med. Svcs. Del. Dept. Correction, 1997—; ednl. diagnostician Dept. Edn., 2001—02; chief regional psychologist First Correctional Med., Del., 2002—. Clin. intern in psychology Allentown Coll. Counseling Ctr., Center Valley, Pa., 1984-87. Contbr. articles to profl. jours. Adult edn. coord. St. Paul's United Meth. Ch., Wilmington, Del., 1988-91, Grace United Meth. Ch., Georgetown, Del., 1974-79, coun. on ministries adminstrv. bd. coord. Christian edn., 1975-79, Birmingham Friends Meeting, 1996—; worship and care std. com. mem. Phila. Yearly Meeting, Quakers, 1999-2000. Recipient Pres. Award for Dissertation, U. Del., Newark, 1984, Runner-up Woodrow Wilson Award for Dissertation, 1984. Mem. NOW (pres. Bucks County chpt. 1986-87), APA, Pa. Psychol. Assn. Democrat. Office: MPCJF Delaware DOC 1301 E 12th St Wilmington DE 19802-5315

BOSTON, WILLIAM LAWRENCE, elementary educator, administrator; b. Balt., July 16, 1951; s. William Lawrence and Elizabeth (Coates) B.; 1 child, Tyrell Franklin. BS, Coppin State Coll., 1983; MS, Johns Hopkins U., 1989. Tchr. Balt. City Pub. Schs., 1970—. Presenter workshops in field; mem. theater curriculum development team Md. State Dept. Edn.; drama instr. Learning Through the Arts; mem. supt.'s com. to organize citywide parent/community conf., 1990-91. Bldg. rep. Baot. Tchrs. Union, 1977—; mem. community choirs The Majestics, Interfaith Community Singers; mem. Arena Players. Democrat. Mem. African Methodist Episcopal Ch. Avocations: singing, writing, travel, modeling. Office: Balt City Pub Schs 1500 Imla St Baltimore MD 21224-6142

BOSWELL, FRED C. retired soil science educator, researcher; b. Monterey, Tenn., Aug. 20, 1930; s. Ferdando Cortez and Julia Ann (Speck) B.; m. Marjorie Sue Brown, Sept. 3, 1954; children: Elaine Joy Boswell King, Julia Alma Boswell Merry. BS, Tenn. Tech., 1954; MS, U. Tenn., 1956; PhD, Pa. State U., 1960. Asst. agron U. Tenn., Knoxville, 1955-56; asst. soil chemist Ga. Agrl. Experimental Sta., Experimental, Ga., 1956-57; asst. prof. U. Ga., Athens, 1960-82, prof., head agronomy dept., 1982-89, prof. Griffin, 1989-91, prof. emeritus, 1991—; adj. prof. U. Tenn., 1993—. Contbr. chpts. to numerous books and sci. jours. on agrl. concerns; mem. editorial com. Fertilizer Technology and Use, 1985. Mem. com. State of Ga. Goals for Ga., 1971; chmn. subcom. Griffin Spalding Co., Ga., 1988. With U.S. Army, 1951-53. Fellow Am. Soc. Agronomy, Soil Sci. Soc. Am. (bd. dirs. 1978-80, so. branch pres. 1983-84), Toastmasters (v.p. 1972). Achievements include research related to certain micronutrients nitrification transformation and nitrogen movement and nitrification inhibitors; published/researched in environmental science, emphasis on land treatment waste materials. Home: 748 Russell Strausse Cookeville TN 38501-4515

BOSWELL, JAMES AURTHUR, JR., English language educator; b. Pitts., Mar. 21, 1953; s. James A. and Pauline R. B.; m. Olivia. BA summa cum laude, Slippery Rock U., 1975, MA, 1980. Ops. mgr. Hills Dept. Store, York, Pa., 1975-77; fin. trainee GE, Erie, Pa., 1977-78; mgmt. trainee Montgomery Ward, Meadville, Pa., 1978-79; educator Harrisburg (Pa.) Area C.C., 1981—. Writing lab. coord. Harrisburg C.C., 1981-88, 93—; presenter at numerous ednl. seminars and workshops, 1984—. Contbr. articles to profl. jours., poetry to mags; editor: (poetry) The World According to Siggy, 1988. Vol. instr. reading, writing, Melrose Project; instr. in report writing to high sch. engring. students; mem. United Way Com., Harrisburg; active Adult Choir, deacon Ch. Brethren. Recipient Recgnition Svc. cert. Faculty Coun., Harrisburg C.C., Gratitude award from Black Student Union mems, Nat. Instr. award of merit Internat. Assn. Automotive Svc. Ednl. Program, 1998. Mem. MLA, Pa. Assn. Devel. Educators, Nat. Coun. Tchrs. English, Mid-Atlantic Writing Ctrs. Assn., Assembly for Tchg. English Grammar. Home: 676 S 82nd St Harrisburg PA 17111-5533 Office: Harrisburg Area CC 1 Harrisburg Area CC Dr Harrisburg PA 17110

BOSWELL, TOMMIE C. retired middle school educator; b. Gainesboro, Tenn., Nov. 8, 1942; d. Tommy and Ethel (Draper) Cassetty; m. Neal Stanley Boswell, Aug. 28, 1965; children: Brian Andrew, James Travis. AA, Cumberland U., Lebanon, Tenn., 1962; BS, Tenn. Technol. U., 1965; MAT, Rollins Coll., Winter Park, Fla., 1980, EdS, 1984. Cert. tchr. English, social studies; cert. adminstrv. supr. Tchr. English and social studies Beaumont Middle Sch., Kissimmee, Fla., 1965-72, tchr. social studies, 1978-89, Neptune Middle sch., Kissimmee, 1989-99; ret. Team leader 8th Grade Acad. Team "Challengers", Kissimmee, 1994—. Founding pres. Canterbury Lane Neighborhood Assn., Kissimmee, 1988; mem. N.M.S. Program Improvement Coun., Kissimmee, 1994—. Named Social Studies Tchr. of the Yr., Fla. Coun. for Social Studies, 1984, 86, 89, Outstanding Tchr. of Am. History, Joshua Stevens chpt. DAR, Kissimmee, 1982; Delta Kappa Gamma scholar, 1980. Mem. Fla. Trails Assn. Appalachian Trail Conf., Jackson County Tenn. Hist. Soc. Republican. Methodist. Avocations: geneology, reading, bottle and stamp collecting, hiking.

BOSWORTH, BRUCE LEIGHTON, school administrator, educator, consultant; b. Buffalo, Mar. 22, 1942; s. John Wayman and Alice Elizabeth Rodgers; children: David, Timothy, Paul, Sheri, Skyler. BA, U. Denver, 1964; MA, U. No. Colo., 1970; EdD, Walden U., 1984. Elem. tchr. Littleton (Colo.) Pub. Schs., 1964-67, 70-81; bldg. prin. East Smoky Sch. Divsn. 54, Valleyview, Alta., Can., 1967-70; pres., tchr. St. Michael's-of-the-Mountains Sch., Littleton, 1981—. Adoption cons. hard-to-place children; ednl. cons. spl. needs children Warren United Meth. Ch. Mem. ASCD, Coun. Exceptional Children, Masons, Shriners, York Rite. Home and Office: 3500 S Lowell Blvd Apt 316 Denver CO 80236-6168 E-mail: misterb@yahoo.com.

BOSWORTH, THOMAS LAWRENCE, architect, architecture educator; b. Oberlin, Ohio, June 15, 1930; s. Edward Franklin and Imogene (Rose) B.; m. Abigail Lumbard, Nov. 6, 1954 (div. Nov. 1974); children: Thomas Edward, Nathaniel David; m. Elaine R. Pedigo, Nov. 23, 1974; stepchildren: Robert Haden Pedigo, Kevin Ian Pedigo. BA, Oberlin Coll., 1952, MA, 1954; postgrad., Princeton U., 1952-53, Harvard U., 1956-57; MArch, Yale U., 1960; PhD Honoris Causa (hon.), Kobe U., Japan, 2003. Draftsman Gordon McMaster AIA, Cheshire, Conn., summer 1957-58; resident planner Tunnard & Harris Planning Cons., Newport, R.I., summer 1959; designer, field supr. Eero Saarinen & Assocs., Birmingham, Mich., 1960-61, Hamden, Conn., 1961-64; individual practice architecture Providence, 1964-68, Seattle, 1968—; asst. instr. architecture Yale U., 1962-65, vis. lectr., 1965-66; asst. prof. R.I. Sch. Design, 1964-66, asso. prof., head dept., 1966-68; prof. architecture U. Wash., Seattle, 1968-98, prof. emeritus, 1998—, chmn. dept., 1968-72; chief architecture Peace Corps Tng. Program, Tunisia, Brown U., summers 1965-66; archtl. cons., individual practice Seattle, 1972—; dir. multidisciplinary program U. Wash., Rome, Italy, 1984-86. Vis. lectr. Kobe U., Japan, Oct., 1982, Nov., 1990, Apr., 1993, May, 1995, June, 1998; Pietro Belluschi Disting. Vis. Prof. U. Oreg., 1996; dir. arch. in Rome program U. Wash., Rome, 1996. Bd. dirs. N.W. Inst. Arch. and Urban Studies, Italy, 1983-90, pres., 1983-85; dir. Pilchuch Glass Sch., Seattle, 1977-80, trustee, 1980-91, adv. coun., 1993—; mem. Seattle Model Cities Land Use Rev. Bd., 1969-70, Tech. Com. Site Selection Wash. Multi-Purpose Stadium, 1970, Medina Planning Commn., 1972-74, steering adv. com. King County Stadium, 1972-74, others; chmn. King County (Wash.) Environ. Devel. Commn., 1972-74, King County Policy Devel. Commn., 1974-77; bd. dirs. Arcade Mag., 1988-2002, pres. 1988-2000; bd. mgrs. YMCA Camping Svcs., 1998-2002; adv. bd. U. Wash Rome Ctr., 1999—. With U.S. Army, 1954-56. Winchester Traveling fellow Greece, 1960; assoc. fellow Ezra Stiles Coll. Yale U.; mid-career fellow in arch. Am. Acad. in Rome, 1980-81, vis. scholar, Spring 1988. Fellow AIA (Seattle medal 2003); mem. Monday Club (Seattle), Bohemian Club (San Francisco), Tau Sigma Delta. Home: 2411 25th Ave E Seattle WA 98112-2610 Office: U Wash Dept Architecture PO Box 355720 Seattle WA 98195-5720

BOSWORTH, WILLIAM POSEY, physician, physical education educator; b. Valdosta, Ga., Mar. 23, 1935; s. Paul Brooks and Myra Mae (Posey) B.; m. Wanda Marie Grimm; 1 child, Lynne Marie. BS, U. Tampa, 1957; MEd, Springfield (Mass.) Coll., 1961; postgrad., Orlando (Fla.) Jr. Coll., 1968; DO, U. Health Scis., Kansas City, Mo., 1972. Phys. edn. tchr., jr. high sch. tchr. Duval County Sch. Bd., Jacksonville, Fla., 1959—62; intern U.S. Naval Hosp., Phila., 1972—73; gen. practice medicine Jacksonville, 1974—. Physician athletic team, 1975—. Mem. Duval County Sch. Bd., Jacksonville, 1986—90, Jacksonville Sports Com., 1981—86, chmn., 1986; mem. Duval County Hosp. Authority, 1982—86, chmn., 1986; mem. Fla. Gov.'s Coun. on Phys. Fitness and Sports, 1985—93, Fla. Sunshine State Games Found., 1990—99, Sports in Fla. Found., 2000—. With USMCR, 1953—58, with USNR, 1969—99, capt. M.C., 1988—. Decorated Navy Commendation medals (2), Meritorious Svc. medal; named Gen. Practitioner of Yr., Fla. Soc. Am. Coll. Family Physicians, 1982, Health Educator of the Yr., Duval County Coalition Against Tobacco, 1991; recipient Physician's Recognition award, AMA, 1988, 1991, 1994, 1997, 1999, 2002, Vol. Svc. 35 yr. gold pin award, AAU/USA, 1988. Mem.: PTA (hon. life-Fla. 2000, Nat. 2001), Freedoms Found. at Valley Forge (pres. Jacksonville chpt. 1995—97), Assn. Mil. Surgeons U.S., Duval County Acad. Family Physicians (pres. 1984), Duval County Med. Soc., Fla. Soc. Sons of Am. Revolution (pres. 1980, 2000, Meritorious Svc. medal 1986, Disting. Svc. medal 2001), Fla. Med. Assn., Rotary Club of Mandarin (charter mem. 1975, pres. 1985—86), Rotary Club of San Jose (charter mem. 2003), Am. Legion 40/8 Honor Soc. (Voyageur of Yr. 1990). Office: 9765 San Jose Blvd Jacksonville FL 32257-4402

BOTSTEIN, LEON, academic administrator, conductor, historian; b. Zurich, Switzerland, Dec. 14, 1946; s. Charles and Anne (Wyszewianski) Botstein; m. Jill Lundquist, 1970 (div.); children: Sarah, Abigail(dec.); m. Barbara Haskell, 1982. BA (Woodrow Wilson fellow, Danforth Found. fellow, Sloan Found. fellow, Rockefeller fellow), U. Chgo., 1967; MA, Harvard U., 1968, PhD, 1985. Teaching fellow Harvard U., 1968—69; lectr. history Boston U., 1969; asst. to pres. N.Y.C. Bd. Edn., 1969—70; pres. Franconia Coll., 1970—75, Bard Coll., Annandale-On-Hudson, 1975—, Simon's Rock Coll. Bard, Great Barrington, Mass., 1979—; founder, artistic dir. Bard Music Festival, 1990—; music dir. Am. Symphony Orch., N.Y.C., 1992—, Jerusalem Symphony Orch., 2003—; artistic dir. Am. Russian Young Artists Orch., 1995—. Founder, prin. condr. White Mountain Music and Art Festival, NH, 1973—75; condr. Hudson Valley Philharm. Chamber Orch., 1989—92; guest condr. London Philharmonic, 1986—99, Philharmonia Orch., 1986, Pro Arte Chamber Orch. of Boston, 1988—89; other guest conducting appearances in Korea, Japan, Czech Republic, Philippines, Austria, Brazil, Lithuania, Romania, Scotland, Germany, Switzerland, Russia; past chmn. N.Y. Coun. Humanitites, Assn. Episc. Colls., Harper's Mag. Found.; vis. prof. Hochschule fur angewandte Kunst, Vienna, 1988; vis. faculty Manhattan Sch. Music, 1986; chmn. Salzburg Seminar, 1987; mem. nat. adv. com. Yale-New Haven Tchrs. Inst. Author: (novels) Jefferson's Children: Education and the Promise of American Culture, 1997; editor: (book) The Compleat Brahms, 1999, Musical Quar., 1992—; contbr. articles to profl. publs.; conductor: albums. Recipient Berlin Prize Fellowship; grantee Rockefeller fellow. Fellow: Am. Acad. Arts & Scis. Office: Bard Coll Office of Pres Annandale On Hudson NY 12504

BOTTOM, DORIS ALLENE, secondary school educator; b. Weatherford, Okla., Aug. 4, 1936; d. Aubrey Daniel and Buena Vista (Wilson) Shewmaker; m. George Grayson Bottom, Oct. 9, 1955; children: Earl Grayson, Paula Allene, Allen Elwood, Jo Ann. BS in Elem. Edn., Southwestern Okla. State U., 1969, BS in Bus. Edn., 1986, MEd, 1987; postgrad., U. Fla., 1973-75. Cert. tchr. Fla., Okla. Tchr. Duvall Pub. Sch., Jacksonville, Fla., 1969, Baker County Pub. Sch., Macclenny, Fla., 1969-81; prin. Sew-N-Nook, Macclenny, Fla., 1977-79; tchr. Hammon (Okla.) Pub. Sch., 1981—. Evening instr. Okla. State U., 1990-91, 91-92. Mem. NEA, Okla. Edn. Assn., Fla. Edn. Assn. (bd. dirs. 1977), Okla. Edn. Microcomputer Assn. (pres.), Nat. Bus. Edn. Assn., Assn. Classroom Tchrs., Okla. Bus. Edn. Assn., Delta Kappa Gamma. Democrat. Mem. Ch. Christ. Office: Hammon Pub Sch 8th & Common St PO Box 279 Hammon OK 73650-0279

BOTTOMLEY, PAUL ARTHUR, radiology educator; b. Ivanhoe, Victoria, Australia, Mar. 14, 1953; BS with honors, Monash U., 1975; PhD, U. Nottingham, Eng., 1978. Rsch. assoc. Johns Hopkins U., Balt., 1978-80; physicist G-E R&D Ctr., Schenectady, N.Y., 1980-94; Russell H. Morgan prof. radiology Johns Hopkins U., Balt., 1994—, dir. Divsn. MR Rsch., 1997—. Bd. dirs. Surgi-Vision Inc. Mem. editl. bd. Magnetic Resonance in Medicine, Magnetic Resonance Imaging, Magnetic Resonance Materials in Physics Biology & Medicine; contbr. more than 125 refereed articles to profl. jours. Coolidge fellow G-E R&D Devel. Ctr., 1990. Fellow Soc. Magnetic Resonance in Medicine (Gold medal 1989). Achievements include key role in development of high-field magnetic resonance imaging and localized magnetic resonance spectroscopy, including human applications; 29 patents in field. Office: Johns Hopkins U Dept Radiology 601 N Caroline St Ste 4221 Baltimore MD 21287-0843

BOTTOMS, BRENDA PINCHBECK, elementary education educator; b. South Hill, Va., Sept. 30, 1958; d. Bernard Irving Jr. and Laura Etta (Rogers) Pinchbeck; m. Franklin Keith Bottoms, Apr. 20, 1984; children: David Keith, Heath Brennan. BS in Elem. Edn., Longwood Coll., Farmville, Va., 1979. Cert. 4-7 tchr., Va.; cert. talented and gifted tchr., 1997. Substitute tchr. Nottoway County Schs., Blackstone, Va., 1979-80; mid. sch. tchr. Greensville County Schs., Emporia, Va., 1981-83, elem. tchr., 1983—. 6th grade chmn. Belfield Elem. Sch., Emporia, 1990-93; Hugs tutorial tchr., 1987; cert. Spaulding tchr., 1989, reading in the content areas tchr. Participant Quality Schs. Com., 1993-94. Recipient Parent Vol. award Greensville County Schs., 1991, Women's Leadership award Greensville County, 1990, 91. Avocations: reading, crocheting, sports, children. Home: 2351 Zion Church Rd Emporia VA 23847-7347 Office: Belfield Elem Sch 515 Belfield Rd Emporia VA 23847-8065

BOTTOMS, ROBERT GARVIN, academic administrator; b. Birmingham, Ala., June 28, 1944; s. Dalton Garvin and Mary Inez (Cruce) Bottoms; m. Gwendolynn Jean Vickers, June 14, 1968; children: David Timothy, Leslie Clair. BA, Birmingham So. U., 1966; BD, Emory U., 1969; D of Ministry, Vanderbilt U., 1972. Chaplain Birmingham (Ala.) So. Coll., 1972—74, asst. to pres., 1974—75; asst. dean, asst. prof. church and ministry Vanderbilt U., Nashville, 1975—78; v.p. for univ. rels. DePauw U., Greencastle, Ind., 1978—79, exec. v.p. external rels., 1979—83, exec. v.p. of univ., 1983—86, acting pres., 1985, pres., 1986—. Cons. Arthur Vining Davis Found., Jacksonville, Fla., 1978—79, Luth. So. Sem., Columbia, SC, 1979—80; cons. theol. edn. The Lilly Endowment, Indpls., 1979—82; cons. Fund for Theol. Edn., N.Y.C., 1981—82; chmn. audit com. Centel Cable TV Co., Oak Brook, Ill., 1987—89; Am. ctr. for internat. leadership organizer Edn. Policy Commn. U.S.-USSR Emerging Leaders Summit, Phila., 1988. Author: Lessons in Financial Development, 1982. Chmn. com. on ch. and coll. Episcopal Diocese Ind., 1979—84; bd. advisors Vanderbilt Div. Sch., 1980—93; bd. trustees Seabury-Western Theol. Sem., 2001—; bd. dirs. Joyce Found., 1994—2002, G.M. Constrn. Inc., Indpls., 1998—, The Posse Found., 2001—, Women in Govt., Washington, 2001—. Recipient CASE V Chief Exec. Leadership award, 2000. Mem.: NCAA (coun. 1989—95, subcom. eligibility appeals), Ind. Colls. Ind. Found. (bd. dirs. 1987—, nominating com. 1990—), Women in Govt. (bd. dirs. 2001—), Great Lakes Colls. Assn. (bd. dirs. 1987—, chair 1994—96), Ind. Colls. of Ind. (bd. dirs. 1987—, exec. com. 1991—), Am. Coun. Edn. (commn. on women in higher edn. 1990—91), Assn. Governing Bds. Univs. and Colls. (coun. pres. 1997—), Nat. Assn. Schs. and Colls. United Meth. Ch. (bd. dirs. 1987—91), Nat. Assn. Ind. Colls. and Univs. (task force increasing participation of minorities in ind. higher edn. 1989—95), Nat. Coun. Chs. (governing bd. 1985—91), Chgo. Club., Cosmos Club (Washington), Univ. Club of N.Y.C., Columbia Club (Indpls.). Avocation: boating. Home: 125 Wood St Greencastle IN 46135 Office: DePauw Univ Office of Pres 313 S Locust St Greencastle IN 46135-0037

BOUCHARD, THOMAS JOSEPH, JR., psychology educator, researcher; b. Manchester, N.H., Oct. 3, 1937; s. Thomas and Florence (Charest) B.; m. Pauline Marina Proulx, Aug. 13, 1960; children: Elizabeth, Mark. BA, U. Calif., Berkeley, 1963, PhD, 1966. Asst. prof. U. Calif., Santa Barbara, 1966-69, U. Minn., Mpls., 1969-70, assoc. prof., 1970-73, prof., 1973—, chmn. dept. psychology, 1985-91. Dir. Minn. Ctr. Twin and Adoption Rsch., U. Minn., 1980—. Editor (assoc.): (jour.) Jour. Applied Psychology, 1977—80, Behavior Genetics, 1982—86; contbr. articles jours. over 150 articles to profl. jours. With USAF, 1955-58. Fellow AAAS, APA, Am. Psychol. Soc.; mem. Phi Beta Kappa, Sigma Xi. Home: 1860 Shoreline Dr Wayzata MN 55391-9771 Office: Univ of Minn Dept Psychology 75 E River Rd Minneapolis MN 55455-0280 E-mail: bouch001@tc.umn.edu.

BOUCHELLE, HENRY ELLSWORTH WIRT, III, planetarium director, educator; b. Wilmington, Del., July 15, 1949; s. Henry Ellsworth Wirt Jr. and Evelyn Elizabeth (Gray) B.; m. Mary Christine Baker, Dec. 27, 1970 (div.); children: Henry Mitchell, Samuel Stuart. BA, Johns Hopkins U., 1971; EdD, Wilmington Coll., 2002; MS, Johns Hopkins U., 1976. Diplomate Am. Watchmakers Inst.; cert. tchr. Tchr. Gibson Island (Md.) Sch., 1973-76; reading specialist Charlotte (N.C.) Country Day Sch., 1976-78; instr. Winthrop Coll., Rock Hill, S.C., 1978-81; tchr. Pilot Sch., Wilmington, Del., 1981-86; planetarium dir. Colonial Sch. Dist., New Castle, Del., 1986—. Dir. Project Starwalk, Colonial Sch. Dist., New Castle, 1986—; agt. Project SPICA, NSF/Harvard Ctr. for Astrophysics, Cambridge, Mass., 1989—. Astromoner-in-residence Ashland Nature Ctr., Hockessin, Del., 1992—. Tchr. in Space finalist, NASA, Washington, 1985. Mem. Del. Astron. Soc. (pres. 1992—), Am. Assn. Variable Star Observers, Nat. Sci. Tchrs. Assn., Mid. Atlantic Planetarium Soc., Del. County Acad. of Sci., Phi Delta Kappa. Avocations: astronomy, amateur rocketry, antique clocks. Home: 1320 W 7th St Wilmington DE 19805-3223 Office: Starwalk Planetarium Colonial Sch Chase Ave New Castle DE 19720 E-mail: hbouchel@udel.edu.

BOUCHER, LAURENCE JAMES, educator, chemist; b. Yonkers, N.Y., Sept. 16, 1938; s. Edward Joseph Boucher and Matilda Ann (Klicska) Higgins; m. Susan Ann Calkins, Aug. 15, 1964; children: Amy Elizabeth, Stephen Edward. AAS in Indsl. Chemistry, Westchester C.C., White Plains, N.Y., l958; BS in Chemistry, Mich. State U., l960; MS in Chemistry, U. Ill., l962, PhD Inorganic Chemistry, l964. Resident rsch. assoc. Argonne (Ill.) Nat. Lab., l964-66; asst. prof. chemistry Carnegie-Mellon U., Pitts., 1966-7l, assoc. prof., l97l-76; titular prof. U. Autonoma Metropolitana, Mexico City, l976-78; prof. chemistry, head dept. Western Ky. U., Bowling Green, l978-85; dean Coll. Arts and Scis., Ark. State U., Jonesboro, 1985-90; dean Coll. Natural and Math. Scis. Towson (Md.) U., 1990-97, prof. chemistry, 1997—. Prof. Exxon Rsch. Co., Linden, N.J., l973; rsch. chemist U.S. Dept. Energy, Bruceton, Pa., l976; Fulbright lectr., Colombia, l98l. Contbr. numerous articles to profl. jours. Mem. Am. Chem. Soc., Sigma Xi, Phi Kappa Phi, Alpha Sigma Lambda. Democrat. Episcopalian. Avocation: latin american studies. Office: Towson U Dept Chemistry 8000 York Rd Towson MD 21252-0001 E-mail: laurenceboucher@netscape.net., lboucher@towson.edu.

BOUCHER, RAYMOND JOSEPH, retired secondary school educator; b. Central Falls, R.I., Nov. 11, 1933; s. Elzear and Roseanna (Carrignan) B.; m. Potenciana Cruz Santos, July 4, 1963; children: Raymond M., Ronald J., Richard Eric. BA, St. Joseph Coll., Spring Hill, Ala., 1954; MEd, Loyola U., Chgo., 1958; MA, Ateneo de Manila U., Quezon City, The Philippines, 1971; postgrad., SUNY, Buffalo, 1971-72. Cert. tchr., N.Y., N.M. Tchr. Mt. St. Charles Acad., Woonsocker, R.I., 1953-57, Cath. Mission ednl. system, Alexishafen Vicariate, New Guinea, 1958-63; instr. gen. and ednl. psychology Far Eastern U., Manila, Philippines, 1963-64; tchr., head tchr., supr. elem. schs. Trust Territory Pacific Islands, Truk, Palau, 1964-68; tchr. chemistry and English as a second lang. Palau High Sch., Western Caroline Islands, 1969-71; sci. tchr. Marshall Islands High Sch., 1972-76; tchr. sci. and electronics Gallup (N.Mex.) High Sch., 1976-80, tchr. math., 1980-98; ret., 1998. Instr. math. U. N.Mex., Albuqerque, 1980—: mem. systemic change com. NSF, 1991-92; tchr./developer developmental math. program Coll. of Marshall Islands, 1995—. Apptd. mem. Coun. Advancement Math. and Sci. Edn., 1991-92; mem. math curriculum com. N.M. Dept. Edn., 1992. Mem. Nat. Coun. Tchrs. Math., Am. Math. Soc., N.Mex. Coun. Tchrs. Math. (pres. 1990-92, mem. exec. coun. 1992-94). Roman Catholic. Avocations: amateur radio, carpentry, gardening. Home: PO Box 1258 Majuro MH 96960-1258

BOUCHER, THOMAS OWEN, engineering educator, researcher; b. Providence, June 25, 1942; s. Joseph William and Anne Marie (Byrne) B.; m. Unn Gunnerus Jermstad, Mar. 30, 1974. BSEE, U. R.I., 1964; MBA, Northwestern U., 1970; PhD in Indsl. Engring., Columbia U., 1978. Sr. project engr. Continental Can Co., Chgo., 1967-69; sr. staff cons. ABEX Corp., N.Y.C., 1970-72; asst. prof. Cornell U., Ithaca, N.Y., 1978-81, Rutgers U., New Brunswick, N.J., 1981-87, assoc. prof., 1987-94; prof., 1994—. Author: Computer Automation in Manufacturing, 1996; co-author: Analysis and Control of Production Systems, 2d edit., 1994; dept. editor IIE Transactions, 1987-91; area editor Engring. Economist, 1989-93; assoc. editor Jour. Productivity Analysis, 1989-91; mem. editl. bd. Internat. Jour. Flexible Automation and Integrated Mfg., 1992-2000, Jour. Engring. Valuation and Cost Analysis, 1995—. 1st lt. U.S. Army, 1965—67, Vietnam. Grantee NSF, Def. Logistics Agy. Mem. IEEE (sr.), SME (sr.), Am. Soc. for Engring. Edn. (chmn. engring. econ. dir. 1986-87), N.Y. Acad. Scis., Inst. Indsl. Engrs. (sr. mem., Wellington award 2002), Sigma Xi. Roman Catholic. Achievements include research in manufacturing automation, computer integrated manufacturing systems, production planning and control, and engineering economics. Home: 65 Douglas Rd Glen Ridge NJ 07028-1227 Office: Rutgers U Sch Engring 96 Frelinghuysen Rd Piscataway NJ 08855-0909

BOUCHILLON, JOHN RAY, education coordinator; b. Covington, Ga., Sept. 3, 1943; s. John Ray and Mary Reid (Death) B.; m. Martha Jo Logue, Dec. 18, 1965; children: Trey, Monica, Beth. BA, LaGrange Coll., 1965; MEd, Ga. Coll., 1969. Tchr. chemistry Baldwin County, Milledgeville, Ga., 1965-71, career coord., 1971-72; dir. career edn. Liberty County, Hinesville, Ga., 1972-75; career edn. cons. Ga. Dept. Edn., Atlanta, 1975-86, quality basic edn. field adminstr., 1986-87, coord. local strategic planning, 1987-92, sch. support team leader, 1992-98, ret., 1998. Dir. sch. support svcs., asst. dir. sch. improvement and tng. divsn. Ga. Dept. Edn., 1996-98; chmn. career edn. adv. com. Ga. So. Coll., Statesboro, 1972-73; dir.-at-large guidance div. Ga. Vocat. Assn., Atlanta, 1976; sec.-treas. Ga. Vocat. Guidance Assn., 1976, pres., 1979. Co-editor: (newsletter) Ga. Pupil Personnel, 1975; editor: (newsletter) Ga. Personnel and Guidance, 1977-78; mem. editl. bd. Jour. Career Edn., 1978-80, Future Mag., 1978, Chronicle Guidance Corp., 1987-89. Mem. Ga. Sch. Counselors Assn. (Gov.'s award for Govt. Svc.), Internat. Soc. Ednl. Planners (bd. dirs. 1987-91). Democrat. Methodist. Avocations: photography, woodworking. Home: 4276 Village Green Cir Conyers GA 30013 E-mail: raybou@worldnet.att.net.

BOUDART, MICHEL, chemical engineer, chemist, educator, consultant; b. Belgium, June 18, 1924; came to U.S., 1947, naturalized, 1957; s. Francois and Marguerite (Swolfs) B.; m. Marina D'Haese, Dec. 27, 1948; children: Mark, Baudouin, Iris, Philip. BS, U. Louvain, Belgium, 1944, MS, 1947; PhD, Princeton U., 1950; D honoris causa, U. Liège, U. Notre Dame, U. Nancy, U. Ghent. Research asso. James Forrestal Research Ctr., Princeton, 1950-54; mem. faculty Princeton U., 1954-61; prof. chem. engring. U. Calif., Berkeley, 1961-64, adj. prof. chem. engring., 1994—; prof. chem. engring. and chemistry Stanford U., 1964-80, Keck prof. engring., 1980-94, Keck prof. engring. emeritus, 1994—. Co-founder Catalytica, Inc.; Humble Oil Co. lectr., 1958; AIChE lectr., 1961; Sigma Xi nat. lectr., 1965; chmn. Gordon Rsch. Conf. Catalysis, 1962. Author: Kinetics of Chemical Processes, 1968, (with G. Djéga-Mariadassou) Kinetics of Heterogeneous Catalytic Reactions, 1983; editor: (with J.R. Anderson) Catalysis: Science and Technology, 11 vols., 1981-96, (with Marina Boudart and René Bryssinck) Modern Belgium, 1990; mem. adv. editl. bd. Catal. Letters, 1989—, Catalysis Rev., 1968—, Jour. Molecular Catalysis, 1995—, Cattech, 1996—. Recipient Curtis-McGraw rsch. award Am. Soc. Engring. Edn., 1962, R.H. Wilhelm award in chem. reaction engring., 1974, Chem. Pioneer award Am. Inst. Chemists, 1991; Belgium-Am. Ednl. Found. fellow, 1948, Procter fellow, 1949; Fairchild disting. scholar Calif. Tech. Inst., 1995. Fellow AAAS, Am. Acad. Arts. and Scis., Calif. Acad. Scis.; mem. NAS, NAE, Am. Chem. Soc. (Kendall award 1977, E.V. Murphee award in indsl. and engring. chemistry 1985), Catalysis Soc., Am. Inst. Chem. Engrs., Chem. Soc., Académie Royale de Belgique (fgn. assoc.), French Nat. Acad. Pharmacy (fgn.). Home: 228 Oak Grove Ave Atherton CA 94027-2218 Office: Stanford U Dept Chem Engring Stanford CA 94305 Fax: 650-723-9780. E-mail: mboudart@stanford.edu.

BOUDINOT, FRANK DOUGLAS, dean; b. New Brunswick, NJ, Mar. 31, 1956; s. Frank Lins and Dorothy Jean (Libourel) B.; m. Sarah Garrett, Sept. 1992; 1 child, Frank Garrett. BS in Biology, Springfield Coll., 1978; PhD in Pharmaceutics, SUNY, Buffalo, 1986. Vet. technician Afton Animal Hosp., Williamsville, N.Y., 1978-79; rsch. technician SUNY-Millard Fillmore Hosp., Buffalo, 1979-80; grad. asst. SUNY, 1980-85; asst. prof. pharmaceutics U. Ga., Athens, 1986-90, assoc. prof., 1990-98, head dept. pharm., 1992-98, prof., head dept. pharm. & biomed. scis., 1998-99, prof. dept. pharm. and biomed. scis., 1998—, assoc. dean grad. sch., 1999—2001, sr. assoc. dean Grad. Sch., 2001—02; dean Sch. Grad. Studies Va. Commonwealth U., Richmond, 2002—, prof. Dept. Pharmaceutics, 2002—. Scientific adv. bd. Pharmassett Ltd., 1999—; adj. prof. Dept. Pharma. and Biomed. Scis., U. Ga., 2002—. Mem. editl. bd.: Jour. Pharmacy Tchg., 1989—2001, Biopharm. and Drug Disposition, 1994—, Antimicrobiol. Agts. and Chemotherapy, 1998—2001, Archives of Pharmacal Rsch., 1999—2001, referee: Jour. Pharm. Scis., 1988—, Jour. Pharm. Rsch., 1989—, N.Am. editor: Jour. Biopharmaceutics and Drug Disposition, 1998—; contbr. over 100 articles to profl. jours. Vice chair govt. svcs. subcom. Oconee 2000, Watkinsville, Ga., 1986—87; vol., event svcs. agt. Summer Olympics, Athens, Ga., 1996; rollerhockey coach Athens YMCA, 2001—02; Little League baseball coach Midlothian, Ga., 2003—; del. Ga. State Rep. Conv., Atlanta, 1989, 1991, 1992; bd. dirs. Oconee Animal Shelter, Watkinsville, Ga., 1986—88. Named one of Outstanding Young Men of Am., 1987. Mem. AAAS, Am. Assn. Pharm. Scientists (mem. abstract screening com., 2001-02, rsch. achievement com., 2002), Am. Assn. Coll. Pharmacy (del. 1989-90, profl. affairs com. 1990-91, tchr. mentoring com., 2002—), Am. Soc. Microbiology, Coun. Grad. Sch., So. Conf. Grad. Sch. (award com. 2002), mem. Rho Chi: Pharmaceutical Hon. Soc.; mem. Phi Kappa Phi (v.p. for scholarships and awards, 2003-). Episcopalian. Achievements include research in pharmacokinetics of antiviral drugs, effects of age in drug disposition, veterinary pharmacokinetics, and drug pharmacodynamics. Office: Va Commonwealth U Sch Grad Studies PO Box 843051 Richmond VA 23284-3051 E-mail: fdboudinot@vcu.edu.

BOUDREAU, ROBERT DONALD, meteorology educator, retired; b. North Adams, Mass., Mar. 9, 1931; s. Lucien Albert and Rose Elizabeth (Franceschini) B. BS with honors, Tex. A&M U., 1962, MS, 1964, PhD, 1968. Cert. cons. meteorologist; cert. instrument and multi engine flight instr., airline transport pilot. Research meteorologist Atmospheric Scis. Lab., Ft. Huachuca, Ariz., 1965-68, Deseret Test Ctr., Salt Lake City, 1968-70, Meteorol. Satellite Lab., Washington, 1970-71; sr. atmospheric scientist Earth Resources Lab. NASA, Bay St. Louis, Miss., 1971-75; prof., chmn. meteorology dept. Metro. State Coll., Denver, 1976-97, ret., 1997, prof. emeritus. Contbr. articles to profl. jours. Mem. Am. Meteorol. Soc., Nat. Weather Assn. (v.p. 1995), U.S. Pilots. Assn., Pilots. Internat. Assn. Internat. Meteorology Aviation and Electronics Inst. (pres. 1982-86), Sigma Xi. Republican. Mem. Unitarian Ch.

BOUDREAUX, GLORIA MARIE, nursing educator; b. Lafayette, La., May 2, 1935; d. Simon Zepherin and Orta Marie (Pierret) B. Diploma, Charity Hosp. Sch. Nursing, 1962; BA maxima cum laude, St. Edward's U., 1974; MS in Psychiat.-Mental Health Nursing, Tex. Women's U., 1976. Head surg., med. nurse Lafayette Charity Hosp., 1962-65; commd. 1st lt. U.S. Army, 1965, advanced through grades to col. Nurse Corps, 1983, ret., 1995; psychiat. staff nurse VA Hosp., New Orleans, 1968-72; psychiat. nurse U.S. Army Nurse Corp., San Francisco and Augusta, Ga., 1966-67; instr. Tex. Woman's U. Sch. Nursing, Houston, 1976-80; clin. specialist VA Med. Ctr., Houston, 1980-87; psychiat. nursing coord. Spring Shadows Glen, Houston, 1987-88; instr. assoc. degree nursing program Houston CC, 1988-91; asst. prof. nursing La. State U., Eunice, 1992-96; with Cmty. Rehab. Hosp. Counseling, 1997-99. Clin. specialist, cons. in psychiat.-mental health nursing. Vol., bd. dirs. local chpt. ARC Disaster health and Mental Health Svcs.; with La. ARC State Svc. Coun. and state lead for disaster mental health; cert. instr. ARC Disaster Svcs. Recipient Nat. Def. Svc. medal, 1968, Army Res. Component medal, 1972, Armed Forces Res. medal, 1977 (10-yr. device 1988), Army Commendation medal, 1978, Army Meritorious Svc. medal, 1990, Presdl. Sports award, 1989, 90, 91, Acadia Red Cross Outstanding Vol. award for disaster svcs., 1998. Mem.: ANA (cert. in psychiat. mental health nursing), Internat. Crit. Incident Stress Found. and Acadiana CISM for Fire Dept., Assn. Mil. Surgeons U.S., Res. Officers Assn., Am. Psychiat. Nurses Assn., Ret. Officers Assn., Ret. Army Nurse Corps Assn., Vietnam Vets. Assn., Sigma Theta Tau. Avocations: music, photography, walking, bicycling, reading. Home: 307 Meadow Ln Lafayette LA 70506-6323

BOUDREAUX, SUSAN CASTRO, elementary school educator; b. Baton Rouge, Mar. 28, 1951; d. Philip Michael and Grace Agnes (O'Rillion) Castro; m. Jimmie Joseph Boudreaux, June 19, 1976; children: Suzanne Michelle, Stacy Elizabeth. BS, La. State U., 1973, MEd, 1975. Title 1 reading tchr. Ascension Parish, Prairieville, La., 1975-97, 2d grade tchr., 1997-99, tchr. 1st grade reading, 1999—2001, tchr. physical edn., 2001—. Mentor, assessor Ascension Parish, Prairieville, 1998—. Grantee La. State Dept. Edn., 1997-98, Ascension Fund, 1998—. Mem. La. Assn. Health, Physical Edn., Recreation and Dance. Democrat. Roman Catholic. Avocation: tennis.

BOUÉ, DANIEL ROBERT, pediatric pathologist, neuropathologist, educator; b. N.Y.C., June 22, 1958; s. Robert Charles and Dorothea Anna B.; m. Julie Marie Borgerding; children: Rachel Hope, Jenna Elizabeth, AnnaMarie Monique, Sarah Jane. BA cum laude, Carleton Coll., 1980; PhD, U. Minn., 1988, MD, 1991. Diplomate in anat. and clin. pathology and pediatric pathology Am. Bd. Pathology. Intern U. Calif., San Diego, 1991-92, resident in pathology, 1992-94, chief resident-elect, 1994-95; attending physician U. Calif./San Diego Med. Ctr., 1994-95; clin. instr. U. Calif., San Diego, 1994-95; fellow pediat. pathology Columbus Childrens Hosp., 1995-96; clin. instr. Ohio State U., Columbus, 1995—97, clin. asst. prof. pathology, 1998—; fellow pediat. neuropathology Columbus Childrens Hosp., 1996; staff pathologist, dir. Neuropathology program Childrens Hosp., Columbus, 1997—; dir. surg. and autopsy neuropathology, muscle and nerve biopsy svcs. Interim dir perinatal pathology and autopsy svc. U. Calif., San Diego, 1994-95; rev. pathologist Biopathology Ctr., Children's Hosp. Rsch. Found.; prin. investigator multiple grants; presenter in field. Contbr. articles to profl. jours.; referee med. jour. publs. Med. Scientist scholar U. Minn., 1982-91, G.T. Evan scholar Dept. Lab. Medicine and

Pathology, 1982-85, Life & Health Ins. Med. Rsch. Fund, scholar, 1985-90; recipient J.T. Livermore Hematology award Minn. Med. Found., 1988, undergrad. med. student rsch. award 1991, Dr. Vernon D.E. Smith award, 1990. Fellow Am. Coll. Pathology, Am. Soc. Clin. Pathologists (Sheard-Sanford award 1988), Coll. Am. Pathologists; mem. Soc. Pediat. Pathology, Alpha Omega Alpha. Office: Columbus Childrens Hosp Dept Lab Med 700 Childrens Dr Columbus OH 43205-2664

BOUGHAN, ZANETTA LOUISE, music educator; b. Grantham, Eng., Mar. 22, 1959; arrived in U.S., 1964; d. Peter Leonard and Alyda Venita Maria (Bellord) Snowden; m. Robert William Boughan, Nov. 3, 1995. Student, George Mason U., 1977—78, U. Alaska, 1985—87, Cochise Coll., 1999—, Wayland Bapt. U., Sierra Vista campus, 2003—. Pvt. piano and violin instr., Sierra Vista, Ariz., 1988—. Concertmaster Cochise Coll. Orch., Sierra Vista, 1999—2001, Pima Coll. Orch., Tucson, 2001—02; first violinist Sierra Vista Sym. Orch., 2001—02. Vol. Sierra Vista Police Dept., 2002—; ct. apptd. spl. adv. vol. State Ariz., 2002—; vol. in Police Svc., 2002—; mem. Citizens Police Acad. Assocs., 2003—. With USN, 1979—84. Mem.: Ariz. Music Tchrs. Assn., Nat. Music Tchrs. Assn., Cochise Music Tchrs. Assn. (chmn. fundraising com. 1997—, sec. 1998—2000, treas. 2001—03, pres. 2003—, Profl. Develop. grant 2001). Home: 4924 Marconi Dr Sierra Vista AZ 85635 E-mail: zboughan@earthlink.net.

BOURG, LOUISE JANETTE, retired secondary school educator; b. Chgo., Oct. 2, 1947; d. Harry Francis and Alice Louise (Bate) De Boer; m. Leo J. Bourg., July 31, 1971. BA, Greenville Coll., 1969; MA, Gov.'s State U., Ill., 1973; admnstrn. cert., Gov.'s State U., 1986. Cert. tchr. secondary sch., gen. adminstrn., Ill. Tchr. French and English, internal/external rev. teams Tinley Park (Ill.) HS, 1969—2002; ret., 2002. Sec. S. Interconf. Assn. Mem. NEA, ASCD, Ill. Edn. Assn., Am. Assn. Tchrs. of French., Am. Coun. Tchrs. of Fgn. Lang. Avocations: reading, physical fitness, gardening, golf, tennis. Home: 47491 Lakeview Dr Lawrence MI 49064

BOURGOIN, DAVID L. lawyer, real estate broker, trade broker, educator, video/television producer; b. Jersey City, Mar. 5, 1946; s. Louis Joseph and Irene Mary Bourgoin. BS, St. Peter's Coll., Jersey City, 1968; MBA, UCLA, 1970; JD, U. San Diego, 1987. Bar: Hawaii 1988, Pa. 1989, U.S. Ct. Appeals (fed. cir.) Hawaii 1988, U.S. Internat. Ct. Appeals. Fin. mgr. Mattel Toys, Hawthorne, Calif., 1969—71; music prodr. Topanga Canyon Records, Redondo Beach, Calif., 1971-76; stock broker Dean Witter, L.A., 1976-78, 2003; prof. U. Hawaii, Honolulu, 1978-80; trade broker Hawaii chi Trading Co., Honolulu, 1978—; pvt. practice Honolulu, 1988—; real estate broker Realty Offices of D.L.B., Honolulu, 1991—. Prof. U. Md., Heidelburg, Germany, 1983-95; vis. prof. mgmt. & internat. studies U. Hawaii, 2003; prodr. TCR Prodns. Capt. USAR, 1973-85. Mem. Hawaii State Bar, Japanese C. of C., K. of C. Avocations: culture, music, sports. Office: 1188 Bishop St Ste 2010 Honolulu HI 96813-3308 E-mail: theofficesnet@yahoo.com.

BOURHAM, MOHAMED ABDELHAY, nuclear and electrical engineering educator; b. Mehalla, Gharbeia, Egypt, Apr. 18, 1944; arrived in U.S., 1987; s. Abdelhay Mohamed Bourham and Badria Ahmed Ghida; m. Laila Gadel Hak, Mar. 22, 1966 (div. 1977); 1 child, Ahmed Mohamed; m. Doria Mahmoud Wafa, Mar. 22, 1987; 1 stepchild, Samir Sami. BSc, Alexandria (Egypt) U., 1965; MSc, Cairo U., 1969; PhD, Ain Shams U., Cairo, 1976. Registered profl. engr. Sr. researcher, asst. prof., then prof. Nuclear Rsch. Ctr., Cairo, 1965-91; vis. assoc. prof. N.C. State U., Raleigh, 1987-91, rsch. assoc. prof. nuclear engring., 1991-95, assoc. prof., 1995-97, prof., 1997—, undergrad. adminstr., 1999. Contbr. scientific papers to sci. publs. Maj. arty. Egyptian Army, 1968—74. Recipient George Blessis Outstanding Undergrad. Advisor award, 2003; grantee, U.S. Army, 1989—, U.S. Dept. Energy, 1992, USN, 1995—, Nat. Textile Ctr., 1999—, USDA, 2001—. Mem.: AAAS, AIAA, IEEE (publs. chair Internat. Conf. Plasma Sci. 1998), Am. Assn. for Engring. Edn., Nat. Assn. of scholars, Am. Assn. Engring. Edn., Am. Soc. Engring. Edn., Nat. Assn. Scholars, Electric Launcher Assn., Fusion Power Assocs., Univ. Fusion Assn., N.Y. Acad. Scis., Am. Nuc. Soc. (tech. chair fusion meeting 1998, exec. com. 1998—), Am. Phys. Soc., U.S. Naval Inst. (life), Nat. Def. Indsl. Assn. (life), Sigma Xi. Moslem. Achievements include research in in plasma microinstabilities and electromagnetic emission from core plasmas in magnetically confined fusion devises; plasma torches for waste disposal; development of of magnetically collimated electron beams for microeletronics; techniques in pulsed power systems for eletrothermal and electro thermal chemical launchers; of diagnostics methodology and techniques for hyper-volocity plasma launchers; database on plasma-facing components; of database for plasma-material interactions under combustion environment; methodology for disruption parameters and surface erosion of fusion tokamaks and methodology for accident scenarios in future large magnetic fusion reactors; research and development of plasma treatment of material surfaces and textile fabrics and non-wovens; research in on plasma-fabric treatment at atmospheric pressures and surface sterilization and decontamination, nano structures and nanoparticulates implantation, x-ray sources for imaging; plasma application to insects control. Office: NC State U Dept Nuclear Engring Raleigh NC 27695-0001 E-mail: bourham@ncsu.edu.

BOURLAND, D(ELPHUS) DAVID, JR., linguist, educator; b. Wichita Falls, Tex., June 6, 1928; s. Delphus David and Margaret (Hawley) B.; m. Elizabeth Jagush, Oct. 16, 1981; children by previous marriages: David III, Meda, Ruskin, Ileana. AB, Harvard U., 1951, MBA, 1953; lic. in English linguistics, U. Costa Rica, 1973. Ops. analyst Ops. Evaluation Group MIT, Washington, 1955-61; with various corps., 1961-65; pres. IR Assocs., Inc., San Diego, 1965-69, Semantics Rsch. Corp., Washington, 1969-71; from instr. to assoc. prof. U. Costa Rica, San Jose, 1971-80; pres. Semantics Rsch. Corp., Wichita Falls, Tex., 1994—. Trustee Inst. Gen. Semantics, 1964-89. Author: Introduccion a la Tagmemica, 1974; co-author: An Advanced Course in Squirrelly Semantics: A Coloring Book for Some Adults, 1993, Not So Great Moments in the Lives of Great Men and Women, 1994; editor Gen. Semantics Bull., 1964-70; co-editor: To Be or Not: An E-Prime Anthology, 1991, More E-Prime: To Be or Not II, 1994, E-Prime III!, 1997; contbr. numerous articles to profl. publs. Lt. USNR, 1953-65. Korzybski fellow Inst. Gen. Semantics, 1949-50. Mem. Inst. Gen. Semantics, Internat. Soc. Gen. Semantics (contbg. editor Et Cetera, bd. dirs. 1993—, v.p. devel. 1995-97, pres. 1998—, assoc. editor 2000—), Am. Legion (comdr. dept. Panama Canal 1979-81, post comdr. Costa Rica 1980-84), Sons Am. Legion (nat. adjutant 1985, 86), Forty and Eight (nat. exec. com. 1983-86), Harvard Faculty Club, Harvard Club Boston, Wichita Falls Country Club, Sons. Confederate Vets., Wichita Falls Yacht Club. Republican. Avocation: power lifting. Home: 1517 Celia Dr Wichita Falls TX 76302-3515

BOURNE, CAROL ELIZABETH MULLIGAN, biology educator, phycologist; b. Rochester, N.Y., May 4, 1948; d. William Thomas and Ruth Townsend (Stevens) Mulligan; m. Godfrey Roderick Bourne, Dec. 21, 1968. BA in Botany/Bacteriology, Ohio Wesleyan U., 1970; MS in Botany, Miami U., Oxford, Ohio, 1978; PhD in Natural Resources, U. Mich., 1992. Lab. asst. Ohio Wesleyan U., Delaware, 1968-70; biol. lab. tech. USDA-Forest Svc., Delaware, 1970-73; grad. rsch. asst. botany dept. Miami U., Oxford, 1973-75; electron microscopist coll. medicine U. Cin., 1975-76; rsch. asst. sch. pub. health U. Mich., Ann Arbor, 1978-80, rsch. assoc. coll. medicine, 1981-83, grad. rsch. asst. sch. natural resources, 1983-86, grad. teaching asst. dept. biology, 1987; postdoctoral scientist U. Fla., Ft. Lauderdale, 1990-92; adj. instr. ecology Fla. Atlantic U. Coll. Liberal Arts, Davie, 1992-93. Adj. asst. prof. dept. biology U. Mo., St. Louis, 1994—, Washington U., St. Louis, 1994—2000, Pierre Laclede Honors Coll., U. Mo., St. Louis, 1997—; bd. dirs. CEIBA Biol. Ctr., Inc. Contbr. articles to scholarly jours. Grantee NSF, 1987-89. Mem.: Soc. for Study of Evolution, Internat. Soc. for Diatom Rsch., Phycological Soc. Am., Am. Inst. Biolog. Scis. Office: U Mo at St Louis Dept Biology 8001 Natural Bridge Rd Saint Louis MO 63121-4499 E-mail: BourneC@msx.umsl.edu.

BOURNE, KATHERINE DAY, journalist, educator; b. Lynn, Mass., Sept. 11, 1938; d. Schuyler Vandervort and Elsie Marie (Mayo) Day; m. William Nettleton Bourne; children: William Alexander, Katherine Loring. BS in Edn., Keene Tchrs. Coll., 1960; MEd, Harvard U., 1984. Tchr. Wachusett Regional High Sch., Holden, Mass., 1960-61; arts editor Bay State Banner, Boston, 1966—; dir. edn. Suffolk County House of Correction, Boston, 1979-84; edn. coord. Dept. Transitional Asst., Mass., 1984—2002, ret., 2002—. Contbr. music revs. to Christian Sci. Monitor. Dir. rels. Crime-out, Boston, 1983; mem. Gov.'s Commn. on Status of Women, 1970-74; co-founder, dir. Harvard-Radcliffe Forum Theatre, Cambridge, 1964-68; bd. dirs., mem. ARC Greater Boston, 1987-95, NAACP Boston, 1978-81. NEH journalism fellow, 1978; recipient Melnea A. Cass award Greater Boston YMCA, 1984. Mem. NAACP (life). Avocations: collecting african-american literature, aerobics, photography, stamps, art relating to black history and life. Home: 52 High St Brookline MA 02445-7707 Office: Bay State Banner The Fargo Bldg 68 Fargo St Boston MA 02210-2122

BOURQUE, ANITA MARY, social services administrator; b. Fitchburg, Mass., Nov. 22, 1942; d. Arthur E. and Yvonne Blanch (Hebert) Leclerc; m. Joseph Gerard Bourque, June 28, 1969; 1 child, Craig. BS in Elem. Edn. and Spl. Edn. magna cum laude, Fitchburg State Coll., 1974; MA in Counseling Psychology summa cum laude, Anna Maria Coll., Paxton, Mass., 1980. Cert. tchr. K-8, Mass. Tchr. 6th-8th grades St. Mary Sch., Putnam, Conn., 1963-65; tchr. 4th-8th grades Immaculate Conception Sch., Fitchburg, 1965-71, St. Joseph Sch., Fitchburg, 1971-79; in bus. mgmt. Foamtech, Fitchburg, 1979-84; owner, mgr. Homestead Realty, Fitchburg, 1984-86, Bourque Video and Photo, Leominster, Mass., 1986-94; religious edn. adminstr. St. Joseph Sch., Fitchburg, 1984-86, prin., 1991-95; prin., health facility adminstr. Fla. Inst. Neurologic Rehab., Inc., Wauchula, Fla., 1995-97; dir., asst. v.p. human svcs. Gulfstream Goodwill, West Palm Beach, Fla., 1997—. Organizer mktg. devel. com. St. Joseph Parish Coun. 1992, gen. chair St. Joseph 100th Centennial Com., 1994; mem. parents com. St. Joseph's Scouting. Mem. Nat. Cath. Edn. Assn., Mass. Reading Assn., Video Software Dealers Assn., Woman's Coun. of Realtors (pres.), North Worcester Bd. Realtors. Home: 4248 SE Sweetwood Way Stuart FL 34997-2265

BOURQUE, BOYD D. secondary education educator; Secondary tchr. Hahnville High Sch.; instr. TCP/IP and phys. networking La. State U., Baton Rouge. Recipient Tchr. Excellence award Internat. Tech. Edn. Assn., 1992.*

BOUSFIELD, EDWARD LLOYD, biologist, educator; b. Penticton, B.C., Can., June 19, 1926; s. Reginald H. and Marjorie F. (Armstrong) B.; m. Barbara Joyce, June 20, 1953 (dec. Apr. 1983); children: Marjorie Anne, Jessie Katherine, Mary Elizabeth, Kenneth Lloyd; m. Joyce Burton, Feb. 11, 1994. BA, MA, U. Toronto, 1948; PhD in marine biology, Harvard U., 1954. Invertebrate zoologist Nat. Mus. of Natural Sci., Ottawa, Ont., Can., 1950-64, chief zoologist, 1964-74, sr. scientist, 1974-86, curator emeritus, 1986-90. Rsch. assoc. Royal Ont. Mus., Toronto, 1984—, Royal B.C. Mus., Victoria, 1990-95. Author: Canadian Atlantic Sea Shells, 1960, Shallow-water Gammaridean Amphipoda of New England, 1973, History of the Canadian Society of Zoologists: The First Decade, 1974, Cadborosaurus, Survivor from the Deep, 1995; mng. editor: Amphipacifica, 1994-98, 2000—; contbr. articles to profl. jours. Recipient Outstanding Achievement award Civil Service Can., 1985. Fellow Royal Soc. Can.; mem. Ottawa Field Naturalists Club (hon., pres. 1959-61), Can. Soc. Zoologists (hon., pres. 1979-80, archivist 1971-91, hon. mem. 1993—), Crustacean Soc., New Eng. Estuarine Rsch. Soc., RA Curling Club (pres. 1972-73) (Ottawa), Victoria Curling Club, Highland Park Lawn Bowling Club (pres. 1978-79, 89-90), Victoria Lawn Bowling Club, Granite Curling Club, Sigma Xi. Mem. Can. Alliance Party. Avocations: musical instruments, lawn bowling, curling. Home: 1710-1275 Richmond Rd Ottawa ON Canada K2B 8E3 E-mail: elbousf@magma.ca.

BOUTELLE, JANE CRONIN, fitness consultant; b. Arlington, Mass., Nov. 3, 1926; d. William Francis and Sara (Gillis) Cronin; m. G. William Boutelle, 1953 (dec. 1973); children: Jeanne E., William R., James G. BS, Boston U., 1948; MA, Columbia U., 1953. Cert. tchr., Mass. Tchr. dance and health edn. Newton (Mass.) H.S., 1948-51, Scarsdale (N.Y.) H.S., 1951-55, Marymount Coll., Tarrytown, N.Y., 1955-58, Manhattanville Coll., Purchase, N.Y., 1958-59; pres., fitness cons. The Boutelle Method, Inc., Greenwich, Conn., 1973—. Author: Lifetime Fitness for Women, 1978; contbr. articles to mags. Mem. nat. alumni bd. Boston U., 1981—85, mn. 40th reunion; pres. Westchester Dance Coun., Westchester County, NY, 1956—57; mem. woman's com. Lighthouse, Westchester County, 1983. Recipient Bravo award Greenwich YWCA, 1978. Mem.: AAUW (chmn. edn. 1963—68), Greenwich Assn. Pub. Schs. (chmn. 1968—73), Assn. Women in Phys. Edn., Soroptimists Internat. (chmn. scholarship com.), Greenwich Woman's Club Gardeners (chmn. 1996—2000). Office: The Boutelle Method Inc 6 Huckleberry Ln Greenwich CT 06831-3341

BOUVIER, JANET LAUBACH, secondary education educator; b. Benton, Pa., Nov. 27, 1930; d. Jonathan Paul and Ethel Irene (Bray) L.; m. Roland Joseph Bouvier, Sept. 29, 1930; children: Ann, Caroline, Susan. BA, Wilson Coll., 1952; MS in Edn., Temple U., 1973, EdD, 1988. Legal correspondent Pa. Bur. Motor Vehicles, Harrisburg, Pa., 1952-53; tchr. Columbus High Sch., Columbus, Ga., 1954-55; English tchr. Mechanicsburg (Pa.) Area Sch. Dist., 1967—. Instr. of "Women in Politics" More Women Candidates, Harrisburg, 1986. Mem. Mechanicsburg Edn. Assn. (v.p. 1988—), Phi Delta Kappa, Omicron Tau Theta. Republican. Avocations: reading, gardening, interior design. Home: 307 W Green St Shiremanstown PA 17011-6522

BOVE, PATRICE MAGEE, elementary education educator; b. Fort Madison, Iowa, Apr. 29, 1946; d. Claude and Susie T. Magee; m. Roger E. Bove, Aug. 6, 1983; 1 child, Jonna. MusB, U. Iowa, 1968; M of Music Edn., Temple U., 1976. Tchr. elem. instrumental music Birmingham (Mich.) Sch. Dist., 1968-69; tchr. elem. music T-E Sch. Dist., Berwyn, Pa., 1969—. Co-author: Philadelphia Orchestra Student Concert Books, 1994—; contbr. MENC (Strategies for Teaching Elementary Music), 1996. Educator, writer edn. adv. com. Phila. Orch., 1994—; accompanist chorus, Wayne, Pa., 1995, Suzuki Concerts, Immaculata, Pa., 1994-97. Mem. AAUW, Nat. Assn. Music Therapy, Music Tchrs. Assn., Gordon Inst. Music Learning, Suzuki, Kodaly, Orff, Pa. Music Edn. Assn. (dist. 12 co-host elem. songfest 1995), Music Educators Nat. Conf. Avocations: reading, computers, cooking. Home: 325 Holly Rd West Chester PA 19380-4614

BOVEE, COURTLAND LOWELL, business educator; b. Red Bluff, Calif., Oct. 4, 1944; s. Courtney Van and Shirley Patricia (Safford) B. AA, Shast Coll., 1965; BS, U. N.D., 1967; MS, U. Tenn., 1968. Mem. faculty Grossmont Coll., El Cajon, Calif., 1968—, now prof. business; prin., v.p. Bovee & Thill L.L.C., Las Vegas, Nev., 1997—. Co-author: Bus. in Action, 2004, (textbooks) Bus. Today, 10th edit., 2001, Excellence in Business Communication, 5th edit., 2001, Bus. Communication Today, 7 edit., 2002. Mem. Assn. for Bus. Comm. Avocations: photography, travel. Office: Bovee & Thill LLC 2950 E Flamingo Rd Las Vegas NV 89121-5208 E-mail: bovee@dc.rr.com.

BOVEE, EUGENE CLEVELAND, protozoologist, emeritus educator; b. Sioux City, Iowa, Apr. 1, 1915; s. Earl Eugene and Martha Nora (Johnson) B.; m. Maezene B. Wamsley, May 18, 1942 (div. 1967); m. Elizabeth A. Moss, May 9, 1968; children— Frances, Gregory, Matthew; stepchildren— Lynne, Lisa. BA, U. No. Iowa, 1939; MS, U. Iowa, 1948; PhD, UCLA, 1950. Instr. zoology Iowa U., 1940-41; biology tchr. Greene (Iowa) H.S., Iowa, 1941-42; instr. biology U. No. Iowa, 1946-48; journalist Iowa Rev. Greene, 1945—46; instr. zoology UCLA, 1948-50, research zoologist, 1962-68; asst. prof. biology Calif. Poly. U., 1950-52; assoc. prof. zoology, dept. chmn. N.D. State U., 1952-53; asst. prof. biology U. Houston, 1953-55; assoc. prof. U. Fla., 1955-62; prof. physiology and cell biology U. Kans., Lawrence, 1968-85, prof. emeritus, 1985—. Owner arts and crafts bus., 1985-96; cons. Am. Type Culture Collection, 1980-82, W.C. Brown, Pub., 1978-82. Author: (books of poems) Give Back My Body, 1994, To Tartarus and Back, 1999, Sette Bellos, 2000, A Cinquain Zoo, 2000, Old Olympian Games, 2000, Pundamonium, 2001, Biblical Limericks, 2002, Sonnets for Various Reasons, 2002, Historical Limericks, 2003, The Common Gene Pool, 2003; co-editor, co-author: An Illustrated Guide to the Protozoa, 1985; co-author: How to Know the Protozoa, 2d edit., 1979; Microscop. Anat. Invert., Vol. 1, 1991; editor Kans. Sci. Bull., 1974-79; contbr. chpts. to books, articles to sci. jours.; contbr. to small press lit. jours. 1st lt. U.S. Army, WWII. Research grantee NIH, 1957-62, NSF, 1970-74, NIH, NSF and ONR, 1962-68, Kans. Fed. Water Resources Inst. and U. Kans., 1968-81; recipient Disting. Alumni award U. No. Iowa, 1980. Fellow Iowa Acad. Sci.; mem. Soc. Protozoologists (hon., pres. 1979-80, v.p. 1970-71, treas. 1972-78, exec. com. 1970-81), Am. Microscop Soc. (mem.-at-large exec. com. 1959-62), Western Soc. Naturalists, Kans. Acad. Sci. (life mem., pres. 1979-80, exec. com. 1975-81), Acad. Am. Poets, Kans. State Poetry Soc., Kans. Authors Club (Writing Achievement award 1996), Nat. Woodcarvers Assn., United Amateur Press Assn. Am., Sigma Xi. Home: 808 Mississippi St Lawrence KS 66044-2659

BOVEY, LISA DAWN, special education educator; b. Martinsburg, W.Va., Dec. 19, 1959; d. Noah Leon Jr. and Jane Carlene (Canby) B. BA in Elem. Edn., Shepherd Coll., 1982; MA in Spl. Edn., W.Va. U., 1988. Cert. elem. edn. tchr., 1-6, spl. edn. learning disabilities K-12, W.Va. Regular substitute Berkeley County Schs., Martinsburg, 1982-83, tchr. Gerrardstown Elem., 1983-87, spl. edn. tchr., 1987-89, spl. edn. tchr. Valley View Elem., 1989—. Mem. Sci. Olympiad Com., Martinsburg, 1984-87, W.Va. on-site rev. bd. Randolph County Dept. Edn., Charleston, W.Va., 1986; yearbook coord. Valley View Elem., 1989-90, referral agt., 1989—; W.Va. U. Practicum Tchr., Morgantown/Martinsburg, 1990, 92, 93, 96; adv. student coun. Valley View Elem. Sch., 1992-96; mentor tchr. Berkeley County Schs., 1992-93, others. Mem. Tuscarora Presbyn. Ch., Martinsburg, 1970—, dir. Christmas Internat. House, 1988, 89, 91; bd. dirs. Martinsburg Alumni Assn., 1988-91; chmn. Jump Rope for Heart Valley View Elem. Am. Heart Assn., 1993; chmn. check-in com. Am. Heart Walk, 1992, others. Nominee for Outstanding Young Educators Jaycees, 1986; recipient Outstanding Svc. award Am. Student Coun. Assn., 1993-94, Golden Apple Achievement award Ashland Oil Co., 1995. Mem. NEA, Berkeley County Edn. Assn., W.Va. Edn. Assn., Phi Delta Kappa (sec. 1994-95). Republican. Avocations: arranging dried flowers, biking, reading, swimming. Home: 1413 W Martin St Martinsburg WV 25401-2058 Office: Valley View Elem Sch RR 4 Box 269 Martinsburg WV 25401-9419

BOWDEN, ANN, bibliographer, educator; b. East Orange, N.J., Feb. 7, 1924; d. William and Anna Elisabeth (Herrstrom) Haddon; m. Edwin Turner Bowden, June 12, 1948; children: Elisabeth Bowden Ward, Susan Turner, Edwin Eric; m. William Burton Todd, Nov. 23, 1969. BA, Radcliffe Coll., 1948; MS in Library Services, Columbia U., 1951; PhD, U. Tex., 1975. Cataloger, reference asst. Yale U., 1948-53; manuscript cataloger, rare book librarian, librarian Humanities Research Ctr., librarian Acad. Ctr., U. Tex., Austin, 1958-63, lectr., sr. lectr. Grad. Sch. Library and Info. Sci., 1964-85, 88-89; coordinator adult services Austin Pub. Library, 1963-67, asst. dir., 1967-71, dep. dir., 1971-77, assoc. dir., 1977-86; bd. dirs. Tex. Info. Exchange, Houston, 1977-78; bd. dirs. AMIGOS Bibliog. Council, Dallas, 1978-82, chmn. bd., 1980-81, trustee emeritus, 1986—; chmn. AMIGOS '85 Plan, 1984-86; scholar in residence Rockefeller Found. Villa Serbelloni, Bellagio, Italy, 1986, Ransom Ctr. scholar U. Tex., Austin, 1990—; Zachariah Polson fellow Libr. Co. of Phila., 1990. Author (with W.B. Todd) Tauchnitz International Editions in English, 1988, Sir Walter Scott: A Bibliographical History, 1998; editor: T.E. Lawrence Fifty Letters: 1921-1935, 1962; Maps and Atlases, 1978; assoc. editor Papers of the Bibliographical Soc. Am., 1967-82; contbr. articles to profl. jours. Served as cpl. USMC Women's Res., 1944-46. Mem. ALA (council 1975-79), Assn. Coll. and Research Libraries (chmn. rare book and manuscript sect. 1975-76), Tex. Library Assn. (chmn. publs. com. 1965-71), Bibliog. Soc. Am., Phi Kappa Phi, Kappa Tau Alpha. Club: Grolier (N.Y.C.). Died May 23, 2001.

BOWDEN, NANCY BUTLER, school administrator; d. Rogers Davis and Lilla Ann (Yarbrough) B.; m. Robert C. Bowden. 1970 (div. 1981); 1 child, Linda Camille. BA in English, Spanish, Southwest Tex. U., 1964; MEd in Counseling, U. Houston, 1972, EdD in Curriculum Instrn., 1978, postgrad., 1979. Cert. profl. mid-mgmt. adminstrv., Tex., profl. supr., Tex., profl. reading specialist, Tex., profl. coun., Tex., elem. gen. English Spanish, Tex., high sch. English Spanish, Tex. Tchr., Spanish, English, reading Bowie Jr. High Sch., Odessa, Tex., 1964-65; tchr., reading Nimitz Jr. High Sch., San Antonio, 1965-66; tchr., Spanish Chofu High Sch., Tokyo, 1966-68; tchr., English, speech Carverdale High Sch., Houston, 1966-69; tchr., English Clear Creek High Sch., League City, Tex., 1969-71; instr., curriculum instrn. dept. U. Houston, University Park, 1974-75, 76-77; asst. prof. U. Houston at Clear Lake, Clear Lake, 1978-86; asst. prin. Travis Elem. Sch., Baytown, Tex., 1986-92; reading specialist Metcalf Elem. Sch., Houston, 1992-93; asst. prin. Holmsley Elem. Sch., Houston, 1993—2001, Lieder Elem. Sch., Houston, 2001—. Adj. faculty mem. U. Houston, 1989, 90, 99—, lectr., 1975-76, 77-78; presenter in field. Contbr. articles to profl. jours. Mem. Nat. Assn. Elem. Sch. Prins., Nat. Coun. Tchrs. English, Internat. Reading Assn., Tex. Elem. Sch. Prins. Suprs. Assn., Tex. State Reading Assn., Greater Houston Area Reading Coun., Bay Area Reading Coun. (past. pres.), Assn. Supervision Curriculum Devel., Kappa Delta Pi. Office: Lieder Elem Sch 17003 Kieth Harrow Houston TX 77084

BOWDISH, COLETTE ELIZABETH, educator; b. Denver, Dec. 31, 1949; d. William Bickett and Marguerite Katherine (Tank) Bastien; m. David Spencer Bowdish, Feb. 20, 1971; 1 child, Lara Elise. BA in Psychology, U. Colo., Boulder, 1970; BA in Biology with distinction, U. Colo., Denver, 1986, MA in Biology with distinction, 1988. Cert. tchr., Colo. Mgr., v.p. Bastien's Restaurant, Inc., Denver, 1971—; tchg. asst. U. Colo., Denver, 1986-88; tchr. Denver Pub. Sch., 1984-89; rating bd. specialist VA, Denver, 1989—. Troop leader Girl Scouts Am., Denver, 1986—. Recipient Regent's scholarship, U. Colo., 1967, Colo. Scholars' scholarship, 1985-87. Republican. Roman Catholic. Avocations: training horses, collecting and pressing flowers, camping, travel. Home: 15720 E Mercer Pl Aurora CO 80013-2540 also: 144 Van Gordon St Denver CO 80225-1808

BOWEN, ALICE FRANCES, school system administrator; b. Worcester, Mass., Apr. 14, 1948; d. Vincent Francis and Alice Frances (Gray) B. BS in Edn., Worcester State Coll., 1971, MS in Math. Edn., 1973, MS in Computer Sci. Edn., 1985. Cert. prin., math. and social studies tchr., Mass. Tchr. math. Worcester Pub. Schs., 1971-83, tchr. computer sci., 1983-92, asst. prin., 1992—. Instr. SAT prep. Ctrl. New Eng. Coll., Worcester, 1980-85; mem. Greater Worcester Urban Math. Collaborative Alliance for Edn., 1992-95. Leader Montachusetts coun. Girl Scouts U.S.A., 1968-85. Recipient St. Anne award Montachusetts coun. Girl Scouts U.S.A., 1978. Mem. ASCD, AAUW (bd. dirs. Worcester br. 1972-75, 90-96, Eleanor Roosevelt tchr. fellow 1991, Turtle award Worcester br.), Alliance for Edn.,

Delta Kappa Gamma, Phi Delta Kappa (Adminstr. of Yr. 2002). Democrat. Roman Catholic. Avocations: travel, crafts, reading. Home: 43 Sheridan Dr Shrewsbury MA 01545-3865 Office: Burncoat Mid Sch 135 Burncoat St Worcester MA 01606-2405

BOWEN, AUDREY LYNN HARRIS, elementary education educator; b. Kew Gardens, N.Y., Feb. 1, 1955; d. Roy Hartley and Margaret PEarl (Pitnam) Harris; m. Phillip Darrell Bowen, Aug. 9, 1980 (div. May 1987); 1 child, Meghan Elizabeth. AA, St. Mary's Coll., 1975; BA in Edn., Elon Coll., 1978. Tchr. 2d grade Onslow County Schs., Richlands, N.C., 1978-79; classroom asst. Wake County Schs., Wendell, N.C., 1980, substitute tchr. Raleigh, N.C., 1981-82; tchr. kindergarten North Hills Child Care Ctr., Raleigh, N.C., 1982-83; tchr. primary reading Forsyth County Schs., Winston Salem, N.C., 1987-88; tchr. Stokes County Schs., King, N.C., 1988-89, tchr. 1st grade, 1989-90; tchr. 4th grade Caswell County Schs., Yanceyville, N.C., 1992—; tchr. Master's in Reading program A & T State U., Greensboro, N.C., 1994-96. Author of poems. Recipient Outstanding Svc. award Wake County Big Sister Program, 1981-83. Mem. Nat. Assn. Learning Disabled, N.C. Assn. Learning Disabled, N.C. Assn. Educators, Royal Order of Moose. Republican. Methodist. Avocations: flute, singing, writing poetry, cross-stitch, skiing. Office: Caswell County Schs PO Box 160 Yanceyville NC 27379-0160

BOWEN, DOUGLAS GLENN, electrical engineer, consultant; b. Spanish Fork, Utah, May 6, 1951; s. William Morgan and Ferne (Davis) B.; m. Jarleen Ottesen, Dec. 28, 1972; children: Erica Anne, Emily Elizabeth, David, Summer. BSEE, MSEE, U. Wyo., 1975; MBA, Brigham Young U., 1993. Enlisted USAF, 1972, advanced through grades to capt., 1977, engr., 1975-81, resigned, 1981; prin. engr. Martin Marietta, Littleton, Colo., 1981-83; sr. engr. Sperry Corp., Salt Lake City, 1983-85; from staff engr. to chief engr. Unisys Corp., Salt Lake City, 1985-94; dir. DWD Enterprises, Inc., Salt Lake City, 1994; tech. dir. Loral Corp., Salt Lake City, 1995-97, ops. dir. L-3 comm. sys., 1997-98, chief engr. L-3 comm.-West, 1998—. Instr. Weber Coll., Ogden, Utah, 1987-88, U. Northrup, Inglewood, Calif., 1976-78; cons. USAF, Office of Sec. Air Force and Def. Support Projects Office, Pentagon, Washington, 1988—; mem. steering com. Utah Ctr. for Excellence; mem. curriculum adv. com. U. Utah, 1994—, mem. indsl. adv. bd. Coll. Engring., 1995—; assoc. U. Phoenix, 1996—; mem. NASA-Air Force Space Comm. & Telemetry Study Group, 1996—; mem. NATO Air Group IV, 1996—; adj. faculty U. Phoenix, Utah Campus, 1996—. Patentee in field. Bd. dirs. Spanish Fork Utility Bd., 1986—, Utah Mcpl. Power Assn., Provo, 1990, DWD Enterprises, 1994, Utah Ctr. for Excellence, 1995; chmn. Spanish Fork City Telecomms. Com., 1999—. Mem. Am. Legion, Old Crows, Air Force Assn. (v.p. 1988-89), Tau Beta Phi. Avocations: piano, gardening. E-mail: DGBowen@aol.com., douglas.g.bowen@L-3com.com.

BOWEN, JEWELL RAY, chemical engineering educator; b. Duck Hill, Miss., Jan. 9, 1934; s. Hugh and Myrtle Louise (Stevens) B.; m. Priscilla Joan Spooner, Feb. 4, 1956; children: Jewell Ray, Sandra L., Susan E. BS, MIT, 1956, MS, 1957; PhD, U. Calif., Berkeley, 1963. Asst. prof. U. Wis., Madison, 1963-67, assoc. prof., 1967-80, prof. chem. engring., 1970-81, chmn. chem engring. dept., 1971-73, 78-81, assoc. vice chancellor, 1972-76; prof. chem. engring. U. Wash., Seattle, 1981-2000, prof. emeritus, 2001—, dean coll. engring., 1981-96. Cons. in field; adviser NSF, Dept. Def.; vis. prof. Kyoto U. Internat. Innovation Ctr., 2002. Contbr. articles to profl. jours.; editor: 7th-10th Internat. Colloquia on Dynamics of Explosions and Reactive Systems, 1979, 81, 83, 85, chmn. program com. 18th; bd. dirs. Inst. for Dynamics of Explosions and Reactive Sys., 1989—, pres., 1989-95, treas. 1995—. Bd. dirs. Wash. Tech. Ctr., 1983-97, interim exec. dir., 1989-91; mem. Wash. High Tech. Coordinating Bd., 1983-87. Recipient SWE Rodney Chipp award, 1995; NATO-NSF postdoctoral fellow, 1962-63, sr. postdoctoral fellow, 1968; Deutsche Forschungsgemeinschaft prof., 1976-77. Fellow AIAA, AAAS (com. on coun. affairs 1995-97, sect. chmn. 1996-97), Am. Soc. Engring. Edn. (deans coun. 1985-92, chmn. 1989-91, bd. dirs. 1989-94, 1st v.p. 1991, pres.-elect 1992, pres. 1993); mem. AIAA, AIChE, Am. Phys. Soc., Combustion Inst., Sigma Xi, Tau Beta Pi, Beta Theta Pi. Home: 5324 NE 86th St Seattle WA 98115-3922 Office: U Wash Dept Chem Engring PO Box 351750 Seattle WA 98195-1750 E-mail: bowen@engr.washington.edu.

BOWEN, JIMMIE CARL, vocational education educator; b. Palmdale, Calif., Dec. 27, 1955; s. Charles Richard and Majorie Elizabeth (Cole) B.; m. Marsha Corrine Nuckolls, Apr. 30, 1978; 1 child, Allison Tiffany. AA, Antelope Valley Coll., Lancaster, Calif., 1988; AS, Antelope Valley Coll., 1989; Diploma Computerized Acctg., Diploma in Word Processing, Ameritech Colls., Inc., Van Nuys, Calif., 1988. 1st asst. mgr. Thrifty Corp.-Thrifty Drug and Discount, Lancaster, Calif., 1974-88; software cons. Calif. Freeware, Palmdale, 1989-90, Barbara's Choice Software, Lancaster, 1991—; computer/software instr. A-1 Computer Sch., Lancaster, 1992—; hardware/software cons. Bowen's Computer Cons., Palmdale, 1991—; bus. edn./computer instr. Ameritech Colls., Inc., Van Nuys, 1988-93; hardware/software instr. and cons. ABC Computer Learning Ctrs., Lancaster and Van Nuys, Calif., 1992-94, Computer Sci. Corp., Edwards AFB, 1994-96; tng. supr. GTE, 1996—. Hardware/software trainer. Contbr. articles to profl. jours. Mem. Nat. Assn. Desktop Pubrs., Antelope Valley Microcomputer Users Group, L.A. Amiga Users Group, Antelope Valley Commodore Users Group (pres., newsletter editor 1990—). Avocations: hiking, camping, travel. Home: 38739 5th St E Apt 1 Palmdale CA 93550-3774

BOWEN, PATRICIA LEDERER, dental educator; b. Evanston, Ill., July 5, 1943; d. John Arthur and Edna Virginia Lederer; m. Clarence Henry Metzner, Jr., June 1, 1963 (div. Feb. 1972); children: Donald Frederick Metzner, John Henry Metzner; m. Steven Casto Bowen, Mar. 31, 1973. Dental Hygienist, U. Louisville, 1972; B in Health Edn., U. Ky., 1982; MPA, Western Ky. U., 1985. Pvt. practice dental hygienist, various locations, 1972-75; pub. health dental hygienist U.S. Army, Berlin, 1975-78; cmty. health dental hygienist U.S. Army Dental Activity, Ft. Knox, Ky., 1978-95, U.S. Army Health Svcs. Command, Ft. Knox, Ky., 1981-95; pub. health dental hygienist Meade County (Ky.) Sch. Sys., 1995-96, LaRue County (Ky.) Sch. Sys., 1995-96; instr. pub. dental health Elizabethtown (Ky.) C.C., 1996-97; asst. dir. Meade County Tourism, 1996-97, dir., 1997—2003. Reporter Meade County Messenger, 1998, news editor, 1999—; lectr. in field. Contbr. articles to profl. jours. Pub. health dental hygienist Lebanon (Ohio) Sch. Sys., 1974—75; pub. health dental program presenter Grand Junction, Colo., 1973—74; CPR instr./instr.-trainer Am. Heart Assn., Ft. Knox, 1985—98, ARC, Ft. Knox, 1978—87. Decorated Order of Mil. Med. Merit U.S. Health Svcs. Command; recipient Patriotic Civilian Svc. award, Dept. of Army, 1986, award for Excellence, Delta Dental Ins. Co., 1991, 1994. Mem.: Ky. Oral health Consortium (exec. sec.-treas. 1991—96, chair 1995—96), Ky. Dental Hygiene Assn. (chair pub. health dental hygiene 1980—84), Louisville Dental Hygiene Assn. (chair legislation 1982), Am. Assn. Pub. Health Dentistry, Am. Dental Hygiene Assn. (pub. health cons. Ky. 1979—80), Meade County C. of C. (dir. 1998, Vol. of the Yr. 1998), Assn. U.S. Army (v.p. publicity 1994—). Avocations: photography, travel, snorkeling, hiking, reading. Home: 348 Greenbriar Ct Brandenburg KY 40108-9153 E-mail: pbowen@bbtel.com.

BOWEN, RAY MORRIS, academic administrator, engineering educator; b. Ft. Worth, Mar. 30, 1936; s. Winfred Herbert and Elizabeth (Williams) B; m. Sara Elizabeth Gibbens, July 5, 1958; children: Raymond Morris, Marguerite Elizabeth. BS in Mech. Engring., Texas A&M U., 1958, PhD in Engring., 1961; MS in Mech. Engring., Calif. Inst. Tech., 1959. Registered profl. engr., Tex., Ky. Assoc. prof. Mech. Engring. La. State U., Baton Rouge, 1965-67; prof. Mech. Engring. Rice U., Houston, 1967-83, chmn. dept., 1972-77; dir. divsn. NSF, Washington, 1982-83, from acting asst. dir., engr. to dep. asst. dir., engr., 1990-91; prof. Engring., dean U. Ky., Lexington, 1983-89; v.p. acad. affairs Okla. State U., Stillwater, Okla., 1991-93, interim pres., 1992—94; pres. Tex. A&M U., College Station, 1994—2002, pres. emeritus, 2002—. Mem. staff Sandia Corp., Albuquerque, summers 1966, 67, 72, cons., 1970-78; cons. U.S. Army Ballistic Rsch. Lab, Aberdeen Proving Ground, Md., 1970, Sun Oil Co., Albuquerque, 1974-75. Author: Introduction to Continuum Mechanics for Engineers, 1989; co-author: Introduction to Vectors and Tensors, Vols. I and II, 1976; contbg. author: Rational Thermodynamics, 1984; contbr. articles to profl. jours. Capt. USAF, 1961-64. Fellow Johns Hopkins U., 1964-65 Soc. Scholars Johns Hopkins U., Nat. Sci. Bd., 2002-, Tau Beta Pi, Phi Kappa Phi, Sigma Xi. Office: Tex A&M Univ Evans Library Annex 252C College Station TX 77843-5000

BOWEN, THOMAS LEE, academic administrator; b. Elyria, Ohio, Aug. 18, 1965; s. Dorothy Ann (Hayes) B. BA in History, Morehouse Coll., 1990. Asst. Atlanta Daily World Newspaper, 1985-89; archives asst. Nat. Archives - S.E. Region, E. Point, Ga., 1989-90; asst. dir. Upward Bound Program Oberlin (Ohio) Coll., 1991-92; community coord. Elyria Ministerial Alliance, 1992—. Coord. Project Malcolm, Elyria, 1990-92. Mem. City of Elyria M. L. King Commn., 1992, Leadership Lorain County, 1993; bd. dirs. Elyria City Schs., 1992—, Lorain County Urban League, 1993—. Named Man of Yr. Elyria Club Negro Bus. and Profl. Women's Clubs Inc., 1993. Mem. NAACP (exec. bd. Elyria chpt.), Lorain County Alliance Black Sch. Educators (exec. com.), Mid-Am. Assn. Ednl. Opportunities programs Personnel, Kemet Frat. (co-founder). Baptist. Avocations: African and African-Am. culture. Home: 233 Warden Ave Elyria OH 44035-2649

BOWEN, WILLIAM GORDON, economist, educator, foundation administrator; b. Cin., Oct. 6, 1933; s. Albert A. and Bernice (Pomert) B.; m. Mary Ellen Maxwell, Aug. 25, 1956; children: David Alan, Karen Lee. BA, Denison U., 1955; PhD, Princeton U., 1958. Mem. faculty Princeton (N.J.) U., 1958-88, prof. econs., 1965-88, dir. grad. studies Woodrow Wilson Sch. Pub. and Internat. Affairs, 1964-66, provost, 1967-72, pres., 1972-88, Andrew W. Mellon Found., N.Y.C., 1988—. Bd. dirs. Merck and Co., Inc., Am. Express Co., Univ. Corp. for Advanced Internet Devel. Internet, JSTOR; bd. overseers Tchrs. Ins. and Annuity Assn.-Coll. Ret. Equities Fund.; chmn. bd. dirs. Ithaka Harbors, Inc.; lectr. U. Oxford, 2000. Author: The Wage-Price Issue: A Theoretical Analysis, 1960, Wage Behavior in the Postwar Period: An Empirical Analysis, 1960, Economic Aspects of Education: Three Essays, 1964, (with W. J. Baumol) Performing Arts: The Economic Dilemma, 1966, (with T. A. Finegan) The Economics of Labor Force Participation, 1969, Ever the Teacher, 1987, (with J. A. Sosa) Prospects for Faculty in the Arts and Sciences, 1989, (with Neil L. Rudenstine) In Pursuit of the PhD, 1992, Inside the Boardroom: Governance by Directors and Trustees, 1994, (with T. Nygren, S. Turner, E. Duffy) The Charitable Nonprofits, 1994, (with Derek Bok) The Shape of the River: Long-Term Consequences of Considering Race in College and University Admissions, 1998, (with James L. Shulman) The Game of Life: College Sports and Educational Values, 2001, (with Sarah A. Levin) Reclaiming the Game: College Sports and Educational Values, 2003. Trustee Ctr. for Advanced Study in Behavioral Scis., 1978-84, 89-92, Denison U., 1992-2000; regent emeritus Smithsonian Instn. Recipient Joseph Henry medal Smithsonian Instn., 1996, (with Derek Bok) Grawemeyer award in edn. U. Louisville, 2001. Mem. Am. Econs. Assn., Indsl. Rels. Rsch. Assn., Coun. on Fgn. Rels., Phi Beta Kappa. Office: Andrew W Mellon Found 140 E 62nd St New York NY 10021-8124

BOWENS, GLORIA FURR, educational administrator; b. Detroit, Apr. 15, 1927; d. Leon Lewis and Iva Rose (Talbot) Furr; B.S., Tufts Coll., 1947; Ed.M., State Coll. Boston, 1968; Ed.D., Harvard U., 1975; 1 dau., Stephanie T. Sci. tchr. Boston Pub. Schs., 1961-71, asst. to the dir. orientation for integration, 1971-73, acting dir. personnel mgmt., 1981-82, instr. med. tech., 1982— ; asst. supt. schs. Roosevelt (L.I., N.Y.) Sch. Dist., 1974-77; asst. dir. urban schs. collaborative Northeastern U., Boston, 1977-79, dist. IX coordinator curriculum and competency resources, 1979-81; ptnr. antique shop, Pickering Wharf, Salem, Mass., 1982—; pres. Horizons Extended Ednl. Consulting, 1992-98. Mem. Nat. Council Adminstrv. Women Edn. (exec. bd. 1970-73), Am. Assn. Sch. Adminstrs., North Shore Antiques Assn. (treas.), Phi Delta Kappa, Alpha Kappa Alpha.

BOWERFIND, EDGAR SIHLER, JR., physician, medical administrator; b. Cleve., May 7, 1924; s. Edgar Sihler and Edna (Strong) B.; m. Maria Washington Tucker, Apr. 28, 1956; children— Edgar Sihler III, Ellis Tucker, Jane Strong, William Minor Lile Student, Creighton U. Med. Sch., 1945-47; MD, Western Res. U., 1949. Diplomate Am. Bd. Internal Medicine. Intern Univ. Hosps. of Cleve., 1950-51, resident in medicine, 1954-56; practice medicine specializing in internal medicine Cleve., 1957-92; mem. faculty Case Western Res. U. Sch. Medicine, Cleve., 1956-92, asst. prof. medicine, 1965-92, dir. health clinics, utilization rev., 1965-92, asst. prof. emeritus, 1992—; chief med. services Horizon Ctr. Hosp., Cleve., 1981-83. Sec. Citizens Commn. on Grad. Med. Edn., 1964-66 Sub-deacon Episcopal Diocese Ohio, 1970—; trustee The Sihler Mental Health Found. Served with AUS, 1943-46, to capt. USAF, 1951-53. Decorated Bronze Star; Ogelbay fellow in medicine U. Hosps. Cleve., 1955-56 Home: Ste 915 2181 Ambleside Dr Cleveland OH 44106

BOWERMAN, ANN LOUISE, writer, genealogist, educator; b. Branch County, Mich., June 4, 1933; d. George Allen and Mary (Thomas) Hubbard; m. Virgil Lee Bowerman, June 4, 1954 (div. 1977); children: William Lee, Sally Ann; m. Virgil Wayne Dunkel, Jr., May 23, 1987 (div. Dec. 1996). BA, Western Mich. U., 1966, MSLS, 1971, MA, 1976. Cert. tchr. K-8, Mich., libr. sci. Tchr. Bethel #6 Sch. Dist., Coldwater, Mich., 1953—55; tchr. kindergarten Union City (Mich.) Schs., 1963-64; children's libr. Sturgis (Mich.) Pub. Libr., 1971-72; libr./media specialist Coldwater H.S., 1972-91; field rep. U.S. Census Bur., 2000—02; media specialist libr. Union City (Mich.) Schs., 2002—03; retired, 1991. Mem. programming com., mem. ann. scholarships telethon com., camera staff, video editor Cable TV Channel 31, Coldwater, 1983-90. Author: The Bater Book, 1987, A Bowerman Family History, 1998, Historic Howe, Indiana Walking Tour, 1998, The William (6) Bowerman Family of Conneaut Township, 1998; co-author: Recommendations for High School Media Centers in Michigan, 1980 (booklet); contbr. articles to profl. jours. Mem., chair governing bd. Woodlands Libr. Coop., Albion, Mich., 1973-74, 83-86; adv. coun. Calhoun and Branch Counties Regional Ednl. Media Ctr., Marshall, Mich., 1972-91; com. mem. So. Mich. Region of Coop., Albion, 1989-91; leader All Around 4-H Club, Union City, 1954-74; mem. Sullivan Lady's Aid Soc., Union City, 1955-74, Twin Lakes Cmty. Assn., 1997—; chair winter program com. Tibbits Arts Found., Coldwater, 1980-90; mem. Coldwater Hist. Preservation Assn., 1978-86; del. Mich. Rep. State Conv., Detroit, 1986; candidate for Branch County Commr., Coldwater, 1988; mem. Mich. Assn. for Computer Users in Learning, 1975-91; mem. cultural arts com., mem. walking tour com. Howe (Ind.) Cmty. Assn., 1996—. Recipient Cert. of Appreciation, Mich. Assn. for Media in Edn., 1980, 91, Golden Apple Retirement award Coldwater H.S., 1991. Mem. Soc. of Genealogists (London), New England Hist. Geneal. Soc., Descendants of Founders of Ancient Windsor, Ctrl. N.Y. Geneal. Soc., DAR (good citizen selection com., treas. Coldwater br. 1997-2002), Mich. Assn. Ret. Sch. Pers., Schenectady County Hist. Soc., Old Brutus Hist. Soc., Union City Geneal. Soc., St. Joseph County Hist. Soc. (advisor to Land Office Mus. com. 1997—), Crawford County Geneal. Soc., Coldwater Edn. Assn. (sec. 1980-90), Beta Phi Mu. Avocations: travel, coin collecting, tennis. Home: 1820 W 600 N Howe IN 46746-9406 E-mail: abowerma@ligtel.com.

BOWERS, CAROLYN POWERS, county official, educator; b. Clarksville, Tenn., Dec. 11, 1945; d. Carl Liberty and Margaret Eudora (Poyner) Powers; m. William Michael Bowers, June 27, 1963; chlidren: Laurie Lynn Bowers Swift, Margaret Alice Bowers Hooper. BS, Austin Peay State U., 1967, MA in Edn., 1975; postgrad., U. Tenn. Cert. tchr., Tenn. Tchr. bus. and office edn. Clarksville (Tenn.) High Sch., 1969-74, 94—, tchr. stenography lab, compuerized acctg. software tools, 1974-84; tchr. data processing Clarksville Vo-Tech Ctr., 1984-94, liason staff, 1990-93; elected trustee Montgomery County, 1998—. Mem. state steering com. Tenn. Tchrs. Study Coun., 1980-82; pres., v.p., sec. Curriculum Coordinating Com., 1983-89; advisor Bus. Profls. Am., Clarksville High Sch. and Vocat. Tech. Ctr. chpt., 1984-94. Tchr. CCD Immaculate Conception Ch., Clarksville, 1971-72, mem., 1964—; sponsor Future Tchrs. Am., 1994-95; sec., treas. Middle Tenn. Trustees Assn. Mem. NEA, Nat. Bus. Edn. Assn., Am. Vocat. Assn., Tenn. Bus. Edn. Assn., Tenn. Edn. Assn., Tenn. Vocat. Assn. (bd. dirs. bus. edn. 1992-94), Tenn. Office Edn. Tchrs. Assn. (pres. 1995-96), County Officials Assn. Tenn., Clarksville Rotary Club, Clarksville Montgomery County Edn. Assn. (v.p., sec., treas., editor newsletter, Adopt-A-Sch. Coun. 1990—), Clarksville C. of C. Avocations: swimming, music, gardening, reading. Office: Montgomery County Trustees Office 350 Pageant Ln Clarksville TN 37040-8606 Address: 400 Savannah Trace Dr Clarksville TN 37043-5442

BOWERS, GLORIA MILLS, secondary education art educator; b. Brookville, Pa., May 9, 1951; d. James Arthur and Geraldine Evelyn (Huffman) Mills; m. Ralph Gordon Bowers, July 2, 1977; 1 child, Amy Lynn. BS in Art Edn. with distinction, Pa. State U., 1973. Elem. art tchr. Jersey Shore (Pa.) Elem. Sch., 1973-76; secondary art tchr. Lock Haven (Pa.) H.S., 1982-95; secondary and elem. art tchr. Sugar Valley Elem. and H.S., Loganton, Pa., 1995-96; elem. art tchr. Woolrich (Pa.) Elem. Sch., 1995-96, Lamar Twp. Elem. Sch., Salona, Pa., 1995-96; secondary art tchr. Bald Eagle-Nittany H.S., Mill Hall, Pa., 1996—. Mem. AAUW, Pa. State U. Alumni Assn., Assn. Clinton County Educators, Pi Lambda Theta, Beta Sigma Phi (v.p. Jersey Shore chpt. 1982, pres. 1983, Woman of Yr. 1984, 85). Democrat. Avocations: antiques, drawing, reading, swimming, Pa. State U. football. Home: 402 W Water St Lock Haven PA 17745-1112

BOWERS, LINDA HERALD, secondary education educator; b. Pitts., Oct. 6, 1948; d. Harry McBride and Alice Rose (Shiring) Herald; Tammy, Eddie, Patty. BS, St. Bonaventure (N.Y.) U., 1970; MA, Boston Coll., 1972. Cert. secondary math. tchr., Miss.; nat. bd. cert. tchr. Tchr. math. Arlington (Mass.) High Sch., 1972-73, Corinth (Miss.) High Sch., 1973-76, 1979-80, Alcorn Cen. High Sch., Glen, Miss., 1981—2001, Grafton H.S., York, Va., 2001—03, Sewickley (Pa.) Acad., 2003—. Sponsor Nat. Honor Soc., 2001—03. Named Tchr. of Yr., Radio Shack, 2000; named to, Miss. STAR Tchr. Hall of Fame, 1997; recipient Presdl. award, 1995. Mem.: NEA, Nat. Coun. Tchrs. Math., Mu Alpha Theta. Avocations: swimming, basketball. Home: 1016 Irwin Dr Pittsburgh PA 15236-2331

BOWERY, WARREN E. music educator; b. Wheeling, W. Va., May 11, 1959; s. Warren E. and Gertrude (Gross) B.; m. Susan C. Waybright, Aug. 10, 1985. BA with hons., West Liberty State Coll., 1981. Substitute tchr. Marshall County Schs., Moundsville, W.Va., 1982-84; band, choir and music tchr. Ottoville (Ohio) Local Schs., 1985—. Com. mem. Putnam County Music Edn. Com., Ottawa, Ohio, 1986, 91, 96, 2001. Composer (musical theater): The Bloody Bridge, 1994, You Can't Get There From Here!, 1995. Mem. Music Educator's Nat. Conf., Ohio Music Edn. Assn., Ohio Edn. Assn. (Outstanding Treas. award 1995), Ottoville Local Edn. Assn. (treas. 1989-90, 2002—). Lutheran. Avocations: pub. svc. monitoring, musician, All-Ohio Scanner Club, target shooting. Office: Ottoville HS PO Box 248 Ottoville OH 45876-0248

BOWIE, PHYLLIS, secondary education educator; Tchr. secondary geography S.A.V.E. High Sch., Anchorage. Recipient Disting. Tchr. K-12 award Nat. Coun. for Geog. Edn., 1992. Office: SAVE HS 410 E 56th Ave Anchorage AK 99518-1244

BOWLAN, NANCY LYNN, elementary and secondary school educator; b. Walla Walla, Wash., Jan. 16, 1946; d. Ralph Reighard and Irene Elizabeth (Fisher) Nowlen; m. Buel Nathan Bowlan; children: Ronald, Sarah, Sandra, Michelle, John. BA, Ariz. State U., 1968. Cert. reading specialist. Tchr. Seligman (Ariz.) Schs., 1968-71, Page (Ariz.) Schs., 1976-87; tchr., ESL coord. Gila Bend (Ariz.) Schs., 1988-94; tchr. Tucson Unified Sch. Dist., Tucson, 1994—. Leader Girl Scouts Am., Page, Ariz., 1974-75. Mem. Delta Kappa Gamma (chmn. state fin. com. Ariz. 1987—, Alpha Zeta chpt. Casa Grande, Ariz. 1993, treas. Tau chpt., Flagstaff, Ariz. 1992, Lambda chpt., Tucson, 1995—), Ea. Star (Worthy Matron 1990). Republican. Avocations: auto rec. driving, computers, planting, reading. Home: 112 N Players Club Dr Tucson AZ 85745-8916

BOWLBY, LINDA ARLENE, secondary school educator; b. Martins Ferry, Ohio, Sept. 12, 1947; d. Theodore Roosevelt and Jessie Edith (Berry) Nicholls; m. James Keith Bowlby, July 18, 1970. BS in Home Econs., Ohio State U., 1969; MS in Applied Human Ecology, MA in Guidance and Counseling, Bowling Green State U., 1991. Lic. social worker. Tchr. consumer homemaking Wynford H.S., Bucyrus, Ohio, 1969-91, Wynford Satellite, Pioneer Joint Vocat. Sch., Shelby, Ohio, 1991—. Seamstress, sales rep. Korral Kreations, Sycamore, Ohio, 1994—; ind. beauty cons. Mary Kay Cosmetics, 1995—. Co-author: The Sidesaddle Legacy, 1994; author: (booklets) 4-H Manual for Sidesaddles, 2d rev. edit., 1993, Sidesaddles, 1986; editor All Aside newsletter, 1980-89. Leader Girl Scouts U.S., Mansfield/Nevada, Ohio, 1955-72; treas., Sunday Sch. tchr. Brokensword United Meth. Ch. Mem. Am. Vocat. Assn., Am. Quarter Horse Assn., World Sidesaddle Fedn., Inc. (pres., founder 1980—, Mem. of Yr. 1987, 93), Internat. Side Saddle Orgn. (Hall of Fame), Ohio Vocat. Assn., Ohio Quarter Horse Assn. (amateur dir. 1996—), N.W. Ohio Future Homemakers Am. (founding, bd. dirs.), No. Ohio Quarter Horse Assn., Edn. Assn. of Pioneer, Wynford Edn. Assn. (sec.-treas. 1981-91), Wynford Future Homemakers of Am. (advisor). Avocations: raising and showing quarter horses, pygmy goats, sidesaddle horseback riding, crafts, reading. Home: 5619 State Route 19 Bucyrus OH 44820-8971

BOWLES, BETTY JONES, business education educator; b. Richmond, Va., June 10, 1947; d. Robert Lee and Blanche (Williamson) Jones; m. Norman Lee Bowles Sr., Feb. 14, 1970; children: Ruth Anne, Lee, Danny. BS, Va. Commonwealth U., 1969; M Humanities, U. Richmond, 1989. Cert. postgrad. profl., Va. Tchr. Lee Davis H.S., Mechanicsville, Va., 1969-72, 73-74, 84-87; sec. Battlefield Park Elem. Sch., Mechanicsville, 1972-73, Stonewall Jackson Jr. H.S., Mechanicsville, 1982-84, tchr., 1987-91; tchr., dept. chair Atlee H.S., Mechanicsville, 1991—96; tchr. Stonewall Jackson, Mechanicsville, 1996—98, Patrick Henry H.S., Ashland, 1998—, chmn. dept., 2002—. Presenter staff devel. workshop, activities on block scheduling pub. schs. in Va., 1993-94;, Walled Lake, Mich., 1994; Fayetteville, N.C., 1995; mem. Va.-Russia Tchr. Exchange in Moscow, 1995. Lit. sec. Cool Spring Bapt. Ch., Mechanicsville, 1988-98. Named Vocat. Tchr. of Yr. Mechanicsville Rotary Club, 1994. Mem. Nat. Bus. Edn. Assn., So. Bus. Edn. Assn., Va. Bus. Edn. Assn., Va. Vocat. Assn. Baptist. Avocations: opera, exercising, piano. Office: Patrick Henry HS 12449 W Patrick Henry Rd Ashland VA 23005

BOWLES, WALTER DONALD, economist, educator; b. Seattle, Dec. 28, 1923; s. Walter Alexander and Minnie Ellen (Martin) B.; m. Vincenza Pompea Galasso, Dec. 22, 1955; children: Ellen Maria, Walter Donald. BA in Econs, U. Wash., 1949; MA in Econs, Columbia U., 1952, PhD in Econs., 1958; cert. in Soviet economy, Russian Inst., 1952. Editor Research Program on USSR, N.Y.C., 1953-55; fellow Air U., 1955-57; faculty Am. U., Washington, 1957-94, prof. econs., chmn. dept., 1962-65, prof. econs., dean Coll. Arts and Scis., 1965-69, prof. econs., v.p. acad. affairs, 1969-73, prof. econs., 1974—93; on leave as prof. econs., sr. fellow Columbia U.,

1973-74; on leave as economist U.S. AID, 1983-85, cons., 1985-89; prof. econs. Graz Center, Austria, summers 1971-73; prof. emeritus, 1994. Acad. dir. Am. U. London Semester Program, spring, 1991; lectr., dir. African seminars, 1964. With U.S. Army, 1943—46. Mem. AAUP, Am. Econ. Assn., Assn. Study Comparative Econ. Systems, Assn. for Advancement Slavic Studies, Soc. for Internat. Devel. Home: 329 Roosevelt Ave Ventura CA 93003-2589

BOWLING, JOHN ROBERT, osteopathic physician, educator, academic administrator; b. Columbus, Ohio, Feb. 18, 1943; s. Ardyce Saul and Wilma Garcia (Snider) B.; m. Janet Lou Bowman, July 10, 1965; children: Jack Robert, James Richard, Jason Russell. BS, Ohio U., 1965; DO, Kirksville (Mo.) Coll. Osteopathic Medicine, 1969. Diplomate Am. Osteo. Bd. Family Practice; cert. Am. Osteo. Bd. Family Practice. Rotating intern Drs. Hosp., Columbus, 1969—70; gen. practice osteo. medicine Lancaster, Ohio, 1970—88; clin. assoc. prof. Ohio U. Coll. Osteo. Medicine, Athens, 1977—88; med. dir. Lancaster Health Care Ctr., 1980—88; assoc. prof. dept. family medicine U. North Tex. Health Sci. Ctr. Coll. Osteo. Medicine, Ft. Worth, 1988—, interim chmn. dept. family medicine, 1991, vice chmn. dept., 1991—95, course dir. core clin. clerkship in family practice, 1991—2003, mem. steering com. Catchum project, mem. exec. coun. of faculty, 1992, 1996, mem. curriculum com., 1993—, mem. admissions com., 1989—97, dir. student health svcs., 1992—2003, dir. rural curriculum track-family medicine, 1996—2001, dir. predoctoral and rural edn. dept. family medicine, 2001—, phase dir. for integrated clin. curriculum experiences, 1995—. Civ. sr. attending staff Doctors Hosp., 1970—88, co-dir. family practice residency program, 1979, acting dir., 80; chmn. dept. medicine Lancaster Fairfield Cmty. Hosp., 1975, sec. med. staff, 1982—83, pres., 1985; active staff Osteo. Med. Ctr. Tex., 1988—; team physician Bloom Carool (Ohio) Sch., 1973—88; health care workgroup Tex. Tele. Intrastructure Bd., 2001—02. Pres., bd. dirs. Montessori Presch., Lancaster, 1975; chmn. youth basketball com. YMCA; former youth coord., tchr., mem. adminstrv. bd. United Meth. Ch.; mem. chancel chour, men's chorus 1st United Mech. Ch., Grapevine, Tex., 1997—2003; staff parish rels. com. 1st United Meth. Ch., Grapevine, Tex., 2000—01. Named Outstanding Advisor, Tex. Coll. Osteo. Medicine, 1992; recipient Clyde Gallehugh Meml. award, 2002. Fellow Am. Coll. Osteo. Family Physicians (com. on evaluation and edn. 1991—, program chmn. nat. conv. 1995, chmn. resident intern com. 1995-99, Family Physician of Yr. 1996; mem. Am. Osteo. Assn., Ohio Osteo. Assn., Tex. Osteo. Med. Assn. (program chmn. state conv. 1994, 95), Tex. Med. Assn. (preventive medicine task force 1993-94), Tex. Soc. Am. Coll. Osteo. Family Phsyicians (pres. 1999-00). Methodist. Avocations: tennis, golf, photography, music. Home: 550 Timber Ridge Dr Roanoke TX 76262 Office: U North Tex Health Sci Ctr College Osteo Medicine 3500 Camp Bowie Blvd Fort Worth TX 76107-2644 E-mail: jbowling@hsc.unt.edu.

BOWLUS, DALE RICHARD, environmental scientist, educator, consultant; b. Fremont, Ohio, Mar. 31, 1948; s. Dale Roscoe and Margaret Ann (Richard) B.; m. Vicki Marlene Sexton, Dec. 20, 1986; children: Kameron Michele, Lyndsey Nichole, Meganne Oneile. BS, Bowling Green State U., 1970; MS, Morgan State U., 1975. Registered hazardous substances and environ. profl., cert. hazardous materials mgr. Sci. instr. Harford County Bd. Edn., Bel Air, Md., 1970-79, county sci. resource tchr., 1976-78; environ. scientist U.S. Army Environ. Hygiene Agy., Aberdeen Proving Ground, Md., 1977—95, Army hazardous materials spill response team, 1981-90; environ. sci. U.S. Army Ctr. Health Promotion and Preventive Medicine, Aberdeen Proving Ground, Md., 1995—. V.p. Enteco, Inc., Bel Air, 1981-84, A&B Cons., Havre de Grace, Md., 1984-88. Author over 100 waste mgmt. reports, tech. papers and guides; contbr. articles to Municipal and Solid Waste; editl. bd. DOE Newsletter, 1998-02. Exec. bd. Susquehannock Environ. Ctr., Bel Air, 1987-91, v.p., 1988-91; mem. adv. bd. Harford C.C., Bel Air, 1990-94; pres. alumni coun. Harford C.C., 1996-98; founder, original bd. dirs. Ripken Mus., Aberdeen, Md. Recipient Exceptional Performance award U.S. Dept. Def., 1983, 86, 89, 90, Unsung Hero award Susquehannock Environ. Ctr., 1990, Govt. Salute to Excellence award Gov's. Office State Md., 1990, Outstanding Hazardous Waste Mgmt. Support awards Dept. U.S. Army, Air Force NG Bur. 1985, Mass. NG, 1987, U.S. Army, 1987. Mem. ASTM (F-20 subcom. recording sec. 1984-87, v.p. 1987-89), Nat. Environ. Health Assn., Nat. Environ. Tgn. Assn., Bowling Green State U. Alumni Assn., Soc. Risk Analysis (chair Harford County Environ. adv. bd. 1997-2001). Republican. Methodist. Achievements include advanced research in environmental preservation, recycling, health and ecological risk assessment, risk communication and spill response. Home: 909 Leslie Rd Havre De Grace MD 21078-1713 Office: US Army Ctr for Health Promotion and Prev Medicine MCHB-TS-RDE Aberdeen Proving Ground MD 21010-5422

BOWMAN, BARBARA TAYLOR, early childhood educator; b. Chgo., Oct. 30, 1928; d. Robert Rochon and Dorothy Vaugn (Jennings) Taylor; m. James E. Bowman, June 17, 1950, 1 child, Valerie Bowman Jarrett. BA, Sarah Lawrence Coll., 1950; MA, U. Chgo., 1952; DHL (hon.), Bankstreet Coll., 1988, Roosevelt U., 1998, Dominican U., 2002, Gov.'s State U., 2002. Tchr. U. Chgo. Nursery Sch., 1950-52, Colo. Women's Coll. Nursery Sch., Denver, 1953-55; mem. sci. faculty Shiraz (Iran) U. Nemazee Sch. Nursing, 1955-61; spl. edn. tchr. Chgo. Child Care Soc., 1965—67; mem. faculty Erikson Inst., Chgo., 1967—, dir. grad. studies, 1978—94, pres., 1994—2002, prof. early edn., 2002. Mem. early childhood com. Nat. Bd. Profl. Tchg. Stds., 1992-2002; cons. early childhood edn., parent edn.; chair com. on early childhood pedagogy NRC, 1998-99. Contbr. articles to profl. jours. Bd. dirs. Ill. Health Edn. Com., 1969—71, Inst. Psychoanalysis, 1970—73, Ill. Adv. Coun. Dept. Children and Family Svcs., 1974—79, Child Devel. Assoc. Consortium, 1979—81, Chgo. Bd. Edn. Desegregation Commn., 1981—84, Bus. People in Pub. Inst., 1980—, High Scope Ednl. Rsch. Found., 1986—93, Gt. Books Found., 1988—, Cmty.-Corp. Sch., 1988—90; mem. Family Resource Coalition, 1992—96, mem. nat. bd. profl. tchr. stds., 1996—2002. Mem. Ill. Assn. Edn. Young Children, Nat. Assn. Edn. Young Children (pres. 1980-82), Chgo. Assns. Edn. Young Children (pres. 1973-77), Black Child Devel. Assn., Am. Ednl. Rsch. Assn. Achievements include research in early education teaching and school improvement. Office: Erikson Inst 420 N Wabash Ave Chicago IL 60611-3568

BOWMAN, CONNIE JO, secondary education educator; b. Huntington, Ind., Sept. 17, 1949; d. C. Eugene and Geraldine Celeste (Blickenstaff) Howard; m. Thomas Arthur Hess, Aug. 7, 1971 (div. June 1980); 1 child, Audrea Leigh; m. John Ezra Bowman, July 24, 1982; stepchildren: Heather Jane, Howard Thomas. BS, Manchester Coll., 1971; MAT, Purdue U., 1977. Tchr. math. Wabash (Ind.) City Schs., 1971-72, Whitko Community Schs., South Whitley, Ind., 1973-78; part-time instr. Manchester Coll., North Manchester, Ind., 1979-80; tchr. DeKalb Eastern Community Schs., Butler, Ind., 1980—. Chmn. math. dept. Eastside Jr./Sr. High Sch., Butler, 1987—. Mem. NEA, Nat. Coun. Tchrs. Math., Ind. Tchrs. Assn., Ind. Coun. Tchrs. Math. Methodist. Avocations: sewing, reading, church choir. Home: 10231 Garman Rd Leo IN 46765-9217 Office: Eastside Jr/Sr High Sch 603 E Green St Butler IN 46721-1135

BOWMAN, DANIEL OLIVER, psychologist; b. Holly Hill, S.C., Feb. 1, 1931; s. John Daniel and Pansy (Mizzell) Bowman. BA in Music, Furman U., 1951; MEd, U. S.C., 1952; PhD, U. Ga., 1963. Lic. psychologist, S.C. Tchr., English, French Summerville (S.C.) H.S., 1952-53; chmn. English dept., sr. guidance counselor Boys H.S., Anderson, S.C., 1955-61; instr. psychology U. Ga., Athens, 1961-63; asst. prof. psychology The Citadel, Charleston, S.C., 1963-66, assoc. prof. psychology, counselor to corps cadets, 1966-69, prof. psychology, dir. grad. studies, 1969-77, prof., head dept. psychology, 1977-91, Arland D. Williams prof. psychology, 1991-96, prof. emeritus, 1996—. Cons. Charleston County Sheriff's Dept., 1985-94, Berkeley County Sch. System, Moncks Corner, S.C., 1977-89. Chmn. Charleston County Mental Retardation Bd., 1988-90. Mem. APA, AAUP, NASP, Am. Psychol. Soc. (charter), Southea. Psychol. Assn., S.C. Psychol. Assn. (pres. 1990-91, Outstanding Contbrs. Psychology 1988), Phi Kappa Phi (pres. 1979-80), Phi Delta Kappa. Home: 6 Fort Royal Ave Charleston SC 29407-6012

BOWMAN, ELIZABETH SUE, psychiatrist, educator, editor; b. Roanoke, Va., Mar. 9, 1954; d. Edward David and Mildred Lenora B.; m. Philip Meredith Coons, Sept. 5, 1981. BS, Purdue U., 1976; MD, Ind. U., Indpls., 1980; STM summa cum laude, Christian Theol. Sem., Indpls., 1987. Resident in psychiatry sch. of medicine Ind. U., 1980-84, chief resident sch. of medicine, 1984, asst. prof. sch. of medicine, 1984-93, assoc. prof., 1993-00, prof., 2000-01; clin. prof. neurology, 2001—; staff psychiatrist Indpls. VA Hosp., 1986-89. Co-editor-in-chief Jour. Trauma and Dissociation, 1999—; contbr. articles to med. jours., chpts. to books. Fellow Am. Psychiat. Assn. (disting.), Internat. Soc. for Study of Dissociation (treas. 1992-94, pres. 1996, disting.); mem. Am. Med. Women's Assn., Assn. Women Psychiatrists, Ind. Psychiat. Soc. (sec. 1985-86, editor newsletter 1985-88, pres. 1993). Office: 10585 N Meridian St #340 Indianapolis IN 46290

BOWMAN, HAZEL LOIS, retired English language educator; b. Plant City, Fla., Feb. 18, 1917; d. Joseph Monroe and Annie (Thoman) B. AB, Fla. State Coll. for Women, 1937; MA, U. Fla., 1948; postgrad., U. Md., 1961-65. Tchr. Lakeview H.S., Winter Garden, Fla., 1939-40, Eagle Lake Sch., Fla., 1940-41; welfare visitor Fla. Welfare Bd., 1941-42; specialist U.S. Army Signal Corps, Arlington Hall, Va., 1942-43; recreation work, asst. procurement officer ARC, CBI Theater, 1943-46; lab. technician Am. Cyanamid Corp., Brewster, Fla., 1946-47; instr., asst. prof. gen. extension divsn. U. Fla., Fla. State U., 1948-51; freelance writer, editor, indexer N.Y., Fla., 1951-55; staff writer Tampa (Fla.) Morning Tribune, 1956; staff writer, telegraph editor Winter Haven (Fla.) News-Chief, 1956-57; registrar, admissions officer U. Tampa, 1957-59; coll. counselor Atlantic States, 1959-60; registrar, freshman advisor Towson State Tchrs. Coll., Balt., 1960-62; dir. student pers., guidance, admissions Harford Jr. Coll., Bel Air, Md., 1962-64; instr., asst. prof. York (Pa.) Coll., 1965-69, asst. prof. English, journalism, 1966-69; tchr. S.W. Jr. H.S., Lakeland, Fla., 1969-70; tchr. learning disabled Vanguard Sch., Lake Wales, Fla., 1970-82; libr. asst. Polk County Hist. and Geneal. Libr., Bartow, Fla., 1986-91. Editor, Tampa Altrusan, 1958-60, Polk County Hist. Calendar, 1986-90. Mem. Polk County Hist. Commn., 1992-99. Recipient Mayhall Music medal, 1933, Excellence in Cmty. Svc. award Nat. Soc. DAR, 1994, Outstanding Achievement award Fla. State Geneal. Soc., 2002. Mem. AAUW (hon. 50 yr. life), NOW, Nat. Geneal. Soc., Mortar Board, Polk County Hist. Assn. (editor Newsletter 1990-94), Imperial Polk Genealogical Soc., Alpha Chi Alpha, Chi Delta Phi. Home: 511 NE 9th Ave Mulberry FL 33860-2620

BOWMAN, JAMES ARTHUR, JR., obstetrician-gynecologist, educator; b. Cleve., May 3, 1921; s. James Arthur Sr. and Elsie Marie (Hoehn) B.; m. Mabel Elizabeth Bartels, June 10, 1945 (dec. Apr. 1998); children: Jane, Ruth, Mary, Lois. BS in Chemistry, Western Res. U., 1943, MD, 1945. Diplomate Am. Bd. Ob-Gyn. Demonstrator dept. ob-gyn Sch. Medicine Western Res. U. (now Case Western Res. U.), Cleve., 1953-55, clin. instr. Sch. Medicine, 1955-59, sr. clin. instr. ob-gyn, 1959-62, asst. clin. prof. ob-gyn, 1962-84, assoc. clin. prof. ob-gyn, 1984-85, assoc. clin. prof. emeritus dept. reproductive biology. Contbr. rsch. articles to profl. jours. Trustee Med. Alumni Assn., 1982-85. Capt. U.S. Army, 1946-48. Fellow ACOG, Ctrl. Assn. Ob-gyns., Am. Fertility Soc.; mem. AMA, Ohio State Med. Assn., Acad. Medicine, Cleve. Soc. Ob-gyns. (sec. 1974-78, pres.-elect 1978-79, pres. 1979-80). Home: 4902 Lindsey Ln Richmond Heights OH 44143-2930

BOWMAN, JAN MARIE ALBRIGHT, secondary English educator; b. Lancaster, Pa., Nov. 26, 1954; d. Ellsworth W. and Ellen K. Albright; m. Matthew W. Delfert, Sept. 18, 1976 (div. Apr. 1986); 1 child, Erin Lynne; m. Timothy L. Bowman, Aug. 2, 1986; 1 child, Ray Wesley II. BS in Comms. summa cum laude, Lock Haven (Pa.) U., 1976; MEd, Cambridge Coll., 2000. Cert. secondary comm. tchr., Pa. 7-8th grade English instr. Penn Manor Sch. Dist., Lancaster, 1976-77; 9-12th grade English instr. Shade-Ctrl. City Sch. Dist., Cairnbrook, Pa., 1977-85; 12th grade English instr. Conemaugh Twp. Sch. Dist., Davidsville, Pa., 1985—. Tchr.-cons. Southctrl. Pa. Writing Project. Geraldine R. Dodge Found. grantee, 1989, 90, 91. Mem. Nat. Coun. Tchrs. English, Pa. State Edn. Assn. Democrat. Methodist. Home: 4252 Ridge Rd Stoystown PA 15563-9802 Office: Conemaugh Twp Area HS West Campus Ave Davidsville PA 15928 E-mail: bowman@ctasd.org.

BOWMAN, JERRY WAYNE, artist, research scientist; b. Columbia City, Ind., Aug. 3, 1952; s. Wayne Austin and Patricia Ann Bowman; m. Susan Jolie Alexander, Feb. 12, 1988; children: Rachel, Lily. BA magna cum laude, Kalamazoo Coll., 1974. Rsch. scientist Pfizer Inc., Kalamazoo, 1978—. Exhibited in group shows at San Diego Watercolor Soc., 1994, N.W. Watercolor Soc., 1994, Phila. Watercolor Soc., 1995, Grand Exhbn., 1993, 95, Watercolor USA, 1994-96, 98, 2000, 01, 03, Watercolor West, 1992, 94, 96, 97; Rocky Mountain Nat., 1992, 96, 98, 2000, 03, Watercolor Now!, 2003; paintings published in book: Splash 5: Best of Watercolor, 1998, (mag.) Manhattan Arts Internat., 1995. Recipient 1st prize Best of Mich. Show, 1999, 2003, cash prize Watercolor USA, 2000, 03. Mem. Watercolor West (signature, Nat. Watercolor Soc. prize 1997), Rocky Mountain Watermedia Soc. (signature, prize 1998, Daniel Smith award 1991, Golden Palette award 2000), Kalamazoo Inst. Arts, Watercolor USA Honor Soc. Avocations: ornithology, travel, primitive art. Home: 83626 Waldron Dr Lawton MI 49065-7609 E-mail: jerrywbowman@earthlink.net.

BOWMAN, MARIE AGNES, mathematics educator; b. Torrington, Conn., Nov. 2, 1950; d. Joseph John and Teresa Agnes Pasakarnis; m. Ralph Edward Bowman, Aug. 26, 1972; children: Eric, Stephanie. BA, Mass. State Coll., Bridgewater, 1972. Cert. secondary tchr., Mass. Math. tchr. Duxbury (Mass.) Pub. Schs., 1972-75, Hingham (Mass.) Pub. Schs., 1975—. With World Books Ednl. Products, Mass., 1990; pvt. practice mktg., sales and customer svc., Mass., 1990-96; pvt. tutor, Norwell, Mass., 1981-84. Mem. NEA, Nat. Coun. Tchrs. Math., Hingham Tchrs. Assn., Mass. Tchrs. Assn., Assn. Tchrs. Math. in Mass. Avocations: winter skiing, piano, swimming, golf, camping, reading. Home: 6 Mattakeesett Ln Norwell MA 02061-1311

BOWMAN, NAOMA SUSANN, elementary school educator; b. Dublan, Mex., Feb. 17, 1951; d. Samuel Keith and Mary Naoma (Haynie) B. BS in Elem. Edn., Brigham Young U., 1984. Cert. tchr., Utah. Tchr. Escuela Manuel Dublan, 1972-81; tchr. Spanish adult edn. program Mission Tng. Ctr., Provo, Utah, 1981-84, teacher trainer, 1984-85; tchr. Spanish immersion Meadow Elem. Sch., Lehi, Utah, 1985-89, Northridge Elem. Sch., Orem, Utah, 1989—. Asst. dir. Spanish immersion curriculum com. Alpine Sch. Dist., American Fork, Utah, 1986-89, new-tchr. orienter, 1987-92, chair Spanish Immersion Conf., 1989-91, dir. Spanish immersion summer camp, 1991—, rep. Orem Cluster, 1991—, peer evaluator, 1991—, mem. prin. screening com., 1989-90; tchr. summer migrant program, Nebo Sch. Dist., 1992, 93. Grantee Utah Humanities Coun., 1992, City of Orem, 1992. Fellow NEA, ASCD, Alpine Edn. Assn., Utah Edn. Assn., Utah Educators of Tchrs. Assn., Utah Fgn. Lang. Assn. (sec. 1988-90), Utah Fgn. Lang. in Elem. Assn. (pres. 1987-88, Tchr. of Yr. 1989), Phi Delta Kappa. Republican. Mem. Lds Ch. Avocations: making procelain dolls, gardening, sports, travel. Office: Cherry Hill Elem Sch 250 E 1650 S Orem UT 84058-7899

BOWMAN, TILLIAN, educational consultant, writer; b. Mar. 1, 1939; d. Harold Bowman and Sadie Bruskin. MA English Lit., Harvard U., 1964. Writer, editor Meriks Publications, Portland, Maine, 1980—. Recipient Reading Education award, 1965. Mem.: Am. Reading Assn. Office: Meriks Pubs 135 Marginal Way #300 Portland ME 04104-5015

BOWMAN-DALTON, BURDENE KATHRYN, education testing coordinator, computer consultant; b. Magnolia, Ohio, July 13, 1937; d. Ernest Mowles and Mary Kathryn (Long) Bowman; m. Louis W. Dalton, Mar. 13, 1979. BME, Capital U., 1959; MA in Edn., Akron U., 1967, postgrad., 1976-87. Profl. vocalist, various clubs in the East, 1959-60; music tchr. East Liverpool (Ohio) City Shcs., 1959-62, Revere Local Schs., Akron, Ohio, 1962-75, elem. tchr., 1975-80, elem. team leader/computer cons., 1979-85, tchr. middle sch. math., gifted-talented, computer literacy, 1981-92, dist. computer specialist, 1987-93, dist. statis. for standardize local testing, 1987-91, dist. tech. coord., 1993-98, ret., 1998. Local and regional dir. Olympics of Mind, also World Problem Captain for computer problem, 1984-86; cons., workshop presenter State of Ohio, 1987-91, dist. test. coord., 1991-98; coord. for Revere Schs., Ednl. Mgmt. Info. Sys., 1992-98; mem. Citizen Com., Akron, 1975-76; profl. rep. Bath Assn. to Help, 1978-80; mem. Revere Levy Com. 1986, Revere Bond Issue Com., 1991; audit com. BATH, 1977-79; vol. chmn. Antique Car Show, Akron, 1972-81; dist. advisor MidWest Talent Search, 1987-93; dist. statistician of standardized rech. test results. Martha Holden Jennings Found. grantee, 1977-78; Title IV ESEA grantee, 1977-81. Mem. Assn. for Devel. Computer-Based Instrnl. Sys. (dir. 1992-94), Ednl. Mgmt. Info. Sys. and Proficiency Test (coord. for Revere Schs. 1992-2003), Phi Beta. Home: 353 Retreat Dr Akron OH 44333-1623 Office: 3195 Spring Valley Rd Bath OH 44210-0339

BOWSER, GENEVA BEATRICE, secondary school educator, principal; b. Hackensack, N.J., June 20, 1936; d. John Thomas and Earline (Briggs) Schultz; m. Lloyd Thomas Bowser, Dec. 20, 1959; children: Lydell Dana, Lloyd Thomas Jr., Lester Kenneth. BS in Nursing, Johns Hopkins U., 1973; MS in Adminstrn., Supervision, Morgan State U., 1981, EdD, 1989. Staff nurse N.Y. Hosp., Cornell Med. Ctr., N.Y.C., 1957-59, U.S. Pub. Health Hosp., Balt., 1962-67; dir. nursing Community Health Ctr., Balt., 1967-73; tchr. Balt. City Pub. Schs., 1973-82, dept. chair, 1982-89, dept. head, 1989-94, asst. prin. secondary edn., 1994—. Health educator New Shiloh Bapt. Ch., Balt.; mem. Morgan Park Improvement Assn., Project Awareness (Am. Cancer Soc.). Recipient Gov.'s Citation State of Md., 1982, Cert. Merit, Md. Coun. on Vocat. Edn., 1989; nominated Tchr. of Yr., Balt. City Schs., 1989. Mem. ASCD, Vocat. Indsl. Club, Md. Vocat. Assn. Chi Eta Phi, Phi Delta Kappa, Chi Eta Phi. Avocations: reading, travel, mentoring nursing students, working with homeless. Home: 2404 College Ave Baltimore MD 21214-2426 Office: Balt City Pub Schs 100 N Calhoun St Baltimore MD 21223-1867

BOWSER, M. GAYL, special education coordinator; b. St. Louis, Dec. 20, 1948; d. George Winston and Mary Hulda (Bagale) Cloyd; 1 child, Nathan Christopher. BA, U. Mo., 1971; MA, U. Iowa, 1972. Cert. spl. edn. tchr., Oreg. Spl. edn. tchr. Camp Lab. Sch., Cullowhee, N.C., 1971-73; spl. edn. tchr. West H.S., Iowa City, 1974-79, Fir Grove Sch., Roseburg, Oreg., 1979-81, Community Exptl. Edn. Ctr., Iowa City, 1976-79; mainstream specialist Douglas Edn. Svc. Dist., Roseburg, 1981-88; project coord. Oreg. Tech. Access Project, Roseburg, 1988-90; coord. tech. access program Oreg. Dept. Edn., Roseburg, 1990—. Assistive tech. cons., 1986—; mem. transition task force Oreg. Dept. Edn., 1986-88. Author: Computers in Early Intervention, 1988, Computers in Special Education Curriculum, 1989, Computers in Mainstream, 1990, Education Tech Points: A Framework for Assistive Technology Planning, 1998, Assistive Technology Pointers for Parentes, 2000, Hey! Can I Try That?, 2001. Bd. dirs. Coalition for Assistive Tech. in Oreg. Recipient Oreg. Disting. Educator award Milken Nat. Educator Awards, 1993, Disting. Svc. award Coalition in Oreg. for Parent Edn., 1997; named Tchr. of Yr., Oreg. Fedn. Coun. for Exceptional Children, 1992; Transition grantee Oreg. Dept. Edn., 1987-88, project Tech Trans grantee, 1996—, Coop. and Innovative Models grantee, 1988-90. Mem. Internat. Soc. for Tech. in Edn., Assn. for Severely Handicapped Coun. for Exceptional Children (nat. fedn. tech. and media divsn. 1993, Svc. award Nat. fedn. 1993, Tech. and Media Divsn. Svc. award 1992). Avocations: backpacking, music, carpentry. Office: Oreg Tech Access Program 1871 NE Stephens St Roseburg OR 97470-1433

BOWSHER, LAURA KAY, elementary education educator; b. Norwalk, Ohio, Nov. 19, 1967; d. Jack Lee and Caroline Kay (Kiger) B. BS in Edn., Bowling Green State U., 1990, MEd, 1999. Cert. tchr., Ohio. Cook, shift supr. Ranch Steak and Seafood, Bowling Green, Ohio, 1985-93; substitute tchr. Wood County and Hancock County schs., Ohio, 1990-93; tchr. elem. edn. Elmwood Local Sch. Dist., 1993—. Mem.: NEA, Ohio Student Edn. Assn., Ohio Edn. Assn., Golden Key, Kappa Delta Pi. Avocations: cooking, arts and crafts, bicycling, basketball, running. Home: 105 Jackson St Cygnet OH 43413-9791

BOXWILL, HELEN ANN, primary and secondary education educator; b. Washington, Feb. 28, 1946; d. Melvin E. and Ann (Magnotta) Dorenbaum; children: Hope, David, Andre. BA, Dickinson Coll., Carlisle, Pa., 1967; MA, New Sch. Social Rsch., 1976; MS in Adminstrn. and Supervision, Coll. New Rochelle, 1995. Cert. in staff devel.; lic. reading specialist, elem. tchr., English tchr., sch. adminstr., N.Y. Caseworker City of N.Y., 1967-71; dir. Harriet Tubman Day Care Ctr., Bklyn., 1971-73; family counselor Family Inst. for More Effective Living, Westbury, N.Y., 1976-80; elem. tchr. Carousel Day Sch., Hicksville, N.Y., 1980-82, Pub. Sch. 160 Elem. Sch., Queens, N.Y., 1982-83; reading specialist Soterios Ellenos Parochial Sch., Bklyn., 1983-84, Hempstead (N.Y.) Pub. Schs., 1984-90; tchr. SAT The Sch. for Student Achievement, Jericho, N.Y., 1991-93; reading specialist L.I. U., Greenvale, N.Y., 1984-93; reading tchr. Robert Moses Mid. Sch., North Babylon, NY, 1990—93, North Babylon H.S., 1993—; reading coord. Island Park (N.Y.) Pub. Schs., 1999—; prin. Huntington (N.Y.) Sch. Dist., 2001—; prof. Tchr. Tng. Inst., Ethiopia, 2003—. Advisor Sch. Improvement Planning Com., Hempstead, N.Y., 1987-89; mem. Dist. Planning Com., 1993—, Curriculum Adv. Com., 1993—; advisor/advisee com., staff devel. com., lang. arts com., site based mgmt. com. renaissance coord. North Babylon Sch. Dist., 1991-99; tchr., trainer Nassau Tract Tchrs. Ctr., 1985-89, North Babylon Schs., 1991—, Hempstead Schs., 1985-90, insvc. courses Owl Tchrs. Ctr., 1991, 93—; tchr. trainer in Ethiopia through IFESH. Contbr. articles to profl. jours. Advisor Youth of Distinction, Huntington, N.Y., 1991-92; leader Girl Scouts Am., Westbury, 1978; mem. Town of Babylon Anti-Bias Task Force, 1999; mem. 21st Century com. Anti-Defamation League. Grantee City of N.Y. Children's Aid Soc., Tract Ctr., Owl Ctr.; recipient Commty. Svc. award, N.Y. State Tchrs., 1999, award AntiDefamation League Project 21st Century, 2000, Pathfinder award L.I. Bus. Assn. Mem. ASCD, Internat. Reading Assn., Nat. Coun. Tchrs. English, Orton Dyslexia Soc., Nassau Reading Coun. Avocations: swimming, reading, writing, guitar, public speaking on anti-racism. Home: 44 Foxwood Dr E Huntington Station NY 11746-2126 E-mail: helenbox@optonline.net.

BOYAJIAN, TIMOTHY EDWARD, public health officer, educator, consultant; b. Fresno, Calif., Feb. 22, 1949; s. Ernest Adam and Marge (Medzian) B.; m. Tassanee Bootdeesri, Apr. 23, 1987. BS in Biology, U. Calif., Irvine, 1975; M of Pub. Health, UCLA, 1978. Registered environ. health specialist, Calif. Rsch. asst. UCLA, 1978-81; lectr. Chapman U., 29 Palms, Calif., 1982-84, 88-89; refugee relief vol. Cath. Relief Svcs., Surin, Thailand, 1985-86; lectr. Nat. Univ., L.A., 1989-91; environ. health specialist Riverside County Health Svcs. Agy., Palm Springs, Calif., 1991-96; sci. tchr. South Gate (Calif.) H.S., L.A. Unified Sch. Dist., 1999—. Mem. adj. faculty U. Phoenix, 1998—; cons. parasitologist S.

Pacific Commn., L.A., 1979; pub. health cons. several vets. groups, L.A., 1981-84, 97—; cons. Assn. S.E. Asian Nations, Bangkok, Thailand, 1988. Veterans rights advocate, Vietnam Vet. Groups, L.A., 1981-84. With USMC, Vietnam, 1969-71. Recipient U.S. Pub. Health Traineeship, U.S. Govt., L.A., 1977-81. Mem. VFW, United Tchrs. L.A. Avocation: writing. Home: PO Box 740 Palm Springs CA 92263-0740 E-mail: timothy300@aol.com.

BOYAN, NORMAN J. retired education educator; b. N.Y.C., Apr. 11, 1922; s. Joseph J. and Emma M. (Pelezare) B.; m. Priscilla M. Simpson, July 10, 1943; children: Stephen J., Craig S., Corydon J. AB, Bates Coll., Lewiston, Maine, 1943; A.M., Harvard U., 1947, Ed.D., 1951. Instr. U.S. history Dana Hall Sch., Wellesley, Mass., 1946-48; research assoc. Lab. Social Relations, Harvard U., 1950-52; asst. prin. Mineola (N.Y.) High Sch., 1952-54; prin. Wheatley Sch., East Williston, N.Y., 1954-59; assoc. prof. edn., dir. student teaching and internship U. Wis., 1959-61; assoc. prof. edn. Stanford U., 1961-67; dir. div. ednl. labs. U.S. Office Edn., 1967-68, assoc. commr. for research, 1968-69; prof. edn. Grad. Sch. Edn., U. Calif., Santa Barbara, 1969-90, prof. emeritus, 1990—, dean, 1969-80; assoc. in edn. Grad. Sch. Edn., Harvard U., 1980-81; dir. Ednl. Leadership Inst. U. Calif., 1989-91. Vis. scholar Stanford U., 1974, 86; vis. prof. U. Ark. Program in Greece, 1977, Coll. Edn., Pa. State U., summer 1981, Faculty Edn. U. B.C., summer 1983, U. Alta., 1988, UCLA, 1991; cons. numerous U.S. sch. sys., U.S. govt. and Pacific Trust Ters. Co-author: Instructional Supervision Training Program, 1978; mem. editorial bd. Harvard Edn. Rev, 1948-50, Jour. Secondary Edn, 1963-68, Jour. Edn. Research, 1967-82, Urban Edn, 1967-90; cons. editor, contbr. 5th edit. Ency. Ednl. Research, 1982; editor, contbr. Handbook Research on Ednl. Adminstrn., 1988; contbr. articles to profl. jours. Served with USAAF, 1943-46. Recipient Shankland award for advanced grad. study in ednl. adminstrn., 1950, Roald F. Campbell Lifetime Achievement award U. Coun. for Ednl. Adminstrn., 1998. Mem. Am. Ednl. Rsch. Assn. (v.p. div. A 1978-80), Phi Beta Kappa, Phi Delta Kappa. Home: 1031A Calle Sastre Santa Barbara CA 93105-4439 E-mail: nboyan@aol.com.

BOYCE, EMILY STEWART, retired library and information science educator; b. Raleigh, N.C., Aug. 18, 1933; d. Harry and May (Fallon) B. BS, East Carolina U., 1955, MA, 1961; MS in Library Sci., U. N.C., 1968; postgrad., Cath. U. Am., 1977. Librarian Tileston Jr. High Sch., Wilmington, N.C., 1955-57; children's librarian Wilmington Pub. Library, 1957-58; asst. librarian Joyner Library East Carolina U., Greenville, N.C., 1959-61, librarian III, 1962-63; ednl. supr. II ednl. media div. N.C. State Dept. Pub. Instrn., Raleigh, 1961-62; assoc. prof. dept. libr. and info. scis. East Carolina U., 1964-76, prof., 1976-92, chmn. dept., 1982-89; retired, 1992. Cons. So. Assn. Colls. and Schs., Raleigh, 1975-92. Active Asheville YWCA, Mediation Ctr., Botanical Gardens, Literacy Coun. Buncombe County. Mem. ALA, AAUW, N.C. Library Assn., Southeastern Library Assn., Assn. Library and Info. Sci. Educators, Spl. Libraries Assn. Democrat. Home: 30 Creekside Way Asheville NC 28804-1763 E-mail: eboyce@buncombe.main.nc.us.

BOYD, BEVERLY, English literature educator; b. Bklyn., Mar. 27, 1925; d. James Gray and Elspeth Kathleen (Mossop) B. BA, Bklyn. Coll., 1946; MA, Columbia U., 1948, PhD, 1955. Instr. English Bklyn. Coll., N.Y.C., 1947, U. Tex., Austin, 1955-57; prof. English Radford (Va.) Coll., 1957-62; from asst. prof. to prof. English U. Kans., Lawrence, 1962—. Author: The Middle English Miracles of the Virgin, 1963, Chaucer and the Liturgy, 1967, Chaucer and the Medieval Book, 1973, Chaucer According to William Caxton, 1978, Variorum Chaucer fascicle: The Prioress's Tale, 1988, (verse) Philippine's Windows, 1988; contbr. chpts. to books. Recipient Disting. Alumna award Bklyn. Coll., 1979; Guggenheim fellow, 1969; Huntington Libr. fellow, 1960, 75. Avocation: writing poetry. Office: U Kans Dept Of English Lawrence KS 66045-0001

BOYD, CHARLES LEE, horticulture educator; b. Waynesville, N.C., Feb. 5, 1947; s. Jule Jackson and Beulah (Ferguson) B.; m. Linda Charlene Woody, Dec. 12,1971; children: Woody, Brian, Amy. AS, Wingate Coll., 1967; BS in Agriculture Edn., N.C. State U., 1969, MEd, 1972. Vocat.-agriculture instr. Hallsboro (N.C.) High Sch., 1969-71, North Davidson Jr. High Sch., Lexington, N.C., 1971-72, West Davidson High Sch., Lexington, 1972-73; horticultural tech. instr. Blue Ridge Tech. Inst., Hendersonville, N.C., 1973-81, Haywood C.C., Clyde, N.C., 1981-82; horticultural instr. Tuscola High Sch., Waynesville, 1982—. Adv. mem. sounding bd. Haywood County Bd. Edn., Waynesville, 1987. Deacon East Flat Rock Bapt. Ch., Hendersonville, 1981; precint chmn. Re-elect Jim Hunt Campaign, Waynesville, 1992; bd. dirs. Jonathan Creek Fire Dept., Waynesville, 1988—, State Future Farmers Am. Assn., 1988-91; mem. First Bapt. Ch., Hendersonville. Recipient honorary state FFA degree State FFA Assn., 1990. Mem. N.C. Assn. Edn., N.C. Vocat. Agriculture Tchrs. Assn., Haywood County Nurserymen Assn. (pres.), N.C. Nurserymen Assn., N.C. Landscape Contractors Assn., Sun Rise Rotary. Democrat. Avocations: nursery work, landscaping, raising cattle. Home: RR 2 Box 168 Waynesville NC 28785-9802 Office: Tuscola High Sch 350 Tuscola School Rd Waynesville NC 28786-9001

BOYD, CINDY JUNE, secondary mathematics educator, consultant; b. Abilene, Tex., Apr. 29, 1951; d. Claude Fitzgerald and L. Jean (Williams) Huskin; m. Tommy Lee Boyd, Jan. 2, 1970 (div. Mar. 1979); children: Tisha, Le'Ann. BS in Edn., Abilene Christian U., 1973, MEd, 1992; Doctorate (hon.), Rensselaer Poly. Inst., 1997. Tchr. math. Moran (Tex.) Ind. Sch. Dist., 1973-79, Abilene Ind. Sch. Dist., 1979—. Cons. in field; tchr. trainer Tex. Edn. Assn., 1989—. Author: Skit-So-Phrenia, 1989, We Fear-em No Theorem, 1989, Algebra for Everyone...One Card at a Time, 1995, I Feel a Song Coming On!, Books 1-2, 1998, Book 3, 2001, Glencoe: Geometry, 1998, 2d edit. 2003, Scrambled Geometry, Book 1, 1999, Book 2, 2002, Scrambled Algebra, Book 1, 1999, Book 2, 2003; 1 of 2 tchrs. nationwide featured on CNN What's Right About Education. Recipient Walt Disney/McDonald's Nat. Math. Tchr. of Yr. award, 1995, Presdl. award excellence in math., 1994, 95, 96, 97, Tandy Technology prize 1998. Mem. ASCD, Nat. Coun. Tchrs. Math. (Good Neighbor award nat. finalist State Farm 1990-91, math. regional svcs. com. 1995-98), Tex. Coun. Tchrs. Math., Big Country Coun. Tchrs. Math., Tex. State Tchrs. Assn. Mem. Ch. of Christ. Avocations: arts and crafts, swimming, old movies, music. Home: 1417 Coventry Cir Abilene TX 79602-6247 Office: Abilene High Sch 2800 N 6th St Abilene TX 79603-7190

BOYD, CLAUDE COLLINS, educational specialist, consultant; b. Kent, Tex., May 25, 1924; s. Edward Clarke and Nora (Morris) B.; m. Frances Arline Haley, Jan. 22, 1955; children: David Chand, Anese Nasim Boyd Forsyth, Mark Kevin, Kimberly Ann Boyd Surgeon. BA, Tex. A&M U., 1948; MEd, U. Tex., 1957, EdD, 1961. Cert. elem. tchr., prin., supt., Tex. Elem. sch. tchr. Culberson County Ind. Sch. Dist., Van Horn, Tex.; elem. sch. prin. The Austin (Tex.) Ind. Sch. Dist.; elem sch. bilingual tchr. Ector County Ind Sch. Dist., Odessa, Tex.; assoc. prof. Ind. U., Bloomington; curriculum specialist USAID, Guatemala City, Guatemala; project specialist in edn. The Ford Found., N.Y.C.; assoc. prof. edn. Pa. State U., Erie; edn. specialist Devel. Assocs., Inc., Washington; internat. edn. advisor/cons. U.S. Agy. for Internat. Devel., San Salvador, edn. adminstr., curriculum advisor La Paz, Bolivia; Dominican Republic; edn. adminstr., curriculum advisor U.S. Agy. for Internat. Devel., Dominican Republic; free-lance edn. advisor, cons., worldwide svc. Odessa, Tex.; tchr. edn. specialist InterAm. Devel. Bank, Santo Domingo, Dominican Republic. Ednl. supervision specialist InterAmerican Devel. Bank, Santo Domingo, Dominican Republic; substitute tchr. K-12, Ector County ISD, Odessa, Tex. Recipient Grand Order of Edn., Pres. of Rep. of Bolivia. Mem. ASCD, Phi Delta Kappa (past pres. Mu chpt.). Home: 2426 E 21st St Odessa TX 79761-1703

BOYD, DAVID PRESTON, business educator; b. N.Y.C., Oct. 19, 1943; s. David Preston and Mignon (Finch) B.; m. Sally Sparks, Sept. 9, 1989. BA in English Lit., Harvard U., 1965; DPhil in Behavioral Scis., Oxford U., 1973. Asst. headmaster Dedham (Mass.) Country Day Sch., 1965-69; co-owner the Old Cambridge (Mass.) Co., 1973-77; instr. coll. bus. adminstrn. Northeastern U., Boston, 1977-78, asst. prof., 1978-82, assoc. prof., 1982-87, Patrick F. and Helen C. Walsh rsch. prof., 1985-86, chmn. human resources mgmt. dept., 1986-87, prof., 1987—, acting dean, 1987, dean coll. and grad. sch. bus. adminstrn., 1987-94. Author: Elites and Their Education National Foundation for Educational Research, 1973; mem. editl. bd. Internat. Jour. Value-Based Mgmt., Cross-cultural Mgmt., Corporate Governance; contbr. articles to profl. jours. Past trustee Pine Manor Coll.; corporator Brookline Bancorp. Recipient Excellence in Teaching award Northeastern U., 1980; Northeastern U. grantee, 1982-84, Control Data Corp., 1983, NYU, 1985. Fellow Mass. Hist. Soc.; mem. Soc. Colonial Wars, S.R., Oxford Soc., Tennis and Racquet Club, Somerset Club, Mass Hort. Soc. (former trustee), Comml. Club, Beta Gamma Sigma, Phi Kappa Phi. Home: 14 Bristol Rd Wellesley Hills MA 02481-2727 Office: Northeastern U 304 Hayden Hall Boston MA 02115-5000

BOYD, DEN COOK, JR., educational consultant; b. Raven, Va., Sept. 30, 1936; s. Den Cook and Maude (Reynolds) B.; children: Steven Brett, Keith Alan. BS in Math., Emory & Henry Coll., 1961; MS in Secondary Sch. Adminstrn., U. Va., 1967. Cert. sci. tchr., math. tchr., prin. Tchr. math. Osbourn HS, Manassas, Va., 1961-64; asst. prin. Parkside Mid. Sch., Manassas, 1964-67; prin. Parkside Elem. and Mid. Sch., Manassas, 1967-73, Parkside Mid. Sch., Manassas, 1973-83, Woodbridge Mid. Sch., Va., 1983-85; supr. staff devel. Prince William County Pub. Sch., Manassas, 1985-93; cons. Boyd Consulting/Tng. Svc., Fredericksburg, Va., 1994—. Adj. prof. George Mason U., Fairfax, Va., 1991-2000. Co-author: School Based Management: A Training Guide for Site Committees, 1993; participant (video) Training Guide for Site Committees, 1994; conf. presenter/cons./trainer Quality and Site Based Management, 1988—. Named Outstanding Educator Phi Delta Kappa Battlefield chpt., 1989-90, Who's Who in Methodist Ch., 1996, 5th ed. of Who's Who in Am. Ed., 25th ed. of Dictionary of Internat. biography, 12th ed. of tghe Internat. Who's Who of Intellectuals, 14th ed. of Who's Who in the World. Mem. Nat. Staff Devel. Coun. (ann. conf. planning com. 1991-92), So. Assn. Colls. and Schs. (chmn. vis. accreditation teams 1979-. Overseas accreditation team 1994, 2000,2001), Manassas Men's Club (pres. 2000). Methodist. Avocations: golf, shooting pool, travel, beach activities. Home and Office: 12501 Ventura Ln Fredericksburg VA 22407-0117 E-mail: dcboyd930@aol.com.

BOYD, DONALD EDGAR, artist, educator; b. Sparta, Ohio, Feb. 20, 1934; s. Charles William Boyd and Correl Augusta Downing; m. Joyce Martha Hite, June 28, 1964 (div. Mar. 1982); children: Bentley Gale, Laura Dawn, Jonathan Ashley. BFA cum laude, Ohio State U., 1956; MA in Tchg., Harvard U., 1961; MFA in Sculpture, U. Iowa, 1966. Asst. prof., establisher sculpture program Kenyon Coll., Gambier, Ohio, 1966-72; artist-in-residence S.C. Arts Coun., Walterboro, 1973-74; asst. prof. S.D. State U., Brookings, 1974-86; vis. artist Ohio State U., Columbus, 1986-87; adj. prof. Mt. Vernon (Ohio) Nazarene U., 1994—97, adj. prof. art, 2000—; assoc. prof. U. S.D., Vermillion, 1997-98; asst. prof. Muskingum Coll., New Concord, Ohio, 1998-2000. Dir. Fluxus West, 1975—; curator S.D. Exptl. Artists, 55 Mercer St. Gallery, N.Y.C., 1982, Fluxus Columbus, Geoffrey Taber Gallery, 1987; artist in residence S.C. Arts Coun., 1973-74. Exhibited works at Boston Arts Festival, 1962, 64, Dayton Art Inst., 1968 (first prize), Venice Biennale, 1976, Young Fluxus, Artists Space, N.Y.C., catalog, 1982, ArtReach Exptl. Art Gallery, Columbus, 1988, Tulsa U., 1989, Wexner Ctr. for the Arts, 1994, Mus. New Art, 2001, 02; one-man show; Mansfield Art Ctr., Ohio, 2002. Recipient Nat. 1st prize in slides, Buffalo, N.Y., 1970, Best of Show, ArtReach Gallery, Columbus, 1987, All-Ohio Juried Exhbn. at Ohio State U.-Mansfield, 2002, 1st prize, Mansfield Art Ctr., 1990, 2d prize, Zanesville Art Ctr., 1999; grantee, NEA, 1975, S.D. Arts Coun., 1981. Mem. Mansfield Art Ctr., Zanesville Appalachian Art Group. Home: 75 S Main St Fredericktown OH 43019 E-mail: dboyd56@hotmail.com.

BOYD, MONA MANNING, music educator; b. Williamston, N.C., Aug. 1, 1949; d. Thurman Lee and Doris LaDon (Gardner) Manning; m. Ira Hughes Boyd, Nov. 18, 1972; 1 child, Brad Hughes. BMus, East Carolina U., 1971, MMus, 1976. Gen. music tchr., choral dir. Martin County Sch. System, Williamston, N.C., 1971-77, 78—. Vol. pianist Ch., 1967—; mem. alumni bd. East Carolina U., 1991-95. Recipient Young Educator award Jaycees, 1979; named Martin County Tchr. of Yr., 1988-89, Outstanding Educator award East Carolina U. Coun. for Tchr. Edn., 1989. Mem. Am. Choral Dirs. Assn., Music Educators Nat. Conf., Nat. Guild of Piano Tchrs., N.C. Assn. of Educators, Sch. of Music Alumni Profl. Soc. (sec. 1989-91, pres. 1991-95). Mem. Ch. of Christ. Home: 6897 Long Ridge Rd Plymouth NC 27962-9070

BOYD, RICHARD ALFRED, school system administrator; b. Coshocton, Ohio, July 4, 1927; s. Lester Stephenson and Opal Irene (King) B.; m. Marye Joanne McPherson, Aug. 29, 1953; children: Lynne, Julie, Michael, Stephanie. BS in Edn., Capital U., 1951, DHL (hon.), 1984; MA, Ohio State U., 1958; EdD, U. Akron, 1970; LHD (hon.), Cleve. State U., 1997, Baldwin-Wallace Coll., 1997. Rsch. assoc. U. Akron, Ohio, 1968-70; asst. supt. Warren City Schs., Ohio, 1970-71, supt., 1971-75; project dir. Commn. Pub. Sch. Pers. Policies of Ohio, Warren, 1971; supt. Warren Pub. Schs., 1971-75, Lakewood Pub. Schs., Ohio, 1975-84; state supt. edn. Miss. Dept. Edn., Jackson, 1984-89; exec. dir. Martha Holden Jennings Found., Cleve., 1990-95; supt. Cleve. Pub. Schs., 1995-97; interim state supt. State of Miss., 1998; prof. ednl. leadership U. Miss., 1999—; dir. edn. Barksdale Reading Inst., 2000—. Mem. steering com. Edn. Commn. of the States, 1987-90; mem. evaluation panel U.S. Dept. Edn., 1987-89; chmn. Nat. Assessment Governing Bd., 1990-92; dir. edn. programs Barksdale Reading Inst., 2000—. Contbr. articles to profl. jours. Trustee Jr. Achievement of Warren, Cleve. and Jackson; pres. Trumbull County Cmty. Chest, Warren, 1973-75; bd. dirs. Bar Assn. Greater Cleve., 1983-84. Served with USN, 1945-46. Recipient Outstanding Educator award Ohio PTA, 1979, Educator of Yr. award Coun. Exceptional Children, 1981, Outstanding Contbn. to Adult Edn. award Ohio Assn. Adult Educators, 1983, Exec. Educator 100 award N.Am.'s Top 100 Sch. Execs., 1984; named to Coll. Edn. Hall of Fame, Ohio State U., 1995. Mem. Am. Assn. Sch. Adminstrs. (exec. com. 1983-86), Buckeye Assn. Sch. Adminstrs. (pres. 1981-82), Nat. Coun. for Accreditation Tchr. Edn. (exec. com. 1984-89), Coun. Chief State Sch. Officers (bd. dirs. 1988-89), Southeastern Ednl. Improvement Lab. (pres. 1987-89). Episcopalian. Home: 404 Cherokee Dr Oxford MS 38655-2700 Office: 1003 Jefferson Ave Oxford MS 38655 E-mail: rboyd@msreads.org.

BOYD, ROBERT COTTON, English language educator; b. Little Rock, Sept. 20, 1938; s. Robert Hampton and Jessie Leigh (Cotton) B.; m. Katherine Lenore Rock, Jan. 3, 1964; children: Robert Rock, Katherine Anne, Elizabeth Leigh. BA, U. Ark., 1965; postgrad., U. Hamburg, Fed. Republic of Germany, 1965-66; MA, U. Ark., 1967; PhD, Ind. U., 1989. Instr. English Ind. State U., Terre Haute, 1966-70; prof. English St. Louis Community Coll., 1970—, asst. chair english dept., 1993-96; editor Webster Review, 1992-96. Theater critic Sta. KWMU-FM, St. Louis, 1980-94, Sta. KDHX, St. Louis, 1995—; v.p. bd. dirs. River Styx Arts Orgn., 1996—; Fulbright exch. tchr., Germany, 1997—; pres., bd. dirs. River Styx, 1999—. Mem. editl. bd. Gateway Heritage mag., 1996—; contbg. editor River Styx mag., 1996—. Mem. St. Louis-Lyon Sister Cities Com., 1988—, treas., 1993-96; pres. Kirkwood chpt. Am. Field Svc., 1986-87. Recipient Guy Owen Poetry prize So. Poetry Rev., 1991, Poetry award Mo. Writers' Week, 1995. Mem. Nat. Coun. Tchrs. English, Conf. on Coll. Composition and Comm. Democrat. Unitarian Universalist. Avocation: golf. Home: 2243 Village Green Pkwy Chesterfield MO 63017-8119 Office: Saint Louis Community Coll 11333 Big Bend Rd Saint Louis MO 63122-5720

BOYD, ROZELLE, retired university administrator, educator; b. Indpls., Apr. 24, 1934; s. William Calvin Sr. and Ardelia Louise (Leavell) B. BA, Butler U., 1957; MA, Ind. U., 1965. Welfare dept. worker Marion County DPW, Indpls., 1956-57; tchr. Crispus Attucks High Sch., Indpls., 1957-68, adult edn. counselor, 1958-68; asst. dean U. Div., Ind. U., Bloomington, 1968-78, assoc. dean, 1978-82, dir., 1982-98; ret., 1998. Minority leader Indpls. City County Coun.; Dem. nat. committeeman, Dem. Party; mem. coms. Nat. League of Cities. Mem. Alpha Phi Alpha. Presbyterian. Office: Office City-County Council 241 City-County Bldg 200 E Washington St Indianapolis IN 46204-3307

BOYD, WILLARD LEE, academic administrator, educator, museum administrator, lawyer; b. St. Paul, Mar. 29, 1927; s. Willard Lee and Frances L. (Collins) Boyd; m. Susan Kuehn, Aug. 28, 1954; children: Elizabeth Kuehn, Willard Lee, Thomas Henry. BS in Law, U. Minn., 1949, LLB, 1951; LLM, U. Mich., 1952, SJD, 1962. Bar: Minn. 1951, Iowa 1958. Assoc. Dorsey & Whitney, Mpls., 1952—54; from instr. to prof. law U. Iowa, Iowa City, 1954—64, assoc. dean Law Sch., 1964, v.p. acad. affairs, 1964—69, pres., 1969—81, 2002—03, pres. emeritus, 1981—; pres. The Field Mus., Chgo., 1981—96, pres. emeritus, 1996—. Chmn. Nat. Mus. Scis. Bd., 1988—96; adv. com. Getty Ctr. for Edn. in Arts; chair bd. dirs. Harry S Truman Libr. Inst., 1997—2001; past adv. bd. Met. Opera, Ill. Humanities Coun., Ill. Arts Coun., Chgo. Cultural Affairs Bd. Bd. dirs. Nat. Art Inst. Recipient Charles Frankel prize, Nat. Endowment for Humanities, 1989. Mem.: ABA (com. social labor and indsl. legislations 1963—65, chmn. 1965—66, coun. mem. 1975—82, mem. sect. legal edn. and admission to bar chmn. 1980—81, chmn. coun. of sect. on legal edn. and admission), Nat. Commn. Accrediting (past pres.), Am. Assn. Univs. (past chmn.), Nat. Arts Strategies (bd. dirs.), Am. Law Inst., Am. Acad. Arts and Sci., Am. Art Inst., Ill. Humanities Coun., Iowa Bar Assn. Home: 620 River St Iowa City IA 52246-2433 Office: Univ Iowa Law Sch Iowa City IA 52242-1113

BOYD-BROWN, LENA ERNESTINE, history educator, education consultant; b. New Orleans, July 3, 1937; d. Eugene A. and Rosemary (Lewis) Boyd. BA, Xavier U., 1958; MA, Howard U., 1960; EdD, Rutgers U., 1979. History instr. So. U., New Orleans, 1960-61; tchr. D.C. Pub. Schs., Washington, 1961-62; history instr. So. U., Baton Rouge, 1962-63; residence counselor N.C. Cen. U., Durham, 1963-64; counselor, instr. Howard U., Washington, 1964-65; asst. prof. history Grambling (La.) State U., 1965-68, Tuskegee (Ala.) U., 1968-70; assoc. examiner history Ednl. Testing Svc., Princeton, N.J., 1970-79; assoc. prof. history, edn. Dillard U., New Orleans, 1979-88; dir. testing, assoc. prof. history Hampton (Va.) U., 1988-89, assoc. prof. history, dept. history chairperson, 1989-91; assoc. prof. history div. social and polit. sci. Tex. A&M U., Prarie View, 1991-2000. Testing cons. Lincoln (Pa.) U., 1974, So. U., Baton Rouge, 1979, New Orleans, 1986-89, Hampton U., 1988. Contbg. author, editor profl. jours. Martin L. King Jr. fellow, Rutgers U., 1977-78; fellow Howard U., 1958-60, Carnegie-Mellon U., Pitts., 1966-67. Mem. Assn. for Study Negro Life and History, Nat. Coalition of 100 Black Women (New Orleans chpt.), Orgn. Am. Historians, History Edn. Soc., Assn., Phi Alpha Theta, Phi Delta Kappa, Kappa Delta Pi, Alpha Kappa Alpha (Alpha Beta Omega chpt.). E-mail: LIZ37hb@aol.com.

BOYE, ROGER CARL, journalism educator, writer; b. Lincoln, Nebr., Feb. 8, 1948; s. Arthur J. and Matilda J. (Danca) B. BA with distinction, U. Nebr., 1970; MS in Journalism with highest distinction, Northwestern U., 1971. News editor The Quill, Chgo., 1971-73; instr. Medill sch. journalism Northwestern U., Evanston, Ill., 1973-76; vis. prof. journalism Niagara U., Niagara Falls, N.Y., 1976-78; gen. mgr. The Quill, 1980-84, bus. mgr., 1984-86; asst. dean, asst. prof. Medill sch. journalism Northwestern U., 1986-92, asst. dean, assoc. prof., 1992—. Judge various journalism awards and contests, 1970s; master comm. residential coll. Northwestern U., 1989—96. Weekly columnist Chgo. Tribune, 1974-93; contbr. Ency. Britannica Book of the Yr. and the Compton Yearbook, 1982-99; contbg. editor The Numismatist, 2001--. Recipient Maurice M. Gould award Numismatic Lit. Guild, 1981, 92. Mem. Phi Beta Kappa, Kappa Tau Alpha. Office: Northwestern Univ Medill Sch Journalism 1845 Sheridan Rd Evanston IL 60208-0815

BOYEA, RUTHE W. retired educator; b. Waltham, Mass., Sept. 22, 1918; d. George Walter and Ethel Maude Wright; m. Douglas Paul Boyea, 1944; children: Ruthe Priscilla Boyea-Boiczyk, Douglas Paul. B Social Sci., Boston U., 1940; MEd, Ctrl. Conn. State U., 1960; cert. in polit. sci., Trinity Coll., 1970. Cert. elem. tchr., Conn. Dir. religious edn., Springfield, Mass., 1945; tchr. New Britain, Conn., 1945-51; prof. edn. Ctrl. Conn. State U., New Britain, 1951-65, dir., founder Women's Ctr., 1965-85, prof. emeritus, 1985, lectr. on women's issues. Adj. prof. Tunxis C.C., Mattatuck C.C., 1960-70. Commr. Human Rights and Opportunity, City of New Britain; vol., chair bd. dirs. ARC, New Britain; elected mem. Vets. Commn., City of New Britain, 1999. Lt. (j.g.) USN, 1942-45. Named Women's Educator of Yr., YWCA, 1975, Vol. of Yr. United Way, 1999; recipient Women Helping Women award Soroptimist Internat., 1982, Disting. Alumni award Boston U. Sch. Theology, 2002. Mem. AAUW (officer), LWV (bd. dirs.), Nat. Women's Mil. Meml. (founder), Nat. Women's Art Mus., Nat. Women's Hall of Fame. Mem. United Ch. of Christ. Home: 105 Black Rock Ave New Britain CT 06052-1239 Office: Ctrl Conn State U Stanley St New Britain CT 06053

BOYENGA, CINDY A. secondary education educator; b. Elgin, Ill., Aug. 5, 1957; d. Harley J. and Mary Ellen (Johnson) Carlson. BA, Augustana Coll., 1979; MSEd, No. Ill. U., 1989. Cert. tchr., Ill. Tchr. reading Laraway Sch., Joliet, Ill.; tchr. English Custer Park Sch., Braidwood, Ill., Streamwood High Sch., Elgin; tchr. reading and lang. arts Waldo Middle Sch., Aurora, Ill., 1984—. Mem. NAt. Coun. Tchrs. English, Secondary Reading League, Internat. Reading Assn. E-mail: cboyenga@yahoo.com.

BOYER, A(DELINE) NADINE, guidance counselor; b. Franklin, Pa., May 9, 1946; d. Robert Ellsworth and Jean Lucille (Sadler) B. BS in Edn., Ea. Ill. U., 1968, MS in Phys. Edn., 1981, Cert. Edn. Specialist, 1986. Tchr. phys. edn. Freeport (Ill.) H.S., 1968-80; tchr. phys. edn., asst. volleyball coach Lake Land Coll., Mattoon, Ill., 1980-81; guidance counselor Carlyle (Ill.) H.S., 1986-87, Odin (Ill.) H.S., 1986-91, East Richland H.S., Olney, Ill., 1991—. Mem. NEA, Ill. Edn. Assn., East Richland Edn. Assn. Methodist. Avocations: reading, walking, videos. Office: East Richland HS 1200 E Laurel St Olney IL 62450-2545

BOYER, CHERYL MOEN, adult education educator; b. Summit, N.J., Jan. 31, 1948; d. Martin Moen and Marguerite (Weigman) Harris; m. Jerry Boyer, Aug. 16, 1969. Nursing diploma, Mountainside Sch. Nursing, Montclair, N.J., 1969; BS, Millersville (Pa.) U., 1974; MED, Temple U., 1979, EdD, 1988. RN, N.J. Staff nurse Cooper Med. Ctr., Camden, N.J., 1969-71; staff nurse Holy Spirit Hosp., Camp Hill, Pa., 1971-73; instr. Carlisle (Pa.) Hosp. Sch. Nursing, 1974-75, York (Pa.) County Area Vocat. Tech. Sch., 1975-76; dir. edn. Pa. Nurses Assn., Harrisburg, 1977-87; assoc. dir. Common. for C.C.s, Harrisburg, 1987-92; dir. Harrisburg campus, asst. prof. adult edn. Temple U., 1992—. Contbr. articles to profl. jours. Chmn. bd. dirs. Camp Hill Family Health Coun., 1983-86, 91-94; mem. Derry Twp. Planning Commn., Hershey, Pa., 1991-92. Named Outstanding Young Woman Am., 1983; recipient Athena award Harrisburg C. of C., 1994, Outstanding Svc. award Camp Hill Family Health Coun., 1986, 94, Family

Planning Assn. Pa., 1984. Mem. Pa. Nurses Assn. (del. Kansas City, Mo. 1982-86), Pa. Soc. Assn. Execs. (bd. dirs., various coms. 1985-95), Am. Nurses Assn., Pa. Assn. Adult Continuing Edn. (charter, bd. dirs. 1993-95), Continuing Edn. Assn. Pa. Democrat. Presbyterian. Avocations: internat. travel, gourmet cooking, fitness walking. Office: Temple U Harrisburg 223 Walnut St Harrisburg PA 17101-1711

BOYER, KAREN JO ANN, retired secondary gifted education educator; b. Milw., Jan. 8, 1942; d. Hjalmer H. and Elsie I. (Nelson) Anderson; m. Thomas A. Boyer, Apr. 14, 1962; children: Lauren N., Lesley N. BA in English and Edn., Rockford Coll., 1964, MA in Tchg., 1972. Cert. 7-12 tchr., Ill. Tchr. English, Rockford (Ill.) Pub. Schs., 1964-67, substitute tchr., 1967-72, dir. SOURCE vol. program, 1979-84, tchr. English gifted program, 1984—99. Mem. adj. faculty, instr. rhetoric Rock Valley Coll., Rockford, 1980-84; mem. Ill. Writing Project, Evanston, 1990-92. V.p. Jr. League Rockford, 1975-76, cmty. svc. v.p., 1976-77; pres. bd. dirs. Tinker Swiss Cottage, 1982-83. Recipient Holocaust Tchr. award Jewish Fedn. Greater Rockford, 1994. Mem. NEA, AAUW (v.p., treas. Rockford 1974-85), Nat. Coun. Tchrs. English, Ill. Coun. Tchrs. English (Honor Roll of Tchrs. 1986, 95, 96, 97), Ill. Edn. Assn., Rockford Edn. Assn. Avocations: travel, reading, antiques. Home: 229 N Calvin Park Blvd Rockford IL 61107-4604

BOYER, LESTER LEROY, JR., architecture educator, consultant; b. Hanover, Pa., Apr. 6, 1937; s. Lester Leroy and Ruth Florence (Kessler) B.; m. Patricia Barbara Hayes, Dec. 28, 1958; children: Douglas Lester, Blane Edward, Darla Mae. B of Archtl. Engring., Pa. State U., 1960, MS in Archtl. Engring, 1964; PhD in Architecture, U. Calif., Berkeley, 1976. Registered profl. engr., Pa. Instr. archtl. engring. Pa. State U., 1960-64; rsch. engr. Armstrong Cork Co., Lancaster, Pa., 1964-68; course dir. Nat. Soc. Profl. Engrs., 1964-74; sr. cons. acoustics and noise control Bolt Beranek and Newman Inc., Cambridge, Mass., 1968-70; faculty Okla. State U., Stillwater, 1970-84, dir. environ. control program, 1970-84, prof. architecture, 1979-84, Tex. A&M U., College Station, 1984—96, chmn. div. design tech. Coll. Arch., 1988-90, prof. emeritus, 1999—. Fulbright scholar U. N.S.W. and U. Queensland, Australia, 1982, Tech. U., Delft, The Netherlands, 1992; dir. daylighting rsch. NSF, 1985-88; vis. researcher Solar Energy Rsch. Inst., Colo., summer 1985; cons. acoustics, environ. comfort and passive energy design, 1970— ; dir. earth-sheltered bldg. rsch. Control Data Corp. and U.S. Dept. Energy, 1979-81; chair energy rsch. rev. panel on fenestration Office Energy Rsch., U.S. Dept. Energy, Washington, 1988; gen. chmn. Internat. Conf. Earth Sheltered Bldgs., Sydney, Australia, 1983; tech. chmn. Internat. Conf. Earth Sheltered Bldgs., Mpls., 1986; vis. prof., chair dept. arch. Kuwait U., 1997-98; mem. design team Benham Blair & Affiliates, Oklahoma City. Author: Earth Shelter Technology, 1987; editor: Building Design for Environmental Hazards, 1973, Earth Sheltered Building Design Innovations, 1980, Earth Shelter Performance and Evaluation, 1981, Earth Shelter Protection, 1983, Design in Geotecture, 1986, Proceedings of 5th Internat. Conf. on Underground Space and Earth Sheltered Structures, Tech. Univ. Delft, The Netherlands, 1992; contbg. author Simulating Daylight with Architectural Models, 1987. Recipient 1st Pl. Design award Nat. Energy Design competition Calif. State Office Bldg., Sacramento, 1983. Mem. ASHRAE (nat. daylighting symposium organizer 1988), Am. Solar Energy Soc. (nat. coord. passive earth cooling program 1981), Am. Underground Space Assn. (bd. dirs. 1989-92), Illuminating Engring. Soc. Lutheran. Home: HC 68 Box 19 Fort Garland CO 81133-9702 E-mail: llb@fone.net.

BOYER, LILLIAN BUCKLEY, artist, educator; b. Paterson, N.J., Mar. 1, 1916; d. George and Adele (Roomy) Buckley; m. Floyd E. Boyer, Jr., Sept. 7, 1935; 1 child, Karen Boyer Lloyd. BA in Art Edn., U. Ky., 1975. Field interviewer Survey Rsch. Ctr., U. Mich., 1963-68; instr. art U. Ky., Lexington, 1976—2002. Ky. reporter for Sunshine Artists mag., 1976-85. Exhibited in group shows at Grand Theater, Frankfort, Ky., 1983, State Capitol, 1983, Lexington Art League, annually, —, Waller Gallery, Lexington, 1986, Headley-Whitney Mus., 1987—88, 1989, 1990, Gallery IO/IO, Knoxville, 1995, Living Arts and Sci. Ctr., Lexington, 1988, 1989, 1995, 1997, Artists Attic, 1989, Opera House Gallery, 1995, Owensboro Mus. Fine Arts, 2001, others. Crusade chmn. Am. Cancer Soc., Anaheim, Calif., 1958, Orange County, Calif., 1959; active, hon. life mem. PTA, 1950-62; mem. Lexington Arts and Cultural Coun., Ky. Citizens for the Arts, Friends of Ky. Ednl. TV, Headley Whitney Mus., Friends of Lexington Pub. Libr.; pres., life mem. Lexington Art League, 1976-80, 82-83, 84-86. Mem. U. Ky. Alumni Assn., Living Arts and Sci. Ctr., Friends of U.K. Art Mus., Nat. Mus. Women in Arts. Methodist. Address: 969 Holly Springs Dr Lexington KY 40504-3119 E-mail: labinart@aol.com.

BOYER, PATRICIA ANN, social worker, educator; b. St. Paul, Feb. 13, 1934; d. Marvin Harold and Leslye Marilla (Smallidge) Adams; m. Edward Clair Boyer, May 25, 1968. BA, Mankato State Coll., 1958; MSW, U. Pitts., 1964. Lic. clin. social worker, marriage and family therapist, Wyo. Social worker Brown County Welfare Dept., New Ulm, Minn., 1958, Luth. Children's Friend Soc., Mpls., 1958-60, Armstrong County Children's Svc., Kittanning, Pa., 1960-62; psychotherapist Indiana (Pa.) County Guidance Ctr., 1964-65, Ctrl. Wyo. Counseling Ctr., Casper, 1965-70; program dir. Wyo. State Children's Home, Casper, 1975-76; assoc. prof. social work U. Wyo., Laramie, 1970-75, 76—. Marriage and family therapist Casper, 1976—; cons. Platte County Meml. Hosp., Wheatland, Wyo., 1996—, NMI Health Care, Casper, 1997—; instr. Cath. U. Washington, 1990-91, U. Denver, 1985—. Co-author: (with Jason Aronson) A Guide for the Family Therapist, 1984, 2d edit., 1994; contbr. numerous articles to profl. jours. Bd. dirs. Wyo. Med. Ctr., Casper, ethics forum, 1995—, cmty. ethics com., 1996—. Grantee LEAA, 1977-80. Mem. NASW (v.p., chmn. 1967, com. inquiry Wyo. divsn. 1996—, Wyo. Social Worker of Yr. 1987), Am. Family Therapy Acad., Am. Assn. Marriage and Family Therapy (pres. Wyo. divsn. 1979-81, 90-92). Lutheran. Avocations: travel, swimming. Home: 1339 S Mitchell St Casper WY 82601-4436 Office: Univ Wyo Casper Coll Ctr 125 College Dr Casper WY 82601-4612

BOYER-SHICK, KATHY MARIE, special education and mental health consultant; b. Harrisburg, Pa., Jan. 31, 1960; d. William Donald Boyer and Mary Ann Burns; m. Charles W. Shick, Jr., Nov. 19, 1983; 1 child, Charles (Chas) Shick, III. BA in Psychology, U. Md., 1981, MEd in Spl. Edn., 1987, PhD in Spl. Edn. Cert. tchr. spl. edn., Md. Rsch. asst. psychophysiology of sleep Nat. Inst. Mental Health, Bethesda, Md., 1980-81; rsch. asst. dept. psychology U. Md., College Park, 1981, grad. asst. inst. study exceptional children and youth, 1983-85, grad. asst. dept. spl. edn., 1986; clin. asst. dept. behavioral psychology Kennedy Krieger Inst., Balt., 1985-86; rsch. asst. dept. spl. edn. U. Md., 1987, 89-91; spl. edn. resource tchr. Park Elem. Sch., Balt., 1987—95; evaluator dept. spl. edn. Kennedy Krieger Inst., 1988-89, 90—, rsch. intern dept. Cognitive Devel. Neurology, 1990-91; spl. edn. and mental health cons. Balt. City Head Start, 1996—. Presenter in field; lectr. in field; instr. in field. Contbr. articles to profl. jours. Cons. Ednl. Testing Svc., Olney, Md., 1986-87, Kennedy Krieger Inst. Handicapped Children, 1990. Fellow U. Md., 1983-84. Mem. Am. Ednl. Rsch. Assn., Coun. Exceptional Children, Coun. Learning Disabilities. Office: Balt City Head Start 2700 N Charles St Baltimore MD 21218 E-mail: kathy.boyer-shick@erols.com.

BOYETT, JOAN REYNOLDS, arts administrator; b. L.A., May 2, 1936; d. Clifton Faris Reynolds and Jean Margaret (Howard) Hauck; m. Harry William Boyett, Oct. 5, 1956; children: Keven William, Suzanne Marie Boyett Liebherr. Student, Occidental Coll., 1954-55, Pasadena Playhouse, 1955-57. Mgr. youth activities L.A. Philharm. Orch., 1970-79; dir., founder edn. divsn. Performing Arts Ctr. L.A. County, 1979-2001, v.p. edn., 1988-2001. Mem. supt.'s task force on arts edn. Calif. State Dept. Edn., 1997; cons. NEA, Washington; chmn. arts edn. task force Calif. Arts Coun., Sacramento, 1993-95; arts edn. mem. Nat. Working Group, Washington, 1992-95; mem. U.S. Sec. of Edns. Com. on Am. Goes Back to Sch. Active various coms. and task forces, L.A., Sacramento. Named Woman of Yr. L.A. Times, 1976; recipient Labor's award of honor County Fedn. Labor, L.A., 1984, Susan B. Anthony award Bus. and Profl. Women, 1986, Gov.'s award Calif. Arts Coun. and Gov., 1989, R.O.S.E. Outstanding Svc. to Edn. award, U. So. Calif., 1999, Outstanding Arts Educator award Calif. Arts Coun., 2001, Music Ctr. Club 100 Spl. Tribute award, 2001, Women in Ednl. Leadership award, 2002, Ovation award for cmty. svc. Theatre League Alliance, 2002. Mem. Calif. Art Edn. Assn. (Behind the Scenes award 1985), Calif. Dance Educators Assn. (Svc. award 1985), Calif. Ednl. Theatre Assn. (Outstanding Contbn. award 1990, nominated for Nat. Medal Arts 1996, 97). Republican. Presbyterian. Avocations: reading, attending arts events, gardening, swimming. Home: PO Box 1805 Studio City CA 91614-0805 E-mail: jarboyett@earthlink.net.

BOYKIN, CATHERINE MARIE, health care administrator, educator; b. Phila., Dec. 25, 1944; d. William Lee (dec.) and Marie Eleanor (Hewson) B.; m. Walter Miller Morris Jr., Sept. 3, 1977; 1 child, William Martin Boykin-Morris. BSN, Villanova U., 1966; cert. PNP, U. Conn., 1973; MEd, U. Vt., 1997. Cert. PNP, Vt. Pub. health nurse U.S. Peace Corps, Osorno, Chile, 1967-68; coronary care specialist Queen of the Angels Hosp., L.A., 1969-70; pub. health nurse Orthopaedic Hosp., L.A., 1970-72; PNP N.E. Kingdom Mental Health Svcs., Newport, Vt., 1973-75, The Child Health Ctr., St. Johnsbury, Vt., 1975-81; pvt. pediatric nurse practitioner New Directions in Health, St. Johnsbury, 1981-84; PNP The Burke Schs., Burke Hollow, Vt., 1983-84; dir. health, comprehensive health educator Lyndon Inst., Lyndon Center, Vt., 1984—. Chair Vt. Joint Practice Com.: Vt. State Nurses Assn., Vt. State Med. Soc., 1981-83; coord. Drug-Free Schs., Lyndon Inst., Lyndon Center, 1984—; bd. mem. Heart Healthy Vermonter Adv. Bd., St. Johnsbury, 1985-90; pediatric rep. Vt. State Bd. Nursing Nurse Practitioner Adv. Com., 1985—. Vice chairperson Caledonia County Dem. Com., St. Johnsbury, 1990-95, treas., 1995-99, sec. 1999—; Justice of the Peace, Lyndonville, 1990—; chairperson Lyndon Town Dem. Com., Lyndonville, 1991—. Recipient Founding Assoc. award Club de Abstemios Nuevo Amanecer, Osorno, 1968. Mem. ANA, Vt. State Nurses Assn. (chairperson coun. of nursing practice 1975-77), Vt. State Sch. Nurses Assn., Vt. Pediatric Nurse Practitioners (treas. 1987-89, co-chair 1990—), Vt. Nurse Practitioners Inc., Nat. Assn. Sch. Nurses. Roman Catholic. Avocations: computer technology, photography, videography. Home: 645 Diamond Hill Rd Lyndonville VT 05851-8458 Office: Lyndon Institute Lyndon Center VT 05850

BOYKIN, NANCY MERRITT, academic administrator; b. Washington, Mar. 20, 1919; d. Matthew and Mary Gertrude (White) Merritt; m. Ulysses Wilhelm Boykin, Apr. 17, 1965 (dec. 1987); 1 child from previous marriage, Tauyna Lovell Banks. BS, D.C. Tchrs. Coll., 1939; MA, Howard U., 1940, MSW, 1956; PhD, U. Mich., 1976. Employee rels. counselor Office Chief of Fin., U.S. Army, Washington; adminstrv. asst. to civilian aide Sec. of Def., Washington; policewoman Met. Police Dept., Washington; social worker Dept. Pub. Welfare, Washington; adminstrv. asst. to dir. Active Cmty. Teams, Inc., Detroit, 1965—66; dir. continuing edn. for girls program Detroit Pub. Schs., 1966—87; ednl. cons. and cmty. outreach coord. New Health Ctr., Livonia, Mich., 1988—90. Presdl. appointee Nat. Adv. Coun. on Extension and Continuing Edn., 1973—80; cons. U.S. Dept. Edn., 1982. Mem. Mich. Bd. Examiners of Social Workers, 1978—83; gov.'s appointee Mich. Youth Adv. Com., 1984—87, Commn. on Svcs. to Aging, 1992—; mem. Nat. Black Republicans, 1972—, Mich. Rep. Com., 1975—80, 1983—; sec. 1st Rep. Dist., 1973—77; presdl. appointee to nat. adv. bd. C.C. of Air Force, 1984—. Named Educator of Yr., Nat. Black Women's Polit. Leadership Caucus, 1981, Hon. Lt. Col. Aide De Camp in Ala. Militia, Gov. Wallace, 1986, in her honor, The Nancy Boykin Continuing Edn. Ctr., Detroit Pub. Sch. Bd., 1993; recipient Spirit of Detroit award, 1979, Nat. Kool Achiever's award in Edn., Brown and Williams Tobacco Co., 1987, Outstanding Contbns. to Cmty. award, Assn. Black Judges Mich., 1988—90, Cmty. Svc. award, YWCA, 1992, Pioneer award, Frederick Douglas Soc., 1994, others. Mem.: Detroit Assn. Univ. Mich. Women, Detroit Orgn. Sch. Adminstrs., Nat. Assn. Black Sch. Educators, Nat. Assn. Supervision and Curriculum Devel., Profl. Women's Network, Mich. Assn. Concerned with Sch. Age Parents (past pres., Recognition award 1986, Outstanding Svc. award 1993), Wayne State U. Sch. Edn. Alumni Assn. (bd. govs.), U. Mich. Alumnae Assn., Phi Delta Kappa, Alpha Kappa Alpha, Eta Phi Beta (Outstanding Profl. Women award 1992). Home and Office: 1316 Fenwick Ln Apt 513 Silver Spring MD 20910-3503

BOYKIW, NORMA SEVERNE, nutritionist, educator, retired nutritionist; b. Coalmont, Ind., Feb. 3, 1918; d. Charles Edward Goble and Ressa Naomi Johnson; m. Russel Yaroslav Alexis Boykiw, 1948 (dec. Sept. 4, 1992); children: Russel Alexis II, Mark Emerson. BS, Ind. State U., 1941. Registered Med. Asst. 1950. Dietitian asst. Ind. State U., Terre Haute, Ind., 1939—40; tchr. home econ. Wawaka Sch. Sys., Wawaka, Ind., 1941—42; nutrition tchr. Crown Point Sch., Crown Point, Ind., 1942—43; mem. staff patient diabetic diets Wesley Meml. Hosp., Chgo.; writer of diet manuals Pa., 1945—48; office mgr. Russel Boykiw, MD, Clearfield, 1948—92, ret., 1992. Ombudsman Area Agy. on Aging, Clearfield, Pa., 1999—. Compilation author Genealogy for the Goble Family, 1976;, author diet manuals Hosps. Active cmty. devel. Pa. State U., Clearfield, Pa., 1959, 1966; den mother Presbyn. Ch., Clearfield, 1967. Named Woman of the Yr., Bus. and Profl. Women, 1974, Outstanding Citizen of the Yr., Clearfield Rotary Club, 1987; grantee, Ctrl. Pa. Dist. Libr. Bd., 1968—6879. Mem.: AAUW (Outstanding Woman award 1983), Nat. Soc. DF & PA, Nat. Soc. DAR, Clearfield County Hist. Soc. (grant). Democrat. Avocation: yoga. Home: 364 Bailey Settlement Hwy Clearfield PA 16830-3505

BOYLAN, ELIZABETH SHIPPEE, academic administrator, biology educator; b. Shanghai, Nov. 29, 1946; d. Nathan M. and Elizabeth (Little) Shippee; m. Robert J. Boylan, Oct. 2, 1971; children: Elizabeth B., Emily A. AB, Wellesley Coll., 1968; PhD, Cornell U., 1972. Postdoctoral fellow U. Rochester (N.Y.) Sch. Medicine, 1972-73; asst. prof. Queens Coll. CUNY, Flushing, 1973-78, assoc. prof., 1978-82, prof. biology, 1983-95, acting asst. provost, 1988-89, asst. provost, 1989-90, assoc. provost, 1990-92; acting provost Queens Coll. CUNY, Flushing, 1992-93; assoc. provost acad. programs and planning Queens Coll., Flushing, 1994-95; provost and dean of faculty Barnard Coll., N.Y.C., 1995—, prof. biology, 1995—. Chmn. Queens Coll. Acad. Senate, 1985-88; mem. grad. faculty Grad. Ctr. CUNY, N.Y.C., 1977-95; vis. investigator Sloan-Kettering Inst. Cancer Rsch., N.Y.C., 1979-80; trustee N.Y. Met. Ref. and Rsch. Libr. Agy., Manhattan, 1989-97, chmn. fin. com. 1991-97; co-chmn. bd. trustees study com. on secondary edn. CUNY, 1987-88, co-chair vice chancellor's task force on sci., engring., tech. and math., 1988-89; panelist NSF grad. fellowship program, 1992-93; cons. to Nat. Cancer Inst., N.J. Commn. on Cancer Rsch., Endocrine Soc.; mem. breast cancer task force NCI, 1980-84; mem. adv. com. Am. Cancer Soc., 1981-85; Am. Coun. Edn. fellow Pace U., 1993-94; commr. Commn. on Higher Edn., Mid. States Assn. Colls. and Schs., 1999—. Contbr. and reviewer articles to profl. publs.; patentee in field. Grantee Nat. Cancer Inst., 1975-83, Am. Inst. Cancer Rsch., 1987-90, Am. Fedn. Aging Rsch., 1988-89. Mem. AAAS, AAHE, Soc. Devel. Biology, Am. Assn. Cancer Rsch., N.Y. Acad. Scis., Sigma Xi. Office: Barnard Coll Office of Provost 3009 Broadway New York NY 10027-6501

BOYLAN, MERLE NELSON, librarian, educator; b. Youngstown, Ohio, Feb. 24, 1925; s. Merle Nelson and Alma Joy (Kepple) B. BA, Youngstown U., 1950; M.L.S., Carnegie-Mellon U., 1956; postgrad., U. Ariz., 1950-51, Ind. U., 1952. Librarian Pub. Health Library U. Calif., Berkeley, 1956-58; sci. librarian U. Ariz., Tucson, 1958-59; engring. librarian Gen. Dynamics/Convair, San Diego, 1959-61, Gen. Dynamics/Astronautics, 1961-62; assoc. librarian Lawrence Radiation Lab., U. Calif., Livermore, 1962-64, library mgr., 1964-67; chief librarian NASA Ames Research Center, Moffett Field, Calif., 1968-69; asso. dir. libraries U. Mass., Amherst, 1969-70, dir. libraries, Univ. librarian, 1970-72; dir. libraries U. Tex., Austin, 1973-77, U. Wash., Seattle, 1977-89, dir. emeritus, 1989—, prof. Sch. Librarianship, 1982-89; exec. bd. Amigos Bibliographic Council, 1974-77; mem. fin. com., governance com., user's council, computer service council Wash. Library Network, 1978—. Del. Gov.'s Conf. Libraries and Info. Services, 1979; sec. Texas State Bd. Library Examiners, 1974-77; mem. bibliographic networking and resource sharing advisory group Southwestern Library Interstate Coop. Endeavor, 1975-77; sec., chmn. exec. bd. Pacific N.W. Bibliographic Center, 1977-83; mem. com. centralzed acquisitions of library materials for internat. studies Center for Research Libraries.; del. OCLC Users Council, 1981-86. Sec. bd. trustees Littlefield Fund for So. History, 1974-77, Fred Meyer Charitable Trust; mem. adv. bd. Library and Info. Resources for Northwest, 1984-87. Mem. ALA, Assn. Coll. and Research Libraries (legis. com. 1977-81), Assn. Research Libraries (bibliographic control com. 1979-83), Spl. Libraries Assn., Am. Soc. Info. Sci., Beta Phi Mu. Home: 1354 Bellefield Park Ln Bellevue WA 98004-6854 Office: Univ of Wash Libraries Suzzallo Library Seattle WA 98195-0001

BOYLAN, RICHARD JOHN, psychologist, psychotherapist, researcher, anthropologist, educator; b. Hollywood, Calif., Oct. 15, 1939; s. John Alfred and Rowena Margaret (Devine) Boylan; m. Charnette Marie Blackburn, Oct. 26, 1968 (div. June 1984); children: Christopher J., Jennifer April, Stephanie August; m. Judith Lee Keast, Nov. 21, 1987; stepchildren: Darren Andrew Keast, Matthew Grant Keast. BA, St. John's Coll., 1961; MEd, Fordham U., 1966; MSW, U. Calif., Berkeley, 1971; PhD in Psychology, U. Calif., Davis, 1984. Cert. clin. hypnotherapist. Assoc. pastor Cath. Diocese Fresno, 1965-68; asst. dir. Berkeley Free Ch., 1970-71; psychiat. social worker Marin Mental Health Dept., San Rafael, Calif., 1971-77; dir. Calaveras Mental Health Dept., San Andreas, Calif., 1977-85; prof., coord. Nat. U., Sacramento, 1985-86; lectr. Calif. State U., Sacramento, 1985-90, 98-99; instr. U. Calif., Davis, 1984; assoc. prof. Chapman U., Sacramento, 1997-98; instr. Heald Coll., Sacramento, 2000; clin. social worker Dialysis Clinic, Inc., Sacramento, 2000—01. Dir. U.S. Behavioral Health, Sacramento, 1988—89; pvt. practice, Sacramento, 1974—; clin. social worker South Sacramento Dialysis Ctr., 2000—01; clin. cons. Ctr. for Behavioral Health, Sacramento, 2000; adminstrv. supervising social worker Kair In-Home Social Svcs., Inc., 2001—03. Author: (book) Extraterrestrial Contact and Human Responses, 1992, Close Extraterrestrial Encounters, 1994, Labored Journey to the Stars, 1996, Project Epiphany, 1997. Bd. dirs. Marin Mcpl. Water Dist., 1975—77; cons. Calif. State Legis., Sacramento, 1979—80; chmn. Calaveras County Bd. Edn., Angels Camp, Calif., 1981—84; dir. Star Kids Project, Ltd., 2002—. Recipient Geriatric Medicine award, NIH, 1984; Expt. Sta. grantee, USDA, 1983. Mem.: Acad. Clin. Close-Encounter Therapists (founder, v.p.), Nat. Resources Def. Coun., Sacramento Soc. Profl. Psychologists (past pres.), Sacramento Valley Psychol. Assn. (past pres.), Nat. Bd. Hypnotherapy and Med. Anaesthesiology. Democrat. Avocations: hiking, jogging, UFOs, camping. Office: PO Box 22310 Sacramento CA 95822-0310 E-mail: drboylan@sbcglobal.net.

BOYLE, BETSY H. educational administrator; b. Cleve., Feb. 18, 1946; d. John J. Jr. and Lois Frances (Hale) B. BA, Loretto Heights Coll., Denver, 1968; MA, U. No. Colo., 1978, postgrad. Cert. adminstr., Colo. Tchr. Archdiocese of Denver; prin. Presentation of Our Lady Sch., Denver; dir. instrnl. programs Office Cath. Schs., Denver, now assoc. supt., exec. dir. Cath. edn. cons. svcs. Contbr. articles to profl. jours. Mem. ASCD, Nat. Cath. Edn. Assn. (profl. presenter, spc. adv. com.), Cath. Urban Educators, Schs. in Urban Neighborhoods.

BOYLE, EDWARD ALLEN, oceanography educator; b. Aberdeen, Md., May 1, 1949; BA, U. Calif., San Diego, 1971; PhD, MIT, 1976. Postdoctoral fellow U. Edinburgh, Scotland, 1976-77; asst. prof. MIT, Cambridge, 1977-80, assoc. prof., 1980-90, prof., 1990—. NSF fellow MIT, 1971-75, Guggenheim Found. fellow, 1991-92; recipient Huntsman award Bedford Inst. of Oceanography, 1995. Fellow Am. Geophys. Union, Geochem. Soc.(Clair C. Patterson award, 2000), European Union Geosci. Office: MIT E34-258 77 Mass Ave Cambridge MA 02139-4307

BOYLE, JOHN DANIEL, school psychologist; b. Rahway, N.J., Feb. 17, 1955; s. John Daniel Boyle and Norma (Longo) Block; m. Jo Kay Mary Unverferth, Mar. 26, 1983; children: Sean, Kayla. BA, U. Miss., 1977; MS, Northwestern State U., Natchitoches, La., 1982, EdS, 1990. Cert. sch. psychologist, Iowa. Sch. psychologist Sabine Parish Sch. Bd., Many, La., 1981-94, Heartland Area Edn. Agy., Johnston, Iowa, 1994—. Mem. supervision task force La. Dept. Edn., Baton Rouge, 1986-87, mem. gifted task force, 1991-93. Com. co-chmn. Christmas Festival, Natchitoches, 1990. Mem. NASP (La. state del. 1990-94, membership co-chmn. 1992-93, chmn. nominations and elections 1993-95, Iowa state del. 1999—, del. rep. 2000-02), La. Sch. Psychologists Assn. (pres. 1986), KC (grand knight coun. 1357, 1991-93). Roman Catholic. Home: 617 NE Hayes Dr Ankeny IA 50021-2089 Office: Heartland Area Edn Agy 6500 Corporate Dr Johnston IA 50131-1603

BOYLE, JUDITH PULLEN, clinical psychologist, educator; b. Flint, Mich., Aug. 4, 1940; d. Jack Andrew and Patricia Marie (Darby) Coleman; m. Fredric W. Pullen, Aug. 9, 1963 (div. June 1979); children: Fred, Andrea, Thomas.; m. Michael H. Boyle, Feb. 22, 1991. BSBA, Univ. Fla., 1962; MS, St. Thomas Univ., 1990; PhD, The Union Inst., 1994. Elem. tchr. US Sch. System, Tripoli, Libya, North, Africa, 1965-67; asst. librarian Miami Country Day Sch., 1985-86, substitute tchr., 1984-88; counselor Christian Counseling Svc., Ft. Lauderdale, 1991-96; adj. prof. The Union Inst., Miami, 1990—; pvt. practice psychotherapy, 1996—; guidance counselor St. Rose of Lima Sch., 1997—. Bd. dirs. Bayview Ctr. for Mental Health, The Cushman Sch.; adj. prof. St. Thomas U., 1998—. Regent DAR, 1962-76; bd. dirs. Children's Genetic Disease Found., 1993-96. Mem. AAUW, AAUP, Am. Assn. Marriage & Family Therapists, Assn. Christian Therapists, Delta Gamma. Republican. Roman Catholic. Avocations: bible teacher, middleast culture, women's issues, jungian psychology, literature studies. Home: 585 Grand Concourse Miami FL 33138-2464

BOYLE, STEVEN LEONARD, secondary school educator; b. Yakima, Wash., Dec. 6, 1954; s. Leonard Lavern and Lillith Ernestine (Lueck) B.; m. Tracy Lynn Achziger, June 15, 1991. BA in Music Edn., Ctrl. Wash. U., 1979, MA in Adminstrv. Edn., 1992. Cert. K-12 music tchr., Wash. Music tchr. Housel Mid. Sch., Prosser, Wash., 1979-89; 6th-12th grade band tchr. Housel and Prosser H.S., 1989—. Leader Boy Scouts Am., Prosser, 1980—. Mem. NEA, Music Educators Assn., Wash. Music Educators Assn., Prosser Edn. Assn. (pres. 1989-90), Wash. Edn. Assn. (Hon. Mention Tchr. of Yr. 1982). Avocations: outdoor activities, skiing, hiking, camping, travel. Home: 1116 Budd Ave Prosser WA 99350-1306 Office: Housel Mid Sch 2001 Highland Dr Prosser WA 99350-1597 E-mail: boyles@prosserschools.org.

BOYLE, SUSAN JEAN HIGLE, social studies educator; b. Tarrytown, N.Y., June 15, 1956; d. George Edward and Barbara Jean (Deverill) Higle. BA in Psychology, Elem. Edn., Ladycliff Coll., 1978; MS in Learning Disabilities, Fordham U., 1980; EdS in Ednl. Leadership, Stetson U., 1988. Cert. tchr. Fla., social studies tchr. Fla. Tchr. St. Ursula Sch., Mt. Vernon, N.Y., 1978-81, Blue Lake Elem. Sch., DeLand, Fla., 1982-86, Deltona (Fla.) Lakes Elem., 1986-88, Discovery Elem. Sch., Deltona, 1988-89, Tomoka Elem. Sch., Ormond Beach, Fla., 1989-90, Ormond Beach Mid. Sch., 1990—. Eucharistic minister St. Brendan Ch. Named Tchr. of the Quarter, C. of C., Fall 2000, OBMS Tchr. of Yr., 2003; TOPS grantee, 1985,

86, CITE grantee, 2001, Bright Ideas in Newspapers in Edn. grantee, 2001. Mem. Phi Delta Kappa. Avocations: reading, collecting boyd's bears. Office: Ormond Beach Mid Sch 151 Domicilio Ave Ormond Beach FL 32174-3918

BOYLE, THOMAS FRANCIS, educational administrator; b. Coaldale, Pa., Apr. 18, 1947; s. Francis Dennis Boyle and Kathleen (Sheehan) Frankowski; m. Diane Lee Cannizzaro, June 20, 1970; children: Kristen C., Kellie E., Tiffany A. BA, William Paterson Coll., 1969; computer cert., St. Peter's Coll., Jersey City, 1976; Cert. Tax Assessor, Rutgers U., 1978; MA, Kean Coll., 1995; EdD, Nova Southeastern U., 2003. Cert. tchr., N.J.; cert. tax assessor, N.J.; cert. real estate appraiser Nat. Assn. Real Estate Appraisers, Phoenix; cert. prof. assessor Soc. Profl. Assessors; cert. supr., sch. bus. adminstr. Computer coord. Warren (N.J.) Middle Sch., 1986-97; supt. Somerset County Ednl. Svcs. Commn., Raritan, N.J., 1997—. Councilman Borough of Dunellen, N.J., 1978; committeeman Dem. Orgn., So. Plainfield, N.J., 1990. With U.S. Army, 1970-80. Mem. Warren Twp. Edn. Assn. (pres. 1976-78), Somerset County Edn. Assn. (1st v.p. 1980-82, treas. 1982-92), KC, Phi Kappa Phi. Roman Catholic. Home: 901 Garibaldi Ave South Plainfield NJ 07080-3214 Office: Somerset County Ednl Svcs Commn 12 E Somerset St Raritan NJ 08869-2102

BOYLE, WILLIAM CHARLES, civil engineering educator; b. Mpls., Apr. 9, 1936; s. Robert and Daphne Boyle; m. Nancy Lee Hahn, Apr. 11, 1959; children: Elizabeth Lynn, Michele Jenette, Jane Lynette, Robert William. CE, U. Cin., 1959, MS in Sanitary Engring., 1960; PhD in Environ. Engring., Calif. Inst. Tech., 1963. Registered profl. engr., Wis., Ohio. With Milw. Sewerage Commn., 1955-56; civil engr. O. G. Loomis & Sons, Covington, Ky., 1956-59; asst. engr. Ohio River Valley Water Sanitation Commn., summer 1959; asst. prof. dept. engring. U. Wis., Madison, 1963-66, assoc. prof., 1966-70, prof. dept. civil and environ. engring., 1970-96, chmn. dept. civil and environ. engring., 1984-86, assoc. chair, 1988-96, emeritus prof., 1996—. Vis. prof. Rogaland Distriktshogskole, Stavanger, Norway, 1975-76; vis. prin. engr. Montgomery Engrs. Inc., Pasadena, Calif., 1988-89; cons. Procter & Gamble Co., Monsanto Co., S.B. Foot Tanning Co., Wis. Canners & Freezers Assn., Wis. Concrete Pipe Assn., Oscar Mayer & Co., Bartlett-Snow, Hide Service Corp., W.R. Grace & Co., Lake to Lake Dairies, Milw. Tallow, Wausau Paper Co., Packerland Packing Co., Ray-O-Vac, U.S. Army CERL, Owen Ayres & Assocs., Donohue Engrs., Davy Engrs., Carl C. Crane, Green Engring., RSE div. Ayres & Assocs., Schreiber Corp. Inc., Sanitaire, J.M. Montgomery, Engrs., Polkowski, Boyle, & Assocs., Rust E&I; mem. peer rev. panel on environ. engring. EPA; accreditation visitor Accreditation Bd. for Engring. and Tech., 1990—. Contbr. articles to profl. jours. Sr. warden St. Andrews Episcopal Ch., Madison, 1972-74, treas., 1979-85 Recipient Engring. Disting. Alumnus award U. Cin., 1986, Founders award U.S.A. nat. com. Internat. Assn. Water Pollution Rsch. & Control, 1988, commendation EPA, 1989; Mills Found. scholar U. Cin., 1954-59; USPHS trainee, U. Cin., 1959-60; fellow Ford Found., Calif. Inst. Tech., 1960-61, USPHS, Calif. Inst. Tech., 1961-63 Mem. ASCE (life, Wis. chpt., advisor U. Wis. student chpt. 1968-71, chmn. student affairs com. 1970-72, chmn. profl. activities com. 1972-74, nat., control mem. tech. council on codes and standards-environ. standards 1999—, chmn. environ. stds. devel. coun. 1998-2001, chair oxygen transfer standards com., 1975-2002, mem. history and heritage com., reviewer EED Jour., Rudolf Hering medal 1975, Engring. Achievement award from Wis. chpt. 1986, Engr. of Yr. award Wis. sect. 1998), Water Environment Fedn. (life, research com., joint task force-pretreatment of wastewater, tech. practice com.-energy in treatment plant design, author chpt. Manual of Practice Design Wastewater Treatment Plants, author chpt. Ops. Manual on Activated Sludge, chmn. program com., bd. control, 1996-98, jour. reviewer, chmn. tech. practice com. task force on aeration, Radebaugh award 1978, Eddy award com. 1992-98, Harrison Prescot Eddy Rsch. medal 1989, chmn. rsch. symposia, Gordon Maskew Fair medal for environ. engring. edn., 1992, Arthur Sydney Bedell award 2001), Am. Water Works Assn. (life, chmn. task group on oxygen transfer, editl. bd.), Am. Acad. Environ. Engrs. (diplomate, life, accreditation vis. for Accreditation Bd. Engring and Tech., chmn. edn. com. 1993, trustee 1994-97, pres.-elect 1998, pres. 1999-2000, rep. bd. dirs. ABET, 1994-2000, commr. Engr. Accreditation comm. 2001-, Stanley E. Kappe award 2002), Am. Foundrymen's Soc. (com. on waste disposal, Outstanding Rsch. Paper award environ. cen. div. 1989), Sigma Xi, Theta Tau, Phi Eta Sigma, Chi Epsilon, Tau Beta Pi (advisor U. Wis. student chpt. 1994-96). Episcopalian. Avocations: photography, travel. Home: 105 Carillon Dr Madison WI 53705-4614 Office: Univ Wis 2256 Engineering Hall 1415 Engineering Dr Madison WI 53706-1607 E-mail: boyle@engr.wisc.edu.

BOYLE, WILLIAM LEO, JR., educational consultant, retired college president; b. Utica, N.Y., July 23, 1933; s. William Leo and Gladys (Kuney) B. AB, Colgate U., 1955; postgrad., Cornell U. Law Sch., 1960—61; MA, Columbia U., 1964, Profl. Diploma in Ednl. Adminstrn., 1967, EdD, 1969; LLD (hon.), Hawthorne Coll., 1979; postdoctoral, Harvard U., 1979—81; LHD (hon.), Mercy Coll., 1983; LittD (hon.), Curry Coll., 1992. Participant advanced mgmt. program, recruiter, ednl. adviser Procter & Gamble Co., Cin., 1958-60; legis. aide higher edn. com. N.Y. State Senate, Albany, 1961-62; account exec., ednl. cons. Batten, Barton, Durstine & Osborn, N.Y.C., 1962-64; assoc. dir. devel., presdl. asst. Wesleyan U., Middletown, Conn., 1964-65; program cons. Coun. for Aid to Edn., N.Y.C., 1965-70, asst. v.p., 1970-72, v.p., 1972-75; pres. Keuka Coll., Keuka Pk., NY, 1975—78, Curry Coll., Milton, Mass., 1978—92, pres. emeritus, 1992—; part-time practice as ednl. cons. to pvt. colls. and univs., Utica, 1992—. Author: The National Corporate Educational Support Movement, 1954-1966, 1969; contbr. articles to ednl. and profl. jours. Ednl. cons. to Pres. Ford Com., Washington, 1976; vice chmn. nat. bus. and industry com. Colgate U., Hamilton, NY, 1974—, mem. nat. coun., 1975—, ann. fund exec. com., 1975—, Colgate '55 class agt., 1994—, mem. maj. gifts com., established Boyle Scholarship, 1985, Boyle award in polit. sci., 1997; pres., trustee 1036 Park Ave. Corp., N.Y.C., 1970—74; mem. bd. devel. com. Cmty. Found., Utica, 1992—98; established Boyle Individual Fund, Cmty. Found., Utica, 1991, Boyle Parents Meml. Fund, Cmty. Found., Utica, 2002; bd. dirs. Slocum-Dickson Found., Utica, 1991—, Family Svcs. of the Mohawk Valley, Utica, 1992—, House of the Good Shepherd, Utica, 1992—, Oneida County Hist. Soc., Utica, 1994—. Lt. USAF, 1955—58. Decorated Comdr.'s citation USAF. Mem. various ednl. and profl. orgns., also Colgate Univ. Club (N.Y.C.), Columbia Univ. Club (N.Y.C.), Ft. Schuyler Club (Utica) (bd. mgrs.), Sadaquada Golf Club (Utica), Yahnundasis Golf Club (Utica), Rotary. Home: 12 Rose Pl Utica NY 13502-5614

BOYLES, CAROL ANN PATTERSON, career development educator; b. Waverly, N.Y., Aug. 26, 1932; d. Paul Bryan and Ruth Marion (Wilbur) Patterson; widowed 1981; 1 child, Scott Patterson. BA, Keuka Coll., 1953; MEd, U. Fla., 1957. Cert. tchr., Fla. Admissions officer Keuka Coll., Keuka Park, N.Y., 1953-56; residence counselor Fla. State U., Tallahassee, 1957-59; dir. guidance and counseling, assoc. dean student affairs Cen. Fla. C.C., Ocala, 1959-67; asst. dean student activities, orgns., asst. dean women Fla. State U., Tallahassee, 1967-69; dir. guidance Fla. C.C., Jacksonville, 1970-72; from dir. coop. edn., placement dir. experiential learning U. North Fla., Jacksonville, 1972—99, dir. career svcs., 1999—, dir. experiential learning, 1999—2003. Chair Career Expo, Jacksonville, 1977-91; chair, mem. interuniv. sys. com. on career devel., 1972-2003; cons. coop. edn. programs; field reader U.S. Dept. Edn. Chair bd. dirs. Southside Christian Counseling Ctr., 1992-94, 96-97, mem. 1988-94, 96-97; dir. Christian Women's Job Corps., 2000—. Mem. ASTD, Fla. Career Profls. Assn. (hon. life), So. Coll. Placement Assn. (v.p. 1972-73), Southeastern Assn. Colls. and Employers, Fla. Coop. Placement Assn. (pres. 1976-77, John Brownlee Leadership award 1991), Coop. Edn. Assn., Nat. Soc. Exptl. Edn., Jacksonville C. of C. (workforce preparation bd. bus. sch. partnership com., State of Fla. Coll. Acad. Skills Test adv. com. 1994-97, Fla. Dept. Edn. ad hoc com. on placement testing 1995-97), Keuka Coll. Alumni Assn., Kappa Delta Pi. Baptist. Avocations: travel, genealogy, swimming, theater, reading. Home: 7804 Catawba Dr Jacksonville FL 32217-3642

BOYNTON, IRVIN PARKER, retired educational administrator; b. Chgo., Mar. 27, 1937; s. Ben Lynn and Elizabeth (Katterjohn) B.; m. Alyce Jane Coyle, Sept. 3, 1964; children: Gregory Allen, Cathy Lynn, Julie Marie, Michael Irvin, Jonathan David. BA, Ohio Wesleyan U., 1959; BS, U. Akron, 1964; MEd, Wayne State U., 1968; counseling endorsement, Siena Heights Coll., 1988. Cert. tchr., Ohio, Mich. Spl. edn. tchr., acting prin. Sagamore Hills Children's Psychiat. Hosp., Cleve., 1961-64; spl. edn. tchr. Fairlawn Ctr., Pontiac, Mich., 1964-68, Walled Lake (Mich.) High Sch., 1968-71; asst. prin. Oakland Tech. Ctr./Southwest Campus, Wixom, Mich., 1971-98; ret., 1998. Mem. spl. needs guideline com. Mich. Dept. Edn., Lansing, 1973-78; keynote speaker Utah Secondary Conf., Salt Lake City, 1978; evaluator North Cen. Accreditation Assn., Waterford, Mich., 1971-73; adv. com. State Tech.Instn. and Rehab. Ctr., Plainwell, Mich., 1978-85. Pres. Roger Campbell Ministries, Waterford, 1987—. Cited as exemplary spl. needs program U. Wis. Mem. ASCD, Am. Vocat. Assn., Mich. Occupational Edn. Assn., Mich. Occupational Spl. Needs Assn. (Outstanding Spl. Needs Educator), Nat. Assn. Vocat. Spl. Needs Personnel (Outstanding Spl. Needs Program 1975), Phi Delta Kappa. Republican. Home: 4901 Juniper Dr Commerce Township MI 48382-1545 E-mail: irvinboynton@comcast.net.

BOYSEN, THOMAS CYRIL, educational association administrator; b. Sioux Falls, S.D., Nov. 16, 1940; s. Cyril Joseph and Dolores Margaret (Parry) B.; m. PoChan Mar, Aug. 25, 1964 (div. 1980); children: Thomas C., Anne-Marie Lee; m. Laurie Louise Shaffer, June 25, 1983. BA in History, Stanford U., 1962; diploma in grad. edn., Makerere U., Kampala, Uganda, 1964; EdD in Edn. Adminstrn., Harvard U., 1969. Geography master Kabaa H.S., Thika, Kenya, 1964-66; dir. adminstrn. Bellevue (Wash.) Pub. Schs., 1968-70; supt. schs. Pasco Sch. Dist., Wash., 1970-73, Pelham (N.Y.) Pub. Schs., 1973-77, Redlands United Sch. Dist., Calif., 1977-80, Conejo Valley Unified Sch. Dist., Thousand Oaks, Calif., 1980-87, San Diego County Schs., 1987-90, Ky. Commn. Edn., 1991-95; sr. v.p. edn. Milken Family Found., Santa Monica, Calif., 1995—2002; COO L.A. Unified Sch. Dist., 2002—. Bd. trustees Milken Family Found.*

BOZOYAN, SYLVIA, elementary school educator; b. Aleppo, Syria, Feb. 18, 1953; d. Edward Yervant and Takouhi (Knnablian) B. BA, St. Peter's Coll., 1975; MEd, William Paterson Coll., 1978. Cert. elem. tchr., N.J., nursery sch. tchr., N.J. 1st grade tchr. Thomas A. Edison Sch., Union City, N.J., 1975—. Armenian sch. tchr. Holy Cross Armenian Ch., Union City, 1972-80, Sunday sch. tchr., 1969—. Named Outstanding Tchr. Govs. Tchr. Recognition Program, N.J., 1987-88, Outstanding Young Woman of Am., Ala., 1982, 87. Mem. Armenian Gen. Benevolent Union of Am. (sec. N.Y./N.J. Met. chpt. 1985—, sec., dancer ANTRANIG Dance Ensemble/exec. com. 1979—), N.J. Edn. Assn., Hudson County Edn. Assn., Union City Edn. Assn., Kappa Delta Pi, Pi Lambda Theta. Home: 1812 West St Union City NJ 07087-3311

BOZZOMO, WINIFRED KATHRYN, elementary education educator; b. N.Y.C., May 16, 1936; d. John A. and Winifred K. (Dunn) Flynn; m. Robert E. Bozzomo, June 21, 1958; children: Winifred M., Jeanne M., Beth A., Robert E., Hope V., Nancy K. BA magna cum laude, Queens Coll., 1975, MS in Edn., 1976. Tchr. supplemental reading Berkeley Heights (N.J.) Bd. Edn., 1975-77; tchr., 1st, 6th & 8th grades Little Flower Sch., Berkeley Heights, 1977-86; tchr. 1st grade Aquinas Acad., Livingston, N.J., 1986—. Counselor, tchr. Rainbows for all Gods Children, Livingston, 1986—. Vol. chaplains office Overlook Hosp., Summit, N.J., 1979—; vol. soup kitchen St. Joseph's Hosp., Elizabeth, N.J., 1989-92. Mem. N.J. Cath. Tchrs. Assn., N.J. Math. Assn. Roman Catholic. Avocations: reading, golf, fishing, writing, piano.

BRAATEN, LINDA MARIE SKURDELL, secondary education educator; b. Northwood, North Dakota, June 7, 1946; d. Theodore Arnold and Mildred Jeanette (Samnoen) Skurdell; m. Harvey Gordon Braaten, Sept. 3, 1966; children: Susan Marie Braaten Thorson, Jodee Miscielle Braaten Muus, Rachel Elizabeth, Jeffrey Michael. BS in edn., N.D. State U., 1969. lic. vocat. edn., N.D. Food technologist The Pillsbury Co., Mpls., 1970-73; salesperson Pierce Mobile Homes, Fargo, ND, 1974-76; tchr. Northwood Pub. Sch., ND, 1976—. Sec.,treas. Northwood Tchr. Assn., 1978, 85. Mem. NEA, Am. Vocat. Assn., N.D. Edn. Assn., Family, Career and Cmty. Leaders of Am. (dist. advisor 1987, 88, 91-95, 96—), co-state advisor 1996-02, Master Advisor Award 1991, Advisor Mentor Award 1996, hon. mem. N.D. 1997, Outstanding Advisor, 1998, Nat. Spirit of Advising Award, 1998, N.D. Award of Excellence, (FACS Program, 1999), Family and Consumer Sci. (N.D. assn., adv. bd. 1996-02). Avocations: playing piano, traveling, flower gardening. Home: 4735 3rd Ave NE Aneta ND 58212-9605 Office: Northwood Pub Sch 216 S Hougen St Northwood ND 58267-4313 E-mail: hljb@polarcomm.com.

BRACE, C. LORING, anthropologist, educator; b. Hanover, N.H., Dec. 19, 1930; s. Gerald Warner and Huldah (Laird) B.; m. Mary Louise Crozier, June 8, 1957; children: Charles L., Roger C., Hudson H. BA, Williams Coll., 1952; MA, Harvard U., 1958, PhD, 1962. Instr. U. Wis., Milw., 1960-61; asst. prof., then assoc. prof. U. Calif., Santa Barbara, 1961-67; assoc. prof. anthropology U. Mich., Ann Arbor, 1967-71, prof., 1971—, curator phys. anthropology Mus. Anthropology, 1967—. Author: Human Evolution, 1965, 2d edit., 1977, Stages of Human Evolution, 1967, 5th edit., 1995, Atlas of Human Evolution, 1971, 2d edit., 1979, Evolution in an Anthropological View, 2000. With U.S. Army, 1954-56. Fellow AAAS (chmn. sect. H); mem. Am. Ahthrop. Assn., Am. Assn. Phys. Anthropology, Dental Anthropology Assn. (pres. 1988-90), History of Sci. Soc. Home: 1020 Ferdon Rd Ann Arbor MI 48104-3631 Office: U Mich Mus Anthropology 1109 Geddes Ave Ann Arbor MI 48109-1079 E-mail: clbrace@umich.edu.

BRACE, JOAN ELAINE, elementary education educator; b. Houston, Aug. 16, 1943; d. Edward Earl and One Lorene (Brown) B.; m. Charles Albert Brace, Sept. 4, 1965; childrent: Starla Kay, Charla Elaine, Charles Kevin. BS in Provisional Vocat., U. Mary Hardin Baylor, 1966. Home econs tchr. LaFeria (Tex.) Ind. Sch. Dist., 1966-67, Mercedes (Tex.) Ind. Sch. Dist., 1968-70; kindergarten tchr. Galena Park (Tex.) Ind. Sch. Dist., 1977—. Children divsn. dir. Woodforest Bapt. Ch., Houston, 1992—, Sunday sch. tchr., 1980-92; youth dir. Second Bapt. Ch., Galena Park, 1975-80. Grantee Santa Fe RR, 1962; named Outstanding Young Texan Farm Bur., 1965. Mem. Assn. of Tex. Profl. Educators (pres. 1986—, Top 10% Recruiter in state 1992), Kindergarten Tchrs. of Tex., U. of Mary Hardin Baylor Alumni (alumni bd. 1993—, recruiting team 1992), Psi Theta (pres. 1964-65). Republican. Baptist. Avocations: arts and crafts, sewing.

BRACHFELD, JONAS, cardiologist, educator; b. Antwerp, Belgium, Dec. 1, 1924; came to U.S., 1943; s. Chaskiel and Rosa (Spira) B.; m. Rosalind Roth, Apr. 3, 1955; children: Claude A., Renée K., Eric L. BS, Calif. Inst. of Tech., 1947; MD, U. Pa., 1952. Diplomate Am. Bd. Internal Medicine, Am. Bd. Cardiovascular Disease. Chmn. dept. internal medicine Rancocas Hosp., Willingboro, N.J., 1961-94, dir. CCU, 1972-93; founder, CEO Brachfeld Med. Assocs., Willingboro, 1969-94; prof. clin. medicine U. Medicine and Dentistry N.J., Camden, 1993—; dir. Fellows' Clinic, dept. cardiology Univ. Med. Ctr., 1997—. Founder Brachfeld Day Care Ctr. Jewish Geriatric Home, Cherry Hill, N.J., 1972. Fellow Am. Coll. Cardiology, Am. Heart Assn. Avocation: languages (Dutch, Spanish, French, German, and Hebrew). Home: 227 Nicholson Dr Moorestown NJ 08057-2909 Office: U Med Ctr 1103 Kings Hwy N Cherry Hill NJ 08034-1983

BRACKBILL, NANCY LAFFERTY, elementary education educator; b. Lancaster, Pa., Sept. 7, 1938; d. Jacob Martin and Erma Irene Lafferty; m. Albert Landis Brackbill Jr., Aug. 6, 1960; children: Lynn Elizabeth, Lisa Ann. BS in Elem. Edn., Millersville U., 1960, cert. reading specialist, 1981. Tchr. kindergarten Hempfield Sch. Dist., Landisville, Pa., 1960-63; tchr. nursery sch. Zion U.C.C. Nursery Sch., Millersville, Pa., 1971-72; tchr. elem., reading Annville (Pa.)-Cleona Sch. Dist., 1978-79; tchr. reading Palmyra (Pa.) H.S., 1980-81; elem. tchr., reading specialist East Stroudsburg (Pa.) Area Sch. Dist., 1981—, chmn. elem. reading, 1991—. Mem. St. John's Evang. Luth. Ch. Mem. ASCD, Internat. Reading Assn., Colonial Area Reading Educators (legis. chair 1992—, rec. sec. 1994-99), Pa. Edn. Assn., Keystone State Reading Assn. Avocations: tennis, reading, music, bike riding, yoga. Home: 188 Brookside Ln Nazareth PA 18064-9109

BRACKENHOFF, LONNIE SUE, principal; b. Shaw AFB, S.C., Feb. 27, 1957; d. Marshall Alvin Jr. and Marcia Ann Sherrill; m. Charles Robert Brackenhoff, June 18, 1977; children: Christina, Justin. BS in Spl. Edn., East Carolina U., 1978, MA in Edn., 1983; student, Chapman U., 1997; ednl. specialist degree, U. Wyo., 1998; student, Chapman U., 1997. Cert. tchr. and adminstr., Wyo, Calif. Tchr. spl. edn. Edgecombe County Schs., Tarboro, N.C., 1978-84, Laramie County Sch Dist. 1, Cheyenne, Wyo., 1985-92, tchr. elem., 1992-93; prin. Lompoc (Calif.) Unified Sch. Dist., 1993—. Instr. Ea. Wyo. C.C., 1993. Vol. Very Spl. Arts, Cheyenne, 1986, 90-92, coord., 1987-89. Mem. ASCD, Assn. Calif. Sch. Adminstrs., Assn. Lompoc Sch. Adminstrs., Learning Disabilities Assn., Phi Delta Kappa. Avocations: reading, family camping.

BRACKETT, BENJAMIN GAYLORD, physiology and pharmacology educator; b. Athens, Ga., Nov. 18, 1938; s. Ernest Marshall and Julia Claire (Cook) B.; m. Ann Thornton Crawford, Aug. 22, 1959; children: Laura Ellen, Jeffrey Crawford, David Gregory. DVM cum laude, U. Ga., 1962, PhD in Biochemistry, 1966; MA (hon.), U. Pa., 1971. Diplomate Am. Coll. Theriogenologists. Postdoctoral fellow dept. biochemistry U. Ga., Athens, 1962-66, prof. Coll. Vet. Med., 1983—2002, prof. emeritus, 2003—, head dept. physiology/pharmacology, 1983-95; from assoc. to prof. dept. ob.-gyn. Sch. Medicine, U. Pa., Phila., 1966-74; prof. of animal reproduction Sch. Vet. Medicine U. Pa., Phila., 1974-83; also, prof. of rsch. ob.-gyn. Sch. Medicine. Cons. on impacts of applied genetics Office of Tech. Assessment, U.S. Congress, 1979-80, to contraceptive R & D program Ea. Va. Sch. Medicine, Norfolk, 1986-91; pres., chmn. bd. dirs. Reproductive Biol. Assocs., Inc., Atlanta, 1983-88. Editor: New Technologies in Animal Breeding, 1981; contbr. over 275 articles to profl. publs. Grantee, NIH, USDA, others; recipient Rsch. Career Devel. award USPHS/NIH, 1971-76, Disting. Alumnus award Coll. Vet. Medicine, U. Ga., 1998, Internat. award in Animal Reprodn., Lazzaro Spallanzani, 1999. Mem. Internat. Embryo Transfer Soc. (pres. 1984-85, Pioneer award 2004), Am. Soc. Reproductive Medicine, Am. Soc. Andrology, Soc. for Study of Fertility, Soc. for Study of Reproduction (sec. 1982-86), Am. Vet. Med. Assn., Ga. Vet. Med. Assn., Am. Physiol. Soc., Four Chaplains Legion of Honor. Methodist. Achievements include development of in vitro fertilization technology. Office: U Ga Coll Vet Medicine Dept Physiol And Pharm Athens GA 30602

BRACKNER, JAMES WALTER, retired finance educator; b. Selma, Ala., Aug. 6, 1934; s. James Oscar and Ruby Belle (Langston) Brackner; m. Gayle Linton, Sept. 11, 1959; children: James L., Betsy, Joseph L., David L., Susan, Daniel L., Nancy. BS in Acctg., Brigham Young U., 1961, MS in Acctg., 1962; PhD in Accountancy, U. Ala., 1984. CPA, cert. mgmt. acct.; fin. mgmt., fraud examiner. Staff acct. Arthur Andersen, L.A., 1962-65; contr., asst. sec. Teledyne-WIW, L.A., 1965-68; CFO Phaostron Electronics, South Pasadena, Calif., 1968-69, Deseret Mgmt. Corp.-Farms Divsn., Salt Lake City, 1978-81; instr., asst. prof. Brigham Young U., Provo, Utah, 1969-78; from asst. prof. to prof. Utah State U., Logan, 1981-99, prof., 1993-99, Inst. Mgmt. Accts. prof. in residence, 1999—2001, ALCOA prof. acctg.; ret., 2001. Cons., expert witness Richards Brandt Miller Nelson, Salt Lake City, 1988—91; cons. Latvian and Russian Fin. Ministries, 1993, Ministry of Labour and Social Welfare, Govt. of Thailand, 1998—99. Author: (book) Management Accounting/Manufacturing Excellence, 1996; contbr. chapters to books, articles to profl. jours. Scout leader, merit badge counselor Boy Scouts Am., Logan, 1982—. With U.S. Army, 1954—56. Mem.: AICPA, Assn. Cert. Fraud Examiners, Utah Assn. CPAs (chpt. pres. 1995—96), Nat. Contract Mgmt. Assn., Am. Acctg. Assn., Inst. Mgmt. Accts. (mem. ethics com. 1991—94, mem. edn. com. 1994—95, bd. regents 1995—96, nat. v.p. 1996—97, bd. dirs. 1997—, mem. acad. rels. com. 1998, 1999). Republican. Mem. Lds Ch. Avocations: fishing, travel, genealogy. Home: 760 Stewart Hill Dr Logan UT 84321-5690 E-mail: jbracknr@b202.usu.edu.

BRACKS, OSCAR, JR., physician, educator, nuclear chemist; b. Galveston, Tex., Oct. 21, 1947; s. Oscar Sr. and Vivian (Brown) B.; m. Sylvia Ann Robinson, Nov. 24, 1978; children: Derrick D., Jessica A. AS in Biology, Morehouse Coll., Atlanta, 1969; BS in Biology and Chemistry, Ga. State U., Atlanta, 1973; DPM, Ohio Coll. Podiatric Medicine, Cleve., 1978. Diplomate Am. Coun. Cert. Podiatric Physicians and Surgeons; bd. cert. disability analyst; ordained minister, 1975. Head dept. sci. Atlanta Street Acad., 1973-78; rsch. assoc. Tex. Coll. Osteo. Medicine, Ft. Worth, 1978; adj. prof. anatomy Parker Coll. Chiropractic, Dallas, 1986-88; adj. prof. anatomy and physiology Collin County C.C., 1988-80, Brookhaven Coll., 1990-93; dir. instnl. medicine Metroplex Nursing Homes, 1979-89; physician-surgeon North Tex. Podiatry Group, Dallas, 1979—; organic chemist Scientech Inc., Dallas, 1989-90, nuclear chemist, 1990-92. Author: Applied Anatomy of the Back, 1988. Bd. dirs. Sickle Cell Anemia Found., Ft. Worth, 1979-88, Aging Svcs. Commn. III, Ft. Worth, 1984-86, Dallas Bus. Assn., 1991—, Oaklawn Com., Dallas, 1982-88, Tarrant Ministerial Alliance, Ft. Worth, 1989, Lexington Acad. Sci. Fair, Dallas, 1990—. Recipient Martin Luther King award Tarrant County, 1985; named Outstanding Role Model, Tarrant County, Ft. Worth, 1984; named to Outstanding Young Men of Am., 1981. Mem. ASCD, Am. Chem. Soc. (nuclear divsn., medicinal divsn.), Am. Assn. Podiatric Physicians and Surgeons. Avocations: swimming, kiting, water sports, fencing. Office: North Tex Podiatry Group PO Box 810755 Dallas TX 75381-0755

BRADBURN, NORMAN M. behavioral science educator; b. Lincoln, Ill., July 21, 1933; s. Hubert Benjamin and Mary Celeste (Marshall) B.; m. Wendy McAneny, Dec. 15, 1956; children: Isabel Stuart, Andrew Marshall, Laura Humphreys. BA, U. Chgo., 1952, Oxford U., Eng., 1955; MA, Harvard U., 1958, PhD in Social Psychology, 1960. From asst. prof. to assoc. prof. behavioral sci. U. Chgo., 1960-67, prof., 1967—, chmn. dept. behavioral sci., 1973-79, Tiffany and Margaret Blake Disting. Service prof., 1977-99, provost, 1984-89, prof. emeritus, 1999—. Sr. study dir. Nat. Opinion Research Center, Chgo., 1961—, dir., 1967-71, 79-84, 89-92, rsch. dir., 1992-2000; asst. dir. NSF, 2000—. Author: (with D. Caplovitz) Reports on Happiness, 1967, The Structure of Psychological Well-Being, 1970, (with S. Sudman, G. Gockel) Side by Side: A Study of Integrated Neighborhoods, 1971, (with S. Sudman) Response Effects in Surveys, 1974, Asking Questions: A Practical Guide to Questionnaire Construction, 1982, Polls and Surveys: Understanding What They Tell Us, 1988, (with others) Improving Questionnaire Design and Interview Method, 1979, (with S. Sudman and N. Schwarz) Thinking About Answers, 1996. Alexander von Humboldt scholar U. Cologne (Germany), 1970-71 Fellow AAAS, Am. Statis. Assn.; mem. Internat. Statis. Inst., World Assn. Pub. Opinion Rsch., Am. Assn. Pub. Opinion Rsch. (pres. 1991-92), Am. Acad. Arts and Scis. Home: 502 N Abingdon St Arlington VA 22203-2049 Business E-Mail: nbradbur@nsf.gov.

BRADDOCK, DAVID LAWRENCE, health science educator; b. Glendale, Calif., Mar. 10, 1945; s. Mark Perry and Christina Bain Braddock; m. Laura Stanlye Haffer, May 1, 1976; children: Gabriel, Autumn, Adam. BA, U. Tex., 1967, MA, 1970, PhD, 1973. Spl. asst. to dir. sec.'s com. on mental retardation HEW, Washington, 1972; prin. investigator Coun. for Exceptional Children, Reston, Va., 1973-77; cons. White House Conf. on the Handicapped, Washington, 1977-78; rsch. prof., program dir. Inst. Study Devel. Disabilities U. Ill., Chgo., 1979-88, prof. cmty. health scis. Sch. Pub. Health, 1985—2001, prof. human devel., founding head dept. disability and human devel., 1988—2001, assoc. dean for rsch., 1997-98; assoc. v.p. U. Colo. Sys., 2001—; exec. dir. Coleman Inst. for Cognitive Disabilities U. Colo., 2001—; Coleman-Turner chair in cognitive disability, prof. psychiatry U. Colo. Health Scis. Ctr., Coll. Medicine, 2001—. Cons. U.S. Dept. HHS, Washington, 1972—. Author: Federal Policy Toward Mental Retardation, 1987, Residential Services and Developmental Disabilities in U.S., 1992, The State of the States in Developmental Disabilities, 7 edits., Disability at the Dawn of the 21st Century, 2002; co-author: State Law and the Education of Handicapped Children, 1972; contbr. more than 200 articles to profl. jours., monographs in field. Cons. Joseph P. Kennedy Jr. Found.; active in promoting civil and human rights of people with mental retardation and other disabilities.; bd. dirs. Spl. Olympics Internat. Fellow, Nat. Inst. on Disability and Rehab. Rsch., 1988—89; grantee U.S. Dept. HHS, U.S. Dept. Edn., Nat. Inst. on Disability and Rehab. Rsch., 1999—2000; univ. scholar, U. Ill., 1998—2001. Fellow: Am. Assn. on Mental Retardation (pres. 1993—94, editor books and monographs 1997—2002, Career Rsch. award 1998), Delta Omega; mem.: AAAS, Assn. for Retarded Citizens of U.S. (sci. adv. bd. 1987—, Disting. Rsch. award in mental retardation 1987, Franklin Smith award for disting. nat. svc. 2000). Office: Coleman Inst Cognitive Disabilities U Colo SYS 586 4001 Discovery Dr Boulder CO 80309

BRADEMAS, JOHN, retired university president, former congressman; b. Mishawaka, Ind., Mar. 2, 1927; s. Stephen J. and Beatrice Cenci (Goble) B.; m. Mary Ellen Briggs, July 9, 1977. BA magna cum laude (Vets. nat. scholar), Harvard, 1949; D.Phil. (Rhodes scholar), Oxford (Eng.) U., 1954; LL.D. (hon.), U. Notre Dame, Middlebury Coll., Tufts U. (others); L.H.D., Brandeis U., CCNY (others). Legislative asst. to U.S. Senator Pat McNamara; adminstrv. asst. U.S. Rep. Thomas L. Ashley, 1955; exec. asst. to presdl. nominee Stevenson, 1955-56; asst. prof. polit. sci. St. Mary's Coll., Notre Dame, Ind., 1957-58; mem. 86th-96th Congresses from 3d Ind. Dist.; chief dep. majority whip 93d-94th Congresses; majority whip 95th-96th Congresses; mem. com. house adminstrn., com. on edn. and labor, joint com. on Library of Congress; pres. NYU, 1981-92, pres. emeritus, 1992—. Chmn. bd. dirs. Fed. Res. Bank N.Y.; dir. RCA/NBC, Loew's Corp., Scholastic, Inc., N.Y. Stock Exchange, Rockefeller Found.; Past mem. bd. visitors John F. Kennedy Sch. Govt.; bd. overseers Harvard U.; mem. overseers' com. to visit Grad. Sch. Edn.; trustee, mem. adv. council Coll. Arts and Letters U. Notre Dame; bd. visitors dept. polit. sci. M.I.T.; bd. advs. Dumbarton Oaks Research Library and Collection, Woodrow Wilson Center Internat. Scholars; mem. Central Com. World Council Chs.; past mem. Nat. Hist. Publs. Commn., Nat. Commn. on Financing Post-Secondary Edn.; mem. Nat. Commn. Student Fin. Assistance, Study Nat. Needs Biomed. and Behavioral Research NRC, Nat. Acad. Sci. Com. Relations between Univs. and Govt.; bd. dirs. Am. Council Edn.; chmn. N.Y. State Coun. on Fiscal and Econ. Priorities; bd. dirs. Loews Corp., NYNEX, Scholastic Inc., Texaco Inc., Alexander S. Onassis Pub. Benefit Found., N.Y. Stock Exch., Rockefeller Found. Author: Anarcosindicalismo y revolucion en Espana, 1930-37, 1974, Washington, D.C. to Washington Square, 1986; co-author The Politics of Education: Conflict and Consensus on Capitol Hill, 1978. Bd. dirs. Aspen Inst., Berlitz Internat. Inc., Carnegie Endowment Nat. Commn. on Am. and the New World, Nat. Endowment for Democracy, Carnegie Commn. on Sci., Tech. and Govt., chmn. com. on Congress; mem. Nat. Adv. Coun. on the Pub. Svc.; bd. dirs Ctr. for Nat. Policy, chmn. exec. com.; chmn. Nat. Adv. Com. of Fighting Back; trustee U. Notre Dame, Spelman Coll.; bd. dirs. Am. Coun. for the Arts, Acad. for Ednl. Devel., Athens Coll. (Greece), Coun. to Aid Edn.; mem. Smithsonian Nat. Bd.; trustee Com. for Econ. Devel.; mem. Cons. Panel to Comptr. Gen of U.S., Bd. of Advisors of The Carter Ctr. Emory U., Carnegie Coun. on Ethics and Internat. Affairs, Trilateral Commn.; chmn.Internat. Adv. Coun. of Internat. Jewish Com. for Sepharad '92; co-chmn. Due Case Una Tradizione. Served with USNR, 1945-46. Decorated chevalier of Legion of Honor (France, High Knight Comdr. of Honor Order of the Phoenix (Greece); recipient Disting. Service award Inst. Internat. Edn., 1966, Disting. Service award NEA, 1968, Disting. Service award Tchrs. Coll., Columbia U., 1969; Merit award Nat. Council Sr. Citizens, 1972; Disting. Service award Council of State Adminstrs. of Vocat. Rehab., 1973; Disting. Service award Conservation Edn. Assn., 1974; Caritas Soc. award for outstanding contbns. in field of mental retardation, 1975; Gold Key award Am. Congress Rehab. Medicine, 1976; named Humanist of Year Nat. Assn. Humanities Edn., 1978; award for disting. service to arts AAAL, 1978; George Peabody award, 1980; Hubert H. Humphrey award Am. Polit. Sci. Assn., 1984, Ann. Gold medal The Spanish Inst., N.Y.C., 1985, Ellis Island Medal of Honor, 1986, Nat. Gov.s Assn. award, 1988, Athenagoras award for Human Rights, 1990, Gold Medal of Honor of City of Athens, 1991. Fellow Am. Acad. Arts and Scis. (coun.); mem. Am. Legion, Phi Beta Kappa (Senator) Clubs: Masons, Ahepa. Methodist. Office: NYU Office of President 53 Washington Sq S Fl 3 New York NY 10012-1098

BRADEN, MARTHA BROOKE, concert pianist, educator; b. Sturgis, Mich., July 19, 1936; d. Frederick Richard and Laura Clemens (Brooke) B.; m. Edmund Sanford Jones, Mar. 14, 1959 (div. Aug. 1983); children: Carrie Brooke, David Sanford, Christopher Braden, Charles Clemens, Mary Evelyn Reilley. Studied with Frances Oman Clark, Kalamazoo, 1942-60; student, Kalamazoo Coll., 1954-55; MusB, Westminster Choir Coll., Princeton, N.J., 1959; studied with Dr. Julius Hereford, N.Y.C., 1957-59; studied with, David Kraehenbuehl, Princeton, 1959-61, 84-97, Erno Balogh, Washington, 1976-79, Ross Lee Finney, N.Y.C., 1987-88, Madame Ming Tcherepnin, 1979-91, Madeline Bruser, 1999-2000. Cert. directress Montessori primary edn. ages 2 1/2 to 6 Washington Montessori Inst.; cert. of attendance advanced course in Montessori edn. ages 6-12 State Ctr. for Montessori Studies, Bergamo, Italy. Piano tchr. Frances Clark Studios, Kalamazoo, 1951-54; piano faculty piano and prep. depts. Westminster Choir Coll., Princeton, 1956-60; founding faculty mem. New Sch. for Music Study, Princeton, 1960-61; co-founder, Montessori primary dir. Hope Montessori Sch., Annandale, Va., 1963-68; co-founder New City Montessori Sch., Washington, 1969-74; piano faculty New Sch. for Music Study, Princeton, 1978-80; piano tchr./coach Braden Piano Studio, Washington, 1975-78, N.Y.C., 1979—. Artistic dir. The David Kraehenbuehl Soc., 2001—. Featured artist Kalamazoo Symphony, South Bend (Ind.) Symphony, 1954; recitalist (with Doris Martin) Frances Clark Piano Workshops for Piano Tchrs., nationwide, summers 1948-58; N.Y. debut solo recital Carnegie Recital Hall, 1977, Lincoln Ctr. debut solo recital Alice Tully Hall, 1980; solo recitals include Carnegie Recital Hall, N.Y.C., 1979, Abraham Goodman House, N.Y.C., 1981, Merkin Concert Hall, N.Y.C., 1984, 85, NYU Maison Francaise, 1996; artist roster Circum-Arts Found., Inc., 1999—; (recs.) Ross Lee Finney, 1988, Alexander Tcherepnin, 2002, David Kraehenbuehl, 2000, Pocketful of Music, 2003; author, pub.: (with Nancy M. Connors) David Kraehenbuehl, American Composer, 2000; editor, pub.: The Collected Works for Solo Piano by David Kraehenbuehl, 1999, Pocketful of Music, 2003; contbr. articles to Piano and Keyboard, Keyboard Companion. Performer benefit concerts UN Internat. Sch., N.Y., St. Luke's Sch., N.Y., 1999—, Kent Pl. Sch., N.J., 2002. Recipient 2d place award Bartok-Kabalevsky Internat. Piano Competition, Radford Coll., 1992; recipient Tcherepnin award Ibla Internat. Piano Competition, Ragusa, Italy, 1993; grantee concert and tchg. tour of mainland China, Ministry of Culture and Conservatories of Music/The Tcherepnin Soc., 1982, Irving S. Gilmore Found., 1987, Warren Studios, 1998.. Mem.: MENC, Montessori Internat., Nat. Assn. for Music Edn., Music Tchrs. Nat. Assn. Avocations: family, friends, forests. Office: Martha Braden Studio 780 W End Ave Apt 7A New York NY 10025-5548 E-mail: futurenote@earthlink.net.

BRADFORD, DAVID FRANTZ, economist; b. Cambridge, Mass., Jan. 8, 1939; s. Mark Waldo and Matilda (Frantz) B.; m. Gunthild Klaerchen Huober, Feb. 20, 1964; children: Theodore Huober, Catherine Louise. BA magna cum laude (Nat. Merit scholar 1956-60), Amherst Coll., 1960, LHD (hon.), 1985; MS in Applied Math., Harvard U., 1962; Ford Found. dissertation fellow, Churchill Coll., Cambridge U., 1963-64; PhD in Econs, Stanford U., 1966. Econ. cons. Office Asst. Sec. of Def., Germany, Eng. and; Washington, 1964-65; acting instr. econs. Stanford U., 1965-66; asst. prof. econs. Princeton U., 1966-71, assoc. prof. econs. and public affairs, 1971-75, prof. econs. and public affairs, 1975—; assoc. dean Woodrow Wilson Sch., 1974-75, 78-80, 85-88, 89-91, acting dean, 1980, 87. Vis. prof. law Harvard U., 1991; adj. prof. Sch. Law NYU, 1993—; vis. scholar Am. Enterprise Inst., 1993; mem. Pres.'s Coun. Econ. Advisers, 1991-93; dep. asst. sec. for tax policy U.S. Treasury Dept., 1975-76; dir. rsch. in taxation Nat. Bur. Econ. Rsch., 1977-91, rsch. assoc., 1977—. Author: Blueprints for Basic Tax Reform, 1984; Untangling the Income Tax, 1986; contbr. articles to profl. jours. Vice chair N.J. State and Local Expenditure and Revenue Policy Commn., 1985-88; mem. Econ. Policy Coun. N.J., 1985-88, Nat. Commn. on R.R. Retirement Reform, 1989-90. Recipient Exceptional Svc. award U.S. Treasury Dept., 1976; Woodrow Wilson fellow Stanford U., 1960-61, Fulbright fellow Belgium, 1977, fellow Ctr. Advanced Study in Behavioral Scis., Stanford, 1988-89. Mem. Am. Econ. Assn., Econometric Soc., Nat. Tax Assn., Phi Beta Kappa. Office: Princeton U Woodrow Wilson Sch Princeton NJ 08544-1013

BRADFORD, DIANE GOLDSMITH, multimedia marketing and product consultant; b. Provo, Utah, Apr. 20, 1951; d. Howard and Roxey Faye (Rosenbaum) B.; 1 child, Tamara. BS, U. Utah, 1973, MS, 1976, PhD, 1980. Instructional design intern InterWest Regional Med. Edn. Ctr., Salt Lake City, 1979; instr. Algebra divsn. continuing edn. U. Utah, Salt Lake City, 1980-81; project tng. coord. Automated Mfg. Resource Planning Project, O.C. Tanner Co., Utah, 1981-83; data processing dir. VA Med. Ctr., Salt Lake City, 1983-85; asst. dir. tng. and publs. IHC Affiliated Svcs. Inc., Salt Lake City, 1985-88; asst. dir. edn. and tng. GTE Health Systems Inc., Moss Rehab. Hosp., Phila., 1988-89; dir. edn. Wharton exec. edn. U. Pa., Phila., 1989-92; pres. Prime Resources Inc., Aspen, Colo., 1993—. Contbr. articles to profl. jours. Awards judge Coun. Internat. Nontheatrical Events. Mem. Am. Prodn. and Inventory Control Soc. (cert., edn. v.p. 1983-84). Avocations: hiking, skiing, cycling, reading. Home and Office: 1145 Black Birch Dr Aspen CO 81611-1003 also: 255 S 38th St Philadelphia PA 19104-3706

BRADFORD, MARIAH, elementary school educator, consultant; b. Bay Springs, Miss., Sept. 23, 1929; d. Glasco Hunter Bender and Georgianna Holloway; m. Demond Bradford, Sr., Apr. 15, 1960 (div. Sept. 1984); children: Anita, Demond Jr., Kelvin. BS in Home Econs., Jackson Coll., 1953; MS in Edn., Ind. U., 1973; LHD (hon.), Martin U., 1994. Cert. tchr. Miss., 1953, Ind., 1962, Ariz., 1997. Tchr. Scott County Pub. Schs., Forest, Miss., 1953—57, Meridian Mcpl. Separate Schs., Meridian, 1957, 1959—61; county ext. agent Coop. Ext. Dept., Kosciusko, 1958—59; tchr. Ind. Pub. Schs., Indianapolis, 1963—92; sub. tchr. Peoria and Dysart Unified Schs., Peoria and El Mirage, Ariz., 1997—. Sec., bd. dirs. Martin U., Indpls., 1989—94; mem. bd. dirs. Indpls. Edn. Assn., 1970—78; mem. desegregation task force Ind. State Tchrs. Assn., Indpls., 1975—80. Contbr. poems to literary publs. and jours. (Editors' Choice award, 1996). Commr. Planning and Zoning, Surprise, Ariz., 1997—99; big sister Big Brothers/Big Sister, Indpls. and Phoenix, 1987—. Recipient Sagamore of the Wabash, State of Ind., Gov. Evan Bayh, 1994, Golden Apple award, Indpls. Power and Light Co. and Cmty. Leaders Allied for Superior Schs., 1992, Special Human Rights award, Indpls. Edn. Assn. Human Rights Com., 1963, Human Rights award, Indpls. Edn. Assn., 1993; grantee, Indpls. Pub. Schs. Found., 1986, DePauw U. and Dept. of Health Edn. and Welfare, 1977. Mem.: NAACP (life), Assn. Negro Bus. and Profl. Women's Clubs (founder, pres. Madame Walker chpt. 1979—89, Sojourner Truth award 1982), Ch. Nurses Auxiliary (first v.p., nat. missionary Bapt. Conv. Am., Svc. award 1998), Zion Rest Dist. Ch. Nurses Auxiliary (cons.), Household of Ruth (#6851, Grand United Order of Oddfellows). Democrat. Baptist. Avocations: writing, reading, traveling, sewing, volunteering. Home: 18019 N 145th Dr Surprise AZ 85374

BRADICK, ANGELLA VELVET, special education educator; b. Seattle, Sept. 5, 1945; d. George Andrew and Elizabeth Mary (Fath) B.; m. John Francis Raczkiewicz, June 28, 1986. BA, U. Pitts., 1968, MEd, 1969. Cert. tchr., Pa. Spl. edn. tchr. Allegheny Intermediate Unit, Pitts., 1969—. Mem. philosophy and goals self-study com. Brentwood H.S., 1997—, spl. edn. self-study com., 1997-98. Recipient Silver medal-Kata competition Traditional Karate Acad., 1997. Mem. NEA, Pa. State Edn. Assn., Allegheny Intermediate Edn. Assn., Allegheny Flute Assn., Tuesday Mus. Club, Nat. Mus. of Women in the Arts. Office: Brentwood High Sch 3601 Brownsville Rd Pittsburgh PA 15227-3196

BRADLEY, AUDREY LAVERNE, secondary school educator; b. Cresson, Pa., July 18, 1938; adopted d. Gerald Patrick and Audrey P. (Seabolt) Neugebauer; m. Anthony Francis Bradley, Feb. 14, 1960; children: Toni Bradley Kroko, Heather Bradley Mueller, Timothy. BA magna cum luade, St. Francis Coll., 1988, MEd, 1992, BA in English Edn., 1988. Cert. tchr., Pa.; RN, Pa. Staff nurse VA, Wilmington, Del., 1959-60, Mercy Hosp., Altoona, Pa., 1961-63, Commonwealth of Pa., Cresson, 1963-78; tchr. English Bishop Carroll High Sch., Ebensburg, Pa., 1989—; mem. faculty Upward Bound Edn. Program St. Francis Coll., Loretto, Pa., 1988—. Treas. Cresson Jaycettes, 1965; pres. PNA, Cresson, 1967. Mem. Nat. Cath. Tchrs. Assn., Delta Epsilon. Avocations: drama and theater, music, reading, writing, irish genealogy. Home: 21A Sylvan Dr Hollidaysburg PA 16648-2718

BRADLEY, DOUGLAS OLIVER, school principal; b. Richmond, Va., Dec. 29; s. Douglas O. Sr. and Dorothy (Harris) B.; m. Mary Garnett, Aug. 12, 1972. BS, Va. State U., Petersburg, 1972, MEd, 1974, CAGS, 1991; EdD, Va. Tech. U., 1996. Cert. tchr., adminstr., Va. Tchr. Petersburg Pub. Schs., 1972-90, Henrico County Schs., Richmond, 1990-91; asst. prin. Nottoway (Va.) H.S., 1991-92; prin. Nottoway Mid. Sch., 1992—. Treas. Southside Prins. Mid.-Sch. Conf., Va., 1993-94. Served as sgt. USAF, 1965-68. Recipient service and performance awards. Mem. NEA, Va. Edn. Assn., Nottoway Edn. Assn., Nat. Assn. Secondary Sch. Prins., Kappa Alpha Psi. Baptist. Avocations: basketball, softball, football, cards and ping pong. Office: Nottoway Middle Sch PO Box 93 Nottoway VA 23955-0093

BRADLEY, JOSEPH ANTHONY, education program director; b. Albany, N.Y., Mar. 10, 1952; s. John T. and Louise M. (Kuon) B.; m. Judy M. Murphy, May 23, 1987; children: Jennifer Lynn, Joseph Robert. AA, Hudson Valley C.C., 1972; BS, State U. Coll., Plattsburgh, N.Y., 1974. Coord. child support and enforcement Albany County Social Svcs., Albany, N.Y., 1974-78; program analyst N.Y. State Dept. of Mental Hygiene, Albany, 1978-79; program analyst II N.Y. State Higher Edn. Svcs. Corp., Albany, 1979-87, mgr. program rev., 1987-90, asst. dir., 1990-91, dir. program policy and instl. rev., 1991—. Mem. Ancient Order of Hibernians, Elks. Democrat. Roman Catholic. Avocations: sports, reading. Office: NY State Higher Edn Svcs Corp 99 Washington Ave Albany NY 12210

BRADLEY, LEON CHARLES, musician, educator, consultant; b. Battle Creek, Mich., Sept. 8, 1938; s. Leon Harvey and Sigrid Pearl (Anderson) B.; m. Mary Elizabeth, Dec. 23, 1968; children: Kyle Newman, Shannon Sigrid, Karl Norman, Charles Nathan. BA, Mich. State U., 1961; MM Brass Splst., 1967; postgrad., U. Okla., summer 1974, U. Wis., summer 1975. Band dir. Owosso-St. Paul, Mich., 1958-61, Hopkins (Mich.) Pub. Schs., 1961-62, Cedar Springs (Mich.) Pub. Schs., 1962-65; grad. asst. music theory-aural harmony Mich. State U., East Lansing, 1965-67; asst. prof., asst. dir. bands Minot (N.D.) State Coll., 1967-69; assoc. prof. instrumental music, music edn., dir. bands. Coll. of the Ozarks, Point Lookout, Mo., 1969-93, dept. chmn., 1987-89; ret., 1993. Clinician low brass instruments Selmer, Inc., 1979—; founder instrumental ensembles including Am. Concert Band, Xian Conservatory of Music, China, fall 1995; vis. prof. S.W. Bapt. U., 1998—. Performed with Springfield (Mo.) Symphony Orch., 1969-72, 81-98, Springfield Regional Opera Orch., 1981-98, Branson Brass Quintet, 1982—, Coll. of the Ozarks, Mozark Brass Quintet, SMSU Cmty. Band, others; dir. Abou Ben Adhem Shrine Band, 1978-80; contbr. articles to profl. jours. Condr. Republic (Mo.) Cmty. Band, 1999. Recipient Jess Cole Jazz Edn. award, Mo. Jazz Educators Assn., 2003. Mem. Coll. Band Dirs. Nat. Assn. (nat. chmn. Sacred Wind Music commn.), Music Educators Nat. Conf., Internat. Assn. Jazz Educators (state treas. 1980—), Nat. Assn. Wind and Percussion Instrs. (new music reviewer, assn. jour. 1968-71), Mo. Music Edn. Assn., Mo. Bandmasters Assn., Ducks Unltd. (mem. com. 1978-81, chmn. 1981), Masons (Scottish Rite), Shriners, Lions (pres. 1983-84), Phi Mu Alpha. Home: 119 South Dr Branson MO 65616-3708

BRADLEY, MARILYNNE GAIL, advertising executive, advertising educator; b. Rockford, Ill., Apr. 12, 1938; d. Sherwin S. and Lillian (Leopold) Gersten; m. Charles S. Bradley, 1959 (div. Feb., 1994); children: Suzanne, Scott. BFA, Washington U., 1960; MAT, Webster U., St. Louis, 1975; MFA, Syracuse U., 1981; postgrad., St. Louis Tchrs. Acad., 1990. With Essayons Studio, St. Louis, 1968-69; tchr. Webster Groves (Mo.) H.S., 1970-98; instr. Webster Univ., Webster Groves, 1973-82, 97—, supr., 2002; instr. U. Mo., 1980—, St. Louis U., 1978-99, Washington U., St. Louis, 1984-87. Sec. Mo. Art Edn., State of Mo., 1986-87; mem. Tchrs. Acad. 1990-92. Author, illustrator: Arpens and Acres, 1976, Packets on Parade, 1980, illustrator: St. Louis Silhouettes, 1977; editor: (videos) 12 Water Color Lessons, 1987, Techniques of American Watercolor, 1990, The Santa Fe Trail Series, 1993, Over Gauguin's Shoulder, 1994, Aboriginal Art Techniques, 1994, City of Century Homes, 1995, Australian Dreamings, 1996, Aboriginal Art - Past, Present and Future, 1996, Drawing and Painting Techniques, 1997, Line, Shape, Value, 1998, Molas, Snip and Sew: The Kuna Indians, Molas: Panamanian Traditions, 1999, The Katy Trail Series, 2000, Art Along the Katy Trail, 2000, Apre's Paris, 2001, Lewis and Clark Trail, 2001, It's Somewhere in St. Louis, 2002. Bd. govs. Webster Groves Hist. Soc., 1965-72, 94—, v.p., 2002—; mem. St. Louis Philharm. Soc., 1956-72; commr. City of Webster Groves, 1995—; co-chair Hist. Preservation Com., 2002. Named Tchr. of Yr., 1987, Best of Show, Mo. Watercolor Soc., 2000, Southern Watercolor Soc. Silver Brush award, award of Excellence Salute to the Masters. Mem.: Mo. Watercolor Soc. (bd. mem. 2001—), St. Louis Artist Guild (sec. 1985—86, pres. 1989—92, v.p. pres.'s coun. 1995—, Disting. Woman 1987), St. Louis Women Artists, So. Watercolor Soc. (sec. 1978—80, v.p. 2002—, chair 26th ann. exhibit, Silver Brush award, Exceptional Salute to the Masters award), Monday Club (chmn. 1979—83). Avocations: music, art, travel. Home and Office: Bradley & Assocs 817 S Gore Ave Saint Louis MO 63119-4023 E-mail: mgbrad@aol.com.

BRADLEY, RICHARD JAMES, former educational association executive; b. Waltham, Mass., Aug. 18, 1929; s. Bernard E. and Mary E. (Kennedy) B.; BS, Boston U., 1951, MEd, 1959; John Hay fellow Williams Coll., summer 1962; DScEd (hon.), Nasson Coll., 1970; LHD (hon.) Endicott Coll., 1994, Am. Coll. Greece, Deree Coll., 1994; m. Joan Marcia Dick, Dec. 27, 1952; children— Pamela, Michael, Douglas. Penny. Tchr. and prin., N.H., 1954-66; dir. evaluation commn. pub. schs New Eng. Assn. Schs. and Colls., 1966-74, exec. dir., CEO Bedford, Mass., 1974-94; pres. Dick Bradley and Assocs., Inc., Cupertino, Calif., 1995—; cons. U.S. Office of Edn., U.S. Dept. State Office Overseas Schs.; chmn. Nat. Study Sch. Evaluation, 1968-78; spkr. in field. Served in USMC, 1952-54. Mem. N.H. Prins. Assn. (pres. 1964-65), Nat. Assn. Secondary Sch. Prins. (chmn. sch. and coll. rels. com.). Roman Catholic. also: 22652 Silver Oak Ln Cupertino CA 95014-5633 E-mail: mbrad97311@aol.com.

BRADLEY, THOMAS MICHAEL, school system administrator; b. Peoria, Ill., Feb. 22, 1946; s. Thomas Marshall and Waneta Jean (Kinsall) B.; m. Janet Marie Blech, Jan. 28, 1968; children: Angela Michelle, Adam Todd. BA, Bradley U., 1968, MA, 1975; EdD, Ill. State U., 1983. Cert. tchr., bus. ofcl., adminstr., supt., Ill. Tchr. social studies Pekin (Ill.) High Sch., 1968-83, dir. instrn., 1983-88; supt. of sch. Pinckneyville (Ill.) Community High Sch., 1988-92, O'Fallon (Ill.) Twp. High Sch., 1992—. Bd. dirs. Belleville Area Spl. Edn. Dist., St. Clair County Regional Delivery Sys. for Vocat. Edn.; pres. St. Clair County Scholarship Trust. Contbr. papers to profl. publs. Elder Presbyn. Ch. USA, Ill. Synod, 1970—; mem. Pinckneyville C. of C.,1 988-92. Mem. Am. Assn. Sch. Pers. Adminstrs., Am. Assn. Sch. Adminstrs., Ill. Assn. Sch. Adminstrs., Rotary Internat., Phi Delta Kappa, Pi Sigma Alpha. Avocations: tennis, reading, trap shooting. Home: 1106 Elisabeth Dr O Fallon IL 62269-3532 Office: O'Fallon Twp High Sch 600 Smiley St O Fallon IL 62269

BRADSHAW, CYNTHIA HELENE, educational administrator; b. S.I., N.Y., May 9, 1954; d. Frederick Thomas and Audrey Helene (Stetter) B. BS in Elem. Edn., Wagner Coll., 1975; MS in Edn., U. Miami, 1979. Cert. elem. tchr., adminstr., and supr. Tchr. Young Scholars Montessori Sch., S.I., 1975-76, Luth. Schs., Mo. Synod, S.I., 1976, Hialeah and North Miami, Fla., 1976-80, Dade County Pub. Schs., Miami, Fla., 1980-88, Rahway (N.J.) Pub. Schs., Bayonne (N.J.) Pub. Schs., 1988-91; tester, field worker, classroom surveyor Prospects-Chgo., Bklyn., 1991—; prin. Christ Luth. Sch., 1997-98, Calvary Luth. Sch., 1998-99; prin. Calvary Luth. Sch. Luth Scs., Mo. Synod; prin. Balt. City Pub. Schs., 2000—. Reliability study subject Fla. Dept. Edn., Tallahassee, 1984—; participated in 3 videos in cooperation with Wagner Coll., S.I., N.Y., Bayonne (N.J.) Bd. Edn.; co-produced videos with Wagner Coll. and S.I. Continuum, 1988—. Sch. chairperson United Way, Miami, 1983—. Recipient Cert. of Recognition Dade County Pub. Schs., 1984. Mem. United Tchrs. Dade, United Tchrs. Dade Polit. Orgn., Order Ea. Star, U. Miami Sch. Edn. Allied Professions Alumni Assn. (mem. alumni telephone funding campaign 1984), Wagner Coll. Alumni Assn. (alumni telephone funding campaign 1988—), Alpha Delta Kappa. Republican. Lutheran. Avocation: music. Office: Windsor Hills Elem Sch 4001 Alto Rd Baltimore MD 21216 E-mail: CBrad45090@aol.com.

BRADSHAW, ELAINE REYNOLDS, elementary school educator; b. Nashville, Apr. 2, 1954; d. Morgan Boaz Reynolds and Margaret Sanders (Brugh) Roberts; m. Charles Edwin Bradshaw III, Aug. 9, 1975 (div. Dec. 6, 1992). BA, Mercer U., 1975; MEd, U. Ctrl. Fla., 1987. Cert. tchr., adminstrn., supervision, Fla. English tchr. Lake Highland Prep., Orlando, Fla., 1975—. Editor: (newsletter) Leaglance, 1988; asst. editor League Life, 1990; creator, editor (newsletter): Membership Matters, 1991, Jr. League, 1989. Cmty. advisor 4-H Clubs Am., Orlando, 1983-85; pub. edn. com. chmn. Am. Diabetes Assn., Orlando, 1980-81, vol., organizer, 1978-83; chmn. various coms. Jr. League Greater Orlando, 1979—, vol., organizer, 1979—; vol., organizer Orange County Cattlewomens Assn., Orlando, 1982-92. Named one of Outstanding Young Women of Am., 1985; recipient Pres.'s award Jr. League, 1990-91, Outstanding Chmn. award, 1985. Mem. ASCD. Republican. Methodist. Avocations: cooking, gardening, fishing, walking, volleyball. Office: Lake Highland Prep Sch 901 Highland Ave Orlando FL 32803-3295

BRADSHAW, JAMES R. business educator; b. Beaver, Utah, Oct. 26, 1938; s. Lafey LaVel and Ilynn (Christensen) B.; m. Jeanie Bok Dong Chung, Sept. 4, 1964; children: Scott, Lisa, Jonathan, Mibi. BSBA in Edn., CSU, Cedar City, 1968; MS in Bus. Adminstrn./Edn., Utah State U., Logan, 1969; EdD in Bus. Report Writing, Brigham Young U., 1974. Missionary, dist. supr. Latter-Day Ch. Korea, 1958-61; with Mountain Fuel Supply co., Salt Lake City, 1964-66, State Bank of So. Utah, Cedar City, 1966-68, Cache Tractor & Implement Co., 1968-69; vis. prof. MBA program Chaminade U., 1977-85; vis. lectr. Cen. Mich. U., 1983—; prof. internat. bus. Brigham Young U., Hawaii, 1969—. Lectr., presenter Japan, Korea, Hong Kong, Taiwan, Singapore, Jakarta, 1986-92, U.S., Mex., 1982-96; vis. prof. Ctrl. China Normal U., Wuhan, 1997. Contbr. articles to profl. jours. With U.S. Army, 1961-64. Decorated U.S. Army Commendation medal; recipient David L. Sargent Manhood of Yr. award, 1968, NEA Title V fellow Utah State U., 1969, David O. McKay Lectr. award, Brigham Young U., Hawaii, 1987, Disting. Teaching award, Cen. Mich. U., 1987, Outstanding Faculty of Yr. award/Bus. Div., Brigham Young U., Hawaii, 1988, Outstanding Tchr. of Yr. award/Bus. Div., 1988, 90, Disting. Scholar award Korean Acad. Internat. Commerce, 1995. Mem. Acad. Internat. Bus., Acad. Bus. Adminstrn., Nat. Bus. Edn. Assn., Am. Bus. Communications Assn., Hawaii Bus. Edn. Assn., Western Bus. Edn. Assn. Mem. Lds Ch. Avocation: family. Office: Brigham Young U PO Box 1808 Laie HI 96762

BRADSHAW, LINDA JEAN, English language educator; b. Beth Page, N.Y., Nov. 15, 1961; d. Howard Richard and Amy Elaine (Jennings) Corry and Jacque Dolores (Wheat) (stepmother) Corry; m. David Scott Waychoff, May 18, 1985 (div. Apr. 4, 1991); 1 child, Skyler Nicole Waychoff; m. Walter Claburn Bradshaw, Dec. 13, 1991; 1 child, Richard Claburn Bradshaw; 1 stepson, Benjamin Robert Bradshaw. BS in Elem. Edn., S.W. Tex. State U., 1984, MA in English, 1989. Cert. elem. tchr. and secondary tchr., Tex. Learning lab. specialist S.W. Tex. State U., San Marcos, 1984-89; tchr. Judson Ind. Sch. Dist., San Antonio, 1990; project dir. The Psychol. Corp., San Antonio, 1990-91, lang. arts cons., writer, 1991-96; instr. English, lectr. II Sinclair C.C., Dayton, Ohio, 1991-96; dir. ednl. assessments Riverside Pub., Chgo., 1996-2000, test devel. cons., 2000—. Spkr. in field, 1983—. Acting mng. editor: (jour.) Family Relations: Journal of Applied Family and Child Studies, 1993-94. Instr. New Braunfels (Tex.) Ind. Sch. Dist. Cmty. Edn., 1986-88. Recipient Future Tchr. scholarship, 1980. Mem. Nat. Coun. Tchrs. English, Coun. of Coll. Tchrs. of English, Internat. Reading Assn. Avocations: writing, reading, crafts. Office: 425 Spring Lake Dr Itasca IL 60143-2076

BRADSHAW, OTABEL, retired primary school educator; b. Magnolia, Ark., Oct. 27, 1922; d. Grover Cleveland and Mae (Staggs) Peterson; AA, Magnolia A&M Coll., 1950; BS in Edn., So. State Coll., 1953; MS in Edn., Henderson State U., 1975; postgrad. U. Ark.; PhD, Kensington U., 1983; m. Charles Howard Bradshaw, Aug. 14, 1948; children: Susan Charla, Michael Howard. Tchr., English and drama Walkers Creek Schs., Taylor Ark., 1945-46, primary grades Locust Bayou Schs., Camden, Ark., 1946-52, 2d grade Fairview Sch., Camden, 1962-73; tchr. 1st grade Harmony Grove Sch., Camden, 1973-83, coordinator Title IX, gifted children and handicapped; tchr. East Camden Accelerated Sch., 1983-96, ret., 1996; cons. econ. edn. workshop U. Ark., Fayetteville. Life mem., sec., historian chmn. bicentennial com. PTA; active vol. fund-raising drives Am. Cancer Soc., Birth Defects Soc.; leader Missionary Soc., Camden 1st United Methodist Ch.; mem. Camden and Ouachita County Library bd., 1974-77; active Boys Club Aux. Recipient Disting. Alumni Award So. Ark. U., 1981, Valley Forge Tchr. medal and George Washington Honor medal Freedom Found., 1973; Achievement citation Kazanian Found., 1969, citation for ednl. leadership Pres. of U.S., 1976, 77; profl. achievement citation Internat. Paper Co. Found., 1981. Mem. Assn. Supervision and Curriculum Devel. (speaker San Francisco conf.), NEA, Ark. Edn. Assn. (speaker 1969), Harmony Grove Edn. Assn. (pres. 1978-79), Nat. Council for Social Studies (mem. sexism com.), Am. Assn. Adminstrs., Alpha Delta Kappa (outstanding mem.). Club: Tate Park Garden (sec.). Home: 3188 Roseman Rd Camden AR 71701-5533

BRADSHAW, PETER, engineering educator; b. Torquay, Devon, Eng., Dec. 26, 1935; came to U.S., 1988; s. Joseph Newbold and Frances Winifred (Finch) B.; m. Aline Mary Rose, July 18, 1959 (div. 1968); m. Sheila Dorothy Brown, July 20, 1968. BA, Cambridge U., Eng., 1957; DSc (hon.), Exeter U., Eng., 1990. Sci. officer Nat. Phys. Lab., Teddington, Eng., 1957-69; prof. Imperial Coll. Sci. and Tech., London, 1969-88; Thomas V. Jones prof. engring. Stanford U., 1988-95, prof. emeritus, 1995—. Cons. various engring. cos. Author: Introduction to Turbulence, 1971, Momentum Transfer, 1977, Convective Heat Transfer, 1984; author nearly 200 journ. articles on aerodynamics. Recipient Bronze medal Royal Aero. Soc., London, 1971, Busk prize, 1972, Fluid Dynamics award AIAA, 1994. Fellow Royal Soc. London. Avocations: cycling, walking.

BRADSHAW, REBECCA PARKS, academic administrator; b. Chattanooga, Tenn., Dec. 10, 1928; d. Cleve and Rebecca (Brittian) Parks; m. Horace Lee Bradshaw Sr., June 22, 1951; children: Horace Lee Jr., Ronald Cleve, Rebecca Christina, Reneé Sara. BA in Math., Clark Coll., 1949; BS in Edn., D.C. Tchr.'s Coll., 1957; MA in Edn. and Psychology, Howard U., 1968; PhD, Walden U., 1981; MDiv, Howard Divinity Sch., 1992. Cert. tchr., Washington; lic. preacher Bapt. ch.; ordained to min. Bapt. ch., 1993. Census supr. U.S. Govt., Suitland, Md., 1949-59; educator Montgomery County Sch. System, Boyds, Md., 1959-63; educator, adminstr. Dist. Columbia Sch. System, Washington, 1964—. Dean of Students Washington Saturday Coll., 1975-77, dir. student tchrs. Dist. Schs., 1965-80, demonstration tchr. Author: A Descriptive Study on the Effects of Certain Patterns of Parents-Child Relationships on First Grade Readiness, Study I, 1967, Study II, 1981, My Best Friend, 1988, Let's Make a Visible Difference, 1987, Mind, Body, and Soul, 1985. Dir., prin., tchr. Shiloh Bapt. Ch. Sch., Washington, 1952-85, capt. usher bd., 1970-85; mem. Shiloh Child Devel. Ctr., Choir, co-dir. Drama Club, speaker Youth Day, leader Martha Missionary Group, leader Sunshine Circle, sec. Circle Leader's Coun.; bd. mem. Garden Resources of Washington, 1985-86; contact person N.W. Civic Assn., Washington, 1969-75, staff cons. Watkins Sch. PTA, 1965-75; life mem.; contact person, den mother Shiloh Boy Scouts Am., Washington, 1955-60; mem., dir., trainer Cultural and Acad. Programs com. of D.C. Cong. of Tchrs. and Parents; mem. Rainbow Coalition, D.C. Bapt. Conv., D.C. Bapt. Women, So. Bapt. Conv., Nat. Bapt. Conv.; mem. adv. coun. Neighborhood Learning Ctr., 1989; ednl. coord. I Dream a World, 1989; substance abuse coord., 1988-91; coord. Mayor's Citizenship award; Goding Sch. Comty. sponsor clean-up and beautification week and Maxi Arts Gola awards. Named Tchr. of Yr., D.C., 1975, Prin. of Yr., D.C., 1976; recipient Gold Dust in Shiloh award Shiloh Bapt. Ch., 1974, cert. award Washington Saturday Coll., 1975, cert. D.C. Tchrs. Conv., 1986, Outstanding and Dedicated Svc. award Watkins Sch. PTA, 1981, cert. D.C. Women's Hall of Fame/D.C. Commn. for Women, 1989, Outstanding Work in Region D Schs. award, 1988-89, Thomas L. Ayers award, 1989, World Decoration of Excellence award; fellow Waldon U., 1980. Mem. Bus. and Profl. Women (life), D.C. Edn. Assn. of Supervision and Curriculum Devel. (rec. sec.), D.C. Alliance of Black Sch. Educators, Inc., Phi Delta Kappa. Avocations: music, dance, swimming, reading, teaching. Home: 7515 16th St NW Washington DC 20012-1509

BRADT, HALE VAN DORN, physicist, x-ray astronomer, educator; b. Colfax, Wash., Dec. 7, 1930; s. Wilber Elmore and Norma (Sparlin) B.; m. Dorothy Ann Haughey, July 19, 1958; children— Elizabeth, Dorothy Ann. AB in Music, Princeton U., 1952; PhD in Physics, MIT, 1961. Mem. dept. physics MIT, 1961—, prof., 1972-2001, prof. emeritus, 2001—; sci. investigator Small Astronomy Satellite, NASA, 1975-79; co-prin. investigator High Energy Astronomy Obs., 1977-79; prin. investigator Rossi x-ray timing explorer ASM, 1995—2001. Co-editor: X and Gamma Ray Astronomy, 1973, The Active X-ray Sky, 1998; mem. editl. bd. Astrophys. Jour. Letters, 1974-77; auhor: Astronomy Methods, 2003. With USNR, 1952—54. Recipient Exceptional Sci. Achievement medal NASA, 1978, Buechner Tchg. prize, 1990. Mem. Am. Astron. Soc. (sec.-treas. high energy astrophysics divsn. 1973-75, chmn. 1981, Rossi prize HEAD divsn. 1999), Am. Phys. Soc., Internat. Astron. Union, Sigma Xi. Office: MIT 37-587 Cambridge MA 02139

BRADY, CHRISTINE ELLEN, education coordinator; b. Manchester, N.H., Feb. 23, 1943; d. George Lewis and Lucy Eleanor (Broderick) B. BA in English, Manhattanville Coll., 1964; MA in English, U. Pa., 1966; EdD in Curriculum and Instrn., No. Ariz. U., 1987. Cert. tchr., N.Y., Ariz., Mass.; cert. adminstr., N.Y., Ariz. English instr. Bryn Mawr (Pa.) Coll., 1966-67; lang. arts tchr. Tuba City (Ariz.) H.S., 1978-82; asst. dir. Reading/Learning Ctr., Flagstaff, Ariz., 1982-83; supervisory home living specialist Apache Agy. Dept. Indian Affairs, Whiteriver, Ariz., 1983-85; English and edn. lectr. Cortland (N.Y.) State Coll., 1988-89; asst. dir. Tchr. Ctr. Broome County, Binghamton, N.Y., 1990-91; English instr. Broome Cmty. Coll., Binghamton, N.Y., 1989-91; labor svc. rep. N.Y. State Dept. Labor, Ithaca, 1992-94; Title I lang. arts tchr. Highland Residential Ctr. N.Y. State Office Children and Family Svcs., Highland, 1994-98, edn. coord. S.I. Residential Ctr., 1998—2003; edn. supr. Arthur Kill Correctional Facility N.Y. State Dept. Corrections, Staten Island, 2003—. Mem.: AAUW, Assn. Bus. and Profl. Women, Phi Delta Kappa (exec. bd. 1998). Office: Arthur Kill Correctional Facility NY State Dept Correctional Svcs Staten Island NY 10309

BRADY, ELISA GENEVIEVE, special education educator; b. Greensburg, Pa., Feb. 10, 1959; d. Peter Victor and Elsa Maria (Barella) Bonfigli; m. Jon Patrick Brady, Mar. 17, 1984; 1 child, Elise Kathleen. BA in Psychology and Elem. Edn., Seton Hill Coll., Greensburg, 1981; MEd in Mental-Phys. Handicapped Edn., California U. Pa., 1992. Cert. tchr. early childhood, elem., mentally and/or physically handicapped, Pa. Tchr. Diocese of Greensburg, 1981-84, Greensburg-Salem Sch. Dist., 1985-87, Truxal Pre-Sch. Learning Ctr., Greensburg, 1987-88; therapist Centerville Clinics, Fredericktown, Pa., 1988-90; instr. Ctr. for Acad. Rsch. and Enhancement, California, 1991; dir. program ops. Westmoreland Human Opportunities, Greensburg, Pa., 1992—. Mem. St. Paul Sch. Bd., Greensburg, 1990-92. Mem. Coun. for Exceptional Children, Assn. for Direct Instrn., AAUW (Hall of Fame), Sigma Pi Epsilon Delta, Phi Delta Kappa, Beta Sigma Phi. Democrat. Roman Catholic. Avocations: snow skiing, reading. Home: 925 Old Salem Rd Greensburg PA 15601-1334

BRADY, JAMES JOSEPH, economics educator; b. Jersey City, Mar. 2, 1936; s. James and Anna (Shine) B.; m. Sheila Hartney, July 24, 1965; children: Matthew, Michael, James. BA, U. Notre Dame, 1959, MA in Econs., 1963, PhD in Econs., 1969. Profl. baseball player Detroit Tigers, 1955-60; asst. prof. econs. Ind. U., South Bend, 1965-69; asst. prof., assoc. prof., prof. econs. Old Dominion U., Norfolk, Va., 1969-79; dean Coll. Arts and Scis. Jacksonville (Fla.) U., 1979-83, dean Coll. Bus., 1983-84, v.p. acad. affairs, 1984-88, pres.-elect, 1988-89, pres., 1989-95, prof. econs., 1995—. Spl. master Fla. Pub. Employees Rels. Commn., Tallahassee, 1985—; pvt. labor cons., Jacksonville, 1978-88; mem. Fed. Mediation and Conciliation Svc. Labor Panel, 1985—; perm. arbitrator State Fla. dept. mgmt. svcs., 1999-, Social Security Adminstrn. Warner-Ribbins AFB, Fla. Author: Arbitration Principles: Layoffs, 1989; co-author: Transportation Noise Pollution, 1970. With U.S. Army, 1959-61. NASA grantee, Norfolk, Va., 1970. Mem. Am. Arbitration Assn. (labor arbitrator 1965—, comml. arbitrator 1987-89), Indsl. Rels. Rsch. Assn., Soc. Profls. in Dispute Resolution, Jacksonville C. of C. (bd. dirs. 1989—). Avocations: fishing, cooking, tennis. Home: 4454 Maywood Dr Jacksonville FL 32277-1036 E-mail: leftybrady@attbi.com

BRADY, KATHLEEN DEMING, psychologist, occupational therapist, educator; b. Enid, Okla., Jan. 8, 1920; d. Leon J. and Lola Faye (Hendryx) Deming; m. Roland Anderson (dec.); children: Virginia, Leon; m. Frederick S. Brady (dec. Jan. 1999); 1 child, Faye Lillian Burnaman. Student, William & Mary Coll., 1937-38, Arts Student League, NYC, 1938-39; BS cum laude, NYU, 1943; student, Pennsylvania U., 1945, Wayne State U., 1957-59; MA in Exceptional Edn., U. Fla., 1964, EdD in Psychology and Exceptional Edn., 1967. Registered Occupational Therapist, Phila., 1945; Cert. Sch. Psychologist, Occupational Therapist, Guidance. Art tchr., N.Y., Ohio and Mich.; occupational therapist U.S. Army Hosp., 1944-45; dir. occupational therapy Perry Point V.A. Hosp., 1946-55; coord. exceptional edn. program Brevard County, Fla., 1960-64; dir. guidence and counseling Satellite H.S., Brevard County, Fla., 1965-68; dir. guidence Brevard County, 1968-69; dir. guidance and counseling Orange County, 1969; psychologist Learning Disability Ctr. and Gateway Sch., 1970-72; dir. Pupil Personnel Services, High Point, N.C., 1972-73; psychologist Exceptional Edn. Program, Orlando, Fla., 1973-78; dir. Bureau Indian Affairs Special Edn. Program, Washington, 1978-80; psychologist Western Navajo Agency, Tuba City, Ariz., B.I.A. Eastern Navajo, 1983. Tchr. Brevard C.C. Fla., 1964-68, U. Fla. Gainesville, Fla., 1966-68, Fla. Ctrl. U. Orlando, 1969, U. So. Fla. Tampa, Fla., 1971-72, Rollins Coll. Orlando, 1976-77. Author: (booklet on VA rsch.) Occupational Therapy, 1950, Reflections Poems and Pictures, 2001, Renaissance Journey Poetry Book. Pres. Brevard County Coun. Exceptional Children, Brevard County Guidance Assn.; vol., greeter program James A. Haley VA Hosp. Scholar United Cerebral Palsy, U. Fla.; recipient Outstanding Achievement award Veterans Adminstrn. Mem. Nat. Assn. State Dirs. Special Edn. Home: 4000 E Fletcher Ave C-302 Tampa FL 33613-4890 E-mail: k63007@aol.com.

BRADY, MARY ROLFES, music educator; b. St. Louis, Nov. 26, 1933; d. William Henry and Helen Dorothy (Slavick) Rolfes; m. Donald Sheridan Brady, Aug. 29, 1953; children: Joseph William, Mark David, Douglas Sheridan, John Rolfes, Todd Christopher. Student, Stanford U., 1951-54, UCLA, 1967, U. So. Calif., 1972-73; pvt. studies with, Roxanna Byers, Dorothy Desmond, and Rudolph Ganz. Pvt. piano tchr., L.A., 1955—; TV and radio performer. Pres. Jr. Philharmonic Com. L.A., 1975-76; legis. coord., bd. dirs. Philharmonic Affiliates, L.A., 1978-80. Life mem. Good Samaritan Hosp., St. Vincent Med. Ctr., L.A.; trustee St. Francis Med. Ctr., 1984-88; bd. dirs. Hollygrove-L.A. Orphans Home, Inc. Mem. Am. Coll. Musicians Club, Stanford Women's Club (past bd. dirs., pres. L.A. chpt. 1977—), The Muses, Springs Country Club.

BRADY, MARY SUE, nutrition and dietetics educator; b. Sedalia, Mo., Mar. 29, 1945; d. H. Wesley and K. Virginia (McGaw) Steele; m. Paul L. Brady, Sept. 2, 1967; 1 child, Chad W. BA, Marian Coll., Indpls., 1968; MS, Ind. U., Indpls., 1970, DMSc, 1987. Registered dietitian; cert. specialist in pediatric nutrition Am. Dietetic Assn. Pediatric dietitian J.W. Riley Hosp. Children, Ind. U. Sch. Medicine, Indpls., 1970-75, acting dir. pediatric nutrition, 1975-78, 80-82, neonatal dietitian, 1978-80, dir. pediatric nutrition, 1982-96. Asst. prof. Ind. U. Sch. Medicine, Indpls., 1975-88, assoc. prof., 1988-96, prof. 1996—. Contbr. articles to Jour. of Am. Dietetic Assn., Pediatric Pulmonology, Jour. of Pediatrics. Recipient Excellence in Svc. award Ind. U. Sch. Medicine, Sch. Allied Health Scis., 1994, Glenn W. Irwin Jr. Experience Excellence Recognition award IUPUI, 1994, Disting. Alumni award Marian Coll., 1998, Outstanding Educator's award Ind. Dietetic Assn. and Am. Dietetic Assn., 1999. Fellow Am. Dietetic Assn. (charter mem., Excellence in Practice of Clin. Nutrition award 1991, Pediat. Nutrition Practice Group Outstanding Mem. of Yr. 1994, Outstanding Educators award Area 5 Am. Dietetic Assn. and Ind. Dietetic Assn., 1999); mem. Sigma Xi. Office: Ind U Med Ctr Nutrition & Dietetics Ball Residence Hall Rm 112 1226 W Michigan St Indianapolis IN 46202-5212

BRADY, SHERRY SLUDER, guidance counselor; b. Campbellsville, Ky., Oct. 11, 1951; BA, Campbellsville Coll., 1977; MA, Western Ky. U., 1980, Rank I in Edn., 1982. Cert. tchr., secondary guidance, secondary adminstrn., prin. endorsement, Ky. Tchr. English and psychology Casey County High Sch., Liberty, Ky., 1977-85, guidance counselor, 1986—. Instr. psychology Somerset (Ky.) C.C., 1989, liaison acad. counselor, 1989—. Mem. Mid-Cumberland Counselor Assn. (sec.-treas. 1986-88), Ky. Assn. Sch. Adminstrs., Ky. Counselor Assn., Ky. Sch. Counselor Assn., Ky. Assn. Secondary and Coll. Admissions Counselors, Ky. Counseling Assn. (audit chair). Baptist. Avocations: reading, travel. Home: 104 Dandelion Dr Campbellsville KY 42718-3349 Office: Casey County HS 1841 E Ky 70 Liberty KY 42539-9804

BRADY, SYLVIA ELTZ, medical/surgical and pediatric nurse, educator; b. Mobile, Ala., Nov. 6, 1939; d. August and Marie (McQuillen) Eltz; m. Donald William Brady, Sept. 7, 1968; children: Marie Margaret, Donald William, Regina Ann. Diploma, St. Joseph Infirmary, Louisville, 1960; BSN, U. Ala., Tuscaloosa, 1965; MSN, U. Ala., Birmingham, 1979. Instr. South La. Tech. Coll., Houma; head nurse Mobile Infirmary, instr. pediatric nursing; asst. prof. nursing U. Mobile; ret. Mem. Sigma Theta Tau. Home: 2008 Nandina Ct Mobile AL 36693-3604

BRADY-BLACK, WANDALENE, secondary school educator; b. Oklahoma City, Aug. 16, 1938; d. Walter Jacque Brady and Mable Griffin; m. Luke J. Black, Dec. 23, 1957 (dec. 1987); children: Luke J., Eric S., Ieshia L. BS in Oral Comm., U. Ctrl. Okla., 1979. Cert. spl. edn. and oral comm. tchr. Tchr. Oklahoma City Pub. Sch. System, 1980—. Sponsor sr. and jr. classes Douglass High Sch., Oklahoma City, 1984-87, jr. class Capitol Hill High Sch., Oklahoma City, 1993; dir. Capitol Hill Intensity Performance Group, 1990—. Principal artwork includes (paintings) The Lifestyle Series, 1988; author: (short story) The Reunion, 1993. Pres. pack troop 281 Boy Scouts Am., Oklahoma City, 1972-75; deaconess Evang. Bapt. Ch., 1978—, WMU pres. 1979-82, min. edn., 1983-85, dir. activities, 1986-93; fund raiser Disabled Vets., Oklahoma City, 1989—, HIV-AIDS Found., 1991—, Am. Cancer Soc., 1992—; voter registrar Oklahoma County Bd. Elections, 1993. Mem. Alpha Kappa Alpha. Democrat. Office: Capitol Hill High Sch 500 SW 36th St Oklahoma City OK 73109-6699

BRAEUTIGAM, RONALD RAY, economics educator; b. Tulsa, Apr. 30, 1947; s. Raymond Louis Braeutigam and Loys Ann (Johnson) Henneberger; m. Janette Gail Carlyon, July 27, 1975; children: Eric Zachary, Justin Michael, Julie Ann. BS, U. Tulsa, 1969; MSc, Stanford U., 1971, PhD, 1976. Petroleum engr. Standard Oil Ind., Tulsa, 1966—70; staff economist Office of Telecomm. Policy, Exec. Office of Pres., Washington, 1972—73; from asst. to prof. econs. Northwestern U., Evanston, Ill., 1975—; dir. bus. instns. program, 1995—; Harvey Kapnick prof. Bus. Instns. dept. econs. Northwestern U., Evanston, Ill., 1990—, Charles Deering McCormick prof. tchg. excellence, 1997. Vis. prof. Calif. Inst. Tech., Pasadena, 1978-79. Co-author: The Regulation Game, 1978, Price Level Regulation for Diversified Public Utilities, 1989, Microeconomics: An Integrated Approach, 2002; assoc. editor Jour. Indsl. Econs., Cambridge, Mass., 1987-90; mem. editorial bd. MIT Press Series on Regulation, Cambridge, 1980-90, Jour. Econ. Lit., 1987-91, Rev. Indsl. Orgn., 1991—. Coach Skokie (Ill.) Indians Little League, 1985-91, Evanston Youth Baseball Assn., 1991-96. Grantee, Dept. Transp., NSF, Ameritech, Sloan Found., Mellon Found., others; sr. rsch. fellow Internat. Inst. Mgmt., Berlin, 1982-83, 91. Mem. Am. Econ. Assn., Econometric Soc., Internat. Telecommunications Soc. (bd. dirs. 1990-97), European Econ. Assn., European Assn. for Rsch. in Indsl. Econs. (exec. com. 1992—, pres. 1997-99), Soc. Petroleum Engrs. Avocations: travel, music, German lang., French lang. Home: 731 Monticello St Evanston IL 60201-1745 Office: Northwestern U Dept Econs Evanston IL 60208-0001

BRAFF, ROBERT ALAN, cardiologist, educator; b. Bronx, May 9, 1949; s. Louis and Frieda (Margolies) Braff; m. Deborah Charney, May 20, 1973; children: Danielle, Jeremy, JOhanna. BA, Lafayette Coll., Easton, Pa., 1969; MD, SUNY Downstate Med. Ctr., Bklyn., 1973. Diplomate Am. Bd. Internal Medicine, Subsplty. Bd. Cardiovascular Diseases. Intern in medicine St. Vincent's Hosp., N.Y.C., 1973—74, resident, 1974—76, attending physician in medicine, 1978—, dir. exercise lab., 1978—80, dir. noninvasive cardiology, 1980—; fellow in cardiology Georgetown U., Washington, 1976—78; clin. asst. prof. medicine NY Med. Coll., Valhalla, 1979—. Chmn. subcom. stds. coronary care units N.Y.C. Emergency Med. Svcs. Sys., 1979. Fellow: NY Cardiol. Soc., Am. Coll. Cardiology; mem.: NY State Med. Soc., Soc. Critical Care Medicine. Jewish. Office: 36 7th Ave Ste 402 New York NY 10011-6688 E-mail: rbraff@aol.com.

BRAGG, RICK ARLEN, secondary education educator; b. Augusta, Ga., Dec. 25, 1957; s. Richard A., Sr. and Shirley Ann (Starbuck) B.; m. Jane Summers, Oct. 12, 1996; children: Carter David, Chandler Eugene, Casey Ann. BS in English, St. Francis Coll., Ft. Wayne, Ind., 1986; MEd in Health Edn., U. Ala., 1998; EdS in Adminstrn., Lincoln Meml. U., 1999; PhD, U. Argosy, Sarasota, Fla., 2001; EdD in cirruculm and inst., Univ. Sarasoto, 2002. Cert. tchr., Ga.; cert. tchr. Nat. Bd. Profl. Tchg. Stds., 2002. Suspension supr. Columbia City (Ind.) Schs., 1983-86; tchr. Cherokee County Schs., Woodstock, Ga., 1987-90, chair dept. English, 1990—, yearbook advisor, newspaper advisor, 1990-95. Mem. Nat. Edn. Assn., Nat. Coun. Tchrs. English, Internat. Reading Assn., Ga. Assn. Educators, Ga. Scholastic Press Assn., Ga. Athletic Coaches Assn. (Coach of Yr. 1996), Assn. of Sec. Cirriculm Dirs. Republican. Methodist. Avocations: tennis, golf. Home: 135 Copper Ridge Dr Woodstock GA 30188-5738 Office: Cherokee County Schs 4489 Hickory Rd Canton GA 30115-4194

BRAGG, VICKI STEWART, special education educator; b. West Columbia, W.Va., Dec. 23, 1947; d. Guy Thomas and Rosella Almedia (Thomas) Stewart; m. J. Morgan Bragg, May 12, 1972. AB, Marshall U., 1970; MA, W.Va. Coll. Grad. Students, 1976. Cert. tchr. spl. edn., Mich. Trainer, facilitator Wahama High Sch., Mason, W.Va., 1970—. Mem. Spl. Edn. Program Rev. Com., Point Pleasant, W.Va., 1989—; trainer learning strategies U. Kans. Project facilitator Project Heart, Point Pleasant, 1991—. Grantee State W.Va., 1991, 92, 93. Mem. Coun. for Exceptional Children (divsn. learning disabilites, divsn. career devel.). Democrat. Avocations: reading, dancing, gardening.

BRAHMA, CHANDRA SEKHAR, civil engineering educator; b. Calcutta, India, Oct. 5, 1941; came to U.S., 1963; s. Nalinia Kanta and Uma Rani (Bose) B.; m. Purnima Sinha, Feb. 18, 1972; children: Charanjit, Barunashish. B in Engring., Calcutta U., 1962; MS, Mich. State U., 1965; PhD, Ohio State U., 1969. Registered profl. engr. Calif., Utah, N.H., Tex., Wis. Asst. engr. Pub. Works Dept., Calcutta, 1962-63; rsch. asst. Mich. State U., East Lansing, 1963-65; teaching and rsch. assoc. Ohio State U., Columbus, 1965-69; project engr. Frank H. Lehr Assocs., East Orange, N.J., 1969-70; sr. soils engr. John G. Reutter Assocs., Camden, N.J., 1970-72; asst. prof. Worcester (Mass.) Poly. Inst., 1972-74; prin. soils engr. Daniel, Mann, Johnson & Mendenhall, Balt., 1974-79; sr. engr. Sverdrup Corp., St. Louis, 1979-80, cons., 1980—; prof. Calif. State U., Fresno, 1980—2002, prof. emeritus, 2002—. Cons. Expert Resources, Inc., Peoria Heights, Ill., 1981—, The Twining Labs., Inc., Fresno, 1982—, Law Offices Marderosian and Swanson, Fresno, 1985—, Law Offices Hurlbutt, Clevenger, Long and Vortmann, Visalia, Calif., 1988—, Tech. Adv. Svcs. for Attys., Blue Bell, Pa., 1992—. Author: Fundaciones y Mechanica de Suelos, 1986; contbr. articles to profl. jours. Head sci. judge Calif. Cen. Valleys Sci. and Engring. Fairs, Fresno, 1988-2002. Recipient Outstanding Prof. of Yr. award Calif. State U., 1989, Halliburton award Calif. State U., 1991, Calif. Ctrl. Valley Outstanding Profl. Engr. award Calif. Soc. Profl. Engrs., 1993, Disting. Svc. award, 1994, Claude C. Laval Jr. award Innovative Tech. and Rsch. Calif. State U., 1991, 92, Portrait of Success award KSEE 24, Fresno, Calif., 1997, Std. of Excellence award Tau Beta Pi, 1997, Outstanding Prof. award Tau Beta Pi, 1998, Outstanding Prof. award NSPE, 1998; Brahma St. named in City of Bakersfield, Calif., 1989; Fulbright scholar, 1984; Hugh B.

William fellow, Assn. Drilled Shaft Contractors, 1986, others. Fellow ASCE (v.p. 1983-84, pres. 1984-85, Outstanding Engr. award 1985, Disting Svc. award, 1986, Outstanding Prof. award 1985, Edmund Friedman Profl. Recognition award 1993); mem. ASTM, Am. Soc. Engring. Edn. (AT&T Found. award 1991, Outstanding Tchg. award 1997, AT ANDT Found. award for excellence in tchg. and rsch. 1991), Rotary (chair Clovis club 1986—, chair pub. rels. 1987, chair youth svcs. 1989, bd. dirs. 1989). Democrat. Hindu. Avocations: swimming, tennis, music, reading. Home and Office: 561 Houston Ave Clovis CA 93611-7032 E-mail: chandrab@csufresno.edu.

BRAIDEN, ROSE MARGARET, art educator, illustrator, calligrapher; b. LA, Nov. 25, 1922; d. Sylvester and Margaret Mary (Hines) Braiden. BA, Mt. St. Marys Coll., LA; MFA, Calif. Coll. Arts and Crafts. Chmn. art dept. Bishop Montgomery HS, Torrance, Calif., 1958—68; chmn. humanities Mt. St. Mary's Coll., LA, 1968—70; prof. art Santa Barbara City Coll., 1970—. Chmn. photo art dept. Brooks Inst. Photo, 1970—82; chmn. photo dept. Cate Sch., Carpinteria, Calif., 1982—89; staff artist No. Trust Bank, 1996—. Illustrator Choices, 1983, Leah, 1986, The Mystical Ferryboat, 1986, A Mother's Journal, 1990. Founder Los Padres Water Color Soc., 1990. Named Local Hero, Los Padres Water Color Soc., 1997. Democrat. Roman Catholic. Address: 2929 Paseo Tranquillo Santa Barbara CA 93105-2932

BRAIG, BETTY, artist, educator; b. Naylor, Missouri, Apr. 21, 1932; d. Earnest R. and Polly A. (Tyson) Rideout; m. Russell C. Braig, July 27, 1951; one child, Rebecca L. AA, Phoenix Coll., 1964; BA, Ariz. State U., 1970, MA, 1973. Cert. elem. and secondary tchr., Ariz. Tchr., art gallery dir. Phoenix Union High Sch. Dist., Phoenix, 1970-92. Mem. State Adv. Com. on Visual Arts, 1976; gallery dir., South Mountain Ctr. for the Arts, Phoenix, 1988—; examiner Internat. Baccalaureate Program; tchg. art seminars and retreats, 1992 One-woman shows in various galleries; exhibiting artist: Artisimo Gallery, Scottsdale, Ariz., Visions Gallery, Chandler, Ariz.; publs. include Creative Watercolor, 1995, The Best of Watercolor II, 1997, The Best of Composition, 1998. Active Citizens Amb. Program, People to People Internat., Russia and Czechslovakia, 1992. Recipient: Asilomar Faculty Award, Watercolor West, David Gail Award, Western Fedn. Watercolor; Best of Show, Internat. Merit Award, 1998-1999. Mem. Internat. Soc. Exptl. Art, Assn. Am. Watercolor Soc., Ariz. Artist Guild (officer 1978—, Grumbacher award), Ariz. Watercolor Assn. (officer 1975—, Travel Exhbn. award 1978, 80, 83), 22-30 mem. Am. Watercolor Soc., Ariz., Classroom Tchrs. Assn., Wesatern Fedn. Watercolor Soc. Lutheran. Avocations: travel, civic projects. Home: 5271 S Desert Willow Dr Gold Canyon AZ 85218-6950

BRAILEY, SUSAN LOUISE, quality analyst, educator; b. Omaha, Aug. 28, 1939; d. James Burt and Helen Frances B.; m. Hugh Pelham Whitt, Dec. 29, 1990. BS in Edn. with distinction, U. Nebr., Omaha, 1961; postgrad., U. Nebr., Lincoln, 1977-79; MA in Comm., U. Cin., 1970. Cert. quality analyst Quality Assurance Inst., Orlando, Fla. Instr., dir. debate Omaha Pub. Schs., 1965-67; tchr. Walnut Hills H.S., Cin., 1967-69, U. Cin., 1969-72, U. Nebr., Lincoln, 1978; dir. MIS Wayne (Nebr.) State Coll., 1979-80; sr. tech. writer, analyst 1st Data Resources, Omaha, 1981-82, supr. documentation, 1982-83, tng. specialist, 1983-85, sr. analyst quality assurance, 1988-92; tng. specialist Enron Corp., Omaha, 1985-86, sr. analyst quality assurance Houston, 1986-88. Mem. Dem. Nat. Com., 1995—, Dem. Congl. Campaign Com., 2000—. Mem. AAUW, Arthritis Found., Lupus Found, Pi Kappa Delta, Phi Delta Kappa, Phi Delta Gamma. Congregationalist. Avocations: reading, antiques, bridge, music, politics. Home: 9530 Davenport St Omaha NE 68114-3872

BRAILSFORD, JUNE EVELYN, musician, educator; b. Wiergate, Tex., Apr. 11, 1939; d. Lonnie and Jessie (Coleman) Samuel; m. Marvin Delano Brailsford, Dec. 23, 1960; children: Marvin Delano, Keith, Cynthia. BA in Music, Prairie View A & M U., Tex., 1960; MA in Music, Trenton (N.J.) State Coll., 1981; postgrad., Jacksonville State U., summer 1971, Lamar U., Beaumont, Tex., summer 1963, Juilliard Sch., summer 1994. Jr. high music tchr. Lincoln Jr. High Sch., Beaumont, Tex., 1960-61; organist/choir dir. various chs., various locations, 1962-82; dir. adult edn. Morris County Human Resources, Dover, N.J., 1980-82; band and choral dir. Zweibruecken Am. High Sch., Ger., 1982-84. Vocal soloist and pianist Am. Women's Activities, Ger., 1986-87; dir. female choir U.S. Army War Coll., 1978-79, U.S. Air Force Skylarks, Sembach, Ger., 1976-77. Commr., Beaumont (Tex.) Hist. Landmark Commn., 2003; adv. bd., Conv. and Visitors Bur., Beaumont, 2003; hostess/fundraiser Quad City Symphony Guild 75th Ur., Rock Island, 1989, Links, Inc. Beautillion Scholarship, 1989, Installation Vol. Coord. Cons., Ft. Belvoir, Va., 1990-91; minister music First Bapt. Ch., Vienna, Va., 1995; bd. dirs. S.E. Tex. Cmty. Devel. Corp.; active numerous charitable orgns. Recipient Molly Pitcher award U.S. Army F.A. Officers, 1986, Outstanding Civilian Svc. award Dept. Army, 1990, Disting. Civilian Svc. award Dept. Army, 1992. Mem. NAACP (life mem.), Rock Island Arsenal Hist. Soc. (hon. mem.), The Links, Inc., Just Good Friends, Inc., Bible Study Fellowship Internat. Baptist. Avocations: bridge, bid whist, traveling, reading. Home: 7445 Prestwick Cir Beaumont TX 77707

BRAINARD, PAUL HENRY, musicologist, retired music educator; b. Binghamton, N.Y., Apr. 18, 1928; s. George E. and Frances (Weinhauer) B. BA, U. Rochester, 1949, MA, 1951; postgrad., Heidelberg (Germany) U., 1954; PhD, Goettingen (Germany) U., 1960. Research asst. Deutsches Musikgeschichtliches Archiv, Kassel, Germany, 1960; instr. music Ohio State U., 1960-61; faculty Brandeis U., Waltham, Mass., 1961-81, prof. music, 1974-81, chmn. Sch. Creative Arts, 1965-68, chmn. dept. music, 1969-72, 75-77; prof. music Princeton (N.J.) U., 1981-87, Yale Inst. Sacred Music, 1987-93; ret., 1993. Spl. research music history. Author: Le sonate per violino di Giuseppe Tartini, 1975; editor: Neue Bach-Ausgabe, Vols. II/7, 1977, II/8, 1979, I/16, 1981, Cantatas, Easter and Ascension Oratorios, Italienische Violinmusik der Barockzeit, Vols. I, 1987, II, 1988; contbr. articles to profl. jours. Served with AUS, 1951-53. Home: 7 Dover Dr Englewood FL 34223-4637

BRAITHWAITE, BARBARA J. secondary school educator; BA, Ctrl. Mich. U., 1959; MA, U. Mich., 1960. Geography tchr. grade 7 Pocono Mountain Sch. Dist., Swiftwater, Pa. Recipient 1st Place award Am. Express geography competition for tchrs., 1990, Outstanding Secondary Level Tchr. of the Year award Pa. Coun. Social Studies, 1992, Innovative Tchg. award State Farm Ins. Co., 1995. Mem. Pa. Geog. Alliance (steering com., tchr. cons.), Pocono Regional Geog. Alliance (co-founder, chairperson), Nat. Coun. Geog. Edn., Pa. Geog. Soc. (Tchr. Recognition award 1993, Pa. Tchr. of Yr. 1999). Home: 65 Stones Throw East Stroudsburg PA 18301-9694 Office: Pocono Mt Intermediate Sch Swiftwater PA 18370-0254 also: Pocono Mountain Sch Dist Swiftwater PA 18370-0200

BRAITHWAITE, MARGARET CHRISTINE, retired elementary education educator; b. Toledo, Sept. 9, 1945; d. John William and Eleanor Margaret (Gedert) B. BS in Edn., U. Toledo, 1968. Cert. pvt. glider pilot, adv. ground instr. Tchr. 1-8th Toledo Pub. Schs. Resource facilitator for project S.T.A.R., Toledo Pub. Schs. Mem.: Adrian Soaring Club (past pres.), Toledo Fedn. Ret. Tchrs., Lucas Co. Ret. Tchrs. Assn., Ohio Ret. Tchrs. Assn., Soaring Soc. Am., Women Soaring Pilots Assn., Delta Kappa Gamma (chair program of works com.). Avocations: soaring, photography. Home: 3710 Wrenwood Rd Toledo OH 43623

BRAKAS, JURGIS (GEORGE) HOEGH, philosopher, educator; b. Copenhagen, Nov. 14, 1944; arrived in U.S., 1952; s. Martin and Gunhild Hoegh (Bryoe) B. AB in phil., Princeton U., 1968; PhD in phil., Columbia U., 1984. Assoc. prof. philosophy Marist Coll., Poughkeepsie, NY, 1990—. Author: Aristotle's Concept of the Universal, 1988; contbr. articles to profl. jours. Recipient Princeton U. scholarships, 1962-68; Columbia U. fellow, 1972-74; NEH Summer Seminar participant, 2003. Mem. Am.-Scandinavian Found., Am. Phil. Assn., Ayn Rand Soc., Soc. Ancient Greek Phil. Avocations: attending ballets and concerts, films, running, weightlifting. Office: Marist Coll Dept Philosophy Fontaine Hall Poughkeepsie NY 12601 E-mail: jurgis.brakas@marist.edu.

BRAKAS, NORA JACHYM, education educator; b. Schenectady, N.Y., Aug. 9, 1952; d. Thaddeus Michael and Theresa Mary (Patnode) J.; m. Jurgis Brakas, June 15, 1996. BS in Elem. Edn., Plattsburg State U. Coll., 1974; MS in Reading, SUNY, Albany, 1977, Cert. Advanced Study in Reading, 1986, PhD in Reading, 1990. Cert. elem. sch. tchr., reading tchr. Elem. sch. and reading tchr. Lee (Mass.) Ctrl. Sch., 1976-82; reading specialist Guilderland (N.Y.) Sch. Dist., 1988-89; rsch. asst., tchg. asst. SUNY, Albany, 1985-88, instr. reading dept., 1989-90; asst. prof. tchr. edn., reading specialist Southeastern La. U., Hammond, 1990-91, Marist Coll., Poughkeepsie, N.Y., 1991—. Presenter, spkr. in field. Contbr. articles to profl. jours. Student Literacy Corp. grantee U.S. Dept. Edn., 1991, IBM/Marist Joint Study Project grantee, 1992. Mem. Internat. Reading Assn., Soc. Children's Book Writers and Illustrators. Avocations: drawing, writing children's books, collecting antique children's books. Home: PO Box 176 Rhinecliff NY 12574-0176 Office: Marist Coll 388 F Dyson Poughkeepsie NY 12601 E-mail: Nora.Brakas@Marist.edu.

BRAMANTE, FREDRICK J., JR., retail executive; b. Medford, Mass., Nov. 4, 1946; m. Elizabeth Bramante; children: Michael, Candice, Doria, Christopher. BS in Secondary Edn., Keene State Coll., 1970. Sci. tchr. Dolan Middle Sch., Stamford, Conn., 1970—76; founder Daddy's Junky Music Stores, 1972—, pres., CEO, 1972—95, CEO, chmn. bd., 1996—. Mem. N.H. State Bd. Edn., 1992—95, chmn., 2003—; bd. dirs. Salem First Corp., 1995—2000. Named Overall (Nat.) Dealer of Yr., Music and Sound Awards, 1990, Most Effective Dealer/Sound Reinforcement, 1990, Best Svc. Dept. in the U.S.A., 1994—; recipient The New Englander award, Smaller Bus. Assn. New Eng., 1989, Overall Excellence/Ops. Mgmt. award, Music and Sound Awards, 1990, Josiah Bartlett Better Govt. award, 1996, 1998, Best Industry Promotion award, Music and Sound Awards, 1997. Mem.: Am. Music Conf. (bd. dirs. 1983—93, chmn. combo segment 1983—85), Nat. Assn. Music Merchants (bd. dirs. 1984—91, sec. 1987—89, treas. 1989—91, chmn. advt. and promotions com., chmn. combo segment com., Leadership award 1987). Avocations: teaching, current events, boating, writing, public speaking. Home: 587 Bay Rd Durham NH 03824 Office: Daddys Junky Music Stores Inc 1015 Candia Rd Manchester NH 03109*

BRAME, PATTI THOMAS, middle school educator; b. Winston-Salem, N.C., Aug. 18, 1946; d. Raymond Gray and Annie Ruth (Fulk) Thomas; m. John Milam Brame, Aug. 17, 1968; children: Michael Thomas, Jonathan Neal, David Scott. BA, Guilford Coll., Greensboro, N.C., 1968; MEd, U. N.C., Greensboro, 1970. Cert. mid. sch. tchr. comm. skills, math., social studies, N.C. Tchr. Operation Head Start, Walnut Cove, N.C., summer 1968, Prince William County, Dale City, Va., 1968-69, Onslow County, Sneads Ferry, N.C., spring 1969, Morongo Dist., Yucca Valley, Calif., 1970-71, Chesterfield County, Richmond, Va., 1971-73, Surry County, Dobson, N.C., 1982—, mem. sch. improvement team, 1994-96, chmn. sch. improvement team, 1995; tchr. social studies and math. Ctrl. Middle Sch., Dobson, N.C., 1997—. Faculty advisor Battle of Books, Dobson, 1991-99; sponsor MATHCOUNTS, 1999—; participant N.C. Tchg. Acad., 1994-95. Author: Teacher Ideas, 1986, 1990; contbr. Instr. mag., 1989, 90. Ch. trustee Dobson United Meth. Ch., 1990-2002, chmn. Coun. on Ministry, 1988, mem. ch. choir, 1974—; coach for boys and girls tennis team, 1996—. Named Tchr. of Yr., Dobson Elem. Sch., 1986-87, Ctrl. Mid. Sch., 2003. Mem. NEA, N.C. Edn. Assn., Nat. Coun. Tchrs. Math. Avocations: tennis, golf, reading, travel, family activities. Home: 216 Ashley Dr Dobson NC 27017-8401 Office: Central Mid Sch PO Box 768 Dobson NC 27017-0768 E-mail: jpbrame@surry.net.

BRAMMER, BARBARA ALLISON, secondary school educator, consultant; b. Pitts., Sept. 3, 1942; d. Harry Harlan Allison and Valedina J. (Kouloumbrides) Vorkapic; m. Wetsel Jerry Brammer, Jan. 14, 1968; 1 child, Jeffrey Scott. AA, Valencia Community Coll., 1975; BS in Limnology, Fla. Tech. U., 1977; Ms in Adminstrn. and Supervision, Nova U., 1982, postgrad., 1990—. Tchr. Maynard Evans High Sch., Orlando, Fla., 1977-87; facilitator Valencia Community Coll., Orlando, 1987; tchr. Miami Killian Sr. High Sch., 1987-88, Dade County Sci. Zoo Magnet, Miami, Fla., 1988-89; facilitator Miami Dade Community coll., 1989; tchr. Homestead (Fla.) Sr. High Sch., 1989—. Cons. documentary Pub. TV, Orlando, 1982. Author: Marine Science, 1980. Bd. dirs. Butler Chain Conservation Assn., Windermere, Fla., 1983-84. Cpl. USMC, 1960-62. Mem. NSTA, Nat. Marine Educators Assn., United Tchrs. Dade, Fla. Assn. Sci. Tchrs., Fla. Marine Educators Assn. (treas. membership chmn. 1986-88, bd. dirs. 1988-91, S.E. regional bd. dirs. 1996-97, Outstanding Marine Sci. Educator award 1995-96), NOAA Tchr. in the Sea Soc., Beta Sigma Phi. Republican. Avocations: scuba diving, reading, fishing, golf, antique collecting. Home: 15022 SW 74th Pl Miami FL 33158-2139 Office: Homestead Sr High Sch 2351 SE 12th Ave Homestead FL 33034-3511

BRAMMER, BARBARA RHUDENE, retired secondary education educator; b. Dawson, Tex., Aug. 20, 1936; d. William Alpheus and Eunice (Priddy) Hargis; m. Jerry Lane Brammer, Apr. 15, 1960; children: Cathy DeLane Brammer Francis, David Wayne Brammer, Karen Ann Brammer Shelfer. BS in Secondary Edn., U. North Tex., 1958. Cert. math tchr., Tex. Tchr., coach N.W. Ind. Sch. Dist., Justin, Tex., 1957-62; tchr. math. N.W. High Sch., Justin, Tex., 1970-93, dept. head, 1984-93; tchr., coach Decatur (Tex.) Ind. Sch. Dist., 1966-68; substitute tchr. math. dept. N.W. High Sch., Justin, Tex., 1993-95. Coach Acad. Decathlon Team, World Book Ency., 1986-90; advisor Merrill Pub. Co., 1989-91. Recipient Tchr. award Tandy Computers and Tex. Christian U., 1989; named One of 300 Outstanding Tex. Tchrs., Ex Students Assn. U. Tex., Austin, 1989, One of 36 Outstanding Alumnus, Sch. Edn. U. North Tex., 1990; coach of State Champion Acad. Decathlon team, 1988. Mem. NEA, Tex. State Tchrs. Assn. (life), Tex. Ret. Tchrs. Assn., Tex. Math. Tchrs., Rhome Womens Club (pres. 1981-82). Mem. Ch. of Christ. Avocations: collecting math books, riding 4 wheeler, gardening, preserving foods, traveling. Home: 332 Private Rd # 4820 Rhome TX 76078-2217 E-mail: bbrammer@msn.com.

BRAMMER, ELIZABETH HEDWIG, administrator; b. N.Y.C., June 26, 1937; d. Joseph Patrick and Anna Dorothea (Buhner) O'Connor; m. Walter Lee Brammer, Sept. 17, 1955; children: Walter Lee Jr., Victoria Ann Arnao. BS in Elem. Edn., Monmouth Coll., 1974; student, La Salle U., 1982; MS in Spl. Edn., Monmouth Coll., 1985; EdD, Nova U., 1993. Cert. prin., supr., sch. adminstr., adaptive physical edn., reading specialist, learning specialist, youth ministry, elem. edn., tchr. of handicapped. Tchr. St. Mary's Elem. Sch., South Amboy, N.J., 1964-86; learning specialist Arthur Brisbane Child Treatment Ctr., Farmingdale, N.J., 1985-87, Monmouth County Ednl. Svcs. Commn., Eatontown, N.J., 1986-88; prin. Our Lady of Peace Elem. Sch., Fords, N.J., 1988-90; asst. dir. Gateway Sch., Carteret, N.J., 1990-91; LDTC Perth Amboy (N.J.) Pub. Schs., 1991—. Learning specialist, pvt. practice, Cliffwood Beach, N.J., 1985—; evaluator Mid-States Accreditation, Pa., 1989—. Rep. com. woman, Middlesex County; dir. religious edn., St. Lawrence Roman Cath. Ch., Lawrence Harbor, N.J., 1964-84; mem. Mayor's alt. coun., Old Bridge Libr., N.J., 1984; asst. leader Daisy Girl Scouts Am., Cliffwood Beach, N.J., 1984, leader, Girl Scouts Am., Cliffwood Beach, 1968; pres. Lawrence Harbor Little League Womans Aux., 1968. Mem. Internat. Reading Assn., NASA Ednl. Assn., N.J. Assn. Learning Cons., Assn. Supervision and Curriculum Devel., Assn. for Children with Learning Disabilities, Coun. Exceptional Children, Coop. Learning Network, Futurist Soc., Orton Soc., Phi Delta Kappa. Republican. Avocations: chess, politics, philosophy, sculpting, sci.

BRAMS, STEVEN JOHN, political scientist, educator, game theorist; b. Concord, N.H., Nov. 28, 1940; s. Nathan and Isabelle (Tryman) B.; m. Eva Floderer, Nov. 13, 1971; children: Julie Claire, Michael Jason. BS, MIT, 1962; PhD, Northwestern U., 1966. Research assoc. Inst. Def. Analyses, Arlington, Va., 1965-67; asst. prof. polit. sci. Syracuse U., 1967-69; asst. prof. NYU, 1969-73, assoc. prof., 1973-76, prof., 1976—. Vis. prof. U. Rochester, U. Pa., U. Mich., Yale U., U. Calif.-Irvine, U. Haifa, Inst. Advanced Studies, Vienna; cons. in field Author: Game Theory and Politics, 1975, Paradoxes in Politics: An Introduction to the Nonobvious in Political Science, 1976, The Presidential Election Game, 1978, Game Theory and the Hebrew Bible, 1980, rev. edit., 2003; author: (with Peter C. Fishburn) Approval Voting, 1983; author: Superior Beings: If They Exist, How Would We Know?, 1983, Superpower Games: Applying Game Theory to Superpower Conflict, 1985, Rational Politics: Decisions, Games and Strategy, 1985; author: (with D. Marc Kilgour) Game Theory and National Security, 1988; author: Negotiation Games: Applying Game Theory of Moves, 1994; author: (with A.D. Taylor) Fair Division: From Cake-Cutting to Dispute Resolution, 1996; author: The Win-Win Solution: Guaranteeing Fair Shares to Everybody, 1999; co-author: Applied Gamed Theory, 1979, Modules in Applied Mathematics: Political and Related Models, 1983; mem. editl. bd. Pub. Choice, 1973—90, Am. Polit. Sci. Rev., 1978—82, Jour. Politics, 1968—73, 1978—82, 1991—, Math. Social Scis., 1980—, Theory and Decision, 1982—, Jour. Behavioral Decision Making, 1987—90, Jour. Theoretical Politics, 1988—, Group Decision and Negotiation, 1991—, Control and Cybernetics, 1993—, Rationality and Society, 1999—, patentee in field. Social Sci. Rsch. Coun. fellow, 1964-65, Guggenheim fellow, 1986-87; Russell Sage Found. vis. scholar, 1998-99, grantee NSF, 1968-71, 73-75, 80-91, Social Sci. Rsch. Coun., 1968, Ford Found., 1984-85, Sloan Found., 1986-89, U.S. Inst. Peace, 1988-89. Fellow AAAS, Pub. Choice Soc.; mem. Am. Econ. Assn., Am. Polit. Sci. Assn., Internat. Studies Assn. (Susan Strange award 2002), Policy Studies Orgn., Peace Sci. Soc. (pres. 1990-91). Democrat. Jewish. Home: 4 Washington Square Vlg Apt 17I New York NY 10012-1910

BRANCH, BARBARA LEE, elementary education educator; b. Baton Rouge, Sept. 6, 1948; d. Robert Lee and Dorothy Lee (Niquette) B. AB, U. Calif., Davis, 1970, MA, 1976; cert. computer sci., Calif. State U., Sacramento, 1986. Cert. adminstrv. svcs., 1993. Tchr. grades 1-3 Sacramento City Unified Sch. Dist., 1970-81, curriculum and rsch. asst., 1974-90, tchr. 6th grade, 1981-90, mentor tchr., 1986—, math./computer resource specialist, 1990—; tchr. algebra Acad. Talent Search, Sacramento, 1984-86; instr. Nat. U., Sacramento, 1987—; tchr. 7th grade math. and sci. Leonardo da Vinci Sch., Sacramento, 1992-93; prin. elem. sch. Lisbon Elem. Sch., Sacramento, 1993—. Cons. math./computers, Sacramento, 1975—. Named Tchr. of Yr., Sacramento City Unified Sch. Dist., 1990-91; Woodrow Wilson fellow Princeton U. Fellow No. Calif. Math. Project; mem. Nat. Coun. Tchrs. Math., Assn. Sch. Curriculum Devel., Assn. Calif. Sch. Administrs., Math. Alliance for Access and Equity, Calif. Tchrs. Assn., PTA (hon. life). Republican. Methodist. Avocations: bicycling, golf, genealogy. Home: 9296 Linda Rio Dr Sacramento CA 95826-2250 Office: Lisbon Elem Sch 7555 S Land Park Dr Sacramento CA 95831-3863

BRANCH, LAURENCE GEORGE, health policy researcher, educator, gerontologist; b. Cleve., Oct. 31, 1944; s. John Howard and Mercedes (Brachle) B.; m. Patricia Mary Skalski, June 24, 1967; children: Kathryn Helen, Carolyn Mercedes, Daniel Laurence. BA, Marquette U., 1967; MA, Loyola U., Chgo., 1969, PhD, 1971. Program dir. Ctr. Survey Rsch., Boston, 1973-79; assoc. prof. Harvard Med. Sch., 1978-86, Harvard U. Sch. Pub. Health, 1980-86; exec. com. div. aging Harvard U. Med. Sch., 1979-86; assoc. dir. Geriatric Rsch. Edn. and Clin. Ctr. West Roxbury VA Outpatient Clinic, 1982-86; prof., chief health svcs. Boston U. Sch. Pub. Health, 1986-88; prof. Boston U. Sch. Medicine, 1986-95, Duke U. Med. Sch., 1995—. Staff GRECC Bedford VA Hosp, 1986-89; trustee, pres. North Hill Life Care Community, Wellesley, Mass., 1980-89; trustee, pres. Mercy Svcs. for Aging, Farmington Hills, Mich., 1984-89; prins. Later Life Communities, Inc., 1989-92; dir. LTC Res. Abt Assoc., Cambridge, 1989-95; assoc. dir. VA Nat. Ctr. for Health and Promotion, 1995-99; mem. profl. staff Brigham & Women's Hosp., Boston, 1981—; cons. Robert Wood Johnson Found., Princeton, N.J. Mem. editl. bd. Jour. Gerontology, 1981, Jour. Community Health, 1980, Gerontologist, 1982; editor: Jour. Aging and Health, 1988—, Gerontologist, 1999—. Lt. col. USAR, 1968—. Fellow Gerontol. Soc. Am. (sect. chmn. 1989-90); mem. AAAS, Am. Pub. Health Assn. (sect. chmn. 1983-84), Am. Psychol. Assn. Home: 3403 Medford Rd Durham NC 27705-2455 Office: Duke U Aging Ctr PO Box 3003 Durham NC 27710-0001

BRANCH, ROBERT (ROB) HARDIN, radio and television educator, broadcast executive; b. L.A., Oct. 12, 1939; s. C.H. Hardin and Erma Mae (Smith) B.; m. Judy Nilsson, Mar. 1965 (div. June 1980); children: Kirsten Giard, Kelley R.H.; m. Carol Bussy, Mar. 1990 (div. 2001); m. Marva (Myke) Bengtzen, Jan. 2002. BA, Antioch U., 1990. Radio personality Sta. KALL, 1967—70, Sta. KSL, Salt Lake City, 1970-73; asst. news dir. Sta. KOGO, San Diego, 1973-80; reporter Sta. KSDO, San Diego, 1980-84; show host Sta. KTMS, Santa Barbara, Calif., 1984-86; news dir. Sta. KVSD, Vista, Calif., 1986-88; news anchor Sta. KSDO, San Diego, 1988-90; assoc. prof. radio and TV Palomar Coll., San Marcos, Calif., 1990—; gen. mgr. KKSM, San Marcos, 1990—. Staff sgt. U.S. Army, 1958-68. Recipient Golden Mike award So. Calif. Press Assn., L.A., 1974, Alumni of Yr. award Antioch U., Santa Barbara, 1995. Mem. Soc. Profl. Journalists, Radio and TV News Dirs. Assn., San Diego Press Club (bd. dirs. 1974-76, VIP award 1976, Spot News Feature award 1976). Amnesty Internat., Smithsonian Instn., Holocaust Mus. (charter mem.). Home: 5433 Cribari Green San Jose CA 95135 E-mail: rtvprof@highstream.net.

BRAND, ELY, gynecologic surgeon, cancer surgeon, educator; b. Bern, Switzerland, Mar. 29, 1955; BS, MS magna cum laude, Yale U., 1977, MD, 1981. Diplomate Am. Bd. Ob-Gyn., Am. Bd. Gynecologic Oncology. Rotating intern Brigham and Women's Hosp.-Harvard Med. Sch., Boston, 1981-82; resident in ob-gyn. Brigham and Women's Hosp./Mass. Gen. Hosp.-Harvard U., Boston, 1982-85, Mass. Gen. Hosp., Boston, 1982-85; fellow in gynecologic oncology UCLA, 1985-87; dir. U. Colo. Sch. Medicine, Denver, 1988—93; pvt. practice, 1993. Mem. staff Rose Med. Ctr. Med. Ctr. Aurora, Porter and Littleton Hosps., Swedish Hosps., St. Anthony Hosp.; asst. prof. ob-gyn. U. Colo., Denver, dir. ob-gyn. divsn., 1988-93. Mem. ACOG, ACS, AMA, Am. Soc. Clin. Oncology, Soc. Gynecologic Oncology. Office: Denver Gynecologic Oncology 4600 Hale Pkwy Denver CO 80220-4020

BRAND, MYLES, academic administrator; b. N.Y.C., May 17, 1942; s. Irving Philip and Shirley (Berger) B.; m. Wendy Hoffman (div. 1976); 1 child: Joshua; m. Margaret Zeglin, 1978. BS, Rensselaer Poly. Inst., 1964, PhD (hon.), 1991; PhD, U. Rochester, 1967. Asst. prof. philosophy U. Pitts., 1967-72; from assoc. prof. to prof., dept. chmn. U. Ill., Chgo., 1972-81; prof., dept. head U. Ariz., Tucson, 1981-83, dir. cognitive sci. program, 1982-85, dean, social & behavioral scis., 1983-86; provost, v.p. acad. affairs Ohio State U., Columbus, 1986-89; pres. U. Oreg., Eugene, 1989-94, Ind. U., Bloomington, 1994—2002, Nat. Collegiate Athletic Assn., Indpls., 2003—. Author: Intending and Acting, 1984; editor: The Nature of Human Action, 1970, The Nature of Causation, 1976, Action Theory, 1976. Bd. dirs. Ariz. Humanities Coun., 1984-85, Am. Coun. on Edn., Washington, 1992-97. Recipient research award NEH, 1974, 79. Mem. Clarion Hosps. Assn. of Am. Phi, Assn. Am. Univs. (pres. 1999). Office: NCAA PO Box 6222 Indianapolis IN 46206

BRAND, PATRICIA ELIZABETH, secondary education educator, librarian; b. Phila., Mar. 20, 1947; d. Edward J. and Margaret (Scullin) Mahaney; m. Eric A. Brand, June 26, 1971; children: Michelle M., Gregory A., Angela J. BS, Millersville U., 1969; MS, Shippensburg U., 1993. Cert. elem. tchr., libr. sci., supr. elem. edn., elem. prin., secondary prin., Pa. 5th grade tchr. North Penn Sch. Dist., Lansdale, Pa., 1969-71; 4th grade tchr. Pine Grove Area (Pa.) Sch. Dist., 1971-76, substitute tchr., 1977-82; tchr. St. Mary Star of the Sea, Branchdale, Pa., 1982-85, St. Clair (Pa.) Cath. Sch., 1985-91; tchr., libr. Nativity B.V.M. High Sch., Pottsville, Pa., 1991—, Cardinal Brennan H.S., Ashland, Pa., 1992-93. Sr. advisor Girl Scouts U.S.A., Plymouth Meeting, Pa., 1969-71, leader, Pine Grove, Pa., 1977, 84-90; religious edn. tchr. Immaculate Conception Sch., Tremont, Pa., 1979-90. Mem. ASCD, Pa. Assn. for Supervision and Curriculum Devel., Phi Delta Kappa. Roman Catholic. Avocations: sewing, reading, swimming, hiking. Home: RR 4 Box 521 Pine Grove PA 17963-9137

BRANDES, MARGOT, humanities educator, artist; b. Zweibruecken, Germany, Dec. 9, 1930; came to U.S., 1939; d. Eleazar and Martha (Uhlfelder) Bernstein; m. Joseph Brandes, Aug. 16, 1953; children: Cheryl, Lynn Marcia, Susan Michele, Aviva Joy. BS, NYU, 1954; MS, City Coll. N.Y., 1957. Cert. tchr. grades K-8, N.Y., N.J. Instr., curriculum coord. Ramaz Acad., N.Y.C., 1955-56; instr. N.Y.C. Bd. Edn., 1956-58; instr., head tchr. Fair Lawn (N.J.) Jewish Ctr., 1959-89; instr. secular dept. Yavneh Acad., Paramus, N.J., 1968-80, Moriah Acad., Englewood, N.J., 1977-81; instr. ESL Ctr. Acad. Support William Paterson Coll., Wayne, N.J., 1981; lectr., instr. humanities dept. Bergen C.C., Paramus, 1981—. Lectr. Columbia U., N.Y.C., summers 1982, 83; cons. Ednl. Testing Svc., Princeton, N.J., 1990—; evaluator, ednl. programmer N.J. Com. for Humanities, New Brunswick, 1994; book reviewer Prentice Hall; lectr. for acad. and scholarly svc. orgns on art and Judaic sources. Author: (workbook) 'Round the Jewish Year, 1970, 'Round the Jewish Year Sequel, 1974; contbr. to lit. collection September; sculptures exhibited in various instns., including Bergen C. C., William Paterson Coll., Temple Avoda, Barnes & Noble, Radisson Hotel Princeton, Temple Emanuel, Hartford, 2002-03. Mem. regional bd., chair Hebrew Hadassah, Fair Lawn, 1985—; Yale U. archival rsch. assoc. Ramapo (N.J.) Coll., 1991—; creator coffee house for youth Fair Lawn Jewish Community Coun., 1975-78; mem. N.J. State Planning Commn., 1986—, Face Lift Community Improvement Com., End Violence Now, 1991—, N.E. Regional Conf. English, 1989—; interviewer Steven Spielberg Shoah Found., 1993-95. Recipient Scholastic Press award Scholastic Mag., 1978, Original Teaching Aids award Calif. Tchrs. Assn., 1979, State Resolution award Senate, 1988; Melton Rsch. grantee Jewish Theol. Sem., 1986; Brith Abraham fellow NYU, 1954. Mem. Jewish Fedn. North Jersey (bd. trustees, coord. 1979—). Avocations: fencing, synchronized swimming, representational art. Office: Bergen CC 400 Paramus Rd Paramus NJ 07652-1508

BRANDT, B. SHIRLEY BOSCHEE, secondary education educator; b. Lehr, N.D., May 10, 1942; d. Adam and Bertha (Kautz) Boschee; m. James Brandt, June 2, 1963 (dec. June 1994); 1 child, Dana Marie. BS, Valley City State U., 1963; MS, U. Nev., Reno, 1987. Tchr. jr. high sch. English Carson Valley Mid. Sch., Gardnerville, Nev.; tchr. English and phys. edn. Park River H.S., ND; tchr. English Douglas H.S., Minden, Nev. Named Douglas County Tchr. of Yr., 1979, Nev. Tchr. of Yr., 1979, Outstanding K-12 Tchr., Best in Edn. Reno Gazette Jour., Wal-Mart Tchr. of Yr., 2003. Mem. NEA, Nat. Coun. Tchrs. English, Nev. Edn. Assn.

BRANDT, DEBORAH, English educator; BA in English with highest distinction, Rutgers U., 1974; MA in English, Ind. U., 1981, PhD in English, 1983. Assoc. instr.dept. English Ind. U., 1979-81; asst. prof. dept. English U. Wis., Madison, 1983-90, assoc. prof. English, dir. intermediat composition dept. English, 1990—. Rep. Madison campus working group writing instrn. and assessment Alliance Undergrad. Edn., 1988-92; reviewer Harcourt Brace Jovanovich, So. Ill. U. Press, U. Wis. Press, U. Pitts. Press. Author: Literacy as Involvement: The Acts of Writers, Readers, and Texts, 1990, Literacy in American Lives, 2001; co-editor: Written Comm., 1993— (David H. Russell award Disting Rsch. Tchr. Eng. 1993); asst. editor: Coll. English, 1981-83; assoc. editor: First Labor, 1980; poetry editor: Indiana Writers, 1979; contbr. numerous chpts. to books, articles to profl. jours. Literacy vol. project Jamaa, Madison Urban League, Wis. Recipient Louisville Grawe Meyer award, 2003. Mem. Am. Fedn. Tchrs., Nat. Coun. Tchrs. English (exec. com. conf. on coll. composition and comm., Promising Researcher award 1984), Nat. Coun. Rsch. in English, Midwest Modern Lang. Assn. (Writing in Coll. sect. adv. com. 1986-89, sec., acting chair 1984-85). Office: U Wisconsin Dept English 6185 Helen C White Hall 600 N Park St Madison WI 53706*

BRANDT, IRENE HILDEGARD, retired secondary education educator; b. Meriden, Conn., June 6, 1942; d. Walter M. and Hildegard E. Brandt. BS, Ctrl. Conn. State U., 1964, cert. 6th yr. degree, 1989, MS, 1969, postgrad., 1989. Cert. 7-12 math. tchr., K-12 adminstrn. and supervision, intermediate supervision, Conn. Tchr. math. Jefferson Jr. H.S., Meriden, 1964-67, Platt H.S., Meriden, 1967-99; ret., 1999. Substitute tchr. Platt H.S. Active Summit Club, Meriden, 1972-99. Yearbook dedicated to her Platt H.S., 1971, named Oustanding Tchr. by Srs., 1990, 91, 92, 96, 98, 99, 2000. Mem. ASCD, Nat. Coun. Tchrs. Math., New Eng. Math. Tchrs. Assn., Assn. Tchrs. Math. in Conn. (conv. presider 1990-98), Am. Fedn. Tchrs., Conn. Fedn. Tchrs., Meriden Fedn. Tchrs. (sec. 1982-90). Avocations: travel, reading, crossword puzzles, gardening. Home: 70 Genest St Meriden CT 06450-4538

BRANDT, MARYCLARE, interior designer, educator; b. Winona, Minn., Aug. 30, 1950; 1 child, Laran Clare. Student, Academie de Port Royal, Paris, France, 1970-71; BA in Art, Coll. St. Teresa, Winona, 1972; MA in Interior Design, Kans. State U., 1976. Cert. interior designer, Calif. V.p., designer Environ. Concepts, San Marcos, Tex., 1980-86; owner, designer M.C. Brandt, La Jolla, Calif., 1986—. Instr. S.W. Tex. State U., San Marcos, 1985-86, U. Calif., San Diego, 1990-93, San Diego State U., 2002. Works have appeared in numerous mags. including Austin Homes and Gardens, Designer Mag., Better Homes and Gardens, also 3 books. Mem. Am. Soc. Interior Designers (bd. dirs. 1988-90, 94—, pres. San Diego chpt. 1998-99, Outstanding Design award 1990, 1st place award 1990, 2d place award 1994, 99). Office: MC Brandt Interior Design PO Box 8276 La Jolla CA 92038-8276 E-mail: mcbrandt@san.rr.com.

BRANDT, MITZI MARIANNE, retired educational specialist; b. St. Louis, Dec. 21, 1932; d. Vernon Osborn and Kathleen Louisa (Everett) Young; m. William Eugene Brandt Jr., Dec. 16, 1951; children: William Eugene III, Shelley, Susan, Shauna. BS, Wright State U., 1975, M in Reading, 1976; alphabetic phonics therapy cert., Neuhaus Edn. Ctr., Houston, 1993. Tchr. 2d grade Fairborn (Ohio) City Schs., 1975-82; tchr. 3d grade Clear Creek Ind. Sch. Dist., Clear Lake, Tex., 1982-89, ednl. specialist, 1989-93; ret., 1994; pvt. tutor dyslexic students. Mem. advanced dyslexia therapist tng. Neuhaus Edn. Ctr., Houston, 1991; tutor dyslexic children grades 3-9. Rep. Leukemia Soc. of Am., Houston, 1985-90. Mem. Tex. Tchrs. Assn. (chairperson Houston chpt. 1984-87), Clear Creek Educators Assn. (rep. 1983-86), Orton Dyslexic Soc. Avocations: reading, bicycling, crocheting, gardening, research. E-mail: Brandtdyslexia@aol.com.

BRANDT, RONALD STIRLING, retired editor, researcher; b. Neligh, Nebr., Aug. 14, 1932; s. Ferdinand B. and Ruth G. (Thornton) B.; m. Dorothy May Rice, May 13, 1951; children: Rhonda, Rebecca, Bonita. BS, U. Nebr., 1955; MA, Northwestern U., Evanston, Ill., 1960; EdD, U. Minn., 1970. Tchr. Racine (Wis.) Pub. Schs., 1957-62, prin., 1962-64; tchr., cons. No. Nigeria Tchr. Edn. Project, Maiduguri, 1965-66; program coord. Upper Midwest Regional Edn. Lab., Mpls., 1966-68; dir. staff devel. Mpls. Pub. Schs., 1968-70; assoc. supt. Lincoln (Nebr.) Pub. Schs., 1970-78; exec. editor Ednl. Leadership, Alexandria, Va., 1978-96; asst. exec. dir. ASCD, Alexandria, 1995-97; adj. faculty George Mason U., Fairfax, Va., 2003—. Co-author: Dimensions of Thinking, 1986, Dimensions of Learning, 1992, the Language of Learning, 1997; editor: Content of the Curriculum, 1988, Assessing Student Learning, 1998, Education in a New Era, 2000; author: Powerful Learning, 1998. 1st lt. U.S. Army, 1955-57. Inductee EdPress (Ednl. Press Assn.) Hall of Fame, Apr. 1996.

BRANHAM, GRADY EUGENE, principal; b. Birmingham, Ala., June 19, 1947; s. Grady B. and Pauline (Kelley) B.; m. Joy Canavan, Mar. 26, 1983; children: Joy Elizabeth, Gralynn. BS, Birmingham (Ala.) So. Coll., 1969; MEd, Montevallo (Ala.) U., 1976; PhD, U.N.A., St. Louis, 1988. Prin. Dallas Christian Sch., Selma, Ala., 1970-84, Briarwood Christian High Sch., Birmingham, Ala., 1984—. V.p. Community Concert Assn., Selma, 1980-84. Named Patriot of Yr., Patriotic Am. Youth, Jackson, Miss., 1982, Outstanding Alumnae of Yr., Jefferson State C.C., 1999. Mem. Am. Soc. Interior Design. Avocations: travel, design, music. Office: Briarwood Christian High 6255 Cahaba Valley Rd Birmingham AL 35242-4915 E-mail: gbranham@briarwood.org.

BRANHAM, MACK CARISON, JR., retired theological seminary educator, minister; b. Columbia, S.C., Apr. 20, 1931; s. Mack Carison and Laura Pauline (Sexton) Branham; m. Jennie Louise Jones, Dec. 17, 1953; children: Kenneth Gary, Charles Michael, Keith Robert, Laurie Lynn. BS, Clemson U., 1953; MDiv, Luth. Theol. Sem., 1958, STM, 1963; MS, George Washington U., 1968; PhD, Ariz. State U., 1974; DD (hon.), Newberry Coll., 1990; LLD (hon.), Clemson U., 1991. Ordained to ministry Luth. Ch., 1958. Pastor Providence Nazareth Luth. Ch., Lexington, S.C., 1958-59; commd. 2d lt. USAF, 1953, advanced through grades to col., 1959, ret., 1979; adminstrv. asst., registrar Luth. Theol. So. Sem., 1979-81, v.p. adminstrn., 1981-82, pres., 1982-92, pres. emeritus, 1992—. Instr., counselor. Editor Air Force Chaplain newsletter, 1975-77. Decorated bronze star, Legion of Merit; named to Order of Palmetto (S.C.). Mem.: Greater Chapin C. of C. (bd. dirs. 1998—2000, pres. 2000), Rotary. Lutheran. Home: 2839 Old Lexington Hwy Chapin SC 29036-7913

BRANIGAN, HELEN MARIE, educational consultant, administrator; b. Albany, N.Y., Sept. 24, 1944; d. James J. and Helen (Weaver) B. BS in Bus. Edn., Coll. St. Rose, Albany, 1967, MA in English, 1972; postgrad., SUNY, Albany, 1973-81. Tchr., chair dept. bus. edn. S. Colonie Sch. Dist., Albany, 1968-81; assoc. Bur. Bus. Edn. N.Y. State Edn. Dept., Albany, 1981-87; assoc. Bur. Occupational Edn. Program Devel., Albany, 1987-91, Bur. Occupational Edn. Innovation and Quality, Albany, 1991-93, Cen./So. Regional Field Svcs., Albany, 1993-95, North Country/Regional Field Svcs., 1995-98, Regional Sch. Improvement Team, 1998—2003; facilitator Champlain Valley Ednl. Ctr., Plattsburg, 2003—; ednl. cons. The Inst. for Learning Centered Edn., 2003—. Bd. trustees St. Catherine's Found., 1993-97; sr. cons. Internat. Ctr. for Leadership in Edn., Schenectady, N.Y., 1991—; cons. Inst. for Learner-Centered Edn., Potsdam, N.Y., 2003—; bd. dirs. Adirondack Curriculum Project, 2003—; facilitator Champlain Valley Ednl. Ctr., 2003—. Editor: Glencoe Pub., 1986—; contbr. articles to profl. jours. Lay vol. Archdiocese of Anchorage, 1967-68; mem. N.Y. State Staff Devel. Coun. Mem. ASCD, Bus. Tchrs. Assn. N.Y. State, Delta Pi Epsilon. Roman Catholic. Avocations: skiing, mountaineering, golf, reading. Home: 540 New Scotland Ave Albany NY 12208-2318 E-mail: Hbranigan@aol.com.

BRANIN, JOAN JULIA, health services management educator; b. Newark, July 20, 1944; d. Alvin Edwin and Julia (White) B. BA, Newark State Coll., 1966; MA, Calif. State U., 1970; MBA, UCLA, 1979. CFP. Tchr. Los Alamitos (Calif.) Sch. Dist., 1966-70; sales mgr. Calif. Copy Products, 1970-73; pharm. sales rep. Lederle Labs., L.A., 1973-75; med. mktg. analyst Am. Hosp. Supply, Glendale, Calif., 1975-78; corp. loan officer Security Pacific, L.A., 1978-80; v.p. First Interstate Bank, 1980-84; v.p., mgr. Std. Chartered Bank, Chgo., 1984—88; v.p. mgr. Union Bank Pvt. Banking Group, L.A., 1988—89; mgr. Chase Manhattan Pvt. Investment Bank, L.A., 1989—91; fin. planner retirement and estate planning Mass. Mut. Ins. Co., 1991-93; asst. prof. U La Verne, Calif., 1993—, chmn. grad. programs in gerontology, 1997, chmn. health svcs. mgmt. program, 1999—; dept. chair Dept. Health Svc. Mgmt., 1999—. Contbr. articles to profl. jours. Bd. dirs. Area Dance Alliance, Calif. Conf. Arts, Young Musicians Found., UCLA Internat. Student Ctr., 1983-93, Leadership Coun. United Way Med. div., 1989-93. Am. Diabetes Assn., 1989-93, Am. Heart Assn., 1990-93, Music Ctr. Unified Fund Cabinet and Spl. Gifts Com., CSULP Pres. Assocs. exec. bd., 1991-93, Chgo. chpt. Girl Scouts U.S.A., 1987-88, OxBox Summer Sch. Arts Inst., 1987-88. Recipient Disting. Alumni award Calif. State U. Long Beach, 1990, Women of Achievement award YWCA, 1999. Mem. APA, Am. Coll. Healthcare Execs., Am. Evaluation. Assn., Women Health Adminstrn., Healthcare Fin. Mgmt. Assn. (local chpt.), Soc. Behavioral Medicine, Assn. Health Svcs. Rsch., Acad. Health, Women Scholars, Internat. Assn. for Fin. Planning, Gerontol. Soc. Am., Am. Soc. Aging, Phi Kappa Phi, Pi Lambda Theta, Phi Delta Gamma, Kappa Delta Pi. Democrat. Home: 2043 Allen Ave Altadena CA 91001-3423

BRANN, EVA TONI HELENE, archaeology educator; b. Berlin, Jan. 21, 1929; came to U.S., 1942; d. Edgar and Paula (Sklarz) B. BA, Bklyn. Coll., 1950; MA, Yale U., 1951, PhD, 1956; HHD (hon.), Whitman Coll., 1995, Middlebury Coll., 1999. Instr. archaeology Stanford (Calif.) U., 1956-57; tutor St. John's Coll., Annapolis, Md., 1957—, dean, 1990-97; mem. Inst. for Advanced Study, 1958. Mem. U.S Adv. Commn. for Internat. Edn., 1975-77; vis. prof. Whitman Coll., Walla Walla, Wash., 1978-79; honors prof. U. Del., Newark, 1984-86. Author: Protoattic Pottery from the Athenian Agora, 1962, Paradoxes of Education in a Republic, 1979, The World of the Imagination, 1991, What, Then, Is Time, 1999; translator: Greek Mathematics and the Origin of Algebra, 1968; co-translator: Plato's Sophist, 1996, Plato's Phaedo, 1998. Mem. state adv. com. U.S. Commn. on Civil Rights, Md., 1988-96. Woodrow Wilson Ctr. fellow, 1976; NEH grantee, 1987. Mem. Phi Beta Kappa. Democrat. Jewish. Office: St John's Coll PO Box 2800 Annapolis MD 21404-2800

BRANNAN, CLEO ESTELLA, retired elementary education educator; b. Turon, Kans., Feb. 22, 1924; d. Jesse Logan and Nancy Elma (Cox) Zink; m. Raymond Eugene Brannan, Aug. 4, 1946 (deceased); children: Raymond Eugene Jr., Nancy Estelle, Tricia Elaine. BS, Ft. Hays State U., 1964. Cert. elem. edn. educator, Kans. Elem. tchr. Pretty Prairie (Kans.) Schs., 1943-45, Meade (Kans.) Elem. Sch., 1945-48, 58-60, 61-87, substitute secondary sch. tchr., 1987; ret., 1987. Contbr. articles to Meadowlark mag. Trustee Meade Pub. Libr., 1961-65, 90-98, rustee, treas., 1990—; state bd. dirs. Friends of Kans. Librs., 1990-96; Silver Haired legislator, 1999—. Named Kans. State Libr. Friend of the Yr., 2002. Mem. AAUW (local pres. 1985-86), Kans. Ret. Tchr. Assn. (bd. dirs. 1991-99, state pres. 1996-97), Delta Kappa Gamma. Avocations: collecting china, traveling, reading, arranging flowers. Home: PO Box 13 Meade KS 67864-0013

BRANNON, WILLIAM LESTER, JR., neurologist, educator; b. Olar, S.C., Jan. 11, 1936; s. William Lester and Lena Mae (Brigman) B.; m. Darrell Meeks, June 13, 1959; children: Debra Brannon DeMarco, William Bert, Victoria Brannon-Diaz. AB, U. S.C., 1957; MD, Med. U. S.C., 1961. Commd. ensign U.S. Navy, 1960, advanced through grades to capt., 1980; chmn. dept. neurology Nat. Naval Med. Ctr., Bethesda, Md., 1969-79; assoc. prof. neurology Georgetown U. Sch. medicine, Washington, 1969-79; prof. neurology Uniformed Svc. U. Health Scis., Bethesda, 1974-79, chmn. dept. neurology, 1978-79; dir. clin. svcs. Naval Regional Med. Ctr., Charleston, S.C., 1979-80; ret. U.S. Navy, 1980; clin. prof. neurology Med. U. S.C., Charleston, 1979-80; vice chair, dir. neurology U. S.C. Sch. Medicine, Columbia, 1980—2003, clin. prof. neurology, 2003—. Neurology cons. to attending physician U.S. Capitol and White House, 1970-79, to Surgeon Gen. U.S. Navy, 1970-79. Contbr. articles to sci. and med. reports. Fellow ACP, Am. Acad. Neurology, Am. Electroencephalography Soc. Democrat. Methodist. Avocations: tennis, photography, hiking, travel. Office: U SC Sch Medicine 3555 Harden Street Ext Columbia SC 29203-6894 E-mail: wlb@gw.mp.sc.edu.

BRANON, M. SUSAN, school system administrator; b. Milan, Tenn., Sept. 3, 1946; d. Howard Brooks and Mary Louise (Black) Branon; divorced; 1 child, Eric Dean Nelson. BS in Elem. Edn., Lambuth U., 1968; MA in Spl. Edn., Memphis State U., 1974; postgrad., Nat. Coll. of Edn., 1977-80, U. Louisville, 1982, Old Dominion U., 1985, Coll. William and Mary, 1987, U. Ctrl. Ark., 1998-99. Elem. edn. tchr., Orlando, Fla., 1968-70; tchr. learning disabilities Memphis City Sch. System, 1970-74; resource and learning disabilities tchr. Am. Dependent Schs., Fed. Republic Germany, 1974-77; team leader learning disability North Suburban Spl. Edn. Dist., 1977-80; elem. and high sch. tchr. learning disabilities Ft. Knox Ind. Sch. System, 1981-83; learning disabilities developer Norge Elem. Sch., Williamsburg, Va., 1984; learning disability resource and itinerant tchr. Williamsburg James City County Schs., 1984-86; learning disabilities resource tchr., ednl. diagnostician Matthew Whaley Elem. Sch., 1984-87; area supr. spl. edn. sect. Ark. Dept. Edn., Little Rock, 1988-94, coord. comprehensive sys. personnel devel. spl. edn., 1994—96, adminstr. state program devel., 1996—. Asst. in planning state and nat. confs. and insvc. workshops; asst. in developing state program for indirect svc. model; coop. cons. for spl. edn. dept.; program chmn. State Edn. Conf., 1992, 94; state contact for Nat. Assn. State Dirs. of Spl. Edn. ann. meeting, 1993, asst. to developing program ann. meeting, 1995; adj. prof. U. Ctrl. Ark., Conway, 2000-2002; developer paraprofl. tng. modules for Ark, 1997-2002; presenter in field. Vol. adv. Ft. Monroe's Family Mem. of the Handicapped; v.p. United Cerebral Palsy Aux., pres.; bd. dirs., past pres. Indian Hill Condo Assn.; mem. edn. com. Sunday sch. class. Mem. CEC (symposium presenter 1990, 96, sec. divsn. for learning disability Va. chpt.), Ark. Assn. Spl. Edn. Adminstrn. Avocations: entertaining, candy making, baking, walking, travel. Home: 1917 Dakota St North Little Rock AR 72116-4481 Office: Ark Dept Spl Edn 4 State Capitol Little Rock AR 72201-1011 E-mail: sbranon@arkedu.k12.ar.us.

BRANSBY, ERIC JAMES, muralist, educator; b. Auburn, N.Y., Oct. 25, 1916; s. Charles Carson and Lillian Holland (Dowsett) B.; m. Mary Antoinette Hemmie, Nov. 23, 1941; 1 dau., Fredericka Jo. Profl. cert., Kansas City Art Inst., 1938-42; BA, Colo. Coll., 1947, MA, 1949; MFA, Yale U., 1952; DFA (hon.), Park Coll., 1995; DHL (hon.), U. Colo., 1997. Instr. U. Ill., Urbana, 1950-52; asst. prof. art Western Ill. U., Macomb, 1963-65; assoc. prof. art U. Mo., Kansas City, 1965-70, prof., 1970—84, prof. emeritus, 1984—. Cons. on history and theory of mural painting. One-man shows include Okla. Art Ctr., Okla. City, 1973, U. Mo., Kans. City, 1971, 1977, Denver U., 1966, Brigham Young U., 1966, Colo. Springs (Colo.) Fine Arts Ctr., 1968, U. Mo., Columbia, 1979, Loveland Mus., Loveland, Colo., 1989, Pikes Peak Ctr., Colo. Springs, 1995, Ind. State U., Terre Haute, 1999, Colo. Springs Fine Arts Ctr., 2001, exhibited in group shows at Libr. Congress, Smithsonian Instn. (travel), N.Y. Art Students League, Nat. Ctr. for Fine Arts, Moscow, U. Sussex, Eng., N.Y. Archtl. league, murals, U.S. Command and Gen. Staff Sch., 1945, Cossitt Rotunda, Colo. Coll., Colo. Springs, 1949, U. Ill., 1953, NORAD Hdqrs., Colo. Springs, 1956, Brigham Young U., 1958, Mcpl. Bldg., Liberty, Mo., 1982 (Nat. Mural Competition award), Luth. Ch., Mo. Synod, Internat. Ctr., St. Louis, 1983 (Nat. Mural Competition award), planetarium, USAF Acad., Colo. Springs, 1961—70, Western Ill. U., Macomb, 1965, Rockhurst Coll., Kans. City, 1968, F.D. Roosevelt Meml. Competition, 1961, HUD Nat. Cmty. Art Competition, 1974, U. Mo., Kans. City, 1973—75, Mcpl. Bldg., Sedalia, Mo., 1977, Kans. State Capitol Nat. Mural Competition, 1978, St. Paul Sch., Chgo., 1985, Colo. Springs Fine Arts Ctr., 1986, Kans. State U., 1987, Loveland (Colo.) Mus., 1988, Pk. Coll., Kans. City, 1991, Colo. Springs Mus., 1994, Colo. Springs Mcpl. Airport, 1996; contbr. chpt. to book; prodr.: (video tapes in field); in permanent collections; pub.: Art Do-It. Served with inf. AUS, 1942-45. Edwin Austin Abbey Found. mural painting fellow, 1952; grantee applied and theoretical studies in mural painting field U.S., Turkey, Mex., Italy; recipient Veatch creative achievement award U. Mo., 1977, Pres. Benezet alumni achievement award Colo. Coll., 1999; repicient Pollock-Krasner Found. award, 2001-02. Mem. Nat. Soc. Mural Painters, Phi Kappa Phi. Home: 9080 S State Highway 115 Colorado Springs CO 80926-9716 Office: Univ Mo Dept Art Kansas City MO 64110

BRANSCOMB, LEWIS CAPERS, JR., librarian, educator; b. Birmingham, Ala., Aug. 5, 1911; s. Lewis Capers and Minnie Vaughn (McGehee) Branscomb; m. Marjorie Berry Stafford, Jan. 15, 1938 (dec. 1999); children: Lewis Capers III(dec.), Ralph Stafford(dec.), Carol Jean, Lawrence McGehee. Student, Birmingham-So. Coll., 1929-30; AB, Duke U., 1933; AB in Libr. Sci., U. Mich., 1939, AM in Libr. Sci., 1941; postgrad., U. Ga., 1940; PhD, U. Chgo., 1954. Clk. Young & Vann Supply Co., Birmingham, 1933-38; order libr. U. Ga., 1939-41; libr. Mercer U., 1941-42; libr., prof. libr. sci. U. S.C., 1942-44; asst. dir. pub. svc. depts., assoc. prof. libr. sci. U. Ill., 1944-48; assoc. dir. librs., prof., 1948-52; dir. librs., prof. Ohio State U., Columbus, 1952-71, prof. Thurber studies, 1971-81, prof. emeritus, 1981—. Mem. faculty compensation and benefits com. Ohio State U., 1981-90; chmn. Adv. Coun. on Libr. Svcs. and Constrn. Act, Ohio, 1967-70; cons. Punjab Agrl. U., India, 1967, Mansfield (Ohio) Pub. Libr., 1977; mem. adv. coun. Hitachi Found., 1985-88. Author: Ernest Cushing Richardson Research Librarian, Scholar, Theologian, 1993; editor: The Case for Faculty Status for Academic Librarians, 1970; contbr. articles to profl. jours. Mem. Ohio Commn. to Abolish Capital Punishment, 1960-69; bd. dirs. Ctr. for Rsch. Librs., 1953-64, mem. exec. com., 1954-56, chmn. bd. dirs., 1961-62, mem. coun., 1965-71; chmn. bd. trustees Ohio Coll. Libr. Ctr., 1968-70, vice chmn., 1970-72. Mem. AAUP (sec.-treas. U. Ill. chpt. 1947-48; sec.-treas. Ohio State U. chpt. 1948-52, pres. 1953-54; nat. council 1952-55, co-author History of the Ohio Conf. 1949-74, chmn. com. E 1979-91, mem. exec. com. 1981-91), ALA (chmn. nominating com. 1954-55), Assn. Coll. and Research Libraries (dir. 1953-55, v.p. 1957-58, pres. 1958-59), Ohio Library Assn. (chmn. coll. and univ. sect. 1952-53, chmn. library adminstrn. sect. 1969-70, chmn. local conf. com. 1970, chmn. awards and honors com. 1974-75, chmn. notable Ohio librarians com. 1978-79, award of merit 1971, Hall of Fame 1982), Franklin County Library Assn., Acad. Library Assn. Ohio, ACLU (exec. com. Central Ohio chpt. 1958-60, 64-66), Common Cause, Thurber Circle, Thurber House (bd. trustees emeritus 1985—), Friends of Ohio State U. Libraries, Ohio State U. Retirees Assn. (exec. bd. 1983-92), Beta Phi Mu (exec. council 1955-58), Sigma Alpha Epsilon. Democrat. Home: 3790 Overdale Dr Columbus OH 43220-4749 Office: Ohio State Univ Main Libr Columbus OH 43210

BRANSFIELD, JOAN, principal; Prin. Sch. St. Mary, Lake Forest, Ill. Recipient Elem. Sch. Recognition award U.S. Dept. Edn., 1989-90, Nat. Disting. Prin. award, 1998. Office: Sch of St Mary 185 E Illinois Rd Lake Forest IL 60045-1915

BRANSFORD, JOHN D. educational association administrator; BA in psychology, Hamline U., 1966; PhD in cognitive psychology, U. Minn., 1970. Assoc. prof. to prof. Vanderbilt U. Dept. Psychology, 1972—78; sr. scientist Kennedy Ctr., George Peabody Coll., 1980—; prof. George Peabody Coll. Dept. Tchg. and Learning, 1983—; centennial prof. Vanderbilt U. Dept Psychology, 1989—; co-dir. Vanderbilt U. Learning Tech. Ctr., 1984—. Contbr. articles various profl. jours. Co-chair Nat. Acad. Scis. Com.; founding dirs. Ctr. for Innovative Learning Tech. Grantee various rsch. grants. Office: Learning Tech Ctr Vanderbilt U Box 45 Peabody Bldg Rm 043 Nashville TN 37203 Office Fax: 615-343-7556. E-mail: john.bransford@vanderbilt.edu.

BRANSOME, EDWIN DAGOBERT, JR., internal medicine educator; b. N.Y.C., Oct. 27, 1933; s. Edwin Dagobert and Margaretta De Witt (Homans) B.; m. Janet Lee Williams, June 27, 1959; children: Edwin D. III, April Grace. AB, Yale U., 1954; MD, Columbia U., 1958. Intern, resident, rsch. fellow Peter Bent Brigham Hosp., Harvard Med. Sch., Boston, 1958-62; rsch. assoc. Columbia U. Coll. Physicians and Surgeons, N.Y.C., 1962-64; assoc. Scripps Clinic and Rsch. Found., LaJolla, Calif., 1964-66; from asst. prof. to assoc. prof. MIT, Cambridge, Mass., 1966-70; prof. medicine, endocrinology and physiology Med. Coll. Ga., Augusta, 1970—2000, chief sect. endocrinology and metabolism, 1999—2000, prof. emeritus, 2000—; endocrinologist CSRA Renal Svcs., Aiken, SC, 2000—. Com. mem. US Pharmacopoeia, Rockville, Md., 1976-90, trustee, 1990—, pres., 1999-2000; cons. Glaxo-SmithKline, Aventis, Accelerated Pharms., 1999—, Hoechst-Marion-Roussel, 1999—; bd. dirs. Alteon Inc. Mem. editl. bd. Diabetes Care, 2003—; contbr. articles to profl. jours. Bd. dirs. TriDevelopment Commn., Aiken, S.C., 1987-91, treas., 1989-90; bd. dirs. Am. Diabetes Assn., Alexandria, Va., 1986-88. Postdoctoral rsch. fellow NIH, 1959-61, Am. Cancer Soc., 1962-64; recipient Pub. Policy award Ga. affiliate Am. Diabetes Assn., 1990. Mem. AMA, Am. Cancer Soc. (faculty rsch. assoc. 1976-70), Endocrine Soc., others. Achievements include patent (with others) in method of predicting biological activity of compounds by DNA models. Home: 621 Magnolia St SE Aiken SC 29801-4903 Office: CSRA Renal Svcs 755 Medical Park Dr Aiken SC 29801

BRANT, DUANE JAMES, art educator; b. Grand Forks, N.D., Aug. 20, 1951; s. Russell Alan and Elizabeth Rae (Dewey) B.; m. Pip Wilson, Sept. 5, 1974. BA in Art Edn., U. Mont., 1976; MFA in Visual Art, U. Wyo., 1992. Art educator Poplar (Mont.) Mid. Sch., 1976-78, Pinedale Sch., Wyo., 1978-99; prof. Fla. Internat. U., Barry U., Miami, 2000—. Cons. for arts program North Ctrl. Assn., Wyo., 1984-86. Exhbns. include Lincoln Arts Ctr., Calif., 1989, NCECA, Phila., 1992, Tempe (Ariz.) Arts Ctr., 1993, Cesky Krumlov 1st Internat. Ceramic Exhibit, Czech Republic, 1994, Southgate Art Works, London, 1997, Dahl Arts Ctr., Rapid City, S.D., 1998, U. Wyo. Art Mus., 1999, Hoolywood (Fla.) Art Ctr., 2001. Bd. dirs. Pinedale Fine Arts Coun., 1986-88, Teton Learning Ctr., Pinedale, 1985-87, Bike Centennial, Missoula, Mont., 1975-76. Recipient Ft. Lauderdale Mus. Follies award, 1999; Fell-Oskins Fine Art scholar, 1992; Paul Stock grantee, 1992, New Art Forms grantee Nat. Endowment for Arts, 1993; Fulbright fellow, London, 1996-97, Tokyo, 1998, Wyo. Visual Arts fellow, 1997. Mem. Nat. Art Edn. Assn., Nat. Coun. on Edn. for Ceramic Arts, Wyo. H.S. Art Edn. Assn. (pres. elect 1988-89). Avocations: dressage, eventing, mountain biking, sailing, skiing. Home: 1434 Plunkett St Hollywood FL 33020-6432 Office: Fla Internat Univ University Park Miami FL 33199 E-mail: brandtd@fiu.edu.

BRANT, RAYMOND DEAN, elementary education educator; b. Iowa City, Iowa, Mar. 27, 1954; s. Herbert Willis and Beverly Jean (Christee) B. BS in Phys. Edn., U. Iowa, 1976, BA in Elem. Edn., 1980, MA in Elem. Adminstrn., 1990. Cert. tchr., coach, elem. adminstr., Iowa. Elem. tchr. phys. edn. Benton Cmty. Sch. Dist., Van Horne, Iowa, 1976-79; tchr. 5th grade Ctrl. Dallas Sch. Dist., Minburn, Iowa, 1980-85, Riverside Cmty. Sch. Dist., Oakland, Iowa, 1986—. C.H. McCloy scholar, 1976. Democrat. Avocations: jogging, golf. Home: 122 Glass St Apt C4 Oakland IA 51560-4170 Office: Riverside Elem Sch 708 Glass St Oakland IA 51560

BRANTL, SISTER CHARLESMARIE, economics educator; b. Bklyn., Apr. 30, 1929; d. Charles Justin and Edna Marie (Muir) B. BA, Albertus Magnus Coll., 1951; MA, Fordham U., 1959, PhD, 1963. Tchr. N.Y. Diocesan Sch. System, N.Y.C., 1953-61; tchr. Dominican Acad., N.Y.C., 1962-65; prof. Ohio Dominican U., Columbus, 1965-76, Albertus Magnus Coll., New Haven, 1976-90, v.p. acad. affairs, 1990—2002, dir. assessment and instnl. rsch., 2002—. Trustee Ohio Dominican U., Columbus, 1988—; arbitrator Hartford Diocese Arbitration Bd., Hartford, Conn., 1982-88; chmn. bd. dirs. INternat. Assembly Collegiate Bus. Edn., 2003—. Mem. Am. Econ. Assn., Assn. Social Econs., Ea. Econ. Soc., Dominican Order, Tau Pi Phi (nat. gov. 1986-89, trustee 1989-91). Republican. Roman Catholic. Home and Office: Albertus Magnus Coll 700 Prospect St New Haven CT 06511-1224

BRANTON, DANIEL, biology educator; b. Antwerp, Belgium, Jan. 13, 1932; came to U.S., 1941; (parents Am. citizens). AB in Math., Cornell U., 1954; MS in Pomology, U. Calif., Davis, 1957; PhD in Plant Physiology, U. Calif., Berkeley, 1961. Postdoctoral fellow ETH, Zurich, Switzerland, 1961-63; asst., assoc., full prof. botany U. Calif., Berkeley, 1963-73; Higgins prof. biology Harvard U., Cambridge, Mass., 1973—. Vis. scientist La. Molecular Biology, Cambridge, Eng., 1970-71; mem. Molecular Biology Study Sect. NIH, 1974-78. Mem. editl. bd. Jour. Molecular Biology, 1970-73, Jour. Cell Biology, 1970-73, Jour. Membrane Biology, 1973—, Protoplasma, 1973-95. Recipient N.Y. Bot. Garden prize, 1972; NIH fellow, 1959-61, NSF postdoctoral fellow, 1961-62, Miller Found. Rsch. Prof., Berkeley, 1968-69, J.S. Guggenheim fellow, 1970-71; Storer lectr. U. Calif., Davis, 1984, Disting. lectr. Roswell Park Meml. Inst., 1988. Mem. AAAS, NAS (chmn. sect. on cellular and devel. biology), Am. Acad. Arts and Scis., Biophys. Soc., Am. Soc. for Cell Biology (coun. 1972-75, pres. 1984-85), Sigma Xi. Achievements include research in cell biology, protein interactions and molecular organization of erythrocyte and other membranes, cell shape, freeze-etching techniques for electron microscopy. Office: Harvard U Molecular & Cellular Biol 16 Divinity Ave Cambridge MA 02138-2020

BRASCH, WALTER MILTON, journalist, educator; b. San Diego, Mar. 2, 1945; s. Milton and Helen (Haskin) B.; m. Ila Wales (div. 1980); m. Vivian Laughrey (div. 1982); m. Rosemary Renn, Dec. 31, 1983; children: Jeffrey Gerber, Matthew Gerber. AB in Sociology, San Diego State U., 1966; MA in Journalism, Ball State U., 1969; PhD in Mass Comm. and Journalism, Ohio U., 1974. Reporter, editor various daily newspapers, Calif., Ind., Iowa, Ohio, 1965-72; exec. dir. MID Prodns., 1971-74; asst. prof. Temple U., Phila., 1974-76; editor-in-chief Tribune Pubs., L.A., 1976-80; prof. Bloomsburg (Pa.) U., 1980—. Part-time copywriter Maushake Advt., L.A., 1974-85; media analyst Jackson-Walsh, L.A., 1975-84; media cons. to polit. and entertainment clients; media and social issues commentator United Broadcasting Network, 1995-2000; v.p. Scripts Destitute, 1996—; columnist Spectrum Features Syndicate, 1992—; PIO, exec. bd. Columbia County Emergency Mgmt. Agy., 1990—; mem. Pa. Local Emergency Planning Commn., 1995—; mem. regional task force counter terrorism, 2000-. Author: A Comprehensive Annotated Bibliography of American Black English, 1974, Black English and the Mass Media, 1981 (Choice award 1981), Columbia County Place Names, 1983, 2nd edit., 1997, Cartoon Monickers: An Insight into the Animation Industry, 1983, The Press and the State: Sociohistorical and Contemporary Interpretations, 1987 (Choice award 1988), Forerunners of Revolution: Muckrakers and the American Social Conscience, 1990, With Just Cause; Unionization and the American Journalist, 1991, Before the First Snow, 1994, Enquiring Minds and Space Aliens : Wandering Through The Mass Media and Popular Culture, 1996, Brer Rabbit, Uncle Remus and the Cornfield Journalist: The Tale of Joel Chandler Harris, 2000, The Joy of Sax: America During the Bill Clinton Era, 2001 (award Nat. Fedn. of Press Women, 2002), (with Dana Ulloth) Social Foundations of the Mass Media, 2001, Voices from the Couch, 2001, Sex and the Single Beer Can, 2003; editor: A ZIM Self-Portrait, 1988; author (play) Tremor at Sand Creek, 1971, The Face of the Battle, 1972; producer (movie) Ride the Wild Wind, 1976; author, producer In the Beginning (the Indian), 1972, Sounds of the Battle, 1973; contbr. more than 200 articles. Recipient 1st pl. award for column Press Club So. Calif., 1977, for sports, 1980, for revs., 1982, for news feature, 1984, for HM Commentary, 1984, 2nd feature, 1977, 5 awards 2002; 1st pl. award for edn. writing Pacific Coast Press Club, 1982, 2d column award Nat. Soc. Newspaper Columnists, 1995, 96, Herb Caen Meml. award, 2000, 2d col., 2001, 3rd col. award Nat. Fed. Press Women, 2d feature, 2001, 1996, 3rd Feature Story award, 1995, 3rd Feature award, 1995, Outstanding adviser coll. pub., 1996, 99, 2001, 2002, 1st journalism res award, 1997, 2002, 2nd journalism res. award, 1999, 2nd non-fiction book award, 1996, 1st nonfiction book award, 2002, 3rd chpt. in book award, 1999; 1st col. award Pa. Press Club, 1996, 98, 99, 2002, 2nd col. award, 1995, 97, 2000, 2003, 1st feature award, 1995, 96, 2nd feature award, 1997, 2002, 1st, 2002, HM social issues award, 1996, 1st, 2002, 2003, 2nd, 2001, 3rd profile award, 1999, 2nd profile award, 2000, 2nd spl. series award, 1999, 2000, 2nd edn. award, 1996, 1st govt./politics, 2003; HM bus. award, 1996, HM environ. award, 1995, 1st radio talk show award, 1998, 99, 3rd brochure award, 2000, 2nd col. award Pa. Womens Press Assn., 1998, 3rd col. award, 1997, HM, 2002; 1st opinion award Internat. Assn. Bus. Communicators, 1994, 2nd Opinion award, 1999, 2nd media kits award, 1997, San Diego State (Calif.) U., Points of Light award, 1997, 2nd articles award Pennwriters, 1998, Creative Arts award, Bloomsburg (Pa.) U., Dean's Salute to Excellence, 2002, Civil Liberties award ACLU, 1998, Spl. Merit award Lowe Syndrome Soc., 2001. Mem. Soc. Profl. Journalists (pres. Keystone State profl. chpt. 1991-98, dep. regional dir. 1995-97, Dir.'s award 1993, 2d place award for column 1993, 94, 1st pl. sports 1995, HM commentary 1996, 97, 99, 2003, 2nd commentary, 1995, 2000, Nat. Freedom Info. award 1994), Pa. Journalism Educators (pres. 1992-94), Pa. Women's Press Assn. (v.p. 2001-, award 2002), Nat. Soc. Newspaper Columnists, Nat. Writers Union, Newspaper Guild, Author's Guild, Pa. Press Club (Social Issues Reporting award, Govt. Reporting award, Arts and Entertainment Reporting award, Column and General Reporting 2d pl. award, Column and Humor 2d pl. award), Phi Kappa Phi, Kappa Tau Alpha, Alpha Kappa Delta. Jewish. Avocation: collecting political buttons and campaign items. Office: Bloomsburg U 400 E 2nd St BCH # 106 Bloomsburg PA 17815 E-mail: brasch@bloomu.edu.

BRASH, SUSAN KAY, principal; b. Valparaiso, Ind., June 17, 1950; d. Loren Lewis and Naomi Louise (Mundy) Betz; m. Richard Allen Brash, July 8, 1970; children: Jennifer Lea, Julie Christine, Jill Reneé. BS, Ind. U., 1972, MS, 1976, Edn. Specialist, 1989. Cert. adminstrn. and supervision, elem. edn. grades K-8, reading grades K-12, gifted and talented grades K-12. Tchr. grade 1 Portage (Ind.) Twp. Schs., 1971-72; adult basic edn. El-Tip-Wa Vocat., Logansport, Ind., 1976-79; reading tchr. grades 6-8 Ea. Pulaski Schs., Winamac, Ind., 1979-80, reading tchr. grades 9-12, 1980-84, gifted/talented coord., 1984-87, elem. prin., 1987-89, Met. Sch. Dist. Lawrence Twp., Indpls., 1989—. Advisor St. Vincent's Stress Ctr., Indpls., 1993—; presenter and cons. in field. Named Adminstr. of Yr., Ind. Assn. Learning Disabilities, 1990; recipient City Coun./Mayor award, 1994. Mem. ASCD, Nat. Assn. Elem. Sch. Prins. (Nat. Disting. Prin. 1995), Ind. Assn. Sch. Prins. (Ind. Prin. of Yr. 1994), Phi Delta Kappa. Baptist. Office: Met Sch Dist Lawrence Twp 7601 E 56th St Indianapolis IN 46226-1310

BRASHEAR, JOY RAMONA, secondary school educator; b. McKenzie, Tenn., Aug. 18, 1941; d. John Raymond and Lena Beth (Laney) B. BS, Bethel Coll., 1963; MA, Vanderbilt U., 1967, EdS, 1978. Cert. tchr., Tenn. Math. tchr. Grove H.S., Paris, Tenn., 1963-69, Henry County H.S., Paris, Tenn., 1970—. Bd. missions Hopewell Presbytery, N.W. Tenn., 1980-89; mem. jud. concerns com. West Tenn. Presbytery, 1990-96, mem. fin. com., 2001-03. Mem. NEA, Tenn. Tchrs. Math., Nat. Coun. Tchrs. Math., Tenn. Edn. Assn., Henry County Edn. Assn. (treas. 1979-80), Delta Kappa Gamma (pres. 1974-76, 2000-02, scholarship 1975). Avocations: reading, attending theatrical performances. Home: 160 Brashear Rd Mc Kenzie TN 38201-8849 Office: 315 S Wilson St Paris TN 38242-5053

BRASHEAR, ROBERT MARION, retired education educator, consultant; b. Memphis, Jan. 10, 1929; s. Paschal Merlin and Mary Lucile (Lewis) B.; m. Eula Fern Thigpen, Nov. 25, 1952. BS, U. Memphis, 1951; MRE, Southwestern Sem., Ft. Worth, 1956; MEd, Tex. Christian U., 1962; PhD, U. Tex., 1969. Cert. secondary tchr., Tex. Design draftsman Gen. Dynamics, Ft. Worth, 1956-60; math. tchr. Ft. Worth Ind. Sch. Dist., 1960-69; prof. edn., profl. devel. Western Mich. U., Kalamazoo, 1969-90, ret., 1991. Cons. Mich. Emergency Med. Transport, Kalamazoo, 1989—, Western Mich. U. Faculty and Students, 1970—, Nursing divsn. Wayne State U., 1972—, Nazareth Coll. Faculty Adminstrn., 1970—, Union Univ., 1992—; data cons. Reelfoot Coun., Girl Scouts Am., 1996—; adj. faculty dept. leadership Grad. Coll., U. Memphis, 1999—. Contbr. articles to profl. jours. Fund raiser Arthritis Found., Kalamazoo, 1991; bd. dirs., adv. coun. Jackson (Tenn.) Ctr. for Adult Reading Enhancement; bd. dirs., fin. com. Youth Town. With USAF, 1951-54. Mem. ASCD, Am. Ednl. Rsch. Assn., Mich. Acad. Sci., Arts and Letters. Baptist. Avocations: computing, digital photography, gardening. Home: 76 Alta Vista Dr Jackson TN 38305-3142 Office: Western Mich U Kalamazoo MI 49008-3899 E-mail: bobrash@aeneas.net.

BRASS, ERIC PAUL, internal medicine and pharmacology educator; b. Bklyn., Sept. 3, 1952; s. Edward A. and Barbara (Rosen) B.; m. Kathy E. Sietsema, Sept. 3, 1994; children: Carl, Courtney, Alexander. BSChemE, Case Western Res. U., 1974, MSChemE, 1975, PhD in Pharmacology, 1979, MD, 1980. Diplomate Am. Bd. Internal Medicine. Resident in internal medicine U. Wash., Seattle, 1980-82, fellow in clin. pharmacology, 1982-83; asst. prof. medicine and pharmacology U. Colo., Denver, 1983-89; assoc. prof. medicine and pharmacology Case Western Res. U., Cleve., 1989-93; asst. dir. Calif. Clin Trials, 1993-94; prof., chair dept. medicine Harbor-UCLA Med. Ctr., 1994—2000; dir. Harbor-UCLA Ctr. Clin. Pharm., 2000—. Contbr. articles to sci. jours. Recipient Faculty Devel. award Pharm. Mfrs. Assn. Found., 1985; NIH rsch. grantee, 1985, 88, 93. Mem. Am. Fedn. Clin. Rsch., Am. Soc. Pharmacology and Exptl. Therapeutics, Am. Soc. Clin. Pharmacology and Therapeutics (Young Investigator award 1987), Am. Soc. Clin. Investigation. Office: Harbor-UCLA Med Ctr 1124 W Carson St Torrance CA 90502-2004

BRASSELL, ROBERT JAMES, JR., small business owner; b. NYC, Jan. 24, 1972; Student, CUNY, SUNY, L.I. U. Clk. IRS, 2002; owner R.J. Bras Paperwork Svcs., 2002—; founder, CEO Process Handler et al for Hire, Inc., 2002—. Candidate for mem. Bd. Edn. South Huntington Union Free Sch. Dist., Huntington Sta., N.Y., 1997—; founding mem. Com. on Preferred Use Stimson Mid. Sch., 1996, N.Y.C., 1997; field vol. Voter Registration Drive, 1996; election inspector Bd. of Elections in Suffolk County, N.Y., 1996-2001; active Nassau Assn. Continuing/Cmty. Edn., Nassau County, N.Y., 1997—, Friends of Senator D'Amato, Mineola, N.Y., 1997—, Found. Nat. Progress, San Francisco, 1997—, Pub. Concern Found., San Francisco, 1997—, Greenlawn Civic Assn., 1998—, Friends South Huntington Pub. Libr., 1998—, Project Vote Smart, Philipsburg, Mont., 1998—, Common Cause, Washington, 1998—; adv. bd. Huntington Sta. Enrichment Ctr., 1998—; subscribing mem. Radio Sta. WBAI, N.Y.C., 1999—; bd. dirs. Election Leadership Student Govt. Assn. SUNY, Farmingdale, N.Y., 1995-96; asst. summer day camp counselor project PLAY, Town of Huntington, N.Y., 1995; student vol. music dept.; baritone sect. Voices of Walt Whitman; campaign vol. Huntington Twp. Dem. Com., 1996-98, Huntington Twp. Rep. Com., 1998—; mem. Rep. Nat. Com., 1998—, Nat. Rep. Congl. Com., 2002— Mem. ABA, NEA (N.Y. chpt.), ACLU (N.Y. chpt.), NAACP (Huntington Twp. br.), U.S. Libr. Congress Assocs. (charter mem.), Nat. Assn. for Self-Employed, L.I. Assn., U.S. C. of C., Bus. Coun. N.Y. State, Inc., Nat. Treasury Employees Union, Nat. Notary Assn., Ctr. for Def. Info. Home: 40 Lantern St Huntington NY 11743-4744 Mailing: PO Box 131 Greenlawn NY 11740-0131

BRASWELL, JACKIE BOYD, state agency administrator; b. Leon County, Fla., Feb. 15, 1938; d. Chalmer Parks and Kathryn Iris (Johnson) Boyd; m. Fletcher Braswell, Nov. 28, 1957; children: Flecia Lori, Carmen Ethelee. BS, Fla. State U., 1964; M in Ednl. Adminstrn., 1976. edn. cert. Valdosta State Coll., 1968. Lic. tchr., adminstr. Fla. single mgr., ammunition, base clothing fund, security clearance USAF, Moody AFB, 1958-61; tchr. bus. edn. Berrien H.S., Nashville, Ga., 1966-69, Rickards H.S., Tallahassee, 1970-75; bus.-vocat. tchr., chmn. dept. career edn. Lincoln H.S., Tallahassee, 1975-99; dir. ednl. affairs and policy Fla. Lottery, Tallahassee, 1999—. Co-owner, fin. mgr. Rundown Farms, Tallahassee, 1969—; pres. Eight Out Investment Group, 1993-2003; mem. Gov.'s Mentoring Initiative Lottery Mentoring Program, 1999—. Editor: In Touch, 1979-80; contbr. articles to profl. jours. Apptd. to Fla. State Bd. Pub. Schs., Gov. Fla., 1987-90, vice chmn., 1990-91, acting chmn., 1991, Fla. Commn. Edn. Reform and Accountability, 1991-93; invited del. Citizens Amb. Program People Internat., Beijing, Hangzhou, Shanghai, China, 1995; fundraising chmn. Dist. Sch. Supts. Campaign, 1996; sponsorship chair Capital Cultural Ctr., Chukker Challenge, 1997-98; spkr. Fla. Ho. Reps. Recipient Merit award Future Farmers Am., 1974; selectee Harvard Inst., 1991. Mem. Nat. Mus. Women in the Arts (charter), Nat. Bus. Edn. Assn., Fla. Vocat. Assn., Fla. Bus. Edn. Addn., Leon Vocat. Assn. (pres. elect 1987-88, pres. 1988-89), Leon Classroom Tchrs. Assn. (sec.-treas. 1987-88, chair pub. rels., parliamentarian 1988-89, govtl. rels. 1991), Dance Arts Guild, Leon County Farm Bur., Capital Gains Club (treas., 2000), Quill and Scroll, Phi Kappa Phi. Republican. Home: 7006 N Meridian Rd Tallahassee FL 32312-8017 Office: Fla Lottery 250 Marriott Dr Tallahassee FL 32399-4000

BRATRUD, LINDA KAY, secondary education educator; b. Salt Lake City, May 14, 1944; d. Milton Niels and Marian Lucy (Criswell) Peterson; m. Richard L. Settle, Sept. 10, 1965 (div. Sept. 1982); children: Courtney Settle Dodson, Dana R.; m. Jeffrey C. Bratrud, Aug. 27, 1990; children: Jennifer Bratrud Stauffacher, Jeff, John. 1st diploma, U. Grenoble, France, 1964; 2d diploma, U. Paris, 1965; BA, U. Wash., 1966; MBA, U. Puget Sound, 1987. Tchr. French, South H.S., Bakersfield, Calif., 1967-68, Peninsula H.S., Gig Harbor, Wash., 1984-93; instr. French, Tacoma C.C., 1970-71; owner bookstore Smith, Settle, Bingham & Wagner, Tacoma, 1980-82; client exec. asst. Frank Russell Co., Tacoma, 1981-84. Avocations: freelance writing, gardening, golf, tennis, cooking. Address: 353 Gran Via Palm Desert CA 92260-2169

BRATTER, THOMAS EDWARD, psychologist, educator; b. N.Y.C., May 18, 1939; s. Edward Maurice and Marjorie (Polikoff) B.; BA, Columbia Coll., 1961, MA, 1963, EdM, 1969; Columbia U., EdD, 1974; m. Carole Ann Jaffe, Aug. 25, 1963; children: Edward Philip, Barbara Ilyse. Instr. dept. health edn. Tchrs. Coll., Columbia U., N.Y.C., 1969-81; youth resources dir. Village Scarsdale (N.Y.), 1970-72; pvt. practice psychotherapy, 1970-84; dir. City Island Methadone Clinic, Bronx, N.Y., 1972-74; prof. Union Inst., Ohio, 1975-81; pres., founder John Dewey Acad., Gt. Barrington, Mass., 1984—, chmn. adv. bd., 1992—; adj. faculty continuing edn. divsn. dept. psychiatry Harvard U. Med. Sch., Boston, 1995—; cons. Dept. Probation City N.Y., 1973-77, Pan Am Commodities Corp., 1975-78, N. Castle Police Dept., 1978-88; adolescent group psychotherapy cons. Pelham (N.Y.) Guidance Council, 1973-79. Bd. dirs. Odyssey Inst., N.Y.C., 1975-77, Nat. Health Inst., Inc., 1974-76, Nat. Ind. Pvt. Schs. Assn., 1988-91; trustee Daytop Village, Inc., N.Y.C., 1972-84, Forest Inst. Profl. Psychology, Des Plaines, Ill., 1981-84, Gabelli Equity Trust (NYSE), N.Y.C., 1986—, Gabelli Multi-Media Trust, 1994—, Dewey Acad., 1991; chmn. adv. bd. John Dewey Found., 1992; troop master Boy Scouts Am., Scarsdale; varsity basketball coach Sarah Lawrence Coll., 1977-78. Served with NG, 1960-61. Mem. Am. Group Psychotherapy, Am. Psychol. Assn., Am. Assn. Marriage and Family Therapy, Am. Acad. Health Care Providers Addictive Disorders (mem. nat. adv. bd. 1992—), Small Boarding Schs. Assn. (v.p. 1992—), Kappa Delta Pi, Phi Delta Kappa. Author: (with A. Bassin and R.L. Rachin) Reality Therapy Reader, 1976; (with R. and N. Kolodny) How to Survive Your Adolescent's Adolescence, 1984, (with G. Forrest) Alcoholism and Substance Abuse: Strategies for Clinical Intervention, 1985, (with N. and R. Kolodny) Smart Choices, 1986; also over 175 articles on adolescent substance abuse and alcoholism treatment, individual and group psychotherapy and edn.; assoc. editor Jour. Drug Issues, 1970-78; mem. editorial bd. Jour. Corrective and Social Psychiatry, 1974-78, Addiction Therapist, 1975-78, Jour. Specialists in Group Work, 1975-78, Jour. of Mental Health Counseling Assn., 1979-82, Jour. Reality Therapy, 1980-85, Jour. Counseling and Devel., 1983-88, Jour. of Humanistic Education, 1989-93. Home: 53 Logan Rd Salisbury CT 06068-1513

BRATTON, IDA FRANK, retired secondary school educator; b. Glasgow, Ky., Aug. 31, 1933; d. Edmund Bates and Robbie Davis (Hume) Button; m. Robert Franklin Bratton, June 20, 1954; 1 child, Timothy Andrew. BA, Western Ky. U., 1959, MA, 1962. Cert. secondary tchr., Ky. Tchr. math. and sci. Gottschalk Jr. H.S., Louisville, 1959-65; tchr. math. Iroquois H.S., Louisville, 1965-79; tchr. Waggener H.S., Louisville, 1979-2000, chair dept. math., 2000, ret., 2000. Mem. NEA, AAUW, Ky. Edn. Assn., Jefferson County Tchrs. Assn. Democrat. Methodist. Avocations: travel, needle crafts. Home: 304 Paddington Ct Louisville KY 40222-5541 Office: Waggener High Sch 330 S Hubbards Ln Louisville KY 40207-4099

BRAUCH, MERRY RUTH MOORE, gifted education consultant; b. Hubbard, Iowa, Jan. 28, 1920; d. Orville Freneau and Jenny Leona (Thurston) Moore; m. George Pierson Brauch, June 29, 1947. BA, U. Iowa, 1939; MA, Ind. U., 1945; postgrad., Drake U., 1960-61, Western Ill. U., 1965-77. Cert. secondary tchr., spl. supr. lang. arts, Ill. Tchr. Des Moines Pub. Schs., 1954-62; tchr. to gifted, English tchr. Rock Island (Ill.) Pub. Schs., 1962-88; cons. on gifted edn., 1988—; ret. Bd. dirs. Rock Island Art Guild, 1964—, Friends of Chamber Music, 1978-82, Rock Island Pub. Libr., 1990-99, Found. Rock Island Pub. Libr., 2002-; mem. Friends of Art, Davenport Mus. Art, 1968—; tutor Literacy is for Everyone Program, 1990—. Mem. NEA (life), AAUW (br. pres. 1981-83, br. named gift Ednl. Found. 1983-84), Presbyn. Women (life), Etude Music Club (sec. 1986-89), PEO (v.p. 1989-91, pres. 1991-92), Delta Kappa Gamma, Phi Delta Kappa. Republican. Avocations: ensemble and chamber music, piano. Home: 4517 13th Ave Rock Island IL 61201-3132

BRAUDAWAY, GARY WAYNE, secondary school educator, administrator; b. Ft. Worth, Nov. 28, 1955; s. Clarence Albert and Martha Jean (Lutz) B. BA, Hardin-Simmons U., 1982; postgrad., North Tex. State U., 1983, 95; cert. ESL tchr., Tex. Wesleyan U., 1986; postgrad., Middlebury Coll., 1992, U. North Tex.; ME, U. Tex., Arlington, 1998. Cert. secondary tchr., Tex., applied learning tchr. FWISD; mid-mgmt. cert., Tex. Secondary English lang. arts tchr. Ft. Worth Ind. Sch. Dist., 1983-98, asst. prin., 1998—. Presenter Keystone Writing and Reasoning Project, Ft. Worth, 1991-96; cons. Spencer Found., Chgo., 1994, Write to Change, Clemson (S.C.) U., 1994—. Recipient Writing for the Cmty. award Bingham Trust/Clemson U., 1992, Tex. Excellence for Outstanding H.S. Tchr., U. Tex., 1993, Scholastic/Nat. Alliance of Bus. Cmty. award for excellence in edn., 1994, Ednl. Leadership award U. Tex.-Arlington, 1997. Mem. ASCD, NEA, Ft. Worth Edn. Assn., Nat. Coun. Tchrs. English, Tex. State Tchr. Assn., United Educators Assn., Tex. Assn. Secondary Sch. Prins. Baptist. Avocations: restoring classic cars and trucks, cross country running, playing hammer dulcimer and flute. Home: 7704 Trimble Dr Fort Worth TX 76134-4647 Office: Luella Merrett Elem Sch 7325 Kermit Ave Fort Worth TX 76116-9434

BRAUER, ETHEL MAY, secondary education educator; b. Thurmont, Md., June 16, 1946; d. Paul Arthur and Dorothy Virginia (Smith) Alexander; m. Alan Lee Brauer Sr., Apr. 26, 1969; children: Juliann Brauer Frantz, Alan L. Jr., Kelly Lynn. BA in Edn., Frostburg State U., 1968; postgrad., Hood Coll., 1990-92, Mt. St. Mary's Coll., 1994. Cert. social studies tchr. grades 5-12, Md. Tchr. Frederick (Md.) County Bd. Edn., 1968-70, 86-87; newspaper editor Catoctin Enterprise, Thurmont, 1980-83; tchr. social studies grades 6-8 St. John Regional Cath. Sch., Frederick, 1989—. Advisor St. John Regional Cath. Student Coun., Frederick, 1989—; mem. St. John Regional CAth. Sch. Bd., Frederick, 1993—94, Archdiocese Social Studies Curriculum Revision Com., 1994—99, Frederick County Drug-Free Schs.

Com., Newspaper in Edn. County Com. Mem. Am. Legion Aux., Thurmont, 1964—, Thurmont Grange # 409, 1970—; adult leader Thurmont Jr. Grange # 35, 1975—90. Named Young Couple of the Yr., Md. State Grange, Frederick, 1972, Jr. Grange Leader of the Nation, Nat. Grange, Washington, 1979, Outstanding Young Women of Am., 1981. Mem.: Nat. Cath. Edn. Assn., Pi Lambda Theta. Republican. Methodist. Avocations: singing, reading, soccer fan, star trek fan. Home: 9817 4 Points Rd Rocky Ridge MD 21778-9726 Office: St John Regional Cath Sch 114 E 2nd St Frederick MD 21701-5360 E-mail: brauer4@erols.com.

BRAULT, GERARD JOSEPH, French language educator; b. Chicopee Falls, Mass., Nov. 7, 1929; s. Philias J. and Aline E. (Rémillard) B.; m. Jeanne Lambert Pepin, Jan. 23, 1954; children: Francis Gerard, Anne-Marie Welsh, Suzanne Eveline Dannenmueller. AB, Assumption Coll., Worcester, Mass., 1950, DLitt, 1976; AM cum laude, Laval U., 1952; PhD, U. Pa., 1958. Teaching fellow U. Pa., 1954-56, assoc. prof. Romance langs., 1961-65, vice dean Grad. Sch., 1962-65; instr. French Bowdoin Coll., Brunswick, Maine, 1957-59, asst. prof. French, 1959-61; prof. French Pa. State U., University Park, 1965-90, Disting. prof. French and medieval studies, 1990, Edwin Erle Sparks prof. French and medieval studies, 1990-97, head dept. French, 1965-70, Edwin Erle Sparks prof. emeritus French and medieval studies, 1998—. Fellow Inst. Arts and Humanistic Studies, 1976—; dir. NDEA Summer Insts., Bowdoin Coll., 1961, 62, Assumption Coll., 1964; Fulbright fellow, Strasbourg, France, 1956-57, Fulbright rsch. scholar and Guggenheim fellow, Strasbourg, 1968-69; sr. fellow in Can. studies, Quebec City, 1984, Camargo Found. fellow, Cassis, France, 1987, 94. Author: Celestine: A Critical Edition of the First French Translation (1527) of the Spanish Classic La Celestina, 1963, Cours de langue française destiné aux jeunes Franco-Américains, 1963, rev. edits., 1965, 69, Early Blazon, 1972, rev. edit., 1997, Eight Thirteenth-Century Rolls of Arms in French and Anglo-Norman Blazon, 1973 (prix Paul Adam-Even), The Song of Roland: An Analytical Edition (named outstanding book Choice 1979), 2 vols., 1978, La Chanson de Roland: Student Edition, 1984; The French-Canadian Heritage in New England, 1986, Rolls of Arms of Edward I (1272-1307) (Aspilogia III), 2 vols., 1997 (Bickersteth medal, Riquer prize); mem. editl. bd. French Forum, 1975—, Purdue U. Monographs, 1978— ; contbr. articles to profl. jours. Mem. Cath. Commn. on Intellectual and Cultural Affairs, also, Comité de Vie Franco-Américaine, Société Historique Franco-Américaine. Served with CIC, U.S. Army, 1951-53. Decorated Palmes Académiques French Ministry Edn., 1965, officer, 1975; officer, Ordre National du Mérite, 1980, Ordre des Francophones d'Amérique, 1980; recipient Faculty Scholar medal Pa. State U., 1981, Class of 1933 Humanities award, Pa. State U., 1987 Fellow Soc. Antiquaries of London, Heraldry Soc. London, Medieval Acad. Am. (adv. bd. Speculum 1972-75), Académie Internationale d'Héraldique; mem. MLA, Société Rencesvals pour l'étude des épopées romanes (pres. 1985-88, pres. Am.-Canadian br. 1970-73, editorial bd. Olifant 1975—), Am. Assn. Tchrs. French, Middle Atlantic Conf. Canadian Studies (pres. 1981-83), Internat. Arthurian Soc., Harleian Soc. (council 1987-98). Home: 705 Westerly Pky State College PA 16801-4227 Office: Pa State U Burrowes Bldg Rm 325 University Park PA 16802 E-mail: gjb2@psu.edu.

BRAUMAN, JOHN I. chemist, educator; b. Pitts., Sept. 7, 1937; s. Milton and Freda E. (Schlitt) B.; m. Sharon Lea Kruse, Aug. 22, 1964; 1 dau., Kate Andrea. BS, MIT, 1959; PhD (NSF fellow), U. Calif., Berkeley, 1963. NSF postdoctoral fellow UCLA, 1962-63; asst. prof. chemistry Stanford (Calif.) U., 1963-69, asso. prof., 1969-72, prof., 1972-80, J.G. Jackson-C.J. Wood prof. chemistry, 1980—, chmn. dept., 1979-83, 95-96, cognizant dean phys. scis., 1999—2003. Cons. in phys. organic chemistry; adv. panel chemistry divsn. NSF, 1974-78; adv. panel NASA, AEC, ERDA, Rsch. Corp., Office Chemistry and Chem. Tech., NRC; coun. Gordon Rsch. Confs., 1989-95, trustee, 1991-95. Mem. editl. adv. bd. Jour. Am. Chem. Soc., 1976-83, Jour. Organic Chemistry, 1974-78, Nouveau Jour. de Chimie, 1977-85, Chem. Revs., 1978-80, Chem. Kinetics, 1987-89, Accts. Chem. Rsch., 1995-97, 98-2001; bd. trustees Ann. Revs., 1995—, mem. editl. adv. bd.; dep. editor for phys. scis. Sci., 1985-2000, chair sr. editl. bd., 2000—. Alfred P. Sloan fellow, 1968-70, Guggenheim fellow, 1978-79; Christensen fellow Oxford U., 1983-84. Fellow AAAS (chmn. sect. 1996-97, mem.-at-large sect. 1997-99), Calif. Acad. Scis. (hon.); mem. NAS (home sec. 2003—, Award in Chem. Scis. 2001), Am. Acad. Arts and Scis., Am. Chem. Soc. (award in pure chemistry 1973, Harrison Howe award, 1976, R.C. Fuson award, 1986, James Flack Norris award 1986, Arthur C. Cope scholar, 1986, Linus Pauling medal 2002, J. Willard Gibbs medal 2003, exec. com. phys. chemistry divsn., com. on sci. 1992-97), Sigma Xi, Phi Lambda Upsilon. Home: 849 Tolman Dr Palo Alto CA 94305-1025 Office: Stanford U Dept Chemistry Stanford CA 94305-5080

BRAUN, JANICE LARSON, language arts educator; b. Cook, Minn., Mar. 4, 1949; d. Roy Woodrow and Hazel Vivian (Huff) Larson; m. Joseph Edmund Braun, July 17, 1975; 1 child, Elizabeth. BA in English and German, Concordia Coll., Moorhead, Minn., 1971; MEd, St. Mary's U. Minn., 2000. Lang. arts tchr. Dist. 742 Cmty. Schs., St. Cloud, Minn., 1971—, mem. K-12 lang. arts com., 1984—, mem. Tech. H.S. site com., 1988-92. Mem., writer assessment grant com. State of Minn. and Dist. 742, 1993-97, mem. graduation stds. panel, 1997—, mem. dist. gifted and talented task force, 1999—, advisor cultural awareness and racial equity com., lang. arts dept. chair, 2002—; advisor Tech. H.S. chpt. Amnesty Internat., 1987—. Leader Wide Horizons 4-H Club, Benton County, Minn., 1990-98; catechist Bethlehem Luth. Ch., St. Cloud, 1994-96; mem. Archie Givens Origins project St. Cloud State U., 1993-96. Mem. NEA, Minn. Edn. Assn., St. Cloud Edn. Assn., Nat. Coun. Tchrs. English. Democrat. Avocations: reading, walking, skiing, canoeing, camping. Office: Tech HS 233 12th Ave S Saint Cloud MN 56301-4286 E-mail: jbraun@cloudnet.com.

BRAUN, KAZIMIERZ PAWEL, theatrical director, writer, educator; b. Mokrsko Dolne, Kielce, Poland, June 29, 1936; came to U.S., 1985; s. Juliusz and Elzbieta (Szymanowska) B.; m. Zofia M. Reklewska, July 15, 1962; children: Monika Braun Beres, Grzegorz, Justyna. M in Letters, U. Poznan, Poland, 1958, PhD, 1971; MFA in Directing, Theater Acad., Warsaw, Poland, 1962; PhD in Theatre, Wroclaw (Poland) U., 1975; PhD in Directing, Theater Acad., Warsaw, 1988. Prof. Polish State Title, 1992. Prof., dir. Teatr Polski, Warsaw, 1962-64, Teatr Horzycy, Torun, Poland, 1965-67; artistic dir., gen. mgr. Teatr Osterwy, Lublin, Poland, 1967-74, Contemporary Theatre, Wroclaw, 1975-84; head of acting program SUNY, Buffalo, 1987—89, prof. dept theater and dance, 1989—. Prof. Wroclaw U., 1974-85, Sch. Drama, Wroclaw, 1978-85; vis. prof. NYU, 1985, Swarthmore Coll., Pa., 1985-86; regents prof. U. Calif., Santa Cruz, 1986. Dir. 130 plays U.S., Poland, Can., Germany, and Ireland; pub. 31 books theater history, novels, plays, Polish, English transls. Recipient Japanese Found. award, Tokyo, 1981, Guggenheim Found. award, 1990; Best Dir. award, Critics Com., Wroclaw, 1976, 80, 84, 85, Artie award, Buffalo, 1996, Aurum award, Can., 2000, Fulbright award. 2001. Mem. Internat. Theatre Inst. (Young Dir. award 1961), Actors Union Poland, Writers Union Poland, PEN Club. Roman Catholic. Avocation: travel. Office: SUNY Dept Theater and Dance 278 Alumni Arena Amherst NY 14260-5030

BRAUN, LUDWIG, educational technology consultant; b. Bklyn., May 14, 1926; s. Ludwig and Wetie (Schmidt) B.; m. Eva Margaret Taylor, Sept. 7, 1947; children: Barbara Ann, Edith Elizabeth, Anne Catherine, John Ludwig. BEE, Poly. Inst. Bklyn., 1950, MEE, 1955, DEE, 1959. Elec. engr. Allied Control Co., N.Y.C., 1950-51; head electronics dept. Anton Electronics Labs., Inc., Bklyn., 1951-55; from instr. elec. engring. to prof. sys. and elec. engring. Poly. Inst. Bklyn., 1955-72; prof. engring. SUNY, Stony Brook, 1972-82, dir. bioengring. program, 1976-79, dir. personal computers in edn. lab., 1979-82; prof. computer sci., dir. acad. computing lab. N.Y. Inst. Tech., Central Islip, 1982-87; rsch. prof. NYU, N.Y.C., 1987-89; ret., 1989. Sr. fellow C.W. Post Campus, L.I.U., 1998—; dir. Nat. Inst. Microcomputer Based Learning, 1981-87, Intercounty Tchr. Resource Ctr., 1985-87, Mecklenburger Group, 1993-96; lectr., med. scientist Downstate Med. Ctr., 1970-82; cons. ednl. tech., 1990—, Vertol divsn. Boeing Co., GE, Ford Found., NSF, Nat. Inst. Edn., IBM, NET Schs., Inc.; tech. advisor Orton Soc., Suffolk. Author: (with E. Mishkin) Adaptive Control Systems, 1961; contbg. author: Signals and Systems in Electrical Engineering, 1962, Perry's Chemical Engineering Handbook, 1961, System Engineering Handbook, 1965, Computer Techniques in Biomedicine and Medicine, 1973, Vision Test Recommendations for American Education Decision Makers, 1990, Celebrating Success, 1995. Mem. Women's Action Alliance, 1985-88; bd. dirs. Playing To Win, Inc., 1983-90, Internat. Coun. for Computers in Edn., 1987-89. With AUS, 1944-46. First recipient Paul Pair award for contbns. to edn. through tech., Nat. Ednl. Computing Assn. Pioneer award in Ednl. Tech., 1999; fellow Global Village Schs. Inst., 1996-98. Mem. IEEE (sr. 1990), Internat. Soc. for Tech. in Edn. (bd. dirs. 1989-90), Sigma Xi, Tau Beta Pi, Eta Kappa Nu. Home: 11 Parsons Dr Dix Hills NY 11746-5217 E-mail: ludbraun@optonline.net.

BRAUN, MARY LUCILE DEKLE (LUCY BRAUN), therapist, consultant, counselor, educator; b. Tampa, Fla. d. Guthrie "Gus" J. and Lucile (Culpepper) Dekle; children: John Ryan, Matthew Joseph, Jeffrey William, Douglas Edwin. AB, Brenau Coll.; MA, U. Cen. Fla.; EdD, U. Fla. Cert. disability mgmt. specialist, rehab. counselor, victim advocate; lic. mental health counselor; lic. marriage and family therapist; nationally cert. counselor. Coord. Orange County Child Abuse Prevention, Orlando, Fla., 1983-88; cons. Displaced Homemaker Program, Orlando, 1989-94, DCS, Oviedo, Fla., 1990-92. Adj. prof. U. Ctrl. Fla., Orlando, Troy State U.; clin. dir. Response Sexual Abuse Treatment Program, 1993—95; mem. adv. bd. Fla. Hosp. Women's Ctr., Orlando, 1989—; bd. dirs. Parent Resource Ctr., Orlando, Children With Attention Deficit Disorders, Orlando, 1989—91; cons. program devel. for children and adolescent treatment svcs., 1997—98; dir. clin. svcs. Rehab. and Indsl. Counseling, 1997—; cons., counselor contractor VA; counselor Share the Care Program. Author: Someone Heard, 1987, Humor Us Soup, 1989, Child Abuse and Neglect: Resource Guide for Orange County Schools, 1985, 2d edit., 1987; contbg. author: Death from Child Abuse, 1986, Personality Types of Abusive Parents, 1993, Why Children Fight, 1992. Sustaining mem. Jr. League of Greater Orlando. Program recipient Cmty. Svc. award Walt Disney World, 1987. Mem. ACA, Fla. Counseling Assn., Nat. Bd. Cert. Counselors, Phi Kappa Phi, Kappa Delta Pi, Chi Sigma Iota, Alpha Delta Pi. Avocations: scuba diving, sailing, puzzles. E-mail: dr.lucybraun@juno.com.

BRAUN, NORMA MAI TSEN WANG, physician, educator; b. Shanghai, Oct. 30, 1937; came to U.S., 1949; d. Joseph K.C. Wang and Jenina (Soltys) Westman; m. Carl Weineck Braun, June 11, 1961; children: Erich H. P., Aimee C. H. AB, U. Pa., 1959; MD, Columbia U., 1963. Diplomate Nat. Bd. Med. Examiners. Intern in medicine Columbia U. divsn. Bellevue Hosp., N.Y.C., 1963—64, resident in medicine, 1964—65; fellow in cardiopulmonary disease St. Luke's Hosp., N.Y.C., 1967—69; asst. in medicine Coll. Physicians and Surgeons Columbia U., N.Y.C., 1970—72, instr. in medicine, 1972—75, asst. prof. clin. medicine, 1975—86, assoc. prof. clin. medicine, 1986—91, clin. prof. medicine, 1992—. Asst. vis. physician Bellevue Hosp., 1965-67; clin. asst. vis. physicians Grasslands Hosp., Valhalla, N.Y., 1969-70; asst. vis. physician Harlem Hosp., N.Y.C., 1970-73, asst. attending physician, 1974-77; asst. physician Presbyn. Hosp., N.Y.C., 1972-77, asst. attending physician, 1977-83; assoc. attending physician St. Luke's-Roosevelt Hosp. Ctr., N.Y.C., 1982-93, sr. attending physician, 1994—; cons. attending physician Helen Hayes Hosp., Nyack, N.Y., 1980; vis. prof. U. Va., Charlottesville, 1978; lectr., cons. in field. Contbr. articles to profl. jours., chpts. to books. Mabel Mead fellow in medicine Columbia, 1960-63, NIH fellow, 1977-82; Stony-Wold Herbert Lung grantee, 1976-78. Fellow ACP, Am. Coll. Chest Physicians; mem. NY. County Med. Soc., N.Y. State Med. Soc., Am. Women's Med. Assn., Am. Thoracic Soc. (pres. 1989-90, exec. com. 1990, Ea. sect.), Am. Thoracic Soc., Am. Heart Assn., Am. Coll. Chest Physicians, N.Y. Lung Assn. (lectr. 1990, mem. various coms.), N.Y. Acad. Scis., Am. Sleep Disorder Assn., Am. Assn. Home Care Physicians, N.Y. State Thoracic Soc. (exec. com., sec.- treas., v.p., pres.- elect, pres.), N.Y. Trudeau Soc. (chmn. program com. 1977-78, nominating com. 1988-89, membership com. 1990-91, sec. 1992—). Democrat. Office: St Luke's Roosevelt Hosp Ct Ste F 5th Fl 1090 Amsterdam Ave Fl 5 New York NY 10025-1737

BRAUN, PHYLLIS CELLINI, biology educator; b. Bridgeport, Conn., Jan. 19, 1953; d. Rudolph V. and Rose B. (Nappi) Cellini; m. Kevin F. Braun, July 19, 1975; children: Ryan C., Jessica P. BS in Biology, Fairfield U., 1975; PhD in Microbiology, Georgetown U., 1978. Postdoctoral fellow NIH U. Conn. Health Ctr., Farmington, Conn., 1978-79; instr. biology Fairfield (Conn.) U., 1979-80, asst. prof. biology, 1980-84, assoc. prof. biology, 1984-89, prof. biology, 1989—, chair dept. biology, 1993-96. Cons. Miles Pharms., West Haven, Conn., 1984-90, Internat. Schoeffel Industries, N.J., 1984-86, Genetech, San Francisco, 1986; grant reviewer NIH, Bethesda, 1986—. Contbr. articles to profl. jours. Mem. AAAS, Am. Soc. Microbiology, Med. Mycology Assn. Am. Roman Catholic. Avocations: interior decorating, gardening. Office: Fairfield U Dept Biology N Benson Rd Fairfield CT 06430-5152

BRAUNSTEIN, ETHAN MALCOLM, skeletal radiologist, paleopathologist, educator; b. Chgo., June 16, 1945; BA, Dartmouth Coll., 1967; MD, Northwestern U., Chgo., 1970. Instr. radiology U. Mich., Ann Arbor, 1976-81, assoc. prof., 1983-87; asst. prof. radiology Harvard U., Cambridge, Mass., 1981-83; prof. radiology Ind. U., Indpls., 1987-2000, No. Ariz. U., Flagstaff, 2000—. Adj. prof. anthropology Ind. U., Indpls., 1990-00; cons. radiologist Mayo Clinic, Scottsdale, Ariz., 2001—. Contbr. numerous articles to profl. jours., chpts. to books. Bd. dirs. Kelsey Mus. Archeology, Ann Arbor, 1983-87. Mem.: Radiol. Soc. N.Am., Am. Assn. Phys. Anthropologists, Internat. Skeletal Soc. Office: No Ariz U Flagstaff AZ 86011-5200

BRAUTBAR, NACHMAN, physician, educator; b. Haifa, Israel, Oct. 22, 1943; came to U.S., 1975; s. Pinhas and Sabine (Lohite) B.; m. Ronit Aboutboul, Mar. 25, 1968; children: Sigalit, Shirley, Jaques. MD, Med. Sch. Jerusalem, 1968. Diplomate Am. Bd. Internal Medicine, Am. Bd. Nephrology, Am. Bd. Forensic Medicine. Intern Rambam Hosp., Haifa, 1968-69; resident in internal medicine Hadassah Med. Ctr., Jerusalem, 1972-75; fellow in nephrology ULCA Med. Sch., 1975-77, asst. prof. medicine, 1977-78, U. So. Calif., L.A., 1978-83, assoc. prof. medicine, pharmacology and nutrition, 1980-87, clin. prof. medicine, 1987—. Dir. Ctr. for Toxicology and Chem. Exposure; chmn. nephrology sect. Hollywood Presbyn. Med. Center, 1980—; vice chmn. dept. medicine Queen Angeles Hosp.; chmn. pharmacy and therapy; faculty Nat. Jud. Coll., 1998. Author: Cellular Bioenergetics, 1965; editor: Internat. Jour. Occupl. Medicine and Toxicology; contbr. numerous articles, papers to scientific publs. Chmn. rsch. com., pub. rels. com. Kidney Found., L.A., 1980—. Named Hon. Citizen, Los Angeles City Coun., 1984; grantee Am. Heart Assn., 1980—, NIH, 1983. Fellow Collegium Ranazzini; mem. Am. Soc. Nephrology, Am. Soc. Bone and Mineral Rsch., Am. Physiol. Soc., Am. Chem. Soc., Am. Soc. Parenteral Nutrition, Am. Coll. Nutrition, Israeli Soc. Nephrology (hon.). Address: 6200 Wilshire Blvd Ste 1000 Los Angeles CA 90048-5811

BRAVERMAN, RAY HOWARD, secondary school educator; b. Bklyn., Feb. 28, 1947; s. Irving Leonard and Josephine (Segan) B.; divorced; 1 child, Christopher Marc; m. Barbara Diane Braverman, July 30, 1994. BA in History, U. Del., 1969; MA in History, Wash. Coll., 1979; postgrad., U. Del., 1979-85. Cert. tchr., Del. Chmn. history dept., history instr. Dover (Del.) H.S., 1970—. Chmn. history dept. Dover H.S. Recipient Cert. of Appreciation U. Del., 1987, Nat. Coun. History Edn., 1991. Mem. NEA, Nat. Coun. for the Social Studies, Del. Coun. for Social Studies, Nat. Coun. for History Edn., World History Assn., Del. Edn. Assn., Capital Educators Assn., Orgn. of Am. Historians, Am. Hist. Assn. Home: 33 Elizabeth Ave Dover DE 19901-5803 Office: Dover HS One Pat Lynn Dr Dover DE 19904-2853 E-mail: rbraver@capital.k12.de.us.

BRAY, CAROLYN SCOTT, education educator; b. May 19, 1938; d. Alonzo Lee and Frankie Lucile (Wood) Scott; m. John Graham Bray Jr., Aug. 24, 1957 (div. May 1980); children: Caron Lynn, Kimberly Anne, David William. BS, Baylor U., 1960; MEd, Hardin-Simmons U., 1981; PhD, U. North Tex., 1985. Registered med. technologist. Dir. career placement Hardin-Simmons U., 1979-82, adj. prof. bus. comm., 1981-84, assoc. dean students, 1982-85; assoc. dir. career planning and placement U. North Tex., Denton, 1985-95, adj. prof. higher edn. adminstrn., mem. Mentor program; dir. Career Ctr., U. Tex. at Dallas, Richardson, 1995-2000, prof. edn., project mgr. TExES/ExCET, 2000—. Mem. Consortium State Orgn. Tex. Tchr. Edn., 1999—; mem. adv. bd. TxBESS, 2000—. Adult Bible study tchr. 1st Bapt. Ch., Richardson, Tex., 2000—. Mem.: North Ctrl. Tex. Assn. Sch. Pers. Adminstrs. and Univ. Placement Pers. (pres. 1987—88, sec. 1988—95), Nat. Assn. Colls. and Employers (co-chair nat. conf. planning com. 1996—98), Tex. Assn. for Employer Edn. and Staffing (v.p. 1986—87, pres. 1987—88), Am. Assn. for Employment in Edn. (bd. dirs. 1989—94, treas. 1994—95, nat. conf. com. 1999, conf. com. local arrangements 1999, Priscilla A. Scotlan award for disting. svc. 1999), S.W. Assn. Colls. and Employers (life; chair ann. conf. registration 1991—92, vice chair ops. 1992—93, 4-yr. coll. dir. 1998—99, pres.-elect 1999—2000, co-chmn. tech. com.), Leadership Denton (co-dir. curriculum 1988—89, chair membership selection com., steering com. 1990, 1993—94), Denton C. of C. (pub. rels. com. 1988—95), Kappa Kappa Gamma (chpt. advisor, chair adv. bd. Zeta Sigma chpt. 1987—93). Republican. Avocations: skiing, tennis, golf, reading. Office: U Tex at Dallas PO Box 830688 GR22 Richardson TX 75083-0688 E-mail: csbray@utdallas.edu.

BRAY, PATRICIA SHANNON, music educator, musician, small business owner; b. Elkton, Md., Sept. 4, 1953; d. Francis William Shannon and Mary Elizabeth Gardner; m. William Joseph Bray Jr., July 31, 1976; children: Mark William, Eric Joseph. BMEd magna cum laude, East Carolina U., 1975; MS summa cum laude, Med. Coll. Va., Va. Commonwealth U., 1995. Lic. tchr. Va. Tchr., dir. orch. Chesterfield County Pub. Schs., Chesterfield, Va., 1975—. Cellist Richmond Philharm. Orch., Va., 1975—82, Petersburg Symphony, Va., 1987—94, Lynchburg Symphony, Va., 1998—; chair dept. music Salem Ch. Mid. Sch., Richmond, 1998—; owner Talent Edn. Chesterfield, 2000—; adjucator Richard Bland Lions Club, Music Scholarship Competition, Chester, Va., 2000; adjucator Jr. Festival Va. Fedn. of Music Clubs, 2003; presenter in field, 00; co-presenter Suzuki Assn. of the Ams. Conf., 2002; presenter Chesterfield County Pub. Schs. Leadership Conf., 2002. Faculty sponsor Salem Music Boosters, Richmond, 1998—; sch. crisis team Chesterfield County Pub. Schs., 1995—, sch. improvement planning com., 2002—. Scholarship, Theodore Presser Publ. Co. Scholarship, 1973. Mem.: Va. Mid. Sch. Assn., NEA, Am. String Tchrs. Assn., Music Educators Nat. Conf., Suzuki Assn. Americas, Sigma Alpha Iota, Kappa Delta Pi, Phi Kappa Phi. Avocations: hiking, reading, gardening. Home: 918 Dawnwood Rd Midlothian VA 23114 Office: Salem Ch Mid Sch 9700 Salem Church Rd Richmond VA 23237 E-mail: intuitpsb@aol.com.

BRAY, SARAH HARDESTY, newspaper editor, writer; b. Fairmont, W.Va., Jan. 12, 1951; d. Charles Howard and Doris (Wilson) Hardesty; m. William Philip Bray, Sept. 1, 1990; 1 child, Elizabeth Hardesty. BA in English and History, Duke U., 1972; MS in Journalism, Northwestern U., 1973. Copywriter J. Walter Thompson, Chgo., 1973-75; reporter-rschr. Forbes mag., N.Y.C., 1976-78; account exec. Hill and Knowlton, N.Y.C., 1978-80; mem. comm. programs staff Mobil Corp., N.Y.C., 1980-81; v.p. Hill and Knowlton, N.Y.C., 1981-87; dir. comm. Coun. for Advancement and Support of Edn., Washington, 1987-89, v.p. comm., 1989-99; sr. editor opinion sect. Chronicle of Higher Edn., 1999—. Co-author: Success and Betrayal: The Crisis of Women in Corporate America; editor: What People Are Saying About College Prices and College Costs; mem. adv. bd. Duke Mag., 1988—; contbr. Family Weekly mag., 1979-80. Bd. dirs. Lit. Vols. N.Y.C., 1981-86, Eric Hawkins Dance Co., N.Y.C., 1983-86, Horizons Theatre, Washington, 1988-92; mem. vol. com. Circle in the Sq. Theatre, N.Y.C., 1982-83; mem. benefit com. CARE, 1991-94. Mem. Edn. Writers Assn. (bd. dirs. 1989-92). Home: 4501 47th St NW Washington DC 20016-4434 Office: Chronicle of Higher Edn 1255 23rd St NW Washington DC 20037-1125 E-mail: Sarah.bray@chronicle.com.

BRAYBROOKE, DAVID, philosopher, educator; b. Hackettstown, N.J., Oct. 18, 1924; s. Walter Leonard and Netta Rose (Foyle) B.; m. Alice Boyd Noble, Dec. 31, 1948 (div. 1982); children: Nicholas, Geoffrey, Elizabeth Page; m. Margaret Eva Odell, July 1, 1984 (div. 1994); m. Michiko Gomyo, Dec. 22, 1994. Student, Hobart Coll., 1941-43, New Sch. Social Research, 1942, Downing Coll., Cambridge, 1945, Columbia U., 1946; BA, Harvard U., 1948; MA, Cornell U., 1951, PhD, 1953; postgrad. (Am. Council Learned Socs. fellow), New Coll., Oxford, 1952-53; postgrad. (Rockefeller Found. grantee), Balliol Coll., Oxford, 1959-60. Instr. history and lit. Hobart and William Smith Colls., Geneva, N.Y., 1948-50; teaching fellow econs. Cornell U., Ithaca, N.Y., 1950-52; instr. philosophy U. Mich., Ann Arbor, 1953-54, Bowdoin Coll., Brunswick, Maine, 1954-56; asst. prof. philosophy Yale U., New Haven, 1956-63; asso. prof. philosophy and politics Dalhousie U., Halifax, N.S., Can., 1963-65, prof., 1965-88, McCulloch prof. philosophy and politics, 1988-90, prof. emeritus, 1990—; dean liberal arts Bridgeport (Conn.) Engring. Inst., 1961-63; Centennial Commn. chair liberal arts U. Tex., Austin, 1990—. Vis. prof. philosophy U. Pitts., 1965, 66, U. Toronto, Can., 1966-67, Bowling Green State U. (Ohio), 1982, U. Waterloo, 1985; vis. prof. polit. sci. Hill Found., U. Minn., Mpls., 1971, U. Calif., Irvine, 1980, U. Chgo., 1984, Murphy Inst. Pol. Economy Tulane U., 1988; mem. Council Philos. Studies, 1974-79 Author: (with C.E. Lindblom) A Strategy of Decision: Policy Evaluation as a Social Process, 1963, Three Tests for Democracy: Personal Rights, Human Welfare, Collective Preference, 1968, Traffic Congestion Goes Through the Issue-Machine, 1974, Ethics in the World of Business, 1983, Philosophy of Social Science, 1987, Meeting Needs, 1987, (with B. Brown and P.K. Schotch) Logic on the Track of Social Change, 1995; Moral Objectives, Rules and the Forms of Social Change, 1998, Natural Law Modernized, 2001; contbr. articles to profl. jours.; editor: Philosophical Problems of the Social Sciences, 1965; monograph series Philosophy in Canada, 1973-78; Social Rules, 1996; cons. editor Philos. Studies, 1972-76; mem. editl. bd. Am. Polit. Sci. Rev., 1970-72; Ethics, 1979-89; Dialogue, 1974-78, 81-90. Mem. nat. acad. adv. panel Can. Council, Ottawa, 1968-71; chmn. Town Democratic Com., Guilford, Conn., 1961-62. Served with AUS, 1943-46. Guggenheim fellow, 1962-63; Social Scis. and Humanities Research Council Can. fellow, 1978-79, 85-86; vis. fellow Wolfson Coll., Cambridge, 1985-86, Cecil and Ida Green prof. U. B.C., 1986; John Milton Scott prof. Queen's U., 1988. Fellow Royal Soc. Can.; mem. Can. Philos. Assn. (pres. 1971-72), Can. Assn. Univ. Tchrs. (pres. 1975-76), Can. Polit. Sci. Assn., Am. Polit. Sci. Assn. (v.p. 1981-82), Am. Philos. Assn. (exec. com. Eastern div. 1976-79), Am. Soc. Polit. and Legal Philosophy, Friends of the Lake Dist. (life), Amnesty Internat., Phi Beta Kappa. Address: 1500 Scenic Dr Apt 300 Austin TX 78703-2050 also: 1 Prince St #510 Dartmouth NS Canada B2Y 4L3

BRAZELTON, WILLIAM THOMAS, chemical engineering educator; b. Danville, Ill., Jan. 22, 1921; s. Edwin Thomas and Gertrude Ann (Carson) B.; m. Marilyn Dorothy Brown, Sept. 23, 1943; children— William Thomas, Nancy Ann. Student, Ill. Inst. Tech., 1939-41; BS in Chem. Engring, Northwestern U., 1943, MS, 1948, PhD, 1952. Chem. engr. Central Process Corp., 1942-43; instr. chem. engring. Northwestern U., 1947-51, asst. prof., 1951-53, asso. prof., 1953-63, prof., 1963-91, prof.

emeritus, 1991—, chmn. dept., 1955-56, asst. dean Technol. Inst., 1960-61, assoc. dean, 1961-94, acting asst. dean, 1994-96, ret., 1996. Engring. and ednl. cons., 1949— Mem. Prospect Heights (Ill.) Bd. Edn., 1957-61; bd. dirs., exec. com. Chgo. Area Pre-Coll. Program. Recipient Vincent Bendix Minorities in Engring. award ASEE, 1986. Mem. Am. Inst. Chem. Engrs. (chmn. Chgo. sect. 1966-67), Am. Chem. Soc., Am. Soc. Engring. Edn. (chmn. Ill.-Ind. sect. 1963-64, 73-74, Vincent Bendix Minorities in Engring. award, 1986), Soc. for History of Tech., Soc. for Indsl. Archeology, Sigma Xi, Tau Beta Pi, Phi Lambda Epsilon, Alpha Chi Sigma, Triangle. Home: 10 E Willow Rd Prospect Heights IL 60070-1332 Office: Northwestern U Technol Institute Evanston IL 60208-0001 E-mail: wtb@northwestern.edu.

BRAZIER, MARY MARGARET, psychology educator, researcher; b. New Orleans, Feb. 4, 1956; d. Robert Whiting and Margaret Long (Mc Waters) B. BA, Loyola U., New Orleans, 1977; MS, Tulane U., 1985, PhD, 1986. Assoc. prof. Loyola U., 1986—, chair dept. psychology, 1993—, acting assoc. dean Coll. Arts and Scis., 1997-98. Grantee, NSF, 1987, 1999. Mem.: APA, Southwestern Psychol. Assn. (coun. 1988—2000, pres. 2002—), So. Soc. Philosophy and Psychology (exec. coun. 1989—92), Southeastern Psychol. Assn., Am. Psychol. Soc. Roman Catholic. Avocations: gardening, sailing, new orleans cooking and culture, dance. Office: Loyola U Dept Psychology 6363 Saint Charles Ave Dept New Orleans LA 70118-6195 E-mail: brazier@loyno.edu.

BRAZZELLE, MERRY ELIZABETH, special education educator; b. Pensacola, Fla., Dec. 5, 1950; d. Philip Dane and Mary (Rival) Beall; m. James Donald Brazzelle, Oct. 26, 1974; children: Matthew Coby, Meghan Elizabeth. BA, St. Mary's Dominican, 1972; M., Auburn, 1979; cert. in Supervision, Troy State U., 1990; cert. in adminstrn., cert. in Mental Retardation,, 1995. 3rd grade tchr. St. Edward the Confessor Sch., Metairie, La., 1972-73; 2nd grade tchr. Oakhurst Elem. Sch., Milton, Fla., 1973-74; spl. edn. EMR Wicksburg (Ala.) High Sch., 1974-78, spl. edn. tchr. learning disabilities, EMR, OHI grades 1-7, 1978—. Adj. prof., supr. practicum students, Troy State U., Dothan, Ala., 1981, tchr. adv. panel, tchr. liason regional inservice edn. ctr. Tchr. adv. bd. Instr. mag., 1987-89. Houston County rep. Jacksonville State U. Tchr. Hall of Fame, 1990-91. Recipient Outstanding Svc. award St. Jude's Children's Hosp., 1988, Houston County Tchr. of Yr., 1991. Mem. ASCD, Nat. Tchrs. Assn., Ala. Edn. Assn. (rep. 1991-92), Houston County Tchrs. Assn. (rep. 1991-92), Assn. Children with Learning Disabilities (pres. 1990, cert. of appreciation), Ala. Assn. Children with Learning Disabilities (bd. dirs.), Alpha Delta Kappa (pres. Beta Pi chpt. 1990-92). Roman Catholic. Avocations: reading, swimming, crafts, traveling. Home: 1140 Winslette Rd Newton AL 36352-8512 Office: Wicksburg High Sch RR 1 Newton AL 36352-9801

BREAUX, MARION MARY, secondary education educator; b. Raceland, La., June 16, 1950; d. Irby Joseph Breaux and Alvina Doretha (Comardelle) Baudouin, Edwin Joseph Baudouin (stepfather). BA, Nicholls State U., 1972. Cert. tchr. social studies and English edn., La. Tchr. Destrehan (La.) High Sch., 1972-76, Hahnville High Sch., Boutte, La., 1976—. Cons. St. Charles Parish and La. State U. Writing Projects, 1991-98. Author: (poetry) The Red Popsicle, 1991; (prose) I Do, I Do, 1991, Old Wine in New Bottles, 1991. Named Tchr. of Month, Hahnville H.S., 1991, 97, Tchr. of Yr., 1995. Mem. La. Fedn. of Tchrs., St. Charles Parish Fedn. of Tchrs., Nat. Coun. of Social Studies. Avocations: writing, reading. Home: PO Box 279 Boutte LA 70039-0279 Office: Hahnville High Sch 200 Tiger Dr Boutte LA 70039-3520

BREEDEN, BETTY LONETA, secondary school educator; b. Subiaco, Ark., May 29, 1944; d. William Homer and Lillie Mae (Keech) Scrudder; m. Leonard Jerry Breeden, July 11, 1973; 1 child, Sherri Dawn. BS, Ark. Tech. U., 1967; postgrad., Henderson State U., Arkadelphia, Ark., 1969, U. Ark., 1978, 94, U. Ctrl. Ark. Cert. tchr. secondary math., biology, physics, gen. sci., secondary edn., Ark. Tchr. sci. and math. Fourche Valley H.S., Briggsville, Ark., 1966-70, County Line H.S., Branch, Ark., 1970-76, Van Buren (Ark.) Sch. Sys., 1976—. Participant MSM Summer Inst., 1996. Choir mem., tchr., vacation Bible sch. dir. Calvary Missionary Bapt. Ch., Van Buren, 1979—. NSF grantee, 1969; Ark. Sch. for Math. and Sci. AC2E Summer Inst. participant, 1994. Mem. Nat. Coun. Tchrs. Math., Ark. Sch. for Math and Sci. Avocations: reading, playing piano, tutoring. Office: Coleman Jr High Sch 821 E Pointer Trl Van Buren AR 72956-2309

BREEDLOVE, JIMMIE DALE, JR., elementary education educator; b. Pekin, Ill., Jan. 18, 1958; s. Jimmie Dale Sr. and Kay Maria (Goodin) B. BA in Elem. Edn. magna cum laude, Eureka (Ill.) Coll., 1980; MS in Edn., Western Ill. U., 2003. Cert. elem. tchr. K-9, high sch. tchr. 6-12. Homebound instr., learning resource room aide Lewistown (Ill.) Community High Sch., 1980-81; elem. tchr. San Jose (Ill.) Community Unit Sch. Dist. 122, 1981-89, Illini Cen. Community Unit Sch. Dist. 189, 1989—. Geography curriculum, developer; sch. librarian, gifted/talented instr. San Jose Grade Sch. Dir. choir, mem. worship com. San Jose United Meth. Ch. Mem.: NEA, ASCD, Illini Ctrl. Edn. Assn., Ill. Edn. Assn., Internat. Reading Assn., Phi Kappa Phi, Kappa Delta Pi, Alpha Chi. Office: Illini Central Grade Sch Mason City IL 62664

BREEN, VINCENT DE PAUL, bishop; b. Bklyn., Dec. 24, 1936; BA, Cathedral Coll., 1959; Licentiate in Sacred Theology, Gregorian U., 1963. Ordained priest, 1962. Asst. pastor St. Genevieve, Rockaway Point, summer 1963, St. Edmund, Bklyn., 1963-66; asst. supt. schs. Diocese of Bklyn., N.Y., 1966-73, assoc. supt. of schs., 1973-76, supt. of schs., 1976-78, supt. of edn., 1978-94, vicar for edn., 1994-97; bishop Diocese of Metuchen, N.J., 1997—. Chmn. Com. of Nonpublic Sch. Ofcls. of the City of N.Y., 1978-97; mem. adv. com., pub. policy and Cath. schs. U.S. Cath. Conf., 1978-97; past pres. N.Y. State Coun. Cath. Schs. Supts., 1979-80; bd. dirs. Nat. Cath. Ednl. Assn., 1985-88; pres. Nat. Chief Adminstrs. of Cath. Edn., 1985-88; mem. coord. com. N.Y.C. Regional Edn. Ctr. for Econ. Devel.; mem. adv. com. on social policy Diocese of Bklyn., N.Y.; active Interdiocesan Com. on Social Policy, Borough Pres.'s Adv. Panel, Cath. Edn. Leadership Devel., Diocesan Cmmn. on the Elderly, St. John's Univ. Consortium; mem. com. on edn. Nat. Conf. Cath. Bishops, 1998-2001. Mem. Commn. of Elem. Schs. Officers of the Middle States Assn., N.Y. State Gov.'s Edn1. Adv. Com., N.Y. State Com. for Pub. Higher Edn., Commr.'s Adv. Coun. for Pub. Schs., N.Y. State Cath. Conf. Pub. Policy Com., Gov.'s Task Force on Equal Opportunity Edn., N.Y. Alliance for Pub. Schs. Roman Catholic. Office: Roman Cath Diocese Metuchen PO Box 191 Metuchen NJ 08840-0191

BREENE, NORMA WYLIE, special education educator; b. Springfield, Mass., Dec. 22, 1930; d. William James and Lillian (Myers) Wylie; m. Victor Martin, May 30, 1953; children: Dennis, Moira, Paula, Sharon, Lorna. Student, Boston Sch. Occupational Therapy, 1952-54; BS in Zoology, U. Mass., 1953; MEd, Marymount U., Arlington, Va., 1983. Cert. spl. edn., learning disabilities and emotional disturbances K-12. Instructional aide Prince William County Pub. Schs., Woodbridge, Va., 1976-81, tchr. learning disabilities, 1983—. Presenter nat. conf. Coun. for Exceptional Children, New Orleans, 1986, Chgo., 1987. Den mother Boy Scouts Am., 1964-66; brownie leader Girl Scouts U.S., 1966-67, craft advisor, 1967; asst. coach commr. Woodbridge Athletic Assn., 1968-70; karate instr. Fred M. Lynn PTA, 1974-81. Mem. Coun. Exceptional Children, Learning Disabilities Assn., The Orton Dyslexia Soc. Avocations: Karate, music, cartooning. Home: 13810 Botts Ave Woodbridge VA 22191-1937

BREHM, LORETTA PERSOHN, secondary art educator, librarian, consultant; b. New Orleans, Jan. 31, 1954; d. Edwin Joseph and Loretta (Persohn) B. BA, Nicholls State U., Thibodaux, La., 1975, MEd, 1979, postgrad., 1980. Cert. tchr., La. Substitute tchr. Jefferson Parish Sch. Bd., Gretna, La., 1971-74; tchr. art John Ehret Sch., John Ehret High Sch., Marrero, La., 1974-95; art tchr., libr. Westbank Cathedral Acad., 1995-98; cons. Ventures Edn. Sys., 1998—; pub. rels. rep. Jefferson West Higher Edn. Ctr., 1999—. Trustee, chmn. bd. emeritus Jefferson Parish Coun. on Aging; assessor La. State Dept. Edn., 1997—, 1st v.p. Epsilon State, Delta Kappa Gamma Soc. Internat. Ladies aux. Westwego Vol. Fire Co.; historian Westwego Bicentennial; vol. Westwego Com. on Aging, Gumbo Festival, Bridge City, La., ARC, Operation Mainstream, others; founding mem. Jefferson Parish Cmty. Arts Commn.; alumni pres., former sch. advisor Jefferson Parish 4-H Clubs; art dir. Knights of King Arthur Mardi Gras Orgn.; libr. asst. Westbank Cathedral Acad.; choir, set designer Holy Guardian Angels Ch.; trustee Jefferson Parish Coun. on Aging, 1993—; bd. dirs. Westwego Hist. Soc., Jefferson Parish Hist. Soc.; commnr. Westwego Law Enforcement Commn., Westwego Zoning Commn., treas. Westwego Tourist Commn.; treas. Bridge City Cmty. Com. on Aging. Recipient awards from Jefferson Parish Sch. Bd., 1978, Westwego Vol. Fire Co., 1982, 4-H Club, 1983, Am. Automobile Assn. Nat. Sch. Traffic Safety Program, 1987-92, others. Mem. Nat. Art Edn. Assn., La. Art Edn. Assn., Internat. Reading Assn. (chmn. Jefferson Parish coun.), Jefferson Parish Hist. Soc. (charter), New Orleans Mus. Art, La. Children's Mus., Nicholls State U. Alumni Assn., Delta Kappa Gamma, Kappa Kappa Iota, Phi Delta Kappa. Democrat. Avocations: travel, gardening, social work, freelance art work. Home: 250 Louisiana St Westwego LA 70094-4114

BREHM, SHARON STEPHENS, psychology educator, university administrator; b. Roanoke, Va., Apr. 18, 1945; d. John Wallis and Jane Chappel (Phenix) Stephens; m. Jack W. Brehm, Oct. 25, 1968 (div. Dec. 1979) BA, Duke U., 1967, PhD, 1973; MA, Harvard U., 1968. Clin. psychology intern U. Wash. Med. Ctr., Seattle, 1973-74; asst. prof. Va. Poly. Inst. and State U., Blacksburg, 1974-75, U. Kans., Lawrence, 1975-78, assoc. prof., 1978-83, prof. psychology, 1983-90, assoc. dean Coll. Liberal Arts and Scis., 1987-90; prof. psychology, dean Harpur Coll. of Arts and Scis. SUNY, Binghamton, 1990-96; prof. psychology and interpersonal comm., provost Ohio U., Athens, 1996—. Vis. prof. U. Mannheim, 1978, Istituto di Psicologia, Rome, 1989; Fulbright sr. rsch. scholar Ecole des Hautes Etudes en Sciences Sociales, Paris, 1981-82; Soc. for Personality and Social Psychology rep. APA's Coun. of Reps., 1995-2000, finance com., 1999—; chair governing bd. Ohio Learning Network, 1998-99. Author: The Application of Social Psychology to Clinical Practice, 1976, (with others) Psychological Reactance: A Theory of Freedom and Control, 1981, Intimate Relationships, 1985, 2d edit., 1992, (with others) Social Psychology, 1990, 4th edit., 1999, also numerous articles, and chpts. Mem. APA (fin. com. 1999—). Office: Ohio U Office of Provost Cutler Hall Athens OH 45701-2979

BREINES, ESTELLE BORGMAN, occupational therapy educator; b. Bklyn., Mar. 7, 1936; d. Sanford and Sylvia (Goldin) Borgman; m. Ira S. Breines, May 30, 1956; children: Roxanne Gail Breines Sukol, Eric Craig, Jacqueline Ruth Breines Danino. BS, NYU, 1957, PhD, 1986; MA, Kean Coll., 1976; postgrad., Rutgers, 1977-79. Cert. occupational therapist, occupational therapy tchr. Dir. occupational therapy Coney Island Hosp., Bklyn., 1957; sr. occupational therapist Meadowbrook Hosp., East Meadow, N.Y., 1965-67; dir. occupational therapy Brunswick Hosp. Ctr., Amityville, N.Y., 1967-69; pvt. practice N.J., 1971-80; coord. fieldwork Union Coll., Scotch Plains, N.J., 1975-78; pres. Geri-Rehab. Inc., Lebanon, N.J., 1987—; coord. fieldwork Dominican Coll., Blauvelt, N.Y., 1986-87; prof. NYU, 1987-95; chair occupl. therapy programs, asst. to dean health scis. Touro Coll., N.Y.C., 1995—99; chair dept. occupl. therapy Seton Hall U., 1999—. Exec. dir. Devel. Rehab. Svcs., Lebanon, N.J., 1985-91. Author: Perception: Its Development and Recapitulation, 1981, Origins and Adaptations: A Philosophy of Practice, 1986, (assessment tool) Functional Assessment Scale, 1983, (monograph) Proprioceptive Schematic Orientation, 1990, Occupational Therapy Activities From Clay to Computers, 1995, Occupational Therapy Activities for Practice and Teaching, 2003; Am. editor: Israeli Jour. Occupl. Therapy, 1991—; co-editor issue Occupl. Therapy Interant.; columnist OT Advance, 1994—; contbr. articles to profl. jours. Adminstrn. on Aging grantee, 1988. Fellow Am. Occupational Therapy Assn.; mem. N.J. Occupational Therapy Assn. (pres. 2001-, Merit award), World Fedn. Occupational Therapy (del.), Belgian Sheepdog Club Am. (treas. 1989-93), Raritan Belgian Sheepdog Club (pres. 1991). Democrat. Jewish. Avocations: bonsai, dog breeding, gardening, needlecrafts. Home: 15 Hibbler Rd Lebanon NJ 08833-3016 Office: Seton Hall Univ Dept Occupational Therapy 400 S Orange Ave South Orange NJ 07079

BRELAND, KATHLEEN SYLVIA, elementary education educator; b. Washington, July 14, 1946; d. Gerald Hugo and Ella Mary (Hodge) Adams; m. Jake David Breland, June 14, 1969; children: Nicole, Lauren, Mallory, J. Davey. BA, Howard U., 1969; MA, Hofstra, 1974. Tchr. D.C. Pub. Schs., Washington, 1969-71, Hempstead (N.Y.) Head Start, 1971-72, Hofstra U., Hempstead, summer 1972, Uniondale (N.Y.) Pub. Schs., 1972-83, Shaker Heights (Ohio) Pub. Schs., 1985—. Social sci. curriculum writer Shaker Heights Sch., 1989; trainee Gestault Int., Shaker Heights, 1991. Block rep. Onaway Community, Shaker Heights, 1985—; amb. City of Shaker Heights, 1991-95; jr. com. mem. Cleve. Orch. Support, 1991-92; program chair Onaway PTO, Shaker Heights, 1992-93; v.p. women's com. Christ Ch., 1992-93; active women's com. City Club Cleve., 1991-92. Mem. Nat. Assn. for Edn. of Young Children, Assn. for Childhood Edn. Internat. Episcopalian. Avocations: reading, cross-stitch, knitting, exercise, sewing. Home: 15904 Chadbourne Rd Shaker Heights OH 44120-3338 Office: Mercer Elem Sch 23325 Wimbledon Rd Shaker Heights OH 44122-3163

BREM, ANDREW SAMUEL, pediatric nephrologist, educator; b. Worcester, Mass., Nov. 7, 1948; s. Jacob and Martha (Herwitz) Brem; married; children: Matthew Benjamin, Douglas Jacob. BA, Case Western Reserve, 1970; MD, Tufts U., 1974; MA, Brown U., 1989. Intern Maine Med. Ctr., Portland, 1974-75; resident in pediatrics R.I. Hosp. Brown U., Providence, 1975-77; pediatric nephrology-renal physiology fellow Cornell Univ. N.Y. Hosp., N.Y.C., 1977-79; dir. div. pediatric nephrology R.I. Hosp., 1979—. Assoc. prof. pediatrics Brown U., Providence, 1988-95, prof., 1995—; co-chmn. med. rev. bd. Network #1 End Stage Renal Disease, New Haven, 1989-92, bd. dirs., 1995—. Contbr. articles to profl. jours. Fellow Am. Acad. Pediatrics; mem. Am. Soc. Nephrology, Am. Fedn. Clin. Rsch., Am. Soc. Pediatric Nephrology (counselor 1991-95), Soc. Pediatric Rsch., Am. Pediatric Soc., Alpha Omega Alpha.

BREMBECK, WINSTON LAMONT, retired speech communication educator; b. Urbana, Ind., Sept. 28, 1912; s. Paul John and Hulda (Speicher) B.; m. Neva Gloyd, June 20, 1940. BA magna cum laude, Manchester Coll., N. Manchester, Ind., 1936; MA, U. Wis., 1938, PhD, 1947. Instr. Westmar Coll., LeMars, Iowa, 1936-39; tutor Bklyn. Coll., 1939-42; mem. faculty U. Wis., 1947—, prof. communication and pub. address, 1960-83, prof. emeritus, 1983—. Cons. in communications and persuasion to business, profl. and religious groups, 1947— Author: (with W.S. Howell) Persuasion a Means of Social Control, 1952, Persuasion a Means of Social Influence, 1976, also articles. Served with AUS, 1943-46. Recipient A.T. Weaver Outstanding Tchr. award Wis. Speech Assn., 1970 Mem. Speech Assn. Am. (exec. com. 1966-68), Central States Speech Assn. (pres. 1965-66), Wis. Speech Assn. (pres. 1949-50), Delta Sigma Rho, Tau Kappa Alpha, Phi Kappa Phi. Republican. Methodist. Home: 3206 Leyton Ln Madison WI 53713-3405

BRENDLINGER, LEROY R. academic administrator; b. Frederick, Pa., Dec. 14, 1918; s. Claude R. and Elsie May B.; m. Virginia Steltz, Dec. 28, 1941; children: Dawn, Brian, Craig. BS, West Chester State Coll., 1946; MS, U. Pa., 1949; Ed.D., Temple U., 1959. Former tchr., East Greenville, Pa.; Ordnance Officer Candidate Sch., Aberdeen, Md.; former prin. Pottsgrove (Pa.) Schs.; former asst. supt. Montgomery (Pa.) Schs.; pres. Montgomery County Community Coll., now pres. emeritus. Chmn. SCORE, chpt. 594 Tri County area. Author: The Brendlinger Family History 1660-1994, 1995. Past pres. Montgomery County (Pa.) Health and Welfare Coun.; bd. dirs. Montgomery Hosp., Lutheran Children and Family Svc.; pres. Tri-County Area local chpt. Score 594, Pottstown, Pa. With U.S. Army, 1942-46, ETO. Recipient Outstanding Alumnus award West Chester U., 1984. Mem. Am. Assn. Jr. and C.Cs. (past pres. Pa. Commn. C.Cs.). Clubs: Brookside Country (treas. bd. govs.). Office: 340 Dekalb Pike Blue Bell PA 19422-1412

BRENEMAN, CAROL LOU, secondary school educator; b. Lima, Ohio, July 29, 1949; d. Glenn and Ruby Linn Cramer; m. Larry Breneman, Mar. 27, 1970; children: Scott, Ryan. BA in Math., Bluffton Coll., 1970; MEd Math. Edn., U. Ctrl. Fla., 1986, EdD, 1998. Nat. bd. cert. Adolescence and Young Adulthood/Math., 1999. Math. tchr. 7th, 8th grades Bluffton (Ohio) Exempted Village Schs., 1970-71; math. tchr. Upper Scioto Valley High Sch., McGuffey, Ohio, 1971-73; tchr. McComb (Ohio) Local Sch., 1973-79; math. tchr. Lakeview Mid. Sch., Sanford, Fla., 1983-85, Lake Howell High Sch., Winter Park, Fla., 1985—. Sec. Cen. Care Mission Bd. Mem. Nat. Edn. Assn., Nat. Coun. Tchrs. Math., Fla. Edn. Assn., Fla. Coun. Tchrs. Math., Seminole Edn. Assn., Seminole County Tchrs. Math. Avocations: handicrafts, reading. Home: 930 Northern Dancer Way Apt 100 Casselberry FL 32707-6709

BRENNAN, ANN RICHARD, secondary education educator; b. Red Hill, Pa., June 12, 1947; d. Clarence Renninger and Helen Grace (Bucher) Richard; m. Peter Edward Brennan, Mar. 29, 1969; children: Amy Lynn, Wendy Ann. BS in Med. Tech., Lebanon Valley Coll., 1969; MS in Sci. Edn., Fla. State U., 1994. Sci. tchr. Etowah H.S., Woodstock, Ga., 1990—, dept. chair, 1993-2000. Mem. Nat. Sci. Tchr. Assn. (presenter), Ga. Sci. Tchr. Assn. (presenter). Office: Etowah High Sch 6565 Putnam Ford Dr Woodstock GA 30189-1501

BRENNAN, BARBARA MCCARTHY, elementary education educator; b. Bridgeport, Conn. d. John Joseph and Helen Margaret (O'Loughlin) McCarthy; widowed; children: Robert, Steven, Kathleen, Daniel, Deidre, Brian. BS, Wheelock Coll.; MS, postgrad., Cen. Conn. U. Cert. tchr., Conn. Tchr. elem. grades Newington (Conn.) Pub. Schs., 1967—. Rep. Personal Policy Com.; mentor/cooperating tchr. Mem. NEA, AAUW, Conn. Edn. Assn., Newington Tchrs. Assn. Avocations: history, travel, non-fiction reading. Home: 9 Overlook Ter Avon CT 06001-4526

BRENNAN, JOANN, photographer, educator; BFA in Photography, Mass. Coll. Art, 1986, MFA in Photography, 1988. Founder, instr. Progetto Perugia, Studio Arts in Perugia (Italy), 1987—99; photography gallery dir. U. R.I., Kingston, 1988—89, visual arts instr.; photography instr. Mass. Coll. Art, Boston, 1988, Worcester (Mass.) Art Mus., 1988—89; photography lectr. Princeton U., 1990—94, gallery curator program in women's study gallery, 1991—94; asst. prof. photography Coll. Ceramics SUNY, Alfred, 1994—98; asst. prof. photography U. Colo., Denver, 1998—. Photographer (one and two-person shows) Bausch and Lomb Gallery, Corp. Hqrs., Rochester, N.Y., 1998, So. Light Gallery, Amarillo (Tex.) Coll., 2001, Ironton Gallery and Studios, Denver, 2001, Knox Coll., Galesburg, Ill., 2002, 1708 Gallery, Richmond, Va., 2002, U. Arts, Phila., 2003, (group shows) Islep Mus. Art, Long Island, N.Y., 1996, Ball State U. Mus. Art, Muncie, Ind., 1997, Carol Keller Gallery, Denver, 1999, Vincent Price GAllery at E. L.A. Coll., 1999, Tex. Woman's U. Fine Art Gallery, Denton, Tex., 2001, Princeton Art Mus., 2002, Allegheny Coll., Pa., 2002, numerous others, (permanent collections) Danforth Art Mus., Princeton Art Mus., Paine Webber Collection, N.Y.C., N.Mex. State U., Las Cruces. Recipient Purchase award, Danforth Mus. Art, Framingham, Mass., 1992, Commn. award, Miller Performing arts Ctr., N.Y.S.C.C., Alfred, N.Y., 1997; fellow, John Simon Guggenheim Meml. Found., 2003. Mem.: Inst. Electronic Arts, Soc. Photographic Edn. (treas. N.E. region 1994—96, sec. N.E. region 1995—96, chair N.E. region 1996—98, chair S.W. region 2000—01, mem. portfolio rev. com. nat. conf. 2002, conf. com. nat. conf. 2002). Address: 6665 E Jamison Ave Englewood CO 80112*

BRENNAN, LEONARD ALFRED, research scientist, administrator; b. Westerly, R.I., Aug. 2, 1957; s. Leonard Alfred Brennan Jr. and Louise (Gagne) Ladd; m. Teresa Leigh Pruden, Jan. 1, 1980; adopted children: Jessica, Michelle. BS, Evergreen State Coll., 1981; MS, Humboldt State U., 1984; PhD, U. Calif., Berkeley, 1989. Technician USDA Forest Svc., Arcata, Calif., 1984-85; biologist Calif. Dept. Food & Agr., Ukiah, 1985; rsch. asst. U. Calif., Berkeley, 1986-89; lectr. Humboldt State U., Arcata, 1989-90; rsch. scientist dept. wildlife and fisheries Miss. State U., Mississippi State, 1990-93; dir. rsch. Tall Timbers Rsch. Station, Tallahassee, 1993—2001; prof. and endowed chair for quail rsch. Caesar Kleberg Wildlife Rsch. Inst., Tex. A&M U., Kingsville, 2001—. Habitat ecology cons. The Chukar Found., Boise, 1989—. Author: (chpt.) The Use of Multivariate Statistics for Developing Habitat Suitability Index Models, 1986, The Use of Guilds and Guild-Indicator Species for Assessing Habitat Suitability, 1986, Arthropod Sampling Methods in Ornithology: Goals and Pitfalls, 1989, Influence of Sample Size on Interpretation of Foraging Patterns by Chestnut-backed Chickadee, The Habitat Concept in Ornithology: Theory and Applications; editor (with T.L. Pruden) Fire in Ecosystem Management Proceedings 20th Tall Timbers Fire Ecology Conference, 1998, Northern Bobwhite Species Account in Birds of North America Series, 1999; editor The 4th Nat. Quail Symposium, 2000; contbr. articles to profl. jours. U. Calif. fellow, 1987; grantee Calif. Dept. Forestry, Internat. Quail Found., USDA Forest Svc.; San Francisco Bay Area chpt. Wildlife Soc. scholar, 1984; judge Mendocino County Pub. Schs. Sci. Fair, Laytonville, Calif., 1988, Miss. Sci. and Engring. Fair, Miss., 1990-91. Mem. AAAS, Am. Ornithologists' Union, Assn. Field Ornithologists, Cooper Ornithological Soc., Ecol. Soc. Am., Wildlife Soc. (faculty advisor Miss. chpt.), Miss. Wildlife Fedn., Pacific N.W. Bird and Mammal Soc., Wilson Ornithological Soc., Ottawa Field Naturalists' Club. Achievements include design of mathematical sex determination model for the Dunlin, of first data-based habitat suitability index models using multivariate statistics; research on contaminant levels in Dunlins in western Washington state, on factors responsible for long-term Northern Bobwhite population decline, on impact of habitat management for the endangered Red-cockaded Woodpecker on terrestrial vertebrates. Office: Caesar Kleberg Wildlife Rsch Inst Texas A&M Univ Kingsville TX 78363

BRENNAN, MATTHEW CANNON, English literature educator, poet; b. Richmond Heights, Mo., Jan. 18, 1955; s. William Joseph and Suzanne (Simon) B.; m. Laura Lee Fredendall, Aug. 13, 1977 (div. June 1987); 1 child, Daniel William; m. Beverley Simms, May 21, 1994. AB, Grinnell Coll., 1977; MA, U. Minn., Mpls., 1980, PhD, 1984. Editor Golle and Holmes Fin. Learning, Minnetonka, Minn., 1982-84; vis. asst. prof. U. Minn., Mpls., 1984-85; asst. prof. Ind. State U., Terre Haute, 1985-88, assoc. prof., 1988-92, prof. English, 1992—. Author: (poetry) Seeing in the Dark: Poems, 1993, The Music of Exile: Poems, 1994, American Scenes: Poems on WPA Artworks, 2001, (monograph) Wordsworth, Turner, and Romantic Landscape, 1987, The Gothic Psyche, 1997; co-editor: (exhbn. catalog) Is Poetry a Visual Art?, 1993. Ind. Arts Commn. fellow, 1994; Thomas Merton Ctr. Poetry Prize, 1999, Theodore Dreiser Disting. Rsch./Creativity award, 2002; Univ. Rsch. grantee Ind. State U., Terre Haute, 1991, 96, Univ. Arts grantee, 1993, 98, 2001; named to Acad. Am. Poets, U. Minn., Mpls., 1979, 80, 84. Mem. Wordsworth-Coleridge Assn., Phi Beta Kappa, Phi Kappa Phi. Avocations: travel, film. Home: 1013 Maple Ave Terre Haute IN 47804-2936 Office: Ind State U Dept English Terre Haute IN 47809-0001 E-mail: mbrennan@indstate.edu.

BRENNAN, ROBERT LAWRENCE, educational director, psychometrician; b. Hartford, Conn., May 31, 1944; s. Robert and Irene Veronica

(Connors) B. BA, Salem State Coll., 1967; M of Art in Tchg., Harvard U., 1968, EdD, 1970. Rsch. assoc., lectr. Grad. Sch. Edn., Harvard U., Cambridge, Mass., 1970-71; asst. prof. edn. SUNY, Stony Brook, 1971-76; sr. rsch. psychologist Am. Coll. Testing Program, Iowa City, 1976-79, dir. measurement rsch. dept., 1979-84, asst. v.p. for measurement rsch., 1984-92, disting. rsch. scientist, 1990-94. Dir. Iowa Testing Programs, 1994-2002; adj. faculty Sch. Edn. U. Iowa, 1979-94, E.F. Lindquist prof. edn. measurement, 1994—, dir. ctr. for advanced studies in measurement and assessment, 2002—. Author: Elements of Generalizability Theory, 1983, Test Equating Methods and Practices, 1995, Generalizability Theory, 2001; editor: Methodology Used in Scaling the Act Assessment and P-ACT, 1989, Cognitively Diagnostic Assessment, 1995; assoc. editor Applied Psychological Measurement, 1982—, Jour. Ednl. Measurement, 1978-83, 96—; contbr. articles to profl. jours. Harvard U. prize fellow, 1967. Fellow: APA; mem.: Iowa Acad. Edn. (pres. 1996—99), Psychometric Soc., Nat. Coun. Measurement Edn. (bd. dirs. 1987—90, v.p. 1995, pres. 1997—98, Tech. Contbn. award 1997, Career Contbn. award 2000), Am. Statis. Assn., Midwestern Ednl. Rsch. Assn. (pres. 1987—88), Am. Ednl. Rsch. Assn. (v.p. 1994—96, Divsn. D award 1980). Home: 1925 Liberty Ln Coralville IA 52241-1071 Office: U Iowa 297 Lindquist Ctr N Iowa City IA 52242-1533 E-mail: robert-brennan@uiowa.edu.

BRENNAN, STEPHEN JAMES, physical education educator, consultant; BA in Broadcast Journalism and English, U. Nebr., 1973, MEd in Ednl. Adminstrn., 1978, M in Phys. Edn. and Sport Psychology, 1986; PhD in Performance and Health Psychology, U. Nebr., Lincoln, 2001. Tchr., basketball coach Archbishop Ryan H.S., Omaha, 1974-75; tchr., coach Ralston (Nebr.) H.S., 1975-80, Valley (Nebr.) H.S., 1980-84, U. Nebr., Lincoln, 1984-86; founder, pres. Peak Performance Cons., Omaha, 1986—. Performance cons. Kansas City Royals, 1989-94; head basketball coach East All Star Team, Fremont, Nebr., 1981; founder, exec. dir. Midwest Youth Coaches Assn., 1990—, Nat. Assn. Coll. Athletic Recruiters, 1999; exec. dir. The Recruiters Inst., 1993—, The Recruiters Libr., 1993—; pres. Ctr. for Performance Enhancement Rsch. and Edn., 1999—; adj. faculty U. Nebr.-Omaha, 2002—. Author: The Mental Edge: Basketball's Peak Performance Workbook, 1987, 2nd edit., 1993, 3rd edit., 2002, The Sport Performance Report, 1990, Competitive Excellence: The Psychology and Strategy of Successful Team Building, 1990, Competitive Excellence: The Psychology and Strategy of Successful Team Building, 2nd edit., 1995, (with others) Basketball Resource Guide, 1989, 2nd edit., 1995, The Recruiters Bible, 2000, 6 Psychological Factors for Success, 2001; editor: Inside Recruiting: The Master Guide to Successful College Athletic Recruiting, Vol. I, 1998, Vol. II, 1999, Vol. III, 2000; contbr. numerous articles to profl. jours. Mem. AAHPERD, Assn. for Advancement of Applied Sport Psychology, Nat. Assn. Sport and Phys. Edn., Nat. Assn. Basketball Coaches, Nat. Fedn. State H.S. Assns., Nat. Assn. Sports Ofcls., Nat. Fedn. Interscholastic Ofcls. Assn., Nat. H.S. Athletic Coaches Assn., Nebr. Coaches Assn., Midwest Officials Assn., Omaha Met. Area Basketball Coaches Assn. Home and Office: 14728 Shirley St Omaha NE 68144-2144

BRENNAN, THOMAS EMMETT, lawyer; b. Detroit, May 27, 1929; s. Joseph Terence and Jeannette Frances (Sullivan) B.; m. Pauline Mary Weinberger, Apr. 28, 1951; children: Thomas Emmett, Margaret Ann and John Seamus (twins), William Joseph, Marybeth, Ellen Mary. LL.B., U. Detroit, 1952; LL.D., Thomas M. Cooley Law Sch., 1976. Bar: Mich. 1953. Assoc. Kenny, Radom, Rockwell & Mountain, Detroit, 1952-53; ptnr. Waldron, Brennan & Maher, Detroit, 1953-61; judge Detroit Ct. Common Pleas, 1962-63, Wayne County Circuit Ct., 1963-66; justice Mich. Supreme Ct., 1967-73, chief justice, 1969-70; adj. prof. polit. sci. U. Detroit, 1970-72; founder, pres., dean emeritus Thomas M. Cooley Law Sch., Lansing, 1972—; of counsel Riley, Roumell and Connolly, Detroit, 2002—. Mem. Mich. Commn. Law Enforcement and Criminal Justice, 1969-70; bd. dirs. Motor Wheel Corp., 1987-89. Author: Judging the Law Schools, 1997, The Bench, 2000. Founder, commr. Am. Golf League, 2000; bd. dir. Cath. League for Religious & Civil Rights, 1993—. Fellow Am. Bar Found., Mich Bar Found.; mem. ABA, Ingham County Bar Assn., State Bar Mich. (bd. commrs. 1979-83), Mich. Assn. of Professions (Disting. Citizens award 1982), Assn. of Ind. Colls. and Univs. Mich. (bd. dirs., exec. com., sec. 1990, chmn. 1991), Cath. Lawyers Soc. (Thomas More award 1987), Am. Jurisprudence Soc., Inc. Soc., Irish Am. Lawyers, Cooley Legal Author's Soc. (charter), v.p.-treas. 1990—), Mich. State C. of C. (bd. dirs. 1988-94), Walnut Hills Country Club (bd. dirs. 1992-95), Detroit Athletic Club, KC, Delta Theta Phi. Roman Catholic. Office: Thomas M Cooley Law Sch 217 S Capitol Ave Lansing MI 48933-1503 Home: American Golf League 14150 6th Street Dade City FL 33525

BRENNAN, VICTORIA ELIZABETH, chemistry and biology educator; b. Oceanside, N.Y., Dec. 9, 1953; d. William George and Marjorie Elizabeth (Biedermann) Robinson; m. Garrett Thomas Brennan, Aug. 15, 1976; children: Ryan, Alexandra, Annora. BS in Biology, SUNY, Binghamton, 1975; MS in Cell and Molecular Biology, SUNY, Buffalo, 1978, PhD, 1980. Tchr. asst. SUNY, Buffalo, 1975-77, rsch. asst., 1976-80, rsch. asoc., 1980-81; prof. U. New Haven, New London, Conn., 1985-87, 95-96; prof. chemistry and biology Mitchell Coll., New London, 1983—. In sci. curriculum improvement New London Pub. Schs., 1994—. Contbr. articles to profl. jours. Mem. tech. com. New London Pub. Schs., 1995—, mem. planning team, 1995—; mem. cmty. planning team City of New London, 1995—. Mem. AAAS, NOW, Univ. Women, Phi Beta Kappa. Democrat. Episcopalian. Achievements include working to improve science education in the public schools. Office: Mitchell Coll Pequot Ave New London CT 06320

BRENNEMAN, MARY BETH, secondary educator; b. Youngstown, Ohio, Nov. 8, 1950; d. Stanley Earle and Jane M. (Samuel) Babcock; children: Jeffrey Scott, Lisa Marie. BA summa cum laude, Miami U., Oxford, Ohio, 1973; MA, U. Mich., 1975; student, Inst. d'Etudes Francaises, Tours, France. Cert. tchr., Mich.; cert. reality therapy/choice theory. Teaching fellow U. Mich., Ann Arbor, 1973-75; French and German tchr. Sturgis Public Schs., Mich., 1975—. Chaperone for student trips to Wiesloch, Germany, 1977-79, 92; coord. Sturgis-Wiesloch Student Exch. Program, 1979-89; exchange tchr. Realschule Wiesloch, 1994. Mem. Sister Cities Affiliation Bd., 1985-89; flutist Kalamazoo Concert Band and Sturgis Wind Symphony. Mem. Sturgis Edn. Assn., Mich. Edn. Assn., Nat. Edn. Assn., Alpha Lambda Delta, Phi Kappa Phi, Phi Beta Kappa. Methodist. Avocation: flutist in concert band. Home: 408 Maplecrest Ave Sturgis MI 49091-1959 Office: Sturgis Pub Schs 216 Vinewood Ave Sturgis MI 49091-2364

BRENNER, HOWARD, chemical engineering educator; b. N.Y.C., Mar. 16, 1929; s. Max and Margaret (Wechsler) B.; children: Leslie, Joyce, Suzanne; m. Lisa Glucksman, Sept. 8, 1995. BChemE, Pratt Inst., 1950; MChemE, NYU, 1954, D in Engring. Sci., 1957. Instr. chem. engring. NYU, 1955-57, asst. prof. chem. engring., 1957-61, assoc. prof., 1961-65, prof., 1965-66, Carnegie-Mellon U., 1966-77; prof., chmn. dept. chem. engring U. Rochester, N.Y., 1977-81; W.H. Dow prof. chem. engring. MIT, Cambridge, Mass., 1981—. Sr. vis. fellow Sci. Rsch. Coun. Gt. Britain, 1974; Fairchild Disting. scholar Calif. Inst. Tech., 1975-76, Chevron vis. prof., 1988-89; Gulf vis. prof. Carnegie-Mellon U., Pitts., 1991; Lady Davis fellow, Israel, 1995-96; vis. prof. U. Calif., Berkeley, 1996. Author: (with J. Happel) Low Reynolds Number Hydrodynamics, 1965, 2d edit., 1973, Russian edit., 1976; (with D.A. Edwards and D.T. Wasan) Interfacial Transport Processes and Rheology, 1991; (with D. A. Edwards) Macrotransport Processes, 1993; contbr. articles to profl. jours.; co-editor in chief Physico-Chem. Hydrodynamics, 1988-89. Recipient Disting. Alumni award Pratt Inst., 2001, Caribbean Congress Fluid Dynamics award, 2001; Guggenheim fellow, 1988. Fellow AAAS, NAE, AIChE (Alpha Chi Sigma award 1976, Walker award 1985, Lewis award 1999), Am. Acad. Mechanics; mem. NAS, Am. Acad. Arts and Scis., Soc. Rheology (Bingham medal 1980), Am. Phys. Soc. (Fluid Dynamics prize 2001), Am. Chem. Soc. (Kendall award 1988, 11th ann. Honor Scroll Indsl. Engring. Chemistry Divsn. 1961), Am. Soc. Engring. Edn. (Gen. Electric Sr. Rsch. award 1996). Office: MIT Rm 66 564 Dept Of Chem Engring Cambridge MA 02139-4307

BRENNER, LYNNETTE MARY, reading specialist, educator; b. Woodbury, N.J., July 20, 1959; d. Bernhard A. and Anna Rose (Rickert) B. BS in Bible and Elem. Edn., Lancaster (Pa.) Bible Coll., 1981; MEd in Reading, Beaver Coll., 1991. Cert. elem. and reading tchr., N.J., Pa. Elem. tchr. Killian Hill Christian Sch., Lilburn, Ga., 1981-83, Bethel Bapt. Ch. Sch., Cherry Hill, N.J., 1984-92; reading specialist, first grade tchr. Cherry Hill Bd. Edn., 1992—. Adj. faculty Ea. Coll., St. Davids, Pa., 1994-96; mem. steering com. Cherry Hill Tchrs. applying Whole Lang., 1993-95. Sec. missions com. Columbus Bapt. Ch., 1992-97, discipleship ministry, 1993—, Sun. sch. tchr., 1992-94, chmn. missions com., 1992; discipleship leader Precepts Bible study. Recipient recognition for geography awareness N.J. Senate, 1990, recognition Gov.'s Tchr. Recognition Program award, 1995, Celebrate Literacy award Internat. Reading Assn., 1999; named Tchr. of Yr., 1995. Mem. NEA, N.J. Edn. Assn., West Jersey Reading Coun. (bd. dirs. 1995-98, Celebrate Literacy award 1999), N.J. Reading Assn., Internat. Reading Assn. Republican. Baptist. Avocations: Bible study, scrapbooking, stamping, crafts, travel. Office: Joyce Kilmer Elem Sch Chapel Ave Cherry Hill NJ 08002

BRENNER, MARK LEE, academic administrator, physiologist, educator; b. Boston, June 19, 1942; s. Harry D. and Beatrice (Price) B.; m. Ruth Abramson, Aug. 30, 1964; children: Jonathan, Tamara. BS, U. Mass., 1964, MS, 1965; PhD, Mich. State U., 1970. From asst. prof. to prof. horticultural scis. U. Minn., St. Paul, 1970—98, assoc. dean Grad. Sch., 1989-94; assoc. v.p. rsch., 1992-94; v.p. rsch. and dean Grad. Sch., 1994-98; vice chancellor rsch. and grad. edn. Ind. U.-Purdue U., Indpls., 1998—; assoc. v.p. rsch. Ind. U., Bloomington, Ind., 1998—. Cons. Abbott Labs., Chgo., 1988-89; bd. dir. Coun. Govt. Rels., ETS-GRE, Assn. Accreditation Human Rsch. Protection Programs, Inc.; mem. Coun. Rsch. Policy and Grad. Edn., 1999—. Contbr. articles to profl. jours. Fellow Am. Soc. Horticultural Scis. (Outstanding Grad. Educator award 1993); mem. Am. Soc. Plant Physiologists (exec. com. 1986-89), Internat. Plant Growth Substance Assn. (sec.-treas. 1988-91), Minn. Chromatography Forum (pres. 1980-81, Palmer award 1986). Home: 8070 Lynch Ln Indianapolis IN 46250-4222 Office: Office of Vice Chancellor Rsch and Grad Edn Admin Bldg 122 355 N Lansing St Rm 122 Indianapolis IN 46202-2596*

BRENNER, THEODOR EDUARD, academic foundation administration; b. Zurich, Switzerland, May 9, 1942; came to U.S., 1962; s. Eduard and Wally Frieda (Thiele) B.; m. Vivienne Frances Shaw, June 11, 1966 (div.); children: Benedikt Theodor, Tristan Mark. Diploma, Kantonale Handelsschule, Zurich, 1962; LHD (hon.), Pace U., 1986. Dir. summer programs Am. Sch. Switzerland, Montagnola, 1963-65; dir. Inst. for European Studies Fleming Coll., Lugano, Switzerland, 1967-69; adminstrv. dean Franklin Coll., Lugano, 1970-78, pres., 1979-95; dir. gen. Jacobs Found., 1995—. Contbr. articles to profl. jours. Apptd. rep. Consiglio Comunale, Novaggio, Switzerland, 1976-80; mem. Am. Swiss Assn., Inc., N.Y.C., 1985-95. Mem. Assn. Internat. Colls. and Univs. (v.p. 1984-87, 91-95), Swiss-Am. C. of C. (Ticino chpt. bd. dirs. 1987-95), Lions (charter), Canottieri Club (Lugano). Republican. Avocations: crew, photography, film. E-mail: jf@jacobsfoundation.org., brennertheoviv@bluewin.ch.

BRENTLINGER, WILLIAM BROCK, college dean; b. Flora, Ill., Aug. 21, 1926; s. Arthur Kenneth and Frances (Maxwell) B.; m. Barbara Jean Weir, Dec. 29, 1946; children: Gregory, Gary, Rebecca Anne, Garth, Barbara Sue. Student, Washington U., 1946-47; AB, Greenville Coll., 1950; MA, Ind. State U., 1951; PhD, U. Ill., 1959. Instr. speech Greenville Coll., 1951-59, chmn. dept., 1959-62, dean of coll., 1962-69, dean coll. fine arts and comm., 1969-92; interim pres. Lamar U., Beaumont, Tex., 1992-93, asst. to pres., 1993—. Cons. higher edn. Served with USNR, 1944-46. Recipient tchr. study award Danforth Found., 1957 Mem. Internat. Council Fine Arts Deans, Speech Communication Assn. Am., Tex. Speech Assn., Tex. Assn. Coll. Tchrs., Tex. Council Arts in Edn. (pres.), Phi Kappa Phi. Clubs: Rotary (Beaumont). Baptist. Home: 6530 Salem Cir Beaumont TX 77706-5552 Office: Lamar U PO Box 10001 Beaumont TX 77710-0001

BRESLAUER, GEORGE WILLIAM, political science educator; b. N.Y.C., Mar. 4, 1946; s. Henry Edward and Marianne (Schaeffer) B.; m. Yvette Assia, June 5, 1976; children: Michelle, David. BA, U. Mich., 1966, MA, 1968, PhD, 1973. Asst. prof. polit. sci. U. Calif., Berkeley, 1971-79, assoc. prof., 1979-90, prof., 1990—, Chancellor's prof., 1998—2001, chmn. dept., 1993-96, chmn. Ctr. for Slavic and East European Studies, 1982-94, dean of social scis., 1999—. Vice chmn. bd. trustees Nat. Coun. for Soviet and East European Rsch., Washington, 1988-91. Author: Khrushchev and Brezhnev as Leaders, 1982, Soviet Strategy in the Middle East, 1989, Gorbachev and Yeltsin as Leaders, 2002; editor: Can Gorbachev's Reforms Succeed?, 1990, Learning in U.S. and Soviet Foreign Policy, 1991, Russia in the New Century: Stability or Disorder?, 2001. Grantee Ford Found., 1982-84, Carnegie Corp., 1985-94, 97-99. Mem. Am. Assn. for Advancement Slavic Studies (bd. dirs., exec. com. 1990-93). Office: U Calif Dept Polit Sci 210 Barrows Hall Berkeley CA 94720-1950

BRESLOW, RONALD CHARLES, chemist; b. Rahway, N.J., Mar. 14, 1931; s. Alexander E. and Gladys (Fellows) Breslow; m. Esther Greenberg, Sept. 7, 1955; children: Stephanie, Karen. AB summa cum laude, Harvard U., 1952, MA, 1953, PhD, 1955. NRC fellow Cambridge (Eng.) U., 1955—56; mem. faculty Columbia, 1956—, prof. chemistry, 1962—66, S.L. Mitchell prof., 1966—; univ. prof., 1992—. Cons. to industry, 1958—; mem. medicinal chemistry panel NIH, 1964—; mem. adv. panel on chemistry NSF, 1971—; mem. sci. adv. com. GM Corp., 1982—; A.R. Todd vis. prof. Cambridge U., 1982; editor Benjamin, Inc., 1962—. Author: Organic Reaction Mechanisms, 1965, 1969; contbr. articles to profl. jours.; editl. bd. Organic Syntheses, 1964—, Jour. Organic Chemistry, 1969—, Jour. Bio-organic Chemistry, 1972—, Tetrahedron, 1975—, Tetrahedron Letters, 1975—, Procs. NAS, 1984—. Trustee Rockefeller U., 1981—; bd. sci. advisers Alfred P. Sloan Found., 1978—85. Recipient Fresenius award, Phi Lambda Upsilon, 1966, Mark Van Doren award, Columbia U., 1969, Roussel prize, 1978, Great Tchr. award, Columbia U., 1981, T.W. Richards medal, 1984, A.C. Cope award, 1987, G.W. Kenner award, U. Liverpool, Eng., 1988, Paracelsus prize, Swiss Chem. Soc., 1999, Arthur Day award, 1990, Nat. medal of Sci., NSF, 1991, Paracelsus award, New Swiss Chem. Soc., Royal Soc. London, 1990, Mayor's award in Sci., N.Y.C., 2000, Centenary lectr., London Chem. Soc., 1972. Fellow: Indian Acad. Scis. (hon. fgn.), Am. Acad. Arts and Scis., Korean Chem. Soc. (hon.); mem.: NAS (chmn. chemistry divsn. 1974—77, award in chemistry 1989), Royal Soc. Chemistry (London, hon.), New Swiss Chem. Soc. (Paracelsus award 1990), Royal Soc. London (hon.), Chem. Soc. Japan (hon.), Am. Chem. Soc. (pres.-elect 1995—96, pres. 1996, chmn. divsn. organic chemistry 1970, Pure Chemistry award 1966, Baekeland medal 1969, Harrison Howe award 1974, Remsen award 1977, J.F. Norris award 1980, N.Y. sect. Nicholas medal 1989, Priestley medal 1999, Bioorganic Chemistry award 2002), Am. Philos. Soc. (coun. 1987—), Phi Beta Kappa (1st marshall 1952). Home: 275 Broad Ave Englewood NJ 07631-4350 Office: Columbia U Dept Chemistry 116th St & Broadway New York NY 10027

BRESNAHAN, ROGER JIANG, humanities educator, researcher; b. Chicopee, Mass., July 1, 1943; BA, Boston Coll., 1967; MA, NYU, 1968; PhD, U. Mass., 1974. Asst. prof. humanities Voorhees Coll., Denmark, S.C., 1974-78, divsn. chair, 1977-78; Fulbright sr. lectr. in Am. studies U. Philippines, 1976-77; prof. Am. thought and lang., core faculty Asian studies Mich. State U., East Lansing, Mich., 1978—. Editor: In Time of Hesitation, 1981, Conversations with Filipino Writers, 1990, Angles of Vision, 1992. Mem. Coll. English Assn. (hon. life, assoc. exec. sec. 1979-82), Assn. for Asian Studies, Filipino Studies Group (exec. sec. 1993-95), Soc. for Study Midwestern Lit. (corr. sec./treas. 1980—). Office: Dept Writing Rhetoric and Am Cultures Mich State U East Lansing MI 48824-1033

BRESNICK, MARTIN, composer, educator; b. N.Y.C., Nov. 13, 1946; BA in Music Composition, U. Hartford, 1967, MA, 1968, DMA, 1972; student in music composition, Stanford U., Acad. für Musik, Vienna. Compositions include Trio for Two Trumpets and Percussion, 1966, Introit, 1969, Ocean of Storms, 1970, 3 intermezzi, 1971, Musica, 1972, B's Garlands, 1973, Wir Weben, Wir Weben, 1978, Conspriacies, 1979, Der Signal, 1982, High Art, 1983, String Quartet 2 Bucephalus, 1984, Bread and Salt, 1984, Tent of Miracles, 1984, Bag o'Tells, 1984, 3 Choral Songs, 1985, Just Time, 1985, One, 1986, Lady Neils Dumpe, 1987, Trio, 1988, Pontoosuc, 1989; other symphonic ensembles include (orch.) Opere della Musica Povera, Angelus Novus, 1991, 9', Opere dell Musica Povera, Sinfonia, 1992, 15', (orch., mezzo soprano solo) Falling, 1994, 20'; other large chamber ensembles Opere della Music Povera, 8 movements, many versions, 1990-95, 10', On an Overgrown Path, 1996, 25'; other small chamber ensembles include String Quartet #3, 1992, 20',(mezzo soprano, piano) Falling, 1994, 20'; other choral works include Opere della Musica Povera, New Haven, Woodstock, N.Y., 1993, 5'; author: How Music Works; contbr. articles to profl. jours. Fulbright fellow, 1969, Nat. Endowment for Arts grantee, 1975, 79, Conn. Commission on Arts grantee, 1982; recipient Rome prize, 1976, Premio Ancona, 1980, Sinfonia Music prize, 1982, Composers Inc. 1st prize, 1986, Stoeger prize Chamber Music Soc.Lincoln Ctr., 1996. Mem. ASCAP, Conn. Composers Inc. (bd. dirs.), Am. Music Ctr. Office: Yale U Sch Music Yale Sta PO Box 2104A New Haven CT 06520-7440

BRET, DONNA LEE, elementary education educator; b. Pottsville, Pa., Dec. 18, 1950; d. S. Allen and Georgene Katherine (Heiser) Zimmerman; m. Donald Louis Bret, Oct. 11, 1969; 1 child, Thomas Donald. AA, Glendale C.C., 1988; BEd, Ariz. State U., 1990, MEd, 1995. Cert. elem., ESL tchr., Ariz. Kindergarten tchr. Glendale (Ariz.) Elem. Dist., 1991-92, 1st grade ESL tchr., 1992-93, multi-age ESL tchr., 1993—. Rep. Glendale Elem. Assn., 1998-99. Mem. NEA, Ariz. State U. Alumni Assn., Bilingual Club. Office: Glendale Elem Sch Dist 7301 N 58th Ave Glendale AZ 85301-1893

BRETT, MAUVICE WINSLOW, retired educational administrator, consultant; b. Xenia, Ohio, May 24, 1924; d. Perle Alonzo and Lurena Belle (Hamilton) W.; m. John Woodrow Brett, Sept. 20, 1943; children: Diane, John, Anthony, Loretta. BS in Psychology, Howard U., 1944, MS in Psychology, 1946; PhD in English, Union Grad. Sch., Cin., 1978. Tchr. English Hertford County Schs., Winton, N.C., 1959-76, ednl. supr., 1977-80, dir. pers., 1981-87, asst. supt., 1988-89; ret., 1989. Cons. N.C. Coun. English Tchrs., Charlotte, 1979; com. mem. quality assurance program N.C. State Dept. Pub. Instn., Raleigh, 1980-81; bd. visitors Chowan Coll., 1991-97; mem. found. bd. Roanoke-Chowan C.C., 1991-97; adj. prof. psychology Roanoke-Chowan C.C., 1992-97, Chowan Coll., 1993-97, East Carolina U., 1994-97. Sec. Hertford County Arts Coun., 1977; mem. Hertford County 400th Anniversary Com., 1982-83; trustee Elizabeth City State U., 1983-91. Mem. N.C. Assn. Sch. Adminstrs. (dist. rep.), Am. Assn. Sch. Adminstrs., N.C. ASCD, Bus. and Profl. Women's Club, Rotary, Delta Sigma Theta. Home: 1342 Us Highway 13 S Ahoskie NC 27910-8124

BREWBAKER, JAMES LYNN, crop science and genetics educator; b. St. Paul, Oct. 11, 1926; s. Harvey Edgar and Jean (Turner) B.; m. Helen Nazareno (dec. 1969); children: Paul Harvey, Philip Lloyd, Perry Lynn, Pamela Barbara Jean; m. Lilia Verano, 1970 (div.); m. Kathryn Bradley, 1992 (div.). Student, So. Meth. U., 1945, U. Tex., 1945-46; BS in Gen. Sci. cum laude, U. Colo., 1948; PhD in Plant Breeding, Cornell U., 1952. NSF postdoctoral fellow U. Lund, Sweden, 1952-53; asst. prof. agronomy U. Philippines, Los Banos, 1953-55; assoc. geneticist biology dept. Brookhaven Nat. Lab., AEC, Upton, N.Y., 1956-61: assoc. prof. horticulture and genetics U. Hawaii, Honolulu, 1961-64, prof., 1964—. Field staff geneticist Rockefeller Found., Bangkok, 1967-68; cons. IAEA, The Philippines, 1970; vis. prof. dept. plant breeding Cornell U., Ithaca, N.Y., 1974; vis. scientist Internat. Ctr. Tropical Agr., Cali, Colombia, 1978, Nigeria, 1989, Taiwan Agrl. and Forestry Rsch. Insts., 1981, Australia Nat. U., U. Queensland, 1985, 93, Ctr. for Maize and Wheat Rsch., Mex., 1997; cons. in tropical agr. and agroforestry numerous countries, 1970—. Author: Agricultural Genetics, 1962 (trans. into 7 langs.), Experimental Design on a Spreadsheet, 1993, Biometry on a Spreadsheet, 1994, Quantitative Genetics on a Spreadsheet, 1995; editor: Leucaena Rsch. Reports, 1980-90, Nitrogen Fixing Tree Rsch. Reports, 1983-88; mem. editl. bd. several jours.; contbr. over 250 articles to sci. jours. With USNR, 1944-46. Recipient Outstanding svc. award Korean Office Rural Devel., 1978, Excellence in Rsch. award U. Hawaii, 1980, G.J. Watumull Disting. Achievement award Internat. Agr., 1982, recognition Hawaii Senate, 1986, Internat. Inventor's award Swedish Inventors Assn., 1986, Scientist of Yr. award Achievement Rewards for Coll. Students, 1988, Superior Svc. award USDA, 1990, Rsch. award Nat. Coun. Comml. Plant Breeders, 1992, Career award De Kalb Genetics, 1995. Fellow Am. Soc. Agronomy (Crop Sci. Rsch. award 1984), Crop Sci. Soc. Am.; mem. Am. Soc. Hort. Sci., Am. Soc. Forestry, Internat. Soc. Tropical Foresters, Nat. Sweet Corn Breeders Assn. (pres. 1987), Nitrogen Fixing Tree Assn. (founder, pres. 1981-90), Hawaiian Acad. Sci. (pres. 1978), Hawaiian Bot. Soc. (pres. 1967), Hawaii Crop Improvement Assn. (exec. sec. 1969-85), Sigma Xi (pres. Hawaii chpt. 1990), Phi Kappa Phi, Pi Mu Epsilon, Phi Eta Sigma, Phi Sigma, Gamma Sigma Delta (Disting Svc. award 1982). Republican. Presbyterian. Achievements include research in plant breeding, genetics and tropical agriculture, including breeding of field, sweet and supersweet corn, biochemical genetics of crop plants and trees, breeding of Koa, leucaena and tropical N-fixing trees. Office: U Hawaii Dept Tropical Plant and Soil Sci 3190 Maile Way Honolulu HI 96822-2232 E-mail: brewbake@hawaii.edu.

BREWER, A. BRUCE, university administrator; b. Pasadena, Tex., Oct. 18, 1951; s. Leo Louie and Norma Jane (Nabors) Brewer; m. Patricia Anne Lumley, Mar. 12, 1977; 1 child, April Bruce stepchildren: Frand D Hollifield III, Patrick C M. AB in Am. Studies, U. Ala., 1974, MA in Counseling and Guidance, 1975; PhD in Higher Edn. Leadership, Ga. State U., 1988. Asst. dir. admissions Auburn U., Montgomery, Ala., 1976—79, coord. Career Devel. Ctr., 1979-81; coord. cooperative edn. Placement and Cooperative Edn. Office/West Ga. Coll., Carrollton, Ga., 1981-82; dir. dept. career svcs. State U. of West Ga., Carrollton, 1982—. Mem. psychology faculty, coord. orgn. devel. State U. West Ga., Carrollton, 1990—; architect Ga eFair, 2000, Teacher Staffing eFair, 2001; project dir. Ctr. for Traumatology, U. West Ga., Carrollton, 2002—03. Co-editor: (book) Annual Job Search Handbook for Educators, 2000—. Pres Sertoma Civic Club, Carrollton, 1996—97; dist chmn Boy Scouts Am, Carrollton, 1994—95; pres W Ga Indust Leaders Asn, Carrollton, 1995, W Ga Pers Asn, Carrollton, 1992. Mem.: Ga. Assn. Cols. and Employers (pres 2000—01, Founders award 1999). Baptist. Avocations: music, chess, antiques. Office: State Univ West Ga Maple St Carrollton GA 30118-0001 E-mail: bbrewer@westga.edu.

BREWER, CAROL DEAN COAKER, secondary school English language educator; b. Mobile, Ala., Mar. 18, 1949; d. George M. and Cathy (Pennington) Coaker; widowed; 1 child, Jeremy Dean. BA in English, Earlham Coll., 1972; MA in Edn., Ball State U., 1976. Cert. secondary sch. English tchr., Tenn. Tchr. Wernle Children's Home, Richmond, Ind., 1972-73; English tchr. Centerville (Ind.) H.S., 1973-77, Montgomery Bell Acad., Nashville, 1987-91, Father Ryan H.S., Nashville, 1991—, chair

SACS evaluation com., 1993-94; English tchr., chair dept. Marianna (Fla.) H.S., 1977-86. Rsch. tchr. Leonard Bernstein Ctr. for Arts, Nashville, 1994—; coord. summer enrichment program Father Ryan H.S., 1996—. Design cons., 1993-94. Mem. Nat. Coun. Tchrs. English, Bellevue C. of C. (bicentennial mem.). Presbyterian. Home: 122 Morton Mill Cir Nashville TN 37221-6715

BREWER, CHERYL ANN, obstetrician and gynecologist, educator; b. New Rochelle, N.Y., Oct. 31, 1959; d. John Paul and Marie Elizabeth (Royance) B. BS, Miss. U. for Women, 1981; MD, Ind. U., Indpls., 1985. Resident in ob-gyn. SUNY Health Scis. Ctr., Syracuse, 1985-89, asst. prof. ob-gyn., 1989-91; asst. prof. dept. ob-gyn. Ind. U., Indpls., 1991-92; fellow in gynecologic oncology U. Calif., Irvine, 1992-96; asst. prof. ob-gyn., dir. gynecologic oncology Sch. Med. So. Ill. U., 1996-98; asst. prof. U. Ill., Peoria, 1998—. Dir. divsn. gyn. oncology U. Ill., Peoria, 2000—02. Fellow Am. Coll. Ob-Gyn. Home: 59 N Shore Dr Petersburg IL 62675-9778 Office: U Ill Chgo Coll Medicine Dept OG/Divsn Gynecology 515 NE Glen Oak Ave # S5e301 Peoria IL 61603-3136

BREWER, DONALD LOUIS, school superintendent; b. Carbondale, Ill., Nov. 28, 1938; s. Louis Wiliam and Merline Ruth Brewer; m. Wilma Jean Turnage, May 13, 1961; children: Donna Jean Brewer Sanders, Clay Thomas. BS in Edn., So. Ill. U., 1960, MS, 1961. Tchr., coach Alexander County Cen. High Sch., Tamms, Ill., 1961-63; tchr., athletic dir. Egyptian Unit Schs., Olive Branch, Ill., 1963-64; tchr., athletic dir., elem. prin., high sch. asst. prin. Murphysboro (Ill.) Unit Schs., 1964-87; regional supr. Jackson and Perry Counties, Murphysboro, 1987—. Weekly columnist Murphysboro Am., 1982-91. Trustee John A. Logal Coll., Carterville, Ill., 1972—, chmn., 1975-76, 81-87, 93-96; mem. So. Ill. Airport Authority, Carbondale, 1977-86; mem. Mruphysboro Park Bd., 1972—. Elected to Ill. Amateur Softball Assn. Hall of Fame, 1979. Mem. NEA, Assn. Regional Supts., Ill. Athletic Dirs. Assn., Ednl. Coun. of 100, Phi Delta Kappa. Democrat. Methodist. Avocation: promoting softball. Home: 25 Westwood Ln Murphysboro IL 62966-3004 Office: Jackson County Courthouse Regional Supt Schs Murphysboro IL 62966

BREWER, EDITH GAY, librarian, educator; b. Jacksonville, Tex., Aug. 14, 1944; d. Elige Ellis and Jimmie Lee (Durham) Alexander; m. Samuel David Brewer, May 23, 1964; children: Gayla Deeann, Michael David. AA, Tyler (Tex.) Jr. Coll., 1964; BA, Stephen F. Austin State U., 1966, MEd, 1970. Cert. libr., Tex. English tchr., speech tchr. Rusk (Tex.) H.S., 1966-71; English, math, journalism, speech tchr. Whitehouse (Tex.) H.S., 1973-75, libr., 1976—; dist. libr. coord. Whitehouse Ind. Sch. Dist., 1976—. Tech. bd. mem. Whitehouse Ind. Sch. Dist., 1994—; gifted and talented bd. mem. Region VII Edn. Svc. Ctr., Kilgore, Tex., 1996—. Contbr. articles to profl. jours. Bd. dirs. Whitehouse Cmty. Libr., 1985-87; Sunday sch. tchr. First Bapt. Ch., Whitehouse, 1984—, chmn. music com, 1994—, mem. sanctuary choir, 1984—, mem. handbell choir, 1995—; vol. Hospice, 1998—. Recipient Libr. Appreciation award Sunrise Rotary Club, 1994. Mem. Tex. Libr. Assn., Tex. Assn. of Libr. Adminstrs., Am. Libr. Assn. Baptist. Avocations: reading, music, gardening, interior decorating, church activities. Home: 12098 County Road 2175 Whitehouse TX 75791-5024 Office: Whitehouse Ind Sch Dist 108 Wildcat Dr Whitehouse TX 75791-3130

BREWER, EDWARD CAGE, III, law educator; b. Clarksdale, Miss., Jan. 20, 1953; s. Edward Cage Brewer Jr. and Elizabeth Blair (Alford) Little; m. Nancy Corr Martin, Dec. 27, 1975 (div. Sept. 1985); children: Katherine Martin, Julia Blair; m. Laurie Carol Alley, June 27, 1993 (div. Dec. 1999); 1 child, Caroline Elizabeth McCarty; m. Karlyn Ann Schnapp; children: Matthew Karl Schnapp, Andrew Cage Schnapp. BA, U. of the South, 1975; JD, Vanderbilt U., 1979. Bar: Ala. 1980, U.S. Ct. Appeals (5th and 11th cirs.) 1981, U.S. Dist. Ct. (so. dist.) Ala. 1981, Ga. 1982, U.S. Dist. Ct. (no. dist.) Ga. 1982, U.S. Dist. Ct. (so. dist.) Ga. 1988, U.S. Ct. Appeals (3d and 8th cirs.) 1983, U.S. Dist. Ct. (mid. dist.) Ga. 1992, U.S. Supreme Ct. 1996. Law clk. to Hon. Virgil Pittman U.S. Dist. Ct. (so. dist.) Ala., Mobile, 1979-81; law clk. to Hon. Albert J. Henderson U.S. Ct. Appeals (5th and 11th cirs.), Atlanta, 1981-82; pvt. practice Atlanta, 1982-96; instr. Coll. of Law Ga. State U., Atlanta, 1992, 94; adj. prof. legal writing Emory U., Atlanta, 1994-96; asst. prof. law No. Ky. U., Highland Heights, 1996-2000, assoc. prof. law, 2000—02, prof. law, 2002—. Co-author: Railway Labor Act of 1926: Legislative History, 1988, Georgia Appellate Practice, 1996, 2d edit., 2002; author: Powerpoint Materials for Morgan and Rotunda, Professional Responsibility, 1997, 2d edit., 2003; contbr. articles to profl. jours. Mem.: Omicron Delta Kappa, Phi Beta Kappa. Episcopalian. Avocations: choral music, guitar, bicycling, hiking, canoeing. E-mail: brewerec@nku.edu.

BREWER, JUDITH ANNE, special education educator, consultant; b. Pontiac, Mich., Jan. 25, 1952; d. Lorenz Robert and Jane Francis (Behen) Einheuser; m. Randall Edward Brewer, May 17, 1974; children: Michael E., Julie M. BS in Spl. Edn. summa cum laude, Western Mich. U., 1974; MA in Teaching, Oakland U., 1977. Cert. spl. edn. tchr. for emotionally impaired and learning disabled; cert. Project Adventure; cert. advanced stds. Project Adventure. Spl. edn. resource tchr. Mayfield and Woodside Elem. Sch., Lapeer, Mich., 1974-75; learning disabled tchr. Pine Tree Elem. Sch., Lake Orion, Mich., 1976, elem. self-contained learning disabled tchr., 1977-79; spl. edn. resource tchr. Carpenter and Blanche Sims Elem. Sch., Lake Orion, 1976-77; spl. edn. tchr. Lake Orion Middle Sch., 1983-85; spl. edn. tchr., cons. Lake Orion H.S., 1985—, spl. edn. dept. chair, 1992—, interim asst. prin., fall 1994, MATRIX interdisciplinary block program co-chair, tchr., 1994-98. Jr. class advisor Lake Orion H.S., 1985-87, sophomore class advisor, 1987-88, ski club sponsor, 1990-97, sch. improvement com. mem., 1990-94, mem. bldg. coun., 1992—, mem. new bldg. com., 1994-96, mem. block scheduling com., 1995—, mem. insvc. subcom., 1995—, mem. LOHS blue ribbon schs. com., 1999, blue ribbon schs. program evaluator 2000-01, profl. devel. steering com., 2000—; exec. bd. rep. Lake Orion Edn. Assn., 1987-89, 94-95, 98—; student activities chair, sch. improvement team, 1990; high sch. level steering com. North Ctrl. Accreditation, 1989-90, evaluator, 1991, 2000-01, chairperson for LOHS spl. edn. dept. NCA self-study, 1998-99; mem. Cmty. Svc. Com., 1993, mem. portfolio com., 1991; lectr. in field Cath. Social Svcs., Oakland County, Mich., 1985—. Social chmn. Sylvan Manor Homeowners Assn., West Bloomfield, Mich., 1982-84, pres. 1985; sec. Marina Pk. Estates, Subdiv., Lake Orion, 1987-89, soc. chmn., 1991-92. Grantee Lake Orion Bd. Edn., 1990, Durant Funds, 1998. Mem. Mich. Assn. Learning Disability Educators, Oakland County Educators Learning Disabled, Coun. for Exceptional Children. Roman Catholic. Avocations: reading, sewing, swimming, boating. Home: 365 Bay Pointe Rd Lake Orion MI 48362-2572 Office: Lake Orion High Sch 495 E Scripps Rd Lake Orion MI 48360-2249 E-mail: jbrewer1@lakeorion.k12.mi.us.

BREWER, LEWIS GORDON, judge, lawyer, educator; b. New Martinsville, W.Va., Sept. 6, 1946; s. Harvey Lee and Ruth Carolyn (Zimmerman) B.; m. Kathryn Anne Yunker, May 25, 1985. BA, W.Va. U., 1968, JD, 1971; LLM, George Washington U., 1979. Bar: W.Va. 1971, Calif. 1978. Commd. 2d lt. USAF, 1968, advanced through grades to col., 1988, dep. staff judge adv., 1976-78, chief civil law San Antonio Air Logistics Ctr. Kelly AFB, Tex., 1979-83, staff judge adv. MacDill AFB, Fla., 1983-86, chief Air Force Cen. Labor Law Office Randolph AFB, Tex., 1987-88, dep. staff judge adv. Air Tng. Command, 1988-89, staff judge adv. 7th Air Force Osan AFB, Korea, 1989-91, 45 Space Wing Patrick AFB, 1991-93; adminstrv. law judge W.Va. Edn. and State Employee Grievance Bd., Charleston, 1993-2000, mediator, 1994—; legal counsel W.Va. Ethics Commn., Charleston, 2000—. Instr. bus. law No. Mich. U., Marquette, 1972, Solano Coll., Suisun City, Calif., 1978; instr. labor law Webster U., Ft. Sam Houston, 1983. Decorated Air Force Commendation medal, Meritorious Service medal, Legion of Merit. Mem. ABA, Assn. for Conflict Resolution, W.Va. Bar Assn., State Bar Calif., W.Va. U. Alumni Assn., George Washington U. Alumni Assn. Roman Catholic. Home: 528 Sheridan Cir Charleston WV 25314-1063 Office: 1207 Quarrier St Charleston WV 25301-1826 E-mail: Mede8wv@abanet.org., LBrewer@GWMail.state.wv.us.

BREWER, MARJORIE JOY, elementary school educator; b. Chgo., Dec. 4, 1940; d. LeRoy Kenneth and LaVonne Geraldine (Osborn) Moore; m. David Louis Brewer, July 1963 (div. Mar. 1979); children: David Brett, Holly Elaine, Brian Christian. BS in Spl. Edn., Speech and Hearing, Phillips U., 1963; MEd in Elem. Edn., Northeastern State U., 1990. Cert. tchr., Okla. Probation counselor Okla. County Children's Ct., Oklahoma City, 1963—66; elem. tchr. Walt Whitman Magnet Elem. Sch., Tulsa, 1990—92, Waite Phillips Elem. Sch., Tulsa, 1992—2003; tchr. of gifted Phillips Elem. Sch. and Andrew Carnegie Elem. Sch., 2002—03. Mem. editl. com. citizenship edn. com. Okla. Bar Assn., 1992. Ordained deacon Presbyn. Ch. Kirk of the Hills, Tulsa, 1986-89; asst. scoutmaster Troop 16, Boy Scouts Am., New Haven Meth., Tulsa, 1985; pres. Baylor U. Parents League, Tulsa, 1987-88; chmn. 25th class reunion Phillips Univ., Enid, Okla., 1988. Recipient Tchrs. Touching Tomorrow award 1997, award of excellence Tulsa Pub. Schs., 2002, Instructional Excellence in Edn. award Okla. Edn. Assn., 2003; Okla. Bar Assn. scholar, 1991, Okla. Found. for Excellence scholar at Colonial Williamsburg Tchr. Inst., 2002. Mem. Kappa Delta Pi, Delta Kappa Gamma (v.p. Alpha Lambda chpt. 1992-94, pres. 1994-96), Kappa Kappa Iota (sec. Beta Lambda conclave 1996-97, pres.-elect 1997-99, pres. 1999-2002, pres.-elect Tusla Area Coun. 2003—). Republican. Presbyterian. Avocations: readng, sewing, cooking, Bible study, hiking. Home: 6006 S Jamestown Ave Tulsa OK 74135-7844 Office: Waite Phillips Elem Sch 3613 S Hudson Ave Tulsa OK 74135

BREWER, NEVADA NANCY, elementary education educator; b. Balt., Jan. 21, 1949; d. Leo and Rebecca (Johnson) Brewer. BS, Coppin State Coll., 1973, MEd, 1974, MEd, 1981; postgrad., C.C. Balt., 1985. Cert. elem. tchr., spl. edn. tchr. Tchr. Balt. County Adult Edn., Towson, Md., 1973-88; coord. Just Say No to Drugs program Balt. City Sch. Sys., tchr., 2000—01, mgr. summer sch., 2000—02, acad. coach math. and sci., 2002—03, coord. math. elem. lab., 2003—. Coord. Heads Up Program, 1980, math-a-thon program St. Jude Rsch. Ctr., 1993—, 24 Challenge Math. Tournament, 1996—, elem. math. lab., 2003—, academic coach math. and sci. grades prek-5, 2002-03; supr. tchr. for student tchrs. Towson State U., Coll. Notre Dame, Coppin State Coll., 1989—; leadership tchr. STARS sci. program, 1995; participant in Project Future Search Phone-a-Thon to recruit minority students U. Md., College Park., Write to Learn Program, Balt. City Sch. Sys., 1990-91; acad. coach math and sci. grades Pre-K-5, 2002—. Coord. Echo Hill Outdoor Sch., 1988—, mem. adv. bd., 2003—. Recipient Freedom Found. award, 1974. Home: 1616 Wentworth Ave Baltimore MD 21234-6125 E-mail: nbrew@unlonnet.net.

BREWER, PATRICIA ROSE, adult education educator; b. Wilmington, Ohio, Mar. 1, 1953; d. Bertrand Andrew and Leona May (Wilson) Rose; m. Everett Earl Brewer, Sept. 10, 1971; children: Joshua Wayne, Seth Andrew. AB, Wilmington Coll., 1974; MA, Ball State U., Muncie, Ind., 1982; EdD, Columbia U., 1998. Coord., grants mgr. Wilmington Coll., 1980-82; registrar, program dir. Chatfield Coll., St. Martin, Ohio, 1982-85; counselor Ind. U., Richmond, 1987-88, Dayton (Ohio) Edn. Opportunity Ctr., 1988; asst. prof. Sinclair C.C., Dayton, 1988-2000, prof., 2000—01; spl. asst. to provost for adult learners Capital U., Columbus, Ohio, 2001—. E-mail: pbrewer@capital.edu.

BREWER, THOMAS BOWMAN, retired university president; b. Ft. Worth, July 22, 1932; s. Earl Johnson and Maurine (Bowman) B.; m. Betty Jean Walling, Aug. 4, 1951; children: Diane, Thomas Bowman Jr. BA, U. Tex., 1954, MA, 1957; PhD, U. Pa., 1962. Instr. St. Stephens Episcopal Sch., Austin, Tex., 1955-56, S.W. Tex. State Coll., San Marcos, 1956-57; from instr. to asso. prof. North Tex. State U., Denton, 1959-66; asst. prof. U. Ky., 1966-67; asso. prof. Iowa State U., 1967-68; prof. history, chmn. dept. U. Toledo, 1968-71; dean Tex. Christian U., Ft. Worth, 1971-72, vice chancellor, dean univ., 1972-78; chancellor East Carolina U., Greenville, N.C., 1978-82; v.p. acad. affairs Ga. State U., Atlanta, 1982-88; pres. Met. State Coll. of Denver, 1988-93; interim provost U. Alaska, Anchorage, 1995-97. Editor: Views of American Economic Growth, 2 vols, 1966, The Robber Barons, 1969; gen. editor: Railroads of America Series. Home: 104 Javelin Dr Austin TX 78734-5016 E-mail: TBBSR@alumni.utexas.net.

BREWER, WANDA EASTWOOD, retired educator in English, art museum docent; b. Dec. 8, 1926; BFA, U. Denver, 1950; MA, U. No. Colo., 1961, EdD, 1968. Tchr. in English Greeley (Colo.) Ctrl. H.S., 1961-62; prof. English U. No. Colo., 1962-91; docent Denver Art Mus., 1992—.

BRIANT, CLYDE LEONARD, metallurgist, educator; b. Texarkana, Ark., May 31, 1948; s. Clyde Leonard and Bonnie Barbara (Green) B.; m. Jacqueline Louise Duffy, July 16, 1977; children— Paul, Judith, Bonnie. BA, Hendrix Coll., Conway, Ark., 1971; BS, Columbia U., 1971, MS, 1973, Eng. Sc.D., 1974. Postdoctoral fellow U. Pa., Phila., 1974-76; staff metallurgist Gen. Electric Co., Schenectady, NY, 1976—94; prof. engring. Brown U., Providence, 1994—, Otis Randall prof., 2000—, dean engring., 2003—. Vis. scientist Rsch. Inst. for Tech. Physics, Hungarian Acad. Scis., Budapest, 1991. Editor: Embrittlement of Engineering Alloys, 1983; contbr. articles to profl. jours. Recipient Alfred Noble prize, 1980; named one of 100 Most Outstanding Young Scientists in U.S.A., Sci. Digest, 1984; overseas fellow Churchill Coll., Cambridge, Eng., 1987-88. Fellow Am. Soc. Metals; mem. AIME (Robert Lansing Hardy gold medal Metall. Soc. 1977, Rossiter W. Raymond 1979). Democrat. Methodist. Home: 9 Wedgewood Ln Barrington RI 02806-3218 Office: Brown Univ Divsn of Engring Box D Providence RI 02912

BRICE, WILLIAM RILEY, geology educator, planetary science educator; b. Groveland, Fla., Feb. 24, 1936; s. Joseph Vernon and Frances Brice; m. Heather Weidenhofer, Jan. 18, 1964; children: Tania Helen Brice-Coffin, John Armstrong. BS, U. Fla., 1958; Diploma of Edn., U. Tasmania, Australia, 1965; postgrad., Cornell U., 1967-68, MS for Tchrs., 1968, PhD, 1971. Tchr. math., sci. Clermont (Fla.) H.S., 1960-62, 65-67; asst. master sci. Taroona (Tasmania, Australia) H.S., 1962-65; tchg. fellow geol. sci. Cornell U., Ithaca, N.Y., 1968-71; asst. prof. geology and planetary sci. U. Pitts., Johnstown, Pa., 1971-76, assoc. prof. geology, planetary sci., 1976-88, prof. geology, planetary sci., 1988—, chair divsn. natural sci., 1993-97. Vis. assoc. prof. Cornell U., Ithaca, N.Y., 1977-89, vis. prof. geol. sci., 1990-2002; studio tchr. Australian Broadcasting Commn., Hobart, Tasmania, 1963-65. Author: Cornell Geology Through the Years, 1989, Gilbert D. Harris-Life with Fossils, 1996; contbr. articles to profl. jours. 1st v.p. Drake Well Found., v.p., 2001—03, bd. dirs., 1999—2003. With U.S. Army, 1958—60. Named George F. Matthew Rsch. fellow, New Brunswick Mus, 1992, travel grantee, State U. at Campinas (Brazil), 1992, 2001, charter mem., Clermont H.S. Hall of Fame, 1989. Fellow Geol. Soc. Am. (chair history of geol. divsn. 1996, sec.-treas., editor 1999—), Nat. Assn. Geosci. Tchrs. (sec., treas. eastern sect. 1976-92, chair disting. svc. award com. 2000—, Disting. Svc. award 1999), History of Earth Sci. Soc. (pres.-elect 2001-2002, pres. 2003—), Petroleum History Inst. (pres. 2003—), Drake Well Found. (bd. dirs. 1998-2003, 2d v.p. 2001-2003), Petroleum History Inst. (bd. dirs. 2003—, inaugural pres. 2003—, editor 2003—). Avocations: theater lighting, photography, singing. Office: U Pitts at Johnston Geology and Planetary Sci Johnstown PA 15904 E-mail: wbrice@pitt.edu.

BRICKMAN, JANE PACHT, history educator; b. N.Y.C., Feb. 5, 1946; d. Sol and Beatrice (Lereah) Pacht; m. John M. Brickman, Feb. 26, 1972; children: Elizabeth A., Suzanna P. BA, Queens Coll., 1968, MA; PhD, CUNY, 1978. Part-time tchr. Hofstra U., Queens Coll., Pace U., U.S. Mcht. Marine Acad., 1970-83; asst. prof. history U.S. Mcht. Marine Acad., Kings Point, N.Y., 1983-86, assoc. prof. history, 1986-93, women's advisor, 1983-94; prof. history, 1993—; head dept. humanities, 1994—. Contbr. articles to profl. jours. Trustee Am. Mcht. Marine Mus., 1999—. Office: US Mcht Marine Acad Kings Point NY 11024

BRIDGER, TERESA LYNNE, education educator; b. Oneonta, N.Y., Oct. 7, 1962; d. James Albert and Janice Elaine (Markham) B.; 3 children. BS in Spl. and Elem. Edn., Ind. (Pa.) U., 1983; MEd in Internat. Multicultural Studies, U. Pitts., 1988; PhD, George Mason U., 1997. Cert. spl. edn. and elem. tchr., supr., adminstr., Md. Spl. edn. tchr. Craig House-Technoma, Pitts., 1984-87; from spl. edn. tchr. to elem. tchr. Prince George's County Pub. Schs., Upper Marlboro, Md., 1987-91, multicultural edn. specialist, 1991-95; owner consulting business, 1990—; part-time kindergarten tchr., 1995-96; dir. elem. edn. tchg. program U. Md., 1996—2002; assoc. prof. early childhood edn. Prince Georges (Md.) C.C., 2002—. Cons. in field. Named Tchr. of Yr. City of Bowie, Md., 1988-89. Mem. ASCD, Mid-Atlantic Assn. for Coop. in Edn., Internat. Assn. for the Study Coop. in Edn., Nat. Assn. for Multicultural Edn., Md. Multicultural Coalition. Avocations: cooking, reading, walking, travel.

BRIDGES, CHRISTINE E. elementary education educator; b. Springfield, Mass., Nov. 4, 1954; d. Claude Thomas and Rita Christina (Banim) Myers; m. Garry C. Bridges, Sept. 25, 1976; 1 child, Kevin Michael. BS in Edn., Westfield State U., 1986. Cert. early childhood edn., kindergarten to 3d. Tchr. DeBerry Elem. Sch., Springfield, Mass.; Homer St. Elem. Sec. decision-making team; faculty and student coun. coord. PTO; cert. megaskills leader Home and Sch. Inst. Mem. Mass. Tchrs. Assn., Springfield Tchrs. Club (early childhood curriculum com. mem.), Kappa Delta Pi.

BRIDGES, EDWIN MAXWELL, education educator; b. Hannibal, Mo., Jan. 1, 1934; s. Edwin Otto and Radha (Maxwell) B.; m. Marjorie Anne Pollock, July 31, 1954; children: Richard, Rebecca, Brian, Bruce. BS, U. Mo., 1954; MA, U. Chgo., 1956, PhD, 1964. English tchr. Bremen Community High Sch., Midlothian, Ill., 1954-56; asst. prin. Griffith (Ind.) High Sch., 1956-60, prin., 1960-62; staff assoc. U. Chgo., 1962-64, assoc. prof., 1967-72; assoc. dir. Univ. Coun. for Edn. Adminstrn., Columbus, Ohio, 1964-65; asst. prof. Washington U., St. Louis, 1965-67; assoc. prof. U. Chgo., 1967-72; prof. U. Calif., Santa Barbara, 1972-74; prof. edn. Stanford (Calif.) U., 1974—. Mem. nat. adv. panel Ctr. for Rsch. on Ednl. Accountability and Tchr. Evaluation, 1990-95; external examiner U. Hong Kong, 1990-92; vis. prof. Chinese U., Hong Kong, 1976, 96; disting. vis. prof. Beijing U., 2002; cons. World Bank, China, 1986, 89; dir. Midwest Adminstrn. Ctr., Chgo., 1967-72. Author: Managing the Incompetent Teacher, 1984, 2d edit., 1990, The Incompetent Teacher, 1986, 2d edit., 1991, Problem Based Learning for Administrators, 1992; co-author: Introduction to Educational Adminstration, 1977, Implementing Problem-based Leadership Development, 1995. Recipient of the R.F. Campbell Lifetime Achievement award, 1996; named Outstanding Young Man of Ind., C. of C., 1960; named hon. prof. and cert. of honor So. China Normal U., 1989, Citation of Merit for Outstanding Achievement and Meritorious Svc. in Edn., U. Mo. Coll. Edn., 1999. Mem. Am. Ednl. Rsch. Assn. (v.p. 1974-75). Office: Stanford U Sch Edn Stanford CA 94305 E-mail: bridges@stanford.edu.

BRIDGES, JAMES A. vocational school educator; Pres. Valdosta (Ga.) Tech. Inst. Named Outstanding Vocat. Educator, 1993. Office: Valdosta Tech Inst PO Box 928 Valdosta GA 31603-0928

BRIDGES, JUDY CANTRELL, gifted and talented education educator; b. Dallas, Feb. 17, 1947; d. William and Jewel Alexandria (Autrey) C.; m. Gary L. Bridges, Aug. 17, 1969; children: John Drewry, Judith Alexandria. BA, Tex. Tech. U., 1969; gifted/talented endorsement, Sul Ross State U., Alpine, Tex., 1992, MEd, 1993; cert. in mid-mgmt., Sul Ross State U., 1994. Lic. secondary edn. math. and English. Tchr. New Deal (Tex.) Ind. Sch. Dist., 1969—70, Indpls. Pub. Schs., 1970, USDESEA, Zweibruecken, Germany, 1971—73, Lubbock (Tex.) Ind. Sch. Dist., 1973—76, Ector County Ind. Sch. Dist., Odessa, Tex., 1976-85, 87-90, tchr. gifted spl. edn., 1990—92, gifted/talented coord., 1992—97, dir. advanced acad. svcs., 1977—2001; ednl. cons., self employed Odessa, 2001—02; prin., dir. gifted programs Midland Ind. Sch. Dist., 2002—. Acct. Walter Smith CPA, Odessa, 1977—82; real estate appraiser Appraisal Assocs., Odessa, 1985—87; vis. lectr. Sul Ross State U., Odessa, 1994, Odessa, 1997—98, Odessa, 2001; mem. gifted/talented adv. com. Region 18 Edn. Svc. Ctr., Midland, Tex., 1993—2001. Author: (poem) Paradigm Shifts in the West Texas Sand, 1991. Advisor, officer Jr. League of Odessa, Inc., 1980—, treas./treas. elect, 1986—88; treas. Campaign to Elect County Judge, Odessa, 1991; mem. bd. Permian H.S. Football Booster Club, 1993; dir. region I Tex. Acad. Decathlon, 1999, 2000; bd. dirs. ECISD Edn. Found., 2002—; treas., asst. treas., bd. dirs. Odessa Symphony Guild, 1996—98, sec.-treas., 2002, bd. dirs., 1999—2000; dir. Tex. Assn. for the Gifted and Talented, 1999—2001; chairperson math. Gifted/Talented Performance Stds. Com. Tex., 2000; mem. State Bd. for Educator Cert. Math. Stds. Com., 2000; sec., treas. Tex. Assn. for the Gifted and Talented, 2002. Recipient Dept. of Def. Commendation, U.S. Dependent Edn. System, Zweibruecken, 1973, Cert. of Appreciation-Stop of Felony Odessa Police Dept., 1992. Mem. ASCD, NEA, Tex. State Tchrs. Assn. (treas. Ector County unit 1991-92), Tex. Assn. Gifted and Talented, Am. Creativity Assn., Nat. Coun. Tchrs. Math. Baptist. Avocations: snow skiing, flora design, reading, travel. Home: 4243 Lynbrook Ave Odessa TX 79762-7146 Office: 409 N Texas Ave Odessa TX 79761 E-mail: bridgesjc@hotmail.com.

BRIEGER, GERT HENRY, medical historian, educator; b. Hamburg, Germany, Jan. 5, 1932; arrived in U.S., 1938, naturalized, 1943; s. Carl Helmuth and Ylse (Fuchs) Brieger; m. Katharine Crenshaw, July 2, 1955; children: Heidi E., William N., Benjamin C. AB, U. Calif., Berkeley, 1953; MPH, Harvard U., 1962; PhD, Johns Hopkins U., 1968. Intern UCLA Med. Ctr., 1957—58; asst. prof. history of medicine Johns Hopkins U. Sch. Medicine, Balt., 1966—70; assoc. prof. cmty. health scis., assoc. prof. history Duke U., Durham, NC, 1970—75; prof. history of health scis., chmn. dept. U. Calif., San Francisco, 1975—84; William H. Welch prof., dir. Inst. History of Medicine Johns Hopkins U., Balt., 1984—2001, chair dept. hist. sci. med. and tech., 1993—2001, disting. svc. prof., 2002—. Author (with A.M. Harvey, S.L. Abrams and V.A. McKusick): A Model of Its Kind, A Centennial History of Johns Hopkins Medicine, 1989; editor: Medical America in the Nineteenth Century, 1972, Theory and Practice in American Medicine, 1976; co-editor Bull. of the History of Medicine, 1990—. Served to capt. U.S. Army, 1958—61. Mem.: History of Sci., Am. Assn. History of Medicine (pres. 1980—82). Home: 10 E Lee St Baltimore MD 21202-6003 Office: Johns Hopkins U Welch Med Library Rm 320 1900 E Monument St Baltimore MD 21205-2167 E-mail: gbrieger@jhmi.edu.

BRIEND-WALKER, MONIQUE MARIE, French and Spanish language educator; b. Lamballe, France, Nov. 21, 1946; came to U.S., 1970; d. Francis Marie and Maria Françoise (Auffray) Briend; m. Robert A. Walker, Apr. 21, 1979; children: Charlotte Marie, Robert Anselle, Alexander Francis. Licence-es-lettres, U. Rennes, France, 1969; Maîtrise de lettres, U. Rennes, 1971. Asst. prof. U. Rochester, N.Y., 1970-71; prof. English and art Ecole Privée Louise de Bettignies, Paris, 1972-77; sr. lectr. U. Dartmouth, Hanover, N.Y., 1982-87; tchr. French St. Albans Sch., Washington, 1988-89; tchr. French and Spanish Landon Sch., Bethesda, Md., 1989—. Asst. in mktg. CBS Records, Paris and N.Y., 1978-82; dir. summer cultural and linguistic program London-in-Europe, Bethesda, 1989—. Fulbright scholar U. Rochester, 1970-71. Roman Catholic. Avocation: watercolors. Office: Landon Sch 6101 Wilson Ln Bethesda MD 20817-3199

BRIGANCE, ALBERT HENRY, educational writer, publisher; b. Keota, Okla., Sept. 13, 1932; s. Otto Elias and Okla Lillian (Christenberry) B.; m. Pat June Hicks, Mar. 31, 1956; children: Rebecca Jean, Royce Dean; 1 foster child, Dee Damron. BS in Elem. Edn., Southeastern Okla. State U., Durant, Okla., 1955; MA in Elem. Adminstrn., Calif. State U., Fresno, 1960; cert. in sch. psychology, Calif. State U., L.A., 1965. Elem. tchr. Pacific Union Sch., Fresno, Calif., 1957-60, Hudson Sch. Dist., La Puente, Calif., 1960-65; sch. psychologist Humboldt County Schs., Eureka, Calif., 1965-78; writer Curriculum Assocs., North Billerica, Mass., 1976—. Assoc. prof. Calif. State U.-Humboldt, Arcata, Calif., 1975-76; adj. prof. U. Tenn., Knoxville, 1991. Author: BRIGANCE Inventories, 1976-82, BRIGANCE Screens, 1980-98, BRIGANCE Prescriptive Teaching Material, 8 books, 1985-95, High-Interest Low-Vocabulary Reading Program, 16 books and digital CD, 2002. Staff sgt. USAF, 1953-57. Named to Hall of Fame, Keota High Sch., 1991; named Disting. Alumnus of Southeastern Okla. State U., 1999. Mem. Coun. for Exceptional Children. Republican. Methodist. Avocations: genealogy, hiking in smoky mountains. Home and Office: 278 Royal Oaks Dr Maryville TN 37801-9614

BRIGGS, CYNTHIA ANNE, educational administrator, clinical psychologist; b. Berea, Ohio, Nov. 9, 1950; d. William Benajah and Lorraine (Hood) B.; m. Thomas Joseph O'Brien, Nov. 28, 1986; children: Julia Maureen, William Thomas. B Music Edn., U. Kans., 1973; MusM, U. Miami, 1976; D. Psychology, Hahnemann U., 1988. Lic. psychology, Mo.; bd. cert. music therapist. Music therapist Parsons (Kans.) State Hosp., 1973-74; grad. asst. U. Miami, Coral Gables, Fla., 1974-76; asst. prof., dir. Hahnemann U., Phila., 1976-85, asst. prof., 1985-91; psychology resident Assocs. in Psychol. and Human Resources, Phila., 1988-91; clin. dir. Child Ctr. of Our Lady, St. Louis, 1991—; adj. faculty Lindenwood U., 2000—. Mem. editl. bd. Jour. Music Therapy, 1997-2001; adj. faculty LIndenwood U., 2000—; contbr. chpts. to books, articles to profl. jours. Mem. Am. Assn. Music Therapy (pres. 1987-89), Nat. Coalition Arts Therapies Assns. (chair 1991-93). Democrat. Avocations: cooking, piano, music, theatre. Office: Child Ctr of Our Lady 7900 Natural Bridge Rd Saint Louis MO 63121-4628

BRIGGS, HENRY PAYSON, JR., headmaster; b. Boston, Apr. 14, 1932; s. Henry Payson Sr. and Eleanor Temple (Smith) B.; m. Charlin Shoenberger Devanney, Nov. 28, 1987; children from previous marriage: Payson Stewart, Heather Kavanagh. BA, Harvard U., 1954, MAT, 1959. Dir. admissions and fin. aid Harvard U., Cambridge, Mass., 1956-66; headmaster Western Res. Acad., Hudson, Ohio, 1966-76, Seven Hills Sch., Cin., 1976—95; interim head St. James' Sch., L.A., 1995—96; dir. major gifts Cin. Opera, 1996-99; interim head The Potomac Sch., McLean, Va., 1999-2000, The Norfolk (Va.) Acad., 2000-01, The Ft. Worth CDS, 2001—02, St. Timothy's Sch., Balt., 2002—. Steering com. Leadership Cin., 1990—; bd. dirs. Queen City Found.; vestryman, warden, mem. com. Christ Episcopal Ch. Cathedral, Cin., 1977—. 1st lt. U.S. Army, 1954-56. Mem. Headmasters Assn. (officer), Country Day Sch. Headmasters Assn.(v.p.), Literary Club, Univ. Club, Tennis Club Cin. (pres.), Williams Club (N.Y.C.). Avocations: education, sports, outdoors, politics. Home: 7937 Bar Harbor Dr Cincinnati OH 45255-4430

BRIGGS, PHILIP JAMES, political science educator, author, lecturer, reviewer; b. N.Y.C., July 28, 1938; s. Philip Edward and Florence Marie (Fulham) B.; m. Candace Rae Kohn, Jan. 30, 1971; children: Nicola Fulham, Adam Kohn. BS, SUNY, Oswego, 1960; MA, Maxwell Sch. Citizenship and Pub. Affairs, Syracuse U., 1962, PhD, 1969. Asst. prof. social sci. SUNY Coll. Tech., Delhi, 1963-65; part-time admissions counselor Syracuse (N.Y.) U., 1967; assoc. prof. polit. sci. East Stroudsburg (Pa.) U., 1968-72, prof. polit. sci., 1972-99, dept. grad. coord.and chmn., 1977-95, faculty Fulbright adviser, 1981-82, disting. prof., faculty emeritus, 2000—. Foxhowe lectr., 1980; Commonwealth spkr. Pa. Humanities Coun., 1984—86, 1996—99; invited del. Sci. Rsch. Coun., Acad. Sci. USSR, 1979; invited participant seminar Georgetown U., 1983; invited scholar Presdl. Conf. Com., Hofstra U., 1984, 85, 87; panel co-chair Internat. Polit. Sci. World Congress, Paris, 1985, panel chair, Berlin, 94; manuscript referee Armed Forces and Soc., Chgo., 1979, Chgo., 93; cons. McGraw-Hill Book Co., N.Y.C., 1981. Author: Making American Foreign Policy, President-Congress Relations from the Second World War to Vietnam, 1991, 1992, Making American Foreign Policy, President-Congress Relations from the Second World War to the Post-Cold War Era, 1994, 1995, 1997; contbg. author: series The Congress of the United States, 1789-1989; editor: Politics in America, Readings and Documents, 1972; contbr. articles and revs. to profl. publs.; (TV appearances on) C-Span, 1987, Blue Ridge Cable and Pennarama, 1991, Action News 24, Erie, Pa., 1999. Exec. sec. Rsch. Com. on Armed Forces and Soc. Internat. Polit. Sci. Assn., 1985; panel chmn. rsch. com. Fundacion Jose Ortega y Gasset, Madrid, 1990; mem., panel participant Ctr. for Study of Presidency, 1995, 96; spkr. cmty. groups, Pa., NJ, NY, 2000-03. With USCG, 1962, USCGR, 1962-70. Mem. Pa. Polit. Sci. Assn. (panel chmn. ann. meetings 1993-99), Pi Sigma Alpha.

BRIGGS, WINSLOW RUSSELL, plant biologist, educator; b. St. Paul, Apr. 29, 1928; s. John DeQuedville and Marjorie (Winslow) B.; m. Ann Morrill, June 30, 1955; children: Caroline, Lucia, Marion. BA, Harvard U., 1951, MA, 1952, PhD, 1956; Doctorate (hon.), U. Freiburg, Germany, 2002. Instr. biol. scis. Stanford (Calif.) U., 1955-57, asst. prof., 1957-62, asso. prof., 1962-66, prof., 1966-67; prof. biology Harvard U., 1967-73, Stanford U., 1973—; dir. dept. plant biology Carnegie Instn. of Washington, Stanford, 1973-93. Author: (with others) Life on Earth, 1973; mem. editl. bd. Ann. Rev. Plant Physiology, 1961-72; contbr. articles on plant growth and devel. and photobiology to profl. jours. Recipient Alexander von Humboldt U.S. Sr. Scientist award, 1984-85, Sterling Hendricks award USDA Agrl. Rsch. Svc., 1995, DeWitt award for partnership Calif. State Pks., 2000, Finsen medal Assn. Internat. Photobiology, 2000; John Simon Guggenheim fellow, 1973-74, Deutsche Akademie der Naturforscher Leopoldina, 1986. Fellow AAAS; mem. NAS, Am. Soc. Plant Physiologists (pres. 1975-76, Stephen Hales award 1994), Calif. Bot. Soc. (pres. 1976-77), Am. Acad. Arts and Scis., Am. Inst. Biol. Scis. (pres. 1980-81), Am. Soc. Photobiology, Bot. Soc. Am., Nature Conservancy, Sigma Xi. Home: 480 Hale St Palo Alto CA 94301-2207 Office: Carnegie Inst Washington Dept Plant Biology 260 Panama St Palo Alto CA 94305-4101

BRIGHT, DAVID FORBES, academic administrator, classics and comparative literature educator; b. Winnipeg, Man., Can., Apr. 13, 1942; s. John Hamilton and Pauline Murray (Forbes) B.; m. Marlene Joanne Mayercik, Feb. 20, 1965; children: Jennifer, Sarah. BA (hons.), U. Man., 1962; AM, U. Cin., 1963, PhD, 1967. Asst. prof. classics Williams Coll., Williamstown, Mass., 1967-70; from asst. to assoc. prof. classics U. Ill., Urbana-Champaign, 1970-85, prof. classics and comparative lit., 1985-89, chmn. dept. classics, 1977-81, 85-88, dir. comparative lit. dept., 1986-88, acting dean Coll. Liberal Arts and Scis., 1988-89; dean Coll. Liberal Arts and Scis. Iowa State U., Ames, 1989-91; dean, v.p. for arts and scis. Emory U., Atlanta, 1991-97, prof. classics and comparative lit., 1991—, chmn. dept. classics, 1999—, dir. comparative lit., 1999-2001. Author: Haec mihi fingebam. Tibullus in his World, 1978, Elaborate Disarray: The Nature of Statius' Silvae, 1980, Miniature Epic in Vandal Africa, 1987, The Academic Deanship, 2001; editor: Classical Texts and Their Traditions, 1984. Bd. dirs. Atlanta Ballet Co., Savoyards Light Opera, Coun. of Colls. of Arts and Scis., pres. 1996-97. Woodrow Wilson Found. fellow, 1962, U. Cin. travel fellow Am. Acad. in Rome, 1965-66, Am. Council Learned Socs. fellow, 1981-82; Rsch. scholar Delmas Found., 1987. Mem. Am. Philol. Assn., Classical Assn. Middle West and South (exec. com. 1985-89, pres. 1989), Vergilian Soc. (trustee 1983-86), Soc. of Fellows Am. Acad. Rome. Episcopalian. Home: 2646 Rangewood Dr NE Atlanta GA 30345-1516 Office: Emory U Dept Classics 221F Candler Libr Atlanta GA 30322-0001 E-mail: dbright@emory.edu.

BRIGMAN, DOROTHEA JANE PENGELLY, secondary and elementary education educator; b. Limerick, Pa., Feb. 3, 1940; d. William Radford and Clarissa Roth (Grubb) Pengelly; m. Benny Lee Brigman, Jan. 30, 1960 (div. Oct. 1976); children: Benny Lee, Rita Elizabeth, Lloyd James. BS, Ursinus Coll., 1962; MEd in Reading, West Chester U., 1984; cert. in Advanced Study in Tech., Johns Hopkins U., 1987, EdD, 1995. Cert. reading specialist Pa.; cert. in elem. edn. and mentally and/or physically handicapped. Supr./demonstrator Dutchmaid, Inc., Ephrata, Pa., 1963-78; co-founder/tchr. Holy Trinity Parish Day Sch., West Chester, Pa., 1978-79; tchr. Upland Country Day Sch., Kennett Square, Pa., 1978-90, dir. tech., 1990—; adj. prof. West Chester U., 1996—99. Mem. staff curriculum devel. for tech. Upland Country Day Sch., Kennett Square, 1990—. Active vestry, dir. altar guild, lay reader, chalice bearer, choir mother, inquirer's class Ch. of The Holy Trinity, West Chester, Pa., 1962—; hostess Chester County Hosp., West Chester, 1976—, YWCA, West Chester, 1986—; active catechumenate process Episcopal Diocese of Pa., Phila., 1994-95; hostess Gilbert & Sullivan Soc., West Chester, 1995—; chmn. group of vols. Chester County Hosp. May Festival; vol. St. Paul's Chapel at Ground Zero. Mem. Alpha Upsilon Alpha (charter Epsilon chpt., sec. 1986-88), Phi Delta Kappa. Republican. Avocations: cooking, sewing. Home: 905 Sheridan Drive West Chester PA 19382-5410 Office: Upland Country Day Sch 420 W Street Rd Kennett Square PA 19348-1193 also: West Chester U Dept Childhood Studies West Chester PA 19383-0001

BRIGNONI, GLADYS, foreign language educator; b. Ponce, P.R., Apr. 9, 1965; d. Angel Manuel and Gladys Alejandrina (Roman) B. BA, Purdue U., 1987; MAT, Ind. U., 1992, PhD, 1996. Cert. in Spanish and ESL for secondary sch., Ind. Assoc. instr. Spanish dept. Ind. U., Bloomington, 1988—, Spanish instr. Continuing Studies, 1992—, instr. fgn. lang. methods, 1993-94, Spanish instr. Ctr. Internat. Bus. & Rsch., 1993-94, rsch. asst. Ctr. for Reading and Lang. Studies; asst. prof. Spanish Old Dominion U., Norfolk, Va., 1996—. Spanish tchr. Internat. Ednl. Sys., Nashville, Ind., 1991-92; Spanish grammar instr. Ind. U. Honors Program in Mex., 1991-92; tchr. Spanish Bloomingh H.S. South, 1993-94; curriculum specialist, cons. Office of Workforce Devel., Gov.'s Commn. on Adult Literacy, Little Rock, 1994-95; Spanish translator Pan Am. Games, Indpls., summer 1987; presenter in field. Mem. Latinos Unidos, 1989-94; VITAL tutor for ESL Learners, Bloomington, 1994-95; Spanish instr. Older Am. Ctr., Bloomington, summer 1995. Ind. U. scholar, 1988-95. Mem. Ind. Fgn. Lang. Tchrs. Assn., Internat. Soc. for Intercultural Edn., Tng. and Rsch., Am. Coun. Tchg. Fgn. Langs., Sigma Delta Pi. Roman Catholic. Avocations: playing piano, music, reading, jogging. Home: 4557 Sawgrass Ct Alexandria VA 22312-3152

BRILL, DONALD MAXIM, educator, writer, researcher; b. Elk Mound, Wis., Sept. 8, 1922; s. John James and Grace Darling (Mayo) B.; m. Meredith Joy Wright, June 25, 1955; children: John Richard, Rebecca Jean, Linda Marie, Susan Elizabeth. BS, Stout State U., 1947; MA, U. Minn., 1949; PhD, U. Wis., 1973. Tchr. Mpls. Pub. Schs., 1949-50, Eau Claire (Wis.) Pub. Schs., 1950, Chippewa Valley Tech. Coll., 1951-58; supr. Wis. Tech. Colls., Madison, 1958-65; coord. Great Cities Program for Sch. Improvement Rsch. Coun., Chgo., 1965-67; supr. rsch. Wis. Tech. Colls., Madison, 1967-70, asst. state dir., 1970-83. Adj. prof. U. Wis., Stout, 1983-86. Mem. state com. for employment support of Guard and Res., 1983-86; mem. Eau Claire Dist. Sch. Bd., 1989-92; founding bd. dirs. Fourth Dimension, Inc., WHEM-FM, 1994-98; primary candidate 3d Congl. Dist., Wis., 1994. With U.S. Army, 1942-45, ETO. Mem. DAV, VFW, SAR, Am. Vocat. Assn. (life), The Mayflower Soc. Republican. Baptist. Avocations: writing, genealogy, poetry, travel, restored victorian home. Home: W 2745 Mitchell Rd Eau Claire WI 54701-8603 E-mail: dmb316@aol.com.

BRILLIANT, ELEANOR LURIA, social work educator; b. Bklyn., Nov. 25, 1930; d. Joseph and Leah (Cohen) Luria; m. Richard Brilliant, June 24, 1951; children: Stephanie, Livia, Franca, Myron. BA, Smith Coll., Northampton, Mass., 1952; MS, Bryn Mawr (Pa.) Coll., 1969; DSW, Columbia U., 1974. Asst. in prodn. course Harvard Bus. Sch., Cambridge, Mass., 1952-54; instr. Bryn Mawr Coll., 1969-71; adminstr., dir. Lower East Side Family Union, N.Y.C., 1974-75; dir. planning/evaluation United Way of Westchester, White Plains, N.Y., 1975-78, assoc. exec. dir., 1978-80; asst. prof. Columbia U., N.Y.C., 1980-84, assoc. prof., 1984-85; assoc. prof. social work Rutgers U., New Brunswick, N.J., 1986-95, prof., 1995—, mem. women's studies faculty, 1992—; dir. BSW program Rutgers U. Livingston Coll., New Brunswick, 1987-89; chair, adminstr. policy and planning area MSW program Rutgers U. Sch. Social Work, New Brunswick, 1992-97. Cons. United Way of Westchester, White Plains, 1980, Family Info. and Referral Svc. Teams, Inc., White Plains, 1980-83, 87, James Bell Assoc., 1994-96. Author: The Urban Development Corporation: Private Interests and Public Authority, 1975, The United Way: Dilemmas of Organized Charity, 1990, Private Charity and Public Inquiry: A History of the Filer and Peterson Commissions, 2000. U.S. Fulbright grantee, 1972-73, NIMH grantee 1968-69; fellow Douglass Coll., Rutgers U., 1992—. Mem. NASW (rep. to del. assembly 1987, 90, nat. treas. 1989-91), Assn. for Rsch. on Non-Profit Orgns. and Vol. Action (v.p. adminstrn./sec. 1997-99, bd. mem.-at-large 1999-01), Internat. Soc. for Third-Sector Rsch., Assn. for Cmty. Orgn. and Social Adminstrn. Avocations: travel, reading, swimming. Home: 10 Wayside Ln Scarsdale NY 10583-2908 Office: Rutgers U Sch Social Work 536 George St New Brunswick NJ 08901-1167

BRIMIJOIN, KAY ROTHGEB, education educator; b. Washington, June 13, 1945; d. Wade Lee and Marjorie Katherine (Miller) Rothgeb; m. Mark Pierce Brimijoin, June 23, 1967; children: William Armstrong II, Katharine Perry. BA, Conn. Coll., 1963-67; MEd, Lynchburg Coll., 1989; PhD, U. Va., 2002. Elem. tchr. Amherst Acad., Va., 1976-80, Amherst County Pub. Sch., 1982-88, coord. enrichment programs, 1988—2000. Adj. faculty U. Va., 1998—, Faculty Sweet Briar Coll., 2000—. Grantee Va. Dept. of Ed., 2000, 2002; Commn. Arts, 1994-96, US Dept. Edn., 1989. Mem. ASCD, Am. Edn. Rsch. Assn., Nat. Assn. Gifted Children (Nat. Curriculum award 1999, Doctoral Student Award, 2002), Va. Assn. for Gifted (bd. mem. 1989-98, sec. 1993-96, pres.-elect 1996-98, pres. 1998-99), Phi Delta Kappa. Avocations: piano, cooking, hiking, reading.

BRINK, DEAN CLIFFORD, secondary school educator; b. Billings, Mont., June 24, 1936; s. Leon Arthur and Felicia Ellen (Baker) B.; m. Carol Jean Cameron, Aug. 16, 1958; children: Kathryn, Constance, Stephen. BS in Edn., Mont. State U., 1958; MA in History, U. Wash., 1966, PhC in History, 1973. Cert. tchr. Wash. Am. history tchr. Roosevelt H.S., Seattle, 1961—, chair history dept., 1985-98. Cons. The Coll. Bd., N.Y.C., 1982—; vis. lectr. history dept. U. Wash., Seattle, 1970-71, 73-74, Coll. Edn., 1974-83; mem. faculty Advanced Placement Summer Inst., Stanford U., 1997—. Co-author: A History of Our American Republic, 1978, Legacy of Freedom: A History of the United States, 1986; contbr. articles to profl. jours. Recipient Outstanding H.S. History Tchr. award U. Wash., 1982, Lifetime Outstanding H.S. History Tchr. award U. Wash., 1990, Excellence in Edn. award Seattle Com. for Excellence Edn., 1986, Outstanding Tchr. award U. Chgo., 1992, Class Act Tchr. award KSTW-TV, 1993, Top of the Class award Seattle Times, 1998. Home: PO Box 82192 7123 NE 162nd St Kenmore WA 98028-0192 Office: Roosevelt HS 1410 NE 66th St Seattle WA 98115-6744

BRINK, STUART JAY, pediatric endocrinologist, educator; b. N.Y.C., May 13, 1947; s. Morris and Gertrude (Kulik) B.; 1 child, Marcy Ann. BS, Bklyn. Coll., 1968; MD, U. So. Calif., L.A., 1972; PhD (hon.), U. Timisoara, Romania, 1999. Diplomate Am. Bd. Pediat., Am. Bd. Pediat. Endocrinology. Pediat. intern L.A. County/U. So. Calif. Med. Ctr., 1972-73, jr. resident in pediatrics, 1973-74, sr. resident in pediatrics, 1974-75, chief resident in pediatrics, 1975-76; fellow pediatric endocrinology Children's Hosp. Boston, Harvard Med. Sch., 1976-77; fellow diabetes Joslin Clinic, Harvard Med. Sch., Boston, 1977-78; sr. pediatrician Joslin Clinic, Boston, 1978-83; med. dir. DTCA Waltham (Mass.)-Weston Hosp., 1985-94; dir. pediat. and adolescent diabetes and endocrinology Newton (Mass.) Wellesley Hosp., 1994—2000. Clin. instr. pediats. Harvard Med. Sch., Boston, 1976—; sr. endocrinologist New Eng. Diabetes and Endocrinology Ctr., Waltham, Mass., 1984—; assoc. clin. prof. pediats. Tufts U. Sch. Medicine, Boston, 1995—. Fellow: Lawson Wilkins Pediat. Endocrine Soc., Am. Acad. Pediats.; mem.: Internat. Pediat. Diabetology (Eli Lilly award 2003), Ambulatory Pediat. Assn., Internat. Soc. Pediat. and Adolescent Diabetes, Soc. Dominicana de Endocrinologia y Nutricion (hon.), Internat. Diabetes Fedn., Juvenile Diabetes Found. (Ann Wolfe award 1987), Am. Diabetes Assn. (pres. Mass. affiliate 1992—94, 1995—96, Nat. Youth Svc. award 1990, Lilly Internat. Partnership in Diabetes award 2003). Jewish. Home: 196 Pleasant St Newton Centre MA 02459-1815 Office: New Eng Diabetes & Endocrinology Ctr 40 Second Ave Ste 170 Waltham MA 02451-1136 E-mail: stubrink@aol.com.

BRINKLEY, PHYLLIS, program artist, educator; b. Madison, Wis., May 28, 1926; d. Reynale R. and Florence (Jarvis) Crosby; m. William Malry, Jr., Aug. 5, 1949. BA in Speech and English, U. Wis., 1948, postgrad., 1949. Tchr. speech, 1951—56; spkr., program artist, 1956—. Current programs First Ladies of Our Land, Women of Worth, A Walk with Mr. Lincoln, Mary and Abraham, Stained Glass: Gift of Light, Eleanor Roosevelt: Innovator; interpretative reader, 1950—58; radio artist Focus on Books Sta. WHA, 1967—72. Author: (book) Abraham Lincoln and His Wife, Mary: Two Human Beings, 1975, The Lincolns: Targets for Controversy, 1986. Chmn. Little Sisters Sisters of St. Benedict, 1986—87; tchr. Bible Norway Grove Luth. Ch., DeForest, Wis., 1990—94; vol. hosp. aux.; pub. affairs chmn. Madison Civics Club; pres. Madison Women's Mcpl. Golf League; tutor literacy students, 1991—. Named Hon. Cannoeer, St. Louis Civil War Roundtable; recipient award of excellence, Wis. Fedn. Women's Clubs. Mem.: AAUW (chmn. antiques group 1991—93), Nat. League Am. Pen Women, Internat. Platford Assn., Women's Club Madison (pres. 1997—2000). Home: 6115 Imperial Dr Waunakee WI 53597-9686

BRINKMAN, JOHN ANTHONY, historian, educator; b. Chgo., July 4, 1934; s. Adam John and Alice (Davies) B.; m. Monique E. Geschier, Mar. 24, 1970; 1 son, Charles E. AB, Loyola U., Chgo., 1956, MA, 1958; PhD, U. Chgo., 1962. Rsch. assoc. Oriental Inst., U. Chgo., 1963, dir. inst., 1972-81, asst. prof. Assyriology and ancient history, 1964-66, assoc. prof., 1966—70, prof., 1970—84, Charles H. Swift disting. svc. prof., 1984—2001, chmn. dept., 1969—72, Charles H. Swift disting. svc. prof. emeritus, 2001—. Ann. prof. Am. Schs. Oriental Rsch., Baghdad, 1968-69; chmn. Baghdad Schs. Com., 1970-85, chmn. exec. com., 1973-75, trustee, 1975-90; chmn. vis. com. dept. Near Ea. langs. and civilizations Harvard U., 1995-2001. Author: Political History of Post-Kassite Babylonia, 1968, Materials and Studies for Kassite History, Vol. I, 1976; Prelude to Empire, 1984; editorial bd. Chgo. Assyrian Dictionary, 1977—, State Archives Assyria, 1985—; editor in charge Babylonian sect. Royal Inscriptions of Mesopotamia, 1979-91; contbr. numerous articles to profl. jours. Fellow Am. Research Inst., in Turkey, 1971; sr. fellow Nat. Endowment Humanities, 1973-74; Guggenheim fellow, 1984-85 Fellow Am. Acad. Arts and Scis.; mem. Am. Oriental Soc. (pres. Middle West chpt. 1971-72), Am. Schs. of Oriental Rsch., Brit. Inst. Persian Studies, Brit. Sch. Archaeology in Iraq, Deutsche Orient Gesellschaft, Brit. Inst. Archaeology at Ankara. Roman Catholic. Home: 1321 E 56th St Apt 4 Chicago IL 60637-1762 Office: U Chgo 1155 E 58th St Chicago IL 60637-1569

BRINKMEYER, MARY FOSS, school system administrator; b. Cin., Sept. 28, 1949; d. Edward Henry and Amelia Louise (Hamberg) Foss; m. Joseph Edward Brinkmeyer, July 1, 1972; children: Lauren, Joseph Edward III. AB, Trinity Coll., 1971; MEd, Xavier U., 1972, postgrad. in Ednl. Adminstrn., 1989-91. Cert. sch. supt., Ohio. Tchr. Children's World, Schaumburg, Ill., 1972-74; directress Summit Country Day Sch., Cin., 1974-78, asst. to headmaster, 1989—, chmn. ednl. orgn. study, 1992-93; chmn. Educating for Character program, 1993—. Mem. prin.'s ctr. Harvard Grad. Sch. Edn. Fellow Inst. Devel. Ednl. Activities (Disting. Edn. award 1992-94, chmn. strategic planning com.); mem. ASCD, Am. Montessori Soc., Jr. League Cin., NAFE, Nat. Inst. Bus. Mgmt., ASCDX, Nat. Ctr. for Effective Schs. R&D, Ctr. for Advancement Ethics and Character. Roman Catholic. Avocations: ice skating, physical fitness, travel. Office: Summit Country Day Sch 2161 Grandin Rd Cincinnati OH 45208-3300

BRINKMEYER, ROBERT HERMAN, JR., American literature and Southern studies educator; b. Washington, July 7, 1951; s. Robert Herman and Mary (Yarbrough) B. BA, Duke U., 1973; MA, U. N.C., 1975, PhD, 1980. From instr. to asst. prof. N.C. Cen. U., Durham, 1975-86; asst. prof. Tulane U., New Orleans, 1986-88; assoc. prof. Am. lit. and So. studies U. Miss., Oxford, 1988-91, prof., 1991—. Author: Three Catholic Writers of the Modern South, 1985, The Art and Vision of Flannery O'Connor, 1989; mem. editorial bd. Miss. Quar., 1988—; contbr. articles to profl. jours. Mem. MLA, South Atlantic MLA, Coll. English Assn., Soc. for Study of So. Lit., Phi Beta Kappa, Phi Eta Sigma. Home: 417 E Sutton St Fayetteville AR 72701-4335 Office: Dept English U Miss University MS 38677

BRISKO, CYNTHIA BELL, primary education educator; b. Dallas, July 16, 1956; d. Charles Edward and Ethelyn Mary (Szad) Bell; m. Thomas A. Brisko, June 23, 1984. BS in Edn. magna cum laude, U. North Tex., 1979, MEd, 1982. Cert. elem. edn. grades 1-8, elem. English, kindergarten, Tex. Kindergarten tchr. Plano (Tex.) Ind. Sch. Dist., 1980-90, Coppell (Tex.) Sch. Dist., 1990—. Workshop presenter Tex. Assn. for Gifted and Talented, Houston, 1990; Kindergarten team leader Coppell Sch. Dist., 1993—. Mem. NEA, ASCD, Nat. Assn. for the Edn. Young Children, So. Assn. on Children Under Six, Assn. Childhood Edn. Internat., Kindergarten Tchrs. Tex., Collin County Assn. for the Edn. Young Children, Tex. State Tchrs. Assn., Phi Kappa Phi. Presbyterian. Avocations: reading, snow skiing, water aerobics, antique shopping.

BRISTOL, STANLEY DAVID, mathematician, educator; b. Mankato, Minn., Dec. 30, 1948; s. Robert Frederick Bristol and Ruth Charlotte (Buckeye) Bristol Bond; m. Elaine Metzer, Jan. 30, 1970; children: Thomas Alan, Jennifer Elise. BS, Ariz. State U., 1969, MA, 1970. Cert. secondary tchr. with gifted edorsement. Math. tchr. Saguaro HS, Scottsdale, Ariz., 1973-74, Poston Jr. HS, Mesa, Ariz., 1974-77, Corona del Sol HS, Tempe, Ariz., 1977—, chair math. dept., 1990—2003; math. tchr. Ariz. State U., Tempe, 1989—. Sunday sch. tchr. 1st United Meth. Ch., Tempe, 1983—93. With U.S. Army, 1970—73. Named Tchr. of the Yr., Diablos C. of C., 1987, 1998, Tribune Educator of Yr., 1995, Honored Educator, Flinn Found., 1997, Outstanding Adj. Facult, Rio Salado Coll., 2000; recipient Presdl. award for excellence in math. tchg., 1990. Mem.: NEA, Math. Assn. Am., Ariz. Assn. Tchrs. Math., Nat. Coun. Tchrs. Math., Ind. Order Foresters. Avocations: photography, reading, bowling, computers. Office: Corona del Sol High Sch 1001 E Knox Rd Tempe AZ 85284-3204 E-mail: sbristol.cds@tuksd.k12.az.us.

BRISTOW, CAROLYN LUREE CUMMINGS, library media specialist; b. Jackson, Mich., Feb. 20, 1943; d. Leon Dewitt and Lulu Luree (Boyle) Cummings; m. Michael Barry Bristow, June 21, 1964; children: Michael Christopher, Jeffery Alan, Benjamin Aaron. AA, Jackson Jr. Coll., 1963; BA, Western Mich. U., 1965; postgrad., UCLA, 1969; MEd, Wright State U., Dayton, Ohio, 1996. Cert. tchr. 1-8, ed. tech. specialist K-12, Ohio. Libr. elem. sch. Portage (Mich.) Pub. Schs., 1965-67; substitute tchr. Redondo Beach (Calif.) City Schs., 1967, libr. elem. sch., 1968, libr. cons., 1968-69; dir. ednl. media svcs. Troy (Ohio) City Schs., 1975-78; libr. elem. sch. Bethel Local Schs., Tipp City, Ohio, 1974-75, K-8 media specialist,

1982-92, tech. coord., 1992—. Youth music leader LDS Ch., Huber Heights, Ohio, 1976—; coun. tng. chmn. Boy Scouts Am., Springfield, Ohio, 1978-90; pres. Menlo Park PTO, Huber Heights, 1982-84. Recipient dist. award of merit Boy Scouts Am., 1986, Silver Beaver award, 1988; Tchr. of Yr. award Bethel Local Schs., 1987; 21st Century grantee Bethel Bd. Edn., 1992; Jennings scholar Martha E. Jennings Found., 1993. Mem. Ohio Ednl. Libr. Media Assn., Greater Miami Valley Ednl. Tech. Coun. Avocations: playing mountain lap dulcimer, piano, church organist and choir director, reading, gardens. Home: 932 Lakeshore Dr Medway OH 45341-1510 Office: Bethel Local Schs 7490 State Route 201 Tipp City OH 45371-7316

BRISTOW, MICHAEL, cardiologist, researcher, medical educator; b. West Palm Beach, Fla., Nov. 8, 1944; s. Julius Cyrus and Rosemary Logsdon Bristow; m. Karyn A. Kowalski, June 28, 1978; children: Justin, Nathan, Jacques. BS in Vet. Scis., U. Ill., 1966; MD, U. Ill., Chgo., 1970, PhD in Pharmacology, 1971. Diplomate Am. Bd. Internal Medicine, cert. Am. Bd. Cardiovascular Disease. Asst. prof. cardiology Stanford (Calif.) U. Sch. Medicine, 1983—84; assoc. prof. cardiology U. Utah Sch. Medicine, Salt Lake City, 1984—88, prof. internal medicine (cardiology), 1988—91; dir. Temple Hoyne Buell Heart Ctr. U. Colo. Health Scis. Ctr., Denver, 1991—; head divsn. cardiology U. Colo. Sch. Medicine, Denver, 1991—, S. Gilbert Blount endowed chair cardiology, 2000—; acting dir. U. Colo. Cardiovascular Inst., Denver, 1998—. Sole practitioner Nat. Health Svc. Field Sta. (USPHS Nat. Health Corps), West Yellowstone, Mont., 1972—74; founder, sci. co-founder Myogen, Inc., Westminster, Colo., 1996, bd. dirs., 1998—, chmn. sci. adv. bd., 2000—; mem. sci. adv. bd. Cardiovasc. Clin. Rsch., 2000—, Genzyme, 2000—, Covalent, 2000—, CVRx, 2000—; founder ARCA Discovery, Inc., Aurora, Colo., 2001. Patentee in field. Named top heart failure investigator, Sci. Watch, 1999; recipient Therapeutic Frontiers award, Am. Coll. Clin. Pharmacy, 1993. Fellow: Am. Coll. Cardiology, Am. Heart Assn. (Desert/Mountain Affiliate Rsch. Com. 2001—, Ed Ricketts award 2000); mem.: Assn. Am. Physicians, Assn. Univ. Cardiologists, Am. Fedn. Clin. Rsch., Am. Soc. Clin. Investigation, Heart Failure Soc. Am. (exec. coun. 1999—, founding), Coun. on Basic Cardiovascular Scis. Avocations: skiing, basketball, hiking. Office: U Colo Health Scis Ctr 4200 E 9th Ave B130 Denver CO 80262

BRITES, JOSÉ BAPTISTA, secondary education educator, writer, artist; b. Alcorochel, Torres Novas, Portugal, June 7, 1945; came to U.S., 1970; s. José and Ludovina (Guia) B.; m. Olga M. Boyd; children: David Joseph, Kevin Daniel. BA in Art, BA in Lang., Brown U., 1981, MEd, 1982. Cert. secondary tchr., R.I. Interpreter Davies Vocat. High Sch., Lincoln, R.I., 1983-86, bilingual tchr., 1986-87, LEP tchr., coord., 1987-96, guidance counselor, 1997—. LEP state adv. bd., Providence, 1990-92; vice dir. Immigrants Cultural Found., Lisbon, Portugal, 1988-91; co-founder Peregrinação-Arts/Letters, Lisbon, 1983-91, Sol XXI Arts/Letters, 1992—; founder, pres. Peregrinação Publs., 1995; apptd. Gov. Bruce Sundlum to bd. R.I. State Coun. Arts, 1993-97; guest poet II and III Internat. Symposium on Poetry, U. Coimbra, Portugal, 1995, 98; mem. Portuguese-Am. Leadership Coun. of U.S., Washington. Author: (poetry) Poemas Sem Poesia, 1975, Imigramar, 1981, (short stories) Imigramantes, 1984, Estórias Para A História de Alcorochel, 1994, Twenty Five Years of Poetry, 1995, Coisas e Loisas das nossas terras, 1996, Coisas do Coiso e da Coisa, 1996, Do Ribatejo ao Além-Tejo, 1998, (novel) De Casa para o Inferno, 2000, Cantigas ao Desafio na Diáspora, 2001, Cantigas ao Desafio n América do Norte e Açores, 2001, Portugal e a Saudade, em Verson, 2001—, Cantigas Do Desafio Velhas E Desgarradas, 2002, Jasco Aguiar, Meio Seculo A Cantar Cantigas, 2002; editor: Ronnie, A Smiling Life With Down Syndrome, 2002; singer Portuguese Heritage Choral, Pawtucket, R.I.; staff writer Portuguese Times, New Bedford, Mass., Portuguese Tribune, San Jose, Calif., O Emigrante, Lisbon, O ALMONDA, Torres Novas, O Mirante, Chamusca, O Ribatejo, Santarèm LUSO-AMERICANO, The Portuguese Post, Newark, Correio dos Açores, Azores, Português na Austrália, Voice, Can. Recipient Community award Portuguese Am. Citizens, 1984, 1st prize in several poetry contests, citations from Sen. Claiborne Pell, 1984, Gov. Joseph Garrahy, 1984, Mayor Henry S. Kinch, 1979, New Bedford Mayor Rosemary Tierney; honored by CASA DA SAUDADE Libr., 1995. Mem. Portuguese Writers Assn., Am. Acad. Poets. Avocations: painting, sculpting (metal), book reviews, travel. Home: 36 Brayton Ave Rumford RI 02916-2513 Office: Davies Jr HS Jenckes Hill Rd Lincoln RI 02865 E-mail: jbrites@peregrinacao.com.

BRITT, MARGARET MARY, finance educator; b. Balt., Jan. 21, 1951; d. Joseph John and Lottie Elizabeth (Zielinski) Britt. BA in Elem. Edn., U. Mass., 1972; BSBA, Boston U., 1979, M in Human Resource Edn., 1990; DBA in Human Resource Mgmt., Nova Southeastern U., 2002. Cert. tchr. elem. edn., music Mass., Va., N.C., vocat. tech. educator in bus. mktg. Mass. Internal auditor Digital Equip. Corp., Maynard, Mass., 1979-82, sr. fin. analyst FDP, 1982-83, sr. fin. analyst sales Stow, Mass., 1983-85, cons. trainer Maynard, 1985-87, fin. cons., trainer, 1987-90, mgr. corp. fin. edn., 1990-94; automated office instr. Mass. Job Tng., Worcester, 1995-97; sci. tchr. Holden Christian Acad., Eastern Nazarene Coll., Worcester, 1997—, instr. dept. bus. Quincy, Mass., 1998-2000, assoc. prof. dept. bus., 2000—02, asst. prof. bus. adminstrn., 2002—; assoc. prof. dept. bus. Mt. Vernon (Ohio) Nazarene U., 2003—. Part-time instr. fin. continuing edn. dept. Syracuse U., 1990—91; adj. prof. bus. Eastern Nazarene Coll., Quincy, Mass., 1994—; bd. dirs. Am. Biog. Inst.; spkr. in field. Sec. Parsons Hill Homeowners Assn., Worcester, 1985—90; presenter time mgmt. workshop MIT-Soc. Women Engrs. and Alumnae, Cambridge, 1988, 1989. Named Outstanding Young Women of Am., 1984. Mem.: AAUW, NAFE, ASTD, Nat. Mus. Women in the Arts, Inst. Internal Auditors. Avocations: walking, reading, singing, cooking. Home: 387 Nantasket Ave Apt 5 Hull MA 02045-2748 Office: Eastern Nazarene Coll 23 E Elm Ave Quincy MA 02170-2905

BRITTAIN, SISTER JANELLE ANN, parochial school educator; b. Coffeyville, Kans., Sept. 10, 1939; d. Earl Eugene and Annie Mary (Wishall) B. BS in Elem. Edn., Sacred Heart Coll., 1964; MA in Classroom Reading, Cardinal Stritch Coll., 1973. Cert. elem. tchr., Kans.; joined Sisters of St. Joseph, Roman Cath. Ch., 1959. Primary grades tchr. St. Clements, Hayward, Calif., 1962-64, St. Michael's Sch., Mulvane, Kans., 1964-66, St. Mary's Sch., Ulysses, Kans., 1966-69, Wichita, Kans., 1969-71, Sacred Heart Sch., Dodge City, Kans., 1971-78, Holy Name Sch., Winfield, Kans., 1978-81, Holy Savior Sch., Wichita, 1981-82, St. Felicitas Sch., San Leandro, Calif., 1982-87, St. Mary's Sch., Ponca City, Okla., 1987-92, Holy Name Sch., Coffeyville, Kans., 1992—. Mem. Internat. Reading Assn., Ea. Hills Reading Assn., Kans. Reading Assn. Avocations: tutoring, walking, corresponding with friends. Office: Holy Name Sch 406 Willow St Coffeyville KS 67337-4899 Home: 409 Willow St Coffeyville KS 67337-4835

BRITTELL-WHITEHEAD, DIANE PEEPLES, secondary education educator, addiction counselor; b. Binghamton, N.Y., Feb. 2, 1950; d. Berbie Winfred and Vera (Bufano) Peeples; m. Edward James Brittell, June 14, 1975 (div. 1991); children: Jesse, Aimeé, Jeneé; m. Paul Whitehead, July 20, 1996. BS in Mental Health, Hahnemann U., 1974; MEd, cert. reading specialist, Widener U., 1987, MEd. Cert. in spl. edn., allied addictions practitioner, Pa.; cert. criminal justice specialist. Cashier Pantry Pride Markets, Norristown, Pa., 1964-74; tchr. Parkway Day Sch., Phila., 1973-77; diagnostic tchr. Sleighton Farms, Wawa, Pa., 1984-85; tchr., reading specialist Ridley Sch. Dist., Ridley Park, Pa., 1987—. Assoc. prof. Neumann Coll. Grad. Sch. Wilkes U., Pa., 1999—; mental health worker, tchr. Hahnemann Hosp., Phila., summers 1988-94; addictions counselor Crozer Chester (Pa.) Med. Ctr., 1991—, Keystone Rehab. Ctr., Chester, 1993—; tutor, Chester, 1985-87; lectr. state tchrs. convs., Pa., N.J., 1986-88, various rehab. workshops, 1986—. Contbr. articles to various publs. Vol. St. Mary's Orphanage, Ambler, Pa., 1967-69. Mem. NEA, ASCD, AAUW, Nat. Assn. Drug Abuse Counselors, Pa. Edn. Assn., Pa. Assn. Drug Abuse Counselors. Republican. Avocations: shark research, scuba diving, writing, reading, music. Home: 400 E Hinckley Ave Ridley Park PA 19078-2518 Office: Ridley Mid Sch Ridley Park PA 19078

BRITTON, CHARLES VALENTINE, secondary education educator; b. Kingsport, Tenn., Jan. 18, 1947; s. Charles E.C. and Nancy (Blanchard) B.; m. Rose Patryce Guthrie, Mar. 23, 1968; 1 child, Rose Patryce. BS, Duke U., 1969; PhD, U. Fla., 1977. Computer analyst/cons. to automotive industry, 1977-80; tchr. physics N.C. Sch. Sci. and Math., Durham, 1980—, dept. chmn., 1981-84. Master tchr., instr. Woodrow Wilson Nat. Fellowship Found., Princeton, N.J., 1988—. Contbr. articles to profl. jours. With U.S. Army, 1970-72. Tandy Tech. scholar, 1997. Mem. Am. Phys. Soc., Am. Assn. Physics Tchrs. (physics teaching resource agt. 1986—), N.C. Sci. Tchrs. Assn. (bd. dirs. 1993—). Office: NC Sch Sci and Math 1219 Broad St Durham NC 27705-3577

BRITTON, RUTH ANN WRIGHT, elementary educator; b. Ft. Smith, Ark., Apr. 4, 1943; d. Ralph M. and Margaret E. (Reising) Wright; m. Joseph D. Britton, Sept. 25, 1965; children: Beth, Meg, Jo. BA in Elem. Edn., Concordia Tchrs. Coll., River Forest, Ill., 1965; MS, Kans. State U., 1978. Cert. in reading K-12, elem. 1-6, developmental reading K-12, developmental edn. Tchr. 5th grade Pickens (S.C.) Sch. Dist., 1966-68; Tchr. grades 5 and 2 Manhattan (Kans.) City Schs., 1969, 77-78; Chpt. I reading tchr. Montgomery County Schs., Christianburg, Va., 1982-86; Dir. Jr. HS reading lab. Hillsborough County Schs., Tampa, Fla., 1986-92; Instr., dept. head Cochise Coll., Douglas, Ariz., 1993—. Co-author: Reading Handbook for Parents, Making Connections, a sociology and reading handbook. Recipient Helping Hands award for vol. svc. U.S. Army 7th Corps in Germany, 1980, Excellence in Edn. by Nat. Inst. for Staff and Organizational Development, 1997-98; named Outstanding Instr. Cochise Coll., 1999-2000, Tchr. of Yr. TCJS, 1989-90. Mem. Internat. Reading Assn., Literacy Vols., Coll. Reading and Learning Assn., Governor's Commn. for Svc. Learning and Volunteerism, 2002-. Office: Cochise Coll 4190 West Highway 80 Douglas AZ 85607

BRIXEY, SHAWN ALAN, digital media artist, media educator, director; b. Springfield, Mo., Jan. 23, 1961; s. Alan M. and Mary Lou (Peters) B.; m. Sonja Max, 1998. BFA in New Media, Kansas City Art Inst., 1985; MS in Advanced Visual Studies, MIT, 1988. Grad. tchg. asst. dept. arch. MIT, Cambridge, 1985-87; Leonardo fellow, inaugural vis. fellow Leonardo Project U. Mich., Ann Arbor, 1988; adj. faculty, lectr. CAVS dept. arch. MIT, Cambridge, 1989; asst. prof., dir. media arts program art U. Ky., Lexington, 1990, grad. faculty, assoc. mem. Coll. Fine Arts, 1991; asst. prof., chair cross-disciplinary arts program Sch. Art U. Wash., Seattle, 1994, grad. faculty Coll. Arts and Scis., 1995-98; disting. fellow Inst. for New Media San Francisco State U., 1997-98; asst. prof. digital media/new genre U. Calif., Berkeley, 1998—2002, dir. Ctr. Digital Art and New Media Rsch., 1998—2002; assoc. prof. U. Wash., Seattle, 2002—, assoc. dir. ctr. digital arts and experimental media, 2002—. Dir. exptl. media lab. dept. art U. Ky., Lexington, 1992; dir. studio for media arts rsch. and techs. lab U. Wash., Seattle, 1994-98, co-dir. lab animation for arts, 1995-98, acting dir. Ctr. Advanced Rsch. Tech. in the Arts and Humanities, 1996-97; Disting. mentor in multimedia San Francisco State U., 1997; keynote spkr. Mayor's Internat. Tech. Summit, San Francisco, 1998; mem. U. Calif., Pres.'s Planning Group on Digital Art, 1998; dir. critical hist. issues net art Nat. Symposium U. Calif., Berkeley, 2000; keynote spkr. KC Jubilee Internat. Film Festival, Kansas City, Mo., 2000, Internat. Planetworks Conf., Presidio, San Francisco, 2000; spkr. 0/0/01 exhbn. San Francisco Mus. of Modern Art, 2001; judge Art Future award, Taiwan, 2000; spkr. in field. Exhbns. include Documenta 8, Kassel, Germany, 1987, 85th Anniversary of the German Art Union, Badischer, Kunstverein, Karlsruhe, Germany, 1988, Cranbrook Acad. Art Mus., Bloomhill Hills, Mich., 1990, Contemporary Art Ctr., Cin., 1991, State Mus., Columbia, S.C., 1992, MIT Mus., Cambridge, Mass., 1995, Del. Ctr. Contemporary Art, Wilmington, 1996, Internat. Symposium Electronic Art ISEA 97, Chgo., Cultural Olympiad, 1998, Winter Olympics Nagano, Japan, 1999, Design and Architecture Triennial, Cooper Hewitt Nat. Design Mus., N.Y.C., 2000, Inst. for Studies in the Arts, Ariz. State U., 2000, Henry Art Gallery, U. Wash., Seattle, 2001; prodr. "Digital Dreams" (Pacific Film Archives/Premiere Student Digital Films), Berkeley, 2000, Sea Changes (Pacific film Archives/Digital Film Festival), Berkeley, Calif., 2001; interviewee Springboard (PBS TV), 2001. Mentor advanced placement new media and digital video/audio courses Fayette County H.S. Sys., Lexington, Ky., 1990-93; bd. dirs. Ctr. for Contemporary Art, Seattle, 1996-98; keynote spkr. Seattle-Northshore Sch. Dist. Leadership Conf., 1998. Recipient Major Equip. award Silicon Graphics Industries, 1994, Apple Computer Inc., 1994, Newport/Klinger, 1996, Intel Corp., 1997, Boxlight Corp., 2000; New Media fellow Rckefeller Found., 2003. Democrat. Episcopalian. Avocations: scuba diving, tennis, collecting old film, media electronics, electric toys. Office: Univ of Wash Ctr for Digital Arts & Experimentl Media 3 Thompson Hall Seattle WA 98195 Home: 5622 Keystone Pl N Seattle WA 98103 Office Fax: 206-616-1746. E-mail: shawnx@u.washington.edu.

BRIZENDINE, ANTHONY LEWIS, civil engineering educator; b. Bluefield, W.Va., Apr. 27, 1962; s. Donald Lewis B. and Erma Louise Havens; m. Laora Eugenia Dauberman, July 13, 1991; children: Lauren Renia, Elizabeth Kaitlyn, Courtney Elaine. AAS, Wytheville C.C., 1987; BS, Bluefield State Coll., 1989; MSCE, Va. Poly. Inst. and State U., 1990; PhD, W.Va. U., 1997. Draftsman, detailer Peters Equipment Co., Inc., Bluefield, 1981-85, design engr., 1985-87, project civil engr., 1987-89; instr. Wytheville (Va.) C.C., 1991, Fairmont (W.Va.) State Coll., 1991-93, asst. prof., 1993-95, dir. honors program, 1994—, assoc. prof., 1996-99, prof., 1999—. Cons. U.S. Army Corps Engrs., Vicksburg, Miss., 1992-94; advisor ASCE Student Orgn. Fairmont State Coll., 1991—. Grantee NSF/WV EPSCOR, 1993, 94, 95; recipient W.Va. Young Civil Engr. of Yr. award, 1995, Technol. Accreditation Commn. Accreditation Bd. for Engring. and Technol., 1998—. Mem. ASTM, ASCE (nat. tech. curricula and accreditation com. 1996-2000, v.p. W.Va. sect. 1994, treas., 1997—, v.p. W.Va. No. br. 1994, 98, sec./treas. 1993, del. mgmt. conf. 1995, chairperson W.Va. sect. continuing edn., pres. No. W.Va. br. 1996, pres.-elect 1995), Am. Soc. Engring. Educators, Am. Soc. Hwy. Engrs., Internat. Soc. Soil Mechanics and Found. Engrs. Home: PO Box 1043 Fairmont WV 26555-1043 Office: Fairmont State Coll 1201 Locust Ave Fairmont WV 26554-2451

BROAD, CYNTHIA ANN MORGAN, special education educator, consultant; b. Toledo, Ohio, Apr. 19, 1947; d. James Glenn and Elaine Louise (Morris) Morgan; m. Alan Hugh Broad, Aug. 2, 1975; children: Travis Alan, Trevor Morgan. BS in Edn., Bowling Green State U., 1969, MEd, 1970, Accomplished Grad. (hon.), 1993. Cert. spl. edn. tchr., elem. tchr. Tchr. remedial reading ednl. therapy unit Toledo (Ohio) State Hosp., 1970; spl. edn. tchr. Green Elem. Sch. L'Anse Creuse (Mich.) pub. schs., 1970-81, spl. edn. tchr. Lobbestael Elem. Sch., 1982-95, spl. edn. cons., 1989-95, spl. edn. tchr. Higgins Elem. Sch., 1995—. Contbr. articles to profl. jours.; developer talking animal idea telephone teachng tool, 1978. Fellow Masters Level Bowling Green State U., 1969-70; recipient Tchr. of Yr. State of Mich. Dept. Edn., 1989-90, Nat. Educator award Milken Family Found., 1990, Burger King Disting. Svc. to Edn. award, 1990. Mem. NEA, Mich. Edn. Assn., Mich. Reading Assn., Mich. Assn. Children with Learning Disabilities, Coun. Exceptional Children (Golden Nugget award 1989), Delta Kappa Gamma, Kappa Delta Pi. Avocations: technology, golf, biking, telecommunications, reading. Home: 71 S Deeplands Rd Grosse Pointe Shores MI 48236-2643 Office: L'Anse Creuse Higgins Elem Sch 29901 24 Mile Rd Chesterfield MI 48051-1760

BROADY, FANNIE MARIE, vocational school educator; b. Marshall, Tex., Feb. 1, 1931; d. Mitchell and Minnie U. (Pylant) Turner; m. Edward Cortez Broady, Sept. 19, 1971. B in Social Sci., Bishop Coll., 1949. Cert. Office Tech., Ky., High Sch., Tex. Sec. Harrison County Well-Child Clinic, Marshall, Tex., 1950; house parent Fannie Walls Children's Home, Oakland, Calif., 1951; accounts receivable clk. Bishop Coll., Marshall, 1953; Sec. Jarvis Christian Coll., Hawkins, Tex., 1954-55, 57-58, Tex. Blind, Deaf, and Orphan Sch., Austin, 1955-57; acting dir. pub. rels. Jarvis Christian Coll., 1959-60; sec. Tex. So. U., Houston, 1960-61; instr. W. Ky. Vocat. Sch., Paducah, 1965-93, substitute tchr., 1993; ret., 1993. Owner Marie's Sec. Svcs., Marshall, 1943-61, Houston, 1961-65. Organizer state conf. Ky. State NAACP, Paducah, 1977. Named Duchess of Paducah City of Paducah, 1982; recipient Pres'. Svc. awd. Ky. Branch NAACP, 1977. Mem. Am. Vocat. Assn., Ky. Vocat. Assn., First Dist. Vocat. Assn., Ky. Court Reporters' Assn. (assoc.), Nat. Court Reporters' Assn. (assoc.), Delta Pi Epsilon, Phi Beta Kappa (Gamma Pi chpt. co-hostess regional mtg. 1982). Democrat. Baptist. Avocations: piano, speaking and operating shorthand machine. Home: 1006 Round Table Ct Louisville KY 40222-4422

BROBECK, DAVID GEORGE, middle school administrator; b. Rochester, Pa., Nov. 7, 1953; s. Stanley Clark and Jane Kirk (McBurney) B.; m. Gretchen Ann Bricker, June 18, 1977; children: Melissa Ann, Emily Elizabeth, Lauren Rebecca, Sarah Jane. BA, Calif. Luth. U., 1975; MEd, Kent State U., 1978, PhD, 1998. Cert. reading and English tchr., Ohio; cert. elem. and secondary prin., Ohio; cert. supt., Ohio. Tchr. Kent (Ohio) City Schs., 1975-92; asst. football coach Roosevelt High Sch., Kent, 1975-92, summer prin., 1987-92, head track coach, 1990-92; track coach Davey Middle Sch., Kent, 1978-89, asst. prin., 1992-96; prin. Woodridge Mid. Sch., Peninsula, Ohio, 1996—. Guest lectr. Kent State U., 1985-98, Akron U., 1997, Ursuline Coll., 1996-98; presenter in field. Bd. dirs. Kent Credit Union, 1981-90; coun. pres. Trinity Luth. Ch., Kent, 1986-87; dir. Kent Youth Ctr., 1986. Named Metro League Coach of Yr., Record Pub., 1990, 91, 92, Akron Dist. Coach of Yr., Akron Area Track Coaches Assn., 1991; recipient Bowman fellow Kent State Univ., 1993-94. Mem. ASCD, Ohio Middle Sch. Assn. (exec. bd. 1998—), Nat. Middle Sch. Assn., Ohio Assn. Secondary Sch. Prins., Nat. Assn. Secondary Sch. Prins., Ohio Assn. Elem. Sch. Prins., Phi Delta Kappa (IDEA fellow). Democratic. Avocations: jogging, woodworking, playing guitar, singing, reading. Office: Woodridge Mid Sch 4451 Quick Rd Peninsula OH 44264-9706 Home: 1875 Pearce Cir Salem OH 44460-1861

BROCK, ANGELA EULENE DOUGLASS, education educator; b. McMinnville, Tenn., Apr. 16, 1972; d. John Douglass, Shirley Eulene (McGee) Douglass; m. Tyson Lynn Brock, June 26, 1993; children: Allison Victoria, Jonathan Hunter. BS, Mid. Tenn. State U., 1993, MEd, 1995. Tchr. F.C. Boyd, Sr. Christian Sch., McMinnville, Tenn., 1994—99; adj. faculty Motlow State C.C., McMinnville, 2000—. Leader Girl Scouts U.S., 2002—; Bible tchr. Ctrl. Ch. of Christ, McMinnville, 1987—, event coord., 1998—. Mem.: DAR, AAUW. Avocations: camping, crafts, travel, sewing. Home: 1668 Fairview Rd Mc Minnville TN 37110

BROCK, GERALD WAYNE, telecommunications educator; b. Hanford, Calif., Mar. 31, 1948; s. Aston A. and Leila L. (McAtee) B.; m. Ruth Carol Reisner, June 27, 1971; children: Jane, Sara, David, James. BA, Harvard U., 1970, PhD, 1973. Asst. prof. U. Ariz., Tucson, 1973-78; assoc. prof. Bethel Coll., St. Paul, 1978-79; econ. cons. Brock Econ. Rsch., St. Paul, 1979-83; economist FCC, Washington, 1983-86, chief acctg. and audits divsn., 1986-87, chief common carrier bur., 1987-89; prof. telecom. George Washington U., Washington, 1990—. Author: The U.S. Computer Industry, 1975, The Telecommunications Industry, 1981, Telecommunication Policy for the Information Age, 1994. Office: George Washington U Telecommunications Program 805 21st St NW Washington DC 20052 E-mail: gbrock@gwu.edu.

BROCK, JAMES WILSON, drama educator, playwright, researcher; b. Greensfork, Ind., May 23, 1919; s. Virgil Prentiss and Blanche (Kerr) B.; m. Martha Faught, June 1942 (div. Mar. 1956); m. Patricia Anne Clemons, Mar. 1956 (div. Nov. 1966); children: Lisa Anne, Tamsen Lee, Julie Michele; m. Marjorie Mellor, Feb. 1, 1969 (dec. Jan. 1995); m. Esther Arzoo, Dec. 18, 1996. AB, Manchester Coll., 1941; MA, Northwestern U., 1942, PhD, 1950. Assoc. prof. Albion (Mich.) Coll., 1946-56; asst. prof. Mich. State U., East Lansing, 1956-57, U. Mich., Ann Arbor, 1957-58; assoc. prof. Fla. State U., Tallahassee, 1958-59; prof. Calif. State U., Northridge, 1959-89. Mng. dir. Plymouth (Mass.) Drama Festival, 1956-58. Author: (plays) Modern Chancel Dramas, 1964, (musical dance drama) The Summons, 1964; contbr. articles to profl. jours. Sgt. USAAF, 1942-45, Middle East, ETO. Decorated Bronze Star; fellow Ch. Soc. for Coll. Work, Eng., 1964; rsch. grantee Calif. State U. Found., 1964, 66, 67. Mem. Am. Soc. Theatre Rsch., Nat. Theatre Conf., Nat. Trust for Historic Preservation, Internat. Found. Theatre Rsch., Theta Alpha Phi (sec.-treas. 1952-57), Delta Sigma Rho. Democrat. Episcopalian. Avocations: travelling, collecting, gardening. Home: Simi Valley, Calif. Died Jan. 22, 2002.

BROCK, LORI ANNE SOWAR, special education educator; b. Mableton, Ga., Sept. 9, 1970; d. Douglas Alan and Trudy Teresa (White) Sowar; m. Russell Hill Brock, June 13, 1992. Student, U. Ga., 1988-90; BS in Spl. Edn., Ga. Coll., 1992. Cert. tchr., Ga. Spl. edn. tchr., tech. coord. Greene-Taliaferro Mid. Sch., Greensboro, Ga., 1992—. Varsity and mid. sch. cheerleading coach Greene-Taliaferro H.S. and Mid. Sch., 1993-95; mem. Project 2061-AAAS, Greene County, Greensboro, 1994-95. Mem. ASCD, Nat. Coun. Tchrs. Math. Roman Catholic. Avocations: waterskiing, arts and crafts, computers, reading. Office: Greene-Taliaferro Mid Sch 1002 S Main St Greensboro GA 30642-1216

BROCK, LUCY RAY BRANNEN, science educator; b. Atlanta, July 23, 1950; d. Rupert Guy and Madge Rabena (Williams) Brannen; m. Michael Levin Brock, May 1, 1983; stepchildren: Eric James, Jason Leon. BS, U. Ga., 1972; MS, N.C. State U., 1975, PhD, 1981. Lab. dir., rsch. assoc. Ctr. Reproductive Rsch. and Testing, Raleigh, N.C., 1981-85; tchr. Wake Christian Acad., Raleigh, 1985-86, head dept. sci., 1986—, dir. spl. projects, 1990—96. Owner Scholastic Concepts, Raleigh, 1993—. Author: Study Strategies for Students, Books 1 and 2, 1993, Biology Study Guide, 1994, revised yearly; contbr. articles to profl. jours. Active WCA Faculty Handbell Choir, 1994—. Mem. N.C. Sci. Tchrs. Assn., Nat. Assn. Biology Tchrs., Sigma Xi Rsch. Soc. Republican. Baptist.

BROCKENBROUGH, THOMAS WILLIAM, civil engineer, educator; b. Buena Vista, Va., July 14, 1920; s. Bernard Jeremiah and Myrtle (Orr) Brockenbrough; m. Mary Lou Kocher, Aug. 1954; children: Thomas William, Mary Alice. BSCE, Va. Poly. Inst., 1942; MS in Civil Engring., MIT, 1946. Registered profl. engr., Del. Asst. prof. civil engring. Va. Poly. Inst., Blacksburg, 1949—53; assoc. prof. U. Del., Newark, 1953—64, asst. dean Coll. Engring., 1964—74, prof., 1974—87, chmn. dept. engring., 1984—87, prof. emeritus, 1988—. Cons. engr. E.I. DuPont de Nemours, Wilmington, Del., 1980—. Contbr. articles to profl. jours. Chmn. bd. appeals City of Newark, 1973—; elder First Presbyn. Ch., Newark, 1958—. Named Del. Engr. of Yr., Del. Soc. Profl. Engrs., 1979. Mem.: ASCE (pres. 1964), Del. Acad. Scis. (pres. 1978), Am. Concrete Inst., Am. Soc. Engring. Edn., Blue and Gold Club (bd. dirs.), Omicron Delta Kappa, Sigma Xi, Tau Beta Pi, Chi Epsilon. Democrat. Avocations: gardening, photography. Home: 5 S Dillwyn Rd Newark DE 19711-5543

BROCKET, JUDITH ANN, elementary education mathematics educator; b. Muscatine, Iowa, Feb. 3, 1942; d. Kenneth McKay and Dorothy Pearl (Stewart) Uebe; m. Raymond Gene Brocket, July 28, 1963; 1 son, Jamie.

AA, Muscatine Jr. Coll., 1962; BA, Parsons Coll., 1965; grad., Children's Inst. of Lit., 1987. Cert. tchr., Iowa. Swim instr. for handicapped ARC, Burlington, IA, 1965; 3d grade tchr. Burlington Community Sch. Dist., 1965-68, 5th grade tchr., 1970-80, chpt. I math. tchr., 1980—; 4th grade tchr. West Burlington (Iowa) Community Sch. Dist., 1968-70. Presenter in field; mem. North Cen. Accreditation Com., 1984-87; mem. Lit. Mag. Com., 1988—. Contbr. articles to profl. publs.; author math. workbooks, curriculum guide. Pres. Burlington PTA, 1981-82, treas., 1988-89; mem., spokesperson Burlington Sch. Dist. Adv. Com., 1980—; mem. Burlington Parent Adv. Com., 1980—; nom. coun. Messiah Lutheran Ch. Recipient cert. of merit U.S. Dept. Edn., 1987; Fed. Govt. grantee, 1983, 84. Mem. NEA, Iowa State Edn. Assn., Burlington Edn. Assn., Burlington Art Guild, Alpha Delta Kappa. Democrat. Lutheran. Avocations: reading, oil painting, bridge, golf, sewing. Home: 2819 Shamrock Dr Burlington IA 52601-2318

BROCKETT, RALPH GROVER, adult education educator; b. Toledo, Ohio, Feb. 22, 1954; s. Ralph Grover and Hazel Anna (Frederick) B.; m. Patricia Anne Roney, Aug. 3, 1979 (div. Jan. 1997); 1 child, Megan Roney Brockett; m. Mary Florence Rowden, July 20, 2002. BA, U. Toledo (Ohio), 1976, MEd, 1977; PhD, Syracuse (N.Y.) U., 1982. Cert. gerontology, 1982. Continuing edn. project asst. SUNY, Albany, 1978-79; adminstrv. asst. adult edn. program Syracuse U., 1979-81, asst. prof. adult edn., 1982-84; project devel. coord. End Stage Renal Disease Network 26, East Syracuse, N.Y., 1981-82; asst. prof. adult edn. Mont. State U., Bozeman, 1984-88; assoc. prof. adult edn. U. Tenn., Knoxville, 1988-96, prof. adult edn., 1996—, coord., 1993—. Editor: Continuing Education in the Year 2000, 1987, Ethical Issues in Adult Education, 1988, Professional Development for Educators of Adults, 1991; co-editor Overcoming Resistance to Self-Direction in Adult Learning, 1994, The Power and Potential of Collaborative Learning Partnership, 1998; co-author: Self-Direction in Adult Learning: Perspectives on Theory, Research, and Practice, 1991, The Profession and Practice of Adult Education (Houle award for outstanding lit. in adult edn. 1997), 1997, Toward Ethical Practice, 2003; mem. editl. bd. Adult Edn. Quar., 1986-93, 2002—; editor-in-chief New Directions for Adult and Continuing Edn., 1989-98; co-editor Adult Learning, 2001—; contbr. articles to profl. jours. Advisor Jr. Achievement of Northwestern Ohio, Toledo, 1972-75. Recipient Charters award Syracuse U. Sch. Edn., 1986. Mem. Am. Assn. Adult and Continuing Edn. (bd. dirs. 1988-90, unit chair 1980-81, 90-91, Meritorious Svc. award 1981, 88, 90), Commn. Profs. Adult Edn. (bd. dirs. 1985-87, chair 1992-94), Mountain Plains Adult Edn. Assn., Juvenile Diabetes Rsch. Found. (bd. dirs. E. Tenn. chpt. 2002—). Avocations: music, reading, writing, history. Home: 6531 Deane Hill Dr Apt 50 Knoxville TN 37919-6012 Office: U Tenn Dept Ednl Psychology and Counseling A520 Claxton Complex Knoxville TN 37996

BROCKETT, ROGER WARE, engineering and computer science educator; b. Seville, Ohio, Oct. 22, 1938; s. Roger Lawrence and Grace Ester (Patch) B.; m. Carolann Christina Riske, Aug. 20, 1960; children: Mark William, Douglas Matthew, Erik Roger. BS in Engring. Sci., Case Western Res. U., 1960, MS in Instrumentation Engring., 1962, PhD, 1964; MS (hon.), Harvard U., 1969. Asst. prof. MIT, Cambridge, Mass., 1963-67, assoc. prof., 1967-69; Gordon McKay Prof. Applied Math. Harvard U., Cambridge, Mass., 1969-90, Wang prof., 1990—. Cons. Lincoln Lab., Lexington, Mass., 1965-78, GE, Schenectady, N.Y., 1989-90, ORNL, 1990—. Author: Finite Dimensional Linear Systems, 1970. Recipient Donald P. Eckman award Am. Automatic Control Coun., 1974, Richard Bellman award, 1989; John Simon Guggenheim fellow, 1976-77. Fellow IEEE (Control Systems Sci. and Engring. award 1991); mem. NAE, Am. Math. Soc., Soc. Indsl. and Applied Math, Sigma Xi. Office: Harvard U Pierce Hall 33 Oxford St Cambridge MA 02138-2901

BROCKHAUS, ROBERT HEROLD, SR., business educator, consultant; b. St. Louis, Apr. 18, 1940; s. Herold August and Leona M. (Stutzke) B.; m. Joyce Patricia Dees, June 13, 1970; children: Cheryl Lynn, Robert Herold. BS in Mech. Engring., U. Mo.-Rolla, 1962; MSIA, Purdue U., 1966; PhD, Washington U., St. Louis, 1976. Mgr. Ralston-Purina, St. Louis, 1962-69; pres. Progressive Mgmt. Enterprises, Ltd., St. Louis, 1969—; asst. prof. mgmt. sci. St. Louis Univ., 1972-78, assoc. prof., 1978-84, prof., 1984—; chair in entrpreneurship Coleman Found., 1991—; dir. Small Bus. Inst., St. Louis Univ., 1976-86, Inst. Entrepreneurial Studies, St. Louis Univ., 1987-90; treas. CORO Found., 1987-92; exec. dir. Jefferson Smurfit Ctr. for Entrepreneurial Studies, 1990—; 1st v.p. Mo. Inventors Assn., 1988-94; state adminstr. Mo. Small Bus. Devel. Ctr., St. Louis, 1982-86; state dir. Mo. Small Bus. Devel. Ctrs., St. Louis, 1987-89. Schoen prof. entrepreneurship Baylor U., 1981; McAninch prof. entrepreneurship Kans. State U., 1985—87; vis. scholar So. Cross U., Australia, 1995; del. White House Conf. on Small Bus., 1986, 95; alderman City of Sunset Hills, 1998—; nat. rsch. adv. SBA, 2003. Co-author: Encyclopedia of Entrepreneur, 1982: Building a Better You, 1982; Nursing Concepts for Health Promotion, 1979, Art and Science of Entrepreneurship, 1985, Entrepreneurship in the 1990's, 1991, The State of the Art of Entrepreneurialship, 1992; editor Journal of Consulting, 1988-90; co-editor: Frontiers of Entrepreneurship Research, 1990, Advances in Entrepreneurship, Firm Emergence and Growth, 1993, 95, Entrepreneurship Education, 2001; editor Family Bus. Rev., 1993-97; also contbr. articles to profl. jours. Bd. dirs. City Venture, St. Louis, 1982-86; v.p. United Ch. of Christ, 1991-92, pres., 1992-93; chair troop 25 Boy Scout Am., 1990-93, vice chair Gravois Trail Coun., 2000—; chair, pres. Eastern Mo. Small Bus. Week, 2002. Named extraordinary prof., Potchefstroom U., South Africa, 2000—03, Lindbergh Leader, 2001; recipient Outstanding Svc. award, Boy Scouts Am., 1994, Disting. Svc. award Gravois Trl. Coun., 2002, award of excellence, NASDAQ; Fulbright fellow, U. Waikato, New Zealand, 1985. Fellow Internat. Coun. for Small Bus. (sr. v.p. 1981-83, internat. pres. 1983-84, bd. dirs. 1983, v.p. 1986, exec. dir. 1987—), Nat. Small Bus. Inst. Dirs. Assn. (nat. v.p. 1980-82, 96-97, nat. pres. 1982-83, Disting. Mentor award 2000), U.S. Assn. for Small Bus. Entrepreneurship; mem. Assn. Collegiate Entrepreneurs (internat. bd. dirs., exec. com. 1991-93, recipient outstanding entrepreneurship educator awd., 1992), Acad. Mgmt. (nat. prog. chmn. 1977-78, exec. com. 1993-95), Inventor's Assn. St. Louis (bd. dirs. 1989-94, 1st v.p. 1991), Family Firm Inst. (internat. conf. chair, 1995), Fenton Jaycees (treas.), Exec. Club (St. Louis, moderator 1973-86), Pi Kappa Alpha (dist. pres. 1969-74, faculty adv. 1990—, recipient disting. svc. award 1972, bd. dirs., treas., endowment found. nat. coun. for youth and religion, 1994—). Avocations: swimming, sailing, camping. Home: 10000 Hilltop Dr Saint Louis MO 63128-1512 E-mail: brockhau@slu.edu.

BROD, ROY DAVID, ophthalmologist, educator; b. Phila., Oct. 8, 1957; s. Kenneth Lester and Carlene Marcy (Chalick) B.; m. Janice Hope Prossack, May 7, 1983; children: Jamie, Rebecca. BS in Biochemistry magna cum laude, Tulane U., 1979; MD with honors, Temple U., 1983. Diplomate Am. Bd. Ophthalmology. Intern Presbyn. U. Pa. Med. Ctr., Phila., 1983-84; resident in ophtholmology La. State U. Eye Ctr., New Orleans, 1984-87; fellow in vitreoretinal Bascom Palmer Eye Inst., Miami, Fla., 1987-88; assoc. vitreoretinal surgeon Geisinger Med. Ctr., Danville, Pa., 1988-91; pvt. practice Lancaster, Pa., 1991—. Asst. prof. Thomas Jefferson U. Sch. Medicine, Phila., 1991-92; clin. asst. prof. Pa. State U. Sch. Medicine-Hershey Med. Ctr., 1992-95, clin. assoc. prof., 1995—; presenter in field. Contbr. articles to med. jours., chpts. to books. Recipient Outstanding Tchr. award Geisinger Med. Ctr., 1990, 91; Tulane scholar, 1976, E.J. and Sarah Evans scholar, 1979, scholar Measy Found., 1982; named among Best Doctors in Am., 2000. Fellow Am. Acad. Ophthlmology (Honor award 1998); mem. AMA, Assn. for Rsch. in Vision and Ophthalmology, Vitreous Soc. (exec. com.), Retina Soc., Rsch. To Prevent Blindness, Soc. for Contemplation Fascinating Fluorescein Angiograms, Atlantic Coast Vitreoretinal Study Group, Atlantic Coast Fluorescein Angiography Club, Pa. Med. Soc., Pa. Acad. Ophthalmology, Phi Beta Kappa, Alpha Omega Alpha, Phi Eta Sigma, Alpha Epsilon Delta, Omicron Delta Kappa. Avocations: sailing, tennis, bicycling. Office: PO Box 3200 Ste 310 2108 Medical Offices Lancaster PA 17604-3200 E-mail: RYJN@aol.com.

BRODEN, THOMAS FRANCIS, III, French language educator; b. South Bend, Ind., Nov. 19, 1951; s. Thomas F. and Joanne Marjorie (Green) B.; m. Marcia C. Stephenson, Oct. 14, 1989. AB, U. Notre Dame, Ind., 1973; AM, Ind. U., 1976, PhD, 1986; postgrad., Coll. France, Paris, 1979-80. Asst. d'anglais Lycee Henri IV and Inst. Nat. Telecomm., Paris, 1979-80, Lycee St.-Louis and Inst. Nat. Agronomique, Paris, 1981-82; lectr. French U. Notre Dame, Ind., 1984-87; vis. asst. prof. Tulane U., New Orleans, 1987-88; asst. prof. French U. Nebr., Lincoln, 1988-91, Purdue U., West Lafayette, Ind., 1991-97, assoc. prof. French, 1997—, chmn. French sect., 1999—2001. Editor Newsletter for Paris-Greimassian Semiotics, 1990-92, 97, La Mode en 1830, 2000. Notre Dame scholar, 1969-73; Rotary fellow, 1973-74, French Govt. fellow, 1981-82, PRF summer rsch. fellow; NEH grantee, 1990, Maude Hammond Fling Faculty Summer fellow, 1991. Mem. Am. Assn. Tchrs. French, Semiotic Soc. Am. (exec. bd. 1992-94), Simone de Beauvoir Soc., N.Am. Assn. for History of Lang. Scis., Toronto Semiotic Cir., Can. Semiotic Assn., Assn. Internat. de Semiotique Visuelle. Avocations: jogging, biking, gardening. Office: Purdue U Fgn Langs Stanley Coulter Hall West Lafayette IN 47907

BRODERICK, JAMES ALLEN, art educator; b. Chgo., July 25, 1939; s. James and Catherine (Cahill) B.; m. Alice Moehelenhof, Aug. 24, 1963 (div. June 1977); children: Brian, Mark; m. Cindy Gambell, Dec. 21, 1978; children: Victoria, Catherine, Maureen. BA, St. Ambrose Coll., Davenport, Iowa, 1962; MA, U. Iowa, 1966. Asst. prof. N.W. Mo. U., Maryville, 1966-76, dir. art gallery, 1967-76, chmn. art dept., 1970-76; prof. art Tex. Tech U., Lubbock, 1976-83, chair art dept., 1976-83; prof. art U. Tex., San Antonio, 1983—, dir. visual arts divsn., 1983—2002, prof. emeritus, 2003—. Photographer, painter, etcher; exhibited works throughout U.S., 1960s—. Mem. Nat. Assn. Schs. Art and Design (v.p. 1996-99, pres. 1999-02, accreditation reviewer 1977—), Nat. Coun. Art Adminstrs. (bd. dirs. 1994—). Democrat. Home: 2511 Old Gate San Antonio TX 78230-5230 Office: U Tex San Antonio 6900 N Loop 1604 W San Antonio TX 78249-1130

BRODIE, CATHERINE ANNE, music educator; b. Marshall, Mich., Mar. 11, 1948; d. Stephen Frank and Ernestine Viola (Lake) Trupiano; m. William Brodie, Sept. 4, 1970; children: Matthew Ian, Andrew Benjamin, Brian Patrick. BS in Music Performance, Eastern Mich. U., 1970, MA in Music Edn., 1973. Grad. asst. Ea. Mich. U., Ypsilanti, 1970-73, asst. condr. Madrigal Singers, 1972-73; choir dir. St. Ursulas Cath. Ch., Ypsilanti, 1972-77; pvt. voice and pinao instr. Ypsilanti, 1972-79; music educator Monroe (Mich.) Pub. Schs., 1980—. Choral condr. Oakland Singers, Bloomfield Hills, Mich., 1990—. Vocalist Parker Choral, Grosse Ile, Mich., 1988—95, John Tyner Chorale, 1996, dist. mgr., 1996—98, exec. bd., 2001—; choir mem. St. Paul's Meth. Ch., Monroe, 1984—. Recipient Tchr. of Yr., Mich. Music Educators Assn., 1996—97. Mem.: Mich. Educators Assn., Mich. Music Educators Assn. (Tchr. of the Yr. 1996—97), Am. Choral Dirs. Assn., Music Educators Nat. Conf., Mich. Sch. Vocal Music Assn. (honors choir chmn. 1990—94, honor choir dir. 1994—95, 2001—02). Office: Monroe High Sch 901 Herr Rd Monroe MI 48161-9744

BRODIE, HARLOW KEITH HAMMOND, psychiatrist, educator, past university president; b. Stamford, Conn., Aug. 24, 1939; s. Lawrence Sheldon and Elizabeth White (Hammond) B.; m. Brenda Ann Barrowclough, Jan. 26, 1967; children: Melissa Verduin, Cameron Keith, Tyler Hammond, Bryson Barrowclough. AB, Princeton U., 1961; MD, Columbia U., 1965; LLD hon., U. Richmond, 1987; LHD (hon.), High Point U., 1992. Diplomate Am. Bd. Psychiatry and Neurology. Intern Ochsner Found. Hosp., New Orleans, 1965-66; resident in psychiatry Columbia-Presbyn. Med. Center, N.Y.C., 1966-68; clin. assoc. intramural research program NIMH, 1968-70; asst. prof. psychiatry, dir. gen. clin. research center Stanford U. Med. Sch., 1970-74; prof. psychiatry, chmn. dept. Duke U. Med. Sch., 1974-82, James B. Duke prof. psychiatry and behavioral scis., 1981—, prof. dept. psychology, prof. law, 1980—; psychiatrist-in-chief Duke U. Med. Center, 1974-82; chancellor Duke U., 1982-85, pres., 1985-93, pres. emeritus, 1993—. Mem. Pres. Biomed. Rsch. Panel, 1975; mem. Carnegie Coun. on Adolescent Devel., 1986-97; trustee Com. for Econ. Devel., 1986-93, mem. subcom. on edn. and child devel., 1990; trustee Nat. Humanities Ctr., 1988-93; mem. nat. rev. and adv. panel for improving campus race rels. Ford Found., 1990-94; mem. subcom. on Edn. on Child Devel. Com., 1990; bd. dirs. Inst. of Medicine, Mental Health and Behavioral Medicine, 1981-83, chmn., 1981-82; chmn. Com. on Substance Abuse and Mental Health Issues in AIDS Rsch., 1992-95; mem. com. on leadership devel. Am. Coun. on Edn., 1990-93. Co-author: The Importance of Mental Health Services to General Health Care, 1979, Modern Clinical Psychiatry, 1982; co-editor: American Handbook of Psychiatry, vols. 6, 7 and 8, 1975, 81, 86, Controversy in Psychiatry, 1978, Psychiatry at the Crossroads, 1980, Critical Problems in Psychiatry, 1982, Signs and Symptoms in Psychiatry, 1983, Consultation-Liaison Psychiatry and Behavioral Medicine, 1986, AIDS and Behavior: An Integrated Approach, 1994, Keeping an Open Door: Passages in a University Presidency, 1996; assoc. editor Am. Jour. Psychiatry, 1973-81. Recipient Disting. Med. Alumni award Columbia U., 1985, Disting. Alumnus award Ochsner Found. Hosp., 1984, Strecker award Inst. of Pa. Hosp., 1980, N.C. award for sci., 1990, William C. Menninger Meml. award ACP, 1994. Fellow: Royal Soc. Medicine; mem.: NAS, Internat. Soc. Sport Psychiatry, Soc. Biol. Psychiatry (A.E. Bennet Rsch. award 1970), Royal Coll. Psychiatrists, Inst. Medicine, Am. Psychiat. Assn. (sec. 1977—81, pres. 1982—83). Home: 63 Beverly Dr Durham NC 27707-2223 Office: Duke U Office of Pres Emeritus 205 E Duke Bldg Durham NC 27708

BRODKIN, ADELE RUTH MEYER, psychologist; b. N.Y.C., July 8, 1934; d. Abraham J. and Helen (Honig) Meyer; m. Roger Harrison Brodkin, Jan. 26, 1957; children: Elizabeth Anne Brodkin Brauer, Edward Stuart. BA, Sarah Lawrence Coll., 1956; MA, Columbia U., 1959; PhD, Rutgers U., 1977. Lic. psychologist N.J. Sch. psychologist pub. schs., 1961—73; assoc. dir. Infant Child Devel. Ctr. St. Barnabas Med. Ctr., Livingston, N.J., 1977-79; clin. asst. prof. dept. psychiatry U. Medicine and Dentistry N.J., Newark, 1979-90, clin. assoc. prof., 1990-2001. Vis. scholar Hasting Ctr. for Life Scis., NY, 1979; sr. child devel. cons.; cons. Scholastic, Inc., 1988—. Author: Fresh Approaches to Working with Problematic Behavior, 2001, The Lonely Only Dog, 1998, Between Teacher and Parent, Supporting Young Children As They Grow, 1994; author: (with A.T. Jersild and E.A. Lazar) The Meaning of Psychotherapy in the Teacher's Life and Work, 1962; contbr. articles to profl. jours. Fellow, NIMH, 1962; Adelaide M. Ayer fellow, Columbia U., 1962—63, Louis Bevier fellow, Rutgers U., 1976—77. Fellow: Am. Orthopsychiat. Assn.; mem.: APA, Am. Sociol. Assn., N.J. Psychol. Assn. Home and Office: 2 Trevino Ct Florham Park NJ 07932-2724

BRODKIN, ROGER HARRISON, dermatologist, educator; b. Newark, July 31, 1932. A.B. Lafayette Coll., Easton, Pa., 1954; M.D., Jefferson Med. Coll., 1958; M.M.S. in Dermatology, NYU, 1967. Diplomate Am. Bd. Dermatology. Intern, Lenox Hill Hosp., N.Y.C., 1958-59; resident in dermatology NYU and Bellevue Hosp., N.Y.C., 1959-62; teaching asst. NYU, 1962-64, instr. dermatology, 1964-66; clin. asst. prof. U. N.J. Med. and Dental Sch., Newark, 1966-69, clin. assoc prof., 1969-79, clin. prof., 1979—; pres. Ctr. Dermatology, West Orange, N.J. Named Best Drs. in N.Y. N.Y. Mag. Fellow ACP, Am. Acad. Dermatology, Royal Soc. Medicine, Sigma Psi. Office: Ctr Dermatology 101 Old Short Hills Rd West Orange NJ 07052-1000

BRODY, DAVID, artist, educator; b. N.Y.C., Feb. 16, 1958; s. Jules and Roxane (Offner) B. BA, Bennington (Vt.) Coll., 1981; MFA, Yale U., 1983. Vis. prof. Carnegie Mellon U., Pitts., 1990-91; head grad. studies Studio Art Ctr. Internat., Florence, Italy, 1992-96; asst. prof. painting and drawing U. Wash., Seattle, 1996-2000, assoc. prof., chmn. dept., 2000—. One-man shows include Gallery NAGA, Boston, 1989, 92, 94, 96, Hewlett Gallery, Carnegie Mellon U., Pitts., 1991, Galeria Gilde, Guimarães, Portugal, 1996, Esther Claypool Gallery, Seattle, 1999, 2001, 2002; exhibited in group shows Chgo. Ctr. for Print, 1985, FPAC Gallery, Boston, 1986, Bridgewater Gallery, N.Y., SixToSix Gallery, N.Y.C., 1987, Gallery NAGA, Boston, 1989, 95, Mills Gallery, Boston Ctr. for Arts, 1989, 90, 91, Hewlett Gallery, 1990, Fitchburg Art Mus., Mass., 1991, 93, Limner Gallery, N.Y.C., 1992, Tribeca Gallery 148, N.Y., Decordova Mus., Lincoln, Mass., 1994, RipArte Art Fair, Rome, Italy, 1995, FAC Art Fair, Lisbon, Portugal, 1995, Trevi Flash Art Mus., Italy, 1996, The Painting Center, N.Y.C., 1996, The Alternative Mus., N.Y.C., 1996, Mus. Fine Arts, Fla. State U., Tallahassee, 1997, ARCO Art Fair, Madrid, 1996, 97, 99, Ctr. on Contemporary Art, Seattle; selected pubs.: David Brody, Selected Paintings, 1985-1994, David Brody, Selected Paintings, 2001-2002. Grantee Guggenheim Found., N.Y.C., 1991, Fulbright Found., Washington, 1992, Elizabeth Found. for Arts, N.Y.C., 1994, Basil H. Alkazzi award, 1998. Office: U Wash PO Box 353440 Seattle WA 98195-3440 E-mail: brody@u.washington.edu.

BRODY, HAROLD, neuroanatomist, gerontologist; b. Cleve., May 15, 1923; s. Julius and Esther (Barowitz) B.; m. Anne Pertz, Mar. 24, 1951; children: David Andrew, Evan Barrett. Student, L.I. U., 1941-43; BS, Western Res. U., 1947; PhD, U. Minn., 1953; MD, U. Buffalo, 1961. Instr. anatomy U. Minn., Mpls., 1949-50; asst. prof. U. N.D., Grand Forks, 1950-54, U. Buffalo, 1954-59; assoc. prof. SUNY (merger with U. Buffalo 1961), 1959-63, prof., 1963-95, disting. tchg. prof., 1995—; asst. dean SUNY, Buffalo, 1968-69; assoc. dean SUNY (merger with U. Buffalo 1961), 1969-70, Buswell rsch. fellow, 1970—, chmn. dept. anat. scis., 1971-92. Acting dir. Ctr. for Study of Aging, SUNY, Buffalo, 1977-80, organizer, curator Mus. Neuroanatomy, 1994—; vis. prof. neurophthalmology St. Mary's Hosp., Rochester, N.Y., 1965-75, U. Copenhagen, 1987, 90, 91, 92, 93, 95; Anthes Wilson Abernathy disting. lectr. U. Toronto, Ont., Can., 1987; mem. com. on rsch. and demonstration White House Conf. on Aging, 1971; mem. biology coun. Canisius Coll., Buffalo, 1969; mem. sci. bd. Buffalo Otol. Found., 1968-73; mem. nat. adv. coun. Nat. Inst. on Aging, NIH, 1975-79. Abstractor, Excerpta Medica Sect. Gerontology and Geriat., 1959—; sci. referee Science, 1956—, Jour. Morphology, 1958—; sci. referee Jour. Gerontology, 1957-73, assoc. editor, 1973-75, editor-in-chief, 1975-80; editor Neurobiology of Aging, 1981—; mem. editl. bd. Gerontology and Geriat. Edn., 1980—, Exptl. Gerontology, 1984—. Trustee Erie County Meals on Wheels, Legal Svcs. for Elderly; pres. Friends of Health Scis. Med. Libr. SUNY, Buffalo, 1999. With M.C., AUS, 1943-46. Recipient NSF travel award, 1957, Robert W. Kleemeier Rsch. award in gerontology Gerontol. Soc. Am., 1978; co-recipient Lyn Millane Cmty. Svc. award Amherst (N.Y.) Sr. Citizens' Found., 1998-99; Fulbright sr. rsch. scholar, Copenhagen, 1963. Mem. AAAS, Roswell Park Med. Club (pres. 1978-79), Am. Assn. Anatomists, Am. Assn. Anatomy Chmn., Am. Geriat. Soc., Am. Aging Assn. (trustee 1970-77), Gerontol. Soc. Am. (mem. exec. com. 1961-63, 68-71, pres. 1974-75), Buffalo Neuropsychiat. Soc. (pres. 1967-68), Alpha Omega Alpha. Achievements include research on effects of aging on human central nervous system. Home: 50 Stahl Rd Apt 301 Getzville NY 14068-1554 Office: SUNY Buffalo Main St Campus Dept Pathology and Anat Scis Rm 204 Sherman Hall Buffalo NY 14214

BRODY, WILLIAM RALPH, academic administrator, radiologist, educator; b. Stockton, Calif., Jan. 4, 1944; m. Wendy Brody; 2 children. BSEE, MIT, 1965, MSEE, 1966; MD, Stanford U., 1970, PhD in Elec. Engring., 1975. With Nat. Heart, Lung, and Blood Inst., USPHS, Balt., 1973—75; intern, then resident and fellow dept. cardiovasc. surgery Sch. Medicine Stanford U., Calif., 1970—73, tng. med. fellow cardiovasc. surgery, resident diag. radiol., 1975—77, from assoc. prof. to prof. dept. radiology, dir. rsch. labs., 1977—86; prof. Stanford U., 1982—84; founder, pres., CEO Resonex, Inc., 1984—87, chmn. bd. dirs., 1987—89; radiologist-in-chief Johns Hopkins Hosp., Balt., 1987—94; prof. radiology, provost U. Minn. Acad. Health Ctr., 1994—96, spl. asst. to pres., 1996; mem. staff depts. elec., computer engring., biomed. engring. Sch. Medicine Johns Hopkins U., 1987—94, Martin Donner prof., dir. dept. radiology, 1987—94; pres. Johns Hopkins U., 1996—. Contbr. articles to profl. jours. Fellow coun. cardiovasc. radiology Am. Heart Assn.; mem. internat. adv. bd. Inst. Sys. Sci., NAt. U. Singapore, 1994—97; mem. internat. acad. adv. panel, 1997; mem. sci. adv. com. Whitaker Found., 1992—97, governing com., 1997—; bd. dirs. Greater Balt. Com., 1997; trustee Goldseker Found., 1996, Balt. Mus. Art, 1997. Recipient Established Investigator award, Am. Heart Assn., 1980—84. Fellow: NAS (Inst. Medicine), IEEE, Am. Inst. Med. and Biomed. Engring. (founding), Am. Coll. Cardiology, Am. Coll. Radiology. Achievements include patents in field. Office: Johns Hopkins Univ 242 Garland Hall 3400 N Charles St Baltimore MD 21218-2680

BROGAN, FRANK T. former lieutenant governor; m. Courtney Strickland. BA magna cum laude, U. Cin.; M in Ednl. Leadership, Fla. Atlantic U. m. Courtney Brogan. Supt. schs. Martin County Sch. Dist., Fla., 1988-94; commr. edn. Fla. Dept. Edn., Tallahassee, 1994-99; lt. gov. State of Fla., Tallahassee, 1999—2003; pres. Florida Atlantic U., 2003—. Former tchr., dean of students, asst. prin., prin. Martin County Sch. Dist.; chair task force Fla. Classrooms First; mem. development team Tech Prep program. Named Supt. of yr., Fla. Legislature, 1992. Republican. Office: Florida Atlantic Univ PO Box 3091 777 Glades Rd Boca Raton FL 33431-0991

BROGGI, BARBARA ANN, elementary education educator, staff developer; b. New Brunswick, N.J., Jan. 8, 1945; d. Alexander Robert and Dorothy Sheldon (Smith) G.; m. John Victor Broggi, June 10, 1967; children: John A., Kristin M., Jeffrey M. BA, William Paterson Coll., 1967. Tchr. South Brunswick (N.J.) Bd. Edn., 1967-69, Creative Nursery Kindergarten, Highland Park, N.J., 1972-78, Highland Park Bd. Edn., 1979-97, libr./media specialist, staff developer, 1990-97, media specialist, 1997—. Owner, mgr. JKJ Sports Collectibles, Highland Park, 1981; mem. Bellcore Tchr. Inst., 1991—; participant Met. program Met. Opera Guild, 1990—; mem. sci. teams Consortium for Edn. Equity, Rutgers U., 1989—; ednl. cons. Kendall Hunt Pub. Co., 1994—. Contbr. to college textbook. Recipient Tchr. Recognition award, N.J. Gov., 1991, 94. Mem. ASCD, N.J. Edn. Assn., N.J. Assn. for Supervision and Curriculum Devel., Highland Park Edn. Assn. Home: 206 Exeter St Highland Park NJ 08904-3734 Office: Bartle Sch Mansfield St Highland Park NJ 08904

BROISMAN, EMMA RAY, economist, retired international official; b. Boston, July 11, 1922; BA in Sociology, U. Maine, 1944; MA in Econs., Columbia U., 1946. Rsch. asst., libr. Internat. Labour Orgn. Liason Office with UN, N.Y.C., 1947—57; program fellowship officer Internat. Labor Orgn. Asian Field Office, Bangalore, India, 1957-63; program officer Internat. Labor Orgn., Geneva, 1964-68, Internat. Labor Orgn. Reg. Office for Asia and the Pacific, Bangkok, 1969, sr., pers. fin. and adminstrn. officer, 1970-72; chief rels. and info. sect. Internat. Labour Office, Bangkok, 1973-75, dep. dir. New Delhi, 1975-78; coord. women and youth programs Internat. Labour Orgn., Bangkok, 1978-83; UN rep. Internat. Coun. Women, 1985—. Assoc. Ctr. for Study of Women and Soc., Grad. Ctr., CUNY, 1989—; internat. devel. cons., 1983—; UN rep. to Internat. Coun. Women, 1984—. Contbr. articles to profl. jours. Recipient Women of the Yr. award N.Y. League Bus. and Profl. Women, 2000. Mem. LWV (dir. 1986-90), Nat. Coun. Women (sec., bd. dirs. 1991-94), Pan Pacific South-East Asia Women's Assn. (bd. dirs.), Am. Com. on Fgn. Policy, Acad. Coun. on UN Sys. Avocations: art, music, golf. Home: 301 E 48th St Apt 16B New York NY 10017-1720

BROITMAN, SELWYN ARTHUR, microbiologist, educator; b. Boston, Aug. 30, 1931; s. Julius Z. and Sara (Sallus) B.; m. Barbara Merle Shwartz, June 13, 1953; children: Caryn Beth, Jeffrey Z. BS, U. Mass., 1952, MS, 1953; PhD, Mich. State U., 1956. Dir. Biotech. Assocs., 1959-62; research instr. dept. pathology Boston U. Sch. Medicine, 1963-64, asst. prof. dept. microbiology, 1965-69, assoc. prof. dept. microbiology, 1969-75, prof., 1975—, prof. pathology and lab. medicine, 1983—, asst. dean med. sch. admissions, 1983—; assoc. prof. nutritional scis. Henry Goldman Sch. Grad. Dentistry Boston U., 1974—. Assoc. medicine dept. medicine Harvard Med. Sch., 1969-74; rsch. assoc. Mallory Inst. Pathology, Boston City Hosp., Gastro Intestinal Rsch. Lab., 1956-71; assoc. in medicine Thorndike Meml. Lab., 1969-74; chair, co-chair of various admission programs Boston U. Sch. Medicine; adv.-at-large Acad. of Advisors, 2003. Contbr. articles to profl. jours. Founding mem. Digestive Disease Found. Served with AUS, 1952-66; advisor Boston U. Sch. Medicine, 2003. Recipient Outstanding Teaching award Boston U. Sch. Medicine 1st Yr. Class, 1976 Fellow Am. Coll. Gastroenterology; mem. AAAS, Am. Soc. for Investigative Pathology, Am. Soc. for Nutritional Scis., Am. Assn. for Cancer Rsch., Am. Fedn. for Med. Rsch., Am. Soc. Microbiology, Soc. Applied Bacteriology (Eng.), Soc. Exptl. Biology and Medicine, Nutrition Today Soc. (founding), Am. Gastroent. Assn., Boston Gastroent. Soc., Nat. Acad. Scis. (com. diet, nutrition and cancer 1980-83), N.Y. Acad. Scis., Boston Bug Club (pres. 1976), Sigma Xi. Office: 80 E Concord St Boston MA 02118-2307

BROLSMA, CATHERINE, secondary education educator, educational administrator; b. Paterson, N.J., Aug. 21, 1936; d. Nicholas and Jennie (Guidone) Cantisano; m. Walter Brolsma, Jr., June 21, 1958; children: Sharon Brolsma Craig, Patricia Brolsma Iulo, Cindy Brolsma. BS in Edn., William Paterson Coll., Wayne, N.J., 1958, MA in Social Sci., 1975, postgrad., 1980, Montclair (N.J.) State Coll., 1980. Cert K-8 tchr., K-12 social studies tchr., prin., N.J. Elem. tchr. Hawthorne (N.J.)-Roosevelt Sch., 1958, Ryerson Sch. and Anthony Wayne Jr. High Sch., Wayne, 1966-68, Lincoln Sch., Pompton Lakes, N.J., 1968-76; elem. and mid. sch. tchr. Lakeside Sch., Pompton Lakes, 1976—; tchr. history Pompton Lakes High Sch.; supr. K-12 social studies Pompton Lakes Schs., 1990—. Tchr. adult edn. Pompton Lakes Sch. System, 1970-80; co-chair middle states self-study com. Pompton Lakes High Sch., 1990 ; mem. middle states evaluation team New Milford (N.J.) High Sch., 1993. Campaign worker John Anderson for Pres., Hackensack, N.J., 1980, also other Dem. campaigns, 1984-92. Recipient award for excellence in teaching Gov. State of N.J., 1988; scholar William Paterson Coll., 1954-58. Mem. NEA, Prins. and Suprs. Assn., N.J. Edn. Assn. (chmn. nominating com. 1980-83, ethics com. 1970-73), Greater Bergen Suprs. Assn., Nat. Coun. for Social Studies, N.J. Coun. for Social Studies, North Jersey Acad. Alliance World History (co-chmn. 1992—). Avocations: reading, playing piano, embroidery, singing, cooking. Home: 525 Lincoln Ave Pompton Lakes NJ 07442-1306 Office: Pompton Lakes High Sch 44 Lakeside Ave Pompton Lakes NJ 07442-1734

BROM, LIBOR, journalist, educator; b. Ostrava, Czechoslovakia, Dec. 17, 1923; came to U.S., 1958, naturalized, 1964; s. Ladislav and Bozena (Bromova) B.; m. Gloria S. Mena, Aug. 31, 1961; 1 son, Rafael Brom. Ing., Czech Inst. Tech., 1948; JUC, Charles U. Prague, 1951; postgrad., San Francisco State Coll.; MA, U. Colo., 1962, PhD, 1970. V.p. Brom, Inc., Ostrava, 1942-48; economist Slovak Magnesite Works, Prague, Czechoslovakia, 1948-49; economist, chief planner Vodostavba, Navika, Prague, 1951-56; tchr. Jefferson County Schs., Colo., 1958-67; prof., dir. Russian area studies program U. Denver, 1967-91, prof. emeritus, 1992—; journalist, mem. editorial staff Denni Hlasatel-Daily Herald, Chgo., 1978-96; editorial staff Jour. of Interdisciplinary Studies, 1988—. Pres. Colo. Nationalities Council, 1970-72; comptroller Exec. Bd. Nat. Heritage Groups Council, 1970-72; mem. adv. bd. Nat. Security Council, 1980-85; acad. bank participant Heritage Found. Author: Ivan Bunin's Proteges, Leonid Zurov, 1973, Alexander Zinoviev's Concept of the Soviet Man, 1991; co-author: Has the Third World War Already Started, 1983, Christianity and Russian Culture in Soviet Society, 1990, The Search for Self-Definition in Russian Literature, 1991; translator: Problems of Geography, 1955; author: (in Czech) In the Windstorm of Anger, 1976, Time and Duty, 1981, Teacher of Nations and Our Times, 1982, The Way of Light, 1982, On the Attack, 1983, Between the Currents, 1985, Homeland After 50 Years Nazi & Communist Occupation, 1992. V.p. Colo. Citizenship Day, 1968-69; pres. Comenius World Coun., 1976-85, World Representation of Czechoslovak Exiles, 1976-84; pres. Czech World Union, 1985-94; gen. sec. Czechoslovak Rep. Movement, 1980-91. Recipient Americanism medal DAR, 1969, Disting. Service award Am. by Choice, 1968, Kynewisbov Pioneer award Denver U., 1989; named Tchr. with Superlative Performance MLA, 1961, Outstanding Faculty mem. Omicron Delta Kappa, 1972, The Order of M.R. Stefanik Provisional Czechoslovak Govt. in Exile, Order of Judr. Karel Kramar, Nat. Dem. Party, Czech Republic. Mem. Am. Assn. Tchrs. Slavic and Ea. European Langs. (v.p. 1973-75), Rocky Mountain Assn. Slavic Studies (sec./treas. 1975-78, v.p. 1978-81, pres. 1982-83), Czechoslovak Christian Dem. Movement in Exile (ctrl. com. 1970-79), Dobro Slovo (hon.), Slava (hon.), Nat. Rep. Nationalities Coun. (co-chmn. human rights com. 1979-81), Phi Beta Kappa (hon.). Republican. Roman Catholic. Home: 434 A Woodview Rd Barrington IL 60010-1770 Office: U Denver Denver CO 80208-0001 E-mail: lbrbrm@aol.com.

BROMBAL, DOUGLAS NEREO, retired university official, consultant; b. Windsor, Ont., Can., May 18, 1930; s. Nereo and Johanna (Lausch) B.; m. Margaret Anne Howard, Aug. 1, 1953 (div. Feb. 1980); children: David Scott, Karen Elaine; m. Agnes Calcutt Garrison, May 3, 1986. BA, U. Windsor, 1969. Buyer Ford Motor Co. Can., Windsor, 1949-59; sales engr. F.F. Barber Machinery Co., Toronto, Ont., 1959-60, Gardner-Denver Co., Toronto, 1960-61; purchasing and maintenance mgr. Essex Coll., Assumption U., Windsor, 1961-63; asst. to treas., purchasing mgr. U. Windsor, 1963-67, asst. to v.p. adminstrn., 1967-70, asst. v.p. adminstrn., 1970-72; dir. adminstrv. svcs. Carleton U., Ottawa, Ont., 1972-93, dir. pension fund mgmt., 1993-96; cons., 1996—; hon. chmn. Comstat Capital Scis., Inc., Can., 1997-99; acting exec. dir. Canadian Assn. Univ. Bus. Officers, 1996-97. Mem. pres.'s adv. com. on campus revs. U. Alta, Edmonton, 1987; cons. Brock U., St. Catherines, Ont., 1989. Treas. Can. Red Cross, Windsor, 1968-72; bd. dirs. Can. Assn. Christians and Jews, Windsor, 1970-72; bd. mgmt. Ch. of the Ascension, Diocese of Huron, Windsor, 1964-72, synod del., 1964-72. Mem. Assn. Can. Pension Mgmt. (treas. 1984-87), Can. Pension and Benefits Conf. (regional coun. 1987-90), Pension Investment Assn. Can., Ea. Assn. Coll. Aux. Svcs. (bd. dirs. 1988-94, pres. 1992-93), Nat. Assn. Coll. Aux. Svcs. (Silver Torch award 1994), Italian Wine Soc. Can. (nat. pres.). Avocations: downhill skiing, reading, wine tasting. Home: 1226 Stanton Rd Ottawa ON Canada K2C 3E2

BROMBERT, VICTOR HENRI, literature educator, author; b. Germany, Nov. 11, 1923; came to U.S., 1941, naturalized, 1943; s. Jacques and Vera B.; m. Beth Anne Archer, June 18, 1950; children: Lauren Nora, Marc Alexis. BA, Yale U., 1948, MA, 1949, PhD, 1953; postgrad., U. Rome, 1950-51; HHD (hon.), U. Chgo., 1981, U. Toronto, 1997. Faculty Yale U., New Haven, 1951-75, from assoc. prof. to prof., 1958-75, Benjamin F. Barge prof. Romance lits., 1969-75, chmn. dept. Romance langs. and lit., 1964-73; Henry Putnam univ. prof. romance and comparative lit. Princeton (N.J.) U., 1975—99, dir. Christian Gauss seminars in criticism, 1984-94, chmn. Coun. Humanities, 1989-94. Summer prof. Middlebury Coll., 1951-53, Institut d'Etudes Françaises, Avignon, 1962, 64, 73, U. Colo., 1965; Christian Gauss Seminar in criticism Princeton U., 1964; vis. prof. Scuola Normale Superiore, Pisa, Italy, 1972, U. Calif., 1978, Johns Hopkins U., 1979, Columbia U., 1980, NYU, 1980, 81, U. P.R., 1983, 84, U. Bologna, Italy, 1984, Yale U., 1985; Phi Beta Kappa vis. scholar, 1986-87, 89-90; lectr. Alliance Française, humanities U. Kans., 1966; lectr. Collège de France, 1991; mem. Fulbright screening com., 1965; dir. fellowships in residence NEH, Princeton U., 1975-76, dir. summer seminar, 1979, 82, 84, 86, 88; mem. adv. com. for humanities Libr. of Congress, 1976; mem. Yale U. Coun., 1977-83; mem. ednl. adv. bd. Guggenheim Found., 1982— Author: (Literary Critiques) The Criticism of T. S. Eliot, 1949, Stendhal et la Voie Oblique, 1954, The Intellectual Hero, 1961, The Novels of Flaubert, 1966, Stendhal: Fiction and the Themes of Freedom, 1968, Flaubert par lui-même, 1971, La Prison Romantique, 1976, The Romantic Prison: The French Tradition, 1978, Victor Hugo and the Visionary Novel, 1984, The Hidden Reader, 1988, In Praise of Antiheroes, 1999, Trains of Thought: Memories of a Stateless Youth, 2002; editor: Stendhal: A Collection of Critical Essays, 1962, Balzac's La Peau de Chagrin, 1962, The Hero in Literature, 1969, Flaubert's Madame Bovary, 1969, The World of Lawrence Durrell, 1962, Ideas in the Drama, 1964, Malraux, 1964, Instants Premiers, 1973, Romanticism, 1973, Literary Criticism, 1974, Die Romanische Novelle, 1977, The Author in His Work, 1978, Essais sur Flaubert, 1979, Writers and Politics, 1983, Flaubert and Postmodernism, 1984, Writing in a Modern Temper, 1984, Literary Theory and Criticism, 1984, Hugo le Fabuleux, 1985, 19th Century Literary Criticism, 1985, Charles Baudelaire, 1987, Albert Camus, 1989, André Malraux, 1989, Gustave Flaubert, 1989, Dilemmes du Roman, 1989, Ninteenth Century French Poetry, 1990, Literature, Culture and Society in the Modern Age, 1991, Literary Generations, 1992, Dix Etudes sur Baudelaire, 1993, George Sand et son temps, 1994, Pratiques d' écriture, 1996, Stendhal et le comique, 1999, 500 Years of Theater History:, 2000; contbr. articles to profl. jours. Served with M.I. AUS, 1943-45. Decorated officer Ordre des Palmes Académiques; recipient Harry Levin prize in comparative lit., 1978, Howard T. Behrman award for disting. achievement in humanities, 1979, Wilbur Lucius Cross medal for outstanding achievement, Yale Univ., 1985, Médaille Vermeil de la Ville de Paris, 1985, The Pres. award for disting. tchg., 1999; fellow Fulbright fellow, 1950—51, Guggenheim fellow, 1954—55, 1970, sr. fellow, NEH, 1973—74, Rockefeller found. resident fellow, Bellagio, Italy, 1975, 1990; grantee Am. Coun. Learned Socs., 1966. Fellow Am. Acad. Arts and Scis.; mem. MLA (editl. adv. comm. 1979-83, pres. 1989), Am. Assn. Tchrs. French, Am. Comparative Lit. Assn., Am. Philos. Soc., Soc. des Etudes Françaises, Soc. des Etudes Romantiques, Acad. Lit. Studies (pres. 1983), Soc. d'Histoire Littéraire de la France, Soc. U. per gli Studi di Lingua e Letteratura Francese, Inst. Romance Studies, Elizabethan Club (pres. 1968-70), Yale Club, Phi Beta Kappa. Office: Princeton U 303 E Pyne Princeton NJ 08544-0001 Home: 49 Constitution Hill W Princeton NJ 08540-6774

BROMLEY, DAVID ALLAN, physicist, engineer, educator; b. Westmeath, Ont., Can., May 4, 1926; s. Milton Escort and Susan Anne (Anderson) Bromley; m. Patricia Jane Brassor, Aug. 30, 1949 (dec. Oct. 1990); children: David John, Karen Lynn. BS in Engring. Physics, Queen's U., Kingston, Ont., 1948, MS in Physics, 1950; PhD in Nuclear Physics, U. Rochester, 1952; MA (hon.), Yale U., 1961; D of Natural Philosophy (hon.), U. Frankfurt, 1978; Docteur (Physique) (hon.), U. Strasbourg, 1980; DSc (hon.), Queen's U., 1981, U. Notre Dame, 1982, U. Witwatersrand, 1982, Trinity Coll., 1988; LittD (hon.), U. Bridgeport, 1981; Dott. (hon.), U. Padua, 1983; LHD (hon.), U. New Haven, 1987; DSc (hon.), Rensselaer Polytechnic Inst., 1990; LHD (hon.), Ill. Inst. Tech., 1990; DSc (hon.), Lehigh U., 1991, Bklyn. Polytechnic Inst., 1991, U. Guelph, 1991, Fordham U., 1991, Northwestern U., 1991, Coll. of William and Mary, 1991; D Engring. Tech. (hon.), Wentworth Inst., 1991; DSc (hon.), SUNY, U. Mass., Adelphi U., 1993; DHL (hon.), Mt. Sinai Med. Ctr., 1993; D. Eng. (hon.), Colo. Sch. Mines, 1992; DSc (hon.), Fla. State U., 1993, Mich. State U., 1994, Mt. Sinai Med., 1996, U. Pitts., 1997, U. Toronto, 1998; Tex. Tech. U. (hon.), 2001. Oper. engr. Hydro Electric Power Commn. Ont., 1947—48; rsch. officer Nat. Rsch. Coun. Can., 1948; instr., then asst. prof. physics U. Rochester, 1952—55; sr. rsch. officer, sect. head Atomic Energy Can. Ltd., 1955—60; assoc. prof. physics, asso. dir. heavy ion accelerator lab. Yale U., 1960—61, prof. physics, dir. A. W. Wright Nuclear Structure Lab., 1961—89, chmn. physics dept., 1970—77, Henry Ford II prof. physics, 1972—93, Sterling prof. scis., 1994—, dean engring., 1994—2000; asst. to Pres. for sci. and tech. Washington, 1989—93; dir. Office of Sci. and Tech. Policy, Washington, 1989—93; chmn. Pres.'s Coun. Advisers on Sci. and Tech., Washington, 1989—93, Fed. Coordinating Coun. Sci., Engring. and Tech., Washington, 1989—93, Nat. Critical Materials Coun., Washington, 1990—92. Cons. Brookhaven, Argonne, Berkeley and Oak Ridge Nat. Labs., Bell Telephone Labs., IBM, GTE; mem. panel nuc. physics NAS, 1964, chmn. com. on nuc. sci., 1966—74, chmn. physics survey, 1969—74; mem.-at-large, mem. exec. com. divsn. phys. scis. NRC, 1970—74, mem. exec. com., assembly phys. and math. scis., 1974—78, mem. naval sci. bd., 1974—78; mem. high energy physics adv. panel ERDA, 1974—78; mem. nuc. sci. adv. panel NSF and Dept. Energy, 1980—89; mem. White House Sci. Coun., 1981—89, Nat. Sci. Bd., 1988—89; bd. dirs. MBARI, Monterey, Calif., Echlin Inc., New Haven, Thermo Vision, Cambridge, Mass., Sci. Applications Internat., Paris; founding ptnr. Washington Adv. Group, 1997. Editor: Physics in Perspective, 5 vols., 1972, Large Electrostatic Accelerators, 1974, Nuclear Detectors, 1978, Heavy Ion Science, 8 vols., 1981—84, A Century of Physics, 2001; co-editor: Proceedings of the Kingston International Conference on Nuclear Structure, 1960, Facets of Physics, 1970, Nuclear Science in China, 1979, The President's Scientists: Reminiscences of a Presidential Science Advisor, 1993; assoc. editor Annals of Physics, 1968—89, Am. Scientist, 1969—81, Il Nuovo Cimento, 1970—89, Nuclear Instruments and Methods, 1974—89, Science, Technology and the Humanities, 1978—89, Jour. Physics, 1978—89, Nuclear Science Applications, 1978—89, Technology in Soc., 1981—89, cons. editor McGraw Hill Series in Fundamentals of Physics, 1967—89, McGraw Hill Ency. Sci. and Tech. Oak Ridge Assoc. Univs., 1977—80; U. Bridgeport, 1981—86; Sheffield Scientific Sch., 1995—. Decorated Comdr.'s Cross Order of Merit Fed. Rep. of Germany; recipient Disting. Alumnus award, U. Rochester, 1986, U.S. Nat. medal of Sci., 1988, Presdl. medal, N.Y. Acad. Scis., 1989, Yale medal in Sci. and Engring., 1991, Disting. Svc. award, IEEE, 1991, Louis Pasteur medal of Sci., U. Strasbourg, 1991, Harvey medal, Pierce Found., 1991, Disting. Svc. medal, NSF, 1992, Pub. Svc. medla, Ctr. Study of Presidency, 1992, Exec. Yr. award, R&D Mag., 1992, Disting. Scholar medal, U. Rochester, 1993; fellow Timothy Dwight Coll., 1961, Guggenheim, 1977—78, Humboldt, 1978, 1985, 1986, Benjamin Franklin Royal Soc. Arts, London, 1979, Sheffield, Yale U., 2001. Fellow: Am. Phys. Soc. (mem. coun. 1967—71, v.p. 1995, pres.-elect 1996, pres. 1997, Nicholson medal 2001), Washington Adv. Group (sr.); mem.: NAS, AAAS (chmn. physics sect. 1977—78, pres.-elect 1980, pres. 1981—, chmn. bd. 1982—, William Carey medal 1993, Philip Abelson prize 1997), Am. Assn. Engring. Edn. (bd. dirs. 1995—), Am. Soc. for Engring. Edn. (bd. dirs. 1995—), Coun. Engring. Deans (bd. dirs. 1994—, 1994—), Coun. on Fgn. Rels., Southeastern U. Rsch. Assn. (bd. dirs. 1984—89), Internat. Union Pure and Applied Physics (U.S. nat. com. 1969—, chmn. 1975—76, v.p. 1975—81, pres. 1984—87), Conn. Acad. Sci. and Engring., N.Y. Acad. Arts and Scis. (bd. govs. 1994—), Conn. Acad. Arts and Scis. (coun. 1976—78), European Phys. Soc., Can. Assn. Physicists, Sigma Xi. (pres. Yale 1962—63). Home: 35 Tokeneke Dr North Haven CT 06473-4348 Office: Yale Univ PO Box 208124 New Haven CT 06520-8124 also: Wright Nuc Structure Lab 272 Whitney Ave Rm 207 New Haven CT 06520

BRONARS, JOSEPH CHARLES, JR., philosophy educator; b. Chgo., Aug. 3, 1925; s. Joseph Charles Sr. and Mary Barbara (Krawczyk) B.; m. Joanne Reynolds, Jan. 27, 1968; 1 child, Kristin. Student, DePaul U., 1942-43, 46-47; BA, St. Mary's Sem., Perryville, Mo., 1950; MA, Catholic U. of Am., 1955, PhD, 1957. Lectr., asst. prof. St. Mary's Seminary, Perryville, Mo., 1955, 61-62; instr., asst. prof. DePaul U., Chgo., 1957-61, 65-67; asst. prof., acad. dean and registrar Cardinal Glennon Coll., Shrewsbury, Mo., 1962-65; asst. prof. Queens Coll., CUNY, Flushing, N.Y., 1968-97. Senator U. Faculty Senate, CUNY, N.Y.C., 1988-91, Queens Coll. Acad. Senate, Flushing, 1970-73; pres. AAUP, Queens Coll., 1969-72; cons. Comp. Edn. Soc. in Europe, 1968-69. Contbr. articles on edn. in profl. jours. Served with USNR, 1943-46. Fellow Philosophy Edn. Soc. Democrat. Avocation: violin.

BRONKAR, EUNICE DUNALEE, artist, art educator; b. New Lebanon, Ohio, Aug. 8, 1934; d. William Dunham and Helen Kate (Hypes) Connor; m. Charles William Bronkar, Jan. 26, 1957; 1 child, Ramona. BFA, Wright State U., 1971, M in Art Edn., 1983, postgrad. art studies, 1989, Dayton Art Inst., 1972. Cert. art tchr., Ohio. Part time tchr. Springfield (Ohio) Mus. of Art, 1967-77; adjunct instr. Clark State C.C., Springfield, 1974-84, lead tchr., 1984-94, adj. asst. prof., 1998-2000, asst. prof., 1989-94; ret., 1994; artist private practice, Urbana, Ohio, 1995—. Edn. chmn. Springfield Mus. Art, 1973-74; image banks participant, Ohio Arts Coun., Columbus, Visual Arts Network, Dayton, Ohio, 1994—; affiliated with The Art Ctr. of St. Augustine, Fla. Art Scene, Little Gallery, Springfield, Ohio, The Frame Haven Gallery, Springfield, Ohio. One-woman shows include in Springfield, Ohio: Polo Club, Upper Valley Mall Cinema, Security Nat. Bank, Mr. C's Beauty Salon, Lakewood Beach, Springfield Mus. of Art, Clark State C.C.; Dayton, Ohio: Miami Valley Hosp., High St. Gallery, Stoeffer's Restaurant, Wegerzyn Garden Ctr., Meml. Hall, Wright State Univ., Urbana, Ohio: Champaign County Arts Coun., Urbana Cinema; South Charleston, Ohio: Cmty. Park Dedication, Philip Caldwell spl. guest spkr., Chmn. of the Bd. and CEO Ford Motor Co; 4-person show Springfield Mus. Art, 1999, Zanesville (Ohio) Art Ctr., 2000; accepted in over 100 area, state, regional, and nat. juried exhbns., including Ohio Water Color Soc.'s Ann. Traveling shows 1983-84, 86-87, Western Ohio Watercolor Soc., Hon. Mention 1983, 2001, Chase Patterson award, 1985, Spl. Merit award, 1990, 1st, 1995, 1st, 2000, Merit award 1997, 98; Springfield Mus. of Art: awards 1965, 68; 2d pastel 1972, 2d pastel and 1st drawing 1976, Jurors award pastel 1979, 1st drawing 1986, 3d drawing 1987, 2d drawing 1989, 1st drawing 1990, 1st drawing, 1991, 2d painting 1991, 1st drawing 1992, 2d, 1998, 2d pastel 1998, 1st drawing 2000, 2d painting, 2003, 1st painting, 2002, 2nd painting, 2003; Dayton Soc. Painters and Sculptors: Best of Show 1974, 2000, 1st painting, 2d painting 3d drawing 1978, Hon. Mention 1979, 3d Graphic 1980, Best of Show drawing 1981, 1st pastel 1981, 1st drawing 1991, 3d painting 1993, 2nd drawing 1993, Spl. Merit award for balance, 2001, Merit award, 2001, 03; Champaign County Fair: Best of show drawing and 1st pastel 1968; Miamisburg, Ohio 2003 (Best of Show drawing, 1st in painting); drawings and paintings in Am. Artist Renown, 1981, Shades of Gray, 1983, 84, 86, 87, 90, 91, 93, 94, 97, 1st painting, Harrisburg Gallery, Ohio, 2003 (Best of Show drawing); group shows include Wilson Gallery, Sidney, Ohio; represented in six pub. and numerous pvt. collections. Cleaned and restored art collections at Springfield Pub. Schs., Hist. Soc. in Springfield, Logan County Hist. Soc., Champaign County Hist. Soc., Warder Pub. Libr., Foos Manor Bed & Breakfast and the Masonic Temple, Penn House and Mus. of Art in Springfield, 1970-00, Calumet Antiques, Yellow Springs, Ohio, other groups and numerous pvt. collections, 1970—; mem. adv. com. comml. art, Clark County JVS Sch., Springfield, 1991-2003; judge more than 10 pub. h.s. art shows, 1970s-90s; judge Logan County (Ohio) Fair Fine Art Show profl. and amateur, 1998, Champaign County Fair Art Show, 2001. Recipient medal Bicentennial Com. and 4H Found. of Ohio, Springfield, 1976, Outstanding Tchr. award Clark State C.C., 1992, commd. to paint 2 past pres. Generals of the Natl. Soc. Daughters of the Amer. Revolution, which hangs in Continental Hall, Washington. Mem. Western Ohio Water Color Soc, Springfield (Ohio) Mus. of Art, Dayton Soc. Painters and Sculptors, Cin. Art Club, Ohio Water Color Soc., Nat. Mus. Women in Arts, Ohio Pleen Air Painters, Audubon Artists Soc., Pastel Soc., St. Augustine (Fla.) Art Assn., Portrait Soc. Ames, others. Avocations: swimming, walking, sewing, flower arranging, travel to Europe, Caribbean, Russia, Israel and Ireland.

BRONNER, DEBRA ANN, secondary school educator; b. Little Falls, N.Y., Jan. 17, 1961; d. Darwin Eugene and Martha (Hoke) B. BS, St. Lawrence U., 1983, MEd, 1986. Sci. tchr. Indian River Ctrl. Sch., Phila., 1984-87, Owen D. Young, Van Hornesville, NY, 1990—2001, James A. Green Ctrl. Sch., Dodgeville, NY. Chemistry mentor Coll. Finger Lakes, N.Y., 1999—; mem. com. Rural Partnership for Sci., Cooperstown, N.Y., 1991-96. Sec. Bd. Volleyball Ofcls., Utica, N.Y., 1988-92. Fellow Genentech, 1994, mentor, 1996; rsch. fellow Am. Soc. Biochemists and Microbiologists. Mem. Nat. Earth Sci. Tchrs. Assn., Nat. Assn. Sci. Tchrs., Nat. Biology Tchrs., Sci. Tchrs. Assn. N.Y. State. Office: James A Green HS Slawson St Ext Van Hornesville NY 13475 E-mail: dabronner@aol.com.

BRONSON, FRANKLIN H. zoology educator; b. Pawnee City, Nebr., Apr. 6, 1932; s. Harry and Vida (Shanklin) B.; m. Virginia Rowe, Nov. 14, 1951 (div. 1975); children— Barbara Ann, Steven Michael; m. Rebecca Barnett, Nov. 16, 1978 BS, Kans. State U., 1956, MS, 1957; PhD, Pa. State U., 1961. Assoc. staff scientist Jackson Lab., Bar Harbor, Maine, 1961-65, staff scientist, 1965-68; assoc. prof. U. Tex., Austin, 1968-72, prof., 1972—, dir. Inst. Reproductive Biology, 1978—. Cons. NIH, NSF Author: Mammalian Reproductive Biology, 1989; contbr. articles to profl. jours. Avocation: fly fishing. Home: 2725 Trail Of The Madrones Austin TX 78746-2344

BRONSON, JOHN ORVILLE, JR., retired librarian; b. Memphis, Apr. 6, 1937; s. John Orville and Elinor (Sutherland) B.; m. Patricia Ann Packer, June 11, 1962; 1 stepchild, Richard Wayne McCoy; children: Victoria Patricia Elizabeth, Glenn Charles. Student, N.E. Miss. Jr. Coll., 1957-59; BS, Miss. State U., 1961; MLS, U. Miss., 1965. Field sec. Miss. Libr. Commn., 1961-63, Acacia Nat. Frat., 1963-65; instr. U. Miss., 1965-66; head libr. Calhoun Jr. Coll., Decatur, Ala., 1965-67, Chesapeake Coll., Wye Mills, Md., 1967-82, telecomms. specialist, 1982-91, coord. media tech., 1991-2000. Pres. Wye Milling Co., Inc. Editor Ala. Jr. Coll. Librarian, 1966-67. Historiographer, Easton diocese Episcopal Ch., 1980-83; pres. Talbot County Dem. Club, 1984-85; v.p., sec. congl. coun. St. Marks Luth. Ch., 1999—; del. Del.-Md. synod ELCA, 1998-99; bd. dirs., Integrity, Cathedral of the Annunciation, Episcopal Diocese of Md., Balt., 1999-2003. Served with USAFR, 1955-63. Mem. ALA, Md. Libr. Assn., Ala. Libr. Assn., Md. Assn. Jr. Colls., Congress Acad. Librs., Old Wye Mill Soc. (treas.) Soc. for Preservation Md. Antiquities (dir.), Upper Shore Geneal. Soc. (founder), Acacia, Masons. Home: 7288 Shirley Dr Easton MD 21601-4804

BRONSON, OSWALD PERRY, SR., religious organization administrator, clergyman; b. Sanford, Fla., July 19, 1927; s. Uriah Perry and Flora (Hollingshed) B.; m. Helen Carolyn Williams, June 8, 1952; children— Josephine Suzette, Flora Helen, Oswald Perry. BS, Bethune-Cookman Coll., 1950; B.D., Gammon Theol. Sem., 1959; PhD, Northwestern U., 1965. Ordained to ministry Meth. Ch., 1957; pastor in Fla., Ga. and Rock River Conf., Chgo., 1950-66; v.p. Interdenominational Theol. Center, Atlanta, 1966-68, pres., 1968-75, Bethune-Cookman Coll., 1975-. Dir. Fla. Bank and Trust Co.; Past trustee Carrie Steel Pitts Home, Atlanta; past pres. and chmn. bd. edn. Ga. Conf., Central Jurisdiction, United Meth. Ch.; now mem. bd. ministry DeLand dist., also Fla. Ann. Conf., mem., univ. senate, past chmn. div. ministry, mem.-at-large bd. global ministries; mem. Pres.'s Bd. Advisors HBCU, USAF Bd. Advisors HBCU. Bd. dirs. United Meth. Com. on Relief; past mem. Volusia County (Fla.) Sch. Bd., Fla. Gov.'s Adv. Council on Productivity; past mem. exec. com. So. Regional Edn. Bd.; mem. adv. com. Fla. Sickle Cell Found., Inc.; past mem. council presidents Atlanta U. Center; mem. Fla. Bd. Ind. Colls. and Univs.; past trustee Hinton Rural Life Center; past bd. dirs. Inst. of Black World, Wesley Community Center, Atlanta, Martin Luther King Center Social Change, Work Oriented Rehab. Center, Inc., Fund Theol. Edn.; mem. nat. selection com. Rockefeller Doctoral Fellowships in Religion; bd. dirs. Am. Nat. Red Cross, United Way, Nat. Assn. Equal Opportunity in Higher Edn., United Negro Coll. Fund; also mem. fund raising strategy adv. com. Ga. Pastors' Sch.

Crusade scholar, 1957-64. Mem. Am. Assn. Theol. Schs. (v.p. 1968-70), Ministerial Assn. of Halifax Area, Religious Edn. Assn. (past pres., past chmn. bd. dirs.), Mid-Atlantic Assn. Profs. Religious Edn., Fla. Assn. Colls. and Univs. (pres. 1997—), Atlanta Theol. Assn. (past vice chmn.), AAUP, Daytona Beach area C. of C., NAACP, Theta Phi (past dir. internat. soc.), Alpha Kappa Mu, Phi Delta Kappa, Sigma Pi Phi, Alpha Phi Alpha. Clubs: Rotary, Daytona Beach area Execs, Daytona Beach Quarterback. Methodist. Office: Bethune-Cookman Coll 640 Dr Mary Mcleod Bethune Blv Daytona Beach FL 32114-3012

BROOK, JUDITH SUZANNE, psychiatry and psychology researcher and educator; b. N.Y.C., Dec. 31, 1939; d. Robert and Helen E. (Zimmerman) Muser; m. David W. Brook, Dec. 15, 1962; children: Adam, Jonathan. BA, Hunter Coll., 1961; MA in Psychology, Columbia U., 1962, EdD in Devel. and Ednl. Psychology, 1967. Lic. psychologist, N.Y. Asst. prof. psychology Queens Coll., CUNY, Flushing, 1967-69; rsch. assoc. Columbia U., N.Y.C., 1969-77, sr. rsch. assoc., 1977-80; assoc. prof. psychiatry Mt. Sinai Sch. Medicine, N.Y.C., 1980-90, adj. prof., 1990-94; prof. N.Y. Med. Coll., Valhalla, N.Y., 1990-94; prof. cmty. and preventive medicine Mt. Sinai Sch. Medicine, 1994—. Rsch. scientist devel. award Nat. Inst. on Drug Abuse, 1982-90, sr. rsch. scientist, 1992—, ad hoc reviewer, 1989—, chair study sect. epidemiology, prevention and rsch., 1995-2000; ad hoc reviewer NIMH, NSF, 1992—; adj. prof. psychiatry N.Y. Med. Coll., 1994-2001. Author: (Psychology book) The Psychology of Adolescence, others; contbr. chpts. to books and more than 200 articles to profl. jours. Recipient 1st ann. Dean's Disting. Rsch. award N.Y. Med. Coll., 1992; grantee Nat. Inst. on Drug Abuse, 1979—. Fellow: Am. Psychopathol. Assn.; mem.: APA, NY State Psychol. Assn., Assn. for Med. Edn. & Rsch. in Substance Abuse, Am. Psychol. Soc. (liaison officer 1989—), Coll. on Problems of Drug Dependence. Office: Mt Sinai Sch Medicine Dept Cmty & PrevMed Box 1044A One Gustave Levy Pl New York NY 10029

BROOKE, DOLORES ANN, special education educator; b. Livingston, Ill., July 27, 1937; d. Joseph Francis and Tillie (Pelko) Dalla-Riva; m. Eddie Wayne Brooke, Dec. 22, 1956; children: Todd Wayne, Tari Jo Brooke Cerentano. BS in Elem. Edn. with highest honors, So. Ill. U., Edwardsville, 1971; MS in Spl. Edn., So. Ill. U., 1975. Cert. nat. bd. cert. tchr. 2002. Tchr. learning disabled Edwardsville Dist. 7, 1971-73, 3rd grade tchr., 1973-74, 2nd grade tchr., 1974—2003, kindergarten tchr., 2003—. Pres. Village of Livingston, 1985-89; mem. Holy Cross Luth. Choir, choir dir., dir. Christmas Nativity and Easter Passion plays, nat. bd. cert. tchr. Recipient Excellence in Teaching award 1992; named semi-finalist Thanks to Tchrs., 1990. Mem. NEA, Ill. Edn. Assn., Edwardsville Edn. Assn., Lewis and Clark Reading Coun., Madison, Jersey and Calhoun Coordinated Bargaining Coun., Internat. Reading Assn., Internat. Platform Assn., Delta Kappa Pi. Democrat. Lutheran. Avocations: swimming, reading, bike riding, traveling, walking. Home: PO Box 82 Livingston IL 62058-0082

BROOKES, CAROLYN, early childhood education educator; b. Orlando, Fla., June 16, 1946; d. Thomas M. and Hilda Marie (Hanson) Jessen: m. Edward N. Brookes, Aug. 8, 1970 (dec. Oct. 1990); 1 child, Donna Marie. BA, U. So. Fla., 1969; MS, Nova U., 1990. Asst. dir., dir. lower schs. Gables Acad., Winter Park, Fla., 1973-83; tchr. Orange County Pub. Schs., Orlando, 1983-98, early childhood resource tchr., high-scope trainer, 1983-92, coord. edn. homeless children and youth program, 1992-95. Coord. mentor tchr. program U. Ctrl. Fla. and Orange County Pub. Schs., 1993-96; regional specialist State Dept. of Edn., 1997-98; parent educator, adj. instr. U. Ctrl. Fla.; ednl. cons.; literacy first trainer distance educator Ednl. Mgmt. Group, Phoenix, 1994-96; trainer Staff Devel. for Educators, Implications Brain Rsch., Literary First, Loving Guidance; pres. People to People, 1992-99; literacy coach U. North Fla., 1998-2000.; project cons. staff devel. CD programs, Jensen Learning Corp., 2002. Co-author presch. literacy curriculum, 2001. Mem. ASCD, Internat. Reading Assn., Nat. Staff Devel. Coun., Assn. for Childhood Edn. Internat., Nat. Assn. for Edn. Young Children, So. Early Childhood Assn., Orange County Assn. for Edn. Young Children, Delta Kappa Gamma Soc. Internat. for Key Women Educators, Phi Delta Kappa. Home: 6316 Grand Bahama Cir Tampa FL 33615-4204 Office: Carolyn Jessen Brookes Ednl Cons 6316 Grand Bahama Cir Tampa FL 33615-4204 E-mail: cjbrookes@aol.com.

BROOKES, MONA E. author, lecturer, art educator; b. L.A., May 9, 1937; d. John Arthur Brookes and Mary Elizabeth Baker Boles; m. Charles Hall, Jan. 1966 (div. Aug. 1968); 1 child, Mark Evan. BA in Art and Psychology magna cum laude, George Pepperdine U., L.A., 1959. Founder Monart Drawings Schs. (30 locations), Ojai, Calif., 1981—. Cons. in field; condr. seminars in field; lectr. in field. TV talk show guest Daybreak L.A., 1982, Disney Mag., 1983, Today Show, 1987, ABC Home Show, 1988. Author: Drawing with Children, 1986, Drawing for Older Children and Teens, 1991; contbr. articles to profl. jours. Adv. bd. Nat. Learning Ctr., Washington, 1989-91. Calif. Arts Coun. grantee, 1980-83. Home and Office: PO Box 1630 Ojai CA 93024-1630

BROOKINS, DOLORES, educational consulting organization executive; b. Memphis, Mar. 10, 1948; d. Adolphus Sr. and Katherine (Pierson) B. BA in Elem. Edn., Lane Coll., 1970; MS in Guidance and Counseling, Tenn. State U., 1973; PhD in Ednl. Adminstrn., Ohio State U., 1982. Cert. tchr., prin. grades Kindergarten through 9, Tenn; cert. counselor grades kindergarten through 12, D.C.; cert. HUD cons. Elem. tchr. Memphis City Schs., 1970-73; ednl. cons. Memphis Area Schs. and Tenn. State U., 1970-92; head resident counselor Tenn. State U., Nashville, 1973, test supr./counselor III, 1974-76; asst. dean students, dir. counseling ctr. Lane Coll., Jackson, Tenn., 1976-78; rsch. assoc., dir. evening fin. aid, night bldg. mgr. Ohio State U., Columbus, 1978-82; asst. dean students, dir. minority affairs U. Ark., Fayetteville, 1982-85; assoc. dir. instrnl. svcs., assoc. rschr. Ill. Cmty. Coll. Bd., Springfield, 1985-87; legis. aide/rschr. to chmn. appropriation II com. Ill. Gen. Assembly, Springfield, 1987-88; asst. to dir. budget, mgmt. acct. II City of Springfield, 1988, exec. dir. human rels. commn., fair housing bd., 1988-91; ednl. cons. B&A, Memphis, 1970-80, sr. ednl. cons., 1981-91, CEO, sr. ednl. cons. Washington, 1992-94. Adj. prof. Sch. Social Work, U. Ill., 1988-91; assoc. grad faculty Coll. Grad. Studies, Ctrl. Mich. U. Author: (manual) Administrative Burnout: A Latent Dysfunction of Roles, Goals Disjunction and Organizational Routinization, 1982, Smile: A Peer Counseling Manual, 1985. Election judge, pollwatcher, Washington, 1994. Named one of Outstanding Young Women of Am., 1983; named Outstanding Female Exec., NAFE, Washington. Mem. ASTD, Nat. Assn. Human Rights Workers (mem. com. 1989-91), Rotary, Phi Delta Kappa. Baptist. Avocation: sewing. Home and Office: 5294 Louise Rd Memphis TN 38109-6923

BROOKS, ARLENE SHEFFIELD, secondary education educator; b. High Point, N.C., Apr. 3, 1939; d. Sandy B. and Geneva M. (McCaskill) Sheffield; m. James Nash Brooks, July 18, 1964; children: James Timothy, Terry Sheffield. AB, Guilford Coll., 1961; MA, Longwood Coll., 1967. Tchr. social studies Bluestone Sr. High Sch., Skipwith, Va., 1961-64; tchr. Park View Sr. High Sch., South Hill, Va., 1964-67, 80—, Park View Jr. High Sch., South Hill, Va., 1976-80. Mem. Order Ea. Star, Delta Kappa Gamma (2d v.p. 1982-84, rec. sec. 1984-86, pres. 1992-94). Baptist. Avocations: reading, cross stitch, piano, travel. Home: 506 N Brunswick Ave South Hill VA 23970-1602 Office: Park View Sr High Sch 205 Park View Cir South Hill VA 23970-5031

BROOKS, BENJAMIN RIX, neurologist, educator; b. Cambridge, Mass., Dec. 1, 1942; s. Frederic Manning and Miriam Adelaide (Rix) B.; m. Susan Jane Whitmore, May 31, 1970; children: Nathaniel Phillips, Alexander Whitmore, Joshua Cushing. AB cum laude, Harvard U., 1965, MD magna cum laude, 1970. Diplomate Am. Bd. Psychiatry and Neurology, Am. Bd. Internal Medicine. Intern, asst. resident Harvard Med. Svc., Boston City Hosp., 1970-72; resident in neurology Mass. Gen. Hosp., Boston, 1972-74; clin. assoc. med. neurology br. Nat. Inst. Neurolog. Diseases and Stroke, Bethesda, Md., 1974-76; rsch. fellow neurovirology div. Johns Hopkins Med. Sch., Balt., 1976-78, asst. prof. neurology dept., 1978-82; assoc. prof. neurology and med. microbiology U. Wis. Med. Sch., Madison, 1982-87, prof., 1987—; staff neurologist William S. Middleton Meml. VA Hosp., Madison, 1982-84, chief neurology svc., 1984—. Examiner Am. Bd. Psychiatry and Neurology, Evanston, Ill., 1980—; chmn. neuropharmacologic drugs adv. com. FDA, Rockville, Md., 1982-85; vis. prof. various schs., U.S., Eng., Fed. Republic Germany, Japan, Spain. Editor: Amyotrophic Lateral Sclerosis, 1987, Brain Rsch. Bull., 1980-90; contbr. papers, revs., abstracts to profl. publs., chpts. to books. Mem. ushers com. Grace Episcopal Ch., Madison, 1983—; mem. talented and gifted evaluation com. Madison Sch. Bd., 1986; mem. com. on VA manpower of the Inst. of Medicine of the Nat. Acad. Scis. Lt. comdr. USPHS, 1974-76. Recipient Nat. Rsch. award Nat. Inst. Neurolog. and Communicative Disorders and Stroke, 1976-78, Tchr.-Investigator Devel. award, 1978-82. Mem. Am. Acad. Neurology (chair govt. svcs. sect. 1995—, mem. animal rsch. com. 1990-95), Am. Neurolog. Assn., Wis. Neurolog. Soc. (sec.-treas. 1985-87, v.p. 1988, pres.-elect 1989, pres. 1990), Soc. for Neurosci., N.Am. ALS Care Registry (adv. com.), Soc. Exptl. Neuropathology, Am. Soc. Microbiology, Internat. Soc. Neuroimmunology, Assn. VA Neurologists (pres. 1994-96, councilor 1996—), Soc. In Vitro Biology, Tissue Culture Assn., World Fedn. Neurology Rsch. Group on Motor Neuron Diseases (steering com.). Republican. Avocations: running, sailing, swimming, bicycling, hiking. Office: Wm S Middleton Meml VA Hosp 2500 Overlook Ter Madison WI 53705-2254

BROOKS, CLIFTON ROWLAND, SR., pediatrician, educator, enviromental medicine; b. Louisville, Ky., May 8, 1923; s. Herbert Berwick and Ella Tatum (Rowland) B.; m. Agnes Joan McVeigh, June 21, 1947 (dec. 1991); children: Clifton Rowland, Daniel R., Gordon B., Philip H.; m. Berverly Frances Thrower Persons, Feb. 14, 1993. BS, U. Wis., 1944, MD, 1946; MPH, UCLA, 1970. Diplomate Am. Bd. Pediat., Am. Bd. Environ. Medicine, Internat. Bd. Environ. Medicine, Calif. State Cred. K-12 (life), Cert. Health-related subjects, Calif. Cmty. Coll., Cert. Flight Instr., FAA, ASMEL; SES, Gliders, Ground Instrn.: Airplanes, Gliders, Instruments. Pvt. practice, Newark, 1950-60, Metro Washington, 1960-70, Orange County, Calif., 1970-83; clin. br. mgr. FAA, U.S. Dept. Transp., Oklahoma City, 1983-87; exec. dir. Am. Bd. Environ. Medicine, Norman, Okla., 1988-93, Internat. Bd. Environ. Medicine, Norman, Okla., 1988-93, Carl Albert Indian Health Facility, Ada, Okla., 1991. Founder Am. and Internat. Accrediting Bd. Environ. Medicine, 1988, Harriet Lane Home 1954-60; founder, 1st pres. Am. Bd. Environ. Medicine & Internat. Bd. Environ. Medicine; instr. Epilepsy Clinic, Allergy Clinic, Johns Hopkins Hosp., Balt.; asst. prof. cmty. medicine Georgetown U., Washington; assoc. prof. pediat. U. Calif., Irvine; prof. oral surgery Loma Linda (Calif.) Dental Sch.; prof. health edn. Coll. Allied Health Scis., Health Scis. Ctr., Oklahoma City, 1987-99; various mil. instr. positions. Author: Audiovisual Training Programs, 1973; editor: Registers for the Boards, 1989-90; contbr. articles to profl. jours. Mem. Montgomery County (Md.) Safety Bd., 1962; mem. sci. adv. bd. U.S. EPA, Washington, 1976-80. Tng. officer (19 yrs.) USAR, comd. AeroMed Squadrons, USAFR, 1968—77, supr. to tng. officers USAFR, 1968—77, ret. ARNG, 1977—83. Fellow APHA, AMA, Augustan Soc., Am. Coll. Allergy and Immunology, Am. Coll. Chest Physicians, Am. Coll. Preventive Medicine, Am. Coll. Occupl. and Environ. Medicine, Am. Acad. Environ. Medicine, Royal Soc. Medicine (UK), Am. Coll. Genealogy (cert.), Huguenot Soc. London, Soc. Antiquarians (Scot); mem. Manorial Soc. Gt. Britain. Presbyterian. Avocations: teaching genealogy, freemasonry. Home: 10717 Sunset Blvd Oklahoma City OK 73120-2437

BROOKS, DANA D. dean; b. Hagerstown, Md., Aug. 1, 1951; s. Fred and Helen (Brooks) Miles. AA, Hagerstown Jr. Coll., 1971; BS, Towson State Coll., 1973; MS, W.Va. U., 1976, EdD, 1979. Asst. prof. W.Va. U., Morgantown, 1979-83, assoc. prof., 1983-88, prof., 1988—, acting asst. dean, 1986-87, acting dean, 1988, assoc. dean, 1987-92, interim dean, 1992-93, dean, 1993—. Recipient Rev. Dr. Martin Luther King, Jr. Achievement award W.Va. U., 1997, Social Justice award W.Va. U., 1992, Cheikh Anata DIOP award for outstanding African-Centered Rsch.; fellow Am. Acad. Kinesiology and Phys. Edn., 1999; scholar W.Va. U., 1999, Minority scholar Ill. State U., 2003; grantee in field; named to Hagerstown Jr. Coll. Sport Hall of Fame, 2003, named Hall of Fame, Hagerston C.C., 2003. Mem. AAHPERD (Young Profl. award 1982), Midwest APPHERD (v.p. 1988-89, pres.-elect 1993, pres. 1994-95, Svc. award 2000), W.Va. Assn. Health, Phys. Edn. and Recreation (pres. 1983-84, Ray O. Duncan award 1991), Golden Key (hon.), Phi Delta Kappa. Avocations: tennis, fencing. Home: 811 Timberline Morgantown WV 26505-1120 Office: W Va U 257 Coliseum Morgantown WV 26506

BROOKS, DEBRA L. healthcare executive, neuromuscular therapist; b. Cedar Rapids, Iowa, Dec. 10, 1950; d. Rex L and Phyllis M (Harman) Brooks; children from previous marriage: Brei, Benjamin, Bryan. BA, Coe Coll., 1973; MS, Clayton Coll., 1999, PhD, 2000. Cert. neuromuscular therapy Fla., natural therapeutics specialist N.Mex. Tchr. Cedar Rapids Cmty. Sch. Dist., 1973-92; COO NeuroMuscular Therapy Ctr., Walford, Iowa, 1994—. Educator Helping Hands Seminars, Cedar Rapids, 1992—2000, Debra Brooks' Seminars, Walford, 1993—; bus and educ consult Brooks Consults, Cedar Rapids, 1990—; mem Iowa Bd Examiners, 2001—03; chair adv. bd. ABLE, 2001—02; mem., chair Nat. Alliance State Bds., 2001—02; editl. bd. Momentum Media. Contbr. articles to profl jours and newsletters. Fundraiser, performer in musicals St Luke's Hosp, Cedar Rapids, 1978—91; fundraiser, performer in Follies Cedar Rapids Symphony, 1981—99; fundraiser, performer in telethons Variety Clubs Am, Cedar Rapids, 1989—91; mem Walford Community Develop, 1994—98; editl. bd. Tng. and Conditioning Mag. Named Outstanding Mentor of the Yr, YWCA, 2001; recipient First in Nation in Educ Award, State of Iowa, 1991, Tribute to Women of Achievement Award, YWCA, 2001. Mem.: Am. Coll. Healthcare Execs. (chmn. 2002—03), Am. Massage Therapy Assn. (state v.p., edn. dir. 1992—94, nat. trustee Found. 1994—98, nat. bd. dirs. 1994—2002, cert), Profl. Women's Network. Avocations: singing, painting, pianist, power walking, philosophy. Office: NeuroMuscular Therapy Ctr PO Box 8267 Cedar Rapids IA 52408-8267 E-mail: montanadebrabrooks@yahoo.com.

BROOKS, GERLDINE MCGLOTHLIN, elementary school educator; b. Luling, Tex., Feb. 9, 1932; d. Fred Augusta and Bessie (Rutherford) McGlothlin; m. Kenneth A. Brooks, Nov. 27, 1952; children: Richard E., Kenneth A. BS in Elem. Edn., S.W. Tex. State U., 1962; postgrad., Tex. A&I U. Cert. in elem. edn., Tex. Classroom tchr. New Braunfels (Tex.) Ind. Sch. Dist., 1962-65, Pearsall (Tex.) Ind. Sch. Dist., 1965-81, Gonzales (Tex.) Ind. Sch. Dist., 1981—98, Cuero Christian Acad., 1998—2000. Composer (songs) Blubonnetts All Over Texas, How Amazing is His Grace, Hemmed in by the Mountains, Take That Tree, In Our Greatest Losses, You're Not Alone. Mem. Nat. Fedn. Music Cubs (local pres., dist. v.p. 1989-91, treas. 1990—98), Classroom Tchrs. Nat. Edn. Assn., Tex. Ret. Tchrs. Assn. (dist. pres., 2002—, pres. Gonzales county chpt., 2000-02), Gonzales Art League, Delta Kappa Gamma (chpt. pres. 1988-90, Local Achievement award 1988). Office: Gozales Ind Sch Dist 1615 St Louis St Gonzales TX 78629-4330

BROOKS, JERRY CLAUDE, safety engineer, educator; b. College Park, Ga., Apr. 23, 1936; s. John Bennett and Mattie Mae (Timms) B.; m. Peggy Sue Thornton, Feb. 26, 1961; children: Apryll Denise, Jerry Claude, Susan Vereen. BS, Ga. Inst. Tech., 1958. Safety engr. Cotton Prodrs. Assn., Atlanta, 1959-64, dir. safety and loss control, 1964-70; dir. corp. protection Gold Kist, Inc., Atlanta, 1970-81; dir. corp. safety J.P. Stevens, 1981-84, dir. safety and security, 1984-86, dir. health and safety, 1986-88; dir. loss control Am. Yarn Spinners Assn., 1988-89; dir. safety Spring Industries, Inc., 1989-2000; cons. Occupational Safety Cons., 2000—. Instr., Ga. Safety Inst., Athens, Ga., 1971-78. Bd. dirs. Greater Lithonia (Ga.) Homeowners Assn., Ga. Soc. Prevention of Blindness, Ga. Safety Coun. Served with AUS, 1958-59. Mem. Am. Soc. Safety Engrs. (chpt. pres. 1968-69, regional v.p. 1974-76), Nat. Safety Coun. (gen. chmn. fertilizer sect. 1969-70, gen. chmn. textile sec. 1985-87, Disting. Svc. to Safety award 1989, Palmetto chpt. pres. 1994), So. Safety Conf. (v.p. bus. and industry 1968-74, pres. 1974), Am. Textile Mfrs. Inst. (chmn. safety and health com. 1991-93, Donald B. Hayes lifetime achievement award 2000), Am. Soc. Indsl. Security, S.C. Occupl. Safety Coun. (bd. mem. 1994-99), Ga. Bus. and Industry Assn. (dir., named outstanding mem. 1981), Internat. Assn. Hazard Control Mgrs. (chpt. pres. 1979-80), Masons, Rosicrucians, Exch. Club (pres. 1969-70, Book of Golden Deeds award 1981) (Lithonia). Home: 100 Woodmere Ln Columbus NC 28722-4408 E-mail: jbrooks@aol.com.

BROOKS, JOSEPH RUSSELL, educational administrator; b. Charlotte, N.C., Aug. 18, 1931; s. Brown W. and Grace M. (Allen) B.; m. Iris Fern Shrader, July 22, 1954; children: Elizabeth, Mark, Jane. BA, Aurora (Ill.) U., 1953; MEd, U. N.C., 1959, EdS, 1964; EdD, U. N.C., Greensboro, 1984. Cert. English tchr., supt., prin., N.C. Tchr. Charlotte Schs., 1953-61; prin. Bethune Sch., 1961-62, Midwood Sch., Charlotte, 1962-64, Devonshire Sch., Charlotte, 1964-67, Albemarle Rd. Jr. H.S., Charlotte, 1967-71; asst. supt. secondary schs. Greensboro Schs., 1971-78, asst. supt. pers., 1978-82, asst. supt. mid. schs., 1982-85, interim supt., 1985-87; supt. Aiken County Pub. Schs., Aiken, S.C., 1987-95; interim supt. Laurens Dist. #56, SC, 2001, Saluda Sch. Dist., SC, 2002. Coll. instr. U. N.C., Greensboro, 1975-87, U. S.C., Aiken, 1995-98; assessor N.C. Prins.' Assessment Ctr., Raleigh, N.C., 1982-87; cons. in field. Mem. Greater Augusta (Ga.) Arts Coun., 1987-95, Aiken County Commn. Higher Edn., 1987-95, Aiken County Tech. Commn. Aiken Tech. Coll., 1987-95, N.C. Humanities Com., 1985-87. IDEA fellow Kettering Found., 1966, 68. Mem. Am. Assn. Sch. Adminstrs., Greater Aiken C. of C., Rotary (Aiken bd. dirs. 1995-98, pres. 1999-2000), Phi Delta Kappa. Presbyterian. Home: 114 Hemlock Dr Aiken SC 29803-2612 E-mail: joefern@duesouth.net.

BROOKS, LEANNE RUTH HURT, secondary school educator; b. Muncie, Ind., Nov. 11, 1961; d. H. Terrence Hurt and Ruth Margaret (Hunter) Morgan; m. Ivan Roderick Brooks, Sept. 1, 1984. BA, Anderson U., Ind., 1984; MS summa cum laude, Ill. State U., 2003. Dist. mgr. Sujen, Chattanooga, 1984-87; tchr. computer aide Sch. Dist. 61, Decatur, Ill., 1987-90; ednl. facilitator Job Tng. Partnership, Decatur, 1990—2000. Part-time GED instr. Richland C.C., Decatur, 1993—. Mem. Mensa, Camarada Club, Kappa Mu Epsilon, Phi Eta Sigma, Sigma Zeta, Alpha Chi, Delta Mu Delta, Kappa Delta Pi. Republican. Ch. of God. Avocations: creative writing, piano. Home: 1061 Bunker Ln Decatur IL 62526-9318

BROOKS, LILLIAN DRILLING ASHTON (LILLIAN HAZEL CHURCH), adult education educator; b. Grand Rapids, Mich., May 27, 1921; d. Walter Brian and Lillian Church; m. Frederick Morris Drilling, 1942 (div. Apr. 1972); children: Frederick Walter, Stephen Charles, Lawrence Alan, Lynn Anne; m. Richard Moreton Ashton, Aug. 25, 1973 (dec. 1990); m. Ralph J. Brooks, May 21, 1994. Student, Grand Rapids Jr. Coll., 1939-41, Wayne State U., 1941-42, Grand Rapids Art Inst., 1945-49, UCLA, 1964-69, Loyola Marymount Coll., Westchester, Calif., 1970-73; life tchg. credential, U. So. Calif., Long Beach, 1973. Life teaching credential, Calif. Decorator John Widdicomb Furniture Co., 1945-49; tchr. art Inglewood (Calif.) Sch. Dist., 1965-73; tchr. adult edn. art Downey (Calif.) Unified Sch. Dist., 1973-95; tchr. art Assn. Retarded Citizens and Mentally Disadvantaged Students Downey Cmty. Health Ctr., 2001—02. Art tchr. institutionalized adults ages 18 to 60, 2000—; lectr. Downey Art League, 1990-92, Whittier (Calif.) Art Assn., 1991, h.s. and mid. sch. lectr., 1994-95; judge Children's Art Exhibit, Downey, 1992; participant Getty Found., San Francisco, 1993, Getty Found., Cranbrook, 1994, Getty Conf. on Aesthetics, 1995, Cin. U., 1992, El Segundo, 1994; mem. state accreditation com. Inglewood and Downey United Sch. Dists., 1966-70, 75-80, 85—; owner A & B Furniture Svc. Ctr., 1995—. One-woman shows include El Segundo Mcpl. Libr., 1965, Pico Rivera Art Gallery, 1978, Downey Art Mus., 1999; exhibited in group shows at Fairlane Show, Dearborn, Mich., 1959, Jane Lessing Art Gallery, 1966, Westchester Mcpl. Libr., 1971, Inglewood City Hall, 1973, Aegina Sch., Greece, 1973, Downey Mus. Art, 1992, 99-2000; represented in permanent collection U. Mich., Calif. Senate Bldg. Pres. bd. dirs. Downey Art Mus., 1996-2002, dir. Mus., 1998, vol. dir., 1999, bd. dirs. 1998-2000; art commr. City of Dearborn, Mich., 1954-59; former pres. Dearborn Art Inst., Pacific Art Guild; pres. Downey Art League, 1991-94, v.p., 1999-2000; pres. Exhbn. Ch., 1995, v.p. 1996-98; vol. dir. Art Mus., 1998-99; lectr. on art as a career local Downey high and mid. schs.; juried children's art shows; vol. tchr. basic art; judge art shows. Recipient Certs. of Appreciation for contbn. of leadership Coord. Coun. Downey, Downey Governing Bd., Downey Bd. Edn., 1997, 2002, Cmty. Svc. award for Outstanding Svc. Downey Rotary, 1994, Cert. of Recognition Calif. State Assembly, 1999, Downey Coord. Coun., 1998-99, award 2002; named Tchr. of Yr., Masons, Downey, 1986; painting chosen to represent dist. in state capital, 1999-2001. Mem. Calif. Coun. on Art Edn. (parliamentarian Downey 1990-92, Calco Excellence in Tchg. award 1991, various certs.). Avocations: reading, hiking, internat. travel, photography, painting. Home: 9318 Fostoria St Downey CA 90241-4020

BROOKS, LLOYD WILLIAM, JR., osteopath, interventional cardiologist, educator; b. Amarillo, Tex., Nov. 4, 1949; s. Lloyd William and Tina Margaret (Roe) B.; m. Ann Nettleship, Apr. 3, 1987. BS, U. Tex., 1972; DO cum laude, U. North Tex., 1985. Diplomate Am. Osteo. Bd. Internal Medicine; bd. cert. in internal medicine & cardiology. Intern Dallas-Ft. Worth Med. Ctr., 1985; resident in internal medicine Ft. Worth Osteo. Med. Ctr., 1986-88; fellow in cardiology Detroit Heart Inst.; fellow in angioplasty and interventional cardiology Riverside Meth. Hosp., Columbus, Ohio; pvt. practice Ft. Worth, 1990—, Heart Place; chief of medicine, chief of staff Osteo. Med. Ctr. of Tex. Clin. asst. prof. U. North Tex. Health Sci. Ctr., Ft. Worth, 1991—. Contbr. articles to med. jours. Fellow Am. Coll. Cardiology, Am. Coll. Osteo. Internists; mem. AMA, Am. Osteo. Assn., Am. Coll. Osteo. Internists (diplomate). Avocations: photography, music, woodworking, sailplaning, scuba diving. Office: Ft Worth Heart & Vascular 1002 Montgomery St Ste 212 Fort Worth TX 76107-2693

BROOKS, LORRAINE ELIZABETH, retired music educator; b. Port Chester, N.Y., Mar. 10, 1936; d. William Henry Brooks and Marion Elizabeth Brooks. BS in Music Edn., SUNY, Potsdam, 1958; M of Performance, Manhattan Sch. Music, 1970; cert. in Religion EPS, Trinity Coll., 2000. Dir. Camp Spruce-Mountain Lakes, North Salem, N.Y., 1964-73; youth adviser St. Peter's Episcopal Ch., Port Chester, N.Y., 1964-65, St. Andrew's-St. Peter's Ch., Yonkers, N.Y., 1970-73; v.p. South Yonkers Youth Council, 1970-76; assoc. Sisters Charity of N.Y., Scarsdale, 1978—; eucharistic minister, lector Our Lady of Victory Ch., Mt. Vernon, N.Y., 1981-93, eucharistic minister lector, 1981—93; asst. chaplain White Plains Hosp. Ctr., NY, 1981—2000; chaplain for renal patients St. Joseph's Med. Ctr., Yonkers, NY, 2000—. Cons. Quincy Tenants Assn., Mt. Vernon, 1986—; workshop presenter in kidney hemodialysis transplant; music educator cons., 2000—; chaplain for renal pts. St. Joseph Med. Ctr., Yonkers, NY, 2000—; choral dir. Elem. Middle Sch. Soloist Greenhaven Correctional Facility retreat, N.Y., 1994; recital St. Mary's Ch. Outreach Program, 1994. Vestrywoman St. Andrew's Episc. Ch., Yonkers, 1971-75; contralto soloist St. Peter's Episc. Ch., Port Chester, 1959-69, Cape Cod Roman Cath. Charismatic Conf., 1993; mem. Collegiate Chorale, N.Y.C., 1958-68; svc. team mem. Charismatic Cmty., Scarsdale, 1975-91; v.p. Willwood Tenant Assn., Mt. Vernon, 1981-82, pres., 1982-84; vol. speaker N.Y. Regional Transplant Program, 1992—; active Montefiore Med. Ctr.

TRIO, 1991—, presenter kidney transplant program, 1995; active Teen/Twenty Encounter Christ, 1990-92; soloist concert Holy Spirit Episcopal Ch., Orleans, Mass.; facilitator Our Lady of the Cape, Brewster, Mass.; inspirational spkr. St. Joan of Arc, Orleans, Mass., 2002; lector, eucharistic min. St. Mary's Roman Cath. Ch., 1993—, facilitator RENEW program, 1994—, CORE team mem., 1996, coord. prayer group Day of Reflection, elected leader prayer group, 1998—, adviser young adults ministry, 1998-2002; asst. coord. RENEW, St. Mary's Ch., Mt. Vernon, N.Y., leader Charismatic Prayer Group, 1998-2000, cons. to Charismatic group, 2000—; coord. Life in the Spirit Program, 1997; trustee Edn. Parish Svc. Program, Trinity Coll., 2000; vol. chaplain for renal patients St. Joseph's M.C., Yonkers, N.Y., 2001—; team mem. Women's Cursillo-English, N.Y. Archdiocese; active Christopher Leadership course Gabriel Richard Inst., N.Y., 2000; vol. chaplain for renal patients St. Joseph's Med. Ctr., Yonkers, N.Y. Mem. Westchester County Sch. Music Assn. (exec. bd.), Scarsdale Tchrs. Assn. (exec. bd.), Music Educators Nat. Conf., West Cmty. Sch. Music Assn (exec. bd. 1967-70). Democrat. Roman Catholic. Avocations: swimming, reading, walking, organic cooking, concerts. E-mail: Brookhem@aol.com.

BROOKS, PATRICIA SCOTT, principal; b. St. Louis, July 19, 1949; d. John Edward and Doris Louise (Webb) Scott; m. John Robert Brooks, May 22, 1986; 1 child, Ollie. BS, W.Va. State Coll., 1971; MA, Marshall U., 1974; adminstrv. cert., Ind. U., 1990. Cert. tchr., Ind. Tchr. spl. edn. Huntington (W.Va.) State Hosp., 1971; tchr. elem. edn. Kanawha County Sch., Charleston, W.Va., 1971-78, Washington Twp., Indpls., 1979-82, tchr. mid. sch., 1982-90, adminstrv. intern, 1989-90, asst. coord., 1990, 92, asst. prin., 1990-93; prin. Pike Twp., Indpls., 1993-2000, New Pike Twp. Sch.-Snacks Crossing Elem., 2001. Participant Ind. U. Tchr. as a Decision Maker Program, Bloomington, 1989; mem. Human Rels. Com., Indpls., 1996; presenter U.S. Dept. Edn. Panelist State PTA Conv. Recipient Tchr. Spotlight award Topics Newspaper, 1983; named one of 100 Outstanding Black Women in State of Ind., Nat. Coun. Negro Women, 1990, Ctr. for Leadership Devel. award, 2002; Danforth fellow Ind. U., 1989. Mem. Ind. Assn. for Elem. and Mid. Sch. Prins., Phi Delta Kappa, Delta Sigma Theta. Methodist. Avocations: tennis, cooking, reading, dancing. Home: 2432 Laurel Lake Blvd Carmel IN 46032-8902

BROOKS, PETER (PRESTON), French and comparative literature educator, department chair, writer; b. N.Y.C., Apr. 19, 1938; s. Ernest and Mary Caroline (Schoyer) B.; m. Margaret Elisabeth Waters, July 18, 1959 (div. 1995); 3 children; m. Rosa Ehrenreich, May 15, 2001. BA, Harvard U., 1959, PhD, 1965; postgrad., U. Coll. London, 1959-60, U. Paris, 1962-63; MA (hon.), Yale U., 1975; Doctor (hon.), Ecole Normale Supérieure, 1997; MA (hon.), U. Oxford, 2001. Instr. French Yale U., 1965-67, asst. prof., 1967-72, assoc. prof., 1972-75, prof. French and comparative lit., 1975—, Chester D. Tripp prof. humanities, 1980-2001, dir. The Lit. Major, 1974-79, dir. Whitney Humanities Ctr., 1980-91, 96-01, chmn. dept. French, 1983-88, chmn. dept. comparative lit., 1991-97, Sterling prof. comparative lit. and French, 2001—. Vis. prof. Eastman U. Oxford, 2001—02. Author: The Novel of Worldliness, 1969, The Child's Part, 1972, The Melodramatic Imagination, 1976, Reading for the Plot, 1984, Body Work, 1993, Psychoanalysis and Storytelling, 1994, World Elsewhere, 1999, Troubling Confessions, 2000; co-editor: Law's Stories, 1996, Whose Freud?, 2000; contbg. editor Partisan Rev., 1972-88; mem. editl. bd. Yale French Studies, 1966—; chmn. Yale Jour. Criticism, 1987—. Acad. advisor Marlboro Co., 1975—; regional chmn. Mellon Fellowships in Humanities, 1982-84; trustee Hopkins Sch., New Haven, 1983-88; mem. adv. coun. West European program The Wilson Ctr.; mem. adv. bd. Stanford Humanities Ctr., 1996-2001; mem. humanities adv. coun. N.Y. Pub. Libr. Decorated Officier des Palmes Académiques, 1986; Marshall fellow, 1959, Morse fellow, 1967, Guggenheim fellow, 1973, Am. Coun. Learned Socs. fellow, 1980, NEH fellow, 1988. Fellow Am. Acad. Arts and Scis.; mem. MLA (exec. coun. 1993-97), Am. Phil. Soc., Yale Club, Elizabethan Club (New Haven), Century Assn. Democrat. Office: Yale U Dept Comparative Lit PO Box 208299 New Haven CT 06520-8299 E-mail: peter.brooks@yale.edu.

BROOKS, PHILIP RUSSELL, chemistry educator, researcher; b. Chgo., Dec. 31, 1938; s. John Russell and Louise Jane B.; children: Scott, Robin, Christopher, Steven. BS, Calif. Inst. Tech., 1960; PhD, U. Calif., Berkeley, 1964. Rsch. assoc. physics dept. U. Chgo., 1964; from asst. to assoc. prof. chemistry Rice U., Houston, 1964-75, prof., 1975—. Editor: State-to-State Chemistry, 1977. Vol. Boy Scouts Am., Houston, 1970—. Recipient Humboldt prize Alexander von Humboldt Found., 1985; predoctoral fellow NSF, 1960-63, postdoctoral fellow, 1963-64, Alfred P. Sloan fellow, 1970-74, John Simon Guggenheim fellow, 1974-75, Vis. Erskine fellow U. Canterbury, 1991, JSPS fellow Japan Soc. Promotion Sci., 1992. Fellow Am. Phys. Soc.; mem. Am. Chem. Soc. Achievements include research on chemical reaction dynamics. Home: 1026 Glourie Cir Houston TX 77055-7504 Office: Rice U Chemistry Dept MS60 6100 Main St Houston TX 77005-1892 E-mail: brooks@python.rice.edu.

BROOKS, SHARON LYNN, dentist, educator; b. Detroit, Oct. 19, 1944; d. Edward Haggit Doubleday and Ila Annabelle (Bobier) Kitamura; m. David Howard Brooks, Aug. 29, 1965. ABEd, U. Mich., 1965, DDS, 1973, MS, 1976, 84, 89. Diplomate Am. Bd. Oral and Maxillofacial Radiology, Am. Bd. Oral Medicine. Pvt. practice, Ann Arbor, 1973-76; clin. instr. dentistry U. Mich., Ann Arbor, 1973-76, asst. prof., 1976-80, assoc. prof., 1980-86, prof., 1986—, assoc. prof. radiology Sch. Medicine, 1992—; chair oral radiology sect., 1993-94. Vis. prof. U. Rochester (N.Y.), 1991.; cons. VA Med. Ctr., Ann Arbor, 1981—, Allen Park, 1983—; nat. bd. test constructor dental hygiene Joint Commn. Nat. Dental Examinations, Chgo., 1986-91. Contbr. articles to profl. jours. Rep. U. Mich. Senate Assembly, Ann Arbor, 1981-84, 87-91; bd. dirs. Ann Arbor YWCA, 1985-88; mem. Senate Assembly Com. on U. Affairs, 1989-90. Mem. ADA, Mich. Dental Assn., Washtenaw Dist. Dental Soc. (pres. 1990-91), Orgn. Tchrs. Oral Diagnosis (pres. 1988-89), Am. Assn. Dental Schs. (chair oral diagnosis sect. 1991-92, oral radiologist sect. 1993-94), Internat. Assn. Dental Rsch., Am. Bd. Oral Medicine (bd. dirs. 1990—), Am. Acad. Oral and Maxillofacial Radiology (bd. dirs. continuing edn. 1985-88), Internat. Assn. Oral Maxillofacial Radiology, Health Physics Soc. Avocations: swimming, hiking, nature study, reading, needlework. Office: U Mich Sch Dentistry Dept Oral Med Pathology Surgery Ann Arbor MI 48109-1078

BROOKS, SHELLEY, middle school educator; b. Boston, Aug. 20, 1955; d. Bernard and Carol Florence (Klass) B. BEd, U. Miami, Coral Gables, Fla., 1977; cert. in reading, U. Fla., Gainesville, 1978; postgrad., U. Tex., Dallas, 1990, U. Nev., Las Vegas, 1993. Cert. early childhood edn., elem., K-12 reading tchr., Nev. Elem. curriculum libr. U. Miami, 1977-78; classroom tchr. Citrus County Sch. Dist., Homosassa, Fla., 1978-80; reading tchr. Dallas Ind. Sch. Dist., 1982-90, Clark County Sch. Dist., Las Vegas, 1990—. Tchr. rep. Clark County Sch. Dist., 1991-93, Dallas Ind. Sch. Dist., 1982-90. Mem. Internat. Reading Assn. Jewish. Avocations: skiing, tennis. Office: James Cashman Mid Sch 4622 W Desert Inn Rd Las Vegas NV 89102-7115

BROOKS, VERNON BERNARD, neuroscientist, educator, author; b. Berlin, May 10, 1923; s. Martin and Margarete (Hahlo) B.; m. Nancy Fraser, June 29, 1950; children— Martin Fraser, Janet Mary, Nora Vivian. BA, U. Toronto, 1946, PhD, 1952; M.Sc., U. Chgo., 1948. Lectr., asst. prof. McGill U., Montreal, Que., Can., 1950-56; asst. prof., assoc. prof. Rockefeller Inst., N.Y.C., 1956-64; prof. physiology N.Y. Med. Coll, 1964-71, chmn. dept., 1964-69; prof., chmn. dept. physiology U. Western Ont., London, Can., 1971-76. Vis. fellow Australian Nat. U., Canberra, 1954-55; Disting. vis. prof. dept. movement and sci. Columbia U. Tchrs. Coll., 1985-86; fellow The Neuroscis. Inst., Rockefeller U., N.Y.C.; vis. prof. Inst. for Brain Rsch., Kyoto (Japan) U.; life mem. chancellor's coun. Victoria Coll., U. Toronto, 1993—. Author: The Neural Basis of Motor Control, 1986; co-editor: Exptl. Brain Rsch., 1980-92; mem. editl. bd. Jour. Motor Behavior, 1981-89; autobiography in The History of Neuroscience in Autobiography, vol. 3, 2001. Mem. Am. Physiol. Soc. (editorial bd. jour. 1962-65, editor sect. neurobiology 1969-71, editor vol. on motor control Handbook of Physiology Series 81), Canadian Physiol. Soc. (asso. editor 1969-73), Soc. Neurosci., Internat. Brain Research Orgn., Can. Assn. U. Profs. Unitarian Universalist. Spl. research brain mechanisms in motor control and motor learning. Home: 99 Euclid Ave London ON Canada N6C 1C3

BROOKS-TURNER, MYRA, music educator; b. Knoxville, Tenn., Jan. 13, 1933; d. Paul David and Lilli Ray Brooks; m. Ronald J. Turner, June 11, 1960; children: Stacy Turner Steele, Cheryl Turner Walker, Teresa Turner Basler. Student of piano, voice and composition, Juilliard Sch. Music, 1945—51; BMus in Piano, So. Meth. U., 1955, MusM in Theory and Composition, 1956, postgrad. in Piano, 1957—58. Educator Dallas Indep. Schs., Tex., 1956—60; choral music specialist Knoxville City Schs., Tenn., 1960—65; composer-in-residence Birmingham Children's Theatre, Ala., 1965—68; music instr. Mercer U. Music Prep. Sch., Atlanta, 1975—77; instr. composition Maryville Coll. Pres. Sch. of the Arts, Tenn., 1978—80; music instr. U. Tenn., Knoxville, 1990—92; owner Myra Brooks Turner Studio of Music, Knoxville, Tenn., 1992—. Freelance writer, pub. MBT Productions, Knoxville, 1993—. Composer, producer : (musicals) Make Way for Love, 1955; Uh-Uh, 1956; Javaho Junction, 1958; composer, dir. The Green Dragon, 1965—68 (Seattle Nat. Playwriting First Place award); contbr. articles to profl. publs. and jours. Music worship leader Epis. Ch. of Ascension, Knoxville, Tenn., 1992—93. Recipient Cultural Arts award, Tenn. Arts Commn., 1982. Mem.: Tenn. Fed. Music Clubs (state jr. counselor 1978—88, officer, state bd. 1978—89, Ea. Tenn. divisional v.p. 2002—, officer, state bd. 2002—, East Tenn. divsn. jr. counselor 2002—, editor State Piano Competition Book 2003, 2004—06), Nat. Fed. Music Clubs (jr. festivals bulletin advisor 1982—90), Knoxville Music Tchrs. Assn. (sec., bd. mem. 2000—01, Composer of Yr. 1978, 2001), Tenn. Music Tchrs. Assn., Nat. Music Tchrs. Assn., Ossoli Circle, Knoxville Writer's Group, Tuesday Morning Musical Club (pres. 1990—91), U. Tenn. Faculty Women's Club, Pi Kappa Lambda Nat. Music Honorary, Mu Phi Epsilon Internat. Frat. (pres. 1973—74, pres. Atlanta Alumnae, Music Therapy award 1974), Alpha Delta Pi. Republican. Episcopalian. Achievements include published 350 original piano solos, duets, art songs and anthems from 1993 to 2003. Avocations: study of French, study of Italian, lessons in computer graphics and finale, interior decorating, photography.

BROPHY, DENNIS RICHARD, psychology and philosophy educator, administrator, clergyman; b. Milw., Aug. 6, 1945; s. Floyd Herbert and Phyllis Marie (Ingram) B. BA, Washington U., 1967, MA, 1968; MDiv, Pacific Sch. Religion, 1971; PhD in Indsl. & Orgnl. Psychology, Tex. A&M U., 1995. Cert. coll. tchr., Calif. Ednl. rschr. IBM Corp., White Plains, NY, 1968—71; edn. minister Cmty. Congl. Ch., Port Huron, Mich., 1971—72, Bethlehem United Ch. Christ, Ann Arbor, Mich., 1972—73, Cmty. Congl. Ch., Chula Vista, Calif., 1974; philosophy instr. Southwestern Coll., Chula Vista, 1975; assoc. prof. psychology & philosophy Northwest Coll., Powell, Wyo., 1975—96, prof., 1996—, assessment testing coord., 1999—. Chmn. social sci. divsn., 1992-95; religious edn. cons. Mont.-No. Wyo. Conf. United Ch. of Christ. Mem. APA (Daniel Berlyne award 1996), Wyo. Coun. Humanities, Soc. Indsl. Orgnl. Psychology, Soc. Tchg. of Psychology, Yellowstone Assn. United Ch. Christ, Phi Beta Kappa, Phi Kappa Phi, Sigma Xi, Omicron Delta Kappa, Theta Xi, Golden Key Nat. Honor Soc. Faculty Outstanding Svc. award, 2003. Home: 533 Avenue C Powell WY 82435-2401 Office: Northwest Coll 231 W 6th St Powell WY 82435-1898 E-mail: brophyd@northwestcollege.edu.

BROPHY, JERE EDWARD, education educator, researcher; b. Chgo., June 11, 1940; s. Joseph Thomas and Eileen Marie (Sullivan) B.; m. Arlene Marie Pintozzi, Sept. 21, 1963; children: Cheryl, Joseph. BS in Psychology, Loyola U., Chgo., 1962; MA in Human Devel., U. Chgo., 1965, PhD in Human Devel., 1967. Rsch. assoc., asst. prof. U. Chgo., 1967-68; from asst. to assoc. prof. U. Tex., Austin, 1968-76; staff devel. coord. S.W. Ednl. Devel. Lab., Austin, 1970-72; prof. Mich. State U., East Lansing, 1976-92, co-dir. Inst. for Rsch. on Tchg., 1981-93, univ. disting. prof., 1993—. Co-author: Teacher-Student Relationships: Causes and Consequences, 1974; editor (book series) Advances in Research on Teaching, 1989—. Fellow Ctr. for Advanced Study in the Behavioral Scis., 1994. Fellow: APA, Internat. Acad. Edn., Am. Psychol. Soc.; mem.: Nat. Soc. for the Study of Edn., Nat. Coun. for the Social Studies, Nat. Acad. Edn., Am. Ednl. Rsch. Assn. (Palmer O. Johnson award 1983, Presdl. citation 1995). Office: Mich State U 213B Erickson Hall East Lansing MI 48824-1034

BROPHY, SUSAN DOROTHY, adapted physical education educator; b. Waltham, Mass., Nov. 9, 1954; d. Lawrence A. and Dorothy M. (Furbush) B. BS, U. Mass., 1976; MS, U. Wis. La Crosse, 1981. Cert. tchr. phys. edn., adapted phys. edn. tchr., Mass. Substitute tchr. Waltham, Weston and Lexington (Mass.) Sch. Depts., 1976-77; supr. recreation, in-svc. trainer W. E. Fernald State Sch., Waltham, 1978-80; cons. adapted phys. edn. East Cen. Ohio Spl. Edn. Regional Resource Ctr., Dover, 1981-82; tchr. adapted phys. edn. Heartland Area Edn. Agy., Newton, Iowa, 1982-86, Lawrence (Mass.) Sch. Dept., 1986—2001, Andover Pub. Schs., Mass., 2001—. Co-chmn. Adapted Phys. Edn. State Com., Mass., 1986—, cert. com. phys. edn. Dept. Edn., Mass., 1989-92. Co-author: (assessment test) Heartland Gross Motor Evaluation, 1985. Coach Newton YMCA Swim Team, 1985-86, Waltham (Mass.) Youth Basketball Assn., 1993-2001; co-founder Stephanie's Toy Box, Newton, 1984. Fed. Govt. grantee, 1980-81, Horace Mann grantee, 1988-89 Mem. AAHPERD (mem. local arrangements com. 1998-99), Mass. Assn. Health, Phys. Edn., Recreation and Dance (co-chair com. adapted phys. edn. 1989—, Adapted Phys. Edn. Tchr. of the Yr. award 1997, mem. honor awards com. 2001—). Avocations: horticulture, antiques, bicycling, traveling. Home: 48 Marianne Rd Waltham MA 02452-6218 Office: Andover Pub Schs South Sch 55 Woburn St Andover MA 01810

BROSTROM, THERESA ANNE, home educator; b. St. Paul, June 17, 1967; d. George Donald and Jeanne Louise (Momberger) Koran; m. Mark Stanley Brostrom, Aug. 1, 1992; children: Matthew, Christoph, Dominic, AnnElise, Caleb, Magdalene. BS, Mankato State U., 1989, MS, 1994. Cert. elem. edn., educable mentally retarded, trainable mentally retarded, emotional behavioral disordered, work experience coord. Resident counselor Ramsey County, Shoreview, Minn., 1986—; behavior analyst Merrick Co. Inc., Maplewood, Minn., 1989-90; spl. edn. tchr. Hennepin Tech. 287, Maple Grove, Minn., 1991-92, Osseo Sch. 279, Brooklyn Park, Minn., 1992—2000. Mem. Options Com., Maple Grove, Minn., 1992-93, Transition Support Person, Brooklyn Park, 1993-98; co-chair Staff Devel., Brooklyn Park, 1993-97, Cmty. Transition Interagy. Com., Robbinsdale, Minn., 1994-98. Mem. Hall Govt., Mankato State U., 1985-89, Circle K., Mankato State U., 1988-89; mem. family formation core team Ch. of St. Paul, Ham Lake, Minn., 2002—. Roman Catholic.

BROTHERSON, MARY LOU NELSON, education educator; b. N.Y.C., Oct. 9, 1933; d. Harry David and Estelle Molly (Cohen) Nelson; m. Donald E. Brotherson, July 19, 1959; children: Nancy, Elizabeth. B of Edn. magna cum laude, U. Miami, 1955; MEd, U. Ill., 1967, EdD, 1982. Tchr. elem. sch. Dade County Schs., Miami Beach, Fla., 1955-59, Champaign (Ill.) Unit 4, 1959-61; prof., dir. tchr. edn. Parkland Coll., Champaign, 1969-93; adj. prof. edn. St. Thomas U., North Miami, Fla., 1993—96; cons. in field, 1996—2003; adj. prof. grad. tchr. edn. Nova Southeastern U., 1996—2003; undergrad. adv. bd. Barry U., 2000—03. Interviewer and educator, Holocaust Documentation and Edn. Ctr., Miami, 1994-2003. Author: New Careers in Education: Teacher Aide Handbook, 1971; author/editor: Teacher Aide Manual for Special Education, 1982. Chair East Ctrl. Holocaust Edn. Com., 1989-93; bd. dirs. Sinai Temple, Champaign, 1983-86, Temple Sinai, North Miami Beach, 1996-03, Ctrl. Agy. Jewish Edn., Miami, 1994-97. Recipient Quality of Life award Champaign-Urbana Jewish Fedn.; U. Miami scholar, 1955; E.P.D.A. Nat. Leadership fellow U. Ill., 1977-80. Mem. Nat. Coun. Tchrs. English, Nat. Assn. Edn. Young Children (validator), Kappa Delta Pi (nat. Point of Excellence award), Delta Kappa Gamma. Independent. Jewish. Avocations: reading, music, art, storytelling. Home and Office: 3640 Yacht Club Dr Apt 810 Miami FL 33180-3571

BROTT, BARBARA JO, gifted and talented education educator; b. Chgo., May 29, 1947; d. Walter David Berry and Joann Berry Manka; m. T. Michael Brott, Feb. 23, 1981. BA, U. Ill., 1968, MEd, 1981. Cert. tchr., libr. sci.-media specialist, Ill. Tchr. Sch. Dist. 230, Orland Park, Ill., 1968-69, Sch. Dist. 135, Orland Park, 1969—. Cons. edn. of gifted, talented various sch. dists., 1985—. Monthly columnist Jour. Journies, Writing! mag. Bd. dirs. Andrew Scholarship Found., Orland Park, Ill., 1989—; bd. dirs. Children's Rsch. Found., Western Springs, Ill., 1991—. Mem. S. Suburban Reading Coun., Orland Coun. Edn. (officer). Office: Sch Dist 135 8851 151st St Orland Park IL 60462-3450

BROUDO, JOSEPH DAVID, art educator; b. Balt., Sept. 11, 1920; s. Wolfe and Sarah (Novick) B.; m. Beatrice Tuchin, Oct. 10, 1943 (dec. 1962); children: Lonna Susan, Robert Jeffrey; m. Barbara Fitzgerald, Nov. 22, 1963. BFA, AlfredU., 1946; MEd, Boston U., 1950. Chmn. art dept. Endicott Coll., Beverly, Mass., 1946—, disting. prof. emeritus, 1995. Exhibited paintings and ceramics in numerous shows; represented in permanent collections Internat. Mus. Ceramics, Italy, Prieto, Mills Coll., Calif.; pvt. collections throughout the world. Mem. City Dem. Com., Beverly, 1984-93. With U.S. Army, 1942-43. Avocations: teaching, ceramics, painting. Home: 5 Gary Ave Beverly MA 01915-1103 E-mail: broudo@endicott.edu.

BROUSSEAU, GEORGIA COLE, school principal; b. Balt., June 25, 1945; d. George E. and Laura Jane (Canrike) Kline; m. C. Eugene Cole, June 26, 1963 (div. 1977); m. Edwin C. Brousseau, Dec. 17, 1977; 1 child, Russell Eugene Cole. AA, Pima C.C., Tucson, 1972; BA, U. Ariz., 1974, MEd, 1979. Cert. elem. tchr., supr., prin., Ariz. Instrnl. tech. trainer, writing specialist K through 12 Tucson Unified Sch. Dist.; prin. Wheeler Elem. Sch., Tucson. Lectr. Chapman Coll., Tucson; former lectr. continuing edn. opportunities for women U. Ariz., Tucson; adj. faculty Pima C.C. Former trustee, bd. govs. Pima Community Coll.; commr., vice chair Pima County Merit Comsn., 1991—. Recipient Outstanding Svc. award Tucson Trade Bur., 1972, Cmty. Svc. award Pima County Bd. of Supervisors, 1996. Mem. NEA, ASCD, Ariz. Edn. Assn., Tucson Edn. Assn. (v.p. 1993-94), Pima C.C. Alumni Assn. (past pres.), Phi Delta Kappa (Friend of Edn. award 1982). Home: 7374 E Calle Lugo Tucson AZ 85710-5734

BROWDER, FELIX EARL, mathematician, educator; b. Moscow, July 31, 1927; s. Earl and Raissa (Berkmann) Browder; m. Eva Tislowitz, Oct. 5, 1949; children: Thomas, William. SB, MIT, 1946; PhD, Princeton U., 1948; MA (hon.), Yale U., 1962; D (hon.), U. Paris, 1990. C.L.E. Moore instr. math. MIT, 1948—51, vis. assoc. prof., 1961—62, vis. prof., 1977—78; instr. Boston U., 1951—53; asst. prof. Brandeis U., 1955—56; from asst. prof. to prof. Yale U., 1956—63; prof. math. U. Chgo., 1963—72, Louis Block prof. math., 1972—82, Max Mason disting. svc. prof., 1982—87, chmn. dept., 1972—77, 1980—85; v.p. rsch. Rutgers, The State U. NJ, 1986—91; univ. prof. Rutgers U., New Brunswick, 1986—. Vis. mem. Inst. Advanced Study, Princeton (N.J.) U., 1953—54, 1963—64; vis. prof. Princeton U., 1968, Inst. Pure and Applied Math., Rio de Janeiro, 1960, U. Paris, 1973, 1975, 1978, 1981, 1983, 1985; sr. rsch. fellow U. Sussex, 1970, 1976, England; Fairchild Disting. visitor Calif. Inst. Tech., Pasadena, 1975—76; spkr. Internat. Congress of Math., 1970, Sci. Bd. Santa Fe Inst., 1986—98, U.S. Nat. Med. Sci., 1999. Contbr. theorems to books, including Nonlinear Problems, 1966, Functional Analysis and Related Fields, 1970, Nonlinear Operators and Nonlinear Equations of Evolution in Banach Spaces, 1976, Nonlinear Functional Analysis and Its Applications, 1986. With U.S. Army, 1953—55. Fellow Guggenheim, 1953—54, 1966—67, Sloan Found., 1959—63, NSF sr. postdoctoral fellow, 1957—58. Fellow: AAAS (chmn. sect. A 1982—83); mem.: NAS (coun. mem. 1992—95), Math. Assn. Am., Am. Math. Soc. (editor bull. 1959—68, 1978—83, mem. coun. 1959—72, 1978—83, mng. editor 1964—68, 1980, exec. com. counl 1979—80, colloquium lectr. 1970, pres. 1999—2001), Am. Acad. Arts and Scis., Sigma Xi (pres. chpt. 1985—86). Achievements include development of linear and nonlinear partial differential equations; nonlinear functional analysis and fixed point and mapping theorems. E-mail: browder@math.rutgers.edu.

BROWDER, OLIN LORRAINE, legal educator; b. Urbana, Ill., Dec. 19, 1913; s. Olin Lorraine and Nellie (Taylor) B.; m. Edna Olive Forsythe, Sept. 9 1939 (dec. Nov. 1993); children: Ann Browder Sorensen, Catherine Browder Morris, John; m. Aleeta Swantner, May 17, 1997. AB, U. Ill., 1935, LL.B., 1937; S.JD, U. Mich., 1941. Bar: Ill. 1939. Practiced in Chgo., 1938-39; asst. prof. bus. law U. Ala., 1939-41; asst. prof. law U. Tenn., 1941-42; mem. legal dept. TVA, 1942-43; spl. agt. FBI, 1943-45; prof. law U. Okla., 1946-53, U. Mich., Ann Arbor, 1953-79, James V. Campbell prof. law, 1979-84, prof. emeritus, 1984—. Author: (with others) American Law of Property, 1953, (with L.W. Waggoner) Family Property Transactions, 1965, 3d edit., 1980, (with R. A. Cunningham, G.S. Nelson, W.B. Stoebuck, D.A. Whitman) Basic Property Law, 1966, 5th edit., 1989, (with L. W. Waggoner and R. V. Wellman) Palmer's Cases on Trusts and Succession, 4th edit., 1983. Mem. Order of Coif, Phi Beta Kappa, Beta Theta Phi, Phi Alpha Delta, Phi Kappa Phi. Home: 1520 Edinborough Rd Ann Arbor MI 48104-4128

BROWER, DAVID JOHN, lawyer, urban planner, educator; b. Holland, Mich., Sept. 11, 1930; s. John J. and Helen (Olson) B.; m. Lou Ann Brown, Nov. 26, 1960; children: Timothy Seth, David John, II, Ann Lacey. BA, U. Mich., 1956, JD, 1960. Bar: Ill. 1960, Mich. 1961, Ind. 1961, U.S. Supreme Ct. 1971. Asst. dir. div. community planning Ind. U., Bloomington, 1960-70; rsch. prof. dept. city and regional planning U. N.C., Chapel Hill, 1970—, assoc. dir. Ctr. for Urban and Regional Studies, 1970-94; pres. Coastal Resources Collaborative, Ltd., Chapel Hill and Manteo, N.C., 1980—; counsel Robinson & Cole, Hartford, Conn., 1986—. Vis. prof., Vt. Law Sch., South Royalton, summers, 1994—. Author: (with others) Constitutional Issues of Growth Management, 1978; Growth Management, 1984, Managing Development in Small Towns, 1984, Special Area Management, 1985, Catastrophic Coastal Storms, 1989, Understanding Growth Management, 1989, Coastal Zone Management: An Evaluation, 1991, An Introduction to Coastal Zone Management, 1994, rev. edit. 2002, Natural Hazard Mitigation, 1999. Fellow Am. Inst. Cert. Planners (Coll. of Fellows); mem.Am. Planning Assn. (bd. dirs. 1982-85, chmn.-founder planning and law div. 1978, co-chmn. substainable devel. group 1995—). Democrat. Episcopalian. Home: 612 Shady Lawn Rd Chapel Hill NC 27514-2009 Office: U NC CB # 3140 Chapel Hill NC 27599-0001 E-mail: brower@email.unc.edu.

BROWN, ABBIE HOWARD, education educator, researcher; b. Bklyn., Mar. 5, 1960; s. Ronald Wallace and Shirley Ann B. MA, Columbia U., 1988; PhD, Ind. U., 1999. Tchr. Bank Street Sch. for Children, N.Y.C., 1985-88, Ridgewood (N.J.) Pub. Sch., 1988—95; assoc. instr. Ind. U., Bloomington, 1995—99; asst. prof. edn. Wash. State U., Pullman, 1999—2002; assoc. prof. edn. Calif. State U., Fullerton, 2002—. Faculty mem. Walden U., Mpls., 1996—. Author: Multimedia Projects inthe Classroom, 2002; contbr. articles to profl. jours. Avocations: science fiction, comic books.

BROWN, ANN HERRELL, secondary school educator; b. Alexandria, Va., July 17, 1942; d. Richard Edward and Mary Elizabeth (Simpson) Herrell; m. George Thomas Brown, Jan. 31, 1970. BA in Modern Fgn. Lang., The King's Coll., 1964; postgrad., Georgetown U., 1972, U. Va., George Mason U. Cert. tchr. Va. Tchr. Spanish, French Thomas Jefferson High Sch., Fairfax, Va., 1964-67; instr. Spanish Barrington (R.I.) Coll., 1967-68; tchr. Spanish George Washington High Sch., Alexandria, Va., 1968-70, Francis C. Hammond High Sch., Alexandria, 1970-72, 1972-81, tchr. Spanish, dept. chair, 1981-93; tchr. Spanish Minne Howard Sch., Alexandria, 1993—. Sec., treas. Fairfax County Sr. Citizens Day Care Assn., 1986-91, bd. dirs., 1986-94. Mem. ASCD, NEA, Edn. Assn. Alexandria, Va. Edn. Assn., Am. Coun. Tchrs. Fgn. Langs., Alpha Delta Kappa, Beta Gamma (historian 1994-96, pres. 1992-94, v.p. 1990-92, sec. 1988-90). Avocations: reading, traveling, animals. Home: 6803 Galax Ct Springfield VA 22151-3836 Office: Minnie Howard Sch 3801 W Braddock Rd Alexandria VA 22302-1904

BROWN, BARBARA JEAN, special and secondary education educator; b. Midland, Tex., Nov. 3, 1945; d. John Joseph and Sarah Beryl (Seely) Sury; m. Samuel Bradford Brown III, June 30, 1984. BA in English, U. Tex., Arlington, 1967, MAT in English and Humanities, 1979. Cert. gifted and English tchr., Tex., Fla. With Euless (Tex.) Jr. H.S./Hurst-Euless-Bedford Ind. Sch. Dist., 1967-84, Edgewater High Sch./Orange County Sch. Bd., Orlando, Fla., 1984-86; tchr. Lakeview Mid. Sch./Seminole County Sch. Bd., Sanford, Fla., 1986-98, Lake Mary (Fla.) H.S./ Seminole County Sch. Bd., 1998—. Curriculum writer Hurst-Euless-Bedford Ind. Sch. Dist., Hurst, mem. curriculum and dist. policy devel. com.; curriculum writer Seminole County Sch. Bd.; presenter Tex. Gifted Conf., Houston. Seminole County Sch. Bd. grantee, 1987-88, Svc. award, 1991, finalist, 1989-93; recipient Tchr. Merit award Walt Disney World Co., 1990-92; named Prominent Educator of Tex., 1983, Tchr. of the Yr., Coun. for Exceptional Children, 1991. Mem. NEA, PTA, Nat. Assn. Gifted Children, Seminole County Tchrs. English, Coun. Reading Tchrs., Fla. Scholastic Press Assn., Orlando Area City Panhellenic, Phi Mu (pres. Winter Park-Orlando chpt. 1988-91, nat. state day chmn. 1993-94), Sigma Tau Delta, Sigma Delta Phi. Roman Catholic. Home: 107 Hatfield Ct Longwood FL 32779-4606

BROWN, BARBARA MAHONE, communications educator, poet, consultant; b. Chgo., Feb. 27, 1944; d. Loniel Atticus and Anne (Savage) Mahone. BA, Wash. State U., 1968; MBA, U. Chgo., 1975; PhD, Stanford U., 1988. Dir. corp. comm. NBC, N.Y.C., 1975-77; assoc. prof. dept. bus. adminstrn. and econs. Clark Coll., Atlanta, 1978-84; assoc. prof. depts. journalism and advt. U. Tex., Austin, 1988-91; assoc. prof. dept. mktg. San Jose (Calif.) State U., 1990—. Pres. Elbow Room Cons., 1994—; cons. The Fielding Inst., Santa Barbara, Calif., 1995—; evaluator Western Assn. Schs. and Colls., Oakland, Calif., 1993—; cons. KQED-TV (PBS), San Francisco, 1991; OBAC Poet, Orgn. Black Am. Culture, Chgo., 1970-75; mentor Ctr. for Devel. Women Entrepreneurs, 1995-97; founding faculty Fielding Inst. ODE Program, 1996. Author: (vol. poetry) Sugarfields, 1970; writer-rschr. pub. affairs documentary, WMAQ-TV (NBC Chgo.) 1973, WNET-TV (PBS N.Y.C.) 1971; contbr. articles to profl. acad. jours. Bd. dirs. Kids in Common, San Jose, 1997-98; trustee Hillbrook Sch., Los Gatos, Calif., 1995-98; vestry St. Edward's Episcopal Ch., San Jose, 1994-96; steering com. UN Mid-Decade of Women, Southeast Regional Conf., 1980. Regents fellow in comm., U. Tex. at Austin, 1989; tchr.-scholar San Jose State U., 1993. Mem. Delta Sigma Pi, Beta Gamma Sigma. Episcopalian. Avocations: art, literature, orchids, photography. Office: San Jose State U BT-750 One Washington Sq San Jose CA 95192-0069

BROWN, BERNICE LEONA BAYNES, foundation consultant, educator, consultant; b. Pitts., June 19, 1935; d. Howard Leon and Henrietta Lydia (Hodges) Baynes; m. James Brown, May 4, 1964; 1 child, Kiyeseni Anu. BFA, Carnegie Mellon U., 1957; MEd, U. Pitts., 1966. Tchr. Pitts. Pub. Schs., 1957-65; lectr. Carlow Coll., Pitts., 1964-67; edn. specialist Bay Area Urban League, San Francisco, 1967-68; asst. prof. San Francisco Coll. for Women, 1968-72; dean students Lone Mountain Coll., San Francisco, 1972-76; dir. San Francisco Pub. Schs. Commn., 1976; program exec. San Francisco Found., 1977-86; ednl. cons. San Francisco, 1987—; found. adminstr. Clorox Co. Found., 1989-91; dean of faculty and staff devel. City Coll. of San Francisco, 1991-98; dean Workforce Edn./Calworks Edn. and Tng., 1998—. Vis. scholar Stanford (Calif.) U., 1987-88. Mem. bd. of govs. Calif. Cmty. Colls., 1975-81, Calif. Post Secondary Edn. Commn., Sacramento, 1978-80, State Supt's Adv. Com. on Black Am. Affairs, Calif., 1985—; chair Found. Cmty. Svc. Cable T.V., San Francisco, 1982-84; trustee Schs. of Sacred Heart, San Francisco, 1982-87; bd. dirs. Urban Econ. Devel. Corp., 1988-2000, High/Scope Ednl. Rsch. Found., 1990-98, Network for Elders, 1997—, Cmty. Bds., Inc., 2000—; trustee Howard Thurman Ednl. Trust, 1989-94, Uprising Cmty. Credit Union, San Francisco, 2001—. Recipient Milestone award Citizen's Scholarship Found. of Am., 1995, Profl. Women of Yr. award, San Francisco Bus. & Profl. Women, Inc. Mem. San Francisco LWV (bd. mem. 2000—), Women and Founds. Corp. Philanthropy (bd. dirs. 1985-87), Assn. Black Found. Execs. (bd. dirs. 1978-82), Commonwealth Club of Calif. (bd. gov. 1988-91). Home: 1271 23d Ave San Francisco CA 94122-1605 Office: City Coll San Francisco Ocean Phelan 50 Phelan Ave San Francisco CA 94124-9411 E-mail: bbrown@ccsf.org.

BROWN, BEULAH LOUISE, retired elementary educator; b. Warren County, Ohio, Feb. 21, 1917; d. Fred Austin and Roba E. (Doughman) Birmingham; m. William Dale Brown, Aug. 14, 1942 (dec. Apr. 1984). Student, Ohio U., 1937-39, BS in Edn. cum laude, 1957. Cert. tchr., Ohio. Tchr. 2d grade Bainbridge (Ohio) Village Sch., 1939-43; rsch. lab. asst. Mead Paper Corp., Chillicothe, Ohio, 1944-45; tchr. 2d grade Chillicothe City Schs., 1945-46, Marysville (Ohio) Schs., 1946-49; tchr. 1st grade Riley Twp. Sandusky County Schs., Fremont, Ohio, 1951-52; tchr. 2d grade Fremont City Schs., 1952-59, Lancaster (Ohio) City Schs., 1959-64, tchr. 1st grade, 1966-75; tchr. 2d grade Ashland (Ohio) City Schs., 1964-66. Supervising tchr. Bowling Green (Ohio) State U., 1955-59, Ohio U., Athens, 1960-64, 66-75, Ashland Coll., 1964-66. Mem. AAUW, Farifield County Ret. Tchrs., Ohio Ret. Tchrs., Clionian Literary Club, Kappa Delta Pi, Delta Kappa Gamma. Republican. Methodist. Avocations: reading, travel.

BROWN, BEVERLY JEAN, educator; b. Pensacola, Fla., Jan. 24, 1943; d. Elisha and Melanie Alfreda (Creal) Jones; m. Ozie Marion Portis, May 1, 1963 (div. Apr. 1976); 1 child, Diedra LaShalle; m. Ernest Arnell Brown, Oct. 13, 1979. BS, Fla. A&M U., 1966; M of Edn., U. North Fla., 1986. Cert. in adminstrn. and supervision. Tchr. Meriwether County Sch. Dist., Greenville, Ga., 1966-67, Hamilton County Sch. Dist., Jasper, Fla., 1968-69, Duval County Sch. Dist., Jacksonville, Fla., 1969-82, primary resource tchr., 1982-87; adminstrv. intern Duval County Sch. Bd., 1987-88, tchr. instructional support, 1988-90, vice prin., 1990—95, prin., 1995—2000; re., 2000. Mem. Retired Duval Adminstrs., Fla. Ret. Educators, Duval Ret. Educators. Democrat. Home: 11133 Aristides Way Jacksonville FL 32218-6217

BROWN, BILLY CHARLIE, secondary school educator; b. Cookeville, Tenn., Feb. 20, 1947; s. Joe Homer and Sallie Mable (Hendrickson) B. BS in Forestry, BS in Edn., U. Tenn., 1969, EdD in Curriculum and Instruction, 1979; MA in Secondary Sci. Edn., Tenn. Tech. U., 1973, EdS in Secondary Sci. Edn., 1976. Cert. secondary sci. tchr., Ga., Tenn., Ky. Tchr., dept. chair Westwood Jr. High Sch., Manchester, Tenn., 1970-77; tchr., coach Feldwood High Sch., College Park, Ga., 1979-84; tchr., sci. Shiloh High Sch., Lithonia, Ga., 1984-87; coord. environ. energy sci. edn. ctr. U. Tenn., Knoxville, 1987-88; assoc. prof. Ky. Wesleyan Coll., Owensboro, 1990-93; with Cobb County Schs., Marietta, Ga., 1993—98; sci. edn. cons. Oak Ridge Nat. Lab., 1993-99; assoc. prof. edn., Insnl. EPSB Programs coord. Lindsey Wilson Coll., Columbia, Ky., 1999—. Vis. asst. prof. U. Tenn., Knoxville, 1988-90; co-dir. Ctr. for Environ./Energy/Sci. Edn., U. Tenn., Knoxville, 1988-90; sci. cons. area sch. dists. Ky. Wesleyan Coll., Owensboro, 1990-93; dir. Elem. Sci. Leadership Inst., Oak Ridge Nat. Lab., 1993—. Contbr. articles to profl. jours. Named Outstanding Classroom Tchr., Tenn. Edn. Assn., 1975. Mem. Nat. Sci. Tchr. Assn. (Outstanding Sci. Educator nominee 1991), Nat. Coun. Tchrs. Math., Mid-East Regional Assn. Educators Tchrs. Sci. Avocations: cultural music, sports coaching, writing, hiking. Home: 86 Edmonton Rd Columbia KY 42728-9422

BROWN, BRUCE JOSEPH, medical technology educator; b. Madison, Wis., 1942; s. Frederick E. and Marcella M. Brown; m. Susan C. Brown; children: Christi, Julie, Molly. BS, Xavier U., Cin., 1965; MS, U. Ariz., 1974; EdD, W.Va. U., 1993. Registered med. technologist, specialist in clin. and pub. health microbiology. MLT program coord. So. W.Va. C.C., Logan, 1974-79; med. lab. technician, technologist program dir. Marshall U., Huntington, W.Va., 1979—. Pres. Ironton Arts Coun. Capt. Med. Svcs. Corps U.S. Army, 1965-72. Mem. Am. Soc. Clin. Pathology (assoc.), Am. Soc. Clin. Lab. Sci. Avocation: playing violin. Office: Marshall Univ One John Marshall Dr Huntington WV 25755-0003

BROWN, BURTON ROSS, humanities educator, university administrator; b. Mapleton, Utah, Jan. 14, 1940; s. June Wells and Muriel Fay (Curtis) B.; m. Sylvia Lynne Hamilton, June 26, 1963; children: David, Heidi, Stacey, Richard, Elisabeth, Catherine, Shelly. MusB, Brigham Young U., Provo, Utah, 1967; MA, U. No. Colo., Greeley, 1971, D of Mus. Edn., 1979. Dir. choral music, instr. German Western High Sch., Las Vegas, Nev., 1967-69; dir. choral music South High Sch., Pueblo, Colo., 1972-73, East High Sch., Pueblo, 1973-76; asst. prof. humanities No. Ariz. U., Flaggstaff, 1976-85, assoc. prof., 1985—, dir. performing arts series, 1981-90, dir. office profl. devel., 1990-92. Contbr. articles to profl. jours. Adjudicater state choral, solo and ensemble festivals, Greeley and Flagstaff, 1973-85. With USNR, 1957-60. Univ. Presdl. fellow No. Ariz. U., 1988. Mem. Nat. Assn. for Humanities Edn., Assn. for Integrated Studies, Medieval & Renaissance Assn., Phi Mu Alpha Sinfonia, Sigma Gamma Chi (advisor 1984-86). Mem. Lds Ch. Avocations: chess, racquetball, languages, computer programming. Home: 601 Whipple Rd Flagstaff AZ 86001-3051 Office: No Ariz U Dept Humanities PO Box 6031 Flagstaff AZ 86011-0001

BROWN, CARLOS, secondary education educator, psychology educator; b. Chgo., June 17, 1946; s. Nancy Brown. BA in Bus. Adminstrn., Graceland Coll., Lamoni, Iowa, 1973; BS in Phys. Edn., U. Ill., Chgo., 1986; MS in Phys. Edn., Chgo. State U., 1992, MS in Psychology, 1994. Cert. phys. edn. tchr., Ill.; cert. alcoholism counselor, cert. therapeutic recreation counselor. Phys. dir. Chgo. Boys Club, 1973, Chgo. Youth Ctr., 1973-76; paraprofl. Boy Scouts Am., Chgo., 1977; social worker Off the Street Club, Chgo., 1978; counselor, recreational therapist Tom Seay Ctr./Salvation Army, Chgo., 1979-81; recreational therapist Forkosh Hosp., Chgo., 1981-84; dir. phys. edn. Sears YMCA, Chgo., 1984-86; tchr. Chgo. Park Dist./Jackson Park, 1986-88, Chgo. Bd. Edn., 1988—; psychology/counselor, 1995-96. Instr. psychology Harold Washington Coll., Chgo.; phys. edn. instr. Triton Coll. Water safety instr. ARC, 1973—. Served with USMC, 1966-69, Vietnam. Recipient certs. and awrds ARC, 1983, 86, 90. Mem. AAHPERD, ACA, Ill. Counseling Assn., Ill. Assn. for Health, Phys. Edn., Recreation and Dance. Home: 910 W Vermont Ave Chicago IL 60643-6631 Office: Triton Coll 2000 N 5th Ave River Grove IL 60171-1907

BROWN, CAROL ANN, elementary education educator; b. Glen Ridge, N.J., Sept. 18, 1942; d. Henry and Marie (Capelli) Minasian; m. Simpson Brown Jr., July 12, 1969. BA, Kean Coll., 1964, postgrad., 1981-84. Tchr. 2d grade Washington Sch., Nutley, N.J., 1964-87; tchr. reading clinic Fairleigh Dickinson U., Rutherford, N.J., 1968-74; tchr. kindergarten The O'Neal Sch., Southern Pines, N.C., 1988-90; tchr. 1st grade Episcopal Day Sch., Southern Pines, N.C., 1990—. Mem. NEA, Internat. Reading Assn. (Moore County coun.), N.J. Edn. Assn. Avocations: crafts, sewing, golf. Home: PO Box 416 Pinehurst NC 28370-0416 Office: Episcopal Day Sch 340 E Massachusetts Ave Southern Pines NC 28387-6198

BROWN, CHERYL ANN, high school counselor; b. Cin., Jan. 15, 1950; d. Emmett A. and Rosalyn (Grieb) Brown; divorced; children: Courtney Pelz, Hayley Pelz. BS in Elem. Edn. cum laude, U. Cin., 1972; MEd in Guidance, Xavier U., 1975. Lic. profl. counselor. Tchr. Beechwoods Elem. Sch., Cin., 1972-74, Greenhills Mid. Sch., Cin., 1974-75; counselor Reading City Schs., Cin., 1975-77, Hamilton County Bd. Edn., Cin., 1980-83; mid. sch. counselor Indian Hill Mid. Sch., Cin., 1983-86; h.s. counselor Fairfield (Ohio) H.S., 1986—. Mem. citizens resource com. Princeton Bd. Edn., Cin., 1982-85; mem. staff-parish rels. com. Ch. of the Saviour, Montgomery, Ohio, 1993—; mem. strategic planning com. Venture Capital, in-svc. com.; mem. Critical Incident Stress Mgmt. Team. of Southwestern Ohio; emergency med. technician, firefighter City of Sharonville. Recipient Amb. award Fairfield Bd. Edn., 1994, Apple awards, 1994-2000, Tchr. award Cin. Gas & Elec. Co., 1994. Mem. ACA, NEA, Ohio Edn. Assn., Ohio Counseling Assn., Greater Cin. Counseling Assn. Avocations: antiques, travel, collecting nancy drew and dara girls originals. Home: 3877 Cornell Rd Cincinnati OH 45241-2679 Office: Fairfield HS 8800 Holden Blvd Fairfield OH 45014-2100

BROWN, CHRISTOPHER PATRICK, health care administrator, educator; b. Phoenix, June 7, 1951; s. Charles Francis and R. Patricia (Quinn) B.; m. Tracey Ann Wallenberg, May 23, 1987; 1 child, Ryan Matthew. AA in Biol. Scis., Shasta Coll., Redding, Calif., 1976; AS in Liberal Arts, SUNY, Albany, 1977; grad. Primary Care Assoc. Program, Stanford U., 1978; BA in Community Svcs. Adminstrn., Calif. State U., Chico, 1982; M. in Health Svcs., U. Calif., Davis, 1984. Gen. mgr. Pacific Ambulance Svc., El Cajon, Calif., 1974; primary care assoc. Family Practice, Oregon-Calif., 1978-82; cons. Calif. Health Profls., Chico, 1982-84; bus. ops. mgr. Nature's Arts, Inc., Seattle, 1985-86; instr. North Seattle C.C., 1984-89, program dir., 1986-89; asst. dir. Pacific Med. Clinic North, Seattle, 1990-92; dir. Pacific Med. Clinic Renton (Wash.), Pacific Med. Ctr., 1992-95; dir. ops./physician svcs. St. Luke's Regional Med. Ctr., Boise, Idaho, 1995-97, adminstr. ambulatory care, 1997-98; adminstr. St. Luke's Meridian (Idaho) Med. Ctr., 1997-98; COO, sr. v.p. Medford (Oreg.) Clinic, 1998-2000; pres./cons. Integra Healthcare Solutions, 2000—. Mem. Butte County Adult Day Care Health Coun., Chico, 1982-84; bd. dirs., pres. Innovative Health Care Svcs., Chico, 1982-84; bd. dirs. Highline W. Seattle Mental Health Ctr., 1985-90, v.p. 1988-90; tech. adv. com. North Seattle C.C., 1992-93; bd. dirs. ARC, 1997-98. Mem. Internat. Platform Assn., Soc. Ambulatory Care Profls., Med. Group Mgmt. Assn., Multispecialty Group Exec. Soc., Accreditation Assn. for Ambulatory Health Care (accreditation surveyor 1996-97). Avocations: gardening, woodworking, church activities. Home: 345 Orth Dr Central Point OR 97502 E-mail: cbrown3394@aol.com.

BROWN, CLARENCE FLEETWOOD, comparative literature educator; b. Anderson, S.C., May 31, 1929; s. Clarence Fleetwood and Mildred McCorkle (Cunningham) B.; m. Jacqueline Duquesne; children: Katherine, Christopher. BA, Duke U., 1950; MA, U. Mich., 1956; PhD, Harvard Coll., 1962. Prof. Russian lit. Princeton (N.J.) U., prof. comparative lit.; prof. emeritus Princeton U., 1999—. Mem. exec. com. Nat. Translation Ctr., Austin, Tex., 1966-73; mem. exec. bd. Translation Ctr., Columbia U., 1987-91; mem. fiction jury Creative Arts Awards, Brandeis U., 1991. Author newspaper column Ink Soup, 1991—. With U.S. Army, 1951-54, ETO. Recipient Christian Gauss award in Lit. Criticism, Phi Beta Kappa, 1974.

BROWN, D. ROBIN, elementary school educator; b. Cleve., Oct. 31, 1949; d. William Michael and Darla G. (Carlson) Linsenmann; m. Ross H. Brown, Aug. 21, 1971. BA cum laude, W.Va. Wesleyan U., 1971; MA, Ashland U., 1988, postgrad., 1988-90, Ohio State U., 1989-90. Cert. elem. tchr., Ohio, W.Va. Tchr. Lost Creek Elem. Sch., Clarksburg, W.Va., 1971-72, Leesburg (Va.) Middle Sch., 1972-75, Northmoor Elem. Sch., Dayton, Ohio, 1975-79, Jonathan Alder Local Schs., Plain City, Ohio, 1979—. Active TWIG # 158, Columbus, Ohio, 1990—, Salvation Army, Columbus, 1990—, Worthington Hills Women's Club, Columbus, 1985—. Recipient Sci. award Exxon, 1974. Mem. Internat. Reading Assn., Reading Recovery, Kappa Delta Pi, Sigma Eta Sigma, Pi Gamma Mu, Tri Beta. Avocations: golf, reading, travel, sports, volunteer work. Home: 825 Highview Dr Columbus OH 43235-1232 Office: Jonathan Alder Local Schs 4331 Kilbury Huber Rd Plain City OH 43064-9064

BROWN, DALE SUSAN, government administrator, educational program director, writer; b. NYC, May 27, 1954; d. Bertram S. and Beatrice Joy (Gilman) Brown. BA, Antioch Coll., 1976. Rsch. asst. Am. Occupational Therapy Assn., Rockville, Md., 1976-79; writer Pres.' Com. on Employment of People with Disabilities, Washington, 1979-82, program mgr. handicapped concerns com., 1982—85, program mgr. labor com., 1985, 96-98, program mgr. work environment and tech. com., 1988-94, program mgr. com. on libr. and info. svcs., 1984-86, youth devel com., 1986-88, new products devel. team, 1987-90, agy. rep., 1991-93, with interagy. tech. assistance coordinating team, 1992-94; program mgr. Job Accomodation Network, 1997-99; mgr. Nat. Conf. of Youth with Disabilities, 2000; policy advisor Office Disability Employment Policy Dept. Labor, 2001—, mem. youth team, 2002—. Cons. in field, gen. assembly speaker nat. conv. Gen. Fedn. Women's Clubs, 1981, mem. Rehab Svcs. Adminstrn. Task Force on Learning Disabilities, 1981-83. Author: Steps to Independence for People with Learning Disabilities, 1980, Pathways to Employment for People with Learning Disabilities, 1991, Working Effectively with People Who Have Learning Disabilities and Attention Deficit Hyperactivity Disorder, 1995, I Know I Can Climb the Mountain, 1995, Learning Disabilities and Employment, 1997, Learning A Living Guide to Planning Your Career and Finding A Job for People with Learning Disabilities, Attention Deficit Disorder and Dyslexia, 2000, Job-Hunting Tips for the So-Called Handicapped, 2001, (films) They Could Have Saved Their Homes, 1982; dir.: (videotape) Part of the Team People with Disabilities in the Workforce, 1990; co-editor: Learning Disabilities Quar. Americans with Disabilities Act and Learning Disabilities, 1992; mem. editl. bd. Perceptions, 1981—83, Learning Disabilities Focus, 1988—90, In the Mainstream, 1994—98; guest editor: Learning Disabilities Rsch. and Practice, 1990—96; guest editor Learning Disability and Career Development, 2002; guest editor: Career Planning and Adult Devel. Jour., 2002. Bd. dirs. Closer Look Nat. Info. Ctr., Washington, 1980—83; bd. dir. Am. Coalition for Citizens with Disabilities, 1985—86; congrl. task force Rights and Empowerment of Ams. with Disabilities, 1988—90; profl. adv. bd. Nat. Attention Deficit Disorder Assn., 1996—99; bd. dir. Coun. on Quality and Leadership, 2000—; adv. bd. Internat. Ctr. for Disability Resources on the Internet, 2003—; chair conf. on Info. Tech. for User With Disabilities, 1989; spl. asst. for people with disabilities Federally Employed Women, 1991—92; blue ribbon panel Nat. Telecomm. Access for People with Disabilities, 1989—94; pres. Assn. Learning Disabled Adults, Washington, 1979—80; del. Nat. Writer's Union, 1999; rep. com. on fed. govt. as model employer, com. on youth with disabilities Presdl. Task Force on Employment of Adults with Disabilities, 1999—2002; judge, Ten Outstanding Young Ams. U.S. Jr. C. of C. Jaycees, 2003. Named one of Ten Outstanding Young Ams., U.S. Jr. C. of C. Jaycees, 1994; recipient, Margaret Byrd Rawson award, 1989, Personal Achievement award Women's Program USDOL, 1989, Individual Achievement award, Nat. Coun. on Communication Disorders, 1991, Spl. Achievement award, Pres.'s Com. on Employment of People with Disabilities, 1991, Gold Screen award, Nat. Assn. Gov. Communicators, 1991, Arthur S. Fleming award, 1992; grantee, Found. for Children with Learning Disabilities, 1982. Mem.: Inter Agency. Com. on Handicapped Employees (rep. 1989—91), Learning Disabilities Assn. Am. (bd. dirs. 1986—91), Nat. Assn. Govt. Communicators (Blue Pencil award 1986), Nat. Network of Learning Disabled Adults (founder, pres. 1980—81, rep. inter-agy. com. on comuter support handicapped employees 1998—99), ALA. Democrat. Office: Office Disability Employment Policy Dept Labor S1011 200 Constitution Ave NW Washington DC 20210

BROWN, DAVID EDWARD, elementary and environmental education educator; b. Quincy, Ill., Feb. 27, 1965; s. Jerry Lee and Rose Ann (Strieker) B. AA, John Wood C.C., 1985; BS in Elem. Edn., Spl. Edn., Quincy Coll., 1988. Cert. tchr., Fla., Ill. Nature dir. Boy Scouts Am., Mendon, Ill., 1983-86; park ranger U.S. Army C.E., Quincy, Ill., 1987; tchr. Moody Elem. Sch., Bradenton, Fla., 1988-91, Wakeland Elem. Sch., Bradenton, 1991—. Tchr. edn. coord. Fla. Div. Forestry, 1991—, project Learning Tree facilitator, 1991—; facilitator Project Wild, Fla. Game and Freshwater Fish Commn., 1990—, biodiversity facilitator, 1993—; co-dir. environ. edn. Wakeland Elem. Sch., 1992; facilitator 4-Rs cirriculum and biodiversity Fla. Dept. Edn., 1993; facilitator S.W. Fla. Water Mgmt. Dist., 1993; regional dir. Fla. Project Learning Tree. Contbg. author: (curriculum) Water Watcher Guide, 1992, (booklet) Florida Division Forestry Environmental Education Resource Manual. Coach Manatee Lightning Soccer Club, Bradenton, 1991; asst. leader Bradenton area Boy Scouts Am., 1992. Grantee Fla. Environ. Edn. Found., 1992; recipient Program of Excellence award Fla. Dept. Edn., 1993; named Conservation Tchr. of Yr., Nat. Assn. Conservation Dists., 1990, Rookie Facilitator of Yr., Fla. Game and Freshwater Fish Commn., 1991, Wakeland Elem. Tchr. of Yr., 1993, Environ. Tchr. of Yr., AT&T, 1994, One of 5 Top Ednl. Tchrs., Gov. of Fla., 1993, 94, others. Mem. ASCD, Nat. Audubon Soc., Nat. Sci. Tchrs. Assn., Am. Assn. Zoo Keepers, Nat. Wildlife Fedn., Lowry Park Zoo Docent Orgn. Democrat. Roman Catholic. Avocations: volleyball, photography. Home: 3210 Castleton Dr Bradenton FL 34208-5327 Office: 3316 Fox Run E Quincy IL 62301-6254

BROWN, DAVID RICHARD, school system administrator, minister; b. Manhattan, Kans., Oct. 22, 1929; s. Marion Arthur and Dorothy (Bailey) B.; m. Jeanette Christine Phoenix, July 28, 1962; children: David M., Mark, Thomas. BA, U. So. Calif., 1951; MDiv, U. Chgo., 1955; postgrad., U. So. Calif., 1956, 57. Ordained minister, Presbyn. Ch. Assoc. pastor Federated Community Ch., Flagstaff, Ariz., 1957-59; minister of edn. Lakeside Presbyn. Ch., San Francisco, 1959-62; pastor of edn. 1st Presbyn. Ch., Medford, Oreg., 1962-69, pastor Newark, Calif., 1969-75; founder, pastor Community Presbyn. Ch., Union City, Calif., 1975-89; founder, supt. Christian Heritage Acad., Fremont, Calif., 1984—2000; organizing pastor New Life Presbyn. Ch., Fremont, 1989—99; asst. prof. Chabot Coll., Hayward, Calif., 1975-80; pastor New Life Presbyn. Ch., Castro Valley, Calif., 1999—. Moderator Presbytery of No. Ariz., 1959, Presbytery of No. Calif., 2001—02; religion editor The Valley Citizen, Danville, Calif., 2000—. Dir.: (various Shakespearian theatrical prodns.), 1982—84 (Thesbian award, 1984). Pres. Boys Christian League, L.A., 1953-54, Coconino Assn. for Mental Health, Flagstaff, 1958-59; chaplain Mozumdar YMCA Camp, Crestline, Calif., 1952-56; chmn. Tri-City Citizens Action Com., 1986-90. Recipient plaque KC, 1989. Mem. Rotary (chpt. pres. 1988-89, Paul Harris fellow 1989). Avocations: skiing, stamps, choir, drama.

BROWN, DEBORAH JOYCE, special education educator; b. Ft. McPhearson, Ga., Dec. 4, 1954; d. Bud Lawrence and Betty Jean (Moore)_ B. BS, Appalachian State U., 1977, MA, 1988. Cert. communication disorders specialist, learning disabilities tchr., emotionally handicapped tchr. Resource tchr. Caldwell County Schs., Lenoir, N.C., 1978-79; communication disorders specialist Cherokee County Schs., Murphy, N.C., 1980—. Supr. House of Lloyd, Kansas City, Mo., 1988; mem. Mountain Area Writing Project, summer 1998. Mem. Alcohol and Drug Def., ASCD, Wednesday

Revolution (chairperson pupil svcs. 1989-90), Dare to Say No Club (leader 1989-91), Collaborative Edn. (implementer/trainer/tchr. 1991—), Writing 4 & 6 (co-trainer/trainer/tchr. 1991—), Safety Patrol (leader trainer 1992-93, creative writing corrd., staff devel. tchr. 1995—, chairperson staff devel. 1999-00). Avocations: art, reading, bible study and prayer, aerobics, missions work.

BROWN, DELORES JEAN, retired elementary school educator; b. Enid, Okla., June 6, 1938; d. Jesse M. and Bessie M. (Veley) Smith; m. Gerald E. Brown, May 31, 1958; children: Kristin (Brown) Hancock, Craig E. BS in Elem. Edn., Phillips U., 1975. Cert. elem. tchr., Okla. Tchr. Glenwood Elem. Sch., Enid, Okla., 1975—98; ret., 1998. Cons. book author, 1994. Mem. Okla. Coun. Tchrs. of Math., Kappa Kappa Iota (treas.) Republican. Baptist. Home: 2609 Robin Rdg Enid OK 73703-6424

BROWN, DIANA HAYES, elementary education educator; b. Leesburg, Fla., Dec. 5, 1950; d. Autrey Johnson and Dorothy (Scott) Hayes; m. Jerry David Brown, Aug. 5, 1972; children: Brandon David, Gavin Scott. BEd, Fla. Tech. U., 1972; MEd, U. Ctrl. Fla., 1977. Cert. tchr., Fla. Tchr. Lake County Sch. Bd., Tavares, Fla., 1971-85, coord. program, 1987—. Adv. panel office of edn. rsch. improvement Nat. Dept. Edn., 1990. Pres. Clermont Jr. Woman's Club, 1974-75; bd. dirs. YMCA, Clermont, Fla., 1985-86; nominating com. 1st United Meth. Ch., Clermont, 1992—; citizens adv. Clermont High, 1992—. Recipient Nat. Staff Devel. award Nat. Coun. States Insvc. Edn. N.Y., 1991, Edn. award Lake County League of Cities, 1992. Mem. ASCD, Nat. Coun. States on Insvc. Edn., Am. Fedn. Tchr., Fed. Edn. Assn., Lake County Edn. Assn., Invitational Edn. Alliance, Delta Kpapa Gamma. Methodist. Avocations: writing humorous poetry, reading, beach activities, traveling, working with people. Home: 1732 Disston Ave Clermont FL 34711-3412 Office: Lake County Schs Howey Ctr 510 S Palm Ave Howey In The Hills FL 34737-3904

BROWN, DIANA L. elementary education educator; b. Bklyn., Oct. 9, 1946; d. Elva Jane Brown. AAS, N.Y.C. Community Coll., Bklyn.; BS, CCNY, 1980; postgrad., Nova U., Ft. Lauderdale, Fla. Cert. educator, Fla.; class cert. behavior analysis. Supr. outpatient clinics N.Y. Health and Hosps. Corp., N.Y.C.; asst. dir. Toddlers Country Club, Orlando, Fla.; tchr. Friends Sem., N.Y.C.; tchr. 3d grade Dover Shores Elem. Sch./Orange County Sch. Bd., Orlando, Fla.; 3d grade tchr. Shingle Creek Elem. Sch., 1993, 5th grade tchr., 1993-95, curriculum resource tchr., dean, 1995-97; alternative edn. tchr. Dover Shores Elem. Sch., 1997; 5th grade tchr. Tangelo Park Elem., 1997—2002; trainer for new tchrs., great beginnings induction Orange County Sch. Bd., 2001—; tch. applied behavior analysis Rocklake Elem. Sch., 2002—, dean, 2002—. Sch.-based care team for students at risk; state sci. textbook adoption com., 1994-95; county sci. curriculum writing team, 1994-95.; trainer new tchrs. Great Beginnings Program, 2001—. Author: Afro-Amercan Artists: A Bio-Bibliographical Directory. Named Tchr. of Yr. Dover Shores, 1990-91; Coun. of Black Faculty and Staff scholar. Mem.: NEA, Nat. Sci. Tchrs. Assn.

BROWN, DONALD ROBERT, psychology educator; b. Albany, NY, Mar. 5, 1925; s. J. Edward and Natile (Rosenberg) B.; m. June Gole, Aug. 14, 1945; children: Peter Douglas, Thomas Matthew, Jacob Noah. AB, Harvard U., 1948; MA, PhD, U. Calif.-Berkeley, 1951. Mem. faculty Bryn Mawr Coll., 1951-64, prof. psychology, 1963—. Sr. research cons. Mellon Found., Vassar Coll., 1953-63; part-time vis. prof. Swarthmore Coll., U. Pa., also U. Calif.-Berkeley, 1953-61; fellow Center Advanced Study Behavioral Scis., 1960-61; prof. psychology, sr. research scientist, dir. Center Research Learning and Teaching, U. Mich., 1964— ; cons. Peace Corps, 1965-71; hon. research fellow Univ. Coll., London, 1970-71; Fulbright sr. research fellow Max Planck Inst., Berlin, 1982; Netherlands Basic Sci. fellow, Leyden, 1983 Author: articles, chpts. in books; editor: Changing Role and Status of Soviet Women, 1967, Frontiers of Motivational Psychology, 1986; co-editor: Frontiers of Mathematical Psychology, 1990. Served with AUS, 1943-46, ETO. Fellow Am. Psychol. Assn., Chinese Acad. Sci.; mem. Soc. Psychol. Study of Social Issues, AAAS, AAUP, Sigma Xi, Psi Chi. Home: 2511 Hawthorne Rd Ann Arbor MI 48104-4031

BROWN, DONALD VAUGHN, technical educator, engineering consultant; b. Fairfield, Maine, May 16, 1919; s. Walter C. and Hazel (Fogg) Brown; m. Christine R. Bishop, Mar. 14, 1945 (dec. Oct. 2000); 1 child, Donald V. Jr.; m. Wanda Jean Grant, June 1, 2002. BS, U. Maine, Orono, 1943; MS, Brigham Young U., 1963; EdD, Utah State U., 1965. Registered profl. engr., Maine. Apprentice engr. U.S. Steel Corp., Elwood City, Pa., 1943-47; works metallurgist Aluminum Co. of Am., Alcoa, Tenn., 1947-55; asst. v.p. Penobscot Fibre Co., Old Town, Maine, 1955-60; assoc. prof. Inst. Paper Chemistry, Appleton, Wis., 1960-62; instr. Brigham Young U., Provo, Utah, 1962-63, Utah State U., Logan, 1963-65; dean Fla. Keys C.C., Key West, 1965-66; dean, prof. Western Piedmont C.C., Morganton, N.C., 1966-68; prof. U. Tenn., Knoxville, 1968—. Cons. Assn. Am. States, Washington, 1976—, San Jose Costa Rica, S.A., Tenn. State Dept. Edn., Nashville, 1970—84, Maine State Libr., Augusta, 1970—; coord. Surname Index Project, 2001, Am. Adventure, Inc., Orlando, Fla., 1986—96, Thousand Trails Resorts, 1989—95, Coast to Coast Camping, Inc., Washington, 1986, Lincoln Acad., New Castle, Maine, 1994; cons. Capetown South Africa Mission, 2003—05; bd. dirs. Goodwill-Hinckley, Maine. Author: A Teaching Partnership, 1972, Metallurgy Basics, 1978; contbr. articles to profl. jours.; patentee 4 chemical processes. Scoutmaster Boy Scouts Am., Elwood City, Pa. and Alcoa, Tenn., 1946-52, scout commr., Massena, N.Y. and Orono, Maine, 1952-60; trustee Hinkley (Maine) Sch., 1978—. Lt. USN, 1944-46, 50-52, PTO, WW II, Korean War. Recipient Presdl. USN Unit citation, 1945. Mem. Am. Vocat. Assn., Am. Tech. Edn. Assn., Engring. Edn. Assn. (editing bd. 1968-79). Avocations: photography, sailing, hiking, camping. Home: 6423 Honeywood Knoxville TN 37918

BROWN, DOROTHEA WILLIAMS, technology consulting company executive; b. Austin, Tex., Dec. 23, 1918; d. Van Wilford and Ethel Lee (Connor) Williams; m. Ira Harper Brown, Aug. 23, 1943; 1 child, Michele Brown Scott. BA, Huston-Tillotson Coll., Austin, 1939; MA, John Carroll U., 1959; PhD, U. Akron, 1980. Cert. counselor, supr., adminstr., Ohio. Tchr., counselor, prin. Cleve. Pub. Schs., 1952-70; chief program officer Kent Ctr. for Ednl. Devel. and Strategic Svcs., Kent (Ohio) State U., 1970-75; dean, dir. Cuyahoga Community Coll., Cleve., 1975-79; assoc. dir. Nat. Inst. Staff and Orgn. Devel., U. Tex., Austin, 1979-82; dir., cons., co-owner TAPIT, Inc. (Theory and Practice in Tech.), Washington and Newark, 1983—. Cons. Cleve. Commn. for Higher Edn., 1968-71; sec. vol. com. Austin Ind. Sch. Dist., 1987-89; mem. task group 4 Tex. Commn. for Bus. and Edn., 1990-91; participant White House Initiative for Hist. Black Colls. and Univs., Washington, 1990; mem. com. to select outstanding women in mgmt. State of Tex., 1990; chmn. Z.B. Sikes teaching excellence award Huston-Tillotson Coll., Austin, 1989—; com. mem., mem. cmty. rels. adv. bd. U. Tex. Contbg. editor New Lady, 1963-70; contbr. articles to ednl. jours. Mem. nat. bd. dirs. Girl Scouts U.S., 1977-83, bd. dirs., chmn. nominating com. lone star coun. Girl Scouts Mirrors Program, 1981-85, 1993—; chmn. Austin Commn. for Women, 1981-85; v.p. Laguna Gloria Art Mus., Austin, 1983—; mem. Higher Edn. Commn. Austin, 1983—; observer Internat. Social Workers Group, Kenya, Egypt, Ethiopia, others; study tour mem. Ctr. Study Socialist Edn. Keet State U., China, 1984-85, U.S.S.R. 1986; trustee Cen. Tex. chpt. ARC, 1988—; community advisor Jr. League of Austin, 1987-89; docent Tex. Gov.'s mansion, 1983-87, Lyndon Baines Johnson Libr./Mus., 1988—, Am. Inst. for Learning (Creative Rapic Learning Ctr.); sec. Women and World Issues, 1984-87, Austin Mus. Art; bd. dirs., trustee Adopt-A-Sch., 1990—; bd. dirs. Austin Child Guidance Ctr., 1991—; mem. Austin's Great Decision Group; cmty bd. dirs. KLRU; com. mem. Foster Care Project. Recipient Martin Luther King Community award Bergstrom AFB, Austin, 1984, Woman of Austin award Austin Commn. for Women, 1989, Outstanding Woman award Girl Scouts U.S., 1989, cert. of appreciation U.S. Office of Edn., 1993, Spl. Recognition award for Vol. Svcs., 1992; named to Austin Women Hall of Fame, 1985, 87; numerous other awards. Mem. AAUW (chmn. fellowship awards to doctoral students 1987-90), Links (pres. Austin chpt. 1984-92, 91-93, program dir. western area 1987-89, contbn. award 1987), Order Ea. Star (bronze star award Mt. Olive grand chpt. 1987), Pi Lambda Theta, Alpha Kappa Alpha, Phi Delta Kappa. Episcopalian. Avocations: reading, writing, needlework, foreign travel. Home: 13900 Shaker Blvd Apt 610 Cleveland OH 44120-1566 Office: TAPIT Inc 109 Linden Hall Ln Gaithersburg MD 20877-3461

BROWN, ELMIRA NEWSOM, retired elementary school educator; b. Proctor-Crittenden, Ark., May 31, 1907; d. Emanuel Newsom and Tennessee Johnson; m. James Jefferson Brown, Nov. 19, 1942. BS, U. Ark., Pine Bluff, 1950; MS, U. Ark., Fayetteville, 1954. Tchr. Wynoka (Ark.) Elem. Sch., 1930-34, Mildred Jackson Elem. Sch., Hughes, Ark., 1934-42; prin. McCrory (Ark.) Elem. Sch. (now Elmira N. Brown H.S.), 1943-50; tchr. Scipio A. Jones H.S., North Little Rock, Ark., 1950-53, Howard Elem. Sch., Ft. Smith, Ark., 1954-60, Goldstein Elem. Sch., Hot Springs, Ark., 1960-67, Langston H.S., Hot Springs, 1967-68; ret., 1968. Interim exec. dir. Coun. Econ. Opportunity, Hot Springs, 1968—. V.p. Woodland Shores Cmty. Action, Royal, Ark., 1983-92; mem. Dem. Nat. Com., Washington, 1992-97; chairperson task force Dem. Congl. Campaign Com., Royal, 1992-96; mem. women's missionary soc. African Meth. Episcopal Ch., dir. connectional skill shops WMS, 1980. Mem. AAUW, LWV, Ch. Women United, U. Ark. Alumni Assn., Zeta Phi Beta. Mem. African Meth. Episcopalian Ch. Avocations: softball, basketball, fishing, boating, gardening.

BROWN, FREDERICK GRAMM, psychology educator; b. Madison, Wis., Apr. 6, 1932; s. Fred E. and Meda I. (Gramm) B.; m. Barbara A. Thaller, June 23, 1956; children: Jeffrey S., Kirk F., Daniel H. BA, U. Wis., 1954, MA, 1955; PhD, U. Minn., 1958. Asst. prof. U. Mo., Columbia, 1958-61; asst. prof. psychology Iowa State U., Ames, 1961-64, assoc. prof. psychology, 1964-68, prof. psychology, 1968—97, Univ. prof., 1993—97, Univ. prof. emeritus, 1997—; vis. scholar Ednl. Testing Service, 1985-86. Author: Measurement and Evaluation, 1971, Guidelines for Test Use, 1980, Measuring Classroom Achievement, 1981, Principles of Educational and Psychological Testing, 3d edit., 1983 Fellow Ctr. for Advanced Study in Behavioral Scis., 1967-68, U.S. Office Edn., 1967-68 Fellow APA, Am. Psychol. Soc.; mem. Am. Ednl. Rsch. Assn., Nat. Coun. Measurement in Edn., Phi Beta Kappa. Home: 2616 Kellogg Ave Ames IA 50010-4725

BROWN, GARY SANDY, electrical engineering educator; b. Jackson, Miss., Apr. 13, 1940; s. John Leo and Welma (Kelley) B.; m. Mary Kathleen Connaughton, Mar. 16, 1970; children: Joshua John, Nathan Matthew. BSEE, U. Ill., 1963, MS, 1964, PhDEE, 1967. Grad. rsch. asst. Antenna Lab. U. Ill., Urbana, 1963-67; mem. tech. staff TRW Systems Group, Redondo Beach, Calif., 1969-70; sr. engr. Rsch. Triangle Inst., Durham, N.C., 1970-73; sr. scientist Applied Sci. Assocs., Apex, N.C., 1973-85; prof. elect. engring. Va. Poly. Inst. and State U., Blacksburg, 1985—, apptd. Bradley disting. prof. electromagnetics, 2002. With Wallops Flight Facility, NASA, Wallops Island, Va., 1974; cons. Naval Rsch. Lab., Washington, 1988-91, Decision Scis. Applications, Arlington, Va., 1988-91, DTI Inc., Torrance, Calif., 1987-91, Applied Physics Lab., Laurel, Md., 1987-88, Waste Policy Inst., Blacksburg, Va., 1991—, Motorola Corp., Chandler, Ariz., 1991-93; mem. NATO AGARD Electromagnetic Propogation Panel, 1993—; dir. Electromagnetic Interactions Lab. Contbr. chpts. to books, articles to profl. jours. Capt. U.S. Army, 1967-69. Recipient Best Paper awards R.W.P. King, 1978, Schelkunoff, 1999, Bradley Disting. Prof. Electromagnetics, 2002. Fellow IEEE (Third Millenium award 2000); mem. Antennas and Propagation Soc. of IEEE (pres. 1988), Am. Geophys. Union (editor's citation Radio Sci., Am. sects. 1986), Internat. Union of Radio Sci. (mem.-at-large 1987, sec. U.S. nat. com. 1997-99, chair U.S. nat. com. 2000-2002), NATO AGARD Sensors and Propagation Panel. Avocations: backpacking, jogging. Office: Va Poly Inst & State U Bradley Dept Elec Engr Blacksburg VA 24061

BROWN, GEORGE E. judge, educator; b. Hammond, Ind., July 27, 1947; s. George E. and Violet M. (Matlon) B.; m. Patricia A. Schneider, June 6, 1970; children: Janet M., Elizabeth A. BS, Ball State U., 1969; JD, DePaul U., 1974; grad., Ind. Jud. Coll., 1996. Bar: Ind. 1974, Ill. 1974, U.S. Dist. Ct. (no. dist.) Ind. 1979, U.S. Supreme Ct. 1977, U.S. Tax Ct. 1977. Pvt. practice, LaGrange & Lake Counties, Ind., 1974-84; judge LaGrange County Ct., 1984-87, LaGrange Superior Ct., 1988—. Part-time chief dep. prosecutor LaGrange County, 1975—77; adj. faculty Tri-State U., Angola, Ind., 1991—. Vol. Jr. Achievement, 1997—. Mem.: ABA, Nat. Conf. State Trial Judges (criminal justice com.), Ind. Judges Assn. (com. protective orders), LaGrange County Bar Assn. (pres. 1978), Ind. State Bar Assn. (ho. of dels., com. on improvements in the jud. sys.), Rotary (past dir., v.p. 1999—2000, pres. 2000—01, bd. dirs. 2002—). Office: Lagrange Superior Ct Courthouse Lagrange IN 46761

BROWN, GREGORY NEIL, university administrator, forest physiology educator; b. Detroit, Feb. 10, 1938; s. Robert Octavus and Dorothy Etta May (Kingsbury) B.; m. Patricia Lee Talbott, Dec. 16, 1961 (div. 1974); children: Kathryn Duket, Julie Ann, Deborah Louise; m. Janeth Christine Hartman, May 24, 1974 (dec. 1997); children: Kimberly Suzanne, Kevin Scott; m. Laura Jean Dale, June 27, 1998. BS, Iowa State U., 1959; MF, Yale U., 1960; DF, Duke U., 1963. Plant physiologist Oak Ridge Nat. Lab., 1963—66; asst. prof. forestry to prof. U. Mo.-Columbia, 1966—77, dir. grad. studies Sch. Forestry, 1969—74; prof. Iowa State U., Ames, 1977—78; dept. head, prof. U. Minn.-St. Paul, 1978—83; dean, prof. U. Maine-Orono, 1983—86, acting v.p. acad. affairs, 1986-87, 91-92, v.p. rsch. and pub. svc., 1987—92; dean, prof. Coll. Natural Resources, Va. Poly. Inst. and State U., Blacksburg, 1992—, interim dean Coll. Agrl. and Life Scis., 2003. Assoc. dir. Maine Agrl. Exptl. Sta., Orono, 1983-86, acting pres., 1992; assoc. dir. Va. Agrl. Exptl. Sta., Blacksburg, 1992—, interim provost, 1995; chair, bd. dirs. Powell River Project, 1996—; mem. sci. adv. bd. Nat. Ctr. Housing and the Environment, 2002—. Author-editor: Seedling Physiology and Reforestation Success, 1984; editor: International Directory of Woody Plant Physiologists, 1974-84, Jour. Forest Sci., 1979-82; editl. bd.: Renewable resources Jour., 2002—. Contbr. articles to profl. jours. Scoutmaster Boy Scouts Am., 1965-66; mem. Forestry Rsch. Adv. Coun., U.S. Sec. Agr., 2000-2002. Mem. Soc. Am. Foresters (chmn. physiology working group 1983-84), Nat. Assn. Profl. Forestry Schs. and Colls. (north Ctrl. rsch. chmn. 1981-82, nat. sec. treas. 1984-85, nat. pres. elect 1986-87, 94-95, pres. 1996-97), Internat. Union Forest Orgns. (chmn. working parties 1970-86), Nat. Assn. State Univs. and Land-Grant Colls. (chair bd. on natural resources 1997, chair U.S. geol. survey partnership com. 1997-2000), Soc. for Preservation and Encouragement of Barbershop Quartet Singing in Am. (pres. 1973-74), Sigma Xi, Xi Sigma Pi, Gamma Sigma Delta (jr. faculty award 1971). Lutheran. Home: 1810 Mountainside Dr Blacksburg VA 24060-9202 Office: Va Poly Inst and State U Coll Natural Resources 324 Cheatham Hall Blacksburg VA 24061 E-mail: browngn@vt.edu.

BROWN, HARLEY PROCTER, JR., zoology educator, entomology researcher; b. Uniontown, Ala., Jan. 13, 1921; s. Harley Procter Brown and Martha Ida (McGinniss) Brown Coleman; m. Laura Clifford Williams, June 1, 1942 (dec. 1989); 1 child, Mary Hamilton Brown Catron; m. Marie Magdalen Jenkins, Dec. 20, 1989 (dec. 1997); m. Dorothy Ellis McGregor, Oct. 26, 1997. AB, AM, Miami U., Oxford, Ohio, 1942; PhD, Ohio State U., 1945. Grad. asst. in zoology Ohio State U., Columbus, 1942-45; instr. zoology U. Idaho, Moscow, 1945-47, Oreg. Inst. Marine Biology, Charleston, 1946; instr. biology Queens Coll., Flushing, N.Y., 1947-48; asst. prof., then assoc. prof. U. Okla., Norman, 1948-62, prof. zoology, 1962-84, prof. emeritus, 1984—; curator of invertebrates Stovall Mus. Sci. & History (now S.N. Okla. Mus. Natural History), Norman, 1962—. Rsch. prof. Franz Theodore Stone Inst., Put-In-Bay, Ohio, 1949. Author: Aquatic Dryopoid Beetles of the U.S.A., 1972; editor: Highlights and Lowlights, 1981; contbr. chpts. to Immature Insects, vol. 2, 1991; contbr. over 100 articles to biol. jours. Instl. rep., mem. dist. com., counselor Norman area Boy Scouts Am., 1949-70. NSF fellow, 1964, 70. Fellow AAAS (life); mem. Am. Inst. Biol. Scis. (governing bd.), Am. Microscopical Soc. (pres. 1975-76), N.Am. Benthological Soc., Sigma Xi, Phi Eta Sigma, Phi Sigma (nat. v.p. 1980—). Democrat. Presbyterian. Achievements include discovery of new genera and species of wasps (Pteromalidae, Eulophidae, Diapriidae) and water beetles (Elmidae, Dryopidae, Psephenidae, Lutrochidae, Limnichidae); research in life histories of various aquatic insects and their insect parasites (Sisyrids, Psephenids). Home: 504 Dakota St Norman OK 73069-7013

BROWN, HERBERT CHARLES, chemistry educator; b. London, May 22, 1912; arrived in U.S., 1914; s. Charles and Pearl (Gorinstein) Brown; m. Sarah Baylen Brown, Feb. 6, 1937; 1 child, Charles Allan. AS, Wright Jr. Coll., Chgo., 1935; BS, U. Chgo., 1936, PhD, 1938, DSc (hon.), 1968; doctorate (hon.), Wayne State U., 1980, Lebanon Valley Coll., 1980, L.I. U., 1980, Hebrew U. Jerusalem, 1980, Pontificia Universidad de Chile, 1980, Purdue U., 1980; doctorates (hon.), U. Wales, 1981, U. Paris, 1982, Butler U., 1982, Ball State U., 1985, Nicolas Copernicus U., Torun, 1998. Asst. chemistry U. Chgo., 1936—38, Eli Lilly post-doctorate rsch. fellow, 1938—39, instr., 1939—43; asst. prof. chemistry Wayne U., 1943—46, assoc. prof., 1946—47; prof. inorganic chemistry Purdue U., 1947—59, Richard B. Wetherill prof. chemistry, 1959, Richard B. Wetherill rsch. prof., 1960—78, emeritus, 1978—. Vis. prof. UCLA, 1951, Ohio State U., 1952, U. Mex., 1954, U. Calif. at Berkeley, 1957, U. Colo., 1958, U. Heidelberg, 1963, SUNY, Stony Brook, 1966, U. Calif., Santa Barbara, 1967, Hebrew U., Jerusalem, 1969, U. Wales, Swansea, 1973, U. Cape Town, South Africa, 1974, U. Calif., San Diego, 1979; Harrison Howe lectr., 53; Friend E. Clark lectr., 53; Freud-McCormack lectr., 54; Centenary lectr., England, 55; Thomas W. Talley lectr., 56; Falk-Plaut lectr., 57; Julius Stieglitz lectr., 58; Max Tishler lectr., 58; Kekule-Couper Centenary lectr., 58; E.C. Franklin lectr., 60; Ira Remsen lectr., 61; Edgar Fahs Smith lectr., 62; Seydel-Wooley lectr., 66; Baker lectr., 69; Benjamin Rush lectr., 71; Chem. Soc. lectr., Australia, 72; Armes lectr., 73; Henry Gilman lectr., 75; others; hon. prof. Organomet Chem. Chinese Acad. Scis., 1994; chem. cons. to indsl. corps.; rschr. phys., organic and inorganic chemistry relating chem. behavior to molecular structure, selective reductions, hydroboration and chemistry of organoboranes. Author: Hydroboration, 1962, Boranes in Organic Chemistry, 1972, Organic Synthesis via Boranes, 1975, The Nonclassical Ion Problem, 1977; co-author: (with A.W. Pelter and K. Smith): Borane Reagents, 1988; co-author: (with P.V. Ramachandran) Organoboranes for Syntheses, 2001; co-author: (with G. W. Kramer, A.B. Levy, and M. Mark Midland) Organic Syntheses via Boranes, Vol. 1, 2001; co-author: (with M. Zaidlewicz) Organic Syntheses via Boranes, Vol. 2, 2001; co-author: (with A. Suzuki) Organic Syntheses via Boranes, Vol. 3, 2003; contbr. articles to chem. jours. Bd. govs. Hebrew U., 1969—90; co-dir. war rsch. projects for U.S. Army, Nat. Def. Rsch. Com., Manhattan Project U. Chgo., 1940—43. Decorated Order of the Rising Sun, Gold and Silver Star Japan; named one of Top 75 Disting. Contbrs. to Chem. Enterprise, Chem. & Engring. News, 1998; recipient Purdue Sigma Xi rsch. award, 1951, Nichols medal, 1959, award, Am. Chem. Soc., 1960, S.O.C.M.A. medal, 1960, H.N. McCoy award, 1965, Linus Pauling medal, 1968, Nat. medal of Sci., 1969, Roger Adams medal, 1971, Charles Frederick Chandler medal, 1973, Chem. Pioneer award, 1975, CUNY medal for sci. achievement, 1976, Elliott Cresson medal, 1978, C.K. Ingold medal, 1978, Nobel prize in Chemistry, 1979, Priestley medal, 1981, Perkin medal, 1982, Gold medal award, Am. Inst. Chemists, 1981, G.M. Kosolapoff medal, 1987, NAS award in chem. scis., 1987, Oesper award, Cin. sect. Am. Chem. Soc., 1990, Herbert C. Brown medal and award for creative rsch. in synthetic methods, Am. Chem. Soc., 1998; fellow (hon.) U. Wales Swansea, 1994. Fellow: AAAS, Indian Nat. Sci. Acad. (fgn.), Royal Soc. Chemistry (hon.); mem.: NAS, Chinese Acad. Sci. (hon. prof. 1994), Indian Acad. Sci., Chem. Soc. Japan, Pharm. Soc. Japan (hon.), Am. Chem. Soc. (chmn. Purdue sect. 1955—56), Am. Acad. Arts and Sci., Sigma Xi, Phi Beta Kappa, Alpha Chi Sigma, Phi Lambda Upsilon (hon.). Office: Purdue U Dept Chemistry Lafayette IN 47907

BROWN, HILTON, visual arts educator, artist, writer; b. Momence, Ill., Sept. 22, 1938; s. Oswald E. and Maud M. (Shronts) B. Student, Goodman Theater/Art Inst. Chgo, 1956-58, U. Chgo., 1959-60, U. Ill., Chgo., 1961-62; cert. in fine arts, 1962; Diploma in Fine Arts, BFA in Painting, Sch. of Art Inst. Chgo., 1962, MFA in Painting, 1963. Instr. drawing/painting Sch. Art Inst. Chgo., 1962-65; asst. prof. fine art Sch. Fine Arts Washington U., St. Louis, 1965-68; asst. prof. fine arts Goucher Coll., Towson, Md., 1968-70, assoc. prof. fine arts, 1970-75, prof. and chair dept. visual arts, 1975-78; vis. assoc. prof. art history U. Del., 1974-78, prof. art conservation, 1978-84, Mayer prof. artists techniques, 1984-88, prof. art, art history and art conservation, 1988-92, Harriet T. Baily prof. art, art conservation, art history and mus. studies, 1992—. Cons., lectr. Nat. Tchr. Inst./Nat. Gallery of Art, Washington, 1990—. Author: (exhbn. catalog) The Art and Archives of Ralph Mayer, 1984; co-author (exhbn. catalog) Milk and Eggs: The American Revival of Tempera Painting, 1930-1950, 2002; co-curator (exhbn.) Brandywine River Mus., Akron Art Mus., Spencer Mus., U. Kans., 2002; one person show Susan Isaacs Gallery, Wilmington, Del., 1990, work in mus. collections Balt. Mus. of Art. Sec. bd. dirs. Gay and Lesbian Alliance of Del., Wilmington, 1991-93; co-chair Lesbian, Gay, Bisexual Caucus of Commn. to Promote Racial and Cultural Diversity, U. Del., 1992-99, chair faculty senate com. on diversity and affirmative action, 1993-95, 97-98. Democrat. Anglo-Catholic. Avocations: reading, gardening. Office: Univ of Delaware Mus Studies 301 Old College Hall Newark DE 19716 E-mail: hilton@udel.edu.

BROWN, ILENE DE LOIS, special education educator; b. Wichita, Kans., Aug. 17, 1947; d. Homer DeWitt and Estella Lenora (Cleland) Rusco; m. Gale Robert Aaroe, Nov. 23, 1967 (div. July 1983); 1 child, Candice Yvonne. BEd in Elem. Edn., Washburn U., Topeka, 1969; MS, Nazareth Coll. Rochester, 1979. Cert. tchr. Idaho. Emotionally disturbed trainer Rochester Mental Health Ctr., Greece, N.Y., 1970-71, West Ridge, Greece, 1971-72; tutor kindergarten through grades 6 Craig Hill, Greece, 1978-79; resource rm. tchr. math. English Village, Greece, 1979-80; resource rm. tchr. grades 4-6 Lakeshore, Greece, 1980; tutor, translator Guadalajara, Mex., 1980-82; tchr. grade 1 English John F. Kennedy Sch., Guadalajara, 1982-83; tchr. various grades Greenleaf (Idaho) Friends Acad., 1983-89; resource tchr., high sch. spl. edn. community work coord. Middleton (Idaho) Primary Sch., 1989-91, tchr., 1991—, tchr. 2d grade, 1990—. Sunday sch. tchr. Mem. Coun. for Exceptional Children, Coun. for Children with Behavior Disorders and Learning Disabilities (officer, sec. state chpt. 1991-92), Middleton Profl. Devel. Com. (chairperson profl. devel. com. 1992-95—), Idaho Edn. Assn., Middleton Edn. Assn., Phi Delta Kappa. Avocations: bicycling, traveling, reading, birdwatching. Office: Mill Creek Elem Sch 500 N Middleton Rd Middleton ID 83644-5499 E-mail: ibrown@msd134.org.

BROWN, JACQUELINE REYNELL, primary school educator; b. Florence, Ala., Aug. 30, 1955; d. Grady Reynolds and Emma Helen (Ezell) Patton; m. Marvin Randall Brown, June 24, 1977; children: Bethany Ann, Laura Ashley. BS, U. N. Ala., 1977, MA, 1988; cert. dental hygiene, U. Ala., 1976. Kindergarten tchr., Florence, Ala., 1978—. Mem. NEA, Ala. Ednl. Assn., Beta Sigma Phi, Kappa Delta Pi. Avocation: geneology. Home: RR 7 Box 53 Florence AL 35634-9807

BROWN, JAMES ALLISON, anthropology educator; b. Evanston, Ill., Jan. 16, 1934; s. Richard Paul and Olive (Harris) B.; m. Constance Margaret Kimball, Aug. 5, 1967 (div. 1975); 1 child, Douglas Alfred Kimball; m. Judith Quinn Drick Toland, Oct. 1, 1978 (div. 1981); m. Ruth Aizuss

Migdal, Jan. 29, 1997; 1 child, Samuel James Migdal-Brown. AB, U. Chgo., 1954, MA, 1958, PhD, 1965. Asst. prof. Anthropology and Computer Inst. Stovall Mus. Okla., 1965-66; asst. prof. dept. anthropology and computer instrn. soc. sci. rsch. Mich. State U., 1966-69, assoc. prof., 1967-71, rsch. assoc., 1967-71; assoc. prof. dept. anthropology Northwestern U., Evanston, Ill., 1971-79, prof., 1979—, chair, 1989-95. Rsch. assoc. Field Mus. Natural History, Chgo., 1989—; editor Ill. Archaeol. Survey, Urbana, 1966-78, bd. dirs., 1978-85, 88-91, pres., 1991-93; vis. fellow Clare Hall Coll., Cambridge, 1987-88, life fellow, 1989—; advisor dir. registration and edn. State of Ill., 1977, NSF, NEH, Nat. Geographic Soc., AAAS, Time-Life Books, Readers Digest Books, Smithsonian Press, U. Chgo. Press; scientific advisor on redesign Mus. of Ocmulgee Nat. Monument, Macon, Ga., 1978-80. Author: (with others) Pre-Columbia Shell Engravings from Craig Mound at Spiro, Oklahoma, Vols. 1-6, 1975-83, Ancient Art of the American Woodland Indians, 1985; author: Aboriginal Cultural Adaptations in the Midwestern Prairies, 1991, The Spiro Ceremonial Center, 1996; editor: Essays on Archaeological Typology, 1982, Archaic Hunters and Gatherers in the American Midwest, 1983, Prehistoric Hunters and Gatherers: The Emergency of Cultural Complexity, 1985. Sec. Found. for Ill. Archaeology/Ctr. for Am. Archaeology, 1973-83, bd. dirs., 1973—, mem. exec. com., 1984—; mem. Ill. and Mich. Canal Nat. Heritage Corridor Commn., 1985-87, 98—; bd. dirs. Ill. State Mus., 1985-99, chmn. bd., 1995-99; bd. dirs. Mississippi Valley Archaeol. Ctr., 1986-2003. With U.S. Army, 1957-59. Grantee NSF, 1970, 72, 74, 77, 87, Nat. Park Svc., 1980, 86, Ill. Dept. Transp., 1978, Ill. Historic Preservation Agy., 1980, 85, 86, Am. Philos. Soc., 1973, Wenner-Gren Found., 1974; fellow NEH; recipient Disting. Svc. award Soc. Am. Archaeology, 1999. Fellow AAAS, Am. Anthrop. Assn.; mem. Current Anthropology (assoc.). Home: 2238 N Geneva Ter Chicago IL 60614-3716 Office: Northwestern U Dept Anthropology 1810 Hinman Ave Evanston IL 60208-0809

BROWN, JAY MARSHALL, retired secondary school educator; b. Bklyn., July 26, 1933; s. Sidney and Bertha (Swirsky) Brown; m. Merle Thelma Kaminsky, Nov. 4, 1956; children: Sidney Matthew, Ellen Beth Factor. BS in Journalism, NYU, 1955, MA in Am. Civilization, 1960; postgrad., Yeshiva U., 1958-60, U. Conn., West Hartford, 1968-70; 6th yr. profl. diploma, So. Conn. State Coll., 1977. Pub. rels. dir, asst. credit mgr. Colonial Sand & Stone Co., N.Y.C., 1955-60; employment counselor N.Y.C. Dept. Welfare, 1960-63; attendance tchr. Bd. Edn., N.Y.C., 1963-65; youth dir. Jewish Community Ctr., Rochester, N.Y., 1965-67; exec. dir. Conn. Valley Regional B'nai B'rith Youth, New Haven, 1967-70; resource tchr. Sheridan Mid. Sch., Bd. Edn., New Haven, 1970-72; learning ctr. tchr. Bd. Edn., New Haven, 1972-74; social studies tchr. Troup Mid. Sch., Bd. Edn., New Haven, 1974-80; history tchr. Hillhouse HS, Bd. Edn., New Haven, 1980-93; ret., 1993. Tchr. U.S. history New Eng. Acad. Jewish Studies, New Haven, 1984—85; specialist audio-visual and media Quinnipiac Coll., Hamden, Conn., 1982. Contbr. articles to profl. jours. Chmn. clear sch. mission com. Hillhouse HS, New Haven, 1984, mem. effective sch. steering com., 1984, mem. sch. planning and mgmt. team, 1988—91, coord. teenagers adv. program, 1989—91, mem. faculty senate, 1991—93; acting pres. Alliance Mentally Ill, 1993—94, pres., 1995—; mem. Commn. on Disabilities Town of Hamden, 2001—, chair Commn. on Disabilities, 2002—; corr. sec. Jewish Hist. Soc., New Haven, 1980—81; v.p. Regency Hills Condo Assn., 1994—95; active Mental Health Month Com., 1995—99; mem. Family resource Ctr. com. Consultation Ctr., 1994—98; coord. Mental Health Network Spkrs. Bur., 1996—97, 1998; facilitator Journey of Hope Ednl. Program, 2002—; vice chmn. Regional Mental Health Bd., Catchment Area 7, 1997—2002; mem. rev. and evaluation team State Regional Mental Health Bd. Dist. 2, 1996—2000, vice chmn., 1997—2000; bd. govs. Inst. Learning and Retirement, 1998—2000; coord. New Haven County's Mental Illness Awareness Week, 1998—, People Helping People Program, 1998—; mem. Hamden Commn. Disability Rights and Obligation, 2001—; chmn. Hamden Commn. Disability Rights, 2002—03; mem. Hamden Dem. Town Com., 1974—76; pres. Brotherhood Mishkan Israel, 1976—78, 1983—87, 1988—89, 2001—02, sec., 1997—98, treas., 1998—2001; asst. treas. Congregation Mishkan Israel, 1983—84, chmn. budget com., 1987—88, chmn. house and property com., 1979—84, trustee, 1978—84, 1986—92, 1994—2003, mem. pers. com., 1996—2002, mem. abatement com., 1997—98, libr., archivist, 1981—84, mem. ops. com., 1999—2002. Recipient Man of Yr. award of Merit, Congregation Mishkan Israel's Brotherhood, 1978, People Helping People award, Sears and NAMI, 2001. Mem.: New Haven County Ret. Tchrs. Assn. (v.p. 1994—95, sec. 1997—2003), Phi Delta Kappa. Democrat. Jewish. Avocations: philately, polit. items, sports items, cmty. svc.. Home: 25 Wright Ln Hamden CT 06517-2126 E-mail: jay_m_brown@sbcglobal.net., jmb25@juno.com.

BROWN, JEANNE PINKETT, physical education educator; b. Washington, Mar. 19, 1935; d. Alfred Shelton and Leland H. (Chapple) Pinkett; m. Maurice Alvin, Apr. 17, 1960; chidlren: Maurice Jr., Mark Anthony. BS, Va. State U., 1957. Tchr. Portsmouth (Va.) Bd. Edn., 1957-58; attendance officer Washington Bd. Edn., 1958-59, tchr., 1959-61, Arlington (Va.) Bd. Edn., 1961—, track coach, 1979—. Vol. Children's Ctr. Dept. Human Svcs., Washington, 1960-87. Mem. AAPEHRD, Nat. Edn. Assn., Arlington Edn. Assn., Va. Educators Assn., Nat. Edn. Assn. Avocations: artistic framing, art collecting, window treatments. Home: 2011 30th St SE Washington DC 20020-3305

BROWN, JOAN HALL, elementary school educator; b. Montgomery, Ala., Sept. 12; d. Leo Nathaniel and Bertha (Glaze) Hall; m. Tyrone Brown, Aug. 25, 1984. BS in Elem. Edn. cum laude, Ala. State U.; MEd cum laude, Auburn U., Montgomery, 1989. Cert. tchr., Ala. Tchr. Resurrection Sch., Montgomery, 1985-89, St. John the Bapt. Cath. Sch., Montgomery, 1989-91; tchr., former asst. prin. St. John Resurrection Cath. Sch., Montgomery, 1991-94; tchr. Highland Gardens Elem. Sch., Montgomery, 1994—. Mem. sch. bd. Resurrection Sch., 1987-88, advisor, editor sch. newspaper; textbook com. Mobile Diocese, Montgomery, 1985-87, mem. English proficiency com., 1991-92; coord. State Spelling Bees, 1989, St. John the Bapt. Cath. Sch., 1990-91, St. John Resurrection Cath. Sch., 1991-94, textbook com. 1993-94; fin. com. Highland Gardens Sch., v.p. programs. Mem. Resurrection Cath. Ch.; mem. Montgomery County PTA. Grantee Arts Coun. Montgomery, 1991, 93, 94. Mem. NEA, Ala. Edn. Assn., Capitol Area Reading Educator, Nat. Honor Soc., Deka Philos. Svc. Orgn. (v.p. 1985—), Internat. Reading Assn., Kappa Delta Pi. Democrat. Roman Catholic. Avocations: reading, bicycling, volleyball, calligraphy, aerobics. Home: 705 N Pass Rd Montgomery AL 36110-2906

BROWN, JOAN RENEE, music educator; b. East St. Louis, Ill., Nov. 20, 1950; d. Dorris Lee Boyle and Mable Cotton; m. Edward Brown, Aug. 20, 1972; children: Katherine Kine, Arama Mara. MB, So. Ill. U., Edwardsville, 1972. Tchr. music, choir dir. King Jr. High Sch., East St. Louis, Lincoln Sr. High Sch., East St. Louis, Normandy Sr. High Sch. Recipient Boys & Girls Club of Am. award, Appreciation award, Ch. of God, Apple for the Tchr. award, Iota Phi Lambda, 2000. Mem. Nat. Assn. Jazz Educators, Music Educators Nat. Conf., Am. Choral Dir. Assn., Ill. Music Edn. Assn., Sigma Gamma Rho (appreciation award). Home: 1475 Gaty Ave East Saint Louis IL 62201-3210

BROWN, JOHN S. educational association administrator; BA, Brown U.; MS, PhD, U. Mich. Dir. Xerox, Palo Alto Rsch. Ctr., Calif., 1990; chief scientist Xerox Corp., 1992; bd. mem. Nat. Acad. Edn., NYC, 2003—. Co-founder Inst. for Rsch. and Learning. Co-author (with Paul Duguid): The Social Life of Information. Fellow: Am. Assn. Artificial Intelligence; mem.: Nat. Assn. Edn. Office: Nat Acad Edn NYU Sch Edn 726 Broadway 5th Fl New York NY 10003-9580 also: 5 Cambridge Ctr 8th Fl Cambridge MA 02142 E-mail: nae.info@nyu.edu.

BROWN, JOHN WALTER, vocational education supervisor; b. Waverly, Va., Dec. 13, 1937; s. Wilburt Herman and Martha Ann (Holmes) B. BS in Vocat. Indsl. Edn., Va. State U., 1968; MEd in Vocat. Indsl. Edn., Pa. State U., 1970; cert. advanced study in edn., Johns Hopkins U., 1973; PhD in Vocat. Indsl. Edn., Pa. State U., 1976. Cert. tchr., advanced profl., prin., supr., supt., vocat. edn., Md. and Pa. Drafting instr. Peabody Sr. High Sch., Petersburg, Va., 1962-63; electronics instr. Hampstead Hill Jr. High Sch., Balt., 1965-66, Calverton Jr. High Sch., Balt., 1966-73, dep. prin., 1975-80; vice prin. Carver Vocat. Tech. Sr. High Sch., Balt., 1975; ednl. specialist Balt. City Pub. Schs., 1974, coord., 1980-84, div. specialist, 1984-89, curriculum specialist, 1989-93; prin. House One Rowland Intermediate Sch., Harrisburg, Pa., 1993-94; coord. profl. pers. devel. Pa. State Dept. of Edn., Harrisburg, 1994—2003, coord. profl. pers. devel. and acting mgr., divsn. product devel., 2001—. Instr. Va. State U., Petersburg, 1962-63, Coppin State Coll., Balt., 1972-73; mem. Balt. City Adv. Coun. on Vocat. Edn. and trade adv. subcoms. With U.S. Army, 1963-65. Named to Va. State U. Sports Hall of Fame. Mem. Am. Vocat. Edn. Assn., Nat. Assn. Indsl. and Tech. Edn., Pub. Schs. Adminstrs. and Suprs. Assn., Johns Hopkins Alumni Assn., Pa. State U. Alumni Assn., Va. State U. Alumni Assn., Iota Lambda Sigma, Phi Delta Kappa. Methodist. Avocations: sports, reading, travel, writing, gardening. Home: 5914 Charnwood Rd Baltimore MD 21228-1205 Office: Pa State Dept Edn Bur of Career and Tech Edn 333 Market St Harrisburg PA 17101-2210 E-mail: jobrown@state.pa.us.

BROWN, JULIA ANNE, elementary school educator; b. Tulsa, Nov. 19, 1947; d. Clint George Jr. and Marjorie (Pulver) Garrett; m. Henry Christopher Noll, June 24, 1972 (div. June 1980); 1 child, Christopher Overstreet; m. Darryl Howard Brown, July 22, 1983; 1 child, Kelly Garrett. BS in Elem. Edn., Okla. State U., 1970. Cert. elem. tchr., Okla. 3d grade tchr. Wash. Elem. Sch., Ponca City, Okla., 1978-80; sch. libr. Roosevelt Elem. Sch., Ponca City, Okla., 1980-91, 3d grade tchr., 1991—, mem. bldg. level team, 1992-95. Mem. Assn. Classroom Tchrs. (rep. Ponca City chpt.). Republican. Methodist. Avocations: gardening, reading, being with my children.

BROWN, JULIE BALDWIN, nursing educator; b. Richmond, Ky., Sept. 6, 1964; d. Charles Earl and Patricia Earlene (Cornellson) Baldwin; m. Scott Grady Brown, Nov. 28, 1987; children: Mallory Katherine, Thomas Christopher. BSN, Ea. Ky. U., 1986; MSN, Bellarmine Coll., 1995. RN, Ky., ambulatory women's health care. Staff nurse U. Ky. Med. Ctr., Lexington, 1987-88, head nurse, clin. rsch. ctr., 1988-91; asst. prof. med. assisting tech. Ea. Ky. U., Richmond, 1991—. Childbirth educator, Lexington, 1986—. Mem. Am. Assn. Med. Assts. (site surveyor and Task Force on Test Constrn.), Ky. Assn. Med. Assts., Sigma Theta Tau, Chi Omega (advisor 1990—), Delta Kappa Gamma. Baptist. Avocation: collecting christmas ornaments. Office: Ea Ky U Med Assisting Dizney # 229 Richmond KY 40475

BROWN, JUNE DYSON, elementary education educator, administrator; b. Petersburg, Va., July 28, 1949; d. James Elmer Sr. and Clara (Foster) Dyson; m. Robert Wendell Brown, Apr. 10, 1971; children: Jason, Joshua, James-Robert. BA in English, Emory & Henry Coll., 1971; MEd in Early Childhood Edn., U. Ga., 1993; EdS, U. Ga, 1998. Cert. elem. tchr., Ga. Tchr. DeKalb County Schs., Decatur, Ga., 1971-72, 76-78, Newton County Schs., Covington, Ga., 1972-74, 80-84, 85-88, Henry County Schs., McDonough, Ga., 1984-85; tchr., grade mgr. Gwinnett County Schs., Berkeley Lake, Ga., 1988-90; tchr., learner support strategist Cobb County Schs., Marietta, Ga., 1990-96, asst. adminstr., 1996—2000; Prin. Lamar County Elem. Sch., 2000—; prof. Piedmont Coll., 2000—. Active North Ga. Conf. Min.'s Wives, Atlanta, 1990-93; pres. Atlanta/Marietta Min.'s Wives, 1991-93 Mem. ASCD, DAR, Internat. Reading Assn., Profl. Assn. Ga. Educators, Kappa Delta Pi, Phi Kappa Phi. Methodist. Avocations: sewing, reading, beachcombing. Home: 811 Avalon Rd Thomaston GA 30286-4011

BROWN, KAREN LUCILLE, elementary school educator; b. Breese, Ill., Sept. 6, 1951; d. Edward William and Mary Ann (Haar) Ford; m. James Kevin Brown, June 30, 1973; children: James, Mark, Ann. BS, So. Ill. U., Edwardsville, 1973. Cert. tchr., Ill. Tchr. Wesclin Community Unit 3, Trenton, Ill., 1973-90; tchr. kindergarten Trenton Elem. Sch., 1991—. Mem. NEA, Ill. Edn. Assn., Wesclin Edn. Assn., St. Mary's Altar Sodality, St. Mary's Cath. Ch. Democrat. Roman Catholic. Avocations: painting, crafts, reading, piano. Office: Trenton Elem Sch 308 N Washington St Trenton IL 62293-1244 Address: 343 Chrysler Dr Fenton MO 63026-2806

BROWN, KAREN RIMA, orchestra manager, Spanish language educator; b. N.Y.C., Apr. 26, 1943; d. Alexander and Leona (Rosenfeld) Jaffe; m. Russell Vernon Brown, Aug. 13, 1966; children: Stephanie Leona and Gregory Russell. BA, Colby Coll., 1965; MA, U. Wis., 1966. Teaching asst. U. Wis., Madison, 1965-66, instr. Spanish Janesville, 1966-68, Baraboo, 1968-70, Eau Claire, 1970-71, Ohio U., Zanesville, 1978-98, assoc. prof., 1998—; mgr. Southeastern Ohio Symphony, New Concord, 1977-99. Lectr. Spanish Muskingum Coll., New Concord, 1984, 97-99; mem., music panelist Ohio Arts Coun., Columbus, 1979-83, 90-93; pres. S.E. Ohio Regional Arts Coun., Zanesville, 1978-80. Bd. dirs. Muskingum County Visitors and Conv. Bur., Zanesville, 1987-90, bd. sec., 1989-90; bd. dirs. Assn. of Two Toledos, 1984-87, Ohio Citizens Com. for Arts, Canton, 1979-84; mgr. emeritus Southestern Ohio Symphony Orch., 1999—. Mem. Am. Assn. Tchrs. Spanish and Portuguese, Ohio Valley Fgn. Lang. Assn., Bus. and Profl. Women, Phi Beta Kappa, Phi Sigma Iota, Sigma Delta Pi (hon.). Democrat. Avocations: travel, consultant to arts organizations, mentor for gifted high school students. Office: Ohio Univ-Zanesville 1425 Newark Rd Zanesville OH 43701-2695

BROWN, KATHLEEN, elementary school educator, consultant; b. Phila., Apr. 25, 1950; d. Charles Vincent and Angela (Piscitello) S.; children: Irene Rochelle Myers-LeGoff, Brian Gregory Myers. AS, Camden County Coll., Blackwood, N.J., 1978; BA, Glassboro State Coll., 1980; MA, Rowan Coll. N.J., 1992. Cert. nursery sch. and elem. edn. tchr. Math. specialist, tchr. 6th grade, 3d grade, 2d grade, gifted and talented class Lindenwold (N.J.) Sch. Dist., 1980—, instr. GED, 1989-90. Cons. Shanahan Edn. Assocs., Gloucester City, N.J., 1990—, Ednl. Info. Resource Ctr., Sewell, N.J., 1991. Sci. fellow Glassboro State Coll., 1987. Mem. NSTA, Nat. Coun. Tchrs. Math. (presenter), Assn. Math. Tchrs. N.J. (presenter), N.J. Edn. Assn., N.J. Math Coalition, Assn. Suprs. and Curriculum Dirs. (presenter), Kappa Delta Pi. Avocations: theater, travel. Office: Lindenwold Sch 550 Chews Landing Rd Lindenwold NJ 08021-3796 Home: 12 Saint Johns Ln Mullica Hill NJ 08062-9646

BROWN, KEVIN L. special education administrator; b. Bronx, N.Y. s. Lawrence Henry and Helen Anna (Kraft) B.; m. Maureen E. Sauer; children: Jason L., Russell K. BBA, Pace U., 1969, MBA, 1973; MS in Edn., L.I. U., 1992; PhD in Sch. Adminstrn. with honors, CUNY, 1997. Cert. spl. edn. tchr., N.Y. Market rsch. zone mgr., sales supv. Am. Greetings Corp., Cleve., 1973-86; mktg. mgr. Action Auto Inc., N.Y.C., 1986-90; asst. chairperson com. on spl. edn., D-13 spl. edn. coord. Boys and Girls High Sch., N.Y.C. Bd. Edn., Bklyn., 1990—. Adj. prof. SUNY-Empire State Coll., L.I., 1988—. Mem. Coun. for Exceptional Children, Kappa Delta Pi. Avocations: travel, camping, bicycling. Home: 150 Rockaway Ave Rockville Centre NY 11570-5924 Office: Boys and Girls High Sch 57 Willoughby St # Std-13 Brooklyn NY 11201-5290 E-mail: keubrown@ix.netcom.com.

BROWN, LAUREN EVANS, zoologist, researcher, educator; b. Waukesha, Wis., Sept. 4, 1939; s. Winston Dever and Julianne Evelyn Brown; m. Jill Rae Hollingshead, Feb. 21, 1968; children: Lara Nell, Kara Anne Nash, Evan Saxon. BS, Carroll Coll., 1961; MS, So. Ill. U., Carbondale, 1963; PhD, U. Tex., Austin, 1967; postgrad., U. Melbourne, Australia, 1968. Rsch. asst. biochem. Dairyland Food Lab., Waukesha, 1960; tchg. asst. Mark Twain Inst., St. Louis, 1961; tchg. and rsch. asst. So. Ill. U., Carbondale, 1961—63; rsch. asst. Pine Hills Field Sta., Pine Hills Swamp, Ill., 1963; tchg. and rsch. asst. U. Tex., Austin, 1963—67; asst. prof. to assoc. prof. Ill. State U., Normal, 1967—77, prof., 1977—; chair sect. ecology, evolution, ethology and systematic biology Ill State. U., 1978—79, chair interdisciplinary studies, 1996—. Endangered species and environ. cons., 1966—; chair undergrad. and grad. curriculum coms. Ill. State U., 1974—83, athletic coun., rsch. grant evaluation com., 1992—95, curriculum infusion program mem., 1995—2002, libr. com., 1997—2002, chair libr. com., 1998—2002, hon. libr., 2002—; mem. Houston Toad Recovery Team US Fish and Wildlife Svc., 1978—84, 1998—; interdisciplinary studies, 1996; affiliate profl. scientist Ill. Natural History Survey, 1997—; presenter in field. Editor: Herpetologica, 1978—81, Alytes, 2000—; mem. editl. bd.: Ill. Natural History Survey, 1999—; contbr. articles to profl. jours. and chapters to books. Grantee in field, 1962—, Rsch. Grant Evaluation Com., 1992—95. Mem.: Council Biology Editors, Internat. Soc. Study and Conservation Amphibians (mem. editl. bd. 2000—), Am. Soc. Ichthyologists and Herpetologists, Declining Amphibian Populations Task Force, Soc. Study Amphibians & Reptiles (conservation com.), Herpetologists' League (bd. trustees 1979—80), Am. Rabbit Breeders Assn. (chair libr. com. 2001—02). Achievements include rediscovery of the near extinct Houston Toad in Lost Pines. Avocations: swimming, hiking, breeding and rearing animals. Home: 15958 E 2550 North Rd Hudson IL 61748-9391 Office: Ill State Univ Dept Biological Sci Campus Box 4120 Normal IL 61790-4120

BROWN, LAURIE MARK, physicist, educator; b. Bklyn., Apr. 10, 1923; s. William and Elvira (Fleischman) B.; m. Judith Kobrin, Dec. 27, 1942 (dec. May 1963); children: Joanna Lisa, Julie Elena; m. Brigitte Dziumbla-Winzeler, June 6, 1969; children: Judith, Jean. AB, Cornell U., 1943, PhD, 1951. Mem. faculty physics Northwestern U., Evanston, Ill., 1950—, prof., 1961-93, prof. emeritus, 1993—. Mem. Inst. for Advanced Study (NSF fellow), Princeton, 1952-53; cons. Argonne Nat. Lab., 1960-70; vis. prof., Vienna, 1966, Rome, 1967, São Paulo, 1972-73 Editor and author profl. books; contbr. articles to profl. jours. Fulbright research scholar Italy, 1958-60 Fellow Am. Phys. Soc. (chmn. div. history of physics 1983-84, 2001-2002). Home: 724 Noyes St Evanston IL 60201-2847

BROWN, LEON CARL, history educator; b. Mayfield, Ky., Apr. 22, 1928; s. Leon Carl and Gwendolyn (Travis) B.; m. Anne Winchester Stokes, Aug. 29, 1953; children: Elizabeth Boone, Joseph Winchester, Jefferson Travis. BA, Vanderbilt U., 1950; postgrad., U. Va., 1950-51, London Sch. Econs., 1951-52; PhD, Harvard, 1962. Fgn. Svc. officer., Beirut, 1954-55, Khartoum, Sudan, 1956-58; asst. prof. Mid. Ea. studies Harvard U., Cambridge, Mass., 1962-66; assoc. prof. Nr. Ea. history and civilization Princeton (N.J.) U., 1966-70, Garrett prof. fgn. affairs, 1970-93, Garrett prof. emeritus, 1993—, chmn. dept. Nr. Ea. studies, 1969-73, dir. program Nr. Ea. studies, 1969-73, 80-93. Author: (with C.A. Micaud and C.H. Moore) Tunisia: The Politics of Modernization, 1964, The Tunisia of Ahmad Bey, 1974, International Politics and the Middle East, 1984, Religion and State: The Muslim Approach to Politics, 2000; editor: State and Society in Independent North Africa, 1966, From Madina to Metropolis: Heritage and Change in the Near Eastern City, 1973, (with Norman Itzkowitz) Psychological Dimensions of Near Eastern Studies, 1977, Centerstage: American Diplomacy Since World War II, 1990, (with Cyril E. Black) Modernization in the Middle East, 1992, Imperial Legacy: The Ottoman Impact On The Balkans & The Middle East, (with Matthew Gordon) Franco-Arab Encounters, 1996, Diplomacy in the Middle East, 2001; translator with commentary: The Surest Path; The Political Treatise of a 19th Century Muslim Statesman, 1967. Served with USAAF, 1945-46. Mem. Middle East Studies Assn. (pres. 1975-76) Home and Office: 191 Hartley Ave Princeton NJ 08540-5613 E-mail: lcbrown@princeton.edu.

BROWN, LILLIAN HILL, retired academic administrator; b. Newport News, Va., Nov. 24, 1932; d. Charlie Wyatt and Caroline Melinda (Rowlett) Hill; m. Louis Franklin Brown, June 30, 1956; children: Avery L., Colin H. BS, Va. State Univ., 1955; MS, U. Bridgeport, 1967, profl. 6th yr. degree, 1983; post grad., So. Conn. State Univ., 1985. Chmn. guidance and pers. svcs. Wilby H.S., Waterbury, Conn., team mem. student assistance team, coord. natural helpers program, proctor SAT coll. bds. prog. Mem. pres.'s adv. bd. Teikyo Post U.; admission advisor com. Naugatuck Valley Comty.-Tech. Coll.; adv. bd. to bd. govs. for higher edn. in Waterbury; adv. panel Racial Imbalance Regulations of Pub. Schs. in Conn.; regional adv. bd. dirs. Bank Boston. Bd. trustees St. Margaret's-McTernan Sch.; bd. dirs., chmn. nominating com. Waterbury Symphony Orch.; trustee, chair nominating com. The Antiquarian and Landmark Soc.; bd. dirs. Children's Comty. Sch.; chmn. bd. dirs. Waterbury chpt. ARC; bd. trustees, chmn. scholarship com. The Waterbury Found.; bd. mgrs., mem. The Waterbury Club; mem. devel. com. Waterbury Hosp. Health Network, Inc.-Waterbury Hosp.; mem. oral history project African Ams. in Waterbury; co-chair Leavenworth Soc./United Way; vestry bd., chalice bearer St. John's Episcopal Ch.; life mem. NAACP; mem. Waterbury chorale; co-founder In Search of Excellence A Scholarship Fund for African Am. Students; incorporator Child Guidance Clinic; co-chair United Way-Leavenworth Soc.; adv. regional bd. Bank Boston. Recipient Plaque for Outstanding Leadership in Cmty., Tribute to Conn. Women, Plaque for Outstanding Leadership in Cmty., Alpha Kappa Alpha, Achievement award Nat. Assn. Negro Bus. and Profl. Woman's Clubs, Inc., Cmty. Svc. award Waterbury Jaycees, 1991, St. John's Order of the Eagle, 1995, Humanitarian Svc. award Anderson's Boys Club, 1999, Cmty. Svc. Vol. of Yr. United Way CNV, 2001. Mem. NEA (life), Conn. Edn. Assn., Waterbury Tchr. Assn., Pupil Pers. and Guidance Assn., The Sch. Counselor (Conn. chpt.), Phi Delta Kappa (Plaque for Dedicated Svc. to U. of Conn. chpt. 1993), Delta Sigma Theta (charter mem. New Haven alumnae chpt., Waterbury alumnae chpt. v.p. 2001)., Waterbury Chorale (v.p.), The Links, Inc. (charter mem. Waterbury chpt.). Avocations: domestic and foreign travel, collecting lladro porcelain, chorale singing, collecting porcelain dolls of color. Home: 59 Timber Ln Waterbury CT 06705-3608

BROWN, LILLIE HARRISON, music educator; b. Cin., July 7, 1937; d. James Albert and Lucille Elizabeth Harrison; m. Frederick Brown, Apr. 12, 1958 (dec. June 1996); children: Kevin Frederick(dec.), Gyll Renee Simpson, Carla Y. BS in Music Edn., U. Cin. Coll. Conservatory of Music, 1961. Music specialist Cin. Pub. Schs., 1961—91, 1999—2002; minister of music, ch. musician Bethel Bapt. Ch., Cin., 1956—. Nominating com. chmn. Coll. Conservatory Alumnae Bd., Cin., 1995—2001; music com. chmn. Hamilton County Ret. Tchrs., Cin., 1992—; mem. NAACP, 1994—. Mem.: Alpha Kappa Alpha (regional music chmn., dir., pres. 1972—76). Home: 1935 Crane Ave Cincinnati OH 45207

BROWN, LILLIE MCFALL, elementary school principal; b. Feb. 29, 1932; d. Clayton and Septertee (Dewberry) McFall; m. Charles Brown, Oct. 4, 1958; 1 child, Eric McFall. BA in Home Econ., Sci., Langston Univ., 1956; MA in Spl. Edn., Chgo. Tchrs. Coll., 1964; MA in Adminstrn., Seattle Univ., 1976. Home econ. tchr. Altue (Okla.) Separate Pub. Schs., 1955-56, first grade tchr., 1956-57, fourth grade tchr., 1957-60; middle sch. tchr. Chgo. Pub. Sch.s, 1960-64; spl. edn. primary tchr. Seattle Pub. Schs., 1966-67, spl. edn. intermediate tchr., 1967-68, program coord., 1968-71, elem. asst. prin., 1971-76, elem. prin., 1976—. Mem. Project READ, Seattle, 1968; chairperson Eighteenth Coll. Fair, Seattle, 2001. Contbr. articles to profl. jours. Treas. African Am. Alliance, 1980—; historian Wash. Alliance Black Sch. Educators, 1991—; vol. Olympic Games, Seattle, 1990; participant First African-African Am. Summit, Ibidjian, Cote d'Ivoire, 1991-92; mem. rsch. bd. advisors Am. Biog. Inst., 1995—; chair 18th Coll. Fair, Seattle, 2001. Sears Found. grantee, 1967; recipient Disting.

Alumni award Nat. Assn. for Equal Opportunity in Higher Edn., 1997. Mem. NAACP, Nat. Assn. Elem. Sch. Prins., Assn. Wash. Sch. Prins., Elem. Prins. Assn. Seattle Pub. Schs., Prins. Assn. Wash. State, Prin. Assn. Seattle Pub. Schs., Ednl. Leadership, Phi Delta Kappa, Kappa Delta Pi, Delta Sigma Theta. Democrat. Baptist. Avocations: swimming, dance, bicycling, travel, reading.

BROWN, LINDA LOCKETT, nutrition management executive, nutrition consultant; b. Jacksonville, Fla., Jan. 8, 1954; d. Willie James and Katie Lee (Taylor) Lockett; m. Thomas Lee Brown, Dec. 18, 1982; children: Ashanti, William, Timothy. BS in Agr., U. Fla., 1975, M in Agr., 1981. Lic. profl. nutritionist; cert. food svc. dir., Ill.; registered dietitian; cert. lifestyle counselor in stres and weight mgmt. Chemist, microbiologist Green Giant Co., Alachua, Fla., 1975-77; lab. technologist II U. Fla., Gainesville, 1977-81, ext. agt. I Ft. Myers, 1981-85, ext. agt. II, 1985-87, West Palm Beach, 1987-88; pres. CINET, Inc., West Palm Beach, 1985—; dir. food & nutrition svcs. Alachua Gen. Hosp., 2002—. Nutritionist Head Start, Jacksonville, Fla.; area supr. Palm Beach County Sch. Food Svc., 1988—90; adj. prof. Palm Beach C. C., Palm Beach, Fla., 1990, Fla. C. C., Jacksonville, 1993—; dir. sch. food svc. St. Johns County, Fla., 1990—; cons. in field; vis. prof. U. Fla. Coop. Ext. Svc., Clay County, Fla., 1996—; instr. U. N. Fla., 1999—2001. Columnist Palm Beach Post, 1989—, Fleming Island News, 2002; contbr. articles to profl. jours.; host nutrition digest radio show Sta. WZNZ-AM, Jacksonville, 1996—. Diabetes educator Diabetes Treatment Ctr. Am., Jacksonville, Fla., 1997—; mem. exec. bd. Cmty. Coordinating Coun., Ft. Myers, Fla., 1985, Am. Heart Assn., Palm Beach, Fla., 1989—90; co-founder Friends of Hearing Impaired Youth, Gainesville, Fla., 1976; tutor-coord. Sampson, Gainesville, 1973; mem. Jr. League, Ft. Myers, 1987, Palm Beach, 1987—90, mem. edn. tng. com., 1989—90, mem. cmty. rsch. com., 1989—90; mem. nutrition com. Am. Heart Assn., Palm Beach, 1989—; mem. Clay County Children's Commn., 2000—, chmn., 2001—02; elected vice chmn. Fla. Health & Human Svcs. Bd., 1993—94, chmn., 1994—96. State U. Sys. Bd. Regents grantee, 1980. Mem.: NAFE, Jacksonville Dietetic Assn., Sch. Food Svcs. Assn., Caloosa Dietetic Assn. (sec.), Palm Beach Dietetic Assn. (cmty. nutrition chair 1988—89, chair legis. com. 1989—90), Am. Dietetic Assn. (network of blacks in nutrition, chair legis. com. 1988—89, chair nominating 1989, sec. 1989—90, state profl. recruitment coord.), Fla. Dietetic Assn. (chair minority issues com., chair membership 1987—88, chair edn. & registration 1988—90, state profl. recruitment coord. rep. Fla. chpt., chair nominating com. 1994—), Am. Diabetes Assn. (mem. profl. adv. com. Jacksonville affiliate 1996), Soc. Nutrition Edn. (legis. network chmn.), Am. Soc. Tng. & Devel., Internat. Food Svc. Execs. Assn. (treas. St. Augustine chpt. 1993—), N. Fla. Profl. Spkrs. Assn., Nutrition Today Soc., Greater Palm Beach Bus. & Profl. Women (minority student mentor, role model mentor), Nat. Spkrs. Assn., Internat. Platform Assn., Nat. Assn. Ext. Home Econs. Agts., Nat. Spkrs. Assn., Epsilon Sigma Phi, Alpha Zeta. Avocations: singing, violin. Office: 1651 Glen Laurel Dr Middleburg FL 32068-8228 E-mail: cinet_inc@msn.com.

BROWN, LINDA M. elementary education educator; b. Alton, Ill., Oct. 13, 1951; d. James E. and Virginia A. (Holm) Meyers; m. Michael C. Brown, Dec. 28, 1974; 1 child, Emilie Lynne. BS in Edn., Ill. State U., Normal, 1974; MAT, Webster U., Kansas City, Mo., 1984. Cert. in gifted edn. Tchr. grades 1-8 Loretto Sch., Kansas City; tchr. 5th and 6th grades Pembroke-Hill, Kansas City, Center Schs., Kansas City, tchr. gifted and talented; computer tchr. K-8 Montessori Sch., Lake Forest, Calif. Recipient Bus. and Edn. Working Together award Joliet C. of C. Mem. Assn. for Supervision and Curriculum Devel.

BROWN, LINDA WEAVER, academic administrator; b. Pottsville, Pa., Aug. 29, 1941; d. Robert Roland and Blanche (Cox) Weaver; m. Harold Lewis Brown Jr., June 9, 1962; children: Garth Weaver, Blythe Elizabeth, Grant Christian. BA, Gettysburg Coll., 1963; MEd, U. Hawaii, 1965; MA, Carnegie-Mellon U., 1970, PhD, 1972. Faculty Point Park Coll., Pitts., 1967-68, asst. dean admissions, 1968-69; faculty Allegheny C.C., Pitts., 1969-72, U. Santa Clara, Calif., 1976-80, Bentley Coll., Waltham, Mass., 1986-88; chair humanities Endicott Coll., Beverly, Mass., 1988-89; v.p. comms. Brown Assoc., Concord, Mass., 1989-91; dir. edn. Bunsai Gakuen Boston Inst Intercultural Comm., Lincoln, Mass., 1991-93; divsn. chair English and ESL Roxbury C.C., Boston, 1994-96; v.p. Brown Assocs., Concord, Mass., 1997—. Cons., spkr. in field. Author book rev. New Perspectives on Down Syndrome, 1989. Bd. dirs. Mental Health Assoc., Middlesex County, 1985-89, Minuteman Assn. for Retarded Citizens, Concord, 1990-92. Named Outstanding Young Woman from Hawaii, Bus. and Profl. Women, 1966; faculty grantee Allegheny C.C., 1969, 70, 71, U. Santa Clara, 1978, 79, 80. Mem. AAUP, AAUW, Alpha Psi Omega. Avocations: music, advocacy, reading, cross cultural studies. Home: 384 Caterina Hts Concord MA 01742-4752 Office: Brown Assocs 384 Caterina Hts Concord MA 01742-4752

BROWN, LLOYD DAVID, association executive, management educator; b. New Haven, Conn., Mar. 22, 1941; s. Lloyd and Laura Whitney (Dodge) B.; m. Jane Gibson Covey, June 14, 1969; children: Rachel Covey, Nathan Lloyd. BA in Social Rels., Harvard Coll., 1963; LLB, MPhil in Organizational Behavior, Yale U., 1969, PhD in Organizational Behavior, 1971. Community organizer Peace Corps, Dessie, Ethiopia, 1963-65; from asst. to assoc. prof. organizational behavior Case Western Res. U., Cleve., 1971-80; pres., chmn. Inst. Devel. Rsch., Boston, 1980—2001; from assoc. prof. to prof. Boston U. Sch. Mgmt., 1981-2001, chmn. organizational behavior, 1981-86, 97-99, faculty dir. doctoral program, 1993-95. Fulbright vis. lectr. Pub. Enterprise Ctr. for Continuing Edn., New Delhi, India, 1979-80; cons. Ford Found., WHO, World Bank, USAID, Asia and Africa, 1980—; vis. prof. pub. policy Kennedy Sch. Govt., Harvard U., 1999-2001, lectr., 2001—; dir. internat. programs Hauser Ctr. for Non-Profit Orgn., 1999—. Author: Learning From Changing, 1974, Managing Conflict at Organizational Interfaces, 1983, The Struggle for Accountability: NGO'S, Social Movements and the World Bank, 1998, Practice-Research Engagement for Civil Society in a Globalizing World, 2001; contbr. articles to profl. jours. Assoc. Synergos Inst., N.Y.C., 1987-99; mem. adv. coun. Vol. Fgn. Aid, Washington, 1997-2001; bd. dirs. World Edn. Inc., 2001—, Inst. for Devel. Rsch., 1980-2001, PRIA Internat., 1995—, Oxtam Am., 2002—, Consensus Bldg. Inst., 2002. Mem. Acad. Mgmt. (pres. organizational devel. div. 1984-85), Assn. for Rsch. on Nonprofit Orgn. and Vol. Action, Internat. Assn. for Third Sector Rsch. Democrat. Avocations: skiing, tennis, science fiction. Office: Harvard Univ Hauser Ctr Nonprofit Orgns 79 JFK St Cambridge MA 02138 E-mail: dave_brown@harvard.edu.

BROWN, LOWELL SEVERT, physicist, educator; b. Visalia, Calif., Feb. 15, 1934; s. Volney Clifford and Anna Marie Evelyn (Jacobson) B.; m. Shirley Isabel Mitchell, June 23, 1956; 1 son, Stephen Clifford. AB, U. Calif., Berkeley, 1956; PhD (NSF predoctoral fellow 1956-61), Harvard U., 1961; postgrad., U. Rome, 1961-62, Imperial Coll., London, 1962-63. From rsch. assoc. to assoc. prof. physics Yale U., 1963-68; mem. faculty U. Wash., Seattle, 1968—, prof. physics, 1970-2001, prof. emeritus, 2001—; mem. staff Los Alamos (N.Mex.) Sci. Lab., 2001—. Vis. prof. Imperial Coll., London, 1971-72, Columbia U., N.Y.C., 1990; vis. scientist Brookhaven Nat. Lab., summer, 1965-68, Lawrence Berkeley Lab., summer 1966, Stanford Accelerator Ctr., summer, 1967, CERN, Geneva, summer, 1979, Inst. for Theoretical Physics, U. Calif., Santa Barbara, winter 1999; mem. Inst. Advanced Study, Princeton, N.J., 1979-80; cons. Los Alamos Nat. Lab., spring 1999, vis. scientist, 1991; vis. physicist Deutches Elektronen-Synchrontron, Hamburg, 1986 Author: Quantum Field Theory, 1992; mem. editl. bd. Phys. Rev., 1978-81; editor Phys. Rev. D, 1987-95; contbr. articles to profl. publs. Trustee Seattle Youth Symphony Orch., 1986—95. Postdoctoral fellow NSF, 1961-63; sr. post-doctoral fellow, 1971-72; Guggenheim fellow, 1979-80 Mem. Ferrari Club of Am. (dir. Northwest region 1999—). Home: 621 Halona Santa Fe NM 87505 Office: X-7 MS F699 PO Box 1668 Los Alamos NM 87545 E-mail: lowellb@ferrariclub.com.

BROWN, MARGUERITE JOHNSON, music educator; b. El Paso, Tex., Mar. 31, 1940; d. Don Lee and Eloise (Watson) Johnson; m. R. Don Lumley, Dec. 1961 (div. July 1982); children: Jessica Lumley Rodela, Jeffrey Tate Lumley; m. Gilbert Bivins Brown, Oct. 27, 1989; 1 stepchild, Erich Michael. MusB in Piano Pedagogy with honors, U. Tex., 1962; M in Liberal Arts with honors, So. Meth. U., 1974. Tchr., group piano Dallas Ind. Sch. Dist., 1965-72; tchr. music theory Canal Zone Coll., Panama Canal Zone, 1977-79, musical theater accompanist, 1975-79; tchr. class piano Del Mar Coll., Corpus Christi, Tex., 1980-82; tchr., edn. dir. piano & keyboard Coast Music Co., Corpus Christi, Tex., 1982-87; tchr. class piano, theory Del Mar Coll., Corpus Christi, Tex., 1987-90, performance accompanist, 1993-94; owner, piano tchr. pvt. Studio 88, Corpus Christi, Tex., 1994—2001; resident music dir. Monastery St. Clare, Brenham, Tex., 2001—. Mem.: Nat. Guild Piano Tchrs. (adjudicator), Nat. Guild Piano Tchrs., Dallas Music Edn. Assn. (pres. piano divsn. 1969—71), Music Tchrs. Nat. Assn., Corpus Christi Music Tchrs. Assn. (pres. 1995—97), Nat. Fedn. Music Clubs. Office: Monastery Saint Clare 9288 Hwy 105 Brenham TX 77833-7269 Home: 9280 Highway 105 Brenham TX 77833-7269

BROWN, MARTHA WOLFE, elementary school educator; b. Milton, Fla., July 28, 1962; d. Walter Stanley and Lois Anne (Haines) W. BA, Fla. So. Coll., 1985. Cert. elem. tchr., Fla. Tchr. Hernando Elem. Sch., Citrus County Sch. Bd., Fla. Active in ch. and community orgns. Mem. Kappa Delta Pi, Delta Kappa Gamma (scholar), Order Ea. Star, Lioness Club. Home: 3530 E Buffalo Ln Hernando FL 34442-4113

BROWN, MELBOURNE THOMAS, SR., elementary education educator; b. Elizabeth, N.J., June 29, 1941; s. Melbourne Amos and Winifred (O'Connor) B.; m. Deanna Elena Davies, Oct. 8, 1961; children: Melbourne T. Jr., Mathew Timothy. AA, Moorpark Coll., 1971; BA, Calif. State U., Northridge, 1973, MEd, 1980. CLU. Ins. underwriter various agys., L.A., 1962—; tchr. Simi Valley (Calif.) Unified Sch. Dist., 1974-76, L.A. Unified Sch. Dist., 1976—. Speaker ednl. confs., 1987—. Author, inventor (learning system books and game) Wonder Number, 1986. Pres. Young Dems., L.A., 1968; chair Neighborhood Coun., Simi Valley, 1984. Cpl. USMC, 1958-61. Fellow NEA, VFW, ACLU. Methodist. Avocations: reading, bike riding, traveling. Home and Office: Interactive Dimensions 1825 Gaviota Ct Simi Valley CA 93065-2207

BROWN, NANCY ELLEN, language educator, writer; b. Inglewood, Calif., May 2, 1960; d. Robert Alexander and Elizabeth (Collins) B.; life ptnr. Susan Mary Allen. AA in Gen. Studies, Cypress (Calif.) Coll., 1985; BA in French, Calif. State U., Fullerton, 1986; MA in Multicultural Edn., Calif. State U., Dominquez Hills, 1991. Profl. clear multi-subject credential with lang. emphasis, Spanish bilingual cultural specialist credential, Calif.; nat. bd. cert. tchr. Bilingual tchr. L.A. Unified Sch. Dist., 1986—, mem. site leadership coun., 1989—, grant and proposal writer, 1990—. Pvt. cons. Best Practice Partnership, 1998—. Mem. ASCD, Calif. Assn. for Bilingual Edn., United Tchrs. L.A. (chpt. chmn. 1989—). Democrat. Home: 6714 La Marimba St Long Beach CA 90815 Office: Hawaiian Avenue Sch 540 Hawaiian Ave Wilmington CA 90744-4998 E-mail: sinetag@earthlink.net.

BROWN, NANCY MILLER, school system administrator; b. Dayton, Ohio, Jan. 24, 1931; d. Nathan Edgar and Treva (Heath) Miller; m. Ermon Royal Brown, Jan. 30, 1954; children: Craig(dec.), Kyle, April. BS in Edn., Miami U., 1953; postgrad., Wright State U., U. Dayton, Sinclair CC, Dayton. Cert. elem. edn. grades K-8. Tchr. Dayton City Schs., 1953-89, mem. bd. edn., 1994-2001, v.p., 1995—97, pres., 1998. Mem., bd. dirs. Dayton Area Sch. Employees Fed. Credit Union, 1981—, chmn. bd. dirs., 1988, chair supervisory com., 1994—; profl. conf. day coord. Dayton City Schs., 1985—86, 1986—87; mem. com. initial stds. guide talented and gifted Ohio Dept. Edn., Columbus; mem. evaluation team Nat. Coun. Accredit Tchr. Edn., Washington; mem. adv. coun. Coll. for Srs. Sinclair CC, 2001—03. Bd. dirs., adv. bd. Voluntary Action Ctr., Dayton, 1990—93; mem. loan and investment com. Citywide Devel. Corp., Dayton, 1990—; mem. City of Dayton Neighborhood Leadership Inst., 1983, rec. sec. alumni assn., 1999—2001, pres., 2002—03; bd. govs. Ctr. Health Cmtys., Wright State U., 1990—, chair, 2001—; sec., treas. Miami Valley Leadership Alumni, 1990—95. Mem.: Western Ohio Edn. Assn. (chair 1989—93, 2002—, founder, ret.), Ohio Edn. Assn.-Ret. (adv. coun., vice chair 1993—97, chairperson 1997—2000, chmn. 2001—). Avocations: reading, volunteering, camping, embroidery. Home: 4121 Banning Ct Dayton OH 45405-5202 E-mail: wickedwitch70@juno.com.

BROWN, NORA M. private school educator; Tchr. Dr. James H. Naylor Sch., Hartford, Conn., 1973—; area coord., sec., third v.p. Hartford Fed. of Tchrs., 1994—2000. Office: Dr James H Naylor Sch 639 Franklin Ave Hartford CT 06114-3089

BROWN, PAMELA ANN, chemical engineering educator; b. Bakersfield, Calif., Mar. 10, 1955; m. Harvey William Brown. BS, SUNY, Albany, 1977; SM, MIT, 1979; PhD, Polytech. U., 1989. Rsch. chem. engr. Am. Cyanamid, Stamford, Conn., 1978-80; staff scientist Pall Corp., Glen Cove, N.Y., 1980-81; cons., instr., rsch. asst. Polytech. U., Bklyn., 1984-92; instr. Barnard Coll., Manhattan, N.Y., 1992-93; asst. prof. Stevens Inst., Hoboken, N.J., 1993-98; assoc. prof. NYC Tech. Coll., Bklyn., 1998—. Cons. P.M. Brown Engring., Baldwin, N.Y., 1989—; advisor Woman Engr. mag., Hauppage, N.Y., 1994—; chairwoman Mini Tech. Conf., Hoboken, 1995-96. Contbr. articles to profl. jours. including Indsl. and Engring. Chemistry, AIChE Jour., Chem. Engring. Edn. Candidate 19th AD NY, 1996; committewoman Dem. Party, Baldwin, NY, 1995-99. Mem. Am. Chem. Soc. (faculty advisor student chpt. 1998—), Phi Beta Kappa. Achievements include development of method of terephthalic acid purification. Home: 3356 Bertha Dr Baldwin NY 11510-5025

BROWN, PETER DAVID GILSON, German language educator; b. Alton, Ill., Oct. 18, 1943; s. Weir Messick and Vivian Virginia (Bauer) B.; m. Elaine Greenblatt, Sept. 10, 1966 (div. Aug. 1970); 1 child, Stephanie; m. Susan Roberta Jensen, Sept. 11, 1970 (div. Mar. 1992); 1 child, Andrew J.B. BA summa cum laude, Columbia Coll., 1964; MA, Columbia U., 1965, PhD, 1971. Instr. of German Columbia U., N.Y.C., 1967-71, Barnard Coll., N.Y.C., 1968-71; asst. prof. German SUNY, New Paltz, 1971-74, assoc. prof. German, 1974-86, prof. German, 1986—99, disting. svc. prof. German, 1999—. Dir. SUNY Acad. Summer Program, Hamburg/Stade, Fed. Republic Germany, 1974-98; mem. editorial adv. bd. Peter Lang Pub., N.Y.C., 1986—. Author: Oskar Panizza: His Life and Works, 1983; editor: (series of 100 vols.) Studies in Modern German Literature, 1985—, Studies in German Jewish History, 1995—, Women in German Literature, 1997—; contbr. articles to profl. jours. Chmn. Mid-Hudson Nuclear Opponents, New Paltz, N.Y., 1974-80; legis. coord. Safe Energy Coalition of N.Y. State, Albany, 1974-75; bd. dirs. Environ. Planning Lobby, Albany, 1976-77, Hudson River Sloop Clearwater, Poughkeepsie, N.Y., 1981-83. Recipient Advanced German Studies Prize German Consulate, 1963, Experienced Faculty Travel award NYS/UUP, 1987; Woodrow Wilson fellowship Woodrow Wilson Found., 1964; Tech. Assistance Study grant U.S. Dept. Energy, 1980, Chancellor's Award for Excellence in Teaching, 1993, Bundesverdienstkreuz, 1999, Tchr. of Yr. award, 2000. Mem. Am. Assn. of Tchrs. of German, Modern Lang. Assn. of Am. Avocations: writing poetry, piano playing, photography. Office: SUNY Dept Fgn Langs 414 Jacobson Faculty Tower New Paltz NY 12561-2499

BROWN, RADIE LYNN, secondary school educator; b. Stuart, Fla., Nov. 14, 1962; d. Albert R. III and Martha Katherine (Brooks) Krueger; m. Richard G. Brown, Jan. 2000; 1 child, Travis. AB, Ga. Wesleyan Coll., 1984; postgrad., U. Cen. Fla. Tchr. English Brevard County Sch. System, Melbourne, Fla., 1984-86; bank officer, tng. dir. First Nat. Bank and Trust, Stuart, 1987-90; dir. Christian edn. 1st Presbyn. Ch., Stuart, 1990-91; prof. English, Indian River Community Coll., Ft. Pierce, Fla., 1990-91; employment comm. cons. Curtis and Assocs., Grand Island, Nebr., 1992-93; exec. dir. Community HelpCenter, Grand Island, 1993, Martin County Literacy Coun., Stuart, Fla., 1993-94; mgr. ednl. svcs. The Palm Beach Post subs. Cox Enterprises, Inc., West Palm Beach, Fla., 1994-95; with audiotext advt./programming dept. The Stuart (Fla.) News, 1995-96; lang. arts tchr. Southport Middle Sch., Port St. Lucie, Fla., 1996—2002; h.s. English tchr. Lincoln Park Acad., Ft. Pierce, Fla., 2002—. Republican. Lutheran. Avocations: gardening, golf, equestrian sports. Home: 3505 SW Buckskin Trl Okeechobee FL 34974

BROWN, RAQUEL LYNN, elementary school educator; b. Frankfurt, Germany, Sept. 3, 1966; Came to U.S., 1974; d. Rufus Lee and Estella (William) B. BS, Hampton U., 1989; MA in Elem. Edn., Regent U., 1993, postgrad., 2000. Elem. tchr. Newport News Pub. Schs., Va., 1999—2001; asst. prin. McIntosh Elem. Sch., 2001—. Avocations: reading, tutoring, swimming.

BROWN, RHODERICK EDMISTON, biochemistry researcher, educator; b. Hendersonville, N.C., Apr. 7, 1953; s. Rhoderick Edmiston and Jane Patterson (Servais) B.; m. Laura Strippel Brown, Sept. 12, 1981; children: Caroline Finley, Christopher Hamilton. AB in Chemistry and Zoology, U. N.C., 1975; PhD in Biochemistry, Wake Forest U., 1981. Rsch. assoc. dept. biochemistry U. Va., Charlottesville, 1981-86; asst. prof. Hormel Inst., U. Minn., Austin, 1986-92, assoc. prof., 1993-98, prof., 1999—. Grad. faculty dept. biochemistry/molecular biology Mayo Grad. Sch., Mayo Clinic, Rochester, Minn., 1989—. Mem. editl. bd. Chemistry and Physics of Lipids, 1996—; contbr. articles to profl. jours., chpt. to book. Mem. AAAS, Am. Heart Assn. (coun. on basic rsch.), Am. Soc. Cell Biology, Biophys. Soc., Microscopy Soc. Am., Minn. Acad. Scis. Achievements include research on biochemical, cell biological and molecular biological glycolipid transfer protein from mammalian cells, spontaneous transfer of glycolipids between membranes, monolayer film characterization of sphingolipids and their interactions with other lipids and proteins, sphingolipid-sterol interactions and structural basis of raft or microdomain formation, freeze fracture and freeze etch electron microscopic characterization of lipid mesomorphic structure, structural basis of glycolipid nanotube formation and facilitation of 2D protein crystallization, model membrane surface structure and localization of toxins and lectins bound to glycolipids in membranes. Office: U Minn Hormel Inst 801 16th Ave NE Austin MN 55912-3679

BROWN, ROBERT ALAN, atmospheric science educator, research scientist; b. LA, June 11, 1934; s. Carl Clayton and Olive (Hirst) B.; m. Marcia Louise Jobe, Dec. 12, 1957; children: Vanessa, Morgan, Tristin. BS, U. Calif., Berkeley, 1957, MS, 1963; PhD, U. Wash., 1969. Fellow U. Wash., Seattle, 1969-70, Nat. Ctr. Atmospheric Sci., Boulder, Colo., 1970-71; rsch. prin. investigator U. Wash. Polar Sci. Ctr., Seattle, 1971-73; prof. atmospheric sci. U. Wash., Seattle, 1983—. Adj. prof.: Naval Postgrad. Sch., 1983, Fraunhofer Inst., Garmish, Germany, 1991, U. Concepcion, Chile, 1996, 2003, Ecole Poly., Paris, 1997. Author: Analytic Methods in Planetary Boundary Layer Models, 1973, Fluid Mechanics of the Atmosphere, 1991, The Tree, 2003; co-author: The Panzaic Principle, Microwave Remote Sensing for Ocean and Marine Weather Forecast Models, Ency. of Earth System Science, Surface Waves and Fluxes: Current Theory, Polar Oceanography, 1990; editor Pacific Ocean Remote Sensing Congress book series, 1992—, Remote Sensing of the Pacific Ocean with Satellites, 1998; contbr. over 80 articles to profl. jours. 1st lt. U.S. Army, 1957-59. Recipient Disting. Sci. award, Pan Ocean Remote Sensing Confs., 2000. Fellow Am. Meteorol. Soc.; mem. Am. Geophys. Union, Am. Oceanographic Soc., Sigma Xi, Phi Kappa Psi. Democrat. Office: U Wash Dept Atmospheric Sci PO Box 351640 Seattle WA 98195-0001

BROWN, ROBERT ARTHUR, chemical engineering educator; b. San Antonio, July 22, 1951; s. Ralph and Lillian (Rilling) B.; m. Beverly Ann Lamb, June 22, 1972; children: Ryan Arthur, Keith Andrew. BS, U. Tex., 1973, MS, 1975; PhD, U. Minn., 1979. Instr. U. Minn., Mpls., 1978; asst. prof. chem. engring. MIT, Cambridge, 1979-82, assoc. prof., 1982-84, prof., 1984—, Warren K. Lewis prof., 1992—, exec. officer dept. chem. engring., 1987-88, head dept. chem. engring., 1989-96, dean Sch. of Engring., 1996-98, co-dir. supercomputer facility, 1989-94, provost, 1998—. Cons. Lincoln Labs., Lexington, Mass., 1985-87, Mobil Solar Energy, Waltham, Mass., 1982-93. Contbr. over 160 articles to profl. jours. Recipient Outstanding Jr. Faculty award Amoco Oil Co., 1981, Camille and Henry Dreyfus Tchr.-Scholar award 1983; named one of Outstanding Young Texans-Execs. U. Tex., 1991. Mem. AAAS, NAE, NAS, AIChE (Allen P. Colburn award 1986, Profl. Progress award 1996), Soc. Indsl. and Applied Math., Am. Assn. Crystal Growth (Young Author award 1985), Am. Phys. Soc., Am. Acad. Arts and Scis. Office: MIT 3-208 Cambridge MA 02139 E-mail: rab@mit.edu.

BROWN, ROBERT DALE, wildlife science educator, department head; b. Red Bluff, Calif., July 31, 1945; s. Charles Arthur and Carol Joyce (Dale) B.; m. Regan Mensch, June 30, 1981; children: Alex, Jason, Adam. Student, U. Calif., Davis, 1963-65; BS, Colo. State U., 1968; PhD, Pa. State U., 1975. From asst. prof. to assoc. prof. Tex. A&I U., Kingsville, 1975-81; from assoc. rsch. scientist to rsch. scientist C. Kleberg Wildlife Rsch. Inst., Kingsville, 1981-87; dept. head Miss. State U., Starkville, 1987-93, Tex. A&M U., College Station, 1993—, coord. Gulf Coast coop. ecosys. studies unit, 2002—. Dir. Inst. for Renewable Resources, College Station, 1995—. Editor: Antler Development in Cervidae, 1983, Translocation of Wild Animals, The Biology of Deer, 1991. Lt. col. USMCR, 1968-93. Mem. Am. Inst. Nutrition, Wildlife Soc. (v.p.), Am. Fisheries Soc., Nat. Assn. Univ. Fish and Wildlife Programs (past pres.), Soc. for Range Mgmt. Episcopalian. Avocations: scouting, hunting, fishing, scuba, sailing. Office: Tex A&M U # 2258 Dept Wildlife Fisheries Sci College Station TX 77843-2258 E-mail: rdbrown@tamu.edu.

BROWN, ROBERT WALLACE, retired mathematics educator; b. Portland, Oreg., May 20, 1925; s. Bert and Stella (Conway) B.; m. Doris Arrilda Burroughs, Sept. 4, 1948; children: Robert Wallace, Janice Dianne. BS, Pacific U., 1950; MS, Oreg. State U., 1952, PhD, 1958. Mathematician, Nat. Bur. Standards, Corona, Calif., 1952-54; Mathematician Boeing Co., Seattle, 1958-66; vis. asso. prof. Oreg. State U., Corvallis, 1966-67; prof. math. U. Alaska, Fairbanks, 1967-82, head dept., 1967-77, 79-82; vis. prof. math. Lewis and Clark Coll., Portland, Oreg., 1982-85; ret., 1985. Contbg. author: Error in Digital Computation, 1965. With USNR, 1942—45. Mem. Math. Assn. Am., Am. Math Soc., AAAS, Sigma Xi, Pi Mu Epsilon, Sigma Pi Sigma. Home: 20755 SW Prindle Rd Tualatin OR 97062-9701

BROWN, ROGER DALE, academic administrator; b. Durant, Okla., Sept. 16, 1943; s. Paul Bruce and Blanch Elizabeth (Barr) B.; m. Judie Ann MacDermott, June 18, 1944; children: Roger Dale Jr., Jeffrey Alan. BA in Edn., Southea. State U. Okla., 1967; MEd, Ctrl. State U., Edmond, Okla., 1973; EdD, East Tex. State U., 1982. Dir. choir Beaver (Okla.) Pub. Sch., 1967-70, Borger (Tex.) Pub. Sch., 1970-73; dir. choir, chairperson dept. music Frank Phillips Coll., Borger, 1973-91, coll. dean, 1991—97; pers. and tng. mgr. H.B. Zachary Co., 1997—98; v.p. for acad. affairs Western Okla. State Coll., Altus, 1999—. Pres. Tri-City Concert Assn., Borger, Tex., 1976-78, Magic Plains Arts Coun., Borger, 1983-85.; U.S. fed. govt. funds to Tex. higher edn. coordinating bd. grant to Frank Phillips Coll.; bd. dirs.

Southwestern Okla. Workforce Investment Bd., 1999—; mem. Okla. State Regents for Higher Edn., Coun. on Instrn., 1999—. Carl Perkins grantee in vocat. edn., 1991—. Mem. Tex. Adminstrs. of Continuing Edn. (chmn. West Tex. region 1993-96, state bd. dirs. 1993-96, chmn. Panhandle tech-prep consortium bd. dirs. 1996—), Okla. Two-Year Chief Acad. Officers (chair 2002-03), Rotary Internat. (mem. bd. vocat. svc. Borger club 1994-95, song leader 1982-85), Phi Delta Kappa. Methodist. Avocations: reading, gardening, singing. Office: Western Okla State Coll 2801 N Main St Altus OK 73521

BROWN, RUBYE GOLSBY, secondary education educator, artist; b. Youngstown, Ohio; d. Clifford and Augusta Bell (Blalock) Golsby; m. Robert L. Brown (dec.); children: Harlean J. Preston, Charles, Louis, Carson, Gloria, Robin, Debbie. BA in Edn., Youngstown (Ohio) State Coll., 1956, BS, 1979, MS in Sociology, Edn. and Adminstrn., 1981; Cert. in History and Govtl. Econs., Youngstown State U., 1989. Credit mgr. Klivan's, Youngstown, 1953-56; sec. City Hall, Treasurer's Office, Youngstown, 1956; substitute tchr. Chaney High Sch., Youngstown, 1981-92; tchr. Round Rock High Sch., 1992—; instr. Austin (Tex.) Community Coll., 1993—; owner Custom Craft, Austin, 1993—. Instr. in art, pub. speaker on crime and drug abuse. Mem. Ohio Bd. Health, 1980—; pres. Mahoning County Courtwatch, 1987—; ednl. specialist Police Dept. Task Force, Youngstown, 1989—; vol. Olin E. Teaque Detention Ctr.; former v.p. Cmty. Action Bd. Youngstown; former mem. Welfare Agy., Youngstown; former mem. Welfare Bd. Mahoning County; former v.p. Health Sys. Agy. Ea. Ohio; former 5th ward committeewoman Youngstown Dem. Com. Recipient Health Care award, Columbus State Bd. Health, 1988. Mem. ASCD, Am. Univ. and Coll. Women, Cedar Park C. of C. Democrat. Baptist. Avocations: reading, crafts and ceramics, art work.

BROWN, SANDRA LEE, art association administrator, watercolorist; b. Chgo., July 9, 1943; d. Arthur Willard and Erma Emily (Lange) Boettcher; m. Ronald Gregory Brown, June 21, 1983; 1 child, Jon Michael. BA in Art and Edn., N.E. Ill. U., 1966; postgrad., No. Ill. U. Cert. K-9 tchr., Ill. Travel agt. Weiss Travel Bur., Chgo., 1959-66; tchr. Chgo. Sch. Sys., 1966-68, Schaumburg (Ill.) Sch. Dist. 54, 1968-94, creator coord. peer mentoring program for 1st-yr. tchrs., 1992-96; cons. Yardstick Ednl. Svcs., Monroe, Wis., 1994—2003; exec. dir. Monroe Arts Ctr., 1996—2001, Monroe Area Coun. for the Arts, Madisonville, Tenn., 2002—03; arts mgmt. cons. Helping Hands, Non-Profit Consulting, Knoxville, Tenn., 2003—. Mem. adv. bd. Peer Coaching and Mentoring Network, Chgo. suburban region, 1992-94; peer cons. Schaumburg Sch. Dist. 54, 1988-94. Exhibited in group shows Court House Gallery, Woodstock, Ill., Millburn (Ill.) Gallery, Gallerie Stefanie, Chgo., Monroe Arts Ctr., 1997. Campaign chmn. for mayoral candidate, Grayslake, Ill., 1989; campaign chmn. for trustee Citizens for Responsible Govt., Grayslake, 1991. Mem. Lakes Region Watercolor Guild, Delta Kappa Gamma (chmn. women in arts Gamma chpt. Ill. 1992-94, Alpha Mu chpt. 1995-97), Cmty. Arts League (Athens, Tenn.). Avocations: gardening, musician for barn dances, pre-war Appalachian, blues and cajun music, research collecting 78 rpm records. Home and Office: Helping Hands Non-Profit Consulting PO Box 1456 Athens TN 37371

BROWN, SARAH RUTH, accountant, educator; b. Chattanooga, July 3, 1956; d. Elmon Huey Sr. and Janie Margaret (Stevens) B. BS, Athens State Coll., 1977; MBA, U. North Ala., 1981; D of Bus. Adminstrn., Miss. State U., 1990. CPA, Ala. Staff acct. Garrard, Humphries, and Snow CPAs, Muscle Shoals, Ala., 1978-80; div. acct. State of Ala. Hwy. Dept., Tuscumbia, 1980-84; grad. asst. Miss. State U., Starkville, 1984-85; instr. U. North Ala., Florence, 1985-90, asst. prof., 1990-92, assoc. prof., 1992-97, eminent scholar chair sch. bus., 1994-95, prof., 1997—. Rsch. grant, U. North Ala., 1987. Mem. AICPA, AAUP, Inst. Mgmt. Accts. (dir. ednl. projects 1986-87, comty. responsibilities 1987-89, v.p. profl. edn. 1990-91), Am. Acctg. Assn., Midsouth Inst. Accts., Ala. Assn. Acctg. Educators, Pi Tau Chi, Beta Gamma Sigma, Phi Kappa Phi. Methodist. Avocations: tennis, swimming, biking, reading, canoeing. Office: U North Ala PO Box 5206 Florence AL 35632-0001 Business E-Mail: srbrown@una.edu.

BROWN, SCOTT WILSON, educational psychology educator; b. Greenwich, Conn., Dec. 1, 1952; s. Vernon Watson and Elizabeth (Rounds) B.; m. Mary Margret pearson, July 28, 1974; children: Matthew, Melissa, Steven. AB in Psychology, Boston U., 1974; MS in Psychology, Montana State U., 1975; PhD in Psychology, Syracuse U., 1980. Prof. ednl. psychology U. Conn., Storrs, 1980—, chair dept. psychology, 1994—2000. Mem. editl. bd. Computers in Schs. jour., 1985—, Internat. jour. Inst. Media, 1995—; contbr. articles to profl. jours. Grantee: IBM, 1991, U.S. Ctrs. for Disease Control, 1991-98, Conn. Dept. Health Svcs., 1992, NSF, 2001-, OERI, 2001-. Mem. APA, Am. Psychol. Soc., Am. Ednl. Rsch. Assn., Northeastern Ednl. Rsch. Assn. (pres. 1991-92). Congregationalist. Home: 26 Cowles Rd Willington CT 06279-1704 Office: U Conn 249 Glenbrook Rd Storrs Mansfield CT 06269-2064

BROWN, SHARI K. special education educator; b. Detroit Lakes, Minn., Nov. 5, 1973; d. Kermit and Marie Schultz; m. Christopher A. Brown, June 20, 1998. BA, Concordia Coll., 1996; postgrad., Moorhead State U., 1997. Lic. specific learning disabilities. Tchr. specific learning disabilities Moose Lake (Minn.) Cmty. Schs., 1997—98, Sebeka (Minn.) Pub. Schs., 1999—. Mem.: Edn. Minn.-Sebeka.

BROWN, SHERI LYNN, artist, poet, educator; b. Bluefield, W.Va., Nov. 22, 1968; d. James H. and Rosa B. Wilkes. BA Comml. Art and Advt., Concord Coll., 1992. Owner T.J. Cool Advt., 1992—; writer Hill Top Records, Hollywood, Calif., 2001. Author numerous poems in anthologies. Mem. I Am His choir Scott St. Bapt. Ch., 1983—87. Mem.: Internat. Soc. Poets. Avocations: art, writing, trumpet, french horn, mellophone. Home: 120 Russell Terr Bluefield WV 24701-2932

BROWN, STEVEN E. retired educational association administrator; b. Manitowoc, Wis., Oct. 26, 1951; s. Norman J. and Marda Brown; m. Lillian Pastina, Feb. 14, 1992; m. Jeannine Desmarais, June 9, 1974 (div. May 9, 1984); 1 child, Aimée. BA, U. Ariz., 1973; MA, N.Mex. State U., 1976; PhD, U. Okla., 1981. Instr. U. Okla., Norman, 1981—82; consumer skills coord. Ind. Living Project, Norman, Okla., 1982—84; disability programs specialist Office of Handicapped Concerns, Oklahoma City, 1984—87; exec. dir. Progressive Ind., Norman, 1987—90; tng. dir. World Inst. on Disability, Oakland, Calif., 1990—93; co- founder Inst. on Disability Culture, Las Cruces, N.Mex., 1994. Adj. prof. U. San Francisco, 1993—96; poet in residence Another Planet, Las Cruces, 1999—2001; co-founder Inst. on Disability Culture, Las Cruces, N.Mex., 1994; resident scholar U. Hawaii at Manou, Ctr. on Disability Studies. Author: Independent Living: Theory & Practice, 1994, Investigating a Culture of Disability: Final Report, 1994, Pain, Plain and Fancy Rappings: Poetry from the Disability Culture, 1995, Voyages: Life Journeys, 1996, Celebrating Passion, Relentlessness and Vision: The Manifesto Editorials, 2001, The Goddess Approaches Fifty: Poems, 2001, Dragon Files in Paradise: An Activists Partial Poetic Autobiography, 2001, A Celebration of Diversity: An Annotated Bibliography about Disability Culture, 2nd edit., 2002, Love Into Forever: A Tribute to Heroes, Martyrs, Friends and Colleagues, 2002, Freedom of Movement: Independent Living History and Philosophy, 2003, Movie Stars and Sensuous Scars: Essays on Journey from Disability Shame to Disability Pride, 2003. Bd. of dir. Hawaii Ctrs. for Ind. Living, 2003—; bd. dirs. Hawaii Ctrs. Independent Living, 2003—; Regional Representative National Council on Independent Living, Washington.

BROWN, SUSAN ELIZABETH S. secondary school educator; b. Niagara Falls, NY, Feb. 25, 1940; d. Harold Marvin and Thelma A. (Lowenberg) Sonnichsen; m. Edward J. Hehre, Jr., June 22, 1963 (div. Apr. 1977); children: Nancy Elizabeth, Edward James III; m. Robert Goodell Brown, July 30, 1988 (div. Jan., 1999). BA, Cornell U., 1963; student, L.I. U., 1970-73; MALS, Dartmouth Coll., 1986; student, U. Geneva, Switzerland. Cert. profl. educator level II, Vt., libr./media specialist level I, Vt. Latin and French tchr. Pinkerton Acad., Derry, N.H., 1964-67; adminstrv. sec. New Eng. Bd. Higher Edn., New Eng. Coun. Higher Edn. Nurses, Durham, N.H., 1968; French tchr. Shelter Island (N.Y.) H.S., 1972; Latin, French, Journalism tchr. Woodsville (N.H.) H.S., 1974-88; Latin, French tchr. Thetford (Vt.) Acad., 1988—2003, telecomm. coord., 1993-94. Alternative cert. bds., N.H., Vt.; adj. prof. English Composition N.H. Comty. Tech. Coll., Claremont, 1998, 99, Littleton, 2000; adv. com. Nat. Latin Exam, 1999; mem. adv. coun. N.H. Coun. on Humanities, 1999. Contbr. articles to profl. jours. Trustee, chair Haverhill (N.H.) Libr. Assn., 1978-88, 2002--; moderator Haverhill U.C.C., 1985; treas. Latham Libr., Thetford, 1992-98. Mem. New Hampshire Classics Assn. (pres. 1966-68, hon. 1970, treas. 1977-87)), Classics Assn. New Eng. (exec. bd. 1981-87, 92-93, 2000-02, Matthew I. Wiencke award for excellence in secondary sch. tchrs. 2000), Sigma Tau Delta. Avocations: singing, library vol., sewing, reading, travel. Home and Office: 1260 Dartmouth Coll Hwy North Haverhill NH 03774 E-mail: roaringcreekfarm@valley.net.

BROWN, THEODORE LAWRENCE, chemistry educator; b. Green Bay, Wis., Oct. 15, 1928; s. Lawrence A. and Martha E. (Kedinger) B.; m. Audrey Catherine Brockman, Jan. 6, 1951; children: Mary Margaret, Karen Anne, Jennifer Gerarda, Philip Matthew (dec.), Andrew Lawrence. BS in Chemistry, Ill. Inst. Tech., 1950; PhD, Mich. State U., 1956. Mem. faculty U. Ill., Urbana, 1956—, prof. chemistry, 1965-93, prof. chemistry emeritus, 1993—, vice chancellor for rsch., dean Grad. Coll., 1980-86, dir.Beckman Inst. for Advanced Sci. and Tech., 1987-93. Vis. scientist Internat. Meteorol. Inst., Stockholm, 1972; Boomer lectr. U. Alta., Edmonton, Can., 1975; Firth vis. prof. U. Sheffield, Eng., 1977; mem. bd. govs. Argonne Nat. Lab., 1982-88, Mercy Hosp., Urbana, 1985-89, Chem. Abstracts Svc., 1991-96, Arnold and Mabel Beckman Found., 1994—, Am. Chem. Soc. Pub., 1996-2001. Author: (with R.S. Drago) Experiments in General Chemistry, 3d edit., 1970, General Chemistry, 2d edit., 1968, Energy and the Environment, 1971, (with H.E. LeMay and B.E. Bursten) Chemistry: The Central Science, 1977, 9th edit., 2003, Making Truth: Metaphor in Science, 2003; assoc. editor Inorganic Chemistry, 1969-78; contbr. articles to profl. publs. Mem. Govt.-Univ.-Industry Roundtable Coun., 1989-94; bd. dirs. Champaign County Opportunities Industrialization Ctr., 1970-79, chmn. bd. dirs., 1975-78. With USN, 1950-53. Sloan rsch. fellow, 1962-66, NSF sr. postdoctoral fellow, 1964-65, Guggenheim fellow, 1979. Fellow AAAS, Am. Acad. Arts and Scis.; mem. Am. Chem. Soc. (award in inorganic chemistry 1972, award for disting. svc. in advancement of inorganic chemistry 1993), Sigma Xi, Alpha Chi Sigma. Home: 10741 Crooked River Rd Unit 101 Bonita Springs FL 34135-1726

BROWN, THOMAS GLENN, psychology educator; b. Portsmouth, Va., Aug. 10, 1948; s. Harold Clifford and Mary Alice (Rorie) B.; m. Civita Ann Caruso, Jan. 6, 1979; children: Amy Elizabeth Brown, Megan Glenn Brown. BA, U. Va., Charlottesville, 1970; MA, Hollins Coll., Roanoke, Va., 1972; PhD, U. Maine, Orono, 1975. Asst. prof. Utica Coll. Syracuse U., Utica, N.Y., 1975-79, assoc. prof., 1979-84, prof. psychology, 1984—, chmn. div. behavioral studies, 1983-88, dean, 1988—, v.p., 1990-99, pres., 1998, disting. prof., 1999—. Contbr. articles to profl. jours. NIMH grantee. Mem. AAUP, Ea. Psychol. Assn., Ft. Schuyler Club, Ctr. Casaurian Studies (pres.), Psi Chi, Pi Kappa Phi. Methodist. Home: 1321 Graffenburg Rd New Hartford NY 13413-3602 Office: Syracuse U Utica Coll 1600 Burrstone Rd Utica NY 13502-4857

BROWN, VALERIE ANNE, psychiatric social worker, educator; b. Elizabeth, N.J., Feb. 28, 1951; d. William John and Adelaide Elizabeth (Krasa) B. BA summa cum laude (fellow), C.W. Post Coll., 1972; MSW (Silberman scholar), Hunter Coll., 1975; PhD, Am. Internat. U., 1996. Diplomate Am. Bd. Examiners, Am. Bd. Clin. Social Work, Nat. Assn. Social Work; cert. addictions specialist; cert. master hypnotherapist; cert. psychophilogic integration therapist. Social work intern Greenwich House Counseling Ctr., N.Y.C., 1973-74, Metro Cons. Ctr., N.Y.C., 1974-75; sr. psychiat. social worker, co-adminstr. Essex County Guidance Ctr., East Orange, N.J., 1975-80; pvt. practice psychiat. social work, psychotherapy, 1979—. Sr. psychiat. social worker John E. Runnells Hosp., Berkeley Heights, N.J., 1980-86; dir. social work Northfield Manor, West Orange, N.J., 1987; clin. coord. Project Portals East Orange Gen. Hosp., 1987-88; asst. dir. ARS/Century House Riverview Med. Ctr., Red Bank, N.J., 1988-93; sr. clin. case mgmt. specialist Prudential Ins. Co., Woodbridge, N.J., 1993; clin. dir. Greenhouse-KMC, Lakewood, N.J., 1994-2000, Shoreline-KBH, Toms River, N.J., 1996-2000; tech. advisor Nat. Comm. Network, 1988—; mental health clinician III UMDNJ-UBHC, Edison, N.J., 2000—; instr. Brookdale Coll., 1991—; co-founder Women's Growth Ctr., Cedar Grove, N.J., 1979; counselor Passaic Drug Clinic, 1978-80; field instr. Fairleigh Dickinson U., Madison, N.J., 1981-86, Brookdale Coll., 1989-92; field supr. Union Coll., Cranford, N.J., 1986; instr. Sch. Social Work, NYU, N.Y.C., 1980-83, asst. prof., 1983-85; evaluator Intoxicated Driver Resource Ctr., Essex County, N.J., 1987-88. Alt. Monmouth County profl. adv. bd. Named Dist. Alumnae Mother Seton Regional H.S., Clark, N.J., 1997. Mem. NASW (Whittman Lifetime Achievement nominee 1997-98), Psi Chi, Pi Gamma Mu, Sigma Tau Delta. Avocations: reading, swimming, travel. Office: 20 Ellsworth Ct Red Bank NJ 07701-5403

BROWN, VIRGINIA SUGGS, writer, language arts educator, consultant; b. St. Louis, July 14, 1924; d. Clarence and Viola (Hampton) Suggs; m. Charles F. Brown, Jan. 24, 1947. BA, Stowe Tchrs. Coll., 1947; MA, Washington U., St. Louis, 1952; PhD, St. Louis U., 1979. Tchr. elem. edn. St. Louis Pub. Schs., 1945-56, reading tchr. Banneker Clinic, 1956-60, supr., 1960-65; dir. head start office of econ. opportunity St. Louis Human Devel., 1965-66; dir., exec. editor McGraw-Hill Book Co., Manchester, Mo., 1966-89; ednl. cons. Zaner-Bloser, Inc., Columbus, Ohio, 1989-93. Trustee Danforth Found., St. Louis, 1976—; trustee Logan Coll. Chiropractic, Chesterfield, Mo., 1987-97, chmn., 1995-97; mem. com. Westlake Scholarship Found., St. Louis, 1981-84. Sr. author: (textbook series) Skyline Series, 1965; co-author: The New "Discovery" Technique for Art Instruction, 1976, (teaching units) Literacy Plus, 1992-93; editor, contbr. (mag.) Teaching Pre K-8 "Green Pages", 1971— (Ed-Press award 1973). Mem. exec. com. United Way of Greater St. Louis, 1975-83; bd. dirs. Mo. State Bd. Chiropractic Examiners, Jefferson City, Mo., 1982-86; trustee Long Term Care Ombudsman Program, St. Louis, 1988-92; active St. Louis U. Alumni Coun., 1984-87. Recipient Hannah G. Solomon award Nat. Coun. Jewish Women, 1966, Outstanding Svc. award Mo. State Bd. Chiropractic Examiners, 1986, Disting. Svc. award Logan Coll. Chiropractic Alumni, 1991. Mem. ASCD, Internat. Reading Assn., Nat. Assn. for Edn. of Young Children, Pi Lambda Theta (bd. dirs. 1980-86, 1st v.p. 1982-86, Outstanding Svc. award 1985), Phi Delta Kappa. Avocation: bridge. Home and Office: 11717 Westport Crossing Dr Saint Louis MO 63146-4233

BROWN, WARNELLA CHARLIE, speech and language pathologist; b. Summit, Miss., Jan. 4, 1962; d. Richard and Charlie B. (Lee) B. BS, U. So. Miss., 1980; MS, Columbia U., 1990; postgrad., L.I. U., 1993—. Speech therapist N.Y.C. Bd. Edn., 1982-83; elem. tchr. Redeemer Bapt. Sch., L.A., 1984-85; speech therapist N.Y.C. Bd. Edn., 1986—, St. Mary's Hosp. for Children, 1993—; supr. speech improvement tchrs. CSD # 23. Speech therapist Vis. Nurses Assn., Bklyn., 1992. Active PTA United Fedn. Tchrs. of N.Y.C., Bridgestreet AME Ch. Mem. ASCD, NAESP, AAUW, Am. Speech and Hearing Assn., Nat. Assn. Secondary Sch. Prins., Nat. Black Speech, Lang. and Hearing Assn., Nat. Coalition Black Women, N.Y. State Speech, Lang. and Hearing Assn., N.Y.C. Black Speech, Lang. and Hearing Assn., Univ. So. Miss. Alumni Assn., Tchrs. Coll. Alumni Assn., Phi Delta Kappa, Eagles (chpt. 68), Amanath Ct., Queen of South Palace, Alpha Kappa Alpha. Avocations: singing, tennis, drama, writing.

BROWN, WARREN DONALD, adult education educator, retired police officer; b. Bklyn., June 2, 1952; s. William and Connie Lee (Walker) B.; children: Tarnell, Cameron. BA, St. Thomas U., Miami, Fla., 1974; MPA, Fla. Internat. U., 1989; PhD in Conflict Resolution and Analysis, Nova Southeastern U., 2000. Cert. tchr., cert. tchr. adult edn., cert. in police standards, Fla. Substitute tchr. Dade County Pub. Schs., Miami, 1975-76, Paterson (N.J.) Bd. Edn., 1976-77; vet.'s coord. Passaic County C.C., Paterson, 1976-78; tchr. ESL L.A. Unified Sch. Dist., 1979-80; tchr. sci. and English Westview Jr. H.S., Dade County Pub. Schs., Miami, 1980-86; part-time instr. Miami-Dade C.C., 1980-84; tchr. adult edn. Krome Detention Ctr./Sunset H.S., Miami, 1990-91, Am. Adult Edn., Dade County Pub. Schs., 1992—; police officer, ret. sgt. City of Hialeah, Fla.; adj. prof. Criminal Justice Inst., Nova Southeastern U., Union Inst. and Univs.; project mgr. AKAL Security, Inc. Instr. police tng. Sch. of Justice and Safety Adminstrn., Miami, 1992—. Mem./advisor People United to Lead Struggle for Equality, 1994—. Bateman grantee Biscayne Coll., Miami, 1994; recipient Safety Belt award U.S. Dept. Transp., Washington, 1993. Mem. United Tchrs. of Dade, Dade County Police Benevolent Assn., Internat. Chief of Police Assn., Fla. Internat. U. Alumni, St. Thomas U./Biscayne Coll. Alumni. Republican. Words Of Life Ch. Avocations: sports, reading, travel, computers, music. Home: 630 NW 186th St Miami FL 33169-4460

BROWN, WENDY WEINSTOCK, nephrologist, educator; b. N.Y.C., Dec. 9, 1944; d. Irving and Pearl (Levack) Weinstock; m. Barry David Brown, May 2, 1971 (div. Sept. 1995); children: Jennifer Faye, Joshua Reuben, Julie Aviva, Rachel Ann. BA, U. Mass., 1966; MD, Med. Coll. of Pa., 1970; MPH, St. Louis U., 1999. Diplomate Am. Bd. Internal Medicine. Intern U. Ill. Affiliated Hosps., Chgo., 1970-71; resident in internal medicine The Med. Coll. Wis. Affiliated Hosps., Milw., 1971-74; gen. practitioner Vogelweh (W. Germany) Health Clinics, 1975-76; fellow in nephrology Med. Coll. of Wis. Milw. County Med. Complex, Milw., 1976-78; staff physician St. Louis VA Med Ctr., 1978—2003, acting chief, hemodialysis sect., 1983-85, chief dialysis/renal sect., 1985-90; dir. clin. nephrology, 1990—2003; staff physician St. Louis U. Hosps., 1978—2003, St. Louis City Hosp., 1982-85, St Mary's Health Ctr., St. Louis, 1994—2003; chief of staff VA Tenn. Valley Healthcare Sys., Nashville, 2003—. Assoc. prof. internal medicine St. Louis U. Health Sci. Ctr., 1985—98, prof. internal medicine, 1998—2003; prof. medicine Meharry Med. Coll.. Vanderbult Univ., 2003—. Reviewer Clin. Nephrology, Nephrology, Dialysis and Transplantation, Am. Jour. Nephrology, Am. Jour. Kidney Disease, Jour Am. Geriatric Soc., Jour. Am. Soc. Nephrology, Geriatric Nephrology and Urology, Kidney Internat.; med. editor NKF Family Focus; mem. editl. bd. Clin. Nephrology, Geriatric Nephrology, Internat. Urology and Nephrology; contbr. articles to profl. jours. Mem. adv. coun. Mo. Kidney Program, 1985-91, chmn., 1988-89; numerous positions Nat. Kidney Found., 1984—, nat. chmn., 1995-97; bd. dirs. United Way, St. Louis, 1994-2003, Nat. Kidney Found. Ea. Mo. and Metro East, Inc., 1980-94; bd. dirs. Combined Health Appeal Greater St. Louis, Inc., 1988, pres., 1989-92; bd. dirs. Combined Health Appeal Am., 1991-98, sec., 1992-96, vice chmn., 1996-98; editor-in-chief Advances in Replacement Theraoy, 2004—. Named Casual Corner Career Woman of Yr., 1986, Combine Health Appeal of Am. Vol. of Yr., 1991, Olympic Torch Bearer, 1996, St. Louis Health Profl. of Yr., 1997; recipient Upjohn Achievement award, Med. Coll. Wis. Affiliated HOsps., 1972, Cert. of Leadership, St. Louis YWCA, 1989, Chmn.'s award, Nat. Kidney Found. of Ea. Mo. and Metro East, 1990, award of excellence, 2002, Chmn.'s award, Nat. Kidney Found., Washington, 1990, Martin Wagner award, Nat. Kidney Found., 1999, award of excellence, Nat. Kidney Found. Ea. Mo. and Metro East, 2002. Fellow ACP; mem. Am. Soc. Nephrology, Internat. Soc. Nephrology, Coun. on Kidney in Cardiovascular Disease, Am. Heart Assn., St. Louis Soc. Am. Med. Women's Assn., St. Louis Internists (v.p. 1983-84, pres. 1984-85), Women in Nephrology (pres. 2000-02), Internat. Soc. for Peritoneal Dialysis, Am. Geriatrics Soc., Soc. for Exec. Leadership in Acad. Medicine (bd. dirs., program chair 1999—), Alpha Omega Alpha. Home: 100 Frontenac Frst Saint Louis MO 63131-3235 Office: VA Tenn Valley Healthcare Sys 1310 24th Ave S Nashville TN 37212-2637 E-mail: wendy.brown@med.va.gov.

BROWN, WILBUR C. college director; b. Prosperity, S.C., Dec. 20, 1926; s. James F. and Mattie Lee (Suber) B.; 1 child, Grace Marsha Brown-Burns; m. Willie Mae Mayer, Dec. 10, 1950; 1 child, Barbara Brown-Floyd. BS, Benedict Coll., 1950; MA, Columbia U. Tchrs. Coll., 1963; EdD, U. So. Miss., 1976. Math. and sci. tchr. Sch. Dist. # 1, Marion, S.C., 1950-55, from math. and sci. tchr. to prin. Anderson County, S.C., 1955-84; pvt. practice electronic repair Greenville, S.C., 1984-87; coord. resources Morris Coll., Sumter, S.C., 1987-89, coord. elem. edn., 1989-94, coord. resources, faculty devel., 1989—; vol. math. and sci. tchr. Fuller Normal Indsl. Inst., Greenville, S.C., 1994—. Libr. adv. bd., Anderson County, S.C. Nomination com. S.C. Prin. Assn., Columbia, 1976, program com., 1977; com. to elect gov. Dem. Party, Anderson County, 1978. With USAF, 1945-47. Mem. S.C. Assn. Tchr. Educators (recruitment com. 1987), Phi Delta Kappa (sec. 1986-87). Democrat. Baptist. Avocations: electronics, gardening, furniture refinishing. Home: 146 Glenn Rd Greenville SC 29607-2231 Office: The Greenville News PO Box 1688 Greenville SC 29602-1688

BROWN, WILLIAM SAMUEL, JR., communication sciences and disorders educator; b. Pottstown, Penn., Apr. 25, 1940; s. William Samuel and Elizabeth (Gallager) B.; m. Elaine Kay Whitehouse, Aug. 18, 1962; children: William Samuel III, Allen Reed. MA, SUNY, Buffalo, 1967, PhD, 1969. Speech therapist Crawford Cty. Schools, Meadville, Penn., 1962-65; rsch. asst. SUNY, Buffalo, N.Y., 1965-68; prof. U. Fla., Gainesville, Fla., 1970—. Contrib. numerous publications to scientific jours. Postdoctoral fellow U. Fla, Gainsville, 1968-70. Fellow Internat. Soc. Phonetic Sci. (coun. rep. 1980—), Am. Speech-Lang.-Hearing Assn., Acoustical Soc. Am.; mem. Am. Assn. Phonetic Sci. (exec. sec. 1980—). Republican. Presbyterian. Office: U Fla IASCP Dauer 63 Gainesville FL 32611

BROWN, ZANIA FAYE, elementary education educator; b. Muskogee, Okla., Sept. 22, 1954; d. Aaron L.Z. and Teleatha (Sanford) Mahone; m. Benjamin Brown Jr., Oct. 5, 1985. BA in Elem. Edn., U. Mo., 1976, MA in Reading Edn., 1980. Cert. elem. edn. and reading edn., Mo. Elem. tchr. Kans. City Sch. Dist., Mo., 1977—, tchr. chpt. I basic skills, 1990—, Title 1 instrnl. facilitator, 1995-96, mem. profl. devel. team, 1995—96, Title 1 instrnl. facilitator, 1997—; mem. profl. devel. team Kansas City (Mo.) Sch. Dist., 1997—. Mem. Kansas City Equity Cadre, 1996—, profl. devel. team, 1997, co-sec. mentor steering com. for new and beginning tchrs., 1997—; reading recovery tchr., 1999; instrl. coach KCMO Sch. Dist., 2000-03; mentor in field; presenter in field. Site coord. Reading Is Fundamental, 1995—; instrnl. coach Kansas City (Mo.) Sch. Dist., 1999, 2002-03, reading recovery tchr., 1999. Recipient For Kids' Sake Caring award Kansas City TV 5, 1990; named one of Outstanding Young Women of Am., 1980. Mem. Internat. Reading Assn., Nat. Assn. Negro Profl. and Bus. Women, U. Mo. Kansas City Alumni Assn. (life), Alpha Kappa Alpha (corr. sec. Kansas City chpt. 1986-88, treas. 1976, sgt.-at-arms 1984-85), Phi Delta Kappa (v.p. 1993, 2003—, chmn. reading power, 1984, 97, 99, 2001-03, sec. 1991, corr. sec. 1992-93, 2001-03, pres. 1995-97, exec. advisor 1997—, regional chair 1999-2003); mem. Phi Lambda Theta, Ednl. Hon. Society, 2003; Assn. for supervision and curriculum devel. (ASCD). Office: 1211 Mcgee St Kansas City MO 64106-2416

BROWN-EKUE, MAVIS ICILDA, elementary education educator; b. Kingston, Jamaica, Mar. 20, 1945; d. Eustace and Dearest (Dacres) Brown; divorced; Children; Abigail, Matthew. AA, N.Y.C. Cmty. Coll., 1973; BS, Medgar Evers Coll., 1976; MS, L.I. U., 1979; postgrad., Columbia U. Cert. elem. tchr., N.Y. Tchr. elem. Morant Bay (Jamaica) Sch., 1966-70; tchr. Day Care Centre, Bklyn., 1974-77, N.Y.C., 1977-81, Pub. Sch. 191M, N.Y.C., 1981-85, Pub. Sch. 153M, N.Y.C., 1985—. Co-instr. Malcolm-King Coll., N.Y.C., 1980. Contbr. articles to profl. jours. Tutor N.Y.C. Lit. Vol., 1981. Mem. Am. Fedn. Tchrs., United Fedn. Tchrs., Phi Delta Kappa (editor Theta talks). Democrat. Baptist. Avocations: reading, art and crafts, sewing, cooking. E-mail: cildaa@netscape.com.

BROWNELL, BLAINE ALLISON, university administrator, history educator; b. Birmingham, Ala., Nov. 12, 1942; s. Blaine Jr. and Annette (Holmes) B.; m. Mardi Ann Taylor, Aug. 21, 1964; children— Blaine, Allison BA, Washington and Lee U., 1965; MA, U. N.C., 1967, PhD, 1969. Asst. prof. Purdue U., West Lafayette, Ind., 1969-74; assoc. prof., chmn. dept. U. Ala., Birmingham, 1974-78, prof., 1980-90, dean grad. sch., 1978-84, dean social and behavioral scis., 1984-90; provost, v.p. for acad. affairs U. North Tex., Denton, 1990-98; exec. dir. Ctr. Internat. Programs and Svcs. U. Memphis, 1998-2000; pres. Ball State U., Muncie, Ind., 2000—. Sr. fellow Johns Hopkins U., Balt., 1971-72; Fulbright lectr. Hiroshima U., Japan, 1977-78; dir. U. Ala. Ctr. Internat. Programs, 1980-90. Author: The Urban Ethos...., 1975, City in Southern History, 1977, Urban America, 1979, 2d edit., 1990, The Urban Nation 1920-80, 1981; editor Jour. Urban History, 1976-90, assoc. editor, 1990-95. Mem. Birmingham City Planning Commn., 1975-77, Jefferson County Planning Commn., 1975-77, Dallas Com. Fgn. Rels., 1990-98; chmn. Birmingham Coun. on Fgn. Rels., 1988-90. Mem. Am. Hist. Assn., Orgn. Am. Historians, So. Hist. Assn., Philos. Soc. Tex. Presbyterian. Office: Ball State U Office Of Pres Muncie IN 47306-0001

BROWNELL, GORDON LEE, physicist, educator; b. Duncan, Okla., Apr. 8, 1922; s. Roscoe David and Mabel (Gourley) B.; m. Anna-Liisa Kairento; children: Wendy Silverman, Peter G., David L., James K., Piia Kairento, Janne Kairento. BS, Bucknell U., Lewisburg, Pa., 1944; PhD, Mass. Inst. Tech., 1950. Mem. faculty MIT, 1950—, prof., 1970-91, prof. emeritus, 1991—; dir. Physics Rsch. Lab., Mass. Gen. Hosp., Boston, 1950—. Bd. dirs. Neuroresearch Fund. Served to lt. (j.g.) USNR, 1944-46. Fellow Am. Phys. Soc., Am. Nuclear Soc., Am. Coll. Radiology (hon.); mem. Am. Assn. Physicists in Medicine (Coolidge award 1987), Soc. Nuclear Medicine (Paul C. Aebersold award 1975), European Soc. Nuclear Medicine (de Hevesy medal 1979, 2003) Clubs: Union Boat (Boston). Home: 45 Warren St Salem MA 01970-3132 Office: Mass Gen Hosp Physics Rsch Lab Boston MA 02114 also: MIT Cambridge MA 02139 E-mail: g.brownell@verizon.net.

BROWNELL, KELLY DAVID, psychologist, educator; b. Evansville, Ind., Oct. 31, 1951; s. Arnold Buffum and Margaret Elizabeth (Egly) Brownell; m. Mary Jo Gabriele, Aug. 20, 1977; children: Matthew Joseph, Kevin David, Kristy Elizabeth. BA, Purdue U., 1973; PhD, Rutgers U., 1977. Lic. clin. psychologist Conn. Postdoctoral fellow Brown U., Providence, 1977; from asst. prof. to assoc. prof. U. Pa., Phila., 1977—87, prof., 1987-90; prof. psychology Yale U., New Haven, 1991—, prof. epidemiology and pub. health, chair dept. psychology, 2003—, dir. Yale Ctr. Eating and Weight Disorders, 1994-2000, master of Silliman Coll. Author: (book) Handbook of Eating Disorders, 1986, Handbook of Behavioral Medicine, 1988, Eating Disorders in Athletes, 1991, Eating Disorders and Obesity, 1995, vol. 2, 2002, Behavioral Medicine and Women, 1998; contbr. articles to profl. jours. Recipient Cattell award, N.Y. Acad. Scis., 1978, Choice award, ALA, 1989. Fellow: APA (pres. divsn. health psychology 1989—90), Acad. Behavioral Medicine Rsch., Soc. Behavioral Medicine (pres. 1988—89); mem.: Assn. Advancement Behavior Therapy (pres. 1988—89). Office: Yale U Dept Psychology Box 208205 Yale Sta New Haven CT 06520-8205

BROWNFIELD, SALLY ANN, education educator; b. Shelton, Wash., May 6, 1950; d. Kenneth W. and Frances E. (Brown) Selvidge; m. Michael L. Brownfield, Sept. 27, 1968; children: Jess D., Toby J. BA, The Evergreen State Coll., Olympia, Wash., 1982; MEd, Pacific Luth. U., Tacoma, Wash., 1989. Cert. elem. and secondary tchr., Wash. With Indian edn. program Shelton Sch. Dist., 1979-80; chpt. I dir., instr. We-He-Lute Indian Sch., Olympia, Wash., 1983-85; instr. Olympic Coll., Bremerton, Wash., 1985-87; classroom tchr. Hood Canal Sch. Dist., Shelton, 1986—2002; mem. faculty Wash. State U., 2002—. Chairperson multicultural edn. com. Hood Canal Sch. Dist., officer Indian edn. parent com., 1987-94; presenter Rural Edn. Assn. NAt. Conv., 1984; curriculum and facilities devel. com. for Bldg. Shelton Campus of Olympia Coll., Bremerton, Wash., 1993-95. GED instr., 1995; bd. dirs. Mason County Cmty. Network, 1994-95, South Puget Intertribal Planning Agy. Cmty. Network, 1995. Mem.: N.W. Regional. Ednl. Lab. (bd. dirs. 1996—2002), Wash. State Indian Edn. Assn. (bd. dirs. 1995—), Western Wash. Native Am. Edn. Consortium. Avocations: travel, crafts, boating, photography, historiography.

BROWNING, LESLIE O. middle school educator; b. New Site, Ala., Nov. 4, 1937; s. Roy and Vertis (Oliver) B.; m. Adalia Moore, May 1, 1959; children: Kerry, Kenny. BS, Jacksonville U., 1960; Masters, Ala. A & M U., 1970. Head coach Gray YMCA, Gadsden, Ala., 1959-63; head coach football All County John Jones Sch., Gadsden, 1963-66, Sand Rock (Ala.) High Sch., 1966-67; offensive coord. Gaston High Sch., Gadsden, 1967-68; line coach Southside High Sch., Gadsden, 1968-69; head coach football Hinson Jr. High. Sch., Attalla, Ala., 1969-77; coach football Etowah High Sch., Attalla, 1977-78, Etowah Middle Sch., Attalla, 1978-85, indsl. arts tchr. Attalla City, Ala., 1986—. Named Most Valuable Player, Ala. ASA, 1982. Baptist. Avocations: football, basketball, baseball. Home: 123 Larkhaven Dr Rainbow City AL 35906-3007

BROWNLEE, WILSON ELLIOT, JR., history educator; b. Lacrosse, Wis., May 10, 1941; s. Wilson Elliot Sr. and Pearl (Woodings) B.; m. Mary Margaret Cochran, June 25, 1966; children: Charlotte Louise, Martin Elliot. BA, Harvard U., 1963; MA, U. Wis., 1965, PhD, 1969. Asst. prof. U. Calif., Santa Barbara, 1967-74, assoc. prof., 1974-80, prof. history, 1980—2002, spl. advisor to systemwide provost, 1995, assoc. systemwide provost, 1996, prof. emeritus, 2002—. Vis. prof. Princeton (N.J.) U., 1980-81; chmn. dept. history U. Calif., Santa Barbara, 1984-87, acad. senate, 1983-84, 88-90, systemwide acad. senate, 1992-93; dir. U. Calif.-Santa Barbara Ctr., Washington, 1990-91; chmn. exec. com. dels. Am. Coun. Learned Socs., N.Y.C., 1988-90, bd. dirs.; bd. dirs. Nat. Coun. on Pub. History, Boston; bicentennial lectr. U.S. Dept. Treasury, 1989; faculty rep. U. Calif. Bd. Regents, 1991-93; adj. prof. history Calif. State U., Sacto., 1997-99; mem. bd. control, U. Calif. Press, 1996-99; co-organizer Conf. On History of Reagan Presidency U. Calif., Santa Barbara and Vanderbilt U., 2002. Author: Dynamics of Ascent, 1974, 2nd edit., 1979, Progressivism and Economic Growth, 1974, Federal Taxation in America: A Short History, 1996; co-author: Essentials of American History, 1976, 4th edit., 1986, America's History, 1987, 3rd edit., 1997; editor: Women in the American Economy 1976, Funding the American State, 1996; co-editor: The Regan Presidency: Pragmatic Conservatism and Its Legacies, 2003; contbr. numerous articles to profl. jours., chpts. to books. Chmn. schs. com. Harvard Club, Santa Barbara, 1971-80, 85, 86; pres. Assn. for Retarded Citizens, Santa Barbara, 1982-84; 1st v.p. Assn. for Retarded Citizens Calif., Sacramento, 1983-84; pres. Santa Barbara Trust for Hist. Preservation, 1986-87, 95-97, 2002-03; trustee Las Trampas Inc., 1994-97, Calif. State Parks Found., 2002-03. Charles Warren fellow Harvard U., 1978-79, fellow Woodrow Wilson Ctr., Washington, 1987-88; recipient Spl. Commendation, Calif. Dept. Pks. and Recreation, 1988, Oliver Johnson award for Disting. Svc. U. Calif. Acad. Senate, 1998. Mem. Am. Hist. Assn., Orgn. Am. Historians, Econ. History Assn., Am. Tax Policy Inst. Office: U Calif Dept History Santa Barbara CA 93106 Business E-Mail: brownlee@history.ucsb.edu.

BROWN-ZEKERI, LOLITA MOLANDA, elementary school educator; b. Stephens County, Mar. 15, 1963; d. James and Doris (Phillips) Brown; m. Austin Zekeri, Nov. 21, 1998; 1 child: Annabelle Lola. BS with honors, North Ga. Coll., 1985, MEd, 1989, EdS, 1994. Cert. tchr. Tchr., 2nd grade Jackson County Bd. Edn., Nicholson, Ga., 1985-87, chpt. 1 tchr., 1987—98, third grade tchr., 1998—. Chmn. grade level Jackson County Bd. Edn., 2002—03. Author: Exploring Blue Highways, 1995; co-author: Making Learning Funner, So People Want To Learn, A Longitudinal Study of Students' Perceptions About Schooling. Active Paradise AME Ch. trustee 1986-99, asst. Sun. Sch. sec. 1986-99, Sun. Sch. sec., 1999—, young adult choir mem. 1987-2001, Christian Edn. Youth Dept. 2d v.p. 1988—, Vacation Bible Sch. art coord. and tchr. 1986—. Mem. Ga. Edn. Assn., Assn. Childhood Educators Internat., North Ga. Coll. Union Bd. (chmn. decorations/hospitality com. 1983-84, sec. 1984-85), Benton Parent/Tchr. Orgn.

BROXMEYER, HAL EDWARD, medical educator; b. Bklyn., Nov. 27, 1944; s. David and Anna (Gurman) B.; m. C. Beth Biller, 1969; children: Eric Jay, Jeffrey Daniel. BS, Bklyn. Coll., 1966; MS, L.I. U., 1969; PhD, NYU, 1973. Postdoctoral student Queens U., Kingston, Ont., Can., 1973-75; assoc. researcher, rsch. assoc. Meml. Sloan Kettering Cancer Ctr., N.Y.C., 1975-78, assoc., 1978-83, assoc. mem., 1983; asst. prof. Cornell U. Grad. Sch., N.Y.C., 1980-83; assoc. prof. Ind. U. Sch. Medicine, Indpls., 1983-86, prof. medicine, microbiology and immunology, 1986—; sci. dir. Walther Oncology Ctr., Indpls., 1988—, chmn. microbiology and immunology, 1997—. Mem. hematology II study sect. NIH, Bethesda, Md., 1981-86, 95-2000, chair, 1997-2000; adv. com. NHLBI, NIH, Bethesda, 1991-94; chmn. bd. sci. counselors Nat. Space Biomed. Rsch. Inst., 1998—; mem. coun. Nat. Space Biomed. Rsch. Inst., 1999—, MSAB, Viacell Corp.; bd. dirs. Nat. Disease Rsch. Interchange. Assoc. editor Exptl. Hematology, 1981-90, Jour. Immunology, 1987-92, Stem Cells, 1996-97, Brit. Jour. Haematology, 1998—; editor Jour. LeuKocyte Biology, 1995—; sr. editor Jour. Hematotherapy and Stem Cell Rsch., 2000—; mem. editl. bd. Blood, 1983-87, Biotech. Therapeutics, 1988-95, Internat. Jour. Hematology, 1991—, Jour. Lab. Clin. Medicine, 1992—, Jour. Exptl. Medicine, 1992—, Annals Hematology, 1993—, Cell Transplantation, 1994—, Critical Rev. Oncology/Hematology, 1995—, Stem Cells, 1998—, Jour. Blood and Marrow Transplantations, 1998—, Cytokines, Cellular and Molecular Therapy, 1998—l contbr. over 550 papers to prof. publs. Mem. ednl. com. Leukemia Soc. Am., Indpls., 1983—, nat. career devel. study sect., N.Y., 1991-95, 2000—. Recipient Founder's Day award NYU, 1973, Merit award Nat. Cancer Inst., 1987-95, Spl. Fellow award, 1976-78, and Scholar award, 1978-83, Gold medal City of Paris, 1993, World of Difference award Ind. Health Industry Forum, 1997, Leukemia Soc. Am., Landsteiner award Am. Assn. Blood Banks, 2002, Health Care Heroes award Indpls. Bus. Jour., 2002. Mem. AAAS, N.Y. Acad. Scis., Soc. for Leukocyte Biology, Am. Assn. Cancer Rsch., Am. Assn. Immunologists, Internat. Soc. Exptl. Hematology (pres. 1990-91), Am. Soc. Hematology (coun. mem. 2000—), Am. Fedn. Clin. Rsch., Am. Soc. Blood and Marrow Transplantation. Avocation: competitive Olympic-style weightlifting. Home: 1210 Chessington Rd Indianapolis IN 46260-1630 Office: Ind U Sch Medicine 950 W Walnut St Rm 302 Indianapolis IN 46202-5181 Fax: 317-274-7592. E-mail: hbroxmey@iupui.edu.

BROYLES, ARTHUR AUGUSTUS, physics educator, researcher; b. Atlanta, May 16, 1923; s. Richard Johnson and Mary Ruth (Jones) B.; m. Jenna Anne Schneider, Dec. 25, 1943; children: Rhea Diane, David Charne, Bonnie Sue Rote, Frances Eileen Hare. BS with high honors, U. Fla., 1942; PhD, Yale U., 1949. Asst. prof. U. Fla., Gainesville, 1949-50, assoc. prof., 1959-61, prof., 1961-86, prof. emeritus, 1986—; staff physicist Los Alamos (N.Mex.) Sci. Lab., 1950-53; sr. physicist in rsch. RAND Corp., Santa Monica, Calif., 1953-59; cons. Lawrence Livermore (Calif.) Nat. Lab., 1986—90. Vis. prof. U. Adelaide, Australia, 1980; mem. subpanel, nuclear physics panel Nat. Rsch. Co./Nat. Acad. Scis., Washington, 1969. Mem. resource bd. Am. Jour. of Physics, 1974-76; contbr. over 52 articles to profl. jours. Pres. Am. Civil Def. Assn., Starke, Fla., 1962-65, mem., 1965—. Lt. USNR, 1943-45. Fellow Am. Phys. Soc.; mem. Am. Assn. Physics Tchrs., Phi Beta Kappa. Home: 3716 SW 6th Pl Gainesville FL 32607-2901 Office: U Fla Physics Dept Gainesville FL 32611

BROYLES, BONITA EILEEN, nursing educator; b. Ross County, Ohio, Sept. 29, 1948; d. Arthur Runnels and Mary Elizabeth (Page) Brookie; m. Roger F. Broyles, Dec. 29, 1984; children: Michael Richard Brown, Jeffrey Allen Brown. BSN, Ohio State U., 1970; MA with honors, N.C. Cen. U., Durham, 1988; EdD summa cum laude, LaSalle U., 1996. ADN instr., CPR instr. Piedmont C.C., Roxboro, N.C.; instr. nursing Watts Sch. Nursing, Durham; res. float staff nurse Durham County Gen. Hosp., Durham; dir. practical nursing edn., instr. Piedmont C.C., Roxboro, N.C.; maternity patient tchr. Mt. Carmel Med. Ctr., Columbus, Ohio. Second-level coord. assoc. degree nursing faculty Piedmont Community Coll., 1990—. Co-author: Test Manual for Bowden, Dickey, Greenberg Children and Their Families: The Continuum of Care, 1998; author: Clinical Companion for Ashwill and Droske Nursing of Children: Principles and Practice, 1997; author: (with Reiss and Evans) Pharmacological Aspects of Nursing Care, revised 6th edit., 2002; author: Dosage Calculation Practice for Nurses, 2003. Named ADN Educator of Yr. N.C. Assoc. Degree Nursing Coun., 1993; recipient nat. tchg. excellence award Nat. Inst. Staff Orgnl. Devel., U. Tex., Austin, 1998, Faculty Excellence award Piedmont Cmty. Coll., 2001. Office: Piedmont CC Sch Nursing College St Roxboro NC 27573

BROYLES, MICHAEL LEE, geophysics and physics educator; b. Corpus Christi, Tex., Apr. 3, 1942; s. Ned Lee and Marion (Richardson) B.; m. Laura Ruth Ferguson, July 30, 1983; 1 child, William Matthew. BA in Phys. Sci., San Francisco State U., 1965; MST in Physics, U. Wis., Superior, 1972; MS in Geophysics, U. Hawaii, 1977; EdD in Higher Edn., Tex. A&M U., Commerce, 1999. Cert. sec. sch. tchr. Tchr. sci. and math. Upper Lake and Sonoma (Calif.) Pub. Schs., 1966-72; geophys. rschr. Hawaii Inst. Geophysics, Honolulu, 1973-79; rsch. geophysicist Amoco Prodn. Co., Tulsa, 1979-80; exploration geophysicist Mobil Oil Corp., Dallas, 1980-86; prof., chmn. dept. physics and astronomy Collin County C.C., Plano, Tex., 1986—. Mem. editl. bd.: UFO Phenomena Mag., Bologna, Italy, 1976-79; contbr. Sci. Ency., 1979-96; edit bd., Ctrl. European Jour of Physics, 2003, contbr. articles to profl. jours. Grantee NSF, 1991—. Mem. Am. Assn. Physics Tchrs., Tex. Jr. Coll. Tchrs. Assn., Mutual UFO Network (state dir. Hawaii 1975-79, state sect. dir. Dallas County 1987-92). Methodist. Achievements include geothermal research and developing teaching methodologies for physics. Office: Collin County CC 2800 E Spring Creek Pky Plano TX 75074-3300 E-mail: mbroyles@ccccd.edu.

BROYLES, RUTH RUTLEDGE, retired principal; b. Sullivan County, Tenn., July 15, 1912; d. Floyd Lylburn and Ethel Sally (Gross) Rutledge; m. David Lafayette Broyles, Aug. 15, 1937 (dec. Oct. 1980); children: Nancy Ann Broyles McCracken, Edwin Joseph, Dava Lee Broyles Russell. BS, East Tenn. State U., 1934, MA, 1968. Cert. English and biology tchr., Tenn., elem. edn. supr., supt. cert. Tchr. English Jonesborough (Tenn.) High Sch., 1934-38; tchr. 3d and 4th grades Telford (Tenn.) Elem. Sch., 1956-57; tchr. 3d grade Midway Elem. Sch., Jonesborough, 1957-62; tchr. 5th grade Jonesborough Elem. Sch., 1962-67; supr. tchr. corp. program East Tenn. State U., Johnson City, 1967-69; prin. Cherokee Elem. Sch., Johnson City, 1969-78, ret., 1978. Chair person Coun. for Appalachian Christian Village. County commr. Washington County Ct., 1980-90; chair Jonesborough Civic Trust, 1982-85, Watauga Regional Libr. Bd., Washington County, 1982-87, Washington County/Jonesborough Mus., Jonesborough, 1984—, Tenn. Homecoming 1986, 1985-86; mem. Washington County Libr. Bd., 1991—; mem. expansion com. Washington County/Jonesboro Libr., 1997—; mem. Washington County Oak Hill Sch. Edn. Project, 1998—; mem. fin. com. Washington County Bd. Edn., 1991-95; historian Washington County, 1991—; elder, Sunday sch. tchr., chair Christian edn. com. Jonesborough (Tenn.) Presbyn. Ch., 1989-91; moderator Presbyn. Women, chair adminstrv. com. Holston Presbytery, Kingsport, Tenn.; historian Synod of Living Waters Presbyn. Women, Brentwood, Tenn.; mem. Synod of Living Waters Ministry Divsn., Brentwood; mem. ch. coun. Tusculum Coll., Greenville, Tenn.; mem. Bicentennial com. for Washington County State of Tenn., 1993-97; mem., vice-chmn. Appalachian Christian Village Resident Coun., 1998—, chair, 1999—; mem. Washington County Mus. Com. on Oak Hill sch. project, 1998—; mem. expansion com. Jonesborough Libr., Washington County, 1998—. Recipient E. Harper Johnson Human Rels. award for edn. Tenn. Edn. Assn., 1997; named Woman of the Yr., Bus. and Profl. Women, Jonesborough, Tenn. 1975, Hon. Col., State of Tenn., 1989; Ruth Rutledge Broyles Scholarship Fund for tng. tchrs. named in her honor, 1994. Mem. Tenn. Ret. Tchrs. (state pres. 1985-86, Nashville 1978—, legis. asst. East Tenn. 1991-95, Plaque 1985-86), N.E. Tenn. Tourism Coun. (chair, Silver Tray 1989, Outstanding Svc. award 1993), Tenn. Congress Parents and Tchrs. (v.p. Nashville 1948-69), Tenn. Libr. Assn. (trustee Nashville 1984-85), Washington County Ret. Tchrs. (life, chmn. scholarship com. 1991—), Tenn. Ret. Tchrs. Assn., Washington County Hist. Soc. (pres. 1994-96). Presbyterian. Avocations: traveling, historian, preservationist. Home: Jonesborough, Tenn. Died Jan. 17, 2002.

BRUCE, ROBERT JAMES, retired academic administrator; b. Aug. 12, 1937; s. Andrew Carson and Ruth Lillian (Barr) B.; m. Judith Ann Garland, Aug. 29, 1959; children: Kimberley Bruce Campbell, Scott Garland. AB, Colby Coll., 1959; MA, U. Mass., Boston, 1964; postgrad., Boston U., 1964; LHD (hon.), Widener U., 1992, Wilkes U., 2001, Holy Family Coll., 2001. Devel. officer Colby Coll., Waterville, Maine, 1965-70; v.p. Bard Coll., Annandale-on-Hudson, N.Y., 1970-74, acting pres., 1974; v.p. univ. rels. Clark U., Worcester, Mass., 1975; v.p. devel. Widener U., Chester, Pa., 1975-81, pres., 1981—2001, pres. emeritus, 2002—, also trustee. Lectr. Queen Anne's Coll., U.K., Chorley Tchrs. Coll., U.K.; instr. Colby Coll.; chmn. Crozer-Keystone Health System; chmn. Univ. Tech. Park; trustee Episcopal Acad. Trustee Episcopal Acad. Recipient Bard Coll. medal, 1975, Disting. Alumnus award Colby Coll., 1985, Liberty Bell award; Fulbright grantee U.K., 1964-65. Mem.: Assn. Ind. Colls. and Univs. (past chmn.), Pa. Assn. Colls. and Univs., Am. Assn. Higher Edn., Nat. Assn. Ind. Colls. and Univs. (past chmn. bd.), Am. Assn. Colls., St. Andrew's Soc. Pa., Castine Golf Club (Maine), Winter Harbor (Maine) Yacht Club, Union League (Phila.), Phi Kappa Phi. Episcopalian. Home: 670 Heatherton Lane West Chester PA 19380 Office: Widener U Office Pres Emeritus Chester PA 19013

BRUCE, VERONICA HELENE, nursing educator; b. Los Angles, Sept. 20, 1954; d. Estanislau Cruz Lopez and Minnie Delores Moore Lopez; m. Daniel Alexander Bruce, Nov. 6, 1986; children: Kathryn Lee, Rebecca Leigh. BA, UCLA, 1977; BSN, Calif. State U., 1992. RN Calif., Nev., cert. pub. health nurse, Calif., Nev. Nurse L.A. County Clinic, 1992—93, pub. health nurse, 1993—96, El Dorado County, South Tahoe, Calif., 1997, Washoe Tribe, Gardnerville, Nev., 2000—01; health educator, rschr., treatment rschr. Bilingual Health Educators & Rsch., South Tahoe, Calif., 2001—. HIV counselor, L.A. County, 1993—96; supr. pediatric clinic, L.A., 1992—93. Author: Euthanasia, 1990, The Gypsy Culture, 1995; co-author: Manual for Pregnant Teens, 1992. Mem., Child Abuse Resource Team, L.A., 1995. Recipient Perseverance Award, U.S. Army Nurse Corp., 1992; Audrienne Moseley Scholar, UCLA, 1996—97. Mem.: Christian Healing Team, Am. Sch. Health Assn. (scholar 1991), Sigma Thete Tau. Avocations: running, skiing, water-skiing, volleyball. Home and Office: 3313 W River Park Dr South Lake Tahoe CA 96150-5192

BRUCH, JOHN CLARENCE, JR., engineer, educator; b. Kenosha, Wis., Oct. 11, 1940; m. Susan Jane Tippett, Aug. 19, 1967. BCE, U. Notre Dame, 1962; MCE, Stanford U., 1963, PhD in Civil Engring., 1966. Acting instr. engring. Stanford (Calif.) U., 1966; asst. prof. engring. U. Calif., Santa Barbara, 1966-74, assoc. prof. engring., 1974-78, prof. engring., 1978—. Grantee, NSF, 1987—93, 1999—2003, NASA, 1997—2004. Mem. ASCE, Am. Sci. Affiliation, Sigma Xi, Tau Beta Pi. Avocations: golf, jogging. Office: U Calif Mech Engring Dept Santa Barbara CA 93106

BRUCK, ARLENE FORTE, secondary education educator; b. Kingston, N.Y., June 26, 1945; d. Machileo and Lillian (Turco) Forte; m. Laurence J. Bruck; children: Jennifer Lynn, Jason Scott. BA in Latin, Coll. Mt. St. Vincent, Riverdale, N.Y., 1967; MS in Psychology, SUNY, New Paltz, 1971. Cert. in social studies, Latin, elem. edn. Tchr. 2d grade Kingston Schs. Consol., 1967-74, tchr. Latin, psychology and sociology, 1984—. Mem. Mid-Hudson Social Studies Coun., 1992—. Placement chair Jr. League, Kingston, 1982-84; vol. Girl Scouts, Tillson, N.Y., 1981-86, Athletes Against Drugs, Kingston, 1984-87. NEH fellow, 1992; recipient Gender Equity fellowship, Mary Dodge McCarthy award for gen. excellence, 1967, Mid-Hudson Social Studies Coun. Excellence in Tchg. award, 1994, Nat. Honor Soc. Tchr. Recognition award, Wall of Tolerance honoree, Southern Poverty Law Ctr.; named Outstanding Young Woman, 1974, Internat. Biog. Ctr. Woman Yr., 1996-97; N.Y. State Regents scholar, 1963-67, AAUW scholar, 1963-67. Mem. APA, AAUW (v.p. 1970-74, sec. 1975-77, pres. program 1994, pres. 1995-96), N.Y. State Assn. Fgn. Lang. Tchrs. Roman Catholic. Avocations: reading, gourmet cooking, travel. Home: 39 Beth Dr Kingston NY 12401-6148 Office: Kingston High Sch 403 Broadway Kingston NY 12401-4617

BRUCKER, ROBIN RAE, secondary education art educator; b. Cleve., Oct. 13, 1956; d. Robert Ray and Dorothy Jean (Gross) Switzer; m. James Merrill Brucker, July 30, 1983; children: Robert Merrill, Jamie Lee. BA, Mt. Union Coll., 1978; MA, Coll. Mt. St. Joseph, 1988. Instr. art 7-12th grades Northmor Local Schs., Galion, Ohio, 1978-80; instr. art 7th, 9-12th grades Mt. Gilead (Ohio) Exempted Village Schs., 1980—. Tchr. counselor Am. Leadership Study Group, Europe, 1979, 88; advisor Mt. Gilead High Sch. Art Club, 1980—, jr. class, 1986-88; mem. Inservice Com., Mt. Gilead, 1985—, Prin.'s Adv., 1986—; mem. program com. Beta Programs, 1995. Instr. Hobby Horse Craft Shop, Mt. Gilead, 1980-86; juror Morrow County, Marion County community activities and art shows, 1980—; pres. Morrow County Fine Arts Guild, Mt. Gilead, 1984-86, 87—; mem. Mt. Gilead Citizens for Zoning Campaign, 1986. Recipient 1st place award Morrow County Fine Arts Fine Craft Show, Mt. Gilead, 1985, 2d place award, 1986; named one of Outstanding Young Women of Am., 1985. Mem. NEA, Ohio Edn. Assn., Ohio Art Edn. Assn. (rep. publicity 1985-86, North Cen. Outstanding Art Tchr. award 1986). Republican. Methodist. Avocations: traveling, calligraphy, drawing. Office: Mt Gilead High Sch Park Ave Mount Gilead OH 43338

BRUCKNER, MARTHA, academic administrator; Bachelor's degree, Master's degree, U. Nebr., Omaha; Doctorate, U. Nebr., Lincoln. Assoc. supt. for ednl. svcs. Millard (Nebr.) Pub. Schs.; tchr. h.s., asst. prin., prin. pub. schs.; assoc. prof., chairperson ednl. adminstrn. U. Nebr., Omaha. Contbr. articles to profl. jours. Recipient award, Nebr. Coun. Sch. Adminstrs., Nebr. Schoolmasters Orgn. Mem.: ASCD (pres.-elect 2003—, bd. dirs., budget liaison, organizer student chpt. U. Nebr., Omaha). Office: Don Stroh Adminstrn Ctr 5606 S 147th St Omaha NE 68137*

BRUDVIG, GARY W. chemistry educator; b. Grand Forks, N.D., May 10, 1954; s. Glenn L. and Myrna W. Brudvig; m. Colleen M. Brudvig, July 31, 1976; children: Lars, Erik, Karin. BS, U. Minn., 1976; PhD, Calif. Inst. Tech., 1981. NIH predoctoral trainee Calif. Inst. Tech., Pasadena, 1976-80;

Miller postdoctoral fellow U. Calif., Berkeley, 1980-82; asst. prof. Yale U., New Haven, 1982-87, assoc. prof., 1987-91, prof., 1991—, chmn. dept. chemistry, 2003—. Chmn. Eastern Regional Photosynthesis Conf., Woods Hole, Mass., 1985; review panelist Dept. Energy, Washington, 1985, 93,, Dept. Agrl., Washington, 1987, NIH, Washington, 1992, 93, 95, 96, 97, 98; external examiner Oberlin (Ohio) Col., 1996; mem. phys. biochemistry study section NIH, Washington, 2000—. Contbr. numerous articles to profl. jours.; editor: (with others) Photosynthesis Rsch., Am. Scientist, Biospectroscopy; asoc. editor Biochemistry, 2000—. Recipient Scholar award Searle Found., 1983-86, rsch. fellowship Alfred P. Sloan Found. 1986-88, teacher-scholar award Camille and Henry Dreyfus Found., 1985-90. Fellow AAAS; mem. Am. Chem. Soc., Biophys. Soc. (exec. com., bioenergetics subgroup 1994-97), Am. Soc. Photobiology, Internat. Soc. Photosynthesis Rsch., Tau Beta Pi, Phi Beta Kappa. Avocations: canoeing, soccer, guitar. Office: Yale Univ Dept Chemistry PO Box 208107 New Haven CT 06520-8107

BRUESCHKE, ERICH EDWARD, physician, researcher, educator; b. nr. Eagle Butte, S.D., July 17, 1933; s. Erich Herman and Eva Johanna (Joens) B.; m. Frances Marie Bryan, Mar. 25, 1967; children: Erich Raymond, Jason Douglas, Tina Marie, Patricia Frances, Susan Eva. BS in Elec. Engring, S.D. Sch. Mines and Tech., 1956; postgrad., U. So. Calif., 1960-61; MD, Temple U., 1965. Diplomate Am. Bd. Family Practice, also cert. in geriatrics. Intern Germantown Dispensary and Hosp., Phila., 1965-66; mem. tech. staff Hughes Research and Devel. Labs., Culver City, Calif., 1956-61; practiced gen. medicine Fullerton, Calif., 1968-69; dir. research Ill. Inst. Tech. Research Inst., Chgo., 1970-76; research asst. prof. Temple U. Sch. Medicine, 1965-69; mem. staff Mercy Hosp. and Med. Center, Chgo., 1970-76; vis. prof. Rush Med. Coll., Chgo., 1974-76, prof., chmn. dept. family practice, 1976—, program dir. Rush. Christ family practice residency, 1978-93, vice dean, 1992—, acting dean, 1993-94, dean, 1994-2000, v.p. univ. affairs, 2000—02; trustee Anchor HMO, 1976-81, v.p. med. and acad. affairs, 1981—; trustee Synergon Health Systems, 1993-98; vice chmn., bd. dirs. Rush Presbyn. St. Lukes Health Assocs., disting. prof. medicine, 2002—, Rush Med. Coll. of Rush U., 2002—. Sr. attending Presbyn.-St. Luke's Hosp., Chgo., 1976—; med. dir. Chgo. Bd. of Health West Side Hypertension Ctr., 1974—78; bd. dirs. Comprehensive Health Planning Met. Chgo., 1971—74, Fedn. of Ind. Ill. Colls. and Univs., West Suburban Higher Edn. Consortium; adv. com. Edn. to Careers, Health and Medicine/Chg. Bd. Edn. Editor-in-chief Disease-a-Month, 1998—; assoc. editor Primary Cardiology, 1979-85; cons. editor for family practice Hosp. Medicine, 1986—; med. editor World Book/Rush Presbyn. St. Lukes/Med. Ency., 1987—; contbr. articles to profl. jours. Served with USAF, 1966-68. Named Physician Tchr. of Yr. Ill. Acad. Family Physicians, 1988, alumni of yr. Temple U. Sch. Medicine, 1996. Fellow Am. Acad. Family Physicians, Inst. of Medicine of Chgo.; mem. IEEE (chmn. Chgo. sect. Engring. in Medicine and Biology group 1974-75), Internat. Soc. for Artificial Internal Organs, Am. Fertility Soc., Am. Occupational Med. Assn. (recipient Physician's recognition award 1969, 72, 75), Chgo. Med. Soc., Am. Heart Assn., Assn. for Advancement Med. Instrumentation, N.Y. Acad. Scis., Sigma Xi, Phi Rho Sigma, Eta Kappa Nu, Alpha Omega Alpha. Home: 319 N Lincoln St Hinsdale IL 60521-3442

BRUGAM, RICHARD BLAIR, biology educator; b. Phila., Dec. 23, 1946; s. Richard Jerrom and Margaret Suzanne (Blair) B.; m. Ella Suzanne Oren, Aug. 1, 1970; children: Amy Susann, Matthew Richard. BA in Biology, Lehigh U., 1968; M Philosophy, Yale U., 1974, PhD in Biology, 1975. Rsch. assoc. Limnol. Rsch. Ctr. U. Minn., Mpls., 1975-78; asst. prof. So. Ill. U., Edwardsville, 1978-84, assoc. prof., 1984-90, prof., 1990—; vis. scholar U. Wash., Seattle, 1984-85. Chair dept. biol. scis. So. Ill. U., Edwardsville, 1996-2002. Mem. editl. bd.: Jour. of Paleolimnology, 1998—; contbr. articles to Ecology, Archiv fur Hydrobiologie, Jour. of Paleolimnology, Holocene. Sgt. U.S. Army, 1969-72. Recipient J. Willard Gibbs prize Yale U., 1968; grad. fellowship NSF, 1968. Mem. AAAS, Ecol. Soc. Am., Am. Quaternary Assn., Ill. Acad. Scis., Phi Beta Kappa, Sigma Xi (grant 1973). Achievements include discovery that recently deposited sediment of lakes can be used to reconstruct pollution histories of the lakes, that acid lakes on coal mine sites eventually neutralize, that land clearance and watershed development in Pacific Northwest caused lakes to become more alkaline, that the addition of organic matter to acid coal mine lakes causes them to neutralize, that water levels in lakes and bogs in the Upper Peninsula of Michigan have risen in the last 4.000 years due to increase in available moisture. Home: 1400 Lantz Ct Edwardsville IL 62025-3901 Office: So Ill U PO Box 1651 Edwardsville IL 62026-1651

BRUGGE, DIANE ELIZABETH, secondary education educator; b. Ann Arbor, Mich., June 8, 1953; d. Philip Brandin and Olive Elfreda (Saethre) Brugge; m. Steven Edward Miller, July 2, 1977; children: Jason Steven, Sarah Elizabeth, Trevor Philip. BA in Biology, Augustana Coll., 1975; MS in Sci. Edn., U. Iowa, 1983. Cert. secondary edn. tchr., Iowa. Tchr. biology Bettendorf H.S., Iowa, 1975—. Del. leader People to People Youth Sci. Exch., Russia, 1991-92, Australia, 1993-94, 96, 2002, Costa Rica, 1995, France, Austria, Switzerland, Italy, 2003; marine biology/zoology del. to Australia/New Zealand, 1993, 96, 2002; tchr. exch. program, Cramlington, Eng., 2001; organizer student exch. program Bettendorf HS/Cramlington Cmty. H.S., 2002; presenter in field. Bd. dirs. Scott County Resource Enhancement and Protection, 1990—, Bettendorf Trees Are Us; com. mem. Bettendorf Tree Walk, 2002—. Recipient Eddy award, River Action Com., Scott County Tchr. of Yr. award, Scott County Soil and Water Conservation Dist., 1999. Mem. Math. and Sci. Tchrs. Assn. (rep. Scott County 1986-90, pres. 1991-92), Iowa Conservation Edn. Coun., Quad City Engring. and Sci Coun. (co-v.p. tech. edn., scholarships, awards). Lutheran. Avocations: swimming, skiing, sailing, canoeing, backpacking. Home: 3328 S Hampton Dr Bettendorf IA 52722-2650 Office: Bettendorf High Sch 3333 18th St Bettendorf IA 52722-2700 E-mail: dbrugge@bettendorf.k12.ia.us.

BRULL, CAROL JEAN, elementary school educator; b. Hays, Kans., Oct. 30, 1947; d. Hilarius and Henrietta (Leiker) Dinkel; m. Randolph F. Brull, July 26, 1969; children: Christopher, Peter, Jeffrey. BS, Ft. Hays State U., 1969, MS, 1973. Cert. elem. sch. tchr., Kans. Tchr. 4th grade Carey Sch., Newport, R.I., 1969-71; tchr. Title I reading Wilson Sch., Hays, Kans., 1974; tchr. English Wakeeney (Kans.) Grade Sch., 1974-75; tchr. grades 4 and 5 St. Mary's Sch., Ellis, Kans., 1976-85; tchr. lang. arts, math., social studies and sci. grades 6 through 8 Kennedy Mid. Sch., Hays, 1985-98; tchr. grade 5 Holy Family Elem. Sch., Hays, 1998—. Sponsor collection of student writing and art Irish Image, 1994—98; sponsor chess club Holy Family Elem. Sch., 2003—, mem. NCA steering com., vis. team mem. Club/project leader Ellis Sunflowers 4-H Club, 1978—89; dir. Thomas More Prep-Marian Folk Chorus, Hays, 1991—95; dir./organist ch. choir St. Mary's Ch., Ellis, 1973—91. Grantee, McDonald's Corp., 1989, 2000, 2002. Mem. Nat. Coun. Tchrs. of English, Kans. Assn. Mid. Level Educators (mem. state bd. 1987-88), Alpha Delta Kappa. Avocations: reading, counted cross-stitch, quilting.

BRUMFIELD, WILLIAM CRAFT, Slavic studies educator; b. Charlotte, N.C., June 28, 1944; s. Lewis F. and Pauline Elizabeth (Craft) B. BA, Tulane U., 1966; PhD in Slavic langs., U. Calif., Berkeley, 1973. Vis. lectr. U. Wis., Madison, 1973-74; asst. prof. Harvard U., Cambridge, Mass., 1974-80; assoc. prof. Tulane U., New Orleans, 1984-91, prof. Slavic langs., 1992—. Resident dir. Am. Coun. Tchrs. of Russian Pushkin Inst. Program, Moscow, 1979-80; co-dir. Summer Inst. for Coll. Faculty, NEH, 1994; lectr. on architecture, photography and lit. at museums and univs throughout U.S. and Europe. Author: Gold in Azure: One Thousand Years of Russian Architecture, 1983, The Origins of Modernism in Russian Architecture, 1991, A History of Russian Architecture, 1993, An Archtl. Survey of St. Petersburg: 1840-1916, 1994, Lost Russia: Photographing the Ruins of Russian Architecture, 1995, Landmarks of Russian Architecture: A Photographic Survey, 1997; editor, contbr.: Reshaping Russian Architecture: Western Technology, Utopian Dreams, 1990, Christianity and the Arts in Russia, 1991, Russian Housing in the Modern Age: Design and Social History, 1993, Commerce in Russian Urban Culture: 1861-1914, 2001, Zhilishche V Rossii: vek XX, 2001, Predprinimatelstrov i gorodskaia kultura V Rossii, 2002; contbr. articles to profl. jour.; represented in permanent collections at Photographic Archives, Nat. Gallery Art, Washington; elected to Russian Acad. of Architecture, 2002. Woodrow Wilson fellow, 1966, NEH fellow Nat. Humanities Ctr., 1992-93, fellow Harvard Russian Rsch. Ctr., 1980-81, Guggenheim fellow, 2000-2001; NEH Collaborative Fellowship Am. Coun. for Internat. Edn., 2001-02; sr. exch. scholar Internat. Rsch. Exchs. Bd./Am. Coun. Learned Socs. U.S.-USSR Exch., Moscow, 1983-84, rsch. scholar Kennan Inst., Washington, 1989; grantee Samuel H. Kress Found., 1996-97, grantee Nat. Coun. for Eurasian and East European Rsch., 1999-2000; elected to Russian Acad. Architecture, 2002. Mem. Am. Assn. Advancement Slavic Studies, Soc. Archtl. Historians, Inst. Modern Russian Culture (head photography sect.), Am. Coun. Tchrs. of Russian, Soc. of Historians of East European and Russian Art and Architecture, Russian Acad. Architecture. Office: Tulane U Slavic Dept New Orleans LA 70118 E-mail: brumFiel@tulane.edu.

BRUNER, JEFFREY BENHAM, foreign language educator; b. Holdenville, Okla., Mar. 20, 1961; s. Eugene and Billye Jo B.; m. Deborah Elaine Wilkinson, June 16, 1984 (div. Feb. 1995); m. Twyla Anne Meding, Dec. 22, 1995. BA in Spanish, Okla. Bapt. U., 1983; MA in Spanish, Rutgers U., 1986, PhD in Spanish, 1990. Asst. prof. Trenton (N.J.) State Coll., 1988-90, W.Va. U., Morgantown, 1990-96, assoc. prof., 1996—, chair dept. fgn. langs., 2002—. Mem. adv. bd. W.Va. U. Phil. Papers, 1994—. Contbr. articles to profl. jours. V.p., bd. dirs. Maintain People's Coop., Morgantown, 1996-2000. Recipient Radiol. Cons. Assn. award, Morgantown, 1992; Riggle fellow, W.Va. U., 1992. Mem. ACLU, MLA (del. assembly 2003—), N.E. MLA, So. Comparative Lit. Assn., 20th Century Spanish Soc. Avocations: cross country skiing, cycling, hiking, travel. Office: WVa U Dept Fgn Langs Chitwood Hall Morgantown WV 26506-6298

BRUNER, JEROME S. law educator; BA, Duke U., 1937; PhD, Harvard U., 1941. Prof. NYU, Sch. of Law, NYC, 1998—; prof. Psychology Harvard U.; watts prof. Oxford U.; Meyer vis. prof. NYU Sch. of Law, NYC, 1991. Founder Head Start. Author: The Process of Education, 1961. Recipient Internat. Balzan prize, CIBA Gold medal for Dist. Rsch., Dist. Scientific award, Am. Psychological Assn. Mem.: Pres. Sci. Adv. Com., Nat. Acad. Edn. Office: NYU Sch of Law Fuchsberg Hall 249 Sullivan St 3rd Fl New York NY 10012-1099

BRUNING, JAMES LEON, academic administrator, educator; b. Bruning, Nebr., Apr. 1, 1938; s. Leon G. and Delma Dorothy (Middendorf) Bruning; m. E. Marlene Schaff, Aug. 24, 1958; children: Michael, Stephen, Kathleen. BA, Doane Coll., 1959; MA, U. Iowa, 1961, PhD, 1962. Chmn. dept psychology Ohio U., Athens, 1972-76, acting dean arts and scis., 1976-77, assoc. dean, 1977-78, vice provost, 1978-81, provost, 1981-93, trustee prof., 1993—, v.p. regional higher edn., 1998—99, dir. Enterprise project, 2002—03. Planning cons. NCHEMS, Boulder, Colo., 1979—80; provost Shawnee (Ohio) State U., 1996. Author: (book) Computational Handbook of Statistics, 1997, Research in Psychology, 1970; contbr. articles to profl. jours. Chair task force Ohio Bd. Regents, 1994—95. Grantee, Esso, 1963—64, NIMH, 1963—66, EPDA, 1974—75, OBOR, 1989—91. Mem.: APA (vis. scientist), AAAS, Midwestern Psychol. Assn., Sigma Xi. Democrat. Lutheran. Home: 6148 Melnor Dr Athens OH 45701-3577 Office: Ohio U Psychology Dept Athens OH 45701 E-mail: bruningj@ohio.edu.

BRUNJES, PETER CRAWFORD, neurobiology educator; b. Columbus, Ohio, June 19, 1953; s. Thomas Hilbert and Marie Elizabeth (Baker) B.; m. Victoria Lee Manning, July 31, 1976; children: Benjamin Manning, Lee Manning, Samuel Manning. BS, Mich. State U., 1974; PhD, Ind. U., 1979. Postdoctoral fellow U. Ill., Champaign, 1980; asst. prof. psychology U. Va., Charlottesville, 1981—86, assoc. prof. psychology, 1986-93, prof., 1993—, commonwealth prof., 2001—, assoc. dean for grad. program and rsch., 2002—. Contbr. articles to profl. jours. Recipient Takasago award Assn. for Chemoreception Scis., 1990, Outstanding faculty award U. Va., 1991. Mem. AAAS, Soc. for Neurosci., Assn. for Chemoreception Rsch. (Takasago award 1990). Office: U Va Dept Psychology 102 Gilmer Hall Charlottesville VA 22904-4400

BRUNO, AUDREI ANN, nurse educator, administrator; b. Pitts., Oct. 31, 1946; d. Vincent Joseph and Julia Elizabeth (Karaffa) Mataya; m. Edward Orlando Bruno, Apr. 30, 1966; children: Brent Edward, Bradley Edward. AA, Community Coll. Allegheny County, 1976; BSN, Pa. State U., 1984; MSN, U. Pitts., 1988. Cert. nurse adminstr. Psychiat. nursing supr. Western Psychiat. Clinic and Inst., Pitts., 1976-81; staff charge nurse Magee Women's Hosp., Pitts., 1981-82; charge team leader Central Med. Pavillion, Pitts., 1982-84; clin. specialist Vis. Nurse Assn. of Allegheny County, Pitts., 1984-92. Rschr. U. Pitts.; speakers bur. C.C. Allegheny County; project developer WPIC Adolescent Module, 1980-81; CEO Psycho-Ednl. Cons., 1996; coord. grant Putting Cmty. Health into AD Curriculum, 1993-96; bd. dirs. Theos Internat.; mem. Nurses' Health Study II, Harvard Sch. Pub. Health, 1989-99. Chmn. North Huntington (Pa.) Suicide Awareness and Prevention Com., 1986-88; fieldworker Project Star, Pitts., 1986-88; mem. Pa. Task Force on Elder Abuse, Nurses Interest in Care of Elderly; mem. adv. com. Nat. Project DART; bd. dirs. Am. Found. Suicide Prevention. Mem. Nursing Quality Assurance (cons.), Sigma Theta Tau. Home: 707 Duncan Ave Apt 401 Pittsburgh PA 15237-5025

BRUNO, GRACE ANGELIA, accountant, retired educator; b. St. Louis, Oct. 11, 1935; d. John E. and Rose (Goodwin) B. BA, Notre Dame Coll., 1966; MEd, So. Ill. U., 1972; MAS, Johns Hopkins U., 1983; PhD, Walden U., 1985. CPA, Mo., Md., N.J. Tchr. Sch. Sisters of Notre Dame (SSND) of St. Louis, 1962-80; pres. Bruno-Potter, Inc., Avon By The Sea, N.J., 1981—. Asst. treas., instr. acctg. Coll. of Notre Dame of Md., Balt., 1978-80, treas., 1979-80; asst. prof. acctg. Georgian Ct. Coll., Lakewood, N.J., 1985-91; fin. advisor James Harry Potter gold medal award ASME, N.Y.C., 1980—. Elected to Internat. Platform Assn., 1987. Mem. AICPA, N.J. Soc. CPAs, St. Louis Bus. Educators (treas. 1972-73), Inst. Bus. Appraisers, Inc., Johns Hopkins Univ. Faculty Club. Democrat. Roman Catholic. Home and Office: 419 3rd Ave Avon By The Sea NJ 07717 E-mail: gbruno4u@monmouth.com.

BRUNO, LOUIS VINCENT, special education educator; b. Allegheny County, Pa., Feb. 10, 1959; s. Thomas E. and Anna Marie (Lavra) B. BS in Elem. Edn., U. Pitts., 1981, MEd in Mentally/Physically Handicapped, 1982, cert. secondary prins., 1990. Cert. tchr. expectations and student achievement/gender/ethnic expectations and student achievement coord., learning potential assessment device instr., instrumental enrichment trainer. Tchr. Steel Valley Sch. Dist., Munhall, Pa., 1981-82; adult living program instr. United Cerebral Palsy Assn., Pitts., 1982; from learning disabilities tchr. to asst. prin. Wilkinsburg (Pa.) Sch. Dist., 1982—98, asst. prin. Wilkinsburg (Pa.) Mid. Sch., 1998—; prin. 8th Linton Mid. Sch., Pitts., 1999—. Mem. adv. bd. TV and Video Tchrs. Assn. of Western Pa. Home: 301 Mcgregor Dr Verona PA 15147-3433 E-mail: loubruno@aol.com., lbruno@phsd.k12.pa.us.

BRUNSDALE, MITZI LOUISA, (MALLARIAN), English language educator, book critic; b. Fargo, N.D., May 16, 1939; d. Gregory Starn and Phyllis (Grobe) Mallarian; m. John Edward Brunsdale, Dec. 2, 1961; children: Margaret Louisa, Jean Ellen and Maureen Lois, twins. BS(hon.), N.D. State U., 1959, MS, 1961; PhD, U. N.D., 1976; post grad., Ind. U., 1976. Grad. asst. Ind. U., 1959-60; instr. English and French Mayville State Coll., ND, 1961; instr. English Mayville State Coll., ND, 1975-76; asst. prof. Mayville State Coll., ND, 1976-78, assoc. prof., 1978-83; prof. Mayville State U., ND, 1983—, chmn. divsn. liberal arts, 1998—2003. Book critic, Houston Post, 1971-85; book reviewer, Chgo. Tribune, 1987—, The Armchair Detective, 1995-98, Publishers Weekly, 1996—, The Strand Mag., 1998—; state sec., treas. N.D. Am. Coun. on Edn. Nat. Identification Program Bd. Author: Sigrid Undset: Chronicler of Norway, 1988, Dorothy L. Sayers: Solving the Mystery of Wickedness, 1991, James Joyce: The Short Fiction, 1993, James Herriot, 1996, Student Companion to George Orwell, 2000. Contbr. articles to profl. jour. and reference ency. Sec. twentieth Dist. N.D. Rep. Com., 1963-70; chmn. N.D. Humanities Coun., 1980, 81-82; grant rev. panelist NEH; corr. sec. N.D. Fedn. Rep. Women, 1990-92. Mem., MLA, D.H. Lawrence Soc., Am. James Joyce Soc., Phi Kappa Phi, Sigma Alpha Iota, Kappa Alpha Theta. Home: RR 1 Box 9 Mayville ND 58257-9706 Office: Mayville State Coll Dept English Mayville ND 58257

BRUNSON, KENNETH WAYNE, cancer biologist; b. Chico, Tex., Sept. 18, 1936; s. George Starr and Gwendolyn Laverne (Mount) B.; m. Myrna Marquerite Lapré, Jan. 26, 1963; children: Gregory Sean, Geoffrey Gordon. BA in Biology, Chemistry, U. N. Tex., 1964, MA in Biology, Chemistry, 1966; PhD in Microbiology, Biochemistry, U. Minn., 1973; postdoctoral Tumor Biology, The Salk Inst., San Diego, Calif., 1974-77. Lectr. U. Calif., Riverside, 1974-75; rsch. assoc. The Salk Inst., La Jolla, Calif., 1974-77; asst. specialist U. Calif., Irvine, 1977-79; asst. prof. Sch. Medicine Ind. U., Indpls., Gary, 1979-84, assoc. mem. grad. sch. Bloomington, 1979-84; sr. rsch scientist Pfizer Inc, Groton, Conn., 1984-91; assoc. prof. Sch. Medicine U. Pitts., 1991-99; affiliate mem. U. Pitts. Cancer Inst., 1991-94, mem., 1994-99, dir. Tumor Model Lab., 1995-99, dir. in vivo preclin. rsch. for health scis., 1996-99, sect. head cancer metastasis biology program, 1991—95; dep. dir. Inst. for Cancer Rsch. U. North Tex. Health Sci. Ctr., Ft. Worth, 1999—2002, dir., 2002—03, adj. prof. dept. molecular biology and immunology, 2000—01, mem. grad. faculty microbiology and immunology program, 2001—03, rsch. prof. dept. molecular biology and immunology, 2001—03; sr. dir. Sopherion Therapeutics, Inc., New Haven, 2003—. Mem. expert panel workshop Exptl. Metastasis: Designing New Strategies, 1988; founding mem. sci. edn. com. Pfizer, Inc., Groton, Conn., 1987—91. Mem. editl. bd.: In Vivo, 2002—, sci. advisor: 10-vol. treatise Cancer Growth and Progression, 1986—89; contbr. articles to profl. jours. including Cancer Rsch., In Vivo, Jour. Nat. Cancer Inst., Jour. Nat. Cancer Inst. Mem. planning com. Regional Health Adminstrn. Conf., Ind., 1984; mem. exec. bd. Shadyside Action Coalition, Pitts., 1993—96, chmn. parking and transp. com., 1993—95; mem. Lake Country Place Assn., 2001—; bd. dirs. Tarrant County unit Am. Cancer Soc., 2002—03, bd. dirs.Lake County unit, 1981—84; bd. dirs. Pa. Soc. Biomed. Rsch., 1997—99. With U.S. Army, 1958—61. Recipient XVI Internat. Cancer Congress award Internat. Union Against Cancer, New Delhi, India, 1994. Mem. Am. Assn. for Cancer Rsch., Am. Assn. Immunologists, Am. Soc. Cell Biology, Metastasis Rsch. Soc., Am. Soc. for Microbiology, (chmn. edn. com., Ind. br.), Am. Inst. Biol. Scis., Pa. Soc. Biomed. Rsch. (bd. dirs. 1997-99). Achievements include pioneering research in cancer metastasis models, some of which has been described in Sci. Am., Mar., 1979, Proceedings of Nat. Acad. of Sci., 1980, Cancer Growth and Progression, 1989, and Biologic Therapy of Cancer, 1995. Home: 49 Hampton Rd Hamden CT 06518 Office: Sopherion Therapeutics Inc 300 George St New Haven CT 06511

BRUNSTAD, MICHAEL LEWIS, elementary education educator; b. Aberdeen, Wash., Nov. 17, 1956; s. William Ray and Diane (Mason) B.; m. Kathleen Rochelle Close, Apr. 8, 1989; children: Roger Russell Tryon, Mason Ray. Student, Grays Harbor Coll., 1975-77; BA in Edn., Western Wash. U., 1981; postgrad., Ctrl. Wash. U., 1984-86, U. Alaska, 1992—. Cert. tchr. Alaska, Wash. Subs. tchr. Renton (Wash.), Kent (Wash.) and Auburn (Wash). Sch. Dists., 1981-84; tchr. jr.-sr. high sch. Wishram (Wash.) Sch. Dist., 1984-86; tchr. phys. edn. K-12 Quinault Lake Sch. Dist., Amanda Park, Wash., 1986-87; mgr. Nautilus Fitness Ctr., Aberdeen, 1987-88; recreation supr. Clallam Bay (Wash.) Correction Ctr. for Men, 1988-90; tchr. elem. edn. Cape Flattery Sch. Dist., Sekiu, Wash., 1990-91, Anchorage (Alaska) Sch. Dist., 1991—. Head coach girl's basketball team Wishram High Sch., 1984-85, head coach volleyball team, 1984, 85; head coach football team Lake Quinault High Sch., Amanda Park, 1986; asst. coach wrestling Clark Jr. High Sch., Anchorage, 1992; summer Day camp dir. Anchorage Parks and Recreation, Municipality of Anchorage, 1993; asst. football coach Nea Bay (Wash.) H.S., 1990. Contbr. articles to profl. jours. Soccer and football coach Boys & Girls Club, 1993—. Named Eagle Scout Boy Scouts Am., 1973. Mem. Elks (dir. hoop shoot lodge # 1351 1995—). Avocations: powerlifting, camping, skiing, fishing, hunting. Office: Anchorage Sch Dist 4600 Debarr Rd Anchorage AK 99508-3126 Home: Spc 521 2221 Muldoon Rd Anchorage AK 99504-3631

BRUSCH, JOHN LYNCH, physician, educator, hospital administrator; b. Boston, Nov. 3, 1943; s. Charles and Margaret Agnes (Lynch) Brusch; m. Patricia Gahan, May 12, 1973; children: Amy Claire, Meaghan, Patrick. BS, Tufts U., 1965, MD, 1969. Diplomate Am. Bd. Internal Medicine, Am. Bd. Infectious Disease, Am. Bd. Geriatrics. Intern New Eng. Med. Ctr., Boston, 1969-70, resident in medicine, 1970-71, resident in infectious disease, 1971-74; asst. chief medicine Brighton Pub. Health Svc. Hosp., Boston, 1974-76; pvt. practice physician Cambridge, Mass., 1976—; chief medicine Youville Hosp., Cambridge, 1991—, dir. cmty. medicine, 1995—; clin. assoc. medicine Mass. Gen. Hosp., Boston, 1996—; med. dir. transitional care unit, chief medicine Somerville Hosp., 1999—. Assoc. chief medicine Cambridge Health Alliance, 1999—, dir. hosp. bd., 2003—; asst. prof. medicine Harvard Med. Sch., 2001—; bd. dirs. North Cambridge Coop Bank. Co-author: (book) Infective Endocardits; assoc. editor: Infectious Disease Practice, 1984—, mng. editor: Emedicine, 2001—; contbr. articles to profl. jours. With USPHS, 1974—76. Decorated knight of the Holy Sepulchre. Fellow: ACP; mem.: Am. Soc. Microbiology, Longwood Cricket Club. Home: 52 Radcliffe Rd Belmont MA 02478-3340 Office: Cambridge Hosp 1493 Cambridge St Cambridge MA 02139-1099 E-mail: jbruschmd@aol.com.

BRUSH, STEPHEN GEORGE, historian, educator; b. Bangor, Maine; s. Edward Newcomb and Lillian Maynard (Hatfield) B.; m. Phyllis Egbert; children: Denise, Nicholas. AB in Physics, Harvard U., 1955; DPhil in Physics, Oxford (Eng.) U., 1958. Postdoctoral fellow Imperial Coll., London, 1958-59; physicist Lawrence Radiation Lab., Livermore, Calif., 1959-65; rsch. assoc. Harvard Project Physics, Cambridge, Mass., 1965-68; lectr. Harvard U., Cambridge, Mass., 1966-68; assoc. prof. U. Md., College Park, 1968-71, prof., 1971—, Disting. univ. prof. History of Sci., 1995—. Author: The Kind of Motion We Call Heat, 1976, Statistical Physics and the Atomic Theory of Matter, 1983, History of Modern Science, 1988, History of Modern Planetary Physics, 1996; co-author: Physics, The Human Adventure: From Copernicus to Einstein and Beyond, 2001; co-author: Introduction to Concepts and Theories in Physical Science, 1973, 2d rev. edit.; author, editor: Kinetic Theory, 1965, vol. II, 1966, Vol. III, 1972. Rhodes scholar, Oxford U., 1955-58; NSF grantee, 1965—; Guggenheim fellow, 1999-2000. Fellow AAAS, Am. Phys. Soc. (councillor 1987-90); mem. History of Sci. Soc. (pres. 1990-91, Pfizer award 1977, Hazen Edn. prize 2001). Achievements include theoretical research calculation showing that a system of charged particles (plasma) will condense from gas to solid under conditions of high pressure and low temperature. Office: U Md Dept History Inst Phys Sci and Tech College Park MD 20742-0001

BRUSHABER, GEORGE KARL, academic administrator, minister; b. Milw., Dec. 15, 1938; s. Ralph E. and Marie C. (Meister) B.; m. N. Darleen Dugar, Jan. 27, 1962; children: Deanna Lyn Dalberg, Donald Paul. BA, Wheaton Coll., 1959, MA, 1962; MDiv, Gordon-Conwell Theol. Sem.,

1963; PhD, Boston U., 1967. Ordained to ministry Bapt. Gen. Conf., 1966. Prof. philosophy, chair dept. Gordon Coll., Wenham, Mass., 1963-72; dir. admissions and registration Gordon-Conwell Theol. Sem., 1970-72; v.p., acad. dean Westmont Coll., Santa Barbara, Calif., 1972-75; v.p., dean of coll. Bethel. Coll., St. Paul, 1975-82; pres. Bethel Coll. & Theol. Sem., St. Paul and San Diego, 1982—. Staley Found. lectr. Anderson U., Sioux Falls Coll.; sec. for higher edn. Bapt. Gen. Conf., Arlington Heights, Ill., 1982—; cons., evaluator Minn. Humanities Commn., St. Paul. Editor Gordon Rev., 1965-70; pub., founding editor Christian Scholar's Rev., 1970-79; exec. editor Christianity Today, 1985-90, chmn. sr. editors, 1990-2000; contbr. articles to religious jours. Bd. dirs. Youth Leadership, Mpls., 1982—, Fairview Elders' Enterprises Found., 1989—, Scripture Press Ministries Found., 1994—; adv. bd. Mpls./St. Paul Salvation Army, 1992--; chair bd. Scripture Press Ministries, 1994—; adv. coun. Evang. Environ. Network, 1994—; mem. Commn. on Minorities in Higher Edn. Am. Coun. Edn., 1995-99. Mem. Christian Environ. Assn., Christian Coll. Consortium (bd. dirs.), Nat. Assn. Evangs. (trustee 1982—), Minn. Pvt. Coll. Coun. (bd. dirs. 1982—), Minn. Consortium Theol. Sems. (bd. dirs. 1982—), Cook Comm. Internat. (bd. dirs. 1998—), Coun. Ind. Colls. (bd. dirs. 1984-89), Am. Philos. Assn., Evang. Theol. Soc., Am. Assn. Higher Edn., Swedish Coun. Am. (bd. dirs. 2000—), Soc. Christian Philosophers, Fellowship Evang. Sem. Pres., Minn. Club, North Oaks Country Club. Home and Office: Bethel Coll and Theol Sem 3900 Bethel Dr Saint Paul MN 55112-6902

BRUSKY, LINDA L. middle school mathematics and science educator; b. Chgo., Sept. 22, 1948; d. Ervin and Elizabeth (Martinek) Lange; m. George F. Brusky, Mar. 13, 1971. BA in Elem. Edn., Northeastern Ill. State Coll., Chgo., 1970; MA in Gen. Adminstrn., Northeastern Ill. U., 1998. Cert. tchr. K-9, Ill., gen. adminstr., Ill., 1998. Tchr. St. Mary of the Angels Sch., Chgo., 1970-98, tchr. jr. high sch. math. and sci., 1987-93, tchr. mid. sch. math., 1993-98; prin. St. James Sch., Chgo., 1998—2002, Our Lady of Charity Sch., Cicero, Ill., 2002—. Charter mem. Statue of Liberty Ellis Island Found., Inc., N.Y.C., 1985—; site coord. Joyce Found. Magnet Summer Sch., 1991, DeWitt-Wallace/Readers Digest Found. Magnet Ctr. Summer Sch., 1992. Recipient Cardinal Bernadin Tchr. Achievement award 1992; Joyce Found. scholar, 1987-91, Weber H.S. Tchr. Recognition award, 1998. Fellow Nat. Assn. Watch and Clock Collectors; mem. ASCD, Ill. Assn. for Supervision and Curriculum Devel., Nat. Coun. Tchrs. Math., Nat. Cath. Edn. Assn. (Disting. Grad. award 1995), Ill. Coun. Tchrs. Math., Archdiocesan Prins. Assn., Nat. Assn. of Elem. Sch. Principals, Psi Chi. Roman Catholic. Avocations: opera, collecting antique clocks and watches. Office: Our Lady of Charity Sch 3620 S 57th Ct Cicero IL 60804

BRUYA, JOHN ROBERT, art educator; b. Oakland, Calif., Aug. 17, 1941; s. William Clement and Margurite Alene (Giesa) B.; m. Marilyn Catherine Rosera; children: Sara Allison, Kristen Catherine. BA in Edn., Eastern Wash. U., 1963; MFA, U. Wash., 1970. Tchr. art Wendler Jr. High Sch., Anchorage, 1964-67; instr. U. Wash., Seattle, 1970-71; prof. art Slippery Rock (Pa.) U., 1971—. Mem. craft adv. com. Pa. Coun. Arts; sabbatical rschr., France, 1999-2000. Recipient Top Ten Sr. Yr. Eastern Wash. U., Cheney, 1963; named Artist of Yr. Butler County (Pa.)/Music & Arts Festival, 1985. Mem. Am. Craft Coun., Soc. N.Am. Goldsmiths, Pa. Art Edn. Assn. (Outstanding Pa. Higher Edn. Art Educator 1994), Associated Artists Pitts. (bd. dirs. 1972-75), Pitts. Craftsmen's Guild (bd. dirs. 1971-75). Democrat. Roman Catholic. Avocations: gourmet cooking, raising Bonsai. Home: 326 State St Grove City PA 16127-1629 Office: Slippery Rock U Art Dept Slippery Rock PA 16057 E-mail: robert.bruya@sru.edu.

BRYAN, GINA GRAY, middle school educator; b. Goldsboro, N.C., Oct. 24, 1965; d. Lloyd C. Gray and Gloria (Uzzell) Lee; m. Joseph Paul Bryan, Jan. 15, 1993. BS cum laude in Edn., N.C. State U., 1987, MEd, 1994. Tchr. Wayne County Schs., Goldsboro, 1987—. Mem. Nat. Coun. Tchrs. English, Kappa Delta Pi, Alpha Delta Kappa (Tchr. of Yr. award 1992). Home: 324 Ryan Blvd Goldsboro NC 27534-8682 Office: Greenwood Mid Sch 3209 E Ash St Goldsboro NC 27534-4545

BRYAN, HENRY COLLIER, clergyman, retired secondary school educator; b. Atlanta, Apr. 10, 1941; s. Thomas Harper and Rubye (Collier) B. Student, Temple U., 1959-63, 64, 70; BEd, Cheyney U., 1962; postgrad., Va. Union U., 1965-66; MDiv, Ea. Bapt. Theol. Sem., 1968; postgrad., Howard Law Sch., 1962-63, U. Alaska, Juneau, 1990. Cert. math. tchr., Phila.; ordained to ministry Am. Bapt. Ch., 1968. Tchr. math. Masterman Demonstration Sch., Phila., 1968-71, Phila. High Sch. for Girls, 1971-97; ret., 1997. Chaplain Alpha Phi Alpha Fraternity, Phila, 1968—. Assoc. min. Zion Bapt. Ch., 1967-68; asst. min. Wynnefield United Presbyn. Ch., 1969-72; Charter mem. North br. Y's Men Assn., Phila., 1972—; bd. dirs. Cherry Hill (N.J.) Civic Assn., 1992—. Recipient Outstanding Young Men Am. award Wynnefield Presbyn. Ch., Phila., 1971. Mem.: ASCD, NAACP (life), NSTA (life), Pa. Coun. Tchrs. Math., Pa. Coun. Suprs. Math., Nat. Coun. Suprs. Math., Math. Assn. Am., Phila. Fedn. Tchrs. (bldg. rep. Girls' H.S. 1996—97), Phila. Health Computer Users Group (life), Am. Baptist Mins. Coun. (life), Nat. Coun. Tchrs. Math. (life), Assn. Tchrs. Math. Phila. (life), Alpha Phi Alpha (life), Phi Delta Kappa (life). Avocations: computers, electronics, sports, chess, world travel. Home: 17 W Brook Dr Cherry Hill NJ 08003-1109

BRYAN, JOHN LELAND, retired engineering educator; b. Washington, Nov. 15, 1926; s. George W. and Buena (Youe) B.; m. Sarah Emily Barton, June 7, 1950; children: Joan Marie, Steven Leland. AA, Okla. State U., 1950, BS, 1953, MS, 1954; D.Ed., Am. U., 1965. Field rep. Grain Dealers Mut. Ins. Co., Indpls., 1950, Jackson, Miss., 1950-52; sr. instr. U. Md., 1954-56, prof., 1956-93; ret., 1993. Fire prevention engr., civil engring. div. U.S. Coast Guard, Washington, summers 1960-64 Author: Fire Detection and Suppression Systems, 1973, 3d edit., 1993, Automatic Sprinkler and Standpipe Systems, 1976, 3d rev. edit., 1997. Mem. Soc. Fire Protection Engrs., Nat. Fire Protection Assn., ASTM, Iota Lambda Sigma, Psi Chi, Kappa Delta Pi, Phi Kappa Phi. Home: 2399 Bear Den Rd Frederick MD 21701-9328

BRYAN, MARY JO W. realtor, artist, art educator; b. Dumas, Tex., Apr. 12, 1944; d. Edwin Franklin and Martha Lou (Workman) Williams; m. Gary W. Bryan, June 4, 1966; children: Mark William, Stacy Lynn. BS in Edn., Tex. Tech U., 1966; MEd in Guidance and Counseling, North Tex. U., 1969; MA in Art, West Tex. A&M U., 1994. Cert. tchr., all-level counselor, Tex. Tchr. Lubbock (Tex.) Ind. Sch. Dist., 1966, Irving (Tex.) Ind. Sch. Dist., 1966-68, Dallas Ind. Sch. Dist., 1968-69, counselor, 1969-71; bus. mgr. Gary W. Bryan, M.D., P.A., Amarillo, Tex., 1977—2002; artist Amarillo, 1994—; mgr. Prudential Ada Realtors, 2003—. Organizer Healthtreat, Med. Alliance, 1988; speakers chmn. Med. Alliance AIDS Program, 1992-96; mem. Leadership Amarillo, C. of C., 1989-90. Mem. Polk Street United Meth. Ch., class program com., 1988, 90, 93, 95, 96, chair Role and Status of Women feminist theology, 1995-2001; bd. friends Amarillo (Tex.) Pub. Libr., 1997-2003, v.p., 2001-02; bd. dir. Panhandle Art Ctr., 2003. Mem.: Amarillo Watercolor Assn. (pres. 2002—04), Lone Star Pastel Soc., Amarillo Fine Arts (chair Fall Art Show 2002), Potter-Randall County Med. Alliance (pres. 1988—89, sec.-treas. healthreat, Svc. award 1989), Tex. Med. Alliance (chair AIDS and sexually transmitted disease 1995—99), Am. Med. Alliance, Med. Mgrs. (v.p. 1989—90, Svc. award 1989).

BRYAN, RICHARD ARTHUR, retired special education educator; b. Atlanta, Apr. 10, 1941; s. Thomas Harper and Rubye (Collier) B. BE, Cheyney U., 1962; postgrad., West Chester (Pa.) U., 1963, Howard U., 1962-63, Temple U., 1968-88. Masters Equivalency, Pa., 1975. Tchr. spl. edn. Elkin Sch., Phila., 1969-96, tchr. in charge, 1973-96, tchr. resource edn., 1984-96, tchr. program suppt. liason dist. 5, 1991-96; ret., 1996. Charter mem. North Br. YMCA, Phila., 1972; treas. Phila. Heath Users Group, Phila., 1980, charter, 1983—. With U.S. Army, 1963-65. Summer Tchr. fellow Sch. Dist. Phila., 1971. Mem. NAACP (life), Phila. Fedn. Tchrs., Phila. Heath User (charter, treas. 1980), Phi Delta Kappa (life), Alpha Phi Alpha (life). Roman Catholic. Avocations: religious studies, computers, electronics, writing. Home: 17 W Brook Dr Cherry Hill NJ 08003-1109

BRYANT, ANNE LINCOLN, educational association executive; b. Jamaica Plain, Mass., Nov. 26, 1949; d. John Winslow and Anne (Phillips) B.; m. Peter Harned Ross, June 15, 1986; stepchildren: Charlotte Ross, George Ross. BA in English, Secondary Edn., Simmons Coll., 1971; EdD in Higher Edn., U. Mass., 1978. Intern U. Mass., Amherst, 1972; asst. to dean Springfield Tech. C.C., 1972-74; dir. Nat. Assn. Bank Women Ednl. Found., Chgo., 1974-86; v.p. P.M. Haeger, Chgo., 1978-86; exec. dir. AAUW, Washington, 1986-96, also exec. dir. Ednl. Found., Legal Advocacy Fund; exec. dir. Nat. Sch. Bds. Assn., Washington, 1996—. Contbr. articles to profl. jours. Mem. exec. com. Simmons Coll., Boston, 1971—; adv. commr. Edn. Commn. States, 1986—; mem. bd. govs. UNA of U.S.A., 1991—, Ind. Sector, 1988-94, Hosp. Corp. Am., 1993-94. Recipient William H. Cosby Jr. award U. Mass., 1983; named Woman of Yr. for Edn., YWCA, 1976. Fellow Am. Soc. Assn. Execs. (bd. dirs. 1985-88, Key award 1992); mem. Am. Assn. for Higher Edn. (bd. dirs. 1980-87). Episcopalian. Avocations: tennis, skiing, reading, walking.*

BRYANT, DARYL LESLIE, painter, educator; b. L.A., Feb. 11, 1940; d. Colin Willis and Virginia Rousseau (Graves) Timmons; m. Dennis Rourke Murphy, 1960 (div. 1972); children: John Ashley, Sarah; m. Daniel Walster Bryant, 1985. Student, U. So. Calif., Acad. Arts, Florence, Italy; AA, Valley Coll., Van Nuys, Calif. Asst. designer Koret Calif., San Francisco, 1959-60; freelance artist Studiowork, Studio City, Calif.; art dir. Brentwood (Calif.) Publs., 1978-87; painter, graphic designer South Pasadena, Calif., 1987—; tchr. Creative Arts Group, Sierra Madre, Calif., 1996—. Works published in books and mags. Mem. Mid Valley Arts League (bd. dirs. 1993—), Nat. Watercolor Soc. (signature), Watercolor West (signature), Calif. Art Club (signature). Avocations: swimming, hiking, travel, journal keeping.

BRYANT, EVELYN CHRISTINE, elementary education educator; b. Lakeview, S.C., Aug. 1, 1942; d. Jasper L. and Marcella (William) Page; m. James A. Bryant, Feb. 1, 1964; children: James Jr., Marc C., Linda E. AAS in Gen. Edn., Fayetteville Tech. C.C., Fayetteville, N.C., 1987; BS in Elem. Edn., Fayetteville State U., 1990, MA in Spl. Edn., 1994. Tchr.'s aide spl. edn. Ashley Sch., Fayetteville, 1976-81; substitute tchr. Cumberland County/Ft. Bragg, Fayetteville, 1989-90; data processor Census Bur., Fayetteville, 1990; tchr. chpt. I reading Midway Elem., Dunn, N.C., 1990-95, Cliffdale Elem. Sch., Fayetteville, N.C., 1995—. Active Parents Autism Children, 1970—, Mother's Mar. Dimes, 1990-91. Mem. NEA, Order Eastern Star (asst. sec. 1986-87), Heroine Jericho, Daus. of Zion, Kappa Delta Pi. Baptist. Avocations: tennis, creative writing, cooking, hiking. Home: 725 Glensford Dr Fayetteville NC 28314-0843

BRYANT, GAIL ANNETTE GRIPPEN, nurse, educator; b. Mason City, Iowa, Mar. 30, 1935; d. Charles Meredith and Velma Josephine Elaine (Bookhart) Grippen; children: David Allen, Kimberly Lynn. BSN, U. Mich., 1957; MSN, U. Tex., 1978. Cert. rehab. RN, cert. rehab. nurse. Instr., asst. prof. dept. nursing Coll. Santa Fe, 1980-87, assoc. prof., coord. Assoc. Degree and BSN programs, 1987-88, acting chair dept. nursing, 1988—; freelance writer, reviewer Glorieta, N.Mex., 1990. Lectr. in field. Sec.-treas. Glorieta Estates Water Coop.; mem. rehab. team St. Vincent Hosp., Santa Fe, 1991-99. Mem. ANA (dist. sec. 1986-91, 92-94), CRRN, Nat. Assn. of Orthopedic Nurses, Sigma Theta Tau.

BRYANT, GWENDOLYN LANA, elementary education educator; b. Cleve., Aug. 23, 1955; d. Oscar Lewis and Willie Dell (Long) Berry; m. Robert Dale Bryant, Jan. 3, 1985 (div.); 1 child, Adrian Brian. BS in Elen. Edn., U. Akron, 1977, postgrad., 1989, U. Ashland, 1993—. Cert. tchr. elem. sch. Ohio. Tchr. elem. sch. Canton (Ohio) City Schs., 1977-78; job counselor Stark City Schs., Canton, 1979-82 summers, JPTA, Canton, 1984-90 summers; tchr. adult edn. Canton City Schs., 1984-83; tchr. elem. sch. Akron (Ohio) Pub. Schs., 1979—. Mem. Akron Edn. Assn. Jr. League Akron, Akron Cultural Exch. (bd. dirs. 1990—), Young Adult Missionaries Soc. (v.p., sec. 1992—), U. Akron Black Alumni Assn. (bd. dirs. 1984-85), Delta Kappa Gamma. Avocations: collecting children's books & african prints, reading.

BRYANT, JANICE ANN, special education department administrator; b. Ada, OK, Mar. 11, 1955; d. Virgil and Corine Townsend; m. Larry Paul Bryant, Mar. 16, 1985; children: Samuel Paul, Mark Nathaniel. BS in Edn, E Ctrl Univ, Ada, OK, 1973—77, MEd, 1978—80. Cert. tchr. mental retardation OK, elem. edn. OK, 7th/8th gr. Social Studies OK, learning disabilities tchr. OK, reading specialist OK. Mem.: Oklahoma Dirs. Spl. Svcs. Baptist. Avocations: gardening, needlecrafts, cooking.

BRYANT, MARTHA JEAN, reading specialist; b. Jersey Shore, Pa., May 3, 1949; d. Paul E. and Carolina M. (Vairo) B. BS in Health and Phys. Edn., Lock Haven U., 1975; AA in Gen. Studies, AS in Bus. Acctg., AS in Bus. Mgmt., Williamsport Area C.C., 1977, AA in Individual Studies, 1978; MBA, Wilkes U., 1990; MEd, Bloomsburg U., 1997. Cert. health and phys. edn. tchr., Pa., secondary bus. edn. tchr., Pa., reading specialist, Pa. Office worker Citizens Cable Co., Williamsport, Pa., 1967-71, Lock Haven (Pa.) U., 1973-74; accounts payable clerk Williamsport Area C.C., 1977-78, sec. gen. svcs., 1978-83, sec. transp., 1983-86; acct. I West Branch Drug and Alcohol Abuse Commn., Williamsport, 1986-88; acct. Radiant Steel Products Co., Williamsport, 1988-90; staff acct. Divine Providence Hosp., Williamsport, 1990-96. Instr. personal computer Williamsport Area CC, 1984-85; title I reading specialist Athens (Pa.) Area Sch. Dist., 1997-99; reading specialist Jersey Shore Sch. Dist., 1999--. Developer (computer programs) Departmental Budget Tracking, 1984, Patient Information System, 1987. Dir. swimming YWCA Day Camp, Williamsport, 1971-72, swim instr., 1975-84, YMCA, Williamsport, 1985-92; coach varsity field hockey Williamsport Area C.C., 1978-91; vol. ARC 15 yrs.; cantor St. Boniface Ch., 1983-93; mem. Williamsport Civic Chorus, 1984-91, 97—, pres., 1986-88; cast mem. Cmty. Theatre League, Williamsport, 1986-91; mem. Wst. Br. Chorale, 1991-96; mem. Susquehanna Valley Chorale, 1993-97; soloist Williamsport area; project Literacy Lycoming County, 1997; active North Ctrl. Reading Coun. Recipient Bishop Hafey award St. Lawrence Ch. Cath. Daus., 1965; ARC 15 yr. pin. Mem. Williamsport Music Club (treas. 1989-92), Repasz Band, Imperial Teteque Band, Jersey Shore Town Band, Internat. Reading Assn., N. Ctrl. Reading Assn., Pa. State Edn. Assn., Keystone State Reading Assn. Democrat. Roman Catholic. Avocations: music, bowling, stitchery. Home: 330 E Mountain Ave Williamsport PA 17702-7733

BRYANT, WILBERT, government counselor; b. Goulds, Fla. BS in math., Fla. Agr. Mech. U.; M in edn., Howard U.; attended, Nat. War Coll. Dept. asst. sec. US Dept. Edn. Off. Higher Edn. Programs, Off. Postsecondary Edn., Wash., 2001; counselor to sec. White House Initiative on Hist. Black Coll. and U., Wash., 2003—; dep. sec. to sec. of edn. State of Va., 1994—2001. Vp for student affairs Va. Union U. Bd. mem. Va. Workforce Coun., Va. Adv. Coun. Adult Edn. and Literacy, Edn. Leaders Coun., Commn. on Info. Tech., Commn. on Edn. Infrastructure, Va., Ad. Coun. Va. Bus. Edn. Partnership, Govenor's Blue Ribbon Commn. Higher Edn., Govenor's Commn. Sch. Constrn.; bd. of trustees Jamestown-Yorktown Found.; bd. mem. Governor's Distance Learning Steering Com., Va., Va. Environ. Edn. Adv. Com., Va., Va. Nat. Guard Diversity Adv. Com., Va.; bd. of trustees Fla. A&M U.; bd. mem. Va. Rsch. and Tech. Adv. Commn. 2nd lt. U.S. Army. Decorated Legion of Merit; recipient Hon. Doctorate of Humane Letters, Va. State U., Shaw U. NC. Office: US Dept Edn Off Postsecondary Edn 1990 K St NW Washington DC 20006*

BRYK, ANTHONY S. education educator; BS Summa Cum Laude, in chem., Boston Coll., 1970; EdD, Harvard Grad. Sch. Edn., 1977. Instr. to asst. to assoc. prof. Harvard Grad. Sch. Edn., 1973—85; vis. assoc. prof. U. Chgo., Edn. and Sociology Dept., 1984—85; assoc. prof. to prof. U. Chgo, Dept. Edn. and Coll., 1985—2000; Marshall Field IV prof. U. Chgo., Dept Sociology, 1997—; fellow Stanford U., Ctr. for Advanced Studies in Behavioral Sci., 2002—. Founding dir. Consortium on Chgo. Sch. Rsch.; prin. investigator Ctr. for Rsch. Edn of Students at Risk, Johns-Hopkins U., Howard U. Recipient Sch. Reform Achievement award, Chgo. Assn. Local Sch. Coun., 1998, Philomethia Club Boston Coll. award, 1970, The Palmer A. Johnson award, Am. Ednl. Rsch. Assn., 1991, Willard Waller award, Am. Sociol. Assn., 1991—93. Mem.: Nat. Acad. Edn., Am. Statis. Assn., Am. Ednl. Rsch. Assn., Am. Sociol. Assn., Sigma Xi, Alpha Sima Nu. Office: Harvard U 1313 E 60th St 23A Chicago IL 60637*

BRYNILDSEN-SMITH, KRISTINE ANN, principal; b. Seattle, Feb. 24, 1950; d. Rudolph Wyman and Shirley Ann (Atkinson) Neuser; m. Richard Stephen Brynildsen, June 3, 1972 (div. 1980); 1 child, Erik Brynildsen; m. Albert Joseph Smith Jr., June 25, 1983; children: Gregory Smith, Margaret Smith. BA, U. Wash., 1972, MA, 1975; EdD, Seattle U., 1984. Cert. continuing adminstr./prin.; cert. continuing tchr. Tchr. Benson Hill Elem., Renton, Wash., 1972-81, Lake Ridge Elem., Renton, 1981-84, Hazen H.S., Renton, 1984-86; prin. St. Catherine Elem., Seattle, 1986-93, Holy Cross H.S., Everett, Wash., 1993—. Mem. assessment team Cath. Schs., Seattle, 1990-93; tchr. trainer Here's Looking at You 2000, Seattle, 1991-93; adj. prof. Pacific Luth. U., Tacoma, 1979-86; workshop designer, presenter Highline Sch. Dist., Burien, Wash., 1983; participant Cath. Prin.'s Acad., 1989; spkr. NEA Conf. on Human and Civil Rights, 1979. Mem. oral bd. Seattle Fire Dept., 1992; conf. chair World Affairs Coun., Seattle, 1985; mem. adv. com. U. Wash. Coll. of Edn., Seattle, 1983-85; mem. human rels. commn. Wash. Edn. Assn., Federal Way, 1979-81. Recipient 10 Yrs. Adminstrv. Svc. award Cath. Archdiocese of Seattle, 1996, Outstanding Svc. award Archdiocese of Seattle, 1987, Spl. Svc. Recognition award Wash. Edn. Assn., 1984. Mem. ASCD, Rotary, Phi Delta Kappa (charter mem.). Democrat. Roman Catholic. Avocations: reading, music, ballet, theater. Home: 2224 Broadway E Seattle WA 98102-4136 Office: 12911 39th Ave SE Everett WA 98208-6159

BRYNSKI, CHRISTINA HALINA, school system administrator, consultant, educator; b. Detroit, June 2, 1940; d. Halina J. (Zawadzki) B. BA, Wayne State U., 1962, MA, 1984. Cert. secondary education tchr. Lang. arts tchr. Livonia (Mich.) Pub. Schs., 1962-74, learning specialist, 1974-85, social studies coord., 1982-85, staff devel. coord., 1985—; cons. Ednl. Support Systems, Inc., Farmington Hills, Mich., 1992—. Cons. Right to Read, Washington, 1971-72, Mid. Cities Assn., Lansing, Mich., 1985-89, various counties in Mich., 1985-90; adj. prof. Madonna U., Livonia, Mich., 1994—. Contbr. articles to profl. jours. Mem. ASCD, Nat. Staff Devel. Coun., Effective Instrn. Consortium, Phi Delta Kappa, Pi Lambda Theta. Avocations: knitting, reading, gardening. Home: 17547 Fairfield St Detroit MI 48221-2740

BRYSON, PAULA KAY, secondary school educator; b. New Albany, Ind., Oct. 4, 1945; d. Paul Lomax and Sarah (Shope) B.; m. Walter Randall Scruggs, Oct. 2, 1965 (div. 1983); children: Randall Scott Scruggs, Vance Andrew Bryson. BSBA in Mktg., Western Carolina U., 1971, cert. in Teaching, 1988, MA in Edn., 1989. Cert. secondary sch. tchr., N.C. Area sec. N.C. State Hwy. Commn., Waynesville, 1966-67; dep. sec. Western Carolina U., Cullowhee, N.C., 1967-71; office mgr. Akzo Am., Asheville, N.C., 1971-88; tchr. Asheville H.S., 1989-97, T.C. Roberson H.S., Asheville, 1997—. Instr. A-B C.C., Asheville, 1990—. Sponsor Maggie BMW Nat. Motorcycle Rally. Mem. N.C. Bus. & Profl. Women (pres. Asheville chpt. 1990-91, state bd. dirs. 1991-93, dist. dir. 1992-93, Woman of Yr. 1991), Nat. Bus. Edn. Assn., Am. Vocat. Assn., Nat. Mktg. Edn. Assn. (state commn. 1999-2000), N.C. Assn. Edn., N.C. Bus. Edn. Assn., N.C. Vocat. Assn., Western Carolina Women's Coalition (v.p. 1992-94), N.C. State Dept. Pub. Instruction (program leadership coun. bus. edn.), Kappa Delta Pi, Beta Sigma Phi. Methodist. Avocations: bmw motorcycle touring, traveling, camping, volunteer work. Home: 16 W Baird Mountain Rd Asheville NC 28804-1126 Office: TC Roberson HS 250 Overlook Rd Asheville NC 28803-3317

BRZEZINSKI, ZBIGNIEW, political science educator, author; b. Warsaw, Mar. 28, 1928; came to U.S., 1953, naturalized, 1958; s. Tadeusz and Leonia (Roman) B.; m. Emilie Anna Benes, June 11, 1955; children: Ian, Mark, Mika. BA with 1st class honors in Econs. and Polit. Sci., McGill U., 1949, MA in Polit. Sci., 1950; PhD, Harvard U., 1953. Inst. govt. and research fellow Russian Research Center, Harvard U., 1953-56; asst. prof. govt., research assoc. Russian Research Center and Center Internat. Affairs, Harvard U., 1956-60; assoc. prof. public law and govt. Columbia U., 1960-62, prof., 1981-89. Dir. Rsch. Inst. Internat. Change, 1962-77; mem. faculty Russian Inst., 1960-77; dir. Trilateral Commn., 1973-76; asst. to pres. U.S. for nat security affairs, 1977-81; ofcl. Nat. Security Coun., 1977-81; counselor Ctr. Strategic and Internat. Studies, 1981—; prof. Nitze Sch. Advanced Internat. Studies, Johns Hopkins U., 1989—; mem. policy planning coun. U.S. Dept. State, 1966-68, Pres.'s Fgn. Intelligence Adv. Bd., 1987-91; mem. Joint Com. Contemporary China, Social Sci. Rsch. Coun., 1961-62; guest lectr. numerous pvt. and govt. instns. 1953—, participant internat. confs., 1955—. Author: The Permanent Purge-Politics in Soviet Totalitarianism, 1956, The Soviet Bloc— Unity and Conflict, 1960, Ideology and Power in Soviet Politics, 1962, Alternative to Partition, 1965, Between Two Ages, 1970, The Fragile Blossom, 1971, Power and Principle, 1983, Game Plan, 1986, The Grand Failure: The Birth and Death of Communism in the Twentieth Century, 1989, Out of Control, 1993, The Grand Chessboard, 1997; co-author: Totalitarian Dictatorship and Autocracy, 1957, Political Power: USA/USSR, 1964 (German edit. 1966), also numerous articles.; editor, co-author, contbr.: Political Controls in the Soviet Army, 1954; Editor, co-author, contbr.: Africa and the Communist World, 1963, Dilemmas Of Change In Soviet Politics, 1969, Dilemmi Internazionazionali In Un-epoca. Teconetronica, 1969; columnist: Newsweek, 1970-72; co-editor: Russia and the Commonwealth of Independent States: Documents, Data and Analysis, 1997. Mem. hon. steering com. Young Citizens for Johnson, 1964. Recipient Presdl. Medal of Freedom, 1981, U Thant award, 1995, Order of White Eagle, Poland, 1995. Fellow AAAS; mem. Coun. Fgn. Relations. Clubs: Metropolitan (Washington). Office: Ctr Strategic & Internat Studies 1800 K St NW Washington DC 20006-2202

BUBASH, PATRICIA JANE, special education educator; b. St. Louis; d. Emil John and Anne Marie (Candrl) B. BA in Deaf Edn., Fontbonne U., 1974; postgrad., St. Louis U., 1975-76, U. Mo., Columbia, 1982-84, U. Mo., St. Louis, 1984; MA in Edn., Washington U., 1996. Life cert. K-12 tchr. of deaf, learning disabilities, emotional and behavior disorders, K-8 elem. tchr., Mo. Tchr. of deaf Spl. Sch. Dist. St. Louis County, 1974—. Mem. curriculum devel. action com. Drug Free Schs.; character plus com., profl. devel. com. bldg. rep. Drug Edn. Task Force. Mem. Jr. League St. Louis, 1989—; mem. bd. jr. divsn. St. Louis Symphony Soc., co-chmn. membership, 1991-92, 92-93; co-chmn. Gypsy Caravan Vols., St. Louis, 1991, 92-93; leader Boy Scouts Am., 1984—, Explorer Scouts, 1990, Girl Scouts U.S.A., 1984—, Just Say No Club, 1987—; mem. The Troupe of Dance St. Louis, 1991—; mem. Step Up St. Louis, 1991—; active Alliance Francaise; mem. bd. dir. St. Louis-Lyon Sister Cities, Inc., 2002. Named Tchr. of Month, Spl. Sch. Dist. St. Louis County, 1987, 2000-01; recipient Spl. Needs Tchr. award Boy Scouts Am., 1989, 96, Classroom Scouting,

2002, Outstanding Leader of Yr., 2002, Commitment to Kids award Spl. Sch. Dist. St. Louis County, 2001, Spl Amb. award, 2003; Fulbright scholar Tchr. Exch., U.S./U.K., 2002-03. Mem. Coun. for Exceptional Children, Mo. Edn. Assn., Alexander Graham Bell Assn. for Deaf, Coun. Edn. of Deaf, St. Louis Ski Club, St. Louis Skating Club. Roman Catholic. Avocations: french, dancing, swimming, tennis, snow skiing. Office: Spl Sch Dist St Louis County 12110 Clayton Rd Saint Louis MO 63131-2516

BUCCI, MARY RUTH, primary education educator; b. New Castle, Pa., July 21, 1948; d. David Feyling and Mary Ann (Bintrim) Clausen; m. Richard Alan Bucci, May 24, 1975; children: Melissa Kay, Jeffrey Michael, Keren Ann. BS in Edn. cum laude, Slippery Rock U., 1971, MEd magna cum laude, 1974; MA in Edn. summa cum laude, Regents U., 1988. Cert. tchr., reading specialist, curriculum supr., Pa. Tchr. lang. arts Shenango Elem. Sch., New Castle, 1971-76; tchr. kindergarten Rhema Christian Sch., Coraopolis, Pa., 1984-95, curriculum specialist, 1988-91, tchr. computer sci., 1991-95; coord. gen. studies Hillel Acad. of Pitts., 1995-97; dir. curriculum and instrn. New Brighton (Pa.) Area Sch. Dist., 1997—. Pvt. tutor, home sch. evaluator; mem. sec. Rhema Christian Sch. Bd., Aliquippa, Pa., 1986-89. Mem. ASCD, Alpha Xi Delta (chpt. dir. 1976-77, province collegiate dir. 1974-76). Republican. Home: 206 Windy Hill Dr Coraopolis PA 15108-1146 Office: New Brighton Area Sch Dist 3225 43d St New Brighton PA 15066

BUCEY, CONSTANCE VIRGINIA RUSSELL, retired elementary school educator, education educator; b. Miami, Aug. 22, 1936; d. Mose and Lillian (Jones) Russell; m. Henry Lee Bucey. BS Virginia State Coll., 1959, postgrad. U. Miami, 1961—63; postgrad. Fla. A&M U., Tallahassee, 1962—63; postgrad. UCLA, 1970; MA and Reading Specialist Credential, Pepperdine U., 1976. Tchr. J.R.E. Lee Elem. Sch., South Miami, Fla., 1959—67, Margaret Duff Elem. Sch., Rosemead, Calif., 1974—82, Hillcrest Elem. Sch., Monterey Park, Calif., 1982—95; ret., 1995; part-time prof. Calif. State U. Charter Sch. Edn., L.A., 1998—, univ. supr. in divsn. curriculum and instrn., 1998—. Bd. pres., v.p., dir. First Fin. Fed. Credit Union, 1973—82, dir., 1985—. Los Angeles Ct. juror docent. Recipient Vol. Achievement Filene award, 1997, awards for oil paintings, various exhbns. Mem.: AAUW, NEA, Nat. Assn. Credit Union Presidents, Ret. Tchrs. Calif., Garvery Sch. Tchrs., Calif. Tchrs. Assn., Reading Specialists of Calif., Women Aware, Southland Art Assn., Bus. and Profl. Womens Club, Am. Legion Aux., Alpha Kappa Alpha. Home: 871 Ashiya Rd Montebello CA 90640

BUCHAN, RUSSELL PAUL, publisher, gas company executive, entrepreneur; b. St. Petersburg, Fla., May 24, 1947; s. Charles Joseph and Amelia (Petraca) B. BS in Econs. magna cum laude, Stetson U., 1969; MA, Vanderbilt U., 1975. Asst. to pub. Trend Publs., Tampa, Fla., 1971-74; book editor South Mag., Tampa, 1973-74; owner Buchan Gas Co., St. Petersburg, 1968—. Pub. Buchan Publs., St. Petersburg, 1980—96; pres. Buchan Gas Co., Grills Parts Dist., 1986—. Host Radio Sta. WTAN, Clearwater, Fla.; co-author: Florida: A Guide to the Best Restaurants, Resorts, Hotels, 1992, Florida Weekends, 1991, rev. edit., 1994; pub.: Florida's Best Beach Vacations, Florida County Inns, 1993. Mem. Pinellas County Gas Adv. Bd., 1979-88, vice-chmn., 1982-83, chmn. 1986-87; bd. dirs. Eckerd Coll. Library Friends, 1971-85, 91-95, chmn., 1982. Named Res. Grand champion Fla. State Barbecue Championship, 1995; Woodrow Wilson fellow, 1969. Mem. Pinellas County Gas Assn. (sec.-treas. 1977-78, pres. 1979-80), Fla. Young Gassers (dist. dir. 1979-81), Nat. LP Gas Assn., Fla. LP Gas Assn. (dir. 1979-81), Fla. Mag. Assn. (treas. 1974-75), Tampa Bay Econs. Forum, Kansas City Barbecue Soc., Internat. Wine and Food Soc. (br. chmn. St. Petersburg 1979-80), Wine Friends, WineBuffs, Brotherhood Knights of Vine, Order of Dali. Republican. Roman Catholic. Office: Buchan Gas Co 6150 49th St N Saint Petersburg FL 33709-2116

BUCHANAN, BENNIE LEE GREGORY, special education educator; b. Bells, Tenn., Mar. 24, 1928; d. Walter Homer and Hassie Mae (Herron) Gregory; m. Shannon Mill Buchanan, Sept. 10, 1951 (dec. 1989); children: Michael Keith, Shannon M. Jr., Sandra J., Greg ory E. Student, A&I State Coll., 1948-51; BA, Lane Coll., 1955; MEd, Memphis State U., 1977. Tchr. Haywood County Bd. Edn., Brownsville, Tenn., 1956-59, Hardeman County Bd. Edn., Bolivar, Tenn., 1959-89; owner, dir. Bennie's Family Day Care Home, Bolivar, 1991—, tchr. jr. high sch. spl. edn., 1972-88; owner, dir. Bennies Group Day Care Home, Bolivar, 1993—. Den leader Bolivar area Boy Scouts Am., 1972-74; chair Jr. High Band Boosters, Bolivar, 1973. Mem. ASCD, NAACP, Hardeman County Homemakers Club, Eastern Star, Daus. of Isis. Democrat. Baptist. Avocations: reading, sewing, crafts. Home: 431 S Jones St Bolivar TN 38008-2547

BUCHANAN, RELVA CHESTER, engineering educator; b. Port Antonio, Portland, Jamaica, Apr. 10, 1936; came to U.S., 1958; s. Stephen Eleazor and Imogene (Reid) B.; m. Bernice Brown, Jan. 11, 1957 (div. 1967); 1 child, Annette Lorraine. BS, Alfred (N.Y.) U., 1961; PhD, MIT, 1965. Mgr. Glass Scientific Co. Indsl. Dev. Corp., Kingston, Jamaica, 1956-58; sr. research engr. IBM Corp., Poughkeepsie, N.Y., 1964-74; prof. engring., chair ceramics div. U. Ill., Urbana, 1988-92; prof., head dept. materials sci. and engring. U. Cin., 1992—. Author, editor Electronic Ceramic Applications, 1986, 2nd edit. 1991. Fellow Am. Ceramic Soc. (trustee); mem. Electrochem. Soc., Materials Rsch. Soc. Home: 7651 Brannon Dr Cincinnati OH 45255-3089 Office: U Cin Dept Materials Sci/Engring 498 Rhodes Hl Cincinnati OH 45221-0001

BUCHANAN, WALTER WOOLWINE, electrical engineer, educator, academic administrator; b. Lebanon, Ind., Oct. 6, 1941; s. Eugene Neptune and Amy Malvina (Woolwine) B.; m. Carol Ann Saunders, Dec. 28, 1968 (div. 1978); children: William Saunders, John Douglas; m. Charlotte Jane Drake, 1985. BA, Ind. U., 1963, JD, 1973, PhD, 1993; BS in Engring., Purdue U., 1982, MS in Elec. Engring., 1984. Bar: Ind.; registered profl. engr., Ind., Fla., Tenn., Oreg., Mass. Aerospace engr. Martin Co., Denver, 1963-64, Boeing Co., New Orleans, 1964-65; audit coord. Ind. Tax Bd., Indpls., 1970-73; atty. VA, Indpls., 1973-79; electronics engr. Naval Avionics, Indpls., 1979-86; asst. prof. Ind. U.-Purdue U., Indpls., 1986-93, U. Ctrl. Fla., Orlando, 1993-95; assoc. prof., chair Mid. Tenn. State U., Murfreesboro, 1995-96; prof., dean Oreg. Inst. Tech., Klamath Falls, 1996-99; prof., dir. Northeastern U., Boston, 1999—. Cons. Benjamin/Cummings Pubs., Menlo Park, Calif., Holt, Rinehart & Winston, N.Y.C., Houghton Mifflin Co., Boston, MacMillan Pub. Co., Columbus, Delmar Pub. Co., Albany, Prentice Hall, Simon & Schuster, Columbus, Oxford U. Press, N.Y.C., Discovery Press, L.A., Springer-Verlag, Ltd., London, Inst. for Sci. Info., Phila., Microsoft Corp., Redmond, Wash., Utah Bd. Regents, Pa. State U., Altoona, Excelsior Coll., Albany, NY, Springer-Verlag-Ltd., London; evaluator Accreditation Bd. for Engring. and Tech., Balt.; mem. Tech. Accreditation Commn., 1998—2003; grants reviewer NSF, Washington; mem. editl. bd. Internat. Jour. of Modern Engring. Mem. editl. bd. Jour. Engring. Tech.; contbr. over 90 articles to profl. publs. Past chmn. theater adv. bd. Ind. U.-Purdue U., Indpls., faculty coun., 1989-92, exec. com., 1991-92; fundraiser Ind. U. Found., Indpls.; tech. com. Ind. Bus. Modernization Corp., Indpls., 1990-93; vestry St. Paul's Ch., Klamath Falls, Oreg., 1998-99. Lt. comdr. USN, 1965-69, Vietnam. Recipient Glenn W. Irwin award, Peter Marbaugh award Ind. U.-Purdue U. Indpls., 1988; Wright scholar Ind. U., 1961; Rsch. grantee Ctr. on Philanthropy, 1992, Fla. Engring. and Indsl. Experimentation Sta., 1993. Fellow: Am. Soc. for Engring. Edn. (exec. bd. ednl. rsch. and methods divsn. 1986—92, exec. com. engring. tech. divsn. 1994—, past chair, internat. engring. tech. Listserv adminstr., bd. dirs., Centennial award 1993, Frederick J. Berger award 2000, James H. McGraw award 2003, rsch. grantee); mem.: NSPE (educator, exec. bd., past sec., Profl. Engr. in Edn. award 1993, 1997), IEEE (sr.; com. tech. accreditation activities, past chair, press electronics tech. editl. bd.), Indpls. Sci. and Engring. Found. (bd. dirs. 1988—92), Profl. Engrs. in Oreg. (chair engring. edn. 1997—99, pres. elect 1999), Tenn. Soc. Profl. Engrs. (chair engring. edn. 1996), Soc. Mfg. Engrs. (sr.), Fla. Engring. Soc. (chair engring. edn. 1993—95), Ind. Soc. Profl. Engrs. (chair engring. edn. 1988—92), Engring Tech. Leadership Inst. (exec. coun., past chair), Univ. Faculty Club (bd. dirs. 1988—93), Scientech Club (bd. dirs. 1990—92), Order of Engr., Engring. and Sci. Hall of Fame, Phi Beta Delta, Delta Phi Alpha, Tau Alpha Pi (pres.). Republican. Episcopalian. Achievements include systems test evaluation on the Apollo booster rocket. Office: Northeastern U Sch Engring Tech 120 Snell Engring Ctr Boston MA 02115-5000 Fax: 617-373-2501. E-mail: buchanan@coe.neu.edu.

BUCHER, DOROTHY ANN, secondary education English educator; b. East St. Louis, Ill., Apr. 14, 1951; d. Edward Arthur and Margaret Louise (Christenson) B. BS in Edn., Eastern Ill. U., 1973; MS in Ednl. Adminstrn., So. Ill. U., 1986. Cert. secondary educator, adminstr., Ill. Tchr. St. Martin of Tours Sch., Washington Park, Ill., 1973-79, tchr., prin., 1979-85; tchr. English Collinsville (Ill.) H.S., 1988—. Com. mem. for the devel. of the prin. intern program Diocese of Belleville, Ill., 1980. Mem. NEA, Nat. Coun. Tchrs. English, Ill. Edn. Assn., Collinsville Edn. Assn. Home: 3 N Shore Ln Collinsville IL 62234-5537 Office: Collinsville H S 2201 S Morrison Ave Collinsville IL 62234-1449

BUCHER, KATHERINE TOTH, education educator, librarian; b. Shickshinny, Pa., July 30, 1947; d. George Washington and Edith May (Laidacker) Toth; m. Glenn Allen Bucher, June 10, 1970. BS, Millersville State Coll., 1969; MLS, Rutgers U., 1970; EdD, Auburn U., 1976. Elem. libr. Benton (Pa.) Area Schs., 1969; curriculum materials libr. Radford (Va.) Coll., 1970-71; head libr. Macon County-Tuskegee (Ala.) Pub. Libr., 1971-74; tchg. asst. Auburn (Ala.) U., 1974-75; adj. faculty Cath. U., Washington, 1979-84, U. N.C., Chapel Hill, 1979-82; prof. graduate program, dir. of elementary and middle sch. edn. Old Dominion U., Norfolk, Va., 1975—. Author: Computers and Technology in School Library Media Centers, 1994, 2d rev. edit., 1998, (with M. Lee Manning) Teaching in the Middle School, 2001, (with M. Lee Manning) Classroom Manangement, 2003; children's lit. cons. WAVY-TV, Norfolk, 1992—, WVEC-TV, Norfolk, 1992—; contbr. articles to profl. jours. Mem. adv. com. Norfolk Pub. Libr., 1990—; mem. Va. Auctioneers Assn., Richmond, Va., 1992—. Mem. Am. Libr. Assn., Am. Assn. Sch. Librs., Va. Ednl. Media Assn. Avocations: needlework, antiques and collectibles, rail fan. Office: Old Dominion Univ Dept Edn Curriculum Norfolk VA 23529-0161 E-mail: kbucher@odu.edu.

BUCHER, RICHARD DAVID, sociology educator; b. New Haven, Connecticut, Apr. 13, 1949; s. Charles Augustus and Jacqueline (Dubois) B.; m. Patricia Lawrence, July 28, 1973; children: James, Kathryn, Suzette. BA in Sociology, Colgate U., 1971; MA in Sociology, NYU, 1974; PhD in Sociology, Howard U., 1983. Instr. sociology Rock Valley Coll., Rockford, Ill., 1972-73; prof. sociology Balt. City C.C., Md., 1974—, coord. sociology, 1982-89, dir. Inst. Intercultural Understanding, 1991-96. Campus liaison Am. Assn. C.Cs./Kellogg Beacon Coll. project Promoting Intercultural Awareness and Understanding in Md. Cmty. Coll., 1992-94. Co-author: Recreation for Today's Society, 1974, 2d edit., 1984; author: Diversity Consciousness: Opening Our Minds to People, Cultures, and Opportunities, 2000. Chair Carroll County Cmty. Rels. Commn. Westminster, Md., 1990-91; chair pers. parish rels. com. Wesley-Freedom Ch., Eldersburg, Md., 1982-84. Grantee Fund for Improvement Post-Secondary Edn., Washington, 1989-90; recipient tchg. excellence award Nat. Inst. Staff and Orgnl. Devel., 1994, Ann. award Carroll County Human Rels. Commn., 2002; named Carnegie Found. for Advancement of Tchg./Case Md. Prof. of Yr., 2000. Mem. Am. Sociol. Assn., So. Sociol. Soc., Soc. for Disability Studies. Democrat. Methodist. Avocations: walking, swimming, family recreation. Home: 2538 Vance Dr Mount Airy MD 21771-8814 Office: Balt City C C 2901 Liberty Heights Ave Baltimore MD 21215-7807 E-mail: rdbucher@aol.com.

BUCHERT, STEPHANIE NICOLE, music educator; b. Seaford, Del., Sept. 2, 1976; d. John George and Connie Lee Chapis; m. Todd Michael Buchert; 1 child, Colby Skyler. student, BS in Music Edn., West Chester U., 1998. Cert. music tchr. Choir dir., asst. band dir. Cape Henlopen H.S., Lewes, Del., 1998—2002; choir dir., music tchr. Lewes Mid. Sch., 2002—. Mem. Delaware Jr. All State Chours Com., 2002—03. Mem.: Del. State Educators Assn., Del. Music Educators Assn. Avocations: singing, reading, drawing. Home: 18547 Whaleys Corner Road Georgetown DE 19947 Office: Lewes Mid Sch 820 Savannah Rd Lewes DE 19958

BUCHHOLZ, WILLIAM JAMES, communications executive, educator; b. Ladysmith, Wis., July 17, 1945; s. James Fossegard and Hazel Winnefred (Crandell) B.; m. Dorothy Ann Kostka, June 17, 1967; children: Christopher, Jeffrey. BA, U. Wis., Eau Claire, 1967; MA, Ohio U., 1968; PhD, U. Ill., 1976. Grad. asst. U. Ill., Urbana, 1972-76; asst. prof. English, bus. communication, info. design Bentley Coll., Waltham, Mass., 1976-83, assoc. prof., 1983-91, prof., 1991—, dir. undergrad./grad. bus. communication programs, 1988-95, co-chmn. dept. English, 1993; chmn. dept. English, 1995-2000; cons. in corp. comm. and internet, 1978—; chmn. dept. info. design and corp. comm., 2001—. Mgr. pubs. Scholastech Inc., Cambridge, Mass., 1983-9; cons. in field. Author: (with others) Truth and Taste: Revisiting High Ethical Standards, 1994, Writing in Business and Manufacturing, 1998; editor, author: Communication Training and Consulting in Business, Industry and Government, 1983; co-editor, contbr.: The Challenge of Change, Managing Communications and Building Corporate Image in the 1990s, 1989, Global Communications: Applying Resources Strategically, 1990; co-editor: New Corporate Relationships, 1991; contbr. articles to profl. jours., chpts. to books. With USN, 1968-72. Grantee FIPSE, 1986, 87; fellow NDEA-IV, 1967-68, inst. fellow Bentley Coll., 1991-92. Mem.: Boston IA, Phi Sigma Epsilon. Roman Catholic. Avocations: personal computing, swimming, cross-country skiing, reading, travel. Home: 44 Raffaele Dr Waltham MA 02452-0313 Office: Bentley Coll Grad Ctr 175 Forest St Waltham MA 02452-4713 E-mail: wbuchholz@bentley.edu.

BUCHIN, JEAN, psychologist, educator; b. N.Y.C., Aug. 15; d. Mac and Celia Jacobs; children: Peter J., John D. BA, CUNY; MA, Columbia U.; PhD, NYU. Tchr. N.Y.C. Pub. Schs.; counselor, asst. prof. CUNY. Mem. Nat. Bd. Cert. Counselors, Nat. Bd. Cert. Career Counselors; asst. prof. coord. Which Way With Women program Baruch Coll.; vis. asst. prof. NYU; cons. N.Y.C. Tchrs. Consortium; mem. Spkrs. Bur., Child Abuse Ctr.; mgmt. tng. cons. Met. Life Ins. Co., N.Y.C.; cons. assessment programs N.Y.C. Divsn. Pers., Sci. and Tech. Adv. Bd.; cons. N.J. Human Resources Divsn.; career cons. AARP; lectr., leader workshops 53d St. Y., NYU, Queens Coll., A.W.E.D., leader workshops Marymount Coll.; mediator ABA; cons. Child Abuse Ctr. Author: Singular Parent, Noah's Ark Minus One. Washington Sq. Coll. fellow. Mem. AAUP, ACA, APA (pres. Tri State chpt. divsn. 35), Ea. Psychol. Assn., Met. N.Y. Assn. for Applied Psychology, Bus. and Profl. Women, Career Devel. Specialists Network.

BUCHIN, STANLEY IRA, management consultant, finance educator; b. N.Y.C., Sept. 7, 1931; s. K. and Bertha (Handman) B.; m. Jacqueline Thurber Chase, Sept. 14, 1957; children: Linda C., David L., Gordon T. SB, MIT, 1952; MBA, Harvard U., 1956, DBA, 1962. Asst. to treas. Bay State Abrasives, 1956-58; rsch. asst. Harvard Bus. Sch., 1958-59, rsch. assoc., 1959-60, instr., 1960-61, lectr., 1961-62, asst. prof., 1962-66, assoc. prof., 1966-69; pres. Applied Decision Sys., Wellesley, Mass., 1969-78; v.p. Temple, Barker & Sloane, Inc., Lexington, Mass., 1975-80, sr. v.p., 1980-90; prin. Arthur D. Little, 1991-99. Pres. Boston-Bermuda Cruising Ltd., 1992-97, Gen. Ship Cruising Corp., 1994-97; vis. lectr. Templeton Coll. Oxford (Eng.), 1991-93; prof. Arthur D. Little Sch. Mgmt., 1992—; assoc. prof. Boston U., 1997—; chmn. acad. policy com. Met. Coll., long-range planning com. Mass. Sch. Profl. Psychology. Author: E-Book about Business Strategy, 2000, E-Book about Marketing, 2001. Trustee, chmn. long range planning com. Mass. Sch. Profl. Psychology. With Chem. Corps, U.S. Army, 1952-54. IBM fellow, 1962-63; George F. Baker scholar, 1956. Mem. Am. Mktg. Assn., Inst. Mgmt. Sci., Fin. Mgmt. Assn., Harvard Club Boston, Tau Beta Pi. Republican. Congregationalist. Home: Union Wharf # 304 Boston MA 02109-1206 Office: 808 Commonwealth Ave Boston MA 02215-1206 Business E-Mail: sbuchin@bu.edu.

BUCINELL, RONALD BLAISE, mechanical engineer, educator; b. Johnson City, N.Y., Feb. 3, 1958; s. Felix James and Irene Mary (Novak) B.; m. Jill Bucinell, Aug. 24; children: Ryan Michael, Benjamin David. AAS, Rochester Inst. Tech., 1978, BS, 1981; MS, Drexel U., 1983, PhD, 1987. Registered profl. engr., N.Y. Engr. Boeing Aerospace, Seattle, 1979-80; rsch. asst. Dyna East Corp., Wynnewood, Pa., 1983-85; rsch. analyst Hercules Aerospace, Magna, Utah, 1987-89; rsch. engr. Materials Scis. Corp., Blue Bell, Pa., 1989-93; v.p. Innotech, Schenectady, N.Y., 1991—. Adj. asst. prof. Temple U., Phila., 1991—, U. Utah, Salt Lake City, 1988-90; assoc. prof. Union Coll., Schenectady, 1993—, dir. Composite Material Mfg. & Evaluation Lab.; creator virtual internat. design studio. Publ. reviewer: Jour. Composite Materials, 1988—; co-editor Jour. Composite Tech. and Rsch.; contbr. articles to profl. jours. Initiated a pilot hands-on sci. program for 1st-5th graders, later adopted, Schenectady Schs., mem. PTO, mem. Shared Decision Making Com. Fellow NASA. Mem. AIAA, Soc. Exptl. Mechs., ASME, ASM, ASTM (chmn. task group, chmn. subcom.), Am. Soc. Engring. Edn., KC (4th deg.), Sigma Xi. Achievements include the development of methodology for altering failure modes in composite overwrapped pressure vessels; scaling methodology for response of composite materials; stochastic damage progression model for composite materials; test procedures and fixtures for evaluating the behavior of composite materials; developer of the international virtual design studio concept in engineering education. Home: 1063 Merlin Dr Schenectady NY 12309-1633 Office: Union Coll Steinmetz Hall Schenectady NY 12308 E-mail: bucinelr@union.edu.

BUCINSKI, JANICE KAY, secondary education educator; b. Poplar Bluff, Mo., Mar. 24, 1952; d. John Wiley and Sylvia (Brown) Smith; 1 child, Wesley Alexander. BA in History and Edn., U. Ark., 1974; MS in Edn., Ea. Ill. U., 1991. Lic. tchr., Ill., Mo. Social studies tchr. Bryant (Ark.) H.S., 1974-77, Meml. H.S., Evansville, Ind., 1981-82; market support rep. Van Ausdall and Farrar, Evansville, Ind., 1983-86; adminstrv. asst. Farm Credit Svcs., Effingham, Ill., 1986-87; social studies tchr. Effingham H.S., 1987-92, Cmty. H.S. Dist. # 218, Oak Lawn, Ill., 1992—. Girl's track and field coach Effingham H.S., 1989-92; asst. girl's cross-country coach Eisenhower H.S., Blue Island, Ill., 1992; yearbook advisor Polaris Sch., Oak Lawn, 1993—. Active Friends of the Libr., Art Inst. Chgo., Chgo. Hist. Soc. Mem. NEA, Ill. Edn. Assn., Aircraft Owners and Pilots Assn., Internat. Women's Pilot Assn., Phi Delta Kappa. Avocations: aviation, golf, reading, travelling, sports, aerobic dance. Home: 10223 S Central Park Ave Evergreen Park IL 60805-3717

BUCK, CATHERINE ANN, special education educator; b. Chgo., Oct. 6, 1961; d. Chester U. and Betty J. (Terry) Buck. BA in Spl. Edn., Northeastern Ill. U., 1984, MA in Spl. Edn., 1988. Cert. tchr., Ill. Tchr. Chgo. Bd. Edn., 1984—, reading instr., 1990-91, 1999—2001. Tchr. art after sch. program Chgo. Bd. Edn., 1987; tchr. spl. edn. Molloy Sch., Morton Grove, Ill., 1989—91, Morton Grove, 1994—96. Mem. Coun. for Exceptional Children, Alpha Chi, Delta Kappa Gamma. Democrat. Avocations: dancing, swimming. Home: 4535 N Long Ave Apt 3B Chicago IL 60630-3531

BUCK, DONALD TIRRELL, retired finance educator; b. Manchester, N.H., Nov. 17, 1931; s. Harry Forrest and Gladys (Tirrell) B.; m. Marion Gilmour, Aug. 2, 1969; children: Marianne Elizabeth, Elizabeth Allison Tirrell Buck Rizzo. BS, U. N.H., 1955, MA, 1961. Analyst New England Mut. Life Ins. Co., Boston, 1957-59; instr. fin. U. Pa. Wharton Sch. Bus., Phila., 1961-65; asst. prof. econs. and fin. So. Conn. State Coll., New Haven, 1965-74; assoc. prof. So. Conn. State U., New Haven, 1975-80, prof., 1981-97, emeritus prof., 1998—, mem. faculty senate, 1968-76, chmn. dept. acctg. fin., 1984-85. Pub. mem. investment adv. coun. to treas. State of Conn., Hartford, 1983-92. Contbr. articles to profl. publs. Mem. adv. coun. bd. Higher Edn. State of Conn., 1983-85; participant econ. workshop hearings legis. fin. com. Gen. Assembly, Conn., 1978-83. With U.S. Army, 1955-57. Mem. AAUP (pres. So. Conn. State U. chpt. 1981-83), SAR (pres. Nathan Hale chpt. 1993-96, auditor Conn. State chpt. 1993-99), Am. Econ. Assn., Soc. Colonial Wars in State of Conn., Boston Athenaeum (life mem.). Congregationalist. Home: Old Town St Hadlyme CT 06439-0129 Office: So Conn State U 501 Crescent St New Haven CT 06515-1330

BUCK, JANE LOUISE, psychology educator; b. Reading, Pa., Mar. 10, 1933; d. C. Robert and Viola Louise (Berger) B.; m. Leo Laskaris, Oct. 7, 1954 (div. Aug. 1978); 1 child, Julie. BA, U. Del., 1953, MA, 1959, MEd, 1966, PhD, 1971. Instr. U. Del., Newark, 1964-66; rsch. assoc. Rsch. for Better Schs., Phila., 1967-68; asst. prof. Del. State U., Dover, 1969-73, assoc. prof., 1973-77, prof. psychology, 1977-98. Cons. in stats. E.I. duPont de Nemours, Wilmington, Del., 1983-93; vis. prof. Ctr. for Sci. and Culture, U. Del., 1986; bd. dirs. The Blvd. and Beyond, Wilmington. Author: Specifying the Risk, 1985; contbr. articles to profl. jours. Speaker, evaluator Del. Humanities Forum, 1980-88; pres. Del. Gerontol. Soc., Newark, 1987-88; mem. town coun. Chesapeake City, Md., 1998-2000; commr. parks and recreation, Chesapeake City, Md., 1998-99; bd. dirs. Friends of Cecil County Libr., 2000. Mem. AAAS (mem. sr. scientists and engrs.), AAUP (nat. coun. 1987-90, 93-99, pres. Del. State U. chpt. 1976-80, 95-98, chief negotiator 1982-98, mem. nat. com. on historically Black colls. and univs. and status of minorities in the profession 1988-91, 1998-2000, interim sec. Del. Conf 1991-92, pres. Del. conf. 1993-2000, mem. nat. com. govtl. rels. 1994-97, Sternberg award for collective bargaining 1994, nat. pres. 2000—), Am. Psychol. Soc., Coun. Tchrs. Undergrad. Psychology, Humanities and Tech. Assn., Am. Statis. Assn. (v.p. Del. chpt. 1999-2000), Danforth Assocs., Kappa Delta Pi, Psi Chi, Alpha Chi Omega. Avocations: classical music, reading, gardening, sewing, computer graphics. E-mail: buck@count.com.

BUCK, LAWRENCE PAUL, academic administrator, educator; b. Pittsburg, Kans., Oct. 6, 1944; m. Judy L.; children: David L., Laura T. BA, Wichita State U., 1966; MA, Ohio State U., 1967, PhD in History, 1971. Asst. prof. Widener U., Chester, Pa., 1971-77, assoc. prof. history, 1977-85, prof. history, 1985—, dean Coll. Arts and Scis., 1981-84, acad. v.p., provost, 1984—, acting pres., 1994, 2001—02. Author: Die Haltung der Nurnberger Bauernschaft im Bauernkrieg, 1970, Opposition to Tithes in the Peasants' Revolt, 1973, Civil Insurrection in a Reformation City, 1976, Demands for Reform by Urban Dissidents During the German Peasants' Revolt, 1977, The Reformation, Purgatory, and Perpetual Rents in the Revolt of 1525 at Frankfurt am Main, 1985; translator: Monemvasia: The Town and Its History, 1981; co-editor: The Social History of the Reformation; contbr. articles to profl. jours., book chpts. Rsch. grantee Am. Philos. Soc., 1973, NEH, 1974. Mem. Am. Soc. Reformation Rsch., 16th Century Study Conf. Office: Widener U Office of the Provost One University Pl Chester PA 19013 E-mail: lawrence.p.buck@widener.edu.

BUCK, LORI ANN, special education educator; b. Dayton, Ohio, Nov. 16, 1966; m. Bobby Ray Buck; children: Travis, Jason, Cassie, Paige. BEd magna cum laude, Wright State U., 1989; M in Reading, U. Dayton, 1996. Learning disabilities tchr. Miamisburg (Ohio) City Schs., 1990, West Carrollton (Ohio) City Schs., 1990—. Ind. beauty cons. Mary Kay. Mem. Miamisburg Assembly of God. Avocations: horseback riding, swimming, camping.

BUCK, RICHARD PIERSON, chemistry educator, researcher; b. L.A., July 29, 1929; s. Richard Maurice and Lucile Frances (Pierson) B.; m. Mary Ann Kenney, May 23, 1959; children: Nancy Elizabeth Buck McKenna, Pierson Kenney, Margaret Ruth Bok. BS, Calif. Inst. Tech., 1950, MS, 1951; PhD, MIT, 1954. Teaching asst. MIT, Cambridge, 1951-52, NSF fellow, 1952-53, Dupont teaching fellow, 1953-54; rsch. chemist Chevron Rsch. Corp., Richmond, Calif., 1954-61, asst. to gen. mgr., 1956-58; prin. rsch. chemist Bell & Howell Rsch. Ctr., Pasadena, Calif., 1961-65; sr. scientist Beckman Instrument Co., Fullerton, Calif., 1965-67; assoc. prof. chemistry U. N.C., Chapel Hill, 1967-75, prof., 1975—, adj. prof. biomed. engring. and math. Sch. Medicine, 1990—99, prof. emeritus, 1999—. Kenan prof.-on-leave U. Bristol, Eng., 1976-77; vis. prof. Imperial Coll., London, 1987, Bundeswehr U. Munich, 1989-91; cons. Eastman Kodak, Rochester, N.Y., 1969-77, E.I. duPont de Nemours & Co., Wilmington, Del., 1979-84; mem. adv. bd. I-Stat Corp., Princeton, N.J., 1984-90, HemoSense, Inc., San Jose, Calif, 1998—, NIH resource at Case Western Res. U., Cleve., 1977-84, Ctr. for Solid State Sensors, U. Pa. Moore Sch. Engring., Phila., 1980-84; chmn. A Nomenclature Commn., Internat. Union Pure and Applied Chemistry, 1991—. Author: (with V.V. Cosofret) Pharmaceutical Applications of Membrane Sensors, 1992; mem. editorial bd. 4 internat. chemistry jours.; contbr. over 350 articles to sci. jours. Recipient C.N. Reilley award Soc. Electroanalytical Chemistry, 2000; Von Humboldt grantee, Bonn, Germany, 1989-91, grantee Advanced Rsch. Projects Agy., 1967-71, NSF, 1971—, N.C. Biotech. Ctr., 1990-94. Fellow Electrochem. Soc. (div. chmn., outstanding achievement award sensor divsn. 1996); mem. Am. Chem. Soc., Internat. Soc. Electrochemistry (bd. dirs. 1988-91), Bohemian Club (San Francisco). Avocations: performing chamber music, solo piano playing. Home: 101 Creekview Cir Carrboro NC 27510-4111 also: 139 Elliott Dr Menlo Park CA 94025-2622 Office: U NC Dept Chemistry CB 3290 Venable Hl Chapel Hill NC 27599-0001

BUCKELEW, CAROLYN ROSE PIERCE, nursing educator; b. Norfolk, Va., May 23, 1946; d. William Patrick and Rose Veronica (McHugh) Pierce; m. Paul Thomas Buckelew, Mar. 7, 1969; 1 child, Heather Lael. BSN, Va. Commonwealth U., 1970; MA in Edn., Seton Hall U., 1978. RN, Va., N.J.; cert. Nat. Bd. Cert. Counselors; cert. clin. specialist in adult psychiat. mental health nursing ANCC; cert. hypnotherapist; lic. clin. specialist, prescriptive practice. Indsl. nurse United Engrs., Linden, N.J., 1970; staff nurse Carrier Found., Belle Meade, N.J., 1972, 73-74; instr. nursing Charles E. Gregory Sch. Nursing, Raritan Bay Med. Ctr., Perth Amboy, NJ, 1973—2003; pvt. practice, 1985—. Cons. Ctr. for Life Dynamics, West Orange, N.J., 1984—. D. Loren Southern, M.D., Princeton, N.J., 1989-94; workshop spkr., 1986—; presenter radio programs Roles in Nursing, Sta. WCTC, 1990; 1st spkr. Masters in Residence on AIDS, Spkrs. Bur. Carrier Found., Raritan Bay Med. Ctr., 1990-93, Raritan Bay, 1990-2003; reviewer textbooks; spkr. in field; presenter N.J. Nursing Students Conv. Contbr. articles to profl. jours. Vol. Health Fairs, East Brunswick, Old Bridge, N.J., 1975—, Hand-in-Hand, Middlesex C.C., Edison, N.J., 1986-99, Cystic Fibrosis, East Brunswick, 1988; speaker family asthma program Am. Lung Assn., Freehold, N.J., 1982-87; sec. exec. bd. St. Thomas Parish Coun., Old Bridge, 1988-92. Recipient vol. recognition award Marlboro Psychiat. Hosp., 1988. Mem. Assn. Diploma Schs. Profl. Nursing (nomination com. 1988-89, sec. exec. bd. 1988-93), Interant. Assn. Counselors, Nat. League Nursing, N.J. State Nursing Assn., N.J. League Nursing, Social Cert. Clin. Specialist exec. bd. (treas. 1999—), Nat. Assn. Cert. Hypnotists, Raritan Bay Med. Ctr. Old Br. Aux. (exec. bd. 1989-2001, treas. 1999-2003), E. Hanson Aux. (spkr. on stress mgmt. 1992, therapeutic touch 1994-2003, insomnia mgmt.), Carrier Found. Aux. Avocations: hiking, crocheting, biking, reading. Home: 79 Hilliard Rd Old Bridge NJ 08857-1535 Office: Charles E Gregory Sch Nursing 530 New Brunswick Ave Perth Amboy NJ 08861-3674

BUCKELLEW, WILLIAM FRANKLIN, retired education educator; b. Georgetown, Ill., June 10, 1928; s. Frank and Verla (Haworth) B.; m. Lois Soliah, Apr. 9, 1952; children: Michael, Mark, Jon. BS, N.D. State U., 1953; MS, U. Ill., 1954; EdD, U. Ark., 1968. Cert. tchr., coach, Ill. Tchr., coach Kanakaee (Ill.) Pub. Schs., 1954-56; athletic dir. Lake Park High Sch., Medinah, Ill., 1956-62; asst. prof. phys. edn. Ea. Ill. U., Charleston, 1962-68, assoc. prof. teaching, rsch. and kinesiology, 1968-70, prof., chmn. dept. phys. edn., 1970-77, coord. grad. program dept. health, phys. edn. and recreation, 1977-88, acting dean Coll. Health, Phys. Edn. and Recreation, 1986-88, adviser to postgrad. students Coll. Edn., 1988-93; ret., 1993. Mem. com. on assessment Ill. Office Edn., Springfield, 1973-75, com. on competency-based tchr. edn. program, 1975-78; ednl. cons. to Ill. sch. dists., 1960-82; cons., evaluator Nat. Coun. Accreditation of Tchr. Edn., 1973, 85; speaker, rsch. cons. Asian Phys. Edn. and Sport Rsch. Assn., Kaoshiung, Taiwan, 1984; chmn. Ill. Athletic Coaching Cert. Program, 1985-86; presenter at profl. confs. Contbr. articles to Ill. Jour. Health, Phys. Edn. and Recreation, Asian Jour. Phys. Edn., others. With USAF, 1946-49. Mem. NEA, AAHPERD, Ill. Assn. Health, Phys. Edn., Recreation and Dance, N.Am. Soc. Psychology of Sport and Phys. Edn., Ill. Edn. Assn., Ill. Assn. Higher Edn., Fishing Tackle Collectors Ill., Nat. Fishing Lure Collectors Club, Masons, Scottish Rite, Shriners, Phi Epsilon Kappa, Phi Delta Kappa, Sigma Alpha Epsilon. Methodist. Avocations: hunting, fishing, collecting hunting and fishing artifacts. Home: 1602 Shaffer Pl Charleston IL 61920-3163

BUCKINGHAM, BARBARA RAE, social studies educator; b. Union City, Ind., Jan. 27, 1932; d. Ray E. and Edith A. (Wagner) B. BA cum laude, Hanover Coll., 1954; MA, Ind. Univ., 1956. Tchr. City Sch. Dist., Marion, Ohio, 1956-64, social studies educator Rochester, NY, 1966—. Editor: Revonah, 1954; art work Aldelphean, 1959. Vol. Peace Corps, Ethiopia, 1964-66, Mary Cariola Children's Ctr., Christian Heritage Homes, Hope Hall, Congresswomen Louise Slaughter Campaign, 1996-97, 96-98; gov. bd. Rochester Returned Peace Corps Vols., 1968-76; election com. mem. Councilwoman Letvin, Gates, N.Y., 1980; steering com. Pub. Affairs Forum, Hanover, 1952, DAR. Mem. AAUW (pres. 1958-59), DAR, Nat. Peace Corps Assn., Friends of Ethiopia, Rochester Tchr. Assn., Pi Gamma Mu (Outstanding Grad. award 1954), Gamma Sigma Pi, Alpha Phi Gamma. Democrat. Presbyterian. Avocations: travel, art work. Home: 64 Lyellwood Pkwy Rochester NY 14606-4532

BUCKLAND, MICHAEL KEEBLE, librarian, educator; b. Wantage, Eng., Nov. 23, 1941; came to U.S., 1972; s. Walter Basil and Norah Elaine (Rudd) B.; m. Waltraud Leeb, July 11, 1964; children: Anne Margaret, Anthony Francis. BA, Oxford U., 1963; postgrad. diploma in librarianship, Sheffield U., 1965, PhD, 1972. Grad. trainee Bodleian Library, Oxford, Eng., 1963-64; asst. librarian U. Lancaster (Eng.) Library, 1965-72; asst. dir. for tech. svcs. Purdue U. Libraries, West Lafayette, Ind., 1972-75; assoc. prof. Sch. of Info. Mgmt. and Sys. U. Calif., Berkeley, 1976-79, dean, 1976-84, prof., 1979—, asst. v.p. library plans and policies, 1983-87; v.p. Ind. Coop. Library Svcs. Auth., 1974-75. Co-dir. Electronic Cultural Atlas Initiative, 2000—; vis. scholar Western Mich. U., 1979; vis. prof. U. Klagenfurt, Austria, 1980, U. New South Wales, Australia, 1988. Author: Book Availability and the Library User, 1975, (with others) The Use of Gaming in Education for Library Management, 1976, Reader in Operations Research for Libraries, 1976, Library Services in Theory and Context, 1983, 2d edit., 1988, Information and Information Systems, 1991, Redesigning Library Services, 1992; editor: Historical Studies in Information Science, 1998, Robert Gitler and the Japan Library School, 1999. Fulbright Rsch. scholar U. Tech., Graz, Austria, 1989. Mem. ALA, Am. Soc. Info. Sci. (pres. 1998), Assn. Libr. and Info. Sci. Edn., Calif. Libr. Assn. Office: U Calif Sch Info Mgmt And Sys Berkeley CA 94720-0001

BUCKLEITNER, WARREN WILLIAM, editor, former elementary school educator; b. St. Joseph, Mich., Sept. 30, 1958; s. Eric and Mary Lee (Hoos) B.; m. Ellen Wolock, July 15, 1991; children: Sarah, Jenna. BS in Elem. Edn., Ctrl. Mich. U., 1981; MA in Human Devel., Pacific Oaks Coll., Pasadena, Calif., 1986; postgrad., Mich. State U., 1992—. Cert. tchr., Mich. Tchr. Susnet Elem. Sch., Vicksburg, Mich., 1982, McKinley Elem.Sch., Cadillac, Mich., 1983; sr. cons. High/Scope Edn. Rsch. Found., 1983-93; editor Children's Software Revue, Ypsilanti, Mich., 1993—. Cons. in field. Contbr. numerous articles to profl. jours. Recipient Codie award for best software reviewer Software Pubs. Assn., 1995. Office: Children's Software Revue 120 Main St Flemington NJ 08822-1411

BUCKLER, MARILYN LEBOW, school psychologist, educational consultant; b. N.Y.C., Mar. 18, 1933; d. Herman and Gertrude (Abolitz) Lebow; m. Sheldon A. Buckler, June 1, 1952 (div. 1978); children: Julie, Eve, Sarah Buckler Welcome. BS cum laude, NYU, 1954; MEd in Counseling, Northeastern U., 1970. Cert. ednl. psychologist, Mass.; sch. guidance counselor, Mass., sch. psychologist, Mass. Kindergarten tchr. Washington Pub. Schs., 1955-56, Stamford (Conn.) Pub. Schs., 1956-58; guidance counselor Framingham (Mass.) Pub. Schs., 1969-70; sch. psychologist, guidance counselor Carlisle (Mass.) Pub. Schs., 1970-95; parent program cons. Reach out to Schs. program Wellesley Coll.-Stone Ctr., 1993—. Tchr. parenting course Middlesex C.C., Bedford, Mass., 1990—, cons. LEAP program, 1992-93; workshop leader, creator parenting courses, various pvt. schs. and orgns., Mass., 1990—; spl. project cons., workshop specialist "Families First" Wheelock Coll., 1995—. Mem. ACA, Mass. Sch. Counselor Assn., Mass. Sch. Psychologists Assn., Pi Lambda Theta. Avocations: films, cooking, traveling, reading.

BUCKLEW, NEIL S. educator, past university president; b. Morgantown, W.Va., Oct. 23, 1940; s. Douglas Earl and Lanah L. (Martin) B.; children—Elizabeth, Jennifer, Jeffrey. AB, U. Mo.; MS, U. N.C.; PhD (grad. fellow), U. Wis. Dir. personnel Duke U., 1964-66; dir. employee relations U. Wis., 1966-70; prof., v.p. Central Mich. U., Mt. Pleasant, 1970-76; prof., provost Ohio U., Athens, 1976-80; pres. U. Mont., Missoula, 1981-86, W.Va. U., 1986-95, prof., 1995—. Vis. rsch. fellow Pa. State U.; arbitrator in field. Author: Public Sector Collective Bargaining, Planning in Higher Education. Mem. Nat. Assn. State Univs. and Land Grant Colls. Office: West Va U PO Box 6025 Morgantown WV 26506-6025 E-mail: nbucklew@wvu.edu.

BUCKLEY, EDWARD JOSEPH, retired academic dean; b. Belleville, Ont., Can., Aug. 28, 1920; s. William John and Mary Jane (Conlin) B. BA, U. Ottawa, Ont., 1952, MA, 1958. Tchg. master Ont. Coll. Edn., Toronto; treas. Famous Players Can. Corp., Belleville, 1940-60; dir. Fed. Govt. Adult Tng. Program, Belleville, 1960-70; dir. tech. divsn. Loyalist Coll. Applied Arts and Scis., Belleville, 1970-75, dean continuing edn., 1976-85. Author: History of St. Michael's Paris: 1829-1979, 1983. Mem., chmn. Belleville Separate Sch. Bd., 1943-60; bd. dirs. Belleville Dept. Health, 1949-56; mem. Belleville Retarded Children's Authority, 1952-59. Decorated Knight Equestrian Order Holy Sepulchre, Knight Sovereign, M.I. Order Malta. Mem. K.C. (state dept. Ont. 1978-80, dir. New Haven 1983-90). Liberal. Roman Catholic. Home: 153 Dundas St W Belleville ON Canada K8P 1A7

BUCKLEY, MYRNA J. secondary school educator; b. Bangor, Me., Aug. 17, 1946; d. Maurice Arthur and Marie Ruth (Oak) Eastman (dec.); m. J. Larry Buckley, Oct. 14, 1967; children: Blake Morris, Benton James. BS, West Tex. A&M U., 1990, MEd, 1994. Cert. elem. sch. tchr., Tex. Tchr. grade 6 Hereford (Tex.) Independent Sch. Dist., 1991; tchr. English grade 8 Hereford (Tex.) Jr. H.S., 1991—98, tchr. speech grade 7, 8, 1994—98; tchr. English grade 8 Littlefield (Tex.) Jr. H.S., 1998—. Rep. Leadership Team Hereford (Tex.) Jr. H.S., 1993-95, Middle Sch. Conf., 1993, 94; Tex. rep. Ea. N. Mex. U. writing project, Portales, N. Mex., 1992-95; English rep. pilot team Hereford (Tex.) Jr. H.S., 1993; tchr., organizer, dir. plays Hereford Jr. H.S.-Students Articulately Speaking, 1993. Mem. Nat. Coun. Tchrs. English, Tex. Coun. Tchrs. English, Tex. A&M Aggie Mothers' Club, Tex. Classroom Tchrs. Assn., Tex. Middle Sch. Assn., Kappa Delta Pi (sec. 1994-95). Home: RR 1 Box 179 Littlefield TX 79339-9552 Office: Littlefield Jr H S 105 N Lake St Littlefield TX 79339

BUCKLEY, REBECCA HATCHER, physician, educator; b. Hamlet, N.C., Apr. 1, 1933; d. Martin Armstead and Nora (Langston) Hatcher; m. Charles Edward Buckley III, July 9, 1955; children: Charles Edward IV, Elizabeth Ann, Rebecca Kathryn, Sarah Margaret. BA, Duke U., 1954; MD, U. N.C., 1958. Intern Duke U. Med. Ctr., Durham, N.C., 1958-59, resident, 1959-61, pediat. allergist and immnologist, 1961—. Dir. Am. Bd. Allergy and Immunology, Phila., 1971-73, chair exam. com., 1971-73, co-chair bd. dirs., 1982-84; chair Diagnostic Lab. Immunology, 1984-88; mem. staff Duke U. Med. Ctr.; asst. prof. pediat. and immunology, 1968-72, assoc. prof. pediat., 1972-76, prof. pediat., 1976-79, assoc. prof. immunology, 1972-79, prof. immunology, 1979—, J. Buren Sidbury prof. pediat., 1979—. Contbr. articles to profl. jours. Recipient Allergic Diseases Acad. award Nat. Inst. Allergy and Infectious Diseases, 1974-79, Merit Rsch. award NIH, 1987-97, Nat. Bd. award Med. Coll. Pa., 1991, Clemons von Pirquet award Georgetown, 1993, Disting. Tchr. award Duke U. Med. Alumni Assn., 1993, Lifetime Achievement award Immune Deficiency Found., 1994, Disting. Svc. award Am. Acad. Allergy and Immunology, 1996, Disting. Faculty award Duke U. Med. Alumni Assn., 1998. Fellow AAAS (chair med. scis. sect. 2001-03), Am. Acad. Allergy and Immunology (exec. com. 1975-82, pres. 1979-80, hon. fellow award 1999); mem. Am. Assn. Immunologists, Soc. Pediatric Rsch., Am. Acad. Pediatrics (Bret Ratner award 1992), Southeastern Allergy Assn. (pres. 1978-79), Am. Pediatric Soc. (coun. mem. 1991—, pres. 1999-2000, chmn. immune deficiency found. med. adv. com. 2003—). Republican. Episcopalian. Home: 3621 Westover Rd Durham NC 27707-5032 Office: Duke U Med Ctr PO Box 2898 Durham NC 27710-2898 E-mail: BUCKL003@mc.duke.edu.

BUCKLIN, LOUIS PIERRE, business educator, consultant; b. N.Y.C., Sept. 20, 1928; s. Louis Lapham and Elja (Barricklow) B.; m. Weylene Edwards, June 11, 1956; children: Randolph E., Rhonda W. Student, Dartmouth Coll., 1950; MBA, Harvard U., 1954; PhD, Northwestern U., 1960; PhD with honors (hon.), Stockholm Sch. Econs., 2001. Asst. prof. bus. U. Colo., Boulder, 1954-56; instr. in bus. Northwestern U., Evanston, 1958-59, assoc. dean Grad. Sch. Bus. Adminstrn., 1981-83; prof. bus. adminstrn. U. Calif., Berkeley, 1960-93, prof. emeritus, 1993—. Mem. ASUC Aux. Enterprise Bd., 1999—, chmn., 2000-2001; vis. prof. Stockholm Sch. Econs., 1983, INSEAD, Fontainebleau, France, 1984, Erasmus U., Rotterdam, Netherlands, 1993-94, Cath. U. Leuven, Belgium, 1994; prin. Bucklin Assocs., Lafayette, Calif., 1975—; adv. bd. Gemini Cons., San Francisco, 1987-94. Author: (books) A Theory of Distribution Channel Structure, 1966, Competition Evolution in the Distrubutive Trades, 1972, Productivity in Marketing, 1979; editor: Vertical Marketing Systems, 1971, (books) Channels and Channel Institutions, 1986, (journal) Jour. of Retailing, 1996—2001. Mem. City of Lafayette Planning Commn., 1990-93. Capt. USMC, 1951-53, Korea. Recipient Alpha Kappa Psi Found. award for best paper in Jour. Mktg., 1993, Lifetime Recognition for scholarly contbns. to retailing Soc. for Mktg. Advances, 2001. Mem. Inst. for Ops. Rsch. Mgmt. Scis., Am. Mktg. Assn. (Paul D. Converse award 1986), Soc. for Mktg. Advances (Lifetime Achievement award 2001). Democrat. Avocations: travel, microcomputers, photography. Office: U Calif Haas Sch Bus Berkeley CA 94720-0001 E-mail: pbucklin@haas.berkeley.edu.

BUCK-MOORE, JOANNE ROSE, nursing administrator, educator; b. Cambridge, Mass., Jan. 3, 1939; d. Joseph J. and Louise L. (Buck) Verrochio; m. C. Edwin Buck (dec.); m. Donald P. Moore (dec.); children: Marie-Louise, Victoria, Katrina, Edwin. ASN, Middlesex C.C., Bedford, Mass., 1977; BSN magna cum laude, Worcester (Mass.) State Coll., 1980; MSN, U. R.I., 1983. RN, Mass. Dir. nursing Ctr. for Rehab. at Columbus, East Boston, Mass., Mt. Pleasant Hosp., Lynn, Mass.; nurse mgr. and program dir. Commonwealth of Mass. Dept. of Mental Health, Boston. Course instr. Palm Beach C.C., Fla. Atlantic U.; lectr. at schs., clubs, seminars, confs.; legal cons. and expert witness. Author: Management by Objective: A Handbook for Nurses. Mem. ANA (cert. mental health nurse), Sigma Theta Tau. Home: 18 Faulkner Hill Rd Acton MA 01720-4211

BUCKNER, JOHN CRAWFORD, psychologist, educator; b. Boston, Oct. 3, 1957; s. Philip Franklin and Ann Haswell (Smith) B.; m. Elizabeth Hall Cousins, July 16, 1983; children: Kimberly Cousins, Mila Ann. BA, Stanford U., 1979; MA, U. Hawaii, 1981; PhD, U. Md., 1986. Clin. psychology intern Crownsville (Md.) Hosp. Ctr., 1983-84; postdoctoral fellow Johns Hopkins U., Balt., 1986-89; extramural rsch. staff fellow NIMH, Rockville, Md., 1989-91; lectr. on psychiatry Harvard U., Boston, 1991—; assoc. dir. rsch. The Better Homes Fund, Newton, Mass., 1991-94, dir. rsch., 1994-98; instr. psychiatry Harvard Med. Sch., Boston, 1999—. Mem. editl. bd. Am. Jour. Cmty. Psychology, 1994—; rsch. editor Am. Jour. Orthopsychiatry, 1994-99. Contbr. articles to profl. jours. NIMH fellow Johns Hopkins U., 1987, 88; NIMH grantee 1994—. Mem. APA, APHA, Am. Orthopsychiat. Assn. Office: Children's Hosp Dept Psychiatry 300 Longwood Ave Boston MA 02115-5724

BUCKNER-REITMAN, JOYCE, psychologist, educator; b. Benton, Ark., Sept. 25, 1937; d. Waymond Floyd Pannell and Willie Evelyn (Wright) Whitley; m. John W. Buckner, Aug. 29, 1958 (div. 1970); children: Cheryl, John, Chris; m. Sanford Reitman, Aug. 13, 1994. BA, Ouachita Bapt. Coll., 1959; MS in Edn., Henderson State U., 1964; PhD, North Tex. State U., 1970. Lic. psychologist, Tex., marriage and family therapist; cert. Nat. Registry Health Svc. Providers in Psychology; master trainer in imago relationship therapy. Assoc. prof. U. Tex., Arlington, 1970-80, chmn. dept. edn., 1976-78; pvt. practice psychology, Arlington, 1974—. Dir., chief profl. officer Southwest Inst. Relationship Devel., Weatherford, Tex.; author, profl. speaker; appeared on internat. TV shows, including Oprah Winfrey Show. Mem. APA, Nat. Assn. for Imago Relationship Therapy (pres.), Nat. Speakers Assn., Am. Assn. Marital and Family Therapy. Avocations: dancing, travel, art. Home: 2208 Farmer Rd Weatherford TX 76087-6964 E-mail: JoyBuckner@aol.com.

BUCKWALTER, JOHN DAVID, biologist educator; b. Strasburg, Pa., Feb. 10, 1951; s. Robert Denlinger and Faith Martin (Steffy) B.; m. Laurel Jo Grastorf, Nov. 26, 1971; children: Janna, Rachel, Martha, Jewel, Esther. BS, Houghton Coll., 1973; MA, SUNY, Geneseo, 1980. Cert. tchr. biology and chemistry 7-12, N.Y. Grad. tchg. asst. SUNY, Geneseo, 1975-76; tchr. sci. Bible Acad., Nazareth, Ethiopia, 1976-79, Andover (N.Y.) H.S., 1980-82; prof. biology SUNY, Alfred, 1982—. Cons. Penn-York Energy Corp., Wellsville, N.Y., 1987-88. Mem. sch. bd. Alfred-Almond (N.Y.) Ctrl. Sch., 1988-99, Wellsville (N.Y.) Christian Sch., 1984-89. Recipient Outstanding award Outstanding Young Men Am., 1986, Excellance award Nat. Inst. for Staff and Orgnl. Devel., 1993; named Tchr. of Yr. SUNY Alfred Alumni Assn., 1991. Mem. Am. Sci. Affiliation, Empire State Assn. of Two Yr. Coll. Biologists. Republican. Mennonite. Office: Life Sci Dept SUNY Coll Tech Alfred NY 14802 E-mail: buckwajd@alfredstate.edu.

BUCZYNSKI, MARY FRANCES, speech therapist; b. Wilkes Barre, Pa., June 1, 1954; d. Frank Edward and Mary (Waslowski) B. BS, Pa. State U., 1976; MS summa cum laude, Bloomsburg (Pa.) U., 1986. Speech-lang. clinician Luzerne Intermediate Unit #18, Kingston, Pa., 1976-92; speech therapist Novacare, King of Prussia, Pa., 1988—; speech-lang. clinician Hanover Area Sch. Dist., Wilkes Barre, Pa., 1992—; speech therapist Therapy Care/Team Rehab., Williamsport, Pa., 1992—; home health speech therapist Allied-John Hienz, Wilkes Barre, Pa., 1992—. Speech therapist Crossroads Thearapy, Pocono Mountain, Pa., 1993-95, Step-by-Step Inst. of Human Rels., Kingston, 1985-88, Inst. of Human Rels., Wilkes Barre, 1977-78. Mem. St. Joseph's Ch., Wilkes Barre, 1954—, Rep. Nat. Party, Wilkes Barre, 1976—, Wilkes Barre Ballet Co., 1982-92, MADD, Wilkes Barre, 1990—, WVIA Channel 44, Wilkes Barre, 1991—, Lee Park PTA, Hanover Twp., Pa., 1993-95, FM Kirby Ctr., Wilkes Barre, 1993—, Mem. Am. Speech and Hearing Assn., N.E. Speech and Hearing Assn., PSEA, HEAA, Pa. Speech and Hearing Assn. Republican. Avocations: weight training, running, swimming, tennis, art, poetry. Home: 75 Wesley St Forty Fort PA 18704-4115

BUDALUR, THYAGARAJAN SUBBANARAYAN, chemistry educator; b. India, July 14, 1929; came to U.S., 1969, naturalized, 1977; s. Subbanarayan Subbuswamy and Parvatham (Gopalakrishnan) B.; children: Chitra, Poorna, Kartik. MA, U. Madras, 1951, M.Sc., 1954, PhD, 1956. Reader organic chemistry U. Madras, 1960-68; prof. chemistry U. Idaho, Moscow, 1968-74; prof. chemistry, dir. div. earth phys. sci. U. Tex., San Antonio, 1974-2000, emeritus prof., 2000—. Lectr. in field. Author: Mechanisms of Molecular Migrations; Selective Organic Transformations; Editorial bd. chem. jours.; contbr. articles to profl. jours.; 3 patents in field. Recipient Intra Sci. Research award, 1966 Fellow Am. Chem. Soc.; mem. Chem. Soc. London, Soc. Cosmetic Chemistry N.Y. Acad. Sci., Am. Inst. Chemists, Sigma Xi, Phi Kappa Phi. Clubs: Lions. Home: 6119 Amble Trl San Antonio TX 78249-2108

BUDD, NANCY J. lawyer, school system administrator; b. Glendale, Calif., Dec. 28, 1951; d. Arthur Richard Budd and Claire (Jorgensen) Budd Brooks; m. Joe F. Calhoun, Aug. 14, 1982; 1 child, Lauren Noelani. BA magna cum laude, Calif. State U., Chico, 1974; JD, U. Calif., Davis, 1979. Bar: Hawaii 1980, Calif. 1980, U.S. Dist. Ct. Hawaii 1980, U.S. Ct. Appeals (9th cir.) 1982. Prin. Law Offices Nancy J. Budd, Lihue, Hawaii, 1980-82, 87—; mng. lawyer Legal Aid Soc. Hawaii, Lihue, 1982-87. Pres., v.p. for legislation King Kaumauali'i Elem. Sch., Hanamaulu, Hawaii, 1989—; arbitrator ct. annexed arbitration program Circuit Ct. of 5th Cir., State of Hawaii, 1987—. Co-producer video on sch. reform. Bd. dirs. Kauai (Hawaii) Cmty. Housing Resource Be., 1986—, Hawaii State Parent Tchr. Student Assn. Bd. Mgrs., Honolulu, 1989-92, Salvation Army Adv. Bd., Lihue, 1991—; vice chair, bd. dirs. Kauai Housing Devel. Corp., 1992—; bd. dirs., pres. Kauai Children's Fund, Inc., Lihue, 1989—; pres., bd. dirs. Kauai Dist. Parent Tchr. Student Assn., Lihue, 1989—; mem. legacy planned giving com. Am. Cancer Soc., Kauai, 1991—; of counsel Kauai Acad. of Creative Arts; cmty. rep. State Found. on Culture and the Arts in Public Places Project King Kaumualii Elem. Sch., 1993—. Mem. ABA, Hawaii Bar Assn., Kauai Bar Assn. (v.p. 1983-84, pres. 1985-86). Avocations: hiking, photography, tennis, swimming, canoeing. Office: 4374 Kukui Grove St Ste 103 Lihue HI 96766-2007

BUDELMANN, BERND ULRICH, zoologist, educator; b. Hamburg, Germany, Apr. 1, 1942; came to the U.S., 1987; s. Gunther and Minna (Siemssen) B. PhD, U. Munich, 1970; degree, U. Regensburg, 1975. Asst. prof. U. Regensburg, Germany, 1973-78, assoc. prof., 1978-87, Heisenberg fellow, 1979-84; assoc. prof. U. Tex., Galveston, 1987-93, prof., 1993—, chief div. biol. marine resources, 1996-2000. Mem. sci. adv. bd. Stazione Zoologica Anton Dohrn, Naples, Italy, 1992-2000; exec. sec. Cephalopod Internat. Adv. Coun., 1994-2000. Contbr. articles to Nature, Philos. Transactions of Royal Soc., Jour. Comparative Physiology. Bd. dirs. Galveston Symphony Orch., 1994—. Grantee Deutsche Forschungsgemeinschaft, 1979-85, NIH, 1989—, Wellcome Trust, 1991, NSF, 1997—. Mem. Am. Soc. Gravitational and Space Biology, Assn. for Rsch. on Otolaryngology, Barany Soc., Deutsche Zoologische Gesellschaft, Gesellschaft Deutscher Naturforscher und Arzte, Internat. Soc. Neuroethology, J.B. Johnson Club, Neurotological and Equilibriometric Soc., Soc. for Exptl. Biology, Soc. for Neurosci., Verband Deutscher Biologen, Rotary Club Galveston (bd. dirs. 1999-2001, officer 2002—), Sigma Xi (sec. chpt. 1988—). Lutheran. Home: 1823 Bayou Shore Dr Galveston TX 77551-4336 Office: U Tex Med Br Marine Biomed Inst Galveston TX 77555-1069 E-mail: bubudelm@utmb.edu.

BUDIG, GENE ARTHUR, former chancellor, professional sports executive; b. McCook, Nebr., May 25, 1939; s. Arthur G. and Angela (Schaaf) B.; m. Gretchen VanBloom, Nov. 30, 1963; children: Christopher, Mary Frances, Kathryn Angela. BS, U. Nebr., 1962, MEd, 1963, EdD, 1967; LLD, Ill. State U., 1982; LHD, U. Nebr., 1989, Baker U., 1995. Exec. asst. to gov. Nebr., Lincoln, 1964-67; adminstrv. asst. to chancellor, asst. prof. ednl. adminstrn. U. Nebr., Lincoln, 1967-70, asst. vice chancellor acad. affairs, prof. ednl. adminstrn., 1970, asst. v.p., dir. pub. affairs, 1971; v.p., dean univ. Ill. State U., Normal, 1972, pres., 1973-77, W.Va. U., Morgantown, 1977-81; chancellor U. Kans., Lawrence, 1981-94; pres. Am. Baseball League, N.Y.C., 1994—. Author: (with Dr. Stanley G. Rives) Academic Quicksand: Expectations of the Administrator, 1973; editor, contbr. chpts. to Perceptions in Public Higher Education, 1970, Dollars and Sense: Budgeting for Today's Campus, 1972, Higher Education - Surviving the 1980s, 1981, A Higher Education Map for the 1990s, 1992; editorial cons. chpts. in Phi Delta Kappan, 1976—; contbr. articles to profl. jours. Mem. Intergovtl. Coun. on Edn., 1980-84; trustee Nelson-Atkins Mus. Art, Kansas City, Mo.; bd. dirs. Truman Libr. Inst., Midwest Rsch. Inst., Univ. Field Staff Internat. Maj. gen. Air N.G., 1985-92; asst. to chief of staff N.G. Bur., 1990-92. Named One of 10 Outstanding Young Persons, Ill. Jaycees, 1975, One of Top 100 Leaders in Am. Higher Edn., Change mag. and Am. Coun. on Edn., 1979, One of 75 Outstanding Young Men and Women Educators Am., Phi Delta Kappa, 1981; recipient Disting. Svc. award Baker U., 1990. Office: Am Baseball League 245 Park Ave Fl 28 New York NY 10167-0002

BUDNIK, PATRICIA MCNULTY, retired elementary education educator; b. Riverside, N.J., July 2, 1936; d. Norbert E. and Mabel E. (Seifert) McNulty; divorced; children: Barry J., Scott D. BEd, U. Miami, Coral Gables, Fla., 1967, MEd, 1972; EdD, Nova U., 1991. Elem. tchr. Dade County Pub. Schs., Miami, Fla., 1967-2001; ret., 2001. English prof. Hunan Edn. Coll., Changsha, China, summer terms, 1994, 95, 96, 97, 99, 2000, 2001, Hunan Normal U., summer 2002; adj. faculty Nova Southeastern U., Ft. Lauderdale, Fla. Contbr. articles to profl. jours. Mem. choir, Evangelism Explosion Team St. Andrews Presbyn. Ch., Sunday sch. supt. With U.S. Army. Grantee Found. Excellence Pub. Edn., 1986, 87, Broward Community Found., 1990. Mem. Nat. Assn. Edn. Young Children, Assn. Childhood Edn. Internat., Internat. Reading Assn., Fla. Reading Assn., United Tchrs. Dade (bldg. steward). Home: 1820 N 45th Ave Hollywood FL 33021-4104

BUEHLER, MARILYN KAY HASZ, secondary education educator; b. Garden City, Kans., July 19, 1946; d. Benjamin Bethel and Della Marie (Appel) Hasz; m. Brice Edward Buehler, July 23, 1966. BA in English, Washburn U., 1970; MA in Reading Edn., Ariz. State U., 1976; DHL (hon.), No. Ariz. U., 1989. Cert. tchr. English and secondary edn. Vol. probation officer, co-facilitator Maricopa County Probation Office, Phoenix, 1972; adult edn. tchr. Phoenix Union High Sch., 1972-73; tchr. English Trevor G. Browne High Sch., Phoenix, 1973; tchr. Title I Carl Hayden High Sch., Phoenix, 1974; tchr. English Camelback High Sch., Phoenix, 1975, Central High Sch., Phoenix, 1976-85, North High Sch., Phoenix, 1985—2003; ret., 2003. Chmn. awareness facilitator Phoenix Union High Sch. System, 1986-95; speaker Partnrships in Edn., Phoenix, 1991—, adv. bd. Phoenix Coll. Creative Writing, 1995—; internat. baccalaureate examiner, 1998; edn. cons. working on sec, sch. counseling degree, 2003. Bd. dirs. Ariz. Edn. Found., Phoenix, 1990-95, North High-Ariz. Pub. Svc. Partnership Com., 1991-95. Named Ariz. State Tchr. of Yr., State of Ariz./AEF, 1989; recipient award of honor for outstanding contbns. to edn. Nat. Sch. Pub. Rels. Assn., 1989, others. Mem. NEA, Nat. Coun. Tchrs. English, Classroom Tchrs. Assn., Nat. Writers Club, Nat. State Tchrs. of Yr., Ariz. State Tchrs. of Yr. (pres. 1993-95), Phoenix Zoo Bd. (edn. com, 1995-96). Democrat. Avocations: reading, writing, fishing, swimming. Office: North High Sch 1101 E Thomas Rd Phoenix AZ 85014-5476 Home: 212 East Bethany Hone Rd Phoenix AZ 85012-1229

BUELL, JON ALFRED, education and curriculum development administrator; b. Oak Park, Ill., Dec. 20, 1939; s. Alfred Leslie and G. Ruth (Rickman) B.; m. Sandy Wheat, June 9, 1962; children: Wendy Louise, Shelley Lynn, Jon Robert. BA in Comm. Arts, U. Miami, 1961; cert., Stanford U., 1984; cert. Stanford Pub. Course, Med. Inst. for Sexual Health, 1993. U. Miami (Fla.) campus dir. Campus Crusade for Christ, 1962-65, ctrl. Tex. dist. dir., 1965-68, southeastern regional dir. Birmingham, Ala., 1968-72; v.p. Probe Ministries Internat., Dallas, 1973-80; pres. and bd. dirs. Found. for Thought & Ethics, Dallas, 1981—. Participant White House Conf. on the Family, Washington, 1988; bd. dirs. Inherit a Blessing, Richardson, Tex.; organizer sci. symposium Darwinism: Scientific Inference or Philos. Preference, Dallas, 1992; presenter and spkr. in field. Editor: The Mystery of Life's Origin, 1984; editor (symposium procs.) Darwinism: Science or Philosophy?, 1994; editor 7 books. Program participant Richardson (Tex.) Observance of Meml. Day, 1974; active Dallas Ind. Sch. Dist. Religion Task Force, Dallas, 1991—. Mem. ASCD, Am. Sci. Affiliation (assoc.).

BUELL, LAWRENCE INGALLS, English language educator; b. Bryn Mawr, Pa., June 11, 1939; s. Clarence Addison and Marjorie (Henderson) B.; m. Phyllis Kimber; children: Denise, Deirdre. AB, Princeton U., 1961; MA, Cornell U., 1962, PhD, 1966. From asst. prof. to prof. English Oberlin (Ohio) Coll., 1966-90; prof. dept. English Harvard U., Cambridge, 1990—, dean undergrad. edn, 1992-96. Dir. Summer Inst. for High Sch. Tchrs., NEH, Oberlin, 1984-85; vis. prof. English U. Chgo., 1986; mem. faculty Bread Loaf Sch. English, 1987-88. Author: Literary Transcendentalism, 1973, New England Literary Culture, 1986, The Environmental Imagination, 1995, Writing for an Endangered World, 2001, Emerson, 2003; mem. editl. bd. Am. Quar., Phila., 1979-82, Am. Lit., Durham, N.C., 1983-86, PMLA, 1994-96. Trustee, officer Oberlin Shansi Meml. Assn., 1972-87. Woodrow Wilson Found. fellow, 1961-62; Howard Found. fellow, 1969-70; NEH Rsch. fellow, 1979-80, 2002; Guggenheim Found. fellow, 1987-88. Mem. Modern Language Assn., Am. Studies Assn. Democrat. Mem. United Ch. of Christ. Avocations: nature, sports. Office: Harvard U Dept English Cambridge MA 02138

BUENAFLOR, JUDITH LURAY, secondary education educator; b. Phila., Mar. 11, 1949; d. James and Dorothy Tawney (Riley) Arnao; m. Michael Vincent Buenaflor, July 7, 1973 (dec. 1996); children: Amy, Katherine, Ryan. BA, Rosemont Coll., 1971; MA in English, Kutztown U., 1998. Tchr. Ctrl. Cath. High Sch., Allentown, Pa., 1991-97; adminstrv. asst. St. Thomas More Sch., Allentown, 1999-2000, principal, 2000—. Advisor Odyssey of the Mind, Allentown, 1989-91, Nat. Honor Soc., 1991-97; part-time prof. Allentown Coll.; Allentown Coll. MEd program, 1999. Author: (writing seminar) The Influential Writer, 1999. Mem. tower ball com. Sacred Heart Hosp., Allentown, Pa., 1987-89; pres. women's guild, St. Thomas More, Allentown, 1986; mem. bd. assocs. Sacred Heart Hosp. Mem. Nat. Assn. Tchrs. English, Women's Guild, Alpha Epsilon Lambda (hon.). Roman Catholic. Avocations: writing, historical fiction. Home: 1128 Valley View Dr Allentown PA 18103-6042 E-mail: JLBSTM@hotmail.com.

BUETOW, PAUL ELMER, principal; b. Bay City, Mich., Oct. 18, 1942; s. Elmer Otto and Esther Alma (Rohloff) B.; m. Barbara Louise Slack, June 18, 1966; children: Michelle Carolyn, John Eric. AA, Concordia Jr. Coll., Milw., 1962; BA, Concordia Sr. Coll., Ft. Wayne, 1964; MA, U. Minn., 1973. Tchr., coach Concordia Luth. High Sch., Ft. Wayne, 1966-69, asst. prin., tchr., 1979-85; prin., tchr. Luth. High Sch., Mpls., 1970-73, Luth. High Sch. Sch. South Fla., Davie, 1973-79; prin. Luth. High Sch., Metairie, La., 1985—. Mem. Fla./Ga. Bd. Parish Edn., Orlando, 1975-79, chmn. so. dist., New Orleans, 1990—; chmn. Ind. Dist. Gifted Edn. Task Force, Ft. Wayne, 1983-85; mem. North Ctrl. Accrediting Teams, Ft. Wayne, 1979-85. Editor: Models for Gifted/Talented Education, 1983. Bible class leader, ch. com. mem. Luth. chs. in Minn., Ind., Fla., Mich., La., 1964—; bd. mgrs. YMCA, Metairie, 1989—. U.S. Office Edn. fellow in classical langs. U. Minn., Mpls., 1969-70. Republican. Lutheran. Avocations: coaching, tennis, golf. Home: 24770 Perdido Beach Blvd Orange Beach AL 36561-3010 Office: Luth High Sch 3864 17th St Metairie LA 70002-4499

BUFFINGTON, AUDREY VIRGINIA, educator, consultant, author; b. Westminster, Md., Oct. 6, 1931; d. Martin Luther and Elsie Virginia (Heltibridle) Myers; m. John David Buffington, June 20, 1953 (div. 1963); 1 child, A. Virtina Buffington Hunter. BA, Western Md. Coll., 1952; MEd, Pa. State U., 1968. Cert. tchr., supr., Md., Mass. Tchr. math. Carroll County Pub. Schs., Westminster, 1952-68, supr. math., 1968-73; state math. supr. Md. Dept. Edn., Balt., 1973-79; program mgr. Ginn & Co., Lexington, Mass., 1979-81; tchr. math Wayland (Mass.) Pub. Schs., 1982-94, ret., 1994. Speaker, workshop leader numerous local and state edn. meetings. Author: Meters, Liters and Grams, 1973, textbook series Merrill Mathematics, 1985, 87, math. comic books King Features Comic Math. Libr., 1979, You are My Mommy/You are My Daddy, 1998; creator NASCO Algebra Models. Pres. Carroll County Gen. Hosp. Aux., Westminster. Recipient Math. Educator of Yr. award Md. Coun. Tchrs. Math., 1978, Trustee Alumni award Western Md. Coll., 1979. Republican. Lutheran. Avocations: collecting Uncle Wiggily items and works of F. Earl Christy, bridge. Home: PO Box 386 South Thomaston ME 04858-0386

BUFFONI, FRANCA, pharmacology educator; b. Firenze, Italy, May 6, 1925; d. Giovanni and Egle (Scuffi) B. D in Pharmacy, U. Firenze, 1947. Asst. prof. U. Firenze, 1951-70, tchr., 1957-70, prof., 1970-95, emeritus prof., 1998—. Mem. AAAS, N.Y. Acad. Scis., Biochem. Soc. (London), Soc. Italian Pharmacologia. Office: U Firenze Dept Pharmacology Viale G Pieraccini 6 50139 Firenze Italy E-mail: fbuffo@box.tin.it.

BUFFUM, WILLIAM ERWIN, social worker, educator; b. Grand Rapids, Mich., Dec. 11, 1944; s. Erwin Clair and Sena (Lucas) B.; m. Valerie Jane Regetz, Feb. 20, 1973; 1 child, Lindsay Louise. BA, Calvin Coll., 1966; MSW, U. Mich., 1970; PhD, Case Western Reserve U., 1981. Prof. U. Houston Sch. Social Work, 1999—2002; assoc. dean Barry U. Sch. Social Work, 1999—2003; dir. Aurora U. Sch. of Social Work, Ill., 2003—. Mem. editorial bd. Jour. Sociology and Social Welfare, Jour. Community Practice. Bd. dirs. Refugee Svc. Alliance, Houston, 1988-99. Mem. NASW, Coun. on Social Work Edn., Assn. Community Orgn. and Social Adminstrn. Democrat. Avocations: running, sailing. Home: 231 Abington Ln North Aurora IL 60542 Office: Aurora U Sch Social Work 347 S Gladstone Ave Aurora IL 60506-4892 E-mail: wbuffum@aurora.edu.

BUFORD, RONETTA MARIE, music educator; b. Kansas City, Mo., Sept. 17, 1946; d. Joseph Ronald and Violet Katheryne (Jennison) Coursey; 1 child, Frederick Kenyatta. Bachelor of Music Edn., Lincoln U. of Mo., 1968; M in Liberal Arts, Baker U., 1996. Cert. vocal and instrumental music tchr., Mo. Chmn. vocal music M.L. King Jr. High Sch., Kansas City, 1968-71; chmn. music dept. Southeast Jr. High Sch., Kansas City, 1971-75; chmn. fine arts Paseo High Sch., Kansas City, 1975-90; vocal music specialist Met. Advanced Tech. H.S., Kansas City, 1990-98, asst. girls basketball coach, asst. cross country coach, 1992-98; owner Buford's Day Care, 1996-97, Buford's Mini Univ.; TRAC music instr. Crispus Attucks Elem. Sch., 2001—. Summer music specialist Horace Mann Elem. Sch., Kansas City, 1972; mentor Students at Risk, Kansas City, 1988; vis. lectr. Lincoln U., Jefferson City, Mo., 1980, 85, 87, NE Mo. State U., Kirksville, 1986; panelist Sta. KPRS, Kansas City, 1987; Title One mentor K.C. Mo. Sch. Dist.; min. music N.W. Mo. Conf. A.M.E. Ch., Kansas City, 1984-91, choir dir., 1985—; dir. sr. choir Ward Chapel A.M.E. Ch., KAnsas City, 1985-87; instr. of choir, band and orch. N.E. Law, Pub. Svc. and Mil. Sci. H.S., 1998-99; girl's varsity asst. basketball coach, girl's jr. varsity basketball coach, drill mistress N.E. Lady Vikings Drill Team, fine arts dept. chairperson. Author: (curricula) Junior High Learning Task, 1972, Motivating the Unmotivated, 1986. Asst. troop scoutmaster Boy Scouts Am.; spl. cons. music United Meth. Ch. Women; active NAACP; parent chaperone Kansas City Marching Cobras Drill Team, 1993—. Recipient Meritorious Service award Lincoln U. Vocal Ensemble, 1985, Outstanding Tchr. award Black Archives Mid-Am., 1987; named one of Outstanding Young Women of Am., 1983. Mem. NAACP, AAUW, MADD, Am. Choral Dirs. Assn., Am. Fedn. Tchrs., Am. Assn. Retired Persons, Music Educators Nat. Conf., Nat. Assn. Negro Women, Order Eastern Star, Order Cyrenes, Heroines of Jericho, Daus. of Isis, Tri-M Music Honor Soc., Order Golden Circle, Nat. Coaches Assn., Bethel A.M.E. Ch. (life), Bethel Missionary Soc., Mass Choir and Parsonage Club, Licoln U. Mo. Alumni Assn., Vocat. Indsl. Clubs Am., "C" Scholarship Club, Alpha Kappa Alpha, Phi Delta Kappa, Sigma Alpha Iota. Avocation: photography. Home: 3610 E 26th St Kansas City MO 64127-4321 Office: Kansas City Sch Dist 1211 Mcgee St Kansas City MO 64106-2416

BUFORD SPEIGHT, VELMA RUTH, retired alumni affairs director; b. Snow Hill, N.C., Nov. 18, 1932; d. John Thomas and Mable Lee (Edwards) S.; m. Howard H. Kennedy, 1953 (div. 1961); 1 child, Chineta; m. William B. Buford, 2002. BS, N.C. A&T U., 1953; MEd, U. Md., 1965, PhD, 1976. Cert. counselor, tchr., Md. Tchr. math. and French, Kennard H.S.igh Sch., Centreville, Md., 1954-60, counselor, 1960-66; coord. guidance dept. Queene Anne's County H.S., Centreville, 1966-69; adv. specialist in civil rights Md. Dept. Edn., Balt., 1969-72, supr. guidance, 1972-76, dep. asst. state supt., 1976-82, asst. state supt., 1982-86; dir. EEO recruitment U. Md., College Park, 1972; coord. guidance and counseling U. Md. Ea. Shore, Princess Anne, 1986-87; assoc. prof. counselor edn. East Carolina U., Greenville, 1989; chmn. dept. edn., coord. grad. prog. guidance and counseling U. Md., Ea. Shore, Greenville, 1989-93, chmn. dept. edn., 1990-94; dir. alumni affairs N.C. A&T U., Greensboro, 1993-97; ret., 1997. Adj. prof. Loyola U., Balt., 1976-80, Johns Hopkins U., Balt., 1980; cons., 1987—; speaker numerous seminars; elected to bd. trustees N.C. A&T State U., 1998. Mem. Nat. Coalition for Chpt. I Parents, Washington, 1980-87, Human Rights Commn., Howard County, Md., 1987—; chmn. Gov.'s com. Studying Sentencing Alternatives for Women, Annapolis, Md., 1987; founder, chmn. Mothers to Prevent Dropouts, Centreville; trustee N.C. A&T State U., 1998—. Recipient Early Childhood Edn. award Japanese Govt., 1984, Md. State Tchrs'. Assn. Minority award Black Chs. for Excellence in Edn.; Fulbright Hayes scholar, 1991. Mem. Am. Counseling Assn., Nat. Alliance Black Educators, Assn. for Supervision and Curriculum Devel., Assn. Tchr. Edn., Md. Assn. Coll. Tchr. Edn., Md. Counseling Assn., N.C. A&T U. Alumni Assn. (nat. pres. 197983, Excellence award 1983), Tchr. Edn. and Profl. Standards Bd. Clubs: Community Action (Centreville). Democrat. Presbyterian. Avocations: reading, cooking, sewing, bicycling. Home: 11 Carissa Ct Greensboro NC 27407-6366

BUHAIN, WILFRIDO JAVIER, medical educator; b. Bacoor, Cavite, Philippines, Oct. 12, 1940; m. Carlota Torres; children: Ronald, Edgar. AA, BS, U. Philippines, 1959, MD, 1964. Diplomate Am. Bd. Internal Medicine, Am. Bd. Pulmonary Diseases. Rsch. fellow in cardiology U. Philippines, Philippine Gen. Hosp., 1964-65; rotating intern Queens Hosp. Ctr., N.Y.C., 1965-66, resident in internal medicine, 1965-68; clin. fellow in pulmonary diseases Hosp. of U. Pa., 1968-69, chief pulmonary function lab. dept. medicine, 1971-72; rsch. fellow in pulmonary diseases Hosp. of U. Pa., VA Hosp., Phila., 1969-71; assoc. in medicine, cardiovascular-pulmonary div. med. dept. U. Pa. Sch. Medicine, 1971-72; assoc. in medicine, dept. medicine Mt. Sinai Sch. Medicine, CUNY, 1972-74; clin. instr. medicine Georgetown U., 1976-95. Chief pulmonary function lab. dept. medicine Mt. Sinai Hosp. Svcs./City Hosp. Ctr. at Elmhurst, 1973-74; med. dir. respiratory therapy dept. Mt. Vernon Hosp., 1978—, chmn. dept. medicine, 1987-88, pres. med. staff, 1996-98; mem. exec. com. Alexandria Hosp., 1983; trustee, chmn. med. affairs coun. Inova Health Sys., 1998-99. Contbr. articles to profl. jours. Queensborough Soc. grantee; Pa. Thoracic Soc. grantee. Fellow ACP, Am. Coll. Chest Physicians; mem. Am. Soc. Internal Medicine, Alexandria Med. Soc., Va. Med. Soc., Philippine Med. Assn. (exec. dir., past pres. Metro-Washington), Assn. Philippine Physicians in Am. (v.p.). Avocations: tennis, golf, ballroom dancing. Office: 6300 Stevenson Ave Ste B Alexandria VA 22304-3554

BUI, KHOI TIEN, college counselor; b. Binh Dinh, Vietnam, Dec. 23, 1937; came to U.S., 1975; naturalized, 1982; s. Luu and Quang Thi (Tran) B.; m. Yen Kim Nguyen, Dec. 7, 1962; children: Khanh, Huy, Huan. BS in Agri., Agrl. Coll., Vietnam, 1962; BS, Law U., Vietnam, 1965; MS, Polit. and Bus. Mgmt. U., Vietnam, 1972, PhD; DLitt (hon.), London Inst. for Applied Rsch., 1991; DE (hon.), World Acad., 1997; PhD (hon.), Inst. Affairs Internat., 1997. With Ministry Agri., Republic of Vietnam, 1962-75; counselor Houston C.C., 1976—, chmn. Indochinese Culture and Refugee Info. Ctr., 1981—. Nat. Planner Tng., Taiwan, 1963, Philippines, 1965, Australia, 1968, Japan, 1970, Thailand, 1971. Author: (poetry books) America My First Feelings, 1981, 20 Poems and 1000 Thoughts, 1994; contbr. to other poetry books, novel and textbook in Vietnamese. Founder, moderator radio sta. The Voice of Free Vietnam, Houston, 1980—; chmn. Indochinese and Refugee Info. Ctr., Houston Community Coll. Decorated knight Order of Templars, officer de l'ordre des Arts et des Lettres; recipient Nat. Lit. prize Republic Vietnam, 1966, Houston's Poet Laureate award, 1984, Golden Poet award World of Poetry, 1985, Edn. award, 1985, Men of Achievement award, 1989, Medal of Honor, 1990, One-in-a-Million Medal, 1991, Most Admired Man of the Decade award, 1992, Twentieth Century award for Achievement, 1992, various medals Govt. of the Republic of Vietnam; named Man of Yr., 1990, Internat. Man of Yr., 1992, Albert Einstein medal, 1996, Literature medal, 1996. Fellow Royal Soc. Lit.; mem. Leadership Houston Assn., Pen Am. Ctr. Avocations: writing poetry, reading, swimming. Home: 13715 Towne Way Dr Sugar Land TX 77478-1652 Office: Houston CC 1300 Holman St Houston TX 77004-3834 E-mail: buihuyluc@hotmail.com.

BUI, TY VAN, computer programmer, systems analyst; b. Cai Tau Ha, Sadec, Vietnam, Dec. 7, 1959; came to U.S., 1988; s. Tu Van and Nhung Thi (Ha) B.; m. CamVan Nguyen, Feb. 15, 1986; 1 child, Quoc Trung Dinh. BS in Secondary Edn., Edn. Coll., Vietnam, 1980; BS in Computer Sci. and Applied Math., U. Wis., Oshkosh, 1992. Tchr. math. Cao Lanh (Vietnam) High Sch., 1980-82; tchr. physics Sadec High Sch., 1982-84; chief comm. sect. UN High Commn. for Refugees, The Philippines, 1986-87; computer programmer Wis. Dept. Revenue, Madison, 1990, systems analyst, 1991; cons. computer lab. U. Wis., 1990-92, computer programming cons. English dept., 1992; computer programmer, cons. Kag Labs. Internat., Inc., Oshkosh, 1992; sr. programmer analyst Northwestern Mut. Life Ins., Milw., 1993-96, system analyst, 1995-96; staff analyst CASE Corp., Racine, Wis., 1996-98, bus. system cons., 1998, sr. bus. system cons., team leader IT storage mgmt., 1999—. Software engr. Mgmt. Control System, 1991; programmer An Invention or Idea Generating Program, 1992, Case's Unix Standards for Batch Processing, 1997,, Case's Worldwide Infrastructures for Client/Server Environment, 1998. Mem. Assn. for Computing Machinery, Math. Assn. Am., Alpha Lambda Delta. Avocations: tennis, reading, canoeing. Home: 7046 Evans Dr Franklin WI 53132-8908

BUIS, DIANNA LOVINS, elementary education educator, guidance counselor; b. Blanchester, Ohio, Jan. 23, 1961; d. Dean Edward and Mary Gethaline (Hyden) Lovins; m. Douglas Edward Buis, Sept. 2, 1983; children: Shaun Douglas, Cristopher Michael. AD in Fine Arts, Somerset (Ky.) C.C., 1980; B in Elem. Edn., U. Ky., 1983; M in Edn. Counseling, Ea. Ky. U., Richmond, 1991, postgrad., 1993. Cert. elem. guidance counselor, Ky.; rank I endorsement for individual intellectual assessment Ea. Ky. U. Tchr. Waynesburg Elem. Sch., Ky., 1982-91; elem. guidance counselor Lincoln County Bd. Edn., Stanford, Ky., 1991—2000; tchr. Eubank Elem. Sch., Eubank, Ky., 2001—; employed Pulaski County Bd. of Ed., Somerset, Ky. Asst. coach Acad. Team, Waynesburg, 1983-85; trainer, counselor-on-call Project XL-Summer Sch., Stanford, 1994; coach Olympics of the Mind, Waynesburg, 1984; individual intelligence assessment, counselor Lincoln County Sch. Sys., 1993-2000. Youth group leader for Mid./HS; youth group leader, membership com. chair Christian Ch. Mem. Ky. Assn. Sch. Adminstrn., Ctrl. Ky. Counseling Assn., Ky. Coun. on Adminstrs. of Spl. Edn., mem. Ky. Ed. Assoc., 2001-pres., Profl. Assn. Diving Instrs. Scuba Divers. Mem. Christian Ch. (Disciples Of Christ). Home: 12095 N Highway 1247 Eubank KY 42567-9005 E-mail: dscbuis@aol.com.

BUIS, PATRICIA FRANCES, geology educator, researcher; b. Jersey City, Dec. 29, 1953; d. George Herman Buis and Marie Agnes Fitzsimmons. BA in Geology, Rutgers U., 1976; MA in Geology, Queens Coll., 1983; PhD in Geology, U. Pitts., 1988; MS in Mining Engring., Mich. Tech. U., 1994, PhD in Mining Engring., 1995. Coal quality geochemist Pa. Geologic Survey, Harrisburg, 1989-91; asst. prof. U. Miss., Oxford, 1994-96, Japanese Sci. and Tech. Mgmt. Program scholar, 1996-97; lectr. environ. sci. MTI Coll. Bus. Tech., Sacramento. Vis. asst. prof. mining engr. dept. U. Alaska, Fairbanks, 1997-98; vis. lectr. earth sci. dept. N.E. Ill. U., Chgo., 1998-99; cons., reviewer of sci. textbooks prior to pub. Winston-Rinehart, Austin, Tex., 1994—; vis. prof. environ. geology Lander U., Greenwood, SC. Dept. Edn. doctoral fellow in mining Mich. Tech. U., 1991-95, Provost Predoctoral fellow U. Pitts., 1988; Dept. Edn. grantee Mich. Tech. U., 1993; nat. merit scholar Schering-Plough, Rutgers U., 1971-75. Mem. Soc. Exploration Geochemistry, Nat. Water Wells Assn., Am. Mineralogist, Sigma Xi. Home: 3810 Madison Ave Apt 12 North Highlands CA 95660

BUKONDA, NGOYI K. ZACHARIE, health care management educator; b. Lubumbashi, Shaba, Zaire, Feb. 14, 1951; came to U.S., 1987; s. Munyuka Kalambayi and Tumba (Tshileo) Marie; m. Muyumba Kapinga Agnes, Aug. 29, 1975; children: Munyuka Ngoyi, Muyumba Ngoyi, Kalambayi Ngoyi, Tshileo Ngoyi, Kashala Ngoyi, Ntumba Gloria Ngoyi. BS in Health Systems Mgmt., U. Kinshasa, Zaire, 1981; Diploma in Teaching, U. Zaire, 1983; MPH, U. Minn. Sch. Pub. Health, 1989; PhD, U. Minn., 1994. Hosp. adminstr. Gen. Hosp., Bukavu, Zaire, 1975-76; dep. chmn. Med. Tech. Inst., Kindu, 1976-78; chief of bur. Ministry of Health Zaire, Kinshasa, 1981-83, chief div., 1983-87; health planner Sanru B.P. 3355 Kinshasa, Kinshasa, 1987; asst. prof. Inst. Superieur de Techniques Medicales, Kinshasa, 1981-87; grad. fellow African Am. Inst., N.Y.C., 1987-94; grad. tchg. asst. Grad. Program in Social and Adminstrv. Pharmacy, Mpls., 1991-94; asst. prof. health care mgmt. So. Ill. U., Carbondale, 1994-97; asst. prof. pub. and cmty. health No. Ill. U. Sch. Allied Health Professions, DeKalb, 1997—2003, assoc. prof., 2003—. Acad. sec. Inst. Superieur de Techniques Medicales, Kinshasa, 1983—86; cons. Joint Commn. Worldwide Consulting, 1999—; prin. investigator Zambia Hosp. Accreditation Descriptive Study; rsch. cons. Botswana-Harvard Partnership Inst. for HIV Rsch. and Edn., 2000—; co-investigator Male Involvement in Prevention of Mother-to-Child Transmission of HIV/AIDS in Botswana, 2001; mem. Press Bd., No. Ill. U., 2001—, mem. adv. bd. Ctr. for Black Studies, 2002—, mem. faculty senate, 2002—, chair faculty rights and responsibilities com., 2003—, mem. undergrad. acad. environ. com., 2003—, mem. responsible conduct of scholarship com., 2003—; rsch. cons. Peters Inst. for Pharm. Care, U. Minn. Coll. Pharmacy, 2002—; mem. dean award com. Coll. Health & Human Scis., No. Ill. U., 2002—; cons. HIV care Divsn. of Netcare Group, South Africa, 2003—; cons. NIMH-MRISP faculty devel. project in mental health rsch. Morehouse Coll., 2003—. Reviewer: Pub. Health Nursing, 1996—, mem. editl. bd.: Selected Health Sys. of Africa, 1999—; editor: Leja Bulela Newsletter. Mem. health and human scis. curriculum com. No. Ill. U., 2000—02; fed. pres. Union for Democracy and Social Progress, 1999—2003. Named Hon. Citizen of Louisville, 1986; recipient Plaque for Outstanding Work for Mems. of Leja Bulela, 2000—01, Recognition plaque, Internat. African Students Assn. and Yale African Students Assn., 2001; grantee, Mac Arthur Interdisciplinary

Program on Peace Internat., 1991; Afgrad fellow, African Am. Inst., 1987, Melendy Grad. fellow Coll. of Pharmacy, 1991, Lilian Cobb Faculty Internat. Travel fellow, No. Ill. U., 2003, Grad. Sch. Summer fellow, 2003. Mem. APHA, Internat. Assn. HIV/AIDS, Am. Pharmacy Assn., Assn. des Adminstrs. Gestionnaires (pres. 1981-87). Roman Catholic. Home: 956 Quail Run Dekalb IL 60115-6116 Office: No Ill U Sch Allied Health Profs Dekalb IL 60115 E-mail: nbukonda@niu.edu., ngoyizacharie@juno.com.

BUKOVEC, JOSEPH ALOYSIUS, special education educator; b. Hoboken, N.J., Nov. 9, 1929; s. Alois and Sophie (Draksler) B.; m. Adeline Nicole Cinotti, Aug. 17, 1964 (dec. Jan. 9, 1985); m. Linda Lee Torrisi, Apr. 14, 1991. BA, Seton Hall U., 1951; MA, Jersey City State Coll., 1967; EdD, Columbia U., 1971. Cert. secondary English, reading, Latin, handicapped tchr., prin./supr., N.J. Tchr. Bd. Edn., Teaneck, NJ, 1962-97, co-project dir./project coord. The Comm. Workshop, 1978-97; adj. prof. Jersey City State Coll., Jersey City, 1972-75, Fairleigh Dickinson U., Teaneck, 1981-84, 98-99, Felician Coll., Rutherford, NJ, 1998-99. Author: Monitoring Student Activities, 1978, Monitoring Student Programs, 1979; co-author: Annotated Bibliography on Professional Education of Teachers, 1969; contbr. articles to profl. jours.; appeared in passion play Park Theatre, Union City. With U.S. Army, 1954-56. Recipient William A. Liggitt award for ednl. excellence Phi Delta Kappa, 1978, Exemplary Project award N.J. State Dept. Edn., 1978. Mem. NEA, Internat. Reading Assn., N.J. Edn. Assn., Teaneck Tchrs. Edn. Assn., Bergen County Edn. Assn. Avocations: acting, photography. Home and Office: 11 Hampton Pl Nutley NJ 07110-2813

BUKOWINSKI, MARK STEFAN TADEUSZ, geophysics educator; b. Trani, Italy, Oct. 17, 1946; came to U.S., 1962; s. Stanley K. and Jadwiga Teresa (Jezierski) B.; m. Halina V. Mudy, June 20, 1970; children: Katherine, Anne, John, Christopher. BS in Physics, UCLA, 1969, PhD in Physics, 1975. Asst. rsch. geophysicist Inst. Geophysics and Planetary Physics, UCLA, 1975-78; asst. prof. U. Calif., Berkeley, 1978-82, assoc. prof., 1982-89, prof., 1989—, vice chmn. dept. geology and geophysics, 1997—99. Mem. editl. bd. Jour. Geophys. Rsch., 1988-91, Phys. Earth Planetary Interiors, 1992-2002; contbr. over 60 articles to profl. jours. NSF grantee, 1976—, Inst. Geophysics and Planetary Physics. Mem. AAAS, Am. Geophys. Union (mem. mineral physics com. 1988-90), Mineralog. Soc. Am. (mem. publs. com. 1988-91, chair 1991-92, elected fellow 1995). Avocations: hiking, photography, computers. Home: 5738 Laurelwood Pl Concord CA 94521-4807 Office: U Calif Berkeley Dept Earth and Planetary Sci Berkeley CA 94720-0001

BUKOWSKI, ELAINE LOUISE, physical therapist, educator; b. Phila., Feb. 18, 1949; d. Edward Eugene and Melanja Josephine (Przyborowski) B. BS in Phys. Therapy, St. Louis U., 1972; MS, U. Nebr., 1977. Lic. phys. therapist, N.J.; diplomate Am. Bd. Disabilities Analysts (sr. analyst, profl. adv. coun. 1995—). Clk. City of Phila., 1967; staff phys. therapist St. Louis Chronic Hosp., 1973, Cardinal Ritter Inst., St. Louis, 1973-74; dir. campus ministry musicals Creighton U., Omaha, 1974-75; tchg. asst. U. Nebr. Med. Ctr., Omaha, 1975-76; lectr. in anatomy U. Sci. and Tech., Kumasi, Ghana, 1977-78; chief phys. therapist Holy Family Hosp., Berekum, Ghana, 1978-79; coord. info. & guidance The Am. Cancer Soc., Phila., 1979-81; staff phys. therapist Holy Redeemer Vis. Nurse Assn., Phila., 1981-83, rehab. supr. Swainton, N.J., 1983-87; asst. prof. phys. therapy Richard Stockton Coll. N.J., Pomona, 1987-96, assoc. prof., 1996—2002, prof., 2002—03. Bd. dirs. The Bridge, Phila., 1979-80; vacation relief phys. therapist, N.J., summer 1988—; mem. profl. adv. coun. Holy Redeemer VNA, Swainton, N.J., 1982-93, chmn., 1985-91, mem. pers. com., cons. hospice program, 1985-87, rehab. cons., 1987-88; legis. adv. coun. subcom. on edn. and health care Cape May & Cumberland Counties, 1988-90; utilization rev. cons. rehab. svcs., 1990; mem. fitness screening team N.J. State Legislature, 1990; mem. geriatric rehab. del. Citizen Amb. Program, China, 1992; middle states accreditation team evaluator, 1997-98. Co-author slide study program, (video) Going My Way? The Low Back Syndrome, 1976; author: Muscular Analysis of Everyday Activities, 2000. Vol. Am. Cancer Soc., Phila., 1979-82, Walk-a-Day-in-My Shoes prog. Girl Scouts Am., Cape May County, N.J., 1983-86; task force phys. therapy prog. Stockton State Coll., Pomona, N.J., 1985-88. U.S. Govt. trainee, 1971, 72; Physical Therapy Fund grantee, 1975, 76; recipient Vol. Achievement award Am. Cancer Soc., 1981. Mem. Am. Phys. Therapy Assn. (edn. sect., orthop. sect., vice chmn. so. dist. 1993-96, 99-2001, chmn. 1996-98, bd. dirs., ho. of dels. 1994-97, key contact voting dist. 2, mem. N.J. legis. network 1989-96, 1999-2002, mems. mentoring program 1998—, chair nominating com. 2002—, key act voting dist., Phys. Therapy Club (sec. 1971-72), N.J. Phys. Therapy Assn. (rsch. com. 1995-97). Avocations: gardening, music, reading, poetry. Office: Richard Stockton Coll NJ Phys Therapy Program Jim Leeds Rd Pomona NJ 08240 E-mail: elaine.bukowski@stockton.edu.

BUKOWY, STEPHEN JOSEPH, accounting educator; b. Phila., May 24, 1949; s. Stephen and Ida Teresa (Zigman) B.; m. Joy Coughenour, Oct. 14, 1950; 1 child, Catherine Alexis. BS in Acctg., Pa. State U., 1971; MBA, Coll. William & Mary, 1976; M Forest Resources, U. Ga., 1989, PhD in Acctg., 1993. CPA, Va. Grad. asst. Coll. William and Mary, Williamsburg, Va., 1975-76; acct., auditor GAO, Washington, 1976-82; asst. prof. Emory (Va.) and Henry Coll., 1982-84; grad. asst. U. Ga., Athens, 1984-88; asst. prof. Bradley U., Peoria, Ill., 1988-92; acct. Darts & Pool, Peoria, 1992-93; sr. fin. analyst U.S. Coast Guard, Washington, 1993—94; MBA dir. U. NC, Pembroke, 1994—99, assoc. prof. acctg., 1994—. Comdr. USCGR, 1971-95. Mem. AICPA, Res. Officers Assn. (pres. Pa. chpt. 1991-92), Inst. Mgmt. Accts., Am. Acctg. Assn., Soc. Am. Foresters, Beta Alpha Psi, Beta Gamma Sigma. Avocations: stamp collecting, reading, woodworking. Office: U NC Pembroke PO Box 1510 1 University Rd Pembroke NC 28372-8699

BULL, BRIAN STANLEY, pathology educator, medical consultant, business executive; b. Watford, Hertfordshire, Eng., Sept. 14, 1937; came to U.S., 1954, naturalized, 1960; s. Stanley and Agnes Mary (Murdoch) B.; m. Maureen Hannah Huse, June 3, 1963; children: Beverly Velda, Beryl Heather. BS in Zoology, Walla Walla Coll., 1957; MD, Loma Linda (Calif.) U., 1961. Diplomate: Am. Bd. Pathology. Intern Yale U., 1961-62, resident in anat. pathology, 1962-63; resident in clin. pathology NIH, Bethesda, Md., 1963-65, fellow in hematology and electron microscopy, 1965-66, staff hematologist, 1966-67; research asst. dept. anatomy Loma Linda U., 1958, dept. microbiology, 1959, asst. prof. pathology, 1968-71, assoc. prof., 1971-73, prof., 1973—, chmn. dept. pathology, 1973—, chmn. dept. pathology and human anatomy, 1993—, assoc. dean for acad. affairs sch. medicine, 1993-94, dean sch. medicine, 1994—2003. Cons. to mfrs. of med. testing devices; mem. Internat. Commn. for Standardization in Hematology, pres., 1997-99. Mem. bd. editors Blood Cells, Molecules and Diseases, 1995—; contbr. chpts. to books, articles to med. jours.; patentee in field; editor-in-chief Blood Cells N.Y. Heidelberg, 1985-94. Served with USPHS, 1963-67. Nat. Inst. Arthritis and Metabolic Diseases fellow, 1967-68; recipient Merck Manual award, 1961, Mosby Scholarship Book award, 1961; Ernest B. Cotlove Meml. lectr. Acad. Clin. Lab. Physicians and Scientists, 1972; named Alumnus of Yr., Walla Walla Coll., 1984, Honored Alumnus, Loma Linda U. Sch. Medicine, 1987, Humanitarian award, 1991, Citizen Yr., C. of C., Loma Linda, 1997, President's award, Luma Linda U. Adventist Health Scis. Ctr., 2003. Fellow Am. Soc. Clin. Pathologists, Am. Soc. Hematology, Coll. Am. Pathologists, FDA Panel on Hematology and Pathology Devices, Nat. Com. on Clin. Lab. Standards, N.Y. Acad. Scis.; mem. AMA, Calif. Soc. Pathologists, San Bernadino County Med. Soc. (William C. Cover Outstanding Contbn. to Medicine award 1994), Acad. Clin. Lab. Physicians and Scientists, Am. Assn. Pathologists, Sigma Xi, Alpha Omega Alpha. Seventh-day Adventist. Achievements include patents in field of blood analysis instrumentation; development of quality control algorithms for blood analyzer calibration; origination of techniques and instrumentation for the measurement of thrombosis risk and for regulation of anti-coagulation during cardiopulmonary bypass. Office: Loma Linda U Sch Medicine 11234 Anderson St Loma Linda CA 92354-2871 E-mail: bbull@som.llu.edu.

BULL, INEZ STEWART, special education, gifted music educator, coloratura soprano, pianist, editor, author, curator; b. Newark, Apr. 13, 1920; d. Johan Randulf and Aurora (Stewart) B. Diploma in piano, Juilliard, 1946; cert., Chautauqua Inst. Sch. Music, 1940-46; diploma, U. Oslo Grad. Sch., Norway, 1955; MusB, N.Y. Coll. Music, 1965; MA, NYU, 1972, EdD, 1979. Piano tchr. Juilliard Inst. Musical Art, NY, NY, 1942-43; chmn. music dept. Casement's Coll., Ormond Beach, Fla., 1949-50; dir. music Essex County Girls Vocat. & Tech. HS, Newark, 1953-57; dir. music, organist State of N.J. Institution for Retarded Girls North Jersey Tng. Sch., Totowa, NJ, 1953-68; spl. edn. gifted coord. Jefferson Magnet Sch. Pub. Sch. Sys., Union City, NJ, 1956-95; dir. Upper Montclair Music Sch., Montclair, NJ, 1945—, Ole Bull Music Sch., Potter County, Pa., 1952-68. Adjudicator Lycoming Coll., Williamsport, Pa., 1948—; conductor Whippany Symphony Orch., 1951-52; curator, builder Ole Bull Mus., Carter Camp, Pa., 1968—; dir. youth chorus Jefferson Sch., Union City, 1956-95; dir. Hudson County Elem. Choral Festival, 1971—; artist-in-residence, Union City; guest lectr. Columbia U., N.Y.C., Yale U. Grad. Sch. Music, Hartford, Conn., NYU, Lycoming Coll., Williamsport, Pa., Mansfield U., Pa., Princeton U., NJ, U. Scranton, Pa., Jersey City State Coll. Author: 27 books; editor: various newsletters and mag.; author: (song) Evening Prayer, 1934, I Will Bow and Be Humble, 1954, Voice of Am., 1952; recording artist Educo Records, soloist WFMB radio sta., Daytona Beach, Fla., 1949—50, NBC, Hartford, Conn., WNJR, Union, N.J., 1952—68, WNBT-ABC, Wellsboro, Pa., 1997—2002, Norsk Rikskringkasting, Oslo, Radio and TV Franchise, Paris, recitals, France, Norway, Eng., Switzerland, S. Am., US. Choir dir. First Congl. Ch., 1940-43, Holy Trinity Luth. Ch., Nutley Luth. Ch., 1953-55; organist, choir dir. North Jersey Tng. Sch. Chapel, 1952-68; founder, dir. Ole Bull Music Festival, 1952—; dep. gov. and mem. rsch. bd. advisors Am. Biog. Inst., Raleigh; US State Dept amb. of goodwill to Norway by order of Pres. Dwight D. Eisenhower, 1953, Norwegian Goodwill amb. to US by order of King Haakon VII, 1953. Recipient Freedom medal-Eisenhower medal, 1953, Sterling Silver plaque King Olav V of Norway, 1966, NJEA award, 1970, Performing Arts Prestige award in Edn., 1976, Olympic Gold medal Norwegian Govt., 1992, Silver medal of Honor, 1991, Gold medal of Honor, 1992, Pa. Senate Legis. citation, 1992, Outstanding Tchr. of the Handicapped in the U.S. Nat. Rsch. Coun., 1970, Woman of Distinction honorable mention award Girl Scout Coun. of Greater Essex County, 1996, Artisan award Oakeside Bloomfield Cultural Ctr., 1996, 50 Women You Should Know award Internat. YWCA, 1996, inducted into Millenium Hall of Fame, Am. Biog. Inst., 1998; named Am. Biog. Inst. World Laureate, 1999, St. Olav medal King Harald V (Norway), 1999, Outstanding Woman in Arts award World History Project/Twp. of Montclair, 2000, key to the City Renovo award, Pa., 2000, 2002, Am. Medal of Honor award Pres. of U.S., 2001, Nobel Peace prize, 2002, Congl. Medal of Merit, 2003, World Laureate Am. Biog. Inst., 1999, Congl. Medal of Excellence, Am. Biog. Inst., 2003; Fulbright scholar U. Oslo (Norway) Grad. Sch., 1955; film made in her honor A Child is Waiting, 1963. Mem. Ole Bull Hist. Soc. (pres. 1972—), Phi Delta Kappa (pres. 1984-86, newsletter editor 1984-92), Kappa Delta Pi (pres. 1984—, newsletter editor 1984—, counselor NYU Beta Pi chpt. 1996), Pen & Brush Club, Internat. Percy Grainger Soc. (v.p.), NYU Alumnae Club Inc. (bd. dirs., rec. sec., newsletter editor, 1979—). Republican. Avocations: concert pianist, soprano, writer. Home: 172 Watchung Ave Montclair NJ 07043-1737 Home (Summer): 79 S Cherry Springs Rd Galeton PA 16922 Office: Robert Waters Sch 2800 Summit Ave Union City NJ 07087-2329

BULLARD, JUDYANN DEPASQUALE, elementary education educator; b. Copaigue, N.Y., Oct. 7, 1952; d. Nicholas and Marie (Daole) DePasquale; married; 1 child, Robin Ann. AB in English, Ga. State U., 1973, postgrad., 1985—; MEd, Mercer U., Macon, Ga., 1984. Tchr. Robins AFB Sch. System, Warner Robins, Ga., summers 1980-84; tchr. grades 5, 7 and 8 Christ the King Sch., Atlanta, 1984-89; tchr. grade 5 Warren T. Jackson Sch., Atlanta Pub. Sch. System, 1989—. Supervising tchr. Mercer U., Atlanta, 1992; dir. Rainbows for All Children: Support Program for Children in Grief, 1986-88. North Atlanta Parents for Pub. Schs. grantee, 1991. Mem. ASCD, Nat. Coun. Tchrs. English (workshop presenter 1991), Ga. Coun. Tchrs. English (workshop presenter 1989, 91, 92, 93), Profl. Assn. Ga. Educators, Atlanta Jr. C. of C., Ga. Assn. Educators, Kappa Delta Pi. Office: Warren T Jackson Sch 1325 Mount Paran Rd NW Atlanta GA 30327-3705

BULLARD, LINDA LANE, elementary school educator; b. Orlando, Fla., Sept. 4, 1947; d. Charles Mather and Nevard S. (Vartanian) Lane; m. Henry Milton Bullard III, Aug. 22, 1986. AA, Vernon Ct. Jr. Coll., Newport, R.I., 1967; BA, Nathaniel Hawthorne Coll., Antrim, N.H., 1969; MS, So. Conn. State U., New Haven, 1974. Cert. tchr. nursery through 8th grade. Kindergarten tchr. North Branford (Conn.) Sch. Sys., 1970—. Cons. nursery sch. Nursery on Notch Hill, North Branford, Conn. Campaigner Republican party, Branford, 1994; ch. sch. tchr. Zion Episcopal Ch., North Branford, 1990—. Mem. Kindergarten Assn. Conn. (corr. sec. 1973, pres. 1989-90, Pin 1989-90), Shoreline Assn. Edn. Young Children (v.p.), Alpha Kappa. Avocations: playing the flute, singing in church choir. Home: 83 Cedar Knolls Dr Branford CT 06405-6008

BULLARD, PAMELA, writer, educational consultant; b. Norwood, Mass., Sept. 14, 1948; d. Richard Kendall and Nancy (Stone) B. BA, NYU, 1970; MSL, Yale U., 1978. Reporter, editor Boston Herald Am., 1971-74; reporter WGBH-TV PBS, Boston, 1974-79; producer, dir. WCVB-TV, Boston, 1979-81; exec. producer WNEV-TV, Boston, 1981-83, WCVB-TV, 1981-84, 1983-84; asst. prof. Emerson Coll., Boston, 1985-87; freelance writer, ednl. cons., 1987—. Asst. prof. Boston U. Sch. Pub. Communications, 1977, 79, 80, Kennedy Inst., Harvard U., 1977. Co-author: (with Judith Stoia) The Hardest Lesson, 1979 (Christopher award), (with Barbara Taylor) Making School Reform Happen, 1993, Keepers of the Dream, 1994; The Revolution Revisited: Effective Schools and Systemic Reform, 1995; author: More Than Dreams, 1987. Recipient numerous awards, including Emmy, UPI award. Mem. Authors Guild, NOW, World Wildlife Fedn.

BULLEN, THERESA ANN, special education coordinator; b. Union City, Pa., July 27, 1965; d. Michael and Candace L. (Turner) Kirik; m. Charles E. Bullen, Jr., Aug. 21, 1987; 1 child, Michael. BA, Mercyhurst Coll., Erie, Pa., 1987; MS in Adminstrn., Cen. Mich. U., 1993. Cert. tchr., Pa., N.D. Counselor Perseus House, Inc., Spartansburg, Pa., 1985-87; therapeutic foster parent North Cen. Human Svcs., Minot, N.D., 1988-90; tchr. spl. edn. Dakota Boys Ranch, Minot, 1989-93, staff coord., 1990-93; spl. edn. coord. The Dakota Ctr., Minot, 1994—. Mem. Am. Bus. Women's Assn., Coun. for Exceptional Children, Alpha Phi Sigma. Republican. Methodist. Avocations: softball, camping, bowling, t-ball coach. Home: PO Box 5007 Minot ND 58702-5007 Office: The Dakota Ctr PO Box 5007 Minot ND 58702-5007

BULLOCK, CHARLES SPENCER, III, political science educator, author, consultant; b. Nashville, July 22, 1942; s. Charles Spencer and Elenor Alice (Davis) B.; m. Frances Lee Mann, Sept. 10, 1965; children—Georgia Beth, Judith Rebecca Lee. AB, William Jewell Coll., 1964; MA, Washington U., St. Louis, 1967, PhD, 1968; postgrad., Emory U., 1964-65. Asst. prof. U. Ga., Athens, 1968-72, assoc. prof., 1972-75; prof. U. Houston, 1975-77; prof. polit. sci. U. Ga., Athens, 1977—, Richard B. Russell chair polit. sci., 1980—, research fellow Inst. Behavioral Research, 1977-84. Adj. prof. U. Okla., 1987—. Co-author or co-editor: Black Political Attitudes, 1972, The New Politics, 1970, Law and Social Change, 1972, Racial Equality in America, 1975, Coercion to Compliance, 1977, Public Policy in the Eighties, 1983, PublicPolicy and Politics in America, 1978, 84, Implementation of Civil Rights Policy, 1984, Governing a Changing America, 1984, Georgia Political Almanac, 1991, Runoff Elections in the United States, 1992, Forest Resource Policy, 1993, Georgia Political Almanac, 1993-94, 1993, Georgia Political Almanac, 1995-96, 1995, David Duke and the Politics of Race in the South, 1995, New Politics of the Old South, 1998, rev. 2d edit. 2003, Open Seat Elections to the U.S. House, 2000. Mem. Ga. adv. com. to U.S. Commn. on Civil Rights; mem. Leadership Athens, 1992-93. Recipient citation for achievement William Jewell Coll., 1983, William A. Owens award for creativity in social sci. rsch., 1991, V.O. Key award for best book on so. politics, 1993, Outstanding Tchg. award, 1987, 1993, 95, 99, 2003; grantee NSF, 1973-75, Nat. Inst. Edn., 1973-76. Mem. Am. Polit. Sci. Assn. (exec. coun. 1989-91), Southwestern Polit. Sci. Assn. (Outstanding Paper award 1975, Jewell Prestage Best Paper award 2003), Midwest Polit. Sci. Assn., So. Polit. Sci. Assn. (pres. 1985-86, Scott-Foresman award 1984, award for best paper on women and politics 1988-89), Ga. Polit. Sci. Assn. (pres. 2001-02), Legis. Study Group (chmn. 1983-85), Rotary. Episcopalian. Home: 1011 River Run Bishop GA 30621-1663 Office: U Ga Dept Polit Sci Athens GA 30602

BULLOCK, LYNDAL MARVIN, special education educator; b. Bixby, Okla. s. V.E. and Cordie Mae (Nance) B. BS, Southwestern Coll., 1956; BA, Okla. City U., 1959; MEd, U. Okla., 1963; EdD, U. Kans., 1968. Tchr., counselor Okla. City Pub. Schs., 1959-63, Wichita (Kans.) Pub. Schs., 1963-66; asst. prof. Cen. State U., Edmond, Okla., 1968-69; assoc. prof. U. Fla., Gainesville, 1969-75; prof. U. Okla., Norman, 1975-77, U. Louisville, 1977-78, U. North Tex., Denton, 1979—. Contbr. over 100 articles, books, chapters and monographs. Named Regents Prof., U. N. Tex., 1991; recipient Outstanding Contbr. to Behavioral Disorders, Midwest Symposium for Leadership, 1995, J.E. Wallin award, Internat. Coun. Exceptional Children, 1995, Excellence in Tchg. award, 2002. Mem. Tchr. Educators for Behavior Disorders (pres. 1977-78), Coun. for Children with Behavior Disorders (pres. 1978-79), Coun. for Exceptional Children (v.p., pres.-elect, pres. 1980-84, v.p., pres.-elect, pres. tchr. edn. div. 1988-91). Office: U North Tex PO Box 13857 Denton TX 76203-6857

BULLOCK, MOLLY, retired elementary school educator; d. Wiley and Annie M. Jordan; m. George Bullock; children: Myra A. Bauman, Dawn M. BS in Edn., No. Ariz. U., 1955, postgrad., 1958, LaVerne U., 1962, Claremont Grad. Sch., 1963, Calif. State U. L.A., 1966. Tchr. Bur. Indian Affairs, Kaibeto, Ariz., 1955-56, Crystal, N.Mex., 1956-59, Covina (Calif.) Valley Unified Sch. Dist., 1961-95, supervising master tchr. trainees LaVerne U. and Calif. State U. - L.A., 1961-71, mem. curriculum devel. adv. bd., 1977-79; ret., 1995. Cons. Bauman Curry Co., PR; mem. voting com. Excellence in Edn. awards Lawry's Foods; attendee reading conf. Claremont (Calif.) Grad. Sch. Author: (poems) A Tree (Golden Poet, 1991), What is Love (Golden medal of honor), The Change of Seasons (Dimond Homer trophy, 1999, Poet of the Yr. medallion). Vol. visitor area convalescent hosps.; mentor to former students. Mini grantee, Hughes/Rotary Club/Foothill Ind. Bank, 1986—90. Mem.: NAFE, Covina Unified Edn. Assn., Internat. Platform Assn., Internat. Soc. Poets (hon.). Avocations: poetry, collecting jewelry, dolls, paintings.

BULLOUGH, VERN LEROY, sexologist, historian, nursing educator, researcher; b. Salt Lake City, July 24, 1928; s. D. Vernon Bullough and Augusta Rueckert; m. Bonnie Uckerman, Aug. 2, 1947 (dec. 1996); children: David(dec.), James, Steven, Susan, Michael; m. Gwen Brewer, Aug. 15, 1998. BSN, Calif. State U., Long Beach, 1981; BS, U. Utah, 1951; MA, U. Chgo., 1951, PhD, 1954. Assoc. prof. Youngstown (Ohio) U., 1954-59; from asst. prof. to prof. Calif. State U., Northridge, 1959—79; dean faculty natural and social scis. SUNY Coll., Buffalo, 1980-89, disting. prof., 1988-93, disting. prof. emeritus, 1993—. Adj. prof. U. So. Calif., 1994—2003, Ctr. for Sex Rsch., Calif. State U., Northridge, 1994—; fellow Ctr. for Medieval-Renaissance Studies UCLA, 1995—. Author, co-author: more than 50 books; editor (sr. editor): Free Inquiry; mem. editl. bds.: 8 jours., 2003—; contbr. more than 200 articles to profl. jours. Active in civil liberties and civil rights orgns.; founding mem. first fair housing group in U.S., 1959. With Security Agency U.S. Army, 1946—48. Named Outstanding Prof, Calif Stat Univ sys, Disting Prof, SUNY; recipient Kinsey award, numerous other awards for rsch. into sexuality, history, medicine, nursing and cmty. svcs. Fellow: Coun. for Sci. Medicine and Mental Health, Com. for Sci. Investigation of Claims to the Paranormal, Internat. Humanist and Ethical Union (past pres.), Acad. Humanism (laureate), Soc. Sci. Study Sex (past pres.), Am. Acad. Nursing. E-mail: vbullough@csun.edu.

BUNCE, ROBERT WINFORD, literature educator; b. Raleigh, NC, Mar. 23, 1948; s. Robert Winford and Marjorie Zell Bunce; m. Vanita Beth Hazlewood, Aug. 1, 1987; children: Sarah, Kate. BA, U. N.C., 1972; MA, Miss. State U., 1986; PhD, U. Miss., 1994. Instr. English N.W. Miss. C.C., Senatobia, 1989—. Editor (contbr.): (book) Unknown Southern Poets, 2002. Mem. Motorcycle Owners Am. Cpl. USMC, 1967—70, Vietnam. Mem.: BMW Motorcycle Owners Am. Home: Apt 9E 200 Moore Ave Senatobia MS 38668 Office: Northwest Miss Cmty Coll 4975 Highway 51 N Senatobia MS 38668 Personal E-mail: rwbunce@northwestms.edu.

BUNCH, DALE, academic administrator; Pres. Midstate Coll. Office: Office of the President Midstate Coll Peoria IL 61602

BUNCH, KATHY LYNN, secondary education educator; b. Louisville, June 29, 1956; d. Herbert H. and Jean (Harper) B. BS, Western Ky. U., 1978, MA, 1981, postgrad., 1984, 86. Cert. Home Econs. Nutritionist So. Ky. Headstart, Bowling Green, 1978-79; home econs. tchr. Metcalfe County High Sch., Edmonton, Ky., 1979—; teen parent coord. Metcalfe County Bd. Edn., Edmonton, 1985—; dir., owner Kid's World Day Care, Glasgow, Ky., 1990—. Mem. Nat. Assn. for Edn. Young Children, Ky. Assn. for Early Childhood Edn., Child Care Coun., Nat. Certification Day Care Ctrs. (treas. Region IV), Am. Home Econs. Assn., Am. Vocat. Assn., Ky. Vocat. Assn., Ky. Assn. Vocat. Home Econs. Tchrs., Am. Spl. Vocat. Edn. Assn., Ky. Spl. Vocat. Assn., Metcalfe County Edn. Assn. (bldg. rep. 1980-81, 85-86, chmn. evaluation com. 1989-90), Ky. Home Econs. Tchrs. Assn., Phi Eta Sigma, Phi Upsilon Omicron. Democrat. Methodist. Avocations: cooking, sewing, bicycling, skating, dancing. Home: 24 Love Knob Rd Glasgow KY 42141-9521 Office: Metcalfe County Bd Edn Edmonton KY 42129

BUNCH, MICHAEL BRANNEN, psychologist, educator; b. Miami, Fla., Oct. 19, 1949; s. Edwin Bunch and Janet (Morgan) Bradley; m. Kathryn Ann Campbell, Jan. 17, 1970; children: Melissa Anne, Amy Kathryn. BS, U. Ga., 1972, MS, 1974, PhD, 1976. Tests and measurement specialist Mountain Plains Corp., Glasgow, Mont., 1975-76; rsch. psychologist Am. Coll. Testing Program, Iowa City, 1976-78; sr. profl. NTS Rsch. Corp., Durham, N.C., 1978-82; v.p. Measurement Inc., Durham, N.C., 1982—. Mem. Durham Pub. Edn. Task Force, Durham, 1983-90; chmn. Durham Math. Coun., 1985-90; adj. faculty N.C. Ctrl. U., Durham, 1988-93. Mem. Am. Psychol. Soc., Am. Ednl. Rsch. Assn., Nat. Coun. Measurement in Edn., Ga. Ednl. Rsch. Assn., Sigma Xi. Home: 6 Fernwood Ct Durham NC 27713-7547 Office: Measurement Inc 423 Morris St Durham NC 27701-2128

BUNDY, HALLIE FLOWERS, biochemist, educator; b. Santa Monica, Calif., Apr. 2, 1925; d. Douglas and Phyllis (Flowers) B. BA in Chemistry, Mt. St. Mary's Coll., L.A., 1947; MS in Biochemistry, U. So. Calif., 1955, PhD in Biochemistry, 1958. Instr. sch. medicine U. So. Calif., L.A., 1959-60; asst. prof. Mt. St. Mary's Coll., 1960-63, assoc. prof., 1963-66, prof. biochemistry, 1966-90, emeritus prof., 1990—. Asst. program dir. undergrad. rshc. participation NSF, Washington, 1965-66. Contbr. rsch. articles to profl. jours. USPHS predoctoral fellow, 1955-57; NSF Sci.

Faculty fellow, 1969-70; grantee NIH, 1960-66, 86-89, NSF, 1961-78, 87-89, Grad. Women in Sci., 1974. Mem. Am. Chem. Soc., Pacific Slope Biochem. Conf., Sigma Xi. Achievements include research in isolation, characterization and comparison of enzymes from diverse plant and animal species; the use of dyes to monitor protein folding.

BUNDY, JANE BOWDEN, artist, educator; b. Jersey City, N.J., Mar. 14, 1922; d. John Stanley and Caroline (White) Bowden; m. Wendell Stimpson Brown Jr., June 20, 1942 (dec. Aug. 1992); children: Wendell S. Brown, Caroline E. Calbos, Barbara J. Valentine, Jeffrey L. Brown, Cynthia J. Brown; m. Donald Lawson Bundy, Oct. 15, 1999 (dec. Sept. 2000). BS in Phys. Edn., Douglass Coll., 1942; studies with Betty Abel, Little Silver, N.J., 1962; studies with John Terelak, Marblehead, Mass., 1968-70; studies with Amelia James, Atlanta, 1975-82, studies with Ouida Canaday, 1982-94, studies with Joseph Perrin, 1994. Cert. tchr. phys. edn. and sci. K-12. Substitute tchr. Elem. Sch., Little Silver, N.J., 1965-68, Title I tchr., 1967-68; substitute tchr. Marblehead and Lynn, Mass., 1968-70, DeKalb County, Decatur, Ga., 1970—2002. Publicity chmn., sec., v.p. DeKalb County Art Ctr., Atlanta, 1976—; sec., v.p. Artists Atelier of Atlanta, 1993—. Exhibitions include acrylics, watercolors, collages and drawings, animal portraits; contbr. articles to profl. jours. V.p., sec., bd. dirs. PTA, Little Silver, 1958-70; bd. dirs. AAUW, Little Silver, 1960-70. Mem. Callanwolde Guild (bd. dirs. 1976—), Atlanta Artists Club (Merit award 1995). Republican. Presbyterian. Avocations: tennis, bridge, reading, gardening, bowling. Home: 2110 Gunstock Dr Stone Mountain GA 30087-1621 Studio: Artists Atelier Atlanta 800 Miami Cir NE Ste 200 Atlanta GA 30324-3048 E-mail: janebundy@prodigy.net.

BUNDY, KELLY JANE, learning disabilities educator, consultant; b. Bedford, Ind., Nov. 15, 1958; d. Webster Herschel and Sarah Ann (Chambers) B. BA in Elem. Edn., Oral Roberts U., 1982, MA in Reading, 1986, postgrad. in Learning Disabilities, Psychometry, 1985-86. Tchr. 3rd grade St. Vincent Cath. Sch., Bedford, Ind., 1982-85; tchr. 4th grade Metro Christian Acad., Tulsa, Okla., 1986-87; elem. sch. tutor Diagnostic Instrn. Ctr., Tulsa, Okla., 1986-87; learning disabilities tchr. K-6 Parkview Primary, Intermediate Schs., Bedford, Ind., 1987-90; learning disabilities cons., tchr. OLJM Joint Svcs, Parkview Primary Sch., Bedford, 1990-92, OLJM Joint Svcs, Bedford Jr. High Sch., 1992—. Co-presenter Conf. Okla. Assn. for Children and Adults with Learning Disabilities, Tulsa, 1987; presenter at in-service, meetings on Attention Deficit Disorder, Bedford, Ind., 1992-93. Mem. Learning Disabilities Assn., Children Having Attention Deficit Disorders, Read Coun., Coun. for Exceptional Children. Republican. Avocations: boating, fishing, piano, reading, computers. Home: PO Box 1015 Bedford IN 47421-1015 Office: OLJM Joint Svcs 1501 N St Bedford IN 47421-3715

BUNDY-DESOTO, TERESA MARI, language educator, vocalist; d. Jose Jesus Avila-Carrillo and Maria del Pilar Lozano Avila; m. Glendon B. Bundy, Oct. 15, 1972 (div. May 20, 1987); children: Pete Hernandez Bundy, Angelita Dianne Bundy, Crystal Lorraine Bundy-Schwabenland, Ivan Glen Bundy; m. John B. Soto, Mar. 31, 1996. AA magna cum laude, Fresno City Coll., 1976; BA summa cum laude, Calif. State U., Fresno, 1978; Spanish and bilingual tchg. credential, 1979. Master tchr., trainer Proteus Adult Edn., Visalia, Calif., 1967—73; tchr. trainer Fresno City-County Manpower Commn., Calif., 1973—76; tchr. Spanish, mentor tchr. Ctrl. Unified Sch. Dist., Fresno, 1979—86; dept. chairperson Madera Unified Sch. Dist., Calif., 1986—89; tchr. Spanish, English Hoover HS/Fresno Unified Sch. Dist., 1989—. Rschr., trainer Office of Edn., Washington, 1968—74; adult edn. tchr. Chavez Adult Edn. Ctr.; alt. chief examiner ofcl. GED testing ctr. Gen. Ednl. Devel. Testing Svc., 1999—; spkr. in field. Singer: recorded 2 CDs and mus. videos under stage name Luz De Luna. Profl. radio announcer Spanish Radio Stas., Fresno, 1978—96; TV model Spanish TV Univision, Fresno, 1980; judge Miss Laverkin, Utah, 1982. Recipient Miss El Futuro C.U., 1967, 1972. Mem.: Am. Coun. on Edn., Calif. Tchr. Assn. Democrat. Mem. Lds Ch. Home: 1149 E San Bruno Ave Fresno CA 93710 E-mail: luzdeluna@comcast.net.

BUNDY-IANNARELLI, BARBARA ANN, educational administrator; b. Niagara Falls, N.Y., June 13, 1947; d. Leo Charles and Norma June (Lamberson) B. BS in Edn., State Coll. U., Buffalo, 1965, MS in Edn., 1970; MS in Reading Edn., SUNY, Buffalo, 1974, PhD in Edn., Rsch., Evaluation, 1982. Cert. tchr. elem. edn., reading, adminstrn., N.Y. Tchr. 4th grade Niagara Falls City Sch. Dist., 1970-72, tchr. remedial reading, 1972-76, project dir., 1976-81, reading resource tchr., 1981-83, tchr. spl. assignment, 1983-84, supr. elem. edn., 1984-91, supr. curriculum and staff devel., 1991-93, elem. prin., 1993—. Adj. prof. Niagara U., Lewiston, N.Y., 1989—, State Univ. Coll., 1990-91, SUNY, 1990; cons., presenter, speaker various confs., clubs and workshops. Bd. dirs. campaign cabinet United Way Niagara, 1987—, campaign chair, 1993, Boys and Girls Club, 1991-93, Bootstrap Niagara, Inc., Niagara Falls. Named Outstanding Vol. Everywoman Opportunity Ctr., 1988, Community Person of the Day, Sta. WBFO, 1990, Niagara County Woman of Yr., 1993; recipient Good Neighbor award Niagara Falls Anthony Bax Meml., 1990, Outstanding Alumni award SUNY, 1989. Mem. Western N.Y. Women in Adminstr., Niagara Falls Adminstrv. and Supervisory Coun. (bd. dirs. 1986—, pres. 1987-91, 95—), Niagara Frontier Reading Coun. (pres., past conf. chair, membership chair 1984—), Phi Delta Kappa. Avocations: reading, computer, movies, music, writing. Home: 929 Creekside Dr Niagara Falls NY 14304-2531 Office: Hyde Park Elem Sch 1620 Hyde Park Blvd Niagara Falls NY 14305-3206

BUNGER, ROLF, physiology educator; b. Hamburg, Germany, Oct. 19, 1941; came to U.S., 1979; s. Heinz Johannes Albert and Helga (Franz) B.; m. Margriet Akkerman, Dec. 14, 1973; children: Nils, Frank. MD, U. Hamburg, 1969, U. Heidelberg, Germany, 1970; MD habil., U. Munich, 1979. Intern Heidberg Infirmary, Hamburg, 1970; asst. of physiology U. Aachen, Germany, 1970-75, U. Munich, 1975-79; asst. prof. dept. physiology F. E. Hebert Med. Sch., USUHS, Bethesda, Md., 1979-82, assoc. prof., 1983-92; prof. USUHS, Bethesda, Md., 1992—; prof. of molecular and cellular biology US Univ. Health Svc., Bethesda, Md., 1994—, prof. anesthesiology, 2000—. Cons. U. Buffalo, 1983, U. Ala., 1986-89, U. Tex., Ft. Worth, 1990—, AAALAC, 1997—; referee, editl. reviewer domestic and fgn. sci. med. rsch. jours. and instns., including NIH, VA, NSF, HFSP, Dutch Heart Found., MRC, 1994—; vis. prof. Erasmus U., Rotterdam, 1992; lectr. in field. Mem. editl. bd. Internat. Jour. Purine and Pyrimidine Rsch., 1989-93, Internat. Jour. Angiology, 1991-95, Am. Jour. Physiology, 1999—, Heart and Circulation; guest referee editor Jour. Applied Physiology, 1998—. Webelo leader Boy Scouts Am., McLean, Va., 1986-87, packmaster, 1987-89. Capt., German Air Force Med. Corp. Grantee, Uniformed Svcs. U. Health Scis., 1979—, NIH, 1982—2000, Dept. Def., 1995—99. Fellow Am. Heart Assn.; mem. Am. Physiol. Soc., Deutsche Physiol. Gesellschaft. Achievements include clarification of adenylate compartments in myocardium; demonstration of energy-linked and work dependence of myocardial pyruvate dehydrogenase flux, of interstitial free AMP in myocardium; research in metabolic enhancement of isolated and in-situ preischemic and postischemic heart preparations; metabolic protection of cytosolic phosphorylation potential by pyruvate and adenosine during myocardial reperfusion and stunning; adenylate-related theory of metabolic coronary control, energy linked control of sarcoplasmic reticulum Ca 2+ - ATPase; pyruvate protection against apoptosis infarct size and hemorrhagic shock, Redox control of NADH oxidase; patents in field. Home: 1922 Kenbar Ct Mc Lean VA 22101-5321 Office: USUHS Dept Physiology 4301 Jones Bridge Rd Bethesda MD 20814-4799

BUNIAK, RAYMOND, educational professional; b. Sao Paulo, Mar. 21, 1955; came to U.S., 1959; s. Wasyl and Katharina (Kurpita) B.; m. Karen Sue Harbecke, Apr. 28, 1957. BA in Edn., Northeastern Ill. U., Chgo., 1977; MMus, DePaul U., 1981; EdD in Curriculum and Instrn., Loyola U., 2004. Cert. tchr. K-12, 6-12 music, Ill. Profl. musician/trombone and euphonium player, condr., Chgo. metro area, 1973—; studio tchr. of brass instruments various, Chgo. metro area, 1979—, band dir. New Trier West High, Northfield, Ill., 1981-82, O.L.P.H. Sch., Glenview, Ill., 1986-94; instrnl. devel. and grants officer/tchr. Kelly H.S., Chgo., 1994—. Grant writer for tech., instrnl. program improvements, coord. Internat. Baccaleureate Program, Kelly H.S., 1997—, coord. AP program, also coord. ILCA program. Author: A 20th Century Treatise on the Trombone, 4 vols., 1984. Recipient Univ. Talent scholarship Northeastern Ill. U., 1974-77. Mem. ACDS, Francis Galpin Soc., Internat. Trombone Assn., Nat. Cath. Bandmaster's Assn., Music Educators Nat. Conf., Chgo. Fedn. of Musicians. Avocations: household renovation, auto repair, bible tchr. Home: 105 N Western Ave Bartlett IL 60103-4030 Office: Thomas Kelly High Sch 4136 S California Ave Chicago IL 60632-1817 E-mail: rbuniak@cps.k12.il.us., RayBuniak105@msn.com.

BUNKER, BERYL H. retired insurance executive, community volunteer; b. Chelsea, Mass., Aug. 18, 1919; d. Albert Crocker and Eva Agnes (Norris) Hardacker; m. John Wadsworth Bunker, Oct. 31, 1942. Student, Simmons Coll., 1936-38, Boston Coll. Law, 1948-49; grad., Bentley Sch. Acctg., Boston, 1958; BBA with highest honors, Northeastern U., 1962, MBA, 1967; D of Humane Svc. (hon.), Simmons Coll., 2001. CFA. Legal rsch. clerk Frank Shepard Co., N.Y.C., 1938-43; cost acct. Johns Manville Corp., Pittsburg, Calif., 1943-46; studio mgr. Wheelan Studios, Boston, 1946; clerical supr. Columbian Purchasing Group, Boston, 1946-48; office mgr. Wellesley (Mass.) Coll., 1948-51; statistician Eastman Kodak Co., Rochester, N.Y., 1951-53; investment officer John Hancock Mut. Life, Boston, 1953-74; sr. v.p. John Hancock Advisers, Boston, 1974-84. Nat. bd. dirs. YWCA of the U.S.A., 1988-94, hon. bd. dirs., 1998—, mem. World Svc. Coun., 1992—; pres. bd. dirs. Boston YWCA, 1985-87, active 1977-96; chair bd. Vis. Nurses Assn. Cape Cod Found., South Dennis, Mass., 1995; bd. dirs. Old South Meeting House Mus., Boston, 1989-92; trustee Simmons Coll., 1994-2000, chair centennial com. 1999-2000, corporator, 2000—; mem. women's coun. exec. com. Pine St. Inn, 1992—; bd. visitors Women's Edn. and Ind. Union, 2000—; adv. com. Boston Women's Fund, 2001—; mem. adv. com. On The Rise, 1997—; mem. Ct. for Women in Politics and Public Policy, Assocs. of the Boston Pub. Libr. Bd., The Coll. Club of Boston, 1998—, Cambridge YWCA, Neighborhood Assn. of the Back Bay; honoree Pine St. Inn Women's Coun., 2000. Recipient Philanthropy award Women in Devel., 1990, Disting. Alumni award Bentley Coll., 1994; named Woman of Achievement, Cambridge YWCA, 1991, Lifetime Service to Women award, On The Rise, 1998, Lifetime Achievement award, College Club, 1998, Outstanding Alumna North Eastern U., 2000. Mem. AARP, LWV, NOW, AAUW, Assn. Investment Mgmt. Rsch., Mass. Action for Women, Mass. Women Polit. Caucus, Boston Security Analysts Soc. (treas. 1973-76), Mass. Women's State Wide Legis. Network (dir. 1987), Simmons Coll. Alumnae Assn. (pres. 1989-91, Alumnae Svc. award 1984, Planned Giving award 1993), Older Women's League, The Internat. Alliance, Harwich Hist. Soc., Project Vote Smart, Women's Ednl. and Indsl. Union, Friday Forum, Eire Soc., Wellesley Ctrs. for Women. Avocations: fundraising, theater, reading. Home: 790 Boylston St Apt 22F Boston MA 02199-7921 E-mail: berylb@mailstation.com.

BUNKER, DEBRA J. elementary education educator; b. Oshkosh, Wis., Sept. 19, 1955; d. Donald and Dawn E. (Fischer) B. BSEd, U. Wis., Oshkosh, 1977, MSE in Reading, 1984. Cert. elem. edn. grades 1-6, reading grades K-12, reading tchr., reading specialist. Chpt. 1 reading tchr./specialist Oshkosh (Wis.) Area Sch. Dist. Mem. Citizen Amb. Reading Delegation to Hungary and Russia, 1993; presenter at early childhood and reading confs. Founder, coord. Bookends Reading Club. Mem. ASCD, Internat. Reading Assn. (Community Svc. award), Wis. State Reading Assn. (chair pub. com., reading conf.), Fox Valley Reading Coun. (v.p. elect., v.p., past pres., chair, parents and reading com., pub./memberships com., historian), Bookends Reading Club (founder, coord.), Kappa Delta Pi.

BUNNELL, PETER CURTIS, photography and art educator, museum curator; b. Poughkeepsie, N.Y., Oct. 25, 1937; s. Harold Curtis and Ruth (Buckhout) B. BFA, Rochester Inst. Tech., 1959; MFA, Ohio U., 1961; MA, Yale U., 1965. Curator of photography Mus. Modern Art, N.Y.C., 1966-72; prof. history of photography and modern art Princeton (N.J.) U., 1972—2002, prof. emeritus, 2002—. Curator of photography Art Mus. Princeton U., 1972-02, dir., 1973-78, 98-2000. Author; Clarence H. White, 1987, Minor White: The Eye That Shapes, 1989, Degrees of Guidance, 1993, Thomas Joshua Cooper, 1995, Ruth Bernhard: Photographs, 1996, Aaron Siskind: The Bond and The Free, 1997, Walter Chappell: Time Lived, 2000, Remembering Limelight, 2001, Edward Ranney: The Character of the Place, 2003; editor: A Photographic Vision, 1980, The Art of Pictorial Photography, 1992, Photography at Princeton, 1998. Guggenheim fellow, 1979, Asian Cultural Coun. Rsch. fellow, 1984. Fellow Royal Photographic Soc. (hon.); mem. Soc. for Photog. Edn. (chmn. 1973-76), The Friends of Photography (pres. 1978-87, chmn. 1987-92), Century Assocs. Club. Office: Princeton U Dept Art And Archaeology Princeton NJ 08544-1018

BUNNETT, JOSEPH FREDERICK, chemist, educator; b. Portland, Oreg., Nov. 26, 1921; s. Joseph and Louise Helen (Boulan) B.; m. Sara Anne Telfer, Aug. 22, 1942; children: Alfred Boulan, David Telfer, Peter Sylvester (dec. Sept. 1972). BA, Reed Coll., 1942; PhD, U. Rochester, 1945. Mem. faculty Reed Coll., 1946-52, U. N.C., 1952-58; mem. faculty Brown U., 1958-66, prof. chemistry, 1959-66, chmn. dept., 1961-64; prof. chemistry U. Calif., Santa Cruz, 1966-91, prof. emeritus, 1991—. Erskine vis. fellow U. Canterbury, N.Z., 1967; vis. prof. U. Wash., 1956, U. Wurzburg, Germany, 1974, U. Bologna, Italy, 1988; rsch. fellow Japan Soc. for Promotion of Sci., 1979; Lady Davis vis. prof. Hebrew U., Jerusalem, Israel, 1981; mem. adv. coun. dept. chemistry Princeton (N.J.) U., 1985-89; mem. NRC com. on alternative chem. demilitarization techs., 1992-93; mem. Dept. Def. panel on Gulf War Health Effects, 1993-94; co-chmn. peer rev. com. Russian-Am. Joint Evaluation Program, 1995-96; co-chmn. NATO Advanced Rsch. Workshop on Chem. Problems Associated with Old Arsenical and Mustard Munitions, Lodz, Poland, 1996; working group chem. weapons destruction, scientific adv. bd. Orgn. Prohibition Chem. Weapons, 1999—. Co-editor: Arsenic and Old Mustard: Chemical Problems in the Destruction of Old Arsenical and Mustard Munitions, 1998; contbr. articles to profl. jours. Trustee Reed Coll., 1970-97, trustee emeritus, 1997—. Fulbright scholar U. Coll., London, 1949-50, U. Munich, 1960-61; Guggenheim fellow U. Munich, 1960-61; recipient James Flack Norris award in phys. organic chemistry Am. Chem. Soc., 1992; named hon. mem. Societa Chimica Italiana. Fellow AAAS, Internat. Union Pure and Applied Chemistry (chmn. commn. phys. organic chemistry 1978-83, sec. organic chemistry divsn. 1981-83, v.p. 1983-85, pres. 1985-87, chmn. task force on sci. aspects of destruction of chem. warfare agts. 1991-95, chmn. com. on chem. weapon destruction 1995-2001, fellow, 2002.); mem. Am. Acad. Arts. and Scis., Am. Chem. Soc. (editor jour. Accounts of Chem. Rsch. 1966-86), Royal Soc. Chemistry (London), Pharm. Soc. Japan (hon.), Acad. Gioenia (U. Catania, hon.), Soc. Argentina de Investigaciones en Quimica Organica (hon.). Home: 608 Arroyo Seco Santa Cruz CA 95060-3148 Office: U Calif Dept Chemistry Santa Cruz CA 95064 Fax: 831-459-2935. E-mail: bunnett@chemistry.ucsc.edu.

BUNTING, CAROLYN ELLEN, educational consultant, writer; b. Durham, NC, Jan. 4, 1943; d. Glenn Woodburn and Emma Lucille (Garrard) B. BA, U. N.C., Greensboro, 1965; MEd, Duke U., 1971, PhD, 1977. Cert. social studies tchr., curriculum specialist, supr./adminstr., N.C. Tchr. Greensboro Pub. Sch., 1965-68, Durham Pub. Sch., NC, 1969-71; supr. student tchrs. Appalachian State U., Boone, NC, 1973-74; pvt. practice pub. sch. cons., 1974-75; tchr., supr. Sampson County Schs., Clinton, NC, 1975-77; prof. edn. Campbell U., Buies Creek, NC, 1977-87; exec. NC Assn. Sch. Adminstr., Raleigh, NC, 1987-89; mid. sch. adminstr. Durham Pub. Sch., NC, 1990-95; ind. ednl. cons. and writer. Contbr. articles to numerous jours. Mem. ASCD, Nat. Mid. Sch. Assn., Kappa Delta Pi, Phi Kappa Phi, currently working on a collection of classroom stories as told by tchr. Avocations: reading, gardening, cooking, decorating. Home: 214 Morreene Rd Durham NC 27705-6105

BUNTING, DAVID CUYP, economics educator, consultant; b. Chgo., Sept. 22, 1940; s. Van Asmus and Jane (Whittemore) B.; m. Susan Jean Wilkins, Oct. 28, 1978; children: Maxwell C., Henri N. BS, Ohio State U., 1962, MA, 1964; MS, U. Wis., 1966; PhD, U. Oreg., 1972. Asst. prof. Ea. Wash. U., Cheney, 1971-76, assoc. prof., 1976-80, prof., 1980—. Cons. Bonneville Power Adminstrn., Spokane, Wash., 1985-99. Author: Rise of Large American Corporations, 1987; contbr. articles to profl. jours. Soccer coach Spokane Youth Sports Assn., 1985-94. Mem. Am. Econ. Assn., Royal Econ. Soc., Internat. Health Economists Assn., Soc. for Advancement of Socio-Econs. Democrat. Home: 2311 E 17th Ave Spokane WA 99223-5121 Office: Ea Wash U PAT 300 Dept Economics Cheney WA 99004 E-mail: dbunting@ewu.edu.

BUONO, ANTHONY FRANCIS, business educator; b. Bronx, N.Y., Sept. 13, 1947; s. Frank Dominic and Jeannette (Gehl) B.; BS, U. Md., 1975; MA, Boston Coll., 1977, PhD, 1981; m. Mary Alice Keyl, Jan. 11, 1970; 1 child, Christopher Keyl. Rsch. assoc. Lab. Psychosocial Studies, Boston Coll., 1976-78, lectr. dept. orgnl. studies, 1977-79; instr. Nat. Assn. Bank Women Inst., Simmons Coll., summers 1979-85; asst. prof. dept. mgmt. Bentley Coll., Waltham, Mass., 1979-84, assoc. prof., 1985-89, prof., 1990—, dept. chair, 1989-94, rsch. fellow ctr. for bus. ethics, 1992—; orgn. devel. cons. in field. With USAF, 1969-75. NIMH grantee, 1976-78. Mem. Acad. Mgmt., Eastern Acad. Mgmt., Am. Sociol. Assn., Roman Catholic. Author: (with James L. Bowditch) Quality of Work Life Assessment: A Survey Based Approach, 1982; A Primer on Organizational Behavior, 1985, 5th edit., 2001, The Human Side of Mergers and Acquisitions: Managing Collisions Between People, Culture and Organizations, 1989; (with Lawrence T. Nichols) Corporate Policy, Values and Social Responsibility, 1985; editor: Current Trends in Management Consulting, 2001; Developing Knowledge and Value in Manangement Consulting, 2002, Enhancing Inter-Firm Networks and Interorganizational Strategies, 2003; asst. editor Bus. and the Contemporary World, 1987-96; contbr. articles to profl. jours. Home: 15 Virginia Ridge Rd Sudbury MA 01776-1053 E-mail: abuono@bentley.edu.

BUONO, FREDERICK J. secondary school educator; b. Syracuse, N.J. s. Albert Buono; m. Nancy Sykes, Aug. 1, 1964. BS, Syracuse U., 1961, MS, 1964, PhD, 1967. Rsch. scientist Rohm & Haas, Bristol, Pa., 1967-72; dir. rsch. Tenneco Chems., Piscataway, NJ, 1972-85; tchr. Lenape Regional H.S., Medford, 1986—. Contbr. articles to profl. jours. NIH fellow, 1964-67. Mem. Am. Soc. Microbiology, N.J. Edn. Assn. Avocations: reading, gardening. Home: 18 Edgewood Rd Robbinsville NJ 08691-1128

BUOTE, ROSEMARIE BOSCHEN, retired special education educator; b. Jamaica, NY, Nov. 13, 1939; d. George Frederick and Mary (Bernadick) Boschen; m. Victor Roy Buote, June 27, 1964; children: Kristine Enos, Alissa Cassidy. BA, Barrington (R.I.) Coll., 1962; MEd, R.I. Coll., Providence, 1985, Fitchburg (Mass.) State Coll., 1991. Cert. spl. edn. and elem. tchr. Elem. tchr. Town of Barrington, 1962-68, 69-70; resource rm. instructional aide Town of Rehoboth, Mass., 1983-84; spl. edn. tchr., behavior mgmt. specialist Dept. of Edn. Tri-County Dist., Ednl. Svcs. in Instnl. Schs., Taunton, Mass., 1985—2002; ret., 2002. Sec. Conservation Commn., Town of Dighton, 1971—74, Friends of the Taunton Libr. B d.; lay eucharistic minister Pastoral Outreach Commn., Episcopal Diocese Mass.; bd. dirs. Gordon Coll. Alumni Bd., Wenham, Mass., 1989—92, Am. Cancer Soc. S.E. Mass. Mem.: AAUW (Mass. state v.p. for membership 2003—, sec., Taunton area br. past pres.), Mass. Computer Using Educators, Coun. for Children with Learning Disabilities, Coun. Children with Behavioral Disorders, Coun. Exceptional Children, Southeastern New Eng. Marine Educators, Nat. Marine Educators Assn., Red Hat Soc., Dighton Garden Club (pres. 1979—82), Delta Kappa Gamma (pres. 2002—). Avocations: reading, writing, gardening, theater. Home: 1690 Wellington St Dighton MA 02715-1000 Fax: (508) 669-5894. E-mail: Rosemariebuote@aol.com.

BURAKOFF, STEVEN JAMES, immunologist, educator; b. N.Y.C., Oct. 13, 1942; s. Jack and Adelene (Van Praag) B.; m. Suzanne Weindling, Sept. 3, 1965; 1 child, Alexis. BA, Lehigh U., 1964; MA, Queens Coll., Flushing, N.Y., 1965; MD, Albany Med. Coll. Union U., 1970; MA (hon.), Harvard U., 1984; DHL hon., Spertus Inst., Chgo., 2002. Diplomate Am. Bd. Internal Medicine. Intern, resident N.Y. Hosp., Cornell Med. Ctr., 1970-73.; instr. Harvard Med. Sch., Boston, 1976-77, asst. prof., 1977-80, assoc. prof., 1980-83, prof., 1983—2000; chief pediat. oncology Dana Farber Cancer Inst., Boston, 1985-2000; Margaret M. Dyson prof. pediat. Harvard Med. Sch., Boston, 1998-2000; Laura and Isaac Perlmutter prof. NYU Sch. Medicine, 2000—. Ted Williams sr. investigator, Dana Farber Cancer Inst., 1995-2000; dir. Skirball Inst. for Biomolecular Medicine, 2000—, NYU Cancer Inst., 2000—; bd. dirs. The Med. Found. Contbr. over 300 articles to profl. jours. Recipient Sr. Faculty award Am. Cancer Soc., 1980-85. Mem. Am. Soc. Clin. Investigation, Am. Assn. Immunologists (head program com. 1985-86), Assn. Am. Physicians, Transplantation Soc.

BURBANK, STEPHEN BRADNER, law educator; b. NYC, Jan. 8, 1947; s. John Howard and Jean (Gedney) B.; m. Ellen Randolph Coolidge, June 13, 1970; 1 child, Peter Jefferson. AB, Harvard U., 1968, JD, 1973. Bar: Mass. 1973, Pa. 1976, U.S. Supreme Ct. 1977. Law clk. Supreme Jud. Ct. of Mass., Boston, 1973-74, Chief Justice Warren Burger, Washington, 1974-75; gen. counsel U. Pa., Phila., 1975-80, asst. prof. law, 1979-83, assoc. prof. law, 1983-86, prof. law, 1986—, Fuller prof. law, 1991-95; Berger prof. law, 1995—. Reporter 3rd Cir. Jud. Discipline Rules, Phila., 1981-82, 84, 3rd Cir. Task Force on Rule 11, Phila., 1987-89; mem. Nat. Commn. on Jud. Discipline and Removal, 1991-93; mediator, arbitrator Ctr. for Pub. Resources, NY, 1986—; cons. Dechert, Price & Rhoads, Phila., 1986—; mem. CPR Arbitration Commn., 1997-2000; spl. master NFL, 2002—. Mem. Com. to Visit Harvard and Radcliffe Coll., Cambridge, Mass., 1979-85; mem. adv. bd. Inst. Contemporary Art, Phila., 1982-99; charter trustee Phillips Acad., Andover, Mass., 1980-97. Mem. Am. Law Inst. (life, adviser transnational rules of civil procedure 1997—, adviser internat. jurisdiction and judgments 1999—). Am. Arbitration Assn. (mem. panel of arbitrators 1985—), Century Assn., Am. Jud. Soc. (mem. exec. com. 1997-2002, v.p. 1997-99), Phi Beta Kappa. Avocations: swimming, travel, tennis. Office: U Pa Sch Law 3400 Chestnut St Philadelphia PA 19104-6204 E-mail: sburbank@law.upenn.edu.

BURBRIDGE, ANN ARNOLD, music educator, choir director; b. Galesburg, Ill., Sept. 13, 1947; d. Adis Michael and Janet Louise (Frymire) Arnold; m. Robert Arthur Burbridge, June 27, 1970; children: Britt, Michael, Mark. BMEd, Augustana Coll., 1969; MMEd, Tex. Tech. U., 1987, postgrad.; Kodaly cert. levels 1, 2 and 3, Silver Lake Coll., 1990; advanced Kodaly cert., U. North Tex., 1993; postgrad., Tex. Tech U.; Choral Music Experience level I cert., London; Choral Music Experience level II cert., No. Ill. U., 1995, Choral Music Experience level III cert., 1996, Choral Music Experience level IV cert., 1997, Choral Music Experience artist-tchr., 1998. Tchr. Washington Jr. High Sch., Chicago Heights, Ill., 1969-70, Magnolia Sch., Valdosta, Ga., 1970-71; music tchr. Mountain Home AFB (Idaho) Presch. and Kindergarten, 1971-82, Christ the King Cathedral Sch., Lubbock, Tex., 1982-84; tchr. music Nat Williams Elem. Sch. Lubbock Ind. Sch. Dist., 1985-99; music instr. Lubbock Christian U., 1997-99; dir. choir Madison H.S., San Antonio, 1999—2001, Brackenridge

H.S., San Antonio, 2001—02; fine arts adminstr. for elem. music and secondary choral San Antonio Ind. Sch. Dist., 2002—. Mem. campus performance objectives com., author curriculum materials for elem. music; dist. mentor; scorer Tex. Master Tchr. Exam; validator Nat. Bd. Profl. Tchg. Stds., 2002; fine arts team writer Tex. Edn. Agy.; fine arts team writer Tex. Essential Knowledge and Skills: Web Resources and Tex. Curriculum Tex. Edn. Network; founder, past artistic dir. Lubbock Children's Choir; clinician, presenter in field; author, cons. Glencoe McGraw Hill Pub. Co., Macmillan Publ. Co.; mem. team writing guidelines and models of integrated arts and interdisciplinary studies Nat. Consortium Arts. Author: Fundamentals of Music, 1987; author, cons. Silver Burdett Ginn Publ. Co. Bd. mem. Llano Estacado Friends of Piano Found.; mem. Nat. Integrated Arts and Interdisciplinary Studies com. Nat. Consortium of Arts; clinician, cons. TEA Fine Arts Cadre, 2002—. Recipient Disting. Svc. award Lubbock Jaycees, Innovative Teaching Strategy award, LISD. Mem. Am. Choral Dirs. Assn., Orgn. Am. Kodaly Educators, Music Educators Nat. Conf. (nat. registered and cert.), Kodaly Educators Tex., Tex. Music Educators Assn. (state chair elem. music 1995-97, past region XVI chair), Tex. Classroom Tchrs. Assn. (rep.), Lubbock Elem. Music Tchrs. Assn. (treas.), Tex. Music Educators Conf. (state pres. 2000-02), Tex. Coalition Music Advocacy (past state pres.), Phi Delta Kappa (past v.p. programs and del. Llano Estacado chpt.). E-mail: Ann@SATX.RR.com., aburbridge@SAISD.net.

BURCH, SUSAN ANN, human resource developer, educator; b. DeKalb, Ill., Sept. 18, 1946; d. Leon David and Dorothy Rose (Schade) Larson; m. Thomas Lee Burch, Oct. 10, 1970; children: Lee Thomas, Shannon Joy. BA, No. Ill. U., 1968, MS in Edn., 1982, ABD, 1993. English tchr. Dist. 129, Aurora, Ill., 1968-72; adminstrv. asst. Dean's Grant, Dekalb, 1981-82; instr. psychology, coord. gifted Waubonsee C.C., Sugar Grove, Ill., 1982-97, mgr. children's programs, 1984-97, grant writer, 1989—; program dir. fashion merchandising Internat. Acad. Merchandising and Design, chgo., 1997-98; human resource developer Acxion Corp., Chgo., 1998—. Freelance cons., Sugar Grove, 1986-97, corp. trainer, 1990—; field reader U.S. Dept. Edn., 1993-95. Advisor ednl. Found., Plano, Ill. 1989-90. Mem.: Ill. Assn. for Gifted Children, Am. Soc. Tng. and Devel., Assn. for Applied and Therapeutic Humor, Am. Assn. Adult Continuing Edn., Internat. Soc. Performance Improvement (Chgo. chpt.), Kappa Delta Pi. Avocations: writing, reading, dancing, music, sewing. Home: 3S 515 Marion Cir Sugar Grove IL 60554

BURCHELL, JEANNE KATHLEEN, primary school educator; b. Queens, N.Y., May 14, 1930; d. Nicholas A. and Florence M. (Doscher) B. AB, Manhattanville Coll., 1951; MS, Fordham U., 1952, postgrad., 1952-58, St. John's U., 1969. Cert. childhood edn. tchr., sch. adminstr., supr., N.Y. Tchr. Gwendoline N. Alleyne Sch. Pub. Sch. 152, Queens, 1954-88, early childhood coord., 1988—. Assoc. editor Courier P.S. 152 PTA, 1960—. Recipient Award of Merit, Queensborough Fedn. Parents Clubs, Inc., Dist. 1, 1981, 92, Sch. of Edn. Alumni Achievement award Fordham U., 1994, Anne de Xainctonge Disting. Alumna award Notre Dame Sch. Manhattan, 1997. Mem. Assn. Tchrs. N.Y. (Educator of Yr. 1988), Fordham U. Sch. Edn. Alumni Assn. (bd. dirs. 1992—), Notre Dame Sch. Alumnae Assn. (pres. 1990-94). Home: 84-09 35th Ave Apt 2E Jackson Heights NY 11372-5402 Office: Pub Sch 152 33-52 62nd St Woodside NY 11377-2236

BURCHENAL, JOAN RILEY, science educator; b. N.Y.C., Dec. 11, 1925; d. Wells Littlefield and Bertha Barclay (Fahys) Riley; m. Joseph Holland Burchenal, Mar. 20, 1948; children: Elizabeth Payne Burchenal Paul (dec.), Joan Littlefield Burchenal Nycum, Barbara Fahys Burchenal Landers, Caleb Wells, David Holland, Joseph Emory Barclay; 1 stepchild, Mary Holland Burchenal Nottebohm. BA, Vassar Coll., 1946; MAT, Yale U., 1971; MA, Fairfield U., 1981. Sci. tchr. New Canaan (Conn.) Country Sch., 1968-69, Low Heywood Sch., Stamford, Conn., 1968-69, The Thomas Sch., Rowayton, Conn., 1972-73, Darien Bd. Edn., Conn., 1973-91, ret. Mem. panel on grants for tchrs. enhancement program NSF, 1987, 92; K-12 sci. curriculum com., 1994-2000. Hon. chmn. Darien Sci. Fair, 1986; mem. steering com. Holly Pond Saltmarsh Conservation Com., 1968—71; mem. acad. courses com. Darien Cmty. Assn., 1964—71, chmn., 1971; trustee Garrison Forest Sch., 1959—62; rep. Town Meeting of Darien, 1993—, mem. edn. com., 1993—, chair edn. com., 1995—97, rules com., 2000—; cmty. rep. K-12 Sci. Curriculum Com., 1994—2000; elder First Presbyn. Ch. of New Canaan, 1994—97, Stephen min., 1994—; bd. dir., chmn. standards com. A Better Chance, Darien, Conn., 1985—99; bd. dir. Darien Nature Ctr., 1975—91, Darien Audubon Soc., 1978—86, Darien LWV, 1951—62, Alumnae and Alumni Vassar Coll. Recipient Presdl. award for excellence in sci. teaching Nat. Sci. Tchrs. Assn., NSF, Washington, 1985. Mem. AAAS, N.Y. Acad. Sci., Nat. Assn. Biology Tchrs., Nat. Sci. Tchrs. Assn., Assn. Presdl. Awardees in Sci. Teaching (nominating com. 1987-90), Cosmopolitan Club, Ausable Club, Noroton Yacht Club, Phi Beta Kappa. Republican. Presbyterian. Avocations: reading, travel, trekking, birding. Home: 18 Juniper Rd Darien CT 06820-5707 E-mail: jhbjrb@aol.com.

BURCHFIEL, BURRELL CLARK, geology educator; b. Stockton, Calif., Mar. 21, 1934; s. Beryl Edward and Agnes (Clark) B.; children: Brian Edward, Brook Evans, Benjamin Clark, Halsey Royden. BS, Stanford U., 1957, MS, 1958; PhD, Yale U., 1961. Prof. geology Rice U., 1961-76, MIT, 1977-84, Schlumberger prof. geology, 1984—. Served with U.S. Army, 1958-59. Fellow Geol. Soc. Am., Am. Acad. Arts and Scis., Nat. Acad. Scis., Am. Geophys. Union, European Union Geoscis. (hon. fgn.); mem. Geol. Soc. Australia, Am. Assn. Petroleum Geologists, Chinese Acad. Scis. (fgn.). Home: 9 Robinson Park Winchester MA 01890-3717 Office: MIT 77 Massachusetts Ave # 54-1010 Cambridge MA 02139-4307 E-mail: bchurch@mit.edu.

BURCHFIELD, JERRY LEE, artist, educator, author; b. Chgo., July 28, 1947; s. Darrell and Margaret (Reames) B.; m. Barbara Jane Blaha, Aug. 24, 1968; 1 child, Brian. BA, Calif. State U.-Fullerton, 1971, MA in Art, 1976. One-man shows include Laguna Beach (Calif.) Mus. Art, 1974, Arco Ctr. Visual Art, L.A., 1976, Tyler Sch. Art, Phila., Laguna Beach Sch. Art, 1977, Eastern Wash. U., 1978, Foto Gallery, N.Y.C., L.A. Mcpl. Art Gallery, Barnsdall Park, Hollywood, 1979, Susan Spiritus Gallery, Newport Beach, Calif., Yuen Lui Gallery, Seattle, Ufficio Dell Arte, Paris, France, 1980, No. Ill. U., Colo. Coll., 1981, George Eastman House, Rochester, N.Y., Orange Coast Coll., Gallery Graphics, San Diego, 1982, Golden West Coll., 1983, Irvine (Calif.) Fine Arts Ctr., 1985, Amarillo (Tex.) Coll., 1985, Andover (Mass.) Gallery, 1984, Osaka Contemporary Art Ctr., Japan Min Gallery, Tokyo, 1988, Long Beach Mus. of Art, Calif., 1989, Calif. State U., Fullerton, La., 1990, Newport Harbor Art Mus., Calif., 1993, Orange County Ctr. Contemporary Art, 1993, Irvine Valley Coll., Calif., 1998, Laguna Art Mus., Ga., 2000, UCR/Calif. Mus. Photography, 2003; group exhbns. include Rochester Inst. Tech., Chgo. Art Inst., Bowers Mus., Santa Ana, Calif., Sioux City (Iowa) Art Ctr., L.A. Ctr. for Photog. Studies, Franklin Inst., Phila., L.A. County Mus. Art, George Eastman House, Rochester, Am. House, Berlin, Fed. Republic Germany, Columbia Coll., Chgo., Newport Harbor Mus., Ufficio Dell Arte, Harvard U., Kicken Gallery, Koln, Fed. Republic Germany, Fla. State U., Tallahassee, 1984, Pavillion Des Arts de La Ville de Paris, 1984, New Photo Montage, Chgo. Art Inst., 1984, Calif. State U. Long Beach Art Mus., 1985, John Michael Kohler Arts Ctr., Sheboygan, Wis., 1985, Clarence Kennedy Gallery, Cambridge, Mass., 1985, Gallery Min, Tokyo, 1986, La Ctr. for Photo Studies, L.A., 1986, Laguna Beach (Calif.) Mus., 1986, Photo Resource Ctr., Boston, 1986, U. So. Calif., L.A., 1986, Photokina, Germany, 1986, La Joua Mus. Contempart, L.A., 1987, L.A. County Mus., 1989, Pomona Coll., 1990, Calif. Mus. Photoge, Riverside, 1992, Laguna Art Mus., Calif., 1993, UCLA Armand Hammer Mus., 1995, Mus. Fine Arts, Fla. State U., 1997, Orange County Mus. Art, Calif., 1997, Biola U., L.A., 1997, Mt. St. Mary's Coll., L.A., 1997, Mus. Photographic Art, San Diego, 2003; represented in permanent collections in L.A. County Mus. Art, Oakland, Mus., George Eastman House, Long Beach State U., Bibliotheque Nationale, Paris, Bellevue (Wash.) Art Mus., Denver Art Mus., Security Pacific Bank, Chase Manhattan Bank, Ea. Wash. U., St. Louis Mus. Art, Newport Harbor Art Mus., U. Calif.-Riverside Mus., Photography, Mus. Photog. Arts, San Diego, Laguna Beach Mus. and So. Coast Plz., Mountain Bell, Gould Corp., Chgo., Ctr. Creative Photography, Tuscon; cons. KOCE-TV, Huntington Beach, Calif., 1983, Laguna Beach Mus., 1982—; author: Darkroom Art, 1981, Photography in Focus, 1996, Light as Substance, 1998, Habitat, 2000, In Transition, 2003; editor: No Mo Po Mo Mag., 1995-98; illus., contbr.: The Basic Darkroom Book, 1978; contbr. articles to photog. mags. Recipient Excellence award Nat. Inst. for Staff and Orgnl. Devel., Faculty Devel. award Cypress Coll., 1996, Out of Box Thinkers award Calif. C.C. League, 1999, Outstanding Individual Artist award Orange County, 2001, Outstanding Contrbn. to Arts award Cypress Cultural Arts Commn., 2001 Mem. L.A. Ctr. for Photog. Studies, Friends of Photography, Soc. Photog. Edn., Laguna Beach Arts Alliance (dir. 1980). Home: 6 Meade Irvine CA 92620-2623 Office: Cypress Coll 9200 Valley Vw Laguna Beach CA 92630

BURD, JOHN STEPHEN, academic administrator, music educator; b. Lock Haven, Pa., Apr. 6, 1939; s. John Wilson and Lily (Fye) B.; m. Patricia Ayers, June 3, 1961; children: Catherine Elizabeth, Emily Susanne. B in Music Edn., Greenville Coll., 1961; MS in Sacred Music, Butler U./Christian Theo. Sem., 1964; PhD, Ind. State U., 1971. Adj. music instr. Rose Hulman Inst. Tech., Terre Haute, Ind., 1969-71; assoc. prof. Greenville (Ill.) Coll., 1971-76; prof. edn. Lindenwood Coll., St. Charles, Mo., 1976-80; v.p. acad. affairs Maryville U., St. Louis, Mo., 1980-85; pres. Brenau U., Gainesville, Ga., 1985—. Team evaluator Nat. Coun. Accreditation Tchr. Edn., 1979-84; mem. exec. coun. Women's Coll. Coalition, 1989-92, NAICU Commn. on State Rels. Bd., 1991—; adv. bd. Wachovia Bank, Gainesville. Editor: New Voices in Education, 1969-71; contbr. articles to profl. jours. Choir dir. Ctr. Presbyn. Ch., St. Louis, 1984-85, Maryville U., St. Louis, 1983-85; v.p. Christian Arts, Inc., N.J., 1965—; adv. bd. N.E. Ga. Med. Ctr.; bd. dirs. Gainesville Symphony, 1991-94, Crawford W. Long Mus.; chair Gainesville Redevel. Authority, Chicopee Park Commn. Recipient Outstanding Young Alumnus award Greenville Coll., 1982, Disting. Alumnus award, 1991. Mem. Am. Assn. Tchr. Edn., Am. Assn. Higher Edn., So. Assn. Women's Colls. (pres. 1988-89), Ga. Found. Ind. Colls. (exec. bd. 1986—, vice chmn. 1993), Ga. Assn. Colls. (pres. 1989-90, 2003—), Gainesville C. of C. (bd. dirs.), Ga. Found. Ind. Colls. (vice chmn. 1993, 2003). Methodist. Avocations: tennis, travel, art. Office: Brenau U 1 Centennial Cir Gainesville GA 30501-3697 E-mail: jburd@lib.brenau.edu.

BURDETT, BARBRA ELAINE, biology educator; b. Lincoln, Ill., Mar. 18, 1947; d. Robert Marlin and Klaaska Johanna Baker; m. Gary Albert Burdett, Sept. 27, 1968; children: Bryan Robert, Heather Lea, Amanda Rose. AA, Lincoln Coll., 1981; postgrad., Ill. State U. Edn. Core, 1982-83; BS, Millikin U., 1985; postgrad., Western U., 1994-95, U. Ill., Springfield, 1997, Quincy (Ill.) U., 1998. Cert. tchr., Ill. Tchr. advanced placement biology, botany and human physiology Brown County H.S., Mt. Sterling, Ill., 1985-95; tchr. zoology, botany, environmental sci. Pleasant Plains (Ill.) H.S., 1995-97; tchr. biology Quincy (Ill.) H.S., 1997-98; owner Wild Winds Pub. Co., 1999—. Dir. Drama Club, Brown County H.S., 1988-90, dir. sci. fairs; ednl. advisor Nat. Young Leaders Conf. Author: Misty White, 1991, Possums Sing, 1994; co-author: The Last Button on Gabe's Coat, 1999, Derthro—Meet Mrs. Claus, 1999. Sponsor Children, Inc., Richmond, Va., 1985—, Internat. Wildlife Coalition, North Falmouth, Mass., 1991—; commdr. club, silver leader., 1988—. Mem. ASCD, Nat. Assn. Biology Tchrs. (Biology Tchr. of Yr. in Ill. 1994), Ill. Sci. Tchrs. Assn., Phi Delta Kappa (newsletter editor 1990), Phi Theta Kappa. Episcopalian. Avocation: classical guitar.

BURDICK, GLENN ARTHUR, physicist, engineering educator; b. Pavilion, Wyo., Sept. 9, 1932; s. Stephen Arthur and Mary Elizabeth (McClerg) B.; m. Joyce Mae Huggett, July 14, 1951; children: Stephen Arthur, Randy Glenn. BS, Ga. Inst. Tech., 1958, MS, 1959; PhD, MIT, 1961. Registered profl. engr., Fla. Office mgr. Statewide Contractors, Las Vegas, Nev., 1955-56; spl. tool designer Ga. Inst. Tech., Atlanta, 1954-55, instr., 1956-59; sr. mem. rsch. staff Sperry Microwave, Oldsmar, Fla., 1961-65; prof. elec. engring. U. So. Fla., Tampa, 1965—, dean Coll. Engring., 1979-86, prof. elec. engring., 1965-86, disting. prof. engring., 1986—, dean emeritus, 1986—; pres. Burdick Engring. and Sci., Inc., 1983—. Invented underground pipeline leak detector, 1956, sail boat mast insulation, 1981. Mem. Tampa Bay Fgn. Affairs Com., 1981-88, Pinellas County (Fla.) High Speed Rail Task Force, 1982-91, Gov. of State of Fla. Energy Task Force, 1980-85; vice chmn. Fla. Task Force for Sci. Energy and Tech. Svc. to Industry, 1981-82. Tex. Gulf scholar, 1957-58; NSF fellow, 1958-61, Woodrow Wilson fellow, 1958-59; named Engring. Faculty Mem. of Yr. State of Fla., 1986. Fellow Am. Assn. Forensic Sci., Nat. Fire Protection Agy., Am. Bd. Forensic Examiners, Nat. Acad. Forensic Engrs.; mem. Fla. Engring. Soc. (Engr. of Yr. award 1981), Internat. Soc. Hybrid Microelectronics (nat. pres. 1974), IEEE (sr. mem., Engr. of Yr. award 1980), Nat. Acad. Forensic Engring., N.Y. Acad. Sci., U.S. Profl. Engrs. Edn. (vice-chmn. SE region, 1986-88), Clearwater Tennis Club (pres. Fla. chpt. 1965, 69), Downtown Club. Home: 18728 Lake Iola Rd Dade City FL 33523-6117 Office: Burdick Engring and Sci Inc 18530 Lake Iola Rd Dade City FL 33523-6149

BURDICK, LARRY ELDON, retired science educator; b. Omaha, Dec. 12, 1933; s. Ralph St. Elmo and Gladys Irene (Mincks) B.; m. Nancy Ruth Shaff, Aug. 31, 1963 (div. 1979); children: Julie, David; m. Jean Marie Rosser, Oct. 9, 1982; stepchildren: Russell, Deborah, Steven (dec.), Dean Rahn. BS, Ill. State U., 1965; MA, Rockford Coll., 1978. Cert. tchr. Tchr. English and sci. A. Lincoln Jr. High Sch., Rockford, Ill., 1965-78; tchr. sci. B.W. Flinn Middle Sch., Rockford, Ill., 1978—. Monk Cistercian order, Dubuque, Iowa, 1959-62. 3d class petty officer USN, 1952-56. Mem. Ill. Sci. Tchrs. Assn., Rockford Edn. Assn. (area bd. dirs. 1985-89), Rockford Divers Assn. (v.p. 1970-74). Avocations: scuba diving, traveling, bible study, study of arthurian legends. Office: Flinn Middle Sch 2525 Ohio Pkwy Rockford IL 61108-7599

BURDICK, LARRY G. school system administrator; Supt. Pryor (Okla.) Pub. Schs. State finalist Nat. Supt. Yr., 1992. Office: Pryor Pub Schs 521 SE 1st St Pryor OK 74361-4600 E-mail: burdickl@pryor.k12.ok.us.

BURG, FREDRIC DAVID, physician, university dean; b. Chgo., May 23, 1940; s. Paul S. and Muriel C. (Buchsbaum) B.; m. Nancy Green, Oct. 5, 1997; children: Benjamin, Bethanny, David, Kathryn, Paul James, Jennifer Margaret. BA cum laude, Miami U., 1961; MD with distinction, Northwestern U., 1965. Diplomate Am. Bd. Pediatrics. Intern, resident, chief resident in pediatrics Northwestern U. Med. Sch., Chgo., 1965-68; cons., sr. surgeon Bur. Community Environ. Mgmt., USPHS, 1968-70; Kellogg fellow Ctr. for Teaching in Higher Edn. Northwestern U., 1970-71; assoc. exec. sec., dir. evaluation and research Am. Bd. Pediatrics, Chgo. and Phila., 1971-77; adj. assoc. prof. U. Pa., 1976-80, assoc. prof., 1980-82, prof. pediatrics, 1982-97, prof. emeritus, 1997—, assoc. dean for acad. programs, 1980-89, vice dean for edn., dir. office acad. programs, 1989-95; prof., assoc. dean U. Ala. Sch. medicine, Huntsville, 1996—; exec. dir. U. Ala. Huntsville Health Ctr. Pres., CEO, Valley Found., Huntsville, Ala., 2003—; trustee, bd. overseers U. Pa. Sch. Medicine, 1992-95; assoc. dir. Nat. Bd. Med. Examiners, Phila, 1971-78, v.p., dir. dept. grad. and continuing med. evaluation, 1976-80, mem. Part III com., 1981-87, cons., 1988-89, also mem. NBME task force computer based testing; cons. ACP, 1983-92, chmn. MKSAP/PMP com.; mem. Fgn. Med. Sch. Panel, State of N.J., 1983-90, State of N.Y.; bd. dirs. Children's Sea Shore House. Phila., Martha Lloyd Cmty. Svcs., Troy, Pa.; v.p., pres. & chief exec. officer Valley Found., Huntsville, Ala.; nat. chair Orgn. Regional Med. Campuses, 2001. Sr. editor Current Pediatric Therapy, 1992—, Pediatrics-A Problem Based Review; mem. editl. bd., publs. com. Joint Commn. Accreditation of Hosps., 1983-87; contbr. articles to med. jours. Served with USPHS, 1968-70. Sr. fellow Inst. for Rsch. in Higher Edn., 1996-99. Fellow Am. Acad. Pediat.; mem. Ambulatory Pediatrics Assn. (sec.-treas. 1977-80, pres. 1983-84), Assn. Am. Med. Colls. (chmn. N.E. group on med. edn., nat. steering group med. edn., nat. chmn. 1989-90, project dir. Robert Wood Johnson Commn. on Sci. and Med. Edn., 1990-92, chair group on regional med. campuses 2003—), Internat. Pediat. Assn. (steering com. 1985-97), Am. Edn. Rsch. Assn., Pa. Med. Soc. (chmn. coun. on accreditation 1986-87), Phila. Pediat. Soc. (treas. 1980-82) Office: U Ala Sch Medicine 301 Governors Dr Huntsville AL 35801 E-mail: burgf@uasomh.uab.edu.

BURGER, HENRY G. vocabulary scientist, anthropologist, publisher; b. N.Y.C., June 27, 1923; s. B. William and Terese R. (Felleman) B.; m. Barbara G. Smith, Nov. 29, 1991. BA with honors (Pulitzer scholar), Columbia Coll., 1947; MA, Columbia U., 1965, PhD in Cultural Anthropology (State Doctoral fellow), 1967. Indsl. engr. various orgns., 1947-51; Midwest mfrs. rep., 1952-55; social sci. cons., 1956-67; anthropologist Southwestern Coop. Ednl. Lab., Albuquerque, 1967-69; assoc. prof. anthropology and edn. U. Mo., Kansas City, 1969-73, prof., 1973-93, prof. emeritus, 1993—, founding mem. univ. wide doctoral faculty, 1974-93; founder, pub. The Wordtree, Overland Park, Kans., 1984—. Lectr. CUNY; adj. prof. ednl. anthropology U. N.Mex., 1969; anthrop. cons. U.S. VA Hosp., Kansas City, 1971—72; spkr. in field; columnist linguistic column New Times, New Verbs, 1988—. Author: Ethno-Pedagogy, 1968, 2nd edit., 1968; editor, compiler: The Wordtree, a Branching Dictionary for Solving Phys. and Social Problems, 1984, selected for exhibit at 3 insts., selected as topic Cambridge Ency. of the English Lang., 1995—, 7 time citee Oxford English Dictionary, —, mem. editl. bd. Coun. Anthropology and Edn., 1975—80; contbr. to anthrologies, articles; interviewee Voice of America, 2002. Capt. AUS, 1943-46. NSF Instl. grantee, 1970. Fellow World Acad. Art and Sci., Am. Anthrop. Assn. (life), Royal Anthrop. Inst. Gt. Britain (life); mem. European Assn. for Lexicography, Internat. Assn. Semiotic Studies, English-Speaking Union (v.p. Kansas City chpt. 1995-96), Dictionary Soc. N.Am. (life, terminology com.), Kans. Acad. Sci. (life), Assn. Internationale de Terminologie, Academie Europeenne des Scis., Arts et Lettres (corr.), Columbia U. Club, Phi Beta Kappa. Achievements include discovery of the branchability of processes (corresponding, for materials, to the periodic table of elements); research on computerized causality and reasoning. Office: The Wordtree 10876 Bradshaw St Overland Park KS 66210-1148 E-mail: burger@cctr.umkc.edu.

BURGESS, NANCY JO, elementary education educator; b. Alva, Okla., Jan. 11, 1953; d. Leonard Ray and Helena Bertha (Schick) Nelson; m. Dennis Wayne Burgess, May 20, 1975 (dec. Sept. 1992); children: Justin Dallas, Tia Denise. B in Music Edn., Southwestern Okla. State U., 1975. Music tchr. grades K-12 Aline/Cleo Springs, Okla., 1976-77; music tchr. grades 1-5 Hickok Sch. Unified Sch. Dist. 214, Ulysses, Kans., 1977-78; music tchr. grades 1-5 and trainable mentally handicapped Red Rock Sch. Unified Sch. Dist. 214, Ulysses, 1980—; music tchr. grades 6 and TMH Joyce/Kepley Sch., Ulysses, 1983-99; music tchr. grades K-8 Unified Sch. Dist. 312, Haven, Kans., 1999—2001; music tchr. USD 313, Buhler, Kans., 2001—. Dir. ch. choir Grace Luth. Ch., Ulysses, 1987-90, Christian bd. edn., 1990-94, youth sponsor, 1992-98; site coun. mem. H.S., Ulysses, 1993-99. Named Outstanding Educator, Grant County C. of C., 1987. Mem. NEA, Kans. Nat. Edn. Assn., Grant County Tchrs. Assn., Kans. Music Educators Assn. Avocations: gardening, reading, music.

BURGESS, RUTH LENORA VASSAR, speech and language educator; b. Pune, India, Aug. 6, 1939; d. Theodore R. and F. Estelle (Barnett) Vassar; m. Stanley Milton Burgess, Feb. 26, 1960; children: John Bradley, Stanley Matthew, Scott Vassar, Heidi Amanda Elizabeth, Justin David. BS in Edn., Tex. Tech. U., 1960; MA, U. Mo., 1968, PhD, 1979. Speech therapist Inkster (Mich.) Pub. Schs., 1961-62; mid. sch. tchr. Strafford (Mo.) Pub. Schs., 1962-63; speech therapist Fulton (Mo.) Pub. Schs., 1967-68; speech-lang. clinician Springfield (Mo.) Pub. Schs., 1963-66; asst. prof. Evangel Coll., Springfield, 1968-76; prof. Sch. Tchr. Edn. S.W. Mo. State U., Springfield, 1976—, dir. Ctr. Rsch. and Svc., 1990-97. Mem. sci. adv. bd. Internat. Ctr. Enhancement of Jerusalem, Israel, 1993—; field reviewer Dept. Edn., Washington, 1993-96, U.S. Vocat. Rehab., Washington, 1993, 94, 96,99; mem. evaluation team Title I Springfield Schs., 1994. Author: The Status of the Educational Resource Teacher, 1981; editor The Learner in the Process, 1978-80; contbr. articles to profl. jours. Ex-officio bd. dirs. Orphanage Assn., Pune, 1968—; mem. Kodaikanal-Woodstock Alumni Assn., Atlanta, 1956—; mem. Women Issues Network, Springfield, 1993—. Grantee Dept. Edn., 1978-83, 90-92, Dept. Elem. and Secondary Edn., 96, Mellon Found., 1988-90. Mem. AAUW, ASCD, Am. Speech, Lang. and Hearing Assn. (cert.), Internat. Assn. for Cognitive Edn. (field editor 1990-94). Avocations: literary group, hiking, creative writing, travel, advocacy. Office: SW Mo State U 901 S National Ave Springfield MO 65804-0088 E-mail: rvb649f@smsu.edu.

BURGHDUFF, JOHN BRIAN, mathematics educator; b. Augusta, Ga., July 16, 1958; s. Richard Dean and Betty Kay (Hebeler) B. BS in Applied Maths., Tex. A&M U., 1980; MS in Maths., Ohio State U., 1982; PhD in Math., U. Houston, 1994. Teaching asst. Tex. A&M U., College Station, 1978-80, Ohio State U., Columbus, 1980-82; instr. San Jacinto Coll., Houston, 1982-88, U. Houston, 1988-92; prof. Kingwood Coll., 1992—2003; chair dept. math and philosophy Cypress-Fairbanks Coll., Tex., 2003—. Vol. youth dir. League City (Tex.) Ch. of Christ, 1982-86; faculty sponsor San Jacinto Coll. Bapt. Student Union, Houston, 1982-86; vol. Magnificat House Homeless Shelter, Houston, 1989—. Mem. Math. Assn. Am., Am. Math. Soc., Inst. for Combinatorics and its Applications. Democrat. Episcopalian. Achievements include research in spectra of graphs and permanents of matrices. Home: 4122 O'Meara Dr Houston TX 77025-5423 Office: Cypress-Fairbanks Coll Dept Math and Philosophy Cypress TX 77433 E-mail: john.burghduff@nhmccd.edu.

BURGIN, WALTER HOTCHKISS, JR., educational administrator; b. Harrisburg, Pa., Apr. 14, 1935; s. Walter Hotchkiss and Wilhelmina (Buntin) B.; m. Barbara Isabelle Waddell, June 15, 1957; children: Christine, Jennifer. AB, Dartmouth Coll., 1957; postgrad., Princeton U., 1957-59; EdM, Harvard U., 1964. Tchr. math. Phillips Exeter (N.H.) Acad., 1964-72, Mercersburg (Pa.) Acad., 1959-64, chmn. dept., 1961-64, headmaster, 1972-97; tchr. math. Sidwell Friends Sch., Washington, 1997-98; exec. dir. Edward E. Ford Found., Washington, 1998—2002; tchr. math. Maret Sch., Washington, 2002—. Mem. Pa. Bd. for Pvt. Acad. Schs., 1973-94. NSF fellow, 1957-59, Shell fellow, 1964. Mem. Math. Assn. Am., Nat. Assn. Prins. Sch. for Girls, Headmasters Assn. (treas. 1993-96, v.p. 1996-97), Nat. Coun. Tchrs. Math., Nat. Assn. Ind. Schs. (bd. dirs. 1989-96, sec. 1992-96), Pa. Assn. Ind. Schs. (exec. com. 1980-90). Democrat. Mem. United Ch. of Christ. Home: 2153 California St NW Apt 402 Washington DC 20008-1845 E-mail: whburgin@aol.com.

BURGOS-SASSCER, RUTH, chancellor emeritus; b. N.Y.C., Sept. 5, 1931; m. Donald Sasscer, June 14, 1958; children: Timothy, James, Julie, David. BA, Maryville (Tenn.) Coll., 1953; MA, Columbia U., 1956; PhD, Fla. State U., 1987. Mem. faculty Inter-Am. U., P.R., 1968-71; dept. chair U. P.R., Aguadilla, 1972-76, dir. non-traditional programs Cen. Adminstrn. Regional Coll., 1976-81, dir., dean, chief exec. officer, 1981-85; v.p. faculty and instrn. Harry S. Truman Coll., Chgo., 1988-93; pres. San Antonio Coll., 1993-96; chancellor Houston C.C. Sys., 1996-2000; sr. fellow U. Houston Law Ctr. Inst. of Higher Edn Law and Goverance, 2001—. Bd. dirs. Nat. Hispanic Coun. C.C.s. Bd. dirs. Greater Houston Partnership, Houston Read Commn., City of Houston Ethics Com., Am. Assn. C.C., Internat. Consortium for Ednl. and Econ. Devel., Laredo Nat. Bank, Houston. Mem. Am. Assn. C.C., Internat. Consortium for Ednl. and Econ. Devel. Presbyterian. Home: 530 Bolton Pl Houston TX 77024-4601 E-mail: ruthburgossas@hotmail.com.

BURGOYNE, BARBARA ELIZABETH, elementary education educator; b. Rockford, Ill., Aug. 21, 1966; d. George William and Marilyn (Triebel) B. BA, U. Ill., 1988, MEd, 1991. Cert. elem. tchr. Ill. Elem. tchr. Rockford Sch. Dist., 1993—; pools mgr. Rockford Park Dist., 1988—2001; elem. tchr. Cherry Valley Elem. Sch. Dist., 2003—. Instr. Internat. Red Cross, Nat. Pool and Waterpark Lifeguard Tng. Program. Mem. ASCD, Jr. League Rockford (past pres.), Kappa Delta Pi, Zeta Tau Alpha. Avocations: outdoor recreation, reading, drum corps, stamp collecting.

BURGOYNE, EDWARD EYNON, chemistry educator; b. Montpelier, Idaho, Sept. 26, 1918; s. Sidney Eynon and Beatrice (Holmes) B.; m. Mary Ida Ream, June 30, 1950 (dec. July 1995); children: Mary Anne (Mrs. William Worsnop), Elaine (Mrs. Mark A. LeVan), Edward Ream, Bryce William; m. Millicent Elaine Barclay. Student, Idaho State U., 1937-39; BS, Utah State U., 1941; postgrad., U. Chgo., 1942-43; MS, U. Wis., 1947, PhD, 1949. Research chemist Phillips Petroleum Co., Bartlesville, Okla., 1949-51; asst. prof. Ariz. State U., Tempe, 1951-56, assoc. prof., 1956-59, prof. chemistry, 1959-83, prof. emeritus, 1984—. Author: A Short Course in Organic Chemistry, 1979, translated into Spanish, Italian, Japanese; Contbr. articles to profl. jours. Served with USAAF, 1942-46, PTO; lt. col. USAFR; ret. Fellow AAAS; mem. Am. Chem. Soc., Ariz. Acad. Sci., Sigma Xi. Mem. Ch. of Jesus Christ of Latter-day Saints. Achievements include patents in field. Home: 3035 E Menlo St Mesa AZ 85213-1679

BURGWYN, ANNA POOLE, English language educator; b. May 20, 1950; d. W.H.S., Jr. and Anna Lucille (Poole) B. AA, St. Mary's Jr. Coll., Raleigh, N.C., 1970; BA in English, Salem Coll., Winston-Salem, N.C., 1972. English tchr. Northeast Acad., Lasker, N.C. Mem. NCTE. Home: PO Box 418 Woodland NC 27897-0418

BURISH, THOMAS GERARD, academic administrator; b. Peshtigo, Wis., May 4, 1950; s. Bennie Charles and Donna Mae (Willkom) B.; m. Pamela Jean Zebrasky, June 19, 1976; children: Mark Joseph, Brent Christopher. AB summa cum laude, U. Notre Dame, 1972; MA, U. Kans., 1975, PhD, 1976. Lic. psychologist, Tenn. Asst. prof. psychology Vanderbilt U., Nashville, 1976-80, assoc. prof., 1980-86, prof., 1986—2002, dir. clin. tng., 1980-84, chair dept. psychology, 1984-86, assoc. provost, 1986—92, provost, 1992—2002; pres. Washington and Lee U., Lexington, Va., 2002—. Mem. cancer rsch. manpower rev. com. Nat. Cancer Inst., 1991-96; co-chair Bridge task force com. Am. Cancer Soc., 1994-96; mem. breast cancer rsch. panel US Army Med. Rsch., 1995-2001. Co-editor: Coping with Chronic Disease, 1983, Cancer, Nutrition and Eating Behavior, 1985; co-author: Behavior Therapy, 1987, Health Psychology, 1991. Chmn. St. Mary's Sch. Bd., Nashville, 1982-83; participant Leadership Nashville, 1989-90; vice chair, bd. dir. Am. Cancer Soc. Fellow Am. Psychol. Assn., Am. Psychol. Soc.; mem. Acad. Behavioral Medicine Rsch., Phi Beta Kappa. Roman Catholic. Office: Washington and Lee U Washington Hall Lexington VA 24450

BURKART, JEFFREY EDWARD, communications educator; b. Chgo., Sept. 12, 1948; s. Irwin John and Florence Henrietta (Drzich) B.; m. Martha Louise Gaertner, Aug. 13, 1972; children: Jonathan, David, Andrew. BA, Concordia Tchrs. Coll., 1971; MA, U. Nebr., 1977; PhD, U. Minn., 1988. Cert. elem. and secondary sch. tchr., Ind., Mo. Wis., Nebr. Organist, choral dir., youth dir. St. John's Luth. Ch., Bingen, Ind., 1969-70; tchr. Wyneken Meml. Luth. Sch., Decatur, Ind., 1969-70; residence counselor Concordia Coll., River Forest, Ill., 1970-71; instr. Luth. High Sch. North, St. Louis, 1971-72, Martin Luther High Sch., Greendale, Wis., 1972-75; tchr. St. John's Luth. Sch., Seward, Nebr., 1975-77; prof. ednl. communications/media, dir. audiovisual svcs. Concordia U., St. Paul, 1977-97, media cons., 1997—, assoc. dean for Christian ministry, 1999—, assoc. dean Coll. Vocation and Ministry, 1999—. Cons. Luth. Ch.-Mo. Synod, St. Louis; ednl. cons. St. Paul Pub. Schs., 1989, Elk River (Minn.) Sch. Dist., 1988-89; dir. European study Am. Inst. Fgn. Study, Greenwich, Conn.; editor-at-large and Christian edn. specialist Concordia Pub. Ho., 1996. Author: The Sonday School Book, 1995, Sure You Can Use a Little Good News!, 1996, Creative Worship, 1996, The Seeds That Grew and Grew, 1997, The Man Who Couldn't Speak, 1998, A Surprise in Disguise, 1999, Down Through the Roof, 1999, Don't Get Burned (musical), 1999, (video tape) The Hospital Zone, 2000, Camel's Hair and Honey, 2000; composer contemporary ch. music; author articles on children's lit. and early childhood edn., also drama and music articles; author religious video, filmstrip series; presenter in field; author, composer: (musical) Man Overboard, 1995; composer, lyricist In League with Our Lord, 1999, Jesus Cares for China's Children, 2000, We're In Jesus' Company, 1999, Anyone Who Welcomes, 2000, (children's book) The Hidden Prince, 2002; (CDs) Oh, Come, Lord Jesus, 2001, Oh, Come, Emmanuel, 2002, Oh, Come Risen One, 2003. Mem. Assn. for Supervision and Curriculum Devel., Luth. Edn. Assn.,, Assn. of Luth. Ch. Musicians, Phi Delta Kappa. Avocations: music, photography, reading, astronomy, travel. Office: Concordia Univ 275 Syndicate St N Saint Paul MN 55104-5494 E-mail: jburkart@csp.edu.

BURKE, BERNARD FLOOD, physicist, educator; b. Boston, June 7, 1928; s. Vincent Paul and Clare (Brine) B.; m. Jane Chapin Pann, May 30, 1953 (dec. Aug. 1993); children: Geoffrey Damian, Elizabeth Chapin, Mark Vincent, Matthew Brine; m. Elizabeth King Platt, Oct. 28, 1998. SB, MIT, 1950, PhD, 1953. Staff mem. terrestrial magnetism Carnegie Instn. of Washington, 1953-65, chmn. radio astronomy sect., 1962-65; prof. physics, Burden prof. astrophysics MIT, 1965-2001, prof. physics, Burden prof. emeritus, 2001—. Vis. prof. U. Leiden, Netherlands, 1971-72, U. Manchester, Eng., 1992-93; trustee N.E. Radio Obs. Corp., 1973-95, vice chmn., 1975-82, chmn., 1982-95; cons. NSF, NASA, Dept. Transp.; Oort lectr. U. Leiden, 1993; Karl Jansky lectr. NAt. Radio Astronomy Obs., 1998. Trustee Associated Univs., Inc., 1972-90; mem. Nat. Sci. Bd., 1990-96; commr. Marsh Conservation Dist., Cambridge, 2001—. Recipient Helen Warner prize Am. Astron. Soc., 1963; Rumford prize Am. Acad. Arts and Scis., 1971; Sherman Fairchild scholar Calif. Inst. Tech., 1984, Smithsonian Regents fellow, 1985; sr. fellow Carnegie Instn. of Washington, 1997. Fellow AAAS; mem. NAS, Am. Acad. Arts and Scis., Am. Phys. Soc., Am. Astron. Soc., Royal Astron. Soc., Internat. Astron. Union, Internat. Astron. Fedn. (Pecek lectr. 1993), Internat. Sci. Radio Union, Merle Tuve Sr. fellow Carnegie Instn. of Washington. Achievements include research on microwave spectroscopy, radio astronomy, galactic structure, antenna design, cosmology. Office: MIT Dept Physics Cambridge MA 02139

BURKE, JANET LOIS, business consultant, computer science educator; b. Chgo., Jan. 3, 1951; d. Joseph and Lorine Carol (Kalvin) Orenstein; m. Joseph D. Burke, Aug. 5, 1978; children: Kynan Neville, Alison Lyn, Owen Joseph. AAS in Liberal Arts, Westchester C.C., Valhalla, N.Y., 1976; BA in Psychology and Biology, SUNY, Purchase, 1978; cert. tchg., Lee Coll., 1993. Cert. tchr. grades 7-12 gen. sci., chemistry, biology, math., Tenn. Cert. trainer thematic/integrated curriculum, Nat. Sch. Conf. Inst.; cert. p.c. troubleshooting essential instr. Mainframe computer operator Pergamon Press, Inc., Elmsford, N.Y., 1977-78; programmer, documentation analyst Kane-Miller Inc., Tarrytown, N.Y., 1978-79; sys. analyst, on-line programmer Combe, Inc., White Plains, N.Y., 1979-81; sys. analyst, sr. programmer Technicon, Inc., Tarrytown, 1981-83; tchrs. aide Little Seaters Nursery, Belvidere, N.J., 1987-89; technology instr., sys. cons. Chattanooga-Hamilton Country Schs., Tenn., 1994-98; small bus. cons., 1994—; owner Eclectik Framing & Art Ltd., 2001—. Substitute tchr. various pub. elem. schs., Warren County, N.J., Chattanooga, Hamilton County, Tenn., 1987-94; personal computer applications support ComputerWorld, Dover, Del., 1983-85; vol. libr. Hamilton County Schs., Chattanooga, 1989-91; gifted tchr. Bradley County Sch., Cleveland, Tenn., 1993. Bd. dirs. Chattanooga City Coun. PTAs, 1993-94, unification analyst com. chair, 1993-94; pres. White Twp. PTO, 1987-89; organizer White Twp. Concerned Parents Group, 1988-89; chair Chattanooga Sch. Liberal Arts Enrichment Com., 1993-94. Recipient Pres.'s Vol. Action award WhiteHouse, 1994; minigrantee Edna McConnell Clark Found., 1994, Pub. Edn. Found., Libr. Power, 1994, 95, 96. Mem. AAUW, Profl. Picture Framers Assn. Avocations: fabric art, quilting, landscaping, camping, hiking. Home: 1562 Treadway Pl Columbus OH 43235-1151

BURKE, JOHN PATRICK, internist, educator; b. Marshalltown, Iowa, Jan. 19, 1940; s. Raphael Eggleston and Marjorie N. (Busch) B.; m. Andrea Marie Keane, May 9, 1970; children: Paul, Matthew, Edward, Erin. BA, summa cum laude, U. Iowa, 1961, MD, 1964. Diplomate Am. Bd. Internal Medicine, Am. Bd. Infectious Disease. Intern Yale-New Haven Hosp., 1964-65, resident in medicine, 1965-67; rsch. fellow Harvard med. unit Boston City Hosp., 1968-70; chief infectious disease sect. LDS Hosp., Salt Lake City, 1970—; epidemic intelligence svc. officer Ctr. for Disease Control and Prevention, 1967—70. Asst. prof. medicine U. Utah, Salt Lake City, 1970-75, assoc. prof., 1975-83, prof., 1983—, Mark Presdl. endowed chair in medicine, 1999—; spl. reviewer NIH, Bethesda, Md., 1978, 80; mem. tech. panel on infections within hosps. Am. Hosp. Assn., 1996; cons. Inst. Medicine, NAS, 1998—, Ctrs. for Disease Control and Prevention, 1994, 99, Nat. Patient Safety Found., 1999, Lewin Group, 1999-2000; mem. sci. adv. coun. Heart and Lung Inst. LDS Hosp. Found., 1990—; co-founder TheraDoc, Inc., 1999. Mem. editl. bd. Am. Jour. Infection Control, 1981-97, Infection Control and Hosp. Epidemiology, 1979-88, 2003-; contbr. numerous articles to med. jours., chpts. to books. Surgeon USPHS, 1967-70. NIH-Nat. Inst. Allergy and Infectious Disease grantee, 1974-79, 79-82, 83-85, 86-89, FDA, 1999. Fellow Infectious Disease Soc. Am., ACP; mem. Soc. for Healthcare Epidemiology Am. (councillor 1981-82, treas. 1985-88, v.p. 1991, mem. bd. dirs. 1991-93, pres. 1992), Utah Med. Assn. (del. 1975-77), Am. Epidemiol. Soc., Alpha Omega Alpha, Phi Beta Kappa. Mem. Christian Ch. Home: 1966 Yale Ave Salt Lake City UT 84108-1827 Office: LDS Hosp Med Office Bldg Ste 204 370 9th Ave Salt Lake City UT 84103 E-mail: john.burke@hsc.utah.edu.

BURKE, JOSEPH C. former university official; b. New Albany, Ind., Mar. 20, 1932; s. Dennis F. and Beatrice V. (McDevitt) B.; m. Joan Thompson, Sept. 1, 1956; children: Maura, Colleen. BA, Bellarmine Coll., Louisville, 1954; MA, Ind. U., 1958, PhD, 1965. Instr. Ohio Wesleyan U., Delaware, 1960-62; asst. prof. to prof. history Duquesne U., Pitts., 1962-70; prof. history Loyola of Montreal, 1970-73, acad. v.p., 1970-73, SUNY Coll., Plattsburgh, 1973-74, pres., 1974-85; provost, vice chancellor for acad. affairs SUNY Sys., Albany, 1985-95; pres. Rsch. Found. SUNY, Albany, 1990-95, interim chancellor, 1994; sr. fellow, dir. higher edn. prog. Nelson A. Rockefeller Inst. Govt., Albany, 1956. Cons. leadership adn planning for colls. and univs. Contbr. books, monographs, chpts. and articles to profl. jours., chpts. to books on higher edn. Trustee Miner Found. Rsch.; chmn. bd. Miner Agrl. Inst. Grantee Pew Charitable Trusts Luce Found., 1996—, Ford Found., 1996—. E-mail: burkejo@rockinst.org.

BURKE, RITA HOFFMANN, educational administrator; b. N.Y.C., Dec. 22, 1925; d. George William and Beatrice (Kearney) Hoffmann; m. Francis Joseph Burke, Oct. 4, 1952; children: Francis J., Patrick G., Joseph P., Rosemary Childs, Jeanmarie R., Gerard W., Christopher M., Maurita B. BA in Econs., Hunter Coll., N.Y.C., 1951; postgrad., Corning (N.Y.) Community Coll., 1985. Cashier Bloomingdale's Dept. Store, N.Y.C., 1943; jr. actuary Equitable Life Assurance Soc., N.Y.C., 1944-48; jr. acct. Steuben Glass, N.Y.C., 1948-53; controller E. R. Wolcott, Inc., Big Flats, N.Y., 1973-78; library asst. Notre Dame High Sch., Elmira, N.Y., 1978-85, bus. mgr., 1985—. Mem. sch. bd. St. Mary Our Mother Sch., Horseheads, N.Y., 1970-76; mem., v.p., sec. parish coun. St. Mary Ch., Horseheads, 1973-76; historian Cinderella, 1973. Mem. Nat. Newman Hon. Soc. Democrat. Roman Catholic. Avocation: volunteering. Home: 16 Brookside Cir Elmira NY 14903-9387

BURKE, ROBERT HARRY, surgeon, educator; b. Cambridge, Mass., Dec. 22, 1945; s. Harry Clearfield and Joan Rosalyn (Spire) B.; m. Margaret Cauldwell Fisher, May 4, 1968; children: Christopher David, Catherine Cauldwell. Student, U. Mich. Coll. Pharmacy, 1964—67; DDS, U. Mich., 1971, MS, 1976; MD, Mich. State U., 1980. Diplomate Am. Bd. Oral and Maxillofacial Surgery, Am. Bd. Cosmetic Surgery. Pvt. practice cosmetic and reconstructive surgery, Ann Arbor, Mich. House officer oral and maxillofacial surgery U. Mich. Sch. Dentistry, U. Mich. Hosp., Ann Arbor, 1973-76; clin. asst. prof. dept. oral surgery U. Detroit Sch. Dentistry, 1976-77; adj. asst. rsch. scientist Ctr. Human Growth and Devel. U. Mich., 1976-77, adj. rsch. investigator, 1982-85; clin. asst. prof. Mich. State U., East Lansing, 1978-80, 1987—; house officer surg. emphasis St. Joseph Mercy Hosp., Ann Arbor, 1980-81; adj. rsch. investigator dept. anatomy U. Mich. Med. Sch., 1982-85; adj. clin. asst. prof. oral and maxillofacial surgery U. Mich., 1984-86, 2002-2003, adj. clin. assoc. prof. maxillofacial surgery, 2003—; lectr. U. Detroit Sch. Dentistry, 1986, assoc. clin. prof. oral and maxillofacial surgery, 1987-90; cons., lectr. dept. occlusion U. Mich. Sch. Dentistry, 1986, asst. clin. prof. dept. maxillofacial sugery, 2002, assoc. adj. clin. prof., 2002—; head sect. dentistry and oral surgery dept. gen. surgery St. Joseph Mercy Hosp., 1982-87, mem. exec. com. dept. gen. surgery, 1984-87; chmn. com. emergency care rev. Beyer Meml. Hosp., Ypsilanti, Mich., 1986, also active, 1987, 1990-2000; active staff St. Joseph Meml. Hosp.; courtesy staff Saline (Mich.) Cmty. Hosp., 1978-88; Chelsea (Mich.) Med. Ctr., 1978-88, 90-92, McPherson Cmty. Hosp., Howell, Mich., 1984-87, Herrick Meml. Hosp., 1998—, Bixby Hosp., 1998—, Annapolis Hosp., 2000-2002, Oakwood Hosp., 2000-2002; dir. Mich. Ctr. Cosmetic Surgery. Mem. editl. bd. Topics in Pain Mgmt., 1985—; contbg. editor Am. Jours. Cosmetic surgery, 1990-91; sect. editor Internat. Jour. Aesthetic and Restorative Surgery, 1992-95, 96-2000, Internat. Jour. Cosmetic Surgery and Aesthetic Dermatology, 2000—. Campaign chmn. med. and dental sects. United Way Washtenaw County, Ann Arbor, 1982, dental sect. 1983; profl. adv. com. March of Dimes Genesee County Valley Chpt., Flint, 1979; pres. Huron Pkwy. Pla. Condominium, 1984—. Fellow: Am. Acad. Aesthetic and Restorative Surgery, Am. Coll. Oral and Maxillofacial Surgeons, ACS, Internat. Coll. Surgeons; mem.: Inst. Study Profl. Risk, Washtenaw County Med. Soc., European Assn. for Cranio-Maxillofacial Surgery, Chalmers Lyons Acad. oral Surgery, European Soc. Aesthetic Surgery and Liposuction, Internat. Soc. Cosmetic Laser Surgeons, Am. Assn. Craniomaxillofacial Surgeons, Am. Assn. Cosmetic Maxillofacial Surgeons, AMA, Pres.'s Club, Victor's Club, Omicron Kappa Upsilon. Congregationalist. Office: 2260 S Huron Pky Ann Arbor MI 48104-5151 E-mail: info@robertburke.com.

BURKES, LIONEL SEATON, science educator, writer, researcher; b. Hindsville, Ark., Mar. 25, 1933; s. Elmo C. and Bernie Ethel (Cook) B.; m. Pansy Lenora Hobbs Burkes, Dec. 24, 1961; children: Geoffrey Dion (dec.), Eric Kevin, Cynthia Michele, Aaron Shane, Mark Alan. BSE, U. Ark., 1960; MA in Biol. Sci., U. Mont., 1964. Cert. adminstrn. and sci., Ark., Iowa; sci. N. Mex. Instr. sci. and sociology Corona (N. Mex.) Mcpl. Schs., 1960-62; instr. sci. Albuquerque (N. Mex.) Pub. Schs., 1964-66; instr. biology and zoology U. Wis., Whitewater, 1966-69; asst. prof. edn. Mo. We. State Coll., St. Joseph, 1970-71; asst. campus dir. Southeastern Cmty. Coll., West Burlington, Iowa, 1971-75; dir. Inst. Mgmt. and Continuing Edn. Iowa Wesleyan Coll., Mt. Pleasant, 1977-78, 83-84; staff devel. specialist and tng. cert. officer La. Dept. Health and Human Resources, Office Mental Retardation, Ruston (La.) State Sch., 1982—83; instr. scis. Ft. Smith (Ark.) Pub. Schs., 1985-94; ret., 1995; rschr., writer, 1995—. Spl. rschr. Sandia Nat. Labs., Albuquerque, summers 1985-87. Contbr. articles to profl. jours. Leader U.S. delegation People to People Youth Sci. Exchange, Russia, Ukraine, 1990, China, Hong Kong, 1991, New Zealand, Australia, 1992; judge sci. fair pub. schs. N. Mex. and Ark., 1984-95; spkr. Career Days Westark C. C., Fort Smith, Ark., 1991-93. Nat. Sci. Found. Fellow U. Mont., 1961-64; recipient Nat. Security Clearance U.S. Dept. Energy, 1986, Outstanding Tchr. Proclamation Mayor of Fort Smith, Ark., 1995. Avocations: writing, reading, research, traveling abroad, hiking.

BURKHARDT, ANN, occupational therapist, clinical educator; b. Providence, Dec. 21, 1954; d. Kenneth Ralph and Betty Jane (Neale) B. BA in Psychobiology, Wheaton Coll., 1976; MA in Occupl. Therapy, NYU, 1979. Lic. occupl. therapist, N.Y., R.I., Mass. Staff therapist Charlton Meml. Hosp., Fall River, Mass., 1979; staff therapist, sr. therapist Columbia U.-Harlem Hosp., N.Y.C., 1979-84; staff therapist, burn specialist Cornell Med. Ctr.-N.Y. Hosp., N.Y.C., 1984-86; dir. occupl. therapy Greater Harlem Nursing Home, N.Y.C., 1986-87; chief occupl. therapist Meml. Sloan-Kettering Cancer Ctr., N.Y.C., 1987-92; asst. dir. occupl. therapy N.Y. Presbyn. Hosp.-Columbia Presbyn., N.Y.C., 1992-99, 1992—99, dir. occupl. therapy, 1999—; clin. instr. Columbia U., N.Y.C., 1993—, assoc. clin. instr., 1999—; pvt. practice N.Y.C., 1984—; clin. assoc. Mercy Coll., Dobbs Ferry, NY, 1998—. Del. Coll. of Occupl. Therapists, Edinburgh, Scotland, 1995, World Fedn. Occupl. Therapists, London, 1994, Montreal, Can., 1998, Stockholm, 2002; spkr. in field. Author: Occupational Therapy Intervention in Recreational Settings in Acute Care, 1993; co-editor, co-author: Stroke Rehabilitaton: A Function Based Approach, 1997; (pamphlet) Lymphedema: Self-Care and Treatment, 1992; co-author: A Therapists Guide to Oncology, 1996; contbr. articles to profl. jours., chpts. to books; columnist O.T. Week, The Sacred Fire Newsletter. Svc. award Touro Coll., N.Y., 1996. Fellow Am. Occupl. Therapy Assn. (cert., alt. rep. to rep. assembly 1992-94, polit. action com. 1994, dir., bd. dirs. 2002-, Recognition of Achievement award 1997, Svc. award 1997, 99, editor Quarterly adminstrn. and mgmt. spl. interest sect. 2001-2002); mem. Am. Occupl. Therapy Assn., N.Y. State Occupl. Therapy Assn. (alt. rep. 1992-94, pres.-elect. 1994-95, pres. 1995-99, Merit award 1990, Svc. award 1999, news editor 1999-), Metro N.Y. Dist. Occupl. Therapy Assn. (bd. dirs., sec. 1990-96, Abreu award 1998), Am. Congress Rehab. Medicine, N. Am. Soc. Lymphology, Internat. Soc. Lymphology, Am. Phys. Medicine, Am. Soc. Assn. Execs., Am. Med. Writers Assn., Am. Burn Assn., Congress of Rehab. Medicine. Avocations: kyacking, singing, theater going, traveling, writing. Home: 160 E 91st St Apt 4B New York NY 10128-2458 Office: Milstein Hosp Bldg 8 Garden North 407 177 Fort Washington Ave New York NY 10032-3713

BURKHART, JOHN ERNEST, theology studies educator; b. Riverside, Calif., Oct. 25, 1927; s. Joseph Ernest and Lockie Louisa (Dryden) B.; m. Virginia Bell French, Sept. 16, 1951; children: David Aaron, Audrey Elizabeth, Deborah Ann. BA, Occidental Coll., 1949; BD, Union Theol. Sem., 1952; PhD, U. So. Calif., 1959; DD, Occidental Coll., 1964. Ordained to ministry United Presbyn. Ch., 1952. Pastor Presbyn. U. U. So. Calif., L.A., 1953-59, from instr. to prof. of Theology, 1959-1990; prof. Systematic Theology McCormick Theol. Sem., Chgo., 1990-93, prof. emeritus, 1993—. Vis. prof. Garrett Theol. Sem. Evanston, Ill., 1966, DePaul U., Chgo., 1970. Author: Kingdom, Church, and Baptism, 1959, Understanding the Word of God, 1964, Worship, 1982; contbr. articles to profl. jours. 1st lt., chaplain USAF, 1952-53. Fellow Royal Anthrop. Inst., Soc. for Values in Higher Edn.; mem. Am. Acad. Religion, Cath. Theol. Soc. of Am., N.Am. Acad. Liturgy, Am. Theol. Soc. (pres. 1969-70), Midwest Alumni Club (v.p. 1985-90), Quadrangle Club, Blue Key, Rotary, Phi Beta Kappa. Democrat. Presbyterian. Home: 569 Woodland Ridge Dubuque IA 52003 E-mail: burkhart@mchsi.com.

BURKHOLDER, GRACE ELEANOR, archaeologist, educator; b. Sumas, Wash., Sept. 21, 1920; d. George Lewis and Leah (Benke) Welch; m. Warren Stanford Burkholder, June 4, 1938 (div. Apr. 1957); children: Warren Stanford, Carol Joyce Brackett. BEd cum laude, U. Miami, Fla., 1956; MEd, U. Okla., 1980. Tchr., Laurel Sch., Oceanside, Calif., 1956-58; elem. tchr. U.S. Navy, Kwajalein, M.I., 1958-59, Transport Co. Tex., Kwajalein, 1959-60, Arabian Am. Oil Co., Dhahran, Saudi Arabia, 1960-80. Author: An Arabian Collection: Artifacts from the Eastern Province, 1984, Perceptions of the Past: Solar Phenomena in Southern Nevada, 1995; author: (with others) Rock Art Papers, vol. 7, 1990, vol. 8, 1991, vol. 9, 1992, vol. 10, 1993, vol. 12, 1995, American Indian Rock Art, vol. 17, 1992; rsch., publs. on Ubaid sites and pottery in Saudi Arabia. Active San Diego Mus. Man, Mus. No. Ariz., Clark County Heritage Mus., Lost City Mus. Mem. Am. Rock Art Rsch. Assn., Nev. Archael. Assn. (Ting-Perkins Outstanding Contrbns. award 1995).

BURKOFF, JOHN MICHAEL, law educator, lawyer; b. Louisville, Nov. 16, 1948; s. Stanley Thomas and Joyce Ann (Switow) B.; m. Nancy Mammen, Aug. 17, 1969; children: Amy Nicole, David Michael. AB, U. Mich., 1970, JD, 1973; LLM, Harvard U., 1976. Bar: Mich. 1974, Pa. 1979. Law clk. to justice Mich. Supreme Ct., Detroit, 1973-75; adj. prof. law Wayne State U., Detroit, 1974-75; instr. law Boston U., 1975-76; asst. prof. U. Pitts., 1976-79, assoc. prof., 1979-82, prof., 1982—, assoc. dean, 2000—. Of counsel Marcus & Shapira, Pitts., 1976—2000; mem. faculty Pa. Coll. of Judiciary, 1983—; reporter Prosecution Function and Def. Function Stds. Task Force, ABA, 1988-93. Author: Criminal Offenses and Defenses in Pennsylvania, 1984, 2d edit., 1989, 4th edit., 2000, Criminal Defense Ethics: Law and Liability, 1986, 2d edit., 2002, Search Warrant Law Desk Book, 1987, Ineffective Assistance of Counsel, 1993, Readings in Criminal Law, 1998, Criminal Law: Cases, Problems and Exercises, 2002, Criminal Procedure: Cases, Problems and Exercises, 2000; editor Search and Seizure Law Report. Del. Dem. Nat. Conv., N.Y.C., 1980; chair Pitts. Citizens Police Rev. Bd., 1997-99. Named Hon. Chief Police City of Louisville, 1980; Ford Found. fellow, 1976. Mem. ABA (chair trial judge standards task force 1997-2000), ACLU, Pa. Bar Assn., Assn. Am. Law Schs. (chair criminal justice sect. 1980, exec. coun. 1977-82), U.S. Supreme Ct. Hist. Soc., Am. Judicature Soc. Democrat. Jewish. Home: 6104 Kentucky Ave Pittsburgh PA 15206-4213 Office: U Pitts Sch Law Pittsburgh PA 15260 E-mail: burkoff@pitt.edu.

BURMAN, SHEILA FLEXER ZOLA, special education educator; b. N.Y.C., May 1, 1935; d. Jack and Edna (Eagle) Flexer; m. Eugene Lee Zola, July 7, 1957 (div. Aug. 1973); children: Leslie Sheldon, Sharon Joanne; m. Milton Burman, Mar. 19, 1978 (dec. Apr. 1999). Student, Hunter Coll., 1952-55; BA in Edn., BS, UCLA, 1957, 85, spl. edn. cert. for learning handicapped, 1985; and severely handicapped; MS in Counseling, U. LaVerne, 1983; resource specialist cert., Calif. Luth. U., 1988. Cert. tchr., spl. edn. tchr., resource specialist, pupil pers. credential. Tchr. L.A. Unified Sch. Dist., 1957-62, tchr. 3rd grade gifted, 1977-81, spl. edn. tchr., 1981-88, mid. sch. resource tchr., 1987—89, elem. resource tchr., 1989—96, spl. edn. coord., 1997—. Cert. tchr., spl. edn. tchr., resource specialist, pupil pers. credential. Pres. L.A. chpt. Brandeis U. Nat. Women's Com., 2000-02, western region v.p. membership, 2000—; bd. dirs. U. Women, U. of Judaism. Grantee CTIP 1988, Computer 1989. Mem. Coun. for Exceptional Children, Assn. Ednl. Therapists, United Tchrs. L.A., Calif. Tchrs. Assn., UCLA Alumni Assn., UCLA Grad. Sch. Edn. Alumni Assn., Hunter Coll. Alumni Assn., Pi Lambda Theta. Avocations: swimming, reading, needlepoint. Home: 15455 Hamner Dr Los Angeles CA 90077-1802 Office: 4525 Irvine Ave North Hollywood CA 91602-1915

BURMASTER, ELIZABETH, school system administrator; b. Balt., July 26, 1954; B Music Edn., U. Wis., 1976, MS, 1984. Music and drama tchr.; prin. Madison West H.S., 1992—2001; state supt. pub. instrn. State of Wis., Madison, 2001—. Mem. bd. regents U. Wis., Wis.; mem. Edn. Commn. U.S., Wis. Tech. Coll. Sys. Bd., Ednl. Comms. Bd., Very Spl. Arts Wis.,

Gov.'s Work-Based Learning Bd.; bd. dirs. TEACH Wis. Mem.: Coun. of Chief State Sch. Officers, SAI-Music Assn., Tempo Internat., Assn. Wis. Sch. Adminstrs. Mailing: PO Box 7841 Madison WI 53707-7841

BURMEISTER, VIRGINIA ELIZABETH, retired secondary educator; b. Danville, Ill., Oct. 27, 1926; d. Carl J. and Ruby M. (Ludwig) B. BSEd, Eastern Ill. U., 1949; MA, U. Colo., 1960. Tchr. sci. Cumberland Unit Dist., Toledo, 1949-54; Bellwood Sch. Dist., 1954-59; tchr. sci. Ladue Sch. Dist., St. Louis, 1959-89; ret., 1989. Mem. PEO, Mo. State Tchrs. Assn. (past pres.), Delta Kappa Gamma, Kappa Kappa Iota. Home: 1610 Redbird Cv Saint Louis MO 63144-1122

BURNETT, CASSIE WAGNON, middle school educator; b. Atlanta, Aug. 31, 1950; d. Lovic Pierce and Virginia (Slaughter) Wagnon; m. Irvin D. Burnett, Sept. 26, 1970; children: Bryan, Brittany. BA, Oglethorpe U., 1971; MEd, Ga. State U., 1975. Tchr. elem. sch. Dekalb County Bd. Edn., Decatur, Ga., 1971-81; tchr. jr. high sch. Greater Atlanta Christian Sch., Norcross, Ga., 1982—. 6th grade sponsor History Club, 1992-94; co-sponsor Joy Club, 1990-92. Named Star Tchr. for Gwinnet Co., 1995. Office: Greater Atlanta Christian Sch PO Box 4277 Norcross GA 30091-4277

BURNETT, PATRICIA HILL, portrait artist, author, sculptor, lecturer; b. Bklyn. d. William Burr and Mimi (Uline) Hill; m. William Anding Lange, 1944 (div. 1947); 1 child, William Hill; m. Harry Albert Burnett III, Oct. 9, 1948 (dec. 1979); children: Harry Burnett III, Terrill Hill, Hillary Hill; m. Robert L. Siler, 1989. Student, U. Toledo, 1937-38, Goucher Coll., 1939-41, MA program Inst. D'Allende, Mex., 1967, Wayne State U., 1972; pvt. studies with, John Carroll, Detroit, 1941-44, Sarkis Sarkisian, 1956-60, Wallace Bassford, Provincetown, Mass., 1968-72, Walter Midener, Detroit, 1960-63. Actress Long Ranger and Green Hornet prgrams, Radio Blue Network, 1941-46; tchr. painting and sculpture U. Mich. Extension, Ann Arbor, 1965—. Lectr. N.Y. Speakers Bur., 1971—; propr. Burnett Studios, Detroit, 1962-88, mgr., 1962—; appt. to Mich. Quarter Commn. by gov. Engler, 2002. Numerous one-woman shows of paintings and sculptures include Scarab Club, Detroit, 1971, Midland (Mich.) Art Ctr., Wayne State U., Detroit, The Gallery, Ft. Lauderdale, Fla., Agra Gallery, Washington, Salon des Artes, Paris; numerous group shows include: Palazzo Pruili Gallery, Venice, 1971, Detroit Inst. of Arts, 1967, Butler Mus., Cleveland, 1972, Windsor (Ont., Can.) Art Ctr., 1973, Weisbaden (Germany) Gallery, 1976, Retrospective Show: Birmingham Bloomfield Art Assn., 1997; represented in permanent collections: Detroit Inst. Arts, Wayne State U., Wooster (Ohio) Coll., Ford Motor Co., Detroit, Bloomfield Art Assn., Bloomfield Hills, Mich., Henry Ford Hosp. Collection, Fed. Ct. Appeals in Washington, City-County Bldg., Detroit, Mich. State Capitol Bldg., Royal Acad. of Art, London, Moscow Mus., Moscow, Russia, Mich. State Capital, Lansing, Mich., Royal Palace of India, New Delhi, Palace of The Philippines, Manila, Mansion of Prime Minister, Greece; also pvt. collections: numerous portrait paintings including Indira Ghandi, Benson Ford, Joyce Carol Oates, Mrs. Edsel Ford, Betty Ford, Mayor Roman Gribbs, Princess Olga Mrivani, Lord John Mackintosh, Marlo Thomas, Viveca Lindfois, Betty Freidan, Gloria Steinem, Congresswoman Martha Griffiths, Margaret Papandreou, Valentina Tereshkova, Barbara Walters, Margaret Thatcher, Corazon Aquino, Violetta Chamarra, Jackie Joyner Kersee, Mayor Dennis Archer, Wayne U. pres. David Adamany, author Kate Millett, Michele Engler and triplets, Patricia Ireland, Rosa Parks, others; mem. editl. bd. Am. Portrait Soc.; author: True Colors: An Artist's Journey from Beauty Queen to Feminist. Chairwoman of Mich. Women's Commn., 1972—; pres. Detroit House of Correction Commn., 1975—; treas. Rep. Dist. 1 of Mich., 1973—; mem. Issues com., Rep. State Ctrl. Com., 1975-76; sec. Rep. State Ways and Means com., 1975—, Detroit Libr. Commn., 1980-85, Detroit Human Rights Commn., 1976-80, Detroit City Planning Commn., 1985-90; mem. Mich. State Adv. Coun. vocat. Edn.; mem. Mich. Arts in Edn. Coun., 1978—; mem. New Detroit Arts Com., 1979—; chmn. World Feminist Commn., 1974—; life mem. NAACP. Recipient Silver Salute award Mich. State U., 1976, Most Popular award San Diego Sculpture Show, 1971, First prize award Cape Cod Artists Show, 1968, State of Mich. award for creativity Gov. John Engler, 1999, Life Accomplishment award Mich. Women's Found., 2001; named Disting. Woman of Mich., Bus. and Profl. Women's Orgn., 1974, Disting. Woman Northwood Inst., 1977, Artist of Yr., Mich. Art Train, 1989, Disting. Woman award Mich. Bus. and Profl. Women Internat.; named to Ohio Hall of Fame, 1987, Mich. Women's Hall of Fame, 1988, one of Most Outstanding Women in Mich., Women in Advt., 1998, one of 10 People with Most Clout Outside of County, Detroit Free Press, 1998, one of 95 Most Powerful Women in Mich., Corp. Mag., 2002; elected to Internat. Hall of Fame, 2002. Mem. Mich. Women's Forum (founder 1989, bd. dirs. 1989-99, Internat. Women's Forum, bd. dirs. 1989-99), Detroit Inst. Arts (dir. membership com. 1958—), Nat. Assn. Commns. for Women (pres. 1976-78), Mich. Acad. of Arts, Detroit Soc. Women Painters and Sculptprs, Women in the Arts, Scrab Club (dir. 1962-63), Ibex Club (pres. 1951), NOW (nat. bd. 1971-75, del. UN conf. Mex., 1975, Feminist of Yr.), Coun. Leading portrait Painters (elect), Women's Econ. Club, N.Y. Portrait Club (nat. adv. bd. 1977—), French-Am. C.of C. (v.p.), Alpha Phi, Zonta, Detroit Econ. Club (bd. dirs.) Episcopalian. Home: 13 Oaks Ct Bloomfield Hills MI 48304-2120

BURNETT, SUZANNE KATHERINE, education educator; b. St. Louis, June 6, 1952; d. John L. Casey and Alice Lovan Tourville; m. Michael J. Burnett, Dec. 29, 1973; children: Thomas, Katherine. BS in Math. Edn., U. Mo., 1973; MEd in Ednl. Psychology, U. Hawaii, 1976; MA in Ednl. Tech., Pepperdine U., 2001. Cert. secondary tchr., Tenn. GED math. instr. St. Louis H.S., Honolulu, 1974-75, Olympic Coll., Barbers Point, Hawaii, 1975-76, Palatine (Ill.) Dist. 211, 1983-84; parent effectivenes instr. self-employed, Chgo. and Memphis, 1981-86, math. tutor, 1983-92; computer coord./tchr. Hutchison Sch., Memphis, 1988—2001; technology coord. St. George's Sch., Germantown, Tenn., 2002—. PTA officer Germantown (Tenn.) Elem. Sch., 1985-88; chmn. tennis league Welcome Wagon, Germantown, 1986-88; pres. Homeowners' Orgn., Germantown, 1991-92; mem. Leadership Germantown, 2002. Mem.: Nat. Coun. Tchrs. Math., Internat. Soc. for Tech. in Edn., Kappa Delta Pi. Roman Catholic. Avocations: walking, reading, gardening, tennis. Office: St George's Sch 8250 Poplar Ave Germantown TN Home: 2691 Sweet Oaks Cir Germantown TN 38138-6253

BURNEY, BETTY SEABROOK, educational administrator; b. Jacksonville, Fla., Apr. 19, 1956; d. Oliver and Helen (Robinson) Seabrook; m. Calvin L. Burney, Sept. 3, 1983; children: Calvin Jr., Craig. BA, U. Miami, Coral Gables, Fla., 1977; MA, No. Ill. U., 1979. Mgr. mgmt. systems Jacksonville Planning Dept., 1979-81; asst. v.p. Fla. Nat. Bank, Jacksonville, 1981-85; dir. human resources Mazda Motors Am., E., Jacksonville, 1985-87; dir. Kidsville Learning Ctr., Jacksonville, 1987—. Cons. Kidsville, USA, Jacksonville, 1988—; adviser Jax Black Youth Program, Jacksonville,1 990, Ctr. for Excellence, Jacksonville, 1991. Mem sch. adv. com. Martin L. King Elem. Sch., 1993; pres. PTA Martin L. King Elem. Sch., 1993-94. Recipient Community Leadership award Urban League, Jacksonville, 1989, 90, 91, Community Svc. award Nurses for Christ, Jacksonville, 1990, 91, Bus. Leadership award 1st Bapt. Ch., Jacksonville, 1990. Home: 5626 International Dr Jacksonville FL 32219-3627 Office: Kidsville Learning Ctr 2553 Soutel Dr Jacksonville FL 32208-2050

BURNHAM, STEVEN JAMES, physician, educator; b. Atlanta, June 29, 1947; s. James Harrison and Virginia (Brown) B.; m. Judith Swain, Feb. 26, 1972 (div. 1983); children: Christopher, Laura; m. Cynthia Ann Billings, May 24, 1986 (div. 1995); m. Cathy Lee Rustad, July 13, 2002. BA, Vanderbilt U., 1969, MD, 1972. Intern, then resident Vanderbilt U. Hosps., Nashville, Tenn., 1972-77; asst. prof. U. N.C., Chapel Hill, 1979-83, assoc. prof, 1983-91, prof., 1991—. Vascular Surgery fellow Northwestern U., 1978-79. Mem. ACS. Home: 30156 Pharr Dr Chapel Hill NC 27517 Office: U NC Chapel Hill 210 Clin Sci Bldg Chapel Hill NC 27514 E-mail: stburnhm@med.unc.edu.

BURNHAM, TOM, school system administrator; b. Jackson, Miss., May 5, 1946; 1 child, Cassandra Burnham Vanderford. BSBA, Miss. Coll., Clinton, 1969, MEd, 1975; EdS, Delta State U., Cleveland, Miss., 1983, EdD, 1985. Cert. in social studies adminstrn., Miss., sch. adminstrn., Miss. Tchr., dept. chair Pearl (Miss.) High Sch., 1969-72; asst. prin. McLuarin Jr. High, Pearl, 1973-81; asst. dean cont. edn. Delta State U., Cleve., Miss., 1981-86; prin. Solomon Jr. High, Greenville, Miss., 1986-87; supt. Biloxi (Miss.) Pub. Schs., 1987-92; state supt. edn. Miss. Dept. Edn., Jackson, 1992-97; exec. dir. Gulf Coast Edn. Consortium, Long Beach, Miss., 1998-99; supt. Henderson County Schs., NC, 1999—. Mem. Am. Assn. Sch. Adminstrs., Miss. Profl. Educators, Miss. Assn. Sch. Supts., Phi Delta Kappa. Baptist. Office: 414 4th Ave W Hendersonville NC 28739*

BURNIM, MICKEY L. academic administrator; Provost Elizabeth City State U., N.C., 1995—. Office: Elizabeth City State U Campus Box 790 1704 Weeksville Rd Elizabeth City NC 27909-7806

BURNINGHAM, KIM RICHARD, former state legislator; b. Salt Lake City, Sept. 14, 1936; s. Rulon and Margie (Stringham) Burningham; m. Susan Ball Clarke, Dec. 19, 1968; children: Christian, Tyler David. BS, U. Utah, 1960; MA, U. Ariz., 1967; MFA, U. So. Calif., 1977. Cert. secondary tchr., Utah. Tchr. Bountiful (Utah) High Sch., 1960-88; mem. Utah Ho. of Reps., Salt Lake City, 1979-94; cons. Shipley Assocs., Bountiful, 1989-94, Franklin Covey, 1994—. Gubernatorial appointee as exec. dir. Utah Statehood Centennial Commn., 1994-96; mem. Utah State Bd. Edn., 1999-2000, vice chmn., 2000-01, chmn., 2001—; bd. dirs. Nat. Assn. State Bds. Edn., 2000-2001 (pres. 2003-). Author dramas for stage and film, also articles; columnist, Davis County Clipper, 2000—. Mem. state strategic planning com. Utah Tomorrow, 1989—. Recipient Carl Perkins Humanitarian of Yr. award, ACTE, 2002. Mem. NEA, PTA (life), Utah Edn. Assn., Davis Edn. Assn., Nat. Forensic League. Mem. Lds Ch. Avocations: gardening, history. Home: 932 Canyon Crest Dr Bountiful UT 84010-2002 E-mail: krb84010@aol.com.

BURNISKE, RICHARD WILLIAM, JR., education educator; b. Montague City, Mass., Feb. 27, 1960; s. Richard William and Penelope Joan Burniske; m. Jacqueline Wines, June 19, 1982; children: Justin Wines, Christopher Wines. BA, U. N.C., 1982; MA, Middlebury Coll., 1989; PhD, U. Tex., 2001. Tchg. cert., N.Y. Tchr. Cairo (Egypt) Am. Coll., 1982-83; English tchr. Deerfield (Mass.) Acad., 1983-87; asst. prin. Academia Cotopaxi, Quito, Ecuador, 1987-92; English tchr. Internat. Sch. Kuala Lumpur, Malaysia, 1992-96; asst. instr. U. Tex., Austin, 1997-99; asst. prof. Coll. Edn. U. Hawaii-Manoa, Honolulu. Cons., tng. specialist World Bank Inst., Washington, 1998-2003; project coord. Inst. for Tech. Learning, Austin, 1996-97; assoc. editor Jour. Online Learning, Austin, 1997-99; examiner Internat. Baccalaureate Orgn, Kuala Lumpur, 1993-95. Author: (book) Breaking Down the Digital Walls, 2000, Literacy in the Cyber Age, 2000, (anthology chpt.) The Nearness of You, 1996, The Learning Highway, 1998, Taking Sides, 2000. Fundraiser March of Dimes, Austin, 1999; grant writer Inst. Technology and Learning, Austin, 1996-97; vol. cons. Austin Learning Acad., 1997-99. Univ. fellow U. Tex., 1996-98, NEH fellow, 1990, 91; Morehead scholar U. N.C., 1978-82. Mem. MLA, Internat. Soc. for Tech. in Edn. (bd. dirs. 1996—), Am. Ednl. Rsch. Assn., Nat. Coun. Tchrs. English. Roman Catholic. Avocations: sailing, bicycling, hiking, camping, traveling. Office: Univ Hawaii Dept Ednl Tech-Wist Hall 228 1776 University Ave Honolulu HI 96822 E-mail: burniske@hawaii.edu.

BURNLEY, KENNETH STEPHEN, school system administrator; m. Eileen Burnley; children: Traci, Trevor, Jonathan, Tyler. BS, MA, PhD, U. Mich. Tchr. various schs., Mich.; asst. track coach U. Mich.; tchr., coord., asst. prin., prin., dir. Ypsilanti Bd. Edn.; instr. Ea. Mich. U.; asst. supt. instrn. Waverly Bd. Edn.; supt./CEO Fairbanks (Alaska) North Star Borough Sch. Dist.; supt. schs. Colorado Springs (Colo.) Sch. Dist. 11, 1987—2000; CEO Detroit Pub. Schs., 2000—. Speaker in field. Bd. dirs. Colo. Nat. Bank Exch. Named Supt. of Year, Am. Assn. Sch. Adminstrs., 1993. Mem. Colo. Springs C. of C. (bd. dirs.). Avocations: exercising, weight training, boxing, reading, chess. Office: 3011 West Grand Blvd Fl 14 Detroit MI 48202*

BURNS, BRENDA CAROLYN, retired special education administrator, chemical dependence counselor; b. Scalf, Ky., July 22, 1947; d. Lindberg and Ina Jean (Mills) Bingham; m. Michael Burns (div. 1985). BA in English, Wright State U., Dayton, OH, 1968, BA in Spanish, 1971, MEd in Spanish, English and Edn., 1973; MEd in Counseling, Cleve. State U., Cleve., 1985; MAEd in Sch. Psychology, U. Akron, 1985. Cert. in Spanish, English, counseling, sch. psychology, sch. social work, pupil pers., Ohio; cert. chem. dependence counselor. Tchr. Spanish Centerville (Ohio) City Sch., 1971-73; tchr. Spanish and English Rocky River (Ohio) City Sch., 1973-78; sch. counselor Brooklyn (Ohio) City Sch., 1978-84; intern sch. psychologist Westlake (Ohio) City Sch., 1984-85; sch. psychologist Brooklyn City Sch., 1985-87, sch. psychologist, coord. student svcs., 1987-97, dir. pupil svcs., 1997-99; ret., 1999. Adv. coun., chair Cuyahoga Spl. Edn. Svc. Ctr., Cleve., 1991-92; chem. dependency counselor Oakview at S.W. Gen. Health Ctr. Avocations: reading, raising dogs, walking, movies.

BURNS, CAROLYN DIANE, music educator; b. Alton, Ill., Apr. 29, 1950; d. Robert Milton and Emma Rosalie (Weigand) Krase; m. Robert Joseph Burns, Aug. 14, 1982; children: Emily, Austin. Student, Cin. Coll. Music Conservatory, 1972-75; BA, Rocky Mountain Coll., 1980; M of Music Edn., U. Mont., 1987; postgrad., Mont. State U., 2002—. Cert. music tchr. K-12., Mont. Sec., staff edn. Good Samaritan Hosp., Cin., 1973-76; asst. dir. pub. rels. St. Vincent Hosp., Billings, Mont., 1976-78; sec. Luth. Social Svcs., Billings, Mont., 1978-80; tchr. music Sch. Dist. #14, Shelby, Mont., 1980—. Adv. bd. Cadenza Mag., Mont., 1994—; cons. Fine Arts Curriculum, Shelby, 1995. Contbr. articles to Cadenza Mag., 1990-93. Choir dir. Sunshine Singers, Shelby, 1984—, Meth. Ch., Shelby, 1993—; dir. Luth. Ch. handbell choirs, 1999—. Recipient scholarship Bus. & Profl. Women, 1987, Mont. Arts Coun. grant, 1993; Soroptomist scholarship, 2002, Delta Kappa Gamma State Scholarship, 2003, Internat. Scholarship, 2003. Mem. Mont. Gen. Music Tchrs. (pres. 1990-92, spkr. 1993), Mont. Music Educators Assn. (exec. bd. mem. 1990-92), Soc. for Gen. Music (symposium participant 1993), Delta Kappa Gamma (rsch. chmn. 1993-97). Lutheran. Avocations: reading, composing, sewing, swimming, tennis. Office: Meadow Sch 141 6th Ave N Shelby MT 59474-1802

BURNS, DIANE, elementary education educator; b. N.Y.C., Feb. 20, 1946; d. John A. and Virginia Mae (Ridenour) De Gaetano; 1 child, Michele Young; m. Frank Anthony Burns, Apr. 6, 1980; 1 child, Michael John. BA, SUNY, New Paltz, 1968; MEd, U. Ctrl. Fla., 1984. Cert. tchr. elem., early childhood and gifted edn., Fla. Tchr. grade 3 Three Village Sch. Dist., Setauket, N.Y., 1968-69; reading tchr. Am. Heritage Sch., Hollywood, Fla., 1971-74; tchr. various grades Oak Park Elem., Leesburg, Fla., 1975-87; tchr. gifted 3d and 4th grades Dabney Elem., Leesburg, 1987-95; tchr. 3d grade Treadway Elem. Sch., Leesburg, Fla., 1995—. Pvt. tutor, Leesburg. Author, editor: The Time Shifters, 1990 (Fla. Assn. of Gifted grant). Soloist, choir mem. Chancel Choir-Morrison United Meth. Ch., Leesburg, 1986—. Named Fla. Merit Master tchr. State of Fla., Tallahassee, 1983. Mem. Fla. Assn. Gifted, Lake County Edn. Assn., Lake County Reading Coun., Alpha Delta Kappa (chaplain 1986-88). Republican. Avocations: sewing, reading, needlecrafts, traveling, scrapbooking. Office: Treadway Elem Sch 10619 Treadway School Rd Leesburg FL 34788-4680

BURNS, JAMES W. education educator; b. New Haven, Jan. 24, 1937; s. James W. and Helen M. (Wieliesz) B.; children: Amy, Kristin, Katherine. BS, Ctrl. Conn. State U., 1958; MEd, Pa. State U., 1964, EdD, 1969. Tchr. Greenwich (Conn.) Pub. Schs., 1958-64; dir. Curriculum Ctr. Pa. State U., University Park, 1964-68; prof. edn., reading recovery tchr. and leader trainer Western Mich. U., Kalamazoo, 1968—. Mem. Internat. Reading Assn., Nat. Coun. of Tchrs. of English, Mich. Reading Assn., NGA. Home: 5093 Century Ave Kalamazoo MI 49006-5713 Office: 3414 Sangren Hall Kalamazoo MI 49007

BURNS, JOHN FRANCIS, state official, educator; b. Joliet, Ill., Sept. 13, 1945; s. Francis J. and Agnes A. (Vidmar) B.; m. Melinda A. Peak, 1995; 1 child, Alyssa Marie. BA in History, Lewis Coll., 1967; MA in History, Wash. State U., 1972; cert., Western Wash. U., 1977, Acad. Cert. Archivists, 1989. Cert. tchr. Calif. Instr. Skagit Valley Coll., Mt. Vernon, Wash., 1972-75; Pace prof. Chapman Coll., Orange, Calif., 1975-76; instr. Western Wash. U., Bellingham, 1976; project adminstr. Wash. State Records Bd., Olympia, 1977-81; chief of archives State of Calif., Sacramento, 1981-95; dir. Calif. State Archives and Golden State Mus., 1995-97; history and social sci. cons., online course models project dir. Calif. Dept. Edn., 1997—. Cons. and lectr. in field; adj. prof. history Calif. State U., Sacramento, 1987—; adj. prof. libr. sci. San Jose State U., 1999--. Author: Approaching the Millenium: Prospects and Perils in California's Archival Future, 1992; editor: Historical Records of Washington State, 3 vols., 1980-81, Guide to the Los Angeles Police Department Records of the Robert F. Kennedy Assassination Investigation, 1993, Social Studies Review, 1999, History of Sacramento, 1999, Capital Dreams: The Transformation of Sacramento, 2003; co-editor Washington State Guide to Governor's Papers, 1977, Taming the Elephant: Politics, Government and Law in Pioneer California, 2003; contbr. chpts. to books, articles to profl. jours. Sec. Calif. Heritage Preservation Commn., Sacramento, 1981-97; coord. Calif. Hist. Records Adv. Bd., Sacramento, 1981-97; chmn. Nat. Steering Com. of State Records Coord., Sacramento, 1983-85; mem. Calif. Hist. State Capitol Commn., Sacramento, 1984-97, exec. dir. Calif. State Archives Found., 1987-97; mem. Sacramento Commn. History and Sci., 1993-99; mem. adv. bd. Calif. Internat. Studies Project, 1998--. Lt. USN, 1967-70, Vietnam. Recipient Calif. State Govt. Mgmt. award, 1986, 89, Calif. Mil. History Medal award, 1997, Publs. award Sacramento County Hist. Soc., 1999, Spl. Achievement award Sacramento County Hist. Soc., 2000, Resolution of Hon. award Sacramento County Bd. Suprs., 1999-2000, Presdl. award Calif. Coun. Soc. Studies, 2001-02, Diane Brooks award, 2003; grantee Nat. Hist. Publ. and Records Commn., Washington, 1977-86, U.S. Dept. Edn., 1998-2001. Mem. Nat. Assn. Govt. Archives and Records Adminstrs. (v.p. 1986-88, bd. dirs. 1983-85, pres. 1988-90), Soc. Am. Archivists (chmn. com. goals and priorities 1987-90), Calif. Com. for Promotion of History (steering com. 1984-87, award of merit 1989), Spindex Users Network (chmn. 1979-81), Orgn. Am. Historians, Soc. Calif. Archivists (cert. recognition 1989), Calif. Coun. for the Social Studies (dept. rep. 1998—), Nat. Coun. for the Social Studies, Am. Assn. for State and Local History (host com. chair 1998), Nat. Coun. for History Edn. (host com. chair 2000). Office: Calif Dept Edn Stds and Assessment 1430 N St Ste 5408 Sacramento CA 95814 E-mail: jburns@cde.ca.gov.

BURNS, JOHN LUTHER, psychologist, educator; b. Walland, Tenn., May 25, 1932; s. John Luther and Hattie Leona (Hatcher) B.; m. Naomi Jean Staley, June 29, 1957; children: Martha Kay, Alan Scott. BS, U. Tenn., 1956, MS, 1957; PhD, U. Tex., 1969. Asst. to dean students U. Tenn., Knoxville, 1957-66; asst. prof. of counselor edn. and psychology Ark. State U., Jonesboro, 1969-72, assoc. prof., 1972-78, prof., 1978-94, prof. emeritus, 1994—; pvt. practice Jonesboro, 1984-90. Contbr. articles to profl. jours. With USNR, 1952-54. University fellow U. Tex., 1966-69, Presidents fellow Ark. State U., 1984-85. Mem. APA, MidSouth Ednl. Rsch. Assn. (bd. dirs. 1991-93), MidSouth Ednl. Rsch. Found. (bd. dirs. 1992—), Phi Kappa Phi (chpt. pres. 1974-75). Baptist. Avocation: golf. Home: 212 University Dr Jonesboro AR 72401-8482

BURNS, MARIE T. retired secondary education educator; b. Nashua, N.H. d. Charles Henry and Eleanor Agnes (Martin) O'Neil; m. Thomas M. Burns; children: Ann Burns Pelletier, Mary Burns Powlowsky, Catherine Burns Patten. BA, Regis Coll.; postgrad., Rivier Coll. Cert. tchr., N.H. Tchr. English Pelham (N.H.) Sch. Dept., City of Nashua. Former trustee, chmn. of house com., sec. bd. dirs. Mary A. Sweeney Home; judge, participant River Coll. Literacy Festival. Mem. Nashua Tchrs. Union (mem. secondary grouping practices com. Nashua Sch. Dist.), N.H. Ret. Tchrs., Nashua Ret. Tchrs.

BURNS, MARY W. school system administrator; b. Liberty, Miss., Feb. 4, 1941; d. Ruban and Rhodie (Allen) Williams; m. Lucius Hurst, Dec. 18, 1959 (div. 1969); m. Milton Burns, Aug. 25, 1969; children: Michael (dec.), Deborah, Gregory, Shedrick, Tiffany. BA Elem. Edn., So. U. New Orleans, 1979; MA, Xavier U., 1987, postgrad. Cert. Mental Retardation, Early Childhood Edn., Mild Moderate Elem., Secondary, Assessment tchr. Tchr. aide, math tutor Orleans Pub. Schs., 1966-79; tchr. mathematics Derham Jr. High Sch., 1979-81; spl. edn. tchr. William J. Guste Elem., New Orleans, 1981-83; spl. edn. tchr. mild moderate F.W. Gregory Jr. High, New Orleans, 1983-88; sch. adminstr. New Orleans Pub. Schs., 1988—; Chpt. I reading specialist, reading recovery tchr. Lafayette Elem. Sch., 1989—. Dir. Tech Prep Youth Inst. Delgado C.C., 1989; mem. Blue Ribbon scoring com. for New Core Battery; dept. chair spl. edn. Gregory Jr. High Sch., 1985-86; bldg. rep. United Tchrs. New Orleans, 1976-79; exec. coun. paraprofl. chpt., 1975-79. Mem. NAACP, NEA, Nat. Coun. Negro Women, Coun. Exceptional Children, Assn. Supr. and Curriculum Devel., Edn. Week, United Tchrs. New Orleans, Black Caucus Social Educators. Home: 2769 Pressburg St New Orleans LA 70122-6450 Office: Lafayette Elem Sch 2727 S Carrollton Ave New Orleans LA 70118-4338

BURNS, MARYANN MARGARET, elementary education educator; b. Portland, Maine, Mar. 4, 1944; d. William and Emma (Greco) B. Finishing sch. grad., Chandler Sch. for Women, Boston, 1963; BS in Edn. and English summa cum laude, U. Maine, 1974. Cert. elem. tchr., Maine. Pvt. sec. IBM, L.A., 1968-70; learning lab. tchr. Sch. Adminstrv. Dist. # 6, Bar Mills, Maine, 1974—, Frank Jewett Sch., W. Buxton, Maine. Mem. NEA, Maine Tchrs. Assn., U. Maine Alumni Assn., Polit. Action Com. Democrat. Roman Catholic. Home: 17 Wild Rose Ave South Portland ME 04106-6619 Office: Sch Adminstrv Dist 6 PO Box 38 Bar Mills ME 04004-0038

BURNS, ROBERT IGNATIUS, historian, educator, clergyman; b. San Francisco, Aug. 16, 1921; s. Harry and Viola Marie (Whearty) B. BA, Gonzaga U., 1945, MA, 1947, Fordham U., 1949; Phil.B., Jesuit Pontifical Faculty, Spokane, Wash., 1946, Phil.Lic., 1947; S.Th.B., Jesuit Pontifical Faculty, Alma, Calif., 1951, S.Th.Lic., 1953; postgrad., Columbia U., 1949, Oxford (Eng.) U., 1956-57; PhD summa cum laude, Johns Hopkins U., 1958; Doc.ès Sc.Hist., Fribourg (Switzerland) U. (double summa cum laude), 1961; hon. doctorates, Gonzaga U., 1968, Marquette U., 1977, Loyola U., Chgo., 1978, Boston Coll., 1982, Georgetown U., 1982, U. San Francisco, 1983, Fordham U., 1984, U. Valencia, 1985. Mem. Jesuit order; ordained priest Roman Catholic Ch., 1952. Asst. archivist Jesuit and Indian Archives Pacific N.W., Province, Spokane, 1945-47; instr. history dept. U. San Francisco, 1947-48, asst. prof., 1958-62, assoc. prof., 1963-66, prof., 1967-76; sr. prof. dept. history UCLA, 1976—, named overscale (chair), 1987—; dir. Inst. Medieval Mediterranean Spain, 1976—; prof. methodology, faculty history Gregorian U., Rome, 1955-56. Guest lectr. humanities honors program Stanford U., 1960; vis. prof. Coll. of Notre Dame, Belmont, Calif., 1963; James chair Brown U., Providence, 1970; faculty mem. Inst. Advanced Study, Princeton, N.J., 1972; Levi della Vida lectr. UCLA, 1973; vis. prof., Hispanic lectr. U. Calif. at Santa Barbara, 1976; staff UCLA Near Eastern Center, 1979—, UCLA Center Medieval-Renaissance Studies,

1977—; Humanities Coun. lectr. NYU, 1992; Columbus Quincentennial Commn. of Calif. State Legislature, 1992. Author: The Jesuits and the Indian Wars of the Northwest, 1966, reprinted 1985, The Crusader Kingdom of Valencia: Reconstruction on a Thirteenth-Century Frontier, 1967, Islam Under the Crusaders: Colonial Survival in the Thirteenth-Century Kingdom of Valencia, 1973, Medieval Colonialism: Post-Crusade Exploitation of Islamic Valencia, 1975, Moors and Crusaders in Mediterranean Spain, 1978, Jaume I i els Valencians del segle XIII, 1981, Muslims, Christians and Jews in the Crusader Kingdom of Valencia, 1983, El reino de Valencia en el siglo XIII, 1983, Society and Documentation in Crusader Valencia, 1985, The Worlds of Alfonso the Learned and James the Conqueror, 1985, Emperor of Culture: Alfonso X, 1990, Foundations of Crusader Valencia, 1991, rev. transl. Els fonaments del regne croat de València, 1995, El Regne Croat de Valencia, 1994, Jews in the Notarial Culture, 1996, Negotiating Cultures: Bilingual Surrender Treaties in Muslim Crusader Spain, 1999, El papel de Játvia, 1999, Las Siete partidas of Alfonso X, 5 vols., 2000; bd. editors: Trends in History, 1979—, Anuario de Estudios Medievales (Spain), 1985—, Bull. of the Cantigueiros, 1986—, Catalan Rev., 1986—, Medieval Encounters, 1998—; co-editor: Viator, 1980-93; assoc. editor Ency. of Medieval Iberia; mem. editl. bd. U. Calif. Press, 1985-88, chair, 1987-88, mem. bd. of control, 1987-88; contbr. articles to profl. jours. Trustee Hill Monastic Manuscript Library, 1977-81; mem. adv. bd. Am. Bibliog. Center, 1982— . Recipient Book award Am. Hist. Assn. Pacific Coast Br., 1968, Am. Assn. State Local History, 1967, Am. Cath. Hist. Assn., 1967, 68, Book award Inst. Mission Studies, 1966, Am. Cath. Press Assn., 1975, Phi Alpha Theta, 1976; Haskins medal Medieval Acad. Am., 1976; Premi de la Critica, 1982; Premi Catalonia, 1982, Premi Internacional Llull, 1988; Cross of St. George Catalan Govt., 1989; Guggenheim fellow, 1963-64; Ford Found. and Guggenheim grantee, 1980; NEH fellow, 1971, 73, 75-83, 88, Am. Coun. Learned Socs. fellow, 1972; travel grantee, 1975; Robb Publ. Grantee, 1974; Darrow Publ. grantee, 1975; Consejo Superior de Investigaciones Cientificas (Spain) travel grantee, 1975, 82; Valencia province and Catalan region publ. grantee, 1981; Del Amo Grantee, 1983; U.S.-Spain treaty grantee, 1983-85; grantee Consejo Superior de Investigaciones Cientificas (Spain), 1985; Mellon Publ. grantee, 1985, U.S.-Spain Treaty grantee, 1999. Fellow Medieval Acad. Am. (trustee 1975-77, prize com. 1980, scribe 1987—), Accio Cultural del Pais Valencia; mem. Hispanic Soc. Am. (hon.), Am. Cath. Hist. Assn. (pres. 1975, coun. 1976—), Soc. Spanish Portuguese Hist. Studies (exec. coun. 1974-77), Am. Hist. Assn. (del. Internat. Congress Hist. Scis. 1975, 80, pres. Pacific Coast br. 1979-80, exec. coun. 1981-83), Medieval Assn. Pacific (exec. coun. 1975-77), Acad. Rsch. Historians Medieval Spain (pres. 1976), N.Am. Catalan Soc., Tex. Medieval, Inst. Catalan Studies, Barcelona (elected). Office: UCLA History Dept Los Angeles CA 90095-0001

BURNS, SANDRA, lawyer, educator; b. Bryan, Tex., Aug. 9, 1949; d. Clyde W. and Bert (Rychlik) B.; 1 son, Scott. BS, U. Houston, 1970; MA, U. Tex., 1972, PhD, 1975; JD, St. Mary's U., 1978. Bar: Tex. 1978; cert. tchr., adminstr., supr. instrn., Tex. Tchr. Austin (Tex.) Ind. Sch. Dist., 1970-71; prof. child devel./family life and home econs. edn. Coll. Nutrition, Textiles and Human Devel. Tex. Women's U., Denton, 1974-75; instrnl. devel. asst. Office of Ednl. Resources divsn. instr U. Tex. Health Sci., San Antonio, 1976-77; legis. aide William T. Moore Tex. Senate, Austin, fall 1978, com. clk.-counsel, spring 1979; legal cons. Colombotti & Assocs., Aberdeen, Scotland, 1980; corp. counsel 1st Internat. Oil and Gas, Inc., 1983; contracted atty. Humble Exploration Co., Inc., Dallas, 1984; assoc. Smith, Underwood, Dallas, 1986-88; pvt. practice Dallas, 1988—; mem. grad. faculty Tex.A&M U., Commerce. Atty. contracted to Republic Energy Inc., Bryan, Tex., 1981-82, ARCO, Dallas, 1985; vis. lectr. Tex. A&M U., fall 1981, summer, 1981; lectr. home econs. Our Lady of the Lake Coll., San Antonio, fall, 1975. Contbr. articles on law and edn. to profl. jours. Mem. Coll. of the State Bar of Tex., Phi Delta Kappa. Office: Preston Commons West 300 8117 Preston Rd Dallas TX 75225 E-mail: burns@attorney-mediator.com.

BURNS, THOMAS SAMUEL, history educator; b. Michigan City, Ind., June 7, 1945; m. Carol Ann Morris, June 29, 1968; 1 child, Catherine Elizabeth. AB, Wabash Coll., 1967; postgrad., Am. Sch. Classical Studies, Athens, summer 1967; MA, U. Mich., 1968, PhD, 1974. Asst. prof. history Emory U., Atlanta, 1974-80, assoc. prof., 1980-85, Samuel Candler Dobbs prof. history, 1985—, chmn. dept. history, 1989-92. Dir. summer seminar for sch. tchrs. NEH, 1985, 88; adj. prof. U. Windsor, Ont., summer 1978, 79; vis. research prof. Kommission für alte Geschichte und Epigraphik des deutschen archäologischen Instituts in München, spring 1982; vis. research prof. Römisch-Germanische Kommission des deut. arch. Instituts, Frankfurt, spring 1982; Gastprof. Universität Augsburg, 1986. Author: The Ostrogoths: Kingship and Society, 1980, A History of the Ostrogoths, 1984, (with B.H. Overbeck) Rome and the Germans as Seen in Coinage, 1987, Barbarians within the Gates of Rome, 1994, (with J.W. Eadie) Urban Centers and Rural Realities, 2000, Rome and the Barbarians 100 B.C.-A.D. 400, 2003; co-dir. of Archaeological excavations in Passau, Germany, 1978-79, Manching, Germany, 1985, Pecs, Hungary, 1998; contbr. articles to profl. jours. With U.S. Army, 1969-71. Recipient Emory Williams Disting. Teaching award Emory U., 1982; Fulbright fellow Fed. Republic Germany, 1986, Boak fellow in ancient history U. Mich., 1971-74; Disting. Vis. scholar-in-residence U. Adelaide, Australia. Mem. Medieval Acad. Am. (nominating com. 1987-88), Ga. Classical Assn., AAUP (pres. Emory U. chpt. 1983-84), Am. Canoeing Assn., Phi Beta Kappa, Omicron Delta Kappa. Avocations: camping, fishing, wilderness canoeing, travel. Home: 268 Woodview Dr Decatur GA 30030-1037 Office: Emory U Dept History Atlanta GA 30322-0001

BUROW, SHARON RUTH, education educator; b. Cleve., Feb. 6, 1952; d. Warren and Ruth Catherine (Schenk) Hamula; m. Michael M. Burow, June 6, 1976; children: Matthew, Katherine. BS in Elem. Edn., Dr. Martin Luther Coll., 1976; MS in Early Edn., Concordia U., Mequon, Wis., 1993. Cert. early childhood tchr., Wis. 5th grade tchr. Ocean Dr. Luth. Sch., Pompano Beach, Fla., 1976; 2nd and 3rd grade tchr. Peace Luth. Sch., Hartford, Wis., 1976-77, substitute tchr., 1977-83, K-8 spl. edn. tchr., 1983-85, presch. tchr., 1985-89, adminstr., kindergarten tchr., 1989—; owner, operator, tchr., adminstr. St. Paul's Little Learner Smile Ctr., St. Paul's Luth. Ch., Slinger, Wis., 1985-89. Early edn. instr. Moraine Park Tech. Coll., Hartford, 1992—; prof. in early edn. Concordia U., 1994—, Wis. Luth. Coll., Milw., 1995—. Author: And I Can Go and Tell, 1995, Counting on Christmas, 1995, Jellybean Easter Storeis, 1995, Who Is Martin Luther, 1995; producer, dir., writer (video) And I Can Go And Tell, 1995. Bd. dirs. Slinger Libr., 1988-90. Named Tchr. of Yr., County Lion's Club, 1994. Mem. ASCD, Nat. Assn. for Edn. of Young Children, Assn. for Childhood Edn. Internat., Luth. Educators of Young Children, Phi Delta Kappa. Republican. Lutheran. Avocations: writing, crafts, walking, reading.

BURR, JOHN ROY, philosophy educator; b. Oshkosh, Wis., July 18, 1933; s. Lester John and Dorothy Viola (Hoffman) B.; m. Marjorie Jean Bakirakis, July 4, 1963; children: Michael John, Christopher Scott, Kara Jean. BA, U. Wis.-Madison, 1955; MA (Univ. grantee), Columbia U., 1956, PhD, 1959. Adj. faculty Franklin and Marshall Coll., 1959-61; asst. prof. philosophy Hood Coll., 1961-64; faculty dept. philosophy U. Wis.-Oshkosh, 1964-66, assoc. prof., 1966-68, prof., 1968—, John McN Rosebush univ. prof., 1984—, chmn. dept., 1966-76, 2002—, chmn. humanities div., 1966-76, asst. dean letters and sci., 1976-79, mem. faculty senate, 1981-96, 97-99, pres. faculty senate, 1983-84, 87-88; chmn. univ. acad. policies com. U. Wis., Oshkosh, 1996—98. Editor: Handbook of World Philosophy: Contemporary Developments Since 1945, 1980, (with Milton Goldinger) Philosophy and Contemporary Issues, 8th rev. edit., 2000, 9th rev. edit., 2004, World Philosophy: A Contemporary Bibliography, 1993; contbr. to Ency. of Unbelief, 2 vols., 1985; contbr. articles to profl. jours. Pres. Oshkosh Community Players, 1968-69, bd. dirs., 1966-69; pres. Wis. Assn. Children and Adults with Learning Disabilities, 1984-88. Ford Found. grantee, 1963-64; Wis. State U. Regents Research grantee, 1971-72; Sabbatical grantee, 1987. Mem. Am. Philos. Assn., Metaphys. Soc. Am., Assn. Asian Studies, AAUP (chpt. pres. 1975-76, 80-82, successively sec., 1985-88, v.p., 86-88 to pres. Wis. conf. 1989-90), Wis. Acad. Scis., Arts and Letters, Candlelight Club, Masons, Phi Beta Kappa, Phi Kappa Phi, Phi Eta Sigma, Delta Sigma Rho, Pi Kappa Delta. Home: 2114 Doemel St Oshkosh WI 54901-2546

BURRELL, E. WILLIAM, retired university adminstrator, educator; b. Providence, Apr. 28, 1927; s. Edward John and Helene Agnes (Kelly) B.; m. Barbara Mary O'Connor, Apr. 18, 1953; children: Jason Edwin, Mary Elizabeth. Student, Providence Coll., 1945-47; AB, Fordham U., 1949; MA, Boston U., 1959; EdD, Harvard U., 1964; HLD honoris causa, Salve Regina U., 1996. Tchr. Providence Sch. Dept., 1957-65; prof. English and edn. Salve Regina U., Newport, R.I., 1965-96, chmn. dept. edn., 1967-73, dean of coll., 1974-77, v.p., dean of faculty and grad. studies, 1977-95, emeritus prof., 1996—. Mem. accreditation team, sometime chmn. New Eng. Assn. Schs. and Colls., Winchester, Mass., 1975-86. Mem. allocations panel United Way Southeastern New Eng., Providence, 1976-93; bd. dirs. Samaritans of R.I., Providence, 1985-90. Mem. R.I. Coun. Tchrs. English (life; founder 1959, pres. 1965-67), Barnard Club (pres. 1971-72), Phi Delta Kappa.

BURRILL, KATHLEEN R. F. (KATHLEEN R. F. GRIFFIN-BURRILL), Turkologist, educator; b. Canterbury, U.K., Mar. 8, 1924; d. William Henry and Ruby Amy (Webber) Griffin; children: Anne Ruth, Jane Ruth. AM, Columbia U., 1957, PhD, 1964; cert., Mid. East Inst., Columbia U, 1959. Officer of Brit. Coun., Ankara, Turkey, U.K., 1947-55; lectr. to prof. Middle East and Asian langs. and cultures Columbia U., N.Y.C., 1957-2000, prof. emerita, 2000—. Author: The Quatrains of Nesimi, Fourteenth-Century Turkic Hurufi Poet; co-editor Archivum Ottomanicum, 1984-95; contbr. articles to profl. jours. and encys. Recipient rsch. and travel award, Coun. Rsch. Humanities, 1966—67; fellow, Columbia U., 1957—59, Ford Found., 1959—60, Am. Rsch. Inst. in Turkey, summers, 1967, 1975. Fellow: Mid. East Studies Assn. (dir. 1974—76, founding fellow); mem.: Am. Assn. Tchrs. Turkic Langs. (pres. 1986—2002, hon. pres. 2003—), Mid. East Inst. (Washington), Brit. Soc. Mid. East Studies, Inst. Turkish Studies (governing bd. 1995—2001, founding assoc.), Turkish Studies Assn. (dir. 1974—76).

BURRIS, ANN, nursing educator; b. Salt Lake City, Feb. 27, 1952; d. Wesley Theodore and Elizabeth Ann (Scrowther) B.; 1 child, Julie Ann. ADN, Weber State Coll., 1977; BSN, U. Phoenix, 1993. Staff nurse ICU and critical care unit Logan (Utah) Regional Hosp., insvc. edn. coord. Affiliate faculty Weber State U./Utah State U. coop. nursing program. Mem. Am. Assn. Critical Care Nurses. Home: PO Box 456 Smithfield UT 84335-0456

BURRIS, BOYD LEE, psychiatrist, psychoanalyst, physician, educator; b. Knoxville, Tenn., Jan. 28, 1930; s. Fred Roosevelt and Mildred Blanche Burris. BS, U. Tenn., Knoxville, 1951; MD, U. Tenn., Memphis, 1952. Diplomate in psychiatry Am. Bd. Psychiatry and Neurology; cert. in psychoanalysis. Tng. and supervising analyst Balt.-Washington Inst. for Psychoanalysis, Washington, 1974—, co-dir., 1980-86; clin. prof. psychiatry and behavioral scis. George Washington U. Sch. Medicine, Washington, 1983—; clin. prof. psychiatry Georgetown U. Sch. Medicine, Washington, 1990—; mem. bd. trustees Ctr. for Advanced Psychoanalytic Studies, Princeton, N.J., Aspen, Colo., 1982—, pres. bd. trustees and dir., 1994—2003; pvt. practice psychiatry and psychoanalysis Washington, 1960—. Active staff George Washington U. Hosp., 1963-96; cons. Potomac Found. for Mental Health, Bethesda, Md., 1969-78, St. Elizabeth's Hosp., Washington, 1969-88. Contbr. chpt. to book, articles to profl. jours. Lt. comdr. M.C., USN, 1954-56. Mem. Am. Psychiat. Assn. (chair tellers com. 1987-88), Am. Psychoanalytic Assn. (bd. on profl. standards 1982-86, 2000-2002), Balt./Washington Soc. for Psychoanalysis (pres. 1978-79). Home: 3100 Rolling Rd Chevy Chase MD 20815-4038 Office: 4545 42nd St NW Ste 310 Washington DC 20016-4623

BURRIS, CRAVEN ALLEN, retired college administrator, educator; b. Wingate, N.C., Sept. 11, 1929; s. Craven Cullom and Virginia Neulin (Currie) B.; m. Jane Russell Burris, June 19, 1955; children: Christa Cullom, David Allen. AA, Wingate Coll., 1949; BS, Wake Forest U., 1951; BDiv, Southeastern Bapt. Sem., Wake Forest, N.C., 1958; MA, Duke U., 1959, PhD, 1964. Prof. history and govt. Gardner-Webb U., Boiling Springs, N.C., 1958-66; prof. history, govt. and interdisciplinary studies St. Andrews Presbyn. Coll., Laurinburg, N.C., 1966-69; v.p., dean of coll., prof. history and politics Meredith Coll., Raleigh, N.C., 1969-98, ret., 1998, acting pres., 1971. Contbr. articles to profl. jours. Precinct ofcr. State Conv. del., N.C. Dem. Party, 1969, 71; pres., dir. Tammy Lynn Found./Retarded Children, Raleigh, 1980—; chmn. Raleigh Hist. Dists. Commn., 2000-2001. Lt. USNR, 1951-55, Italy and Atlantic Fleet. Recipient Disting. Alumni award Wingate U., 1983, Fulbright Study Trip, U.S. Govt., Pakistan, 1973, Study Trip USSR, 1988, Rsch. Brit. Mus. and Libr., 1963, 97. Mem. Civitan Internat. (v.p. bd. dirs. 1970—), Lions Club (editor 1965), Masons. Baptist. Avocations: choral singing, tennis, racquetball, golf, sailing, gardening. Home: 1322 Duplin Rd Raleigh NC 27607-3721 Office: Meredith Coll 3800 Hillsborough St Raleigh NC 27607-5237

BURRIS, JAMES FREDERICK, federal research administrator, educator; b. Mauston, Wis., Apr. 15, 1947; s. James Duane and Margaret Katherine (Jones) B.; m. Christine Tuve, July 3, 1971; 1 child, Cameron William Tuve. AB, ScB, Brown U., 1970; MD, Columbia U., 1974. Diplomate Am. Bd. Internal Medicine, Subspecialty Bd. Geriatrics, Am. Bd. Clin. Pharmacology. Intern Roosevelt Hosp., N.Y.C., 1974-75; resident in internal medicine Georgetown U. Med. Ctr., Washington, 1977-79; fellow in hypertension VA Med. Ctr., Washington, 1979-81; asst. prof. Sch. Medicine, Georgetown U., Washington, 1981-86, assoc. prof., 1986-91, coord. MD/PhD program, 1988-94, prof., 1991-97; clin. prof., 1997—; asst. dean Sch. Medicine, Georgetown U., Washington, 1987-90; assoc. dean Sch. Medicine Georgetown U., 1990-97, dir. continuing profl. edn., 1994-97; dep. chief R&D officer Vets. Health Adminstrn., U.S. Dept. Vets Affairs, Washington, 1997—2003; chief cons. Geriatrics and Extended Care, Vets. Health Adminstrn, US Dept. Vets. Affairs, Washington, 2003—. Bd. dirs. Inst. for Clin. Rsch., Washington, 1989-92; bd. regents Am. Bd. Clin. Pharmacology, 1992-98, 2002—; rsch. adminstr. cert. coun.; rsch. assoc. hypertension unit VA Med. Ctr., Washington, 1981-92; vis. investigator Centre Hospitalier, U. Vaudois, Lausanne, Switzerland, 1982-83; dir. clin. rsch. Cardiovasc. Ctr. No. Va., Falls Church, 1988-92; under-sec. health's exec. performance award U.S. Dept. of Vet. Affairs, 1999, 2000, Commendation award, 2003-. Mem. editl. bd. Jour. Clin. Pharmacology, Jour. Am. Geriat. Soc., Clin. Pharmacology and Therapeutics; contbr. over 250 articles to profl. jours. Cubmaster Boy Scouts Am., 1995-98, asst. scoutmaster, 1998—. Lt. comdr. USPHS, 1975-77 (active duty), 1977-(inactive reserve). Recipient svc. award ARC, 1970, outstanding svc. citation DAV, 1987, meritorious svc. award Am. Heart Assn., 1994, Cubmasters award Boy Scouts Am., 1998, James E. West award, 1997, Scouter's Tng. Key award, 2000, Vicennial medal Georgetown U., 2000; commd. officer student tng. and extern program scholar USPHS, 1973-74; rsch. fellow Found. for Rsch. of Cardiovascular Diseases, Lausanne, 1983. Fellow: ACP, Am. Coll. Cardiology, Am. Coll. Clin. Pharmacology (bd. regents 1990—95, 1998—2003, hon. regent 2003, Disting. Svc. award 1992), Am. Coll. Preventive Medicine, Am. Geriatrics Soc.; mem.: AMA (physician's recognition award 1982, 1985, 1988, 1991, 1994, 1997, 2001), Am. Heart Assn. (chmn. rsch. peer rev. com. 1992—94, rsch. com. 1994—96, bd. dirs. Nation's Capital affiliate 1994—97, v.p. 1995—96, fellow couns. on high blood pressure rsch., circulation, epidemiology, coun. clin. cardiology), Sigma Xi. Achievements include education and research in hypertension, hyperlipidemia, preventive cardiology and clinical pharmacology; grants and contracts management and regulatory affairs and technology transfer administration; direction of continuing professional education programs; federal clinical and research policy development and program implementation. Office: Vets Health Adminstrn (114) Dept VA 810 Vermont Ave NW Washington DC 20420-0001 E-mail: james.burris@hq.med.va.gov.

BURRIS, JOHN EDWARD, academic administrator, biologist, educator; b. Feb. 1, 1949; s. Robert Harza and Katherine (Brusse) Burris; m. Sally Ann Sandermann, Dec. 21, 1974; children: Jennifer, Margaret, Mary. AB, Harvard U., 1971; postgrad., U. Wis., 1971—72; PhD, U. Calif., San Diego, 1976. Asst. prof. biology Pa. State U., University Park, 1976—83, assoc. prof. biology, 1983—85, adj. assoc. prof., 1985—89, adj. prof., 1989—2001; pres. Beloit College, Beloit, Wis., 2000—. Dir. bd. biology NRC, Washington, 1984—89; exec. dir. Commn. Life Scis., 1988—92, mem., 1993—97; dir., CEO Marine Biol. Lab., Woods Hole, Mass., 1992—2000; pres.-elect Am. Inst. Biol. Scis., 1995, pres., 96; chmn. adv. com. student sci. enrichment program Burroughs Wellcome Fund, 1995—2002; life and microgravity scis. and applications adv. com. NASA, 1997—2001; trustee Krasnow Inst., 1999—2002; bd. dirs. Radiation Effects Rsch. Found., Wis. Found. Ind. Colls. Trustee Grass Found., 2001—. Mem.: AAAS (bd. dirs. 2002—), Naples Stazione Zoologica, Consiglio Sci., Phi Beta Kappa. Office: 700 College St Beloit WI 53511 E-mail: burrisj@beloit.edu.*

BURROUGHS, BLANCHE EDWINA, retired elementary school educator; b. Grand Rapids, Minn., Feb. 7, 1934; d. John Charles and Dorothy Lucille (Doran) Kopitke; m. George Bouschor, June 4, 1956 (div. Dec. 1959); m. Robert Raymond Burroughs, Dec. 1959); children: Bradley, Barbara, Brian. BA magna cum laude, Hamline U., 1956. Cert. elem. tchr. 2d grade tchr. Manistique (Mich.) Pub. Schs., 1956-58; 6th and 7th grade tchr. St. Paul Pub. Schs., 1958-64, 65-66; 2d grade tchr. Manchester (Conn.) Pub. Schs., 1968; 3d and 6th grade tchr. St. Paul Pub. Schs., 1970—96. Mem. adv. bd. Twin City Area Writing Project, St. Paul, 1980-85, Environ. Learning Ctr., Isabella and Finland, Minn., 1984-88; tchr. educator Tchr. Expectations Student Achievement, St. Paul, 1990-96; facilitator Who Are We? program, St. Paul, 1990-96. Mem. ASCD, City of St. Paul Edn. Assn. Republican. United Methodist. Avocations: golf, bridge, church youth work, Appalachia svc. project, Habitat for Humanity. Home: 2309 Taft St NE Minneapolis MN 55418-4131

BURROUGHS, TAMMY WESTBERRY, elementary education educator; b. Jesup, Ga., Aug. 28, 1961; d. Bryant L. and Annette (Taylor) Westberry; m. Nick Allen Burroughs, July 25, 1987. BS, Valdosta (Ga.) State Coll., 1983, MS, 1985, EdS in Early Childhood Edn., 1992; MS in Administrn., West Ga. State U., EdS in Administrn., 1993. Tchr. Pine Grove Elem. Sch., Valdosta, 1983-87, Lake Harbin Elem. Sch., Morrow, Ga., 1987—93; asst. prin. Riverdale Elem. Sch., Ga., 1993—2000; prin. McGarrah Elem. Sch., Morrow, Ga., 2000—. Baptist. Home: 140 Windsong Dr Stockbridge GA 30281-6421 Office: McGarrah Elem Sch 2201 Lake Harbin Rd Morrow GA 30260

BURROWAY, JANET G. English language educator, novelist; b. Phoenix, Sept. 21, 1936; m. Walter Eysselinck, 1961 (div. 1973); children: Timothy Alan, Tobyn Alexander; m. William Dean Humphries, 1978 (div. 1981); m. Peter Ruppert, 1993. AB cum laude, Barnard Coll., 1958; BA with honors, Cambridge U., 1960, MA, 1965; student, Yale Sch. Drama, 1960-61. Instr. English Harpur Coll., Binghamton, N.Y., 1961-62; lectr. U. Sussex, Eng., 1965-70; assoc. prof. English Fla. State U., Tallahassee, 1972-77, prof. English, 1976-86, McKenzie prof. English, 1986-95, Robert O. Lawton Disting. prof., 1995—2002, emerita, 2002—. Vis. lectr. U. Iowa, 1980, Carolyn Benton Cockefair Disting. Writer in Residence U. Mo., 1995. Author: Descend Again, 1960, The Dancer from the Dance, 1965, Eyes, 1966, The Buzzards, 1970, The Truck on the Track, 1970, The Giant Jam Sandwich, 1972, Raw Silk, 1976, Writing Fiction, 1982, 6th edit., 2002, Opening Nights, 1985, Cutting Stone, 1992, Medea with Child, 1997, Sweepstakes, 1999, Embalming Mom, 2002, Imaginative Writing, 2002; fiction reviewer New Statesman mag., London, 1970-71, 75, Phila. Inquirer, 1986—, N.Y. Times Book Rev., 1990—; author numerous poems and short stores; contbr. articles to profl. jours. Bd. dirs. Assoc. Writing Programs Am., 1987-90, v.p., 1988-89. Scholar U. Ariz., Elk's Club, KP, 1954-55, Barnard Coll. Alumni, 1955-58, Marshall, 1958-60; fellow RCA/NBA, 1960-61, Nat. Endowment Arts, 1976, Yaddo Residency, 1985, 87, Lila Wallace Reader's Digest fellow, 1994-95; grantee Fla. Fine Arts Coun., 1983-84. Office: Fla State U Dept English Tallahassee FL 32306-1580 E-mail: jburroway@english.fsu.edu.

BURROWS, BERTHA JEAN, retired academic administrator; b. Brush, Colo., June 15, 1930; d. John and Marie Pabst; m. Leslie R. Burrows, Sept. 2, 1951; children: Paul Eric, Amy Susan, Julie Diane, David Arthur. BA in Bus., U. Colo., 1952. Sec. Dental Found. Colo., Denver, 1969—70, John Boswick, MD, Denver, 1970—72; adminstrv. cons. dept. contg. edn. U. Colo. Sch. Dentistry, Denver, 1975—76; asst. dir. vol. svcs. U. Colo. Health Sci. Ctr., 1977—80; sec. Denver Neurosurg. Assn., Denver, 1981—83, ret., 1983. Part-time bookkeeper Clark & Co., Denver, 1981—83; mem. various coms. U. Colo. Hosp., Denver, 1999—. Vol. U. Colo. Hosp., Denver, 1970—; treas. U. Colo. Hosp. Gift Shop, 1997—, bd. mgrs., 1987—. Mem.: Colo. Assn. Healthcare Auxilians and Vols. (treas. 2000—01, chmn. gift shop 2002—03, pres.-elect 2003—), U. Colo. Srs. Assn. (pres. 2002—). Home: 6911 E Iliff Place Denver CO 80224

BURROWS, ELIZABETH MACDONALD, religious organization executive, educator; b. Portland, Oreg., Jan. 30, 1930; d. Leland R. and Ruth M. (Frew) MacDonald. Certificate, Chinmaya Trust Sandeepany, Bombay; PhD (hon.), Internat. U. Philosophy and Sci., 1975; ThD, Christian Coll. Universal Peace, 1992. Ordained to ministry First Christian Ch., 1976. Mgr. credit Home Utilities, Seattle, 1958, Montgomery Ward, Crescent City, Calif., 1963; supr. Oreg. dist. tng. West Coast Tele., Beaverton, 1965; pres. Christ Ch. of Universal Peace, Seattle, 1971—, prof. religion, also bd. dirs.; pres. Archives Internat., Seattle, 1971—; v.p. James Tyler Kent Inst. Homeopathy, 1984-95; sec. Louis Braille Inst. for the Blind, 1995—. Author: Crystal Planet, 1979, Pathway of the Immortal, 1980, Odyssey of the Apocalypse, 1981, Harp of Destiny, 1984, Commentary for Gospel of Peace of Jesus Christ According to John, 1986, Seasons of the Soul, 1995, Voyagers of the Sand, 1996, The Song of God, 1998, Hold the Anchovies, 1996, Pilgrim of the Shadow, 1998, Maya Sangh and the Valley of the White Ones, 2001, The Secret Jesus Scroll, 2002, Poetry Chapbook, 2002, Visions, 2002, Maya Sangh and the Valley of the White One. Recipient Pres. award for literary excellence CADER, 1994, 95, 97, Diamond Homer award Famous Poets Soc., 1998, Pub.'s Choice award Poets of the New Era, 2002. Mem. Internat. Speakers Platform, Internat. New Thought Alliance, Cousteau Soc., Internat. Order of Chivalry, The Planetary Soc. Home: 10529 Ashworth Ave N Seattle WA 98133-8937 E-mail: Starbase2001@earthlink.net.

BURSLEY-HAMILTON, SUSAN, secondary school educator; b. Redbank, N.J., May 6, 1955; d. Robert Kelly and Irene Magdolin (Connell) Bursley; m. Raymond Hamilton, June 20, 1981; 1 child, Robert. BA in Edn., No. Ariz. U., 1978, MA, 1988. Asst. prin. Kingman Jr. High Sch., Ariz. Order Eastern Star scholar. Mem. Am. Fedn. Tchrs.

BURSTEIN, JOYCE HOPE, elementary education educator; b. San Jose, Calif., Jan. 12, 1960; d. Carroll Jay and Olivia (Chang) Biggerstaff; m. Steven Michael Burstein, Mar. 26, 1988; children: Alexander, Cameron,

Natalie. AA, West Valley Coll., 1980; BA, UCLA, 1984; MA with honors, U. Calif., Northridge, 1995. Tchr. elem. sch. L.A. Unified Sch. Dist., 1987-92; tchr. elem. sch., curriculum writer social studies Stephen S. Wise Elem. Sch., L.A., 1992-94; elem. tchr., portfolio specialist Burton St. Sch., Panorama City, Calif., 1994—. Cons. in field. Recipient Bank of Am. Music award, San Jose, 1978. Mem. Nat. Coun. Tchrs. English, Nat. Coun. for Social Studies, UCLA Alumni Assn. Avocation: violin. Home: 24143 Highlander Rd West Hills CA 91307-1243

BURSTYN, JOAN NETTA, education educator; b. Leicester, Eng., Mar. 6, 1929; d. David Edward and Nellie (Wachman) Jacobs; m. Harold L. Burstyn, Aug. 19, 1958; children: Judith, Gail, Daniel. BA with honors, U. London, 1950, cert. of edn., 1952, acad. diploma in edn., 1958, PhD, 1968. Tchg. fellow edn. Harvard U., Cambridge, Mass., 1959-64; lectr. U. Pitts., 1967; lectr. psychology and edn. Carnegie Mellon U., Pitts., 1967-68, instr., 1968, asst. prof., 1969-74, dir. tchr. edn., 1970-74; assoc. prof., chairperson dept. edn. Douglass Coll., Rutgers U., New Brunswick, N.J., 1974-81, prof. edn., 1981-85, dir. women's studies program, 1981-85; dean sch. edn. Syracuse (N.Y.) U., 1986-89, prof. cultural founds. of edn. and of history, 1986—2003, sr. rsch. assoc., 2002—03, dir. violence prevention project, 1997-98, prof. emeritus, rsch. prof. edn., 2003—. Co-dir. Fund for Improvement of Post-Secondary Edn. Grant, 1983-85; vis. prof. Monash U., Australia, summer 1989; Emens disting. prof. Ball State U., 1996; dir. Nat. Endowment for Humanities Pilot grant, 1980-82; seminar rsch. assoc., Syracuse (N.Y.) U., 2002-03 Author: Song Cycle, 1976, Victorian Education and the Ideal of Womanhood, 1980, Waiting for the Lame Horse, 1987; co-author: Preventing Violence in Schools: A Challenge to American Democracy, 2001; editor: Preparation for Life?, 1986, Desktop Publishing in the University, 1991, Educating Tomorrow's Valuable Citizen, 1996; editor-in-chief Past and Promise: Lives of New Jersey Women, 1990; contbr. articles to profl. jours.; assoc. editor Signs: Jour. of Women in Culture and Soc., 1974—80; mem. editl. bd.: Jour. Women in Culture and Soc., 1980—89, History of Edn. Quar, 1982—86, History of Higher Edn. Ann., 1989—, Issues in Edn., 1983—87, Syracuse U. Press, 1991—94, Ednl. Founds., 2000—, Jour. Sch. Violence, 2001—. Mem. adv. bd. nurse-midwifery ednl. program U. Medicine and Dentistry N.J., 1978-83; bd. dirs. Children's Sch. Sci., Woods Hole, Mass., 1977-80; assoc. dir. N.E. Council Women in Devel., 1981-82; mem. joint com. Am. Hist. Assn. and Can. Hist. Assn., 1978-81. Recipient grant-in-aid John F. Kennedy Sch. Govt. and Bunting Inst., 1964-65; Marion Talbot fellow AAUW, 1965-66; recipient Faculty Merit award Rutgers U., 1977, 81. Fellow AAAS; mem. AAUW, Am. Hist. Assn., Am. Ednl. Rsch. Assn. (com. on freedom of inquiry and human rights 1984-86, pubs. com. 1986-89), History of Edn. Soc. U.S. (pres. 1985-86), Am. Ednl. Studies Assn. (chmn. publs. com. 1984-85, v.p. 1993-94, pres.-elect 1994-95, pres. 1995-96). Office: Syracuse U Sch Edn 350 Huntington Hl Syracuse NY 13244-0001 E-mail: jburstyn@syr.edu.

BURT, AURELIA THOMAS, educational administrator, middle school consultant; b. Balt., Jan. 9, 1937; d. Wade Purcell and Caroline Catherine (Brown) Thomas; m. Richard C. Burt, Oct. 10, 1959; children: David Richard, Thomas Barrington. BA, U. Md., 1959; MEd, Loyola Coll., Balt., 1968. Tchr. Balt. City Pub. Schs., 1959-60, St. Louis Pub. Schs., 1960-62, Framingham (Mass.) Pub. Schs., 1962-63; tchr., adminstr. Roland Park Country Sch., Balt., 1965-93; adminstr. Notre Dame Prep. Sch., Balt., 1993—; counselor, cons. St. Ignatius Loyola Acad., Balt., 1993—. Evaluator Blue Ribbon Schs. Program, Dept. Edn., Washington, 1993—; evaluator Mid. State Assn., Assn. Ind. Schs., Mid-Atlantic States, 1982—; workshop leader, cons. schs. in U.S. and Japan, 1984—. Edn. chairperson Balt.-Kawasaki Sister City Com., Balt., 1984-94; co-founder, bd. dirs. Parents Coun. Balt., 1983-92; mem. adv. bd. Solomon Schecter Sch., Balt., 1990-92. Mem. Assn. Ind. Md. Schs. (pres. 1981-82, dir. beginning tchrs. inst. 1993—), Nat. Assn. Ind. Schs. (elem. and mid. schs. com. 1984-88, conf. presenter 1984, Workshop Leader), Nat. Mid. Sch. Assn. Roman Catholic. Avocations: traveling, tennis, golf, reading.

BURT, ROBERT AMSTERDAM, lawyer, educator; b. Phila., Feb. 3, 1939; s. Samuel Matthew and Esther (Amsterdam) B.; m. Linda Gordon Rose, June 14, 1964; children: Anne Elizabeth, Jessica Ellen. AB, Princeton U., 1960; BA in Jurisprudence, Oxford (Eng.) U., 1962, MA, 1968; JD, Yale U., 1964, MA (hon.), 1976. Bar: D.C. 1966, Mich. 1973, U.S. Supreme Ct. 1971. Law clk. to chief judge U.S. Ct. Appeals D.C., 1964-65; asst. gen. counsel Office President's Spl. Rep. Trade Negotiations, 1965-66; senatorial legis. asst., 1966-68; assoc. prof. law U. Chgo. Law Sch., 1968-70; assoc. prof., then prof. law U. Mich. Law Sch., 1970-76; prof. law in psychiatry U. Mich. Med. Sch., 1973-76; Southmayd prof. Yale U. Law Sch., 1976-93, Alexander M. Bickel prof., 1993—. Spl. master U.S. Dist. Ct. Conn., 1987-92, 95. Bd. dirs. Benhaven Sch. Autistic Persons, New Haven, 1977—, chmn., 1983-96; bd. dirs. Judge David L. Bazelon Ctr. for Mental Health Law, 1985—, chmn., 1990-2000; mem. adv. bd. Project on Death in Am., Open Soc. Inst., 1994—; bd. dirs. Slifka Ctr. for Jewish Life at Yale, 1996—. Rockefeller fellow, 1976, John Simon Guggenheim fellow, 1997-98. Mem. Inst. Medicine (coun. 1992-94). Democrat. Jewish. Home: 66 Dogwood Cir Woodbridge CT 06525-1254 Office: Yale U Sch Law PO Box 208215 127 Wall St New Haven CT 06511-6636 E-mail: robert.burt@yale.edu.

BURTON, AMY JUNE, retired elementary education educator; b. Iva, S.C., June 14, 1936; d. Emory Goss and Olivia (Copeland) B. Assoc. Secretarial Sci., Anderson (S.C.) Coll., 1960; BA in Edn., U. S.C., 1970, postgrad., 1971-92, Clemson U., 1972-93. Cert. elem. tchr., S.C. Adminstrv. asst./sec. S.C. Highway Dept., Anderson, 1960-63; adminstrv. asst./sec. S.C. Dept. Social Svcs., Anderson, 1963-67; 3rd grade tchr. Anderson Sch. Dist. 3, 1970-97, ret., 1997. Magnet homebound tchr., 1980-81; mem. math. com. Basic Skills Assessment Program, Office Rsch. S.C. Dept. Edn., 1979-84. Rschr. for pictorial history of Iva, S.C., 1998-99; tchr. Vacation Bible Sch. 1st Bapt. Ch. of Iva, 1981, 83, 84, Children's Sunday Sch., 1982-84, Adult Sunday Sch., 1974-76; ch. clk. 1st Bapt. Ch. Iva, 1965-67; sec./genealogist Burton Reunion Com., 1972, 1991-2003. Mem.: Ret. Tchrs. Assn. Anderson County, S.C. Avocations: gardening, sewing, music, travel, genealogy. Home: 627 W W Burton Rd Iva SC 29655-8802

BURTON, BARRY LAWSON, librarian, educator; b. Ulverston, Cumbria, Eng., Dec. 30, 1942; s. William Lawson and Runah (Sandwell) B.; m. Wendy Fay Monks, Dec. 4, 1970 (dec. Oct. 1997); children: Jodi, Nigel Robin, Simon Lawson. BA, U. Keele, 1965. Reference office Flinders U., Australia, 1966-67; chief libr. Salisbury Coll. Advanced Edn., 1968-71; dep. univ. libr. Makerere U., Uganda, 1972; libr. Hong Kong Polytechnic U., 1973—. Pres. Internat. Fedn. for Info. and Documentation, Commn. for Asia and Oceania, 1981-88. Editor Directory of Professional Associations and Learned Societies in Hong Kong, 1988—; contbr. articles to profl. jours. Mem. Hong Kong Libr. Assn. (chmn. 1975), Libr. Assn. Australia (assoc.), Chartered Mgmt. Inst., Chartered Inst. Libr. and Info. Profls., Hong Kong Wine Soc. (chmn. 1983—). Avocation: wine judging. Home: 1811 Convention Plaza Apts 1 Harbour Rd Wanchai Hong Kong Office: Hong Kong Polytech U Univ Librarian Kowloon Hong Kong E-mail: lbbarry@polyu.edu.hk.

BURTON, ERLIE P. academic administrator; b. Walnut Ridge, Ark., Mar. 1, 1926; s. George Washburne and Ollie Maya (Brandon) Patterson; m. William Herman Burton, July 24, 1949; children: William, Marcus, Craig, Robin. AA with honors, Loop Coll., 1964; BS with honors, Chgo. State U., 1966; MEd., Loyola U., 1968. Distbn. clk. U.S. Post Office, Chgo., 1959-65; math. tchr. Chgo. Bd. Edn., 1966-68, adjustment tchr., 1968-69; asst. prof. behavioral scis. Malcolm X Coll., Chgo., 1969-75, chairperson, 1975-77, acting dean arts sci., 1977-78, chairperson behavioral sci., 1978—. Cons. MEBS, Inc. Chgo., 1977—; v.p. Soon & Burton Internat. Traders, 1979-83. Mem. Jackson Park Highlands Assn., 1967, Women's Dem. Network, Chgo. 1983—, Women to Save South Shore, 1987, Mothers Against Drunk Drivers, Alliance Against Intoxicated Motorists, 1989, Nat. Trust for Hist. Preservation, 1989, Nat. Geographic Soc., 1989, Ill. Pub. Action Campaign for Toxic Safety, 1989. Mem. Am. Fed. Tchrs., Ill. Fed. Tchrs., Am. Assn. Retired Persons, Cook County Coll. Tchrs. Union, Nat. Coun. Negro Women, Anthropology Club, Magnificant 7 Club. Presbyterian. Avocations: antiquing, gardening, reading, writing, poetry, interior decorating. Home: 6737 S Cregier Ave Chicago IL 60649-1019 Office: Malcolm X Coll Dept Behavioral Sci 1900 W Van Buren St Chicago IL 60612-3145

BURTON, JOHN BRYAN, music educator; b. Lubbock, Tex., Nov. 10, 1948; s. John Clark and Geraldine (Wolf) B. B in Music Edn., West Tex. State U., 1970; MA, Western State Coll. Colo., 1973; D in Music Edn., U. So. Miss., 1986. Dir. bands, humanities Jal (N.Mex.) Schs., 1978-79; dir. bands, gen. music Bronte (Tex.) Schs., 1979-80; dir. bands Comfort (Tex.) Schs., 1980-82; dir. high sch. band, music coord. Kirbyville (Tex.) Ind. Schs., 1982-84; grad. asst. U. So. Miss., Hattiesburg, 1984-86; asst. prof. music, dir. bands, music theatre dir. Frostburg (Md.) State U., 1986-91; prof. music edn. West Chester (Pa.) Univ., 1991—, coord. grad. studies, 1997—, dir. post baccalaureate tchr. cert. program, 2001—. Panelist Symposium on Native Am. Musics, Coll. Music Soc. 33d Nat. Meeting, Washington, 1990; curriculum cons. Prince Georges County Schs., Upper Marlboro, Md., 1991, other Mid-Atlantic schs.; guest condr. Allegany County Honor Band, Tri-State Honor Band, 1986-87, Allegany County Band, Bedford County Band, Mineral County Band, 1987-88, Allegany Solo and Ensemble Festival Harford County Intermediate Bands Festival, 1990-91; presenter conf. Ea. divsn. Music Educators Nat. Conf., 1993, 95, 97, 99, 2001, 03, So. divsn., 1994, Internat. Kodaly Soc. Conf., Am. Orff-Schulwerk Assn., Orff 100 Internat. Conf. on Music and Dance, Melbourne, Australia, 1995, Internat. Soc. for Music Edn., Amsterdam, 1996, Internat. Soc. for Music Edn. Commn. on Cmty. Music Making, Liverpool, 1996, many others; lectr. nat. meeting Music Educators Nat. Conf., 1992, 94, 96; cons. Native Am. music, 1993, 94, nat. chair, editor Social Scis. Rsch. Group Soc. for Rsch. in Music Edn., 1994-96; edit. adv. bd. mem. Tchg. Music, 1996-98; keynote lectr. World Conf. Internat. Soc. Music Edn., 1994, 96, 98, 2000, 01, 02; mem. ISME Commn. on cmty. music activity, Durban, South Africa, 1998; mem. exec. bd. Soc. for Music Tchr. Edn. (ea. rep.), 1998—; presenter and lectr. in field; vis. prof. U. Washington, 1995, Ga. State U., 1995, Trenton State Coll., 1996, U. Okla., 1996, U. Nebr., 1997, U. Sioux Falls, 1997, Rider U., 1998. Assoc. editor: Scholars, 1994-2001; author: moving Within the Circle: Contemporary Native American Music and Dance, 1993, Music of the Minority Nationalities of the People's Republic of China, 1989, When the Earth Was Like New: Songs and Stories of the Western Apache, 1994, Songs of A Living Apache Tradition: The Musical Life of Chesley Goseyun Wilson, 1994, (with Maria P. Kreiter) Native American Flute Music, 1997; co-author: Welcome to Mussomeli: Italian Children's Songs, 1999; contbg. author: Multicultural Perspectives in Music Education, 2d edit., 1996, Getting Started with Teaching Multicultural Music, 1996, Making Connections: Multicultural Traditions and the National Standards in Music Education, 1996, Strategies for Teaching: General Music K-4, 1996, Strategies for Teaching: General Music 5-8, 1996, Strategies for Teaching: General Music 9-12, 1996, Strategies for Teaching: Beginning and Middle Level Band Grades 5-8, 1996, Strategies for Teaching: High School Band, 1996, Strategies for Teaching: College Methods Class, 1996, Strategies for Teaching: High School Chorus, 1996, Many Seeds, Different Flowers--The Music Education Legacy of Carl Orff, 1997, On the Sociology of Music Education, 1997; mem. editl. bd. Music Edn. Internat., 2001--; contbr. songs to World of Children's Song, 1993, lessons and photographs to The Music Connection, 1995, songs and lessons to Share the Music, 1995, World Music and Music Education: Facing the Issue, 2002, Making Music (classroom music texttbook series), song transcriptions to OAKE Multicultural Songs, Dances and Games, 1995, articles to profl. jours. Mem. Nat. Band Assn., Music Educators Nat. Conf. (presenter nat. meeting 1992, 94, 96, 98, 2000, 2002), Australia Soc. Music Educators, Pa. Music Educators Assn., Coll. Band Dirs. Nat. Assn., Coll. Music Soc., Soc. for Ethnomusicology (chair edn. com. 1999—), Associated Photographers Internat., Audubon Soc., Amnesty Internat., Phi Mu Alpha, Alpha Chi, Kappa Delta Pi, Kappa Kappa Psi. Avocations: photography, travel, gardening. Home: 441 Webb Rd Chadds Ford PA 19317-9125 Office: West Chester U Sch Music West Chester PA 19383-0001 E-mail: jburton3@wcupa.edu.

BURTON, JUNE ROSALIE KEHR, history educator; b. North Wildwood, N.J., June 19, 1941; d. Harry Ludwick and Mary Laura (Hawk) Kehr. AB, Stetson U., 1965, MA, 1967; PhD, U. Ga., 1971; LLD (hon.), Stetson U., 1992. Workshop leader high sch. tchrs. advanced placement course in European history Ednl. Testing Svcs., Princeton, N.J.; lic. real estate agt., Ohio. Tchr. New Smyrna Beach (Fla.) High Sch., 1966-67; teaching asst. dept. history U. Ga., Athens, 1968-71; prof. history U. Akron, Ohio, 1971-94, prof. emeritus, 1994. Akron rep. to the faculty adv. com. to the Chancellor of the Ohio Bd. Regents, 1990-94; adv. com. to the Pres. of the U. Akron, 1992-93; AP cons. Coll. Bd. AP, Princeton, N.J.; workshop presenter in field. Author: Napoleon and Clio, 1979; assoc. editor: Historical Dictionary of Napoleonic France, 1985; editor: Essays in European History, Vol. 1, 1989, Vol. II, 1995, Adrienne Lafayette as Medical Patient, 1999; contbg. editor Napoleon Mag., 1996-98; assoc. editor Napoleon Jour., 1998-2001; contbr. articles to profl. jours. Recipient Legion of Merit, Internat. Napoleonic Soc., 1999, Svc. Award, Enno Kraehe, 2000; Ford M.A.-3 fellow, Stetson U., 1964—67, Humanities grantee, Rockefeller Found., 1976—78, Dorothy Danforth Compton fellow, Inst. Study World Politics, 1977—78. Mem.: AAUP (chpt. pres. 1978, 1988), European History Sect. (chmn. book prize com. 1995, 2002, chmn. 1992, nominating com. 1983—84), So. Hist. Assn. (exec. coun. 1989—92, nominating com. 1995). Methodist. Avocation: painting. Home: 64 Waldorf Dr Akron OH 44313-6226

BURTON, KAY FOX, retired secondary education educator, guidance counselor; b. Ottawa, Ill., Jan. 4, 1938; d. Andrew Owen and Hattie L. (Rasmusson) Fox; m. Edward John Burton, Dec. 26, 1966. BA, St. Xavier U., Chgo., 1960; MEd, Loyola U., Chgo., 1967. Instr. math. Coll. of St. Benedict, St. Joseph, Minn., 1960-61; tchr. math. Gage Park High Sch., Chgo., 1962-74; tchr., coord. math. dept. Westmont (Ill.) High Sch., 1974-94, coll. counselor, 1980-90, ret., 1994. Counselor Coll. of DuPage, Glen Ellen, Ill., 1982-83. Contbg. author Elementary Mathematics Series, 1964-68. Mem. NEA, Nat. Coun. Tchrs. Math., Ill. Coun. Tchrs. Math., Ill. Assn. Coll. Admissions Counselors, Ill. Edn. Assn. (chpt. treas. 1986-90), Delta Kappa Gamma (v.p. Beta Phi chpt. 1990-92, treas. 2001—). Roman Catholic. Avocations: collecting advertising rulers and antique mathematics books, travel. Home: 5S 517 Allison Ln Naperville IL 60540

BURTON, RICHARD IRVING, orthopedist, educator; b. Providence, Sept. 18, 1936; s. Kenneth Gould and Edith Irving (Vayro) B.; m. Margaret Ann Leaman, Apr. 5, 1961; children: Thomas Kenneth, Douglas Leaman. BA, Amherst Coll., 1958; MD, Harvard U., 1962. Diplomate Am. Bd. Orthopaedic Surgery (examiner 1980—, bd. dirs. 1989-98). Intern U. Rochester, N.Y., 1962-63, resident in surgery, 1963-64; resident in orthopedic surgery Harvard U., 1966-70; fellow in hand surgery Roosevelt Hosp., N.Y.C., 1970-71; asst. prof. Cleve. Clinic Found., 1971-72, head sect. surgery of hand, 1971-74, assoc. prof., 1973-74; mem. faculty U. Rochester Med. Sch., 1974—, head sect. surgery of hand, 1974—2003, prof. orthopedics, 1979—, Marjorie Strong Wehle prof. orthopedics, 1995-2000, dean's prof., 2000—02, assoc. chmn. dept. orthopedics, 1981-88, chmn., 1988—2000, acting chmn. dept. neurol. surgery, 2000—02, sr. assoc. dean for acad. affairs, 2002—; sr. assoc. orthopedist Strong Meml. Hosp., Rochester, 1974-79, orthopedist, 1979—; sr. assoc. dean for acad. affairs U. Rochester Med. Sch., 2002—. Chmn. cert. of added qualifications com. Am. Bd. Orthopaedic Surgery, 1994-98. Assoc. editor Jour. Hand Surgery, 1980-84; contbr. articles to profl. jours., chpts. to books. Mem. exec. com. Monroe County chpt. Am. Arthritis Found., 1983-86; elder Presbyn. Ch. Buswell Disting. Svc. fellow, U. rochester, 1980-81. Recipient Exec. of Yr. award Profl. Secs. Internat., Flower City chpt., 1981. Mem. ACS, AAAS, Am. Acad. Orthopedic Surgeons (chmn. hand and wrist com. 1986-89, orthopedic resources com. 1989-91), Am. Bd. Orthop. Surgery (dir. 1988-98), Am. Bd. Med. Specialties (voting rep. 1995-98), Am. Soc. Surgery of the Hand (coord. divsn. edn. 1982-85, coun. 1985-89, chmn. membership com. 1991, v.p. 1990, pres.-elect 1991, pres. 1992), Am. Orthopedic Assn. (exec. com. 1986, resident rsch. conf. com. 1987-89, chair 1989, membership com. 1989-92, chmn. 1992, exec. com. 1992, forward planning com. 1996-99), Interurban Orthopedic Soc., Am. Rheumatism Assn., Eastern Orthopedic Assn., Monroe County Med. Soc., N.Y. State Med. Soc., Rochester Acad. Medicine, Rochester Orthopedic Soc., Soc. N.Y. State Orthopedic Surgeons, J. William Littler Soc., Amherst Alumni Assn., Harvard U. Med. Sch. Alumni Assn. Home: 7869 Hidden Oak Pittsford NY 14534-9607 Office: U Rochester Med Ctr Deans Office Box 706 601 Elmwood Ave Rochester NY 14642-0001

BURTON, SHARON ILENE, elementary educator; b. Spencer, W.Va., Mar. 31, 1945; d. Nolan and Gladys (Drake) Foglesong; m. Donald Duane Burton, June 17, 1970. AB magna cum laude, Glenville State Coll., 1967; AM, W.Va. U., 1971. Cert. tchr., W.Va. Tchr. 1st and 4th grades McKinley Elem. Sch., Parkersburg, W.Va., 1967-72; tchr. Chpt. I reading lab. Washington Jr. High Sch., Parkersburg, 1972-90; Chpt. I reading/math. specialist Tygart Elem. Sch., Parkersburg, 1990-93, Waverly (W.Va.) Elem. Sch., 1990-93; tchr. 3rd grade Franklin Elem. Ctr., Parkersburg, 1993—99, title 1, 1999—2001; ret., 2001. Mem. Wood County Reading Coun. (past chairperson pub. rels., pres., past v.p.), Am. Fedn. Tchrs., W.Va. Fedn. Tchrs. (past mem. exec. bd., sec.), Wood County Fedn. Tchrs. (sec.-treas.), Wood County Tchrs. Acad.

BURTON, SHARON K. primary education educator; b. Harlan, Ky., Apr. 2, 1965; d. Eugene and Imogene B. AAS in Bus. and Data Processing Tech., S.E. C.C., Cumberland, Ky., 1985; BS in Elem. Edn., Ea. Ky. U., 1988; MA in Elem. Edn., Morehead State U., 1990. Cert. Rank I Elem. Ed., Guidance, Counseling, 1991. Instrnl. asst. Letcher County Bd. Edn., Arlie Boggs Elem., Eolia, Ky., 1985-87; substitute tchr. Letcher County Bd. Edn., Whitesburg, Ky., 1987-89; 6th-8th health, spelling and phys. edn. tchr. Letcher County Bd. Edn., Cowan Elem., Whitesburg, 1989-90, remedial educator, 1990-92, ungraded primary educator, 1992—. Mem. tech. com. Letcher County Bd. Edn.-Cowan Elem., Whitesburg, 1992-96; participant Commonwealth Inst. for Tchrs. program Ky. Edn. Tech. Systems, 1993-94, Ky. Early Learning Profile Field Study, 1993-94; presenter in field. Storyteller, Tales from the Hills and Hollers group. Mem. Primary Club (media specialist 1992-93), Attendance Com., Textbook Adoption Com. 1993-94; primary liaison, 2002-; chairperson, Literacy Com., 2003-. Home: 15846 Highway 119 S Partridge KY 40862-6419

BURTON, VALERIE DIANE, elementary school educator; b. East Orange, N.J., Aug. 5, 1947; d. Theodore R.and Elsie E. (Brown) Smith; m. Clifford R. Burton, Oct. 18, 1969; children: Celeste, Corey, Victoria. BA, U. Pitts., 1969. Cert. elem. edn. and social studies tchr., N.J. Employment counselor State of N.J., Newark, 1970-71; tchr. Morris Sch. Dist., Morris Twp., N.J., 1972—. Multicultural specialist; adv. coun. rep. Morris Sch. Dist., Morristown, 1974-77, mem. negotiating team, 1981-85, elem. rep. social studies curriculum, 1985-86, gifted and talented rep., 1989-92; master tchr. summer intern, 1993. Feature writer Long Beach (Calif.) Times Newspaper, 1988. Mem. edn. com. Jack & Jill, Inc., Morris County, 1982—mem. parent adv. com. Morristown (N.J.) H.S., 1992—; tutor, ednl. liaison Neighborhood House Vols., 1993—; gospel chorus leader. Mem. ASCD, NAACP (edn. com. Morristown chpt. 1983-84), Urban League (edn. com. Morristown chpt. 1988-89), Delta Sigma Theta (mem. in-take com. 1990—, program com., Delteen mentoring chair). Democrat. Baptist. Avocations: bridge, bid whist, travel. Home: 21 Stonehenge Rd Morristown NJ 07960-2649

BURTT, ANNE DAMPMAN, special education educator; b. Phila., Nov. 22, 1950; d. Elmer and Anne (Scott) Dampman; m. James Burtt, Aug. 5, 1972. BS in Edn. cum laude, Duquesne U., 1972; MEd, U. Pitts., 1976, Temple U., 1985. Cert. spl. edn., elem. tchr., reading specialist. Tchr. Pitts. Pub. Schs., 1972-77; tchr. Montgomery County (Pa.) Intermediate Unit, 1997—2000, Archdiocese of Phila. Schs., 2000—; archdiocese Phila. Schs., 2000—. Mem. PTO, 1972—, Chpt. Attention Deficit Disorders, 1989—, CHADD Bux-Mont. Divsn., Behavioral Disorders/Learning Disorders. Recipient Pius X award Archdiocese Phila., Most Successful Grad. 25th Yr. Reunion West Phila. Cath. Girls' H.S. Mem. Pa. State Edn. Assn., Coun. for Exceptional Children, Behavior Disorders and Learning Disabilities. Home: 131 Maple Ave Willow Grove PA 19090-2902

BUSBEE, KLINE DANIEL, JR., law educator, lawyer; b. Macon, Ga., Mar. 14, 1933; s. Kline Daniel and Bernice (Anderson) B.; children: Rodgers Christopher, Jon Edward. BBA, So. Meth. U., 1961, JD, 1962. 70ptnr. Worsham, Forsythe, Sampels & Busbee, Dallas, 1962; ptnr. Locke, Purnell, Rain & Harrell, P.C., Dallas, 1970-98, Gibson, Dunn & Crutcher, Dallas, 1998-99. Adj. prof. law So. Meth. U. Sch. Law, 1974—83, 1992, 2003, sr. fellow Inst. Internat. Banking and Fin., 2001—; adj. prof. pub. internat. law U. Tex. Grad. Sch. Mgmt., Dallas; bd. dirs. Atmos Energy Corp.; vis. sr. fellow Ctr. for Comml. Law Studies, Queen Mary U. London, 2001—, Brit. Inst. Internat. and Comparative Law, Russell Sq., 2001—. Mem.: ABA, Dallas Com. on Fgn. Rels., Tex. Bar Assn., Dallas Petroleum Club, Snowmass Club, Dallas Country Club. Home: 4360 San Carlos St Dallas TX 75205-2052 E-mail: danbusbeelaw@msn.com.

BUSCH, BRITON COOPER, historian, educator; b. LA, Sept. 5, 1936; s. Niven and Phyllis (Cooper) B.; m. Deborah B. Stone, Aug. 16, 1958 (div. 1984); children: Philip Briton, Leslie Cooper; m. S. Jill Harsin, June 4, 1985. AB, Stanford U., 1958; MA, U. Calif. at Berkeley, 1960, PhD, 1965. Instr. Colgate U., 1963-65, asst. prof. history, 1965-68, assoc. prof. history, 1968-73, prof., 1973-78, William R. Kenan, Jr. prof., 1978—2003, dept. chmn., 1980-85, dir. div. social scis., 1985-91, William R. Kenen Jr. prof. emeritus, 2003—. Mem. coun. Internat. Commn. of Maritime History, 1996-2000. Author: Britain and the Persian Gulf, 1894-1914, 1967, Britain, India and the Arabs 1914-1921, 1971, Mudros to Lausanne: Britains Frontier in West Asia 1918-1923, 1976, Master of Desolation: The Reminiscences of Capt. Joseph J. Fuller, 1980, Hardinge of Penshurst: A Study in The Old Diplomacy, 1980, Alta California 1840-1842: The Journal and Observations of William Dane Phelps, Master of the Ship Alert, 1983; The War Against the Seals: A History of the North American Seal Fishery, 1985; Fremont's Private Navy: the 1846 Journal of Capt. W.D. Phelps, 1987, Whaling Will Never Do For Me: The American Whaleman in the 19th Century, 1994, (with B.M. Gough) Fur Traders From New England: The Boston Men, 1787-1800, 1996; editor: Canada and the Great War: Western Front Association Papers, 2003; book rev. editor Am. Neptune, 1991-2003. Woodrow Wilson fellow, 1963; Nat. Endowment for the Humanities fellow, 1967-68; Social Sci. Research Council fellow, 1968-69 Mem. Am. Hist. Assn., Royal Soc. Asian Affairs, Mid. East Inst., Mid. East Studies Assn., Western Front Assn., Soc. Mil. History (book prize com. 1996-98, chair 1998-2000), N.Am. Soc. Oceanic History (exec. coun. 1983-88, v.p. 1988-91, pres. 1991-92, 95-98, chmn. book award com. 1987-92, book prize 1984, 86, 94, 97). Home: PO Box 154 Hamilton NY 13346-0154 Office: Colgate U Dept History 13 Oak Dr Hamilton NY 13346-1383

BUSCH, FREDERICK MATTHEW, writer, literature educator; b. N.Y.C., Aug. 1, 1941; s. Benjamin and Phyllis (Schnell) B.; m. Judith

Burroughs, Nov. 29, 1963; children: Benjamin, Nicholas. BA, Muhlenberg Coll., Allentown, Pa., 1962, LittD (hon.), 1980; MA, Columbia U., 1967. Writer for mags., N.Y.C., and Greenwich, Conn., 1966—; from instr. to prof. Colgate U., Hamilton, N.Y., 1966-87, Fairchild prof. lit., 1987—2003, writer in residence, 2003—. Acting dir. Program in Creative Writing U. Iowa, Iowa City, 1978-79. Author: 25 books including Sometimes I Live in the Country, 1986, Absent Friends, 1989, Harry and Catherine, 1990, Closing Arguments, 1991, Long Way From Home, 1993, The Children in the Woods: New and Selected Stories, 1994 (PEN/Faulkner award nomination, 1995), Girls, 1997, (essays) A Dangerous Profession, 1998, (novel) The Night Inspector, 1999 (PEN/Faulkner award nomination, NBCC award nomination, 2000); editor: (anthology) Letters to a Fiction Writer, 1997, (stories) Don't Tell Anyone, 2000, A Memory of War, 2003; numerous other essays and short stories. Recipient Nat. Jewish Book award for fiction, Jewish Book Coun., 1986, Fiction award, AAAL, 1986, PEN/Malamud, 1991, Award of Merit, AAAL, 2001; fellow, Guggenheim Found., 1981—82, Ingram Merrill Found., 1981—82. Mem.: AAAS, PEN, Am. Acad. Arts & Scis., Authors Guild Am., Writers Guild Am.

BUSECK, LARRY ALLEN, music educator; b. Huntingdon, Pa., Feb. 20, 1948; s. Jessey Gerald and Helen Jean (Schields) B. BS in Music Edn., Indiana U. Pa., 1970. Registered "R" judge. Elem. music tchr. Blairsville (Pa.)-Saltsburg Sch. Dist., 1970—2002. Author: Introduction to Freestyle, 1989. Elder Presbyn. Ch., Saltsburg, 1981. Mem. Am. Horse Shows Assn. (recorded "r" judge 1991), U.S. Dressage Fedn. (bronze medal 1989, silver medal 1991), U.S. Equestrian Team, Am. Hanoverian Soc., Western Pa. Dressage Assn. (pres. 1980—, most valuable mem. 1984, 85). Home: 2274 Rte 380 Saltsburg PA 15681-9802

BUSER, CAROLYN ELIZABETH, correctional education administrator; b. St. Paul, June 14, 1946; d. Jerome Alfred and Ella Caroline (Anderson) B.; m. Richard John Ward, Sept. 17, 1977; children: John Jerome Buser Ward, Carl Alfred Buser Ward. BA in English, Carleton Coll., 1968; MS in Spl. Edn., U. Md., 1985, PhD in Ednl. Policy and Adminstrn., 1996. Correctional tchr. Md. Div. Correction, Hughesville, 1970-74, Balt., 1974-76; correctional edn. supr. Md. Dept. Edn. Md. Penitentiary, Balt., 1976-80, Md. Correctional Instn., Jessup, 1980-88; correctional edn. supr. Md. Dept. Edn., Md. correctional pre-release program Md. Correctional Instn. for Women, Jessup, 1988-94; field coord. correctional edn. Md. Dept. Edn., 1994-2001, dir. correctional edn., 2001—. Cons. Am. Correctional Assn., Laurel, Md., 1980; Md. state dir. Correctional Edn. Assn., Laurel, 1988-90; program supr. Prison Literacy, Nat. Inst. Corrections, Washington (designated exemplary program, 1986), mem. editl. rev. bd. Jour. Correctional Edn., 2002—. Mem. editl. rev. bd. Jour. Correctional Edn., 2002—. Fellow Edn. Behaviorally Disordered Students, U. Md., 1985. Mem.: Md. Assn. Adult Cmty. and Continuing Edn., Correctional Edn. Assn. (sec. 1986, edit. bd. Jour. Correctional Edn. 2002—), Phi Kappa Phi. Office: Md State Dept Edn 200 W Baltimore St Ste 1 Baltimore MD 21201-2595 E-mail: cbuser@msde.state.md.us.

BUSH, DEBORAH LEE, communications technology educator; b. Kingston, Pa., Apr. 13, 1952; d. Maurice and Lillian (Reed) Howells; m. R. Steven Bush, June 25, 1983; children: Stephanie Lee, David Michael. BA, Marshall U., 1974, MA, 1976. Dir. continuity news programming Sta. WJLS-AM, Beckley, W.Va., 1976-78; dir. continuity Sta WCIR-AM, Beckley, 1978-82; instr. Coll. W.Va., Beckley, 1982—; instr. communications tech. Raleigh County Vocat.-Tech. Ctr., Beckley, 1982—. Cons. W.Va. cemetary Assn., Charleston, 1991—. Sec. Curtain Callers, Inc., Mt. Hope, W.Va., 1978-92; dir. missions Oak Hill (W.Va.) Bapt. Ch., 1992—. Mem. Beckley Bus. and Profl. Women (past pres.), Beta Sigma Phi. Avocation: community theater. Office: Raleigh County Vocat Tech 410 1/2 Stanaford Rd Beckley WV 25801-3144

BUSH, MARJORIE EVELYNN TOWER-TOOKER, educator, media specialist, librarian; b. Atkinson, Nebr., Mar. 12, 1925; d. Albert Ralph and Vera Marie (Rickover) Tower-Tooker; m. Louis T. Genung, Feb. 2, 1944 (dec. Jan. 1982); 1 child, Louis Thompson; m. Laurence Scott Bush, Sept. 22, 1984; 1 stepchild, Roger A. Student, U. Nebr., 1951, Wayne State Coll., 1942-47; BA, Colo. State Coll., 1966, U. No. Colo., 1970; postgrad., Doane Coll., 1967-68, U. Utah, 1973-74, PhD (hon.), 1973; MA in Tchg., Hastings (Nebr.) Coll., 2000. Elem. tchr. Atkinson Pub. Schs., 1958-69; adminstr. libr. and audiovisual comm. Clay County Dist. I-C, Fairfield, Nebr., 1972-81; media specialist Albion (Nebr.) City Schs., 1981—. Mem. Neb. Gov.'s White House Conf. on Libraries. Chmn. edn. adminstrv. bd. Park Hill United Meth. Ch., Denver, also pres.; sec. Denver Symphony Guild, Colo. Symphony Guild, 1990-96. Mem. NEA (life), ALA, AAUW, ASCD, Nat. Coun. Tchrs. English, Nebr. Edn. Assn., Colo. Edn. Assn., Nebr. Libr. Assn., Nebr. Ednl. Media Assn., Mountain Plain Libr. Assn., Assn. Childhood Edn. Internat., Assn. Ednl. Comm. & Tech., Internat. Visual Literacy Assn., Nat. Coun. Exceptional Children, Alumni Assn. U. No. Colo. (life charter), Women Educators Nebr., United Meth. Women (pres.), Am. Legion Aux., Nebr. Lay Citizens Assn. (exec.), Am. NAt. Cowbelles, Nebr. Cowbelles, Internat. Platform Assn., LWV, Women's Soc. Christian Svc., Ak-Sar-Ben, Windsor Gardens Club (Denver), Opti-Mrs. Club (pres.), Optimists Internat., Columbine Optimists (pres. 1987-88), Ea. Star. Address: 1003 E 9th St Hastings NE 68901-4140

BUSH, SANDI TOKOA, elementary school educator; b. Albany, Ga., Aug. 1, 1953; d. Charlie and Beauty (Miller) Bush; 1 child, Allen. BS, Barry U., Miami, 1983; MS, Nova U., 1987; PhD, Union Inst., 2001, U. Cin., 2001. Cert. tchr. Fla. Counselor Health and Rehab. Svcs., Miami, Fla., 1979-86; tchr. Dade County Pub. Schs., Miami, 1986—. Tchr., tutor Ind. Children's Group, Miami, 1987—; co-chmn. Hall of Fame Dade County Sch. Bd., 1986—, world difference, 1987—. Author: (book) World of Poetry Anthology The Sun, 1991; co-author: Experiences with Discrimination: From Deep Within, 1998; contbr. articles to profl. jours. Mem.: Nova U. Assocs., Nova U. Alumni Assn. (mem. recruitment com. 1987—88, Recognition award 1988), Smithsonian Assocs. (Recognition award 1988), Am. Mus. Natural History (assoc.). Avocations: reading, classical music, walking, jogging, tennis.

BUSHWAY, RODNEY JOHN, food science educator; b. Milo, Maine, June 23, 1949; s. Alfred Joseph and Dorothy Elizabeth (Landers) B.; children: Nicholas David, Meghan Elizabeth. BS, U. Maine, 1971; MS, Tex. A&M U., 1973, PhD, 1977. Rsch. analytical chemist Phillips Petroleum, Bartlesville, Okla., 1977-78; prof. food sci. U. Maine, Orono, 1978—. Sci. adv. bd. Immuno Systems, Scarborough, Maine, 1991—; cons. for food and chem. industries; lectr. in field. Author: (with others) HPLC Analysis of Presticide Residues in Food, 1991; contbr. 100 articles to refereed sci. jours. including Food Chemistry Bull. Environ. Contamination and Toxicology; mem. editl. bd. Jour. Food Protection, 1991—. Judge sch. sci. fairs, Maine, 1980—, mem. sch. bd.; mem. Gov.'s Com. State of Maine Human Health Effects of Pesticides, 1994. USDA grantee, 1983-84, 86-95. Mem. Inst. Food Technologists, Am. Potato Assn., Am. Chem. Soc., Assn. Official Analytical Chemists (assoc. referee 1980—). Roman Catholic. Achievements include devel. of an official analytical method for analysis of Rotenone in pesticide formulations; devel. of several analytical methods using HPLC and immunoassay techniques for pesticide residues in food and water. Office: U Maine Dept Food Sci 5736 Holmes Hall Orono ME 04469-5736

BUSINGER, JOOST ALOIS, atmospheric scientist, educator; b. Haarlem, Netherlands, Mar. 29, 1924; came to U.S., 1956; s. Leopold Joost Eduard and Helena Margareta (Schimpf) B.; m. Judith Businger, May 21, 1949 (div. June 1983); children: Ferdi, Steven, Margaret Anne; m. Marianne Kooiman, Jan. 1987. Candidaats, U. Utrecht, Netherlands, 1947, Doctoraat, 1950, PhD, 1954. Sci. officer Inst. Hort. Engring., Wageningen, Netherlands, 1951-56; research assoc. U. Wis., Madison, 1956-58; asst. to prof. atmospheric sci. U. Wash., Seattle, 1958-83, prof. emeritus, 1983—; chmn. dept. atmospheric sci., 1982-83; vis. scientist Nat. Ctr. Atmospheric Research, Boulder, Colo., 1983-86, sr. scientist, 1986-89, retired. Author: An Introduction to Atmospheric Physics, 1963, 2d edit., 1980, Atmosphere-Ocean Interaction, 2d edit., 1994. Precinct committeeman Democratic Party, Seattle, 1970-71. Sr. fellow NRC, Australia, 1965-66; sr. scientist Koninklijk Nederlands Meteorologisch Instituut, 1974-75; recipient(Vilhelm Bjerknes award European Geophysical Soc., 2003. Fellow AAAS (chmn. sect. Atmospheric and Hydrospheric Scis., 1992, sec. 1994—2003), Nat. Acad. Engring., Am. Meteorol. Soc. (Half Century award 1979); mem. Am. Geophys. Union, Royal Acad. Scis. (Netherlands) (corr.), AAUP (pres. Seattle chpt. 1972-73, nat. councillor 1974-76) Home: PO Box 541 Anacortes WA 98221-0541

BUSKIRK, BRUCE DAVID, marketing educator; b. Lawrence, Kans., Jan. 28, 1952; s. Richard H. and Barbara Jean (Lusk) B.; m. Sheryl Ann Cunningham, June 17, 1978; children: Brian Scott, Robert William, Kathleen Sarah. BS in Mktg., U. So. Calif., 1974; MS in Mktg., La. State U., 1976; PhD in Mktg., Mich. State U., 1983. Instr. U. S.C., Columbia, 1976-78, Mich. State U., East Lansing, 1978-81; asst. prof. Kent (Ohio) State U., 1981-86, Northwestern U., Evanston, Ill., 1986-89; assoc. prof. Bryant Coll., Smithfield, R.I., 1990-92; prof. mktg. and econs., head dept., dir. MBA program Valdosta (Ga.) State Univ., 1992-96; prof. mktg. Pepperdine U., chair mktg., econs. and quantifiable methods. Author: Retailing, 1979, Direct Marketing, 1989, Selling, 13th edit., 1992. Mem. Beta Gamma Sigma, Alpha Mu Alpha. Office: Geo L Graziado Sch Bus and Mgmt 400 Corp Pt Culver City CA 90230

BUSKIRK, ELSWORTH ROBERT, physiologist, educator; b. Beloit, Wis., Aug. 11, 1925; s. Ellsworth Fred and Laura Ellen (Parman) B.; m. Mable Heen, Aug. 28, 1948; children: Laurel Ann Buskirk Wiegand, Kristine Janet Buskirk Hallett. Student, U. Wis., 1943; BA, St. Olaf Coll., Northfield, Minn., 1950; MA, U. Minn., 1951, PhD, 1954. Lab. and tchg. asst. Lab. Physiol. Hygiene, U. Minn., 1951-53; rsch. fellow Life Inst. Med. Rsch. Fund, 1953-54; physiologist Environ. Rsch. Ctr., Natick, Mass., 1954-57, Nat. Inst. for Arthritis, Metabolic and Digestive Diseases, NIH, Bethesda, Md., 1957-63; prof. applied physiology Pa. State U., University Park, 1963-92, dir. Lab. Human Performance Rsch., 1963-92, Marie Underhill Noll prof. Human Performance, 1988-92, emeritus, 1992—. Mem. sci. adv. com. Pres.' Coun. on Phys. Fitness, 1959-61; mem. applied physiology study sect. divsn. rsch. grants NIH, 1964-68, 76-80; mem. com. on interplay of engring. with biology and medicine NAS-NAE, 1968-74, 82-88; mem. rsch. com. Pa. Heart Assn., 1970-73, 82-86, 87-89, 90-95; mem. Pa. Gov.'s Coun. on Phys. Fitness and Sports, 1978-82; mem. com. on mil. nutrition rsch. NAS/NRC, 1982-90; mem. clin. scis. study sect. divsn. rsch. grants NIH, 1989-92, spl. reviewer, 1992-99; mem. Def. Women's Rsch. Com. IOM, NAS-NRC, 1995. Sect. editor Jour. Applied Physiology, 1974-78, assoc. editor, 1978-84; co-editor Sci. and Medicine in Sports and Exercise, 1974, editor, 1973-75; editor-in-chief, 1984-88, cons., editor, 1989-94; mem. editl. bd. Physician and Sports Medicine, 1974-85, Jour. Cardiopulmonary Rehab., 1980-2000, Underseas and Hyperbaric Medicine, 1988-95, Am. Jour. Clin. Nutrition, 1982-92, Jour. Gerontology, 1982-92, Exptl. Gerontology, 1989-98; also over 250 articles on physiology, revs. to sci. jours. Bd. visitors Sargent Coll., Boston U., 1976-92; bd. dirs. Ctr. Cmty. Hosp., Pa., 1966-70, sec., 1971-72, v.p., 1973, pres., 1974-75. Served with U.S. Army, ETO. Recipient Disting. Alumni award St. Olaf Coll., 1969, Daggs Svc. award Am. Physiol. Soc., 2000; rsch. grantee NIH, 1963-92, U.S. Olympic Com., 1965-68, USAF, 1965-69, Pa. Dept. Health, 1966-67, Pa. Heart Assn., 1966, 76-80, NSF, 1968-70, Nat. Inst. Occupl. Safety and Health, 1969-74; NATO sr. fellow in sci., 1977; named to Athletic Hall of Fame, St. Olaf Coll., 2000. Mem. AAAS, AAPHERD, ASHRAE, Aerospace Med. Assn., Am. Acad. Phys. Edn., Am. Coll. Sports Medicine (citations 1973, 75, Honor award 1984, editl. award 1989, 93, Mid-Atlantic regional chpt. Svc. award 1991), Am. Inst. Nutrition, Am. Physiol. Soc. (pres. environ. and exercise sect. 1987-91, com. on coms. 1988-92, Honor award environ. exercise physiology sect. 1993, Daggs award 2002), Am. Heart Assn. (coun. on epidemiology), N.Y. Acad. Scis., NIH Alumni Assn., Pa. Heart Assn. (rsch. com. 1988-94), Am. Diabetes Assn., Coun. Biology Editors (Healthy Am. Fitness Leaders award 1992), Centre Hills Country Club. Lutheran. Home: 216 Hunter Ave State College PA 16801-6947 Office: Pa State U 119 Noll Lab University Park PA 16802-6900

BUSOVICKI, JOHN FRANCIS, secondary education educator; b. Clymer, Pa., Dec. 10, 1939; s. John and Blanche (Cernik) B.; m. Rose Ann Felichko, Aug. 11, 1962; children: John, Joseph, David, Lisa. BS in Math. Edn., Indiana U. Pa., 1965; MS in Math., U. Notre Dame, Ind., 1969. Laborer Youngstown (Ohio) Sheet & Tube, 1958-61, Magas Welding, Clymer, 1961-65; tchr. math. United H.S., Armagh, Pa., 1965-68, Indiana U. of Pa., 1969-2000. Bd. dirs. Hist. Soc. Indiana County, Indiana Coin Club, Indiana County Sports Hall of Fame; math. textbook reviewer West, Saunders, Macmillan Pub., Addison-Wesley Pub., 1980—; numismatic advisor and appraiser, 1969—. Author: Postcard History of Indiana County, 2003. Vol. Dem. Party, Indiana County, Pa., 1961—, United Way, Heart Fund, Indiana County, 1976—; merit badge adviser coins and stamps Boy Scouts Am., Indiana County, 1975—; hist. adviser Clymer and Indiana County, 1976—. NSF Acad. Yr. Inst. grantee U. Notre Dame, 1968. Mem. Nat. Coun. Tchrs. Math., Pa. Coun. Tchrs. Math., Indiana U. Pa. Alumni Club, Notre Dame Alumni Club, Am. Numis. Assn., Pa. Assn. Numis., Liberty Seated Coin Soc., Indiana Coin Club. Roman Catholic. Avocations: hunting, fishing, postcards, coin and stamp collecting, antique cars, guns. Home: 510 Walcott St Clymer PA 15728-1427

BUSS, DAVID MICHAEL, psychology educator; b. Indpls., Apr. 14, 1953; s. Arnold Herbert and Edith Hertha B.; children: Ryan P., Tara P. BA, U. Tex., 1976; PhD, U. Calif., Berkeley, 1981. Asst. prof. Harvard U., Cambridge, Mass., 1981-85; assoc. prof. psychology U. Mich., Ann Arbor, 1985-91, prof., 1991-96, U. Tex., Austin, 1996—. Author: The Evolution of Desire, 1994/2003, Evolutionary Psychology: The New Science of the Mind, 1999, The Dangerous Passion, 2000. Fellow APA (Early Sci. Career Contbn. award 1988, G. Stanley Hall award 1990); mem. Human Behavior and Evolution Soc. (coun. 1994—), Am. Psychol. Soc., Internat. Consortium Personality and Social Psychologists (bd. dirs. 1993—). Avocations: squash, tennis, disc golf, movies, music. Office: U Tex Dept Psychology Austin TX 78731

BUSS, LEO WILLIAM, biologist, educator; b. Alexandria, Va., Sept. 27, 1953; s. Leo Alfred and Margaret (Nyhan) B.; m. Jane Moore, June 12, 1982; children: Evan Daniel, Blake William. BA, Johns Hopkins U., 1975, MA, 1977, PhD, 1979; MA (hon.), Yale U., 1990. Asst. prof. dept. biology Yale U., New Haven, 1979-84, assoc. prof., 1984-90, assoc. prof. dept. geology and geophysics, 1988-90, prof. dept. biology, 1990-96, prof. dept. ecology and evolutionary biology, 1996—, chmn. program in organismal biology, 1990-95, dir. Inst. Biospheric Studies, 1991-96. Curator Peabody Mus. Nat. History, New Haven, 1979—; dir. Sears Found. Marine Rsch., 1992—. Author: The Evolution of Individuality, 1987; co-editor: Population Biology and Evolution of Clonal Organisms, 1985. John Simon Guggenheim fellow, 1984, Prize fellow John D. and Catherine MacArthur Found., 1989.

BUSS, SAMUEL RUDOLPH RUDOLPH, mathematics educator, researcher; b. New Haven, Conn., Aug. 6, 1957; s. Martin John and Nancy Jane (Macpherson) B.; m. Teresa Paula Thacker, June 7, 1980; children: Stephanie, Ian. BS in Math. and Physics, Emory U., 1979; MA in Math., Princeton U., 1982, PhD in Math., 1985. VLSI engr. Proximity Designs Corp. (now Franklin Electronic Pub.), 1980-82; researcher Math. Scis. Rsch. Inst., Berkeley, Calif., 1985-86; instr. U. Calif., Berkeley, 1986-88, asst. prof. math. San Diego, 1988-90, assoc. prof., 1990-93, prof. math., 1993—. Co-organizer workshop on feasible math., Ithaca, 1989; organizer workshops on proof theory, complexity and logic, San Diego, 1990, Prague, 1991. Author: Bounded Arithmetic, 1986, 3D Computer Graphics: A Mathematical Introduction with Open GL, 2003; editor: Archive for Mathematical Logic, Lecture Notes in Logic; co-editor: Feasible Mathematics, 1990; author, editor: Handbook of Proof Theory, 1998; patentee in field; contbr. articles to profl. jours. NSF fellow, 1979-80, 82-84, 85-88, Sloan Found. fellow, 1984-85; NSF grantee, 1988—. Mem.: American Mathematical Society, Association for Computing Machinery, IEEE Computer Society, Association for Symbolic Logic. Achievements include patents on associative memory circuit system and method, on methods for minimum-cost matchings. Office: U Calif San Diego Math Dept La Jolla CA 92093

BUSSE, EILEEN ELAINE, special education educator; b. Green Bay, Wis., Oct. 16, 1957; d. Ervin F. Dohl and Elaine I. (Behnke) Richmond; m. John F. Busse, July 5, 1980; children: Jessica Lynn, Jeremy John. BS in Elem. and Spl. Edn., U. Wis., Eau Claire, 1979; MS in Spl. Edn., U. Wis., Whitewater, 1985. Cert. tchr. elem. and spl. edn. Tchr. spl. edn.-mentally retarded Ithaca (Wis.) Pub. Schs., 1979-80; spl. edn. tchr. Walworth County CDEB, Whitewater, Wis., 1980—, Lakeview Elem. Sch., 1991-2000, Whitewater H.S., 2000—; summer sch. instr. St. Thomas U., 2003. Coop. tchr. U. Wis., Whitewater, 1988—; summer sch. tchr. U. St. Thomas, St. Paul, Minn., 2003. Author: Student Owned Spelling, 1991, II, 1992, III, 1994. Mem. First English Luth. Ch. edn. com., Whitewater, 1990-95, 98—, chmn. edn. com., 1993-95, mem. ch. coun., 1993-94, 97—; active Girl Scouts U.S.A., 1992-2000; advisor sr. high youth 1st English Luth. Ch., 1998—. Recipient Excellence in Edn. award U.S. Dept. Edn., 1984-85, Recognized spl. educator, 1998. Mem. Coun. for Exceptional Children, Wis. Assn. Children with Behavioral Disorders, Milw. (Wis.) County Zool. Soc., Delta Kappa Gamma. Avocations: reading, travel, gardening. Home: 455 Ventura Ln Whitewater WI 53190-1548 Office: Whitewater HS 534 S Elizabeth St Whitewater WI 53190

BUSTAMANTE, DOLORES MORALES, elementary education educator; b. El Paso, Tex., May 23, 1950; d. Hector M. Morales and Gloria Lightbourn; m. Daniel Ray Bustamante, Sept. 21, 1979; children: Rosalinda Danielle, Adrian Ramon. BA, U. Tex., El Paso, 1973; MSW, U. Houston, 1978. Rsch. asst. Southwestern Schs. Study, El Paso, 1971-73; caseworker Mental Health Retardation, El Paso, 1974-76; intern in pub. affairs Gulf Oil Corp., Houston, 1977-78; rsch. cons. Tex. Commn. on Alcoholism, Houston, 1978-79; dir. yough svcs. SER-Jobs for Progress, Houston, 1979-81, conf. coord., 1982; asst. dir. INROADS/Houston, Inc., 1983-88; tchr. elem. sch. Houston Ind. Sch. Dist., Houston, 1992—. Tech. translator CRS Group Engrs., Houston, 1981-82; audience developer Soc. Performing Arts, Houston, 1982. Mem. Minority Women's Assn., Trabajadores Sociales de Aztlan, Cultural Arts Coun. Houston. Roman Catholic. Home: 4309 Leeland St Houston TX 77023-3017 Office: River Oaks Elem Sch 2008 Kirby Dr Houston TX 77019-6016

BUTCHER, AMANDA KAY, retired university administrator; b. Lansing, Mich., Oct. 25, 1936; d. Foster Eli and Mayme Lenore (Taft) Stuart; m. Claude J. Butcher, Aug. 24, 1957; 1 child, Mary Beth. BS in Bus., Cen. Mich. U., 1981. Office asst. Dept. Dairy Sci., East Lansing, Mich., 1966-76; bus. mgr. dept. pathology Coll. Vet. Medicine Mich. State U., East Lansing, 1976-96. Mem. Adminstrv. Profl. Suprs. Assn. (v.p. 1982), Adminstrv. Profl. Assn. East Lansing (pres. 1976-80). Avocations: photography, antiques, bowling. Home: 610 Emily Ave Lansing MI 48910-5404

BUTCHER, ANN PATRICE, elementary school educator; b. Aurora, Ill., May 14, 1965; d. Harry Neal and Patsy JoAnn (Smith) Patterson; m. Steven James Butcher, July 14, 1990; children: Todd Merrill, Seth Richard-James, Zacharry Neal. BA, Aurora U., 1989; MA, No. Ill. U., 1994; EdD in Leadership in Curriculum and Instrn., Aurora U., 2003. Cert. in elem. edn., curriculum and supervision. Elem. sch. tchr. Sch. Dist. #129, Aurora, 1989—; gifted tchr. Aurora U., 1993—. Tchr. Adv. Bd. for Sci. Edn., Sci.-Tech./Physics of Aquatic Animals, Aurora; Impact II adv. bd. Ill. Math. and Sci. Acad., Aurora, 1991, Leadership Inst. Integrating Internet, Instrn. and Curriculum participant, instr. Fermi Acceleration Lab., Batavia, Ill.; mem. consortium Aurora Cmty. Edn., 1996—; dir. programs Scholars program Aurora U., 1996—. Recipient Impact II grant, Ill. Math. and Sci. Acad./State of Ill., 1991, 1992, Best in West award, 2001, Honor Roll of Tchrs. award, Assn. Sci. and Tech. Ctrs., Washington, 1996; grantee, Aurora Found., 1993. Mem. NEA, Ill. Edn. Assn., Ill. Sci. Tchrs. Assn., Ill. Reading Coun., Aurora Cmty. Edn. Consortium, Kappa Delta Pi. Lutheran. Avocations: physical fitness, aerobics, running, weight training. Home: 805 Acorn Dr North Aurora IL 60542-3030 Office: Fearn Elem Sch 1600 Hawksley Ln North Aurora IL 60542 E-mail: butch4@interaccess.com.

BUTCHER, HARRY WILLIAM, educational administrator, educator, historian; b. Frederick, Okla., May 15, 1948; s. Harry William Hobbs and Alice Marie (Brownrigg) Butcher Able; m. Susan Mary Howell, Nov. 11, 2000; children: Jonathan Hobbs, Megan Rachel. BS, Okla. State U., 1970, postgrad., 1971. Cert. tchr. Tex., 2002. Agt. Pinkerton, Inc., Oklahoma City, 1971-73, mgr. investigation Dallas, 1973-75, mgr. Baton Rouge, 1975-77, Memphis, 1977-78, mgr., dist. Houston, 1978-79, v.p. Mark Lipman Divsn. Memphis, 1979-84, regional dir. Dallas, 1984-88, dir., group investigation Ft. Worth, 1988-89, dir. nat. accounts, 1990-91; v.p. domestic and internat. sales, 1991-96; sr. v.p. domestic and internat. sales Pinkerton, Inc., Ft. Worth, 1996-99, sr. v.p. strategic accounts, 1999-2000; founder, exec. dir. Ctr. for Edn., 2000—; educator Ft. Worth Ind. Sch. Dist., 2000—. Mem. Am. Mgmt. Assn. (pres.'s assn.), Pres.'s Club (Minot Dodson award for outstanding leadership 1997), Tex. Hist. Soc., Golden Key Soc., Nat. Trust Historic Preservation, Phi Alpha Theta. Republican. Episcopalian. Avocations: teaching young people, gardening, historical studies.

BUTH, DONALD GEORGE, biology educator; b. Chgo., Feb. 23, 1949; s. Werner George and Arlene Dolores (Kreier) B. BS in Zoology, U. Ill., 1971, AB in Anthropology, 1972, MS in Zoology, 1974, PhD in Ecology, Ethol. and Evolution, 1978. Research, teaching asst. U. Ill., Urbana, 1971-78; postdoctoral researcher UCLA, 1978-79, instr. biology, 1980, asst. prof., 1980-86, assoc. prof., 1986-92, prof., 1992—. Coord. bd. U. Calif. Water Resources, 1990-97. Contbr. articles to profl. jours. Fellow AAAS, Willi Hennig Soc. (councilor 1981-82); mem. Am. Soc. Ichthyologists and Herpetologists (bd. govs. 1984-98, 2003—, exec. com. 1983-86, assoc. editor COPEIA, 1985-93, 2002-, editl. bd. 1993-96, 99-2000), So. Calif. Acad. Sci. (bd. dirs. 1992-96). Office: Dept Organismic Biology Ecology and Evolution UCLA Los Angeles CA 90095-1606 E-mail: dbuth@ucla.edu.

BUTHOD, MARY CLARE, school administrator; b. Tulsa, Aug. 20, 1945; d. Arthur Paul and Mary Rudelle (Dougherty) B. MA in Teaching, Tulsa U., 1969; M Christian Spirituality, Creighton U., 1981. Joined Order of St. Benedict. Asst. tchr. HeadStart, Tulsa, 1966; tchr. Madalene Parish Sch., Tulsa, 1968-69, Monte Cassino Pvt. Sch., Tulsa, 1969-79; prin. Monte Cassino Elem. Sch., Tulsa, 1979-86; dir. Monte Cassino Sch., Tulsa, 1986—. Mem. convent coun. Benedictine Sisters, Tulsa, 1975-88, dir. formation programs, 1983—. Mem. State Congl. Ednl. Com., Tulsa, 1989-90; co-chair for edn. and human devel. Tulsa Coalition Against Illegal Use of Drugs, 1990-91; mem. adv. com. Okla. State Schs. Attuned, 2002—. Recognized for Excellence in Edn. U.S. Dept. Edn., 1993-94. Mem. Tulsa Reading Coun. (sec. 1975-77), Nat. Cath. Edn. Assn., Delta Kappa Gamma. Home: 2200 S Lewis Tulsa OK 74114-3117 Office: Monte Cassino Sch 2206 S Lewis Ave Tulsa OK 74114-3109

BUTLER, ARTHUR MAURICE, university administrator; b. Osaka, Japan, Mar. 18, 1947; came to U.S. 1949; s. John Elzie Jr. and Connie Mae (Hartzel) B.; m. Celine Marie Bell, Sept. 19, 1970. BA in Polit. Sci., Calif. State Coll., San Bernadino, 1977. Asst. dir. pub. safety Calif. State Coll., 1975-81, dir. pub. safety, 1981-87, dir. adminstrv. svcs., 1987—; exec. dir. Found. for Calif. State U., San Bernardino, 1987—. Bd. dirs. Western Assn. Coll. Aux. Svcs., Calif., Inland Bus. Coun. on Emergency Preparedness, San Bernadino. Vice chair City Personnel Bd., Riverside, Calif., 1981-88; chair Selective Svc. Bd., Riverside, 1980—; active Calif. Rep. Cen. Com. Sacramento, 1982-84; bd. dirs. Calif. State U. Risk Mgmt. Authority, 1996—. Mem. Nat. Assn. Coll. Aux. Svcs. (dir. region 1 1988-89), Newcomen Soc., Serra Club (trustee, sec. Riverside chpt. 1985-90), Victoria Club, Pi Sigma Alpha. Roman Catholic. Avocations: skiing, fly fishing. Office: Calif State U San Bernardino 5500 University Pkwy San Bernardino CA 92407-2318

BUTLER, BILLIE RAE, educational administrator; b. Waverly, Tenn., Aug. 2, 1941; d. Clifford Ronald and Pauline Elizabeth (Forsythe) Hunter; m. E.D. Longest (div.); children: Tamara Dianne, Teresa Denise, Tanya Darlene; m. William R. Butler, Dec. 16, 1979. AA, Hartnell Coll., Calif., 1973; BA, Chapman Coll., Calif., 1978. Cert. life permit Children's Ctr., Calif. Commn. for Tchr. Prep. and Licensing. Tchr. Monterey County Office of Edn., Salinas, Calif., 1973-78, coord., 1978-80, program dir., 1980—. Mem. Monterey County Child Care Planning, 1992—; bd. dirs., officer Monterey Bay Parents as Tchrs., Monterey County, 1990-96. Mem., officer Salinas Valley Child Abuse Prevention Coun., Monterey County, 1980-84; mem. Family Self-Sufficiency Coord. Coun., Monterey Coun. Mem. AAUW, Calif. Head Start Assn. (bd. dirs. 1991-93), Cen. Coast Assn. for Edn. of Young Children (bd. dirs. 1984-90). Avocations: flower arranging, cooking/regional and ethnic cuisines, history, travel. Office: Monterey County Office Edn 901 Blanco Cir Salinas CA 93901-4401 Address: 927 Campbell Cir Woodland CA 95776-9352

BUTLER, DOUGLAS M, state agency administrator, educator; b. Bronx, N.Y., Sept. 28, 1954; s. John Marshal and Dorothy (Goodman) B. BA in Psychology, Manhattan Coll., 1977; MS in Clin.-Sch. Psychology, City College, N.Y.C., 1979; MEd in Ednl. Psychology, U. Tex. at Austin, 1984, PhD in Learning Disabilities, 1993. Rsch. asst. N.Y.C. Youth Bd., 1977, 78, 79, 80-81; activity therapist Bellevue Psychiat. Hosp., N.Y.C., 1978-79; grad. teaching asst. City Coll., 1978-79; teaching asst. U. Tex. at Austin, 1981; program evaluator office rsch. and evaluation Austin Ind. Sch. Dist., 1983-85; tutor after sch. programs Carver Libr., Austin, 1985-88; disability examiner Tex. Rehab. Comsn., Austin, 1985-88; ednl./fiscal program specialist Tex. Edn. Agy., Austin, 1988—. Mem. numerous state coms.; mentor elem. sch., 1991—. Mem. NASP, Coun. Exceptional Children. Avocations: exercise, running, travel, reading. Office: Tex State Dept Edn Tex Edn Agy 1701 Congress Ave Austin TX 78701-1402

BUTLER, EVELYN ANNE, writer, educator, editor; b. Norfolk, Va., Aug. 17, 1940; d. James Timothy and Janette Laura (Boardman) Kelly; m. Gerald Joseph Butler, Feb. 14, 1964; children: James Dale, Marian Margaret Cade, Wayne Anthony. BA, U. Calif., Berkeley, 1963; MA, NYU, 1966; PhD, U. Calif., San Diego, 1985. Mem. faculty lit. Chapman Coll., Orange, Calif., 1972-81, San Diego State U., 1984—2003, U. Paris-Dauphine, 1990-91. Reviewer Children's Lit., 1970—, Recovering Lit., Fiction Internat. Author: (novels) Fire, 1992, Going Away, 1996; editor in-chief Blue Daylight Books, 2000—; asst. editor jour. Fiction Internat., 1985-89. Fellow Woodrow Wilson Fellowship Com., 1963-64, NDEA U. Calif., San Diego, 1968-72. Mem. AAUP, MLA, Phi Beta Kappa. Avocations: languages, travel. Home and Office: PO Box 805 Alpine CA 91903-0805

BUTLER, GEOFFREY SCOTT, systems engineer, educator, consultant; b. Jacksonville, Fla., July 19, 1958; s. George Lauritzen and Mary Elizabeth (Cox) B.; m. Diana Lynn Martin, Aug. 29, 1987. BS in Aerospace Engring., U. Fla., 1981; MS in Aerospace Engring., San Diego State U., 1986; MS in Aerospace Systems, West Coast U., 1988. Engr. Lockheed Missiles & Space Co., Sunnyvale, Calif., 1981-83; engring. specialist Convair div. Gen. Dynamics, San Diego, 1983-92; project mgr. Horizons Tech., Inc., San Diego, 1992-95, BAE Systems, Inc., 1995—. Tech. program chmn. 13th Applied Aerodynamics Conf., chmn. missile sys. tech. com., 2002-2003; cons. WEB Engring., San Diego, 1992—. Contbr. articles to profl. publs. Mem. AIAA (sr. mem., MSTC chmn. 2001). Republican. Roman Catholic. Achievements include conception and direction of first tests of store separation at hypersonic speeds within a ballistic range, specialized software development activities. Office: Bae Systems PO Box 509008 San Diego CA 92150-9008

BUTLER, JAMES NEWTON, chemist, educator; b. Cleveland, Ohio, Mar. 27, 1934; s. Clyde Henry and Margaret (Manor) B.; m. Nancy Elizabeth Close, Aug. 31, 1957 (div.); 1 son, Christopher J.; m. Rosamond Hatch Bee, Dec. 10, 1966; stepchildren: Alden G. Bee, Kenneth M. Bee. BS, Rensselaer Poly. Inst., 1955; PhD, Harvard U., 1959. Staff scientist NACA Lewis Lab., Cleve., summers 1952-57, MIT Lincoln Lab., summer 1958; instr. U. B.C., Vancouver, 1959-61, asst. prof., 1961-63; sr. scientist Tyco Labs., Inc., Waltham, Mass., 1963-66, dept. head, 1966-71; from lectr. to prof. emeritus Harvard U., Cambridge, Mass., 1970—2000, prof. emeritus, 2000—; cons. Tyco Labs., Inc., Waltham, Mass., 1962-63, 71-73. Mem. steering com. co-author report Petroleum in the Marine Environment, Nat. Acad. Scis.— NRC, 1973-75, 80-82; mem. tech. panel, report drafting com. Com. on Environ. Decision-Making, 1975-77; chmn. com. on effectiveness of oil spill dispersants, NRC, 1985-89; cons. EPA, 1978—, NOAA, 1981—. Author: Ionic Equilibrium, 1964, rev. edit., 1998, Solubility and pH Calculations, 1964, The Calculus of Chemistry, 1965, Problems for Introductory University Chemistry, 1967, Pelagic Tar from Bermuda and the Sargasso Sea, 1973, Carbon Dioxide Equilibria and Their Applications, 1982, reprinted, 1991, Studies of Sargassum and the Sargassum Community, 1983, Using Oil Spill Dispersants on the Sea, 1989, The Exxon Valdez Oil Spill: Fate and Effects in Alaskan Waters, 1995; also articles. Trustee Bermuda Biol. Sta., 1972-97, v.p., 1985-86, 89-93, pres., 1986-89, life trustee, 1997—. NSF Faculty Sci. fellow, 1977; Alumni scholar Relsselaer Poly. Inst., 1955, NSF fellow, GE fellow Harvard U., 1959. Mem. Am. Chem. Soc., AAAS, Am. Soc. Limnology and Oceanography, Internat. Soc. Electrochemistry, Electrochem. Soc. N.Y. (chmn. Boston sect.), Gordon Research Conf. on Electrochemistry (chmn.), Assn. Harvard Chemists (pres.), Sigma Xi, Phi Lambda Upsilon. Office: Harvard U Div Engring and Applied Scis Pierce Hall 29 Oxford St Cambridge MA 02138-2901 E-mail: butler@deas.harvard.edu.

BUTLER, JANET BABINGTON, assistant principal; b. Hagerstown, Md., Apr. 25, 1966; d. Kenneth B. and Carolyn V. (Cox) Babington; m. Charles E. Butler III, June 23, 1990. BS in Edn., Ga. So. Coll., 1988; MEd, Armstrong State Coll., 1990; EdS, Ga. So. U., 1994, EdD in Curriculum Studies, 2001. Cert. tchr., Ga. Elem. tchr. Lanier Elem. Sch., Pembroke, Ga., 1988-95, Bryan County Elem. Sch., Pembroke, Ga., 1995-98, tech. specialist, 1998—2002, mem. curriculum devel. com., 1998—2002. Mem. ASCD, Ga. Assn. Educators, Kappa Delta Pi, Phi Kappa Phi. Republican. Roman Catholic. Avocation: micronesian studies. Home: PO Box 1461 Pembroke GA 31321-1461 Office: Bryan County Elem Sch 104 Ash Branch Rd Pembroke GA 31321

BUTLER, JOAN MARIE, physical education educator; b. Hanover, N.H., Jan. 22, 1958; d. James Francis and M. Jean (Chagnon) B. BS in Phys. Edn. magna cum laude, Keene State Coll., 1980. Cert. tchr., N.H. Phys. edn. instr. Keene (N.H.) State Coll. Lab. Sch., 1981; phys. edn. instr. and athletic dir. Chesterfield (N.H.) Cen. and Westmoreland Elem. Schs., 1981-82; phys. edn. instr. Hanover St. and Sch. St. Schs., Lebanon, N.H., 1983-87; phys. edn. instr. Prince William County Sch. Dist., Dumfries, Va., 1987-89, Grantham Village (N.H.) Sch., 1989-90, Canaan (N.H.) Elem. Sch. and Enfield (N.H.) Village Sch., 1990—. Children's daycare programmer and waterfront supr., LaSalette, Enfield, summer, 1981-84; water safety swimming instr. Lebanon Meml. Pool, summer, 1985-87, S. Run Recreation Ctr., Burke, Va., Jan.-July, 1989; cultural arts activity com. chair person, Hanover Str. Elem. Sch., Lebanon, 1985-87; cross-country ski instr. Eastman Ski Touring Ctr., Grantham (N.H.), Dec.-Mar., 1989—; water safety swimming instr., swim team coach, Eastman Recreation Dept., Grantham, June-Aug., 1989-93; water safety instr. Colby Sawyer Coll., New London, 1993—. Sec. Lebanon Recreation Adv. Bd., Lebanon, N.H., 1987. Recipient Golden Apple Tchr. award, Enfield Village Sch., 1992. Mem. AAHPERD, N.H. Assn. Health, Phys. Edn., Recreation and Dance (Tchr. Merit award 1992). Home: PO Box 45 Georges Mills NH 03751-0045 Office: Canaan Elem Sch School St Canaan NH 03741

BUTLER, JODY TALLEY, gifted education educator; b. Columbus, Ga., Mar. 14, 1958; d. Bill Ray and Jacqueline (Hay) T.; m. Danny Butler. BS in Edn., West Ga. Coll., 1979, MEd, 1982; EdD, Auburn U., 1988. Cert. tchr., Ga. Tchr. Cen. Primary Sch., Carrollton, 1979-88; tchr. gifted student program QUEST Cen. Middle School, Carrollton, 1988-98; co-owner Hay's Mill Antiques, Ga., 1994—; QUEST tchr. Roopville Elem., Mt. Zion Elem., 1998-2000; tchr. of gifted Carrollton Elem. Sch., 2000—. Mem. handbell choir Carrollton Presbyn. Ch. Mem. Internat. Reading Assn., Profl. Assn. Ga. Educators, Carroll County Cmty. Chorus, Phi Delta Kappa (Dissertation of Yr. award 1989), Phi Kappa Phi, Alpha Gamma Delta. Presbyterian. Avocations: antiques, travel, music, writing, guitar. Office: Carrollton Elem Sch 401 Ben Scott Blvd Carrollton GA 30117

BUTLER, JOHN EDWARD, biomedical sciences educator, consultant; b. Rice Lake, Wis., Jan. 10, 1938; s. Edward W. and Ida (Fredrick) B.; children: Kirsten Diane Butler Bennett, Brian Miller. BS in Chemistry and Biology, U. Wis., River Falls, 1961; PhD in Zoology and Biochemistry, U. Kans., 1965. Ranger, naturalist U.S. Nat. Park Svc., Crater Lake, Oreg., 1961-63; tchg. asst. U. Kans., Lawrence, 1961-66; rsch. biologist USDA, Washington, 1968-71; asst. prof. microbiology U. Iowa, Iowa City, 1971-74, assoc. prof., 1974-80, prof., 1980—, dir. Iowa biotech. tng. program, 1984-89, dir. grad. studies dept. microbiology, 1996—. Cons. devel. immunology. Editor: The Ruminant Immune System, 1981, Immunochemistry of Solid-phase Immunoassay, 1991; mem. editl. bd.: Analytical Biochem., Develop. & Comparative Immunology; contbr. more than 180 articles and revs. to sci. jours. Recipient citation Inst. for Sci. Info., 1983; Max Planck fellow, Mariensee, Germany, 1972-74, Fogarty internat. fellow NIH-Fogarty Ctr., 1981-82. Mem.: Soc. Mucosal Immunity, Am. Assn. Immologists, Stearman Restorers Assn. Avocations: flying, bicycle touring. Office: U Iowa Dept Microbiology Bowen Sci Bldg 51 Newton Rd Iowa City IA 52242-1109 E-mail: john-butler@uiowa.edu.

BUTLER, MARIE GLADYS, nursing educator; b. Chester, Pa., June 12, 1951; d. Joseph Francis and Juanita Marie (Spear) B. Diploma, LPN, James Martin, 1983; AGS, C.C. of Phila., 1989; BSN, Thomas Jefferson U., 1991. Cert. rehab. nurse. LPN Care Pavillon of Walnut Park, Phila., 1983-84, Supior Care, Phila., 1984-85, Norrell, Jenkintown, Pa., 1986-87, Health Force, Jenkintown, 1987-91, Proto Call, Phila., 1990-91; staff nurse VA Med. Ctr., Phila., 1991-93; case mgr. Nursing Unlimited Homecare, 1993; RN staff nurse Brinton Manor Subacute Rehab., 1993-95, Nurse Power, 1993-97, Maxim Healthcare, 1995—; home care RN Absolute Nursing Care, Landsdown, Pa., 1995—96; PRN pool Taylor Hosp. Transitial Care Unit, 1995-96; RN Camp Sunshine, Thorton, Pa., 1995, 98; clin. nursing instr. James Martin Sch. of Practical Nursing, Phila., 1996; unit mgr. St. Ignatius Nursing Home, Phila., 1996-97; RN, unit mgr. CareParish, Phila., 1997; case mgr. Aspen Home Health Care, Phila., 1997—98; tele. svc. rep. TV Guide, Radnor, Pa., 1998—2001; CNA instr. Am. Trade Bus. Sch., Phila., 1999—2000; RN Ctrl. Health Svcs., Media, Pa., 2001—02, Pulmonary Care Inc., Havertown, Pa., 2002—03; instr. Harrison Career Inst., Phila., 2003—. Regional coord. Student Nurses Assn. Pa., Harrisburg, 1990-91; co-chair mentoring com. C.C. Phila. Alumni Assn., 1992; mem. mentor and shadowing program Thomas Jefferson U., Phila., 1992; RN Camp Sunshine, 1995. Mem. Ladies Aux. of VFW, Phi Theta Kappa (C.C. of Phila. chpt.), Sigma Theta Tau (membership com. Delta Rho chpt. 1992, 94, v.p. 1993-95, del. biannual conv. 1993, chmn. membership com. 1995—). Roman Catholic. Avocations: gardening, sewing, crocheting, walking, traveling. Home: 5522 N Mascher St Philadelphia PA 19120-2918 Office: Harrison Career Inst 1619 Walnut St Philadelphia PA 19103

BUTLER, MARY MARGARET, secondary education educator; b. Austin, Tex., Jan. 18, 1949; d. Joseph Cronin and Lucille Ann (Sager) B. BA, Tex. Tech. U., 1970, MA, 1976; MEd, Sam Houston State Coll., 1975. Cert. secondary English/polit. sci. tchr., mid-mgmt. supr., supt. Tchr. Livingston (Tex.) Ind. Sch. Dist., 1972-83; bldg. prin. Livingston Mid. Sch., 1984-89; tchr. McCullough H.S., The Woodlands, Tex., 1989—. Chmn. child welfare bd. Polk County Child Welfare, Livingston, 1988-89; cons. region X Edn. Svc. Ctr., Dallas, 1989-90, mem. com. region VI, Huntsville, 1988; cons. San Houston Acad. Sam Houston State U., Huntsville, 1992. Contbr.: (curriculum guide) Sam Houston: A Citizen of His Time An Instructional Guide, 1992. Recipient for God and Youth award Diocese of Beaumont (Tex.) Cath. Youth Orgn., 1979, award Optimist Club, Livingston, 1989. Mem. ASCD, Nat. Coun. Tchrs. English, Nat. Coun. Social Studies, Tex. Assn. Staff Devel., Delta Kappa Gamma, Phi Delta Kappa. Home: 91 N Deerfoot Cir The Woodlands TX 77380-1523 Office: JL McCullough HS 3800 S Panther Creek Dr The Woodlands TX 77381-2732

BUTLER, NANCY TAYLOR, gender equity specialist, program director; b. Newport, RI, Oct. 31, 1942; d. Robert Lee and Roberta Claire (Brown) Taylor; m. Edward M. Butler, Aug. 22, 1964; children: Jeffrey, Gregory, Katherine. AB, Cornell U., 1964. Asst. dir. Career Equity Assistance Ctr. for Tng. Coll. of N.J., 1990-98; owner Equity Resources, Tinton Falls, N.J., 1993—. Mem. N.J. Dept. Edn. Gender Equity Adv. Comm., 1995—, sec., 1996-2000, chair, 2000—. Editor Equity Exch., 1991—. Monmouth County dist. ethics com. Supreme Ct. N.J., 1987-91; pres. Vol. Ctr. Monmouth County, Red Bank, 1985-89; mem. Cornell U. Coun., Ithaca, N.Y., 1987-91, 94—, adminstrv. bd., 1996—, vice-chair, 2001—; dir. Cornell Assn. Class Officers, 1991-97; chair Cornell Alumni Trustee Nominating Com., 1994. Recipient Woman of Achievement award Commn. on Status of Women, 1988, Women's History Tribute NOW-N.J., 1995, Woman Leader award N.J. Assn. Women Bus. Owners, 1996. Mem. AAUW (life; pres. N.J. chpt. 1988-90, Edn. Found. Named Gift 1982, 83, 84, 86, 87, 89, 91), Nat. Coalition for Sex Equity in Edn. Home: 20 Cedar Pl Tinton Falls NJ 07724-2807

BUTLER, ORTON CARMICHAEL, earth science educator, climatologist; b. Millersburg, Ohio, June 9, 1923; s. Maxon Henry Butler and Atossa Ruth Carmichael; m. Betty Ellen Johnson, Sept. 15, 1951; children: Marilyn Jean, Kathryn Ellen. BA, Oberlin Coll., 1948; MA, Clark U., 1951; PhD, Ohio State U., 1969. Rsch. analyst, China specialist U.S. Army Engr. Strategic Intelligence, Washington, 1951-60; prof. Memphis State U. (now U. Memphis), 1960-81; prof. emeritus U. Memphis, 1981. Author: (book) An Introductory Soils Laboratory Handbook, 1979, other publs. Cpl. U.S. Army, 1942-46, PTO. Mem. Masons. Republican. United Ch. of Christ. Avocations: tree farming, gardening, golf.

BUTLER, PAUL THURMAN, retired religious studies educator; b. Springfield, Mo., Nov. 17, 1928; s. Willard Drew and Verna Lois (Thurman) B.; m. Gale Jynne Kinnard, Nov. 20, 1948; children: Sherry Lynne, Mark Stephen. ThB, Ozark Bible Coll., 1961, M Bibl. Lit., 1973; ThD, Theol. U. Am., 1990. Ordained to ministry Christian Ch., 1958. Noncommd. officer USN, 1946-56; mem. staff Amphibious Forces Pacific, 1947-50; mem. CTF 90 Korean War, 1950-51; mem. guided missile unit 41 Guided Missile Unit 41, Point Mugu, Calif., 1951-56; ret., 1956; min. Washington Christian Ch., Lebanon, Mo., 1958-60; registrar Ozark Christian Coll., Joplin, Mo., 1960-92, prof. Bible and philosophy, 1960-98; ret., 1998. Min. Westside Christian Ch., 1960-63, North Joplin Christian Ch., 1969-71. Author: The Gospel of John, 1961, The Minor Prophets, 1968, Daniel, 1976, Isaiah, 3 vols., 1978, Esther, 1979, The Gospel of Luke, 1981 (transl. into Korean, French, Portuguese, East Indian-Tamil), Revelation, 1982, I Corinthians, 1984, II Corinthians, 1986, What the Bible Says about Civil Government, 1990, Approaching the New Millennium—An Amillennial Look at A.D. 2000, 1997; also author 8 geneal. family histories: Butlers, Thurmans, Ganns, Alleys, Painters, Kinnard, Driefuses, Vincents. Recipient Outstanding Alumnus award Ozark Christian Coll., 1992. Mem. SAR (nat. chaplain gen. 1991-92, pres., sec. Mo. Soc. chpt., pres. Sgt. Ariel Nims chpt.), Nat. Soc. Sons. Colonial New Eng., Nat. Soc. Sons and Daus. Pilgrims, Ret. Officers Assn. (hon.), Am. Legion, Mo. Territorial Pioneers, Mo. Geneal. Soc., Tenn. Geneal Soc., Tenn. Pioneer Ancestors, Joplin Hist. Soc., Gann Family Hist. Soc. (pres. 1993-95). Republican. Home: 2502 Utica St Joplin MO 64801-1246

BUTLER, ROBIN ERWIN, retired vocational technical educator, consultant; b. St. Louis, May 16, 1929; s. Erwin and Florence Katherine Butler; m. Marie Day, Aug. 22, 1947; children: Lawrence Robin, Nicki Ruth; m. Linda Koenig, June 12, 1993. BA, Alma Coll., 1960; MDiv., U. Dubuque, 1964; postgrad., U. Wis., 1981—, Pacific Western U., Los Angeles, 1986—. Cert. vocat., tech. and adult edn. tchr. Printer, journalist various corps., Ohio, Ky., Ind., Iowa, 1945-64; asst. pastor presby. Ch., Manitowoc, Wis., 1964-67; program dir. YMCA, Manitowoc, 1968-69; owner operator Butler & Son Contractors, Manitowoc, 1969-72; supr. Mirro Corp., Manitowoc, 1972-81; adult educator Lakeshore Tech. Inst., Cleve., 1981-97, lead instr. mgmt. tech., 1985-86; ednl. cons. Rebcon, Manitowoc, Wis., 1997—. Adj. prof. mgmt. Cardinal Stritch Coll., Milw., 1985—, Silver Lake Coll., Manitowoc, 1999—; cons. accelerated adult edn., consensus building, human rels. skills, 1986—. Author: Andragogical Guidelines, 1985; columnist: The Midwest Flyer, 1981-85. Mem. Gov's. Task Force on Aero. Revenues, Madison, 1981. Served to sgt. U.S. Army, 1948-49. Mem. Am. Mgmt. Assn., Internat. Alliance for Learning, Wis. Regional Writers Assn. Roman Catholic. Home and Office: Rebcon 1408 Columbus St Manitowoc WI 54220-5602 E-mail: linrob@lsol.net.

BUTLER, SUSAN LOWELL, educational association executive, writer; b. Bklyn., Feb. 10, 1944; d. John William and Catherine (Mauro) Yost; m. Horace Hamilton Lowell (div. 1982); m. James Thomas Butler, Feb. 12, 1983; stepchildren: James, Kevin, Michael. BA, Lycoming Coll., 1965; postgrad., U. Pa., 1965-67. Tchr. English and Journalism Bristol Twp. Schs., Levittown, Pa., 1967-70; field rep. Nat. Edn. Assn., Washington, 1970-74, dir. comm., 1974-80, dir. western states region Austin (Tex.) and Denver, 1980-84; acct. supr. Dale Chrisman & Assocs., Austin, 1984-86; pvt. cons. Austin, 1986-88; exec. v.p. Women in Comm., Inc., Washington, 1988-91; nat. exec. dir. Nat. Women's Hall of Fame, Seneca Falls, NY, 1991-96; dir. Coalition For America's Children, Washington, 1996—97; managing partner Butler Pub. Affairs, 1998—; sr. dir. pub. edn. Nat. Mental Assn., 2000—; v.p. comms. and public affairs The Hospices of Nat. Capital Region, Fairfax, Va., 2000—. Mem. bd. The Media Inst., Washington, 1989-91, mem. family lodge steering com. NIG, 2000—. Author: National Education Association: A Special Mission, 1987, Handbook of Association Communications, 1987, Pressing Onward: The Women's Historical Biography of the National Education Association, 1996. V.p. pub. affairs Mental Health Assn. of Tex., Austin, 1987-88; bd. dirs. Nat. Women's Hall of Fame, Ovarian Cancer Nat. Alliance, 1997—; co-chair Ovarian Cancer Coalition Greater Washington, 1997—; dirs. consumer liaison group Nat. Cancer Inst. Dirs. Consumer Liaison Group, 1997—; adv. bd. Nat. Archives History Project, 1995-96; active Alexandria (Va.) Commn. for Women, 1996—, 250th Anniversary Commn., 1997—; bd. dirs. Ovarian Cancer Nat. Alliance, 1997—. Mem. Am. Soc. Assn. Execs., Pub. Rels. Soc. Am. (accredited), Women in Comm. Inc. Episcopalian. Avocations: skiing, photography. Home and Office: Butler Pub Affairs 406 Skyhill Rd Alexandria VA 22314-4920

BUTLER, VICKIE BURKHART, college official; b. Knoxville, Tenn., May 22, 1955; d. James Claude and Ruth Adelia (Pratt) B.; m. Benjamin Larry Butler, Jan. 7, 1984; 1 stepson, Benjamin Brent. BS, Carson-Newman Coll., 1976; MS, U. Tenn., 1979. Cert. tchr. Tchr. Knox County Sch. System, Knoxville, 1976-82; state vol. coord. Tenn. Dept. Human Svcs., Nashville, 1982-89; dir. alumni rels. Carson-Newman Coll., Jefferson City, Tenn., 1989—. Mem. Tenn. Advancement Resources Coun., 1989—; cons.; workshop leader; program builder; grad. Tenn. Leadership, 1990. Author: (manual) DHS Volunteer Services, 1982. Pianist, dir. bell choir 1st United Meth. Ch., Newport, 1985—, sec. nominations and personnel com. mem. Fellow Lab. for Learning; mem. Gamma Sigma Sigma, Phi Lambda Theta, Kappa Delta Pi. Avocations: piano, cooking, singing, reading. Office: Carson Newman Coll Russell Ave Jefferson City TN 37760

BUTLER-NALIN, KAY, secondary school educator; b. Kalamazoo, Mich., Nov. 25, 1948; d. Donald Thomas and Barbara (Little) Butler; m. Paul M. Nalin, Aug. 28, 1971; children: Alethea Lauren, Amelia Meagan. BA, Ctrl. Coll., 1971; MA, Stanford U., 1978, PhD, 1985. Compensatory reading project facilitator Ednl. Testing Svc., Princeton, 1972-78; assoc. rschr. Stanford (Calif.) U., 1985-88; asst. prof. composition Coll. San Mateo, Calif., 1988-90; asst. prof. English edn. U. No. Iowa, Cedar Falls, 1990—97, 1999—2003; rschr. grad. sch. edn. U. Calif., Santa Barbara, 1999—2001. Rschr. The Pangaea Network. Author poems, revs.; contbr. articles to profl. jours. and chpts. to books. Avocations: swimming, gardening, moonlore, technology.

BUTORAC, FRANK GEORGE, librarian, educator; b. Crosby, Minn., Feb. 12, 1927; s. Frank and Mary (Paun) B.; m. Mary Regis McGowan Ratigan, Apr. 8, 1972; stepchildren: Helen Elizabeth, Nicholas. AB, U. Mich., 1950, AM, 1956, AMLS, 1958; postgrad., Cornell Law Sch., 1950-51, Harvard U., 1953; postgrad. in philosophy, U. Notre Dame, 1959, 60-62; postgrad. in theology, Holy Cross Coll., 1962-66; postgrad., Cath. U., 1963, Georgetown U., 1965, NYU, 1968-70, 79-81, Cambridge U., 1975, Oxford U., 1989, postgrad., 1995, postgrad., 2003, Trinity Coll., Dublin, 1990. With exec. tng. program U.S. Rubber, Mishawaka, Ind., 1952-53; tchr. 6th grade Jefferson Sch., Wayne, Mich., 1953-54; tchr. social studies Slauson Jr. H.S., Ann Arbor, Mich., 1954-55; supervising tchr. social studies Lincoln Consol. H.S., Ea. Mich. U., Ypsilanti, 1955-57; circulation libr., engring. libr. U. Mich., Ann Arbor, 1958-59; joined Congregation of Holy Cross, 1959; postulant U. Notre Dame, 1959; seminarian and temporary profession, 1959-66; novice Sacred Heart Novitiate, Jordan, Minn., 1959-60; registrar Mercer C.C., Trenton, N.J., 1966-68, asst. dir. cmty. and ext. svcs., 1968-70, dir. evening and ext. ops., 1970-71, dir. spl. programs, 1971-74, dir. libr. svcs., 1974-84, chmn. libr. tech. program, 1974-84, dir. libr. devel., 1984-87, libr., 1987—. Cons. libr. edn., libr. mgmt. Pres. U. Mich. Clubs Coun. 2d Dist., 1991-93; chmn. U. Mich. Newman Ctr. Fund Drive, 1958; professed Secular Franciscan Order Monastery of St. Clare, Bordentown, N.J., 1984, 3d Order Dominican, 2003—; ann. participant Yale U.-Hopkins summer seminar program, 2000—. Bd. dirs. U. Mich. Alumni Assn., 1995-98; chmn. Anna B. Stokes Found., Trenton, 1972; dean's adv. com. Cornell Law Sch., 1972-73; mem. N.J. State Adv. Com. on Aging, 1971; mem. Mich. State Ctrl. Com. Young Democrats, 1949-50. Served with USN, 1944-47. Recipient Tall Cedars of Lebanon award for Cmty. Svc., Trenton, 1974. Mem. ALA, N.J. Libr. Assn. (exec. bd. 1977-78), Purnell Sch. Parents Assn., Cornell Law Assn., Bennington Coll. Parents Assn., Pine Manor Coll. Parents Assn., U. Mich. Ctrl. N.J. (pres. 1987-91), Mensa, English Speaking Union, Nassau Club (Princeton, N.J.), Princeton Club (N.Y.C.), Trenton Lions Club (pres. 1972), Trenton Torch Club (pres. 1972), Cornell Club Ctrl. N.J. (pres. 1977-78), Marines' Meml.

Club (San Francisco), Cath. Alumni Club Trenton (pres. 1968), Theta Delta Chi, Phi Delta Phi, Phi Delta Kappa, Kappa Delta Pi, Alpha Phi Omega. Republican. Roman Catholic. Home: 6 Mercer St Princeton NJ 08540-6808 Office: 1200 Old Trenton Rd Princeton Junction NJ 08550-3407

BUTT, HUGH ROLAND, gastroenterologist, educator; b. Belhaven, N.C., Jan. 8, 1910; s. Harry Frederick and Maybelle (Jarvis) B.; m. Mary Dempwolf, Apr. 8, 1939; children: Selby, Lucy, Charles, Frances. Student, Va. Poly. Inst., 1927-29; MD, U. Va., 1933; MS, U. Minn., 1937. Diplomate: Am. Bd. Internal Medicine (mem. bd., subsplty. gastroenterology). Intern St. Luke's Hosp., Bethlehem, Pa., 1933-34; fellow medicine Mayo Found., 1934-37, 1st asst., 1937-38, instr., 1938-43, asst. prof., 1943-47, assoc. prof., 1947-52, prof., 1952-82. Cons. physician Mayo Clinic, St. Mary's Hosp., 1938-80; chmn. sci. counselors Nat. Cancer Inst., 1961-62; mem. Nat. Adv. Cancer Coun., 1966-74, chair residency review com., 1959-60; v.p. Nutrition Found.; chmn. sci. adv. com. Ludwig Inst. Cancer Rsch., 1971-86; pres. Assn. for Study Liver Disease, 1961-62. Author: (with Snell) Vitamin K, 1941; papers, monographs. Served as lt. comdr. M.C. USNR, 1942-46. Recipient John Horsley Meml. prize U. Va., 1938 Master ACP (pres. 1971-72, Alfred Stengel Meml. award 1975); mem. Royal Coll. Physicians (London), Royal Coll. Physicians (Ireland and Scotland), Am. Soc. Clin. Investigation, Am. Gastroent. Assn. (pres. 1960, Julius Friedenwald medal 1979), Assn. Am. Physicians, Am. Assn. Study Liver Diseases (pres. 1956). Episcopalian. Home: 1014 7th St SW Rochester MN 55902-2004

BUTTERFIELD, CHARLES EDWARD, JR., educational consultant; b. Urbana, Ill., Mar. 31, 1928; s. Charles E. and Bessie J. (Winters) B.; m. Gayle Coberley, Jan. 27, 1952; children: Jeffrey M., Carey J. BS in Biology, Chemistry, Physics, Psychology, Edn., U. Ill., 1951, MS, 1953; postgrad., Duke U., 1958, No. Ill. U., 1958-59, Mich. State U., 1959, 64-65, 72, Knox Coll., 1962, Fla. State U., 1969, U. Colo., 1970. Field exec. Nottawa Trails coun. Boy Scouts Am., Battle Creek, Mich., 1953-54; instr. sci. Gardner (Ill.)-South Wilmington Twp. H.S., 1954-59; pub. rels. cons., edn. cons. Dresden Nuclear Power Plant, Consol. Edison, Braidwood, Ill., 1958—60; biology coord. Lake Park H.S., Medinah, Ill., 1959-65; sr. sci. project editor Singer/Random House Pub. Co., N.Y.C., 1965-68; sci. supr. K-12 Ramsey (N.J.) Pub. Schs., 1968-82; sci. edn. cons., 1981—; pres., CFO, Shield Cons., 1977—. Instr. radiation physics N.W. Cmty. Hosp., Arlington Heights, Ill., 1963-65; cons. Rand McNally Pubs., 1972-80; peer reviewer NSF proposals, 1979-84; mem. sci. adv. bd. Raintree Publs., Milw., 1981-86; assoc. Thomas A. Edison Found., 1981-88; condr. various workshops for sci. tchrs., 1965—. Contbg. author: NSSA Sourcebook for Science Supervisors, 2nd edit., 1976, 3rd edit., 1988. Pres. Bd. Edn., Gardner, Ill., 1956-57; pres. Foxwood Village Fedn. Mfrd. Home Owners of Fla., 1988-90; co-project dir., fin. officer suprs. programs NSF/NSSA/PEEC, 1979-83; treas., bd. dirs. Highland Fairways Property Owners Assn., 1993-96, 99-2002, fin. cons., 1996—; judge Seiko Youth Challenge, 1994, 95. With USN and USMC, 1946-48. Recipient Allendale (N.J.) Cmty. Lifesaving award, 1976; NSF/AAAS fellow Mich. State U., 1964-66, fellow 1st Southeastern NASA Aerospace Conf., 1961. Fellow AAAS; mem. NEA, ACLU, Nat. Sci. Ednl. Leadership Assn. (mem. exec. com. 1974-80, pres. 1977-78, sr. staff mem. various other confs. U. Calif. at San Diego, 1979, U. Iowa 1979-80, supr. nat. elections 1982-2000, mem. editl. adv. bd. 1986-91, Outstanding Svc. award 1990, 98, 1st hon. lifetime exec. bd. mem. award for outstanding svc. 2000—), Nat. Sci. Tchrs. Assn. (exec. bd. 1977-78, Disting. Svc. Sci. Edn. citation 1981), Am. Humanist Assn., N.J. Sci. Tchrs. Assn., N.J. Sci. Suprs. Assn. (Disting. Svc. award 1982), Ramsey Suprs. Assn. (founding pres. 1980-81), Bergen County Sci. Suprs. Assn. (pres. 1971-73, Outstanding Svc. award 1974, 78), Sch. Sci. and Math. Assn., Am. Inst. Biol. Scis. (cons. biological sci. curriculum study 1965—), Nat. Assn. Biol. Tchrs., Coun. Elem. Sci. Internat., Assn. Edn. Tchrs. Sci., N.J. Prins. and Suprs. Assn., Am. Assn. Notaries, Nat. Notary Assn., U. Ill. Alumni Assn., Fla. So. Coll. Sixth Man Club, Cmty. Assns. Inst., 1st Marine Divsn. Assn., Fleet Marine Force Combat Med. Pers. Assn., Am. Legion, USN Meml. Found., Lakeland (Fla.) C. of C., Mensa, Masons, DeMolay Internat. (chevalier), Order of Ea. Star, Humanist Assn. West Ctrl. Fla. (charter), Norwalk H.S. Alumni Assn., U. Ill. Alumni Assn., Psi Chi. Office: 22 Spring Ave Oakland NJ 07436-1930 E-mail: chargayb2@earthlink.net.

BUTTERFIELD, KAREN, educational association administrator; EdD. Art tchr. Coconino H.S.; founder, dir. Flagstaff Arts and Leadership Acad., 1996—. Named State Tchr. Yr. Ariz., 1993, Disney Am. Tchr. award, 1993.*

BUTTERFIELD, STEPHEN ALAN, education educator; b. Middlebury, Vt., Sept. 10, 1948; s. Stewart Ellsworth and Mary Elizabeth (Coursey) B.; m. Jeanne Allison Zong, June 20, 1970; children: Sarah, Jason, Scott. BS, Springfield (Mass.) Coll., 1971; MEd, Keene State Coll., 1980; PhD, Ohio State U., 1984. Tchr. 4th grade Whitingham Sch., Jacksonville, Vt., 1971-72; prin., tchr. Halifax Sch., West Halifax, Vt., 1972-73; tchr. phys. edn. Austine Sch. for the Deaf, Brattleboro, Vt., 1973-81; prof. edn. and spl. edn. U. Maine, Orono, 1984—. Project dir. Nat. Youth Sports Program, state coord.; chmn., mem. Maine Task Force on Adapted Phys. Edn. Editor Maine Jour. Health, Phys. Edn., Recreation and Dance, 1988-96; contbr. articles to profl. jours. Bd. dirs. Bangor (Maine) YMCA, 1990-92, Maine Adapted Sports and Recreation, 1994-98; mem. Gov.'s Coun. Phys. Fitness and Sports, 1996-98, 2000-2004; mem. nat. stds. com. Adapted Phys. Edn., 2000-2002; mem. adv. bd. U.S. Sports and Fitness Ctr. for Disabled. Recipient Meritorious award for Exceptional Project Performance, Nat. Youth Sports Program; state, fedn. found. grantee. Mem. AAHPERD (ea. dist. merit award for phys. edn. 1989), Maine Assn. Health, Phys. Edn., Recreation and Dance (pres. 1986-87, Honor award for disting. leadership 1989), Nat. Consortium Phys. Edn. Recreation for Individuals with Disabilities (bd. dirs. 1997-99, editor The Advocate 1994-96). Republican. Avocation: military history. Home: 277 14th St Bangor ME 04401-4454 Office: U Maine 5740 Lengyel Hall College Ave Orono ME 04469-5740 E-mail: steve.butterfield@umit.maine.edu.

BUTTERS, JOHN PATRICK, travel company executive, educator; b. Janesville, Wis., Jan. 11, 1933; s. John William and Mary Helen (Tracey) B.; m. Collette Helen Jung, Apr. 20, 1963; children: Blair John, Laura Lisbeth. BA, U. Wis., 1955. cert. travel counselor. Traffic supr., field training Pan Am. Airways, Chgo., 1958-64; ops. mgr. incentives Lerios/E.F. MacDonald, San Francisco, 1964-67; retail agy. mgr. Bungey Travel, Palo Alto, Calif., 1967-68; dist. sales mgr. Lissonne Lindeman, San Francisco, 1968-71; group travel mgr., Wis. div. Am. Automobile Assn., Madison, 1971-75; owner, v.p., sec. Travel/ease Inc., Madison, 1975-88; owner, pres. Travel Learn, Ltd., Madison, 1981-90; sr. curriculum specialist Inst. Cert. Travel Agts., Wellesley, Mass., 1989-93; free lance tour coord., tour escort Gretchen Petersen Tours, Inc., Madison, Wis., 1993-2000, Van Galder Tour and Travel, Janesville, Wis., 1996—. Cons. Madison Area Tech. Coll., 1982-88, Rockford (Ill.) Bus. Coll., 1988-90; treas. Capital Area Travel Soc., Madison, 1973-77. Editor: Travel Industry Mktg., 1990, Travel Industry Bus. Mgmt., 1992, U.S.A.-Can., 1992, Pacific Rim, 1993, Latin Am., 1994; contbr. articles to profl. jours. Program chmn. The Travel Club, Madison, 1973-77; bd. trustees St. Andrew's Soc., Madison, 1976-88 (treas. 1975-79); chmn. mus. svc. coun. Rock County Hist. Soc., Janesville, Wis., 1985-89; trustee Schumacher Farm Conservancy, Waunakee, Wis., 1984—. Mem. Inst. Cert. Travel Agts. (life), U. Wis. Alumni, Madison Club. Avocations: travel, reading, geneology, history, geography. Home: 1328 Oakland Ave Janesville WI 53545-4243 Office: Van Galder Tour and Travel 20 S Main St Janesville WI 53545-3959

BUTTON, CAROL DRUSILLA, elementary education educator; b. Nelson, Pa., Nov. 6, 1941; d. Weldon Reed and Erma Goldie (Preston) Pease; m. Llewellyn Dallas Button, June 26, 1965; 1 child, Carol Lynn. BS, Mansfield U., 1963; MEd, Pa. State U., 1965. Cert. elem. tchr., Pa. Tchr. No. Tioga Sch. Dist., Elkland, Pa., 1963—98, substitute tchr., 1998—. Mem. State Scholarship Com., Delta Kappa Gamma, 1985-91. Mem. Pa. State Edn. Assn., No. Tioga Edn. Assn. (exec. bd. 1984-90), Order Eastern Star, Shakespeare Club, Delta Kappa Gamma (Pi chpt.), Nat. Ed. Assn. (Ret.), Pa. Assn. of Sch. Retirees. Home: 408 W Main St Elkland PA 16920-1008 Office: No Tioga Sch Dist Coates Ave Elkland PA 16920-1306

BUTTS, GEORGIA LEBRENDELLE, secondary education educator; b. Elizabeth, N.C., July 24, 1943; d. George Lee and Erma (Basnight) Moore; m. Clifton Tiberous Butts, Oct. 30, 1968; children: Lloyd Christopher, Tonja, Sonja Yvette, Clifton Tiberous. BA, Norfolk State U., 1978, MA, 1993. Cert. collegiate profl., Va. Tchr. various subjects Portsmouth Pub. Schs., Isle of Wight County Schs.; tchr. math. and sci. Tabernacle Prayer Christian Sch., Norfolk, Va.; owner Butts Tutorial/Tng. Svcs. Bible tchr. Charity House Adult Facility, Va., 1990—, Corner Stone Baptist Ch., 1989—; dir. Bible edn. Cornerstone Missionary Bapt. Ch., Elizabeth City, N.C. Recipient Graduate scholar Norfolk State U., 1983-84, Kelloge grantee Norfolk State U., 1977-78. Mem. Assn. Supervision and Curriculm Devel. Avocations: singing, sewing, fishing. Home: 2229 Lansing Ave Portsmouth VA 23704-5439

BUTZ, GLORIA K. elementary education educator; b. Salem, Oreg., Aug. 29, 1951; d. Mary Carolyn (Davis) Mann; m. Loren O. Butz, Aug. 18, 1973; children: Janiess Dielle, Karel Trevor. BA Music Edn., Seattle Pacific U., 1973, MEd, 1981. Cert. elem./secondary tchr., Wash.; profl. cert. Assn. Christian Schs. Internat. Music tchr., grades K-6 Auburn (Wash.) Sch. dist. #408, 1973-75, tchr. sixth grade, 1975-77; reading tutor Valley Christian Sch., Auburn, 1983-84, elem. tchr., fifth/sixth grades, 1984—; head tchr. Valley Christian Mid. Sch., Auburn, 2000—03, prin., 2003—. Mem. sch. bd. Valley Christian Sch., 1982-84; young author's camp staff mem., Seattle Pacific U., Wash., 1981-83. Dir. Vacation Bible Sch., Auburn Free Meth. Ch., 1987, 89, 92, 94. Mem. Internat. Reading Assn., Washington Orgn. for Reading Devel. Republican. Avocations: piano, flute, travel, gardening, sewing. Home: 1505 24th St SE Auburn WA 98002-7837

BUTZ, MARY, principal; b. Bklyn., Jan. 5, 1948; d. John and Eva (Cewe) B. BA, St. Joseph's Coll. Women, 1969; MA, Bklyn. Coll., 1972. Tchr. N.Y.C. Bd. Edn., 1969-82; asst. prin. E.R. Murrow H.S., N.Y.C., 1982-88; staff devel. specialist U.F.T., N.Y.C., 1988-90; staff devel. borough coord. Queens (N.Y.) High Sch., 1990-92; assoc. dir. ednl. issues Am. Fedn. Tchrs., Washington, 1992-93; dir., founder Manhattan Village Acad., N.Y.C., 1993-94, prin., 1994-99; prin. mentor New Visions for Pub. Schs., 1999-2000; exec. dir. for prin./leadership tng. N.Y.C. Bd. of Edn., 1999—2003. Cons. in field. Kellog Found. fellow, 1988-91. Mem. Coalition Network. Avocations: furniture refinishing, cooking, biking, reading, wine collecting. Office: PO Box 1288 Southold NY 11971

BUTZ, OTTO WILLIAM, political science educator; b. Floesti, Romania, May 2, 1923; came to U.S., 1949, naturalized, 1959; s. Otto E. and Charlotte (Engelmann) B.; m. Velia DeAngelis, Sept. 13, 1961. BA, U. Toronto, 1947; PhD, Princeton U., 1953. Asst. prof. polit. sci. Swarthmore Coll., 1954-55; asst. prof. politics Princeton U., 1955-60; asso. editor Random House, N.Y.C., 1960-61; prof. social sci. San Francisco State Coll., 1961-67; academic v.p. Sacramento State Coll., 1967-69, acting pres., 1969-70; pres. Golden Gate U., 1970-92; pres. emeritus, 1992—. Author: German Political Theory, 1955, The Unsilent Generation, 1958, Of Man and Politics, 1960, To Make a Difference— A Student Look at America, 1967. Recipient Calif. State Colls. Outstanding Tchr. award, 1966 Mem. Am. Polit. Sci. Assn. Office: 536 Mission St San Francisco CA 94105-2921

BUUS, LINDA LEE PANNETIER, secondary education educator; b. Rapid City, S.D., Aug. 23, 1949; d. Max Pannetier and Pansy A. (Francisco) Robison; m. David V. Buus, Aug. 1, 1970 (div. Apr. 1988); children: Baend J., Yuri D. BS in Secondary Edn., Black Hills State, 1973; MEd, Lesley Coll., 1988. Cert. tchr. English, social studies, libr.-media specialist, Wyo. Tchr.'s aide Taipei (Taiwan) Am. Sch., 1971-72; 7th and 8th grade social studies tchr. Our Lady of Perpetual Help Sch., Rapid City, 1973-74; 7th and 8th grade English and spelling tchr. Newcastle (Wyo.) Jr. H.S., 1974-75; 9th grade social studies, English tchr. Campbell County Jr. H.S., Gillette, Wyo., 1975-76; 9th grade social studies tchr. Twin Spruce Jr. H.S., Gillette, 1976-81, Sage Valley Jr. H.S., Gillette, 1982—; chairperson dept. social studies Twin Spruce Jr. H.S. and Sage Valley Jr. H.S., 1979-91, 94—. Mem. liaison task force Campbell County Sch. Dist., 1983-86, mem. curriculum coordinating coun., 1987-90; student tchr. supr. U. Wyo., Laramie, 1980-93. Participant Wyo. Gov.'s Youth Conf./Legis. Youth Forum, Cheyenne, 1979-81. Fellow Taft Inst. Govt., 1985, Nat. Humanities Summer History, 1991. Mem. NEA (del. to rep. assembly 1986), Campbell County Edn. Assn. (faculty rep. 1983-88, v.p. 1986-87, mem. leadership team 1994—), Wyo. Edn. Assn. (senate liaison legis. dinner 1985, mem. profl. standards and practices comm. 1994—), Wyo. Coun. of Social Studies, Nat. Coun. of Social Studies, Kappa Delta Pi, Sigma Kappa (pres. 1970), Phi Kappa Phi (mem. Wyo. chpt.). Roman Catholic. Avocations: counted cross stitch, reading, hiking, traveling. Home: PO Box 488 Moorcroft WY 82721-0488 Office: Sage Valley Jr H S 1000 W Lakeway Rd Gillette WY 82718-5633

BUYANOVSKY, SOPHIA, linguist, educator; b. Moscow, Nov. 17, 1956; d. Michael and Lubor Yakobishvili; m. Lev Buyanovsky, Aug. 27, 1977; children: Michael, Paul, Daniel. BA, MA, Moscow State U. Tchr. of Russian S.I. Tech. H.S., N.Y.C., 1989—. Home: 52 Blue Hills Dr Holmdel NJ 07733

BUZZELLI, CHARLOTTE GRACE, special education educator; b. Mar. 21, 1947; d. Edmund Albert and Sarah Agnes (Russo) Buzzelli. BS, U. Akron, 1969, MS in Edn., 1976. Tchr. St. Anthony Sch., Akron, 1969-76; program coord., tchr. Akron Montessori Sch. Continuing Edn. Program, Eastwood Ctr., Akron, 1976-77; dir. edn. Fallsview Psychiat. Hosp., Ohio Dept. Mental Health, Cuyahoga Falls, 1977-92, developer job tng. partnership grant program and spl. needs handicapped grant program, 1992-97; tng. coord. N.E. regional & program educator children svcs. Ohio Dept. Mental Health State Operated Svcs., 1992—97. Spl. edn. svcs. developer and educator cmty svcs. div. North Coast Behavioral Healthcare Sys., Ohio Dept. Mental Health, 1997-2002; tchr. adult basic lit. edn. program Akron City Sch. Dist., 1992—; developer Akron City Schs. Project Rise Homeless Youth Family Learning Literacy Program, 2001—; cons. in field; pioneered first spl. edn. program in Ohio for adult state psychiat. hosp.; developed 1st community-based adult basic edn. program in state instn. in Ohio; program cons. state operated svcs. State of Ohio; participant U. Hawaii Study Tours Rsch. Projects, Internat. Edn. and East Asia Pi Lambda Theta Orient Study Tour, Manoa campus, 1990, spl. edn. rsch. U. Akron, 1976. Developer literacy evaluation program Project Rise Homeless Youth, Akron, Ohio, 1991—; mem. gospel meets Symphony chorus Akron Symphony Orch. Gospel Choir, 1996—; mem. choir Diocese of Cleve., St. John's Cathedral, Mass of Jubilee Gospel Choir, 1998, 2000. Named Ohio Tchr. of Yr., 1979; recipient A Key award, U. Akron, Urban Light award for outstanding svc., 2001, Cmty. Svc. Achievement award, Italian Am. Soc., Cmty. Collaboration award, Summit County Housing Network, 2003. Mem. CEC (coun. pres.), ASCD, Assn. Children with Learning Disabilities, Internat. Reading Assn., U. Akron Alumni Assn., Univ. Club, Akron Women's City Club, Coll. Club of Akron, Pi Lambda Theta (pres.), Phi Delta Kappa, Delta Kappa Gamma, Gamma Beta (pres.), Kappa Kappa Iota. Avocations: pet therapy to children and adults with disabilities, reading, travel, writing, singing, creating community resources for spl. edn. students and mental health clients. Home: 662 Dayton St Akron OH 44310-2301 Office: Adult Basic Literacy Edn Profl Devel Acad 785 Carnegie Ave Akron OH 44314

BYASSEE, MARGARET FOLEY, art educator, poet, vocalist; b. Newport, R.I., Jan. 17, 1922; d. Edward B. and May (Cruickshank) Foley; m. Ivan Byassee, Oct. 1, 1950 (dec.). Student, Wheaton Coll., 1947-49; BA, U. Tenn., Knoxville, 1952; MEd, U. Tenn., Chattanooga, 1984. Cert. tchr. Art tchr. Oak Ridge (Tenn.) City Sch. Sys., 1953-61, Chattanooga (Tenn.) City Sch. Sys., 1962-82, Sweetwater (Tenn.) City Schs., 1984-85, artist-in-residence. Author numerous poems; one-woman shows Gallery 210, Chattanooga, Ariel Galleries, N.Y., among others. Mem. Artist Guild, Newport, R.I., 1998-99, Newport Art Mus., 1998-99; pres. Chattanooga Civic Arts League, Authors and Artists, Chattanooga. Sgt. U.S. Army, 1943-46. Named to Internat. Soc. Poetry Hall of Fame, 1996; recipient Editor's Choice award Nat. Libr. Poetry, 1995, 96, 2000. Mem. Women in the Arts, Internat. Soc. Poetry, Assn. Visual Arts, Chattanooga Tenn. Authors and Artists. Avocations: tennis, golf, camping, soloist with island senior chorus, painting. Home: 2 Donna Dr Portsmouth RI 02871-1133 E-mail: MargarByas@aol.com.

BYERS, ELIZABETH, education educator; b. Cedar Rapids, Iowa, Mar. 22, 1964; d. Charles A. Byers and Mary Ann Hetherington-Byers. BA in Music, BA in English and Speech, Coe Coll., 1986; MA in Rhetorical Studies, U. Iowa, 1988, MA in English Edn., 2002. Tchg. asst. in pub. speaking U. Iowa, Iowa City, 1987—88, rsch. asst., 1987, tchg. asst. bus. and profl. speaking, 1987—88, art history teaching asst., 2000; English/speech instr. Kirkwood C.C., Iowa City, 1988—89; English and speech instr. Mt. Mercy Coll., Cedar Rapids, 1989—93; elem. edn. instr. Iowa Wesleyan Coll., Mt. Pleasant, 2001—. ESL tutor Kirkwood C.C., Iowa City, 1988—93, Mt. Mercy Coll., 1988—93; pub. speaking cons., Iowa City, 1988—93. Grad. student editor: Basil Blackwell Companion, 1989; editor: Communicating, 1992, author web page for postsecondary tchrs. Vol. Habitat for Humanity, Iowa City, 1999—2001, Cath. Worker House, Cedar Rapids, 1990—93. Mem.: DAR (Good Citizenship award 1982), Mu Phi Epsilon, Pi Lambda Theta (Teaching Excellence award 2001), Phi Beta Kappa. Home: PO Box 156 Morning Sun IA 52640-0156

BYERS, MARY MARGARET (PEG BYERS), systems educator; b. Munhall, Pa., May 20, 1953; d. Gerald J. B. and Florence B. (Luty) Byers-Steiner. BA, U. Pitts., 1982; MS, Nova U., 1993. Office conversion mgr. Franklin Interiors, Pitts., 1979-82; astrological cons. pvt. practice, Pitts., 1982-87; tng. cons. Elcomp Systems, Greentree, Pa., 1987-88; system sales Computer Renaissance, Pitts., 1988-89; instr. Duff's Bus. Inst., Pitts., 1989-91; bus. owner Byers Computer Svcs., Jeffersonboro, Pa., 1988-92; systems cons. pvt. practice, Jeffersonboro, Pa., 1993-96; systems coord. Mellon Bank, Pitts., 1996-97; dir. edn. Computer Learning Ctrs., Monroeville, Pa., 1997—. Mem. Hi-Tech. Coun., Pitts. Author: Introduction to Computers, 1994, PC Trouble Shooting, 1996; co-author: Into to Guidesign Using, 1996. Mem. NAFE, High Tech. Coun., Mensa. Avocations: reading, collecting music, astrology, metaphysics. Office: Computer Learning Ctrs Inc 777 Penn Center Blvd Fl 3D Pittsburgh PA 15235-5927

BYLSMA, CAROL ANN, environmental education and science education consultant; b. L.A., Dec. 5, 1941; d. Carl Minke and Anna (Testa) Bylsma; m. Leo C. Jones Jr., June 23, 1961, (div. Nov., 1979); children: Lauran Marie, Lynell Ann. BS, U. Colo., Boulder, 1970; MA, U. No. Colo., Greeley, 1978; postgrad., U. Colo., 1984, Rocky Mountain Bio Lab., Gothic, Colo., 1984. Tchr. Douglas County Schs., Castle Rock, Colo., 1970-79, Cherry Creek Schs., Englewood, Colo., 1979-81; naturalist Colo. Divsn. Parks & Recreation, Denver, 1978-81; dir. Barr Lake Nature Ctr., Brighton, Colo.; instr. Met. State Coll., Denver, 1982-84; environ. edn. cons. Aerie Nature Series, 1982-85; dir. environ. edn. Colo. Divsn. Wildlife, Denver, 1985-94, coord. aquatic edn., 1990-94; pres., CEO Nature Adventures Internat., Denver, 1985-94; dir. edn. Aspen (Colo.) Global Change Inst., 1994-95; pres., CEO Forest Song Assocs., Phoenix, Ariz., 1995—. Bd. dirs. Wild Colo. Fund, 1987-94; faculty affiliate Colo. State U., Colo. Sch. Mines, 1990—, U. Phoenix, 1996—; co-prin. investigator water chemistry GLOBE program U. Ariz., 1995—, project coord., 1995; project dir. Environ. Ednl. Outreach Program, Four Corners Sch. of Outdoor Edn., Monticello, Utah, 1995, 96; adv. coun. Internat. Environ. Mgmt. Inst. of Am. Grad. Sch. Internat. Bus., Phoenix, 1995—; sci. edn. cons. Durango (Colo.) 9R Sch. Dist., 1996—. Actor: Cottonwood Kid, 1986; featured (documentary) By Grace of Man, 1981; contbr. WILD Aquatic Guide, 1987 (Dir.'s Award for Excellence 1990, Spl. Recognition for Excellence award); editor (newsletter) Wild Colorado, 1985-94; feature page Outdoors Colorado; ednl. cons., co-producer (video series) A Home for Pearl, 1989, (10 part TV series) Water Wonders, 1992. Pres. Western Interpreters Assn., Denver, 1981-83; coor. field trips Denver Audubon Soc., 1979-82; bd. dirs. Colo. Alliance for Environ. Edn., 1988-90; mem. nat. steering com. Project WILD, 1987-90, nat. steering com. Aquatic Edn. for the Deaf, 1992; tech. cons. Nat. WILD Sch. Sites Program, Western Regional Environ. Edn. Coun., 1993—; mem. adv. coun. Internat. Environ. Mgmt. Inst., 1995—. Recipient svc. award Western Regional Environ. Edn. Coun., 1988, Nat. Leadership award Project WILD, 1990, Outstanding Achievement award EPA Region 8, 1992. Mem. N.Am. Environ. Edn. Assn., Nat. Sci. Tchrs. Assn., The Wildlife Soc. (Profl. Achievement award in Wildlife Edn. Colo. chpt. 1992), Save the Rainforests, Nat. Assn. Curriculum and Supervision, Xerces Soc., Universal Pantheist Soc. Avocations: adventure traveling, photography, organic gardening, landscaping, backpacking. Office: Forest Song Assocs 4747 E Elliot Rd # 29-488 Phoenix AZ 85044-1627

BYNAGLE, HANS EDWARD, library director, philosophy educator; b. Ruurlo, The Netherlands, Feb. 24, 1946; came to U.S., 1956; s. Cornelius Adrian and Maria (Kalfsbeek) B.; m. Janet Mae Monsma, June 27, 1969; children: Maria Elizabeth, Derek Johannes. BA, Calvin Coll., 1968; PhD, Columbia U., 1973; MLS, Kent State U., 1976. Asst. prof. philosophy Union Coll., Schenectady, N.Y., 1972-73, Coll. Wooster, Ohio, 1974-75; dir. learning resources Friends U., Wichita, Kans., 1976-82; dir. library Eckerd Coll., St. Petersburg, Fla., 1982-83; dir. library, prof. Whitworth Coll., Spokane, Wash., 1983—. Author: Philosophy: A Guide to the Reference Literature, 1986, 2nd edit., 1996; mem. editl. bd. Christian Scholar's Rev., 1992—; numerous rev. to profl. jours. Named one of Outstanding Young Men of Am., 1982. Mem. ALA, Assn. Coll. and Research Libraries (chmn. Kans. chpt. 1980-81). Presbyterian. Avocation: music. Home: 1122 W Bellwood Dr Spokane WA 99218-2907

BYNUM, HENRI SUE, education and French educator; b. Columbia, Miss., Feb. 7, 1944; d. George Milton and Lois Marie (Newsom) Dearing; m. James Lamar Bynum Jr., Feb. 28, 1965; children: James Wesley, Charles Drew. BA, U. So. Miss., 1967, MEd, 1977, PhD, 1979. Cert. tchr., Fla. Tchr. French, Spanish, modern dance Natchez (Miss.) Adams Pub. Schs., 1972—76; tchr. ESL U. So. Miss., Hattiesburg, 1977—79, coord. academic programs English Lang. Inst., 1979—81, adj. prof., 1980—81; dir. internat. edn. So. Ctr. for Rsch. and Innovation, Hattiesburg, 1981—82; chmn., asst. prof. dept. ESL U. So. Ala., Mobile, 1982—85; tchr. French, Spanish Moss Point (Miss.) High Sch., 1985—86; tchr. French Vero Beach (Fla.) Jr. High, 1986—87; prof. edn., French, chair edn. dept., dean Arts and Scis. Indian River C.C., Ft. Pierce, Fla., 1987—. Adj. prof. Mobile Coll., 1986; cons. for curriculum devel. Colegio LaCruz, Puerto LaCruz, Venezuela, Escuela Anaco (Venezuela); co-dir. ESL curriculum Workshop, Assn. Venezuelan Am. Schs., Anaco. Cons. Safe Space, Inc., Vero Beach, 1989—; mem. bd. dirs. Fla. Fund for Minority Tchrs., Inc., 1998—. Mem. Phi Delta Kappa, Kappa Delta Pi. Republican. Avocations: reading, gourmet cooking, cross stitching. Office: Indian River Community Coll 3209 Virginia Ave Fort Pierce FL 34981-5541

BYNUM, JUDITH LANE, gifted and talented education educator; b. Forrest City, Ark., Jan. 21, 1948; d. Herbert Sydney and Corine (Traweek) Lane; m. Barton Alan Bynum; children: Judith Ann, Alan Woodrow. BSE, Ark. A&M Coll., 1969; MEd, U. Ark., Little Rock, 1991. Cert. tchr. sec.

math., English, gifted and talented, Ark. Tchr. Monticello (Ark.) Pub. Sch., 1969-70, Dermott (Ark.) Sch. Dist., 1970-71, Montrose (Ark.) Acad., 1972-75, 80-87; tchr. gifted and talented Fountain Hill (Ark.) Sch. Dist., 1987-88; tchr., coord. gifted and talented Drew Ctrl. Sch. Dist., Monticello, 1988—, curriculum coord., 1993—. Insvc. presenter Mind-Mapping Multiple Intelligences, 1992—. Illustrator: Catch Them Learning, 1993, The Pre-Adolescent, 1997; artist calendars, 1995, 96. Coord. Pride of Dermott Festival, 1989. Named Ark. Oldsmobile Tchr. of the Yr., Ark. Oldsmobile Assn., 1990; recipient Disting. Leadership award Ark. Leadership Acad., 1995, Master Educator award Union Bank, Monticello, 1997. Mem. Agate Gifted and Talented Educators (nomination com. 1996-98). Avocations: writing, reading, artwork, music. Home: 476 Collins Line Rd Dermott AR 71638-8768

BYNUM, MAGNOLIA VIRGINIA WRIGHT, retired secondary school educator; b. Waynesboro, Ga., Jan. 10, 1934; d. George and Edith Arilee (Williams) Wright; m. Marvin Bynum, Sept. 17, 1955 (dec. Oct. 1977). BS in Bus. Edn., N.C. A&T State U., Greensboro, N.C., 1956; postgrad., NYU, 1964—65; MS in Edn., CUNY, Bklyn., 1985, Adv. Cert. Guidance & Counseling, 1986. Engring. adminstr. Radio Receptor Co., Bklyn., 1957—59; data processing staff NYU, N.Y.C., 1959—64; tchr., dean, counselor Lincoln H.S., Jersey City, 1964—92; ret., 1992. Adj. prof. CUNY, Bklyn., 1986—90; asst. to Congressman Edolphus Towns, 10th Congl. Dist., Bklyn., 1982—90; counselor incentive program dept. human resources Bklyn. Coll., 1992—93; cons. Parent Advocacy, Medgars Evers Coll., Bklyn., 1984—85. Editor-in-chief (newsletter) Cornerstone Torch, 1993—97. Mem. Cmty. Coalition for Edn., Greensboro, NC, NAACP; spearheaded Hard of Hearing campaign, Bklyn.; women's day chairperson New Zion Missionary Bapt. Ch., Greensboro, NC; chairperson bd. dirs. Chama Child Devel., Bklyn., 1983—91, Cornerstone Day Care Ctr., Bklyn., 1991—97. Named to Faculty Achievement Hall of Fame, Lincoln H.S., 1981; recipient Outstanding Cmty. Svc. award, Bklyn. Coll. Grad. Students, 1984, citations, Congl. Record, 1990, 1997; scholar Myers Jacob Guidance & Counseling scholar, 1984. Mem.: Alpha Kappa Alpha, Phi Delta Kappa, Kappa Delta Pi. Baptist. Avocations: reading, travel, singing. Home: 563 Summerwalk Rd Greensboro NC 27455

BYRD, ELLEN STOESSER, school nurse administrator; b. Dayton, Tex., Dec. 10, 1941; d. Edward Joseph and Nina Mae (Cannon) Stoesser; m. C. Robert Byrd, June 6, 1964; children: Byron, Preston, Aaron, Robyn. BSN, Baylor U., 1964. RN, Tex. Nurse Parkland Hosp., Dallas, 1964-65; nurse gyn. svcs. Baylor U. Med. Ctr., Dallas, 1965-66; charge nurse med./surg. Collin Meml. Hosp., McKinney, Tex., 1967-68; nurse newborn nursery St. Paul Hosp., Dallas, 1972; pvt. duty nurse Dist. 4 Tex. Nurse Assn., Dallas, 1976; sch. nurse Dallas Ind. Sch. Dist., 1989-90; home health nurse Rehab Home Care, DeSoto, Tex., 1994-98; dermatology nurse Dallas Bapt. U., 1999—2001, dir. health svcs., campus nurse, 2001—; sch. nurse Richardson (Tex.) Ind. Sch. Dist. Mem. adv. bd. Baylor U. Sch. Nursing, Dallas, 1994—, chmn. adv. bd. 1999—; advisor Baylor U. Woman's Coun., Dallas, 1995—, pres., 1994-95. Author: History of Dallas CPA Wives, 1983, Biography of Mae Stoesser, 1988, Byrd Family 25 Years, 1990. Program chmn. Freedom Found. Valley Forge, Dallas, 1986-89; centennial circle chmn. Dallas County Heritage Soc., Dallas; deacon Cliff Temple Bapt. Ch., 1988; v.p. DeSoto Svc. League, 1990; pres. Dallas CPAs Wives Club, 1984-85; mem. Richardson Jr. League. Recipient W.T. White Meritorious Svcs. award Baylor U. Alumni Assn., 1996. Mem. Richardson Jr. League, Presbyn. Presby Ptnrs. Repubican. Baptist. Avocations: european travel, grandchildren. Home: 304 Prince Albert Ct Richardson TX 75081-5059 Office: Dallas Bapt Univ 3000 Mountain Creek Pkwy Dallas TX 75211-9299 Fax: 972-234-8448.

BYRD, GWENDOLYN PAULINE, school system superintendent; b. Mobile, Ala., July 21, 1943; d. Marley and Frances (Ramsay) B. BS in History, Marillac Coll., St. Louis, 1966; MA in Sch. Adminstrn., DePaul U., 1975. Tchr. St. Matthias Sch., St. Louis, 1966-70; prin., tchr. Cathedral Elem. Sch., Natchez, Miss., 1970-74; prin. St. Francis De Sales Sch., Lake Zurich, Ill., 1974-77; curriculum coord. for sch. system Archdiocese of Mobile, 1977-83, sch. supt., 1983—. Chairperson Little Flower Liturgy Com., Mobile, 1980—; pvt. sch. rep. to adv. com. on tchr. edn. State of Ala., 1983—; adv. bd. Cath. Svc. Ctr., Mobile, 1989—; v.p. bd. dirs. Mobile Mental Health Assn., 1990—; bd. dirs. L'Arche Cmty., 1992—. Named Outstanding Career Woman, Gayfer's Career Club, 1985, Outstanding Supt., Ala. Assn. Learning Disabilities, 1988, Disting. Diocesan Leader Today's Cath. Tchr. Mag., 1992. Mem. Nat. Cath. Edn. Assn., Chief Adminstrs. Cath. Edn. (regional rep. and chair schs. adv. 1995), CACE (exec. com. 1996), Phi Delta Kappa. Office: Office Cath Schs PO Box 129 Mobile AL 36601-0129

BYRD, MARY JANE, education educator; b. Topeka, Apr. 21, 1946; d. Vernon Thomas and Mary Elizabeth (Caldwell) Wharton; m. Gerald David Byrd, June 24, 1965; children: Kari, Juli, Cori. BS, U. So. Ala., 1980, MBA, 1984; D of Bus. Adminstrn., Nova Southeastern U., 1991. Dental asst. Gerald E. Berger, DMD, Mobile, Ala., 1963-65; dental hygenist Robert P. Hall, DMD, Mobile, Ala., 1965-66; teller Am. Nat. Bank, Mobile, Ala., 1972-75; office mgr. Byrd Surveying, Inc., Mobile, Ala., 1975-80; div. acct. cafeteria Morrison, Inc., Mobile, Ala., 1980-82; mgmt. cons. pvt. practice Mobile, Ala., 1982-84; lectr. acctg. U. South Ala., Mobile, Ala., 1984; asst. prof. acctg. & mgmt. Univ. Mobile, Mobile, Ala., 1984-89; assoc. prof. acctg. and mgmt. Mobile Coll., 1989-95; prof. mgmt., 1995—. Reviewer Internat. Jour. Pub. Adminstrn., 1991—; dir. Nat. Assn. Accts., Mobile, 1986-89. Author: Supervisory Management Study Guide/Southwestern, 1993, 97, Small Business Management; An Entrepreneur's Guide to Success/Irwin, 1994, 4th edit. 2003, Human Resource Management, Dame, 1995; contbr. articles to profl. jours. Named Assoc. of the Month, Home Builders Assn., 1986, Charles S. Dismukes Outstanding Mem., Nat. Assn. Accts. Mem. AAUW, Acad. Mgmt., Am. Bus. Women Assn., Mortgage Lenders Assn., So. Acad. Mgmt. Office: Univ Mobile PO Box 13220 Mobile AL 36663-0220 E-mail: janebyrd@free.umobile.edu.

BYRNE, DANIEL WILLIAM, biostatistician, educator; b. Bklyn., Jan. 21, 1958; s. Thomas Edward and L.M. (Collins) B.; m. Loretta Marie May, June 22, 1985; children: Michael, Virginia. BA in Biology, SUNY, Albany, 1983; MS in Biostatistics, N.Y. Med. Coll., 1991. Programmer, med. software dept. surgery N.Y. Med. Coll., Valhalla, 1983-84; computer/data analyst N.Y. Med. Coll., Westchester County Med. Ctr. and affiliate hosps., 1984-87; rsch. asst. prof. dept. surgery N.Y. Med. Coll., Valhalla, 1988-98, rsch. asst. prof. dept. cmty. and preventive medicine, 1996-99; founder, med. rsch. cons. Byrne Research, Ridgefield, Conn., 1989-99; dir. biostats. GCRC Vanderbilt U., 1999—. Author: Publishing Your Medical Research Paper: What They Don't Teach in Medical School, 1997; author, programmer various software including Trauma Management System, 1990, Occupational Stress Database, 1990, contbr. numerous articles to med. jours. Mem.: Biometric Soc., Am. Statis. Assn. Roman Catholic. Home: 407 Landrake Close Franklin TN 37069-4347 Office: AA-3228 Med Ctr N 1161 21st Ave S Nashville TN 37232-2195

BYRNE, JOHN MICHAEL, energy and environmental policy educator, researcher; b. Chgo., Nov. 2, 1949; s. Michael Thomas and Mabel Victoria (Cranford) B.; m. Elizabeth Maria Garey, Aug. 9, 1975; children: Brian, Tara. BA in Econs., U. Del., 1971, MA, 1973, PhD in Urban Affairs and Pub. Policy, 1980. Asst. prof. Coll. Urban Affairs and Pub. Policy, U. Del., Newark, 1982-86, assoc. prof., 1986-92, prof., 1992—, dir. Energy Policy Rsch. Group, 1981-84, dir. Ctr. for Energy and Environ. Policy, 1984—, chair Urban Affairs and Pub. Policy grad. program, 1992-96. Apptd. environ. policy advisor Korea Nat. Assembly, 1998—; co-exec. dir. Joint Inst. for a Sustainable Energy and Environ. Future, 1999—. Co-editor: Energy and Cities, 1985, The Politics of Energy R&D, 1986, Energy and Environment: The Policy Challenge, 1992, Governing the Atom: The Politics of Risk, 1996, Environmental Justice, 2002; mem. editl. bd. Bull. of Sci., Tech. and Soc., 1995—; contbg. author: 2nd and 3rd Assessment Reports of the Intergovtl. Panel on Climate Change, 1995—. Bd. dirs. Urban Environ. Ctr., 1997—, Environ. Market Solutions, Inc., 2002—. Grantee ESMAP/World Bank, 1990-91, U.S. Dept. Energy/Nat. Renewable Energy Lab., 1991-2001, UNIDEL Found., 1992, U.S. EPA, 1994, 97-2001, Asia Found., 1995, Inst. Internat. Edn., 1996-97, W. Alton Jones Found., 1997-2002, U.S. Dept. Energy, 2002—, Blue Moon Fund, 2003—; recipient Fulbright Sr. Lectr./Rschr. award, 1995. Mem. IEEE Social Implications of Tech. Affiliate, Nat. Assn. Sci., Tech. and Society (adv. bd. 1991—). Avocations: music, woodworking, hiking. Office: U Del Ctr Energy & Environ Policy Newark DE 19716-7301

BYRNE, JOHN VINCENT, higher education consultant; b. Hempstead, N.Y., May 9, 1928; s. Frank E. and Kathleen (Barry) B.; m. Shirley O'Connor, Nov. 26, 1954; children: Donna, Lisa, Karen, Steven. AB, Hamilton Coll., 1951, JD (hon.), 1994; MA, Columbia U., 1953; PhD, U. So. Calif., 1957. Research geologist Humble Oil & Refinery Co., Houston, 1957-60; assoc. prof. Oreg. State U., Corvallis, 1960-66, prof. oceanography, 1966—, chmn. dept., 1968-72, dean Sch. Oceanography, 1972-76, acting dean research, 1976-77, dean research, 1977-80, v.p. for research and grad. studies, 1980-81, pres., 1984-95; adminstr. NOAA, Washington, 1981-84; pres. Oreg. State U., 1984-95; higher edn. cons. Corvallis, 1996—. Program dir. oceanography NSF, 1966-67; exec. dir. Kellogg Commn. on Future of State and Land Grant Univs., 1996-2000; dir. Harbor Br. Ocean Inst., Oregon Coast Aquarium. Recipient Carter teaching award Oreg. State U., 1964. Fellow AAAS, Geol. Soc. Am.; mem. Geol. Soc. Am., Am. Geophys. Union, Sigma Xi, Chi Psi. Home: 3190 NW Deer Run St Corvallis OR 97330-3107 Office: Autzen House 811 SW Jefferson Ave Corvallis OR 97333-4506 E-mail: john.byrne@orst.edu.

BYRNE, MARY MARGARET (MEG BYRNE), elementary education educator; b. Bronx, N.Y., Feb. 25, 1939; d. Peter Joseph and Margaret Mary (Coyle) Walsh; m. Edmond A. Byrne, Dec. 20, 1969; children: Bernadette, Peter, Ned. BS in Edn., Fordham U., 1966; postgrad., Columbia Basin Coll., 1980-82; MS in Gifted Edn., Coll. New Rochelle, 1989. Cert. tchr., N.Y., N.J., Mich. Ednl. rep. IBM, N.Y.C., 1960-64; tchr. M.L. Vetter Sch., Eatontown, N.J., 1965-70; design cons. Keeney Assocs. Ltd., Pasco, Wash., 1980-83; tchr. St. Christopher Sch., Marysville, Mich., 1983-85, Mechanicstown Sch., Middletown, N.Y., 1986—. Tchr. educator Middletown Tchr. Ctr.; coord. Head Start program, Eatontown, 1966-68; coach Odyssey of the Mind, 1989; mem. sch. improvement team, Middletown, 1991-92, lang. arts assessment com., 1991—. Troop leader Mt. Kisco (N.Y.) area Girl Scouts U.S.,1 976-77; coord. Youth Group, Marysville, 1983-84; parent advocate Parents of Children with Learning Disabilities, Marysville, 1984-85; actress local theater group, 1990; coach election debate group, 1992. Mem. ABC Reading Coun., Middletown Tchrs. Assn. (bldg. rep. 1991). Avocation: oil painting. Office: Mechanicstown Elem Sch E Main St Middletown NY 10940

BYRNES, CHRISTOPHER IAN, academic dean, researcher; b. N.Y.C., June 28, 1949; s. Richard Francis and Jeanne (Orchard) B.; m. Catherine Morris, June 24, 1984; children: Kathleen, Alison, Christopher. BS, Manhattan Coll., 1971; MS, U. Mass., 1973, PhD, 1975; D (hon.) of Tech., Royal Inst. Tech., Stockholm, 1998. Instr. U. Utah, Salt Lake City, 1975-78; asst. prof. Harvard U., Cambridge, Mass., 1978-81, assoc. prof., 1981-85; rsch. prof. Ariz. State U., Tempe, 1985-89; prof., chmn. dept. systems sci. and math. Washington U., St. Louis, 1989-91, dean engring. and applied sci., 1991—. Adj. prof. Royal Inst. Tech., Stockholm, 1985-90; cons. Sci. Sys., Inc., Cambridge, 1980-84, Sys. Engring., Inc., Greenbelt, Md., 1986; sci. advisor Sherwood Davis & Geck, 1996-98, Aucsyn Venture Capital Cernium Inc., 2002-; mem. NRC; bd. dirs., chmn. compensation com. Belden Inc.; chmn. bd. dirs. Ctr. for Emerging Techs.; pres., bd. dirs. WUTA, Inc. Editor: (book series) Progress in Systems Control, 1988—01, Foundations of Systems and Control, 1998—2001; Nonlinear Synthesis, 1991, 13 other books; contbr. numerous articles to profl. jours., book revs. Recipient Best Paper award, IFAC, 1993. Fellow: IEEE (Geroge Axelby award 1991), Acad. Sci. St. Louis, Japan Soc. for Promotion Sci.; mem.: AAAS, Regional Chamber for Growth Assn. (vice chmn. tech., chmn. Tech. Gateway Alliance 2000—03), Royal Swedish Acad. Engring. Sci. (fgn.), Am. Math. Soc., Soc. Indsl. Applied Math. (program com. 1986—89), Tau Beta Pi, Sigma Xi. Avocations: cooking, fishing, travel. Office: Washington U Sch Engring and Applied Sci 1 Brookings Dr Saint Louis MO 63130-4899 E-mail: Chrisbyrnes@seas.wustl.edu.

BYRNES, LAWRENCE WILLIAM, dean; b. Windsor, Ont., Can., June 17, 1940; s. Carl Wilfred and Alice Hendrie (Thomson) B.; m. Margaret Amelia Snavely, June 26, 1965; children: Andrew Carl, Mary Margaret. BA in Social Sci., Mich. State U., 1963, MA in History, 1967, PhD in Edn., 1970. Tchr. social studies Grosse Pointe (mich.) Schs., 1963-66; prof. Calif. State U., Northridge, 1969-78; dean edn. Southeastern La. U., Hammond, 1978-83, Moorhead (Minn.) State U., 1983-88, Edinboro (Pa.) U., 1988-91; dir. Ctr. for Teaching and Learning U. So. Colo., 1991-95; dean Coll. Edn. and Tech. Eastern N.Mex. U., Portales, 1995—. Ptnr., cons. ML Byrnes and Assocs., Erie, Pa. Author: Religion and Republic Education, 1975; co-author: Total Quality Management in Higher Education, 1991, The Quality Teacher: Implementing TQM in the Classroom, 1992. Mem. Gov.'s Steering Com. on Strengthening Quality in Schs., N. Mex. Mem. Am. Assn. Colls. Tchr. Edn. (chmn. global and internat. tchrs. edn. com.), N. Mex. Assn. Colls. Tchr. Edn. (pres.), Phi Delta Kappa (pres. Moorhead chpt. 1987-88, historian Erie chpt. 1991—. hist. South Colo. chpt. 1994—) Democrat. Episcopalian. Avocations: running, drums, music. Home: 416 E 17th Ln Portales NM 88130-9266 Office: ENMU Coll Edn & Tech Portales NM 88130

BYROM, JACK EDWARDS, private school administrator; b. San Antonio, Mar. 2, 1929; s. Charley Emmett and Mary Elizabeth (Edwards) B.; m. Bobbie LaRue Massey, Aug. 30, 1953; children: Deborah Elizabeth, Mary LaRue, James Edwards. BA, Baylor U., 1950; MDiv, Southwestern Bapt. Theol. Sem., Ft. Worth, 1954; DD (hon.), U. Mary Hardin-Baylor, 1972. Ordained to ministry Bapt. Ch., 1947. Pastor lst Bapt. Ch., Christine, Tex., 1947-50, Maypearl, Tex., 1950-52, Water Street Bapt. Ch., Waxahachie, Tex., 1952-55, Grace Temple Bapt. Ch., Corpus Christi, Tex., 1955-57, lst Bapt. Ch., Carrizo Springs, Tex., 1957-61, San Marcos, Tex., 1961-65; pres. San Marcos Bapt. Acad., San Marcos, 1965—. Chmn. standards com. Accrediting Commn. Tex. Assn. Bapt. Schs., 1986-88, pres. 1988-90, 92-93; dir. Christian Edn. Coordinating Bd., Dallas, 1983-84, 92-93; pres. San Antonio Ednl. TV, Inc., 1991-92. Pres. San Marcos United Fund, 1969; bd. dirs. Heritage Assn., San Marcos, 1976-90, San Antonio TV, Inc., 1985-90; mem. Hays County Farm Bur., 1990; mem. futures com. Sch. Edn. Baylor U., 1994, adv. bd. mem.. Named lt. col. Tex. State Guard, 1965-71; recipient Outstanding Ex-Student award Somerset (Tex.) High Sch., 1976, Beautify San Antonio award San Antonio Beautification Assn., 1982, Outstanding Profl. Man award Hays County Soil and Water Conservation Dist., 1988, comdrs. award for pub. svc. U.S. Army Third Region, 1990. Mem. Ind. Schs. Assn. S.W. (fin. com. 1969-90), Tex. Bapt. Sch. Adminstrs. Assn. (pres. 1982-84, 92-93), San Marcos C. of C. (pres. 1968-69), Baylor U. Alumni AAssn. Democrat. Avocations: golf, boating. Home and Office: San Marcos Bapt Acad 2801 Ranch Road 12 San Marcos TX 78666-2437

CAAMANO, KATHLEEN ANN FOLZ, gifted and talented educator; b. Rozellville, Wis., Dec. 20, 1944; d. Joseph and Isabel Ann (Brost) Folz; m. Gerald J. Caamano, Aug. 10, 1968; children: Michelle, David. BS, U. Wis., Stevens Point; MA, Ctrl. Mich. U. Cert. tchr., Ill. Tchr. Midland (Mich.) Pub. Schs., 1968-74, Newark (Ohio) City Schs., 1974-77, Minooka (Ill.) Sch. Dist., 1986—, coord. gifted edn. Pres. Camelot Homeowners Assn., Joliet, Ill.; tutor Big Bros./Big Sisters Assn. Will County; voter registrar Will County, Joliet. Recipient Those Who Excel award Ill State Bd. Edn. Mem. Internat. Reading Assn., Ill. Edn. Assn. (tchr. rep), Gifted Edn. Coun., Ill. Assn. Ednl. Rsch. and Evaluation, Will County Reading Coun., Delta Kappa Gamma (v.p.), Beta Sigma Phi (pres.). Roman Catholic. Avocations: travel, reading, golf, bridge. Home: 22257 S Galahad Dr Joliet IL 60431-7611

CABANAS, ELIZABETH ANN, nutritionist, educator; b. Port Arthur, Tex., Oct. 27, 1948; d. William Rosser and Frances Merle (Block) Thornton. BS, U. Tex., 1971; MPH, U. Hawaii, 1973; PhD, Tex. Woman's U., 2001. Registered dietitian; cert. diabetes educator. Clin. nutritionist Family Planning Inst. Kapiolani Hosp., Honolulu, 1972-74; dietitian Kauikeolani Children's Hosp.-Pacific Inst. Rehab. Medicine, Honolulu, 1974-75; asst. food service adminstr. San Antonio Ind. Schs., 1975-89; coord. equipment and facilities Dallas Ind. Sch., 1990-91; nutritionist SureQuest Solutions in Software, Richardson, Tex., 1990-91; nutritionist div. endocrinology, metabolism and hypertension, clin. studies unit rsch. nutritionist, asst. prof. dept. health promotion & gerontology U. Tex. Med. Br., Galveston, 1991—2002. Lectr. nutrition U. Hawaii, Honolulu, 1974-75, St. Mary's U., San Antonio Coll., 1984-90; adj. faculty Tex. Woman's U., 1994; cons. nutritionist, 1980—; presenter in field. Contbr. papers to profl. jours. Vol. ARC, Brooke Army Med. Ctr., Saddle Light Ctr. for Therapeutic Riding, Habitat for Humanity. Recipient diabetes educator recognition Eli Lilly & Co., 1994. Mem. Am. Dietetic Assn., Am. Assn. Diabetes Educators (chair holistic care specialty practice group 1997-98), Assn. Sch. Bus. Ofcls. Internat., Nutrition and Food Svc. Mgmt. Com., Am. Diabetes Assn. (adv. com. U. Tex. Med. Br. children's diabetes mgmt. program 1993-98, mem. Galveston County diabetes support group 1991-99, Disting. Svc. award 1995, mem. Galveston County Outreach adv. com., UTMB rep. 1996-98), Coun. Nutritional Scis. and Metabolism (profl. sect., non-peer rev. com. 1993-94), Tex. Sch. Food Svc. Assn. (dist. bd. dirs. 1977-78), Tex. Nutrition Coun. (nominating com. 1996-97, 2d v.p. 1997-99, sports and cardiovasc. nutritionists practice group, Tex. gerontol. nutritionists practice group), Houston Area Dietetic Assn. (legis. network com. 1995-99), San Antonio Dietetic Assn., San Antonio Sch. Food Svc. Assn. (com. chmn. 1975-89), Tex. Assn. Sch. Bus. Ofcls., Tex. Restaurant Assn., San Antonio Area Food Svc. Adminstrs. Assn. (pres. 1989-90), Assn. Profls. in Positions of Leadership in Edn., Dallas Dietetic Assn. (cons. nutritionists practice group, chmn. 1990-91), Harris County Biofeedback Soc., San Antonio Mus. Assn., Randolph C. of C., Grand Opera House, Galveston (patron), Galveston Hist. Found., Phi Kappa Phi. Avocations: perpetuation of Hawaiian culture, nordic skiing, equestrian sports, art, dixieland jazz.

CABAUP, JOSEPH JOHN, geology educator; b. Bronx, N.Y., Nov. 5, 1940; s. Joseph Christopher and Angelina (DeVenuta) C.; m. Barbara Louise Mellor, June 26, 1965 (div. Dec. 1987); children: Joseph E., Jean M.; m. Nancy Ann Peters, July 2, 1993. BA in Physics, Hunter Coll., 1962; MS, U. N.C., 1969. Cert. geologist, Maine. Asst. prof. chemistry and physics Winthrop Coll., Rock Hill, S.C., 1967-70; tchr. Franconia (N.H.) Coll., 1970-71, Dartmouth High Sch., North Dartmouth, Mass., 1971-72; asst. prof. physics R.I. Jr. Coll., 1972-74; prof. geology N.H. Tech. Coll., Berlin, 1974—. Environ. cons. Environ. Survey and Analysis, Whitefield, N.H., 1971—. Mem., past pres. Bethlehem Conservation Commn., 1984-93; bd. dirs. Weeks State Pk. Assn., 1986-94. Mem. AAAS, Geol. Soc. Am. Home: 15 Terrace St Whitefield NH 03598-3015 Office: NH Tech Coll 2020 Riverside Dr Berlin NH 03570-3717

CABRERA, CARMEN, secondary education educator; b. Havana, Cuba, Dec. 31, 1948; came to U.S., 1962; d. Armando and Carmen (Gomez) C. AA, East L.A. Coll., 1970; BA, Calif. State U., L.A., 1972; MA, Calif. State U., 1975. Cert. tchr., Calif. Tchr. Sacred Heart of Mary H.S., Montebello, Calif., 1973-91, acad. dean, 1989-91; tchr., curriculum dir. Cantwell Sacred Heart of Mary H.S., Montebello, 1991-98, advanced placement/honors courses tchr., chair fgn. lang., 1998—. Instr. East L.A. Coll., Monterey Park, Calif., 1974-77; chairperson dept. fgn. lang. Sacred Heart of Mary H.S., 1980-91, Cantwell Sacred Heart of Mary H.S., 1991-93, 95—. Assoc. Beverly Hosp. Found., Montebello, 1990-93. Mem. ASCD, Am. Assn. Tchrs. Spanish and Portuguese (contest dir. 1987-89), Am. Coun. on Tchg. Fgn. Langs., Nat. Cath. Ednl. Assn., Phi Kappa Phi. Office: Cantwell Sacred Heart Mary 329 N Garfield Ave Montebello CA 90640-3803

CACCIATORE SINNOTT, ANN FRANCES, special education educator; b. Phila., Mar. 26, 1953; m. Frank I. Cacciatore, Sept. 12, 1975; 1 child, Alice C. BS, U. Tampa, 1974; postgrad., U. South Fla., 1976-78, Fla. Co. U., 1979-81, U. Cen. Fla., 1988. Cert. tchr., Fla. Remedial tchr. Hillsborough County Pub. Schs., Tampa, Fla., 1975; lead tchr. gifted edn. program Polk County Pub. Schs., Winter Haven, Fla., 1976-79, tchr. of emotionally handicapped Dundee, Fla., 1979-80, tchr. spl. edn. Lakeland, Fla., 1980-82; lead tchr. spl. edn. Palm Beach County Pub. Schs., Lake Worth, Fla., 1983-85, behavior specialist, instrnl. support tchr., program asst. Orange County Pub. Schs., Orlando, Fla., 1990—. Co-author: Resource Manual for Emotionally-Handicapped Teachers, 1982; author learning games; developer Affective Curriculum Guide, Grades K-12. Grantee FDLRS, 1980, Coun. Exceptional Children, 1991-92; Found. Computer grante, 1992-93. Fellow Coun. Exceptional Children, Coun. for Children with Behavior Disorders; mem. PTA, Peace Found., Autistic Soc. Avocations: reading, travel, antiques. Office: Orange County Pub Schs 445 W Amelia St Orlando FL 32801-1128

CACOSSA, ANTHONY ALEXANDER, Romance languages educator; b. Newburgh, NY, Jan. 29, 1935; s. Salvatore and Franceschina (Scicchitano) C.; m. Anna Iaccino, Apr. 10, 1969. BA, Johns Hopkins U., 1955; MA, Syracuse U., 1956; D Modern Langs., U. Catania, Italy, 1969. Teaching asst. Syracuse (N.Y.) U., 1956-57; asst. prof., chmn. fgn. langs. Coppin State Coll., Balt., 1959-65; asst. prof. to prof. modern langs., coord. Italian studies Towson State U., Balt., 1965-83; adj. prof. Romance langs. and ESL Greenwich U., Hilo, Hawaii, 1989—2000; core faculty advisor in edn. Walden U., Mpls., 1990—96. Vis. tchr. Newburgh (NY) Free Acad., 1956; vis. lectr. Loyola Coll., Balt., 1967; accredited and chartered profl. cons. fgn. lang. edn. and curriculum design, Balt., 1983—; Fulbright lectr. Colombia, 1965, Italy, 1968-69, Costa Rica, 1972-73. Author: A Bergamask Parody of Guarini's Il Pastor Fido, 1972, Italian trans., 1973; contbr. articles to profl. jours. Fellow in Italian NEH, Stanford (Calif.) U., 1979; East European studies fellow Am. Coun. Learned Socs., UCLA, 1986. Mem. AAUP, Sigma Delta Pi (hon.). Home and Office: 316 E Melrose Ave Apt B Baltimore MD 21212-2913 E-mail: antalfra@aol.com.

CADE, TONI MARIE, medical educator; b. St. Martinville, La., Dec. 5, 1957; d. Dennis Peter and Susie Ann (Benoit) Hulin; m. Robert William Cade, June 9, 1978; children: Chelsea Lynn, Brittany Marie, Haley Elizabeth. BS, U. Southwestern La., 1979, MBA, 1991. Reg. health info. adminstr.; cert. coding specialist. Receptionist Surgery Ctr., Lafayette, La., 1976-77; supr. utilization review profl. stds. Rev. Orgn., Lafayette, La., 1979-80; coding supr. Our Lady of Lourdes Regional Med. Ctr., Lafayette, La., 1980-86, cons. health info. dept., 1987-88; cons. med. record OPTION Care, Lafayette, La., 1991; instr. med. record adminstrn. U. Southwestern La., Lafayette, 1987-92, instr. health info. mgmt., 1992-94, asst. prof. health info. mgmt., 1994—. Cons. in field. Author: Medical Terminology Instructor's Resource and Activity Kit, 1994. Mem.: La. Health Info. Mgmt. Assn. (bylaws-strategy mgr. 1990—91, state convention project mgr. 1992—93, coding roundtable project mgr. 1995—96, 2001—02, sec. 1996—97, pres.-elect 1997—99, pres. 1999—2000, past pres. 2000—02), Southwest Dist. Health Info. Mgmt. Assn. (pres. 1992, dist. rep. 1993, treas. 1994—95), Am. Health Info. Mgmt. Assn. (del. 1992, 1994, 1995, 1997, 1998, 1999). Roman Catholic. Avocation: travel. Office: U La at Lafayette PO Box 41007 Lafayette LA 70504-0001

CADNEY, CAROLYN, secondary education educator; b. Port Gibson, Miss., Jan. 27, 1952; d. Norman and Mary Viola (Rogers) C. BS, Alcorn State U., 1972; MEd, U. So. Miss., 1978. Cert. adult edn. Tchr. Fernwood Jr. H.S., Biloxi, Miss., 1972-73, Nichols Jr. H.S., Biloxi, Miss., 1973-80, Biloxi H.S., Miss., 1980—. Adj. instr. Jefferson Davis Jr. Coll. Miss. Gulf Coast C.C., Biloxi, 1988—; tchr. adv. com. Southeastern Regional Vision for Edn., Greensboro, N.C., 1993—. Recipient Enhancement award Biloxi Bay Chamber, Miss., 1995; named Outstanding Educator Biloxi Rotary Club, Miss., 1993, Miss. State Tchr. of Yr. State of Miss., 1994, Outstanding Woman of Yr. New Horizons, Gulfport, Miss., 1995. Mem. Miss. Profl. Educator (outstanding mem. award 1994), Delta Sigma Theta (v.p. 1990-92, woman of yr. 1993). Baptist. Avocation: tennis. Office: Biloxi High Sch 1424 Father Ryan Ave Biloxi MS 39530-3598

CADY, ELWYN LOOMIS, JR., medico legal consultant, educator; b. Ames, Iowa, Feb. 21, 1926; s. Elwyn Loomis Sr. and Annabel (Lacey) C.; m. Jane Carolyn Elliott, Jan. 27, 1964 (dec. Dec. 1989); children: James Anson, Kathryn Anne; stepchildren: Martin Norman Jensen III, Paul Elliott Jensen. BS in Medicine, U. Mo., 1955; JD, Tulane U., 1951. Bar: Mo. 1951, U.S. Supreme Ct. 1965. Sci. comml. tchr., athletic dir. and coach Vermillion (Kans.) Rural High Sch., 1948-49; pvt. practice Kansas City, St. Louis, Independence, Mo., 1951—; dir. law-medicine program U. Kansas City, 1951-56; asst. dir. Law-Sci. Inst. U. Tex., Austin, 1956-57, sec. Law-Sci. Acad. Am., 1956-57; of counsel Koenig & Dietz, St. Louis, 1959-74; gen. counsel Elliott Oil, Inc., Independence, 1966—, Overland Park Dry Cleaners, Inc. Mem. com. on mgmt. Ea. Jackson County Planned Parenthood Clinics, Independence, 1970-75. Author: (book) Law and Contemporary Nursing, 1961, 1st. rev. edit., 1963; Author: (with others) Immediate Care of the Acutely Ill and Injured, 1974, Cardiac Arrest and Resuscitation, 1958, 4th rev. edit., 1974, West's Federal Practice Manual, 1960, rev. 2nd edit., 1989, Gradwohl's Legal Medicine, 1954; book reviewer: sci. books and films. Legal Counsel Friends of the Truman Campus, U. Mo.-Kansas City, Independence, 19 87-97, Cmty. Assn. for the Arts, Independence, 1991—; charter mem. Friends of Nat. Frontier Trails Ctr., Independence, 1990—, Independence Hist. Trails City Com., 1991—. With U.S. Army, 1944-45, ETO. Fellow Harry S. Truman Libr. Inst. for Nat. and Internat. Affairs (hon.), Am. Acad. Forensic Sci. (ret.); mem. AAAS (life), Nat. Geog. Soc. (life), Am. Legion (past comdr., judge adv., chaplain, chmn. state blood donor program, chmn. dist. oratorical contest), Mo. Writers' Guild (past pres., historian), Soc. Mayflower Descs. (gov. Heart of Am. colony), Phi Alpha Delta (life), Phi Beta Pi, Tau Kappa Epsilon. Home and Office: 1919 Drumm Ave Independence MO 64055-1836

CAFFIN, LOUISE ANNE, library media educator; b. N.Y.C., Feb. 15, 1943; d. Milton D. and Tinette C. Caffin. BS, NYU, 1964; MLS, L.I. U., 1966. Tchr. N.Y.C. Bd. Edn., 1966—. Author: (manuscripts) Outward Bound, 1985, Californa Vs. Caryl Chessman, 1948-60 and Beyond, 1984, The Untrammelled Road He Chose: William O. Douglas, 1983, Invictus, 1985, Automobiles, Alcohol Abuse and Traffic Safety Curriculum, 1986, Tribute to Anne Frank, 1985, Private Letters and Public Works, 1987, If...Covert Operations in World War II, 1988. Member B'nai B'rith. Mem. Schoolmen and Schoolwomen's Lodge. Avocations: reading, painting, research, writing. Office: Frank D Whalen Middle Sch 135 2441 Wallace Ave Bronx NY 10467-9215

CAFRITZ, PEGGY COOPER, communications executive; b. Mobile, Ala., Apr. 7, 1947; d. Algernon Johnson and G. Catherine (Mouton) C.; married; 2 children. BA in Polit. Sci., George Washington U., 1968, JD, 1971. Bar: D.C. 1972. Founder Workshops for Careers in Arts, Washington, 1968; developer, chmn. bd. Duke Ellington Sch. Arts., Washington, 1968-84; dir. Arrowstreet, Architects and Planners Inc., Cambridge, Mass., 1972-74, Washington, 1972-74; spl. asst. to pres. Post-Newsweek Stas. Inc., Washington, 1974-77; programming exec., producer documentary films Sta. WTOP-TV, Washington, 1974-77. Cons. arts critic pub. TV show Around Town, 1986—. Cultural arts critic (PBS TV show) Around Town, 1986—. Mem. exec. com. D.C. Commn. Arts and Humanities, 1970-75, chmn., 1979-87, chmn. emeritus, 1987—; trustee Am. Film Inst., 1972-74, Pratt Inst., 1991; bd. govs. Corcoran Gallery Art, Washington, 1972-74; exec. dir. gt. issue program D.C. Bicentennial Commn., 1974; bd. dirs. Washington Performing Arts Soc., 1983—, Kennedy Ctr. Performing Arts, 1986—, Women's Project, 1987—, Nat. Guild Community Schs. of Arts, 1976-80, Pennsylvania Ave. Devel. Corp., Washington, 1979-87, Atlanta U., 1983-86, Washington, Am. Place Theater, N.Y.C.; co-chmn. Mayor's Blue Ribbon Task Force on Cultural and Econ. Devel., 1987-88; mem. exec. bd. Nat. Assembly State Arts Agys., 1979-86, planning com., 1986-87; mem. conv. staff Dem. Nat. Com., 1972, 76; mem. steering com. Carter-Mondale, Washington, 1976; mem. nat. panel Arts, Edn. and Ams., 1975-79; mem. internat. com. UNICEF, 1976-79; chair Smithsonian Cultural Edn. Com., 1989—; co-chair Smithsonian Cultural Equity Com., 1988—; mem. African-Am. Instnl. study adv. com. Smithsonian Instn., 1990— pres., D.C. St. Bd. of Education, 2001-. Fellow Woodrow Wilson Internat. Ctr. for Scholars, 1971; recipient John D. Rockefeller III award, 1972, George F. Peabody award U. Ga., 1976, Emmy award, 1977, 27th Ann. Broadcast Media award, 1977, Zeta Phi Beta award for outstanding contbn. in the arts, 1974, N.Y. Black Film Festival award, 1976, Women's Achievement award Pub. TV, 1984, Brava award for Outstanding Contbn. to Arts in Washington, 1988, Mayor's Art award for excellence in svc. to arts, 1991, 20th Malcolm X DayAnniversary award Arts Advocacy, 1991, Ann. Cultural Alliance award, 1992; named Washingtonian of Yr. Washingtonian mag., 1972, Woman of Yr. Mademoiselle mag., 1973, and numerous other awards. Mem. ABA, D.C. Bar Assn. Home and Office: 3030 Chain Bridge Rd NW Washington DC 20016-3410

CAGALA, M. THERESE, assistant principal; b. Evergreen Pk., Ill., Jan. 14, 1952; d. Frank Anthony and Marie (Nugent) Burns; m. Robert Michael Cagala, Sept. 16, 1973; children: Brian, Tracy. BS in Phys. Edn., U. Ill., Chgo., 1974; M in Ednl. Adminstrn., Govs. State U., 1994. Phys. edn. tchr. Chgo. Bd. of Edn., 1974-77; owner/mgr. Nautilus Fitness, Naperville, Ill., 1979-81, mgr. Hickory Hills, Ill., 1981-82, Golds Gym, Orland Pk., Ill., 1982-83; phys. edn. tchr. grades K-8 St. Patricia Sch., Hickory Hills, 1983-95, asst. prin., 1992-95, Kolmar Sch., Midlothian (Ill.) Sch. Dist. 143, 1995—. Mem., advisor St. Patricia Sch. Bd., 1992-95; home-sch. rep. St. Cletus Sch. Bd., La Grange Park, Ill., 1989-91. Soccer coach Hickory Hills Pk. Dist., 1986-92; volleyball coach St. Cletus Sch., 1991-93; pres. St. Cletus Home-Sch. Assn., 1990-91, v.p. 1989-90. Ill. State scholar, 1970, Govs. State U. Alumni scholar, 1994; recipient Archdiocese Heart of the Sch. award Chgo. Archdiocese, 1994, Svc. to Mankind award Sertoma, 1995. Mem. AAHPERD, Nat. Assn. Secondary Sch. Prins., Ill. Prin. Assn., U. Ill. Alumni Assn. (life). Roman Catholic. Avocations: volleyball refereeing, walking, aerobics, reading. Office: Kolmar Sch 4500 143rd St Midlothian IL 60445-2612

CAGGINS, RUTH PORTER, nursing educator; b. July 11, 1945; d. Henry Chapelle and Corinne Sadie (Baines) Porter; m. Don Randolph Caggins, July 1, 1978; children: Elva Rene, Don Randolph Jr., Myles Thomas Chapelle. BS, Dillard U., New Orleans, 1967; MA, NYU, 1973; PhD, Tex. Woman's U., 1992. Staff nurse Montefiore Hosp., Bronx, 1968—70, head nurse, 1970—72; nurse clinician Met. Hosp., N.Y.C., 1973—74, clin. supr., 1974—76; asst. prof. U. So. La., Lafayette, 1976—78; assoc. prof. Prairie View A&M U. Coll. Nursing, Houston, 1986—. Apptd. project dir.LIFT Ctr. Active The Links Inc., Houston, 1982—, Nat. Black Leadership Initiative on Cancer, Houston, Family and Cmty. Violence Prevention; family life ctr. dir. Prairie View AUM U. Coll. Nursing; active Pine Oak Cornerstone Bapt. Ch.; bd. dirs. Houston Achievement Pl. Recipient Tchg. Excellence award, Nat. Inst. Staff and Orgnl. Devel., 1992—93, 1995—96, 1996—97; grantee, Prairie View A&M Univ., 1994—95, 1996—97. Mem.: ANA (clin. ethnic/racial minority fellow 1989—92, post doctoral proposal devel. program 1995), Assn. Black Nursing Faculty in Higher Edn. (Dissertation award 1990), A.K. Rice Inst. (assoc. Ctrl. States Ctr., Tex. Ctr.), Nat. Black Nurses Assn., Chi Eta Phi, Delta Sigma Theta, Sigma Theta Tau. Democrat. Avocations: singing, sewing, traveling, aerobics, writing. Home: 5602 Goettee Cir Houston TX 77091-4523 Office: Prairie View A&M U Coll Nursing 6436 Fannin St Houston TX 77030-1519

CAHALEN, SHIRLEY LEANORE, retired secondary education educator; b. LaHarpe, Kans., Aug. 20, 1933; d. Hugh E. and Irma Eunonia (Russell) Pearman; m. Keith E. Cahalen, Sept. 2, 1953; 1 child: Keith P. Student, Iola Jr. Coll., 1951-52, McPherson Coll., 1952-53, Pratt C.C., 1963-64; BS, Northwestern State U., Alva, Okla., 1966; MS, Kans. State U., 1981; postgrad., Emporia State U., 1982-86. Cert. spl. edn. tchr., Kans. With Kans. Power & Light Co., McPherson, 1952-53, State Farm Ins. Co., Jacksonville, Fla., 1957-59, Kans. Fish and Game Commn., Pratt, 1960-62; tchr. home econs. Kirby-Smith Jr. H.S., Jacksonville, Fla., 1966-67, Unified Sch. Dist. 254, Medicine Lodge, Kans., 1968-71, Sch. Dist. 259, Wichita East, Wichita, Kans., 1971-73, Dist. 490, El Dorado, Kans., 1975-82; tchr. spl. edn. Augusta (Kans.) Sr. H.S., 1982-93; ret., 1993. Sec. IDP Unified Sch. Dist. 490, 1986-88, dirs. coun., 1987-93, effective sch. track com., 1990-93; mem. abuse intervention team Unified Sch. Dist. 402, 1989-91. Mem. edn. com. First United Meth. Ch., 1981-87. Mem. Walnut Valley Edn. Assn., Kans. Edn. Assn. (state rep.), NEA (El Dorado chpt.), Butler County Spl. Edn. Assn., ADK, AAUW (pres. 1979-81), Coun. for Exceptional Children, Am. Legion Aux., Kappa Delta Pi. Methodist. Home: 205 N Main St Apt 6 El Dorado KS 67042-2057

CAHILL, GERARD ALBIN, university educator; b. N.Y.C., Dec. 21, 1936; s. Albin G. and Susan E. (Maschenic) C.; m. Lea D. Chandler, Jan. 29, 1993. BS in Elec. Engring., Manhattan Coll., 1958; MBA, CCNY, 1962; PhD, NYU, 1973. Registered profl. engr., N.Y. With Lucent Tech., N.Y.C., 1959-67; divsn. contr. Gen. Dynamics Corp., Orlando, Fla., 1967-68; corp. contr. Smithfield Corp., Washington, 1968-69; v.p. HETRA Co., Melbourne, fla., 1969-71, CODI Corp., Fairlawn, N.J., 1971-73; v.p. fin., treas. Cablecom-Gen. Inc., Denver, 1973-81; sr.v.p. Capital Cities Cable Inc., Bloomfield Hills, Mich., 1981-82; sr. v.p. Simmons Comm., Inc., Stamford, Conn., 1982-85; prof. Westfield (Mass.) State Coll., 1986-87, Fla. Inst. Tech., 1987—. Cons. in field. Ford Found. fellow, 1965. Mem. NSPE, Nat. Assn. Forensic Economists, Ea. Econ. Assn., Suntree Country Club. Office: 208 Versailles Dr Melbourne FL 32951 E-mail: gcahill@fit.edu.

CAHILL, THOMAS ANDREW, physicist, educator; b. Paterson, N.J., Mar. 4, 1937; s. Thomas Vincent and Margery (Groesbeck) C.; m. Virginia Ann Arnoldy, June 26, 1965; children: Catherine Frances, Thomas Michael. BA, Holy Cross Coll., Worcester, Mass., 1959; PhD in Physics; NDEA fellow, U. Calif., Los Angeles, 1965. Asst. prof. in residence U. Calif., Los Angeles, 1965-66; NATO fellow, research physicist Centre d'Etudes Nucleaires de Saclay, France, 1966-67; prof. physics U. Calif., Davis, 1967-94; acting dir. Crocker Nuclear Lab., 1972, dir., 1980-89. Dir. Inst. Ecology, 1972-75; cons. NRC of Can., Louvre Mus. UN Global Atmospheric Watch, 1990—; mem. Internat. Com. on PIXE and Its Application, Calif. Atty. Gen., Nat. Audubon Soc., Mono Lake Com. Author: (with J. McCray) Electronic Circuit Analysis for Scientists, 1973; editor Internat. Jour. Pixe, 1989—; contbr. articles to profl. jours. on physics, applied physics, hist. analyses and air pollution. Prin. investigator IMPROVE Nat. Air Pollution Network., 1987-97; co-dir. Crocker Hist. and Archeol. Projects; head U. Calif. Delta Group, Davis, 1997-. OAS fellow, 1968, Japanese Nat. Rsch. fellow, Kyoto, 1992. Mem. Am. Phys. Soc., Air Pollution Control Assn., Am. Assn. Aerosol Rsch., Sigma Xi Democrat. Roman Catholic. Home: 1813 Amador Ave Davis CA 95616-3104 Office: U Calif Dept Applied Sci One Shields Ave Davis CA 95616

CAHN, STEVEN MARK, philosopher, educator; b. Springfield, Mass., Aug. 6, 1942; s. Judah and Evelyn (Baum) C.; m. Marilyn (Ross), May 4, 1974. AB, Columbia U., 1963, PhD, 1966. Vis. instr. Dartmouth Coll., 1966; vis. prof. U. Rochester, NY, 1967; asst. prof. philosophy Vassar Coll., Poughkeepsie, NY, 1966-68, NYU, N.Y.C., 1968-71, assoc. prof., 1971-73, dir. grad. studies, 1972, dir. under grad. studies, 1971-73; prof., chmn. dept. philosophy U. Vt., Burlington, Vt., 1973-80, adj. prof. philosophy, 1980-83; dean grad. studies, prof. philosophy Grad. Sch. and Univ. Ctr., CUNY, 1983—, provost, v.p. for acad. affairs, 1984-92, acting pres., 1991; program officer Exxon Edn. Found., N.Y.C., 1978-79; assoc. dir. Rockefeller Found., N.Y.C., 1979-81, acting dir. humanities, 1981-82; dir. div. gen. programs NEH, Washington, 1982-83. Pres. John Dewey Found., 1983— ; cons., panelist NEH, 1975-82 Author: Fate, Logic, and Time, 1967, 82, A New Introduction to Philosophy, 1971, 86, The Eclipse of Excellence: A Critique of American Higher Education, 1973, Education and the Democratic Ideal, 1979, Saints and Scamps: Ethics in Academia, 1986, rev. 1994, Philosophical Explorations: Freedom, God and Goodness, 1989, Puzzles & Perplexities: Collected Essays, 2002; editor: (with Frank A. Tillman) Philosophy of Art and Aesthetics: From Plato to Wittgenstein, 1969, The Philosophical Foundations of Education, 1970, Philosophy of Religion, 1970, Classics of Western Philosophy, 1977, 6th edit., 2002, New Studies in the Philosophy of John Dewey, 1977, Scholars Who Teach: The Art of College Teaching, 1978, (with David Shatz) Contemporary Philosophy of Religion, 1982, (with Patricia Kitcher and George Sher) Reason at Work: Introductory Readings in Philosophy, 1984, 3d edit., 1995, Morality, Responsibility and the University: Studies in Academic Ethics, 1990, Affirmative Action and the University: A Philosophical Inquiry, 1993, (with Joram G. Haber) Twentieth Century Ethical Theory, 1995, The Affirmative Action Debate, 1995, 2nd edit., 2002, Classic and Contemporary Readings in the Philosophy of Education, 1997, Classics of Modern Political Theory: Machiavelli to Mill, 1997, (with Peter Markie) Ethics: History, Theory, and Contemporary Issues, 1998, 2nd edit., 2001, Exploring Philosophy: An Introductory Anthology, 2000, Classics of Political and Moral Philosophy, 2002, (with David Shatz) Questions About God, 2002, (with Tziporah Kasachkoff) Morality and Public Policy, 2003, (with Maureen Eckert and Robert Buckley) Knowledge and Reality, 2003, Philosophy for the 21st Century: A Comprehensive Reader, 2003; gen. editor Issues in Acad. Ethics, 1994—, Critical Essays on the Classics, 1997—, Blackwell Philosophy Guides, 2001—, Blackwell Readings in Philosophy, 2001—. Chmn. standing com. on tchg. philosophy Am. Philos. Assn., 1985-90, del. Am. Coun. Learned Socs., 1998-2002. Home: 100 W 57th St New York NY 10019-3302 Office: CUNY Grad Sch U Ctr 365 5th Ave New York NY 10016-4334

CAI, X. SEAN, physical education educator; b. Guiyang, Guizhou, People's Republic of China, Feb. 14, 1963; came to U.S., 1990; s. Yonglu Cai and Yuhua Qiu. Bachelor's degree, S.W. China Normal U., Chongqing, 1984; Master's degree, Shanghai Inst. Phys. Edn., 1987; PhD, U. Ark., 1995. Lic. in Chinese martial arts. Tchr. phys. edn. Yu Ying Elem. Sch., Guiyang, 1977-80; asst. prof. Shanghai Inst. Phys. Edn., 1987-90; vis. scholar Calif. State U., Sacramento, 1990-91; lectr. U. Ark., Fayetteville, 1991-95; asst. prof. U. Akron, Ohio, 1995—. Contbr. rsch. articles to profl. jours. Martial arts athlete, Guiyang Youth Athlete's Sch., 1975-79. Mem. AAHPERD (chairperson rsch. divsn. Ohio br.), Nat. Assn. Sports and Phys. Edn., Ohio Assn. Health, Phys. Edn., Recreation and Dance (chair divsn. rsch. in higher edn.), Chinese Students and Scholars Assn. (pres. 1993-94), Martial Arts Assn. (advisor 1993-94), Badminton Club (advisor 1996—). Office: U Akron Dept Phys & Health Edn Akron OH 44325-0001

CAIN, B(URTON) EDWARD, chemistry educator; b. Batavia, N.Y., Sept. 11, 1942; s. Burton Leo and Bettie S. (Williams) C. BA, SUNY, Binghamton, 1964; PhD, Syracuse U., 1971. Biochemist Onondaga County (N.Y.) Pub. Health Labs., Syracuse, N.Y., 1971-72; chemist O'Brien & Gere Cons. Engrs., Inc., Syracuse, N.Y., 1972-74; asst. prof. chemistry Nat. Tech. Inst. Deaf, Rochester (N.Y.) Inst. Tech., N.Y., 1974-80, assoc. prof. dept. chemistry, 1980-84, prof., 1984—; asst. chemistry dept. head Rochester Inst. Tech., 1981-87, 88—. Reader Advanced Placement chemistry exams. Ednl. Testing Svc., June 1987, 88, 89, 90, 91, 92. Author: The Basics of Technical Communicating, 1988; contbr. articles to profl. jours. Reviewer grant proposals coll. sci. instrument program NSF, 1987, instrumentation and lab. improvement program NSF, 1992. Recipient Eisenhart Outstanding Tchr. award, 1980. Mem. Am. Chem. Soc., AAAS, AAUP, Nat. Sci. Tchrs. Assn., Nat. Assn. Deaf, Conf. Am. Instrs. for Deaf, Registry of Interpreters for Deaf, Sigma Xi, Phi Lambda Upsilon, Gamma Epsilon Tau (Tchr. of Yr. award 1983). Home: 200 East Ave Apt 1105 Rochester NY 14604-2633 Office: 85 Lomb Memorial Dr Rochester NY 14623-5603 E-mail: becsch@rit.edu.

CAIN, CLIFFORD CHALMERS, chaplain, educator; b. Zanesville, Ohio, Feb. 15, 1950; s. Clifford Chalmers Sr. and Ethel Virginia (Bokelman) C.; m. Louise E. Lueckel, June 7, 1975; children: Rachel Mariël, Zachary Matheüs. BA, Muskingum Coll., 1972; M Div., Princeton Theol. Seminary, 1975; postgrad., Rijksuniversiteit te Leiden, The Netherlands, 1975-78; D in Ministry, Vanderbilt U., 1981; PhD, Rikkyo U., Tokyo, 1994. Ordained to ministry Am. Bapt. Ch., 1975. Assoc. pastor The Am. Protestant Ch., The Netherlands, 1975-78; chaplain Muskingum Coll., New Concord, Ohio, 1978-81; chaplain, assoc. prof. Franklin (Ind.) Coll., 1981—, dean of the chapel, 1993—, prof., 1994—. Pres. Met. Indpls. Campus Ministry, 1984-85, Ind. Office for Campus Ministries, 1985-88. Author: Faith Faces the World, 1989, Growing in Grace: Theological Stories for Children, 1992, What Manner of Person?, 1995, Envisioning Respect, 2001, The Earth Is The Lord's, 2003; contbr. articles to profl. jours. and book revs.; contbg. editor: The Intersection of Mind and Spirit, 1985; contbg. author: Stewardship, 1998, Keeping the Faith, 2003. V.p. The Am. Community Council, The Hague, The Netherlands, 1977-78; bd. dirs. Evergreen Village, New Concord, Ohio, 1980-81. Mem. Am. Acad. Religion, Soc. Bibl. Lit., Bapt. Peace Fellowship N.Am., Nat. Assn. Coll. and U. Chaplains (bd. dirs., v.p., pres.). Avocations: photography, music, traveling, sports, archaeology. Home: 300 W Jefferson St Franklin IN 46131-2110 Office: Franklin Coll East Monroe St Franklin IN 46131

CAIN, KAREN MIRINDA, musician, educator; b. Anna, Ill., Feb. 25, 1944; d. James Paul and Margaret Camilla (Sinks) C. MusB, So. Ill. U., 1966, MusM in Voice and Choral Conducting, 1967; postgrad., Trinity Coll., Washington, 1985. Cert. music tchr., Md. Choral music tchr., Prince George's County, Md., 1969-71; music tchr. class piano Montgomery County, Md., 1972-89; music tchr., founder of studio Rockville, Md., 1972—; co-founder, dir., arranger, profl. madrigal ensemble The Renaissance Revelers, 1985—. Choral music dir. and soloist various chs. and synagogues, Rockville, Md., 1972-92; soprano soloist, sect. leader Grace Luth. Ch., Washington, 2000—; singer Paul Hill Chorale, Washington, 1982-90, mem. chorale staff, music theory instr., 1984-90; contbr. minstrel and history guilds, performer, mem., Md. Renaissance Festival, 1987—. Dir., editor: (CD) Renaissance Romance, 1994 (CD) Journey into Light, 2002; arranger choral works featured on Renaissance Romance, Journey Into Light; dir.: performances at The Lutheran Reformation Svc. held at The Washington Nat. Cathedral, 1995, The White House, Kennedy Ctr.; co-author (with John Sinks): Sinks: A Family History, 1980. Mem. AAUW, Md. Music Tchrs. Assn., Montgomery County Class Piano Tchrs. Assn., Mu Phi Epsilon. Home and Office: 862 College Pkwy # T-1 Rockville MD 20850-1938

CAIN, SANDRA KAY, secondary education educator; b. Beardstown, Ill., Mar. 30, 1949; d. Roy Martin and Helen Faye (Leatherman) Doll; m. Rodney Lee Cain, June 22, 1975; children: Matthew Martin, Philip John. BA, MacMurray Coll., 1971. Cert. edn., spl.-music grades K-12. Jr. and sr. high choir Virden (Ill.) Sch. Dist., 1971-74; sr. high vocal music Harlem H.S., Machesney Park, Ill., 1974-77; music and choir tchr. grades K-12 Faith Acad., Rockford, Ill., 1979-82, 84-85; jr. high vocal music tchr. Harlem Jr. High, Loves Park, Ill., 1985-88; sr. high vocal music and drama tchr. Harlem H.S., Machesney Park, 1988—. Music dir. Faith Ctr., Rockford, 1978-89, Grace Family Ch., Belvidere, Ill., 1989—. Merit badge counselor Boy Scouts Am., Machesney Park, 1989-94. Recipient Those Who Excell Recognition, State Bd. Edn. Ill., 1990; named Most Inspirational Tchr., Western Ill. U., 1994, 97. Mem. Am. Choral Dirs. Assn., Ill. Music Educators Assn., Music Educators Nat. Conf., Tri-M Music Honor Soc. (state chair 1992-99). Independent. Avocation: collecting antiques. Home: 4630 Illinois St Loves Park IL 61111-5851 Office: Harlem High Sch One Huskie Cir Machesney Park IL 61115 E-mail: scain@harlem122.org.

CAIN, WILLIAM STANLEY, experimental psychologist, educator, researcher; b. N.Y.C., Sept. 7, 1941; s. William Henry and June Rose (Stanley) Cain; m. Claire Murphy, Oct. 30, 1993; children: Justin, Alison-stepchildren: Michael, Jennifer, Courtney. BS, Fordham U., 1963; MSc, Brown U., 1966, PhD, 1968. From asst. fellow to fellow John B. Pierce Lab., New Haven, 1967-94; from instr. to assoc. prof. dept. epidemiology, pub. health, and psychology Yale U., New Haven, 1967-84, prof., 1984-94; prof. otolaryngology U. Calif., San Diego, 1994—. Mem. sensory disorders study sect. NIH, Bethesda, Md., 1991—95; mem. sci. adv. bd. Ctr. Indoor Air Rsch., Linthicum, Md., 1991—99. Mem. editl. bd. Chem. Senses, 1985—94, mem. editl. adv. bd. Indoor Air, 1990—2000, Physiology and Behavior, 1995—96; editor: 5 books, 1971—; contbr. articles to profl. jours. Recipient Jacob Javits/Claude Pepper award, NIH, 1984, Sense of Smell Rsch. award, Fragrance Rsch. Fund, 1986. Fellow: ASHRAE (Crosby Field award 1984), APA, Acad. Indoor Air Rsch.; mem.: N.Y. Acad. Scis. (pres. 1986), Assn. Chemoreception Scis. (exec. chmn. 1983—84). Home: 4459 Nabal Dr La Mesa CA 91941-7168 Office: U Calif Dept Surgery 9500 Gilman Dr Rm Mc957 La Jolla CA 92093-0957

CAIN, WILLIAM VERNON, academic administrator; b. Atlanta, Jan. 28, 1942; s. Clarence Wilmer and Mamie (Lynch) C.; m. Janice Faye Blair, Aug. 22, 1970; children: Katherine Susanne, William Christopher. BS, West Ga. Coll., 1967, MEd, 1969; postgrad., U. Ga., 1970-71, U. No. Fla., 1984-86; EdD, U. Ala., 1975. Tchr. Cobb County Schs., Marietta, Ga., 1967-68; instr. Ga. Retardation Ctr., Athens, Ga., 1969-71; sch. psychometrist Cobb County Schs., Marietta, Ga., 1971-72; intern, program coord. Ala. Staet Dept. Edn., Montgomery, 1972-74; field coord. S.E. Regional Resource Ctr., Montgomery, 1974-76, program coord., asst. dir., 1977-80; dir. spl. edn. Montgomery County Schs., 1976-77; cons. Fla. Diagnostic & Learning Resources System, Tallahassee, 1980-81, tng. facilitator, supr., coord. presch. project, 1980-87; dir. Multi-System Evaluation Ctr., Anniston, Ala., 1987—. Contbr. articles to profl. jours. Treas. Ala. Coun. for Exceptional Children, Montgomery, 1975-76; chmn., deacon Westside Bapt. Ch., Jacksonville, Ala., 1988-92; v.p. Ala. Head Injury Chpt., Calhoun County, Ala., 1992. Mem. Nat. Assn. Sch. Psychologist, Coun. for Exceptional Children, Alpha Theta (Hall of Fame). Baptist. Home: 1201 7th Ave NE Jacksonville AL 36265-1113 Office: Multi System Evaluation Ctr PO Box 2084 1024 Us Highway 431 N Anniston AL 36206-2089

CAINE, STANLEY PAUL, college administrator; b. Huron, SD, Feb. 11, 1940; s. Louis Vernon and Elizabeth (Holland) C.; m. Karen Anne Mickelson, July 11, 1964; children: Rebecca, Kathryn, David. BA, Macalester Coll., 1962; MS, U. Wis., 1964, PhD, 1967; LLD, Hanover Coll., 2000; LittD, MacMurray Coll., 2003. Asst. prof. history Lindenwood Coll., St. Charles, Mo., 1967-71; from asst. to assoc. prof. history DePauw U., Greencastle, Ind., 1971-77; prof. history, v.p. for acad. affairs Hanover (Ind.) Coll., 1977-89; pres. Adrian (Mich.) Coll., 1989—. Bd. dirs. NCAA Coun., 1995-96, vice chair mgmt. coun. divsn. III, 1997-99, pres.'s coun., 1999-2002; cons., evaluator North Ctrl. Assn., 1984—. Author: The Myth of a Political Reform, 1970; contbr. to book The Progressive Era, 1974; co-editor: Political Reform in Wisconsin, 1973. Bd. dirs. Nat. Assn. Schs., Colls. and Univs. of United Meth. Ch., 1994-97, 2000—, pres., 2002-03; mem. Lenawee Tomorrow, Adrian, 1989—. Recipient D.C. Everest prize

Wis. State Hist. Soc., 1968; Woodrow Wilson fellow, 1962-63, Nat. Presbyn. fellow Presbyn. Ch. U.S., 1963-65 Mem. Orgn. Am. Historians, Nat. Assn. Ind. Colls. Univs. (bd. dirs. 1997-2000), Rotary. Methodist. Avocations: sports, reading. Office: Adrian Coll Office of Pres 110 S Madison St Adrian MI 49221-2518

CAIRE, WILLIAM, biologist, educator; b. Savannah, Ga., Nov. 3, 1946; s. James Andrew and Anna Elizabeth (Rahn) C.; children: William James, Jacob Wooldridge, Samuel Rahn. AA, Howard Coll., Big Spring, Tex., 1966; BS, Tex. Tech. U., 1969; MS, U. North Tex., 1972; PhD, U. N.Mex., 1978. Tchr. math. and sci. J.L. Long Jr. High Sch., Dallas, 1969-70; biologist U.S. Fish and Wildlife Svc., Ft. Collins, Colo., 1974; rsch. assoc. U. Mo., Sullivan, 1975-76; prof. biology U. Ctrl. Okla., Edmond, 1976—, asst. dean Coll. Math. and Sci., 1992-96, dean Coll. Math. and Sci., 2000—. Cons., spkr. in field. Author: Mammals of Oklahoma, 1989; reviewer jour. articles; contbr. articles to profl. jours. Grantee NSF grant, U. Ctrl. Okla. Mem. Southwestern Assn. Naturalists, Am. Soc. Mammalogists, Okla. Acad. Sci. Avocations: golf, woodworking, gardening. Home: 10774 Coyote Cir Arcadia OK 73007-9206 Office: U Ctrl Okla Dept Biology Edmond OK 73034 E-mail: wcaire@wcok.edu.

CAIRNS, ELTON JAMES, chemical engineering educator; b. Chgo., Nov. 7, 1932; s. James Edward and Claire Angele (Larzelere) C.; m. Miriam Esther Citron, Dec. 26, 1974; 1 dau., Valerie Helen; stepchildren: Benjamin David, Joshua Aaron. BS in Chemistry, Mich. Tech. U., Houghton, 1955; BS in Chem. Engring, 1955; PhD in Chem. Engring. (Dow Chem. Co. fellow, univ. fellow, Standard Oil Co. Calif. grantee, NSF fellow), U. Calif., Berkeley, 1959. Phys. chemist GE Rsch. Lab., Schenectady, 1959-66; group leader, then sect. head chem. engring. div. Argonne (Ill.) Nat. Lab., 1966-73; asst. head electrochemistry dept. GM Rsch. Labs., 1973-78; assoc. lab. dir., dir. energy and environment divsn. Lawrence Berkeley Nat. Lab., Calif., 1978-96, C.D. Hollowell meml. lectr., 1996, head, Energy Conversion and Storage Program, 1982—; prof. chem. engring. U. Calif., Berkeley, 1978—. Cons. in field; mem. numerous govt. panels; Croft lectr. U. Mo., 1979. Author: (with H.A. Liebhafsky) Fuel Cells and Fuel Batteries, 1968; mem. editor bd. Advances in Electrochemistry and Electrochm. Engring., 1974—; divsn. editor Jour. Electrochem. Soc., 1968-91; regional editor Electrochimica Acta, 1984-99, editor, 2000—; contbr. articles to profl. jours.; patentee in field. Recipient IR-100 award, 1968, Centennial medal Case Western Res. U., 1980, R&D 100 award, 1992, Melvin Calvin medal of distinction Mich. Technol. U., 1998; named McCabe lectr. U. N.C., 1993; grantee DuPont Co., 1956. Fellow Am. Insts. Chemists, Electrochem. Soc. (chmn. phys. electrochem. divsn. 1981-84, v.p. 1986-89, pres. 1989-90, Francis Mills Turner award 1963); mem. AIChE (chmn. energy conversion com. 1970-94), AAAS, Am. Chem. Soc., Internat. Soc. Electrochemistry (chmn. electrochem. energy conversion divsn. 1977-85, U.S. nat. sec. 1983-89, v.p. 1984-88, pres. 1999-2000), Intersoc. Energy Conversion Engring. Conf. (steering com. 1970—, gen. chmn. 1976, 90, 97, program chmn. 1983, co-chair internat. meeting on lithium batteries 2002), Sigma Xi (pres. Berkeley chpt. 2002-03). Home: 239 Langlie Ct Walnut Creek CA 94598-3615 Office: Lawrence Berkeley Nat Lab 1 Cyclotron Rd Berkeley CA 94720-0001 E-mail: ejcairns@lbl.gov., cairns@cchem.berkeley.edu.

CAIRNS, SARA ALBERTSON, physical education educator; b. Bloomsburg, Pa., July 18, 1939; d. Robert Wilson and Sara (Porter) Albertson; m. Thomas Cairns, Apr. 13, 1968. BS in Edn., Pa. State U., 1961; MS in Edn., West Chester U., 1965. Cert. tchr., Pa., Del., prin., Del.; adaptive p.e. specialist. Phys. edn. tchr., coach Cen. Columbia County High Sch., Bloomsburg, Pa., 1961-64; phys. edn. tchr. Christina Sch. Dist., Newark, Del., 1964—, coord. adult edn., 1998—. Cons. U. Del., Newark, 1984—, coop. tchr., 1965—; area coord. New Castle (Del.) County Parks and Recreation, 1973—; presenter in field. Contbr. articles to profl. pubis. Chair Leasure Elem. Sch. campaign United Fund, 1987-91. Recipient Outstanding Svc. award New CAstle County Parks and Recreation, 1985. Mem. NEA, AAUW, AAHPERD, Del. Assn. Health, Phys. Edn., Recreation and Dance (v.p. dance 1991-94, exec. bd.), Del. State Edn. Assn. Democrat. Presbyterian. Avocations: toy poodles, beach, walking. Home: 40 Vansant Rd Newark DE 19711-4839 Office: Leasure Elem Sch 1015 Church Rd Newark DE 19702-5102

CALABRESI, GUIDO, judge, law educator; b. Milan, Oct. 18, 1932; s. Massimo and Bianca Maria (Finzi Contini) C.; m. Anne Gordon Audubon Tyler, May 20, 1961; children: Bianca Finzi Contini, Anne Gordon Audubon, Massimo Franklin Tyler BS in Analytical Econs., Yale U., 1953, LLB, 1958, MA (hon.), 1962; BA in Politics, Philosophy and Econs., Oxford U., 1955, MA in Politics, Philosophy and Econs., 1959; LLD (hon.), Notre Dame U., 1979, Villanova U., 1984, U. Toronto, 1985, Boston Coll., 1986, Cath. U. Am., 1986, U. Chgo., 1988, Conn. Coll., 1988, Chgo.-Kent-I.T.T., 1989, William Mitchell Coll. Law, 1992, Princeton U., 1992, Detroit Mercy Sch. Law, 1994, Seton Hall U., 1995, Albertus Magnus Coll., 1995, Lewis and Clark Coll., 1996, St. John's U., 1997, Pace U., 1998, Iona Coll., 1998, Roger Williams U., 1999, Hofstra U., 1999, N.Y. Law Sch., 1999, Skidmore Coll., 2000, Colby Coll., 2001, U. San Diego, 2001; Dott. Ius SD (hon.), U. Turin, Italy, 1982; JD (hon.), U. Pavia, Italy, 1987, U. Stockholm, 1993; PhD (hon.), U. Haifa, Israel, 1988; DPhil, U. Tel Aviv, 1998; LHD (hon.), U. New Haven, 1989, Williams Coll., 1991, Quinnipiac Coll., 1993; DSc in Politics (hon.), U. Padua, Italy, 1990; Dott. Jur. (hon.), U. Bologna, Italy, 1991, U. Milan, 1998. Bar: Conn. 1958. Asst. instr. dept. econs. Yale U., New Haven, Conn., 1955-56; law clk. to Hon. Hugo Black U.S. Supreme Ct., Washington, 1958-59; asst. prof. Yale U. Law Sch., 1959-61, assoc. prof., 1961-62, prof., 1962-70, John Thomas Smith prof. law, 1970-78, Sterling prof. law, 1978-95; prof. emeritus, lectr. Yale U., 1995—; dean Yale U. Law Sch., 1985-94, Sterling prof. law emeritus, lectr., 1995—; judge U.S. Ct. Appeals 2d cir., New Haven, 1994—. Fellow Timothy Dwight Coll., 1960—; vis. prof. Harvard U. Law Sch., 1969-70, Japan Am. Studies Seminar, Kyoto-Doshisha Univs., summer 1972, European U. Inst., Florence, Italy, 1979; Arthur L. Goodhart prof. legal sci. Cambridge U., also fellow St. John's Coll., 1980-81. Author: The Costs of Accidents: A Legal and Economic Analysis, 1970; (with P. Bobbitt) Tragic Choices, 1978; A Common Law for the Age of Statutes, 1983 (ABA citation of merit, Order of Coif Triennial Book award); Ideals, Beliefs, Attitudes and the Law: Private Law Perspectives on a Public Law Problem (Silver Gavel award ABA), 1985; contbr. articles to profl. jours. Hon. trustee Hopkins Grammar Sch., pres. 1976-80; trustee St. Thomas More Chapel, Yale U.; vice-chmn. bd. trustees Carolyn Found., Minn. Rhodes scholar, 1953; named one of Ten Outstanding Young Men Am., U.S. Jaycees, 1962; recipient Laetare Medal, U. Notre Dame, 1985, Marshall-Wythe medal Coll. William and Mary, 1985, award for outstanding rsch. in law and govt. Fellows of Am. Bar Found., 1998, Thomas Jefferson medal in law Jefferson Found./U. Va. Law Sch., 2000. Fellow Am. Acad. Arts & Scis., Associazione Italiana di Diritto Comparato, Brit. Acad. (corr.), Royal Swedish Acad. Scis. (fgn.), Nat. Acad. dei Lincei (fgn.), Acad. delle Sci. di Torino (fgn.); mem. Conn. Bar Assn., Assn. Am. Law Schs. (exec. com. 1986-89), Am. Philos. Soc. Home: 639 Amity Rd Woodbridge CT 06525-1206 Office: US Ct Appeals 2d Cir 157 Church St New Haven CT 06510-2100*

CALAME, KATHRYN LEE, microbiologist, educator; b. Leavenworth, Kans., Apr. 23, 1940; d. Jay O. and Marjorie B.; m. Byron Edward Calame, June 9, 1962; children: Christine Lee, Jonathan David. BS, U. Mo., 1962; MS, George Washington U., 1965, PhD, 1975. Asst. prof. biol. chemistry UCLA, 1980-85, assoc. prof., 1985-88, prof., 1988; prof. microbiology Coll. Physicians and Surgeons Columbia U., N.Y.C., 1988—. Mem. sci. rev. bd. Howard Hughes Med. Inst., 2002—. Exec. editor: Nucleic Acids Rsch., 1992-98; mem. bd. rev. editors: Sci. Mag., 1988-2000; assoc. editor Jour. Clin. Investigation; contbr. articles to profl. jours. Bd. trustees Leukemia Soc. Am., N.Y.C., 1992—, chair grant rev. com., 1992-96; bd. scientific counselors Nat. Inst. Child Health and Devel., 1999—. Recipient Stohlman award Leukemia Soc. Am., 1989, Faculty Alumni award U. Mo., Columbia, 1996; disting. lecture in basic sci., Columbia Physicians and Surgeons, 1998. Fellow: AAAS; mem.: Am. Acad. Arts & Sci., Am. Assn. Biochemistry and Molecular Biology (chair pub. com. 1992—93). Democrat. Avocations: cooking, gardening, reading, antiques. Office: Columbia U Dept Microbiology 701 W 168th St New York NY 10032-2704

CALANDRA, LINDA CLAUDIA, special education educator; b. Trenton, N.J., Apr. 20, 1953; d. Vito Joseph (dec.) and Saba Joan (Del Favero) C. BA, Georgian Court Coll., 1975; MA, Rowan U., 1992. Cert. elem. and spl. edn. educator, N.J.; cert. sch. bus. adminstr., prin., supr., N.J. Tchr. of handicapped Sister Georgine Learning Ctr., Trenton, 1975-78, Clearview Regional Jr. High Sch., Mullica Hill, N.J., 1978-96, Clearview Regional H. S., Mullica Hill, N.J., 1996—. Mem.: N.J. Edn. Assn. (profl. devel. com. 2003), Gloucester County Edn. Assn. (rep. 2003—, 1st v.p. 2002—), Clearview Edn. Assn. (rep. 1988—2002). Roman Catholic. Avocations: tennis, swimming, travel, crafts. E-mail: calandrali@mail.clearviewregional.edu., lcc@comcast.net.

CALAWAY, JAMES, elementary education educator; Secondary tchr. conservation sci. MacArthur Jr. High Sch., Lawton, Okla. Recipient Conservation Tchr. award (South Central, Nat. Assn. Conservation Dist., ICI Americas, 1992. Office: MacArthur Jr High Sch 510 NE 45th St Lawton OK 73507-6199

CALDERA, LOUIS EDWARD, academic administrator, former federal official; b. El Paso, Tex., Apr. 1, 1956; s. Benjamin Luis and Soledad (Siqueiros) C.; m. Eva Orlebeke Caldera. BS, U.S. Mil. Acad., 1978; JD, MBA, Harvard U., 1987. Bar: Calif. 1987. Commd. 2nd lt. U.S. Army, 1978, advanced through ranks to capt., 1982, resigned commn., 1983; assoc. O'Melveny & Myers, L.A., 1987-89, Buchalter, Nemer, Fields & Younger, L.A., 1990-91; deputy county counsel County of L.A., 1991-92; mem. Calif. State Assembly, 46th Dist., L.A., 1992-97, chmn. banking and fin. com.; mng. dir., COO Corp. for Nat. Svc., Washington, 1997-98; Sec. of the Army Washington, 1998—2001; vice chancellor, univ. advancement Calif. State U., 2001—03; pres. Univ. New Mexico, Albuquerque, 2003—. Democrat. Roman Catholic. Office: Univ New Mexico Albuquerque NM 87131*

CALDWELL, ANN WICKINS, academic administrator; b. Rochester, N.Y., Dec. 3, 1943; d. Ralph Everett and Constance Ann (McCoy) Wickins; m. Herbert Cline Caldwell, Sept. 17, 1966; children: Constance Haley Blacklow, Robert James. BA in English Lit., U. Mich., 1965. Reporter Democrat & Chronicle, Rochester, 1961-64; asst. to dean Harvard Grad. Sch. of Edn., Cambridge, Mass., 1965-70, editor alumni quarterly, 1968-71; freelance editor, writer Harvard U. and Radcliffe, Cambridge, 1971-73; assoc. sec. Philips Acad., Andover, Mass., 1973—80; v.p. for planning and resources Wheaton Coll., Norton, Mass., 1980-90; assoc. dir. Mus. Fine Arts, Boston, 1990-91; v.p. for devel. Brown U., Providence, 1991-97; pres. MGH Inst. Health Professions, Boston, 1997—. Chair bicentennial com. Newburyport, Mass., 1974—76; citizens adv. com. Pub. Sch., Newburyport, 1979—80; bd. dirs. Am. Laryngological Voice Rsch. & Edn. Found.; trustee Women's Edn. and Indsl. Union, Boston, 1988—91, John Hope Settlement Ho., Providence, 1997—. Mem.: Women in Devel. Boston (founder, pres. 1984—86), Coun. for Advancement and Support of Edn. (trustee, sec. dist. 1 1985—87, trustee, sec. nat. 1987—89), Boston Club, Chilton Club, Phi Delta Kappa. Avocations: sailing, skiing, travel, reading. Office: Charlestown Navy Yard 36 First Ave Boston MA 02129-4724 E-mail: acaldwell@mghihp.edu.

CALDWELL, BARRETT SCOTT, industrial engineering educator; b. Phila., Sept. 25, 1962; s. Shirl C. and Jacqueline H. (Horsey) C.; m. Shanta Wilson Hartsough, Sept. 1, 1986 (div.); children: Piers Hartsough C., Kyrie Eleison Hartsough C. BS in Aero. & Astronautics, BS in Humanities, MIT, 1985; MA in Psychology, U. Calif., Davis, 1987, PhD in Social Psychology, 1990. Grad. student lectr. U. Calif., Davis, 1985-90; asst. prof. U. Wis., Madison, 1990-97, assoc. prof., 1997—2000, Purdue U., West Lafayette, Ind., 2000—. Author: (book) Social Processes in Isolated Groups of U.S. Park Service Rangers, 1990; contbr. articles to Behavior and Info. Tech. and Human Factors. Mem. ministry and counsel Madison Quakers Monthly Meeting, 1992-94; dir., Ind Space Grant Consortium, 2001—. Recipient Minority Rsch. Initiation award NSF, Madison, 1994, grad. fellowship NSF, Davis, 1985, Ameritech Faculty fellowship, Madison, 1991. Mem. Human Factors and Ergonomics Soc. (co-chair tech. program com.). Avocation: rowing. Office: Purdue U-Sch of Indsl Engring 315 N Grant StRm 228D Lafayette IN 47907-2023

CALDWELL, DAN EDWARD, political science educator; b. Oklahoma City, May 12, 1948; s. John Edward and Hester Evelyn (Kiehn) C.; m. Lora Jean Ferguson, Mar. 21, 1970; children: Beth Christine, Ellen Claire, John Ferguson. BA in History, Stanford U., 1970, MA in Polit. Sci., PhD in Polit. Sci., 1978; MA in Internat. Rels., Tufts U., 1971. Staff mem. Office Emergency Preparedness, Exec. Office of Pres., Washington, 1972; rsch. and teaching fellow Stanford (Calif.) U., 1975-78; assoc. dir. Ctr. for Fgn. Policy Devel., Brown U., Providence, 1982-84; prof. polit. sci. Pepperdine U., Malibu, Calif., 1978-82, 84—, pres. faculty orgn., 1980-81, 89-90. Dir. Forum for U.S.-Soviet Dialogue, Washington, 1984—, pres., 1989-91. Author: American-Soviet Relations, 1981, The Dynamics of Domestic Politics and Arms Control, 1991, World Politics and You, 2000; editor: Henry Kissinger, 1985. Elder Pacific Palisades (Calif.) Presbyn. Ch. With USN, 1971-74. Named Prof. of Yr., Pepperdine U. Student Alumni Assn., 1992.; rsch. fellow U.S. Inst. Peace, 1987, Pew faculty fellow Harvard U. Kennedy Sch. Govt., 1990. Mem. Internat. Inst. Strategic Studies (London), Am. Polit. Sci. Assn., Internat. Studies Assn. (sect. exec. com. 1982-87, dir. sect. on Am.-Soviet rels. 1984-86, fellow 1977), Coun. on Fgn. Rels. Avocations: tennis, skiing. Home: 654 Radcliffe Ave Pacific Palisades CA 90272-4331 Office: Pepperdine U Social Sci Divsn 24255 Pacific Coast Hwy Malibu CA 90263-0002 E-mail: dan.caldwell@pepperdine.edu.

CALDWELL, HOWARD BRYANT, English language educator; b. London, Ky., Jan. 28, 1944; s. Stratton and Linda Emily (Bryant) C. BA, Berea (Ky.) Coll., 1966; MA, U. Calif., Berkeley, 1977. Cert. adult edn. tchr. Tchr. L.A. Unified Sch. Dist., 1977—. Mem. L.A. County Mus. Art, N.Y. Met. Mus. Art, L.A. World Affairs Coun. With USAF, 1966-70, The Philippines. Mem. United Tchrs. L.A., London Victory Club. Republican. Baptist. Avocations: international travel, languages, classical music.

CALDWELL, JO ANN KENNEDY, elementary educator; b. Franklin, Va., Oct. 31, 1937; d. Benjamin and Bertha (Cicacco) Kennedy; m. Charles Gary Caldwell, Dec. 23, 1962; 1 child, Richard Blair. BA, Baylor U., 1959; MS, No. Mich. U., 1969, MA, 1970. Cert. tchr., Tex., Mich., Calif. Tchr. Univ. Jr. High Sch./Waco (Tex.) Sch. Dist., Gwinn (Mich.) Middle Sch., No. Mich. Lab. Sch., Marquette, Fairfield (Calif.)-Suisun Unified Sch. Dist. Mentor tchr.; presenter workshops; cons. creative oral langs. activities, choral reading, storytelling Readers Theatre. Recipient Solano County's Celebrate Literacy award, 1994. Mem. NEA, ASCD, Internat. Reading Assn., Calif. Reading Assn., Calif. Tchrs. Assn., Delta Kappa Gamma, Phi Delta Kappa.

CALDWELL, JUDITH, horticultural educator; Prof. Clemson U., S.C. Recipient Outstanding Undergrad. Educator award, 1992. Office: Dept of Horticulture Rm D136 Pool EGG Ctr Clemson U Clemson SC 29634-0375*

CALDWELL, MARY ELLEN, English language educator; b. El Paso, Ark., Aug. 6, 1908; d. Clay and Mabel Grace (Coe) Fulks; m. Robert Atchison Caldwell, Feb. 22, 1936; 1 child, Elizabeth. PhB, U. Chgo., 1931, MA, 1933. Instr. English U. Ark., Fayetteville, 1940-42, U. Toledo, 1946-48; from instr. to asst. prof. to assoc. prof. U. N.D., Grand Forks, 1952-79, assoc. prof. emeritus, 1979—, prof. ext. divsn., 1979-2000. Author: North Dakota Division of the American Association of University Women, 1930-63, A History, 1964; co-author: The North Dakota Division of the American Association of University Women, 1964-84, 2d vol., 1984; contbr. revs. and articles to scholarly jours. Sec. citizen's com. Grand Forks Symphony Assn., 1960-66. Mem. AAUW (life, N.D. state pres. 1968-70), P.E.O., MLA (life), Soc. for Study of Midwestern Lit. (bibliography staff 1973-2002, MidAm. award for disting. contbns. to study of midwstern lit. 2000), Linguistic Cir. of Man. and N.D. (pres. 1981), Melville Soc. Democrat. Episcopalian. Home: 514 Oxford St Grand Forks ND 58203-2847

CALDWELL, NAOMI RACHEL, librarian, library media specialist, educator; b. Providence, Mar. 31, 1958; d. Atwood Alexander II and Juanita (Johnson) Caldwell; 1 child, William Earl Wood. BS, Clarion State Coll., 1980; MSLS, Clarion U. Pa., 1982; postgrad., Tex. A&M U., 1986-87, Providence Coll., 1990-92; PhD in Libr. and Info. Studies, U. Pitts., 2002. Cert. tchg. libr.; cert. libr. media specialist. Asst. dir., adult svcs. libr. Oil City (Pa.) Pub. Libr., 1984-85; microtext reference libr. Sterling C. Evans Libr., Tex. A&M U., College Station, 1985-87; libr. media specialist Nathan Bishop Mid. Sch., Providence, 1987-92; libr. sci. doctoral fellow dept. libr. sci. Sch. Libr. and Info. Sci. U. Pitts., 1992-94; sch. library media specialist Feinstein H.S. for Pub. Svc., Providence, 1994-99; asst. prof. U. R.I. Grad. Sch. Libr. Info. Studies, 2002—. Mem. discovery award com. U.S. Bd. on Books for Young People, 1994; mem. com. R.I. Children's Book Award, 1990—92, R.I. Read-Aloud, 1990—92; participant Native Am. and Alaskan Native Pre-Conf. to White House Conf. on Librs. and Info. Scis., Washington, 1991, George Washington U. Nat. Indian Policy Ctr. Forum on Native Am. Librs. and Info. Svcs., Washington, 1991; participant, spkr. Internat. Indigenous Librs. Forum, Auckland, New Zealand, 1999; hon. del. White House Conf. on Libr. and Info. Svcs., Washington, 1991; bd. dirs. Ocean State Freenet; mem. exec. bd. R.I. Ednl. Media Assn., 1996—97; cons. Am. Coll. Testing, 1995—; mem. exec. bd. Native Am. child literacy program If I Can Read, I Can Do Anything, 2001—; mem. Coalition Libr. Advocates, 2002—; presenter in field. Mem. editl. adv. bd., reviewer : Multicultural Rev., 1991—; mem. adv. bd. Native Ams. Info. Dir., 1992, OYATE, 1992—, Gale Ency. Multicultural Am., Native N.Am. Ref. Libr.; mem. exec. bd.: OYATE, 2001—; reviewer Clarion Books, Greenwood Press, Random House, Harcourt Brace Trade Divsn., Browndeer Press, Oryx Press; contbr. articles to profl. jours. Mem. State of R.I. Libr. Bd., 1996-97, Spl. Presdl. Adv. Com. on Libr. of Congress, 1996-97; mem. nominating com. R.I. chpt. Girl Scouts of Am., 1998-99. Mem.: ALA (councilor-at-large 1992—96, chmn. com. on status of women in librarianship 1995—97, nominating com. 1996—97, legis. assembly 1996—98, councilor-at-large 1996—2000, assembly on planning and budget 1998—99, presdl. task force spectrum program, com. on coms. 1999—2000, spectrum jury com. 2001—02, com. on diversity 2001—03, pres.'s adv.com. 2003—), R.I. Coalition of Libr. Advs. (sec. 2003), Native Am. N.E. Librs., Worcraft Cir. Native Writers and Storytellers, Windwalker Coalition, Libr. Adminstrn. Mgmt. Assn., Spl. Librs. Assn., Am. Assn. Sch. Librs., Am. Indian Libr. Assn. (new mems. round table publicity com. 1986, new mems. round table minority recruitment com. 1986—88, OLOS libr. svcs. for Am. Indian people subcom. 1986—88, ALCTS micropub. com. 1988—90, OLOS libr. svcs. for Am. Indian people subcom. 1990—91, pres. 1990—94, mem. coun. com. on minority concerns 1991—92, chmn. 1992—94, sec. 1994—96, mem. coun. com. on minority concerns 1994—96, book award task force 2002—03). Home: 475 Sowams Rd Barrington RI 02806-2745 Office: U RI Grad Sch Libr and Info Studies 11 Rodman Hall Kingston RI 02881 E-mail: inpeacencw@aol.com.

CALDWELL, PATRICIA FRANCES, financial consultant, lecturer; b. Columbus, Ohio, Aug. 21, 1942; d. Richard and Elizabeth Frances (McQuiniff) Smith; m. Terry Edward Caldwell, Dec. 19, 1970; children: Carrie Elizabeth, Christina Leigh. BS, Otterbein Coll., 1964; MEd, U. Okla., 1967; PhD, U. Calif., Riverside, 1981. Cert. secondary edn. tchr., Calif., Ohio. Secondary tchr. Copley (Ohio) Jr. High Sch., 1964-65, Apple Valley (Calif.) Jr. High Sch., 1967-68; tchr., counselor Victor Valley Coll., Victorville, Calif., 1968-74; dean of students San Bernardino (Calif.) Valley Coll., 1974-78; lectr. Calif. State U., San Bernardino, 1979-82, 85-86, La Verne U., Victorville, 1983-84, U. Redlands, Calif., 1988—; pvt. practice mgmt. cons. Victorville, 1987—. Cons. Victor Valley Coll., Victorville, Palomar Coll., San Marcos, Calif., San Bernardino Valley Coll., 1992—, John Deere Corp., Moline, Ill., 1992—, Allan Hancock Coll., Santa Maria, Calif., 1994—, Victor Valley Union H.S. Dist., Victorville, 1993—, Pacific Oaks Coll., 1994, Barstow Coll., 1995—, Network Calif. C.C. Founds., 1995—, Western Fairs Assn., 1989—, Western Wash. Fair, 1992—, Pacific Nat. Exhbn., Vancouver, B.C., Can., 1990—, Calif. Assn. Racing Fairs, 1993-94, Calif. Constrn. Authority, 1994—, numerous county and state fairs. Leader Girl Scouts U.S., Victorville, 1980-93; pres. San Gorgonio Girl Scout coun., 1984-87; bd. dirs. Oro Grande Found., Victorville, 1984—; pres. Victor Valley Coll. Found., Victorville, 1994-96; pres. Victor Elem. Bd. Trustees, 1980-90. Recipient Lifetime Achievement award Desert Communities United Way, 1993; named Soroptomist Woman of Distinction, 1992. Mem. Nat. Sch. Bds. Assn., Am. Assn. Sch. Adminstrs., Calif. Sch. Bds. Assn., Victorville C. of C. (v.p., bd. dirs. 1994-96), Rotary. Republican. Presbyterian. Avocations: sailing, skiing, reading. Home: 13993 Burning Tree Dr Victorville CA 92392-4353 Office: 15476 W Sand St Victorville CA 92392-2314

CALDWELL, ROSSIE JUANITA BROWER, retired library service educator; b. Columbia, S.C., Nov. 4, 1917; d. Rossie Lee and Henrietta Olivia (Irby) Brower; m. Harlowe Evans Caldwell, Aug. 6, 1943 (dec. 1983); 1 adopted dau., Rossie Laverne Caldwell Jenkins. BA magna cum laude, Claflin U., 1937; MS, S.C. State Coll., 1952; MSLS, U. Ill., 1959. Tchr. libr. Reed St. H.S., Anderson, S.C., 1937-39, Emmett Scott H.S., Rock Hill, S.C., 1939-42, Wilkinson H.S., Orangeburg, S.C., 1942-43, libr., 1945-57; civilian pers. War Dept., Tuskegee Army Air Field, 1943-45; asst. prof., then assoc. prof. libr. svc. dept. S.C. State U., Orangeburg, 1957-83. Co-editor (mag.) Trinity United Meth. Women; contbg. author book in field; author articles. Assoc. mem. Orangeburg Regional Hosp. Aux.; mem. Historical Soc. S.C.; trustee, Christian adv. United Meth. Ch. in S.C., 1978—86; co-chair history and archives com. Trinity United Meth. Ch. Recipient Presdl. citation Claflin Coll., 1989, Links award for cmty. achievement, 1998, numerous ann. vol. work citations; Founders Day honoree, 1994, Heritage Club award Claflin U., 2000; named to Claflin Coll. Hall of Fame, 1997; Woman of Yr., United Meth. Women, 2003. Mem. NAACP (life), ALA (continuing life mem.), ALA Black Caucus (emeritus), AAUP (emeritus), VFW Aux. (life), Nat. Women's History Mus. (charter, Washington), S.C. Libr. Assn. (hon.), AAUW (editor Orangeburg br. bull.), Friends of the Libr. (Orangeburg County), Palmetto Med. Dental Pharm. Assn. Aux. (historian, state pres., Woman of Yr. 1972, Spl. Longevity award 2003), Links Club (archivist, historian), As You Like It Bridge Club, Daus. of Isis, Claflin Univ. Forerunners Club (coord., founder 1987), Golden Scholarship Club (co-founder 1987), Sigma Pi Phi (archousa, Claflin queen 1935-37, emeritus queen 1999), Phi Delta Kappa (emeritus mem.), Alpha Kappa Alpha (life mem.; Golden Soror 2001), Omega Psi Phi (Omega Lambda Sigma chpt. Scroll of Honor 1988), Beta Phi Mu (mem. internat. Libr. hon. soc., mem. libr. sci. soc.). Home: 1320 Ward Ln NE Orangeburg SC 29118-1342 E-mail: bojal@hotmail.com.

CALDWELL, STRATTON FRANKLIN, kinesiology educator; b. Mpls., Aug. 25, 1926; s. Kenneth Simms and Margaret Mathilda (Peterson) C.; m. Mary Lynn Shaffer, Aug. 28, 1955 (div. May 1977); children: Scott Raymond, Karole Elizabeth; m. Sharee' Deanna Ockerman, Aug. 6, 1981; 1 stepchild, Shannon Sharee' Calder. Student, San Diego State Coll., 1946-48; BS in Edn. cum laude, U. So. Calif., 1951, PhD in Phys. Edn., 1966; MS in Phys. Edn., U. Oreg., 1953. Teaching asst. dept. phys. edn. UCLA, 1953-54, assoc. in phys. edn., 1957-65, vis. asst. prof. phys. edn., 1967; dir. phys. edn. Regina (Sask., Can.) Young Men's Christian Assn., 1954-56; tchr. sec. grades, dir. athletic Queen Elizabeth Jr.-Sr. High Sch., Calgary, Alta., Can., 1956-57; asst. prof. phys. edn. San Fernando Valley State Coll., Northridge, Calif., 1965-68, assoc. prof., 1968-71; prof. phys. edn. dept. kinesiology Calif. State U., Northridge, 1971-90, prof. kinesiology, 1990-92, prof. kinesiology emeritus, 1992. Vis. asst. prof. phys. edn. UCLA, 1967; vis. assoc. prof. phys. edn. U. Wash., Seattle, 1968, U. Calif., Santa Barbara, 1969. Author (with Cecil and Joan Martin Hollingsworth) Golf, 1959, (with Rosalind Cassidy) Humanizing Physical Education: Methods for the Secondary School Movement Program, 5th edit., 1975; also poetry, book chpts., articles in profl. jours., book revs. With USN, 1944-46. Recipient Meritorious Performance and Profl. Promise award Calif. state U., 1986, 87, 89, Disting. Teaching award, 1992; AAPHERD fellow, 1962, Am. Coll. Sports Medicine fellow, 1965, Can. Assn. for Health, Phys. Edn., and Recreation fellow, 1971. Fellow Am. Alliance for Health, Phys. Edn., Recreation and Dance (Centennial Commn. 1978-85, cert. appreciation 1985), Am. Coll. Sports Medicine; mem. Calif. Assn. for Health, Phys. Edn., Recreation and Dance (pres. L.A. coll. and univ. unit 1969-70, v.p. phys. edn. com. 1970-71, mem. editorial bd. CAHPER Jour. 1970-71, mem. forum 1970-71, Disting. Svc. award 1974, Honor award 1988, Verne Landreth award 1992), Nat. Assn. for Phys. Edn. in Higher Edn. (charter), Sport Art Acad., Nat. Assn. for Sport and Phys. Edn., N.Y. Acad. Scis., N.Am. Soc. for Sports History, Sport Lit. Assn., Acad. Am. Poets, Phi Epsilon Kappa (Svc. award 1980), Alpha Tau Omega (charter, Silver Circle award 1976, Golden Circle award 2001), Phi Delta Kappa, Phi Kappa Phi, others. Republican. Mem. Christian Ch. Avocations: reading, writing. Home: 80 N Kanan Rd Oak Park CA 91377-1105

CALDWELL, WILLARD E. psychologist, educator; b. Flushing L.I., N.Y., July 10, 1920; s. Howard Eugene and Lillian (Warner) C. AB in Psychology, U. Fla., 1940, MA in Psychology, 1941; PhD in Psychology, Cornell U., 1946; postgrad., Washington Sch. Psychiatry, 1948-53. Lic. psychologist, D.C. Grad. asst. psychology U. Fla., Gainesville, 1940-41; teaching asst. Psychology Dept. Cornell (N.Y.) U., 1943-46; prof. psychology, dept. chmn. Mary Baldwin Coll., Staunton, Va., 1947-48; asst. prof., assoc. prof., prof. psychology The George Washington U., Washington, 1948-85, prof. emeritus psychology, 1985—. Psychotherapist. Editor, contbg. author: Principles of Comparative Psychology, 1960; contbr. over 50 articles to profl. jours. Pvt. U.S. Army, 1941-42. Mem. APA, Am. Psychol. Soc., D.C. Psychology Assn., Internat. Soc. Biometeorology. Republican. Episcopalian. Avocations: swimming, gardening, traveling. Home: Apt 316 1101 New Hampshire Ave NW Washington DC 20037-1509

CALDWELL, WILLIAM EDWARD, educational administration educator, arbitrator; b. Providence, Aug. 18, 1928; s. James E. and Eva E. (Barker) C.; m. Doris E. Parlee, June 17, 1950; children: William E., Donna E., Allen E. BA in Math., Ea. Nazarene Coll., 1950; MEd in Secondary Edn., U. N.H., 1957; PhD in Ednl. Adminstrn., NYU, 1968. Cert. prin., supt., arbitrator. Tchr. math., dir. music, coach pub. schs., Berwick, Maine, 1950-54; tchr. math., supr. pub. schs. Valley Stream, N.Y., 1954-61; guidance counselor, prin. pub. schs. Manchester, Conn., 1961-67; dir. secondary tchr. tng. U. Hartford, Conn., 1967-69; exec. dir. Pa. Sch. Study Coun., University Park, 1970-78; prof. ednl. adminstrn. Pa. State U., University Park, 1969—, pres. faculty coun., 1985-86, ombudsman Coll. Edn., 1986-90, chmn. edn. adminstrn. program, 1987-90, chmn. adminstrn., policy, founds. and internat. edn., 1990-93, prof. emeritus, 1993—. State dir. mediation Commonwealth of Pa., Harrisburg, 1979-80; conciliator, fact finder Pa. Labor Rels. Bd., Harrisburg, 1971—; arbitrator AAA, FMCS, Pa. Labor Rels. Bd., 1971—. Author: Collective Negotiation in Public Education, 1970, Agreement, Policy for Principal/Supervisor, 1983; mem. editl. bd. Jour. Individual Employment Rights, 1993—; contbr. articles to profl. jours., chpts. to books, author reports. Nat. del. Am. Assn. Sch. Adminstrs., Washington, 1976, 77, 79; bd. dirs. Fed. Credit Union, Manchester, Conn., 1963-67, Appalachian Ednl. Lab., Charleston, W.Va., 1970-78; examiner Pa. Civil Svc. Commn., Harrisburg, 1972-79. Lt. col. USMCR, ret. 1988. Recipient Commendation award Pa. Sch. Bds. Assn., 1980, Acad. Achievement award NYU, 1969, Outstanding Svc. award Commonwealth Pa., 1973, Outstanding Svc. award Pa. Dept. Labor, 1987, Excellence in Instrn. award Pa. Sch. Study Coun., 1994, William E. Caldwell Excellence in Adminstrn. award Pa. Sch. Study Coun., 1997—. Mem. Am. Ednl. Rsch. Assn. (presenter), Pa. Assn. Secondary Sch. Prins. (rsch. chmn., Commendation award 1983, Excellence in Edn. award 1986).

CALDWELL PORTENIER, PATTY JEAN GROSSKOPF, advocate, educator; b. Davenport, Iowa, Sept. 28, 1937; d. Bernhard August and Leontine Virginia (Carver) Grosskopf; m. Donald Eugene Caldwell Mar. 29, 1956 (dec. Feb. 1985); children: John Alan, Jennifer Lynn Caldwell; m. Walter J. Portenier, Oct. 3, 1992. BA, State U. Iowa, 1959. 2d grade tchr. D.B. Hoffman Sch., East Moline, Ill., 1959—60; 3d grade tchr. McKinley Sch., Moline, Ill., 1963—66; K-6 sub. tchr., spl. edn. tchr. Moline, 1970—84; hearing officer Ill. State Bd. Edn., Springfield, 1979-91, Appellate Court, 1986-91. Pres., bd. dirs. Tri-County Assn. for Children With Learning Disabilities, Moline, Ill., 1972-79, adv. vol., Iowa and Ill., 1979-91; mem. adv. coun. Prairie State Legal Svcs., Inc., Rock Island, Ill., 1984-91; mem. profl. svcs. com. United Cerebral Palsy N.W. Ill., Rock Island, 1986-88; arbitrator Am. Arbitration Assn., Chgo., 1986-91, Better Bus. Bur., Davenport, 1986-91. Founder, pres. Quad Cities Diabetes Assn., Moline, 1969-72, bd. dirs., 1973—; mem. com. Moline Internat. Yr. Disabled, 1981; mem. Assn. for Retarded Citizens, Rock Island, 1987; mem. vol. Coun. on Children at Risk, Moline, 1988-91; reader for the blind Sta. WVIK, Rock Island, 1989-91; bd. dirs. First United Meth. Ch. Nursery Sch., Santa Monica, 1997-99; docent Petersen Automotive Mus., L.A., 1997—. Mem. Ill. Assn. for Children with Learning Disabilities (bd. dirs., adv. 1980-83). Presbyterian. Avocations: travel, reading, crocheting. Home and Office: 2443 La Condesa Dr Los Angeles CA 90049-1221 Fax: 310-472-8327. E-mail: p-jportenier@beachnet.com.

CALENDAR, RICHARD LANE, biochemistry educator; b. Hackensack, N.J., Aug. 2, 1940; s. Howard L. and Jean (Wappler) C.; m. Gunilla Viola Jansen, Jan. 6, 1969 (div. Sept. 1983); children: Hugo Raphael, Johanna Magdalena. BS in Chemistry, Duke U., 1962; PhD in Biochemistry, Stanford U., 1967. Helen Hay Whitney fellow Karolinska Inst., Stockholm, 1966-68; mem. faculty dept. cell and molecular biology U. Calif., Berkeley, 1968—, asst. prof. to prof., 1968—76. Alexander von Humboldt fellow, Munich, 1973, Guggenheim fellow, Stockholm, 1979-80. Home: 940 Euclid Ave Berkeley CA 94708-1436 Office: U Calif 401 Barker Hall Berkeley CA 94720-3208

CALFAPIETRA, ELIZABETH ANNE, special education educator; b. Bklyn., Oct. 12, 1945; d. Vincent Guy and Anna Mary Calfapietra. BS in Edn. magna cum laude, Brentwood Coll., 1969; MS in Religious Edn., Fordham U., 1976; MS in Spl. Edn., Bklyn. Coll., 1984. Cert. elem., secondary and spl. edn. tchr., N.Y. Elem. tchr. St. Pius X Sch., Plainview, N.Y., 1969-71, St. Therese of Lisieux, Bklyn., 1980-82; secondary tchr. Our Lady of Mercy Acad., Syosset, N.Y., 1971-74, Mercy High Sch., Riverhead, N.Y., 1978-80; spl. edn. tchr. Bklyn. Diocese Dept. Edn., 1982-85, independence coord., 1985-90; spl. edn. tchr. Mary McDowell Ctr. for Learning, Bklyn., 1990-92, Catherine McAuley High Sch., Bklyn., 1992—. Lectr. in field. Mem. Nat. Assn. for Mentally Retarded Persons, Nat. Network Spl. Needs Ministry (founder, pres. 1990), Coun. for Exceptional Children. Avocations: birding, camping, writing, hiking, trumpet.

CALFEE, ROBERT CHILTON, psychologist, educational researcher; b. Lexington, Ky., Jan. 26, 1933; s. Robert Klair and Nancy Bernice (Stipp) C.; m. Nel Pearl Little, June 30, 1991. BA, UCLA, 1959, MA, 1960, PhD, 1963. Asst. prof. psychology U. Wis., 1964-66, assoc. prof., 1966-69; assoc. prof. edn. Stanford U., 1969-71, prof., 1971-98, prof. emeritus, 1998—; assoc. dean research and devel., dir. Center for Ednl. Research, 1976-80; dean Sch. Edn. U. Calif., Riverside, 1998—. Cons. and speaker in field; vice-chmn. State of Calif. Commn. for Establishment of Acad. Content and Performance Stds., 1996—; mem. com. on equivalancy and linkage of ednl. tests NRC/NAS, 1998—. Author: Human Experimental Psychology, 1975, Cognitive Psychology and Educational Practice, 1982, Experimental Methods in Psychology, 1985, Handbook of Educational Psychology, Teach Our Children Well, 1995, (with Marilyn J. Chambliss) Textbooks for Learning, 1999; editor: Jour. Ednl. Psychology, 1984-90, Ednl. Assessment, 1992—. Trustee Palo Alto (Calif.) Sch. Dist., 1984-88; vice chair Calif. Commn. for Ednl. Stds. Guggenheim Meml. fellow, 1972; fellow Center for Advanced Study in Behavioral Scis., 1981-82 Fellow AAAS, APA; mem. Am. Ednl. Rsch. Assn., Internat. Reading Assn. (named to Hall of Fame), Nat. Conf. Rsch. in English, Psychonomic Soc., Nat. Coun. Tchrs. English, Nat. Soc. Study of Edn. (bd. trustees), Sigma Xi. Home: 215 Bathurst Rd Riverside CA 92506-6129 Office: U Calif Sch Edn 1207 Sproul Hl Riverside CA 92521-0001 Fax: 909-787-3942. E-mail: robert.calfee@ucr.edu.

CALGAARD, RONALD KEITH, university president; b. Joice, Iowa, July 29, 1937; s. Palmer O. Calgaard and Orrie (Beatrice) Nessa-Calgaard; m. Gene Rae Flom, June 14, 1959; children: Lisa Rae, Kent David. BA, Luther Coll., 1959, LLD, 1988; MA, U. Iowa, 1961, PhD in Econs., 1963; LLD, Tex. Luth. Coll, 1987. Instr. in econs. U. Iowa, 1961-63; asst. prof. econs. U. Kans., Lawrence, 1963-65, assoc. prof., 1967-72, prof., 1972-79, assoc. vice chancellor, 1974-75, vice chancellor acad. affairs, 1975-79; postdoctoral fellow in Latin Am. studies Santiago, Chile, 1965-67; pres. Trinity U., San Antonio, 1979—. Bd. dirs. Valero Energy Corp. Author: Economic Planning in Underdeveloped Countries, 1962. Active S.W. Rsch. Inst., San Antonio, United Way San Antonio and Bexar County, Ind. Colls. and Univs. Tex., 1993—; bd. visitors Air U.; trustee So. Assn. Colls. and Schs., 1991-93; elder First Presbyn. Ch., San Antonio; bd. Higher Edn. Coun. San Antonio, pres., 1996; chair So. Collegiate Athletic Conf., Associated Colls. of the South; bd. govs. YMCA San Antonio and Hill Country; adv. bd. Cystic Fibrosis Found.; active San Antonio Acad. Tex., Tex. Rsch. Tech. Found., Philosophical Soc. Tex., San Antonio Med. Found.; pres. Trinity U., 1979-99. Woodrow Wilson fellow, 1959-60; recipient W.T. Bondurant Sr. Disting. Humanitarian award San Antonio Acad., 1997. Mem. Assn. Presbyn. Coll. and Univs., Assn. Tex. Colls. and Univs. (pres. 1996). Office: Austin Calvert Flavin Office of Pres 755 E Mulberry San Antonio TX 78212-7200

CALHOON, ROBERT ELLSWORTH, biology educator; b. L.A., Dec. 29, 1938; s. Robert Moats and Leva (Conner) C.; m. Janette Mattox, June 18, 1969. BA, San Diego State U., 1961, MS, 1967; PhD, Purdue U., 1972. Assoc. prof. biology Queens Coll., CUNY, 1973—. Chmn. Columbia U. Sem. Population Biology, 1987-88. Contbr. articles to Can. Jour. Zoology, Jour. Animal Ecology, Exptl. and Molecular Pathology, Reproductive Toxicology, Anthrozoo's. Rsch. grantee CUNY, 1989-2002. Office: Queens Coll CUNY Dept Biology Flushing NY 11367

CALHOUN, JOAN MARIE, elementary education educator, resource specialist; b. Long Beach, Calif., June 10, 1969; d. Robert Warren and Barbara Ann C. BA summa cum laude in Diversified Edn., Mt. St. Mary's Coll., L.A., 1991; MS Lang. Lit./Learning summa cum laude, Calif. State U., Long Beach, 1997, MS in Spl. Edn. summa cum laude, 2000. Cert. elem. tchr., Calif. Child care worker Long Beach Unified Sch. Dist., 1987-91, recreation leader spl. edn., 1989-95; 4th grade tchr. Anaheim (Calif.) City Sch. Dist., 1991-92; 3rd grade tchr. St. Cyprian Sch., Long Beach, 1992-97; resource specialist Long Beach Unified Sch. Dist., 1997—. Pvt. tutor, Long Beach. Recipient Paul Douglas scholarship Aid of Student Commissioning, Sacramento, 1988-90, Pres. award Calif. State U. Mem. Delta Sigma Epsilon. Avocations: accomplished pianist, flutist, outdoors exercise.

CALHOUN, MARY LYNNE, dean; b. Huntington, W.Va., June 15, 1945; d. Boyd and Mary Katherine (Estler) Jarrell; m. Lawrence Gibson, Feb. 3, 1968; children: Eliza, Mary Laura. AB, Randolph-Macon Woman's Coll., 1967; MEd, U. Ga., 1971, PhD, 1975. Tchr. Cin. Pub. Schs., 1968-70; diagnostic tchr. Mott Children's Health Ctr., Flint, Mich., 1971-72; demonstration tchr. U. Ga., Athens, 1972-73; asst. prof. spl. edn. Winthrop Coll., Rock Hill, S.C., 1974-77; coord. of interdisciplinary tng. Human Devel. Ctr., Winthrop U., Rock Hill, 1977-82; prof. spl. edn. U. N.C., Charlotte, 1982—, chmn. dept. counseling, spl. edn. and child devel., 1994-99, dean Coll. Edn., 1999—. Author: (with others) Charlotte Circle Intervention Guide for Parent-Child Interactions, 1991; contbr. articles to profl. jours. Named Educator of Yr. N.C. Assn. for Retarded Citizens, 1985; U.S. Dept. Edn. grantee, 1985, 88, 91, 96. Mem. Coun. for Exceptional Children, N.C. Divsn. for Early Childhood (pres. 1989-90, Leadership award 1990), Am. Ednl. Rsch. Assn. Democrat. Presbyterian. Office: U NC Coll of Edn Charlotte NC 28223

CALHOUN, OLLIE ARLENE, elementary school educator; b. L.A., Aug. 4, 1939; d. Noah Edgar and Ollie B. (Wade) McDaniels; m. Verdie B. Calhoun, June 21, 1961 (div. 1964); children: Kevin Bernard Calhoun, Kimberlyn Arlene Battle. AA, L.A. City Coll., 1959; BA, Calif. State U., L.A., 1961, MA, 1974; EdD, U. San Francisco, 1983. Cert. elem. tchr., adult edn., adminstr. svc., Calif. Tchr. L.A. Unified Sch. Dist. Parmelee Ave Sch., 1961-72, community liason, 1972-74, bilingual and ESL resource tchr., 1974-76; bilingual and ESL coord. L.A. Unified Sch. Dist. Westminster Ave. Sch., 1976-78; dist. adviosr L.A. Unified Sch. Dist. Bd. Edn., 1978-82; bilingual master tchr. L.A. Unified Sch. Dist. Hyde Park Sch., 1982-85; bilingual mentor tchr. L.A. Unified Sch. Dist. Raymond Ave. Sch., 1985-87, L.A. Unified Sch. Dist. M.L. King Elem. Sch., 1987—. Dist. rep., sec. Florence, Firestone Community Coun., L.A., 1972-74; tchr. cons. TRW Corp., El Segundo, Calif., 1986-87, State Dept. Edn., Sacramento, 1991-92; mentor, rep. mem. Supts. Blueprint for Action Com., L.A., 1989-91; founder, coord. Ten Sch. Program, Academic Tentahlon, 1991. Author: (dist. brochure) Black Contbrns. in Music, (Rsch. award) 1973. Mem. Dem. Assn. Club, 1978-86, Black Women's Forum, L.A., United Negro Coll. Fund Com., 1987-91, Inglewood Neighborhood Preservation Com., 1990-91. Recipient Outstanding Svc. award, Proficiency in English Program, L.A., 1980, Ideal Tchr. award, L.A. Unified Sch. Dist., Region C, 1985, Ctr. for Acad. Interinstl. Progress award UCLA Grad. Sch. of Edn., 1991, Excellence in Edn. award, N.Y. Stock Exchange, L.A., 1992. Mem. NEA, ASCD, Profl. Women in Leadership (vice chmn. edn. com. 1981-83), United Tchrs. of L.A., Univ. So. Calif. Edn. Alumni. Democrat. Avocations: motor home camping, arts and crafts and challenging table games. Home: 3305 W 83rd St Inglewood CA 90305-1754 Office: LA Unified Sch Dist ML King Elem Sch 3989 S Hobart Blvd Los Angeles CA 90062-1124

CALHOUN, PATRICIA HANSON, secondary education educator; b. Detroit, Apr. 29, 1940; d. James William and Gordie Eugenia (Wiggins) H.; m. Hubert Calhoun, Jr., July 27, 1956; children: Phillip Wayne, Debra Jean, Donna Marie. BS in Comprehensive Bus. Edn., West Georgia Coll., 1981, MEd in Comprehensive Bus. Edn., 1982, EdS in Comprehensive Bus. Edn., 1984. Cert. tchr., performance based tchr., comprehensive bus. educator, Ga. Tchr. bus. edn. Bowdon (Ga.) H.S., 1982, Carroll County (Ga.) Vocat.-Tech. Sch., 1982-85, Chattahoochee Tech. Inst., Marietta, Ga., 1986-91, Paulding County H.S., Dallas, Ga., 1982-91, East Paulding H.S., Dallas, 1991—, also coord. coop. bus. edn., head dept. vocat. edn., 1991—. Advisor Future Bus. Leaders Am., Dallas, 1984—. Mem. NEA, Ga. Assn. Educators, Ga. Bus. Edn. Assn., Nat. Bus. Edn. Assn., Nat. Vocat. Assn., Ga. Vocat. Assn., Phi Kappa Phi, Kappa Delta Pi. Republican. Home: 724 Burns Rd Carrollton GA 30117-2518 Office: East Paulding High Sch 3320 E Paulding Dr Dallas GA 30157-3210

CALIFANO, JOSEPH ANTHONY, JR., lawyer, public health policy educator, writer; b. Bklyn., May 15, 1931; s. Joseph Anthony and Katherine (Gill) C.; m. Hilary Paley Byers, 1983; children by previous marriage: Mark Gerard, Joseph Anthony III, Claudia Frances; stepchildren: Brooke A. Byers, John Fredric Byers IV. BA, Holy Cross Coll., 1952; LLB, Harvard U., 1955. Bar: N.Y. 1955, U.S. Supreme Ct. 1966, D.C. 1969. With firm Dewey Ballantine, N.Y.C., 1958-61; spl. asst. to gen. counsel Dept. Def., 1961-62; spl. asst. to sec. Army, 1962-63; gen. counsel Dept. Army, 1963-64; spl. asst. to sec. and dep. sec. Def., 1964-65; spl. asst. to Pres. of U.S., 1965-69; ptnr. Arnold & Porter, Washington, 1969-71, Williams, Connolly & Califano, Washington, 1971-77; sec. HEW, 1977-79; ptnr. Califano, Ross & Heineman, Washington, 1980-82; sr. ptnr. Dewey Ballantine, Washington, 1983-92; prof. pub. health policy Columbia U. Schs. Medicine and Pub. Health, N.Y.C., 1992—; chmn., pres. Nat. Ctr. on Addiction and Substance Abuse at Columbia U., N.Y.C., 1992—. Bd. dirs. ADP, Inc., Viacom Inc.; gen. counsel Dem. Nat. Com., 1971—72. Author: The Student Revolution: A Global Confrontation, 1969, A Presidential Nation, 1975, Governing America: An Insiders Report from the White House and the Cabinet, 1981, The 1982 Report on Drug Abuse and Alcoholism, America's Health Care Revolution, 1986, The Triumph and Tragedy of Lyndon Johnson, 1991, Radical Surgery: What's Next for America's Health Care, 1995, (with Howard Simons) The Media and the Law, 1976, The Media and Business, 1978. Trustee Urban Inst., Am. Ditchley Found., Century Fund, Nat. Health Mus.; bd. govs. N.Y. and Presbyn. Hosp. Inc.; chmn. Inst. Social and Econ. Policy in Mid. East, Harvard U., 1983-98. Recipient Distinguished Civilian Svc. award Dept. Army, 1964; Man of Year award Justinian Soc. Lawyers, 1966; Disting. Pub. Svc. medal Dept. Def., 1965; named One of Ten Outstanding Young Men of America, 1966. Mem. N.Y. State Bar Assn., D.C. Bar Assn., Met. Club (Washington), Century Assn., Univ. Club.

CALINGAERT, PETER, computer scientist, educator; b. N.Y.C., Aug. 12, 1931; BA, Swarthmore Coll., 1952; postgrad., U. Nancy, France, 1952-53; AM, Harvard U., 1954, PhD, 1955. Rsch. assoc., then instr. Harvard U., Cambridge, Mass., 1955-57, asst. prof., 1957-62; staff systems planner IBM, Poughkeepsie, N.Y., 1962-63, devel. planner, 1963-66; systems planning mgr. Sci. Rsch. Assocs., Chgo., 1966-68; prof. computer sci. U. N.C., Chapel Hill, 1968-95, prof. emeritus, 1995—. Cons. Hewlett-Packard Co., Palo Alto, Calif., 1981-82; v.p. Microelectronics Ctr. N.C., Research Triangle Park, 1982-83. Author: Principles of Computation, 1965, Assemblers, Compilers, and Program Translation, 1979, Operating System Elements, 1982, PC-DOS Fundamentals for Diskette-Based Operation, 1986, Program Translation Fundamentals, 1988; contbr. articles to various jours. Mem. IEEE, (fellow) AAAS, Phi Beta Kappa, Sigma Xi. Achievements include patent for IBM System/360 Data Processing System. Office: Univ NC CB # 3175 Chapel Hill NC 27599-3175

CALKIN, JOY DURFÉE, healthcare executive, consultant, educator; b. Wolfville, N.S., Can., Apr. 7, 1938; came to U.S., 1970; d. Garth Longworth and Rena Coffin (Cox) C. BSN, U. Toronto, 1960; MSN, U. Wis., 1968, PhD, 1980; DSc (hon.), U. N.B., Can., 1997. Nurse various hosps., Toronto, N.S.and Aberdeen, Scotland, 1960-63; instr. U. N.B., Fredericton, Can., 1963-66, asst. prof., 1968-70; from asst. to assoc. to prof. Sch. Nursing, U. Wis., Madison, 1970-85; from asst. to assoc. to full prof. nursing Faculty Medicine, Dept. Preventive Medicine, 1980-85; dean, prof. sch. nursing U. Calgary, Alta., Can., 1985-89, assoc. acad. v.p., 1989-90, acad. v.p., provost, 1990-97; pres., CEO Extendicare Inc., Markham, Ont., Can., 1997-99, dep. chmn., CEO, 1999—. Vis. prof. health scis. U. Oreg., Portland, 1980; cons. Troll Assocs., Madison, 1976-80, Thorne, Stevenson & Kellogg, Edmonton, 1985-86; mem. Premier's commn. on future health care for Alberta. Mem. editorial bd. Recent Advances in Nursing, U.K.; reviewer various nursing jours.; contbr. articles to profl. jours. Bd. dirs. Alberta Found. Nursing Rsch., 1988-91, Alberta Family Life and Substance Abuse Found., 1992-93; v.p. Muttart Found., 1993—, v.p., 1996-99, pres., 1999—; bd. dirs. Extendicare, 1995—. Grantee in field. Mem. Am. Nurses Assn., Can. Nurses Assn. (various coms.). Office: Extendicare Inc 3000 Steeles Ave E Markham ON Canada L3R 9W2

CALKINS, DAVID ROSS, physician, medical educator; b. Kansas City, Kans., May 27, 1948; s. Leroy Adelbert and Emily Virginia (Kyger) C.; m. Susan Spalding Rice, Sept. 22, 1989; 1 child, Christopher Ross. AB, Princeton (N.J.) U., 1970; MD, MPP, Harvard U., 1975. Diplomate Am. Bd. Internal Medicine. Intern U. Wash., Seattle, 1975-76; resident in medicine Beth Israel Hosp., Boston, 1976-78, from asst. to assoc. in medicine, 1981-96; fellow White House, Washington, 1978-79; spl. asst., dep. exec. sec. HHS, Washington, 1979-81; from instr. to asst. prof. medicine Harvard Med. Sch., Boston, 1981-96; from instr. to asst. prof. Harvard Sch. Pub. Health, Boston, 1985-96, dir. profl. programs dept. health policy and mgmt., 1985-96; chief div. gen. internal medicine, med. dir. ambulatory svc. New Eng. Deaconess Hosp., Boston, 1991-96; assoc. dean for primary care U. Kans. Sch. Medicine, Kansas City, 1996-98, from assoc. prof. to prof. internal and preventive medicine, 1996-99, sr. assoc. dean for edn., 1998-99; assoc. prof. medicine Harvard Med. Sch., Boston, 1999—, assoc. dean for clin. programs, 1999—2003. W.K. Kellogg Found. fellow, 1987. Office: 25 Shattuck St Boston MA 02115-6027 Business E-Mail: david_calkins@hms.harvard.edu.

CALKINS, HUGH, foundation executive; b. Newton, Mass., Feb. 20, 1924; s. Grosvenor and Patty (Phillips) C.; m. Ann Clark, June 14, 1955; children: Peter, Andrew, Margaret, Elizabeth. AB, LLB, Harvard U., 1949, D in Law (hon.), 1985. Bar: Ohio 1950. Law clk. to presiding judge U.S. Ct. Appeals (2d cir.), N.Y.C., 1949-50; law clk. to justice Felix Frankfurter U.S. Supreme Ct., Washington, 1950-51; from assoc. to ptnr. Jones, Day, Reavis & Pogue, Cleve., 1951-90; tchr. elem. schs. Cleve. City Sch. Dist., 1991-94. Contbr. articles on fed. income tax to profl. jours. Mem. Cleve. Bd. Edn., 1965-69; assoc. dir. Pres.'s Commn. on Nat. Goals, Washington, 1960; mem., pres., fellow Harvard U., 1968-85; mem. task forces Cleve. Summit on Edn., 1990-94; pres., trustee Initiatives in Urban Edn., 1991—. Capt. USAF, 1943-46. Mem. ABA (chmn. tax sect. 1985-86), Am. Law Inst. (coun.), City Club, Cleve. Skating Club, Rowfant Club, Phi Beta Kappa. Democrat. Unitarian Universalist. Home and Office: 3345 N Park Blvd Cleveland OH 44118-4258

CALKINS, RICHARD W. former college president; b. June 3, 1939; BA in Music, Albion Coll., 1960; MA in Edn., Mich. State U., 1966, MA, 1971, postgrad., 1972—; Doctorate (hon.), Ferris State U., 1992. Vocal music tchr. Ridgeview Jr. High Sch., 1961-64, Creston High Sch., 1964-68, asst. dir. pers., 1968-71, gen. assoc. supt., 1971-74, asst. supt. pers. and community svcs., 1974-75; pres. Grand Rapids (Mich.) C.C., 1975-98; ret., 1998. Cons. in field. Bd. dirs. religious activities Epworth Assembly, Ludington, Mich., 1960-82; mins. music Eastminster Presbyn. ch., Grand Rapids, 1964-93; v.p. planning, mem. exec. com. Downtown Mgmt. Bd., 1985-91; pres. Grand Rapids C.C. Found., 1978—; bd. dirs. Mich. Info. Tech. Network, 1988—; mem. Mid Am. Training Group, 1989—, Downtown Planning Com., 1991, Nat. Modernization Forum, 1990-91, Nat. Coalition Advance Tech. Ctrs., 1990—, Alliance for Mfg. Productivity, 1990—, IBM CIM Higher Edn., 1990—; bd. dirs., mem. pub. policy and pers. coms. YMCA, 1989-92; chair edn. div. United Way Kent County, chair major accounts, 1992; founding bd. dirs. Noorthoek Acad., 1989—; bd. dirs. edn. and summer facility coms. Grand Rapids Symphony, 1989— Mem. Indsl. Tech. Inst., Am. Assn. Community and Colls., Assn. C.C. Trustees, Assn. Tchr. Educators, Mich. Assn. Sch. Adminstrs., Mich. Assn. Pub. Adult Continuing Educators, Mich. Assn. Tchr. Educators, Mich. C.C. Assn. (chair polit. action com. 1983—, exec. com. 1987-90, v.p. 1987-88, past pres. 1989-90, treas. 1990-91), C.C. Assn. for Tech. Transfer, Grand Rapids Dunkers Club, Peninsular Club Grand Rapids, Phi Delta Kappa. Home: 2519 Riveredge Dr SE Grand Rapids MI 49546-7450 Office: Grand Rapids Community Coll 143 Bostwick Ave NE Grand Rapids MI 49503-3201

CALLAGHAN, JOHN JOSEPH, orthopaedist, surgeon, educator; b. Rio de Janiero, Jan. 15, 1954; came to U.S., 1956; s. Donald Francis Callaghan and Regina Bernat; m. Kim L. McDougall, May 28, 1983; children: Patrick, Katharine. BS, U. Notre Dame, 1976; MD, Loyola U., 1978. Resident in orthop. U. Iowa, Iowa City, 1978-83, assoc. prof. dept. orthop., 1990-92, prof. dept. orthop. and biochem. engring., 1992—, Lawrence and Marilyn Dorr Chair, 2000—; fellow adult hip reconstructive surgery Hosp. Spl. Surgery, N.Y.C., 1983-84; asst. prof. Duke U., Durham, NC, 1988-90. Editor: The Adult Hip, 1998, Adult Hip and Knee Reconstruction, 1995, The Adult Knee, 2002; contbr. articles to Jour. Bone Jt. Surgery. Maj. U.S. Army, 1984-88. Grantee NIH, 1995-97; Am. British Can. fellow Orthop. Assn., 1991. Fellow Am. Acad. Orthop. Surgeons (bd. dirs.); mem. Hip Soc. (program chair 1996-97, sec. 1998—, Frank Stinchfield award 1985, 94, 96, 97, John Charnley award 1999), Knee Soc. (Mark Coventry award 2001, Orthop. Rsch. Soc., Am. Assn. Arthritic Hip Knee Surgeons (sec. 1995-98, pres. 2001-02), Am. Bd. Orthop. Surgeons (bd. dirs. 2000—), Mid.Am. Orthop. Assn. (pres. 2000—). Roman Catholic. Achievements include long term follow up, biomechanical study of and design of hip and knee replacement implants. Home: 3012 Forest Gate Cir NE Iowa City IA 52240-7907 Office: Dept Orthop 200 Hawkins Dr Iowa City IA 52242-1009 E-mail: john-callaghan@uiowa.edu.

CALLAGHAN, MARY ANNE, secondary school educator; b. Seattle, Mar. 14, 1947; d. John Joseph and Catherine Clara (Emard) C.; m. David Michael Buerge, Mar. 8, 1975; children: David John, Catherine Emily. BA in English Lit., U. Wash., 1970, Teaching Cert., 1973. Standard Wash. state teaching certification. Tchr. tng. intern Hazen H.S., Renton, Wash., 1968-70, tchr. English, 1970-71; tchr. English, theology Forest Ridge Sch. of the Sacred Heart, Bellevue, Wash., 1971-93, dean of students, 1988-92; tchr. English, theology Holy Cross H.S., Everett, Wash., 1993—, student life v.p., 1995-98, Archbishop Murphy H.S. (formerly Holy Cross H.S.), 1999. Chair English dept. Forest Ridge H.S. and Holy Cross H.S., 1980—; mem. accreditation team Holy Name Acad., Seattle, 1991, O'Dea H.S., Seattle, 1995; insvc. presenter for Archdiocese of Seattle, 1992, 93, 98. Vol. Christian Movement for Peace, Montreal, Quebec, 1972; sch. bd. mem. St. Catherine Parish, Seattle, 1984-90. Recipient grants to initiate ethnic awareness programs Religious of the Sacred Heart, 1982, grant to study Asian lit. NEH, 1988. Mem. Nat. Cath. Edn. Assn., Nat. Coun. Tchrs. English. Roman Catholic. Avocations: film, hiking, teaching classes on grief. Office: Archbishop Murphy HS PMB # 6132 12911 39th Ave SE Everett WA 98208-6159 E-mail: mcallaghan@archbishopmurphyhs.org.

CALLAHAN, FRANCIS PATRICK, JR., social studies educator; b. Danville, Pa., Dec. 30, 1946; s. Francis Patrick and Mildred (Kwiatkowski) C.; m. Janet Carolyn Gehlhaus, Aug. 23, 1969; 1 child, Steven Frederick. BA, Bloomsburg U., 1969, Trenton State Coll., 1973. Cert. tchr., Pa. Tchr. elem. sch. Boyertown (Pa.) Sch. Dist., 1969; tchr. social studies Cedar Cliff High Sch., Camp Hill, Pa., 1969-71, Cen. Bucks East High Sch., Buckingham, Pa., 1971—. Mem., chmn. profl. standards and practices commn. Pa. Dept. Edn., Harrisburg, 1982-88, learning coord., 1992. Basic edn. coord. Gov. Thornburgh's re-election campaign, Harrisburg, 1981; dep. campaign chmn. Jim Greenwood for State Senator, Doylestown, Pa., 1986; adviser World Affairs Coun., Doylestown, 1989-92. Grantee World Affairs Coun., 1992-93. Mem. NEA, Pa. State Edn. Assn., Cen. Bucks Edn. Assn. (legis. chmn., pres. 1976-78), Pa. State Social Studies Orgn., Nat. Social Studies Orgn. Avocations: fishing, politics, running. Home: 3980 Landisville Rd Doylestown PA 18901-1100 Office: Cen Bucks East High Sch Holicong And Anderson Rd Buckingham PA 18912

CALLAHAN, TANYA DENISE, art educator; b. Balt., Apr. 14, 1962; d. Reginald Jerome and Catherine Delores (Williams) Hicks; m. Samuel Paul Callahan Jr., Aug. 8, 1981; 1 child, Samuel Paul III. AA in Fine Art, Anne Arundel C.C., Arnold, Md., 1984, cert. day care, 1987; career diploma interior decorating, Internat. Corr. Sch., Pa., 1990; BS in Art Edn., Bowie (Md.) State U., 1990, M.Ed, 1993. Cert. art tchr., Md. Long-term art substitute Anne Arundel County Bd. Edn., Annapolis, Md., 1990, art tchr., 1991—. Mem. ASCD, Nat. Art Edn. Assn., Tchr's. Assn. Anne Arundel County, Md. Hall for Creative Arts, Md. Art Edn. Assn., Alpha Kappa Alpha (achievement award 1990), Alpha Kappa Mu, Kappa Delta Pi Democrat. Avocations: reading, decorating, art.

CALLAN, RICHARD JOHN, elementary school educator; b. Indpls., Dec. 8, 1953; s. John B. and Bernice (Burns) C. BS, Ind. U., Indpls., 1977, MS, 1985. Cert. elem. tchr. Tutor Indpls. Pub. Schs., 1974-76, tchr., 1977-81; tchr. 3d grade Franklin Twp. Schs., Indpls., 1981—. Edn. cons. Ind. Dept. Edn., summer, 1990, 98, mem. proficiency guide writing team, 1991, 97; lectr. various workshops, seminars; co-chmn. "Make and Take It" com. Nat. Coun. Tchrs. of Math. conv., 1994; trainer Math. Assessment: The Hoosier Alternative, 1994; mem. edn. expert panel in sci. and math. U.S. Dept. Edn., 1998—; lectr. in math. edn. Franklin (Ind.) Coll. Author: (with others) Improving Students' Learning and Attitudes, Multi-Cultural Education, 1992, Indiana Department of Education Mathematics and Assessment Guide, 1992, Mathematics Assessment, The Hoosier Alternative (M.A.T.H.A.), 1994, Mission Mathematics: Workshops on Linking Aerospace and the NCTM Standards, 1997, Math, Literature and Unifix, 2001, Math, Literature and Manipulation, 2001. Faculty rep. Bunkerhill PTO 1989-92. Grantee Ind. Dept. Edn., 1990—; recipient William J. Garrett award, 1976, Outstanding Young Men of Am. award Ind. U., Presdl. award for Excellence NSF and Ind. Dept. Edn., 1993, Presdl. award for Excellence in Sci. and Math. Teaching, 1995, NASA Ednl. Workshop for Elem. Sch. Tchrs. award, 1995. Mem. NEA, ASCD, Ind. State Tchrs. Assn., Ind. Coun. Tchrs. Math. (exec. bd. 1992-96, reviewer jour. 1993, co-chair fall conf. 1997—, profl. devel. chair 2000—), Nat. Coun. Tchrs. Math. (arithmetic tchr. referee 1990-96, chair ctrl. regional program 2003), Franklin Twp. Edn. Assn. (pres. 1989-90, 91-92, 98-2000, cen. discussion team 1989-92), Ind. U. Alumni Assn., Cen. Ind. Coun. Tchrs. Math. (exec. bd. 1992—, pres. 1991), South Ctl. Ind. Coun. Tchrs. Math., Ind. State Tchrs. Assn., Ind. U. Edn. Alumni Assn. (steering com., chair 1978-79), Soc. Elem. Presdl. Awardees (math. rep. 1997-2003). Fax: (317) 882-0067. E-mail: rcallan@iquest.net.

CALLAN, TERRANCE DENNIS, JR., dean, religious studies educator; b. Helena, Mont., Feb. 6, 1947; s. Terrance Dennis and Mary Phyllis (Mack) C.; m. Jane Dolores Williams, June 20, 1981; children: Terrance Dennis III, Anne Kathleen. BA with honors, Gonzaga U., 1969; MPhil, Yale U., 1972, PhD, 1976. Asst. prof. Xavier U., Cin., 1975-80; dir. religious edn. St. Clement Parish, St. Bernard, Ohio, 1980-83; asst. prof. Athenaeum of Ohio, Cin., 1983-86, assoc. prof., 1986-92, prof., 1992—, acad. dean, 1989—. Author: Forgetting the Root, 1986, Psychological Perspectives on the Life of Paul, 1990, The Origins of Christian Faith, 1994; contbr. articles to profl. jours. Fellow Woodrow Wilson Found., 1969. Mem. Soc. Bibl. Lit., Cath. Bibl. Assn., Eastern Gt. Lakes Bible Soc. (pres. 1990). Roman Catholic. Avocations: reading, geneaology, computers. Office: Athenaeum of Ohio 6616 Beechmont Ave Cincinnati OH 45230-2000 E-mail: tcallan@mtsm.org.

CALLANDER, KAY EILEEN PAISLEY, business owner, retired education educator, writer; b. Coshocton, Ohio, Oct. 15, 1938; d. Dalton Olas and Dorothy Pauline (Davis) Paisley; m. Don Larry Callander, Nov. 18, 1977. BSE, Muskingum Coll., 1960; MA in Speech Edn., Ohio State U., 1964, postgrad., 1964-84. Cert. elem., gifted, drama, theater tchr., Ohio. Tchr. Columbus (Ohio) Pub. Schs., 1960-70, 80-88, drama specialist, 1970-80, classroom, gifted/talented tchr., 1986-90, ret., 1990; sole prop. The Ali Group, Kay Kards, 1992—. Coord. Artists-in-the Schs., 1977-88; cons., presenter numerous ednl. confs. and sems., 1971—; mem., ednl. cons. Innovation Alliance Youth Adv. Coun., 1992—. Producer-dir., Shady Lane Music Festival, 1980-88; dir. tchr. (nat. distbr. video) The Trial of Gold E. Locks, 1983-84; rep., media pub. relations liason Sch. News., 1983-88; author, creator Trivia Game About Black Americans (TGABA), exhibitor of TGABA game at L.A. County Office Edn. Conf., 1990; presenter for workshop by Human Svc. Group and Creative Edn. Coop., Columbus, Ohio, 1989. Benefactor, Columbus Jazz Arts Group; v.p., bd. dirs. Neoteric Dance and Theater Co., Columbus, 1985-87; tchr., participant Future Stars sculpture exhibit, Ft. Hayes Ctr., Columbus Pub. Schs., 1988; tchr. advisor Columbus Coun. PTAs, 1983-86, co-chmn. reflections com., 1984-87; mem. Columbus Mus. Art, Citizens for Humane Action, Inc.; mem. supt.'s adv. coun. Columbus Pub. Schs., 1967-68; presenter Young Author Seminar, Ohio Dept. Edn., 1988, Illustrating Methods for Young Authors' Books, 1986-87; cons. and workshop leader seminar/workshop Tchg. About the Constitution in Elem. Schs., Franklin County Ednl. Coun., 1988; sponsor Minority Youth Recognition Awards, 1994. Named Educator of Yr., Shady Lane PTA, 1982, Columbus Coun. PTAs, 1989, winner Colour Columbus Landscape Design Competition, 1990; Sch. Excellence grantee Columbus Pub. Schs.; Commendation Columbus Bd. Edn. and Ohio Ho. of Reps. for Child Assault Prevention project, 1986-87; first place winner statewide photo contest Ohio Vet. Assn., 1991; recipient Muskingum Coll. Alumni Disting. Svc. award, 1995. Mem. ASCD, AAUW, Assn. for Childhood Edn. Internat., Ohio Coun. for Social Studies, Franklin County Ret. Tchrs. Assn., Nat. Mus. Women in the Arts, Ohio State U. Alumni Assn., U.S. Army Officers Club, Navy League, Liturgical Art Guild Ohio, Columbus Jazz Arts Group, Columbus Mus. Art, Nat. Coun. for Social Studies, Columbus Art League, Columbus Maennerchor (Damen sect.). Republican. Avocations: painting, photography, swimming, golfing, playing piano and organ. Home: 9131 Indian Mound Rd Pickerington OH 43147 E-mail: pais1609@aol.com.

CALLARD, CAROLE CRAWFORD, librarian, educator; b. Charleston, W.Va., Aug. 8, 1941; d. William O. and Helen (Shay) Crawford; children: Susan Lynne, Annie Laurie. BA in Am. History, U. Charleston, 1963; MLS, U. Pitts., 1966; MA in Social Founds., Ea. Mich. U., 1978; grad., Nat. Inst. for Geneal. Rsch., 1997. Tchr. Blessed Sacrament Sch., South Charleston, W.Va., 1962-64; grad. trainee W.Va. Libr. Commn., Charleston, 1964-65; reference libr. Tompkins County Pub. Libr., Ithaca, N.Y., 1966-69; head libr. U.S. Embassy, Addis Ababa, Ethiopia, 1969-70; head govt. documents Haile Sellassie U., Addis Ababa, 1970-71; br. libr. Ann Arbor (Mich.) Pub. Libr., 1973-83; documents libr. U. Mich., Ann Arbor, 1983-84; pub. svcs. supr. Libr. of Mich., Lansing, 1984-95; depository libr. inspector Govt. Printing Office, 1995-96; librarian Allen Co. Pub. Libr., Ft. Wayne, Ind., 1996-97; specialist Libr. of Mich., Lansing, 1997—; adj. prof. libr. info. sci. Wayne State U., Mich., 2003—; instr. Nat. Inst. for Geneal. Rsch., 1999, adj. prof., 2003—. Chair around the world, around the campus U. Mich. Faculty Women's Club, Ann Arbor, 1974-76; tchr. genealogy Holt Pub. Schs., Okemos Pub. Schs., 1990-92, Lansing Cmty. Schs., 2000, Washtenaw C.C., 1992-94; lectr., Libr. Info. Sci., Wayne State U., 2003; judge Mich. history Day, 1991, 93, 94; genealogy chair Abrams Found., 1997—. Author: Index to 150th Anniversary Issue Ithaca Jour., 1967, Guide to Local History, Sources in the Huron Valley, 1980; editor: Sourcebook of Michigan, 1986, Michigan Cemetery Atlas, 1991, Michigan 1870 Census Index, 1991-95, Michigan Cemetery Sourcebook, 1994, Government Documents for Genealogists Historians and Archivists, 1998; column editor Mich. History Mag. and Chronicle; contbr. articles to profl. jours. Membership chair LWV, Ann Arbor; v.p. Geneal. Soc. Washtenaw County, Mich., 1993, pres., 1993-94; v.p. Palatines to Am., 1987-90, Washtenaw Libr. Club, 1982-83; pres. Mich. Staff Assn., Lansing, 1985-86; pres. Govt. Documents Roundtable of Mich., pres., 1992-93; pres. Mich. Data Base Users Group, 1992-93; chmn. book sale Friends of Ann Arbor Pub. Libr. Recipient Notable Document award Govt. Documents Roundtable of Mich., 1991, Paul Thurston Documents award Govt. Documents Roundtable of Mich., 1993, Cert. of Merit Assn. State and Local History, 1995, Mich. Geneal. Coun., Libr. of Mich. Found. and Abrams Found. award, 1996, P. William Filby award for genealogy librarianship, 2003; grantee U. Pitts., 1966, prof. staff grantee Ann Arbor Pub. Schs., 1980, edn. found. grantee Mich. Libr. Assn., 1982. Mem. ALA (state and local documents com., mem. genealogy com. 2000—, instr. genealogy pre-conf. 2001—, mem. local history com. 2002-, chmn. genealogy pre-conf. 2003—), AAUW (corr. sec., historian 1973-74, 82-83), DAR (corr. sec. Lansing chpt., Sarah Angell Caswell chpt. chair, registrar CAR Seimes Microfilm), Children of Am. Revolution, Internat. Soc. Brit. Genealogy (trustee 1994-96), Mich. Libr. Assn. (chmn. govt. documents sect. 1982-84, leadership acad. 1991-93), Spl. Librs. Assn., D.C. Libr. Assn., Va. Libr. Assn., Fedn. Genealogy Socs. (del., corr. sec. 1986-87, v.p. regional affairs 1989-92), Nat. Genealogy Soc. (instr. devel. com. 1988-90, chmn. instns. com. 1992—, archives and libr. com. 1993-94), Mich. Geneal. Coun. (ofcl. good will ambassador 1995—, P. William Filby award 2003), Mich. Libr. Assn. Avocations: storytelling, reading, travel, genealogy. E-mail: ccallard@michigan.gov.

CALLAWAY, LINDA MARIE, special education educator; b. Upland, Calif., June 21, 1940; d. Elwyn T. and Fladger Idell (Flake) Bice; m. David Barry Callaway, May, 1957 (div. sept. 1962); children: Tess Callaway Tyler, Darren Francis. B in English, Calif. State U., Fullerton, 1975; MEd Adminstrn., Calif. State U., L.A., 1991. Cert. tchr. L.A. County Office Edn., 1984—88; resource specialist spl. edn. Pomona (Calif.) Unified Sch. Dist., 1990—. Presenter U. St. Petersburg, Russia, 2002. Mem. Soc. Of Friends. Avocations: traveling, jewelry making. Home: 2225 Brescia Ave Claremont CA 91711-1807 Office: Pomona HS Pomona Unified Sch Dist 475 Bangor St Pomona CA 91767-2449

CALLEN, JEFFREY PHILLIP, dermatologist, educator; b. May 30, 1947; s. Irwin R. and Rose P. (Cohen) C.; m. Susan B. Manis, Dec. 21, 1968; children: Amy, David. BS, U. Wis., 1969; MD, U. Mich., 1972. Diplomate Am. Bd. Internal Medicine, Am. Bd. Dermatology. Intern, resident in internal medicine U. Mich., Ann Arbor, 1972-75, intern, resident in dermatology, 1975-77; from asst. clin. prof. to dir. residency tng. program U. Louisville Sch. Medicine, 1977-84, dir. residency tng. program, 1984-88; chief dermatology svc. Louisville VA Hosp., 1984-93, prof., chief dermatology divsn., 1988—. Author: Manual of Dermatology, 1980, Cutaneous Aspects of Internal Disease, 1981, Neurology Clinics North America, 1987, Dermatologic Signs of Systemic Disease, 1988, 3d edit., 2003, Color Atlas of Dermatology, 1993, 2d edit., 2000, Current Practice of Dermatology, 1995; editor: Clinics in Rheumatic Disease, 1982, Dermatologic Clinics, 1985, 89, 2002, Medical Clinics of North America, 1982, 84, 86, 89; editor-in-chief Dermavision video program; mem. editl. bd. Internat. Jour. Dermatology, 1990-95; assoc. editor Internat. Jour. Dermatology, 1993-95, Jour. Am. Acad. Dermatology, 1995-; editor spl. issues of jours. in field. Bd. dirs. Actor's Theater of Louisville, 1982-91, 92-98, 2000—, sec., 1986-87, Ky. Arts and Crafts Found., 1991-97; bd. govs. JB Speed Art Mus., 1995-2003. Fellow ACP, Am. Acad. Dermatology (chmn. audio/visual edn. com., task force therapeutic agts., internal med. symposium 1978-83, chmn. sci. and tech. exhibits 1986-89, dir. various symposiums, mem. coun. sci. assembly 1993-98, chair 1997-98, chair com. to evaluate ann. meeting, 1999-2003, vice chair coun. on edn. 2002-2003, chair coun. on edn. 2003—, v.p.-elect 2003—, bd. dirs. 1995-99, mem. exec. com. 1997-99, co-chair program for 21st century 1999-2000, chair psoriasis edn. conf. 2002), Am. Coll. Rheumatology (founder, chair skin disease study group 1996-98, 2000-02); mem. AMA, Am. Fedn. Clin. Rsch., Am. Dermatol. Assn., Dermatology Found. (trustee 1984-90), Louisville Theatrical Assn. (bd. dirs. 1999-2002). Achievements include research on condition in which systemic disease has cutaneous manifestations, lupus erythematosus, psoriasis, dermatomyositis. Office: U Louisville Dept Dermatology 310 E Broadway Ste 200 Louisville KY 40202-1745

CALLENDER, NORMA ANNE, psychology educator, counselor; b. Huntsville, Tex., May 10, 1933; d. C.W. Carswell and Nell Ruth (Collard) Hughes Bost; m. B.G. Callender, 1951 (div. 1964); remarried 1967 (div. 1973); children: Teresa Elizabeth, Leslie Gemey, Shannah Hughes, Kelly Mari; m. E Purfurst, June 1965 (div. Aug. 1965). BS, U. Houston, 1969; MA, U. Houston at Clear Lake, 1977; postgrad., U. Houston, 1970, Tex. So. U., 1971, Lamar U., 1972-73, U. Houston-Clear Lake, 1979, 87, 89-93, St. Thomas U., 1985, 86, Aerospace Inst., NASA, Johnson Space Ctr., 1986, U. Houston-Clear Lake, summer 98, San Jacinto Coll., 1988—99, postgrad., 1994, postgrad., 2001—03. Cert. profl. reading specialist, Tex.; lic. profl. counselor. Tchr. Houston Ind. Schs., 1969-70; co-counselor, instr. Ellington AFB, Houston, 1971; tchr. Clear Creek Schs., League City, Tex., 1970-86; owner, dir. Bay Area Tutoring and Reading Clinic, Clear Lake City, Tex., 1970—, Bay Area Tng. Assocs., 1982-98, Bay Area Family Counseling, 1995—; cons., LPC intern Guidance Ctr. Pasadena (Tex.) Ind. Sch. Dist., 1993-95. Part-time instr. San Jacinto Coll., Pasadena, 1980-81, 91-93; univ. adj. U. Houston, Clear Lake, 1986-91; founder, editor BATA Books Pub., 1997—; cons. in field. Contbr. poetry to profl. jours. State advisor U.S. Congl. Adv. Bd., 1985-87; vol., bd. dirs. Family Outreach Ctr., 1989-92; vol. Bay Area Coun. on Drugs and Alcohol, Nassau Bay, Tex., 1993-94; bd. dirs. Ballet San Jacinto, 1985-87; adv. bd. Cmty. Ednl. TV, 1990-92. Recipient Franklin award U. Houston, 1965-67; Delta Kappa Gamma/Beta Omicron scholar, 1967-68, PTA scholar, 1973, Berwin scholar, 1976, Mary Gibbs Jones scholar, 1976-77, Found. Econ. Edn. scholar, 1976, Insts. Achievement Human Potential scholar, Phila., 1987. Mem.: ACA, Internat. Reading Assn., Clear Creek Educators Assn. (past, honorarium 1976, 1977, 1985), Leadership Clear Lake Alumni Assn. (charter, program and projects com. mem. 1986—87, edn. com. 1985), U. Houston Alumni Assn. (life), Phi Theta Kappa, Phi Delta Kappa, Kappa Delta Pi, Psi Chi (life), Phi Kappa Phi (life). Mem. Life Tabernacle Ch. Office: 1234 Bay Area Blvd Ste R Houston TX 77058-2538

CALLEO, DAVID PATRICK, history, political, economy and international relations educator; b. Binghamton, N.Y., July 19, 1934; s. Patrick and Gertrude (Crowe) C.; m. Avis Thayer Bohlen. BA, Yale U., 1955, MA, 1957, PhD, 1959. Instr. polit. sci. Brown U., Providence, 1959-60; from instr. to asst. prof. polit. sci. Yale U., New Haven, 1961-67; rsch. fellow Nuffield Coll., Oxford U., 1966—67; cons. to undersec. for polit. affairs U.S. Dept. of State, Washington, 1967-68; prof., dir. European studies Nitze Sch. Advanced Internat. Studies Johns Hopkins U., Washington, 1968—, Dean Acheson chair Nitze Sch. Advanced Internat. Studies, 1988—, Univ. prof., 2001—; sr. Fulbright lectr. Fed. Republic Germany, 1975; assoc. fellow Jonathan Edwards Coll, Yale U., New Haven, 1972—; v.p. Lehrman Inst., N.Y.C., 1972-87; project dir. The Twentieth Century Fund, N.Y.C., 1981-85. Project dir. The 20th Century Fund, N.Y.C., 1993-99; assoc. Centre d'Etudes et de Rsch. Internat., 1993-94; enseignant invité Inst. d'études politiques de Paris, 1993-94; invited prof. Inst. U. de hautes études Internat., Geneva, 1999. Author: America and the World Political Economy, 1973 (Gladys M. Kammerer award Best Book Analyzing Am. Nat. Policy, Am. Polit. Sci. Assn. 1973), The German Problem Reconsidered, 1978, The Imperious Economy, 1982, Beyond American Hegemony, 1987, The Bankrupting of America, 1992, Rethinking Europe's Future, 2001. Trustee, Jonathan Edwards Trust, 1972—. Guggenheim fellow, 1966-67. Mem. Am. Polit. Sci. Assn., Coun. on Fgn. Rels., Brooks' (London), Met. Club Washington, Century Assn. (N.Y.C.), Internat. Inst. for Strategic Studies, Literary Soc. (Washington). Avocations: gardening, squash, opera. E-mail: dcalleo@jhu.edu.

CALLESEN-GYORGAK, JAN ELAINE, special education educator; b. Manistee, Mich., Sept. 21, 1959; d. Carl Wayne and Patsy Arlene (Haglund) Callesen; m. Gregg Gyorgak, Oct. 27, 1990; children: Danielle Marie, Nathaniel Charles, Kristen Lynn, Wayne Anthony. BS in Edn., Bowling Green State U., 1981; M in Curriculum and Instrn., Cleve. State U., 1988. Lic. elem. edn., spl. edn., libr. and media scis. Montessori tchr. Children's Home of Parma (Ohio), 1981-82; kindergarten tchr., coord. Murton's Child Devel. Ctr., Fairview Park, Ohio, 1983-85; spl. edn. tchr.-learning disabilities Cleve. Pub. Schs., 1985—. Advisor Safety Patrol, Cleve., 1986—. Mem. ASCD, Cleve. Tchrs. Union, Coun. for Exceptional Children (divsn. learning disabilities). Avocations: needlepoint, embroidery, collecting precious moments figurines. Home: 6283 Surrey Dr North Olmsted OH 44070-4813 Office: Walton Elem Sch 3409 Walton Ave Cleveland OH 44113-4942

CALVERT, DAVID RANDALL, educational interpreter, consultant; b. Indpls., June 6, 1961; s. Cecil Wayne Calvert and Dianne Marie (Medenwald) Thomas; m. Lorraine Marie Jones, Aug. 14, 1982; 1 child, Corbin Randall. AA cum laude, Vincennes U., 1995; postgrad., Ball State U., 1995—. Sales clk. J.C. Penney, Greenwood, Ind., 1979-80; proofreader Hunt Type, Indpls., 1980-83; media conversion specialist Photo Comp, Brownsburg, Ind., 1983-84, PR Graphics, Indpls., 1984-85; tech. support mgr. Shaffstall Corp., Indpls., 1985-90; interpreter cons. Cmty. Svcs. for the Deaf, Indpls., 1990-91; ednl. interpreter Purdue U., West Lafayette, Ind., 1991-92, Carmel/Clay Schs., Noblesville, Ind., 1992—. Cons. ednl. issues, State of Ind., Indpls., 1994. Editor (newsletter) Insights, 1991-93 (Recognition award 1993); contbr. articles to profl. jours. Interpreter Hendricks County Civic Theatre, Danville, Ind., 1992—, Bradley United Meth. Ch., Greenfield, Ind., 1992—, Specialized Interpreting Svcs., Indpls., 1992—. Recipient Shining Star Nominee award Sta. WTHR and Star Nat. Bank, 1994. Mem. ASCD, Registry of Interpreters for the Deaf (chairperson edn. interpreter 1994—, state liaison edn. 1992—, editor Ind. chpt. 1992—coord. ann. silent retreat 1992), Ind. State Tchrs. Assn. (assoc., panelist, coord., 1990, Svc. award 1993), Ind. Assn. for the Deaf. Republican. Methodist. Avocations: college basketball, professional football, soccer, tennis, music. Office: Noblesville HS 18111 Cumberland Rd Noblesville IN 46060-5650 Home: 14736 White Tail Run Noblesville IN 46060-7883

CALVERT, JACQUELINE CLAIRE, elementary education educator; b. Milan, Tenn., Aug. 16, 1944; d. John Clark and Iris (Pierce) Fisher; m. Thomas Leon Calvert Jr., Apr. 27, 1968; children: Grant, Matthew, Amanda. BS, U. Tenn., 1966; MEd, Trevecca Nazarene Coll., 1993. Cert. tchr., Tenn. Asst. divsn. mgr. pers. dept. NLT Corp., Nashville, Tenn., 1966-73; elem. tchr. Lawrence County Bd. Edn., Lawrenceburg, Tenn., 1982—. Mem. Tchr. Study Coun., Tenn., 1989; chair Sch./Cmty. Accreditation Team, 1990; tchr. Tutor At-Risk Students, 1994—; mem. rsch. group Appalachia Ednl. Lab.-QUILT Program, 1991—. Grantee Lawrence County 21st Century Coun., 1994. Mem. Lawrence County Edn. Assn. (faculty rep. 1990—), Tenn. Edn. Assn. (del. to rep. assembly 1994). Office: Ethridge Elem Sch 33 Main St Ethridge TN 38456-2040

CALVIN, TERESA ANN B. secondary education educator; b. Annapolis, Md., Sept. 18, 1931; d. Lawrence Edward and Lovey L. (Hall) Blackstone; m. James C. Calvin, Dec. 18, 1952 (dec. Dec. 1969); children: Jamesetta Teresa, Ann Elizabeth, Lavenia Manina, Lenora Angelica Hope. Student, Howard U., Washington, 1948-51; AB, Va. U., Richmond, 1952; postgrad., Ohio State U. Cert. tchr. Md., La. Substitute tchr. Bossier Parish, Caddo Parish, Shreveport, La., 1954-56; tchr. French Community Ctr., Alexandria, La., 1959-61; substitute tchr. Opelousas (La.) Sch. Dist., 1961-63, Orleans Parish Sch., New Orleans, 1963-72; tchr. social studies Anne Arundel County, 1972-93. Presenter in field. Writer worships. Judge attys. State of

Md. Essays for Md. Bicentennial; story teller Kunta Kute Com., Annaplis, 1990; mem. women of color bd. YCWA, 1993; founder Living Edn. Ctr. Mus., Annapolis House Relics, 1803-1993; mem. social studies Am. team to Vietnam Am. Citizen Ambs., 1993. Ford scholar, 1984; recipient Outstanding Community Leadership award Mt. Moriah Ch., 1986; cited by Tchrs. Anne Arundel County for Human Rels., 1993. Mem. NEA, Md. Tchrs. Assn., Internat. Platform Assn., Herbert Frisby Hist. Soc., Kiwanis, Delta Sigma Theta (chaplain 1989-92, chair arts and letters Annapolis chpt.). Republican. Methodist. Avocations: travel, writing, music. Home: 767 Fairview Ave Apt B Annapolis MD 21403-2936

CALVO, RHONDA LYNNE, special education educator; b. Upland, Calif., Jan. 31, 1960; d. Ronald Thurl and Marilyn Brown Smith; m. Chuck M. Calvo, May 30, 1981; children: C.J., Christian. BA in Social Sci., Azusa Pacific U., 1982; degree, Prescott Coll., 1994. Lic. tchr. Ariz., 1994, Nev., 1998. Spl. edn. tchr. Lake Havasu Unifed Sch. Dist., Lake Havasu City, Ariz., 1994—98, Clark County Sch. Dist., Boulder City, Nev., 1998—99, spl. edn. tchr. facilitator, 1999—. Adv. Nat. Jr. Honor Soc., Garrett, Miss., 1999—2002; mem. various com. Boulder City H.S., 2000—02. Recipient Caring Enough to Make a Difference award, STOP DUI, 2002; grantee Least Restrictive Environ. grant, Clark County Sch. Dist., 2001—02. Republican. Avocations: boating, swimming, water sports. Office: Boulder City High School 1101 Fifth St Boulder City NV 89005

CAMACHO, JAMES, JR., mathematician, educator; b. N.Y.C., June 17, 1956; s. James and Pascuala (Franqui) C. BS, Polytechnic Inst. N.Y., 1978, MS, 1980; PhD, Polytechnic U., 1987. Adjunct teaching fellow, lectr. Polytechnic U., Bklyn., 1982-87; asst. prof. Jersey City State Coll., 1987-96; assoc. prof. New Jersey City U., Jersey City, 1996—. Active Coun. Hispanic Affairs Jersey City State Coll., 1987—; speaker at profl. meetings; grad. coord. math. dept., N.J. City U., 1997-, tutoring coord. math. dept., 2000-. Contbr. articles to profl. jours. Jersey State Coll. grantee, 1990-93. Mem. Am. Math. Soc., Math. Assn. Am. Roman Catholic. Avocations: cinema, astronomy. Home: 33 Hamilton Ave Edison NJ 08820-3934 Office: New Jersey City Univ Math Dept 2039 John F Kennedy Blvd Jersey City NJ 07305-1527 E-mail: jcamacho@njcu.edu.

CAMARA, PAULINE FRANCOEUR, secondary school educator, principal; b. Somerset, Mass., May 3, 1962; d. Rene L. and Anita E. (Cadoret) Francoeur; m. Robert P. Camara, Aug. 9, 1986; children: Kalyn E., Kyle R. AS in Bus. Adminstrn., Bristol C.C., Fall River, Mass., 1982; student, Bryant Coll., Smithfield, R.I., 1982-84; BS in Acctg., U. Mass., Dartmouth, 1987; M.Ednl. Leadership Adminstrn., Bridgewater State Coll., 1997. Cert. tchr. bus. edn., 5-12, prin. 9-12, info. tech. specialist K-12. Sr. acct., acct., mgr. Elbe-Cesco Inc., Fall River, Mass., Bank of Boston; tchr. Our Lady of Fatima H.S., Warren, R.I., 1994; acad. coord., instr. Westport (Mass.) H.S., 1994-98; tchr. Somerset H.S., 1998—, vice prin., 2000—. Adj. tchr. bus. and tech. Bristol C.C., 1997; coach Providence Coll., 1996—98; site coord. Schs. That Work, 1998—2000. Vice pres. Somerset Chace Stret Sch. PTO, 1996-97; bd. dirs. Town of Somerset Spectrum Program, 1996-99; mem. schools-That-Work, 1994—; mem. PALMS, 1995—. Mem. Nat. bus. Educators Assn., New Eng. Bus. Educators Assn., Mass. Bus. Educators Assn. (pres. 1999-2000, v.p. 1997-99, bd. dirs. 1995—), Mass. Cheer Coaches Assn. (treas. 1987-89). Office: Somerset HS Grandview Ave Somerset MA 02726

CAMARDA, HARRY SALVATORE, physics educator, researcher; b. N.Y.C., Sept. 23, 1938; m. Judith Susan Silberberg, Aug. 20, 1964; children: Ilene, Alexander. BS in Physics, NYU, 1963; PhD in Physics, Columbia U., 1970. Rsch. assoc. Columbia U., N.Y.C., 1970-71, Nat. Bureau Standards, Gaithersburg, Md., 1971-73; sr. physicist Lawrence Livermore (Calif.) Nat. Lab., 1974-79; prof. physics Pa. State U., Media, 1979—. Cons. Lawrence Livermore Nat. Lab., 1979—. Contbr. numerous articles to profl. jours. Mem. Am. Phys. Soc., N.Y. Acad. Scis., Sigma Xi. Office: Delaware County Campus Pa State U Media PA 19063

CAMBERS, PHILIP WILLIAM, pastor, music minister, music educator; b. Kansas City, Mo., May 5, 1957; s. William Hammond Cambers and Mary Elisabeth (Sharp) Kehrer; m. Sharon Kay Thompson, Apr. 28, 1984; children: Ashley Carmen, Jeffrey Philip, Scott William. B of Music Edn., BA of Sci. Edn., Cen. Mo. State U., 1979. Lic. to preach Assemblies of God, 1987; cert. tchr. music and French. Youth min. First Assembly of God, St. Joseph, Mo., 1982; min. of music Calvary Assembly of God, Toledo, 1982-85, First Assembly of God, Mobile, Ala., 1985, N. Highland Assembly of God, Columbus, Ga., 1985-86, Southside Assembly of God, Jackson, Miss., 1986-92; with First Assembly of God, Honolulu, 1992-94, 1st Assembly of God Ch., East Lansing, Mich., 1994-95; sr. pastor New Life Assembly of God Ch., Ann Arbor, Mich., 1995—; tchr. music Truman Mid. Sch., St. Joseph, Mo., 1979-82, Calvary Christian Sch., Toledo, Ohio, 1982-85, Briarcrest Christian Sch., Columbus, Ga., 1985-86, Southside Christian Sch., Jackson, Miss., 1986-92. Dist. music dir. Miss. Dist. Coun., Assembly of God, Jackson, 1986-92, Hawaii Dist. Coun., 1992-94; host Miss. Dist. Coun. Choral Workshop, Jackson, 1987; adjudicator Nat. Fine Arts Festival Assembly of God, Springfield, Mo., 1988, 90, 99, 2000; choral clinician Evangel Assembly of God, Columbus, Miss., 1988-90; prodr. Melody on Ice, Ann Arbor Figure Skating Club, 1998; sec.-treas. Metro South sect. Assemblies of God, 1999-2002. Contbr. articles to profl. jours. Choir dir. Children's Choir & Handbell Choir (for nursing homes), Jackson, 1989-90; handbell choir dir. TV comml. Sta. WAPT-TV, Jackson, 1990; sec. Ann Arbor Figure Skating Club, 1999-2002. Recipient First Place Nat. Assn. Tchrs. Singing, 1979. Mem. Am. Guild English Handbell, Am. Choral Dir.'s Assn. Home: 2112 Ann Arbor Saline Rd Ann Arbor MI 48103-9710 Office: New Life Assembly of God Ch 2118 Ann Arbor Saline Rd Ann Arbor MI 48103-9710

CAMEL, PEGGY THURSTON, guidance counselor; b. Ft. Jay, N.Y., June 1, 1938; d. Joseph Donald and Eileen Rose (McCoy) Thurston; m. James T. Camel, Sept. 12, 1959; children: Renée Michelle Camel Meaux, Simone P., Jacques J., André Jean, Etienne P. Diploma, Charity Sch. Nursing, New Orleans, 1959; BA in Psychology, Stephens Coll. for Women, 1976; MEd, U. Southwestern La., 1983. Cert. tchr., La.; RN, La.; cert. emergency med. tech. Staff nurse USPHS Hosp., New Orleans, 1959-60, Barstow (Calif.) Community Hosp., 1960-61, Abrom Meml. Hosp., Kaplan, La., 1962-63; DON Vermilion Nursing Home, Kaplan, La., 1963-69; instr. nursing, dept. head Gulf Area Tech. Inst., Abbeville, La., 1969-88, guidance counselor, 1988—; staff nurse Abbeville Gen. Hosp., 1978—. Chair Kaplan chpt. ARC, 1974-76; bd. dirs. Acadiana Bd. Nursing, Lafayette, La., 1984-88, Home Health Nursing Adv. Com., Abbeville, 1984-89, Gulf Area Tech. Inst. Adv. Com., Abbeville, 1989—. Mem. Vermilion Parish CPR Awareness Com., 1984-88. Mem. Am. Vocat. Assn., La. Vocat. Assn. (health occupation educator of yr. 1983), Trade and Industry Assn. La. Vocat. Assn. (sch. rep. 1986—), Health Occupations Educators Assn. (treas. 1982-83), Am. Bus. Women Assn. (pres. Kaplan chpt. 1982, Bus. Woman of Yr. 1983). Roman Catholic. Avocations: arts and crafts, oil painting, self-improvement courses, travel, music. Home: 1800 N Herpin Ave Kaplan LA 70548-5623 Office: Gulf Area Tech Inst 1115 Clover St Abbeville LA 70510-3811

CAMERIUS, JAMES WALTER, marketing educator, corporate researcher; b. Chgo., June 14, 1939; s. Wilbert Albert and Violet Elna (Johnson) C. BS, No. Mich. U., 1961; MS, U. N.D., 1963; postgrad., U. Okla., 1974-77. From instr. to assoc. prof. No. Mich. U., Marquette, 1963-90, prof. mktg., 1990—. Lectr. in field; mem. adv. bd. S.E. Advanced Tech. Edn. Consortium. Newsletter editor N.Am. Case Rsch. Assn.; bd. rev., editl. rev. bd. Bus. Case Jour.; mem. internat. editl. adv. bd. Jour. SMET Edn. Cir. lay rep. Luth. Ch.-Mo. Synod, 1987-89; pres. Redeemer Luth. Ch., Marquette, 1989-90, sec. to ch. coun., 1990-92, bd. elders, 1993-98, v.p., 2000-2001, pres. 2001-02; mktg. track chair N.Am. Case Rsch. and Mktg. Assn., 1997-2003. Recipient MAGB Disting. Prof. award, 1995; Rsch. grantee Direct Selling Edn. Found., 1987-2002, Walker L. Cisler Sch. No. Mich. U., 1990, Filene Rsch. Inst., 1994; named Outstanding Case Reviewer, Case Rsch. Jour., 1998. Fellow Acad. Mktg. Sci.; mem. Am. Mktg. Assn., Soc. Case Rsch. (v.p. 1990-91, case workshop dir. 1999, pres.-elect 2000, pres. 2001-2002, archivist 2002—), N.Am. Case Rsch. Assn. bd. dirs. (midwest rep.), World Assn. for Case Method Rsch. and Application (case colloquium dir. 1997—), WACRA Adv. bd., Econ. Club, Alpha Kappa Psi (Alumni award). Democrat. Home: 171 Lakewood Ln Marquette MI 49855-9543 Office: No Mich U Mktg Dept Marquette MI 49855

CAMERON, ALASTAIR GRAHAM WALTER, astrophysicist, educator; b. Winnipeg, Man., Can., June 21, 1925; came to U.S., 1959, naturalized, 1963; s. Alexander Thomas and Airdrie Edna (Bell) C.; m. Elizabeth Aston MacMillan, June 11, 1955. B.Sc., U. Man., 1947; PhD, U. Sask., 1952, D.Sc. (hon.), 1977; A.M. (hon.), Harvard U., 1973. Asst. prof. physics Iowa State Coll., Ames, 1952-54; asst., asso. and sr. research officer Atomic Energy Can., Ltd., Chalk River, Ont., 1954-61; sr. research fellow Calif. Inst. Tech., Pasadena, 1959-60; sr. scientist Goddard Inst. Space Studies, N.Y., 1961-66; prof. space physics Yeshiva U., 1966-73; prof. astronomy Harvard U., Cambridge, Mass., 1973-97, Donald H. Menzel prof. astrophysics, 1997-99, Donald H. Menzel rsch. prof. astrophysics, 1999—; sr. rsch. scientist Lunar and Planetary Lab., U. Ariz., 2000—. Chmn. Space Sci. Bd., 1976-82, Nat. Acad. Scis. Contbr. articles to profl. jours. Recipient J. Lawrence Smith medal NAS, 1988, Disting. Pub. Service medal NASA, 1983. Mem. NAS, AAAS, Am. Phys. Soc., Am. Geophys. Union (Harry H. Hess medal 1989), Am. Astron. Soc. (Russell lectr. 1997), Internat. Astron. Union, Meteoritical Soc. (Leonard medal 1994). Office: Lunar and Planetary Lab 1629 E University Blvd 527A Tucson AZ 85721 E-mail: acameron@lpl.arizona.edu.

CAMERON, DOUGLAS WINSTON, parochial education educator, writer; b. Cin., Oct. 29, 1947; s. Benjamin Franklin and Ruth (Anders) C.; m. Ann Templeton, Nov. 30, 1968; children: Robert Handly, Jennifer Rebecca. AB, Harvard U., 1969. Cert. EMT, wilderness EMT, CPR instr. Am. Heart Assn. Writer, v.p. Outdoor Enterprises, Inc., Sewanee, Tenn., 1970-73; chmn. history dept. St. Andrews (Tenn.) Sch., 1973-76; tchr., dir. summer sch. St. Andrews-Sewanee Sch., St. Andrews, 1988-96; dir. spl. student programs The Univ. of the South, Sewanee, Tenn., 1976-79, dir. the Bishop's Common, 1979-85; exec. dir. Gov.'s Commn. on Tenneseans Outdoors, Nashville, 1985-87. Bd. dirs. John Templeton Found., Tenn. Environ. Coun.; instr. Wilderness Med. Assocs. Co-author: (guide books) N.Y. Times Guides to Outdoors, U.S.A., 1972, 73, Under the Sun at Sewanee, 1977; co-editor commn. report Tennesseans Outdoors, 1986. Asst. chief Sewanee Fire Dept., 1976—; dir. Sewanee Emergency Med. Svc., 1988-91; rep. Sewanee Community Coun., 1976-84, 86—; community rep. (budget and affordable housing com.) to Bd. trustees, U. of the South, 1989-91; chmn. Tenn. Scenic Rivers Celebration, Nashville, 1984; mem. Leadership Franklin county Franklin County Found. for Ednl. Excellence; canoe and kayak instr. Camp Merrie Woode; canoe team coach, EMT instr. U. of the South. Named Citizen of Yr. Sewanee Civic Assn., 1986, Dist. 10 Soccer Coach of Yr., 1990, Hero in Am. Edn. Readers Digest, 1996. Mem. Am. Canoe Assn. (coun. 1982-84, mem. conservation com. 1988—, chair 1988-90), Nat. Slalom and Wildwater Com. (chmn. 1980-84). Episcopalian. Avocations: whitewater canoeing, hiking, bird watching, sailing, reading. Home: 900 Can Tex Dr Sewanee TN 37375-2835

CAMERON, GUY N. biologist, educator; b. San Francisco, May 1, 1942; BS, U. Calif., Berkeley, 1963; MS, Calif. State U., Long Beach, 1965; PhD, U. Calif., Davis, 1969. Asst. prof. U. Houston, 1971-76, assoc. prof., 1977-83, prof., 1984—; prof. and dept. head U. Cincinnati, 1998—. Contbr. more than 100 articles to profl. jours. Trustee Armand Bayou Nature Ctr., Houston, 1991-98, Houston Arboretum, 1990-98. Grantee NSF, NIH, DOE Mem. Tex. Soc. Mammalogists (pres. 1988-89), Am. Soc. Mammalogists (editor 1990—, bd. dirs. 1983-86, 2000-02, pres.-elect 2002-), Ecol. Soc. Am., British Ecol. Soc. Office: Dept Biological Scis U Cincinnati PO Box 210006 Cincinnati OH 45221-0006

CAMERON, JUDITH LYNNE, secondary education educator, hypnotherapist; b. Oakland, Calif., Apr. 29, 1945; d. Alfred Joseph and June Estelle (Faul) Moe; m. Richard Irwin Cameron, Dec. 17, 1967; 1 child, Kevin Dale. AA in Psychol., Sacramento City Coll., 1965; BA in Psychol., German, Calif. State U., 1967; MA in Reading Specialization, San Francisco State U., 1972; postgrad., Chapman Coll.; PhD, Am. Inst. Hypnotherapy, 1987. Cert. tchr., Calif. Tchr. St. Vincent's Cath. Sch., San Jose, Calif., 1969-70, Fremont (Calif.) Elem. Sch., 1970-72, LeRoy Boys Home, LaVerne, Calif., 1972-73, Grace Miller Elem. Sch., LaVerne, Calif., 1973-80, resource specialist, 1980-84; owner, mgr. Pioneer Take-out Franchises, Alhambra and San Gabriel, Calif., 1979-85; resource specialist, dept. chmn. Bonita H.S., LaVerne, Calif., 1984; mentor tchr. in space sci. Bonita Unified Sch. Dist., 1988-99, rep. LVTV; owner, therapist So. Calif. Clin. Hypnotherapy, Claremont, Calif., 1988—. Bd. dirs., recommending tchr., asst. dir. Project Turnabout, Claremont, Calif.; Teacher-in-Space cons. Bonita Unified Sch. Dist., LaVerne, 1987-99; advisor Peer Counseling Program, Bonita High Sch., 1987—; advisor Air Explorers/Edwards Test Pilot Sch., LaVerne, 1987—; mem. Civil Air Patrol, Squadron 68, Aerospace Office, 1988-92; selected amb. U.S. Space Acad.-U.S. Space Camp Acad., Huntsville, Ala., 1990; named to national (now internat.) teaching faculty challenger Ctr. for Space Edn., Alexandria, Va., 1990; regional coord. East San Gabiel Valley Future Scientists and Engrs. of Am.; amb. to U.S. Space Camp, 1990; mem. adj. faculty challenger learning ctr. Calif. State U., Dominguez Hills, 1994, state sch. accreditation team, 2000; rep. ceremony to honor astronauts Apollo 11, White House, 1994; exec. bd. Bonita Unfied tchrs. assoc., 1995— (negotiating team, 1998—); flight dir. mission control, Challenger learning ctr., Long Beach, Ca., 2002—. Vol. advisor Children's Home Soc., Santa Ana, 1980-81; dist. rep. LVTV Channel 29, 1991; regional coord. East San Gabriel Valley chpt. Future Scientists and Engrs. of Am., 1992; mem. internat. invesigation Commn. UFOs, 1991; field mem. Ctr. for Search for Extraterrestrial Intelligence, 1996; tchr., leader Ctr. for the Study Extraterrestrial Intelligence, 1997—. Recipient Tchr. of Yr., Bonita H.S., 1989, continuing svc. award, 1992; named Toyolaa Tchr. of Yr., 1994. Mem. NEA, AAUW, Internat. Investigations Com. on UFOs, Coun. Exceptional Children, Am. Psychol. Assn., Calif. Assn. Resource Specialists, Calif. Elem. Edn. Assn., Calif. Tchrs. Assn., Calif. Assn. Marriage and Family Therapists, Planetary Soc., Mutual UFO Network, Com. Sci. Investigation L5 Soc., Challenger Ctr. Space Edn., Calif. Challenger Ctr. Crew for Space Edn., Orange County Astronomers, Chinese Shar-Pei Am., Concord Club, Rare Breed Dog Club (L.A.), gardening club of Am., ctr. for the extraterrestrial intelligence, diplomat, 1997. Republican. Avocations: skiing, banjo, guitar, flying, astrophotography. Home: 3257 La Travesia Dr Fullerton CA 92835-1455 Office: Bonita High Sch 115 W Allen Ave San Dimas CA 91773-1437

CAMMACK, ANN, librarian, secondary school educator; b. Akron, Ohio, Sept. 24, 1947; d. Matthew John and Anna (Maxim) Klinovsky; m. Robert Floyd Cammack, Sept. 27, 1969; children: Lisa Ann, Holly Ann, Noël Ann, Monica Ann. BA, Youngstown State U., 1969; MLS, Tex. Woman's U., 1995, PhD, 2001. Cert. tchr. secondary sch. Ohio, elem. and secondary sch., Tex. English tchr. Struthers (Ohio) City Schs., 1969-83; asst. cataloger Amon Carter Mus., Ft. Worth, 1997, 2000—01. Life mem. Tex. Parent Tchrs. Assn., historian Arlington, 1991-92. Doctoral fellow Tex. Woman's U., 1996. Mem. AAUW, ALA, Ladies Aux. VFW, Tex. Libr. Assn., Youngstown State U. Alumni Assn., Beta Phi Mu. Avocation: golf.

CAMMARATA, JOAN FRANCES, Spanish language and literature educator; b. Bklyn., Dec. 22, 1950; d. John and Angelina Mary (Guarnera) Cammarata; m. Richard Montemarano, Aug. 9, 1975. BA summa cum laude, Fordham U., 1972; MA, Columbia U., 1974, MPhil, 1977, PhD, 1982. Preceptor Columbia Coll., NYC, 1974-82; adj. instr. Fordham U., NYC, 1980-81; adj. asst. prof. Iona Coll., New Rochelle, NY, 1982-84; asst. prof. Manhattan Coll., Riverdale, NY, 1982-90, assoc. prof., 1990-96, prof., 1996—. Author: Mythological Themes in the Works of Garcilaso de la Vega, 1983; editor: Women in the Discourse of Early Modern Spain, 2003; mem. editl. bd. Modern Lang. Studies; editl. reviewer D.C. Heath; contbr. articles and revs. to profl. jours. Fellow arts and sci. Columbia U., 1972-75; grantee Manhattan Coll., 1985, 91, NEH, 1987, 88, Spain's Min Edn. Culture, 1997—; Rsch. Fellowship grantee NYU Faculty Seminars, 1992, 94; named univ. assoc. Faculty Resources Network Program NYU, 1985—; Andrew Mellon Found. vis. scholar, 1990; scholar-in-residence NYU, 1991-92, 97-98. Mem.: MLA (mem. del. assembly), N.Y. State Assn. Fgn. Lang. Tchrs., Am. Assn. Tchrs. Spanish and Portugese, Assn. Internat. de Hispanistas, Renaissance Soc. Am., Inst. Internat. de Lit. Iberoamericana, South Atlantic, South Ctrl. and Midwest MLA, N.E. MLA (rsch. fellow 1991, v.p. 1997—98, pres. 1998—), Am. Coun. Tchg. of Fgn. Langs, Cervantes Soc. Am., Hispanic Inst. Roman Catholic. Avocations: piano, gardening, writing, needlework. Office: Manhattan Coll Bronx NY 10471

CAMMAROSANO, JOSEPH RAPHAEL, economist, educator; b. Mt. Vernon, NY, Mar. 12, 1923; s. Louis Raphael and Mary Nancy (Sansone) C.; m. Rosalie Nancy Esposito, Nov. 22, 1952; children: Louis, Nancy, Joseph. Student, Stanford U., 1943-44; BS cum laude, Fordham U., 1947, PhD, 1956; MA, N.Y.U., 1949. Insp. U.S. Bur. Customs, 1948-50; asst. prof. Iona Coll., 1950-55, Fordham U., Bronx, N.Y., 1956-60, assoc. prof., 1962-67; dir. Inst. Urban Studies, 1964—84, prof. econs., 1967—93, prof. emeritus, chmn. dept. econs., 1969, exec. v.p., 1969-75, 85-88, acting fin. v.p., treas., 1984-85; fiscal economist U.S. Bur. of Budget, Washington, 1961-62. Fiscal cons. N.Y. State Temp. Commn. on Constl. Conv., 1957—58, N.Y. State Spl. Legis. Com. on Revision and Simplification of the Constn., 1958—60, N.Y. State Tax Structure Study Com., 1962—70, N.Y. State Temp. Commn. on the Constn., 1966—67, N.Y. Bell Tel. Co., 1960; cons. N.Y.C. Econ. Devel. Adminstrn., 1969, Cmty. Coun. Greater N.Y., 1971—74; vice chmn. Regional Manpower Adv. Com. to U.S. Secs. Labor and HEW, 1970—73, chmn., 1973—74; cons. ACTION, Fed. Agy. for Vol. Svc., 1976, N.Y.C. Pub. Devel. Corp., 1979—81, Office of Edn. Roman Cath. Diocese of N.Y., 1981—87; mem. adv. com. Ind. Budget Office City of N.Y., 1990—92; higher edn. cons. U. Md., 1980, Malcolm-King Coll., 1982—89, Manhattan-Marymount Coll., 1987—89. Author: Highway Finance in New York State, 1958, A Profile of the Bronx Economy, 1967, A Plan for the Redevelopment of the Brooklyn Navy Yard, 1968, The Long Range Forecasting of Telephone Demand, 1960, Industrial Activity in the Inner City: A Case Study of the South Bronx, 1981, The Contributions of John Maynard Keynes to Foreign Trade Theory and Policy, 1987. Trustee Fordham Rd. Devel. Corp., 1969—85, St. Joseph's Coll., Bklyn., 1974—80, Cathedral Coll., Douglaston, NY, 1969—85, Bronx Inter-Neighborhood Housing Corp., 1975—88, AAPC; mem. ednl. policies com. bd. trustees L.I. U., Greenvale, NY, 1977—85. With U.S. Army, 1943—46, ETO. Mem. Am. Econ. Assn., Phi Delta Kappa. Home: 120 Archer Ave Apt 2C Mount Vernon NY 10550-1423

CAMMAROTA, MARIE ELIZABETH, nursing educator; b. Phila., Oct. 12, 1943; d. Angelo J. Cardile and Angeline M. Cardile; m. Charles C. Cammarota, Aug. 14, 1965; 1 child, Sharon Marie. AS, Orange County Coll., Middletown, N.Y., 1963; BA, Glassboro State Coll., 1977, MA, 1981; EdD, Nova Southeastern U., 1995. Cert. sch. social worker, sch. nurse, pupil personal svcs., supr., FNP, sch. nurse practitioner, N.J.; RN, N.J., N.Y., Pa. Staff nurse to asst. head nurse Thomas Jefferson U. Hosp., Phila., 1963-65; instr. St. Joseph's Hosp., Sch. Nursing, 1965-66; sch. nurse Gloucester County Vocat. Tech. Sch., Sewell, N.J., 1974-88; asst. prof. Rowan U., Glassboro, N.J., 1988—. Adj. prof. Gloucester County Coll., Sewell, 1985-95, Glassboro (N.J.) State Coll., 1986-88; cons. com. on sch. health N.J. Acad. Pediatrics, Trenton, 1986—; cons. Edn., Info. and Resource Ctr., Sewell, 1989—; spkr. in field; state advisor N.J. Health Occupations Am. Recipient Golden Apple award Edn., Info. & Resource Ctr., Sewell, 1991. Mem. ANA, Am. Acad. Pediatrics (affiliate sect. sch. health), Am. fedn. Tchrs., Gloucester County Sch. Nurse Assn. (pres. 1983-85), Phi Delta Kappa (Zeta Nu chpt. v.p. membership 1993-96, historian 1996—, Outstanding Leadership award 1984). Avocations: traveling, reading, arts and crafts. Home: 44 Bryant Rd Turnersville NJ 08012-1447

CAMMISA, FRANK P., JR., surgeon, educator; b. Waterbury, Conn., Jan. 18, 1956; m. Gail McGovern; children: Anne Katherine, Frank P. III, John Patrick. BS summa cum laude, Tufts U., 1978; MD, Columbia U., 1982. Diplomate Nat. Bd. Med. Examiners, Am. Bd. Orthopaedic Surgery. Resident in gen. surgery The Presbyn. Hosp., Columbia-Presbyn. Med. Ctr., N.Y.C., 1982-83; resident in orthopaedic surgery The Hosp. for Spl. Surgery, N.Y.C., 1983-87; fellow in spinal surgery U. Miami (Fla.)-Jackson Meml. Med. Ctr., 1987-88; asst. scientist rsch. divsn. The Hosp. for Spl. Surgery, N.Y.C., 1988-99, asst. attending surgeon, 1988-99, chief spine svc., 1995—, assoc. scientist rsch. divsn., assoc. attending surgeon, 2000—, dir. spine care Inst., 1999—. Vis. clin. fellow surgery Coll. of Physicians and Surgeons, Columbia U., N.Y.C., 1982-83; clin. assoc. surgery Cornell U. Med. Coll., N.Y.C., 1983-87, instr. orthopaedic surgery, 1988-89, asst. prof. orthopaedic surgery, 1990-99, assoc. prof. clin. orthopaedic surgery, 2000—; attending surgeon VA Hosp., Miami, 1987-88; asst. attending surgeon The N.Y. Hosp., N.Y.C., 1988-99; attending surgeon spinal cord injury svc. Burke Rehab. Ctr., White Plains, N.Y., 1988—; attending surgeon VA Hosp., Bronx, N.Y., 1988—; assoc. attending surgeon N.Y. Presbyn. Hosp., 2000—; presenter in field; cons. Meml. Sloan Kettering Cancer Ctr., N.Y.C., 1988—; spinal cons. St. John's U. Athletic Teams, 1988—, N.Y. Knights World League of Am. Football, 1991-92, Phoenix Alliance, 1993, N.Y. Racing Assn., 1993. Editorial bd.: Orthopaedic Product News, 1990-91; contbr. chpts. to books and articles to profl. jours. Grantee The Hosp. for Spl. Surgery, 1986, Acromed Corp., 1988, Orthopaedic Rsch. and Edn. Found., 1991-92; recipient Harvard Book prize Harvard Club So. Conn., 1974, Tufts Psychology Soc. Rsch. award Tufts U., 1978, Resident award N.Y. Acad. Medicine, Sect. Orthopaedic Surgery, 1986, 87, Lewis Clark Wagner award Hosp. for Spl. Surgery, N.Y.C., 1986; N.Am. Traveling fellowship Am. Orthopaedic Assn., 1989; Ofcl. citation Gen. Assembly State of Conn., 1992. Mem. ACS, ACP, Am. Acad. Orthopaedic Surgeons, Internat. Coll. Surgeons, Am. Coll. Spine Surgery; mem. AMA, N.Am. Spine Soc., Am. Spinal Injury Assn., Internat. Soc. for Study of Lumbar Spine, Cervical Spine Rsch. Soc., Scoliosis Rsch. Soc., Med. Soc. State N.Y., N.Y. State Soc. Orthop. Surgeons, N.Y. County Med. Soc., Alumni Assn. The Hosp. for Spl. Surgery, Assn. of the Alumni, Coll. Physicians and Surgeons, Columbia U., The Irish-Am. Orthop. Soc., Ea. Orthop. Assn. (Fellow scholar award 1988, Spinal Rsch. award 1989), Groupe Internat. Cotrel-Dubousset, N.Y. Athletic Club, Winged Foot Golf Club, Phi Beta Kappa, Psi Chi, Alpha Omega Alpha, Delta Tau Delta. Office: Hosp for Spl Surgery 535 E 70th St New York NY 10021-4898

CAMP, ROGER ORTHO, fine arts educator, artist, photographer; b. Colfax, Wash., Feb. 19, 1945; s. Ortho O. and Helen E. (Minnassian) C.; m. Susan E. Lee-Warren, Dec. 22, 1982; children: Jason Hibbs, Ashley Hibbs. BA, U. Calif., Goleta, 1967; MA, U. Tex., 1968, U. Iowa, 1973, MFA, 1974. Instr. Ea. Ill. U., Charleston, 1968-69; asst. prof. Columbus (Ohio) Coll. Art and Design, 1974-76; prof. Golden West Coll., Huntington Beach, Calif., 1977-95, chair dept. fine arts, 1996—. Contract photographer Black Star, N.Y.C., 1987—, Graphistock, N.Y.C., 1995—; artist Yancey Richardson Gallery, N.Y.C., 1990—. Photographer: Swimmers, 1988, Graphis Photo 94, 1994, Exploring Color Photography, 1995, At The Water's Edge,

1995, Shoreline: The Camera, 1996; photographer, designer Butterflies in Flight, 2002. Guest curator Huntington Beach Art Ctr., 1995; mem. Friends of South Coast Repertory, Costa Mesa, Calif., 1980—; assoc. Performing Arts Ctr., Costa Mesa, 1990. Named Artist of Yr., City of Huntington Beach, 1992; recipient Leica medal of Excellence, Leitz/New Sch., N.Y.C., 1989, Best Sports Photograph award Agfa/Graphis, 1995; Fulbright Hays fellow Fulbright Found., Brazil, 1988, Richard Florsheim fellow Fine Arts Work Ctr., Provincetown, 1982-83. Mem. Soc. Photographic Educators. Avocations: travel, gardening. Office: Golden West Coll 15744 Golden West St Huntington Beach CA 92647

CAMPAGNA, TIMOTHY NICHOLAS, institute executive; b. Chgo., June 8, 1957; s. Nicholas and Dorothy (Hoffmeister) C.; m. Diana Lynn Czarny, Aug. 1, 1981; children: Maria, Joseph. BA, Lewis U., Romeoville, Ill., 1980, MA, 1985. Basketball referee NCAA and Ill. High Sch. Assn., 1976-95; asst. dir. housing Lewis U., 1978-80; tchr. Fairmont Jr. High Sch., Lockport, Ill., 1979-80; tchr., therapist Guardian Angel Home, Joliet, Ill., 1980-82; assoc. dean students DeVry Inst. Tech., Lombard, Ill., 1982-84, dean students, 1984-87, dean adminstrv. svcs. Irving, Tex., 1987-93, dean evening coll., dir. Ctr. Bus. and Industry Ednl. Svcs., 1993-95, dean enrollment mgmt. and mktg., 1994-95; v.p. Am. Inst. Commerce, Davenport, Iowa, 1995-97; pres. Westwood Coll. Tech., 1997-2000, Denver Tech. Coll., 2000-01, DeVry U., 2001—. Mem. sch. bd. Holy Family Nazareth; mem. nominating bd. Outstanding Men and women of Am. Coach Nativity of Our Lord Basketball Team, Hyland Hills Youth Hockey Team, St. Louis 2001 Planning Com.; vol. YMCA. Named Tchr. of Yr., Fairmont Jr. High Sch., 1980, Adminstr. of Yr., DeVry Inst. Tech., 1984. Mem. Nat. Assn. Student Pers. Adminstrs., Am. Assn. Coll. Registrars and Admissions Officers, Nat. Assn. Fgn. Student Advisors, Nat. Assn. Coll. and Univ. Bus. Officers, Denver C. of C., CEO Network. Roman Catholic. Avocations: golf, travel. Office: DeVry Univ 1870 W 122d Ave Westminster CO 80234 E-mail: tcamp@rmi.net., tcampagna@den.devry.edu.

CAMPANA, PHILLIP JOSEPH, German language educator; b. Jersey City, Apr. 10, 1941; s. Ralph Joseph and Alberta Alphonsine (Lepis) C.; m. Paulette Monique Beauregard, Apr. 20, 1968 (div. Apr. 19, 1978); children: Lisa Marie, Michael Phillip. BA in German magna cum laude, St. Peters Coll., Jersey City, 1962; postgrad. (Fulbright scholar), U. Saarbrücken, Germany, 1962-63; PhD, Brown U., 1970. Instr. German St. Peter's Coll., Jersey City, summer 1964; grad. asst. in German Brown U., Providence, 1965-67; assoc. prof. German Tenn. Tech. U., Cookeville, 1970-74, prof. German, 1974—, chmn. dept. fgn. langs., 1970—2003, founder and 1st dir. English Lang. Inst., 1977, dir. Interactive Videodisc Project, 1984-94. State chmn. So. Conf. on Lang. Tchg., 1981-85; reviewer grant proposals (EESA, Title II) Tex. Coord. Bd. for Higher Edn., 1986, U.S. Dept. Edn., 1987; evaluator Nat. Tchrs. Exam in German for Ednl. testing Svc., 1990; lectr., presenter in field. Assoc. editor Schatzkammer, 1980-89, cons. editor, 1990-93, editl. bd., 1993—; evaluator: the materials Ctr. of Am. Assn. Tchrs. German, 1980-81, Modern Lang. Jour., Fgn. Lang. Annals, Seminar; mem. editl. bd. Unterrichtspraxis, 2000—; book rev. editor Unterrichtspraxis, 2002—; contbr. numerous articles and revs. to profl. jours. Mem. faculty adv. group on master plan for higher edn. Tenn. Higher Edn. Comm., 1973, steering com. on tchr. edn., 1983-84; chmn. Tenn. Bd. Regents Task Force on Improvement of Quality in Tchr. Edn., 1982; mem. Com. on Bus. and Fiscal Affairs, Tenn. Bd. Regents, 1975-76. Recipient Outstanding Faculty award in Tchg., Tenn. Tech. U., 1976, Goethe-Inst. award, 1977, 84, 99, Nat. Endowment for the Humanities, 1981, Meritorious Svc. award Nat. Coun. State Suprs. of Fgn. Langs., 1981, Svc. award Rural Educators Alliance for Lang., 1993, Outstanding Faculty award for Profl. Svcs., Tenn. Tech. U., 1995; Fulbright scholar, 1962-63, 80, 88; Woodrow Wilson fellow, 1962-64, NDEA fellow, 1963-66; grantee Tenn. Tech., 1984, 86-87, 87-88, 88-89, Govt. of Germany, 1983, Tenn. Higher Edn. Commn., 1986-87, 88, 89, 97, 98, 99, Tenn. Bd. Regents, 1989, Tenn. Humanities Coun., 1990. Mem. AAUP, MLA, Am. Assn. Tchrs. German (Tenn. chpt. pres. 1975-77, treas. 1980-92, cert. of Merit award 1982), Tenn. Fgn. Lang. Tchg. Assn. (bd. dirs. 1974-77, 80-81, 82-85, 98-2001, pres. 1977-80, mem. com. 1990-96, rep. Ctrl. States Conf. bd. 1990-93, Jacqueline C. Elliott award 1984), Ctrl. States Conf. on Tchg. Fgn. Langs. (chmn. 1984-87, bd. dirs. 1979-80, 81-84, 91-94, adv. coun. 1978—, co-editor annual volume 1995, co-chair Leadership CSC, 1995-96), Am. Coun. on Tchg. Fgn. Langs. (exec. coun. 1985-86, 91-94, chmn. pub. com. 1993-94, Florence Steiner award 1987), Tenn. Fgn. Lang. Inst. (bd. govs. 1986-2001, v.p., sec.-treas.), Tenn. Coun. Internat. Edn. (bd. dirs. 1976-78), Ill. Fgn. Lang. Tchrs. Assn. (mem. adv. bd. 1986-88, nominating com. 1987-88, Land of Lincoln Svc. award 1986, 87), Consortium for German in S.E. (founding mem., treas. 1991-96), Omicron Delta Kappa. Roman Catholic. Home: 1135 Meadow Rd Cookeville TN 38501-2035 Office: Tenn Tech U Dept Fgn Langs PO Box 5061 Cookeville TN 38505-0001 E-mail: pcampana@tntech.edu.

CAMPANY, SARAH WILSON, special education educator; b. Morganton, N.C., July 27, 1932; d. George Moran and Ruth Josephine (Franklin) Wilson; m. Howard Gene Whitley, Sept. 5, 1952 (div. 1963); children: Myron Gene, Howard Moran; m. Hiram Lee Roberts, Sept. 25, 1982 (dec. 1991); m. A.N. Campany, Nov. 20, 1992. BS in Psychology, Catawba Coll., 1953; MS in Deaf Edn., Appalachian State U., 1959, MA in Spl. Edn., 1967. Cert. tchr., N.C., Miss. Tchr. Fayetteville (N.C.) Ctr. for Handicapped, 1953-56; tchr., tchr. trainer N.C. Sch. for the Deaf, Morganton, 1956-63; prin. Western Carolina Ctr., Morganton, 1963-70; dir. edn. Western Correction Ctr., Morganton, 1970-73; edn. specialist West Tenn. Sch. for Deaf, Jackson, 1973-83; tchr. Sherard Sch., Coahoma County, Miss., 1990—. Instr. Delta State U., Cleveland, Miss., 1990—; mem. Adv. Coun. for Hearing Impaired;vol. tchr. children's sign lang. workshop Bolivar County Pub. Libr., 1982-90; speaker at civic orgns. Contbr. articles to profl. publs. Mem. Nat. Assn. of Deaf, Coun. Exceptional Children, Alexander Graham Bell Assn. for Deaf, Tenn. Edn. Assn., Tenn. Speech and Hearing Assn., West Tenn. Coun. Exceptional Children, Tenn. Assn. for Deaf, Tenn. Registry of Interpreters for the Deaf (Jackson Area subdiv.), Conv. Am. Instrs. of Deaf, Conf. Execs. of Am. Schs. for Deaf, Coun. on Edn. of Deaf, Alpha Delta Kappa. Methodist. Avocations: reading, knitting, walking, quilting, crafts. Home: PO Box 990 Shelby MS 38774-0990

CAMPASINO, ELLEN MARIE, elementary school educator; b. Titusville, Pa., Aug. 30, 1950; d. Frank and Helen (Lowicki) Campasino. BS in Elem. and Early Childhood Edn., Edinboro U., 1972, cert. in elem. and early childhood edn., 1978. 1st grade tchr. St. Titus Sch., Titusville, 1975-76, 4th grade tchr., 1976-77, 3rd grade tchr., 1977—. Coaching tchr. St. Titus Tchr. Induction Program, Titusville, 1989—90, asst. to prin., 1993—; mentor tchr., 2000—01. Mem. ministry tng. program Diocese of Erie; min. hospitality St. Walburga Parish, Roman Cath. Ch., Titusville. Recipient Svc. award, Diocese of Erie, 1988, 1990, 1996, 25 Yrs. of Svc. award, 2000—01. Avocations: reading, doll collecting, embroidery. Office: St Titus Sch 528 W Main St Titusville PA 16354-1598

CAMPBELL, ABE WILLIAM, music educator; b. St. Louis, Jan. 22, 1950; s. Thomas Edward and Dorothy Caroline (Strauss) C.; m. Joanne Marie Hutchinson, June 19, 1971; children: Bob, Amy, Anne, Molly. B of Music Edn., So. Ill. U., 1972. Dir. band & choir Mercy High Sch., St. Louis, 1972-76, Pattonville R-3 Dist., St. Louis, 1976-80; tchr. music, social studies Immaculate Heart of Mary, St. Louis, 1981-83, Little Flower Sch., St. Louis, 1983-86; tchr. St. Louis Prep Sem., 1986-87; tchr. 6th grade Our Lady Lourdes, St. Louis, 1987-88; substance abuse counselor St. Clare Hosp., Alton, Ill., 1988-91; tchr. music St. Gregory Sch., St. Louis, 1991—96, asst. prin., 1993—96, JFK H.S., 1996—97, St. Thomas Aquinas-Mercy H.S., 1997—. Mem. sch. bd. Little Flower Cath. Sch., St. Louis, 1981-83; mem. parish coun. Little Flower Ch., St. Louis, 1987-90. Mem. NAt. Cath. Edn. Assn., Nat. Mid. Sch. Assn., Music Educators Nat. Conf. Roman Catholic. Avocations: acting, gardening, bowling. Home: 1131 Ralph Ter Richmond Heights MO 63117-1528

CAMPBELL, ALLAN MCCULLOCH, bacteriology educator; b. Berkeley, Calif., Apr. 27, 1929; s. Lindsay and Virginia Margaret (Henning) C.; m. Alice Del Campillo, Sept. 5, 1958; children— Wendy, Joseph. BS in Chemistry, U. Calif. at Berkeley, 1950; MS in Bacteriology, U. Ill., 1951; PhD, 1953; PhD hon. degree, U. Chgo., 1978, U. Rochester, 1981. Instr. bacteriology U. Mich., 1953-57; research asso. Carnegie Inst., Cold Spring Harbor, N.Y., 1957-58; asst. prof. biology U. Rochester, N.Y., 1958-61, assoc. prof., 1961-63, prof., 1963-68; prof. biol. sci. Stanford (Calif.) U., 1968—, Barbara Kimball Browning prof. humanities and scis., 1992—. Author: Episomes, 1969; co-author: General Virology, 1978; editor Gene, 1980-90, mem. editl. bd., 1990—; assoc. editor Virology, 1963-69; assoc. editor Ann. Rev. Genetics, 1969-84, editor, 1984—; spl. editor Evolution, 1985-88; editl. bd. Jour. Bacteriology, 1966-72, Jour. Virology, 1967-75, New Biologist, 1989-92. Served with AUS, 1953-55. Recipient Research Career award USPHS, 1962-68 Mem. Nat. Acad. Scis., Am. Acad. Arts and Scis., Am. Soc. Microbiology, Soc. Am. Naturalists, Genetics Soc. Am., AAAS, Am. Acad. Microbiology. Democrat. Home: 947 Mears Ct Stanford CA 94305-1041 Office: Stanford U Dept Biol Scis Stanford CA 94305 E-mail: AMC@stanford.edu.

CAMPBELL, ALMA JACQUELINE PORTER, elementary education educator; b. Savannah, Ga., Jan. 5, 1948; d. William W. and Gladys B. Porter. BS in Elem. Edn., Savannah State Coll., 1969; MEd, SUNY, Brockport, 1971, cert. advanced study in adminstrn. magna cum laude, 1988. Cert. permanent elem. tchr., N.Y. Elem. tchr., Savannah, 1969-70, 71-74; tchr. intern project unique Rochester (N.Y.) City Sch. Dist., 1970-71, tchr., 1974-88, adminstrv. intern chpt. 1 office, 1988; mem. student progress task force, 1994; mem. coun. elem. leadership, mem. instrnl. com.; basic skills cadre Francis Parker Sch., Rochester, 1988—, lead tchr. mentor, 1991—; lead tchr., mentor tchr., basic skills cadre John Walton Spencer Elem. Sch. No. 16, 1992—; vice prin. Theodore Roosevelt Sch # 43, 1993-94, prin., 1994-99; apptd. mem. Profl. Devel. Acad. Adv. Bd., 1999. Demonstration tchr., 1987-88; active Effective Parenting Info. and Children program, 1987-89; active coop. tchr. program Nazareth Coll. and Rochester City Sch. Dist., 1987; mem. policy bd. Rochester Tchr. Ctr., 1994, adminstrv. rep. to policy bd., 1995-97; adv. com. N.Y. State Systemic Iniative, 1994, sch. quality reviewer; coord., presenter ednl. workshops; apptd. mem. Student Progress Task Force, 1995; asst. WXXI Broadcasting Partnership and Sch. Number 43; coord. Sch. Quality Rev. Initiative, 1996-97; establisher partnership with Urban Schs. Inst. in conjunction with U. Rochester, 1996-97; mem. Supt. Janey's Profl. Devel. Focus Group, 1997; apptd. vis. practitioner Prin.'s Ctr. Harvard U., 2000; mem. Oxford Round Table, St. Anthony's Coll. Author: (with McGriff) Quick Reference Manual for Teachers, 1989-90; co-author: A Quick Reference Manual for Teachers and Absolutely Jam-Packed With Super Teaching Tips, 1991-92. Mem. Martin Luther King Commn. on Edn., Rochester, 1988-89, Francis Parker Sch. PTA, 1988—; mental health asst. Curriculum Task Force, Rochester City Sch. Dist., 1991, coop. learning tchr., trainer, 1990, 91-92; asst. dir. Meml. A.M.E. Zion Ch., 1979-82, dir. summer camp, 1982-85, asst. sec. bd. Christian edn., 1987-89; bd. dirs. Hamm House, Jefferson Area Child Devel. Ctr., 1990-91; active United Way; mem steering com. African Am. Devel. Program. Mem. ASCD (assoc.), NAFE (sub-adv. com. Strong Mus. sch. programs), Am. Assn. Sch. Adminstrs., Internat. Reading Assn., Rochester Coun. Elem. Leadership, Phi Delta Kappa (treas. 1996-97), Alpha Kappa Alpha (chair nominating com. 1988-89, Ivy Leaf reporter 1992—, Cert. of Achievement 1988). Democrat. Avocations: reading, travel, collecting mugs, visiting amusement parks. Home: 40 Menlo Pl Rochester NY 14620-2718 also: Meml AME Zion Ch Clarissa St Rochester NY 14604 Office: Theodore Rossevelt Sch 1305 Lyell Ave Rochester NY 14606-2119 also: Harvard U 536 Leverett House Mail Ctr 28 De Wolfe St Cambridge MA 02138 E-mail: ACampbel43@netscape.net.

CAMPBELL, CATHERINE LYNN, elementary school educator; b. Lynchburg, Va., Mar. 16, 1961; d. Tomie Eawell Campbell and Barbara (Arthur) McCraw. BA, Sweet Briar Coll., 1983; MEd in Adminstrv. and Supervision, U. Va., 2003. Cert. elem. tchr., NK-8 tchr. VA. Tchr. Amherst (Va.) County Pub. Schs., 1984—. Mem. Va. Real Estate Bd. Common Interest Properties. Mem.: ASCD, Va. Edn. Assn., NEA, Nat. Honor Soc. Avocations: horseback riding, raising quarter horses. Home: 139 Cedar Crest Dr Ste 107 Madison Heights VA 24572-2366 Office: Amherst County Pub Schs Amherst VA 24521

CAMPBELL, DAVID NEIL, physician, educator; b. Peoria, Ill., Dec. 1, 1944; s. William Neil and Lillian May (Hunter) C.; m. Charlyn Harris, Nov. 16, 1968; children: Scott, Chris, Brad. BA, Northwestern U., 1966; MD, Rush Med. Sch., 1974. Resident in gen. and cardiothoracic surgery U. Colo. Health Sci. Ctr., Denver, from asst. prof. to prof. surgery, 1988-95, prof. surgery, 1995—. Cons., Denver, Colo., 1986—. Lt. U.S. Army, 1966-67, Korea. Office: U Colo Health Sci Ctr 4200 E 9th Ave # C310 Denver CO 80220-3706

CAMPBELL, EDWARD FAY, JR., religion educator; b. New Haven, Jan. 5, 1932; s. Edward Fay and Edith (May) C.; m. Phyllis Kletzien, Sept. 4, 1954; children: Thomas Edward, Sarah Ives. BA, Yale U., 1953; BD, McCormick Theol. Sem., 1956; PhD, Johns Hopkins U., 1959. Ordained to ministry Presbyn. Ch., 1956. Asst. pastor 1st Presbyn. Ch., Balt., 1956-58; from instr. to Francis McGaw prof. McCormick Theol. Sem., Chgo., 1958-97, prof. emeritus, 1997; parish asssoc. Lake View Presbyn. Ch., Chgo., 1997—2001. Mem.-at-large ch. and soc. com. Chgo. Presbytery, 1987-96; dir., coord. archeological expedition to Tell Balatah/Shechem, Palestine, 1966—; bd. trustees Maine Coun. Chs., 2001—; mem. Protestants for the Common Good, Ill., 1997—. Author: The Chronology of the Amarna Letters, 1964, Anchor Bible: Ruth, 1975, Shechem II: Profile of a Hill Country Vale, 1991, Shechem III: Stratigraphy and Architecture, 2002; (with others) Harper Bible Dictionary, The Oxford Companion to the Bible, 1993, The New Encyclopedia of Archaeological Excavations in the Holy Land, 1993, The Oxford History of the Biblical World, 1998; co-editor: (with David Freedman) Biblical Archaeologist Reader 2, 3, 4; contbr. articles and revs. to profl. jours. Bd. trustees Maine Coun. Chs., 2002—. Am. Coun. Learned Socs. fellow, 1972-73. Mem. Cath. Bible Assn., Soc. Bibl. Lit. (sr. editor monograph series 1989-93), Am. Sch. Oriental Rsch. (trustee 1972-82, 95-98, v.p. 1973-81, Ann. Prof. 1964-65). Democrat. Home: Apt J322 15 Piper Rd Scarborough ME 04074-7546

CAMPBELL, ELAINE JOSEPHINE, retired educational director, writer, critic, educator; b. Phila., Pa., Aug. 6, 1932; d. William Maxwell and Anna Marie (Roller) Bauer; m. John Bruce Campbell, Dec. 21, 1957; children: Jennifer Ann, Rebecca Ellen, Sabrina Frances. BA with maj. honors (Univ. scholar), U. Pa., 1954; MA, Simmons Coll., 1973; PhD (Univ. scholar), Brandeis U., 1981; MEd, Boston U., 1993. Tchg. fellow dept. English and Am. lit. Brandeis U., 1974-80; lectr. English Regis Coll., Weston, Mass., 1980-81, asst. prof. English, dir. freshman writing program, 1981-84; writer-editor The MITRE Corp., Bedford, Mass., 1984-86; lectr. in writing MIT, Cambridge, 1986—2001, ret., 2001; staff devel. specialist MITRE Inst., 1986-88, inst. affairs staff, 1988-91, dir. spl. programs, 1992-94; ptnr. Campbell Consulting, 1995-98; lectr. Port Enrichment Celebrity Cruises, 1995—. Author: ESL Resourcebook for Engineers and Scientists, 1995, (introduction) The Orchid House (P. Allfrey), 1982; editor: The Whistling Bird: Writing by Caribbean Women, 1998; contbr.; Studies in Modern Commonwealth Literature, Subjects Worthy Fame, Fifty Caribbean Writers, Studies in Commonwealth Literature, A Double Colonization: Colonial and Post-Colonial Women's Writing, Dictionary of Literary Biography; book reviewer World Literature Written in English, Kunapipi; contbr. articles, revs., reports to profl. jours., US, Can., Jamaica, Denmark, India, Eng., S.Am.; panelist at profl. meetings, convs. Mem. MLA, Caribbean Studies Assn., European Assn. Commonwealth Lit. and Lang. Studies, Assn. Caribbean Women Writers and Scholars, Kappa Delta, Pi Lambda Theta. Home: 63 Puritan Ln Sudbury MA 01776-2424 also: PO Box 1703 Cruz Bay VI 00831-1703

CAMPBELL, JILL FROST, university official; b. Buffalo, July 29, 1948; d. Jack and Elaine Mary (Hamilton) Frost; m. Gregory H. Campbell, May 31, 1969; children: Geoffrey, Kimberly, Kristina. BS, SUNY, Brockport, 1970, MSED, 1981; PhD, U. Buffalo, 1997. From acct. clk. bursar's office to asst. v.p. SUNY, Brockport, 1974—2003, asst. v.p. student affairs, 2003—. Chmn. web redesign com. SUNY, Brockport; mem. enrollment ops. group SUNY, Brockport, 1997-99, mem. metroctr. com. for student svcs., 1997-98, chair campus com. on profls.' roles and rewards, 1997-98, campus jud. officer, 1997-99, mem. coll. rev. panel, 1995—, coll. com. profl. evaluation, 1995—, strategic planning com., 1995-97, mem. retention com., 1998—, mem. presdl. scholars com., 1998-99, mem. strategic planning implementation com. on retention, 1999-2000, mem. strategic planning implementation com. on systemic change, 1999-2000, mem. alumni follow-up survey adv. com., 1999-2000, coord. alumni placement survey, 2000-, mem. transfer articulation group, 1999—, mem. acad. advisement task force, 2000-01, mem. enrollment mgmt. divsn. budget rev. com., 2000, chmn. alumni survey consulting group, 2000-02, mem. coll. tech. coun., 2003-. Mem. exec. com. Nativity Home Sch. Assn., Nativity Blessed Virgin Sch., Brockport, 1985-87, mem. sch. pub. rels. and mktg. com., 1985-88, mem. ch. festival com., 2001—; mem. Friends of Brockport Athletics, 1985-2000; coach Brockport Youth Summer Soccer, 1988-91; host family Assn. for Teen-Age Diplomats, 1995-96; mem. com. Chancellor's Award for Excellence in Profl. Svc., Brockport, 1989-90; liaison Brockport Child Care Ctr., 1995-96. Grantee United Univ. Professions, 1985, 90, 93, 94, 2000, 01. Mem. NAFE, Nat. Assn. Instl. Rsch. (mem. exec. com., co-originator and discussion leader books and current issues 1985-87, co-author profl. file, presenter papers, presenter panels 1979-87), SUNY Assn. Instl. Rsch. and Planning Officers (mem. exec. com., presenter papers, presenter panels 1984-87), North East Assn. Instl. Rsch. (mem. exec. com., sec. 1985-87, presenter papers, presenter panels 1978-87), Nat. Coun. Univ. Rsch. Adminstrs., Internat. Conf. for Women in Higher Edn. (presenter 1992), SUNY Brockport Alumni Assn., Brockport Profl. Women's Group, Rsch. Found. Cen. Office (users group 1987-90, sponsored program comm. com. 1990-97, 4-yr. rsch. coun. 1988-93, vice chmn. 1991, chmn. 1992, univ. colls. rsch. coun. 1993-97), N.Y. State Transfer Articulation Assn. (presenter 1998, 2003, mem. conf. com. 2001-03, nominations com., 2001-02, registration 2001-03), N.Y. State/United Univ. Professions (Excellence award 1990, 2003). Home: 5129 Redman Rd Brockport NY 14420-9601 Office: SUNY Brockport Seymour 224 350 New Campus Dr Brockport NY 14420

CAMPBELL, JOHN ROY, animal science educator, academic administrator; b. Goodman, Mo., June 14, 1933; s. Carl J. and Helen (Nicoletti) C.; m. Eunice Vieten, Aug. 7, 1954; children: Karen L., Kathy L., Keith L. BS, U. Mo., 1955; MS, U. Mo., Columbia, 1956, PhD, 1960. Instr. dairy sci. U. Mo., Columbia, 1960-61, asst. prof., 1961-65, assoc. prof., 1965-68, prof., from 1968; assoc. dean, dir. resident instrn. Coll. Agr. U. Ill., Urbana-Champaign, 1977-83, dean Coll. Agr. Urbana, 1983-88; pres. Okla. State U., Stillwater, 1988-93. Author (with J.F. Lasley): The Science of Animals That Serve Humanity, 1969, The Science of Animals That Serve Humanity, 3d edit., 1985; author: In Touch with Students, 1972; author: (with R.T. Marshall) The Science of Providing Milk for Man, 1975; author: Reclaiming A Lost Heritage...Land-Grant and Other Higher Education Initiatives for the Twenty-First Century, 1985, Dry Rot in the Ivory Tower, 2000; author: (with M.D. Kenealy and K.L. Campbell) Animal Sciences...The Biology, Care and Production of Domestic Animals, 2002. Recipient Superior Tchg. award Gamma Sigma Delta, 1967, Internat. award for disting. svc. to agr., 1985, Disting. Svc. award Coll. Osteo. Medicine Okla. State U., 1992. Fellow Am. Dairy Sci. Assn. (dir. 1975-78, 80-86, pres. 1980-81, Ralston Purina Disting. Tchg. award 1973, Award of Honor 1987); mem. Nat. Assn. Coll. Tchrs. Agr. (Ensminger Interstate Disting. Tchr. award 1973, Teaching fellow 1973, Disting. Educator award 1990, Nat. Assn. State and Univ. and Land-Grant Colls. (commns. on home econs. and vet. medicine, com. on water resources, coun. of presidents), Okla. Futures, Gamma Sigma Delta. Office: Okla State U 201AS Stillwater OK 74078-0001 Personal E-mail: jcampbell.author.educator@mchsi.com. Business E-Mail: bale@okstate.edu.

CAMPBELL, JOHN YOUNG, economics educator; b. London, May 17, 1958; came to U.S., 1979; s. Alexander Elmslie and Sophia Anne (Sonne) C.; m. Susanna Peyton, Apr. 28, 1984; children: Graham, Malcolm, Naomi, Sophia. BA, Oxford (Eng.) U., 1979; PhD, Yale U., 1984. Asst. prof. econs. Woodrow Wilson Sch. Princeton (N.J.) U., 1984-89, prof. econs. and pub. affairs Woodrow Wilson Sch., 1989-94; Otto Eckstein prof. applied econs. Harvard U., Cambridge, Mass., 1994—; mng. ptnr. Arrowstreet Capital, LP. Contbr. articles to profl. jours. NSF grantee, 1988; Alfred P. Sloan rsch. fellow, 1989. Fellow Am. Acad. Arts and Scis.; mem. Am. Econ. Assn., Am. Fin. Assn., Econometric Soc. Avocation: choral singing. Office: Harvard U Dept Econs Littauer Ctr 213 Cambridge MA 02138

CAMPBELL, KATHLEEN CHARLOTTE MURPHEY, audiology educator, administrator, researcher; b. Sioux Falls, S.D., Mar. 20, 1952; d. Chester Humphrey and Ruth Maxine (Thompson) Murphey; m. Craig Anthony Campbell, Nov. 15, 1975. BA, S.D. State U., 1973; MA, U. S.D., 1977; PhD, U. Iowa, 1989. Cert. audiologist. Clin. grad. asst. dept. communication U. S.D., Vermillion, 1976-77; regional audiologist II British Columbia Ministry Health, Cranbrook, 1977-82; audiologist II dept. otolaryngology head and neck U. Iowa, Iowa City, 1983-88, rsch. asst. dept. speech, pathology and audiology, 1985; doctoral fellow Health Svcs. R&D, VA, Iowa City, 1987-88; prof. div. otolaryngology dept. surgery So. Ill. U. Sch. Medicine, 1989—, prof., 1996—. Cons. Packer Engring., Naperville, Ill., 1992—. Editorial cons. Am. Jour. Audiology, 1992; reviewer Annals of Otolaryngology, 1992; contbr. articles to profl. jours. Mem. Midamerica Playwrights Theatre, Springfield, Ill., 1989—, Sierra Club, Springfield, 1989—. Recipient Clin. Investigator Devel. Award grant NIH, 1990, Small Bus. Innovative Rsch. grant NIH, 1990, Ctrl. Rsch. Coun. grant So. Ill. U., 1991, Children's Miracle Network award So. Ill. U., 1991, 92, Alzheimer Disease Ctr. grant So. Ill. U. Sch. Medicine, 1992, James A. Shannon Dir.'s award NIH, 1997-99. Mem. Am. Speech-Lang.-Hearing Assn., Am. Acad. Audiology, Assn. Rsch. in Otolaryngology, Am. Acad. Otolaryngology-Head/Neck Surgery (assoc.), Mensa. Achievements include development of of a device for treatment of Meniere's disease; research in in electrocochleography and perilymphatic fistual; patents for for otoprotective agents for ototoxicity. Office: SIU Sch Medicine PO Box 19629 Springfield IL 62794-9629

CAMPBELL, LINZY LEON, molecular biology researcher, educator; b. Panhandle, Tex., Feb. 10, 1927; s. Linzy Leon and Eula Irene (McSpadden) C.; m. Alice P. Dauksa, Feb. 7, 1953. BA in Bacteriology and Chemistry, U. Tex., 1949, MA, 1950, PhD, 1952. Rsch. scientist U. Tex., 1947-51; predoctoral rsch. fellow NIH, 1951-52; postdoctoral rsch. fellow Nat. Microbiol. Inst., U. Calif. at Berkeley, 1952-54; asst. prof., then assoc. prof. Wash. State U., 1954-59; assoc. prof. Western Res. U. Sch. Medicine, 1959-62; sr. rsch. fellow USPHS, 1959-62; prof. microbiology U. Ill. at Urbana, 1962-72, head dept., 1963-71, dir. Sch. Life Scis., 1971-72; prof. microbiology, provost and v.p. acad. affairs U. Del., Newark, 1972-88, univ. rsch. prof. molecular bioscis., 1988-89, Hugh M. Morris rsch. prof. molecular bioscis., 1989—. Editorial bd.: Jour. Bacteriology, 1961-65; editor, 1964-65, editor-in-chief, 1965-77; Contbr. articles to profl. jours. Served with USNR, 1944-46. Fellow AAAS; mem. Am. Soc. Microbiology (chmn. publ. bd. 1965-80, councilor at large 1962-64, v.p. 1972-73, pres. 1973-74), Am. Soc. Biochemistry and Molecular Biology. Office: U Delaware Dept Biology 400 Morris Library Newark DE 19717 E-mail: campbell@udel.edu.

CAMPBELL, SISTER MAURA, religious studies and philosophy educator; b. Bayonne, N.J. d. Patrick John and Helena Marie (Collins) C. BS, Seton Hall U., 1940, MA, 1945, Providence Coll., 1953, D in Religious Edn. (hon.), 1985; PhD, St. Mary's Sch. Theology, Notre Dame, Ind., 1955; postgrad., Marquette U., Ottawa U., 1969, Cath. U. Am., 1970-71. Joined Dominican Order, Roman Cath. Ch., 1927. Tchr. elem. and secondary schs., 1930-42; dir. postulants Mt. St. Dominic, Caldwell, NJ, 1955-59, dir. scholastics, 1959-69; mem. faculty Caldwell Coll., 1955—, prof. religious studies, 1957-86, prof. emerita, 1986—, chmn. dept., 1969—89, pres. faculty counsel, 1986-89. Permanent rep. internat. Cath. edn. office UN Non-Govtl. Orgns., 1969—; cons. Thomas Edison State Coll., 1962-2002; v.p. internat. Cath. orgns. N.Y. Info. Ctr., 1978, pres., 1987-90; permanent rep. World Assembly Internat. Cath. Edn. Office, Bangkok, 1982; participant Women's Forum, Nairobi, Kenya, 1985, Mexico City, 1986, Madrid, 1993, Rome, 1994; participant World Congress of Office of Cath. Internat. Edn., Rome, 1994; del. Fourth Internat. UN Conf. Women, Beijing, 1995; Roman Catholic rep. World Coun. Religions, 1986-88. Mem. editl. bd. The Cath. Adv. Mem. Ecumenical/Interfaith Commn. Archdiocese of Newark, 1986-90; elected mem. exec. bd. Non-Govtl. Orgn./Dept. Pub. Info. at UN, 1988-90. Recipient Recognition award for outstanding achievement in higher edn. State of N.J., 1989, Jubilee medal Archdiocese of Newark, 1994, Disting. Svc. award Sacred Heart Inst., 1994, Peace Initiative award First Dominican Sisters, 1995, Jubilee Medal Pro Meritis, Archdiocese of Newark, 1995, Office of Cath. Internat. Edn. award for representation at UN, 1998, Redemptors Mater award 1999, Woman of Distinction award Soroptimist Internat., 2000, Fidelity to Mission award Cath. Internat. Edn. Conf., Brazil, 2002; named Ambassador for Peace, World Fedn. Women for Peace, 2002. Mem. Dominican Edn. Assn. (past pres.), Coll. Theology Soc. (past v.p., sec.), Am. Acad. Religion, Religious Edn. Assn., Cath. Theology Soc., Coun. Religion and World Affairs, Theta Alpha Kappa (hon. mem. alumnus 1989, Veritas award 1989, Outstanding Prof. award 1989). Home: St Catherine Convent 7 Ryerson Ave Caldwell NJ 07006-6199 Office: Caldwell Coll 9 Ryerson Ave Caldwell NJ 07006-6109 E-mail: smaura@caldwell.com.

CAMPBELL, MAYNARD THOMAS, English language educator; b. Atlanta, Mar. 23, 1917; s. James Wiley and Florence (Thomas) C.; m. Shirley I. Hare, July 14, 1960; stepchildren: Michael R. Hare, Kathleen D. Rogers, Kevin S. Hare. BS, Ohio State U., 1942; postgrad., Claremont Grad. Sch., 1957, 58, 59; MEd, U. Ariz., Tucson, 1952, EdD, 1967. Tchr. Salt Creek Twp. Schs., Pickaway County, Ohio, 1937-40; tchr., prin. Venice (Ohio) Elem. Sch., 1942-44, Sasebo (Japan) Dependents Sch., 1954-55, Upper Secondary Comml. Japanese High Sch., Sasebo, 1954-55; tchr., counselor Tucson Pub. Schs., 1944-81; tutor in English for spkrs. of other langs., 1981—. Vis. instr. Kurume U., Kyushu, Japan, fall 1985. Author: Campbell, Evans, Hosler and Thomas Family Tress of Ohio, 1973. Mem. staff Ohio State Archeol. and Hist. Soc., 1941-42. Mem. NEA (life), ASCD, Ariz. Counselors Assn., George Washington Masonic Nat. Mel. Assn. (life), Ariz. State Geneal. Soc. (life), Pickaway County Hist. Soc., Internat. Platform Assn. (bd. govs. 1989—), Tucson Y's Men's Club (pres. and dist. gov. 1952), Masons, Phi Delta Kappa (life, chpt. pres. 1965-66). Unitarian Universalist. Home: Apt 522 1668 W Glendale Ave Phoenix AZ 85021-8966

CAMPBELL, PATRICIA BARBARA, educational research company executive, consultant; b. Worcester, Mass., Dec. 9, 1947; d. Philip Stephen and Barbara M. (McCarthy) C.; m. Tom R. Kibler, Jan. 19, 1976; 1 child, Kathryn Campbell-Kibler. BS in Math., LeMoyne Coll., 1969; MS in Instrnl. Tech., Syracuse U., 1971, PhD in Tchr. Edn., 1973. Rsch. programmer Thomas J. Watson Rsch. Ctr. IBM, Yorktown Heights, N.Y., 1968-69; instr. computer uses in edn., asst. to dir. rsch. Syracuse (N.Y.) U., 1970-72; evaluator Tchr. Cons. Inc., Syracuse, 1971-72; asst. prof., assoc. prof. ednl. founds. Ga. State U., Atlanta, 1973-77; dir. project on sex stereotyping in edn. Women Educators, Red Bank, N.J., 1976-79; dir. grants, rsch. and acad. devel. William Paterson Coll., Wayne, N.J., 1979-80; dir. Campbell-Kibler Assocs., Groton, Mass., 1980—. Program and evaluation cons. to numerous orgns., including Bklyn. Coll., CUNY, Rutgers U., Harvard U., Urban Inst., Cities in Schs., Youth Bur. City N.Y., pub. schs.,Boston, N.Y., N.J., nonprofit groups throughout Am. and Africa. Co-author: What Will Happen If. . .Young Children and the Scientific Method, 1985, The AAUW Report: How Schools Shortchange Girls, 1992; author (monograph) The Hidden Discriminator, 1989; contbr. articles to profl. jours., chpts. to books. Recipient merit award Ednl. Press Assn. Am., 1987, Betty Vetter Rsch. award Women in Engring. Program Advs. Network, 1998; grantee U.S. Dept. Edn., 1976-90. Mem. Am. Ednl. Rsch. Assn. (chmn. com. on spl. interest groups 1984-85, bd. dirs. profs. ednl. rsch. 1975-78, Willystein Goodsell award 1990, editor Rsch. News & Comments Ednl. Rschr. 1995-98), Women Educators (chmn. 1976-78, 85-86). Office: Groton Ridge Heights Groton MA 01450 E-mail: campbell@campbell-kibler.com.

CAMPBELL, PATRICIA ELAINE, elementary education educator; b. Cin., Dec. 3, 1943; d. Jake T. and Margaret O. (Hunter) C.; 1 child, Andre. BA in Elem. Edn., Andrews U., 1968; MA in Edn., U. Cin., 1978. Cert. elem tchr., prin. and supr., Ohio. Tchr. elem. Cin. Pub. Schs., 1968—, consulting tchr. Math. Assessment Devel., 1988—. Curriculum writer gifted and talented, career edn., programs in math. and sci.; mentor; youth program leader. Chmn. bd. Pvt. Parochial Sch., Cin., 1991-95. Mem. Ohio Maths. Group, Cin. Maths. Group, Nat. Coun. Tchrs. Maths. Adventist. Office: Cin Pub Schs 230 E 9th St Cincinnati OH 45202-2174

CAMPBELL, SARAH, elementary school educator, special education educator; b. Altavista, Va., Jan. 4, 1940; d. Charlie and Emma Francis (Morgan) Dalton; m. James Campbell, June 12, 1961; children: Saunta, Sidra. AA, Altantic Community Coll., 1976; BA magna cum laude, Glassboro State Coll., 1978; nursery sch. cert., Rutgers U.; spl. edn. cert., Glassboro State Coll., 1986; grad., Garden State Bible Sch., Pleasantville, N.J., 1994. Cert. tchr., NJ; asst. chaplain, Bapt. Ch.; ordained to ministry Bapt. Ch., 1995. Tchr. Head Start program Atlantic Human Resources, Inc., Atlantic City; ednl. area supr. Head Start program Adriatic Day Care Ctr., Atlantic, N.J.; head tchr., mgr. Atlantic Human Resources, Ind./Adriatic Day Care Ctr., Atlantic. Edn. con. Pleasantville (N.J.) Day Care Ctr. Past pres. dist. 8 Second Bapt. Ch.; choir libr. Gt. Choir; co-dir. children's ministry; tchr. Bible studies Greater Exodus Missionary Bapt. Ch. Mem. ASCD, Nat. Assn. Edn. Young Children.

CAMPBELL, SHANNON, school executive director; BS in Mental Retardation, Western Ill. U., 1978; MS in Diagnostic Teaching, Fla. Internat. U., 1982; Edn. Specialist degree, Nova U., 1989. Cert. administrn. and supervision, menatlly handicapped, specific learning disabilities, emotionally hanicapped. Tchr., 1978-82; head tchr., administr., 1982-84; exec. dir. The Learning Experience Sch., Coral Gables, Fla., 1984--. Bd. dirs. The Growing Place, The Learning Experience Sch., Presch. Handicapped Interagency Coun.; adv. bd. FIU Edn. Programs. Recipient KC award 1991; named Jaycee Young Outstanding Floridian 1989. Mem. Fla. Ind. Sch. Assn. (bd. dirs.), Community Com. for Developmental Handicaps, Coun. for Exceptional Children, Fla. Assn. Ind. Spl. Ednl. Facilities, Nat. Down Syndrome Congress. Office: Learning Experience Sch 536 Coral Way Coral Gables FL 33134-4915

CAMPBELL, SONYA BETH, elementary school educator; b. Tucson, Nov. 22, 1966; d. Frank Adam and Susie Joyce (Musgrove) C. BS in Edn., Cen. Mo. State U., 1989; MEd, Drury U., 1994; Specialist in Edn., S.W. Mo. State U., 2000; postgrad., St. Louis U. Supr. homework program Dept. Def., 1995—97; 1st grade tchr. Waynesville R-VI Dist., Ft. Leonardwood, Mo., 1989—94, 2d grade tchr., 1994—99, remedial reading tchr., 1999—2000, intern adminstr., 2000—01, asst. prin., 2001—; instr. Drury U., 2001—. Presenter in field. Named Citizen of Yr., 1994, Tchr. of Mo., 1997; recipient Outstanding Achievement in Autism award, 1990—2001, Tech. award, Tech. in Edn., 2002, Newspaper in Edn. award, Laclede Elec. Coop., 2003. Mem.: ASCD, Coun. for Exceptional Children, Learning Disability Assn., Am. Ednl. Rsch. Assn., Rsch. Assn. Minority Profs., Cmty. Tchrs. Assn., Mo. State Tchrs. Assn., Mo. Assn. Elem. Sch. Prins., Nat. Assn. Elem. Sch. Prins., Pride Investment Group, Dau. of Iris, Order Ea. Star, PTO, Coalition for Progress, NAACP, Kappa Delta. Baptist. Avocations: reading, crafts, sports, bottle collector, walking. Home: 16343 Thiltgen Ln Saint Robert MO 65584 Office: Pence Elem Sch 6824 Pulsaki Ave Fort Leonard Wood MO 65473 E-mail: sonyacampbell@waynesville.k12.mo.us.

CAMPBELL, SUSAN CARRIGG, secondary education educator; b. Copaigue, N.Y., Dec. 8, 1946; d. Richard Carrigg and Mildred Josephine (Schneider) C. BS cum laude, SUNY, Oswego, 1968; MA, Adelphi U., 1992. Cert. secondary tchr., N.Y. Tchr. Brentwood (N.Y.) Pub. Schs., 1968—2002. Co-developer learning skills program Brentwood (N.Y.) Pub. Schs., 1985-89, co-chairperson sch. improvement team, 1990-92, 93-94, 95, mem. summer curriculum writing project, 1993, adv. program com., 1993-94, conflict resolution trainee, 1994; adv. Student Leaders Club, Brentwood, N.Y., 1991; coord. Art Enrichment Show, 1986-91. Named Tchr. of Yr. Brentwood East Mid. Sch. PTA, 1995-96. Mem. L.I. Coun. Social Studies, Brentwood Tchrs. Assn., Kappa Delta Pi, Pi Gamma Mu. Democrat. Lutheran. Avocations: reading, walking beaches, gardening.

CAMPBELL, WILLIAM JOSEPH, academic director; b. Bklyn., N.Y., Nov. 26, 1944; s. William Joseph and Loretta Jane (Graessle) C. BA in Philosophy, U. Dayton, 1966; MS in Edn., Fordham U., 1972; MA in Theology, St. John's U., 1977; MA in Pvt. Sch. Adminstrn., U. San Francisco, 1986; EdD in Ednl. Mgmt., U. LaVerne, 1990. Cert. sch. adminstr., Calif.; cert. guidance counselor, N.Y. Tchr., dean students Most Holy Trinity H.S., Bklyn., 1966-68; tchr., coach Charlotte (N.C.) Cath. H.S., 1968-69; tchr., dir. freshman guidance Chaminade H.S., Mineola, N.Y., 1969-82; tchr., counselor Junipero Serra H.S., Gardena, Calif., 1982-84; academic asst. prin. Archbishop Riordan H.S., San Francisco, 1984-87; prin. Chaminade Coll. Prep., West Hills, Calif., 1987-90; dir. edn. Marianists, Cupertino, Calif., 1990-95; asst. supt. Archdiocese of Portland, Oreg., 1996—. Bd. dirs. Regis H.S., Staton, Oreg.; chmn. bd. regents Chaminade U., Honolulu. Mem. ASCD, Nat. Assn. Secondary Sch. Prins., Nat. Cath. Edn. Assn., World Future Soc., Assn. for Religious and Values Issues in Counseling, Phi Delta Kappa. Avocations: golfing, reading, cooking. Office: Archdiocese of Portland 2838 E Burnside St Portland OR 97214-1895

CAMPENNI, CAROL M. special education educator; b. Phila., Jan. 3, 1957; d. Angelo A. and Jacqueline (Colantuono) Masciantonio; m. Robert Campenni, May 21, 1976; children: Jessica Lynn, Jonathan Robert, Jaclyn Christine. BS in Edn., West Chester U., 1980, MEd, 1993. Cert. elem., spl. edn. tchr., Pa. Spl. edn. tchr Upper Darby (Pa.) schs., 1982-83, Marple Newtown (Pa.) schs., 1983-84, Delaware County Intermediate Unit, Media, Pa., 1984-86, Chester County Intermediate Unit, Exton, Pa., 1986-88, Unionville Chadds Ford Sch., Kennett Square, Pa., 1988—. Instrn. support mem. Unionville Sch. Dist., Kennett Square, 1990—, mem. student assistance team, 1992—. Active local PTO. Mem. Pa. State Edn. Assn. (bldg. rep. 1988-89), Pa. Mid. Schs. Assn., Downingtown Spirit Soccer Club, Kappa Delta Pi. Avocations: public relations, gardening, reading. Home: 1226 Cranberry Ln Coatesville PA 19320-4708 E-mail: ccampen@ucf.k12.pa.us.

CAMPHOR, JAMES WINKY, JR., educational administrator; b. Balt., Mar. 16, 1927; s. Emma Rosetta (Lewis) Butler; m. Lillie Mae Gilliard (div. Sept. 1976); children: Yvonne, Michael, Yolande; m. Florine Alston Camphor, Aug. 10, 1980. BS, Coppin Coll., 1951; MA, Coppin State Coll., 1971. Tchr. Dept. Edn., Balt., 1951-53, Dept. Juvenile Svcs., Chettenham, Md., 1953-75, demonstration tchr., 1972-75; behavior specialist Dept. Health and Mental Hygiene, Montgomery County, Md., 1975-87, ednl. supr., 1987—. Cons. Fantastic Buddies Travel, Balt., 1980-94. Co-author: (study) Social Studies in the Training School, 1963. Mem. adv. bd. Foster Grandparents Assn., Prince George County, Md., 1991—94, Nat. Assn. Sickle Cell Disease, Balt., 1984—94, chmn. Walk-A-Thon, 1991; pres. Am. Fedn. State County Mcpl. Employees Assn., Assn. State County Employees Montgomery County, 1991; mem. adv. com. capital campaign Coppin State Coll., 1998—2002, mem. cmty. fundraising coalition, 2002—, pres. nat. alumni assn., 2002—; supt. Sunday sch. Emmanuel Cmty. Ch., Balt., 1945. Recipient Comty. Svc. award Nat. Assn. Sickle Cell Disease, 1988, Presdl. citation Nat. Assn. in Higher Edn., 1992, Gov.'s Citation award William Donald Shafer, Annapolis, Md., 1994, Commitment to Edn. award City Coun. of Balt., 1994. Mem. Black Profl. Men Inc., Bus. and Profl. Coun. (pres. 1989-94), Comty. Men (comty. mem., bus. mgr. 1985-92), Lucky Ten Inc. (charter, pres. 1990-94), Elks, Phi Beta Sigma (pres. 1990-94). Democrat. Avocations: reading, tutoring, traveling, collecting pipes, singing. Home: 3308 Lauri Rd Baltimore MD 21244-1324 Office: Dept Health and Mental Hygiene 3100 Gracefield Rd Silver Spring MD 20904-1870

CAMPION, THOMAS CLIFFORD, secondary school educator; b. Detroit, Aug. 23, 1949; s. Bruce and Mildred Reis (Warner) C.; m. Mary Spellbring, June 3, 1972; children: Jason S., Amanda S. AA, Prince George's C.C., Largo, Md., 1969; BS, Towson State U., 1971; MS, Bowie State U., 1977. Cert. adv. profl. educator, Md. Tchr. U.S. history Prince George's County Pub. Schs., Lanham, Md., 1971—. Dept. history team leader Prince George's County Pub. Schs, 1981-93, chairperson 1974-93. Author/illustrator supplemental ednl. material, 1985, 87; contbr. articles to profl. publs.; creator polit. cartoons. Bd. dirs. Bowie (Md.) Boys and Girls Club, 1987-89; bd. dirs., tennis chmn. Belair Bath and Tennis Club, Bowie, 1989-92. Mem. Nat. Orgn. Regular Men (bd. dirs. 1991—). Avocations: tennis, golf, softball, reading, travel. Home: 12734 Buckingham Dr Bowie MD 20715-2463 Office: Thomas Johnson Mid Sch 5401 Barker Pl Lanham Seabrook MD 20706-2499

CAMPOS, JERI LARUTH, elementary education educator; b. Lamesa, Tex., July 21, 1940; d. A.E. and Edith LaRuth (McGregor) Helstrom; m. Ralph Leon Campos, Aug. 25, 1973; children: Christopher, Aimee. BA, San Diego State U., 1972, postgrad. Cert. elem. tchr., Calif., Tex. Tchr. Bonsall (Calif.) Union Sch. Dist., 1973-77, 87-90, Lorena (Tex.) Elem. Sch., 1990—; prin., tchr. Rawhide Christian Sch., Bonsall, 1984-85. Mem. Tex. Fedn. Tchrs. (nominee Disney Tchr. of Yr.), Tourette Syndrome chpt. City of Hope, No. County Parents Orgn. San Diego Citizens Found. scholar, 1973, and various others. Mem. Ch. of Christ. Avocations: recreational vehicle camping, choral singing, home crafts.

CANARINA, OPAL JEAN, nurse, administrator, educator, consultant, lecturer; b. Geneva County, Ala., Mar. 21, 1936; d. O. Lee and L. Ellen (Box) Peacock; m. Miles Steven Bajcar, June 27, 1953 (div.); children: Debra Lynn-Wilson; Wayne Steven; m. Arnold R. Canarina, June 19, 1965 (dec. 1998); children: Catherine Mary, Christopher John, Charles Benjamin. B.S.N. summa cum laude, George Mason U., Fairfax, Va., 1976, M.S.N., Vanderbilt U., 1981. R.N., Va., Tenn., Ky., Okla., Utah, Miss., Fla. Staff and charge nurse Georgetown U. Hosp., Washington, 1976; charge nurse ob-gyn Vanderbilt U. Hosp., Nashville, 1976-77; charge nurse labor and delivery svc. Baptist Hosp., Nashville, 1977-80; asst. prof. dept. baccalaureate nursing Austin Peay State U., Clarksville, Tenn., 1981-83; dir. nursing svcs. Meml. Hosp., Guymon, Okla., 1983-85; dir. Women's Ctr./Maternal-Child Nursing, McKay-Dee Hosp. Ctr., Ogden, Utah, 1985-87; dir. nursing Jeff Anderson Regional Med. ctr., Meridian, Miss., 1987-89, program mgr., dir. Women's Ctr. Univ. Community Hosp., Tampa, Fla., 1989-91; adminstrv. dir. women's health svcs. Scripps Meml. Hosp., La Jolla, Calif., 1991-92; asst. adminstr., prof. Hart County Hosp., Hartwell, Ga., 1992-94; cons. to middle Tenn. and No. Utah areas health and nursing issues; cons. quality assurance Al Hada Hosp, TAIF, Saudi Arabia, 1992, assoc. adminstr. nursing, 1992-99, ret., 1999. Recipient cert. of excellence R.N.s on campus George Mason U., 1976. Mem. ANA (cert. in nursing adminstrn. 1989), NAFE, Am. Orgn. Nurse Execs., Am. Coll. Health Care Execs. (internat. assoc.), Tenn. Nurses Assn. (legis. chmn. dist. 13, 1982-83, pres. 1982), Va. Nurses Assn. (Student Nurse of Yr. award 1975), Sigma Theta Tau, Alpha Chi.

CANCER, CATHY LYNN, elementary education educator; b. Vidalia, Ga., July 10, 1963; d. Jessie and Hattie Lee Hunt; m. Anthony Gerald Cancer, June 8, 1990; children: Hunter Tyrez, Oshjiah Lynn. BBA, Savannah State U., 1987; Tchg. Cert., Ga. So. U., 1989, MEd in Sch. Counseling, 1996. MED in sch. counseling. Elem. tchr. Toombs County Bd. Edn., Lyons, Ga., 1989-97, Burke County Bd. Edn., Waynesboro, Ga., 1997—. Bus. cons. H&K Package Store, Lyons, 1989—. Fellow ASCD, GSCA. Avocations: music, reading, card games. Home: PO Box 1223 Lyons GA 30436-6223

CANCRO, ROBERT, psychiatrist, educator; b. NYC, Feb. 23, 1932; s. Joseph and Marie E. (Cicchetti) C.; m. Gloria Costanzo, Dec. 8, 1956; children: Robert, Carol. Student, Fordham U., 1948-51; MD, SUNY, 1955. Intern Kings County Hosp., Bklyn., 1955-56, resident in psychiatry, 1956-59; attending staff Gracie Sq. Hosp., N.Y.C., 1959-66; clin. instr. SUNY Downstate Med. Ctr., Bklyn., 1959-66; staff psychiatrist Menninger Found., Topeka, Kans., 1966-69; cons. Topeka State and VA Hosps., 1967-69; prof. dept. psychiatry U. Conn. Health Ctr., Farmington, 1970-76; prof., chmn. dept. psychiatry NYU Med. Ctr., 1976—; dir. N.S. Kline Inst. Psychiat. Research, 1982—. Cons. psychiat. edn. br. NIMH; biol. scis. sect. NIMH. Editor 10 books.; Contbr. articles on schizophrenia to profl. jours. Recipient Freida Fromm-Reichmann award, 1975, Strecker award, 1978, Dean award, 1981, Lehmann award, 1992. Fellow A.C.P., Am. Coll. Psychiatrists, Am. Psychiat. Assn.; mem. Am. Psychol. Assn., Assn. Am. Med. Colls., Am. Assn. Social Psychiatry (pres. 1984-86), N.Y. Acad. Scis., AAAS, AMA. Home: 118 Mclain Rd Mount Kisco NY 10549-4932 Office: NYU Med Ctr 550 1st Ave New York NY 10016-6402 E-mail: robert.cancro@med.nyu.edu.

CANDELARIA, ANGIE MARY, special education educator; b. Durango, Colo., July 13, 1939; d. Angelo and Lucia (Mattevi) Dallabetta; m. David Candelaria, Sept 24, 1958 (div. Mar. 1964); children: David D., Craig D.; m. Richard James McMullen, July 3, 1982 (dec. Mar. 1999). BA, Ft. Lewis Coll., Durango, 1965; postgrad., U. North Colo., 1997-99. Cert. tchr. spl. edn., Colo. Tchr. Sch. Dist. R25, Loveland, Colo., 1967-68; tchr. spl. edn. Sch. Dist. 9R, Durango, 1968-98, mem. profl. devel. com., 1990-97; ret., 1998. Ind. rschr. Josten Integrated Computer Edn. Co. Colo. Dept. Edn. spl. edn. grantee, 1966, cross-cultural inst. grantee, 1972-74, Sch. Dist. 9R grantee, 1992. Mem. ASCD, NEA, Colo. Edn. Assn., Durango Edn. Assn., Internat. Reading Assn., VFW Aux. (life), Am. Legion Aux., Elks, Colombo Lodge. Republican. Roman Catholic. Avocations: computers, travel, reading, animals. Home: 16B 1741 Tustin Ave Apt 16B Costa Mesa CA 92627-3294 also: PO Box 472 Durango CO 81302-0472

CANDELAS, TERESA BUSH, special education educator; b. Ft. Eustis, Va., Jan. 28, 1956; d. John Gilbert and Juanita Margaret (Ingram) Bush; m. Jose Antonio Candelas, May 21, 1979 (dec.); children: Deanna, Tony, John, Kristopher, Angelina. BA in Edn., U. Fla., 1993, MEd in Spl. Edn., 1998. Cert. tchr. spl. edn., learning disabilities, mental retardation. Tchr. self-contained mentally handicapped Sch. Bd. Alachua County, Archer, Fla., 1993—. Mem. sch. adv. bd. Archer Cmty. Sch., 1994—; host family Spanish Heritage, Gainesville, Fla., 1992-96. Mem. PTA, Coun. for Exceptional Children, U. Fla. Alumni Assn., Alachua County Edn. Assn. Roman Catholic. Avocations: woodworking, sewing, camping. Home: 13600 Copper Croft Run Apt D Blacksburg VA 24060-6044

CANDELMO, LEE FRANCE, special education educator; b. Orange, N.J., Jan. 17, 1941; s. John and Ruth Claire (France) C.; m. Mary Lariccia, Oct. 20, 1962; children: Robert, Lori, Kristen. BA in English Lit., Rutgers U., 1962; MA in Student Personnel Svcs., Kean Coll., Union, N.J., 1975. English tchr. Bernards Twp. Bd. Edn., Basking Ridge, N.J., 1966-72, counselor, 1972-78; tchr. adult handicapped East Brunswick (N.J.) Bd. Edn., 1978-85, counselor adult and youth handicapped, 1985—. Author: An English Course of Study, 1968, The Intergration of Beadleston Classified Adolescents into a Regular Junior High School, 1975; contbr. book chpt. Recipient award for svc. to disabled persons Nat. Sch. Bd., 1986, U.S. Sec. Edn. award for vocat. edn. for handicapped youth, 1986. Mem. NEA, Rutgers U. Alumni Assn. Presbyterian. Avocations: reading, volunteer work, stamp collecting, photography. Office: East Brunswick High Sch Adult Edn Office Cranbury Rd East Brunswick NJ 08816

CANDLIN, FRANCES ANN, psychotherapist, social worker, educator; b. Phila., July 18, 1945; d. Francis Townley and Wilma (David) C. BA magna cum laude, Loretto Heights Coll., Denver, 1967; MSW with honors, St. Louis U., 1971. Diplomate Am. Bd. Clin. Social Work; cert. social worker; lic. clin. social worker, Colo. Recreational therapist trainee Jewish Hosp., St. Louis, 1970-71; social worker trainee Jefferson Barracks VA Hosp., St. Louis, 1970-71; social worker Adams County Juvenile Probation, Brighton, Colo., 1972-74, Boulder (Colo.) County Social Svcs., 1974-75; sch. social worker Adams County Sch. Dist. #50, Westminster, Colo., 1975-80; workshop presenter Human Enrichment Cons., Denver, 1980-90; pvt. practice Denver, 1980—; dir. Madison St. Counseling Ctr., Denver, 1991-97; founder, dir. Women's Mysteries Tour Co., 1993, Enneagram Ctr. of Colo., 1997—. Cons. Mountain Plains Regional Ctr., Denver, 1981-85, Dept. Edn., Topeka, 1981-87, Dept. Spl. Edn., Nebr., Colo., Mo., N.Mex., Utah, 1982-86. Bd. dirs. Denver Sch. for Gifted, 1982-86, Weaver Found., 1985-86, St. Mary's Acad., Englewood, Colo., 1985-88. Recipient stipend NIMH, 1969, VA Social Work Trainee, 1970. Mem. NASW, NOW, Acad. Cert. Social Workers, Internat. Enneagram Assn., Assn. Transpersonal Psychology, Colo. Assn. Clin. Social Workers, Vajra Soc. (bd. dirs. 1990—). Avocations: world travel, women's issues, spiritual devel. Office: Enneagram Ctr Colo PO Box 933 Glenwood Springs CO 81602

CANHAM, PRUELLA CROMARTIE NIVER, retired educator; b. Statesboro, Ga., Dec. 4, 1924; d. Esten Graham and Mary Lee (Jones) Cromartie; m. Robert E. Niver June 4, 1946 (div. 1965) m. David L. Canham July 26, 1985; 1 child, Peddy Niver Hayhurst Moran. BS in Bus. and Music, Ga. So. U., 1944; postgrad., various univs. tchr. voice, piano, chorus and bus. career maths. North Ft. Myers H.S., Fla.; former sec. Statesboro Air Base, Ga., Warner Robbins Air Base, Macon, Ga.; former tchr. Westside Sch., Bulloch County, Ga., Southside Sch., Opelika, Ala. Mem. Singers Club of L.I.; guest spkr., panelist various cultural orgns. in Fla. and so. states; soloist various chs. and schs.; music cons. local theater groups; mem. Fla. State Secondary Music Instructional Materials Coun. Nominee Gannett Found. Heart of Gold Humanatarian award, 1981; named Vocal Solo. Lit. Music Specialist State of Florida, Lee County Florida Tchr. of the Year, 1987, nominee Nat. Tchr. Hall of Fame, 1998; recipient Nat. Libr. Poet's Editor's Choice award, 1994; cert. Appreciation Nat. Park Trust, 1995, Lee County Sch. Dist. Fla., 1991, numerous awards in 2002, including: ABI Hall of Fame, Great Minds of 21st Century, Poet of Year, Internat. Poet Merit and Honored Mem., 500 Founders of 21st Century, Internat. Biographical Ctr. Living Legions, 1000 Great Scholars, Worlds Lifetime Achievement award, Companion of Honor, Internat. Peace Prize,

Am. Medal of Honor; Nobel Prize for Oustanding Achievement and Contbr. to Humanity, 2002. Mem. AAAS, Am. Ch. Dirs. Assn., Fla. Music Educator Assns., Music Educator's Nat. Conf., Lee County Alliance of the Arts (charter), Fla. Vocal Assn. (past coord., state bd.), Nat. Assn. of Tchrs. of Singing in Am. and Cand., So. Fla. Symphony and Chorus Assn., Am. Guild of Organists, Fla. League of the Arts (past pres. and bd. dirs., hon. life, 1998—), Lee County Retired Tchrs. Assn., Fla. Vocal Assn., Am. Choral Assn., Internat. Soc. Poets (disting. mem. 1994, merit award, 1995), Profl. Women's Adv. Bd., others. Home: 1271 Burtwood Dr Fort Myers FL 33901-8711

CANIPE, JAMES BOYD, economics educator; b. Gastonia, N.C., Jan. 9, 1950; s. Boyd Navey and Janie Louise (Roberts) C.; m. Nealie Kaye Trent, June 12, 1977; children: Jennifer, Cheryl. AA, Wingate (N.C.) Coll., 1970; BSBA, U. N.C., 1972; MA in Econs., East Tenn. State U., 1976; postgrad., U. Tenn. Instr. of econs. Steed Coll., Johnson City, Tenn., 1976-79, Union Coll., Barbourville, Ky., 1980-81; asst. prof. of econs. Clinch Valley Coll., Wise, Va., 1985-91. Adj. instr. of econs. Walters State C.C., Morristown, Tenn., 1978-80, 83-86, Carson-Newman Coll., Jefferson City, Tenn., 1982, S.E. C.C., Middlesboro, Ky., 1992—. Mem. Johnson City Masons, Knoxville Scottish Rite Bodies, Jericho Shrine Temple, Gideons Internat. Avocations: reading, walking, traveling.

CANIZARES, CLAUDE ROGER, astrophysicist, educator; b. Tucson, June 14, 1945; s. Orlando and Stephanie (Bolan) C.; children: Kristen, Alexander. BA, Harvard U., 1967, MA, 1968, PhD, 1972. From rsch. staff to assoc. provost MIT, Cambridge, 1971—2001, assoc. provost, 2001—. Assoc. dir. NASA-Chandra X-ray Obs. Ctr.; chair NRC Space Studies Bd., 1994-2000; chair space sci. adv. com. NASA, 1993-94, mem. Space Earth Sci. Adv. Com., Washington, 1986-88; mem. adv. coun. NASA, 1992-2000; mem. astron. and astrophysics survey com. NRC, Washington, 1989-91; trustee Assoc. Univs., Inc., 1997—; mem. Air Force Sci. Adv. Bd., 1999—; mem. bd. on physics and astronomy NRC, 2001—. Contbr. articles over 170 to profl. jours. Royal Soc. vis. fellow, Cambridge, Eng., 1981-82, Alfred P. Sloan Found. fellow, 1980-84; NASA grantee, 1975—. Fellow Am. Phys. Soc.; mem. NAS, AAAS, Am. Astron. Soc., Internat. Astron. Union, Internat. Acad. Astronautics, Phi Beta Kappa, Sigma Xi. Achievements include first implementation of studies in x-ray spectroscopy and plasma diagnostics of supernova remnants, clusters of galaxies. Office: MIT 77 Massachusetts Ave 3-234 Cambridge MA 02139-4309 E-mail: crc@mit.edu.

CANN, SHARON LEE, retired health science librarian; b. Ft. Riley, Kans., Aug. 14, 1935; d. Roman S. and Cora Elon (George) Foote; m. Donald Clair Cann, May 16, 1964. Student, Sophia U., Tokyo, 1955-57; BA, Calif. State U., Sacramento, 1959; MSLS, Atlanta U., 1977; EdD, U. Ga., 1995. Cert. health scis. libr. Recreation worker ARC, Korea, Morocco, France, 1960-64; shelflister Libr. Congress, Washington, 1967-69; tchr. Lang Ctr., Taipei, Taiwan, 1971-73; libr. tech. asst. Emory U., Atlanta, 1974-76; health sci. libr. Northside Hosp., Atlanta, 1977-85, libr. cons., 1985-86; libr. area health edn. ctr., learning resource ctr. Morehouse Sch. Medicine, 1985-86; edn. libr. Ga. State U., 1986-93; dir. libr. svcs. Ga. Bapt. Coll. Nursing, 1993-99, ret., 1999. Author: Life in a Fishbowl: A Call To serve, 2003; editor Update, publ. Ga. Health Scis. Libr. Assn., 1981; contbr. articles to publs. Chmn. Calif. Christian Youth in Govt. Seminar, 1958. Named Alumni Top Twenty Calif. State U., Sacramento, 1959. Mem. ALA, Med. Libr. Assn. (bookkeeper So. chpt. 1996-98, credentialing com. 1996-2000, nursing and allied health sect. continuing edn. chair 1998-2000, hon. life), Spl. Libr. Assn. (dir. South Atlantic chpt. 1985-87), Ga. Libr. Assn. (spl. libr. divsn. chmn. 1983-85), Ga. Health Scis. Libr. Assn. (chmn. 1981-82, hon. life), Atlanta Health Sci. Libr. (chmn. 1979, 95), Am. Numis. Assn., ARC Overseas Assn., Audubon Soc., Women in Mil. Svc. for Am., Suncity Hilton Health Computer Club (v.p. 2003). Home: 69 Plymouth Ln Bluffton SC 29909-5062 E-mail: sharoncann@aol.com.

CANNELL, CYNDY MICHELLE, elementary school principal; b. Salt Lake City, Utah, July 27, 1948; d. Nick M. and Eugenie E. (Pfanmuller) Fasselin; m. Peter Anthony Cannell, Oct. 13, 1973; children: Peter John, David. BA, U. Utah, 1970, MA, 1973. Cert. adminstr., supr. severly handicapped, spl. edn., emotionally handicapped, gifted and talented. Tchr. Hab Ctr., 1973-74, Hill View Elem Sch., 1974-78; coord. spl. needs. Granite Sch. Dist., Salt Lake City, 1978-79, tchr. leader youth in custody, 1979-80, coord. spl. edn., 1980-84; asst. prin. Western Hills Elem. Sch., Salt Lake City, 1984-85; prin. Webster Elem. Sch., Salt Lake City, 1985-90, Plymouth Elem. Sch., Salt Lake City, 1990-95, Twin Peaks Elem. Sch., Salt Lake City, 1995—2000; field asst. Utah State Office Edn., 2000—01; coord. spl. edn. unit Cottonwood Heights Elem., 2002. Mem. state strategic planning com. for edn., 1990-91, elem. prin. adv. com., 1990-96, spl. edn. strategic planning com., 1990-91, exec. class size steering com., 1990, ptnrs. in edn. com., 1985—, sch. lunch com., 1989-91, emer. preparedness com., 1989-90; mem. Women's State Legis. Coun., Utah, 1991-92; co-coord. Corp. Games, 1988—. Contbr. articles to profl. mags. Prin. rep. to state PTA Community Involvement Commn., 1989-90, Oquirrh South PTA Coun., 1989; mem. Utah Youth Village Scholarship Com., 1996—. Named Outstanding Educator of Yr. Nat. PTA Phoebe Apperson Hearst, 1990, Outstanding Adminstr. Utah Congress of Parents and Tchrs., 1989-90, Region V PTA, 1988-90. Mem. Granite Assn. Elem. Sch. Prins. (sec. 1998—, Innovator of Yr. 1997-98), Granite Assn. Sch. Adminstrs. (sec., treas. 1990-91) Utah Assn. Sch. Adminstrs., Nat Assn. Elem. Adminstrs., Granite Assn. Sch. Adminstrs. Avocations: skiing, reading, tennis, golf, travel. Home: 10331 S 2375 E Sandy UT 84092-4422 Office: Cottonwood Heights Elem 2415 E Bengal Blvd Salt Lake City UT 84121

CANNELLA, DEBORAH FABBRI, accountant; b. Statesville, N.C., Sept. 7, 1949; d. Raymond Joseph and Sylvia (Sides) Fabbri; m. S.J. Garciga, Apr. 16, 1970 (div. 1990); children: Jennifer, Melissa, Bryan; m. Frank Cannella, July 1, 1994. Student, U. So. Fla., 1970, 91—; Presch. Edn. degree, Montessori Inst. Am., 1984; BS in acctg., U. So. Fla., 1995; postgrad., U. South Fla., 1995-98. Cert. Montessori Presch. Edn., Kansas City, Mo.; CPA. Tchr. presch. Montessori Acad. of Temple Terr., Fla., 1982-87; tchr. 1st grade St. John's Parish Day Sch., Tampa, Fla., 1987-99; acct. Pender, Newkirk & Co., CPAs, 1999—. Facilitator Bay Area Assn. Ind. Schs. Profl. Day, 1990, mem. program com., 1990-92; bd. dirs. Tampa Prep. Parent's, grad. reception, 1987-88. Mem. AICPA, Fla. Inst. CPAs, Tampa Mus. of Art, Tampa Bay Performing Arts Ctr., Mus. Sci. and Tech. Episcopalian. Avocations: walking, reading, baking. Office: St John's Parish Day Sch 906 S Orleans Ave Tampa FL 33606-2941

CANNELLA, NANCY ANNE, educational administrator; b. Franklin Square, N.Y., Feb. 26, 1951; d. Philip and Nina (Vecchiano) Calabrese; m. Joseph L. Cannella, Jan. 10, 1950; children: Kimberly, Jonathan, Ashley. BS in Elem. Edn., St. John's U., 1973, MS in Curriculum Devel., 1975. Tchr. elem. sch. Bklyn. Dioceses, 1972-76; program devel. specialist Farifax County (Va.) Pub. Schs., 1976-80; exec. dir. Armonk (N.Y.) Children's Corner, 1982—; coll. field supr. Manhattanville Coll., Harrison, N.Y., 1990-93, Columbia U. Tchrs. Coll., St. Rose Coll. Bd. dirs., pres. Harrison Youth Coun., Westchester, 1995—; consulting trainer Wellsley Coll., Mass., 1998. Co-pres. Louis M. Klein Mid. Sch. PTA, Harrison, 1990-93, 96, 97, v.p., 1995; treas. Harrison Ave. Sch. PTA, 1986-88, v.p. ways 'n means, 1984-86; bd. dirs. Harrison Day Ctr., 1993—; bd. dirs. N.Y. State Childcare Coalition, 1997—. Mem. Westchester Assn. Edn. Young Children (bd. dirs. 1989-92, sec. 1991-92), Harrison Parent Tchr. Coun. (v.p. 1993, co-pres. 1994-96), Sch. Age Dir.'s Network (pres. 1988-90, v.p. 1991-93). Avocation: tennis. Home: 26 Sunny Ridge Rd Harrison NY 10528-2206 Office: Armonk Children's Corner PO Box 601 Armonk NY 10504-0601 E-mail: ncanel@aol.com.

CANNITO, MICHAEL PHILLIP, speech language pathologist, educator; b. Patterson, N.J., May 30, 1952; s. Ralph Theodore and Rose (Angelica) C.; children: Caitlin, Laurel Tess. BA, Lamar U., 1975, MS, 1980; PhD, U. Tex., Dallas, 1986. Cert. speech lang. pathologist. Asst. prof. Our Lady of the Lake U., San Antonio, 1986-87, U. Texas, Austin, 1987-92; assoc. prof. U. South Ala., Mobile, 1992-94, U. Memphis, 1994-99, prof., 1999—. Rsch. scientist Ctr. for Rsch. Initatives and Stratagies for the Communicatively Impaired, Memphis, 1994—; rsch. cons. Harry Jersig Ctr., Our Lady of the Lake U., San Antonio, 1990-96; coord. Speech Sc. Lab. Coll. of Comm., U. Tex., 1988-90., adj: assoc. prof. U. Tenn., Memphis, 1996-Co-editor: Neuro-Motor Speech Disorders, 1997, Treating Disordered Speech Motor Control, 1991; series editor Pro Ed Pub., Austin, Tex., 1996—; assoc. editor Jour. of Speech, Lang. and Hearing Rsch., 1997—2000. Grantee NIH, 1996. Mem. Am. Speech, Lang. and Hearing Assn. (1st award for Sci. Merit 1983). Achievements include the documentation of neurol. and psychological characteristics of individuals with spasmodic dysphonia (laryngeal dystonia), and evaluation of the influence of botulinum toxin on spasmodic dysphonic speech. Office: Sch Audiol/Speech Pathology U Memphis 807 Jefferson Ave Memphis TN 38105-5042

CANNON, BENNIE MARVIN, physical education educator; b. Goshen Pike, Ala., Aug. 20, 1942; s. L.D. and Gussie Lee (Canty) C.; m. Vercilla Brown, Aug. 27, 1966; children: Steven Marvin, Jonathan Benjamin, Noah Christopher. AA, Chgo. City Coll., 1964; BS, Upper Iowa U., 1968; postgrad., U. Ill., 1971-76. Cert. phys. edn., safety and driver edn. tchr., Ill. Tchr. elem. phys. edn. Chgo. Pub. Schs., 1968-69, tchr. gen. sci., 1969-71, tchr. secondary phys. edn., driver's edn., 1971-78, 79—. Fitness specialist del. Dwight David Eisenhower Found., Spokane, Wash., 1992, Driver Edn. Profl. del. Dwight David Eisenhower Found., Spokane, 1996. Mem. AAPHERD, Ill. Assn. Health, Phys. Edn., Recreation and Dance (Quarter Century award Chgo. dist. 1993, Quarter Century Club award state dist. 1994), Nat. Sci. Tchrs. Assn., Ill. H.S. and Coll. Driver Edn. Assn., Nat. Fedn. News, Am. Fedn. Tchrs., Phi Zeta Tau. Democrat. African Methodist Episcopal. Avocations: baseball, basketball, skating, tennis, bicycling. Home: 8419 S Indiana Ave Chicago IL 60619-5606

CANNON, BRYAN CEDRIC, physical education educator; b. Boston, June 29, 1968; s. Mabel Cannon. BS, U. R.I., 1990; postgrad., Towson (Md.) State U., 1992—. Cert. health tchr. Phys. edn. instr. Balt. County Bd. of Edn., Towson, 1991—. Vol. Senator Edward Kennedy, Boston, 1994. Lt. U.S. Army, 1990. Recipient Gold Cert. of Excellence Govs. Prevention Initiative, 1994. Mem. AAHPERD, Md. State Tchrs. Assn., Tchr. Assn. of Balt. County, Nat. Guard Assn. of U.S., Nat. Guard Assn. of Md. Democrat. African Methodist Episcopalian. Avocations: reading, traveling, family, running, weight lifting. Office: Winfield Elem Sch 8300 Carlson Ln Baltimore MD 21244-1309

CANNON, DANNIE PARKER, special education educator; b. Knoxville, Tenn., Sept. 19, 1951; d. Tommie Isaac and Mary (Halliburton) Parker; m. Robert Kyle Cannon Sr., Aug. 2, 1975; children: Thomas Parker, Jonathan Ray, Robert Kyle Jr.; m. Holly Overton; 1 child, Laura Lee; m. Mike Regan; 1 child, Daniel Cameron. BS in Edn., U. Tenn., 1973, MS, 1975. Cert. tchr. emotionally disburbed, neurologically impaired, learning and behavior disorders. Tchr. 2d and 3d grade Farragut Primary, Knoxville, 1973-75; elem. resource tchr. Brown Sch., Louisville, 1975; spl. edn. resource tchr. Waggener High Sch., Louisville, 1975-95; tchr. 2nd and 3d grades St. Matthews Elem. Sch., Louisville, 1995—. Tchr. exptl. program U. Tenn., Knoxville, 1972-73; project tchr. CAEVEP-CSDC Project, Louisville, 1977-78. Sunday sch. tchr. Hurstbourne Bapt. Ch., Louisville, 1984-86, Pleasant Grove Bapt. Ch., Louisville, 1987-90. Recipient Amgen award, Jefferson County Ky. Program, 2000. Fellow NEA, Parents Tchrs. Students Assn., Ky. Edn. Assn., Jefferson County Tchrs. Assn. Republican. Avocations: piano, doll collecting, antiques, genealogy, reading. Home: 10611 Kinross Ct Louisville KY 40243-1760 Office: St Matthews Elem Sch 601 Browns Ln Louisville KY 40207-4043

CANNON, ELIZABETH ANNE, special education educator; b. Chgo., May 22, 1946; d. Peter Francis and Mary Patricia (Tangney) Foley; m. Martin Francis Cannon, July 10, 1982. BSEd, Chgo. Tchrs. Coll., 1969; MS in Spl. Edn. Learning Disabilities, Chgo. State U., 1982, MA in Edn. Adminstrn. and Supervision, 1988; postgrad., Northeastern Ill. U., 1988, Colo. State U., 1992-94, U. Denver, 1992-94. Cert. elem. and secondary tchr., adminstr., spl. edn., EMH, TMH, ED, BD, LD, gifted, supervision and adminstrn. spl. edn., Ill., Colo. Sch. clk. Chgo. Pub. Schs., summer 1965-69, tchr. spl. edn. mentally handicapped, 1969-90, tchr. regular and spl. summer schs., 1970-76; tchr. adult edn. City Colls. Chgo., 1971-81; tchr. spl. edn. Lake Mid. Sch. Denver Pub. Schs., 1992—. Cooperating tchr. trainer Chgo. State U., Roosevelt U., U. Ill., Denver Metro Coll., U. Colo.; mem. local sch. coun., 1974-90, prin.'s adv. coun., 1974-90, mem. PTA Chgo. Bd. Edn., 1969-90. Leader Girl Scouts Chgo. St. Barnabus Sch., 1968-72; mem. Archbishop's Guild (Denver) Mother of Perpetual Help Circle. Recipient Gov.'s Master Tchr. award State of Ill., Springfield, 1983, Tchr. of Merit award Chgo. Bd. Edn., Dists. 16, 19, 1974-88, PTA, Chgo., 1974-88. Mem. ASCD, AAUW, Coun. Exceptional Children (Ill. chpt.), Am. Fedn. Sch. Adminstrs., Colo. Assn. Sch. Execs., Coun. Learning Disabilites, Kappa Delta Pi, Delta Kappa Gamma Internat. (Denver chpt.). Democrat. Roman Catholic. Avocations: swimming, hiking mountain trails, camping, bike riding, arts and crafts. Home: 2041 S Wolff St Denver CO 80219-5044

CANNON, LENA FERRARA LEE, retired education educator; b. Morgantown, W.Va., Oct. 12, 1918; d. Emil and Philomena (Purificato) Ferrara; m. Robert Young Cannon, June 10, 1948; children: Emilie, Robert Y. Jr., Leigh. BS, W.Va. U., 1940, MS, 1944; postgrad., U. Wis., 1945-48. Tchr. Osage (W.Va.) Jr. High Sch., 1941-45; rsch. asst. U. Wis., Madison, 1945-48; asst. prof. Auburn (Ala.) U., 1948-70, asst. producer, host Ala. Pub. TV, 1955-84, specialist in foods nutrition, 1970-84; retired, 1984. Weekly TV program PBS-TV, 1955-84, weekly columns Montgomery Adv., 1979-84, Columbus Enquirer, 1960-65. Author: Today's Home, Vols. 1-3, 1953-84, Southern Living's Quick and Easy Cookbook, 1979; contbr. articles to profl. jours. Bd. dirs. Commn. Aging, Montgomery, Ala., 1981-83, Apobonna Commn. Aging, 1979-83; adv. bd. Auburn U. Theatre. Mem. Internat. Platform Assn., Am. Home Econs. Assn., Am. Women Radio TV, Women in Communications, Phi Upsilon Omicron. Roman Catholic. Avocations: cooking, dancing, entertaining, bridge, reading.

CANNON, MAJOR TOM, special education educator; b. Anniston, Ala., Nov. 11, 1932; s. Thomas Albert and Sallie Mae (James) C. BA in Liberal Arts, Samford U., 1961; postgrad., So. Bapt. Theol. Sem., 1961-62, Tulane U., 1962-63, Auburn U., 1963-64; MEd in Counseling, U. Ga., 1968; postgrad., U. S.C., 1971, 81, 84, Francis Marion Coll., 1979—80, Western Md. Coll., 1980, S.C. State Coll., 1981-85, U. Charleston, 1993, The Citadel, Charleston, S.C., 1996-97, Charleston So. U., Francis Marion Coll., 2000, postgrad., 2003. Cert. prin., guidance counselor, spl. edn. tchr., psychology, S.C. English tchr. North Whitfield H.S., Dalton, Ga., 1964-65, Savannah (Ga.) H.S., 1965-66; guidance counselor Savannah Pub. Schs., 1966-79; dir. spl. svcs. Marlboro County Sch. Dist., Bennettsville, S.C., 1979-80, coord. programs for handicapped, 1980-81; tchr. trainable mentally retarded Edisto Mid. Sch., Orangeburg, S.C., 1981-86; tchr. learning disabled Norman C. Toole Mid. Sch., Charleston, S.C., 1986-88, Berkeley Mid. Sch., Moncks Corner, S.C., 1988-97, chmn. dept. spl. edn., 1991-94; specialist learning disabilities Berkeley County Sch. Dist., Moncks Corner, 1995-97; resource C.E. Murray H.S., Greeleyville, S.C., 1997—. Labor resources technician City of Savannah, 1979; presenter in field; mem. Strategic Planning Com. for Berkeley County Sch. Dist., 1993-97, Sch. Improvement Coun., 1996-97. Contbr. poetry to Great Poems of the Western World, 1990, Our World's Favorite Gold and Silver Poems, 1991, Perceptions, 1994, Am. Poetry Annual, 1994; author resource manuals and videotaped lessons. Charter Rep. Nat. Com., 1992—, Rep. Presdl. Task Force, 1989—, Rep. Nat. Commn. on Am. Agenda, 1996, Nat. Rep. Senatorial Com., 1990—; at-large del. Rep. Party Platform Planning Com.; mem. Ga. Com. on Children and Youth, 1968. With USN, 1953-57. Recipient Nat. Def. Edn. award U.S. Office of Edn., 1966-67, GE Found. award, 1971, Rep. Presdl. Legion of Merit, 1992-2001, Rep. Presdl. award, 1994, Rep. Presdl. Order of Merit, 1997. Mem. ASCD, ASPCA, AARP, Acad. Am. Poets, Nat. Authors Registry, Coun. for Exceptional Children, Am. Pers. and Guidance Assn., Am. Sch. Counselors Assn. (Ga. coord.), Nat. Assn. Sch. Counselors., Am. Legion, VFW (life), Ga. Assn. Educators, Ga. Pers. and Guidance Assn., Palmetto Tchrs. Assn., Sierra Club, Nature Conservancy, Nat. Resources Def. Coun., World Wildlife Soc., Defenders of Wildlife, Rainforest Alliance, Ocean Conservancy, Nat. Trust for Hist. Preservation, Civil War Preservation Trust, Environ. Def., Heritage Found., Nat. Pks. Conservancy Assn., Humane Soc. U.S., Phi Delta Kappa, Kappa Delta Pi. Republican. Baptist. Avocations: coin collecting, pets, scientific experiments, historical studies. Home: 324 Tulane Dr Ladson SC 29456-6235

CANNON, TYRONE, dean; BS in Child Devel. and Family Rels., U. Conn., 1973, MSW, 1975; MLS, U. Pitts., 1981; postgraduate, U. San Francisco. Clin. social worker, 1975—80; social scis. libr. U. Tex., Arlington, 1981—83; social work libr. Columbia U., N.Y.C., 1984—88, acting instructional svcs. libr., 1987—88; head social scis. divsn. Okla. State U., 1988—89; head reference Thomas P. O'Neill Jr. Libr. Boston Coll., 1989—91, acting. univ. libr., 1993, sr. assoc. univ. libr., 1991—95; dean univ. librs. U. San Francisco, 1995—. Mem.: Assn. Coll. Rsch. Librs. (v.p., pres.-elect 2002—03). Office: U San Francisco 2130 Fulton St San Francisco CA 94117-1080*

CANOVA, JOHN RICHARD, educational administrator; b. Rockford, Ill., Feb. 17, 1941; s. John Joseph and Leona Rose (Sorrentino) C.; m. Roseann Sacco, June 5, 1965; children: Kimberly Ann, Joseph Robert, John Michael. BS, No. Ill. U., 1963, MS, 1970. Cert. tchr., secondary adminstr., chief sch. bus. ofcl., Ill. Tchr. Boylan Ctrl. Cath. High Sch., Rockford, 1963-70, dean of students, 1970-74, dir. bus. affairs, 1974-82; bus. mgr. Bensenville (Ill.) Elem. Sch. Dist. # 2, 1988-91; asst. supt. bus. svcs. Harlem Consolidated Sch. Dist. # 122, Loves Park, Ill., 1991—. Active Consolidated Day Com., Rockford, 1979, Nat. Italian-Am. Sports Hall of Fame, Arlington Heights, Ill., 1991, Harlem Community Ctr., Loves Park, 1992; charter mem. Festa Italiana, Rockford, 1979. NSF grantee, 1970. Mem. Assn. Sch. Bus. Ofcls., Ill. Assn. Sch. Bus. Ofcls., Manh Nah Tee See Country Club. Avocation: golf. Home: 23 Johns Woods Dr Rockford IL 61103-1608 Office: Harlem Consolidated 8605 N 2nd St Machesney Park IL 61115-2003

CANTILLI, EDMUND JOSEPH, safety engineering educator, translator, writer, consultant; b. Yonkers, N.Y., Feb. 12, 1927; s. Ettore and Maria (deRubeis) C.; m. Nella Franco, May 15, 1948; children: Robert, John, Teresa. AB, Columbia U., 1954, BS, 1955; cert., Yale Bur. Hwy. Traffic, 1957; PhD in Transp. Planning and Engring., Poly. Inst. Bklyn., 1972; postgrad. in urban planning and pub. safety, NYU, 1968-71. Registered profl. engr., N.Y., N.J., Calif.; profl. planner, N.J.; bd. cert. safe ty profl. (BCSP); bd. cert. planner (AICP); bd. cert. forensic engr. (BCFE). Supervising engr. safety rsch. and studies Port Authority of N.Y. & N.J., 1955-69; prof. transp. and safety engring. Poly. U., N.Y.C., 1969-90; pres. Urbitran Assocs., 1973-81; exec. dir., chmn. bd. Internat. Inst. for Safety Trans., Inc., 1977—; pres. EJC Safety Assocs., Inc., 1989—. Tchr. Italian, algebra, traffic engring., urban planning, transp. planning, urban and transp. geography, land use planning, aesthetics, environment, indsl., traffic and transp. safety engring., human factors engring., ethics for engrs.; cons. transp. and traffic safety engring., community planning, traffic engring., transp. planning, accident reconstrn., environ. impacts, 1969—; vis. prof. transp. safety engring. Inst. Superior Técnico, Lisbon, 1987-97; advisor to doctorate students Poly. U., CUNY, 1969-94, Politecnico di Milano, U. Trieste, Italy, 1980—; consulting forensic engr., accident reconstructionist, expert witness transp. accident litigation including hwy. traffic, railroad, rail rapid transit, pedestrian accidents, 1969—. Translator (Italian-English autobiog. Joseph Tusiani): The Difficult Word; The New Word; The Ancient Word, 1988; author: Programming Environmental Improvements in Public Transportation, 1974, Transportation and the Disadvantaged, 1974, Transportation System Safety, 1979; editor: Transportation and Aging, 1971, Pedestrian Planning and Design, 1971; editor, contbr.: Traffic Engineering Theory and Control, 1973; editor and calligrapher There Is No Death That Is Not Ennobled by So Great A Cause, 1976; contbr. over 200 articles to profl. jours. and trade jours.; developer daylight running lights, methods of severity evaluation of accidents, identification, priority-setting and treatment of roadside hazards, transp. system safety methodology; expert systems for improving traffic safety; introduced diagrammatic traffic signs, collision energy-absorption devices. With U.S. Army, 1945-49, 50-51. Fellow ASCE, Inst. Transp. Engrs., Nat. Acad. Forensic Engrs.; mem. NSPE, Am. Planning Assn. (charter), Am. Inst. Cert. Planners (cert.), Am. Soc. Safety Engrs., N.Y. Acad. Scis., Nat. Assn. Profl. Accident Reconstrn. Specialists, Internat. Assn. for Accidents and Traffic Medicine, Human Factors Soc., N.Y. Acad. Scis., System Safety Soc., Sigma Xi. Home: 134 Euston Rd West Hempstead NY 11552-1024 Office: PO Box 63 Franklin Square NY 11010-0063 E-mail: ejcsafety@aol.com., insafetran@aol.com., cantoxxv@aol.com.

CANTLIFFE, DANIEL JAMES, horticulture educator; b. N.Y.C., Oct. 31, 1943; s. Sarah Lucretia Keesler C.; m. Elizabeth F. Lapetina, June 5, 1965; children: Christine, Deanna, Danielle, Cheri. BS, Delaware Valley Coll., Doylestown Pa., 1965; MS, Purdue U., 1967, PhD, 1971. Asst. prof. horticulture U. Fla., Gainesville, 1974-76, assoc. prof., 1976-81, prof., 1981—, asst. chair dept., 1983-84, acting chair dept., 1984-85, chmn. dept., 1985-92, acting chair dept. fruit crops, 1991-92, chair dept. hort. scis., 1992—. Vis. prof. U. Hawaii, Honolulu, 1979-80; sci. cons. Sun Seeds Genetics, Hollister, Calif., 1987, Pillsbury Co., 1987—, Teltech Inc., Bloomington, Minn., 1988—, DNAP, Monsanto, Seed Dynamics, Ball Seed Co., Sybron Chem., Dow Agro Scis. Contbr. articles to profl. jours. and conf. procs., chpts. to books. Recipient rsch. award Fla. Fruit and Vegetable Assn., Orlando, 1986, Alumni Achievement award Delaware Valley Coll., Doylestown, 1990, Distinguished Agrl. Alumni award Purdue Univ., 1999. Fellow Am. Soc. Hort. Sci. (v.p. rsch. 1991-92, pres.-elect 1993-94, pres. 1994-95, chmn. 1995-96, Outstanding Grad. Educator award 1991, Best Paper Vegetable Sect. 1992, Membership Recruitment award 1996, Outstanding Rsch. award 1997, vegetable publ. award 1997, So. Region Leadership and Adminstrn. award 2000), Crop Sci. Soc. Am. (Seed Sci. award 1997); mem. Fla. State Hort. Soc. (v.p. vegetable sect. 1984-85, pres. 1991-92, chmn. exec. com. 1992-93, best paper vegetable sec. 1990, 92, 93, 2001, 2003, profl. excellence program award 1996, USDA Group Hon. award for Excellence 1997, Internat. Soc. Hort. Sci. (chair sect. of vegetables), Crop Sci. Soc. Am., Fla. Seed Assn. (hon.), Internat. Soc. Horiculture, Am. Soc. Plant Physiologists, Am. Soc. Agronomy, Internat. Soc. Tropical Horticulture, Bot. Soc. Am., N.Am. Strawberry Growers Assn., Plasticulture Soc. Am., Sigma Xi, Delta Tau Alpha, Phi Kappa Phi, Gamma Sigma Delta, Phi Beta Delta. Office: U of Fla Hort Scis Dept PO Box 110690 1251 Fifield Hall Gainesville FL 32611-0690

CANTOR, NANCY, academic administrator; b. NYC; m. Steven Brechin; children: Maddy, Archie. AB, Sarah Lawrence Coll., 1974; PhD in Psychology, Stanford U., 1978. Faculty, chair dept. psychology Princeton (NJ) U., 1991—96; dean Horace H. Rackham Sch. Grad. Studies, vice provost for acad. affairs U. Mich., Ann Arbor, 1996—97, provost, exec. v.p. acad. affairs, 1997—2001; chancellor U. Ill.-Urbana-Champaign, 2001—. Mem. adv. bd. NSF; mem. com. on nat. needs in biomed. and behavioral sci. rsch. NRC, mem. com. on women in sci. and engring. Co-author (or co-editor): 3 books; contbr. 50 articles to profl. jours., chpts. to books. Recipient Woman of Achievement award, Anti Defamation League. Fellow: Soc. for Personality and Social Psychology, APA (Disting. Sci. award for early career contbn. in psychology), Am. Psychol. Soc.; mem.: Am. Assn. for Higher Edn. (vice chair bd. dirs.), Am. Acad. Arts and Sci., Inst. of Medicine of NAS. Office: Univ Ill-Urbana-Champaign 320 Swanlund Adminstrn Bldg 601 E John St Champaign IL 61820

CANTORE GREEN OEHLER, JEAN, secondary education educator; b. Alexandria, Va., Aug. 16, 1953; d. Thomas Anthony and Dorothy Joan (Mahony) Cantore; m. Gregory Michael Oehler, Dec. 7, 2002; children: Thomas Scott Green, Jared Andrew Green. BA in English summa cum laude, SUNY, Albany, 1974, MA in English summa cum laude, 1976; student, Albany Law Sch., 1978-79. Cert. secondary sch. tchr. English and Spanish, N.Y., Mass. English tchr. Niskayuna Schs., Schenectady, N.Y., 1976-77, East Greenbush (N.Y.) Schs., 1977-78, Brighton Ctrl. Schs., Rochester, N.Y., 1979—. Asst. prof. English, SUNY, Albany, 1979. Coach Little League Brighton Baseball, Rochester, 1991—; mem. ALS Therapy Devel. Found. Recipient Tchr. of Yr. award Tufts U., 1986, Outstanding Educator award Cornell U., 1987, Outstanding Tchr. Tribute, Tufts U., 1995, Univ. Rochester Phi Beta Kappa Tchr.-Scholar Recognition award, 1982, 94. Mem. NEA, Nat. Coun. Tchrs. English, Autism Soc. Am., Parent-Tchr.-Student Assn., Parents Advocation Support Svcs., ALS Assn. Am., Phi Beta Kappa. Avocations: gardening, writing, art collecting, music, swimming. Office: Brighton High Sch 1150 Winton Rd S Rochester NY 14618-2299

CANTRELL, DOUGLAS EUGENE, history educator, author; b. Whitewood, Va., May 24, 1959; s. Charles Anderson Cantrell and Norma Lovus Davis; m. Lisa Ann Sanders, July 29, 1988. BA, Berea Coll., 1982; MA, U. Ky., 1985. Student tchr. Harlan (Ky.) High Sch., 1983; grad. asst. U. Ky., Lexington, 1983-87, instr. history, 1988, Elizabethtown (Ky.) C.C., U. Ky., 1987-91, asst. prof. history, 1991—96, assoc. prof., 1996—2003, prof., 2003—. Presenter in field. Author: American Dreams and Realities: A Retelling of the American Story, The Western Dream of Civilization, HIstorical Perspectives: A Reader and Study Guide; co-editor: Ky. History Jour., 1987; contbr. articles to profl. jours. Mem. Ky. Hist. Soc., Ky. Assn. Tchrs. History (mem. exec. bd. 1991—, pres. 1994—), Orgn. Am. Historians, So. Hist. Assn., Appalachian Studies Assn., Filson Club. Avocations: breeding tropical fish, bass fishing. Home: 220 Ruby Dr Elizabethtown KY 42701-4632 Office: Elizabethtown CC 600 College Street Rd Elizabethtown KY 42701-3053

CANTRELL, SHARRON CAULK, principal; b. Columbia, Tenn., Oct. 2, 1947; d. Tom English and Beulah (Goodin) Caulk; m. William Terry Cantrell, Mar. 18, 1989; 1 child, Jordan; children from previous marriage: Christopher, George English, Steffenee Copley. BA, George Peabody Coll. Tchrs., 1970; MS, Vanderbilt U., 1980; EdS, Mid. Tenn. State U., 1986. Tchr. Ft. Campbell Jr. High Sch., Columbia, Tenn., 1970-71, Whitthorne Jr. High Sch., Columbia, Tenn., 1977-86, Spring Hill (Tenn.) High Sch., 1966—. Mem. NEA, AAUW (pres. Tenn. divsn. 1983-85), Maury County Edn. Assn. (pres. 1983-84), Tenn. Edn. Assn., Assn. Preservation Tenn. Antiquities, Maury Alliance, Friends of Children's Hosp., Rotary (bd. dirs.), Phi Delta Kappa. Mem. Ch. of Christ. Home: 5299 Main St Spring Hill TN 37174-2495 Office: Spring Hill High Sch 1 Raider Ln Columbia TN 38401-7346

CANTU, DINO ANTONIO, secondary education history educator; b. Savanna, Ill., Sept. 25, 1961; s. Alfonso A. and Bonnie L. (Wills) C.; m. Sandra Lou Smith, May 12, 1984; children: Derek Anthony, Dylan Alex. AS in Social Sci., Highland C.C., Freeport, Ill., 1981; BSE in Social Sci. Edn., Ark. State U., 1983, MA in History, 1984, specialist in C.C. Edn., 1989; PhD in Curriculum & Instrn., So. Ill. U., 1996. Tchrs. Cert. Social Studies 7-12, Mo. Tutor PASS Program Ark. State U., Jonesboro, 1982-83, grad. asst. History Dept., 1983-84; military intelligence officer U.S. Army, Ft. Knox, Ky., 1984-88; history instr. Ark. State U., Jonesboro, 1988-89; tchr. Am. history, chair dept. social studies Ste. Genevieve (Mo.) High Sch., 1989—; adj. faculty 1-8-1-8 program St. Louis U., Ste. Genevieve, Mo., 1991—. Chmn. Social Sci. Curriculum Com., Ste. Genevieve, Mo., 1991; evaluator North Ctrl. Vis. Com., Ste. Genevieve, Mo., 1992; cooperating tchr. S.E. Mo. State U., Ste. Genevieve, Mo., 1992; rep. NCSS Textbook Com., Washington, 1992—; rep. Governor's Task Force Environ. Edn., 1993-94; rep. ad hoc com. performace stnds. Mo. Dept. Elem. and Secondary Edn., 1994; v.p. Mo. Coun. for the Social Studies, 1996-97, pres-elect, 1997—. Presenter Civil War Prison Camp, 1984, Rural Traditions, 1991. Commr. Ste. Genevieve (Mo.) Landmarks Commn., 1992—; bd. dirs. Found. for Restoration of Ste. Genevieve, 1993-94; rep. steering com. Ste. Genevieve Hist. Preservation and Tourism, 1993-94. Capt. U.S. Army, 1984-88. Recipient Social Sci. award Highland C.C., Freeport, Ill., 1981, George C. Marshall ROTC award U.S. Army, Ark. State U., 1984, Military Intelligence Acad. award U.S. Army, Ft. Huachuca, Ariz., 1985, Army Commendation medal U.S. Army, Ft. Knox, Ky., 1988; named Outstanding Young Educator, Jaycees, Ste, Genevieve, Mo., 1992, Mo. Social Studies Tchr. of Yr., Mo. Coun. Social Studies, 1994. Mem. Nat. Coun. History Edn. (Mo. com. corr.), Am. Sociol. Assn., Nat. Coun. Social Studies (chmn. sociology spl. interest group 1993-95, instruction com., 1995-96), Mo. Coun. Social Studies (v.p.), Mo. Hist. Soc., Orgn. Am. Historians, Pi Gamma Mu, Sigma Phi Epsilon, Kappa Delta Pi, Phi Kappa Phi, Phi Alpha Theta. Home: 4609 W Sandpiper Dr Muncie IN 47304-2895 Office: St Genevieve H S 715 Washington St Sainte Genevieve MO 63670-1237

CANTU, KATHLEEN MARIE, academic administrator; b. Gary, Ind., May 23, 1956; d. John and Nellie Rose (Lopez) C. BS in Retail Mgmt., U. Wis., 1982. Page Wis. State Senate, Madison, 1980; store mgr. Fanny Farmer Candy Shops, Inc., Madison, 1980-85; recruiter, advisor Office of Admissions U. Wis., Madison, 1985-90, program mgr. Sch. Nursing, 1990—. Commr. City of Madison Cmty. Svcs. Commn., 1990—; bd. dirs. Dane County Human Svcs. Bd., Madison, 1993-98; cmty. mem. Cmty. Assessment for Health and Human Svcs. Planning in Dane County, Madison, 1993, Latino Adv. Com. to U.S. Senator Russ Feingold, Madison, 1994—. Continuing adult edn. grantee U. Wis., 1991; recipient George Washington Carver award in chemistry, U. Wis.-Madison, 1992. Mem. Nat. Coalition of Hispanic Health and Human Svcs. Orgn., Wis. Indian Edn. Assn., Nat. Assn. Hispanic Nurses. Democrat. Roman Catholic. Avocations: travel, jogging, theater, horseback riding, reading. Office: U Wis Sch Nursing K6 252 Clin Sci Ctr 600 Highland Ave Madison WI 53792-0001

CAPASSO, FRANK LOUIS, secondary school educator; b. N.Y.C., Apr. 30, 1943; s. Louis and Marie Francis (Fiermonte) C.; m. Diane Patricia Webster, July 8, 1967; children: Ann Marie, Eleanor, Elizabeth. BA in History, Iona Coll., 1964; MS in Edn., Fordham U., 1976, MA in History, 1995. Tchr. Intermediate Sch. 148, N.Y.C., 1965-92, Truman H.S., N.Y.C., 1992—. Mentor N.Y.C. Bd. Edn., 1993-97; acting chairperson Intermediate Sch. 148, 1985-91, cooperating tchr., 1997. Mem. Nat. Coun. Social Studies, Mid. State Coun. Social Studies, United Fedn. Tchrs. (chpt. leader 1986-91, Ely Tractenberg award 1975-76). Democrat. Roman Catholic. Home: 48 Pratt St New Rochelle NY 10801-4339

CAPERTON, RICHARD WALTON, photographer, automobile repair company executive, educator, consultant; b. Waynesburg, Pa., Jan. 11, 1948; s. Walton Greene Caperton and Sareta (Campbell) Garetson; children: Richard Walton Jr., Christa Elizabeth, Joseph Allen, Stephanie Gabrielle; m. Linda L. Burgess, July 4, 1999; 1 stepchild: Melinda Carlson. Grad. high sch., Naples, Fla. Asst. mgr. W.T. Grant Co., Naples, 1967-75; pres., chief exec. officer, gen. mgr. R&R Automotive Inc., Naples, 1975-95, CEO, 1996; pres., chief exec. officer AAMGO Auto Parts Inc., Naples, 1987-91; pres. Caperton Properties, 1977—2000, Nu U Mktg., 1991-95, Caperton Consulting, 1994-96. Instr. Walker Tech. Inst., 1996-97; advt. cons. Edwards Publs., 1998; owner Rick Caperton Photography, Anderson, S.C., 2000—. Bd. dirs. East Naples Civic Assn., 1979-80; v.p. Fla. Sports Park, Naples, 1997, pres., 1997-98, bd. dirs., 1987—, dir. emeritus; mem. adv. bd. Walker Tech. Inst., 1991-95; apptd. to Fla. New Motor Vehicle Arbitration Bd., 1994-97. Fellow Automobile Svc. Assn., Rotary (bd. dirs. Naples East 1987-96, v.p. Naples East 1990-91, pres. 1996-97), mem. Greater Anderson Rotary. Republican. Methodist. Avocations: golf, scuba diving, boating, shooting. Office: 1701 Broadway Lake Rd Anderson SC 29621 E-mail: rikcapertonphoto@cs.com.

CAPERTON, W. GASTON, former governor, educational association administrator; b. W.Va., 1940; m. Rachael Worby; children: Gat, John. Grad., Univ. N.C., 1963. Pres. McDonough Caperton Ins. Group, 1976—; gov. W.Va., 1989-97; dir. Inst. Edn. & Govt. Columbia U., N.Y.C., 1997—99; pres. Coll. Bd., 1999—. Founder, past pres. W.Va. Edn. Fund. Office: The Coll Bd 45 Columbus Ave New York NY 10023

CAPETILLO, CHARLENE VERNELLE, music educator, special education educator; b. Streator, Ill., Sept. 18, 1944; d. Miles Bryan and Lillian Mae Baker; m. Benjamin Capetillo, July 20, 1963; children: Christiana, Matthew Bryan, Susannah Carlina. Photography cert., Woodland Hills Occupl. Ctr., 1979; student, Pierce Coll., 1985, student, 1987. Sales staff Avon, Pasadena, Calif., 1963—78; pvt. seamstress Calabasas, Calif., 1963—; piano and voice tchr. pvt. and pub. schs., Conejo and L.A., 1978—; singer L.A. Opera, Opera Pacific, 1985—95, L.A. Camerata Orch., 1985—; owner, pres. Hollywood Angels Childrens' Photography, L.A., 1994—; spl. edn. tchr. L.A. Unified Sch. Dist., 1999—; dir. sales Neo-Life Diamite Health Products, 1985—. Actor: (poems and essays); performer: Carnegie Hall, 1999, 2001, 2003, (soloist) China Tour, 2003. Vol. performer various retirement homes, L.A., 1992—; soloist numerous chs., L.A.; choir mem. Grace Cmty. Ch., Sun Valley, Calif., 1994—96. Mem.: Phi Beta, Pi Alpha Theta. Achievements include 4th great grandaughter of Daniel Boone. Avocations: traveling, hiking, quilting, art. Home: 6519 W 87th Pl Westchester CA 90045

CAPITOL-JEFFERSON, VIOLA WHITESIDE, secondary education art educator; b. Greenville, Pa., Feb. 23, 1947; d. Claude Henry Sr. and Geraldine (Carter) Whiteside; m. William H. Capitol Jr., Aug. 29, 1970 (div. 1982); m. Porter James Jefferson, Sept. 17, 1983. BS in Art Edn., Youngstown State U., 1971; MA in Art Edn., Trinity Coll., 1977. Cert. tchr. art, Md. Gen. office staff Greenville Hosp., 1965-70; pvt. sec. Gibbs Paving and Demolition, West Middlesex, Pa., 1970-71; tchr. art Lackey High Sch., Indian Head, Md., 1971-76; tchr. art, chair dept. McDonough High Sch., Pomfret, Md., 1976-88; tchr. art Surrattsville High Sch., Clinton, Md., 1988-90, 91-92, Largo High Sch., 1990-91; art tchr., chair dept. Friendly High Sch., Ft. Washington, Md., 1992—. Multi-cultural curriculum writer Prince George's County, Upper Marlboro, Md., 1988—; multicultural liaison, Friendly H.S., Ft. Washington, Md., 1993—; sr. class sponsor, 1992-93; resource person Black Male Achievement Program, Prince George's County, 1990—, Cultural Experiences Program, 1988—; spkr., presenter ann. Md. Art Edn. Vol. Photo Archive, Nat. Mus. African Art, Washington, 1987, docent, 1985—; vol. Cross-Cultural Ctr., Washington, 1989—; sponsor youth ministries in assn. with Terry and Assocs., Inc., Wyo., Mich., 1992. Recipient Disting. Svc. award Charles County Tchr. of Yr., Jaycees, 1982, Cert. of Outstanding Svc. Mid. States Assn. Colls. and Secondary Schs., 1974-89, Educator of Yr. award Prince George's Art Coun., 1995. Mem. NEA, Nat. Art Edn. Assn. (J. Eugene Grigsby award 1995), Md. Tchrs. Assn., Md. Art Edn. Assn. (COMC rep. exec. com. 1992—, Outstanding New Art Tchr. in Prince George's County 1989), Smithsonian Assocs., Black Women United for Action, Delta Sigma Theta. Avocations: reading historical novels, writing poetry, interior decorating. Home: 9200 Genoa Ave Fort Washington MD 20744-3777

CAPLAN, ARTHUR, university program director, educator; b. Boston, Mar. 21, 1950; s. Sidney and Natalie (Fluke) C.; m. Margaret Brennan; 1 child, Zachary. BA, Brandeis U., 1971; MA, Columbia U., 1973, MPhil, 1975, PhD, 1979. Staff assoc. in ethical issues in sci. and medicine The Hastings Ctr., 1975-76, assoc. for humanities, 1977-84, assoc. dir., 1985-87; instr. Sch. of Pub. Health Columbia U., N.Y.C., 1977-78, assoc. for social medicine, 1978-81; prof. philosophy, surgery; dir. Ctr. for Biomedical Ethics U. Minn., Mpls., 1987-94; dir. U. Pa. Ctr. for Bioethics, Phila., 1994—. Vis. prof. U. Pitts., 1986: adv. bd. Poynter Inst., Nat. Marrow Donor Program, ARC. Author: Moral Matters, 1995, Prescribing Our Future: Ethical Challenges in Genetic Counseling, 1993, If I Were a Rich Man Could I Buy a Pancreas and Other Essays on Medical Ethics, 1992, When Medicine Went Mad: Bioethics and the Holocaust, 1992, Everyday Ethics: Resolving Dilemmas in Nursing Home Life, 1990, Beyond Baby M, 1990; contbr. articles to profl. jours.; lectr., commentator in field. Mem. Clin. Health Care Task Force, Wash. (vice chmn. ethics working group 1993-94); cons. Office of Tech. Assessment U.S. Congress, Minn. Dept. Health, Am. Found. for AIDS Rsch., NIH, Dept. Health and Human Svcs., Nat. Marrow Donor Program, Lifesource-Organ Procurement Org., Nat. Acad. Scis.-Inst. Medicine, state legis. Pa., Minn., N.Y., N.J. Recipient Commr.'s award Dept. Health and Human Svcs., 1993. Mem. Am. Assn. Bioethics (pres. 1993-95), Ctrl. Soc. for Clin. Rsch. Avocation: tennis. Office: U Pa 3401 Market St Philadelphia PA 19104-3318

CAPLAN, LOUIS ROBERT, neurology educator; b. Balt., Dec. 31, 1936; s. Carl Clarence and Bess Pauline (Cohen) C.; m. F. Brenda Fields, Nov. 28, 1963; children: Laura, Daniel, Jonathan, David, Jeremy, Benjamin. BA cum laude, Williams Coll., 1958; MD summa cum laude, U. Md., 1962. Diplomate Am. Bd. Internal Medicine, Am. Bd. Psychiatry and Neurology. Intern to jr. asst. resident Boston City Hosp., 1962-64; resident Harvard Neurol. Unit, Boston, 1966-69; cerebrovascular fellow Mass. Gen. Hosp., Boston, 1969-70; neurologist Beth Israel Hosp., Boston, 1970-78; asst. prof. Harvard Med. Sch., Boston, 1970-78, prof. neurology, 1999; chief neurologist Michael Reese Hosp., Chgo., 1978-84; prof. neurology U. Chgo., 1980-84; chief neurologist New England Med. Ctr., Boston, 1984-97; prof., chmn. dept. neurology Tufts U., Boston, 1984-97, prof. medicine, 1989-97; neurologist Beth Israel Deaconess Med. Ctr., Boston, 1998—; prof. neurology Harvard Med. Sch., 1999—. Author: stroke: A Clinical Approach, 1986, 3rd edit., 2000, Consultations in Neurology, 1987, The Effective Clinical Neurologist, 2nd edit., 2001, Vertebrobasilar Arterial Disease, 1993; author: (with others) Cerebral Small Artery Disease, 1993; author: Management of Persons with Stroke, 1993, Brainstem Localization and Function, 1993, Intercerebral Hemmorhage, 1994, Family Guide to Stroke, 1994, Brain Ischemia-Basic Concepts and Clinical Relevance, 1995, Stroke Syndromes, 2nd edit., 2001, Posterior Circulation Disease, 1996, Neurologic Disorders: Course and Treatment, 1996, 2d edit., 2003, Primer on Cerebrovascular Diseases, 1997; author: (with others) Clinical Neurocardiology, 1999; author: Uncommon Causes of Stroke, 2001, Striking Back at Stroke--A Doctor-Patient Journal, 2003; contbr. over 500 articles to profl. jours.; contbr. more than 500 articles to profl. jours. Bd. dirs. Solomon Schecter Day Sch., Boston, 1977-78, Chgo., 1983-85. Capt. U.S. Army, 1962-64. Recipient House Officer Teaching prize Michael Reese Hosp., 1980. Fellow Am. Acad. Neurology, Am. Neurol. Assn., Stroke Coun. Am. Heart Assn. (chmn. 1987-89, sci. adv. com. 1990—), Royal Soc. of Medicine; mem. Coun. Med. Specialties Socs. (rep. 1982-90), Chgo. Neurol. Soc. (chmn. 1984-85), Boston Soc. Neurology and Psychiatry (pres. 1988-89), Chgo. Heart Assn. (chmn. stroke com. 1979-84), Australian Neurol. Soc. (hon.), German Neurol. Assn. (hon.), Phi Beta Kappa, Alpha Omega Alpha. Democrat. Jewish. Office: Beth Israel Deaconess MC Dept Neurology 330 Brookline Ave Palmer 127 Boston MA 02215-5400

CAPLIN, MORTIMER MAXWELL, lawyer, educator; b. N.Y.C., July 11, 1916; s. Daniel and Lillian (Epstein) C.; m. Ruth Sacks, Oct. 18, 1942; children: Lee Evan, Michael Andrew, Jeremy Owen, Catherine Jean. BS, U. Va., 1937, LLB, 1940; JSD, NYU, 1953; LLD (hon.), St. Michael's Coll., 1964. Bar: Va. 1941, N.Y. 1942, D.C. 1964. Law clk. to Hon. Armistead M. Dobie U.S. Ct. Appeals (4th cir.), Richmond, 1940-41; assoc. Paul, Weiss, Rifkind, Wharton & Garrison, N.Y.C., 1941-42, 45-50; prof. law U. Va., Charlottesville, 1950-61, vis. prof. law, 1965-87, prof. emeritus, 1988—; ptnr. Perkins, Battle & Minor, Charlottesville, 1952-61; U.S. commr. IRS, Washington, 1961-64; sr. ptnr. Caplin & Drysdale, Washington, 1964—. Mem. Pres.'s Task Force on Taxation, 1960; bd. dirs. Danaher Corp., Washington, Fairchild Corp., Dulles, Va., Presdl. Realty Corp., White Plains, N.Y., Environ. and Energy Study Inst.; mem. pub. rev. bd. Arthur Andersen & Co., Chgo., 1980-88; reorgn. trustee Webb & Knapp, Inc., 1965-72. Author: Proxies, Annual Meetings and Corporate Democracy, 1953, Doing Business in Other States, 1959; editor-in-chief Va. Law Rev., 1939-40; contbr. numerous articles on tax and corp. matters to profl. jours. Past chmn. bd. dirs. Nat. Civic Svc. League, Am. Coun. on Internat. Sports; past chmn. nat citizens adv. com. Assn. Am. Med. Colls.; trustee Arena Stage, U. Va. Law Sch. Found., Wolf Trap Found. Performing Arts, Shakespeare Theatre, Washington, Arena Stage, Washington, Peace Through Law Found., Washington; bd. overseers U. V.I.; chmn. adv. bd. Hospitality and Info. Svc., Washington; hon. chmn. Coun. for Arts, U. Va.; past pres. Atlantic Coast Conf.; emeritus trustee George Washington U.; mem. bd. visitors U. Va., 1992-97; pres., bd. dirs. Indigent Civil Litigation Fund; mem. governing coun. U. Va. Miller Ctr. Pub. Affairs. Decorated mem. initial landing force Normandy Invasion USN; recipient, Va. State Bar and Va. Soc. CPAs award, 1960, Achievement award, Tax Soc. of NYU, 1962, Judge Learned Hand Human Rels. award, Am. Jewish Com., 1963, 1993, Alexander Hamilton award, U.S. Treasury Dept., 1964, Disting. Svc. award, Tax Execs. Inst., 1964, medal in law, U. Va. Thomas Jefferson Found., 2001. Fellow Am. Bar Found., Am. Tax Policy Inst., Am. Coll. Tax Counsel; mem. ABA (ho. of dels. 1980-92, mem. fed. jud. com. 1993-96, ALI-ABA com. continuing profl. edn., chair DC Fellows), Nat. Conf. of Lawyers and CPAs, Am. Law Inst. (life), N.Y. State Bar Assn., Va. Bar Assn., D.C. Bar Assn., D.C. Bar Found. (adv. com.), Univ. Club (Washington), Fed. City Club (bd. govs.), Colonnade Club (Charlottesville), Order of Coif, Phi Beta Kappa, Phi Beta Kappa Assocs., Omicron Delta Kappa. Democrat. Jewish. Avocations: swimming, tennis, hiking. Home: 5610 Wisconsin Ave Apt 18E Chevy Chase MD 20815-4415 Office: One Thomas Circle NW Washington DC 20005-5802 E-mail: mmc@capdale.com.

CAPLOW, THEODORE, sociologist, educator; b. N.Y.C., May 1, 1920; s. Samuel Nathaniel and Florence (Israel) C.; m. Margaret Mary Pettit, 1981. AB, U. Chgo., 1939; PhD, U. Minn., 1946; LLD, Ball State U., 2003. Mem. faculty U. Minn., 1945-60; prof. sociology Columbia U., 1961-70; chmn. dept. sociology U. Va., Charlottesville, 1970-78, 84-86, Commonwealth prof., 1973—. Vis. prof. U. Bordeaux, France, 1950, U. Aix-Marseille, France, 1951, U. Utrecht, Netherlands, 1954-55, Stanford, 1957, P.R., 1959, U. Bogota, Colombia, 1962, Sorbonne, Paris, France, 1968-69, Institut d'Etudes Politiques, Paris, 1983, U. Rome, 1984, U. Oslo, 1986; pres. Mendota Research Group Inc., 1957-65 Author: Sociology of Work, 1954, Principles of Organization, 1964, Two Against One, 1968, L'Enquête Sociologique, 1970, Toward Social Hope, 1975, Peace Games, 1989, American Social Trends, 1991, Perverse Incentives, 1994; sr. author: The Academic Marketplace, 1957, The Urban Ambience, 1964, Middletown Families, 1982, All Faithful People, 1983, Recent Social Trends in the United States, 1960-90, 1991, Systems of War and Peace, 1995, Sociologie Militaire, 2000, The First Measured Century, 2001, Leviathen Transformed, 2002. With AUS, 1943-45, PTO. Decorated Purple Heart. Mem. Tocqueville Soc. (pres. 1979-83), Am. Sociol. Assn. (sec. 1983-86), Farmington Hunt Club Albemerle Yacht Club,(Charlottesville), Century Club (N.Y.C.), Tarratine Club (Dark Harbor, Maine). Home: Twin Springs 793 Reas Ford Rd Earlysville VA 22936-2306 E-mail: tc@virginia.edu.

CAPORINO, GRACE CONNOLLY, education educator, consultant; b. Red Bank, N.J. d. Daniel Joseph and Mary Agnes (Martinez) Connolly; m. Gabriel Anthony Caporino, July 19, 1960 (dec. Mar. 1974); children: Melanie Brezovsky, Pamela. BA in Lit., Purchase Coll., 1974; MA in Secondary English, Manhattanville Coll., 1978. Grad. prof. edn. Manhattan Coll., Purchase, N.Y., 2000—. Lit. cons. Advanced Placement English Lit. Exam Reader, The Coll. Bd., Princeton, N.J., 1988—; cons. Tchr. Task Force, U.S. Holocaust Meml. Mus., Washington, 1990—; project dir. NEH masterwork grant CUNY Grad. Ctr., N.Y.C., 1989-91; project dir. NEH Humanities Focus Grant Holocaust Perspectives: The Word and the Image, Manhattanville Coll., Purchase, N.Y., 1995-96, adj. prof. edn.; adj. prof. Manhattanville Coll., 2000; vis. lectr. Fitchburg (Mass.) State Coll., 2001—. Contbg. author: pamphlets Guidelines for Teaching the Holocaust, 1993, Teacher's Guide for Artifact Poster Series, 1993, Teaching for a Tolerant World, 1999; author: Testimonies from the Aryan Side, 2001, Jewish Catholics in the Warsaw Ghetto, Remembering for the Future: The Holocaust in the Age of Genocide, 2001. Summer fellow Haifa U. and Yad Vashem, Jerusalem, Israel, 1987, summer NEH fellow Hollins Coll., Roanoke, Va., 1988; recipient Louis Yavner Teaching award Regents of SUNY, 1991, Robert Goldman award for excellence in Holocaust Edn., N.Y.C., 1999; Mandel fellow Edn. Dept. U.S. Holocaust Meml. Mus., 1998-99. Mem. Nat. Coun. Tchrs. English (mem. Tchg. about Genocide and Intolerance com. 1994—), Internat. Consortium Nat. Coun. Tchrs. English (host European profs. English U.S. visit 1994), N.Y. State United Tchrs. Avocations: international travel, film, theater, art collecting, reading, classical music. Home: 213 California Rd Yorktown Heights NY 10598-4907 Office: Manhattanville Col 2900 Purchase St Purchase NY 10577

CAPPELLI, MARY ANTOINETTE, principal; b. Rome, Lazio, Italy, July 27, 1938; came to U.S., 1962; d. Angelo and Antonia (Parente) C. Teaching diploma, U. Rome, Italy, 1960; BA, Annhurst Coll., 1968; MA, So. Conn. State U., 1972, postgrad., 1982. Cert. adminstr., supr., Conn.; joined Sisters of Our Lady of the Garden, Roman Cath. Ch. Elem. tchr. Scuola Pontificia, Rome, 1960-61; libr. Marianapolis Prep. Sch., Thompson, Conn., 1964-68; spl. edn. tchr. Stonegate Sch., Durham, Conn., 1968-75; tchr. St. Brendan Sch., New Haven, Conn., 1975-76, prin., 1976-95. Coord. Community Svcs. Whalley Bus. Dist., New Haven, 1980—. Mem. Nat. Cath. Edn. Assn. Democrat. Avocations: gardening, sewing, reading, environmentalist. Home: 455 1/2 Whalley Ave New Haven CT 06511-3011 Office: Saint Brendan Sch 342 Ellsworth Ave New Haven CT 06511-7103

CAPPIELLO, MIMI, elementary school educator; b. Atella, Potenza, Italy, Feb. 3, 1952; d. Giovanni Turro and Rosa Maria Palese; m. Gerard Cappiello; children: Jessica, Vera, Andrew John. Degree in bus. mgmt., Eckerd Coll., St. Petersburg, Fla., 2000. Cert. grade sch. tchr. Tchr. Scoula Elem. Statale, Atella, Italy, 1972—74; bus. mgr. All-lfemcare Ob-Gyn Ctr., Clearwater, Fla., 1983—96; sch tchr. Elem. Sch., 1992—. Mem.: Holy Sepulchre (Lady Commander 1992—2002). Roman Catholic. Avocations: gardening, painting, gourmet cooking, archaeology. Home: 1965 Lynnwood Ct Dunedin FL 34698 Home Fax: 727-786-4905. Personal E-mail: Anjeve @aol.com.

CAPPS, DENNIS WILLIAM, retired secondary school educator, artist; b. Phila., Mar. 14, 1944; s. William Hoyle and Alice Gertrude Capps; children: Andrea Diane, Adrienne Kathleen. BSBA, Fairmont State Coll., 1968; MEd, Miami U., Oxford, Ohio, 1975, postgrad., 1991-92, U. Cin., 1991-92, Wright State U., 1992. Cert. secondary tchr. math., visual arts, Ohio. Secondary schs. tchr. math. Mason (Ohio) City Schs., 1968-89, secondary schs. tchr. visual arts, 1989-98; ret., 1998. Asst. cultural arts dir. Middfest Internat., 1997-; chmn. Youth Arts Exhbn., Summerfair, Cin., 1991-97; mem., ofcl. photographer Multi-cultural On-site Curriculum Writing

Project, Mex., summer 1993; mem. regional evaluating team North Ctrl. Accrediting Assn. One-man shows include Artique Gallery, Middletown, Ohio, 1997; 4-man show Agora Gallery, N.Y.C., 1998, Base Gallery, Cin., 1999, Middfest Internat., 2003, Main Cross Gallery, Lexington, Ky., 2003; exhibited in group shows, including Miami U., 1975, Middletown Fine Arts Ctr., 1980, 96, 97, 98, Fitton Ctr. for Arts, Hamilton, Ohio, 1996, 97, 98, 99, San Giuseppe Gallery, Coll. of Mt. St. Joseph, Cin., 1997, Hargis Unique Gallery, Pomona, Calif., 1997, Cin. Art Acad., 1997, Pendleton Art Ctr., Cin., 1998; represented by Hargis Unique Gallery, 1996-97, Agora Gallery, 1997-98, Base Gallery, Cin., 1999-2001, Main Cross Gallery, Lexington, Ky., 1999—. Recipient Jennings Scholarship award Martha Holden Jennings Found., Dayton, Ohio, 1974-75, Golden Apple Tchr. award, Mason City Sch. System, 1988. Mem. NEA, Ohio Edn. Assn., Mason Edn. Assn. (treas. 1975-76, v.p. 1979-80), Nat. Art Edn. Assn., Ohio Art Edn. Assn. (state bd. dirs. 1993-95, presenter conv. 1993, 94, local conv. coord., 1995), S.W. Ohio Art Edn. Assn. (regional dir. 1993-95), Am. Mensa Soc., Intertel, Cin. Art Mus., Contemporary Arts Ctr. Democrat. Avocations: photography, drawing, painting, pocket billiards. Home: 11761 Percivale Ct Cincinnati OH 45241-5907

CAPPS, LARRY LYNN, school librarian; b. Liberal, Kans., Aug. 27, 1950; s. Charles Andrew and Mary Edna Capps; m. Janet Sue Smith, Jan. 9, 1971; children: Heather Lynn, Larry Lynn Capps II. BA in Edn., Northeastern State U., 1972; MLS, U. Okla., 1980. Tchr. H.S. French and English Weleetka (Okla.) Pub. Schs., 1972—73; tchr. H.S. English, libr. Bowlegs (Okla.) Pub. Schs., 1973—83; libr., yearbook, acad. bowl teams Dale (Okla.) Pub. Schs., 1983—. Mem.: NEA, Okla. Jr. Acad. Bowl Assn. (treas., membership chmn. 1997—), Okla. Acad. Coaches Assn., Okla. Edn. Assn. Republican. Baptist. Avocations: stamp collecting, coin collecting, television, movies, music. Office: Dale Pub Schs 300 Smith Ave Dale OK 74851

CAPRIO, ANTHONY S. academic administrator; b. Providence, Apr. 12, 1945; s. Salvatore and Esther (Iafrati) C. BA, Wesleyan U., 1967; MA, Columbia U., 1969, PhD, 1973; BA (hon.), Western New Eng. Coll., 2000. Asst. prof. langs. and fgn. studies Lehman Coll., CUNY, Bronx, 1971-76; assoc. prof. Cedar Crest Coll., Allentown, Pa., 1976-80; prof., adminstr. Am. U., Washington, 1980-89; provost Oglethorpe U., Atlanta, 1989-96; pres. Western New Eng. Coll., Springfield, Mass., 1996—. Mem. Nat. Humanities Faculty, 1977—. Author: Reflets de la femme, 1973, En Français, 1976, 3d edit., 1985; contbr. over 100 articles to profl. jours., chpts. to books. Trustee Willie Ross Sch. for the Deaf, 1999—, Springfield Symphony Orch., 1998—; bd. dirs. Springfield Adult Edn. Coun., 1999-2002, Greater Springfield Convention and Visitors Bureau, 1999—, Pioneer Valley Econ. Devel. Coun., 2000—, Springfield Sch. Vols., 2000—, Tuition Exch. Inc., 1994—, Mass. Mentoring Partnership, 2001—; exec. com. Assn. Ind. Colls. and Univs. in Mass., 1999-2002; mem. cabinet Cmty. United Way of Pioneer Valley, 1998—; co-chair Leadership Coun. of Springfield Mentoring Partnership, 1998—; corporator Springfield Libr. and Mus. Assn., 1998—; task force on workforce devel. Pioneer Valley Planning Commn., 1998—; pres. Cooperating Colls. of Greater Springfield, 2000—; accreditation com. ABA, 2002—. Recipient Adminstr.-Faculty award for outstanding performance Am. U., 1984, Disting. Adminstr. and Educator award Greater Washington Assn. Fgn. Lang. Educators, 1986. Mem. Am. Translators Assn., Am. Assn. Higher Edn., Am. Assn. Univ. Adminstrs., Soc. Coll. and Univ. Planning, Phi Beta Kappa, Omicron Delta Kappa, Phi Beta Delta, Phi Beta Kappa (fellow), others. Office: Western New Eng Coll Office of President 1215 Wilbraham Rd Springfield MA 01119-2612

CAPUANO, REGINA MARIE, hydrogeologist, geochemist educator; d. Dominick Louise and Mary Capuano; m. Stephen John Naruk; 1 child, John Capuano Naruk. BS cum laude, SUNY; MS, U. Ariz., PhD, 1988. Geochemist, project mgr. U. Utah Rsch. Inst., Salt Lake City, 1978-84; rsch. assoc. Bur. of Econ. Geology, U. Tex., Austin, 1987-89; asst. prof. U. Houston, 1989-96, assoc. prof., 1996—. Mem editl. bd. Ground Water Monitoring and Remediation, 1998—. Contbr. articles to profl. jours. including Ground Water, Geomicrobiology Jour., Am. Assn. of Petroleum Geologists, Geochimica Cosmochimica Acta, others. Grantee Gulf Coast Hazardous Substance Rsch. Ctr., 1989-93, Tex. Advanced Rsch. Program, 1989, 94, 96. Mem. Geochem. Soc., Am. Assn. of Petroleum Geologists, Assn. of Ground Water Scientists and Engrs. Office: U Houston Dept Geoscis 312 Sci and Rsch Bldg 1 Houston TX 77204-5007

CAPUTO, ANNE SPENCER, knowledge and learning programs director; b. Eugene, Oreg., Jan. 14, 1947; d. Richard J. and Adelaide Bernice (Marsh) Spencer; m. Richard Philip Caputo, July 15, 1977 (dec. Sept. 1997); 1 child: Christopher Spencer Caputo. BA in History, Lewis and Clark Coll., Portland, Oreg., 1969; MA, U. Oreg., 1971; MALS, San Jose State U., 1976. Librarian San Jose State U., Calif., 1972-76; online instr. DIALOG Info. Svcs., Palo Alto, Calif., 1976-77, chief info. scientist Washington, 1977-85, mgr. classroom instrn. program, 1986-89, dir. acad. programs, 1990-96; sr. dir. prof. devel. Knight-Ridder Info., Arlington, Va., 1996-97; sr. dir. acad. and profl. market devel. The Dialog Corp., Arlington, 1998; dir. info. pro and acad. programs Dow Jones Interactive Pub., Washington, 1998—. Asst. prof. info. sci. Cath. U. Am., Washington, 1978—2000; online cons. Nat. Com. Library-Info. Sci., Washington, 1980—82; adj. prof. U. Md. Coll. Info. Studies, 2000—. Author: Brief Guide to DIALOG Searching, 1979; contbr. articles to profl. jours. Named Info. Sci. Tchr. of Yr. Catholic U. Am., 1983. Mem.: ALA, Am. Assn. Sch. Librarians, D.C. Library Assn., Am. Soc. for Info. Sci. (officer, chair Potomac Valley chpt. 1985—86), Spl. Library Assn. (pres.-elect 2001). Episcopalian. Avocation: photographing architectural details on national trust buildings. Home: 4113 Orleans Pl Alexandria VA 22304-1618 Office: Factiva 1400 L St NW Ste 460 Washington DC 20005-3509 E-mail: anne.caputo@factiva.com

CAPUTO, JANETTE SUSAN, clinical neuropsychologist, educator; b. Detroit, Nov. 16, 1946; d. Anthony John and Sarah Rose (Mancuso) C.; m. Thomas Aloysius Closurdo, Oct. 29, 1971 (div. Jan. 1981); m. Kenneth Joseph Bruza, Aug. 4, 1981. BA, Wayne State U., 1968, MLS, 1969, PhD, 1976; MA, Ctrl. Mich. U., 1985, D in Psychology, 1989. Dir. librs. St. Joseph Mercy Hosp., Pontiac, Mich., 1971-77; libr., head. sci. libr. Wayne State U., Detroit, 1977-81; dir. Saginaw Health Sci. Libr. Saginaw (Mich.) Coop Hosps., 1981-83; contract psychologist Midland (Mich.) Mental Health, 1985, Dow Chem. Co., Midland, 1985-87; predoctoral fellow Rusk Inst. Rehab. Medicine, N.Y.C., 1987-88; clin. neuropsychologist Mid. Mich. Regional Med. Ctr., Midland, 1988-90; staff neuropsychologist Mary Free Bed Hosp., Grand Rapids, Mich., 1990-91; pres. Rehab. Strategies, P.C., Alma, Mich., 1991—. Adj. asst. prof. Mich. State U., 1995—; vis. prof. Alma Coll., 2000—. Author: The Assertive Librarian, 1984, Stress and Burnout in Library Service, 1990; contbr. articles to profl. jours. Mem. APA, Am. Viola Soc., Am. Congress Rehab. Medicine, Am. Acad. Neurolgy, Nat. Acad. Neuropsychology, Internat. Neuropsychology Soc., Rotary (Alma-St. Louis). Avocation: semi-professional violist. Home: 5651 N Luce Rd Alma MI 48801-9503 Office: Rehab Strategies PC 245 E Warwick Dr Alma MI 48801-1026

CARAM, DOROTHY FARRINGTON, educational consultant; b. McAllen, Tex., Jan. 14, 1933; d. Curtis Leon and Elena (Santander) Farrington; m. Pedro C. Caram, June 7, 1958 (dec. Aug. 2000); children: Pedro M., Juan D., Hector L., Jose M. BA, Rice U., 1955, MA, 1974; EdD, U. Houston, 1982; postgrad., U. Madrid, 1957. Tchr. Houston Ind. Sch. Dist., 1955-56, 56-60, St. Mark's Episcopal Ch., Houston, 1964-65; substitute tchr. St. Vincent De Paul Cath. Sch., Houston, 1965-68; mgr. med. office Houston, 1983; dir. Fed. Home Loan Bank, Little Rock, 1976-82; pres. Inst. Hispanic Culture, Houston, 1983, 93, chmn. bd., pres., 1984; with Houston Ednl. Excellence Program, 1980. Mem. task force Tex. Edn. Agy., 1981-83; mem. adv. coun. Nat. Inst. Neurol. and Communicative Disorders and Stroke, 1972-76; pres. IDM Satellite Comm. of Tex. Divsn., Inc., 1990, chmn. bd., 1998—99 asst. to pres. U. Houston, 1991-94, ret., 1994. Mem. coun. Miller Theater, Houston, 1976—, adv. bd. emeritus, 2000-; bd. dirs. Houston Pops, 1983-87, United Way Tex., 1991-94; mem. task force Quality Integrated Edn., Houston, 1972; bd. dirs. United Way Tex., Gulf Coast, 1989-95, mem. exec. bd., sec.; mem. Civil Commn. Houston, 1983-85; bd. mgrs. Harris County Hosp. Dist., 1988-90; founder, bd. dirs. Houston Hispanic Forum, 1985, pres., 1989-90; chmn. bd. Teatro Bilingue de Houston, 1989-90; pres. Mexican Cultural Inst. Houston, Inc., 1997; bd. dirs. Southmain Ctr. Assn., 1998—, Harris County Hosp. Dist. Found., 1997—, Houston Ind. Sch. Dist. Found., 1996-2002, chmn. peer com. magnet and vanguard schs., 1996—; mem. adv. bd. Theater Under Stars, Career and Recovery, Jobs for Progress of Tex. Gulf Coast, Inc., AAMA; bd. dirs. Majestic Seas Aquarium, 1998-99; bd. dirs., treas. Colonial Homes Found. for Youth, 1999; mem. Mil. and Hospitler Order of St. Lazarus of Jerusalem, 1982-; pres. Braes Rep. Women, 2002—, precinct judge, 1998—; v.p. edn. bd. Houston Grand Opera, 2001—. Recipient Willie Velasquez Outstanding Hispanic Citizenship award, 1994, Dorothy F. Caram Leadership award Blueprint-United Way Tex. Gulf Coast, 2000, 2001-02, Woman of Vision award Delta Gamma Found., 2003; named Vol. of Yr., United Way Tex. Gulf Coast, 1992, Outstanding Alumnus, Coll. Edn. U. Houston, 2000, Woman of Vision, Delta Gamma Found., 2003; decorated Lady in Court of Isabel La Catolica by King Carlos (Spain), 1984. Mem. Cedars Club (pres. 1978). Roman Catholic. Home: 2603 Glen Haven Blvd Houston TX 77025-2132 E-mail: dcaram@worldnet.att.net.

CARAM, EVE LA SALLE, English educator, writer; b. Hot Springs, Ark., May 11, 1934; d. Raymond Briggs and Lois Elizabeth (Merritt) La Salle; m. Richard George Caram, Apr. 19, 1965 (div. Apr. 1978); 1 child, Bethel Eve. BA, Bard Coll., 1956; MA, U. Mo., 1977. English instr. Stephens Coll., Columbia, Mo., 1974,79-82; fiction writing grad. instr. Sch. Profl. Writing U. So. Calif., L.A., 1982-87; English lit. and writing instr. Calif. State U., Northridge, 1983—; sr. fiction writing instr. The Writers' Program UCLA, 1983—. Fiction contest judge Calif. State U., Long Beach, 1992, 94, writer's conf. spkr., 1985-87, 94; spkr., mem. panel Tex. Am. Studies Assn., Wichita Falls, 1998. Author: (novel) Dear Corpus Christi, 1991, 2d edit., 2001, Wintershine, 1994, Rena, A Late Journey, 1999; editor: Palm Readings, Stories from Southern California, 1998; fiction editor West/Word, 1991. Mem. AAUP, Assn. Calif. State Profs., Nat. Assn. Tchrs. English, Poets and Writers, PEN Ctr. U.S.A. West. Democrat. Avocations: swimming, beach walks, outdoors. Home: 3400 Ben Lomond Pl Apt 121 Los Angeles CA 90027-2952 Office: UCLA Ext The Writers' Program 10995 Le Conte Ave Los Angeles CA 90095-3001 also: Calif State U English Dept 1811 Nordoff Northridge CA 91330-0001 E-mail: ecaram1@earthlink.net.

CARAMAZZA, ALFONSO, psychology educator; b. Aragona, Agrigento, Italy, June 22, 1946; came to U.S., 1970; s. Carmelo and Emma (Zammuto) C.; children: Pierre, Simone, Francesca. BA in Psychology, McGill U., Montreal, Can., 1970; MA, Johns Hopkins U., 1972, PhD, 1974; Doctor (hon.), U. Catholique de Louvain, Belgium, 1993. From asst. prof. to assoc. prof. Johns Hopkins U., Balt., 1974-81, prof., 1981-93, chair, 1987-92; David T. McLaughlin Disting. prof. Dartmouth Coll., Hanover, N.H., 1993-95; prof. Harvard U., 1995—. Adv. bd. Jour. Cognitive Neuroscience, 1988—, Jour. of Neurolinguistics, 1992—, and others; editor: Cognitive Neuropsychology, 1996—; lectr. in field. Author: (with E. Zurif) The Acquisition and Breakdown of Language: Parallels and Divergencies, 1978, Cognitive Neuropsychology and Neurolinguistics in Models of Cognitive Function and Impairment, 1990, Issues in Reading Writing and Speaking: A Neuropsychological Perspective, 1991; contbr. articles to profl. jours., chpts. to books. Recipient Javits Neuroscience Investigator award NIH, J.L. Signoret Prize in Biology. Home: 28 Marshall St Brookline MA 02446-5468 Office: Harvard Univ Dept Psychology William James Hall Cambridge MA 02138

CARBERRY, EDWARD ANDREW, chemistry educator; b. Milw., Nov. 20, 1941; s. Edward Andrew Carberry Sr. and Sophie Teresa (Hologa) Ryall; m. Linda Lee Querry, July 22, 1967; children: Daniel Edward, Cristin Lee. BSChemE, Marquette U., 1963; PhD in Inorganic Chemistry, U. Wis., Madison, 1968. Prof. chemistry S.W. State U., Marshall, Minn., 1968—. Lectr. Higher Coll. of Chemistry Russian Acad. of Scis., 1992. Author: Chemistry in our Daily LIves, 1999, Glassblowing: An Introduction to Scientific and Artistic Frameworking, 2003; contbr. articles to profl. jours. Mem. Am. Chem. Soc., Am. Scientific Glassblowers' Soc., Mendeleev Chem. Soc. (Moscow), Assn. for Advancement of Chem. Edn. (Moscow). Home: 700 1st St S Marshall MN 56258-1758 Office: SW State Univ Dept Chemistry Marshall MN 56258

CARBIA, JOSE ELISEO, elementary school principal, educator; b. Miami, July 9, 1948; s. Joe and Rosa (Lesassier) C.; m. Vilma Cueto, Dec. 25, 1987; children: Sharon, Vanessa, Maria, Jose Guillermo. B of Music, Fla. State U., 1970; BS in Elem. Edn., Fla. Atlantic U., 1972; MS in Adminstrv. Supervision, Fla. Internat. U., 1979; EdD in Ednl. Leadership, Nova U., 1989. Cert. tchr. elem. edn., reading, adminstrn., supervision, Fla. Tchr. Dade County Pub. Schs., Miami, 1972-81, asst. prin., 1981-84; prin. Coconut Grove Elem. Sch., Miami, 1984-90, Coral Reef Elem. Sch., Miami, 1990-95, Kendale Elem. Sch., Miami, 1995—. Mem. Paideia Group, Chapel Hill, N.C., 1990—. Mem. ASCD, Fla. Assn. Sch. Adminstrs., Internat. Reading Assn., Dade County Adminstrs. Assn. (bd. dirs. 1989-91), S. Fla. Ctr. for Exec. Educators (bd. dirs. 1988-92), Pers. and Guidance Assn. (Adminstr. of Yr. 1985). Republican. Roman Catholic. Avocations: music, fishing, travel. Office: Kendale Elem Sch 10693 SW 93rd St Miami FL 33176-2698

CARBO, TONI (TONI CARBO BEARMAN), information scientist, educator; b. Middletown, Conn., Nov. 14, 1942; d. Anthony Joseph and Theresa (Bauer) Carbo; m. David A. Bearman, Nov. 14, 1970 (div. Nov. 1995); 1 child, Amanda Carole Bearman Rochon; m. Clark Coolidge, July 7, 1962 (div. Apr. 1966). AB, Brown U., 1969; MS, Drexel U., 1973, PhD, 1977. Bibliog. asst. Am. Math. Soc., Math. Revs., 1962-63; supr. Brown U. Phys. Scis. Library, Providence, 1963-66, 67-71; subject specialist U. Wash. Engring. Library, Seattle, 1966-67; teaching and research asst. Drexel U., Phila., 1971-74; exec. dir. Nat. Fedn. Abstracting and Info. Svcs., Phila., 1974-79; cons. for strategic planning and new product devel. Instn. Elec. Engrs., London, 1979-80; exec. dir. U.S. Nat. Commn. on Libraries and Info. Sci., Washington, 1980-86; prof. U. Pitts. Sch. Info. Sci., 1986—, dean, 1986—2002. Adv. com. U.S. Dept. Commerce, Patent and Trademark Office, 1987—90; trustee Engring. Info., Inc., 1985—87; Lazerow lectr. U. Ind., 1984, U. Toronto, 1999; Schwing lectr. La. State U., 1988; lectr. No. Ohio Am. Soc. Info. Spl. Librs. Assn., 1990; lectr. Beta Phi Mu, Phila., 1992; Sigma chpt. lectr. Drexel U., Phila.; U.S. adv. coun. Nat. Info. Infrastructure, 1994—96; U.S. del. G-7 Info. Soc. Conf.; bd. dirs. Pa. Info. Hwy. Consortium; Miles Conrad lectr. Nat. Fedn. Abstracting & Info. Svcs., 1997; Biennial Srygley lectr. Fla. State U., 1997; Nasser Sharify lectr. Pratt U., 1997; mem. Nat. Conf. Lawyers and Scientists, 2000—; Cunningham lectr. Vanderbilt U., 2002; lectr. in field. Co-editor: Internat. Info. and Libr. Rev., 1989—92; editor, 1993—; mem. editl. bds. profl. jours.: ; contbr. articles to profl. jours. Mem. presdl. adv. com. Carnegie Libr. Pitts.; bd. dirs. Greater Pitts. Literacy Coun. Recipient Disting. Alumni award, Drexel U. Coll. Info. Studies, 1984, 100 Most Disting. Alumni award, 1992, 100th Anniversary medal, Drexel U., 1992, Silver Anniversary award, U.S. Nat. Commn. Librs. & Info. Sci., 1996, Leadership award in Sci. and Tech., YWCA Greater Pitts., 2000; fellow Madison Coun., Libr. Congress, 2002—03. Fellow: AAAS (chmn. sect. T 1992—93, coun. 1997—99), Spl. Librs. Assn. (rsch. com. 1987—92, internat. rels. com. 1991), Inst. Info. Scientists, Nat. Fedn. Abstracting and Info. Svcs. (hon.); mem.: ALA (coun. 1988—92, 50th Anniversary Honor Roll 1996), Internat. Women's Forum Western Pa., Assn. Libr. and Info. Sci. Edn. (bd. dirs. 1996—2000, pres. 1997—98, Profl. Contbn. to Libr. and Info. Sci. Edn. award 2002), Internat. Fedn. Info. and Documentation (co-chair U.S. nat. com. 1990—2000, chair global info. infrastructure and superhighways taskforce 1993—96, mem. coun., chair info. structures and policies com. 1997—2000), Nat. Info. Stds. Orgns. (bd. dirs. 1987—90), Pa. Libr. Assn. (adv. bd. Pa. Gov.'s Conf. libr. and info. svcs. 1996, Disting. Svc. award 1996), Am. Soc. Info. Sci. and Tech. (chmn. networking com., chmn. 50th ann. conf., pres. 1989—90, chmn. planning and nominations com. 1990—91, SIG III cabinet rep. 2003—, Watson Davis award 1983), 3 Rivers Connect (bd. dirs., exec. com. 1998—, vice chair 1999, interim chair 2003), Ctr. Democracy and Tech. (bd. dirs. 1996—, chair 1999—2002), Laurel Initiative (bd. dirs. 1990—93). Home: 263 Maple Ave Pittsburgh PA 15218-1523 Office: 135 N Bellefield Ave Pittsburgh PA 15213-2609 Fax: 412-648-7001. E-mail: tcarbo@mail.sis.pitt.edu.

CARBON, CLINTON LEROY, headmaster; b. Detroit, Jan. 22, 1954; s. Thurman and Anna Mildred (Stubbs) C. BFA, Howard U., 1978; MA, U. Mich., 1983. Artistic dir. Howard U. Children's Theatre, Washington, 1976-84; founding dept. head, instr. St. Andrew's Episcopal Sch., Bethesda, Md., 1978-84, Episcopal High Sch., Bellaire, Tex., 1984-90, assoc. headmaster, 1990-92. Founding mem. Master Tchr. Bd. Dir. (musical) Godspell, 1991, Little Shop of Horrors, 1993, Once on This Island, 1994; founder (children's theatre) Children's Living Arts Summer Session, 1991. Sponsor Internat. Thespian Soc. Troupe. Mem. ASCD, Am. Alliance for Theatre and Edn., Tex. Ednl. Theatre Assn., Tex. Thespian Soc. (chmn. adv. bd. 1991-92), U. Mich. Alumni Assn. Office: Episc H S 4621 Fournace Pl Bellaire TX 77401-2505

CARBON, MAX WILLIAM, nuclear engineering educator; b. Monon, Ind., Jan. 19, 1922; s. Joseph William and Mary Olive (Goble) C.; m. Phyllis Camille Myers, Apr. 13, 1944; children: Ronald Allen, Jean Ann, Susan Jane, David William, Janet Elaine. BSME, Purdue U., 1943, MS, 1947, PhD, 1949. With Hanford Works divsn. GE, 1949-55, head heat transfer unit, 1951-55; with rsch. and advanced devel. divsn. Avco Mfg. Corp., 1955-58, chief thermodynamics sect., 1956-58; prof., chmn. nuclear engrng. and engrng. physics dept. U. Wis. Coll. Engring., Madison, 1958-92, emeritus prof., collateral faculty, 1992—, acting assoc. dean for rsch., 1995-96. Group leader Ford Found. program Singapore, 1967-68; mem. adv. com. on reactor safeguards, 1975-87; chmn. spl. com. for integral fast reactor U. Chgo., 1984-94, chmn. spl. adv. com. for nuclear tech. program Argonne (Ill.) Nat. Lab., 1995-2002; mem. INPO Nat. Nuclear Accrediting Bd., 1990-94; mem. nuclear safety rev. and audit com. Kewaunee Nuclear Power Plant, 1993-96. Author: Nuclear Power: Villain or Victim, 1997. Capt. ordnance dept. AUS, 1943-46. Named Disting. Engrng. Alumnus, Purdue U. Fellow Am. Nuclear Soc.; mem. AAAS, Sigma Xi, Tau Beta Pi. Office: U Wis Engrng Rsch Bldg Madison WI 53706 E-mail: carbon@engr.wisc.edu.

CARDENAS, DIANA DELIA, physician, educator; b. San Antonio, Tex., Apr. 10, 1947; d. Ralph Roman and Rosa (Garza) C.; m. Thomas McKenzie Hooton, Aug. 20, 1971; children: Angela, Jessica. BA with highest honors, U. Tex., 1969; MD, U. Tex., Dallas, 1973; MS, U. Wash., 1976, MHA, 2001. Diplomate Nat. Bd. Med. Examiners, Am. Bd. Phys. Medicine & Rehab., Am. Bd. Electrodiagnostic Medicine. Asst. prof. dept. rehab. medicine Emory U., Atlanta, 1976-81; instr. dept. rehab. medicine U. Wash., Seattle, 1981-82, asst. prof. dept. rehab. medicine, 1982-86, assoc. prof. dept. rehab. medicine, 1986-92, prof. rehab. medicine, 1992—. Med. dir. rehab. medicine clinic U. Wash. Med. Ctr., Seattle, 1982—99; project dir. N.W. Regional Spinal Cord Injury Sys., Seattle, 1990—; mem. Accreditation Coun. for Grad. Med. Edn. Residency Rev. Com., 1995—96; chief of svc. rehab medicine U. Wash. Med. Ctr., 2002—. Editor: Rehabilitation & The Chronic Renal Disease Patient, 1985, Maximizing Rehabilitation in Chronic Renal Disease, 1989; acad. editor Archives of Phys. Medicine and Rehab., 1997-99; contbr. articles to profl. jours. Co-chairperson Lakeside Sch. Auction Student Vols., Seattle, 1991; bd. dirs. CONSEJO Counseling & Referral Svc. Mem.: Inst. of Medicine Nat. Acad. Sci. (com. on assessing rehab. sci. and engring. 1996—97, com. on injury prevention and control 1997—99), Nat. Inst. Child Health and Human Devel. (rsch. subcom. 1996—99), Am. Assn. Electrodiagnostic Medicine, Am. Congress of Rehab. Medicine (chairperson rehab. practice com. 1981—83, bd. govs. 2003—, Ann. Essay Contest winner 1976), Am. Acad. Phys. Medicine and Rehab. (chairperson rsch. adv. and advocacy com. 1997—99), Am. Spinal Injury Assn. (chairperson rsch. com. 1990—94, bd. dirs. 1994—2000, co-chair internat. rels. com. 1995—98, chair internat. rels. com. 1999—2002, chair mktg. com. 2000—03), Assn. Acad. Physiatrists (chair awards com. 1993—99). Avocations: art collecting, sewing, painting. Office: Univ Wash Dept Rehab Med Box 356490 1959 NE Pacific St Seattle WA 98195-0001

CARDENAS, RAUL RODOLFO, JR., engineering executive, educator; b. Galveston, Tex., Feb. 5, 1929; s. Raul Rodolfo and Clementina (Munoz) C.; m. Mary R. Gaglio, Nov. 23, 1961; children: Dianne, Randolph, Patricia. BA, U. Tex.-Austin, 1951, postgrad., 1955-57; MS in Environ. Health Sci., NYU, 1963, PhD, 1970. Asst. rsch. scientist NYU, N.Y.C., 1961-63, asst. prof., 1966-72; rsch. assoc. Manhattan Coll., 1963-66; prof. dept. civil engrng. Poly. Inst. N.Y., Bklyn., 1972-87; pres. Internat. Technol., Inc., Northvale, N.J., 1997—, also bd. dirs. Northvale, N.J., Tel Aviv, Israel. Bd. dirs. Advanced Compost Technol (ACT), v.p., tech. dir.; lab. dir. sewage dist. Rockland County; adj. prof. Hunter Coll., Polytech U., Cooper Union Coll., CCNY; lectr., cons. in field. Contbr. articles to profl. jours. and books. First chmn. elect PCB Settlement Com., N.Y. State, 1974-76; chmn. bd. dirs., pres. Carpenter Environ. Assoc., Inc., 1980-91; gov.'s tech. adv. bd. State of N.J., 1985; mem. pres. adv coun. Dominican Coll. 1st lt. U.S. Army, 1952-54. Fellow Scientists Inst. for Pub. Info.; mem. Water Environ. Assn. (Outstanding Analyst Achievement award 1996), Am. Soc. Microbiology, AAAS, Interam. Assn. San. Engrs., N.Y. Explorers Club, Sigma Xi. Home and Office: 66 Pine Tree Ln Tappan NY 10983-2112

CARDIFF, ROBERT DARRELL, pathology educator; b. San Francisco, Dec. 5, 1935; s. George Darrell and Helen (Kohfield) C.; m. Sally Joan Bounds, June 23, 1962; children: Darrell, Todd, Shelley. BS, U. Calif., Berkeley, 1958, PhD, 1968; MD, U. Calif., San Francisco, 1962. Intern King's County Hosp., Bklyn., 1962-63; resident in pathology U. Oreg., Portland, 1963-66; NIH fellow U. Calif., Berkeley, 1966-68, mem. faculty med. sch. Davis, 1971—, prof. pathology med. sch., 1977—, chair dept. pathology, 1990-96; dir. Ctr. for Med. Informatics U. Calif. Davis Healthcare System, Davis, 1996-98; chair Med. Informatics Grad. Group, 2002—; faculty Ctr. for Comparative Medicine U. Calif. Davis Healthcare System, Davis. Mem. sci. adv. bd. Contra Costa Cancer Fund, Walnut Creek, Calif., 1985-99; mem. Univ.-Wide AIDS Task Force, Berkeley, 1984-87; vis. prof. Sun-Yat Sen U. Med. Sci., Peoples Republic of China, 1985, 93, Harvard Med. Sch., 1990, U. Calif. San Diego, 1998-99. Mem. editorial bd. Human Pathology, 1992—, Tumor Markers, 1992—, Internat. Jour. Oncology, 1992—, Jour. Mammglnd Biol. and Neoplasia, 1998—; contbr. articles to profl. jours. Lt. col. U.S. Army, 1968—71. Recipient Triton Rsch. award Triton Bioscis., Inc., 1985, Kaiser Found. Teaching award U. Calif. Med. Sch., Davis, 1985, Disting. Teaching award U. Calif., Davis, Sadusk award Peralta Cancer Inst., 1986, Faculty Rsch. award U. Calif. Med. Sch., 1988, Affirmative Action award U. Calif. Davis Med. Ctr., 1991., others. Master: AAUP (exec. com. 1983—85); mem.: No. Calif. Pathology Soc. (pres. 1990—96), Sacramento Pathology Soc. (bd. dirs. 1985—96), Internat. Assn. Breast Cancer (bd. dirs. 1984—96), Internat. Acad. Pathology, Pluto Soc., Sigma Xi. Avocations: basketball, skiing, jogging. Office: U Calif-Davis Ctr for Comparative Medicine 98 County Rd & Hutchison Dr Davis CA 95616

CARDIN, SUZETTE, nursing educator; b. Attleboro, Mass., Feb. 4, 1950; d. Wilfred W. and Vera E. (Broadbent) C.; m. Edward R. Barden, May 10, 1986; children: Luke Edward, Helen Elizabeth. Diploma, Children's Hosp. Sch. Nursing, Boston, 1970; BSN, Southeastern Mass. U., 1974; MS, U. Md., 1978; DNSc, UCLA, 1995. RN, Calif. Nursing instr. Fall River (Mass.) Diploma Sch. Nursing, 1974-76; staff nurse SICU Johns Hopkins Hosp., Balt., 1977-78; dir. critical care nursing Med. Ctr. Hosp. Vt., Burlington, 1978-83; nurse mgr. UCLA Med. Ctr., 1984-98, performance improvement coord., 1998-99; asst. adj. prof. UCLA Sch. Nursing, 1998—. Co-editor: Personnel Management in Critical Care Nursing, 1989, Critical Care Nursing, 1992, 96; mem. editl. bd. Dimensions of Critical Care Nursing, 1989—, Clin. Issues in Critical Care Nursing, 1989-92, AONE Leadership Perspectives, 1993-96. Recipient award Profl. Businesswomen, 1973, award Maxicare Ednl. & Rsch. Found., 1993, Nurse Mgr. Leadership Excellence award AONE, 1994. Fellow Am. Acad. Nursing, Am. Heart Assn. (coun. cardiovasc. nurses comm. com. 2001-03, advocacy com. 2003—); mem. AACN (chair various coms., co-editor CCRN newsletter 1985-86, cert. com. 1984-85, liaison AANN cert. bd. 1986-88, pres. Vt. chpt. 1979-81, program com. 1987-88, NTI com. 1987-88, leadership devel. workgroup 1999-2002), Children's Hosp. Alumnae Assn., Sigma Theta Tau (co-editor newsletter Gamma Tau chpt. 1987-89, rsch. com. 2003--). Home: 2102 Farrell Ave Redondo Beach CA 90278-1819 E-mail: scardin@sonnet.ucla.edu.

CARDINAL-COX, SHIRLEY MAE, education educator; b. Morann, Pa., May 6, 1944; d. Thomas Joseph and Mary Louise (Nemish) Giza; m. Leland Dean Cox, May 9, 1998; children: Julie Ann, Karen Lee. BS, Lock Haven U., 1966; MEd, Pa. State U., 1970. Tchr. Bald Eagle Nittany Corp., Mill Hall, Pa., 1966-68; tchr., supr. Pa. State U., University Park, 1968-76; tchr., chairperson State Coll. (Pa.) Area Schs., 1968-76; primetime educator Oregon-Davis Corp., Hamlet, Ind., 1984—. Instr., cons. Dept. Edn., Indpls., 1979—, cons. energy edn., 1980—85, educator linker, 1981—, rep. prime time, 1987—2000; prof. Ancilla Coll., Donaldson, Inc., 1976—; chair for evaluation North Ctrl. Accreditation Assn., 1988—89, mem. leadership team, 1996, North Ctrl. Regional Lab., 1991—92, 1993—, mem. steering com., 1996—97; mem. leadership team Fermi Nat. Accelerator Lab., 1994—. Author: Energy Activities with Learning Skills, 1980. Chmn. publicity com. Rep. Orgn. Plymouth, Ind., 1983—; mem. Teacher Talk, Ind. Gov's. Com., 1988-89; usher capt. dept. athletics Notre Dame U., 1997—. Recipient Mankind and Edn. award U.S. Jaycees and Ind. Jaycees, 1981. Mem. Ind. State Tchr. Assn., Marshall County Reading Assn., Pa. State U. Club, Proficiency Bd. Accreditation (chairperson 1996), Phi Delta Kappa (v.p. programs South Bend chpt. 1992-93, v.p. membership 1994-95), Pi Lambda Theta, Sigma Kappa (chmn. Parent Club), Tri Kappa. Roman Catholic. Avocations: reading, aerobics, jogging, biking, tennis. Home: 10101 Turf Ct Plymouth IN 46563-9494

CARDOSO, ANTHONY ANTONIO, artist, educator; b. Tampa, Fla., Sept. 13, 1930; s. Frank T. and Nancy (Mesina) C.; m. Martha Rodriguez, 1954; children: Michele Denise, Toni Lynn. BS in Art Edn., U. Tampa, 1954; BFA, Minn. Art Inst., 1965; MA, U. South Fla., 1975; PhD in Art, Elysion Coll. Calif., 1981. Art instr., head fine arts dept. Jefferson H.S., Tampa, 1952-67, Leto H.S., Tampa, 1967—; supr. art and humanities Hillsborough County Sch., Tampa, 1985—91. Bd. dirs., supr. art Hillsboro County Schs.; rep. Tampa Art Council; artist, 1952-87. One-man shows include Warren's Gallery, Tampa, 1974, 75, 76, Tampa Realist Gallery, Tampa, 1975; group shows include Rotunda Gallery, London, End., 1973, Raymon Duncan Galleries, Paris, France, 1973, Brussells (Belgium) Internat., 1973; represented in permanent collections Minn. Mus., St. Paul, Tampa Sports Authority Art Collection, Tampa Arts' Coun.; executed murals Tampa Sports Authority Stadium, 1972, Suncoast Credit Union Bldg., Tampa, 1975. Recipient Prix de Paris Art award Raymon Duncan Galleries, 1970, Salon of 50 States award Ligoa Duncan Gallery, NYC, 1970, Latham Found. Internat. Art award, 1964, XXII Bienniel Traveling award Smithsonian Instn., 1968-69, Purchaase award Minn. Mus., 1971, 1st award Fla. State Fair, 1967, Gold medal Accademia Italia, 1981-82, Medallion Merit, Internat. Parliament, Italy, 1984, Statue of Vittoria award for centro studi and richerche, Italy, 1988, Accademia D'Europa, Premio Palma D'Oro D' Europa, Italy, 1989—, El Prado Gallery, 1990—, Merit award Festival Arts Hillsborough County Tampa, 1994-2002, El Prado Gallery, Tampa, 1999-2003. Democrat. Roman Catholic. Office: El Prado Art Gallery 3208 W Nassau St Tampa FL 33607-5145

CARDULLO, ROBERT JAMES, theatre educator; b. Bklyn., Apr. 27, 1948; s. Francesco Santo and Angela Helen (Fattorusso) C.; m. Kirsi Birgitta Virtanen, June 11, 1993; children: Kia, Emil. BA, U. Fla., 1973; MA, Tulane U., 1982; MFA, Yale U., 1985, DFA, 1989. Free-lance dramaturg and theatre critic Cornell U., Fla. State U., various newspapers, 1973-80; tchg. asst. Tulane U., New Orleans, 1980-82; tchg. fellow Yale U., New Haven, 1982-86; vis. asst. prof. La. State U., Baton Rouge, 1986-87; asst. prof. U. Richmond, Va., 1987-90, U. Mich., Ann Arbor, 1990-95, assoc. prof., 1995—2000, prof., 2000—03; vis. prof. Hunter Coll., CUNY, 2003—; adj. prof. NYU, 2003—. Mem. theatre adv. panel NEH, Washington, 1994; Fulbright lectr., Finland, 1996. Author: Film Chronicle: Critical Dispatches from a Forward Observer, 1987-92, 1994, The Crommelynck Mystery, 1997, Vittorio De Sica, 2002; editor: Film Criticism of Vernon Young, 1990, What Is Dramaturgy?, 1995, Playing to the Camera, 1998, Theater of the Avant-Garde, 1890-1950, 2001, Conversations with Stanley Kauffmann, 2003; translator German-Language Comedy, 1992, Bazin at Work, 1997, The Theater of Fernand Crommelynck, 1998; cons. editor The Explicator, 1987-91; contbg. editor New Orleans Rev., 1987-93, The Hudson Rev., 1988—; editl. bd. mem. Studies in the Humanities, 1987—. Louis B. Mayer scholar Yale Sch. of Drama, New Haven, 1984-85; summer fellow La. State U., Baton Rouge, 1987, U. Mich., Ann Arbor, 1995. Mem. Phi Beta Kappa. Roman Catholic. Avocation: baseball. Office: Hunter Coll Theatre Dept 522 Hunter North 695 Park Ave New York NY 10021

CARDWELL, JESSIE WOMACK, elementary education educator; b. Greensboro, N.C., Aug. 26, 1938; d. Daniel and Mary (Bedenbaugh) Womack; m. Leo Maurice Cardwell Sr., Aug. 26, 1954; children: Cynthia Alston, Leo Jr., Michael, Sharon. BS, Bennett Coll., 1967; MA, A & T State U., 1977. Tchrs. N.C. Grammar Grad. cert. Tchr. Greensboro (N.C.) City Schs., 1967—. Dir. White Oak Grove Recreation, Joe & Kathleen Bryan Enrichment Fund, Greensboro, 1970-74; reading tchr. Upward Bound, A & T State U., Greensboro, 1970-84; career counselor Upward Bound, U. N.C., Greensboro, 1975-80; staff devel. tchr. Greensboro City Schs., 1990-92. Dist. supt. Ctrl.-Western Dist. of Western N.C. Conf., AME, Greensboro-Asheville, N.C., 1980—; appointed to Area Mental Health and Substance Abuse Bd., Guilford County, Greensboro, 1993—. Named Tchr. of Yr., Parent Mag., Parent Inst., 1969. Mem. NAACP, NEA, Internat. Reading Assn., Nat. Sci. Assn., N.C. Assn. Educators (rep., com. profl. rights and responsibilities). Avocations: reading, gardening. Home: 4503 Southall Dr Greensboro NC 27406-8550

CARDWELL, SANDRA GAYLE BAVIDO, university admissions professional; b. Vinita, Okla., July 14, 1943; d. Amos Calvin Wilkins and Gretta Odell (Pool) Wilkins Kudlemyer; m. Phillip Patrick Bavido, Nov. 26, 1964 (div. Dec. 1973); 1 child, Phillip Patrick Bavido Jr.; m. Max Loyd Cardwell, Jan. 18, 1979 (div. Apr. 1992). AA, Tulsa Jr. Coll., 1973; BS cum laude, U. Tulsa, 1975. Sec. with various cos., 1966-69; sec. U.S. Dept. Fgn. Langs., West Point, N.Y., 1969-70; dep. ct. clk. civil div. Tulsa County Dist. Ct., Tulsa, 1975-76, dep. ct. clk. U.S. Passport Office, 1976-77; broker-assoc. Gordona Duca, Inc., Realtors, Tulsa, 1977-91; mem. admissions staff St. Francis Hosp., Tulsa, 1997—2000; univ. admissions profl. Oral Roberts U., Tulsa. Mem. Polit. Action Com., Tulsa, 1980—; vol. children's rights and child abuse legis. and statutes.; bd. of trustees Asbury United Meth. Ch., 2003—. Mem. AAUW, Tulsa Met. Bd. Realtors, Okla. Bd. Realtors, Tulsa Christian Women's Club (contact advisor 1988-89), Stonecroft Ministries (life publs. 1987-88), United Meth. Women (bd. dirs. 1986-87), Phi Theta Kappa (pres.), Pi Sigma Alpha (treas. 1974). Republican. Methodist. Avocations: piano, boating, gardening, reading, walking. Home: 3908 S St Louis Tulsa OK 74105-3317 Office: Oral Roberts U 7777 S Lewis Ave Tulsa OK 74171

CARE, NORMAN SYDNEY, philosophy educator; b. Gary, Ind., Dec. 20, 1937; s. J. Norman and Anne (Baron) C.; m. Barbara Lou Bassett, Aug. 17, 1958; children: Steven Brooks, Jennifer Lorraine. BA, Ind. U., 1959; MA, U. Kans., 1961; postgrad., Oxford U., 1962-63; PhD, Yale U., 1964. Instr. Yale U., New Haven, 1964-65; asst. prof., assoc. prof., prof. philosophy Oberlin (Ohio) Coll., from 1965. Author: On Sharing Fate, 1987, Living with One's Past, 1996, Decent People, 2000; editor: Readings in Theory of Action, 1968; author essays and revs., 1965—. Recipient Teaching Excellence award Sears-Roebuck Found., 1991. Mem. AAUP, Am. Philos. Assn. Home: Oberlin, Ohio. Died Sept. 4, 2001.

CAREY, CATHERINE ANITA, artist, art educator; b. Washington, Sept. 27, 1960; d. Charles William Carey and Geraldine Elizabeth Sheil; m. Brian Elliot Sinofsky. Student, Corcoran Sch. Art, 1976—78; BFA, Va. Commonwealth U., 1982. Fine art painter, Escondido, 1982—; graphic artist Circuit City Stores, Inc., Richmond, Va., 1985—87, Circuit City stores, Inc., Walnut, Calif., 1987—89; art dir. W. Coast Cmty. Newspapers, Encinitas, Calif., 1989—91; freelance art dir. Elements Graphic Design, Escondido, 1991—; tchr. Art Methods and Materials Show, Pasadena, Calif., 1998—; workshop leader Golden Door, Escondido, 2001—; tchr., owner The Glass House Art Studio, Escondido, 2001—. Workshop leader Daler-Rowney Art Mfr., 1998—; workshop demonstration artist Savoir Faire, San Diego, 2000—. Exhibitions include Paintings from Giverny France, La Jolla, Calif., 2000, Paintings by Cathy Carey, Escondido, Calif., 2001, Impressions of Mission Trails, San Diego, 2002, Color Harmony and Contrast, Escondido, Calif., 2003, one-woman shows include Expressive Colors, Escondido Artists Gallery, 2003; author: The Philosophy of Color, 2003. Organizer art shows for children, Encinitas, 1990—91, San Diego, 1999—2000, 2000—01. Recipient Blue Ribbon, San Dieguito Art Club, 1990, Honorable Mention, San Diego Watercolor Soc., 2000, Escondido Art Assn., 2001. Master: Scripps Ranch Art Club (pres. 2000—01, founder 2000). Avocations: hiking, photography, swing dancing, gardening, cooking. Office: Glass House Studio 2048 Ridgecrest Pl Escondido CA 92029 Fax: 760-489-9149. E-mail: element@abac.com.

CAREY, GERALD JOHN, JR., retired research institute director emeritus, former air force officer; b. Bklyn., Oct. 1, 1930; s. Gerald John and Madeline (McNamara) C.; m. Joan Bennett, Apr. 24, 1954; children: Gerald John, III, Cathleen, John Kevin, Daniel. BS, U.S. Mil. Acad., 1952; MS in Aero. Engring, Tex. A&M U., 1961. Commd. 2d lt. USAF, 1952, advanced through grades to maj. gen., 1978; pilot trainee Victoria, Tex., 1953; flight instr. Laredo, Tex., 1954-56; asst. air attache Tokyo, 1958-61; aero. engr. Air Force Systems Command, Andrews AFB, Md., 1963-66; flight comdr. Seymour Johnson AFB, 1967; ops. officer Udorn, Thailand, 1969-70; wing comdr. 1st and 56th Tactical Fighter Wings, Tampa, Fla., 1973-75; asst. dep. chief of staff ops. Tactical Air Command Hdqrs., Langley AFB, Va., 1975-78; comdr. USAF Tactical Air Warfare Center, Eglin AFB, Fla., 1978-81; ret., 1981; emeritus assoc. dir. Rsch. Inst. Ga. Inst. Tech., Atlanta, 1981—. Mem. USAF Sci. Adv. Bd., 1995. Decorated Legion of Merit, D.S.M., D.F.C. with 2 oak leaf clusters. Mem. Air Forces Assn., Daedalians, Tau Beta Pi, Sigma Gamma Tau. Office: Ga Inst Tech Rsch Inst Atlanta GA 30332-0001

CAREY, GRAHAM FRANCIS, engineering educator; b. Cairns, Queensland, Australia, Nov. 14, 1944; came to U.S., 1968; s. Lionel Dudley and Alma Lilian Carey; m. Kira Iljins, Jan. 13, 1968; children: Varis, Tija. BS, U. Queensland, 1965, BS with honors, 1966; MS, U. Wash., 1970, PhD, 1974. Registered profl. engr., Tex. Research engr. Boeing Co., Seattle, 1968-70; research prof. U. Wash., Seattle, 1974-76; prof. aerospace enging. U. Tex., Austin, 1977—, dir. Computational Fluid Dynamics Lab., 1986—. U.S. rep. Fenomech Conf., Germany, 1978, U.S.-Germany, Germany, 1981; lectr. Summer Rsch. Inst., Australia, 1984; Cray lectr., Adelaide, Australia, 1991; plenary lectr. Finite Element Meeting, Finland, 1993, summer grad. program, 1995, Finland Conf., 1996; keynote lectr. CTAC '97, Australia, 1996, Brazil Conf., 1997, EMAC '98, Australia, 1998; adj. fellow Minn. Supercomputer Inst., Mpls., 1986; Richard B. Curran Centennial chair in engring., 1998—; lectr. in field. Author: Introduction to Finite Element Methods, 1974, Finite Element Series, vols. I-VI, 1980-86, Circuit Device and Processes Simulation, 1996, Computational Grids: Generation, Adaptation and Solution Strategies, 1997; editor: Finite Elements in Fluids, 1984, Parallel Supercomputing: Methods, Algorithms and Applications, 1989, Finite Element Modeling of Environmental Problems, 1995; editor (internat. jour.) Comms. in Numerical Methods in Engring., 1984—; contbr. numerous articles to profl. jours. Recipient Ex-Student's Assn. Tchg. Excellence award, 1995 Mem. AIAA, Soc. for Indsl. and Applied Math., Am. Acad. Mechanics, Soc. for Engring. Sci., Soc. for Computer Simulation, U.S. Assn. for Computation of Mechanics, Internat. Assn. for Computational Mechanics (fellows award 1998). Office: U Tex Austin Dept Aerospace Engring WRW 111 Computational Fluid Dy Austin TX 78712

CAREY, JANET L. physical education educator; b. Johnson City, N.Y., Jan. 8, 1949; d. Charles B. and Mary Jane (Pritchard) W.; m. Howard J. Barner, July 10, 1971 (div.); children: Stacy Patrice, Christie Suzanne; m. Clifford W. Carey, July 28, 1984; 1 child, Colleen Alice. BA in Math. and Secondary Edn., SUNY, Oswego, 1970; postgrad., SUNY, New Paltz, 1976—. Cert. tchr. math. grades 7-12, phys. edn. grades K-12, N.Y. Tchr. math. Marcellus (N.Y.) Ctrl. Sch., 1970-71, Liberty (N.Y.) Cen. Sch., 1971-81; tchr. GED Sullivan County Boces, Liberty, 1976-85; tchr. phys. edn. Jeffersonville (N.Y.)-Youngsville Cen. Sch., 1981-87; dir. tennis Browns Resort Hotel, Loch Sheldrake, N.Y., 1979-89; tennis profl. Stevensville Resort Hotel, Loch Sheldrake, 1990; tchr. phys. edn. Fallsburg (N.Y.) Cen. Sch., 1987—. Assoc. adj. instr. phys. edn. Sullivan County C.C., Loch Sheldrake, N.Y., 1976—; mem. ad hoc adv. com. N.Y. Dept. Edn., Albany, 1990-92; instr. cross country and alpine skiing Pines Resort Hotel, 1976-94, tech. dir., 1980-94, ski sch. dir., 1993-94; tech. dir. ski sch. Granit Hotel Winter Fun Park, 1994-98, dir. ski sch., 1995-98, dir. cross country, 1999—; N.Y. State phys. best coord. AAHPERD, Cooper Inst., 1991—; dir. ski sch. Pines Resort Hotel, 1997-98, cross country dir., 1997-98; dir. ski sch. Spring Glen Resort, 1998—. Mem. Sullivan County Youth Bur., Monticello, 1987—, Tri-Valley Youth Commn., Grahamsville, NY, 1982—96, tennis instr., 1992—, swimming dir., 1990—; co-chair Sullivan County Aquatic Com., Monticello, Town of Fallsburg Swim Programs; swimming coord. Town of Fallsburg, 1985—; dir. Town of Neversink Parks and Recreation, 1992—; coach Hudson Valley Girls Tennis Empire State Games, 1992—94; coach varsity boys skiing Fallsburg H.S., 1989—90, varsity girls tennis, 1991—, varsity boys tennis, 1994—, coach varsity girls skiing, 1985—, co-chair health, wellness com., 1992—96, super team advisor, 1994—96; state tennis chair Empire State Games, 1994—; CPR instr. Am. Heart Assn. Mem.: ARC (vol., instr. water safety 1969—, instr. trainer 1976—, lifeguard instr., first aid safety instr., safety trainer 1968—), AAHPERD (coord. Alliance State Fitness 1991—, nat. del. 1995, 1996, 1997, aquatic coun.), AAUW, N.Y. State Ski Racing Assn. (Alpine coach 1999—), N.Y. State Coaches Assn., U.S. Ski Coaches Assn., U.S. Ski Instrs. Am., Nat. Profl. Bus. Womens Assn., N.Y. State Pub. H.S. Athletic Assn. (aquatic cons. state safety com., sect. 9 safety chmn. 1983—, sect. 9 chairperson boys tennis 1994—), Aquatic Exercise Assn. (instr.), Nat. Water Fitness Assn. (instr. 1990—, coord. 1991—), Nat. Ski Patrol, Ea. Profl. Ski Instrs. Assn., N.Y. State Assn. for Health, Phys. Edn., Recreation and Dance (program planner secondary edn. 1992—, secondary pres.-elect 1994—95, exec. coun. 1995—, secondary pres. 1995—96, bd. dirs. 1996—, aquatic sect. program planner 1997—, chair bd. dirs. 1998—99, Aquatics sect. pres. 1999—). Office: Fallsburg Ctrl Sch Brickman Rd Fallsburg NY 12733

CAREY, MARTIN CONRAD, gastroenterologist, molecular biophysicist, educator, medical geneticist; b. Clonmel, Ireland, June 18, 1939; came to U.S., 1967; s. John Joseph and Alice (Broderick) C.; m. Garcia Antonieta Fernandez, July 1, 1972 (div. 1987); children: Julian Albert, Dermot Martin. MB, BCh BAO with 1st class honors, Nat. U. Ireland, 1962, MD, 1981, DSc, 1984; AM (hon.), Harvard U., 1989; LLD (hon.), Nat. U. Ireland, 1992. Intern St. Vincent's Hosp., Dublin, Ireland, 1962-63, resident, 1965-67, Nat. Maternity Hosp., Dublin, Ireland, 1963, St. Luke's Hosp., Dublin, Ireland, 1964, Queen Charlotte's Hosp., London, 1964; asst. prof. medicine Boston U. Sch. Medicine, 1973-75, Harvard U. Med. Sch., Boston, 1975-79, assoc. prof., 1979-88, Lawrence J. Henderson assoc. prof. health sci. & Tech., 1979-88, 88-91, faculty mem. grad. sch. arts & scis., 1983—, assoc. mem. dept. cellular & molecular physiology, 1983—, prof. medicine, 1988—, prof. health sci. & tech., 1991—. Mem. staff Brigham and Women's Hosp., Boston, 1975—; McIlrath guest prof. Royal Prince Alfres Hosp., U. Sydney, Australia, 1987; cons. Gipharmex S.A., Milan, 1984—87, Dow Chem. Co., Midland, Mich., 1984—87, Merix, Inc., Needham, 1986—96, Oculon, Cambridge, 1987—95, Ciba-Giegy, Summit, NJ, 1988—93, Labs. Fournier, Dijon-Diax, 1992—93, Hoechst AG (now Aventis), Frankfurt, 1993—2002, GelTex, Inc., 1993—, Merck & Co., 2001—, Dublin (Ireland) Molecular Medicine Centre, 2001—, Mpex Biosci., Inc., San Diego, 2002—, Chrysalis Biotech., Inc., Galveston, Tex., 2003—. Author: Bile Salts and Gallstones, 1974, Hepatic Excretory Function, 1975; assoc. editor Jour. Lipid Rsch., 1978-81; mem. editl. bd. Am. Jour. Physiology, 1976-81, Gastroenterology, 1983-88, Hepatology, 1981-84; contbr. articles to profl. jours.; patentee in field. Recipient Acad. Career Devel. award NIH, 1976, Merit award, 1986, Adolf Windaus prize Falk Found., 1984, Huddinge Sikhuis medal Karolinska Inst., Stockholm, 1992, Fitzgerald medal U. Coll., 1993, Ismar Boas medal German Soc. for Digestive and Metabolic Diseases, 2002; hon. fellow med. faculty Nat. U. Ireland, Dublin, 2003; postdoctoral fellow Boston U. Sch. Medicine, 1968-73, Guggenheim Found. fellow, 1974, Fogarty Internat. fellow NIH, 1968, Fulbright fellow, 1967-68. Fellow AAAS, Royal Coll. Physicians Ireland; mem. Gastroenterology Rsch. Group (vice chmn., steering coms.), Am. Soc. Clin. Investigation, Am. Gastroent. Assn. (disting. achievement award 1990, William Beaumont prize 2000), Am. Oil Chemists Soc., Biophys. Soc., Interurban Clin. Club, Am. Assn. Physicians, Royal Irish Acad. (hon.), St. Botolph Club (Boston). Roman Catholic. Office: Brigham and Womens Hosp Div Gastroenterology 75 Francis St Boston MA 02115-6106 E-mail: mccarey@rics.bwh.harvard.edu.

CAREY, RICHARD GWYNN, principal; b. Jacksonville, Fla., Dec. 18, 1945; s. John Dick and Betty (Marshall) C.; m. Bonnie Lou Richardson, June 8, 1970; children: Merrilyn, Allison. BS in Community Svcs., So. Coll., 1969; MA in Ednl. Adminstrn., Andrews U., 1980. Cert. tchr., Kans. Tchr. Louisville jr. Acad., 1969-70; prin. Ridgetop Sch., Nashville, 1970-72; tchr. H.J. Detwiler Sch., Washington, 1972-75; prin. Columbia Jr. Acad., S.C., 1975-79, Midland Adventist Sch., Shawnee, Kans., 1980-85, Redding Adventist Sch., Calif., 1985-89, Sacramento Adventist Acad., 1989—. Computer cons. Mem. ASCD, Nat. Assn. Sch. Prins., Nat. Assn. Sec. Sch. Prins. Republican. Seventh-day Adventist. Home: 818 71st St Darien IL 60561-4026 Office: Sacramento Adventist Acad 5601 Winding Way Carmichael CA 95608-1212

CAREY, ROBERT MUNSON, medical educator, physician; b. Lexington, Ky., Aug. 13, 1940; s. Henry Ames and Eleanor Day (Munson) C.; m. Theodora Vann Hereford, Aug. 24, 1963; children: Adonice Ames, Alicia Vann, Robert Josiah Hereford. BS, U. Ky., 1962; MD, Vanderbilt U., 1965; Doctor Honoris Causa, Fed. U. Ceara, Brazil, 1998. Diplomate Am. Bd. Internal Medicine, Am. Bd. Endocrinology and Metabolism, Nat. Bd. Med. Examiners. Intern in medicine U. Va. Hosp., Charlottesville, 1966; jr. asst. resident in medicine N.Y. Hosp.-Cornell Med. Ctr., N.Y.C., 1968-69, sr. asst. resident, 1969-70; instr. endocrinology, dept. medicine Vanderbilt U. Sch. Medicine, Nashville, 1970-72; postdoctoral fellow in medicine St. Mary's Hosp. Med. Sch., London, 1972-73; asst. prof. internal medicine, endocrinology and metabolism U. Va. Sch. Medicine, Charlottesville, 1973-76, assoc. prof., 1976-80, prof., 1980—, James Carroll Flippin prof. medical sci. and dean, 1986—2002, prof. u., 2002—, David A. Harrison III disting. prof. medicine, 2002—, assoc. dir. Clin. Rsch. Ctr., 1975-86, prof., dean emeritus, 2002—, head. div. endocrinology and metabolism, dept. internal medicine, 1978-86, chmn. gen. faculty, chmn. med. adv. com., chmn. exec. com., 1986—. Attending staff U. Va. Hosp., Charlottesville, 1973—, pres. clin. staff, 1977-79, vice chmn. med. policy com., 1986—, adv. bd. 1986—; mem. study sect. on exptl. cardiovascular scis. NIH, 1982-85; mem. cardiovascular and renal adv. com. USDA, 1988—; vis. prof. div. nephrology, U. Miami Med. Sch., Fla., 1979, 83, 84, Hosp. das Clinicas da Univ., Fed. do Ceara, Forteleza, Brazil, 1981, hypertension div. Mt. Sinai Sch. Medicine, N.Y.C., 1981, div. pediatric endocrinology N.Y. Hosp.-Cornell Med. Ctr., 1981, dept. endocrinology St. Vincent's Hosp., Univ. Coll., Dublin, Ireland, 1982, depts. physiology and endocrinology Mayo Grad. Sch. Medicine, Rochester, Minn., 1984, div. rsch. Cleve. Clinic Found., 1984, Genentech, Inc., San Francisco, 1984, divs. endocrinology and metabolism U. Mass., U. Pa. Sch. Medicine, Boston U. Med. Sch., 1984, U. N.C. Sch. Medicine, 1985, Harvard Med. Sch., Boston, 1987, Jefferson Med. Coll., 1988; Bley Stein vis. prof. endocrinology U. So. Calif., 1987; Pfizer vis. prof. in pharmacology U. Chgo., 1988; co-organizer 3d Internat. Meeting on Peripheral Actions of Dopamine, Charlottesville, 1989; v.p. Va. Ambulatory Surgery, Inc., 1986—; speaker, presenter numerous nat. and internat. profl. meetings and congresses. Author: (with E.D. Vaughn) Adrenal Disorders, 1988; co-editor: Hypertension: An Endocrine Disease, 1985; mem. editorial bd. Jour. Clin. Endocronlogy and Metabolism, 1981-84, Hypertension jour., 1983-84, Am. Jour. Physiology: Heart and Circulatory Physiology, 1987-89, Am. Jour. Hypertension, 1987—; author over 150 articles, revs., papers for profl. jours., contbr. 19 chpts. to books. Mem. exec. com. and fin. com. U. Va. Health Services Found., 1986—; bd. dirs. Va. Kidney Stone Found., Inc., 1986—, The Harrison Found., Inc. U. Va., 1986—, Dyslexia Ctr., Charlottesville, 1986—. Surgeon (lt. comdr.) USPHS, 1966-68, res., 1968—. Recipient Attending Physician of Yr. awrd dept. internal medicine U. Va. Med. Ctr., 1983-84, Disting. Alumnus award and Founder's medal Vanderbilt U.; USPHS fellow Vanderbilt U., 1970-72; recipient numerous NIH grants as co-prin. and prin. investigator, 1972—; named to Hall Disting. Alumni, U. Ky., 2000. Master ACP (program com. regional meeting 1987); fellow Coun. for High Blood Pressure Rsch. AHA (program com. 1984-86, exec. and long rang planning coms. 1992—; chair-elect 2002-); mem. Inst. Medicine of NAS, Am. Heart Assn. (established investigator 1975-80), Va. affiliate Am. Heart Assn. (bd. dirs. 1977-83, pres. 1979-80, Disting. Service award), The Endocrine Soc. (fin. com. 1988—, chair devel. com. 1991-92), Am. Fedn. Clin. Rsch. (so. sect. councilor 1978-81, nominating com. 1982), So. Soc. Clin. Investigation (nominating com. 1982, sec.-treas. 1985-86), Inter-Am. Soc. for Hypertension, Am. Soc. Clin. Investigation, Am. Clin. and Climatol. Assn., Am. Soc. Hypertension (intersocietal affairs com. 1986—), Internat. Soc. Hypertension, Assn. Am. Physicians, AMA, Albemarle County Med. Soc., Med. Soc. Va., Assn. Am. Med. Coll.s Coun. of Deans, Inst. of Medicine, Nat. Acad. of Scis., The Raven Soc., Alpha Omega Alpha (Disting. Med. Alumnus award Vanderbilt U. 1994). Home: Pavilion Vi East Lawn Charlottesville VA 22903 Office: U Va Sch Medicine PO Box 801414 Charlottesville VA 22908-1414

CAREY, VAN PATRICK, mechanical engineering educator, researcher; b. Syracuse, N.Y., May 18, 1952; s. Lee Francis and Marylyn Jane (Palgrave) C.; m. Judith Anne Reichert, July 12, 1975; children: Elizabeth Megan, Sean Wesley. BS, Cornell U., 1974; MS, SUNY, Buffalo, 1976, PhD, 1981.

Project engr. Gen. Motors Corp., Lockport, N.Y., 1976-78, sr. project engr., 1980-82; asst. prof. mech. engring. U. Calif., Berkeley, 1982-85, assoc. prof., 1985-90, prof., 1990—. Cons. Redwood Microsys., Redwood City, Calif., 1997, Behr Automobiltechnik, Stuttgart, Germany, 1996-97; mem. assoc. faculty Lawrence Berkeley (Calif.) Lab., 1984—. Author: Liquid-Vapor Phase-change Phenomena, 1992, Statistical Thermodynamics and Microscale Thermophysics, 1999; contbr. articles to profl. jours.; patentee in field. Recipient Excellence in Teaching award Pi Tau Sigma, 1985, Pres. Young Investigator award NSF, 1985, Clifford C. Furnas Meml. award U. Buffalo, 2001; research grantee U. Calif., 1982-83, NSF, 1983-85, 1985-86, 91-95, NASA, 1994-95, 98—, Aradigm Corp., 1997-98, Alcoa Found., 1998-99; summer fellow NASA-Ames, 1991, Sandia Nat. Lab., 1995, 96. Fellow AAAS, ASME; mem. ASHRAE, AIAA, Soc. Automotive Engrs. (Teetor award 1984), Am. Soc. Engring. Edn. Avocations: skiing, photography, running. Office: U Calif Dept Mech Engring 6123 Etcheverry Hall Berkeley CA 94720-1741

CARFORA, JOHN MICHAEL, economics educator, academic administrator; b. New Haven, Conn., July 24, 1950; s. John Michael and Rose Mary (Mitro) C.; m. Linda Louise Palmer, July 22, 1972; 1 child, Rachel Ellen. BS, U. New Haven, 1973, MPA, 1975; MS in Econs. and Polit. Sci., London Sch. Econs., 1978; AM, Dartmouth Coll., 1985; EdM, Harvard U., 1993. Rsch. asst. London Sch. Econs. and Polit. Sci., 1980-81; lectr. polit. sci. Albertus Magnus Coll., New Haven, 1982-83; lectr. econs. and quantitative analysis U. New Haven, 1982-83; program cons. Dartmouth Coll., 1984-85, asst. prof. internat. econ. Sch. Internat. Tng., 1985-90; v.p. rsch. and acad. affairs, dir. Soviet-Am. projects Global-Genesis, Internat. Cons., 1989-91, dir. east and west projects, 1992-94; asst. dean for rsch. and sponsored programs Ind. State U., Terre Haute, 1994-95; dir. grants and sponsored programs Simmons Coll., Boston, 1995-97; assoc. dir. grants and contracts Dartmouth Coll., Hanover, NH, 1997—2002; dir. office rsch. & sponsored programs Boston Coll., 2002—. Ednl. cons. USSR Acad. Mgmt., Moscow, 1991-92; vis. asst. prof. U.S. Dept. Def., Europe, 1979-80; vis. sr. lectr. Poly. of Ctrl. London, 1980; vis. asst. prof. internat. rels. So. Conn. State U., New Haven, 1982; cons. Commonwealth Acad. Mgmt., Moscow, 1992-94; lectr. in field. Editl. bd. Rsch. Mgmt. Rev.; contbr. articles to profl. jours. With USAR, 1970-76. Recipient Roy E. Jenkins award, 1972; fellow Radio Free Europe-Radio Liberty, 1979, Internat. Rsch. and Exchs. Bd., 1981-84. Mem. ASTD, AAUP, Am. Assn. Advancement Slavic Studies, Nat. Assn. Fgn. Student Advisors (internat. educators), Am. Acad. Polit. Sci., Am. Econ. Assn., Am. Polit. Sci. Assn., Am. Assn. for Higher Edn., Am. Assn. for Adult and Continuing Edn., Nat. Coun. Univ. Rsch. Adminstrs., Acad. Polit. Sci., N.E. Slavic Assn., Soc. Rsch. Adminstrs., Royal Acad. Pub. Adminstrn. (Eng.), Atlantic Econ. Soc., Am. Friends of the London Sch. Econs. (Conn. program chmn. 1981-85, N.H.-Vt. program chmn. 1985-87, alumni bd. dirs. 1983-92). Office: Office Sponsored Programs Boston Coll Chestnut Hill Chestnut Hill MA 02467 E-mail: carfora@bc.edu.

CARICO, OPAL LEE, retired elementary school educator; b. New Tazewell, Tenn., May 9, 1929; d. Raleigh David and Myrtle Rose (Bunch) Lester; m. Joyce Darrell Carico, Nov. 25, 1956; 1 child, Thomas Darrell. BS cum laude, East Tenn. State U., 1977, MEd, 1982, postgrad., 1989—. Cert. elem. and spl. reading tchr. Sec. Tenn. Eastman co., Kingsport, Tenn., 1958-62; tchr. Sullivan County Bd. Edn., 1978—94; math. tchr., coach math bowl team, 1989—94; ret., 1994. Participant Fantasy Lit. Workshop Nat. Inst. for the Humanities, Johnson City, Tenn., 1985, Mathcaps Workshop Nat. Sci. Found., Johnson City, 1987, 88. Vol. tchr. Spl. Class for Gifted Students, Blountville, Tenn., 1985, 86. Recipient Who's Who Among America's Tchrs., 1992. Mem. Tenn. Edn. Assn., Nat. Edn. Assn., Sullivan County Edn. Assn., Phi Kappa Phi. Avocations: gardening, reading, decorating. Home: 412 Meadow Ln Kingsport TN 37663-2546

CARIGNAN, CLAUDE, astronomer, educator; b. Montreal, Dec. 20, 1950; s. Philippe and Gilberte (Frenette) Carignan; m. Lucie Houde, Aug. 1972 (div. Oct. 1985); children: Stephanie, Veronik, Marilis; life ptnr. Monique Mujawamariya. MSc, U. Montreal, 1978; PhD, Australian Nat. U., Canberra, 1983. Fellow Kapteyn Lab., Groningen, Holland, 1983-85; rsch. fellow U. Montreal, 1985-90, asst. prof., 1990-91, assoc. prof., 1991-97, prof., 1997—. Dir. de L'Observatoire Du Mont Megantic; bd. dirs. CFHT. Contbr. articles to profl. jours. Mem. Can. Astron. Soc. (bd. dirs. 1992-96, future radio astronomy nat. facility com. 1995-97), Am. Astron. Soc. Achievements include research in neutral hydrogen in galaxies from radio synthesis observations, detailed kinematics, mass distribution and properties of dark matter in spiral and dwarf galaxies. Home: 290 ch Des Mille-Feuilles St St Sauveur PQ Canada J0R 1R7 Office: U Montreal Dept Physics CP 6128 Succ Centre Ville Montreal QC Canada H3C 3J7

CARL, HAROLD FRANCIS, theology educator; b. Marion, Ill., Nov. 18, 1958; s. Philip N. and Marian Minerva (Rhoads) C.; m. Gwendolyn S. Wolfley, June 7, 1980; 1 child, Joshua Spencer. BS in Mus. Edn., Malone Coll., Canton, Ohio, 1981; MDiv, Gordon-Conwell Sem., South Hamilton, Mass., 1987; PhD in Systematic Theology, Westminster Sem., Phila., 1992. Ordained to ministry Evang. Friends Ch., 1983. Pastor Evang. Friends Ch., Portsmouth, R.I., 1981-87; assoc. prof. theology, mem. adminstrv. coun. Houston Grad. Sch. Theology, 1992-97; chaplain, lectr. religion Berry Coll., Rome, Ga., 1998—2002; chaplain LeTourneau U., Longview, Tex., 2002—, lectr. in religion, 2002—. Contbr. articles to religious publs. James H. Montgomery scholar Westminster Sem., 1987. Mem. Evang. Theol. Soc. Avocations: computers, electronics, music, scuba diving. Office: LeTourneau Univ Box 7001 Longview TX 75607-7001

CARLETON, MARY RUTH, development professional, consultant; b. Sacramento, Feb. 2, 1948; d. Warren Alfred and Mary Gertrude (Clark) Carleton; m. Bruce A. Hunt, Jan. 21, 1989. BA in Polit. Sci., U. Calif., Berkeley, 1970, MJ, 1974; postgrad., San Diego State U. TV news anchor, reporter Sta KXAS-TV, Ft. Worth, 1974-78, Sta. KING-TV, Seattle, 1978-80, Sta. KOCO-TV, Oklahoma City, 1980-84, Sta. KTTV-TV, L.A., 1984-87; news anchor Sta. KLAS-TV, Las Vegas, 1987-91, Sta. KNV-TV, 1991-93, Sta. UNLV-TV, 1993-94; broadcast instr. Okla. Christian Coll., 1981-84, UCLA, 1985-87; broadcast instr., dir. Women's Ctr. U. Nev., Las Vegas, 1991-94, news dir. univ. news Sta. UNLV-TV, 1992-94; asst. dean devel. San Diego State U., 1994-97; v.p., dir. devel. Scripps Found., 1997-99; v.p. instl. advancement Holy Names Coll., Oakland, Calif., 1999-2001; assoc. v.p. advancement U. San Francisco, 2001—. V.p. exec. com. West Coast Conf.; cons. in field. Bd. dirs. World Neighbors, Oklahoma City, 1984-89, Allied Arts Coun. So. Nev., Las Vegas, 1988-94, Nev. Inst. for Contemporary Art, 1988-94, Las Vegas Women's Coun., 1993-94, Friends of Channel 10, 1991-94, United Way, Las Vegas, 1991-94, secret witness bd., 1991-94; bd. dirs. Case Dist. VII, 1998—, conf. chair, 2003. Recipient Broadcasting award UPI, 1981, Nat. award for best documentary, 1990, Tri-State award for best newscast, 1990, Emmy award, L.A., 1986, L.A. Press Club award, 1986, 90, Nat. awaad for documentaries UPI, 1990, Woman of Achievement Media award Las Vegas C. of C., 1990; named Best Environ. Reporter, Okla. Wildlife Fedn., 1983, Disting. Woman of So. Nev., Woman of Achievement, Las Vegas Women's Coun., 1990. Mem. AARP (mem. nat. econ. issues team 1992-94, state legis. com.), Women in Comm. (Clarion award 1981, Best Newscaster 1990), Soc. Profl. Journalists, Press Women, Investigative Reporters, Calif. Alumni Assn. (bd. dir. 2002—), Sigma Delta Chi. Democrat. Roman Catholic. Avocations: tennis, gourmet cooking. Office: Univ San Francisco 2130 Fulton St San Francisco CA 94117-1080

CARLIN, BETTY, education educator; b. N.Y.C. d. Samuel and Rose Sara (Bernstein) Grossberg; m. Arthur S. Carlin, July 18, 1953 (dec.); children: Lisa Anne Skinner, James Howard. BA, UCLA, 1952; MA, U. Calif., Berkeley, 1955. Educator L.A. Sch. Dist., 1952-55; owner Carlin's Shoes, L.A., 1952-68; educator Berkeley (Calif.) Sch. Dist., 1957-58; master tchr. spl. programs Calif. State Coll., Hayward, 1967-84; educator U. Calif., Berkeley, 1984-86; tchr. demonstrator C.V.U. Sch. Dist.; student tchr. supr. Calif. State U., Hayward. Co-owner Art-Car Corp., 1978-88. Creator ednl. videos for children Study in Characteristics of an Effective and Loving Mother, Children's Play as Related to Intelligence, An Eclectic Approach to Teaching Reading. Mem. Nat. Tchrs. Assn., Calif. Tchrs. Assn., Commonwealth Club, San Francisco Opera Guild. Avocations: swimming, opera, theater, gardening, vocal study.

CARLIN, CAROL RUTH, education educator; b. Milw., Nov. 12, 1946; d. Robert and Ruth A. (Walsh) C. BS in Social Studies/English, U. Wis., 1969; MA in Communication, U. Wis., Milw., 1975. Tchr. Waterford (Wis.) High Sch., 1969-72, Badger High Sch., Lake Geneva, Wis., 1972—2002; adj. prof. Viterbo U., 2002—. Organizer Leadership Dynamics Program, Lake Geneva, 1992—2002; vol. assessor level III Alverno Coll., Milw., 1990—98; Women in Edn. del. U.S.-China Joint Conf. on Women's Issues, 1995. Recipient Robert J. Webster Mentor award Screen Printing Assn. Internat., 1992, Wis. Women Leaders in Edn., AAUW, 1996; Christa McAuliffe fellow, 1995-96; Kohl fellow, 2000. Mem. NEA (bd. dirs. 1981-87), Wis. Edn. Assn. Coun. (bd. dirs. 1981-87, vol. grass roots organizer 1976—). Democrat. Avocations: political/community organizing, reading. Home: 6914 W Coldspring Rd Greenfield WI 53220-2911

CARLISLE, CASEY ALLEN, chemist, educator; b. Trenton, Fla., Sept. 20, 1949; s. Eddie Roy and Meveree Martha Carlisle; m. Marianne M. Bonnell, Aug. 6, 1970; children: Jonathan Edward, Allen Bryce, Kerry Brett, Kristofer Robin, John Paul. AA, Fla. Coll., Temple Terrace, 1969; BA in Edn., U. Fla., 1974, MA in Edn., 1976; Ednl. Specialist in Sci. and Computers, Nova U., 1986. Cert. in chemistry, biology, mid. sch. sci., health edn., elem., ednl. supervision and leadership, Fla. Tchr. Trenton (Fla.) Elem. Sch., 1974-76; tchr. sci. Dixie County H.S., Cross City, Fla., 1976-90, chmn. dept. sci., 1984-90; tchr. chemistry/sci. Santa Fe High sch., Alachua, Fla., 1990—, chmn. dept. sci., 1994—98. Instr. sci. Lake City C.C., 1984-90. Minister Old Town Ch. of Christ, 1990—; mem. sch. bd, Gilchrist County, Trenton, Fla., 1978—82. Avocations: farming, computers, home improvement. Home: 4022 SE 17th Trl Trenton FL 32693-4611 Office: Santa Fe High School 16331 US Highway 441 Alachua FL 32615-5281

CARLISLE, JAY CHARLES, II, lawyer, educator; b. Washington, Apr. 8, 1942; s. Jay C. and Opal Fiske C.; m. Frances Bell, Nov. 22, 1970 (div.); 1 child, Marie Bell; m. Janessa C. Nisley, June 22, 1984. AB, UCLA, 1965; JD, U. Calif., Davis, 1969; postgrad., Columbia U., 1969-70. Bar: N.Y. 1970, N.Mex. 1972, U.S. Dist. Ct. (so., ea. and we. dists.) N.Y. 1971, U.S. Ct. Appeals (2d cir.) 1975, U.S. Supreme Ct. 1975. Asst. trial counsel ITT, Hartford, 1970-71; assoc. Bigbee, Bryd, Carpenter & Crout, Santa Fe, 1971-73; pvt. practice law, 1973-75; asst. dean faculty of law SUNY, 1975-78; from asst. prof. to prof. of law Pace Univ., White Plains, N.Y., 1978—. Spl. master N.Y. Supreme Ct., 1980—; commr. N.Y. Task Force on Women and Cts., 1984-86; adj. prof. Fordham U., 1987-88, 90-91, N.Y. Law Sch., 1993—, Quiniplae Law Sch., 2001—; referee N.Y. State Commn. on Jud. Conduct, 1999—. Apptd. chair pub. adv. coun. N.Y. Temp. Commn. on Local Govt. Ethics, 1992-94; mem. Yonkers Police Profl. Stds. Rev. Bd., 1993-95; commr. N.Y. Task Force on Cameras In the Cts., 1996-97. Recipient Harrison Tweed award ABA/Am. Law Inst. Fellow: Am. Bar Found.; mem.: Assn. of Bar of City of N.Y., N.Y. State Bar Assn., Hudson Rotary (pres. 2002—03). Republican. Episcopalian. Office: Pace U Sch Law 78 N Broadway White Plains NY 10603-3796

CARLISLE, MARIBETH SHIRLEY, mathematics educator; b. Indpls., July 20, 1951; d. Robert Lee and Luann (Burwell) Shirley; m. Robert Douglas Carlisle, June 10, 1978; 1 child, Nancy Beth. BA, Mich. State U., 1973. Cert. secondary sch. math. tchr. Tchr. math. Union City (Mich.) Cmty. Schs., 1973-77, Irving (Tex.) Pub. Schs., 1977-79, Hastings (Mich.) Area Schs., 1979-80, Boone County Schs., Madison, W.Va., 1980-83, Centreville (Mich.) Pub. Schs., 1985—. U.S. del. U.S./Russia Joint Conf. on Edn., Moscow, 1994. Mem. Math. Assn. Am., Nat. Coun. Tchrs. Math., Mich. Coun. Tchrs. Math. Avocations: sailing, travel, music, refinishing furniture. Office: Centreville Pub Schs Box 158 190 Hogan Centreville MI 49032

CARLO-MELENDEZ, ARNALDO, mathematics educator; b. Mayaguez, P.R., Oct. 1, 1953; s. Asdrubal Ali and Herolida (Melendez) Carlo; divorced; 1 child, Arnaldo Ali. BA, U. S. Fla., 1975. Cert. math. tchr., grades 6-12, Fla. Math. tchr. U.S. Peace Corps., Washington, Montverde (Fla.) Acad. Mem. ASCD, Nat. Coun. Tchrs. Math., Phi Kappa Phi. Home: PO Box 560469 Montverde FL 34756-0469 E-mail: mva2math@hotmail.com.

CARLQUIST, SHERWIN, biology and botany educator; b. Los Angles, July 7, 1930; s. Robert William and Helen (Bauer) C. BA, U. Calif., Berkeley, 1952, PhD, 1956; post grad, Harvard U., 1956. Assoc. prof. Claremont Grad. Sch., Calif., 1967-93, asst. prof. botany, 1956-61; prof. biology Pomona Coll., Claremont, Calif., 1976-93. Author: Japanese Festivals, 1965; Island Life, 1965; (Gleason Award N.Y. Bot. Garden); Comparative Plant Anatomy, 1961; Hawaii: A Natural History, 1970; Island Biology, 1974; Ecological Strategies of Xylem Evolution, 1975; Comparative Wood Anatomy, 1988; Man/Natute, 2002; Tarweeds and Silverswords, 2003; Natural Man, 1991, Man Naturally, 1996, Outsiders, 1996, The Natural Male, 1999; contbg. articles to profl. jour. Recipient Gleason Award N.Y. Bot. Garden, 1967; Career Award Bot. Soc. Am., 1977; Allerton Award, 1992; Asa Gray Award Am. Soc. Plant Taxonomists, 1993; Margaret Getman Svc. to Students Award U. Calif., Santa Barbara, 1996; Fellows' Medal Calif. Acad. Sci., 1996; Career Award Santa Barbara Bot. Garden, 1996; Man and Nature in Art award, 1999; Botanical Medal, Linnean Soc. of London, 2002.

CARLS, ALICE CATHERINE, history educator; b. Mulhouse, France, June 14, 1950; came to U.S., 1977; d. Victor Adrien Clement and Lise Simone (Ebersolt) Maire; m. Stephen Douglas, June 25, 1977; children: Philip, Elizabeth, Paul. BA, Sorbonne U., Paris, 1970, MA, 1972, PhD, 1976. Asst. prof., polit. sci. Lambuth Coll., Jackson, 1985-88, asst. prof., history, polit. sci., 1988-92; asst. prof. history U. Tenn., Martin, 1992-96, chmn. dept. history, 1997-2000, assoc. prof. history, 1996-2001, prof. history, 2001—, chmn. long-range planning com. on Civil Rights Conf., 2001—. Ea. European corr. Ctr. Pub. Justice, Washington, 1981—97, mem. editl. bd., 1998—. Author: The Free City of Danzig in Crisis, 1938-1939, 1982; translator (Jan Kochanowski): A Life of One's Own, 1992; translator: (Wladyslaw Grzedzielski) The Polish Rider, 1991; translator: (Jozef M. Rostocki) Escaping Death, 1995, A Fly in My Soup, 1998; translator: (Jozef Wittlin) The Salt of the Earth, 2000; translator: (Stephen D. Carls) Louis Loucheur, 1872-1931, Engineer, Statesman, Technocrat; translator: (Anna Frajlich) The Wind, Anew, Searches for Me, 2003; contbr. articles to profl. jours. Mem. Bicentennial Com., Ad-hoc Bicentennial Com., Jackson, 1987; alt. dir. Ad-hoc Com. Memories Life Bemis Jackson, 1991-92; dir. Ad-hoc Com. Polish Week, Sterling, Kans., 1982. Grantee Herbert Hoover Instn. for War, Revolution and Peace, 1984, Herbert Hoover Pub. Libr. 1979, Deutscher Akademischer Austausch Dienst 1975, French Ministry Fgn. Affairs 1973-75; recipient Internat. Scholar award U. Tenn., Martin, 1999. Cunningham award U. Tenn., Martin, 2002; featured scholar U. Tenn., Martin, 1999. Mem.: Am. Hist. Assn., Ctr. for Pub. Justice, So. Hist. Assn. (Simpson and Smith awards com. of the European history sect. 2001—, sec.-treas. European history sect. 2002—), Polish Inst. Arts and Sci., Am. Assn. for Advancement of Slavic Studies, Polish-Am. Hist. Assn. (exec. com. 1989—91, mem. editl. bd. 1991—93), UN Assn.-USA, Am. Hist. Assn., Pi Delta Phi, Phi Kappa Phi. Presbyterian.

CARLSEN, JAMES CALDWELL, musicologist, educator; b. Pasco, Wash., Feb. 11, 1927; s. Theodore N. and Eunice (Caldwell) C.; m. Mary Louisa Baird, May 1, 1949; children: Philip C., Douglas A., Susan A., Kristine L. BA, Whitworth Coll., 1950; MA, U. Wash., 1958; PhD, Northwestern U., 1962. Pub. sch. tchr., Almira, Wash., 1950-53; pub. sch. tchr. Portland, Oreg., 1953-54; mem. faculty Whitworth Coll., 1954-63, U. Conn., 1963-67; prof. music U. Wash., Seattle, 1967-92, head div. systematic musicology, 1968-92, ret., 1992, emeritus prof. music, 1992—. Rsch. assoc. Stäatliches Institut für Musikforschung, West Berlin, Germany, 1973-74; adj. prof. psychology U. Wash., 1979-92; vis. lectr. Instituto Investigaciones Educativas, Buenos Aires, 1981, Ind. U., 1985, Centro de Investigacion en Educacion Musical del Collegium Musicum, Buenos Aires, 1994; vis. scholar U. Bergen, Norway, 1986; disting. vis. prof. music Aichi U. Edn., Japan, 1992; Housewright eminent scholar chair in music Fla. State U., 1998. Author: Melodic Perception, 1965; editor Jour. Research in Music Edn, 1978-81; assoc. editor Psychomusicology, 1980-01; cons. editor Jour. Music Perception and Cognition, Japan, 1998—. Condr. Spokane Symphonic Band, Wash., 1957-60; music dir. Walla Walla Choral Soc., 1997. Served with AUS, 1945-47. Danforth Tchr. Study grantee, 1960-61; grad. fellow Presbyn. Ch., 1961-62; Fulbright-Hays grantee, 1973-74; recipient Soc. Rsch. in Music Edn. Sr. Researcher award, 1994. Mem. AAUP, Music Educators Nat. Conf., Music Edn. rsch. Coun. (past chmn.), Coll. Music Soc., Soc. for Music Perception and Cognition, Internat. Soc. Music Edn. (chmn. rsch. commn. 1976-80), Internat. Soc. Music Edn. Rsch. Commn. Seminars (hon. life), Internat. Soc. Music Edn. (hon. life), Walla Walla Symphony Soc. (bd. dirs. 1997-2003). Home: 845 Fern Ct Walla Walla WA 99362-8857 E-mail: carlsen@wwics.com.

CARLSON, ARTHUR EUGENE, accounting educator; b. Whitewater, Wis., May 10, 1923; s. Paul Adolph and Dorothy Adeline (Cooper) C.; m. Lorraine June Bronson, Aug. 19, 1944; 1 child, George Arthur. EdB, U. Wis., Whitewater, 1943; MBA, Harvard U., 1947; PhD, Northwestern U., 1954. Instr. Ohio U., 1947-50; lectr. Northwestern U., 1950-52; from asst. prof. to prof. acctg. Washington U., St. Louis, 1952-88, prof. emeritus, 1988—. Vis. prof. U. Hawaii, 1963-64. Author: College Accounting, 1967, 7th edit., 1993, Accounting Essentials, 1973, 5th edit., 1991. Chmn. Robert Meml. Endowment Fund, University City, Mo., 1972-2003, trustee Police and Fire Pension Bd., 1979-88. Mem. Inst. Mgmt. Accts. (past pres.), Assn. Sys. Mgmt. (past pres., Disting. Svc. award 1973), Soc. Profs. Emeriti Washington U. (pres. 1995, disting. bus. alumni awards com. 1998—), Kiwanis (pres. 1969). Republican. Episcopalian. Avocations: bowling, gardening. Home: 801 S Skinker Blvd # 9A Saint Louis MO 63105-3228 E-mail: carlson@olin.wustl.edu.

CARLSON, CHARLES EVANS, university official; b. Savanna, Ill., Aug. 25, 1941; s. Gustave Bert and Agnes Loretta (Johnson) C.; m. Nancy Jane Wahl, Aug. 10, 1963; children: Courtney E., Darrin C. BA, Carthage Coll., 1963; MA, U. Ill., 1965. Tchr. Polo (Ill.) Community High Sch., 1963-65; instr. history Ctrl. Mich. U., Mt. Pleasant, 1966-72, regional assoc. dir. Detroit campus, 1987—, coord. spl. projects, acad. advisor. Contbr. articles to profl. publs. Mem. Optimist Club. Avocation: golf. Office: Ctrl Mich U Cel North Mount Pleasant MI 48859-0001 E-mail: charles.e.carlson@cmich.edu.

CARLSON, DALE ARVID, university dean; b. Aberdeen, Wash., Jan. 10, 1925; s. Edwin C.G. and Anna A. (Anderson) C.; m. Jean M. Stanton, Nov. 11, 1948; children: Dale Ronald, Gail L. Carlson Manahan, Joan M. Carlson Lee, Gwen D. Carlson Lundgren. AA, Grays Harbor Coll., 1947; BSCE, U. Wash., 1950, MS, 1951; PhD, U. Wis., 1960. Registered profl. engr., Wash., 1955. Water engr. City of Aberdeen, 1951-55; asst. prof., assoc. prof., prof., chmn. dept. civil engring. U. Wash., Seattle, 1955-76, dean (Coll Engring.), 1976-80, dean emeritus, 1980—, dir. Valle Scandinavian Exch., 1980—2002; chmn. dept. civil engring. Seattle U., 1983-88, acting dean sci. and engring., 1990, dean sci. and engring., 1990-92. Vis. prof. Tech. U. Denmark, Copenhagen, 1970, Royal Coll. Agr., Uppsala, Sweden, 1976, 78 Contbr. articles to profl. jours. Exec. bd. Pacific N.W. Synod Luth. Ch. in Am., chmn. fin. com., 1980-84, treas., 1986-87, bd. edn., fin. com. Evang. Luth. Ch. in Am., 1987-91; v.p. Nat. Luth. Campus Ministry, 1988-91; treas. N.W. Washington synod Evang. Luth. Ch. in Am., 1996-2000, mem. synod candidacy com., 2001—; exec. bd. Nordic Heritage Mus., 1981-86; bd. dirs. Hearthstone Retirement Ctrs., 1984-93, Evergreen Safety Coun., 1980-86. With AUS, 1943-45. Named Outstanding Grad. Weatherwax High Sch., Aberdeen, 1972, Outstanding Grad. Grays Harbor Coll., 1947; guest of honor Soppeldagene, Trondheim, 1978 Mem. ASCE, Internat. Water Acad., Am. Soc. Engring. Educators, Am. Acad. Environ. Engring., Am. Water Works Assn., Am. Scandinavian Found., Swedish Am. C. of C. (bd. dirs. 1994-99), Norwegian Am. C. of C., Rainier Club, Rotary, Phi Beta Kappa, Sigma Xi, Chi Epsilon. Home: 9235 41st Ave NE Seattle WA 98115-3801 E-mail: dcarlson@engr.washington.edu.

CARLSON, DAVID CHARLES, media specialist, secondary school educator; b. Grand Rapids, Minn., Nov. 17, 1942; s. Charles Albert and Jeannette Kathryn Marie (Stram) C.; children: Kristine Michelle, Mindy Sue, Jacky Lyn. AS, Itasca Cmty. Coll., 1962; BS, Bemidji State U., 1964, MS, 1974. Cert. 7-12 math. and physics tchr., jr. h.s. specialist, Minn. Algebra and math. tchr. Big Fork (Minn.) High Sch., 1967-99; instrument man, survey crew Grand Rapids (Minn.) City Engrs., 1979-90; math. and sci. tchr. Mansfield (Wash.) High Sch., 1965-67, Walker (Minn.) High Sch., 1964-65; media specialist ICTV Television Studios, Grand Rapids, 1990—. Sec., pres. Range Area Volleyball Official, Minn., 1974-94; evaluator, cons. Minn. Computer. Contbr. articles to profl. jours. Mem. Minn. State High Sch. League. Democrat. Mem. Lds Ch. Avocations: hunting, fishing, hockey, high school sports fan. Home: 802 NE 7th Ave Grand Rapids MN 55744-3041 Office: Bigfork High Sch Bigfork MN 56628 E-mail: dcsquare@hotmail.com.

CARLSON, ELIZABETH BORDEN, historian, educator; b. Fall River, Mass., Oct. 5, 1937; d. Richard and Elizabeth McGinley Borden; m. William C. Badger, Sept. 14, 1957 (div. July 1974); children: Christopher C. Badger, Lisa A. Badger; m. Robert F. Carlson, May 5, 1985. Student, Radcliffe Coll., Cambridge, Mass., 1955—57; BA cum laude, Harvard U., 1975; MA with honors, U. Calif., Santa Barbara, 1983, PhD with honors, 1988. Assoc. and contbg. editor The Carlisle Gazette, Mass., 1975—80; head pub. relations Gregory Fossella Assocs., Boston, 1978—80; tchr. Westmont Coll., Santa Barbara, Calif., 1986—90; pres. The Ednl. Design Found., Norwich, Vt., 1991—. Contbr. over 100 articles to profl. jours. Mem. Master Planning Com., Carlisle, Mass., 1974—78; Carlisle rep. Master Planning Com. of Greater Boston, 1978—80; bd. dirs. The Fenn Sch., Concord, Mass., 1969—73; pres. PTA, Carlisle, 1967—69. Mem.: Soc. of Archtl. Historians. Avocations: reading, birdwatching, tennis, swimming, skiing. Home: 502 Plaza Rubio Santa Barbara CA 93103 Office: The Ednl Design Found PO Box 25 66 Old Coach Rd Norwich VT 05055

CARLSON, GARY PATRICK, toxicologist, educator; b. Buffalo; s. Ralph S. and Eileen M. (O'Day) C.; m. Judith A. Pierucci, Sept. 7, 1968; children: Barbara, Eric, Matthew, David. BS, St. Bonaventure (N.Y.) U., 1965; PhD, U. Chgo., 1969. Asst. prof. pharmacology U. R.I., Kingston, 1969-75; assoc. prof. toxicology Purdue U., West Lafayette, Ind., 1975-80, prof. toxicology, 1980—, assoc. head Sch. of Health Scis., 1997—. Adj. prof. pharmacology and toxicology Ind. U. Med. Sch., Indpls., 1982—; mem. sci. adv. bd. U.S. EPA, Washington, 1986-93, health effects rev. panel, 1980-93; mem. toxicology study sect. NIH, Washington, 1982-86; mem. nat. toxicology program bd. of scientific counselors Nat. Toxicology Program, Research Triangle Park, N.C., 1995-99. Assoc. editor Fundamental and

Applied Toxicology, 1986-91, Jour. Toxicology and Environ. Health, 1982—; contbr. articles to profl. jours. Grantee, NIH, EPA. Office: Purdue University Sch Health Scis Civil Engring Bldg 550 Stadium Mall Dr West Lafayette IN 47907-2051

CARLSON, JANET FRANCES, psychologist, educator; b. Newport, R.I., Oct. 3, 1957; d. Robert Carl and Alice Marion (Orina) Carlson; m. Kurt Francis Geisinger, Sept. 22, 1984. BS summa cum laude, Union Coll., Schenectady, 1979; MA in Clin. Psychology, Fordham U., 1982, PhD in Clin. Psychology, 1987. Lic. psychologist NY, cert. sch psychologist NY. Clin. psychology intern Conn. Valley Hosp., Middletown, Conn., 1983-84; rsch. fellow Schering-Plough Found., Bronx, N.Y., 1984-85; psychologist I Creedmoor Psychiat. Ctr., Queens Village, N.Y., 1985-86; psychologist Hallen Sch., Mamaroneck, N.Y., 1986-88; asst. prof. psychology Fordham U., Bronx, N.Y., 1988-89; asst. prof. sch. and applied psychology Fairfield (Conn.) U., 1989-93, dir. sch. and applied psychology programs, 1989-90; from asst. prof. counseling and psychol. svcs. to prof. SUNY, Oswego, 1993—2002, assoc. dean Sch. Edn., 1998-2001; prof. psychology, head dept. gen. academics Tex. A&M U., Galveston, 2002—. Cons. N.Y.C. Bd. Edn. Office Rsch., Evaluation and Assessment, 1988—92; vis. asst. prof. psychol. LeMoyne Coll., Syracuse, NY, 1992—93; dir. Office Tchg. Resources in Psychol., 2001—. Recipient Sugarfree scholarship, 1984—85; grantee Sigma Xi, 1984—85. Fellow: APA; mem.: NASP, N.Y. Assn. Sch. Psychologists, Northeastern Ednl. Rsch. Assn. (ed newsletter 1988—91, bd dirs. 1990—93, pres. 1995—96), N.Y. State Psychol. Assn., Eastern Psychol. Assn., Am. Ednl. Rsch. Assn., Sigma Xi, Psi Chi, Phi Kappa Phi (pres. 1995—96). Avocations: wildlife preservation, conservation issues.

CARLSON, KAREN GLINERT, principal; b. Chgo., May 29, 1952; d. Allen W. and Ann (Hirsch) Glinert; m. John R. Carlson, Dec. 1, 1974; children: Kristina, Erika. BA, Northwestern U., Evanston, Ill., 1973; MEd, Nat. Louis U., Evanston, Ill., 1982; postgrad., Northwestern U., Evanston, Ill., 1989—, DePaul U., 1987-88. Tchr. Headstart Santa Maria Adolorata, Chgo., 1974-77; bilingual edn. specialist Chgo. Pub. Schs., 1977-78; tchr. bilingual learning disabilites Pilsen Acad., Chgo., 1980-81; Spanish tchr. Baker Demonstration Sch. Nat. Louis U., Evanston, 1982-85; tchr. bilingual spl. edn. Dist. 65, Evanston, 1984-88; supr. learning disabilites and behavior disorders Dist. 28, Northbrook, Ill., 1988-89; rsch. asst. Northwestern U., Evanston, 1989-90; cons. Prescott Elem. Sch., Chgo., 1990, prin., 1990—. Mem. local sch. coun. Prescott Sch., Chgo., 1990—; mem. Supt.'s Think Tank Chgo Pub. Schs., 1991—. Commr. Evanston Human Rels. Commn., Evanston, 1989-91; apptd. Mayors Drug Task Force, Evanston, 1989-90; co-chairperson Residential Crime Prevention Com., Evanston, 1988-91; bd. dirs. Evanston Latin Am. Assn., 1984-89. Recipient Gov.'s Community Crime Prevention award Ill Criminal Justice Authority, 1988, Ill. Bell Ameritech LSC award, 1990, Quest Sch. award CTU, 1992, Am.'s Best Sch. Project award Redbook Mag., 1993, Am. Hero in Edn. aware Reader' Digest, 1993; Chgo. Community Trust grantee, 1992; named Urban Sch. Leader, NCREL, 1992, Outstanding Chgo. Pub. Sch. Adminstr., Citizens Schs. Com., 1993. Mem. ASCD, Am. Edn. Rsch. Assn., Am. Assn. Sch. Adminstrs., Nat. Assn. for Bilingual Edn., Coun. for Exceptional Children, Ill. Assn. for Multicultural Edn., Tchrs. Acad. Math. and Sci. (bd. dirs. 1992), Phi Delta Kappa (Educator of Yr. 1992). Home: 1022 Wesley Ave Evanston IL 60202-1161 Office: Prescott Sch 1632 W Wrightwood Ave Chicago IL 60614-1970

CARLSON, LAWRENCE ARVID, retired English language educator, real estate agent; b. San Diego, Dec. 29, 1935; s. Arvid Fritiof and Ruth Mathilda (Hedman) C.; m. Patricia Catherine Barlow, Sept. 8, 1963; children: Lawrence Stephen, Janine Catherine. BA in History, Roanoke Coll., 1957; MS in Edn., S.D. State U., 1962; MA in English, Calif. State U., Fullerton, 1966; grad., Realtor Inst., 2002. Cert. e-PRO Internet Profl. Tchr. Edison Jr. High Sch., L.A., 1962—63, Anaheim (Calif.) High Sch., 1963—66; prof. English Orange Coast Coll., Costa Mesa, Calif., 1966—2001; ret., 2001; instr. karate Orange Coast Coll., Costa Mesa, 1984—95. Sales assoc. Real Estate Offices, San Juan Capistrano, Calif., 1994—. Host, writer (ednl. TV show) Creative Writers Viewpoint, 1975. Horseback riding tour leader Rock Creek Pack Sta., Bishop, Calif., 1990-95; leader 4-H, Orange County, Calif., 1983-93; vol. Liberty Walk, Dana Point, Calif., 1997. Maj. USMCR, 1957-67. Recipient Excellence award Nat. Inst. Staff Orgnl. Devel., 1993. Mem. Nat. Assn. Realtors, Calif. Assn. Realtors, Orange County Assn. Realtors, Faculty Assn. Calif. C.C.'s. Democrat. Lutheran. Avocations: horseback riding, Karate, surfing. Home: PO Box 1266 Rancho Carrillo 10871 Verdugo Rd San Juan Capistrano CA 92693 Office: Ste A-102 32241 Camino Capistrano San Juan Capistrano CA 92675 Personal E-mail: ranchcarlson@earthlink.net. Business E-Mail: carlsons@larandpat.com.

CARLSON, LINDA MARIE, language arts educator, consultant; b. St. Paul, Dec. 24, 1951; d. Kenneth Leroy Carlson and Margaret Berget. BS in English and Polit. Sci., U. Minn., Duluth, 1973, MEd in Rhetorical Theory, 1979; MBA, U. St. Thomas, 1987; postgrad., Rensselaer Poly. Inst., 1992—. Cert. Myers-Briggs Type Indicator adminstrn., cert. tchr., Minn. Tchr. English, curriculum leader Ind. Sch. Dist. 13, Columbia Heights, Minn., 1973-76, publs. advisor, coach, 1974-76; exec. asst. to provost Univ. Minn., Duluth, 1977-80; tech. editor EG and G (U.S. Dept. Energy), Idaho Falls, Idaho, 1980-89; tchr. English, gifted and talented Ind. Sch. Dist. 11, Coon Rapids, Minn., 1980—, lang. arts curriculum developer, 1981—, publs. advisor, 1982-84, learning styles cons., 1986—, assessment cons., 1989—. Performance assessment cons. Minn. State Dept. Edn., St. Paul, 1990-98; writing assessment cons. Minn. State Graduation Rule Pilot Site, St. Paul, 1994-98; lang. arts cons., curriculum design cons., multicultural cons. pvt. and pub. schs. Minn., 1987—. Mem. Minn. Arthritis Found., St. Paul, 1981-90, Commn. on Health and Healing, Mpls., 1984-86. Recipient Golden Apple Teaching award Ashland Oil Co., 1994; All-Univ. scholar Rensselaer Poly. Inst., 1992. Mem. NEA, ASCD, Am. Ednl. Rsch. Assn., Nat. Coun. for Tchrs. of English, Anoka-Hennepin Edn. Assn. (pub. rels. com. 1980-85), Coll. Compositional Comm. Avocations: jewelry making, hiking, white-water rafting, travel. Home: 11117 Cottonwood St NW Coon Rapids MN 55448-3385

CARLSON, MARVIN ALBERT, theater educator; b. Wichita, Kans., Sept. 15, 1935; s. Roy Edward and Gladys (Nelson) C.; m. Patricia Alene McElroy, Aug. 20, 1960; children— Geoffrey, Richard. BS, U. Kans., 1957, MA, 1959; PhD, Cornell U., 1961. Instr. speech and drama Cornell U., Ithaca, N.Y., 1961-62, asst. prof., 1962-66, assoc. prof. theatre arts, 1966-73, prof., 1973-79, chmn. dept., 1966-68, 73-78; dir. Cornell U. (Univ. Theatre), 1963-64, 65-66; prof. theatre and drama Ind. U., Bloomington, 1979-86, prof. comparative lit., 1984-86, disting. prof., 1986—; exec. officer PhD program in theatre Grad. Ctr. CUNY, 1986-95; Sidney E. Cohn chair in theatre CUNY, 1988—. Walker-Ames lectr. U. Wash., 1994. Author: Andre Antoine's Memories of the Theatre-Libre, 1964, The Theatre of the French Revolution, 1966, The French Stage in the Nineteenth Century, 1972, The German Stage in the Nineteenth Century, 1972, Goethe and the Weimar Theatre, 1978, The Italian Stage from Goldoni to D'Annunzio, 1981, Theories of the Theatre, 1984, The Italian Shakespearians, 1985, Places of Performance, 1989, Theatre Semiotics, 1990, Deathtraps, 1993, Performance, 1996, Voltaire and the Theatre of the Eighteenth Century, 1998, The Haunted Stage, 2001. Recipient George Jean Nathan award, 1994, ATHE Career Achievement award, 1995, Calloway prize, 2001; Guggenheim fellow, 1968, Ind. U. Soc. for Humanities fellow, 1993. Fellow Am. Theatre Assn.; mem. Am. Soc. Theatre Rsch. (Outstanding Achievement award 2000), Internat. Assn. Theatre Critics, Am. Theatre in Higher Edn., Internat. Fedn. Theatre Rsch., Nat. Theatre Conf. Home: 20 E 35th St New York NY 10016 Office: CUNY Grad Grad Ctr Program in Theatre 365 Fifth Ave New York NY 10016-4334 E-mail: mcarlson@gc.cuny.edu.

CARLSON, NORA, elementary school educator; b. Pasadena, Calif., Apr. 5, 1956; d. Charles T. and Geraldine (Wood) C. BA, Wash. State U., 1978; MEd, Eastern Wash. U., 1981. Cert. elem. edn., spl. edn., Wash. Elem. tchr. Marysville (Wash.) Sch. Dist., 1978—99, Edmonds Sch. Dist., 1999—2000, Northshore Sch. Dist., 2000—. Recipient Golden Acorn award, PTSA. Mem. Alpha Delta Kappa.

CARLSON, ROBERT CODNER, industrial engineering educator; b. Granite Falls, Minn., Jan. 17, 1939; s. Robert Ledin and Ada Louise (Codner) C.; children: Brian William, Andrew Robert, Christina Louise. BSME, Cornell U., 1962; MS, Johns Hopkins U., 1963, PhD, 1976. Mem. tech. staff Bell Tel. Labs., Holmdel, N.J., 1962-70; asst. prof. Stanford (Calif.) U., Stanford, 1970-77, assoc. prof., 1977-82, prof. indsl. engring., 1982-2000, prof. mgmt. sci. & engring., 2000—. Program dir., lectr., cons. various spl. programs U.S., Japan, France, 1971—; cons. Japan Mgmt. Assn., Tokyo, 1990—, Boeing, L.A., 1998--, GKN Automotive, London, 1989—, Rockwell Internat., L.A., 1988—; vis. prof. U. Calif., Berkeley, 1987-88, Dartmouth Coll., Hanover, N.J., 1978-79; vis. faculty Internat. Mgmt. Inst., Geneva, 1984, 88. Contbr. articles to profl. jours. Recipient Maxwell Upson award in Mech. Engring. Cornell U., 1962; Bell Labs. Systems Engring. fellow, 1962-63, Bell Labs. Doctoral Support fellow, 1966-67. Mem. INFORMS (chmn. membership com. 1981-83), Inst. Indsl. Engrs., Am. Soc. Engring. Edn., Am. Prodn. and Inventory Control Soc. (bd. dirs. 1975-81), Confrerie des Chevaliers du Tastevin, Tau Beta Pi, Phi Kappa Phi, Pi Tau Sigma. Avocations: wine tasting, travelling. E-mail: r.c.carlson@stanford.edu.

CARLSON ARONSON, MARILYN A. English language and education educator; b. Gothenburg, Nebr., July 24, 1938; d. Harold N. and Verma Elnora (Granlund) C.; m. Paul E. Carlson, July 31, 1959 (dec. Sept. 1988); 1 child, Andrea Joy; m. David L. Aronson, July 8, 1995. BS in Edn., English and Psychology, Sioux Falls Coll., 1960; MA in History, U. S.D., 1973, MA in English, 1992, EdD in Ednl. Adminstrn., 1997. Tchr. English and social scis. curriculum coord. Beresford (S.D.) Pub. Sch., 1960-78; tchr. English and social scis. Sioux Empire Coll., Hawarden, Iowa, 1979-85; instr. English and ESL, Midwest Inst. for Internat. Studies, Sioux Falls, S.D., 1985-89; asst. prof. English Augustana Coll., Sioux Falls, 1989-97, asst. prof. English and edn., 1997-2000; acad. affairs coord. acad. evaluation U. S.D., Vermillion, 2000—02; assoc. acad. dean Nat. Am. U., Sioux Falls, 2002—03, acad. dean, 2003—. Part time instr. psychology Northwestern Coll., 1985; part time instr. English and lit. Nat. Coll., 1985-88; part time instr. English and history Augustana Coll., 1986-89; presenter in field. Author: Visions of Light: Flannery O'Connor's Themes and Narrative Method, 1992, A Higher Education Perspective: Themes and Narrative Methods of Flannery O'Connor and Eudora Welty, 1997; Plains Goddesses: Heroines in Willa Cather's Prairie Novels, 1995; contbr. articles and revs. to profl. publs. including The Social Sci. Jour., others. Humanities Scholar evaluator Rainbow Project and Increasing Cultural Understanding Seminar, 2000; evaluator Profl. Devel. Conf. Native Am. Curriculum, Rapid City, S.Dak., 2001; mem. S.D. Humanities Coun., 2003—. Recipient Internat. Prof.'s Exch. award Sor Trondelag Coll., Trondheim, Norway, Jan. 1999; named Tchr. of Yr. Beresford (S.D.) Pub. Schs., 1976; S.D. Humanities scholar, 1993—; Bush mini-grantee, 1993, Internat. Studies grantee, 1994, 98, 99, S.D. Humanities Spkr.'s Bur. grantee, 1996—. Mem.: Delta Kappa Gamma. Home: 29615 469th Ave Beresford SD 57004-6457 Office: Nat Am U 2801 S Kiwanis Ave Sioux Falls SD 57105 E-mail: mcarlson@national.edu.

CARLSON-PICKERING, JANE, gifted education educator; b. Providence, Sept. 17, 1954; d. Arthur Julius and Laura Helen (Extovicz) Carlson; m. Allan Thomas Pickering, Nov. 2, 1980; children: Lauren, Taylor. BS in Art Edn., R.I. Coll., 1976, MEd in Art and Indsl. Arts Edn., 1983. Cert. elem. tchr., gifted edn. tchr., R.I. Profl. photographer Ted Pickering Studios, Warwick, R.I., 1973—; calligraphy tchr. Warwick Adult Edn., 1978; secondary tchr. graphics arts Warwick Sch. Dept., 1976-78, secondary tchr. gifted program, 1978-83; elem. gifted program coordinator and tchr. Chariho Sch. System, Wyoming, R.I., 1983-94, multiple intelligences program dir., tchr. M.I. Smart!, 1994—; computer coord. Chariho Elem. Schs., 1998—; multiple intelligence specialist Learning Network's Teachervision.com website, 2000-2001. Mem. Commr.'s Task Force on Vocat. and Indsl. Arts Edn., Providence, 1984-85, Commr.'s Task Force on Gifted and Talented Edn., 1991-92, Chariho K-12 Curriculum Coun., 1992—, tech. com., 1993—; aerial photographer for Aerovisions, 1988-92; adj. faculty R.I. Coll., 1996—; cons. R.I. Dept. Edn., 1996—; tchr. R.I. Found. Tchrs. in Tech. Program, 1998. Recipient First Pl. award photography Warwick Arts Found., 1984, Tchr. award Invent Am., 1991, Lunar Disc Program Tchr. Tng. Cert. NASA, 1991, Sci. Tchr. of Yr. award Amgen Biotech. Co., 2003; grantee R.I. Found. Tchrs. Tech. Pilot Program, 1997; R.I. Tchrs. in Tech. fellow, 1999-2003. Mem. NEA, ASCD, State Advs. Gifted Edn., Nat. Student Art Edn. Assn. Club (treas. 1971-72), Nat. Sci. Tchrs. Assn., Epsilon Pi Tau. Avocations: photography, golf, biking, travel. Home: 209 Blueberry Ln West Kingston RI 02892-1818 Office: Chariho Sch Dept Switch Rd Wood River Junction RI 02894 E-mail: jcpic@chariho.k12.ri.us., rif00227@ride.ri.net.

CARLTON, DOREEN CHARLOTTE, special education supervisor and administrator; b. Bklyn., Oct. 8, 1931; d. Harry and Roselle (Janis) Goldman; children: Brian, Scott, Alison. AA, Suffolk County C.C., Seldon, N.Y., 1977; BA in Social Scis., Adelphi U., 1979, MS in Spl. Edn., 1980; PhD in Ednl. Leadership and Adminstrn., L.I. U., 1982. Lic. sch. adminstr. and supr., sch. dist. adminstrn., spl. edn. Spl. Edn. tchr. Devel. Disabilities Inst., Smithtown, N.Y., 1969-85; program coord. The Shield Inst., N.Y.C., 1985—. Office: The Shield Inst 144-61 Roosevelt Ave Flushing NY 11354-6252

CARMAN, DARREN L. middle school educator; b. Louisville, Oct. 1, 1968; s. Donald L. and Doris L. (Dowell) C. BS, Ea. Ky. U., 1990; MS, U. Louisville, 1994. Grad. asst. dept. sci. Ea. Ky. U., Richmond, 1991; tchr. sci. Meade County Schs., Brandenburg, Ky., 1991—, asst. coach acad. team, 1993-94. Recipient Gladys Perry Tyng award Coll. of Edn., Ea. Ky. U., 1990. Mem. Nat. Sci. Tchrs. Assn., Phi Delta Kappa, Alpha Upsilon Alpha, Kappa Delta Pi (v.p. 1989-90). Democrat. Methodist. Avocations: hiking, reading, travel, fishing, music. Home: 46 Loblolly Ln Brandenburg KY 40108-9122 Office: Stuart Pepper Middle Sch Old Ekron Rd Brandenburg KY 40108

CARMAN, JOHN HERBERT, elementary education educator; b. New Brunswick, NJ, Feb. 5, 1937; s. John Herbert and Lillian Elizabeth (Twyman) C.; m. Linda Kyle, Aug. 26, 1979. BA in Bus. Adminstrn., Rutgers U., 1960, postgrad., 1977-85; elem. teaching cert., Trenton State Coll., 1965; postgrad., Kean Coll., 1979-81. Cert. K-8 tchr., N.J. Tchr. Jr. HS, New Brunswick, NJ, 1961-81, Lincoln Elem. Sch., New Brunswick, NJ, 1981-98; substitute tchr. Mt. Desert Island H.S., 2000—03. Baseball coach St. Peter's Grammar Sch., 1971-1995; coord. summer playgrounds New Brunswick Recreation Dept., 1956-89 Trustee Rutgers U., New Brunswick, 1986-92, 1996-2002; elected Trustee Emeritus, Rutgers U, 2002-, mem. Kirkpatrick Chapel com., 1981-85, mem. St. Michaels Chapel com., 1981-83, treas., 1991-98, mem. bd. trustees exec. com., 2000-2001; co-chair Friends of the Geology Mus., 1995—; active Procter Found., 1992—. With U.S. Army, 1962. Recipient Loyal Son of Rutgers award Rutgers U., 1978, New Brunswick,NJ African-Am. Pioneer Award, 2002, Rutgers Meritorious Svc. award, 1991, Gov.'s Tchr. Recognition award, 1998, Middlesex County Vocat. Schs. award, 1998, Alumni Trustees award Rutgers U., 2000; named New Brunswick Citizen of Week, 1980, Alec Baker award KC, 1984, Colgate-Palmolive award for edn. achievement, 1992; 1937 state scholar Rutgers U., 1956-60; named to St. Peter's Hall of Fame, 1996. Mem. NJ Edn. Assn., Middlesex County Edn. Assn., New Brunswick Edn. Assn., St. Peter's Athletic Assn., Rutgers Coll. Alumni Assn. (corr. sec., v.p., pres.-elect 1982-85, pres. 1985-86, Phonothon All Star Team 1991-97, Hall of Fame 1997). Episcopalian. Avocations: sports, reading, theater, musical programs. Home: PO Box 602 Mount Desert ME 04660-0602 Office: Kyles Keep 110 Main St Bar Harbor ME 04609-1873

CARMAN, MARY ANN, retired special education educator; b. Kerrville, Tex., July 12, 1941; d. William Earl and Virginia (Tracy) Gregg; m. Douglas Gary Carman, July 20, 1968; 1 child, Christina Tracy. BA in Psychology, So. Meth. U., 1959-63; MS in Spl. Edn., E. Tex. State U., 1971. Cert. spl. edn. tchr., Iowa; teaching credential, Tex. Salesperson James K. Wilson Clothing Store, Dallas, 1963; sec. psychology dept. So. Meth. U., Dallas, 1964; EEG technician Dr. Paul Levin, Neurologist, Dallas, 1965-68; sec. geography dept. E. Tex. State U., Commerce, 1968-70; tchr. pilot program early childhood edn. Farmers Br. (Tex.) Sch. Dist., 1971; chair dept. spl. edn. U. Dubuque, Iowa, 1972-75; tchr.'s aide Crockett Elem. Sch., San Marcos, Tex., 1978, 79; spl. edn. tchr. Travis Elem. Sch., San Marcos, 1980—2000, ropes course facilitator campus improvemnt team, 1994-95, tchr. class-within-a-class 2d and 3d gr. levels, presenter project math 2d gr. campus improvement team, ropes course facilitator, 1995-96. Mem. dist. ednl. improvement coun. San Marcos Consol. Ind. Sch. Dist., 1991, participant strategic planning workshop, 1991, learning styles tng. course, 1992, chmn. sight based mgmt. team, 1991; facilitator ROPES course, 1993. Winant vol. Episcopal Ch., E. India Dock, London, 1963; coach state meet Spl. Olympics team San Marcos Consol. Ind. Sch. Dist., 1981, ofcl. at state games, 1988; facilitator exptl. edn. TRUST (Teamwork, Responsibility, Understanding for Students and Tchrs.), 1993. Recipient 1st place Bill Gray award Tex. Assn. Bus., The Spl. Kid's Co., 1991, Teaching Excellence award Lions Club San Marcos, 1991. Mem. ASCD, Phi Delta Kappa. Home: 817 Willow Creek Cir San Marcos TX 78666-5061

CARMAN, ROBERT EUGENE, secondary school educator; b. Malden, Mo., July 21, 1940; s. Beauford Lav and Margaret Lav (Wiseman) C.; m. Betty Ann Robertson, July 1963 (div. 1968); m. Nada Joyce Shoemaker, Nov. 2, 1968; children: Jason Austin, Justin Aaron (dec.). BS in Edn., Southeast Mo. State Coll., 1962; MS in Combined Scis., U. Miss., 1966, cert., 1988. Cert. tchr., Mo. Tchr. math. Malden (Mo.) High Sch., 1962-67, Hazelwood Jr. High Sch., Florissant, Mo., 1967-72, supr. math., 1972-92, ret., 1992; early childhood and elem. edn. instr. U. Mo., St. Louis, 1993-95. Mid. level specialist SMILE Inst., St. Louis, 1989; cons. pub. schs., St. Louis, 1989-91, 96-99, St. Genevieve, Mo., 1990, Riverview Gardens Sch. Dist., St. Louis County, Mo., 1990, Mehlville, Mo., 1990-95, St. Charles, Mo., 1991, Wentzville, Mo., 1994, others, including Glencoe Pub. and Mimosa Pub., Milliken Pub.; program cons. Math. and Sci. Edn. Ctr., 1986-91. Author: Using Cooperative Techniques and Manipulatives to Teach Core Competence and Key Skills, 1989, Supermarket Math, 1993, Knowledge Works, 1996; editor books, software, manipulatives, articles, Math. Tchr., 1984-92. Named Hazelwood Jr. High Sch. Tchr. of Yr., 1992-93. Mem. ASCD, Math. Educators Greater St. Louis (bd. dirs. 1984-86, pres. 1988-89, newsletter editor 1986-88, Educator of Yr. 1991-92, chmn. student support spring conf. 1995, mem. chair 1996—, jour. com. 2002—), Mo. Coun. Tchrs. Math. (pres. 1992-93, exec. bd. 1988-90, chmn. jr. h.s. math. contest 1988-90, chair contest test writing, 1998—, gen. chmn. spring meeting 1991, Educator of Yr. 1991-92), Nat. Coun. Tchrs. Math. (chmn. student exhibit St. Louis Cen. Regional conf. 1988, chmn. mid grades conf. program 1991, chmn. workshop support Springfield Cen. Regional conf. 1995), Am. Philatelic Soc. Avocation: stamp collecting. Home: 3125 Matlock Dr Florissant MO 63031-1519 E-mail: bobcarman@aol.com.

CARMI, SHLOMO, mechanical engineering educator, scientist; b. Cernauti, Romania, July 18, 1937; came to U.S., 1963, naturalized, 1978; s. Shmuel and Haia (Marcovici) C.; m. Rachel Aharoni, Dec. 23, 1963; children: Sharon, Ronen-Itzhak, Lemore. Student, Technion, Haifa, Israel, 1958-60; BS cum laude, U. Witwatersrand, Johannesburg, South Africa, 1962; MS, U. Minn., 1966, PhD, 1968. Research engr. W. Rand Gold Mining Co., Krugersdorp, South Africa, 1962-63; research asst., research fellow U. Minn., 1963-68; asst. prof. mech. engring. Wayne State U., Detroit, 1968-70, 72-73, assoc. prof., 1973-78, prof., 1978-86; prof. and head mech. engring. and mechanics dept. Drexel U., Phila., 1986-96; prof., dean Coll. Engring. and Info. Tech. U. Md. Baltimore County, Balt., 1996—. Sr. lectr. Technion, Israel Inst. Tech., 1970-72, sabbatical I. Taylor chair, 1977-78; Congl. fellow sci. adv. to Sen. Carl Levin, 1985-86; rsch. specialist Ford Motor Co., summers 1973, 74, 76, 77, Detroit Edison Co., summer 1983; spkr. in field; chair Nat. Mech. Engring. Dept. Heads Com., 1996-97. Editor three books in field; contbr. articles and revs. to profl. jours.; assoc. editor Jour. Fluids Engring., 1981-84. Served in Israeli Army, 1956-58. South African Technion Soc. scholar, 1960-62; recipient prize Transvaal Chamber of Mines, 1961, faculty rsch. award Wayne State U., 1970; rsch. grantee Dept. Energy, U.S. Army Rsch. Office, NSF, Nat. Inst. for Standards and Tech., NIH, Advanced Rsch. Project Agy., Air Force Office of Sci. Rsch. Fellow ASME (v.p. engring. edn. 2000-03; mem. Am. Soc. Engring. Edn. (dean's coun. 1996—), Am. Phys. Soc., Accreditation Bd. for Engring. and Tech. (evaluator mech. engring. programs 1988-96), Golden Key, Sigma Xi, Tau Beta Pi, Pi Tau Sigma, Phi Kappa Phi. Home: 2 Aston Ct Owings Mills MD 21117-1439 Office: U Md Baltimore County Coll Engring Baltimore MD 21250-0001

CARMICHAEL, PAUL LOUIS, ophthalmic surgeon; b. July 8, 1927; s. Louis and Christina Ciamaichela; m. Pauline Cecilia Lipsmire, Oct. 28, 1950; children: Paul Louis, Mary Catherine, John Michael, Kevin Anthony, Joseph William, Patricia Ann, Robert, Christopher. BS in Biology, Villanova U., 1945; MD, St. Louis U., 1949; MS in Medicine, U. Pa., 1954. Diplomate Am. Bd. Ophthalmology; cert. isotope methodology Hahnemann Med. Coll. Rotating intern St. Joseph's Hosp., Phila., 1949-50; resident in ophthalmology Phila. Gen. Hosp., 1952-54; asst. prof. ophthalmology Hahnemann Med. Coll., Phila., 1960-66, clin. assoc. prof. nuclear medicine, 1974-90. With radioactive isotope dept. Wills Eye Hosp., Phila., 1956-61, sr. asst. surgeon, 1961-65, assoc. surgeon, 1966-72, assoc. surgeon retinal svc., 1972-90; attending ophthalmologist Holy Redeemer Hosp., Meadowbrook, Pa., 1963-65; assoc. ophthalmologist Grand View Hosp., Sellersville, Pa., 1958-75; instr. ophthalmology Grad. Sch. Medicine, U. Pa., Phila., 1956-63; clin. assoc. prof. ophthalmology Temple U., Phila., 1967-72; clin. assoc. prof. ophthalmology Thomas Jefferson U. Sch. Medicine, Phila., 1971-90; chief ophthalmology North Pa. Hosp., Lansdale, 1959-90, pres. staff, 1959; pres. Ophthalmic Assocs., Lansdale, 1969-90. Co-author: Nuclear Ophthalmology, 1976; contbr. chpts. to books, papers to profl. confs., articles to publs. in field. Pres. bd. dirs. North Pa. Symphony, 1976-78. Capt. M.C., U.S. Army, 1950-51. Named Outstanding Young Man of Yr., Lansdale Jaycees, 1959, Outstanding Young Man, State of Pa. Jaycees, 1960. Fellow ACS, Internat. Coll. Surgeons, Coll. Physicians Phila.; mem. AMA, Montgomery County Med. Soc., Pa. Med. Soc., Am. Acad. Ophthalmology, Pa. Acad. Ophthalmology, Assn. Rsch. in Ophthalmology, Inter-County Ophthalmol. Soc. (co-founder, pres. 1975-78), Ophthalmic Club Phila. (pres. 1964), Delaware Valley Ophthalmic Soc. (pres. 1985-89). Roman Catholic. Home: Box 680308 2567 Columbine Ct Park City UT 84068 E-mail: pplcsr@cs.com.

CARMICHAEL, WILLIE FRANKLIN, JR., science educator; b. Atlanta, Mar. 18, 1939; s. Willie Franklin and Inez Yvonne (White) C. BA, Morris Brown Coll., 1961; MA, Atlanta U., 1965, EdS, 1967. Cert. tchr. Ga. Tchr. sci. Winder City Bd. Edn., Ga., 1961-63, Atlanta Bd. Edn., 1963-97, Washington Evening Sch., Atlanta, 1971-94. Staff biomed. scis. program Emory U., Atlanta, 1980-83; mem. faculty STAR-Lab., Morris Brown Coll., summers, 1992, 93; cons. on central cities Atlanta Bd. Edn., summer, 1968; tchr. Price Cmty. Sch., Atlanta, 1967-68. Author: (with others) Atlanta Pub. Schs. Rev. Biology Curriculum Guide, 1978. Founder Assn. to Revive

Grant Park, Atlanta, 1973; co-founder Dogwood City Landmarks, Atlanta, 1981; mem. No In-Town Piggyback Coalition, Atlanta, 1984; trustee Historic Oakland Cemetery, Inc., Atlanta, 1984; advisor to student winners Ga. PTA Safety Contest; advisor Fulton H.S. chpt. Jr. Engring. Tech. Soc.; Fulton H.S. chairperson Southeastern Consortium for Minorities in Engring. Named Tchr.-of-Yr., Fulton H.S., Atlanta, 1974, Outstanding Secondary Educator of Am., 1974; recipient Tchr. Spotlight award Washington High Evening Sch. newspaper, 1974, Sci. Project Sponsor award Am. Soc. Microbiology, 1976, Student Tchr. Achievement Recognition award Kiwanis Club Atlanta, 1981, 82, 83, Fire Prevention award Atlanta Fire Bur., 1982, 83, 84, 85, 86, 87, 88, 90, 90, 92, Disting. Svc. Citation Atlanta-Fulton County Emergency Mgmt. Agy., 1985, Parents Tchrs. Students Assn. award Fulton H.S., 1993; subject of yearbook dedication Fulton H.S., 1978; grantee Apple Corps., 1988, Ga. PTA, Ecology Grant, 1992. Mem. CIRCA, NEA, Atlanta Preservation Ctr., Nat. Trust Historic Preservation, Victorian Soc. of Am., Ga. Ornithology Soc., Nat. Audubon Soc., Ga. Trust Historic Preservation, Thomasville Cemetery Preservation Soc., Sierra Club, Omega Psi Phi, Phi Delta Kappa (Clark-Atlanta U. chpt.). Mem. Mt. Carmel African Meth. Episcopal. Ch. Home: 1225 Hosea L Williams Dr SE Atlanta GA 30317-1603

CARNESALE, ALBERT, academic administrator; b. Bronx, NY, July 2, 1936; m. Robin Gerber, Apr. 6, 2002; children: Keith, Kimberly. BME, Cooper Union, 1957; MS, Drexel U., 1961, LLD (hon.), 1993; PhD, N.C. State U., 1966, LLD (hon.), 1997; AM (hon.), Harvard U., 1979; ScD (hon.), N.J. Inst. Technology, 1984. Prof. N.C. State U., Raleigh, 1962—69, 1972—74; chief Def. Weapons Systems U.S. Arms Control and Disarmament Agy., Washington, 1969—72; prof. John F. Kennedy Sch. of Govt. Harvard U., Cambridge, Mass., 1974—97, acad. dean John F. Kennedy Sch. of Govt., 1981—91, dean John F. Kennedy Sch. of Govt., 1991—95, provost, Lucius N. Littauer Prof. Pub. Policy and Adminstrn., 1994—97; chancellor UCLA, 1997—. Author: Nuclear Power Issues and Choices: Report of the Nuclear Energy Policy Study Group, 1977, Living with Nuclear Weapons, 1983, Hawks, Doves and Owls: An Agenda for Avoiding Nuclear War, 1985, Superpower Arms Control: Setting the Record Straight, 1987, Fateful Visions: Avoiding Nuclear Catastrophe, 1988; co-author: New Nuclear Nations: Consequences for US Policy, 1993. Recipient Gano Dunn award Outstanding Profl. Achievement, Cooper Union, N.Y.C. Fellow: Am. Acad. Arts and Scis.; mem.: L.A. World Affairs Coun., Internat. Inst. for Strategic Studies, Coun. on Fgn. Rels. Office: UCLA Office of Chancellor 405 Hilgard Ave Los Angeles CA 90095-1405

CARNEY, ANN VINCENT, retired secondary education educator; b. Slippery Rock, Pa., Feb. 17, 1933; d. Arthur Porter and Leila Felicia (Watson) Vincent; m. Charles Lucien Carney Jr., Dec. 15, 1954 (div. 1974); children: Adrienne Ann, Stephen Vincent. BS, Drexel Inst. Tech., 1955; MEd, U. Pitts., 1972. Cert. tchr., reading specialist, Pa. Tchr. English Allegheny Valley Sch. Dist., Springdale, Pa., 1957-62; reading specialist Gateway Sch. Dist., Monroeville, Pa., 1972-98. Mem. AAUW, Internat. Reading Assn., Keystone State Reading Assn., Three Rivers Reading Coun., Phi Kappa Phi, Omicron Nu. Republican. Avocations: reading, travel, needlework, cooking, gardening. Home: 4013 Impala Dr Pittsburgh PA 15239-2705

CARNEY, MARK, financial executive; b. Girard, Ohio; m. Deborah Frances Finnerty; children: Deidre, Caitlin. BA summa cum laude in polit. sci., Ohio U., 1980; M in pub. admin., Ohio State U., 1982. Dep. chief fin. off. US Dept. of Edn., Wash., DC, 1999—; mgmt. intern Fed. Exec. Inst., 1998; dir. US Small Bus. Admin. Comml. Loan Servicing Ctr., Fresno, Calif., US Small Bus. Admin. Nat. Fin. Ctr., Denver. Named Dist. Fed. Mgr., Denver, 1995; recipient Credit Mgmt. Distinction award, US Dept. Treas., Debt Collection Distinction award, Payments Mgmt. Distinction award. Democrat. Office: US Dept of Edn 400 Maryland Ave Washington DC 20202 Office Fax: 202-401-0006. E-mail: mark.carney@ed.gov.*

CARNEY, THOMAS QUENTIN, academic administrator, educator, pilot; b. Crawfordsville, Ind., Feb. 26, 1949; s. Quentin Ruel and Alice Laverne (Silvey) C.; m. Karen Sue Rippy, Mar. 28, 1970; children: Catherine Anne, Cheryl Lynn, Allison Elaine. AS, Purdue U., 1970, BS, 1971; MS, Purdue U., W. Lafayette, 1977, PhD, 1984. Lic. airline transport pilot; cert. flight instr.; cert. aviation safety counselor. Temporary instr. Dept. of Aviation Tech., W. Lafayette, Ind., 1971-72; flight instr. Reid Airways, Inc., W. Lafayette, 1972; instr. dept. of aviation tech. Purdue U., W. Lafayette, 1972-81, academic coord., dept of aviation tech., 1981-84, asst. prof., asst. dept. head dept. aviation tech., 1984-85, assoc. prof., asst. dept. head aviation tech., 1985-88, prof., assoc dept. head aviation tech., 1989—2002, prof., dept. head, 2002—. Cons. in field. Sr. author: Hazardous Mountain Winds and Their Visual Indicators; editor: Collegiate Aviation Rev.; mem. editl. bd. Jour. Aviation/Aerospace Edn. and Rsch., Jour. Aerospace Transp. Worldwide; contbr. articles to profl. jours. Deacon, elder, Immanuel United Ch. of Christ, Lafayette; rep. United Ch. of Christ. Grantee Airway Sci., Fed. Aviation Adminstrn., Wash., 1986. Mem. Univ. Aviation Assn. (bd. dirs. ctrs. of excellence, pubs. com.), Am. Meterol. Soc. (past com. aviation, range, and aerospace meteorology), Aircraft Owners and Pilots Assn., Coun. Aviation Accreditation (bd. dirs., chair stds. com., treas.), Purdue Book Great Tchrs., Phi Eta Sigma, Phi Kappa Phi (James G. Dwyer award for outstanding undergrad. tchg., William A. Wheatley award for outstanding contbn. to aerospace edn.). Avocations: speleology, woodworking, snow skiing, reading. Home: 2301 Wigeon Dr Lafayette IN 47905-4084 Office: Purdue U Dept Aviation Tech West Lafayette IN 47907-2015 E-mail: tcarney@purdue.edu.

CARNEY-DALTON, PAT, elementary education educator; b. Hatboro, Pa., July 1, 1950; d. James A. and Mary (McGrath) Carney; m. Richard W. Dalton; children: Sean, Chris and Keith Ohrberg. BS, Gwynedd Mercy Coll., 1978; MEd, Beaver Coll., Glenside, Pa., 1981. Cert. tchr., program specialist, Pa. Elem. edn. tchr. Assumption Blessed Virgin Mary Sch., Feasterville, Pa., 1968-71, St. John Bapt. Sch., Ottsville, Pa., 1973-74; tchr. of gifted Bucks County IV # 22, Doylestown, Pa., 1978—; tchr. cons. Pa. Writing Project, West Chester, 1988—; artist-in-residence Quakertown (Pa.) Sch. Dist., 1990-91; tchr. of insvc. Pa. Insvc. Coun., Doylestown, 1990—. Tchr. insvc. Kutztown (Pa.) Sch. Dist., 1992, Ctrl. Sch. Dist., Doylestown, 1992, Bristol (Pa.) Twp. Sch. Dist., 1992-93. Contbr. poetry to publs., articles to profl. jours. Fellow Pa. Writing Project; mem. ASCD, Pa. Assn. for Gifted Edn., Nat. Coun. Tchrs. English, Nat. Coun. for Social Studies. Avocations: reading, writing, walking. Home: 270 Paine St Doylestown PA 18901-4026

CARNOCHAN, WALTER BLISS, retired humanities educator; b. N.Y.C., Dec. 20, 1930; s. Gouverneur Morris and Sibyll Baldwin (Bliss) C.; m. Nancy Powers Carter, June 25, 1955 (div. 1978); children— Lisa Powers, Sarah Bliss, Gouverneur Morris, Sibyll Carter; m. Brigitte Hoy Fields, Sept. 16, 1979. AB, Harvard, 1953, A.M., 1957, PhD, 1960. Asst. dean freshmen Harvard U., 1954-56; successively instr., asst. prof., assoc. prof., prof. English, Stanford (Calif.) U., 1960-94, prof. emeritus, 1994—, chmn. dept. English, 1971-73, dean grad. studies, 1975-80, vice provost, 1976-80, dir. Stanford Humanities Ctr., 1985-91, Anthony P. Meier Family prof. humanities, 1988-91, Richard W. Lyman prof. humanities, 1993-94, Richard W. Lyman prof. emeritus, 1994—, acting dir. Stanford Humanities Ctr., 1999. Mem. overseers com. to visit Harvard Coll, 1979-85, mem. bd. advisors Ehrenpreis Ctr. for Swift Studies, 1984—. Author: Lemuel Gulliver's Mirror for Man, 1968, Confinement and Flight: An Essay on English Literature of the 18th Century, 1977, Gibbon's Solitude: The Inward World of the Historian, 1987, The Battleground of the Curriculum: Liberal Education and American Experience, 1993, Momentary Bliss: An American Memoir, 1999. Trustee Mills Coll., 1978-85, Athenian Sch., 1975-88, Berkeley (Calif.) Art Mus., 1983-96, 98-2001. Home: 138 Cervantes Rd Portola Valley CA 94028-7725 E-mail: carnochan@stanford.edu.

CAROTHERS, ROBERT LEE, academic administrator; b. Sewickley, Pa., Sept. 3, 1942; s. Robert Fleming and Mary (Skinner) C.; children: Robert Kennedy, Shelley Rye, Matthew K. Ruane. BS, Edinboro U., 1965; MA, Kent State U., 1966, PhD, 1969; JD, U. Akron, 1980. Bar: Pa. 1981. Prof. English, dean, v.p. Edinboro U., 1968-83; pres. S.W. State U., Marshall, Minn., 1983-86; chancellor Minn. State U. Sys., St. Paul, 1986-91; pres. U. R.I., Kingston, 1991—. Author: Freedom and Other Times, 1972; John Calvin's Favorite Son, 1980. Served with AUS, 1960-68. Avocation: fishing. Home: 56 Upper College Rd Kingston RI 02881-2022 Office: URI Office of the Pres Green Hall 35 Campus Ave Kingston RI 02881-1303

CARPENTER, DOROTHY SCHENCK, special education educator; b. Tewksbury, Mass., Feb. 17, 1942; d. William Edmond and Grace (Scott) Schenck; m. Booker Stephen Carpenter, Sept. 12, 1964; children: B. Stephen II, Sean D., Dreux S., Seth B. BA, George Washington U., 1987; MS, Johns Hopkins U., 1996. Cert. tchr., sch. counselor, Md. Sec. U.S. Dept. State AID, Washington, 1960-67; spl. edn. instr. asst. Montgomery County, Md. Pub. Schs., Gaithersburg, 1980-87, spl. edn. tchr. Rockville, 1987—. Ballot box judge Mont. Co. Md. Bd. Elections, Clarksburg, 1980-87. Bd. Trustees grantee George Washington U., 1986, Columbia Women's scholar, 1986; Montgomery Coll. grantee, 1979, 80. Mem. NEA, Nat. Art Edn. Assn., Coun. for Exceptional Children, Mont. Co. Edn. Assn., Pi Lambda Theta (sec. 1989-90). Home: 12200 Greenridge Dr Boyds MD 20841-9032

CARPENTER, J. SCOTT, vocational educator; Supr. Penta County Career Ctr., Perrysburg, Ohio, supr. student svcs. & admissions. Named Nat. Vocat. Tchr. of Yr., 1993, Nat. Bus. Tchr. of Yr. Office: Penta County Career Ctr 30095 Oregon Rd Perrysburg OH 43551-4533 E-mail: scarpenter@pentanet.k12.oh.us.

CARPENTER, JOHN EVERETT, retired principal, educational consultant; b. Tarrytown, N.Y., Nov. 27, 1923; s. Everett Birch and Mary (Avery) C.; student Union Coll., 1943; B.A., Iona Coll., 1946; M.A., Columbia, 1949, profl. diploma, 1961; m. Marie F. McCarthy, Nov. 14, 1944; 1 son, Dennis Everett. Tchr., Blessed Sacrament High Sch., New Rochelle, N.Y., 1946-50; tchr., adminstr. Armonk (N.Y.) pub. schs., 1950-62; dir. guidance Ridge Street Sch., Port Chester, N.Y., 1962-64; counselor Rye (N.Y.) High Sch., 1964-66, prin., 1966-78, ret.; guest lectr. Served to lt. USNR; now lt. comdr. ret. Res. Decorated Bronze Star medal. Mem. Middle States Assn. Colls. and Schs. (commn. on secondary schs.), Am. (life), Westchester-Putnam-Rockland (past pres.) personnel and guidance assns., NEA, Am. Legion (past comdr.), Phi Delta Kappa, Kappa Delta Pi. Rotarian (past pres., Paul Harris fellow). Clubs: Tarrytown Boat (past commodore). Home: Green Valley, Ariz. Died Oct. 30, 2001.

CARPENTER, MARGARET MARY, state legislator, information technology manager; b. Detroit, Aug. 3, 1950; m. C.A. Bryant, Jr. (dec. Mar. 1985); m. Dale Richard Carpenter, June 25, 1988; 1 child, Heather. BS, U. Ala., 1975; MEd, U. South Ala., 1989, postgrad., 1995. Cert. tchr. spl. edn., Ala. Kindergarten tchr. Gila Bend (Ariz.) Schs., 1976-77; tchr. 1st grade Dept. of Def. Overseas Schs., Okinawa, Japan, 1977-79; spl. edn. tchr. Selbyville (Del.) Middle Sch., 1980-81; dir. religious edn. Corpus Christi Ch., Mobile, Ala., 1990-93; spl. edn. tchr. Mobile County Schs., 1981-92; PhD asst. U. South Ala., Mobile, 1992-95; mgr. tng. and devel. Teledyne Continental Motors, Mobile, 1995—99; legislator State of N.C., 2000—02; internet bus. owner. Cons. Ala. Rsch. and Insvc. Ctr., Mobile, 1988-89; presenter papers at convs. Religion tchr. Corpus Christi Ch., Mobile, 1981-94. Mem. Coun. for Exceptional Children, Nat. Coun. for Children with Behavioral Disorders, Ala. Coun. for Children with Behavior Disorders, Kappa Delta Pi (Outstanding Student of the Yr. 1994). Roman Catholic. Avocations: golf, relaxation training, cross stitch. Home: PO Box 893 Waynesville NC 28786-0893

CARPENTER, MARK WARREN, social sciences educator; b. Long Beach, Calif., Nov. 11, 1949; s. Philip Benham and Nancy Anne (Banchor) C. BA in Comm., Calif. State U., Fullerton, 1974, MPA, 1977; MA in Behavioral Sci., Calif. State U., Dominguez Hills, 1982; MA in Edn., U. Calif., Riverside, 1994. Life cert. tchr. cmty. coll. sociology; life cert. FCC. Editor, rsch. analyst, project coord. Govt. edn. Ctr., L.A., 1975-76; rsch. fellow Calif. State U., Dominguez Hills, 1980-81, mem. staff registrar's office Fullerton, 1984-87; tchg. asst. U. Calif., Riverside, 1987-88; lectr., mem. faculty dept. sociology Riverside C.C., 1989—. Founder, World Citizens Institute, 1986. Author/compiler: (ednl. directory) After Work in Los Angeles, 1976; author, editor: (gen. plan element) Torrance Energy Awareness Monograph, 1978. Sgt. U.S. Army, 1969-71, Vietnam. Mem. Am. Ednl. Rsch. Assn., Am. Soc. Pub. Adminstrn. (mem. higher edn. and govt. rels. com.), Sociology of Edn. Assn., Assn. Environ. Profls., Calif. Coop. Edn. Assn., Internat. Assn. Cognitive Edn., Internat. Platform Assn., Com. for Expanded Ednl. Opportunity, So. Calif. Assn. Govts., Mensa. Avocations: surfing, writing. Home: PO Box 8116 Moreno Valley CA 92552-8116 Office: Riverside C C 4800 Magnolia Ave Riverside CA 92506-1242 E-mail: markc@rccd.cc.ca.us.

CARPENTER, PAMELA PRISCO, bank officer, foreign language educator; b. Norwood, Mass., July 12, 1958; d. Francis Joseph and Helene Louise (Swartz) Prisco; m. Charles Gilbert Carpenter, Oct. 18, 1981; children: Charles, Craig, Cameron. BA summa cum laude, Harvard U., 1980; grad. cert., U. Salamanca, Spain, 1980; postgrad., Boston State Coll., 1980-81. Cert. Spanish tchr., Mass.; lic. real estate sales assoc., Mass. V.p. global fin. instns. Fleet Nat. Bank, 1980—; bilingual edn. substitute tchr. Boston English H.S., 1979-80; grades K-2 Spanish tchr. IES Lang. Sch., Westwood, Mass., 1991-92; pvt. Spanish and French tutor. Pres. parent adv. bd. Mulberry Childcare and Pre-sch. Ctr., Norwood, 1991-94; mentor Bank of Boston/Hyde Park H.S. Partnership, 1990; sec. C.J. Prescott Elem. Sch. PTA, 1995-97. Radcliffe Club of Boston scholar, 1976. Mem. Phi Beta Kappa. Home: 549 Neponset St Norwood MA 02062-5201

CARPENTER, RAYMOND LEONARD, information science educator; b. Watertown, N.Y., Dec. 1, 1926; s. Raymond Leonard and Ethel Marian (Smith) C.; m. Patricia Ann Anderson, June 22, 1962; 1 child, Christopher. AB in Sociology, St. Lawrence U., 1949; MA in Sociology, U. N.C., 1951, MS in Library Sci., 1959, PhD in Sociology, 1968. Gen. library asst., then head of searching sect. U. N.C., Chapel Hill, 1956-58, vis. instr., 1958-59, lectr., 1960-68, assoc. prof., 1968-81, prof. Sch. Info. and Library Sci., 1981—, acting dean Sch. Info. and Library Sci., 1970-72; bibliographer Duke U. Library, Durham, N.C., 1959; mem. Inst. Rsch. in Social Sci., Chapel Hill, 1981—. Cons. Nat. Inst. Standards Orgn., Washington, 1988-89. Author: Public Library Patrons in North Carolina, 1975, Statistical Methods for Librarians, 1978; author numerous articles, revs., monographs. With U.S. Army, 1944-45. Fulbright-Hays rsch. scholar, Italy, 1974. Mem. ALA (rep. Internat. Fedn. Library Assn., Netherlands, 1989-93, dir. standards study, Chgo., 1979-81, chmn. panel on Italy, Chgo., 1978—), Assn. Library and Info. Sci. Edn., Am. Sociol. Assn., AAUP, Internat. Assn. Social Sci. Info. Svc. and Technology, Beta Phi Mu, Alpha Kappa Delta. Home: 108 Silver Cedar Ln Chapel Hill NC 27514-1659

CARPER, BARBARA ANNE, nursing educator; BSN, Tex. Women's U., 1959; clin. cert. in anesthesia, U. Mich., 1962; MEd, Columbia U., 1966, EdD, 1975. Instr. U. N.Mex. Coll. Nursing, Alburquerque, 1966-69; assoc. prof. Tex. Women's U. Coll. Nursing, Denton, 1976-80, prof., coord. doctoral program, 1980-82; prof. grad. program U. So. Maine Sch. Nursing, Portland, 1982-84; prof., chairperson dept. nursing Colby-Sawyer Coll., New London, N.H., 1984-88; prof. Regents Coll., SUNY, Albany, 1985-89; assoc. prof., coord. undergrad. program U. N.C. Coll. Nursing, Charlotte, 1989-91, interim dean, 1991-92, prof., assoc. dean for acad. affairs, 1992—99, prof., 1994—99, prof. emeritus. Vis. scholar Harvard U., 1981-82; mem. Nursing Theory Think Tank, 1982; mem. exec. bd., chmn. project com. New Eng. Orgn. Nursing, 1986-88; vis. prof. Marion A. Buckley Sch. Nursing, Adelphi U., 1989-90; Green Chair honor prof. Harris Coll. Nursing, Tex. Christian U., 1980-81; Margaret D. McLean lectr. Meml. U. Nfld., Can., 1990; numerous consultations, workshops, lectures, seminars and speeches in field. Mem. editorial bd. Jour. Advances in Nursing Sci., 1978-99, Asian Jour. Nursing Studies, 1993-95; contbr. articles to profl. jours. Bd. dirs., mem. exec. com., mem. patient and cmty. svcs. com. Nat. Kidney Found. N.H., 1987-89; bd. dirs. Hospice at Charlotte, 1991-97, co-chairperson ethics adv. com., 1995-97, vice chair at large 1996-97; bd. dirs. Cmty. Health Svcs., 1991-94. Fellow Am. Acad. Nursing (co-chair ethics/legal adv. com. 1983-86, mem. planning com. 1988, Ann. Sci. Sessions of Acad., mem. expert panel on ethics 1991—); mem. ANA (coun. nurse rschrs.), N.C. State Nursing Assn., Sigma Theta Tau (Disting. lectr. 1994-95), Phi Kappa Phi. Office: U NC Coll Health and Human Svcs 9201 University City Blvd Charlotte NC 28223-0002

CARPER, KENNETH LYNN, architect, educator; b. Colfax, Wash., Nov. 2, 1948; s. Emery C. and Marjorie A. (Hain) C.; m. Tanya J. Corcoran, June 9, 1970; children: Brent, Corin, Daren. BArch, Wash. State U., 1972, MSCE, 1977. Registered architect, Wash. Architect, designer Sylvester Assocs., Spokane, Wash., 1968-74; prof. architecture Wash. State U., Pullman, 1974—. Author: Why Buildings Fail, 2001, Forensic Engineering, 1989, 2nd edit. 2001, Construction Failure, 1997; editor: Forensic Engineering: Learning from Failure, 1986; founding editor Jour. of Performance of Constructed Facilities, 1986—; contbr. articles to profl. jours. Facilities adv. com. pub. schs. Pullman, 1985—. Named Outstanding Prof. Coll. Engring. & Arch., Wash. State U., 1985, Sch. Arch., 1983, 84, 85, 92, 98, 2000, 2001, Engr. of Yr. award ASCE Inland Empire Section, 1994; recipient Outstanding Faculty award N.W. Coop. Edn. Assn., 1992, All-Univ. Pres.'s Faculty Excellence award, Wash. State U., 1994. Mem. ASCE (Nat. Forensic Engring. award 1997, Richard R. Torrens award 1991, Daniel Mead award 1983, chair tech. coun. on forensic engring. 1990, chair pubs. com. 1986—, chair com. on dissemination of failure info. 1985), Am. Soc. Engring. Edn. Democrat. Office: Wash State U Coll Engring and Arch Sch Of Arch and Constrn Mgmt Pullman WA 99164-2220

CARPER, WILLIAM BARCLAY, management educator; b. Winchester, Va., Apr. 3, 1946; s. Roy Silas and Evadnyr Joyce (Arthur) C.; m. Brenda Carol Campbell, Aug. 20, 1966 (div. Sept. 1994); children: Melissa Paige, Jonathan Barclay; m. Andrea Lynn Sikes, Mar. 15, 1997; 1 stepson, Christopher Paul Sikes. BA, U. Va., 1968; MBA, Coll. William & Mary, 1976; PhD, Va. Poly. Inst. and State U., 1979. Instr. Va. Poly. Inst. and State U., Blacksburg, 1976-79; asst. prof. Auburn (Ala.) U., 1979-81, George Mason U., Fairfax, Va., 1981-87; assoc. prof. mgmt. Ga. So. U., Statesboro, 1987-92, prof., 1992-95, dept. head, 1987-90, assoc. dean., 1989-95; dir. ctr. for mgmt. devel., 1993-94; dean Coll. U. West Fla. Coll. Bus., Pensacola, 1995-2000; prof. mgmt. U. West Fla., Pensacola, 1995—, assoc. v.p. for acad. affairs, 2000—03, dep. EEO/AA officer, 2000—03. Dir. small bus. programs George Mason Inst., 1983-85; pres. Strategic Mgmt. Systems, Inc., Statesboro and Pensacola, Fla., 1987—; cons. Nat. Health Advisors, Ltd., McLean, Va., 1983-95, Can. Mfrs. Inst., Washington, 1986-95; vis. prof. bus. Ecole Supérieure du Commerce Extérieur, Paris, 2001. Jour. reviewer Acad. Mgmt. Rev., Jour. Mgmt., Rev. Bus. and Econ. Rsch., Mgmt. Sci.; mem. editl. bd. Jour. Global Info. Mgmt., Jour. of Mktg. Theory and Practice; contbr. articles to profl. jours. USAFR advisor Montgomery County Composite Squadron CAP, Blacksburg, 1977-79; coach Youth League Soccer and Football, Auburn, Ala. and Vienna, Va., 1980-86; mem. exec. com. cub scouts Boy Scouts Am., Vienna, 1982-83; pres. Statesboro High Sch. Quarterback Club, 1991-92; mem. Leadership Pensacola, 1998-99. Pilot, USAF, 1968-74. Pilot USAF, 1968—74. Decorated DFC, Air medal with 3 oak leaf clusters; recipient Disting. Faculty Mem. award George Mason U., 1984; grantee SBA, 1983-84, Commonwealth of Va., 1984-86, State of Ga., 1994-95. Mem. Acad. Mgmt. (dissertation award com.), Ea. Acad. Mgmt., So. Mgmt. Assn. (program com. 1981-82, bd. dirs. 1989-92, mem. teaching excellence com. 1992-94), Decision Scis. Inst. (program com. 1991-92, v.p., 2003—, bd. dirs., 2003—, Alpha Iota Delta liaison com. 2003—), S.E. Region Decision Scis. Inst. (program com. 1985-86, v.p. industry liaison 1986-87, v.p. planning and devel. 1987-88, sec. 1990-91, coun. mem. 1992-2003, coun. chair 1994-98, nominations com. 1996, program chair, 2003—), Inst. Mgmt. Sci. (editor Southeastern chpt. Proceedings Jour. 1987, coun. 1986—, program chmn. 1986-87, sec.-treas. 1987-88, v.p. 1988-89, pres. 1989-90, Disting. Svc. award 1992), So. Bus. Adminstrn. (bd. dirs. 1998-2000), Soc. Advancement Mgmt. (Disting. Svc. award 1985), Aircraft Owners and Pilots Assn., Mid-Day Optimist Club (membership dir. 1989-91, bd. dirs. 1989-91), 5 Flags Rotary, Leadership Pensacola, U. Va. Alumni Assn. (Pensacola chpt. treas. 1997—, bd. dirs. 1997—, pres. 1998-2000), Pensacola Navy Flying Club, Delta Sigma Phi, Beta Gamma Sigma (pres. chpt. 1995-2002), Phi Kappa Phi. Methodist. Avocations: scuba diving, golf, flying/air transport. Office: U West Fla Dept Mgmt Bldg 76 Pensacola FL 32514-5750

CARPINELLI, JOHN DOMINICK, computer engineering educator; b. Clifton, NJ, Sept. 12, 1961; s. Dominick D. and Nina (Nasissi) C. B Engring., Stevens Inst. Tech., 1983; M Engring., Rensselaer Poly. Inst., 1984, PhD, 1987. Spl. lectr. N.J. Inst. Tech., Newark, 1986-87, asst. prof. elec. and computer engring., 1987-93, assoc. dir. computer engring., 1992-94, dir. computer engring., 1994-96, assoc. prof. elec. and computer engring., 1993—. Tech. adv. bd. Cauldron Corp., Bethesda, Md., 1992—. Author: Computer Systems Organization and Architecture, 2001; contbr. articles to profl. jours. Mem. IEEE (sr.), IEEE Computer Soc., IEEE Edn. Soc., Am. Soc. Engring. Edn. Office: NJ Inst Tech University Heights Newark NJ 07102-1982

CARR, BESSIE, retired middle school educator; b. Nathalie, Va., Oct. 10, 1920; d. Henry C. and Sirlena (Ewell) C. BS, Elizabeth City Coll., N.C., 1942; MA, Columbia U. Tchrs. Coll., 1948, PhD, 1950, EdD, 1952. Cert. adminstr., supr., tchr. Prin. pub. sch., Halifax, Va., 1942-47, Nathalie-Halifax County, Va., 1947-51; prof. edn. So. U., Baton Rouge, 1952-53; supr. schs. Lackland Schs., Cin., 1953-54; prof. edn. Wilberforce U., Ohio, 1954-55; tchr. Leland Sch., Pittsfield, Mass., 1956-60; chair math. dept., tchr. Lakeland Mid. Sch., N.Y., 1961-83. Founder, organizer, sponsor 1st Math Bowl and Math Forum in area, 1970-76; founder Dr. Bessie Carr award Halifax County Sr. High Sch., 1962. Mem. Nat. Women's Hall of Fame. Mem. AAUW (auditor 1970-85), Delta Kappa Gamma (auditor internat. 1970-76), Assn. Suprs. of Math. (chair coordinating council 1976-80), Ret. Tchrs. Assn., Black Women Bus. and Profl. Assn. (charter mem. Senegal, Africa chpt.). Democrat. Avocations: travel, photography, souvenirs.

CARR, CYNDA ANNETTE, elementary education educator; b. Harper, Kans., June 6, 1948; d. Don Edward and Raquel Ann (Daniels) C. BA, Wichita (Kans.) State U., 1974, MEd, 1980. Tchr. Unified Sch. Dist. 361, Anthony, Kans., 1974—. Steering com. Kans. Tchr. of Yr., 1995—; tchr. cons. Kans. Geographic Alliance, 1992—, Delta Kappa Gamma, 1981—, state editor, 1993—. Trainer Wheatbelt area coun. Girl Scouts U.S., Hutchinson, Kans., 1980—83, 1985—92, bd. dirs., 1987—91, active various coms. and task forces, neighborhood chmn. Anthony coun., 1985—91, troop leader, 1976—84, 1988—89; bd. dirs. Harper County chpt. Am. Cancer Soc., Anthony, 1986—98, Anthony United Way, 1987—89; mem. Leadership Harper County, 1994—95; activities counselor Camp

Hope/Am. Cancer Soc., 1987; sponsor Kids for Saving Earth, 1991—98; mem. Soil Conservation Earth Team, 1992—; participant Golden Gift Leadership/Mgmt. Seminar, 1995; Young Careerist Anthony Bus. and Profl. Women's Club, 1976; Sunday sch. tchr., mem. choir 1st Congl. Ch., 1990—2001. Named Tchr. of Yr. Harper County Conservation Dist., 1992; recipient Silver Pen award Kans. Edn. Assn., 1987, Thanks Badge award Girl Scouts U.S., 1988, Contbn. to Conservation award Anthony Republican, 1992, Nat. Educator award Milken Family Found., 1994, Diana award Epsilon Sigma Alpha, 1985. Mem. Anthony Bus. and Profl. Women's Club. Avocations: calligraphy, collecting hippos. Home: 401 S Kansas Ave Anthony KS 67003-2624 Office: Anthony Elem Sch 215 S Springfield Ave Anthony KS 67003-2550

CARR, GWENN CLAIRE, instructional technology consultant, educator; b. Darby, Pa., Jan. 7, 1950; d. Donald f. and Anna Marie (Murphy) Phillips; children: Tara, Rebecca. BS in Elem. Edn., St. Joseph's U., 1974; MEd, Chestnut Hill Coll., 1983. Cert. educator, Pa. Vision therapist Drs. Marcus & Seiderman, King of Prussia, Pa., 1986-88; computer tchr. Compu-Tech, Mt. Laurel, N.J., 1986-88; tchr. Archdiocese of Phila., 1968-92; computer instr. Ctr. for Tech. Studies, Norristown, Pa., 1990—; acad. instr. PECO Energy Co., Plymouth Meeting, Pa., 1992-94, project mgr. rollout of tng. for customer fullfillment Norristown, 1994—. Resident resource assoc. Temple U., 1993—; adj. prof. Allentown Coll., 1994-96, Chestnut Hill Coll., 1996—; mem. benefit com. Montgomery County Libr., Norristown, 1986-88; mem. middle states rev. com. Archdiocese of Phila., 1988-92; cons. on CES Compu-Tech, Mt. Laurel, 1986-88. Author: (jour.) Technology & Learning, 1991; co-authors articles to profl. publs. Sec. Peter Wentz Farmstead Soc., Worcester, Pa., 1991-94. Edn. Alumni-St. Joseph's U., Phila., 1992-94. Mem. ASTD (mem. adv. bd. Ctr. for Tech. Studies 1992—), Peter Wentz Farmstead Soc., Edn. Chpt. Alumni St. Joseph's U. Roman Catholic. Office: Price Waterhouse LLP The Learning Ctr 30 S 17th St Philadelphia PA 19103-4001

CARR, JACQUELYN B. psychologist, educator; b. Oakland, Calif., Feb. 22, 1923; d. Frank G. and Betty (Kreiss) Corker; children: Terry, John, Richard, Linda, Michael, David. BA, U. Calif., Berkeley, 1958; MA, Stanford U., 1961; PhD, U. So. Calif., 1973. Lic. psychologist, Calif; lic. secondary tchr., Calif. Tchr. Hillsdale High Sch., San Mateo, Calif., 1958-69, Foothill Coll., Los Altos Hills, Calif., 1969—. Cons. Silicon Valley Companies, U.S. Air Force, Interpersonal Support Network, Santa Clara County Child Abuse Council, San Mateo County Suicide Prevention Inc.,Parental Stress Hotline, Hotel/Motel Owners Assn.; co-dir. Individual Study Ctr.; supr. Tchr. Edn.; adminstr. Peer Counseling Ctr.; led numerous workshops and confs. in field. Author: Learning is Living, 1970, Equal Partners: The Art of Creative Marriage, 1986, The Crisis in Intimacy, 1988, Communicating and Relating, 1984, 3d edit., 1991, Communicating with Myself: A Journal, 1984, 3d edit., 1991; contbr. articles to profl. jours. Vol. US Peace Corps., Sri Lanka, 1997. Mem. Mensa. Clubs: Commonwealth. Home: # 5-2G 390 N Winchester Blvd Santa Clara CA 95050-6563 Office: Foothill College 12345 El Monte Rd Los Altos CA 94022-4597

CARR, LES, psychologist, educator; b. Bklyn., Mar. 7, 1935; s. Sam and Sara (Berman) Carr; children: Lincoln Damian, Sharon Rose, Lewis Wade, Faith Theresa. BA, NYU, 1957; MA, New Sch. for Social Rsch., N.Y.C., 1959; PhD, Vanderbilt U., 1963. Diplomate Am. Bd. Med. Psychotherapists (fellow); lic. psychologist, Calif.; cert. psychologist R.I. Rsch. and clin. intern Rockland State Hosp., N.Y.C. Dept. Mental Hygiene, 1958-59; cons. clin. psychologist to sr. clin. psychologist Ctrl. State Hosp., Nashville, 1962-64; sr. coord. psychol. svcs. U. R.I., Providence, 1963-68; prof., chmn. psychology dept., dean Summer Sch., Salve Regina Coll., Newport, R.I., 1966-70, v.p. acad. affairs, 1969-71; project dir. Newport Hosp., 1967-71; pres. Lewis U., Lockport, Ill., 1971-76; dean of faculty Columbia Pacific U., San Rafael, Calif., 1977—2000; pres. Columbia Commonwealth U., 2000—. Pres., dir. Elder 100 Plus, Inc., Somerset, Calif.; staff psychologist San Quentin State Prison, 1989—2000; former edn!. cons. to sultan and min. of edn., Oman; staff psychologist No. Calif. Women's Facility, 2000—03. Past chmn. R.I. Gov.'s Task Force on Mental Health Rehab.; chmn. bd. dirs. Sr. U., Richmond, Can.; mem. nat. adv. coun. Profl. Children's Sch., N.Y.C.; past chmn. adv. bd. dirs. Comprehensive Mental Health Ctr., Newport; past bd. dirs. Regional Ballet Soc., Joliet, Ill., R.I. Rehab. Assn.; past chmn. bd. trustees St. Mary's Acad., Nauvoo, Ill.; past mem. exec. com. R.I. Gov.'s Commn. on Vocat. Rehab. With U.S. Army, 1958. Mem. APA, Calif. Psychol. Assn. Home: 7900 Shenandoah Ln Somerset CA 95684-9597 Fax: 530 620-6427.

CARR, MARSHA HAMBLEN, elementary school principal; b. Dunlap, Tenn., Nov. 28, 1961; d. Jackie Robert and Molly Ann (Johnson) Hamblen; m. Lonnie Gerron Carr, Feb. 26, 1980; 1 child, Gerra Sheree. BS in Spl. Edn. magna cum laude, Tenn. Tech. U., 1989, MA in Supervision of Instrn., 1992, ednl. specialist degree Edn. Leadership, 1997. Resource tchr. Sequatchie County Bd. Edn., Dunlap, 1989-90; early childhood spl. edn. tchr. Project CHILD Sequatchie County Bd. Edn., Dunlap, 1990-91, coord., 1991-97; principal Griffith Elem. Sch., Dunlap, Tenn., 1997—. Presenter Tenn. Young Children Assn., Chattanooga, 1992—; mem. adv. bd. Tenn. Early Intervention System, Chattanooga, 1990—; behavior mgmt. cons., Dunlap, 1990—; presenter Am. Edn. Rsch. Assn., San Diego. Active First Bapt. Ch. of Dunlap; Title I Sch. Support Svc. Facilitator. Mem. NEA, Tenn. Edn. Assn., Sequatchie County Edn. Assn., Assn. Supervision and Curriculum, Internat. Platform Assn., Phi Kappa Phi, Delta Kappa Gamma (1st v.p., Internat. Xi state mem. chair), Pi Lambda Theta, Kappa Delta Pi. Democrat. Baptist. Avocations: reading, oil painting, travel, old movies. Home: 1043 Tram Trl Dunlap TN 37327-4446 Office: Griffith Elem Sch PO Box 819 Dunlap TN 37327-0819 Fax: (423) 949-6872.

CARR, MICHELE PAIGE, dental hygienist, educator; b. Queens, N.Y., Jan. 10, 1963; d. Michael Barry and Celia Barbara Zeitlin; m. John Joseph Carr, Aug. 31, 1986; children: Drew, Bailey. BS, Ohio State U., 1984, MA, 1993. Registered dental hygienist, 1984. Dental hygienist various dental offices, Columbus, Ohio, 1984—89; faculty coord. Nisonger Ctr., Columbus, 1989—96; asst. prof. dental hygiene Ohio State U., Columbus, 1996—. Contbr. articles to profl. jours. Named Dental Hygiene Outstanding Instr., Ohio State U. Coll. of Dentistry, 1999; fellow Rsch. fellow, Am. Assn. Dental Schs./Warner Lambert, 1998; grantee, Ohio Devel. Disabilities Coun., 2001—. Mem.: Am. Dental Edn. Assn., Am. Dental Hygienists Assn., Am. Assn. of Dental Rsch., Ohio State U. Dental Hygiene Alumni Soc. (treas. 1999—), Sigma Phi Alpha. Avocation: tennis. Home: 1463 Harrison Rd SW Pataskala OH 43062 Office: Ohio State University 305 W 12th Ave #179 Columbus OH 43218-2357 Office Fax: 614-292-8013. Personal E-mail: carr.3@osu.edu. E-mail: carr.3@osu.edu.

CARR, STEPHEN HOWARD, materials engineer, educator; b. Dayton, Ohio, Sept. 29, 1942; s. William Howard and Mary Elizabeth (Clement) C.; m. Virginia W. McMillan, June 24, 1967; children: Rosamond Elizabeth, Louisa Ruth. BS, U. Cin., 1965; MS, Case Western Res. U., 1967, PhD, 1970. Coop. engr. Inland divsn. GM, Dayton, 1960-65; asst. prof. materials sci. and engring. and chem. engring. Northwestern U., Evanston, Ill., 1970-73, assoc. prof., 1973-78, prof., 1978—, dir. Materials Rsch. Ctr., 1984-90, asst. dean engring., 1991-93, assoc. dean engring., 1993—. Cons. in field. Contbr. articles to profl. jours. Recipient Outstanding Alumni Achievement award U. Cin. Coll. Engring., 1993. Fellow Am. Soc. for Metals Internat., Am. Phys. Soc.; mem. AIChE, Soc. Automotive Engrs. (Ralph R. Teetor award 1980), Plastics Inst. Am. (Ednl. Svc. award 1975), Am. Chem. Soc., Soc. Plastics Engrs., Materials Rsch. Soc. Achievements include patents in plastics and textiles fields. Home: 2704 Harrison St Evanston IL 60201-1216 Office: Northwestern U 2145 Sheridan Rd Evanston IL 60208-0834

CARRAHER, MARY LOU CARTER, art educator; b. Cin., Mar. 9, 1927; d. John Paul and Martha Leona (Williams) Carter; m. Emmett Carraher, Nov. 6, 1943 (div. July 1970); children: Candace Lou Holsenbeck-Smith, Michael Emmett, Cathleen C. Kruska. Student, U. Cin., 1946-48, Calif. State U., 1973-74. Lifetime credential in adult edn.: art, ceramics, crafts, Calif. Substitute tchr. Cobb County Schs., Smyrna, Ga., 1961-63; art tchr. pvt. lessons Canyon Country, Calif., 1968-72; adult edn. art tchr. Wm. S. Hart H.S. Dist., Santa Clarita, Calif., 1973-97; children's art and calligraphy cmty. svcs. Coll. of the Canyons, Santa Clarita, Calif., 1976-96. Fine arts coord. Santa Clarita Sr. Ctr., 1998—; founder, bd. dirs. Santa Clarita Art Guild, 1972-80; art dir. European tours Continental Club, Canyon Country, 1977-81; art tour guide and travel cons. Northridge (Calif.) Travel, 1981-91; vol. art tchr. stroke patients Henry Newhall Meml. Hosp., Valencia, Calif., 1993-96; craft tchr. for respite care program, Newhall, Calif., 1995-96, Respite Care Ctr., Santa Clarita Valley Sr. Ctr., 1995-96; art tour guide, Andulusia, Spain, 1997, 99. Artist, author History of Moreland School District, San Jose, California, 1965; prin. works include Paintings for each season of Church Year, 1970's, Baptismal painting, 1988, Sr. Ctr. Watercolors Ctr. Scenes, 1993, Watercolors of Christmas Charity Home Tour, 1993, Henry Mayo Newhall Meml. Hosp., 1997, 1999, 2001, 2002, 2003, murals painted for Christian Ch. and Sr. Ctr., 1997—99, mall st. painting for charity, 2000. Tchr., mem. Santa Clarita United Meth. Ch., 1966-96; judge for art contests and exhibits, Santa Clarita, 1973-96; mem. Santa Clarita Valley Hist. Soc., 1989-96; mem. Alumni Assn., Norwood (Ohio) City Schs., 1993-96; leader art tours to Spain, 1997, 99, 2002, Italy, 2001, Portugal, 2002, Australia, New Zealand and Fiji, 2003; designer certs, with scenes of Sr. Ctr., Cir. of Friends certs. Recipient Bravo award nomination for Outstanding Achievement in Art, 1995, Sr. of Yr. Santa Clarita Valley Sr. Ctr. and Svc. Newspaper "The Signal", 1995, Christian Svc. award Santa Clarita United Meth. Ch., 1988; invited by Citizen Amb. Program of People to People Internat. to join U.S. del. to assess bus. and trade opportunities of the craft industry in China. Mem. Santa Clarita Valley Arts Coun., Hosp. Home Tour League, Nat. Women in the Arts (charter, Washington). Republican. Methodist. Avocations: travel, art related crafts, reading.

CARRAHER, SHAWN MICHAEL, management educator; b. Kansas City, Kans., Nov. 9, 1966; s. Charles E. and Loyalea Velda (Zimmerman) C.; m. Sarah Carlene Laine, July 6, 2001; 1 child, Shawn, Jr. BBA with honors, Fla. Atlantic U., 1987; MBA, U. Cin., 1988; PhD, U. Okla., 1992. Delivery specialist Dayton Daily News, Beavercreek, Ohio, 1980-85; pres., owner Carraher & Sons, Beavercreek, 1982-87; tchr. U. Kans., Lawrence, 1988; rschr. Fla. Atlantic U., Boca Raton, 1989-90, U. Okla., Norman, 1990-92; vis. asst. prof. U. Wis., Milw., 1992-94; assoc. prof. Calif. State U., Chico, 1994-95, Ind. State U., Terre Haute, 1995-98, Ind. U., Bloomington, 1998-2000; prof. mgmt. and global entrepreneurship Tex. A&M U., Commerce, 2000—. Pres. Carraher & Carraher Cons. Group, 1997—; cons. City of Norman, 1990-91, USAF, 1990-92, Pratt & Whitney, West Palm Beach, Fla., 1990; spkr. at more than 600 profl. presentations on goal-setting and mgmt. devel., including U. Okla., Norman, 1992; rep at large Southwest Acad. Mgmt., 1998-2001, program chair elect, 2001—02; bd. dir. Southern Mgmt. Assn., 2000-03, program chmn., 2002-03; International Mgmt. and Bus. track chair Acad. Internat. Bus.; Mgmt. History and Future Trends track chair Southern Mgmt. Assn.; chair elect Acad. Mgmt., 2000-01; chair elect, sec. U.S. Assn. for Small Bus. and Entrepreneurship, 2000-01, program chair internat. divsn., 2001—02; asst. v.p. program chair Acad. Internat. Bus., divns. chmn., 2002-03, competitive papers chmn., 2003—; dir. Internat. Family Bus. Ctr., Tex. A&M U., 2002—. Author: (12 video tapes) Industrial Psychology, 1992; contbr. 80 articles to profl. jours. Pres. Christians In Action, Beavercreek, 1984-85; treas. Campus Crusade for Christ, Norman, 1991-92. Shuman fellow U. Okla., 1991; recipient Outstanding Reviewer award for Careers Divsn. of the Acad. of Mgmt., SW Acad. Mgmt. Disting. Reviewer award, 1997, 2000, Midwest Acad. Mgmt. Disting. Reviewer award, 2000, Southern Mgmt. Assn. Outstanding Reviewer award, 2000. Mem. Acad. Mgmt., Am. Ednl. Rsch. Assn., Am. Psychol. Soc., So. Mgmt. Assn., S.W. Acad. Mgmt., U.S. Assn. for Small Bus. and Entrepreneurship (Fulbright sr. specialist, 2002), Acad. Internat. Bus. Avocations: research, speaking on goal-setting, martial arts, weight-lifting, cooking. Office: Tex A&M U-Commerce Dept Mgmt and Mgmt PO Box 3011 Commerce TX 74529-3011

CARREL, MARIANNE EILEEN, music educator; b. Greenville, Pa., Aug. 28, 1957; d. Francis Raymond Cremi, Betty Hutton Cremi; m. Marion Lee Carrel. Student, Clarion U. Pa., 1975—76; BS, Edinboro U., 1979, MEd, 1985. Cert. elem. tchr. Ohio. Substitute tchr. Greenville and Reynolds Sch. Dists., Greenville, Pa., 1979—80; tchr. music Webster County Schs., Cowen, W.Va., 1980—84; grad. asst. Edinboro U., Edinboro, Pa., 1984—85; tchr. music Madison Local Schs., Madison, Ohio, 1985—86; tchr. music Geneva Area City Schs., Geneva, Ohio, 1986—. Sec. All-Am. Judges Assn., Ohio, 1989—. Named Assoc. of Yr., Am. Bus. Women's Assn., 2000-2001. Mem.: NEA, Internat. Double Reed Soc., Music Educators Nat. Conf., Ohio Edn. Assn., Kappa Delta Pi, Sigma Alpha Iota (life). Home: 4850 Boughner Rd Rock Creek OH 44084 Office: Geneva Area Schs 839 Sherman St Geneva OH 44041 Personal E-mail: mandmcarrel@direcway.com.

CARRELL, HEATHER DEMARIS, school system administrator; b. Bryn Mawr, Pa., Jan. 4, 1951; d. Jeptha J. and J. Demaris (Affleck) C.; m. Peter F. Brazitis, June 27, 1981; children, Evan, Victoria. BA, Oberlin Coll., 1973; MEd, U. Wash., 1976, PhD, 1982. Cert. tchr., Wash. Head tchr., trainer Exptl. Edn. Unit U. Wash., Seattle, 1976-80, tchr. trainer, 1976-80, supr. early childhood and spl. edn. tchrs. in tng., 1980, coord. classrooms behavior disorders, 1980-81, coord. interdisciplinary tng., 1979-82, asst. prin., 1981-82, cons. Transition Rsch. Problems Handicapped Youth, 1986-88; self-employed cons., 1983-96; adminstr. North Kitsap Sch. Dist., Paulsbo, Wash., 1997—. Cons. North Kitsap Sch. Dist., Poulsbo, Wash., 1984; presenter edn. and spl. edn. various groups from U.S., Can., Australia, 1977-82; pres., co-founder Hansville (Wash.) Coop. Presch., 1982, 84-89; mem. diversity and multicultural advocacy team Wash. State Sch. Dirs. Assn.; rep. to U. Wash. Tchr. Profl. Edn. Adv. Bd., 1992-95; mem. WSSDA Fin. Task Force, 1994; mem. Intertribal Coun. Com. on Racism, North Kitsap, Wash., 1993-94. Author: (with others) The Experimental Education Training Program, 1977; contbr. articles to profl. publs. Commr. North Kitsap Dept. Parks and Recreation, 1983-84; dir. North Kitsap Sch. Bd., 1990-95, v.p., 1992-93, pres., 1993-95; trustee North Kitsap Tchr. of Yr. Found., 1989-90; bd. dirs. North Kitsap Juvenile Diversion Bd., 1987-91; co-founder, v.p. bd. dirs. Kitsap Cmty. Found., 1993-96. Bur. Edn. Handicapped fellow, 1974-75, 77-78.

CARRERE, CHARLES SCOTT, law educator, judge; b. Dublin, Ga., Sept. 26, 1937; 1 son, Daniel Austin. BA, U. Ga., 1959; LLB, Stetson U., 1961. Bar: Ga. 1960, Fla. 1961. Law clk. U.S. Dist. Judge, Orlando, Fla., 1962-63; asst. U.S. Atty. Middle Dist. Fla., 1963-66, 68-69, chief trial atty., 1965-66, 68-69; ptnr. Harrison, Greene, Mann, Rowe & Stanton, 1970-80; judge Pinellas County, Fla., 1980-96; vis. prof. law Stetson Coll. Law, 1997-98, Cumberland Law Sch., 1998-99. Recipient Jud. Appreciation award St. Petersburg Bar Assn., 1996, Alumnus of Yr. award Stetson Student Bar Assn., 1998. Mem. State Bar Ga., Fla. Bar, Phi Beta Kappa. Presbyterian. Address: PO Box 22034 Gateway Mall Sta Saint Petersburg FL 33742 Fax: 727-395-0444.

CARREY, NEIL, lawyer, educator; b. Bronx, N.Y., Nov. 19, 1942; s. David L. and Betty (Kurtzburg) C.; m. Karen Krysher, Apr. 9, 1980; children: Jana, Christopher; children by previous marriage: Scott, Douglas, Dana. BS in Econs., U. Pa., 1964; JD, Stanford U., 1967. Bar: Calif. 1968. Mem. firm, v.p. corp. DeCastro, West, Chodorow, Inc., L.A., 1967-97; of counsel Jenkens & Gilchrist, L.A., 1998—. Instr. program legal paraprofls., U. So. Calif., 1977-89; lectr. U. So. Calif. Dental Sch., 1987—, Employee Benefits Inst., Kansas City, Mo., 1996; legal cons. 33rd Dist. Calif. PTA, 1997—. Author: Nonqualified Defered Compensation Plans-The Wave of the Future, 1985. Treas. Nat. Little League, Santa Monica, Calif., 1984—85, pres., 1985—86, coach, 1990—95; referee, coach Am. Soccer Youth Orgn., 1989—95; officer Vista Del Mar Child Care Ctr., L.A., 1968—84; coach Bobby Sox Softball Team, Santa Monica, 1986—88, bd. dirs., 1988, umpire in chief, 1988; various positions The Santa Monica Youth Athletic Found., 1995—; dir. The Small Bus. Coun. of Am., 1995—, Santa Monica H.S. Booster Club, 1995—97; active various positions Santa Monica Police Activities League, 1995—; pres. Gail Dorin Music Found., 1994—; v.p. Sneaker Sisters, 1996—2001; pres. Santa Monica Jr. Rowing, 1997—2002; legal cons. 33d Dist. Calif. PTA, 1997—99; recreation and parks commr. City of Santa Monica, 1999—; sec. Santa Monica Leaders Club, 1999—2000; mem. U. Pa. Women's Sports Adv. Bd., 1998—; pres. Chris Carrey Charitable Found., 2000—; v.p. bd. Ivan and Sam Found., 2002—; active numerous coms. Santa Monica-Malibu Sch. Dist., 1983—; bd. dirs. Padres Contra el Cancer, 2001—03, v.p., 2002—03, pres., 2003—. Mem.: LWV (dir. 1997—), Children's Hosp. L.A. (adv. coun. 2001—), Children's Ctr. for Cancer and Blood Diseases, U. Pa. Alumni Soc. (pres. 1971—79, dir. 1979—87), Mountaingate Tennis Club, Alpha Kappa Psi (life). Jewish. Home: 616 23d St Santa Monica CA 90402-3130 Office: 12100 Wilshire Blvd Fl 15 Los Angeles CA 90025-7120 E-mail: ncarrey@aol.com., ncarrey@jenkens.com.

CARRICK, CYNTHIA ANNE, special education educator, educational administrator; b. Cleve., Nov. 7, 1953; d. Donald John and Elizabeth Julia (Feigi) Deucher; m. John Paul Carrick, Dec. 14, 1974; children: Jennifer Lynn, Jessica Elizabeth. BS, U. Akron, 1974, MS, 1986. Cert. tchr., Ohio. Learning disabilities tchr. Medina (Ohio) City Schs., 1974-77; spl. edn. tchr. Bklyn. City Schs., 1977-79, Brunswick (Ohio) City Schs., 1979-83; tchr., mentor tchr., coord. Berea (Ohio) City Schs., 1983-91; spl. edn. tchr. Medina City Schs., 1991—, wellness coord., 1992—. Facilitator Summit County Children's Svcs. Bd., Akron, Ohio; lectr. Cleve. State U., U. Akron, Berea Children's Home; presenter Ohio Assn. Child Care Agys., Columbus; key note speaker Ohio Women's Network. Bd. trustee United Ch. Christ Congregational, Medina, Medina City Schs. Levy Campaign Com.; leader strategic planning com. Medina City Sch. Dist., Medina, 1992-93. Jennings scholar Jennings Found., 1991-92. Mem. ASCD, Nat. Coun. for Self Esteem, Kappa Delta Pi, Pi Lambda Theta. Avocations: backpacking, parasailing, auto crossing. Home: 3350 E Smith Rd Medina OH 44256-8785 Office: Medina City Schs 777 E Union St Medina OH 44256-1970

CARRICK, ELAINE LEET, kindergarten educator; b. Hancock, N.Y., Feb. 13, 1952; d. Clinton Herald and Lorraine (Westcott) Leet; divorced; children: Roy Douglas, Casey Bruce. BS, Shippensburg (Pa.) U., 1974. Cert. in early childhood edn. and English, Pa., Alaska. Tchr., dir. Paupack (Pa.) Nursery Sch., 1987-90; kindergarten tchr. Delaware Valley Elem. Sch., Milford, Pa., 1992—. Tchr. Sunday sch. Paupack United Meth. Ch., 1981-90; leader 4-H Dog Care and Tng., Pike County, 1988. Mem. Nat. Assn. for Edn. of Young Children, Nat. Coun. Tchrs. Math., Phi Delta Kappa. Avocation: writing short stories and plays. Home: 738 Maple Ave Honesdale PA 18431-1451

CARRICO, DEBORAH JEAN, special education teacher; b. East St. Louis, Ill., Dec. 6, 1948; d. Leo Anthony and Edna Linda (Willett) C. BS, Murray State U., 1972; MA, Calif. State U., L.A., 1978. Cert. tchr., Calif. Tchr. Bonita Unified Sch. Dist., San Dimas, Calif., 1973-74, L.A. County Office Edn., Downey, 1974—. Mentor L.A. County Office of Edn., 1989—. Bd. dirs. Hope House, Anaheim, Calif., 1988—. Mem. Coun. for Exceptional Children, Phi Kappa Phi. Democrat. Roman Catholic. Avocations: photography, videography, educational technology. Office: LA County Office Edn 9300 Imperial Hwy Downey CA 90242-2813

CARRIER, FRANCE, medical educator; b. Beauport, Que., Can., June 9, 1961; d. Philippe Carrier and Therese Pare; m. Steven I. Hirschfeld, June 9, 1950. PhD, U. Montreal, 1988. Postdoctoral fellow Biotechnology Rsch. Inst., Montreal, 1988—89; vis. assoc. NIH, Bethesda, Md., 1989—91; vis. scientist Nat. Cancer Inst. NIH, Bethesda, 1991—98; asst. prof. U. of Md., Balt., 1998—. Mem. Greenebaum Cancer Ctr., Balt.; instr. med. and grad. schs. Contbr. articles to profl. jours., chapters to books. Rsch. grantee (R01), NIH, 1999—2003, Rsch. grantee, Am. Cancer Soc., 2000—02, Rsch. grantee (STTR), NIH, 2001—02, Rsch. grantee, A-T Children's Project, 2003—, Internat. fellow, Human Frontier Sci. Program Orgn., 1990. Mem.: Am. Assn. for Cancer Rsch. (sponsor, Brigid Leventhal award 2002), N.Y. Acad. Scis., Cosmos Club (Elected mem. 1999). Achievements include patents for methods for determining the presence of functional p53 in mammalian cells; research in genotoxic stress-response, cancer progression, chromatin remodeling. Office: U Md 108 N Greene St Baltimore MD 21201-1503 Home Fax: 301-879-0776; Office Fax: 410-706-8297. Personal E-mail: fcarr001@umaryland.edu. Business E-Mail: fcarr001@umaryland.edu.

CARRIER, RONALD EDWIN, academic administrator, director; b. Bluff City, Tenn., Aug. 18, 1932; s. James Murphy and Melissa (Miller) C.; m. Edith Marie Johnson, Sept. 7, 1955; children: Michael Lavon, Linda Lois Carrier Frazee, Jennine Marie. BS, Ea. Tenn. State U., 1955; MS in Econs., U. Ill., 1957, PhD in Econs., 1960. Assoc. prof. econs. U. Miss., Oxford, 1960-63; dir., prof. Bur. Bus. and Econ. Research, Memphis U., 1963-66, provost, v.p. acad. affairs, 1966-71; pres., chancellor James Madison U., Harrisonburg, Va., 1971—2002, pres. emeritus, 2002—; pres. Ctr. for Innovative Tech., Herndon, Va., 1986-87. Bd. visitors Va. State U., Sorensen Inst., Integic, Inc.; mem. adv. bd. Assn. Small Bus. Devel. Ctrs.; chancellor Romanian Am. U. Author: Plant Locations: A Theory and Explanations, 1968; contbr. articles and monographs to profl. publs. Mem. White House Conf. Balance Econ. Growth; mem. Va. Indsl. Facilities Study Commn., 1972-75; chmn. Va. Land Use Adv. Com., 1974-77, Va. Gov.'s Electricity Costs Commn., 1975—; mem. Va. Gov.'s Energy Resource Adv. Commn., 1975-76, Gov.'s Regulatory Reform Adv. Bd., 1983, Joint Subcom. to Study Coal Slurry Pipeline Feasibility, 1983, ethics com. Senate Va., 1999, Va. Higher Edn. Steering Commn., 2002. Earheart fellow 1958-60; recipient Ben Franklin award Memphis Printing Industry, 1966, faculty award East Tenn. State U., 1955, Disting. Svc. award Jr. C. of C., 1965, Virginian of Yr. award Va. Assn. Broadcasters, 1982; named Outstanding Virginian, FHA, 1990; cultural laureate Va.; named Outstanding Virginian FFA, 1991. Mem.: Sigma Phi Epsilon, Omicron Delta Gamma, Omicron Delta Kappa. Methodist. Home: PO Box 570 Basye VA 22810-0570 Office: James Madison U MSC 5760 Med Arts E Ste 2 Harrisonburg VA 22807

CARRIERE, BROTHER WILLIAM JOSEPH, school system administrator; b. Detroit, Mar. 26, 1943; s. Leon Simon and Josephine Mary (Diguigno) C. BA, Loyola U., Chgo., 1970; MA, Seton Hall U., 1973; PhD, U. Ariz., 1982. Cert. tchr., sch. adminstr. Tchr. various Cath. schs., 1965-75, adminstr., 1975-80; prof. St. Mary's Coll., Moraga, Calif., 1983-86; assoc. supt. Diocese of Orange, Calif., 1986-90, supt., 1990—. Dir. tchr. edn. for Christian brs. St. Mary's Coll., Moraga, 1983-86, sch. adm. master's program dir. Cath. schs., 1983-86. Recipient Disting. Svc. to Cath. Edn., Today's Cath. Tchr. Mag., 1987. Mem. Nat. Cath. Ednl. Assn. (exec. com. 1989-93). Roman Catholic. Home: 214 W Alberta St Anaheim CA 92805-2607 Office: Dept Cath Schs PO Box 14195 Orange CA 92863-1595

CARRINGER, ROBERT, English language and film educator; b. Knoxville, Tenn., May 12, 1941; m. Sonia Raysor, Sept. 7, 1968. AB, U. Tenn., 1962; MA, Johns Hopkins, 1964; PhD, Ind. U., 1968. Asst. prof. English U. Ill., Urbana, 1970-76, assoc. prof. English, 1976-84, prof. English and film, 1985—, disting. prof., 1985. Author: Ernst Lubitsch, 1978 (Choice Outstanding Acad. Book award 1979), The Making of Citizen Kane, 1985, rev.

edit., 1996, Magnificent Ambersons: A Reconstruction, 1993; editor: The Jazz Singer, 1979; contbr. articles to profl. jours.; prodr. laserdiscs. Mem. editl. bd.: Am. Studies, Quar. Rev. Film and Video, Cinema Jour. Recipient Instrnl. Tech. awards Amoco Corp., 1980, Apple Computer, 1988; Rsch. grantee NEH, 1986-87; fellow in cognitive psychology U. Ill., 1990-91; Getty scholar Getty Rsch. Inst., 1996-97. Mem.: MLA (chmn.film divsn. exec. com. 1981), Phi Beta Kappa, Phi Kappa Phi. Home: 50 County Rd 1675N Seymour IL 61875 Office: U Ill 608 S Wright St Urbana IL 61801 E-mail: fergus@uiuc.edu.

CARRINGTON, J.P. (JOSSIF PETER BARTOLOTTI), nutritionist, psychoanalyst, research scientist, educator; b. N.Y.C., Mar. 13, 1948; s. Nicholas S. and Yolanda Virginia (Luisi) B.; 1 child, Joseph Nicholas. Cert. advanced study, N.Y. Inst. Advanced Study, 1974; EdM, Harvard U., 1985; postgrad. in nuclear engring., MIT, 1985. Cert. psychol. assessment/analysis provider; lic. nutritionist. Med. nutritionist, N.Y., 1970—; psychoanalyst, psychotherapist, 1985—; sr. fellow, prof. med. nutrition and theoretical physics N.Y. Inst. Advanced Study, N.Y.C., 1980—; founder Eugenics Corp., Del., 1994—. TV and radio guest ABC Nat. Network, 1992; host of Carrington Nutrition radio programs, WNN Radio, WSHE Radio, Fla., 1989. Electorate sr. governing bd. Harvard U. Fellow N.Y. Inst. Advanced Study (sr., pub. info. dir. on NASA 1983—, Albert Einstein Gold medal of Sci. 1985); mem. N.Y. Acad. Sci., Harvard Alumni Assn., Harvard Club, Phi Delta Kappa. Avocations: theoretical physics, Chinese medicine, natural scis., relativity, nutritional eugenics. Office: Eugenics Corp PO Box 770514 Coral Springs FL 33077-0514

CARRINGTON, PAUL DEWITT, lawyer, educator; b. Dallas, June 12, 1931; s. Paul and Frances Ellen (DeWitt) C.; m. Bessie Meek, Aug., 1952; children: Clark DeWitt, Mary Carrington Coults, William James, Emily Carrington. BA, U. Tex., 1952; LLB, Harvard U., 1955. Bar: Tex. 1955, Ohio 1962, Mich. 1967. Practice, Dallas, 1955; teaching fellow Harvard U., 1957-58; asst. prof. law U. Wyo., 1958-60, Ind. U., 1960-62; assoc. prof. Ohio State U., 1962-65; prof. U. Mich., 1965-78; dean Duke U. Sch. Law, Durham, N.C., 1978-88, prof., 1978—. Reporter civil rules adv. com. Jud. Conf. of U.S., 1985-92. Author: (with Meador and Rosenberg) Justice on Appeal, 1977, (with Meador and Rosenberg) Appeals, 1994, (with Babcock) Civil Procedure, 1977, 3d edit., 1983, Stewards of Democracy, 1999. Mem. Ann Arbor (Mich.) Bd. Edn., 1970-73; pres. Pvt. Adjudication Ctr., Inc., 1988-94, chmn., 1995-2002. With U.S. Army, 1955-57. Guggenheim fellow, 1988-89. Fellow: Am. Acad. Appellate Lawyers, Am. Acad. Arts and Scis., Am. Bar Found.; mem.: ABA, Am. Law Inst. Episcopalian. Office: Duke U Sch Law Durham NC 27708-0362 E-mail: pdc@law.duke.edu.

CARRITHERS, JOSEPH EDWARD, English composition and literature educator; b. Red Bay, Ala., July 28, 1963; s. Edward Walden and Dessie Lee McClure. BA in Comm./Journalism, Miss. State U., Starkville, 1985, BA in English/History, 1987, MA in English, 1990, U. So. Calif., 1992, PhD in English, 2003. Reporter Comml. Dispatch, Columbus, Miss., 1985-88; mng. editor Starkville Daily News, 1988-90; asst. lectr. U. So. Calif., L.A., 1990-94; ESL instr. Don Martin Coll., Monterey Park, Calif., 1991; part-time prof. Mt. San Antonio Coll., Walnut, Calif., 1991-94; lectr. Woodbury U., Burbank, Calif., 1993-94; assoc. prof. English Fullerton (Calif.) Coll., 1994—. Mem. faculty senate Fullerton Coll. 1996-2002, pres. 1998-2001, mem. Planning and Consultative Coun., Fullerton Coll., 1997-2002, 2003—. Contbr. poetry to Forum; contbr. articles to Frontiers, Men's Fitness, Jour. Popular Film and TV. Mem. MLA, United Faculty, Nat. Coun. Tchrs. English, Am. Studies Assn., Gay and Lesbian Assn. Dist. Employees, Lambda Soc. (advisor). Office: Fullerton Coll 321 E Chapman Ave Fullerton CA 92832-2011

CARROLL, CLAIRE BARRY, special education educator; b. N.Y.C., Aug. 31, 1927; d. John Michael and Antonia (LeTarte) Barry; m. Felix P. Carroll, Oct. 2, 1948; children: Catherine, Mary, Theresa. Student, St. Johns U., 1947-49, Keane Coll., 1965-67; BS, Cheyney (Pa.) Coll., 1974; MS, Pa. State U., 1976. Cert. spl. edn. supr. Substitute tchr. Delaware County Dists., Pa., 1967-77; resource, learning disabilities specialist Delaware County Intermediate Unit 25, Media, Pa., 1977-92, transition/support tchr., 1990-93; ret., 1993. Edn. cons. learning disabilities and behavior modification, 1994—; dir. preschool Cheyney (Pa.) Coll., 1972-74; mem., chair Coun. for Learning Disabilities, Reston, Va., 1982-85; vol. religious instr. Don Guanella Sch. and St. Joseph, Springfield, Aston, 1987-92; co-dir. summer program Don Guanella Sch., Springfield, 1991. Dir. recreation program Woodbrook Summer Program, Aston, 1968-80; newsletter editor Woodbrook Civic Assn., Aston, 1968-81; girl scout leader Girl Scouts Am., Aston, 1968-81; vol. Dem. Candidates, Media, Pa., 1986-90, Horizons Unlimited; vol. counselor Apprise. Mem. Nat. Ret. Tchr.'s Assn., Coun. for Exceptional Children, Quota Club Internat. (pres., v.p. 1982-94), Del. County Group Hard of Hearing, Self Help Hard of Hearing People, Inc., Alpha Phi Sigma, Kappa Delta Pi, Alpha Kappa Mu. Democrat. Roman Catholic. Home: 22 Blackthorne Ln Aston PA 19014-2626

CARROLL, CYRIL JAMES, speech communication and theatre educator; b. Phila., Sept. 28, 1933; s. Michael James and Sara (Timony) C.; m. Ann Cary Sanson, Dec. 18, 1965; 1 child, Deborah. BA in Theatre Arts, Pa. State U., 1959; MA in Dramatic Arts, U. Md., 1970. Tchr. Gwynn Park Sr. H.S., Brandywine, Md., 1959-64, Crossland H.S., Camp Springs, Md., 1964-69; teaching fellow in speech U. Md., College Park, 1969-70; adj. prof. speech Prince George's C.C., Largo, Md., 1968-70, prof. speech and theatre, 1970—, program coord., theatre, 1992—. Cons. to various pub. schs. Prince George's County, Upper Marlboro, Md., 1971—; mem. adv. bd. Suitland (Md.) H.S. of Performing Arts, 1987-89. Served with U.S. Army, 1956-58, France. Named Outstanding Play Dir., Md. Drama Assn., 1966, 67, 68. Mem. Am. Theatre in Higher Edn., Speech Comm. Assn., Ea. Comm. Assn., Md. Comm. Assn. (v.p., pres. 1976-80), East Ctrl. Theatre Assn., Pa. State U. Alumni Assn. Democrat. Roman Catholic. Avocations: acting, tennis, golf. Office: Prince George's CC 301 Largo Rd Upper Marlboro MD 20774-2109 E-mail: cc71@pgstumail.pg.cc.md.us.

CARROLL, EDWARD PERRY, instrumental music educator, conductor; b. Sarasota, Fla., Dec. 17, 1934; s. Oliver Henry Perry and Sarah Theodosia (Amsden) C.; m. Rosa Marion Harvey, Dec. 30, 1965; 1 child, Kathryn Susan. MusB, Baylor U., 1957; M of Ch. Music, So. Bapt. Sem., 1970; EdD in Ch. Music, New Orleans Bapt. Sem., 1979. Bandsman USAF, U.S. and Spain, 1957-66; coll. instrumental tchr. Brewton Parker Coll., Mt. Vernon, Ga., 1970-73; prof. music Anderson (S.C.) Coll., 1975—. Condr. Anderson Symphony Orch., 1975—; mus. dir. Anderson Cmty. Theatre, 1976-94. Mem. wing staff CAP, Anderson & Columbia, S.C., 1986-99, mid. east. regional staff, 1999—. With USAF, 1957-66. Mem. Music Educators Nat. Conf., Nat. Assn. Coll. Wind and Percussive Instrs., Hymn Soc. U.S. and Can., Internat. Trombone Assn., So. Bapt. Music Conf., Coop. Bapt. Fellowship Ch. Music Conf., Kappa Kappa Psi (life mem., pres. 1956-57), Phi Mu Alpha (life mem., pledgemaster 1955-56). Avocations: softball, photography. Home: 126 Foxcroft Way Anderson SC 29621-2547 E-mail: mhcarroll@carol.net.

CARROLL, FRANCES LAVERNE, librarian, educator; b. Scammon, Kans., Dec. 6, 1925; d. Robert Allen and Truda Hilda (Flanagan) C. BS in Ed., Kans. State Tchrs. Coll., 1948; MA in Libr. Sci., U. Denver, 1956; postgrad., Western Res. U., 1957; PhD in Edn., U. Okla., 1970. Bookkeeper Baxter Springs Bank, Kans., 1944; tchr. English and journalism high sch. Caney, Kans., 1947-49; libr. Field Kindley Meml. HS, Coffeyville, Kans., 1949-54; librarian Coffeyville Jr. Coll., 1954-62; supr. elem. sch. libraries Coffeyville, 1957-62; asst. prof. library sci. U. Okla., Norman, 1962-67, assoc. prof., 1972-75, acting dir. sch. library sci., 1974-75, prof., 1975-86, emeritus, 1986—. Head library studies Nedlands Coll. Advanced Edn. (formerly Western Australian Secondary Tchrs. Coll.), Perth, 1977-81; guest lectr. Drexel Inst. Tech., Phila., 1964, U. London, 1972, Pahlavi U., Shiraz, Iran, 1976, Beijing Fgn. Studies U., 1992; dir. US Office Edn. Inst., 1966, 67, 69. Author: (with Mary Meacham) The Library at Mount Vernon, 1977, Exciting, Funny, Scary, Short, Different and Sad Books Kids Like, 1984, More Exciting, Funny, Scary, Short, Different and Sad Books Kids Like, 1992, (with Pat Beilke) Guidelines for the Planning and Organization of Sch. Libr. Media Ctr., 1979, Guidelines for Planning and Organization of Library Media Centers, 1990, Arabic translation, 1995, Recent Advances in Sch. Librarianship, 1981, (with John Harvey) Internationalizing Libr. Ed., 1987; nat. series editor: Reading for Young People, 1979-85; editor: (with Philip Schwartz) Biog. Directory of Nat. Librarians, 1989, Destination Discovery! Activities and Resources for Studying Columbus and Other Explorers, 1994, (with Susan Houck) Internat. Biog. Directory of Nat. Archivists, Documentalists and Librarians, 1996, (with John Harvey and Susan Houck) Internat. Librarianship, 2001; contbr. articles to profl. jour. US Office Edn. grantee, 1969 Mem. AAUW, AAUP, ALA, Okla. Student Libr. Assn. (state sponsor 1963-84), Okla. Libr. Assn., Internat. Rels. Round Table (chmn. membership 1970-74), Internat. Fedn. Libr. Assn. (chmn. sect. sch. libr. 1973-77), Delta Kappa Gamma, Phi Delta Kappa, Beta Phi Mu. Office: Sch Library & Info Studies 401 W Brooks St Norman OK 73019-6032

CARROLL, GEORGE JOSEPH, pathologist, educator; b. Gardner, Mass., Oct. 14, 1917; s. George Joseph and Kathryn (O'Hearn) C. BA, Clark U., Worcester, Mass., 1939; MD, George Washington U., 1944. Diplomate Am. Bd. Pathology. Intern Worchester City Hosp., 1944-45; resident in medicine Doctors Hosp., Washington, 1945-46; resident in pathology Sibley Hosp., Washington, 1948-49, VA Hosp., Washington, 1949-50; asst. pathologist D.C. Gen. Hosp., 1950-51, assoc. pathologist, 1951-52; pathologist Louise Obici Meml. Hosp., Suffolk, Va., 1952—, sec. med. staff, 1956-59, chief of staff, 1959-60, 67-69; pathologist Chowan Hosp., Edenton, N.C., 1952-71, Southampton Meml. Hosp., Franklin, Va., 1952—, Greensville Meml. Hosp., Emporia, Va., 1961—. Instr. pathology Georgetown U. Sch. Medicine, 1950-52; instr. bacteriology Am. U., Washington, 1950-51; assoc. clin. prof. pathology Med. Coll. Va., Richmond, 1968-70; clin. prof. pathology Va. Commonwealth U., 1970— ; prof. dept. pathology Eastern Va. Med. Sch., Norfolk, 1974— ; sec.-treas. Va. Bd. Medicine, 1967-86, treas., 1971-86. Contbr. articles to med. jours. Served with U.S. Army, 1946-48. Fellow ACP, Coll. Am. Pathologists, Am. Soc. Clin. Pathologists (bd. dirs. 1969—, pres. 1977—), Internat. Acad. Pathology; mem. AMA, So. Med. Assn. (Va. councilor 1965-70, pres. 1973-74), Med. Soc. Va., 4th dist. Med. Soc. (pres. 1968-70), Seaboard Med. Soc. (pres. 1957), George Washington Med. Soc., Tri-County Med. Soc. (pres. 1971-73), Am. Soc. Clin. Pharmacy Therapeutics, Va. Soc. Pathology (pres. 1973-74), Soc. Nuclear Medicine, Am. Assn. Blood Banks, Am. Cancer Soc. (bd. dirs. Va. div. 1955-62), Va. Med. Svc. Assn. (bd. dirs. 1960-71), Rotary. Home: 219 Northbrooke Ave Suffolk VA 23434-6647

CARROLL, HARVEY FRANKLIN, retired chemistry and nutrition educator; b. New Haven, Aug. 25, 1939; AB, Hunter Coll., CUNY, 1961; PhD, Cornell U., 1969. Sr. chemist Uniroyal Chem., Naugatuck, Conn., 1968-69; prof. phys. scis. Kingsborough C.C./CUNY, Bklyn., 1969—2003, prof. emeritus, 2003—. Vis. prof. Hebrew U., Jerusalem, 1979-80. Mem. Am. Chem. Soc., Sigma Xi. E-mail: hcarroll@kbcc.cuny.edu.

CARROLL, JAMES JOSEPH, electrical and computer engineering educator; b. Phila., Apr. 1, 1967; s. James Joseph Sr. and Mary Ann Carroll. BSEE, Syracuse U., 1989; MSEE, Ga. Inst. Tech., 1990; PhD in Elec. Engring., Clemson U., 1993. Intern engr. GE, Schenectady, 1986, Eastman Kodak Co., Rochester, N.Y., 1988; rsch. asst. Ga. Inst. Tech., Atlanta, 1989-90; R&D engr. Westinghouse Savannah River Co., Aiken, S.C., 1991, 92; teaching and rsch. asst. Clemson (S.C.) U., 1990-93; Air Force Office Sci. Rsch. summer faculty rschr. Wright Lab., Wright Patterson AFB, Ohio, 1994, 95; assoc. prof. Clarkson U., Potsdam, N.Y., 1993—. Contbr. articles to profl. jours., chpt. to book. Pres.'s fellow Ga. Tech., 1989, NASA fellow, 1991, EPSCOR/Dept. Energy fellow, 1993. Mem. IEEE (chmn. CDC session 1994, 95, mem. red ribbon panel 1994, 95, asst. to robotics and automation program chair 1993), Eta Kappa Nu (faculty advisor 1994—), Tau Beta Pi, Phi Kappa Phi. Achievements include Westinghouse Savannah River site invention disclosure entitled Impedance Control System for a Commercial Manipulator to be Used During Circular Saw Cutting. Home: Bingham Hill Apts Apt B Box 354 Hannawa Falls NY 13647 Office: Clarkson U Dept Elec & Computer Engr PO Box 5720 Potsdam NY 13699-0001

CARROLL, KAREN, art educator; Dir. grad. programs in art edn. Md. Inst. Coll. Art, Balt. Named Nat. Higher Edn. Art Educator, Nat. Art Edn. Assn., 1992. Office: Maryland Inst Coll of Art 1300 W Mount Royal Ave Baltimore MD 21217-4134*

CARROLL, LUCY ELLEN, choral director, music coordinator, educator; b. NYC, Oct. 11; d. Edward Joseph and Lucy Sophie (Czapszys) C. B in Music Edn., Temple U., 1968; MA, Trenton State Coll., 1973; D in Musical Arts, Combs Coll. Music, Phila., 1982. Cert. tchr. music, N.J., Pa., Nat. Cert., 1991. Tchr. music Log Coll. Jr. High Sch., Pa., 1968-72, Ind. (Pa.) High Sch., 1972-73, William Tennent High Sch., Warminster, Pa., 1973-98, dir. mus. theater, 1973-98; choir dir. St. John Bosco Parish Choir, 1999—2001; organist, dir. Carmelite Monastery, Phila., 1996—. Music coord. Centennial Schs., 1991-98; founder, dir. Madrigal Singers, Warminster, Pa., 1971-98; choral dir. Cabrini Coll., Radnor, Pa., 1974-77, First Day Singers, Phila., 1979-83, Combs Coll. Music, Phila., 1981-84, 87-88; choral adjudicator various Music festivals, 1973-98; theatre dir., Villa Joseph Marie (Holland), 1998-99; del. Internat. Arts Conf., Cambridge, Eng., 1992; adj. assoc. prof. Westminster Choir Coll., Princeton, 2002—; lectr. in field. Singer (operas Ambler Festival) Street Scene, 1970, Death of Bishop of Brindisi (premiere); (Robin Hood Dell) La Boheme; dir. (jazz theater piece N.Y.C.) Murder of Agamemnon, 1980, (drama) Power of Love (1705), 1986, (outdoor music theater) Vorspiel (Pa. Historic Commn. 1989); editor The Monastery Hymnal, 2002; columnist Polyphony mag., Adoremus Bulletin, 2002—; creator Churchmouse Squeaks cartoons, Monastery Mice cartoons; contbr. articles to profl. jours., and mags. Dir. Monastery Choir, Phila., 2001—. Recipient awards Writers of Future, 1985, 87, Andrew Ferraro award Combs Coll. Music, 1989, plaque for svc. to music Bucks County Commr., 1991, Disting. Citizen medal Southampton Twp., 1994, Harmony award Country Gentlemen Nat. Soc. for Preservation and Encouragement Barbershop Quartet Singing in Am., 1994; Scholar-In-Residence, Pa. Hist. and Museum Commn.; named Humanities Spkr. for 2000, Pa. Humanities Coun. Mem. Am. Choral Dirs. Assn., Sci. Fiction Fantasy Writers of Am., Am. Musicol. Soc., Am. Guild Organists, Organ Hist. Soc., Latin Liturgy Assn., Del. Valley Composers (choral cons. 1988-90), Hist. Soc. Pa., Smithsonian Assocs., Musical Fund Soc. of Phila., The Soc. for Am. Music, Pa. Music Educators Assn. (adv. bd. 1986-87, contbg. writer Spotlight on Tchg. Chorus 2003), Nat. ASsn. State Tchrs. of the Yr., Ephrata Cloister Assocs., Sigma Alpha Iota. Republican. Roman Catholic. Avocation: travel. Home: 712 High Ave Hatboro PA 19040-2418 E-mail: LucyCarroll@att.net.

CARROLL, MARILYN JEANNE, medical technologist, educator; b. San Pedro, Calif., Feb. 20, 1950; d. Wayne E. and Katherine M. (Hepburn) Arnold; m. Shawn Michael Carroll, Aug. 21, 1971; children: Michael J., Megan J. AA, L.A. Harbor Coll., Wilmington, Calif., 1970; BA, Calif. State U., Dominiguez, 1972. Med. technologist Martin L. King Hosp., L.A., 1975, Harbor Gen. Hosp., Torrance, Calif., 1975-79, Rsch. and Edn. Inst., Torrance, 1979-88; teaching asst. UCLA, 1980-88; v.p., lab. mgr. J.A. Turner Diagnostic Parasitology Lab., Carson, Calif., 1984—. Lectr. Harbor-UCLA Med. Ctr., Torrance, 1975-90. Mem. Am. Soc. Microbiology, Am. Soc. Clin. Pathologists, Am. Soc. Parasitologists, So. Calif. Soc. Parasitologists, Sports Car Club Am. Democrat. Avocations: racquetball, automobile racing, needlecrafts. Office: Turner Parasitology 519 W Carson St Ste 104 Carson CA 90745-2642

CARROLL, MICHAEL M. academic dean, mechanical engineering educator; b. Thurles, County Tipperary, Ireland, Dec. 8, 1936; came to U.S. 1960; s. Timothy and Catherine (Gleeson) C.; m. Carolyn F. Gahagan, Oct. 31, 1964; children— Patricia, Timothy J. BA, Univ. Coll., Galway, Ireland, 1958, MA, 1959; PhD, Brown U., 1965; DSc, Nat. U. Ireland, 1979, LLD (hon), 1992. Asst. prof. mech. engring. U. Calif., Berkeley, 1965-69, assoc. prof., 1969-73, prof., 1973-83; Shell disting. chair Shell Cos. Found., 1983-88; dean George R. Brown Sch. Engring., Burton J. and Ann McMurtry prof. engring. Rice U., Houston, 1988-98, prof. engring., 1998—. Bd. dirs. Daniel Industries Inc.; cons. TerraTek Labs., Salt Lake City, 1976-84, Thoratec Lab., Berkeley, Calif., 1976-84, Sci. Applications Internat., La Jolla, Calif., 1984—, JAG Industries, Trinidad, Calif., 1984—, Sandia Labs., Albuquerque, 1991—, Brit. Petroleum, Houston, 1991—, Adams Golf, 1998—. Contbr. articles to profl. jours.; mem. editorial bds. of tech. jours. Fellow ASME, Am. Acad. Mechanics (pres. 1994-95), Am. Acad. Arts and Scis.; mem. NAE, Am. Soc. Engring. Edn. (gov. bd., deans coun. 1992—), Soc. Engring. Sci. (bd. dirs., v.p., pres.), Sigma Xi. Roman Catholic. Avocations: crossword puzzles, golf, play writing. Home: 48 T Huxley Ln Missouri City TX 77459-1901 Office: Rice U Sch Computational & Applied Math PO Box 1892 MS 134 Houston TX 77251-1892

CARROLL, ROBERT C. principal; b. Jan. 29, 1944; Office: Carmel H S 1 Carmel Pkwy Mundelein IL 60060-2499*

CARROLL, ROSEMARY FRANCES, historian, educator, lawyer; b. Providence, Oct. 15, 1935; d. Francis Edward and Katherine Loretta (Graham) C. AB, Brown U., 1957; MA, Wesleyan U., 1962; PhD, Rutgers U., 1968; JD, U. Iowa, 1983. Bar: Iowa 1983. Asst. prof. history Notre Dame Coll., N.Y.C., 1968-70; vis. asst. prof. history Denison U., Granville, Ohio, 1970-71; asst. prof. history Coe Coll., Cedar Rapids, Iowa, 1971-75, assoc. prof. history, 1975-84, prof. history, 1984—2000, chair dept. history, 1988—2000, affirmative action officer, 1973-98, prelaw advisor, 1988-98, rep. Truman Found., 1988, faculty rep. Rhodes Scholarship Trust, 1993-98, faculty rep. Brit. Marshal Scholarship, 1996-98, Henry and Margaret Hagg disting. prof. history, 2000—01, Henry and Margaret Hagg disting. prof. history emerita, 2001—. Contbr. articles to profl. jours. Vol. lawyer Legal Services Corp. Iowa, Cedar Rapids, 1984—2003, mem. adv. coun., 1985—2003. Olmsted fellow Hoover Presdl. Libr. Assn., 1987-92, Hoover grantee, 1992-94, NEH grantee, 1992-93. Mem. ABA, AAUP, AAUW, Iowa Bar Assn. (legal heritage com. 1988—), Linn County Bar Assn. (continuing legal edn. com. 1990-2002), Linn County Women Atty. (treas. 1990-91), Orgn. Am. Historians (membership com. 1978), So. Hist. Assn. (membership com. 1986-87, 88-89, 96-98), So. Assn. Womens Historians (pres. 1975-76, membership com. 1987-88, 89-90, 96-98), Phi Kappa Phi. Roman Catholic. Avocations: bicycling, swimming. E-mail: rfcarroll1@aol.com.

CARROLL, ROY, retired academic administrator; b. England, Arkansas, Dec. 8, 1929; m. Eleanor Kate Moorefield, 1953; children: Jane, Linda. BA cum laude, Ouachita Bapt. U., 1951; MA, Vanderbilt U., 1959, PhD, 1964. Math. tchr. Baker High Sch., Columbus, Ga., 1955; asst. prof. history and polit. sci. Mercer U., Macon, Ga., 1959-65; prof. history, chmn. dept. history and polit. sci. Armstrong State Coll., Savannah, Ga., 1965-69; prof. history, chmn. dept. history Appalachian State U., Boone, N.C., 1969-79; v.p. planning gen. adminstrn. U. N.C. System, 1979-90, 91-96, sr. v.p., v.p. acad. affairs, 1996-99, ret., 1999; interim chancellor U. N.C., Asheville, 1990-91. Mem. N.C. Justice Edn. and Tng. Standards Commn., 1979-90, chmn. Planning Com. of the Commn., 1981-88; mem. adv. bd. Inst. Transp. Rsch. and Edn., Rsch. Triangle Park, 1980—; bd. dirs. Western N.C. Devel. Assn., 1990-91, N.C. State Employees Credit Union, 1990-91, Rsch. Triangle Inst., 1996-2000; trustee Appalachian State U., 2000—. Contbr. articles to profl. jours. Inf. officer U.S. Army, 1951-53, Japan, Korea. Fulbright scholar, Eng., 1958-59. Home: 6811 Huntingridge Rd Chapel Hill NC 27517-8673 Office: U North Carolina Gen Adminstrn PO Box 2688 Chapel Hill NC 27515-2688 E-mail: rcl@ga.unc.edu.

CARROTHERS, GERALD ARTHUR PATRICK, environmental and city planning educator; b. Saskatoon, Sask., Can., July 1, 1925; BArch, U. Man., Can., 1948, MArch, 1951; MCP, Harvard U., 1953; PhD, MIT, 1959. Lectr. architecture U. Man., Winnipeg, 1948-52; research asst. regional sci. Mass. Inst. Tech., Cambridge, 1953-56; asst. prof. town and regional planning U. Toronto, Ont., Can., 1956-60; assoc. prof. to prof. city planning U. Pa., Phila., 1960-67, chmn. dept. city planning, 1961-65; founding dir. Inst. Environ. Studies, 1965-67; prof. York U., Downsview, Ont., 1968—, founding dean faculty environ. studies, 1968-76. Chmn. U. Toronto-York U. Joint Program in Transp., 1971-78; adviser Central Mortgage and Housing Corp., Can., 1967-77; vis. prof. U. Nairobi, Kenya, 1978-80; mem. founding bd. dirs. Can. Urban Inst., 1988. Fellow World Acad. Art and Sci., Royal Archtl. Inst. Can., Can. Inst. Planners (founding editor Plan Can., 1959, councillor 1968-70); mem. Am. Inst. Cert. Planners (life), Regional Sci. Assn. (founding mem., founding editor Papers 1954, pres. 1970-71), Ont. Assn. Architects (life), Ont. Profl. Planners Inst. (founding registrar, founding bd. dirs. 1985). Home: 24 Bertmount Ave Toronto ON Canada M4M 2X9 Office: York U Fac Environ Studies 4700 Keele St Toronto ON Canada M4M 2X9

CARSON, BARBARA GILBERT, education educator, consultant; b. Lancaster, Pa., July 7, 1941; d. Joe Capp and Anna Elizabeth Gilbert; m. Cary Carson, June 19, 1965; 1 child, Anna Purcell. AB, Brown U., 1963; MA, U. Del., 1965. Assoc. prof., lectr. Am. Studies The George Washington U., 1975—99; adj. prof. Coll. William and Mary, Williamsburg, Va., 1982—. Author: The Gov. Palace, 1982, Ambitious Appetites, 1991. Office: American Studies College of William and Mary Williamsburg VA 23187

CARSON, BETH H. nursing educator; b. Chesnee, S.C., May 31, 1949; d. Thomas Jay and Nell V. (Burnett) Hollifield; m. J. Hugh Parris, Sept. 28, 1968 (div. Sept. 1982); children: Robin, Jonathan; m. Harrold H. Carson, Aug. 11, 1988; children: Benjamin, Samuel. ADN, U. S.C., 1978; BSN, 1995. RN; BLS instr., ACLS instr. Med. sec. Internal Med. Assocs., Spartanburg, S.C., 1968-78, nurse, 1978-88; nurse cardiac rehab. part-time Spartanburg Med. Ctr., 1980-88, staff nurse, charge nurse progressive care unit, 1988-94, clin. unit educator post cardiovasc. unit, 1994—. Mem. policy & procedure com. Spartanburg Regional Med. Ctr., 1993—, mem. cardiovasc. critical care com., 1994—, mem. cardiovasc. divsn. edn. com., 1994—. Vol. staff nurse St. Luke's Free Med. Clinic, Spartanburg, 19—93—. Mem. AACN, ANA, Piedmont Dist. Nurses Assn., Sigma Theta Tau. Avocations: piano, skiing, hiking, reading, biking. Home: 313 Slopingwood Ln Spartanburg SC 29301-2434

CARSON, JUANITA ELAINE, biologist, educator; b. Ridge Spring, S.C., Dec. 5, 1940; d. James Padgett and Rosalind Vermelle (Scott) C.; m. Kenneth M. Chitwood, June 9, 1963 (div. Apr. 1983); children: Ami, Kira Susanne. AA, North Greenville Coll., 1960; BS in Biology, U. S.C., 1962; MS in Biology, Mich. State U., 1967; EdD in Sci. Edn., Temple U., 1977. Tchr. sci. Myrtle Beach (S.C.) High Sch., 1962-65, Richland County Schs., Columbia, S.C., 1965-68; coord. sci. & staff devel. Newton County Bd. Edn., Covington, Ga., 1977—97, adminstrv. asst. staff devel. evaluation, 1977—98; prof. edn. Wesleyan Coll., Macon, Ga., 1998—. Presenter in field. Fellow Temple U., Phila., 1974-77. Mem. Ga. Assn. Edn. Leaders, Ga. Staff Devel. Coun. (bd. dirs. 1988-91), Ga. Sci. Tchrs. Assn. (pres. 1980-82,

Disting. Svc. award 1983), Met. Atlanta Tchr. Edn. Group (pres. 1987-88), Phi Delta Kappa. Democrat. Methodist. Avocations: running, hiking, travel. Home: 456 Adrian Pl Macon GA 31204-1702 Office: Wesleyan Coll 4760 Forsyth Ave Macon GA 31210

CARSON, LINDA MARIE, elementary school educator; b. La Salle, Ill., Aug. 3, 1947; d. Francis Harold and Dorothy (Dalton) Groleau; m. Randolph William Carson, Aug. 20, 1971; children: Sean, Kevin, Bethany. BS in Edn., No. Ill. U., 1969, MS in Edn., 1978. Cert. elem. tchr., Ill. Elem. tchr. Dist. 300, Dundee, Ill., 1969-85; instr. ESL, Elgin (Ill.) Community Coll., 1986; tchr. Dist. 15, McHenry, Ill., 1986—. Instr. ACT rev. McHenry County Coll., Crystal Lake, Ill., 1991. Co-pres. Eastview Sch. PTO, Algonquin, Ill., 1981-82; pres. Algonquin Women's Club, 1987-89. Home: 631 Webster St Algonquin IL 60102-2869 Office: Valley View Sch 6515 W State Route 120 Mchenry IL 60050-7450

CARSON, MARY SILVANO, career counselor, educator; b. Mass. d. Joseph and Alice V. Silvano; m. Paul E. Carson (dec.); children: Jan Ellen, Jeffrey Paul, Amy Jayne. BS, Simmons Coll., 1947; MA, U. Chgo., 1970, postgrad., 1971, 72, Ctr. Urban Studies, 1970, DePaul U., 1980. Cert. acad. counselor, Ill.; nat. cert. counselor. Mgr. S.W. Youth Opportunity Ctr., Dept. Labor, Chgo., 1964-68; careers counselor Gordon Tech. H.S., Chgo., 1971-74; dir. Career and Assessment Ctr., YMCA Coll., Chgo., 1974-81; project coord. Career Ctr., Loop Coll., Chgo., 1981-85; pvt. practice San Francisco, 1990—. Mem. adv. bd. City-Wide Coll. Career Ctr.; bd. dirs. Loop YWCA, Chgo., coord. employment project, 1985-87; ESL tchr., Greece, 1990. Mem. ACA, TESOL, Am. Ednl. Rsch. Assn., Nat. Career Devel. Assn., Internat. Counseling Assn., Internat. Lyceum (London), Browning Soc., World Coun., English Speaking Union, Met. Club, Commonwealth Club, Pi Lambda Theta (chpt. pres. 1975).

CARSON, MICHAEL, secondary school educator, music educator; b. Suffolk, Va., Jan. 15, 1960; s. James Lee and Mary Ann Carson; children: Chiquita Watford, Teneisha Faulks. MusM, Norfolk (Va.) State U., 1988, BS in Music Edn., 1982. Cert. tchr. instrumental music K-12. Band dir. John Yeates H.S. / Driver Intermediate, Suffolk, Va., 1982—90, Nansemond River H.S. / John Yeates Mid., Suffolk, 1990—99, Western Br. Mid. Sch., Chesapeake, Va., 1999—. Band leader, mgr. N-TREGUE, Chesapeake, 1994—. Musician local jazz-pop band. Mem.: Music Educators Nat. Conf. Office: Western Br Mid Sch 4201 Hawksley Dr Chesapeake VA 23321

CARSON, REGINA E. healthcare administrator, geriatric specialist, pharmacist, educator; b. Washington; BS in Pharmacy, Howard U.; MBA in Mktg., MBA in Health Care Adminstrn., Loyola Coll., Balt., 1987. Asst. prof., asst. dir. pharmacy U. Md., Balt., 1986-88; asst. prof., coord. profl. practice Howard U., Washington, 1988-95; prin. Marrell Cons., Randallstown, Md., prin., mng. ptnr., 1993—; exec. dir. Sunrise Assisted Living, Fairfax, Va., 1997-99. Drug utilization rev. cons. Md. Pharmacy Assn., Balt., 1986—90; cons. pharmacist Baltimore county Adv. Coun. Drug Abuse, Towson, Md., 1984—86; edn. cons. ADWHE, Accra, Ghana, 1999; program evaluator Train Pharm., UMF-Cluj, Romania, 1999—2002. Bd. dirs. N.W. Hosp. Ctr. Aux., Randallstown, Joshua Johnson Coun., Balt. Mus. Art, Alzheimers Assn. Ctrl. Md.; trustee C.C. of Baltimore County, 1997—. Named Outstanding Alumni, Howard U. Coll. Pharmacy, 1992; recipient Gregor T. Popa medal, UMF-Iasi, Romania, 2000. Fellow: Am. Soc. Cons. Pharmacists; mem.: Nat. Assn. Retail Druggists (adv. com., long-term care com.), Nat. Pharm. Assn. (life, Outstanding Women in Pharmacy 1984), Am. Assn. Colls. Pharmacy, Nat. Assn. Health Svc. Execs. Avocation: Avocations: pharmacognosy, Windsor chairs, American art.

CARSON, STEVEN LEE, newspaper publisher; b. N.Y.C., Mar. 23, 1943; s. Harold and Mathilde (Seidel) C.; m. Yvonne DeDrozizhki, Aug. 8, 1971 (dec. Feb. 1980). BA, NYU, 1964, MA, 1965. Archivist, conf. dir. Nat. Archives, Washington, 1967-73; chmn. White House Conf. Pres. & Children, Washington, 1974; editor, writer Manuscript Soc. News, Washington, 1987—; conf. dir. The Manuscript Soc., 1974-80. Dir. history pavilion Hall of Fame Great Am., N.Y.C., 1964; editor Pres. Commn. Civil Disorders, Washington, 1968; mem. (charter) Hildene Robert Todd Lincoln estate; TV commentator; spkr. in field. Author: Maximilien Robespierre, 1988; (plays) The Last Lincoln, Princess Alice; contbr. articles to profl. jours. Speechwriter The White House, U.S. Congress, Md. Ho. Dels., 1974—; historian Rock Creek Cemetery, Washington, 1997—. Recipient NYU Heights Daily News Alumni award, 1964, Archival medal, Republic of Korea, 1972, Internat. Psychohistory Assn. award, 1983, Lincoln Group of N.Y. award, 1988, 1992, Man of the Month award, Washington Bus. Jour., 1989, Surratt Soc. award, 1993, delivered ofcl. Lincoln Day Address, Ford's Theatre, Washington, 1996, Smithsonian lectr., 1999—; grantee, Md. Commn. Humanities, 1986, 1987, U.S. Dept. Interior, 1985; Ford Found. fellow, 1964, Johns Hopkins U. Chas Carroll Fulton fellow, 1965. Fellow: The Manuscript Soc.; mem.: Washington Ind. Writers, Nat. Writers Union, Nat. Press Club, NYU Soc. of the Torch, Abraham Lincoln Inst. (trustee 1997—), Lincoln Group D.C. (pres. 1985—88, Lincoln Recognition award 2003), Lincoln Forum (trustee 1997—), Lincoln Group III (trustee 1986—91), NYU Perstare et Praestare, NYU Hon. Soc. Avocation: collecting historic manuscripts & letters. Office: The Manuscript News 8811 Colesville Rd Ste 506 Silver Spring MD 20910-4332

CARSON, WILLIAM STUART, music educator, music administrator; b. Mpls., Dec. 14, 1956; s. Herbert L. and Ada Lou (Siegel) C.; m. Laura Jean Herzstock, Dec. 28, 1986; children: Marissa Michelle, Eric Jonathan. BA, Macalester Coll., St. Paul, 1979; MMusic, So. Ill. U., Carbondale, 1981; D of Musical Arts, Ariz. State U., Tempe, 1992. Teaching asst. So. Ill. U., 1979-81; music dir. Carbondale Cmty. High Sch., 1981-83; music coord., band dir. West Lafayette (Ind.) Cmty. Schs., 1983-84; asst. prof. music Plymouth (N.H.) State Coll., 1984-88; teaching asst. Ariz. State U., Tempe, 1988-90; dir. bands Coe Coll., Cedar Rapids, Iowa, 1990—, chair dept. music, 2002—. Bus. mgr. Cedar Rapids Mcpl. Band, 1992—; prin. guest condr. Ea. Iowa Brass Band, Mt. Vernon, 1991—; freelance woodwind performer with orchs., bands and jazz bands, 1979—; guest condr./adjudicator bands and jazz bands, 1979—. Author: On the Path to Excellence: The Northshore Concert Band, Paynter, Buhelman, and Beyond, 2003; contbr. articles to profl. jours. Recipient Music Sweepstakes award Ill. High Sch. Music Assn., 1982, Outstanding Dissertation award Coun. for Rsch. in Music Edn., 1994. Mem. Iowa Bandmasters Assn., Music Educators Nat. Conf., Coll. Band Dirs. Nat. Assn., Nat. Band Assn. (Iowa state chair), Phi Kappa Phi (chpt. pres. 1993-94). Avocations: hiking, camping. Home: 5029 Broadview Dr SE Cedar Rapids IA 52403-3270 Office: Coe Coll 1220 1st Ave NE Cedar Rapids IA 52402-5008 E-mail: wcarson@coe.edu., band@coe.edu.

CARSTENSEN, LAURA LEE, gerontology educator; b. Phila., Nov. 2, 1953; d. Edwin Lorenz Carstensen and Pam. McDonald; m. Ian H. Gotlib, Aug. 27, 1995; 1 child, David Joseph Pagano. BS, U. Rochester, 1978; MA, W.Va. U., 1980, PhD, 1983. Asst. prof. Ind. U., Bloomington, 1983-87, Stanford (Calif.) U., 1987-94, assoc. prof., 1995—. Sci. cons. Max Planck Inst. Human Devel. & Edn., Berlin, 1992—; assoc. dir. Terman gifted project Stanford U., 1994—. Author book chpt.; co-author Psychology: The Study of Human Experience, 1991; co-editor: Handbook of Clinical Gerontology, 1987. Recipient First Investigator award Nat. Inst. Aging, 1987. Fellow Gerontol. Soc. Am. (mem.-at-large 1994—, Kalish Innovative Publication award 1993); mem. APA, Am. Psychol. Soc. Office: Stanford U Dept Psychology Bldg 420 Jordan Hall Stanford CA 94305-2130

CARSWELL, VIRGINIA COLBY, retired primary school educator, special education educator; b. Manchester, N.H., Aug. 10, 1923; d. Aretas Putnam and Lucille (Ford) Colby; m. Elwin Dow Carswell, Jan. 26, 1946 (dec. July 1997); children: Susan Lee Carswell-Hurdis, Debra Ann Carswell Roberts. Diploma, Elliot Hosp. Sch. Nursing, 1945; BS in Spl. Edn.-Elem. Edn., Brenau Coll., 1977, postgrad., 1978-80. Asst. dietitian Elliot Hosp., Manchester, N.H., 1946-58; tchr., head instr. Hi Hope Svc. Ctr., Lawrenceville, Ga., 1970-87; presch. tchr. Buford (Ga.) Meth. Presch., 1987—. Child devel. internship Gainsville (Ga.) Coll., 1988-89. Vol. numerous ch. activities. Recipient Outstanding Citizen award Woodman of the World Life Ins. Soc., 1981, Golden Rule award, J.C. Penney, 1984, Gene Willis award, Gwinnett County Assn. Retarded Citizens, 1987, Svcs. to Handicapped, Gwinnett Mental Health Assn., 1983, Leadership award Girl Scouts Am., 1970, Merit Mother award Am. Mothers Assn., 1980. Mem. Coun. Exceptional Children (Outstanding Profl. award 1987), Ga. Presch. Assn. (Disting. Cert. of Recognition 1998), So. Assn. Children under Six, Nat. Assn. Edn. Young Children (Disting. Cert. Recognition Profl. 1998), Am. Red Cross (instr. 1970—). United Methodist. Avocations: cooking, sewing, bowling, reading. Home: 1525 Laurel Crossing Pkwy Apt 1114 Buford GA 30519

CART, PAULINE HARMON, minister, educator; b. Jamestown, Ky., Nov. 3, 1914; d. Preston L. and Frances L. (Sullivan) Harmon; m. William C. Cart, July 3, 1936; children: Charles W., David N. (dec.). BS Berea Coll., 1955; MA U. Mich.-Ann Arbor, 1957, postgrad., 1957; postgrad. Ea. Mich. U., 1957, Nanjing Coll. Traditional Medicine, 1987, PhD in Homeopathic Philosophy. Cert. Tuina instr.; lic. Asatar master tchr. Mgr., owner Gen. Store, Beattyville, Ky., 1936-41; def. worker GM, Dayton, Ohio, 1941-46; tchr. Ann Arbor Pub. Schs., 1955-83, Leads Sch., Eng., 1963-64; myomassologist Coll. Natureopathic Physicians, St. Louis, 1959-84; min., counselor Ch. of Universology, Ann Arbor, 1972—; master tchr. Star's Edge Internat., Altamonte Springs, Fla., 1991—; prof. nutrition and body balancing Inst. Natural Health Scis., Mich., also bd. dirs, 1994—; ind. travel agent, 1995; rep. Systemic Formulas of Ogden, Utah, 1995—; CEO Cart's Cosmic Health Rsch., 1996—; lectr. in the field, 1995—. Contbr. poems and short stories to mags. Instr. Touch for Health Found., Pasadena, Calif., 1972—, Iridology, Escondido, Calif., 1972—; Gua Sha instr., Aruba, Mich., N.C.; bd. dirs. Music in Trauma Release Touch for Health in Profl. Health Practitioner; mem. Conservative Caucus, Washington, 1973-95. Mem. NEA (del. 1959, cons. 1987—), Am. Nutrition Counselors Am., Internat. Myomathetics Fedn. (sec. edn. 1985—), Mich. Myomassology Assn. (pres. 1990-91), Assn. Mich. Myomassologists Inc. (v.p. 1987-88), Am. Assn. Univ. Women, Federated Organic Garden & Farming of Mich. (v.p. 1985-86), Alumni Assn. U. Mich. (life), Berea Alumni Assn., Delta Kappa Pi. Republican. Avocations: painting, quilting, crafts, writing, world traveler. Died Jan. 31, 1998. Home: 2564 Hawks Rd Ann Arbor MI 48108-1311 Office: 2450 Hawks Rd Ann Arbor MI 48108-1311

CARTER, AMY HARPSTER, special education educator; b. Lewistown, Pa., Dec. 5, 1964; d. Harry Rodgers and Shirley (Hess) Harpster; m. Donald L. Carter, Oct. 3, 1992; 2 children. BEd, Lock Haven U., 1987; M Learning Disabilities, Shippensburg U., 1991. Itinerant learning support tchr. West Perry Sch. Dist., Elliottsburg, Pa., 1987—. Bible sch. tchr. Messiah Luth. Ch., Elliottsburg, 1992—. Mem. Coun. Exceptional Children, Kappa Delta Pi, Phi Kappa Phi. Avocations: painting, ceramics, gardening, travel. Home: 239 W Main St New Bloomfield PA 17068-9618 Office: West Perry Sch Dist RR 1 Elliottsburg PA 17024-9801

CARTER, ASHTON BALDWIN, physicist, educator, government agency executive; b. Phila., Sept. 24, 1954; s. William Stanley and Ann Baldwin C.; m. Ava Clayton Spencer, Aug. 6, 1983; children: William A., Ava Clayton. BA in Physics, BA in Medieval History, Yale U., 1976; PhD in Theoretical Physics, Oxford (Eng.) U., 1979. Analyst Office of Technology Assessment, Washington, 1980-81; rsch. analyst Office of Sec. Def., Washington, 1981-82; rsch. fellow MIT, Cambridge, 1982-84; asst. prof. Kennedy Sch. Govt., Harvard U., Cambridge, 1984-86, assoc. prof., 1986-88, Ford Found. prof. Sci. and Internat. Affairs, assoc. dir. Ctr. for Sci. and Internat. Affairs, 1988-90, dir. Ctr. for Sci. and Internat. Affairs, 1990-93; asst. sec. for internat. security policy U.S. Dept. Def., Washington, 1993-96; Ford Found. prof. Kennedy Sch. Govt., Harvard U., Cambridge, Mass., 1996—. Mem. Def. Sci. Bd., Washington, 1990-93, 97—; mem. Def. Polit. Bd., Washington, 1997—; advisor NAS, 1990—, AAAS, 1988—, White House Office of Sci. and Technology Policy, 1990-93, Joint Chiefs Staff; trustee MITRE Corp. Author: Directed Energy Missile Defense in Space, 1984; co-author: Ballistic Missile Defense, 1984, Managing Nuclear Operations, 1987, Beyond Spinoff: Military and Commercial Technologies in a Changing World, 1991, Soviet Nuclear Fission: Control of the Nuclear Arsenal in a Disintegrating Soviet Union, 1991, A New Concept of Cooperative Security, 1992, Cooperative Denuclearization: From Pledges to Deeds, 1993, Global Engagement: Cooperation and Security in the 21st Century, 1994, Preventive Defense: A New Security Strategy for America, 1999. Rhodes scholar, 1976; named Outstanding Young Man of Am., U.S. Jaycees, 1987. Mem. Am. Phys. Soc. (Forum award 1988), Coun. Fgn. Rels., Internat. Inst. Strategic Studies, Phi Beta Kappa. Office: Harvard U JFK Sch of Govt 79 JFK St Cambridge MA 02138-5801

CARTER, BARRY EDWARD, lawyer, educator, administrator; b. L.A., Oct. 14, 1942; s. Byron Edward and Ethel Catherine (Turner) C.; m. Kathleen Anne Ambrose, May 17, 1987; children: Gregory Ambrose, Meghan Elisabeth. AB with great distinction, Stanford U., 1964; M.P.A., Princeton U., 1966; JD, Yale U., 1969. Bar: Calif. 1970, D.C. 1972. Program analyst Office of Sec. Def., Washington, 1969-70; mem. staff NSC, Washington, 1970-72; rsch. fellow Kennedy Sch., Harvard U., Cambridge, Mass., 1972; internat. affairs fellow Coun. on Fgn. Rels., 1972; assoc. Wilmer, Cutler & Pickering, Washington, 1973-75; sr. counsel Select Com. on Intelligence Activities, U.S. Senate, Washington, 1975; assoc. Morrison & Foerster, San Francisco, 1976-79; assoc. prof. law Georgetown U. Law Ctr., Washington, 1979-89, prof., 1989-93, 96—; exec. dir. Am. Soc. Internat. Law, Washington, 1992-93; acting undersec. for export adminstrn. U.S. Dept. Commerce, Washington, 1993-94, deputy undersec., 1994-96. Vis. prof. law Stanford U. Law Sch., 1990; bd. dirs. RWE Nukem, Inc., 1998—; chmn. adv. bd. Def. Budget Project, 1990—93; mem. UN Assn. Soviet-Am. Parallel Studies Project, 1976—87; adv. coun. Zurich Emerging Markets Solutions, 2001—. Author: International Economic Sanctions: Improving the Haphazard U.S. Legal Regime, 1988 (Am. Soc. Internat. Law Cert. of Merit 1989); co-author: International Law, 4th edit., 2003; co-editor: Internat. Law: Selected Documents, 2003—; contbr. articles to profl. jours. With U.S. Army, 1969-71. Mem.: ABA, Am. Soc. Internat. Law (hon. v.p. 1993—99, counselor 1999—2000), Coun. on Fgn. Rels., DC Bar Assn., Calif. Bar Assn., Am. Law Inst., Am. Bar Found., Phi Beta Kappa. Democrat. Roman Catholic. Home: 2922 45th St NW Washington DC 20016-3559 Office: Georgetown U Law Ctr 600 New Jersey Ave NW Washington DC 20001-2075 E-mail: carter@law.georgetown.edu.

CARTER, CATHERINE LOUISE, retired elementary and middle school educator; b. Oakland, Calif., Mar. 31, 1947; d. Robert Collidge and Mae (Reidy) C. BA, Ohio Wesleyan U. Tchr. Barclay Elem. Sch., Cherry Hill, N.J., 1969-72, Malberg Elem. Sch., Cherry Hill, 1972-80, Beck Mid. Sch., Cherry Hill, 1980-89, 94-95, Carusi Jr. H.S., Cherry Hill, 1989—94, 1995—2002. Coord. Nat. Women's History Month Cherry Hill Jr. Schs., 1993-2002. Advisor Mother Earth and Friends Environ. Club, 1989-2000; mem. dist. Recycling Program Cherry Hill Pub. Schs., 1990-94, Womyn and Religion Untarian Universalist Ch. Cherry Hill, 1994—, Nat. Mus. Women Arts, 1996—, Women's Philharm., 1997—; sponser Childreach, 1997—. Mem. Nat. Ret. Tchr. Educators Assn., N.J. Ret. Tchr. Edn. Assn., Camden County Ret, Tchr. Edn. Assn., Cherry Hill Ret. Tchr. Edn. Assn., NOW,World Wildlife Fedn., Global Fund for Women, Planned Parenthood, Alice Paul Centenial Found., Seeking Edn. Equity and Diversity (study group 1994), Freedom from Hunger, Population Comms. Internat. Avocations: foreign travel, foreign films, arts, nature, jazz. Home: 10 Brookwood Dr Voorhees NJ 08043-4757

CARTER, CONNIE BEVERLY, education consultant; b. Walla Walla, Wash., Aug. 12, 1926; d. Rowland Averill Yeend and Geraldine (McEvoy) Davis; m. Forest Taylor Carter, 1943 (div. 1984); children: Gordon D., Kathy Jo Altman, Michael J. BA, U. Nev., 1969, M in Curriculum, postgrad., U. Nev., 1972, M Counseling, 1982. Cert. tchr., Nev. With real estate sales dept. Bartsas Realty, Las Vegas, Nev., 1960; tchr. Clark County Sch. Dist., Las Vegas, 1969-90. Dir. Edn. Cons. Svcs., Las Vegas, 1987—; owner, dir. La Madre Mountain Sch., 1996—. Mem. Dem. Cen. Com., Las Vegas, 1985—; advocate ct. apptd. spl. advocate, Las Vegas, 1984—; v.p. United Ch. of Women, Las Vegas, 1959; pres. PTA, Las Vegas, 1958, 62; mem., trustee Nat. Kids Campus, Las Vegas, 1987. Mem. Clark County Classroom Tchrs. Assn. (bd. dirs., serving on negotiations team 1977), Orton Dyslexic Soc., Assn. Children with Learning Disabilities, Assn. Supervision and Curriculum Devel., Am. Assn. for Counseling and Devel. Baptist. Avocations: reading, dancing, basketball fan, travel. Home: 4147 Melody Ln Las Vegas NV 89108

CARTER, DAVID GEORGE, SR., university administrator; b. Dayton, Ohio, Oct. 25, 1942; s. Richard Walter and Esther Mae (Dunn) C.; children: Ehrika Aileen, Jessica Faye, David George Jr. BS, Cen. State U., 1965; MEd, Miami U., 1968; PhD, Ohio State U., 1971. Cert. elem. tchr., Ohio. Prin. Dayton Pub. Schs., 1969-70, supr., 1970-71, unit facilitator, dist. supt., 1971-73; asst. and assoc. prof. Pa. State U., State College, 1972-77; assoc. dean and prof. edn. U. Conn., Storrs, 1977-82, assoc. v.p. acad. affairs, 1982-88; pres. East Conn. State U., Willimantic, 1988—. Corporator Liberty Bank, 1999—, dir., 2000—, Marine Corps Univ. Mem., bd. of visitors, 1998, chair-elect, 2001. Contbr. articles to profl. jours. Bd. dirs. New England Regional Exch., Framingham, Mass., 1981-86, Haitian Health Found.; mem. Gov.'s Task Force on Jail and Prison Overcrowding; bd. visitors, Marine Corps U. Named Young Man of Yr. Dayton C. of C., 1973, Disting. Alumnus Ctrl. State U., Wilberforce, Ohio, 1988, Man of Yr., African Am. Affairs Commn., 2000—; inducted into Donald K. Anthony Achievement Hall of Fame Ctrl. State U., 1993; recipient Roy Wilkins Civil Rights award NAACP, 1994; 39th Americanism award Conn. Am. Legion, 1994; recipient Greater Hartford NAACP award of honor, 2001, Good Citizen award, Conn. Grand Lodge Order Sons of Italy in Am., 2001, Educator of Yr. award Greater Hartford Assn. of Negro Bus. and Profl. Woman's Club, 2003, Whitney M. Young Jr. Svc. award Urban Scouting Com. Conn. Rivers Coun. Boy Scouts Am., 2003. Mem. Nat. Orgn. Legal Problems of Edn. (bd. dirs. 1980-83), NCAA (chair pres.' commn. divsn. III 1995-97, pres.'s commn. 1991-97), Am. Ednl. Rsch. Orgn., Phi Delta Kappa, Pi Lambda Theta, Phi Kappa Phi, Sigma Pi Phi. Home: 9 Charles Ln Storrs Mansfield CT 06268-2308 Office: East Conn State U 83 Windham St Willimantic CT 06226-2211

CARTER, DOROTHY ANNIS, secondary school educator; b. Roanoke, Va., Feb. 11; d. Edward Kenneth and Annie (Fowler) C.; m. Edward Lee Carter, Aug. 5, 1955. BS, Bluefield State Tchrs. Coll., 1953; MA, Federal City Coll., 1975; EdD, Nova Univ., 1985. Cert. tchr., Va., Md. Music tchr. Kennard High Sch., Dillwyn, Va., 1953-55; history, music tchr. Carter G. Woodson High Sch., Centreville, Md., 1955-58; music tchr. Roosevelt High Sch., Washington, 1960; history tchr. Banneker Jr. High Sch., Washington, 1960; open space coord., acting adminstr. Shaw Jr. High Sch., Washington, 1961-92; community sch. tchr. GED Shaw Jr. High Sch., Washington, 1980. Tutor Outreach Program, Shaw Community Sch., Washington, 1985-92; program coord. Adopt-A-Sch. Prometheans, Washington, 1977-87; program coord. Partners In Edn., Washington, 1987-92; presenter various workshops and confs. Author: ERS Spectrum, 1993. Dir youth choral Vermont Ave. Baptist Ch., Washington, 1965-80; tchr. rep. community sch. Shaw Neighborhood Coun., 1985; vol. coord. Supr. Of DCPS, Washington, 1990. Recipient Exemplary Svc. award Washington Pub. Schs., 1984; U.S. Diamond award United to Serve Am., 1991. Mem. Nat. Assn. Black Educators, Alpha Kappa Appha (Golden Girl award 1985). Baptist. Avocations: reading, flower gardening, ceramics, listening. Office: Shaw Jr High Sch 925 Rhode Island Ave NW Washington DC 20001-4140

CARTER, EDITH HOUSTON, statistician, educator; b. Charlotte, N.C., Oct. 12, 1936; d. Z. and Ellie (Hartsell) Houston; m. Fletcher F. Carter, Apr. 2, 1961. BS, Appalachian State U., 1959, MA, 1960; PhD, Va. Poly. Inst. and State U., 1976. Transcript analyst Fla. Dept. Edn., Tallahassee, 1961-65; instr. Radford U., 1969-70, 91-94, asst. prof., 1994—. Prof. New River C.C., Dublin, Va., 1970-83, dir. instl. research, 1974-78, asst. dean Coll. Arts and Scis., 1978-79, statistician, 1979-83. Editor Community Coll. Jour. Research and Planning, 1981-93, Am. Assn. Community Colls. Jour. (rsch. review editor 1991-95), Newsletter Southeastern Assn. C.C. Research, 1972—; mem. editorial bd. C.C. Rev., 1990-93. Violist New River Valley Symphony, Va. Poly. Inst. and State U. Orch., Radford U. Orch., S.W. Va. Opera Soc. Orch., summer mus. Enterprise ORch., 1999—; sec./treas. Radford New River Valley chpt. Am. Sewing Guild, 1991-94, pres., 1994-96. Mem. Am. Ednl. Rsch. Assn., State and Regional Ednl. Rsch. Assn. (sec./treas. 1989-93, pres. 1993-95, svc. chmn. 1995—, Leadership award 1995, 2002-03), Assn. Instl. Research (exec. bd. 1976-78), Southeastern Assn. C.C. Rsch. (exec. bd. 1976-78, Outstanding Service award, Disting. Service award 1981), Nat. Coun. Rsch. and Planning (Outstanding Svc. award 1992, James R. Montgomery Svc. award, 2001), Coll. Music Soc., Am. String Tchrs. Assn., Va. Ednl. Rsch. Assn. (pres. 1997), Va. Fedn. Women's Clubs (dir. 1968-70), Va. Tech. U. Alumni (pres. New River Valley chpt. 1982-83), So. Assn. for Instnl. Rsch., Radford Jr. Woman's Club (pres. 1967-68), Phi Delta Kappa (pres. New River Valley chpt. 1997-99). Presbyterian. Home: 6924 Radford Univ Radford VA 24142 Office: Radford U Russell Hall Radford VA 24142 E-mail: ecarter@radford.edu.

CARTER, EVELYN ADKINS, secondary education educator; b. Boykins, Va., Sept. 22, 1954; d. Hugh and Hattie (Rogers) Adkins; m. Herman Leon Carter, July 23, 1979; children: Jarrett, Jamelah, Jason. BA in English, Va. State U., 1976; postgrad., Trinity Coll., U. Va., Charlottesville; MEd of Adminstrn./Supervision, Bowie State U., 1990. Cert. tchr., Md. Tchr. English Campbell County Schs., Rustburg, Va.; instr. English King George County Coll., King George, Va.; tchr. English Friendly High Sch., Ft. Washington, Md., Suitland (Md.) Univ. High Sch. Participant mentoring program Suitland Univ. High Sch., mentor new tchrs., sponsor Write-A-Book, mem. holistic writing com. Mem. ASCD, PTA, Va. Edn. Assn., Md. Edn. Assn.,Campbell County Edn. Assn., King George Edn. Assn., Md. State Tchrs. Assn., Alpha Kappa Alpha.

CARTER, FLETCHER FAIRWICK, university administrator, education educator; b. Bagdad, Fla., Feb. 12, 1930; s. Ollie Martin and Florence Lista (Owens) C.; m. Edith J. Houston, Apr. 2, 1961. BA in Polit. Sci., U. Fla., 1953; MA in Social Scis., Appalachian State U., 1960; PhD in Higher Edn. Adminstrn., Fla. State U., 1965. Tchr. Santa Rosa County Pub. Schs., Milton, Fla., 1955-61, jr. H.S. math. and sci. tchr., 1957-61; instr. in geography Appalachian State U., Boone, N.C., 1961; analyst Fla. State Dept. Edn., Tallahassee, 1961-62; registrar Mitchell Coll., Statesville, N.C., 1963-64; instr., student tchg. supr. Fla. State U., Tallahassee, 1964-65; prof. edn. Radford (Va.) U., 1965—, asst. dean Sch. Edn., 1967-72, dir. instnl. rsch. and analyses, 1968—2001, prof. ednl. studies, 2001—. Tchg. fellow Appalachian State U., Boone, N.C., 1959-60; mem. com. on program costing State Coun. for Higher Edn. in Va., 1974, mem. com. on reporting practices, 1981, cons. on facilities, 1986, mem. com. on rsch. facilities, 1988-90 Chmn. bd. trustees Radford Pub. Libr., 1986-2002. 1st lt. U.S. Army, 1952-55, Korea. Kellogg fellow Fla. State U., 1961-63. Mem. Va.

Assn. for Mgmt., Analysis and Planning (charter, bd. dirs. 1969—), So. Assn. Instnl. Rsch. (charter, nominating com.), Assn. Instnl. Rsch. (assoc. clubs com., paper com. 1997), Am. Ednl. Rsch. Assn., Masons (40 yr. cert. 1993), Lions (pres., sec., 25 Yr. cert. 1994), Phi Eta Sigma, Phi Delta Kappa (pres., sec.), Pi Gamma Mu. Methodist. Home: 305 Fairway Dr Radford VA 24141-3909 Office: Radford U PO Box 6924 Radford VA 24142-6924 E-mail: fcarter@radford.edu.

CARTER, FRANCES MONET, nursing educator; b. Mayfield, Ky., Aug. 6, 1923; d. Orlando Lee and Hattie Lois (Buckingham) C.; m. Carl Baker; Donald Matthies, Henry Evans. RN, Louisville Gen. Hosp., 1944; cert. advanced psychiat. nursing instrn., U. Minn., 1945; BS, UCLA, 1948; MA, San Francisco State U., 1957; EdD, U. San Francisco, 1978. RN, Calif. Supr., instr. Herrick Meml. Hosp., Berkeley, Calif.; instr. Compton (Calif.) Sanitarium; prof. U. San Francisco, prof. emerita. Author: The Role of the Nurse in Community Mental Health, 1968, Psychosocial Nursing: Theory and Practice in Hospital and Community Mental Health, 1971, 2d edit., 1976, 3d edit., 1981. First alumni fellow U. Louisville, 1990, World Health Orgn. fellow, 1961-62, 70. Fellow Am. Acad. Nursing; mem. ANA, World Fedn. for Mental Health, Sigma Theta Tau, Alpha Sigma Nu.

CARTER, GALE DENISE, elementary education educator; b. N.Y.C., Sept. 5, 1953; d. Albert Edward and Josephine (Hernandez) D'Ambrosio; m. David Samuel Carter, Apr. 3, 1976; children: Stephanie, David, Jennifer, Michelle. BS, U. Md., 1975, MEd, 1992. Tchr. 7th grade Mt. Calvary Sch., Forestville, Md., 1975-77; tchr. 6th and 7th grades Mother Catherine Spaulding Sch., Helen, Md., 1986-87; substitute tchr. St. Mary's County Pub. Schs., Leonardtown, Md., 1987-88, tchr. 3rd grade, 1988-90, tchr. 6th grade, 1990-95, reading specialist Margaret Brent Middle Sch., 1995-99; tchr. reading Lemon Bay (Fla.) H.S. Leader Girl Scouts U.S., Washington. Recipient Marian Medal award Archdiocese of Washington/Cath. Girl Scouting, 1968. Mem. PTA, Md. Tchrs. Assn., Internat. Reading Assn. (Md. chpt.). Democrat. Roman Catholic. Avocations: reading, girl scouting activities. Home: 9382 Impala Cir Port Charlotte FL 33981-3117

CARTER, GENE RAYMOND, professional association executive; b. Staunton, Va. BA, Va. State U.; MA, Boston U.; EdD, Columbia U., 1973; LLD (hon.), Va. State U.; LittD, Old Dominion U. Various teaching and ednl. adminstrv. pos., 1960-92; exec. dir. ASCD, 1992—. Cons. various colls. and univs. Trustee Va. Wesleyan Coll.; bd. dirs. Norfolk So. Corp.; mem. adv. bd. Edn. Commn. of the States. Recipient Brotherhood citation Nat. Conf. of Christians and Jews, 1985, Presdl. citation Nat. Assn. Equal Oppty. in Higher Edn., 1985, Outstanding Sch. Supt. in Va. in 1985 award John F. Kennedy Ctr. for the Performing Arts, 1985, Nat. Supt. of the Yr. award Am. Assn. Sch. Adminstrs., 1988, Annual Leadership for Learning award Am. Assn. Sch. Adminstrs., 1990, Disting. Alumni award Teacher's Coll. Columbia U., 1991. Office: ASCD 1703 N Beauregard St Alexandria VA 22311-1714 Home: 10910 Chatham Ridge Way Spotsylvania VA 22553 E-mail: gcarter@ascd.org.

CARTER, JAMES CLARENCE, pastor, educator; b. N.Y.C., Aug. 1, 1927; s. James Clarence and Elizabeth (Dillon) C. BS in Physics, Spring Hill Coll., 1952; MS in Physics, Fordham U., 1953; STL in Theology, Woodstock Coll., 1959; PhD in Physics, Cath. U. Am., 1956. Ordained priest Roman Cath. Ch., 1958. Instr., asst. prof. Physics Loyola U., New Orleans, 1960-67, assoc. prof. of Physics, 1967—, v.p., 1970-74, pres., 1974-95, chancellor, 1995-2001; pastor Immaculate Conception Parish, New Orleans, 2001—. Bd. dirs. Met. Area Com.; mem. higher edn. facilities com. State La., 1971-73, Am. Council's Commn. on Leadership in Higher Edn., 1975-78; bd. trustees Loyola U. Chgo., 1981-90; chmn. Mayor's Com. Ednl. Uses CATV, 1972. Contbr. articles to profl. jours. Mem. adv. com. New Orleans Pub. Library for the NEH Grant, 1975; bd. dirs. Greater New Orleans Area United Way, 1976-82, La. Ednl. TV Authority, 1977-83; bd. trustees Regis U., 1980-90, 94—, U. San Francisco, 1991-2000, St. Joseph's U., 1993—. Recipient Torch of Liberty award Anti-Defamation League of B'nai B'rith, 1983. Mem. Palmes Academiques, So. Assn. of Colls. and Schs. (exec. council of the commn. on colls.), Am. Phys. Soc., Am. Assn. Physics Tchrs., Assn. Jesuit Colls. and Univs. (chmn. acad. v.p. conf. 1971-74, chmn. 1991-94, exec. dir. 1996), Nat. Assn. Ind. Colls. and Univs. (bd. dirs. 1977-82), Am. Council Edn., Sigma Xi. Office: Jesuit Ch 130 Baronne St New Orleans LA 70112

CARTER, JOHN JEFFERSON, government educator, author; b. Wheaton, Mo., Apr. 28, 1955; s. John Jefferson and Donna Deloris (Clark) C.; m. Jerri Lynn Walker, Aug. 19, 1978; 1 child, Elizabeth Anne. BA in Polit. Sci., U. Mo., 1977; MA in Polit. Sci., Ctrl. Mo. State U., 1978; PhD in Polit. Sci., U. Mo., 1981. Asst. prof. history and govt. Ctrl. Meth. Coll., Fayette, Mo., 1980-84, assoc. prof. govt., 1984-88, prof. govt., 1988—, Barker-Oakes disting. prof. social scis., 1991—97. Polit. cons., Fayette, 1981—. Author: Covert Operations and the Emergence of the Modern American Presidency 1920-1960, 2003, Covert Operations as A Tool of Presidential Foreign Policy from 1800 to 1920, 2000; contbr. chpt. to book, articles to profl. jours. Contbg. mem. Dem. Nat. Com., Washington, 1993-2000; mem. Mo. Dem. Party, Jefferson City, 1978-20034. Recipient John F. Kincaid Edn. Achievement award Ctrl. Meth. Coll., 1994, Wye summer fellowship Aspen Inst., 1993. Mem. Am. Polit. Sci. Assn., Am. Acad. Polit. Sci., Mo. Polit. Sci. Assn., Masons, Pi Gamma Mu (appointed regional gov. 1992, Disting. Svc. award 1991), Phi Kappa Phi, Pi Sigma Alpha. Methodist. Avocation: chess. Home: PO Box 449 Fayette MO 65248-0449 Office: Ctrl Meth Coll 411 Central Methodist Sq Fayette MO 65248-1129 E-mail: jcarter@cmc.edu.

CARTER, JULIA MARIE, secondary education educator; b. Topeka, May 2, 1958; d. Jack Earnest and Bonita Aileen (Hatfield) Estes; m. Dan W. Carter; children: John-Thomas, Jessica Raye. BA, Ouachita Bapt. U., 1982; MBA, U. Phoenix, 2003. Cert. tchr. K-12, Ark., Fla., Md., Va., Pa., Mich., Ohio, Iowa. Tchr. French Dunbar Jr. High, Little Rock, 1989-91; tchr. Mt. Vernon (Ark.) Schs., 1991; tchr. French Cathedral Sch., Little Rock, 1991-92; tchr. St. Mark's Episcopal Sch., Oakland Park, Fla., 1992-93; tchr. French Miramar (Fla.) High Sch., 1993-96, Benjamin Franklin Sch., 1996—98, West Village Acad., 1999—2000, Detroit Public Sch., 2000—01, Bettendorf (Iowa) Pub. Schs., 2001—, Davenport (Iowa) Pub. Schs., 2003—. Owner Carter's Ednl. Svcs.; author, presenter in field. Vol. Chicot Elem., Little Rock, 1989-90, Silver Lake Mid. Sch., North Lauderdale, Fla., 1992-93, Miramar High Sch., 1993-95; mem. Ednl. Materials Equality Com., Little Rock, 1990-91. Fullbright scholar, 1989. Mem. Am. Assn. Tchrs. French (Prof. du Laureat 1989, 92), Am. Fedn. Tchrs. Democrat. Methodist. Avocations: traveling, historic research, writing.

CARTER, KIMBERLY FERREN, nursing educator; b. Wheeling, W.Va., July 15, 1963; d. Donald Ray and Nan Shaw Ferren; m. Gregory Lawrence Carter; children: Leanna, Brandon. Diploma, Ohio Valley Gen. Hosp. Sch. Nursing, Wheeling, W.Va., 1984; BSN, Radford U., 1986; MSN, U. Va., 1987, PhD, 1997. Cert. breast health facilitator Am. Cancer Soc.; RN; cert. 2nd Degree Reiki practitioner. Pub. health nurse educator Cen. Shenandoah Health Dist., Staunton, Va., 1987—88; nursing edn. specialist edn. and health promotion Kennestone Regional Health Care Sys., Marietta, Ga., 1988—90; asst. prof. nursing West Ga. Coll., Carrollton, Ga., 1990—92; from instr. to asst. to assoc. prof. Radford U., Va., 1992—. Bd. dir. Salem Rsch. Inst.; bd. rev. Advances in Nursing Sci., Fredericksburg, 1999—; rsch. cons. VA Med. Ctr., Salem, 1997—2002. Contbr. profl. stds. document Essentials of Baccalaureate Nursing Ed. for Entry Level Cmty./Pub. Health Nursing (C/PHN)., 2000; author: (book) Documenting health assessment findings: an applications module, 1995, Instructor's Guide and Test Bank for Sims, 1995. Mem. Roanoke Valley Task Force on Homelessness, Roanoke, 1996—. Recipient Am. Cancer Soc. award for Outstanding Svc. and Commitment to Breast Cancer Detection, 1999; grantee curriculum devel. grant, Helene Fuld Health Trust, 2001—03, faculty seed grantee, Radford U., 1999, faculty rsch. grantee, 1997. Mem.: Phi Kappa Phi, Sigma Theta Tau (corr. sec. 1996—2000, 2002—). Office: Radford U Box 6964 Radford VA 24142 Office Fax: 540-831-7716. Business E-Mail: kcarter@radford.edu.

CARTER, MAE RIEDY, retired academic official, consultant; b. Berkeley, Calif., May 20, 1921; d. Carl Joseph and Avis Blanche (Rodehaver) Riedy; m. Robert C. Carter, Aug. 19, 1944; children: Catherine, Christin Ann. BS, U. Calif., Berkeley, 1943. Ednl. adviser, then program specialist div. continuing edn. U. Del., Newark, 1968-78; asst. provost women's affairs, exec. dir. status of women Office Women's Affairs, U. Del., 1978-86; mem. adv. bd. Rockefeller Family Grant Project, 1979-83. Regional v.p. Del. PTA, 1960-62; pres. Friends Newark Free Library, 1968-69; mem. fiscal planning com. Newark Spl. Sch. Dist., 1972. Author: Research on Seeing and Evaluating People, 1982, (with Geis and Butler) Seeing and Evaluating People, 1982, revised, 1986, (with Haslett and Geis) The Organizational Woman: Power and Paradox, 1992, also papers and reports in field. Recipient Outstanding Svc. award Women's Coordinating Coun., 1977, 79, Spl. Recognition award Nat. U. Extension Assn., 1977, award for credit programs, 1971, Creative Programming award, 1971, medal of distinction U. Del., 1998; AAUW grantee, 1968; Fulbright grantee, 1976; named to Del. Women Hall of Fame, 1995. Mem. AAUW (past br. pres.), LWV, NOW, Women's Legal Def. Fund, Nat. Women's Polit. Caucus. Democrat. Home: 604 Dallam Rd Newark DE 19711-3110

CARTER, MARTHA ELOISE, retired curriculum specialist, reading consultant; b. Fulton, Miss., Aug. 9, 1935; d. Charles Tilmon and Vola Mae (Warren) Cooper; m. Hubert W. Carter, Aug. 3, 1957 (div.); 1 child, Bryan W. BS, U. Wis., 1957, MA, 1971. Classroom tchr. Milw. Pub. Schs., 1957-73, reading supr., 1973-76, generalist, supr., 1976-83, curriculum specialist in reading, 1983-95. Cons. New Reading Program, N.Y.C., 1993-94; adv. bd. Cardinal Stritch Coll., Milw., 1992-94; mem. tchrs. as readers com. Internat. Reading Assn., Newark, Del., 1994-97. Sunday sch. tchr., choir mem. Bapt. ch. Recipient Celebrate Literacy award Internat. Reading Assn. and Milw. Area Reading Coun., 1992; named Woman of Yr., Bd. Christian Edn., 1990. Mem. ASCD, Wis. State Reading Assn., Milw. Area Reading Coun., Phi Delta Kappa, Delta Kappa Gamma (corr. sec. 1994-95). Home: 3867 N 68th St Milwaukee WI 53216-2009 Office: Mt Zion Child Devel Ctr PO Box 12545 Milwaukee WI 53212-0545

CARTER, PAMELA LEE, program administrator; b. Indpls., Sept. 29, 1949; d. Bernard Marsh and Virginia Lee (Rigsby) Fisher; m. Michael Carter, Aug. 19, 1975. BS in Elem. Edn., Ball State U., 1971, MA, 1973; postgrad., various univs. Cert. tchr., Mich. Kindergarten tchr. Lynn (Ind.) Elem. Sch., 1971-74, Padgett Elem. Sch., Lakeland, Fla., 1974; substitute tchr. Farmington (Mich.) and Clarenceville (Mich.) Pub. Schs., 1975-76; kindergarten tchr. Waverly Community Schs., Lansing, Mich., 1976-86, K-12 curriculum coord., 1985-96, dir. strategic planning, 1996-2000; dir. healthy families program Women's Resource Ctr. of Livingston County, Brighton, Mich., 2000—. Nat. lecture staff Gesell Inst. Human Devel., New Haven, Conn., 1986—; resource counselor Willoway Summer Day Camp, Wixom, Mich., 1976; assoc. dir. Meadowbrook Woods Learning Ctr., Novi, Mich., 1975; child devel. cons. Northland Pioneer Coll., Holbrook, Ariz., 1975. Contbr. articles to profl. jours. Named Outstanding Early Childhood Specialist Cen. Mich. Assn. for Edn. Young Children, 1985, Outstanding Young Educator Waverly Jaycees, 1980, Gov.'s Quality Care award Waverly Cmty. Schs. Child Care Program, 2000. Mem. ASCD, Nat. Assn. Edn. Young Children, Assn. for Childhood Edn. Internat., Sierra Club. Avocations: reading, hiking, cross country skiing, bicycling, travel. Office: Womens Resource Ctr Livingston County 2980 Dorr Rd Brighton MI 48116 E-mail: pcarter@wrc-livingston.org .

CARTER, PAULA STANLEY, special education educator; b. Wilmington, N.C., Nov. 29, 1950; d. Lawrence Paul and Theresa Olivia (Bullard) S.; m. Stanley Wayne Carter, Sept. 13, 1975; 1 child, Marina Kostyleva (dec.). Student, U. N.C., 1969-71; BA in Theology, Berkshire Christian Coll., 1974; MEd, U. North Fla., 1979. Cert. K-12 spl. learning disabilities, gifted and acad. talented tchr., ESOL tchr.; cert. mentor internship program; cert. clin. effectiveness trainer. Tchr., vol. assoc. Ogden Christian Acad., Wilmington, N.C., 1972-73; thcr. pre-sch. neurol. impaired Southbury (Conn.) Tng. Sch., 1973-74; GED tchr. Fla. Jr. Coll., Jacksonville, 1975-76; presch. tchr. United Cerebral Palsy, Jacksonville, 1976-78; career counselor City of Jacksonville, 1978-81; exceptional edn. tchr. Duval County Schs., Jacksonville, 1981—, tchr., 1998—2002. Cons., advisor Nursing Home Adv. Bd., Jacksonville, 1986-88; rep. Duval Tchrs. Assn., Jacksonville, 1992-93. Author: Parent-Student Handbook John Love Elementary, 1991, Elementary Government - Magnet Program Course, 1991, Tips for Teachers of E.S.E. Students, 1993, Classroom Motivator Henry F. Kite Elementary School, 1994. Pres. Advent Christian Youth Assn., Wilmington, 1967-69; pres. Coun. on Aging/Advocates, Jacksonville, 1986-88; v.p. Opportunity Devel., Inc., Jacksonville, 1985-90; rep. Telethon Easter Seals Assn., Jacksonville, 1981-90; rep., vol. Duval Assn. Retarded Citizens Spl. Olympics, Jacksonville, 1974-79; vol. civic, polit., tchr. assns., 1974—; host parent Edn. Exch. Program, 1981-96; tchr. single adult denomination Sunday Sch.; active Under BluePrint 2000 Goal V, Fla., 1995-96; chair Victory Over Violence program Duval County Sch. # 37, 1995-96, safety patrol dir., chair Zeroing Prevention Drug Abuse; pres. PTA, 2001—. Fellowship grantee Advent Christian Delegation, Wilmington, 1969; recipient Supt.'s Bronze Key Club award United Way Assn., Jacksonville, 1991-92, Cert. of Achievement Am. Fedn. Tchrs., AFL-CIO, 1993-94. Mem. ASCD, Coun. Exceptional Children, Dinsmore Improvement Assn., Delta Kappa Gamma (v.p. 1994-96, coord. coun. 1994-96, pres. 1992-96, pres. coord. coun. 1996-98, Pres.'s award 1994, pres. Beta Pi chpt. 1996-2001). Democrat. Baptist. Home: 7335 Thien St Jacksonville FL 32219 Office: Henry F Kite Magnet Elem Sch Gifted and Academ Talented 9430 Lem Turner Rd Jacksonville FL 32208-1569

CARTER, RICHARD DUANE, business educator; s. Herbert Duane and Edith Irene (Richardson) C.; m. Nancy Jean Cannell, Sept. 3, 1955; 1 child, Erich Richardson. AB, Coll. William and Mary; MBA, Columbia U.; PhD, UCLA, 1968. Sr. advisor, dir. Taiwan Metal Industries Devel. Ctr. (under auspices of ILO), 1966-67; dir. UNDP, cons. svcs., Taiwan, 1966-67; chief exec. officer Human Resources Inst., Baton Rouge, La., 1968-70; liaison advisor Internat. Inst. Applied Systems Analysis, Vienna, Austria, 1975; U.S. rep., dir. indsl. mgmt. and cons. svcs. program UN Indsl. Devel. Orgn., Vienna, 1970-75; mem. East-West Trade and Mgmt. Commn., 1973-75; sr. advisor, dir. Korean Inst. Sci. and Tech. (under auspices of UN), Seoul, 1974-75; dean Sch. Bus. Quinnipiac Coll., Hamden, Conn., 1977-80; chmn. bd. TCG Industries, Inc., N.Y.C., 1980—; prof. mgmt., program coord. Fairfield (Conn.) U., 1980-84; founder, mng. dir. Internat. Mgmt. Consortium, Vienna, Westport and Millerton, N.Y., 1975—; assoc. mem. Seminar on Orgn. and Mgmt. Columbia U., 1975-89, vice-chmn. Seminar on Orgn. and Mgmt., 1976-89, chmn. rsch. and publ. com. Seminar on Orgn. and Mgmt., 1983-89; mng. dir. Wainwright & Ramsey Securities, Inc., N.Y.C., 1985—. Mem. editorial bd. Indian Adminstrv. and Mgmt. Rev., New Delhi, 1974-76; author: Management: In Perspective and Practice, 1970, The Future Challenges of Management Education, 1981; also numerous articles and revs. Trustee Dingletown Community Ch., Greenwich, Conn., 1978-87; mem. adv. coun. Calif. Coll. Tech., L.A., 1978—. Recipient Disting. Alumni medallion (Olde Guarde), Coll. William and Mary, 2001. Fellow Internat. Acad. Mgmt.; mem. Acad. Mgmt., Am. Mgmt. Assns. (pres.'s council, dir. 1976-77), N.Am. Soc. Corp. Planning, N.Am. Mgmt. Coun. (bd. dirs. 1983-87), Soc. Internat. Orgn. Devel., Mensa, Triple Nine Soc., Explorers Club, Sharon (Conn.) Country Club, Beta Gamma Sigma.

CARTER, ROBERTA ECCLESTON, therapist, counselor; b. Pitts. d. Robert E. and Emily B. (Bucar) Carter; divorced; children: David Michael Kiewlich, Daniel Michael Kiewlich. Student, Edinboro State U., 1962-63; BS, California State U. Pa., 1966; MEd, U. Pitts., 1969; MA, Rosebridge Grad. Sch., 1987. Tchr. Bethel Park Sch. Dist., Pa., 1966-69; writer, media asst. Field Ednl. Pub., San Francisco, 1969-70; educator, counselor, specialist Alameda Unified Sch. Dist., Calif., 1970—. Master trainer Calif. State Dept. Edn., Sacramento, 1984—; personal growth cons., Alameda, 1983—. Author: People, Places and Products, 1970, Teaching/Learning Units, 1969; co-author: Teacher's Manual Let's Read, 1968. Mem. AAUW, NEA, Calif. Fedn. Bus. and Profl. Women (legis. chair Alameda br. 1984-85, membership chair 1985), Calif. Edn. Assn., Alameda Edn. Assn., Charter Planetary Soc., Oakland Mus., Exploratorium, Big Bros of East Bay, Alameda C. of C. (svc. awsard 1985). Avocations: aerobics, gardening, travel. Home: 1516 Eastshore Dr Alameda CA 94501-3118

CARTER, SALLY PACKLETT, elementary education educator; b. Clovis, N.Mex., May 15, 1948; d. Charles Everett and Marion Jamie Gee; m. Leonard Gene Carter, Mar. 7, 1969; 1 child, Dale Lee. BS in Edn., Ctrl. Mo. State U., 1969, MS in Edn., 1981. Cert. vocat. home econs. grades 7-12, elem. edn. grades K-6, Mo., K-8 elem. edn., home econs. grades 7-12, Ariz., EA/sci., nat. bd. cert. tchr. Home econ. tchr. Deepwater (Mo.) High Sch., 1969-71; tchr. grade 7 Deepwater (Mo.) Sch., 1971-73; tchr. grades 1 and 2 Davis R-12, Clinton, Mo., 1974-80; tchr. grade 5 Southeast Elem., Clinton, 1980-96; substitute tchr. Mesa, Ariz., 1996-97; tchr. grade 6 Fountain Hills (Ariz.) Middle Sch., 1997—. Mem. Mo. State Tchrs. (pres. ctrl. dist. 1989-90), Clinton Tchrs. Assn. (pres. 1985, 90, 92), Ariz. Edn. Assn., VFW Ladies Aux. Post 1894, Delta Kappa Gamma (1st v.p. Mu. chpt. 1992-94, pres. Mu. chpt. 1994-96, Alpha Epsilon chpt. 1996—, 1st v.p. 2002—), Phi Kappa Phi. Avocations: reading, fishing, cooking, sewing. Home: 6316 E Quartz St Mesa AZ 85215-0943

CARTER, SHIRLEY RAEDELLE, retired elementary school educator; b. Pueblo, Colo., Oct. 28, 1937; d. John Clay and Velda Edythe (Bussard) Apple; m. Carrol Joseph Carter, Apr. 26, 1958; children: Margaret Carol, Norma Katherine, Michael Clay. AA in Edn., Pueblo Jr. Coll., 1957; BA in Elem. Edn., Adams State Coll., 1960, MA in Elem. Edn., 1971. Cert. tchr., Colo. 2d and 3d grade tchr. Beulah (Colo.) Elem. Sch., 1957-58; 3d grade tchr. Westcliffe (Colo.) Elem. Sch., 1961-62; substitute tchr. Dist. RE 11J, Alamosa, Colo., 1974-77; 6th grade English tchr. Evans Intermediate Sch., Alamosa, 1977-78, 5th grade English tchr., 1978-80; 5th grade tchr. Evans Elem. Sch., Alamosa, 1980-90, 4th grade tchr., 1990-95; ret., 1995. Owner Shirley's Selectables Joe's Junk, Creede, Colo., 1993—.k Editor, pub. newspaper Evans Eagle, 1984, newspaper anns. Tasanti, 1957, El Conquestor, 1959. Leader San Luis Valley Girl Scout Columbine Coun., 1972-77, adult trainer, 1974-87; dir. San Luis Valley Girl Scout Camp, 1974-75, program dir., 1976-87; parish Coun. Sacred Heart Ch., Alamosa, Colo., 1982-84. Mem. Creede C. of C. (bd. dirs. 1994-96), Internat. Reading Assn. (bd. dirs. San Luis Valley chpt. 1980-90, pres., 1983-84, presenter Colo. Coun. 1982-88, Sweetheart 1985-86, 90-91). Democrat. Roman Catholic. Avocations: reading, wood carving, collecting. Home: PO Box 53 Creede CO 81130-0053

CARTER, TERRI GAY MANNS, Latin language educator; b. Centralia, Ill., Jan. 8, 1954; d. William Henry and Alfrieda (Kramer) Manns; m. Jerry William Carter, July 16, 1977; children: Emily Ann, Jerry William. BA, Tex. Tech U., 1975; MEd, U. North Tex., 1991, EdD, 1997. Secondary sch. Latin tchr. Big Spring (Tex.) Ind. Sch. Dist., 1975-78, Conroe (Tex.) Ind. Sch. Dist., 1978-89, Grapevine (Tex.)-Colleyville Ind. Sch. Dist., 1989-98, curriculum writer, 1991—, insvc. preparer, 1992, chair dept. fgn. lang., 1994-98, asst. prin., 1998—. Lay minister Emmanuel Presbyn. Ch., Bedford, Tex., 1991-92. Mem. Classical Assn. So. U.S., Tex. Classical Assn., Am. Classical League, Tex. Fgn. Lang. Assn., Tex. Assn. for Gifted and Talented. Democrat. Avocation: reading. Home: 2600 Knoll Trl Euless TX 76039-2044 Office: Grapevine High Sch 3223 Mustang Dr Grapevine TX 76051-5998

CARTER, T(HOMAS) BARTON, law educator; b. Dallas, Aug. 6, 1949; s. Sydney Hobart and Josephine (Wren) C.; m. Eleonore Dorothy Alexander, June 3, 1978 (div. 1988); 1 child, Richard Alexander. BA in Psychology, Yale U., 1971; JD, U. Pa., 1974; MS in Mass Communication, Boston U., 1978. Bar: Mass. 1974, U.S. Dist. Ct. Mass. 1975, U.S. Ct. Appeals (1st cir.) 1975. Asst. prof. law Boston U., 1979-85, assoc. prof., 1985-96, prof., 1996—; pvt. practice Boston, 1974—. Pres. Tanist Broadcasting Corp., Boston, 1981—2001. Co-author: The First Amendment and the Fourth Estate, 1985, 8th edit., 2000, The First Amendment and the Fifth Estate, 1986, 6th edit., 2003, Mass Communications Law in a Nutshell, 1988, 5th edit., 2000. Mem. ABA, Assn. for Edn. in Journalism and Mass Comm. (clk. 1981-82, asst. head 1982-83, head 1983-84), Broadcast Edn. Assn. (chair law and policy divsn. 1989-90), Fed. Comm. Bar Assn., Univ. Club. Avocation: bridge. Home: 109 Commonwealth Ave Apt 6 Boston MA 02116-2345 Office: Boston U 640 Commonwealth Ave Boston MA 02215-2422 E-mail: comlaw@bu.edu.

CARTER, YVONNE JOHNSON, writer, editor, English educator; d. John Miller and Lorraine Johnson; m. Vernon L. Carter, Jr.. BA cum laude, St. Paul's Coll., 1971; MA, U. Md., 1979; PhD, Howard U., 1994. Contract specialist Dept. Def., Richmond, Va., 1972-75; edn. reporter Washington Afro-Am. Newspaper, 1980-82; writer-editor U.S. Army Engr. Sch., 1982-83, U.S. Dept. Army, Alexandria, Va., 1983-84; sr. editor Nat. Def. U., Washington, 1984-85; writer-editor USIA, Washington, 1985-91; lectr. Bowie (Md.) State U., 1994-96; writer-editor U.S. EEOC, Washington, 1995—. Mem. Fed. Comm. Network, Washington, 1997—. Editor: The United States and the World Economy, 1984; editor (periodical) The Civil Rights Movement and the Legacy of Dr. King, 1989, (periodical) Two Cultures, Shared Values: Nigeria and the U.S., 1990; author (periodical) EEOC Mission, 1995—. Mem. Habitat for Humanity, Atlanta, 1999, Corcoran Gallery Art, Washington, 1999, Nat. Hist. Preservation Soc., Washington, 1999, Smithsonian, Washington, 1999, Libr. of Congress Assocs., 1999, Fed. Comms. Network, Washington, 1999. Fellow U. Md., 1978; Ivan Earle Taylor scholar Howard U., 1992. Mem. AAUP, AAUW, Alpha Kappa Alpha. Democrat. Baptist. Office: EEOC 1801 L St NW Washington DC 20036-3811

CARTER-JONES, SHEILA LORRAINE, secondary school educator; b. Pitts., May 12, 1950; d. D. Frank and Marcia Lavine (Mason) Carter; m. Bruce Arnold Jones, July 28, 1985. BA, Carnegie-Mellon U., 1972; MEd, U. Pitts., 1980, postgrad., 1992—. Tchr. English Bd. Pub. Edn., Pitts., 1972—. Site liaison for student tchrs. Bd. Pub. Edn., Pitts., 1994—; cons. SGI Culture Dept., 1990—, Scholastic Reading Achievement, Tchr. Expectation and Student Achievement, Pitts., 1980-83; tchr. cons. Western Pa. writing project, Pitts., 1989—, Braddock Hist. Soc., Pitts., 1990—. Contbr. poems to Tri-state Anthology, 1991, Pennsylvania Review, 1994, Pittsburgh Quarterly, 1994. Mem. Nat. Coun. Tchrs. English (sessions coord. 1994). Avocations: water coloring, refinishing antiques, tile-mosaic murals. Home: 118 Dunlap St Pittsburgh PA 15214-2023

CARTLIDGE, SHRILEY ANN BELL, school administrator; b. Indianola, Miss., July 26, 1940; d. Albert and Betty (Newsome) Bell; 1 child, Carol W. Rowe; m. Arthur J. Cartlidge. BS, Miss. Valley State U., Itta Bena, 1964; MEd, Delta State U., Cleveland, Miss., 1975. Tchr. English Greenville (Miss.) Pub. Schs., 1964-93, chmn. dept. English, 1971-87, dist. chmn. dept. English, 1987-93; instr. supr. Yazoo City (Miss.) Schs., 1993-94, chpt. 1 coord., 1994-96; dir. fed. programs, 1996—. Tchr./cons. Writing Across the Curriculum, MAS (state testing sys.). Bd. dirs. Miss. PTA, 1987—, v.p. edn., 1993-95, editor bull., 1993-95, state treas., 1995—. Mem. NEA, Nat. Coun. Tchrs. English, Internat. Reading Assn., Miss. Assn. Sch. Adminstrs.,

Eta Phi Beta (past pres., sec.). Baptist. Avocation: reading. Office: Yazoo City Mcpl School 1133 Calhoun Ave Yazoo City MS 39194-2939

CARTMAN, SHIRLEY ELEISE, retired music educator; b. Chgo., June 27, 1931; d. Johnny Theophilus Cartman and Hattie Lee Marshall. BS in Music Edn., U. Ill., 1950—53; M in Bus. Mgmt. and Supervision, Ctrl. Mich. U., 1977—78. Cert. tchg. cert. Wash., 1960, provisional tchg. cert. Gary Cmty. Sch. Corp., 1966, life tchg. cert. Ga. Dept. Edn., 1987. 4th grade tchr. Clover Park Sch. Dist., Tacoma, 1960—64; strings tchr. Gary (Wash.) Cmty. Sch. Co-op., 1965—70; music tchr. Prince Georges C.C., Camp Springs, Md., 1973—74; orch. tchr. Dekalb County Bd. of Edn., Decatur, Ga., 1989—91; string ensemble prof. Spelman Coll., Atlanta, 1998—99; music conservatory directress Chapel Hill Harvester Ch., Decatur, Ga., 1992—96; strings instr. New Birth Missionary Bap. Ch. Faith Acad. Sc., Decatur, Ga., 1997—2000. Talent coord. for talented Youth of Gary, Ind., 1968—70; cons. "Jackson Five" Steel Town Record C., Gary, 1967—68; mgr. New Generation Band, New Experience Bank, Decatur, 1985—87; first lady of gospel violin various churches throughout Atlanta area, 2000—01; pt. time strings instr. DeKalb County (Ga.) Bd. Edn., 2000—01; creator, designer The Cartman Fun Music Curriculum Greenforest McCalep Early Learning Ctr., Decatur, Ga. Musician (profl. entertainer): Shelia Carr, 1970; musician: (songwriter) (songs) Lonely Heart, 1968 (Sung by the Jackson Five, 1972); author: (children's short story collection) Stolen Key, 1974, A Teacher Remembers the Jacksons, 1987, 4 children's music books; designer and creator (songs books and teaching aids) The Cartman Fun Music Method, 2002; author: tiny-tot music books for children. SP4 U.S. Army, 1974—75, Fort Mead, Md. Mem.: NAACP (life; ACT-SO chairperson 2000—02, Plaque for Svc. as ACT-SO chairperson 2000—01). Democrat. Avocation: travel. Home: 3945 Johns Hopkins Ct Decatur GA 30034 Office: Cartman Music Studio 3945 Johns Hopkins Ct Decatur GA 30034 Office Fax: 678-418-0166.

CARTON, CRISTINA SILVA-BENTO, elementary educator; b. Santiago, Beira Alta, Portugal, Jan. 23, 1928; came to U.S. Jan. 4, 1936; d. Mario Antunes and Alice (Silva) Bento; m. Jorge Luis Rodriguez; children: A. James DeCosta, Robert J. DeCosta, Wanda Rodriguez. BA, Queens Coll., 1968, MS, 1973; MA, SUNY, Stony Brook, 1983. Cert. elem. tchr. N.Y., Fla., ESOL tchr. Fla. Tchr. Our Lady of Loretto, Hempstead, N.Y., 1961-66, Hempstead Pub. Schs., Hempstead, 1968-70, Cen. Islip (N.Y.) Pub. Schs., 1970-87, Broward County Pub. Schs., Ft. Lauderdale, Fla., 1988—2000; drop out prevention coord., lead tchr. Pines Mid. Sch., 1990—92, tchr. ESL coord., 1992—96; drop out prevention 6th grade tchr. Silver Trail Mid. Sch., 1996-98, 6th grade health and sci. tchr., 1998—99, tchr., 1999—2000; ret., 2000. Instr. philosophy Barry U., Miami, 1989-90. Mem. Nat. Cancer Assn., Stony Brook, N.Y., 1971-73; internat. chairperson AAUW, Stony Brook, 1970-73; fund raiser Dem. Party, Selden, N.Y., 1976. Recipient Fellowship for Study Abroad Gulbenkian Found., 1967. Mem. Nat. Edn. Assn., N.Y. State Tchrs. Assn., Cen. Islip Tchrs. Assn., Parent Tchrs. Assn. (membership chair 1970-75), Kappa Delta Pi, Phi Delta Kappa. Democrat. Avocations: travel, painting, reading, opera, ballet. Home: 410 NE 45th St Fort Lauderdale FL 33334-2314

CARTWRIGHT, CAROL ANN, university president; b. Sioux City, Iowa, June 19, 1941; d. Carl Anton and Kathryn Marie (Weishapple) Becker; m. G. Phillip Cartwright, June 11, 1966; children: Catherine E., Stephen R., Susan D. BS in Early Childhood Edn., U. Wis., Whitewater, 1962; MEd in Spl. Edn., U. Pitts., 1965, PhD in Spl. Edn., Ednl. Rsch., 1968. From instr. to assoc. prof. Coll. Edn. Pa. State U., University Park, 1968-72, from assoc. prof. to prof., 1972-79, dean acad. affairs, 1981-84, dean undergrad. program, vice provost, 1984-88; vice chancellor acad. affairs U. Calif., Davis, 1988-91, prof. human devel., 1988-91; pres. Kent (Ohio) State U., 1991—. Trustee Akron Reg. Devel. Bd., 1991—, Akron Gen. Med. Ctr., 1991—; bd. dirs. First Energy Corp. (formerly Ohio Edison), Akron, 1992—, Republic Engineered Steels, Inc., Massillon, Ohio, 1992—. Editorial bd. Topics in Early Childhood Special Education, 1982-88, Exceptional Education Quarterly, 1982-88. Pres., bd. dirs. Child Devel. Coun. of Center County, Title XX Day Care Contractor, 1977-80; bd. dirs. Center County United Way, State College, Pa., 1984-88, Urban League of Greater Cleve., 1997—; bd. mem. Davis (Calif.) Art Ctr., 1988-91, Davis Sci. Ctr., 1989-91; bd. dirs. Ohio divsn. Am. Cancer Soc., 1993-2000, nat. bd. dirs., 1993—. Mem. AAUW, Am. Coun. Edn., Am. Ednl. Rsch. Assn., Am. Assn. for Higher Edn., Nat. Assn. State Univs. and Land-Grant Colls., Coun. for Exceptional Children. Roman Catholic. Avocations: walking, reading, traveling. Home: 1703 Woodway Rd Kent OH 44240-5917 Office: Kent State U Office of the President PO Box 5190 Kent OH 44242-0001 E-mail: carol.cartwright@kent.edu.

CARTWRIGHT, TALULA ELIZABETH, writing and leadership educator, consultant; b. Asheville, N.C., Oct. 25, 1947; d. Ralph and Sarah Helen (Medford) C.; m. Edwin Byram Crabtree, May 23, 1976 (div. Sept. 1984); children: Charity, Baxter; m. Richard Thomas Legan, Apr. 27, 1986; 1 child, Isaac. BA, U. N.C., 1971, MEd, 1974, EdD, 1988. Instr. McDowell Tech. Inst., Marion, N.C., 1972-73, Guilford Tech. C.C., Jamestown, N.C., 1973-89, Guilford Coll., Greensboro, N.C., 1982-87, U. N.C.-Greensboro, 1982-87, N.C. A&T State U., Greensboro, 1984-85. With Communication Assocs., Lenoir, Shelby, Asheboro, Greensboro, 1981—; dean continuing edn. Caldwell C.C., Lenoir, N.C., 1989-92; v.p. acad. programs Cleve. C.C., 1992-95; sr. faculty and program mgr. Ctr. for Creative Leadership, Greensboro, N.C., 1996—; bd. dirs Carolinas Quality Consortium, 1993-95, N.C. Quality Coun., 1994-95; chmn. bd. dirs. Cleve. Abuse Prevention Coun., 1993-95. Tchr. of Yr. award Guilford Tech. C.C. Edn. Assn., 1982, Edn. Honor Roll award 1989; winner Human Rights Writing Contest, 1988, 89. Mem. NCAE (pres. local unit 1988-89, chmn. higher edn. commn. 1989-90, 92-95), Am. Assn. Women in C.C., Women's Adminstrs. in N.C. (exec. bd. 1995).

CARUANA, JOAN, educator, psychotherapist, nurse; b. Bklyn., Dec. 11, 1941; d. Gaetano and Fanny Caruana. BS, Boston Coll., 1964; MA, NYU, 1975; grad., Psychoanalytic Psychotherapy Study Ctr., 1992. RN, N.Y.; cert. clin. specialist in adult psychiat. mental health nursing, psychiat. nurse practitioner. Instr. St. Vincent's Hosp. Sch. Nursing, N.Y.C., 1965-99; psychotherapist N.Y.C., 1987—. Mem. St. Vincent's Hosp. Sch. Nursing Alumnae Assn. (editor newsletter 1978—, pres. 1998—). Office: 153 Waverly Pl 5th Fl New York NY 10014-3872

CARUSO, JOHN, JR., education and educational psychology educator; b. N.Y.C., Sept. 6, 1940; BA in History, U. Conn., 1962, MA in History, 1963, PhD, 1974; MS in Sociology, So. Conn. State U., 1974, MS in Counseling, 1979, MA in Ednl. Tech., 1986. Cert. 7-12 social studies tchr., N.Y., elem. edn. supr., Conn. Chair edn. and ednl. psychology Western Conn. State U., Danbury, 1969—, dir. Ctr. Profl. Devel., 1997—. Vis. prof. U. Md., Asia, 1974-75, U. So. Calif., Asia, 1976-77; dir. internat. programs U. Nev., Las Vegas, 1982-83. Served to 1st lt. U.S. Army, 1963-65. Fulbright scholar Yonsei U., Seoul, Korea, 1981; recipient doctoral fellowship State of Conn., 1968, fellowship NEH, 1979, fellowship Yale U., 1986, 87, Goethe award FCI, 1974. Mem. Phi Delta Kappa, Phi Alpha Theta, Phi Kappa Phi. Office: WCSU 181 White St Danbury CT 06810-6826 Business E-Mail: carusoj@wcsu.edu.

CARUSO, KAY ANN PETE, elementary education educator; b. New Orleans, Sept. 23, 1944; d. John R. and Dorothy E. (LeBlanc) Pete; m. Frank J. Caruso III, Nov. 11, 1967; 1 child, Brian Joseph. BA, Southeastern La. U., 1966; MEd, U. New Orleans, 1981. Tchg. cert. La. Elem. tchr., libr., tchr. 5th grade reading Jefferson Parish Pub. Sch. Sys., Metairie, La., 1966—. Sec. Brother Martin H.S. Parent Club, New Orleans, 1992-94; tchr. rep. Alice Birney Sch. Parent/Tchr. Group, Metairie, 1979-83, 96-97; vol. Rep. Nat. Conv., New Orleans, 1990. Named tchr. of yr. Jefferson Parish C. of C. 1988, 95-96; recipient Barbara McNamara award for reading promotion Reading Is Fundamental program, 1989, Disting. Tchg. award Gifted and Talented Program Northwestern State U., 1995. Mem. AAUW (sec. 1996-98, v.p. 1998—), Jefferson Librs. Assn. (v.p., pres. 1984-88), Jefferson Fedn. Tchrs. (librs. chpt. rep. 1985-87, Ret. Tchrs. chpt. sec. and charter mem.), So. Assn. Colls. and Schs. (evaluator, com. chair 1980-98), AAUW (chpt. sec. 1996-98, v.p. 1998—, name grant honoree 1996), Jefferson Geneal. Soc. (sec. 2001—), Delta Kappa Gamma (chpt. sec. 1984-86, v.p. 1988-90, pres. 1994-98, dir. South dist. 1997—, state treas. 2001—). Avocations: reading, travel, geneaology. Office: Alice Birney Elem Sch 4829 Hastings St Metairie LA 70006-2676

CARVER, DOROTHY LEE ESKEW (MRS. JOHN JAMES CARVER), retired secondary education educator; b. Brady, Tex., July 10, 1926; d. Clyde Albert and A. Maurine (Meadows) Eskew; m. John James Carver, Feb. 26, 1944; children: John James, Sheila Carver Bentley, Chuck, David. Student, So. Oreg. Coll., 1942-43, Coll. Eastern Utah, 1965-67; BA, U. Utah, Hayward, 1968; MA, Cal. State Coll. at Hayward, 1970; postgrad., Mills Col., 1971. Instr. Rutherford Bus. Coll., Dallas, 1944-45; sec. Adolph Coors Co., Golden, Colo., 1945-47; instr. English Coll. Eastern Utah, Price, 1968-69; instr. speech Modesto (Calif.) Jr. Coll., 1970-71; instr. personal devel. men and women Heald Bus. Colls., Oakland, Calif., 1972-74, dean curricula Walnut Creek, Calif., 1974-86; instr. Diablo Valley Coll., Pleasant Hill, Calif., 1986-87, Contra Costa Christian H.S., 50 1992; ret., 1992. Communications cons. Oakland Army Base, Crocker Bank, U.S. Steel, I. Magnin, Artec Internat.; presenter in field. Author: Developing Listening Skills. Mem. Gov.'s Conf. on Higher Edn. in Utah, 1968; mem. finance com. Coll. Eastern Utah, 1967-69; active various cmty. drives; bd. dirs. Opportunity Ctr., Symphony of the Mountain;; pres. adv. bd. Walnut Creek Srs., 1998—. Mem. AAUW, Bus. and Profl. Womens Club, Nat. Assn. Deans and Women Adminstrs., Delta Kappa Gamma. Episcopalian (supt. Sunday Sch. 1967-69). Clubs: Soroptimist Internat. (pres. Walnut Creek 1979-80, sec., founder region 1978-80); Order Eastern Star. Home: 20 Coronado Ct Walnut Creek CA 94596-5801

CARVER, M. KYLE, secondary education educator; Tchr. sci. A.C. Reynolds Mid. Sch., Asheville, N.C., 1976-2000. Mem. bd. trustees Mars Hill Coll., 1977—, N.C. Ednl. Coun. for Exceptional Children, 1986-94. First runner-up Outstanding Earth Sci. Tchr. N.C., 1992. Office: A C Reynolds Middle Sch 2 Rocket Dr Asheville NC 28803-9100

CASAD, ROBERT CLAIR, legal educator; b. Council Grove, Kans., Dec. 8, 1929; s. Clair L. and Eula Imogene (Compton) C.; m. Sally Ann McKeighan, Aug. 20, 1955; children: Benjamin Nathan, Joseph Story, Robert Clair, Madeleine Imogene. AB, U. Kans., 1950, MA, 1952; JD with honors, U. Mich., 1957; S.JD, Harvard U., 1979. Bar: Kans. 1957, Minn. 1958, U.S. Dist. Ct. Kans. 1957; U.S. Ct. Appeals (10th cir.) 1985. Instr. law U. Mich., Ann Arbor, 1957-58; assoc. firm Streater & Murphy, Winona, Minn., 1958-59; asst. prof. law U. Kans., Lawrence, 1959-62, assoc. prof., 1962-64, prof., 1964-81, John H. and John M. Kane prof. law, 1981-97; John H. and John M. Kane prof. law emeritus, 1997. Vis. prof. UCLA, 1969—70, U. Ill., 1973—74, U. Calif., Hastings, 1979—80, U. Colo., 1982, U. Vienna, 1986, U. Mich., 1986, U. Valladolid, 1988, Chuo U., 1992, U. Salamanca, 1995, Emory U., 2001—02. Author: Jurisdiction and Forum Selection, 1988, 2d edit., 1999, Jurisdiction in Civil Actions, 1983, 2d edit., 1991, (with Richman) 3d edit., 1998, Expropriation Procedures in Central America and Panama, 1975, (with others) Kansas Appellate Practice, 1978, Civil Judgment Recognition and the Integration of Multiple State Associations, 1982, Res Judicata in a Nutshell, 1976; (with Fink and Simon) Civil Procedure: Cases and Materials, 2d edit., 1989, (with Gard) Kansas Code of Civil Procedure Annotated, 3rd edit., 1997, (with Clermont) Res Judicata: A Handbook on its Theory, Doctrine and Practice, 2001; contbr. numerous articles to legal jours. Mem. civil code adv. com. Kans. Jud. Coun. 1st lt. USAF, 1952-53. Recipient Coblentz prize Sch. Law, U. Mich., 1957, Rice prize U. Kans. Law Sch., 1976, 83, 84, 88, 89, medal Dana Fund for Internat. and Comparative Legal Studies, 1981, Balfour Jeffrey Rsch. prize U. Kans., 1984; Ford fellow, 1965-66, fellow in law Harvard U., 1965-66, OAS fellow, 1976, NEH fellow, summer 1978; grantee Dana Fund for Internat. and Comparative Legal Studies. Mem. Am. Law Inst., ABA, Kans. Bar Assn., Order of Coif. Democrat. Home: 1130 Emery Rd Lawrence KS 66044-2515 E-mail: casad@ku.edu., crobkan@cs.com.

CASAMENTO, MARIA M. speech pathology/audiology services professional, special education educator; b. Hoboken, N.J., June 24, 1955; d. John Anthony and Margaret (Lilli) Mastromarino; m. Anthony Dominick Casamento, Aug. 22, 1987; 1 child, Keith Anthony. BA in Speech Pathology, Montclair State Coll., 1977. Speech correctionist Learning Ctr. for Exceptional Children, Ft. Lee, N.J., 1977-78; spl. edn. tchr. Fairview (N.J.) Pub. Schs., 1978-87; history and sci. educator Middlesex County Vocat. High Sch., Piscataway, N.J., 1987-88; speech specialist East Windsor (N.J.) Pub. Schs., 1988-89; art coord., cons. Attuned Images, Arlington, Tex., 1990—; speech, language pathologist Arlington (Tex.) Pub. Schs., 1991—. Project share developer, cons. Bergen County Dept. Edn., Leonia, N.J., 1982; mentor Arlington (Tex.) C. of C., 1991—. Mem. Autism Soc. Ft. Worth (recipient Mid-Cities chpt. award 1994). Avocation: art and dance enthusiast.

CASASENT, DAVID PAUL, electrical engineering educator, data processing executive; b. Washington, Dec. 8, 1942; s. Harold Kane and Delta (Fletchall) C.; m. Paula Timko; children: Candace, Erin, Maureen, Tod, Jon. BSEE, U. Ill., Urbana, 1964, MS, 1965, PhD, 1969. Prof. elec. engring. Carnegie Mellon U., Pitts., 1969—; pres. Unicorn Systems, Inc., Pitts., 1983—. Dir. Ctr. for Optical Data Processing, Pitts. Editor: Optical Data Processing, 1978; contbr. more than 600 articles to tech. jours. Recipient Thomas K. Benedict award AIAA, 1979; named George Westinghouse prof. Carnegie-Mellon U., 1980. Fellow IEEE (local pres. 1971-72, Barry Carlton award 1976), Optical Soc. Am. (local pres. 1975-77), Soc. Photo-Optical Instrumentation Engrs. (gov. 1982-85, 87-90, pres. 1993, exec. bd.), Internat. Neural Network Soc. (gov. 1992-95, 1998-00, pres. 1999). Republican. Roman Catholic. Avocations: travel, basketball, volleyball. Home: 133 Woodland Farms Rd Pittsburgh PA 15238-2021 Office: Carnegie Mellon U Dept Elec & Computer Engring Pittsburgh PA 15213-3890

CASAS-PARDO, JOSE, economics educator; b. Fonelas, Spain, Sept. 16, 1938; s. Eugenio Casas-Martinez and Eulalia Pardo-Pardo; m. Johanna Broda, Jan. 4, 1943 (div. 1976); 1 child, Ana; m. Amelia Garcia-Valdecasas Jimenez; children: Luis, Elena. LLB, Law Sch. of Granada, Spain, 1960, PhD in Law, 1967; BSc in Econs., London Sch. Econs., 1964; PhD, Madrid Sch. Econs., 1972. Asst. prof. Law Sch. of Granada, 1964-66; asst. econ. officer UN Secretariat, N.Y.C., 1967-68; assoc. prof. U. Valencia, Spain, 1968-69, prof. econs., 1978-81, 84—; assoc. prof. Autonomous U. Madrid, 1969-75, prof. econs., 1982-84; assoc. prof. Complutense U., Madrid, 1976-77; prof. econs. U. Salamanca, Spain, 1980-81, Open U., Madrid, 1981-82, also dir. dept. applied econs., Law Sch., 1988—. Econ. adviser, Bank of Granada, 1964-65; sec.-gen., Generalitat Valenciana, 1978-79; cons. European Expertise Svc.; sr. cons. Ukrainean Govt. Tacis Office European Commn., 1997. Author: Curso de Economia, 1981, Analisis Economico de lo Politoco, 1984; editor: Economia y Politica, 1987, Economic Effects of the European Expansion 1492-1824, 1992, Nueva Economia del Bienestar, 1995, Current Issues in Public Choices, 1995, New Welfare Economics, 1995, Las Limitaciones del Paradigma de la Elección Racional: Las Ciencias Sociales en la Encrucijada, 1998; contbr. articles to profl. jours. Lt. Spanish Army, 1958-61. Grantee, Spanish-Am. Com., Madrid, 1979-84, Liberty Fund, 1980, Brit. Coun., 1988, Erasmus Programme, European Community, Brussels, 1988. Fellow Institucio Valenciana d'Estudi e Investigacio; mem. Am. Econs. Assn., London Sch. Econs. Soc., European Pub. Choice Soc. (pres. 1994-95). Avocations: literature, films, travel. Home: Arquitecto Mora 3-2a 46010 Valencia Spain Office: U de Valencia Dept Economia Politica Edificio Dept Occidental Nou Campus Tarongers 46022 Valencia Spain Fax: 34-96-3828206. E-mail: jose.casas@uv.es.

CASCADDEN, CORINNE ELIZABETH, elementary school administrator; b. Berlin, N.H., Mar. 3, 1953; d. Henry T. and Noella (Bourbeau) Cote; m. Neil Cascadden; children: Joshua, Zachary. BS, Plymouth State Coll., 1975, MEd, 1982. Cert. elem. edn. tchr., elem. sch. prin., bilingual edn., N.H. Tchr. French, social studies, grades 5-8 Berlin Regional Cath. Sch., 1975-77; bilingual aide Burgess Sch., Berlin, 1977-78, tchr. grade 5, 1978-80; tchr. grade sch. Brown Sch., Berlin, 1980-86; prin. Berlin Pub. Schs., 1986—. Mentor N.H. Tchr. Induction, Concord, 1990—; leader Local N.H. Sch. Improvement Program, Concord, 1989-92; judge Odyssey of the Mind, 1991, 92. Contbr. to handbook: Franco American Studies, 1981. Recipient N.H. Outstanding Community Vol. award for Leathers Lane Community Playground, Gov. of N.H., Gold Circle Partnership Achievement award N.H. P.I.E., 1992, Blue Ribbon Achievement award, 1991, 92; N.H. Dept. Edn. grantee, 1987-88, No. N.H. Found./N.H. Charitable grantee, 1991. Mem. ASCD, New Eng. Reading Assn. (state rep. candidate exec. bd. 1993), Nat. Assn. Elem. Sch. Prins., N.H. Assn. Sch. Prins. Avocations: downhill skiing, reading, playing piano. Home: 1787 Hutchins St Berlin NH 03570-3509 Office: Brown Elem Sch 190 Norway St Berlin NH 03570-3049

CASE, ELIZABETH JOY, special education administrator; b. Phila., Oct. 12, 1948; d. Edward N. and Helene (LeBlanc) C. BS in Edn./Spl. Edn., Ashland Coll., 1970; MA in Spl. Edn., Fairfield U., 1975; PhD, U. N.Mex., 1985. Cert. tchr. spl. edn. K-12, regular edn. K-12, adminstr. Tchr. second grade Mansfield (Ohio) Pub. Schs., 1969-70; supr., tchr. spl. edn. Greenwich (Conn.) Pub. Schs., 1970-78; cons. Nat. Learning Disabilities Assistance Project, Washington, 1976-78; instr. Fairfield (Conn.) U., 1975-79; grad. asst., fellow U. N.Mex., Albuquerque, 1978-81, instr., 1980-85; cons. IBM, White Plains and Arwork, N.Y., 1976-81; asst. prin. Albuquerque Pub. Schs., 1981-82, coord. spl. edn., 1989—93; dir. rsch. Harcourt/Psychol. Corp. Cons. Office of Spl. Edn., U.S. Dept. Edn., Washington, 1980—; dir. regional large sch. testing programs, mid-continent Harcourt Edn. Measurement, 1999—; dir. grants and devel. Minn. Dept. Children, Families, and Learning; dir. Minn. Assessment Project; presenter in field. Contbr. articles to profl. jours./publs. Chmn. Gov.'s Com. on the Concerns of the Handicapped, Santa Fe, N.Mex., 1988—; pres. Civitan/Sierra Vista, Albuquerque, 1989, Albuquerque Wheelchair Tennis Assn., 1985, World Inst. on Disabilities, 1997-98; adv. bd. Protection and Advocacy, Albuquerque, 1988-90; vice-chmn. N.Mex. Vols. for the Outdoors, Albuquerque, 1988-91; bd. dirs. Very Spl. Arts, 1984—, Easter Seal Fundraiser, 1976—, Spl. Olympics, 1986—. Named Vol. of the Yr., N.Mex. Vols. for the Outdoors, 1988, Nat. Woman's Single Champion/Nat. Wheelchair Tennis Assn., Irvine, Calif., 1985, Most Inspirational Tennis Player, 1985, Outstanding Leader in Elem. Edn., Ashland, Ohio, 1976, Conn. Outstanding Young Woman, Hartford, 1976. Mem. N.Mex. Coun. Exceptional Children (treas. 1990-92), Am. Ednl. Rsch. Assn., Phi Delta Kappa (pres. local chpt. 1990-91).

CASE, LARRY D. agricultural education specialist; b. Norborne, Mo., Aug. 8, 1943; s. Burr Jr. and Eva Marie (Harper); m. Joy Leona Vandivort, June 18, 1966; children: Jeffrey Dale, Rebecca Joy, Matthew Edward. BS in Agriculture, U. Mo., 1966, MEd, 1972, EdD, 1983; LHD (hon.), SUNY, Cobleskill, 1990. Life cert. agriculture tchr. Tchr. Northwestern High Sch., Mendon, Mo., 1966, Orrick (Mo.) Sch. Dist., 1966-69, Lexington (Mo.) R-V Sch. Dist., 1969-73, vocat. dir., 1973-74; dir. vocat. edn. Lexington La-Ray Area Vocat. Sch., 1974-77; supr. agrl. edn. Mo. Dept. Elem. & Sec. Edn., Jefferson City, 1977-78, state dir. agrl. edn., 1978-84; ednl. program specialist-agriculture U.S. Dept. Edn., Washington, 1984—. Chmn. bd. Future Farmers Am., Alexandria, 1984, Nat. Coun. for Vocat. Tech. Edn. in Agr., Alexandria, 1984-93, Nat. Postgrad. Agrl. Students Orgn., Alexandria, 1984; pres. Future Farmers Am. Found., Alexandria, 1984; adj. prof. Pa. State U., University Park. Contbr. articles on agrl. edn. and internat. travel related to agrl. edn. Active deacon Fredericksburg (Va.) Bapt. Ch., 1984—, Sunday sch. tchr., 1984—; pres. Motts Row Property Owners Assn., 1988-89. Recipient Hon. Am. Farmer degree Future Farmers Am., 1984, Citation of Merit, U. Mo. Coll. of Agr., 1990. Mem. Future Farmers Am. Alumni Assn. (life), Am. Vocat. Assn., Nat. Assn. State Suprs. Agrl. Edn. (sec. 1980-84), Nat. Vocat. Agr. Tchrs. Assn. (life), Nat. Planning Assn. (food and agr. com.), Phi Delta Kappa, Alpha Gamma Rho (nat. hon. mem.). Office: US Dept Edn OVAE 330 C St SW Washington DC 20202-0001*

CASE, PENNY LU, elementary education educator; b. Upper Sandusky, Ohio, Nov. 23, 1953; d. Robert Ward and Ruthe Virginia (Mayer) C. BS in Edn. summa cum laude, U. Findlay, Ohio, 1975; M in Curriculum and Instrn., Ashland (Ohio) U., 1986. Cert. tchr. K-8, Ohio. Substitute tchr. Area Schs., Sycamore, Carey, others, 1976; tchr. 2d grade Eden Elem. Sch., Upper Sandusky, 1976-90; tchr. 2d grade gifted and talented students East Elem. Sch., Upper Sandusky, 1990—. Chmn. Family Literacy Program, Upper Sandusky, 1991—; speaker in field. Martha Holden Jennings scholar, 1990. Mem. NEA, Ohio Edn. Assn. (sec.), Ohio Reading Assn., Friends of the Libr., Order Ea. Star, Sigma Kappa. Republican. Mem. United Ch. of Christ. Avocations: decorative painting, travel. Home: 3732 County Highway 43 Upper Sandusky OH 43351-9157 Office: East Elem Sch 401 3rd St Upper Sandusky OH 43351-1105

CASEBEER, DEANNA FERN GENTRY, elementary education educator; b. Albert Lea, Minn., July 18, 1945; d. Floyd Chester and Evelyn Vera (Bressel) Gentry; m. Roger Ned Casebeer, Oct. 2, 1965; children: Nita Ankrom, John Casebeer. BS in Edn., So. Mo. State U., 1969, MS in Edn., 1985. Elem. tchr. Nicholes Junction Sch., Willard, Mo., 1969-70, West Ctrl. Sch., Joplin, Mo., 1970-72, Raymondville (Mo.) Pub. Schs., 1972-78, Houston (Mo.) Pub. Sch., 1978-81, Marion C. Early Sch., Morrisville, Mo., 1981-84, Bolivar (Mo.) Pub. Schs., 1986—95, Starr tchr. dept. of elem. and secondary edn., 1995—97; edn. specialist Polk County Soil and Water Dist., 2000—. Pvt. edn. cons., 1999—; Starr tchr. Dept. Elem. and Secondary Edn., 1995-97; edn. specialist Polk County Soil and Water Dist., 2001—; cons. Edn. Unltd., Inc., St. Louis. Mem. James River Assembly. Mem. Internat. Reading Assn. (sec. 1994). Republican. Avocations: needle work, swimming, reading, painting, scuba diving. Home and Office: 1223 E 473rd Rd Bolivar MO 65613-8166

CASERTA, JEAN KILSHEIMER, elementary education educator, family counselor; b. Charleston, W.Va., Feb. 8, 1954; d. John Robert and Elizabeth (Carraher) Kilsheimer; m. Michael Joseph Caserta, Oct. 11, 1975; children: James, John, Julie. BA in French and Edn., Immaculata Coll., 1975; MS in Family Therapy, Nova Southeastern U., 1993. Cert. tchr., Fla. Substitute tchr. Mamaroneck (N.Y.) High Sch., 1976-78; tchr. elem. Broward County Sch. Bd., Ft. Lauderdale, Fla., 1980—, intern family therapist Coral Springs, Fla., 1992-93; tchr. 3-4th grade Forest Hills Elem., Coral Springs, Fla., 1992—. Editor newpaper Immaculatan, 1973-75. Tchr. CCD, St. Malachy and St. Elizabeth Ann Seton Chs., St. Andrews Ch., Ft. Lauderdale, Fla., 1980—; vol. Coral Springs Nat. Little League, 1985—, Taravella Booster Club, Coral Springs, 1990—; mem. PTA. Mem. AAUW, Kappa Gamma Pi, Lambda Iota Tau, Delta Epsilon Sigma. Republican. Roman Catholic. Avocations: tennis, reading, needlepoint, swimming, family activities. Home: 8397 NW 14th St Coral Springs FL 33071-6777 Office: Forest Hills Elem 3100 NW 85th Ave Coral Springs FL 33065-4616

CASEY, BEVERLY JANE, special education educator; b. Le Mars, Iowa, July 3, 1951; d. Francis C. and Jane F. (Lanzendorf) Homan; m. Richard D. Casey, Aug. 11, 1973; children: Courtney, Ryan, Molly. BS in Spl. Edn., BS in Elem. Edn., U. S.D., 1974. Cert. elem. and spl. edn. tchr., S.D. Tchr. fifth grade St. Agnes Sch., Vermillion, S.D., 1974-77; tchr. Madison (S.D.) Preschool, 1977-79; spl. educator ECCO, Madison, 1981-86; tchr. fourth grade Little Flower Sch., Sioux Falls, S.D., 1987-90; resource tchr. Sioux Falls Pub. Schs., 1990—93, 5th grade tchr., 1993—. Grant evaluator ECCO, Madison, 1987. Co-developer (retirement program) The Golden Years, 1983. Avocations: golf, skiing. Office: Lincoln Elem Sch 1116 W 9th St Sioux Falls SD 57104-3401

CASEY, BONNIE MAE, artist, educator; b. Chgo., Ill., Aug. 1, 1932; d. Edward Frances Kusch, Bessie Elaine (Moulding) Kusch; m. George Daniel Casey, Feb. 21, 1953; children: Cheryl Ann, Stuart Evan, Charles Alan. Student, Am. Acad. Art, Chgo., Harper Jr. Coll., Schamburg, Ill. Instr. Village Art Sch., Skokie, Ill., 1965—80, Art Barn, Elk Grove Village, Ill., 1978—83, Mountain Artists Guild, Prescott, Ariz., 1985—2000, Pima Coll., Green Valley, Ariz. Bd. dirs. Southwestern Artists Assn.; mem. visual arts com. Prescott Fine Arts Assn., 1995—2003; bd. dirs. Prescott Arts and Humanities, 1986—99; tchr. Vaison la Romaine, France, San Mignel del Allende, Mexico; instr. in field; organizer, arts curator Open Space Alliance, 2001. Contbr. articles to Fine Art Collector mag. ., Wine and Dine mag.; prin. works include painting 9-11-01, 2001, logo design, Arts and Humanities Coun., Prescott, Town of Chino Valley, Ariz., mural design, History of Chino Valley, one-woman shows include Mitchell Mus., Trinidad, Colo., 1992, 50 Yr. Art Retrospective, 2003, exhibited in group shows at Phippen Mus. Named Curator of Yr., Prescott Fine Arts Assn.; recipient Grumbacher Gold medal, 1992, 1996, Gov.'s award nominee, Ariz. Commn. on Arts; featured artist 50 Yrs. of Art Retrospective, Prescott Fine Arts Gallery, 2003. Mem.: Southwestern Artists Assn., Western Acad. Women Artists (historian), Oil Painters Am., Phippen Western Art Mus., Prescott Art Docents (docent auditor 1996—2003). Avocation: travel. Home: 3380 N Yuma Dr Chino Valley AZ 86323

CASEY, DARLA DIANN, elementary school educator; b. West Linn, Oreg., Mar. 21, 1940; d. Karl F. and Lucille Iona (Wilson) Lettenmaier; m. Charles Emerson Casey, July 30, 1965; children: John, Michael, Kim. BSEd, U. Wis., Milw., 1965; MEd, postgrad., Oreg. State U., U. Oreg., West State, Port State. Cert. tchr. grades K-9, basic art grades 1-12. Tchr., grade 3, swimming instr., grades 4-6 Lakeside (Oreg.) Elem.; tchr., readiness rm. K-1 Siuslaw Elem., Florence, Oreg.; tchr., grades K and 1st, spl. reading, art Washington Elem., Canon City, Colo.; tchr., grade 1 Sam Case Elem. Sch., Lincoln County Sch. Dist., Newport, Oreg. Mentor tchr. N.W. Sci. Survey Com.; aerospace sci. tchr. 3d through 5th and 4H Young Astronauts 3d through 5th NASA's Space Down to Earth Program, 1998; speaker in field. Contbr. articles to profl. jours. Named Oreg. Elem. Sci. Tchr. of Yr. Am. Electronics Assn. and Dept. Edn., 1989; NASA scholar (Nasa ednl. workshop for elem. sci. tchrs. program), 1992, 95, Oreg. Cadre for All tchrs. of Sci. scholar, 1993, NASA Flight Opportunities for Sci. Tchr. Enrichment Project scholar, 1995, Am. Astron. Soc. Tchr. Resource Agt., 1996, ASTRA scholar U. Tex. and McDonald Observatory, 1996. Mem. Oreg. Sci. Tchrs. Assn., Oreg. Reading Assn., Oreg. Seacoast Reading Coun. (past pres.), Oreg. Math. Tchrs. Assn., Phi Delta Kappa. E-mail: dasey1@harborside.com.

CASEY, ELBERTA, secondary education educator; b. Frankfort, Ky., Feb. 20, 1956; d. James Vernon and Meta Bush (Dowden) C. BA, Transylvania U., Lexington, Ky., 1978; M in Secondary Edn., U. Ky., 1986. Tchr. sci. at middle sch. level Fayette County Schs., Lexington, 1978—. Mem. NEA, Ky. Edn. Assn., Nat. Middle Sch. Assn., Nat. Sci. Tchrs. Assn., Nat. Middle Level Sci. Assn., Fayette County Edn. Assn. Christian. Office: Crawford Middle Sch 1813 Charleston Dr Lexington KY 40505-2596

CASEY, GENEVIEVE M. librarian, educator; b. Mpls., July 13, 1916; d. Eugene James and Cecelia (Malerich) C. BS, Coll. St. Catherine, St. Paul, 1937; MA, U. Mich., 1956. Mem. staff Detroit Pub. Library, 1937-46, 48-61, chief extension dept., 1948-61; Mich. State librarian Lansing, 1961-67; prof. library scis. Wayne State U., 1967-83. Fulbright prof. U. Brasilia, 1979; librarian U.S. Army Libraries, ETO, 1946-47; scholar in residence U. Mo. Sch. Library and Informational Sci., 1985. Author: Library Service to the Aging, 1983, Father Clem Kern, Conscience of Detroit, 1989. Named Mich. Librarian of Yr. 1978. Mem. ALA (pres. Assn. Hosp. and Instn. Libraries 1961-62, pres. library edn. div. 1970-72), Pub. Library Assn. (pres. 1976-78), Mich. Library Assn., Am. Assn. Library Schs. (pres. 1979) Address: 1121 Torrey Rd Grosse Pointe MI 48236-2358

CASEY, H(ORACE) CRAIG, JR., electrical engineering educator; b. Houston, Dec. 4, 1934; s. H.c. and Mae (Walls) C.; m. Jean Anne Merritt, June 14, 1960 (div. 1983); children: Anne, Michael; m. Jacqueline Lucas, Jan. 22, 1983. BSEE, Okla. State U., 1957; MSEE, Stanford U., 1959, PhD, 1964. Devel. engr. Hewlett-Packard, Palo Alto, Calif., 1957-62; mem. tech. staff Bell Labs., Murray Hill, N.J., 1964-79; chmn. dept. elec. engring. Duke U., Durham, N.C., 1979-94, prof. elec. engring., 1979—. Mem. Dept. of Def. Adv. Group Electron Devices, Washington, 1975-79; bd. dirs. Acme Elec., 1984-91. Author: Heterostructure Lasers, 1978, Devices for Integrated Circuits: Silicon and III-V Compounds, 1999. Fellow IEEE (pres. Electron Devices Soc. 1988-89, editor centennial issue Trans. on Electron Devices 1984); mem. Am. Phys. Soc. Office: Duke U Dept Elec Engring Durham NC 27706 E-mail: hcc@ee.duke.edu.

CASEY, JOHN DUDLEY, writer, English language educator; b. Worcester, Mass., Jan. 18, 1939; s. Joseph Edward and Constance (Dudley) C.; m. Jane Barnes, June 10, 1967 (div. 1980); children: Maud, Nell; m. Rosamond Pinchot Pittman, June 27, 1982; children: Clare, Julia. BA, Harvard U., 1962, LLB, 1965; MFA, U. Iowa, 1968. Prof. English U. Va., Charlottesville, 1972-92, U. Iowa, 1998, U. Va., 1999—. Lit. executor Estate of Breece D'J Pancake, 1979—; resident scholar Am. Acad. in Rome, 1990-91. Author: An American Romance, 1977 (runner up Ernest Hemingway award 1977), Testimony and Demeanor, 1979 (Friends Am. Lit. award 1980), Spartina, 1989 (Nat. Book award 1989), Supper at the Black Pearl, 1995, The Half-life of Happiness, 1998; co-translator: You're an Animal, Viskovitz (By A. Boffa), 2002; contbr. stories (O. Henry award 1989), essays maj. nat. mags. including New Yorker, Esquire. With USAR, 1959-60. Guggenheim fellow, 1979-80, Nat. Endowment for Arts fellow, 1983, resident Am. Acad. in Rome, 1990-91; grantee Strauss living AAAL, 1992-97. Mem. PEN. Avocation: rowing. Office: U Va Dept English Bryan Hall Charlottesville VA 22903-3289 also: Michael Carlisle Carlisle & Co 24 E 64th St New York NY 10021-7201

CASEY, MURRAY JOSEPH, physician, educator; b. Armour, S.D., May 1, 1936; s. Meryl Joseph and Gladice (Murray) C.; m. Virginia Anne Fletcher; children: Murray Joseph Jr., Theresa Marie, Anne Franklin, Francis Xavier, Peter Colum, Matthew Padraic. Student, Chanute Jr. Coll., 1954-55, Rockhurst Coll., 1955-56; AB, U. Kans., 1958; MD, Georgetown U., 1962; postgrad., Suffolk U. Law Sch., 1963-64, Howard U., 1965, U. Conn., 1977; MS in Mgmt., Cardinal Stritch Coll., 1984; MBA, Marquette U., 1988; cert. in Theology, Creighton U., 2003—. Diplomate Nat. Bd. Med. Examiners, Am. Bd. Ob-Gyn. Intern USPHS Hosp.-Univ. Hosp., Balt., 1962-63; staff physician USPHS Hosp., Boston, 1963-64; rsch. staff Lab Infectious Diseases, Nat. Inst. Allergy and Infectious Diseases, NIH, Bethesda, Md., 1964-66; virologist, resident physician Columbia-Presbyn. Med. Ctr. also Francis Delafield Hosp., N.Y.C., 1966-69, USPHS sr. clin. trainee, 1969-70; fellow gynecol. oncology, resident dept. surgery Meml. Hosp. Cancer and Allied Diseases, Meml. Sloan-Kettering Cancer Ctr., N.Y.C., 1969-71; Am. Cancer Soc. fellow, 1969-71; ofcl. observer in radiotherapy U. Tex. M.D. Anderson Hosp. and Tumor Inst., Houston, 1971; vis. scientist Radiumhemmet Karolinska Sjukhuset and Inst., Stockholm, 1971; asst. prof. ob-gyn U. Conn. Sch. Medicine, 1971-75, assoc. prof., 1975-80, dir. gynecologic oncology, 1971-80, also mem. med. bd.; Linson fellow Am. Coll. Surgeons Commn. on Cancer, 1979—89, 1995—; prof., assoc. chmn. dept. ob-gyn U. Wis. Med. Sch., 1980-89; prof., chmn. dept. ob-gyn. Creighton U., Omaha, 1989-94; chief ob-gyn. and dir. gynecologic oncology St. Joseph Hosp., Creighton U. Med. Ctr., Omaha, 1989-94; dir. gynecologic oncology Creighton Cancer Ctr., 1996—. Faculty coun. Creighton U., 1992—93, 1995—, acad. coun., 1992—93, 1995—, instrnl. rev. bd. dirs., 1994—, rank and tenure com., 1998—2001, cancer ctr. adv. bd., 1994—, sr. appts. and tenure com., 1998—, prin. investigator Cancer Ctr., 2001—02; bd. dirs. Mo. Valley Consortium, Cmty. Coop. Oncology Program; chief ob-gyn Mt. Sinai Med. Ctr., Milw., 1980—82, dir. gynecologic oncology, 1980—89, also mem. med. exec. com.; chmn. research adv. com., mem. council Conn. Cancer Epidemiology Unit; 8. Editor, contbr. articles in sports medicine to profl. jours., chpts. to books; rsch. in oncogenesis and tumor immunology. Bd. dirs., mem. exec. com., chmn. profl. edn. com. Hartford unit Am. Cancer Soc., dir. Milw. divsn., exec. com. 1985-87, v.p., 1985-86, pres.-elect, 1986-87, 1st v.p. exec. com. Wis. divsn. 1987-89, bd. dirs., chmn. profl. edn. com., 1987-89, bd. dirs., 1989-96, exec. com. Nebr. divsn., 1989-93, pub. edn. and communications com., profl. edn. com. vice chair, 2nd v.p., 1990-91, 1st v.p., pres.-elect, 1991-92, pres., 1992-93, bd. dirs. Douglas County unit, 1993—; mem. mayor's adv. com. Cancer Survivors Park, City of Omaha, 1991-92; mem. Parks and Recreation Bd., City of Omaha, 1993-94; mem. med. svcs. 1980 Winter Olympic Games, Lake Placid, N.Y.; mem. med. supervisory team U.S. Nordic Ski Team. Lt. (j.g.) USPHS, 1962-64, lt. comdr., 1964-66; col. USAR, 1988-93. Fellow: ACS, Am. Coll. Ob-Gyn; mem.: AAAS, Omaha Ob-Gyn. Soc., Milwaukee Gynecologic Soc., Assn. Mil. Surgeons, Am. Urogynecol. Soc., Lake Placid Sports Medicine Soc. (v.p. 1981—84, pres. 1984—86), Soc. Meml. Gynecol. Oncologists (exec. bd. 1979—84, pres. 1982—83), Internat. Assn. for Advancement of Humanistic Studies in Medicine, N.Am. Menopause Soc., Internat. Menopause Soc., Am. Soc. Clin. Oncology, Am. Radium Soc., Internat. Gynecol. Cancer Soc., New Eng. Assn. Gynecol. Oncologists (pres. 1980—81), European Soc. Gynecol. Oncologists, Soc. Gynecol. Oncologists, Am. Fertility Soc., Am. Assn. Gynecologic Laparoscopists, Am. Soc. Colposcopy, N.Y. Acad. Scis., Am. Coll. Sports Medicine, Cen. Assn. Ob-Gyns., Soc. of Gynecol. Surgeons, St. George Soc., Cedarburg C. of C. (dir. 1983—85, Ambassadors com. 1983—89, chmn. bus. indsl. program com. 1985, 1987—89), Beta Gamma Sigma. Office: Creighton U Sch Medicine Dept Ob-Gyn 601 N 30th St # 4810 Omaha NE 68131-2137

CASH, DEANNA GAIL, retired nursing educator; b. Coatesville, Pa., Nov. 28, 1940; Diploma, Jackson Meml. Hosp., 1961; BS, Fla. State U., 1964; MN, UCLA, 1968; EdD, Nova U., Ft. Lauderdale, Fla., 1983. Staff and relief charge nurse Naples (Fla.) Comty. Hosp., 1961-62; staff nurse Glendale (Calif.) Comty. Hosp., 1964-65; instr. Knapp Coll. Nursing, Santa Barbara, Calif., 1965-66; staff nurse, team leader Kaiser Found. Hosp., Bellflower, Calif., 1968-69; prof. nursing El Camino Coll., Torrance, Calif., 1969-96, ret., 1996. Coord., instr. Internat. RN Rev. course, L.A., 1974-76; mentor statewide nursing program, Long Beach, Calif., 1981-88; clin. performance in nursing exam. evaluator Western Performance Assessment Ctr., Long Beach, 1981-96. Mem. ANA.

CASH, LISA FREEMAN, elementary education educator; b. Oberlin, Ohio, Dec. 10, 1959; d. Roger Lee Freeman and Patricia Ann (Swesey) Lott; m. Jeffrey Clayton Lamb, May 8, 1982 (div. 1985); m. R. Todd Cash, Mar. 27, 1988; children: Rebecca, Rachel. BA, Fla. So. Coll., 1982; MS, Nova U., 1988. Cert. tchr., Fla. Tchr. Hornbeck (La.) High Sch., 1982-84, Chester A. Moore Elem. Sch., Ft. Pierce, Fla., 1985-92, tchr. bilingual devel. kindergarten, 1989-91, reading tchr., 1991-92; dropout prevention specialist Parkway Elem. Sch., Port St. Lucie, Fla., 1992—, asst. prin., 1993—. Mem. ASCD, Nat. Coun. Tchrs. English, Internat. Reading Assn., Alpha Delta Kappa (v.p. 1990—), Phi Delta Kappa, Alpha Delta Pi Alumnae Assn. (charter, v.p. 1990-92). Republican. Presbyterian. Avocations: cross-stitch, reading, sailing. Home: 4845 River Oak Ln Fort Pierce FL 34981-4423 Office: Parkway Elem Sch 7000 NW Selvitz Rd Port Saint Lucie FL 34983-8203

CASHEN, ELIZABETH ANNE, elementary school educator; b. Norwalk, Ohio, July 15, 1938; d. Charles Robert and Mildred Ethelyn (Bacon) Cissne; m. Ronald Edward Cashen, May 28, 1960; children: Janet Kaye Cashen Crawford, Robert Edward. BS, Bowling Green State U., 1974, MEd, 1979. Cert. tchr., Ohio. Primary tchr. Genoa Area Schs., Clay Center, Ohio, 1974—; head tchr. Allen Elem., 1993—. Mentor Mentorship Program; presenter restructuring program Genoa Area Schs., 1992. Pres. Mobile Meals, Genoa, 1984-90 Mem. Genoa Area Edn. Assn. (pres. 1989), Delta Kappa Gamma (chmn. membership com. 1992-93). Mem. United Ch. of Christ. Avocations: singing, reading. Office: Allen Cen Sch 4862 N Genoa Clay Center Rd Curtice OH 43412-9617

CASHMAN, SUZANNE BOYER, health services administrator, educator; b. Phila., Apr. 14, 1947; d. Vincent Saul and Ethel (Wolf) Boyer; m. Daniel Cashman, Jan. 16, 1971; children: Adam, Rebecca, David. BA, Tufts U., 1969; MS, Cornell U., 1973; ScD, Harvard U., 1980. Sr. analyst Urban Sys. Rsch., Cambridge, Mass., 1979-82; cons. Mass. Dept. Pub. Health, Boston, 1982-83; spl. asst. to v.p. Brigham and Women's Hosp., Boston, 1983-85; assoc. dir. rsch. Boston U. Office Spl. Projects, 1985-89; asst. prof. Boston U. Sch. Pub. Health, 1985-96; evaluator Cmty. Oriented Primary Care, Boston, 1989-91; assoc. dir. Ctr. for Cmty. Responsive Care, Boston, 1991-97; pub. health cons. U. Mass. Med. Ctr., Worcester, 1998; assoc. prof. dept. family medicine, cmty. health Med. Sch. U. Mass., Worcester, 1999—, asst. dir. preventive medicine residency, 1999—. Cons. Acad. Health Ctrs., Derby, Conn., Columbia, SC, Atlanta, Balt., 1995—97; conf. planner New. Eng. Rural Health Roundtable. Co-editor: Community Oriented Primary Care, 1998; contbr. articles to profl. jours. Mem. leadership tng. program., sec. alumni orgn. com. NCCJ, Boston, 1995—2002; sec. bd. exec. com., conf. planner Cmty.-Campus Partnerships for Health and New England Rural Health Roundtable; bd. mem. Assn. Tchrs. of Preventive Medicine; mem. bd. dirs. Cmty. Ptnrs., Inc.; mem. task force Healthy People 2010 Curriculum. Mem. APHA, Assn. Tchrs. Preventive Medicine (conf. planner, bd. dirs.), Mass. Pub. Health Assn. Avocations: ballet dancing, sewing, cooking, jogging, gardening. Home: 17 Calvin Rd Newtonville MA 02460-2104 Office: U Mass Med Ctr Dept Family Medicine 55 Lake Ave N Worcester MA 01655-0002 E-mail: suzanne.cashman@umassmed.edu.

CASKEY, OWEN LAVERNE, retired psychology educator; b. Corsicana, Tex., Mar. 10, 1925; s. Price Hamilton and Esma Eulysses (Lisman) C.; m. Shirley Jean Larned, Apt. 10, 1981; children: Leigh Ann, Deborah Jane. BS, Tex. Tech U., 1947, MEd, 1948; EdD, U. Colo., 1952. Lic. psychologist, Tex.; lic. profl. counselor, Tex. Tchr. Lubbock (Tex.) Pub. Schs., 1941-43; instr. Tex. Tech U., Lubbock, 1947-50, prof. ednl. psychology, 1964-83, prof. emeritus, 1983—, v.p. student affairs, 1968-70, assoc. v.p. acad. affairs, 1970—73, dir. instrnl. rsch., 1974-81, assoc. dean Coll. Edn., 1976-78. Asst. prof. Colo. State U., 1950-53, assoc. prof., 1954-58; counseling psychologist VA, Denver, 1954; cons. psychologist Rohrer, Hibler & Replogle, Dallas, 1958-63; assoc. prof. Okla. State U., 1963-64; psychologist El Paso (Tex.) Pub. Schs., 1981-87; cons. to state and govt. agys. including El Paso Police Dept., 1981-87. Contbr. numerous articles to profl. jours. Chmn. Cmty. Planning Coun., 1973-75; bd. dirs. United Way, 1973-75, mem. budget com., 1973-79, mem. long-range planning com., 1978-80; bd. dirs. South Plains Health Sys., 1976-81, mem. exec. com., 1978-81. Served to lt. (j.g.) USN, 1943-46, ETO. VA fellow, 1954, U. Colo. fellow, 1954; recipient numerous rsch. grants, 1966-68. Mem. APA, Soc. for Accelerated Learning and Tchg. Methodist. Home: 3320 E Dowling Mill Ct Boise ID 83706

CASLER, FREDERICK CLAIR, SR., academic administrator, law enforcement educator; b. Corry, Pa., Mar. 7, 1946; s. Clair O. and Helen M. (Church) C.; m. Janice L. Newrick, Nov. 26, 1983; 1 child, Frederick Clair Jr. AA, Miami-Dade Jr. Coll., 1970; BGS, Rollins Coll., 1975, MS in Criminal Justice, 1979; cert., Kissimmee Police Acad., 1974, 88; PhD in Bus. Adminstrn., Fla. Christian U., 2002. Cert. tchr., Fla. Tchr. criminal justice Orange County Schs., Orlando, Fla.; tchr., work experience coord. Osceola County Schs., Kissimmee, Fla., dep. sheriff, dep. sheriff sgt. res.; police-sch. liaison officer Kissimmee Police Dept./Osceola County Schs.; vocat. adult and community education tchr. Kissimmee Police Acad./Osceola Dist. Schs.; coord., dep. dir. Kissimmee Criminal Justice Acad.; dep. dir. Criminal Justice Acad. Adviser various youth orgns. including SADD, Just Say No Club; cubmaster Boy Scouts Am.; res. dep. sheriff, sgt. Osceola County Sheriff's Office; mem. Osceola County Rep. Exec. Com. Mem.: AARP, NEA, AFL-CIO, NRA (life), U.S. Army-Vets Assn., Law Enforcement Officers Christ, U.S. Dep. Sheriff's Assn., Fla. Sheriff's Assn., Am. Fedn. Tchrs., Am. Criminal Justice Assn., Internat. Conf. Police Chaplains, Fla. Peace Officers Assn., Fla. Criminal Justice Tng. Officers Assn., Osceola County Tchrs. Assn., Fla. Tchrs. Assn., Fla. Assn. Sch. Resource Officers, Nat. Assn. Chiefs of Police, Am. Soc. Law Enforcement Trainers, Internat. Conf. of Police Officers, Am. Fedn. of Police, Son Vets. Fgn. Wars, U.S. Army Vietnam-Era Vets. Assn. (assoc.), Police Acad. Alumni Assn., Am. Police Hall of Fame, Sons Confederate Vets., Sons the Am. Legion, Law Enforcement Officers for Christ, Am. Assn. Christian Counselors, Fla. Police Benevolent Assn., Sons Union Vets. Civil War, Sons VFW of the U.S., Kiwanis (dir.), Moose, Scottish Rite, Shriners, Am. Legion (post comdr. 1973), Masons, Elks, York Rite, Alpha Omega Epsilon (chpt. pres. 1996), Lambda Alpha Epsilon.

CASMIR, MINA G. HALLIDAY, speech educator, consultant; b. Hamburg, Iowa, Oct. 16, 1945; d. Ralph Hoover and Florence (Hummel) Halliday; m. Fred L. Casmir. BS, Northwest Mo. State U., 1967; MS, So. Ill. U., 1968. Cert. secondary edn. tchr. and supr. Teaching asst. So. Ill. U., Carbondale, 1967-68; tchr. Belleville (Ill.) West High Sch., 1968-73; edn. cons. Ill. State Bd. Edn., Springfield, 1973-86; pvt. practice cons. Los Angeles, 1986—99, Flagstaff, Ariz., 1999—. Active SCA Summer Conf. on Coll. Sophomore Speaking/Listening Competencies, 1987, Springfield Area Arts Council, 1981-85; advisor Ill. Arts Council, 1981-86, Ill. High Sch. Theatre Festival, 1975-86. Editor: Teaching Speech Today, 1979, The Arts: A Basic Component of General Education, 1983; (book series) Basic Oral Communication, 1981-82; contbr. articles on communication edn. to profl. jours. Mem. ASCD, Nat. Comm. Assn., Am. Alliance Theatre and Edn. Assn. (pres. Secondary Edn. div. 1985-86, bd. dirs. 1986-87, sec. 1987), Ill. Theater Assn. (Ann. Recognition award 1980), Ill. Speech and Theatre Assn. (Edith Harrod award 1979, Sanders Life award 1986), Internat. Comm. Assn., Ill. Alliance Arts Edn. (exec. sec. 1975-86, Arts Edn. Svc. award 1987). Democrat. Mem. Church Of Christ. Avocations: reading, painting, traveling. Home and Office: 8950 Koch Field Rd Flagstaff AZ 86004-3277

CASON, NICA VIRGINIA, nursing educator; b. Edna, Tex. 1 child, Cynthia Diane. Diploma, Lillie Jolly Sch. Nursing, 1965; BSN, U. Tex. Med. Br., Galveston, 1967; MSN, U. So. Miss., 1981. RN, Miss. Pub. health nurse Miss. State Dept. Health, Pascagoula, 1978; nursing instr. Miss. Gulf Coast Community Coll.-Jackson County Campus, Gautier, 1981-84, chair ADN program, 1984—. Col. USAFR, ret. Mem. NOADN, Nat. League Nursing, Sigma Theta Tau, Phi Kappa Phi.

CASPAR, DONALD L.D. biophysics and structural biology educator; b. Ithaca, N.Y., Jan. 8, 1927; s. Caspar V. and Blanche (Dvorak) C.; m. Gwladys Williams, Dec. 20, 1962; children: Emma, David. BA in Physics, Cornell U., 1950; PhD in Biophysics, Yale U., 1955. Postdoctoral fellow Calif. Inst. Tech., 1954-55, MRC Lab. Molecular Biology, Cambridge, Eng., 1955-56; instr. biophysics Yale U., New Haven, 1956-58, asst. prof., 1958-59; rsch. assoc. Harvard U., Cambridge, Mass., 1962-63; lectr. Harvard Med. Sch., Boston, 1963-73; rsch. assoc. in pathology Children's Hosp. Med. Ctr., Boston, 1959-73; prof. of physics, rsch. prof. of structural biology Rosenstiel Basic Med. Scis. Rsch. Ctr., Brandeis U., Waltham, Mass., 1972-94, acting dir., 1987-88; prof. biol. scis. Inst. Molecular Biophysics Fla. State U., 1994—. Mem. biophysics and biophys. chem. study sect. NIH, 1969—73; guest rsch. assoc. in biology Brookhaven Nat. Lab., 1973—, chmn. biology dept. vis. com., 1974—77, mem., 1996—99, mem. neutron users adv. com. biology dept., 1980—81, 1991—97, mem. adv. com. scanning transmission electron microscope facilty, 1985—96, mem. program adv. com. high flux beam reactor physics dept., 1992—97, Haworth disting. scientist, 1994—96; mem. nat. laser users facility steering com. Lab. Laser Energetics U. Rochester, NY, 1981—84; mem. sci. adv. com. European Molecular Biology Lab., Heidelberg, Germany, 1976—81; mem. sic. adv. com. structural biology ctr. Argonne Nat. Lab., 1989—94; mem. adv. bd. Nat. Ctr. Macromolecular Imaging Baylor Coll. Medicine, 1995—2000; mem. editl. com. Ann. Revs. Biophysics and Bioengring., 1970—73; vis. prof. Inst. Molecular Biophysics Fla. State U., 1994; rsch. fellow Japan Soc. Promotion Sci. Inst. Molecular Biology Nagoya U., 1984. Contbr. articles, rsch. papers to profl. publs. Grantee NIH, 1969-88, 2001—, NSF, 1983-86, Guggenheim fellowship, 1994; recipient Outstanding Investigator award Nat. Cancer Inst., 1988-2002. Fellow Am. Acad. Arts and Scis., Biophys. Soc. (pres. 1991-92, nat. lectr. 1985, charter fellow 1999); mem. NAS, Am. Crystallographic Assn. (Fankuchen award 1992). Achievements include research in structural biology of viruses, membranes and protein adaptability. Home: 911 Gardenia Dr Tallahassee FL 32312-3001 Office: Fla State U Inst Molecular Biophysics Tallahassee FL 32306-4380

CASPER, GERHARD, law educator, former academic administrator; b. Hamburg, Germany, Dec. 25, 1937; s. Heinrich and Hertha C.; m. Regina Koschel, Dec. 26, 1964; 1 child, Hanna. LL.M., Yale U., 1962; Dr.iur., U. Freiburg, Germany, 1964; hon. degree, Yale U., 2000, Uppsala U., 2000; legal state exam, U. Frieburg, U. Hamburg, 1961. Asst. prof. polit. sci. U. Calif., Berkeley, 1964—66; assoc. prof. law and polit. sci. U. Chgo., 1966—69, prof., 1969—76, Max Pam prof. law, 1976—80, William B. Graham prof. law, 1980—87, William B. Graham Disting. Svc. prof. law, 1987—92, dean law sch., 1979—87, provost, 1989—92; prof. law Stanford (Calif.) U., 1992—, pres., 1992—2000, pres. emeritus, 2000—; Peter and Helen Bing prof., 2000—. Vis. prof. law Cath. U., Louvain, Belgium, 1970, U. Munich, 1988, 91. Author: Realism and Political Theory in American Legal Thought, 1967, (with Richard A. Posner) The Workload of the Supreme Court, 1976; co-editor: The Supreme Ct. Rev., 1977-91, Separating Power, 1997. Successor, trustee Yale U., 2000—; bd. dirs. Am. Acad. in Berlin, 2000—. Fellow Am. Acad. Arts and Scis.; mem. Internat. Acad. Comparative Law, Am. Bar Found. (bd. dirs. 1979-87), Coun. Fgn. Rels., Am. Law Inst. (coun. 1980—), Oliver Wendell Holmes Devise (permanent com. 1985-93), Am. Philos. Soc., The Trilateral Commn., 1996—. Office: E114 Encina Hall Inst for International Studies Stanford CA 94305-6055 E-mail: gcasper@stanford.edu.*

CASPER, LEONARD RALPH, American literature educator; b. Fond du Lac, Wis., July 6, 1923; s. Louis and Caroline (Eder) C.; m. Linda Velasquez-Ty, June 2, 1956; children: Gretchen Gabrielle, Kristina Elise. BA, U. Wis., 1948, MA, 1949, PhD, 1953. Grad. asst. U. Wis., 1949-51; instr. Cornell U., 1952-53; asst. prof. U. Philippines, 1953-56, Fulbright lectr., 1962-63, summer 1973; mem. faculty Boston Coll., 1956—, prof. contemporary Am. lit., 1963-93, prof. emeritus, 1993—99; lectr. RSVP, 2001—. Dir. creative writing U. RI, 1958; lectr. in field. Author: Robert Penn Warren: The Dark and Bloody Ground, 1960, The Wayward Horizon: Essays on Modern Philippine Literature, 1961, The Wounded Diamond: Studies in Modern Philippine Literature, 1964, New Writing from The Philippines: A Critique and Anthology, 1966, A Lion Unannounced: 12 Stories and a Fable, 1971, Firewalkers: Concelebrations 1964-1984, 1987,

In Burning Ambush: Essays, 1985-90, 1991, The Opposing Thumb: Decoding Literature of the Marcos Regime, 1995, Sunsurfers Seen From Afar: Critical Essays, 1991-96, 1996, The Blood Marriage of Earth and Sky: The Later Novels of Robert Penn Warren, 1997, The Circular Firing Squad, 1999, Green Circuits of the Sun: Studies in Philippine and American Literature, 2002; contbg. author prefaces: 13 Kalisud, 1955, Brother, My Brother, 1960, The Selected Stories of Francisco Arcellana, 1963, A Stun of Jewels, 1963, Godkissing Carrion, 1964, Selected Stories of N. V.M. Gonzalez, 1964, After This Exile, 1965, Black or Otherwise, 1969, Scent of Apples, 1979, Distances: in Time, 1983, Salimbibig: Philippine Vernacular Literature, 1984, Ethnic Houses and Philippine Artistic Expression, 1988, Morning Song, 1990, Literature and Politics, 1993, Gentle Woman: Mary to the Filipinos, 1997; editor: Six Filipino Poets, 1955, Modern Philippine Short Stories, 1962; co-editor: (with T.A. Gullason) The World of Short Fiction: An International Collection, 1962; contbg. editor Panorama, Manila, 1965-61, Drama Critique, 1956-62, Solidarity, Manila, 1966-78, Literature East and West, 1969-81, Aquila, 1975-79, Pilipinas, 1987-2002. Served with F.A., AUS, 1943-46. Recipient Ford Found. Pub. award, Nat. Coun. on Arts award, 1970, Rockefeller Found. Residency award, Bellagio, Italy, 1994; Stanford Creative Writing fellow, 1951-52; Bread Loaf Creative Writing scholar, 1961; rsch. grantee Am. Coun. Learned Socs.-Social Sci. Rsch. Coun., 1965, Asia Soc., 1965; Creative Writing grant Boston Coll.; rsch. travel grantee Am. Philos. Soc., 1968-69. Home: 54 Simpson Dr Framingham MA 01701-4076

CASPER, MARIE LENORE, middle school educator; b. Honesdale, Pa., Mar. 26, 1954; d. Frank J. and Ellenore L. (Austin) Shedlock; m. Gerald Joseph Casper, Oct. 9, 1976 (dec. Oct. 1998); children: Julia Anne, Jennifer Marie. BA, Marywood Coll., 1976; masters equivalency cert., State of Pa., 1982. Cert. elem. and secondary social studies tchr., Pa. Substitute tchr. Western Wayne Sch. Dist., South Canaan, Pa., 1976-81, secondary and elem. tchr., 1981-86, chpt. 1 math. specialist, 1986-90, middle sch. social studies tchr., 1990—; social studies tchr. Wallenpaupack Area Sch. Dist., Hawley, Pa., 1980-81. Coord. Western Wayne Middle Sch., WWII commemorative com. Contbr. articles to profl. jours. Active PTA Wilson Sch., Western Wayne Mid. Sch. Mem. NEA, Pa. State Edn. Assn., Pa. Mid. Sch. Assn., Waymart Hist. Soc., Western Wayne Edn. Assn., Wayne County Hist. Soc., Smithsonian Instn., Audubon Soc., Nat. Geog. Soc., Platform Assn., Am. Legion Aux. (life). Republican. Roman Catholic. Avocations: piano and vocal music, needlecraft, reading, antiques, genealogy. Home: PO Box 31 Lake Quinn Rd South Canaan PA 18459-0031 Office: Western Wayne Mid Sch RR 8 Box 8170 Lake Ariel PA 18436-9802

CASS, BARBARA FAY, elementary school educator; b. Vernon, Tex., Jan. 24, 1949; d. Jester Earl and Sylvia Louise (Bowden) Hunt; m. Millard Don Cass, Jan. 21, 1966; 1 child, Paula Sue Cass Threatt. BS, Tex. Tech U., 1985. Sec. Dr. Johnson, Plainview, Tex., 1973; receptionist Dr. T.M. Trimble, Wylie, Tex., 1973-75, Dr. Thomas Neal, Lubbock, Tex., 1987-88; bookkeeper Aledo (Tex.) Counter Top, 1976-77; receptionist med. records and ins. clk. care unit Trinity Oaks Hosp., Ft. Worth, 1977-78; substitute tchr. Lubbock Ind. Sch. Dist., 1986-87, DeSoto (Tex.) Ind. Sch. Dist., 1988-89; kindergarten tchr. home econs. Tyler St. Christian Acad., Dallas, 1989-94; tchr. 1st grade Robinwood Christian Acad., Seagoville, Tex., 1994-97; tchr. kindergarten Hope Christian Sch., Tijeras, N.Mex., 1998—2002; kindergarten tchr. Eastern Hills Christian Acad., Tijeras, 2002—, on campus adminstr., 2002—. Baptist. Home: 9032 Walter Bambrook Pl NE Albuquerque NM 87122-2711

CASS, DAVID, economist, educator; b. Honolulu, Jan. 19, 1937; s. Phil and Muriel (Dranga) C.; m. Janice Vernon, Sept. 14, 1959 (div. July 1983); children— Stephen, Lisa BA, U. Oreg., 1958; PhD in Econs. and Stats., Stanford U., 1965; D (hon.), U. Geneva, 1994. From asst. to assoc. prof. Yale U., New Haven, 1964-70; prof. econs. Carnegie-Mellon U., Pitts., 1970—74, U. Pa., Phila., 1974-88, Paul F. and E. Warren Shafer Miller prof. econs., 1988—, dir. Ctr. for Analytic Rsch. in Econs. and the Social Scis. Prof. econs. European Union Inst., Italy, 1996—97. Contbr. articles to profl. jours.; co-editor: Selected Readings in Macroeconomics from Econometrica, 1974; The Hamiltonian Approach to Economics, 1976. 1st lt. USAR, 1959-65. Guggenheim fellow, 1970-71; recipient Morgan prize U. Chgo., 1976; Sherman Fairchild Disting. Scholar Calif. Inst. Tech., 1978-79; NSF grantee, 1971-91. Fellow Am. Econ. Assn.(disting. fellowship), Econometric Soc., Am. Acad. Arts and Scis.; mem. Phi Beta Kappa. Office: Univ Pa 435 McNeil/6297 3451 Walnut St Philadelphia PA 19104

CASS, RONALD ANDREW, dean; b. Washington, Aug. 12, 1949; s. Millard and Ruth Claire (Marx) C.; m. Valerie Christina Swanson, Aug. 24, 1969; children: Laura Rebecca, Alexander Stephan. BA with high distinction, U. Va., 1970; JD with honors, U. Chgo., 1973. Bar: Md. 1973, D.C. 1974, U.S. Dist. Ct. D.C. 1974, U.S. Ct. Appeals (D.C. cir.) 1974, U.S. Supreme Ct. 1977, Va. 1979. Law clk. to chief judge U.S. Ct. Appeals (3d cir.), Wilmington, Del., 1973-74; assoc. Arent, Fox, Kintner, Plotkin & Kahn, Washington, 1974-76; asst. prof. law U. Va. Sch. Law, Charlottesville, 1976-81; assoc. prof. law Boston U., 1981-83, prof., 1983-95; dean Boston U. Law Sch., 1990—; Melville Madison Bigelow prof. Boston U., 1995—; legal advisor Office Plans and Policy, FCC, Washington, 1987-88; mem. U.S. Internat. Trade Commn., Washington, 1988-90, vice chmn., 1989-90. Cons. comm. program Aspen (Colo.) Inst., 1977-78, Adminstrv. Conf. U.S. Washington, 1980-87, Helsell, Fetterman, Martin, Todd & Hokanson, Seattle, 1984-85, Assn. Trial Lawyers Am., Phila., 1985-87, UN Conf. Trade and Devel., Geneva, 1991, U.S. Dept. Justice, 1998, Microsoft Corp., 1998-; spl. cons. Nat. Econ. Rsch. Assn., Cambridge, Mass., 1990-94; arbitrator Biogen v. Schering-Plough, 1999-2000, Telesia Sistemas v. Lucent Tech., 2000-2002, UPS v. Canada, 2001-; adj. scholar Am. Enterprise Inst., Washington, 1993-; sr. fellow Internat. Ctr. Econ. Rsch., Turin, 1996-97, 99-2002; sesquicentennial assoc. Ctr. Advanced Studies U. Va. Law Sch., 1980-81; mem. nat. adv. bd. Case Western Res. U. Sch. Law, 1996-97; disting. lectr. U. Francisco Marroquin, Guatemala City, 1996, IMADEC Internat. Bus. Sch., Vienna, 2000, U. Aix en Provence, 2002, Boston U. London Program, 2002. Author: Revolution in the Wasteland: Value and Diversity in Television, 1981, (with Colin S. Diver) Administrative Law: Cases and Materials, 1987, (with Colin S. Diver and Jack M. Beermann) Administrative Law: Cases and Materials, 2nd edit., 1994, 3d edit., 1998, 4th edit., 2002, (with John R. Haring) International Trade in Telecommunications, 1998, The Rule of Law in America, 2001, (with Michael Knoll) International Trade Law, 2003; contbr. articles and essays to profl. jours., also chpts. to books. Bd. dirs. Northwestern Va. Health Systems Agy., Culpeper, 1980; bd. govs. Sightsavers Internat., Washington, 1989-91; bd. dirs. Telecomm. Policy Rsch. Conf., Washington, 1989-91, sec.-treas. 1989-90, vice chmn., 1991-92; bd. dirs. New Eng. Legal Found., 1994-2002, New England Coun., 1995-; bd. overseers Boston Bar Found., 1992-94, Supreme Jud. Ct. Hist. Soc., 1997-2000; sr. Europe Discussion Group, Ctr. for Strategic and Internat. Studies, 1989-96; bd. advisors George Mason U. Law Sch. Law & Econs. Ctr., 1996-99, Inst. Dem. Comm., Boston, 1991-92, Fundación de la Commn. Social, Madrid, 1995-, IMADEC Internat. Bus. Sch., Vienna, 1999-2001, Legal Issues in Econ. Integration, Amsterdam, 2000-. Fellow Am. Bar Found.; mem. ABA (adminstrv. law and regulatory practice sect., coun. 1993-95, chair 1998-99, legal edn. and admission bar sect., review commn. 1994-95, ho. of dels. 2000-02), Am. Law Inst., Am. Law Deans Assn. (bd. dirs. 1995—, pres. 1995-97), Mont Pelerin Soc., Boston Bar Assn. (coun. 1992-95), Adminstrv. Conf. U.S. (pub. mem. 1990-95, govt. mem. 1988-90), Transatlantic Policy Network (U.S. Working Group), Spring Valley C. C., Order of Coif, Phi Beta Kappa, Bay Club, Federalist Soc., Internat. Law (exec. com. 2001-). Republican. Jewish. Home: 250 Hammond Pond Pkwy #205 S Chestnut Hill MA 02467-1517 Office: Boston U Sch Law 765 Commonwealth Ave Boston MA 02215-1401

CASSCELLS, SAMUEL WARD, III, cardiologist, educator; b. Wilmington, Del., Mar. 18, 1952; s. Samuel Ward and Oleda (Dyson) C.; m. Roxanne Bell, Feb. 10, 1990; children: Sam, Henry, Lillian. BS cum laude, Yale U., 1974; MD magna cum laude, Harvard U., 1979. Intern then resident Beth Israel Hosp., Boston, 1979-82; cardiology fellow Mass. Gen. Hosp., Boston, 1982-85; Kaiser fellow clin. epidemiology Brigham and Women's Hosp. and Harvard Sch. Pub. Health, 1984-85; rsch. fellow Nat. Heart, Lung, and Blood Inst., Bethesda, Md., 1985-91; vis. scientist Scripps Inst. Medicine and Sci., LaJolla, Calif., 1991-92; chief cardiology, T.R. and M. O'Driscoll Levy prof. medicine U. Tex. Med. Sch., Houston, 1994-2000; John E. Tyson Disting. prof. medicine and public health U. Tex. Health Scis. Ctr., Houston, 2000—, v.p. biotech., 2001—. Chief cardiology Hermann Hosp., Houston, 1994-2001; assoc. dir. cardiol. rsch. Tex. Heart Inst. and St. Luke's Episc. Hosp., Houston, 1992—; med. dir. U. Tex. Telemedicine; founder Prizm Pharms., La Jolla, 1992—, Selective Genetics, La Jolla, Delphi Dignostics, Houston, Volcano Therapeutics, Laguna Hills, Calif., LifeSentry Inc., Houston, Vertical Ventures, Washington; cons. FDA, US Army; founder Pres. Bush Ctr. Cardiovasc. Health, Houston; dir. Lifeline Systems; mem. adv. bd. U. Houston Law Ctr. Health Law and Policy Inst., 1999-2001. Mem. editl. bd. Circulation, 1992—, Am. Jour. Cardiology, 1992—, Tex. Heart Inst. Jour., 1992—, Vascular Medicine, 1995-2001, U.T. Lifetime Newsletter, 1996—, Jour. Royal Soc. Medicine 1999—, Heart Watch, 2001--; contbr. numerous articles to profl. jours. Mem. Bush-Cheney HHS Transition Adv. Com., 2001—; pres. George W. Bush Healthcare Adv. Com., 2001—; mem. mayor's adv. com. to Med. Strike Force, 2001--; mem Gov.'s Coordinating Coun. on Health and Bioterrorism; mem. task force on bioterrorism Ctr. for Strategic and Internat. Studies, 2001--; bd. dirs. CapCURE; mem. prostate cancer adv. bd. M.D. Anderson Cancer Ctr.. Recipient First Harvard/CIMIT award for med. innovation, 2001. Mem.: Am. Clin. and Climatological Assn., Assn. Profs. Cardiology (bd. dirs.), Assn. Univ. Cardiologists, Am. Coll. Cardiology, Houston Cardiology Soc. (pres. 1995—96), Soc. Vascular Biol. Medicine (bd. dirs. 1997—2000), Am. Heart Assn. (Houston bd. dirs. 1992—2001), The Siasconset Casino Assn., The Dancers, Tejas Breakfast Club, Bidermann Golf Club (Centerville, Del.), Coronado Club, Houston Country Club, City Tavern Club (Washington), Farmington Country Club (Charlottesville, Va.), Vicmead Hunt Club (Wilmington, Del.), Union Boat Club (Boston), Chevy Chase (Md.) Club. Office: U Tex Med Sch 6431 Fannin St Houston TX 77030-1501 E-mail: s.ward.casscells@uth.tmc.edu.

CASSELMAN, SHARON MAE, recreational specialist; b. Cin., June 27, 1954; d. Alvin Maurice and Rosella Ann (Ruhe) C. Grad high sch., Cin. Instr. aquatics Powell Crosley YMCA, Cin., 1970-79; instr. phys. edn. St. John the Bapt. Elem. Sch., Cin., 1976-84; asst. aquatic dir., coach Jewish Cmty. Ctr., Cin., 1979-81; aquatic dir. City of Springdale, Cin., 1979-86; coach Roger Bacon High Sch., Cin., 1984-86; product cons. sales mktg. World Wide Aquatics, Inc., Cin., 1984-86; asst. dir. sports info. for women Vanderbilt U., Nashville, 1986-91, head coach men's and women's diving, 1986-91; program supr. recreation City of Springdale (Ohio), 1991—. Mem. spl. events com. City of Springdale, 1992-95; pres. Nashville Diving League, 1989-91; cons. in field. Vol. Big Bros., Nashville, 1990, Fund Raisers for Youth Sports, Springdale, 1994, 95; sponsor Muscular Dystrophy Assn. Lock-Up, Cin., 1995. Recipient Bronze medal Sports Challenge Cystic Fibrosis Found., Nashville, 1989; named Regional Champion U.S. Volleyball Assn., 1976, All Tournament Team U.S. Slow-Pitch Softball Assn., Cin., 1986. Mem. Ohio Parks and Recreation Assn. (aquatic sect.), Greater Cin. Pool Operators Assn. (advisor). Republican. Lutheran. Avocations: golf, tennis, racquetball, music, gardening. Office: City of Springdale Parks & Recreation 11999 Lawnview Ave Cincinnati OH 45246-2341

CASSENS, BARBARA ANN, mathematics and computer educator, consultant; b. Vienna, Mo., Dec. 11, 1943; d. Alex J. and Lucy G. (Volmert) Arunski; m. Simon Patrick Cassens, Dec. 29, 1962; children: Edward Gerard, Mary Alesia. BS in Math., St. Louis U., 1964, MS, 1968; postgrad., SUNY, Oswego, 1970-75, Central State U., Edmond, Okla., 1980-83. Cert. tchr., N.Y., Mo. Tchr. math. Villa Duchesne Sch., St. Louis, 1964-65; lectr. math. SUNY, Oswego, 1968-70; tchr. math. City Sch. Dist., Oswego, 1970-77, Watervliet (N.Y.) City Sch. Dist., 1977-79; Chpt. I math. specialist Edmond Sch. Dist., 1979-87; tchr. math. high sch., 1987-94; tchr. h.s. math Sarcoxie (Mo.) Sch. Dist., 1994—, chair dept. math. Ind. computer programmer, 1982—; workshop presenter. Mary Clemens scholar, 1961-64; named Outstanding Secondary Math. Tchr., Pitts. State U., 2002. Mem. Nat. Coun. Tchrs. Math., Pi Mu Epsilon. Democrat. Roman Catholic. Home: PO Box 1273 Joplin MO 64802-1273

CASSY, CATHERINE MARY, elementary school educator; b. Granite City, Ill., Aug. 12, 1949; d. George Joseph and Margaret Mary (Pieper) Crawshaw; m. Gene Herschel Cassy, June 5, 1971. BS in Edn., So. Ill. U., 1971; MS, Lindenwood Coll., 1987. Cert. lifetime elem., instrumental music, vocal music tchr., reading specialist, Mo., elem. tchr., Ill. Tchr. music Fowler Elem. Sch., Phoenix, 1972-73; tchr. 5th grade Parkview Elem. Sch., Granite City, 1973-82; tchr. of gifted Maryville Sch., Granite City, 1982-83; tchr. 6th grade and vocal music Henderson Jr. High Sch., St. Charles, 1984-86; tchr. 6th grade, tchr. vocal music Barnwell Jr. High Sch., St. Charles, Mo., 1986-87; tchr. 6th grade M.G. Henderson Elem. Sch., St. Charles, 1987-97; curriculum facilitator Francis Howell Sch. Dist., St. Charles, 1997—. Cycle chairperson Henderson Sch., 1991—. Mus. dir., performer Showtime Express, Inc., Granite City, 1989-96; chair Great Rivers Environ. Edn. Network, 1994-96. Named Tchr. of Yr. Barnwell Jr. High Sch., 1987; recipient Travis Hack Meml. award, 1993, Excellence in Teaching award Emerson Electric, 1993; Nat. Elem. Sci. Leadership grantee Nat. Sci. Resource Ctr., 1993, 96-97; Mo. Dept. Elem. and Secondary Edn. grantee, 1996-97. Fellow Tchr.'s Acad.; mem. ASCD, NSTA, NEA, Internat. Reading Assn., Nat. Coun. Tchrs. Math., Mo. Coun. Tchrs. Math., Mo. Sci. Tchrs. Assn., Acad. Sci. St. Louis, Nature Conservancy, Phi Delta Kappa. Avocations: music, community theater, computers, astronomy. Home: 2191 Shirlene Dr Granite City IL 62040-2564

CASTAÑEDA, JAMES AGUSTIN, language educator, golf coach; b. Bklyn., Apr. 2, 1933; s. Ciro Castañeda and Edna May Sincock; m. Terrill Lynn McCauley, Sept. 14, 1957; 1 child, Christopher James; m. Clara Luz Gutiérrez, Dec. 9, 1991. BA summa cum laude, Drew U., 1954; MA, Yale U., 1955, PhD, 1958; Certificat d'Aptitude à l'Enseignement du Français à l'Etranger, Université Paris, 1957; postgrad., Universidad de Madrid, 1957—; student summer inst. tchrs. fgn. langs., Purdue U., 1959. Asst. to assoc. prof. Spanish and French Hanover (Ind.) Coll., 1958-61; asst. prof. Spanish Rice U., Houston, 1961-63, assoc. prof. Spanish, 1963-67, prof. Spanish, 1967—. Vis. prof. Spanish U. So. Calif., 1959, U. N.C., 1962, 68, Western N.Mex. U., 1970; Florence Purington vis. prof. Mt. Holyoke Coll., 1976-77; prof. summer program Hispanic studies in Spain Rice U., 1979, 82, 83-90, head freshman baseball coach, 1962-67, asst. varsity coach, 1962-83, chmn. dept. Classics, Italian, Portuguese, Russian and Spanish, 1964-72, moderator television series, 1964-67, 68-69, head golf coach, 1983-98; lectr., dir., adviser and sponsor numerous acad. and other coms. in field. Author: A Critical Edition of Lope de Vega's "Las paces de los reyes, y Judía de Toledo", 1962, introducción, edición, 1971, Agustín Moreto, 1974, Mira de Amescua, 1977, El esclavo del demonio, 1980; contbr. numerous articles to profl. jours. Chmn. interview team in Europe Kent Fellowship Program, 1968; active Internat. Good Neighbor Coun. Rose Meml. scholar Drew U., 1950-54, Varsity Club scholar, Alumni Assn. Meml. scholar, Fulbright scholar Université de Paris, 1956-57, scholar Instituto de Cultura Hispánica, 1971; Danforth fellow Yale U., 1954-58, teaching fellow 1958—; named Miembro Titular, Instituto de Cultura Hispánica de Madrid, 1972, Hon. Master Will Rice Coll., 1976, Spanish Tchr. of Yr. and Fgn. Lang. Tchr. of Yr., Tex. Fgn. Lang. Tchrs.' Assn., 1982; recipient Drew U. Alumni Achievement award in Humanities, 1973, Will Rice Coll. James St. Fulton Svc. award 1973, Bklyn. Cadets Alumni Assn. Achievement award, 1976, Spanish Heritage award 1982, Disting. Svc. award Assn. Rice Alumni, 2000; named to Drew U. Athletics Hall of Fame, 1997. Mem. Am. Assn. Spanish and Portugese (numerous coms. and offices), Am. Assn. Tchrs. French, Am. Coun. Tchrs. Fgn. Langs. (del. affiliate assembly, 1970-75), S. Ctrl. Modern Lang. Assn. (various coms. and offices), Houston Area Tchrs. Fgn. Langs. (various coms. and offices), Modern Lang. Assn. (various coms. and offices), Inst. Hispanic Culture Houston (founding mem. 1966, numerous other coms. and offices), Sigma Delta Pi (hon. pres. 1998). Office: Rice Univ 6100 Main St Houston TX 77005-1892 E-mail: spangolf@rice.edu.

CASTEEN, JOHN THOMAS, III, university president; b. Portsmouth, Va., Dec. 11, 1943; s. John Thomas and Naomi Irene (Anderson) C.; children: John Thomas IV, Elizabeth, Lars. BA with high honors, U. Va., 1965, MA, 1966, PhD, 1970; LLD, Shenandoah Coll. and Conservatory Music, 1984; DHL, Bentley Coll., 1992; hon. degree, Piedmont (Va.) C.C., 1992; DPA, Bridgewater Coll., 1993; D honoris causa, U. Athens, Greece, 1996; DHL (hon.), Transylvania U., 1999. Asst. prof. English U. Calif., Berkeley, 1970—75; assoc. prof., dean admissions U. Va., Charlottesville, 1975—82; adj. prof. Va. Commonwealth U., Richmond, 1982—85; prof. English, pres. U. Conn., Storrs, 1985—90; pres. U. Va., 1990—, George M. Kaufman presdl. prof. of English, 1990—. Bd. dirs. NCAA, Wachovia, Inc., Sallie Mae, Ctrl. Va.'s Pub. Broadcasting; mem. Assn. Acad. Health Ctrs.' Coun. Health Scis. and Univ.; mem. com. Nat. Inst. on Alcohol Abuse and Alcoholism and Misuse on Coll. Campuses; chair Coun. for Higher Edn. Accreditation, 2000—. Author: 16 Stories, 1981; contbr. articles to various publs.; mem. editl. adv. bd. The Presidency. Sec. edn. Commonwealth of Va., Richmond, 1982-85; trustee Mariner's Mus., 1990—, Coll. Entrance Exam Bd., N.Y.C., 1980-90, chmn. 1986-88; mem. So. Regional Edn. Bd., 1982-85. New Eng. Bd. of Higher Edn., 1986-90; mem. nat. adv. com. Nat. Domestic Violence Media Campaign, 1992—; dir. Am. Coun. on Edn., 1993-96. Recipient Outstanding Virginian award, 1993, Gold medal award Nat. Inst. Social Scis., 1998. Mem. Assn. Am. Univs. (exec. com.), So. Assn. Colls. and Schs. (chair commn. on colls. 1995-97, pres.-elect 1997, pres. 1998), Assn. Governing Bds. Colls. and Schs. (coun. of pres. 1992—), Keswick Club, Farmington County Club, Commonwealth Club (Richmond), Phi Beta Kappa. Episcopalian. Office: P O Box 400224 Charlottesville VA 22904 E-mail: jtc@virginia.edu.

CASTELGRANT, ELIZABETH ANN SAYLOR, physical education educator, consultant; b. Neshanic Station, N.J., Jan. 9, 1951; d. Clement Joseph and Dorothy Ann (Wargo) Saylor; m. Daniel Peter Castelgrant, Apr. 20, 1991. BS, East Stroudsburg U., 1972. Phys. edn. tchr. West Amwell Sch., Lambertville, N.J., 1972-87, Lebanon (N.J.) Borough Sch., 1978-88, Flemington (N.J.) Raritan Schs., 1987—. Steering com. Juvenile Task Force, Flemington, 1980-83; mem. task force Sch. Health and Edn. Resource Ctr., Flemington, 1983-85; cons. North Hunterdon In-Svc. Day, Clinton, N.J., 1983; mem. EIC Tchr. Adv. Bd., Morristown, 1983-86; training cons. N.J. Edn. Assn., 1993—; in-svc. cons. Hunterdan County, 1999. Editor: Hunterdon County Edn. Assn. Bulletin, 1976-97. Publicity chair Hunterdon County Spl. Olympics, 1973-77; chair Camp Isabel Internat. Food Festival, Flemington, 1979, Tchrs. to Re-elect Meyner, Florio, McConnel, Foran, Weidel, 1976-90, South County Sr. Citizen's Program, Hunterdon County, 1978-82; vol. LVW, Hunterdon County, 1980-85, local bicentennial com., Lambertville, 1976, Deborah Hosp. Fund Drive, Flemington, 1984-86, Big Bros./Sisters, Flemington, 1983-86; mem. Flemington Tenants' Orgn., 1984-86, Hunterdon/Somerset Bus. and Edn. Partnership Adv. Coun., 1990—, Hunterdon County Dental Health Commn., 1989—, chair, 1995—; steering com. Hunterdon County Staff Devel. Coop., 1996—, paradigm pioneer com., 1993—; decision making com. Flemington Raritan Participatory, 1996—. Mem. AAUW, NEA, AAHPERD, N.J. Edn. Assn. (mem.'s rights com. 1972—, chair 1975—, chair Be Heard Campaign, 1980, mem. fair play com. 1983—, del. assembly 1978-83, 90-92, 98—), Hunterdon County Edn. Assn. (pres. 1978-82, 90-92, v.p. 1992—), Flemington-Raritan Edn. Assn. (v.p.-at-large 1987—, shared decision making com. 1993—), Hunterdon-Somerset County Bus. and Edn. Partnership (adv. bd., steering com. 2001/SCANS project 1991-97), Delta Kappa Gamma (1st v.p. Rho chpt.), Alpha Omicron Pi. Avocations: helping others, reading, quiet times. Home: 223 Longview Rd Bridgewater NJ 08807-2091 Office: Desmares Sch 16 Old Clinton Rd Flemington NJ 08822-5700 also: NJEA Region 13 47 E Main St Flemington NJ 08822-1216

CASTELLANO, SANDRA LORRAIN, principal; b. Elizabeth, N.J., Feb. 17, 1944; d. George and Florence (Malinowsky) Miller; m. Robert F. Castellano, Dec. 27, 1962 (div. Jan. 2000); children: Nicci, Anthony, Maria. BA, Newark State Coll., 1970; MEd in Early Childhood Edn., U. South Fla., 1997; EdD, Nova Southeastern U., 2004. Cert. elem. edn., N.J. Tchr. grade 1 Linden (N.J.) Pub. Schs., 1970-73, pilot tchr. open ct. reading series, 1971-72, supr. coll. interns, 1973-76, tchr. grade 3, 1973-81, asst. to bldg. prin., 1976-81; tchr. various grades Aberdeen Prep., Seffner, Fla., 1981-91, dir. curriculum Temple Terrace, Fla., 1992—, dir. after sch. activities, dir. pub. rels., 1991-92, owner. Head cons. Ednl. Devel. Resources, Temple Terrace, 1992—. Coach Bay Area Youth Soccer League, Brandon, 1984; local coord. Brandon Elks Hoop Shoot, 1988-92. Mem. NAFE, ASCD, Nat. Assn. for Edn. Young Children, Hillsborough County Child Care Assn., Temple Terrace C. of C.(sec. to bd. dirs.). Avocation: reading. Home: 524 Lantern Cir Tampa FL 33617-3724

CASTENELL, LOUIS ANTHONY, academic administrator; b. N.Y.C., Oct. 2, 1947; s. Louis Anthony Sr. and Marguerite (Barzon) C.; m. Mae Beckett, May 3, 1975; children: Louis Calvin, Elizabeth M. BA, Xavier U., 1968; MS, U. Wis., Milw., 1973; PhD, U. Ill., 1980. Cert. counselor and tchr. Elem. tchr. Orleans Parish Schs., New Orleans, 1968; academic advisor U. Wis., Milw., 1970-74; alumni dir. Xavier U., New Orleans, 1974-77, dean Grad Sch., 1980-89; dean Coll. Edn. U. Cin., 1990-99, U. Ga., 1999—. Cons. in field. Contbr. chpts. to books and articles to profl. jours. Mem. edn. commn. Nativity Sch., Cin., 1990, NAACP, 1990; mem. steering com. Cin. Youth Collabarative, 1990; bd. dirs. Tri-State Edn. and Tech. Found., Cin., 1990. Sgt. U.S. Army, 1968-69, Korea. Recipient Presdl. Citation, Assn. Multicultural Counseling, Washington, 1983. HEW fellow, 1978-80. Mem. AACD, Am. Edn. Rsch. Assn., Am. Assn. Colls. Tchrs. Edn. (chmn. bd. dirs. 2001—), Nat. Bd. Profl. Tchg. Stds., Assn. Tchr. Educators, State U. Deans Edn., Kappa Delta Pi, Phi Delta Kappa. Democrat. Roman Catholic. Avocations: reading, travel, photography. Home: 1320 Beverly Dr Athens GA 30606-7610 Office: U Ga Coll Edn Aderhold Hall G-3 Athens GA 30602 E-mail: lcastene@coe.uga.edu.*

CASTERLOW, GILBERT, JR., mathematics educator; b. Rich Square, N.C., Oct. 28, 1948; s. Gilbert and Juanita (Joyner) C.; m. Patricia Ann Vaughan, June 2, 1979; children: Bonita K., Laveda M., Marquita V. BS in Math. Edn., N.C. A&T State U., Greensboro, 1970, MS in Math. Edn., 1971; PhD in Curriculum and Instrn., Pa. State U., State College, 1980. Grad. asst. N.C. A&T State U., Greensboro, 1970-71, instr. math., 1971-77, math/computer edn. coord., 1980—, math. cons., 1984—, assoc. prof., 1986-91, prof., 1991—; adj. instr. Bennett Coll., Greensboro, 1973-74, Winston Salem (N.C.) State U., 1981-83; grad. asst. Pa. State U., State College, 1977-80; math. edn. coord. Saturday Acad. Program, Greensboro, 1981-94; bd. dirs., 1994—; math. edn. coord. Greensboro Area Math. and Sci. Edn. Ctr., 1984—. Math. edn. cons. Bennington Corp., State Dept. Pub. Instrn., Greensboro Coll., 1980—; presenter various local, state & nat. confs.; bd. govs. U. N.C. System. Co-author: The AM-BC Saturday Academy, 1988; contbr. articles to profl. jours.; condr. rsch. in the use of calculators, computers and other technologies to enhance math. instruction. Vol. Greensboro-Guilford County Area Schs., 1970—, Income Tax Assistance Program, Greensboro, 1980—; pres., v.p., chmn. Gen. Greene and Lincoln Mid. Schs. and Dudley H.S., Greensboro, 1985—; mem., tutor,

Sunday sch. tchr., trustee East White Oak Bapt. Ch., Greensboro, 1992—. Recipient Excellence in Teaching award U. N.C. Bd. Gov's., 1996, Disting. Alumni award N.Am. Fedn. for Equality of Opportunity, 1997; several funded grants, numerous appreciation and svc. awards from schs. and orgns. Mem. NAACP, ASCD, Math. Assn. Am. (regional rep. 1986—), Nat. Coun. Tchrs. Math. (testbook reviewer 1988—), N.C. Coun. Tchrs. Math. (v.p. colls. 1985-87, pres. Ctrl. Region 1993-95, W.W. Rankin Meml. award for excellence in math. edn. 1994), Am. Bowling Congress, Greater Greensboro Bowling Assn., Triad Scratch Bowling League (pres.), Kappa Delta Pi (Presdl. Excellence award 1977), Pi Mu Epsilon, Phi Delta Kappa, Alpha Kappa Mu. Democrat. Baptist. Avocations: Karate, bowling. Home: 4229 Queen Beth Dr Greensboro NC 27405-6360 Office: NC AT&T U Dept Math Marteena Hl Greensboro NC 27411-0001

CASTETTER, WILLIAM BENJAMIN, retired education educator, educational director; b. Shamokin, Pa., Aug. 31, 1914; s. Edward Franklin and Stella (Zimmerman) C.; m. Roberta Vera Breitmeyer, Aug. 6, 1947. BS, U. N.Mex., 1936, MA, 1937; PhD, U. Pa., 1948. Cert. tchr. sci. and fgn. langs., Pa. Tchr., prin. Melrose (N.Mex.) Sch. Dist., 1937-40; prof. Lebanon Valley Coll., Annville, Pa., 1947-49, U. Pa., Phila., 1949-81, dir. edn. svc. bur., 1970-81. Author: (textbook) The Human Resources Function in Educational Administration, 1950—; contbr. articles to profl. jours. Capt. U.S. Infantry, 1941-45. Recipient Tchg. and Svc. award Phi Delta Kappa, U. Pa. Chpt., Phila., 1980. Republican. Episcopalian. Avocations: wood working, gardening. Home and Office: Waverly Heights Villa 33 1400 Waverly Rd Gladwyne PA 19035-1254

CASTIGNETTI, DOMENIC, microbiologist, biology educator; b. Boston, Sept. 22, 1951; s. Andrew and Anna (Guarino) C.; m. Dorothy Ann Papalia, June 22, 1975; children: Nancy, Lisa, Michael. BA, Merrimack Coll., 1973; MS, Colo. State U., 1977; PhD, U. Mass., 1980. Post-doctoral fellow Brandeis U., Waltham, Mass., 1980-82; asst. prof. Loyola U., Chgo., 1982-88, assoc. prof., 1988—98, prof., 1999—. Recipient grant Cystic Fibrosis Found., Bethesda, Md., 1989. Mem. AAAS, Am. Soc. for Microbiology, Sigma Xi (pres. Loyola U. chpt. 1991-92). Roman Catholic. Achievements include first publ. of rsch. establishing that microbial iron chelators, siderophores, were present during a clinical infection of humans/cystic fibrosis patients. Office: Loyola Univ Chgo Biology Dept 6525 N Sheridan Rd Chicago IL 60626-5344

CASTILE, NORA FAYE PARKS, retired secondary education educator; b. Fitzgerald, Ga., Aug. 3, 1938; d. Murray Arthur and Sadie Louise (Butler) Parks; m. Harold Dean Castile, July 31, 1960; 1 child, Joseph David. BS in Edn., Ga. State Coll. for Women, Milledgeville, 1960; MS in Edn., U. North Fla., Jacksonville, 1979. Cert. tchr., Va., Fla. Tchr. Norview H.S., Norfolk, Va., 1962-65, Orange Park (Fla.) H.S., 1965-71, Clay H.S., Green Cove Springs, Fla., 1971-96. Vol. Mus. So. History, Jacksonville, Fla. Mem. United Daus. Confederacy (pres. Eliz. Gaines chpt. 1992-96, dist. II dir. 1996-98, Fla. divsn. historian 1998-2000, Fla. divsn. 2d v.p. 2000-02, v.p. 2002—), Nat. Soc. So. Dames Am. (Jacksonville chpt.). Methodist. Home: 3627 County Road 218 Middleburg FL 32068-5705

CASTILLO, MARIO ENRIQUE, artist, educator; b. Rio Bravo, Mexico, Sept. 19, 1945; came to U.S., 1955, naturalized, 1965; s. Manuel Castillo and Maria Enriquez de Allen. Cert., Ill. Inst. Design, 1964; BFA, Sch. of Art Inst., Chgo., 1969; MFA, Calif. Inst. Arts, 1972; postgrad., U. So. Calif., 1969-70, Pasadena City Coll., 1977, Calif. State U., L.A., 1980-81, Calif. State U., Dominguez Hills, 1986-88, East L.A. City Coll., 1982, Nat. U., Inglewood, Calif., 1990, Columbia Coll., Chicago, Il, 1996. Designer J.M. Pateros Studios, Inc., Chgo., 1965, Lukas & Assocs., Chgo., 1966; instr. Pilsen Settlement House, Chgo., 1967; comml. artist Chgo. Bd. Edn., 1968; instr. United Christian Cmty. Svc., Chgo., 1968-69; mural dir. Halsted Urban Progress Ctr., 1968, Dept. Human Resources, Chgo., 1969, McHenry Coll., Crystal Lake, Ill., 1992, No. Ill. U., DeKalb, 1993, Joliet Jr. Coll., Ill., 1994, Coll. of Lake County, Grayslake, Ill., 1994, U. Guadalajara, Ocotian, Mex., 1995, SAIC & Lincoln Park Cultural Ctr., Chgo., 1996, Bemis Found., Omaha, 1996, Triton Coll., River Grove, Ill., 1997; tchg. asst. Calif. Inst. Arts, Valencia, 1970-72, instr., 1972-73, Santa Monica (Calif.) City Coll., 1973; mem. faculty dept. art U. Ill., Champaign, 1973-76; comml. artist L.A., 1977; instr. art Immaculate Heart Coll., Hollywood, Calif., 1979-80, Pacific Asian Consortium in Edn., 1980-81, E.C.F. Art Ctr., L.A., 1986-90, L.A. Unified Sch. Dist., 1986-90, Instituto Comercial Artistico, Maywood, Calif., 1987, Lexicon Sch. Languages, 1987-88, Plaza de la Raza, 1989-90; mem. faculty art dept. Columbia Coll., Chgo., 1990—. Panelist at Northeastern Ill. U., Chgo., 1974, Coll. Art Assn., Chgo., 1975, Columbia Coll., Chgo., 1992, 94, 96, Chgo. Artist Coalition, 1993, Nat. Assn. Chicano Studies, Chgo., 1994, 96, Suburban Fine Arts Ctr., Highland Park, Ill., 1995, U. Guadalajara, Jalisco, 1995; presenter workshop Human Rights Portfolio, Chgo., 1994, Chgo., 1995; guest lectr. Galeria J.M. Velazco, Mexico City, 1975, Centro de la Causa, Chgo., 1975, Latino Cultural House, Champaign, 1975, U. Ill., Champaign, 1975, 76, Corpus Christi (Tex.) State U., 1978, McHenry County Coll., 1991, 92, Northwestern U., 1991, Columbia Coll., Montebello Sch. Dist., 1990, No. Ill. U., DeKalb, 1993, Triton Coll., River Grove, Ill., 1993, 94, Prospectus Gallery, Chgo., 1993, Joliet (Ill.) Jr. Coll., 1994, St. Cloud (Minn.) State U., 1994, MacMurry Coll., Jacksonville, Ill., 1994, Coll. of Lake County, 1994, Nat.-Louis U., Chgo., 1995, Melrose Park (Ill.) Pub. Libr., 1995, Mobil Art Gallery, Jacksonville, Ill., 1994, Northeastern U., Chgo., 1995, Harold Washington Libr., Chgo., 1995, Munster Ind. Cultural Ctr., 1995, U. Guadalajara, Ocotlan, Jalisco, 1995, 96, CCC Art Gallery, Chgo., 1995, Winnetka (Ill.) Cultural House, 1995, No. Ill. U., DeKalb, 1995, U. Guadalajara, La Barranca Campus, 1996, Lincoln Park Cultural Ctr., Chgo., 1996, Triton Coll., River Grove, 1996, 97; art juror Weisman Scholarship CCC, Chgo., 1993, Old Town Art Fair, Chgo., 1994, Hokin Gallery CCC, Chgo., 1995, Weisman Best of Show, Chgo., 1996; curator art exhibitions U. Ill., Champaign, 1975, Columbia Coll., Chgo., 1994, 95, Triton Coll., 1995, No. Ind. Arts Assn., Munster, 1995, 11th Street Art Gallery CCC, 1995, Hokin Ctr. Gallery, Columbia Coll., 1996; interior designer El Mercado Co., L.A. 1981-83; regular performer musical program Noches Rancheras, East L.A., Calif., 1981-83; cons. in field. One-man shows include Scholarship and Guidance Assn., Chgo., 1968, Calif. Inst. of the Arts, Burbank, 1971, Valencia, Calif., 1972, Latino Cultural House, U. Ill., Champaign, 1976, Inst. for Hispanic Cultural Studies, Santa Monica, Calif., 1989, Orlando Gallery, Sherman Oaks, Calif., 1989, Sangre De Cristo Arts and Conf. Ctr., Pueblo, Colo., 1991, Prospectus Gallery, Chgo., 1991, 93, McHenry County Art Gallery, 1991, No. Ill. U. Art Gallery, DeKalb, 1993, Atwood Art Ctr., St. Cloud U., 1994, MacMurry Coll., Jacksonville, Ill., 1994; numerous group shows including Fresno Art Mus., Calif., 1991, San Francisco Art Mus., 1991, San Francisco Mus. of Modern Art, 1991, Albuquerque Mus., 1991, Denver Art Mus., 1991, 93, Expo, 1993, San Antonio Mus. of Art, 1993, Nat. Mus. of Am. Art, 1993, Chgo., 1993, 94, Chgo. Latino Film Festival, 1994, Las Artes Galeria, Omaha, 1994, Open Windows Gallery, Chgo., 1994, S. Suburban Coll., South Holland, Ill., 1994, Columbia Coll., Chgo., 1994, 95, J.R. Shapiro Gallery, Oak Park, 1994, Cath. Theol. Union, Chgo., 1995, John Linsey Dallery, Oak Park, 1995, Hokin Gallery CCC, Chgo., 1995, Oak Park Art League, 1995, Pilsen Artist to Artist, Chgo., 1996, Prospecturs Gallery, Chgo., 1998, CCC Faculty Exhbn., Chgo., 1996, Richard Love Gallery, Chgo., 1996, La Llorona Gallery, Chgo., 1997, Prospectus Art Gallery, Chgo., 1997, Mexican Fine Arts Ctr. Mus., 1997, Chgo. Hist. Soc., 1996, 97, Mus. Contemporary Art, Chgo., 1996, 97, numerous others film screenings U.S., Europe, and Mexico; commd. muralist in public locations and pvt. residences; represented in permanent collections: Sara Lee Corp., Chgo., Mexican Mus. of Fine Arts, Chgo., San Francisco Mus. of Art, San Francisco Mus. of Contempory Art, Tucson Mus. of Art, Latino Inst., Chgo., Columbia Coll., Chgo., Bell Telephone Co., Chgo., Lake Meadows Assn., Chgo., Scholarship and Guidance Assn., Chgo., City of Chgo., San Antonio Art Mus., Guadalupe Cultural Arts Ctr., Denver, Evergreen State Coll., Olympia, Wash., Chgo. Humanities and Art Coun., Denver, Ariztlan, Inc., Phoenix, Mira, Chgo., Centro Cultural de La Raza, San Diego, San Diego Art Mus, Albuquerque Mus., San Francisco Art Mus., San Diego Mus. Contemporary Art, Denver Art Mus., Mex. Mus., San Francisco, Portland Art Mus., Nat. Mus. Am. Art, Washington, numerous group exhibitions include: Norris Gallery Cultural Arts Ctr., 1997, Instituto Cultural Puertoriqueno, 1998, Chgo. Athenaeum, Schaumburg, 1998, Ill. State Museum, 1999, Guadalupe Cultural Ctr., 2000; also numerous pvt. collections. Contbr. articles to numerous publications. Active contributor to cultural organizations. Recipient numerous awards including nat. gold medal, gold keys and certs. Scholastic Mag., 1963-65, cert. of merit N.Y. Times, 1965, 1st Prize award, Chgo. Police Dept., 1964, 1st Prize award Chgo. Assn. Commerce & Industry, 1965, 1st Pl. award U. Ill. Chgo. LASP design competition, 1st prize Maldef Art Competition, 1989, 1st pl. ESDC's Archtl. Relief Design Competition for New Homes in Chgo., 1992; artist to represent Midwest in nat. workshop, UCLA, 1988, artist to represent Latino culture in Spanish TV comml., 1989, 1st prize Homewood (Ill.) C. of C., 1967, 1st prize Fiesta del Quinto Sol, Chgo., 1974, 1st prize Mus. Sci. and Industry, Chgo., 1975, 1st prize for 18th St. banner design, Chgo., 1994; Am. Film Inst. grantee, 1972; Oakley fellow U. So. Calif., 1969-70; Scholarship and Guidance Assn. grantee, 1965-68, Ford Found. grantee, 1975; named Artist of Yr., Latino Inst., 1991. Achievements include rsch. in Perceptualism (the phenomena of after-images and optical illusions in paintings to create the feeling of the 4th dimension and alterations in color perception, visual investigations into discovering peculiar ways of presenting the human condition on this planet using superimposed layers of different states of realities and warping images and space so as to turn them "up-side-down"; composing numerous songs. Home: 10101 S Avenue M Chicago IL 60617-5925 Office: Columbia Coll Dept Art & Design 600 S Michigan Ave Chicago IL 60605-1900 E-mail: mc@mariocastillo.com.

CASTILLO, SUSAN, school system administrator; b. L.A., Aug. 14, 1951; m. Paul Machu. BA, Oreg. State U., 1981. Mem. staff Oreg. Pub. Broadcasting Radio, 1979-82; journalist, reporter legis. sessions Sta. KVAL-TV, Salem, 1991, 93, 95, journalist, reporter Eugene, 1982-97; mem. Oreg. State Senate, Salem, 1997—2002, vice chair edn. com., mem. health and human svcs. com., mem. transp. com., asst. Dem. leader legis. sessions, 1999, 2001, supt. pub. instrn., 2003—. Leader Oreg. Women's Health & Wellness Alliance. Mem. Gov.'s Task Force on DUII, 1997, Gov.'s Task Force on Cmty. Right to Know; bd. dirs. Oreg. Commn. on Hispanic Affairs, 1997, Birth to Three, Oreg. Environ. Coun.; mem. adv. com. Oreg. Passenger Rail Adv. Coun.; mem. Labor Comm.'s Adv. Com. on Agrl. Labor; vice-chair Farm Worker Housing Task Force. Democrat. Achievements include being the first Hispanic woman to serve in Oregon legislature. Office: Oregon Dept Education 255 Capitol St NE Salem OR 97301-0203*

CASTLE, EMERY NEAL, agricultural and resource economist, educator; b. Eureka, Kans., Apr. 13, 1923; s. Sidney James and Josie May (Tucker) C.; m. Merab Eunice Weber (dec.), Jan. 20, 1946; 1 child, Cheryl Diana Delozier; m. Betty Thompson, Mar. 18, 2000. BS, Kans. State U., 1948, MS, 1950; PhD, Iowa State U., 1952, LHD (hon.), 1997. Agrl. economist Fed. Res. Bank of Kansas City, 1952-54; from asst. prof. to prof. dept. agrl. econs. Oreg. State U., Corvallis, 1954-65, dean faculty, 1965-66, prof., head dept. agrl. econs., 1966-72, dean Grad. Sch., 1972-76, Alumni disting. prof., 1970, prof. univ. grad. faculty econs., 1986—, dir. rural studies program, 2001—03; v.p., sr. fellow Resources for the Future, Washington, 1976-79, pres., 1979-86. Vice-chmn. Environ. Quality Commn. Oreg., 1988-95; pres. Acad. for Lifelong Learning, Oreg. State U., 2002-03. Editor: The Changing American Countryside: Rural People and Places, 1995; mem. editl. bd. Land Econs., 1969—. Recipient Alumni Disting. Service award Kans. State U., 1976; Disting. Service award Oreg. State U., 1984 Fellow AAAS, Am. Assn. Agrl. Economists (pres. 1972-73), Am. Acad. Arts and Scis. Home: 1112 NW Solar Pl Corvallis OR 97330-3640 Office: Oreg State U 227 Ballard Corvallis OR 97331

CASTLEBERRY, JAMES NEWTON, JR., retired law educator, dean; b. Chatom, Ala., Dec. 28, 1921; s. James Newton and Nellie (Robbins) C.; m. Mary Ann Blocker, Feb. 12, 1944 (dec.); children: Jean, Nancy, James III (dec.), Elizabeth, Cynthia, Robert, Mary Ann. JD magna cum laude, St. Mary's U., 1952; diploma in comparative law, Nat. U. Mex., 1960; diploma in tchg. of comparative law, Strasburg, 1963. Bar: Tex. 1952. Asst. atty. gen. State of Tex., 1953-55; prof. law St. Mary's U., San Antonio, 1955-92, dean, 1978-89, dean emeritus, 1989—, ret., 1992. Dir. St. Mary's U. Summer Program in Internat. and Comparative Law, Innsbruck, Austria, 1986-89; exec. dir. Tex. Ctr. for Legal Ethics and Professionalism, 1990-92; lectr. comparative law fgn. legal study tours Corp. for Profl. Confs., 1990—. Co-author: Water & Water Rights, 1970; contbr. articles to law jours. Bd. dirs. Preservation Tex., San Antonio Conservation Soc.; trustee Tex. Supreme Ct. Hist. Soc. Mem. ABA, Am. Bar Found., San Antonio Bar Assn., Tex. Bar Found., San Antonio Bar Found., Tex. State Bar, Phi Delta Phi (internat. pres. 1977-79). Home: 7727 Woodridge Dr San Antonio TX 78209-2223

CASTOR, CAROL JEAN, artist, teacher; b. Bend, Oreg., Feb. 3, 1944; d. Keith and Lena (Morara) Morrison; 1 child, William Franklin. BFA, U. Okla., 1967; postgrad., U. Tulsa, summer 1976, Art Student's League of N.Y., N.Y.C., summer 1984. Benedictine Oblate with Osage Monastery, Sand Spring, Okla. Dir. art dept. Jefferson Jr. High Sch., Oklahoma City, 1967-68; art instr. Vinita (Okla.) High Sch., 1976-80; profl. artist specializing in commd. portraiture Carol Castor Art Studio, Vinita, 1980—, profl. portrait artist: also paints Native Ams., cowboys, Americana, landscapes and sacred subjects, 1980—; maintains art studio Vinnie Ream Cultural Ctr. Bd. dirs. Craig Gen. Hosp.; artist-in-residence mural project Vinita Pub. Sch. Alternative Sch., 1998, landscape project, 2000, Sculpture Park Garden, 2001, Collage, 2003; artist-in-residence Vinita Pub. Schs. Arts Experience, 1998-99, 2001-03; artist collage project, 2002, 03, 04. Represented in permanent collections at Vinita Pub. Libr., Craig Gen. Hosp., Vinita, 1st Nat. Bank & Trust, Vinita, Cowgirl Hall of Fame and Western Heritage Ctr., Ft. Worth, Okla. Hall of Fame, Oklahoma City, Okla. U. Med. Sch., Oklahoma City, Oklahoma U. Law Sch., Norman, Okla. U. Pharmacy Sch., Oklahoma City, Columbia Presbyterian Med. Ctr., N.Y., Nat. Cmty. Pharmacists Assn., Alexandria, Va.; featured in 2nd edit. of American Artists: An Illustrated Survey of Leading Contemporaries; portraits represented by Grand Ctrl. Galleries, N.Y.; artist cover illustration Oklahoma's Guide to Grand Lake, P.E.O Record, 2003; contbr. illustration to Labor of Love: The Life and Times of Vinnie Ream; cover artist for Mar.-Apr. 2003 issue P.E.O. Record. Mem. Mayor's Adv. Com., Vinita, 1972-74; mem. bldg. com. Vinita Pub. Libr., 1974-75; charter mem. Vinita chpt. Okla. Alliance for Mentally Ill, 1986—; organizer, mem. com. Young Life, Vinita, 1987-89; mem. com. for chronically and mentally ill Vinita Day Ctr. Inc., 1987—; organizer Ea. Trails Art Assn., 1972-84, chmn. Art Invitational '98, '99, '00, '01, Vinita; bd. dirs. Craig Gen. Hosp., 1995—; chmn. Med. Svcs. Corp., 1998-2000, Attuck Alternative Acad., 2002; mem. Benedictine Oblate of Osage Monastery. Recipient Cmty. Svc. award Vinita C. of C., 1984, named to Hall of Fame, 1993. Mem. AAUW (pres. Vinita chpt. 1972-74, Best banner award nat. conv. 1979, Women of Achievement award 1985, pres. Vinnie Ream Cultural Ctr. Found. 2000-03; bd. dirs.), P.E.O., Am. Soc. Portrait Artists. Democrat. Roman Catholic. Avocations: song writing, reading, piano, writing, poetry. Home: 121 Jennie Ln PO Box 411 Vinita OK 74301 E-mail: castorart@junct.com.

CASTRO, MARIA GRACIELA, medical educator, geneticist, researcher; b. Buenos Aires, Mar. 2, 1955; d. Nestor Antonio Castro and Maria Esther Rodriquez; m. Pedro Ricardo Lowenstein, Jan. 12, 1988; 1 child, Elijah David Lowenstein. BSc 1st class in Chemistry, Nat. U. La Plata, Argentina, 1979, MSc in Biochemistry, 1981, PhD in Biochemistry, 1986. Fogarty postdoctoral fellow Lab. Neurochem. & Neuroimmunol. Nat. Inst. Child Health and Human Devel. NIH, Bethesda, Md., 1986-88; sr. rsch. fellow Lab. Molecular Endocrinology Dept. Biochemistry and Physiology U. Reading, England, 1988-90; lectr. dept. molecular and life scis. U. Abertay, Dundee, Scotland, 1991-92; lectr. in neurosci., dept. physiology U. Wales Coll. Cardiff, 1991-95; sr. lectr. medicine Sch. Medicine U. Manchester, England, 1995-98, prof. molecular medicine, 1998—, dir. molecular medicine and gene therapy unit, 1996—. Expert Women in Sci. Tech., Sheffield, England, 1996—; neurosci. panel Wellcome Trust, England, 1999—; co-dir. dept. molecular medicine Cedar-Sinai Med. Ctr., 2001—; co-dir. bd. govs. Gene Therapeutics Rsch. Inst., Cedars Sinai Med. Ctr., 2001—; prof. medicine UCLA, 2002—. Mem. editl. bd.: Jour. Endocrinology, Jour. Molecular Endocrinology, Current Gene Therapy, Gene Therapy, Pituitary, 2000, Neuro Molecular Medicine, 2001—; contbr. articles to profl. jours. Rsch. grantee, Brit. Heart Found., 1997, Med. Rsch. Coun., 1998, Biotechnology and Biol. Rsch. Coun., 1999—2000, Wellcome Trust, 1999, NIH, 2003—. Mem.: NIH, Nat. Inst. Neurol. Disorders and Stroke (mem. study sect., grant award), Internat. Soc. Nerovirology (founding mem.), Soc. Neuroscience, Endocrine Soc., Am. Gene Therapy Assn. Achievements include patents in field; research in program development of gene therapy for chronic neurological diseases and brain cancer. Fax: 310-423-7308. E-mail: castromg@cshs.org.

CASTRO, STEPHANIE L. business management educator; b. San Antonio, Tex., Mar. 8, 1968; d. Reuben Riley and Mary Jaquelyn Loeffler; m. Erik Ricardo Castro, Aug. 21, 1993; 1 child, Cole Anthony. BBA, Fla. Internat. U., 1993; PhD, U. Miami, 1998. Asst. prof. La. State U., Baton Rouge, 1998—2000; vis. asst. prof. U. Miami, 2000—02; asst. prof. Fla. Atlantic U., 2002—. Mem.: APA, Acad. Mgmt., Soc. Indsl. Orgnl. Psychologists. Home: 17411 SW 61st Ct Fort Lauderdale FL 33331-1715

CASTRO-KLAREN, SARA, Latin American literature educator; b. Arequipa, Sabandia, Peru, June 9, 1942; d. José Andrés and Zoila Rosa (Rivas) Castro-Valdivia; m. Peter F. Klaren, Sept. 3, 1962; 1 child, Alexandra. BA, UCLA, 1962, MA, 1965, PhD, 1968. Asst. prof. Dartmouth Coll., No. Hampshire, N.H., 1970-84; chief Hispanic div. Lib. of Congress Fed. Govt., Washington, 1984-86; prof. Latin Am. lit. Johns Hopkins U., Balt., 1986—. Dir. program Latin Am. Studies, JHU. Author: El Mundo Magico de J.M. Arquedas, Lima, 1973, Mario Vargas Llosa, Analisis Introductorio, Lima, 1988, Escritura Sujeto y Transgresión, Mexico, 1989, Understanding Mario Vargas Llosa, U. S.C., 1990, Women's Writing in Latin America, 1991, Latin American Women's Narrative: Practices and Theoretical Perspectives, 2003. Fellow Woodrow Wilson Ctr. for Scholars, Washington, 1977-78. Mem. MLA, AAUP, Latin Am. Studies Assn., Ibero-americana, Soc. Hispanists, Am. Assn. Colls. and Univs. Avocation: gardening. Home: 9438 Rabbit Hill Road Great Falls VA 22066

CASTRO-POZO, TALIA, dancer, educator; b. Lima, Peru, Oct. 2, 1975; came to U.S., 1995; d. Jose and Renée Castro. Profl. degree in Ballet and Modern Dance, Nat. Ballet Sch., Lima, Peru, 1992; studied with Sergei Radchenko, Mabel Silvera Studio, Buenos Aires, 1992; student, Sch. Am. Ballet, 1995-96. Soloist Nat. Ballet, 1992-95; supr. Stepping Out Studios performing, tchr. ballroom dancing, 1999—. Rep. Internat. Ballet Competition, U.S.A., 1994, World Ballet Competition, Osaka, Japan, 1995, 30th Course of Ballet and Modern, Varna, Bulgaria. Dancer in classical, contemporary, modern pieces including Don Quixote, Spring Waters, Spartacus, A Solas; featured dancer in film Summer of Sam; choreographer in ind. film Angela, 1999. Dancer/choreographer Korean Army Festivities, Lima, 1992; dancer First Festival for Children's Rights, Lima, 1995. Recipient 1st Place award Latin Am. competition, 1989; Best Dancer of Yr. award Peruvian Press, 1991. Mem. Nat. Assn. Writers and Artists.

CASWELL, FRANCES PRATT, retired English language educator; b. Brunswick, Maine, June 25, 1929; m. Forrest Wilbur Caswell, June 30, 1956; children: Lucy Caswell Hilburn, Helen Caswell Watts, Harold F. BA, U. Maine, 1951; MA, U. Mich., 1955. Tchr. English, Bridgton (Maine) High Sch., 1951-54, Grosse Point (Mich.) High Sch., 1955-56; instr. South Maine Tech. Coll., South Portland, 1968-84, chmn. dept., 1984-93. Bd. dirs. Maine Vocat. Region 10, 1993-2003. Author: Growing Through Faith, A History of the Brunswick United Methodist Church, 1821-1996, 1996; contbg. author: Brunswick, Maine, 250 Years A Town, 1989. Pres. United Pejepscot Housing Inc., Brunswick, 1987-93. Mem. AAUW, Casco Bay Art League. Methodist. Avocations: painting, gardening.

CATA, ISABELLE MARIE GROS, foreign language educator; b. Boulogne Billancourt, France, Jan. 27, 1961; arrived in U.S., 1984; d. Claude Raoul and Ginette (Naudin-Spagnol) G. BA in English/Spanish, U. Paris III, 1982; MA in French, U. So. Calif., 1987, PhD in French, 1993. Asst. prof. Grand Valley State U., Allendale, Mich., 1993-99, assoc. prof. French, 1999—. Contbr. articles to profl. jours. Josephine de Karman fellow, 1991-92; Grand Valley State U. summer rsch. grantee, 1993, Circle Tchg. grantee, 1997-98, 98-99, 99-2000, 2000—. Mem.: MLA, Conseil Internat. d'Etudes Francophones, Women in French, Assn. Victor Segalan, Pi Delta Phi. Buddhist. Avocations: reading, yoga, dancing. Home: 501 Pleasant St SE Grand Rapids MI 49503 Office: Grand Valley State Univ 1 Campus Dr Allendale MI 49401 E-mail: catai@gvsu.edu.

CATALDI, SUZANNE LABA, philosophy educator; b. Somerville, NJ, Nov. 9, 1951; d. Michael and Ann (Bialy) Laba. BA, George Mason U., Fairfax, Va., 1981; PhD in Philosophy, Rutgers U., New Brunswick, N.J., 1991. Asst. prof. Moorhead (Minn.) State U., 1991-95; assoc. prof. So. Ill. U., Edwardsville, 1995—. Author: Emotion, Depth and Flesh: A Study of Sensitive Space, 1993. Office: So Ill U Edwardsville IL 62026 E-mail: scatald@siue.edu.

CATANESE, ANTHONY JAMES, academic administrator; b. New Brunswick, N.J., Oct. 18, 1942; s. Anthony James and Josephine Marlene (Barone) C.; m. Sara Jean Phillips, Oct. 23, 1968; children: Mark Anthony, Michael Scott, Mark Alexander. BA, Rutgers U., 1963; M in Urban Planning, NYU, 1965; PhD, U. Wis., 1968. Asst. prof. city planning Ga. Inst. Tech., Atlanta, 1967-78, assoc. prof., 1968-73, chmn. doctoral studies com., 1970-73; James A. Ryder prof. transp. and planning, dir. Ryder program in transp. U. Miami, Coral Gables, Fla., 1973-75; dean Sch. Architecture and Urban Planning U. Wis., Milw., 1975-82; prof. architecture and urban planning, provost Pratt Inst., N.Y.C., 1982-84; dean Coll. Architecture, U. Fla., Gainesville, 1984-89; pres. Fla. Atlantic U., Boca Raton, 1989—2002, pres., prof., 1990—2002; pres. Fla. Inst. Tech., Melbourne, 2002—. Sr. Fulbright prof., Colombia, 1971-72; sr. cons. State of Wis., 1965-67, sr. planner State of N.J., 1963-67; pres. A. J. Catanese & Assocs., Inc., 1967—; mem. pres. commn. NCAA, 1991-93. Author: Scientific Methods of Urban Analysis, 1972, New Perspectives on Urban Transportatio Research, 1972, Systematic Planning-Theory and Applications, 1970, Planners and Local Politics: Impossible Dreams, 1973, Urban Transportation in South Florida, 1974, Personality, Politics and Planning, 1978, Introduction to Urban Planning, 1979, Introduction to Architecture, 1979, The Politics of Planning and Development, 1984, Uban Planning, 1988; contbr. articles to profl. jours. Chmn. Mid. DeKalb County Dem. Party, 1969-71, mem. 5th Congl. Dist. Dem. caucus, 1971; aide-de-camp Gov.'s Office, State of Ga., 1971-72; mem. Ga. Dunes Studies Commn., 1972-73; bd. dirs. Archtl. Rsch. Ctrs. Consortium, 1976—; mem. Urban Policy Task Force, Carter presdl. campaign, 1976, 80; pres. Park West Redevel. Corp., 1976-78; chmn. Milw. City Plan Commn., 1978-82; bd. dirs. Goals for Milw. 2000, 1978-82, Environ. Edn. Found. Fla.; chmn. Gainesville (Fla.) Planning Bd., 1986-89. With USAR, 1961-63. Recipient fellowships State of N.J. Act of 1927, 1962-63, Werner Hegemann Found., 1963-65, Wis. Alumni Rsch. Found., 1965-68, Richard King Mellon Trust,

1966-67, Ford Found., 1967, Nat. Endowment Arts, 1980. Mem. Am. Inst. Planners (bd. govs., v.p. 1971-74), Am. Inst. Cert. Planners (mem. exec. com. 1971-74), Am. Planning Assn., Transp. Rsch. Bd., Regional Sci. Assn., Am. Acad. Polit. and Social Scis., Assn. Coll. Schs. Planning, Heritage Club, Wycliff Club, Tower Club. Office: Fla Inst Tech 150 W University Blvd Melbourne FL 32901

CATCHINGS, YVONNE PARKS, artist, educator; d. Andrew Walter and Hattie Marie (Brookins) Parks; m. James A.A. Catchings, May 30, 1960 (dec.); children: Andrea Yvonne Hunt Warner, Wanda Elaine Hunt McLean, James Albert A. AB in Art, Spelman Coll., 1955; MA in Art Edn., Columbia U., 1958; MA in Mus. Practice, PhD in Edn., U. Mich., 1970; MA, Wayne State U., 1994. Cert. art therapist. Tchr. art Atlanta Bd. Edn., 1955—59; instr. in art Spelman Coll., 1956—57; tchr. art Detroit Bd. Edn., 1959—75, art specialist, 1976—77, reading specialist, 1987—. Asst. prof. art Valdosta State Coll., 1987—88; lectr. Marygrove Coll., 1970—72. One-woman shows include Black Artist South, Huntsville (Ala.) Mus., 1978, exhibited in group shows at Forever Free: Art by African Am. Women 1862-1980, traveling show, 1981, Westbeth Art Gallery, NY, 1993, N.C.A. Mich-Gallery, 1993; author: You Ain't Free Yet Notes From a Black Woman, 1976; subject of: American Negro Art by Cedric Dover, 1960, Black Artist on Vol. 2 by Samella Lewis, 1970, Black Personalities of Detroit, 1975, Builders of Detroit by Anne Russell, 1978, The Art of Black American Women by Robert Henkes, 1993; author: Gumbo Ya Ya: Anthology of Contemporary African American Women Artists, 1995. Trustee Afro Am. Mus., 1970—72; program chmn. Nat. Aux. to Nat. Dental Assn., 1966, chmn. art and craft, 1976; chmn. reception com. United Negro Coll. Fund, Detroit, 1980. Recipient Fulbright Hayes grant for study, Zimbabwe, 1982, Spirit of Detroit award, Detroit Common Coun., 1978, Mayor's award of Merit, City of Detroit, 1980, James D. Parks Art award, Nat. Conf. Art, 1979. Mem.: Am. Art Therapy Assn., Mich. Art Therapist Assn., Your Heritage House Mus., Nat. Conf. Artists, Nat. Art Edn. Assn., Carrousels Club, Links Club, Smart Set Club, Moles Club, Delta Sigma Theta (chmn. Founders Day 1965, nat. chmn. heritage and archives, mem. nat. exec. bd.), Phi Delta Kappa. Home: 1306 Joliet Pl Detroit MI 48207-2834

CATCHPOLE, JUDY, state official; m. Glenn Catchpole; children: Glenda, Fred, Katie. BA in Edn., U. Wyo. Former state supt. pub. instrn. State Dept. Edn., Cheyenne, Wyo.; mem. Wyo. Higher Edn. Assistance Authority, 2002—. Exec. dir. Wyoming Rep. Party; mem. Wyoming Land and Investment bd., CCSSO bd. dirs., U. Wyo. bd. trustees, Edn. Commn. of the States Commr., STARBASE bd. dirs. (pres.). Mem. Wyo. Sch. Bds. Assn. (past vice chmn.), Wyo. Early Childhood Assn. (past pres.). Office: Wyo Dept Edn 2300 Capitol Ave Fl 2 Cheyenne WY 82002-0050*

CATEFORIS, DAVID CHRISTOS, art history educator; b. Balt., Apr. 16, 1964; s. Vasily Christos and Mary-Ann Augusta (Baugh) C.; m. Elizabeth Ritchie Seale, Sept. 16, 1989; 1 child, Alexander Christos. BA with distinction, Swarthmore Coll., 1986; MA in art history, Stanford U., 1988, PhD in art history, 1992. Asst. prof. art history U. Kans., Lawrence, Kans., 1992-98, assoc. prof., 1998—. Author: Willem De Kooning, 1994; collaborating author: Art History, 2d edit., 2002; editor Decade of Transformation: American Art of the 1960's, 1999; contbr. articles to profl. jours. and art mus. catalogs. Mem. Coll. Art Assn., Midwest Art History Soc., Phi Beta Kappa. Avocation: jogging. Office: U Kans Art History Dept 1301 Mississippi St Rm 209 Lawrence KS 66045-7500 E-mail: dcat@ku.edu.

CATES, DENNIS LYNN, education educator; b. Dallas, Nov. 25, 1946; s. Robert N. and Wanda June (Boyd) C.; m. Sue Anne Sadler, Aug. 9, 1975. BA, Tex. Tech U., 1968, MEd, 1976, EdD, 1986; MA, Sul Ross State U., 1981. Cert. secondary edn. tchr., deficient vision, learning disabilities, mental retardation, supervision, mid-mgmt., orientation and mobility instr. Tchr. Eagle Pass (Tex.) Ind. Sch. Dist., Beeville (Tex.) Ind. Sch. Dist., Levelland (Tex.) Ind. Sch. Dist.; tchg. asst. Tex. Tech. U., Lubbock; asst. prof. West Tex. State U., Canyon, 1986-89, U. S.C., Columbia, 1989-95, dir. Ctr. for Excellence in Spl. Edn. Tech., 1992-93; assoc. prof. Cameron U., Lawton, Okla., 1995-2000, prof., 2000—. Presenter numerous profl. confs.; field reviewer edn. jours. and pubs. Contbr. articles to profl. jours. Sgt. USAF, 1969-73. Grantee Consultation Tchrs. grant, 1981—82. Mem.: AAUP, ASCD, Assn. Tchr. Edn., Assn. Edn. and Rehab. for Blind and Visually Impaired (chmn. Divsn. 3 1998—2000, past chmn. 2000—02, newsletter editor Divsn. 3), Am. Coun. for Rural Spl. Edn. (chmn.-elect 2000—02, chmn. 2002—03, past chmn. 2003—, 2003—, bd. dirs., chmn. commn. com., past chmn. 2003—), Coun. for Exceptional Children (pres. Okla. chpt. 2001—02, treas. Okla. subdivsn. devel. disabilities divsn. 2001—, past pres. 2002—03, past pres. Okla. chpt. 2002—03, past pres. 2002—03), Am. Ednl. Rsch. Assn., Internat. Assn. Spl. Edn., Am. Assn. Mental Retardation, Nat. Coun. Geog. Edn., Nat. Coun. for Social Studies, Phi Delta Kappa. Office: Cameron U Dept Edn Lawton OK 73505 E-mail: dennisc@cameron.edu.

CATES, MICHELLE RENEE, air force reserve officer, consultant; b. Peoria, Ill., June 30, 1956; d. Roy Frederick and Dorothy Eleanor (Powell) C. BS in Phys. Edn., Taylor U., Upland, Ind., 1978; MA in Curriculum and Instrn., Chapman U., Orange, Calif., 1991. Par profl. West Chicago (Ill.) High Sch., 1978-79; tchr. lang. arts 1st Bapt. Christian Sch., Downers Grove, Ill., 1979-80; grad. asst. Whitworth Coll., Spokane, Wash., 1980; teaching fellow N.W. Nazarene Coll., Nampa, Idaho, 1981-83; commd. officer USAF, 1983-92, advanced through grades to capt., 1989; intelligence officer Operation Desert Shield and Storm, King Fahd Air Base, Saudi Arabia, 1991; ret. USAF, 1992; asst. prof. aerospace studies U. Ariz., Tucson, 1992; tactical officer Comdt.'s Office, Tex. A&M U., College Station, 1992; resigned from active duty. Sr. cons. with Booz Allen & Hamilton, 1995—. Maj. USAR. Democrat. Baptist. Avocations: weight lifting, bicycling, running, team sports. Home: 1308 Lakeshore Cir San Jose CA 95131-3596

CATES, SUE SADLER, educational diagnostician; b. Ft. Worth, Aug. 7, 1947; d. Randall and Mary Jo (Merkt) Sadler; m. Dennis Lynn Cates, Aug. 9, 1975. BA, Baylor U., 1970; MEd, Sul Ross State U., 1977. Cert. tchr., counselor, ednl. diagnostician, Tex. Tchr. spl. edn. Eagle Pass (Tex.) Ind. Sch. Dist., 1974-76, Beeville (Tex.) Ind. Sch. Dist., 1976-80; supr., ednl. diagnostician Sinton (Tex.) Ind. Sch. Dist., 1980-81; counselor, diagnostician Snyder (Tex.) Ind. Sch. Dist., 1981-86; ednl. diagnostician Pampa (Tex.) Ind. Sch. Dist., 1987-89; elem. counselor Richland County Sch. Dist., Columbia, S.C., 1989-95; ednl. diagnostician Wichita Falls (Tex.) Ind. Sch. Dist., 1995-97, Graham (Tex.) Ind. Sch. Dist., 1997-98, Carrollton-Farmers Branch (Tex.) Ind. Sch. Dist., 1998-2000, Cedar Hill Ind. Sch. Dist., 2000-01, Arlington (Tex.) Ind. Sch. Dist., 2001—02, Ft. Worth (Tex.) Can! Acad. Charter Sch., 2002—, Ft. Worth Can! Acad. Charter Sch., 2002, Van Zandt/Rains County SSA-Edgewood ISD, 2003—. Bd. dirs. Scurry County Sheltered Workshop, 1981-85, Tex. Assn. Children with Learning Disabilities, 1976-77, 81-83; coach Tex. Spl. Olympics, Beeville, amd Sinton, 1978-81; mem. sanctuary choir Floral Heights United Meth. Ch., Wichita Falls, 1995-98, Stephen min., 1992-2003; tchr. Sunday sch., youth coordinator, various other positions. Mem. Tex. Ednl. Diagnosticians' Assn., Council Exceptional Children, Council Ednl. Diagnosticians, Assn. Supervision and Devel., Nat. Assn. Workshop Dirs., NEA, Tex. State Tchrs. Assn., Tex. Classroom Tchrs. Assn., Am. Assn. Counseling and Devel., Tex. Assn. Counseling and Devel., Tex. Ednl. Diagnosticians Assn., AAUW, Phi Delta Kappa, Zeta Phi Eta. Avocations: swimming, coin collecting, travel, singing, jewelry. Home: 4402 York St Wichita Falls TX 76309-4014 Office: Edgewood Ind Sch Dist Van Zandt/Rains County SSA PO Box 727 Edgewood TX 75117

CATHEY, MARY ELLEN JACKSON, religious studies educator; b. Florence, S.C., Jan. 12, 1926; d. John William and Mary Ellen (Heinrich) Jackson; m. Henry Marcellus Cathey, May 31, 1958; children: Mary Emily Cathey Ewell, Henry Marcellus Jr. AB, Winthrop Coll., 1947; MRE, Presbyn. Sch. Christian Edn., Richmond, Va., 1953. Cert. Christian educator. Tchr. English, drama Jenkins Jr. High Sch., Spartanburg, S.C., 1947-51; dir. Christian edn. First Presbyn. Ch., Anderson, S.C., 1953-56, Bethesda (Md.) Presbyn. Ch., 1956-59; organizer, dir. Co-op Nursery Sch., Bethesda Presbyn. Ch., 1967-70; dir. Christian edn. Potomac Presbyn. Ch., Potomac, Md., 1977-83, Bethesda Presbyn. Ch., 1983-85, Nat. Presbyn. Ch., Washington, 1985-88; freelance cons. and educator Nat. Capital Presbytery, Washington, 1988—. Edn. cons. Covenant Presbyn. Ch., Arlington, Va., 1987, First Presbyn. Ch., Arlington, 1989-91, Lewinsville Presbyn. Ch., McLean, 1990; elder Nat. Presbyn. Ch., 1990—; elder commr. Gen. Assy., Presbyn. Ch., Milw., 1992. Author hymn text: God Almighty, God Eternal, 1956, others, numerous poems; co-author: Confirmation Guidebook, 1988, The Circle of Wholeness, 1991. Mem. Nat. Leadership Ctr., Washington, 1999—2000; mem. pres.;s adv. coun. Union Sem.-Presbyn. Sch. Christian Edn., Richmond, Va.; pub. trustee Washington Theol. Consortium; elder Presbyn. Ch. USA, copmmr. gen. assembly, 1992. Recipient Sparkler Award Presbyn. Sch. of Christian Edn. Alumni/ae Coun., 1991. Mem. Hymn Soc. U.S. and Can., Presbyn. Writers' Guild, Presbyn. Assn. Musicians, Assn. Presbyn. Ch. Educators, Nat. Capital Presbytery Educators. Avocations: travel, theatre, music, dancing, writing. Home and Office: 1817 Bart Dr Silver Spring MD 20905-4418

CATHEY, WADE THOMAS, retired electrical engineering educator; b. Greer, S.C., Nov. 26, 1937; s. Wade Thomas Sr. and Ruby Evelyn (Waters) C.; children: Susan Elaine, Cheryl Ann. BS, U. S.C., 1959, MS, 1961; PhD, Yale U., 1963. Group scientist Rockwell Internat., Anaheim, Calif., 1962-68; from assoc. prof. to prof. elec. engring. U. Colo., Denver, 1968-85, chmn. dept. elec. engring. and computer sci., 1984-85, chmn. faculty senate, 1982-83, prof. Boulder, 1985-97, rsch. prof., 1997—2003, ret., 2003. Pres. CDM Optics, 1996—; dir. NSF Ctr. Optoelectronic Computing Sys., Boulder, 1987-93; cons. in field, 1968—. Author: Optical Information Processing and Holography, 1978; contbr. articles to profl. jours.; inventor in field. Fellow Croft, U. Colo., 1982, Faculty, U. Colo., 1972-73. Fellow IEEE, Optical Soc. Am. (topical editor 1977-79, 87-90), Soc. Photo-Optic Instrumentation Engrs. Achievements include extend focal depth and passive ranging in imaging systems, rsch. on matching image acquisiton and signal processing systems. Home: 248 Alpine Way Boulder CO 80304-0406 Office: U Colo Dept Elec Engring Boulder CO 80309-0425 also: CDM Optics Inc 4001 Discovery Dr Ste 2110 Boulder CO 80303 E-mail: tomc@cdm-optics.com.

CATHEY-GIBSON, SHARON SUE RINN, school principal, college administrator; b. Reed City, Mich., June 11, 1940; d. Sherwood and Ellen (Hutson) Rinn.; children: Joel A., Julie A.; Sharon Sue Rinn Cathey-Gibson, Aug. 27, 1996; m. Warren Gibson, Aug. 27, 1996. BA in Edn., San Francisco State U., 1962; postgrad., U. Mich., 1972-74, U. Calif., 1975-77; MA in Edn., U. Nev., 1988, EdD in Curriculum and Instrn., 1991. Tchr. Laguna Salada Union Sch. Dist., Pacifica, Calif., 1962-64, Redwood City (Calif.) Sch. Dist., 1964-66, Lapeer (Mich.) Sch. Dist., 1970-74; tchr., choral dir. Pine Middle Sch., Reno, 1978-84; tchr. Washoe County Sch. Dist., Reno, 1985—, adminstrv. elem. edn. cons., 1991-92; adminstrv. cons. Nev. State Dept. Elem. Edn., Carson City, 1990—; prin. Anderson Elem. Sch., Reno, 1992—, Elizabeth Lenz Elem. Sch., 1994, Libby Booth Sch., Reno, 1994-97; prof., adminstr. Sierra Nev. Coll., 1994—2002, adminstr., 1997—2002, ret., 2002; asst. prof. U. Nev., Reno, 2002—, cons. for literacy, 2001—03; cons., ptnr., editl. staff Superior Edn. and Leadership Inc. Adminstr. Sierra Advocates for Family Equity; statewide exec. dir. tchr. edn. Thompson Learning Ctr., Reno, 1987—89, diagnostician, 1987—89; asst. U. Nev., 1988—90; cons. Nev. State Be. Elem. Edn., 1990, Computer Users Educators of No. Nev.; adminstr., prof. and coord. sch. based programs, dir. tchr. edn. dept. Sierra Nev. Coll.; CASA worker; cons., editor Superior Learning & Leadership Corp.; presenter in field; ptnr. Superior Learning Co. Adminstr. Sierra Advocates for Family Equity. Recipient Celebrate Literacy award, Internat. Reading Assn., 2003; grantee, Nev. ESSA, 1977. Mem.: AAUW (pres. 1976—78), Nev. Assn. Coll. Tchrs. Edn., Nat. Coun. Tchrs. English, Nat. Reading Assn., Internat. Reading Assn. (state pres. 1992, local pres. 1993—94, Literacy award 1995, Celebrate Literacy award 2003), Washoe County Tchrs. Assn., Kiwanis (Reno Sunrisers chpt. sec. 1995—98, pres. 2001—02), Kappa Delta Epsilon (adviser), Delta Kappa Gamma (state pres. 1989—91), Phi Kappa Phi. Republican. Episcopalian. Avocations: music, art, swimming. Home: 2550 Comstock Dr Reno NV 89512-1347

CATLETT, ROBERT BISHOP, economics educator; b. Grand Junction, Colo., Aug. 29, 1952; s. Charles William and Hellen Kathrine (Bishop) C.; m. Lorraine Elizabeth Arsenault, Sept. 9, 1977; children: Mariah Elizabeth, Johanna Kathrine, Emma Christine. AB, U. Nebr., 1974, AM, 1975, postgrad., 1980-81. Lectr. econs. Emporia (Kans.) State U., 1976-78, asst. prof., 1978—, dir. Ctr. Econ. Edn., 1988—. Econ. model developer U.S. Dept. Agr., Emporia, Kans., 1982-88; program evaluator Assn. Collegiate Bus. Schs. and Programs, 1991, 92, 93, Chgo. Bd. Trade Judge of 1992 Commodity Challenge; con. Econ. Conditions Analysis-S.E. Kans., U. Kans., Kans. Inc., Fed. Res. Bank Kansas City, 1993; participant NSF program on exptl. econs. U. Ariz., 1991; bd. dirs. FCI; judge NASDAQ Ednl. Found. Nat. Tchg. Awards, 1999, 2002. Author: Microeconomics, Principles and Applications Test Bank, 1998, Macroeconomics, Principles and Applications Test Bank, 1998, Microeconomics: A Contemporary Introduction-Test Bank, 1997, Economics: A Contemporary Introduction-Test Bank, 1997; contbg. author Strategies for the Future, 1990, Human Energy Facing the Future, 1991, others; contbr. articles to profl. jours.; manuscript and book reviewer Southwestern Pub. Co., 1991—; manuscript reviewer Harper Collins Coll. Pubs., 1994, West Pub. Co., 1995, Blackwell Pub. Co., 1997, Simon & Schuster, 1998, 99, Prentice Hall, 1999, McGraw Hill, 2003, Addison Wesley Lang., 2003; referee Jour. of Risk and Ins., 1998-2002. Named Outstanding Prof. Phi Delta Theta, Emporia, 1987. Mem. AAUP (Emporia State U. chpt. exec. com.), Am. Econs. Assn., Nat. Assn. Econ. Educators (chair legal and legis. com. 2002-03), Kans. Econs. Assn. (pres. 1986-87), Kans. Coun. on Econ. Edn. (exec. com. 1990, bd. dirs. 1999-2002), Mo. Valley Econs. Assn. Avocations: victorian house restoration, cycling, skating, sports. Home: 405 Exchange St Emporia KS 66801-3817 Office: Emporia State U 1200 Commercial St Emporia KS 66801-5087

CATO, GLORIA MAXINE, retired secondary education educator, school program administrator; b. Covington, La., Mar. 22, 1942; d. Dan and Roxieana (Washington) Smith; widowed; 1 child, Mark. BS, Southern U., 1965; MS, Pepperdine U., 1974. Tchr. Los Angeles Unified Sch. Dist., 1965-81, counselor, magnet program coordinator, 1981—, PUSH for Excellence program coordinator, 1978-80, student activities coordinator, 1982-84, coll. advisor, 1984-85, personnel specialist, tchr. advisor, 1986-87, asst. prin., 1992—99; ret., 1999. Edn./counselor cons. L.A. Unified Sch. Dist. Trustee L.A. Ednl. Allance Restructuring Now. Recipient Community-Sch. Service award City of Los Angeles, 1978; named to Top Ladies of Distinction, 1992. Charter mem. NEA, Nat. Assn. Biology Tchrs. (finalist Tchrs. award 1978), Magnet Counselor Assn., Los Angeles Counselors Assn.; mem. United Tchrs. Los Angeles, Associated Adminstrs. L.A., Assn. Calif. Sch. Adminstrs., Asst. Prin. Secondary Counseling Svcs. Orgn., Phi Delta Kappa, Alpha Kappa Alpha (Mu Beta Omega chpt.). Democrat. Baptist. Home: 3661 Kensley Dr Inglewood CA 90305-2230

CATTANDO-HELD, DONNA, school director; b. Chicago Heights, Ill., June 13, 1949; d. Frank and Betty Cattando; m. Edward A. Held, May 10, 1979; 1 child, Julia Held. BA cum laude, San Francisco State U., 1975. Tchr. Sch. Without Walls, San Francisco, 1974, Discovery Ctr., San Francisco, 1975-77; dir. Newbridge Elem. Sch., L.A., 1977-90, The Country Sch., North Hollywood, Calif., 1990-92; adminstr. Children Now, L.A., 1992; founder, head sch. Tarzana Hills Elem. Sch., Tarzana, Calif., 1992—, tech. and sci. specialist, 1993—. Vol. George Moscone senate-gubernatorial and mayorial campaigns, San Francisco, 1971-76.

CATTANEO, JACQUELYN ANNETTE KAMMERER, artist, educator; b. Gallup, N.Mex., June 1, 1944; d. Ralph John and Gladys Agnes (O'Sullivan) Kammer; m. John Leo Cattaneo, Apr. 25, 1964; children: John Auro, Paul Anthony. Student, Tex. Woman's U., 1962-64. Portrait artist, tchr., Gallup, N.Mex., 1972. Coord. Works Progress Adminstrn. art project renovation McKinley County, Gallup, Octavia Fellin Performing Arts wing dedication, Gallup Pub. Libr.; formation com. mem. Multi-Modal/Multi-Cultural Ctr. for Gallup; exch. with Soviet Women's Com. USSR Women Artists del., Moscow, Kiev, Leningrad, 1990; Women Artists del. and exch., Jerusalem, Tel Aviv, Cairo, Israel; mem. Artists Del. to Prague, Vienna and Budapest; mem. Women Artists Del. to Egypt, Israel and Italy, 1992, artist del., Brazil, 1994, Greece, Crete, Turkey, Spain, 1996, N.S. and Ont., N.B., PEI, Can., 2000. One-woman shows include Gallup Pub. Libr., 1963, 66, 77, 78, 81, 87, Gallup Lovelace Med. Clinic, Santa Fe Sta. Open House, 1981, Gallery 20, Farmington, N.Mex., 1985—, Red Mesa Art Gallery, 1989, Soviet Retrospect Carol's Art & Antiques Gallery, Liverpool, N.Y., 1992, 97, N.Mex. State Capitol Bldg., Santa Fe, 1992, Lt. Govt. Casey Luna-Office Complex, Women Artists N.Mex. Mus. Fine Arts, Carlsbad, 1992, Rio Rancho Country Club, N.Mex., 1995; exhibited in group shows including Navajo Nation Libr. Invitational, 1978, Santa Fe Festival of the Arts Invitational, 1979, N.Mex. State Fair, 1978, 79, 80, Catharine Lorrilard Wolfe, N.Y.C., 1980, 81, 84, 85, 86, 87, 88, 89, 90, 91, 92, 4th ann. exhbn. Salmagundi Club, 1984, 90, 98, 3d ann. Palm Beach Internat., New Orleans, 1984, Fine Arts Ctr., Taos, 1984, The Best and the Brightest O'Brien's Art Emporium, Scottsdale, Ariz., 1986, Gov.'s Gallery, 1989, N.Mex. State Capitol, Santa Fe, 1987, Pastel Soc. West Coast Ann. Exhbn., Sacramento Ctr. for Arts, Calif., 1986-90, gov.'s invitational Magnifico Fest. of the Arts, Albuquerque, 1991, Assn. pour la Promotion du Patrimone Artistique Française, Paris Nat. Mus. of the Arts for Women, Washington, 1991, Artists of N.Mex., Internat. Nexus '92 Fine Art Exhbn., Trammell Corw Pavillion, Dallas, Carlsbad (N.Mex.) Mus. Fine Art; represented in permanent collections Zuni Arts and Crafts Ednl. Bldg., U. N.Mex., C.J. Wiemar Collection, McKinley Manor, Gov.'s Office, State Capitol Bldg., Santa Fe, Hist. El Rancho Hotel, Gallup, Sunwest Bank, Fine Arts Ctr., Taos, Armand Hammer Pvt. Collection, Wilcox Canyon Collections, Sadona, Ariz., Galaria Impi, Netherlands, Woods Art and Antiques, Liverpool, N.Y., Stewarts Fine Art, Taos, N.Mex., Rehoboth McKinley Christian Hosp. & Sacred Heart Cathedral, Gallup, NM. Mem. Dora Cox del. to Soviet Union-U.S. Exch., 1990. Recipient Cert. of Recognition for Contbn. and Participation Assn. pour la Patrinome du Artistique Français, 1991, N.Mex. State Senate 14th Legislature Session Meml. # 101 for Artistic Achievements award, 1992, Award of Merit, Pastel Soc. West Coast Ann. Membership Exhbn., 1998, award N.Mex. State Ho. Reps. for Artistic Achievement, 2001, Holbein award for excellence in painting Pastel Soc. West Coast Internat. Juried Exhbn.; honored for preservation of WPA Dept. Edn. N.Mex. State Ho. of Reps., 2001. Mem. Internat. Fine Arts Guild, Am. Portrait Soc. (cert.), Oil Painters of Am., Pastel Soc. of West Coast (cert., Hobein award, award of excellence mem.'s show 1999), Mus. N.Mex. Found., N.Mex. Archtl. Found., Mus. Women in the Arts, Fechin Inst., Artists' Co-op (co-chair), Gallup C. of C., Gallup Area Arts and Crafts Coun. (nat. and internat. artist of distinction award 1997), Am. Portrait Soc. Am., Pastel Soc. N.Mex., Catharine Lorillard Wolfe Art Club of N.Y.C. (oil and pastel juried membership), Oil Painters of Am., Pastel Soc. N.Mex., Soroptomists (Internat. Woman of Distinction 1990), Salmagundi Art Club. Address: 210 E Green St Gallup NM 87301-6130 E-mail: cattaneo@cnetco.com.

CATZ, BORIS, endocrinologist, educator; b. Troyanov, Russia, Feb. 15, 1923; came to U.S., 1950, naturalized, 1955; s. Jacobo and Esther (Galbmilion) C.; m. Rebecca Schechter; children: Judith, Dinah, Sarah Lea, Robert. BS, Nat. U. Mex., 1941, MD, 1947; MS in Medicine, U. So. Calif., 1951. Intern Gen. Hosp., Mexico City, Mex., 1945-46; prof. sch. medicine U. Mex., 1947-48; instr. medicine U. So. Calif., 1952-54, asst. clin. prof., 1954-59, 1959-83, clin. prof., 1983—; pvt. practice L.A., 1951-55, Beverly Hills, Calif., 1957—. Chief Thyroid Clinic L.A. County Gen. Hosp., 1955-70; sr. cons. thyroid clin. U. So. Calif., L.A. Med. Ctr., 1970—; clin. chief endocrinology Cedars-Sinai Med. Ctr., 1983-87. Author: Thyroid Case Studies, 1975, 2d edit., 1981; contbr. numerous articles on thyroidology to med. jours. Capt. U.S. Army, 1955-57. Rsch. fellow medicine U. So. Calif., 1949-51; Boris Catz lectureship in his honor Thyroid Rsch. Endowment Fund, Cedars Sinai Med. Ctr., 1985. Fellow ACP, Am. Coll. Nuclear Medicine (pres. elect 1982), Royal Soc. Medicine, Am. Thyroid Assn. (Disting. Svc. award 2001); mem. AMA, AAAS, Cedars Sinai Med. Ctr. Soc. History of Medicine (chmn.), L.A. County Med. Assn., Calif. Med. Assn., Endocrine Soc., Am. Thyroid Assn., Soc. Exptl. Biology and Medicine, Western Soc. Clin. Rsch., Am. Fedn. Clin. Rsch., Soc. Nuclear Medicine, So. Calif. Soc. Nuclear Medicine, N.Y. Acad. Scis., L.A. Soc. Internal Medicine, Collegium Salerni, Cedar Sinai Soc. History Medicine, B'nai B'rith Club, The Profl. Man's Club (past pres.), Phi Lambda Kappa. Home: 300 S El Camino Dr Beverly Hills CA 90212-4212 Office: 435 N Roxbury Dr Beverly Hills CA 90210-5027

CAULFIELD, JAMES BENJAMIN, pathologist, educator; b. Mpls., Jan. 1, 1927; s. Linus Joseph and Olive Bell (Curtis) C.; m. Virginia Walsh, Jan. 28, 1950; children: Ann, John, Clare. BA, Miami U., Oxford, Ohio, 1947; BS, U. Ill., 1948, MD, 1950. Intern Henrotin Hosp., Chgo., 1950-51; resident U. N.C., Chapel Hill, 1951-52, U. Kans. Med. Ctr., Kansas City, 1954-55; vis. investigator Rockefeller Inst., N.Y.C., 1955-56; instr. pathology Harvard U., 1959-64, asst. prof., 1964-70, assoc. prof., 1970-75; asst. pathologist Mass. Gen. Hosp., Boston, 1960-64, assoc. pathologist, 1964-75; prof., chmn. dept. pathology U. S.C., 1975-85; prof. pathology U. Ala., Birmingham, 1985—. Adj. prof. Med. U. S.C., Charleston, 1981-85; rsch. on collagen network of heart and changes associated with alterations in the network. Contbr. articles to profl. jours. Served with USN, 1944-46, 52-54. Mem. Am. Soc. Cell Biology, Am. Soc. Pathology, Internat. Acad. Pathology, Fedn. Exptl. Pathology, Electron Microscopy Soc., Internat. Study Group for Heart Research (treas. Am. sect. 1972-85), N.Y. Acad. Scis., Harvard Club, Boston Athenaeum Club, Sigma Xi, Phi Eta Sigma. Office: U Ala Dept Pathology 506 Kracke Bldg 619 19th St S Birmingham AL 35233-0001

CAULKINS, DAVID DOUGLAS, anthropology educator; b. Rapid City, S.D., Aug. 28, 1940; s. David P. and Helen J. (Smythe) C.; m. Lorna J. Wilson Caulkins, June 14, 1963. BA, Carleton Coll., Northfield, Minn., 1962; PhD, Cornell U., 1982. Prof. Anthropology Grinnell (Iowa) Coll., 1970—. Contbr. articles and chpts. to profl. jours. Grantee, NSF, 1993—95, 2002—. Mem. Am. Anthrop. Assn. Office: Grinnell College PO Box 805 Grinnell IA 50112-0805 E-mail: caulkins@grinnell.edu.

CAURAUGH, JAMES H. physical education educator; b. Potsdam, N.Y., Feb. 4, 1952; s. Jess H. and Doris M. (Bishop) C.; m. Kathryn L. Hosmer, Aug. 3, 1974; 1 child, Kirstin L. BS, SUNY, Brockport, 1974; MS, Pa. State U., 1977; PhD, Fla. State U., 1984. Cert. tchr., N.Y. From instr. to asst. prof. Pa. State U., University Park, 1975-81; grad. rsch. asst. Fla. State U., Tallahassee, 1981-84; asst. prof. U. Okla., Norman, 1984-88, U. Fla., Gainesville, 1988-91, assoc. prof. phys. edn., 1991—, dir. Motor Behavior Lab., 1988—, co-dir. ctr., 1988—. Mem. editorial bd. ACTA Psychologica, Amsterdam, The Netherlands, 1991—; contbr. articles to profl. jours. Chmn. 10K race McKeesport (Pa.) Hosp., 1979-81. Fellow AAHPERD;

mem. N.Am. Soc. for Psychology of Sport and Phys. Activity (conf. coord. 1994), Can. Soc. Psychomotor Learning and Sport Psychology, Internat. Soc. for Sport Psychology. Avocations: running, bicycling, reading, travel with family.

CAUSEY, SUSAN MARIE, retired health educator; b. Walker Park, Ga., Aug. 8, 1947; d. Harold Bates and Keturah Elizabeth (Burgess) C. BS in Health, Phys. Edn. and Recreation, Ga. Coll., 1968; postgrad., various schs., 1971—95. Cert. tchr., Ga. Tchr. health, phys. edn. Lakeshore High Sch., College Park, Ga., 1968-88, chair dept., 1978-88; tchr. health Roswell (Ga.) High Sch., 1988—98; ret., 1998—. Sponsor, coach Lakeshore and Roswell High Schs., 1988-98. Author, editor (newsletter) Physical Expressions, 1968-98. Counselor Camp Juliette Low, Cloudland, Ga., 1965-87, dir., 1974-76, bd. trustees, 1985—; vol., mem., instr. CPR courses ARC, 1980—; sponsor, coord. Red Ribbon Week and Great Am. Smokeout, Roswell, 1988—; sponsor drug-free group Choice, Roswell, 1988-95, PHAR (Peer Helpers at Roswell), 1990-96. Recipient Cert. Dedication award Camp Juliette Low Bd. Trustees, 1975. Mem. NEA, AAHPERD, Ga. Assn. Educators, Ga. Assn. Health, Phys. Edn., Recreation and Dance (Health Educator of Yr. award 1992), Fulton County Assn. Educators. Avocations: piano, camping, reading, canoeing, collecting musical instruments.

CAVALIERE, FRANK JOSEPH, lawyer, educator; b. N.Y.C., Dec. 29, 1949; s. Alfred and Margaret Joan Cavaliere. BA in Econs., Bklyn. Coll., 1970; BBA in Acctg., Lamar U., 1976; JD, U. Tex., 1979. Bar: Tex. 1979. Atty. Coke & Coke, Dallas, 1979-81, Weller, Wheelus & Green, Beaumont, Tex., 1981-84; pvt. practice law Beaumont, 1985—; from asst. to full prof. bus. law Lamar U., Beaumont, 1985—. Mem. editl. adv. bd. CPA Tech. and Internet Advisor, 2000—; tech. advisor Am. Law Inst.-ABA, 1998—, also continuing legal edn. spkr. Author (column) Web-Wise Lawyer, The Practical Lawyer, 1996; contbr. articles to profl. jours. Advisor Pi Kappa Alpha Fraternity, Beaumont, 1987-90, Delta Sigma Pi Fraternity, Beaumont, 1994-97. Lt. USNR, 1970-75. Mem. ABA, Tex. Bar Assn., Coll. of the State Bar Tex., Jefferson County Bar Assn., Phi Beta Kappa. Office: 148 S Dowlen Rd PMB 683 Beaumont TX 77707-1755 E-mail: cavfj@prodigy.net., cavalierfj@hal.lamar.edu.

CAVALLARO, MARY CAROLINE, retired physics educator; b. Everett, Mass., Feb. 2, 1932; d. Joseph and Domenica Cavallaro. BS, Simmons Coll., 1954, MS, 1956; EdD, Ind. U., 1972; postgrad., Tufts U., 1980-81. Inst. math. and physics Sweet Briar (Va.) Coll., 1955-56; instr. physics Simmons Coll., Boston, 1956-58, Randolph-Macon Woman's Coll., Lynchburg, Va., 1958-59; lectr. Boston U., 1960-61; asst. prof. physics Framingham (Mass.) State Coll., 1961-63; prof. physics Salem (Mass.) State Coll., 1963-94; ret., 1994. Cons. Introductory Phys. Scis. group Edn. Devel. Ctr., Newton, 1966; asst. to dean grad. studies Salem State Coll., 1971-78, coord. pre-engring. program, 1980-89, coord. secondary edn. program, 1989-91; vis. scholar Harvard U. Grad. Sch. Edn., Cambridge, Mass., 1989-90. Grantee, NSF, 1962. Mem.: MTA, NEA, AAUW, Am. Inst. Physics, Am. Assn. Physics Tchrs., Am. Phys. Soc., Ind. U. Alumnae Assn., Simmons Coll. Alumnae Assn., Pi Lambda Theta. Avocations: travel, reading, swimming. Home: 14 Winford Way Medford MA 02155-1526

CAVANAGH, GERALD FRANCIS, business educator; b. Cleve., Sept. 13, 1931; s. Gerald Francis and Margaret Mildred (Gilmore) C. BS in Engring., Case Western Res. U., 1953; MBA, St. Louis U., 1958, Licentiate in Philosophy, 1959, MEd, 1960; Licentiate in Theology, Loyola U., Chgo., 1965; D in Bus. Adminstrn., Mich. State U., 1970; PhD, LHD (hon.), Loyola U., Balt., 1989, Siena Heights U., 1998. Ordained Jesuit Cath. priest, 1964. Assoc. prof. Wayne State U., Detroit, 1970-79; chair bus. ethics Santa Clara (Calif.) U., 1979-80; prof. U. Detroit, 1980-86; Gasson chair Boston Coll., 1986-87; acad. v.p. U. Detroit Mercy, 1989-92, provost, chancellor, 1992-95, chair bus. ethics, 1995—. Trustee Fordham U., N.Y.C., 1974-80, Xavier U., Cin., 1981-84, Santa Clara U., 1991-2003, Holy Cross, Mass., 2001—; bd. chair U. Detroit, 1975-77; presenter in field. Author: Blacks in the Industrial World: Issues for the Manager, 1972, The Businessperson in Search of Values, 1976, American Business Values in Transition, 1976, Ethical Dilemmas in the Modern Corporation, 1988, American Business Values with International Perspectives, 4th rev. edit., 1998; contbr. articles to profl. jours. Mem. bd. ethics City of Detroit, 1994-2000. Mem. Internat. Assn. for Bus. and Soc., Acad. Mgmt. (Sumner Marcus award 1990), Soc. for Bus. Ethics, Theta Tau, Blue Key, Alpha Phi Omega (advisor), Beta Gamma Sigma, Tau Kappa Alpha, Alpha Sigma Nu. Office: Univ Detroit Mercy Lansing-Reilly Hall PO Box 19900 Detroit MI 48219-0900 E-mail: cavanagf@udmercy.edu.

CAVANAGH, PETER ROBERT, academic administrator, department chairman, science educator, researcher; b. Wolverhampton, Staffordshire, Eng., July 31, 1947; came to U.S., 1972; s. John Joseph and Dorothy Ann (Stokes) C.; m. Magda Margalova, Dec. 21, 1968 (div. 1979); 1 child, Sasha; m. Ann Elizabeth Vandervelde, Apr. 18, 1981; children: Drew, Chris, Jennifer. BEd, U. Nottingham, Loughborough Coll., 1968; PhD, U. London, Royal Free Hosp. Sch. Med., 1972. Rsch. asst. Royal Free Hosp. Sch. Med., London, 1968-72; asst. prof. Pa. State U., University Park, 1972-75, assoc. prof., 1975-81, prof. biomechanics, 1981—86, prof. locomotion studies, 1986—2002, dir. Ctr. Locomotion Studies, 1986—2002, prof. biobehavioral health, 1989—2002, rsch. dir. Diabetic Foot Clinc, 1989—2002; prof. medicine Pa. State U. Coll. Med., Hershey, 1993—2002; prof. orthopaedic surgery and rehabilitation Pa. State U., 1994—2002, disting. prof. kinesiology, medicine, orthopedics & rehabilitation and biobehavioral health, 1993—2002; v.p. rsch. DIApedia LLC, State Coll., Pa., 1999—; rsch. dir. Diabetic Foot Clinic, Milton S. Hershey Med. Ctr., Hershey, 1993—2002; Virginia Lois Kennedy chmn. biomedical engring. dept. & acad. dir. Diabetic Foot Care Program Cleveland Clinic Found., 2002—. Vis. prof. U. Dept. Med., Manchester Royal Infirmary, U. Manchester, United Kingdom, 1990-91; cons. U.S. Olympic Com., Colorado Springs, Colo., 1984-90, NASA, Houston, 1986—, various athletic shoe and biomedical cos., U.S., Japan, Germany, 1978—; expert witness for patent and trademark, diabetic foot, foot injury, footwear and footprints; trustee Mus. Contemporary Art, Cleveland, 2003-. Author: The Running Shoe Book, 1980; co-author: Biomechanics and Physiology of Cycling, 1978, The Biomechanics of Distance Running, 1990, The Foot in Diabetes: A Bibliography, various edn. 1992, 2000, The Foot in Diabetes, 2d and 34d edn., 1994, 2000; mem. editl. bd. Posture and Gait, Foot & Ankle Internat., 1994—, Internat. Journ. Lower Extremity Wounds, 2001-. Mem. Internat. Soc. Biomechanics (pres. 1995-97, Muybridge medal 1987), Am. College Sports Medicine (fellow 1983, trustee 1987-90, Wolffe lectr. 1987, Citation award 1997, Dill lectr. 2001), Am. Soc. Biomechanics (pres. 1986-87, Borelli award 1994), Am. Diabetes Assn. (chmn. foot coun. 1997-99, Pecoraro lectr. 2002), Aerospace Med. Assn., Orthopedic Rsch. Soc., European Assn. Study Diabetes, Am. Soc. Bone and Mineral Rsch., Am. Orthopaedic Foot and Ankle Soc. (hon.), Melpomene Inst. Adv. Bd., IOC Olympic Acad. Sport Sci. Avocations: running, music, flying. Office: Cleveland Clinic Found 9500 Euclid Ave ND20 Cleveland OH 44195

CAVANAGH, RICHARD EDWARD, research policy organization executive; b. Buffalo, June 15, 1946; s. Joseph John and Mary Celeste (Stack) C.; m. Patricia Sypher, 1995; 1 child. BA, Wesleyan U., Middletown, Conn., 1968; MBA, Harvard U., 1970. Assoc. McKinsey & Co. Inc., Washington, 1970-77, ptnr., 1980-88; exec. dir. fed. cash mgmt. U.S. Office Mgmt. and Budget, Washington, 1977-79; exec. dean Kennedy Sch. Govt. Harvard U., Cambridge, Mass., 1988-95; pres., CEO The Conference Board, Inc., N.Y.C., 1995—. Cons. Carter-Mondale Presdl. Transition, 1976-77; domestic coord. Pres.' Reorgn. Project, The White House, Washington, 1978-79; mem. exec. com. Pres.' Pvt. Sector Survey on Cost Control, Grace Commn., 1982-83. Co-author: (with Donald K. Clifford Jr.) The Winning Performance: How America's High-Growth Midsize Companies Succeed, 1985, 2d edit., 1988 (pub. in 11 fgn. langs.). Mem. bd. judges Dively Award, Harvard U., 1984-94; trustee Ctr. for Excellence in Govt., 1985, 96—, Drucker Found., 1998-2002, Ednl. Testing Svc., 1997—, vice chair, 2002-; trustee Wesleyan U., 1988-2000, vice chair, 1997-2000; trustee, dir. Black Rock Mut. Funds, 1994—; dir. Fremont Group, 1997—, The Guardian Ins., 1998—, Arch Chems., Inc., 1996—, Airplanes Group and Aircraft Fin. Trust, 1999—. With U.S. Army, 1968. Recipient Presdl. commendation, 1979, 80, 83; John Reilly Knox fellow, 1969, Clark fellow, 1969. Mem. Am. Soc. Pub. Adminstrn., Acad. Polit. Sci., Coun. on Fgn. Rels., Raimond Duy Baird Assn., Wesleyan U. Alumni Assn. (chmn. 1985-87), Met. Club (D.C.), Harvard Club (N.Y.C., Boston), Siwanoy Country Club (Bronxville, N.Y.), The Links (N.Y.C.), Beta Theta Pi. Democrat. Roman Catholic. Office: The Conference Board Inc 845 3rd Ave New York NY 10022-6600

CAVAT, IRMA, artist, educator; b. Bklyn. children: Karina Cavat-Gore, Nika Cavat-Hoffman. Student, NYU, 1956, Alexander Archipenko Sch., Woodstock, N.Y., 1959, New Sch. for Social Rsch., N.Y.C., 1960-62. Prof. art U. Calif., Santa Barbara, 1964-91. One-woman shows include Pollock Fine Art, Summerland, Calif., 2002, Gallery Sistina, Rome, 1961, 63, Santa Barbara Mus. Art, 1966, Phoenix Art Mus., 1967, Kennedy Gallery, N.Y.C., 1972, 74, 78, Arwin Galleries, Detroit, 1982, 84, 87, Feingarten Gallery, L.A., 1991, Cline Gallery, Santa Fe, 1995, Fielding Inst., Santa Barbara, Calif., 1996, Arts and Letters Gallery, Santa Barbara, 1999, others. Fulbright fellow, Rome, 1957-59. Avocations: poetry, travel. Office: Univ of California Dept Art Santa Barbara CA 93106

CAVE, LILLIAN JOANN, school system administrator; b. Union City, N.J., Sept. 29, 1942; d. George Thomas and Leatha Willie (Shelton) C. BA, Paterson State Coll., 1964; MA, Jersey City (N.J.) State Coll., 1978, MA, 1982; EdD, Seton Hall U., 1992. Tchr. of secondary math. West N.Y. (N.J.) Bd. Edn., 1964-78, secondary guidance counselor, 1978-85, dir. guidance, 1985-92, dir. student pers. svcs., 1992—; counselor West N.Y. Juvenile Aid Bur., 1981—. Chairperson West N.Y. Juvenile Conf. Com., 1979—; trustee West N.Y. Libr. Bd., 1992—. Recipient Cert. of Merit N.J. State Dept. of Edn., 1982. Mem. ASCD, NEA, N.J. Prins. and Suprs. Assn., Am. Ednl. Rsch. Assn., Phi Delta Kappa, Delta Sigma Theta. Avocations: public speaking, record collection. Office: West New York Bd of Edn 5501 Park Ave West New York NJ 07093-3523

CAVE, MAC DONALD, anatomy educator; b. Phila., May 14, 1939; s. Edward Joseph and Adeline Roberta (MacDonald) C.; m. Donna Kay Brainard, Jan. 1, 1989; children: Eric MacDonald, Heidi Lee, Anne Elizabeth. BA, Susquehanna U., 1961; MS, U. Ill., 1963, PhD, 1965. Instr. dept. anatomy U. Ill. Coll. Medicine, Chgo., 1964-65; asst. prof. U. Pitts. Sch. Medicine, 1967-72; assoc. prof. anatomy U. Ark. Med. Ctr., Little Rock, 1972-79, prof. anatomy, 1979—. Contbr. numerous articles to profl. jours. Am. Cancer Soc.-Swedish Am. exchange fellow, 1966; USPHS postdoctoral fellow Max Planck Inst., Tubingen, W. Ger., 1966-67 Mem. AAAS, Am. Assn. Anatomists, Am. Soc. Cell Biology, Am. Soc. for Microbiology, Sigma Xi, Pi Gamma Mu. Home: 5220 Crestwood Dr Little Rock AR 72207-5404 Office: U Ark Med Scis Dept Anatomy and Neurobiology 4301 W Markham St Little Rock AR 72205-7101

CAWLEY, SISTER MAUREEN ANN, school principal; b. Newark, Aug. 25, 1931; d. Michael James and Julia E. (McKeon) C. BS in Edn., Coll. of St. Elizabeth, Convent Station, N.J., 1961; MLS in Comm., Rutgers U., 1968; postgrad., Notre Dame U., 1974, Boston Coll., 1986. Cert. tchr., media specialist, tchr., N.J.; joined Sisters of Charity, Roman Cath. Ch. Tchr. St. Aloysius, Jersey City, 1951-56, Star of the Sea Sch., Long Branch, N.J., 1956-61, good Counsel Elem. Sch., Washington Twp., N.J., 1961-63; tchr., asst. prin. St. Peter's Elem. Sch., New Brunswick, N.J., 1963-77, prin., 1977-93; instr. Coll. of St. Elizabeth, 1972-74; interim supt. Diocese of Metuchen, N.J., 1982; dir. planning and devel. St. Peter's Schs., New Brunswick, 1989-93; prin. St. Peter's H.S., New Brunswick, 1993—. Mem. New Brunswick Tomorrow Edn. Task Force, 1987—; mem. Sisters of Charity Edn. Bd., Paterson, N.J., 1985-94; mem. Cultural Ctr. Edn. Com., New Brunswick, 1990-93; mem. Rutgers/New Brunswick Math Project, 1989-92. Editor, author newsletter The Spirit, 1990-92; editor St. Peter's Alumni Directory, 1992. Mem. Sister Cities, New Brunswick, 1992—; grad. Leadership Inst., New Brunswick, 1990. Named Adminstr. of Yr. Title I Parents, 1979, Prin. of Month Today's Cath. Tchr., 1986; recipient U.S. Sch. of Excellence award U.S. Dept. Edn., 1987, Religious Activity award KC, 1988. Mem. Nat. Cath. Edn. Assn., Metuchen Diocese Prin. Assn. Avocations: classical music, travel, spectator sports, reading, beachwalking. Home: 90 Somerset St New Brunswick NJ 08901-1220 Office: St Peter's HS 175 Somerset St New Brunswick NJ 08901-1944

CAWOOD, THOMAS FRED, retired music therapist; b. Monroe, Mich., Aug. 29, 1952; s. Fred and Mona Ruth (West) C.; m. Alice Jane White, Aug. 24, 1974; children: Johanes Frederick, Amber Diane, Cassandra Jean. B Music Performance, U. Mich., 1975; BFA, Mich. State U., 1977; postgrad., Ea. Mich. U. Registered music therapist; cert. Bd. Music Therapy. Music therapy intern Essex County Hosp. Ctr., Cedar Grove, N.J., 1977; music therapist Oakdale Regional Devel. Ctr., Lapeer, Mich., 1978-79; clinician Schulmerich Handbell Co., Sellerville, Pa., 1992—95; entertainer Musicians Local 542, Flint, 1991—; music therapist Genesee Intermediate Sch. Dist., Flint, 1979—2001; mus. dir. Grace Episcopal Ch., Lapeer, Mich., 1989—92; ret., 2001—. Participant Nat. Assn. Music Therapy Spl. Project Music Edn./Therapy for Severely/Profoundly Handicapped Children, 1981; nat. and regional conf. presenter, 1982, 84-85, 88, 90; music therapist pvt. clients; entertainer Autoworld and Waterstreet pavilion, Flint; presenter in field. Contbr. articles to profl. jours. Recipient Team Spirit award United Way Campaign, Genesee County, 1985. Mem. Am. Assn. Music Therapy (approved clin. internship dir. 1980, chmn. music therapists in schs. 1989—, internship 1989-2001), Am. Guild Organists, Am. Fedn. Musicians, Coun. Exceptional Children.. Home: 409 Lou Alice Dr Columbiaville MI 48421-9705 Office: Genesee Intermediate Sch Dist 2413 W Maple Ave Flint MI 48507-3429

CAWS, MARY ANN, French language and comparative literature educator, critic; b. Wilmington, NC, Sept. 10, 1933; d. Harmon Chadbourn and Margaret Devereux (Lippitt) Rorison; m. Peter Caws, June 2, 1956 (div. 1987); children: Hilary, Matthew. BA, Bryn Mawr Coll., 1954; MA, Yale U., 1956; PhD, U. Kans., 1962; D.Humane Letters, Union Coll., 1983. Asst. instr. Romance Langs. U. Kans., Lawrence, Kans., 1957-62, asst. editor Univ. press, 1957-58, vis. asst. prof., spring 1963; lectr. Barnard Coll. Columbia U., NYC, 1962-63; mem. faculty Sarah Lawrence Coll., Bronxville, NY, 1963-64, Hunter Coll. CUNY, NYC, 1966-88; prof. Grad. Sch. CUNY, NYC, 1969-88, exec. officer comparative lit. program Grad. Sch., 1977-79, exec. officer French program Grad. Sch., 1979-86, Disting. prof. French and comparative lit. Grad. Sch., 1983—, prof. English, 1985—, Disting. prof. French, comparative lit., English Grad. Sch., 1987—. Phi Beta Kappa vis. scholar, 1982-83; dir. NIH summer seminars for coll. tchrs., 1978, 85; mem. faculty Sch. of Criticism and Theory, Dartmouth U., 1988, Sch. Visual Arts, 1993; professeur associé Université de Paris VII, 1993-94; co-chair Henri Peyre Inst. for the Humanities, 1980-1996, French Inst., 1997-2002; lectr. NY Coun. for Humanities, 1992-96. Author: Surrealism and the Literary Imagination, 1966, The Poetry of Dada and Surrealism, 1970, The Inner Theatre of Recent French Poetry, 1972, The Presence of René Char, 1976, René Char, 1977, The Surrealist Voice of Robert Desnos, 1977, La Main de Pierre Reverdy, 1979, The Eye in the Text, Essays on Perception, Mannerist to Modern, 1981, André Breton, 1982, 96, The Metapoetics of the Passage, Architextures in Surrealism and After, 1982, Yves Bonnefoy, 1984, Reading Frames in Modern Fiction, 1988, Edmond Jabès, 1988, The Art of Interference: Stressed Readings in Visual and Verbal Texts, 1989, Women of Bloomsbury, 1991, Robert Motherwell: What Art Holds, 1996, Carrington and Lytton: Alone Together, 1996, The Surrealist Look: An Erotics of Encounter, 1997, Picasso's Weeping Woman: The Life and Art of Dora Maar, 2000, Virginia Woolf: Illustrated Life, 2002, Robert Motherwell with Pen and Brush, 2003, Marcel Proust: Illustrated Life, 2003; co-author: Bloomsbury and France: Art and Friends, 1999; editor: Dada-Surrealism, 1972, co-editor, 1980-2002, Le Siècle éclaté, 1974-78, About French Poetry from Dada to Tel Quel, 1974, Selected Poetry Prose of Stéphane Mallarmé, 1982, Selected Poems of St.-John Perse, 1983, Writing in a Modern Temper, 1984, Textual Analysis, 1986, Perspectives on Perception: Philosophy, Art, and Literature, 1989, City Images, 1992, Joseph Cornell's Theater of the Mind: Selected Diaries, Letters and Files, 1994, Manifesto: A Century of Isms, 2001, Mallarme in Prose, 2001, Surrealist Painters and Poets, 2001, Surrealist Love Poems, 2002, Vita Sackville-West: Selected Writings, 2002; co-editor: Selected Poems of René Char, 1992, Contre-Courants: Les femmes s'écrivent à travers les siècles, 1994, Écritures de femmes: Nouvelles Cartographies, 1996; translator: Poems of René Char, 1976, Approximate Man and other Writings of Tristan Tzara, 1975, Mad Love, 1987, The Secret Art of Antonin Artaud, 1998, Ostinato, 2002; co-translator: Poems of André Breton, 1984, Communicating Vessels, 1990, Break of Day, 1999; chief editor Harper Collins World Reader, 1994, Manifesto: A Century of isms, 2001, Surrealist Painters and Poets, 2001, Mallarmé in Prose, 2001; contbr. articles to profl. jours. Decorated officier Palmes Académiques, France; fellow Guggenheim Found., 1972-73 NEH, 1979-80, Fulbright traveling fellow, 1972-73, Rockefeller Found. fellow, 1994; Getty scholar, 1990. Mem. MLA (exec. coun. 1973-77, v.p. 1982-83, pres. 1983-84), Am. Assn. Tchrs. French, Assn. for Study Dada and Surrealism (pres. 1982-86), Internat. Assn. Philosophy and Lit. (exec. bd. 1982—, chmn. 1984), Acad. Lit. Studies (pres. 1985), Am. Comparative Lit. Assn. (exec. com. 1981, v.p. 1986—, pres. 1989-91). Home: 140 E 81st St New York NY 10028-1805 Office: CUNY Grad Ctr 365 Fifth Ave New York NY 10016

CAWS, PETER JAMES, philosopher, educator; b. Southall, Eng., May 25, 1931; came to U.S., 1953; naturalized, 1995; s. Geoffrey Tulloh and Olive (Budden) C.; m. Mary Ann Rorison (div.); children: Hilary, Matthew; m. Nancy Breslin, Nov. 28, 1987; 1 child, Elisabeth. BS, U. London, 1952; MA, Yale U., 1954, PhD, 1956. Instr. natural sci. Mich. State U., 1956-57; asst. prof. philosophy U. Kans., 1957-60, assoc. prof., 1960-62, chmn. dept., 1961-62, Rose Morgan vis. prof., 1963; vis. prof. U. Costa Rica, 1961; exec. assoc. Carnegie Corp. N.Y., 1962-65, cons., 1965-67; prof. philosophy Hunter Coll., N.Y.C., 1965-82, chmn. dept., 1965-67; exec. officer Ph.D. program in philosophy CUNY, 1967-70, 81-82; Univ. prof. philosophy George Washington U., 1982—, dir. PhD Program in Human Scis., 1991-93; vis. prof. NYU, spring 1982, U.Md., spring 1985; tchr. New Sch. Social Research, 1965-67; mem. adv. bd. Learning Corp. of Am., 1968-74. Vis. scholar U. Kent, Canterbury, Eng., 1993-94; lectr. Smithsonian Resident Assocs. Program, 1988-95; mem. Coun. Philos. Studies, 1965-71; bd. dirs. Coordinating Coun. Lit. Mags., 1969-70; mem. Scientists Inst. for Pub. Info., 1967-94, treas., 1969-72, fellow, 1972-94, dir., 1975-80, vice chmn., 1975-79; mem. editl. bd. Environment, 1972-78; mem. bd. advisers, history of physics program Am. Inst. Physics, 1966-75; mem. NRC, 1967-70, Assembly Behavioral and Social Scis., 1973-77; nat. lectr. Sigma Xi, 1975-77; dir. Bicentennial Symposium of Philosophy; cons. in humanities LWV, 1978; vis. scholar Phi Beta Kappa, 1983-84; 1st Philip Morris Disting. lectr. in bus. and soc. Baruch Coll., N.Y.C., 1986; sr. fellow Christina River Inst., 2001—. Author: The Philosophy of Science, Systematic Account, 1965, Science and the Theory of Value, 1967, Sartre, 1979, Structuralism: A Philosophy for the Human Sciences, 1997, Yorick's World: Science and the Knowing Subject, 1993, The Capital Connection, 1993, Ethics from Experience, 1996; editor: Two Centuries of Philosophy in America, 1980, The Causes of Quarrel: Essays on Peace, War and Thomas Hobbes, 1989; mem. editl. bd. Jour. Enterprise Mgmt., 1976-81, Philosophy Documentation Ctr., mem. cmty. adv. bd. The News Jour., Wilmington, Del., 1998—2001. Recipient Pres.'s medal Grad. Sch., CUNY, 1978; Am. Council Learned Socs. fellow Paris, 1972-73; Rockefeller Found. humanities fellow, 1979-80 Fellow AAAS (v.p. 1967); mem. Am. Philos. Assn. (dir., chmn. com. on internat. coop. 1974-84), Fedn. Internat. des Socs. de Philosophie (commn. on policy 1979-88, comité dir. 1978-88), Philosophy of Sci. Assn. (del.), Soc. Gen. Systems Rsch. (pres. 1966-67), Soc. Am. de Philosophie de Langue Française (v.p. 1989-92, pres. 1992-94), Elizabethan Club, Washington Philosophy Club (pres. 1988-89), Phi Beta Kappa (hon. Alpha chpt. D.C.). Home: 237 Cheltenham Rd Newark DE 19711-3617 Office: George Washington U Dept Philosophy Washington DC 20052-0001 E-mail: pcaws@gwu.edu.

CAYLEFF, SUSAN EVELYN, women's studies educator, department chairman; b. Boston, Mar. 4, 1954; d. Nathan and Frieda C. BA, U. Mass., 1976; MA, Sarah Lawrence Coll., 1978, Brown U., 1979, PhD, 1983. Tchg. fellow Brown U., Providence, 1981-83; asst. prof. Inst. for the Med. Humanities, U. Tex. Med. Br., Galveston, 1983-87; assoc. prof. dept. women's studies San Diego State U., 1987—, faculty advisor varsity women's crew team, 1988—, prof. dept. women's studies, 1992—, prof., chair dept. women's studies, 1997—. Adj. faculty Inst. for the Med. Humanities, U. Tex. Med. Br., 1987—; humanities rep. com. for the protection of human subjects San Diego State U., 1988-97. Author: Wash and Healed..., 1987, Wings of Gauze: Women of Color and the Experience of Health and Illness, 1993, Babe: The Life and Legend of Babe Didrikson Zaharias, 1995 (Pulitzer Prize nominee 1995-96, Outstanding Book award Gay and Lesbian Alliance Against Defamation), Babe: The Greatest All-Sport Athlete of All Time, 2000; editl. cons. Tex. Medicine, 1985-87; mem. editl. bd. Med. Humanities Rev., 1986-87. Nat. Endowment for Humanities grantee, 1984, Babe Didrikson Zaharias Meml. Found. grantee, 1986, San Diego State U. Found. grantee, 1988, 98, Kennedy Inst. for Bioethics scholar Georgetown U., 1984, Calif. State U. scholar, 1989—; named Outstanding Prof. San Diego State U. Assoc. Students, 1993, prof. nominee San Diego State U. Trustees, 1994. Nat. Endowment for Humanities grantee, 1984, Babe Didrikson Zaharias Meml. Found. grantee, 1986, San Diego State U. Found. grantee, 1988, Kennedy Inst. for Bioethics scholar Georgetown U., 1984, Calif. State U. scholar, 1989—; named Outstanding Prof. San Diego State U. Assoc. Students, 1993, San Diego State U. Trustees, 1994, Outstanding Grad.'s Most Influential Faculty, 2000. Mem. Am. Assn. for the History of Medicine, Nat. Women's Studies Assn., Coordinating Group for Women in the Hist. Profession, Western Assn. for Women's Historians, Soc. for Menstrual Cycle Rsch., Brown U. Alumni Assn., Phi Kappa Phi, Phi Beta Delta. Democrat. Jewish. Avocations: collecting antiques, weightlifting, running, Native-Am. and African artifacts, sports. Office: San Diego State U Dept Womens Studies San Diego CA 92182

CAYWOOD, BARBARA MAY, artist, educator; b. Long Beach, Calif., July 24, 1921; d. Herbert Abram and Juliette (Bagby) Shutt; m. Phillip Kinnie Caywood, Oct. 21, 1940 (div. Feb. 1974); children: Wayne, Nancy, Darryl, Juliette, David. Student, Cuesta Coll., 1974-76. Cert. pre-sch.-kindergarten edn. Meth. Ch. Bd. Edn.; cert. Inst. Children's Lit. Lab. tchr. Meth. Ch. Bd. Edn., L.A., 1965-69; artist various locations, 1975-80, 1987-89, 1981-89; artist, tchr. Morgan City (La.) Housing Authority, 1989—. Sec. South Bay Artist's Guild, L.A., 1970-72; tchr. Laubach Literacy Act, Los Osos, Calif., 1988-89; tchr., artist Morgan City Goal #2000 Sch. Bd., 1991-97. Author: (children's books) Teaching Creativity, 1993, Andy's Day; exhibited in group shows South Bay Artists Guild, 1971, 72, Los Angeles County Mus., 1972, Cambria, Calif., 1976, San Luis Obispo, Calif., 1974-76, Siracusa, Sicily, 1982, Los Osos, Calif., 1982-83, Morgan City, La., 1993, 94, 95, 96, 97, others. Charter mem. Friends of Morgan City Pub. Libr., 1993; bd. dirs. Morgan City Visions, 1993-97.

Tchg. grantee Morgan City, 1994. Mem. Artists Guild United (children's show chmn. 1991), Nat. Mus. Women in Arts (charter), La. Watercolor Soc., Sierra Club, Wilderness Soc. Avocations: hiking, sailing. Home: 109 El Bosque Dr San Jose CA 95134-1607

CAYWOOD, CLARKE LAWRENCE, marketing educator, public relations executive; b. Madison, Wis., Mar. 13, 1947; s. Fred Lawrence and Marjorie Caroline (Clarke) C.; m. Mary Margaret Westing, Dec. 15, 1973; children: Matthew Shields, Emily Margaret, Graham Clarke. BBA, U. Wis., 1969, PhD, 1985; MPA, U. Tex., 1972. Asst. to gov. Exec. Office, Madison, 1969-70; research assoc. Lyndon Baines Johnson Sch. Pub. Affairs, U. Tex., Austin, 1971-72; legis. officer Office of Atty. Gen., Madison, 1972-74; exec. dir. Friends of Channel 21, Sta. WHA-TV, Madison, 1975-76; lectr. U. Wis., Whitewater, 1976-78; asst. prof. Marquette U., Milw., 1978-87; vis. asst. prof. U. Wis., Madison, 1987-89; assoc. prof. and dir. Medill Sch. Journalism, Pub. Rels., Integrated Mktg. Comm. Northwestern U., Evanston, 1989—. Bd. dirs. Biz360, DevLab, Direct Selling Edn. Found., Washington, Nat. Telemedia Coun., Madison; cons. Sony, Emerson Electric, Nat. Pub. Radio, IBM Corp., Scania, Kreab, Dairy Mgmt., Inc., Budgetel Corp., Wis., IBM-Europe, State of Wis. Author: The Handbook of Strategic Public Relations and Integrated Communication, 1997; pub. Jour. Integrated Comm.; contbr. articles to profl. jours. Adv. council Office of Lt. Gov., Madison, 1988; del. Wis. Rep. Party Conv., 1974-88; campaign dir. Scott McCallum, Wis., 1986; trustee Mus. Contemporary Art, Chgo.; bd. dirs. Chgo. Symphony. Mem. Am. Acad. Advt., Am. Mktg. Assn., Assn. Edn. on Jour. and Mass Comm., Arthur W. Page Soc. (trustee), Pub. Rels. Soc. Am. (Silver Anvil co-chair, Educator of the Yr.), Beta Gamma Sigma. Republican. Presbyterian. Home: 100 Old Green Bay Rd Winnetka IL 60093-1512 Office: Northwestern U Medill Sch Evanston IL 60208-0001 E-mail: c-caywood@northwestern.edu.

CAZAYOUX, EDWARD JON, architect, educator; b. New Roads, La., Feb. 15, 1943; s. Michel Anthony and Mary Elsie (Powers) C.; m. Elizabeth Faye Chustz, Oct. 23, 1944; children: Kurt Gerard, Michel Anthony, Corrie Elizabeth, Jonathan Edward. BArch, U. Southwestern La., 1970; M. City Planning, MArch, Ga. Inst. Tech., Atlanta, 1972. Registered architect, Colo., La. Asst. prof. arch. Ga. Inst. Tech., Atlanta, 1971-72; intern architect Roark Assocs., Denver, 1972-75; archtl. pvt. practice Renaissance Design, Denver, 1975-76; architect EnvironMental Design, Breaux Bridge, La., 1976—; asst. prof. arch. U. Southwestern La., Lafayette, 1976-82, assoc. prof., 1982-87, prof. arch., 1987—, head dept. arch., 1985-94, dir. Sch. Arch., 1994—, dir. ULL Bldg. Inst. in the Sch. of Architecture and Design, 2003—. Author: Natural Louisiana Architecture, 1989, A Manual for the Environmental and Climatic Responsive Restoration and Renovation of Older Houses in Louisiana, 2003 ; designer climate responsive homes. Chair hist. com. Vermilionville, Lafayette, 1992-93. With U.S. Army, 1961-64. Recipient U.S. Dept. Energy award for energy innovation, 1984, Charles E. Peterson prize Hist. Am. Bldg. Survey Nat. Park Svc., Athenaeum of Phila., 2000; Hay Found. grantee, 1988, Dept. Natural Resources grantee, 1982, 91, 2002. Mem. AIA of South La. (pres. 1993, Pres. award, 1998, design awards 2002), Constrn. Specification Inst. (Acadiana chpt. pres. 1993-94), Am. Solar Energy Soc., Vernacular Arch. Forum, Artist Blacksmith Assn. of N.Am, Phi Kappa Phi. Roman Catholic. Avocations: gardening, bee keeping, photography, travel. Office: Univ of La School Of Architecture Lafayette LA 70504-3850 Home: 1025 Green Ln Breaux Bridge LA 70517-6747

CAZDEN, COURTNEY B(ORDEN), education educator; b. Chgo., Nov. 30, 1925; d. John and Courtney (Letts) Borden; m. Norman Cazden (div. 1971); children: Elizabeth, Joanna. BA, Radcliffe Coll., 1946; MEd, U. Ill., 1953; EdD, Harvard U., 1965. Elem. tchr. pub. schs., N.Y., Conn., Calif., 1947-49, 54-61, 74-75; asst. prof. edn. Harvard U., Cambridge, Mass., 1965-68, assoc. prof., 1968-71, prof., 1971-95, Charles William Eliot prof. emerita, 1996—. Vis. prof. U. N.Mex. summer 1980, U. Alaska, Fairbanks, summer 1982, U. Auckland, N.Z., spring 1983, Bread Loaf Sch. of English, Vt., 1986—; chairperson bd. trustees Ctr. Applied Linguistics, Washington, 1981-85. Author: Child Language and Education, 1972, Classroom Discourse: The Language of Teaching and Learning, 2d edit., 2001, Whole Language plus Essays on Literacy in the US and New Zealand, 1992; co-editor: Functions of Language in the Classroom, 1972, English Plus: Issues in Bilingual Education, 1990; editor: Language in Early Childhood Education, rev. edit., 1981. Trustee Highland Ednl. and Rsch. Ctr., New Market, Tenn., 1982-84; bd. dirs. Feminist Press, Old Westbury, N.Y., 1982-84; clk. New Eng. regional office Am. Friends Svc. Com., Cambridge, 1989-92. Recipient Alumna Recognition award Radcliffe Coll., 1988; fellow Ctr. Advanced Study in Behavioral Scis., Stanford, Calif., 1978-79; Fulbright research fellow, New Zealand, 1987. Mem. Nat. Acad. Edn., Coun. on Anthropology and Edn. (pres. 1981, George & Louise Spindler award 1994), Am. Assn. Applied Linguistics (pres. 1985), Nat. Conf. on Rsch. in English (pres. 1993-94), Am. Ednl. Rsch. Assn. (exec. com. 1981-84, award for disting. contbns. to ednl. rsch. 1986). Mem. Soc. Of Friends. Office: Harvard U Grad Sch Edn Appian Way Cambridge MA 02138

CAZEL, HUGH ALLEN, industrial engineer, educator; b. Asheville, N.C., Aug. 6, 1923; s. Fred Augustus and Agnes (Petrie) C.; m. Edna Faye Hawkins, Sept. 2, 1944; children: Audre Elizabeth, Hugh Petrie, Susan Margaret, Steven Sidney. BS in Indsl. Engring., N.C. State U., 1948, M in Indsl. Engring., 1972. Registered profl. engr., N.C., Ga. Svc. mgr. Cazel Auto Svc. Co., Asheville, 1948-51; sales rep. Snap-On Tools Corp., Kenosha, Wis., 1951; estimator, cost acct. Std. Designers, Inc., Asheville, 1951-52; designer Robotyper Corp., Hendersonville, N.C., 1952-53; engr. Western Electric Co., Burlington, N.C., 1953-74; alt. rep. configuration mgmt. subcom. Electronic Industries Assn., 1970-72; mgr. engring. BellSouth Telephone Co., Atlanta, 1974-79; ret., 1979; ptnr. Engring. Unltd., 1963—. Instr. math. Elon Coll., 1956-59; instr. engring. graphics and design Ga. Inst. Tech., 1977-87, ret., 1987; instr. constrn. blue print reading DeKalb C.C., 1981-87; project engr. Dept. Def. Election poll worker, 1960-93. Re. candidate N.C. Ho. of Reps., 1964; mem. Dekalb County (Ga.) Adv. Com., 1979-82; dir. Glendale Townhouses Assn., chmn, 1979-80; mem. adminstrv. bd. 1st United Meth. Ch., Decatur, 1976-86; interviewer Decatur Emergency Assistance Ministry, 1990-92; lay mem. Ea. N.C. Ann. Conf. United Meth. Ch., 1965-73; vol. Dept. Vets. Affairs Med. Ctr., Durham, N.C., 1993-97, ambulance driver chpt. 20 Disabled Am. Vets., Guilford County; active Muir's Chapel United Meth. Ch., 2002—. With AUS, 1943-46, ETO. Mem. NSPE, AAAS, Am. Inst. Indsl. Engrs. (pres. Raleigh, N.C. chpt. 1963-64), Profl. Engrs. N.C. (pres. North Piedmont chpt. 1972-73, state bd. dirs. 1970-73), Ga. Profl. Engrs. in Industry (chmn. 1976), Ga. Soc. Profl. Engrs. (energy com. 1979-86, Ga. Engr. of Yr. in Industry 1976), Tel. Pioneers Am. (life, pres. Dixie chpt. 1991-92), Rep. Club, Odd Fellows, Rotary, Lions (local sec. 1991—2003). Achievements include patent for ultra low frequency sound generator for deep sea, 1972. Home: 801 Meadowood St Apt 24 Greensboro NC 27409-2831

CAZENAVE, ANITA WASHINGTON, secondary school educator; b. Austin, Tex., Nov. 9, 1948; d. Willis Hunt and Henry Etta Washington Littleton; m. Noël Anthony Cazenave, July 20, 1971; 1 child, Anika Tené. BA in Early Childhood/Elem. Edn., Dillard U., New Orleans, 1971; MEd in Reading Edn., Loyola U. of New Orleans, 1976; PhD in Psychology of Reading Edn., Temple U., 1993. Cert. tchr., La., Pa.; cert. reading tchr., adminstr., Conn. Dir. Second Bapt. Day Nursery, Ann Arbor, Mich., 1971-72; reading cons. New Orleans Pub. Schs., 1972-78; reading instr. Temple U., Phila., 1979-80; reading specialist Operation Re-Entry Career Svcs., Inc., Phila., 1980-81; coord. ednl. svcs. Phila. O.I.C. Project new Pride, 1981; reading and math. tchr. Reading Edn. and Diagnostic Svcs. Inc., Phila., 1981-84; lang. arts/reading tchr. FitzSimons Middle Sch., Phila., 1985-91; reading tchr. Putnam (Conn.) Middle Sch., 1991-92; reading cons. Bloomfield (Conn.) H.S., 1992-98, Carmen Arace Mid. Sch., Bloomfield, 1998—2002, Manchester (Conn.) H.S., 2002—. Presenter workshops Bloomfield Bd. Edn., 1993-94, others; reader SAT II writing tests Ednl. Testing Svcs.; adj. prof. English Manchester Cmty. Tech. Coll., 1997. Leader Girl Scouts U.S., New Orleans, 1977-78, Brownie troop leader, 1983-90; Sunday sch. supt. Mt. Airy United Meth. Ch., Phila., 1980-82; campaign worker Wilson Goode for Mayor, Phila., 1982; dir. ministry Acolyte Min. met. A.M.C. Zion Ch., Hartford, Conn.; asst. supt. of youth Met. A.M.E. Zion Ch., 2000. Named Outstanding Leader, Troop Parents Girl Scouts, Phila., 1985. Mem. ASCD, Internat. Reading Assn., Phila. Coun. of Internat. Reading Assn. (com. chair 1983-85), Greater Hartford Coun. Internat. Reading Assn. (recording sec. 1994—), Delta Sigma Theta (Hartford Alumnae chpt. chaplain and collegiate advisor 1994—, parliamentarian 1996—, chair state coun. chpts. heritage & archives 1994—, chair SAT tng. com. 1995—). Democrat. Avocations: reading, sewing, travel, camping, old movies. Home: 37 Storrs Heights Rd Storrs Mansfield CT 06268-2305 Office: Manchester HS 134 E Middle Turnpike Manchester CT E-mail: anitacazenave@hotmail.com.

CEBULA, MARY ANN ANTIONETTE, special education educator, speech correctionist; b. Orange, N.J., Oct. 20, 1950; d. Dominic and Frances (Romano) Cianci; m. Charles Michael Cebula, July 28, 1973; 1 child, Jessica Ann. BA, Kean State Coll., Union, N.J., 1972; MA, Georgian Ct. Coll., Lakewood, N.J., 1991. Cert. nursery sch. tchr. handicapped, learning disability tchr. cons. Resource room and speech tchr., reading recovery specialist St. Anthony's Sch., Belleville, NJ, 1972-73, mid. sch. tchr., 1973-78; elem. tchr. Our Lady of Mt. Carmel Sch., Orange, N.J., 1982-86, Holy Family Sch., Lakewood, 1986-88; tchr. spl. edn. Stafford Twp. Sch., Manahawkin, N.J., 1988—. Asst., helper Tournament of Champions, Toms River, 1991. Co-author curriculum for multiply handicapped students, 1991. Asst., helper Spl. Olympics, Toms River, 1988—. Mem. N.J. Edn. Assn., Learning Disabled Assn., N.J. Coun. Learning Disabled, Stafford Twp. Edn. Assn. Roman Catholic. Avocations: reading, crafts. Home: 123 Oak Hill Dr Toms River NJ 08753-1729

CECCHETTI, STEPHEN GIOVANNI, economics educator; b. Berkeley, Calif., Aug. 18, 1956; s. Giovanni A. and Ruth Elizabeth (Schwabacher) C.; m. Ruth M. Charney, Sept. 6, 1986; children: Daniel A., Ethan B. SB in Econs., MIT, 1977; MA in Econs., U. Calif., Berkeley, 1979, PhD in Econs., 1982. Rsch. assoc. Nat. Bur. Econ. Rsch., 1986—2003; prof. econs. Ohio State U., Columbus, 1987—2002; exec. v.p., dir. rsch. Fed. Res. Bank, 1997—99; prof. internat. econs. and fin. Brandeis U., Waltham, Mass., 2003—. Rsch. assoc. fellow Nat. Bur. Econ. Rsch., 1986—; cons. Fed. Res. Banks, Fed. Res. Bd., Fgn. Ctrl. Banks. Editor Jour. Money Credit and Banking, 1992-2001; referee and editl. bd. dirs. numerous profl. jours.; contbr. articles to profl. jours., chpts. to books and Fin. Times. Office: Graduate Sch of Internat Econ and FIn Brandeis Univ Mail Stop 32 Waltham MA 02454-9110 E-mail: steve@cecchetti.net.

CECCHI, DAVID ROBERT, graphic designer; b. Holyoke, Mass., July 29, 1964; s. Robert Joseph and Emily Helen (Dynia) C.; m. Laurie Anne Martin, Nov. 4, 1989; children: Joseph Erminio, J. Bailey Martin. BFA, RISD, 1986. Asst. prodn. mgr. Reminder Publs., East Longmeadow, Mass., 1986-87; prin. Cecco, Feeding Hills, Mass., 1987-97; graphic designer Darby O'Brien Advt., Springfield, Mass., 1987-90; art dir. De Witt Anthony, Northampton, Mass., 1990-94; design dir. The Super Market, East Longmeadow, Mass., 1995-97; creative dir. TSM Design, Springfield, Mass., 1997—. Mem. Anne Sullivan Meml. Com., Agawam, 1989-94, Agawam (Mass.) Sch. Com., 1989-91, vice chmn., 1989, sec., 1990; chmn. Agawam Hist. Commn., 1993—; mem. Agawam Italian Sister City Commn. Recipient Merit award The One Show, N.Y., 1989, Print's Regional Design ann. Print Mag., Md., 1990-93, Simpson Paper Design contest Simpson Paper Co., San Francisco, 1992, Silver award Conn. Art Dirs. Club, 1996. Mem. Am. Ctr. for Design, Am. Inst. Graphic Arts, Advt. Club Western Mass. (bd. dirs. 1993-94, pres. 1994-96, chmn. Charles A. Stein award 1994, 1st pl. newspaper campaign 1989-93, Best of Show award 1992, 93, Charles A. Stein award 1996).

CECIL, BONNIE SUSAN, elementary education educator; b. Louisville, Sept. 29, 1951; d. Robert Lawrence and Mary Hedwig (Kluesner) C. BA in Edn., U. Ky., 1973; MS in Edn., Ind. U., 1978; postgrad., U. Louisville, 1988—. Tchr. grades 1-4 Roosevelt Cmty. Sch., Jefferson County, Ky., 1972-80; tchr. ages 6 and 7 Wandle Primary Sch., London, 1980-81; tchr. 1st grade Foster Elem. Sch., Jefferson County, 1981-82; tchr. ages 5-8 Brown Sch. Primary, Jefferson County, 1982—. Co-dir., instr. writing process for tchrs. Ky. Writing Insts. I and II, Boone County, 1986-88; instr. writing process insvc. Jefferson County Pub. Schs., 1988-89, workshop presenter on environ. edn., 1990, 92, supr. student tchrs., 1989-90, 92, 94, 95, 97; instr. lang. arts U. Louisville, 1990-91; participant Fulbright Tchr. Exch. Program, London, 1980-81, Brown Sch. Dream Team, 1992; presenter ann. conf. Ky. Assn. Edn. Young Children-Louisville Assn. for Children Under Seven, 1990; presenter Cmty. Learning Resource Conf., 1992; participant Louisville Writing Project, 1984-85, premier class Leadership Edn., 1986-87. Tchr. rep. J. Graham Brown Sch. PTSA, 1983-90, 92-97; tchr. rep. site-based decision making coun., 1996—; bd. dirs. Roosevelt Cmty. Sch., Inc., 1973-76; creator, dir. summer reading and writing program Portland Mus., Louisville, 1985; treas. Louisville Homefront Performances, Inc., 1986-87, sec., 1988-90, bd. dirs. 1984-96; state bd. dirs. Cmty. Farm Alliance, 2001-2002, v.p. Henry County chpt., 2001-. Recipient Golden Apple Achievement award Ashland Oil Co., 1989, Individual Tchr. Achievement award, 1992, Nat. Educator award Milken Family Found., 1994, ExCel award WHAS-TV and PNC Bank, 1995; named Jefferson County Elem. Tchr. of Yr., 1992, Ky. Elem. Tchr. of Yr., 1993, Ky. Tchr. of Yr., 1993, Milken Family Nat. Educator Project Mentor, 1998; grantee Ky. Arts Coun., 1986-87, Jefferson County Pub. Schs.-U. Louisville, 1989-91, U. Louisville, 1991, Rosenbaum Found., 1998; named Milken Virtual Workspace Mentor, 1998; inducted into The Commonwealth Inst. for Tchrs., 1998. Mem. ASCD, NEA, Assn. Childhood Edn. Internat., Nat. Coun. Tchrs. English (conf. presenter 1988, chmn., presenter nat. conf. 1992), Ky. Edn. Assn., Jefferson County Tchrs. Assn., Leadership Edn. Alumni Assn. Avocations: music, gardening, pets. Office: J Graham Brown Sch 546 S 1st St Louisville KY 40202-1816 E-mail: bcecil2@jefferson.K12.ky.us.

CECIL, ELIZABETH JEAN, writer; b. Biloxi, Miss., Apr. 13, 1938; d. Dudley Charles and Margaret Jean (Gilchrist) Andrews; m. Anthony Francis Cieslewicz (Cecil), Nov. 22, 1962; children: Stephen Charles, Sarah Jean. BA, Colo. State Coll., Greeley, 1959; MA, Stanford U., 1963. Cert. speech and lang. pathologist, Wis. Speech-lang. pathologist Racine (Wis.) Unified Sch. Dist., ret., 2003. Author: (booklet essays) Jean's Stuff, 1993; author series of pictorial geneal. books. Office Vocat. Rehab. fellow Stanford U. Mem.: Assn. Supervision and Curriculum Devel. Presbyterian.

CEDERBERG, JAMES, physics educator; b. Oberlin, Kans., Mar. 16, 1939; s. J. Walter and Edith E. (Glad) C.; m. Judith Ness, June 10, 1967; children: Anna Sook, Rachel Eun. BA, U. Kans., 1959; MA, Harvard U., 1960, PhD, 1963. Lectr., rsch. assoc. Harvard U., Cambridge, Mass., 1963-64; from asst. prof. to prof. St. Olaf Coll., Northfield, Minn., 1964—80, prof., 1980—92, Grace A. Whittier prof. sci., 1992—. Councilor Coun. on Undergrad. Rsch., 1985-91, 92-95, pres. physics coun., 1985-88; summer rsch. assoc. U. Mich., 1967, Harvard U., 1980; fellow Duke U., 1969-70, Harvard U., 1976-77; vis. prof. U. Washington, 1991-92, U. Canterbury, Christchurch, New Zealand, 1998-99. Recipient Distinguished Service Citation awd., Am. Assn. of Physics Teachers, 1993; fellow NSF, Woodrow Wilson fellowship; grantee various corps., NSF, RUI. Fellow: Am. Phys. Soc. (Undergraduate Rsch. prize 2002); mem.: Am. Assn. Physics Tchrs. (mem. coun. on undergraduate rsch.), Sigma Xi, Pi Mu Epsilon, Sigma Pi Sigma, Phi Beta Kappa. Lutheran. Office: St Olaf Coll 1520 Saint Olaf Ave Northfield MN 55057-1098 Fax: 507-646-3968. E-mail: ceder@stolaf.edu.*

CELANT, ATTILIO, geographer, educator; b. Polcenigo, Pordenone, Italy, Dec. 28, 1942; s. Arturo and Elsa (Nadin) C.; m. Alberta Migliaccio, May 1, 1975; children: Simone, Chiara, Lucia. Grad. econ., U. La Sapienza, 1967. Asst. prof., assoc. prof. U. Rome, 1971-86; prof. U. Udine, Italy, 1987-91, U. Rome, 1991—, head dept. regional analysis, 1994—2002, dir. M in Econs. and Mgmt. of Tourism, 2000—. Head dept. geography Inst. Ency. Italy, Rome, 1968—; pres. coll. of dirs. of depts. U. La Sapienza, 1998-2002, bd. dirs., 1998-2002, dean faculty of econs., 2002—. Author: Geografia Degli Squilibri, 1994, Geografia Dei Divari Territoriali, 1986, Fondamenti Della Geografia, 1990; editor: Sahel - Geografia Di Una Sconfitta, 1995, Commercio Estero e Competitività Internazionale, 1999, Competizione Territoriale nelle Regioni Italiane, 2002. Mem. Assn. Am. Geographer, Soc. Geography Italy (advisor), Assn. Study Geography (advisor). Home: via Collina 48 00187 Rome Italy Office: Dept di Analisi Regionale via Castro Laurenziano 9 00161 Rome Italy Personal E-mail: attilio.celant@uniroma1.it.

CELESTE, RICHARD F. academic administrator, former ambassador, former governor; b. Cleve., Nov. 11, 1937; s. Frank C.; m. Dagmar Braun, 1962; children: Eric, Christopher, Gabriella, Noelle, Natalie, Stephen; m. Jacqueline Lundquist; 1 child; 6 stepchildren. BA in History magna cum laude, Yale U., 1959; Ph.B. in Politics, Oxford U., 1962. Staff liaison officer Peace Corps, 1963, dir., 1979-81; spl. asst. to U.S. amb. to India, 1963-67; mem. Ohio Ho. of Reps., Columbus, 1970-74, majority whip, 1972-74; lt. gov. State of Ohio, Columbus, 1974-79, gov., 1983-91; mng. ptnr. Celeste & Sabety, Ltd., Columbus, Ohio, 1991—97; amb. to India New Delhi, 1997—2001; co-chair, Homeland Security Proj. The Century Found., 2002—; pres. Colorado Coll., 2002—. Mem. Ohio Dem. Exec. Com. Rhodes scholar Oxford U., Eng. Mem. Am. Soc. Pub. Adminstrn., Italian Sons and Daus. Am. Methodist. Office: Office Pres Colorado Coll 14 E Cache La Poudre St Colorado Springs CO 80903*

CENTERBAR, ALBERTA ELAINE, education educator, research specialist; b. Ilion, N.Y., Dec. 8, 1949; d. Raymond A. and Gladys J. (Orcutt) Pettengill; m. Richard E. Centerbar, Nov. 2, 1985. BFA, Fla. Atlantic U., 1971, MEd, 1975, EdS, 1993, EdD, 1995. Tchr. 3d grade St. Anastasia Sch., Ft. Pierce, Fla., 1971-74; spl. edn. tchr. St. Lucie County Schs., Ft. Pierce, 1975-80, music specialist, 1980—; adminstr./dir. First United Meth. Ch., Ft. Pierce, 1971-81. Adj. prof. (undergrad.) Fla. Atlantic U., Boca Raton, 1990—, adj. prof. law & fin. (grad.), rsch. specialist, 1993—; tchr. evaluator Fla. performance mgmt. cert. St. Lucie County Schs., 1990—; evaluator, rsch. specialist, sch. law, sch. fin. specialist S.E. Assn. Colls. and Schs., Fla., 1993; revised state cert. tchr. exam. Guest organist chs. from Fla. to Ga., 1981—; accompanist local theater and state band groups, 1975—; adminstrv. bd. First United Meth. Ch., Ft. Pierce, 1971—; chair and vice chair edn. leadership adv. coun. Fla. Atlantic U., 1991-94, co-chair Prof. of Yr. selection com., 1993. Phi Kappa Phi Nat. Grad. scholar, 1992—. Mem. AAUW, ASCD, Fla. Music Educators Assn. Avocations: computers, travel, tennis, horseback riding. Home: 1923 S Ocean Dr Fort Pierce FL 34949-3362 Office: Village Green Elem School 1700 SE Lennard Rd Port Saint Lucie FL 34952-6599 also: Fla Atlantic Univ 500 NW University Dr Port Saint Lucie FL 34986-2221

CENTNER, CHARLES WILLIAM, lawyer, educator; b. Battle Creek, Mich., July 4, 1915; s. Charles William and Lucy Irene (Patterson) C.; m. Evi Rohr, Dec. 22, 1956; children: Charles Patterson, David William, Geoffrey Christopher. AB, U. Chgo., 1936, AM, 1938, 39, PhD, 1941; JD, Detroit Coll. Law, 1970; LLB, LaSalle Extension U., 1965. Bar: Mich. 1970. Asst. prof. U. N.D., 1940-41, Tulane U., New Orleans, 1941-42; liaison officer for Latin Am., Dept. State at Lend-Lease Adminstrn., 1942; assoc. dir. Western Hemisphere divsn. Nat. Fgn. Trade Coun., N.Y., 1946-52; exec. Ford Motor Co., Detroit, 1952-57, Chrysler Corp. and Chrysler Internat. S.A., Detroit and Geneva, Switzerland, 1957-70. Adj. prof. Pace U., N.Y.C., 1950-52, Wayne State U., Detroit, 1971-78, U. Detroit, 1970-72, Wayne County C.C., 1970-2001. Author: Great Britian and Chile, 1810-1914, 1941. Lt. comdr. USNR, 1942-45, Res., 1945-75. Mem. ABA, State Bar Mich., Oakland County Bar Assn., Masons. Republican. Episcopalian. Home: 936 Harcourt Rd Grosse Pointe Park MI 48230-1874

CEPIELIK, ELIZABETH LINDBERG, elementary school educator; b. Syracuse, N.Y., Sept. 18, 1941; d. Herman Elroy and Kathryn Emily (Karl) Lindberg; m. Michael A. Zemel, Apr. 22, 1967 (div. Jan. 1973); 1 child, Molly; m. Martin Joseph Cepielik, Mar. 10, 1973; children: Jeffrey, Kristina, Julie. AA, Stephens Coll., Columbia, Mo., 1961; BA, San Jose State Coll., 1963; postgrad., Calif. State U., L.A., 1963-67. Tchr. Humphreys Ave. Sch., L.A., 1963-71; math. specialist Non-Pub. Schs. Program, L.A., 1971-84; tchr. Sheridan Street Sch., L.A., 1984—2003; receptionist Weight Watchers, Arcadia, Calif., 1987—. Editor News of Polonia. Vol. Sta. KPCC, Pasadena, Calif., 1988-94. Mem.: DAR, Swedish Am. Ctrl. Assn. (auditor 1987—90, sec. 1989—), Polish Nat. Alliance (sec. lodge 1980—, sec. coun. 1983—93, treas. Woman's divsn. 1992—93), Polish Am. Congress (sec. 1990—93, auditor, bd. dirs. 2001—), Skandia (auditor, sec. Pasadena lodge 1983—), Stephens Coll. Alumnae Club (pres. Pasadena chpt. 1967—68), Swedish Am. Women's Club. Republican. Presbyterian. E-mail: polishnews@earthlink.net.

CERE, RONALD CARL, languages educator, consultant, researcher; b. N.Y.C., Oct. 22, 1947; s. Mindie Anthony and Edvige Clelia (Ruggero) C. BA, CUNY, 1968; MA, Queens Coll., 1969; PhD, NYU, 1974. Asst. prof. SUNY, Old Westbury, 1974-77, U. Ill., Urbana, 1977-80, U. Nebr., Lincoln, 1980-83, Gettysburg (Pa.) Coll., 1983-85; prof. Ea. Mich. U., Ypsilanti, 1985-90, 1990—. Cons. Trinity Dynamics, N.J., Harcourt Brace Jovanovich, Harper & Collins, D.C. Heath, Prentice-Hall, Random House, Scott Foresman Pub. Cos., 1985—; speaker, presenter in field. Author: Los Fabulistas, 1969, Exito Comercial, 3d edit., 2001; contbr. articles to profl. jours. Recipient James C. Healy award NYU, 1974. Mem. MLA, ASTD, Am. Assn. Tchrs. Spanish and Portuguese (dir. career svcs.), Am.Coun. Teaching Fgn. Langs., Soc. for Intercultural Edn., Tng. and Rsch., Southern Conf. Lang. Teaching (bd. advisors). Home: 2245 Glencoe Hills Dr Apt 7 Ann Arbor MI 48108-3017 Office: Ea Mich U Dept Fgn Langs 219 Alexander Hall Ypsilanti MI 48197-2255 E-mail: fla_cere@online.emich.edu.

CERNERA, ANTHONY JOSEPH, academic administrator; b. Bronx, N.Y., Mar. 21, 1950; children: Anthony, Philip, Thomas, Anne Marie. BA in History and Theol., Fordham U., 1972, MA in Religious Edn., 1974, PhD in Theology, 1987. Tchr./chmn. Aquinas High Sch., Bronx, N.Y., 1972-77; asst. exec. dir. Bread for the World Ednl. Fund, 1977-80, exec. dir., 1980-81; exec. asst. to pres. Marist Coll., Poughkeepsie, N.Y., 1981-84, asst. v.p. acad. affairs, dean acad. programs & svcs., 1984-85, v.p. coll. advancement, 1985-88; pres. Sacred Heart U., Fairfield, Conn., 1988—. Bd. dirs. Mt. St. Michael Acad., Fairfield County Cmty. Found.; also bus. adv. com., Commn. on Children Bus. Adv. Com. State of Conn., NCCJ Regional Chpt., Conn. Hospice, Inc.; v.p. exec. com. Conn. Conf. Ind. Colls. Office: Sacred Heart U Office of Pres 5151 Park Ave Fairfield CT 06432-1000

CERNY, JOSEPH CHARLES, urologist, educator; b. Apr. 20, 1930; s. Joseph James and Mary (Turek) C.; m. Patti Bobette Pickens, Nov. 10, 1962; children: Joseph Charles, Rebecca Anne. BA, Knox Coll., 1952; MD, Yale U., 1956. Diplomate Am. Bd. Urology. Intern U. Mich. Hosp., Ann

Arbor, 1956-57, resident, 1957-62; practice medicine specializing in urology Ann Arbor and Detroit, 1962—. Instr. surgery (urology) U. Mich., Ann Arbor, 1962-64, asst. prof., 1964-66, assoc. prof., 1961-77, clin. prof., 1971—; chmn. dept. urology Henry Ford Hosp., Detroit, 1971—, chmn. emeritus urology Henry Ford Hosp., 1998; pres. Resistors, Inc., Chgo., 1960—; cons. St. Joseph Hosp., Ann Arbor, 1973—; chief urology sect., dept. surgery Ann Arbor VA Hosp., 1999—; mem. instnl. rev. bd. for rsch. U. Mich. Med. Sch., 2001. Mem. editl. bd. Am. Jour. Kidney Diseases, 1988—; contbr. articles to profl. jours., chpts. to books. Bd. dirs., trustee Nat. Kidney Found. Mich., Ann Arbor, 1988—, chmn. urology coun., 1987—, exec. com., 1987—, pres., 1988—, emeritus trustee, 1997; bd. dirs. Ann Arbor Amateur Hockey Assn., 1980-83; pres. PTO, Ann Arbor Pub. Schs., 1980; chmn. capital campaign Nat. Kidney Found. Mich., 2002. Lt. USNR, 1956-76. Recipient Disting. Svc. award Transplantation Soc. Mich., 1982, Disting. Svc. award Nat. Kidney Found. Mich., 1993, Champion of Hope award Nat. Kidney Found., 1997, Disting. Career award Henry Ford Hosp. Alumni, 2000. Fellow ACS (pres.-elect Mich. br. 1984-85, pres. 1985—); mem. Am. Acad. Med. Dirs., Am. Coll. Physician Execs., Internat. Soc. Urology, Am. Urol. Assn. (pres. Mich. br. 1980-81, pres. North Cen. sect. 1985-86, manpower com. 1987-88, 90-92, jud. rev. com. 1987-91, tech. exhibits 1987-88, fiscal affairs rev. commn. 1985-89, audit commn. 1992-96, chmn. 1995, exec. commn. 1993—, bd. dirs. 1994—, work force com., publs. com. 1995—, chmn. publs. com. 1999, Best Sci. Exhibit award 1978, Best Sci. Films award 1980, 82, audio-visual com. 1994—, program rev. com. 1994—, urology work force com. 1995—, jud. and ethics com. 1997—), Transplantation Soc. Mich. (pres. Mich. 1983-85), Am. Assn. Transplant Surgeons, Endocrine Surgeons, Soc. Univ. Urologists, Am. Assn. Urologic Oncology, Am. Fertility Soc., Am. Coll. Physician Execs., Am. Acad. Med. Dirs., S.W. Oncology Group, Barton Hills Country Club, Ann Arbor Racquet Club. Avocations: tennis, fishing, civil war. Home: 2800 Fairlane St Ann Arbor MI 48104-4110 Office: U Mich Health Sys Sect Urology Dept Surgery 1500 E Medical Center Dr Ann Arbor MI 48109-0005 E-mail: jocerny@umich.edu.

CERONE, DAVID, academic administrator; m. Linda Sharon Cerone. Dir. and mem. summer faculty Meadowmount Sch. Music; prof. violin Oberlin Conservatory, 1962—71; chmn. string dept. and Kulas prof. Cleve. Inst. Music, 1971—81, pres., 1985—, Mary Elizabeth Callahan pres. chair; mem. violin faculty Curtis Inst. Music, 1975—85, head violin dept., 1981—85. Founder Cleve. Chamber Music Seminar, 1974; co-founder and dir. ENCORE Sch. Strings; bd. advisors Astral Artistic Svcs.; juror various violin competitions; bd. dirs. Univ. Cir., Inc., Avery Fisher Artist Program. Cleve. Orch. debut, 1987, former mem. Cleve. Chamber Players; musician: (violin and chamber ensemble) Donald Erb's View of Space and Time, 1987, Canterbury Trio, 1984—89. Mem. Leadership Cleve. Class of 1989. Named Person of Yr., Am. Italian Heritage, 1994; recipient No. Ohio Live Award of Achievement, 1986. Mem.: Suzuki Assn. (aux. dir. internat. bd.). Office: Cleve Inst Music 11021 East Blvd Cleveland OH 44106-1705*

CESEÑA, CARMEN, education educator, education administrator; b. Ensenada, Calif., July 16, 1947; d. Teodoro L. Ceseña and Guadalupe (Miranda) Carrillo; m. Rogelio A. Cardenas, Feb. 16, 1978; children: Maya-Ixel Ceseña-Cardenas. BA, San Jose State, 1969, standard elem. credential, 1972, MA, 1975; postgrad., Claremont Grad. Sch., 1986—. Cert. community coll. life credential. Lectr. U. Calif., Berkeley, 1975-86; lectr., supr. Sonoma State U., Rhonert Park, Calif., 1978-79; instr. Stanislaus State U., Turlock, Calif., 1982-84, Victor Valley Coll., Victorville, Calif., 1990—. Mem. acad. senate Victor Valley Coll., Victorville, 1991—; dist. advisory mem. Victor Elem. Sch. Dist., Victorville, 1990—; chairperson dept. Victor Valley Coll. Gain Program, Victorville, 1991-93; site coun. chair Del Rey Elem. Sch., Victorville, 1990—. Founding mem. Calif. Assn. Bilingual Edn., San Jose, 1970, High Desert Latino Coalition, 1993; mem. Victor Valley Little League, 1988—; Kaleidoscope Leadership trainer Nat. Inst. for Leadership Devel., 1994; bd. dirs. A Better Way Shelter for Domestic Abuse, Victor Valley Coll., 1994-95. Recipient WHOO (We Honor Our Own) award; Kellogg fellow Univ. Austin, 1993-94. Mem. AAUW, Assn. for Study of Higher Edn., Nat. Assn. Pers. Adminstrs., Am. Assn. Women in Community and Jr. Colls., Pi Lambda Theta. Avocations: reading, gardening, traveling, antique collecting. Home: 15852 Inyo Ct Victorville CA 92392-3479 Office: Victor Valley Coll 18422 Bear Valley Rd Victorville CA 92392-5850

CETTEL, JUDITH HAPNER, artist, secondary school educator; b. Langley, Va., Aug. 28, 1945; d. Francis S. and Mary Louise (Ellers) Hapner. BFA, Miami U., Oxford, Ohio, 1967, MEd, 1972; student, La Varenne Cooking Sch., Paris, 1976, Alliance Francais, 1976. Cert. tchr. art K-12, Ohio. Artist WMUB TV, Miami U., Oxford, Fla., 1966-67; grad. tchg. asst. Miami U., Oxford, Fla., 1971-72; graphic designer, asst. to editor Miami U. Dept. Alumni Affairs, Oxford, Fla., 1967-69; tchr. art Mason HS, Ohio, 1969—; chair dept. fine arts K-12 Mason City Sch., Mason, Ohio, 1980—99; ptnr. Life Style Designs, Cin., 1978—; chair visual arts dept., K-12 Mason City Sch., Mason, Ohio, 1999—. Graphic designer/advt. dir. Hurrah! Gourmet Kitchenware and Cooking Sch., Cin., 1973—80; freelance fine artist, Cin., 1967—; mem. crisis intervention team Mason City Sch., Mason, Ohio, 1993—95, mem. faculty adv. bd., 1994—96, coord. curriculum fine arts, 1995—99, mem. bldg. design team, 1994, Mason, 99, mem. fine arts coun., 1998—; commd. artist Big Pig Gig, Cin., 1999—2000. Artist murals in various comml. and residential settings, 1982—; represented in pvt. collections, Ohio, Ohio, N.H., N.J., N.C., Va.; featured in article Arts and Activities Mag., 1994. Mem., vol. Mt. Adams Civic Assn., Cin., 1976—, Mt. Adams Garden Club; adv. coun. mem. Assn. for Advancement of Arts in Edn., 1995-98, mem. long range planning team, 1996—; mem. planning team Vis. Artists' Alliance. Recipient Golden Apple award Mason City Schs., 1988, Shining Star award, 1995, 96, Contemporary Design award Homerama-Cin. Home Builders Assn., 1980, Martha Holden Jennings Master Tchr. award, 2002; Arts in Edn. grantee Ohio Arts Coun., 1987; grantee Arts Connection Pilot Sch., 1996—, Harvard Inst. for Sch. Leadership, 2001. Mem. NEA, Ohio Edn. Assn., Mason Edn. Assn., Nat. Art Edn. Assn., Ohio Art Edn. Assn., S.W. Ohio Art Edn. Assn., Assn. Advancement Arts Edn. Avocations: scuba diving, cooking, travel, historic restoration, painting murals and large canvases. Office: 1224 Ida St Cincinnati OH 45202

CEVERA, EILEEN LEVY, special education educator; b. Balt., June 29, 1952; d. Julius and Jean Feinstein Levy; children: Jason Adam, Jonathan Lucas. BS in Spl. Edn. and Elem. Edn., U. Md., 1974; MS in Comm. Disorders, Johns Hopkins U., 1982. Tchr. moderate lang. disorders Baltimore County Pub. Sch., Towson, Md., 1974-75; tchr. comm. disorders Anne Arundel County Pub. Schs., Annapolis, Md., 1975-81; tchr. handicapped Mercer County Spl. Svcs. Sch. Dist., Trenton, N.J., 1982-92; tchr. resource room Carroll County Pub. Schs., Westminster, Md., 1989-89; tchr. handicapped West Windsor-Plainsboro Sch. Dist., Princeton Junction, N.J., 1992—. Coord. prodn. Through The Broken Looking Glass interdisciplinary inclusion project. Producer Through the Broken Looking Glass, an Inclusion prodn., 1995. Vol., supporter Spl. Olympics, N.J., 1991—. Recipient N.J. gov.'s tchr. recognition award, 1987, 94. Home: 422 Clarksville Rd Princeton Junction NJ 08550-1515 Office: West Windsor-Plainsboro Mid Sch 55 Grovers Mill Rd Plainsboro NJ 08536-3105

CEYER, SYLVIA T. chemistry educator; Grad. summa cum laude, Hope Coll., Holland, Mich.; PhD, U. Calif., Berkeley. Postdoctoral fellow Nat. Bur. Standards; faculty mem. dept. chemistry MIT, Cambridge, Mass., 1981—, J.C. Sheehan prof. chemistry. Recipient Recognition award for young scholars AAUW Ednl. Found., 1988, Nobel Laureate Signature awd. for Graduate Education in Chemistry, Am. Chemical Soc., 1993. Fellow NAS (chmn. chemistry sect.), Am. Phys. Soc., Am. Acad. Arts and Scis. Office: MIT 6-217 Dept Chemistry 77 Mass Ave Dept Cambridge MA 02139-4307

CHA, SOYOUNG STEPHEN, mechanical engineer, educator; b. Inchon, Korea, June 25, 1944; arrived in U.S., 1974; s. Sang O. and Sook S. (Lee) C.; m. Young W. Park, Sept. 4, 1974. BS, Seoul (Korea) Nat. U., 1969; MS, Mich. State U., 1976; PhD, U. Mich., 1980. Project rsch. engr. Northrop corp., Rsch. Triangle Park, N.C., 1979-84; prof., dir. opto-mech. lab. U. Ill., Chgo., 1984—. Spkr. in field; co-chair Beijing Optical Diagnostics Symposium, 2002. Editor numerous procs. vols., Optics Lasers in Engineering; contbr. more than 130 articles to profl. jours. Dept. of Energy fellow, 1987, NASA fellow, 1994, USAF fellow, 1996. Fellow Internat. Soc. Optical Engrng. (conf. chair, co-chair 1991—), ASME (tech. com. 1983-87), Am. Soc. Aeronautics and Astronautics (tech. com. 1994-97, 1998—), Visualization Soc. Japan (conf. co-chair 1998, 2002). Methodist. Achievements include patent for holographic velocimetry.

CHACE, WILLIAM MURDOUGH, former university administrator; b. Newport News, Va., Sept. 3, 1938; s. William Emerson and Grace Elizabeth (Murdough) Chace; m. JoAn Elizabeth Johnstone, Sept. 5, 1964; children: William Johnstone, Katherine Elizabeth. BA in English, Haverford Coll., 1961; MA in English, U. Calif., Berkeley, 1963; PhD in English, U. Calif., 1968; LLD (hon.), Amherst Coll., 1990, William Coll., 1992. Instr. Stillman Coll., Tuscaloosa, Ala., 1963—64; teaching asst. U. Calif., Berkeley, 1964—66, acting instr., 1967—68; asst. prof. English Stanford U., 1968—74, assoc. prof., 1974—80, prof., 1980, assoc. dean Sch. Humanities and Scis., 1981—85, vice provost for acad. planning and devel., 1985—88; pres. Wesleyan U., Middletown, Conn., 1988—94, Emory U., Atlanta, 1994—2003. Dir. Sun Trust Banks; cons. Hewlett-Packard, Hallmark Cards, Inc., Hawaiian Ednl. Fund, Midwestern Mgmt. Assn.; vis. prof. The Coll. Aboard the Delta Queen, 1979, 80, 82, The Coll. in Western Europe and Brit. Isles, 1985; lectr. to libr. assocs. Stanford U., 1976; lectr. 6th Internat. James Joyce Symposium, Dublin, 1977, MLAL Ann. Conv., 1977, 78, Tufts Symposium, 1978, English Conf. U. Calif., Berkeley, 1979, Eighth Internat. James Joyce Symposium, Dublin, 1982, IBM Internat. Bus. and Acad. Conf., Monte Carlo, 1984, Ezra Pound Centennial Colloquium, San Jose State U., 1985, Ann. Meeting of Assn. of Grad. Liberal Studies Programs, St. Louis, 1986, Chico State U., La. State U., 1987, U. Utah Sch. Medicine Pub. Lecture series, 1987, No. Calif. Sci. Meeting Am. Coll. Physicians, Monterey, Calif., 1987, 13th Internat. James Joyce Symposium, 1992; presenter Joyce and History conf. Yale U., 1990; spkr. Fleur Cowles Flair Symposium, U. Tex., Austin, 2000. Author: James Joyce: A Collection of Critical Essays, 1973, The Political Identities of Ezra Pound and T.S. Eliot, 1973, Lionel Trilling: Criticism and Politics, 1980; co-author: Graham Greene: A Revaluation, 1990; co-editor: Justice Denied: The Black Man in White America, 1970, An Introduction to Literature, 1985; co-editor: (with JoAn E. Chace) Making It New, 1972; contbr. articles to profl. jours.*

CHACKO, GEORGE KUTTICKAL, systems science educator, consultant; b. Trivandrum, India, July 1, 1930; came to U.S., 1953. s. Geevarghese Kuttickal and Thankamma (Mathew) C.; m. Yo Yee, Aug. 10, 1957; children: Rajah Yee, Ashia Yo Chacko Lance. MA in Econs. and Polit. Philosophy, Madras U., India, 1950; postgrad., St. Xavier's Coll., Calcutta, India, 1950-52; B in Commerce, Calcutta U., 1952; cert. postgrad. tng., Indian Stat. Inst., Calcutta, 1951; postgrad., Princeton U., 1953-54; PhD in Econometrics, New Sch. for Social Rsch./New School U., N.Y.C., 1959; postdoctoral, UCLA, 1961. Asst. editor Indian Fin., Calcutta, 1951-53; comml. corr. Times of India, 1953; dir. mktg. and mgmt. rsch. Royal Metal Mfg. Co., N.Y.C., 1958-60; mgr. dept. ops. rsch. Hughes Semicondr. div., Newport Beach, Calif., 1960-61; cons., 1961-62; ops. research staff cons. Union Carbide Corp., N.Y.C., 1962-63; mem. tech. staff Research Analysis Corp., McLean, Va., 1963-65, MITRE Corp., Arlington, Va., 1965-67; sr. staff scientist TRW Systems Group, Washington, 1967-70; asst. in rsch. Princeton U., 1953—54; cons. def. systems, computer, space, tech. systems and internat. devel. systems, assoc. in math. test devel. Ednl. Testing Service, Princeton, N.J., 1955-57; asst. prof. bus. adminstrn. UCLA, 1961-62; lectr. Dept. Agr. Grad. Sch., 1965-67; asst. professorial lectr. George Washington U., 1965-68; professorial lectr. Am. U., 1967-70, adj. prof., 1970; vis. prof. def. systems Mgmt. Coll., Ft. Belvoir, Va., 1972-73; vis. prof. U. So. Calif., 1970-71, prof. systems mgmt., 1971-83, prof. systems sci., 1983-94, prof. emeritus, 1994; prof. mgmt. U. Pertanian/U. Putra, Malaysia, 1996—2000; prin. investigator IRPA project U. Pertanian, Malaysia, 1996-97; prof. U. Putra, Malaysia, 1997—; prof. tech. mgmt. Malaysian Grad. Sch. Mgmt., 1997—; founder, chmn. Joint MIT-MGSM Pan-Asian Program in Mgmt. of Tech., 1997—2000; prof. mgmt. tech. Multimedia U., Selangor, 2001—; chmn. Centre of Excellence of Mgmt. Tech., 2001—02, sr. advisor, 2002—; sr. consultant to Profitera Corp. Malaysian Govt. Multimedia Development Corp. R&D Project: Electronic Enhancement of Receivables Realization, 2002—; consultant ptnr. Natl. Info. Tech. Coun., Govt. of Malaysia, 2003—; chmn., CEO George Chacko Mgmt. Sdn. Bhd., Kuala Lumpur, Washington D.C., 2003—. Sr. Fulbright prof. Nat. Chengchi U., Taipei, 1983-84, sr. Fulbright rsch. prof., 1984-85; prin. investigator and program dir. Tech. Transfer Project, Taiwan Nat. Sci. Coun., 1984-85; disting. fgn. expert lectr. Taiwan Ministry Econ. Affairs, 1986; sr. vis. rsch. prof. Taiwan Nat. Sci. Coun. Nat. Chengchi U., Taipei, 1988-89; sr. vis. rsch. prof. Dah-Yeh Inst. Tech., Dah-Tsuen, Chang-Hwa, Taiwan, 1993-94; vis. prof. Nat. Chengchi U., Taipei, 1993-94; v.p. program devel. Systems and Telecom. Corp., Potomac, Md., 1987-90; chief sci. cons. RJO Enterprises, Lanham, Md., 1988-89; cons. Med. Svcs. Corp. Internat., vector biology and control project U.S. Agy. for Internat. Devel., 1991; guest lectr. Tech. Univs. Tokyo, Taipei, Singapore, Dubai, Cairo, Warsaw, Budapest, Prague, Bergen, Stockholm, Helsinki, Berlin, Madras, Bombay, London, 1992, Yokohoma, Taipei, Hong Kong, Kuala Lampur, Madras, Bombay, Alexandria, Jerusalem, Cairo, Paris, London, 1993-94, Madrid, Bologna, Milan, Monte Carlo, Amsterdam, Vienna, Austria, Kuala Lampur, Bangkok, 1994; Bogta, Quito, Lima, Santiago, Buenos Aires, Rio De Janeiro, Johannesburg, Kuala Lumpur, 1996; USIA sponsored U.S. sci. emissary to Egypt, Burma, India, Singapore, 1987; USIA sponsored U.S. expert on tech. transfer and military conversion 1st Internat. Conf. on Reconstrn. of Soviet Republics, Hannover, Germany, 1992; keynote speaker 2d annual conf. on mgmt. edn. in China, Taipei, Taiwan, 1989, world conf. on transition to advanced market economies, Warsaw, Poland, 1992, annual conv. Indian Inst. Indsl. Engring., Hyderabad, India, 1993, First Sino-South Africa Bilateral Symposium on Tech. Devel., Taipei, 1994, First Asia-Pacific Convention on Bus. mgmt. Edn., Kuala Lumpur, 1996, Annual Conf. of Malaysian Soc. of Ops. Rsch. and Mgmt. Scis, 1997; keynote spkr. Portland Intl. Conf. on Mgmt. of Engring. and Tech., 2003; mem. internat. adv. com. on restructuring strategies for electronics info. industry Asian Inst. Tech. Workshop, 1994, Technological Forecasting and Social Change, 1996—; mem. First Convention on Bus. and Mgmt. Edn., Kuala Lumpur, 1996, mem. Asian-Pacific Conf. on Mgmt. Sci., Malaysia, 1997. Author: 31 books in field including Applied Statistics in Decision Making, 1971, Computer Aided Decision Making, 1972, Systems Approach to Public and Private Sector Problems, 1976, Operations Research Approach to Problem Formation and Solution, 1976, Management Information systems, 1979, Trade Drain Interperative of Technology Transfer: U.S. Taiwan Concomitant Coalistions, 1985, Robotics/Artificial Intelligence/Productivity U.S.-Japan Concomitant Coalitions, 1986, Technology Management: Applications to Corporate Markets and Military Missions, 1988, The Systems Approach to Problem-Solving: From Corporate Markets to National Missions, 1989, Toward Expanding Exports Through Technology Transfer: IBM Taiwan Concomitant Coalitions, 1989, Dynamic Program Management: From Defense Experience to Commercial Application, 1989, Decision-Making Under Uncertainty: An Applied Statistics Approach, 1991, Operations Research/Management Science: Case Studies in Decision Making Under Structured Uncertainty, 1993, Invoking Intercessory Prayer Power: Mediating Modern-day Miracles, 1997, Targeting Strategies for Continuous Competitiveness: 33 Corporate, Country, and Cross-Country Applications for Information Technology (IT) Industry, 1988, Half-Indian, Half-Chinese, and All American, 1998, Synergizing Invention and Innovation for Missions and Markets: 31 Corporate, Country and Cross Country Applications in Integrating Technology and Territory within and Between Corporations and Countries, 1999, Survival Strategies of Hitech Corporations: Applicable Insights from 20th Century Eminent Executive Narratives, 1999; columnist: The Sunday Star, 1998-2003, Bus. Times, 2003, Asian Beacon, 2003—; contbr. articles to profl. pubs.; editor, contbr. 25 books including The Recognition of Systems in Health Services, 1969, Reducing the Cost of Space Transportation, 1969, Systems Approach to Environmental Pollution, 1972, National Organization of Health Services-U.S., USSR, China, Europe, 1979, Educational Innovation in Health Services-U.S., Europe, Middle East, Africa, 1979, Management Education in the Republic of China: Second Annual Conference, 1989, Expert Systems: 1st World Congress Proceedings, 1991, Transition to Advanced Market Economics: Internat. Conf. Proceedings, 1992, Industrial Engineering Interfaces: Inndian Nat. Conf. Proceedings, 1993, Technological Development: 1st Sino-South Africa Bilateral Symposium Proceedings, 1994, Lenten Daily Devotions, 1996, Asia Pacific Convention on Dynamism and Invention in Management Education Proceedings, 1996, Foundations of Game Theory, 1997; guest editor Jour. Rsch. Comm. Studies, 1978-79; assoc. editor Internat. Jour. Forecasting, 1982-85; mem. internat. editl. bd. Malaysian Jour. Mgmt. Scis., 1996-98. Active Nat. Presbyn. Ch., Washington, 1967-84, mem. ch. coun., 1969-71, mem. chancel choir, 1967-84, co-dean ch. family camp, 1977, coord. life abundant discovery groups, 1979; chmn. worship com. Taipei Internat. Ch., 1984, founder, dir. Intercessory Prayer Power, 1984, mem. adult choir, 1983-85, 88-89, 93-96, chmn. membership com., 1985, chmn. stewardship and fin. com., 1985, chmn. com. Christian edn., 1988, Sunday Sch. supt., 1989, adult Sunday sch. leader, 1993; adult Sunday Sch. leader 4th Presbyn. Ch., Bethesda, Md., 1986-87, mem. sanctuary choir, 1985—; participant 9th Internat. Ch. Mus. Festival, Coventry Cathedral, 1992; mem. Men's Ensemble, 1986-93; mem. Ministry Com. Men of 4th Rep. to Session, 1990—; founder, dir. Prayer Power Partnership, 1990—; adult Sunday sch. leader Kuala Lumpur Internat. Ch., 1996—; mem. internat. adv. bd. Technol. Forecasting and Social Change, 1996—; charter mem. IndUS Entrepreneurs, Malaysian chpt. 2002—. Recipient Gold medal Inter-Collegiate Extempore Debate in Malayalam U. Travancore, Trivandrum, India, 1945, 1st pl. Yogic Exercises Competition U. Travancore, 1946, Jr. Lectureship prize Physics Soc. U. Coll., 1946, 1st prize Inter-Varsity Debating Team Madras, 1949, NSF internat. sci. lectures award, 1982, USIA citation for invaluable contbr. to America's pub. diplomacy, 1992, Commendation for 2 books on U.S. - Taiwan Technology Transfer by Presidential Palace, Taipei, 1993; Coll. scholar St. Xavier's Coll., 1950-52; Inst. fellow Indian Stat. Inst., 1951, S.E. Asia Club fellow Princeton U., 1953-54, Univ. fellow UCLA, 1961. Fellow AAAS (nat. coun. 1968-73, chmn. or co-chmn. symposia 1971, 72, 74, 76, 77, 78), Am. Astronautical Soc. (v.p. publs. 1969-71, editor Tech. Newsletter 1968-72, mng. editor Jour. Astronautical Scis. 1969-75)); mem. Ops. Rsch. Soc. Am. (vice chmn. com. of representation on AAAS 1972-78, nat. coun. tech. sect. on health 1966-68, editor Tech. Newsletter on Health 1966-73), Washington Ops. Rsch. Coun. (trustee 1967-69, chmn. tech. colloquia 1967-68, editor Tech. Newsletter 1967-68, Banquet chmn. 1992-93), Inst. Mgmt. Scis. (rep. to Internat. Inst. for Applied Systems Analysis in Vienna, Austria 1976-77, session chmn. Athens, Greece 1977, Atlanta 1977), World Future Soc. (editl. bd. publs. 1970-71), N.Y. Acad. Scis., Soc. Scientific Mgmt. and Ops. Rsch. (Egypt, 1st hon. fgn. mem.), Inst. for Ops. Rsch. and the Mgmt. Scis. (founding, INFORMS 1994); Kiwanis (charter 1st v.p., Life-time Hickson fellow 1995), Costa Mesa North Club (charter 1st v.p., dir.), Friendship Heights Club (charter pres., dir., Outstanding Svc. award 1972-73, Life award), Bethesda Club (disting. divsn. one svc. award, 1968, 70, capital dist. chmn. 1967, 69-70, 71-72, inter divsn. chmn. Green Candle of Hope Dinner, 1965-82), Capital dist. Found. 1982, Taipei-Keystone Club (disting. dir., spl. rep. of internat. pres. and counselor to dist. of Republic of China 1983-86, Pioneer Premier Project award Asia-Pacific conf. 1986, Legion of Honor 1985), Bethesda Club (dir. 1967-69, 95, chmn. internat. rels. 1991—, chmn. hon. com. 1992—, numerous coms. 1966—). Democrat. Office: U So Calif Inst Safety And Sys Mgmt Los Angeles CA 90089-0001

CHADWELL, JIM F. principal; BA, Tex. Christian U., 1991, M of Sch. Adminstrn., 1996. Program specialist, crisis call counselor Charter Hosp., Grapevine, Tex., 1991—98; intern Gymnasium Hochrad, Hamburg, Germany, 1993; tchr. sociology, psychology, German N.W. Ind. Sch. Dist., Justin, Tex., 1993—97, asst. prin. h.s., 1997—99, prin. h.s., 1999—. Mem. North Tex. Fulbright Exch. Peer Rev. Com., 1997—. Bd. dirs. Tarrant County Courage to Teach; mem. Light House Schs. Consortium. Named Adminstr. of Yr., Tex. Ednl. Theatre Assn.; recipient Nat. Youth Leaders Conf. award, 1999. Mem.: ASCD, Tex. Assn. for Supervision and Curriculum Devel., Nat. Assn. Secondary Sch. Prins., Tex. Assn. Secondary Sch. Prins., Pi Sigma Alpha.

CHAE, YOON KWON, minister, educator; b. Seoul, Korea, Feb. 13, 1932; came to U.S., 1973; s. Sang H. and Bong Soo (Cho) Chae (Choi); m. Geon Min, Mar. 3, 1981 (dec.); m. Kook Ja Park, Dec. 4, 1982; 1 child, John Wooshik. BA, San Jose Bible Coll., 1960; MA, Lincoln Christian Sem., 1961; DD, Am. Bible Inst., 1968; ThD, Immanuel Bapt. Sem., 1976. Ordained to ministry Christian Ch., 1960. Pastor numerous Christian Chs., Korea and U.S., 1962—; pres., chancellor Korea Christian Coll., Seoul, 1965—. Prof. San Jose Christian Coll., 1985—; bd. dirs. Geon Christian Children's Home, Seoul, 1966—, Korea Gospel Mission, San Jose, 1974—. Author: My Dear American Friends I, 1973, II, 1982, III, 1989, The Shattered Cross I, 1972, II, 1978, III, 1985, Yoon Kwon Chae Column, 1988, Sermons for 52 Weeks, 1987. 1st lt. Korean Army, 1953-56. Mem. Kiwanis (pres. Seoul 1983-84, gov. 1987-88). Republican. Home: 1043 Forest Knoll Dr San Jose CA 95129-3015 Office: San Jose Christian Coll S 12th and Virginia San Jose CA 95112

CHAFFEE, STEVEN, communication educator; b. South Gate, Calif., Aug. 21, 1935; s. Edwin W. and Nancy M. Chaffee; m. Sheila McGoldrick, 1966 (div. 1987); children: Laura, Adam, Amy; m. Debra Lieberman, 1989; 1 child, Eliot. s. Edwin W. and Nancy M. Chaffee; m. Sheila McGoldrick, 1959 (div. 1986); children: Laura, Adam, Amy; m. Debra Lieberman, 1989; 1 child, Eliot. BA in History, U. of Redlands, 1957; MS in Journalism, UCLA, 1962; PhD in Comm., Stanford U., 1965. News editor Angeles Mesa News-Advertiser, L.A., 1957; reporter Santa Monica (Calif.) Evening Outlook, 1962; from asst. prof. to full prof. U. Wis., Madison, 1965-81; prof. comm. Stanford (Calif.) U., 1981-99, U. Calif., Santa Barbara, 1999-2001. Author: Communication Concepts I: Explication, 1991; co-editor: Handbook of Communication Science, 1987; co-author: Television and Human Behavior, 1978; editor: Political Communication, 1975. Lt. (j.g.) USN, 1957-61. Fellow Internat. Comm. Assn. (pres. 1981); mem. Assn. for Edn. in Journalism and Mass Comm., Am. Polit. Sci. Assn. Democrat. Avocation: hiking. Home: Santa Barbara, Calif. Died May 15, 2001.

CHAGNON, JOSEPH V. school system administrator; b. Newark, Mar. 28, 1929; m. Placidia Irma Rodrigeuz; children: Elaine, Joseph, David, Raymond, John. BS in Edn., N.J. State Tchr. Coll., 1954; MA, Columbia U., 1958; cert. pub. sector mgmt. labor rels., Rutgers U., 1983, cert. equal employment opportunity, 1984, cert. human resource mgmt., 1987. Tchr. Newark Pub. Schs., 1954-65, adminstr., 1965-92. Assessor N.J. Assessment Ctr. for Prins.; mentor for prins. and vice prins. N.J. Dept. Edn., 1992—; chmn. Coun. Union Employees Bd. Edn., Newark, 1990—; mem. labor adv. bd. Essex County Coll., 1992—; v.p. Essex West Hudson Labor Coun.,

1993—; trustee United Labor Agy., Essex County, 1994—; bd. dirs. Newark Bd. Edn. Employees Credit Union. Commr. East Brunswick, N.J. Sewage Authority, 1970-88, 97—, sec., 1971, 79-81, vice chmn., 1972, 81, chmn., 1974, 82-88; pres. East Brunswick Mus. Corp., 1978-81, trustee, 1978—, sec. 1994-96, commr., 1997—; trustee East Brunswick Pub. Libr., 1978—, sec., 1986—; mem. East Brunswick Recreation and Pks. Adv. Bd., 1966-80, chmn., 1974-80, mem. emeritus; mem. East Brunswick Planning Bd., 1988-91; mem. labor adv. bd. Essex County Coll., 1992—; v.p. Essex-West Hudson Labor Coun.; trustee United Labor Agy. Essex County. Recipient Ednl. Leadership award Benedette Crocé Ednl. Soc., 1982, Ednl. Svc. award Essex County and State N.J., 1991, Leadership award Orgn. Afro-Am. Adminstrs., 1994. Commr. East Brunswick (N.J.) Sewage Authority, 1970-88, sec., 1971, 79-81, vice chmn., 1972, 81, chmn., 1974, 82-88; pres. East Brunswick Mus. Corp., 1978-81, trustee, 1978—; trustee East Brunswick Pub. Libr., 1978—, sec., 1986—; mem. East Brunswick Recreation and Parks Adv. Bd., 1966-80, chmn., 1974-80; mem. labor adv. bd. Essex County Coll., 1992—; mem. Essex-West Hudson Labor Coun.; trustee United Labor Agy. Essex County; bd. dirs. Newark Bd. Edn. Employees Credit Union, 1995—. Home: 7 Carol Ct East Brunswick NJ 08816-4405 Office: 624 Bloomfield Ave Bloomfield NJ 07003-2510

CHAGNON, LUCILLE TESSIER, workforce development and literacy specialist; b. Gardner, Mass., June 1, 1936; d. Fred G. Tessier and Alfreda C. (Ross) Noel; m. Richard J. Chagnon, Sept. 16, 1978; children: Daniel, David. BMus, Rivier Coll., Nashua, N.H.; cert. in human resource mgmt. and cmty. devel., Inst. Cultural Affairs, Chgo., 1969; MEd, Boston Coll., 1972. Educator, N.H., 1960-73; internat. cons. Inst. Cultural Affairs, Chgo., 1973-79; staff tng. dir. CO-MHAR, Inc., Phila., 1979-81; pres., owner Chagnon Assocs., Collingswood, N.J., 1981-86; prin. Sacred Heart Sch., Camden, N.J., 1986-87; founder, dir. Lifeline Literacy Project, 1988-94; literacy and developmental learning specialist Rutgers U., Camden, 1989-99; coord. work readiness, Workforce Devel. Inst. Drexel U., Phila., 1999-2000. Adj. grad. faculty dept. counseling psychology Temple U. Sch. Edn., Phila., 1985—90; sr. project staff Right Assocs., Phila., 1982—91, 2001—. Author (with Richard J. Chagnon): The Best is Yet to Be: A Pre-Retirement Program, 1985; author: Easy Reader, Learner, Writer, 1994, Voice Hidden, Voice Heard: A Reading and Writing Anthology, 1998, You, Yes YOU, Can Teach Someone to Read, 2004. Bd. dirs. Camden County Literacy Vols. of Am., 1987—91, Handicapped Advocates for Ind. Living, 1987—; mem. Collingswood (N.J.) Bd. Edn., 1985—89. Mem.: ASCD, Internat. Reading Assn., Internat. Alliance for Learning, Inst. Cultural Affairs, Brain-Based Edn. Network, Nat. Learning Found. (adv. bd. 1997—). Home and Office: 408 River Rd Wilmington DE 19809-2731 Fax: 302-762-0285. E-mail: lifeline248@aol.com.

CHAI, WINBERG, political science educator; b. Shanghai, Oct. 16, 1932; came to U.S., 1951, naturalized, 1973; s. Ch'u and Mei-en (Tsao) C.; m. Carolyn Everett, Mar. 17, 1966 (dec. 1996); children: Maria May-lee, Jeffrey Tien-yu. Student, Hartwick Coll., 1951-53, LittD, 2002; BA, Wittenberg U., 1955; MA, New Sch. Social Rsch., 1958; PhD, NYU, 1968; DHL, Wittenberg U., 1997; DL, Hartwick Coll., 2002. Lectr. New Sch. Social Rsch., 1957-61; vis. asst. prof. Drew U., 1961-62; asst. prof. Fairleigh Dickinson U., 1962-65, U. Redlands, 1965-68, assoc. prof., 1969-73, chmn. dept., 1970-73; prof., chmn. Asian studies CCNY, 1973-79; disting. prof. polit. sci., v.p. acad. affairs, spl. asst. to pres. U. S.D., Vermillion, 1979-82; prof. polit. sci., dir. internat. programs U. Wyo., Laramie, 1988—. Hmn. Third World Conf. Found., Inc., Chgo., 1982—; pres. Wang Yu-fa Found., Taiwan, 1989—. Author: (with Ch'u Chai) The Story of Chinese Philosophy, 1961, The Changing Society of China, 1962, rev. edit., 1969, The New Politics of Communist China, 1972, The Search for a New China, 1975; editor: Essential Works of Chinese Communism, 1969, (with James C. Hsiung) Asia in the U.S. Foreign Policy, 1981, (with James C. Hsiung) U.S. Asian Relations: The National Security Paradox, 1983, (with Carolyn Chai) Beyond China's Crisis, 1989, In Search of Peace in the Middle East, 1991, (with Cal Clark) Political Stability and Economic Growth, 1994, China Mainland and Taiwan, 1994, revised edit. 1996, Hong Kong Under China, 1998; co-translator: (with Ch'u Chai) A Treasury of Chinese Literature, 1965; co-author (with May-Lee-Chai) The Girl from Purple Mountain, 2001; contbg. editor: Encyclopedia of Modern Asia, 2003. Haynes Found. fellow, 1967, 68; Ford Found. humanities grantee, 1968, 69, Pacific Cultural Found. grantee, 1978, 86, NSF grantee, 1970, Hubert Eaton Meml. Fund grantee, 1972-73, Field Found. grantee, 1973, 75, Henry Luce Found. grantee, 1978, 80, S.D. Humanities Com. grantee, 1980, Pacific Culture Fund grantee, 1987, 90-91. Mem. AAAS, AAUP, NAACP, Am. Polit. Sci. Assn., Am. Assn. Chinese Studies (pres.1978-80), N.Y. Acad. Scis., Internat. Studies Assn. Democrat. Home: 1071 Granito Dr Laramie WY 82072-5045 Office: PO Box 4098 Laramie WY 82071-4098 E-mail: WinbergChai@aol.com.

CHAIKLIN, AMY LYNN, childhood education program developer; b. Hartford, Conn., Nov. 6, 1968; d. Michael Bland and Miriam Ellen (Bloom) C. BSC, U. Miami, 1990; MA, George Washington U., 1993. Rschr. Mailman Ctr. for Child Devel., Coral Gables, Fla., 1990; tchr., trainer Child Assault Prevention Project South Fla., Miami, 1990-91; head infant tchr. Meeting House Coop. Presch., Alexandria, Va., 1991-92; child devel. specialist comprehensive child devel. program Edward C. Mazique Parent Child Center, Washington, D.C., 1992-94; early intervention prototyper Army Exception Family Mem. Dept. Landstuhl (Germany) Regional Med. Ctr., 1994-95; early intervention specialist Air Force Svcs. for Exceptional Children, Rota, Spain, 1995—. Rsch. asst. dept. tchr. preparation and spl. edn. George Washington U., Washington, 1992-93. Home: Nuestras Senora del Mar 29 11500 El Manantial Puerto de Santa Maria Spain Office: AFSEC Unit 50085 Box 1917 Fpo AE 09645-5085

CHAIKLIN, HARRIS, retired social work educator; b. Bridgeport, Conn., June 27, 1926; s. David and Victoria (Spector) C.; m. Sharon Udren, June 5, 1955; children: Seth, Matthew, Martha, Nina. BA with distinction, U. Conn., Storrs, 1950; MA in Sociology, U. Conn., 1952; MS in Social Work, U. Wis., 1953; postgrad. in Sociology, NYU, 1953-55; PhD, Yale U., 1961. Lic. social worker, Md., Acad. Cert. Social Workers. Psychiat. social worker, caseworker Jewish Bd. of Guardians, N.Y.C., 1953-56; caseworker Jewish Family Svc., New Haven, Conn., 1958-59; instr. sociology U. Conn., 1959-60; asst. prof. Smith Coll., Northampton, Mass., 1960-62, U. Md., Balt., 1962-64, assoc. prof., 1964-71, prof., 1971-97, asst. dean Informatics, 1990-97, prof. emeritus, 1998; caseworker Jewish Family and Children's Svc., Balt., 1963-76; pvt. practice, 1977—. Caseworker John F. Kennedy Inst. Family Ctr., 1984-86; clin. assoc. prof. psychiatry U. Md. Med. Sch., 1974—; assoc. John F. Kennedy Inst. for Handicapped Children; vis. prof. Haifa U., 1976-77, 80-81, 86-87, Morgan State U., 1977-78; tchr. U. Calif, Berkeley, U. Conn. Sch. Social Work, Hartford Coll., U. Mass., U. Vt., others. Editor: Marian Chace: Her Papers, 1975, Inventory of Research, 1963-65; (with others) Aides for Research Teachers: I-IV, 1969; (with Ralph Segalman) Symbolic Interaction and Social Welfare, 1979; contbr. articles to profl. jours.; mem. editl. bds. Recipient Harry Greenstein award Balt. Associated Jewish Charities, 1986, Md. Higher Edn. Assn. award of Merit, 1991; named Commonwealth Fund fellow, Yale U., 1956-58, Sr. Fulbright Hays lectr., Haifa U., 1976-77. Mem. NASW (Social Worker of Yr., Md. 1973, Social Work Pioneer 2001), Am. Sociol. Assn., Am. Orthopsychiat. Assn., Coun. on Social Work Edn. Home: 5173 Phantom Ct Columbia MD 21044-1318 E-mail: hchaikli@comcast.net., hchaikli@erols.com.

CHAIM, LINDA SUSAN, special education administrator; b. Detroit, May 20, 1950; d. Donald J. and Shirley R. (Dennis) McCarthy; 1 child, Jeremy Chaim. B Edn. and Psychology, Concordia U., Montreal, Que., Can., 1978; MEd in Psychology, McGill U., 1992; cert. in Autism Spectium Disorders, U. Vt. Adolescent clin. tchr., team leader McGill-Montreal Children's Hosp. Learning Ctr., 1976—; clin. tchr., cons. team leader Lansdowne Ctr., Montreal, 1982—; dir. student svcs. Vanguard Intercultural Sch., Montreal, 1986—; dir. student support svcs. Franklin West Supervisory Union, Fairfax, Vt., 1994-96; spl. edn. adminstr. Franklin N.W. Supervisory Union, 1996—. Mem. adv. bd. for behaviorally challenged children Vt. Dept. Edn., Montpelier, 1995—96; dir., founder, advisor camp for spl. needs Camp Sitara, Montreal; cons., cook Camp Tournesol, Montreal; mem. Vt. Rural Autism project U. Vt., Montpelier, 1997—; mem. exec. bd. Northwestern Counselling and Support Svcs., 2002. Mem. rev. panel devel. disabilities State of Vt. Human Rights Commn., 2002—; active Scouts Can., 1989—93; mem. exec. bd. dirs. Vt. Parents and Info. Ctr., 1997—. Recipient Spl. Edn. Adminstr. of Yr., State of Vt., 2000—01, Cmty. Partnership award on behalf of children with devel. disabilities Franklin and Grand Isle County, State Autism Task Force, 2000—01. Mem. Coun. for Exceptional Children, Assn. Mediators Families Que., Assn. Camps Que. Avocations: cooking for large groups, camping, writing children's books. Office: Franklin NW Supervisory 21 Church St Swanton VT 05488-1434

CHAIM, ROBERT ALEX, dean, educator; b. Stockton, Calif., Oct. 25, 1947; s. Alex Jr. and Carmen Lorraine (Rodriques-Lopez) C.; m. Diane Leonora Gregonis, May 30, 1971 (dec. 1973); m. Linda Jean Riley, Dec. 22, 1976. AA, San Joaquin Delta Coll., 1967; BA, Sacramento State Coll., 1970; cert. in secondary teaching, U. Pacific, 1972, ArtsD, 1980. Instr. English lang. U. Pacific, Stockton, 1973-77, lectr. lang. of law Sacramento, 1977-95; asst. to dean McGeorge Sch. Law, Sacramento, 1977-81, asst. dean students, 1981-95; dean students Roger Williams U. Sch. Law, Bristol, R.I., 1995-98. Cons. grammar, usage and linguistics numerous law orgns. and pvt. law firms, Calif. and R.I., 1978—; mem. curriculum com. law sch. U. San Fernando, Calif., 1979; mem. ABA/Assn. Am. Law Schs./Law Sch. Admission Coun. Joint Task Force on Fin. Aid, 1991-93. Editor-in-chief Stauffer Legal Rsch. Series, 1978-95; contbr. articles to scholarly books and profl. jours. Mem. Elk Grove (Calif.) Community Planning Adv. Couns., 1986-88, vice-chmn., 1987; mem. scholarship com. Centro Legal de Calif., Sacramento, 1987-90, curriculum adv. com. Elk Grove Unified Sch. Dist., 1988, scholarship com. Sacramento Country Day Sch., 1988; lectr., campus coord. Oak Park Sports and Edn. Found., Inc., 1989-95; bd. advisors St. Hope Acad. Youth Orgn., 1991-98. Recipient Meritorious Svc. award Asian-Am. Law Students Assn., Sacramento, 1986, 87, Outstanding Svc. award La Raza Law Students Assn., 1988. Mem. ABA (assoc., legal edn. and bar admissions sect.), Nat. Assn. Fgn. Student Affairs, Assn. Am. Law Schs. (mem. legal rsch. and writing sect., student svcs. sect., student svc. com. 1990-91, law admission coun. joint task force on fin. aid 1991-94), Lions Club (judge 53rd ann. multiple dist. four, final spkr. contest, 1990). Avocations: golf, cabinetry, gardening.

CHAISSON, ERIC JOSEPH, astrophysicist, science administrator, educator; b. Lowell, Mass., Oct. 26, 1946; m. Lola Judith Eachus; children: Megan Lyra, Paul Cygnus, Bridget Aquila. BS cum laude, U. Mass., Lowell, 1968; AM, Harvard U., 1969, PhD, 1972. NAS/NRC post-doctoral fellow Smithsonian Astrophys. Observatory, 1972-74; rsch. assoc. Harvard Coll. Observatory, 1972-74; staff mem. Harvard-Smithsonian Ctr. for Astrophysics, 1974-82; asst. prof. Harvard U., 1974-79, assoc. prof., 1979-82; prof. of astronomy and physics Haverford Coll., 1982-86; sr. rsch. physicist MIT Lincoln Lab., 1986-87; sr. scientist, dir. ednl. programs Space Telescope Sci. Inst., Balt., 1987-92; adj. prof. physics and astronomy Johns Hopkins U., 1987-92; assoc. dir. Johns Hopkins U. Space Grant Coll., 1987-92; dir. Wright Ctr. for Sci. Edn., Tufts U., Medford, Mass., 1992—; prof. physics and astronomy, prof. edn. Tufts U., Medford, 1992—; co-dir. MIT Space Grant Consortium, 1992—. Non-resident tutor Mather House Harvard Coll., 1979-82, Quincy House Harvard Coll., 1986-87; assoc. Harvard Coll. Observatory, 1986—; Shapley vis. prof., Amer. Astron. Soc., 1979-83; adj. prof. Wellesley Coll., 1986-87; mem. sci. adv. com. Hayden Planetarium, Boston Mus. Sci., 1975-82; bd. overseers Boston Mus. Sci., 2001—; mem. com. on acad. studies Harvard Astronomy Dept., 1975-82, chmn., 1978-82; mem. com. on pub. edn. Harvard-Smithsonian Ctr. for Astrophysics, chmn., 1978-82; mem. users' com. Nat. Radio Astronomy Observatory, 1978-81; mem. sci. working group on extra-terrestrial intelligence NASA, 1979-90; mem. Bowdoin Prize com. Harvard U., 1979-82; mem. panel NAS, 1988-90; mem. adv. com. NSF, 1989; nat. lectr. Phi Beta Kappa, 1995-96; lectr. in field. Author: Cosmic Dawn: The Origins of Matter and Life, 1981 (Phi Beta Kappa award 1981, Am. Inst. Physics-U.S. Steel Found. award 1981, Nat. Book award finalist 1982), La Relativita, 1983, The Life Era: Cosmic Selection and Conscious Evolution, 1987, Relatively Speaking: Black Holes, Relativity and the Fate of the Universe, 1988, Universe: An Evolutionary Approach to Astronomy, 1988, (with Steve McMillan) Astronomy Today, 1993, 96, 99, 2002, (with George B. Field) The Invisible Universe: Probing the Frontiers of Astrophysics, 1985, The Hubble Wars: Astrophysics Meets Astropolitics in the Two-Billion Struggle Over the Hubble Space Telescope, 1994 (Am. Inst. Physics award 1995), (with Steve McMillan) Astronomy: A Beginner's Guide to the Universe, 1995, 98, 2001, (with T. Kim) The 13th Labor: Improving Science Education, 1999, Cosmic Evolution: The Rise of Complexity in Nature, 2001; mem. editl. bd. Zygon: The Jour. Religion and Sci., 1982—; bd. editors World Futures: The Jour. Gen. Evolution, 1986—; contbg. editor Air and Space Mag.; sci. advisor PBS "Search for Solutions"; co-writer PBS "Starfinder"; co-writer (IMAX movie) Cosmic Voyage, 1992-94. Bd. dirs. Found. for the Future, 1997—; mem. bd. overseers Boston Mus. Sci., 2001—. Capt. U.S. Air Force, 1969-73. Rsch. fellow Alfred P. Sloan Found., 1976-79; recipient Bok prize Harvard U., 1977, Smith-Weld prize, Harvard U., 1978, Hubble Space Telescope Project cert. Merit NASA, 1993. Mem. AAAS, Am. Inst. Physics (com. on pub. edn. and info. 1981-83, book award 1981, 95), Am. Astron. Soc. (edn. adv. bd. 1985-89, Harlow Shapley vis. prof. 1979-83), Am. Assn. Physics Tchrs., Internat. Astron. Union, Internat. Union Radio Sci., Fedn. Am. Scientists, Authors Guild, Authors League of Am., Emerson Soc., Thoreau Soc. Achievements include research on the origins and evolution of material systems throughout the universe. Home: 77 Walden St Concord MA 01742-2508 Office: Tufts U Wright Ctr for Sci Edn 4 Colby St Medford MA 02155-6013 E-mail: eric.chaisson@tufts.edu.

CHAIT, ANDREA MELINDA, school psychologist; b. Buffalo, May 7, 1970; d. Marvin and Rochelle (Benatovich) C. BS in Health Edn., Ithaca (N.Y.) Coll., 1992; MEd in Spl. Edn., U. Fla., 1995, MA in Edn., 2001, PhD in Sch. Psychology, 2002. Nat. cert. sch. psychologist. Substitute tchr. Cortland (N.Y.) H.S., 1992; tchrs. aid, substitute Stanley G. Falk, Cheektowaga, N.Y., 1993; pvt. spl. edn. tutor Buffalo and Gainesville, 1992—99; behavioral disorders tchr. Paul D. West Middle Sch., East Point, Ga., 1995-96; chair discipline com. spl. edn. dept. Paul P. West Middle Sch., East Point, Ga., 1995—; grad. tchg. asst. U. Fla., 1998-99; sch. psychologist internal sub. Browar Co. Pub. Schs., 2001—02. Adj. mem. faculty Santa Fe C.C., 2000—; clin. coord. LEAP program Kennedy Krieger Inst., 2002—. Vol. Task Force for Battered Women, Ithaca, 1991, Human Rights Orgn., Gainesville, 1993-94. Mem. APA, Nat. Assn. Sch. Psychologists, Pi Lambda Theta, Kappa Delta Pi, Phi Kappa Phi. Jewish. Avocations: reading, drawing, game development. Home: 1600 Trebor Ct Lutherville MD 21093

CHAJET, LORI MENSCHEL, secondary education educator; b. N.Y.C., May 26, 1971; d. Clive and Bonnie Sue (Loeb) C. BA in Ednl. Studies and Pub. Policy, Brown U., 1993; MEd, Columbia U., N.Y.C., 1995. Project asst. Nat. Ctr. for Rsch. in Vocat. Edn., U. Calif., Berkeley, 1993-94; rsch. asst. Nat. Ctr. for Restructuring Edn., Schs. and Tchg., N.Y.C., 1994-95; tchr. East Side Cmty. H.S., N.Y.C., 1995—. Big sister Brown Community Outreach, Brown U., 1989-93; coord., tchr. Sat. Sch. Project, 1990-91, English tchr., Monteverde Inst., Costa Rica, 1992; literacy/GED tutor Travelers Aid Soc., Providence, 1990-91; project asst. Coalition of Essential Schs., Providence, 1991-92. McGraw fellow grant Brown U., 1992. Democrat. Jewish. Avocations: photography, outdoor sports, hiking, camping, running.

CHAKRAVORTY, RANES CHANDRA, surgeon, educator; b. Calcutta, India, Jan. 9, 1929; came to U.S., 1952; s. Pares Chandra and Sivani (Mazumdar) C.; m. Chitra Adhikari, Nov. 10, 1955; children: Aryaa, Agnis. MB, BS, U. Calcutta, 1949; MEd, Va. Poly. Inst. & State U., 1992. Cert. Royal Coll. Surgeons. Internship and residency U. Calcutta, 1949-52; resident Mt. Sinai Hosp., Chgo., 1952-53; from asst. resident to chief resident and fellow Meml. Sloan Kettering Cancer Ctr., N.Y.C., 1953-59; registrar Hammersmith Hosp., U. London, 1955; stagiaire Jules Bordet Cancer Ctr, Brussells, 1959, Gustave Roussy Cancer Ctr., Seine, France; asst. prof. surgery Inst. Postgrad. Med. Edn. and Rsch., Calcutta, 1960-62, prof., 1970-71; surgeon Chittaranjan Cancer Hosp., Calcutta, 1962-70; head dept. oncology RKM Sevapratishthan, Calcutta, 1961-70; asst. prof. Med. Coll. Va., Richmond, 1971-74; assoc. prof. U Va. Med. Sch., Charlottesville, 1974-80, prof., 1980-99; chief surgery VA Med. Ctr., Salem, Va., 1974-94; ret. U. Va. Med. Sch., Charlottesville, 1999. Dir. Health Care Ctr., Trinity Luth. Ch., Roanoke, Va., 1982-84; Squibb-Olin observer Meml. Sloan-Kettering Cancer Ctr., N.Y.C., 1966; adj. prof. anatomy Coll. of Health Scis., Roanoke, Va., 1999—. Author, editor: Core Concepts in Cancer, 1983; editor Scalpel and Tongs, Am. Journal of Medical Philately, 1973—; mem. editl. bd. Vets. Health Systems Jour., 1997—, Jour. Indian Med. Assn., 1997—; also chpts. to books. Recipient Vth Subbarow Oration award Andhra State Med. Assn., 1968, Subodh Mitra medal 1st All India Chemotherapy Congress, 1980, GIECO Pub. Svc. cert., 1991, Calvert medal, 1995, A.K. Sen medal, 1995, J.B. Chatterjea medal, 1995, Disting. Alumnus Radha Govinda Kar Med. Coll., Calcutta U., 1997. Fellow ACS (liaison fellow commn. on cancer 1974-94), Royal Coll. Surgeons (Eng.); mem. Soc. Surg. Oncology Soc. Head and Neck Surgeon, Am. Assn. for Cancer Edn., Brit. Assn. Surg. Oncology, Am. Assn. History of Medicine, Internat. Soc. History of Medicine, French Soc. for History of Medicine (fgn.), Va. Philatelic Fedn. (sec. 1981-82, pres. 1984-85, 92-93), Am. Topical Assn. (disting. topical philatelist 1992), AAPI (trustee 1990—), Univ. Calcutta Med. Alumni Assn. (pres. 1990-91), Am. Assn. Physician India, Rotary (chmn. internat. svcs. 1984-86). Democrat. Vedantist. Avocations: medical philately, astronomy, photography, computers, travel. Home: 5049 Cherokee Hills Dr Salem VA 24153-5848 Office: VA Med Ctr Salem VA 24153

CHALFANT-ALLEN, LINDA KAY, retired Spanish language educator; b. New Kensington, Pa., Oct. 9, 1943; d. Fred and Evelyn V. (Peters) C.; m. Charles V. Utley, Sr., Jan. 26, 1963 (div.); children: Charles V. Utley, Yvette Melissa Utley; m. Simon Allen, Feb. 13, 1998. BA in Child Study, Vassar Coll., 1965; MS in Spanish and Linguistics, Georgetown U., 1971. Cert. tchr., N.Y., D.C. Bilingual rsch. asst. Georgetown U., Washington, 1966-71; curriculum writer D.C. Pub. Schs., 1969-70, 91; asst. prof., rsch. assoc. U. D.C., 1982-85; asst. to dir. Latin for Modern Sch., McLean, Va., 1968-94; tchr. D.C. Pub. Schs., 1965-95, ret., 1995; freelance cons., editor, 1961—; bilingual legal sec. Wilkinson, Barker, Knauer & Quinn, Washington, 1996-97; legal sec. Thelen Reid & Priest, 1998-2000. Proposal review panelist Nat. Endowment for Humanities, Washington, 1984, 87, 89, U.S. Dept. Edn., Washington, 1986. Founder, 1st pres. Fgn. Lang. Action Group, Washington, 1978-79; Sunday sch. tchr., Washington, 1972-93. Recipient Grad. Study fellowship King Juan Carlos Found., Spain, 1994, Travel grant Spain '92 Found., 1994. Roman Catholic. Avocations: travel, reading, bowling, baking, exercise, crochet. E-mail: lindachalfant@msn.com.

CHALFIN, SUSAN ROSE, psychologist, educator; b. Phila., Apr. 26, 1956; d. Harry Herbert and Arlene Sybil (Abrams) C.; m. Thomas Arthur Dughi, May 22, 1983. BA, Columbia U., 1978; postgrad., Wayne State U., 1978-79; MA, Clark U., 1982, PhD, 1990. Lic. psychologist, Fla. Rsch. asst. dept. psychology Barnard Coll., Columbia U., N.Y.C., 1976-78; grad. asst. Wayne State U., Detroit, 1978-79; psychometrican Spl. Edn. Program, Balt., 1984; family therapist, psychometrician Frederick County Spl. Edn. and Treatment Program, Frederick, Md., 1984-87; psychology assoc. Psychol. Counseling & Consultation Ctr., Glen Burnie, Md., 1987-88; behavioral specialist div. psychology Jackson Meml. Hosp., Miami, Fla., 1989-90; asst. prof. U. Miami, 1994—2002; clin. psychologist Jackson Meml. Hosp., 2002—. Cons. Hughes-Gaeda Ctr., Miami, 1989-90, Alliance for Psychol. Svcs., Miami, 1990-94; vol. faculty U. Miami, 2002—. Contbr. articles to profl. jours. Univ. scholar Clark U., 1979-80, Univ. fellow, 1980-81, rsch. fellow, 1981-82; fellow NIMH, 1982-83. Mem. APA. Avocations: swimming, jogging, photography, bicycling. Office: 1695 NW 9th Ave Rm 1425 Miami FL 33136-1005

CHAMBERLAIN, CHARLES FRANK, retired artist, educator; b. Brockton, Mass., Aug. 7, 1942; s. William Smith and Bertha Louise (Hansler) C.; m. Linda Chloe Cheney, Jan. 3, 1968; children: Gabrielle Elizabeth, Pamela Chloe. BFA, Mass. Coll. Art, Boston, 1964; MFA, SUNY, Alfred, 1967. Instr. U. N.H., Durham, 1966-67; prof. art East Carolina U., Greenville, NC, 1967—2003, ret., 2003—. Chair arts commn. Episcopal Diocese of East Carolina, Kinston, N.C., 1988—. Exhibitor pottery at Crafts Multiples, Washington, 1978; exhibitor ceramic art at Rocky Mt. Art Ctr., 1996, Henri Gallery, Washington, 1965; artist Stations of the Cross, St. Paul's Ch., Greenville, N.C., 1965. Mem. Nat. Coun. Edn. Ceramic Art. Democrat. Office: East Carolina U Sch Art Greenville NC 27858-4353

CHAMBERLAIN, JENNIFER RUTH, elementary school educator; b. Pensacola, Fla., Mar. 13, 1970; d. Thomas Harold and Gloria Jean (Stanley) C. Post grad., Auburn (Ala.) U., 1988-91. Mem. Auburn Wind Symphony, Auburn Symphony Orch., Auburn Women's Chorus. Mem. Auburn Assn. for Childhood Edn., Auburn U. Marching Band. Republican. Mem. Ch. of Christ. Avocations: music, cars, softball, football. Home: 309 S Gay St Auburn AL 36830-7433

CHAMBERLAIN, KATHRYN BURNS BROWNING, retired career officer; b. Rapid City, S.D., Jan. 17, 1951; d. George Alfred III and Mildred Doty Browning; m. Thomas Richard Masker, Apr. 19, 1975 (widowed Sept. 1978); m. Guy Caldwell Chamberlain III, Mar. 25, 1980 (div. Oct. 1988); children: Burns Doty, Anne Caldwell. BA, La. Tech. U., 1973; postgrad., Naval Postgrad. Sch., Monteray, Calif., 1978-79; MA, Auburn U., 1984; postgrad., U. Ill., 1994-96, Govs. State U., 1995-96. Ensign USN, 1974, lt. jg., 1976, lt., 1978, advanced through grades to comdr., 1983, surface warfare designation, 1980, joint staff officer, 1986, comdg. officer Mil. Sealift Command Office, 1986-88; comdr., exec. officer USNAVFAC, Newfoundland, Nfld., Can., 1991-94; cmty. planner City of Montgomery, 1998—. Mem. AAUW, Am. Planning Assn., Urban and Regional Info. Sys. Assn. Home and Office: 364 Felder Ave Montgomery AL 36104-5616 E-mail: kchamberlai1@earthlink.net.

CHAMBERS, CAROL TOBEY, elementary school educator; b. L.A., July 17, 1947; d. Joseph Richard and Jean Doris (Neal) Tobey; m. Joseph Price Chambers, June 8, 1973; 1 child, Ryan Leigh. Student, Ohio State U., 1965-67; BS in Edn., George Peabody Coll. Tchrs., 1969; postgrad., U. Tenn., 1971, Belmont U., 1971, 88, 96, Tenn. State U., 1980-83, Vanderbilt U., 1986, 92, Trevecca Coll., 1978, 89, 90, Tenn. Arts Acad., 1989, 94-96; arts seminar, workshop, Coll. of Santa Fe, 1997. Cert. tchr. elem. edn., K-12 art, Tenn. Tchr. 4th grade Metro-Nashville Pub. Sch., Nashville, 1969-70, tchr. art, music, 1970-71; tchr. 5th grade Harding Acad., Nashville, 1971-75, tchr. art K-8, 1977-2000, tchr. art K-5, 2000—, chmn. fine arts com. Presenter workshops Mid-So. Assn. Ind. Schs., Nashville, 1971—75; vis. com. Oak Hill Sch. So. Assn. Colls. and Schs., Nashville, 1990; vis. com. St. Bernard Acad., 1991; chair planning com. Harding Acad., Nashville, 1992—94, mem. 25th ann. com., chmn. fine arts com.; fine arts chair St.

Cecilia Acad. Parents Club, Nashville, 1991—93, mem. Parents Club; co-founder Art Tchrs. Guild, Nashville; organizer Youth Art Month Exhibit, Nashville, 1992—. V.p. in charge of art Children's Internat. Edn. Ctr., Nashville, 1985-90; mem. edn. coun. Frist Fine Arts Ctr.; mem. Cheekwood Fine Arts Ctr. and Bot. Gardens, Nashville, 1987—; prodr. parent's seminar 1st Bapt. Ch., 1986; charter mem. Frist Mus. for Visual Arts. Recipient C. of C. award for best spl. project/display for Artworks 9, 2000; Outstanding Tchr. of Humanities grantee Tenn. Humanities Couns., 1988; named Tenn. Elem. Art Tchr. of Yr., Tenn. Art Edn. Assn., 2001. Mem. Nat. Art Edn. Assn., Tenn. Art Edn. Assn., Nat. Mus. Women in the Arts (charter). Baptist. Avocations: watercolor and calligraphy, traveling, singing, piano. Home: 722 Starlit Rd Nashville TN 37205-1210 Office: 170 Windsor Dr Nashville TN 37205-3719 E-mail: chambersc@hardingacademy.org.

CHAMBERS, IMOGENE KLUTTS, school system administrator, financial consultant; b. Paden, Okla., Aug. 6, 1928; d. Odes and Lillie (Southard) Klutts; m. Richard Lee Chambers, May 27, 1949. BA, East Ctrl. State U., 1948; MS, Okla. State U., 1974, EdD, 1980. High sch. math. tchr. Marlow (Okla.) Sch. Dist., 1948-49; with Bartlesville (Okla.) Sch. Dist., 1950-94; asst. supt. bus. affairs, treas. Ind. Sch. Dist. 30, 1977-87, treas., 1985-94; fin. acctg. cons. Okla. State Dept. Edn., 1987-92; dir. Plz. Bank, Bartlesville, 1984-93. Adv. dir. Bank Okla., 1994-96. Treas. Okla. Schs. Ins. Assn., 1982—97, adminstr., 1993—97; bd. dirs. Mutual Girls Club, 1981—. Mem. Okla. Assn. Sch. Bus. Ofcls., Assn. Sch. Bus. Ofcls. Internat., Okla. Ret. Educators Assn., Washington County Ret. Educators Assn., Okla. State U. Alumni Assn., East Ctrl. U. Alumni Assn. (bd. dirs. 1994-96). Democrat. Methodist. Home: 911 SE Greystone Pl Bartlesville OK 74006-5141 E-mail: ikcgene@bartnet.net.

CHAMBERS, JERRY RAY, school system administrator; b. St. Joseph, Mo., Oct. 1, 1947; s. Ray Linden and Betty Allene (Roach) C.; m. Jacqueline Kaye Thomas, Feb. 11, 1967; children: Sandra Kaye, Jennifer Lynn. AS, Mo. Western State Coll., 1967; BA, U. Mo., Kansas City, 1969, MA in Edn. Adminstrn. and History, 1971; postgrad., U. Madras, India, 1974; PhD in Edn. Adminstrn., U. Mo., Kansas City, 1986. Tchr. Lillis High Sch., Kansas City, Mo., 1969; high sch. tchr. Sch. Dist. St. Joseph, Mo., 1969-80, dir. media svcs., 1980-90; supt. schs. Sch. Dist. Washington, Mo., 1990-2001, Wolf Br. Sch. Dist., Swansea, Ill., 2001—. Coun. pres. ITV Kansas City Pub. TV, 1981-90; assessor Mo. Prin. Assess Ctr., DESE, Jefferson City, Mo., 1987-90; bd. dirs. 353 Econ. Devel. Corp. Washington, 1991-2000, Network Ednl. Devel., St. Louis, 1993-96; exec. com. Coop. Sch. Dists. St. Louis. Author: Missouri Students Tune IN, 1987, History of Missouri Instructional Television, 1986, Beyond the Bullet Hole, 1988. Bd. dirs. Regional Bluffs Libr., St. Joseph, 1989, United Fund, Washington, 1992-95; campaign co-chmn. Earnings Tax Com., St. Joseph, 1988; chmn. edn. divsn. United Way, St. Joseph, 1986-89, bd. dirs. 1992; bd. dirs. Tri-County Fine Arts Ctr., 1992-97. Recipient Alumni Achievement award U. Mo., Kansas City, 1988, Disting. Alumni award Mo. Western State Coll., 1990, Disting. Leadership award Nat. Assn. Com. Leadership, 1988, Key to City award City of St. Joseph Mayor, 1990, Mo. Supt. of Yr. award, 1999, Pearce award 1999; Fulbright scholar, 1974. Mem. Am. Assn. Sch. Adminstrs., Ill. Assn. Sch. Adminstrs., Lions Club (Washington chpt., 1990-2003, St. Joseph Host Club pres. 1989-90, chmn., exec. com. Cooperating Sch. Dists. Greater St Louis, 1996-98, pres. CSD 1999-2000). Avocations: basketball, tennis, reading, model railroading, nostalgia, baseball. Home: 2 Winchester Ct Washington MO 63090-5314 Office: School Dist Wolf Br 410 Huntwood Rd Swansea IL 62226

CHAMBERS, JOAN LOUISE, retired librarian, retired dean; b. Denver, Mar. 22, 1937; d. Joseph Harvey and Clara Elizabeth (Carleton) Baker; m. Donald Ray Chambers, Aug. 17, 1958 BA in English Lit., U. No. Colo., Greeley, 1958; MS in L.S., U. Calif.-Berkeley, 1970; MS in Systems Mgmt., U. So. Calif., 1985; cert., Coll. for Fin. Planning, 1989. Libr. U. Nev., Reno, 1970-79; asst. univ. libr. U. Calif., San Diego, 1979-81, univ. libr. Riverside, 1981-85; dean librs., prof. Colo. State U., Ft. Collins, 1985-97, emeritus dean and prof., 1997—. Mgmt. intern Duke U. Libr., Durham, N.C., 1978-79; sr. fellow UCLA Summer, 1982; cons. tng. program Assn. of Rsch. Libraries, Washington, 1981; libr. cons. Calif. State U., Sacramento, 1982-83, U. Wyo., 1985-86, 94-95, U. Nebr., 1991-92, Calif. State U. System, 1993-94, Univ. No. Ariz., 1994-95. Contbr. articles to profl. jours., chpts. to books. Bd. dirs. Consumers Union, 1996—. U. Calif. instl. improvement grantee, 1980-81; State of Nev. grantee, 1976, ARL grantee, 1983-84. Mem.: PEO, Colo. Mountain Club, Phi Kappa Phi, Kappa Delta Phi, Phi Lambda Theta, Beta Phi Mu. Avocations: hiking, snow shoeing, skiing, cycling, tennis. Home and Office: PO Box 1477 Edwards CO 81632-1477 E-mail: chambers@vail.net.

CHAMBERS, JOHN WHITECLAY, II, history educator; b. West Chester, Pa., Aug. 6, 1936; s. John McCausland and Le-Arie P. Chambers; m. Dorothy Roman, 1958; children: John Bret, Jeffrey Mark, Michael Adam; m. Amy Russo Piro, 1982; 1 child, Tacy Elizabeth. Reporter Pasadena (Calif.) Ind. Star-News, 1958-60, San Rafael (Calif.) Ind.-Jour., 1960-61; news and documentary writer/prodr. KRON-TV, San Francisco, 1961-65; asst. prof. history Barnard Coll., Columbia U., N.Y.C., 1972-82, Rutgers U., New Brunswick, N.J., 1982-87, assoc. prof., 1987-93, prof., 1993—2002, disting. prof., 2002—, dept. chair, 1997-98. Fulbright lectr. U. Rome, spring 1982; project dir. Rutgers Ctr. Hist. Analysis, 1993-95; vis. lectr. U. Tokyo, 1997. Author: Three Generals on War, 1973, Draftees or Volunteers, 1975, The Eagle and the Dove: The Peace Movement and U.S. Foreign Policy, 1900-1922, 1976, 2d edit., 1991, The Tyranny of Change: America in the Progressive Era, 1890-1920, 1980, 3d edit., 2000; author: (with Warren Susman) American History Reading Lists, 3 vols., 1983; author: To Raise an Army: The Draft Comes to Modern America, 1987 (Best Book award Soc. Mil. History, 1988, Best Book on Mil. History, 1987); author: (with Charles C. Moskos) The New Conscientious Objection: From Sacred to Secular Resistance, 1993; author: (with David Culbert) World War II Film and History, 1996; author: (with G. Kurt Piehler) Major Problems in American Military History, 1998; editor in chief Oxford Co. to Am. Mil. History, 1999 (Disting. Ref. Book award Soc. Mil. History, 2001). NEH grantee, 1974; humanities fellow Rockefeller Found., 1981-82, vis. fellow Inst. Advanced Study, Princeton, 1995-96. Mem.: Soc. Mil. History, Orgn. Am. Historians, Am. Hist. Assn., Peace History Soc. (pres. 1975—77). Office: Rutgers U 16 Seminary Pl New Brunswick NJ 08901-1108 E-mail: chamber@rci.rutgers.edu.

CHAMBERS, JOHNNIE LOIS (TUCKER CHAMBERS), elementary school educator, rancher; b. Crocket County, Tex., Sept. 28, 1929; d. Robert Leo and Lois K. (Slaughter) Tucker; m. R. Boyd Chambers; children: Theresa A., Glyn Robert, Boyd James, John Trox. BEd, Sul Ross State U., Alpine, Tex., 1971. Tchr. 1st and 2d grades Candelaria (Tex.) Elem. Sch., 1971-73; head tchr. K-8 Ruidosa (Tex.) Elem. Sch., 1973-77, Presidio Ind. Sch. Dist. at Candelaria Elem. Sch., 1977-91, tchr. 2d and 3d grades, 1991-93, tchr. pre-kindergarten, kindergarten and 1st grade, 1993-98; acting prin. Candelaria Elem. and Jr. High, 1995-98, head tchr. pre-K to 8th grades, 1996-98, tchr. pre-K, kindergarten, 1st and 2d grades, 1996—99, ret., 1999; tchr. Redford (Tex.) Elem. Sch., 2001—, tchr. pre-K-6, 2001—01. Mem. sight-base decision making, Presidio, 1991-94; mem. Chihuahuan Desert Rsch. Inst., Alpine, 1982-94. Leader Boy Scouts Am., Ruidosa and Candelaria, 1973-91, Cub Scout leader, 1973-91; chpt. mem. Sheriffs Assn. Tex., Austin, 1980; bd. dirs. Big Bend Regional Hosp. Dist., 2001—; mem. Ctr. for Big Bend Studies. Recipient awards Boy Scouts Am., 1969, 83, winner Litter Gitter award, 1994-95. Mem. Tex. State Tchrs. Assn., Tex. Fedn. Rep. Women, The Archaeol. Conservancy, Phi Alpha Theta. Avocations: hiking, camping, anthropologic digs, cave exploring, cooking. Home: 99 Retirement Cir Marfa TX 79843 E-mail: johnnieltc@brooksdata.net.

CHAMBERS, RICHARD LEON, retired Turkish language and civilization educator; b. Brundidge, Ala., Sept. 27, 1929; s. Cody Leon and Eunice Gertrude (Logan) Chambers. BS in History, U. Ala., Tuscaloosa, 1950, MA in History, 1955; BS in Fgn. Svc., Georgetown U., 1951; MA in History and Oriental Studies, Princeton U., 1958, PhD in Near Ea. Studies, 1968. Lectr. history Am. U. in Cairo, 1958-59; asst. in instrn. Princeton (N.J.) U., 1960; instr. history St. Lawrence U., Canton, N.Y., 1960-62; instr. Turkish lang. and civilization U. Chgo., 1962-65, asst. prof., 1965-71, assoc. prof., 1971-95, dir. Ctr. for Mid. Ea. Studies, 1979-85, assoc. prof. emeritus, dir. devel. Ctr. for Mid. Ea. Studies, 1995—2000. Co-founder, dir. Am. Rsch. Inst. in Turkey-Bosphorus U. summer Turkish lang. program, Istanbul, 1982-88; pres. Am. Rsch. Inst. in Turkey, Chgo. and Phila., 1985-88. Co-editor: Beginnings of Modernization in the Middle East: The 19th Century, 1968, Contemporary Turkish Short Stories, 1977; contbr. articles to profl. jours. and Ency. Brit. Recipient edn. award Am.-Turkish Coun., Washington, 1997, Svc. award Mid. East Studies Assn., 1998; fellow German Acad. Exch. Svc., Munich, 1951-52, Ford Found., Princeton, 1955-57, rsch. fellow Am. Rsch. Inst. in Turkey, Istanbul, 1965. Mem.: Turkish Studies Assn. (sec./treas. 1997—99), Am. Assn. Tchrs. Turkic Langs., Mid. East Studies Assn. N.Am., Internat. Assn. Mid. Ea. Studies, Am. Oriental Soc., Am. Hist. Soc. Avocations: travel, reading, gardening, antiques. Home: 1243 Westmoreland Ave Montgomery AL 36106-2017 Office: U Chgo Ctr for Mid Eastern Studies 5828 S University Ave Chicago IL 60637-1515 E-mail: rlc3@mailstation.com.

CHAMBERS, ROBERT HUNTER, III, college president, American studies educator, consultant; b. Winston-Salem, N.C., Oct. 24, 1939; s. Robert Hunter and Hildred (MacDonald) C.; m. Alice Louise Grant, Aug. 18, 1962 (div. 1995); children: Lisa, Grant. AB, Duke U., 1962; B.D., Yale U., 1965; PhD, Brown U., 1969. Asst. prof., dean Davenport Coll. Yale U., New Haven, 1969-74; vis. fellow Clare Coll., Cambridge U., Eng., 1972-73; prof., dean Coll. Arts and Scis. Bucknell U., Lewisburg, Pa., 1975-84; vis. scholar Doshisha U., Kyoto, 1982; pres., prof. English Western Md. Coll., Westminster, 1984—2000; sr. cons. Marts & Lundy, Inc., Gainesville, Fla., 2001—. Founding dir. Wellway Ctrs., Inc., Ft. Worth, 1984—88, WMC Devel. Corp., 1985—88; presdl. chmn. Centennial Conf., Md. and Pa., 1986, 1998—99; mem. segmental adv. com. State Bd. Higher Edn., Annapolis, Md., 1985—88; mem. internat. adv. coun. U. Buckingham, England; mem. cmty. bd. Carroll Co. Health Svcs., Inc., 1988—2000; assoc. fellow Davenport Coll., Yale U. Author, editor: Twentieth Century Interpretations of All the King's Men, 1977. Contbr. articles to profl. jours. Bd. dirs. Ind. Coll. Fund of Md., Balt.,1984—; mem. coun. on grad. edn. Brown U., 1989; mem. City of Westminster Mayoral Task Force, 1990; co-chair spl. gifts Am. Heart Assn.; mem. task force on assessment Nat. Assn. Ind. Colls. and Univs., 1991-92, mem. commn. on state rels., 1992-95; mem. Gov.'s Edn. Policy Transition Team, 1994-95; mem. Md. Citizens for Arts; bd. dir. Coun. of Ind. Colls., 1997—. Rockefeller Brothers fellow, 1962-63; Nat. Endowment for the Humanities grantee, 1978, U.S.-Japan Friendship Commn. grantee, 1982; recipient Balt. Regional Coun. Govts. award, 1989. Mem.: NCAA (pres. coun. 1999—2000), MLA, Internat. Assn. Univ. Presidents, Coun. on Econ. Edn. in Md. (trustee 1), Am. Studies Assn., Md. Ind. Coll. and Univ. Assn. (bd. dirs. 1984—2000, exec. com. 1985—88, 1991—2000, budget com. 1985—89, 1991, chair 1994—98), Mid. States Assn. Colls. and Schs. (commr. 1985—91, exec. com. 1986—91, vice chair 1987—89, chair 1990), Higher Edn. Commn., The Japan Soc., Nat. Assn. Ind. Colls. and Univs. (policy com. 1998—2000), Center Club, Yale Club, Rotary (hon. 1990), Phi Beta Kappa Assocs., Phi Beta Kappa. Avocations: running, reading, traveling. Office: Marts & Lundy Inc 10040 SW 52d Rd Gainesville FL 32608 E-mail: robertgam@netline.com., changers@martsandlundy.com.

CHAMBERS-MANGUM, FRANSENNA ETHEL, special education educator; b. Meridian, Miss., June 27, 1957; d. Forrest S. and Betty (Wade) Chambers; 1 child, Richard Jomar Sullivan. BS, Jackson State U., 1979, MA, 1980, EdS, 1986. Cert. tchr., Miss., secondary adminstr., Miss. Chpt. tchr. Meridian Pub. Schs., 1979; tchr. spl. edn. Magee (Miss.) Pub. Sch., 1980-84; speech pathologist Heritage Sch. Learning Disability, Jackson, Miss., 1984-85, Canton (Miss.) Pub. Schs., 1985-86, spl. edn. tchr., 1986-88, pre-sch. coord., 1988-89; tchr. spl. edn. lang. delayed Jackson (Miss.) Pub. Schs., 1989-90, tchr. spl. edn., 1990—, mid. sch. reading tchr., 1993—. Miss. Writing Project cons. tchr., 1989—, Adult Edn. tchr. (ages 16-65). Writer and editor poems. Mem. Miss. Registrar Voters Com., Jackson, 1975—, Vista/Peace Corps, Jackson, 1980, NAACP, Jackson, 1982-85; bd. dirs., sec. and coord. Roshea Recovery Ctr., 1993—; tchr. Sunday sch., Jackson, 1992. Named Miss Miss. Elks, 1972-74, Miss Miss. Congeniality, Jaycees, 1972; Black Women's Assn. partial scholar, 1975. Mem. Miss. Writers of Am., Miss. Assn. Colls. and Evaluator Univs., Miss. Assn. Tchrs. (evaluator 1986—, Educator of Yr.), Learning Disabled Assn. Miss., Miss. Assn. Edn., Eastern Star, Daus. of Isis. Democrat. Avocations: writing poetry, public relations. Home: 1772 Casteel Dr Jackson MS 39204-3508

CHAMBERS-MCCARTY, LORRAINE, painter, educator; b. Detroit, Aug. 17, 1920; Student, Detroit Art Acad., 1938, Stephens Coll., 1940, Wayne State U., 1942; studied with, Glen Michaels, Emil Weddidge, Robert Wilbert, Guy Palazzola, Ray Fleming, Edgar Yaeger, Hughie Lee Smith, Bertold Schweitz, Thomas Hart Benton, Carol Wald, Adolph Dehn. Mem. faculty Flint Inst. Arts, Mich., 1970-85, Grosse Point (Mich.) War Meml., 1972-90; pvt. tchr. art Royal Oak, Mich.; mem. faculty Muskegon (Mich.) Inst. Arts, 1978-80, Flint Inst. Arts, 1978—; artist in residence Stephens Coll., Columbia, Mo., 1981; now juror, critic, lectr., tchr. pvt. profl. students. Advisor, designer Internat. Women's Air & Space Mus., Ohio, 1986-00, Okla., juror, critic in field, lectr.in field; ofcl. artist USAF, 1981-99; instr. Birmingham Bloomfield (Mich.) Art Assn., Islanders of St. Loud-Workshop Retreats in No. Mich., 1979-94, Paint Creek Ctr. for Arts, Rochester, Mich., Mt. Clemens Ctr. for Arts, Mich., Flint Inst. Arts,, Muskegon Mus. of Art, Jesse Besser Mus., Alpena, Ella Sharpe Mus., Jackson, Mich, Ctr. for Creative Studies, Detroit, Art League, Marco Island, Fla., Blue Water Art Assn., Stephens Coll., Mo., Milford Fine Arts Assn., Mich., 1990-00, Sanibel-Captiva Art Assn., Fla. others; cons. Greenfield Village Mus., 1991-00; mentor U. Mich., 1992, Cranbrook Art Acad.; trustee, designer Internat. Women's Air and Space Mus., Cleve., 1997—. Numerous one woman shows including Midland Arts Coun., 1978, Dayton Art Inst., 1978, Flint Inst. Arts, 1980, Nat. Acad. Arts and Letters, 1980, Stephens Coll., 1981; numerous group shows including Women '71, DeKalb, Ill., Butler Mus. Am. Art, Youngstown, Ohio, Detroit Inst. Arts, 1980, Ohio Arts Coun. Nat. Traveling Show, 1982; represented in permanent collections including Smithsonian Nat. Air and Space Mus., Muskegon Mus. Art, Butler Mus. Am. Art, Dow Chem. Co., Midland, Mich., No. Ill. U., DeKalb, K Mart Internat. Hdqrs., Troy, Mich., Capital City Airport, Lansing, R.L. Polk Co., Detroit, Bohn Aluminum and Brass, Southfield, Mich., Jug Pilots P047s, N.Y.C., Am. Natural Resources Hdq., Beech Aircraft, Wichita, Cessna Aircraft Corp., Dennos Mus., Federal Aviation Admintsrn., Flint Inst. Arts, Internat. Women's Air and Space Mus., Mich. Dept. Aviation, Renaissance Ctr.; commns. include murals for Gen. Dynamics Landsystems 1 Mich., Alpena Light & Power Co., art works for Lear Siegler Seating Co., Mich., 4 H Hdqrs., Washington, Trusswall Internat., Mich., R.L Polk Co., Mich., Capitol City Airport, Mich., Gerald Behaylo, Mich., Upjohn Pharm. Hdqs., Mich., Dow Chem. Co., Mich., Internat. Women's Air and Space Mus., Hi-Lex Corp., Mich. and Japan; producer TV series The Artist in You; inventor, designer Artist's Eye: Visual Aid for Artists. Mem. exec. com. Oakland County Cultural Coun. Recipient numerous awards including Purchase prize Butler Mus. Am. Art, 1969, Grand Jury award 16th Ann. Mid-Mich., Best Painting by a Woman award Detroit Inst. Arts, 1971, Disting. Alumnae award Stephens Coll., 1982, 1st place award Nat. Fedn. Local Cable Programmers, 1984; recipient grant Lester Hereward Cooke Found., 1984, Ossabaw Island Project, 1965, 67, 72; named creative artist, Mich. Coun. Arts, 1983, master to apprentice, Mich. Coun. Arts, 1983, artists consultancy, Mich. Coun. Arts, 1983. Mem. Detroit Soc. Women Painters and Sculptors, All Women Transcontinental Air Race Assn., Mich. Watercolor Soc., Artists Equity Assn., Mich. Acad. Arts Sci. Letters. Home: 1112 Pinehurst Ave Royal Oak MI 48073-3370

CHAMBLISS, CHARLOTTE MARIE, secondary education educator; b. Dallas, May 4, 1956; d. Wallace C. and Betty H. (Duncan) C. BFA cum laude, U. North Tex., 1984. Supr., dispatcher Direct Couriers Am., Dallas, 1978-85; from instr. visual arts to test devel. com. B.T. Washington High Sch., Dallas, 1989—2002; test devel. com. advanced placement studio art B.T. Washington H.S. for Performing and Visual Arts, Dallas, 2002—; visual art instr. Hillcrest H.S., Dallas, 1994-95. Grader Advanced Placement Studio Art, 2000—03, mem. test devel. com., 2002—. O'Donnell Found. grantee, 1994-2001; recipient Fulbright Meml. Fund, 2001 Avocations: camping, hiking, reading. Home: 2547 Valwood Pkwy Farmers Branch TX 75234-3413

CHAMIS, CHRISTOS CONSTANTINOS, aerospace scientist, educator; b. Sotira, Greece, May 16, 1930; arrived in U.S., 1948; s. Constantinos and Anastasia (Kyriakos) C.; m. Alice Yanosko, Aug. 20, 1966; children: Chrysanthie, Anna-Lisa, Constantinos. BS in Civil Engring., Cleve. State U., 1960; MS, Case Western Res. U., 1962, PhD, 1967. Draftsman, designer Cons. Engring., Cleve., 1955-60; rsch. asst. Case Western Res. U., Cleve., 1960-62, rsch. assoc., 1964-68; rsch. mathematician B.F. Goodrich, Brecksville, Ohio, 1962-64; aerospace engr. Glenn Rsch. Ctr. NASA, Cleve., 1968-78, sr. rsch. engr., 1978-86, sr. aerospace scientist, 1986—. Cons. Lawrence Livermore Labs., Calif., 1974-79; adj. prof. Cleve. State U., 1968—, Akron U., 1980—, Case Western Res. U., 1984—. Editor: Composites Analysis/Design, 1975, Test Methods and Design Allowables for Composites, 1979, 89; mem. editl. bd. Jour. Composites Rsch. and Tech., Reinforced Plastics and Composites, Internat. Jour. Damage Mechanics, Theoretical and Applied Fracture Mechanics; contbr. numerous articles to sci. jours.; patentee in field for Intraply Hybrid Composites and Exoskeletal Engine Concepts; rschr. in hygrothermal composite micromechanics, computational composite mechanics-computer codes, high-temperature composite structures, structural tailoring of engine structures, computational simulation of progressive fracture, engine structures computational simulations, computational simulation/tailoring of coupled multi-discipline problems, and probabilistic structural analysis. Served with USMC, 1952-53. Fellow ASME, AIAA (assoc. editor 1986-88), ASCE, ASTM, Soc. Advancement Materials and Process Engring., Soc. Automotive Engrs.; mem. Soc. Exptl. Mechanics, Am. Soc. Metals, Am. Soc. Composites, Soc. Engring. Sci., Am. Ceramic Soc., Sigma Xi, Dodoni Club, Hellenic U. Club. Home: 24534 Framingham Dr Cleveland OH 44145-4902 E-mail: christos.c.chamis@nasa.gov.

CHAMLEE, ANN COMBEST, music educator; b. Waco, Tex., Jan. 5, 1934; d. Otis Carter Ray and Hazel Meharg; children: Ann Alisabeth Chamlee, Margaret Carter Chamlee Zabcik. BM, Baylor U., 1969, MM, 1987; postgrad., Sam Houston State U., 1978-82. Exec. sec. Rocketdyne, McGregory, Tex., 1953-56; legal sec. Brown Assocs., Temple, Tex., 1977-80; fashion salesperson The Rosebud, Temple, Tex., 1980-85; choir master, organist Covenant Luth. Ch., Temple, Tex., 1984-89; piano tchr. Temple, Tex., 1964-87; music educator Temple Coll., 1988—. Artist in schs. Cultural Activities Ctr., Temple, 1980—. Author: Music Fundamentals Workbook, 1989, Two Halves Make a Whole, 1985. Performer with Linda Kowalski Cmty. Concert Tour, Ind., 1978; music dir. Gatesville/Milam County Tex.; bd. dirs. City Fedn. Womens Club, Temple, Temple Civic Theatre, 1998—. Recipient Outstanding Cmty. Vol. award City Fedn. of Womens Club, 1991, U2 award Child Help, Inc., 1991, Musician of Yr. award Wildflower Guild, 1994. Mem. Nat. Music Tchrs. Assn., Tex. Coalition for Quality in Arts Edn. (bd. dirs. 1995—), Music Club of Temple (past pres. 1968-89), Ctrl. Tex. Music Tchrs. Assn. (past pres. 1970-72, 94-96), Tex. Music Tchrs. Assn. (conv. presenter 1993, 97), Nat. Piano Guild (judge 1980-97), Lions (bd. dirs. 1993-95, Hon. Lion or Yr. 1970, Lion of Yr. 1993). Office: Temple Coll 2600 S 1st St Temple TX 76504-7435

CHAMORRO MELÉNDEZ, DIGNA, education educator; b. Ponce, P.R., Mar. 8, 1954; d. Victor J. Chamorro and Digna Meléndez. BA in Edn., U. Interamericana P.R., Ponce, 1977. Special education specialist P.R. Dept. Edn., Ponce, 1977—; instr. spl. edn. U. Interamericana de P.R., San Germán, 1990—. Diocese v.p. Juventud Acción Catolica, Ponce, 1976. Mem. Coun. Exceptional Children, Teaching Exceptional Children, Educadores Puertorriqueños en Accion. Roman Catholic. Home: Glenview Gardens W26 D1 Ponce PR 00731

CHAMPAGNE, DUANE WILLARD, sociology educator; b. Belcourt, N.D., May 18, 1951; m. Carole Goldberg; children: Talya, Gabe, Demelza. BA in Math., N.D. State U., 1973, MA in Sociology, 1975; PhD in Sociology, Harvard U., 1982. Teaching fellow Harvard U., Cambridge, Mass., 1981-82, rsch. fellow, 1982-83; asst. prof. U. Wis., Milw., 1983-84, UCLA, 1984-91, assoc. prof., 1991-97, prof., 1997—. Publs. dir. Am. Indian Studies Ctr., UCLA, 1986-87, assoc. dir., 1990, acting dir., 1991, dir., 1991-02, affiliate faculty UCLA Native Nations Law and Policy Ctr., 2003—; adminstrv. co-head interdepartmental program for Am. Indian studies UCLA, 1992-93; mem. grad. rsch. fellowship panel NSF, 1990-92, minority fellowship com. ASA; cons. Energy Resources Co., 1982, No. Cheyenne Tribe, 1983, Realis Pictures, Inc., 1989-90, Sta. KCET-TV, L.A., 1990, 92, Salem Press, 1992, Book Prodns. Systems, 1993, Readers Digest, 1993, Rattlesnake Prodns., 1993. Author: American Indian Societies, 1989, Social Order and Political Change, 1992, The ACCIP Community Service Report: A Second Century of Dishonor-Federal Inequities and California Indians, 2002; editor: Native American Studies in Higher Education: Models for Collaboration Between Indigenous Nations, 2002, Special Issues on Indigenous Issues: Hagar, International Social Science Review, 2001, Native North American Almanac, 1994, Native North American Almanac, 2d edit., 2001, Chronology of Native North American, 1994; co-author: Native America: Portrait of the Peoples, 1994, A Second Century of Dishonor: Federal Inequities and California Tribes, 1996, Service Delivery for Native American Children in Los Angeles County, 1996; editor: Native Am. Studies Assn. Newsletter, 1991—92; co-editor: Native American Activism: Alcatraz to the Longest Walk, 1997, Contemporary Native American Cultural Issues, 1999; book rev. editor: Am. Indian Culture and Rsch. Jour., 1984—86; editor, 1986—2002; series editor: Contemporary American Indian Issues, 1998—; editor: The Native North American Almanac, 2d edit., 2001, Native American Studies in Higher Education, 2002; contbr. numerous articles to profl. jours. Mem. city of L.A. Cmty. Action Bd., 1993, L.A. County/City Am. Indian Commn., 1992-2000, chair, 1993, 95-97, 2000-02, sec., 2002, vice chair, 1997-2000; mem. subcom. for cultural and econ. devel. L.A. City/County Native Am. Commn., 1992-93; bd. dirs. Ctr. for Improvement of Child Caring, 1993—; bd. dirs., Greater L.A. Am. Indian Culture Ctr., Inc., 1993, incorporator, 1993; trustee Southwest Mus., 1994-97, Nat. Mus. Am. Indian, 1998—; master Coll. Humanities and Social Sci., N.D. State U., 1996. Recipient L.A. Sr. Health Peer Counseling Cmty. Vol. Cert. of Recognition, 1996; Writer of Yr. award Cir. Native Writers and Storytellers, 1999; honoree Nat. Ctr. Am. Indian Enterprise, 1999; grantee Rockefeller Found., 1982-83, U. Wis. Grad Sch. Rsch. Com., 1984-85, Wis. Dept. Edn., 1984-85, 87-88, 88-89, NSF, 1985-88, 88-89, Nat. Endowment for Arts, 1987-88, 91-92, NRC, 1988-89, Nat. Sci. Coun., 1989-90, John D. and Catherine T. MacArthur Found., 1990-91, Hayes Found., 1990-91, 92-93, Calif. Coun. for Humanities, 1991-92, Ford Found., 1990-92, Gale Rsch. Inc., 1991-93, 93-95, Rockwell Corp., 1991-93, GTE, 1992-93, Kellog Found., 1997-2000, Pequot Mus. and Rsch. Ctr., 1997-2002, So. Calif. Indian Ctr., 1998; Fund for the Improvement of Post Secondary Edn., 1998-2003, Nat.

Endowment for Humanities, 2002—, Dept. Justice, 2001—; Am. Indian scholar, 1973-75, 80-82, Minority fellow Am. Sociol. Assn., 1975-78, RIAS Seminar fellow, 1976-77; Rockefeller Postdoctoral fellow, 1982-83, NSF fellow, 1985-88, Postdoctoral fellow Ford Found., 1988-89. Avocations: chess, jogging. Home: 2152 Balsam Ave Los Angeles CA 90025 Office: UCLA Native Nations Law and Policy Ctr Dept Sociology 264 Haines Hall Los Angeles CA 90095-1551 E-mail: champagn@ucla.edu.

CHAMPAGNE, RONALD OSCAR, academic administrator, mathematics educator; b. Woonsocket, R.I., Jan. 2, 1942; s. George Albert and Simone (Brodeur) C.; m. Ruth Inez DesRuisseux, Nov. 25, 1970 BA, Duquesne U., 1964; MA, Cath. U. Am., 1966, Fordham U., 1970, PhD, 1973. Instr. math. Sacred Heart U., Bridgeport, Conn., 1966-69; asst. prof. math. Manhattanville Coll., Purchase, N.Y., 1969-75, dir. advanced studies program, 1973-75; prof. math., v.p., dean of faculty Salem Coll., W.Va., 1975-82; prof. math., pres., trustee St. Xavier U., Chgo., 1982-94, pres. emeritus, 1994—; prof. philosophy, v.p. for devel. Roosevelt U., Chgo., 1996—. Bd. dirs. Chgo., Tchrs. Acad. for Math. and Sci. Author: LP Spaces of Complex Valued Functions, 1966; A Formalization of the Dialectical Development of Intelligence, 1974 Mem. Mat. Assn. Am., Philosophy of Sci. Assn., Carlton Club, Econs. Club Chgo., Exec. Club Chgo. Roman Catholic. Office: Roosevelt Univ 430 S Michigan Ave Chicago IL 60605-1394

CHAMPION, ANN LOUVERTA, secondary school educator; b. Experiment, Ga., Dec. 12, 1939; d. Hubert Sr. and Arwillow (Crafter) C. BS, Morris Brown Coll., 1964; MEd, Ga. Coll., 1977. Cert. tchr., tchr. support specialist, Ga. Home econs. tchr. Henderson High Sch., Jackson, Ga., 1964-69, Henderson Jr. High Sch., Jackson, 1969-71, Jackson High Sch., 1971-83, Griffin (Ga.) High Sch., 1983-96, ret., 1996. Nutritionist Westbury Convalescent Home, Jackson, 1966-67; mem. nutrition Am. Cancer Soc., Griffin, 1992—. Vol. Griffin Spalding Regional Hosp., 1985—; mem. Com. Family 2000, Griffin, 1989; treas. Artistic Focus, Griffin, 1983. Mem. Alpha Kappa Alpha (v.p. 1986-88, Hodegos 1989-91), Phi Delta Kappa (scholar). Democrat. African Methodist. Avocations: working with senior citizens and youth groups, shopping, travel, interior design. Home: 448 Brook Ln Griffin GA 30224-4451 Office: Griffin High Sch 1617 W Poplar St Griffin GA 30224-2093

CHAMPION, NORMA JEAN, communications educator, state legislator; b. Oklahoma City, Jan. 21, 1933; d. Aubra Bell (dec.) and Beuleah Beatrice (Flanagan) Black; m. Richard Gordon Champion, Oct. 3, 1953 (dec.); children: Jeffrey Bruce, Ashley Brooke. BA in Religious Edn., Cen. Bible Coll., Springfield, Mo., 1971; MA in Comm., S.W. Mo. State U., 1978; PhD in Tech., U. Okla., 1986. Producer, hostess The Children's Hour, Sta. KYTV-TV, NBC, Springfield, 1957-86; asst. prof. Cen. Bible Coll., 1968-84; prof. broadcasting Evangel U., Springfield, 1978—; mem. Springfield City Coun., 1987-92, Mo. Ho. of Reps., Jefferson City, 1993—2002, Mo. Senate, 2003—. Adj. faculty Assemblies of God Theol. Sem., Springfield, 1987—, pres. coun.; bd. dirs. Global U.; mem. Commn. on Higher Edn., Assemblies of God, 1998—; frequent lectr. to svc. clubs, ednl. seminars; seminar spkr. Internat. Pentecostal Press Assn. World Conf., Singapore, 1989; announcer various TV commls. Contbr. numerous articles to religious publs. Mem. bd Mo. Access to Higher Edn. Trust, 1990—, Boys & Girls Town of Mo.; regional rep. Muscular Dystrophy Assn.; mem. adv. bd. Chameleon Puppet Theater, 1987; mem. exec. bd. Univ. Child Care Ctr., 1987; hon. chmn. fund raising Salvation Army, 1986; also numerous other bds., hon. chairmanships.; judge Springfield City Schs. Recipient commendation resolution Mo. Ho. of Reps., 1988; numerous awards for The Children's Hour; Aunt Norma Day named in her honor City of Springfield, 1976. Mem. Nat. Broadcast Edn. Assn., Mo. Broadcast Edn. Assn., Nat. League Cities, Mo. Mcpl. League (human resource com. 1989, intergovtl. rels. com. 1990), Nat. Assn. Telecom. Officers and Advisors, PTA (life). Republican. Mem. Assemblies of God Ch. Avocations: gardening, reading, interior decoration. Home: 3609 S Broadway Ave Springfield MO 65807-4505 Office: Evangel Univ 1111 N Glenstone Ave Springfield MO 65802-2125 E-mail: mchampio@servics.state.mo.us.

CHAMPNEY, LINDA LUCAS, reading educator; b. El Paso, Tex., Dec. 18, 1946; d. William Franklin and Caroline (Clements) Lucas; m. Rod Wayne Champney, Aug. 4, 1967; children: Kimberley Anne, Krisa Marie, Kari Lyn. BA, U. Tex., 1968; MEd, U. Colo., 1989. Cert. lang. arts and elem. edn. educator; nat. bd. cert. tchr. early adolescent lang. Tchr. MacArthur Jr. H.S., El Paso, 1968-69, 78-79; dir., tchr. St. Paul's United Meth. Ch., El Paso, 1976-78; subs. tchr. Irvine (Calif.) Unified Sch. Dist., 1981; reading tutor Mark Twain Elem. Sch., Littleton, Colo., 1982-83; lang. arts, reading tchr. Powell Mid. Sch., Littleton, 1983-93; mid. sch. reading specialist Littleton Pub. Schs., 1996-97. Instr. C.C. Aurora, Colo., 1990-91, C.C. Denver, Colo., 1995—. Mem. ASCD, Internat. Reading Assn. (chairperson secondary rog. com.), Littleton Edn. Assn. (faculty rep.). Avocations: reading, traveling, movies, family. Home and Office: 1657 W Canal Ct Littleton CO 80120-4515

CHAMPY, WILLIAM, JR., mathematician, educator, researcher, scientist, writer, biologist, chemist, inventor, physicist; b. Orangeburg, S.C., July 23, 1949; s. Buster and Mamie (Brown) Champy. BS in Profl. Chemistry, S.C. State Coll., 1977, MEd, 1985, postgrad.; cert. prodn. operator, Orangeburg-Calhoun Tech. Coll., Orangeburg, S.C., 1990; cert. computer operator, Orangeburg-Calhoun Tech. Coll., 1997. Cert. critical needs tchr. in sci. and math.; lic. bus driver, S.C., armed security guard, small bus. owner, operator. Mgr., owner Champy's Night Club, Orangeburg, S.C., 1968-84; tchr. chemistry, physics, sci. Quinas H.S., Augusta, Ga., 1980; instr. math. Orangeburg-Calhoun Tech. Coll., Orangeburg, S.C., 1985-87; tchr. math Branchville (S.C.) H.S., 1987; coord. devel. lab., math instr. Denmark (S.C.) Tech. Coll., 1989-90; lab. mgr., adminstr., instr. biology/chemistry and physics lab. Voorhees Coll., Denmark, SC, 1991-92; math instr. Midlands Tech. Coll., Columbia, S.C., 1994; security officer Security Force, Inc., 1992-94, Spartan Security, 1995-96, Pinkerton, Inc., 1988—, Sizemore Security, Columbia, 1996—; rsch. asst. dept. energy, divsn. ecology S.C. State U., Orangeburg, unit mgr. dormatory, student svc. program coord. I, 1999—; with U.S. Census, 2000. Truck driver, laborer City of Columbia, 1980; edgefiler, tool sharpener Utica Tool Co., Inc., Orangeburg, 1982; security officer Wells Fargo, Orangeburg, 1990-92, Security Force, Inc., 1992-94, others; substitute tchr., bus driver Orangeburg Sch. Dist. # 5, 1988—; freelance personal income tax preparer, 1998—; coord. Swapop Tutoring Program S.C. State U./NASA, Orangeburg, 1998—; press operator, blademaker Frigidaire Corp., Orangeburg, 1998—; saw operator, laborer, inspector N.Am. Container, Orangeburg, 1996. Holder 20 copyrights, 2 patents in field. Census enumerator, summer 1990; custodian, maint., set-up helper Episcopal Ch. of the Redeemer, 1997; field rep. U.S. Census Bur., 1997; security officer Am. Security, Inc. Mem. AAAS, ACS, NAACP, Nat. Assn. Physics Students, Nat. Inst. Sci., Am. Mgmt. Assn., S.C. State U. Nat. Alumni Assn., S.C. Tech. Edn. Assn., Nat. Inst. Sci., Nat. Soc. Black Engrs., Nat. Assn. Black Engrs., Ernest E. Just Sci. Club, Chem Phi Chem Chemistry Club, Masons (sec.), Phi Delta Kappa, Omega Psi Phi. Avocations: pocket billiards, reading, fishing, hunting, checkers. Home and Office: PO Box 2669 Orangeburg SC 29116 E-mail: wchampy@scsu.edu.

CHAN, LAWRENCE SIU-YUNG, dermatologist, educator; b. Hong Kong, Dec. 10, 1949; came to U.S., 1975; s. Cheong-Yin Chan and Chun-Fun Wu. AA, Montgomery Coll., Takoma Park, Md., 1978; student, Messiah Coll., Grantham, Pa., 1978-79; BS, BS, MIT, 1981; MD, U. Pa., 1985. Diplomate Am. Bd. Dermatology, Nat. Bd. Med. Examiners. Intern Rutgers Med. Sch., Camden, N.J., 1986-87; resident U. Mich., Ann Arbor, 1987-91; asst. prof. Wayne State U., Detroit, 1991-93, Northwestern U., Chgo., 1993—2002, dir. immunodermatology divsn., 1993—2002; assoc. prof. U. Ill., 2002—, dir. immunology rsch., 2002—. Adj. lectr. U. Mich., 1991-93. Editor: (sci. textbook) Animal Models of Human Inflammatory Skin Disease, 2003. Recipient Clin. Investigator award, NIH, Bethesda, 1996; grantee Merit Rev., VA Rsch. Com., 1996; Small Project, High-risk Project and Rsch. Project grantee, NIH, 2001. Fellow Am. Acad. Dermatology; mem. Soc. Investigative Dermatology, Ctrl. Soc. Investigative Dermatology (chmn. 1995), Dermatology Found. (Career Devel. award 1993), Am. Assn. Immunologists, Am. Soc. Investigative Pathology, Alpha Omega Alpha. Achievements include identification of a novel skin basement membrane component, generation of an animal model of atopic dermatitis, generation of an animal model of an autoimmune hairloss disorder alopecia areata. Office: U Ill Dept Dermatology 808 S Wood Chicago IL 60612-3010 E-mail: larrycha@uic.edu.

CHAN, SIU-WAI, materials science educator; b. Hong Kong, Feb. 27, 1958; m. Kung Yip Cheung, July 6, 1984; children: L.Y., K.Y. BS, Columbia U., 1980; ScD, MIT, 1985. Summer instr. IBM, Fishkill, N.Y., 1979, 80; rsch. assoc. MIT, Cambridge, 1980-85, tchg. asst., 1981; mem. tech. staff Bellcore, Murray Hill, N.J., 1985-86, Red Bank, N.J., 1986-90; assoc. prof. materials sci. Columbia U., N.Y., 1990—. Edn. coord. Chinese Sch. of CCC N.J., 1991-93. Presdl. Faculty fellow Nat. Sci. Found., 1993. Office: Columbia U Sch Engring & Applied Sci 510 Mudd Bldg, MC 4714 500 W 120th St New York NY 10027-8031

CHAN, TAK HANG, chemist, educator; b. Hong Kong, June 28, 1941; s. Ka King and Ling Yee (Yick) C.; m. Christina W.Y. Hui, Sept. 6, 1969; children: Juanita Y., Cynthia S. BA, U. Toronto, 1962; MA, Princeton U., 1963, PhD, 1965. Rsch. assoc. Harvard U., 1965-66; asst. prof. McGill U., Montreal, Que., Can., 1966-71, assoc. prof., 1971-77, prof. chemistry, 1977—, chmn. dept., 1985-91, dean sci., 1991-94; v.p., 1994-99; Tomlinson chair prof., 2000—; chair prof. Hong Kong Poly. U., 2001—. Vis. chair prof. Hong Kong Poly. U., 2001. Contbr. articles to profl. jours. Killam fellow, 1983-85; recipient R.U. Lemieux award Can. Soc. Chem., 1993, Merck, Sharp and Dohme award, 1982. Fellow Royal Soc. Can., Third World Acad. (assoc.); mem. Chem. Inst. Can., Am. Chem. Soc., Royal Soc. Chemistry. Office: 801 Sherbrooke St Montreal West Montreal QC Canada H3A 2K6 E-mail: tak-hang.chan@mcgill.ca.

CHAN, WAI-YEE, geneticist, educator; b. Canton, China, Apr. 28, 1950; arrived in U.S., 1974; s. Kui and Fung-Hing (Wong) Chan; m. May-Fong Sheung, Sept. 3, 1976; children: Connie Hai-Yee, Joanne Hai-Wei, Victor Hai-Yue, Amanda Hai-Pui, Bessie Hai-Lui. BSc with first class honors, Chinese U. of Hong Kong, 1974; PhD, U. Fla., 1977. Tchg. asst. dept. biochemistry and molecular biology U. Fla., Gainesville, 1974-77; rsch. assoc. U. Okla., Oklahoma City, 1978-79, asst. prof. dept. pediats., 1979-82, assoc. prof., 1982-89, asst. prof. dept. biochemistry and molecular biology, 1979-82, assoc. prof., 1982-89; prof. dept. pediats., biochemistry, molecular biology and cell biology Georgetown U., Washington, 1989—. Staff affiliate pediat. endocrine metabolism and genetic svc. Okla. Children's Meml. Hosp., Oklahoma City, 1979—89, dir. Clin. Trace Metal Diagnostic Lab., 1979—85, asst. sci. dir. Biochem. Genetics and Metabolic Screening Lab., 1980—87; co-dir. State of Okla. Tchg. Hosp., 1982—87. Editor: 2 books and monograph, Jour. Endocrine Genetics, Jour. Am. Coll. Nutrition, Jour. Current Molecular Medicine; contbr. articles to profl. jours. Assoc. mem. Okla. Med. Rsch. Found., Oklahoma City, 1987—89. Recipient Okla. Med. Rsch. Found. Merrick award, 1988; fellow NATO, 1979; scholar, Chinese U. Hong Kong, 1972—74, 1973—74. Mem.: Am. Coll. Nutrition, Endocrine Soc., Am. Assn. Immunology, Soc. Pediat. Rsch., Am. Soc. Cell Biology, Am. Soc. Human Genetics, Am. Soc. Biochem. Molecular Biology, Am. Inst. Nutrition. Achievements include patents for for application of pregnancy-specific glycoproteins; development of of in-vitro diagnostic method for Wilson's Disease. Home: 10708 Butterfly Ct North Potomac MD 20878-4209 Office: LCG NICHD NIH Bldg 49 Rm 2A08 49 Convent Dr MSC 4429 Bethesda MD 20892-4429 E-mail: chanwy@mail.nih.gov.

CHANCE, JANE, English literature educator; b. Neosho, Mo., Oct. 26, 1945; d. Donald William and Julia (Mile) C.; m. Dennis Carl Nitzsche, June, 1966 (div. Mar. 1969); 1 child, Therese; m. Paolo Passaro, Apr. 30, 1981,(div. May 2002); children: Antony Damian, Joseph Sebastian. BA in English with honors and highest distinction, Purdue U., 1967; AM in English, U. Ill., 1968, PhD in English, 1971. Lectr. U. Saskatchewan, Can., 1971-72, asst. prof., 1972-73; asst. prof. English, Rice U., Houston, 1973-77, assoc. prof., 1977-80, prof., 1980—; hon. rsch. fellow U. Coll. U. London, 1977-78. Sec., Scientia, 1982-83, acting dir., 1983-84; dir. NEH Summer Seminar for Coll. Tchrs. on Chaucer and Mythography, 1985, NEH Inst. for Coll. Tchrs. on Medieval Women, 1997; pres., founder TEAMS, 1986-89; founder, dir. med. studies program Rice U., 1986-92; founding mem. Rice U. Commn. on Women, 1986-88; resident Rockefeller Found., Bellagio, Italy, 1988; mem. Sch. Hist. Studies Inst. for Advanced Study, Princeton U., 1988-89; vis. rsch. fellow Inst. for Advanced Studies in Humanities, U. Edinburgh, summer, 1994; Eccles fellow Humanities Ctr., U. Utah, 1994-95; plenary spkr. Rocky Mountain Med. and Renaissance Assn., 1995; 2d annual lectr. on Italian archaeology Friends of Archaeology U. St. Thomas/Fedn. Italian Assns., Houston, 1997; semi-plenary spkr. 4th annual meeting Internat. Soc. for the Classical Tradition, 1998; plenary spkr. Medieval Studies Forum, Fu Jen Cath. U., Taipei, Taiwan, 2000, Tex. Medieval Assn., Baylor U., Waco, 2000. Author: The Genius Figure in Antinquity and the Mid. Ages, 1975, Tokien's Art: A Mythology for Eng., 1979, Woman as Hero in Old English Lit., 1986, The Lord of the Rings: The Mythology of Power, 1992; : rev. edit., 2001, Medieval Mythography: From Roman North Africa to the Sch. of Chártres, AD 433-1177 (South Ctrl. MLA book prize, 1994), The Mythographic Chaucer: The Fabulation of Sexual Politics, 1995, Medieval Mythography, vol. 2: From the Sch. of Chártres to the Ct. at Avignon, 1177-1350, 2000; translator: Christine de Pizan's Letter of Othea to Hector, 1990; editor: The Mythographic Art: Classical Fable and the Rise of the Vernacular in Early France and Eng., 1990, Medievalism in the Twentieth Century, Studies in Medievalism, vol. 2:2, 1983, The Inklings and Others, vol. 3:3, 1990, Gender and Text in the Later Mid. Ages, 1986, pt. pb., 2003, The Assembly of Gods, 1999, Tolkien the Medievalist, 2002, Tolkien and the Invention of Myth: A Reader, 2004; co-editor: Mapping the Cosmos, 1985, Approaches to Tchg. Sir Gawain, 1986; gen. editor: Focus Libr. of Medieval Women, 1988—, Boydell & Brewer Libr. of Medieval Women, 1997—, series editor: Greenwood Guides to Hist. Events in the Medieval World, 2001—, Praeger Series on the Mid. Ages, 2003—, mem. editl. bd.: Coll. Lit., 2002—. Bd. dirs. Rice U. Press, 1981-88. NEH fellow, 1977-78, Guggenheim fellow, 1980-81, ACLS Travel grantee, 1982, Mellon leave Rice U., 1988, Disting. Faculty Tchg. fellow, 1995, Ctr. for Study Cultures fellow, 1998, NEH Fellow, St. Louis Univ. Ctr. for Med. Studies, 2003, Mellon Fellow, Pope Pius Vatican Film Libr., 2003; recipient Women's Ctr. IMPACT award Rice U., 1998. Mem. AAUP (Rice U. chpt. sec., treas. 1975-76), MLA, Scientia (acting dir. 1983-84, sec. 1982-83), Internat. Soc. Classical Tradition, Internat. Neo-Latin Soc. Avocations: book collecting, photography, travel. Office: Rice U Dept English MS 30 PO Box 1892 Houston TX 77251-1892 E-mail: jchance@rice.edu.

CHANCE, PATTI LYNN, school leadership educator; b. Oklahoma City, July 13, 1955; d. Claude R. and Margaret M. (Altman) Bruza; m. Edward W. Chance, Mar. 20, 1976. BA with highest honors, U. Okla., 1977; MEd, S.D. State U., 1987; PhD, Univ. Okla., 1992. Cert. elem. tchr., adminstr., secondary social studies tchr. Counselor Youth Svcs., Chickasha, Okla., 1977-80; elem. tchr. Lindsay (Okla.) Pub. Schs., 1980-81; jr. high tchr. Bethel (Okla.) Pub. Schs., 1981-84; coord. gifted and talented program Henryetta (Okla.) Pub. Schs., 1984-85, Grove Sch., Shawnee, Okla., 1985-86; instr. S.D. State U., Brookings, 1987-88; acad. counselor U. Okla., Norman, 1988-89; middle sch. tchr. Norman (Okla). Pub. Schs., 1989-90; elem. asst. prin. Deer Creek Pub. Schs., Edmond, Okla., 1990-92, elem. prin., 1992-95; gifted edn. program specialist Clark County Sch. Dist., Las Vegas, 1995-98; asst. prof. Dept. Ednl. Leadership U. Nev., Las Vegas, 1998—. Presenter, cons. in field. Contbr. articles to profl. publs. Mem. Coun. of Profs. of Instrl. Supervision, Nat. Assn. for Gifted Children, Nat. Assn. Elem. Sch. Prins., Nat. Middle Sch. Assn., Phi Beta Kappa. Office: U Nev Dept Ednl Leadership Rm 453002 4505 S Maryland Pky Las Vegas NV 89154-9900

CHANDLER, ALICE, higher education consultant, university president; b. Bklyn., May 29, 1931; d. Samuel and Jenny (Meller) Kogan; m. Horace Chandler, June 10, 1954; children: Seth, Donald, Barnard C. AB, Columbia U., 1951, MA, 1953, PhD, 1960; LHD, Kean U., 1997, Ramapo Coll., 2001. Instr. Skidmore Coll., 1953-54; lectr. Columbia U. Barnard Coll., 1954-55, Hunter Coll., CUNY, 1956-57; from instr. to prof. CCNY, 1961-76, v.p. instl. advancement, 1974-76, v.p. acad. affairs, 1974-76, provost, 1976-79, acting pres., 1979-80; pres. SUNY Coll., New Paltz, 1980-96; interim pres. Ramapo Coll., 2000-2001. Cons. in higher edn., 1996—; bd. dirs. Mohonk Mountain House, N.J. Coun. Humanities. Author: The Prose Spectrum: A Rhetoric and Reader, 1968, The Theme of War, 1969, A Dream of Order, 1970, The Rationale of Rhetoric, 1970, The Rationale of the Essay, 1971, From Smollett to James, 1980, Foreign Student Policy: England, France, and West Germany, 1985, Obligation or Opportunity: Foreign Student Policy in Six Major Receiving Countries, 1989, Access, Inclusion and Equity: Imperatives for America's Campuses, 1997, Public Higher Education and the Public Good: Public Policy at the Crossroads, 1998, Paying the Bill for International Education: Programs, Purposes, and Possibilities at the Millenium, 1999. Lizette Fisher fellow. Mem. Lotos, Phi Beta Kappa.

CHANDLER, ARTHUR BLEAKLEY, pathologist, educator; b. Augusta, Ga., Sept. 11, 1926; s. Clemmons Quillian and Mary Isabella (Bleakley) Chandler; m. Jane Stoughton Downing, Sept. 2, 1953; children: Arthur Bleakley, John Downing. Student, U. Ga., 1943-44; MD, Med. Coll. Ga., 1948. Diplomate Am. Bd. Pathology. Intern Baylor U. Hosp., Dallas, 1948-49; resident in pathology, NIH trainee in cancer dept. pathology Med. Coll. Ga., 1950-51, asst. in pathology, 1949-50, mem. faculty, 1949—, prof. pathology, 1962-2000, chmn. dept., 1975-2000, emeritus prof., emeritus chmn., 2001—. Com. mem. Nat. Heart, Lung and Blood Inst., 1969—93. Mem. editl. bd. Haemostatis, 1975—83, Pathology Rsch. and Practice, 1987—2001;, author papers in field; contbr. chapters to books. Trustee Young Mens Libr. Assn. Fund, 1962—72, Historic Augusta, Inc., 1966—69, Augusta-Richmond County Mus., 1965—87, Dan Printup Meml. Trust, 1985—2000, Acad. Richmond County, 1984—. Officer AUS Med. Corps, 1951—53. Fellow Commonwealth Fund, Norway, 1963—64. Mem.: AMA, Sch. Medicine Alumni Assn. Med. Coll. Ga. (pres. 1996—97), Richmond County Med. Soc. (trustee 1984—2002, sec. 1987, v.p. 1988), Med. Assn. Ga., Ga. Heart Assn., Ga. Assn. Pathologists (pres. 1984—85), Am. Heart Assn. (chmn. coun. on thrombosis 1978—80, chmn. com. on coronary lesions and myocardial infarctions 1980—82, fellow coun. arteriosclerosis), Am. Soc. Hematology, Am. Assn. Pathologists, Coll. Am. Pathologists, Am. Assn. History Medicine, Internat. Soc. for History of Medicine, Internat. Soc. Thrombosis and Haemostasis, Internat. Acad. Pathology, Alpha Omega Alpha. Episcopalian. Home: 803 Milledge Rd Augusta GA 30904-4351 Office: Med Coll Ga Dept Pathology Augusta GA 30912

CHANDLER, CHARLES LEE, JR., school system administrator; b. Roanoke, Va., Dec. 18, 1950; s. Charles L. Sr. and Sadie E. (Simpson) C.; m. Judy K. Bailey, May 14, 1974; children: Lee, Jonathan. BSEd, Concord Coll., Athens, W.Va., 1973; MA, W.Va. Grad. Coll., Institute, 1986; EdD, Nova Southeastern U., Ft. Lauderdale, Fla., 1995. Lic. tchr., adminstr. Tchr. Rockbridge County Schs., Lexington, Va., 1973-75; adminstr. Mercer County Schs., Princeton, W.Va., 1975-95; supt. Hancock County Schs., New Cumberland, W.Va., 1995—. Grantee Nat. and Community Svc. Act, Wade Elem., 1992. Mem. Masons, Eastern Star (grand organist W.Va. 1991-92). Presbyterian. Office: Hancock County Schs PO Box 1300 New Cumberland WV 26047-1300 Address: 333 Forest Dr Belle Vernon PA 15012-9675

CHANDLER, DAVID, scientist, educator; b. Bklyn., Oct. 15, 1944; SB, MIT, 1966; PhD, Harvard U., 1969. Research assoc. U. Calif., San Diego, 1969-70; from asst. prof. to prof. U. Ill., Urbana, 1970-83; prof. U.Pa., Phila., 1983-85, U. Calif., Berkeley, 1986—. Vis. prof. Columbia U., N.Y.C., 1977-78; vis. scientist IBM Corp., Yorktown Heights, N.Y., 1978, Oak Ridge Nat. Lab., 1979; cons. Los Alamos Nat. Labs., 1987-90; Miller rsch. prof., 1991; dir. de recherche Ecole Normale Superieure de Lyon, France, fall 1992; Christensen vis. fellow Oxford U., winter 1993, Hinshelwood lectr., 1993; Kolthoff lectr. U. Minn, 1994; faculty chemist Lawrence Berkeley Nat. Lab., 1996—, Miller rsch. prof., 1999-2000; Mulliken lectr. U. Chgo.; Lennard-Jones lectr. Royal Chem. Soc., Eng., 2001. Editor Chem. Physics, 1985—; mem. editl. bd. Jour. Statis. Physics, 1976-78, 94-96, Jour. Chem. Physics, 1978-80, Chem. Physics Letters, 1980-82, 91-2001, Molecular Physics, 1980-87, Theoretica Chimica Acta, 1988-89, Jour. Phys. Chemistry, 1987-92, Procs. NAS, 2001-02, Phys. Rev. E, 1995-2001, Adv. Chem. Phys., 1995—; mem. editl. adv. bd. PhysChemComm, 1999—, Proceedings Nat. Acad. Sci., 2000-01; author books in field; contbr. articles to profl. jours. Recipient Bourke medal, Faraday divsn. Royal Chem. Soc., Eng., 1985, Hirschfelder Theoretical Chemistry prize, U. Wis., 1998, Humboldt Rsch. award, 1999; fellow, Alfred P. Sloane Found., 1972—74, vis. fellow, Merton Coll., Oxford, 2001. Fellow AAAS, Am. Phys. Soc.; mem. NAS, Am. Acad. Arts and Scis., Am. Chem. Soc. (chmn. divsn. theoretical chemistry 1984, chmn. divsn. phys. chemistry 1990, Joel Henry Hildebrand award 1989, Theoretical Chemistry award 1996). Avocations: tennis, piano. Office: Dept Chem 1460 U Calif Berkeley Berkeley CA 94720-1460 E-mail: chandler@cchem.berkeley.edu.

CHANDLER, JAMES BARTON, international education consultant; b. Conway Springs, Kans., May 27, 1922; s. James Perry and Bessie May (Stone) C.; m. Madeleine Racoux, July 27, 1946; children: Paul A., Peter R., Michele A. Chandler Dore. AB, U. Kans., 1947, MA, 1949; postgrad., U. Mich., 1950—54. Asst. prof., fgn. student advisor Ea. Mich. U., 1953-55, 57-58; lang. edn. advisor Okla. A&M/Ethiopia, 1955-57, U. Mich./Laos, 1958-60; tchr. edn., advisor U.S. AID-Laos, Vientiane, Laos, 1960-61, edn. div. chief, 1961-63, asst. dir. manpower, industry, pub. administrn., 1965-69, deputy mission dir., 1969-73; higher edn. advisor U.S. AID-Tunisia, Tunis, Tunisia, 1963-65; dir. Office of Edn. AID, Washington, 1973-76, assoc. asst. adminstr., 1976-77; dir. Internat. Bur. Edn. UNESCO, Geneva, 1977-83; cons. Ann Arbor, 1983-88; St. Louis, 1989—. With Rotary, Vientiane, Laos, 1966-73, sec. 1968-69. Capt. U.S. Army, 1943-47, ETO. Decorated Bronze Star, 1945; recipient Meritorious Honor award AID, 1973, Disting. Career Svc. award, 1977, Cert. Appreciation Pres. Gerald Ford, 1975, Letter Appreciation Dir. Gen. UNESCO, Geneva, 1983; S.L. Whitcomb fellow U. Kansas, 1948-49; fellow Ford Found., 1951-52. Mem. AAUP, Am. Acad. Social and Polit. Sci., Am. Fgn. Svc. Assn., NRA, Nat. Icarian Soc., Nat. Assn. Scholars, Nat. Parks and Conservation Assn., Am. Assn. Retired Persons, Nat. Wildlife Fedn., Archaeol. Inst. Am., Ind. Rights Found., Comparative and Internat. Edn. Soc., Diplomatic and Consular Officers Ret. (regional corr.), Nat. Assn. Ret. Fed. Employees (pres. Ann Arbor chpt. 1986-89, v.p. St. Louis chpt. 1989-90, pres. 1991-93, bd. dirs. 1992-93), Mo. Hist. Soc., Richmond Heights Srs. (v.p., pres.), Smithsonian Assocs., World Affairs Coun., Wilson Ctr. Assn., Nature Conservancy, Assn. Former Internat. Civil Servants, VFW, Am. Legion, 4th Cavalry Assn., Austrian Soc. of St. Louis, Soc. Francaise St. Louis (bd. dirs., v.p., pres., sec., sgt.-at.-arms), Ctr. for Internat. Understanding., Alliance Francaise, St. Louis-Lyon Sister Cities Com., Rotary (bd. dirs., officer 1992-2001, mid-County chpt. 2001—), St. Louis Discussion Club, Great Decisions

Discussion Group, UN Assn. U.S.A., Phi Beta Kappa, Pi Delta Phi, Phi Kappa Phi. Roman Catholic. Avocations: bowling, bridge, billiards, oil painting, writing memoirs, stamps and coins. Home and Office: 7449 Rupert Ave Richmond Heights MO 63117

CHANDLER, JAMES JOHN, surgeon, educator; b. Dayton, Ohio, Nov. 13, 1932; s. James Kapp and Margaret Bertha (Paulson) Chandler; m. Fleur Elizabeth Varney, July 23, 1955; 1 child, Jennifer Hauge. AB, Dartmouth Coll., 1954, diploma in medicine, 1955; MD cum laude, U. Mich., 1957. Diplomate Am. Bd. Surgery. Intern Harvard Surg. Svc., Boston City Hosp., 1957-58, jr. asst. resident, 1958; resident, chief resident in surgery, clin. fellow Am. Cancer Soc. U. Oreg. Hosps., Portland, 1961-64, instr. surgery, 1964; courtesy staff, chmn. surgery Med. Ctr. at Princeton, NJ, 1972—92, pres. med. and dental staff, 1993-94; clin. prof. surgery U. Medicine and Dentistry N.J.-Robert Wood Johnson Med. Sch., Piscataway, 1976—; active staff Robert Wood Johnson U. Hosp., New Brunswick, NJ, 2000—. Cons. in surgery Princeton U.; trustee Med. Ctr. Princeton, 1993—94. Contbr. chapters to books, articles to profl. jours. Bd. dirs. Trinity Counseling Svc., 1968—, chmn., 1968—72; pres. Princeton Day Sch. PTA, 1976—78, trustee, 1976—81; mem. alumni coun. Dartmouth Med. Sch., 1981—86, Dartmouth Coll., 1983—86; active All Sts. Episcopal Ch., Princeton, 1965—. Lt. USN, 1958—60, served to lt. comdr. USNR, 1960—61. Fellow: ACS (pres. N.J. chpt. 1976—77, gov. 1981—87), Soc. Surg. Oncology, Am. Coll. Chest Physicians; mem.: AMA, Soc. Internat. Surgery, Soc. Surg. Alimentary Tract, Collegium Internationale Chirurgiae Digestivae, Med. Soc. N.J. (sec., chmn. surgery sect. 1967—69), Soc. Surgeons N.J., Am. Soc. Clin. Oncology, Gatineau Fish and Game Club, Bedens Brook Club, Nassau Gun Club (pres. 2001—02), Alpha Omega Alpha. Home: 95 Russell Rd Princeton NJ 08540-6729 Office: 1 Robert Wood Johnson Pl New Brunswick NJ 08903-0019 E-mail: chandljj@umdnj.edu.

CHANDLER, JOHN WESLEY, educational consultant; b. Mars Hill, N.C., Sept. 5, 1923; s. Baxter Harrison and Mamie (McIntosh) C.; m. Florence Gordon, Aug. 25, 1948; children: Alison, John, Jennifer, Patricia. Student, Mars Hill Coll., 1941-43; AB, Wake Forest Coll., 1945, L.H.D. (hon.); B.D., Duke U., 1952, PhD, 1954; LL.D., Hamilton Coll., 1968, Colgate U., 1968, Williams Coll., 1973, Amherst Coll., 1974, Wesleyan U., 1978, North Adams State Coll., 1983; L.H.D., Wake Forest U., 1968, Trinity Coll., 1982, Middlebury Coll., 1983, Bates Coll., 1983, Beaver Coll., Duke U., 2002. Instr. philosophy Wake Forest Coll., 1948-51, asst. prof., 1954-55; asst. prof. religion Williams Coll., 1955-60, assoc. prof., chmn. dept., 1960-65, Cluett prof. religion, 1965-68, acting provost, 1965-66, dean faculty, 1966-68; pres. Hamilton Coll., Clinton, N.Y., 1968-73, Williams Coll., Williamstown, Mass., 1973-85, Assn. Am. Colls., Washington, 1985-90; ednl. cons. Korn/Ferry Internat., Washington, 1990-91, Acad. Search Cons. Svc., Washington, 1992—. Contbg. author: Miscellany of American Religion, 1963, Masterpieces of Religious Literature, 1963, also jour. articles and revs. Trustee Williams Coll., 1969-73; bd. visitors Wake Forest Coll., 1971-77, 79-91; bd. dirs. Williamstown Theatre Festival, 1973-85, Sterling and Francine Clark Art Inst., 1973-85; pres. New Eng. Assn. Schs. and Colls., 1977-78, Assn. Ind. Colls. and Univs. Mass., 1977-79; chmn. New Eng. Colls. Fund, 1978; trustee Duke U., 1985-94, chmn., 1993-94; trustee Randolph-Macon Woman's Coll., 1985-88, Phillips Collection, 1997-2001; dir. Value Line Funds, 1991—. Fulbright fellow India, 1963; Kent fellow. Mem. Phi Beta Kappa. Mem. United Ch. of Christ. Clubs: Williams; Cosmos (Washington). Office: Williams Coll Oakley Ctr Williamstown MA 01267 E-mail: John.W.Chandler@williams.edu.

CHANDLER, KAREN REGINA, career guidance specialist; b. Billings, Mont., Nov. 10, 1937; d. James Daniel Romine and Regina (Graham) Middleton; m. Dave Chandler, June 28, 1959; children: Dan, Lance, Trina. BS in Social Sci., Mont. State U., 1959; cert. summa cum laude, Seattle U., 1982. Employment specialist Magna & Assocs. Vocat. Rehab., Federal Way, Wash., 1983-84; instr., employment specialist Pvt. Industry Coun., Auburn, Wash., 1985; career guidance specialist Kent (Wash.) Pub. Schs., 1986—. Chmn. LWV, Kent, 1978. Mem. Wash. Career specialist Assn. (legis. chmn. 1986—, founder), Wash. Vocat. Assn. (sec. 1993-94, Occupational Info. Specialist award 1993), Wash. State Guidance Task Force, Wash. Vocat. Assn. Guidance (sec. 1993-94, pres.-elect 1994-95, pres. 1995—), Wash. Guidance & Counseling Plan (mem. writing team), W.Va. Guidance Assn. (pres. 1995-96). Democrat. Presbyterian. Avocations: reading, horseback riding, gourmet cooking, collecting antiques. Home: PO Box 129 Hysham MT 59038-0129 Office: Kent Pub Schs 12430 SE 208th St Kent WA 98031-2231

CHANDLER, KIMBERLEY LYNN, educational administrator; b. Waynesboro, Va., Sept. 28, 1961; d. Alden Hugh and Cecille Frances (Brooks) C. BA in Elem. Edn., Coll. William and Mary, 1984, MA in Edn./Gifted Edn., 1992, postgrad. Lic. educator, Va. Tchr. Fredericksburg (Va.) Pub. Schs., 1984-87, Henrico County Pub. Schs., Richmond, Va., 1987-98; gifted edn. resource specialist Hanover County Pub. Schs., Richmond, Va., 1998-2000; supr. enrichment programs, coord. of sci. K-12 Amherst County Pub. Schs., Va., 2000—03; cert. curriculum cons. Ctr. for Gifted Edn., 2002—; panel reviewer Jacob K. Javits Grant Program, U.S. Dept. Edn., 2002; postdoctoral fellow, curriculum coord. Ctr. for Gifted Edn. Coll. of William and Mary, Williamsburg, Va., 2003—. Summer sch. coord. Henrico County Pub. Schs., 1996, 97, staff devel. presenter, 1996, 97; curriculum cons. Coll. of William and Mary, Williamsburg, Va., 1996; presenter in field.; mem. gifted edn. staff devel. talent bank, mem. tchr. stds. com. Va. Dept. Edn.; mem. peer coaching program, Prin.'s Acad.; sch. renewal planning team facilitator Hanover County Pub. Schs.; mem. adj. faculty U. Va. Sch. Continuing and Profl. Studies, 2001—; instr. Casenex, Inc.; participant David L. Clark Grad. Student Seminar, 2003. Author: (curriculum unit) Literary Reflections, 1992; author: (with others) Aiming for Excellence-Gifted Program Standards: Annotations to the NAGC Pre-K-Grade 12 Gifted Program Standards, ERIC Research Report, 2002, (book review) Gifted and Talented International; editor (newsletter): Va. Assn. for the Gifted, 1999—. Vol. Hanover Humane Soc., 1994—, Habitat for Humanity Global Village Program, Nicaragua Disaster Relief Mission Team, 1999, Brazil VBS Mission Team, 2000; mem. Habitat for Humanity Global Village Team to South Africa, 2001. Recipient Doctoral Student award Nat. Assn. for Gifted Children, 2002, Hollingworth Rsch. award, 2003; grantee Henrico Edn. Found., 1997, Henrico Gifted Adv. Coun., 1997, Pntrs. in Arts grantee Richmond Arts Coun., 1996, Hanover Edn. Found., 1999, Coll. William and Mary, 2003; postdoctoral fellow Ctr. Gifted Edn., Coll. William and Mary, 2003—. Mem.: Va. Assn. for the Gifted (ex officio bd. dirs.), Va. Soc. for Tech. in Edn., Hanover County Prins. Acad., Nat. Assn. for Gifted Children (sec./treas. technol. divsn. 1997—99, sec./treas. profl. devel. divsn. 1997—99, chair profl. devel. divsn. 2003—, Harry Passow Classroom Tchr. scholarship 1997, Outstanding Curriculum award 2000, Doctoral Student award 2002, Hollingworth award 2003), Delta Kappa Gamma, Kappa Delta Pi (chpt. sec.). Home: 11444 New Farrington Ct Glen Allen VA 23059-1629 Office: Coll William and Mary Ctr for Gifted Edn PO Box 8795 Williamsburg VA 23187-8795 E-mail: kchan11444@aol.com.

CHANDLER, PATRICIA ANN, retired special education educator; b. Stow, Maine, May 25, 1929; d. Herbert Raymond and Tressia May (Walker) Harmon; m. Robert Leslie Chandler, Mar. 25, 1949 (dec. June 1991); children: Rose Ann Chandler Savage, Alexander Michael. BS, U. Maine, Portland, 1965; MEd, U. So. Maine, 1978. Tchg. prin. Annie Heald Sch., Lovell, Maine, 1954—70, New Suncook Sch., Lovell, Maine, 1970, Sadie Adams Sch., North Fryeburg, Maine, New Suncook Sch., Lovell, Maine; ret., 1983. Contbr. articles to profl. jours. Mem.: Oxford County Ret. Tchrs. Assn., Maine Assn. of Retirees, Inc. (licentiate). Republican. United Ch. Of Christ Congl. Avocations: cooking, travel, writing, painting. Mailing: 434 Roosevelt Trail Casco ME 04015-3515

CHANDLER, VICTORIA JANE, elementary school educator, writer; b. Chestnut Hill, Pa., Oct. 27, 1954; d. Roland Jay and Elisabeth Ann (Renton) Turner; m. Howard Steven Chandler, June 24, 1978; children: Christopher, Robert. BS, Kutztown State U., 1976; postgrad., Loyola Coll., Towson, Md., 1977, 79; MEd, Beaver Coll., Glenside, Pa., 1991. Cert. tchr., Pa. Tchr. spl. edn. Md. Sch. for Blind, Balt., 1976-80; tchr. 2nd grade Lehigh Christian Acad., Phila., 1986-91; tchr. vision support Montgomery County IU #23, Norristown, Pa., 1991-92; tchr. instructional support team Sch. Dist. of Springfield Twp./Montgomery County, Oreland, Pa., 1992-94; spl. edn. tchr. Council Rock Sch. Dist., 1994-95; dir. instrn., elem. prin. Calvary Christian Acad., Phila., 1995—. Asst. dir. Mustard Seed Farm Camp for Handicapped, Spring City, Pa., 1980—. Active Ch. Sunday Sch. Calvary Chapel, Feasterville, Pa., 1992—. Active Ch. Sun. sch. Berachah, Cheltenham, Pa., 1982-90. Avocations: photography, educational board games. Home: 509 Brook Ln Warminster PA 18974-2719

CHANDRA, PRAMOD, art history educator; b. Varanasi, India, Nov. 2, 1930; came to U.S., 1964; s. Moti and Shanti (Devi) C.; m. Mary Carmen Lynn, 1981; children: Abhijit, Sasanka. BS, Georgetown U., 1951; PhD, U. Bombay, 1964. Asst. curator Prince of Wales Mus. of Western India, Bombay, 1954-60, curator art and archaeol. sects., 1960-64; assoc. prof. U. Chgo., 1964-71, prof., 1971-80; George P. Bickford prof. Indian and South Asian art Harvard U., Cambridge, Mass., 1980—. Founder, dir. Ctr. for Art and Archaeology, Am. Inst. Indian Studies, 1965-71; founder, pres. Am. Com. South Asian Art, 1963-71; hon. advisor on archaeology and mus. Govt. of Madhya Pradesh, India; hon. advisor Govt. of Chattisgarh, 2000--; guest curator Sculpture of India exhbn. Nat. Gallery Art, Washington, 1985. Author: Bundi Painting, 1959, Stone Sculpture in the Allahabad Museum, 1971, Studies in Indian Temple Architecture, 1974, The Cleveland Tutinama and the Origins of Mughal Painting, 1976, On the Study of Indian Art, 1983, Sculpture of India 3000 BC-1300 AD, 1985 Recipient Bharat Kala Bhavan award Banaras Hindu U., India; grantee NEH, 1976-80. E-mail: pchandra@fas.harvard.edu.

CHANDRAS, KANANUR V. psychology educator; b. Bangalore, India, Jan. 1, 1935; s. K. and Parvathamma Veerabhadraiah; children: Tara, Kiran, Sunil. BS, Mysore U., Karnataka, India, 1958; MA, Hindu U., 1958; MS, PhD, Southern Ill. U., 1962, 1968; MS, Valdosta State U., 1978, EdS, 1979. Lic. counselor, Ga.; cert. criminal justice specialist; nat. cert. counselor. Prof. edn. McGill U., Montreal, Can., 1968-71; prof. counseling psychology, head dept. Ft. Valley (Ga.) State U., 1972—. Vis. prof. edn. U. Northern Iowa, Cedar Falls, Fla. A&M U., Tallahassee. Author 13 books; contbr. articles to profl. jours.; editl. bd. Jour. Counselor Edn. & Supervision, 1992—, Counseling and Devel. Jour. Recipient numerous awards and honors; Can. Coun. grantee. Mem. AAUP, Am. Counseling Assn., Am. Sch. Counselors Assn., Am. Mental Health Counselors Assn., Assn. Counselor Edn. and Supervision, Mental Health Counselor Assn., Adult Devel. Aging & Counseling Interest Network (chair), Ga. Mental Health Counseling Assn., Internat. Assn. Addictions and Offender Counselors. Office: Ft Valley State U Fort Valley GA 31030 E-mail: chandrak@mail.fvsu.edu.

CHANDRASEKARAN, BALAKRISHNAN, computer and information science educator; b. Lalgudi, Tamil Nadu, India, June 20, 1942; came to U.S., 1963; s. Srinivasan and Nagamani Balakrishnan; m. Sandra Mamrak, Oct. 21, 1978; 1 child, Mallika. B in Engring., Madras U., Karaikudi, India, 1963; PhD, U. Pa., 1967. Devel. engr. Smith Kline Instruments, Phila., 1964-65; rsch. specialist Philco-Ford Corp., Blue Bell, Pa., 1967-69; asst. prof. computer and info. sci. Ohio State U., Columbus, 1969-71, assoc. prof., 1971-77, prof., 1977-95; sr. rsch. scientist, 1995—; dir. Lab. for Artificial Intelligence Rsch., Columbus, 1983—. Co-chmn. Symposium on Potentials and Limitations of Mech. Intelligence, Anaheim, Calif., 1971; chmn. Norbert Wiener Symposium, Boston, 1974; sci. dir. Summer Sch. on Computer Program Testing, SOGESTA, Urbino, Italy, 1981; vis. scientist Lawrence Livermore Nat. Lab., Livermore, Calif., summer 1981, cons. fall 1981; vis. scientist MIT Computer Sci. Lab., 1983; dir. NIH Artificial Intelligence in Medicine Workshop, 1984; organizer panel discussion on artificial intelligence and engring. ASME, 1985; vis. scholar Stanford U., 1990-91; keynote spkr. World Congress on Expert Sys., Mexico City, 1998, Internat. Conf. on Diagrammic Reasoning, Callaway Gardens, Ga., 2002. Editor: Diagrammatic Reasoning, 1995; co-editor Computer Program Testing, 1981; editor ACM Sigart Spl. Issue on Structure, Function, and Behavior, 1985; assoc. editor Artificial Intelligence in Engring., 1986—; mem. bd. editors Internat. Jour. Pattern Recognition & Artificial Intelligence, Med. Expert Systems, Artificial Intelligence in Engring.; assoc. editor Internat. Jour. Human-Computer Interactions, 1996—. Recipient Outstanding Paper award Pattern Recognition Soc., 1976; Moore fellow U. Pa., 1964-67. Fellow IEEE (editor-in-chief Expert Jour. 1990-94), Am. Assn. for Artificial Intelligence (chmn. workshops on diagrammatic reasoning 1992), Assn. for Computing Machinery; mem. Sys. Man and Cybernetics Soc. IEEE (v.p. 1974-75, pattern recognition com. 1969-72, assoc. editor Trans. 1973—, guest editor spl. issue on distributed program solving 1981). Democrat. Avocation: travel. Home: 2053 Iuka Ave Columbus OH 43201-1415 Office: Ohio State U Dept Computer and Info Sci 2015 Neil Ave Columbus OH 43210-1210 E-mail: chandra@cis.ohio-state.edu.

CHANEY, RONALD CLAIRE, environmental engineering educator, consultant; b. Tulsa, Okla, Mar. 26, 1944; s. Clarence Emerson and Virginia Margaret (Klinger) C.; m. Patricia Jane Robinson, Aug. 11, 1984. BS, Calif. State U., Long Beach, 1969; MS, Calif. State U., 1970; PhD, UCLA, 1978. Prof. engr., Calif., Oreg.; lic. geotech. engr., Calif. Structural engr. Fluor Corp. Ltd., LA, 1968-70; rsch. engr. UCLA, 1972-74; lab. mgr. Fugro Inc., Long Beach, 1974-79; assoc. prof. Lehigh U., Bethlehem, Pa., 1979-81; dir. Telonicher Marine Lab. Humboldt State U., Trinidad, Calif., 1996—2000, prof. Arcata, Calif., 1981—. Geotech. engr. LACO Assoc., Eureka, Calif., 1988—; panel mem. Humboldt County Solid Waste Appeals, Eureka, 1992-96; mem. shipboard measurement panel Joint Oceanog. Instn., Washington, 1991-96. Co-editor Symposium on Marine Geotechnology and Nearshore/Offshore Structures, 1986, Symposium on Geotechnical Aspects of Waste Disposal in the Marine Environment, 1990, Symposium on Dredging, Remediation and Containment of Contaminated Sediments, 1995, 2d Internat. Symposium on Contaminated Sediments, 2003; editor Marine Geotech. Jour., 1981-92; co-editor Marine Georesources and Geotech. jour., 1992—, ASTM Geotech. Testing Jour., 1996-2002. Fellow ASTM (Hogentogler award 1988, Std. Devel. award 1991, Outstanding Achievement award 1992, 2003, Dudley medal 1994, Award of Merit 1995, vice chmn. D18, 1995-2001), Seismological Soc. Am., Earthquake Engring. Rsch. Inst., Sigma Xi, Phi Kappa Phi. Office: Humboldt State U Dept Environ Resources Engring Arcata CA 95521

CHANG, AMOS IH-TIAO, retired architecture educator; b. Dist. Pu-nin, Kwangtung, China, Dec. 2, 1916; came to U.S., 1967; s. Sia-tee and Sok-gat (Lin) C.; m. Jennie Ming chio, Aug. 3, 1938; children: Chung Yue, Chung Tsiang, Chung Ling, Songsri. BS in Civil Engring., Nat. Chung King U., 1939; MFA in Architecture, Princeton U., 1949, PhD in Architecture, 1951. Cert. architect Nat. Coun. Archtl. Registration Bds.; registered architect Kans., N.Y., Mo. Archt. engr., China, 1934-46; tchr., architect Princeton Grad. Sch., N.J., 1951-52; architect Bangkok, Thailand, 1952-67; tchr., archt. Kans. State U., 1967-73, assoc. prof. archt., 1974, prof., 1974-87; retired, 1987. Author: The Tao of Architecture, 1956; co-author: The Routledge Companion to Contemporary Architectural Thought, 1993; prin. works include Bangkok Christian Coll., U.S. Embassy extension Bangkok, Linn State Bank, Kans.; patentee hexagonal non-stop traffic pattern. Chang Gallery named in his honor Kans. State U. Mem. AIA, Internat. Sco. Chinese Philosophy, Internat. Shell Structure Assn., Chinese Soc. Engrs. U.S.A. (Paul Harris fellow), Rotary Club, Phi Tau Phi, Tau Sigma Delta. Presbyterian. Avocation: violin. Home and Office: 701 Harris Ave Manhattan KS 66502-3613

CHANG, CHING MING (CARL CHANG), engineering executive, mechanical engineer, educator; b. Nanking, China; came to U.S., 1967; m. Birdie S.C. Chang, Dec. 18, 1964; children: Andrew L.P., Nelson L.A., Michele Chang. Dipl. Ing., Technol. U. Aachen, Germany, 1962; PhD, Technol. U. Aachen, 1967; MBA, SUNY, Buffalo, 1985. Registered profl. engr., N.Y., Va. Asst. prof. N.C. State U., Raleigh, 1968-73; sr. engr. to sr. devel. assoc. Praxair, Inc. (formerly Union Carbide Indsl. Gases), Tonawanda, N.Y., 1973-95, bus. devel. mgr., 1995-98; pres. CarlChang LLC Bus. Cons., Amherst, N.Y., 1998—; dir. analytical engring. O'Mara Cons. Engrs., Buffalo, 2001—. Adj. prof. engring. SUNY, Buffalo, 1979—. Author: (book) Managerial Challenges for Engineers in the New Millennium, 2004; contbr. articles to profl. jour. Named Person of Yr. Tech. Soc. Coun., Buffalo, 1986. Mem. NSPE (pres. Erie-Niagara chpt. 1980-81, Disting. Svc. award 1981, Basinsky award 1984, Engring. Educator of Yr. award 1990, Praxair Special Recognition award for Technol. Leadership, 1992, Basinski-Wohler award 1994). Achievements include inventor; holder of five U.S. patents. Avocations: tennis, travel, computer games, mahjong. also: SUNY Buffalo Dept Indsl Engring 323 Bell Hall Buffalo NY 14260 E-mail: CChangLLC@aol.com.

CHANG, CHING-JER, medicinal chemistry educator; b. Hsinchu, Taiwan, China, Oct. 17, 1942; came to the U.S., 1968; s. Tin-lian and Awei (Lai) C.; m. Shu-fang Kuo, Dec. 25, 1978; children: Philip, Sylvia. BS, Nat. Taiwan Cheng Kung U., 1965; PhD, Ind. U., 1972. Asst. prof. Purdue U., West Lafayette, Ind., 1973-78, assoc. prof., 1978-84, prof., 1984—. Mem. bioorganic and natural products chemistry study sect., NIH, Bethesda, Md., 1986-90, spl. study sect., 1991—; editl. adv. bd. Jour. Natural Products, 1989-99; assoc. editor: Jour. Asian Nat. Products; reviewer Human Frontier Sci. Program, Strassbourg, France, 1992—, Hong Kong Govt. Rsch. Grant Coun., 1997—. Contbr. articles to profl. jours. Mem. Am. Soc. Pharmacognosy (exec. com. 1993-97), Am. Chem. Soc., Am. Assn. for Cancer Rsch., Phytochem. Soc. N.Am., Argentinian Soc. Organic Chemistry (hon. mem.). Achievements include patents in field. Office: Dept Medicinal Chemistry Purdue Univ West Lafayette IN 47907-2091 E-mail: cjchang@pharmacy.purdue.edu.

CHANG, HOWARD FENGHAU, law educator, economist; b. Lafayette, Ind., June 30, 1960; s. Joseph Juifu and Mary Hsueh-mei C. AB in Govt. cum laude, Harvard Coll., 1982; M in Pub. Affairs, Princeton (N.J.) U., 1985; JD magna cum laude, Harvard U., 1987; SM in Econs., MIT, 1988, PhD in Econs., 1992. Bar: N.Y. 1989, D.C. 1989. Law clk. to hon. Ruth Bader Ginsburg U.S. Ct. of Appeals, Washington, 1988-89; asst. prof. law U. So. Calif. Law Sch., L.A., 1992-94, assoc. prof. law, 1994-97, prof. law, 1997-99, U. Pa., Phila., 1999—. Vis. assoc. prof. law Georgetown U. Law Ctr., Washington, 1996-97; prof. law Stanford Law Sch., 1998. Supervising editor Harvard Law Rev., Cambridge, 1986-87. John M. Olin fellowship Dept. Econs. MIT, 1987, 90, 91; nat. merit scholar IBM, 1978. Mem. Am. Econ. Assn., Am. Law and Econs. Assn. Office: U Pa Law Sch Law Sch 3400 Chestnut St Philadelphia PA 19104-6204

CHANG, ISABELLE C. librarian, educator, writer; b. Boston, Feb. 20, 1924; d. Que Wah Chin and June Hall; m. Min Chueh Chang, May 28, 1948; children: Francis Hugh, Claudia, Pamela. BS in Lib. Sci., Simmons Coll., 1946; MA in English, Clark U., 1967; MA in Psychology, Anna Maria Coll., 1982. Lib. trustee Shrewsbury (Mass.) Pub. Lib., 1958-59, 65-68, lib. dir., 1959-64; tchr. English, audio visual and media coord., librarian Shrewsbury (Mass.) Schs., 1964-91, guidance counselor, 1980-91. Author: What's Cooking at Changs, 1959, Chinese Fairy Tales, 1965, Tales from Old China, 1969, Gourmet on the Go, 1970, The Magic Pole, 1977, Spag: The American Dream, 1992, Artemas Ward, 2002. Shrewsbury Town Rep., 1997—. Recipient award for Disting. Writing Chandler Greene, 1966. Mem. ALA (life), NEA (life), AAAS (life), AARP (dir. 1995—), Nat. Acad. Scis. (life), Mass. Tchrs. Assn. (life), Shrewsbury Hist. Soc. (life), Worcester Art Mus. (life). Home: 15 Fiske St Shrewsbury MA 01545-2721 E-mail: isabellechang@aol.com.

CHANG, JAE CHAN, hematologist, oncologist, educator; b. Aug. 29, 1941; arrived in U.S., 1965; s. Tae Whan and Kap Hee (Lee) Chang; m. Sue Young Chung, Dec. 4, 1965; children: Sung-Jin, Sung-Ju, Sung-Hoon. MD, Seoul (Korea) Nat. U., 1965. Diplomate Am. Bd. Internal Medicine, Hematology, Med. Oncology, Am. Bd. Pathology (Hematology). Intern Ellis Hosp., Schenectady, NY, 1965—66; resident Harrisburg (Pa.) Hosp., 1966—69, fellow in nuclear medicine, 1969—70; fellow in hematology and oncology, instr. U. Rochester, 1970—72; chief hematology sect. VA Hosp., Dayton, Ohio, 1972—75; hematopathologist, co-dir. hematology lab. Good Samaritan Hosp., Dayton, 1975—2002, dir. oncology unit, 1976—2001, chief hematology and oncology sect., 1976—2003; clin. prof. medicine U. Calif., Irvine, Calif., 2003—; mem. Chao Family Comprehensive Cancer Ctr., U. Calif., Irvine, 2003—. Asst. clin. prof. Ohio State U., Columbus, 1972—75; assoc. clin. prof. Wright State U., Dayton, 1975—80, clin. prof., 1980—99, prof., 1999—2003, co-dir. hematology and med. oncology fellowship program, 1993—98; cons. hematology VA Hosp.; adv. com. Greater Dayton Area chpt. Leukemia Soc. Am., 1977; trustee Montgomery County Soc. Cancer Control, Dayton, 1976—85, Dayton Area Cancer Assn., 1985—88, Cmty. Blood Ctr., 1982—86, Hipple Cancer Rsch. Crt., 1999—2002. Contbr. articles to profl. jours., columns in newspapers. Recipient Med. Econ. Essay Competition award, 1990, Wright State U. Acad. of Medicine award, 1985, Laureate award, APC-ASIM Ohio Chpt., 2001, Spl. Commendation, Ohio Senate, 2002. Fellow: ACP; mem.: AAAS, Montgomery Med. Soc. (dir. 1990—93), Dayton Soc. Internal Medicine (pres. 1989), Am. Soc. Clin. Oncologists, Am. Soc. Hematology. Home: 230 City Blvd W #303 Orange CA 92868 Office: UCI Med Ctr Div Hematology/ Oncology Chao Family Comp Cancer Ctr 101 The City Dr Orange CA 92868 E-mail: jaec@uci.edu.

CHANG, JEFFREY CHAI, dentist, educator, researcher; b. Canton, China, Dec. 19, 1946; came to U.S., 1967; s. Po Wing and Wai Ming (Chan) C.; m. Frances Fuhnan Liang; children: Sheila Sai, Kenneth Kiu. BA with honors, Northeastern U., 1971; DDS, Georgetown U., 1976; MS in Dentistry, U. Tex. Dental Br., Houston, 1996. Commd. 2d lt. U.S. Army, 1976, advanced through grades to maj.; gen. dental officer Dental Corps Ft. Bliss, Tex., 1976-79; officer-in-charge Dental Clinic U.S. Army, Pusan, Korea, 1979-80, asst. chief clinician dental activity Ft. Momouth, N.J., 1980-83, chief dental emergency svc. dental activity Ft. Hood, Tex., 1983—85, resigned, 1985; clin. asst. prof. Dental Sch. U. Calif., San Francisco, 1985-88; clin. asst. prof. NYU Coll. Dentistry, N.Y.C., 1988-90; asst. prof. U. Tex. Dental Br., 1990-92, assoc. prof., 1992—. Cons. VA Med. Ctr., San Francisco, 1987-88, St. Barnabas Hosp., Bronx, N.Y., 1988-90, VA Med. Ctr., Houston, 1993—, ADA Coun. on Sci. Affairs, 1996—; scientist Houston Biomaterials Rsch. Ctr., 1996—. Contbr. 40 articles, 20 abstracts to profl. jours. Col. USAR, 1996—. Master Acad. Gen. Dentistry; fellow Am. Coll. Dentists, Acad. Dentistry Internat., Internat. Coll. Dentists; mem. ADA, Am. Assn. Dental Rsch., Internat. Assn. Dental Rsch., Chinese Am. Drs. Assn. (bd. dirs. 1994-2001), Am. Legion, Omicron Kappa Upsilon, Delta Sigma Delta. Avocations: soccer, stamps, contemporary music, photography, hi-fi systems. Home: 4123 Custer Creek Dr Missouri City TX 77459-1545 E-mail: drjeffchang@hotmail.com.

CHANG, KWANG POO, microbiology educator; b. Taipei, Republic of China, Nov. 12, 1942; came to U.S., 1972; s. W.C. and H.H. (Lo) C.; m. Chin Shen, Apr. 13, 1971; 1 child, Patrick. BSc in Entomology, Nat. Taiwan U., Taipei, 1965; MSc in Cell Biology, U. Guelph, Ont., Can., 1968, PhD in

Cell Biology, 1972; postgrad., Rockefeller U., 1972-74. Rsch. assoc. Rockefeller U., N.Y.C., 1974-76, asst. prof., 1976-79; assoc. prof. Rockefeller U., N.Y.C., 1979-83; prof. microbiology U. Health Scis. Chgo. Med. Sch., North Chicago, Ill., 1983—. Mem. U.S. Army Med. Rsch. Parasitic Diseases Rev. Panel, 1984-89; mem. study sect. on tropical medicine and parasitology NIH, 1987-91. Contbr. articles to sci. jours. Recipient Pres.'s award Can. Soc. Entomol. Ont., 1968, Irma T. Hirschl career scientist award, 1977, Morris E. Parker award U. Health Scis. Chgo Med. Sch., 1985, Seymour Hutner award Soc. Protozoologists, 1987. Office: U Health Scis Chgo Med Sch 3333 Green Bay Rd North Chicago IL 60064-3037 Fax: 847-578-3349. E-mail: changk@finchcms.edu.

CHANG, LYDIA LIANG-HWA, social worker, educator; b. Wuhan, Hubei, China, Sept. 25, 1929; came to U.S., 1960; d. Shu-Tze Yu-Rou and Jian-Bung (Young) C.; m. Norman Stock, Aug. 20, 1998; children: Elizabeth Shu-Mei L. Ip, George Shu-Ang Lee. Diploma in Spanish and Lit., U. Sorbonne, Paris, 1959; MSW, NYU, 1963; cert. in advanced social work, Columbia U., N.Y.C., 1977, PhD in Social Work, 1980. Cert. social worker, cert. sch. bilingual social worker, N.Y. Supr. Cath. Charities, N.Y.C., 1969-71; dir. mental health cons. ctr. Univ. Settlement, N.Y.C., 1971-73; psychotherapist Luth. Med. Ctr., Bklyn., 1974-78; assoc. prof. U. Cin., 1978-80; asst. prof. Borough of Manhattan C.C., N.Y.C., 1983-86; bilingual sch. social worker N.Y.C. Bd. Edn., 1987-98, instr. for staff devel. program, 1991-98; psychotherapist Western Queens (N.Y.) Consultation Ctr., 1998—. Govt. ofcl.; cmem. mty. sch. bd. Dist. 30 N.Y.C. Bd. Edn., 1999—; cons. Cath. Social Svc. Bur., Cin., 1978-80; faculty advisor Borough of Manhattan C.C., 1983-86. Contbr. articles and poetry to various publs. Mem. adv. bd. Pub. Sys. of Schs., Cin., 1978-80, Orange County Asian Am. orgn., Goshen, N.Y., 1980-82; treas. U.S.-China Ednl. Fund, Hastins-on-Hudson, N.Y., 1994—; mem. Asian-Am. Dem. Assn., Queens, 1993—, Am. Voters Assn., Queens, 1986—; founder of the Shu-Tze Chang and Jian-Bung Young Chang Ednl. scholarship fund, China, 1996. Mem. NASW, Nat. Assn. Sch. Social Workers, Columbia Alumni Assn., Nankai Alumni Assn. (v.p. 1991-94). Episcopalian. Avocations: flute, tai-chi-chuang, swimming, reading. Home: 77-11 35th Ave Apt 2P Jackson Heights NY 11372

CHANG, SHIRLEY LIN (HSIU-CHU CHANG), librarian, educator; b. Chia-yi, Taiwan, June 22, 1937; came to U.S., 1962; naturalized, 1977. d. Tzu-kun and Ying (Chang) Lin; m. Parris H. Chang, Aug. 3, 1963; children: Yvette Y., Elaine Y., Bohdan P. BA, Nat. Taiwan U., Taipei, 1960; postgrad., U. Wasn., 1962-63; MLS, Columbia U., 1967; MA, Pa. State U., 1988. Libr. asst. Yale U., New Haven, 1964-67; asst. ref. libr. Pa. State U., University Park, 1971-75; cataloguer Australian Nat. U., Canberra, 1978; catalog/ref. libr. Lock Haven U., 1979—, asst. prof., 1982-88, assoc. prof., 1988—. Reference libr., reference catalog/desk coord. Lock Haven U., Pa. Author: Taiwan's Brain Drain and Its Reversal, 1999. Mem. ALA, Chinese-Am. Librs. Assn. (chmn. awards com. 1982-83), Asian/Pacific Am. Librs. Assn., Assn. for Asian Studies, Pa. Libr. Assn., Phi Beta Delta Honor Soc. Home: 1221 Edwards St State College PA 16801 Office: Lock Haven U Stevenson Libr Lock Haven PA 17745 E-mail: schang@lhup.edu.

CHANG, SYLVIA TAN, health facility administrator, educator; b. Bandung, Indonesia, Dec. 18, 1940; came to U.S., 1963. d. Philip Harry and Lydia Shui-Yu (Ou) Tan; m. Belden Shiu-Wah Chang, Aug. 30, 1964 (dec. Aug. 1997); children: Donald Steven, Janice May. Diploma in nursing, Rumah Sakit Advent, Indonesia, 1960; BS, Philippine Union Coll., 1962; MS, Loma Linda (Calif.) U., 1967; PhD, Columbia Pacific U., 1987. Cert. RN, PHN, ACLS, BLS instr., cmty. first aid instr., IV, TPN, blood withdrawal. Head nurse Rumah Sakit Advent, Bandung, Indonesia, 1960-61; critical care, spl. duty and medicine nurse, team leader White Meml. Med. Ctr., L.A., 1963-64; nursing coord. Loma Linda U. Med. Ctr., 1964-66; team leader, critical care nurse, relief head nurse Pomona (Calif.) Valley Hosp. Med. Ctr., 1966-67; evening supr. Loma Linda U. Med. Ctr., 1967-69, night supr., 1969-79, adminstrv. supr., 1979-94; sr. faculty Columbia Pacific U., San Rafael, Calif., 1986-94; dir. health svc. La Sierra U., Riverside, Calif., 1988—. Site coord. Health Fair Expo La Sierra U., 1988-89; adv. coun. Family Planning Clinic, Riverside, 1988-94; blood and bone marrow drive coord. La Sierra U., 1988—. Counselor Pathfinder Club Campus Hill Ch., Loma Linda, 1979-85, crafts instr., 1979-85, music dir., 1979-85; asst. organist U. Ch., 1982-88. Named one of Women of Achievement YWCA, Greater Riverside C. of C., The Press Enterprise, 1991, 2000, Safety Coord. of Yr. La Sierra U., 1995. Mem. Am. Coll. Health Assn., Pacific Coast Coll. Health Assn., Adventist Student Pers. Assn., Sigma Theta Tau. Republican. Seventh-day Adventist. Avocations: music, travel, collecting coins, shells and jade carvings. Home: 1025 Crestbrook Dr Riverside CA 92506-5662 Office: 4700 Pierce St Riverside CA 92515-8247 E-mail: schang@lasierra.edu.

CHANG, WILLIAM SHEN CHIE, electrical engineering educator; b. Nantung, Jiangsu, China, Apr. 4, 1931; s. Tung Wu and Phoebe Y.S. (Chow) C.; m. Margaret Huachen Kwei, Nov. 26, 1955; children: Helen Nai-yee, Hugh Nai-hun, Hedy Nai-lin. BSE, U. Mich., 1952, MSE, 1953; PhD, Brown U., 1957. Lectr., rsch. assoc. in elec. engring. Stanford (Calif.) U., 1957-59; asst. prof. elec. engring. Ohio State U., 1959-62, assoc. prof., 1962-65; prof. dept. elec. engring. Washington U., St. Louis, 1965—79, chmn. dept., 1965-71, dir. Applied Electronic Scis. Lab., 1971-79, Samuel Sachs prof. elec. engring., 1976-79; prof. dept. elec. and computer engring. U. Calif., San Diego, 1979—, chmn. dept., 1993-96. Author: Principles of Quantum Electronics, 1969, RF Photonic Technology in Optical Fiber Links, 2002; Contbr. articles to profl. jours. Fellow Am. Optical Soc., IEEE; mem. Am. Phys. Soc. Achievements include research on quantum electronics and guided wave optics. Home: 12676 Caminito Radiante San Diego CA 92130 Office: U Calif San Diego MS-0407 Dept Elec/Computer Engring La Jolla CA 92093-0407 E-mail: wchang@ucsd.edu.

CHANG, Y. AUSTIN, materials engineer, educator; m. P. Jean Ho, Sept. 15, 1956; children: Vincent D., Lawrence D., Theodore D. BS in Chem. Engring, U. Calif., Berkeley, 1954; PhD in Metallurgy, U. Calif., 1963; MS in Chem. Engring, U. Wash., 1955. Chem. engr. Stauffer Chem. Co., Richmond, Calif., 1956-59; postdoctoral fellow U. Calif.-Berkeley, 1963; metall. engr. Aerojet-Gen. Corp., Sacramento, 1963-67; assoc. prof. U. Wis.-Milw., 1967-70, prof., 1970-80, chmn. materials dept., 1971-78, assoc. dean research Grad. Sch., 1978-80; prof. dept. materials sci. and engring. U. Wis., Madison, 1980—, chmn. dept., 1982-91, Wis. Disting. prof., 1988—. Mem. summer faculty Sandia Labs., Livermore, Calif., 1971; vis. prof. Tohuku U., Sendai, Japan, fall 1987, MIT, Cambridge, fall 1991; NRC Disting. lectr. in material sci. Nat. Cheng Kung U., Tainan, Taiwan, 1987-88; adj. prof. U. Sci. Tech., Beijing, 1987—, hon. prof., 1995-96, adv. bd., 1996—; hon. prof. Ctrl. South U. Technology, Changsha, Hunan, 1996—, S.E. U., Nanjing, 1997, N.E. U., Shenyang, 1998; Winchell Lectr., Purdue U., 1999; summer faculty Quantum Structure Resh. Initiative, Hewlett-Packard Laboratories, Palo Alto, 1999; Belton Lectr. CSIRO, Clayton, Victoria, Australia, 2000. Co-author four books on phase equilibria and thermodynamic properties; co-editor four books; contbr. 300 scholarly articles in metall. and materials field to profl. jours. Mem. bd. Goodwill Residential Cmty., Inc., Milw., 1978-80; mem. Wis. Gov.'s Asian Am. Adv. Coun., 1980-82, Nat. Acad. Engring., 1996. Recipient Outstanding Instr. award U. Wis., Milw., 1972, Byron Bird award U. Wis., Madison, 1984, Alloy Phase Diagram Internat. Comm. Best Paper award, 1999; named hon. prof. Southeast U. Nanjing, 1997, Northeast U., Shenyang, 1998. Fellow Am. Soc. Metals Internat. (Fellow award 1978, trustee 1981-84, Hall of Fame award Milw. chpt. 1986, Albert Easton White Disting. Tchr. award 1994, Albert Sauveun Achievement award 1996), Minerals, Metals and Materials Soc. (v.p., 1999, pres. 2000, William Hume-Rothery award 1989, Educator award 1990, Extraction and Processing lectr. award 1993, Mathewson award 1996, John Bardeen award 2000); mem. NSPE, NAE, Orgn. Chinese Ams. (chpt. pres. 1979-81), Nat. Assn. Corrosion Engrs., Electrochem. Soc., Materials Rsch. Soc., Am. Phys. Soc., Chinese Acad. Scis. (fgn. academician, 2000), Sigma Xi, Tau Beta Pi, Phi Tau Phi, Alpha Sigma Mu (pres. 1984-85, hon. life). Office: U Wis 1509 University Ave Madison WI 53706-1538*

CHAO, JAMES LEE, chemist, educator; b. Lafayette, Ind., Sept. 4, 1954; s. Tai Siang and Hsiang Lin (Lee) Chao; m. Juliana Meimei Ma, Apr. 4, 1992; 1 child, Jamie. BS in Chemistry, U. Ill., 1975, MS in Chemistry, 1976; PhD in Chemistry, U. Calif., Berkeley, 1980. Applications scientist IBM Instruments, Inc., Danbury, Conn., 1980-87; vis. assoc. prof. dept. chemistry Duke U., Durham, N.C., 1986-87, adj. asst. prof. dept. chemistry, 1987-91, adj. assoc. prof., 1992-2000, adj. prof., 2000—; adv. scientist Materials Engring. Lab., IBM, Research Triangle Park, N.C., 1987-2000, program mgr. for strategic IP licensing, 2000—02, IBM alphaworks emerging tech. strategist, 2002—. Cons. Lab. for Laser Energetics, U. Rochester, N.Y., 1979-80; postdoctoral fellow Lab. for Chem. Biodynamics, Lawrence Berkeley Lab., 1980; referee Applied Spectroscopy, 1982—, Applied Physics Letters, Jour. Applied Physics, 1989—; grant referee N.C. Biotech. Ctr., 1991—. Contbr. articles to profl. jours. Edmund James scholar, 1972-75, Dow Chem. scholar, 1977. Fellow N.Y. Acad. Scis., Am. Inst. Chemists; mem. ASTM, Am. Chem. Soc. (chmn. N.C. sect. 1991, councilor 1993—, mem. internat. activities com. 1998-2001, assoc. mem. patents and related matters 2002--, editl. bd. ACS Job Spectrum 2002--, Marcus E. Hobbs svc. award 1995), Soc. for Applied Spectroscopy, Coblentz Soc., Triangle Coun. Engring. and Sci. Socs. (treas. 1992-94), Sigma Xi. Achievements include development of step-scan implementation for FT-IR spectrometers to study photothermal and time-resolved spectroscopies; stds. project authority for IBM environmental gaseous corrosion testing. Home: 7424 Ridgefield Dr Durham NC 27713-9503 Office: IBM Corp Dept WUOA/667 PO Box 12195 RTP Durham NC 27709

CHAO, JASON, family physician, educator; b. Chgo., July 18, 1955; s. Jen-Hung and Julia (Yu) C.; m. Betsy Charlene Wolf, July 27, 1984; 1 child, Elysa Wolf Chao. BS, Northwestern U., 1977, MD, 1979; MS, Case Western Res. U., 1984. Registerd physician, Ohio; diplomate Am. Bd. Family Practice. Resident family practice U. Iowa Hosps. and Clinics, Iowa City, 1979-82; fellow family medicine Case Western Res. U., Robert Wood Johnson Faculty Devel., Cleve., 1982-84; asst. prof. Case Western Res. U., Cleve., 1984-93, assoc. prof., 1993—. Attending physician U. Hosps. of Cleve., Ohio, 1984—, med. dir. dept. family practice, 1991-95; trustee Ohio Group Against Smoking Pollution, 1986-89; exec. com. Clin. Sci. Program, Case Western Res. U. Med. Sch., Cleve., 1990-92; assoc. med. dir. QualChoice Health Plan, 1995-97, med. dir., 1997-99; curriculum dir. Year 1-2 primary care track Case Western Res. U. Med. sch., Cleve., 1999—, predoctoral divsn. dir. dept. family medicine, 2000—. Author: (computer instrnl. materials) MED-CAPS Diagnostic Problem Cases, 1989; contbr. articles to profl. jours. Vol. physician Cleve. (Ohio) Free Med. Clinic, 1982—; bd. dirs. Chinese Student and Alumni Svcs., 1984-86; systems operator Family Medicine Area of Cleve. Freenet, 1985-99; mem. all-star volleyball team Euclid Ch. League, Cleve., 1988, 89, 91, 95, 96, 97, 98, 99, 2000, 2002. Recipient Community Svc. award Northwestern U. Med. Sch., Chgo., 1979, grant for predoctoral tng. in family medicine USPHS, 1987-90, 2001—. Fellow Am. Acad. Family Physicians; mem. Ohio Acad. Family Physicians (rsch. advisor 1987-93, Merit award 1988), Cleve. Acad. Family Physicians, Soc. Tchrs. Family Medicine, N.Am. Primary Care Rsch. Group, Physicians for Social Responsibility (treas. NEO chpt. 1984-2000, pres. NEO chpt. 2000—), Chinese Am. Med. Soc. Methodist. Avocations: computers, volleyball, downhill skiing. Office: 11100 Euclid Ave Cleveland OH 44106-1736

CHAPANIS, ALPHONSE, human factors engineer, ergonomist; b. Meriden, Conn., Mar. 17, 1917; s. Anicatas and Mary (Barkevich) Chapanis; m. Marion Amelia Rowe, Sept. 23, 1941 (div. 1960); children: Roger, Linda Chapanis Fox; m. Natalia Potanin, Mar. 25, 1960 (div. 1987); m. Vivian Woodward, Nov. 24, 2001. BA, U. Conn., 1937; MA, Yale U., 1942, PhD, 1943; DSc, U. Conn., 1998. Cert. Human Factors Profl. Prof. psychology The Johns Hopkins U., Balt., 1946-82; prof. emeritus, from 1999; pres. Alphonse Chapanis, PhD, P.A., Balt., 1974-99. Mem. tech. staff Bell Labs., Murray Hill, N.J., 1953-54; mem. adv. panel USAF Office Sci. Rsch., Washington, 1956-59; mem. com. on human factors NRC, Washington, 1980-85; liaison scientist Office Naval Rsch., Am. Embassy, London, 1960-61; cons. IBM, Yorktown Heights, N.Y. and Bethesda, Md., 1960-95, Loral Fed. Sys., Bethesda, 1995-96. Author: Research Techniques in Human Engineering, 1959, Man-Machine Engineering, 1965, Human Factors in Systems Engineering, 1996, The Chapanis Chronicles; 50 Years of Human Factors Research, Education, and Design, 1999; co-author: Applied Experimental Psychology, 1949; editor: Ethnic Variables in Human Factors Engineering, 1975; co-editor: Human Engineering Guide to Equipment Design, 1963; contbr. over 175 articles to profl. jours. Capt. USAAF, 1943-46. Recipient Disting. Contbn. for Applications in Psychology award APA, 1978, Outstanding Sci. Contbn. to Psychology, Md. Psychol. Assn., 1981, Outstanding Achievement in Behavioral and Social Sci. award Wash. Acad. Sci., 1997. Fellow AAAS, Soc. Engring. Psychologists (Franklin V. Taylor award 1963), Human Factors and Ergonomics Soc. (Paul W. Fitts award 1973, Pres.' Disting. Svc. award 1987), Ergonomics Soc. (hon.), Internat. Ergonomics Assn. (Outstanding Contbn. award 1982). Achievements include patent (with others) on Correlation of Seismic Signals. Home: Baltimore, Md. Died Oct. 4, 2002.

CHAPEL, ROBERT CLYDE, stage director, theater educator; b. June 25, 1945; married. BA in TV, U. Mich., 1967, MA in Theatre, 1968, PhD in Theatre, 1974. Asst. prof. dept. theatre U. Ala., 1974-75; profl. actor LA, 1975-77; dir. devel. Force Ten Prod., LA, 1977-78; v.p. prodn. Trans-Atlantic Enterprises, LA, 1978-81; actor, dir. LA, 1981-83; dir. BFA mus. theatre program U. Mich., Mich., 1983-84; coordinating dir. MFA mus. theatre program Tisch Sch. of Arts NYU, NYC, 1984—86; co-prodr. Shubert Archives Series Lyceum Theatre, NYC, 1984-86; artistic dir. Music Theatre North, Potsdam, NY, 1986; freelance dir. NYC, 1986—88; dir. mus. theatre program San Diego State U., San Diego, 1988-90; prof., chair dept. drama U. Va., Va., 1990—; mng. dir. Heritage Repertory Theatre, Charlottesville, Va., 1990-94, prodr., artistic dir., 1995—; exec. dir. Va. Film Festival, Va., 1996—2000. Chmn. pres. commn. on fine arts and performing arts U. Va., 1998-2001. Mem. SAG, AFTRA, Assn. for Theatre in Higher Edn., Nat. Assn. Schs. of Theatre, Actors Equity Assn., Soc. Stage Dirs. and Choreographers. Home: 1029 Hazel St Charlottesville VA 22902-4904 E-mail: rcc2u@virginia.edu.

CHAPEL, SALLY JO, behavioral scientist, nurse, educator, minister; b. Chgo., June 13, 1937; d. Clyde Charles and Elizabeth (Lynk) Knudson; m. James Harrington Richards, Sept. 3, 1958; children: Jill Louise, Jeffrey James; m. James Harold Moore, Aug. 5, 1978; m. Charles Bruce Baucom, Feb. 3, 1998. AA, RN, Hennipen State Coll., 1974; BA in Bus., Human Svcs., Met. State U., 1979, MA in Religion, 1983; PhD in Behavioral Sci., Nat. Christian U. Mo., 1983. Ordained min. Light of Christ Sem., 1983. Surgical technician No. Meml. Hosp., Golden Valley, Mn., 1973-74; RN U. Minn., 1974-75, Sacred Heart Med. Ctr., Spokane, Wa., 1975-76, St. Mary's Hosp., Mpls., 1976-78; internat. speaker, pres. Braintree, Mpls., 1977-94; pres. Personal Growth Found., Mpls., 1978-85; RN Golden Valley (Minn.) Health Ctr., 1980-86; psychotherapist, 1986-94; nurse U. Colo., 1994-95, Boulder (Colo.) Mental Health Ctr., 1994-96, Luth. Med. Ctr., Colo., 1995; field nurse Total Care, Charlotte, N.C., 1996; child and adolescent svcs. nurse supr. Mecklenburg County, NC, 1996—2001; nursing supr. My Brother's House, 2001—. Apprentice Sioux Medicine Woman, 1989; master practitioner neuro-linguistics, 1991, Level IV transformational kinesiology, 1992; clin. pastoral edn., Denver, 1995; victim advocate Boulder County Sheriff's Dept., 1995. Author: Patterns for Change, 1982, The Pentagonal Brain, 1984, Intuition-How to Develop and Trust It, 1984, Color Sense, 1984, Inner Space, 1986, Wakankana-Keeper of the Sun, 1989, Seasons of the Red Bear, 1991, Onion Peelings, 1992, Love Me and Let Me Go, 1995; founder, dir. Peers Optimal Health Program, 1992-94. Office: 2614 Springs Dr Charlotte NC 28226-3015

CHAPELLE, SUZANNE ELLERY GREENE, history educator; b. Phila., Sept. 21, 1942; d. John Channing and Jessie Horn (Myers) Ellery; m. Michael Thomas Greene, Sept. 15, 1972 (dec. 1973); 1 child, Jennifer; m. Francis Oberlin Chapelle, Apr. 14, 1984 (dec. 1999). BA, Harvard U., 1964; MA, Johns Hopkins U., 1966, PhD, 1970. Asst. prof. Am. history Towson State U., Balt., 1969-71; assoc. prof. Am. history Morgan State U., Balt., 1971-75, prof., 1975—. Author: Books for Pleasure, 1976, Baltimore: An Illustrated History, 1980, 2d rev. edit., 2000; sr. author: Maryland: A History of its People, 1986; revisions author: A Child's History of the World, 1994, African American Leaders of Maryland, 2000, The Maryland Adventure, 2001; mem. publs. bd. Md. Hist. Soc. Bd. dirs. Md. Interfaith Coalition for the Environment, 1997-2001, v.p., 1999-2001; bd. dirs. Md. Conservation Coun., 1999-2000, Irvine Nature Ctr., 2001—. Mem. Am. Hist. Assn., Am. Studies Assn. (mem. exec. bd. Chesapeake chpt. 1988-90), Popular Culture Assn. (bd. dirs. 1980-82), Orgn. Am. Historians, Md. Hist. Soc. (publs. com. 1998—), Mid-Atlantic Popular Culture Assn. (pres. 1977-80), Balt. County League Environ. Voters (exec. bd. 1992-96), Episcopal Diocese of Md. Com. on the Environ. (sec. 1994—), Ruxton-Riderwood Assn. (bd. govs. 1987-91), The Johns Hopkins Club, The Harvard-Radcliffe Club Md. Episcopalian. Home: 6021 Lakeview Rd Baltimore MD 21210-1033 Office: Morgan State U Hist Dept Baltimore MD 21251-0001 E-mail: schapelle@moac.morgan.edu., suechapelle@hotmail.com.

CHAPIN, JUNE ROEDIGER, education educator; b. Chgo., May 19, 1931; d. Henry and Stephanie L. (Palke) Roediger; m. Ned Chapin, June 12, 1954; children: Suzanne, Elaine. BA in Liberal Arts, U. Chgo., 1952, MA in Social Sci., 1954; EdD in Edn., Stanford U., 1963. Tchr. credentials, Calif., Ill. Tchr. Chgo. (Ill.) Pub. Schs., 1954-56, Redwood City (Calif.) Schs., 1956-60, San Francisco (Calif.) State U., 1963-65, U. Santa Clara, Calif., 1965-67; prof. edn. Coll. Notre Dame (now Notre Dame de Namur U.), Belmont, Calif., 1967—. Author, co-author twelve books. Recipient Hilda Taba award Calif. State Social Studies Coun., 1976. Mem. Am. Sociol. Assn., Am. Ednl. Rsch. Assn., Nat. Coun. for the Social Studies, Social Sci. Edn. Consortium, Phi Delta Kappa. Avocations: swimming, stamp collecting. Home: 1190 Bellair Way Menlo Park CA 94025-6611 E-mail: JuneChapin@aol.com.

CHAPIN, KENNETH LEE, middle school educator; b. Bridgeport, Conn., May 28, 1942; s. Melvin Leroy and Katherine (Hurley) C.; m. Lois Kimberley, June, 1990; children: Keith Allen, Kristine; children from previous marriage: Dawn-Marie, Kenneth Lee Jr., Dana Lee, Debra-Lynn. BS, U. Bridgeport, 1972, MA, 1974. Cert. tchr., Conn., Fla. Tchr. advanced math. and remedial reading East Elem. Sch., New Canaan, Conn., 1972-88; tchr. sci. Saxe Mid. Sch., New Canaan, 1988-89; tchr. social studies Sugarloaf Mid. Sch., Monroe County Schs., Sugarloaf Key, Fla., 1990-96; tchr. advanced geography Westwood Mid. Sch., Gainesville, Fla., 1996—. Pres., CEO Connlab Media Prodns., Inc., Trumbull, Conn., 1977-82; owner K.L. Chapin Builders, Monroe County, 1982-89; team leader Rawlings Elem. Sch., 1992-96. Mem. Breezeswept Beach Estates Civic Assn., Ramrod Key, Fla., 1989-93. With USN, 1961-63. Named Exceptional Student Edn. Mainstreaming Tchr. of Yr., Exceptional Student Edn. Parents Local of Exceptional Student Edn. Orgns. Fla., Monroe County, 1991. Mem. Nat. Coun. for Social Studies, Fla. Coun. for Social Studies (Tchr. of Yr. 1992). Republican. Mem. Lds Ch. Avocations: international travel, philately, gourmet cooking, gardening, graphic arts. Home: 12630 SE 16th Ln Morriston FL 32668-2203 Office: Westwood Mid Sch 3215 NW 15th Ave Gainesville FL 32605-5097

CHAPLEAU, MARK WILLIAM, physiologist, educator; b. Hartford City, Ind., Feb. 27, 1955; s. Craig William and Florene Helen (Gibbons) C.; children: Gina Marie, Nicole Calia, Riley Craig. BS, U. Wis., Whitewater, 1977; PhD, La. State U. Med. Ctr., 1985. Postdoctoral rsch. fellow dept. internal medicine U. Iowa, Iowa City, 1985-87, asst. rsch. scientist dept. internal medicine, 1987-89; rsch. health sci. specialist VA Med. Ctr., Iowa City, 1988—; asst. prof. cardiovasc. diseases, dept. internal medicine U. Iowa, Iowa City, 1989-97, assoc. prof. cardiovasc. diseases, dept. internal medicine, 1997, assoc. prof. dept. physiology and biophysics, 2003—. Reviewer profl. jours., 1988—. Mem. editl. bd. Hypertension, 1991-96, Primary Sensory Neuron, 1995-98, Am. Jour. Physiology, 1999-2002, Clin. Autonom. Rsch., 2001-03, Hypertension, 2001-03; contbr. articles to profl. jours. Fellow Am. Physiol. Soc. (cardiovasc. sect.), Am. Heart Assn. (coun. high blood pressure rsch., coun. on basic cardiovasc. scis.); mem. AAAS, Soc. Neurosci., Am. Fed. Med. Rsch., N.Y. Acad. Sci., Internat. Soc. Autonom. Neurosci., Am. Soc. Hypertension, Am. Autonomic Soc. (bd. dirs.). Office: U Iowa Coll Medicine E327-1 General Hosp Iowa City IA 52242 E-mail: mark-chapleau@uiowa.edu.

CHAPMAN, ALLEN FLOYD, management educator, college dean; b. Dawson, N.Mex., Apr. 14, 1930; s. Thomas and Velma (Sylva) C.; m. Ann Bunker; children: Margaret Ann, Nancy Elizabeth. BS, U. Colo., 1951; D Bus. Adminstrn., Harvard U., 1965; MBS, Hartford Grad. Ctr., 1982. Commd. ensign USN, 1951, advanced through grades to lt., resigned, 1960; rsch. assoc. Harvard U., Boston, 1961-63; dean grad. sch. bus. C.W. Post Ctr., L.I. U., Greenvale, N.Y., 1963-77; prof. mgmt. Hartford (Conn.) Grad. Ctr., 1977-96, dean Sch. of Mgmt., 1977-79, 81-84, 87-89; prof. mgmt. Sch. Mgmt. Rensselaer at Hartford, 1996—. Pres., founder various pvt. corps., N.Y., Conn., 1965—; cons. to various corps. and depts. and agys. of U.S. Govt. Patentee in field. Recipient Cert. for Patriotic Civilian Svc. U.S. Army, 1973. Home: 64 Great Hl Pond Rd Portland CT 06480-1315

CHAPMAN, DELORES, elementary education educator; b. Chgo., June 22, 1945; d. John Calvin and Julia (Frazier) C. AA, Kennedy-King Coll., 1966; BA, Northeastern Ill. U., 1968, MA, 1979. Tchr. Chgo. Bd. Edn., 1968—; v.p. Chapman's Security Systems, Inc., Country Club Hills, Ill., 1990—. Chpt. I reading tchr. Fed. Govt./Chgo. Bd. Edn., Chgo. Archdiocese, 1982-85; mem. profl. poers. adv. com. Carver Primary Sch., Chgo., 1990—, chmn. sci. fair, 1987-91; chmn. Emmanuel Christian Sch. Bd., Chgo., 1996—. Vice chmn. Emmanuel Christian Sch. Bd., Chgo., 1992-96; dir. Emmanual Bapt. Ch. Children's Choir, 1973—. Chgo. Found. for Edn. grantee, 1992. Mem. NAACP, ASCD, Nat. Sci. Tchrs. Assn., Ill. Sci. Tchrs. Assn., Northeastern Ill. U. Alumni Assn., Ill. Coun. Tchrs. Math. Avocations: playing the piano, reading. Home: 18600 Village West Dr Hazel Crest IL 60429-2462

CHAPMAN, GENEVA JOYCE, entrepreneur, educator, writer; b. Calvert, Tex., Sept. 23, 1951; d. John Henry and Deborah Betty Chapman. BA, Cameron U., 1973; MEd, Wichita State U., 1976; EdSp in early intervention edn., U. Toledo, 1997. Cert. tchr., Ohio. Tchr.'s aide Newton (Kans.) Pub. Schs., 1973-74; classroom tchr. Wichita (Kans.) Pub. Schs., 1976-83; ednl. cons. Ginn and Co., Columbus, Ohio, 1984-86; vol. coord. Friends of the Homeless Shelter, Columbus, 1986-88; family life educator Pilot Program, Toledo, 1988-89; journalist Toledo Jour., 1989-91; behavior mgmt. specialist Lucas County Bd. Mental Retardation/Devel. Disabilities, Toledo, 1991—98, spl. edn. tchr., 1998—99, habilitation specialist, 1999—; CEO TALMAR, Toledo, 1993—. Dir. Showcase Prodns. divsn. TALMAR. Newspaper columnist Chit-Chat, 1990; reporter The Sojourner's Truth Newspaper, 2002; editor The Holland Herald, 2002; author (musical): A Marvel, A Miracle, America; founder a Capella duo Two Voices Only, 1991; creator Ms. Hipps comic strip, 1984; featured playwright Chgo. Dramatist Workshops, 1993-94; writer, dir., prodr. original musical drama: Juneteenth, 1993. Founder Toledo Blackstage Theatre Co., 1990, playwright-in-residence; founder For Colored Girls Repertory Co., 1994. Recipient Community Svc. Fine Arts award Save Our Children, 1993. Mem. NEA (bldg. supr. 1974-79), NAFE, Am. Fedn. Tchrs., Nat. Assn. to Advance Fat Acceptance. Avocations: acting, writing and directing plays, singing.

CHAPMAN, JOYCE EILEEN, court reporting educator, administrator; b. Red Bluff, Calif., June 11, 1940; d. Joseph L. and Elaine C. (Potter) Cole; m. William H. Chapman, July 15, 1961; 1 child, Gregory W. AA in Bus. Edn., Shasta Coll., Redding, Calif., 1960; BA in Bus. Edn., Chico (Calif.) State Coll., 1962; MA in Edn. with distinction, Calif. State U., Chico, 1991. Cert. C.C. instr., office svcs. and related techs., banking, fin., ct. reporting, office adminstr. Calif. Tchr. bus. edn. Red Bluff (Calif.) Union H.S., 1962-63; traffic mgr. WOHP Radio, Bellefontaine, Ohio, 1963; tchr. bus. edn. Indian Lake H.S., Lewistown, Ohio, 1963-64; adminstrv. and transp. supr. Tumpane Co., Inc., Adana, Turkey, 1964-66; telephone claims rep. Allstate Ins. Co., San Antonio, Tex., 1966-70; tchr. vocat. office edn. Somerset (Tex.) H.S., 1975-80; instr. bus. edn. Shasta Coll., Redding, Calif., 1980-94; instr. office info. systems Butte Coll., Oroville, Calif., 1987-90, instr. ct. reporting, 1990—. Mem. Butte Coll. Curriculum Com. Oroville, 1990-91; facilitator ct. reporting Adv. Com., Oroville, 1990—, Butte Coll. Ct. Reporting, Oroville, 1990—; mem. Butte FLEX Com. (staff devel.), Oroville, 1993-96. Author: Introduction to Computer-Aided Transcription, 1991, (degree program) Court Reporting: A Macro Curriculum for Butte C.C. Dist., 1990, (instrnl. text) Transcription Skills, Medical Terminology, Legal Terminology, General Vocabulary. Mem. ASCD, NEA, Nat. Ct. Reporters Assn., Calif. Ct. Reporters Assn., Calif. Tchrs. Assn., North State Ct. Reporters Assn., Reporting Assn. Pub. Schs. Calif. (sec.-treas.). Republican. Avocations: travel, jewelry mfg., reading, golf. Office: Butte Coll 3536 Butte Campus Dr Oroville CA 95965-8303

CHAPMAN, KATHY, secondary school educator; b. Columbus, Ohio, Jan. 2, 1950; d. Donald Ray and Anna Frances (Tackett) Hayes; m. Gary Dean Chapman, Dec. 28, 1971; children: Jennifer, Rebecca. BA, So. Meth. U., 1972. Tchr. Tyler Street Christian Acad., Dallas, 1972—, also Holocaust edn. coord. Condr. seminars Assn. Christian Schs. Internat., Dallas, 1983-85, 2000-03. Vol. Ballet Dallas, 1987-96; mem. Dallas Jr. Fine Arts, 1980-88; adv. Nat. Jr. Honor Soc., Nat. Honor Soc. Recipient Golden Oak award, Oak Cliff C. of C., 1998; Mandel fellow, US Holocaust Meml. Mus., 2001. Methodist. Avocations: reading, writing, sewing, painting. Home: 1150 N Windomere Ave Dallas TX 75208-3505 Office: Tyler Street Christian Acad 915 W 9th St Dallas TX 75208-5026 E-mail: kathy-chapman@webtv.net.

CHAPMAN, LENORA ROSAMOND, day care provider, social service organization director; b. Bklyn., N.Y., Feb. 22, 1922; d. William Leon and Rosamond Cecile (Walker) C.; m. Thomas Leftwich, Oct. 12, 1968 (div. 1972). BA, Brooklyn Coll., 1944; MEd, NYU, 1957; cert. in mgmt. of non-profit orgns., Hofstra U. Cert. tchr., N.Y. Tchr. N.Y.C. Pub. Schs., 1944-67, Hempstead (N.Y.) Pub. Schs., 1967-79, tchr. adult basic edn., 1980-83; tchr., tutor Hofstra U., Hempstead, 1982-89; tchr. NOAH program comm. arts and math Hofstra Univ., Hempstead, 1982-84, tchr., Upward Bound Program Comm. Arts, 1984-89, tutor psychology and basic study skills New Coll., 1987-88; directress Jackson Meml. Day Care Ctr., Hempstead, 1983-84, 88-94. Tchr., tutor Hempstead Homebound Students, 1977-83, Catholic Guardian Soc.-Foster Care Children, 1979-89. Chairperson Nassau County Dept. Sr. Citizens Foster Grandparent program, 1988-94; rep. Sr. Citizens Village of Hempstead Citation Foster Grandparent Program, 1992. Mem. NAACP, ASCD, Assn. Childhood Edn. Internat., Nat. Assn. Edn. Young Children, Ctrl. Nassan Negro Bus. and Profl. Women's Clubs Inc., Phi Delta Kappa (Svc. award for membership), Kappa Delta Pi. African Methodist Episcopal Zion. Avocations: singing, dancing, sewing, operas, arts and crafts. Home and Office: 108 Glenmore Ave Hempstead NY 11550-6630

CHAPMAN, LORING, psychologist, physiology educator, neuroscientist; b. L.A., Oct. 4, 1929; s. Lee E. and Elinore E. (Gundry) Scott; m. Toy Farrar, June 14, 1954 (dec.); children: Robert, Antony, Pandora (dec.). BS, U. Nev., 1950; PhD, U. Chgo., 1955. Lic. psychologist, Oreg., N.Y., Calif. Rsch. fellow U. Chgo., 1952-54; rsch. assoc., asst. prof. Cornell U. Med. Coll., N.Y.C., 1957-61; rsch. dir. Music Rsch. Found., N.Y.C., 1958-61; assoc. prof. in residence Neuropsychiat. Inst., UCLA, 1961-65; rsch. prof. U. Oreg., Portland, 1965; br. chief NIH, Bethesda, Md., 1966-67; prof., chmn. dept. behavioral biology, joint prof. human physiology Sch. Medicine U. Calif., Davis, 1967-81, prof. psychiatry and head Divsn. of Clin. Psychology, 1981-91, prof. emeritus, from 1991, prof. neurology, 1977-81, prof. human physiology, 1977-81, asst. dean, rsch. affairs, 1972-74; vice chmn. div. of sci. basic to medicine, 1976-79. Lic. psychologist, Calif. Author: Pain and Suffering, 3 vols, 1967, Head and Brain 3 vols, 1971, (with E.A. Dunlap) The Eye, 1981; assoc. editor courtroom medicine series updates, 1965-91; contbr. sci. articles to pubis. Fogarty Sr. Internat. fellow, 1980; grantee NASA, 1969-80; grantee NIH, 1956-91; grantee Nat. Inst. Drug Abuse, 1971-80; recipient Thorton Wilson prize, 1958, Career award USPHS, 1964, Commonwealth Fund award, 1970. Mem. Am. Acad. Neurology, Am. Physiol. Soc., Am. Psychol. Assn., Royal Soc. Medicine (London)., Am. Neurol. Assn., Am. Assn. Mental Deficiency, Aerospace Med. Assn., Soc. for Neurosci. Died May 24, 2001.

CHAPMAN, MARY JOYCE, school librarian; b. Aransas Pass, Tex., Jan. 15, 1952; d. Alex and Jewel D. (Jefferson) Vincent; m. Michael O'Larry Chapman, Aug. 27, 1983; 1 child, Michael Jeorel. BS in Elem. Edn., Tex. A&I U., Kingsville, 1974; postgrad., Chgo. State U. Cert. tchr., Tex., Ill.; cert. in bilingual tng., Tex. Tchr. Woodlawn Hills Elem. Sch., San Antonio, 1974-75; bilingual music tchr. Saenz and Noonan Elem. Sch., Alice, Tex., 1975-76; substitute tchr. Chgo. Bd. Edn., 1976-77; head tchr. Emmanuel Christian Sch., Chgo., 1977-85; tchr. W. Harvey-Dixmoor Sch. Dist. # 147, Harvey, Ill., 1985-91, libr., 1991—. Sponsor Spanish Club Emmanuel Christian Sch., 1980-85, student coun., 1984-85, mem. yearbook com., 1984-85; sponsor cheerleaders M. L. King Sch., Harvey, 1989-91. Ch. musician in Chgo., Zion Hill M.B. Ch., 1977-82, Murchison Temple, 1983-88, Divine Temple of God, 1992, First Christian M.B. Ch., 1994-95; active PTA. Mem. ASCD, Alpha Kappa Alpha. Baptist. Avocations: music, bowling, volleyball. Home: 16905 Langley Ave South Holland IL 60473-3068 Office: M L King Sch 14600 Seeley Ave Dixmoor IL 60426-1052

CHAPMAN, RONALD THOMAS, musician, educator; b. Bklyn., Dec. 16, 1933; s. William Leon and Rosamond (Walker) C.; m. Joyce Elaine Chase, Dec. 1966 (dec. May 1973); adopted child, Debra Anne (dec. July 1992); m. Virginia Marie Knochenhauer, Feb. 14, 1975 (dec. July 1989); stepchildren: Suzanne, Michael. BS cum laude, CUNY, 1982; MA in Teaching, Lehman Coll., 1983; PhD in Music in Higher Edn., NYU, 1989. Cert. tchr. music, N.Y., tchr. Spanish, N.Y. Toured with Leonard dePaur Infantry Chorus, 1953-55; mem. trio The Versatones, U.S. and Can., 1955-59; vocalist, 1978—; asst. dir. men's choir Kingsborough Community Coll., 1980-82; asst. to dir. mixed chorus Lehman Coll., CUNY, 1982-83; instr. voice NYU, N.Y.C., 1986—; instr. computer music for music teachers N.Y. Inst. Tech., N.Y.C., 1987; music tchr. Hempstead Sch. Dist., 2002—. Pvt. instr. voice, piano, guitar, computerized music, music theory, sight singing and music lit., 1980—; substitute tchr. Hempstead (N.Y.) Sch. Dist., 1983-85, 2002—, mem. faculty, 1988-89, tchr. adult edn., ESL, 1993—, tchr. group piano, group voice in continuing adult edn. program, 1993—, substitute music tchr., 2002-03; instr. voice NYU, 1986—; bd. dirs. Cultural Environ, Queens, N.Y.; adjudicator N.Y. Singing Tchrs. Assn., 1995. Performed in Spain, Japan, Thailand, The Philippines, Eng., Jamaica, Can., Vietnam, P.R., Fed. Republic of Germany, Laos, Portugal and U.S. including N.Y.C., Atlanta and Miami; TV appearances on Johnny Carson Show, Arthur Godfrey Talent Scouts, Gary Moore Show, Tex and Jinx Falkenburg Show, many others; rec. artist for Columbia Records, RCA Records, Island in the Sun soundtrack; appeared in Broadway play Kwamina; appearing nightly Fox Hollow, 1978-93, Caterer/Restaurant, Woodbury, N.Y., 1978—; starred in Playboy Club and Hotel Chain, 1960-67, (movies) Rueda de Sospechosos, 1963, (revue) The Ronnie Chapman Show, 1968-69; debuted by singing and accompanying himself on piano a medley of Broadway Show Tunes and Internat. Art Songs in various langs. Carnegie Hall, 1991, 92, 93, 94, 95, 96; Cafe Trilussa, 1996-97, J. DeCarlos Restaurant, Huntington, N.Y., 1998—. Bd. dirs. Cultural Environment, Queens, N.Y., 1978—; apptd. dep. gov. Am. Biog. Inst. Rsch. Assn., 1992. Mem. Internat. Assn. for Rsch. in Singing (rsch. assoc. Found. for Rsch. Singing), Nat. Assn. Tchrs. of Singing, N.Y. Singing Tchrs. Assn., N.Y. State Sch. Music Assn. (cert. to adjucate "Voice"), Internat. Assn. Jazz Educators, Chopin Found. N.Y., Am. Assn. Choral Dirs., Music Educators Nat. Conf., Music Tchrs. Nat. Assn., Assoc. Music Tchrs. League N.Y., Internat. Platform Assn., Am. Choral Dirs. Assn., Phi Delta Kappa (v.p. programs NYU chpt. 1988-89), Pi Kappa Lambda, Kappa Delta Pi (chpt. 3d v.p. 1994—). Achievements include being awarded a design patent for invention of a portable back rest/supporter, 1993. Home and Office: 108 Glenmore Ave Hempstead NY 11550-6630 E-mail: drchapman@ronchainc.com.

CHAPMAN, RUSSELL LEONARD, botany educator; b. Bklyn., May 30, 1946; s. Russell Hood and Helen C.; m. Melanie Anne Chapman, June 28, 1969; children: Christopher John, Timothy Sean. BA, Dartmouth Coll., 1968; MS, U. Calif., Davis, 1970, PhD, 1973. NSF grad. fellow dept. botany U. Calif., Davis, 1971-73; asst. prof. dept. botany and plant biology La. State U., Baton Rouge, 1973-77, assoc. prof. dept. botany, 1977-83, prof. dept. botany, 1983—95, prof. dept. biol. sci., 1995—, assoc. dean Coll. of Arts and Scis., 1979-83, assoc. dean Coll. of Basic Scis., 1983-84, chmn. dept. botany, 1988-94, assoc. vice chancellor Office of Rsch. and Econ. Devel., 1994-96, interim exec. dir. Ctr. for Coastal, Energy and Environ. Res, 1995-96, exec. dir. Ctr. for Coastal, Energy and Environ. Resources, 1996-2001, dean Sch. of the Coast and Environment, 2001—, adj. prof. dept. oceanography and coastal scis. Mem. editl. bd.: Jour. of Phycology, Algologia, Molecular Phylogenetics and Evolution; assoc. editor Am. Jour. of Botany, 1995—; author book chpts. in field; contbr. articles to profl. jours. Bd. dirs. Baton Rouge Earth Day, Inc., 1990-92; mem. Found. for Hist. La., Baton Rouge, 1973—; trustee Johnston Sci. Found., 2000- (bd.dirs. 2001-). Recipient Outstanding Undergrad. Teaching award Amoco Found., Inc., 1978, Disting. Faculty award La. State U. Alumni Fedn., Baton Rouge, 1981; Paul Harris fellow, 2000. Fellow Linnean Soc. London; mem. Phycol. Soc. Am. (sec., v.p., pres. 1985-90, bd. trustees 1994—), Botanical Soc. Am. (chmn. phycol. sect. 1983-85, fin. adv. com. 2000—), British Phycol. Soc., Internat. Phycol. Soc. (exec. coun. 2001—), Internat. Soc. for Evolutionary Protistology, Willie Hennig Soc., La. Soc. Electron Microscopy (treas., pres. 1976-80), Environ. Rsch. Consortium La. (bd. trustees 1998—, pres. 1999-2000, sec.-treas. 2000-01), Phi Kappa Phi, Sigma Xi, Omicron Delta Kappa. Episcopalian. Home: 6920 Bayou Paul Rd Saint Gabriel LA 70776-5602 Office: La State U Sch Coast & Environ 1002 R Energy Coast and Environ Bldg Baton Rouge LA 70803-4110 E-mail: chapman@lsu.edu.

CHAPPELL, MICHELLE R. elementary education educator; b. Jackson Heights, N.Y., Oct. 6, 1941; d. Ogden Morris and Lucille M. (Gendron) Randel; m. William Richard, Aug. 10, 1963 (div.); children: Jeffrey David, Eric Michael; m. Paul William Chappell, July 8, 1978 (dec.). AA, Green Mountain Jr. Coll., 1961; BS, Syracuse U., 1963. Cert. tchr., Ohio, N.Y. Tchr. Portsmouth (R.I.) Pub. Schs., 1963-64, Quonset Elem. Sch., North Kingstown, R.I., 1964-67, Maisie Quinn Elem. Sch., West Warwick, R.I., 1968-70, Gahanna (Ohio) Middle Sch. West, 1975-78, 79—, Hannah Penn Middle Sch., York, Pa., 1979. Ch. coun. Reformation Luth. Ch., Columbus, Ohio, 1989—. Named Jenning scholar Gahanna Jefferson Sch. and Martha Holden Jennings Found., 1989-90. Mem. NEA, Met. Ednl. Coun. Lutheran. Avocations: travel, camping, needlework, crafts. Office: Gahanna Middle Sch W 350 N Stygler Rd Gahanna OH 43230-2438

CHAPPELL, MILES LINWOOD, JR., art history educator; b. Norfolk, Va., June 6, 1939; s. Miles Linwood Sr. and Melrose Clarice (Debnam) C.; m. Marcial Cassada, July 23, 1966; children: Ashley, Oliver, Picot. BS in Chemistry, Coll. William and Mary, 1960; PhD in Art History, U. N.C., 1971. Prof. art history dept. art and art history Coll. William and Mary, Williamsburg, Va., 1971—; chair dept. Chancellor prof. art history Coll. William and Mary, 1987; artistic adv. bd. Interlochen Ctr. for Arts. Author: Cristofano Allori, 1984, Lodovico Cigoli, Disegni, 1992, The Fine Art of Drawing, 1993; co-author: Disegni dei Toscani, 1979, Lodovico Cigoli, tra manierismo e barocco, 1992, Renascence of the Florentine Baroque in "Dialoghi di storia dell'arte", 1998, The Artistic Education of Maria de'MEdici, 2003; formulator and co-author: Form, Function and Finesse: Drawings from the Herman Found., 1983; asst. editor: Studies in Iconography, 1978-80; adv. editor: Eighteenth-Century Life, 1980-84, 85—; contbr. articles on Renaissance, Baroque and Am. art to profl. jours. Mem. internat. survey of Jewish monuments, U. Ill., 1978. Harvard U. Ctr. for Italian Renaissance Studies fellow, Florence, 1980; Cité Internat. des Arts, 1995; recipient numerous rsch. grants. Mem. Kunsthistorisches Institut Florence, Phi Beta Kappa (Alpha chpt. award for scholarship 1987, v.p. 1992-93). Avocations: drawing, painting, music. Home: 139 Ridings Cv Williamsburg VA 23185-3903 Office: Coll William & Mary Dept Art History Williamsburg VA 23187 E-mail: mlchap@wm.edu.

CHAPPELL, SHIRLEY ANN, elementary school educator; b. Montgomery, Ala., June 23, 1951; d. Abe and Laura (Brown) Ch. AA, Springfield (Mass.) Tech. C..C., 1974, Holyoke (Mass.) C.C., 1987; BA magna cum laude, Am. Internat. Coll., 1989; cert., Nat. Acad. for Paralegal Studies, 1990. Clerical temp. mortgage dept. S/S Bank, Springfield, 1985; telemarketer ARC, Springfield, 1988-89; substitute tchr. Springfield Pub. Schs., 1992—. Contbr. articles to newspapers. Vol. Ted Kennedy Senate Campaign, Springfield, 1970, Youth Voters Participation, Springfield, 1971; organizer Crime Watch Group Seymour Ave., Springfield, 1990; vol. English tutor Holyoke Community Coll., 1987. Polit. scholar Am. Internat. Coll., Springfield, 1989; recipient Silver Poet award World Poetry-Jubilee, Orlando, Fla., 1986. Mem. Am. Internat. Coll. Alumni Assn. (com. mem. 1989-90, 93-94). Democrat. Baptist. Avocations: reading, writing, travel, newswatching, cooking. Home: 46 Garvey Dr Springfield MA 01109-1513

CHARALAMBOUS, SUSAN F. nursing educator, consultant; d. Richard G. and Helene (Cahn) Strassburger; m. C. Harry Charalambous, Jan. 3, 1999. ASN, Miami Dade C.C., 1970; BS in Edn., Fla. Internat. U., 1972, MS in Edn., 1982, BSN, 1984; MSN, Barry U., 1992; EdD, Nova-Southeastern U., 1996. RN, Fla. Staff nurse Mt. Sinai Med. Ctr., Miami Beach, Fla., 1970—, cardiovasc. perfusionist, 1972—; staff nurse surgery Jackson Meml. Hosp., Miami, 1972-75; nursing educator, clin. nurse specialist Meml. Hosp., Hollywood, Fla., 1980-85; nursing educator CNS-surgery Broward Gen. Med. Ctr., Ft. Lauderdale, Fla., 1985-89; asst. prof. nursing Barry U., Miami Shores, Fla., 1989-99; assoc. prof. nursing Fla. Internat. U., N. Miami, 1999—. Perioperative nursing, exec. dir., sr. nursing educator, cons. Ednl. Design Sys., Inc., Hollywood, 1985—; assoc prof Miami Dade C.C. Sch. Nursing, 2001—. Author: Perioperative Nursing--Principles and Practice, 1993, 2d edit., 1997, Comprehensive Review for Perioperative Nursing, 1995. Mem. ANA (cert. med.-surg. nurse), AACN (cert.), Assn. Oper. Perioperative Reg. Nurses, Fla. Coun. Oper. Rm. Nurses, Pi Kappa Alpha, Sigma Theta Tau (Lamda Chi). Avocations: classical music, opera, horses.

CHARAP, STANLEY HARVEY, electrical engineering educator; b. N.Y.C., Apr. 21, 1932; s. William and Esther Charap; m. Marilyn Novick, Aug. 7, 1955; children: Joshua David, Lawrence Gordon. BS in Physics, Bklyn. Coll., 1953; PhD in Physics, Rutgers U., 1959. Mem. rsch. staff IBM T.J. Watson Rsch. Ctr., Yorktown Heights, N.Y., 1958-64; rsch. scientist Rsch. div. Am.-Standard Inc., Piscataway, N.J., 1964, supr. solid state physics, 1965-66, mgr. physics and electronics, 1966-68; assoc. prof. elec. and computer engrng. Carnegie Mellon U., Pitts., 1968-71, prof., 1971-96; prof. emeritus, 1997—; assoc. head dept. Carnegie Mellon U., Pitts., 1980-85, acting head dept., 1981-82, vice chmn. faculty senate, 1972-73, chmn. faculty senate, 1986-87, assoc. dir. Data Storage Systems Ctr., 1990-96. Cons. Westinghouse Rsch. Ctr., Pitts., 1969-84; mem. tech. staff Bell Labs., Whippany, N.J., summer 1973; sr. vis. fellow U. Wales, Cardiff, spring 1976; vis. scientist Control Data Corp., Mpls., summer 1987. Editor: Physics of Magnetism, 1964; contbr. to Magnetism & Metallurgy, 1969; contbr. over 60 tech. articles to profl. jours. V.p. Sch. Advanced Jewish Studies, Pitts., 1989-91. Recipient Tech. Achievement award Nat. Storage Industry Consortium, 1998. Fellow IEEE (fellow com. 1997-99, Millennium medal 2000); mem. IEEE Magnetics Soc. (sec.-treas. 1987-88, v.p. 1989-90, pres. 1991-92, past pres. 1993-94, editor-in-chief IEEE Trans. on Magnetics 1982-86, editl. bd. IEEE Press 1989-91, IEEE Tech. activities bd., liaison coun. 1993, gen. chmn. Joint INTERMAG-MMM conf. 1994, Disting. Lectr. 1996, Achievement award 1998), Am. Inst. Physics, Conf. on Magnetism and Magnetic Materials (treas. 1981-83, gen. chmn. 1986). Office: Carnegie Mellon U Dept Elec-Computer Engring 5000 Forbes Ave Pittsburgh PA 15213-3890 E-mail: s.charap@ieee.org.

CHARATZ, PEARL EILEEN, educational administrator; b. Bklyn., Dec. 29, 1951; d. Sidney L. and Sylvia G. (Okun) Katz; m. Philip Mitchell Charatz, Oct. 27, 1973; children: Seth Stuart, Heather Joy. BA, Fairleigh Dickinson U., 1972; MA, Kean Coll., 1977. Cert. tchr., supr., N.J. Tchr. Harbor Sch., Red Bank, N.J., 1972-75, Matawan (N.J.) Bd. Edn., 1975-79, Coastal Learning Ctr., Morganville, N.J., 1979-82, Keyport (N.J.) High Sch., 1982-85; learning disabilities tchr./cons. Monmouth County Ednl. Svcs. Commn., Eatontown, N.J., 1985-86; learning cons. Tinton Falls (N.J.) Bd. Edn., 1986; student assistance specialist East Brunswick (N.J.) Bd. Edn., 1986—. Dir. Study Skills Clinic, Holmdel, N.J., 1991—; tchr. Congregation B'nai Israel Hebrew High Sch., Rumson, N.J., 1989—. Mem. Assn. Student Assistance Profls., N.J. Assn. Learning Cons. Jewish. Avocations: skiing, dancing, reading, music. Home: 4 Woodhollow Dr Holmdel NJ 07733-1663 Office: East Bruswick Bd Edn Hammarskjold Sch Rues Ln East Brunswick NJ 08816

CHARENDOFF, MARK STUART, educator; b. Toronto, Aug. 21, 1963; s. Nathan and Lillian (Zaid) C.; m. Susan Frances Cohen, Sept. 7, 1992. B Hebrew Letters, Darche Noam Coll., Jerusalem, 1985. Ordained rabbi, 1986. Asst. regional dir. B'nai B'rith Youth Orgn., Toronto, 1986—88, cons., 1994—95; dir. Judaic Cultural Devel. Jewish Cmty. Ctr. Toronto, 1988—94; program cons. Charles R. Bronfman Found., Montreal, Canada, 1992—95; dir. Jewish Ednl. Svcs. Jewish Cmty. Ctrs. Assn. N.Am., N.Y.C., 1994—98; v.p. Andrea and Charles Bronfman Philanthropies, N.Y.C., 1998—2002; pres. Jewish Funders Network, N.Y.C., 2002—. Mem. adv. bd. Washington Inst. for Jewish Leadership and Values, 1996—, Nat. Ctr. for Hebrew Lang., 1997—; chmn. Forum Jewish Educators, N.Y.C., 1990-93. Editor: Jewish Education and the Jewish Community Center, 1974. Bd. dirs. Coalition for Advancement Jewish Education, 1997—, Edah, 1999—. Jewish. Avocations: sailing, biking, travel. Office: Jewish Funders Network 300 7th Ave 18th Fl New York NY 10001

CHAREST, GABRIELLE MARYA, educational administrator; b. Westfield, Mass., Jan. 3, 1943; m. Leonard Kenneth Charest, Aug. 21, 1965 (div.); children: Leonard Kenneth Jr., Douglas John. BA, St. Joseph Coll., West Hartford, Conn., 1964; MEd, Westfield State Coll., 1978; EdD, U. Mass., 1996. Cert. tchr., adminstr., Mass., Vt., N.H., Conn., Calif. Tchr. French, West Springfield (Mass.) Jr. H.S., 1964-65, Agawam (Mass.) Jr. H.S., 1967-69; tchr. French, Latin, Spanish, and English Agawam H.S., 1973-81, chmn. dept. fgn. langs., 1981, asst. prin., 1981-95; prin. Springfield (Vt.) H.S., 1996—99, Plainfield (Conn.) Ctrl. Sch., 1999—2001; interim prin. Haddam-Killingworth H.S., Higganum, Conn., 2001—02; mgr. profl. devel. San Jose (Calif.) Unified Sch. Dist., 2002—. Adj. faculty Westfield State Coll., 1986-96; rsch. asst. U. Mass., Amherst, 1991-92; workshop presenter on mentoring, 1990; chmn. steering com. for re-evaluation by New England Assn. Schs. and Colls., 1986-88; presenter profl. devel. workshops Agawam Pub. Schs., 1992-93, restructuring sys. analysis, 1994, at Huntington, Mass. for Gateway Regional Schs., 1995, Belchertown (Mass.) Schs., 1996. Sec. West Springfield Conservation Commn., 1971-73; active Friends West Springfield, Libr., 1990-96, Springfield Libr. and Mus., 1994-96, Friends of the Springfield Town Libr., 1996-99. Grantee New Eng. Assn. Schs. and Colls., 1991-92, Three River Valley (Vt.) Sch. to Work, 1997. Mem.: ASCD, Nat. Staff Devel. Coun., Calif. ASCD, Phi Delta Kappa. Avocations: herb gardening, travel, genealogical research, interior decorating, sewing. Home: 1136 Francisco Ave Apt 3 San Jose CA 95126-1303 E-mail: gabri_charest@yahoo.com.

CHARLES, BLANCHE, retired elementary education educator; b. Spartanburg, S.C., Aug. 7, 1912; d. Franklin Grady and Alice Floride (Hatchette) C. BA, Humboldt State U., 1934. Tchr. Mt. Signal and El Centro schs., 1934—48, Calexico (Calif.) Unified Sch. Dist., 1958-94; libr. Calexico Pub. Lib., 1948—59; ret., 1994. Elem. sch. named in her honor, 1987. Mem. NEA, ACT, Calif. Tchrs. Assn., DAR, Nat. Soc. Daus. of Confederacy, Delta Kappa Gamma. Avocations: gardening, reading. Home: 37133 Hwy 94 Space 3 Boulevard CA 91905-9524

CHARLES, JOSEPH GLENN, middle school educator; b. Laredo, Tex., Dec. 13, 1957; s. Juan Aguillion and Alicia (Maldonado) Charles. BS in Biology, U. Tex., San Antonio, 1981, postgrad., 1986, U. Tex., 1982-83. Cert. secondary sci. tchr., Tex. Head dept. Meml. Mid. Sch., Laredo, Tex., 1983-85, 86-87; tchr. St. Augustine Sch., Laredo, 1987-89; head dept. Dr. J.G. Cigarroa Mid. Sch., Laredo, 1989—, master tchr., 1994—, mem. site base decision coun., 1993—, chair curriculum, 1999—. Sci. fair coord. Laredo Ind. Sch. Dist., 1990—, textbook adoption chair, 7th grade sci., 2001. CCD tchr., co-dir. local Roman Cath. Ch., 1983-86. Mem. Sci. Tchr. Assn. Tex., Tex. State Tchr. Assn., Nat. Sci. Tchr. Assn., Tex. Classroom Tchrs. Assn. Avocations: gardening, walking. Home: 1719 Gustavus St Laredo TX 78043-2332 Office: Laredo Ind Sch Dist Dr J G Cigarroa Mid Sch 2600 Palo Blanco St Laredo TX 78046-8219 E-mail: jcharles@laredo.k12.tx.us.

CHARLESWORTH, ARTHUR THOMAS, mathematics and computer science educator; b. Gainesville, Fla., Nov. 8, 1944; s. Arthur Riggs and Martha Jean (Hamilton) C.; m. Josephine Ann Owenby, Sept. 10, 1966; 1 child, Jonathan David. BS in Math., Stetson U., 1966; AM in Math., Duke U., 1968, PhD in Math., 1974; MS in Computer Sci., U. Va., 1983. Trajectory analysis engr. Apollo support dept. GE, Daytona Bch., Fla., 1966-67; instr. Jacksonville (Fla.) U., 1968-69, Randolph-Macon Coll., Ashland, Va., 1969-71; asst. prof. Queens Coll., Charlotte, N.C., 1974-76, U. Richmond, Va., 1976-82, assoc. prof., 1982-89, prof., 1989—. Sec. astronomy, math., physics sect. Va. Acad. Sci., 1977-78, chmn., 1978-79; treas. Md., D.C., Va. sect. Math. Assn. Am., 1980-82. Contbr. articles to profl. jours. Chmn. Trinity Meth. Comsn. on Missions, Richmond, 1981. Research grantee NASA Langley Rsch. Ctr., Hampton, Va., 1987, 88, 89, 90, 91, 92. Mem. IEEE, Assn. Computing Machinery, Omicron Delta Kappa, Sigma Xi. Avocations: hiking, rock collecting. Office: U Richmond Dept Math/Computer Sci Richmond VA 23173

CHARLESWORTH, MARION HOYEN, secondary education educator; b. Lowell, Mass.; d. Francis Emmanuel and Elizabeth (Donabed) Hoyen; A.A. in Acctg. summa cum laude, Worcester Jr. Coll., 1950; B.A. in English cum laude, Worcester State Coll., 1976; m. Donald W. Charlesworth, Sept. 7, 1952 (dec. May 24, 1974); 1 son, Donald W. Jr. Office mgr. Worcester Shoe Co. (Mass.), 1945-46; asst. fin. sec. YMCA Worcester, 1946-56;

substitute tchr. Haverhill High Sch. (Mass.), 1965—, tchr. acctg., evening div. Haverhill High Sch., 1979-85, tchr. English evening divsn., 1985-89. Vol. clk. Haverhill Pub. Library Fund Raising, 1966-69, vol. pub. libr. gift shop, 1989-91; mem. Haverhill Skating Rink Com., 1969-70; vol. Merrimack Wastewater Mgmt. Study, U.S.C.E., Commonwealth of Mass. and Merrimack Valley Planning Commn. in cooperating with EPA, 1973-75; vol. ARC Home Nursing, 1942; Haverhill Recycling, 1971-75, Haverhill Cmty. meals, 1983—; vol. hostess USO, 1941-52; fin. sec. 1st Presbyterian Ch., Worcester, 1942-46; sec. Planetary Minds, Worcester YWCA, 1951, treas. Bus. and Profl. Girls, 1951; deacon First Congregational Ch., Haverhill, 1967-70, 74-75, 81-83, mem. outreach com., 1978-81, auditor women's guild, 1987—; bd. dirs. Steven-Bennett Home, Inc., Haverhill, 1977—, Winnekenni Found., Inc., 1977—, sec. 1991-93; vol. USD Ctr., Worcester, Mass., WWII; bd. dirs. Children's Aid and Family Soc. of Haverhill, 1987-97, clk. of bd., 1992-93; mem. Hale Hosp. Aux., Haverhill, 1971—, Haverhill Growth Alliance, 1979-82, Haverhill Neighborhood Coalition, 1979-82, Friends of Haverhill Pub. Libr., 1979—, vol., 1989-91, Merrimack River Watershed Council, 1980—, Northeast Cultural Arts Ctr., 1982-93; charter mem. Statue of Liberty Ellis Island Found., 1984—; mem. Widowed Life Line Program Affiliate Children's Aid and Family Soc., 1974-88, vol., 1983-88. Mem. NAM, Mature Students Orgn. (chmn. parliamentary procedure 1974), Haverhill Parent Tchr. Assns. (exec. bd. 1964-71); pres. Caleb Dustin Hunking PTA, 1968-71; Mass. Congress PTA, Worcester State Alumni Assn., Tau Lambda Omega (sec. 1950-52). Clubs: Haverhill Garden (pres. 1973-75, chmn. pub. relations 1972-84, dir. 1975-82), Women's City of Haverhill (2d v.p. 1971-73, life mem. 1985, pres. 1997-99); Assyrian-Am. Ind. (treas. 1948-72) (Worcester). Mass. reporter The Assyrian Star, 1963-64. Recipient Cert. appreciation Haverhill Kiwanis Club, 1986, Citation Commonwealth of Mass. State Senate, 1988. Instrumental while club pres. in numerous awards being bestowed on Haverhill Garden Club, including regional, state and nat. awards, 1979, also nat. publicity award from Nat. Council of State Garden Clubs and Sperry and Hutchinson Co., 1979, 80. Home: 35 Columbia Park Haverhill MA 01830-3303

CHARLETON, MARGARET ANN, child care administrator, consultant; b. Orange, Calif., Aug. 3, 1947; d. Arthur Mitchell and Isabelle Margaret (Esser) C.; (div. Sept. 1985). AA in Liberal Arts, Orange Coast Coll., 1968; BA in Psychology, Chapman U., 1984. Head tchr. Presbyn. Ch. of the Master, Mission Viejo, Calif., 1977-81; child care program adminstr. Crystal Stairs, Inc., L.A., 1981—2001. Mem. adv. bd. Children's Home Soc., Santa Ana, Calif., 1982-83; cons. Calif. Sch. Age Consortium, Costa Mesa, 1987, Calif. State Dept. of Edn., 1988; trainer preschool edn. program Sesame Street PBS, 1994-96; lectr. in field; presenter Western Regional Child Care Food Program Conf., San Francisco, 1997, Save the Children Conf., Atlanta, Ga., 1998, 10th Ann. Child Care Food Program Sponsor's Conf., 2001. Contbr. articles to profl. jours. Mem. South Orange County Community Svc., Mission Viejo, 1983—; liaison Family Svcs.-Marine Base, El Toro, Calif., 1989—; mem. adv. bd. Dept. Social Svc., 1997—. Recipient Plaque of Recognition, Vietnamese Community of Orange County, 1984. Mem. NAFE. Roman Catholic. Avocations: sailing, skiing, traveling, wine. Office: Child Nutrition Program So Calif 7777 Alvarado Rd Ste 700 La Mesa CA 91941

CHARLEY, MARILYN ROSE, special education educator; b. Shiprock, N.Mex., Nov. 1, 1956; d. Phillip and Irene Tsosie (Begay) C. AA, Bacone Jr. Coll., Muskogee, Okla., 1977; BSE, Eastern N.Mex. U., 1982; MA in Edn., No. Ariz. U., 1988. Tchr. spl. edn. and resource Cen. Consol. Sch., Shiprock. Recipient Am. Legion award, 1977, Presdl. award 1977. Mem. NEA, Phi Theta Kappa. Office: Generations Personal Care 817 N Tucker Ave Farmington NM 87401

CHARLSON, ROBERT JAY, atmospheric sciences educator, scientist; b. San Jose, Calif., Sept. 30, 1936; s. Rolland Walter and Harriet Adele (Stucky) C.; m. Patricia Elaine Allison, Mar. 16, 1964; children: Daniel Owen, Amanda Marcella. BS in Chemistry, Stanford U., 1958, MS in Chemistry, 1959; PhD in Atmospheric Scis., U. Wash., 1964; postgrad. (Fulbright scholar), London U., 1964-65; PhD (hon.), Stockholm U., 1993. Rsch. engr. Boeing Co., Seattle, 1959-62; rsch. asst. prof. dept. civil engring. U. Wash., Seattle, 1965-69, assoc. prof. atmospheric chemistry, 1969-71, assoc. prof. civil engring. and geophysics, 1971-74, prof. atmospheric chemistry in civil engring. geophysics and environ. studies, 1974-94, prof. atmospheric scis., 1985-98, adj. prof. chemistry, 1985-96, prof., 1996-98, prof. emeritus, 1998—; King Carl XVI Gustaf prof. environ. sci. Sweden, 1999-2000. Author: (with S.S. Butcher) An Introduction to Air Chemistry, 1972; assoc. editor: Jour. Applied Meteorology, 1971-73; co-editor: Global Biogeochemical Cycles, 1992; Earth System Science: From Biogeochemical Cycles to Global Change, 2000; mem. editorial bd. Jour. Boundary Layer Meteorology, 1971-86, Water, Air and Soil Pollution, 1971-85; contbr. articles on atmosphere chemistry to profl. jours.; patentee in field. Co-recipient Gerbier-Mumm award World Meteorol. Orgn., 1988; grantee USPHS, EPA, NSF, NASA, NOAA. Fellow Am. Meteorol. Soc., Am. Geophys. Union; mem. AAAS, Am. Chem. Soc., Sigma Xi, Phi Lambda Upson (hon.). Office: U Wash Dept Atmospheric Scis PO Box 351640 Seattle WA 98195-0001

CHARLTON, SHIRLEY MARIE, educational consultant; b. Nashville, Nov. 20, 1934; d. Ottis Ruby and Irene Lenoir (Cabler) C.; children: David Matthew Christian Sironen, Charlton Gwynn Cabler Sironen. BS, George Peabody Coll. Tchrs., 1954; MA in Ednl. Adminstrn. and Supervision, U. Tenn., Chattanooga, 1970. Cert. supr., Tenn. Classroom tchr. Albany (Ga.) Pub. Schs., 1954-55, 56-57, Orlando (Fla.) Pub. Schs., 1960-61, Grand Forks (N.D.) Pub. Schs., 1962-65; TV and resource tchr. Chattanooga Publ Schs., 1965-67, supr., 1967-97; cons., 1997-99. Mem. NEA, Tenn. Edn. Assn., Chattanooga Edn. Assn. (charter mem. negotiating team 1979-81), Alpha Delta Kappa (v.p. 1981-83). Episcopalian. Avocations: history, genealogy, acting, art, music.

CHARNER, IVAN, educational sociologist; b. NYC, May 11, 1949; s. Hilliard Daniel and Geraldine (Resnick) C.; m. Kathleen Hammond, May 7, 1971; children: Megin Hammond, Sam Hammond. BA, Harpur Coll., 1970; MA, Ont. Inst. for Studies in Edn., 1972. Rsch. asst. Ont. Inst. for Studies in Edn., 1970-73; rsch. assoc. Nat. Inst. Edn., Washington, 1973-78; sr. rsch. assoc. Nat. Inst. Work and Learning, Washington, 1978-79, dir. rsch., 1979-90, dir., 1990—; sr. program officer Acad. for Ednl. Devel., Washington, 1988-93, v.p., 1993—. Cons. U.S. Dept. Edn., Md. State Dept. Edn., Rockwell Internat., 1978, Nat. Alliance Bus., 1985, Tchrs. Coll. Columbia U., 1985, Washington Hosp. Ctr., Va. C.C., ASTO, 1986, Control Data Corp., Ky. Fried Chicken Corp., Va. Tech. U., Office Ednl. Rsch. and Improvement, Nat. Ctr. Rsch. in Vocat. Edn., Control Data Corp., 1987, Jefferson County (Ky.) Schs., Anchorage Schs., 1991, Bell South Found., 1994, Mich. Sch.-to-Work Office, 1994, Jobs for the Future, 1995, Nat. Ctr. for Edn. Stats., 1995, Nat. Ctr. for Rsch. in Vocat. Edn., 1996, Iowa Sch.-to-Work Office, 1996-98, Capital Region Workforce Devel. Bd., 1999, N.J. Dept. Edn., 1999-2000. Nat. Youth Employment Coalition, 1998-2000, UAW-GM Ctr. for Human Resources, 1998-2000, Office of Vocat. and Adult Edn., 2002-03, Carnegie Corp. of N.Y., 2002—, Ford Found., 2002—, Annenberg Found., 2002—. Author: An Untapped Resource: Negotiated Tuition Aid in the Private Sector, 1978, Lifelong Learning and the World of Work, 1979, Patterns of Adult Participation in Learning Activities, 1980, Investing in Your Employees Future, 1980, Union Subsidies to Workers for Higher Education, 1980, Greater Resources and Opportunities for Working Women, 1981, Motivating Adult Learning Through Planned Change, 1981, Employment Based Tuition Assistance, 1982, Supporting Educational Opportunities for Workers, 1982, Fast Food Jobs, 1984, HRD Tomorrow, 1984, Different Strokes for Different Folks: Access and Barriers to Adult Education and Training, 1984, Postsecondary Responses to a Changing Economy, 1985, Translating Experiences into a New Credential for Youth Transitions, 1986, Variations by Theme: The Life Transitions of Clerical Workers, 1986, Higher Education Partnerships: Practices, Policies and Problems, 1986, The Career Passport: Student Workbook and Leader's Guide, 1987, The Future of Work in America: Workers, the Workplace and Technological Literacy, 1987, Youth and Work: What We Know, What We Don't Know, What We Need to Know, 1987, Human Resources Implications of an Aging Workplace, 1987, Responding to the Educational Needs of Today's Workplace, 1987, Union Retirees: Enriching Their Lives Enhancing Their Contribution, 1988, The Development of Work Attitudes Among Adolescents, 1988, Employability Credentials: A Key to Successful Youth Transition to Work, 1988, Motivation for Educational Participation by Retirees: The Expressive Instrumental Continuum Revisited, 1989, Improving Workplace Literacy Through Community Collaboration: Workbook and Leader's Guide, 1989, Options and Opportunities: Overcoming Barriers to Worklife Education and Training, 1989, Premature Retirement: Does a Positive Attitude Ensure a Successful Transition?, 1989, Responding to Needs: An Assessment of the NCCE Parent HELPLINE and ACCESS Clearing House, 1990, Increasing Educational Attainments: An Evaluation of the Hispanic Student Success Program, 1990, Worker Awareness and Participation in Education and Training Programs, 1991, Youth Opportunities Unlimited Evaluation, 1991, Coming to the Edge: To Fly or to Fall, 1991, Challenging Our Communities: Purposeful Action for Youth Transition, 1993, Key Organizational Issues in Intergenerational Mentoring, 1993, The Benefits of Mentoring: Outcomes for Mentors and Youths, 1994, Minor Laws of Major Importance: A Guide to Federal and State Child Labor Laws, 1994, Everbody's Business Nobody's Responsibility: National School to Work Transition Initiatives with Implications for Educational Restructuring, 1994, School-to-Work Transition: A Mosaic in Search of A System, 1994, Reforms of the School-to-Work Transition: Findings, Implications and Challenges, 1995, School-to-Work Opportunities: Prospects and Challenges, 1996, School-to-Work Opportunities Through the Lens of Youth Development, 1996, Learning from Experience: A Cross Case Comparison of School-to-Work Transition Reform Initiatives, 1996, Zen and the Art of School-to-Work Maintenance, 1996, Everything You Always Wanted to Know About School-to-Work But Didn't Know Who to Ask: The School-to-Work Learning Center, 1996, Building School-to-Career Systems: Lessons Learned, 1997, Using the Twelve Building Blocks of a School-to-Work System, 1997, "We Need To Be In It For All 9 Innings", Lessons from Employer Participation in School-to-Careers in Colorado, 1998, New Bottle or New Wine: Unique Policy Features of the School-to-Work Opportunity Act, 1998, The Site Visit as Technical Assistance: A User's Guide, 1998, System Building in School-to-Work, 1998, School-to-Work: How Do We Make It Last, 1999, Measuring School-to-Career Effectiveness, 1999, Job Corps and the Workforce Investment Act: Implications for Performance Assessment, 1999, Applying National Data to Evaluation and Communication Issues, 1999, Integrated Curriculum: Bridging the Academic-Vocational Divide, 2001, School-to-Work Outcomes: A Synthesis of National School-to-Work Studies, 200, others; editor: Education and Work in Rural America: The Social Context of Early Career Decisions and Achievement, 1978. Grantee HEW, 1978-80, U.S. Dept. Labor, 1979, 86, 95-99, Women's Ednl. Equity Act, 1979—, U.S. Dept. Edn., 1981-82, 84-86, 91—, 94-97, 99-2000, 2002—, U.S. Dept. Def., 1983-86, U.S. Dept. Labor, 1985-87, Corp. for Nat. Svc., 1995-96, PEW Charitable Trusts, 1994-96, UAW-GM Ctr. for Human Resources, 1992-2000, Nat. Inst. for Literacy, 1993-99, Nat. Youth Employment Coalition, 1998-2000, Carnegie Corp. N.Y., 2002—, Ford Found., 2002—, Annenberg Found., 2002—; Ont. Inst. for Studies in Edn. fellow, 1972. Mem. ASTD, Am. Ednl. Rsch. Assn., Am. Sociol. Assn. Home: 8406 Cedar St Silver Spring MD 20910-5537 Office: 1825 Connecticut Ave NW Washington DC 20009-5708 E-mail: icharner@aed.org.

CHARNEY, CAROLYN JEAN, school administrator, elementary education educator; b. Ft. Collins, Colo., Nov. 6, 1965; d. F. J. and Patricia (Pearson) C. BS, Tex. A&M, 1987; MEd, U. Tex., 1992. Cert. tchr., Tex. Tchr. elem. edn. Austin (Tex.) Ind. Sch. Dist., 1987-94, asst. prin., 1992-94, Whitestone Elem. Sch., Leander, Tex., 1994—. Author: Camp Takatoka Ropes Manual. Mem. Kappa Delta Phi, Phi Delta Kappa, Phi Kappa Phi. Avocations: outdoor sports, music.

CHARNEY, JONATHAN ISA, law educator, lawyer; b. NYC, Oct. 29, 1943; s. Wolfe R. and Rita Dorothy (Greenfield) Charney; m. Sharon Renee Lehman, June 12, 1966; children: Tamar, Adam, Noah. BA, NYU, 1965; JD, U. Wis., 1968. Bar: Wis. 1968, Tenn 1974, NY 1980, US Supreme Ct. 1971. Atty., Land and Natural Resources div. Dept. Justice, Washington, 1968—71; atty., chief marine resources sect., 1972; asst. prof. law Vanderbilt U., Nashville, 1972—75; assoc. prof., 1978—. Cons. in field; vis. prof. U. Pa., 1989. Contbr. articles profl. jour. Mem.: Order of Coif, Internat. Boundary Rsch. Unit (mem. bd. adv. 1993—), Assn. Am. Law Sch. (chmn. internat. law sect. 1985), Am. Jour. Internat. Law (bd. editors 1986—, editor in chief 1998—), Am. Soc. Internat. Law (exec. council 1982—85, v.p. 1994—96), Am. Law Inst., Coun. Fgn. Rels., Am. Br. Internat. Law Assn. (chair com. on formation of internat. law 1986—90), ABA (chair internat. law sect. internat. ct. com. 1988—89, dep. vice chair sect. on internat. law, pub. internat. law div. 1988—90), Wis. Law Rev. (bd. editors 1966—68), Ocean Develop. and Internat. Law (bd. editors 1985—, editor in chief 1998—), Marine Policy Ctr. (sr. advisors com. 1987—96, chair 1991—96), Woods Hole Oceanographic Inst. Office: Vanderbilt University Law School 131 21st Avenue South Nashville TN 37203-1181

CHARPENTIER, GAIL WIGUTOW, private school executive director; b. N.Y.C., Mar. 10, 1946; d. Jacob M. and Ethel (Israel) Wigutow; m. Peter Jon Charpentier; children: Elisabeth Marie, Matthew Kyle. BA, CUNY, 1967; MA, New Sch. Social Research, N.Y.C., 1976; PhD, LaSalle U., 2002. Lic. social worker; cert. adminstr. of spl. edn. Tchr. Spl. Service Pub. Sch., Bronx, N.Y., 1967-73; adminstr. Boston City Hosp., 1973-76; dir. Monson Devel. Ctr., Palmer, Mass., 1976; residential dir. Kolburne Sch., New Marlboro, Mass., 1976-79; exec. dir. Berkshire Meadows, Housatonic, Mass., 1979—. Rschr. Nat. Opinion Rsch. Ctr., N.Y.C. and Boston, 1973-76; trainer residential child care, Mass., 1978—; mem. human rights bd. Oakdale Found., Great Barrington, 1980-90. Recipient Community Criminal Justice award Justice Resource Inst., 1984. Mem. NAFE, Am. Assn. Mental Retardation, Mass. Assn. Approved Pvt. Schs. (bd. dirs. 1982-84, ins. trustee 1984-87, svc. award 1982), New Eng. Assn. for Child Care, Rotary, Berkshire Profl. Women, Hop Brook Club (pres.). Avocations: skiing, tennis, sailing, bass fishing, golf. Home: Orchard House PO Box 406 Tyringham MA 01264-0406 Office: Berkshire Meadows 249 N Plain Rd Housatonic MA 01236-9736 E-mail: gcharpentier@jri.org.

CHARPENTIER, KEITH LIONEL, school system administrator; b. Attleboro, Mass., Mar. 6, 1959; s. David L. and Matilda (Marchand) C. AS, Mitchell Coll., 1980; BS, Plymouth State Coll., 1982, MEd in Guidance and Counseling, 1992, cert. advanced studies adminstrn./supr., 1999. Cert. phys. edn. and health sci. tchr., N.H.; cert. reality therapist; cert. guidance dir., N.H.; rsch. for better tchg. cert. observing and analyzing tchrs. Health, sci. tchr. SAU #23 Sch. System, Woodsville, N.H., 1982-84; counselor F.L. Chamberlain Sch., Lyman, N.H., 1984-86; spl. edn. tchr. Blue Mt. Union Sch., Wells River, Vt., 1985-86; dean of students, counselor Pike (N.H.) Sch. Inc., 1986-93; guidence counselor New Found Mid. Sch., Bristol, N.H., 1993-98, dean students, vice prin., 1998—. Instr. assoc. level Crisis Prevention Inst., Brookfield, Wis., 1989—, Drug/Alcohol Edn., Meredith, N.H., 1988—, Life Skills Edn., Granville, Ohio, 1987—; pvt. provider outpatient counseling Divsn. Children, Youth and Families, Dept. Health and Human Svcs., State of N.H., 1992—. Vol. firefighter, capt. Haverhill Corner Fire Dept. Recipient Mitchell Coll. Athletic Trainers award, 1980. Mem. ASCD, ACA, Nat. Athletic Trainers Assn., Nat. Mid. Sch. Assn., N.H. Assn. of Sch. Princpals, Nat. Assn. of Secondary Sch. Principals, Phi Delta Kappa. Avocations: sports, coaching, skiing, fishing, hunting, photography, gardening. Home: 214 Rockcreek Dr North Haverhill NH 03774

CHARSKY, THOMAS ROBERT, elementary education educator; b. Binghamton, N.Y., Feb. 20, 1952; s. Matthew J. and Margaret L. (Katusak) C. BM, Cath. U. Am., 1974, MM, 1986. Cert. music tchr., N.J. Vocal music tchr. Clifton (N.J.) Bd. Edn., 1981—. Adj. prof. music William Paterson U., Wayne, NJ, 2001—. Recipient Gov.'s Tchr. Recognition award; named Passaic County Tchr. of Yr., 1988-89. Mem.: NEA, Clifton Tchrs. Assn. (pres., Educator of Yr. 1993), N.N.J. Orff-Schulwerk Assn. (membership sec., treas., v.p., pres.), Am. Orff-Schulwerk Assn. (nat. trustee, region V rep.), N.J. Music Educators Assn., Music Educator Nat. Conf., N.J. Edn. Assn., Phi Mu Alpha. Home: 54 Beverly Hill Rd Clifton NJ 07012-1402

CHASE, BARBARA LANDIS, school administrator; b. Hershey, Pa., May 6, 1945; d. Floyd and Ruth Landis; m. David William Chase; children: Ashley Lawrence, Katherine Landis Chase. AB in History, Brown U., 1967; MLA, Johns Hopkins U., 1990. Tchr. 3rd grade Moses Brown Sch., Providence, R.I., 1967-68; tchr./dir. admissions Wheeler Sch., Providence, 1973-80; headmistress Bryn Mawr, Baltimore, Md., 1980-94; head of sch. Phillips Acad., Andover, Mass., 1994—. Contbr. articles to profl. jours.; presentations in field. Trustee Pike Sch., 1996-99, Sch. Yr. Abroad, 1994—, Tower Hill Sch., 1990-94, Brown U. 1995-2000; mem. Baltimore Ednl. Scholarship Trust, 1987-94, Baltimore Consortium Tchg. Am. History, 1987-90. Mem. Nat. Assn. Independent Schs. (bd. dirs. 1989-93, cons. 1988-89, chair sch. heads adv. com. 1986-88), Assn. Independent Md. Schs. (pres. bd. trustees 1986-88), The Headmasters Assn., Country Day Sch. Headmasters' Assn. U.S., Nat. Assn. Principals Schs. Girls, Headmistresses Assn. East.

CHASE, EUGENE THOMAS, secondary school educator; b. Clark AFB, Philippines, May 25, 1968; s. Paul Edward and Marsha Ann (Skinner) Jakola. BA in Polit. Sci., U. Okla., 1990; MA in Polit. Sci., U. Ctrl. Okla., 1994. Cert. tchr. social studies, govt., history, Okla.; nat. bd. cert. tchr., 2001. Substitute tchr. Mid-Del Schs., Midwest City, Okla., 1991-92; tchr. govt. Edmond (Okla.) North H.S., 1992—. Acad. team coach Meml. H.S., Edmond, 1993-94. Mem. steering com. Okla. Closeup Found., Oklahoma City, 1993-94; parliamentarian Parkview Neighbor Assn., Oklahoma City, 1992; voter registrar Okla. County Election Bd., 1994. Named Tchr. of Yr., Edmond North H.S., 2002—03. Mem. Nat. Coun. for Social Studies, Phi Theta Kappa. Democrat. Mem. Christian Ch. (Disciples Of Christ). Avocations: politics, music, computers, reading, hockey. Office: Edmond North High Sch 215 W Danforth Rd Edmond OK 73003-5206

CHASE, JEANNE NORMAN, artist, educator; b. Spokane, Wash., Feb. 15, 1929; d. John Henry and Violet Inez (Crosby) Norman; m. David Carl Chase, July 4, 1964. BFA in Painting, Calif. State U., Northridge, 1959. Instr. painting and drawing Ringling Sch. Art and Design, Sarasota, Fla., 1978-94, chmn. fine arts dept., 1983-85. Condr. workshops Ringling Workshop Series, Wildacres Retreat, N.C., 1984, 85; lectr. in field. Group and one-woman shows include Rauchbach Gallery, Bal Harbour, Fla., 1981, 83, Boca Grande (Fla.) Gallery, 1982, Tatem Gallery, Ft. Lauderdale, 1986, 87, St. Boniface Conservatory of Arts, Sarasota, 1988, Helios Gallery, Naples, Fla., 1989, Manatee C.C. Fine Arts Gallery, 1988, Phillips Gallery, Sanibel, Fla., 1991, Mickelson Gallery, Washington, 1989-94, Venice Art Gallery, Fla., 2003, others; nat. and internat. juried competitions Ridge Crest Art Assn., Winter Haven, Fla., 1980, Mason Keane Gallery, N.Y.C., 1981 (Best of Show), Tampa (Fla.) Mus. of Arts, 1982, El Paso Mus. Art, 1982, Columbia-Greene C.C., Hudson, N.Y., 1982, Edison C.C., Ft. Myers, Fla., 1982, 85, The Soc. of the Four Arts, Palm Beach, Fla., 1982, 87, The Capitol Gallery, Tallahassee, Fla., 1986, Tampa Mus., 1988, Binnewater Arts Ctr., N.Y.C., 1988, others.; represented in permanent collections former Pres. Jimmy and Roslyn Carter, Grace Lemon (collector), Indonesia, Bendix Avionies, Dr. and Mrs. Victor Maitland, Fla., Ringling Sch. Art and Design, Mr. and Mrs. E. Howland Swift III, Va., Chatahoochie Mus. Art, Ga., Dr. Artine Artinian, Fla., George Whitman, Shakespeare and Co., Paris, Veroingue Rabin Le Gall E'cole des Beaux-Arts, Paris, Donahoe Swift Assn., N.Y.C., Chonquing Mus., China, Spencer Mus. of Art, Kanas City; works published in book American Artists, an Illustrated Survey of Leading Contemporary Americans, 1986; subject in books: Female Artists in the United States: a Research and Resource File, 1986, 88, Artists and Their Cats, 1990, Drawings, Hylton-Leech Gallery, Sarasota, Fla., 1996; subject numerous newspaper articles; TV and video interviews: Focus on the Arts, Channel 4, 1980, A Fabric of Our Own Making, Ga. State U., 1981, Introduction to Jeanne Norman Chase, local sta., St. Augustine, Fla., 1991. Mem. Fla. Artists Group. Recipient Merit award Foster Harmon Gallery, Sarasota, 1991. Mem. Fla. Artists Group. Avocations: writing, piano, traveling. Studio: 1817 Ingram Ave Sarasota FL 34232

CHASE, KAREN HUMPHREY, middle school education educator; b. New Bedford, Mass., Nov. 17, 1948; d. Clifton Humphrey and Alice (Duffy) C. BA in Sociology, Stonehill Coll., 1970; MA in Edn., Lesley U., 2003. Cert. tchr. K-8, Mass. Elem. tchr. Minot (Maine) Consol. Sch., 1970-72; tchr. social studies George R. Austin Mid. Sch., Lakeville, Mass., 1972—2002, co-coord. students as mediators program, 1996—98; tchr. social studies Freetown-Lakeville Mid. Sch., 2002—. Dept. leader social studies, Austin Mid. Sch., Lakeville, 1976-80; supt. search team Freetown-Lakeville Sch. Dist., 1995. Actor/dir.: Your Theatre, Inc. New Bedford, Mass., 1985—; mem. Marion Arts Ctr., 1973—; 2nd v.p. Educators Assn. Freetown-Lakeville, 1991-93, 1st v.p., 1993-2003. Named Young Careerist of Yr., Bus. and Profl. Women, Wareham, Mass., 1979. Mem. Plymouth County Educators Assn. (Significant Svc. Honor award 1995), Mass. Tchrs. Assn., NEA, Nat. Coun. for Social Studies. Avocations: travel, reading, hiking, gardening, theatre. Home: 196 Clapp Rd Rochester MA 02770-4000 Office: Freetown-Lakeville Mid Sch 96 Howland Rd Lakeville MA 02347

CHASE, KAREN SUSAN, English literature educator; b. St. Louis, Oct. 16, 1952; d. Stanley Martin and Judith C.; m. Michael H. Levenson, Dec. 30, 1984; children: Alexander Nathan, Sarah Sophie. BA, UCLA, 1974; MA, Stanford U., 1977, PhD, 1980. Asst. prof. U. Va., Charlottesville, 1979-85, assoc. prof., 1985-91, prof., 1992—. Author: Eros and Psyche, 1984, George Eliot's Middlemarch, 1990; co-author: The Spectacle of Intimacy: A Public Life For The Victorian Family, 2000 Office: Univ of Va English Department 219 Bryan Hall Charlottesville VA 22903

CHASE, OSCAR G(OTTFRIED), law educator, consultant, author; s. Sidney and Helen G. Chase; m. Jane Monell, June 12, 1969; children: Arlo M., Oliver G. BA (hon.), NYU, 1960; JD, Yale U., 1963. Bar: N.Y. 1963, U.S. Dist. Ct. (so. and ea. dists.) N.Y. 1968, U.S. Ct. Appeals (2nd cir.) 1970, U.S. Supreme Ct. 1972, U.S. Ct. Appeals (D.C. cir.) 1975. Staff mem voter edn. project SNCC, Jackson, Miss., 1963-64; counsel Lower West Side Cmty. Corp., N.Y.C., 1966-67; lawyer M.F.Y. Legal Svcs., Inc., 1967-68; asst. gen. counsel, dir. law reform, 1968-72; prof. law Bklyn. Law Sch., 1972-78; vis. prof. law NYU, 1978-79; prof. law, 1979—. Assoc. dean law sch., 1990-94, vice dean law sch., 1994-99. Author: CPLR Manmual, rev. edit., 1980, Civil Litigation in New York, 1983, end. edit., 1990, 4th edit., 2002, New York Practice Guide: Negligence, 4 vols., 1989; co-author: Cases and Materials on Civil Procedure, 1987; contbr. New York Practice, bi-monthly column for N.Y. Law Jour., 1982-84; contbr. articles to profl. jours. Bd. dirs. Untapped Resources, Inc., 1970—81; mem. adv. com. ACLU Reproductive Freedom Project, 1977—82; mem. civil litigation com. Ea. Dist. N.Y.; mem. joint AALS, ABA, Law Sch. Admission Coun. on Fin. Aid, 1991—94; bd. dirs. Inst. Judicial Adminstrn., 1992, co-exec. dir., 2000—. Office: NYU Sch Law 40 Washington Sq S New York NY 10012-1099

CHASE, WILLIAM JOHN, history educator; b. Glen Cove, N.Y., Sept. 4, 1947; s. William J. and Frances S. (Storen) C.; m. Donna M. Schaefer; children: Matthew, Alexander. BA in History, Lafayette Coll., 1969; MA in Russian Studies, Boston Coll., 1973, PhD in Russian/Modern European History, 1979. History instr. Boston Coll., 1976-79; asst. prof. history U. Pitts., 1979-85, assoc. prof. history, 1985—2000, prof. history, chair dept. history, 2000—, dir. Ctr. for Russian and East European Studies, 1989-91, mem. com. Ctr. for Russian and East European Studies, 1979—, mem. adv. bd. Univ. Honors Coll., 1980-82. Co-dir. The Soviet Data Bank, Data Archive on the History of Soviet Society and State; hist. cons. Pitts.-Donetsk Oral History Project, Perestroika from Below film, 1989; conf. organizer Restructuring USA/USSR, U. Pitts., 1991; presenter in field. Author: Workers, Society and the Soviet State: Labor and Life in Moscow, 1918-1929, 1987, Enimies Within the Gates? The Comintern and the Stalinist Repression, 1934-1939, 2001; co-editor: The Carl Beck Papers in Russian and East European Studies, 1982—, (with E.A. Tiurina, S.V. Prasolova and A.K. Sokolov) Research Guide to the Russian State Archive of the Economy, 1993; mem. editorial bd., prodn. editor Russian Archives Series; mem. editorial bd. Russkoe Proshoe, 1991—; contbr. articles to profl. jours. Sgt. USMCR, 1969-75. Grantee Social Sci. Rsch. Coun., 1991, Am. Coun. Learned Socs., 1990, Internat. Rsch. and Exchs. Bd., 1990, Kennan Inst. for Advanced Russian Studies, 1990, Dept. Edn., 1991; fellow Am. Coun. Learned Socs., 1981, W. Averell Harriman Inst. for Advanced Study of the Soviet Union, Columbia U., 1982, NEH, 1985-85, Nat. Coun. for Soviet and East European Rsch., 1983-84, 85-86, 95-96, Hewlett Rsch., U. Pitts., 1993. Office: U Pitts Dept History Pittsburgh PA 15260

CHASEK, ARLENE SHATSKY, academic director; b. Newark, N.J., June 1, 1934; d. Herman and Rose (Sporn) Shatsky; m. Marvin B. Chasek, Apr. 10, 1960; children: Pamela S., Laura N., Daniel J. BA, Cornell U., 1956; MA, Columbia U., 1957; postgrad., U. N.D., 1972-74, Rutgers U., 1981-91. Tchr. English and journalism Elizabeth (N.J.) Pub. Schs., 1978-80, Summit (N.J.) Pub. Schs., 1978-80; coord. MA program Fairleigh Dickinson U., Teaneck, N.J., 1979-81; editor AT&T, Murray Hill, N.J., 1980-81; project coord. Consortium for Ednl. Equity, Rutgers U., New Brunswick, N.J., 1981-85, project dir., 1985-88, dir. spl. projects, 1988-93, dir. family involvement programs in math., sci. and tech., 1993-95, dir. Ctr. for Family Involvement in Schs., 1995—. Mem. steering com., N.J. coord. Am. Goes Back to Sch. initiative U.S. Dept. Edn., 1997. Author, editor: Rutgers Family Tools and Technology, 1994, Rutgers Family Science, 1993, Mathematics in Art/Art in Mathematics, 1986 (U.S. Dept. Edn. award 1987), From Jumping Genes to Red Giants: A Guide to High School Science Research; author: The Recruitment and Retention Challenge, 1982, Futures Unlimited, 1985 (Curriculum award am. Ednl. Rsch. Assn. 1986). Recipient Golden Apple award for Family Involvement Programs, Working Mother mag., U.S. Dept. Edn., and Tchrs. Coll. Columbia U., 1996. Mem. AAUW, LWV, NSTA, Nat. Assn. Equity Educators, Coop. Learning Assn., Internat. Tech. Edn. Assn., Assn. Math. Tchrs. N.J. Home: 9 Schindler Pl New Providence NJ 07974-1738 Office: Rutgers Univ Center for Math, Science, and Computer Busch Campus, SERC New Brunswick NJ 08903

CHASKELSON, MARSHA INA, neuropsychologist; b. Brookline, Mass., Jan. 6, 1950; d. Hyman and Doris (Sacks) C.; m. Allen Noah Elgart, July 8, 1973; children: Jonah Elgart, Benjamin Elgart, Sarah Elgart. BA in Psychology, U. Mass., 1971; MEd in Spl. Edn., Boston Coll., 1972, PhD Counseling Psychology, 1985. Lic. psychologist; cert. sch. psychologist; cert. provider. Resource room specialist for emotionally disturbed Acton-Boxborough Regional Jr. High Sch., Acton, Mass., 1972-76; faculty mem., on-site facilitator Boston Coll., Chestnut Hill, Mass., 1976-77; in-patient coord., out-patient staff psychologist Kennedy Meml. Hosp., Brighton, Mass., 1977-80; contracted sch. psychologist Beverly (Mass.) Pub. Schs., 1981; contracted staff psychologist Human Resource Inst., Franklin, Mass., 1980-82, mental retardation coord., 1982-83; clin. specialist Alternatives, Unltd., Whitinsville, Mass., 1981-87; dir. Lexington Psychol. & Ednl. Resources, Lexington, Mass., 1987—. Psychology intern psychology dept. Kennedy Meml. Hosp., Brighton, 1976-77, post-doctoral psychologist Children's Hosp. Med. Ctr., Boston, 1984-85; post-doctoral neuropsychologist New Eng. Rehab. Hosp., Woburn, Mass., 1985-86; co-chairperson Lexington A.D.D. Parent Group, 1987-88. Mem. Am. Psychol. Assn., Assn. Higher Edn. and Disability., Coun. for Exceptional Children, Mass. Psychol. Assn., Mass. Assn. for Children with Learning Disabilities. Democrat. Jewish. Office: Lexington Psychol & Ednl Resources 76 Bedford St Ste 26 Lexington MA 02420-4641

CHASSE, EMILY SCHUDER, librarian, educator; b. Paducah, Ky., June 10, 1953; d. Charles Bernard and Ann (Sidwell) Schuder; m. William Chasse, Aug. 30, 1980; 1 child, Sarah Ann Schuder Chasse. Student, Iowa State U., 1972-74; BA in Elem. Edn., Antioch Coll., 1976; MLS, U. R.I., 1979. Cert. tchr., Conn. Child care worker Walker Home & Sch., Needham, Mass., 1975-78; children's libr. Plainville (Conn.) Pub. Libr., 1979-82; part-time instr. in children's lit. Manchester (Conn.) Community Coll., 1981-83; asst. curriculum lab. libr. Cen. Conn. State U., New Britain, 1982-89, libr. on-line search svcs., 1989—. Freelance storyteller, 1980—. Contbr. articles to profl. jours. Mem. ALA, Conn. Libr. Assn., Conn. Storytelling Assn., Hither & Yon Storytellers. Democrat. Mem. Soc. Of Friends. Office: Cen Conn State U Burritt Libr 1615 Stanley St New Britain CT 06053-2439

CHASSMAN, KAREN MOSS, educational administrator; b. Bklyn., Aug. 18, 1946; d. Bernard and Esther (Steier) Kahn; m. Robert Moss (div. 1973); 1 child, Jeff; m. Richard Chassman, Oct. 31, 1992 (dec. Feb. 1994). BA, Hunter Coll., 1967; MS in Edn., Bklyn. Coll., 1969, advanced cert. in lang. arts, 1978. Tchr. nursery, kindergarten and grades 1-6 Common Branches, 1967-78; sales rep., real estate broker various cos., 1978-91; dir., owner The Reading Improvement Ctr., East Islip, N.Y., 1991—. Mem. Islip C. of C., Islip Rotary (ednl. scholar 1992—). Avocations: aerobic exercise, antiques, travel. Office: Reading Improvement Ctr 2545 Middle Country Rd Centereach NY 11720 Address: 234 E Main St East Islip NY 11730 Office: Reading Improvement Ctr 268 East Main St East Islip NY 11730

CHASTAIN, KENNETH DUANE, retired foreign language educator; b. Salem, Ind., July 20, 1934; s. Lloyd Lionel and Cristal Louise (Hoke) C.; m. Mary Janice McFadden, June 14, 1959; children: Kevin Duane, Brian Duane, Michael Allen. BS, Ind. U., 1956; MA, Ball State U., 1962; PhD, Purdue U., 1968. Tchr. Seymour HS, Ind., 1956-62, Columbus HS, Ind., 1962-64; grad. instr., prof. Purdue U., Lafayette, Ind., 1964-72; prof. Asbury Coll., Wilmore, Ky., 1972-73, U. Va., Charlottesville, Va., 1973-95, prof. emeritus, 1995—. Author: Developing S-L Skills, 1988, Imaginate, 1991, Spanish Grammar in Review, 1993, Exploraciones en la Literatura Hispanica, 1993, The Money Chase: Counting the Cost, 2000, Social Security and More: Comments on Government, 2001, English as a Communication System, 2001. With U.S. Army, 1957-58. Recipient Florence Steiner Leadership in Fgn. Lang. Edn. award Am. Coun. Teaching Fgn. Langs., 1989. Avocations: exercise, gardening, nature, travel. Home: 2674 Bakers Chapel Church Rd Big Sandy TN 38221-5318 E-mail: jkchas@compu.net.

CHATER, SHIRLEY SEARS, health educator; d. Norman and Edna Sears; m. Norman Chater, Dec. 5, 1959 (dec. Dec. 1993); children: Cris, Geoffrey. BS, U. Pa., 1956; MS, U. Calif., San Francisco, 1960; PhD, U. Calif., Berkeley, 1964. Asst., assoc., prof. dept. social and behavioral scis. Sch. Nursing U. Calif.-San Francisco, Sch. Edn.-Berkeley, 1964—86; asst. vice chancellor acad. affairs U. Calif., San Francisco, 1974—77, vice chancellor acad. affairs, 1977—82; council assoc. Am. Council Edn., Washington, 1982—84; sr. assoc. Presdl. Search Consultation Svc. Assn. Governing Bds., Washington, 1984—86; pres. Tex. Woman's U., Denton, 1986—93; chair Gov's health policy task force State of Texas, 1992; commr. Social Security Adminstrn., Washington, 1993—97; Regent's prof. Inst. for Health and Aging U. Calif., San Francisco, 1997—98. Vis. prof. Inst. Health & Aging U. Calif., San Francisco, 1998—. Mem. commn. on women Am. Coun. on Edn.; bd. dirs. Carnegie Found. for Advancement of Tchg., United Educators Ins. Risk Retention Group, Denton United Way, 1986—93. Mem.: Nat. Acad. Nursing, Nat. Acad. Social Ins., Nat. Acad. Pub. Adminstrn., Internat. Alliance, San Francisco Women's Forum West, Inst. Medicine NAS. Office: Inst Health and Aging 3333 California St Ste 340 San Francisco CA 94118-1944

CHATFIELD, SCOTT PATRICK, secondary school art educator; b. Manchester, N.H., Mar. 17, 1962; s. Oliver James and Maureen (Flanagan) C.; m. Andrea Grilli, Aug. 3, 1991. BFA, Alfred U., 1984; MEd, Notre Dame Coll., 1991. Cert. tchr. art, elem., secondary, N.H. Tchr. elem. schs. art Cuba (N.Y.) Cen. Sch., 1984-86; tchr. secondary sch. art Coe-Brown Northwood (N.H.) Acad. Sponsor Nat. Art Honor Soc., Northwood, 1990—; art therapist Coe-Brown Northwood Acad., 1991—. Exhibited paintings and drawings in group shows at N.H. Art Assn. Gallery, Manchestr, 1989, 91. Recipient Excellence in Edn.: Visual Arts award Coe-Brown Northwood Acad., 1993, 94, 95, Outstanding Achievement for Art Edn., 1995. Mem. Nat. Art Edn. Assn., N.H. Art Educators Assn. (regional v.p., treas. 1993-96; Art Educator of Month 1991), New Eng. Assn. Art Therapists (profl.), N.H. Art Therapy Assn., Am. Art Therapy Assn. (profl.). Avocations: photography, calligraphy, running, gardening, cooking. Office: Coe-Brown Northwood Acad RR 1 Box 158A Northwood NH 03261-9801

CHATMAN, ELEANOR LOUISE, secondary school educator; b. Nashville, Aug. 30, 1959; d. Donald Leveritt and Eleanor Scrutchions Chatman. BA, Oberlin Coll., 1982; MA, Ea. Mich. U., 1991. Substitute tchr. Chgo. Pub. Schs., 1984—87, Spanish/French tchr., 1991—; grad. asst. Ea. Mich. U., Ypsilanti, 1989—91; Spanish tchr. Diversified Ednl. Svcs., Detroit, 1990. Singer: (TV series) The Tonight Show, 1996. Singer Christ Universal Temple, 1994; mem. Christ Universal Temple Ensemble, 1994—99. Scholar, Nat. Bd. for Profl. Tchg. Stds., 2002. Avocations: singing, dancing, religious study.

CHATO, JOHN CLARK, mechanical and bioengineering educator; b. Budapest, Hungary, Dec. 28, 1929; s. Joseph Alexander and Elsie (Wasserman) C.; m. Elizabeth Janet Owens, Aug. 1954; children: Christine B., David J., Susan E. ME, U. Cin., 1954; MS, U. Ill., 1955; PhD, MIT, 1960. Co-op student, trainee Frigidaire div. GMC, Dayton, Ohio, 1950—54; grad. fellow U. Ill., Urbana, 1954—55; grad. fellow, inst. MIT, Cambridge, 1955—58, asst. prof., 1958—64; assoc. prof. U. Ill., Urbana, 1964—69, prof., 1969—96, prof. emeritus, 1996—, chmn. exec. com. bioengrng. faculty, 1972—78, 1982—83, 1984—85, asst. dean of engring., 1997—98. Cons. Industry and Govt., 1958—; dir., founder Biomed. Engrng. Systems Team, Urbana, Ill, 1974-78; assoc. editor Jour. Biomech. Engrng., 1976-82. Patentee in field; contbr. articles to profl. jours., chpts. to books on heat transfer, bio-heat transfer, refrigeration, air conditioning, cryogenics, and thermal systems. Com. mem. troop 6 Boy Scouts Am., Urbana, 1984—86; com. mem. Urbana Plan Commn., 1973—78; mem. adv. com. Urbana Park Dist., 1981—84; 2nd v.p. Champaign County Izaak Walton League, 1986, 1st v.p., 1987, pres., 1988—92, bd. dirs., state dir., 1992—; mem. Urbana Postal Customer Adv. Coun., 2002—; trustee 1st Presbyn. Ch., Urbana, 1976—78, 1999—2001, elder, 1982—85; bd. dirs. Univ. YMCA, Champaign, Ill., 1976—78, 1987—90. Recipient Tobin award Champaign County Izaak Walton League, 1992, Cmty. Svc. award Urbana Park Dist., 1996, Russell Scott Meml. award, Cryogenic Engrng. Conf., 1979; named Disting. Engrng. Alumnus, U. Cin., 1972, NSF fellow 1961, Fogarty Sr. Internat. fellow 1978-79; Japan Soc. Promotion of Sci. fellow, 1997. Fellow: ASHRAE (treas. East Ctrl. Ill. chpt. 1984, sec. 1985, 1987, 1st v.p. 1988, pres. 1989), ASME (exec. com. bioengrng. divsn. 1992—96, sec. 1993—94, chmn. 1994—95, Charles Russ Richards Meml. award 1978, N.R. Lissner award 1992, Dedicated Svc. award 2000), Am. Inst. Med. and Biol. Engrs.; mem.: IEEE (sr.), Am. Soc. Engrng. Edn., Internat. Inst. Refrigeration (assoc.), Audubon Soc. Champaign County (bd. dirs. 1988—89, v.p. 1990, treas. 1991—93, v.p. 1995—96, treas. 1998—99, pres. 2000—02, bd. dirs. 2002), Exch. Club Urbana (bd. dirs. 1989—91, 1995—96, pres.-elect 1996—97, pres. 1997—98, dist. dir. 2001—). Achievements include research in fields of heat transfer, bio-heat transfer, refrigeration, air conditioning, cryogenics, and thermal systems. Office: U Ill Dept Mech Indsl Engring 1206 W Green St Urbana IL 61801-2906 E-mail: jbchato@staff.uiuc.edu.

CHATTERJEE, AMITAVA, finance educator, consultant; b. Calcutta, India, Jan. 10, 1961; came to U.S., 1986; s. Nepal and Shila Chatterjee; m. Rupa Bhattacharjya, Dec. 15, 1993; 1 child, Anirudha. BS, U. Calcutta, 1983, MS, 1985; postgrad. diploma in operational rsch., Ops. Rsch. Soc. India, Calcutta, 1985; PhD, U. Miss., 1992. Cert. cash mgr. Assn. Fin. Profls., 2002. Jr. rsch. fellow U. Calcutta, India, 1985—86; tchg. and rsch. asst. U. Miss., University, 1987-90, 1990-92; coord. area econs. and fin., asst. prof. fin. Lemoyne Owen Coll., Memphis, 1992-96; asst. prof. fin. Fayetteville (N.C.) State U., 1996-99, assoc. prof. fin., 1999—2001; prof. fin. Tex. So. U., Houston, 2001—. Advisor Econs. and Fin. Club, Fayetteville, 1996—2001. Co-author: Principles of Finance, 2d edit., 1998—; contbr. articles to profl. jours. Named All India Nat. scholar of merit, Govt. Of India, 1977, All India Jr. Rsch. fellow, 1985, Grad. fellow, Internat. Fedn. Operational Rsch., 1985—, Tchr. of Yr., Fayetteville (N.C.) State U., 2000; recipient citation of excellence, Anbar Electronic Intelligence, 1998, Disting. Rsch. Award, Allied Academies, 2001; Classroom Tchg./Learning grantee, Carolina Colloquy for Univ. Tchg., Cullowhee, N.C., 1999, Rsch. grantee, Tex. So. U., 2001, 2002. Mem.: Acad. Econs. and Fin. (bd. dirs. Hattiesburg, Miss. 1996—, track chair 1999, 2000, 2001), Acad. Fin. Case Rsch. (founder, mem. editl. bd. jour. 1999—), Fin. Mgmt. Assn., Am. Fin. Assn. Hindu. Avocations: reading, cooking. Home: PO Box 16665 Sugar Land TX 77496 Office: Texas Southern U Sch of Bus 3100 Cleburn Ave Houston TX 77004 E-mail: chatteramit@hotmail.com.

CHATTON, BARBARA ANN, education educator; b. San Francisco, Aug. 4, 1948; d. Milton John and Mildred (Vick) C.; m. Andrew M. Bryson, May 1, 1993. BA, U. Calif., Santa Cruz, 1970; MLS, UCLA, 1971; PhD, Ohio State U., 1982. Libr. John Steinbeck Pub. Libr., Salinas, Calif., 1971-79; prof. U. Wyo., Laramie, 1982—. Author: Using Poetry Across the Curriculum, 1993; co-author: Creating Connections, 1986, Blurring the Edges, 1999. Mem., past chair Friends of Libr., Albany County, Wyo., 1989—. Recipient Ellbogen award U. Wyo., 1990. Mem. ALA, Nat. Coun. Tchrs. English, Internat. Reading Assn., Phi Delta Kappa. Office: U Wyo Coll Edn PO Box 3374 Laramie WY 82071-3374 E-mail: bchat@uwyo.edu.

CHATZKY, HERBERT, music educator; b. Balt., Apr. 8, 1935; s. Samuel and Sonia (Greenspun) C.; m. Sally Anne Rush, Feb. 13, 1973; children: Christine, Lisa, David. BS, Juilliard Sch. of Music, 1957; MS, 1958, postgrad., 1959. Cert. tchr. music, Conn. Accompanying staff Juilliard Sch. Music, N.Y.C., 1952-57, tchr. class piano, 1958-60; instr. in piano Bowling Green (Ohio) State U., 1960-61; asst. prof. piano and accompanying Hart Coll. Music, Hartford, Conn., 1961-72; music staff South Windsor (Conn.) Sch., 1972-97; choirmaster Hartford (Conn.) Symphony Chorale, 1972-73, ofcl. pianist, 1962-73; dir. 2nd Congregational Ch., Manchester, Conn., 1967-86, North United Meth. Ch., Manchester, 1986—. Dir. Manchester Young Artist Competition, Conn., 1974—; music dir., sr. organist, Temple Beth Israel, Conn., 1986-98, dir. Jewish music competition; mem. Scehovic-Chatzky Piano Duo; dir. Newcomb Friends for Music Concerts, Newcomb Young Composer Contest. Composer: (symphonic composition) Night Music for Orchestra, 1952, Variations, 1952 (hon. mention N.Y. Philharmonic 1952), Music for Orchestra and Chorus: 29th Psalm, 1973; arranger for organ; Lincoln Portrait, 1978; performed concert series Lake Placid Synagogue. Performer holocaust music, Conn. Pub. Radio, Hartford, 1970, 2nd Congregational Ch., Manchester, 1978; dir. concert series, 2nd Congregational Ch., 1975-86; lectr. on sight-reading, New Eng. Piano Tchrs. Assn., 1967; trustee Newcomb United Meth. Ch.; v.p. Newcomb C. of C.. Sgt. USANG, 1960-70. Recipient full piano scholarship Juilliard Sch. Music, 1952-57, french-horn scholarship, 1952-57; award of Philo-Music Soc., N.Y.C., 1955; winner of concerto competition, Juilliard Sch. of Music, 1958; concerto soloist under Arthur Fiedler, Hartford Symphony Orchestra, 1972. Jewish. Avocations: mountain climbing, hiking, reading, travel in motorhome. Home: PO Box 214 Newcomb NY 12852-0214 also: 5461 Rte 28N Newcomb NY 12852 E-mail: hchatzky@capital.net.

CHAUDHRY, HUMAYUN JAVAID, physician, medical educator, flight surgeon, writer; b. Karachi, Pakistan, Nov. 17, 1965; came to U.S., 1971, naturalized, 1978; s. Hukam Dad and Riffat Sultana (Bhatti) C.; m. Nazli Tabasum Iqbal, June 7, 1992; children: Shaun Hatim, Haris Iqbal. BA, NYU, 1986, MS, 1989; DO, N.Y. Coll. Osteo. Medicine, 1991; SM, Harvard Sch. of Pub. Health, 2001. Diplomate Nat. Bd. Osteo. Med. Examiners, Am. Bd. Internal Medicine; lic. physician, surgeon, N.Y. Intern St. Barnabas Hosp., Bronx, NY, 1991-92; resident in internal medicine Winthrop-U. Hosp., Mineola, NY, 1992-95, chief med. resident, 1995-96; asst. prof. medicine N.Y. Coll. Osteo. Medicine, Old Westbury, 1997—2003, chmn. dept. medicine, 2001—, med. dir., 2003—, assoc. prof. medicine, 2003—; attending physician, dir. med. edn. Long Beach (N.Y.) Med. Ctr., 1996-2001; attending physician Island Park Med. Care, 1996-98, Family Care Ctr., Long Beach, N.Y., 1996-99, Academic Health Care Ctr., N.Y. Coll. Osteopathic Medicine, 2001—; mem. staff Winthrop U. Hosp., 2001—. Reporter, news editor, TV anchorman Third World Broadcasting Network, N.Y.C., 1986-95; asst. clin. instr. medicine SUNY Stony Brook Sch. Medicine, 1995-96. Mem. editl. bd. New Physician, Reston, Va., 1991-99; contbr. articles to profl. jours. Bd. mem. Multifaith Forum of LI. Capt. USAF Res., 1999—2002, maj. USAF Res., 2002—. Regents Coll. scholar State of NY, Albany, 1982; recipient Essay Competition award N.Y.C. Fire Dept., 1979. Fellow: ACP (Nassau West dist. pres. 2000—), Am. Coll. Osteo. Internists, Nassau Acad. of Medicine, Royal Soc. Medicine UK; mem.: AMA, Nassau County Med. Soc. (bd. dirs. 2002—03), So. Poverty Law Ctr., Am. Acad. Osteopathy, Med. Soc. State of NY, Islamic Soc. N.Am., Nassau Soc. Internal Medicine (bd. dirs. 1996—98, v.p. 1998—99, pres. 1999—2000), NY State Osteo. Med. Soc., Assn. Osteo. Dirs. Med. Educators (bd. dirs. 2001—03, treas. 2003—), Islamic Med. Assn. N.Am., Am. Coll. Osteo. Internists (founding pres. NY chpt. 1998—, bd. dirs. 1999—), NY State Soc. Internal Medicine (pres. resident physicians sect. 1995—96, bd. dirs. 1996—2000), World Wildlife Fund, Islamic Ctr. LI, NY Coll. Osteo. Medicine Alumni Assn. (sec. bd. dirs. 1995—98, pres. 1998—2000, bd. dirs. 2000—02), Amnesty Internat. Muslim. Avocations: reading, cinema, travel. Home: 53 Timber Ridge Dr Commack NY 11725-1739 Office: NY Coll Osteo Medicine Dept Medicine Hannah & Charles Serota Acad Ctr Rm 121 Old Westbury NY 11568-8000 E-mail: hchaudhr@nyit.edu.

CHAUDOIR, JEAN HAMILTON (JEAN HAMILTON), educator; b. Lake Charles, La., July 31, 1945; d. John Gardiner and Nora (Alford) Hamilton; divorced; 1 child, Elizabeth Jean. BS, La. State U., 1967, MEd, 1986, postgrad., 2002. Tchr. 3d grade St. Pius X Sch., Baton Rouge, 1967-69; tchr. 2d grade St. Francis Cabrini Sch., Alexandria, La., 1969-75; tchr. 3d grade St. Theresa Sch., Shreveport, La., 1975-76; tchr. 4th grade Sacred Heart Sch., Baton Rouge, 1976-79, West Baton Rouge Parish, Brusly, La., 1979-80; tutor Ed-U-Care, Baton Rouge, 1987-88; with summer program East Baton Rouge Parish, Baton Rouge, 1990-91, tchr. Chpt. 1 summer sch., 1993, 94; part time tchr. Modern Curriculum Press, Baton Rouge, 1995—; tchr. for instrnl. support Lanier Elem. Sch., Baton Rouge, 1997—2002, chair improvement team. Chair Adopt-A-Sch. at Park Forest Elem., Baton Rouge, 1986-94; chair mktg. com. Park Forest Elem. Sch., Baton Rouge, La., 1986-94, mem. adv. coun., 1993-94, chair monitoring com., 1993-94; mem. Title 1 Sch. Wide Com., 1995. Sustaining mem. Jr. League Baton Rouge, 1985—2001. Mem.: Delta Kappa Gamma (pres.). E-mail: jchaudoir@ebrpss.k12.la.us.

CHAUHAN, SUNEET BHUSHAN, medical educator; b. Rewa, India, Mar. 28, 1958; came to U.S., 1971; s. Sushila (Singh) C.; m. Laurie Pitchford, Jan. 19, 1985; children: Tara, Kiren. BA in Chemistry/Biology summa cum laude, Beaver Coll., Gleside, Pa., 1979; MD, Thomas Jefferson U., Phila., 1983. Lic. physician, Miss., Ill., Ga. Intern Naval Hosp., Portsmouth, Va., 1983-84, resident, 1986-89; fellow U. Miss., Jackson, 1992-94; asst. prof. U. Ill., Peoria, 1994-95, Med. Coll. Ga., 1995-98. Contbr. articles to Jour. Inorganic Nuclear Chemistry, Am. Jour. Ob/Gyn., Jour. Reproductive Medicine, Jour. Miss. State Med. Assn., Jour. Maternal Fetal Investigation, Perinatol, South Med. Jour. Lt. comdr. USNR, 1979-92. Decorated Navy Commendation medal; Armed Forces Health Professions scholar, 1979-83. Mem. Lambda Delta Alpha, Phi Kappa Phi. Achievements include research in estimate of birth weight among diabetic patients, newborn electrolyte response to amnioinfusion with lactated ringer's versus normal saline, remote umbilical arterial blood pH analysis. Office: Spartanburg Regional Healthcare Sys 853 N Church St Ste 403 Spartanburg SC 29303-3064

CHAVES, JUAN CARLOS, mechanical engineering educator, consultant, researcher; b. San Jose, Costa Rica, Aug. 22, 1961; s. Cipriano and Carmen (De Ona) C.; m. Carolina Evans, July 5, 1986; children: Gloriana, Juan Ignacio. BS, U.S. Mil. Acad., 1983; MME, Rensselaer Poly. Inst., 1985; MBA, SUNY, 1990, PhD in Mfg. Engring., 2002. V.p., cons. Ingetec SRL, San José, 1985—; univ. prof. mech. engring. U. Costa Rica, San Pedro, 1986—; supt. prodn. planning Magma s.A., San Jose, 1985-86; maintenance mgr. Empaques Tecnicos, San Jose, 1986-87; cons., CEO Costarrican Electricity Inst., San Jose, 1987-88; supr. microcomputer lab. Sch. of Bus., SUNY, Albany, 1989-90; dir. Hotel Amb., San Jose, 1990—; asst. dir. sch. mech. engring. U. Costa Rica, 1994, adj. prof., dir. grad. studies sch. mech. engring., 1999—. Scholarship U.S. Mil. Acad., 1979-83, Orgn. of Am. States, 1983-85. Mem. ASME, Fed. Sch. Engrs. and Archs. Costa Rica, Soc. Mfg. Engrs., Beta Gamma Sigma. Office: Interlink #574 7801 NW 37th St Miami FL 33166 Home: APDO 685-1200 Pavas San Jose Costa Rica E-mail: jcchaves@wpi.edu.

CHAVEZ, DOROTHY VAUGHAN, elementary school educator, environmental educator; b. Columbus, Miss., Jan. 13, 1942; d. Robert Clayton and Sara (Harris) Vaughan; m. Samuel Patrick Chavez, Nov. 18, 1961; children: Sarah Rose, Samuel Clayton. BS, Miss. U. for Women, 1962; MEd, U. North Tex., 1968; PhD, Tex. A&M U., 1995. Cert. tchr., supr., Tex. Tchr. Littleton (Colo.) Ind. Sch. Dist., 1962-64, Albuquerque Ind. Sch. Dist., 1964-65, Richardson (Tex.) Ind. Sch. Dist., 1965-69, Austin (Tex.) Ind. Sch. Dist., 1973-89, 92, Round Rock (Tex.) Ind. Sch. Dist., 1992-97; instrnl. coord. Outdoor Edn. Ctr. Houston Ind. Sch. Dist., 1997—. Curriculum dir. Outdoor Sch., Marble Falls, Tex., 1996—; instructional coord. Outdoor Edn.Ctr., Houston Ind. Sch. Dsit., 1997—. Author: Nature's Classroom: Locations and Programs in Texas, 1991; editor: Directory of Environmental Education and Interpretive Centers, 1992, Take Children to the Wilds... to Discover Wildflowers and Native Plants, 1993; contbr. articles to environ. publs. Dir. vol. ushers staff Austin Symphony Orch. Soc., 1991-95. Mem. Tex. Assn. Environ. Edn. (editor 1991-93, Outstanding Contbns. award 1992), Tex. Edn. Agy (environ. edn. adv. com.), Tex. Outdoor Edn. Assn., Nat. Sci. Tchrs. Assn., Tex. Sci. Tchrs. Assn., N.Am. Environ. Edn. Assn., Am. Nature Study Soc., Roger Tory Peterson Inst., Tex. PTA (hon. life), Alpha Delta Kappa, Delta Kappa Gamma, Gamma Sigma Delta. Avocations: wildflower and grass study, canoeing, camping, backpacking, outdoor recreation. Home: RR 4 Box 4185 Trinity TX 75862-9323 Office: Houston Ind Sch Dist Outdoor Edn Ctr RR 2 Box 25B Trinity TX 75862-9475

CHAVEZ, MARY LYNN, pharmacy educator; b. Detroit, May 8, 1950; d. Gilbert E. and Dorothea J. (Munro) Van Sickle; m. Pedro I. Chavez, May 12, 1973; children: Pedro C., Stephen J. BS in Pharmacy, U. Tex., 1973; PharmD, Purdue U., 1985. Instr. Coll. Pharmacy U. P.R., San Juan, 1983-84, 87-88, asst. prof. pharmacy practice, 1988-92, clin. pharmacy specialist Med. Sch.-Pediat. Oncology Group, 1990-93, assoc. prof. pharmacy, 1990-93; assoc. prof. dept. pharmacy practice Chgo. Coll. Pharmacy, Midwestern U., Downers Grove, Ill., 1993-98, acting asst. chmn. clin. edn., 1997-98; dir. didactic edn. Midwestern U. Coll. Pharmacy, Glendale, Ariz., 1998—; dir. complementary therapies Rsch. Ctr. Advancement Pharmacy Practice, Glendale, 1998—, prof. pharmacy practice, 1999—. Writer pharmacy exam. CAT-NAPLEX/NABPLEX Licensure, Park Ridge, Ill., 1996; reviewer posters and presentations Am. Assn. Health Sys. Pharmacies, Bethesda, Md., 1996—; reviewer manuscripts Annals of Pharmacotherapy, Cin. Therapeutics, Am. Jour. Pharm. Edn., Jour. Pharmacy Tech., Am. Jour. Health Sys. Pharmacy, 1995—. Mem. editl. bd. Jour. Am. Pharmacy Assn., Prima Pub., Jour. Herbal Pharmacotherapy; contbg. editor Hosp. Pharmacy. Asst. to cub pack leader area coun. Boy Scouts Am., Naperville, Ill., 1995, 96. Mem. Am. Pharm. Assn., Am. Assn. Colls. of Pharmacy, Am. Soc. Hosp. Pharmacists, Am. Coll. Clin. Pharmacists, Sigma Xi, Rho Chi. Office: Midwestern U Coll Pharmacy Glendale AZ 85308

CHAVIOUS, MARIAN DELORESE, assistant principal; b. Clinton, N.C., Aug. 9, 1950; d. Luther and Sarah Ann (Smith) C. BA, N.C. Cen. U., 1972, MEd, 1979; EdS, East Carolina U., Greenville, N.C., 1991. Employment counselor Office of Employment and Tng., Clinton, 1972-74; tchr. social studies Sanderson High Sch., Raleigh, N.C., 1974; itinerant tchr. Clinton City Schs., 1977-78; tchr. lang. arts Harnett County Schs., Lillington, N.C., 1978-86; media coord. Sampson County Schs., Clinton, 1976-77, industry edn. coord., 1986-92; itinerant tchr. Duplin County Schs., Kenansville, N.C., 1974-75, asst. prin., 1992—. Chairperson Sampson/Clinton Youth Coun., 1988-90. Mem. NCAE (bldg. rep. 1989-90), Am. Legion Aux. (dist. pres. 1972-76), Order Ea. Star (publicity chairperson 1992—), Elks (daughter ruler 1983-85), Order Golden Circle (inner guard 1992). Baptist. Home: RR 1 Box 278 Turkey NC 28393-9733

CHAVOOSHIAN, MARGE, artist, educator; b. NYC, Jan. 8, 1925; d. Harry Mesrob and Anna (Tashjian) Kurkjian; m. Barkev Budd Chavooshian, Aug. 11, 1946; children: J. Dean, Nora Ann. Student, Art Students League, 1943, Reginald Marsh, N.Y.C., 1943, Mario Cooper, 1977. Designer Needlework Arts Co., N.Y.C., 1943-44; illustrator John David Men's Store, N.Y.C., 1944-45; illustrator, layout artist Fawcett Publs., N.Y.C., 1945-47; designer, illustrator Pa. State U., University Park, 1947-49; art tchr. Trenton Pub. Sch., N.J., 1958-68, art cons. Title One Program, 1968-74; painting instr. Princeton Art Assn., N.J., 1974-77, 96, Jewish Cmty. Ctr., Ewing, N.J., 1974-85, Comtemporary Club, Trenton, 1974-85, YMCA, YWCA, Trent Ctr., Trenton, 1974—, various watercolor workshops, N.J., 1990—. Artist-at-large Alliance For Arts Edn., NJ, 1979—80; adj. asst. prof. art instr. Mercer County Coll., West Windsor, NJ, 1985—93; tchr. watercolor workshops Chalfonte, 2001, Cape May, NJ, H. Leeche Studio, Sarasota, Fla., 1998, Sarasota, 99, Art Ctr., Sarasota, 2001, Sarasota, 02. One-woman shows include Rider U., 1974, 2000, Rider Coll., 2002, Jersey City Mus., 1980, N.J. State Mus., 1981, 2001, Trenton City Mus., 1984, 1987, Arts Club, Washington, 1991, Magnolia Rm., Cape May, 1993—2003, Coryell Gallery, Lambertville, N.J., 1993, Chalfonte Cape May, 1993—96, 2001—03, Louisa Melrose Gallery, 2002, exhibited in group shows at Douglas Coll., N.J., 1977, Bergen Mus., Paramus, NJ, 1980—82, Hunterdon Art Ctr., Clinton, N.J., 1982, 1995, Morris Mus., Morristown, N.J., 1984, Allied Artists of Am., 1984, 1986, 1989, 1991—99, Salmagundi Club, N.Y.C., 1988, 1991—92, 1994—99, German Mus., 1995—96, Barron Art Ctr., Woodbridge, NJ, Ridgewood (N.J.) Art Inst., Art Works of Princeton and Trenton, 1995, Hunterdon County Cultural and Heritage Commn. Show, Clinton, N.J., 1995, Trenton City Mus., 2001; actor: others; Represented in permanent collections Mercer County Cultural and Heritage Commn., Arts Club of Washington, N.J. State Mus., Jersey City Mus., Trenton City Mus., Morris Mus., Rider U., Art Mus. San Lazarre, Italy, Bristol Myers Squibb, Johnson and Johnson, Schering Plough Corp., Pub. Svc. Electric and Gas Co., U.S. Trust, N.J. Blue Cross and Blue Shield, Eden Inst., Princeton, N.J., others. Recipient numerous awards Union Coll., E. Jane Given Meml. award, 1996, Pres. award, 1996, Rockport Pubs. Mass. Pub. Inclusion: Best of Watercolor, 1995, Watercolor Places, 1996, Graphic-Sha Pub. Co., The Best of Watercolor, Tokyo, 1996, Landscape Inspirations, 1997, Best of Sketching & Painting, 1998, The Artistic Touch 3, Creative Art Press, 1999, Mercer County Cultural and Heritage Commn. purchase award, 1999, Phillips Mill, Walter E. Martin Meml. award 1992, Patrons award for watercolor 1994, Am. Watercolor Soc., Phila Watercolor Club, Ligorno and Solansky award Hunterdon County Cultural and Heritage Commn., 1991, Cynthia Goodgal Meml. award, Moshe Bahire award Ridgewood Art Inst., 1992, 99, Ruth Ratay award Cmty. Arts Assn. Mid Atlantic Show, 1994, Elliot Liskin Meml. award Salmagundi Open Show, 1995, Thomas Moran Meml. award Salmagundi Open Show, 1999, Mus. award Trenton City Mus., 2000, D. Rodney and DaVinci Paint award Garden State Watercolor Soc., 2000, Dale Meyers medal, Salmagundi Club, NY, 2002, Niece Lumber award, Coryell Gallery, Lambertville, 2003; named Woman of Month Woman's Newspaper of Princeton, 1984, NJ State Coun. Arts fellow, 1979. Fellow Am. Artists Profl. League (Am. Arts Clon award 1973, Winsor Newton award 1980, Gold medal, Barron Art Ctr. award 1991, 93, Merit award 1993, Am. Artists Profl. League award 1994, Best in Show award, Best in Watercolor award 1995, others, representational painting award 1995); mem. Nat. Assn. Women Artists (two yr. nat. travel award 1985, Jeffrey Childs Willis Meml. award, Natl. Assn. Women Artists award 1999), S. Winston Meml. award 1988, (two yr. travel award 1996—), Catherine Lorillard Wolfe Art Club (Bee Paper Co. award 1977, Anna Hyatt Huntington bronze medal, 2000, Cynthia Goodgall Meml. award 1995), Allied Artists Am. (elected mem., Henry Gasser Meml. award 1992), N.J. Watercolor Soc. (Newton Art Ctr. award 1972, Helen K. Bermel award 1984, Howard Savs. Bank award 1986-87, Forbes Mag. award 1997, Lambertville Hist. Soc. award Coryell Gallery, 1995, 2001), Painters and Sculptors Soc. (Medal of Honor, Digby Chandle medal, others), Garden State Watercolor Soc. (Triangle Art Ctr. award 1976, 89, 94, Grumbacher Silver medal 1981, Merit award 1982, Trust Co. award 1987, Triangle award 1994, Art Express award, 1995, Rider U. Gallery award 1995, Cranbury Sta. Art Gallery award 1997, Daler Rowney and Da Vinci paint award 2000), Midwest Watercolor Soc., Nat. Arts Club (John Elliott award 1988), Phila. Watercolor Club (Village Art award 1991), Nat. Watercolor Soc. (signature), Am. Watercolor Soc. (signature). Democrat. Mem. Apostolic Ch. Armenia. Home: 222 Morningside Dr Trenton NJ 08618-4914

CHAWARSKI, MAREK CEZARY, psychologist, researcher, educator; b. Głabczyce, Poland, Sept. 17, 1959; came to U.S., 1989; s. Jan and Stanislawa Chawarski; m. Katarzyna Hildegarda Poetschke, Sept. 17, 1983; children: Szymon, Julian. MA, Jagellonian U., Cracow, Poland, 1987; MS, Yale U., 1992, PhM, 1993, PhD, 1995. Asst. psychologist Psychiat. Clinic of Cracow Med. U., 1983-84; asst. psychologist/therapist Outpatient Psychiat. Clinic of Amalagamated Hosp., Tarnów, Poland, 1985-87; jr. faculty mem., rschr. Jagellonian U., 1987-89; cons. Statis. Lab. Yale U., New Haven, 1992-95, sr. data analyst/mgr. dept. psychiatry, 1995-96, assoc. rsch. scientist, 1996-2000, asst. prof., 2000—. Contbr. articles to profl. publs., chpt. to book. Fulbright Found. scholar, 1989; Yale U. fellow, 1990-95. Mem. APA, AAAS, Polish Psychol. Assn. Office: Yale U Dept Psychiatry CMHC/SAC 34 Park St New Haven CT 06519-1109 E-mail: marek.chawarski@yale.edu.

CHAWNER, LUCIA MARTHA, English educator; b. Ithaca, N.Y., Dec. 2, 1933; d. Lowell Jenkins and Lucia Mary (Soule) C.; m. Movses Guichen Andreassian, Mar. 18, 1967 (div. June 1971). Student, Earlham Coll., 1951-53; BA, U. Colo., 1956; MA, So. Meth. U., 1975. Provisional cert. elem., secondary and talented and gifted, Tex.; profl. cert. reading specialist, Tex. Tchr. grade 7 lang. arts and social studies Stonewall Jackson, Dallas Ind. Sch. Dist., 1959-63; reading clinician Reinhardt, Dallas Ind. Sch. Dist., 1963-66; Reading Resource Pilot Project Lakewood, Dallas Ind. Sch. Dist., 1972-74; devel. curriculum specialist El Centro Coll., Dallas County C.C. Dist., Dallas, 1977-78; English tchr. Health Magnet, Dallas Ind. Sch. Dist., 1979-95; univ. supervising tchr. U. Tex. Dallas, Richardson, 1996—. Part-time instr. El Centro & Richland Colls., Dallas, 1978-88, Brookhaven Coll., Farmers Branch, Tex., 1996-98; mem. English lit. textbook adoption com. Dallas Ind. Sch. Dist., 1988-89; chmn. English dept. Health Magnet, Dallas Ind. Sch. Dist., 1989-94, mgr. innovative grant, 1994-95. Co-leader child and youth study U. Md., Dallas, 1967-69; pres. English-Speaking Union-Dallas Br., 1992-96; mem. Leadership Arts, Dallas Bus. Com. Arts, 1994-95, World Affairs Coun. Greater Dallas; region 7 chmn., nat. bd. mem. English-Speaking Union of USA, 1996-2000. Recipient Instrnl. grant Richland Coll., 1980; Advanced Study grantee Dallas Ind. Sch. Dist., 1973; Named Tchr. of the Yr., Health Magnet, 1991, Rotary Tchr. of the Yr., Health Magnet, 1993, nat. Merit award, English-Speaking Union of USA, 2000. Mem. Dallas Mus. Art League (bd. dirs. 1997—), New Conservatory of Dallas (bd. mem. 1999—, sec. 2002—), Friends SMU Librs. (bd. dirs. 1995-98), Assemblage (pres. 1987-88), Brit. Am. Commerce Assn., Dau. Brit. Empire (sec. 2003¼), Soc. Mayflower Descs., Dallas Knife and Fork Club, Inc. (Bd. Dirs. 2003—), Delta Delta Delta, Phi Delta Kappa, Pi Lambda Theta (Alpha Sigma chpt. pres. 2002—). Avocations: sculpture, needlepoint, fitness exercise, travel. Office: PO Box 141179 Dallas TX 75214-1179

CHAZELLE, BERNARD, computer science educator; b. Clamart, France, Nov. 5, 1955; s. Jean and Marie-Claire (Blanc) C.; m. Celia Martin, June 26, 1982; children: Damien, Anna. Engring. diploma, Ecole Nat. Supérieure des Mines de Paris, 1977; PhD, Yale U., 1980. Rsch. assoc. Carnegie-Mellon U., Pitts., 1980-82; from. asst. prof. to assoc. prof. Brown U., Providence, R.I., 1982-86; assoc. prof. Ecole Normale Superieure, Paris, 1985-86, Princeton (N.J.) U., 1986-89, prof., 1989—. Cons. Xerox Parc, Palo Alto, Calif., 1984, DEC SRC, 1984-93. Editor Algorithmica, Siam Jour. Computing, Jour. Algorithms, Computer Geometry: Theory & Applications, Internat. Jour. Computations Geometry and Applications, Discrete and Computational Geometry, Jour. Assn. for Computing Machinery; contbr. articles to profl. jours. Fellow French Ministry Fgn. Affairs, 1977, J.S. Guggenheim Meml. Found., 1994, NEC, 1998—. Fellow: Assn. for Computing Machinery; mem.: European Acad. Sci. Avocation: blues guitar. Office: Princeton U Dept Computer Sci Princeton NJ 08544-0001

CHEAH, KEONG-CHYE, psychiatrist, educator; b. Georgetown, Penang, West Malaysia, Mar. 15, 1939; came to U.S., 1959; s. Thean Hoe and Hun Kin (Keong) C.; m. Sandra Massey, June 10, 1968; children: Chylynn, Maylynn. BA in Psychology, U. Ark., 1962; MD, U. Ark., Little Rock, 1967, MS in Microbiology, 1968. Diplomate Am. Bd. Psychiatry and Neurology (examiner 1982, 85); cert. Ark. State Sci. Bd., Ark. State Med. Bd. Intern U. Ark. Med. Ctr., 1967-68; resident VA Med. Ctr. and U. Ark. Med. Ctr., Little Rock, 1968-72; chief addiction sect. Little Rock VA Med. Ctr., 1972-73, staff psychiatrist, 1975-80; chief psychiatry American Lake VA Med. Ctr., Tacoma, 1981-86; chief consultation, liason Am. Lake divsn. Puget Sound Health Care Sys., Tacoma, 1986-94; asst. prof. medicine, psychiatry U. Ark., Little Rock, 1975-81; asst. prof. psychiatry and behavioral scis. U. Wash., Seattle, 1981-86, clin. assoc. prof., 1987—2002, clin. assoc. prof. emeritus, 2002—. Mem. dist. br. com. The CHAMPUS, 1977-91; surveyor Jt. Commn. for Accreditation of Healthcare Orgns., 1990-93; site visitor AMA Continuing Med. Edn., 1979-83; book reviewer Jour. Am. Geriatrics Soc., 1984-85; mem. task force alcohol abuse VA Med. Dist. 27, 1984, survey mem. Sytematic External Rev. Process, 1985; mem. mental health plan adv. com. State of Ark., 1976-81, chmn. 1979-81, chmn. steering com., 1979; mem. Vietnamese Resettlement Program, 1979; many coms. Am. Lake VA Med. Ctr. including chmn. mental health coun. 1981-84, utilization rev. com., 1981-86. Contbr. articles and abstracts to profl. jours.; presenter to confs. and meetings of profl. socs. Mem. Parents Adv. Com., Lakes H.S., Wash., 1987-91; mem. Mayor's Budget and Fin. Foresight Com., 1992—, chmn. 1990-92; sch. cons. Child Study Ctr. U. Ark., 1972-74; bd. dirs. Crisis Ctr. Ark., 1974-79, chmn. pub. rels. com., 1975-79, mem. pers. com. 1974, vice chmn. bd. 1977; pres. Chinese Assn. Ctrl. Ark., 1977; mem. gifted edn. adv. coun. Clover Park Sch. Dist. 400, Wash., 1983-85, Parent Tchr. Student Orgn. Recipient U.S. Govt. scholarship 1959, cert. merit State of Ark., 1973, Leadership award, Mental Health Svcs. Divsn., State of Ark., 1980. Fellow Am. Psychiat. Assn. (sec. treas. Asian Am. caucus 1985-87, pres. 1987-94); mem. Assn. Mil. Surgeons U.S., Wash. State Psychiat. Assn. (mem. peer rev. com. 1982-92, chmn. pub. psychiatry com. 1985-93, exec. coun. 1985-93), N. Pacific Soc. Neurology and Psychiatry Assn. (sec.-treas. 1986-99, pres. 1993), S. Puget Sound Psychiat. Assn., Assn. Chinese-Am. Psychiatrists, Chapel of Four Chaplains, Ark. Caduceus Club, Alpha Epsilon Delta, Psi Chi, Phi Beta Kappa, Alpha Omega Alpha. Avocations: reading, target shooting.

CHEATHAM, JOHN BANE, JR., retired mechanical engineering educator; b. Houston, June 29, 1924; s. John Bane and Winnie (Carr) C.; m. Juanita Faye Burns, July 19, 1947; children— Preston, Curtis. BME, So. Methodist U., 1948, MS, 1953; ME, M.I.T., 1954; PhD, Rice U., 1960. Registered profl. engr. Design engr. Linkbelt Co., Dallas and Houston, 1949-50; rsch. engr. Atlantic Refining Co., Dallas, 1950-53; rsch. assoc., head drilling rschr. Shell Devel. Co., Houston, 1954-63; prof. mech. engring. Rice U., 1963-96; chmn. dept. mech. engring. and materials sci., 1994-96; pres. Cheatham Engring. Inc., Houston, 1977-94, Techaid Corp., Houston, 1978-88. Cons. in field. Contbr. to profl. jours.; tech. editor: Jour. Energy Resources Tech, 1979-81. Served to 2d lt. USAAF, 1943-45. Fellow ASME; mem. Am. Inst. Mining and Petroleum Engrs., Am. Soc. Engring. Edn., Sigma Xi. Address: 5671 Longmont Dr Houston TX 77056-2344 E-mail: john_cheatham@hotmail.com.

CHEE, ANN-PING, music educator; b. July 26; came to U.S., 1964; d. To-Khiem Thi and Thanh-Phuc Dong; m. Anthony N.C. Chee, Dec. 27, 1969; children: Andrew, Lawrence. BA in Music cum laude, Conn. Coll., 1970. Tchr. piano, music theory, Houston, 1972—. Named to Piano Guild Hall of Fame, Austin, Tex., 1997. Mem. Nat. Guild Piano Tchrs. (cert.), Music Tchrs. Nat. Assn. (cert.), Tex. Music Tchrs. Assn., Houston Music Tchrs. Assn., Houston Fedn. Music Clubs, Forum Music Tchrs. Assn., Associated Bd. Royal Schs. Music London.

CHEEK, BARBARA LEE, college reading program director, educator; b. Springfield, Mo., Oct. 25, 1935; d. Curtis Earl and Gertrude Helen (Ahonen) Nelson; m. Lee Roy Clyde, June 16, 1961; children: Michael, Paul, Daniel. BA in Edn. cum laude, Pacific Luth. U., 1957; postgrad., U. Wash., Seattle, 1961-62; MA in Elem. Reading Edn., Boise (Idaho) State U., 1982; postgrad., Ea. Oreg. U., 1983, Seattle U., 1989. Cert. elem. and secondary edn. tchr., Wash. Sec. engring. dept. Boeing Aircraft Co., Seattle, 1957; instr. Edmonds (Wash.) Sch. Dist., 1957-61, Clover Pk. Sch. Dist., Tacoma, 1961-62, Payette (Idaho) Sch. Dist., 1970-74; bookkeeper Cheek Dairy Supply, Payette, 1970-71; instr. Ontario (Oreg.) Sch. Dist., 1975-79; prof. Treasure Valley C.C., Ontario, 1979-89, Pierce Coll., Tacoma, 1989-2001, dir. reading dept., 1989-96; dir. Alternative Learning Ctr. at Pierce Coll., Puyallup, Wash., 1996—2001; mem. faculty emeritus Pierce Coll., Puyallup, Wash., 2001—; instr. Profl. Excellence Program Tacoma (Wash.) Sch. Dist., 1994; pvt. reading tutor and cons., 2001—; Stephen min. Luth. Ch., 2003—. Sec. Malheur Reading Coun., Ont., 1986—87; faculty exec. bd. Treasure Valley C.C. Faculty, Ont., 1986—88; mem. Peer Evaluation Oreg. Devel. Edn., Ont., 1986; cons. Tacoma Sch. Dist. Profl. Excellence Program, 1993—; exec. Pharmanex/Nu-Skin Enterprises, 1994—; rep. Avon Cosmetics, 2003—. Moderator Ont. candidate's fair AAUW, 1985, state sec., Payette, 1972-74, sec. N.W. region, 1974, br. pres., 1970-72, 75-77; bd. dirs. Boy Scouts Am., Oregon, Idaho, 1971-84; deacon, v.p. Luth. Ch., 1986; mem. basic literacy steering com. Tacoma, 1992; mem. Pierce County Literacy Coalition, Tacoma, Scandinavian Cultural Ctr., Pacific Luth. U.; asst. min. Luth. Ch., 1984—, Stephen Min. Leader, 2003-, Stephen Min., 2002-. Recipient Faculty Devel. award Higher Edn. State of Wash., 1990-91. Mem. AAUW (chpt. pres. 1970-72), ASCD, Western Coll. Reading Assn., Wash. State C.C., Faculty Devel. (state com.), Wash. Devel. Edn. Assn., Am. Assn. Women in Comty. and Jr. Colls., Wash. Fedn. of Tchrs. (faculty exec. bd.), Coll. Reading and Learning Assn. (pres-elect Washington, Idaho 1998-99, pres. N.W. region 1999-2001), Tchr. English to Spkrs. of Other Langs., Sweet Adelines (pres. Tacoma chpt. 2001-02), Internat., Alpha Delta Kappa (v.p. 1986), N.W. Coll. Reading and Learning Assn. (pres. 1999-2000). Republican. Avocations: handbell choir, soloist, reading, golf, skiing. E-mail: tracinda@worldnet.att.net.

CHELAPATI, CHUNDURI VENKATA, civil engineering educator; b. Eluru, India, Mar. 11, 1933; came to U.S., 1957, naturalized, 1971; s. Lakshminarayana and Anjamma (Kanumuri) Chunduri. B.E. with honors, Andhra U., India, 1954; MS, U. Ill., 1959, PhD, 1962. Jr. engr. Office of Chief Engr., State of Andhra, India, 1954-55; asst. prof. structural engring. Birla Coll. Engring., Pilani, India, 1956-57; research asst. dept. civil engring. U. Ill., 1957-62; asst. prof. engring. Calif. State U., Los Angeles, 1962-65, assoc. prof. Long Beach, 1965-70, prof. civil engring., 1970—96, vice chmn. dept., 1971-73, chmn. dept., 1973-79, coordinator profl. engring. rev. programs, 1972-81, dir. continuing engring. edn., 1982—96, dir. CADDS Research Ctr., 1986—96; pres. C.V. Chelapati & Assos., Inc., Huntington Beach, Calif., 1979—2001. Cons. USN Civil Engring. Lab., 1962—68, 1975—94, Holmes & Narver, Inc., Anaheim, Calif., 1968—73; pres. Profl. Engring. Devel. Publs., 1988—, Continuing Profl. Edn. Inst., 2000—, Irvine Inst. Tech., 2002—. Contbr. articles to profl. jours. Mem. ASCE, Am. Soc. Engring. Edn., Structural Engrs. Assn. So. Calif., Earthquake Engring. Research Inst., Seismol. Soc. Am., Am. Concrete Inst., Am. Inst. Steel Constrn., Sigma Xi, Chi Epsilon, Tau Beta Pi, Phi Kappa Phi. Home: 16292 Mandalay Cir Huntington Beach CA 92649-2107 Office: 8659 Research Dr Irvine CA 92618

CHELSTROM, MARILYN ANN, political education consultant; b. Mpls., Dec. 5; d. Arthur Rudolph and Signe (Johnson) C. BA, U. Minn., 1950; LHD, Oklahoma City U., 1981. Staff asst. Mpls. Citizens Com. Public Edn., 1950-57; coord. policies and procedures Lithium Corp. Am., Inc., Mpls., N.Y.C., 1957-62; exec. dir. The Robert A. Taft Inst. Govt., N.Y.C., 1962-77, exec. v.p., 1977-78, pres., 1978-89, pres. emeritus, 1990—; polit. edn. cons., 1990—; pres. Chelstrom Connection, 1992—. Home: 9600 Portland Ave Minneapolis MN 55420-4564 Office: 155 E 38th St New York NY 10016-2660

CHEN, CATHERINE WANG, provost; b. Chengdu, China, Sept. 19, 1938; came to U.S., 1963; d. S.C. and Y.T. (Chia) Wang; m. Hsuan S. Chen, Sept. 10, 1966; children: James, John. BA, Nat. Taiwan U., Taipei, 1960; MA, U. Minn., 1966, PhD, 1975. Instr. U. Minn., Mpls., 1966-69; lectr. U. Mich., Ann Arbor, 1970-71; reference libr. Northwood U., Middland, Mich., 1971-74, libr. dir., 1974-85, dir. librs., 1985-89, acad. dean, 1989-94, provost, 1994—. Bd. dirs. ARC, Midland, 1992-95, Jr. Achievement, Midland, 1994-96, United Way. Mem. Assn. for Higher Edn. Avocations: theater, reading, travel. Office: Northwood U 4000 Whiting Dr Midland MI 48640-2311 E-mail: chenc@northwood.edu.

CHEN, CHING JEN, mechanical engineering educator, research scientist; b. Taipei, Taiwan, July 6, 1936; came to U.S., 1960; s. I Sung Chen and T. Yen Chen; m. Ruei-Man, Aug. 14, 1965; children— Sandra, Anthony Diploma, Taipei Inst. Tech., 1957; MS in Mech. Engring., Kans. State U., 1962; PhD, Case Western Res. U., 1967. Design engr. Ta-Tung Grinding Co., Taipei, 1959-61; asst. prof. mech. engring. U. Iowa, Iowa City, 1967-70, assoc. prof., 1970-77, prof., 1977-82, chmn., prof. energy div., 1982-84, chmn., prof. dept. mech. engring., 1982-92; sr. rsch. scientist Iowa Inst. Hydraulic Research, 1970-92; mem. exec. com. Iowa Space Grant Coll. Consortium, 1990-92; dean Coll. Engring. Fla. A&M U.-Fla. State U., Tallahassee, 1992—. Cons. govtl. agys., mil. and industry Mem. editorial bd. Altas of Visualization, 1991—96, Atlas of Visualization 1991—; evaluator Accreditation Bd. for Engring. and Tech., 1991—; assoc. editor Jour. Engring. Mechanics, 1990-93; U.S. regional editor Internat. Jour. Visualization, 1997—; mem. editl. bd. Jour. Hybrid Methods in Engring.; contbr. articles to profl. publs. Old Gold fellow Iowa Found., 1968; U.S. sr. Scientist awardee Alexander von Humboldt Fund, Fed. Republic Germany, 1974; hon. prof. Wuhan Inst. of Hydraulic and Elec. Engring, Peoples Republic of China. Fellow ASME, ASCE; mem. AIAA, Am. Soc. Engring. Edn., Internat. Hydraulic Research, Am. Phys. Soc., Soc. Theoretical and Applied Mechanics (hon.) (Taiwan), Japan Soc. Visualization, Sigma Xi. Home: 4643 High Grove Rd Tallahassee FL 32309-2974 Office: FAMU-FSU Coll Engring 2525 Pottsdamer St Tallahassee FL 32310-6046

CHEN, CHUANSHENG, education educator; b. Yongkang, Zhejiang, China, Sept. 2, 1963; s. Lianbu and Xiangqin (Zhang) C.; m. Panfang Fu, May 24, 1990; children: Anthony, Brandon. BS, Hangzhou U., China, 1982; postgrad., Beijing Normal U., 1982-84; MA, U. Mich., 1987, PhD, 1992. Rsch. asst. U. Mich., Ann Arbor, 1985-88, rsch. assoc., 1989-92, teaching asst., 1989-90; asst. prof. U. Calif., Irvine, 1992—96, assoc. prof., 1996—, chmn. dept., 2001—. Contbr. articles to profl. jours. and chpts. to books. Recipient Rsch. award Johann Jacobs Found., 1992-94, Pacific Rim Rsch. Program, 1993-94, U. Calif.-Irvine, 1992—, Spencer fellowship Nat. Acad. Edn., 1993-95. Mem. APA, AAAS, Am. Psychol. Soc., Soc. for Rsch. in Child Devel., Am. Ednl. Rsch. Assn. Avocation: hiking. Office: U Calif Sch Social Ecology Irvine CA 92697

CHEN, EDNA LAU, art educator, artist; b. Lanai City, Hawaii, Apr. 20, 1932; d. George S.H. and Amy Lau; m. Francis F. Chen, Mar. 31, 1956; children: Sheryl Frances, Patricia Ann, Robert Francis. BA, U. No. Colo., 1954; MA, Columbia U., 1955. Cert. tchr., Calif. Tchr. Somerville (N.J.) H.S., 1955-56, Littlebrook Sch., Princeton, N.J., 1956-57, L.A. County Mus., 1978-81, Beverly Hills (Calif.) Adult Sch., 1976—; vol., founder, dir. Garret 21, Warner Sch., L.A., 1971-77. Artist-in-residence Volcano (Hawaii) Art Ctr., 1978, 80. Solo shows include Gallery 100, Princeton, N.J., 1964, 68, 72, 73, Jacqueline Anhalt Gallery, L.A., 1975, Elaine Starkman Gallery, N.Y.C., 1983, Art Loft, Honolulu, 1983, 85, 87. Named Tchr. of Yr., Beverly Hills Kiwanis Club, 1979. Democrat. Unitarian Universalist. Avocations: tennis, triathlon, backpacking, gardening. Home: 638 Westholme Ave Los Angeles CA 90024-3248

CHEN, GUI-QIANG, mathematician, educator, researcher; b. Cixi, Zhejiang, People's Republic of China, May 25, 1963; came to U.S., 1987; parents Zhi-Biao and Jin-Er (Hu) C. BS, Fudan U., Shanghai, People's Republic China, 1982; PhD, Acad. Sinica, Beijing, 1987. Asst. prof. Inst. Systems Sci., Acad. Sinica, 1987; vis. scientist Courant Inst. Math. Scis., N.Y.C., 1987-89; asst. prof. math. U. Chgo., 1989-94; assoc. prof. math. Northwestern U., 1994-96, prof., 1996—. Cons. Argonne Nat. Lab., Chgo., 1989-95. Editor: SIAM Jour. Math. Analysis, Jour. Applied Math. and Physics, Jour. Partial Differential Equations, Acta Math. Sci., Acta Math. Applications Sci., Chinese Annals Math., Comm. Pure and Applied Analysis, Jour. Hyperbolic Differential Equations. Recipient Young Investigator award NSF, Beijing, China, 1987, Nat. Medal of Sci., People's Republic of China, 1989; Alfred P. Sloan Rsch. fellow, 1991, Alexander von Humboldt rsch. fellow, 2003; named Excellent Young Scientist, Beijing Soc. for Sci. and Tech., 1988. Mem.: Soc. for Indsl. and Applied Math. (editor jour.),

Am. Math. Soc. Office: Northwestern Univ Dept Math Evanston IL 60208-2730 E-mail: gqchen@math.northwestern.edu.

CHEN, HO-HONG H. H. industrial engineering executive, educator; b. Taiwan, Apr. 11, 1933; s. Shui-Cheng and Mei (Lin) C.; m. Yuki-Lihua Jenny, Mar. 10, 1959; children: Benjamin Kuen-Tsai, Carl Joseph Chao-Kuang, Charles Chao-Yu, Eric Chao-Ying, Charmine Tsuey-Ling, Dolly Hsiao-Ying, Edith Yi-Wen, Yvonne Yi-Fang, Grace Yi-Sing, Julia Yi-Jiun. Owner Tai Chang Indsl. Supplies Co., Ltd., 1967—; pres. Pan Pacific Indsl. Supplies, Inc., Ont., Can., 1975—, Maker Group Inc., Md., 1986—, Wako Internat. Co., Ltd., Md., 1986—. Prof. First Econ. U., Japan; commr. Overseas Chinese Affairs Commn., Taiwan; chmn. supervisory bd. Global Alliance for Democracy and Peace, Taiwan. Author: 500 Creative Designs for Future Business, 1961; A Summary of Suggestions for the Economic Development in Central America Countries, 1979; Access and Utilize the Potential Fund in Asia, 1980. Mem. Univ. Club (Washington), Kenwood Golf & Country Club (Bethesda, Md.). Office: PO Box 5674 Washington DC 20016-1274

CHEN, HOLLIS CHING, electrical engineering, computer science educator; b. Chekiang, China, Nov. 17, 1935; came to U.S., 1960; naturalized, 1971; s. Yu-Chao and Shui-Tan C.; m. Donna H. Liu, Sept. 3, 1961 (dec. Apr. 1988); children: Deiree, Hollis. BS, Nat. Taiwan U., 1957; MS, Ohio U., 1961; PhD, Syracuse U., 1965. Instr., asst. prof. Syracuse (N.Y.) U., 1961-67; asst., assoc. prof. Ohio U., Athens, 1967-75, prof., 1975—, acting chmn. dept. elec. and computer engring., 1984-86. Author: Theory of EM Waves, 1983, (with others) Research Topics in EM Wave Theory, 1981; contbr. articles to profl. jours. Mem. AAAS, IEEE (sr.), Internat. Union Radio Sci., Am. Soc. for Engring. Edn., Soc. Indsl. and Applied Math., Math. Assn. Am., Am. Geophys. Union, Optical Soc. Am. Home: 1 Ball Dr Athens OH 45701-3621 Office: Ohio U Sch Elec Engring & Computer Sci Athens OH 45701

CHEN, JAMES PAI-FUN, biology educator, researcher; b. Fengyuan, Taichung, Taiwan, May 1, 1929; came to U.S., 1952; s. Chuan and Su-wuo (Lin) C.; m. Metis Hsiu-chun Lin, Dec. 19, 1964; children: Mark Hsin-tzu, Eunice Hsin-yi, Jeremy Hsin-tao. BS, Houghton (N.Y.) Coll., 1955; MS, St. Lawrence U., 1957; PhD, Pa. State U., 1961. From instr. to assoc. prof. Houghton Coll., 1960-64; rsch. assoc. Coll. of Medicine U. Vt., Burlington, 1964-65; rsch. assoc. Sch. of Medicine SUNY, Buffalo, 1965-68; asst. prof. U. Tex. Med. Br., Galveston, 1968-75; sr. rsch. assoc. NASA/Johnson Space Ctr., Houston, 1975-76; rsch. assoc. prof. U. Tenn. Meml. Rsch. Ctr., Knoxville, 1976-78; assoc. prof. Coll. of Medicine U. Tenn., Knoxville, 1978-84, prof. Grad. Sch. of Medicine, 1984—. Rsch. rev. com. Tex. affiliate Am. Heart Assn., Austin, 1974-76; co-investigator Spacelab I project, Johnson Space Ctr., Houston, 1976-83; vis. prof. Trnovo Hosp. Internal Medicine, Ljubljana, Yugoslavia, 1985. Contbr. over 50 articles to profl. jours. including Thrombosis and Haemostasis. Grantee Robert Welch Found., 1970-74, Ortho Rsch. Found., 1971-75, NIH, 1975-82, Am. Heart Assn. Tex. affiliate, 1969-72, 74-75, Am. Heart Assn. Tenn. affiliate, 1984-85, 89-90, U.S. Army Med. Rsch., 1988-91. Fellow Internat. Soc. Hematology; mem. Am. Assn. Immunologists, Am. Soc. Biochemistry and Molecular Biology, Internat. Soc. Thrombosis and Haemostasis, Internat. Fibrinogen Rsch. Soc., Internat. Soc. Fibrinolysis Proteolysis, Am. Bd. Bioanalysis (clin. lab. dir.). Achievements include research in thrombosis and hemostasis; discovery of additional proteolytic fragmentation in the high temperature trypsin cleavage of human IgM; development of a radioimmunoassay for fragment E-neoantigen and applied it to the clinical assay of hypercoagulable state; discovered evidence of the coagulopathy in Pichinde virus-infected guinea pigs; establishment of blood tests to monitor trauma patients for thromboembolism; recognized that hypercoagulability in preterm infants with intraventricular hemorrhage is associated with fibrinolytic shutdown; ascertained that complement and cytokines are responsible for antibody-mediated hypercoagulability in the anti-T-cell therapy of transplantation. Office: U Tenn Med Ctr Dept Med Genetics Box 2 1924 Alcoa Hwy Knoxville TN 37920-1511 E-mail: jchen@mc.utmck.edu., jpaifunchen@yahoo.com.

CHEN, JUDY FAYE, music educator; b. LaJunta, Colo., Jan. 11, 1948; d. Vernon Lafayette and Grace Ama (Young) Boyd; m. Bill Chung-moon Chen, Dec. 26, 1971; children: William, James Thomas. BS in Mus. Edn., Wichita State U., 1971; postgrad. in second lang. edn., U. Houston, 1988, 94. Mgr. credit & office United Jewelers, Houston, 1981-88; substitute tchr. Klein Ind. Sch. Dist., Houston, 1988-90, tchr. elem. sch. music, 1990—. Mem. boys town com. Nitsch Elem. Sch., Houston, 1994, vol. choir dir., 1992-94. Avocations: reading, crocheting, cooking.

CHEN, PETER CONWAY, chemistry educator; b. New Haven, June 3, 1964; s. H.R. and Grace C. Chen; m. Yuko Mizuno, June 12, 1992. AB, Cornell U., 1986; PhD, U. Wis., 1992. Assoc. prof. Spelman Coll., Atlanta, 1992—. Mem. editl. bd. Asian Jour. Spectroscopy. Recipient Reilley-Upjohn award The Upjohn Co., Kalamazoo, Mich., 1992, NASA faculty award for rsch., NSF Careers award. Mem. Am. Chem. Soc., Soc. for Applied Spectroscopy, Sigma Xi, Sigma Pi Sigma. Achievements include research on infrared four wave mixing spectroscopy, laser chemical vapor deposition, SSOPO cars, multiplex cars, GC-Raman, and combustion diagnostics. Office: Spelman Coll Chemistry Dept 350 Spelman Ln SW Atlanta GA 30314-4399

CHEN, PETER PIN-SHAN, electrical engineering, computer science and internet/web educator, data processing executive; b. Taishan, Kwangtung, China, Jan. 3, 1947; came to U.S., 1969; s. Man-See and T.T. Chen; m. Li-Chuang Ho; children: Victoria, Angela, Gloria Lily. BSEE, Nat. Taiwan U., Republic of China, 1968; MS, Harvard U., 1970, PhD, 1973. Student assoc. IBM, Yorktown Heights, N.Y., 1970; teaching fellow Harvard U., Cambridge, Mass., 1970-71; prin. engr. Honeywell, Waltham, Mass., 1973-74; vis. researcher Digital Equipment Corp., Maynard, Mass., 1974; asst. prof. MIT, Cambridge, Mass., 1974-78; assoc. prof. UCLA, 1978-82; Sinclair vis. prof. MIT, 1986-87; Foster Disting. Chair prof. La. State U., Baton Rouge, 1983—. Vis. prof. Harvard U., Cambridge, 1990, MIT, Cambridge, 1990-92; chmn. Chen & Assocs. Inc., Baton Rouge, 1978—; pres. ER Inst., Baton Rouge, 1980—. Author: Entity-Relationship Approach to Logical DB Design, 1978, ER to Systems Analysis, 1980, ER to Information Modeling, 1983; patentee in field. Tech. officer with Republic of China mil. svcs., 1968-69. Named to Data Mgmt. Hall of Fame, 2000; recipient Faculty Career award, UCLA, 1979, Info. Tech. award, Data Adminstrn. Mgmt. Assn., 1990, Gt. Paper in Computer Sci. Achievement award, Data Adminstrn. Mgmt. Assn. Internat., 2000, Stevens award, 2001, Allen Newell award, ACM/AAAI, 2002; Rsch. grantee, NSF, NIST, NIH, Dept. Def., Air Force, Air Force Office Sci. Rsch., Navy, others, 1978—. Fellow: AAAS, IEEE (Harry Goode award 2003), Assn. Computing Machines. Office: La State Univ Computer Sci Dept Baton Rouge LA 70803-0001 E-mail: pchen@lsu.edu.

CHEN, ROGER (RONGXIN CHEN), management educator; b. Shanghai, China, Jan. 20, 1961; m. Hong (Emily) Xu, June 30, 1992; 1 child, Angela. MS, Shanghai Jiao Tong U., 1986; PhD, U. Tex., Dallas, 1995. Lectr. Sch. of Mgmt., Shanghai Jiao Tong U., China, 1986—89; assoc. prof. Sch. of Bus. and Mgmt., U. of San Francisco, San Francisco, 1995—. V.p. Silicon Valley Bus. Forum Inc., Palo Alto, Calif., 1999—. Recipient Silicaon Valley Roundtable Guru award, U.S. Nat. Bus. Econs. Assn. and Silicon Valley Roundtable, 1999, Abramson award for Outstanding Article, (jour.) Bus. Econs., 1998. Mem.: World Affairs Coun., Acad. of Mgmt. Assn. Office: Bus Sch U San Francisco 2130 Fulton St San Francisco CA 94117 Office Fax: 415-422-2502. Business E-Mail: chenr@usfca.edu.

CHEN, SOW-HSIN, nuclear engineering educator, researcher; b. Chia-Yi, Taiwan, Mar. 5, 1935; came to U.S., 1958, naturalized, 1974; s. Pi-Yu Chen and Liang Hsu; m. Ching-Chih Liu, Aug. 19, 1961; children: Anne, Catherine, John. BS in Physics, Nat. Taiwan U., 1956; MS in Physics, Nat. Tsinghua U., 1958; MS in Nuclear Engring., U. Mich., 1962; PhD in Physics, McMaster U., 1964. Postdoctoral fellow AERE Harwell, Berkshire, U.K., 1965; asst. prof. physics U. Waterloo, Ont., Can., 1964-67; rsch. fellow Harvard U., Cambridge, Mass., 1967; asst. prof., then assoc. prof. nuclear engring. MIT, Cambridge, 1968-74, prof. nuclear engring., 1974—. Vis. prof. Tsinghua U., Peking, China, 1982, Ecole Superieure de Physique et Chemie, Paris, 1981, Univ. Konstanz, Germany, 1988, Univ. Bayreuth, Germany, 1988, Univ. Brodeaux I, France, 1991, 93; chmn. Gordon Conf., 1986; co-organizer ACS Conf., Conf. Colloid and Interface Sci.: Trends and Applications, 1985; dir. NATO ASI on Scattering Techniques Applied to Supramolecular and Non-Equilibrium Systems, 1980, Structure and Dynamics of Supramolecular Aggregates and Strongly Interacting Colloids, 1991. Author: Spectroscopy in Biology, Chemistry and Physics-Neutron, X-Ray and Laser, 1975, Scattering Techniques Applied to Supramolecular and Non-Equilibrium Systems, 1981, Micellar Solutions and Microemulsions: Structure: Dynamics and Statistical Thermodynamics, 1990, Structure and Dynamics on Strongly Interacting Colliods and Supramolecular Aggregates in Solution, 1992, Interaction of Photons and Neutrons with Matter-An Introduction, 1997; contbr. 300 articles to sic. jours. Alexander von Humboldt U.S. sr. scientist award Govt. of Germany, 1987-88, 95. Fellow AAAS, Am. Phys. Soc., Japan Soc. for the Promotion of Sci. (Rsch. fellow 1995); mem. Sigma Xi. Home: 1400 Commonwealth Ave Newton MA 02465-2830 Office: MIT 24-209 77 Mass Ave Cambridge MA 02139-4307 E-mail: sowhsin@mit.edu.

CHEN, WAI-KAI, electrical engineering and computer science educator, consultant; b. Nanking, China, Dec. 23, 1936; came to U.S., 1959; s. You-Chao and Shui-Tan (Shen) C.; m. Shirley Shiao-Ling, Jan. 13, 1939; children— Jerome, Melissa BS in Elec. Engring., Ohio U., 1960, MS in Elec. Engring., 1961; PhD in Elec. Engring., U. Ill., Urbana, 1964. Asst. prof. Ohio U., 1964-67, assoc. prof., 1967-71, prof., 1971-78, disting. prof., 1978-81; prof., head dept. elec. engring. and computer sci. U. Ill., Chgo., 1981-2001; vis. assoc. prof. Purdue U., 1970-71; v.p. for acad. affairs Internat. Technol. U., 2000—. Hon. prof. Tianjing U., Peoples Republic of China, 1990, Beijing U. of Posts and Telecomms., Beijing U. of Aeronautics and Astronautics, 1992. Author: Applied Graph Theory, 1970, Theory and Design of Broadband Matching Networks, 1976, Applied Graph Theory: Graphs and Electrical Networks, 1976, Active Network and Feedback Amplifier Theory, 1980, Linear Networks and Systems, 1983, Passive and Active Filters: Theory and Implementations, 1986, The Collected Papers of Professor Wai-Kai Chen, 1987, Broadband Matching: Theory and Implementations, 1988, Theory of Nets, 1990, Linear Networks and Systems: Computer-Aided Solutions and Implementations, 1990, Active Network Analysis, 1991, Modern Network Analysis, 1992, Computer-Aided Design of Comm. Networks World Scientific, 2000; editor: Brooks/Cole Series in Electrical Engineering, 1982-84; editor in chief Advanced Series in Elec. and Computer Engring., World Sci. Pub. Co., Singapore, 1986—, Jour. Circuits, Systems and Computers, 1989—, The Circuits and Filters Handbook, 1995, 2d edit., 2002, The VLSI Handbook, 2000, Design Automation, Languages and Simulations, 2003, VLSI Technology, 2003, Memory, Microprocessor and ASIC, 2003, Analog Circuits and Devices, 2003, Logic Design, 2003; editor The Elec. Engring. Handbook, 1998—, Imperial Coll. Press, 1998—, others; editor The VLSI Series, 2000—; assoc. editor Jour. Circuits, Systems and Signal Processing, 1981—; editor in charge Advanced Series in Circuits and Systems, World Scientific Publ. Co., 1991—; sect. editor Encyclopedia of Physical Science & Technology, 1998-2001; editor-in chief Design Automation, Languages and Simulation, Memory, Microprocessor and ASIC, Analog Circuits and Devices, Logic Design, VLSI Tschmology, CRC Press, 2003. Recipient Lester R. Ford award Math. Assn. Am., 1967, Baker Fund award Ohio U., 1974, 78, Disting. Accomplishment award Chinese Acad. & Profl. Assn. in Mid-Am., 1985, Disting. Guest Prof. award Chuo U., Tokyo, 1987, Outstanding Svc. award Chinese Acad. & Profl. Assn. in Mid-Am., 1988, Outstanding Achievement award Mid-Am. Chinese Sci. & Tech. Assn, 1988, Disting. Alumnus award Elec. and Computer Engring. Dept. Alumni Assn. U. Ill. Urbana-Champaign, 1988, Alexander von Humboldt award Alexander von Humboldt Stiftung, Fed. Republic of Germany, 1985, Rsch. award U. Ill. Chgo. Coll. Engring., 2000, hon. prof. award Nanjing Inst. of Technology and Zhejing U., Peoples Republic of China, 1985, The Northeast U. Tech., East. China Inst. Tech., Nanjing Inst. of Posts & Telecommunications, AnHui U., Chengdu Inst. Radio Engring., Wuhan Univ.; Rsch. Inst. fellow Ohio U., 1972, Japan Soc. for Promotion of Sci., 1986, Sr. U. Scholar award U. Ill., 1986, Ohio U. Alumni Medal Merit for Disting. Achievement in Engring. Edn., 1987, Hon. Prof. award Hangzhan U. of Electronic Tech., China, 1990, Disting. Prof. award Internat. Technol. U., 1995, Hon. Prof. award Taichung U. Healthcare and Mgmt., Taiwan, 2002, Disting. Alumnus award Taipei U. Sci. and Tech., Taiwan, 2002. Fellow IEEE (Circuits and Sys. Soc. Meritorious Svc. award 1997, Edn. award 1998, Golden Jubilee medal 2000, Third Millennium medal 2000), AAAS; mem. NSPE, IEEE Cirs. and Sys. Soc. (adminstrv. com. 1985-87, exec. v.p. 1987, assoc. editor Trans. on Cirs. and Sys. 1977-79, editor 1991-93, pres.-elect 1993, pres. 1994), Md.-Am. Chinese Sci. and Tech. Assn. (bd. dirs. 1984-86, 89-93, pres. 1991-92), Chinese Acad. and Profl. Assn. Mid-Am. (advisor to bd. dirs. 1984-89, pres. 1986-87), Soc. Indsl. and Applied Math., Assn. Computing Machinery, Tensor Soc. Gt. Britain, Sigma Xi (sec.-treas. Ohio U. chpt. 1981), Phi Kappa Phi, Eta Kappa Nu. Office: Internat Technol U 1650 Warburton Ave Santa Clara CA 95050-3714

CHENAULT, SHERYL ANN, elementary education educator; b. Springfield, Mo., May 16, 1953; d. Melvin James and Helenkay (Peterson) Catt; m. Daniel Alden Chenault, June 7, 1975. BS, East Tex. State U., Commerce, 1975; MEd, U. North Tex., Denton, 1987. Resource tchr. Brentfield Elem., Richardson, Tex., 1975-83, Liberty Jr. High Sch., Richardson, 1983-86, Jess Harben Elem., Richardson, 1986-88; tchr. 3rd grade, resource spl. edn., 4th grade Risd Acad., Richardson, 1988-95; tchr. 4th grade Classical Magnet Sch., Richardson, 1995—2000; tchr. 6th grade Richland Elem., Richardson, 2000—02; instrnl. specialist Dover Elem., Richardson, 2002—. Demonstration tchr. reading tchrs., Richardson, 1990; facilitator sch.-based mgmt., Richardson, 1990. Mem. ASCD, Internat. Reading Assn., Tex. Assn. Children and Adults with Learning Disabilities, Assn. Tex. Profl. Educators, Richardson Edn. Assn., Phi Delta Kappa, Kappa Delta Pi Alumnae Assn. (cert. of honor for outstanding svc. 1983), Alpha Delta Pi. Home: 1622 Tynes Dr Garland TX 75042-4701

CHENEY, ELEANORA LOUISE, retired secondary education educator; b. Seneca Falls, N.Y., June 3, 1923; d. Guy Darrell and Alice Augusta (McCoy) Stevenson; m. John C. Dinsmore, Jan. 13, 1941 (div. 1953); children: Patricia Walter, Nancy Shannon, Jon Dinsmore (dec.); m. Daniel Lavern Cheney, Aug. 8, 1959. BA, Rutgers U., 1966; MA, U. Glassboro, 1971. Account clk. GE, Auburn, N.Y., 1953-58; supr. accounts payable Sylvania Electric, Camillus, N.Y., 1958-60; cost acctg. clk. RCA, Cherry Hill, N.J., 1960-64; honors English tchr. Lenape Regional High Sch., Medford, N.J., 1966-74; guidance counselor Shawnee High Sch., 1974-82; owner Another World of Travel, Marlton, N.J., 1984-86; co-founder, trustee, sec. Danellie Found., 1991—. Part-time travel agt., 1986—; myriad pub., 1983—. Counselor Contact Ministries, Moorestown, N.J., 1976—; mem. fin. com., nominating com. Haddonfield (N.J.) United Meth. Ch., 1987-92, supr. ch. sch., 1980-82; bd. dirs. Fellowship House, Camden, N.J., 1994—, Robins' Nest, Glassboro, N.J., 1995—; mem. adminstrv. coun. Haddonfield (N.J.) United Meth. Ch., 1996-99, 2003—, leader small group, 1990—, mem. adminstrv. coun., 2003—; established Jon W. Dinsmore Meml. Math. Scholarship Cherry Hill West, NJ, 1997—. Named to Nat. Woman's Hall of Fame, 1994. Mem. AAUW. Republican. Methodist. Avocations: reading, knitting, gardening. Home: 5 Snapdragon Ln Marlton NJ 08053-4421

CHENEY, LIANA DEGIROLAMI, art history educator; b. Milan, Apr. 24, 1942; d. Ettore Lombroso and Pina (Quarta) DeGirolami; married Aug. 31, 1968 (div. 1987). BS, U. Miami, Fla., 1968, BA, 1970; PhD, Boston U., 1978. Instr. art history U. Lowell, Mass., 1974-78, asst. prof., 1978-82, assoc. prof., 1982—, prof., 1985—, chmn. art dept., 1983—95, chmn. cultural studies dept., 2000. Curator Whistler Art Mus., Lowell, 1984-88; bd. dirs. Interdisciplinary Studio, Lowell, 1981-82; cons. in field. Author: Botticelli's Mythological Paintings, 1985, The Paintings of Casa Vasari, 1985, (with Paul Marks) The Whistler Papers, 1986, (with Edith Burger) Whistler and His Birthplace, 1992, Essays on Italian Mannerism, 1995, Self Portraits by Women Painters, 2000, Neoplatonism and the Arts, 2002, Essays on Women Painters, 2003, Readings in Italian Mannerism, 2003, Vasari's Mythological Paintings, 2003; editor: Vanities and Vanitas, 1992, Pre-Raphaelism in Medieval Art, 1993, Botticelli's Neoplatonic Images, 1993; co-editor: (with Jane Aiken) Peiro's Treatise of Perspective 1492. Grantee T.E. Parker Found., 1986-88, NEH, 1979-89, 90, Lowell Hist. Preservation Commn., 1985-89, Am. Coun. Learned Socs., 1990. Mem. AAIS, Nat. Women Caucus for Art (chair 1986-87), Boston Women Caucus for Art (co-chmn. 1985-87), Coll. Art Assn. Am., Lowell Art Assn., Pre-Raphaelite Soc., Nat. Assn. Schs. Art and Design, Emblem Soc., Renaissance Soc. Am., Victorian Soc. Am., Am. Coun. of the Learned Soc., Wellesley Friends of Art, Phi Beta Kappa. Roman Catholic. Avocations: reading, walking, fencing, astrology, classical music. Home: 112 Charles St Boston MA 02114-3201 Office: U Mass Lowell Cultural Studies Dept Lowell MA 01854

CHENG, CHUEN YAN, biochemist, educator; b. Hong Kong, June 18, 1954; came to the U.S., 1981, naturalized, 1993; s. C. Yin and Tak Ying (Ho) C.; m. Po Lee, Mar. 17, 1978; children; Yan Ho, Chin Ho. BS with honors, Chinese U., Hong Kong, 1978; PhD, U. Newcastle, Australia, 1982. Fellow Population Coun., N.Y.C., 1981-82, rsch. investigator, 1983-84, staff scientist, 1985-87, scientist, 1988-90, sr. scientist, 1991—; assoc. dir. Internat. Consortium on Male Contraception, N.Y.C., 1994-95, dir., 1996—. Asst. prof. Rockefeller U., N.Y.C., 1986-90; prof. U. Rome, 1990—; cons. Angelini Pharms., Inc., River Edge, N.J., 1985-91, Angelini Rsch. Inst., Rome, 1992-93, Fidia Pharms., Inc., Italy, 1997, Bioprogress Pharms., Rome, 2001—. Contbr. over 180 articles to profl. jours. Recipient Sea Horse award, Newcastle U., Australia, 1982. Mem. Am. Soc. Andrology (Best Sci. Paper award 1996), Endocrine Soc. (Richard E. Weitzman Meml. award 1988). Achievements include patents for abnormally glycosylated variants of alpha-2-macroglobulin and serum proteins used to detect autoimmune disease, monoclonal antibody specifically detects abnormal glycosylation site on alpha-1-antitrypsin used to detect autoimmune conditions, testicular protein that regulates androgen production for male fertility control; 3-substituted 1-benzyl-1H indazole derivatives as antifertility agents. Office: Population Coun 1230 York Ave New York NY 10021-6307 E-mail: ycheng@popcbr.rockefeller.edu.

CHENG, GRACE ZHENG-YING, music educator; arrived in U.S., 1982; d. Chang Cheng and Guan-Zhi Fang. B Music, Shanghai Conservatory Music, China, 1980; M Music, U. Nebr., 1985. Tchg. asst. Shanghai Conservatory Music, China, 1976—82, U. Nebr., Lincoln, 1983—85; piano tchr. Freehold (N.J.) Music Ctr., 1985—. Piano soloist Arts in the Aisles, Lincoln, Nebr., 1984, Cecilian Music Club, Monmouth County, NJ, 1986—92; pianist, NJ, 1985—. Recipient Laura R. Conover Pedagogy award Outstanding Tchg., Carnegie Hall, N.Y.C., 1998, 5th Yr. Tchr.'s award, Cecilian Music Club, 1997. Mem.: ASPCA, Nat. Guild Piano Tchrs. (piano adj. 1994—), N.J. Music Tchrs. Assn. (piano adj. 1998), Nat. Music Tchrs. Assn. (piano adj. 1993), Sierra Club. Avocations: internet, travel, photography, gardening. Home: 1 Swallow Ln Howell NJ 07731 Office: Freehold Music Ctr 3681 Unit 4 Rte 9 Freehold NJ 07728 Personal E-mail: gchennj@aol.com.

CHENG, HERBERT SU-YUEN, mechanical engineering educator; b. Shanghai, Jan. 15, 1929; came to U.S., 1949; s. Chung-Mei and Jing-Ming (Xu) C.; m. Lily D. Hsiung, Apr. 11, 1953; children: Elaine, Elise, Edward, Earl. BSME, U. Mich., 1962; MSME, Ill. Inst. Tech., 1956; PhD, U. Pa., 1961. Jr. mech. engr. Internat. Harvester Co., Chgo., 1952-53; project engr. Machine Engring. co., Chgo., 1953-56; instr. Ill. Inst. Tech., Chgo., 1956-57, U. Pa., Phila., 1957-61; asst. prof. Syracuse (N.Y.) U., 1961-62; rsch. engr. Mech. Tech. Inc., Latham, N.Y., 1962-68; assoc. prof. Northwestern U., Evanston, Ill., 1968-74, prof., 1974—, Walter P. Murphy prof., 1987—, dir. Ctr. for Engring. Tribology, 1984-88, 92—. V.p. Gear Rsch. Inst., Naperville, Ill., 1985-90; cons. GM, Chrysler Corp., Deere Co., Nissan, E.T.C., 1970—. Contbr. articles to profl. jours. Deacon South Presbyn. Ch., Syracuse, 1961-62, 1st Presbyn. Ch. Schenectady, N.Y., 1962-68. Named a hon. prof. Nat. Zhejiang (People's Republic of China) U., 1985. Fellow ASME (hon., Mayo D. Hersey award 1990, D.F. Wilcock award 1999), Soc. Tribologists & Lubrication Engrs. (hon., Nat. award 1987, CAP Alfred Hunt award 1997); mem. NAE, Inst. Mech. Engrs. (U.K., Tribology gold medal 1992), Am. Gear Mfrs. Assn. (acad. mem.). Avocations: peking opera, tennis. Office: Northwestern U 219 Catalysis Bldg 2145 Sheridan Rd Evanston IL 60208-0834

CHENG, H(WEI) H(SIEN), soil scientist, agronomic and environmental science educator; b. Shanghai, Aug. 13, 1932; came to U.S., 1951, naturalized, 1961; s. Chi-Pao and Anna (Lan) C.; m. Jo Yuan, Dec. 15, 1962; children: Edwin, Antony. BA, Berea Coll., 1956; MS, U. Ill., 1958, PhD, 1961. Rsch. assoc. Iowa State U., Ames, 1962-64, asst. prof. agronomy, 1964-65; asst. prof. dept. agronomy and soils Wash. State U., Pullman, 1965-71, assoc. prof., 1971-77, prof., 1977-89, interim chmn., 1986-87, chmn. program environ. sci. and regional planning, 1977-79, 88-89, assoc. dean Grad. Sch., 1982-86; prof., head dept. soil, water, and climate U. Minn., St. Paul, 1989—2002, prof. emeritus, 2002—. Vis. scientist Juelich Nuclear Rsch. Ctr., Fed. Republic Germany, 1971-73, 79-80, Academia Sinica, Taipei, Republic of China, 1978, Fed. Agrl. Rsch. Ctr., Braunschweig, Fed. Republic Germany, 1980; mem. acad. adv. coun. Inst. Soil Sci., Academia Sinica, Nanjing, People's Republic China, 1987-2000; mem. adv. bd. Inst. Botany, Academia Sinica, Taipei, 1991-2000; mem. first sci. adv. bd. Dept. Ecology State of Wash., 1988-89; chief tech. advisor project on water-saving agr. for N.W. China, UNDP, 2001—; mem. Nat. Acad. Bd. Agr. and Natural Resources, 2003—. Editor: Pesticides in the Soil Environment: Processes, Impacts, and Modeling, 1990; assoc. editor Jour. Environ. Quality, 1983-89; mem. editorial bd. Bot. bull. Academia Sinica, 1988—, Jour. Environ. Sci. and Health, Part B-Pesticides, Food Contaminants, and Agrl. Wastes, 2000—; cons. editor: Pedosphere, 1991—; contbr. articles to profl. jours. Fulbright rsch. scholar State Agrl. U., Ghent, Belgium, 1963-64. Fellow AAAS, Am. Soc. Agronomy (bd. dirs. 1990-2000, exec. com. 1994-2000, pres. 1998-99), Soil Sci. Soc. Am. (divsn. chair 1985-86, bd. dirs. 1990-93, exec. com. 1994-97, pres. 1995-96, chmn. Smithsonian soils exhibit com. 2002—); mem. Am. Chem. Soc., Soc. Environ. Toxicology and Chemistry, Internat. Soc. Chem. Ecology, Internat. Humic Substances Soc., Coun. for Agrl. Sci. and Tech., Soil and Water Conservation Soc., Inst. Internat. Devel. in Edn. and Agrl. and Life Scis. (chair bd. dirs. 2000—), Sigma Xi (pres. U. Minn. chpt. 1995-96), Phi Kappa Phi, Gamma Sigma Delta (pres. Wash. State chpt. 1988-89, Award of Merit U. Minn. chpt. 2000). Methodist. Office: U Minn Dept Soil Water and Climate 1991 Upper Buford Cir Saint Paul MN 55108-0010 E-mail: hcheng@soils.umn.edu.

CHENG, MEI-FANG, psychobiology educator, neuroethology researcher; b. Kee Lung, Taiwan, Republic of China, Nov. 24, 1938; came to U.S., 1959; d. Chao-Chin Hsieh and Ai Tsu; m. Wen-Kwei Cheng; m. June 7,

1963; children: Suzanne, Po-Yuan, Julie. BS summa cum laude, Nat. Taiwan U., Taipei, 1958; PhD, Bryn Mawr Coll., 1965. Postdoctoral fellow U. Pa., Phila., 1965-68; asst. rsch. prof. Inst. Animal Behavior Rutgers U., Newark, 1969-73, assoc. prof., 1973-79, prof., 1979, acting dir. Inst. Animal Behavior, 1989—91, dir., 1991-95. Cons. NIMH, mem. neurosci. study sect., 1991-95; cons., mem. behavioral neurobiology br. NSF; mem. NIH Reviewers Res., 1995—; cons. numerous granting agys. Author: Advance in the Study of Behavior, 1979; co-editor: Reproduction: A Behavorial and Neuroscientific Perspective, 1986; assoc. editor Hormones and Behavior, 1986-96; cons. Brain Rsch., Sci., others; contbr. articles to profl. jours. Fulbright scholar, 1959; recipient Rsch. Scientist Devel. award NIMH, 1974-79, 79-84, Johnson & Johnson Discovery award, 1989, Hoechst-Celanese Innovative award, 1993, award of excellence in rsch. Rutgers Bd. Trustees, 1998. Mem. Internat. Conf. Neuroethology, Neurosci. Achievements include discovery that a bird's own songs stimulate the endocrine changes; demonstration of the vocal-auditory-endocrine pathways involved in voice and sound mediation of endocrine change, and provide anatomical basis for emotion-sharing theory of vocal communication; discovery of cell loss can trigger neurogenesis in the adult brain and may be harnessed for brain repair and functional recovery. Office: Rutgers U Dept Psychology 101 Warren St Newark NJ 07102-1811

CHENG, RICHARD TIEN-REN, computer scientist, educator; b. Nanjing, China, June 4, 1934; came to U.S., 1961; s. George T. and Elaine M. (Liu) C.; m. Nancy P. Chiang, Jan. 24, 1960; children: James S., Raymond S. BS in Edn., Taiwan Normal U., 1958; MEd, U. Wis., Menomonie, 1963; MS in Elec. Engring., U. Ill., 1969, PhD in Computer Sci., 1971. Instr. Taiwan Normal U., Taipei, 1958-60, Racine (Wis.) Tech., 1963-66; asst. prof. Stout State U., Menominie, 1966-68; rsch. asst. U. Ill., Urbana, 1968-71; asst. prof. U. Wis., Whitewater, 1971-72; asst. prof. Hunter Coll. CUNY, 1972-73; assoc. prof., chair Rochester (N.Y.) Inst. Tech., 1973-74, prof., chair, 1974-79; eminent prof., chair Old Dominion U., Norfolk, Va., 1979-85; chmn., ceo Eastern Computers, Virginia Beach, 1985—. Cons. Western Printing, Racine, 1963-66; sr. cons. Talor Instruments, Rochester, 1980-81, Ministry of Interior, Riyadh, Saudi Arabia, 1980-90; dir., treas. Op. Smile Internat., Norfolk, 1992—; bd. dirs. Nat. Def. U., 1992—, Ctr. Innovative Tech. Va., 1993—, Signet Bank, First Union Bank, SENTARA Health Systems Bd. Contbr. articles to profl. publs. Dir. Marine Sci. Mus., Virginia Beach, 1989—, foundation bd. Norfolk State U., 1992—, Navy League, Norfolk, 1991—, Com. of 100, 1994—; active Boy Scouts Am., 1990—. Recipient medal Pres. Chiang Roc, Taipei, 1961, Founder's award OCA, 1998; named Nat. Minority Bus. Person of Yr., 1991, Pres. George Bush, Entrepreneur of Yr., 1992, K Peat Marwick Group, High Tech. Entrepreneur of Yr., 1992, Ernest Young, Inc., Outstanding Industrialist of Yr. 1998, Outstanding Alumni Taiwan Nat. U. Alumni Assn. Mem. Orgn. Chinese-Am. (founder, pres. 1987-89), Def. Oriental Conf., N.Y. Acad. Sci., C. of C. of Hampton Roads (bd. dirs. 1990—), Cavalian Yacht and Golf Club. Avocations: photography, stamp collecting, gun collecting. Home: 1536 Duke Of Windsor Rd Virginia Beach VA 23454-2504 Office: ECI Systems & Engring 596 Lynnhaven Pky Virginia Beach VA 23452-7303

CHENG, ZHEN-QIANG, research scientist; b. Bengbu, Anhui, China, Sept. 12, 1962; m. Dong-Mei Tian, Sept. 6, 1996; children: Virginia Miaomiao, Jeffrey Junjie. BS, U. Sci. and Tech. China, Hefei, 1985, MS, 1988, PhD, 1991. Lectr. U. Sci. and Tech. China, 1991-93, assoc. prof., 1993-98; rsch. scientist Tex. A&M U., College Station, 1999—. Vis. acad. U. Wales, Cardiff, 1994—95; vis. fellow U. Queensland, Brisbane, 1997—98; vis. rsch. assoc. Va. Poly Inst. and State U., Blacksburg, 1998—99. Contbr. articles to profl. jours. Recipient Presdl. award China Acad. Scis., 1991; sci. grantee U. Sci. and Tech. China, 1993-94, Nat. Sci. Found., Beijing, 1995-97.

CHENHALLS, ANNE MARIE, nurse, educator; b. Detroit, May 26, 1929; d. Peter and Beatrice Mary (Elliston) McLeod; m. Horacio Chenhalls, 1953 (dec.); children: Mark, Anne Marie Chenhalls Delamater. Student, Detroit Conservatory Music, 1946-47; grad., Grace Hosp. Sch. Nursing, 1951; B Vocat. Edn., Calif. State U., L.A., 1967; BS in Nursing, Calif. State U., 1968; MA, Calif. State U., Long Beach, 1985. RN, Calif. Nurse Grace Hosp., Detroit, 1951-52; pvt. duty nurse Mexico City, 1953-54; nurse St. Francis Hosp., Lynwood, Calif., 1957-63; assoc. prof. nursing Compton Coll., Calif., 1964-72; health educator, sch. nurse Santa Ana (Calif.) Unified Sch. Dist., 1972-76, 79—. Med. coord., internat. health cons. Agape Movement, San Bernardino, Calif., 1976-79; instr. community health, Uganda, 1982; med. evaluator Athletes in Action, 1979; pub. health nurse Orange County Health Dept., Calif., 1990-95. Assoc. staff mem. Campus Crusade for Christ; solo vocalist, Santa Ana, Orange, Seal Beach, Dinner Theater, Calif., Civic Light Opera, Buena park, Calif.; acting Master's Repertory Theater, 1990-94, Santa Ana. U.S. govt. grantee, 1968. Mem. Calif. Sch. Nurses Assn., Calif. Tchrs. Assn. Republican. Home: 2601 E Ocean Blvd 810 Long Beach CA 90803-2504 Office: Santa Ana Unified Sch Dist 1601 E Chestnut Ave Santa Ana CA 92701-6322 E-mail: AChenhalls@aol.com.

CHEOROS, EDITH MARIE, elementary school educator; b. Delmont, S.D., Jan. 14, 1940; d. John Louis and Eleanor Sophia (Mosel) Fuchs; m. Peter Joseph Cheoros, Dec. 14, 1941; 1 child, Lisa Maria Cheoros Yamamoto. BS, Concordia Tchrs. Coll., 1962. Tchr. St. John's Luth. Sch., Long Beach, Calif., 1962-69, Wilson Elem. Sch., Lynwood (Calif.) Unified Sch. Dist., 1969—. Participant Oropus (Greece) Project; vis. educator European Inst., Berlin. Writer curriculum Apple, 1975-78. Organist St. John's Ch., Long Beach, 1962-66; life mem. Lynwood PTA. Named Tchr. of Yr., Lynwood C. of C., 1972. Mem. NEA, Nat. Coun. Social Studies, Calif. Tchrs. Assn., Lynwood Tchrs. Assn. (tchr. adv. 1970-76), Cousteau Soc., Friends of Calypso. Lutheran. Avocations: handicrafts, art.

CHERIF, ABOUR HACHMI, biology and science educator; b. Sebha, Libya, Sept. 5, 1953; came to U.S., 1978; s. Hachmi Ahmed Cherif and Fatima (Milad) Ahmed; m. Zachia Middle Child Cherif, Nov. 28, 1981; children: David Tejeda, Nuria Cherif, Zaena Cherif. BS in Biology, Tripoli U., 1972-76; MS in Teaching Biology, Portland State U., 1980-82; PhD in Sci. Edn., Simon Fraser U., 1983-89. Cert. in biology, Libya; cert. leader in environ. issue forums trainers workshops. Biology instr. Sebha Tchr. Inst., Libya, 1976-77; biology lab. instr. Sebha U., Libya, 1976-78; sci. edn. instr. Simon Fraser U., Burnaby, Can., 1986-90; MAT developer in sci. Columbia Coll., Chgo., 1990-91, biology sci. edn. instr., 1990—; sci. instr. Aristotle Acad., Chgo., 1001—; environ. instr. Assn. for Promotion and Advancement of Sci. Edn., Vancouver, Can., 1989-90. Curriculum evaluator The Commonwealth of Learning, Vancouver, Can., 1990; curriculum designer Columbia Coll., Chgo., 1990-91; curriculum developer, dir. rsch. devel. Aristotle Acad., Chgo., 1991—; sci. edn. spl. reviewer acad. stds. exams. numerous pub. schs. dists.; co-chair planning com. 3d Ann. Internat. Conf. of Human Factors in Devel., Chgo., 1998; bd. dirs., exec. com. Internat. Inst. for Human Factor Devel. Soc. Founder, mng. editor Forward to Excellence in Tchg. and Learning newsletter, sci. and math. dept. Columbia Coll., 1993; editor, mem. editl. bd. profl. jours. including Rev. for Human Factors Studies, Am. Biology Tchr.; contbr. numerous articles to profl. jours. Developer MAT Grad. Program, 1991; sci. display, Simon Fraser U., 1988. Recipient Grad. Scholarship award The Ministry of Higher Edn., Tripoli, Libya, 1978-85, Pres'. PhD Rsch. award Simon Fraser U., Burnaby, Can., 1985, Teaching award Aristotle Acad., 1992, Teamwork award 1993; named Personality of Month Mawaheb: Multi-Cultural Mag., Ontario, 1991, 94. Democrat. Avocations: reading, writing, photography, soccer, fishing. Home: 140 Florence Ave Evanston IL 60202-3764 Office: Columbia Coll Chgo 600 S Michigan Ave Chicago IL 60605-1900 Fax: (847) 332-2888. E-mail: artharts@aol.com.

CHERIS, ELAINE GAYLE INGRAM, business owner; b. Ashford, Ala., Jan. 8, 1946; m. Samuel David Cheris, June 8, 1980; 1 child, Zachariah Adam Abraham. BS, Troy State U., 1971. Aquatics dir. Yale U., New Haven, 1976-79; owner, CEO Cheyenne Fencing Soc., Denver, 1980—. Chmn. organizing com. World Fencing Championships, 1989, World Jr./Cadet Fencing Championships, 1993; nat. devel. coord. Modern Pentathlon, 1998, world team fencing coach mens team, 2001, co-chair organizing com. Pentathlon Nation Championship. Author: Handbook for Parents - Fencing, 1988, 2d edit., 1992; editor Yofen Mag., 1988-90, 92—. Mem. Gov.'s Coun. on Sports and Fitness, Colo., 1990-2000; commr. Colo. State Games-Fencing, 1989-95; nat. chair jr. cadet, youth. Modern Penthathlon, 1997—; sec. U.S. Olypmians, Colo. chpt., 1999—. Mem. U.S. Olympic Foil Team, 1980, 88 (6th place fencing), U.S. Olympic Epee Team, 96 (8th place), ranked #1 U.S. Fencing Women's Epee, 1999-2000, mem. U.S. Pan-Am. Games Team, 1987 (Gold medal women's foil team), 1991 (Gold medal women's epee team, 1999, Pan Am. Games Epee Team; named Sportswoman of Yr. Fencing, YWCA, 1980-82, to Sportswoman Hall of Fame, 1982; mem. U.S. World Championship Fencing Team, 1982, 83, 85, 87, 90, 91, 92, 93, 98, 99, U.S. Maccabiah Fencing Team, 1981 (1 Gold, 1 Silver medal, #1 fencer U.S. 2000, 01); U.S. youth world team coach U.S. Modern Penthathlon, 2000, U.S. Pentathlon World Team Coach, 2002, U.S. CISM World Team Coach, 1st Woman, 2001-02; recipient Gold Medal of Honor from Fedn. Internat. d'Escrime, 1993. Mem. AAPHERD, U.S. Fencing Assn. (youth chmn. 1988-90, editor Youth mag., 1988-90, 92—, chmn. Colo. divsn., 1992-94), Fedn. Internat. d'Escrime (chmn. Atlanta fencing project '96, chmn. World Fencing Day 1994). Jewish. Office: Cheyenne Fencing Soc 5818 E Colfax Ave Denver CO 80220-1507 E-mail: elainecheris@coloradofencing.com.

CHERMAK, GAIL DONNA, audiologist, speech and hearing sciences educator; b. N.Y.C., Sept. 30, 1950; d. Martin I. Chermak and Zelda Lax; children: Isaac Martin, Alina Marta. BA in Communication Disorders, SUNY, Buffalo, 1972; MA in Speech and Hearing Sci., Ohio State U., 1973, PhD in Speech and Hearing Sci., 1975. Cert. clin. competency in audiology. Asst. prof. speech So. Ill. U., Edwardsville, 1975-77; assoc. prof. and dir., communication disorders program Wash. State U., Pullman, 1977-89, prof., chmn. dept. speech and hearing scis., 1990—97, 1998—, coord. grad. program dept. speech and hearing scis., 1983-89, interim dean Coll. of Liberal Arts, 1997-98. Feature editor Am. Jour. Audiology, 1991-95, editl. cons., 1994, 95; editl. cons. Ear and Hearing Jour., Cin., 1984, 88, 89, 90, 91, 92, 93, 94, 2001, Internat. Jour. Disability Devel. and Edn., 1991, Lang. Speech and Hearing Svcs. in Schs., 1993, 94, 95, 96, 97, 98, 99, Jour. of Comm. Disorders, 1994; prof. advisor Palowe chpt. Self-Help for Hard of Hearing, Moscow, Idaho, 1984-89. Author: Handbook of Audiological Rehabilitation, 1981, Central Auditory Processing Disorders; New Perspectives, 1997; contbr. articles to profl. jours. Kellogg nat. fellow, 1986-89; Fulbright scholar, 1989-90. Fellow Am. Speech-Lang. Hearing Assn., Am. Acad. Audiology; mem. AAAS, AAUW, Am. Assn. for Higher Edn., Am. Speech, Lang. and Hearing Assn. (cert. clin. competence in audiology), Acoustical Soc. Am., Am. Acad. Audiology, Am. Auditory Soc., Internat. Soc. Audiology, NOW (v.p. Moscow chpt. 1985-86), ACLU (human rights com.), Phi Beta Kappa. Avocations: gardening, jogging, orinthology, skiing. Office: Wash State U Col of Liberal Arts PO Box 642630 Pullman WA 99164-2630 E-mail: chermak@wsu.edu.

CHERNESKY, BARBARA JEAN, special education educator; b. Cleve., June 21, 1950; d. Joseph and Pauline (Rudlosky) C. BS in Edn., Bowling Green (Ohio) State U., 1972; MA in Edn., Columbia U., 1992. Spl. edn. tchr. Logan (Ohio) City/County Schs., 1972-75; spl. edn. tchr., tchr. trainer Sch. of Hope for Mentally Handicapped Children, Jamaica, West Indies, 1975-81; tng. officer Caribbean Inst. Mental Retardation & Other Devel. Disability, Jamaica, 1981-82; tchr. spl. edn. N.Y.C. Bd. Edn., Bklyn., 1982—; ednl. dir. Horace E. Greene Day Care Ctr., Bklyn., 1987-89. Mem. Coun. Exceptional Children (div. mental retardation), Assn. for Gifted (tchr. edn. div., tech. and media div., div. internat. spl. edn. and svcs.). Avocation: advocate for children.

CHERNICOFF, DAVID PAUL, osteopathic physician, educator; b. N.Y.C., Aug. 3, 1947; s. Harry and Lillian (Dobkin) C. AB, U. Rochester, 1969; DO, Phila. Coll. Osteo. Medicine, 1973. Diplomate Nat. Bd. Osteo. Examiners, Am. Osteo. Bd. Internal Medicine, also in Hematology/Oncology. Rotating intern Rocky Mtn. Hosp., Denver, 1973-74; resident in internal medicine Cmty. Gen. Osteo. Hosp., Harrisburg, Pa., 1974-76; fellow in hematology and med. oncology Cleve. Clinic, 1976-78; asst. prof. medicine sect. hematology/oncology Chgo. Coll. Osteo. Medicine, 1978-82, assoc. prof., 1982-89; co-chmn. tumor task force Chgo. Osteo. Med. Ctr., 1978-89, dir. clin. cancer edn., 1978-89; asst. clin. prof. medicine Pa. State U. Coll. Medicine, Harrisburg, 1993—; pvt. practice, 1979. Med. dir. Keystone Peer Rev. Orgn., 1997-2000; chmn. tumor task force Olympia Fields (Ill.) Osteo. Med. Ctr. Trustee, mem. clin. exec. com. Ill. Cancer Coun., 1982-89; bd. dir. Chgo. unit Am. Cancer Soc., 1981-86, chief sec. of Hematology-Oncology Hosp. of Chgo. Coll. Osteo Medicine, 1981-89; carrier adv. com. Xact Medicare Svcs., 1997-2000; med. dir. Keystone Peer Rev. Orgn., 1997-2000. Contbr. articles to med. jours. Fellow Am. Coll. Osteo. Internists, Pa. Osteo. Med. Soc. Ea. Coop. Oncology Group (sr. investigator 1981-89), Am. Soc. Clin. Oncology; mem. Am. Osteo. Assn. Office: 4830 Londonderry Rd Harrisburg PA 17109-5207 E-mail: BronJeffPA@aol.com.

CHERNO, MELVIN, humanities educator; b. El Paso, Feb. 24, 1929; s. Sol and Deborah (Andes) C.; m. Dolores Ellen Himelstein, Dec. 25, 1950; children— Steven Philip, Paige Elise, Julie Rosanne AB, Stanford U., 1950; AM, U. Chgo., 1952; PhD, Stanford U., 1955. Instr. Bakersfield Coll., Calif., 1955-60; successively asst. prof., assoc. prof., prof. Oakland U., Rochester, Mich., 1960-80; Vaughan prof. tech., culture and comm. U. Va., Charlottesville, 1980-2000, Vaughan prof. emeritus humanities, 2001—, prin. second residential coll., 1991-95, 2000-01, co-prin., 1995-96. Co-editor: (4-vol. anthology) Western Society ..., 1967; editor, translator: (essay) Feuerbach on Luther, 1968; contbr. articles on historical topics to profl. jours. Fellow Ford Found., 1953-55, Deutscher Akademische Austauschdienst, 1966, Inst. für Europäische Geschichte, 1966 Mem. Am. Hist. Assn., Am. Soc. Engring. Edn., So. Hist. Assn., Soc. for History of Tech., Soc. for Lit./Sci., Soc. for 19th Century Studies, Phi Beta Kappa. Office: U Va TCC Divsn A237 Thornton Hall PO Box 400744 351 McCormick Rd Charlottesville VA 22904

CHERNOFF, HERMAN, statistics educator; b. N.Y.C., July 1, 1923; s. Max and Pauline (Markowitz) C.; m. Judith Ullman, Sept. 7, 1947; children— Ellen Sue, Miriam Cheryl. BS, CCNY, 1943; Sc.M., Brown U., 1945, PhD, 1948; Sc.D. (hon.), Ohio State U., 1983, Technion, 1984; A.M. (hon.), Harvard U., 1985; laurea (hon.), U. Rome (Sapienza), 1996; PhD (hon.), U. Athens, 1999. Rsch. assoc. U. Chgo., 1948-49; asst. prof. U. Ill., Urbana, 1949-51, assoc. prof., 1951-52, Stanford (Calif.) U., 1952-56, prof. stats., 1956-74; prof. applied math. MIT, Cambridge, 1974-85, prof. emeritus, 1985—; prof. stats. Harvard U., Cambridge, 1985-97, prof. emeritus, 1997—. Researcher in large sample theory, optimal design of expts., sequential analysis, pattern recognition. Author: (with L.E. Moses) Elementary Decision Theory, 1959, Sequential Analysis and Optimal Design, 1972. Recipient Townsend Harris medal CCNY Alumni Soc., 1981. Mem. NAS, Internat. Statis. Inst., Am. Acad. Arts and Scis., Inst. Math. Stats. (pres. 1967-68), Am. Statis. Assn. (Wilks medal 1987, Statistician of Yr. award Boston chpt. 1991). Home: 75 Crowninshield Rd Brookline MA 02446-6777 Office: Harvard U Dept Statistics Cambridge MA 02138 E-mail: chernoff@stat.harvard.edu.

CHERRY, ANDREW LAWRENCE, JR., social work educator, researcher; b. Dothan, Ala., Nov. 11, 1943; s. Andrew L. Cherry and Wyalene Cain; m. Mary Elizabeth Dillon, July 16, 1988. MSW, U. Ala., Tuscaloosa, 1974; D Social Work, Columbia U., 1986. Child welfare worker Escambia County Dept. Pensions and Securities, Brewton, Ala., 1968-72; psychiat. social worker Bryce State Hosp., Tuscaloosa, 1974-79; instr. Salisbury (Md.) State Coll., 1981-85; asst. prof. Marywood Coll. Sch. Social Work, Scranton, Pa., 1986-87; prof. Barry U. Sch. Social Work, Miami, Fla., 1987—2003; prof. mental health Sch. Social Work U. Okla., Tulsa, 2003—, endowed prof. mental health sch. social work, 2003—. Cons. Informed Families Dade County, Miami, 1990—98, Miami Coalition for Care to Homeless, 1991—93, NAACP Minority Media and Telecomm. Coun., 1992—2000; with drug abuse prevention program Cath. Charities, Miami, 1991—2000, Broward Children's Svc., Ft. Lauderdale, 1992—94, The Biscayne Inst., 1994—, St. Luke's Addiction Recovery Ctr., 1995—2000; interim dir. child welfare divsn. Cath. Charities, 1998—2000. Author: The Socializating Instinct: Individual, Family and Social Bonds, 1994, A Research Primer for the Helping Professions: Methods, Statistics, and Writing, 2000, Examining Global Social Welfare Issues Using MicroCase, 2002; co-author: Social Bonds and Teen Pregnancy, 1992; co-editor: Teenage Pregnancy: A Global View, 2001, Substance Abuse: A Global View, 2002; contbr. articles to profl. jours. Scholar, NIMH, 1979. Fellow: Am. Orthopsychiat. Assn.; mem.: NASW, N.Y. Acad. Scis., Conf. Social Work Edn. Achievements include research in and devel. of the social bond theory; extensive work and rsch. among the mentally disabled, homeless, at-risk children and the addicted. Office: U Okla Tulsa Campus 4502 E 41st St Ste 2J02 Tulsa OK 74135-2512 Personal E-mail: alcherry@gbronline.com. Business E-Mail: alcherry@ou.edu.

CHERRY, BARBARA WATERMAN, speech and language pathologist, physical therapist; b. Norfolk, Va., June 25, 1949; d. Robert Bullock and Dorothy Estelle (Walsh) Waterman; m. Albert Glen Cherry, Sept. 17, 1977; 1 child, Dorothy Louise. BS in Phys. Therapy, U. Fla., 1972, MA in Speech-Lang. Pathology, 1982. Lic. phys. therapist, speech and lang. pathologist, Fla.; cert. tchr., Fla. Staff phys. therapist Retreat for the Sick Hosp., Richmond, Va., 1973-75; clin. instr. in phys. therapy Sch. of Rehab. Scis., Tehran, Iran, 1975-76; staff phys. therapist Sulmaniya Hosp., Manama, Bahrain, 1976-77, Cathedral Rehab. Ctr., Jacksonville, Fla., 1978-80; staff speech-lang. pathologist S. Allen Smith Clinic, Jacksonville, 1982-87, Mt. Herman Exceptional Child Ctr., Jacksonville, 1987-91, Duval County Sch. System, Jacksonville, 1991-98, Mt. Herman Exceptional Student Ctr., Jacksonville, 1998—, Brooks Rehab. Hosp., Jacksonville, 2003—. Mem. Am. Speech, Lang., and Hearing Assn., Am. Phys. Therapy Assn., Phi Kappa Phi. Episcopalian. Avocation: Karate (black belt). Home: 8821 Ivey Rd Jacksonville FL 32216-3369 Office: Mt Herman Exceptional Student Ctr 1741 Francis St Jacksonville FL 32209 also: Brooks Rehab Hosp 3599 University Blvd S Jacksonville FL E-mail: cherryab@bellsouth.net.

CHERRY, CAROL LYNN, principal; b. Camden, N.J., Aug. 21, 1948; d. Daniel Joseph and Louise Agnes (Smith) Brown; m. Norman Reddick Cherry, Apr. 19, 1969; children: Talenthea Melaine Cherry Hollis, Aletha Renee Cherry. BS summa cum laude, N.C. AT&T State U., 1974; MEd, Savannah-Armstrong State U., 1979; EdS, U. Ga., 1989; postgrad., Ga. State U., 1992—. Cert. adminstrn. and supervision, early childhood edn., data collector. Tchr. Dept. Def., Babenhausen, West Germany, 1975-77, Chatham County Schs., Savannah, Ga., 1979-80, Clayton County Schs., Jonesboro, Ga., 1980-83, Dept. Def., Fort Buchanan, P.R., 1983-84, Beachwood and University Heights (Ohio) Schs., 1984-86, Houston County Schs., Perry, Ga., 1986-88, instrnl. coord., 1988-94, prin., 1994—. Strategic planning mem. Houston County Schs., Perry, 1990-92; adv. coun. mem. Coop. Ext. Svc., Athens, Ga., 1991-94; leadership acad. Ga. Dept. Edn., Atlanta, 1992-94. Recipient J. Everette DeVaughn Outstanding Doctoral Student award Ga. State U., 1995; named to New Leaders Inst. Ga. Dept. Edn., 1995-96. Mem. NEA, Ga. ASCD, Ga. Assn. Educators, Internat. Reading Assn. (pres. Houston-Peach reading coun. 1990-91), Am. Ednl. Rsch. Assn., Ga. Assn. Elem. Sch. Prins. (sec. 3d dist. 1994-96, pres.-elect 3d dist. 1996—), Nat. Assn. Elem. Sch. Prins. Methodist. Avocation: reading. Home: 102 Cliff Ct Bonaire GA 31005-4308

CHERRY, LAWRENCE EDWARD, JR., computer programming educator; b. Elizabeth City, N.C., Aug. 13, 1965; s. Lawrence Edward and Anne Carolyn (Cobb) C. BS, Elizabeth City State U., 1988; MA in Edn., East Carolina U., 1994. Cert. vocat. bus. edn., computer 9-12 grades. Instr. bus., computers and technology Gates County Schs., Gatesville, N.C., 1989—. Adj. computer instr. Coll. of the Albemarie, Elizabeth City, N.C., 1990-97. Mem. Future Bus. Leaders of Am. (club advisor), Phi Beta Lambda. Republican. Mem. Ch. of Christ. Avocations: piano, reading. Home: 116 S Ashe St Elizabeth City NC 27909-3104 Office: Gates County Schs O88 US Hwy 158 West Gatesville NC 27938-9705

CHERYAN, MUNIR, agricultural studies educator, biochemical engineering educator; b. Cochin, Kerala, India, May 7, 1946; came to U.S., 1968; B. Tech. with honor, Indian Inst. Tech., Kharagpur, 1968; MS, U. Wis., 1970, PhD, 1974. From asst. prof. to assoc. prof. food and biochemical engring. U. Ill., Urbana, 1976-85, prof. food and biochemical engring., 1985—. Cons. UN Devel. Program, 1985—. Author: Ultrafiltration Handbook, 1986, Ultrafiltration and Microfiltration Handbook, 1988; mem. editl. bd. Jour. Food Engring., 1985, Jour. Food Process Engring., 1985—, Internat. Dairy Jour., 1989—, Membrane Tech. Newsletter, 1997—; patentee for protein hydrolysis. Recipient Gardners award Assn. Food Scientists and Technologists, India, 1988, A.D.M. award Am. Oil Chemists Soc., 1984, Rsch. Team award Am. Soybean Assn., 1991, Rsch. and Commercialization award Nat. Corn Growers Assn., 1993. Mem. Am. Inst. Chemical Engrs., Inst. Food Technologists, Am. Chemical Soc., N.Am. Membrane Soc. Office: U Ill Agrl Bioprocess Lab 1302 W Pennsylvania Ave Urbana IL 61801-4714

CHESKY, PAMELA BOSZE, school system administrator; b. Perth Amboy, N.J., June 17, 1942; d. Joseph John and Irene (Konazeski) Bosze; m. Frederick Alan Chesky, Aug. 20, 1966; children: Rick, Scott. BA, Coll. Notre Dame, Balt., 1964; MLS, Rutgers U., 1972. Cert. ednl. media specialist. Tchr. social studies Woodbridge (N.J.) Bd. Edn., 1964-69, ednl. media specialist, 1969-93, supr. librs. guidance and nursing svcs., 1993-95; curriculum specialist for strategic planning Media Ctrs. and Student Assistance Counselors, 1995-97, supr. telecoms. and planning, 1997-99, supr. tech., media ctrs., staff devel. and guidance, 1999—. Membership com. Infolink, Piscataway, N.J., 1995-96, v.p., 1996, pres. 97-98; adv. com. Sch. Commn., Info. Libr. Svc. Rutgers U., 1994—. Contbr. articles to profl. jours. Commr. Woodbridge Cultural Arts Commn., 1992-98; vice-chair Middlesex County Dem. Orgn., New Brunswick, N.J., 1992-95; parliamentarian Woodbridge Dem. Orgn., 1993-97; program co-chair Friends Librs. Woodbridge Twp.; mem. Colonia chpt. Hadassah. Mem. ALA (affiliate assembly), Am. Assn. Sch. Librs. (membership com. 1993-95, chair task force on libr. advocacy 1996-98), Edn. Media Assn. N.J. (pres. 1993-94, scholar 1992, Adminstr. of Yr. 2001), Gamma Phi Beta. Democrat. Roman Catholic. Home: 135 Midwood Way Colonia NJ 07067-3116 Office: Woodbridge Bd Edn PO Box 428 Woodbridge NJ 07095-0428

CHESNUT, NONDIS LORINE, screenwriter, consultant, reading and language arts educator, instructor, counselor; b. South Daytona, Fla., June 29, 1941; d. Anthony Valentine and Myrtle Marie (Allen) Campbell; m. Raymond Otho Chesnut, Aug. 25, 1962; 1 child, Starlina Mintina Chesnut Kladler. BS in English and Speech, Concord Coll., 1962; postgrad., Frostburg U., 1967; MEd, Shippensburg U., 1972; postgrad., W.Va. U., 1973; Advanced Grad. Specialist Degree, U. Md., 1974; postgrad., Md. State Dept. Edn., 1976-95, Inst. Children's Lit., 1995-97, Screenwriters

Unlimited, 1997; writing coursework, Charter Oak State Coll., 2000. Cert. adminstr., secondary prin., elem. prin., reading splist., tchr. English and speech, drama. Tchr. English and speech Harpers Ferry (W.Va.) H.S., 1962-64; with Sears Roebuck, summer 1965; libr. Great Mills (Md.) H.S., 1968-69; tchr. English and reading North Hagerstown H.S., Hagerstown, Md., 1964-73; tchr. South Hagerstown H.S., Hagerstown, 1974-77; reading resource tchr. Woodland Way Elem. Sch., Hagerstown, 1977-83; adj. instr. grad. sch. Hood Coll., Frederick, Md., 1982-83; reading specialist Fountain Rock Elem. Sch., Hagerstown, 1983-85; tchr. Williamsport (Md.) H.S., 1985-95. Reading and lang. arts cons., Md., 1973-95, Fla., 1996-2000; adj. reading instr. Daytona Comm. Coll., 1996-97, Galaxy Middle Sch., 1997-98, drama, lang. arts, reading tchr., 1997-98, key source, 1999; instr. English and writing Bethune-Cookman Coll., fall 2000, ajd. instr. reading, English, Daytona Beach C.C., 2001—; spkr., presenter local, nat. and internat. workshops, 1973-2000; speech and debate coach. Writer for radio programs and advertisements for reading, 1986—, TV programs, 1974-78, 90-91; appeared on TV programs, 1974-78; co-editor column Beckley Post Herald, 1957-59; contbr. articles to newspapers and mags., 1964—; appeared in film Guarding Tess, 1993; screenwriter Heaven on Planet Earth, 2000, Love From Heaven, 2000. Mem. debating team Concord Coll., 1961-62, mem. newspaper staff, 1959-61; mem. Washington County Network of Orgns., 1984-88; co-dir. Billy Bud, 1962; v.p. Women's Ind. Club, 1962, treas., 1961; sec.-treas. Fgn. lang. Club, 1961, Debate Club, 1961-62; treas. Meth. Youth Fellowship, 1961; pres. Tri-Hi-Y, 1959; legis. chairperson State of Md. Reading Coun., 1977-78; active Life in Spirit Group, Emmanuel Meth. Ch., White Sul, 1953-84, St. Ann's Roman Cath. Ch., 1994-95, Grace United Meth. Ch., 1984-95, Lady of Hope Cath. Ch., 1996—; mem. Fla. State Reading Coun., 1996-99. Recipient Pres.'s award State of Md. Reading Coun., 1981, Pres.'s award Washington County Reading Coun., 1981, Guidance Helping award, 1987, Voice of Democracy award VFW/Ladies Aux., 1992, Am. Heritage Writing award Williamsport Lions Club, 1995, numerous others; W.Va. Legislature scholar, 1959-62. Mem. AAUW (ednl. chairperson 1983-85, legis. v.p. 1986-87, cmty. chairperson 1987-89), NEA (publicity and scholarship coms., bldg. rep. 1989-95, del.), ASCD, VFW (chairperson Voice of Democracy 1989-95, VFW award 1989-95), Md. Dist. Am. Heritage Lions (Region II Lions award, Williamsport Am. Heritage Lions award 1995), State of Md. Internat. Reading Assn. Coun. (sec. 1975-79, v.p. elect 1979-80, v.p. 1980-81, pres. 1981-82, nominating chairperson 1982-83), Washington County Tchrs. Assn. (rep., scholarship chair, publicity), Internat. Reading Assn. (sec.-treas. sex differences in reading group 1976-77, 83-85, mem. gender differences in reading group 1985-86, mem. readability interest group, mastery learning interest group, del. convs., internat. rsch. com. 1976-77, 84-85, disabled learners interest group 1975-82), Washington County Reading Assn. (pres. 1981-82), Am. Legion (chairperson oratorial contest 1989-95, speech coach), Fla. Devel. Edn. Assn. (mem. com. registration 1996). Democrat. Avocations: swimming, dancing, travel, psychology, writing. Home: 107 Old Sunbeam Dr Daytona Beach FL 32119

CHESS, SONIA MARY, retired language educator; b. Ashton, Lancashire, Eng., Apr. 14, 1930; came to U.S., 1951, naturalized, 1963; d. Arthur and Sarah Ann (Hulme) Bradburn; m. Joseph Campbell Chess, Nov. 17, 1950; children: Denise Ann, Tanya Marie, Michele Elise, Luana Jo. BA in English Lit., U. Hawaii, Honolulu, 1970, MA, 1973, MA in Am. Studies, 1989, PhD in Am. Studies, 1996. Prof. English U. Hawaii/Honolulu Community Coll., 1971-93, chmn. English dept., 1980-84, div. chairperson lang. arts, 1989-91, ret. Tchr. cons. Hawaii Writing Project, Honolulu, 1983—; tchr. summer sch. Regent, Sandwich Isle chpt. Daus. of Brit. Empire, Honolulu, 1978-80. Recipient Excellence in Teaching medal, U. Hawaii Bd. Regents, 1983; Dickens fellow, Nat. Endowment for Humanities, 1985, Hawaii Writing Project fellow, U. Hawaii Found., 1983. Mem. Hawaii Council Tchrs. English, Assn. Women in Jr. Colls., Humanities Assn. Episcopalian. Avocations: writing, knitting, reading, swimming, travel, gardening.

CHESTER, DANIEL LEON, computer scientist, educator, consultant; b. Albany, Calif., Feb. 26, 1943; s. Frederick Neil and Della Nettie (Zweifel) C. BA in Math., U. Calif., Berkeley, 1966, MA in Math., 1968, PhD in Math., 1973. Asst. prof. math. U. Tex., Austin, 1973-76, asst. prof. computer sci., 1973-80, U. Del., Newark, 1980-85, assoc. prof. computer sci., 1985—. Vis. scientist T. J. Watson Rsch. Ctr., IBM, Yorktown Heights, N.Y., 1978-79; cons. Quantum Leap Innovations, Inc., Newark, Del., 1985—. Mem. IEEE, Assn. for Computing Machinery, Assn. for Computational Linguistics, Am. Assn. for Artificial Intelligence, Cognitive Sci. Soc. Achievements include invention of optimization software. Office: Univ Del Computer and Info Sci Newark DE 19716 E-mail: chester@cis.udel.edu.

CHESTER, MARGARET JANE, special education educator; b. Oklahoma City, Dec. 8, 1947; d. Auston Averon and Hazel Berniece (Price) Daniel. BS, U. Sci. and Arts, 1980; MEd, U. Ctrl. Okla., 1994. Cert. spl. edn. tchr., Okla. Tchr. Tuttle (Okla.) Pub. Schs., 1980—, mem. supt.'s adv. bd., 1993—. Pres. FFA Mother's Club, Tuttle, 1992-94; mem. planning com. Showhill Bapt. Ch., Tuttle, 1994. State of Okla. grantee, 1993. Mem. NEA, Okla. Edn. Assn., Tuttle Edn. Assn. (bldg. rep. 1993-99), Coun. for Exceptional Children. Democrat. Baptist. Avocations: collecting antiques, fishing, gardening, reading, quilting.

CHESTER, NIA LANE, psychology educator; b. L.A., Dec. 8, 1945; d. Thomas Henry and Virginia (Chalmers) Lane; m. C. Ronald Chester, Aug. 9, 1969 (div. July 1988); children: Caben Paul, Ian Thomas. BA magna cum laude, Smith Coll., 1967; MA, Columbia U., 1968; PhD, Boston U., 1981. Tchr. Elmont (N.Y.) Meml. High Sch., 1967-70; master tchr. Ednl. Collaborative Greater Boston, Cambridge, Mass., 1971-75; teaching fellow Harvard U., Cambridge, 1976-78; rsch. assoc. Boston U., 1981-83, 88—; rsch. scholar Radcliffe Coll., Cambridge, 1983-84; assoc. prof. psychology Pine Manor Coll., Chestnut Hill, Mass., 1983—, Lindsey prof., 1990, chair divsn. Natural and Behavioral Scis., 1993-94, dir. internship program, 1994—, dean learning & assessment, 1996-97, dean, 1997—. Reviewer Jour. Personality and Social Psychology, 1985—; vis. prof. Boston U., 1986-88. Co-author: Separating Together: How Divorce Affects Families, 1997; editor: Experience and Meaning of Work in Women's Lives, 1990; contbr. articles to profl. jours., chpts. to books. Bd. dirs. Peabody Aftersch. Program, Cambridge, 1983-85, Tobin Aftersch. Program, Cambridge, 1989—. NIMH fellow, 1979; recipient Ruth Allinger Gibson '26 Teaching award, 1992; Women's Coll. Coalition grantee, 1992. Mem. APA, Ea. Psychol. Asn. (program com. 1989-93). Office: Pine Manor Coll 400 Heath St Chestnut Hill MA 02467-2332

CHESTER, SHARON ROSE, photographer, natural history educator, writer, illustrator; b. Chgo., July 12, 1942; d. Joseph Thomas and Lucia Barbara (Urban) C. BA, U. Wis., 1964; grad., Coll. San Mateo, 1974, U. Calif., Berkeley, 1977, San Francisco State U., 1989. Flight attendant Pan Am. World Airways Inc., San Francisco, 1965; free lance photographer San Mateo, Calif., 1983—; stock photographer Comstock, N.Y.C., 1987-98. Lectr. Soc. Expdns., Seattle, 1985-91, Abercrombie & Kent, Chgo., 1992-94, Seven Seas Cruise Line, San Francisco, 1994-95; owner Wandering Albatross, 1993. Author (checklist) Birds of the Antarctic and Sub-Antarctic, 1986, rev., 1994, Antarctic birds and Seals: A Pocket Guide, 1993, South to Antarctica, 1994, The Northwest Passage, 1994; author and illustrator, Birds of Chile, Aves de Chile, 1995; co-author: The Birds of Chile: A Field Guide, 1993, The Arctic Guide, 1996, The Marquesas Islands: Mave Mai, 1997, Ia Orana Tahiti, 1998, Guide to Maritime Britain and The European North Atlantic, 1999, Guide to Scottish Isles, Faroes and Iceland, 2000, Travel Guides to Namibia and Jordan, 2001, Travel Guides to Egypt and East Africa, 2002; photos featured in Mother Earth Through the Eyes of Women Photographers and Writers, 1992, 10th anniversary edit., 2002; photographer mag. cover Internat. Wildlife Mag., 1985, Sierra Club Calendar, 1986; exhibited photos at Royal Geographic Soc. London. Mem. Calif. Acad. Sci. Avocations: writing, ice dancing, birdwatching. Home: 724 Laurel Ave Apt 211 San Mateo CA 94401-4131

CHEUNG, JOSEPH YAT-SING, biomedical scientist, nephrologist; b. Hong Kong, June 21, 1950; came to U.S., 1972; s. Wah Lun and Wai Ming (Ho) C.; m. Barbara Ann Miller, June 14, 1975. BSc with honors, McGill U., Mont., Can., 1972; MS, Pa. State U., 1974, PhD, 1976; MD, Duke U., 1978. Diplomate Nat. Bd. Med. Examiners, Am. Bd. Internal Medicine, Am. Bd. Internal Medicine and Nephrology. Resident Duke U. Med. Ctr., Durham, N.C., 1978-80; fellow Mass. Gen. Hosp., Boston, 1980-83; instr. in medicine Med. Sch. Harvard U., Boston, 1983-84, asst. prof. medicine, 1984-86; assoc. prof. medicine Pa. State U., Hershey, 1986-91, prof. medicine, 1991—2000; sr. scientist Weis Ctr. for Rsch., Geisinger Med. Ctr., Danville, Pa., 2000—. Mem. editorial bd. Am. Jour. Physiology, 1991-93; assoc. editor Exec. Sports Sci. Rev., 2002—; contbr. articles to Jour. Clin. Investigation, Jour. Biol. Chemistry, New Eng. Jour. Medicine. Grantee Whitaker Found., Juvenile Diabetes Found. Internat., NIH, Am. Heart Assn. Mem. Am. Physiol. Soc., Am. Soc. Nephrology, Am. Soc. Clin. Investigation, Am. Soc. Cell Biology, Biophys. Soc. Republican. Achievements include research in beneficial role of exercise training in postinfarction hearts, phospholemmen regulation of heart function, role of altered calcium regulation in congestive heart failure. Office: Weis Ctr for Rsch Geisinger Med Ctr Danville PA 17822

CHEUNG, JUDY HARDIN, retired special education educator; b. Santa Rosa, Calif., Feb. 3, 1945; d. Robert Stephens and Edna Rozella Hardin. BA, Calif. State U. at Sonoma, Rohnert Park, Calif., 1966; MA, U. San Francisco, 1981. Tchr. St. Thomas (V.I.) Dept. Edn., 1967—71; spl. edn. tchr., basic functional and Ednl. skills to disabled adults Sonoma Devel. Ctr., Eldridge, Calif., 1971—2001; co-adminstr. Redwood Empire Chinese Assn. Sch., 1996—. Co-chair Ednl. Svcs. Profl. Practice Group, Eldridge, Calif., 1989-90, 93-94; pres. Poets of the Vineyard, 1998—. Author, pub.: Acorn to Embers, 1987, Welcome to the Inside, 1984; author, photographer, pub. Captions, 1986. Recipient awards Silver Pegasus, 1983, Poets of the Vineyard, 1986, 87, 2000, 01, Ark. Writers Conf., 1988. Mem. Calif. Fedn. Chaparral Poets (pres. 1989-91, 93-95), Ina Coolbrith Cir. (pres. 1988-90), Calif. Writers Club (treas. Redwood writers br. 1985-86), Artists Embassy Internat. (v.p. 2003—, Amb. of Arts award 1992, 2001), World Congress of Cultures and Poetry (internat. bd. dirs. 1993-2000, Grand Cultures medal 1993, Cert. of merit 2000, medal for Poetic Achievement 2000), Redwood Empire Chinese Assn. (sec., co-adminstr. Chinese Lang. sch. 1996—, Appreciation award for col. svc. 2000). Avocations: photography, reading. Home and Office: 704 Brigham Ave Santa Rosa CA 95404-5245

CHEVALIER, ROBERT LOUIS, pediatric nephrologist, educator, researcher; b. Chgo., Oct. 25, 1946; s. Frank Charles and Marion Helen (Jahnke) C.; m. Janis Julia Slezak, Dec. 23, 1970; 1 child, Juline Arianne. BS, U. Chgo., 1968, MD, 1972. Diplomate Am. Bd. Pediatrics, Bd. Pediatric Nephrology. Pediatric resident U. N.C., Chapel Hill, 1972-75, postdoctoral fellow, 1975-77; nephrology fellow U. Colo., Denver, 1977-78; asst. prof. U. Va., Charlottesville, 1978-83, assoc. prof., 1983-88, prof., 1988—, chief pediatric nephrology, 1978-91, vice chmn. pediatrics, 1988-96, Genentech prof., 1993-97, acting chmn. pediatrics, 1996-97, chmn. pediat., 1997—, Shepherd prof., 1997—. Established investigator Am. Heart Assn., 1983-88. Mem. editl. bd. Renal Failure, 1988—, Pediatric Nephrology, 1995-97, Kidney Internat., 1998—; contbr. numerous articles to profl. jours., chpts. to books. Chmn. med. adv. bd. Nat. Kidney Found. Va., Richmond, 1986-89. Fellow Am. Acad. Pediatrics, Am. Heart Assn.; mem. Am. Pediatric Soc., Am. Physiol. Soc., Am. Soc. Nephrology, Am. Soc. Pediatric Nephrology (pres. 1991-92), Am. Bd. Pediatrics, Internat. Pediat. Nephrology Assn. (councillor 1999—), Soc. Pediatric Rsch., So. Soc. Pediatric Rsch. (pres. 1990-91, chair internat. workshop on devel. nephrology 2001). Office: Univ Va PO Box 386 Charlottesville VA 22902-0386 E-mail: rlc2m@virginia.edu.

CHEVERS, WILDA ANITA YARDE, former state official and educator; b. N.Y.C. d. Wilsey Ivan and Herbert Lee (Perry) Yarde; m. Kenneth Chevers, May 14, 1950; 1 child, Pamela Anita. BA, CUNY, 1947; MSW, Columbia U., 1959, PhD, 1981. Probation officer, Office Probation for Cts., N.Y.C., 1947-55, supr. probation officer, 1955-65, br. chief, 1965-72, asst. dir. probation, 1972-77, dept. commr. dept. probation, 1978-86; prof. pub. adminstrn. John Jay Coll. Criminal Justice, CUNY, 1986-91. Conf. faculty mem. Nat. Council Juvenile and Family Ct. Judges; mem. faculty N.Y.C. Tech. Coll., Nat. Coll. Juvenile Justice; mem. adv. com. Family Ct., First Dept. Sec. Susan E. Wagner Adv. Bd., 1966—70; sec., bd. dirs. Allen Cmty. Day Care Ctr., 1971—75; mem. Las Vegas EMA Ryan White Title I Planning Coun., 1998—2000; chmn., bd. dirs. Allen Christian Sch., 1987—91; bd. dirs. Allen Sr. Citizens Housing, Queensboro Soc. for Prevention Cruelty to Children, Las Vegas LWV. Named to Hall of Fame, Hunter Coll., 1983. Mem. ABA (assoc.), ASPA (coun.), NASW, N.Y. Acad. Pub. Edn., Nat. Coun. on Crime and Delinquency, Acad. Cert. Soc. Workers, Mid. Atlantic States Conf. on Correction, Alumni Assn. Colmbia U. Sch. Social Work, NYU Alumni Assn., NAACP, Counselors, Las Vegas LWV (bd. dirs.), SNCCW (pres. 2002-03), Hansel and Gretel Club (pres. Queens, N.Y. 1967-69), Delta Sigma Theta. Home: 9012 Covered Wagon Ave Las Vegas NV 89117-7010

CHEVRAY, RENE, physics educator; b. Paris, Feb. 6, 1937; came to the U.S., 1962; naturalized U.S. citizen, 1989; s. Robert and Marie-Louise (Fracher) C.; m. Keiko Uesawa, Aug. 9, 1964; children: Pierre-Yves Masaki, Veronique Mie. BS, U. Toulouse, France, 1962; Dipl. Ing. (French Govt. Highest scholar), Ecole Nationale Supérieure d'Electronique, d'Electrotechnique et d'Hydraulique de Toulouse, 1962; MS (Alliance Française of N.Y. fellow), U. Iowa, 1963, PhD, 1967; D.Sc., U. Claude Bernard, Lyon, France, 1978. Product and mfg. engr. Centrifugal Pumps Worthington, Paris, 1963-64; research assoc. Iowa Inst. Hydraulic Research, Iowa City, 1964-67; postdoctoral fellow, lectr. aeronautics Johns Hopkins U., 1967-69; asst. prof. SUNY, Stony Brook, 1969-72, assoc. prof., 1972-79, prof., 1979-82; prof. dept. mech. engring. Columbia U., N.Y.C., 1982-87, chmn. dept. mech. engring., 1987-90. Cons. physics of fluids and instrumentation; vis. prof. Japan Soc. for Promotion Sci., 1975; vis. prof., von. Humboldt fellow U. Karlsruhe, 1975-76 Author: Topics in Fluid Mechanics, 1993; contbr. articles to profl. jours.; rschr. in transport processes in fluids. Recipient Great Tchr. award Soc. Columbia Grads., 1993; Fulbright scholar, 1962-63; grantee NSF, 1970-73, 73-91, Dept. Energy, 1979-89, Office Naval Rsch., 1985-90, Whitaker Found., 1995—; Rsch. Found. SUNY Faculty Rsch. fellow, 1970-71. Mem. Internat. Assn. Hydraulic Rsch., Am. Phys. Soc., N.Y. Acad. Scis., Sigma Xi Home: 300 Riverside Dr Apt 10A New York NY 10025-5239 Office: Columbia U Mech Enging New York NY 10027

CHEW, LYNDA CASBEER, elementary school educator; b. Corpus Christi, Tex., Oct. 1, 1947; d. Joseph Olen and Ethel Jean (Milam) Casbeer; m. Jack H. Chew, Aug. 28, 1976; children: Doise Elizabeth, Charlotte Lee. BA, U. Tex., 1974; MA, S.W. Bapt. Sem., 1975; MEd, U. Tex., El Paso, 1988. Elem. tchr. Sierra Blanca (Tex.) Ind. Sch. Dist., 1979-80, Orange Grove (Tex.) Ind. Sch. Dist., 1987-88, Socorro Ind. Sch. Dist., El Paso, 1988-94, Leander (Tex.) Ind. Sch. Dist., 1994-95, Manor (Tex.) Ind. Sch. Dist., 1995—. Pres. Horizon Heights PTA, El Paso, 1989-90; v.p. Hueco PTO, El Paso, 1990-91, chmn. Dist. PTO/PTA Counc., El Paso, 1989-91. Recipient 4 Regional Ctr. for Minorities sci. grants. Mem. Assn. Tex. Profl. Educators (bldg. rep., adv. com. 1990-92), Assn. for Compensatory Educators Tex., Sci. Tchrs. Assn. Tex., Elem. Sci. Tchrs., U. Tex. Alumni Assn. Baptist. Avocations: reading, softball, fishing, camping. Office: Manor Intermediate Sch PO Box 348 Manor TX 78653-0348 Home: 170 Bailee Cir Poteet TX 78065-4220

CHEW, PAMELA CHRISTINE, language educator; b. Nevada, Mo., Feb. 10, 1953; d. Harry and Delores (Trimmer) C. AA, Cottey Coll., 1973; BA in French, U. Mo., 1975, MA in French Lit., 1977; cert. art criticism, Univ. Internat. dell 'Arte, Florence, Italy, 1981. Admissions counselor Cottey Coll., Nevada, 1976-77; internat. publicist Jim Halsey Co., Tulsa, 1978-79; with archival dept. U. Tulsa, 1980, 81-82; English as second lang. instr. Cath. Social Services, Tulsa, 1981-87. Italian instr. Berlitz Sch. Langs., Tulsa, 1985, U. Tulsa, 1987-90; asst. prof. fgn. lang./ESL Tulsa C.C., 1985—; Italian adj. prof. Oral Roberts U., Tulsa, 2001, ITV Italian Northeastern State U., Broken Arrow, Okla., 2002—, Okla. State U., Stillwater, Okla.; leader middle sch. students to Utsunomiya Japan on Sister City Exch., Tulsa Global Alliance, 2001, 02; Rotary profl. Suva, Fiji, 2003—; presenter in field. Drawings pub. Nimrod Internat. Jour. Prose and Poetry, 1996, Outside the Lines, 2000, 01, 02. Vol. Internat. Council Tulsa, 1985—, Gilcrease Mus. Am. Art & History, Tulsa, 1977-78. Grantee Mimi Atwater Meml. Found., France, 1973-74, Rotary, 1980-81, 2003—, Tomorrow's Tchrs., Tomorrow's Tech., 1999, Rotary scholar, Florence, Italy, 1980-81, U. South Pacific, Fiji, 2003—; recipient cash awards for poetry, 1979, 86, essay, 1981, Excellence in Tchg. award, 1996. Mem. Okla. Tchrs. English as Second Lang., South Cen. MLA (sec. Italian sect. 1986-87), Okla. Fgn. Lang. Assn. (Breck Woman of 90's 1989). Home: PO Box 4193 Tulsa OK 74159-0193 Office: Tulsa CC 3727 E Apache St Tulsa OK 74115-3150 E-mail: pchew@tulsa.cc.ok.us.

CHI, LOIS WONG, emeritus biology educator, research scientist; b. Fuchow, China, May 12, 1921; came to U.S., 1941; d. Leland and Ada (Pang) Wang; m. Henry Chi; children: Lanie, David, Joycelyn. BS, Wheaton Coll., 1945; MS, U. So. Calif., 1947, PhD, 1954. Rsch. fellow Loma Linda (Calif.) U., 1954-57; instr. to assoc. prof. biology Immaculate Heart Coll., L.A., 1957-66; assoc. prof. to prof. biology Calif. State U., Dominguez Hills, 1966-91, rsch. dir., 1979-86, prof. emeritus. Dir. Minority Biomed. Rsch. Program Calif. State U., Dominguez Hills, 1979-86, Minority Honor Program, 1982-86. Contbr. numerous articles to profl. jours. Pres. and v.p. Chinese Am. Faculty Assocs. So. Calif., L.A., Chinese Am. Engrs. and Scientists. Home: 2839 El Oeste Dr Hermosa Beach CA 90254-2234

CHIA, FELIPE HUMBERTO, management marketing educator, author, consultant; b. Lima, Peru, May 17, 1945; came to U.S., 1966; s. Felipe S.G. and Carmen Rosa (Fuseng) C.; m. Mary Elizabeth Davis, Oct. 22, 1971; 1 child, Anne Marie. B in Bus. Mgmt. cum laude, Northwood U., 1970; JD, U. Chgo., 1975; MS, Radford U., 1976; MBA summa cum laude, S.E. Mo. State U., 1979; specialist in cmty. coll. tchg., Arkansas State U., 1981; cert. advanced grad. studies, Coll. William and Mary, 1981; JD, U. Chgo. Data processing mgr. Ctrl. Publs., Lima, 1965-66; adminstrv. asst. data processing svcs. Northwood U., Midland, Mich., 1966-70; stockfitting components supr. Brown Group Industries, Piggott, Ark., 1972-75; adj. instr. bus. New River C.C., Dublin, Va., 1975-76; v.p. mktg. Modern Lands, Inc., Piggott, 1976-79; instr. bus. and econs. Coll. Saint Paul, Lawrenceville, Va., 1979-83; instr. bus. Radford (Va.) U., 1983-88; assoc. prof. mgmt. and mktg. Harrisburg (Pa.) Area C.C., 1988—. Presenter at numerous ednl. seminars and confs., 1979—; judge Dean's Trophy Competition, Randolph, N.J., 1989-93, Distributed Edn., Harrisburg, 1990-95. Author: Study Guide: Management & Organization, 1993, Supervision, 1994; contbr. articles to profl. jours. Bd. dirs. Pa. Assn. for Blind, Harrisburg, 1991—; leader, scoutmaster Boy Scouts Am., 1971-88; supporter 4-H Clubs, 1988-95, United Way, 1983-95. Fellow Wal-Mart Found., 1992, Direct Mktg. Ednl. Found., 1986. Mem. ASTD, Capital Area Mgmt. Devel., Tri-County Pa. Assn. (bd. dirs. 1991—), Bus. Mgmt. Adv. Liaison, Kappa Delta Phi, Phi Beta Lambda (chpt. advisor 1979-96). Avocations: creative writing, do-it-yourself projects, computer applications, poetry, reading books in foreign languages.

CHIANG, FU-PEN, mechanical engineering educator, researcher; b. Oct. 10, 1936; s. Chien-lo and Lien-yin (Mao) C.; m. Jin-lin Li; children: Brian (dec.), Ted, Michelle, Winston. BSCE, Nat. Taiwan U., 1953-57; MS, U. Fla., 1963, PhD in Engring. Sci. and Mechanics, 1966. Civil engr., 1958-62; asst. prof. mech. engring. SUNY, Stony Brook, 1967-70, from assoc. prof. to prof., 1970-87, lead prof., 1987—, dir. Lab. for Exptl. Mechanics Rsch., 1984—, chmn., 1995—. Vis. prof. Swiss Fed. Inst. Tech., Lausanne, 1973-74; sr. vis. fellow dept. physics Cavendish Lab., U. Cambridge, Eng., 1980-81; cons. Army Material and Mechanics Research Ctr., Army Missile Command, Grumann Aerospace Corp., and others. Editor: Internat. Jour. Optics and Lasers in Engring., 1987-93; contbr. articles to profl. jours. Recipient B. J. Lazan award, 1993; postdoctoral fellow Cath. U. Am.; NSF grantee, 1968-73, 76-87, 96—, Air Force of Sci. Rsch. grantee, 1993-98, 2003—, NIH, 2002—. Fellow Soc. Exptl. Mechanics, Optical Soc. Am.; mem. AAAS, ASME, Soc. Photo-Optical Instrumentation Engrs., Am. Acad. Mechanics, N.Y. Acad. Scis. Research on development of optical stress analysis technique such as laser speckles techniques, holographic interferometry, white light speckle techniques, moire methods, photoelasticity, speckle electron microscopy, acoustic speckle techniques and their applications to solid mechanics and biomechanics problems. Office: SUNY Dept Mech Stony Brook NY 11794-0001

CHIANG, GEORGE DJIA-CHEE, retired engineer, educator; b. Shanghai, Sept. 29, 1938; came to U.S., 1963; s. Tai Yei and Wai Yui (Lai) C.; m. Betty Theresa Doue, June 11, 1965; children: Andrew H., Audrey H. BS, Harbin (China) Inst. Tech., 1961; MS, U. Calif., Berkeley, 1965; PhD, Ariz. State U., 1971. Registered profl. engr., Tex. Asst. engr. Harbin Steel Co., 1961-62; rsch. asst. U. Calif., 1964-66; sr. project engr. Sperry Rand Corp., Phoenix, 1966-70; faculty assoc. Ariz. State U., Tempe, 1970-71; head, prof. engring dept. U.S. Army Intern Tng. Ctr., Texarkana, Tex., 1971-77; litigation, tech. cons. Nat. Hwy. Traffic Safety Adminstn., Washington, 1977-94; chief trend and analysis divsn. Nat. Hwy. Traffic Safety Adminstrn., 1994-2001; ret., 2001. Adj. prof. engring. U. So. Calif., Washington, 1977-89; cons. Sperry Rand Corp., Phoenix, 1970-71, Edgewood (Md.) Arsenal, 1972-77. Contbr. articles to tech. jours. Active local PTA; bd. dirs. Potomac Chinese Sch., 1978-81, Chinese Culture and Cmty. Svc. Ctr., 1989-91, pres., 1991-92. Active local PTA; bd. dirs. Potomac Chinese Sch., 1978-81, bd. dirs. Chinese Culture and Community Svc. Ctr., 1989-91, pres., 1991-92. Mem. ASME (tech. adv. com. 1980—), Profl. Engring. Soc., Tau Beta Pi. Democrat. Avocations: reading, tennis, travel. Home: 113 Ivy Arbor Ct Lincoln CA 95648-8631 E-mail: gdchiang@hotmail.com.

CHIANG, SAMUEL EDWARD, theological educator, humanities educator; b. Taipei, Taiwan, Republic of China, Oct. 20, 1959; s. William L. and Gladys (Chao) C.; m. Roberta Jean Bush, Dec. 31, 1987; children: Zachariah Asa, Micah Kaleem, Joni Abigail. B of Commerce, U. Toronto, Can., 1982; MA in Bibl. Studies, Dallas Theol. Sem., 1989. Ordained minister Peoples' Ch., 1990. Writer, rschr. Can. Broadcasting Co., Toronto, Ont., Can., 1980-81; audit automation coord. Can. nat. office Ernst & Young, Toronto, 1982-86; asst. to the pres. Dallas Sem. Found., 1988-91; East Asia regional dir. Ptnrs. Internat., San Jose, Calif., 1991—. Tchr. Applied Principle of Learning-Walk Thru the Bible, 1990—; bd. dirs. Sharp Master Internat. Ltd., Ptnrs. Ltd. Contbr. articles to profl. jours.; editor, contbr. World Christian Perspective, 1988-91. Youth dir. jr. high The Peoples' Ch., Toronto, 1980-82; youth pastor Korean Philadelphia Presbyn. Ch., Toronto, 1983-85; youth dir. Dallas Chinese Fellowship Ch., 1987-90; bd. dirs. Dallas Chinese Ch. Youth Camps, 1987-91; adv. bd. dirs. I Too Have A Dream, Harare, Zimbabwe, 1989—, Foyer Fraternal, Ndjamena, Chad, 1990—, Student Christian Outreach for China, U.S., 1991; bd. dirs. Asian Impact Ministries, 1992-95, SALT, 1996-97, Kingdom Trust, 1992-97, BEE, Inc., 1995-98; advisor The Tear Found., U.K., 1994—; dir. Sharpmaster Internat., 1996—; chmn. Pu Yang Heng Yuan Agritech Devel.

Co. Ltd., 1997—, Olive Advanced Technology Svcs., India, 1997. Mem. Evang. Messiological Soc. Avocations: reading, music, hiking, writing, tennis. Office: PO Box 98583 TST Kowloon Hong Kong China

CHIANG, YUNG FRANK, law educator; b. Taichung, Taiwan, Jan. 2, 1936; came to U.S., 1961; s. Ruey-ting and Yueh-yin (Ho) C.; m. Quay-yin Lin, Nov. 1, 1969; children: Amy P., David H. LLB, Nat. Taiwan U., 1958; LLM, Northwestern U., 1962; JD, U. Chgo., 1965. Bar: Taiwan 1960, N.Y. 1974. Assoc. Yen & Lai Law Office, Taipei, Taiwan, 1960-61; editor The Lawyers Co-op Pub. Co., Rochester, N.Y., 1965; rsch. assoc. Harvard Law Sch., Cambridge, Mass., 1965-67; asst. prof. U. Ga. Sch. Law, Athens, 1967-72; assoc. prof. Fordham U. Sch. Law, N.Y.C., 1972-76, prof., 1976—. Bd. dirs. Taiwan Ctr., N.Y.C.; legal cons., vice-chmn. Asia Bank, N.A., Flushing, N.Y., 1983-88, also bd. dirs.; leader N.Y. judge and lawyers del. to China and Hong Kong, People to People Internat., 1994; organizer, moderator 5 Russian delegations to U.S., People to People Amb. Program, 1994-95; pres. Fordham U. Law Faculty Union, 2000—. Contbr. articles to profl. jours. Organizer, bd. dirs. The Taiwan Mcht. Assn. N.Y., Flushing, 1976-96, pres., 1980-84; pres. N.Y. chpt. Formosan Assn. for Pub. Affairs, Washington, 1991-92. Mem. N.Y. State Bar Assn., N.Am. Taiwanese Profs. Assn. (bd. dirs. 1994-2000, v.p. 1997-98, pres. 1998-99), Nat. Assn. of Securities Dealers (arbitrator 1976-98), Order of Coif. Avocations: reading, skiing, archery, swimming. Office: Fordham U Sch Law 140 W 62nd St New York NY 10023-7407 E-mail: fchiang@mail.lawnet.fordham.edu.

CHICHILNISKY, GRACIELA, mathematician, economist, writer, educator, writer; b. Buenos Aires, Mar. 27, 1946; came to U.S., 1968, naturalized citizen, 1992; d. Salomon Chichilnisky and Raquel Gavensky; children: Eduardo Jose, Natasha Sable. Student, MIT, 1967-68; MA, U. Calif., Berkeley, 1970, PhD in Math., 1971, PhD in Econs., 1976. Postdoctoral fellow Harvard U., 1974, lectr. dept. econs., 1975-77, fellow Harvard inst. internat. devel., 1978; assoc. prof. Columbia U., N.Y.C., 1977-80, prof., 1981—, dir. Program on Info. and Resources, 1994—, prof. stats, 1996—, dir. Columbia Ctr. for Risk Mgmt., 1998—, UNESCO prof. math. and econs., 1995—99. CEO Cross Border Exch. Corp., 1999-2003, chmn. 2003-; mem. presdl. cabinet Banco Ctrl. Republica Argentina, 1971-74; co-prin. investigator Urban Inst., Washington, 1975-77; vis. scholar Internat. Inst. Applied Sys, Analysis Laxenburg, Austria, 1975-77; prin. investigator U.S. Dept. Labor, 1977-78, Rockefeller Found. Project Internat. Rels., 1981-83; project dir. UN Inst. Tng. and Rsch., N.Y., 1979-83; chaired prof. econs. U. Essex, 1980-81; vis. prof. inst. math and its applications U. Minn., 1983-84, U. Siena, Italy, summers, 1991-93, 2002; vis. prof. Stanford Inst. Theoretical Econs., Stanford U., summers, 1991-93, dept. econs., Inst. Internat. Studies, 1993—, vis. prof. depts., econ. and ops. rsch. Stanford U., 1993-94; prof. missionaire U. des Antilles et de la Guyane, spring 1984-85; NSF prof. dept. math. U. Calif., Berkeley, 1985-86; CEO, chmn. FITEL Ltd., 1985-89; exec. dir. Sci. Internat. Ltd., 1989-90; vis. prof. U. Cath. Buenos Aires, Aug. 1993; cons. in field; UNESCO chair in math. and econs., Columbia U., 1995—; Salinbemi chair U. Siena, Italy, 1994-95; CEO Cross Border Exchange, NY, 1999-, chmn. 2003-. Co-author: Catastrophe or New Society? A Latin American World Model, 1976; author: (with G. Heal) The Evolving International Economy, 1986, Oil in the International Economy, 1991, Sustainability: Dynamics and Uncertainty, 1998, Mathematical Economics, 1998, Topology and Markets, 1998, Markets, Information and Uncertainty, 1998, Environmental Markets: Equity and Efficiency, 1999; assoc. editor Jour. Devel. Econs., 1976-86, Advances in Mathematics, 1985, Risk Decision and Policy; mem. various editorial bds.; contbr. articles to profl. jours. Bd. trustees Nat. Resources Def. Coun., N.Y., 1994—. Recipient Internat. Rels. award Rockefeller Found., 1983-84; named Most Disting. Woman Economist, Newcombe Found. and Omega Delta Epsilon, 1991, Leif Johansen award U. Oslo, Norway, 1995; grantee NSF, 1974—; fellow Ford Found., 1967-69, Banco Ctrl. Republica Argentina, 1972-74, spl. fellow UN Inst. Tng. and Rsch., 1977-76. Mem. Coun. Social Choice and Welfare Soc. Office: Columbia U 629 Mathematics New York NY 10027 Mailing: 335 Riverside Dr New York NY 10025

CHIEN, CHIA-LING, physics educator; b. China, Nov. 10, 1942; came to U.S., 1966; s. Ting and An-Hsiu (Wong) C.; m. Christina Yueh Wang, Apr. 15, 1972; children: David, Deborah. BS in Physics, Tunghai U., Taiwan, 1965; MS in Physics, Carnegie-Mellon U., 1968, PhD, 1972. Rsch. assoc. Johns Hopkins U., Balt., 1973-74, assoc. rsch. scientist, 1974-75, asst. prof., 1976-79, assoc. prof., 1979-83, prof., 1983—, dir. materials rsch. sci. and engrng. ctr., 1997—, Jacob L. Hain prof. physics, 2002—. Vis. prof. Johns Hopkins U., Balt., 1975-76; hon. prof. Nanjing U. 2d lt. Air Force, 1965-66, Taiwan. Fellow Am. Phys. Soc.; mem. Materials Rsch. Soc. Office: Johns Hopkins U Dept Physics 3400 N Charles St Baltimore MD 21218-2680 Business E-Mail: clc@pha.jhu.edu.

CHIHARA, CHARLES SEIYO, philosophy educator; b. July 19, 1932; s. George I. and Mary N. (Fushiki) C.; m. Carol J. Rosen, June 14, 1964; 1 child, Michelle N. BS, Seattle U., 1954; MS, Purdue U., 1956; PhD, U. Wash., 1960. Instr. U. Wash., Seattle, 1961-62; asst. prof. U. Ill., Urbana, 1962-63, U. Calif., Berkeley, 1963-68, assoc. prof., 1968-74, prof. philosophy dept., 1974—2000, emeritus prof., 2000—. Author: Ontology and the Vicious-Circle Principle, 1973, Constructibility and Mathematical Existence, 1990, The Worlds of Possibility, 1998, A Structural Account of Mathematics, 2004. NEH fellow for ind. rsch., Paris, 1985-86, U. Calif., 1994-95; postdoctoral fellow Mellon Found., 1964-65, Humanities Rsch. fellow U. Calif., 1967-68; U. Calif. Pres.'s rsch. fellow in humanities, 1996-97. Office: Univ Calif Dept Philosophy Berkeley CA 94720-0001 E-mail: charles1@socrates.berkeley.edu.

CHILA, ANTHONY GEORGE, osteopathic educator; b. Youngstown, Ohio, Dec. 14, 1937; s. Paul and Anne (Jurenko) C.; m. Helen Paulick, Oct. 9, 1965; 1 child, Anne Elizabeth. BA, Youngstown State U., 1960; DO, Kansas City Coll. Osteopathy and Surgery, 1965. Assoc. prof. family medicine Mich. State U. Coll. Medicine, East Lansing, 1977-78, Ohio U. Coll. Medicine, Athens, 1978-83, prof. family medicine, 1983, chief clin. research, 1982; chmn. instl. rev. bd. Ohio U., Athens, 1986-88. George C. Kozma Meml. lectr. Cleve. Acad. Osteo Medicine, 1979, Andrew Taylor Still Meml. lectr., Chgo., 1990, Sutherland Meml. Lectr., San Francisco, 1992. Contbr. numerous articles to profl. jours. Trustee Saint Vladimir's Orthodox Theol. Sem., Tuckahoe, N.Y., 1975-89; active Kootaga Area coun. Boy Scouts Am. Mem.: AAAS, Am. Assn. Orthopaedic Medicine, N.Y. Acad. Scis., Cranial Acad., Am. Acad. Osteopathy (pres. 1983—84, 1985—86, Scott Meml. lectr. Kirksville, Mo. 1984, Thomas L. Northup lectr. Las Vegas 1986, Gutensohn-Denslow award 1995, Andrew Taylor Still medallion of honor 1997), Am. Coll. Gen. Practitioners, Am. Osteo. Assn. (Louisa M. Burns lectr. Clearwater, Fla. 1987), Gen. Charles Grosvenor Civil War Round Table. Republican. Avocations: philately, coin collecting, chess, American Civil War history. Office: Ohio U Coll Osteo Medicine Grosvenor Hall Athens OH 45701

CHILCUTT, DORTHE MARGARET, art educator, artist; b. Fond du Lac, Wis., Jan. 29, 1915; d. John William and Pearl Evelyn (Burnett) Trummer; m. Booth Chilcutt, Feb. 14, 1942; children: Karen Chilcutt Hulett, Booth, Cindy Jo Chilcutt Underhill, Debra Ann Chilcutt-Flippo. BS, U. Wis., 1940, MS, 1952; postgrad., NYU, 1975-78, Instituto Allende, Mex., summer 1958, La Romita Sch. Art, Italy, 1978-96; postgrad. Schohegan Sch., Painting and Sculpture, 1959. Layout artist DeVry Corp., Chgo., 1941-42; tchr. art St. Louis pub. schs., 1951-53, Monroe County Schs., Key West, Fla., 1957-62, Okeechobee Jr. High Sch. (Fla.), 1963-84, Indian River C.C., 1984-99. One woman shows Little Gallery, Key West, 1960, Martello Gallery, Key West, 1963, Ft. Pierce Art Gallery (Fla.), 1970; exhibited in group shows Jacksonville Art Mus. (Fla.), 1959, Tampa Art Mus., 1960, Norton Art Gallery, West Palm Beach, Fla., 1960, Backus Gallery, Ft. Pierce, 1977-98, St. Louis Art Mus., 1951, Wis. Salon of Art, Madison, 1947, Key West Art and Hist. Soc., 1957-90, Key West Art Ctr., 1959; Lighthouse Gallery, Tequesta, 1998; Court House Cultural Ctr., Stuart, 1998; Schacknow Museum of Fine Art, Coral Springs, 1998; represented in permanent collections Ft. Pierce Art Gallery, Martello Galleries; contbr. articles to profl. jours. Recipient Best of Show awards Fla. Fedn. Art, 1974, Ft. Pierce Art Gallery, 1977, Ybor City Ann. Fiesta Day, 1980, Backus Festival, 1992, 1st pl. awards Highlands Art League 8th Ann., 1974, Jensen Beach Ann., Elliot Mus., 1974, 84, Ft. Pierce Scholarship Show, 1972-75, Four-County Art Show, Ft. Pierce, 1972-94, Tchr. of Yr. award Okeechobee County Sch. Bd., 1976, others. Mem. Fla. Watercolor Soc. (sec. 1974-84, bd. dirs. 1984-86), Gold Coast Water Color Soc., Nat. Art Edn. Assn., Fla. Art Edn. Assn. (Career Service award 1986), Miami Watercolor Soc., Treasure Coast Art Soc., Palm Beach Water Color Soc. Democrat. Home: 506 SW 15th St Okeechobee FL 34974-5264

CHILDERS, ANITA FLOWERS, language arts educator; b. Jesup, Ga., Nov. 7, 1939; d. Alberta Flowers; m. Sherman Overton Childers, Sr., June 10, 1956; 1 child, Sherman Overton, Jr. BA, Clark Coll., 1963; MA, Atlanta U., 1973; PhD, The Ohio State U., 1985. Cert. social studies 7-12, reading K-12, middle grades 4-8, Ga. Tchr. William James High Sch., Statesboro, Ga., 1963-64, Liberty County Pub. Schs., Hinesville, Ga., 1964-70, Jesup (Ga.) Jr. High Sch., 1970-74; reading instr. Brunswick (Ga.) Jr. Coll., 1974-75; dir. reading clinic Savannah (Ga.) State Coll., 1975-76; reading coord. Payne Coll., Augusta, Ga., 1978-80; asst. tchr. dept. ednl. theory & practice The Ohio State U., Columbus, 1980-82, grad. administrv. assoc. Univ. Coll., 1982-85; asst. prof. early childhood edn., special asst. to v.p., program mgr. ROTC enchanced skills programs Ft. Valley (Ga.) State Coll., 1985-87; asst. prof. early childhood edn. Ga. Southern Coll., Statesboro, 1987-88, Morris Brown Coll., Atlanta, 1988-89; tchr. lang. arts. Jesup Middle Grades, 1989—. Pvt. reading cons. Jesup, 1976—; coord. oratory Jr. Beta Club of Ga., Jesup, 1992—, sponsor, 1991—. Registrar City Govt., Jesup, 1972; sec. Genesis Housing Com.; pres. Youth Dept. Gen. Freewill Bapt. Ch. Ala., Ga. Recipient Order of Eastern Star, 1991, Missionary award A.M.E. Ch. Waycross Dist., 1992; grantee NSF, 1969, United Negro Coll. Fund, 1981; scholar Presbyn Ch., 1980. Mem. NSF, NEA, Internat. Reading Assn., Assn. of Supervision & Curriculum, Ga. Assn. Educators, Nat. Assn. Negro Bus. & Profl. Womens Club, Progressive Womens Club, Delta Sigma Theta, Phi Delta Kappa. Democrat. Avocations: musicals, theater, reading. Home: 550 N 5th St Jesup GA 31545-1025

CHILDERS, BOB EUGENE, educational association executive; b. Cleveland, Miss., Sept. 16, 1930; s. William Nick and Allie Jeanette (Doty) C.; m. Jo Ann Roberts, May 1, 1953; children: William Frank, Robert Clayton, John Murry, Julia Ann. BA, Union U., 1953; MA, Memphis State U., 1958; EdD, U. Tenn., 1964. Cert. tchr., administr., Tenn. Field engr. RCA, El Paso, Tex., 1955-57; instr. USN, Memphis, 1957-60; prin. Halls H.S., Knoxville, Tenn., 1960-61, McMinn County H.S., Athens, Tenn., 1961-64; asst. commr. Tenn. State Dept. Edn., Nashville, 1964-66; regional dir. USOE, Vocat.-Tech. and Adult Edn., Atlanta, 1966-69; exec. dir. Commn. Occupl. Edn., Atlanta, 1969-82, So. Assn. Colls. and Schs., Atlanta, 1982-92. Cons. U.S. Dept. Edn., Washington, 1963-79, Fla. State Legislature, Tallahassee, 1979, Md. Values Edn. Commn., Annapolis, 1979-80; founder, pres. Childers-Childress Family Assn., 1982-88, 90-96. Editor SACS Procs., 1982-92. Bd. dirs. Boy Scouts Am., Atlanta, 1990-97, Ctr. for Citizenship Edn., Washington, 1978-81; bd. trustees YMCA, Nashville, 1964-66; v.p. Religious Heritage of Am., St. Louis, 1979-86; active Rotary, Atlanta, 1981-92. With U.S. Army, 1953-55. Mem. Am. Vocat. Assn. (life 1966, cons.), Am. Tech. Edn. Assn. (life 1978, pres.1984, v.p. 1983), Am. Vocat. Rsch. Assn., Am. Soc. Assn. Execs., Phi Delta Kappa (past treas. 1960-61, sec. 1960-61), Iota Lambda Sigma, Sigma Alpha Epsilon (pres. 1952). Democrat. Baptist. Avocations: geneology, vitaculture, gardening. Home and Office: 960 River Rd Woodruff SC 29388-9110

CHILDERS, FRANCES CAROLE, nursing director, educator, emergency nurse; b. Middletown, Ohio, Feb. 13, 1945; d. Mark and Elizabeth Frances (O'Flynn) Neu; 1 child, Renee Childers Rupp. ADN, Miami U., Oxford, Ohio, 1979, BSN, 1984; MS in Nursing Adminstrn., Wright State U., 1986. RN, Ohio; cert. in ACLS, Am. Heart Assn. Staff nurse Middletown Regional Hosp., 1979-83, clin. coord., 1983-89; instr. nursing Butler County JVS, Hamilton, Ohio, 1989-92; dir. LNP edn. Miami Valley Career Tech. Ctr., Clayton, Ohio, 1992—; staff nurse, emergency rm. Middletown Regional Hosp., 1991—. Mem. Monroe (Ohio) Hist. Soc.; mem. Smiling Grandmothers, Middletown. Mem. ANA, ASCD, NAFE, Ohio Nurses Assn., Nat. League Nursing, Ohio Vocat. Assn., Ohio Assn. Practical Nurse Educators (chairperson edn. com. 1992—), Soroptimist Internat., Sigma Theta Tau. Roman Catholic. Avocations: golf, reading, needlepoint, piano. Home: 130 E Elm St 1022 Golfview Rd Middletown OH 45042-3460 Office: Miami Valley Career Tech 6800 Hoke Rd Clayton OH 45315-8975

CHILDERS, LAWRENCE JEFFREY, superintendent, personnel director; b. Newport News, Va., Oct. 24; m. Susan; 1 child. BS in Edn., Ohio U., 1972; MEd, Xavier U., Cinn., 1978. Cert. prof. secondary tchr., elem. prin., secondary tchr., local supt. and supt. Tchr. elem., jr. high sch., high sch. Tri-Valley LSD, Dresden, Ohio, 1967-80; head coach boys basketball Ohio U., Zanesville, 1977-80; prin., dir. in-sch. suspension, coach varsity boys basketball Maysville Local Sch. Dist., Zanesville, 1980-82; prin. South Zanesville (Ohio) Sch., 1982-85, Newton Elem. Sch., 1985-89, Millersburg (Ohio) Elem. Sch., West Holmes Local Sch. Dist., 1989-91, dir. spl. edn., prin., 1992-93; county supt. Holmes County Office of Edn., Millersburg, 1993-94; supt. Holmes County Ednl. Svc. Ctr., Millersburg, Ohio, 1995-96; dir. classified pers., site mgr. Tricounty Ednl. Svc. Ctr., Wooster, Ohio, 1997-98; ops. mgr. Tri-county Ednl. Svc. Ctr., Wooster, 1998-99; supt. Crooksville (Ohio) Exempted Village Schs., 1999—. Coach Ohio Regional Campus State Basketball Champions, 1978; developer Parent Vol. Network, 1990, in-sch. post office, 1990—; mem. strategic planning com. for bldg. and grounds improvement West Holmes Local Sch. Dist., 1992-93; spkr. Sch. Study Coun. Ohio, 1992; mem. Tchr. Expectation and Student Achievement; mem. sch. supt.'s adv. coun. Ashland U., 1993, adj. prof., 1995-96; supt.'s rep. Ohio East Regional Tchr. Devel. Ctr., 1994-97; adj. prof. Muskingum Coll., 2001. Mem. adv. bd. Holmes County 4-H, 1990-92; vol. Buckeye Book Fair, 1991, 92, 93; chair Holmes County Interagy, Cluster, 1994-95; mem. exec. bd. Ednl. TV of S.E. Ohio, 2002—; mem. governing bd., S.E. Ohio Spl. Edn. Reg. Resource Ctr., 2002—. Named Ohio Dist. 12 Coach of Yr., 1983, Muskingum Valley League Coach of Yr., 1983, Outstanding Adminstr., Ohio Sch. Bd. Assn. S.E. Region, 2002. Mem. ASCD, Ohio Assn. Elem. Sch. Adminstr., Ohio Sch. Bds. Assn., Buckeye Assn. Sch. Adminstrs., North Ctrl. Buckeye Assn. Sch. Adminstrs., Wayne-Holmes County Prins. Assn., Coun. for Exceptional Children, Sch. Study Coun. Ohio, Holmes County C. of C., Phi Delta Kappa. E-mail: ce_jchilders@seovec.org.

CHILDERS, PAMELA BARNARD, secondary school educator; b. Mt. Holly, N.J., Oct. 11, 1943; d. George W. and Audrey (Clerihue) Barnard; m. Malcolm G. Childers, 1993. BA, Radford Coll., Radford, 1965; MS, Radford U., Radford, 1975; MA, Northeastern U., Boston, 1988; EdD, Nova Southeastern U., 1995. Poetry tchr./cons. Geraldine R. Dodge Found., Morristown, N.J., 1986—; coll. tchr. Woodrow Wilson Nat'l Fellowship Found., Princeton, N.J., 1987-88; Caldwell chair composition The McCallie Sch., Chattanooga, 1991—; English tchr. Red Bank Regional High Sch., Little Silver, N.J., 1966-91, McCallie Sch., Chattanooga, 1991—. Editor The Grapevine, Northeastern U. Writing Newsletter, Boston, 1986-90; mem. editorial bd. The Writing Ctr. Jour., 1987—, Computers and Composition, 1987-90; treas. Assembly of Computers in English; instr. Lesley U., Cambridge, Mass., 2003—; mem. assoc. exec. bd. Internat. Writing Ctrs. Author: Waking Dreams, 1989, The High School Writing Center, 1989, Nat. Directory of Writing Centers, 1992, Waking Dreams II, 1992Programs and Practices, 1994, Articulating: Teaching Writing in a Visual World, 1998. Mem. MLA, Nat. Coun. Tchrs. English (nat. bd. cons.), Internat. Writing Ctrs. Assn. (exec. bd.). Democrat. Presbyterian.

CHILDERS, ROBERT L. secondary education educator; b. Presque Isle, Maine, June 9, 1953; s. Robert L. and Ruth Elizabeth (Chase) C.; m. Sharon Ann Yoder, May 24, 1951; childen; Robert L. III, Lori Lynn, Carrie Ann, Jennifer Lee. BS in Secondary edn., No. State U., 1988. Cert. secondary tchr., S.D. Tchr. sci. Sunshine Bible Acad., Miller, S.D., 1988-89; tcrh. alternative edn. Wayne High Sch., Huber Heights, Ohio, 1989-90; tchr. alternative edn. Weisenborn Intermediate Sch., Huber Heights, Ohio, 1990-91, tchr. social studies, 1991-92, tchr. sci., 1992—. Minister Christian edn. Ch. of the Nazarene, Huber Heights, 1990—. With USAF, 1972-79, Vietnam. Republican. Avocations: ceramic art, bird watching.

CHILDERS, SUSAN LYNN BOHN, special education educator, administrator, human resources and transition specialist, consultant; b. Zanesville, Ohio, Mar. 01; m. Lawrence J. Childers; 1 child. AA, Ohio U., 1978, BS in Edn. cum laude, 1982; MEd in Supervision, Ashland U., 1991. Profl. cert. 1-8 elem. tchr., K-12 edn. handicapped, permanent cert., ; spl. edn. tchr., Ohio. Educator learning disabilities, developmentally handicapped Maysville Local Sch. Dist., South Zanesville, Ohio, 1982-89; work-study coord. Holmes County Office Edn., Millersburg, Ohio, 1990, editor spl. edn. newsletter, 1990-93, cons., supervisor work-study programming, 1991-93; spl. edn. supr. Wayne County Bd. Edn., Wooster, Ohio, 1993-94; adminstr. severe behavior handicapped program, supr. special edn. Ashland-Wayne County Bd. Edn., Wooster, 1994-95; cons. Tri-County Ednl. Svc. Ctr., Wooster, 1996-99; supr. spl. edn., supr. instrn. support Zanesville City Sch., Ohio, 1999-2000; dir. spl. edn. Licking County Ednl. Svc. Ctr., Newark, Ohio, 2000-01; supr. spl. edn. Lancaster City Sch., Ohio, 2001—; pres. Ohio Assoc. Supr. and Coord. of Exceptional Students, 2003. Mem. Holmes County Spl. Edn. Adv. Coun., 1990—93, E. Holmes Local Sch. Dist. Strategic Planning Action Team Job/Life Skills, 1993; rep. Ohio Devel. Handicapped Issues Forum; mem. steering com. Ohio Speaks, 1991—94; mem. strategic planning com. Ashland-Wayne County Bd. Edn., 1994—95; mem. Chippewa Local Sch. Dist. Child Care Bd., 1995—96; chmn. Direct Student Svcs. Strategic Planning Com., 1995—96; mem. safety com. Ashland-Wayne Ednl. Svc. Ctr., 1994—96; mem. svc. coordination com. Wayne County Children and Family First Initiative, 1995, 96, Edn. Rep. Safety Com., Tri-County Ednl. Svc. Ctr., Wooster, 1997—99; mem. exec. com. Licking County Children and Family First Initiative, 2000—01; mem. Licking County Mental Health and Recovery Bd., Newark, 2001, Licking County Behavioral Health Assessment Team, 2000—01, Newark Cmty. Corps Adv. Com., 2001, Fairfield County Children and Family First Clin. Cluster, 2001—02; pres.-elect Ohio Assn. Suprs. and Coords. of Exceptional Students, 2002; spkr. in field. Editor Spl. Edn. Newsletter Holmes County Office Edn., 1990-93. Mem. adv. bd. Holmes County Job Placement, Holmes County Litter Prevention Cmty. Action Plan Com., 1993; vol. Ohio Buckeye Book Fair, 1991—93, 1999, Holmes County Spl. Olympics, 1990—93, chairperson vols., 1993; mem. jr. assembly Bethesda Hosp., 1970—78; mem. Beaux Arts Zanesville Art Ctr., 1972—78; mem. spl. needs adv. bd. Ashland-West Holmes Career Ctr., 1990—93; mem. Transition and Comm. Consortium on Learning Disabilities, Ohio U. Alumni Career Resource Network, Holmes County Abuse Prevention Cmty. Action Plan Com., 1993, Ohio Staff Devel. Coun., Wayne County Family and Children First Coun. (Clin. Cluster), 1994—96; co-chairperson fundraising com. Creating Connections Symposium, Akron, Ohio, 1994; mem. Ashland-Wayne-Holmes Counties Adv. Com. for Tech. and Tng. Subcom., Ohio, 1996—97; adv. com. for tech. 3-county rep. Ashland, Wayne, Holmes, Ohio, 1996—98; A-site tech. tng. com., 1996—97; mem., regional rep. School/Net Communities of Practice, 1996; mem. Licking County Behavioral Health Assessment Team, 2000—01, Licking County Spl. Edn. Collaborative Com., 2000—01, Cmty. Corps Adv. Com., Newark, Ohio, 2001, Licking County Mental Health and Recovery Bd, Newark, 2001, Licking County Fostercare Collaborative Coun., Newark, 2000—01; mem. asst. tech. com., chair speech-lang. dept. Lancaster City Sch., Lancaster, Ohio, 2002—03. Recipient award Muskingum County Office Litter Prevention, 1988, Kids Care Project, 1989, Maysville Bd. Edn. commendation, 1989, Merit award Keep Ohio Beautiful program, 1991, Ohio Future Forum's Exemplary Transition from Sch.-to-Work Model award, 1993, Model Program designation Ohio's Employability Skills Project, 1987, Franklin B. Walter Outstanding Educator award, 1996, 98. Mem. ASCD, AAUW, Career Edn. Assn., Coun. Exceptional Children, Ohio Rural Edn. Assn., Ohio Sch. Supr. Assn., Ohio Assn. Vocat. Edn. Spl. Needs Pers., Ohio Assn. Supr. and Work-Study Coord. (award of Excellence 1992, reg. pres. 1993-94), Wayne-Holmes Elem. Adminstr. Assn., Ohio Pupil Pers. Assn., Ohio Assn. Supr. and Coord. for Exceptional Students (regional pres.-elect 2002, pres. 2003), Phi Delta Kappa. E-mail: s_childers@lancaster.k12.oh.us.

CHILD-OLMSTED, GISÈLE ALEXANDRA, language educator; b. Port-au-Prince, Haiti, Dec. 27, 1946; (parents Am. citizens); d. Daniel McGuire Child and Alice Dejean Child; m. Hans George Bickel, Sept. 1967 (div. Apr. 1984); children: Anna Kristina Villemez, Maia Selena Deubert; m. Jerauld Lockwood Olmsted, June 17, 1988. BA in French with honors, U. Md., 1970; MA in French, Johns Hopkins U., 1978, PhD in Romance Langs., 1981; cert. in translation, Georgetown U. Vis. instr. U. Md., College Park, 1980-81; instr. Johns Hopkins U., Balt., 1981-82; lang. instr. Holton-Arms Sch., Bethesda, Md., 1982-83; asst. prof. dept. modern langs. and lit. Loyola Coll., Balt., 1983-89, assoc. prof., 1989-98, chair dept. modern lang. langs. and lit., 1989-94, prof., 1998—. V.p. faculty coun. Loyola Coll., 1998-2000, mem. steering com. Ctr. for Humanities, 1989-94; organizer, dir. Colloquia on Lang., Lit. and Soc., Balt., 1990, 95, 99, 2002. Author: Jean Genet: Criminalité et Transcendance. 1987; contbr. articles to profl. jours. Faculty rsch. grantee Loyola Coll., 1984, 89, study grantee French Embassy, 1986, 89; Gillman Fellow, 1970-73, 79-80; visitor's scholar U. Cape Town, South Africa, 1995. Mem. MLA (del. Mid-Atlantic region 1992-94, 96-98), Am. Assn. Tchrs. French, Soc. Prof. Français et Francophones d'Amérique, Les Amis de Stendhal, Phi Beta Kappa. Avocations: painting, golf, antiques, classical music, flamenco dancing. Home: 7735 Arrowood Ct Bethesda MD 20817-2821 Office: Loyola Coll 4501 N Charles St Baltimore MD 21210-2601 E-mail: gchildolmsted@loyola.edu.

CHILDS, GAYLE B(ERNARD), retired education educator; b. Redfield, S.D., Oct. 17, 1907; s. Alva Eugene and Dora Amelia (Larsen) C.; AB, Nebr. State Tchrs. Coll., Wayne, 1931; MA, U. Nebr., 1936, PhD, 1949; MEd, Harvard, 1938; m. Doris Wilma Hoskinson, Dec. 22, 1930; children: Richard Arlen, George William, Patricia Ann (Mrs. Ronald Bauers). Tchr. sci. Wynot (Nebr.) High Sch., 1928-30; tchr. sci. Wayne (Nebr.) High Sch., 1931-38, prin., 1938-41; supt. Wakefield (Nebr.) pub. schs., 1941-44, West Point (Nebr.) pub. schs., 1944-46; curriculum specialist U. Nebr. extension div., Lincoln, 1946-49, instr. secondary edn. Tchrs. Coll., also curriculum specialist extension div., 1949-51, asst. prof., 1951-53, asso. prof., 1953-56, prof., head class and corr. instrn., 1956-63, prof., asso. dir. extension div., 1963-66, prof., dir. extension div., 1966-73. Nebr. del. White House Conf. on Aging, 1981; Congl. sr. intern First dist. Congl. Office, Washington, 1981; mem. state curriculum com. Nebr. State Dept. Edn., 1951-55. Sec., bd. dirs. Lincoln chpt. Vols. Intervening for Equity, 1985-86; del. Lancaster County Rep. Party Convs., 1978-90. Fulbright scholar Haile Sellassie I U., Addis Ababa, Ethiopia, 1974. Mem. Nat. Assn. State Univs. and Land Grant Colls. (com. arts and humanities 1963-65), Capitol City Edn. Assn. (pres. 1949-50), Nebr. Edn. Assn. (dist. III sec. 1941-42), Nat. U. Extension Assn. (mem. adminstrv. com., div. corr. study 1956-68, chmn. 1963-65, chmn. research com. 1952-63, assn. dir. 1963-65, mem. joint com. minimum data and definitions 1965-70, chmn. 1971-73; Walton S. Bittner award 1971; establishment Gayle B. Childs award div. ind. study 1969; Gayle B. Childs award 1973), Internat. Council on Corr. Edn. (chmn. com. on research 1957-69, program com. 9th internat. conf. 1971-72), Assn. Univ. Evening Colls. (program com. 1971-72, membership com. 1971-73), Nebr. Schoolmasters Club, Phi Delta Kappa (dist. rep. 1957-63, dir., 1963-69, mem. commn. on edn. and human rights and responsibilities 1964-70, mem. adv. panel on commns. 1970-72; Disting. Service award 1970), North Central Assn. Colls. and Secondary Schs. (cons. def. com. 1953-55, mem. panel vis. scholars 1971-73), Fulbright Alumni Assn., U. Nebr. Emeriti Assn. (pres. 1979-80, bd. dirs 1988-89). Club: Kiwanis (bd. dirs. 1978-81). Contbr. articles to profl. jours. Home: 6500 N Portland Ave # 703 Oklahoma City OK 73116-2035

CHILDS, SALLY JOHNSTON, elementary and secondary education administrator; b. Dover, Ohio, May 22, 1949; d. George W. and Jayne Johnston; m. James William Childs, June 9, 1978; children: Dylan, Karrin. B in Music Edn., Baldwin-Wallace Coll., 1971; MA, Ohio State U., 1973; EdD, U. Akron, 1991. Cert. music tchr., high sch. prin., asst. supt., supervision, Ohio. Dir. band Van Wert (Ohio) Schs., 1973-77, Crestview Schs., Convoy, Ohio, 1977-83, East Holmes Schs., Berlin, Ohio, 1984-85; dir. chorus Green Local Schs., Smithville, Ohio, 1985-88; dir. choir, band, and orch. Akron (Ohio) Pub. Schs., 1988-97, music coord., 1997—. Mem. ASCD, Music Educators Nat. Conf., Ohio Music Edn. Assn., Midwestern Ednl. Rsch. Assn., Kiwanis, Phi Delta Kappa, Pi Lambda Theta, Mu Phi Epsilon, Delta Kappa Gamma. Home: 861 Hampton Ridge Dr Akron OH 44313

CHILTON, BRADLEY STUART, JR., computer information systems educator; b. Abilene, Tex., Apr. 5, 1953; s. Bradley Stuart and Anna Dickie (Negy) C.; m. Caryl Gladney Martin, July 21, 1978; 1 child, Bradley Stuart III. BS, Tex. A&M U., Commerce, 1975, MS, 1977, EdD, 1981. Cert. tchr. math. and biology, cert. middle mgmt. adminstr. Tchr. math. North Mesquite High Sch., Mesquite (Tex.) Ind. Sch. Dist., 1975-78, registrar, asst. prin., 1978-81; assoc. prof. to prof., Regents prof. Tarleton State U., Stephenville, Tex., 1982—, assoc. dean ops., 1987-88, assoc. v.p. student svcs., 1988-91, head, dept. computer info. sys., 2001—. Nat. cons. computer info. systems U.S. of Personnel Mgmt., Va., Pa., Tex., Md., Washington, 1984-90; speaker, workshop chmn. various speeches and workshops, Tex., 1982—; adminstrv. rep. profl. cons. Mesquite Edn. Assn., 1980-81. Contbr. articles to profl. jours. Mem. City of Stephenville Long Range Plan, 1987-88; chmn. City of Stephenville Bldg. Justice Bd., 1989—; chmn. coun. on ministries First United Meth. Ch., Stephenville, 1987-91, chmn. com. edn., 1984-87; elected mem., pres. Stephenville INd. Sch. Dist. Bd. Trustees, 1996-2000; legis. liaison Tex. Legislature for Tex. Sch. Bd. Assn., 1998-2000. Mem. Tex. Computer Edn. Assn., Phi Delta Kappa, Lions Club (life, pres. 1987-88), Omicron Delta Kappa, Delta Mu Delta. Methodist. Avocations: jogging, tennis, golf, numismatics. Home: 121 Byron Nelson Stephenville TX 76401-5920 Office: Tarleton State U PO Box T 0170 Stephenville TX 76402 E-mail: chilton@tarleton.edu.

CHIMENTO, CINDY BROWN, principal; b. New Roads, La., May 20, 1948; d. John Marshall and Marie Blanche (Crosby) Brown; m. Thomas B. Thibaut, June 26, 1971 (div. 1976); m. Roland Joseph Chimento, June 21, 1990; children: Chad, Brittany, Terry. BA, Southeastern La. U., 1971, MEd, 1978, postgrad., 1982. Tchr. Jefferson parish Sch. Bd., Marrero, La., 1972-79, asst. prin. Harvey, La., 1979-83; prin. Harvey Kindergarten Ctr., 1983-84, Vic A. Pitre Elem. Sch., Westwego, La., 1984—. Mem. Libr. Site Location Com., Westwego, 1992; mem. Ednl. Planning Com., Jefferson Parish, 1991-93, asst. supt. planning com., 1991-93, supt. search com., 1992; campaign worker sch. bd. and parish campaigns, 1980—. Named Prin. of the Yr. Jefferson Elem. Adminstrs., 1990, Regional Prin. of the Yr. Dist. I La., 1990; recipient Cert. of Merit Jefferson Parish Coun., 1990. Mem. Jefferson Elem. Adminstrs. (pres. 1991-93), Jefferson Assn. Pub. Sch. Adminstrs. (exec. bd., sec. 1987-89, elem. rep. 1991-93), La. Assn. Prins., So. Assn.Colls. and Schs., La. Assn. Sch. Execs., Nat. Assn. Elem. Sch. Prins. (del. 1992), ASCD, Internat. Reading Assn. Democrat. Roman Catholic. Avocations: reading, travel, swimming. Office: Vic A Pitre Elem Sch 1525 Spruce St Westwego LA 70094-4899

CHIN, ALLEN E., SR., athletic administrator, educator; b. Arlington, Va., Oct. 21, 1950; s. Tung Ock and Hai Ock (Moy) C.; children: Allen Jr., Denise Maria Michelle. BA, George Washington U., 1972, MA, 1974, EdD, 1980. Cert. secondary social studies educator, D.C. Tchr. D.C. Pub. Schs., Washington, 1972-87, 88-91, dir. athletics, 1987-88, 91—. Exec. cons. D.C. Coaches Assn., Inc., Washington, 1988—; exec. dir. AEC-10 Found., Inc., Washington, 1988—. Mem. Jefferson Club, Richmond, Va., 1990-91, Dem. Nat. Com., Washington, 1984—, Dem. Senatorial Campaign Com., Washington, 1984—. Named Athletic Dir. of Yr., NHSACA Region 2, 1995—98; recipient Coach of Yr. award, 1986, 1987, 1988, Disting. Svc. award, NHSACA, 1998. Mem.: Am. Soc. Notaries, Nat. Interscholastic Athletic Adminstrs. Assn., Nat. Coun. for Social Studies, D.C. Coun. for Social Studies, D.C. Coaches Assn. (Hall of Fame 2002), Nat. Geog. Soc., Met. Police Boys & Girls Clubs. Democrat. Avocations: stamp and coin collecting, golf. Home: 6150 Windward Dr Burke VA 22015-3832 Office: Hamilton Sch 1401 Brentwood Pky NE Washington DC 20002 E-mail: aecdciaa@hotmail.com.

CHIN, BEVERLY ANN, literature educator; b. Balt. BA in English, Fla. State U., 1970, MA in English edn., 1971; PhD in reading lang. arts, U. Mass., Coll. Edn., 1972—73, U. Oreg., 1975. Cert. lifetime tchg. secondary English Fla., Ariz., Reading Endorsement Fla. Cmty. Coll. Prof. U. Mont., English Dept., Missoula, Mont., 1981—; dep. dir. field experience program, staff mem. Alternative Sch. Tchr. Edn. Program, Coll Edn., U. Mass., Amherst, Mass., 1972; grad. tchg. fellow U. Oreg., Eugene, 1973—75; asst. prof. U. New Orleans, Elem. Secondary Edn., 1976—77; asst. prof., English Ariz. State U., Tempe, Ariz., 1977—78; adj. asst. prof., English Pinal Cmty. Coll., Mesa, Ariz., 1977—78; vis. prof. edn. U. Oreg., 1978; asst. prof. edn. U. Ctrl. Fla., Orlando, 1978—81. Contbr. articles various profl. jours. Chair Joint Com. on K-16 Composition Standards, 1999—2000; sr. adv. Mont. U. Sys., Writing Proficiency Admissions Standards. Named Outstanding Young Women of Am., 1980. Mem.: Internat. Reading Assn., Assessment Adv. Coun., NW Regional Ednl. Lab., Nat. Coun. Tchrs. of English (pres. 1995—96), Comm. Action Group, Mont. Project Excellence (chair 1988—89), Mont. Assn. Tchrs. English Lang. Arts. (pres. 1984—85), Nat. Bd. Profl. Tchg. Standards, Phi Kappa Phi, Phi Delta Kappa, Kappa Delta Pi, Phi Beta Kappa. Office: U Mont Dept English Rm LA 112 Missoula MT 59812 Office Fax: 406-243-4076. E-mail: bchin@selway.umt.edu.

CHIN, DER-TAU, chemical engineer, educator; b. Zhejiang, China, Sept. 14, 1939; came to U.S., 1963, naturalized, 1977; s. Tsu-Kang and Shou-Chen (Chen) C.; m. Lorna Fe Gencianeo, July 17, 1971; children: Janet G., Lynn G. BSChemE, Chungyuan Coll. Sci. & Engring, 1962; MSChemE, Tufts U., 1965; PhD in Chem. Engring., U. Pa., 1969. Plant engr. Lungyen Sugar Factory, 1962-63; sci. programmer USAF Cambridge (Mass.) Rsch. Lab., Lexington, Mass., 1965; sr. rsch. engr. rsch. labs. GM Corp., Warren, Mich., 1969-75; prof. Clarkson U., Potsdam, N.Y., 1975—. Vis. scientist Brookhaven Nat. Lab., Upton, N.Y., summers 1977, 80, U.S. Army Belvoir Research Devel. Ctr., Ft. Belvoir, Va., summer 1985, U.S. Army Electronics Tech. and Devices Lab., Ft. Mammouth, N.J., summer, 1986, Armstrong Lab. Tyndall Air Force Base, Fla., summer 1995; vis. prof. U. Calif., Berkeley, 1981, Swiss Fed. Inst. Tech., Zurich, 1981, Nat. U. Singapore, 1982, 87, Nat. Tsing Hua UNI, 1989, King Fahd U. Petroleum and Minerals, Dhahran, Saudi Arabia, 2000-2001; cons. Centro de Pesquisas do Energia Electrica, Rio de Janiero, Brazil, summer 1979. Fellow Electrochem. Soc. (Young Authors award 1971); mem. AIChE, Am. Electroplaters Soc., Am. Chem. Soc. Office: Clarkson U PO Box 5705 Potsdam NY 13699-5705 E-mail: chin@clarkson.edu.

CHIN, HONG WOO, oncologist, educator, researcher; b. Seoul, Korea, May 14, 1935; came to U.S., 1974; s. Jik H. and Woon K. (Park) C.; m. Soo J. Chung, Dec. 27, 1965; children: Richard Y., Helen H., KiSik. MD, Seoul Nat. U., 1962, PhD, 1974. Diplomate Am. Bd. Radiology; cert. Korean bd. internal medicine. Resident in radiation oncology Royal Victoria Hosp., Montreal (Que., Can.) Gen. Hosp., 1975-79; asst. prof. U. Ky., Lexington, 1979-86; assoc. dir. Radiarium Found., Overland Park, Kans., 1987-88; clin. prof. radiology U. Mo., Kansas City, 1987-91; chief radiation oncology Va. Med. Ctr., Shreveport, La., 1988; assoc. prof. La. State U., Shreveport, 1988; prof. and dir. radiation oncology Creighton U. Sch. Medicine, Omaha, 1988-90; dir. dept. radiation oncology Creighton U. Cancer Ctr., Omaha, 1988-90; chief radiation oncology Overton Brooks VA Med. Ctr., Shreveport, La., 1990—. Prof. La. State U. Med. Ctr., Shreveport. Author monographs. Lt. comdr. USN, 1967-70. Mem. Pan Am. Med. Assn. (mem. coun. 1984—), AMA, Am. Coll. Radiology, Am. Soc. Therapeutic Radiology and Oncology, Radiation Rsch. Soc., Am. Biograph Assn. (rsch. bd. advisors 1988), Internat. Platform Assn. Roman Catholic.

CHIN, JENNIFER YOUNG, public health educator; b. Honolulu, June 22, 1946; d. Michael W.T. and Sylvia (Ching) Young; m. Benny Chin, Nov. 16, 1975; children: Kenneth Michael, Lauren Marie, Catherine Rose. BA, San Francisco State Coll., 1969; M.P.H., U. Calif., Berkeley, 1971. Edn. asst. Am. Cancer Soc., San Francisco, 1969-70; intern Luth. Med. Ctr., Bklyn., 1971; cmty. health educator Md. Dept. Healht and Mental Hygiene, Balt., 1971-74, N.E. Med. Svcs., San Francisco, 1975; pub. health educator Child Health and Disability Prevention San Francisco Pub. Health Dept., 1975-83; health educator maternal and child health, 1991-95; health educator Breast and Cervical Cancer Control Program, 1995—2000. Grantee USPHS, 1970-71. Mem. Am. Pub. Health Assn., Soc. No. Calif. Pub. Health Edn. (treas. 1976, 77).

CHING, MELVIN CHUNG-HING, retired physiologist, anatomy educator, researcher; b. Honolulu, Feb. 11, 1935; s. Harry S.L. and Roseline Tam (Tom) C.; m. Jane C-A. Hsia, Aug. 21, 1965; children: Mark K-S., Mona M-L. AB, U. Nebr., 1957, MS, 1960; PhD, U. Calif., Berkeley, 1971. Instr. City Coll. San Francisco, 1964-66; instr. anatomy U. Rochester, N.Y., 1971-73, asst. prof., 1973-77; assoc. prof. Med. Coll. Va., Richmond, 1978-82; lectr. biology San Jose (Calif.) State U., 1983; sr. rsch. fellow Nat. Inst. Child Health and Human Devel., NIH, Bethesda, Md., 1983-84; asst. prof. med. anatomy Tex. A&M U., College Station, 1984-85; expert Nat. Inst. Environ. Health Scis., NIH, Research Triangle Park, N.C., 1985-89; asst. prof. vet. anatomy Ohio State U., Columbus, 1989-92; asst. prof. biology James Madison U., Harrisonburg, Va., 1992-95; vis. asst. prof. East Mennonite U., 1996—97. Mem. ad hoc rsch. adv. panel Nat. Inst. Gen. Med. Scis., 1981, 92; adj. prof. biology Mary Baldwin Coll., 1997—; adj. instr. biology John Tyler C.C., 1997-98; personal fin. analyst Primerica Fin. Svcs., Va. Author 2 textbooks on physiology; referee Am. Jour. Vet. Rsch., 1991-93, Am. Vet. Med. Assn., 1992; contbr. chpts. to books, articles to profl. jours. Grantee NIH, 1977-80, Human Growth Found., 1976; NIH sr. rsch. fellow, 1983. Mem. AAAS, Endocrine Soc., Fed. Soc. Explt. Biology, Am. Assn. Anatomists (co-chmn. endocrine session 1982, 87, 92), Am. Assn. Individual Investors (Richmond chpt.. pres. 2002—). Avocations: photography, golf, gardening, music. Home: 12301 Roaringbrook Ct Richmond VA 23233-2106 E-mail: mching@mbc.edu.

CHINNI, ANTHONY PATRICK, special education and industrial education educator; b. Bklyn., May 23, 1955; s. John Anthony and Laura (Pispisa) C.; m. Grace Marie Bradford, Aug. 12, 1978; children: Michael, Christopher. AS, N.Y.C. Tech. Coll., 1975; BS, City Coll. N.Y., 1978; MA, Kean Coll. N.J., 1991. Cert. tchr. indsl. arts, the handicapped, cert. supr., N.J. Tchr. East Brunswick (N.J) High Sch., 1978—, Woodbridge Child Diagnostic and Treatment Ctr., Avenel, N.J., 1986—. Active Vocat. Adv. Com., East Brunswick, 1989—. Mem. Comm. Workers Assn., Spl. Edn. PTA, N.J. Edn. Assn., East Brunswick Edn. Assn., Kean Coll. Alumni Assn. Republican. Roman Catholic. Avocations: model railroads, cars, photography, sports, computers. Office: East Brunswick High Sch 380 Cranbury Rd East Brunswick NJ 08816-3062

CHINULA, DONALD MCLEAN, religious studies educator; b. Bombo Mlowe, Rumphi, Malawi, Mar. 21, 1943; came to U.S., 1964; s. Assie Efron and Mairess (Mhango) C.; m. Torani Sandra Munyenyembe; children: David, Joyce, Maneno. BA, Carleton Coll., Minn., 1968; JD, U. Minn., 1976; LLM, Columbia U., 1977; MDiv, Interdenomination Theol. Ctr., Atlanta, 1985; MA, Sch. Theology, Claremont, Calif., 1991; PhD, Sch. of Theology, Claremont, Calif., 1993. Bar: Minn. 1976, Ark. 1977, D.C. 1977, Ga. 1982. Dep. dir. EEO Macalester Coll., St. Paul, 1969-73; assoc. C & W Legal Svcs., Atlanta, 1977-85; assoc. Christian edn. and youth South Hills, Northkirk and Westminster Presbyn. Chs., Ontario, Calif., 1989-94; assoc. prof. religion Stillman Coll., Tuscaloosa, Ala., 1994—; pastor St. James Presbyn. Ch., Cypress, Ala., 1997—. Adj. prof. legal studies Ga. State U., Atlanta, 1985-94, Chaffey C.C., Alta Loma, Calif., 1989-93; mem. Coun. on Fgn. Visitors, Atlanta, 1979-82. Author The Practical Theology of Martin Luther King Jr., 1997; contbr. articles to profl. jours. Mem. Presbyn. Hunger Com., 1985-87, Self Devel. of People, L.A., 1992-94, Pastoral Care Team, Claremont, 1990-92; sec. Black Lawyers Assn., Little Rock, 1978-79; mem. permanent juc. commn. Presbytery Sheppards, Lapsley, Ala., chmn. new ministries com.; divsn. mission Presbytery Sheppards, Lapsley, Ala. Consortium Global Edn.; faculty rep. bd. trustees Stillman Coll., assoc. chaplain. Fellow African Scholarship Program for Am. Univs., 1964-68, Weyerhauser Ednl. Found., 1976-78. Fellow Internat. Profls. of Ark. (pres. 1978), Internat. Fellows STC (pres. 1987); mem. Am. Assn. Pastoral Counselors, Ga. Bar Assn., Theta Phi. Presbyterian. Avocations: swimming, jogging, golf, tennis.

CHIPMAN, JOHN SOMERSET, economist, educator; b. Montreal, Que., Can., June 28, 1926; s. Warwick Fielding and Mary Somerset (Aikins) C.; m. Margaret Ann Ellefson, June 24, 1960; children: Thomas Noel, Timothy Warwick. Student, Universidad de Chile, Santiago, 1943-44; BA, McGill U., Montreal, 1947, MA, 1948; PhD, Johns Hopkins U., 1951; postdoctoral, U. Chgo., 1950-51; Doctor rerum politicarum honoris causa, U. Konstanz, Germany, 1991, U. Würzburg, 1998; Doctor social and econ. scis., U. Graz, Austria, 2001. Asst. prof. econs. Harvard U., Cambridge, Mass., 1951-55; assoc. prof. econs. U. Minn., Mpls., 1955-60, prof., 1961-81, Regents' prof., 1981—. Fellow Ctr. for Advanced Study in Behavioral Scis., Stanford, Calif., 1972-73; Guggenheim fellow, 1980-81; vis. prof. econs. various univs.; permanent guest prof. U. Konstanz, 1985-91; bd. dirs. Leuthold Funds, Inc., 1995—. Author: The Theory of Intersectoral Money Flows and Income Formation, 1951; editor: (with others) Preferences, Utility, and Demand, 1971, Preferences, Uncertainty and Optimality, 1990, (with C.P. Kindleberger) Flexible Exchange Rates and the Balance of Payments, 1980; co-editor Jour. Internat. Econs., 1971-76, editor, 1977-87; assoc. editor Econometrica, 1956-60, Can. Jour. Stats., 1980-82; mem. adv. bd. Jour. Multivariate Analysis, 1988-92. Recipient James Murray Luck award Nat. Acad. Scis., 1981, Humboldt Rsch. award for Sr. U.S. Scientists, 1992, 2003. Fellow AAAS, Econometric Soc. (coun. 1971-76, 81-83), Am. Statis. Assn., Am. Acad. Arts and Scis., Am. Econ. Assn. (disting.); mem. NAS (chair sect. econ. scis. 1997-2000), Internat. Statis. Inst., Am. Philosophical Soc., Inst. Math. Stats., Can Econ. Assn., Royal Econ. Soc., History of Econs. Soc. Home: 2121 W 49th St Minneapolis MN 55409-2229 Office: U Minn Dept Econs 1035 Heller Hall 217 19th Ave S Minneapolis MN 55455-0400 E-mail: jchipman@econ.umn.edu.

CHIPPAS, DENYSE LEILANI, secondary mathematics educator, travel agent; b. Honolulu, Sept. 30, 1944; d. Richard George and Ann Marie (Martin) Hobbs; m. Ronald Edmund Chippas, June 21, 1969; children: Robin Lynn, Jason Eric. BS, Illinois State U., 1966; MA, Govs State U., 1990. Cert. secondary tchr., Ill. Math. instr. D.D. Eisenhower High Sch., Blue Island, Ill., 1966-71, Marist High Sch., Chgo., 1980—. Agt. Crest Travel Svc., Palos Heights, Ill., 1990—; advisor Marist Math. Team, Chgo., 1991—; moderator pep club Eisenhower High Sch., 1967-69, Eisenhower It's Acad. Team, 1968-70. Dir. Blue Island Park Dist. Day Camp, 1967, '68; leader Brownies Girl Scouts of U.S., Crestwood, Ill., 1977, '78; bd. dirs. PTA Sch. Dist. 130, Crestwood, 1977-80. Mem. Math. Tchrs. Assn., Marist Lay Tchrs. Assn. (bd. dirs.). Home: 5241 137th Pl Crestwood IL 60445-1521 Office: Marist High Sch 4200 W 115th St Chicago IL 60655-4397 also: Crest Travel Svc 7224 W 119th Pl # A Palos Heights IL 60463-1148

CHIROT, DANIEL, sociology and international studies educator; b. Bélâbre, Indre, France, Nov. 27, 1942; came to U.S., 1949; s. Michel and Hélène C.; m. Cynthia Kenyon, July 19, 1974; children: Claire, Laura. BA in Social Studies, Harvard U., 1964; PhD in Sociology, Columbia U., 1973. Prof. internat. studies and sociology Henry M. Jackson sch. U. Wash., Seattle, 1975—, chair internat. studies program. Author: Social Change in a Peripheral Society, 1976, Social Change in the Twentieth Century, 1977, Social Change in the Modern Era, 1986, Modern Tyrants: The Power and Prevalence of Evil in Our Age, 1994, rev. edit., 1996, How Societies Change, 1994; translator: (with Holley Coulter Chirot) Traditional Romanian Villages (Henri H. Stahl), 1980; editor: The Origins of Backwardness in Eastern Europe, 1989, The Crisis of Leninism and the Decline of the Left, 1991, (with Anthony Reid) Essential Outsiders, 1997, (with Martin Seligman) Ethnopolitical Warfare, 2001. John Simon Guggenheim fellow 1991-92. Avocations: skiing, hiking. Office: U Washington Jackson Sch Intl Studies PO Box 353650 Seattle WA 98195-3650

CHITTUM, LORETTA PETTY, federal agency administrator; b. Richmond, Va. m. Warren Chittum, June 2002. BS in crim. justice, polit. sci., sociology, Radford U. Dep. asst. sec. US Dept. Edn., Spec. Edn. and Rehab. Svcs., Wash., 2001—; dir., ctr. for elder rights Va. Dept. of Aging; chief dep. commr. Va. Dept. Rehab. Svcs.; leg. coord. Va. Sec. Health and Human Resources; staff Medicaid Agy., Va., Protection Advocacy Agy., Commonwealth Va. Alter. mem. Fed. Interagency Coord. Coun.; serves Access Bd.; apptd. Va. Devel. Disabilities Coun., Adult Edn., Literacy Coun. Office: US Dept Edn Spec Edn and Rehab Svcs 330 C St SW Mary E Switzer Bldg Rm 3006 Washington DC 20202*

CHITWOOD, HELEN IRENE, elementary education educator; b. Jellico, Tenn., Nov. 3, 1955; d. Earl A. and Helen Louise (Fuson) Douglas; m. Thomas Lee Chitwood, Dec. 29, 1979; children: Thomas Lynn, Paul Harrison, Dana Shoun, Christina Leann. AA, Hiwassee Jr. Coll., Madisonville, Tenn., 1977; BA, Cumberland Coll., Williamsburg, Ky., 1981, MA, 1986. Elem. tchr. Campbell County Schs., Jellico, 1981—. Sunday sch. tchr. 1st Bapt. Ch., Jellico, 1979—. Named Tchr.-Leader of Yr., Campbell County 4-H Club, 1991, 4-H Club of Yr., 1992-93, 93-94, 94-95, Outstanding Young Women Am. Avocations: walking, singing in church choir, working with student clubs and activities. Home: PO Box 424 Jellico TN 37762-0424 Office: Jellico Elem Sch RR 1 Box 236 Jellico TN 37762-9801

CHOATE, JEAN MARIE, history educator; b. Syracuse, N.Y., Dec. 17, 1935; d. Max and Betty (Black) Molyneux; m. Woodrow Choate; children: Anne, Mike, Ruth, Susan. BA, Alma Coll., 1958; MA, U. Wis., 1962; MS, St. Cloud State U., 1972; PhD, Iowa State U., 1992. Instr. Open Bible Coll., Des Moines, 1983-85, Des Moines Area Coll., 1985-97; asst. prof. No. Mich. U., Marquette, 1992-99; assoc. prof. Coastal Ga. C.C., Brunswick, 1999—. Chair women's commn. No. Mich. U., 1996-97. Author: Disputed Ground: Farm Groups that Opposed New Deal Agricultural Programs; book reviewer Jour. of the West, 1996-2000; contbr. articles to profl. jours. Grantee No. Mich. U., 1993, Iowa Found., 1994; Everett Dirksen grantee, 1995, Franklin and Eleanor Roosevelt grantee, 1996, Carl Albert Libr. grantee, 1998, White House Hist. Assn. grantee, 2002. Mem. AAUW (v.p. 1995-97), Agrl. History, Women Historians of Midwest, Orgn. Am. Historians, Am. Hist. Assn., Social Sci. History Assn. Office: Coastal Ga C C Brunswick GA 31520 E-mail: jchoate@bc9000.b.c.peachnet.edu.

CHOBANIAN, ARAM, medical school dean, cardiologist; b. Pawtucket, R.I., Aug. 10, 1929; s. Van and Marina (Arsenian) C.; m. Jasmine Goorigian, June 5, 1955; children: Karin, Lisa, Aram. BA, Brown U., 1951; MD, Harvard U., 1955. Intern, resident Univ. Hosp., Boston, 1955-59, cardiovasc. rsch. fellow, 1959-62; asst. prof. Boston U. Sch. Medicine, 1964-67, assoc. prof., 1967-70, prof. medicine, 1970—, prof. pharmacology, 1975—, John Sandson disting. prof. health scis., 1992—, dir. U.A. Whitaker Labs. for Blood Vessel Rsch., 1973-88, dir. Hypertension Specialized Ctr. Rsch., 1975-95, dir. Cardiovasc. Inst., 1975-92, dean, 1988—, provost Med. Ctr., 1996—, Univ. prof., 1999—. Dir. Nat. Rsch. and Demonstration Ctr. in Hypertension, 1985-90; chmn. FDA Cardiovasc. and Renal Adv. Com., 1978-80, NIH Hypertension and Arteriosclerosis adv. com., 1977-78; chmn. Cardiovasc. Study Sect. B. NIH, 1982-84; chmn. Joint Nat. Com. on Hypertension, NIH, 1990-91, 2003; Sandoz lectr. Royal Coll. Physicians and Surgeons Can., 1989; mem. NIH Nat. Heart, Lung and Blood Adv. Coun., 1993-96; mem. bd. extramural advisers NHLBI, 1999-2002. Author: Heart Risk Book, 1982; mem. editl. bd. New England Jour. Medicine, Hypertension, Jour. Hypertension, Jour. Vascular Biology, Hypertension Rsch., Cardiovasc. Pharmacology. Pres. Am. Heart Assn., Boston, 1974-75; mem. exec. com., trustee Boston Med. Ctr.; bd. dirs. Armenian Culture Soc.; trustee Roger Williams Med. Ctr., Wolfson Found., Quincy Med. Ctr., Mass. Tech. Collaborative, New Eng.Healthcare Inst.; fellow trustee Armenian Assembly of Am. Capt. USAF, 1956-57. Recipient Cmty. Edn. and Disting. Svc. award Am. Heart Assn., Boston, 1975, 78, Eastman Kodak award Nat. Acad. Clin. Biochemistry, 1987, Abbott award Am. Soc. Hypertension. Fellow ACP, Am. Heart Assn. (chmn. coun. high blood pressure rsch. 1984-86, Corcoran lectr. 1989, award of merit 1990, Modern Medicine award 1990, Lifetime Achievement award in hypertension Bristol-Myers Squibb), Nat. Heart, Lung and Blood Inst. (Freis award 1997), Am. Soc. Clin. Investigation, Assn. Am. Physicians, Am. Physiol. Soc., New England Cardiovasc. Soc. (pres. 1985-86), Mass. Med. Soc. (mem. publs. com.), Phi Beta Kappa, Sigma Xi, Alpha Omega Alpha. Home: 5 Rathburn Rd Natick MA 01760-1011 Office: Boston U Sch Medicine 715 Albany St Boston MA 02118-2307

CHOBOTOV, VLADIMIR ALEXANDER, aerospace engineer, educator; b. Zagreb, Yugoslavia, Apr. 2, 1929; came to U.S., 1946; s. Alexander M. and Eugenia I. (Scherbak) C.; m. Lydia M. Kazanovich, June 22, 1957; children: Alexander, Michael. BSME, Pratt Inst., 1951; MSME, Bklyn. Poly. Inst., 1956; PhD, U. So. Calif., 1963. Dynamics engr. Sikorsky Aircraft, Bridgeport, Conn., 1951-53, Republic Aviation, Farmingdale, N.Y., 1953-57, Ramo-Wooldridge, Redondo Beach, Calif., 1957-62; mgr. The Aerospace Corp., El Segundo, Calif., 1962-93; adj. prof. Northrop U., L.A., 1982-91; instr. UCLA, 1984—. Cons. Univ. Space Rsch. Assn., Washington, 1984-85; ad hoc advisor USAF Sci. Adv. Bd., Washington, 1985-87; cons. NASA Space Sta. Adv. Com., Washington, 1990-91; course leader Space Debris, Washington, 1990-91. Author: Spacecraft Attitude Dynamics and Control, 1991; author, editor: Orbital Mechanics, 1991, 3d edit., 2002; contbg. author: Space Based Radar Handbook, 1989, Earth, Sea and Solar System, 1987; contbr. numerous articles and reports to profl. publs. Fellow AIAA (assoc., Achievement award 1993); mem. Internat. Acad. of Astronautics. Achievements include pioneering in the analysis and modeling of space debris. Office: The Aerospace Corp PO Box 92957 Los Angeles CA 90009-2957

CHODOSH, ROBERT IVAN, retired middle school educator, coach; b. Elizabeth, N.J., May 29, 1946; s. Philip Richard and Jean (Landerman) C.; m. Norma Jean Ries, Feb. 14, 1999. BS in Edn., U. Tenn., Knoxville, 1968; MEd, U. Ctrl. Fla., Orlando, 1975. Cert. in phys. edn., health edn. Tchr. Old Dixie Elem. Sch., Titusville, Fla., 1968-78, Surfside Elem. Sch., Satellite Beach, Fla., 1978-79; tchr., basketball and track coach Andrew Jackson

Middle Sch., Titusville, 1979-98; ret., 1998; substitute tchr. Corpus Christi Ind. Sch. Dist., 2002—, Gregory-Portland (Tex.) Ind. Sch. Dist., 2002—. Mem. comprehensive edn. com. Brevard County Schs., Melbourne, Fla., 1990-91. Com. mem. Brevard County Elementary and Secondary Physical Education Guide, 1977, 82, 85, 88. Gray leader, coach North Brevard YMCA, Titusville, 1968-78; recreation leader North Brevard Recreation Dept., 1968-78, summer program leader, 1970-75, 88; scorer, asst. coach, concession stand mgr. Indian River City Little Leauge, 1987, 89. Recipient Tchr. of Yr. award Old Dixie Elem. Sch., Titusville, 1974, Silver Svc. award Brevard County Sch. System. Mem. U. Tenn. Alumni Assn. Democrat. Jewish. Avocations: walking, watching sports, listening to music, swimming, reading. Home: 7721 Hartley Cir Corpus Christi TX 78413-6116 E-mail: bchod39788@aol.com.

CHOHLIS, DANA MARIE, educator, theatre director; b. San Francisco, Dec. 8, 1957; d. Francis P. and Irene Marion (Edwards) Severn; children: Alyssa Katrina, Christina Alexis. BA, Calif. State U., Hayward, 1992, MA, 2000. Cert. English tchr. Tchr. San Leandro (Calif.) Unified Sch. Dist., 1992—; instr. pub. spkg. Peralta C.C., Oakland, Calif., 2000—. Dir. A Midsummer Night's Dream, 1999, Bridge to Terabithia, 1998, Circus in the Wind, 1997, A Case for Two Detectives, 1996, Electra, 2001; performer: Cypress, Taming of the Shrew, Edinburgh Fringe Festival, 2002. Tech. grantee San Leandro Bus. Assn., 1997, 98, 99, Long's Drugs Adopt-a-Class grantee, 2001. Mem. San Leandro Tchrs. Assn. (sec.), No. Calif. Edn. Theatre Assn. (rep.. mem. English/lang. arts stds. com., master tchr., retention program coord.). Avocations: sailing, yacht racing, acting, dancing, hiking. Home: 1448 Church Ave San Leandro CA 94579-1523 E-mail: danabegood@yahoo.com.

CHOI, JONGMOO JAY, finance educator, educator; b. Seoul, Korea, Dec. 4, 1945; arrived U.S., 1969; s. Hyung Joon and Tai Im (Kim) C.; m. B. Eunyup Lee, Mar. 20, 1971; children: Raymond, Jason. BBA, Seoul Nat. U., 1968; MBA, NYU, 1974, PhD, 1980. Instr. NYU, 1979-80; vis. asst. prof. Columbia U., 1980-81; economist Chase Manhattan Bank, N.Y.C., 1981-82; adj. assoc. prof. fin., internat. bus. NYU, 1982-87; Laura H. Carnell prof. fin. and internat. bus. Temple U., 1983—, fin. chair, 1990—91. Vis. faculty U. Pa., U. Hawaii, Internat. U. of Japan, 1987-98; cons. to various corps.; research asst. Nat. Bur. Econ. Research, 1978-79; fin. analyst N.Y.C. Govt. Agy., 1973-75; internat. banking officer Korea Exchange Bank, 1968-73; chair of fin. Temple U. Author: Emerging Capital Markets, 1998, Internat. Trade and Transmission of Inflation: The Japanese Experience, 1985, Asian Financial Crisis, 2000, European Monetary Union and Capital Markets, 2001, Japanese Finance, 2003; mem. editl. bd. Global Risk Management, 2002; editor Internat. Fin. Rev, Jour. of Econ. and Bus., Global Fin. Jour., Multinatl. Fin. Jour., Rev. of Pacific Basin Fin. Markets and Policies, Jour. Internat. Mgmt.; contbr. numerous articles to scholarly jours. Korean-Am. Found. fellow, NYU Multinat. Corps. Project grant; recipient Musser award for Leadership in Rsch. Mem. Am. Econ. Assn., Am. Fin. Assn., Fin. Mgmt. Assn., Acad. Internat. Bus., N.Am. Econ. and Fin. Assn. (pres.), Korea-Am. Fin., Multinational Fin. Soc. (trustee). Home: 516 Lexington Ln Norristown PA 19403-1207 Office: Temple U Fox Sch Bus Management Philadelphia PA 19122 E-mail: jjchoi@temple.edu.

CHOICE, PRISCILLA KATHRYN MEANS (PENNY CHOICE), educational director, international consultant; b. Rockford, Ill., Nov. 8, 1939; d. John Z. and Margaret A. (Haines) Means; m. Jack R. Choice, Nov. 14, 1964; children: William Kenneth, Margaret Meta. BA, U. Wis., 1963; MEd, Nat.-Louis U., 1990; MA, N.E. Ill. U., 1995. Field rsch. dir. Tatham-Laird and Kudner Advt., Chgo., 1964-69; drama specialist Children's Theatre Western Springs (Ill.), 1969-81; gifted teaching asst. Sch. Dist. 181, Hinsdale, Ill., 1980-84; tchr. Sch. Dist. 99, Cicero, Ill., 1984-85; gifted edn. program coord. Cmty. Consolidated Sch. Dist. 93, Carol Stream, Ill., 1985-99; coord. gifted edn. and fine arts Ednl. Svcs. Divsn., Lake County Regional Office Edn., Grayslake, Ill., 1999—. Drama specialist, cons. Choice Dramatics, Hinsdale and Clarendon Hills, Ill., 1976—; producing dir. Mirror Image Youth Theatre, Hinsdale, 1986-88; adj. prof. Coll. DuPage, Glen Ellyn, Ill., 1990-92, Nat.-Louis U., Evanston, Ill., 1991—, Aurora (Ill.) U., 1995—, Govs. State U., University Park, Ill., 1992-93; internat. cons. in gifted edn. and drama-in-edn., 1989—; co-chair advocacy com. Ill. Assn. Gifted Children, 2002—; trustee Friends of the Lake Co. Discovery Mus., 2003—; chair arts divsn. Nat. Assn. for Gifted Children, 2003—. Contbg. author Gifted/Arts Resource Guide, 1990; contbg. editor Ill. Theatre Assn., Followspot News, 1992-95. 96-2002. Mem. gifted adv. com. Ednl. Svc. Ctr., Wheaton, Ill., 1987—90, 1992—95, Regional Office of Edn., Wheaton, 1995—99, Northeastern Ill. U.1993-95., Chgo., 1993—95; bd. dirs. Ill. Theatre Assn., Chgo., 1983—87; chair Arts Divsn. Nat. Assn. for Gifted Children, 2003—; co-chair advocacy Com. Ill. Assn. for Gifted Children, 2002—. Recipient Ill. State Bd. Edn. gifted edn. fellowship, 1988, AAUW continuing edn. scholarship, 1986, 90, Excellence award Ill. Theatre Assn., 1991, Excellence award Ill. Math. and Sci. Acad., 1990, 98, Recognition of Excellence, No. Ill. Planning Commn. Gifted Edn., 1990, Award of Excellence Ill. and Math. Sci. Acad., 1998. Mem. ASCD, World Coun. on Gifted Edn., Nat. Assn. Gifted Children, Ill. Assn. Gifted Children (membership chmn. 1992-94, advocacy com. 1995—, co-chair advocacy com. 2002—), Ill. Coun. Gifted, Am. Assn. Theatre in Edn., Ill. Theatre Assn. (bd. dirs. 1983-87, Outstanding Achievement award 1991), Inst. for Global Ethics, Ill. Alliance Arts Edn., Theatre Western Springs, Phi Delta Kappa. Avocations: swimming, walking, reading. Home: 113 S Prospect Ave Clarendon Hills IL 60514-1422 Office: Lake County Ednl Svcs 19525 W Washington St Grayslake IL 60030-1152

CHOKSY, JAMSHEED KAIRSHASP, historian, religious scholar, language professional, humanities educator; b. Bombay, Jan. 8, 1962; arrived in Sri Lanka, 1962; permanent resident, U.S. 1995, naturalized, 1999. s. Kairshasp Nariman and Freny Kairshasp (Cooper) C.; m. Carol Emma Burnside, Sept. 12, 1993; 1 child, Darius Jamsheed. AB in Mid.-Ea. Langs. and Culture, Columbia U., 1985; PhD in History and Religions, Harvard U., 1991. Tchg. fellow dept. anthropology and archaeology Harvard U., 1988, jr. fellow, 1988-91; vis. asst. prof. depts. history and internat. rels. Stanford U., 1991-93; from asst. prof. to prof. Ind. U., Bloomington, 1993—2001, prof. ctrl. Eurasian studies and history, 2001—. Mem. Sch. Hist. Studies, Inst. for Advanced Study-Princeton, 1993—94; cons. PBS-TV, 1990, L.A. Times, 1998, Am. Mus. Natural History, 1998, Am. Hist. Rev., 1999—; presenter in field. Author: Purity and Pollution in Zoroastrianism, 1989, Conflict and Cooperation, 1997, Evil, Good and Gender, 2002, Archeological Surveys in Pakistan, 1988-90, 1999-2001; contbr. numerous articles to profl. publs. Rsch. fellow Govt. India, Bombay, 1998; John Simon Guggenheim Meml. Found. fellow, 1996-97; resident scholar Ind. U., 1996-97, grantee 1994—, grantee Am. Acad. Religion, 1995-96, Andrew W. Mellon fellow, 1991-93, 2001-02. Fellow: NEH, Royal Asiatic Soc. Great Britain, Ireland, Ctr. for Advanced Study in the Behavioral Scis.; mem.: Cosmos Club (Washington), Explorers Club (NY). Office: Ind U Dept Ctrl Eurasian Studies Goodbody Hall 157 1011 E 3rd St Bloomington IN 47405-7005 E-mail: jchoksy@indiana.edu.

CHOLDIN, MARIANNA TAX, librarian, educator; b. Chgo., Feb. 26, 1942; d. Sol and Gertrude (Katz) Tax; m. Harvey Myron Choldin, Aug. 28, 1962; children: Kate and Mary (twins). BA, U. Chgo., 1962, MA, 1967, PhD, 1979. Slavic bibliographer Mich. State U., East Lansing, 1967—69; Slavic bibliographer, instr. U. Ill., Urbana, 1969—73, Slavic bibliographer, asst. prof., 1973—76, Slavic bibliographer, assoc. prof., 1976—84, head Slavic and East European Libr., 1982—89, head, prof., 1984—2002, dir. Russian and East European Ctr., 1987—89, C. Walter and Gerda B. Mortenson Disting. prof., 1989—2002, dir. Mortenson Ctr. for Internat. Libr. Programs, 1991—2002, prof. emerita, 2003—. Author: Fence Around the Empire: Russian Censorship, 1985; editor: Red Pencil: Artists, Scholars and Censors in the USSR, 1989, Books, Libraries and Information in Slavic and East European Studies, 1986. Chair Soros Found. Network Libr. Program Bd., 1997—2000. Recipient Pushkin gold medal for contbns. to culture, Russian Presdl. Coun. on Culture, 2000. Mem. ALA, Am. Assn. for Advancement of Slavic Studies (pres. 1995), Internat. Fedn. Libr. Assns. and Instns., Phi Beta Kappa. Jewish. Home: 888 S Michigan Ave #403 Chicago IL 60605

CHOMISTEK, CATHERINE, special education educator; b. Detroit, June 30, 1957; d. Stanley J. and Joan H. (Klusowski) Dudek; m. John M. Chomistek, Aug. 4, 1979; children: Emily, Steven, Elizabeth, Ryan. BS, Mich. State U., 1979; MA, Butler U., Indpls., 1982. Cert. tchr. learning disabled, mildly mentally handicapped, emotionally handicapped, Ind. Resource tchr. Sch. 57, Indpls., 1979-82; resource tchr. 1st and 2d grades Grassy Creek Sch., Indpls., 1982-86; resource tchr. Ellis Middle Sch., Elgin, Ill., 1987-88; resource tchr. Inclusion program Grassy Creek Sch., Indpls., 1991—2001; tchr. Daffron Elem. Sch., Plano, Tex., 2001—. Tchr. Exemplary Network, State Dept., 1997-98. Registrar-roadrunner Girl Scouts U.S., 1989-90, troop leader, 1989-93. Recipient Golden Apple award Indpls. Power and Light Co., 1996; State of Ind. 4-Rs grantee, Indpls., 1994. Mem. Ind. Computer Educators, Assn. for Learning Disabilities, Coun. for Exceptional Children. Home: 3812 Neiman Rd Plano TX 75025-4387 Office: Daffron Elem Sch 3500 Preston Meadow Plano TX 75025

CHOMSKY, (AVRAM) NOAM (AVRAM CHOMSKY), linguistics and philosophy educator; b. Phila., Dec. 7, 1928; s. William and Elsie (Simonofsky) C.; m. Carol Doris Schatz, Dec. 24, 1949; children: Aviva, Diane, Harry Alan. BA, U. Pa., 1949, MA, 1951, PhD, 1955, DHL (hon.), 1984, U. Chgo., 1967, Loyola U., Chgo., 1970, Swarthmore Coll., 1970, Bard Coll., 1971, U. Mass., 1973, U. Maine, 1992, Gettysburg Coll., 1992, Amherst Coll., 1995; LLD (hon.), U. Buenos Aires, 1996; DHL (hon.), U. Rovira i Virgili, Catalonia, 1998, U. Guelph, Can., 1999, Columbia U., 1999, U. Conn., 1999, U. Toronto, 2000, U. Western Ont., 2000; LittD (hon.), U. London, 1967, Delhi (India) U., 1972, Visva-Bharati U., Santiniketan, West Bengal, 1980, Cambridge (Eng.) U., 1995; LittD (hon.), U. Calcutta, 2001; Doctorate (hon.), Scuola Normale Superiore, Pisa, Italy, 1999; LLD, Harvard U., 2000; DHL (hon.), McGill U., 1998. Mem. faculty MIT, 1955—, prof. modern langs., 1961—, Ferrari P. Ward prof. modern lang. and linguistics, 1966—, Inst. prof., 1976—. Vis. prof. Columbia U., N.Y.C., 1957-58; mem. Inst. Advanced Study Princeton U., 1958-59; Linguistic Soc. Am. prof. UCLA, summer 1966; Beckman prof. U. Calif.-Berkeley, 1966-67; John Locke lectr. Oxford U., 1969; Bertrand Russell Meml. lectr., Cambridge, 1971; Nehru Meml. lectr., New Delhi, 1972; Huizinga lectr. U. Leiden, 1977; Woodbridge lectr. Columbia U., 1978; Kant lectr. Stanford U., 1979; Jeanette K. Watson disting. vis. prof. Syracuse U., 1982; Pauling Meml. lectr. Oreg. State U., 1995. Author: Syntactic Structures, 1957, Current Issues in Linguistic Theory, 1964, Aspects of the Theory of Syntax, 1965, Cartesian Linguistics, 1966, Topics in the Theory of Generative Grammar, 1966, (with Morris Halle) Sound Pattern of English, 1968, Language and Mind, 1968, American Power and the New Mandarins, 1969, At War with Asia, 1970, Problems of Knowledge and Freedom, 1971, Studies on Semantics in Generative Grammar, 1972, For Reasons of State, 1973, (with Edward Herman) Counterrevolutionary Violence, 1973, Peace in the Middle East, 1974, Logical Structure of Linguistic Theory, 1975, Reflections on Language, 1975, Essays on Form and Interpretation, 1977, Human Rights and American Foreign Policy, 1978, (with Edward Herman) The Political Economy of Human Rights, 2 vols., 1979, Language and Responsibility, 1979, Rules and Representations, 1980, Lectures on Government and Binding, 1981, Concepts and Consequences of the Theory of Government and Binding, 1982, Towards a New Cold War, 1982, Radical Priorities, 1982, Fateful Triangle, 1983, Turning the Tide, 1985, Barriers, 1986, Knowledge of Language, 1986, Pirates and Emperors, 1986, On Power and Ideology, 1987, Language and Problems of Knowledge, 1987, Language in a Psychological Setting, 1987, Generative Grammar, 1987, Culture of Terrorism, 1988, (with Edward Herman) Manufacturing Consent, 1988, Language and Politics, 1988, Necessary Illusions, 1989, Deterring Democracy, 1991, Chronicles of Dissent, 1992, What Uncle Sam Really Wants, 1992, Year 501, 1993, Rethinking Camelot, 1993, Letters from Lexington, 1993, The Prosperous Few and the Restless Many, 1993, Language and Thought, 1994, World Orders, Old and New, 1994, The Minimalist Program, 1995, Powers and Prospects, 1996, The Common Good, 1998, Profits Over People, 1998, The New Military Humanism, 1999, New Horizons in the Study of Language and Mind, 2000, Rogue States, 2000, A New Generation Draws the Line, 2000, Architecture of Language, 2000, 9-11, 2001, Propaganda and the Public Mind, 2001, Understanding Power, 2002, On Nature and Language, 2002, Pirates and Emperors, Old and New, 2002, Middle East Illusions, 2003, Hegemony or Survival, 2003. Named Rsch. Fellow, Harvard Cognitive Studies Ctr., 1964—67; recipient Disting. Sci. Contbn. award, APA, 1984, Kyoto prize, Kyocera Found., 1988, 2001, Benjamin Franklin Inst. award, 1999, George Orwell award, Nat. Coun. Tchrs. English, 1987, 1989, James Killian Faculty award, MIT, 1992, Lannan Lit. award for nonfiction, 1992, Joel Seldin Peace award, Psychologists for Social Responsibility, 1993, Homer Smith award, NYU Sch. of Medicine, 1994, Loyola Mellon Humanities award, Loyola U. Chgo., 1994, Helmholtz medal, Berlin-Brandenburische Akad. Wissenschaften, 1996, Benjamin Franklin Inst. award, 1999, Rabindranath Tagore Centenary award, Asiatic Soc. Calcutta, 2000, Rising Sun of Mehgarh award, Dawn Islamabad, 2001, Adela Dwyer St. Thomas Villanova Peace award, Villanova U., Phila., 2002, Peace award, Turkish Publishers' Assn., Istanbul, 2002, award, Kurdish Human Rights Assn., Dyarbakir, 2002; fellow (Jr.) Soc. Fellows Harvard Univ, 1951—55. Fellow AAAS, Brit. Acad. (corr.), Brit. Psychol. Soc. (hon.), Royal Anthrop. Inst. Gt. Britain, Royal Anthrop. Inst. of Ireland, Utrecht Soc. Arts and Scis. (hon.), Gesellschaft für Sprachwissenschaft (hon.), Am. Acad. Scis., Am. Acad. Philosophy, Royal Soc. Can. (fgn.); mem. APA (William James fellow 1990), NAS, Am. Acad. Arts and Scis., Linguistic Soc. Am., Deutsche Akademie der Naturforscher Leopoldina, Assn. for Edn. in Journalism and Mass Comm. (Profl. Excellence award 1991). Home: 15 Suzanne Rd Lexington MA 02420-1831 Office: 77 Massachusetts Ave Cambridge MA 02139-4301

CHONSKI, DENISE THERESA, primary school educator, artist; b. Albany, N.Y., Jan. 26, 1962; d. Stanley V. and Rosemary K. (Dyda) C. BSBA, BS in Art Edn., Coll. of St. Rose, Albany, N.Y., 1984, MS in Elem. Edn., 1994. Cert. elem., K-12 art tchr.; permanent cert. in elem. edn. N-6 with early childhood annotation, N.Y. K-8 art tchr. St. Luke's Sch., Schenectady, N.Y., 1984-92, Holy Spirit, East Greenbush, N.Y., 1984-85, Vincentian Inst. Grammar Sch., Albany, 1985-86, St. Paul the Apostle, Schenectady, 1986-90, St. Helen's, Niskayuna, N.Y., 1987-89; 5-8 art educator Cohoes (N.Y.) Cath. Schs., 1985-86; 7-12 art educator Notre Dame Bishop Gibbons H.S., Schenectady, 1989-90; pre-K and nursery sch. and K-8 art educator St. Teresa of Avila Sch., Albany, 1990—. Workshop presenter/guest speaker Cath. Sch. Office, Diocese of Albany, 1992—; del. Lakeside Health Inst., Delhi, N.Y., 1993. Mem. Albany Inst. History and Art, 1995—; bd. dirs. Cmty. Maternity Svcs., Albany, 1989-95. Recipient Bldg. Amb. award Edn. Ctr. Inc., 1993-94. Mem. Nat. Assn. Educators Young Children, N.Y. State Art Tchrs. Assn., Nat. Cath. Educators Assn., Kappa Delta Pi. Roman Catholic. Avocations: needlework, art. Home: 64 Hurst Ave Albany NY 12208-1537

CHOOK, EDWARD KONGYEN, academic administrator, medical educator; b. Shanghai, Apr. 15, 1937; s. Shiu-heng and Shuiking (Shek) Chook; m. Ping Ping Chew, Oct. 30, 1977; children from previous marriage: Miranda, Bradman. MD, Nat. Def. Med. Ctr., Taiwan, 1959; MPH, U. Calif., Berkeley, 1964, PhD in Occupl. Health, 1969; ScD, Phila. Coll. Pharmacy & Sci., 1971; JD, La Salle U., 1994. Assoc. prof. U. Calif., Berkeley, 1966-68; dir. higher edn. Bay Area Bilingual Edn. League, Berkeley, 1970-75; prof., chancellor United U. Am., Oakland and Berkeley, Calif., 1975-84; regional adminstr. U. So. Calif., L.A., 1984-90; chancellor Pacific Internat. U., Berkeley and Pomona, Calif., from 1996; pres. Shanghai Internat. Health Ctr., from 1997; chancellor Pacific Internat. U., from 1996; chancellor Bi-Lingual Coll. Media Comm. Hangzhou (China)-Pacific Internat. Joint U., from 1998; pres. Main Coin Investment Mgmt., LTD., Oakland, Calif., from 1999; mem. staff Pacific Internat. U., Guangdong, from 2000; internat. dir. Silver State Air Corp., Las Vegas, Nev.; chancellor Zhejiang TV/Broadcast & Journalism Coll. Huzhon Jr. Coll., from 2002; internat. exec. dir. Zhejiang TV/Movie Prodn. Corp., China, from 2002. Sr. adv. U.S. congl. Adv. Bd.; exec. dir. Internat. Environ. Mgmt. Corp., Asia and Calif., 2002; mem. Presdl. Roundtable Adv. Commn., from 1991; hon. dep. sec. of state State of Calif., 1990—93, spl. adv. to sec. state, from 1991; pres. Pacific Environ. Svc. Corp., from 2001; vis. prof. Nat. Defense Med. Ctr., Taiwan, Taiwan Armed Forces U., from 1982, Tongji U., Shanghai, 1992, Foshan U., China, from 1992; cons. specialist Beijing Hosp., China, from 1988; founder United Svc. Coun., Inc., from 1971; pres. Pan Internat. Acad., Changchun, China, from 1979, San Francisco, from 1979, China Gen. Devel. Corp., from 1992; cons. in field; lectr. in field; adv. Ka Wa Bank, Hong Kong, 1986—96. Editor (assoc.): U.S.-Chinese Times, 1996—98; pub.: Unity Jour./Pwer News, from 1979, China Unity Journ. No. Am. Edit., from 2001; contbr. articles to profl. jours. Goodwill amb. of Asia Federated States of Micronesia, from 1997; pres. Yuen Kong Found. Internat. Understanding, from 1994; trustee Rep. Presdl. Task Force, Washington, from 1978; adv. mainland China affairs Ctrl. Com. Chinese Nationalist Party, Taiwan, 1994—97; pres. Oakland Chinese Nationalist Party, from 1998; mem. senatorial commn. Rep. Senatorial Innter Cir., 1996; deacon Am. Bapt. Ch. Named Aug. 9, 1997 Ed Chook Day, City of Oakland; recipient Presdl. Roundtable Gold medal, 2002. Mem.: World Affairs Coun. San Francisco, Presdl. Roundtable Chamber, Rotary (com. chmn. from 1971), Capital Hill Club. Achievements include research in on hearing conservation program in U.S. Army, criteria to return to work, principles and practices of nuclear, biological and chemical weapons. Home: Oakland, Calif. Died Mar. 27, 2003.

CHOPER, JESSE HERBERT, law educator, university dean; b. Wilkes-Barre, Pa., Sept. 19, 1935; s. Edward and Dorothy (Resnick) C.; m. Mari Smith; children: Marc Steven, Edward Nathaniel. BS, Wilkes U., 1957, DHL, 1967; LLB, U. Pa., 1960. Bar: D.C. 1961. Instr. Wharton Sch. U. Pa., 1957-60; law clk. to Chief Justice Earl Warren U.S. Supreme Ct., 1960-61; asst. prof. U. Minn. Law Sch., 1961-62, assoc. prof., 1962-65; prof. Law Sch. U. Calif., Berkeley, 1965—, dean, 1982-92, Earl Warren prof. Pub. Law, 1991—. Vis. prof. Harvard U., 1970-71, Fordham U., 1999. Author: Constitutional Law: Cases-Comments-Questions, 9th edit., 2001, The American Constitution, Cases and Materials, 9th edit., 2001, Constitutional Rights and Liberties, Cases and Materials, 9th edit., 2001, Corporations, Cases and Materials, 5th edit., 2000, Judicial Review and the National Political Process, 1980, Securing Religious Liberty, 1995; contbr. articles to profl. jours. Mem. AAUP, Am. Law Inst., Am. Acad. Arts and Scis., Order of Coif. Jewish. Office: U Calif Sch Law Berkeley CA 94720-0001

CHOPP, REBECCA S. university president; Dir. grad. studies Inst. for Women's Studies Emory U., Atlanta, dean of faculty and acad. affairs Candler Sch. of Theology, 1993-97. Charles Howard Chandler prof. theology Emory's Grad. Divsn., provost, exec. v.p. for acad. affairs, 1998—2001; dean, Titus Street prof. theology and culture Yale U. Div. Sch., 2001—02; pres., prof. philosophy and religion Colgate U., 2002—. Chair Commn. on Tchg. Emory U., univ. bd. trustees acad. affairs com.; lectr. in field. Author: The Praxis of Suffering: An Interpretation of Liberation and Political Theologies, 1986, The Power to Speak: Feminism, Language, God, 1989, Reconstructing Christian Theology, 1994, Saving Work: Feminist Practices of Theological Education, 1995; theology editor Religious Studies Rev.; editor-at-large Christian Century; editl. bd. Emory Theol. Studies, Religion and Ideology, Jour. of Religion, Word and World, Internat. Jour. of Practical Theology; contbr. articles to profl. publs. Recipient Alumna Achievement award Kans. Wesleyan U., 1990, Disting. Alumna award St. Paul Sch. of Theology, 1991, Founder's Day award Baker U., 1995, Alumna of Yr. award U. Chgo. Divinity Sch., 1997. Mem. Am. Acad. of Religion (pres. southeastern divsn.), Am. Theol. Soc. (chair women in leadership project). Home: 13 Oak Drive Hamilton NY 13346

CHOPPIN, GREGORY ROBERT, chemistry educator; b. Eagle Lake, Tex., Nov. 9, 1927; s. Gilbert P. and Nellie M. (Guidroz) C.; m. Ann M. Warner; children: Denise, Suzanne, Paul, Nadine BS in Chemistry, Loyola U., New Orleans, 1949, DSc (hon.), 1969; PhD in Chemistry, U. Tex, 1953; DSc Tech. (hon.), Chalmers U., Göteborg, Sweden, 1985. Rsch. scientist Lawrence Radiation Lab., Berkeley, Calif., 1953-56; faculty Fla. State U., Tallahassee, 1956—, R.O. Lawton Disting. prof. chemistry, 1968—2001, prof. emeritus, 2001—. Vis. scientist Centre d'Etude Nucleaire Mol, Belgium, 1962-63; vis. prof. Sci. U. Tokyo, 1978; vis. scientist European Transuranium Inst., Karlsruhe, Germany, 1979-80, 95; cons. Argonne Nat. Lab., Los Alamos Nat. Lab., N.Mex., Lawrence Livermore Nat. Lab., Calif., Pacific N.W. Nat. Lab., Wash., Sandia Nat. Lab., N.Mex., Kaiser-Hill Co., Archimedes Tech. Co.; served on panels and coms. of NRC, including bds. chem. sci. and tech. and radioactive waste mgmt. Co-author: Nuclear Chemistry: Theory and Applications, 1980, 2d edit., 1995, 3d edit., 2001; editor: Plutonium Chemistry, 1983, Actinide-Lanthanide Separations, 1985, Lanthanide Probes in Life, Chemical and Earth Sciences, 1989, Principles and Practice of Solvent Extraction, 1992, 2d edit., 2003, Separations of f-Elements, 1995, Chemical Separation Technologies and Related Methods of Nuclear Waste Management, 1999; mem. editl. bd. sci. jours. including Handbook on Physics and Chemistry of Rare Earths; co-discoverer of chemical element 101 Mendelevium; contbr. over 450 articles to sci. jours. Served to cpl. U.S. Army, 1946-48. Recipient Alexander von Humboldt Stiftung award, 1979, Chem. Mfrs. Assn. Edn. award, 1979, Seaborg Actinide Separations Sci. award, 1989, Presdl. citation Am. Nuclear Soc., 1991, Scientist of Yr. award Fla. Acad. of Sci., 1992, Spedding award N.Am. Rare Earth Rsch. Conf., 1996, Chem. Pioneer award Am. Inst. Chemistry, 1997, The Becquerel medal Brit. Royal Soc. Chem., 2000. Fellow AAAS; mem. Am. Chem. Soc. (award Fla. sect. 1973, So. Chemist award 1971, award in Nuclear Chemistry 1985, OESPER award Cin. sect. 1995), Royal Soc. Arts and Sci. (hon. fgn. mem.) (Sweden), Rare Earth Rsch. Conf. (pres. bd. 1981-83, chmn. 16th conf. 1983), Sigma Xi, Phi Beta Kappa. Avocations: sailing, racquetball. Home: 3290 Longleaf Rd Tallahassee FL 32310-6406 Office: Fla State U Dept Chemistry and Biochemistry Dittmer Bldg Tallahassee FL 32306-4390

CHOPRA, ANIL KUMAR, civil engineering educator; b. Peshawar, India, Feb. 18, 1941; came to U.S., 1961, naturalized, 1977; s. Kasturi Lal and Sushila (Malhotra) C.; m. Hamida Banu, Dec. 7, 1976. B.Sc. in Engring, Banaras Hindu U., Varanasi, India, 1960; MS, U. Calif., Berkeley, 1963, PhD, 1966. Design engr. Standard Vacuum Oil Co., New Delhi, India, 1960-61, Kaiser Engrs. Overseas Corps, India, 1961; asst. prof. civil engr. U. Minn., Mpls., 1966-67; mem. faculty U. Calif., Berkeley, 1967—, prof. civil engring., 1976-92, Johnson prof. engring., 1992—. Dir. Applied Tech. Council, Palo Alto, 1972-74; mem. com. natural disasters NRC, 1980-85, chmn., 1982-83; cons. earthquake engring. to govt. and industry. Author: Dynamics of Structures, A Primer, 1981, Dynamics of Structures: Theory and Applications to Earthquake Engineering, 1995, 2001; mem. adv. bd.: MIT Press Series in Structural Mechanics.; contbr. articles to more than 260 profl. pubs. Recipient Gold medal Banaras Hindu U., 1960, Disting. Alumnus award, 1980, certificate of merit for paper Indian Soc. Earthquake Tech., 1974, honor award Assn. Indians in Am., 1985, AT&T Found. award Am. Soc. Engring. Edn., 1987, Disting. Tchg. award Berkeley Campus, 1999. Mem.: ASCE (EMD exec. com. 1981—87, chmn. 1985—86, mem. STD exec. com. 1988—92, chmn. 1990—91, Walter L. Huber prize 1975, Norman medal 1979, Reese rsch. prize 1989, Norman medal 1991, Newmark medal 1993, Howard award 1998, Norman medal 2001), U.S.

Com. on Large Dams, Earthquake Engring. Rsch. Inst. (bd. dirs. 1990—93, George W. Housner medal 2002), Structural Engrs. Assn. No. Calif. (bd. dirs. 1987—89), Seismol. Soc. Am. (bd. dirs. 1982—83), Nat. Acad. Engring. (elected in 1984). Home: 635 Cross Ter Orinda CA 94563 Office: Univ Calif Dept Civil Engring Berkeley CA 94720-0001

CHORONZY, SANDRA, elementary education educator; b. Kingston, Pa., Oct. 29, 1943; d. Alexander William and Genevieve Agnes C. AAS, Hilbert, 1964; BS in Edn., Medaille, Buffalo, 1971; MS in Edn., So. Conn. State Coll., 1977. Cert. elem. educator, Conn. Tchr. Most Precious Blood Sch., Angola, N.Y., 1963-64, St. Sebastian Sch., Dearborn Heights, Mich., 1964-70, St. Anthony Sch., Fairfield, Conn., 1970-71; reading clinic tchr. Hilbert Coll., Hamburg, N.Y., 1971; tchr. St. Michael Sch., Bridgeport, Conn., 1971-73, St. Augustine, Bridgeport, Conn., 1973-87, St. Lawrence, Shelton, Conn., 1987—. Math. curriculum com. Diocese of Bridgeport, 1963, 79, 94, sci. curriculum com., 1995, report card com., 2002-2003. Mem. Sch. Student Team, 2001—03. Mem. Conn. Sci. Tchr.'s Assn., Nat. Sci. Tchr.'s Assn., Nat. Coun. Tchrs. Math., Nath. Cath. Educators Assn. Office: Saint Lawrence Campus 503 Shelton Ave Shelton CT 06484-2821 E-mail: stlawrencescience@hotmail.com.

CHORPENNING, FRANK WINSLOW, immunology educator, researcher; b. Marietta, Ohio, Aug. 17, 1913; s. Roy Albert and Laura Leola (Klintworth) C.; m. Annie Laurie Kay; children: Anne Kay, Jonathan Edward, Kathleen, Janie Cecelia. AB, Marietta Coll., 1939; MSc, Ohio State U., 1950, PhD, 1963. Immunologist USAREUR Med. Lab./US Army, Germany, 1952-55; chief clin. pathology Brooke Gen. Hosp., Ft. Sam Houston, Tex., 1955-61; cons. Nationalist Chinese Army, Taiwan, 1960; from lectr. to prof. Ohio State U., Columbus, 1961-81, prof. emeritus, 1981—. Me. coop. study group WHO, 1953-55. Div. editor Ohio Jour. Sci., 1974-83; editor: Clinical Pathology Procedures, 1959; author: (chpt.) Regulation of Immune Response Dynamics, 1982, Immunology of Bacterial Cell Envelope, 1983; author: The Man from Somerset, 1993; contbr. articles to profl. jours. Mem. Epidemiol. Com., San Antonio, 1949; mem. Rep. Nat. Com., Delaware, Ohio, 1979-97, Rep. Presdl. Task Force, Delaware, 1983-97. Lt. col. US Army, 1941-61. Recipient Commendation, Chinese Surgeon Gen., 1960, C.G. Brooke Gen. Hosp., 1960. Fellow Am. Acad. Microbiology, Ohio Acad. Sci.; mem. Am. Assn. Immunologists, Ohio Acad. Sci., Assn. for Gnotobiotics, Ohio Hist. Soc., Shamrock Club Columbus, Sigma Xi, Beta Beta Beta, Alpha Sigma Phi. Roman Catholic.

CHOUDHURY, DEO CHAND, physicist, educator; b. Darbhanga, India, Feb. 1, 1926; came to U.S., 1955; s. Kapleshwar and Gutainya Choudhury; m. Annette Patricia DuBois, Aug. 3, 1963; 1 son, Raj. BSc, U. Calcutta, 1944, MS, 1946; PhD, UCLA, 1959. Rsch. fellow Niels Bohr Inst., Copenhagen, 1952-55; rsch. asst. physics U. Rochester, N.Y., 1955-56; rsch. and tchg. asst. physics UCLA, 1956-59; asst. prof. physics U. Conn., Storrs, 1959-62; assoc. prof. physics Poly Inst. of N.Y. (now Poly U.), Bklyn., 1962—67; prof. physics Poly Inst. of N.Y., Bklyn., 1967—97, prof. emeritus, 1997—. Vis. asst. physicist Brookhaven Nat. Lab., summer 1960; vis. physicist Oak Ridge Nat. Lab., summer 1962, Niels Bohr Inst., 1978-79. Govt. India Coun. Sci. and Indsl. Rsch. scholar U. Calcutta Coll. Sci., 1947-52. Contbr. chpt. to book, numerous articles on high energy nuclear scattering, nuclear models, structure, reaction, and theoretical astrophysics to profl. publs. Mem. AAAS, Am. Phys. Soc., N.Y. Acad. Scis., Indian Phys. Soc., Sigma Xi, Sigma Pi Sigma. Home: 90 Gold St # 25L New York NY 10038-1833 Office: Poly U Dept Physics 6 Metrotech Ctr Brooklyn NY 11201-3840 Fax: 718-260-3136. E-mail: dchoudhu@duke.poly.edu.

CHOW, CHI-MING, retired mathematics educator; b. Tai-Yuan, Shansi, Republic of China, Nov. 15, 1931; arrived in U.S., 1959; s. Wei-Han Chow and Lu-Tsen Hsu. Cert. tech. officer, Chinese Air Force Tech. Inst., Republic of China, 1954; BS in Math., Ch. Coll. Hawaii, 1962; MS in Math., Oreg. State U., 1965. Tech. officer Chinese Air Force, Republic of China, 1954-59; prof. math. Oakland C.C., Mich., 1965-92, ret., 1992. Author (first author of the proof of the theorem): The sight area A of a moving body is inversely proportional to the square of the distance D between the body and observing point, i.e. A=C/(DxD), where C is a constant; contbr. articles to profl. jours. including The Math. Tchr., 1965. 1st Lt. Air Force of Republic of China, 1954-59. Mem.: Pi Mu Epsilon. Avocation: piloting aircraft. Home: PO Box 903 Novi MI 48376-0903

CHOW, GREGORY CHI-CHONG, economist, educator; b. Macau, South China, Dec. 25, 1929; came to U.S., 1948, naturalized, 1963; s. Tin-Pong and Pauline (Law) C.; m. Paula K. Chen, Aug. 27, 1955; children: John S., James S., Jeanne S. BA, Cornell U., 1951; MA, U. Chgo., 1952, PhD, 1955; hon. doctorate, Zhongshan U., 1986; LLD, Lingnan U., 1994. Asst. prof. MIT, 1955-59; assoc. prof. Cornell U., 1959-62, vis. prof., 1964-65; staff mem., mgr. econ. models IBM Research Center, Yorktown Heights, N.Y., 1962-70, prof., dir. econometric rsch. program, 1970-97; Class of 1913 prof. polit. economy Princeton U., 1979—. Adj. prof. Columbia U., 1965-70; vis. prof. Harvard U., 1967, Rutgers U., 1969; adviser Chinese Natural Sci. Found.; econ. adviser Shandong Provincial Govt. Author: Demand for Automobiles in the United States: A Study in Consumer Durables, 1957, Analysis and Control of Dynamic Economic Systems, 1975, Econometric Analysis by Control Methods, 1981, Econometrics, 1983, The Chinese Economy, 1985, Understanding China's Economy, 1994, Dynamic Economics: Optimization by the Lagrange Method, 1997; co-editor: Evaluating the Reliability of Macro-Economic Models, 1982, Asia in the 21st Century, 1997, The Demand for Durable Goods, 1960, China's Economic Transformation, 2002, Sower of Modern Economics in China: Interview of Gregory C. Chow (in Chinese) by Professor Liu Sufen, 1996, Knowing China, 2004; contbr. articles to profl. jours. Named Hon. Prof., Fudan U., Hainan U., The People's U., Zhongshan U., Shandong U., Nankai U., City U. Hong Kong, hon. pres., Lingnan U., Coll. at Zhongshan U., Nankai U. Fellow Econometric Soc., Am. Statis Assn.; mem. Academia Sinica, Am. Philos. Soc., Am. Econ. Assn., Soc. for Econ. Dynamics and Control (pres. 1979-80). Home: 30 Hardy Dr Princeton NJ 08540-1211 E-mail: gchow@princeton.edu.

CHOW, LEE, physics educator; b. Taipei, Taiwan, Jan. 11, 1950; m. Angie; children: Philip, Andrew. BS in Physics, Nat. Ctrl. U., 1972; PhD in Physics, Clark U., 1981. came to the U.S., 1975. Rsch. assoc. U. N.C., Chapel Hill, 1980-82; asst. prof. U. Ctrl. Fla., Orlando, 1983-88, assoc. prof., 1988-98, prof., 1998—, assoc. chair, 2000—. Vis. asst. prof. U. N.C., 1982-83; dir. Lasersight, Inc., Orlando, 1991-92, Surgilight, Inc., Orlando, 2000—; cons. Quantum Nucleanics Corp., Orlando, 1990-91; pres. Chinese-Am. Scholar Assn. Fla., 1997-98. Inventor in field. Pres. Chinese-Am. Assn. Ctrl. Fla., 1985-86. Rsch. grantee Rsch. Corp., N.Y.C., 1984-86, KEI Laser, Inc., Orlando, 1986-87, DARPA, Washington, 1988-90, NSF, Washington, 1990-92, Lucent Techs., Orlando, 1997-99, Agere Sys., Inc. 2000-02. Mem. Am. Phys. Soc. Office: U Ctrl Fla Dept Physics Orlando FL 32816-2385 E-mail: lc@physics.ucf.edu.

CHOWDHURI, PRITINDRA, electrical engineer, educator; b. Calcutta, July 12, 1927; came to U.S., 1949, naturalized, 1962; s. Ahindra and Sudhira (Mitra) C.; m. Sharon Elsie Hackebeil, Dec. 28, 1962; children: Naomi, Leslie, Robindro, Rajendro. B.Sc. in Physics with honors, Calcutta U., 1945, M.Sc., 1948; MS, Ill. Inst. Tech., 1951; D.Eng., Rensselaer Poly. Inst., 1966. Jr. engr. lightning arresters sect. Westinghouse Electric Corp., East Pittsburgh, Pa., 1951-52; elec. engr. high voltage lab. Maschinenfabrik Oerlikon, Zurich, 1952-53; research engr. High Voltage Rsch. Commn., Daeniken, Switzerland, 1953-56; devel. engr. high voltage lab. GE, Pittsfield, Mass., 1956-59, elec. engr. research and devel. ctr. Schenectady, N.Y., 1959-62, engr. elec. investigations transp. systems div. Erie, Pa., 1962-75; staff mem. Los Alamos (N.Mex.) Nat. Lab., 1975-86; prof. elec. engring. Ctr. Elec. Power Tenn. Technol. U., Cookeville, 1986—. Lectr. Pa. State U. Behrend Grad. Ctr., Erie, 1969-75. Author: Electromagnetic Transients in Power Systems, 1996. Patentee in field. Fellow AAAS, IEEE, Instn. Elec. Engrs. (U.K.), N.Y. Acad. Scis. Democrat. Unitarian Universalist. Home: 690 Valley Forge Rd Cookeville TN 38501-1574 Office: Tenn Technol U Ctr Elec Power PO Box 5032 Cookeville TN 38505-0001 E-mail: pchowdhuri@tntech.edu.

CHRESTMAN, SHIRLEY J. special education educator; b. Rochelle, Ill., Oct. 23, 1948; d. Bernard William and Elizabeth Frances Parsley; m. Walter Glen Chrestman, June 10, 1970; children: Shelly Ann Johnson, Adam Jordan Glen Chrestman. BS in Elem. Edn. and Spl. Edn., Western Ill. U., Macomb, 1970; MS in Ednl. Adminstrn., No. Ill. U., DeKalb, 2000. Elem. tchr. Hiawatha Dist. 426, Kirkland, Ill., 1970-74, spl. edn. tchr., 1975-82, Steward (Ill.) Dist. 220, 1992-96, Ashton (Ill.) Dist. 275, 1996—2000; spl. edn. supervisor Rockford Dist. #205, 2000—. Chmn. Laotian assimilation com. First Congl. Ch., DeKalb, 1985-87; chmn. parent adv. com. Malta (Ill.) Pubs. Schs., 1981-83; mem. family sect. Ogle Co. Habitat Humanity Com. Mem. ASCD, NEA, Ill. Edn. Assn., Ill. Reading Coun., Ill. Prins. Assn., Rockford Prins. Supervisor's Assn. Home: 938 Lincoln Hwy Rochelle IL 61068-1653 E-mail: gcscjc@rochellenet.

CHRISLER, JOAN C. psychologist, educator; b. Teaneck, N.J., Jan. 1, 1953; d. Eugene Reed and Anna Mary (Whalen) C.; m. Christopher Bishop, Nov. 20, 1976. BS in Psychology, Fordham U., 1975; MA, PhD in Exptl. Psychology, Yeshiva U., 1986; cert. in behavior therapy, L.I. U. Asst. prof. Conn. Coll., New London, 1987-93, assoc. prof., 1993-97, prof., 1997—. Vis. scholar The Stone Ctr., Wellesley Coll., 1994; fieldwork in behavior therapy Creedmoor Psychiat. Ctr., Queens Village, N.Y., 1982; group therapist Health Improvement Sys., Cin., 1982-84. Author: (with others) New Directions in Feminist Psychology, 1992, Variations on a Theme: Diversity and the Psychology of Women, 1995, Lectures on the Psychology of Women, 1996, Arming Athena: Career Strategies for Women in Academe, 1998, Charting a New Course for Feminist Psychology, 2002; contbr. numerous articles to profl. jours. Named Woman of Yr., Westchester County, N.Y., 1987; recipient Susan B. Anthony award Westchester NOW, 1987, Christine Ladd-Franklin award AWP, 1996, Disting. Publ. award AWP, 1997. Mem. APA, AAUP (Conn. v.p. 1993-97, pres. 1997-2001), Assn. Women in Psychology (spokesperson 1985-88, conf. coord. 1990, nat. coord. 1992-95), Soc. Menstrual Cycle Rsch. (pres. 2001-03), New England Psychol. Assn. (steering com. 1991-97, treas. 1992-94, pres. 1996), Ea. Psychol. Assn. (bd. dirs. 1997-2000), Internat. Coun. of Psychologists (bd. dirs. 1996-99, 2003—), Psi Chi. Avocations: music, reading, movies, travel. Office: Conn Coll Dept Of Psychology New London CT 06320

CHRISMAN, JAMES JOSEPH, management educator; b. Kansas City, Mo., Oct. 11, 1954; s. James John and Mildred Fay (Nelson) C.; m. Karen Waller, June 11, 1991. AA, Ill. Cen. Coll., 1977; BB, Western Ill. U., 1980; MBA, Bradley U., 1982; PhD, U. Ga., 1986. Machinst WABCO, Peoria, Ill., 1974-78; asst. prof. U. S.C., Columbia, 1986-91; assoc. prof. La. State U., 1991-93; prof. U. Calgary, Canada, 1993—2002, co-dir. venture devel. program, 1996, assoc. dean rsch. and PhD program, 1996-2001, endowed prof. family bus. entrepreneurship, 1999—2002, dir. Ctr. Family Bus. Mgmt. and Entrepreneurship, 1999—2002; prof. Miss. State U., Starkville, 2002—. Cons. UN Devel. Program, 1989-90, Internat. Civil Aviation Orgn., 1990, La. Lottery Corp., 1992, Assn. Small Bus. Devel. Ctrs., 1993—. Editor (assoc.): Case Rsch. Jour., 1984—87; mem. editl. bd.:, 1988—94; editor (case collection): McGraw Hill; editor: (assoc.) Strategic Planning Mgmt., 1987—88; editor: (advt. and circulation) Am. Jour. Small Bus., 1986—88; editor: (promotions) Entrpreneurship Theory and Practice, 1989; mem. editl. bd.:, 1990—94; editor, 1994—98, 2003—; guest editor Entrepreneurship Theory and Practice, 2003—, Jour. Bus. Venturing, 1993—, mem. editl. bd. Jour. Small Bus. Mgmt., 1986—87, guest editor, 2003, mem. editl. bd. Jour. Bus. Strategies, 1993—96, Acad. Mgmt. Jour., 1994—96, Jour. Mgmt., 1995—96, Family Bus. Rev., 1999—, ad hoc reviewer Jour. Mgmt. Studies, —, and many other jours., —; guest editor: Jour. Small Bus. Mgmt., 2003—; contbr. articles to profl. jours. Fellow, The Ctr. for Innovative Studies, 2002—. Fellow U.S. Assn. Small Bus. and Entrepreneurship (competitive papers chmn. 1988, v.p. corp. entrepreneurship 1989, bd. dirs. 1989-93, program chmn. 1991, v.p. rsch. 1992, pres. elect 1993, hon. pres. 1994); mem. N.Am. Case Rsch. Assn. (v.p. publs. 1987, proc. editor 1987, v.p. membership 1988-89, bd. dirs. 1987-89), Internat. Coun. Small Bus. (competitive papers chmn. 1988, v.p. programs 1989, dep. program chmn. 1990, bd. dirs. 1999-2001), Ea. Casewriters Assn. (bd. dirs. 1990), Acad. Mgmt. (exec. com. Entrepreneurship div. 1991-92). Republican. Roman Catholic. Avocations: collecting first edition books, chess, lacrosse, darts, bowling. Home: 1121 Edinburgh Dr Starkville MS 39759 Office: Miss State Univ Coll Bus and Industry Mississippi State MS 39762-9581 Business E-Mail: jchrisman@cobilan.msstate.edu.

CHRIST, CAROL TECLA, academic administrator; b. NYC, May 21, 1944; d. John George and Tecla (Bobrick) Christ; m. Larry Sklute, Aug. 15, 1975 (div. Dec. 1983); children— Jonathan, Elizabeth BA, Douglas Coll., 1966; M.Ph., Yale U., 1969, PhD, 1970. Asst. prof. English U. Calif., Berkeley, 1970-76, assoc. prof. English, 1976-83, prof. English, 1983—, dean dept. English, 1985-88, dean dept. humanities, 1988, acting provost, dean, 1989-90, provost, dean Coll. Letters and Sci., 1990-94, vice chancellor, provost, 1994-2000; pres. Smith Coll., Northampton, Mass., 2002—. Former dir. summer seminars for secondary and coll. tchrs. NEH; former tchr. Bread Loaf Sch. of English; invited lectr. Am. Assn. Univs., Am. Coun. Edn. Author: The Finer Optic: The Aesthetic of Particularity in Victorian Poetry, 1975, Victorian and Modern Poetics, 1984; mem. editl. bd. Victorian Literature, The Victorian Visual Imagination, The Norton Anthology of English Literature; contbr. articles to profl. jours. Mem. MLA Office: Smith Coll College Hall 20 Northampton MA 01063

CHRISTEN, ARDEN GALE, dental educator, researcher, consultant; b. Lemmon, S.D., Jan. 25, 1932; s. Harold John Christen and Dorothy Elizabeth (Taylor) Deering; m. Joan Ardell Akre, Sept. 10, 1955; children: Barbara, Penny, Rebecca, Sarah. BS, U. Minn., 1954, DDS, 1956; MSD, Ind. U., 1965; MA, Ball State U., 1973. Lic. dentist, Ind. Commd. 1st lt. USAF, 1956, advanced through grades to col., 1972; base dental surgeon Zaragoza Air Base, Spain, 1970-73; dental surgeon, cons. preventive dentistry RAF Bentwaters, Eng., 1973-75; air force preventive dentistry officer Sch. Aerospace Medicine, Brooks AFB, Tex., 1978-80; prof., chmn. dept. preventive dentistry Ind. U., Indpls., 1981-93, dir. preventive/cmty. dentistry, 1993-2000, co-dir. nicotine dependence program, 1997—, acting chair oral biology, 2000—. Sr. med. svc. cons. Surgeon Gen., U.S. Air Force, U.S. and Eng., 1974-80; spl. cons. to asst. surgeon gen. for dental svcs., Washington, 1975-80. Co-author: Primary Preventive Dentistry, 4th edit., 1995; contbr. over 250 articles to profl. jours. Bd. dirs. Bexar County chpt. Am. Cancer Soc., San Antonio, 1976-80, Marion County chpt., Indpls., 1980—; mem. Ind. divsn. Pub. Edn. Standing Com., Indpls., 1980. Decorated Service medal with 2 oak leaf clusters, Legion of Merit. Fellow Am. Coll. Dentists; mem. ADA, Am. Acad. Oral Pathology, Internat. Assn. Dental Rsch., Am. Acad. History of Dentistry (v.p. 1984-85, pres. 1986-87). Presbyterian. Avocations: photography, classical music, travel, writing. Home: 7112 Sylvan Ridge Rd Indianapolis IN 46240-3541 Office: Ind U Sch Dentistry 1121 W Michigan St Indianapolis IN 46202-5186 E-mail: achriste@iupui.edu.

CHRISTENSEN, DOUGLAS D. school system administrator; BA, Midland Luth. Coll., 1965; MA, U. Nebr., 1970, PhD, 1978. Tchr. Holdrege (Nebr.) Sr. H.S., 1965-70; h.s. prin. Bloomfield (Nebr.) Cmty. Schs., 1970-74, supt. of schs., 1974-76; county supt. of schs. Knox County Ctr., Nebr., 1975-76; supt. of schs. Colby Pub. Schs. Unified Sch. Dist. #315, 1978-85, North Platte (Nebr.) Pub. Schs., 1985-90; assoc. commr. of edn. Nebr. Dept. of Edn., Lincoln, 1990-92, dep. commr. of edn., 1992-94, commr. edn., 1994—. Presenter, cons. in field. Contbr. articles to profl. jours. Chair North Platte Area Econ. Devel. Task Force, 1986-90, Coun. for Inter-Agy. Cooperation, 1986-90; liturgist First Luth. Ch., 1986-90, chair fin. com., 1988-90; bd. dirs. Mid-Nebr. Cmty. Found., 1989-90; bd. dirs. Mari Sandoz Soc., 1990—; mem. Nebr. Commn. for the Protection of Children, 1994—; advanced planning com. Southwood Luth. Ch., 1994—. Recipient Spirit of PTA award Nebr. PTA, 1997, 98, Cornerstone award Future Farmers Am., 1998, Walter Turner award Am. Assn. Ednl. Svc. Agys., 1998, David Hutchinson award U. Nebr., 1998, Burnham Yates award Nebr. Coun. Econ. Edn., 1999. Mem. ASCD (pres. Kans. affiliate 1984-85), Am. Assn. of Sch. Adminstrs. (Nebr. Supt. of Yr. 1990), Coun. Chief State Sch. Officers (bd. dirs. 1997—), Nebr. Coun. of Sch. Adminstrs., Rotary Internat. (pres. 1981-82), Nebr. Ctr. for Ednl. Excellence (chair 1985-90, bd. dirs. 1989-90), Midland Luth. Coll. Alumni Assn. (pres. 1992-93). Office: Commrs Office Dept of Edn PO Box 94987 Lincoln NE 68509-4987 also: 301 Centennial Mall S Lincoln NE 68509*

CHRISTENSEN, JAMES ARTHUR, middle school educator; b. Santa Monica, Calif., Mar. 31, 1945; s. Arthur Chris and Laura Louise (Wilken) C.; m. Linda J. Carlson, Dec. 19, 1967 (div. Feb. 1986); children: Darcie L., Gretta L., Corry J.; m. Virginia A. Woodruff, June 21, 1986. Student, Oreg. State U., 1963-64; BS in Edn., So. Oreg. State Coll., 1967, postgrad., 1980-82, Coll. of Notre Dame, 1968-69. Cert. elem. tchr., Oreg. 6th grade tchr. Redwood City (Calif.) Sch. Dist., 1967-71; 5th-6th grade tchr. Manzanita Elem. Sch., Grants Pass, Oreg., 1971-75; 9th-10th grade English and reading tchr. Ill. Valley H.S., Cave Junction, Oreg., 1975-76; 8th grade math. and sci. tchr. Laurna Byrne Mid. Sch., Cave Junction, 1976-77; 7th-8th grade math. and sci. tchr. Fleming Mid. Sch., Grants Pass, 1977—. Mem. tech. adv. bd. 3 Rivers Sch. Dist., Murphy, Oreg., 1994-95, mem. staff insvc. adv. bd., 1994-95. Vol. Visitors' Ctr., Grants Pass C. of C., 1993; mem. parish/staff rels. com. United Meth. Ch., Grants Pass, 1994-95. Recipient 3 Rivers Sch. Dist. Tchr. of the Year, 1995, Tech. Learning Challenge grant Through The Earth and Sea Investigators program, 1995—. Mem. ASCD, NEA, Rogue YAcht Club (trustee 1992-96). Democrat. Avocations: sailing, fly fishing. Home: 400 Cumberland Dr Grants Pass OR 97527-9507 Office: Fleming Mid Sch 6001 Monument Dr Grants Pass OR 97526-8515

CHRISTENSEN, RAYMOND LYLE, electrical engineer, educator; b. Winterset, Iowa, July 16, 1920; s. Harry N. and Leta (Bush) C.; m. Fern E. Breakenridge; children: Raymond Lyle Jr., Christena S. BS, Colo. State U., 1964; MS, postgrad., So. Ill. U., 1965—. Journeyman electrician J.B. Decker & Sons, Mason City, Iowa, 1945-50; owner, mgr. Chris Elec. Co., Sumner, Iowa, 1950-52; asst. plant supt. N.W. Ill. Gas & Elec. Co., Savanna, 1952-55; elec. engr. Elec. Energy, Inc., Joppa, Ill., 1955-59; instr. engring. So. Ill. U., Carbondale, 1959-66; assoc. prof. Northwestern State U., Natchitoches, La., 1966—. Cons. Crown Zellerbach Co., USAF, AT&T. Served with USN, 1942-45. Mem. Lions (pres. Natchitoches club, zone chmn., sec., treas., 3d v.p., 2d v.p., dep. dist. gov., dist. gov., 2d v.p. state crippled children's camp, 1st v.p., pres.), Natchitoches Genealogy and Hist. Assn. (1st v.p.), Natchitoches Parish Ret. Educators Assn. (pres.), Phi Delta Kappa (past pres., treas., area coord.). Home: 1017 Oma St Natchitoches LA 71457-5229

CHRISTENSON, CHARLES ELROY, art educator; b. Gary, Ind., Jan. 2, 1942; s. Christian Monroe and Violet May (Kirkland) C.; m. Coral Yvette Demar, Feb. 26, 1966 (div. May 1990); children: Michael Eric, Tessa Diahann, Leah Renee; m. Cheryl Lane Grubb, Mar. 27, 1999. Student, U. Tex., 1960-63; BFA, San Francisco Art Inst., 1966; MFA, U. Wash., Seattle, 1970. Staff artist Taylor Press, Dallas, 1962-63; freelance artist San Francisco, 1963-64, 65-66; comml. artist The Emporium, San Francisco, 1964-65; art educator U. Wash., 1970-71; art instr. Shoreline C.C., Seattle, 1971-75, North Seattle C.C., 1971—, acting chmn. humanities divsn., 1978-79, gallery dir., 1977—. Advisor art group North Seattle C.C., 1978—, head art dept, 1979—; mem. faculty Semester at Sea, 2001; juror Equinox Arts Festival, Everett, Wash., 1981; curator exhbns. Wash. C.C. Humanities Conv., Bellevue, 1986, 87; bd. advisors Noon Star Prodns., Seattle, 1992-95; co-owner, tour leader Sketching and Touring Through France, Seattle, 1992—; co-owner S&E Tours, 2002— . Writer, illustrator: Simple Crafts for the Village, 1968; author poems. Vol. Am. Peace Corps, Andra Pradesh, India, 1966-68; beef leader Riverview Champs-4-H Club, Everett, 1980-81; coach Snohomish (Wash.) Youth Soccer, 1982-88; mem. Seattle Art Mus. Recipient Beyond War Found. award, 1987, Gov.'s Faculty Recognition award, 1987; Seattle C.C. Dist. grantee, 1988, Fulbright grantee India, 1990—, Indonesia, 1994; named to Humanities Exemplary Status, Wash. C.C. Humanities Assn., 1987. Mem. Wash. C.C. Humanities Assn., Smithsonian Inst., Artist's Trust, Seattle C.C. Fedn. Tchrs. (human div. rep. 1977-78), Nat. Coun. for Social Studies, Nat. Campaign for Freedom Expression, Amnesty Internat. Avocations: travel, soccer, skiing, sailing. Office: North Seattle CC 9600 College Way N Seattle WA 98103-3514

CHRISTENSON, GORDON A. law educator; b. Salt Lake City, June 22, 1932; s. Gordon B. and Ruth Arzella (Anderson) C.; m. Katherine Joy deMik, Nov. 2, 1951 (div. 1977); children: Gordon Scott, Marjorie Lynne, Ruth Ann, Nanette; m. Fabienne Fadeley, Sept. 16, 1979. BS in Law, U. Utah, 1955, JD, 1956; SJD, George Washington U., 1961. Bar: Utah 1956, U.S. Supreme Ct. 1971, D.C. 1978. Law clk. to chief justice Utah Supreme Ct., 1956-57; assoc. firm Christenson & Callister, Salt Lake City, 1956-58; atty. Dept. of Army, Nat. Guard Bur., Washington, 1957-58; atty., acting asst. legal adviser Office of Legal Adviser, U.S. Dept. State, Washington, 1958-62; asst. gen. counsel for sci. and tech. U.S. Dept. Commerce, 1962-67, spl. asst. to undersec. of commerce, 1967, counsel to commerce tech. adv. bd., 1962-67, chmn. task force on telecommunications missions and orgn., 1967, counsel to panel on engring. and commodity standards, tech. adv. bd., 1963-65; assoc. prof. law U. Okla., Norman, 1967-70, exec. asst. to pres., 1967-70; univ. dean for ednl. devel., central adminstrn. State U. N.Y., Albany, 1970-71; prof. law Am. U. Law Sch., Washington, 1971-79, dean, 1971-77; on leave, 1977-79; Charles H. Stockton prof. internat. law U.S. Naval War Coll., Newport, R.I., 1977-79; dean, Nippert prof. law U. Cin. Coll. Law, 1979-85, univ. prof. law, 1985-99, prof. emeritus, dean emeritus, 1999—. Assoc. professorial lectr. in internat. affairs George Washington U., 1961-67; vis. scholar Harvard U. Law Sch., 1977-78, Yale Law Sch., 1985-86, Law Sch. U. Maine, Portland, 1997; Wallace S. Fujiyama vis. disting. prof. law Univ. Hawaii Law Sch., 1997; participant summer confs. on internat. law Cornell Law Sch., Ithaca, N.Y., 1962, 64; cons. in internat. law U.S. Naval War Coll., Newport, R.I., 1969; faculty mem., reporter seminars for experienced fed. dist. judges Fed. Jud. Center, Washington, 1972-77. Author: (with Richard B. Lillich) International Claims: Their Preparation and Presentation, 1962, The Future of the University, 1969; Contbr. articles to legal jours. Cons. to Center for Policy Alternatives Mass. Inst. Tech., Cambridge, 1970-81; mem. intergovtl. com. on Internat. Policy on Weather Modification, 1967; Vice pres. Procedural Aspects of Internat. Law Inst., N.Y.C., 1962-2001, trustee, 1962—. Served with intelligence sect. USAF, 1951-52, Japan. Recipient Silver Medal award Dept. Commerce, 1967; fellow Grad. Sch. U. Cin. Mem. Am. Soc. Internat. Law (mem. panel on state responsibility), Utah Bar Assn., Cin. Bar Assn., Order of Coif, Phi Delta Phi, Kappa Sigma. Clubs: Literary (Cin.); Cosmos (Washington). Home and Office: 3465 Principio Ave Cincinnati OH 45208-4242 E-mail: christga@msn.com.

CHRISTESEN, JOHN DENIS, business educator; b. N.Y.C., July 16, 1936; s. Charles Nicholas and Mary Antoinette (Koza) C.; AB, Lehman Coll. CUNY, 1970; MBA with distinction, Pace U., 1975; postgrad. Columbia U., 1976—; Doctor of Industrial Mgmnt. (hon.), U. Industrial Mgmt.; Credit mgr. Butler Lumber Co., 1961-62; fiscal, comptroller, sales staff Lever Bros., 1962-67; contr., sales v.p. Cycle Circus, Inc., 1967-70; v.p. Putnam Bicycle Importers Co., 1970-73; curriculum chmn. bus. adminstrn., prof. mgmt., dept. chmn. bus. adminstrn. & pub. svc. SUNY Westchester C.C., Valhalla, N.Y., 1975—, dir. Mgmt. Inst., chmn. faculty devel. conf., v.p. Faculty-Student Assn., Joseph and Sophia Abeles Disting. chair of bus., 1994—; vis. prof. econs. Mercy Coll., Dobbs Ferry, N.Y.; adj. assoc. prof. mgmt. Iona Coll., New Rochelle, N.Y. bd. dirs. Investment Properties Corp., Computweather Corp., Bio Med. Concepts, Inc.; adv. bd. U. Indsl. Mgmt.; cons. N.Y. State Bd. Regents, N.Y. State Edn. Dept.; chmn. Urba Devel. Corp. of Lewisboro N.Y., Town of Lewisboro Housing Com.; bd. mem. Westchester Minority Devel. Corp., 1983-84. Recipient Medallion Edn. award WCCF. Mem. Am. Acad. Mgmt., Nat. Econs. Club, Am. Inst. Higher Edn., Am. Acad. Polit. and Social Scis., Assn. MBA Execs., N.Y. State Assn. Two-Year Colls. (exec. bd. 1980-84), Nat. Bus. Honor Soc., Alpha Beta Gamma (nat. chmn. 1978-79, nat. devel. chmn. 1980-81, chief exec. officer 1983—), Sigma Lambda, Delta Mu Delta, others. Republican. Roman Catholic. Author: (with R. Wunsch) The Complete Resume Handbook, 1967; Management Miscellany, 1978, 4th edit., 1990; Introduction to Business (film series), 1980; Introduction to Finance (film series), 1982; (with Heinz Weirich) Instructor's Manual for Management, 1984; dir. editor: The Honors Jour., 1995—. Home: 1160 Midland Ave Apt 4C Bronxville NY 10708-6430 Office: Westchester Community Coll 75 Grasslands Rd Valhalla NY 10595-1636

CHRISTIAN, GARY DALE, chemistry educator; b. Eugene, Oreg., Nov. 25, 1937; s. Roy C. and Edna Alberta (Trout) Gonier; m. Suanne Byrd Coulbourne, June 17, 1961; children: Dale Brian, Carol Jean, Tanya Danielle, Tabitha Star. BS, U. Oreg., 1959; MS, U. Md., 1962, PhD, 1964. Rsch. analytical chemist Walter Reed Army Inst. Rsch., Washington, 1961-67; asst. prof. U. Md., College Park, 1965-66, U. Ky., Lexington, 1967-70, assoc. prof., 1970-72; prof. chemistry U. Wash., Seattle, 1972—, acting chmn. dept., 1990, assoc. chmn., 1991-92, divisional dean Arts and Scis., 1993-2001. Vis. prof. Free U. Brussels, 1978-79; invited prof. U. Geneva, 1979; cons. Ames Co., 1968-72, Beckman Instruments, Inc., 1972-84, 88, Westinghouse Hanford Co., 1977-83, Tech. Dynamics, 1983-85, Porton Diagnostics, 1990-91, Bend Rsch., 1992-93, E.I. DuPont de Nemours, Inc., 1993; examiner Grad. Record Exam., 1985-90. Author: Analytical Chemistry, 6th edit., 2003, Instrumental Analysis, 1978, 2d edit., 1986, Atomic Absorption Spectroscopy, 1970, Trace Analysis, 1986, Problem Solving in Analytical Chemistry, 1988, Calculations in Pharmaceutical Sciences, 1993; editl. bd. Analytical Letters, 1971—, Can. Jour. Spectroscopy, 1974-96, Analytical Instrumentation, 1974-93, Talanta, 1980-88 (spl. editor USA honor issue, 1989), Analytical Chemistry, 1985-89, Critical Revs. in Analytical Chemistry, 1985—, The Analyst, 1986-90, Jour. Saudi Chem. Soc., 1995—; editor in chief Talanta, 1989—, Electroanalysis, 1988—, Jour. Pharm. and Biochem. Analysis, 1990-97, Fresenius' Z. Analytical Chem., 1991-93, Laborator Automation, 1992—, Quimica Analitica, 1993—; contbr. articles to profl. jours. Named Fulbright Hays scholar, 1978—79; recipient Medal of Honor, Univ. Libre de Brussels, 1978, Talanta medal, Elsevier Sci., 1995, Commemorative medal, Charles U., 1999, Geoff Wilson medal, Deakin U., 2003. Mem. Am. Chem. Soc. (sect. chmn. 1982-83, chmn. elect divsn. Analytic chemistry 1988-89, chmn. 1989-90, divsn. Analytical Chemistry award for Excellence in Tchg. 1988, Fisher award in analytical chemistry 1996), Soc. Applied Spectroscopy (sect. chmn. 1982), Spectroscopy Soc. Can., Am. Inst. Chemists (cert.), Soc. Electroanalytical Chemistry (bd. dirs. 1993-98). Republican. Home: PO Box 26 Medina WA 98039-0026 Office: U Wash Dept Chemistry Box 351700 Seattle WA 98195-1700 E-mail: christian@chem.washington.edu.

CHRISTIAN, JOE CLARK, medical genetics researcher, educator; b. Marshall, Okla., Sept. 12, 1934; s. Roy John and Katherine Elizabeth (Beeby) C.; m. Shirley Ann Yancey, June 5, 1960; children: Roy Clark, Charles David. BS, Okla. State U., 1956; MS, U. Ky., 1959, PhD, 1960, MD, 1964. Cert. clin. geneticist, Am. Bd. Med. Genetics. Resident internal medicine Vanderbilt U., Nashville, 1964-66; asst. prof. med. genetics Ind. U., Indpls., 1966-69, assoc. prof., 1969-74, prof., 1974-99, assoc. dean basic scis. and regional ctrs., 1996-98, prof. emeritus, assoc. dean emeritus, 1999—. Served with USAR, 1953-60. Mem. AMA, Am. Soc. Human Genetics. Democrat. Methodist. Avocations: bicycling, farming. Office: Ind U Dept Med/Molecular Genetics 975 W Walnut St Dept Med Indianapolis IN 46202-5181 E-mail: jcristi@iupui.edu.

CHRISTIAN, MARIE WASHINGTON ROBERTS, retired elementary school educator; b. Belle Mina, Ala., May 12, 1926; d. Samuel Ward and Althea Tate (Washington) Roberts; m. Jackson Richard Christian, Jan. 28, 1967 (dec.); 2 stepchildren. BS, State Tchrs. Coll., Florence, Ala., 1947; MA, George Peabody Coll., Nashville, 1948; A cert. in elem. edn., U. Ala., 1952, AA cert., 1961. Tchr. history County High Sch., Moulton, Ala., 1948-49; elem. tchr. Riverside Elem. Sch., Decatur, Ala., 1949-53, State Tchrs. Coll., 1953, Verner Elem. Sch., Tuscaloosa, Ala., 1953-68. Tchr. summer sch. Verner Sch., 1954-66. Author: Threads of Many Colors, 1993, 2d edit., 1994; contbr. articles to Limestone Legacy. Hostess Mildred Warner House, Heritage Week, Tuscaloosa, 1982-90; pres. morning group St. Mark United Meth. Ch., Northport, Ala., 1990-91; pres. Suburban Woman's Club, 1983-85. Recipient life writing honors award Shelton State Community Coll., Tuscaloosa, 1990. Mem. AAUW (1st v.p. 1960-61), DAR (1st vice regent 1993-96, 2d vice regent 1982-85), Magna Charta Dames, Alpha Delta Kappa (pres. 1965-66), Kappa Delta Epsilon, Beta Sigma Phi (pres. 1976, 84, Girl of Yr. award 1984, Valentine queen 1970, 80, 86). Avocations: foreign travel, drama, studying spanish, painting, writing. Home: Tuscaloosa, Ala. Died Dec. 24, 2001.

CHRISTIAN, MARY JO DINAN, educational administrator, educator; b. Denver, May 7, 1941; d. Joseph Timothy and Margaret Rose Dinan; m. Ralph Poinsett Christian, Aug. 27, 1966. BA, Loretto Heights Coll., Denver, 1964; MA, George Washington U., 1983. Cert. English educator, adminstrn. and supervision secondary edn. English tchr. Denver Pub. Schs., 1964-67, Prince George's County Pub. Sch., Md., 1967-81; vice-prin. Prince George's County High Sch., Md., 1981-97; program dir. Tchr. Equity Equals Achievement, 1997—99, tchr., mentor, 2002—. Presenter tchr. equity and student achievement Nat. Conf.; Generating Expectations for Student Achievement equity assurance coord. instrs. in-svc. and adminstrs., 1997—99; tchr. mentor, 2002; pres. Tchr. Equity Equals Student Achievement Inc.; owner Independence House Bed and Breakfast, Washington, 2000—. Columnist: WomenSpeak, 1981-91. Rep. Prince George's County Commn. Women UN Fourth World Conf. Women Forum, Beijing, 1995. Md. Ho. of Dels. recognition. Mem. NAFE, ASCD, NEA (chair adminstrs. caucus 1991-93, adminstr.-at-large resolutions com. 1986-92, polit. action com. 1984-86, coord.-at-large women's caucus 1981-91, Creative Leadership award 1989), Md. State Tchrs. Assn. (state coord. Sen. Sarbane campaign 1982, state voter registration coord. 1984, issue coord. Tom McMillen campaign 1986, Women's Rights award 1988), Phi Delta Kappa, Alpha Delta Kappa. Home: 504 Independence Ave SE Washington DC 20003-1143

CHRISTIAN, RICHARD CARLTON, university dean, former advertising agency executive; b. Dayton, Ohio, Nov. 29, 1924; s. Raymond A. and Louise (Gamber) C.; m. Audrey Bongartz, Sept. 10, 1949; children: Ann Christian Carra, Richard Carlton Jr. BS in Bus. Adminstrn, Miami U., Oxford, Ohio, 1948; MBA, Northwestern U., 1949; LLD (hon.), Nat.-Louis U., 1986; postgrad., Denison U., The Citadel, Biarritz Am. U. Mktg. analyst Rockwell Mfg. Co., Pitts., 1949-50; exec. v.p. Marsteller Inc., Chgo., 1951-60, pres., 1960-75; bd. dirs., exec. com. Young and Rubicam, Inc., 1979-84; chmn. bd. Marsteller Inc., 1975-84, chmn. emeritus, 1984—; assoc. dean Kellogg Grad. Sch. Mgmt. Northwestern U., 1984-91, assoc. dean Medill Sch. Journalism, 1991-99. Dir., chmn. Bus. Publs. Audit Circulation, Inc., 1969-75; spkr. in field. Trustee Northwestern U., 1970-74, Nat.-Louis U., Evanston, Ill., 1970-92, James Webb Young Fund for Edn., U. Ill., 1962-95; pres. Nat. Advt. Rev. Coun., 1976-77; bd. adv. coun. mem. Miami U.; mem. adv. coun. J.L. Kellogg Grad. Sch. Mgmt., Northwestern U.; v.p., dir. Mus. Broadcast Comm.; dir. Can. U.S. Ednl. Exch. (Fulbright Found.), 1988-92. With inf. AUS, 1942-46, ETO. Recipient Ohio Gov.'s award 1977, Alumni medal, Alumni, Merit and Svc. awards Northwestern U.; named to the Advt. Hall of Fame, 1991. Mem. Am. Mktg. assn., Indsl. Mktg. Assn. (founder, chmn. 1951), Bus. Profl. Advt. Assn. (life mem. Chgo., pres. Chgo. 1954-55, nat. v.p. 1955-58, G. D. Crain award 1977), U. Ill. Found., Northwestern U. Bus. Sch. Alumni Assn. (founder, pres.), Am. Assn. Advt. Agys. (dir., chmn. 1976-77), Am. Acad. Advt. (1st disting. svc. award 1978), Northwestern U. Alumni Assn. (nat. pres. 1968-70), Mid-Am. Club, Comml. Club, Econ. Club Chgo., Kenilworth Club, Westmoreland Country Club, Alpha Delta Sigma, Beta Gamma Sigma, Delta Sigma Pi, Phi Gamma Delta. Baptist. Home: 2 Arbor Lane Apt 412 Evanston IL 60201

CHRISTIANO, PAUL P. academic administrator, civil engineering educator; b. Pitts., May 12, 1942; s. Natale Anthony and Ida Stella (Lupori) C.; m. Norene Grace DiBucci, Nov. 11, 1967; 1 child, Beth BSC.E., Carnegie Inst. Tech., 1964, MSC.E., 1965; PhD in Civil Engrng., Carnegie-Mellon U., 1968. From asst. prof. to assoc. prof. U. Minn., Mpls., 1967-74; assoc. prof., then prof. Carnegie-Mellon U., Pitts., from 1974, assoc. dean of engrng., 1982-86, head civil engrng., 1986-89, dean engrng., 1989-91, provost, 1991-2000. Co-author: Structural Analysis, 1986; contbr. articles to profl. jours. Mem. ASCE (Prof. of Yr. award Pitts. chpt. 1983) Republican. Roman Catholic. Home: Pittsburgh, Pa. Died June 21, 2001.

CHRISTIANSEN, RAYMOND STEPHAN, librarian, educator; b. Oak Park, Ill., Feb. 15, 1950; s. Raymond Julius and Anne Mary (Fusek) Christiansen; m. Phyllis Anne Dombowski, Nov. 25, 1972; 1 child, Mark David. BA, Elmhurst Coll., 1971; MEd, No. Ill. U., 1974. Dept. dir. Elmhurst (Ill.) Coll., 1971—73; asst. law libr. media svcs. Lewis U., Glen Ellyn, Ill., 1974—77; asst. prof. edn. Aurora (Ill.) U., 1977—90, assoc. prof., 1990—2003, emeritus prof., 2003—, media libr., 1977—82, instnl. developer, 1982—89, dir. univ. media svcs., 1985—2003, dir. ednl. facilities and tech. planning, 2003—; media cons., 1977—. Author: (video series) Rothblatt on Criminal Advocacy, 1975, (book) Index to SCOPE the UN Magazine, 1977. Lic. lay min. Epsicopal Ch., 1990—. Mem.: ASCD, Assn. Tchr. Educators, Assn. Ednl. Comms. and Tech., Phi Eta Sigma, Alpha Psi Omega. Home: 424 S Gladstone Ave Aurora IL 60506-5370 Office: Aurora U Libr 347 S Gladstone Ave Aurora IL 60506-4877

CHRISTIANSEN, SUSAN PUTNAM, artist, educator, consultant; b. Fresno, California, Sept. 4, 1938; d. Murray and Iolene Lazelle (Lund) Putnam; m. Robert Lorenz Christiansen, June 23, 1962; children: Peter Putnam, John Robert (twins), Catherine Sara. BA in biology, art, Stanford U., 1960, MA in edn., 1961. Cert.: secondary tchr., Calif. Tchr. sci. and art Blach Sch., Los Altos, Calif., 1961-62; tchr. art appreciation Jefferson County Schs., Denver, 1963-68; docent Denver Art Mus., 1963-70; docent trainer, classroom aide Palo Alto (Calif.) Sch. Dist. and Cultural Ctr., 1973-84; art cons. Children's Hosp., Stanford, Calif., 1985-90; researcher Creative Svcs., Stanford Alumni Assn., 1989-92; docent Stanford Mus. Art, 1982—. Castilleja Sch. substitute tchr., 1985; docent chair of Stanford Memorial Ch., 1995; freelance artist, illustrator, cons., 1973—; children's art tchr., painter, Hilo Art Ctr., Big Island, Hawaii, 1971-73. Illustrator: signs in Hawaii Volcanoes Nat. Pk., 1971-73; U.S. Geol. Survey, 1977; ; muralist Children's Hosp., 1979-84; painter, illustrator Stanford Centennial exhibit, 1991. Chair Stanford Meml. Ch. docents; chmn. docent group Stanford Meml. Ch., 1996—. Mem. Stanford Alumni Assn. (nomination com. 1970); Nat. Trust for Historic Preservation, Coun. for Arts (v.p. spl. projects com. 1989—); Stanford Hist. Soc., Palo Alto Hist. Assn.; Inst. for Rsch. on Women and Gender; Pacific Art League of Palo Alto. Democrat. Avocations: tennis, piano, gardening, cooking, family geneology. Home: 1118 Harker Ave Palo Alto CA 94301-3420

CHRISTIANSON, MARCIA LARAYE, middle school educator; b. Austin, Minn., June 14, 1947; d. Arnold Raymond and Rayma Arliene (Peterson) C. AA, Austin Community Coll., 1967; BA, Luther Coll., Decorah, Iowa, 1969; MEd in Ednl. Computing, Cardinal Stritch Coll., Milw., 1986. Cert. tchr., Wis. Tchr. Joint Sch. Dist. 1, West Bend, Wis., 1969—. Facilitator, instr. Profl. Improvement Inst., West Bend, 1985-90; co-chair tchr. incentive pilot program, West Bend and Madison, Wis., 1986-88, Dist. Staff Devel. Com., West Bend, 1990—. Bd. dirs. Waubun Girl Scout Coun., 1993-94. Mem. NEA, AAUW, Wis. Edn. Assn. Coun. (bd. dirs., alternate 1992-98), Cedar Lake United Educators (bd. dirs. 1990, vice chair bd. dirs. 1998-2003, pres. bd. dirs. 2003—), West Bend Edn. Assn. (exec. bd., chief negotiator 1982-99), Portside Weavers Guild (past pres.). Lutheran. Avocations: weaving, beading, spinning, tennis, swimming. Home: 125 N University Dr Apt 210 West Bend WI 53095-2948 Office: Badger Mid Sch 710 S Main St West Bend WI 53095-3940

CHRISTIANSON, ROGER GORDON, biology educator; b. Santa Monica, Calif., Oct. 31, 1947; s. Kyle C. and Ruby K. (Parker) Christianson; m. Angela Diane Rey, Mar. 3, 1967; children: Lisa Marie, David Scott, Stephen Peter. BA in Cell and Organismal Biology, U. Calif., Santa Barbara, 1969, MA in Biology, 1971, PhD in Biology, 1976. Faculty assoc. U. Calif., Santa Barbara, 1973-79, staff rsch. assoc., 1979-80; asst. prof. So. Oreg. U., Ashland, 1980-85, assoc. prof., 1985-93, prof., 1993—, coord. gen. biology program, 1980—, chmn. biology dept., 1996, 1997—2003. Instr. U. Calif. Santa Barbara, 1976, 78, 80. Contbr. articles to sci. and ednl. jours. Active Oreg. Shakespeare Festival Assn., Ashland, 1983—87; mem. bikeway com. Ashland City Coun., 1986—88; organizer Bike Oreg., 1982—92, Frontline HS Staff, 1985—2003; short-term mission work Mex. Orphanage, 1986—; ofcl. photographer Ashland H.S. Booster Club, 1987—92; coord. youth program 1st Bapt. Ch., Ashland, 1981—85, mem. ch. life commn., 1982—88, bd. deacons, 1993—95, mem. outreach com., 1994, 1995; youth leader jr. and sr. H.S. students Grace Ch., Santa Barbara, 1973—80. Mem.: AAAS (chair Pacific divsn. edn. sect 1985—2001, coun. Pacific divsn. 1985—, exec. com. Pacific divsn. 1998—, chair local organizing com. Pacific divsn. ann. meeting 2000, chair Pacific divsn. student awards com. 2001, exec. dir. Pacific divsn. 2002—), Assn. for Biology Lab. Edn., Oreg. Sci. Tchrs. Assn., Am. Mus. Natural History, Beta Beta Beta, Sigma Xi (chpt. membership com. 1998—2000). Republican. Avocations: sports, photography, youth work, multimedia presentations, amateur radio operator. Home: 430 Reiten Dr Ashland OR 97520-8762 Office: Southern Oregon U Dept Biology 1250 Siskiyou Blvd Ashland OR 97520-5010 E-mail: rchristi@sou.edu.

CHRISTIE, GEORGE CUSTIS, lawyer, educator, author; b. N.Y.C., Mar. 3, 1934; s. Custis and Sophie (Velimahitis) C.; m. Susan D. Monserud, Apr. 20, 1965 (div. July 1974); 1 child, Constantine George; m. Deborah D. Carnes, Dec. 20, 1974; children: Rebecca Sophia, Nicholas George. AB, Columbia U., 1955, JD, 1957; diploma in internat. law (Fulbright scholar), Cambridge (Eng.) U., 1962; S.JD, Harvard U., 1966. Bar: N.Y. 1957, D.C. 1958. Assoc. Covington & Burling, Washington, 1958-60; Ford Found. fellow in law teaching Harvard U., 1960-61; assoc. prof. law U. Minn., Mpls., 1962-65, prof. law, 1965-66; asst. gen. counsel for Near E. and S. Asia, AID, Dept. State, 1966-67; prof. law Duke U., 1967-79, James B. Duke prof. law, 1979—. Vis. lectr. U. Witwatersrand, South Africa, 1980, Fudan U., China, U. Otago, New Zealand, 1985; fellow Nat. Humanities Center, 1980-81; scholar-in-residence McGuire, Woods & Battle, Richmond, Va., 1983, vis. Freda Alverson prof. law George Washington U., spring 1988; vis. prof. law Northwestern U., 1991-92, U. Athens, Greece, 2000; vis. fellow Rsch. Sch. Social Scis., Australian Nat. U., 2002. Author: Jurisprudence: Text and Readings on the Philosophy of Law, 1973, 2d edit. (with P. Martin), 1995, The Sum and Substance of the Law of Torts, 1980, Law, Norms & Authority, 1982, Cases and Materials on the Law of Torts, 1983, 2d edit. (with J. Meeks), 1990, 3d edit. (with others), 1997, The Notion of an Ideal Audience in Legal Argument, 2000. Served with U.S. Army, 1957. Mem. ABA, Am. Law Inst., Am. Soc. Internat. Law, Phi Beta Kappa. Democrat. Greek Orthodox. Home: 17 Stoneridge Cir Durham NC 27705-5510 Office: Duke U Sch Law PO Box 90360 Durham NC 27708-0360 E-mail: gcc@law.duke.edu.

CHRISTINA, BARBARA ANN, bilingual education administrator; b. Bklyn., June 16, 1947; d. Anthony Michael and Maria Thersa (Spina) Bracco; m. Frank Anthony Christina, July 10, 1971. BA, St. Joseph's Coll., 1968; MA, NYU, 1969; profl. diploma, L.I. U., 1988; EdD, Nova U., 1993. Tchr. French and Spanish John Jay High Sch., N.Y.C., 1969-71, Hampton Bays (N.Y.) High Sch., 1971-72; tchr. ESL Middle Country Sch. Dist., L.I., N.Y., 1973-80, 82-83; tchr. French and Spanish Miller Place (N.Y.) High Sch., 1980-82; tchr. ESL Longwood (N.Y.) Sch. Dist., 1983-89; coord. bilingual/ESL Tech. Assistance Ctr. BOCES I/Suffolk County, Westhampton Beach, N.Y., 1989-95, Western Suffolk BOCES, Lindenhurst, NY, 1995—2003; home office cons. and tchr. trainer, 2003—. Presenter workshops; writer curricula. Contbr. articles to profl. jours. Mem. ASCD, TESOL, Coun. for Exceptional Children, Internat. Reading Assn., Nat. Assn. Bilingual Edn., N.Y. State TESOL, N.Y. State Assn. Bilingual Edn. Home: 47 Highland Down Shoreham NY 11786-1125

CHRIST-JANER, ARLAND FREDERICK, college president; b. Garland, Nebr., Jan. 27, 1922; s. William Henry and Bertha Wilhelmina (Beckman) C.-J.; m. Sally Johnson Grice, Sept. 4, 1975 (dec.).; m. Uta Buehler, Dec. 31, 2002. BA, Carleton Coll., 1943; BD, Yale U., 1949; JD, U. Chgo., 1952; LLD (hon.), Coe Coll., 1961, Carleton Coll., 1967, Colo. Coll., 1971; LHD (hon.), Monmouth Coll., 1967, Curry Coll., 1972; LHD, Cornell Coll., 1999. Asst. to pres. Lake Erie Coll., Painesville, Ohio, 1952-53; asst. to pres. St. John's Coll., Annapolis, Md., 1953-54, tutor, treas., 1954-59, v.p., tutor, 1959-61; pres. Cornell Coll., Mt. Vernon, Iowa, 1961-67, Boston U., 1967-70, Coll. Entrance Exam. Bd., N.Y.C., 1970-73, New Coll., Sarasota, Fla., 1973-75, Stephens Coll., Columbia, Mo., 1975-83, Ringling Sch. Art and Design, Sarasota, Fla., 1984-96, interim pres., 1998-99, pres. emeritus, 1996—; dir. Ringling Ctr. for the Cultural Arts FSU, 2001—. Adv. bd. Sun Bank. Exhibiting artist. Trustee New Coll. Found., U. South Fla., Sarasota, 1973—, Marie Selby Bot. Gardens, 1984—, John and Mable Ringling Mus. Art, 1991-93; bd. dirs. Fla. Ind. Coll. Fund, 1984-96, Fla. Assn. Colls. and Univs., 1984-96. With USAAF, 1943-46. Mem. Am. Acad. Arts and Scis., Assn. Ind. Coll. Art and Design (trustee 1991-96), Nat. Assn. Schs. Art and Design (v.p. 1993-96), Ind. Colls. and Univs. Fla. (bd. dirs. 1984-96), Univ. Club Sarasota, Kiwanis, Phi Beta Kappa (hon.), Phi Delta Theta. Office: Ringling Sch Art and Design 2700 N Tamiami Trl Sarasota FL 34234-5895

CHRISTMAN, DONALD RAY, special education educator; b. Sheridan, Wyo., Aug. 22, 1960; s. Donald C. and Joan Kay (McGlothlin) C. BS in Spl. Edn. and Elem. Edn., Eastern Mont. Coll., 1984. Spl. edn. tchr. Fromberg (Mont.) Schs., 1984-90, Cody (Wyo.) Schs., 1990-93. Asst. coach football Fromberg High Sch., 1984-85, volleyball, 1985-89; coach boys' track, jr. high sch., Fromberg, 1985—; chmn. Community Edn., Fromberg, 1986, Fromberg Tchrs. Assn., 1985-87; educator, trainer Parent Drug Awareness, Teen Leadership Coalition Cody (Wyo.) Schs. Mem. Mont. Edn. Assn., Assn. for Supervision of Curriculum Devel. Roman Catholic. Avocations: research, writing, guitar, art, outdoors. Office: Eastside Sch Bleistein Ave Cody WY 82414

CHRISTMAN, JOLLEY BRUCE, educational research executive, educator; b. Greenville, S.C., Aug. 30, 1947; d. James McDuffie and Mamie (Jolley) Bruce; children: Andrew, Kate, Sarah. BA, Randolph-Macon Woman's Coll., 1969; MS in Edn., U. Pa., 1971, PhD, 1987. Cert. secondary English and social studies tchr., Pa.; cert. prin., Pa. Tchr. Phila. Sch. Dist., 1970-75; lectr., cons. Grad. Sch. Edn. U. Pa., Phila., 1975-84; rsch. assoc. Phila. Sch. Dist., 1985-90, cons., 1990-92; pres. Rsch. for Action, Phila., 1992—. Bd. dirs. Coun. on Anthropology and Edn. Author: Anthropology and Education Quarterly, 1987, (chpt.) Speaking the Language of Power, 1993. Bd. dirs. Community Edn. Ctr., Phila., 1993—, Grad. Sch. Edn. Alumni Assn., U. Pa., Phila., 1990—. Recipient Ethnographic Evaluation award Am. Anthrop. Assn., 1992. Democrat. Episcopalian. Office: Rsch for Action 3701 Chestnut St Philadelphia PA 19104

CHRISTMAN, LUTHER PARMALEE, retired dean, consultant; b. Summit Hill, Pa., Feb. 26, 1915; s. Elmer and Elizabeth (Barnicoat) Christman; m. Dorothy Mary Black, Dec. 5, 1939; children: Gary, Judith, Lillian. Grad., Pa. Hosp. Sch. Nursing for Men, 1939; BS, Temple U., 1948, EdM, 1952; PhD, Mich. State U., 1965; LHD (hon.), Thomas Jefferson U., 1980; DSc (hon.), Grand Valley State U., 1998. Cons. Mich. Dept. Mental Health, Lansing, 1956—63; assoc. prof. psychiat. nursing U. Mich., 1963—67; rsch. assoc. Inst. Social Rsch., U. Mich., 1963—67; prof. nursing and sociology, dean nursing Vanderbilt U., 1967—72; DON Vanderbilt U. Med. Ctr. Hosp., 1967—72; prof. sociology Rush Coll. Health Scis., Chgo.; sr. scientist Rush-Presbyn.-St. Luke's Med. Ctr.; prof. nursing, v.p. nursing affairs Coll. Nursing Rush U., 1972—87; dean Rush U. Coll. Nursing, 1972—87, dean emeritus, 1987—; sr. advisor to pres. Ctr. of Nursing, Am. Hosp. Assn., 1989; pres. Christman-Cornesky & Assocs., 1990—94; adj. prof. Vanderbilt U., 1991—. Chmn. planning com. 1st Midwest Conf. Psychiat. Nursing, Mpls., 1956; cons. cmty. svcs. and rsch. br. NIMH, 1963—66, mem. team to survey mental health facilities of Colo., 1982, mem. team to survey mental health facilities of Ga., 84; psychiat. rsch. project So. Regional Edn. Bd., 1964—67; mem., workshop leader White House Conf. on Children, 1970; nursing panel Nat. Commn. for Study Nursing and Nursing Edn., 1968—70; regional med. programs rev. com. dept. health, edn. and welfare Health Svcs. and Mental Health Adminstrn., 1968—72; cons. dept. medicine and surgery VA Ctrl. Office, 1968—71, 1974—77; panel nurse cons. to com. on nursing AMA, 1968—71; health svcs. adv. com. Am. Assn. Med. Colls., 1968—71; acting com. pub. health Am. Health Found., 1970—72; membership com. Inst. Medicine-NAS, 1972—76, com. on edn. in health professions, 1973—75; mem. S.D. Bd. Nursing, Tenn. Bd. Nursing; cons. in field. Contbr. numerous articles to profl. jours. Named Elinor Frances Reed Disting. Vis. Prof., U. Tenn., Memphis, 2000, Luther Christman Endowed scholar in his honor, Rush Coll. Nursing, 2002; recipient Old Master, Purdue U., 1985, Coun. of Specialists in Psychiat. and Mental Health Nursing award, 1980, Hon. Recognition award, Ill. Nurses Assn., 1987, Edith Copeland Founders award for creativity, 1981, History Makers in Nursing award, Ctr. for Advancement of Nursing Practice, Beth Israel Hosp./Mass. Gen. Hosp., 1992, Lifetime Achievement award, Sigma Theta Tau, 1992, Disting. Alumnus award, Temple U., 1992, Rush U., 1997, Coll. Social Scis. Outstanding Alumnus award, Mich. State U., 1999, Hon. Recognition award, Nat. Academicians of Practice, 1996, Cert. of Appreciation, Marshall County Adult Edn., 1997, Lifetime Achievement award, Tenn. Nurses Assn., 2002. Fellow: AAAS, Soc. Applied Anthropology, Inst. Medicine Chgo., Am. Acad. Nrusing (Living Legend award 1995); mem.: ANA (3d v.p., Jesse M. Scott award 1985), AACN (life Marguerite Rodgers Kinney award 2002), Nat. Acad. Practice (chmn. acad. nursing 1985—92, sec. 1992—96, Disting. Practitioner award 1985, Cert. of Appreciation 1995), Biomed. Engrng. Soc., N.Y. Acad. Scis., Inst. Medicine, Soc. Gen. Sys. Rsch., Am. Sociol. Assn., Mich. Nurses' Assn. (pres. 1961—65), Alpha Kappa Delta, Alpha Omega Alpha (hon.). Home and Office: 5535 Nashville Hwy Chapel Hill TN 37034-2074 E-mail: lchristman@united.net.

CHRISTMAN, SHARON ANN, elementary school educator; b. Greenville, Pa., Sept. 28, 1957; d. Ronald Paul and Dorothy Janet (Ramsey) C. BS in Art Edn., Edinboro State Coll., 1979; MA, U. Ala., Tuscaloosa, 1992; AA EDS, 1995. Nat. bd. cert. tchr. Tchr. art K-6th grade Mountain Brook Schs.,

Birmingham, Ala., 1980—. Designer: (craft book) Christmas Is Coming, 1986, 87, 88, 90, 94. Recipient Fulbright-Hays scholar, Turkey, 1999. Mem. Nat. Art Edn. Assn., Internat. Soc. Edn. through Art, Kappa Delta Pi. Avocations: painting, travel, outdoors. Office: Mountain Brook Elem 3020 Cambridge Rd Birmingham AL 35223-1225

CHRISTMAS, WILLIAM ANTHONY, internist, educator; b. Montreal, June 5, 1939; came to U.S., 1946; s. William Richard and Marcelle (Hudon) C.; m. Maribeth Hanson, July 14, 1962 (dec. Feb. 2001); children: William, Ann, Gillian, Ira; m. Margaret Raye, June 21, 2003. AB, Bowdoin Coll., 1961; MD, Boston U., 1965. Diplomate Am. Bd. Internal Medicine. Mixed medicine intern Sinai Hosp., Balt., 1965-66; resident in internal medicine Med. Ctrs. Hosps. Vt., Burlington, 1966-68; pvt. practice, Bennington, Vt., 1972-77; med. dir. univ. health svcs., asst. prof. medicine U. Rochester, N.Y., 1977-81; NIH fellow in infectious diseases U. Vt., Burlington, 1968-69, dir. Student Health Ctr., 1981-93, clin. asst. prof. medicine, 1983-89, clin. assoc. prof., 1989-93; assoc. clin. prof. cmty./family medicine/dir. student health Duke U., Durham, NC, 1994—2002, clin. prof. cmty./family medicine, 2002—. Sr. assoc. cons. The Spelman & Johnson Group. Cons. editor Jour. Am. Coll. Health, 1985—; contbr. articles to med. jours. Pres., bd. dirs. State Com. Vt. YMCA, Burlington, 1983-91; bd. dirs. Greater Burlington YMCA, 1990-93, Vt. Epilepsy Assn., Rutland, 1990-93; active Vt. Coalition for Disability Rights, 1991-93; chmn. Measles Mumps Rubella Varicella (MMRV) Action Group, Nat. Coalition for Adult Immunizations, 1995-98. Fellow ACP, Am. Coll. Health Assn. (pres. 1987-88, Ruth Boynton award 1989, Edward Hitchcock award 2001), Infectious Diseases Soc. Am. (emeritus); mem. Am. Coll. Health Found. Bd. (chmn. 1998-2003), New England Coll. Health Assn. (pres. 1985-86), Vt. Med. Soc., So. Coll. Health Assn. (pres. 1998-99). Avocations: bread baking, medical history. Office: Duke U Student Health Ctr PO Box 2899 Durham NC 27710-0001 E-mail: bill.christmas@duke.edu.

CHRISTOFIDES, FOTINE, parochial school educator; b. N.Y.C., July 12, 1948; s. Sergios and Theodora C. BA, Queens Coll., Flushing, N.Y., 1970, MA, 1972; PhD, CUNY, 1978; BA in Theology, Ind. Bible Coll., Indpls., 1985. Tchr. Jamaica (N.Y.) Day Sch., 1972—; adminstrv. asst. Bethel United Pentecostal Ch., Old Westbury, NY, 1984—. Mem. Pi Delta Phi. Avocations: singing, songwriting gospel music. also: Jamaica Day Sch 84-35 152nd St Jamaica NY 11432-1972 Home: # 3 4554 Bell Blvd Bayside NY 11361-3355 Office: Bethel United Pentecostal Ch 357 Jericho Tpke Old Westbury NY 11568-1411

CHRISTOPHER, MICHAEL MAYER, secondary education development director; b. Denver, Nov. 3, 1949; s. Charles Harry and Margaret Ann (Mayer) C.; m. Patricia A. Baldwin, Jan. 5, 1980; children: Michelle, Peter, Andrew. MusB, Cornell Coll., 1971; MA, U. Iowa, 1973; ABD, SUNY, Buffalo, 1975. Instr. music theory St. Louis (Mo.) Conservatory of Music, 1975-77, dir. admissions, registrar, 1977-84, assoc. dean, 1984-89, dir. devel., 1989-90, Holland Hall Sch., Tulsa, 1990—. Presenter Alumni Program Coun., N.Y., 1993-94, Ind. Schs. Assn. S.W., Dallas, 1994. Composer of music. Pres. bd. dirs. Sch. Dist. of Affton, St. Louis, 1984-89; v.p. Child Abuse Network, Tulsa; pres. Mill Creek Pond Homeowners Assn., Tulsa. Mem. Coun. for Advancement and Support Edn., Nat. Soc. Fundraising Execs., LEadership Tulsa. Office: Holland Hall Sch 5666 E 81st St Tulsa OK 74137-2099

CHRISTOPHER, RENNY TERESA, liberal studies educator; b. Newport Beach, Calif., Mar. 4, 1957; d. Richard T. and Bebi (Ruhland) C. BA, Mills Coll., 1982; MA, San Jose (Calif.) State U., 1986; PhD, U. Calif., Santa Cruz, 1992. Features editor Horse Lover's Nat. Mag., Burlingame, Calif., 1976-79; prodn. editor Lit. of Liberty, Menlo Park, Calif., 1982; graphic artist Gilroy (Calif.) Dispatch, 1983-84; substitute tchr. Morgan Hill (Calif.) Unified Sch. Dist., 1984-85; lectr. San Jose State U., 1986-87; instr. Cabrillo Community Coll., Aptos, Calif., 1988—; asst. prof. Calif. State U., 1995-98, assoc. prof., 1998—. Film reviewer Matrix Women's Newspaper, Santa Cruz, 1990—; fiction editor Quarry West, U. Calif., 1990-91, advisor Giao Diem/Crosspoint Student Pub., 1991-95. Author: The Viet Nam War/The American War, 1995, Viet Nam and California, 1998; author poems and short story; contbr. articles to profl. jours. Yanklee Meml. fellow San Jose State U., 1985, U. Calif. fellow, 1991. Mem. Modern Lang. Assn., Am. Studies Assn., Popular Culture Assn., Nat. Coun. Tchrs. of English. Avocations: running, bicycling. Office: Calif State U English Dept 1 Univ Dr Camarillo CA 93012

CHRISTOPHERSON, MYRVIN FREDERICK, college president; b. Milltown, Wis., July 21, 1939; s. Fred J. and Inger J. (Haug) C.; m. Anne Christine Marking, June 10, 1967; children: Kirsten, Berit, Bjorn, Nisse. BA, Dana Coll., 1961; MS, Purdue U., 1963, PhD, 1965; DD (hon.), Wartburg Theol. Sem., 1998. Teaching asst., instr. Purdue U., West Lafayette, Ind., 1961-65; asst. prof. speech U. Wis., Madison, 1965-69, assoc. prof. communication Stevens Point, 1969-76, prof. communication, 1976-86, assoc. dean. fine arts and communication, 1970-86; pres. Dana Coll., Blair, Nebr., 1986—. Cons. Wis. Telephone, Milw., 1968-78, AT&T, N.Y.C., 1969-71, 1st Fin. Corp., Stevens Point, 1980-86; commr. Nebr. Coordinating Commn. for Post Sec. Edn., 1989-91; mem. N.E. jud. nominating commn. Ct. Appeals No. 3 Steering Com.; bd. dirs. Found. for Ind. Higher Edn., 2003—; mem. adv. bd. Thrivent Fin. For Lutherans, 2002—. Author: Speaker's Trainer's Guide, 1970, The Company Speaker, 1979; editor: Jour. of the Wis. Communication Assn., 1978—80. Mem. adv. bd. The Lutheran, 1987—94, chmn., 1992—94; bd. dirs. Blair Cmty. Found., 1999—, Planned Giving Svcs., Nebr., chmn., 1992—94; ann. fund appeal chmn. Meml. Cmty. Hosp., 1994; trustee Palmer Chirpractic U., 1998—; mem. coun. pres. Evangel. Luth. Ch. in Am., 1999—, vice chmn., 1999—2000, chmn., 2000—, memls. com. churchwide assembly, 2001; mem. pastoral call com. First Luth. Ch., 1995, mem. ch. coun., 1999; mem. Nebr. Ednl. Fin. Authority, 1991—, chmn., 1992—99, 2001—, vice chmn., 2002—. Inducted into Wall of Honor, Unity High Sch., Polk County, Wis.; fellow Palmer Coll. Chiropractic, Palmer Coll. Chiropractic-West; named Knight of The Order of the Dannebrog, Queen Margrethe II of Denmark, 1997. Mem.: Found. for Independent Higher Edn. (bd. dirs. 2003—), Coun. of Pres., Luth. Edn. Conf. N.Am. (vice chmn. 1994—95, chmn. 1995—96), Nebr. Ind. Coll. Found. (exec. com. 1990—92, vice chmn. 1992—93, chmn. 1994—95), Nebr. Bus. Higher Edn. Forum, Nat. Assn. Intercoll. Athletics (couns. of pres. 1999—), North Ctrl. Assn. Colls. and Schs. (cons.-evaluator 1997—, accreditation rev. coun. 2001—, team chair 2002—), Nebr. Ednl. TV Coun. for higher Edn., Assn. Ind. Colls. Nebr. (chmn. 1992—93), Nat. Assn. Ind. Colls. and Univs. (bd. dirs. 1997—99, 2003—). Avocations: international travel, reading, writing, antique collecting and refinishing, study of theology. Office: Dana Coll Office of Pres Blair NE 68008

CHRISTY, CHARLES WESLEY, III, industrial engineering educator; b. Chester County, Pa., Apr. 29, 1942; s. Charles Wesley Jr. and Violet R. (Pierpont) C.; m. D. Jean Cullmann, Jan. 25, 1972; children: Richard Townsend, Charles Wesley IV, Michael Pierpont. BS, Widener U., 1973; MBA, Temple U., 1980. Chmn. indsl. engring. tech. Del. Tech. and C.C., Newark, 1970—. Pres. Pierpont Industries, Inc., Wilmington, Del., 1985—; adj. assoc. prof. U. Del., Newark, 1994; examiner Del. Quality Award, Wilmington, 1994. Bd. dirs., past pres. Opportunity Ctr., Inc., Wilmington, 1972—. Mem. Am. Inst. Indsl. Engrs. (bd. dirs. Del. chpt. 1970—, past pres.), Am. Soc. Quality Control. Home: 11 Harlech Dr Wilmington DE 19807-2507 Office: Del Tech & CC 400 Stanton Christiana Rd Newark DE 19713-2111 E-mail: cchristy@hopi.dtcc.edu.

CHRISTY, SHELIA, university official, information specialist; b. Mexico, Mo., Feb. 25, 1957; d. William Arch and Gerald Jean (Bailey) Colley; m. Charles David Rumbaugh, Aug. 17, 1974 (div. Jan. 17, 1996); 1 child, Amanda Nicole; m. Patrick Charles Christy, June 14, 1997. BS in Elem. Edn., U. Mo., 1982, MEd in Curriculum and Instrn. Elem., 1984, PhD in Ednl. Tech., 1997. Cert. tchr. grade K-8, media specialist grades K-12. Instr. computing William Woods Coll., Fulton, Mo., 1985-90; edn. tech. Columbia (Mo.) Pub. Schs., 1992-95; cons. PC software installation and tng. U. Mo. Health Scis., ITS Support Analysis, Columbia, 1996-98; edn. and consulting staff devel. specialist U. Mo. Health Scis., Columbia, 1998-2001; staff devel. specialist, UM Morenet U. Mo., Columbia, 2001—. Cons. U. No. Iowa, Cedar Falls, 1993-94, Columbia (Mo.) Cath. Schs., 1994. 4-H project leader Hardin Huslers, Fulton, 1989—. Devel. grantee William Woods Coll., Fulton, 1988-89, Pvt.-Parent Group, Columbia Pub. Schs., 1994-95, Software grantee MicroMedia, U. Mo., 1991-92, NATO researcher workshop tech. grantee, 1994. Mem. Internat. Soc. for Tech. in Edn. (conf. com. 1993-95), Assn. for Ednl. Comm. and Tech. (com. mem. 1994—). Avocations: reading, walking, music, cooking, basket weaving. Home and Office: 8070 Mt Zion Church Rd Hallsville MO 65255 E-mail: christys@missouri.edu.

CHRZANOWSKA-JESKE, MALGORZATA EWA, electrical engineering educator, consultant; b. Warsaw, Nov. 26, 1948; came to U.S., 1985; d. Waclaw and Halina (Siedlanowska) Chrzanowska; m. Witold Norbert Jeske, July 21, 1978; children: Marcin, Olaf. MS in Electronics, Warsaw Tech. U., 1972; MS in Elec. Engring., Tuskegee (Ala.) Inst., 1976; PhD in Elec. Engring., Auburn (Ala.) U., 1988. Rsch. and tchg. instr. Warsaw Tech. U., 1972-75; rsch. and tchg. asst. Tuskegee Inst., 1975-76, Auburn U., 1976-77, rsch. asst., postdoctoral fellow, 1985-89; sr. rschr. Inst. Electron Tech., Warsaw, 1977-82, CAD project leader, 1983-85; asst. prof. Portland (Oreg.) State U., 1989-95, assoc. prof. elec. engring., 1995-2000, prof. elec. engring., 2000—. Cons. Inst. Electron Tech., Warsaw, 1985—; lectr. Tuskegee Inst., 1977; profl/lectr. Oreg. Ctr. for Advance tech., Beaverton, 1991-94. Contbr. articles to profl. jours. Troop leader Polish Scout Assn., Warsaw, 1958-66; sci. and activity com. chmn. Polish Student Assn., Warsaw, 1966-75; mem. Solidarity, Poland, 1980-85. Recipient First Level award Polish Dept. Sci., Higher Edn. and Tech., 1983; named to Women of Distinction in Engring. Columbia coun. Girl Scouts U.S., 1993. Mem. Assn. Computing Machinery, Internat. Conf. on Electronics, Circuits and Sys. (tech. program co-chair 2002), IEEE (sr., Oreg. sect. exec. com. 1994-96, sr. mem.), IEEE Electron Device Soc. (chair edn. com. Oreg. sect. 1989-96), IEEE Circuits and Sys. Soc., Eta Kappa Nu. Achievements include research in low temperature semiconductor device simulation; comprehensive logic and layout synthesis for VLSI and field programmable gate arrays. Office: Portland State Univ Dept Elec Engring 1800 SW 6th Ave Portland OR 97201-5204 E-mail: jeske@ee.pdx.edu.

CHRZANOWSKI, ROSE-ANN CANNIZZO, art educator; b. Bklyn., Mar. 13, 1952; d. Francis Salvatore and Vincenza Pilaro Cannizzo; m. Raymond David Chrzanowski; 1 child, Karen Kuczenski. BA, CUNY, Bklyn., 1974; MS, Fordham U., 1977; postgrad., So. Conn. State U., 1990. Cert. in elem. edn. N.Y. Permanent Tchg. Cert., Conn. Profl. Tchg. Cert., in art Conn. Profl. Tchg. Cert., art EAYA. 3d grade tchr. St. Michael Sch., Bklyn., 1974—78; art tchr. Naugatuck Elem. Schs., Naugatuck, Conn., 1978—90; tchr. City Hill Mid. Sch., Naugatuck, 1990—2000, Naugatuck H.S., 2000—. Tchr., tutor supr. Naugatuck Youth Svcs., 1978—84; edn. program coord. Human Resources Devel. Agy., Naugatuck, 1985—87; adj. prof. Teikyo Post U., Waterbury, Conn., 1996; mem. adv. coun. Celebration Excellence, New Haven, 1998—. Contbg. author: Doing What's Right in the Middle, Promising Practices of Schools with Middle Grades, 1999. Chmn. Naugatuck Arts Commn., 1996—98; nat. tchr. forum rep. State Dept. Edn., 2001. Recipient Emeritus award, Celebration Excellence, 1999. Mem.: NEA, Conn. Art Edn. Assn., Nat. Art Edn. Assn., Phi Delta Kappa. Office: Naugatuck HS 543 Rubber Ave Naugatuck CT 06770 Personal E-mail: rayrochrz@earthlink.net.

CHU, MON-LI HSIUNG, dermatology educator; b. Kwangtung, China, July 27, 1948; came to U.S. 1970; d. Tsun-Shiang and Ah-Wha (Yang) Hsiung; m. Shaw-Chang Chu, Nov. 10, 1972; children: Emily, Andy. BS, Nat. Taiwan U., 1970; PhD, U. Fla., 1975. Adj. asst. prof. U. Med./Dentistry N.J.-Rutgers Med. Sch., Piscataway, N.J., 1979-84, adj. assoc. prof., 1984-86; assoc. prof. Thomas Jefferson U., Phila., 1986-90, prof. molecular biology, 1990-96, prof. dermatology, 1996—. Contbr. over 150 articles to profl. jours. NIH grantee, 1986—. Mem. AAAS, Am. Soc. Biochemistry and Molecular Biology. Achievements include isolation and characterization of cDNAs and genomic DNAs for many human collagens, including Type I, III, VI, XVI collagens; definition of the first deletion mutation in type I collagen in a patient with Osteogenesis Imperfecta. Office: Thomas Jefferson U 233 S 10th St Philadelphia PA 19107-5541

CHU, STEVEN, physics educator; b. St. Louis, Feb. 28, 1948; s. Ju Chin and Ching Chen (Li) C.; children: Geoffrey, Michael. BS in Physics, AB in Math., U. Rochester, 1970; PhD in Physics, U. Calif., Berkeley, 1976. Post doctoral fellow U. Calif., Berkeley, 1976-78; mem. tech. staff Bell Labs., Murray Hill, N.J., 1978-83; head quantum electronics rsch. dept. AT&T Bell Labs., Holmdel, N.J., 1983-87; prof. physics and applied physics Stanford (Calif.) U., 1987—, Frances and Theodore Geballe prof. physics and applied physics, 1990—93, chmn. physics dept., 1999—2001. Morris Loeb lectr. Harvard U., Cambridge, Mass., 1987-88; vis. prof. Coll. de France, fall 1990; Richtmeyer Meml. lectr., 1990. Contbr. papers in laser spectroscopy and atomic physics, especially laser cooling and trapping, and precision spectroscopy of leptonic atoms, polymer and biophysics. Recipient Humboldt sr. scientist award, Sci. for Art prize, 1995; co-recipient King Faisal prize for sci., 1993, Nobel prize for physics, 1997; Woodrow Wilson fellow 1970, doctoral fellow NSF, 1970-74, postdoctoral fellow 1977-78, Guggenheim fellow, 1996. Fellow Am. Phys. Soc. (Herbert P. Broida prize for laser spectroscopy 1987, chair laser sci. topical group 1989, A.L. Schawlow prize 1994), Optical Soc. Am. (William F. Meggars award 1994), Am. Acad. Arts and Scis.; mem. NAS, Academica Sinica, Am. Philos. Soc., Chinese Acad. Sci. (fgn.), Korean Acad. Sci. and Tech. (fgn.).

CHUANG, TSU-YI, dermatologist, epidemiologist, educator; b. Amoy, China, May 21, 1946; s. Hsi and Kia-Ling (Hwang) C.; m. Lydia Ling-Chuan Lee, Dec. 22, 1973; children: Chester, Nancy. B of Medicine, Nat. Taiwan U., Taipei, 1971; MPH, U. Wash., 1978. Diplomate Am. Bd. Dermatology, Am. Bd. Preventive Medicine. From asst. prof. to assoc. prof. dermatology U. Wis., Madison, 1984-92; chief dermatology svc. Middleton VA Med. Ctr., Madison, 1984-90; assoc. prof. dermatology Wright State U., Dayton, Ohio, 1990-95, dir. immunopathology lab., 1994-95; dir. dermatology clinic Frederick A. White Health Ctr., Dayton, 1995; prof. dermatology Ind. U., Indpls., 1995—, med. dir. melanoma program, 1996—, Arthur L. Norins prof., dir. dermatology clinic, 1999—2001. Vis. prof. Nat. Taiwan U., Taipei, 1991-97. Co-author: Conn's Current Therapy, 1992, The Challenge of Dermato-Epidemiology, 1997, Sleisenger & Fordtran's Gastrointestinal and Liver Disease, 2002; editl. cons. Arch Dermatol., Chgo., 1990-99; editor Dermatologica Sinica, Taipei, 1994-96; contbr. over 100 articles to profl. jours. Pres. Rochester (Minn.) Chinese Culture Assn., 1980-82; v.p. Orgn. of Chinese Ams., Madison, 1986-90; pres. Midwest Chinese Christian Assn., Dayton, 1993-94, Indpls., 1996-97. Rsch. grantee U. Wis., 1985-89, VA merit rev. bd. grantee Dept. Vets. Affairs, 1986-88, 90-94; recipient Burdette-Kunkel award Mary Margaret Walther Program for Cancer Care Rsch., 1996-97. Fellow Am. Acad. Dermatology (editl. cons. Am. Acad. Dermatology jour. 1986-2001), Am. Soc. for Dermatol. Surgery; mem. Soc. for Investigative Dermatology, Ind. Chinese Profls. Assn. (pres. 1998). Achievements include first historical cohort study of human papilloma virus infection in U.S. in a defined population, first historical cohort study of genital herpes virus infection in U.S. in a defined population, first incidence study of polymyalgia rheumatica in the U.S. in a defined population, first population-based incidence study of skin cancer in U.S. in two well-defined populations. Office: 1801 N Senate Blvd Ste 745 Indianapolis IN 46202 Home: 7618 Torbay Cir Indianapolis IN 46254-9659

CHUGH, RAM L. economics educator; b. Leiah, Panjab, India, Feb. 5, 1935; came to U.S., 1966; s. Ishwar Das and Hari (Dhingra) C.; m. Seema Gandhi, May 7, 1966; 1 child, Pooja H. BA, Panjab U., 1960, MA in Econs., 1962; PhD in Econs., Wayne State U., 1970. Asst. prof. econs. SUNY, Potsdam, 1970-73, assoc. prof., 1973-79, prof., 1979-91, disting. svc. prof., 1991—, spl. asst. to the pres. for pub. affairs, dir. rural svc., 1990—. Co-author: Black Economy in India, 1986; author: Higher Education and Regional Development, 1992; contbr. articles to profl. jours. Recipient Commr. Outstanding Svc. award N.Y. Dept. Social Svcs., 1993, Cert. Merit N.Y. State Gov.'s award for excellence in rural svc., 1994, Pres.'s award Excellence in Pub. Svc., 1994; sr. rsch. fellow Rockefeller Inst. Govt., Albany, N.Y., 1986. Mem. Am. Econ. Assn., So. Regional Sci. Assn., Adirondack North Country Assn. (bd. dirs. Sarnac Lake, N.Y. chpt. 1984-88), Phi Kappa Phi. Avocations: music, travel, reading, current events. Office: SUNY Potsdam Dept of Economics Potsdam NY 13676

CHUKSORJI, JEAN CAULFIELD, nursing educator; b. New Orleans, Feb. 23; d. Benjamin Caulfield and Alma (Crenshaw) Caulfield Adams; m. Ejimofor Chuksorji; children: Nneze, Blessed. BS, Dillard U.; MSN, U. Wash., 1967; school nurse program, U. Calif., San Francisco; cert. in gerontology, U. So. Calif., L.A.; postgrad., U. Calif., San Francisco. Cert. psychiat. nurse ANA. Clin. instr. Dillard U., New Orleans; supr. Flint Goodridge Hosp.; psychiatric nurse Neuro-Psychiatric Inst., UCLA; staff devel. Mount Zion Hosp., San Francisco, 1969-70; asst. prof./lectr. U. Calif., San Francisco, 1970-77; sch. nurse L.A. Unified Sch. Dist., 1977-78; prof. nursing East L.A. Coll., 1979—. Asst. chmn. nursing dept. East L.A. Coll., 1978—; instr. Calif. State U., San Fransisco Skill Ctr., 1977. Vol. ARC, chaplain Pan Hellanic coun.; mem. ladies aux. St. Peter Claver chpt. KC; bd. dirs. L.A. chpt. Jack and Jill Am., Inc.; active YMCA. Mem. AAUS, AAUP, APHA, LWV, NAACP, Nat. League for Nursing, Calif. Nurses Assn., Calif. Maternal Child Health Assn., Black Woman's Forum, Am. Assn. Women in Cmty. Jr. Colls., Coalition of 100 Black Women (L.A. chpt.), Am. Heart Assn. (past sec., treas.), Sigma Theta Tau. Home: PO Box 781134 Los Angeles CA 90016-9134

CHUKWU, ETHELBERT NWAKUCHE, mathematics educator; b. Mbano, Imo, Nigeria, Nov. 22, 1940; s. Nwachukwu Chukwu Uwaezuoke and Ihejere Theresa; m. Regina Chukwu Nyere, Dec. 26, 1966; children: Chika, Eze, Emeka, Uche, Obioma, Ndubuisi. BSc, Brown U., 1965; MSc, Nsukka U., Nigeria, 1973; PhD, Case Western Res. U., 1972. Asst. lectr. U. Nigeria, Nsukka, 1970; asst. prof. math. Cleve. State U., 1972-76, assoc. prof., 1976-78; prof. U. Jos, Nigeria, 1978-81, dean postgrad. studies, 1977-81; vice chancellor Fed. U. Tech., Yola, Nigeria, 1981-86; prof. math. N.C. State U., Raleigh, 1987—. Mem. Nat. UN Commn. on African Scholarship Program for Am. Univs. fellow, 1962-65. Author 3 books in field; assoc. editor Non-Linear Studies; contbr. articles to profl. jours. Mem. AAAS, Nigerian Math. Soc. (v.p. 1980-82), Math. Assn. Nigeria (pres. 1981-82), Am. Math. Soc., Math Assn. Am., N.Y. Acad. Scis., Am. Assn. for Advancement of Sci., Internat. Fedn. Nonlinear Analysts (mem. global com.), Sigma Xi, Sigma lota Rho. Roman Catholic. Address: NC State U Mathematics Dept Raleigh NC 27695-8205 E-mail: chukwu@math.ncsu.edu.

CHUKWUMERIJE, NKEMDIRIM, medical educator; b. Okigwe, Imo, Nigeria, Dec. 30, 1967; arrived in U.S., 1994; s. Pius and Beatrice Chukwumerije; m. Eukay Chukwumerije, July 14, 2001. NIB, BS, U. Nigeria, Enugu, 1991. Cert. internal medicine. Resident physician Muhlenberg Regional Med. Ctr./ U. Medicine Dentistry N.J.-Robert Wood Johnson Med. Ctr., Plainfield, 1997—2000; physician scholar UCLA Sch. Medicine, 2000—01; acad. hospitalist Cleve. Clinic Found., 2001—. Mem.: ACP (poster presenter 2000), Nat. Assn. Inpatient Physicians (poster presenter 2000). Avocations: reading, travel, soccer. Office: Cleve Clinic Found 9500 Euclid Rd Cleveland OH 44195

CHUMAS, LINDA GRACE, elementary school educator; b. Floral Park, NY, May 3, 1944; d. Vincent Armond and Alisandra (Simonelli) DeAngelis; m. Spero Nicholas Chumas; children: Spero Chris, Kara Alisandra. BS, Ea. Ky. U., 1967; MA, SUNY, New Paltz, 1983. Cert. health and phys. edn. Tchr. phys. edn. Valley Ctrl. H.S., Montgomery, N.Y., 1968-70, varsity girls tennis coach, 1968-70, jr. varsity girls sports coach, 1968-70, tchr. adult edn. and phys. edn., 1968-75; phys. edn. tchr. Leptondale Elem. Sch., Wallkill, N.Y., 1983—; aerobics, line dance tchr. Wallkill H.S. PTO, 1993-96, tchr. ballroom dancing, 1995-96; tchr. ballroom and line dancing Wallkill Reformed Church, Wallkill, 1996-98; tennis tchr. Town of Shawangunk Recreation, Wallkill, 1993-96; tchr. tennis and dance Wallkill Arts Cmty., 1996-98. Jump Rope for Heart coord. Am. Heart Assn., 1983—; mem. Wallkill Ctrl. Sch. Dist. Strategic Planning Com., 1991—; tchr. tennis Walkill Arts Cmty., summer, 1996-98; tchr. ballrm. dancing Mt. St. Mary's Coll., 1999—, Town of Newburgh Recreation program, 2001, Town of Hamptonburgh Sr. Citizens Ctr., 2001. Treas. Am. Field Svc., Wallkill, 1988-93; chair flower sales Am. Heart Assn., Leptondale Elem Sch., 1990-2001; co-dir. road race Shamrock Scramble, Wallkill, 1988-96; mem. Health and Safety Comm., Wallkill Central Sch. Dist., 1991-2001; solicitor Multiple Sclerosis Soc., Capital region, 1990-92, 97-2000, Am. Lung Assn., 1998; coord. Hoops for Heart program Am. Heart Assn., 1997—; mem Walkill Vol. Ambulance Corp., 1999. Recipient Outstanding Devel. award Am. Heart Assn., Kingston, N.Y., 1990, Straight from Heart flowers award 1992-96, Amazing Person award Elem. Physical Edn. Sect. N.Y. Assn. for Health, Physical Edn., Recreation and Dance, 1996. Mem. AAHPERD (mem. coun. svcs. for Ea. dist. assn. 1995-97), N.Y. State Assn. Health, Phys. Edn., Recreation and Dance (sec. 1993-95, Jump Rope for Heart Task Force 1992—, Jump Rope for Heart Catskill zone coord. 1992—, chairperson necrology 1996-98, Amazing Persons award 1996, Hoops for Heart AHA 1997—), N.Y. State United Tchrs. (health ins. rep. Ulster County 1991-2001), Nat. Dance Assn., Wallkill Woman's Club. Democrat. Greek Orthodox. Avocations: volleyball, tennis, gardening, home decorating, ballroom dancing. Home: PO Box 163 Wallkill NY 12589-0163 Office: Leptondale Elem Sch 48 Mill St Wallkill NY 12589-2803 Personal E-mail: LCNY44@aol.com.

CHUN, ARLENE DONNELLY, special education educator; b. Maspeth, N.Y., Dec. 10, 1952; d. William James Jr. and Marguerite Anna (Miller) Donnelly; m. Edward Howard Chun, Aug. 9, 1975; children: Christine, Jennifer, Scott. AA, Luther Coll., 1972; BA, Marymount Manhattan Coll., 1974; MA, C.W Post Coll., 1979; postgrad., Bklyn. Coll., 1989-91. Rsch. asst., adminstrv. asst. LaGuardia C.C., L.I. City, NY, 1975-77; substitute tchr. various sch. dists., Nassau County, NY, 1978-88; family day care provider, 1983-88; speech lang. therapist Sch. for Lang. and Comm. Devel., Glen Cove, NY, 1988—2003, Merrick UFSD, Birch Sch., NY, 2003—. C.W. Post Coll. fellow, 1978-79. Mem. N.Y. State Speech Hearing Lang. Assn., L.I. Speech Hearing Lang. Assn., N.Y. State Day Care Assn., Nassau County Day Care Assn., Coun. Exceptional Children, L.I. U. Alumni Assn. Lutheran. Avocations: crafts, camping, sewing, reading, plate collecting. Office: Sch for Lang and Communication Devel 100 Glen Cove Ave Glen Cove NY 11542-2818 Home: 83 Horn Ln Levittown NY 11756-3408

CHUN, JANG HO, science educator, researcher; b. Koyang, S. Korea, Nov. 23, 1948; s. Oak Bae Chun and Soon Im Min; m. Kyung Won Hong, June 28, 1980; children: Mi Jin, Jin Young. PhD, Stevens Inst.of Tech., N.J., 1980—84. Full prof. Kwangwoon U., Seoul, Korea (South), 1990—. Korea Sci. and Engring. Found. vis. scientist Princeton U., 1988—89; Korea Sci. and Engring. fellow, vis. scientist dept. applied chemistry U. Tokyo, 1994. Contbr. articles to profl. jours. Deacon Shiheung Presbyn. Ch., Seoul, Korea (South), 1993. Lance cpl. Korea Air Force, 1968—71, Osan. Recipient First Prize of Graduation, Kwangwoon U., 1975; Studying Abroad Scholarship, Korea Govt., 1980-1984, May 16 Scholarship, 1972-1974. Mem.: The Electrochem. Soc., Internat. Assn. for Hydrogen Energy, The Korean

Electrochem. Soc. (life; mem. of editl. bd. 2000). Christian. Achievements include research in the phase-shift method for the langmuir and frumkin adsorption isotherms of electroadsorbed hydrogens. Home: 296 Seoksu-dong Manangu Kyunggido Anyang 431-042 Republic of Korea Office: Kwangwoon U Dept Electronic Engring 447-1 Wolgyedong Nowongu Seoul 139-701 Republic of Korea Office Fax: +82-2-942-0107. E-mail: jhchun@daisy.kwangwoon.ac.kr.

CHUNG, ANN JANE ZANE MACDONALD, early childhood education educator, counselor; b. Bradford, Pa., Mar. 26, 1939; d. Robert William and Mildred Fenner (Morgan) Macdonald; m. Richard Paul Chung, Sept. 5, 1964; 1 child, John Robert. BS in Home Econs., Pa. State U., 1961; MA in Elem. Counseling and Guidance, Villanova U., 1977; cert. elem. edn. and early childhood, Temple U., 1973. Tchr. Sch. Dist. Phila., 1961-64, lead tchr., 1965—; elem. guidance counselor Blankenburg Elem. Sch., Phila., 1993-94; lead tchr. Durham Elem. Sch., Phila., 1994—. Cons. early childhood edn., counseling and guidance various schs. Phila. Sch. Dist., 1964—. Tchr. Korean Presbyn. Ch., Chestnut Hill, Pa. Mem. Am. Personnel and Guidance Assn. Avocations: gardening, aerobics, photography. Home: 13 Mary Bell Rd Norristown PA 19403-1937

CHUNG, ED B(AIK), pathologist, educator; b. Kilchoo, Korea, Mar. 16, 1928; came to U.S. 1954; s. Hi Sam and Ok Bong (Lee) C.; m. Ok Hyung Kang, Nov. 9, 1958; children: Sophia M., Jeanne M., Theodore D., Virginia M., Esther K. MD, Severance Union Med. Coll., Seoul, Korea, 1951; MS in Pathology, Georgetown U., 1956, PhD in Pathology, 1958. Diplomate Am. Bd. Pathology in Anatomic Pathology and Clin. Pathology. Resident in pathology Georgetown U. Med. Ctr., Washington, 1954-58; instr. in pathology Georgetown U., Washington, 1958-61, asst. prof. pathology, 1961-63; assoc. prof. pathology Howard U., Washington, 1964-70, prof. pathology, 1970-98; prof. emeritus pathology Howard U. Hosp., Washington, 1999—, attending pathologist, 1964-98, dir. surg. pathology, 1968-98. Cons. Glen Dale (Md.) Hosp., 1968-74, Coroner's Office, Washington, 1969-71; vis. prof. soft tissue pathology, Padua (Italy) U. Inst. Anatomic and Histologic Pathology, 1989. Contbr. numerous articles to profl. jours. Bd. dirs. Washington Korean Community Svc. Ctr., 1974—, vice chmn. 1974-81, chmn. 1981-86; trustee the Korean Sch., Washington, 1971-73; chmn. bd. deacons Washington Korean Bapt. Ch., 1959-69; elder Full Gospel (Assembly of God) First Ch., Washington, 1979—. Capt. Republic of Korea Army Med. Corps, 1952-54. Fellow Am. Soc. Clin. Pathologists, Coll. Am. Pathologists; mem. U.S. and Can. Acad. of Pathology (mem. emeritus), Washington Soc. Pathologists. E-mail: ebchung@juno.com.

CHUNG, KING-THOM, microbiologist, educator; b. Tou Fen, Taiwan, Apr. 25, 1943; came to U.S., 1966; s. Aa-Yuan and Yi-Ing (Buu) C.; m. Lan-Seng Fang, Oct. 27, 1973; children: Theodore, Serena. MA, U. Calif., Santa Cruz, 1967; PhD, U. Calif., Davis, 1972. Scientist Frederick (Md.) Cancer Rsch. Ctr., 1972-77; vis. asst. prof. Food Sci. Inst. Purdue U., West Lafayette, Ind., 1977-78; assoc. prof. Tunghai U., Taichung, Taiwan, 1978-80; prof., chmn. dept. Soochow U., Taipei, Taiwan, 1980-87, dean, 1983-87; vis. scientist U.S. Meat Animal Rsch. Ctr., Clay Center, Nebr., 1987-88; assoc. prof. biology U. Memphis, 1988-93, prof., 1993—. Mem. adv. bd. Dept. Agr. and Forestry, Taiwan Provincial Govt., Taichung, 1982-87; exec. sec. Internat. Symposium on Biogas, Microalgae and Livestock Wastes, Taipei, 1980. Author: (in Chinese) Environment and Pollution, 1987, Intellectuals and Academic Education, 1987, Stories of 25 World Leading Microbiologists, 1996; contbr. articles to profl. jours. Grantee Am. Inst. Cancer Rsch., 1992. Fellow Am. Acad. Microbiology; mem. Am. Soc. Microbiology, Am. Acad. Microbiology, Inst. Food Technologists, Sigma Xi. Achievements include the illustration of the significance of azo reduction in the azo dye mutagenesis and carcinogenesis, quantitative structure activity relationships (QSAR) of aromatic amines, tannins and health, food safety, and history of microbiology. Office: U Memphis Dept Microbiol And Molecular Memphis TN 38152-0001 E-mail: kchung@memphis.edu.

CHUNG, TAE-SOO, physiatrist, educator; b. Tae-Gu, Korea, Feb. 1, 1937; came to U.S., 1964, naturalized, 1978; s. Sang-Taik and Chuwan (Ha) C.; m. Kwangja Park, Apr. 3, 1965; children: Peter, Alexander. MD, Yonsei U., Seoul, 1963. Diplomate Am. Bd. Phys. Medicine and Rehab. Chief resident in rehab. medicine NYU Med. Ctr., N.Y.C., 1967; fellow in rehab. medicine N.Y. Med. Coll., 1968; clin. dir. Children's Rehab. Ctr., St. John's, Nfld., Can., 1969-71; chief spinal cord injury svc., chief children's rehab. unit N.Y. Med. Coll., 1971-75, clin. asst. prof., 1971-80; dir. rehab. unit Newton (N.J.) Meml. Hosp., 1981—. Clin. asst. prof. U. Medicine and Dentistry N.J., Newark, 1976—; mem. N.J. Phys. Therapy Bd., 1995—2001; cons. Sussex County Edn. Commn., 1980—95, Kessler Inst. Rehab., 1998—, Hackettstown (N.J.) Cmty. Hosp., 1999—. Mem. N.J. Soc. Phys. Medicine and Rehab. (sec. 1979-80, pres. 1083-84), Am. Korean Med. Soc. (v.p. N.Y. met. area 1979-80, news editor 1989-90), Am. Acad. Phys. Medicine and Rehab., N.J. Acad. Medicine. Office: 400 W Blackwell St Dover NJ 07801-2525 E-mail: tschungmd@aol.com.

CHUNG, TCHANG-BOK, management analyst, consultant; b. Manchuria, China, May 13, 1942; came to U.S., 1967; s. In-Taek and Yang Rhe (Rhee) C.; m. On Ja Hwang, Nov. 22, 1967. BS, Seoul Nat. U., 1965; M Phys. Edn., Springfield (Mass.) Coll., 1971; MA, Columbia U., 1979, EdM, 1982, EdD, 1986. Cert. pool operator. Dir. phys. edn. Westfield (N.J.) YMCA, 1972-74, sr. program dir., 1974-77; instr. Mont. State U., Bozeman, 1977-78; pool dir. Columbia U. Tchrs. Coll., N.Y.C., 1978-82; assoc. exec. dir. Darien (Conn.) YMCA, 1982-84; pres., cons. The Tchang Group, Springfield, N.J., 1984-86; mgmt. analyst Community and Family Support Ctr. U.S. Army, Seoul, 1987—. Vis. prof. Seoul Nat. U., 1987—; YMCA rep. AAU, 1975-77; tech. officer Seoul Olympic Games, 1988; presenter Olympic Sci. Congresss, Chunan, Republic of Korea, 1988. Contbr. chpt. to book and ency. Mem. Westfield Spl. Pub. Sch. Com., 1973. Scholar Springfield Coll., 1970-71, Columbia U., 1978-81. Mem. AAHPERD, Nat. Recreation and Park Assn., U.S. TangSoo-Do Fedn. (bd. dirs. 1974—), U.S. Judo Assn. (life), Korean Assn. Sport Pedagogy (pres. 1992—), Phi Delta Kappa. Home: Riverside Village B-302 TongBu Ichon-dong Yong San Seoul 140-030 Republic of Korea Office: Psc 303 Box 25 Apo AP 96204-3025

CHUNG, YIP-WAH, engineering educator; b. Hong Kong, Nov. 8, 1950; came to U.S., 1973, naturalized, 1983. BS, U. Hong Kong, 1971, MPhil, 1973; PhD, U. Calif., Berkeley, 1977. Asst. prof. Northwestern U., Evanston, Ill., 1977-82, assoc. prof. material sci. and engring., 1982-85, prof., 1986—, dept. chair, 1992—. Mem. editl. bd. Tribology Letters; assoc. editor ASME Jour. Tribology, 1997—. Active Cmty. Rels. Commn., Wilmette, Ill., Rsch. Grants Coun., Hong Kong; trustee Village of Wilmette, 1997-2001. Lee Pui Hing Meml. scholar, 1970; Earl C. Anthony scholar, 1974; recipient Ralph A. Teetor award, 1990, Tribology divsn. award ASME, 1991. Fellow Japan Soc. for Promotion of Sci., ASM Internat.; mem. ASEE, Am. Phys. Soc., Metal. Soc., Am. Vacuum Soc. (chair Ill. chpt. 1991-94, bd. dirs. 1998-2000), Soc. Tribologists and Lubrication Engrs., ASM Internat. Office: Northwestern Univ Dept Mat Sci & Engring 2225 N Campus Dr Evanston IL 60208-0876

CHURCH, JAY KAY, psychologist, educator; b. Wichita, Kans., Jan. 18, 1927; s. Kay Iverson and Gertrude (Parrish) C.; m. Dorothy Agnes Fellerhoff, May 21, 1976; children: Karen Patrice Turnbull, Caryn Annice Church Casey, Rex Warren, Max Roger. BA, Lipscomb U., 1948; MA, Ball State U., 1961; PhD, Purdue U., 1963. Chemist Auburn Rubber Corp., 1948-49; salesman Midwestern United Life Ins. Co., 1949-52; owner, operator Tour-Rest Motel, Waterloo, Ind., 1952-66; tchr., guidance dir. pub. schs., Hamilton, Ind., 1955-61; counselor Washington Twp. (Ind.) Schs., Indpls., 1961-62; asst. prof. psychology Ball State U., 1963-67, assoc. prof., 1967-71, prof., 1971-88, prof. emeritus, 1988—, chmn. dept. ednl. psychology, 1970-74, dir. advanced grad. programs in ednl. psychology, 1978-81; pvt. practice psychology, 1963—. Mem. APA. Home: 4025 W State Road 28 Ridgeville IN 47380-9068 E-mail: jkchurch@tmcsmail.com.

CHURCH, LILLIAN HAZEL See BROOKS, LILLIAN

CHURCH, RUSSELL MILLER, psychology educator; b. N.Y.C., Dec. 24, 1930; s. Donald E. and Dee (Friedman) C.; m. Ruth Kutz, Apr. 4, 1954; children— Kenneth, Emily. BA, U. Mich., 1952; MA, Harvard U., 1954, PhD, 1956. Mem. faculty Brown U., 1955—, prof. psychology, 1965—, chmn. dept. psychology, 1980-83. Chair faculty exec. com. Brown U., 1995-96. Editor: (with E.E. Boe) Punishment: Issues and Experiments, 1968; editor (with B.A. Campbell) Punishment and Aversive Behavior, 1969. Fellow AAAS, Am. Psychol. Assn. (pres. div. exptl. psychology 1987-88, comparative and physiol. psychology 1991-92); mem. Ea. Psychol. Assn. (pres. 1991-92). Office: Brown U Dept of Psychology 89 Waterman St Providence RI 02912-9079 E-mail: Russell_Church@Brown.edu.

CHURCH, WILLIAM HANDY, chemistry educator; b. Providence, Feb. 3, 1959; s. Henry Clay and Anne Elizabeth (Handy) C.; m. Sheila Ann Moore, Apr. 26, 1986; children: Kimberly Anne-Marie, William Travis. BS, James Madison U., Harrisonburg, Va., 1981; PhD, Emory U., 1987. NIH postdoctoral fellow The Salk Inst., LaJolla, Calif., 1987-88; vis. asst. prof. Trinity Coll., Hartford, Conn., 1988-90; asst. prof. East Carolina U., Greenville, N.C., 1990-95, Trinity Coll., Hartford, Conn., 1995—. Rsch. advisor master's thesis; rsch. mentor undergrads; participant Am. Chem. Soc. Project SEED and Vols. in Pub. Outreach. Contbr. articles to profl. jours. Recipient Cottrell Coll. Rsch. award The Rsch. Corp., Tucson, Ariz., 1993, Rsch. award N.C. Biotech. Ctr., Raleigh, 1993; grantee NIH, 1998—. Mem. Am. Chem. Soc. (pub. rels. officer, coun. com. on pub. rels. 1993-95), Soc. Neurosci., Sigma Xi. Republican. Episcopalian. Achievements include development of chromatographic system to monitor brain chemistry during behavior; research on cocaine effects on dopamine neurochemistry. Office: Trinity Coll Dept of Chemistry Hartford CT 06106

CHURCHWELL, EDWARD BRUCE, astronomer, educator; b. Sylva, NC, July 9, 1940; s. Doris L. Churchwell; m. Dorothy S. Churchwell, June 24, 1964; children: Steven T., Beth M. BS, Earlham Coll., 1963; PhD, Ind. U., 1970. NASA fellow Ind. U., Bloomington, 1963; postdoctoral fellow Nat. Radio Astronomy Obs., Charlottesville, Va., 1970; Heinrich Hertz postdoctoral fellow Max Planck Inst. Radioastronomie, Bonn, Germany, 1970-72, staff scientist, 1972-77; asst. prof. U. Wis., Madison, 1977-79, assoc. prof., 1979-83, prof., 1983—, Alfred E. Whitford prof. astronomy, 2002—. Fellow NASA, 1985, Fulbright Rsch., 1988—89. Mem.: Union Concerned Scientists, Internat. Astron. Union, Am. Astron. Soc. Office: U Wis Washburn Observatory 475 N Charter St Madison WI 53706-1582

CHURGIN, MICHAEL JAY, law educator; b. N.Y.C., Feb. 25, 1948; s. Raphael B. and Sylvia (Nussbaum) C. AB magna cum laude, Brown U., Providence, 1970; JD, Yale U., 1973. Bar: Conn. 1974, Tex. 1975. Supervising atty., teaching fellow Yale Law Sch., New Haven, 1973-75; asst. prof. U. Tex. Sch. Law, Austin, 1975-79, assoc. prof., 1979-81, prof., 1981-90, Raybourne Thompson prof., 1990—. Mem. adv. bd. Advocacy, Inc., Austin, 1985-90; vis. fellow Clare Hall, Cambridge, Eng., 1996; vis. fellow Wolfson Coll., Cambridge, Eng., 1992; Quatercentenary vis. fellow Emmanuel Coll., Cambridge, 2000. Co-author: Toward a Just and Effective Sentencing System, 1977; author: (monograph) Analysis of the Texas Mental Health Code, 1988, 2d edit., 1994; contbr. articles to profl. jours. Mem. pub. responsibility com. Austin Travis County MHMR, 1979-85; bd. dirs. Tex. Hillel, Austin. Fellow W.K. Kellogg Nat. Found., 1980-83. Mem. ABA (bar admissions com. 1998—), Am. Soc. for Legal History (chair com. 1987—), Phi Beta Kappa. Jewish. Home: 4006 N Hills Dr Austin TX 78731 Office: U Tex Sch Law 727 E Dean Keeton Austin TX 78705-3224

CHURUKIAN, GEORGE ALLEN, retired education educator; b. Cleve., June 11, 1932; s. Giragos M. and Helen (Tootikian) C.; m. Carol Ann Jerjisian, July 5, 1958; children: Ann, Martha, Alice. BS, Millikin U., 1955; MS, Hofstra U., 1963; PhD, Syracuse U., 1970. Tchr. Patchogue-Medford Pub. Schs., Patchogue, N.Y., 1959-66; assoc. dir. urban tchr. prep. program Syracuse (N.Y.) U., 1969-71; dir. tchr. edn. Va. Wesleyan Coll., Norfolk, 1971-76; dir. secondary edn. Ill. Wesleyan U., Bloomington, 1976-79, dir. tchr. edn., 1979-90; cons. Bloomington, 1991-93; ret., 1993. Fulbright scholar Kuwait U., 1992.

CHUSED, RICHARD HARRIS, law educator; b. St. Louis, Jan. 31, 1943; s. Joseph and Marie Irene (Steinberg) C.; m. Elizabeth Langer, May 11, 1974; children: Benjamin Langer Chused, Samuel Chused Langer. BA, Brown U., 1965; JD, U. Chgo., 1968. Asst. prof. Sch. of Law, Rutgers U., Newark, 1968-71, assoc. prof., 1971-73, Georgetown U. Law Ctr., Washington, 1973-85, prof., 1985—. Author: Modern Approach to Property, 1978, Cases, Materials and Problems in Property, 1988, 2d edit., 1999, A Property Anthology, 1993, 2nd edit., 1997, Private Acts in Public Places: A Social History of Divorce in the Formative Era of American Family Law, 1994, A Copyright Anthology: The Technology Frontier, 1998; topic and comments editor U. Chgo. Law Rev., 1967-68; contbr. numerous articles to profl. jours. Brown U. Nat. Honor scholar, 1965-68, Bowman C. Lingle fellow, 1966-67. Mem. Soc. Am. Law Tchrs. (bd. govs. 1983-94), Am. Soc. Legal History, Am. Hist. Assn. Democrat. Jewish. Home: 3712 Ingomar St NW Washington DC 20015-1820 Office: Georgetown U Law Ctr 600 New Jersey Ave NW Washington DC 20001-2022 E-mail: chused@law.georgetown.edu.

CHWATSKY, ANN, photographer, educator; b. Phila., Jan. 11, 1942; BS in Art Edn., Hofstra U., 1965, MS, 1971; postgrad., L.I. U., 1973-74. Cert. tchr. Photography editor L.I. Mag., 1976-80; instr. Internat. Ctr. Photography, N.Y.C., 1979-80, Parrish Art Mus., Southampton, N.Y., 1984—. Mem. art faculty NYU, 1991—. Author, photographer: The Man in the Street, 1989; photographer The Four Seasons of Shaker life; photographs featured in Time, Newsweek, Newsday, Manchete, N.Y. Times, MD Med. Times; one person shows include Lincoln Ctr., Buenos Aires, 1983, Photographers Gallery, London, 1985, shakers, Nassau County Mus. Fine Arts, 1987, Greater Lafayette (Ind.) Mus. Art, 1988, Bklyn. Coll., 1990, Kiev, USSR Exhbn. Hall, 1991, Bklyn. Coll., Carrie Haddad Gallery, Hudson, N.Y., 2001; group shows include The Other, Houston Ctr. Photography, 1988, L.I. Fine Arts Mus., 1984, Women's Interart Ctr., N.Y.C., 1976, 80, Parrish Art Mus., Southampton, 1979, Internat. Ctr. Photography, N.Y.C., 1980, 82, Nassau County Mus. Fine Arts, 1983, Soho 20 Gallery, N.Y.C., 1984, New Orleans World's Fair, 1984, Southampton Gallery, 1988, 89, Lizan Tops Gallery, L.I., 1994, Apex Art, N.Y.C., 1995, Am. Mus., Prague, 1997, First Seoul Internat. Tribunal, 1998; represented in permanent collections Forbes N.Y.C., Midtown YWCA, Nassau County Mus. Fine Arts, Susan Rothenberg, others. Recipient Estabrook Disting. Alumni award Hofstra U., 1984; Kodak Profl. Photographers award, 1984; Eastman Found. grantee, 1981-82, Poloroid grantee, 1980. Mem. Assn. Am. Mag. Profls., Picture Profls. Am., Profl. Women Photographers N.Y.C. Studio: 29 E 22nd St Apt 3N New York NY 10010-5305

CHYU, CHI-OY WEI, secondary school educator; b. Kwangtung, China, Dec. 21, 1938; d. Tze-Li and Shui-Hing (Fong) Wei; m. Jih-Jiang Chyu, 1966. BS, Chinese U. Hong Kong, 1959; MS, U. Oreg., 1967; MA, Columbia U., 1986, EdD, 1989. Cert. tchr., N.Y.C., Hong Kong; cert. math. tchr., N.Y., N.J. Tchr. Hong Kong Bd. Edn., 1961-64; dir. Chinese sect. Colegio Diez de Octobre, Lima, Peru, 1964-65; libr. asst. Columbia U., N.Y.C., 1972-80; tchr./adminstr. N.Y.C. Bd. Edn., 1981—. Author booklets; contbr. articles to profl. jours. Recipient Outstanding Svc. awards N.Y. Chinese Sch., 1984, ACE-BE, 1991; Mensius scholar, 1957-59, Fgn. Students scholar, 1965-67; grantee Title VII, 1984-87. Mem. AAAS, ASCD, Nat. Assn. for Asian and Pacific Am. Edn., Assn. Chinese Bilingual Educators (v.p. East Coast U.S.A. 1992—), Nat. Coun. Tchrs. Math., Nat. Assn. Bilingual Edn., Greater N.Y. Assn. for Asian and Pacific Am. Edn. (bd. dirs. 1994—), N.Y. State Assn. Bilingual Edn. Avocations: reading, swimming, traveling, arts.

CIANFARANO, SAM ANTHONY, JR., principal, educator; b. Oswego, N.Y., Mar. 31, 1947; s. Samuel Anthony Sr. and Shirley Arlene (Chillson) C.; m. Lori Ann Nave, June 1981 (div. 1983); m. Linda Ann Easton, Dec. 21, 1985; children: Scott Andrew, Steven Michael. BS in Edn., SUNY, Geneseo, 1969; MEd in Adminstrn., U. Rochester, 1976; EdD in Adminstrn., No. Ariz. U., 1990. Cert. edn. adminstrn. Tchr. Rochester (N.Y.) City Sch. Dist., 1970-75, supervising tchr., sch.-cmty. rels. specialist, counselor, 1975-80; counselor, asst. prin. Murphy Elem. Sch. Dist., Phoenix, 1980-83; middle sch. prin. Osborn Sch. Dist., Phoenix, 1983-84; elem. prin. Deer Valley Unified Sch. Dist., Phoenix, 1984-92, Paradise Valley Unified Sch. Dist., Phoenix, 1992—. Tchr. adminstrn. preperation, tchr. preparation courses U. Phoenix, Ariz., 1989—. Recipient celebrate literacy award Phoenix West Reading Coun., 1995, award for promoting literacy Ariz. State Reading Coun., 1995; named disting. prin. of yr. 1995 State of Ariz. Mem. ASCD, Nat. Assn. Elem. Sch. Prins., Internat. Reading Assn., Phi Delta Kappa. Lutheran. Avocations: running, weight training, racquetball, reading, music. Home: 5114 E Fellars Dr Scottsdale AZ 85254-1029 Office: Paradise Valley USD #69 Liberty Elem Sch 5020 E Acoma Dr Scottsdale AZ 85254-2225

CIANI, ALFRED JOSEPH, language professional, associate dean; b. N.Y.C., June 29, 1946; s. Joseph Alfred and Aurora Smiles (VanOver) C.; m. Sharon Skolkey, Aug. 16, 1968 (div. 1979); children: Mieke Jo, Gabriel Wolf; m. Lesley Lockwood, Aug. 9, 1980; children: Joseph Alfred, Clinton Lockwood. BA, U. Albany, 1969; MA, Coll. of St. Rose, 1972; EdD, Ind. U., 1974. Tchr. Greater Amsterdam (N.Y.) Schs., 1969-72; rsch. asst. Ind. U., Bloomington, 1972-73, assoc. instr., 1973-74; vis. prof. U. Wis., Milw., 1980; asst. prof. U. Cin., 1974-79, assoc. prof., 1979—2002, assoc. dean, info. officer, 1988—2003, prof. emeritus, 2003—. Pres. Ohio Internat. Reading Assn., Columbus, 1981-82; outside cons. State of Miss., Jackson, 1982-84, State of Ky., 1996-99, State of W.Va., 1972-74, 97-98, City of N.Y. Pub. Schs.; cons., U. Oreg. Profl. Devel., Eugene, 1979-80, Nashville Schs., 1982-83, State of W.Va., N.Y.C. Pub. Schs.; mem. Dean's Cabinet; mem. Urban Schs. Task Force. Author: Motivating Reluctant Readers, 1981; editor: (book series) Reading in Content Areas, 1979-81; rev. editor: Rsch. in Mid. Level Edn., 1995—. Grantee Ford Found., 1990, IBM, 1990. Mem. AAUP, Internat. Reading Assn., Am. Ednl. Rsch. Assn. (nat. coms.), Assn. Tchr. Educators (nat. coms.), Nat. Coun. Tchrs. English (nat. coms.), Nat. Mid. Sch. Assn. (nat. coms.), Nat. Reading Coun., Phi Delta Kappa, Kappa Delta Pi (counselor). Democrat. Roman Catholic. Avocations: reading, walking, family oriented activities. Office: U Cin Mail Location 02 Cincinnati OH 45221-0001 E-mail: alfred.ciani@uc.edu.

CIAO, FREDERICK J. school system administrator, educator; b. Phila. married; 3 children. BA, LaSalle U., 1962; MEd, Temple U., 1965; MA, Villanova U., 1972; PhD, Southwest U., 1990. From tchr. to counselor to dept. chmn. N.E. Cath. High Sch., Phila., 1962-73; vice prin. Archbishop Wood High Sch., Warminster, Pa., 1973-85; prin. Bishop McDevitt H.S., Wyncote, Pa., 1985-93, pres., 1993—2003, Archbishop Wood H.S., Warminster, Pa., 2003—. Mem. adj. faculty St. Agnes Hosp. Nursing Sch., Phila., 1963-71, Spring Garden Coll., Phila., 1971-73, Gwynedd Mercy Coll., Gwynedd Valley, Pa., 1976-84, LaSalle U., 1980—; presentor Nat. Diffusion Network, 1992—. Mem. edn. advisor Phila. Orch., 1993—, Italian Lang. Preservation Found., 1999—. Named Man of the Yr., N.E. Cath. Alumni Assn., 1972, Educator of the Yr., Millay Club, 1986; named to Legion of Honor, Chapel of Four Chaplains, 1980; recipient John Neumann medal St. John Neumann High Sch., 1985. Mem. Nat. Assn. Secondary Sch. Prins., Nat. Cath. Edn. Assn., Nat. Coun. Tchrs. of Maths., Maths. Assn. Am., Nat. Assn. Curriculum Devel., Nat. Coun. for Self Esteem, Mid. States Assn. of Colls. (chair). Office: Archbishop Wood HS 655 York Rd Warminster PA 18974

CIARLONE, PATRICIA ANN, elementary education educator; b. West Chester, Pa., Jan. 11, 1949; d. Joseph A. and Mildred Catherine (Brochard) Fennelly; 1 child, Catherine Marie. BSE, West Chester State U., 1970, MSE, 1972; postgrad., various colls., Pa. Cert. tchr., Pa. Elem. tchr. Coatesville (Pa.) Area Sch. Dist., 1970—. Mentor Coatesville Area Sch. Dist., 1991-93. Active Caln Elem. Sch. and Henderson High Sch. PTA, 1986—, Outstanding Svc. award, 1993; campaign worker Citizens to Elect Harry McMullen, Coatesville, 1991-92, Citizens to Elect Robin Garret, West Chester, 1992. Grantee Oakland Found. 1989, 1993. Mem. ASCD, NEA, Nat. Coun. Math. Tchrs., Pa. State Edn. Assn. (legis. contact 1990—), Coatesville Area Tchrs. Assn. (treas. 1986—), PTA Caln Elem. Democrat. Roman Catholic. Avocations: travel, reading, dining out, dancing, computers. Home: 233 Smallwood Ct West Chester PA 19380-1388 Office: Caln Elem Sch 3609 Lincoln Hwy Thorndale PA 19372-1003

CIBOROWSKI, PAUL JOHN, counseling psychology educator; b. NYC, Jan. 15, 1943; s. Paul J. and Mary (Deptuch) C.; m. Doris E. Carlo, June 24, 1973; children: Philip Alan, Kevin Michael. BA, U. Dayton, 1965; MA, NYU, 1969; PhD, Fordham U., 1979. Cert. counselor. Counselor Christ the King H.S., Queens, N.Y., 1967-70; coord. drug edn. Sachem Sch. Dist., Holbrook, N.Y., 1971-73; sr. counselor, grant coord. Sachem Schs., Holbrook, N.Y., 1973-89; mental health counselor, 1980—; assoc. prof. counseling and psychology L.I. U., 1989—. Pres. Stratmar Ednl. Systems; pvt. practice marriage and family therapy; coord. Dept. Counseling and Devel., Brentwood, N.Y.; cons., trainer Family Life Bur., Diocese of Rockville Centre; adv. coun. WSHO radio; contact person for sexual harassment complaints C.W. Post Coll., 2003. Author: The Changing Family I, 1984, 2d edit., 1986, Survival Skills for Single Parents, 1987, Working with Tomorrow's Teens: A 21st Century Challenge, 2000; contbr. articles to profl. jours. Fellow Ctr. for Study of the Changing Family, Port Chester, NY; active Brookhaven Anti-Bias Coalition; co-chair Suffolk County Interfaith Anti-Bias Task Force; chair N.Y. Youth Bd., Western Suffolk Coalition on Child Abuse and Neglect; project dir. Suffolk County Gang Prevention, 2000—, grant coord., 2000—; active Suffolk County Youth in Crisis Task Force, 2003—; chmn. fin. com. St. Mark's Roman Cath. Ch., parish coun.; bd. dirs. Soundview Civic Assn. Grantee in field. Mem.: ACA (com. on children, youth and families), Western Suffolk Counselors Assn. (past treas., past v.p.), Am. Mental Health Counselors Assn. (chmn. spl. interest network on children and adolescents, coord. Child Adv. Network, exec. bd., nat. com. for the rights of children 1992—96), N.Y. State Assn. for Counseling and Devel. (legis. chmn. 1989—92, v.p., state curriculum com. 1981—82), Phi Delta Kappa. Home: 38 Mary Pitkin Path PO Box 284 Shoreham NY 11786-0284

CICCHELLI, JOSEPH VINCENT, principal; b. Jersey City, Sept. 14, 1953; s. Anthony Charles and Julia Marie (Libri) C.; m. Joanne Savino, July 11, 1981; children: Jaime Michele, Jason Michael. AA, Bergen C.C., 1973; BA, William Paterson Coll. of N.J., 1975; MA, Seton Hall U., 1981. Tchr.'s aide Bergen County Spl. Svcs. Sch. Dist., Paramus, 1975-76; tchr. Hackensack High Sch., 1976-98; asst. prin. Fairmount Elem. Sch., Hackensack, 1998—2003, prin., 2003—; educator Hackensack Adult Edn. Ctr., Hackensack, N.J., 1978-92; supr. Hasbrouck Heights Adult Edn. Ctr., Hackensack, N.J., 1987-92, Hackensack Adult Edn. Ctr., 1992-94. Cons. Belville (N.J.) Pub. Sch. Dist., 1987. Active Fairmount Creative Playground Com., Hackensack. Mem. Prins. and Suprs. Assn., N.J. Prins. and Suprs. Assn.,

N.J. Social Studies Coun., Kappa Delta Pi. Roman Catholic. Avocations: photography, fishing, woodcrafting, automobile restoration and shows. Office: Fairmount Elementary Sch 105 Grand Ave Hackensack NJ 07601

CICCI, DAVID ALLEN, aerospace engineer, educator; b. Greensburg, Pa., May 29, 1951; s. Henry and Ann (Bischan) C.; m. Christine Maryanne Smith, July 16, 1977; children: Corey Dylan, Darby Austin. BSME, W.Va. U., 1973; MSME, Carnegie-Mellon U., 1976; PhD in Aerospace Engring., U. Tex., 1987. Registered profl. engr., Pa., Ala. Engr. power systems div. McGraw Edison Co., Canonsburg, Pa., 1973—74; engr. Bettis Atomic Power Lab. Westinghouse Electric Corp., West Mifflin, Pa., 1974—77; sr. engr. Swanson Engring. Assocs. Corp., McMurray, Pa., 1977—81; engring. specialist Bell Helicopter Textron, Ft. Worth, 1981—82; from asst. instr. to rsch. asst. U. Tex., Austin, 1982—87; prof. dept. aerospace engring. Auburn (Ala.) U., 1987—, dir. minority introduction to engring., 1996—2000. Cons. Sverdrup Tech., Inc., Stennis Space Ctr., Miss., 1989-90, Gen. Dynamics Corp., Ft. Worth, 1984, Swanson Engring. Assocs. Corp., McMurray, 1982-83; instr. NASA, Huntsville, Ala., 1989, 90, 92, NSWC, Dahlgren, Va., 2001, U.S. Army, Huntsville, Ala., 2001-02, NRL, Washington, 2002. Contbr. articles to profl. jours. Mem. City Coun., Auburn, Ala., 1998-2002. Mem. AIAA (astrodynamics tech. com. 1991-94, 96—, astrodynamics stds. com. 1991-94), ASME, Am. Astronautical Soc., Tau Beta Pi, Sigma Gamma Tau. Home: 1960 Canary Dr Auburn AL 36830-6902 Office: 211 Aerospace Engring Bldg Auburn U Auburn AL 36849-5338 E-mail: dcicci@eng.auburn.edu.

CICCONE, JOSEPH LEE, criminal justice educator; b. Teaneck, N.J., Jan. 21, 1960; s. Joseph D. and Catherine (Mazzone) C. BS in Police Sci., Jersey City State Coll., 1983, MS in Criminal Justice, 1987; postgrad., Seton Hall U., 1992-93; EdD, Nova Southeastern U., 1996. Supr. N.J. Meadow Lands, East Rutherford, 1978-80; police officer Cliffside Park (N.J.) Police Dept., 1980-83; police sgt. Fairview (N.J.) Police Dept., 1983—; tchr., coach Lincoln Sch., Fairview, N.J., 1987-89; jr. H.S. tchr. Our Lady of Grace Sch., Fairview, 1989-91; prof. sociology, chairperson dept. social sci. Berkeley Coll., Paterson/Waldwick, N.J., 1991-98, dean instrnl. tech., 1998—; prof. criminal justice Monmouth Univ., West Long Branch, N.J., 1991—; sheriff Bergen County Sheriff's Dept., Hackensack, N.J., 1999—. 1st v.p. N.J. State Police Benevolent Assn., East Bergen County, 1983—; instr. Drug Abuse Resistance Edn., Bergen City, N.J., 1989—; chairperson N.J. Gov. Alliance, Fairview, 1990—; acad. trainer Bergen County Police Acad., Mahwah, N.J., 1990—. Author: The Evaluation and Implementation of DARE, 1993, Police Staff Development in Minority Issues; contbr. articles to profl. jours. Mem. Young Dem. Club, Fairview, 1983—, PTA, Fairview, 1989—, Holy Trinity Ch. Choir, 1994, Bd. of Edn., Fairview; exec. bd. N.J. Honor Legion, Hudson City, N.J., 1990—; spkr. in field; sheriff Bergen County, N.J., 1998. Named Police Office of Yr., D.A.R.E. Am., 1990, 93. Mem. Acad. Criminal Justice Sci., Officers Action League, Police Benevolent Assn., Lambda Alpha Epsilon, Phi Delta Kappa. Democrat. Roman Catholic. Avocations: gourmet cooking, bicycling, running, photography, civil rights activist. Office: Bergen County Sheriff's Dept Justice Ctr 10 Main St Hackensack NJ 07601-7000 Home: 450 Wilfred Ter Cliffside Park NJ 07010-1402

CICERO, DIANNE, special education educator; BS, Nazareth Coll. Rochester, 1975; MS, SUNY, Geneseo, 1977. Cert. (permanent) spl. edn., speech and hearing handicapped. PSEN resource rm. tchr. Mt. Morris (N.Y.) Ctrl. Sch., 1978—87; tchr. Steuben-Allegany BOCES, Hornell, NY, 1987—96, Livingston-Wyoming Arc, Geneseo, NY, 1998—.

CICERONE, RALPH JOHN, academic administrator, geophysicist; b. New Castle, Pa., May 2, 1943; married; 1 child. SB, MIT, 1965; MS, U. Ill., 1967, PhD in Elec. Engring. and Physics, 1970. Physicist U.S. Dept. Commerce, 1967; rsch. asst. aeronomy U. Ill., 1967—70; assoc. rsch. scientist aeronomy space physics rsch. lab. U. Mich., Ann Arbor, 1970—78; assoc. rsch. chemist ocean rsch. divsn. U. Calif., San Diego, 1978—80, rsch. chemist Scripps inst. oceanography, 1980—81, Daniel G. Aldrich prof., chair geosci. dept. Irvine, 1989—94, dean Sch. Phys. Scis., 1994—98, chancellor, 1998—; sr. scientist, dir. atmospheric chemistry divsn. Nat. Ctr. Atmospheric Rsch., Boulder, Colo., 1980—89. Lectr., asst. prof. elec. engring. U. Mich., Ann Arbor, 1973—75. Assoc. editor: Jour. Geophysics Rsch., 1977—79; editor, 1979—83. Recipient Bower award for Achievement in Sci., Franklin Inst., 1999. Fellow: AAAS, Am. Geophys. Union (Macelwane award 1979, Revelle medal 2002), Am. Meteorol. Soc., Am. Chem. Soc.; mem.: NAS (elected 1990, mem. com., bd. sustainable devel. 1995—98, com. on women in sci. and engring. 2000—, chair com. on climate sci. 2001), Am. Philos. Soc., Am. Acad. Arts and Scis. Office: U Calif Irvine Chancellors Office 501 Administration Bldg Ofc Irvine CA 92697-1900

CICHOCKI, SHARON ANN, secondary education educator; b. Buffalo, May 15, 1950; d. Arthur Stephen and Jean (Przywuski) Harkiewicz; m. Ronald R. Cichocki, Aug. 22, 1970; children: Gregory, Cindy. BA in Math. and History, SUNY, Buffalo, 1977, EdM in Math. Instrn., 1982. Cert. maths. tchr., N.Y. Tchr. maths. Queen of Heaven Cath. Sch., West Seneca, N.Y., 1970-71; substitute maths. tchr. Depew and Lackawanna Sch. Dists., 1977-79; tchr. Hamburg (N.Y.) Cen. High Sch. Dist., 1979—. Secondary math. coord., Nat. Honor Soc. advisor, svc. club advisor Hamburg (N.Y.) Cen. High Sch. Dist.; prof. math. SUNY, Buffalo. Mem. Nat. Coun. Tchrs. Math., Assn. Math. Tchrs. N.Y. State, Nat. Coun. Suprs. of Math., N.Y. State Assn. Math. Suprs. (past pres., secondary math. coord.), Nat. Assn. Student Activity Advisers. Office: Hamburg High Sch 4111 Legion Dr Hamburg NY 14075-4507

CILELLA, MARY WINIFRED, director; b. Oak Park, Ill., Aug. 24, 1943; d. Charles William Sr. and Theresa Mary (Gilligan) Broucek; m. Salvatore G. Cilella Jr., Aug. 29, 1970; children: Salvatore George III, Peter Dominic. BA, Dominican U., 1965; MAT, U. Notre Dame, 1966; grad. The Prin.'s Inst., Harvard U., 1993; postgrad., U. S.C., 1994-97. Tchr. Miner Jr. H.S., Arlington Heights, Ill., 1966-67; sec. White House, Washington, 1969-70; devel. officer Textile Mus., Washington, 1982-83; dir. meetings and continuing edn. Am. Assn. Mus., Washington, 1983-87; interim lower sch. head, lower sch. head Heathwood Hall Episc. Sch., Columbia, S.C., 1989-94, dir. acad. adminstrn., 1994-95, dir. fin. and adminstrn., 1995-96, asst. head, 1996-98, assoc. head fin. and ops., 1998—2001; cons. Park Tudor Sch., Indpls., 2001—02, dir. Russel and Mary Williams Learning Project, 2002—. Mem. profl. edn. unit adv. com. U. S.C., 1996-2001; mem. U.S. Dept. of Edn.'s Blue Ribbon Schs. Planning Group, 1996; examiner Malcolm Baldrige Nat. Quality award bd. U.S. Dept. Commerce and Nat. Inst. Stds. and Tech., 1999, 2000. Mem. ASCD, Phi Delta Kappa. Roman Catholic. Avocations: gardening, collecting antiques, music, aerobics. Home: 905 Tamarack Cir S Dr Indianapolis IN 46260 Office: Park Tudor Sch 7200 North College Ave Indianapolis IN 46240 E-mail: mcilella@parktudor.org.

CINA, JEFFREY A. chemistry educator; BS, U. Wis., Madison, 1979; PhD, U. Calif., Berkeley, 1985. Postdoctoral MIT, 1985—87; prof. chemistry U. Oreg., Eugene, 1995—, mem. Oreg. Ctr. Optics. Camille and Henry Dreyfus Tchr.-Scholar, 1991—96, James Franck fellow, 1987—88, fellow, John Simon Guggenheim Meml. Found., 2003—. Office: Dept Chemistry 1253 University of Oregon Eugene OR 97403-1253*

CINOTTI, ALFONSE ANTHONY, ophthalmologist, educator; b. Jersey City, Jan. 1, 1923; s. William John Cinotti and Carrie Ilaria; m. Kathleen Dolores Higgins, June 26, 1948; children: Donald, Kathleen, Lawrence, Carol Ann, William. BS, Fordham U., 1943; MD, SUNY, Bklyn., 1946. Diplomate Am. Bd. Ophthalmology. Dir. resident tng. N.Y. Eye and Ear Infirmary, N.Y.C., 1955-59, assoc. dir. Postgrad. Inst., 1956-63; assoc. prof., dir. div. of Ophthalmology N.J. Med. Sch., 1963-72, prof., dir., 1972-74, chmn. faculty, 1974-75; prof., chmn. dept. ophthalmology U. Medicine & Dentistry N.J. Med. Sch., 1974-93; prof., chmn. emeritus U. Medicine & Dentistry, 1993—. Med. dir. Eye Inst. N.J., Newark, 1970-93; trustee N.J. State Commn. for the Blind and Visually Impaired, Newark, 1971-76, 80—, chmn., 1992; founder, mem. Eye Bank of N.J., 1970—. Contbr. articles to profl. jours. Founder Joint Commn. on Allied Health Ophthalmology; mem. adv. bd. Essex County Div. on Aging, Newark, 1984; chmn. med. adv. com., mem. exec. com. Nat. Soc. to Prevent Blindness, N.J. Recipient Outstanding Citizens award Lions 16A, Disting. Alumnus award N.Y. Eye and Ear Infirmary, N.Y.C., Visionary Yr. Eye Inst., N.J., Lions Eyebank, N.J., 1991, Sr. Honors award Am. Acad. Oph., 1991, Master Teaching award Ophth. Alumni Assn. SUNY, Disting. Svc. Award Peter Rodino Law Soc. Seton Hall U. Fellow Am. Coll. Surgeons, Am. Acad. Ophthalmology (bd. councillors 1981-84); mem. AMA (alt. del. 1978-89), Am. Assn. Ophthalmology (pres. 1978, 79), Hudson County Med. Soc. (pres. 1978), N.J. Acad. Ophthalmology and Otolaryngology (pres. 1974). Lodges: Knights of Malta. Republican. Roman Catholic. Avocation: painting. Office: Senior Friendship Center Medical Clinic 811 7th Ave S Naples FL 34102-6715

CINTRON, JUDITH, elementary education educator; b. Mayaguez, P.R., Jan. 28, 1956; d. Angel and Carmen (Castillo) Cintron. BA in Secondary Edn. and Social Studies, Northeastern Ill. U., Chgo., 1980; MA in Ednl. Studies, U. Ill., Chgo., 1990. Cert. elem. and secondary tchr., Ill. Tchr. 8th grade Humboldt Cmty. Christian Sch., Chgo., 1980-83; tchr. 3d grade Jose De Diego Comty. Acad., Chgo., 1983—. Sunday sch. children's supt. Ch. of God, Chgo., 1982-83. Avocations: reading biographies and novels, listening to music--contemporary, christian and popular. Office: Jose De Diego Cmty Acad 1313 N Claremont Ave Chicago IL 60622-2910

CINTRON-FERRER, CARMEN RHODE, educational director; b. San Juan, P.R., May 18, 1952; d. Néstor and Carmen R. (Ferrer) Cintrón-Rivas. BBA in Stats., U. P.R., Río Piedras, 1971, JD in Adminstrv. Law, 1974; MS in Computer Sci., U. Tex., Dallas, 1983. Bar: P.R. 1974, U.S. Dist. Ct. P.R., 1974, U.S. Cir. Ct. (Boston) 1974. Part-time prof. U. P.R., San Juan, 1971-81, U. Sacred Heart, San Juan, 1983-87, dir. planning office, 1983-85, dir. mgmt. info. systems grad. program, 1987—; exec. dir. P.R. Bar Assn., San Juan, 1977-81; teaching asst. U. Tex., Dallas, 1981-83; legal counsel, adminstrv. asst. P.R. Rep. David Noriega, San Juan, 1985-87. Pres. S.I.T.T. (Cons. & Tng. Svcs. in the Computer Industry), Inc., Rio Piedras, 1990—; cons. Jorge Tirado & Assoc., Inc., San Juan. V.p. Inst. del Hogar, San Juan, 1980-81; treas.-pres. Assn. Condóminos de Playas del Yunque, Rio Grande, P.R., 1987-91. GPOP (Grad. Opportunity Program) fellow, 1981-83. Mem. ABA, NAFE, P.R. Bar Assn., Pro-Bono, Inc. (treas. 1983-92), Assn. Computing Machinery, Assn. System Mgmt., Assn. Puertorriqueña de Informática Juridica (treas. 1984-89). Baptist. Address: PO Box 195271 San Juan PR 00919-5271

CIOCIOLA, CECILIA MARY, development specialist; b. Chester, Pa., Feb. 9, 1946; d. Donato Francis Pasqual and Mary Theresa (Dugan) C. BA, Immaculata Coll., 1975; MA, West Chester U., 1984. Tchr. Archdiocese of Phila., 1964-72, Harrisburg Diocese, Pa., 1972-74, Camden Diocese, NJ, 1974-76; tchr., elem. sci. chairperson Archdiocese of Phila., 1976-86; ednl. cons. Macmillan Pub. Co., Delran, NJ, 1986-88; program officer PATHS/PRISM, Phila., 1988-90; mgr. spl. programs minority engring., math., sci. program Prime, Inc., Phila., 1988-99; dir. partnership and cmty. devel. FOUNDATIONS, Inc., 1999-2001; grants adminstr. Chester Cmty. Charter Sch., Pa., 2001—. Tchr. cert. adv. com. U. the Scis., Phila.; cons. Delaware County Intermediate Unit, Media, Pa.; chair elem. (grades 1-8), sci. com. Phila. Archdiocese, 1985-86; coord. Chester County Cath. Schs.: Computer Edn., Pa., 1982-84, Fed. Nutrition Program, St. Agnes Sch., West Chester, Pa., 1982-84, Justice Edn. Teaching Strategies, St. Agnes Sch., West Chester, 1983-84; mem. Mayor's Telecom. Policy Adv. Com., Phila., 1998-2000, Phila. 4-H Program Devel. Com., 1998-2000. Author, editor: (curriculum) Elementary Life and Earth Science, 1984. Mem. adv. com. environ. edn. program Fairmount Pk. Commn., 1998. NSF grantee Operation Primary Phys. Sci., La. State U., 1997—, Project GLOBE, 1997-2000. Mem. ASCD, Nat. Sci. Tchrs. Assn., Pa. Biotech. Assn. (edn. coun.), U. of the Scis. in Phila. (sci. edn. adv. com.), Pa. Sci. Tchrs. Assn. Avocations: poetry, country music, reading, photography, fitness. Office: 214 E 5th St Chester PA 19013-4510

CIOFFI, EUGENE EDWARD, III, retired educational administrator; b. Somerville, N.J., July 26, 1948; s. Eugene E. and Carmela Agnus (Montenegro) C.; m. Ellen Gertrude Coolbaugh, Sept. 12, 1969; children: Christopher, Daniel. BS in Edn., Bloomsburg U., 1970; MEd, Coll. of N.J., 1973. Cert. sch. adminstr., prin., elem. and secondary tchr., N.J. Asst. adminstr., tchr. 6th-8th grades Salah Tawfik Elem. and Mid. Sch., Sunrise, Fla.; chief sch. adminstr., prin. Frelinghuysen (N.J.) Twp. Bd. Edn., 1994-2000; ret., 2000. Pres. Warren County Spl. Svcs. Sch. Dist. Bd. Edn. Mem. ASCD, Warren County Assn. Sch. Adminstrs., N.J. Assn. Sch. Adminstrs., Warren County Prins. and Suprs. Assn., N.J. Sch. Bds. Assn., Phi Delta Kappa.

CIOLLI, ANTOINETTE, librarian, retired educator; b. N.Y.C., Aug. 20, 1915; d. Pietro and Mary (Palumbo) C.; A.B., Bklyn. Coll., 1937, M.A., 1940; B.S. in L.S., Columbia U., 1943. Tchr. history and civics Bklyn. high schs., 1943-44; circulation librarian Bklyn. Coll. Library, 1944-46; instr. history Sch. Gen. Studies, Bklyn. Coll., 1944-50, asst. prof. library dept., 1965-73, assoc. prof., 1973-81, prof. emerita, 1981— ; reference librarian Bklyn. Coll. Library, 1947-59, chief sci. librarian, 1959-70, chief spl. collections div., 1970-81, hon. archivist, 1981— . Mem. ALA, Am. Hist. Assn., Spl. Libraries Assn. (museum group chpt. sec. 1950-51, 52-54), N.Y. Library Club, Beta Phi Mu. Author: (with Alexander S. Preminger and Lillian Lester) Urban Educator: Harry D. Gideonse, Brooklyn College and the City University of New York, 1970; contbr. articles to profl. jours. Home: 31 Tarring St Staten Island NY 10306-4026

CIOTTO, CAROL JEAN MILLER, physical education educator; b. Springfield, Mass., Dec. 30, 1959; d. Bryan E. and Winnifred (Arbo) Miller; m. Paul Joseph Ciotto, Nov. 8, 1986; 1 child, Kristina Marie. BS in Phys. Edn., Cen. Conn. State U., 1981, MS in Adminstrn., Supervision, 1988, 6th-yr. cert. adminstrn., supervision, 1990. Cert. tchr., Conn. Tchr. phys. edn. New Britain (Conn.) Pub. Schs., 1982-83, West Hartford (Conn.) Pub. Schs., 1984—, coach high sch. girls gymnastics, track and field, 1982—, coach high sch. girls' diving, 1982-88, coach high sch. girls' track and field, 1988-90. Presenter at profl. confs. Reviewer Youth Track and Field Manual, 1987. Mem. NEA, AAHPERD, Conn. Assn. health, Phys. Edn., Recreation and Dance (v.p. dance 1985-87, 89-91, Innovative Program award 1984), Nat. Assn. Sports and Phys. Edn. (nat. clinician 1992—), Conn. Assn. High Sch. Coaches, Conn. Edn. Assn. Republican. Avocations: running, singing, ballet, theater, art. Home: 10 Amy Ln Simsbury CT 06070-2702 Office: Webster Hill Sch 125 Webster Hill Blvd West Hartford CT 06107-3799

CIPOLLONE, ANTHONY DOMINIC, judge, educator; b. N.Y.C., Mar. 15, 1939; s. Domenico and Caterina (Brancazio) C.; m. Eileen Mary Patricia Kelly, Sept. 14, 1963; children: Catherine Mary, Kelly Ann, Mary Rose. BA, CCNY, 1961, MA, 1968; JD, Seton Hall U., 1978. Bar: N.J. 1978, Pa. 1978, U.S. Patent Office 1978, Fla. 1980, N.Y. 1984, D.C. 1985, Mass. 1988; cert. civil trial atty. N.J., 1987. Chemist Am. Chicle Co., Long Island City, N.Y., 1961-65; research chemist Denver Chem. Mfg. Co., Stamford, Conn., 1965-66; chem. sales engr. GAF Corp., N.Y.C., 1966-68; nat. acct. rep. Stauffer Chem., N.Y.C., 1968-72; sales mgr. Rhone-Poulenc Inc., South Brunswick, N.J., 1972-78; prosecutor Town of Elmwood Park, N.J., 1981-85, Town of Paramus, N.J., 1982-85; mcpl. ct. judge Town of Paramus (N.J.), 1985-90, Town of Little Ferry (N.J.), 1986-89; atty. planning bd. Twp. Saddle Brook, 1986-87; mcpl. ct. judge Town of Elmwood Park (N.J.), 1991, Town of Saddle Brook (N.J.), 1991-94; atty. Twp. Saddle Brook, 1987-90. Adj. faculty MBA program for chmn. and pharm. mgrs. Fairleigh Dickinson U.; atty. Zoning Bd., City of Hackensack, N.J., 1989-90, atty. Planning Bd., 1991—. Served to sgt. USMC, 1961-66. Mem. ABA, Bergen Bar Assn., N.J. Bar Assn., Pa. Bar Assn., N.Y. Bar Assn., D.C. Bar Assn., Fla. Bar Assn., Mass. Bar Assn., Am. Chem. Soc., Am. Mensa. Roman Catholic. Home: 130 Overlook Ave Hackensack NJ 07601 Office: 15 Main St Ste 215 Hackensack NJ 07601 E-mail: cipollone@aol.com.

CIPRIANI, FRANK ANTHONY, former college president; b. N.Y.C., Sept. 28, 1933; s. Domenico and Maria (DiGiesi) C.; m. Judith Pellathay, Aug. 9, 1959; children: Maria, Frank, Michael, Dominique. AB in Polit. Sci., Queens Coll., 1955; MA in Edn., NYU, 1961, PhD, 1969. Adminstrv. asst. to v.p. bus. affairs NYU, 1961-64; prof. history SUNY Farmingdale, 1964, asst. dean, 1964-67, asst. to pres., 1966-69, v.p. adminstrn., 1969-78, pres. coll., 1978-2000; ret., 2000. Chmn. L.I. Regional Adv. Coun. on Higher Edn.; chmn. bd. dirs. Regional Indsl. Tech. Edn. Coun.; chmn. L.I. Regional Ashfill Bd.; trustee L.I. Power Authority; mem. L.I. Bi-County Planning Bd, L.I. Regional Econ. Devel. Coun. Capt. USAF, 1955-57. Mem. Middle States Assn. Colls. and Secondary Schs., Consortium L.I. Italian Ams., Italian Order Merit. Roman Catholic. Office: SUNY Farmingdale Off of Pres Melville Rd Farmingdale NY 11735

CIRCEO, LOUIS JOSEPH, JR., research scientist, civil engineer; b. Everett, Mass., Aug. 31, 1934; s. Louis Joseph and Matilda (Marotta) C.; m. Brigitta H. Rockstroh, Jan. 26, 1961 (dec. 1986); children: Renata B., Craig L. BS in Engring., U.S. Mil. Acad., West Point, 1957; MS in Soils Engring., 1961; PhD in Civil Engring., Iowa State U., 1963. Registered profl. civil engr., D.C. Commd. 2d lt. U.S. Army, 1957, advanced through grades to col., 1987; rsch. assoc. Lawrence Radiation Lab., Livermore, Calif., 1962-64; civil engr. Bangkok Bypass Road, Thailand, 1965—66; instr. dept. engring. and mil. sci. U.S. Army Engr. Sch., Ft. Belvoir, Va., 1966—68; civil engr. advisor Vietnamese Nat. Mil. Acad., Dalat, Vietnam, 1968-69; rsch. tech. mgr. Def. Atomic Support Agy., Washington, 1969-72; comdr. 20th Engr. Bn., Ft. Campbell, Ky., 1973-75; ops. rsch. analyst nuclear activities br. SHAPE, NATO, Mons, Belgium, 1975-79; dir. U.S. Army Constrn. Engring. Rsch. Lab., Champaign, Ill., 1979-83; dir. Nuclear Survivability, Security and Safety Directorate, Hdqrs. Def. Nuclear Agy., Washington, 1983-87; ret., 1987; dir. Constrn. Rsch. Ctr., Ga. Inst. Tech., Atlanta, 1987—98; prin. rsch. scientist Ga. Tech Rsch. Inst., Atlanta, 1998—. Mem. ASCE, Soc. Am. Mil. Engrs., Assn. U.S. Army, Sigma Xi. Roman Catholic. Achievements include patents for recovery of fuel products from carbonaceous matter using plasma arc; in-situ plasma soil stabilization method and apparatus; in-situ plasma remediation and vitrification of contaminated soils, deposits and buried materials. Avocations: reading, travel. Home: 4245 Navajo Trl NE Atlanta GA 30319-1532 Office: Ga Tech Rsch Inst Atlanta GA 30332-0837 E-mail: lou.circeo@gtri.gatech.edu.

CIRILO, AMELIA MEDINA, educational consultant, supervisor; b. Parks, Tex., May 23, 1925; d. Constancio and Guadalupe (Guerra) Cirilo; m. Arturo Medina, May 31, 1953 (div. June 1979); children: Dennis Glenn, Keith Allen, Sheryl Amelia, Jacqueline Kim. BS in Chemistry, U. North Tex., 1950; MEd, U. Houston, 1954; PhD in Edn. and Nuc. Engring., Tex. A&M U., 1975; cert. in radioisotope tech., Tex. Woman's U., Denton, 1962; cert. in pub. speaking, Dale Carnegie, 1993. Cert. in supervision, bilingual Spanish Tex., permanent profl. tchr. Tex. Tchr. sci. dept. Starr County Schs., Rio Grande City, Tex., 1950—53; elem. tchr. San Benito-Brownsville, Tex., 1953—54, Kingsville (Tex.) Schs., 1954—56; tchr. sci. dept. head chem. physics LaJoya (Tex.) Pub. Schs., 1956—70; tchg. asst. Tex. A&M U., College Station, 1970—74; instr. fire chemistry Del Mar Jr. Coll., Corpus Christi, Tex., 1974—75; exec. dir. Hispanic Ednl. Rsch. Mgmt. Analysis Nat. Assn., Inc., Corpus Christi, 1975—79; head dept. chem. physics San Isidro (Tex.) HS, 1979—82; tchr. chemistry W.H. Adamson HS, Dallas, 1982—84; ednl. cons. Skyline HS, 1992—, tchr. high intensity lang. sci., 1984—86, chmn. faculty adv. com., 1983—84, chemistry tchr., 1986—92. Mem. core faculty Union Grad. Coll., Cin., P.R., Ft. Lauderdale and San Diego, 1975—79; mathematician Well Instrument Devel. Co., Houston, 1950—85; panelist, program evaluator Dept. of Edn., Washington, 1977—79; program evaluator, Robstown, Tex., 1975—79; tchr., trainer Edn. 20 and 2 Region Ctrs., Corpus Christi and San Antonio, 1975—79; rschr., writer Coll. Edn. and Urban Studies Harvard U., Cambridge, Mass., 1978—80; vis. prof. bilingual dept. East Tex. State Coll., Commerce, 1978; ednl. cons. and supr. Adult Basic Edn. Dallas Pub. Schs., 1994—99, kindergarten tchr., 1999—2000, tchr. elem. sci. and math., 2000—02, newcomers ESL tchr., 2002—; conf. presenter program evaluation, 1977—79. Author, rschr. Comparative Evaluation of Bilingual Programs, 1978 (named one of best US books), (poetry) Reflections, 1983; contbr. chapters to books. Mem. Srs. Active in Life adv. com. Dallas City Parks and Recreation; Brazos County advisor Tex. Constl. Revision Commn., 1973—74; sec. Goals for Corpus Christi Com. of 100; Corpus Christi rep. Southwestern Ednl. Authority, Edinburg, Tex., 1977—79; pres. Elem. PTA, 1972—75; mem. Women's Polit. Caucus, Mex. Am. Dems.; exec. bd. Nat. Com. Domestic Violence, 1978—80; bd. trustees Sci. Cluster Skyline HS, 1994—; bd. dirs. Meth. Home for Elderly, Weslaco, Tex., 1968, Am. Cancer Soc. fund drive, College Station, 1971—74; co-founder, bd. dirs. Women's Shelter, Corpus Christi, 1977—78. Named Educator of Yr., Literary Couns. of Greater Dallas, 1997—98; recipient Sr. Salute award for achievements in edn., City of Dallas and NYL Care, 1996; grantee, NSF, The Women's U., 1963—65. Mem.: AAUW, NEA, Metroplex Educators Sci. Assn., Rocky Mountain Sociol. Assn., So. Sociol. Assn., Chem. Soc., Tex. Assn. Bilingual Educators, Tex. Tchrs. Assn., League United Latin Am. Citizens (pres. College Station 1973—74, past dist. dir. Corpus Christi), Pan Am. Round Table, Fiesta Bilingual Toastmasters. Avocations: ballroom dancing, comedy. Home and Office: 5005 Oak Trl Dallas TX 75232-1643

CIRONE, WILLIAM JOSEPH, educational administrator; b. Bklyn., Dec. 27, 1937; s. Joseph Nicholas and Marie Ann (Basile) C.; m. Barbara Jane Skirkie, Dec. 22, 1962; 1 child, Peter Craig. BA, Providence Coll., 1959; MA, NYU, 1960; adminstrv. cert., U. Calif., Santa Barbara, 1977. Tchr. N.Y.C. Pub. Schs., 1960-68; dir. product devel. ednl. divsn. Mead Corp., Atlanta, 1968-70, dir. mktg., 1970-73; founder, dir. Ctr. Cmty. Edn. and Citizen Participation, Santa Barbara, Calif., 1973-82; supt. schs. Santa Barbara County, 1983—. Vis. fellow Chisholm Inst. Tech., Melbourne, Australia, 1986; vis. scholar Ctr. for excellence Tenn. State U., 1986. Host (cable talk shows) Education On-Line-A Line to Learning, Cirone on Schools. Bd. dirs., chair student aide com. Santa Barbara Cmty. Found.; bd. dirs., 1998-; bd. chmn., 2003-; bd. dirs. Cmty. Action Commn., 1973-81, Cmty. Resource Info. Svc., 1978-82, Fin. Crisis Mgmt. Assistance Team, 1993—, Nat. Partnership in Edn., 1998—, S.B. Fightnig Balk, 1994-, chmn.2002-, Calif. Alliance for Arts Edn., 1999—, Ctr. for Learning and Citizenship, Santa Barbara Anti-Defamation League, 2001--; bd. dirs., sec. Pvt. Industry Coun., Santa Barbara, 1999—; bd. dirs. Industry Edn. Coun. Santa Barbara, 1983—, pres., 1990, 99; bd. dirs. Coun. of Alcoholism and Drug Abuse, 1998—, Santa Barbara Lung Assn., 1983-87, Philip Francis Siff Ednl. Found., 1986—; bd. dirs. Impact II, 1989—, pres., 1993-99; bd. dirs. Nat. Comm. Edn. Assn., 1989-92, pres., 1990; regional chair Calif. County Supt. Assn., 1990-96, bd. dirs. media and values, 1989-92; hon. bd. dirs. So. Coast Spl. Olympics; mem. Gov.'s Commn. on Earthquake Hazards, 1981; mem. state bd. Common Cause, 1974-77, organizer and 1st state chmn., Ga., 1970-73; mem. voter accessibility adv. bd. Santa Barbara County, 1986—; mem. adv. bd. CALM, Peace Resource Ctr., Marymount Sch., Women's Cmty. Bldg., Jodi House, Girl Scouts U.S.; comdrs. cmty. liaison com. Vandenberg AFB; mem. Access Theatre; mem. Hon. Commn. for Goleta Hosp.; mem. campaign cabinet Santa Barbara United Way, 1991,

98; adv. bd. Santa Barbara Brand Opera Assn., 1996—; co-chair State Supts. Statewide Arts Task Force, 1997. Recipient Smallheiser award United Fedn. Tchrs., 1968, Hon. Svc. award 15th Dist. PTA, 1979, 81, Intercongregation Orgn. Project Action award, 1995, Anti-Defamation League Santa Barbara Disting. Svc. award, 1996, Meritorious Svc. award Cmty. Action Com., Santa Barbara, 1981, Ind. Living Resource Ctr., 1985, Hon. Svc. award Calif. State PTA, 1995, 99 for '99 award, Santa Barbara C. of C., 1993-99, Profl. Publ. award Calif. County Supts. Assn., Comm. Achievement award Toastmasters Internat., 1999, Santa Barbara Wildlife Care Network award, 2000, Excellence in Svc. award South Coast Bus. and Tech., 2000, Vanguard award, 2002, Calif. Outstanding Art Educators' award Calif. Art's Commn., Emmanus Disting. Cmty. Svc. award, 2002-, Easy Lift Van Guard award, 2002; named Calif. Cmty. Educator of Yr., Calif. Cmty. Edn. Assn., 1984, Pub. Servant of Yr., Santa Barbara County, 1987. Mem. World Future Soc. (life), Am. Assn. Sch. Adminstrs., Assn. Calif. Sch. Adminstrs. (Region XIII Adminstr. of Yr. award 2002), So. Coast Coord. Coun. (past chmn., past exec. com.), Nat. Soc. Fundraising Execs., Automobile Assn. Am. (So. Calif. adv. bd.), Phi Delta Kappa. Democrat. Unitarian Universalist. Home: 953 Elk Grove Ln Solvang CA 93463-9608 Office: PO Box 6307 Santa Barbara CA 93160-6307

CISLER, VALERIE CLARE, music educator, pianist; b. Manitwoc, Wis., June 5, 1958; d. Emil Edward and Diane Clare C.; 1 child, Lauren Clare. BMus magna cum laude, Silver Lake Coll., 1981; MMus, Ea. N.Mex. U., 1983; D Musical Arts, U. Okla., 1993. Grad. asst. Ea. N.Mex. U., Portales, 1981-83, instr. of music, 1983-86; studio tchr., piano Kowalchyk/Lancaster Studio, Norman, Okla., 1987-88, Cisler Piano Studio, Moore, Okla., 1987-94; asst. prof. of music U. Nebr., Kearney, 1994—99, assoc.prof., 1999—. Dir. piano pedagogy program U. Nebr., Kearney, 1994—, chair grad. music program; clinician Alfred Pub. Co., Inc., Van Nuys, Calif., 1996—. Author: (books) Alfred's Basic Piano Libr.-Composition, Level 1A, 1B, 1996, Level 2, 1997, Level 3, 1998. Recipient Profl. Achievement award Silver Lake Coll. Alumni Assn., Manitowoc, Wis., 1996. Mem. Coll. Music Soc., Nebr. Music Tchr.'s Assn. (adjudicator 1994-97), Soc. Am. Music, Music Tchrs. Nat. Assn., Nat. Certification Assn.

CISNA, SUSAN JO, language arts educator; b. Mattoon, Ill., Jan. 24, 1950; d. William F. and Wanda L. (Bartimus) Grimes; m. Dennis E. Cisna, June 6, 1970; children: Michelle, Douglas. BS in Edn., Ea. Ill. U., 1971, MEd, 1992. 4th grade, 5th grade, 8th grade lang. arts tchr. Tuscola (Ill.) Dist. 301, 1970—. Writing cons. Power Writing, Palo Alto, Calif., 1992-94. Citizens cons. com. Villa Grove (Ill.) City Coun., 1993—. Named Ill. Tchr. of Yr. award of excellence, 1994. Mem. Internat. Reading Assn., Nat. Coun. Tchrs. English, Ill. Reading Coun. (regional dir.), Tuscola Edn. Assn., Ea. Ctrl. Reading Coun. (pres. 2000—), Phi. Delta Kappa. Home: 408 Mccoy Ave Villa Grove IL 61956-9770 Office: East Prairie Sch 409 S Prairie St Tuscola IL 61953-1798 E-mail: scisna@tascola.k12.il.us.

CISSELL, WILLIAM BERNARD, health studies educator; b. Fancy Farm, Ky., Apr. 21, 1941; s. James S. and Lucille Marie C.; m. Mary Ellen Siebe, Aug. 26, 1967; 1 child, Lisa Kyung Mi. BS, So. Ill. U., Carbondale, 1967; MS in Pub. Health, UCLA, 1970; PhD, So. Ill. U., 1977. Cert. health edn. specialist. Curriculum coord. Dept. Def. Schs., 1972-75; asst. prin. Teagu (Korea) Am. Sch., 1975-77; asst. prof. U. Tex., Austin, 1977-79, East Tenn. State U., Johnson City, 1979-84, assoc. prof., 1984-89; prof., chmn. health studies Tex. Woman's U., Denton, 1989-98, prof., 1997—; dir. Tex. Statewide Coordinated Statement of Need Project, 1997—2001; chmn. adv. bd. Prairie Area Health Edn. Ctr., 1997—2001. Vis. prof., acting coord. behavioral health promotion and edn. dept. pub. health Jackson State U., 2001-2002; project dir. AIDS Edn. & Tng. Ctr. Tex. and Okla.; mem. joint com. on grad. standards Am. Assn. for Health Edn. and Soc. for Pub. Health Edn., 1993-96; treas. Commn. Nat. Com. for Health Edn. Credentialing, 1989-91; mem. Nat. Task Force for Prep. and Practice of Health Educators, 1986-88; dep. coord. Coalition Nat. Health Edn. Orgns., 2002-; pres. Tenn./Amazonas Ptnrs. of the Ams., 1987-88, Tenn./Amazonas Venezuela Ptnrs. of the Ams., 1981-82. Co-editor: Community Orgn., 1990, (newsletter) SHESIGN, 1989-92, Tenn. So. Pub. Health Edn., 1985-88. Chmn. sch. health com. Am. Lung Assn., Dallas, 1990-92; mem. evaluation com. Smoke Free Class 2000, 1991-93; mem. school site task force Am. Heart Assn., 1985-90. Served with USMC, 1961-64. Mem. Tex. Assn. Health, Phys. Edn., Recreation and Dance (chair cmty. health sect. 1993), Soc. Pub. Health Edn. (historian 1990-92, chair nominating and leadership devel. com. 1991-92, trustee 1995-97, disting. fellow award 1996, co-chmn. history com. 2000-02), Soc. Pub. Health Edn. and Am. Assn. for Health Edn. (baccalaureate approval process com. 1993—), Tenn. Soc. Pub. Health Edn. (pres. 1987-88), Am. Pub. Health Assn. (chmn. SHE sect. 2001-, SHE sect. program com. 2000-02), Tex. Soc. Pub. Health Edn. (pres. 1995-96, Helen Hill Disting. Svc. award 1994, Past Pres. award 1995, Dorothy Huskey Disting. Career award 1997), Golden Key Honor Soc. (co-advisor 1992-97, 2002—), Phi Kappa Phi, Eta Sigma Gamma (co-advisor Alpha Phi chpt. 1992—, disting. svc. award 1997), Denton Breakfast Club (pres.-elect 1999, pres. 2000-01), Kiwanis Internat. (sponsor, U. North Tex. Cir. K 1995-98), Divsn. 39, Tex./Okla. Dist. Kiwanis Internat. (sec. 1993-94), TAMS Key Club (sponsor 1998-2001). Office: Tex Woman's U Dept of Health Studies PO Box 425499 Denton TX 76204-5499

CISZEK, SISTER BARBARA JEAN, educational administrator; b. Berwyn, Ill., June 8, 1946; d. Walter Arthur and Bernice Therese (Demski) C. AB, Loyola U., Chgo., 1971; MA, Concordia U., River Forest, Ill., 1987, CAS, 1994. Cert. tchr., adminstr., supr., Ill. 2d and 4th grade tchr. Our Lady of Mt. Carmel, Melrose Park, Ill., 1968; 1st grade tchr. St. Francis Xavier Sch., LaGrange, Ill., 1968-69; primary tchr. Alexine Montessori Sch., LaGrange Park, Ill., 1971-73, adminstr., tchr., 1973-79; dir. MECA Montessori Sch., Hinsdale, Ill., 1979-86; ednl. cons. CEDA, Chgo., 1988-91; exec. dir. Chgo. Metro Assn. for Edn. of Young Children, 1991-98; prin. Cardinal Bernardin Early Childhood Ctr., Chgo., 1998—. Adj. faculty mem. Concordia U., 1991—; mem. adv. bd. Ctr. for Early Childhood Leadership, Nat. Louis U., Chgo., 1994—. Co-author: Facilitating Montessori All Day, 1989. Mem. ASCD, Nat. Assn. for Edn. of Young Children, Am. Montessori Soc. (cons., cert.), Ill. Montessori Soc. (bd. dirs. 1988-93), Chgo. Assn. for Edn. of Young Children, Nat. Assn. Early Childhood Tchr. Educators. Office: Cardinal Bernardin Early Childhood Ctr 1651 W Diversey Pkwy Chicago IL 60614-1027

CITRON, BEATRICE SALLY, law librarian, lawyer, educator; b. Phila., May 19, 1929; d. Morris Meyer and Frances (Teplitsky) Levinson; m. Joel P. Citron, Aug. 7, 1955 (dec. Sept. 1977); children: Deborah Ann, Victor Ephraim. BA in Econs. with honors, U. Pa., 1950; MLS, Our Lady of the Lake U., 1978; JD, U. Tex., 1984. Bar: Tex. 1985; cert. all-level sch. libr., secondary level tchr. Tex. Claims examiner Social Security Adminstrn., Pa., Fla. and N.C., 1951-59; head libr. St. Mary's Hall, San Antonio, 1979-80; media, reference and rare book libr., asst. and assoc. prof. St. Mary's U. Law Libr., San Antonio, 1984-89; asst. dir. St. Thomas U. Law Libr., Miami, Fla., 1989-96, assoc. dir./head pub. svc., 1996-99, acting dir., 1997-98. Law libr. cons., 2000—. Mem.: ABA, South Fla. Assn. Law Librs. (treas. 1992—94, v.p. 1994—95, pres. 1995—96), S.E. Assn. Law Librs. (newsletter, program and edn. coms. 1991—98), S.W. Assn. Law LIbrs. (continuing edn. com. 1986—88, chmn. local arrangements 1987—88), Am. Assn. Law Librs. (publs. com. 1987—88, com. on rels. with info. vendors 1991—93, bylaws com. 1994—96).

CITTONE, HENRY ARON, hotel and restaurant management educator; s. Joseph and Devora C.; m. Liliane, Oct. 2, 1965; children: Henry Joseph, Marc Ely. Student, Trade and Tech. Coll., L.A., 1971; MS, U. Houston, 1990; postgrad. in edn., Fla. Atlantic U., Boca Raton, 1993-94. Food svc. mgr. U. So. Calif., L.A., 1971; mgr. food and beverage Sheraton Poste Inn, Cherry Hill, N.J., 1972-73; resident mgr. Aruba Caribbean Hotel, Netherlands Antilles, 1973-74, Lima (Peru) Sheraton Hotel, 1974-76; dir. food and beverage Bahia Mar Hotel, Ft. Lauderdale, Fla., 1978-79, Maison Dupuy, New Orleans, 1979-81, Virgin Isle Hotel, St. Thomas, 1981-84; asst. prof. hotel and restaurant mgmt. Galveston Coll. (Tex.), 1984-90; prof. Morehead (Ky.) State U., 1990-92; instr. Coll. V.I., 1983-84, Houston C.C., 1985-90; prof., assoc. dean Fairfax U., La.; dir. food and beverage Gov.'s Club of West Palm Beach, Fla., 2002—. Adj. faculty North Miami (Fla.) Johnson and Wales U., 1994. With Israeli Army, 1956-59. Recipient Cert. Hotal Adminstr. Designation award Ednl. Inst. AH & MA, 1986. Mem. Nat. Restaurant Assn., Am. Hotel and Motel Assn., Internat. Hotel Sales Mgmt. Assn., Internat. Soc. Food and Beverage Execs., Coun. on Hotel, Restaurant, and Instnl. Edn., CHRIE (internat. exch. com.), Conrad Hilton Coll. Alumni Assn. (Disting. Hospitality Educator of Yr. 1988), Global Hoteliers Club. E-mail: CittonHA@msn.com.

CLAIR, THEODORE NAT, educational psychologist; b. Stockton, Calif., Apr. 19, 1929; s. Peter David and Sara Renee (Silverman) C.; m. Laura Gold, June 19, 1961; children: Shari, Judith. AA, U. Calif., Berkeley, 1949, AB, 1950; MS, U. So. Calif., 1953, MEd, 1963, EdD, 1969. Tchr., counselor L.A. City Schs., 1957-63; psychologist Alamitos Sch. Dist., Garden Grove, Calif., 1963-64, Arcadia (Calif.) Unified Sch. Dist., 1964-65; head psychologist Wiseburn Sch. Dist., Hawthorne, Calif., 1966-69; asst. prof. spl. edn., coord. sch. psychology program U. Iowa, Iowa City, 1969-72; dir. pupil pers. svcs. Orcutt (Calif.) Union Sch. Dist., 1972-73; adminstr. Mt. Diablo Unified Sch. Dist., 1973-77; program dir., psychologist San Mateo County Office Edn., Redwood City, 1977-91; assoc. prof. John F. Kennedy U. Sch. Mgmt., 1975-77; pvt. practice as ednl. psychologist specializing in Attention Defecit Disorders Menlo Park, 1978—; pvt. practice marriage and family counselor specializing in Attention Defecit Disorders, 1978—. Dir. Peninsula Vocat. Rehab. Inst., 1978—; psychologist Coll. Counseling Svc., Menlo Park, 1992-2001, Calif. Pacific Hosp., San Francisco, 1993—; mem. adv. bd. Kitty Petty ADD/LD Inst., Palo Alto. Author: Phenylketonuria and Some Other Inborn Errors of Amino Acid Metabolism, 1971; editor Jour. Calif. Ednl. Psychologists, 1992-94; contbr. articles to profl. jours. Served with USNR, 1952-54. Mem. Am. Assn. Marriage & Family Therapy (Calif. divsn.), Calif. Assn. Marriage and Family Therapists, Palo Alto B'nai B'rith Club (pres.), Stanford Club Palo Alto. Home and Office: 56 Willow Rd Menlo Park CA 94025-3654

CLAPS, JUDITH BARNES, educational consultant; b. N.Y.C., Sept. 8, 1938; d. Milton and Marguerite (Goodkind) Tarlau; m. Wayne C. Barnes, July 17, 1957 (div. 1968); children: David, Dan; m. Francis S. Claps, June 25, 1978. BA, Antioch Coll., 1961; MEd, Lehigh U., 1964; AA, William Glasser Inst., Calif., 1984. Tchr. Cedarville (Ohio) Schs., 1960-61, Quakertown (Pa.) Schs., 1961-62, Bethlehem (Pa.) Schs., 1962-95, social worker, 1991-95. In-svc. cons. JB Claps & Assocs., Hellertown, Pa., 1982—; adj. prof. East Stroudsburg U., Pa., 1982-90, De Sales U., Pa., 2001—; pres. Lehigh Valley Coun. for Social Studies, 1990-92; judge Nat. History Day, U. Md., 1989—. Author: Making the Parent Connection, 2001, The Quality School: Tools to Use, 2001, Easy Writer: Learning to Write and Loving It, 2002; creator: pamphlet Rap It Up, 1984, Freemansburg-A Canal Town, 1984, Bethlehem, 1986. Ednl. creator, bd. dirs. Burnside Plantation, Bethlehem, 1982—; mem. adv. coun. Ret. and Sr. Vol. Program. Named History Tchr. of Yr., DAR, Bethlehem, 1984, Pa. Soc. Studies Tchr. of Yr., Pa. Coun. for Social Studies, 1989, nominated for Pa. Tchr. of Yr., 1990. Mem. NEA, William Glasser Inst., Pa. State Edn. Assn., Bethlehem Edn. Assn., Phi Delta Kappa. Avocations: cooking, theater, travel, books, walking. Home: 3430 Drifting Dr Hellertown PA 18055-9601

CLARK, ALAN MARTIN, band director; b. Chattanooga, Tenn., Sept. 1, 1955; s. Leroy B. and Ruth Olene (Martin) C.; m. Barbara Faye Brinkley Johnson, July 19, 1991); 1 child, Stephanie Nickole. BS in Music Edn. magna cum laude, Tenn. Tech. U., 1977; MA in Music Edn. summa cum laude, Western Ky. U., 1979. Cert. educator in instrumental music, Tenn. Grad. asst. Western Ky. U., Bowling Green, 1977-79; band dir., music tchr. Marion County Schs., Jasper, Tenn., 1979-81; performing musician, bus. mgr. Jack Daniels' Original Silver Cornet Band, Nashville, 1981-86; records analyst State of Tenn., Nashville, 1986-93; band dir. Sumner County Schs., Hendersonville, Tenn., 1993—. Performer Sumner County Symphony, 2001—; band dir. Hunters Lane Cmty. Band, Nashville, 1991-96; bd. dirs. Hunters Lane Cmty. Edn., Nashville, 1992-96; pvt. brass instrn. Sumner County Schs., Gallatin, Tenn., 1992—; band camp instr. Hillsboro/Harpeth/Beech High Sch., Nashville, Hendersonville, 1992—. Performer (music/band) Freelance Trombone/Bariton, 1992—, Nashville Wind Ensemble, 1993—, Sumner County Symphony, 2000—. Poll observer CNN/CBS/local affiliates, Nashville, 1991—; mem., treas. Madison Sertoma Club, Nashville, 1992-93. Nat. Soloist finalist Tubists Universal Brotherhood Assn., 1976. Mem. Music Educators Nat. Conf., Tenn. Edn. Assn., Tubists Universal Brotherhood Assn., Middle Tenn. Sch. Band and Orch. Assn., Phi Mu Alpha. Ch. of Christ. Avocations: golf, raquetball, reading, listening to music, radio controlled airplanes. Bus. Office: Merrol Hyde Magnet School 128 Township Drive Hendersonville TN 37075-3821 E-mail: clarka2@k12tn.net.

CLARK, ANN BLAKENEY, educational administrator; b. Greensboro, N.C., May 21, 1958; d. Blake Campbell and Nancy (Hamel) C. BA in English, Davidson (N.C.) Coll., 1980; MEd, U. Va., 1982; postgrad., U. N.C., 1985—. Spl. edn. tchr. Virginia Beach (Va.) Pub. Schs., 1982-83, Devonshire Elem. Sch., 1983-87; asst. prin. Montclare Elem. Sch., 1987-88; prin. Shamrock Gardens Elem. Sch., 1988-90, Alexander Graham Mid. Sch., Charlotte, N.C., 1990-96, Vans H.S., NC, 1996—2001; asst. supt. high schs. Charlotte-Mecklenburg Schs., Charlotte, NC, 2001—. Vice pres. Jr. League of Charlotte, 1988-89; mem. bd. mgrs. Johnston YMCA, Charlotte, 1987—; chmn. bd. A Child's Place, Charlotte, 1989—. Named Nat. Principal of Yr. 1994; named Tchr. of Yr., Devonshire Elem., 1987-88. Mem. ASCD, NAESP, Coun. for Exceptional Children, Coun. for Children, Phi Delta Kappa. Republican. Episcopalian. Avocations: golf, tennis. Home: 7920 Neal Rd Charlotte NC 28262-3226*

CLARK, BARBARA JUNE, elementary education educator; b. Leoti, Kans., May 29, 1934; d. Robert Carter and Adlee Belle (Wilson) C. BS in Edn., Ft. Hays State U., 1958, MS in Edn., 1967. 4th grade tchr. McKinley Elem., Liberal, Kans., 1954—56, Lincoln Elem., Liberal, 1958—61, 5th grade tchr., 1961—62, 4th grade tchr., 1962—2001. Mathfest chmn. Unified Sch. Dist. 480, Liberal, 1987-88, grade level chmn., 1988-89, social studies textbook selection com., 1990-92, intensive assistance team, 89-91, Lincoln Sch. site coun., 1993-94, Lincoln preassessment team, 1992-98, Lincoln strategic action com., 1994-98, reading textbook selection com., 1995-96, others; quality performance accreditation chmn. math team, 1998-2001; with Ft. Hay State U. travel study tours, Hawaii, 1960, Europe, 1962. Editor: Wilson History, 1970—; author Lincoln School History, 1978. Singer Meth. Chancel Choir; pres. Meth Wesleyan Svc. Guild, 1963-66, v.p. 1962-63, treas., 60-62, rec. sec. Meth Dodge City Dist., 1965-68; sponsor, bus. mgr. Meth Ctrl. Kans. Conf. Mission Edn. Tour, 1975-78; rec. sec. United Meth. Ch. Circle 9, 1986-88, v.p., 1996-99; vol. Lincoln Elem., 2002-03. Recipient Representative Young Tchr. award Jr. C. of C., Liberal, 1962, PTA Life Membership, Lincoln Elem., Liberal, 1962, Morale Enhancement award, 2001, Elem. Tchr. of Yr., 2001. Mem. NEA, Kans. NEA, Liberal NEA (Master Tchr. award 1989), Bus. and Profl. Women's Club (pres. 1979-80, treas. 1989-90, 94—, v.p. 1991-94, fin. chair 1992—, Woman of Yr. award 1974), Beta Sigma Phi (Laureate Pi chpt. treas. 1981-91, pres. 1991—, Silver Circle award 1992, Order of Rose award 1974), Delta Kappa Gamma (Phi state conv. registration chmn. 1974, 95, rec. sec. 1986-88, music chmn. 1992-94, pres. 1999-2002, state mem. com. 2001-03, state rsch. com. 2003—), Santa Fe Trail Assn. (charter). Avocations: geneology, history.

CLARK, CAROL RUTH JONES, secondary education educator; b. Thomasville, N.C., Feb. 26, 1949; d. J.C. and Dorothy Darr (Clinard) Jones; m. William David Clark, July 24, 1971; children: Benjamin David, Andréa Ruth. BA in Edn., So. Wesleyan U., 1971. Cert. 4-9 lang. arts tchr., N.C. Tchr. Liberty (S.C.) Elem. Sch., 1971-73, Ridgeway (Va.) Elem. Sch., 1973-74; interim tchr. kindergarten Guilford Primary Sch., Greensboro, N.C., 1982; tchr. lang. arts and Bible Wesleyan Acad., High Point, N.C., 1985—. H.S. sponsor Jr. Civitan Club, 1993-94; sponsor H.S. Student Coun., 1993-97. Tchr. 1st Wesleyan Ch., 1989—, coll. and career leader, 1988-92, tchr. adult class, 1986-96, mem. drama team and music ensemble, 1992-94. Mem. Assn. Christian Schs. Internat. (speaker cheerleading camp 1992, workshop leader 1990, 92). Republican. Avocations: piano, singing, walking, cooking, reading. Office: Wesleyan Acad 1917 N Centennial St High Point NC 27262-7602

CLARK, CHARLES M., JR., medical school administrator; b. Greensburg, Ind., Mar. 12, 1938; s. Charles Malcolm and Mary Louise (Christian) C.; m. Julia Berg Freeman, Jan 27, 1963 (div. 1982); children: Margaret Louise, Brian Alexander; m. Eleanor DeArman Kinney, June 25, 1983; 1 child, Janet Marie Clark. BA, Ind. U., 1960, MD, 1963. From asst. prof. to prof. medicine Ind. U., Indpls., 1969—, from asst. prof. to prof. pharmacology, 1970—; assoc. chief staff rsch. and devel. VA Hosp., Indpls., 1988—2002; dir. Diabetes Rsch. and Tng. Ctr., Indpls., 1977—2002; co-dir. Regenstrief Inst., Indpls., 1993-97; assoc. dean Ind. U. Sch. Medicine, Indpls., 2002—. Chmn. Safety and Quality com. DCCT, 1982-93, Nat. Diabetes adv. bd., 1987-88; chair Nat. Diabetes Edn. Program, 1995-2002; vis. prof. Facultad de Ciencias Medicas, U. Nacional de la Plata, Argentina, 1999-2000. Editor Diabetes Care, 1996-2001; contbr. numerous articles to profl. jours. Lt comdr. USPHS, 1967-69. Mem. ACP, Am. Soc. Clin. Investigation, Internat. Diabetes Fedn., Am. Diabetes Assn. (Banting award 1989). Office: 714 N Senate Ave EF 200 Indianapolis IN 46202 E-mail: chclark@iupui.edu.

CLARK, CLAUDIA J. educational administration, speech, language and learning disabilities professional; b. Bakersfield, Calif., May 18, 1949; d. Norris James and Elizabeth Ann (Nancy) C.; children: Lorin Clark Groshong, Heather Clark Groshong. BA in Linguistics, U. Calif., Riverside, 1970; MS in Communicative Disorders, U. Redlands (Calif.), 1971; PhD in Learning Disabilities, Northwestern U., Evanston, Ill., 1980. Cert. tchr. and adminstr., Oreg. Adj. prof. Calif. State U., Hayward, 1973-74; lang./remediation specialist Lang. Assocs., Orinda, Calif., 1973-75; vis. prof. U. Calif., Berkeley, 1975-76; adj. prof. So. Oreg. Univ., Ashland, 1982—; vis. prof. U. Oreg., Eugene, 1988; resource specialist Helman Sch., Ashland, 1986-87; speech/lang. specialist Medford (Oreg.) Sch. Dist. 549C, 1988-92, asst. dir. spl. edn., 1992—. Rsch. cons. Helman Sch., Ashland, 1987-88; diagnostic cons. Humboldt County Schs., Eureka, Calif., Siskiyou County Schs., Yreka, Calif., 1975. Author: Ambiguity Detection, 1980, Teaching Group Participation Skills, 1988. Pres. Ashland High Arts Advocates, 1992-95. Mem. Learning Disabilities Assn., Oreg. Assn. Supervision and Curriculum Devel., Delta Kappa Gamma, Phi Beta Kappa. Avocations: ballroom dancing, choral singing, travel, skiing, tennis.

CLARK, DEBBIE SUZANNE, secondary school educator; b. Gainesville, Ga., May 21, 1962; d. Don Ewell and Joy Suzanne (Marlowe) C.; m. Jack Cleveland Hurt, Sept. 17, 1988 (div. Oct. 1990). Student, Gainesville Coll., 1979-81; B cum laude, U. Ga., 1983, M, 1986. Cert. tcrh., Ga. Mktg. educator Johnson High Sch., Gainesville, Ga., 1983—. Contbr. articles to newspapers and learning activity packs for marked divsn. of Ohio State U. Facilitator projects Dept. Family Children Svcs., Gainesville, Ga., 1983—, Hall County Humane Soc., 1983—; mem. Hall County Steering Com.; organizer various Red Ribbon Week activities local, county and state level schs., 1988—; organizer various Hall County bus. for reduction of shoplifting, 1983—. Apptd. Hon. Lt. Col.-Aide-de Camp-Gov.'s Office, Ga. Gov. Zell Miller, 1993. Mem. NEA, Distributive Edn. Clubs Am., Am. Vocat. Assn., Ga. Mktg. Edn. Assn. (dir.), Ga. Assn. Educators, Hall County Edn. Assn., Phi Kappa Phi, Kappa Delta Epsilon, Kappa Delta Pi. Republican. Baptist. Home: 2896 Cascade Dr Gainesville GA 30504-5702 Office: Johnson High Sch 3305 Poplar Springs Rd Gainesville GA 30507-8661

CLARK, DIANNE ELIZABETH, religious studies and reading educator; b. Vinton, Iowa, Apr. 20, 1951; d. Edward J. and Bernadine H. (Potthoff) Rhinehart; m. John T. Clark, Oct. 31, 1999; children: Daniel, Craig, Andrea Fullerton. BS/LTD, Concordia Tchr.'s Coll., 1972; MA, U. Iowa, 1986; specialist degree in Christian edn., Concordia Coll., Seward, Nebr., 1991. Cert. classroom tchr. K-9, reading clinician K-12. Dir. Christian edn. Peace Luth. Ch., Hastings, Nebr., 1991—; tchr., reading curriculum com. chair Columbus Community Schs., Columbus Junction, Iowa; tchr. Sylvan Learning Ctr., Coralville, Iowa; substitute tchr. Iowa City Public Schs., Iowa City. Ednl. adv. com. Iowa Wesleyan Coll.; mem. Our Redeemer Preschool Bd.; presenter in field. Mem. NEA, Internat. Reading Assn., Iowa Edn. Assn., Tri-area Reading Assn., Columbus Edn. Assn., Autism Soc. Am., Luth. Edn. Assn. Home: 69 Modern Way Iowa City IA 52240-3068

CLARK, ELIAS, law educator; b. New Haven, Aug. 19, 1921; BA, Yale U., 1943, LL.B., 1947, MA, 1957. Bar: N.Y. 1948, Conn. 1950. Assoc. Cleary, Gottlieb, Friendly & Cox, N.Y.C., 1947-49; mem. faculty Law Sch., Yale U., New Haven, 1949—, prof., 1958—, Lafayette S. Foster prof., 1968-92, Lafayette S. Foster prof. emeritus, 1992—, Myres S. McDougal professorial lectr. law, 1992—. Master Silliman Coll., 1962-81. Co-author: Gratuitous Transfers, 1996, Cases and Materials on Federal Estate and Gift Taxation, 2000; contbr. articles to legal jours. Bd. dirs. Mental Health Conn., 1957-67; bd. dirs. New Haven Found., 1969-76. Mem. Conn. Bar Assn. (Disting. Pub. Service 1959) Home: 1179 Whitney Ave Apt B Hamden CT 06517-3434 Office: Yale U Sch Law SLB 336 127 Wall St New Haven CT 06511-6636

CLARK, EVE VIVIENNE, linguistics educator; b. Camberley, U.K., July 26, 1942; came to U.S., 1967; d. Desmond Charles and Nancy (Aitken) Curme; m. Herbert H. Clark, July 21, 1967; 1 child, Damon Alistair. MA with honors, U. Edinburgh, Scotland, 1965, PhD, 1969. Rsch. assoc. Stanford (Calif.) U., 1969-71, from asst. prof. to assoc. prof., 1971-83, prof., 1983—. Author: Ontogenesis of Meaning, 1979, Acquisition of Romance, 1985, The Lexicon in Acquisition, 1993; co-author: Psychology and Language, 1977. Fellow Ctr. for Advanced Study in the Behavioral Scis., 1979-80, Guggenheim Found., 1983-84. Mem. Dutch Acad. Scis. (fgn.).*

CLARK, FAYE LOUISE, drama and speech educator; b. La., Oct. 9, 1936; m. Warren James Clark, Aug. 8, 1969; children: Roy, Kay Natalie. Student, Centenary Coll., 1954-55; BA with honors, U. Southwestern La., 1962; MA, U. Ga., 1966; PhD, Ga. State U., 1992. Tchr. Nova Exptl. Schs., Ft. Lauderdale, Fla., 1963-65; faculty dept. drama and speech Ga. Perimeter Coll. (formerly DeKalb Coll.), Atlanta, 1967—; chmn. dept., 1977-81. Pres. Hawthorne Sch. PTA, 1983-84. Mem.: Ga. Comm. Assn., Ga. Psychol. Assn., Ga. Theatre Conf. (sec. 1968—69, rep. to Southeastern Theatre Conf. 1969), Nat. Comm. Assn., Atlanta Hist. Soc., Oglethorpe Mus., Thalian-Blackfriars, Atlanta Artists Club (sec. 1981—83, dir. 1983—89), Atlanta Press Club, Friends of Atlanta Opera, Kappa Delta Pi, Sigma Delta Pi, Pi Kappa Delta, Phi Kappa Phi. Home: 2521 Melinda Dr NE Atlanta GA 30345-1918 Office: Ga Perimeter Coll Humanities Dept Dunwoody Campus Dunwoody GA 30338

CLARK, GEORGE WHIPPLE, physics educator; b. Evanston, Ill., Aug. 31, 1928; s. Robert Keep and Margaret (Whipple) C.; m. Elizabeth Kister, Dec. 1956 (div. 1972); children: Katherine, Jacqueline; m. Charlotte Huston

Reischer, Jan. 1988. BA, Harvard U., 1949; PhD, MIT, 1952. Instr. MIT, Cambridge, 1952-54, asst. prof., 1954-60, assoc. prof., 1960-65, prof., 1965-98, Breene M. Kerr prof. physics, 1984-95, prof. emeritus, 1996—. Cons., dir. Am. Sci. and Engring., Inc., Cambridge, 1958-69; dir. Assn. Univs. for Rsch. in Astronomy, Washington, 1982-90. Contbr. numerous articles to profl. jours. Fellow Am. Phys. Soc., Am. Astronomy Soc.; mem. NAS, Am. Acad. Arts and Scis. Office: MIT 37-611 77 Massachusetts Ave Cambridge MA 02139-4301 E-mail: gwc@space.mit.edu.

CLARK, JAMES ALAN, principal; b. Great Lakes, Ill., Sept. 7, 1953; s. Jackie L. and Alvira C. (Garman) C.; m. Suzanne M. Holschbach, Aug. 2, 1986; 1 child, Willis James. BS in Edn., U. Wis., Whitewater, 1975; MS, U. Wis., Milw., 1991. Tchr., coach St. Mary Sch., Janesville, Wis., 1975-77, Medford (Wis.) Jr. High Sch., 1977-79; tchr., prin. St. Patrick Sch., Eau Claire, Wis., 1979-83; prin. St. Paul Sch., Manitowoc, Wis., 1983-89; prin., social studies tchr. St. Frances Cabrini Mid. Sch., Manitowoc, Wis., 1989—. Instr., U. Wis. Ext.; adj. instr., career directed programs, Silver Lake Coll., Manitowoc, Wis.; chmn. accreditation team Diocese of Green Bay (Wis.), 1994, Appleton (Wis.) Cath. Schs., 1993, 96. Mem. Manitowoc Crime Prevention, 1986-89, Gang Task Froce, Manitowoc, 1994—. Mem. ASCD, Nat. Cath. Edn. Assn., Nat. Mid. Sch. Assn., Wis. Assn. Mid. Level. Edn., Diocean Assn. Sch. Adminstrs. (pres. 1992-93, v.p. 1991-92, 2002-2003), Young Men's Christian Assn. Roman Catholic. Avocations: running, reading, sports, politics, family. Home: 522 S 30th St Manitowoc WI 54220-3608 Office: St Frances Cabrini Mid Sch 2109 Marshall St Manitowoc WI 54220-4959

CLARK, JEFFREY WILLIAM, mathematics educator, author; b. Norristown, Pa., Sept. 24, 1961; s. Charles Habby and Martha Margaret (Jones) C.; m. Laura Marie Clark, Oct. 8, 1988. BS, Yale U., 1982, MS, 1985, PhD, 1987. Rsch. analyst Salomon Bros., Inc., N.Y.C., 1987-88; asst. prof. Elon (N.C.) U., 1988—91, 1992—96, assoc. prof., 1996—, chair math. dept., 1994—2000; asst. prof. dept. math. and computer sci. Westminster Coll., New Wilmington, Pa., 1991-92. Author: (with others) Statistics the Easy Way, 1983, Business Statistics, 1985, Quantitative Methods, 1988, Forgotten Statistics, 1998; contbg. author: Dictionary of Business Terms, 1987. Benjamin Silliman fellow Yale U., 1983-85. Mem. Am. Math. Soc., Math. Assn. Am. (S.E. region, dir. N.C. 1997-2000), Assn. Computing Machinery, N.C. Coun. Tchrs. Math. (v.p. colleges, ctrl. region 1997-99). Democrat. Roman Catholic. Avocations: reading, yoga. E-mail: clarkj@elon.edu.

CLARK, JOHN MUNRO, school system administrator; b. Grand Canyon, Ariz., Sept. 16, 1951; s. James K. and Marica Clark; m. Margery Harrision, Aug. 6, 1976; children: Jaime, Preston, Kyndal, Spenser. BA, No. Ariz. U., 1977, MA, 1981. Tchr. Whiteriver (Ariz.) Pub. Schs., 1977-81; asst. prin. Crane Sch. Dist., Yuma, Ariz., 1981-83; prin. Douglas (Ariz.) Pub. Schs., 1983-89; asst. supt. Holbrook (Ariz.) Pub. Schs., 1989-93; supt. Whiteriver (Ariz.) Pub. Schs., 1993—. Presenter in field. With U.S. Army, 1971-73, Viet Nam. Decorated Air medal, Bronze star U.S. Army, Viet Nam, 1971; named Outstanding Young Men of Am., U.S. Army, 1984. Mem. Am. Assn. Sch. Adminstrs., Ariz. Sch. Adminstrs., Ariz. Sch. Svcs. Through Ednl. Tech. (pres. 1994—), Am. Legion, Elks, Masons, Rotary Club. Democrat. Episcopalian. Avocation: collecting old watches and fishing reels. Office: Whiteriver Pub Schs PO Box 190 Whiteriver AZ 85941-0190

CLARK, KATE HELEN, educational administrator; b. Rome, N.Y., Apr. 13, 1945; d. Michael James and Margaret Ellen (Bogan) C. BS, SUNY, Oswego, 1967; MS in Edn., SUNY, Albany, 1971; MS in Spl. Edn., Syracuse U., 1991. Cert. tchr. N-6, spl. edn. N-12, N.Y. Tchr. Schenectady (N.Y.) City Schs., 1967-71, Clinton (Ky.) Ctrl. Schs., 1971-73; pers. and tng. mgr. KMart Corp., Troy, Mich., 1973-90; family educator Consortium for Children's Svcs., Syracuse, N.Y., 1990—. Cons. Project Wrap-A-Round, N.Y. State Dept. Edn., Syracuse, 1993—. Educator/vol. Bike for Life Recreation Program for Adults Without Sight, Liverpool, N.Y., 1990-92; motivator N.Y. State Spl. Olympics, Syracuse, 1994. Recipient Presdl. Fitness awards Nat. Fitness Coun., 1990, 91, 92, 93; N.Y. State Coalition for Young Children with Spl. Needs grantee, 1992. Mem. AAUW, Family Child Care Assn. of Onondaga County, Inc., Onondaga County Child Care Coun., U. Albany Alumni Assn., Am. Profl. Soc. on the Abuse of Children, Am. Orthopsychiat. Assn., Syracuse U. Alumni Assn. Roman Catholic. Avocations: alpine and nordic skiing, biking, race walking, keyboard. Home: 6 E 850 Vine St Liverpool NY 13088 Office: Consortium for Childrens Svc 123 E Water St Syracuse NY 13202-1119

CLARK, KATHLEEN MULHERN, foreign language and literature educator; b. Phila., Oct. 10, 1948; d. John Joseph Jr. and Rosalie (Callahan) Mulhern; m. Robert Lee Clark, Oct. 7, 1972; children: Matthew, Kelly. AB, Immaculata Coll., 1970; MA, Villanova U., 1981; postgrad., U. Laval, Que., Can., 1969, Ecole Francaise des Attachés de Presse, Paris, 1991. Cert. French tchr. French tchr. Great Valley H.S., Devault, Pa., 1971-72, Conestoga Sr. H.S., Berwyn, Pa., 1970-71, 72-78; lectr. fgn. lang. Immaculata (Pa.) Coll., 1973-89, prof. fgn. lang., lit., 1989—, dept. chmn., 1997—. Translator Burroughs Corp., Paoli, Pa., 1976-78; translator, cons. Smith, Kline Animal Health Products, West Chester, Pa., 1985; co-developer, designer Leadership Core Curriculum, Immaculata, 1990—. Class rep. Immaculata Coll. Alumnae Assn., 1970-98, bd. govs. 1996—. Recipient grant U. Laval, 1969, Pew Meml. Trust, 1990. Mem. AAUP, Pa. State MLA (exec. bd. dirs., 1999-2002), Am. Assn. Tchrs. French (v.p. Phila. chpt.), Am. Coun. on Tchg. of Fgn. Langs., Pa. Soc. Tchg. Scholars, Alliance Française, Pi Delta Phi, Lambda Iota Tau. Roman Catholic. Avocations: travel, music. Home: 65 Rossiter Ave Phoenixville PA 19460-2509

CLARK, KATHLEEN VERNON, special education educator; b. Nashville, Apr. 16, 1939; d. Walter Newton Jr. and E. Ruth (Mason) Vernon; m. Stanley Prentiss Clark, Apr. 16, 1962; children: Stanley Martin, Jennifer Kathleen Clark. BA, So. Meth. U., 1961; postgrad., George Peabody Coll., 1975; MA, U. Ala., Tuscaloosa, 1977; EdS, Jacksonville State U., 1986; EdD, U. Ala., Tuscaloosa, 1991. Cert. spl. edn. tchr., Ala. Tchr., spl. olympics coach Piedmont (Ala.) City Schs., 1975-86, testing coord., 1982-86; tchr. Tuscaloosa City Schs., 1986—90, continuing edn. presenter, 1989, chair dept. spl. edn., 1987—89; tchr. Lauderdale County Schs., Florence, Ala., 1990-97. Mem. grad. adv. coun. area of spl. edn. U. Ala., Tuscaloosa, 1989-90; adj. prof. spl. edn. U. No. Ala., 1991-96; spl. edn. tchr. Etowah County Schs., 1997-2001; mem. steering com. So. Assn. Colls. and Schs., sponsor Leo Club. Dir. Meth. Elem. Camps, Sumatanga, Ala., Southeastern Meth. Assembly Grounds; bd. dirs. Lake Junaluska, N.C., 1988-96; pres. Ch. Women United, Decatur, Ala., 1971-72; v.p. United Meth. Women, Northport, Ala., 1988-90; mem. Meth. Commn. on Status and Role of Women, Birmingham, Ala., 1990-92; mem. N. Ala. Meth. Bd. Social Concerns. Mem. NEA, Coun. for Exceptional Children (Tchr. of Yr. 1978), Assn. for Retarded Citizens, Ala. Edn. Assn. (rep. 1988-90, 1999-2001), Kappa Delta Pi, Phi Kappa Phi, Psi Chi. Avocations: reading, traveling. Home: 1001 Clarkview St SW Decatur AL 35601-6203

CLARK, LINDA JANE, elementary school educator; b. Bklyn., Sept. 3, 1963; d. John and Christine D. (Clapp) Bruce; m. Aug. 17, 1991. BS in Elem. Edn. magna cum laude, SUNY, Oswego, 1985; MS in Reading Edn. summa cum laude, SUNY, 1989. Cert. elem., reading edn. tchr., N.Y. Kindergarten tchr. Oswego City Schs., 1985-86; kindergarten tchr. Phoenix (N.Y.) Cen. Schs., 1986-90; tchr. 4th grade Cazenovia (NY) Cen. Schs., 1990—94, tchr. 2d grade, 1996—97, kindergarten tchr., 1999—. Mem. Kappa Delta Pi.

CLARK, M. JUANITA, vocational education evaluator; b. Jackson, Ohio, Apr. 8, 1935; d. James William and Hazel Juanita (Crabtree) Farrar; m. Donald Clark, May 8, 1955; children: Christine, Steven, Bruce, Gregory. BS, Rio Grande Coll., 1977; MS in Edn., U. Dayton, 1984; cert. for vocat. evaluation, Kent State U., 1991—. Bus. edn. tchr. Jackson (Ohio) High Sch., 1977-79; computerized acctg. tchr., fin. assistant Gallia, Jackson, Vinton Joint Vocat. Sch. Dist., Rio Grande, Ohio, 1979-88, tchr. job searching and keeping, 1989-90, vocat. evaluator, 1990—. Southeastern region rep. for Vocational Evaluators State Task Force, Ohio, 1991, '92. Mem. Mem. Am. Vocat. Assn. (Ohio spl. needs div.). Ohio Edn. Assn., Jackson Bus. and Profl. Women's Club (dist. speaker winner 1987, pres. 1993-94). Avocations: oil and water color painting, golf, acting in C.C. plays. Home: 44 Westlawn Ave Jackson OH 45640-1853

CLARK, MARCIA HILEMAN, special education educator; b. Ashland, Ohio, Aug. 18, 1945; d. Wilson Tressler and Betty (Barr) Hileman; m. Terrance W. Clark, Sept. 28, 1968; children: Erin, Adam. BA in Sociology, Mary Washington Coll., 1967; postgrad., No. Ariz. U., 1971-72, Johns Hopkins U., 1991-93. Cert. elem. and spl. edn., Md. Tchr. grade 5 Fairfax (Va.) County Pub. Schs., 1967-69; tchr. grade 3 Flagstaff (Ariz.) County Pub. Schs., 1971-72; music dir. Arlington Echo Camp for Disabled, Millersville, Md., 1973, sci. dir., 1974; sales coord. Avon Products, Inc., Anne Arundel County, Md., 1981-85; spl. edn. tchr. The Harbour Sch., Annapolis, Md., 1985-92, Anne Arundel County Pub. Schs., Annapolis, 1992—. Coach, judge Odyssey of the Mind, 1984-87. Active Crofton Sq. Homeowners Assn. Bd., 1980-85, Crofton Elem. Sch. PTA Bd., 1982-84, Crofton Elem. Sch. Human Rels Com., 1984-85, Crofton Jr. High Sch. PTA Bd., 1987-88, Crofton Middle Sch. Citizen's Adv. Com., 1988-92, Crofton Meadows Elem. Sch. Citizen's Adv. Com., 1989-90, Arundel High Sch. Citizen's Adv. Com., 1990—. Mem. Assn. for Gifted and Talented Youth (bd. mem. 1980-93, pres. 1982-93), Md. Coalition for Gifted and Talented Edn. (sec., liason com. 1991-93, pres. 1993—), Dem. Women of Anne Arundel County. Episcopalian. Avocations: volleyball, reading, collecting antiques. Home: 1501 Farlow Ave Crofton MD 21114-1515

CLARK, MARVETA YVONNE, elementary education educator, consultant, writer; b. Phila., Feb. 23, 1948; d. James Edward Sr. and Louise (Miriam) C. BS, Cheyney State Coll., 1969; MEd., Antioch Coll., 1972. Tchr. William Penn Sch. Dist., Yeadon, Pa., 1969—. Cons. math. curriculum, 1984, reading curriculum, 1986, William Penn Sch. Dist., Darby, Pa.; mem. Am. Women's Econ. Devel. Corp., 1989. Editor-in-chief Milestones Mag. Mem. NEA, Penn. State Edn. Assn., William Penn Edn. Assn. (bldg. rep. 1981-82), Delta Iota chpt. Alpha Kappa Alpha (v.p. Ivy Leaf club 1968), Rho Theta Omega (grad. chpt.). Democrat. Baptist. Home: 502 Evergreen Ln Aston PA 19014-2549

CLARK, MARY TWIBILL, philosopher, educator; b. Phila., Oct. 23; d. Francis S. and Regina (Twibill) Clark. BA, Manhattanville Coll., 1939, L.H.D. (hon.), 1984; MA, Fordham U., 1952, PhD, 1955; postgrad., Yale U., 1968-69; L.H.D. (hon.), Villanova U., 1977. Joined Soc. Sacred Heart, 1939. Tchr., supr. studies secondary schs. Acad. Sacred Heart, Albany, Overbrook, Rochester and N.Y.C., 1941-51; instr. Manhattanville Coll., Purchase, N.Y., 1951-53, asst. prof., 1953-57, assoc. prof., 1957-61, prof. philosophy, 1961-84, chmn. dept., 1962-64, 66-68, 72-79, prof. emeritus, 1984—. Vis. prof. Villanova U., 1980, Fordham U., 1981, 90, 93, St. John Neumann Sem., 1982—, Santa Clara U., 1983, NYU, 1989, SUNY-Purchase, 1991, Fairfield U., 1992, Marquette U., 1993, U. San Francisco, 6 summers; adviser Intercollegiate Assns., Social Action Secretariat, 1956-66; mem. adv. bd. Dionysius, 1977-99, Faith and Philosophy, 1984-87, Personalist Forum, 1985—; fellow Sophia. Author: Augustine, Philosopher of Freedom, 1959, Logic, 1963, Discrimination Today, 1966, Augustinian Personalism, 1970, Augustine: An Introduction, 1984; editor: An Aquinas Reader, 1972, rev. edit., 2000, The Problem of Freedom, 1973; translator Theological Treatises of Marius Victorinus, 1981, Augustine of Hippo's Spirituality, 1984; contbr. articles to profl. jours. Trustee Country Day Sch. of the Sacred Heart, Bryn Mawr, 1993—. Recipient Disting. Alumna award Country Day Sch. Sacred Heart, Bryn Mawr, 1992, Disting. Alumna award Manhattanville Coll., 1999; NEH fellow, 1984-85; hon. mem. Order St. Augustine. Mem. Am. Cath. Philos. Assn. (pres. 1976-77, Aquinas medal 1988), Am. Philos. Assn. (conf. chmn. 1974-76, exec. com. 1988-91), Metaphys. Soc. (exec. com. 1985-88, v.p. 1990-91, pres. 1991-92), Internat. Patristic Assn., Soc. Medieval and Renaissance Philosophy (sec.-treas. 1977-91, v.p. 1991-92, pres. 1992-94, exec. com. 1994—), Internat. Neoplatonic Soc., Conf. Philos. Soc. (exec. com. 1978-86), Soc. Christian Philosophers (exec. com. 1981-84), Cath. Com. Intellectual & Cultural Affairs (exec. com. 1989-92), Kappa Gamma Pi. Address: Manhattanville Coll Purchase NY 10577

CLARK, NANCI, elementary education educator; b. Reno, Apr. 11, 1957; d. Edwin Dail Baggett and Sharon Adair (Patterson) Marks; m. Rodney K. Clark, Oct. 25, 1986; children: Ashley Nichole, Sean Patrick. BS, Calif. State U., 1979, MS, 1983. Bilingual tchr. Moutain View Sch. Dist., 1979; resource specialist, bilingual tchr. Orange (Calif.) Unified Sch. Dist., 1980-88; resource specialist Alvord Unified Sch. Dist., Riverside, Calif., 1988-90, Rialto (Calif.) Unified Sch. Dist., 1990-93, Corona (Calif.)-Norco Unified Sch. Dist., 1993—. Mem. ASCD, Assn. Calif. Sch. Adminstrs. Office: Corona-Norco Unified Sch Dist 1150 Paseo Grande Corona CA 92882-5608 E-mail: clark4@wwdb.org.

CLARK, NOREEN MORRISON, behavioral science educator, researcher; b. Glasgow, Scotland, Jan. 12, 1943; came to U.S., 1948; d. Angus Watt and Anne (Murphy) Morrison; m. George Robert Pitt, Dec. 3, 1982; 1 child, Alexander Robert. BS, U. Utah, 1965; MA, Columbia U., 1972, MPhil, 1975, PhD, 1976. Rsch. coord. World Edn. Inc., N.Y.C., 1972-73; asst. prof. Sch. Pub. Health Columbia U., N.Y.C., 1973-80, assoc. prof., 1980-81, Sch. Pub. Health U. Mich., Ann Arbor, 1981-85, prof., chmn. dept. health behavior and health edn., 1985-95, Marshall H. Becker prof. of pub. health, 1995—, dean, 1995—. Adj. prof. health adminstrn. Sch. Pub. Health Columbia U., 1988—; prin. investigator NIH, 1977—; mem. adv. com. pulmonary diseases Nat. Heart, Lung & Blood Inst., Rockville, Md., 1983-87, mem. adv. com. for prevention, edn. and control, 1987-91, coordinating com. Nat. Asthma Edn. Program, 1991—; assoc. Synergos Inst., N.Y.C., 1987-99; nat. adv. environ. health scis. coun. NIH, 1999—. Co-author: Evaluation of Health Promotion, 1984; editor Health Edn. and Behavior, 1985-97; mem. editorial bd. Women in Health, Advances in Health Edn. and Promotion, Home Health Care Services Quarterly; contbr. articles to profl. jours. Bd. dirs./advisors Aaron Diamond Found., 1990-97, Family Care Internat., N.Y.C., 1987—, Internat. Asthma Coun., Am. Lung Assn., N.Y.C., 1988—, World Edn., Inc., The Healthtrak Found. Prize. Fellow Soc. Pub. Health Edn. (pres. 1985-86, Disting. Fellow award 1987); mem. APHA (chair health edn. sect. 1982-83, Derryberry award in behavioral sci. 1985, Disting. Career award 1994), Am. Thoracic Soc. (Health Edn. Rsch. award Nat. Asthma Edn. Program 1992, Healthtrak Edn. prize 1997), Internat. Union Health Edn., Soc. Behavioral Medicine, Coun. Fgn. Rels., Nat. Acad. Sci. Inst. Medicine, Pi Sigma Alpha. Office: U Mich Sch Pub Health 109 Observatory St Ann Arbor MI 48109-2029

CLARK, PATRICIA RUTH, foreign language educator; b. Lincoln, Nebr., Sept. 26, 1945; d. Martin and Virginia (McDowell) Dunklau; m. Neil B. Clark, Nov. 20, 1965; children: Scott B., Todd B. BA, U. Nebr., 1968. Cert. tchr., Conn. French tchr. Norris H.S., Courtland, Nebr., 1968-69, Canton (Conn.) H.S., 1970; French and Spanish tchr. Renbrook Sch., West Hartford, Conn., 1976—, head of lang. dept., 1980—. Workshop presenter Mid. Sch. Conf., West Hartford, 1991, 93, Advocates of Lang. Learning, Mpls., 1988, Conn. Coun. Lang. Tchrs., 1993-94. Mem. Shelterworks, Bloomfield, 1989-94, bd. dirs., 1994. Recipient Staf Pedagogique award Amb. de France, 1994. Mem. Am. Coun. Tchrs. Fgn. Langs., Conn. Coun. Lang. Tchrs. (Helen Amaral award 1993), Orgn. Progressor Educators, Nat. Network Elem. Lang., Alliance Francaise. Avocations: cycling, gardening, dance. Office: Renbrook Sch 2865 Albany Ave Hartford CT 06117-1899

CLARK, PRISCILLA ALDEN, retired elementary education educator; b. Ray, Ariz., June 4, 1940; d. Edmund A. and Rena F. White; m. Larry C. Clark, Sept. 5, 1959; children: Russell, Kenneth, Clifford, Thomas. BS, Tex. Woman's U., 1987. Cert. elem. tchr., ESL tchr. Tchr. kindergarten and pre-kindergarten, grade level chair Irving (Tex.) Ind. Sch. Dist.; kindergarten tchr. Shady Grove Day Care, Irving; tchr. Irving (Tex.) Sch. Dist.; ret., 2003. Active in ch. and boy scouts; dir. new beginnings Diocese of Dallas and Ft. Worth. Recipient Silver Beaver award. Mem. Sci. Tchrs. Assn. Tex. (dist. sci. trainer), Kindergarten Tchrs. Tex., Assn. Tex. Profl. Educators (state del.), Mortar Bd., Irving Theatre Guild, Pi Lambda Theta (chair nat. com., conf. chair region VII, nat. spkr., internat. v.p. 2001-, pres. Alpha Sigma chpt., pres. Region VII, Region 7 Outstanding award 1996, Internat. Thelma Jean Brown Outstanding Classroom Tchr. award 1997), Alpha Chi, Delta Delta Delta, Omega Rho Alpha, Delta Kappa Gamma (pres. Mu Omicron chpt., Internat. Woman of Yr. 1992-93). Home: 2717 Peach Tree Ln Irving TX 75062-3230

CLARK, RICHARD WALTER, education consultant; b. Mt. Pleasant, Iowa, Apr. 14, 1936; s. Samuel Richard and Floreine Eunice (Walz) C.; m. Rosemary Helma Savage, June 10, 1958; children: Melissa O'Neal, Cameron Clark. BA, U. Wash., 1957, MA, 1963, PhD, 1970. Cert. tchr., prin., supt., Wash. Lectr., grad. asst. U. Wash., Seattle, 1960-61; tchr. Bellevue (Wash.) Pub. Schs., 1961-65, adminstr., 1965-91, dep. supt., to 1991; sr. assoc. Ctr. for Ednl. Renewal, U. Wash., Seattle, 1987—, Inst. for Ednl. Inquiry, Seattle, 1992—; exec. dir. Nat. Network Ednl. Renewal, 2001—. Cons. Pew Charitable Trusts, Phila., 1988-2001, MacArthur Found., Chgo., 1991-92, Coalition of Essential Schs., Brown U., Providence, 1990-97, Ednl Commn. of the States, Denver, 1990-91, Calgary (Alta., Can.) Bd. Edn., 1990-91, others. Author: Effective Speech, 1982, 3d edit., 1994, (with others) Glencoe English 10, 11, 12, 1981, 2nd edit., 1985, (with others) Kids and School Reform, 1997, Effective Professional Development Schools, 1999; contbbr. articles to profl. jours., chpts. to books. Pres. Youth Eastside Svcs., Bellevue, 1972. Capt. USMC, 1957-63. Recipient Outstanding Performance Pub. Svc. award Seattle King County Mcpl. League, 1987; named Educator of Yr., Lions Club, 1991. Mem.: Nat. Soc. Study of Edn., Wash. Assn. Sch. Adminstrs., Am. Edn. Rsch. Assn., Phi Delta Kappa. Methodist. Home and Office: 209 140th Ave Bellevue WA 98005 E-mail: clark@msn.com.

CLARK, ROBERT CHARLES, law educator; b. New Orleans, Feb. 26, 1944; s. William Vernon and Edwina Ellen (Nuessly) C.; m. Kathleen Margaret Tighe, June 1, 1968; children— Alexander Ian, Matthew Tighe. BA, Maryknoll Sem., 1966; PhD, Columbia U., 1971; JD, Harvard U., 1972. Bar: Mass. 1972. Assoc. firm Ropes & Gray, Boston, 1972-74; asst. prof. Yale U. Law Sch., New Haven, 1974-76, assoc. prof., 1976-77, prof., 1977-78; prof. law Harvard Law Sch., Cambridge, Mass., 1979, dean of Law Sch., 1989—2003, disting. svc. prof, Austin Wakeman Scott prof. of law, 2003—. Contbr. articles to profl. jours. Mem. Am. Bar Assn.*

CLARK, ROBERT NEWHALL, electrical and aeronautical engineering educator; b. Ann Arbor, Mich., Apr. 17, 1925; s. Ellef S. and Esther (Baker) C.; m. Mary Quiatt, Aug. 20, 1949; children: Charles W., John R., Timothy J., Franklin T. BSEE, U. Mich., 1950, MSEE, 1951; PhD, Stanford U., 1969. Registered profl. engr., Wash., Minn. Rsch. engr. Honeywell, Inc., Mpls., 1951-57; lectr. Stanford U., 1968; prof. elec. engring. U. Wash., Seattle, 1957—, prof. aeronautics and astronautics, 1986-94; prof. emeritus, 1994—. Vis. scientist Fraunhofer Gesellschaft, Karlsruhe, W.Ger., 1976-77; guest prof. U. Duisburg, W.Ger., 1983-84; cons. analyst Boeing Aerospace Co., Seattle, 1971-92. Author: Introduction to Automatic Control Systems, 1962, Fault Diagnosis in Dynamic Systems, 1989, Control System Dynamics, 1996, Issues of Fault Diagnosis for Dynamic Systems, 2000. With USMC, 1943-46. NSF fellow, 1966-68. Fellow IEEE (life), AIAA (assoc.). Home: 3900 50th Ave NE Seattle WA 98105-5238 Office: U Wash PO Box 352500 Seattle WA 98195-2500

CLARK, RONALD DUANE, chemistry educator; b. Hollywood, Calif., Nov. 21, 1938; s. Marvin Ansel and Elsie Susanna (Appel) C.; m. Rosalind Estelle Proell, Sept. 9, 1967; children: Jennifer, Roger, Kenneth, Stephanie. BS, UCLA, 1960; PhD, U. Calif., Riverside, 1964. Postdoctoral researcher Mich. State U., East Lansing, 1964-65; research chemist Standard Oil Co. Ohio, Warrensville, 1965-69; prof. chemistry N.Mex. Highlands U., Las Vegas, 1969—2000, prof. emeritus, 2002—, dean sch. sci. and tech., 1988-91, dir. rsch. and sponsored projects, 1991—95, dir. computer network svcs. group, 1995—99. Pres. Cycad Products, Las Vegas, 1983—. Author: Chemistry-The Science and the Scene, 1975; contbr. articles to profl. jours. Grantee NSF, Dept. of Energy, NASA. Mem. SPIE, Am. Chem. Soc. (holder offices local chpts.). Republican. Home: 763 Dora Celeste Dr Las Vegas NM 87701-5154

CLARK, ROSE SHARON, elementary school educator; b. Winslow, Ind., Oct. 31, 1942; d. William Noel Fettinger and Mary Emaline Jones; m. Charles Edgar Clark, June 2, 1968; children: Mary Elizabeth, Christopher Edgar. BS, Oakkland City (Ind.) U., 1964; MS, Ind. U., 1968. Elem. edn. tchr. Hendricks Twp. Sch., Shelbyville, Ind., 1964—67, Thomas A. Hendricks, Shelbyville, Ind., 1967—74, 1984—. Mem. bd. First Ch. of the Nazarene, Shelbyville, 1994—, First Ch. of God, Shelbyville, 1969—90; bd. dirs. Bright Star Pre-Sch., Shelbyville, 2001—. Mem.: AAUW (v.p.-treas. 1972—2000), Alpha Delta Kappa. Home: 2466 N Richard Dr Shelbyville IN 46176 Office: Thomas A Hendricks Sch 1111 St Joseph St Shelbyville IN 46176

CLARK, SANDRA MARIE, school administrator; b. Hanover, Pa., Feb. 17, 1942; d. Charles Raymond Clark and Mary Josephine (Snyder) Clark Wierman. BS in Elem. Edn., Chestnut Hill Coll., 1980; MS in Child Care Adminstrn., Nova U., 1985; MS in Ednl. Adminstrn., Western Md. Coll., 1992. Cert. elem. tchr., elem. prin., Pa. Tchr. various elem. schs., Pa., 1962-75; asst. vocation directress Mt. St. Joseph Motherhouse, Chestnut Hill, Pa., 1975-76; tchr. St. Catharine's Sch., Spring Lake, N.J., 1976-77; asst. mgr. Jim's Truck Stop, New Oxford, Pa., 1977-81; adminstr. Little People Day Care Sch., Hanover, 1981-88, sec., treas. bd. dirs., 1985-86; coord. regional resource Magic Yrs. Child Care & Learning Ctrs., Inc., Hanover, 1987-88; prin. St. Vincent de Paul Sch., Hanover, Pa., 1988—. Presenter Hanover Area Seminar for Day Care Employees, 1983-86. Coord. sch. safety patrols St. Vincent's Sch., Hanover, 1969-75, vice-chmn. bd., 1982-84; multi-media instr. first aid ARC, Hanover, 1983-86, bd. dirs., 1984-88; exec. sec. of bd. of dirs. ARC, Hanover, 1988; 1st v.p. Hanover Area Coun. of Chs., 1988, pres., 1989; validator accredidation program Nat. Acad. Early Childhood Programs, Washington, 1987—; bd. dirs. Life Skills Unltd. Handicapped Adults, 1988—; facilitator Harrisburg Diocesan Synod, Hanover, 1985-88, parish del., 1988. Pa. Dept. Pub. Welfare tng. grantee, 1986. Mem. NAFE, Nat. Cath. Ednl. Assn. Clubs: Internat. Assn. Turtles (London). Democrat. Roman Catholic. Avocations: swimming, reading, writing children's stories. Home: 348 Barberry Dr Hanover PA 17331-1302 Office: St Vincent De Paul Sch Hanover PA 17331

CLARK, SHARON ENID, principal; b. Houston, Aug. 7, 1940; d. Olen Otto and Mavis Marie (Godkin) Peterson; m. Philip Blair Crow (div.); 1 child, Shannon Lee Crow; m. Ross Daryl Clark; 1 child, Shelley Enid. BS in Edn., Sam Houston State U., 1961; MEd, Prairie View A&M U., 1976; postgrad., U. St. Thomas, Houston, 1988-92. Cert. elem. and high sch. tchr., adminstr., supr., Tex. Tchr. Spring Br. Ind. Sch. Dist., Houston, 1961-68, 72-73, dir. summer program, 1968; tchr. Albuquerque Pub. Schs., 1969-71, Waller (Tex.) Ind. Sch. Dist., 1973-74, tchr., team leader, 1976-92, sci. advisor, 1989-92, prin., 1992—; team leader Nat. Tchr. Corps Cycle IX, Waller, 1974-76. Facilitator Tex. Elem. Sci. Insvc. Program; trainer Tactics for Thinking, Tex.; presenter in field; staff developer for numerous profl. orgns., Tex., 1976—; co-chair state com. on svc. learning; mentor prin. Tex.

Middle Sch. Network, 1993. Contbr. articles to prof. jours. Recipient Tchrs. Make a Difference award Channel 13/Harris County Dept. Edn., 1988, Tchr. of Yr. award Waller Ind. Sch. Dist., 1988, Outstanding LIfe Sci. Tchr. award Harris County Med. Soc., 1990. Mem. ASCD, Nat. Sci. Tchrs. Assn., Nat. Mid. Sch. Assn., Internat. Reading Assn., Nat. Coun. Social Studies, Tex. Elem. Prins. and Suprs. Assn., Phi Delta Kappa (v.p.). Office: Jones Intermediate Sch Waller Ind Sch Dist PO Box 2877 Prairie View TX 77446-2877

CLARK, SHARON JACKSON, private school administrator; b. Istanbul, Turkey, Feb. 3, 1939; d. John Warren and Maxine Jett (Brient) Jackson; m. Ronald Eugene Clark, June 6, 1959; children: Kristen Anne, Kevin Brooks, Jeffrey Kimball. BFA, Calif. Coll. Arts and Crafts, 1968; MS in Edn., Wheelock Coll., 1978; student, Moore Coll. Art. Co-founder Jowanio, Syracuse, NY, The Thoreau Sch., Salt Lake City, Glen Urquhart Sch., Beverly, Mass.; head, founder Clark Sch. for Creative Learning, Danvers, Mass. Mem. Gifted/Talented Educators North Shore (bd. dir.), Danvers Hist. Soc. (bd. dir.). Home: 487 Locust St Danvers MA 01923-1252

CLARK, SUSAN FRANCES, theater educator; b. Chgo., Mar. 25, 1953; d. Anthony and Frances Frigo. BA, Rockford Coll., 1973; MA, Emerson Coll., 1980; PhD, Tufts U., 1989. Dir. Young People's Theatre, Lincoln, Mass., 1977-80; stage dir. Boston Lyric Opera, 1979-80; designer Middlesex Sch., Concord, Mass., 1975-78, chair theatre dept., 1978-89; mem. faculty theatre dept. Emerson Coll., Boston, 1989-90; asst. prof. theatre U. So. Maine, Portland, 1990-92, Smith Coll., Northampton, Mass., 1992—99; dir. theatre Groton Sch., Mass., 2001—, Malcolm Straham chair English lit. and theatre, 2001—. Exec. dir. Co. of Women, Inc., Boston, 1992-99; artistic dir. Country Summer Theatre, Inc., Concord, 1978-83; adjudicator Am. Coll. Theatre Festival, New Eng., 1990-93, New Eng. Drama Festival, Boston, 1980-89, New Eng. Theater Conf., 1983-90; reader Bunting Inst., Radcliffe Coll., Cambridge, Mass., 1990-93; proposal reader NEH, Washington, 1986. Contbr. chpts. to books in field. Grantee Maine Coun. Arts and Humanities, 1991, U. So. Maine, 1991, Smith Coll., 1993; Nat. Endowment Arts and Humanities summer fellow, 1986, 98, NEH fellow, 1999-2000; Five Colls. Inc. rsch. assoc., 1999—. Mem. MLA, Am. Theater and Drama Soc., New Eng. Theatre Conf. (presenter), Assn. for Theatre in Higher Edn. (presenter), Am. Soc. Theatre Rsch., Theatre Comms. Group, Far West Popular Culture Inst. (referee). Office: Groton Sch Groton MA 01430 E-mail: sclark@groton.org.

CLARK, VIOLET CATHRINE, retired school administrator, volunteer; b. Mpls., Oct. 16, 1915; d. John Albert and Ellen Charlotte (Carlson) Lundgren; m. Robert Edward Clark, May 6, 1944 (div. June, 1954); children: Linda Cathrine Kovach, Sharon Roberta Drake. BS in Horticulture, U. Minn., 1942; MS, U. Minn., St. Paul, 1948. Cert. tchr., adminstr., Calif. Rsch. asst. horticulture U. Minn., Mpls., Duluth, 1942-44; elem. sch. tchr. Elsinore, Calif., 1945-48; elementary sch. tchr. Riverside (Calif.) Pub. Schs., 1953-58, prin., 1958-81. Rschr. raspberries, MMMs Sponsor U. Minn., Duluth, 1942-44. Contbr. articles to newspapers and Hortculture jours., 1942-46. Vol. Ecumenical Ctr. Homeless Shelter and Meals, Oceanside, 1982—, Country Friends, Rancho Santa Fe, 1982—. Reading, Carlsbad, 1991-94, vote solicitor, Carlsbad, 1985-86. Recipient plaque Ecumenical Ctr., 1989, cert., 1995. Mem. Altrusa (com. chair 1943-83), Eastern Star, Alpha Delta Kappa (pres. 1947). Lutheran. Avocations: gardening, golf, volunteering, travel, photography. Home: 4740 Birchwood Cir Carlsbad CA 92008-3706

CLARK, WENDY RODGERS, elementary school educator; b. Middlebury, Vt., Nov. 29, 1947; d. Paul Cochran and Marjorie (Eastman) Welter Rodgers; m. Rowland Vaughn Clark, Aug. 22, 1967; children: Jennifer, Jessica. Student, Conn. Coll., New London, 1965-67; BS, Southampton Coll., 1978, MS, 1982. Cert. elem. tchr., N.Y. Tchr. 6th grade Shoreham-Wading River (N.Y.) Mid. Sch., 1979-81; tchr. 1st grade Shelter Island (N.Y.) Sch., 1981—. Adj. prof. L.I. U., 1997—98. Author childrens fiction, poetry, articles to profl. jours. Bd. dirs. Shelter Island chpt. Nature Conservancy, 1987-90; trustee Shelter Island Pub. Libr., 1988-96. Mem.: ASCD, Nat. Coun. Tchrs. English (rural schs. com.). Avocations: writing, art, folk singing. Home: PO Box 782 Shelter Island NY 11964-0782 Office: Shelter Island Union-Free Schs Rt 114 Shelter Island NY 11964

CLARK, WILLIAM ROGER, artist, educator; b. Altoona, Pa., July 27, 1949; s. Bernard A. and Marion H. (Suter) C.; m. J.C. Lee, Oct. 25, 1986. BFA, Md. Coll. Art, 1971; MEd, Temple U., 1974; MFA, U. Idaho, 1979. Cert. tchr., Pa., N.J. Tchr., coach Cen. Bucks High Sch., Doylestown, Pa., 1974-75; owner, artist Art Art Internat., N.Y.C., 1979-83; sculptor Cath. Fgn. Mission Soc. Am., Seoul, South Korea, 1983-86; adminstr. Mercyhurst Coll., Erie, Pa., 1987-90; prof. Montgomery County Coll., Blue Bell, Pa., 1990—, Bucks County Coll., Newtown, Pa., 1990-94. Dir. Cummings Art Gallery, Erie, 1987-90, Multiple Choice Art Gallery, Blue Bell, 1993—; art cons. St. Justin Martyr Soc., Valley Stream, N.Y., 1991—; artist-in-residence Pa. State Correctional Instn. Graterford, 1992-93. Contbr. articles, illustrations to various publs. Vol. Emmaus Soup Kitchen, Erie, 1987-90, Erie Geriatric Ctr., 1987-90; vol. St. Justin Soc. for Homeless, Valley Stream, 1990—; charter mem. N.J. State Aquarium; active Phila. Mus. Art; vol. St. Michael the Archangel Roman Catholic Ch., mem. folk choir, 1980-83, 90—; vol. Spring Garden Cmty. Theatre, Newtown, Pa. Mem. Nat. Art Edn. Assn., Pa. Art Edn. Assn., Coll. Art Assn., World Wildlife Fund, Nat. Geographic Soc., Oxfam Internat., Wilderness Soc. Roman Catholic. Avocations: music, guitar, singing, aerobics. Home: # 2 675 Harrison Ave Peekskill NY 10566-2343

CLARK, WILMA JEAN MARSHALL, English language educator; b. Akron, Ohio, Apr. 18, 1928; d. Paul Marshall and Laura Mae Haught; m. Gerald F. Clark, Apr. 11, 1947; children: Thomas M., G. Michael, Kathleen S., Deborah J. BA, Akron U., 1961; MA, Morgan State U., 1970; PhD, U. Md., 1980. Tchr. English, Journalism, French Overlea Sr. H.S., 1961-67; tchr. English and Journalism Perry Hall Sr. H.S., 1967-68; chair English dept. Towsontown Jr. H.S., 1968-70; asst. prof. English Dundalk (Md.) C.C., 1970-72; assoc. prof. English Morgan State U., Balt., 1970-94; prof. English Ea. Christian Coll., Belair, Md., 1989-95. Adj. prof. English Lincoln (Ill.) Christian Coll.-East Coast, 1995—; mem. Mountain Christian Sch. Bd., Harford County, Md., 1992—; founding mem. Mountain Christian High Sch., Harford County, 1996—. Contbr. articles to profl. jours. Mem. AAUP, Balt. Alliance of H.S./Coll. Educators, Coll. English Assn. (panel mem. nat. conf., treas./exec. bd. mid-Atlantic group). Home: 11518 Chapman Rd Kingsville MD 21087-1526

CLARKE, CLAIRE DIGGS, academic counselor; b. Long Branch, N.J. d. Jeremiah and LeeBertha (Smith) Diggs; m. David C. Clarke Jr.; 1 child: Caroletta. Student, Livingston Coll., 1948-51; BA, Knoxville Coll., 1955; postgrad., Columbia U., 1961-63; MA in Edn., Hofstra U., 1968; postgrad., U. N.H., Durham, New England Coll., Concord, N.H., 1981. Cert. tchr. English, physical edn. and health edn., counselor edn. Tchr. Charles M. Hall Sch., Alcoa, Tenn., 1955-59, Gilbert Sch., Bklyn., 1959-61; caseworker Bur. Child Welfare of N.Y., 1961-63; tchr., cons. pub. sch. #192, Hollis, N.Y., 1963-69; guidance counselor Winnisquam Regional Sch. Dist., Tilton, NH, 1969—92, specialist assessment intellectual functioning, 1981—. State rep. N.H. House Rep., 2000—. Mem. Merrimack Valley Sch. Bd., 1983-98; police commr. Boscawen Police Dept., 1980—. Mem. Edn. Volunteerism Employment Guild, N.H. Council Vocat. Tech. Edn. (sec. 1976—), Assn. Supervision Curriculum Devel. Lodges: Zonta Internat. (pres. 1979-81). Avocations: fishing, reading, travel, gardening, gourmet cooking. Home: 437 Daniel Webster Hwy Boscawen NH 03303-2411

CLARKE, GARVEY ELLIOTT, lawyer; b. Christ Church, Barbados, May 13, 1935; came to U.S., 1941; s. Elliott and Marion (Gibbs) C.; m. Yvonne E. Hayling, 1961; children: Wendy Y., Garvey H. AB, Dartmouth Coll., 1957; JD, N.Y. Law Sch., 1961. Bar: N.Y. 1963. Attorney legal dept. NBC, N.Y.C., 1963-65; v.p. A Better Chance, Inc., N.Y.C., 1965-75; pres. Nat. Fund for Minority Engring. Students, N.Y.C., 1975-82; v.p. Nat. Action Coun. for Minorities in Engring., N.Y.C., 1982-83; sr. assoc. Right Assocs., N.Y.C., 1983-85; dir. Morehouse Coll. Campaign The Oram Group, Inc., N.Y.C., 1985-86; dir. devel. Project Orbis, N.Y.C., 1986-87; dir. capital campaign United Negro Coll. Fund, N.Y.C., 1987-89; pres. Leadership Edn. and Devel. Progam in Bus., Inc., N.Y.C., 1989—2002; pvt. practice Sarasota, Fla., 2003—. Cons. Edn. Assoc., Washington, 1968-70, Frantzreb and Pray, N.Y.C., 1968-71. Pres. Stuyford Action Coun., Bklyn., 1963-70, Black Alumni of Dartmouth Assn., Hanover, N.H., 1976-78; mem. Dartmouth Alumni Coun., Hanover, 1977-79; bd. dirs. Boys Club of N.Y., N.Y.C., 1970-92; active Greater Centennial A.M.E. Zion Ch. Mem. New York County Lawyers Assn., Dartmouth Lawyers Assn. Home: Lake Ridge Falls 8086 Stirling Falls Cir Sarasota FL 34243

CLARKE, JANICE CESSNA, principal; b. Inglewood, Calif., Sept. 8, 1936; d. Eldon W. and Helen V. Cessna; m. Jack F. Clarke, Mar. 30, 1958; children: Scott Alan, Kristin Ann, Kerry Suzanne. BA, U. of Redlands, 1958; MA in Teaching, Reed Coll., 1963; EdD, U. Nev., Reno, 1993. Cert. tchr., adminstr., Nev. Elem. tchr. Portland (Oreg.) Pub. Schs., 1959-62, Eugene (Oreg.) Pub. Schs., 1964-66; music tchr. Tempe (Ariz.) Pub. Schs., 1969-70, Washoe County Sch. Dist., Reno, 1971-80, tchr. gifted and talented program, 1980-89, coord. gifted and talented program, 1989-93; prin. Brown Elem. Sch., Reno, 1993—. Bd. dirs. Far West Lab. for Ednl. Rsch., San Francisco, 1983-90. Mem. Nev. State Bd. Edn., 1982-90, pres., 1984-86. Recipient Disting. Svc. award Washoe County Tchr. Assn., 1974, Tchr. of Month award Reno/Sparks C. of C., 1984; named to El Segundo High Sch. Hall of Fame, 1989. Mem. NEA, Nev. State Edn. Assn., Nev. Assn. Sch. Adminstrs., Nev. Sch. Bds. Assn. (bd. dirs. 1982-90), Nat. Assn. Elem. Sch. Prins., Phi Delta Kappa, Delta Kappa Gamma. Office: Brown Sch 13815 Spelling Ct Reno NV 89511-7232

CLARKE, JUANITA M. WAITERS, education educator; b. Forkland, Ala., Sept. 29, 1923; d. James Walter and Mary Ellen (McAlpine) Waiters; m. Charles Henry Clarke, Aug. 20, 1946; children: Charles Henry Jr., Charlotte Jean, Jacquelin Marie, Victoria Teresa, Carol Evangeline. BS cum laude, Xavier U., 1944; MA, U. Ala., 1967, EdS, 1974, PhD, 1979. Cert. secondary edn. tchr., Ala.; lic. profl. counselor. English tchr., counselor Holy Family High Sch., Birmingham, Ala., 1954-69; English tchr. Miles Coll., Birmingham, 1969-73, from asst. prof. edn. to assoc. prof., coord. secondary edn., 1974-86; English tchr. Lawson State Community Coll., Birmingham, 1973-74; assoc. prof. edn. Talladega (Ala.) Coll., 1987-89; asst. prof. English Ala. State U., Montgomery, 1989-91; coord. title III, dir. instl. rsch. and planning Miles Coll., Birmingham, Ala., 1992-96, dir. counseling and testing, 1996-97, asst. prof. English, 1997—. Author: The Right Writer, 1990. Mem. Ala. Counseling Assn., Am. Assn. Individual Investors, Alpha Kappa Mu, Delta Sigma Theta. Avocations: sewing, knitting. Home: 1752 Brookfield Ln Birmingham AL 35214-4820 also: PO Box 3800 Birmingham AL 35208-0800

CLARKE, MARIE ELSIE, apparel design educator; b. Vineland, N.J., Aug. 22, 1927; d. John George and Adeline (Mazzi) Vraila; m. Joseph H. Clarke, Jan. 28, 1950 (div. 1986); children: Andrew, Helene. Cert., Pratt Inst., 1948. Stylist Bancroft Sporting Goods, Woonsocket, R.I., 1973-74; asst. dir. design India Imports of R.I., Providence, 1974-76, dir. of design, 1976-80; assoc. prof. apparel design RISD, Providence, 1981-94, prof. apparel design, 1994—99, prof. emeritus, 1999—. Part-time instr. apparel design dept. RISD, 1978-80; cons. Bennett & Co., Newburyport, Mass. and Hong Kong, 1989—, GJM, Newburyport and Hong Kong, 1986-89, New Eng. Mfrs., 1985-87. Guest curator exhibit Newport Hist. Soc., 1985. Mem. Fashion Group Internat., Costume Soc. Democrat. Avocations: hiking, bird watching, swimming.

CLARKE, MARJORIE JANE, environmental educator, consultant, author, researcher; b. Miami, Fla., July 14, 1953; d. Garnet Winston Clarke and Janice Marie (Platt) Johnson. BA in Geology, Smith Coll., 1975; MA in Environ. Sci., Johns Hopkins U., 1978; MS in Energy Tech., NYU, 1982; MPhil, CUNY, 1996, PhD in Earth and Environ. Scis., 1999. Cert. qualified environ. profl., 1994—. Intern EPA, Washington, 1974-75, 76; phys. scientist U.S. EPA, N.Y.C., 1978; sr. economist Tri-State Regional Planning Commn., N.Y.C., 1979-81; policy coord. N.Y. Power Authority, N.Y.C., 1981-83; environ. scientist N.Y.C. Dept. Sanitation, 1984-88; dir. solid waste rsch. INFORM, Inc., N.Y.C., 1988-90; tech. rsch. cons. for four PBS Videos WNET-Channel 13, N.Y.C., 1990; environ. cons. Natural Resources Def. Coun., N.Y.C., 1990—; sr. solid waste cons. INFORM, 1990-94; cons. Air & Waste Mgmt. Assn./Solid Waste Mgmt., 1993-94; rsch. fellow Ctr. for Applied Studies of the Environment, CUNY, 1992—; instr. geography dept. Rutgers U., 1999—2000. Adj. asst. prof. Hunter Coll., 1996, 98, 99, 2001, 2003, Lehman Coll., 2001-, adj. asst. prof., 2002—, scientist in residence, 2001—; cons. Hampshire County (Eng.), Coun., 1994-95; cons. to Commonwealth, 1996; cons., instr. Profl. Recyclers Pa., 2001—2002; mem. steering com. Citywide Recycling Adv. Bd., N.Y.C., 1991—, vice-chair, 2001-2003; mem. Camden County Environ. Tech. Adv. Com., 1993-95; mem. N.J. Dept. Environ. Protection and Energy, Mercury Emission Std.-Setting Task Force, 1992-95; mem. N.Y. State Adv. Bd. on Operating Requirements, Albany, 1988-92; examiner Qualified Environ. Profls. Program, 1995; peer reviewer Environ. Def. Fund, N.Y.C., 1988—, Nat. Resources Def. Coun., N.Y.C., 1988-90; mem. Manhattan Citizens' Solid Waste Adv. Bd., 1990—, chair, 1992-94, vice chair, 1994-96, 2001-2003, chair waste prevention com., 1991—; mem. steering com. N.Y.C. Waste Prevention Coalition, 2000—, vice chair 2001-. Co-author: Burning Garbage in the U.S., 1991, Waste Incineration and Public Health, 1999; contbr. articles to profl. confs. and jours., 1983—; webmaster. Mem. USEPA/Nat. Recycling Coaliton's Nat. Task Force to develop and promote a source reduction procurement strategy, 1996-98; mem. source reduction forum Nat. Recycling Coalition, 1998-2002; founder, pres. Riverside-Inwood Neighborhood Gardens, 1984—, newsletter editor, 1995-2002, webmaster, 1997—; mem. 9/11 Environ. Action Steering Com., 2002—. Recipient citation Dartmouth Coll., 1974, Roy F. Weston award Jour. Solid Waste Tech. and Mgmt., 1997, Cert. of Merit for Best Film by NGO category Environment India's 1998 Internat. Film Festival; featured on cover Money Mag., 1981; U.S. EPA grantee, 1991-95; Gilleece fellow CUNY, 1991-95. Mem. ASME (indsl. and mcpl. waste rsch. com. 1986—, operator cert. com. 1988-98), Nat. Acad. Scis. (nat. rsch. coun. com. health effects waste incineration 1995-99), Air and Waste Mgmt. Assn. (sec. 1988-89, session chair annual meeting 1988—, vice chair 1989-90, chmn. solid waste and thermal treatment com. 1990-92, vice chair solid waste intercom. task force 1992-94, chair integrated waste mgmt. com. 1994-2000, tech. dir. video 1993-94, vice chair mcpl. and med. waste mgmt. divsn. 2000-2003, fellow 2002, chair 2003-), Nat. Recycling Coalition, NRC Source Reduction Forum (steering com.), N.Y. Assn. for Reduction, Reuse and Recycling, N.Y. Cycle Club (ride leader 1982—). Democrat. Avocations: bicycling, photography, guitar, gardening. Home and Office: 1795 Riverside Dr Apt 5F New York NY 10034-5334 E-mail: mclarke@hunter.cuny.edu.

CLARKE, MCKINLEY A. secondary school educator; b. Greensboro, Ala., Oct. 27, 1937; s. Nathaniel and Rebecca (White) C.; m. Cassandra L. Redwood. BA, Miles Coll., 1961; MAT in Teaching, U. Montevallo, 1973; BTh, Bapt. Bible Coll., 1974; AA cert., U. Montevallo, 1984. Ret. tchr. Bessemer (Ala.) Bd. Edn.; English tchr. Jackson S. Abrams High sch., Bessemer; tchr. English and Speech Drake High sch., Thomaston, Ga.; tchr. English and History George W. Carver High Sch., Bessemer. Recipient Cert. of Merit Booker T. Washington Bus. Coll., Award of Recognition State of Ga. Dept. Edn. Mem. NCTE, Ala. Coun. Tchrs. of Compositions, Zeta Phi Lambda. Home: 1011 Valley View Ln Bessemer AL 35020-7348

CLARKE, PEG, physical education educator; b. Artesia, N.Mex., Apr. 18, 1956; BSEd, N.Mex. State U., 1979. Cert. tchr. phys. edn., K-12, Mo. Phys. edn. tchr., 1983-87; phys. edn. specialist K-8 Visitation Sch., Kansas City, Mo., 1988—2001; phys. edn. specialist Kans. City (Kans.) Unified Sch. Dist. 500, 2001—. Co-chair Kansas City Parochial League, Kansas City, Mo.; vice chmn. Parochial League Bd.; bd. dirs. visitation athletic com./volleyball dir.; instr. children's program YWCA, Kans. City, 1987-88. Vol. coach Visitation Sch., Kansas City, North Stars Volleyball Club, U.S. VBA, Spl. Olympics, 1983-87; del. Rep. of Cuba. Mem. AAHPERD, Nat. Assn. Sport and Phys. Edn., Women in Sport, Kans. Assn. Health, Phys. Edn., Recreation and Dance.

CLARKE, ROY, physicist, educator; b. Bury, Lancashire, England, May 9, 1947; BSc in Physics, U. London, PhD, 1973. Rsch. assoc. Cavendish Lab., Cambridge, U.K., 1973-78; James Franck fellow U. Chgo., 1978-79; prof. U. Mich., Ann Arbor, 1979-86; dir. applied physics program, 1986—2002. Co-founder k-Space Assocs. Inc. Editor: Synchrotron Radiation in Materials Research, 1989. Fellow Am. Phys. Soc. Achievements include development of novel methods for real-time x-ray and electron diffraction studies; patent for quasiperiodic optical coatings. Office: U Mich Randall Lab Ann Arbor MI 48109

CLARKE, STEPHAN PAUL, retired language educator, retired writer; b. Watertown, N.Y., Jan. 18, 1945; s. Albert John and Marjory Ruth (Grieb) Clarke; m. Mary Elizabeth Hawley, May 23, 1970; 1 child, Erin Elizabeth. BS in Edn., SUNY, Geneseo, 1966; MA, Bowling Green State U., 1968. Cert. secondary tchr. N.Y. Tchr. English E. J. Wilson HS, Spencerport, NY, 1970-99; ret., 1999. Spkr. N.Y. State Edn. Dept. Writer's Conf., Albany, 1982, Albany, 87. Author: (book) The Lord Peter Wimsey Companion, 1985 (Edgar Allen Poe Spl. award), The Lord Peter Wimsey Companion, rev. edit., 2002, Crimes and Clues, 1977. Chmn. supr. com. Spencerport Fed. Credit Union, 1985—2003, bd. dirs., sec. bd., 1999—; rec. sec. Ch. and Ministry Com. Genesee Valley Assn. United Ch. of Christ, Rochester, 1983—88. Lt. USNR, 1968—70. Recipient Excellence in Secondary Sch. Tchg. award, U. Rochester Grad. Sch. Edn. and Human Devel., 1991. Mem.: SAR (bd. mgrs. Rochester chpt. 1997—, chpt. historian 1999—, chpt. pres. 2001—, War Svc. medal 1996, Silver Good Citizenship medal 1997), Rochester Geneal. Soc., USN Meml. Found., Dorothy L. Sayers Soc. U.K. (spkr. 2002, 1985), Stratford Shakespearean Festival Found. Can., Sons Union Vets Civil War, U.S. Naval Inst. (life). Democrat. Avocations: reading, travel, photography, model railroads, genealogy. Home: 148 Greenway Blvd Churchville NY 14428-9210 E-mail: sclarke@rochester.rr.com.

CLARKE, WALTER SHELDON, independent military consultant, educator; b. Washington, Dec. 28, 1934; s. Walter Clowes and Lena Phoebe (Lovejoy) C.; m. Chantal Aubert, Dec. 26, 1974; children: Philippe, Quentin, Aurélie; 1 stepson, Nicolas Lance. BA, Yale U., 1957; cert. African studies, Northwestern U., 1968. Joined Fgn. Svc., Dept. State, 1958; served in Ruanda-Urundi (Later Kingdom of Burundi), 1960-62, Am. embassy, San Jose, Costa Rica, 1963-65, Bogota, Colombia, 1965-67; desk officer West African affairs Dept. State, 1968-70; chief polit. sect. Am. embassy, Abidjan, Ivory Coast, 1970-72; consul Am. consulate Douala, Cameroon, 1972-74; desk officer Latin Am. affairs Dept. State, 1974-76; info. programmer A/OASIS, 1976-77; consul gen. Djibouti, French Ter. of Afars and Issas, 1977; became charge d'Affaires upon independence of, 1977-80; polit. counselor Am. embassy, 1980-83; dir. intelligence liaison U.S. Dept. State, Washington, 1983-87; instr. Strategy U.S. Naval War Coll., Newport, R.I., 1987, State Dept. advisor to Pres., prof. Dept. Strategy and Policy, 1987-89; counselor of embassy for polit. affairs Am. Embassy, Madrid, 1989-92; prof. internat. rels. U.S. Army War Coll., Carlisle, Pa., 1992-94; ret. State Dept., 1994; sr. advisor Ctr. for Disaster Mgmt. and Humanitarian Assistance, Coll. Pub. Health, U. South Fla., 2003—. Instr. U. Alcala-Henares, 1991-92; dep. chief of mission U.S. Liaison Office, Mogadishu, Somalia, 1993; adj. prof. peace ops. U.S. Army Peacekeeping Inst., Carlisle, Pa., 1994-2003; cons. various mil. commands on peacekeeping, humanitarian ops.; instr. sr. advisor global ctr. disaster assistance and humanitarian Action, U. South Fla., Tampa, 2003—. Contbr. bibliog. and hist. research articles to profl. jours.; co-editor: (with Jeffrey Herbst) Learning from Somalia: Lessons of an Armed Humanitarian Intervention, 1997. Recipient Superior Honor awards Dept. State, 1980, 85, 92, 93, Meritorious Honor award, 1983, U.S. Army Comdr. Pub. Svc. award, 1994. Mem. African Studies Assn. (life), Tampa Bay Com. on Fgn. Rels., U.S. Naval Inst. (life), U.S. Army War Coll. Alumni Assn. (faculty, life). Fax: (813) 909-4156. E-mail: worldata@mindspring.com.

CLARKSON, PHYLLIS OWENS, early childhood educator; b. Spartanburg, S.C., Apr. 3, 1951; d. Thomas Dean and Mary Ann (Turner) Owens; m. Everett Clifford Clarkson Jr., June 6, 1970 (div. Oct. 1989); children: Stacey Daneè, Trey. BA in Edn. magna cum laude, U. S.C., 1993; MEd in Curriculum and Instrn., U. Va., 1999. Substitute tchr. Spartanburg Day Sch., 1984-88, libr. aide, 1988-94; kindergarten tchr. Cedar Road Christian Acad., Chesapeake, Va., 1994-96, office mgr., 1995-96; tchr. 2d and 3d grade Cedar Rd. Christian Acad., Chesapeake, Va., 1996-97, computer lab. asst., 1997-99; tchr. 3d grade Georgetown Primary Sch. Chesapeake Pub. Schs., 1999-2000, tchr. 4th grade Southwestern Elem. Sch., 2000—03, tchr. 5th grade, 2003—. Mem. Cowpens Garden Club, 1988-94. Mem. NEA. Avocations: reading, needlepoint, swimming. Home: 705 Cottage Pl Chesapeake VA 23322-4621 E-mail: poclarkson@aol.com.

CLARY, BRADLEY G. lawyer, educator; b. Richmond, Va, Sept. 7, 1950; s. Sidney G. and Jean B. Clary; m. Mary-Louise Hunt, July 31, 1982; children: Benjamin, Samuel. BA magna cum laude, Carleton Coll., 1972; JD cum laude, U. Minn., 1975. Bar: Minn. 1975, US Dist. Ct. Minn. 1975, US Ct. Appeals (10th cir.) 1977, US Ct. Appeals (8th cir.) 1979, US Ct. Appeals (6th cir.) 1980, US Ct. Appeals (7th cir.) 1981, US Supreme Ct. 1986, US Ct. Appeals (4th cir.) 1989, US Ct. Appeals (9th cir.) 1991. Assoc. Oppenheimer Wolff & Donnelly, St. Paul, 1975-81, ptnr., 1982-2000; legal writing dir. Law Sch. U. Minn., 1999—, clin. prof. Law Sch., 2000—. Adj. prof. Law Sch. U. Minn., Mpls., 1985-99; adj. instr. William Mitchell Coll. Law, St. Paul, 1995-96, 98, adj. prof., 1997, 99. Author: Primer on the Analysis and Presentation of Legal Argument, 1992; co-author: Advocacy on Appeal, 2001, Successful First Depositions, 2001, Successful Legal Analysis and Writing: The Fundamentals, 2003. Vestryman St. John Evangelist Ch., St. Paul, 1978-81, 98-00, pledge drive co-chmn., 1989-90, sr. warden, 2000-2002; mem. alumni bd. Breck Sch., Mpls., 1981-85, 89-96, exec. com., 1991-96, dir. emeritus, 1996—; mem. adv. bd. Glass Theatre Co., West St. Paul, Minn., 1982-87; mem. antitrust adv. panel dept. health State of Minn., 1992-93. Mem. ABA (adv. group antitrust sect. 1987-89, corp. counseling com.), Minn. Bar Assn. (program chmn. antitrust sect. 1986-87, treas. 1987-88, vice-chmn. 1989-90, co-chmn. 1990-92, governing coun. appellate practice sect. 2001--), Phi Beta Kappa. Avocations: tennis, sailing. Office: U Minn Law Sch 229 19th Ave S Rm 444 Minneapolis MN 55455-0400

CLASTER, JILL NADELL, university administrator, history educator; d. Harry K. and Edith Lillian Nadell; m. Millard L. Midonick, May 24, 1979; 1 child from previous marriage, Elizabeth Claster (dec.). BA, NYU, 1952, MA, 1954; PhD, U. Pa., 1959. Instr. history U. Pa., 1956-58; instr. ancient and medieval history U. Ky., Lexington, 1959-61, asst. prof., 1961-64; adj. asst. prof. classics NYU, N.Y.C., 1964-65, asst. prof. history, 1965-68, assoc. prof., 1968-84, prof., 1984—, acting undergrad. chmn. history, 1972-73, dir. M.A. in liberal studies program, 1976-78; assoc. dean

Washington Sq. and Univ. Coll., 1978, acting dean, 1978-79, dean, 1979-86; dir. Hagop Kevorkian Ctr. for Near Eastern Studies, NYU, 1991-96. Appointee N.Y.C. Commn. on Status of Women. Author: Athenian Democracy: Triumph or Travesty, 1967, The Medieval Experience, 1982; Contbr. articles to profl. jours. Danforth grantee, 1966-68; Fulbright grantee, 1958-59 Mem. Am. Hist. Assn., Medieval Acad. Am. Home: 161 W 15th St New York NY 10011-6720 Office: NYU Dept History 53 Washington Sq S Dept History New York NY 10012-1098 E-mail: jill.claster@nyu.edu.

CLAUDIO, MANUEL P.A. medical educator, health facility administrator; b. Manila, June 23, 1938; s. Eduardo L. and Gorgonia A. Claudio; m. Adelina C.B. Claudio, May 1, 1965; children: Basil, Kevin, Kenneth, Liesl. MD, U. E. Ramon Magsaysay Meml. Med. Ctr., Quezon City, The Philippines, 1962; MBA, Northwestern U., 1993. Cert. Am. Bd. Med. Mgmt., Am. Bd. Quality Assurance and Utilization Rev. Physicians. Chmn. dept. medicine Humana Hosp., Hoffman Estates, Ill., 1981—83; chief sect. pulmonary medicine Mercy Hosp. Med. Ctr., Chgo., 1981—2000, med. dir. respiratory care dept., 1988—2000, pres. med. and sci. staff faculty, 1989—91; clin. asst. prof. medicine U. Ill. Coll. Medicine, Chgo., 1983—98; program dir. pulmonary medicine Mercy Hosp. Med. Ctr., Chgo., 1979—98. Contbr. articles to profl. publs. Pres. Philippine Med. Assn. Chgo., 1968; exec. dir. Assn. Philippine Practicing Physician Am., Chgo., 1972; bd. advisors Cath. charities, Chgo., 1986—; Bd. dir., pres. elect Am. Lung Assn., Metro Chgo., Ill., 1992—. Named to Chgo.'s Filipino-Am. Hall of Fame, 1997; recipient Leadership award, Philippine Med. Assn. Chgo., 1968, Disting. Physician award, Philippine Med. Assn., 1992. Fellow: ACP, Inst. Medicine Chgo.; mem.: Am. Thoracic Soc. Roman Catholic.

CLAWSON, JUDITH LOUISE, middle school educator; b. Cleve., Nov. 24, 1938; d. Frank Anthony and Bettie (Cerny) Lisy; m. Robert Wayne Clawson, June 25, 1961; children: Deborah Marie, Gregory Scott. BS in Edn. magna cum laude, Bowling Green State U., 1960; postgrad., UCLA, 1961-65, Kent State U., 1976-80. Cert. secondary sch. math. tchr. Elem. tchr. Long Beach (Calif.) Unified Sch. Dist., 1960-61, L.A. Unified Sch. Dist., 1961-65, Stow (Ohio) City Schs., 1969-78, middle sch. math. tchr., 1978—97; ret., 1997. Cons., presenter in field. Recipient Cert. of Recognition, Martha Holden Jennings Foudn., 1987. Mem. ASCD, AAUW, NEA, LWV, Nat. Coun. Tchrs. of Math., Stow Tchrs. Assn., Ohio Edn. Assn., Ohio Coun. Tchrs. of Math., Delta Gamma (fin. advisor Kent State U. chpt. 1978-90, pres. alumnae chpt. 1987-89, 91-93, Pres.'s award 1987, housing dir. at-large nat. coun. 1997-2001), Kappa Delta Pi. Republican. Methodist. Avocations: golf, tennis, skiing, scuba diving, reading. Home: 7336 Westview Rd Kent OH 44240-5912 Office: Kimpton Mid Sch 380 N River Rd Munroe Falls OH 44262-1331

CLAWSON, ROXANN ELOISE, college administrator, computer company executive; b. Dallas, Oct. 15, 1945; d. Robert Wellington Clawson and Jeannette Irene (Rodenhauser) Clawson Clayton. BFA, Mich. State U., 1968. Library asst. Cooper Union, N.Y.C., 1970-75, asst. librarian, 1976-82, assoc. to dean, 1985—; computer cons., 1986—. Acting appearance in The Dragon's Nest, La MaMa Theatre, 1989. Mem. NAFE, N.Y. Personal Computer Group. Democrat. Lutheran. Avocation: administration.

CLAXTON, HARRIETT MAROY JONES, retired language educator; b. Dublin, Ga., Aug. 27, 1930; d. Paul Jackson and Maroy Athalia (Chappell) Jones; m. Edward B. Claxton, Jr., May 27, 1953; children: E. B. III, Paula Jones. AA with honors, Bethel Woman's Coll., 1949; AB magna cum laude, Mercer U., 1951; MEd, Ga. Coll., 1965. Social worker Laurens County Welfare Bd., Dublin, 1951-56; HS tchr. Dublin, 1961-66; instr. Mid. Ga. Coll., Cochran, 1966-71, asst. prof. English, lit. and speech, 1971-85, assoc. prof., 1985-86, adj. prof., 1987; rsch. tchr. Trinity Christian Sch., 1986, 92, sr. English tchr., 1986-87; ret., 1987. Instr. Ga. Coll., 1987, E. Ga. Coll., 1988—99; weekly columnist Dublin Courier Herald, 1995—. Author: (book) History of Laurens Superior Court; editor: Laurens County History, II, 1987; contbr. articles to profl. jours. and newspapers. Pres., chmn. bd. Mensea/Laurens unit Am. Cancer Soc.; sec. Am. Assn. Ret. Persons, 1987—90; v.p. Dublin Cmty. Concert, 1991—98; mem. preservation com. Hardy Smith House, 1998—2000; bd. dirs. Laurens County Libr., 1960—68, Friends Vets., Heart Ga. Altamaha Regional Devel. Ctr., 1998, sec., 2002—; bd. dir. Laurens County Libr., Dublin-Laurens Arts Coun., 2001—. Named Woman of the Yr., St. Patrick's Festival, Dublin, 1979, Most Popular Tchr., Dublin Ctr., 1985, Olympic Torch Bearer, 1996; recipient Outstanding Svc. award, Cancer Soc., Dublin, 1985, 1993, 1998, Outstanding Alumni award for cmty. svc., Ga. Coll., 1996. Mem.: UDC (chaplain 1999—), DAR (regent, vice regent, historian, state, dist., nat. awards), Dublin Assn. Fine Arts (pres. bd. 1974—76, 1982—84, 1990—98, 2001—03), Dublin Hist. Soc. (pres. 1976—78, 1995—98), Erin Garden Club (pres.), Woman's Study Club (pres.), U.S. Daus. of 1812, Daus. Am. Colonists, Daus. Colonial Wars, Delta Kappa Gamma, Chi Delta Phi (sec.), Phi Theta Kappa (pres.), Alpha Delta Pi (Middle Ga. alumni chpt. 1999—, scholarship plaque 1950), Sigma Mu. Democrat. Baptist. Home: 101 Rosewood Dr Dublin GA 31021-4129

CLAXTON, MELBA SAMMONS, education educator; b. Uvalda, Ga., May 16, 1936; d. Claude Colon and Mildred Rebecca (Gibbs) Sammons; divorced; children: Ralph F. Jr., Carol Anne. AA, Brewton-Parker Coll., Mt. Vernon, Ga., 1970; BS in Edn. cum laude, Ga. So. U., 1972; MEd, *5, 1979; postgrad., Nova Southeastern U., 1993—. Cert. early childhood tchr., Ga. Elem. tchr. Robert Toombs Christian Acad., Lyons, Ga., 1972-77, tchr. kindergarten, 1978-82; bus. mgr. Brewton-Parker Coll., 1960-62, instr. English and reading, 1982-86, asst. prof. edn., 1986-94, assoc. prof., 1995—. State advisor Student Profl. Assn. Ga. Educators, Clarkston, 1988-94. Bd. dirs. Robert Toombs Christian Acad., 1983-85; chmn. food pantry on witness and svc. com. Vidalia (Ga.) Presbyn. Ch., 1991—. Mem. ASCD, Nat. Assn for Edn. Young Children, Internat. Reading Assn., Ga. Assn. for Edn. Young Children, So. Early Childhood Assn., Ga. Assn. Colls. Tchr. Edn., Ga. Assn. Tchr. Educators, Delta Kappa Gamma (editor newsletter 1988-94). Avocations: reading, cooking, sewing, shopping. Home: 122 W College St Ailey GA 30410

CLAY, JOHN HARRIS, JR., secondary school educator; b. Phila., June 7, 1961; s. John H. Sr. and Annie Louise (Jackson) C. BA, Princeton U., 1983; postgrad., Howard U., 1984-85, L.I. U., from 1994, NYU, from 1996. Lic. social studies, bilingual social studies tchr., N.Y. Tchr. Walton H.S., Bronx, N.Y., 1990, Stevenson H.S., Bronx, 1990-91, Evander Childs H.S., Bronx, 1991-92; bilingual social studies tchr. Sarah J. Hole H.S., Bklyn., from 1992. Author: City of Tranquil Light, 1998. Mem. ASCD, Woodrow Wilson Soc. (assoc.), Princeton Alumni Assn., Black Alumni of Princeton, Princeton Club of N.Y. Republican. Buddhist. Avocations: writing, research, hiking, swimming, playing piano and violin. Home: Goochland, Va. Died Nov. 20, 1999.

CLAYTON, INA SMILEY, retired secondary education educator; b. Montrose, Miss., Mar. 2, 1924; d. Oscar Ruben and Leverett (Jones) Smiley; m. Ogia L. Clayton, June 21, 1959; 1 child, Felicia Tulikka. BS, Jackson State U., 1946; MA, Syracuse U., 1955; PhD, U.S. Internat. U., 1977. Head tchr., prin. Smith County Sch., Taylorsville, Miss., 1946-47; supr. Covington County Sch., Collins, Miss., 1947-54; tchr. Nora Dans Sch., Laurel City, Miss., 1955-56; elem. prin., tchr. Oak Park High Sch., Laurel, Miss., 1956-67; tchr. L.A. Sch. Dist., 1967-89. Active NAACP. Mem. NEA, Calif. Tchrs. Assn., Urban League, United Meth. Women (pres., sec.). Home: 5022 W 58th Pl Los Angeles CA 90056-1637 Office: United World Internat Learn Los Angeles CA 90056-1637

CLAYTON, KATY, elementary education educator; b. Bellefonte, Pa., Feb. 21, 1956; d. Everette Lee and Donna June (Trowbridge) Swinney; m. Charles Edward Clayton Jr., July 15, 1977; children: Quinton, Meredith, Zachary. BS in Edn., Southwest Tex. State U., 1978, MEd in Reading, 1983. Tchr. kindergarten Lockhart (Tex.) Pub. Schs., 1978-80; owner pvt. day care San Marcos, Tex., 1980-84; tchr. 1st grade Crockett Elem. Sch., San Marcos, Tex., 1984-89, tchr. 2d grade, 1989-93, reading specialist, 1993—. Dept. leader Crockett Elem. Sch., 1995-2000;, 02— cons. S.W. Tex. Tchr. Ctr., San Marcos, 1991-92; trained Help One Student to Succeed, 1996—. Bd. dirs. Little League, San Marcos, 1987-89, Habitat for Humanity, 2002—; deacon 1st Christian Ch., San Marcos, 1988-92; presenter 23d Annual Tex. State Reading Assn. Conf., The Young Child and Literacy. Recipient Nat. Exemplary award HOSTS, 1997—. Mem.: Reading Recovery Tchrs., Internat. Reading Assn., Tex. Classroom Tchrs. Assn. (pres. 1990—91), San Marcos Bluebonnet Lions Club (sec. 1998—2001). Democrat. Mem. Christian Ch. (Disciples Of Christ). Avocations: reading, needle work, crafts, volksmarching. Home: 513 Willow Creek Cir San Marcos TX 78666-5025 Office: Crockett Elem Sch 1300 Girard St San Marcos TX 78666-2813 E-mail: katy.clayton@san-marcos.isd.tenet.edu.

CLAYTON, PAMELA SANDERS, special education educator; b. Sulphur Springs, Tex., Feb. 8, 1952; d. Carl Louis Sanders, Jr. and Beatrice Coletha Sanders; children: Chad, Cicely. BS, E. Tex. State U., 1974, MEd, 1991. Kindergarten cert., mental retardation cert. Tchr. Saltillo ISD, 1976—77, resource specialist, tchr., 1977—80, Lamar Elem. Sch., Sulphur Springs, 1980—98, Sulphur Springs H.S., 1998—. Dir. student coun., uil prose & poetry dir., taas tutorial coach Sulphur Springs H.S., 1999—2002. Actor: (plays) A Christmas Carol, 1997 (Best Supporting Actress, 1998); singer: (concert) N.E. Tex. Choral Soc., 1998. Mem. allocation com. Hopkins County United Way, Sulphur Springs, 2000—01; bd. dirs. Lakes Regional MHMR, Terrell, Tex., 1997—, Sulphur Springs Pub. Libr., 1994—96. Mem.: Tex. Classroom Tchrs., Delta Kappa Gamma. Methodist. Avocations: poetry, rollercoaster riding, reading, piano. Home: 404 Lamar St Sulphur Springs TX 75482 Office: Sulphur Springs ISD 1200 Connally St Sulphur Springs TX 75482 Office Fax: (903)439-6116. Personal E-mail: pclayton@ssisd.net.

CLEARY, FRANCES MARIE, retired elementary school educator; b. Cleve., Mar. 16, 1945; d. Emil T. and Anne M. (Kan) Suhm; m. John P. Cleary, Oct. 3, 1970; children: Anne, Mary K., John Jr., William II, Patrick, Michael. BS in Edn., St. John's Coll., Cleve., 1967. Cert. tchr. grades 1-8; specialty in computer edn. Tchr. grade 4 St. Francis de Sales, Parma, Ohio, 1967-71; substitue tchr. grades K-9 Warren (Mich.) City Schs., 1971-73; tchr. grades 1 and 4 Holy Family Sch., Parma, 1984—2003. Presenter, John Carroll U., summer 1997. Mem. math curriculum adv. com. Diocese of Cleve., 1991; bd. mem., Diocesan contact, connecting tchrs. to tech. Roman Catholic. Avocations: master seamstress, knitting and designing sweaters, designing costume jewelry. E-mail: hfclass4@hotmail.com.

CLEAVER, DAVID CHARLES, lawyer, educator; b. Sunbury, Pa., Dec. 26, 1941; s. C. Perry and Gertrude Lillian (Clarke) C.; m. JoAnne Irene Sponenberg, Nov. 25, 2000; children: Lisa Eileen, David Clarke, Christopher Perry. Bar: Pa. 1967, U.S. Supreme Ct. 1971. Ptnr. Sharpe Cleaver, Wenger & Townsend, Chambersburg, Pa., 1967-84; sole practice Chambersburg, 1985—. Adj. prof. law Dickinson Sch. Law, Carlisle, Pa., 1971—. Author: Cases and Materials on Wills and Decedent's Estates, 1976, Probate and Estate Administration, The Law in Pennsylvania, 1983, 3d edit., 2000. Past pres., bd. dirs. Chambersburg YMCA; chmn. Franklin County (Pa.) Reps., 1986-92. Mem. ABA, Assn. Trial Lawyers Am., Pa. Trial Lawyers Assn. Lodges: Chambersburg Rotary, Elks, Moose. Home: 455 Overhill Dr Chambersburg PA 17201-3161 Office: 1035 Wayne Ave Chambersburg PA 17201-2986 E-mail: dcleaver@cvn.net.

CLEGHORN, GWENDOLYN MICHAEL, principal, educator; AB, Miss. U. for Women, 1952; MA, Emory U., 1953. Instr. dept. English So. Meth. U., Dallas, 1953-54; tchr. dept. English The Westminster Schs, Atlanta, 1954-55, 60-61, The Westminster Schs., Atlanta, 1967-94, chmn. dept. English, 1967-82, assoc. prin., 1986—; tchr. dept. English Packer Collegiate Inst., Brooklyn Heights, N.Y., 1955-58; asst. prof. dept. English Ga. State U., Atlanta, 1963-67. Coll. counselor, sr. class adviser, grade chmn. The Westminster Schs., 1973-86; instr. div. continuing edn. The U. Ala., 1982; instr. grad. edn. Converse Coll., 1983; ind. schs. rep. Profl. Standards Commn.; examination reader, cons. Advanced Placement English; mem., chair Coun. on Entrance Svcs. of Coll. Bd.; mem. vis. com. So. Assn. Colls. and Schs.; presenter in field. Mem. Nat. Assn. Coll. Admission Counselors (mem. pres.' coun.), So. Assn. Coll. Admission Counselors (pres., chmn. admission practices com.). Home: 51 Peachtree Way NE Atlanta GA 30305-3735

CLELAND, GLADYS LEE, university administrator, adult education educator; b. Schenectady, Feb. 27, 1959; d. Anthony John and Anna Mae (Feight) Campana; m. Michael Joseph Cleland, Aug. 4, 1984. BA in Communications and Edn. cum laude, SUNY, Plattsburgh, 1981; MA summa cum laude, U. Fla., 1986; MS summa cum laude, Syracuse U., 1994. Asst. instr. communications SUNY, Plattsburgh, 1982-83, admissions/media rels. advisor, 1987-88; asst. instr. communications U. Fla., Gainesville, 1985-86; instr. English and communications Clinton Community Coll., Plattsburgh, 1986-87; news cons., acad. liaison Sta. WCFE-TV, Plattsburgh, 1987-88; pub. info. dir. Syracuse (N.Y.) U., 1989-93, pub. rels. coord., 1993-94; spl. projects mgr. SUNY Health Sci. Ctr., Syracuse, 1994-96. News. cons. Sta. WCFE-TV 57, Plattsburgh, 1987-88; producer, rschr. CVPH Med. Ctr., Plattsburgh, 1982-87; freelance talent Sta. WIXT-TV 9, Syracuse, 1988—; press steward Winter Olympic Games, lake Placid, N.Y., 1980; radio announcer, news reporter, sales rep. Sta. WIRY-AM, Plattsburgh, 1980-83; freelance producer, news reporter Sta. WPBT-TV, Miami, Fla., 1983-84. Author: Satellite News Gathering, 1986. Recipient broadcast awards N.Y. State Broadcast Assn., Plattsburgh, 1982-84, Outstanding Talent award Internat. TV Assn., Gainesville, 1986. Mem. Women in Comms. (Woman of Yr. award, 1994), Broadcast Educators Assn., Coll. Media Advisors, RTNDA, Pub. Rels. Soc. Am., Syracuse Press Club, Omicron Delta Kappa, Phi Kappa Chi. Roman Catholic. Avocations: gardening, boating, reading. Home: 4239 Mill Run Rd Liverpool NY 13090-1813 Office: SUNY 103 Charleton Hall Morrisville NY 13408

CLEM, ELIZABETH ANN STUMPF, music educator; b. San Antonio, July 9, 1945; d. David Joseph and Elizabeth Burch (Wathen) Stumpf; m. D. Bruce Clem, June 17, 1972; children: Sean David, Jeremy Andrew. BA in Music Edn., St. Mary-of-the-Woods (Ind.) Coll., 1970; MEd, Drury Coll., Springfield, Mo., 1979. Nationally cert. tchr. music. Music dir., pvt. piano tchr. Precious Blood Parish & Sch., Jasper, Ind., 1968-69; elem. tchr. St. Christopher Sch., Speedway, Ind., 1970-71; elem. and jr. high sch. tchr. Indpls. Sch. System, 1971-72; elem. tchr. Augusta (Ga.) Sch. System, 1972-73, Wabash (Ind.) Sch. System, 1976-77; pvt. practice piano tchr. Wabash, Ind., 1975-77, Honolulu, 1983-86, Burke, Va., 1986-90, Manhattan, Kans., 1990-93, Fayetteville, N.C., 1993-96, Meth. Coll. Performing Arts, Fayetteville, N.C., 1993-96, Ft. Sill, 1996-98. Co-chmn. Manhattan Musicianship Auditions, 1991, chmn., 1992. Dist. fundraiser rep. Wabash chpt. Am. Cancer Soc., 1975; leadership coord. Wabash coun. Girl Scouts U.S.A., 1976; mem. exec. bd. Little Apple Invitational Soccer Tournament, 1992; vol. N.C. Symphony; Red Cross adv. Ft. Campbell, Ky.; rep. NMFA (Nat. Mil. Family Assn.), 1997—2003, Ft. Campbell NMFA, 2001—02; music coord. Ft. Shafter Sacred Heart Chapel, Honolulu, 1985—86. Mem.: Nashville Music Tchrs. Assn., Tenn. Music Tchrs. Assn., Columbus Symphony Womens Assn., Nat. Mil. Family Assn. (rep. 1997—), Nat. Fedn. Music Clubs, Schubert Music Club, Columbus Music Tchrs. Assn., Ga. Music Tchrs. Assn., Lawton Music Tchrs. Assn., Fayetteville Piano Tchrs. Assn. (v.p. 1994, pres. 1995), Raleigh Piano Tchrs. Assn., Okla. Music Tchrs. Assn., N.C. Music Tchrs. Assn. (rep. to nat. assn.), Music Tchrs. Nat. Assn. (cert.), Nat. Guild Piano Tchrs. Republican. Roman Catholic. Avocations: bicycle riding, crafts, reading, walking.

CLEMENDOR, ANTHONY ARNOLD, obstetrician, gynecologist, educator; b. Port-of-Spain, Trinidad, Trinidad, Nov. 8, 1933; came to US, 1954, naturalized, 1959; s. Anthony Arnold and Beatrice Helen (Stewart) C.; m. Elaine Browne, May 31, 1958 (dec. May, 1991); children: Anthony Arnold, David Alan; m. Janat Jenkins, Sept. 23, 1993. AB, NYU, 1959; MD, Howard U., 1963. Diplomate Am. Bd. Ob-Gyn. Intern USPHS, S.I., N.Y., 1963-64; resident Met. Hosp. Ctr., N.Y.C., 1964-68; chief outpatient dept. ob-gyn Metro. Hosp. Ctr., N.Y.C., 1969-73; med. dir. family planning Human Resources Adminstrn., N.Y.C., 1973-74; assoc. dean student affairs, dir. office minority affairs N.Y. Med. Coll., Valhalla, 1974-97, assoc. clin. prof. dept. ob-gyn, 1978-90, prof. clin. ob-gyn, 1990-98; clin. prof. ob-gyn., 1998—. Bd. dirs. Elmcore, Caribbean-Am. Ctr N.Y.C., Nat. Assn. Minority Med. Educators, Inc., 1978-88, Empire State Med. Sci. and Ednl. Found., Inc., Caribbean Am. Ctr. N.Y., 1988-91; mem. Nat. Urban League, N.Y. Urban League; life mem. NAACP. Fellow ACOG, APHA; mem. AMA (mem. survey team liaison com. on med. edn. 1989—, del. N.Y. State 1998—), Am. Fertility Soc., Nat. Med. Assn., N.Y. State Med. Soc. (treas. PAC 1997, councilor 1999-2002, asst. sec. 2002), N.Y. County Med. Soc. (sec. 1989, v.p. 1990, pres. elect 1991, pres. 1992-93, bd. trustees, chmn. bd. trustees 1997-98), N.Y. Acad. Medicine, N.Y. Gynecol. Soc. (v.p. 1986, pres. 1988).

CLEMENS, SYDNEY GUREWITZ, early childhood educator, consultant; b. Washington, Oct. 21, 1939; d. Clarence Darrow Gurewitz and Helen (Levitov) Sobell; children: Alexander Jeremy, Jennifer Martine. BA, U. Chgo., 1959; MA, Columbia U., 1969. Tchr. Bd. of Edn., N.Y.C., 1962-71; co-founder, dir. Discovery Room for Children, N.Y.C., 1969-71; tchr. San Francisco Unified Sch. Dist., 1972-83; mem. faculty Pacific Oaks Coll., Pasadena, Calif., 1988-92; founder, prin. educator, 1st grade tchr. San Francisco Charter Early Childhood Sch., 1993-95; cons., 1995—. Instr. child devel. dept. Merritt Coll., Oakland, 1981; extnsion faculty assocl. prof. Fresno State U., Sonoma State U., Sant Francisco State U., 1985-90; presenter, spkr. in field. Author: Pay Attention to the Children: Lessons for Parents & Teachers from Sylvia Ashton-Warner, 1996, The Sun's Not Broken, A Cloud's Just in the Way; On Child-Centered Teaching, 1983, Centering on the Children, 1985; cons. editor Young Children, Early Childhood Rsch. and Practice, 1997—; contbr. articles to profl. jours. Mem. Pasadena City Commn. on Children, Youth and Families, 1991-92. Avocations: music, Spanish language. Home and Office: 73 Arbor St San Francisco CA 94131-2918 E-mail: aceteacher@earthlink.net.

CLEMENT, BETTY WAIDLICH, literacy educator, consultant; b. Honolulu, Aug. 1, 1937; d. William G. Waidlich and Audrey Antoinette (Roberson) Malone; m. Tom Morris, Jan. 16, 1982; 1 child, Karen A. Brattesani. BA in Elem. Edn., Sacramento State U., 1960; MA in Elem. Reading, U. No. Colo., 1973, MA in Adminstrn., EdD in Edn. & Reading, 1980. Elem. sch. tchr. pub schs., Colo., Calif., 1960-66; reading specialist, title I European area U.S. Dependent Schs., various locations, 1966-75; grad. practicum supr. U. No. Colo. Reading Clinic, Greeley, 1976-77; grant cons. Colo. Dept. Edn., Denver, 1978-81; adult edn. tutor, cons. various orgns., Boulder, Colo., 1983-87; student tchr. supr. U. San Diego, 1989-90; adult literacy trainer for vols. San Diego Coun. on Literacy, 1988—2002; ret., 2002. Adj. prof. U. Colo., Denver, 1981-82, U. San Diego, 1994-1999; adj. prof. comm. arts Southwestern Coll., Chula Vista, Calif., 1990-99; presenter various confs. Co-author, editor: Adult Literacy Tutor Training Handbook, 1990, author rev. edit., 1998. Grantee Fed. Right-to-Read Office Colo. Dept. Edn., 1979, curriculum writing Southwestern Coll., 1992. Fellow San Diego Coun. on Literacy (chair coop. tutor tng. com. 1991-93); mem. Whole Lang. Coun. San Diego, Calif. Reading Assn. Avocation: psychology. E-mail: baclement@cox.net.

CLEMENT, EVELYN GEER, library educator; b. Springfield, Mass., Sept. 1, 1926; d. Elihu and Helen (Schenck) Geer; m. J.R. Clement, Sept. 9, 1946 (div. 1972); children: James Randall, Timothy B., Susan Henson, Marc W., Audrey Ethriedge. BA with honors, U. Tulsa, 1965; MLS, U. Okla., 1966; PhD, Ind. U., 1975. Librarian Tulsa City-County Library, 1960-66; learning resources librarian Oral Roberts U., Tulsa, 1966-68; spl. instr. U. Okla., Norman, 1966-70; prof., chmn. library sci. Memphis State U., 1972-85, dir. Ctr. for Instructional Service and Research, 1985-95, ret., 1995; chmn. acad. senate, 1979-80, mem. faculty tenure and promotion appeals com., 1980-82, mem. standing univ. com. on libraries, 1975-80, 86-87, chmn. women's task force, 1984-85. Editor: Bibliographic Control of Nonprint Media, 1972; contbr. articles to profl. jours. Vol. Red Cross. Doctoral fellow U.S. Office Edn., Title II-B, Ind. U., 1968-71. Mem. ALA, Pi Gamma Mu, Phi Alpha Theta, Beta Phi Mu. Republican. Avocations: microcomputer, needlepoint, exercise, reading. Home: 3914 E 54th St Tulsa OK 74135-4824 E-mail: erren@aol.com.

CLEMENT, PAUL PLATTS, JR., performance technologist, educator; b. Geneva, Ill., Aug. 30, 1935; s. Paul P. and Vera Elizabeth (Dahlquist) C.; m. Susan Alice Aikins, June 7, 1958; children: Paul P. IV, Kathleen Elizabeth. BA in Math., Coe Coll., 1957. Sales tech. rep. Burroughs Corp., Chgo., 1960-63; mgr. EDP, Harding-Williams Corp., Chgo., 1963-65; edn. coord. Standard Oil Co., Chgo., 1965-69; mgr. product planning Edutronics Systems Internat., Chgo., 1969-71; interactive video instrn. specialist Advanced Systems Inc., Chgo., 1971-88; ind. cons. in tng., media use, computers Downers Grove, Ill., 1988; prin. instr., developer UNISYS Corp., Lisle, Ill., 1988-89; mgr. employee devel. CNA Ins. Cos., Chgo., 1990-91; cons. media tng. Internet Systems Corp., Chgo., 1990-93; prin. Clement Consulting Group, Downers Grove, 1993—. Part-time data processing faculty Coll. of DuPage and Coll. extension, Harper Coll., Ill., DeVry Inst., Joliet Jr. Coll.; invited spkr. numerous computer and tng. confs., nat. and internat. assns.; developer, presenter workshops in field; mem. adv. bd. Northeastern Ill. U., Chgo. Developer and pub. 12 animated films with supplementary texts, 84 videotapes, 17 interactive videodiscs and over 7000 pages of expository texts; collaborator 100 other videotapes with supplementary texts; prin. developer micro-computer based People Compatability System, 1983; developer Decision Table Algorithms, 1986, 94th Inf. Div. Assn. Info. System, 1977, Basic Computer Programmer Tng. Curriculum for Eng. Govt., 1979, computerized Data Processing Curricula Devel. System, 1973, Early COBOL Lang. precompiler, 1967, AutoMagic Glossary, 1992; contbr. articles to Datamation Mag., Data Tng. Mag. Capt. USAF, 1958-60. Recipient Silver award WPC, 1996, Gold award, 1998. Home and Office: 4942 Linscott Ave Downers Grove IL 60515-3537 E-mail: PaulClementJr@worldnet.att.net.

CLEMENTE, PATROCINIO ABLOLA, secondary education educator; b. Manila, Philippines, Apr. 23, 1941; s. Elpidio San Jose and Amparo (Ablola) C.; came to U.S., 1965; BSE, U. Philippines, 1960; postgrad. Nat. U., Manila, 1961-64; MA, Ball State U., 1966, EdD, 1969; postgrad. U. Calif., Riverside, 1970, Calif. State Coll., Fullerton, 1971-72. High sch. tchr. gen. sci. and biology, div. city schs., Quezon City, Philippines, 1960-65; doctoral fellow dept. psychology Ball State U., Muncie, Ind., 1966-67, dept. spl. edn., 1967-68, grad. asst. dept. gen. and exptl. psychology, 1968-69; tchr. educable mentally retarded high sch. level Fontana (Calif.) Unified Sch. Dist., 1969-70, intermediate level, 1970-73, dist. sch. psychologist, 1973-79, bilingual edn. counselor, 1979-81; resource specialist Morongo (Calif.) Unified Sch. Dist., 1981-83, spl. day class tchr., 1983-90, tchr. math, sci., Spanish, English, 1990—; adj. assoc. prof. Chapman Coll., Orange, Calif., 1982-91. Adult leader Girl Scouts of Philippines, 1963-65; mem. sch. bd. Blessed Sacrament Sch., Twentynine Palms, Calif. State bd. scholar Ball State U., 1965-66. Fellow Am.

Biographical Inst. (hon. mem. research bd. advisors, life); mem. ASCD, NEA, Coun. for Exceptional Children, Am. Assn. on Mental Deficiency, Nat. Assn. of Sch. Psychologists, Found. Exceptional Children, Assn. for Children with Learning Disabilities, Nat. Geographic Soc., Calif. Tchrs. Assn., Morongo Tchrs. Assn., Smithsonian Inst. Roman Catholic. Home: PO Box 637 Twentynine Palms CA 92277-0637

CLEMENT-FOUTS, SHIRLEY GEORGE, educational services executive; b. El Paso, Tex., Feb. 14, 1926; d. Claude Samuel and Elizabeth Estelle (Mattice) Gillett; m. Paul Vincent Clement, Mar. 23, 1946 (dec. 1997); children: Brian Frank, Robert Vincent, Carol Elizabeth, Rosemary Adele; m. Robert Warren Fouts, Sept. 4, 1998. BA in English, Tex. Western Coll., 1963; postgrad., U. Tex., El Paso, N.Mex. State U., 1988; MEd in Reading, Sul Ross State U., 1987; postgrad. in art history, Paris Am. Acad., 1994-98. Tchr. lang. arts Ysleta Ind. Schs., El Paso, 1960-62; tchr. adult edn., 1962-64; tchr. reading/lang. arts, 1964-77; owner, dir. Crestline Learning Sys., Inc., El Paso, 1980-90; dir. Crestline Internat. Schs., 1980-90; instr. Park Coll., Ft. Bliss, Tex., 1992—, U. Phoenix, 1995—. Dir. tutorial for sports teams U. Tex., El Paso, 1984; bd. dirs. S.W. Inst., pres., 1993; dir. continuing edn. program El Paso Cmty. Coll., 1985; mem. curriculum com. Ysleta Ind. Schs., El Paso, 1974; mem. Right to Read Task Force, 1975-77; mem. Bi-Centennial Steering Com., El Paso, 1975-76; presenter Poetry in the Arts, Austin, Tex., 1992, 97; judge student poetry contest, Austin, Tex., 1995; Poetry Soc. Tex. program presenter Mesilla Valley Writers, 1993-96, El Paso Writers, 1994-2001, Poetry Soc. Tex., 1993-2001; instr. writing Paris Am. Acad., summer 1994, 98; cons. Ysleta Schs., 1995; poetry critic, judge Writers Workshop, Albuquerque, 1999, 2002; lectr. on reading in 4 states; poetry judge E.P. Writers League contest. Author: Writers Organizer, 2000; (poems) Echoes Through the Pass, 1998; co-author: Beginning the Search for God-The Edgar Cayce Approach, 1979; contbr. articles to profl. jours.; contbr. poems to Behold Tex., 1983. Treas. El Paso Rep. Women, 1956; facilitator Goals for El Paso, Rep. Women, 1956;mem. hospitality com. Sun Carnival, 1974, Cotton Festival, 1975. Recipient 1st prize Sky Blue Waters Poetry Contest, 2000, 1st prize EP Writer's League Hist. Memories Contest, 2001. Mem. Internat. Reading Assn. (pres. El Paso County coun. 1973-74, presentor 1978-87), Assn. Children with Learning Disabilities (tchr. 1980), Poetry Soc. Tex. (Panhandle Penwomen's first place award 1981, David Atamian Meml. award 1991, judge 1995), Nat. Fedn. State Poetry Soc. (1st place award ann. contest 1988, 1st prize El Paso Hist. Essay contest 1991, 2nd prize 1995, honorable mention Writer's Digest Contest 1996), Chi Omega Alumnae (pres. 1952-53). Home: 537 Spring Crest Dr El Paso TX 79912-4155 E-mail: clement@elp.rr.com.

CLEMENTS, GREGORY LELAND, physics educator; b. Lincoln, Nebr., Apr. 5, 1949; BS, U. Iowa, 1971, MS, 1976, PhD, 1978. Asst. prof. Dickinson Coll., Carlisle, Pa., 1978-82; systems mgr. SofTec, Iowa City, Iowa, 1982-83; prof. Midland Coll., Fremont, Nebr., 1983—. Mem. Am. Assn. Physics Tchrs. (state pres. 1991). Office: Midland Luth Coll 900 N Clarkson St Fremont NE 68025-4254

CLEMENTS, MARY MARGARET, retired educator; b. Glasgow, Scotland, Dec. 23, 1925; came to U.S., 1928; d. Peter MacIntyre and Margaret Service (Mackay) Somerville; m. Carl Emery Clements, Aug. 28, 1954; children: Robert Peter, Margaret Ann Clements Fleming. BA in Edn., U. Akron, 1946; MA in History, U. Mich., 1950. Permanent cert. tchr., Ohio. Tchr. English, history and Spanish, Brunswick (Ohio) H.S., 1946-47, Covington (Ohio) H.S., 1947-51, Xenia (Ohio) Ctrl. H.S., 1951-58, Notre Dame Acad., Chardon, Ohio, 1970-74; tchr. Spanish, Villa Angela Acad., Cleve., 1968-70; tutor for pupil pers. Euclid (Ohio) Sch. System, 1963-67, 91-94, chmn. English dept. summer sch., 1980-91; ret., 1994; tchr. Spanish, English, and History Euclid (Ohio) Sch. System, 1995-96. Sec., coord. united thank offering Diocesan Episcopal Ch. Women, 1981-94; editor Episcopal Ch. Women's News Notes, 1984-94; mem., host family Am. Field Svc., Euclid, 1961-94; pres. PTA Coun., Euclid, 1974-76; provost Deanery Episcopal Ch., Cleve., 1993-95; trustee Ctr. for Human Svcs., Cleve., 1976-86; mem., past pres. Meridia Euclid Hosp., 1976-94; mem. Women's Caucus, Euclid, 1978-82; circulation mgr. Church Life Episcopal newspaper Diocese of Ohio, 1995; chmn. mission and ministry mem. Com. Against Racism. Recipient award for civic leadership Du Pont, 1980. Mem. AAUW (pres. 1978-80, Faculty Wives Assn. (pres. 1963-65). Home: 55 E 213th St Euclid OH 44123-1064

CLERKIN, LORI SUSAN, primary school educator; b. Jersey City, June 28, 1965; d. Robert John and Mary Margaret (Geraghty) C. BA, Purdue U., 1987. Cert. elem. tchr., N.J. 4th grade tchr. East Orange (N.J.) Bd. Edn., 1990-92, gifted tchr., 1993-94, 1st grade tchr., 1994—, after-school program tchr., 1990—, sci./tech. tchr. K-5, 1995—, math. profl. workshop leader, 1993—, chairperson sch.-based mgmt. bd., 1990-93, mem. math. textbook adoption com., 1992-93. Tchr., trainer Great Ideas in Sci. Montclair State U., 1996—; sci. facilitator, 2000—; mentor tchr., 2001—. Grantee East Orange Bd. Edn., 1994. Mem. East Orange Tchr. Assn. (mem. polit. com. 1993—, Tchr. of Yr. 1996), Essex County Tchr. Assn., N.J. Edn. Assn. Roman Catholic. Avocations: fitness, health, crafting. Home: 1101 Ocean Ave # 16 Bradley Beach NJ 07720-1549 Office: George Washington Carver Inst Sci and Tech 410 N Grove St East Orange NJ 07017-4518

CLERMONT, KEVIN MICHAEL, law educator; b. N.Y.C., Oct. 25, 1945; s. William Theodore and Rita Ruth (Healy) C.; m. Emily Sherwin; 2 children, Adrienne Shaine, Jian Louise. AB summa cum laude, Princeton U., 1967; postgrad., U. Nancy, France, 1967-68; JD magna cum laude, Harvard U., 1971. Bar: Mass. 1971, N.Y. 1974, U.S. Dist. Ct. (so. and ea. dists.) N.Y. 1974, U.S. Ct. Appeals (2d cir.) 1974. Law clk. to judge U.S. Dist. Ct. (so. dist.) N.Y., 1971-72; assoc. Cleary, Gottlieb, Steen & Hamilton, N.Y.C., 1972-74; asst. prof. Sch. Law Cornell U., Ithaca, N.Y., 1974-77, assoc. prof., 1977-80, prof., 1980-89, Flanagan prof. law, 1989—. Vis. prof. Sch. Law Harvard U., Cambridge, 1991. Author: (with another) Res Judicata: A Handbook on Its Theory, Doctrine, and Practice, 2001, Civil Procedure: Territorial Jurisdiction and Venue, 1999, (with others) Materials for a Basic Course in Civil Procedure, 8th edit., 2003, Civil Procedure, 6th edit., 2001, (with others) Law: Its Nature, Functions, and Limits, 3d edit., 1986; editor Harvard Law Rev., 1969-71. Fulbright scholar, 1967-68. Mem. ABA, Assn. Am. Law Schs., Order of Coif, Phi Beta Kappa, Sigma Xi. Home: 100 Iroquois Rd Ithaca NY 14850-2223 Office: Cornell U Sch Law Myron Taylor Hall Ithaca NY 14853 E-mail: kmc12@cornell.edu.

CLERMONT, YVES WILFRID, anatomy educator, researcher; b. Montreal, Que., Can., Aug. 14, 1926; s. Rodolphe and Fernande (Primeau) C.; m. Madeleine Bonneau, June 30, 1950; children— Suzanne, Martin, Stephane B.Sc., U. Montreal, 1949; PhD, McGill U., 1953. Lectr. anatomy McGill U., Montreal, 1953-56, asst. prof., 1956-60, assoc. prof., 1960-63, prof., 1963-97, prof. emeritus, 1997—, chmn. dept., 1975-85. Mem. Nat. Bd. Med. Examiners, Phila., 1979-82; mem. rsch. grant com. Med. Rsch. Coun., Ottawa, 1970-97; cons. WHO, NIH, Ford Found., Fonds pour la formation de chercheurs et l'aide à la recherche, Quebec; sec. Artur Lucian Award Com. for Rsch. in Circulatory Diseases, 1983-97, hon. mem., 1997-2000. Contbr. chpts. to books, numerous articles to profl. jours. Recipient Ortho prize Can. Soc. Study Fertility, 1958, Prix Scientifique Govt. of Que., 1963, S.L. Siegler award Am. Soc. Study Fertility, 1966, Van Campenhout award Can. Fertility and Andrology Soc., 1986, Osler Teaching award McGill U., 1990. Fellow: Royal Soc. Can.; mem.: Can. Assn. Microscopy (v.p. 1982—83), Am. Assn. Andrology (Disting. Andrologist award 1988, Serono award lectureship 1992), Can. Assn. Anatomists (hon. J.C.B. Grant award 1986), Soc. Study of Reprodn., Am. Assn. Anatomists (v.p. 1970—73). Home: 567 Townshend St Saint Lambert QC Canada J4R 1M4 Office: McGill U Dept Anatomy Cell Biol 3640 University St Montreal QC Canada H3A 2B2 E-mail: yves.clermont@mcgill.ca.

CLEVELAND, CEIL MARGARET, writer, journalist, education administrator, English language educator; b. Tex., Jan. 10, 1942; d. Joe Donaldson Cleveland and Margaret Ellen (Gowdy) Slack; m. Donald R. Waldrip; children: Wendy Gentile, James Hardy, Timothy Owen; m. Jerrold K. Footlick, Nov. 24, 1984; stepchildren: Robbyn Footlick, Jill Footlick. BA, Whitworth Coll., 1968; MA magna cum laude, Midwestern U., 1971; postgrad., NYU, Columbia U., 1978-82. Assoc. editor Univ. Press, U. Cin., 1975-77; sr. devel. officer, founding editor-in-chief Columbia mag. Columbia U., N.Y.C., 1976-85; founder, pres. Cleveland Comms., Centerport, N.Y., 1987-91; v.p. instnl. rels. Queens Coll., CUNY, Flushing, N.Y., 1991-95; prof. English, v.p. univ. affairs SUNY, Stony Brook, 1995-98; prof. English N.Y. U., 1998—. Dir. curriculum Cin. Arts and Humanities Consortium, 1972-74; adj. prof. English Xavier U., 1972-77, U. Cin., 1972-77, Queens Coll., 1990—; co-founder Syzygy, Women's Press; founder, pub. fiction and poetry The Mill Pond Press. Author: In the World of Literature, 1991, Whatever Happened to Jacy Farrow: A Memoir, 1997, The Bluebook Solution, a novel, 2002, Your Total Kit for Better Punctuation, 2002; editor: English Musical Culture 1776-1976, 1976; mem. editl. bd.: Liberal Edn., 1987—92. Trustee CNET, Cin., 1973-76, Cin. Symphony, 1973-76, Sch. for Creative and Performing Arts, Cin., 1973-76; founder Inner City Sch. Enrichment Project; mem. Coun. of Racial Equality, 1973-76; active Playhouse in the Park, 1973-76, Internat. Children's Village, Cin., 1973-76. Recipient Writer of Decade and Mag. Editor of Decade, Coun. for Advancement and Support of Edn., 1976—86, Edn. Comms. award, Ed Press, 1993, Internat. Bus. Comms. award, 1994; fellow Va. Ctr. for Creative Arts, 2002. Fellow Woodrow Wilson; mem. MLA, Coun. for Advancement and Support of Edn. (trustee 1981-83), Nat. Edn. Roundtable, N.Y.C. Women Leader's Roundtable, Am. Coun. Edn. (coord. 1994). Home: 11 Prospect Rd Centerport NY 11721-1129 Office: NYU 228 Shimkin Hall 50 W 4th St New York NY 10012-1156

CLEVELAND, CHARLES SIDNEY, secondary education educator; b. Portland, Oreg., Apr. 8, 1951; s. Sidney Charles and Virginia May (Seitzinger) C.; m. Joyce Kristine Nofziger, Nov. 5, 1972; children: Justin Charles, Christpher Joseph Sidney. BS, Portland State U., 1974; MAT, Lewis and Clark Coll., 1980. Geography tchr. Hillsboro (Oreg.) Union High Dist., 1976-98, Hillsborough (Oreg.) H.S., 1998—. Pres. Hillsboro (Oreg.) Active 20-30 Club, 1989, Oreg. Soccer Coaches Assn., 1983-84; asst. scoutmaster Boy Scouts Am., Hillsboro, 1991—; bd. dirs. Oreg. Geog. Alliance, 1987-93, Hillsboro Edn. Assn., 1983-86, 92—. Recipient Instructional Leadership Inst. award Nat. Geog. Soc., 1989; named Oreg. and Region IV Soccer Coach of Yr. by Nat. High Sch. Athletic Coaches Assn., 1984, Outstanding Young Man by Hillsboro C. of C., 1976. Mem. Assn. Am. Geographers, Nat. Coun. Geog. Edn. (Disting. Teaching Achievement award 1992), Nat. Coun. Social Studies, Oreg. Coun. Social Studies (bd. dirs.), Active 20-30 Internat. (life), Elks. Avocations: photography, coaching soccer, scout leader. Office: Hillsborough HS 3285 SE Roodridge Rd Hillsboro OR 97123

CLEWIS, CHARLOTTE WRIGHT STAUB, mathematics educator; b. Pitts., Aug. 20, 1935; d. Schirmer Chalfant and Charlotte Wright (Rodgers) Staub; m. John Edward Clewis, Aug. 11, 1954; 1 child, Charlotte Wright. Student, Memphis State Coll., 1953-54, U. Wis., 1957-59; BA, Newark State Coll., 1963; MAT, Loyola Marymount U., 1974. Asst. dir. to housemother Leota Sch. & Camp, Evansville, Wis., 1957-59; tchr. math. Rahway (N.J.) Jr. H.S., 1963-70, Torrance (Calif.) Unified Sch. Dist., 1970-95, coord. math. dept., 1977-95; mem. instrnl. materials rev. panel State Calif., 1986; instr. Weekend Coll. Marymount-Palos Verdes, 1992-94, math. teams coach. Sec., pres. Larga Vista Property Owners Assn., 1975-84, treas., 2001--; mem. Rolling Hills Estates City Celebration Com., 1975-81; treas. adult leaders YMCA, Metuchen, N.J., 1967-69; bd. dirs. Peninsula Symphony Assn., 1978-84, sec., 1993-97; commr. Rolling Hills Estates Parks & Activities, 1981—, chmn., 1985, 90, 96, 2003; vol. Iditarod Dog Sled Race, 1996—. Recipient appreciation award PTA, 1984, hon. svc. award, 1986. Fellow: Soc. Antiquaries of Scotland; mem.: Clan of the Highlands, Clan MacLeod Soc. U.S.A. Pacific Region. Avocations: camping, reading, horseback riding, computers. Home: 1 Gaucho Dr Rolling Hills Estates CA 90274-5113 E-mail: jclewis2@earthlink.net.

CLICK, GAIL IRENE, middle school educator; b. Shirley, Mass., Jan. 16, 1952; d. Gavin Frederick Hendry and Grace Irene (Holt) Campbell; m. Robert Lynn Click, Dec. 26, 1971; 1 child, Elton Hendrie. BS in Elem. Edn., S.W. Tex. State U., 1973; MS in Edn., Nat. U., 1983. Cert. tchr., Va., Calif. 2d grade tchr. Summersill Elem. Sch., Jacksonville, N.C., 1974-76; 5th, 6th English and history tchr. Beaufort (S.C.) Acad., 1976-78; 2d grade tchr. Makiminato Elem. Sch., Dept. Def. Schs., Okinawa, Japan, 1978-79; tchr. combination 4-8 class Canyon Sch., Vista, Calif., 1981-85; 7th and 8th grade English, math., art and history tchr. Edward Drew Mid. Sch., Stafford, Va., 1985-88, 6th grade tchr., 1990—; 6th and 8th grade English and history tchr. Harris County Mid. Sch., Hamilton, Ga., 1988-90. Recipient Agnes Meyer Outstanding Tchr. award Washington Post Edn. Found., 1991. Mem. NEA, Va. Mid. Sch. Assn., Va. Edn. Assn. Republican. Methodist. Avocations: travel, reading, crafts.

CLICK, JOHN WILLIAM, communication educator; b. Huntington, Ind., Apr. 22, 1936; s. Eric Alger and Ethel (McKenzie) C.; m. Dixie Darlene Brown, Nov. 27, 1960; children: Reid William, Kevin Leon. AB, Ball State U., 1958; MS, Ohio U., 1959; PhD, Ohio State U., 1977. Dir. pub. rels. Findlay (Ohio) Coll., 1959-60; instr. journalism Cen. Mich. U., Mt. Pleasant, Mich., 1960-65; from asst. prof. to prof. Ohio U., Athens, 1965-83; prof., dir. Sch. Journalism La. State U., Baton Rouge, 1983-87; chmn., prof. dept. mass communication Winthrop U., Rock Hill, S.C., 1987—. Cons. Motorola Inc., Franklin Park, Ill., 1968, Portland (Oreg.) State U., 1988, Lenoir-Rhyne Coll., N.C., 1990, U. Tenn. Chattanooga, 1990, Otterbein Coll., 1992; mem. Accrediting Coun. Edn. in Journalism and Mass Comm., 1989-95; 1998-2001. Author: Magazine Editing and Production, 1974-99, Governing College Student Publs., 1980, 93, monograph Ethics and Responsibilities of Advising College Student Publs., 1978, 87, 93; mng. editor: Journalism Quarterly, 1982-91. Recipient Meritorious Course award, 1980, Faculty Svc. award Nat. U. Continuing Edn. Assn., 1983; Medal of Merit, Soc. for Collegiate Journalists, 1979; named to Journalism Hall of Fame, Ball State U., 1987, named Magazine Educator of the Year, 1999. Mem. Soc. Profl. Journalists, Assn. for Edn. in Journalism (Magazine Educator of Yr. 1999), Coll. Media Advisers (pres. 1971-75, Hall of Fame 1994), Soc. for Collegiate Journalists (pres. 1977-79), S.C. Press Assn., Assn. Schs. of Journalism and Mass Comms. (bd. dirs. 1993-95, v.p. 1995-96, pres.-elect 1996-97, pres. 1997-98), Coun. of Comm. Assn. (rep. 1997-98), Kappa Tau Alpha (v.p. 2000-02, pres. 02-04). Office: Winthrop Univ Dept Mass Communication Rock Hill SC 29733-0001

CLIFF, JOHNNIE MARIE, mathematics and chemistry educator; b. Lamkin, Miss., May 10, 1935; d. John and Modest Alma (Lewis) Walton; m. William Henry Cliff, Apr. 1, 1961 (dec. 1983); 1 child, Karen Marie. BA in Chemistry, Math., U. Indpls., 1956; postgrad., NSF Inst., Butler U., 1960; MA in Chemistry, Ind. U., 1964; MS in Math., U. Notre Dame, 1980; postgrad., Martin U., 2000. Cert. tchr., Ind. Rsch. chemist Ind. U. Med. Ctr., Indpls., 1956-59; tchr. sci. and math. Indpls. Pub. Schs., 1960-88; tchr. chemistry, math. Martin U., Indpls., 1989—, chmn. math. dept., 1990—, divsn. chmn. depts. sci. and math., 1993—. Adj. instr. math. U. Indpls., 1991, Ivy Tech State Coll., Indpls., 2002. Contbr. rsch. papers to sci. jours. Grantee NSF, 1961-64, 73-76, 78-79, Woodrow Wilson Found., 1987-88; scholarship U. Indpls., 1952-56, NSF Inst. Reed Coll., 1961, C. of C., 1963. Mem. AAUW, NAACP, NEA, Assn. Women in Sci., Urban League, N.Y. Acad. Scis., Am. Chem. Soc., Nat. Coun. Math. Tchrs., Am. Assn. Physics Tchrs., Nat. Sci. Tchrs. Assn., Am. Statis. Assn., Am. Assn. Ret. Persons, Neal-Marshall-Ind. U. Alumni Assn., U. Indpls. Alumni Assn., U. Notre Dame Alumni Assn., Ind. U. Chemist Assn., Notre Dame Club Indpls., Kappa Delta Pi, Delta Sigma Theta. Democrat. Baptist. Avocations: gardening, sewing. Home: 405 Golf Ln Indianapolis IN 46260-4108 Office: Martin U 2171 Avondale Pl Indianapolis IN 46218-3878

CLIFFORD, CRAIG WILLIAM, physiologist, educator; b. New Orleans, Aug. 25, 1950; s. Samuel John and Dorothy Lillian (Dufau) C.; m. Patricia Ann Lafourcade, Oct. 13, 1973; 1 child, Samantha Louise. BS, La. State U., 1972, MS, 1974, PhD, 1985. Instr. La. State U., Baton Rouge, 1982-85; prof. physiology Northeastern State U., Tahlequah, Okla., 1985—, chair dept. biology, 1196—2001, dean coll. math. sci. nursing, 2001—. Mem. faculty adv. com. Okla. State Regents Higher Edn., Oklahoma City, 1993-95. Recipient Summer Acad. of Sci. award Okla. State Regents Higher Edn., 1991, 93, 94, 96. Mem. Okla. Acad. Scis. (vice chair 1989-90, chair 1990-91 biology sect., pres. 2002-03), Northeastern Faculty Assn. (pres. 1991-93), Arts Coun. of Tahlequah (pres. 1990-92, bd. dirs. 1993-97), Tahlequah Kiwanis Club (pres. 1991-92), Sigma Xi (S.W. regional bd. dirs. 1992-95). Roman Catholic. Home: 1001 S Owens Ave Tahlequah OK 74464-4639 Office: Northeastern State U Tahlequah OK 74464

CLIFFORD, GERALDINE JONCICH (MRS. WILLIAM F. CLIFFORD), education educator; b. San Pedro, Calif., Apr. 17, 1931; d. Marion and Geraldine Joncich; m. William F. Clifford, July 12, 1969 (dec. 1993). AB, UCLA, 1954, M.Ed., 1957; Ed.D., Columbia U., 1961. Tchr., San Lorenzo, Calif., 1954-56, Maracaibo, Venezuela, 1957-58; researcher Inst. Lang. Arts, Tchrs. Coll., Columbia, 1958-61; asst. prof. edn. U. Calif., Berkeley, 1962-67, asso. prof., 1967-74, prof., 1974-94, assoc. dean, 1976-78, chmn. dept. edn., 1978-81, acting dean Sch. Edn., 1980-81, 82-83, dir. edn. abroad program, 1988, 89, prof. grad. sch., 1994—. Author: The Sane Positivist: A Biography of Edward L. Thorndike, 1968, The Shape of American Education, 1975, Ed Sch: A Brief for Professional Education, 1988, Lone Voyagers: Academic Women in Coeducational Universities, 1870-1937, 1989, Equally in View: The University of California, Its Women, and The Schools, 1995. Macmillan fellow, 1958-59, Guggenheim fellow, 1965-66, Rockefeller fellow, 1977-78; recipient Willystine Goodsell award for Contbns. to Women in Edn. Mem. History Edn. Soc., Am. Ednl. Rsch. Assn., Phi Beta Kappa, Pi Lambda Theta. Home: Apt 733 1661 Pine St San Francisco CA 94109-0420

CLIFTON, ANNE RUTENBER, psychotherapist, educator; b. New Haven, Dec. 11, 1938; d. Ralph Dudley and Cleminette (Downing) Rutenber; 1 child, Dawn Anne. BA, Smith Coll., 1960, MSW, 1962. Lic. clin. social worker, Mass.; diplomate Clin. Social Work. Psychiat. case worker adult psychiatry unit Tufts-New Eng. Med. Ctr., Boston, 1962-68, supr. students, 1967-68; pvt. practice psychotherapy, Cambridge and Newton, Mass., 1966—. Supr. med. students, staff social workers out-patient psychiatry Tufts New Eng. Med. Ctr., 1973—, also mem. exec. bd. Women's Resource Ctr., interim co-dir., 1986-88; asst. clin. prof. psychiatry Tufts U. Med. Sch., 1974—, research dept. psychiatry, 1966-68, 73, 77—. Contbr. articles to profl. jours. Mem. NASW, Acad. Cert. Social Workers, Cambridge Tennis Club, Mt. Auburn Tennis Club, Phi Beta Kappa, Sigma Xi. Home: 126 Homer St Newton MA 02459-1518 Office: 59 Church St Ste 4 Cambridge MA 02138-3724 E-mail: annerclifton@aol.com.

CLIFTON, DAVID SAMUEL, JR., research executive, economist; b. Raleigh, N.C., Nov. 15, 1943; s. David Samuel and Ruth Centelle (Paker) C.; m. Karen Lisette Buhrer (div. June 1980); children: Derek Scott, Mark David; m. Eileen Lois Cooley, July 30, 1983; children: Dana Cooley, Michael Cooley. B in Indsl. Engring., Ga. Inst. Tech., 1966; MBA in Econs., Ga. State U., 1970, PhD in Econs., 1980. Customer facilities engr. Lockheed Ga. Co., Marietta, 1966-70; prin. rsch. scientist Ga. Tech. Rsch. Inst., Atlanta, 1970-93, dir. econ. devel. lab., 1979-90, dir. econ. devel. and tech. transfer, 1990-93, dir. Ctr. for Internat. Stds. and Quality, 1991-99; acting exec. assoc. dir. Ga. Tech. Econ. Devel. Inst., Atlanta, 1993-94, group dir. ctrs. Econ. Devel. Inst., 1998-99, group dir. bus. and industry, 1999—2001, prin. rsch. scientist emeriuts, 2001—. Bd. dirs. Sea Adventure Unltd., Inc., Atlanta; cons. UN Indsl. Devel. Orgn., Vienna, 1982, Inst. de Adminstn. Cientifica de los Empreos, Mexico City, 1978; apptd. by gov. So. Tech. Coun., Rsch. Triangle Park, N.C., 1992—. Co-author: Project Feasibility Analysis, 1977; contbr. articles to profl. jours. Mem. Am. Econs. Assn., Atlanta Power Squadron Club, Sigma Xi. Avocations: sailing, navigating. Home: 2486 Williamswood Ct Decatur GA 30033-2810 Office: Ga Tech Ctr Internat Stds & Quality Atlanta GA 30332-0001

CLIFTON, JAMES ALBERT, physician, educator; b. Fayetteville, N.C., Sept. 18, 1923; s. James Albert Jr. and Flora M. (McNair) Clifton; m. Katherine Rathe, June 25, 1949; children: Susan M.(dec.), Katherine Y., Caroline M. BA, Vanderbilt U., 1944, MD, 1947. Diplomate Am. Bd. Internal Medicine (mem. 1972-81, mem. subsplty. bd. gastroenterology 1968-75, chmn. 1972-75, mem. exec. com. 1978-81, chmn. 1980-81). Intern U. Hosps., Iowa City, 1947—48, resident dept. medicine, 1948—51; staff dept. medicine Thayer VA Hosp., Nashville, 1952—53; asst. clin. medicine Vanderbilt Hosp., Nashville, 1952—53; cons. physician VA Hosp., Iowa City, 1965—93; assoc. medicine dept. internal medicine Coll. Medicine, U. Iowa, 1953—54, chief divsn. gastroenterology, 1953—71, asst. prof. medicine, 1954-58, assoc. prof., 1958—63, prof., 1963—91, prof. emeritus, 1991—, traveling fellow, 1964, vis. prof. dept. physiology, 1964, vice chmn. dept. medicine, 1967—70, chmn. dept. medicine Coll. Medicine, 1970—76, Roy J. Carver prof. medicine, 1974—91, Roy J. Carver prof. emeritus, 1991—, dir. James A. Clifton Ctr. Digestive Diseases, 1985—90, interim dean, 1991—93. Investigator Mt. Desert Isle Biol. Lab., Salisbury Cove, Maine, 1964; vis. faculty mem. Mayo Found. and Mayo Clinic, 1966; vis. prof. dept. medicine U. N.C. Chapel Hill, 1970; cons. gastroenterology and nutrition tng. grants com. Nat. Inst. Arthritis and Metabolic Diseases, NIH, 1964—68, chmn., 1965—68; mem. Nat. Adv. Arthritis and Metabolic Diseases Coun., 1970—73; mem. gastroenterology tng. com. VA, Washington, 1967—71, chmn. tng. grants com., 1971—73; mem. med. adv. bd. Digestive Disease Found., 1969—73; vis. prof. gastroenterology U. London (St. Marks Hosp.), 1984—85; mem. sci. adv. com. Ludwig Inst. Cancer Rsch., Zurich, 1984—95. Internat. editl. bd. Italian Jour. Gastroenterology, 1970—90, Gastroenterology, 1964—68. Recipient Disting. Alumnus of Yr. award, Vanderbilt U. Sch. Medicine, 1984, Disting. Alumnus of Yr. Achievement award, U. Iowa Coll. Medicine, 2000, Disting. Mentoring award, 2002; fellow spl. rsch., NIH, USPHS, 1955—56, in medicine, Evans Meml. Hosp., Mass. Meml. Hosps., also Boston U. Sch. Medicine, 1955—56; scholar Phi Connell, Vanderbilt U., 1943—44. Fellow: ACP (bd. regents 1972—79, pres. 1977—78, Alfred Stengel award 1984, Laureate award 1989); mem.: AAUP, AAAS, AMA (liaison com. grad. med. edn. 1976—77), Internat. Soc. Internal Medicine (exec. com. 1978—80), Assn. Profs. Medicine (councillor 1972—73, sec.-treas. 1973—75), Assn. Am. Med. Colls., Am. Physiol. Soc., Soc. Exptl. Biology and Medicine, Assn. Am. Physicians, Am. Clin. and Climatol. Assn. (v.p. 1984), Am. Fedn. Clin. Rsch., Am. Soc. Internal Medicine (Internist of Yr. award Iowa chpt. 1986), Am. Assn. Study Liver Disease, Am. Heart Assn., Am. Gastroent. Assn. (pres. 1970—71), Inst. Medicine NAS, U. Iowa Assn. Emeritus Faculty (pres. 1999—2000), U. Iowa Retirees Assn. (pres. 1999—2000). Home: 39 Audubon Pl Iowa City IA 52245-3437 Office: U Iowa Hosp and Clinics 4 JCP Hawkins Dr Iowa City IA 52242 E-mail: jclifton@uiowa.edu., zylumjim@mchsi.com.

CLINCH, NICHOLAS, assistant principal; b. Tokyo, Dec. 20, 1950; arrived in U.S., 1969; s. Harold Kenneth and Galina (Voevodina) C.; m. Carol Ann Connell, May 27, 1978; children: Michael Alan Clinch, Stephen Alexsei Clinch. BA, Davidson Coll., 1972; MA, Appalachian State U., 1973; EdD, Nova Southeastern U., 2002. Cert. secondary tchr., S.C. Spanish tchr. Gaffney (S.C.) H.S., 1973-74, York (S.C.) Comprehensive H.S., 1974-94; asst. prin. York Jr. H.S., 1994—. Tennis coach York

Comprehensive H.S., 1977-81, soccer coach, 1979-89; home-sch. coord. York County Migrant Program, 1975-81, dir., 1982. Office: York Junior High School 1280 Johnson Rd York SC 29745-2100

CLINE, BETH MARIE, school psychologist; b. San Diego, Apr. 21, 1959; d. Roy Donald and Betty Ruth (Gainey) Hendricks. AAS in Police Sci., Hinds Community Coll., 1979; BS in Criminal Justice, Delta State U., 1981, MEd in Sch. Psychology, 1984, EdS in Sch. Psychology, 1988, D in Edn., 1995. Sch. psychometrist Chattahoochee Flint Regional Edn. Svc. Agy., Americus, Ga., 1984-85, Clarksdale (Miss.) Mcpl. Sch. Dist., 1985-88, sch. psychologist, 1988—2001. Coord. crisis mgmt. team, positive behavioral specialist, sch. psychologist Clarksdale Screening Team, 1988-93; cons. trainer Miss. Dept. Edn., Jackson, 1988-2001, cons., portfolio reviewer, 1990-2001. Mem. adult handbell choirs Clarksdale Bapt. Ch., 1989-2002, mem. adult choir, 1989—, asst. Sunday sch. dir. and tchr., 1990-92, mem. Ladies Ensemble, 1994—, Sunday sch. dir., 1992-94, children's Sunday sch. tchr., 2001—. Mem. Nat. Assn. Sch. Psychologists, Miss. Assn. for Psychology in the Schs. (sec. 1985-87, northern mem.-at-large 1989-91, pres.-elect 1991-92, pres. 1992-93, past pres. 1993-94), Ga. Assn. Sch. Psychologists (chairperson nominations com. 1985, rsch. com. 1985). Baptist. Office: Clarksdale Mcpl Sch Dist PO Box 1088 Clarksdale MS 38614-1088

CLINE, CHARLES WILLIAM, poet, pianist, rhetoric and literature educator; b. Waleska, Ga., Mar. 1, 1937; s. Paul Ardell and Mary Montarie (Pittman) C.; m. Sandra Lee Williamson, June 11, 1966 (div. 1996); 1 son, Jeffrey Charles. Student, U. Cin. Conservatory of Music, 1957-58; AA, Reinhardt Coll., 1957; BA, George Peabody Coll. for Tchrs., 1960; MA, Vanderbilt U., 1963; LittD, World U., 1981; DFA (hon.), Australian Inst. Coordinated Rsch., 1996. Asst. prof. English Shorter Coll., Rome, Ga., 1963-64; instr. English West Ga. Coll., Carrollton, 1964-68; manuscript procurement editor Fideler Co., Grand Rapids, Mich, 1968; assoc. prof. English Kellogg Community Coll., Battle Creek, Mich., 1969-75, prof. English and resident poet, 1975—. Chmn. creative writing sect. Midwest Conf. on English, 1976; condr. poetry readings and workshops. Piano recitals at Internat. Congress on Arts and Comm., 1992, 93, 94, 95, 96, 99; author: Crossing the Ohio, 1976, Questions for the Snow, 1979, Ultima Thule, 1984, (with Amal Ghose and others) Wholeness of Dream, 1989; editor: Forty Salutes to Mich. Poets, 1975; contbr. Gifts of Music, 1994; contbr. poems to jours. and anthologies. Decorated knight comdr. Lofsensischen Unsiniusordens, 1991, knight Order of Knights Templars of Jerusalem, 1991, knight Order of Circulo Nobilario de los Caballeros Universales, 1993, knight Order of Holy Grail, 1996, baron Royal Order of the Bohemian Crown, 1996, count Order of San Ciriaco, 1996; recipient Poetry awards Modus Operandi, 1975, Internat. Belles-Lettres Soc., 1975, Poetry Soc. Mich., 1975, N. Am. Mentor, 1977, 78, Lit. Prize World Inst. Achievement, 1986, 88, Star of Distinction, 19th Internat. Congress on Art and Comm., St. John's Coll., U. Cambridge, 1992, Disting. Participation medallion 20th Congress, Cambridge, Mass., 1993, 26th Congress, Lisbon, 1999, Diplôme d'Honneur en Littèrature et Musique, Inst. des Affaires Internats., 1996; resolutions recognition Kalamazoo City Commn., Mich. Ho. of Reps. and Senate, 1981, others. Fellow World Literary Acad. (founding, prize 1983), Internat. Soc. Lit. (life), Am. Biog. Inst. (life, World Fellowship award 1987, Internat. Hall of Leaders 1988, hon. advisor rsch. bd. advisors nat. divsn. 1994); mem. Tagore Inst. Creative Writing Internat. (life), World Poetry Soc. Intercontinental, Centro Studi e Scambi Internazionali (Poet Laureate award, Diploma di Benemerenza, Diploma d'Onore), Accademia Leonardo da Vinci, Poetry Soc. Am., Poets and Writers Inc., Acad. Am. Poets, Am. Biog. Inst. Rsch. Assn. (dep. gov.), Internat. Biog. Assn. (life patron), World U. Roundtable, Internat. Biog. Ctr. (dep. dir. gen. 1991, 20th Century award for achievement 1992, World Intellectual 1993, cert. of mutual loyalty between dir. gen. and deps. 1999, pictorial testimonial for outstanding scholars of the 20th century 1999), Accademia Internationale di Pontzen (distintivo palmato 1991, lauro d'oro for literary merit 1991, grande medaglia Aurata della fondazione 1997, scettro d'argento 1998), Maison Internat. des Intellectuels, Acad. M.I.D.I., Wordsworth-Coleridge Assn., Assn. Lit. Scholars and Critics. Presbyterian. Office: Kellogg Community Coll 450 North Ave Battle Creek MI 49017-3306

CLINE, DAVID BRUCE, physicist, educator; b. Kansas City, Kans., Dec. 7, 1933; s. Andrew B. Cline and Ella M. Jacks; children: Heather, Bruce, Richard, Yasmin, Daphne. BS, MS, Kansas State Univ., 1960; PhD, Univ. Wis., 1965. Asst. prof. physics Univ. Wis., Madison, 1965-66, assoc. prof. physics, 1966-68, prof. physics, 1969; prof. physics and astronomy UCLA, 1969—. Vis. appts. U. Hawaii, Lawrence Berkeley (Calif.) Lab., Fermilab, CERN; mem. various high energy physics adv. panels and program coms., theory and lab. astrophysics panel, panel on particles NRC Astronomy & Astrophysics Survey Com.; past co-dir. Instit. for Accelerator Physics at U. Wis.; founder Ctr. for Advanced Accelerators, UCLA, 1987. Editor numerous books. With U.S. Army, 1956-58. Recipient Sloan fellow A.P. Sloan Found., 1967. Fellow N.Y. Acad. Scis.; mem. AAAS, Am. Inst. Physics, Phi Beta Kappa. Democrat. Achievements include first search for weak neutical currents that charge flavor; co-discovery of Weak Neutral current at FNAL (HPWF exp) early evidence for charm particle; devise of the antiproton-proton collider; liquid xenon; co-discovery of the W and Z intermediate boson at CERN, Geneva; discovery of B 0 - Bo mixing; patentee for PET medical imagery technique. Office: UCLA Dept Physics 405 Hilgard Ave Los Angeles CA 90095-9000

CLINE, DOROTHY MAY STAMMERJOHN (MRS. EDWARD WILBURN CLINE), education educator, consultant; b. Boonville, Mo., Oct. 19, 1915; d. Benjmain Franklin and Lottie (Ealther) Stammerjohn; m. Edward Wilburn Cline, Aug. 16, 1938 (dec. May 1962); children: Margaret Ann (Mrs. Rodger Orville Bell), Susan Elizabeth (Mrs. Gary Lee Burns), Dorothy Jean; m. Arthur Hugh Deeney, July 11, 1998. Grad. nurse, U. Mo., 1937, BS in Edn., 1939, postgrad., 1966-67; MS, Ark. State U., 1964. Dir. Christian Coll. Infirmary, Columbia, Mo., 1936-37; asst. chief nursing svc. VA Hosp., Poplar Bluff, Mo., 1950-58; tchr.-in-charge staff State Tng. Ctr. No 4, Poplar Bluff, 1959-66, Dorothy S. Cline State Sch. #53, Boonville, 1967-85; instr. U. Mo., Columbia, 1973-74. Cons. for workshops for new tchrs., curriculum revision Mo. Dept. Edn. Mem. Butler County Council Retarded Children, 1959-66; v.p. Boonslick Assn. Retarded Children, 1969-72; sec.-treas. Mo. chpt. Am. Assn. on Mental Deficiency, 1973-75; bd. dirs. Unltd. Opportunities Sheltered Workshop. Mem. NEA, Mo. Tchrs. Assn., Am. Assn. on Mental Deficiency, Coun. for Exceptional Children, AAUW (v.p. Boonville br. 1968-70, 75-77), Mo. Writers Guild, Creative Writer's Group (pres. 1974—), Columbia Creative Writers Group, Eastern Center Poetry Soc., Laura Speed Elliott High Sch. Alumni Assn., Bus. and Profl. Women's Club, Smithsonian Assn., U. Mo. Alumni Assn., Ark. State U. Alumni Assn., PEO, Internat. Platform Soc., Friends Historic Boonville, Delta Kappa Gamma. Mem. Christian Ch. Home: 603 High St Boonville MO 65233-1212

CLINE, JANET E. SAFFORD, school district administrator, desktop publisher; b. London, Aug. 28, 1945; came to U.S., 1946; d. Don F. and Elizabeth G. (Taylor) Safford; m. Raymond D. Cline, Aug. 23, 1966; children: Roger D., Martin A. BA, West Tex. State U., Canyon, 1967. Admissions clk. North Tex. State U., Denton, 1971-72; comms. dir. United Meth. Temple, Port Arthur, Tex., 1973-75; edn. and health reporter Port Arthur News, 1977-82; coord. sch./cmty. rels. Port Arthur Ind. Sch. Dist., 1982-97, dir. comms., 1997—. Owner Janet Cline Pub. Author, editor numerous PAISD Publs.; contbr. articles to profl. jours. Mem. Mayor's Com. on Edn., Port Arthur, 1994-96chmn. Port Arthur Centennial Activities Commn., 1996—; pres. Mid/South Jefferson County chpt. Am. Heart Assn., 1997—, Samaritan Counseling Ctr., Jefferson County, 1997—. Recipient Anson Jones award Tex. Med. Assn., 1983, Silver Star of Tex. award Tex. Hosp. Assn., 1983. Mem. Tex. Sch. Pub. Rels. Assn. (regional v.p. 1988-89, chair com. 1983-97, Bright Idea award 1997), North Port Arthur Rotary Club (v.p. 1997—). Methodist. Avocations: reading, bridge, cross stitch, travel.

CLINE, JANICE CLAIRE, education educator; b. Wausau, Wis., Aug. 22, 1945; d. George Leroy and Irma Olga (Brummond) C.; m. Brent Buell, Jan. 28, 1979. BS, U. Wis., 1967; MA, NYU, 1972; student of Eli Siegel, 1978; student of Ellen Reiss, Aesthetic Realism Found., N.Y.C., 1977—2001; student of Aesthetic Realism Teaching Method, 1977—. Tchr. Hyde Park H.S., Chgo., 1967-69; instr. Chase Manhattan Bank JOB Tng. Program, N.Y.C., 1969-71; evaluator York Coll. Title I Evaluation Team, Jamaica, N.Y., 1972; adj. lectr. N.Y.C. C.C., CUNY, Bklyn., 1971-72, lectr. York Coll. Jamaica, 1972—. Lectr. Aesthetic Realism Assoc., N.Y.C., 1977-2001; guest spkr. WVON, Chgo., 1980. Contbr. articles to profl. jours. Coord. Conf. in Support of the Liberation of S. Africa and Namibia, York Coll., Jamaica, N.Y., 1985, Student/Faculty Consortium on Central Am., York Coll., 1986. Recipient Outstanding Contbn. award Afro-Am. Club, York Coll., 1985, Outstanding Contbn. award Conf. of African People, Jamaica, N.Y., 1986. Mem. AAUP, Profl. Staff Congress (sr. coll. officer, exec. com. 2002—, chpt. chmn.), Internat. Reading Assn., Am. Fedn. Tchrs. (del. 2000—), Nat. Coun. Tchrs. English, CUNY Women's Coalition, Nat. Action Network. Office: CUNY York Coll Dept English 94-20 Guy R Brewer Blvd Jamaica NY 11451-0001

CLINE, PAUL CHARLES, political science educator, state legislator; b. Clarksburg, W.Va., Dec. 26, 1933; s. Kemper Price and Irene (Neff) C.; m. Diane Chilcote, Aug. 10, 1958; children: Alice J. Cline Morris, Camille N. AA, Potomac State Coll., 1953; AB, W.Va. U., 1956, JD, 1957, MA, 1961; PhD in Govt., Am. U., 1968. Bar: W.Va. 1957. Pvt. practive, Huntington, W.Va., 1959-60; asst. prof. polit. sci. James Madison U., Harrisonburg, Va., 1961-68, assoc. prof., 1968-70, coord. fed. grants and program, 1966-67, exec. asst. to pres., 1967-69, head dept. polit. sci. and geography, 1969-71, prof. polit. sci., 1970-95; mem. Va. Ho. of Dels., 1986-87; prof. emeritus polit. sci. James Madison U., Harrisonburg, Va., 1995—. Vis. prof. polit. sci. U. Va., 1986-87. Author: Practical Law, 1978, By the Good People of Virginia, 1991, American Democracy, 1995. Chmn. Harrisburg City Planning Commn., 1971-72; mem. Harrisonburg City Coun., 1972-76; chmn. Harrisonburg Redevel. and Housing Authority, 1979-80. With AUS, 1957-59. Mem. W.Va. State Bar. Home: 408 Valencia Rd Venice FL 34285-2534

CLINE, PAULINE M. educational administrator; b. Seattle, Aug. 25, 1947; d. Paul A. and Margaret R. Cline BA in Edn., Seattle U., 1969, MEd, 1975, EdD, 1983. Cert. tchr., prin., supt., Wash. Tchr. Marysville High Sch., Wash., 1969-70; tchr., adminstr. Blanchet High Sch., Seattle, 1970-78; asst. prin. Edmonds High Sch., Wash., 1978-84; prin. College Place Middle Sch., Edmonds, 1984-85, Mountlake Terrace High Sch., Wash., 1985-93; asst. supt. Mount Vernon Sch. Dist., 1993-2000, Bethel Sch. Dist., 2002—. Recipient Washington award for excellence in edn. Gov. and Supt. Pub. Instruction, 1992, IDEA Kettering fellow, 1984, 86-87, 90-95, 97. Mem. ASCD, Am. Assn. Sch. Adminstr., Rotary (charter mem., past pres. Alderwood club), Phi Delta Kappa. Roman Catholic. Avocations: skiing, kayaking, backpacking, golf.

CLINE, RUTH ELEANOR HARWOOD, translator, historian; b. Middletown, Conn., Oct. 31, 1946; d. Burton Henry and Eleanor May (Cash) Harwood; A.B., Smith Coll., 1968; M.A., Rutgers U., 1969; Ph.D., Georgetown U., 2000; cert. translation from French, Georgetown U., 1978; m. William R. Cline, June 10, 1967; children: Alison, Marian. Reviewer, U.S. Dept. State, Washington, 1979-94. Former v.p. Smith Coll. Class of 1968; rsch. assoc. dept. history Georgetown U., 2002--. Mem. Am. Translators Assn. (cert. in French, Spanish and Portuguese), MLA, Internat. Arthurian Soc. Episcopalian. Translator English verse: Yvain; or the Knight with the Lion (Chretien de Troyes), 1975; Perceval; or the Story of the Grail (Chretien de Troyes), 1983, Lancelot or the Knight of the Cart (Chretien de Troyes), 1990 (Lewis Galantiere Prize 1992), Erec and Enide (Chretien de Troyes), 2000, Cliges (Chretien de Troyes), 2000. Home: 5315 Oakland Rd Chevy Chase MD 20815-6638

CLINE, TIMOTHY BYRON, special education educator; b. Pueblo, Colo., Jan. 23, 1957; s. Richard Dennis and Shirley May (Jones) C. BS in Phys. Edn., U. Colo., 1980, MA in Edn., 1983; grad. cert. in profl. and tech. comm., U. Colo., Denver, 2000. Cert. tchr. phys. edn., ednl. handicapped, Colo. Tchr. self-contained Boulder (Colo.) Valley Schs., 1983-84, day treatment tchr., 1985, tchr. learning disabilities, 1985-86, tchr. h.s. inten., 1986-87, tchr. elem. significant emotional disorders, 1989—; residential treatment tchr. Colo. Christian Home, Denver, 1987-89. Mem. program dept. Centaurus H.S., Boulder Valley Schs., 1986-87. Mem. NEA, Colo. Edn. Assn., Boulder Valley Edn. Assn. Democrat. Roman Catholic. Avocations: swimming, eclectic reading, writing. Home: 10612 Pierson St Broomfield CO 80021-3522 Office: Boulder Valley Sch Dist 6500 Arapahoe Rd Boulder CO 80303-1407 E-mail: clinetb@busd.k12.co.us., tbcline@nyx.net.

CLINEBELL, SHARON KAY, management educator; b. Ozark, Ark., Aug. 3, 1958; d. Raymond C. and Juanelle Wyers; m. John Michael Clinebell. BS, U. Ozarks, 1979; MBA, U. Ark., 1980; DBA, So. Ill. U., 1988. Instr. S.E. Mo. State U., Cape Girardeau, 1981—87; prof. U. No. Colo., Greeley, 1987—. Examiner Malcolm Baldrige Nat. Quality Award, 1997—99. Office: U No Colo Dept Mgmt Greeley CO 80639 Home: 2623 55th Ave Greeley CO 80634

CLINEFELTER, RUTH ELIZABETH WRIGHT, historian, educator; b. Akron, Ohio, Nov. 2, 1930; d. Cyril and Ruth Elizabeth (Dresher) Wright. BA, U. Akron, Ohio, 1952, MA, 1953; MLS, Kent State U., Kent, Ohio, 1956. Serial libr. U. Akron, Akron, Ohio, 1953-61, social sci. rsch. libr., 1961-76, humanities rsch. libr., 1977-83, social sci. humanities bibliographer, 1983—. Lectr. in gen. studies U. Akron, 1960, instr. bibliography, 1956-59, asst. prof. bibliography, 1959-77, assoc. prof. bibliography, 1977-84, prof. bibliography, 1984-99, prof. emeritus, 2000—; resource person NEH, Ohio; mem. joint study com. Am. History Rsch. in Ohio, Ohio Hist. Soc., 1969-70; mem. acad. affairs com. Ohio Faculty Senate, 1971-72; mem. hist. abstracts bibliographic svc. ABC Clio Users Bd., 1978-79. Contbr. articles to profl. jour. Trustee, Akron Area Women's History Project, Summit County Hist. Soc., 1997—; active Citizens Against Sys. Abuse, Humane Soc. Greater Akron, Nat. Trust for Hist. Preservation, Progress Through Preservation, adv. bd, mem., Cascade Locks Park Assn. Recipient Pioneer award for contbns. to women Mortar Board, 1997. Aaron Aren NOW, Woman of the Yr., 2001, mem: AAUP, Am. Hist. Assn., Assn. for Bibliography of History, North Am. Conf. British Studies, History Project Organizational Woman of the Yr., 1993, 1998. Democrat. Episcopalian. Home: 1377 Hadden Cir Akron OH 44313-6505 Office: U Akron Bierce Libr Akron OH 44325-0001

CLINES, CINDY COLLINS, elementary school administrator, educator; b. Lawrenceville, Ga., May 8, 1961; d. David Roger Collins and Mary Wood Verenna; 1 child, Ashleigh Merci Collinwood Clines. BS in Edn. in Early Childhood, U. Ga., 1982, MEd in Reading and Early Childhood, 1988, MEd in Supervision, 1990. Cert. instrnl. supr., early childhood edn. tchr., reading specialist, data collection specialist. Tchr. Auburn (Ga.) Elem. Sch., 1982-92; adminstr., instrnl. lead tchr. Bramlett Elem. Sch., Auburn, 1992—. After sch. program dir. Bramlett Elem. Sch., 1995—, tchr. support specialist supr., 1992—, Barrow County mentor supr., 1994—; mem. Ga. Edn. Leadership Acad., Atlanta, 1992-93. Leader/dir. Girl Scouts, Auburn, 1990-93; Sunday sch. tchr. Harmony Grove United Meth. Ch., Auburn, 1993—, co-chairperson adminstrv. bd., 1993-94, dir. children's ministry, 1995—. Recipient Cert. of Appreciation, Barrow County Assn. Educators, 1992. Mem. Profl. Assn. Ga. Educators, Alpha Delta Kappa, Golden Key Nat. Honor Soc. Democrat. Home: 1427 Harmony Grove Church Rd Auburn GA 30011-2947 Office: WB Bramlett Elem 622 Freeman Brock Rd Auburn GA 30011-2602

CLINTON, BARBARA MARIE, university health services director, social worker; b. Bklyn., May 21, 1947; d. Lawrence Joseph and Kathleen Byrne C.; m. James Edward Selin, Sept. 12, 1981; children: Greta Maureen, Caitlin Carol. Auditor's cert., U. Tunis, Tunisia, 1968; BS, State U. Coll., Buffalo, 1971; student, SUNY, Buffalo, 1970-71; MSW, U. Ga., 1979. Child care worker Gateway United Meth. Youth Ctr., Williamsville, N.Y., 1970; caseworker Erie County Dept. Social Svcs., Buffalo, 1975-76; social worker Orchard Park (N.Y.) Nursing Home, 1976-77; group counselor Erie Med. Ctr., Buffalo, 1976-77; therapist Buffalo Children's Hosp., 1977-78; intern N.E. Ga. Community Mental Health Ctr., Athens, 1980-81; assoc. dir. ctr. health svcs. Vanderbilt U., Nashville, 1981-87, acting dir. ctr. health svcs., 1987-88, dir. ctr. health svcs., 1988—. Lectr. sch. medicine SUNY, Buffalo, 1977-78; gov.'s intern State of Ga., 1978, 79; dir. Maternal Infant Health Outreach Worker Project, 1982-90; adj. lectr. community health sch. nursing Vanderbilt U., 1986—; expert panelist Nat. Resource Ctr. Children Poverty Columbia U., 1987-89, Save The Children Fedn., Westport, Conn., 1992-93, cons.; evaluation advisor Tenn. Commn. Aging, 1991-92; mem. adv. bd. Vanderbilt U. Women's Ctr., 1992-94; presenter in field. Author: (with Mary Porter) Postnatal Home Visit Guide: The Second Year of Life, 1986, (with Toby Barnett) The Emotional Development of Infants: A Discussion Guide for Outreach Workers, 1987; contbr. articles to profl. jours. Active Bring Urban Recycling Nashville Today, Woodbine Community Orgn.; mem. steering com. S.E. Women's Employment Coalition, Lexington, Ky., 1988-91, bd. dirs., 1989-91; bd. dirs. Tenn. Coalition Def. Battered Women, 1990—, Vanderbilt Women's Ctr., 1992—, U. Ky. Coalition on Cancer, Lexington, 1992—. Regents scholar State of N.Y., 1965, 66, 68, 69; grantee Ford Found., 1982-88, J.C. Penny Found., 1983, Robert Wood Johnson Found., 1983-89, van Leer Found., 1986-93, Pub. Welfare Found., 1989-93, Unitarian Universalist Veatch Fund, 1988-93. Mem. APHA, NASW, Nat. Women's Health Network, Internat. Childbirth Edn. Assn., Tenn. Primary Care Assn., Acad. Cert. Social Workers. Home: 313 Peachtree St Nashville TN 37210-4925 Office: Vanderbilt U Ctr Health Svcs Sta 17 Nashville TN 37232-0001

CLINTON, STEPHEN MICHAEL, academic administrator; b. Wichita, Kans., Aug. 21, 1944; s. Thomas Francis and Bettie Lee (Harrison) C.; m. Virginia Ann Schoonover, Aug. 30, 1964; children: Matthew, Michael, Shanna. MA in Philosophy, Trinity Evang. Div. Sch., Deerfield, Ill., 1969, MDiv, 1970; PhD in Theology, Calif. Grad. Sch. Theology, 1979; postgdoc. in philosophy, U. Calif., Riverside, 1985-87, PhD in Edn., 1997; MA in Counseling, Internat. Sch. Theology, San Bernardino, Calif., 1987; MA in Edn., Calif. State U., San Bernardino, 1988. Ordained to ministry Evang. Free Ch. Am., 1973; cert. gifted edn. tchr., Calif. Pastor Lake Zurich (Ill.) EFC, 1967-69, Faith Presbyn. Ch., Wichita, Kans., 1972-74, Highlander Evang. Free Ch., 1974—78, East Cmty. Ch., Orlando, Fla., 1993-94, First Bapt. Ch., St. Cloud, Fla., 1999-2000; dir. extension degree programs Internat. Sch. Theology, 1974-86, assoc. prof., 1978-86; dir. Internat. Leadership Coun., 1986—; pres. Orlando (Fla.) Inst., 1991—, prof. edn. and religion, 1992—; dir. EdD program Iberia-Am. U. Leadership, 1998—. Pres. Ministry Devel., Inc., San Bernardino, 1978-86; chmn. bd. dirs. Masterlife Internat., 1999-2000; bd. dirs. Vision Orlando, 1992—; bd. reference Am. All Stars, 2000—; prof. Belhaven Coll., 2000-01; adj. prof. Moody Bible Inst., Phoenix U., Valenia C.C., Asbury Theol. Sem. Author: The Doctrine of the Christian Life, 1981, Cultural Apologetics, 1983, Calvinism and Arminianism, 1985, The Everlasting God, 1989, Movements Which Changed History, 1993, Theistic Realism, 1998, The Role of the Holy Spirit in Spiritual Development, 2001; also 40 articles. Pres. Advs. for Gifted and Talented Edn., San Bernardino, 1979-85; chmn. state parent coun. Calif. Assn. for Gifted, 1978-83; pres. advocates for gifted and talented edn. San Bernardino Unified Sch. Dist., 1984-87; chmn. bd. dirs. Ctr. for Individuals with Disabilities, San Bernardino, 1984-88; Maitland C. of C., bd. dirs., 2002—. Mem. Evang. Philos. Soc. (editor 1979-81, 84-98, pres. 1983), Evang. Free Ch. Ministerial Assn., Evang. Theol. Soc. (chmn. 1982, 03), John Dewey Soc., Philosophy of Edn. Soc. Office: Orlando Inst 100 Lake Hart Dr Ste 3000 Orlando FL 32832 E-mail: sclinton@toi.edu.

CLOGAN, PAUL MAURICE, English language and literature educator; b. Boston, July 9, 1934; s. Michael J. and Agnes J. (Murphy) C.; m. Julie Sydney Davis, July 27, 1972 (div. 1982); children: Michael Rodger, Patrick Terence, Margaret Murphy. BA, Boston Coll., 1956, MA, 1957; PhD, U. Ill., 1961; F.A.A.R., Am. Acad. in Rome, 1966; MDiv, Blessed John XXIII Sem., 1999. Asst. prof. Duke U., 1961-65; assoc. prof. Case Western Res. U., Cleve., 1965-72; prof. English U. North Tex., Denton, 1972—. Vis. prof. U. Keele, Eng., 1965, U. Pisa, Italy, 1966, U. Tours, France, 1978; vis. mem. Inst. Advanced Study, Princeton, N.J., 1970, 77; cons. Library of Congress, Ednl. Testing Service, NEH, Nat. Acad. Scis., NRC Commn. Human Resources, Nation Rsch. Council Com. for the Study of Rsch.-Doctorate-Programs in the U.S., Am. Council Learned Socs., Nat. Enquiry into Scholarly Communication, Chilton Research Services; mem. Am. Arts Assn., Inst. Internat. Edn., nat. screening com. 1984-88. Author: The Medieval Achilleid of Statius, 1968, Social Dimensions in Medieval and Renaissance Studies, 1972, In Honor of S. Harrison Thomson, 1970, Medieval and Renaissance Studies in Review, 1971, Medieval and Renaissance Spirituality, 1973, Medieval Historiography, 1974, Medieval Hagiography and Romance, 1975, Medieval Poetics, 1976, Transformation and Continuity, 1977, Byzantine and Western Studies, 1984, Fourteenth and Fifteenth Centuries, 1986, The Early Renaissance, 1987, Literary Theory, 1988, Spectrum, 1992, Columbian Quincentenary, 1992, Renaissance and Discovery, 1993, Breaching the Boundaries, 1994, Convergences, 1994, Diversity, 1995, Historical Inquiries, 1997, Transitions, 1998, Civil Strife and National Identity in the Middle Ages, 1999, Literacy and the Lay Reader, 2000, Ethnicity and Self-Identity, 2002, Papal Letters, Manual for Confessors and Romance, 2003; editor: Medievalia et Humanistica, Studies in Medieval and Renaissance Culture, 1970—; contbr. articles to profl. jours. Grantee Duke Endowment 1961-62, Am. Coun. Learned Socs., 1963-64, 70-71, 88, Am. Philos. Soc., 1964-69, U. North Tex., 1972-75, 80-81, 89; sr. Fulbright-Hays postdoctoral rsch. fellow, Italy, 1965-66, France, 1978, fellow Prix de Rome, 1966-67, Bollingen Found., 1966, NEH, 1969-70, 86, 90-91. Mem. Internat. Assn. Univ. Profs. English, MLA (exec. com. 1980-86, del. assembly 1981-86), Internat. Comparative Lit. Assn., Internat. Arthurian Soc., Modern Humanities Research Assn., Medieval Acad. Am. (nominating com. 1975-76, John Nicholas Brown Prize com. 1981-83), Internat. Assn. for Neo-Latin Studies, The New Chaucer Soc., Fulbright Assn. Democrat. Roman Catholic.

CLOHESY, WILLIAM WARREN, philosopher, educator; b. Chgo., July 31, 1946; s. John Cecil and Mary Evelyn (Ahern) Clohesy; m. Stephanie June Jagucki, June 19, 1971. BS, Loyola U., Chgo., 1964-68; MA, So. Ill. U., 1968-71; PhD, New Sch. Social Rsch., N.Y.C., 1981. Instr. Loyola U., Chgo., 1967, asst. prof., 1982-83; tchg. asst. So. Ill. U., Carbondale, 1969; adj. prof. Montclair State Coll., Upper Montclair, NJ, 1981-82; asst. prof. Rochester (N.Y.) Inst. Tech., 1983-86, rsch. assoc., 1986-87; lectr. U. Belgrano, Buenos Aires, 1987; asst. prof. U. No. Iowa, Cedar Falls, 1987-93, assoc. prof., 1993—. BSN adv. com. Allen Coll., Waterloo, Iowa, 1991—2002; instnl. rep. bd. U. No. Iowa, 2002—. Editor: (book) Ethics at Work, 1992; contbr. articles to profl. jours. Recipient Kurt Riezler Meml. award, New Sch. for Social Rsch., 1982, Faculty Excellence award, Iowa Bd. Regents, 2001; fellow Fulbright fellowship to Argentina, 1987; grantee W.K. Kellogg Found., 1995—2001, Iowa Humanities Bd., 1991—92, NEH, 1991—92. Mem.: Soc. Advancement Am. Philosophy, N.Am. Kant Soc., N.Am. Soc. Social Philosophy, Hume Soc., Am. Philos. Assn., Internat.

Soc. 3d Sector Rsch. Democrat. Roman Catholic. Avocation: Irish language, literature, and music. Office: U No Iowa Dept Philosophy & Religion Cedar Falls IA 50614-0501 E-mail: william.clohesy@uni.edu.

CLOPINE, MARJORIE SHOWERS, librarian; b. N.Y.C., June 25, 1914; d. Ralph Walter and Angelina (Jackson) Showers; m. John Junior Clopine, June 19, 1948 (div.); m. Frank Mason Storck, Sept. 14, 1985. BA, Pa. State U., 1935; MS, Drexel U., 1936; MS, Columbia U., 1949. Gen. asst. Libr., Drexel U., Phila., 1937-42; asst. libr. Gen. Chem. Div., Allied Chem. Corp., Morristown, N.J., 1943-46; bibliographer U.S. Office Tech. Svcs., Washington, 1946; med. libr. VA Hosp., Washington, 1946-49; asst. libr. U.S. Naval Obs., Washington, 1949-52, libr., 1952-63; assoc. libr. Bethany (W.Va.) Coll., 1967-69. Alice B. Kroeger Meml. scholar Drexel U., 1935-36. Mem. AAUW, LWV, Inst. Retired Execs. and Profls., Women's Resource Ctr. of Sarasota, Friends of the Arts and Scis., Spl. Libraries Assn., Beta Phi Mu. Contbr. articles to profl. jours. Home and Office: 8400 Vamo Rd Apt 540 Sarasota FL 34231-7816

CLOSE, BEVERLY JEAN, secondary education educator; b. Portland, Oreg., July 1, 1958; d. Bertrand J. and Charlotte J. (Mollett) C. BA in Psychology, U. Oreg., 1980. Cert. English, social studies and journalism tchr., Oreg. Tchr. Glencoe High Sch., Hillsboro, Oreg., 1991, J.B. Thomas Jr. High Sch., Hillsboro, Oreg., 1991-92, Yamhill (Oreg.)-Carlton High Sch., 1992—. Adv. mem. for Reflections (literary mag.), Yamhill-Carlton H.S., 1993—; adviser The Expression (newspaper) Yamhill-Carlton H.S., 1992—. Writer (newspaper) Hollywood Star, 1987-89. Mem. Jr. League of Portland, 1986—; bd. dirs. Friends of Extension, Hillsboro, 1994-95, 4-H (Washington County), Hillsboro, 1994-95. Mem. Nat. Coun. Tchrs. English. Office: Yamhill-Carlton High Sch 275 N Maple St Yamhill OR 97148-7601

CLOSEN, MICHAEL LEE, retired law educator; b. Peoria, Ill., Jan. 25, 1949; s. Stanley Paul and Dorothy Mae (Kendall) Closen. BS, Bradley U., 1971, MS, 1971; JD, U. Ill., 1974. Bar: Ill. 1974; notary pub. Ill. Instr. U. Ill., Champaign, 1974; jud. clk. Ill. Appellate Ct., Springfield, 1974-76, 77-78; asst. states atty. Cook County, Chgo., 1978; prof. law John Marshall Law Sch., Chgo., 1976—2003. Reporter Ill. Jud. Conf., Chgo., 1981—2002; arbitrator Am. Arbitration Assn., Chgo., 1981—; lectr. Ill. Inst. Continuing Legal Edn., Chgo., 1981—2002; vis. prof. No. Ill. U., 1985—86, adj. prof., 1990, St. Thomas U., 1991, Loyola U., Chgo., 1999—2002; vis. prof. U. Ark., 1993, 96; arbitrator Cook County Cir. Ct. Mandatory Arbitration Program, 1990—2002, Will County Cir. Ct. Mandatory Arbitration Program, 1996—2002; dir. Ctr. for Legal Edn., Ltd., 1995—96. Author: (casebook) Agency and Partnership Law, 1984, Agency and Partnership Law, 3d edit., 2000; author: (with others) Contracts, 1984, Contracts, 3d edit., 1992, AIDS Cases and Materials, 1989, AIDS Cases and Materials, 3d edit., 2002, Notary Law and Practice, 1997, Contract Law and Practice, 1998; co-author: (book) The Shopping Bag: Portable Art, 1986, AIDS Law in a Nutshell, 1991, AIDS Law in a Nutshell, 2d edit., 1996, Legal Aspects of AIDS, 1991; contbr. articles to profl. jours. Named One of Outstanding Young Men in Am., 1981; recipient Svc. award, Am. Arbitration Assn., 1984—85, 5-Yr. Cmty. Achievement award, Ill. Politics Mag., 1998. Mem.: ABA, Ill. Bar Assn., Notary Law Inst., Am. Soc. Notaries, Nat. Notary Assn. (Achievement award 1998). Home: 1243 Motorcoach Polk City FL 33868-9774

CLOUD, LINDA BEAL, retired secondary school educator; b. Jay, Fla., Dec. 4, 1937; d. Charles Rockwood and Agnes (Diamond) Beal; m. Robert Vincent Cloud, Aug. 15, 1959 (dec. 1985). BA, Miss. Coll., 1959; MEd, U. So. Fla., 1976; EdS, Nova U., 1982; postgrad., Walden U., 1983. Cert. tchr. Fla. Tchr. Ft. Meade (Fla.) Jr.-Sr. HS, 1959-67, 80-89, Lake Wales (Fla.) H.S., 1967—80, drama coach vocal music dir., conversational Spanish composition, creative writing, English lit.; pres. Cloud Aero Svcs., Inc., Babson Park, Fla., 1992—; owner Diamond Firefox Peruvians. Part-time tchr. Spanish, English Polk County Adult Schs., 1960—76; cons. Fla. Assn. Student Couns. Workshops, 1968—81; instr. Spanish Warner So. Coll., Lake Wales, 1974; instr. vocal music, drama, composition Webber Coll., Babson Park; pvt. tutor in field; writer, dir. numerous pageants for schs.; judge beauty pageants, theatre casting; cons. theatre workshops; guest reader local schs., 2002—03. Contbr. articles to profl. jours. and equine publs., poetry to The Color of Thought. Dir. Imogene Theatre, Milton, Fla., 2001; judge various beauty pageants and talent shows; soloist Babson Park Cmty. Ch., 1970—99, First Bapt. Ch., Jay, 1999—; charter mem., bd. dirs. Lake Wales Little Theatre, Inc., 1976; dir. Four Sq. swing choir; entertainer various orgns.; ring announcer Peruvian and Paso Fino Horse Shows, Naples, Fla. State Fair, 1987—88; mem. Defenders Crooked Lake; vol., dir. candy stripers Lakes Wales Hosp., 1973—79. Recipient Best Actress award, Lakes Wales Little Theatre, Inc., 1978—79. Mem.: AAUW, Fla. Ret. Tchrs. Assn., Fla./Santa Rosa County Ret. Educators Assn., Polk Fgn. Lang. Assn., Polk Coun. Tchrs. English, Fla. Coun. Tchrs. English, Nat. Coun. Tchrs. English, Jay Mural Soc. (bd. dirs.), Jay Hist. Soc., Sassy Singers, Babson Park Womans Club, Southeastern Peruvian Horse Club (life). Republican. Avocations: singing, acting, costume design, horseback riding, Peruvian horse exhibitions and parades. Home: Diamond Firefox Peruvians 4405 Spring St Jay FL 32565

CLOUGH, GERALD WAYNE, academic administrator; b. Douglas, Ga., Sept. 24, 1941; married; 2 children. BSCE, MSCE, Ga. Inst. Tech., 1964; PhD, U. Calif., Berkeley, 1969. Registered prof. engr., Calif., Va. Assoc. prof. to prof. civil engring. Stanford U., Calif., 1974—82; prof. civil engring., coord. geotech. program Va. Polytechnic Inst. and State U., 1982—83, prof. civil engring., head dept. civil engring., 1983—90, dean Coll. Engring., 1990—93; provost, prof. civil engring. U. Wash., Seattle, 1993—94; pres. Ga. Inst. Tech., Atlanta, 1994—. Bd. dirs. Noro-Moseley Ptnrs.; appt. to Pres. Coun. Adv. on Sci. & Tech., 2001—. Trustee Ga. Rsch. Alliance. Mem.: NAE. Office: Ga Inst Tech Office of the Pres 225 N Avae NW Carnegie Bldg Atlanta GA 30332-0001

CLOUGH, LAUREN C. retired special education educator; b. Canton, N.Y., Mar. 17, 1924; s. Hiram William and Lena May (Ladison) C.; m. Margaret Ellen Williamson, June 8, 1951; children: David Wayne, Carol Canty (dec.). BA, U. Ala., 1947; MA in Teaching, U. Jacksonville, 1969; cert. mental retardation, U. Fla.; cert. specific LDEH, U. North Fla. Tchr. Duval County Bd. Pub. Instrn., Jacksonville, Fla., 1964-70; tchr. history Nassau County Bd. Pub. Instrn., Fernandina Beach, Fla., 1970-71, tchr. mentally retarded, 1971-73, specific learning disabled and emotionally handicapped resource tchr., 1973-98; tchr. Hilliard (Fla.) Elem. Sch., 1973-98; ret., 1998; substitute tchr., 1998—. Improvement com. Hilliard Elem. Sch., 1991-98, chmn. sch. pub. rels. com., 1993-95, comm. com., 1994-98, Title I com., 1994-97; sch. accreditation com. SACS, 1995-96, student svcs. com., 1997-98. Alt. mem. adv. com. Fernandina HS, 2001—02, mem. adv. com., 2002—; mem. Cmty. Alliance, 2002. Mem. Nassau County Ret. Educators Assn. (chmn. legislation com. 1999—, pres.-elect 2001-02, pres. 2002-).

CLOUSE, ROBERT GORDON, history educator, minister; b. Mansfield, Ohio, Aug. 26, 1931; s. Garry A. and Marion Katherine (Ost) C.; m. Bonnidell Amelia Barrows, June 17, 1955; children: Gary R., Kenneth D. BA, Bryan Coll., 1954; BD, Grace Theol. Sem., 1957; MA, U. Iowa, 1960, PhD, 1963. Ordained to ministry Brethren Ch., 1958. Min. Grace Brethren Ch., Cedar Rapids, Iowa, 1957-60; prof. history Ind. State U., Terre Haute, 1963—. Min. First Brethren Ch., Clay City, Ind., 1964—; J. Omar Good vis. disting. prof. evang. Christianity Juniata Coll., 1982-83. Author: The Church in an Age of Orthodoxy and Enlightenment, 1980, Two Kingdoms, The Church and Culture Through the Ages, 1993; author, editor: The Meaning of the Millennium, Four Views, 1977, Women in Ministry, Four Views, 1989, War, Four Christian Views, 1991, The New Millennium Manual, A Once and Future Guide, 1999, The Story of the Church, 2002. Dir. Conf. on Faith and History, Terre Haute, 1965—, Eugene V. Debs Found., Terre Haute, 1968—, Cen. Renaissance Conf., 1986—; active Sixteenth Studies Conf. Postdoctoral grantee Folger Shakespeare Libr., 1964; postdoctoral fellow Inst. for Advanced Christian Studies, 1970, Lilly Libr., 1976. Mem. Am. Soc. Ch. History, Calvin Studies Soc., Nat. Fellowship Grace Brethren Mins. Avocations: travel, walking, reading. Home: 2122 S 21st St Terre Haute IN 47802-2634 Office: Ind State U History Dept Terre Haute IN 47809-0001

CLOVER, HAWORTH ALFRED, elementary school educator, historian; b. Woodland, Calif., Feb. 18, 1933; s. Herman Alfred and Anna Margaret (Powell) C.; m. Carol Ann Anderson, June 17, 1961; children: Haworth Alfred, John Allan, Catherine Alette. Student, U. Calif., Davis, 1950-51; MusB, BA, U. of the Pacific, 1957, MA, 1960, EdD, 1977; postgrad., Stanford U., 1962, U. Vt., 1963. Cert. spl. secondary music tchr., gen. elem. tchr., elem. adminstr. Elem. tchr. San Joaquin (Calif.) County Schs., 1957-60, Hillsborough (Calif.) City Sch. Dist., 1960—. Landmark cons. Yolo County Hist. Soc., Woodland, 1984-86; mem. adj. faculty history dept. U. Pacific, 1995—. Author: Hesperian College 1861-1896, 1973; compiler: (book) Haytime, 1974, Hesperian College Landmarks, 1995. Mem. San Francisco Mus. Soc., 1976—, San Francisco Zool. Soc., 1976—. With U.S. Army, 1954-56. Recipient Kirkbridge Calif. History award U. of the Pacific, Stockton, 1957. Mem. NEA, Calif. Sch. Adminstrn. Assn., Calif. and Pa. Geneal. Soc., Hillsborough Tchrs. Assn. (treas. 1961-63), Jedediah Smith Rsch. Assn. (bd. dirs. 1994), Commonwealth Club Calif., Westerner's Internat. (sheriff 1983), San Mateo County Men's Garden Club (pres. 1972-73), U. of the Pacific Alumni (bd. dirs., sec. 1985—), Masons (past master 1986, past patron 1993-94), Phi Mu Alpha, Phi Delta Kappa, Phi Kappa Phi. Republican. Presbyterian. Avocations: wood working, gardening, photography, travel. Home: 2985 Summit Dr Hillsborough CA 94010-6256 Office: Hesperia Press PO Box 1583 Burlingame CA 94011-1583

CLOWER, RICHARD ALLEN, physical education educator; b. Feb. 20, 1929; 2 children. AB cum laude in History/Phys. Edn., Western Md. Coll., 1950; MS in Phys. Edn., Springfield Coll., 1956; EdD in Phys. Edn., W.Va. U., 1965; postgrad., Mich. State U., 1968. Tchr./coach Thurmont H.S., 1950-51, Hampstead H.S., 1953-56; asst. prof., basketball, track and soccer coach Western Md. Coll., 1956-63, assoc. prof., basketball/track coach, dept. head, 1963-65, prof., dept. head, dir. athletics, Lacrosse coach, 1965-75, prof., dir. athletics, dept. head, 1965-84, prof. and head dept. phys. edn., 1984-98; ret. Soccer/basketball ofcl., 1947-63; lectr. in field; cons. in field; condr. workshops in field. Contbr. articles to profl. jours. Bd. visitors Md. Sch. for the Deaf, 1989-93. Decorated Bronze Star medal; Recipient Leadership Citation, The Lacrosse Found., 1979, Cert. of Recognition, ARC, 1979, 88, 89, U.S. Jaycees, 1971, 77. Mem. AAHPERD (archives com. Ea. dist. 1980-84), Md. Assn. for Health, Phys. Edn., Recreation and Dance (historian 1978-80, Presdl. citation 1990), Am. Soc. for Sociology of Sport, AAUP, Am. Canoe Assn., Sports Lit. Assn., N.Am. Soc. for Study of Sport, U.S. Lacrosse Coaches Assn., Phi Delta Kappa, Phi Beta Kappa, Omicron Detla Kappa. Home: 1137 Pinch Valley Rd Westminster MD 21158-2943

CLOYD, HELEN MARY, accountant, educator; b. Austria-Hungary, 1918; came to U.S., 1922, naturalized, 1928; d. Valentine and Elizabeth (Kretschmar von Kienbusch) Yuhasz; m. George S. Smith, Mar. 4, 1939 (dec.); children: George, Nora; m. Chester L. Cloyd, Apr. 16, 1960 (dec.). BS, Eastern Mich. U., 1953; MA, Wayne State U., 1956; PhD, Mich. State U., 1963. CPA, Mich., Ind., W.Va. Pub. acct. Haskins & Sells, Detroit, 1945-53; tchr. Marine City (Mich.) H.S., 1954-59; instr. acctg. Ctrl. Mich. U., Mt. Pleasant, 1959-60; asst. prof. Wayne State U., Detroit, 1960-61; tchr. Grosse Pointe (Mich.) H.S., 1961-64; assoc. prof. acctg. Ball State U., Muncie, Ind., 1964-71; prof. Shepherd Coll., Shepherdstown, W.Va., 1971-76; assoc. prof. George Mason U., Fairfax, Va. Contbr. numerous articles to publs. Recipient McClintock Writing award CPA, Mich., Ind. W.Va. Mem. AICPA, AAAS, Am. Acctg. Assn., Am. Econs. Assn., Assn. Sch. Bus. Ofcls., Delta Pi Epsilon, Pi Omega Pi, Pi Gamma Mu, Order Eastern Star, White Shrine. Home: PO Box 186 Inwood WV 25428-0186

CLOYD, SANDRA GOMEZ, bilingual educator; b. Phoenix, Ariz., Dec. 24, 1956; d. Alberto and Julia (Mendoza) Gomez; m. John Straton Cloyd, May 20, 1978; children: Christopher Gomez, Kimberly Maria, Gabriela Emma. BS in Elem. Edn., Grand Canyon U., 1990. Cert. elem. edn., Ariz. Pers. mgr. U.S. Army, Ft. Bragg, N.C., 1979-80; receptionist Ariz. Fed. Credit Union, Phoenix, 1983-84; adminstrv. asst. Landmark Elem. Sch., Glendale, Ariz., 1984-85; elem. sch. tchr. St. Jerome Sch., Phoenix, 1990-91; bilingual tchr. Cartwright Sch. Dist., Phoenix, 1991—. Home room mother Sine Elem. Sch., Glendale, 1986-89; vol. case worker Cmty. Action Program, Glendale, 1977; polit. activist League United Latin Am. Citizens, Phoenix, 1974-76, Movimiento Estudiantil Chicano de Aztlan, Phoenix, 1975-76. Mem. NEA, Ariz. Edn. Assn., Cartwright Edn. Assn., Westside Reading Conf., Women in Mil. Svc. for Am. Meml. Found. Democrat. Roman Catholic. Avocation: family activities. Home: 7829 W Brown St Peoria AZ 85345-0701 Office: Starlight Park Sch 7960 W Osborn Rd Phoenix AZ 85033-3521

CLUNE, JOHN RICHARD, library administrator; b. Bronxville, N.Y., Nov. 22, 1933; s. Charles Leo and Anne Rose (Murray) C. BA, St. Joseph's Sem., Yonkers, N.Y., 1956; MLS, Pratt Inst. Grad. Libr. Sch., 1966; MA, Long Island U., 1971. Cert. pub. libr., N.Y. Social investigator N.Y.C. Dept. Welfare, 1961-63; English tchr. Walton High Sch., 1963; libr. trainee Bklyn. Pub. Libr., 1964-66; reader svcs. libr. Kingsborough Community Coll., Bklyn., 1966-70, libr.-in-charge mid-Bklyn. location, 1970-71, acting chief libr., 1971-72, dep. chief libr., 1972-77, acting chief libr., 1977-79, chief libr., 1979—. With U.S. Army, 1959-61. Mem. ALA, Libr. Assn. CUNY (v.p. 1971-72, pres. 1973-74), Pratt Grad. Libr. Sch. Alumni Assn., Mid-Bklyn. Newman Club (faculty adviser 1967-71), Beta Phi Mu. Democrat. Roman Catholic. Avocations: reading, baseball fan, listening to classical music. Office: CUNY/Kibbee Libr Kingsborough Community Coll 2001 Oriental Blvd Brooklyn NY 11235-2333

CLUNN, PATRICIA ANN, nursing educator, writer; b. Phila. children: Steven, Jeffrey. BSN, U. Pa., 1964, EdD, 1975; MA, Columbia U.; MEd, Columbia U., 1994, 1975. Cert. clin. specialist in child and adolescent mental health psychiat. nursing ANCC. Dir. psychiat. mental health nursing divsn. ANA, Kansas City, Mo., 1979-80; prof. nursing U. Miami, Fla., 1983-98, prof. emeritus, 1998—. Author: (with D. Payne) Psychiatric Mental Health Nursing (transl. into Polish 1980), (textbook) Child Mental Health Nursing, 1991. Grantee HHRS, U. Miami, 1985-90, HHRS, 1993-96. Mem. ANA (coun. psychiat. mental health nurses, award for contbn. to direct practice 1979), Sigma Theta Tau. Home: 2406 Tamarind Dr Fort Pierce FL 34949-1508

CLUTTER, TIMOTHY JOHN, secondary language arts educator; b. Cin., Jan. 14, 1954; s. Carl Edward and Helen Loretta (Erke) C. BS in Edn., Ohio State U., 1976; M in Linguistics, Yale U., 1980. Cert. tchr. secondary lang. arts, Ohio. Tchr. lang. arts Olentangy Local Sch. Dist., Delaware, Ohio, 1976-78, Forest Hills Sch. Dist., Cin., 1982—. Contbr. articles to profl. jours. Named Most Influential Tchr., 1996. Mem. Nat. Coun. Tchrs. English, Yale Alumni Assn., Phi Kappa Phi, Kappa Phi Kappa. Office: Anderson High Sch 7560 Forest Rd Cincinnati OH 45255-4307

CLYBURN, MICHAEL LEE, secondary school educator; b. San Francisco, June 10, 1948; s. Charles Lee and Billie Jane (Montgomery) C.; m. Carol Sue Harshman, June 4, 1977; 1 child, John Reuben Lee. BA, Mo. So. U., 1971, tchrs. cert., 1982; postgrad., Labette C.C., Parsons, Kans., 1990-91, Pittsburg State U., 1991. Lic. tchr., Kans., Mo., Okla. Substitute tchr., 1989—95; aide Joplin R-8, 1995—2000, tchr. Transitional Learning Ctr., 2000. Mem. North Mid. Sch. Accelerated Schs. Parent Involvement Com., Joplin R-8 Sch. Dist., 1992—. With CAP, Joplin, 1967-70. Avocations: classic car restorations, collecting star trek memorabilia. Home: 1014 Galena Galena KS 66739

CLYDE, WALLACE ALEXANDER, JR., pediatrics and microbiology educator; b. Birmingham, Ala., Nov. 7, 1929; s. Wallace Alexander and Martha Louise (Pou) C.; m. Barbara Jean McClain, Aug. 21, 1953; children: Martha Elizabeth, Susan Ann, Kevin Alexander. BA, Vanderbilt U., 1951, MD, 1954. Intern in pediatrics Vanderbilt Hosp., Nashville, 1954-55, resident, 1956-57, Bapt. Hosp., Winston-Salem, N.C., 1955-56; chief pediatrician U.S. Naval Hosp., Millington, Tenn., 1957-59; fellow in preventive medicine Case Western Res. U., Cleve., 1959-61; instr. in pediatrics U. N.C., Chapel Hill, 1961-62, asst. prof., 1963-67, assoc. prof., 1967-71, prof. pediatrics and microbiology, 1972-93, prof. emeritus, 1993—. Vis. assoc. prof. pathology Yale U., New Haven, 1971-72; assoc. mem. Armed Forces Epidemiol. Bd., Washington, 1963-73; mem. bacteriology-mycology study sect. NIH, Bethesda, Md., 1966-70; dir. Pediatric Pulmonary Specialized Ctr. Rsch., Chapel Hill, 1976-91. Mem. editorial bd. to several sci. jours.; contbr. articles to sci. publs., chpts. to books. Lt. USN, 1957-59. Recipient bronze medal City of Bordeaux (France), 1983, career devel. award NIH, 1964, 69, citation classics award Inst. Sci. Info., 1984, key of City of Birmingham, 1986. Fellow Infectious Diseases Soc. Am.; mem. Internat. Orgn. for Mycoplasmology (sec.-gen. 1980-82, chmn. 1984-86, Presdl. Citation 1990, Kliene-berger Nobel award 1992), Soc. Pediatric Rsch., Am. Soc. Clin. Investigation; mem. S.E. Regional Steering Com.,2003. Democrat. Baptist. Avocations: photography, limericks, video production.

CLYMER, JAY PHAON, III, science educator; b. Lancaster, Pa., June 23, 1951; s. Jay Phaon Jr. and Jeannette (Arnold) C.; m. Elizabeth Teresa Ruddy, June 4, 1988; children: Candace Rose, Colin Jay. BS in Zoology, U. R.I., 1973; MS in Biology, Lehigh U., 1975, PhD in Biology, 1978. Teaching asst. Lehigh U., Bethlehem, Pa., 1973-75, rsch. asst., 1975-78; asst. prof. Marywood U., Scranton, Pa., 1978-83, assoc. prof., 1983—, chmn. sci. dept., 1987-90, v.p. Faculty Senate. Tech. advisor Lackawanna River Corridor Assn., Scranton, 1985—; dir. Riverwatch program, Scranton, 1985—; chmn. edn. com. County Conservation Dist., Clarks-Summit, Pa., 1990—; cons. to environ. firms; rschr. fish survey Wetlands Inst., Stone Harbor, N.J. Author: (booklets) Perspectives on Matter Energy Technology - Study Guide, vol. I, 1987, vol. II, 1991, Ecology - The Science of Nature, vol. I, 1988, vol. II, 1993, Biology - The Study of Life, 1995, Life Science, 1995; contbr. articles to sci. jours. Bd. dirs., v.p. Lackawanna County Conservation Dist., Clarks-Summit, 1990—; coord. fundraising March of Dimes. Mem. Atlantic Estaurine Rsch. Soc. (Grad. award 1979), Internat. Ctr. Environ. Mgmt. Enclosed Coastal Seas, Register of Pa. Biologists, Register of Estaurine Scientists, Lackawanna Fedn. of Sportsmen (officer 1990—), Phi Kappa Phi, Sigma Xi. Avocations: fishing, hunting, woodworking, gardening. Home: 210 Melrose Ave Clarks Summit PA 18411-1440 Office: Marywood U 2300 Adams Ave Scranton PA 18509-1598 E-mail: Clymer@ac.marywood.edu.

CLYMER, JERRY ALAN, educational administrator; b. Easton, Pa., Nov. 3, 1946; s. Wilbur L. and Dorothy M. (Cutsler) C.; m. Theresa M. Merlo, July 26, 1969; children: Shane A., Marc A., Adam T. BA, Moravian Coll., Bethlehem, Pa., 1969; MA, Rider Coll., Lawrenceville, N.J., 1976; postgrad., Trenton (N.J.) State Coll., 1976-80, East Stroudsburg U., 1976-80. Cert. elem. tchr., prin., supr., sch. adminstr., student pers. svcs., N.J. Elem. tchr. Pohatcong Twp. Bd. Edn., Bloomsbury, NJ, 1969—77, asst. prin., 1977—89, chief sch. adminstr., 1989—99, dir. child study team, grants coord., testing coord., 1977—89, supr. summer sch., 1978—79, affirmative action officer, drug free liaison person, 1987—89; supt. schs. Andover Regional Bd. Edn., Newton, 1999—. Coord. N.J. instrnl. child study team dir. for mini grant dist. award FHA and N.J. Dept. Edn., 1989-90. Mem., coach Pohatcong Recreation Assn., 1969—; mem. Pohatcong Centennial Incorporation, 1980-81; chmn. Pohatcong Twp. Sch. Dist. Staff Scholarship Fund, 1971-77. Mem. Am. Soc. Sch. Admin. (N.J. chpt.), N.J. Prins. and Suprs. Assn., Warren Coun. Coun. Sch. Adminstrs., Warren County Elem. Sch. and Mid. Sch. Prins. (v.p. 1981-82, 85-86), Am. Assn. Sch. Adminstrs., N.J. Assn. Sch. Adminstrs. Avocations: camping, swimming, hiking, tennis, basketball. Home: 318 Ohio Ave Phillipsburg NJ 08865 Office: Andover Regional Bd Edn 707 Limecrest Rd Newton NJ 07860-8801 E-mail: jaclymer_08865@yahoo.com.

CMAR, JANICE BUTKO, home economics educator; b. Pitts., Nov. 10, 1954; d. Edward Michael and Ruth Lillian (Pickard) Butko; m. Dennis Paul Cmar, children: Michael, Nicole. BS, Mansfield U., 1976; MS, Duquesne U., 1990. Home econ. tchr. Duquesne (Pa.) Sch. Dist., 1978-83; special edn. tchr. Allegheny Intermediate Unit, Pitts., 1985-95; home econs. tchr. Peters Twp. Sch. Dist., McMurray, Pa., 1995—. Sponsor Duquesne High Sch., Y-Teens and Future Homemakers Am., 1979-83, Pathfinder Student Coun., Bethel Park, Pa., Mon-Valley Secondary Sch. Yearbook and Prom, Jefferson, Pa. Vol. Allegheny County Dept. Cmty. Svcs., Pitts., 1986—97; mem. com. Allegheny County Dem. Orgn.; elected Borough Jefferson Hills Coun., 1997, 2001—, coun. v.p., 2000, 2002; mem. cmty. adv. panel Hercules Corp., 2000; bd. dirs. South Hills Coun. Govts., 2000. Mem. Am. Fedn. Tchrs., Am. Assn. Family and Consumer Scis., State Assn. Family and Consumer Scis., Allegheny County Assn. Family and Consumer Scis. (pres. 1991-92), Phi Delta Kappa, Alpha Sigma Tau. Democrat. Home: 918 Old Hickory Ln Jefferson Hills PA 15025-3437 Office: 625 E Mcmurray Rd Mc Murray PA 15317-3497

COAD, DEREK STEPHEN, statistics educator; b. Redruth, Cornwall, United Kingdom, Mar. 10, 1964; came to U.S., 1993; s. Spencer Derek and Sheila Ann (Lander) C. BSc in Math. Scis., Portsmouth Poly., 1985; MSc in Applied Stats., U. Oxford, United Kingdom, 1986, PhD in Stats., 1989. Temporary lectr. stats. U. Newcastle Upon Tyne, United Kingdom, 1989-90; lectr. stats. U. Sussex, Brighton, United Kingdom, 1990—; vis. asst. prof. stats. U. Mich., Ann Arbor, 1993-95. Tutor Open U., East Grinstead, United Kingdom, 1991-92. Contbr. articles to profl. jours. Grantee Fulbright Commn., 1993-95. Fellow Royal Statis. Soc. (examiner 1995—); mem. Inst. Math. and its Applications (grad. mem., Grad. prize 1985), Inst. Statisticians, Internat. Soc. Clin. Biostatistics, Biometric Soc., Bernoulli Soc. Avocations: learning spanish and russian, travel, reading, snooker. Office: Dept Mathematics University of Sussex Falmer Brighton BN1 9RF England*

COAKLEY, MICHAEL JAMES, university administrator; b. Chgo., Mar. 26, 1954; s. William James and Jane (Wallace) C. BS, U. Ill., 1976; MS in Higher Edn., So. Ill. U., 1978; postgrad., Western Mich. U. Resident dir., instr. health edn. U. Ill., Urbana, 1978-79; complex dir. Western Mich. U., Kalamazoo, 1979-81, asst. dir. residence hall life, 1981-85; dir. residence svcs. Wright State U., Dayton, Ohio, 1985-96; exec. dir. student housing and dining No. Ill. U., Dekalb, 1996—. Founder, developer The Clark Experiment, a residence hall based on Burns Crookston's Intentional Dem. Cmty., U. Ill., 1974; cons., owner Midwest Cons., 1983-85; lectr. in field. Contbr. articles to profl. jours. Chmn. bd. trustees AIDS Found. Miami Valley, Dayton, 1987—; mem. City Priority Bd., Dayton, 1992; bd. dirs. Dayton Art Inst. Guild, 1990-91; mem. cmty. action com. Regional Transp. Authority, 1993—; mem. Friends of Wesleyan Nature Ctr., Dayton, 1992; mem. Dayton AIDS Consortium, 1990-93; mem. City of Kalamazoo Awareness Com., 1982-85. Named Advisor of the Yr., Great Lakes affiliate Nat. Assn. Coll. and Univ. Residence Halls, 1983, Western Mich. U., 1983; recipient Disting. Svc. award Kalamazoo Alcohol and Drug Abuse Coun., 1984, Outstanding Svc. award Great Lakes Assn. Coll. and Univ. Housing Officers, 1984, Disting. Svc. award, 1988, Good Neighbor of the Wk. award EDTN-TV, Dayton, 1990; Coakley scholarship Western Mich. U. Mem.

Assn. Coll. and Univ. Housing Officers (chair task force on regional relationships 1990-92, program chair internat. Automation of Housing workshop 1987), Great Lakes Assn. Coll. and Univ. Housing Officers (mem. visioning com. 1993—, past pres., sec.-treas. 1983-88, editor Trends newsmag. 1981-83), Nat. Assn. Student Pers. Adminstrs., Ohio Housing Officers, Southwestern Ohio Housing Officers, Omicron Delta Kappa. Avocations: music, cooking, speculative fiction. Home: 1181 Golf Ct Dekalb IL 60115-5222 Office: Wright State Univ NIV Student Housing and Svcs Dekalb IL 60115

COALTER, MILTON J., JR., library director, educator; b. Memphis, July 5, 1949; s. Milton J. and Jewel (Mitchel) C.; m. Linda M. Block, May 20, 1973; children: Martha Claire, Siram Jacob. BA, Davidson Coll., 1971; MDiv, Princeton Theol. Sem., 1975, ThM, 1977; PhD in Religion, Princeton U., 1982. Asst. prof. Am. Religion N.C. State U., Raleigh, 1981-82; pub. svcs. libr. The Iliff Sch. Theology, Denver, 1982-84, acting libr. dir., 1984-85; libr. dir., prof. bibliography and rsch. Louisville Presbyn. Theol. Sem., 1985—, acting pres., 2002—03. Acting pres. Louisville Presbyn. Theol. Sem., 2002-03, bd. dirs. Louisville Inst., Scholars Press; gen. assembly coun. task force on ch. membership growth Presbyn. Ch., Louisville, 1989-91, gen. assembly theol. task force for the peace, unity and purity of the ch., 2001-. Author: (with John M. Mulder) The Letters of David Avery, 1979, Gilbert Tennent, Son of Thunder, 1986; (with John M. Mulder and Louis B. Weeks) The Presbyterian Presence in the Twentieth Century, 7 vols., 1989-92, Vital Signs, 1996, Resources for American Christianity, 2002, website for religion divsn. Lilly Endowment, 2000--; editor: (with Virgil Cruz) How Shall We Witness?, 1995; contbr. articles to profl. jours. Mem. Gen. Assembly Task Force on Peace, Unity and Purity of the Ch., 2001—. Recipient Jonathan Edwards award Princeton U., 1977-80, Tchg. award Assn. Princeton Grad. Alumni, 1979-80, Francis Makemie award Presbyn. Ch. Dept. History; Lily Endowment grantee, 1987-90, 99—, N.J. Hist. Commn. grantee, 1979-80, Pew Charitable Trust grantee, 1990-93; Princeton U. Whiting fellow, 1980-81, Mem. Am. Theol. Libr. Assn. (bd. dirs. 1997-2003, pres. 1998-2000), Am. Soc. Ch. History, Am. Acad. Religion. Presbyterian. Office: Louisville Presbyn Theol Sem 1044 Alta Vista Rd Louisville KY 40205-1758

COASE, RONALD HARRY, economist, educator; b. Willesden, Eng., Dec. 29, 1910; arrived in U.S., 1951; s. Henry Joseph and Rosalie (Giles) Coase; m. Marian Ruth Hartung, Aug. 7, 1937. B of Commerce, London Sch. Econs., 1932, DSc in Econs., 1951; Dr. Rer. Pol. honoris causa, Cologne U., Fed. Republic Germany, 1988; D of Social Sci. (hon.), Yale U., 1989; LLD (hon.), Washington U., St. Louis, 1991; LLD (hon.), U. Dundee, Scotland, 1992; DSc (hon.), U. Buckingham, Eng., 1995; DHL (hon.), Beloit Coll., 1996; docteur honoris causa, U. Paris, 1996. Sir Ernest Cassel Travelling scholar, 1931—32; asst. lectr. Dundee Sch. Econs., 1932—34, U. Liverpool, England, 1934—35; from asst. lectr. to lectr. to reader London Sch. Econs., 1935—51; prof. U. Buffalo, 1951—58, U. Va., Charlottesville, 1958—64, U. Chgo., 1964—, now Clifton R. Musser prof. emeritus, sr. fellow in law and econs. Law Sch. Statistician, then chief statistician Ctrl. Statis. Office, Offices War Cabinet, England, 1941—46. Author: British Broadcasting, A Study in Monopoly, 1950, The Firm, the Market and the Law, 1988, Essays on Economics and Economists, 1994; editor: Jour. Law and Econs., 1964—82. Mem. hon. com. Eurosci.; chmn. adv. bd. Contracting and Orgns. Rsch. Inst. U. Mo., Columbia. Named Rockefeller fellow, 1948; recipient Nobel prize in Econs., 1991; fellow Ctr. for Advanced Study Behavioral Scis., 1958—59, sr. rsch. fellow, Hoover Instn., Stanford U., 1977, hon. fellow, London Sch. Econs. Fellow: European Acad., Am. Econ. Assn. (disting.), Brit. Acad. (corr.), Am. Acad. Arts and Scis.; mem.: Internat. Soc. for New Instnl. Econs. (founding pres. 1997), Mont Pelerin Soc., Royal Econ. Soc. Office: U Chgo Laird Bell Law Quadrangle 1111 E 60th St Chicago IL 60637-2776 Home: The Hallmark 2960 N Lake Shore Dr Chicago IL 60637

COATES, SHIRLEY JEAN, finance educator, secondary school educator; b. Nashville, Tenn., Oct. 9, 1944; d. Jerry Baxter Springer and Cora Louise Green; m. Arthur Andrew Coates; children: Andrea, John. BS, Mid. Tenn. State U., 1968; MS, Brigham Young U., 1971. Lic. profl. tchr., cert. tchr. Tenn. career level III. Instr. Young Harris Coll., Young Harris, Ga., 1968—70, U. of Miss., Oxford, Miss., 1971—72; tchr. Dickson County Jr. H.S., Dickson, Tenn., 1972—73, Hickman County H.S., Centerville, Tenn., 1973—. Bus. dept. chmn. Hickman County H.S., Centerville, Tenn., 1994—. Sponsor, Hickman County - Tenn. type-a-thon Leukemia Soc. of Am., BPA Chpt., Nashville, 1989—99; sec. Hickman County H.S. Band Boosters, Centerville, Tenn., 1988—94, Hickman County H.S. Athletic Booster Club, Centerville, Tenn., 1995—96; pageant chmn. Hickman County 4-H Vol. Leaders, Centerville, Tenn., 1990—94; project dir. (head start book dr.) South Ctrl. Human Resources Agy., Centerville, Tenn., 1988—89. Named Tchr. of Yr., Hickman County HS Bd. of Edn., 1990, Bus. Dept. Tchr. of Yr., Hickman County H.S., 2000, Most Disting. H.S. Tchr., Hickman County Tenn. Edn. Assn., 2002; recipient, 2003. Mem.: Bus. Profls. Am. (honor adv. 1991, star advisor 1992), Assn. for Career and Tech. Edn., Daughters of Am. Revolution (asst. registrar, treas. 1998—2002).

COATS, CHARLES F. physics and mathematics educator; b. LaJunta, Colo., Oct. 31, 1949; s. Robert Harold and Edna Lucille (Varner) C. BS in Math., Physics, Southeastern State Coll., 1970; MA in Math., U. Okla., 1977, MS in Physics, 1979, PhD in Physics, 1982. Asst. prof. McPherson (Kans.) Coll., 1979-80, U. Pitts., Bradford, 1980-86, Southeastern Okla. State U., Durant, 1987-89; asst. prof. physics and math. U. Montevallo, Ala., 1989-94, Laredo (Tex.) C.C., 1995—. Prin., Coats Photographic Svcs., Durant, Okla., 1986-89. With U.S. Army, 1971-73. Mem. AAUP, Am. Assn. Physics Tchrs., Math. Assn. Am., Tex. C.C. Tchrs. Assn., Sigma Xi, Kappa Mu Epsilon, Pi Mu Epsilon. Office: Laredo CC Laredo TX 78040

COATS, WENDELL JOHN, JR., political science educator; b. Ft. Sill, Okla., Feb. 11, 1947; s. Wendell John Sr. and Benny Lee (Smith) C.; married; children: Gloria Lee, Karen Evangeline. BA in Polit. Sci., U. Colo., 1969, PhD, 1978. Legis. asst. to Hon. David Stockman U.S. Ho. of Reps., Washington, 1979; asst. prof. polit. sci. Kenyon Coll., Gambier, Ohio, 1981-84; dept. chair, prof. govt. Conn. Coll., New London, 1984—. Lectr. U. Md., Heidelberg, Fed. Republic Germany, 1980-81; vis. fellow Pub. Affairs Conf. Ctr., Kenyon Coll., 1982-83. Author: The Activity of Politics, 1988, A Theory of Republican Character, 1993, Statesmanship, 1995, Oakeshott and His Contemporaries, 2000, Political Theory and Practice, 2003; contbr. articles to profl. jours. Mem. New London Charter Revision Commn., 1985, Gov.'s Task Force on Campaign Fin., 1987. Served to 1st lt. U.S. Army, 1969-72. Mem.: Am. Polit. Sci. Assn., Conf. for Study of Polit. Thought.

COATY, PATRICK CLARK, social sciences educator; b. Janesville, Wis. s. Jerome Clarence and Mary Ellen G. Coaty; m. Ruby Hernandez Coaty, Nov. 18, 2000. BS in edn., Univ. Wis., 1984; MA in internat. studies, The Claremont Grad. Sch., 1992, PhD, 1997. Rsch. assoc. Keck Ctr. for Internat. adn Strategic Studies, Claremont, Calif., 1996-99; instr. Coast Coll. Dist., Costa Mesa, Calif., 1999—. With U.S. Air Force Res., 1982-88. Roman Catholic. Office: Orange Coast Coll 2701 Fairview Rd Costa Mesa CA 92626-5563

COBB, JUDY LYNN, elementary educator; b. Fresno, Calif., July 31, 1940; d. V.W. and Ruth (Benight) Keim; m. Jeffrey, Jay. BA, Calif. State U., Fresno, 1962. Tchr. Fresno (Calif.) Unified Sch. Dist., 1963-68, Lodi (Calif.) Unified Sch. Dist., 1976—2002, chpt. I ESL resource tchr., 1981-87. Designer, implementor curriculum for elem. students; presenter workshops; speaker at profl. confs. Named Mentor Tchr., 1986-88; Title VII grantee. Mem. San Joaquin Reading Assn., Calif. Reading Assn., Internat. Reading Assn. (artist dist. activities). Home: 9531 Springfield Way Stockton CA 95212-2016

COBB, LARRY RUSSELL, ethics educator; b. Clendenin, W.Va., Nov. 7, 1938; s. Ivan O. and Jessie E. Cobb; m. Naomi Faye Cobb, Jan. 19, 1939; children: Michael Kent, Cheryl Lynn. BA in Econs., W.Va. U., 1961; MA in Philosophy and Govt., So. Ill. U., 1963, PhD in Govt., 1967. Instr. Glenville (W.Va.) State Coll., 1963-64; assoc. prof., then prof. Slippery Rock (Pa.) U., 1967-97, prof. emeritus, 1997—. Exec. dir., founder. Ethicsworks Cons., Slippery Rock, 2000—; sec. bd. dirs. Inst. for Values Inquiry, Tulsa, 1990—; bd. dirs., exec. dir. Found. for Philosophy of Creativity, Denton, Tex., 1991—. Contbr. numerous articles to profl. jours., chpts. to books. Bd. dirs. Cmty. Svcs. and Learning Inst., Slippery Rock, 1999—. Mem. Nat. Assn. Housing and Devel. Ofcls. (sec. Mid-Atlantic coun., 1999-2001, Bd. Ethics and Credentialing Trustees, 2000-, v.p. Internat., 2001-, Bd of Govs., 2001-). Democrat. Unitarian Universalist. Avocation: skiing. Home: 250 Slippery Rock Rd Slippery Rock PA 16057 E-mail: ethicsworks@aol.com.

COBB, PAUL, mathematics educator; Cert. Post-Grad. Edn. Bristol U., England, 1977. Math. instr. Headlands Sch., Swindon, England, 1975—76, Brighton, Hove and East Sussex Sixth Form Coll., Brighton, England, 1977—78; asst. prof. to assoc. prof. to prof. Purdue U., Math. Edn., W. Lafayette, Ind., 1983—92; prof. Vanderfilt U., Math. Edn., Nashville, 1992—; adj. prof. edn. So. Cross U., Lismore, Australia, 1998—. Contbr. articles various profl. jours. Adv. Ctr. Rsch. Math. Learning, Copenhagen, 1999—; elected mem. Internat. Com. Internat. Group for Psychology Math. Edn., 1987—91; mem. Rsch. Adv. Com., Nat. Coun. Tchrs. Math., 1995—98. Recipient Outstanding Article, Jour. Rsch Math Edn., 1996; Invited Fellow, Ctr. for Advanced Studies in Behavioral Scis. Mem.: Nat. Acad. Edn., North Am. Chpt. PME, Internat. Group Psychology Math. Edn., AERA Spec. Interest Group Cognitive Structure and Conceptual Change, AERA Spec. Interest Group Rsch Math. Edn., Am. Edn. Rsch. Assn., Nat. Soc. for Study of Edn., Nat. Coun. Tchrs. of Math. Home: 1311 Saxon Dr Nashville TN 37215

COBB, RONALD DAVID, pharmacist, educator; b. Louisville, May 10, 1945; s. Harry D. and Ruth (Roberts) C.; m. Patricia Lee Carroll, Sept. 4, 1964; children: Joy Ruth, Tracy Renee. BS in Pharmacy, U. Ky., 1968, PharmD, 1973. Staff pharmacist Kettering (Ohio) Meml. Hosp., 1968; pharmacist mgr. Lawrence Drugs, Inc., Lexington, Ky., 1969-70; asst. prof. Coll. Pharmacy U. Ky., Lexington, 1973-79, assoc. prof. Coll. Pharmacy, 1980—. Pharmacist cons. Blue Cross/Blue Shield of Ky., Louisville, 1976-90, Market Measures, Inc., West Orange, N.J., 1976-94. Contbr. numerous articles to profl. jours. Bd. dirs. Am. Found. for Pharm. Edn.; trustee Am. Pharm. Assn. Found., 1990-93. Fellow Am. Coll. Apothecaries (assoc.); mem. Blue Grass Pharmacists Assn. (treas. 1969, exec. com. 1969-76, pres.-elect 1970, pres. 1971), Ky. Pharmacists Assn. (bd. dirs. 1972-79, chmn. 1977-78, pres.-elect 1975-76, pres. 1976-77), Am. Inst. History Pharmacy (bd. dirs. 1994-96), Am. Pharm. Assn. (chmn. bd. 1989, pres. 1990, trustee 1985-91), Acad. Pharmacy Practice (pres.-elect 1982-83, pres. 1983-84, bd. dirs. 1980-86). Democrat. Baptist. Avocations: woodworking, photography, traveling, fishing, sports. Home: The Preserve 410 25th Ave SW Vero Beach FL 32962

COBERT, KATHARINE JONES, elementary education educator; b. Balt., Sept. 1, 1941; d. LeRoy E. and Katharine (Diering) Jones; m. G. William Cobert, Aug. 23, 1974. BS, Towson State U., 1963; MEd, Loyola Coll., 1970. Cert. reading specialist, adminstr., supr. Specialist/cons. adult edn. reading Balt. County Bd. Edn., Towson, Md., reading specialist. Instr., part-time mem. faculty Howard C.C., Columbia, Md., 1991-92, Coll. Notre Dame, Md., 1995-99. Mem. Internat. Reading Assn., ASCD, Phi Delta Kappa, Delta Kappa Gamma.

COBLE, DANIEL BRUCE, nursing administrator; b. Spangler, Pa., Nov. 3, 1949; s. Harry Edward and Elizabeth (Klapak) C.; m. Patricia Ann Gibbons, July 2, 1977; children: Matthew Thomas, Timothy Andrew, Amanda Christine (dec. 1999). BMusic, Westminster Coll., 1971; AA in Nursing, Ind. U. S.E., New Albany, 1974; BSN, Regents Coll., Albany, 1982; MS in Nursing, SUNY, Buffalo, 1983; PhD in Nursing Sci., U. Fla., 2000. RN, N.Y., Ky., Pa., Fla. Staff nurse emergency rm. Humana Hosp. Suburban, Louisville, 1974-75; head nurse emergency rm. Cole Meml. Hosp., Coudersport, Pa., 1976-77; staff nurse ICU/CCU Olean (N.Y.) Gen. Hosp., 1977-78, 81-83; staff nurse med. ICU Humana Hosp. Univ., Louisville, 1978-79; staff nurse ICU Lock Haven (Pa.) Hosp., 1979, VA Hosp., Bath, N.Y., 1979-81; nurse mgr. ICU/CCU United Community Hosp., Grove City, Pa., 1983-84; dir. nursing svc. Bethesda Community Hosp., Hornell, N.Y., 1984-85; dir. patient svcs. med./surg. nursing Tampa (Fla.) Gen. Hosp., 1985-95; adj. prof. Nova Univ., Ft. Lauderdale, Fla., 1986—89; vis. instr. U. South Fla., Tampa, 1995-96; asst. prof. U. Tampa, 1996—2002; exec. dir. Fla. Bd. of Nursing, Tallahassee, 2002—. Cons. computerized nursing systems, 1988—. Contbr. articles to profl. jours. Organist St. James United Meth. Ch., Tampa, 1992—2002. Mem. Am. Assembly for Men in Nursing, Am. Guild Organists, Am. Guild English Handbell Ringers, King Internat. Nursing Group, So. Nursing Rsch. Soc., Phi Mu Alpha Sinfonia, Sigma Theta Tau (Delta Beta and Kappa Rho chpt.). Roman Catholic. Avocations: church music, church organist, classical music, baseball, computers. Home: 7806 N St Vincent Tampa FL 33614-3375 Office: 4052 Bald Cypress Way Tallahassee FL 32399-3252 E-mail: dan_coble@doh.state.fl.us.

COBURN, JAMES LEROY, educational administrator; b. Oak Park, Ill., Nov. 21, 1933; s. Forest Edward and Myrtle Emmaline (Clarke) C.; m. Julianne Whitty, Sept. 3, 1955; children: James, Gregory, Julie, Cheryl. BA, North Cen. Coll., Naperville, Ill., 1956; MS, No. Ill. U., 1965; EdD, Vanderbilt U., 1983. Cert. tchr., guidance counselor, supt., Ill. Tchr. Luther South High Sch., Chgo., 1956-58, Maine Township High Sch. East, Park Ridge, Ill., 1958-61, dean, counselor, 1961-64; dir. student pers. svcs. Maine Twp. High Sch. South, Park Ridge, 1964-67; asst. prin. for staff Maine Twp. High Sch. West, Des Plaines, Ill., 1967-73, prin., 1973-97; ret., 1997. Cons. Pitts. Pub. Schs., 1965; chmn. Ill. Blue Ribbon Com. on Edn., Bloomington, 1988; spkr. Internat. Ednl. Symposium, South Korea, 1996. Editor: Growth through Reading, 1960, 61. Pres. Inter-Suburban Assn.; chmn. judges 4th of July Parade, Des Plaines, 1980-86; mem. Des Plaines Beautification Com., 1987, Des Plaines Mayor's Adv. Com., 1989—; Ill. state commr. North Ctrl. Assn., 1992-95; pres. Des Plaines chpt. United Way, 1995—; pres. Twp. Sch. Bd. Caucus, 2002. Recipient Those Who Excel award Ill. Bd. Edn., 1977, Disting. Educator's award Idea Inst., 1984. Mem. Nat. Assn. Secondary Sch. Prins., Am. Assn. Sch. Adminstrs., Ill. Prins. Assn., Intersuburban Assn. Prins. (pres. 1986—), Des Plaines C. of C. (bd. dirs 1980-85, 92-95), Rotary (pres. Des Plaines 1976-77, Most Valuable Mem. award 1979, Paul Harris fellow 1989, John Vaughin excellence in edn. award 1997). Lutheran. Avocations: reading, travel, recreational sports, gardening. Home: 1843 Locust St Des Plaines IL 60018-2326 E-mail: jim0181@attbi.com.

COBURN, MARJORIE FOSTER, psychologist, educator; b. Salt Lake City, Feb. 28, 1939; d. Harlan A. and Alma (Ballinger) Polk; m. Robert Byron Coburn, July 2, 1977; children: Polly Klea Foster, Matthew Ryan Foster, Robert Scott Coburn, Kelly Anne Coburn. B.A. in Sociology, UCLA, 1960; Montessori Internat. Diploma honor grad. Washington Montessori Inst., 1968; M.A. in Psychology, U. No. Colo., 1979; Ph.D. in Counseling Psychology, U. Denver, 1983. Licensed clin. psychologist. Probation officer Alameda County (Calif.), Oakland, 1960-62, Contra Costa County (Calif.), El Cerrito, 1966, Fairfax County (Va.), Fairfax, 1967; dir. Friendship Club, Orlando, Fla., 1963-65; tchr. Va. Montessori Sch., Fairfax, 1968-70; spl. edn. tchr. Leary Sch., Falls Church, Va., 1970-72, sch. administr., 1973-76; tchr. Aseltine Sch., San Diego, 1976-77, Coburn Montessori Sch., Colorado Springs, Colo., 1977-79; pvt. practice psychotherapy, Colorado Springs, 1979-82, San Diego, 1982— ; cons. spl. edn., agoraphobia, women in transition. Mem. Am. Psychol. Assn., Am. Orthopsychiat. Assn., Phobia Soc., Council Exceptional Children, Calif. Psychol. Assn., San Diego Psychological Assn., The Charter 100, Mensa. Episcopalian. Lodge: Rotary. Contbr. articles to profl. jours.; author: (with R.C. Orem) Montessori: Prescription for Children with Learning Disabilities, 1977. Office: 836 Prospect St Ste 101 La Jolla CA 92037-4206 E-mail: mcoburn@san.rr.com.

COCANOUGHER, ARTHUR BENTON, business administration educator; b. Lubbock, Tex., July 6, 1938; s. Arthur Clifton and Bonnie Odell (Ford) C.; m. Dianne Esther Reisenauer, May 27, 1967; children: Carolyn, David. Mgr. Gen. Electric Co., N.Y.C., 1962-67; asst. prof. U. So. Calif., Los Angeles, 1970-72; assoc. prof. So. Meth. U., Dallas, 1972-73; prof. mktg. U. Houston, 1973-75, chmn. dept., 1975-76, dean Coll. Bus., 1976-85, sr. v.p., provost, 1985-87; dean Tex. A&M U. Coll. Bus., College Station, 1987-2001, emeritus, disting. prof. Trustee Investment Series Smith Barney, Citibank Mutual Funds; interim chancellor, Tex. A&M U. system, 2003— ;cons. in field. Contbr. articles to profl. jours. Bd. dirs. Better Bus. Bur., Houston, 1979-87, West Houston Assn., 1984-87. Served to 1st lt. U.S. Army, 1960-62. Recipient Nicholas Salgo award So. Meth. U., 1973, Outstanding Service award U. Houston Alumni Assn., 1982, Disting. Alumnus award Coll. Bus. U. Tex.-Austin, 1981. Mem. Am. Mktg. Assn., Acad. Mktg. Sci. Home: 4409 Nottingham Ln Bryan TX 77802-5904 Office: Tex A&M U Coll Bus Coll Bus 4112 Tamu College Station TX 77843-4112

COCANOUR, BARBARA ANN, anatomy educator; b. Mansfield, Ohio, June 17, 1942; d. Milo Charles and Helen Pauline (Mawhorr) C.; m. Don Hilton, Aug. 23, 1969; children: Kirsten Ann, Eric James. PhD, U. Maine, 1969. Asst. prof. Lowell (Mass.) Tech. Inst., 1969-70, vis. prof., 1971-73, U. Lowell, 1976-81, asst. prof., 1981-86, assoc. prof., 1986-91, prof., 1991—. Author: Flashcards for Human Anatomy and Physiology, 1990, Photographic Atlas, 1995, A Videodisc Index for Slice of Life VI, 1995; co-author: Activities Manual for Anatomy and Physiology, 1990, Laboratory Manual for Human Anatomy and Physiology, 1990; contbr. articles to profl. jours., chapters to books. Mem. AAAS, Nat. Sci. Tchrs. Assn., Human Anatomy and Physiology Soc., Am. Assn. Anatomists. Home: 175 Mass Ave Harvard MA 01451-1709 Office: U Mass Lowell Dept Phys Therapy Lowell MA 01854

COCH, NICHOLAS K. geologist, educator; b. N.Y.C., Mar. 30, 1938; BS, CCNY, 1959; MS, U. Rochester, 1961; PhD, Yale U., 1965. Cert. profl. geologist, Am. Inst. Profl. Geologists. Asst. prof. geology L.I. U., Southampton (N.Y.) Coll., 1965-67; from asst. prof. to prof. geology CUNY, Flushing, 1967-76, prof. geology, 1976—. Lectr. in field. Author: Geohazards, 1995; co-author: Physical Geology, 1982, 91. Fellow Geol. Soc. Am.; mem. Am. Assn. Petroleum Geologists (Meritorious Contbn. in Environ. Geoscis. award, ea. sect., 1996), Am. Meteorology Soc., Soc. Sedimentary Geology. Avocations: photography, scale modeling, cooking, computer graphics, model railroads. Office: Queens Coll CUNY Sch Earth and Environ Sci Flushing NY 11367

COCHÉ, JUDITH, psychologist, educator; b. Phila., Sept. 2, 1942; d. Louis and Miriam (Nerenberg) Milner; m. Erich Coché, Oct. 16, 1966 (dec.); 1 child, Juliette Laura; m. John Anderson, Jan. 1, 1994. BA, Colby Coll., 1964; MA, Temple U., 1966; PhD, Bryn Mawr Coll., 1975. Diplomate Am. Bd. Profl. Psychology; lic. psychologist Pa., Md., N.J., Fla.; cert. in group psychotherapy Nat. Registry Group Psychotherapists. Rsch. asst. Jefferson Med. Coll., 1965-66; diagnostician Law Ct., Aachen, Germany, 1967-68; staff psychologist N.E. Community Mental Health Ctr., Phila., 1969-74; family clinician Inst. Pa. Hosp., 1974-76; instr. psychology Drexel U., 1976-77; lectr. Med. Coll. Pa., 1977-78; asst. clin. prof. Hahnemann Med. Coll., Phila., 1979—; pvt. practice Phila., 1974—, 1985—; assoc. prof. psychiatry U. Pa., 1985—, clin. coord. Psychology, 1999—; assoc. clin. prof. psychology in psychiatry U. Pa. Med. Coll., 1986—; mem. faculty Family Inst. of Phila., 1990—; sr. cons. Phila. Child Guidance Clinic, 1992-96; assoc. clin. prof. psychology in psychiatry U. Pa. Med. Coll., 1986—. Clin. cons. Hilltop Prep Sch., 1977-86; clin. supr. Am. Assn. Marriage and Family Therapy. Co-author: Couples Group Psychotherapy, A Clinical Practice Model, 1990, Co. author Powerful Wisdom: Voices of Distinguished Women Psychotherapists, (1993); contbr. chpts. to books, articles to profl. jours. Bd. dirs. Whitemarsh Art Ctr., 1977-78, Please Touch Museum, 1982-89; mem. prof. adv. bd. Parents Without Ptnrs., 1977-86; mem. adv. com. Pa. Ballet/Shirley Rock. Grantee Del. Children's Bur. Bryn Mawr Coll., 1974-75, Pa. Hosp., 1975-77. Fellow Am. Group Psychotherapy Assn.; mem. APA, Am. Assn. Marriage and Family Therapy (approved supr.), Am. Family Therapy Assn., Phila. Soc. Clin. Psychologists (pres. 1980-81), Family Inst. Phila., Pa. Psychol. Assn. (chmn. legis. com. 1982), Soc. Rsch. in Psychotherapy. Address: Acad House 1420 Locust St Ste 410 Philadelphia PA 19102-4202

COCHIARA, SUZETTE BELSOM, speech pathologist, administrator; b. New Orleans, Sept. 30, 1952; d. Ralph P. and Esther (Pizani) Belsom; m. Jules A. Cochiara, Jr., Aug. 14, 1972; children: Stacey, David. BS, Dominican Coll., 1974; MEd, Our Lady of Holy Cross Coll., 1992. Cert. tchr. La.; lic. speech pathologist, La. Speech pathologist Jefferson Parish Pub. Schs., Harvey, La., 1974-77, '88—; speech pathologist, pvt. therapist to Cath. schs. Marreto, Gretna, La., 1984-88. Mem. sch. bldg. level com. Jean Lafitte Elem. Sch., Lafitte, La., 1991-93, chmn. dyslexia com., 1992-94. Chmn. liturgy bd. St. Anthony Ch., Lafitte, 1990-94; mem. sch. bd. Archbishop Blank H.S., Gretna, La., 1992—, v.p. 1993-94, pres., 1994—. Mem. La. Speech and Hearing Assn., Kappa Delta Pi (pres. 1993—), Kappa Gamma Pi (treas. 1992-93). Home: Rt 1 Box 513 A Lafitte LA 70067 Office: Jefferson Parish Schs Spl Edn 1407 Virgil St Gretna LA 70053-2340

COCHRAN, BETH, gifted and talented educator; b. New Orleans, La., Nov. 2, 1951; d. Hugh Greene Smith, Kathryn Ann Smith; m. Cole Cochran; children: Michael, Steven. B in Music Edn., Ctrl. Mo. State U., 1973; MEd, U. Kans., 1999. Cert. Vocal Music Edn., K-12 1973, Gifted Edn. 2001. Tchr. vocal music Lexington Sch. Dist., Lexigton, Mo., 1973—75; tchr. elem. music North Kansas City Schs., Kansas City, Mo., 1975—77; dir. edn. Tokyo Bapt. Ch., Tokyo, 1984—90; dir. choral music Piper Sch. Dist., Kansas City, Kans., 1990—2000; tchr. vocal music Appleton City Schools, Appleton City, Mo., 2000—02; gifted resource tchr. Appleton City Schs., Appleton City, Mo., 2001—02, Butler Schs., Butler, Mo., 2002—. Min. music First Bapt. Ch., Adrian, Mo., 2001—. Mem.: Gifted Assn. Mo. Baptist. Home: 503 N High St Butler MO 64730 Office: Butler R-5 Schs 4 South High St Butler MO 64730 E-mail: cbcochran@osagevalley.net.

COCHRAN, CAROLYN, library director; b. Tyler, Tex., July 13, 1934; d. Sidney Allen and Eudelle (Frazier) C.; m. Guy Milford Eley, June 1, 1963 (div.). BA, Beaver Coll., 1956; MA, U. Tex., 1960; MLS, Tex. Woman's U., 1970. Libr. Canadian (Tex.) High Sch., 1970-71; rep. United Food Co., Amarillo, Tex., 1971-72; libr. Bishop Coll., Dallas, Tex., 1975-76, St. Mary's Dominican, New Orleans, 1976-77, DeVry Inst. Tech., Irving, Tex., 1978-98, libr. dir. emeritus, 1998—. With Database Searching Handicapped Individuals, Irving, 1983—; vol. bibliographer Assn. Individuals with Disabilities, Dallas, 1982-85. Mem. Am. Coalition of Citizens with Disabilities, 1982-85, Assn. Individuals with Disabilities, 1982-86, Vols. in Tech. Assistance, 1985—, Radio Amateur Satellite Corp., 1985-86; sponsor 500, Inc., 1988-95. Reviewer Libr. Jour., 1974, Dallas Morning News,

1972-74, Amarillo Globe-News, 1970-71. Mem. Dallas regional adv. com. Tex. Commn. for the Blind, 2001. HEW fellow, 1967; honored Black History Collection, Dallas Morning News, Bishop Coll., Dallas, 1973. Mem. ALA, Spl. Libr. Assn., Am. Coun. of Blind (sec. Dallas chpt. 1997-99), Toastmistress Club (pres. 1982-83) (Irving). E-mail: carolyn_cochran@sbcglobal.net.

COCHRAN, LESLIE HERSCHEL, university administrator; b. Valparaiso, Ind., Apr. 24, 1939; s. Robert H. and Dellcena (Marquart) C.; m. Linda Stockman, May 20, 1978; children: Troy, Kirt, Leslee. BS, Western Mich. U., 1961, MA, 1962; Ed.D., Wayne State U., 1968. Mem. faculty Central Mich. U., Mt. Pleasant, 1968-80, assoc. dean, 1970-75, dean fine and applied arts, 1975-76, vice provost, 1976-80; provost S.E. Mo. State U., Cape Girardeau, 1980-92; pres. Youngstown (Ohio) State U., 1992—. Mem. accreditation team North Ctrl. Assn., Chgo., 1982—. Author: Advisory Committee in Action, 1980, Innovative Program in Industrial Education, 1970, Administrative Commitment to Teaching, 1989, Publish or Perish: The Wrong Issue, 1992. Trustee Butler Inst. Am. Art, Western Res. Health Care System, N.E. Ohio Med. Coll. Japan Soc. Promotion of Sci. fellow Tokyo, 1976. Mem. Nat. Assn. Indsl. and Tech. Tchr. Edn. (pres. 1976), Rotary. Office: Youngstown State U Todd Hall Office Of Pres Youngstown OH 44555-0001

COCHRAN, RAYMOND MARTIN, university auditor; b. Passaic, N.J., Aug. 10, 1943; s. Mark and Catherine (Brown) C.; m. Dorothy Parcells; children: Tamara Takoudes, Tania Secor. BS, Farleigh Dickinson U., 1966; MBA, NYU, 1968. CPA, N.Y., N.J. Mgr. audit KPMG, N.Y.C., 1968-79, Engelhard Minerals and Chems. Corp., N.Y.C., 1979-81; dir. internal audit Columbia U., N.Y.C., 1981—. Founder, coord. N.Y. Metro Region Coll. and Univ. Audit Dirs., 1993—. Bd. dirs., treas. Japan Internat. Christian U. Found., Inc., 1985—. 1st lt. U.S. Army, 1969-71. Mem. AICPA, Assn. Coll. and Univ. Auditors (pres. 1999-2000), N.J. Soc. CPAs, Inst. Internal Auditors (pres. N.Y. chpt. 2001-02, bd. govs. N.Y. chpt. 1992—). Home: 818 E Ridgewood Ave Ridgewood NJ 07450-3911 Office: Columbia U 475 Riverside Dr Ste 510 New York NY 10115-0510 E-mail: cochran@columbia.edu.

COCHRANE, WALTER E. academic administrator, music educator, conductor; b. Phila. s. Earl and Martha (Binder) C. BS, MS, U. Pa., Phila.; grad. study, Columbia U., 1959-60. Cert. sch. dist. adminstr., N.Y., Pa., N.J., Mass., Maine, Va.; cert. music supr., N.Y., Pa., Va.; supt. schs., N.Y., Mass.; sch. prin., N.Y., Pa., Mass. Clarinet soloist Phila. Brahms Cycle, 1950; dir. bands Upper Darby Pa. Schs., 1950-51; prof. clarinet and chamber music Phila. Musical Acad., 1950-52; solo clarinetist Phila. Symphonic Band, 1950-58; dir. music Alexandria Va. City Schs., 1951—58; clarinet soloist Alexandria String Quartet, 1952; dist. music dir. Sch. Dist. II, L.I., NY, 1958-60; supr. music N.Y. State Edn. Dept., Albany, 1960-67; conductor NY State Bands, 1960-67; v.p. Found. Am. Art Song, Albany, 1965-70; supr. music Hartford (Conn.) City Schs., 1967-69; instr. music edn. U. Hartford, 1967—69; asst. supt. Sch. Dist. 5, L.I., N.Y., 1970-78; supt. schs. Maine Sch. Adm. Dist. 19, Lubec, Maine, 1978-80; v.p. and dean Inst. Security and Tech., Phila., 1980-87; corp. dir. edn. PTC Career Insts., Phila., 1987; pres. Career Guidance Corp., 1988-91, dir. GED home study program N.Y. State, 1992—. Founder, dir. Stony Brook Conservatory Music, L.I., 1958—61. Author: GED Home Study Program, Meet The Great Composers, The Gulf War, World Wars I and II, Mathematics Mastery Manual, Science Mastery Manual, Understand Music, Women Composers, Literature Mastery Manual, Who Was the Killer Composer?, Clarinet Curriculum, Flute Curriculum, Graded Music for Wind and String Chamber Music, Graded Music for Brass Instruments, Public Schools Can Help You, The AAA Method in American Education-Analysis, Action and Alleviation of Attrition, CATP: Cooperative Analysis of Teacher Performance, Non-Traditional Employment for Women, A Philosophy and Basic Procedures for Supervision, Understanding Students for the Improvement of Learning, Encyclopedia of Conductors. Recipient Humanitarian award Chgo. PTC. Mem. ASCD, NEA, MENC, SAR, NYSSMA (adjudicator, all-state conductor), NASSP, Am. Assn. Sch. Adminstrs., N.Y. Assn. Supr. and Curriculum Devel., Phila. Musical Soc.

COCKE, WILLIAM MARVIN, JR., plastic surgeon, educator; b. Balt., Aug. 2, 1934; s. William M. and Clara E. (Bosley) C.; m. Sue Ann Harris, Apr. 25, 1981; children: Gregory William, Laura Marie, Julie Ann; children by previous marriage: William Marvin III, Catherine Lynn, Deborah Kay, Brian Thomas. BS with honors in Biology, Tex. A&M U., 1956; MD, Baylor U., 1960. Diplomate: Am. Bd. Plastic Surgery (guest examiner 1978). Intern surgery Vanderbilt U. Hosp., Nashville, 1960-61; fellow gen. surgery Ochsner Clinic and Found. Hosp., New Orleans, 1961-64; chief resident surgery Monroe (La.) Charity Hosp., 1963-64; resident reconstructive surgery Roswell Park Meml. Inst., Buffalo, 1965-66; chief resident plastic surgery VA Hosp., Bronx, N.Y., 1966; practice medicine specializing in plastic surgery Nashville, 1968-75, Sacramento, 1976-79; pvt. practice medicine specializing in plastic surgery Bryan, Tex., 1980-92; prof. surgery, head div. plastic/reconstructive surgery Marshall U. Sch. of Medicine, Huntington, W.Va., 1992—. Mem. staff St. Mary's Hosp., Cabell-Huntington Hosp., Huntington Vets. Med. Ctr.; asst. prof. plastic surgery Vanderbilt U. Sch. Medicine, Nashville, 1968-69, asst. clin. prof. plastic surgery, 1969-75; assoc. prof. plastic surgery Ind. U. Sch. Medicine, Indpls., 1975-76; chief plastic surgery service Wishard Meml. Hosp., Ind. U., 1975-76; assoc. prof. surgery U. Calif. Sch. Medicine, Davis, 1976-79, chmn. dept. plastic surgery, 1976-79; prof. surgery, chief div. plastic surgery Tex. Tech. U. Sch. Medicine, Lubbock, 1979-80, dir. Microsurg. Research Lab., 1979-80; clin. prof. surgery Tex. A&M U. Sch. Medicine, 1983-92; prof. plastic surgery, 1986-89; chief plastic surgery svc., dept. surgery, Olin Teague VA Med. Ctr., Temple, Tex., 1986-92; prof. head surgery divsn. plastic and reconstruction Marshall U. Sch. Medicine, 1992—. Author textbooks on plastic surgery; contbr. articles to profl. jours. Served with M.C. USAF, 1966-68. Recipient Dean Echols award Ochsner Hosp. Found., 1963 Mem. ACS, Am. Assn. Plastic Surgeons, Soc. Head and Neck Surgeons, Assn. for Acad. Surgery, Alton Ochsner Surg. Soc. Episcopalian. Home: 45 Olde Farm Rd Ona WV 25545-9747 Office: Marshall U Sch Medicine Dept Surgery 1600 Medical Center Dr Huntington WV 25701-3656

COCKERHAM, KIMBERLY PEELE, ophthalmologist, educator; b. Bellevue, Wash., Apr. 10, 1961; d. Fred Arthur and Dorothy Anne (Cooper) Piontkowski; m. Glenn Cooper Cockerham, Feb. 22, 1997. BA in Biology, U. Calif., San Diego, 1983; MD, George Washington U., 1987. Commd. 2nd lt. U.S. Army, 1983, advanced through grades to maj.; surg. intern Letterman Army Ctr., San Francisco, 1987-88; chief emergency svcs. McDonald Army Hosp., Newport News, Va., 1988-89; neuro-opthalmology cons. Fitzsimons Army Med. Ctr., Denver, 1993-94; resident in ophthalmology Walter Reed Army Med. Ctr., Washington, 1989-92, neuro-ophthalmology fellow, 1992-93, mem. neuro-ophthlamology staff, 1993-94, 95—; orbital disease fellow Allegheny Gen. Hosp., Pitts., 1994-95; dir. orbital disease and oculoplastics Walter Reed Army Med. Ctr., Washington, 1995-98; ret., 1998; ophthalmologist Cockerham Eye Cons., Lock Haven, Pa., 1997—; dir. oculoplastics, orbital disease and reconstrn. Allegheny Gen. Hosp., Pitts., 1999—2002; dir. neuro-ophthalmology and orbital oncology Allegheny Cancer Ctr., Pitts., 2002—. Asst. clin. prof. Uniformed U. Health Scis., Bethesda, Md., 1992-98; instr. neuro-ophthalmology Harvard's Lancaster, U. Houston's Stanford basic ophthalmology courses, 1994—; asst. clin. prof. Drexel U. Sch. Medicine, 2000—; oral bd. examiner Acad. Ophthalmology, 1998—; cons. surg. neuro-ophthalmology U. Pitt. Med. Ctr.; bd. dirs. Vision Svcs.; team opthalmologist Pitts. Pirates baseball team. Author: Practical Diagnois & Management of Orbital Disease, 2001; assoc. editor Jour. of Allegheny Med. Soc.; contbr. articles to profl. jours., chpts. to books. Eye camp doctor Charitable Trust, New Delhi, India, 1996; mem. Surg. Eye Expedition Internat., 1997-99. Fellow ACS, Am. Acad. Ophthalmology, Am. Soc. Ophthalmic Plastic and Reconstructive Surgeons, Am. Soc. Oculofacial Plactics Reconstrn.; mem. N.Am. Soc. Neuro-Ophthalmology, Assn. Rsch. in Vision and Ophthalmology, Orbital Soc., Pa. Med. Soc. (alt. del.), Orbital Soc., Rotary Internat., Alpha Omega Alpha. Avocations: running, writing, tennis, gardening, cooking. Office: Allegheny Ophthalmic & Orbital Assocs 320 E North Ave Ste 116 Pittsburgh PA 15212-4756

COCKERHAM, LORRIS G. radiation toxicologist; b. Denham Springs, La., Sept. 27, 1935; s. Warren Conrad and Leda Frances (Scivicque) C.; m. Patricia Ann Stagg, Aug. 16, 1957; children: Michael B., Richard L., Ann E., Joseph D. BA, La. Coll., 1957; MS, Colo. State U., 1973, PhD, 1979. Diplomate Am. Bd. Forensic Examiners. Commd. 2d lt. USAF, 1961, advanced through grades to lt. col., 1977, instr., 1963-66, squadron electronic warfare officer Fairchild AFB, Wash., 1966-71, asst. prof. dept. chemistry and biology USAF Acad., 1973-77, wing electronic warfare officer, 1977-78, comdr. 416 Munitions Maintenance Squadron, 1978-80; Armed Forces Radiobiology Rsch. Inst., Def. Nuc. Agy., Bethesda, Md., 1980-86; Air Force Office of Sci. Rsch., Bolling AFB, D.C., 1986-87; ret., 1987; exec. dir. NCTR-Associated Univs., Little Rock, 1988-89; pres. The Delta Agy., Little Rock, 1989-93, Phenix Cons. and Svcs. Ltd., Little Rock, 1993—. Dir. Product Safety Labs., East Brunswick, N.J., 1994-95; dir. Toxicol. SITEK Rsch. Labs., Rockville, Md., 1997-99; asst. prof. physiology Sch. Medicine, Uniformed Svcs. U. Health Scis., 1981-87; assoc. prof. U. Ark. for Med. Scis., 1988-89. Troop com. chmn. Iroquois coun. Boy Scouts Am., 1978-80. Decorated D.F.C. (2), Airman's medal, Air medal (12), Air Force Commendation medal, Joint Svc. Achievement medal; Air Force Logistics Command Dioxin Rsch. grantee, 1974-79; recipient Order of Arrow, Boy Scouts Am.; named Disting. Alumnus La. Coll., 1989. Mem. Soc. Neurosci., Internat. Brain Rsch. Orgn., World Fedn. Neuroscientists, Soc. Toxicology, Am. Physiol. Soc., Am. Coll. Toxicology, Sigma Xi, Phi Kappa Phi. Republican. Baptist. E-mail: phenixLtd@aol.com.

CODE, ARTHUR DODD, astrophysics educator; b. Bklyn., Aug. 13, 1923; 4 children. MS, U. Chgo., 1947, PhD, 1950. Asst. Yerkes Obs. U. Chgo., 1946-49; instr. U. Va., Charlottesville, 1950; instr. then asst. prof. astronomy U. Wis., Madison, 1951-56, prof., 1969-92, prof. emeritus, 1992—; mem. staff Mt. Wilson and Palomar Obs. Calif. Inst. Tech., Pasadena, 1956-58, prof., 1958-69; adj. prof. U. Ariz., Tucson, 1992—. Hilldale prof., dir. Space Astronomy Lab. U. Wis. Recipient Disting. Pub. Svc. medal and Pub. Svc. award NASA, Profl. Achievement award U. Chgo. Mem. NAS, Am. Acad. Arts and Scis., Internat. Acad. Astronautics, Assn. of Univs. for Rsch. in Astronomy (chmn. bd. dirs. 1977-80.), Am. Astonomical Soc. (pres. 1982-84). Office: U Wis Madison WI 53714

CODY, FRANK JOSEPH, secondary school educator; b. Detroit, Sept. 13, 1940; s. Burns J. and Margaret (Dowley) C.; m. Shirley Black, May 16, 1992. AB, Loyola U., 1962, PhD, 1965, MA, 1966, MDiv, 1975; PhD, Ohio State U., 1980. Cert. tchr., prin., supr., Ohio, Mich. Headmaster St. Ignatius H.S., Cleve., 1977-81; dir. Chapel Sch., Sao Paulo, Brazil, 1981-83, U. Detroit Ctr. Econ. Edn., 1988-91; assoc. prof., tchr. adminstrv. edn. U. Detroit, 1983-91; adminstr. Grand Rapids Cath. Secondary Schs., 1991-95; headmaster Woodside Priory Sch., Portola Valley, Calif., 1995-97; tchr. Kalamazoo Ctrl. H.S., 1997—, asst. prin., 1998-99; dir. Small Learning Cmtys. Project, 2002—. Trustee Wheeling Coll., 1980-82, mem. Coun. Entrance Svcs. Coll. Bd., 1978-81; mem. Mich. Supt.'s Com. on Accreditation, 1984-88; commr. Nat. Assn. Secondary Sch. Prins./Carnegie Found. Commn. on Future of Am. H.S., 1994-96; dir. rsch. English lang. studies Unified Coll. Guarulhos, Sao Paulo, Brazil, 1998-2002. Co-author: Manual of Educational Risk Management, Escola e Communidade: Uma Parceria Necessaria, O Professor Do Terceiro Milenio; contbr. articles to profl. jours. Trustee Trinity Sch., Menlo Park, Calif., 1996-97; commr. planning commission City of Kalamazoo, 2003—. Mem.: Am. Classical League. Roman Catholic. Office: Kalamazoo Ctrl High Sch 2432 N Drake Rd Kalamazoo MI 49006-1361 E-mail: codyfj@kalamazoo.k12.mi.us.

COE, ELIZABETH ANN, retired elementary education educator; b. El Paso, Tex., Feb. 25, 1944; d. Charles William Murray and Jeanne (Roman) Moore; children: Christopher E. Sanchez, Christine Angela Sanchez. BS in Edn., N.Mex. State U., 1968; postgrad., U. N.Mex., 1987-88; MA in Edn., N.Mex. State U., 1992, MA in Ednl. Diagnostics, 1998; postgrad., East N.Mex. U., 1970-95, U. Phoenix, 1995, Ctr. for Bilingual Multicultural Studies, Cuernavaca, Mex., 1995. Cert. elem. educator, lang. arts. educator Kindergarten thru grade 12, social studies educator Kindergarten thru grade 12, N.Mex. Tchr. Hatch (N.Mex.) Schs., 1968-70, Ruidoso (N.Mex.) Mcpl. Schs., 1970-84; real estate agt., 1978-88; tchr. Tularosa (N.Mex.) Schs., 1988—. Workshop leader Region IX, Ruidoso, 1989, 90; rep. Project L.E.A.D., U. N.Mex., Albuquerque, 1991, N.Mex. State BA Restructuring Conf., Albuquerque, 1990, Mesilla Valley Regional Coun. on Bilingual Edn., 1968-70; co-chair Internat. Reading Assn. Young Authors Conf., Tularosa, 1990-91; cons. N.Mex. State Writing Project, 1993; mem. task force on writing and portfolio assessment N.Mex. State Dept. Edn., 1993—; mem. com. for ednl. plan for student success, Tularosa Mcpl. Schs., mem. bilingual planning com., 1996—. Author: (short story) Los Desesperados, 1989 (1st prize Tri-State award), Tortillitas Quemaditas, 1991 (Honorable Mention). Mem. N.Mex. State Dept. Edn. Task Force on Writing. Mem. NEA, LWV, Phi Kappa Phi. Avocations: studying, brain hemisphericity and learning styles, spanish, creative writing. Home: 800 Hull Rd Ruidoso NM 88345-7717

COE, MICHAEL DOUGLAS, anthropologist, educator; b. N.Y.C., May 14, 1929; s. William Rogers and Clover (Simonton) C.; m. Sophie Dobzhansky, June 5, 1955; children: Nicholas, Andrew, Sarah, Peter, Natalie. AB, Harvard, 1950, PhD, 1959. Asst. prof. U. Tenn., 1958-60; mem. faculty Yale U., 1960—, prof. anthropology, 1968-90, Charles J. MacCurdy prof. anthropology, 1990-94, prof. emeritus, 1994—. Adviser Robert Woods Bliss Collection Pre-Columbian Art, Dumbarton Oaks, Harvard, 1963-80. Author: La Victoria, An Early Site on the Pacific Coast of Guatemala, 1961, Mexico, 1962, The Jaguar's Children: Pre-Classic Art of Central Mexico, 1965, The Maya, 1966, (with Kent V. Flannery) Early Cultures and Human Ecology in South Coastal Guatemala, 1967, America's First Civilization, 1968, The Maya Scribe and His World, 1973, Classic Maya Pottery at Dumbarton Oaks, 1975, Lords of the Underworld, 1978, (with Richard A. Diehl) In the Land of the Olmec, 1980, Young Lords and Old Gods, 1982, (with Dean R. Snow and Elizabeth P. Benson) Atlas of Ancient America, 1986, Breaking the Maya Code, 1992, (with Sophie D. Coe) The True History of Chocolate, 1996, (with Justin Kerr) The Art of the Maya Scribe, 1998, (with Mark Van Stone) Reading the Maya Glyphs, 2001, Angkor and the Khmer Civilization, 2003; contbr. articles to profl. jours. Chmn. bd. Planting Fields Found., 1985— ; pres. Heath Hist. Soc., Mass., 1984-90. Fellow Royal Anthrop. Soc.; mem. NAS, Am. Anthrop. Assn., Conn. Acad. Arts and Scis., Conn. Acad. Scis. and Engring., Limestone Trout Club, The Anglers Club of N.Y., Sigma Xi. Home: 376 St Ronan St New Haven CT 06511-2251 E-mail: olmecC@aol.com.

COELHO, SANDRA SIGNORELLI, secondary school educator, consultant; b. Torrington, Conn., Oct. 19, 1940; d. Ernest J. and Linda M. (Zanolli) Signorelli; m. Walter S. Coelho, July 11, 1964. BS, Cen. Conn. State U., 1962, MS, 1969, postgrad; Intermediate Administration Certification, Cen. Conn. State, 1980- 6th year certificate. Tchr. Torrington Bd. Edn., 1962-65; K-12 tech./math. coord. East Windsor (Conn.) Bd. Edn., 1965—2002; cons. Enfield Town Hall, 2002, Conn. Acad., 2003—, PIMMS, 2003—. Mem. assistive tech. task force State of Conn.; presenter C.A.B.E.;cons. Town of Enfield, Conn. Acad. Chmn. townwide curriculum com. East Windsor; mem. twp. com. Conn. Dept. Edn.; chmn. East Windsor Tech. Com. Recipient Golden Apple award; BEST Mentor-Assessor; Apple Computer scholar; PIMMS fellow. Mem. NEA, Conn. Edn. Assn., Conn. Educators Computing Assn. (adviser), East Windsor Edn. Assn. (past pres.), ATOMIC (sec. exec. bd., past chmn. ann. meeting), Pi Lambda Theta, Phi Delta Kappa (exec. bd.), Delta Kappa Gamma (past v.p. Rho chpt.) Home and Office: 50 Smalley Rd Windsor Locks CT 06096-1134

COFER, SUZANNE MARIE, secondary school educator; b. Wenatchee, Wash., Oct. 29, 1948; d. Earl Raymond Anthony and Wanda Elaine (Haworth) Desilet; m. Donald Frank Cofer, Aug. 30, 1975. BA in English Edn., Wash. State U., 1971; MPA, U. Wash., 1986; postgrad., Western Wash. U., 2002—. Cert. elem. and secondary educator. Tchr. Horsham (Australia) High Sch., 1972-74, Blaine (Wash.) High Sch., 1974-77, Fife (Wash.) High Sch., 1977-78; part-time faculty, program mgr. Pierce Coll., Tacoma, 1978-80; adminstrv. asst. Wash. State Ho. of Reps., Olympia, 1981-84; rsch. analyst Wash State Ho. of Reps., Olympia, 1987-89; coun. mem. City of Tumwater, Wash., 1990-94; tchr. New Century High Sch., Lacey, Wash., 1992—98, Mt. View Elem. Sch., Lacey, 1998—. Del. Dem. Nat. Conv., San Francisco, 1984; chair Pub. Safety Com. City of Tumwater, 1991-92. Wash. Edn. Leadership Intern grantee, 2003—. Mem. Wash. State Hist. Soc., Nat. Trust for Hist. Preservation. Democrat. Avocations: cooking, reading biographies, traveling. Office: 1900 College St SE Lacey WA 98503

COFFEE, GALE FURMAN, musician, educator; b. Oneonta, N.Y., Oct. 20, 1939; d. Delmar Robert and Charlotte Carolyn (Holloway) F.; m. Curtis Webb, June 13, 1961 (div. 1994); children: Nathan Robert, Ellen Jean Coffee Blickhan. MusB, Eastman Sch. of Music, 1961; MusM, Boston U., 1963. Flutist Am. Wind Symphony, Pitts., 1960, 62; piccolo player, 2d flute Spokane (Wash.) Symphony, 1970—; pers. mgr., 1989—; acting prin. flutist, 1990. Adj. instr. Whitworth Coll., Spokane, 1973-93, Gonzaga U., Spokane, 1984-90, Ea. Wash. U., Cheney, 1996—. Mem. Nat. Flute Assn. Home: 1616 E 19th Ave Spokane WA 99203-3716

COFFEY, DONNA HOSKINS, middle school educator; b. Danville, Ky., July 15, 1949; d. James Lish and Evelyn (Allen) Hoskins; m. Donald Stephen Coffey, June 1, 1968; 1 child, James Stephen. BA, U. Ky., 1970; MA, Ea. Ky. U., 1976. Tchr. Hardin County Bd. Edn., Vine Grove, Ky., 1970-72, Boyle County Bd. Edn., Danville, 1972-799; tchr. lang. arts Lincoln County Bd. Edn., Hustonville, Ky., 1970, 1979—2000; ret., 2000; writing cluster leader Hustonville Elem. Sch., Hustonville, Ky., 2002—03, accelerated reading cons., 2000—01; substitute tchr. Lincoln County Sch. Bd., 2001—02, writing cons., 2002—03. Children's dir. Hustonville Bapt. Ch., 1980—. Avocations: gardening, interior decorating. Home: US Hwy 127 S Hustonville KY 40437-9526 Office: Hustonville Sch 93 College St Hustonville KY 40437-9505

COFFEY, KIMBERLY E. secondary school educator; b. Morristown, N.J., Apr. 26, 1973; d. Jeffrey J. and Edith M. Morelock; m. Robert G. Coffey. BA in Math., Hartwick Coll., Oneonta, N.Y., 1995; MA in Math. Edn., Columbia U., 1997; postgrad., N.Y. Inst. Tech. Cert. permanent cert. in secondary math. N.Y. Tchr. math. Clarkstown Ctrl. Sch. Dist., New City, NY, 1997—. Pvt. tutor math., 1997—; curriculum devel. com. Felix Festa Mid. Sch., West Nyack, NY, 1997—. Mem.: Assn. of Math. Tchrs. of N.Y. State (Mem. Scholarship award 1998—), Nat. Coun. Tchrs. Math., Kappa Delta Pi. Office: Felix festa Mid Sch 30 Parot Rd West Nyack NY 10994

COFFEY, MARGARET TOBIN, education educator, county official; b. Binghamton, N.Y., Mar. 30, 1940; d. Henry L. and Mary Margaret (Keenan) Tobin; m. Joseph M. Coffey, Aug. 20, 1968; children: Timothy, Erin, David, Tobin. BA, Manhatten Coll. Sacred Heart, 1962; Cert. Edn., SUNY, Cortland, 1967. Cert. tchr., N.Y. Tchr. Binghamton Sch., 1963-69; early childhood coord. Broome Community Coll., Binghamton, 1971-72; staff caseworker U.S. Rep. Matthew F. McHugh, Washington and Binghamton, 1974-79; dir. Bur. of Census, Binghamton, 1979-80; tchr. adult edn. PROBE Local CBO, Binghamton, 1980-81; tchr. Binghamton City Sch. Dist., 1981-86, coord. VEA, 1986-90, prog. mgr. BCSD adult edn. programs, 1990—. Bd. dirs. Inner City Nursery Sch., Local Devel. Corp., Binghamton; bd. pres. Broome County Coun. Alcoholism, 1986-90; del. N.Y. Dem. Com., Albany, 1970-74; legislator Broome County, 1982—; mem. Children Youth Svcs. Coun., Youth Bur. Bd. Mem. Am. Vocat. Assn., Adult Continuing Edn. Assn., Phi Delta Kappa. Roman Catholic. Home: 30 Davis St Binghamton NY 13905-4318 Office: Binghamton City Sch Dist Columbus Sch Cite PO Box 2126 Binghamton NY 13902-2126

COFFEY, MARK WILLIAM, theoretical physicist, applied mathematician; b. Lincoln, Nebr., Oct. 24, 1957; s. William Davis and Patricia Avalon (Morgan) C. BS, U. Iowa, 1980; MPhil, PhD in Math., N.Y. U., 1983; PhD in Physics, Iowa State U., 1991. Math. instr. N.Y. U., 1980-82; sci. programmer IBM Corp., Palo Alto, Calif, 1983-85, engr., programmer Poughkeepsie, N.Y., 1985-88; rsch. asst. Iowa State U., Ames, 1989-91; NRC postdoctoral fellow Nat. Inst. Stds. and Tech., Boulder, Colo., 1992-94; applied math. instr. U. Colo., Boulder, 1994-95, vis. prof., 1995-97; physicist, sr. systems engr. Gen Dynamics Info. Sys., 1997; sr. scientist TRW, 1998—. Lectr. U. Colo. physics dept., Boulder, 1992-2001; rsch prof physics, Colorado Sch Mines, 2001; vis. prof. Ecole Normale Superieure, Paris, 1994. Contbr. over 80 articles to profl. jours. Recipient Sanxay prize, Davies Meml. Physics award; U. Iowa Honors Found. scholar. Mem. Am. Phys. Soc., Am. Math. Soc., Math. Assn. Am., Soc. Indsl. and Applied Math., Phi Beta Kappa, Sigma Xi, Phi Kappa Phi, Phi Eta Sigma. Achievements include rsch. of electrodynamic and thermodynamic properties of type II superconductors, static and dynamic properties of vortices, forward and inverse problems in magnetic force microscopy, symmetries and exact solutions of nonlinear partial differential equations and cell discretization algorithm for the numerical solution of partial differential equations. Office: Colo Sch of Mines Dept Physics Cb 390 Golden CO 80401-0001 E-mail: mcoffey@stripe.colorado.edu.

COFFIN, BONNIE BREANNE, home economist, educator; b. Pampa, Tex., July 21, 1948; d. Boniface Frank and Francis Louise (Schulze) Rapstine; m. Alan Glen, Jan. 30, 1976; children: Joshua Buck and Mollie Breanne. BS in Home Econs., Texas Tech. Univ., 1971. Cert. tchr. Tex., Fla., child care trainer. Home econs. tchr. Ysletta Sch. Dist., El Paso, Tex., 1971-75; nutrition cons. Dairy Coun. Inc., Amarillo, Tex., 1975-81; appliance demonstrator Amana/Tersco Inc., Amarillo, Tex., 1980-83; instr. Fla. C.C., Jacksonville, 1985-93; nutrition cons. Arlington Head Start, Jacksonville, 1987-89; pre-sch. tchr. Parkwood Bapt. Ch., 1988-89; food demonstrator Henderson Hughey, Atlanta, Ga., 1988-91; substitute & community sch. tchr. Duval County Schs., Jacksonville, 1985-92; home econs. tchr., adult & high sch. Saint Augustine (Fla.) Tech. Ctr., 1989-93; home econs. tchr., middle & high sch. Duval County Sch. Bd., Jacksonville, 1991—. Sponsor Future Homemakers of Am., El Paso, Tex., 1971-75, Jacksonville, 1991, Drug Free/No Compromise Club, 1992—. Author: Housing & Home Furnishings, 1991. Mem., officer PTA, 1982-93, mem. Basket Weavers Guild, 1985-90. Mem. Am. Home Econ. Assn., Am. Vocat. Assn., Fla. Home Econ. Assn., Home Econs. in Bus. (treas., chair 1975-80). Democrat. Methodist. Avocations: crafts, basket weaving, hiking, boating, skiing. Home: 2249 Ivylgail Dr W Jacksonville FL 32225-2042 Office: Paxton High Sch 3239 W 5th St Jacksonville FL 32254-1766

COFFIN, CHARLSA LEE, director, writer, artist; b. Dallas, Nov. 23, 1940; d. Charles Thomas and Zena Madora (Hall) Gaskin; m. Dwight Clay Coffin, June 23, 1964 (div. 1980); 1 child, John Charles. BA, Lawrence U., Appleton, Wis., 1962; postgrad., U. Pitts., 1962-64; Am. Montessori Soc. cert., Rosary Coll., Chgo., 1964. Cert. primary tchr., Am. Montessori Soc., 1984. Asst. to dean of women U. Pitts., 1962-64; directress The Parkside Montessori Sch., Upper Montclair, N.J., 1967—; collaborator (with Dr.

James J. Strain) on chem. imbalance Mt. Sinai Hosp., N.Y.C., 1980—. Author: The State of Focus, 1992, 250 Poems and 250 Songs for Newborn to 8-year old Children, 1993, A Christmas Book: Thoughts of Mother to Son with 2-year old Child, 1996; one-woman show Montclair Libr., 1991. Home: The Rockcliff 10 Crestmont Rd Montclair NJ 07042-1930

COFFMAN, JAY DENTON, physician, educator; b. Quincy, Mass., Nov. 17, 1928; s. Frank David and Etta (Kline) C.; m. Louise G. Peters, June 29, 1955; children: Geoffrey J., Joanne K., Linda J., Robert B. AB, Harvard U., 1950; MD, Boston U., 1954. Diplomate Am. Bd. Internal Medicine. Med. intern Univ. Hosp., Boston, 1954-55, asst. resident in medicine, 1955-56, chief resident in medicine, 1957-58, fellow in cardiovascular disease, 1956-57, sect. head peripheral vascular dept., 1960—; asso. in medicine Boston U. Med. Sch., 1960-65, mem. faculty, 1965—, prof. medicine, 1970—. Author: Raynaud's Phenomenon, 1989; co-author: Ischemic Limbs, 1973, Peripheral Arterial Disease, 2002. Trustee Solomon Carter Fuller Mental Health Center, Boston, 1975-81. Served to capt. M.C. USAR, 1958-60. Mem. ACP, Am. Soc. Clin. Investigation, Am. Fedn. Clin. Rsch., Am. Heart Assn., Begg's Soc., Phi Beta Kappa, Alpha Omega Alpha. Office: 88 E Newton St Boston MA 02118-2308

COFFMAN, (ANNA) LOUISE M. retired elementary education educator; b. Turlock, Calif., Aug. 11, 1924; d. Christopher Ezekial and Annie Laurie (Curtice) Mann; m. Dean Wilton Coffman, Feb. 10, 1945; children: Dane Wilbur, Nancy J. Coffman Hildreth, Janet L. Coffman Dempsey. AA, Modesto Jr. Coll., 1944; BS, Millersville State U., 1961; MEd, Western Md. Coll., 1966. Elem. tchr. Laird Sch. Stanislaus County, Modesto, Calif., 1944-45; tchr. 4th grade Cen. Sch. Dist., York, Pa., 1957-66; tchr. 3d grade Spring Grove (Pa.) Sch. Dist., 1966-84, ret., 1984. Tchr. Grace Acad. Christian Discipleship, York, 1985—; free-lance writer, 1979—; columnist "Notes From the Country," York Sunday News, 1977-88. Author: Abner's Story, 2000, Abner's Escape, 2003. Vol. Bell Shelter, York, 1985—, Access-Shelter for Abused Women, York, 1985—, Women's Rescue Mission Shelter, 1999—; tchr. rep. ARC, York, 1966-84; v.p. women's fellowship St. Paul's-Wolf's United Ch. of Christ, York, 1990-92, pres., 1997-98, editor newsletter, 1985-98, mem. consistory; del. Pa. Ctrl. Conf., 1995, 97-99; mem. United Ch. of Christ Mission and Outreach Com., 1986—, St. Paul's Wolf's United Ch. of Christ, York, 1980. Mem. AAUW (sec. Invest-Hers group 1994-95, write stuff group 1997—, pres. 1998-99), Women in Comm., Inc., Delta Kappa Gamma (Eta chpt., parliamentarian 1987-89, 2d v.p. 1990-92). Republican. Avocations: travel, cooking creatively, writing, local charity work. Home: 3897 Barachel Dr York PA 17402-4403

COFFMAN, TERRENCE J. academic administrator; b. 1945; m. Wallis Coffman. Student, Corcoran Coll. Art and Design, Washington, Lacoste Sch. Arts. Dean then pres. Md. Coll. Art and Design, Silver Spring, 1973—83; pres. Milw. Inst. Art & Design, 1983—. Instr. Smithsonian Instn., Washington. Author: A Walk Through the Wheatfields: The Missing Journals of Vincent van Gogh. Recipient Milw.'s Frank Kirkpatrick award, 2001. Avocation: playing acoustic guitar. Office: Milw Inst Art & Design 273 E Erie St Milwaukee WI 53202-6003*

COGBURN, ALTON O. special education administrator; b. Dublin, Tex., Feb. 1, 1948; s. Alton Ernest and Sarah (Thompson) C.; m. Mary Jan Nelson, Dec. 20, 1969; children: James A., Jonathan N. BS, Abilene Christian, 1972; MEd, Sul Ross, 1977. Cert. provisional high sch. health and phys. edn., provisional high sch. biology, provisional all-level health and phys. edn., provisional all-level lang. and/or learning disabilities, profl. all-level supr., profl. all-level mid-mgmt. adminstr. Tchr., coach Trent (Tex.) Ind. Sch. Dist., 1972-74; tchr. spl. project Sweetwater (Tex.) Ind. Sch. Dist., 1974-75; tchr., coach Sands Ind. Sch. Dist., Ackerly, Tex., 1975-76; spl. edn. tchr. Sweetwater (Tex.) Ind. Sch. Dist., 1976-78, ednl. diagnostician, 1978-80, supr., diagnostician, 1980-86, dir. spl. edn., 1986-93, dir. spl. projects, 1991-93. Developer, dir. Fourteen Pilot/Grant Projects, Sweetwater, Abilene, 1986-93; loan officer Sweetwater (Tex.) Tchrs. Fed. Credit Union, 1986-92; adj. prof. Hardin Simmons U., Abilene, 1988, Abilene (Tex.) Christian U., 1989; com. mem. Regional Alternative Cert. Planning, Abilene, 1990, Regional Screening Alternative Candidates, Abilene, 1991-92; Regional Tech-Prep Adv. Com., Abilene, 1991-92, vice-chmn., 1991-93, Regional Task Force on Emotional Disturbed, Abilene, 1992—; presenter in field. Author: Alternative Curriculum, 1982, 84. Dir. All for One project (citation Directory Partnership Programs, Resources and Couns. 1992); chmn. Mental Health Regional Mgmt. Team, 1993 (Abilene Christian Disting. Alumni citation 1993). Recipient Senate Resolution for PEP Pride award Senate Tex., Austin, 1992. Mem. Am. Vocat. Assn., Tex. Vocat. Tech. Assn., Tex. Coun. Adminstrs. Spl. Edn., Registered Profl. Diagnosticians. Mem. Church of Christ. Avocations: hunting, fishing, grant writing. Home: 113 Neeley Rd Hewitt TX 76643-3754 Office: WCTEC 207 Musgrove St Sweetwater TX 79556-5321 Address: 113 Neeley Rd Hewitt TX 76643-3754

COHEN, ALBERT, musician, educator; b. N.Y.C., Nov. 16, 1929; s. Sol A. and Dora Cohen; m. Betty Joan (Berg), Aug. 28, 1952; children: Eva Denise, Stefan Berg. BS, Juilliard Sch. Music, 1951; MA, NYU, 1953, PhD (hon.), 1959; postgrad., U. Paris, 1956-57. Mem. faculty U. Mich., Ann Arbor, 1960-70, assoc. prof. music, 1964-67, prof., 1967-70; prof. music, chmn. dept. SUNY, Buffalo, 1970-73, Stanford U., 1973-87, William H. Bonsall prof. music, 1974—, prof. emeritus, 2000—. Editor: Broude Bros. Ltd., N.Y.C., Info. Coordinators, Detroit. Author: Treatise on the Composition of Music, 1962, Elements or Principles of Music, 1965; (with J.D. White) Anthology of Music for Analysis, 1965; (with L.E. Miller) Music in the Paris Academy of Sciences, 1666-1793, An Index, 1979, Music in the French Royal Academy of Sciences, 1981, Music in the Royal Society of London 1660-1806, 1987; editor: J.B. Lully, Ballet de Flore, 2001; contbr. articles to profl. jours. Guggenheim fellow, 1968-69; NEH fellow, 1975-76, 82-83, 85-89 Mem. Internat. Musical Soc., Am. Musical Soc., French Musical Soc., Music Libr. Assn. Office: Stanford U Dept Music Stanford CA 94305

COHEN, ANDREW DAVID, language educator, applied linguist; b. Washington, Mar. 14, 1944; s. Harold Jack and Rena (Alpert) C.; m. Sabina Rose Alpert, Mar. 31, 1968; children: Judy Naomi, Daniel Moshe. BA, Harvard U., 1965; MA, Stanford U., 1971, PhD, 1973. Teaching fellow Stanford (Calif.) U., 1970-72; asst. prof. UCLA, 1972-75; assoc. prof. Hebrew U., Jerusalem, 1975-91; prof. ESL U. Minn., Mpls., 1991—. Dir. Ctr. for Applied Linguistics Rsch., Hebrew U., 1981-91, sr. lectr., 1975-79; coord. English lang. placement UCLA, 1972-75; Fulbright lectr., rschr. Cath. Pontifical U., São Paulo, Brazil, 1986-87; dir. Nat. Lang. Resource Ctr., Mpls., 1993—, Inst. Linguistics and Asian and Slavic Langs. and Lits., 1993-2000, Inst. of Linguistics, ESL and Slavic Langs. and Lits., 2000—; Disting. lectr. Temple U., Japan, 1988, scholar of the coll. Coll. Liberal arts, U. Minn., 2002—. Author: A Sociolinguistic Approach to Bilingual Education, 1975, Describing Bilingual Education Classrooms, 1980, Language Learning, 1990, Assessing Language Ability in the Classroom, 1994, Strategies in Learning and Using a Second Language, 1998; co-editor Interfaces Between Second Language Acquisition and Language Testing Research, 1998. Rural cmty. devel. vol. Peace Corps., Bolivia, 1965-67. Sgt. U.S. Army, 1968-74. Mem. Studies in Second Lang. Acquisition (editl. bd. 1985-95), Am. Assn. for Applied LInguistics (sec.-treas. 1993—), Minn. TESOL, Am. Coun. on Tchg. Fgn. Langs., Tchrs. English Fgn. Lang. (rsch. award com.), Internat. Assn. of Applied Linguistics (sec. gen. 1996-2002). Democrat. Jewish. Avocations: squash, music, trumpet, language learning. Office: Univ Minn 315 Pillsbury Dr SE 331 E Nolte Ctr Minneapolis MN 55455 E-mail: adcohen@umn.edu.

COHEN, ARTHUR M. education educator; b. Caldwell, N.J., June 14, 1927; s. Harry Cohen and Rae Berke; m. Florence Brawer. BA, U. Miami, 1949, MA, 1955; PhD, Fla. State U., 1964. Prof. higher edn. UCLA, 1964—. Author: The American Community College, 2003. Avocation: tournament bridge. Office: U Calif 405 Hilgard Ave Los Angeles CA 90095-9000

COHEN, BRIAN JEFFREY, internist, nephrologist, educator; b. N.Y.C., July 29, 1953; s. Franklyn Woodrow and Dee Miriam (Green) C.; m. Lynn Murphy. AB, Harvard U., 1974; MD, U. N.C., 1978; SM in Pub. Health, Harvard U., 1991. Diplomate Am. Bd. Internal Medicine, Am. Bd. Nephrology. Resident in internal medicine U. N.C., 1978-81; postdoctoral fellow dept. physiology Sch. of Medicine Yale U., 1981-83; clin. fellow renal unit Mass. Gen. Hosp., 1983-84; instr. medicine Harvard U. Med. Sch., Boston, 1984-90; staff physician Beth Israel Hosp., Boston, 1984-88, New Eng. Deaconess Hosp., Boston, 1988-90; fellow Div. Clin. Decision-Making New England Med. Ctr., Boston, 1991-93; asst. prof. medicine Tufts U. Sch. Medicine, 1993—. Contbr. articles to med. jours. NIH grantee, 1984-87. Mem. Soc. for Med. Decision Making. Avocation: playing trumpet. Office: New England Med Ctr Box 398 750 Washington St Boston MA 02111-1526 E-mail: bcohen1@tufts-nemc.org.

COHEN, CAROLYN ALTA, health educator; b. Boston, Aug. 25, 1943; d. Haskell Mark and Sarah (Siegal) Cohen. BS, Boston U., 1965; postgrad., Boston State Coll., U. Mass., 1978, Boston Leadership Acad., 1989, Boston Leadership Inst., 1997. Health and phys. edn. tchr., coach, girls athletic coord. Roslindale H.S., Boston, 1965—76; health and phys. edn. tchr., coach, athletic coord. West Roxbury H.S., Boston, 1976—87; asst. dir. health phys. edn. athletics Madison Park Campus, Boston, 1979—87; health educator dept. phys. edn./athletics West Roxbury H.S., Boston, 1989—90, 1990—, lead tchr., 1995—2000; commr. girls' basketball Boston Pub. Schs., 1979—. Cheerleading judge various orgns., 1963, 64, 65, 70, 74, 80, 69-74; coach recreational programs N.E. Deaconess Hosp. Sch. Nursing, 1962-64, Beth Israel Hosp. Sch. Nursing, 1961-64; basketball ofcl. Bay State League, Pvt. Sch. League, Cath. H.S., 1961-80; coach phys. edn. dept. Boston U., 1962-65, 65-68; ofcl. Boston Park and Recreation Dept., 1962-75, summer playgrounds instr., 1961-65; instr. garening, athletic specialist agr. dept. Boston Schs., 1965-76. Trustee Adaptic Environ. Ctr., Boston, 1986—, treas., mem. exec. bd., 1990—; trustee Friends of Boston Harbor Islands, Inc.; instr. ARC, 1965—; rep. Office Children-Area IV, Roslindale, Boston, 1974—76; liaison West Roxbury H.S. and Cmty. Sch. New Move Unltd. Theatre, Boston, 1981—84; liaison spl. arts project West Roxbury H.S., 1993—94. Named to Boston U. Scarlet Key Soc., 1998, N.E. New Agenda Hall of Fame, 2003; recipient Spl. Citation, Boston U. Sargent Coll. Alumni Assn., 1980, Cert. of Appreciation, ARC Mass. Bay, 1986, New Agenda award, Boston Salute to Women in Sport, 1993, Disting. Svc. to Alma Mater award, Boston U., 1994, Citation, Mass. Celebration Women in Sports Day, 2002, citation, Mil. Order of World Wars, 2002, Youth Patriotic & Leadership, 2002. Mem.: Sargent Coll. Alumni Assn. (class sec., editor class newsletter 1965—, Spl. Citation 1980, Black Gold award 1995), Boston U. Nat. Alumni Coun., Boston U. Alumni Assn. (v.p. 1980—82, 1987—89, v.p. cmty. 1995—97, sec. 1997—), Mass. Assn. Health, Phys. Edn., Recreation and Dance (state and exec. com. 1969—74, treas. 1981—94, coord. registration ann. state conv. 1975—94, Honor award recognition 1978, Presdl. Citation 1988, Joseph McKenney award 2002), AAHPERD (bud. mgr. nat. conv. 1988—89), Boston U. Women's Grad. Club (v.p. for scholarship 1981—83, 1985—). Home: 100 Corey St West Roxbury MA 02132-2330

COHEN, DAVID HARRIS, neurobiology educator, university official; b. Springfield, Mass., Aug. 26, 1938; s. Nathan Edward and Sylvia (Golden) C.; m. Arline Wyler, June 17, 1960 (div. Aug. 1980); children: Bonnie, Daniel, Ian; m. Anne Helena Remmes, Jan. 17, 1981; 1 child, Kaitlin BA, Harvard U., 1960; PhD, U. Calif., Berkeley, 1963. Postdoctoral fellow UCLA, 1963—64; asst. prof. physiology Western Res. U., Cleve., 1964—68; assoc. prof. to prof. physiology U. Va. Med. Sch., Charlottesville, 1968—79; prof., chmn. neurobiology SUNY, Stony Brook, 1979—86; v.p. rsch., dean grad. sch. Northwestern U., Evanston, Ill., 1986—91, provost, 1992—95, prof. neurobiology and physiology, 1986—95; v.p. arts and scis., dean of faculty Columbia U., N.Y.C., 1995—2003, prof. biol. scis. and psychiatry, 1995—. Mem. adv. com. directorate biol., behavioral and social scis. NSF, 1982-89; mem. life scis. rsch. adv. bd. Air Force Office Sci. Rsch., 1985-91; mem. bd. govs. Argonne Nat. Lab., 1986-92; bd. dirs. Rsch. Librs. Group, 1993-97, 2001—, Zenith Electronics, Inc., 1990-95, Columbia U. Press, 1996—, Thuris Corp., 2000—, Trevor Day Sch., 2000—. Mem. various edit. bds. profl. jours.; contbr. articles to profl. jours. Bd. overseers Fermi Nat. Accelerator Lab., Batavia, Ill., 1987-94; exec. com. Ill. Gov.'s Sci. Adv. Com., 1989-95; mem. Liaison Com. Med Edn., 1987-89; bd. dirs. N.Y. Structural Biology Ctr., 1999-2003. Mem. Soc. Neurosci. (pres. 1981-82), Pavlovian Soc. (pres. 1978-79), Assn. Neurosci. Depts. and Programs (pres. 1981-82), Nat. Soc. Med. Rsch. (v.p. 1984-85), Nat. Assn. Biomed. Rsch. (bd. dirs. 1985-87), Coun. Acad. Socs. (adminstrv. bd. 1982-87, chmn. 1985-86), Assn. Am. Med. Colls. (exec. coun. 1984-91, chmn. 1989-90), Internat. Brain Rsch. Orgn. (cen. coun. 1978-82). Jewish. Home: 445 Riverside Dr Apt 72 New York NY 10027-6801 Office: Columbia Univ 669 Schermerhorn Ext Mail Code 8545 New York NY 10027

COHEN, DAVID K. education educator; BA in hist. polit. sci., Alfred U., 1956; PhD in European intellectual his., U. Rochester, 1961. Asst. prof. Case Western Reserve U., 1961—66; cons. to gen counsel NAACP, 1964—66; cons. United Presbyn. Ch., United Ch. of Christ, 1964—65; dir. US Commn. on Civil Rights, 1966—67; vis. assoc. Joint Ctr. for Urban Studies, Mass. Inst. Tech., Harvard U., 1967—68; assoc. fellow Metro. Applied Rsch. Ctr., NYC, 1968—70; lectr. to sr. rsch assoc. to assoc. prof. to prof. Harvard Grad. Sch. Edn., 1968—86; pres. Huron Inst., Cambridge, Mass., 1971—86; vis. prof. Yale U., 1976—77; vis. prof. to dist. prof. to interim dean Mich. State U., 1984—91; prof. edn. U. Mich., 1993—. Contbr. articles various profl. jours. Mem.: Nat. Acad. Edn., Math. Scis. Edn. Bd, Nat. Rsch. Coun., Nat. Acad. Scis., Coun. Behavorial Social Sci. Office: U Mich Sch Edn 610 E U Ann Arbor MI 48109-1259 also: 10815 Boyce Rd Chelsea MI 48118 E-mail: dkcohen@umich.edu.

COHEN, DAVID WALTER, academic administrator, periodontist, educator; b. Phila., Dec. 15, 1926; s. Abram and Goldie (Schlein) C.; m. Betty Axelrod, Dec. 19, 1948 (dec. Mar. 1992); children: Jane Ellen, Amy Sue, Joanne Louise. DDS, U. Pa., 1950; DSc (hon.), Boston U., 1975; PhD (hon.), Hebrew U., Jerusalem, 1977, U. Athens, 1979; Dr Honoris Causa, U. Louis Pasteur, Strasbourg, France, 1986; DHL (hon.), U. Detroit, 1989. Diplomate: Am. Bd. Periodontology (chmn. 1972). Research fellow pathology and periodontia Beth Israel Hosp., Boston, 1950-51; mem. faculty U. Pa. Sch. Dentistry, Phila., 1951—, prof. periodontics, 1962-86, chmn. dept., 1962-73; dean Sch. Dental Medicine U. Pa., Phila., 1972-83; dean emeritus U. Pa. Sch. Dentistry, Phila., 1983—; pres. Med. Coll. Pa., 1986-93; chancellor Allegheny U. of Health Scis., 1993-98, chancellor emeritus, 1998—; mem. staff Albert Einstein Med. Center, Phila., Children's Hosp., Phila.; pres. Jewish Publ. Soc., 1993-96. Vis. prof. Boston U. Sch. Grad Dentistry, 1972—; nat. cons. periodontics USAF, 1965-70; bd. govs. Hebrew U., Jerusalem, Betty and Walter Cohen chair in periodontal rsch., 1986; D. Walter Cohen endowed chair in periodontics U. Pa., 1995. Author: (with H.M. Goldman) Periodontia, 1957, (with others) An Introduction to Periodontia, 1959, Periodontal Therapy, 1960, (with R. Genco and Goldman) Contemporary Periodontics, 1990, (with Genco, L. Rose and B. Mealey) Periodental Medicine, 1999; also numerous articles and chpts. V.p. Jewish Publ. Soc., 1985-89, pres., 1993-96; pres. Nat. Mus. Am. Jewish History, Phila., 1996—. Served with USN, 1944-45. Named to Ctrl. H.S. Hall of Fame, 1976; 1st Presdl. scholar U. Calif., San Francisco, 1985-86; named for him Hebrew U. Betty and D. Walter Cohen Chair in Periodontal Rsch., 1986, U. Pa. D. Walter Cohen Endowed Chair in Periodontics, 1995; D. Walter Cohen Mid. East Ctr. for Dental Edn. dedicated by Hebrew U. of Jerusalem, 1997. Fellow AAAS, Am. Acad. Oral Pathology, Am. Acad. Periodontology, Inst. of Medicine of Nat. Acad. Scis.; mem. Am. Soc. Periodontists (pres. 1967), Friends of Nat. Inst. Dental Rsch. (pres. 1998—). Office: Med Coll Pa 3300 Henry Ave Philadelphia PA 19129-1191

COHEN, DIANA LOUISE, psychology, educator, psychotherapist, consultant; b. Phila., Apr. 8, 1942; d. Nathan and Dorothy (Rubin) Blasberg; 1 child, Jennifer. BA, Temple U., 1964, MEd, 1969, PhD, 1996. Lic. psychologist, Pa., N.J.; lic. profl. counselor, N.J.; cert. mental health counselor. Caseworker Phila. Gen. Hosp., 1964-69, staff psychologist, 1969-70, Atlantic Mental Health Ctr., McKee City, N.J., 1970-80, unit dir., 1980-87, v.p. profl. svcs., 1987-91; pvt. practice Pa., N.J., 1991—. Adj. faculty Glassboro (N.J.) State Coll., 1988—; cmty. and family mediator Cmty. Justice Inst., Atlantic County, N.J., 1990—. Com. chmn. Atlantic County Commn. for Missing and Abused Children, 1984—89; co-project dir. Employee Assistance Program, 1994—. Grantee N.J. Dept. Edn., 1988-89, N.J. Job Tng. Partnership Act, 1990. Mem. APA (assoc.), N.J. Counseling Assn., N.J. Mental Health Counselors Assn. (pres.-elect 1996, pres. 1997), South Shore Region Mental Health Counselors Assn. (sec. 1994-97). Avocations: painting, tennis, cross-country skiing. Home: 2 Dee Dr Linwood NJ 08221-1910 Office: 2106 New Rd Ste E1 Linwood NJ 08221-1052

COHEN, ELIZABETH G. education and sociology educator, researcher; b. Worcester, Mass., May 1, 1931; d. Jacob and Anita (Asher) Ginsburg; m. Bernard P. Cohen, Sept. 20, 1953; children: Anita Cohen Williams, Lewis Samuel. BA, Clark U., Worcester, 1953; MA, Harvard U., 1955, PhD, 1958. Lectr. sociology Boston U., 1957-58; lectr. sociology and edu. Stanford U., 1962-66, asst. prof., 1966-69, assoc. prof., 1969-75, prof., 1975—99, dir. Environ. for Teaching, 1970-76, chmn. social sci. in edu., 1970-93, dir. program for complex instruction, 1982—99, prof. emeritus, 1999—. Author: A New Approach to Applied Research, 1968, Designing Groupwork: Strategies for Heterogeneous Classrooms, 2d edit., 1994; contbr. chpts. in books and articles in field to profl. jours. Trustee Clark U., 1986-03. Woodrow Wilson fellow, 1954-55; AAUW fellow, 1956-57; Fulbright fellow, 1972 Mem. Pacific Sociol. Assn. (v.p. 1981-82), Sociology of Edn. Assn. (v.p. 1982-83), Am. Sociol. Assn. (sect. chmn. 1979-80), Am. Ednl. Research Assn., Sociol. Research Assn. Democrat. Jewish. Home: 851 Sonoma Ter Palo Alto CA 94305-1024 Office: Stanford Univ Sch Of Edn Stanford CA 94305

COHEN, HARVEY JAY, physician, educator; b. Bklyn., Oct. 21, 1940; s. Joseph and Anne (Margolin) C.; m. Sandra Helen Levine, June 1964; children: Ian Mitchell, Pamela Robin. BS, Bklyn. Coll., 1961; MD, Downstate Med. Coll., Bklyn., 1965. Diplomate Am. Bd. Internal Medicine, Am. Bd. Hematology. Intern, then resident internal medicine Duke U. Med. Ctr., Durham, N.C., 1965-67, fellow hematology and oncology, 1969-71; chief hematology-oncology VA Med. Ctr., Durham, N.C., 1975-76, chief med. service, 1976-82, assoc. chief of staff-edn., 1982-84, now dir. geriatric research, edn. and clin. ctr.; assoc. prof. medicine Duke U. Med. Ctr., Durham, 1976-80, now prof. medicine, chief geriatric divsn., also dir. Ctr. for Study of Aging, interim chair dept. medicine, 2002—03. Chair bd. sci. counselors Nat. Inst. Aging, 1999—2003. Author: Medical Immunology, 1977; co-author: (with H.G. Koenig) The Link Between Religion and Health: Psychoneuroimmunology and the Faith Factor, 2002, Taking Care After 50, 2000; editor: Cancer I and II, 1987, Jour. Gerontology: Med. Scis., 1988-92, Geriatric Medicine, 1997; contbr. numerous articles to profl. jours. Served as surgeon USPHS, 1967-69. Fellow ACP, Am. Geriatrics Soc. (bd. dirs. 1987-96, chair bd. dirs. 1995-96, sec. 1991-93, ethics com. 1992-96, pres. 1994-95), Gerontology Soc. Am. (clin. sec., rsch. com. 1987-92, chair publs. com. 1996-98, program chair 1994, pres. 2000); mem. Am. Soc. Clin. Oncology, Am. Soc. Hematology, Am. Assn. Cancer Rsch. (cancer and acute leukemia group B, chair cancer in the elderly com.), Assn. Am. Physicians, bd. dirs. Intl. Soc. Geri. Oncology Home: 2811 Friendship Cir Durham NC 27705-5521 Office: Duke U Med Ctr for Study Aging & Human Devel Box 3003 Durham NC 27710-0001

COHEN, JEFFREY ALLEN, neurologist, educator; b. July 3, 1951; BA with honors, Tulane U., 1973; MD, U. Okla., 1977; MS, U. Denver, 1993. Diplomate Am. Bd. Psychiatry and Neurology, Am. Bd. Clin. Neurophysiology. Intern in internal medicine Mt. Sinai Hosp., N.Y.C., 1977—78, resident, chief resident neurology, 1978—81; fellow neurology Mass. Gen. Hosp., Boston, 1981—82, Mayo Clinic, Rochester, Minn., 1985—86; asst. prof. Mt. Sinai Sch. Medicine, N.Y.C., 1982—85; assoc. prof. U. Colo. Sch. Medicine, Denver, 1986—91, clin. prof., 1991—2000; assoc. prof. Dartmouth Med. Sch., Lebanon, NH, 2000—02, assoc. chief neurology, 2000—. Recipient Svc. award, Am. Diabetes Assn., 1996; scholar, Tuland U., 1970—73. Fellow: ACP, Am. Bd. Electrodiagnostic Medicine, Am. Acad. Neurology. Office: Dartmouth-Hitchcock Clinic 1 Medical Center Lebanon NH 03756 E-mail: Jeffrey.A.Cohen@Dartmouth.edu.

COHEN, JUDITH W. academic administrator; b. N.Y.C., May 14, 1937; d. Meyer F. and Edith Beatrice (Elman) Wiles; BA, Bklyn. Coll., 1957, MA, 1960; cert. advanced studies Hofstra U., 1978; MA Columbia U., 1986, postgrad. 1986—. m. Joseph Cohen, Oct. 19, 1957; children: Amy Beth (dec.), Lisa Carrie, Adam Scott Frank, Elyssa Lily. Tchr. N.Y.C. Pub. Schs., Bklyn., 1957-60; tchr. Mid. Country Sch. Dist., Centereach, N.Y., 1970-93, retired 1993; prof. psychology 5 Towns Coll., Dix Hills, N.Y., 1994—. prof. edn. Dowling Coll., Oakdale, N.Y., Title IX compliance officer, 1980-86, team leader 1987-91; dir. Long Island U. Summer Adventure Program, 1994—. Bus. adv. Women's Equal Rights Congress, Suffolk County Human Rights; chmn. bd. edn., Temple Beth David, trustee, 1975-79; pres. CHUMS, 1979-82; Tchr. of Gifted Post-L.I. U. Saturday Program, 1985—; L.I. Writing Project fellow, Dowling Coll., 1979— ; cert. sch. dist. adminstr., supr., adminstr., N.Y. State; adj. prof. Five Towns Coll., 1994—; adj. prof. edn. Dowling Coll., Oakdale, N.Y., 1997—. Mem. Nassau Suffolk Coun. Adminstrv. Women in Edn. (prds. 1979-81), Assn. for Supervision and Curriculum Devel., Assn. Gifted/Talented Edn., Women's Equal Rights Congress Com. (exec. bd.), Suffolk County Coordinating Council Gifted and Talented, Phi Delta Kappa, Delta Kappa Pi. Author: Arts in Education Curriculum in Social Studies and Language Arts, 1981. Home: 35 Gaymor Ln Commack NY 11725-1305

COHEN, JULES, physician, educator, former academic dean; b. Bklyn., Aug. 26, 1931; s. Samuel S. and Dora (Goldstein) C.; m. Doris Eidlin, Mar. 25, 1956; children: Stephen E., David E., Sharon E. AB, U. Rochester, 1953, MD, 1957. Intern Beth Israel Hosp., Boston, 1957-58; resident, fellow in medicine U. Rochester (N.Y.) Strong Meml. Hosp., 1958-60, mem. faculty, 1963—, prof. medicine, 1973—; NIH research asso. Bethesda, Md., 1960-62; research fellow Postgrad. Med. Sch., London, 1962-63; physician in chief Rochester Gen. Hosp., 1976-82; sr. asso. dean med. edn. U. Rochester Sch. Medicine, 1982-97. USPHS research grantee, 1963-69; USPHS research grantee, 74-77; recipient USPHS Research Career Devel. award, 1970-75; Am. Heart Assn. grantee-in-aid, 1969-71 Fellow ACP, Am. Coll. Cardiology; mem. Am. Physiol. Soc., Am. Heart Assn. (fellow coun. on clin. cardiology), Monroe County Med. Soc., N.Y. State Med. Soc., Rochester Acad. Medicine. Jewish. Home: 152 Burkedale Cres Rochester NY 14625-1704 Office: U Rochester Sch Medicine and Dentistry 601 Elmwood Ave Rochester NY 14642-0001 E-mail: Jules_Cohen@urmc.rochester.edu.

COHEN, LAWRENCE BARUCH, neurobiologist, educator; b. Indpls., June 18, 1939; s. Gabriel Murel and Helen (Aronovitz) C.; children: Daniel, Avrum; m. Barbara Ellen Ehrlich; 1 child, Lily Rachel. BS, U. Chgo., 1961;

PhD, Columbia U., 1965. Asst. prof. Yale U., New Haven, 1968-71, assoc. prof., 1971-79, prof. physiology, 1979—. Recipient Elizabeth R. Cole award, Biophys. Soc., 1987, McMaster Award, Columbia U., 1965; named Dist. Lectr., Am. Physiol. Soc., 1998. Office: Yale U Sch Medicine 333 Cedar St New Haven CT 06510-3289 E-mail: lawrence.cohen@yale.edu.

COHEN, LOUIS, medical educator, cardiologist, inventor; b. Chgo., Dec. 5, 1928; s. Harry and Ruth C.; m. Emili Chappie, Mar. 15, 1952; children: Curt, Ruth, Fredric. BS, U. Chgo., 1948, MD with honors, 1953. Diplomate Am. Bd. Internal Medicine. Prof. medicine U. Chgo., 1975—, prof. human nutrition, 1979—. Cons. attending physician cardiology, 1961—; vis. prof. various univs. and hosps., 1968-84; panelist Nat. Acad. Scis., 1980; pres. Med. Inventions Inc., Chgo., 1987—. Author: (with R.J. Jones) The Chemistry of Cardiovascular Diseases, 1964; reviewer sci. and med. jours.; contbr. rsch. articles to profl. jours. on atherogenesis, lipoproteins, enzymes, muscular dystrophy, arrhymogenesis, drug mechanisms and sudden death. Mem. governing bd. Am Heart Assn. of Met. Chgo., 1980—, pres.-elect, 1991, pres. 1992-93; fund raiser Jewish United Fund, 1970—. Lt. commdr. USNR, 1955-57. Am. Heart Assn. rsch. fellow, 1958-62; recipient U.S. Presdl. citation Pres. John F. Kennedy, 1962, Meritorious Svc. award Chgo. Heart Assn., 1973, 90. Fellow ACP, Am. Coll. Cardiology, Am. Coll. Clin. Pharmacology, Am. Heart Assn., Coun. on Arteriosclerosis and Coun. on Clin. Cardiology; mem. Am. Soc. Pharmacology and Exptl. Therapeutics, Ctrl. Soc. for Clin. Rsch., Internat. Soc. for Heart Rsch., Ctrl. Clin. Rsch. Club (pres. 1980-82), Sigma Xi. Jewish. Achievements include patent for intravenous flow regulator and scar reduction. Home: 400 E Randolph St Apt 2603 Chicago IL 60601-5039 Office: U Chgo MC2087 5841 S Maryland Ave Chicago IL 60637-1463

COHEN, LUISA FAYE, primary education educator; b. Pitts., Jan. 2, 1952; d. Emanuel and Mollie (Wise) Bucaresky; m. Howard I. Cohen, July 1, 1979; children: David and Eden (twins). BS with highest honors, Pa. State U., 1973, MS magna cum laude, 1976. Kindergarten tchr. Chartiers Valley Sch. Dist., Pitts., 1973—; realtor FFV Realty Inc., Mt. Lebanon, Pa. Mem. Am. Fedn. Tchrs., Pa. Edn. Assn., Pa. Assn. Supervision and Curriculum Devel., Chartiers Valley Edn. Assn., Early Childhood Educators, Phi Delta Kappa, Chi Omega. Jewish. Home: 1601 Hollow Tree Dr Pittsburgh PA 15241-2960 Office: FFV Realty Inc 1695 Mcfarland Rd Pittsburgh PA 15216-1810

COHEN, MALCOLM STUART, economist, business executive; b. Mpls., Jan. 17, 1942; s. Jack Alvin and Lorraine Ethel (Hill) C.; m. Judith Ann Arenson, Sept. 25, 1965; children: Laura, Randall, Ilona. BA in Econs. summa cum laude, U. Minn., 1963; PhD in Econs., MIT, 1967. Labor economist U.S. Bur. Labor Stats., Washington, 1967-68; lectr. U. Md., Coll. Pk., 1968; asst. to v.p. state rels. and planning U. Mich., Ann Arbor, Mich., 1968-70, various tchr. positions, 1968-85; co-rsch. dir. U. Mich. Inst. of Labor and Indsl. Rels., Ann Arbor, Mich., 1973-80, dir., 1980-93; cons. Corp. Pub. Broadcasting, 1994-97; lectr. indsl. rels. ctr. U. Minn., 1994-96; pres. Employment Rsch. Corp., Ann Arbor, Mich., 1997—. Cons. U.S. Dept. Labor, 1995-2001, EEOC, 1996—, Mich. Senate Fiscal Agy., Lansing, 1988; project dir. various projects Washington, 1968-92; expert witness discrimination and econs. various clients, 1982—. Co-author: A Micro Model of Labor Supply, 1970; contbr. articles to profl. jour.; author: Labor Shortages: As Am. Approaches the 21st Century, 1995; co-author: Global Skill Shortages, 2002. Mem. Nat. Assn. Forensic Economists, Indsl. Rels. Rsch. Assn., Internat. Indsl. Rels. Assn., N.Am. Econ. and Fin. Assn. Avocations: jogging, geneology. Office: Employment Rsch Corp Ste 250 3820 Packard Rd Ann Arbor MI 48108-3348 E-mail: malco@umich.edu.

COHEN, MARIE CAROL, elementary education educator; b. Passaic, N.J., Dec. 24, 1935; d. Salvatore Peter and Marie Camille (DiPietro) Tuzzeo; m. Victor David Cohen; children: Lawrence, Lori, Wendy. BA, William Paterson U., 1960; MS, L.I. U., 1971. Cert. student personnel svcs. 1992. Tchr. elem. Dept. Edn. N.J., Trenton, 1964—. Purchaser antiques ABC Antiques, Garfield, N.J., 1960—. Exhibited in group shows at William Paterson Coll., Wayne, N.J., 1959-60, L.I. Univ., N.Y., 1970-71, Las Vegas Pub. Libr., 1976-77, L.D.S. Ch., Caldwell, N.J., 1985, L.D.S. Ch., Franklin Lakes, N.J., 1986, Louis Bey Libr., Hawthorne, N.J., 1996, one-person exhibit at Half Hollow Hills Libr., Dix Hills, N.Y., 1972-73. Mem. LWV, AAUW (facilitator arts and crafts shows 1992-94), Alumni Assn. William Paterson U., Alumni Assn. L.I. U., Ocean County Art Guild, The Educators Club, Crafters and Artisans Club (pres. Ocean County chpt., faciliator semi-annual show, 2002-03, art show participant), Renaissance Cmty. Democrat. Avocations: opera, classical music, folk dancing, piano, crafts. Home: 4 Drayton Rd Manchester NJ 08759-6052

COHEN, MARSHALL HARRIS, astronomer, educator; b. Manchester, N.H., July 5, 1926; s. Solomon and Mollie Lee (Epstein) C.; m. Shirley Kekst, Sept. 19, 1948; children: Thelma, Linda, Sara. BEE, Ohio State U., 1948, MS, 1949, PhD, 1952. Rsch. assoc. Ohio State U., Columbus, 1950-54; asst. prof. elec. engring. Cornell U., Ithaca, N.Y., 1954-58, assoc. prof., 1958-63, assoc. prof. astronomy, 1963-66; prof. applied electrophysics U. Calif., San Diego, 1966-68; prof. radio astronomy Calif. Inst. Tech., Pasadena, 1968-90, prof. astronomy, 1990-96, exec. officer for astronomy, 1981-84, prof. emeritus, 1996. Prof. associé U. Paris VI, 1989; mem. numerous coms. NSF, NRC, vis. coms. various obs. in U.S., Fed. Republic Germany. Contbr. articles, book revs. to profl. jours.; patentee radio astronomy. With U.S. Army, 1943-46. Co-recipient Rumford medal Am. Acad. Arts and Scis., 1971; Guggenheim Found. fellow Paris Obs., 1960-61, MIT/Inst. Astronomy, Cambridge, Eng., 1980-81; Morrison fellow Lick Obs., 1988. Fellow AAAS; mem. NAS (chmn. sect. astronomy 1989-92), Am. Astron. Soc. (publ. bd. 1980-83), Astron. Soc. Pacific (bd. dirs. 1969-72), Am. Acad. Arts and Scis., Internat. Union for Sci. Radio (chmn. commn. V of U.S. nat. com. 1970-73), Internat. Astron. Union (U.S. nat. com. 1989-92). Avocation: mountain hiking. Office: Calif Inst Tech Dept Astronomy Pasadena CA 91125-0001

COHEN, MARVIN LOU, physics educator; b. Montreal, Que., Can., Mar. 3, 1935; came to U.S., 1947, naturalized, 1953; s. Elmo and Molly (Zaritsky) C.; m. Merrill L. Gardner, Aug. 31, 1958 (dec. Apr. 1994); children: Mark, Susan; m. Suzy R. Locke, Sept. 8, 1996. AB, U. Calif., 1957; MS, U. Chgo., 1958, PhD, 1964. Mem. tech. staff Bell Telephone Labs., Murray Hill, N.J., 1963-64; asst. prof. physics U. Calif., Berkeley, 1964-66, assoc. prof., 1966-69, prof. physics, 1969-95, univ. prof., 1995—, prof. Miller Inst. Basic Resch. in Sci., 1969-70, 76-77, 88, chmn., 1977-81, U. Calif. Faculty Rsch. lectr., 1997—. Chmn. Gordon Rsch. Conf. Chemistry and Physics of Solids, 1972; U.S. rep. to Semicondr. Commn., Internat. Union Pure and Applied Physics, 1975-81; Alfred P. Sloan fellow Cambridge U., Eng., 1965-67; vis. prof. Cambridge U., Eng., 1966, U. Paris, France, 1972-73, summers 68, 75, 87, 88, U. Hawaii, Honolulu, 1978-79, Technion, Haifa, Israel, 1987-88; chmn. planning com. Pure and Applied Sci. Inst. U. Hawaii, 1980—; mem. selection com. Presdl. Young Investigator Awards, 1983; mem. Com. on Nat. Synchrotron Radiation Facilities, 1983-84; chmn. 17th Internat. Conf. on Physics of Semicondrs., 1984; mem. exec. com. Govt.-Univ.-Industry Research Roundtable, 1984—; vice chmn. Govt.-U. Industry Research Roundtable Working Group on Sci. and Engring. Talent, 1984—; mem. rev. bd. for Ctr. for Advanced Materials Lawrence Berkeley Lab., 1986-87; mem. panel on Implications for Mechanisms of Support and Panel on High Temperature Superconductivity, NAS, NSF, 1987; mem. adv. bd. Tex. Ctr. for Superconductivity, 1988-90, vice chair, 1991—; mem. U.S. del. to Bilateral Dialog R&D in the U.S. and Japan, NRC, 1989; mem. sci. policy bd. Stanford Synchrotron Rad. Lab., 1990-92. Editorial bd. Perspectives in Condensed Matter Physics, 1987—; adv. bd. Internat. Jour. Modern Physics B., 1987—, Modern Physics Letters B, 1987—; assoc. editor Materials Sci. and Engring., 1987—; contbr. more than 600 articles to tech. jours. Mem. vis. com. Ginzton Lab., Stanford U., 1991; mem. sci. policy com. Stanford Linear Accelerator, 1993-95. Recipient Outstanding Accomplishment in Solid State Physics award U.S. Dept. Energy, 1981, Sustained Outstanding Rsch. in Solid State Physics award U.S. Dept. Energy, 1990, Cert.of Merit, Lawrence Berkeley Lab., 1991; A.P. Sloan fellow, 1965-67, Guggenheim fellow, 1978-79, 90-91. Fellow AAAS, Am. Phys. Soc. (exec. coun. divsn. solid state physics 1975-79, chmn. 1977-78, Oliver E. Buckley prize for solid state physics 1979, Buckley prize com. 1980-81, chmn. 1981, Julius Edgar Lilienfeld prize 1994, Lilienfeld prize com. 1994—, Isakson Prize com. 1995-98, chmn. 1999); mem. NAS (chmn. condensed matter physics search/screening com. 1981-82, 1988—, chmn. Comstock prize com. 1988, nominating com. for selection of pres., v.p., councilors 1992-93), Am. Acad. Arts and Scis., Nat. Acad. Scis. Home: 201 Estates Dr Piedmont CA 94611-3315 Office: U Calif Dept Physics Berkeley CA 94720-0001*

COHEN, RAYMOND, mechanical engineer, educator; b. St. Louis, Nov. 30, 1923; s. Benjamin and Leah (Lewis) C.; m. Katherine Elise Silverman, Feb. 1, 1948 (dec. May 1985); children— Richard Samuel, Deborah, Barbara Beth; m. Lila Lakin Cagen, Nov. 30, 1986. BS, Purdue U., 1947, MS, 1950, PhD, 1955. Instr. mech. engring. Purdue U., 1948-55, asst. prof., 1955-58, assoc. prof., 1958-60, prof., 1960-98, asst. dir. Ray W. Herrick Labs., 1970-71, dir., 1971-93, acting head Sch. Mech. Engring., 1988-89, Herrick prof. engring., 1994-99, Herrick prof. emeritus engring., 1999—. Cons. to industry. Departmental editor: Ency. Brit., 1957-62; editorial bd. Jour. Sound and Vibration, 1971-87; editor Internat. Jour. of Heating, Ventilating, Air Conditioning and Refrigerating Rsch., 1994-98. Served as sgt. inf. AUS, 1943-46. Recipient Kamerlingh Onnes gold medal, 1995; NATO sr. fellow in sci., 1971 Fellow ASME, ASHRAE; mem. NSPE, Am. Soc. Engring. Edn., Soc. Exptl. Mechanics, Internat. Inst. Refrigeration (chmn. U.S. nat. com. 1992-95, U.S. del. 1992-99), Acoustical Soc. Am., Inst. Noise Control Engring. (pres. 1990), Sigma Xi, Pi Tau Sigma, Tau Beta Pi. Home: 2501 Spyglass Dr Valparaiso IN 46383 Office: Purdue U Ray W Herrick Labs 140 S Intramural Dr West Lafayette IN 47907-2031

COHEN, ROBERT, language educator, writer; b. 1957; Tchr. Iowa Writer's Workshop, U. Houston, Harvard U.; assoc. prof. English Middlebury (Vt.) Coll., 1997—, tchr. Bread Loaf Writers' Conf. Author: The Organ Builder, The Here and Now, 1997, Inspired Sleep, short fiction published in GO, Harper's, Iowa Rev., The Paris Rev., Antaeus, (short stories) The Varieties of Romantic Experience. Recipient Pushcart prize, Editors' Choice: New American Stories, Lila Wallace-Reader's Digest Writers award; fellow, John Simon Guggenheim Meml. Found., 2003. Office: Middlebury Coll English Dept Munore Hall 111 Middlebury VT 05753

COHEN, ROBERT ALAN, agricultural administrator, educator; b. Akron, Ohio, May 7, 1953; s. Ralph and June Laverne (Peck) C.; m. Margaret Elaine Murphy, Dec. 7, 1973 (div. Oct. 1992); children: Benjamin, Daniel, Michael, Karen, Tamara; m. Paula Moyen Bardige, Mar. 19, 1993; children: Marissa, Leigh. BA, U. Akron, 1973; MA, Ohio State U., 1975, student, 1997; MBA, Franklin U., 2001. Cert. secondary tchr., Ohio. Program dir. Sta. WWWJ, Johnstown, Ohio, 1976-80; sales mgr. Sta. WZZT, Johnstown, 1980-83; tchr. Licking Heights Sch. Dist., Summit Station, Ohio, 1983-84; acad. dir. Park Coll., Columbus, Ohio, 1983-91; grad. teaching assoc. Ohio State U., Columbus, 1974-77, instr. dept. comm. Mansfield, 1986—; gen. mgr. Sta. WAPQ, Mansfield, 1990-93; instr. North Ctrl. Tech. Coll., Mansfield, Ohio, 1989-93; regional mgr. ACDI/VOCA (Vol. in Overseas Coop. Assistance), Columbus, 1993—; instr. Agrl. Tech. Inst., Wooster, Ohio, 1990—. Mem. planning com. Nat. Inst. on Coop. Edn., 1997, 2000. Author: Introduction to Cooperatives, 1993; co-author (screenplays) Lost But Not Forgotten, 1990, Dangerous Cartel, 1991. Recipient Thomas J. Evans Teaching Excellence award Ohio State U., Newark, 1988, Coop. Edn. award Yr. award Ohio Coun. Coops., 1994, Pa. Coun. Coops., 1999. Mem. NRA (life), Nat. Coop. Bus. Assn., Nat. Press Club, Coop. Communicators Assn., Assn. Coop. Educators, Ohio Ag Coun., Country Music Assn., Ohio LEAD Alumni Assn. (bd. dirs.). Office: 6161 Busch Blvd Ste 209 Columbus OH 43229-2554

COHEN, ROBERT JAY, biochemistry educator, researcher; b. Milw., May 31, 1942; s. Harry and Mildred C.; m. Carol Neal, Feb. 25, 1968; children: Benjamin, Jonathan, Deborah. BS, U. Wis., Milw., 1964; PhD, Yale U., 1969. Postdoctoral fellow Calif. Inst. Tech., Pasadena, 1969-71; asst. prof. biochemistry U. Fla. Coll. Medicine, Gainesville, 1971-76, assoc. prof. biochemistry and molecular biology, 1976—. Vis. prof. U. Freiburg, Fed. Republic Germany, 1980. Contbr. articles to over 50 sci. publs. Mem. Gainesville Hazardous Materials Com., 1981-87 (chmn. 1984-85). NSF grantee, 1988-92, Office of Naval Rsch., 1988-98. Mem. AAAS, Am. Chem. Soc., Biophys. Soc. Office: U Fla Coll Medicine Dept Biochemistry and Molecular Biology Gainesville FL 32610

COHEN, SAUL G. chemist, educator; b. Boston, May 10, 1916; s. Barnet M. and Ida (Levine) C.; m. Doris E. Brewer, Nov. 27, 1941 (dec. July 1971); children— Jonathan Brewer, Elisabeth Jane; m. Anneliese F. Kissinger, June 1, 1973. AB summa cum laude, Harvard U., 1937, MA, 1938, PhD, 1940; ScD, Brandeis U., 1986. Research fellow Harvard, 1939-40, 41-43, instr., 1940-41; NRC fellow, lectr. U. Calif. at Los Angeles, 1943-44; research chemist Pitts. Plate Glass Co., 1944-45, Polaroid Corp., 1945-50, cons., 1950—98; with Brandeis U., 1950—, prof. chemistry, 1952—, Univ. prof., 1974-86, prof. emeritus, 1986—, chmn. Sch. Sci., 1950-55, dean faculty, 1955-59, chmn. dept. chemistry, 1959-66, 68-72; vis. prof. Havard Med. Sch., 1965, Hebrew U., Jerusalem, 1972. Contbr. articles on reaction mechanisms, free radicals, photochemistry, enzymology to profl. jours. Bd. overseers Harvard U., 1983-89; mem. Joint Com. on Appointments, 1984-89. Fulbright sr. scholar, 1958-59; Guggenheim fellow, 1958-59; Centennial medalist Harvard Grad. Sch. Arts and Scis., 1992. Fellow Am. Acad. Arts and Scis. (council), AAAS; mem. Am. Soc. Biol. Chemists, Am. Chem. Soc. (James F. Norris award 1972, trustee Northeastern sect. 1976-84), Chem. Soc. London, AAUP, Fedn. Am. Scientists, Phi Beta Kappa, Sigma Xi. Achievements include patents in polymers, hyroxylamines as photographic developers, heterocyclic silver solvents, dyedevelopers, diagnostic assays. Home: 90 Commonwealth Ave Boston MA 02116-3040

COHEN, SHIRLEY, musician, educator; b. N.Y.C., Jan. 29, 1918; d. Abraham and Rose (Feldstein) Aronoff; m. Oscar J. Cohen; 1 child, Deborah Natalie Cohen Marcus. Student, NYU; studied piano, composition, harmony, with eminent musician-coaches, 1936-96. Authorized affiliate artist tchr. for SUNY (Purchase) candidates for Master's Degree in piano performance. Music dir. Raquette Lake Girls Club, 1936-38; music tchr. Woodward Sch., Bklyn., 1954-56; tchr. master classes, piano techniques, and interpretation IRPE Bklyn. Coll., Bklyn, 1985-96. Piano debut Steinway Hall, 1935. Recipient Silver medal for piano performance, theory and ear tng., 1934, dramatic arts radio performance WSGH, Bklyn., WLTH, Bklyn., WNYC, Manhattan, 1932-34. Mem. Music Tchrs. Nat. Assn., Bklyn. Music Tchrs. Guild.

COHEN, SHIRLEY MASON, educator, writer, civic worker; b. Jersey City, June 24, 1924; d. Herman and Esther (Vinik) Mason; m. Herbert Leonard Cohen, June 24, 1951; children: Bruce Mason, Annette Pauline, Carol Elyse, Debra Tamara. BA, Rutgers U., 1945; MA, Columbia U., 1946; postgrad., U. Calif., Berkeley, 1946-51. Instr. U. Calif., Berkeley, 1946-51, Am. River Coll., Sacramento, 1962; tchr. various H.S., Sacramento, 1975-92. Mentor tchr. Sacramento City Unified Sch. Dist., 1987-88. Author: Yearning to Breathe Free: The Story of the Vinik, Mason, and Gatkin Families, 1997. Bd. dirs. Sacramento Cmty. Concerts, 1965—. Mem. Phi Beta Kappa. Avocations: theatre, music, tennis, writing, literature.

COHEN, STANLEY NORMAN, geneticist, educator; b. Perth Amboy, N.J., Feb. 17, 1935; s. Bernard and Ida (Stolz) Cohen; m. Joanna Lucy Wolter, June 27, 1961; children: Anne, Geoffrey. BA, Rutgers U., 1956; MD, U. Pa., 1960, ScD (hon.), 1995, Rutgers U., 1994. Intern Mt. Sinai Hosp., N.Y.C., 1960-61; resident Univ. Hosp., Ann Arbor, Mich., 1961-62; clin. assoc. arthritis and rheumatism br. Nat. Inst. Arthritis and Metabolic Diseases, Bethesda, Md., 1962-64; sr. resident in medicine Duke U. Hosp., Durham, N.C., 1964-65; Am. Cancer Soc. postdoctoral rsch. fellow Albert Einstein Coll. Medicine, Bronx, 1965-67, asst. prof. devel. biology and cancer, 1967-68; mem. faculty Stanford (Calif.) U., 1968—, prof. medicine, 1975—, prof. genetics, 1977—, chmn. dept. genetics, 1978-86, K.-T Li Prof., 1993—. Mem. com. recombinant DNA molecules NAS-NRC, 1974; mem. com. on genetic experimentation Internat. Coun. Sci. Unions, 1977—96. Trustee U. Pa., 1997—2002. With USPHS, 1962—64. Named to Nat. Inventors Hall of Fame, 2001; recipient Burroughs Wellcome Scholar award, 1970, Mattia award, Roche Inst. Molecular Biology, 1977, Albert Lasker basic med. rsch. award, 1980, Wolf prize, 1981, Marvin J. Johnson award, 1981, Disting. Grad. award, U. Pa. Sch. Medicine, 1986, Disting. Svc. award, Miami Winter Symposium, 1986, Nat. Biotech award, 1989, de la Vie prize, LVMH Inst., 1988, Nat. Medal Sci., 1988, City of Medicine award, 1988, Nat. Medal of Tech., 1989, Spl. award, Am. Chem. Soc., 1999, Lemelson MIT Prize, MIT, 1996; fellow Guggenheim fellow, 1973; scholar faculty scholar, Josiah Macy, Jr., 1975—76. Fellow: AAAS; mem.: NAS (chmn. genetics sect. 1988—91), Inst. Medicine, Assn. Am. Physicians, Am. Soc. Clin. Investigation, Am. Soc. Pharmacology and Exptl. Therapeutics, Am. Soc. Microbiology (Cetus award 1988), Genetics Soc. Am., Am. Soc. Biol. Chemists, Am. Acad. Microbiology, Phi Beta Kappa, Sigma Xi, Alpha Omega Alpha. Office: Stanford U Sch Med Dept Genetics Rm M-322 Stanford CA 94305

COHEN, STEPHEN FRAND, political scientist, historian, educator, author, broadcaster; b. Indpls., Nov. 25, 1938; s. Marvin Stafford and Ruth (Frand) C.; m. Katrina vanden Heuvel; children: Andrew, Alexandra, Nicola. BS, Ind. U., 1960, MA, 1962; PhD, Columbia U., 1969; cert., Russian Inst., 1969. Instr. Columbia U., N.Y.C., 1965-68; asst. prof. politics Princeton (N.J.) U., N.J., 1968-73; assoc. prof. Princeton U., N.J., 1973-80, prof., 1980-98, prof. emeritus, 1998—, dir. Russian studies, 1973-80, 88-94; prof. Russian studies and History NYU, 1998—. Cons. on Russia, CBS news TV commentator, 1989—; corr., chief cons. PBS WNET films on Russia, 1994-2001; adv. coun. U.S. Acad. Scis., Washington, 1979-82. Author: Bukharin and the Bolshevik Revolution, 1973 (Nat. Book Award nominee 1974, Bukharin prize 1989), Rethinking the Soviet Experience, 1985, Sovieticus: American Perceptions and Soviet Realities, 1985 (Page One award 1985), Failed Crusade: America and the Tragedy of Post-Communist Russia, 2000, 2d edit., 2001; editor: (with Robert C. Tucker) The Great Purge Trial, 1965, (with Rabinowitch and Sharlet) The Soviet Union Since Stalin, 1980, An End to Silence, 1982, (with Katrina vanden Heuvel) Voices of Glasnost: Interviews with Gorbachev's Reformers, 1989; mem. editl. bd. Slavic Rev., 1977-82, Post-Soviet Affairs, 1992-2002; assoc. editor World Politics, 1972-88; columnist The Nation Mag., 1982-87; contbg. editor, 1994—. Bd. dirs. NYU Ctr. for the Media. Recipient Page One award Column Writing, 1985, Ind. U. Disting. Alumn award, 1998, Columbia U. Harriman Inst. Alumnus of Yr. award, 2002; fellow Am. Council Learned Socs., 1971, 72-73; fellow John Simon Guggenheim Found., 1976-77, 88-89, Rockefeller Found., 1980-81; NEH fellow, 1985-86; Fulbright-Hays fellow, 1988-89. Mem. Council Fgn. Relations, Am. Polit. Sci. Assn., Am. Hist. Assn., Am. Assn. for Advancement Slavic Studies. Home: 340 Riverside Dr Apt 8B New York NY 10025-3436

COHEN, SUZETTE FRANCINE, reading specialist; b. Cleve., June 23, 1943; m. Irwin J. Cohen, July 7, 1963 (dec.); children: Kathryn E. Fenton, Gregory M. BA, Cleve. State U., 1975; MEd, John Carroll U., 1979; PhD, Kent State U., 1986. Tchr. English Mayfield Bd. Edn., Mayfield Village, Ohio, 1975-78; tchr. reading South Euclid/Lyndhurst Bd. Edn., Lyndhurst, Ohio, 1978-79; reading specialist Cleve. State U., 1979—. Adj. faculty Ursuline Coll., Pepper Pike, Ohio, 1990, Notre Dame Coll., South Euclid, Ohio, 1994; lectr. John Carroll U., University Heights, Ohio, 1987; field reader dept. edn., Washington, 1992—; textbook reviewer Houghton Mifflin Co., Wadsworth Pub. Co., 1982—, Longman Publ.; seminar leader Adult Gt. Books Found., Chgo., 1990-91; ednl. cons. Ivy Tech. State Coll., Muncie, Ind. Rschr. Rags to Riches Investment Club, Highland Heights, 1993—; active Greater Cleve. PC Users Group, 1994—; leader Investors Spl. Interest Group. Mem. Nat. Investors Assn. (bd. dirs.), Signal Watchers Investment Club, Pi Lambda Theta (pres. Cleve. area chpt. 1988-90, nat. rsch. awards chair 1990-91, Exemplary Projects grantee 1989), Phi Delta Kappa (historian Cuyahoga Valley chpt. 1992-93, rsch. grantee, 1992). Avocation: computers. Home: 6339 Ashdale Rd Mayfield Heights OH 44124-4101 Office: Cleve State U E 2121 Euclid Ave Cleveland OH 44115 E-mail: s.cohen@csuohio.edu.

COHEN, WAYNE ROY, obstetrician-gynecologist, educator; b. N.Y.C., Apr. 27, 1946; s. Eugene Mark and Helene (Paul) C.; m. Marion Boardman, June 9, 1968 (div.); 1 child, Aaron Robert; m. Sharon Rose Ominski, Aug. 24, 1980; children: Daniel Paul, Giselle Rose. AB in Biology, U. Rochester, 1967; MD, Boston U., 1971. Diplomate Am. Bd. Ob-Gyn. Intern Mt. Auburn Hosp., Cambridge, Mass., 1971—72; resident Beth Israel Hosp., Boston, 1973-76; asst. prof. Harvard Med. Sch., Boston, 1976-82; assoc. prof. Albert Einstein Coll. Medicine, N.Y.C., 1983-92, prof., 1992-95; chmn. ob-gyn. Sinai Hosp. Balt., 1995—2000, Jamaica Hosp. Med. Ctr., NY, 2001—; prof. Cornell Med. Coll., 2002—. Editor: Management of Labor, 1983, 2d edit., 1989, Complications of Pregnancy, 2000; contbr. chpts. in books, articles to profl. jours. Mem. Soc. for Gynecologic Investigation, Soc. for Maternal-Fetal Medicine, Am. Fedn. for Clin. Rsch. Democrat. Jewish. Avocation: herpetology. Office: Jamaica Hosp Med Ctr Dept Ob-Gyn 89-06 135th St Ste 6A Jamaica NY 11418 E-mail: wcohen@jhmc.org, wcohen@jhmc.org.

COHEN, WILLIAM JOHN, city and regional planner, educator, photographer; b. Wilmington, Del., July 30, 1941; s. Edward Joseph and L. V. Dolores Cohen; children: Edward Joshua, Rebecca Anne. BA, U. Del., 1964, MA, 1976; M of City Planning, U. Pa., 1999, AM, 2002, PhD, 2003. Rsch. asst. Del. State Planning Office, Dover, 1967-69, sr. planner, 1969-71; dir. planning City of Newark, Del., 1971-77; prin. William J. Cohen and Assocs., Inc., Wilmington, 1977-90, W.J. Cohen Photography, Wilmington, 1985-96; exec. dir. govs. rivers task force Office of Sec. Dept. Natural Resources, Dover, Del., 1992-94, sr. resources planner Office of Sec., 1990-98; city and regional planning cons., 1998—; sr. policy advisor Del. Inst. for Pub. Adminstrn. Instr. in geography U. Del., 1978—2001, adj. instr. in geography, 2001—. Author or co-author over 90 profl. and tech. publs. Exec. dir. Cecil County Md. Arts Coun., 1988-90. Gov.'s Mgmt. fellow, 1993-94; Lewis Mumford scholar Grad. Dept. of City and Reg. Planning, U. Pa., 1996. Mem. Am. Inst. Cert. Planners (charter mem., pres. Del. chpt.1981-83), Del. Assn. for Pub. Adminstrn. (pres. 1976-78). Home and Office: 54 Crooked Rd Bar Harbor ME 04609-7407

COHN, AARON I. anesthesiologist, educator; b. L.A., Sept. 8, 1959; s. Alan Franklin and Louise Christine (Huff) C.; m. Nicola Ann Bernau, July 1984 (div. Aug. 1986). BS, U. Calif. Riverside, 1980; MA, Rice U., 1984; MD, U. Tex. Galveston, 1987. Diplomate Am. Bd. Anesthesiology. Med. intern Montefiore/Univ. Hosp., Pitts., 1987-88; postdoctoral fellow Ctr. for Med. Informatics, Yale U. Med. Sch., New Haven, 1988-90; resident in anesthesiology Yale-New Haven Hosp., New Haven, 1990-91, St. Elizabeth's Med. Ctr., Boston, 1991-93; asst. prof. dept. anesthesiology U. Tex. Med. Br., Galveston, 1993-96; anesthesiologist North Tex. Anesthesia, Dallas, 1996-97; asst. prof. dept. anesthesiology U. Okla., Oklahoma City, 1997-99, U. Colo., Denver, 1999—. Spl. study sect. mem. NIH, Rockville, Md., 1993—; reviewer Jour. Clin. Anesthesia, 1998-99. Contbr. articles to profl. jours. Mem. Internat. Anesthesia Rsch. Soc., Am. Soc. Anesthesiologists, N.Y. Acad. Scis. Republican. Jewish. Avocations: bicycling, pistol shooting, computers, scuba diving, underwater photography. Home: 939 Jersey St Denver CO 80220-4592 Office: U Colo Dept Anes CB B113 4200 E 9th Ave Denver CO 80262-0001 E-mail: aaron_cohn@cyberdude.com.

COHN, JAN KADETSKY, American literature and American studies educator; b. Cambridge, Mass., Aug. 9, 1933; d. Allan Robert and Beatrice (Goldberg) Kadetsky; m. Donald S. Solomon, Feb. 6, 1955 (div. 1968); children: Cathy Rebecca, David Seth; m. William Henry Cohn, Mar. 9, 1969. BA, Wellesley Coll., 1955; MA, U. Toledo, 1961; PhD, U. Mich., 1964. From instr. to asst. prof. U. Toledo, 1964-68; assoc. prof. U. Wis., Whitewater, 1968-70, Carnegie Mellon U., Pitts., 1970-79; prof., dept. chair George Mason U., Fairfax, Va., 1979-87; dean faculty Trinity Coll., Hartford, Conn., 1987-94, G. Keith Funston prof. Am. lit. and Am. studies, 1994—. Cons. in field. Author: The Palace or the Poorhouse, 1979, Improbable Fiction, 1980, Romance and the Erotics of Property, 1988, Creating America, 1989, The Saturday Evening Post (covers), 1995; editor: Henry James, The Portrait of a Lady, 2001. Bd. dirs. Nat. Bldg. Mus., Washington, 1987-91; trustee Norman Rockwell Mus., Sturbridge, Mass., 1997—; exec. bd. dirs. Conn. Pub. Broadcasting, Hartford, 1988-92. Fellow Am. Coun. Learned Socs., 1972, NEH, 1972-73. Mem. Modern Language Assn., Popular Culture Assn., Am. Culture Assn., Am. Studies Assn., Phi Kappa Phi. Democrat. Jewish. Office: Trinity Coll Dept English 300 Summit St Hartford CT 06106-3100

COHN, MARJORIE BENEDICT, curator, art historian, educator; b. N.Y.C., Jan. 10, 1939; d. Manson and Marjorie (Allen) Benedict; m. Martin Cohn, Dec. 19, 1960. BA, Mt. Holyoke Coll., 1960; AM, Radcliffe Coll., 1961; DFA, Mt. Holyoke Coll., 1996. Conservator works of art on paper Art Mus. Harvard U., Cambridge, Mass., 1963-89, lectr. fine arts, 1974-77, sr. lectr., 1977—, print curator, 1989—, acting dir., 1990-91, 2002—. Vis. lectr. Boston U., 1972, 73, Wellesley (Mass.) Coll., 1973; vis. asst. prof. Brown U., Providence, 1975. Author: Wash & Gouache, 1977, A Noble Collection: The Spencer Albums of Old Master Prints, 1992, (with S.L. Siegfried) Works by J.A.D. Ingres in Collection of the Fogg Art Museum, 1980, Francis Calley Gray and Art Collecting for America, 1986, Lois Orswell, David Smith and Modern Art, 2002. Sec. Arlington (Mass.) Hist. Commn., 1972-85. Mem. Am. Acad. Arts and Scis., Print Coun. Am. Democrat. Office: Harvard U Fogg Art Mus 32 Quincy St Cambridge MA 02138-3845 E-mail: cohn@fas.harvard.edu.

COHON, JARED L. academic administrator; m. Maureen Cohon; 1 child, Hallie. BA in Civil Engring., U. Pa., 1969; MA in Civil Engring., MIT, 1972, PhD in Civil Engring., 1973. Legis. asst. for energy and environment U.S. Senator Daniel P. Moynihan, 1997—98; from faculty to assoc. dean engring. to vice provost rsch. Johns Hopkins; prof. environ. systems analysis, dean Sch. Forestry and Environ. Studies Yale U., 1992—97; pres. Carnegie Mellon U., Pitts., 1997—; apptd. chmn. by Pres. Clinton Nuclear Waste Tech. Review Bd., 1997—2002. Recipient Joan Queneay Hodges award, Nat. Audubon Soc. and Am. Assn. Engring. Scis., Pareto-Edgeworth award, Multiple Criteria Decision Making Soc. Office: Carnegie Mellon Univ 5000 Forbes Ave Pittsburgh PA 15213-3890

COIL, CAROLYN CHANDLER, educational consultant; b. Washington, Aug. 22, 1943; d. William Chandler and Charlotte Eleanor (Lanhardt) Hendrix; m. Paul Douglas Coil; children: Paul William, Johnston Allan. BA, U. Md., 1965; MA, U. South Fla., 1985, MEd, 1990. Cert. gifted tchr., secondary tchr., ednl. leadership adminstr. Tchr. Prince Georges County Sch., Upper Marlboro, Md., 1965-71, Ledyard (Conn.) Pub. Schs., 1971-73; insvc. coord. Ednl. TV for S.E. Ohio, Athens, 1977-81; learning resources specialist Fla. Diagnostic and Learning Rsch., Bartow, 1981-92; ednl. cons. Creative Cons. and Tng., Lilburn, Ga., 1992—. Cons., author Pieces of Learning, Marion, Ill., 1991—. Author: Motivating Underachievers, 1992, Motivating Underachievers, rev. edit., 2000, Becoming An Achiever, 1994, Eye on Japan, 1995, Eye on Australia, 1995, Teaching Tools for the 21st Century, 1997, Teaching Tools for the 21st Century, rev. edit., 2000, Tools for Teaching & Learning in the Integrated Classroom, 1997, Hot Topics in Education, 1997, Celebrations, 1998, Encouraging Achievement, 1999, Teacher's Toolbox, 1999, Student Engagement: Raising Achievement for Student Success, 2000, Surviving the MiddleYears, 2001, Solving the Assessment Puzzle, 2001. Mem. exec. bd. New Beginnings for Youth, Orlando, Fla.; mem. cons. commn. Episcopal Diocese of Atlanta. Mem. Phi Delta Kappa, Phi Kappa Phi. Avocations: travel, reading. Home: 4141 Wash Lee Ct SW Lilburn GA 30047-7440 Office: Pieces of Learning 1990 Market Rd Marion IL 62959-8976 E-mail: carolyncoil@aol.com.

COKER, SALLY JO (BOZEMAN), sociology educator; b. Springfield, Ill., Aug. 24, 1956; d. Charles D. and Barbara J. (Bailey) Bozeman; m. Joel Dwain Coker, Nov. 7, 1974; 1 child, Corey Alan. BS, U. Houston, 1992, MA, 1995. Rsch. asst. to prof. psychology U. Houston, 1991; student asst. to dean adminstrn. Lee Coll., Baytown, Tex., 1992; instr. sociology, Am. minorities, social problems, marriage and family, San Jacinto C.C., Pasadena, Tex., 1995—; instr. sociology, Am. minorities, social problems, marriage and family Alvin (Tex.) C.C., 1995-97; instr. sociology, Am. minorities, social problems, orgnl. behavior Lee Coll., 1992—; instr. deviance, social inequality, prins. of sociology Am. minorities U. Houston, 1999—. Human resource mgmt. spkr. H.B. Zachry, Houston, 1995; tng. cons. H.B. Zachry Co., 1999; human resources cons. Mem. AAUP, Am. Sociol. Assn., Tex. C.C. Tchr.'s Assn., Phi Kappa Phi. Democrat. Home: 3607 Trailwood Dr Baytown TX 77521-4835 Office: U Houston Downtown One Main Houston TX 77002 E-mail: sallycoker@cs.com.

COKER, SYBIL JANE THOMAS, counseling administrator; b. Elizabeth, La., Aug. 16; d. Andrew J. and Lillye M. Thomas; m. Charles Mitchell Dolo Coker (dec. Apr. 13, 1983). AA, L.A. City Coll., 1952; BA, Calif. State U., L.A., 1955, Pepperdine U., 1957; MS, Mt. St. Mary's Coll., 1980. Tchr. Barton Hill Sch., 1957—58, 96th St. Sch., 1958—63; tng. tchr., reading specialist Hooper Ave. Sch., 1963—65; reading specialist dept. chair Vermont Ave. Sch., 1965—68; head start tchr. L.A. Urban League, 1966—68; tng. tchr. Hooper Ave. Sch., 1980—87; tng. tchr., tchr. of gifted clusters, grades 4,5,6 Angeles Mesa Sch., 1970—87; Eng. tchr., speech coach Horace Mann Jr. High Middle Sch., 1987—88, speech coach, 1988—90, bilingual coord./ESL, career, college and chap. 1 counselor, 1988—92, 8th grade counselor, career counselor, 1992—94, counselor 8th grade ctr., 1994; counselor David Starr Jordan H.S., L.A., 1995—. Pres., founder The Charles Dolo Coker Jazz Scholarship Found., Inc., L.A., 1983—; freelance wedding coord., cons., 1960—; freelance writer, 1983—; sponsor Motivating Our Students Through Experience, Horace Mann Jr. High Middle Sch., Young Black Profls., Horace Mann Jr. High Middle Sch., USC Med Core, UCLA Partnership, Horace Mann Hr. High Middle Sch. Contbr. columns in newspapers including Pitts. Courier Newspaper, ACC Ch. and Cmty. News, Celebrity Newspaper, L.A. Defender, Herald Dispatch, Watts Times, L.A. Entertainment Digest, CRS Mag., L.A. Gazette, 1950. Founder, dir. Second Baptist Ch. Drama Guild, 1957—67. Named Media Woman of Yr., 1977; recipient Unsung Heroine in Edn. award, Top Ladies of Distinction, 1992, Dist. Svc. award, 2nd Baptist Ch., 1991, Trailblazer award for outstanding contbns. in field of music, Delta Mothers and Sponsors Club, 2002. Mem.: NEA, PTA (life), NAACP (life; subscribing Golden Heritage mem., past bd. mem. L.A. br.), The Soc., Inc., Internat. Assn. Jazz Educators, Counselor's Assn., Black Women's Forum, L.A. Press Club, Soc. Profl. Journalists, Top Ladies of Distinction (L.A. chap., area VI, pub. rels. chair), Nat. Assn. Media Women (nat. recording sec., charter mem. Beverly Hills/Hollywood chap., past pres.), Pol. Action Com. of Educators, United Tchrs. of L.A., Nat. Coun. Negro Women (life), Santa Barbara Jazz Soc., L.A. Jazz Soc., Internat. Assn. Jazz Appreciation, Emanon Birthday and Social Club (charter mem., past pres.), New Frontier Dem. Club, Order of the Ea. Star, Phi Delta Kappa, Delta Sigma Theta (life; Century City alumnae chap., L.A. alumnae chap., Delta Choraliers). Democrat. Baptist. Avocations: creative writing, knitting, singing with the Delta Choraliers, studying piano. Home: 5336 Highlight Pl Los Angeles CA 90016 Office: Charles Dolo Coker Jazz Scholarship Fund 5336 Highlight Pl Los Angeles CA 90016

COLAGE, BEATRICE ELVIRA, education educator; b. Cleveland, Ohio, Aug. 13, 1958; BSEdn., Bowling Green State U., 1980; M of Curriculum, Cleveland State U., 1985. Spanish tchr. Cleveland (Ohio) City Schs., 1980—84, Mayfield (Ohio) City Schs., 1984—85, Solon (Ohio) City Schs., 1985—86, Orange (Ohio) City Schs., 1986—; adult edn. tchr. Mayfield (Ohio) City Schs. Lectr. Italian, Spanish and English. Author: book of 101 poems, 2003. Humanitarian and supporter of arts, civic, social and cultural instns. Mem.: NEA, Il Cenacolo Cleve., Ohio Fgn. Lang. Assoc., Ohio Edn. Assn., Am. Assn. Tchrs. of Spanish and Portuguese.

COLAGRECO, JAMES PATRICK, school superintendent; b. Cliffside Park, N.J., Sept. 12, 1929; s. Anthony Edward and Angelina (Giannantonio) C.; B.A., Muhlenberg Coll., 1953; M.A., Seton Hall U., 1959; postgrad. Montclair Coll., 1960-61, Seton Hall U., 1961-64, Columbia U., 1963-64; m. Gloria Padula, June 8, 1952; children— Janice, Jamie, Anthony, June. Tchr., Cliffside Park Public Schs., 1953—, coach football, basketball, baseball, high sch., 1953-60, prin. elem. and high schs., 1960-72, supt. schs., 1972— ; cons. Dept. Edn. on evaluation, 1971; hearing officer N.J. State Interscholastic Athletic Assn., 1981-82. Bd. dirs. E. Bergen Tchrs. Fed. Credit Union, 1981— ; mem. Cliffside Pk. Library Bd., 1972— ; mem. Middle State Evaluation Com., 1974; chmn. Region VI Spl. Edn. Council for Spl. Edn., 1976; participant N.J. Commr. of Edn. Supts. Acad., 1979; mem. Com. on League Re-Alignment, 1981-82. Drug Edn. grantee, 1974; selected to St. Benedict's Prep. Sch. Hall of Fame, 1986, Man of Yr. Bergen County Leonardo de Vinci Soc., 1991. Mem. N.J. Council of Edn., N.J. Sch. Masters, Bergen County Supts. Assn. (pres. 1985-86), N.J. Assn. Sch. Adminstrs., Am. Assn. Sch. Adminstrs., N.J. Sch. Bds. Assn., Assn. for Supervision and Curriculum Devel. Roman Catholic. Clubs: Cliffside Men's (sec.-treas. 1981-82), Cliffside Park Rotary (pres. 1967), Cliffside Park Lions. Home: 2 Fox Ter Cliffside Park NJ 07010-2906 Office: 525 Palisade Ave Cliffside Park NJ 07010-2914

COLAIACOVO, CHRISTINE MARY, secondary school educator; b. New Britain, Conn., Apr. 12, 1945; d. John Alexander and Rose Irene (Farmer) Drummond; m. Pat Anthony, Dec. 1, 1973; 1 child, Alexander. BS, Cen. Conn. State Coll., 1967; MA, Trinity Coll., 1971; degree in adminstrn., Cen. Conn. State U., 1985. English and sociology tchr. Berlin (Conn.) High Sch., 1968—, head English dept., 1991—. Contbr. poems to profl. pubs. Trinity Coll. fellow, 1967; recipient Celebration of Excellence award State of Conn., 1990. Mem. ASCD, NEA, Conn. Edn. Assn., Berlin Edn. Assn., Nat. Coun. Tchrs. English. Home: 109 Ridge Crest Cir Wethersfield CT 06109-4619 Office: Berlin High Sch 139 Patterson Way Kensington CT 06037-3199

COLARUSSO, ROGER MICHAEL, SR., middle school educator; b. Newark, July 28, 1947; s. Louis and Virginia (Doganiero) C.; m. Mary Ann Colarusso, Dec. 19, 1970; children: Roger Jr., Jamie Anne. BA, William Penn Coll., 1969; MA, Kean Coll., 1988. Tchr. 8th grade Newark Bd. Edn., tchr. 8th grade algebra I, gifted, talented, and math. devel.; math staff developer Newark Pub Schs., 1996—2000, math resource tchr., coord. math dept., 2000—. Student coun. adv. Ann Street Elem. Sch. Master Sgt. USNG, 1971-99. Recipient Gov.'s Recognition award for Tchg., 1995. Mem.: Nat. Coun. Tchrs. Math., Assn. Math. Tchrs. NJ, Am. Assn. Curriculum Devel., Non-Commissioned Officers Assn., Acad. Booster Club. Home: 5 White Ter Nutley NJ 07110-1939

COLASANTI, GEORGETTE ELIZABETH, special education educator; b. Mineola, N.Y., Dec. 4, 1946; d. George Peter and Elizabeth Haskell (Brown) Moyer; m. Regis Joseph Colasanti, Mar. 3, 1979 (div. Apr. 1991); m. John Osher, 1991; children: Meghan Elizabeth, Michael Regis. BA in English, Am. U., 1968; MA Equivalency, U. Md., 1976; MA in Spl. Edn., U. No. Colo., 1992. Cert. secondary edn. educator, Colo. Tchr. English Julius West Jr. H.S., Rockville, Md., 1968-76; tchr. spl. edn., English Place Middle Sch., Denver, 1990-97; tchr. English East H.S., Denver, 1997—2003; tchr. Arrupe Jesuit H.S., Denver, 2003—. Literacy advisor Denver Pub. Schs., 1994-95, 98. Tutor Chapter I, Denver Pub. Schs., 1992, 94. Grantee Coun. for Learning Disabled, 1993. Mem. Coun. for Exceptional Children. Avocations: running, reading, writing, travel. Home: 1664 S Syracuse St Denver CO 80231-2607 Office: Arrupé Jesuit High Sch 4343 Utica St Denver CO 80212 E-mail: gcolasanti@aol.com.

COLBAUGH, RICHARD DONALD, mechanical engineer, educator, researcher; b. Pitts., Oct. 31, 1958; s. Richard Donald and Anne Marie (McCue); m. Kristin Lea Glass, July 18, 1987; 1 child, Allison Collette. BS in Mechanical Engring., Pa. State U., 1980, PhD in Mechanical Engring., 1986. Mechanical engr. McDonnell Douglas Corp., Long Beach, Calif., 1980-81; instr. mechanical engring. Pa. State U., State College, 1981-86; asst. prof. mechanical engring. N.Mex. State U., Las Cruces, 1986-90, assoc. prof. mech. engring., 1990-96, prof. mech. engring., 1996—. Cons. Dept. Energy, Albuquerque, 1987-- Jet Propulsion Lab., Pasadena, Calif., 1988--. Assoc. editor Internat. Jour. of Robotics and Auto., 1991-93, editor-in-chief, 1993—; assoc. editor Internat. Jour. Environ. Conscious Mfg., 1992—, Intelligent Automation and Soft Computing, 1994—; co-author: Robotics and Remote Systems in Hazardous Environ., 1992; contbr. articles to profl. jours.; guest editor numerous jours. Recipient NASA Space Act Tech. Brief award, 1990, 91, 92, 93, 95, 96, Best Paper award Am. Automatic Control Coun., 1990, 93, Best Presentation award Soc. Indsl. and Applied Math., 1995; NASA/ASEE Summer Faculty fellow, 1991, 92. Mem. IEEE, Am. Soc. Mechanical Engrs., Sigma Xi. Achievements include patent for Obstacle Avoidance Redundant Robots Using Configuration Control; development of first real time control algorithm for robots possessing any combination of kinematic of actuator redundancy, one of first adaptive output stabilizing, tracking and compliance controllers for robots, one of first adaptive stabilizers for underactuated mechanical systems. Office: NMex State U Dept Mechanical Engring PO Box 30001 # 3450 Las Cruces NM 88003-8001

COLBERT, BEATRICE HALFACRE, special education administrator; b. Ruleville, Miss., Aug. 21, 1958; d. Marvin Wylie and Julian (Hicks) Halfacre; m. James Eugene Colbert Jr., Nov. 23, 1983; 1 child, Jacob Cale. BS, Miss. State U., Starkville, 1979, MEd, 1982, Ednl. Specialist, 1984. Cert. tchr., Miss. Prevocat. spl. edn. tchr. Natchez (Miss.)-Adams Sch. Dist., 1979-80; elem. spl. edn. tchr., psychometrist Winona (Miss.) Pub. Schs., 1980-86, Moss Point (Miss.) Sch. Dist., 1986-88; spl. edn. dir./program developer, psychometrist, coord. Grenada (Miss.) Sch. Dist., 1988—. Mem. Coun. Exceptional Children, Coun. Adminstrs. Spl. Edn., Learning Disabilities Assn., Miss. Assn. Sch. Adminstrs., Miss. Orgn. Spl. Edn. Svcs. (bd. dirs., sec.). Baptist. Home: 302 Fairground St Winona MS 38967-2106 Office: Grenada Sch Dist 1855 Jackson Ave PO Box 1940 Grenada MS 38902-1940

COLBERT-CORMIER, PATRICIA A. secondary school educator; b. Lake Charles, La., Nov. 12, 1943; 4 children. BS in Biology, U. La., 1965, MS in Microbiology, 1975. Edn. specialist cert. in reading 1978. Tchr. biology dept. Lafayette (La.) H.S., 1975—. Mem. editl. adv. panel Cold Spring Harbor Labs. DNA Learning Ctr. Finalist, Nat. Tchr. Hall Fame; DuPont fellow, 1994, Albert Einstein fellow, NASA, Washington, 2000—01, Disney Ch. Am. Tchr. and Tandy Tech. scholar, 1996. Office: Lafayette HS Biology Dept 3000 W Congress St Lafayette LA 70506*

COLBORN, GENE LOUIS, anatomy educator, researcher; b. Springfield, Ill., Nov. 23, 1935; s. Adin Levi and Grace Downey (Tucker) C.; divorced; children: Robert Mark, Adrian Thomas, Lara Lee Colborn Russell; m. Sarah Ellen Crockett, Aug. 14, 1976; children: Jason Matthew, Nathan Tucker. BA with honors, Ky. Christian Coll., 1957; BS with honors, Milligan Coll., 1962; MS in Anatomy, Wake Forest U., 1964, PhD in Anatomy, 1967. Postdoctoral fellow U. N.Mex. Sch. Medicine, Albuquerque, 1967-68; asst. prof. U. Tex. Health Sci. Ctr., San Antonio, 1968-72, assoc. prof., 1972-75; assoc. prof. anatomy Med. Coll. Ga., Augusta, 1975-88, prof. anatomy, 1988-2000, prof. surgery, 1993-2000, dir. Ctr. for Clin. Anatomy, 1987-2000, dir. med. gross anatomy, 1975—, cons. dept. surgery, 1977-2000, prof. surgery, 1993-2000, emeritus prof. anatomy and surgery, 2000—; clin. prof. surgery Emory U. Sch. Medicine, Atlanta, 1996—; chmn. divsn. anatomical scis. Ross U. Sch. Medicine, Dominica, 2000—01; prof. Am. U. Caribbean Sch. Medicine, St. Maarten, Netherlands Antilles, 2002—, chmn. anatomy, 2002—. Pres. Ga. State Anatomical Bd., 1983-93; cons. Eisenhower Army Med. Ctr., 1990-96. Author: Practical Gross Anatomy, 1982, Surgical Anatomy, 1987, Hernias, 1988, Musculoskeletal Anatomy, 1989, Workbook of Surgical Anatomy, 1990, Clinical Gross Anatomy, 1993, Modern Hernia Repair, 1996, The Embryological and Anatomical Basis of Surgery, 2002; mem. editl. bd.: Clin. Anatomy Jour.; contbr. numerous articles on cardiac conduction, nervous sys., primate anatomy, cell culture and clin. and surg. anatomy to profl. jours. Active San Antonio Symphony Mastersingers, 1970-75, Augusta Opera, 1975—, Augusta Choral Soc., 1975-95; judge Regional Sci. Fairs, Augusta, 1978-90. Recipient Golden Apple award, U. Tex. Health Sci. Ctr., 1975, Outstanding Med. Educator award, Med. Coll. Ga., 1976, 1977, 1978, 1982, 1987, 1988, 1990, 1991, 1997, Disting. Faculty award, 1978, 2000, Excellence in Tchg. award, 1997, 1999, Regents' award in tchg., 1998, others. Mem. AAUP, Am. Assn. Clin. Anatomists (membership chmn. 1982-86, mem. editl. bd. Jour. Clin. Anatomy 1994—), Am. Assn. Anatomists, Columbia County Choral Soc. (founding mem.), KC (4th degree). Republican. Avocations: opera, chorales, chess, tennis, camping. Address: 4115 Columbia Rd Ste 5 Martinez GA 30907-0410 E-mail: glcolb@yahoo.com.

COLBOURN, FRANK EDWIN, communications educator; b. New Haven, Conn., July 5, 1928; s. Ira and Justine (O'Connell) C.; m. Andrea M. Pilato, May 29, 1981; children: Daniel, David, Bruce, Ann Sally. BSBA, Boston U., 1948, JD, 1950; SJD magna cum laude, Bklyn. Law Sch., 1956. Bar: Mass. 1950, Ill. 1952, N.Y. 1956. With mgmt. staff Household Fin., Boston, N.Y.C., Chgo., 1950-52; real estate exec. F.W. Woolworth Co., N.Y.C., 1952-64; assoc. prof. communication Pace U., N.Y.C., 1964-72, prof., 1972—. Pres. Colbourn Communication Cons., Inc., N.Y.C., 1976—; cons. Citizens Campaign Environ., Massapequa, N.Y., 1990. Author: (text and record) The Art of Debate, 1971, How to Judge a Debate, 1973. Head debate coach Pace U., 1980—90, U.S. Merchant Marine Acad., 1968—71. With USN, 1944—46. Mem. AAUP (pres. Pace, N.Y. chpt. 1994-97), Am. Forensic Assn., Internat. Soc. Gen. Semantics, Speech Comm. Assn., Delta Sigma Rho, Phi Alpha Alpha. Avocations: critical thinking instruction, coaching debate and communication, tutoring. Home and Office: 145 Cedar Shore Dr Old Harbor Green Estates Massapequa NY 11758-8133

COLBY, EVELYN JANE, elementary school educator; b. Robinson, N.D., May 11, 1927; d. Henry Johannes Leland and Rachel (Olson) Skar; m. Glenn Wesley Colby (dec. Apr. 1983); children: Janet, Leland, Glenda. BA, Northridge U., 1963; postgrad., C.L.U., 1963-80. Tchr. Union Sch. Dist., Robinson, 1944-45, Tuttle (N.D.) Sch. Dist., 1946-47, Tigard (Oreg.) Sch. Dist., 1947-48, Monango (N.D.) Sch. Dist., 1948-49, Calvary Luth. Sch., Pacoima, Calif., 1960-62, El Rio Sch. Dist., Oxnard, Calif., 1962-63, Conejo Sch. Dist., Thousand Oaks, Calif., 1963-87; ret., 1987. Tchr. PTA, Thousand Oaks, 1962—, mem. mag. com., 1987—; retired sr. mem. Vol. Prog. Goebel Ctr., Thousand Oaks, 1988-2002; treas. Ventu Villa Activity Club, Newbury Park, Calif., 1989—; pres. Ventu Villa GSMOL, Newbury, 1988-2002; treas. Ch. Women United, 1989-2002, pres. 2003—; v.p. Ventura County Coun. Chs., Golden Age Club Thousand Oaks, 1989-2002; active Ventura County Comsn. Children. Mem. Ventura County Retired Tchrs. (life), Sons of Norway (officer 2003). Republican. Lutheran. Avocations: needlepoint, traveling, letter writing, walking, music. Home: 259 Ortega Dr Newbury Park CA 91320-3933

COLBY, LESTINA LARSEN, secondary education educator; b. Mt. Sterling, Ky., Apr. 19, 1937; d. Harold L. and Opal Kearney (Caudel) Larsen; m. Bruce Redfearn Colby, Dec. 28, 1962; children: Charles, Harold, Pamela. BS, U. Chgo., 1958, postgrad., 1958-62. Sci. tchr., debate coach Community High Sch., Midlothian, Ill., 1958-61; biology tchr., debate coach U. Chgo. Lab. Sch., 1961-66; sci. tchr. Springer Jr. High Sch., Wilmington, Del., 1977; biology and math. tchr. McKean High Sch., Wilmington, 1978; biology tchr., debate coach, student coun. advisor U. Liggett Sch., Grosse Pointe, Mich., 1979-93, Edsel B. Ford endowed sci. chair, 1990; biology tchr., chmn. sci. dept. Episcopal High Sch., Jacksonville, Fla., 1993—. Author: Teacher's Manual for Encyclopaedia Britannica's Evolution Unit, 1966, Plants and Animals, 1968. Mem. Nat. Assn. Biology Tchrs. (Mich. Outstanding Biology Tchr. 1990), Nat. Sci. Tchrs. Assn., Fla. Assn. Sci. Tchrs. Baptist. Office: Episcopal HS Jacksonville 4455 Atlantic Blvd Jacksonville FL 32207-2121

COLBY, VIRGINIA LITTLE, retired elementary school educator; b. Saugus, Mass., May 1, 1917; d. Guy L. and Alberta M. (Chadwick) Little; m. Robert E. Colby, Dec. 25, 1951. AB, U. Mass., 1940. Svc. rep. N.E.T. and T. Co. Bus. Office, Lynn, Mass., 1940-63, N.E.T. and T. Co., Concord, N.H., 1963-67; tchr. Shaker Regional Sch. Dist., Belmont, NH, 1967—77, ret., 1977. Author: (book) St. Paul's Episcopal Church Concord New Hampshire: A Guide and Story of its Heritage, Memorabilia for Posterity: The Rev. Dr. Samuel Wood; co-author: Concord Eastside: A History of East Concord, New Hampshire, The Past and Present Here with Blend Highlights from 236 Years of Education in Boscawen, 1761-1997; contbr. articles to profl. jours. Mem.: AAUW (past pres. Concord br.), Boscawen Hist. Soc., Inc. (sec. libr.), Concord Ch. Women United (past pres., v.p.), Lakes Region Ret. Tchrs. Assn. (past pres.), No. N.H. Tel. Pioneers Am. (past pres.), Delta Kappa Gamma (hon.). Home: 134 Mountain Rd Concord NH 03301-6931

COLBY-HALL, ALICE MARY, Romance studies educator; b. Portland, Maine, Feb. 25, 1932; d. Frederick Eugene and Angie Fraser (Drown) C.; m. Robert A. Hall, Jr., May 8, 1976 (dec. 1997); stepchildren: Philip, Diana Hall Goodall, Carol Hall Erickson. BA, Colby Coll., 1953; MA, Middlebury Coll., 1954; PhD, Columbia U., 1962. Tchr. French, Latin Orono (Maine) H.S., 1954-55; tchr. French Gould Acad., Bethel, Maine, 1955-57; lectr. French Columbia U., 1959-60; instr. Romance lit. Cornell U., Ithaca, N.Y., 1962-63, asst. prof., 1963-66, assoc. prof., 1966-75, prof. Romance studies, 1975-97, prof. emerita, 1997—, chmn. Romance studies, 1990-96. Author: The Portrait in Twelfth Century French Literature: An Example of the Stylistic Originality of Chrétien de Troyes, 1965; mem. editl. bd. Speculum, 1976-79, Olifant, 1974—. Fulbright grantee, 1953-54; NEH fellow, 1984-85; recipient Médaille des Amis d'Orange, 1985; decorated chevalier de l'Ordre des Arts et Lettres, 1997. Mem. Modern Lang. Assn., Medieval Acad. Am. (councillor 1983-86), Internat. Arthurian Soc., Société Rencesvals, Académie de Vaucluse, Phi Beta Kappa. Republican. Congregationalist. Home: 308 Cayuga Heights Rd Ithaca NY 14850-2107 Office: Cornell U Dept Romance Studies Ithaca NY 14853 E-mail: amc12@cornell.edu.

COLE, BARBARA ANN, lawyer, educator; b. New Orleans, Sept. 16, 1954; d. Keith Martin Cole and Peggy St. Amant Ducote. BA, Southeastern U., 1976; JD, Loyola U., New Orleans, 1983. Bar: La. 1984, Tex. 1996. Social studies tchr. Slidell (La.) High Sch., 1976-81; instr. Southeastern U., Hammond, La., 1984-85; sole practice Hammond, La., 1983-96; pvt.

practice Kerrville, Tex., 1996—. Drug prosecutor fed. grant bd. dirs. Regional Cath. H.S., 1995—. Pres. Mayor's Commn. on Needs of Women, Hammond, 1985-86; mem. edn. com. Hammond C. of C., 1985-86; chmn. Domestic Violence Task Force, 1985-86; pres. The Citizens Law Ctr.; bd. dirs. Our Lady of Hills Regional Cath. H.S. Mem. La. State Bar Assn. (Young Lawyers sect.), Fed. Bar Assn., La. Assn. Women Attys., La. Trial Lawyers Assn. Lodges: Krewe Iris, Krewe of Omega (captain). Roman Catholic. Avocations: horseback riding, reading, theatre, tennis. Office: 222 Sidney Baker St S Ste 420 Kerrville TX 78028-5983

COLE, DAVID AKINOLA, educational administrator, educator; b. Jan. 8, 1954; s. Nathaniel Jonathan and Betsy (George) C.; m. Claudia Marcella Campbell, Oct. 4, 1980; children: Bryan, Claudette, Lynnette. Student, Milton Margai Tchrs. Coll., 1976-79; BS in Edn. cum laude, Lincoln U., 1985, MEd, 1986; cert. in teaching, U. Ga., 1990, postgrad., 1992, EdD in Ednl. Leadership, 1999. Cert. English tchr., edn. of the gifted, Ga. Asst. tchr. Holy Trinity Boys Sch., Freetown, 1973-76; tchr., asst. libr. S.L. Grammar Sch., Freetown, 1979-82, Lincoln U. Mo., 1983-86; educator Rutland and Clarke County Sch. Dist., Athens, Ga., 1987-89; ednl. therapist Rutland Psychoednl. Svcs./Ga. Psychoednl. Network, Athens, 1989-92; spl. edn. tchr. Burney-Harris-Lyons Sch., Athens, 1992-94; asst. prin. Carver Mid. Sch., Monroe, Ga., 1994-98; asst. prin., Ga. h.s. grad. test coord. Clarke Ctrl. H.S., Athens, Ga., 1998—. Cons. U. Ga., Athens, 1988-90, rsch. asst. nat. rsch. ctr. on the gifted and talented project, 1992-96; mem. adj. faculty Piedmont Coll., Athens; client counselor N.E. Ga. Residential Svcs./Dept. Human Resources, Athens, 1988-95; h.s. instr. Clarke County H.S. Evening Program, 1996—. UNESCO scholar Milton Margai Tchrs. Coll., 1976-79; David A. Cole Outstanding Faculty award established by Clarke Ctrl. H.S., 1998-99. Mem. ASCD, Nat. Coun. Tchrs. English, Coun. for Exceptional Children, Assn. for the Gifted, Coun. for Children with Behavior Disorders, Profl. Assn. Ga. Educators, Ga. Ednl. Rsch. Assn., Psi Chi, Sigma Tau Delta (tchrs. adv. bd. 1992—), Kappa Delta Epsilon (Perfect Scholar award 1992), Pi Lambda Theta. Avocations: reading, travel, music, athletics, tennis. Home: PO Box 5932 Athens GA 30604-5932

COLE, DAVID EDWARD, university administrator; b. Detroit, July 20, 1937; s. Edward Nicholas and Esther Helen (Engman) C.; m. Carol Hutchins, July 9, 1965; children: Scott David, Christopher Carl. BS in Mech. Engring. and Math., U. Mich., 1960, MS in Mech. Engring., 1961, PhD, 1966. Engr. GM, Detroit, 1960—65; prof. U. Mich., Ann Arbor, 1967—, dir. Office for Study of Automotive Transp., 1978—2000; entrepreneur 6 cos., 1975—95; chmn. Ctr. Auto Rsch. and Mgmt., ptnr. The Altarum Inst. Mich, 2000—03; chmn. Ctr. for Automotve Rsch. (ind. not for profit), 2003—. Bd. dirs. MSX Internat., Detroit, Saturn Electronics, Aurburn Hills, Mich., Plastech, Dearborn, R.L. Polk, Southfield, Mich., Campfire Interactive, Ann Arbor, Mich., Mich. Econ. Devel. Corp., Lansing, Cunningham Motors, Livonia, Mich.; mem. energy engring. bd. NRC, 1989-94; select panel U.S.-Can. Free trade Pact, 1988-91. Author: Elementary Vehicle Dynamics, 1972; contbr. articles to profl. jours. Bd. trustees Hope Coll., 1994-98; mem. exec. com., Mich. Economic Devel. Corp.; bd. dirs. Automotive Hall of Fame, Dearborn. Fellow Soc. Automotive Engrs. (dir. 1980-83, 85-88, Teetor award 1969), Engring. Soc. Detroit (Horace H. Rackham medal 2000); mem. Chevalier of the Nat. Order of Merit from France, 1999, Soc. Mktg. Execs. (Mktg. Educator of Yr. 1998, Rene Dubos Environ. award 1998), Nat. Auto Dealers Assn. Found. (Freedom of Mobility award 1993), Swedens Royal Order of the Polar Star. Republican. Presbyterian. Avocations: hunting, fishing, boating, running, golf. Office: Ctr Auto Rsch 3025 Boardwalk Ann Arbor MI 48108-4004 E-mail: dcole@cargrop.org.

COLE, GRACE V. painter, art educator; b. Chgo. d. Peter S. and Katherine Marie (Hill) Ellis. Student, Prairie State Coll., Ecole Albert du Fois, Vihiers, France. Tchr. for pvt. apprentices, Chgo., 1979—; tchr. Prairie State Coll., Chicago Heights, Ill., 1986-95, Old Town Triangle, Chgo., 1990—. Cons. in field, juror, gallery asst., lectr., curator, sales rep., mentor and dir. numerous orgns. Exhibited in group shows at Portraits, Inc., N.Y. Jayson Gallery, Chgo., Clementi House Gallery, London; commd. portraits include Coe Coll., Iowa, Ill. Coll., Medinah Country Club (10 works), Ill., Bank of Louisville (2 works), Bristol Meyers, Ind., Epsicopal Diocese of Chgo. (2 works), MacArthur Found., Chgo. (2 works), U. Tenn., Ill. Coll., Jacksonville, numerous other pvt. and pub. collections. Featured in article in the Artist's Mag., 1984, Today's Chgo. Woman, Jan. 1999; recipient Golden Apple award Prarie State Coll., 1994. Mem. Arts Club Chgo., Nat. Mus. Women in Arts (pres. 2002-2003), Chgo. Artist's Coalition (bd. dirs. 1979-81). Studio: 410 S Michigan Ave Ste 311 Chicago IL 60605-1472 Address: 410 S Michigan Ave Ste 306 Chicago IL 60605-1472

COLE, JEFFREY CLARK, public relations professional; b. Toledo, Jan. 20, 1966; s. Frank Herbert, Jr. and Mary Therese ((Clark)) Cole. BA, U. Toledo, 1989, MEd, 1996. Cert. fund raising exec., Nat. Soc. Fund Raising Execs. Admissions counselor U. Toledo, 1989-92, devel. officer, 1992-97; comm. specialist Dana Corp., Toledo, 1997-99, mgr., pub. rels., 1999-2000, mgr. mktg. com., 2000—. Instr. comm. U. Toledo, 1992-97, adj. prof. comm., 1997—. Editor-in-chief The Collegian, U. Toledo, 1988-89. Pres. student govt. U. Toledo, 1987-88; alumni bd. dirs. St. Francis deSales High Sch., Toledo, 1989-92; bd. mgrs. Univ. YMCA, 1991-95; mem. alumni affiliate steering com. U. Toledo Coll. Arts and Scis., 1992-97; mem. profl. staff coun. U. Toledo, 1993-96, chair, 1995-96; Lucas County Rep. Ctrl. Com., 1996—; exec. com. Lucas County Rep., 1998—; devel. adv. com. St. Francis de Sales H.S., Toledo, 2000—; bd. dirs. Mobile Meals of Greater Toledo, 1999—, vice chair, 1999—; trustee Collegian Media Found., 2001—, chair, 2003—; bd. trustees U. Toledo Student Affairs Com., 2002—, chair, 2003—. Recipient Crystal award for pub. rels. Women in Comm., Inc., 1996; named Outstanding Young Alumnus, U. Toledo, 1999. Mem. Blue Key Nat. Honor Soc. (hon.), Toledo Press Club (award 1989, Excellence in Media award 1995), Internat. Assn. Bus. Communicators, Soc. Profl. Journalists, Toledo Club, Pub. Rels. Soc. Am. (accredited pub. rels.), Omicron Delta Kappa Soc. (adv.). Republican. Avocations: travel, genealogy, writing. Home: 3843 Woodmont Rd Toledo OH 43613-4323 Office: Dana Corp PO Box 1000 Toledo OH 43697-1000 E-mail: jeff.cole@dana.com.

COLE, JONATHAN RICHARD, sociologist, academic administrator; b. N.Y.C., Aug. 27, 1942; s. Richard and Sylvia (Dym) C.; m. Joanna Miller Lewis, June 5, 1968; children: Daniel Lewis, Susanna Dora. BA, Columbia U., 1964, PhD, 1969. Asst. prof. sociology Columbia U., N.Y.C., 1969-73, assoc. prof., 1973-76, prof., 1976—, Quetelet prof. social sci., 1989—2001, dir. Ctr. for Social Scis., 1979-87, v.p. Arts and Scis., 1987-89, provost, 1989-94, provost dean of faculties, 1994—2003, John Mitchell Mason prof., 2002—. Adj. prof. Rockefeller U., 1983-85; pres. Reid Hall Inc.; cons. Ford Found., NSF, Nat. Acad. Scis., Russell Sage Found., AT&T. Author: Social Stratification in Science, 1973, Fair Science: Women in the Scientific Community, 1979, Peer Review in the National Science foundation, Vol. 1, 1978, Vol. 2, 1981, The Wages of Writing: Per Word, Per Price, or Perhaps, 1986, The Outer Circle, 1990, The Research Library in a Time of Discontent, 1994; editor Am. Jour. Sociology; contbr. articles to profl. jours. Recipient Cavaliere Ufficiale Republic Italy, 1996, Commendatore of Gidine al Merito della Repubilica Italiana, 2003; Guggenheim fellow, 1975-76, Ctr. for Advanced Study in Behavioral Scis. fellow, 1975-76. Fellow AAAS, Am. Acad. Arts and Scis.; mem. Am. Sociol. Assn., Internat. Sociol. Assn., Ea. Sociol. Assn., Soc. Rsch. Assn. (hon.), Coun. Fgn. Rels. Home: 404 Riverside Dr New York NY 10025-1861 Office: Columbia U 205 Low Libr 116th & Broadway New York NY 10027

COLE, LOIS LORRAINE, retired elementary school educator; b. Rock Lick, Ky., Oct. 18, 1932; d. Charles Lorraine and Gwendolyn Pearl (Johnson) Blanchard; m. John Hamilton Cole, Jr., July 10, 1953; children: Stephen Wesley, Pamela Cole Winningham, Paula Cole Bruner. BS in Elem. Edn. cum laude, Ind. Wesleyan U., Marion, 1954; postgrad., Miami U., Oxford, Ohio, 1974, 82. Cert. kindergarten and elem. tchr., Ohio. Tutor of handicapped Marengo (Ohio) Elem. Sch., 1955-56; tchr. 6th and 7th grade lang. arts Harmony Elem. Sch., Mingo Junction, Ohio, 1957-59; instr. English God's Bible Sch., Cin., 1963-64; tchr. Parents Coop. Kindergarten, Cin., 1964-68, Mt. Healthy City Schs., Cin., 1968-94, ret., 1994. Tutor PALS, Mt. Healthy, Ohio, 1991, Easley (S.C.) Pub. Schs., 1995-96. Tchr., primary supt. Galbraith Rd. Ch. of God Sunday Sch., Cin., 1970-72, Fairfield Ch. of Nazarene Sunday Sch., Fairfield, Ohio, 1973-77; former local ch. dir. Wesleyan Women Internat., Easley, 1996-99; former 1st v.p. Newcomers' Club, Easley, 1997. Mem. Mt. Health Edn. Assn. (bldg. rep. 1986-87), Ohio Congress Parents and Tchrs. (life). Republican. Wesleyan. Avocations: reading, photography, travel, flower gardening, music. Home: 245 Andover Turn Easley SC 29642-8803 E-mail: jonlo2002@aol.com.

COLE, MARIANNE LEE, secondary education educator; b. New Brunswick, N.J., Nov. 24, 1956; d. Leon Robert and Claire Dorothy (Repei) Chmura; m. David Robert John Cole, Sept. 9, 1978. BA, Trenton State Coll., 1978. Tchr. St. Mary's Sch., South River, N.J., 1978—. Vol. Lacawac Sanctuary, Lakeville, Pa., 1992—. Named Tchr. of Yr. Diocese of Metuchen (N.J.), 1992-93. Mem. Appalachian Mountain Club, Nat. Audubon Soc., Nature Conservancy, Cobbs Lake Preserve (chair Arbor Day com. 1991), Bernese Mountain Dog Club Am. Democrat. Roman Catholic. Avocations: gardening, canoeing, fly-fishing, hiking, cooking. Office: St Marys Sch 22 Holmes Ave South River NJ 08882-1608

COLE, PATRICIA ALUISE, elementary school educator; b. Huntington, W.Va., Dec. 26, 1957; d. Albert James and Nancy Suzanne (Linsenmeyer) Aluise; m. Dennis Franklin Cole, Aug. 1, 1981; 1 child, Dennis Franklin Jr. BA in Elem. Edn./Math. magna cum laude, Marshall U., 1980, MA in Elem. Edn. summa cum laude, 1986. Cert. elem. tchr., math. tchr., W.Va. Bank teller First Huntington Nat. Bank, 1980; elem. and jr. H.S. tchr. Our Lady of Fatima Sch., Huntington, 1980—, tutor, math. olympiad coach and moderator, 1988—. Presenter W.Va. Sci. Tchrs. Convention, Huntington, 1994, OCEA Convention, 1998. Vol. Marshall Artist Series, Huntington, 1982, W.Va. Spl. Olympics, 1988, 89, Huntington Mus. of Art, 1984, 86; sec. Ladies Guild Sacred Heart Ch., Huntington, 1988; area chmn. Heart Fund, Huntington, 1980; mem. River Cities Cultural Coun., Gov.'s Summer Inst., Diocesan Math. Curriculum Com., Instep Tech. Tng., 2001, 02, Mini Soc. Tng., GEMS Tng. Recipient Ashland Oil Tchr. Achievement award, 2002; grantee Diocese of Wheeling, 1991, 95, 2000, 01, 02. Mem. Cabell County Reading Coun., Women's Club of Huntington (com. chmn. 1984-86, treas. 1985, social chmn. 1986, 3d vice chmn. 1987, 2d vice chmn. 1988, 1st vice chmn. 1989, chmn. 1990, Outstanding Chmn. award 1984, 86, Bd. Mem. of Yr. 1987, Dist. Mem. of Yr. 1991), Gamma Beta Phi. Avocations: reading, bible study, exercise, decorating. Home: 5112 Nickel Plate Dr Huntington WV 25705-3134

COLE, ROBERTA CARLEY, retired nursing educator; b. Golden, N.Mex., Feb. 16, 1929; d. Robert and Marie (Davis) Carley; m. Ivan E. Cole, Aug. 3, 1957. BS in Nursing, Calif. State U., L.A., 1974, MS in Nursing, 1977; diploma, St. Joseph Hosp. Sch. Nursing, Phoenix, 1955. Med. nurse St. Joseph Med. Ctr., Burbank, Calif., 1955-57, head nurse, 1957-63, supr. med.-surg. ICU and CCU, 1963-69, rsch. nurse, nursing svc. adminstr., 1969-75; staff nurse per diem Verdugo Hills Hosp., Glendale, Calif., 1985-87; mentor BS in Nursing statewide nursing program Consortium Calif. State U., Dominguez Hills, 1986-88; instr. Pasadena (Calif.) City C.C., 1976-80, asst. prof., 1981-88, assoc. prof., 1988-95, prof., 1995-97, asst. to the chair, 1991-93, interim chair, 1993-94, prof. emeritus, 1997—. Recipient Svc. award ARC. Mem. ANA, NEA, Calif. Nurses Assn., Calif. Tchrs. Assn., So. Calif. Nursing Diagnosis Assn. Home: 10040 Wentworth St Shadow Hills CA 91040-1246 Office: Pasadena City Coll 1570 E Colorado Blvd Pasadena CA 91106-2003

COLEMAN, BARBARA HELENE, educational administrator; b. Chgo., Nov. 13, 1949; d. Alex Martin and Cecil Beatrix (Levine) Berman; m. Morris Kaplan, June 10, 1973 (div. Nov. 1978); 1 child, Sharon Ann; m. Dell Walt Coleman, Dec. 24, 1988. BS in Chemistry, U. Ill., 1970; MA in Chemistry, Rice U., Houston, 1972; EdD, U. Houston, 1994. Cert. supt. mid-mgmt./supervision/ chemistry. Teaching fellow, grad. instr. dept. chemistry Rice U., Houston, 1970-72; chemist dept. urology St. Luke's Hosp., 1972-73; tchr. phys. sci. Northbrook Sr. H.S., 1973-74; tchr. sci. and math. The Kinkaid Sch., Houston, 1977-79; tchr. sci. and math., drill team advisor Marian Christian H.S., Houston, 1979-80; chair sci. dept. Awty Internat. Sch., Houston, 1980-81; jr. analyst Western Geophys. Co., Houston, 1981-89; tchr. phys. sci., biology and math. Bellaire Sr. H.S., Houston, 1989-95; adj. prof. chemistry U. Houston-Downtown, 1994-96; asst. prin. Ryan Mid. Sch., Houston, 1995-96, adminstr. employee appraisal, 1996-98; asst. prin. Fondren Mid. Sch., Houston, 1998—. Presenter staff devel., guest lectr. adminstrn. and supervision Prairie View A&M U., supr. acad. decathlon, asst. asst. prin. Bellaire H.S., 1993-94; sci. safety officer, co-chair phys. sci. dept., chair final exam writing com. Bellaire Sr. H.S., 1991-95; mem. tech. subcom. shared decision making com., sec. ad hoc com. on class ranking Bellaire Sr. H.S. Pers. Com., 1992-95. Editor: (with R. Ritchie) Laboratory Manual: Physical Science, first semester, 1993, second semester, 1994. Grantee U. Houston, Woodrow Wilson Chemistry Program, Eisenhower Phys. Sci. Study Program, 1991. Mem. ASCD, Nat. Sci. Tchrs. Assn., Am. Chem. Soc. (govt. liaison, ctrl. coord. Nat. Chemistry Week. Southeastern Tex. sect. 1991, govt. liaison, mall demonstrator, 1989, dir. sect., chair chem. edn. com. 1982-87, sec. Greater Houston sect. 1994—), Assn. Chemistry Tchrs. Tex., Phi Kappa Phi, Kappa Delta Pi, Phi Delta Kappa, Iota Sigma Pi.

COLEMAN, BERNELL, physiologist, educator; b. Jefferson County, Miss., Apr. 26, 1929; s. Percy and Julia (Nailor) C.; m. Annie C. Richardson, Jan. 30, 1962; children— Rochelle, Ronald. BS, Alcorn A&M Coll., 1952; PhD (Univ. fellow), Loyola U. Stritch Sch. Medicine, Chgo., 1964. Research asst. in biochemistry U. Chgo., 1956-57; research in cancer Hines (Ill.) VA Hosp., 1957-59; instr. St. Louis U. Sch. Medicine, 1963-65, asst. prof. physiology, 1965-67; asst. prof. Chgo. Med. Sch., 1967-69, asso. prof., 1969-76, prof., 1976, Howard U. Coll. Medicine, Washington, 1976—, chmn. dept. physiology and biophysics, 1979—. Lectr. Cook County Grad. Sch. Medicine, U. Ill. Med. Sch.; vis. prof. Rush Med. Coll.; external examiner Godfrey Huggins Sch. Medicine, U. Zimbabwe, Salisbury, 1981; mem. cardiovascular and pulmonary study sect. Nat. Heart, Lung and Blood Inst./NIH, 1982-83, rsch. tng. rev. com., 1990-94. Peer rev. com. Am. Heart Assn., 1988-93, 95—, rsch. com., 1993—. With U.S. Army, 1953-56, Korea. Recipient research award Chgo. Med. Sch. Bd. Trustees, 1975; NIH research fellow, 1960-61; NIH grantee, 1966-68, 69-74, 74-76, 79— ; USPHS fellow, 1961-63; Dept. Def. grantee, 1965-67 Mem.: AAAS, AAUP, Am. Soc. Hypertension (charter), N.Y. Acad. Scis., Internat. Soc. of Hypertension in Blacks, Assn. Black Cardiologists, Fedn. Am. Socs. Exptl. Biology (vis. scientist for minority instns. programs 1982—83, 1989—90), Am. Heart Assn. (basic sci. coun.), Am. Physiol. Soc. (cardiovascular fellow 1985), Phi Rho Sigma, Sigma Xi. Democrat. Achievements include research numerous publs. in cardiovascular physiology. Home: 14200 Myer Ter Rockville MD 20853-2350 Office: 520 W St NW Washington DC 20001-2337 E-mail: bcoleman@howard.edu.

COLEMAN, C. NORMAN, radiation and medical oncologist, researcher, educator; b. N.Y.C., Jan. 24, 1945; s. Samuel A. and Minna (Kramer) C.; m. Karolynn Forsburg, May 25, 1970; children: Gabrielle, Keith. BA, U. Vt., 1966; MD, Yale U., 1970. Diplomate Am. Bd. Internal Medicine, Am. Bd. Radiology, Am. Bd. Med. Oncology. Intern in internal medicine U. Calif., San Francisco, 1970-71, resident in internal medicine, 1971-72; clin. assoc. Nat. Cancer Inst., NIH, Bethesda, Md., 1972-74; clin. fellow therapeutic radiology Stanford (Calif.) U. Med. Sch., 1975-78, asst. prof. dept. radiology and medicine, 1979-84, assoc. prof., 1984-85; prof., chmn. Joint Ctr. for Radiation Therapy, Harvard U. Med. Sch., Boston, 1985-99; dir. radiation oncology sci. program Nat. Cancer Inst., NIH, 1999—, dep. dir. Ctr. for Cancer Rsch., 2001—. Prin. investigator radiation therapy oncology group, chem. modifiers of cancer treatment NIH, 1983-99; chmn. sensitizer protector working group DCT, NIH, Bethesda, 1985-99; mem. radiation study sect. NIH, Bethesda, 1988-92; mem. Nat. Cancer adv. bd. subcom. Nat. Cancer Program, 1993-94; mem. Nat. Cancer Inst. Divsn. of Treatment Bd. of Sci. Councilors, 1995-99. Author: (monograph) Chemical Modifiers of Radiotherapy and Chemotherapy, 1989, Understanding Cancer: Patient's Guide to Diagnosis, Prognosis and Treatment, 1998; editor: (monograph) Interaction of Radiation and Chemotherapy, 1986. Lt. col. USPHS, 1972-74. Fellow ACP, Am. Coll. Radiology, Soc. Chmn. Acad. Radiology Oncology Programs, (pres.), Am. Soc. Therapeutic Radiology and Oncology (bd. dirs. 1996-99), Am. Soc. Clin. Oncology (bd. dirs.), Radiation Rsch. Soc. (counselor 1992-94, pres. 1997); mem. Phi Beta Kappa, Alpha Omega Alpha. Democrat. Avocations: triathlon, family activities. Office: ROSP ROB NIH Bldg 10 B3B69 Bethesda MD 20892 E-mail: ccoleman@mail.nih.gov.

COLEMAN, CHARLES CLYDE, physicist, educator; b. York, Eng., July 31, 1937; came to U.S., 1941; s. Jesse C. and Geraldine (Doherty) C.; m. Sharon R. Slutsky, Aug. 12, 1976; children: Jeffrey Andrew, Matthew Casey. BA, UCLA, 1959, MA, 1961, PhD, 1968. Asst. prof. physics Calif. State U., Los Angeles, 1968-71, assoc. prof, 1971-76, prof., 1976—2002, prof. emeritus, 2002—. Cons. Gen. Dynamics Corp., 1975-77, China Lake Naval Rsch. Labs., 1981; dir. Csula Accelerator Facility; exec. dir. Csula Applied Physics Inst., 1978-83; sr. rsch. fellow Darwin Coll., Cambridge (Eng.) U., 1975-76; project specialist Chinese Provincial Univs. Devel. Project of World Bank, 1987-90; vis. prof. physics U. Istanbul, Turkey, 1969, 72, U. Sydney, Australia, 1977, Arya Mar U., Iran, 1976, U. Natal, South Africa, 1977, UCLA, 1990-91, U. Leicester, U.K., 1995-2001, Hubei U., Wuhan, China, 2002; mem. NASA review panel, 1992. Contbr. articles to sci. publs.; referee Solid State Electronics, Phys. Rev., Phys. Rev. Letters, Jour. Phys. Chem. Solids, Jour. Solid State Chem., Jour. Optical Materials. Trustee Calif. State U. L.A. Found., 1981-85. Grantee NSF, 1976—, Rsch. Corp., 1987-91; NATO Collaborative Rsch. grantee, 1991—; NATO Sr. Rsch. fellow Cavendish Lab. (U.K.), 1983-84, Am. Chem. Soc. Rsch. Faculty fellow, 1990. Fellow Brit. Interplanetary Soc., Royal Philatelic Soc. (London); mem. Am. Phys. Soc., Am. Radio Relay League, Sigma Xi, Phi Kappa Phi, Phi Beta Delta, Sigma Pi Sigma. Office: Calif State U Dept Physics Los Angeles CA 90032 E-mail: ccolema@calstatela.edu.

COLEMAN, COURTNEY STAFFORD, mathematician, educator; b. Ventura, Calif., July 19, 1930; s. Courtney Clemon and Una (Stafford) C.; m. Julia Wellnitz, June 26, 1954; children: David, Margaret, Diane. BA, U. Calif., Berkeley, 1951; PhD, Princeton U., 1955. Asst. prof. Wesleyan U., Middletown, Conn., 1955-58; from asst. prof. to full prof. Harvey Mudd Coll., Claremont, Calif., 1959-98. Lectr. Princeton (N.J.) U., 1954-55; rsch. in field. Author, editor: Differential Equations Models, 1983; editor, translator: Local Methods in Nonlinear Differential Equations, 1988; author: (with others) Differential Equations, 1987, Differential Equations Laboratory Workbook, 1992 (EDUCOM award for best math./computer course materials), Ordinary Differential Equations: A Modeling Perspective, 1998, ODE Architect, 1999 (award of excellence and Gold medal for best CD-ROM in edn.); mem. editl. bd. Jour. of Differential Equations, 1964—, UMAP Jour., 1980—. Mem. Am. Math. Soc., Math. Assn. Am., Soc. Indsl. Applied Math. Office: Harvey Mudd Coll Math Dept 1250 N Dartmouth Ave Claremont CA 91711 E-mail: coleman@hmc.edu.

COLEMAN, DEBRA KAY, special education educator; b. Parkersburg, W.Va. BA, Glenville State Coll., 1979; MA in Spl. Edn., W.Va. U., 1995. Cert. elem. tchr., spl. edn. tchr., learning disabilities, Ohio. Tchr. Warren Local Sch. Dist., Vincent, Ohio, 1981—2001; spl. edn. tchr. Fairland Local Schs., Proctorville, Ohio, 2002—. Mem. altar guild St. John's Episcopal Ch., Huntington, W.Va. Social sci. scholar Parkersburg C.C., 1975-77, Martha Holden Jennings scholar, 1982. Mem. NEA. Avocations: music, reading, writing. Office: Fairland Local Schs Proctorville OH 45669

COLEMAN, ESTHER MAE GLOVER, retired secondary school educator; b. Cleve., Mar. 22, 1932; d. George Emanuel and Ethel Lee (Greggs) Glover; m. Isaiah Francis Coleman, Jan. 16, 1954; children: Aaron Isaiah, Cynthia Denise. BS in Med. Tech., Youngstown State U., 1975, BS in Comprehensive Sci., 1980, postgrad. Cert. tchr., Ohio; cert. med. tech. Med. tech. Trumbull Meml. Hosp., Warren, Ohio, 1960-62, St. Elizabeth Hosp., Youngstown, 1962-72; tchr. chemistry, physics and earth sci. Beaver Locale High Sch., Lisbon, Ohio, 1980-82; tchr. chemistry, biology, earth sci. and gen. sci. Mt. Calvary Christian Acad., Youngstown, 1983-84; comprehensive sci. tchr. Youngstown Pub. Schs., 1984-93; ret., 1993. Tax preparer H & R Block, 1995—. Past pres. Velma Mason Nursery Guild; cheerleading advisor Hayes Jr. High, 1991, 92; trustee Tabernacle Baptist Ch., 2003-. Mem. Ohio Edn. Assn., Youngstown Edn. Assn., Evergreen Garden Club (past pres., treas., historian, libr.), Fellows Riverside Graden, Ohio Ret. Tchrs. Assn., Mahoning Ret. Tchrs. Assn. Baptist. Avocations: gardening, travel, reading. Home: 577 Bennington Ave Youngstown OH 44505-3401

COLEMAN, FRANCES MCLEAN, secondary school educator; b. Jackson, Miss., Feb. 17, 1940; d. Robert Beatty and Dorothy Trotter (Witty) McLean.; m. Thomas Allen Coleman, Aug. 29, 1964; children: James Plemon, Robert McLean, Dorothy Witty McLean, Josiah Dennis, Leonidas McLean. BA, U. Miss., Oxford, 1962; MS, U. Miss., Jackson, 1964, PhD, 1970. Cert. tchr., Miss.; cert. in young adult/adolescent sci., Nat. Bd. Prof. Tchg. Stds. Adolescent/Young Adult Scis. Coord. Title I ESEA Choctaw County, Ackerman, Miss., 1970-73; instr. anatomy and physiology Wood Jr. Coll., Mathiston, Miss., 1977-78; instr. math. Miss. State U., Starkville, 1978-81; tchr. Choctaw City Sch. Dist., Ackerman, 1982—2003, dist. tech. coord., 1995—2003; facilitator PBS Teacherline, 2002—. Adj. faculty Lesley U., Cambridge, Mass., 2002—. Contbr. articles to profl. jours. including Surgery, T.H.E. Jour., Learning and Leading with Tech. Active Miss. State Bd. of Health, Jackson, 1980-94. Recipient Presdl. award for excellence in sci. teaching NSF, 1990, Sci. Tchr. awards Disney, 1993; named to Women Hall of Master Tchrs. Miss. U., 1994; named Educator of Yr. Milken Family Founds., 1991; Tandy scholar, 1991; Tapestry grantee, 1995; Coun. for Basic Edn. Sci.-Math. fellow, 1994, Access Excellence fellow Genentech, 1995, Am. Physiol. Soc. fellow, 1995, Einstein Disting. Educator fellow Dept. of Energy, 2000. Mem. Nat. Sci. Tchrs. Assn., Am. Assn. German Tchrs., Am. Assn. French Tchrs., Am. Assn. Physics Tchrs., Nat. Assn. Biology Tchrs., Miss. Edn. Computer Assn. (Miss. Computer Educator of Yr. 1990, pres.-elect 1995, pres. 1996), Miss. Fgn. Lang. Assn. (pres. secondary sect. 1992-94). Episcopalian. Avocations: reading, travel. Home: PO Box 268 Ackerman MS 39735-0268 Office: Choctaw County Sch Dist PO Box 398 Ackerman MS 39735-0398 E-mail: fcoleman@telepak.net.

COLEMAN, GARY WILLIAM, retired elementary school educator; b. Davenport, Iowa, Dec. 16, 1945; s. Robert Earl and Mildred Margaret (Mast) C.; m. Janice Marie Coleman, Dec. 29, 1973; children: Heidi Marie, Sean Robert. BS in Elem. Edn., U. S.D., 1987; BSBA, Ariz. State U., 1969. Cert. elem. tchr., S.D. Tchr. Marty (S.D.) Indian Sch., 1987-91, Parkston (S.D.) Elem. Sch., 1991-2000, ret., 2000; acct./bookkeeper Ulland Bros Constrn., Austin, Minn.; realtor assoc. Myre-Sorenson Real Estate, Albert Lea, Minn.; bldg. constrn. contractor, landscaper, Alcester, S.D.; site mgr. Heritage Ct. Apts., Oak Leaf Real Estate Mgmt. Ltd., 2001—03; preschool tutor South Ctrl. Edn. Coop., 2002—03; tutor Avon Elem. Sch., SD, 2003—; human resources coord. Boys and Girls Club, Wagner, SD, 2003—.

E.M.T., 1982—2003. Sgt. USAF, 1969-73. Mem. NEA, Parkston Edn. Assn. (v.p. 1995-96, pres. 1996-97, founder scholarship fund 1997), Am. Legion (vice-comdr. S.D. 7th Dist. 2003-2005).

COLEMAN, HENRY EDWIN, art educator, artist; b. Charlottesville, Va., Oct. 26, 1938; s. Albin Clayton and Mary Louise (Nay) C.; m. Charlotte Heyne, Dec. 29, 1962 (dec. 1984); children: Edwin Randolph, Mary Clayton; m. Leslie W. Rose, Jan. 4, 1993; 1 stepson, John A. Rose. AB in Fine Arts, Coll. William and Mary, 1961; MA, U. Iowa, 1963. Instr. art Lawrence Coll., Appleton, Wis., 1963-64; mem. faculty Coll. William & Mary, Williamsburg, Va., 1964-99, prof. fine arts, 1989—91, chair dept. fine arts, 1987—91. Cons. for purchasing CSX Corp. Art Collection, Richmond, Va., 1985. Illustrator: Oscar Wilde's Remarkable Rocket, 1974; one-man shows include Radford Coll., Va., 1975, Gallery II West, St. George, Utah, 1984, U. Maine, Presque Isle, 1989, Andrew & Laura McLain Mus., Florenceville, N.B., Can., 1989, Muscarelle Mus. of Art, William & Mary Coll., Williamsburg, Va., 1999, exhibited in group shows at Patio Show, Iowa City, 1962, 1963, Des Moines Art Ctr., 1963, Lawrence Coll., Appleton, 1964, 20th Century Gallery, Williamsburg, 1964, 1965, 1966, Chrysler Mus., Norfolk, Va., 1972, So. Ill. U. at Carbondale, 1975, Peninsula Art Ctr., Newport News, Va., 1980, Nat. Small Image Exhbn., Spokane, Wash., 1984, Am. Drawing Biennial Muscarelle Mus. of Art, Coll. William and Mary, Williamsburg, 1988, 1990 (Honorable Mention award), 1992, Internat. Cultural Exch. Art Exhibit, Neyagawa, Japan, 1988, Bowery Gallery, N.Y.C., 1988, Invitational D'Art Ctr., Norfolk, 1991, Peninsula Fine Arts Mus., Newport News, 1995, 1996, 2001. Commr. Williamsburg Arts Commn., 1985-91; bd. dirs. Yorktown (Va.) Arts Found., 1989-93; juror Occasion for the Arts, Williamsburg, 1988, 27th Regional Art Exhbn., W.C. Rawls Libr. & Mus., Courtland, Va., 1990; commr. archtl. rev. bd., City Williamsburg, 1994-2000. Summer Rsch. grantee Coll. William & Mary, 1976, Semester Faculty grantee, 1985, Faculty Rsch. grantee, 1991-92. Office: Coll William and Mary Andrews Hall Williamsburg VA 23185

COLEMAN, JULIE KATHRYN, elementary and secondary school educator; b. Peoria, Ill., Sept. 18, 1955; d. John Edward and Mary Ann (Koch) Birdoes Jr.; m. Richard Lee Coleman, Aug. 14, 1976; children: William Casey, Jaime Lee. BS in Edn., Ill. State U., 1977, MS in English, 1986. Cert. elem. educator, secondary English tchr., Ill., Ala., Fla.; nat. bd. cert. tchr. 2001. Tchr. English Norwood Sch., Peoria, Ill., 1977-85; tchr. Saint Pius X Sch., Mobile, Ala., 1985-86, Cora Castlen Elem. Sch., Grand Bay, Ala., 1986-87, Dr. W. J. Creel Elem. Sch., Melbourne, Fla., 1987-89, tchr., team chairperson, 1989-93; 7th and 9th grade lit. tchr. DeLaura Jr. High Sch., Satellite Beach, Fla., 1993—. Adv. bd. Limestone Area Curriculum Adv. Com., Peoria, 1977-85; adv. com. mem. Peoria County Inst. Curriculum Com., 1982-85; presenter in field. Mem. Metro-Mobile Reading Coun., Brevard Reading Coun., Fla. Reading Assn., Delta Kappa Gamma-Beta Sigma. Democrat. Roman Catholic. Avocations: reading, writing, embroidery. Home: 305 Park Ave Satellite Beach FL 32937-3018

COLEMAN, K(ATHERINE) ANN, behavioral psychology educator; b. Plattsburg, N.Y. d. John and Anna C. BS, Elms Coll., 1963; MS, Springfield Coll., 1964; PhD, Boston Coll., 1971; MPH, Harvard U., 1978. Psychologist Exec. Office of the Pres., Washington, 1964-66; rsch. assoc. Harvard U., Cambridge, Mass., 1970-71; asst. prof. SUNY, Stony Brook, 1971-75, assoc. prof., 1975-78, Boston U., 1978—. Owner, pres. La Di Da Properties, Cambridge, 1986—. Co-author: Behavioral Statistics: The Core, 1994, Fundamentals of Behavioral Statistics, 9th edit., 2000; contbr. articles to profl. jours. Fellow APA, Am. Psychol. Soc.; mem. New Eng. Ednl. Rsch. Orgn. (bd. dirs. 1974-86, v.p. 1985-86, pres. 1986-87), Ea. Ednl. Rsch. Orgn. (div. chmn. 1979-91, bd. dirs. 1985-91). Home: 44 Concord Ave Cambridge MA 02138-2380 Office: Boston U Dept Psychology 64 Cummington St Boston MA 02215-2407 E-mail: kaycole@bu.edu.

COLEMAN, KIMBERLY MARIE, elementary educator, special education educator; b. Potsdam, N.Y., Dec. 1, 1955; d. William Douglas and Miriam Elizabeth (Sanford) Krebs; m. Lawrence Brooks Coleman, Feb. 18, 1989; children: Jacquelynn Elizabeth, Melisa Marie, Rebecca Ann. BA cum laude, Brockport (N.Y.) State U., 1976; MS, Syracuse (N.Y.) U., 1983. Cert. in elem. edn., academically gifted, spl. edn.of mentally retarded and visually impaired. Title I team tchr. DeLaWarr Sch. Dist., New Castle, Del., 1977, pre-kindergarten and kindergarten spl. edn. tchr., 1977-81; jr. h.s. tchr. BOCES St. Lawrence County, Canton, N.Y., 1981-82; elem. tchr. Syracuse City Schs., 1982-85; spl. edn. h.s. resource tchr. North Syracuse (N.Y.) Sch. Dist., 1985-89; spl. edn. elem. resource tchr. Scotland County Schs., Laurinburg, N.C., 1991-92, tchr. visually impaired, 1992-2000, acad. gifted tchr., 1998-2000; visually impaired tchr. Chesapeake (Va.) Pub. Schs., 2000—. Tchr. of homebound/hosp.-bound Syracuse and North Syracuse Schs., 1982-89; active Very Spl. Olympics, 1985, 92, 94, 95, 97-99, 2003, Very Spl. Arts Festival, 1984, 85, 94, 95, 97-99. Author/illustrator: (pre-sch. books with tactile pictures for the blind) Tasty Treats, 1993, Good Morning, 1994, The Vegetable Garden, 1994. Dir. crafts Vacation Bible Sch., Laurinburg, 1991-93; dir. children's dept. Nazarene Ch., Syracuse, 1983-88. Mem. Coun. for Exceptional Children (learning disabilities divsn., visual impairment divsn., academically gifted), Scottish Pilot Club of Laurinburg (pres. 1999-2000). Christian. Avocations: skiing, travel, braille.

COLEMAN, MABETH HALLMARK, newspaper publishing professional; b. La Marque, Tex., Aug. 18, 1942; d. T.C. and Cordelia Rebecca (de Cordova) Hallmark; m. Kenneth Wayne Coleman, Mar. 6, 1964; children: Greg, Mark, Sally. BS, Tex. Woman's U., 1964. Tour guide Houston Chronicle, 1980-84, ednl. coord., 1984—. Advisor Harris County Journalism Com., Houston, 1986—. Active Arbor Oaks Civic Club, Houston, 1972—; mem., elder St. Giles Presbyn. Ch., Houston, 1972—; mem., chair Houston Area Model UN, Inc., Houston, 1986—; mem. steering com. Tex. State Citizen Bee, Houston, 1986—; chair steering com. Houston Area Regional Citizen Bee, 1986—; judge Tex. State History Day, Austin, 1989-92. Recipient Red Apple award Spring Br. Edn. Assn., 1989, Friend of Edn. award Clearlake Classroom Tchrs. Assn., 1994. Mem. Nat. Coun. for Social Studies, Nat. Alumnae Assn. Tex. Woman's U., Tex. Profls.-Newspapers in Edn., Tex. Coun. for Social Studies, UN Assn. of USA. Presbyterian. Avocations: traveling, family activities, sewing. Office: Houston Chronicle 801 Texas St Houston TX 77002-2996 Home: 2 Parkway Pl Houston TX 77040-1007

COLEMAN, MALCOLM JAMES, JR., band director, music educator, flute educator; b. Mexia, Tex., Feb. 4, 1947; s. Malcolm James and Wilma (Freeman) C. AAS, Navarro Coll., 1967; MusB, U. North Tex., 1970, M in Music Edn., 1975, PhD, 1987; MusD (hon.), London Inst. Applied Rsch., 1991, Inst. Coordinated Rsch., Australia, 1991, Acad. of Scis. Humanities U., Paris, 1991; DSc (hon.), Collegium Sancti Spiritus, Calif., 1991, The Internat. U., Bombay, 1991; Prof. (hon.), European Sci. & Ednl. Instn., Brussels, 1991; Full Accreditation (hon.), Internat. Cultural Correspondence Inst., Madras, India, 1991; MD (hon.), U. Guadalajara, Mexico, 1993. Lic. profl. counselor, Tex., lic. profl. counselor supr.; cert. sch. counselor, TRT counselor. Flute player NORAD Band, Colo., 1970-73; flute player on temporary duty USAF Acad. Band, 1972; band dir. Hubbard High Sch., Tex., 1974-75, Bremond High Sch., Tex., 1977-79; counselor Pecos-Barstow-Toyah Ind. Sch. Dist., Tex., 1979-84; band dir., flute tchr. Pharr-San Juan-Alamo I.S.D., Tex., 1985—. Lectr. flute U. Tex., Pan Am, 1995—; flute tchr. South Tex. C.C., 1999—; flute player USAF Acad. Band, 1972, N. Am. Air Def. Command Band, 1970-73. Flute and piccolo player, McAllen Town Band, Tex., 1985—, First Baptist Ch., Pecos, 1979-82, flute, piccolo player Rio Grande Valley Wind Symphony, 1994-95; prin. flutist Rio Grande Valley Symphony Orch., 1994-95; flute player Brownsville Cmty. Band, 1990-93. Served with U.S. Army, 1970-73. Recipient Commemorative Lifelong Achievemnt medal of Honor, 1987. Mem. NEA, Tex. Tchrs. Assn. (state del. 1981-82), Pecos-Barstow-Toyah Edn. Assn. (v.p. 1981-82, sec. 1983-84), Tex. Music Edn. Assn., Nat. Flute Assn., Tex. Bandmasters Assn., Internat. Parliament for Safety and Peace, Order KT's Jerusalem, Royal Order of Bohemian Crown (knight and baron), Assn. St. George the Martyr (knight), Holy Cross of Jerusalem (knight), Lofsenic Ursinius Order (knight and comdr.), Legion Aigle de Mer (capt.), Order of San Ciriaco (knight) (Italy), Circulo Nobiliario de los Caballeros (knight) (Spain), Ordre Souverain du Saint Sepulcre (Chevalier grand croix).

COLEMAN, MARY SUE, academic administrator; b. Richmond, Ky, Oct. 2, 1943; m. Kenneth Coleman; 1 child, Jonathan. BA, Grinnell Coll., 1965; PhD, U. N.C., 1969. NIH postdoctoral fellow U. N.C., Chapel Hill, 1969—70, U. Ky., 1971—72, instr., rsch. assoc. depts. biochemistry and medicine, 1972—75, asst. prof. dept. biochemistry, 1975—80, assoc. prof. dept. biochemistry, 1980—85, prof. dept. biochemistry, 1985—90; prof. dept. biochemistry and biophysics U. N.C., Chapel Hill, 1990—93; provost, v.p. for academic affairs, prof. biochemistry U. N.Mex., 1993—95; pres., prof. biochemistry, prof. biol. scis. U. Iowa, Iowa City, 1995—2002; pres. U. Mich., 2002—. Pres. Iowa Health Sys., 1995—2002; vice chancellor grad students and rsch. U. N.C., 1992—93, assoc. provost, dean rsch., 1990—92; trustee U. Ky., 1987—90, assoc. dir. rsch. L.P. Markey Cancer Ctr., 1983—90, dir. grad. studies biochem., 1984—87; acting dir. basir rsch. U. Ky. Cancer Ctr., 1980—83; NSF summer trainee Grinnell Coll., 1962; scientific cons. Abbott Labs., 1981—85, Collaborative Rsch., 1983—88, Life Techs., Inc., 1992; bd. trustees Univs. Rsch. Assn., 1998—; mem. rsch. accountability task force Am. Assn. Univs., 2000—, chair undergrad. edn. com., 1997—, mem. exec. com., 2001—; mem. task force on tchrs. edn. Am. Coun. Edn., 1998—; bd. dirs. Meredith Corp., Am. Coun. Edn.; mem. Big Ten Coun. Pres.'s, 1995—2002; mem. stds. success adv. bd. Am. Assn. Univs. and he Pew Charitable Trusts, 2000—; co-chair Inst. Medicine Com. on Consequences of Uninsurance, 2000—; mem. Gov.'s Strategic Planning Coun., 1998—2000, Imagining Am. Pres.'s Coun., 1999—, Bus.-Higher Edn. Froum, 1999—, Knight Commn., 2000—01; presenter in field. Mem. editl. bd.: Jour. Biol. Chemistry, 1989—93; contbr. articles to profl. jours. Trustee Crinnell Coll., 1996—; mem. bd. govs. Warren G. Magnuson Clin. Ctr., NIH, 1996—2000, State of Iowa Gov.'s ACCESS Edn. Commn., 1997; bd. dirs. United Way, Albuquerque, 1995. Fellow postdoctiral fellow, Clayton Found. Biochem. Inst., U. Tex., 1970—71. Fellow: AAAS, Am. Acad. Arts and Scis.; mem.: Nat. Coll. Athletic Assn. (bd. dirs. 2002—), Nat. Assn. State Univs. ans Land Grant Colls. Coun. Cchief Acad. Officers (exec. com. 1993—95), Am. Soc. Biochem. and Molecular Biology, Am. Assn. Cancer Rsch.

COLEMAN, MATTIE JONES, primary education educator; b. Montrose, Ga., July 28, 1943; m. Alger Shafter Coleman Jr., Nov. 23, 1968; children; Alger Shafter III, Chandra Mattiece. BA, Morris Brown Coll., 1966; MA, Atlanta U., 1971. Cert. elem. tchr., Ga.; tchr. support specialist. Tchr. kindergarten Atlanta Pub. Schs., 1966-70. 80—, lead tchr. day care, 1972-76, tchr. 1st grade, 1977-80. Leadership team chairperson Albright Elem. Sch.; mentor tchr. Author and creator brochure Parent Vols., 1988; author poem. Den master Atlanta region Boy Scouts Am., 1981; mem. adminstrv. com. Phyllis Wheatley YWCA, Atlanta, 1975-77; dep. registrar Fulton County Voters, Atlanta, 1980-84. Nat. Edn. Found. fellow, 1970-71; named Den Master of Yr., South Atlantic Region Boy Scouts Am. Mem. PTA, Am. Fedn. Tchrs. (telephone com. 1984), Nat. Tchr. Corp., Audubon (forest group II, chair children's activities), Order Ea. Star Masons (Worthy Matron), Alpha Kappa Alpha (Kappa Omega chpt., Anti-Grammateus). Democrat. Baptist. Avocations: traveling, reading, listening to music, arts, crafts. Home: 2895 Bob White Dr SW Atlanta GA 30311-3102

COLEMAN, PAUL DARE, electrical engineering educator; b. Stoystown, Pa., June 4, 1918; s. Clyde R. and Catharine (Livengood) C.; m. Betty L. Carter, June 20, 1942; children— Susan Dare, Peter Carter. AB, Susquehanna U., 1940; MS, Pa. State U., 1942; PhD, Mass. Inst. Tech., 1951, D.Sc. (hon.), 1978. Asst. physics Susquehanna U., 1938-40, Pa. State U., 1940-42; physicist USAF-WADC, Wright Field, Ohio, 1942-46, Cambridge Air Research Center, also; grad. research assoc. Mass. Inst. Tech., 1946-51; prof. elec. engring., dir. electro-physics lab. U. Ill. at Urbana, 1951—. Recipient meritorious civilian award USAAF, 1946 Fellow AAAS, IEEE, MTT (Disting. Educator award 1994, Centennial medal 1984), Optical Soc. Am., Am. Phys. Soc.; mem. Sigma Xi, Pi Mu Delta, Pi Mu Epsilon, Eta Kappa Nu. Achievements include research on millimeter waves, submillimeter waves, relativistic electronics, far infrared molecular lasers, beam wave guides and detectors, chem. lasers, nonlinear optics, solid state electronics. Home: 710 Park Lane Dr Champaign IL 61820-7633 Office: Univ Ill 133 Everitt Lab 1406 W Green St Urbana IL 61801-2918

COLEMAN, PAUL JEROME, JR., physicist, educator; b. Evanston, Ill., Mar. 7, 1932; s. Paul Jerome and Eunice Cecile (Weissenberg) C.; m. Doris Ann Fields, Oct. 3, 1964; children: Derrick, Craig. BS in Engring. Math., BS in Engring. Physics, U. Mich., 1954, MS in Physics, 1958; PhD in Space Physics, UCLA, 1966. Rsch. scientist Ramo-Wooldridge Corp. (name now TRW Systems), El Segundo, Calif., 1958-61; instr. math. U. So. Calif., L.A., 1958-61; mgr. interplanetary scis. program NASA, Washington, 1961-62; rsch. scientist UCLA, 1962-66, prof. geophysics, space physics, 1966—; asst. lab. dir., mgr. Earth and Space Scis. divsn., chmn. Inst. Geophysics and Planetary Physics Nat. Lab., Los Alamos, N.Mex., 1981-86; dir. Inst. Geophysics and Planetary Physics UCLA, 1989-92; dir. Nat. Inst. for Global Environ. Change, 1994-96; pres. Univs. Space Rsch. Assn., Columbia, Md., 1981-2000, Girvan Inst. Tech., 2002—. Bd. dirs. Axcess Inc., Dallas, Biocentric Solutions, Inc., Madison, Wis., others; mem. adv. bd. San Diego Supercomputer Ctr., 1986-90, chmn., 1987-88, others; trustee Univs. Space Rsch. Assn., Columbia, Md., 1981-2000, Am. Tech. Alliances, 1990-2002, Internat. Small Satellite Orgn., 1992-96; vis. scholar U. Paris, 1975-76; vis. scientist Lab. for Aeronomy Ctr. Nat. Rsch. Sci., Verrieres le Buisson, France, 1975-76; com. mem. numerous sci. and ednl. orgns., cons. numerous fin. and indsl. cos. Co-editor: Solar Wind, 1972; co-author: Pioneering the Space Frontier, 1986; mem. editorial bd. Geophysics and Astrophysics Monographs, 1970—; assoc. editor Cosmic Electrodynamics, 1968-72; contbr. revs. to numerous profl. jours. Apptd. to Nat. Commn. on Space, Pres. of U.S., 1985, apptd. to Space Policy Adv. Bd., Nat. Space Coun., v.p. of U.S., 1991; bd. dirs. St. Matthew's Sch., Pacific Palisades, Calif., 1979-82, v.p., 1981-82. 1st lt. USAF, 1954-56, Korea. Recipient Exceptional Sci. Achievement Medal NASA, 1970, 1972, spl. recognition for contributions to the Apollo Program, 1979; Guggenheim fellow 1975-76, Fulbright scholar, 1975-76, Rsch. grantee NASA, NSF, Office Naval Research, Calif. Space Inst., Air Force Office Sci. Research, U.S. Geol. Survey. Mem. AIAA, Am. Geophys. Union, Internat. Acad. Astronautics, Bel Air Bay Club (L.A.), Birnam Wood Golf Club (Montecito, Calif.), Cosmos Club (Washington), Valley Club (Montecito, Calif.), Eldorado Country Club (Indian Wells, Calif.), Tau Beta Pi, Phi Eta Sigma. Avocations: flying, skiing, racquetball, tennis, golf. Home: 1323 Monaco Dr Pacific Palisades CA 90272-4007 Office: UCLA Inst Geophysics & Planetary Physics 405 Hilgard Ave Los Angeles CA 90095-9000

COLEMAN, PAUL JOHN, special education educator; b. Newark, May 28, 1964; s. Paul John and Mary A. (Valente) C.; m. Andrea Marie Yanuzzi, July 23, 1994. BA, Jersey City State U., 1986, MA, 1988, MA, 1993. Substitute tchr. Harrison (N.J.) Bd. Edn., 1985-86; H.S. spl. edn. tchr. Montclair (N.J.) Bd. Edn., 1987, Kearny (N.J.) Bd. Edn., 1987—; asst. football coach Kearny (N.J.) H.S., 1987—, asst. wrestling coach, 1988—. Elem. tchr. of handicapped Kearny Summer Sch. Program, 1994; head wrestling coach Harrison H.S., 1985-87. Vol. counselor Camp Fatima, N.J., 1982—; lector, mem. folk mass choir Holy Cross Ch., Harrison; mem. Harrison Halloween Parade Com., 1988—; coach Little League Baseball, Harrison, 1978-82; vol. Kearny Spl. Recreation/Edn. Program, Hudson County Spl. Olympics; mem. com. Hands Across Am.; mem. Harrison Sesquicentennial Parade Com. Fellow Jersey City State Coll., 1986. Mem. ASCD, KC, Moose, Lions, Elks (exalted ruler 1987-88, chmn. scholarship, chmn. hoop shoot, chmn. youth activities, mem. drug awareness com., mem. handicapped com.). Democrat. Roman Catholic. Home: 8 Hamilton St Flemington NJ 08822-3162

COLEMAN, ROBERT GRIFFIN, geology educator; b. Twin Falls, Idaho, Jan. 5, 1923; s. Lloyd Wilbur and Frances (Brown) C.; m. Cathryn J. Hirschberger, Aug. 7, 1948; children: Robert Griffin Jr., Derrick Job, Mark Dana. BS, Oreg. State U., 1948, MS, 1950; PhD, Stanford U., 1957. Mineralogist AEC, N.Y.C., 1952-54; geologist U.S. Geol. Survey, Washington, 1954-57, Menlo Park, Calif., 1958-80; prof. geology Stanford U., Calif., 1981-93, prof. emeritus, 1993—. Vis. petrographer New Zealand Geol. Survey, 1962-63; br. chief isotope geology U.S. Geol. Survey, Menlo Park, 1964-68, regional geologist, Saudi Arabia, 1970-71, br. chief field geochemistry and petrology, Menlo Park, 1977-79; vis. scholar Woods Hole Oceanographic Inst., Mass., 1975; vis. prof. geology Sultan Qaboos U., Oman, 1987, 89; cons. geologist, 1993—; instr. geobotany field sch. Siskiyou Inst., Oreg., 1998-99. Author: Ophiolites, 1977, Geologic Evolution of the Red Sea, 1993, Ultrahigh Pressure Metamorphism, 1995; contbr. articles to profl. jours. Named Outstanding Scientist, Oreg. Acad. Sci., 1977; Fairchild scholar Calif. Inst. Tech., Pasadena, 1980; recipient Meritorious award U.S. Dept. Interior, 1981 Fellow AAAS, Geol. Soc. Am. (coun.), Am. Mineral Soc. (coun., editor), Am. Geophys. Union; mem. Nat. Acad. Scis., Russian Acad. Sci. (fgn. assoc.). Republican. Avocations: wood carving, art. Home: 2025 Camino Al Lago Atherton CA 94027-5938 E-mail: coleman@pangea.stanford.edu.

COLEMAN, ROY EVERETT, secondary education educator, computer programmer; b. Chgo., Oct. 16, 1942; m. Dianna Joy Uchida, Nov. 12, 1988. BS in Physics, Ill. Inst. of Tech., 1964; MS in Physics, DePaul U., 1974; Sci. Edn., Ill. Inst. of Tech., Chgo., 1990; Computer Sci., Chgo. State U., Chgo., 1984. Physics tchr. Morgan Park H.S., Chgo., 1965—, St. Xavier Coll., Chgo., 1977-80; S.M.I.L.E. staff specialist Ill. Inst. of Tech., Chgo., 1982—, computer edn. staff, 1988—. Dir. comp. lit. Chgo. Pub Schs., 1983—84; exec. chair Chgo. Sci. Fair, 2002—. Author: Equipment Evaluation, 1982; co-author: Physics Text Evaluations, 1984. Mem. Pursuit of Excellence Com., Chgo., 1982-88, Scholarship Com., 1985-89; chmn. student sci. fair Chgo. Pub. Schs., 2002—. Recipient Phoebe Aperton Hurst award Nat. PTA, Washington, 1985, Tchr. of Yr. award Chgo. PTA, 1978-80, Presdl. award of Excellence, U.S. Dept. Edn., 1987, Supt. award Chgo. Pub. Schs., 1979, 80, H.S. Tchr. of Astronaut Dr. Mae C. Jemison award, Kohl Internat. Tchg. award, 1994, First pl. Chgo. Rd. Rally Series, 1997, 99; Tandy Tech. scholar, 1995; finalist Golden Apple awards, 1995. Mem.: Am. Assn. Physics Tchrs. (treas., pres. Chgo. chpt.), Sports Car Club Am. (Ind. N.W. region). Avocations: road rallies (rallyemaster, driver scca road rallye), computer games, auto mechanics. Home: 5436 S Kimbark Ave Chicago IL 60615-5284

COLEMAN, SALLYE TERRELL, retired social studies educator; b. Roanoke, Va. d. Glen Watson and Addie (Winstead) Terrell; m. William Daniel Coleman, Apr. 14, 1949. BA, Va. State U., 1941; postgrad., NYU, 1951, U. Va., 1962, 63, Interamerican U., Saltillo, Mex., 1966. Cert. tchr., Va. Tchr. Roanoke Pub. Schs., 1941-70, dir. fed. program, 1970-74. Presenter clinics at profl. meetings. Mem. Roanoke City Sch. Bd., 1984-92, vice-chmn., 1987-90; bd. dirs. United Way, Roanoke, 1984-87, Coun. Community Svcs., Roanoke, 1983-84, Family Svc., Roanoke, 1981-84; mem. Community Hosp. Vol. Aux., Roanoke, 1975—; bd. govs. Found. of Roanoke Valley, 1993—. Recipient Meritorious Teaching award Nat. Coun. Geographic Edn., Atlanta, George Washington Honor medal Freedom Found., Valley Forge, Pa., Edn. award Roanoke NAACP, Image award, 2000, Brotherhood citation NCCJ, Roanoke, Disting. Svc. award Va. Congress Parents and Tchrs.; named Gov. Emeritus Found. for Roanoke Valley. Mem. NAACP (life), Va. Sch. Bds. Assn. (bd. dirs. 1990-92, Excellence in Edn. award 1991), Roanoke City Ret. Tchrs., Zeta Phi Beta (Woman Achiever award 1986). Baptist. Avocations: reading, gourmet cooking, travel, volunteer activities. Home: 4700 Grandin Rd SW Roanoke VA 24018-1928

COLEMAN, SIDNEY RICHARD, physicist, educator; b. Chgo., Mar. 7, 1937; s. Harold Albert and Sadie (Shanas) C. BS, Ill. Inst. Tech., 1957; PhD, Calif. Inst. Tech., 1962. Research fellow dept. physics Harvard U., 1961-63, asst. prof., 1963-66, assoc. prof., 1966-69, prof., 1969—, Donner prof. of sci. Vis. prof. U. Rome, Italy, 1968, Princeton U., 1973, Stanford U., 1979-80, U. Calif., Berkeley, 1989, 95. Author: Aspects of Symmetry, 1985. Trustee Aspen Ctr. Physics. Recipient prize for physics lectures Ettore Majorana Centre Sci. Culture, Boris Pregel award N.Y. Acad. Sci., Disting. Alumnus award Calif. Inst. Tech., Dirac medal Internat. Centre for Theoretical Physics 1990. Fellow NAS (J. Murray Lack award for sci. revs.), Am. Acad. Arts and Sci., Am. Phys. Soc. (Dannie Heineman prize); mem. Lilapa. Home: 1 Richdale Ave Unit 12 Cambridge MA 02140-2610 Office: Harvard U Physics Dept Cambridge MA 02138 E-mail: coleman@physics.harvard.edu.

COLEMAN, TOMMY LEE, soil science educator, researcher, laboratory director; b. Baxley, Ga., Nov. 8, 1952; s. E.C. and Lucille (Fussell) C.; m. Mildred Cross, Dec. 22, 1974 (div. 1977); m. Edna Thompson, Mar. 6, 1982; children: Sherri, Thomas, Brian. BS in Agronomy, Fort Valley State Coll., 1974; MS, U. Ga., 1977; PhD, Iowa State U., 1980. Soil scientist USDA/Soil Conservation Svc., Statesboro, Ga., 1974-77; rsch. assoc. Iowa State U., Ames, 1977-80; postdoctoral fellow in rsch. Ala. A&M U., Normal, 1981-83, asst. prof., 1983-89, assoc. prof., 1989-93, prof. soil sci. and remote sensing, 1993—, dir. remote sensing lab, 1990-95, dir. Ctr. for Hydrology, Soil Climatology and Remote Sensing, 1995—; rsch. phys. scientist USGS, Reston, Va., 1992-93; dir. Ctr. Hydrology, Soil Climatology, and Remote Sensing, 1995—. Cons. Abiola Farms Ltd., Lagos, Nigeria, 1988, U.S. AID-Botswana, Gaborone, 1989-91, 1993—, INRAN-DRE and U.S. AID-Niger, Niamey, 1990. Contbr. articles to profl. jours. Mem. Am. Soc. Agronomy, Soil Sci. Soc. Am., Am. Soc. Photogrammetry and Remote Sensing, NAACP, Profl. Soil Classifiers of Ala., Minorities in Agrl., Natural Resources and Related Scis., North Ala. Golf Club (pres. Huntsville chpt. 1987-92), Omega Psi Phi (Xi Omicron chpt., chair scholarship com. Huntsville chpt. 1986-90). Democrat. Baptist. Office: Ala A&M U Dept Plant & Soil Sci PO Box 1208 Normal AL 35762-1208

COLER, MYRON A(BRAHAM), chemical engineer, educator; b. N.Y.C., Mar. 30, 1913; s. Marcus and Bertha (Bebarfald) C.; m. Viola Ethel Buchbinder, Nov. 15, 1942 (dec. Jan. 1993); children: Mark D., Sandra Coler Carson; m. Lena Amark, Feb. 16, 1996 (div. Mar. 1998). AB, Columbia U., 1933, BS, 1934, ChE, 1935, PhD, 1937; postgrad., NYU, Bklyn. Poly. Inst. With NYU, N.Y.C., 1941-75, prof., dir. surface tech. program dir. creative sci. program. Supr., rsch. scientist Manhattan Project, 1943-45; founder, pres., dir. chmn. bd. Markite Co., Markite Corp., Markite Engrng. Co., 1948-67, Coler Engring. Co., 1967—, The Vulcan Press Divsn., Valmath, 1988—; sponsor-in-residence Franklin Inst. Rsch. Labs., 1975-81; cons. numerous cos. and govt. agys. Author: Aircraft Engine Finishes, 1941; editor, contbg. author: Essays on Creativity in the Sciences, 1963, Essays on Invention and Education, 1977; numerous articles to profl. jours.; patentee in field. Bd. dirs. Marcus and Bertha Coler Found.; mem. adv. com. dept. phys. and engring. metallurgy Polytechnic Inst. N.Y.; mem. pres.'s com. for Sch. Continuing Edn., NYU; appointee Nat. Inventors Coun., 1966-74; mem. state tech. svc. com. Dept. Commerce; with divsn. cultural studies UNESCO-Dept. State, 1982. Named hon. prof. Polytechnic Inst. N.Y.; Weston fellow Electrochem. Mem. AAAS, Am. Math. Soc., Materials Rsch. Soc., Am. Nuclear Soc., N.Y. Acad. Sci., Electrochem. Soc., Am. Ceramic Soc., Am. Chem. Soc., Am. Soc. for Metals, Am. Def.

Preparedness Assn., Internat. Precious Metals Inst., Sigma Xi, Phi Beta Kappa, Phi Lambda Upsilon, Tau Beta Pi, Epsilon Chi. Address: Empress Hotel 7766 Fay Ave La Jolla CA 92037-4309

COLES, ANNA LOUISE BAILEY, retired university official, nurse; b. Kansas City, Kans., Jan. 16, 1925; d. Gordon Alonzo and Lillie Mai (Buchanan) Bailey; children: Margot, Michelle, Gina. Diploma, Freedmen's Hosp. Sch. Nursing, 1948; BSN, Avila Coll., Kansas City, Mo., 1958; MSN, Cath. U. Am., 1960, PhD in Higher Edn., 1967. Instr. VA Hosp., Topeka, 1950—52, supr. Kansas City, Mo., 1952—58; asst. dir. in-service edn. Freedmen's Hosp., Washington, 1960—61, adminstrv. asst. to dir. nursing, 1961—66, assoc. dir. nursing services, 1966—67, dir. nursing, 1967—69; dean Howard U. Coll. Nursing, Washington, 1968—86, dean emeritus, 1986—; cons. pvt. practice, Kansas City, Kans.; dir. minority devel. U. Kans., 1991—95. Pres. Nurses Examining Bd., 1967—68; cons. Gen. Rsch. Support Program, NIH, 1972—76; mem. Inst. Medicine, NAS, 1974—; cons. VA Ctrl. Office continuing edn. com., 1976—; mem. D.C. Health Planning Adv. Com., 1967—68, Tri-State Regional Planning Com. for Nursing Edn., 1969, Health Adv. Coun., Nat. Urban Coalition, 1971—73; bd. dirs. Hilton Grand Vacation CLub Seaworkd Internat. Ctr. Contbr. articles to profl. jours. Trustee Cmty. Group Health Found., 1976—77, cons., 1977—; bd. regents State Univ. Sys. Fla., 1977; adv. bd. Am. Assn. Med. Vols., 1970—72; bd. dirs. Iona Whipper Home for Unwed Mothers, 1970—72, Nursing Edn. Opportunities, 1970—72. Recipient Sustained Superior Performance award, HEW, 1962, Meritorious Pub. Svc. award, Govt. of D.C., 1968, medal of honor, Avila Coll., 1969, Disting. Alumni award, Howard U. Nat. Assn. for Equal Opportunity in Higher Edn., 1990, Cmty. Svc. award, Black Profl. Nurses Kansas City, 1991, Lifetime Achievement award, Assn. Black Nursing Faculty in Higher Edn., 1993, Svc. award, Midwest Regional Conf. on Black Families and Children, 1994. Mem.: ANA, Am. Assn. Colls. Nursing (sec. 1975—76), Am. Congress Rehab. Medicine, Nat. League Nursing, Societas Docta (charter, pres. 1996—99), Freedmen's Hosp. Nursing Alumni Assn., Alpha Kappa Alpha, Sigma Theta Tau. Home: 15107 Interlachen Dr Apt 205 Silver Spring MD 20906-5627

COLES, LORI JANE, secondary school educator; b. Elkhart, Kans., Mar. 5, 1963; d. Lawrence R. and Elma Ruth Smith; m. Lyn Mark Coles, June 30, 1984; children: Jamie, Jason. Student, Emporia State U., 1981—84; BS, Cameron U., 1985; MS, Pittsburg State U., 1996. Cert. tchr. Kans. Sci. instr. Cherokee (Kans.) Unified Sch. Dist. 247, 1989—97, Plains (Kans.)-Kismet Unified Sch. Dist. 483, 1997—99, Meade (Kans.) Unified Sch. Dist. 226, 1999—. Mem. sch. improvement com. Cherokee USD 247, 1992—97, Meade USD 226, 1999—; presenter in field. Vol. Boy Scouts Am., Cherokee, Meade, 1991—. Grantee Students in Free Enterprise grant, Pittsburg State U., 1995, 1996, Excellence in Edn. grant, Wolf Creek Nuc. Corp., Burlington, Kans., 1998, 2000. Mem.: Kans. Assn. Tchrs. Sci., Nat. Sci. Tchr. Assn. Avocations: needlecrafts, reading, crafts, camping. Office: Meade HS Unified Sch 226 Box 400 Meade KS 67864

COLES, ROBERT, child psychiatrist, educator, author; b. Boston, Mass., Oct. 12, 1929; s. Philip and Sandra (Young) C.; m. Jane Hallowell; children— Robert, Daniel, Michael. AB, Harvard U., 1950; MD, Columbia U., 1954; MD (hon.), Temple U., Notre Dame U., Bates Coll., 1972, Wayne State U., 1973, Western Mich. U., Holy Cross Coll., 1974, Hofstra U., 1975, Coll. William and Mary, Bard Coll., U. Lowell, U. Cin., 1976, Stonehill Coll., Lesley Coll., Rutgers U., 1977, Wesleyan U., Columbia Coll., Knox Coll., Cleve. State U., Wooster Coll., 1978, U. N.C., Manhattan Coll., St. Peter's Coll., Coll. New Rochelle, Pratt Inst. and Sch. Design, 1979, Berea Coll., Bklyn. Coll., Emmanuel Coll., 1980, Colby Coll., 1981, Sienna Heights Coll., Salem State Coll., Williams Coll., 1983, Beloit Coll., 1984, Emory U., Fairfield U., Macalaster Coll., Colgate U., 1986, Dartmouth Coll., 1987. Intern U. Chgo. Clinics, 1954-55; resident in psychiatry Mass. Gen. Hosp., Boston, 1955-56, McLean Hosp., Belmont, Mass., 1956-57, Judge Baker Guidance Center-Children's Hosp., 1957-58; mem. staff children's Unit Met. State Hosp., Waltham, Mass., 1957-58; mem. staff alcoholic clinic Mass. Gen. Hosp.; teaching fellow in psychiatry, mem. psychiat. staff and clin. asst. in psychiatry Harvard Med. Sch., 1955-58; research psychiatrist Harvard U. Health Services, 1963—; lectr. gen. edn. Harvard U., 1966—, prof. psychiatry and med. humanities, 1977—; founder and editor DoubleTake Magazine, 1995—. Child psychiat. fellow Judge Baker Guidance Center, Children's Hosp., Boston, 1960-61; mem. Nat. Adv. Com. on Farm Labor, 1965— ; cons. Appalachian Vols., 1965—, Rockefeller Found., 1969—, Ford Found., 1969— ; mem. Inst. of Medicine, Nat. Acad. Scis., 1973-78; vis. prof. public policy Duke U., 1973— ; cons. supr. dept. psychiatry Cambridge (Mass.) Hosp., 1976— ; cons. Center for Study of So. Culture, U. Miss., 1979— ; bd. dirs. Ctr. for Documentary Studies, Duke U.; vis. prof. psychiatry, Dartmouth Coll., 1989. Author: Children of Crisis: A Study of Courage and Fear, 1967, Dead End School, 1968, Still Hungry in America, 1969, The Grass Pipe, 1969, The Image is Yours, 1969; Wages of Neglect, 1969, Uprooted Children: The Early Lives of Migrant Farmers, 1970, Teachers and the Children of Poverty, 1970, Erik H. Erikson: The Growth of His Work, 1970, The Middle Americans, 1970, Migrants, Sharecroppers and Mountaineers, 1972, The South Goes North, 1972, Saving Face, 1972, Farewell to the South, 1972, A Spectacle Unto the World, 1973, Riding Free, 1973, The Darkness and the Light, 1974, The Buses Roll, 1974, Irony in the Mind's Life: Essays on Novels by James Agee, Elizabeth Bowen and George Eliot, 1974, Headsparks, 1975, The Mind's Fate, 1975, Eskimos, Chicanos and Indians, 1978, Privileged Ones, Vol. V of Children in Crisis book series, 1978, (with Jane Hallowell Coles) Women of Crisis Lives of Struggle and Hope, 1978, Walker Percy: An American Search, 1978, Flannery O'Connor's South, 1980, Women of Crisis; Lives of Work and Dreams, 1980, Dorothea Lange: Photographs of a Lifetime, 1982, (with Ross Spears) Agee, 1985, The Political Life of Children, 1986, Dorothy Day: A Radical Devotion, 1987, Simone Weil: A Modern Pilgrimage, 1987, Times of Surrender: Selected Essays, 1988, Harvard Diary, 1988, That Red Wheelbarrow, 1988, The Call of Stories: Teaching and the Moral Imagination, 1989, Rumors of Separate Worlds, 1989, The Spiritual Life of Children, 1990; contbg. editor: The New Republic, 1966—, Am. Poetry Rev, 1972—, Aperture, 1974—, Lit. and Medicine, 1981—, New Oxford Rev, 1981— ; mem. editorial bd.: Integrated Edn., 1967—, Child Psychiatry and Human Devel., 1969—, Rev. of Books and Religion, 1976—, Internat. Jour. Family Therapy, 1977—, Grants mag., 1977—, Learning mag., 1978—, Jour. Am. Culture, 1977—, Jour. Edn., 1979— ; bd. editors: Parents' Choice, 1978— ; editor: Children and Youth Services Rev., 1978— . Bd. dirs. Field Found., 1968— ; trustee Robert F. Kennedy Meml., 1968—, Robert F. Kennedy Action Corps, State of Mass., 1968—, Miss. Inst. Early Childhood Edn., 1968—, Twentieth Century Fund, 1971— ; bd. dirs. Reading is Fundamental, Smithsonian Inst., 1968—, Am. Freedom from Hunger Found., 1968—, Am. Parents Com., 1971— ; mem. corp. Boston Children's Service, 1970; mem. adv. council Inst. for Nonviolent Social Change of Martin Luther King, Jr. Meml. Center, 1971—, Ams. for Children's Relief, 1972— ; mem. nat. com. for Edn. of Young Children, 1972— ; mem. nat. adv. council Rural Am., 1976— ; trustee Austen Riggs Found., Stockbridge, Mass., 1976— ; mem. nat. adv. com. Ala. Citizens for Responsive Public Television, 1976— ; mem. adv. com. Nat. Indian Edn. Assn., 1976— ; visitor's com. mem. Boston Mus. Fine Arts, 1977; bd. dirs. Boys Club Boston, 1977; vis. com. Boston Coll. Law Sch., 1977; adv. Center for So. Folklore, 1978— ; mem. children's com. Edna McConnell Clark Found., 1978— ; bd. dirs. Lyndhurst Found., 1978— ; mem. nat. adv. bd. Foxfire Fund, Inc., 1979— . Recipient Ralph Waldo Emerson prize Phi Beta Kappa, 1967; Anisfield-Wolf award in race relations Saturday Rev., 1968; Hofheimer award Am. Psychiat. Assn., 1968; Sidney Hillman prize, 1971; Weatherford prize Berea Coll. and Council So. Mountains, 1973; Lilliam Smith Award So. Regional Council, 1973; McAlpin medal Nat. Assn. Mental Health, 1972; Pulitzer prize, 1973 (all received for Children of Crisis, Vols. II, III); disting. scholar medal Hofstra U., 1974; William A. Shonfeld award Am. Soc. Adolescent Psychiatry, 1977; MacArthur Found. award, 1981; Josepha Hale award, 1986; fellow Davenport Coll., Yale U., 1976— Fellow Am. Acad. Arts and Scis., Inst. Soc., Ethics and the Life Scis.; mem. Am. Psychiat. Assn., Am. Orthopsychiat. Assn. (past dir.), Acad. Psychoanalysis, Nat. Orgn. Migrant Children. Office: Harvard U Univ Health Svcs 75 Mount Auburn St Cambridge MA 02138-4960

COLES, WILLIAM HENRY, ophthalmologist, educator; b. Rochester, N.Y. BA, Ohio Wesleyan U., 1958; MD, Emory U., 1962; MS, La. State U., 1970. Diplomate Am. Bd. Ophthalmology. Intern Grady Hosp., Atlanta, 1962-63; resident Charity-La. State U., New Orleans, 1966-70; prof. ophthalmology Emory U., Atlanta, 1980-86, dir. postgrad. edn., 1981-86; prof. ophthalmology SUNY, Buffalo, 1986—, chmn. dept., 1986—. Clin. assoc. prof. Med. Univ. S.C., Charleston, 1980-86; chief of svc. Grady Meml. Hosp., Atlanta, 1981-84; chief ophthalmology svc. VA Hosp., Atlanta, 1984-86; chmn. adv. coun. Ophthalmic Surgery, 1998. Author: Ophthalmology: A Diagnostic Text, 1989; sect. editor: Medicine for the Practicing Physician, 1984 (Med. Textbook of Yr. award). Dir. Inst. Health Assessment, 1997—. Nat. Eue Inst. grantee, 1975-78. Mem. AMA, ACS (chair adv. coun. 1997—, regent 1998-), AAUP, Am. Acad. Ophthalmology (Disting. Svc. award 1989, sr. honor award 1998), Med. Soc. State of N.Y., Assn. Rsch. and Vision in Ophthalmology, Assn. Univ. Profs. in Ophthalmology (trustee, pres. 1996-97). Home: 120 Donegal Dr Chapel Hill NC 27517

COLE-SCHIRALDI, MARILYN BUSH, occupational therapy educator; b. N.Y.C., Jan. 29, 1945; d. George Lyman and Theis (Maurer) Bush; m. Carl E. Cole, Aug. 31, 1968 (div. June 1981); children: Charlot E. Sleeper, Bradley Eric Cole; m. Martin M. Schiraldi Sr., July 3, 1982. BA, U. Conn., 1966; grad. cert., U. Pa., 1969; MS, U. Bridgeport, 1982. Registered occupational therapist, Conn. Staff occupational therapy Ea. Pa. Psychiat. Inst., Phila., 1968-69; dir. occupational therapy Middlesex Meml. Hosp., Middletown, Conn., 1973-76; supervising occupational therapist Lawrence & Meml. Hosps. Day Treatment Ctr., New London, Conn., 1976-79; staff occupational therapist Newington Children's Hosp., Newington, Conn., 1980-82; asst. prof. occupational therapy Quinnipiac Coll., Hamden, Conn., 1982-95, assoc. prof., tenured, 1995—. Vis. faculty fellow Yale U., 1999-2001; cons. psychiat. svcs. VA Med. Ctr., West Haven, Conn., 1983-91; cons. Fairfield Hills Hosp., Newtown, Conn., 1989-91. Author: (textbook) Group Dynamics in Occupational Therapy, 1993, 3d edit., 2003; co-author Structured Group Experiences, 1982; contbr. chpts. to books, articles to profl. jours. Grantee Quinnipiac Coll, 1986; recipient Best Seller award Slack, Inc., 1999. Fellow: Am. Occupl. Therapy Assn. (Comms. award 1976, Svc. awards 1998, cert.); mem.: AAUW (cultural chair 1972, publicity chair 1973—76, edn. chair 1989—91, nominations 1993—96, membership treas. 1998—2001), Ctr. Study Sensory Integrative Dysfunction (cert. 1979), World Fedn. Occupl. Therapists, Conn. Occupl. Therapy Assn. (sec. 1978, nominations chair 1982—89, state mental health chair spl. interest sect. 1999—), U.S. Sailing Assn., U.S. Power Squadron, Sigma Xi. Republican. Episcopalian. Office: Quinnipiac U Dept Occupl Therapy 275 Mount Carmel Ave Hamden CT 06518-1961 E-mail: marilyn.cole@quinnipiac.edu.

COLETTA, NANCY JOY, vision scientist, educator; b. Pawtucket, R.I., Sept. 3, 1955; d. Armand Anthony and Nora Afton C. BS, Providence Coll., 1977; OD, Pa. Coll. Optometry, 1981; PhD, U. Calif., Berkeley, 1985. Guest worker Nat. Eye Inst., Bethesda, Md., 1980-81; rsch. assoc. Ctr. for Visual Sci. U. Rochester, N.Y., 1985-87; asst. prof. optometry U. Houston, 1988-94, assoc. prof. optometry, 1994—. Grant referee NSF, 1988-90; jour. referee Vision Rsch., 1985—, Jour. Physiology, 1990, Jour. Optical Soc., 1987—, Investigative Ophthalmology and Visual Sci., 1989—, Visual Neurosci., 1991—, Optometry and Vision Sci., 1994—. Contbr. articles to Applied Optics, Archives of Ophthalmology, Investigative Opththalmology and Visual Sci., Jour. Optical Soc. Am., Ophthalmic and Physiol. Optics, Vision Rsch. Recipient Harold Kohn award Am. Optometric Found., 1981, Chancellor's Patent Fund award U. Calif., Berkeley, 1985, Best Post award Houston Soc. for Engring. in Medicine and Biology, 1991; grantee SPIE, 1988, NIH, 1989, 91, Nat. Eye Inst., 1992—. Fellow Am. Acad. Optometry; mem. AAAS, Optical Soc. Am., Assn. for Rsch. in Vision and Ophahtlmology, Sigma Xi, Beta Sigma Kappa. Achievements include research in optical effects on night vision, in visual perceptual effects due to spatial sampling of retinal image by cone photoreceptors, non-invasive technique to measure cone spacing, and interactions between rod and cone mechanisms in human flicker sensitivity.

COLEY, BRENDA ANN, elementary education educator; b. Indpls., Sept. 17, 1958; d. Jack Louis Mullis and Margaret Ann (Crites) Farris; m. Keith Alan Coley, Feb. 17, 1978; children: Amy Michelle, Jared Wesley, Adam Jacob. B Music Edn., Ind. U., 1981; MS in Music Edn., Ind. State U., 1987. Tchr. music Clay Community Sch. Corp., Staunton, Ind., 1981-84; choral dir. Spencer (Ind.)-Owen Community Sch. Corp., 1984-90, tchr. music, 1990—2000; asst. prin. McCormick's Creek Elem. Sch., Spencer, Ind., 2000—. Composer children's musical: Up! Up to the Moon!!, 1992; composer gospel music., founder "Jubilation in Christ", gospel singing group, 1997-. Choir dir. 1st Christian Ch., Spencer. Mem. NEA, Music Educators Nat. Conf., Ind. Music Educators Assn., Spencer-Owen Edn. Assn., Order Ea. Star, Kappa Kappa Kappa, Pi Lambda Theta, Delta Theta Tau. Democrat. Avocations: singing, sports, bowling. Home: 40 Mozart Ln Spencer IN 47460-9344 Office: McCormick's Creek Elem Sch 1601 Flatwoods Rd Spencer IN 47460-1499

COLEY, LINDA MARIE, retired secondary school educator; b. Albany, Ga., Apr. 19, 1945; d. Leonard Earl and Hazel (Brady) C. BS in Math., Piedmont Coll., 1966; MS in Math., U. Ga., 1972, postgrad. Cert. tchr., Ga.; certed gifted tchr. Tchr. Toccoa (Ga.) Pub. Schs., 1966-67, Hall County Sch. Dist., Gainesville, Ga., 1967-68, Clarke County Sch. Dist., Athens, Ga., 1968—2001. Sec., 1st v.p. Clarke County Dem. Com., Athens, 1981—, Gov.'s Club. Mem. NEA, Ga. Edn. Assn., Clarke County Assn. Educators (treas., sec.), Alpha Delta Kappa (treas., sec., pres., dist. treas.), Phi Delta Kappa. Democrat. Baptist. Home: 135 Ravenwood Pl Athens GA 30605-3344

COLFACK, ANDREA HECKELMAN, elementary education educator; b. Yreka, Calif., July 17, 1945; d. Robert A. Davis and June (Reynolds) Butler; m. David Lee Heckelman, Sept. 5, 1965 (div. Nov. 1982); children: Barbara, Julie; m. Neal Cleve, Jan. 1, 1984; 1 stepchild, Karl. AB, Calif. State U., L.A., 1966; MA, Calif. State U., Fresno, 1969. Life std. elem. credential, Calif. cert. competence: Spanish, Calif.; ordained to ministry Faith Christian Fellowship Internat., 1987; Calif. preliminary adminstrv. credential, 1995. Tchr. Tulare (Calif.) City Schs., 1966-67, Palo Verde Union Sch. Dist., 1967-70, Cutler-Orosi (Calif.) Union Sch. Dist., 1979-82, Hornbrook (Calif.) Union Sch. Dist., 1982-84; sales mgr. Tupperware, Fresno, Calif., 1973-79; bilingual tchr. West Contra Costa (Calif.) Unified Sch. Dist., 1984-95, prin. Bayview Elem. Sch., 1995—2000; prin. Rosa Parks Elem. Sch., Berkeley Unified Sch. Dist., 2000—01; prin. E.M. Downer Elem. Sch., West Contra Costa Unified Sch. Dist., 2001—. Site mentor Bayview Elem. Sch., Richmond, 1990-92; ELD mentor, Richmond, 1992-94, mentor selection com., 1994-95; summer sch. prin. Grant Elem. Sch., Richmond, 1995. Co-author: Project Mind Expansion, 1974. Recipient Calif. Dist. Sch. award, 1998; East Bay C.U.E. Tech. grantee, 1995. Mem. Calif. Assn. Bilingual Educators (sec. Richmond 1990-91), AAUW (pres. Tulare br. 1967-68), Calif. Assn. Sch. Adminstrs., Richmond Assn. Sch. Adminstrs. Democrat. Pentecostal. Avocation: leading music and home bible studies. Home: 5461 Hackney Ln Richmond CA 94803-3830 Office: EM Downer Elem Sch 1777 Sanford Ave San Pablo CA 94806

COLIJN, GEERT JAN, academic administrator, political scientist; b. Naarden, The Netherlands, Sept. 23, 1946; came to US, 1969; s. Izak and Aaltje Cornelia (Rozeboom) C.; m. Sarah Ellen Griffith, Jan. 4, 1986; 1 child, Cornelia Alice. Kandidaat, U. van Amsterdam, 1969; MA, Temple U., 1971, PhD, 1977. From asst. prof. to assoc. prof. polit. sci. Richard Stockton Coll. NJ, Pomona, NJ, 1978-91, prof., 1991—, chmn. social and behavioral sci., 1982-85, dean of gen. studies, 1988—. Trustee Internat. House, Phila., 1990-2002; steering com. Visions of Higher Edn. Conf., Zurich, Switzerland, 1988-94; vis. fellow U. Warwick, 1987-88 Co-editor: Confronting the Holocaust, 1997, From Prejudice to Destruction, 1995, Hearing the Voices, 1999; mem. editl. bd. Jour. Genocide Studies; contbr. articles to profl. jour. Mem. exec. com. Holocaust Resource Ctr., Pomona, 1988—; trustee Community Justice Inst., Atlantic City, NJ, 1982-85; mem. nat. adv. coun. Anne Frank Ctr., 1992-94. Avocations: classical music, speedskating, travel. Home: 135 Old New York Rd Port Republic NJ 08241-9739 Office: Richard Stockton Coll NJ Jimmie Leeds Rd Pomona NJ 08240 E-mail: jan.colijn@stockton.edu.

COLIZ, JAMES RUSSELL, university administrator, telecommunications consultant; b. Orange, N.J., May 7, 1948; s. James T. and Eleanor Louise (Cragle) C.; m. Donna S. Coliz, Dec. 17, 1977 (div. 1995); 1 child, Rebecca Elizabeth. BS in Econs., U. Wis., Stevens Point, 1973; MS in Telecomm., Colo. U., Boulder, 1986; PhD in Telecomm., Ind. U., 1990. Sr. staff asst. Mut. Benefit Life, Kansas City, Mo., 1973-79; agy. office mgr. New Eng. Life, Denver, 1979-84; lectr. Ind. U., Bloomington, 1988-89; asst. prof. Syracuse (N.Y.) U., 1989-96, dir. M.S. program in telecomm., 1992-96; asst. prof. SUNY, 1996—; dir. Telecomm. Inst., SUNY, Utica, 1997—; mng. ptnr., dir. rsch. Silver Plume Rsch. Group, 1997—. Senator Syracuse U. Senate, 1991-96, chmn. senate com. on student life, 1994-96; cons. mem. No. Telecom. Cons. Liaison Program, Richardson, Tex., 1994—; mem. bd. grad. studies Syracuse U., 1994—. Contbr. articles to profl. jours. Staff sgt. U.S. Army, 1970-71, Vietnam. Ameritech fellow Ind. U., Bloomington, 1988-89; grantee Syracuse U., 1992, 94. Mem. Telecomm. Mgrs. Assn., Ctrl. N.Y. Comm. Assn. Democrat. Mennonite. Home: 376 Grant Blvd # 326 Syracuse NY 13206-2601 Office: 376 Grant Blvd # 326 Syracuse NY 13206-2601

COLKER, MARVIN LEONARD, classics educator; b. Pitts., Pa., Mar. 19, 1927; s. Philip Marcus and Sarah (Grodner) C.; m. Hazel Robinson, Nov. 28, 1959; 1 son, Philip Ian. BA summa cum laude, U. Pitts., 1948; PhD, Harvard U., 1951; LittD (hon.), U. Dublin, 1987. Sheldon fellow Harvard U., 1951-52; Fulbright fellow U. Paris, 1951-52; Instr. classics U. Va., 1953-56, asst. prof., 1956-59, asso. prof., 1959-68, prof., 1967-98, chmn. dept. classics, 1963-68, prof. emeritus, 1998—. Cataloguer Mediaeval manuscripts U. Dublin, Ireland, 1958-88, lectr. patristics, Mediaeval Latin, 1962-63; co-dir. Mediaeval manuscripts course standing conf. Nat. and Univ. Librarians, Dublin, 1968 Author: Fulcoii Belvacensis Epistolae, 1954, Henrici Augustensis Planctus Evae, 1956, Richard of S. Victor and the Anonymous of Bridlington, 1962, Analecta Dublinensia: Three Medieval Latin Texts in the Library of Trinity College, Dublin, 1975, Galteri De Castellione Alexandreis, 1978, America Rediscovered in the Thirteenth Century, 1979, Trinity Coll. Dublin Library: Descriptive Catalogue of the Mediaeval and Renaissance Latin Manuscripts, 2 vols., 1991, A Previously Unpublished Hist. of the Trojans, 1998, Previously Unpublished Letters Ascribed to Saint Jerome, 2000, Michael of Belluno and His Speculum Conscientie: the Unique Manuscript Recently Discovered, 2003; mem. editl. bd. Medievalia et Humanistica; assoc. editor Retiarius. Grantee Am. Philos. Soc., Trinity Trust, NEH, U. Dublin Fund; ACLS fellow, 1962-63, Sesquicentennial Rsch. Assn. fellow U. Va., 1973-74, Ctr. Advanced Studies rsch. assoc. U. Va., 1992-93, Guggenheim fellow, 1973-74, Fulbright fellow to London and Dublin, 1987-88, Bibliog. Soc. Am. fellow, 1996. Mem. Am. Philol. Assn. (medieval Latin studies group), Mediaeval Acad. Am. (former councillor) Assn. for Manuscripts and Archives in Rsch. Collections, Medieval Latin Assn. N.Am., Classical Assn. Mid. West and South, Phi Beta Kappa. Home: 105 Westminster Rd Charlottesville VA 22901-2229 Office: U of Va 401 Cabell Hall Charlottesville VA 22903

COLL, EDWARD GIRARD, JR., university president; b. Pitts., Aug. 9, 1934; s. Edward G. and Alive V. (Ebeling) C.; m. Carole Hulse, Feb. 3, 1958; children— Thomas, Jean Coll Mendenhall, Peter, Karen, Kelly. BA, Duquesne U., 1960, LHD (hon.), 1983, Alfred U., 2000. Div. dir. United Fund Allegheny County, Pitts., 1959-61; asst. to exec. v.p. United Fund Dade County, 1961-63; asst. to v.p. for devel. affairs U. Miami, Fla., 1963-66, dir. corp. and found. relations, 1966-67, dir. devel., 1967-72, sec. univ. corp., 1972-73, v.p. for devel. affairs, 1973-82; pres. Alfred U., N.Y., 1982-2000; ret., 2000. Bd. dirs. Steuben Trust Co.; lectr. in field. Contbr. articles to profl. jours. Chmn. zoning bd. appeals Dade County, 1973-82; bd. dirs. Nat. Ctr. Child Abuse and Neglect, 1985-90; pres. com. NCAA, 1988-92, coun. mem. 1993-97, vice-chair divsn. III, 1990, v.p., 1994-96; trustee Coun. for Support and Advancement Edn., Washington, 1981-82, 87-89, chair, 1991-92. With U.S. Army, 1953-56. Univ. Adminstr. Fulbright fellow U. Warwick, Coventry, Eng., 1985. Mem. Ind. Colls. and Univs. N.Y. (bd. dirs. 1982-86), Duquesne Univ. Alumni Assn., Am. Mktg. Assn. (hon.), Miami Club, University Club, Genesee Valley Club, Wellsville Country Club, Delta Mu Delta, Phi Kappa Phi, Beta Gamma Sigma. Roman Catholic. Office: PO Box 121 Alfred Sta Alfred NY 14803 E-mail: coll@alfred.edu.

COLLETT, JENNIE, principal; Prin. OB Whaley Sch., San Jose, Calif., 1995—. Recipient Elem. Sch. Recognition award U.S. Dept. Edn., 1989-90. Office: O B Whaley Sch 2655 Alvin Ave San Jose CA 95121-1609

COLLIER, ALBERT M. pediatric educator, child development center director; b. Elba, Ala., May 3, 1937; s. Milford William and Ida Ruth C.; m. Mary Gaynell Wehler, July 17, 1960; children: Albert Mark, Dennis Murray, Jonathan Lee. BS, U. Miami, 1959, MD, 1963. Pediatric resident U. Miami, Coral Gables, Fla., 1963-66; infectious diseases fellow U. N.C., Chapel Hill, 1968-70, from asst. prof. to assoc. prof., 1971-80, prof., 1980—, divsn. chief infectious disease, 1980—, assoc. dir. ctr. environ. med. lung bio, 1980—, acting dir. Frank Porter Graham Child Devel. Ctr., 1990-92, assoc. chmn. of pediatrics for rsch., 1997—, med. sch. sci. integrity officer, 2000—. Contbr. over 100 articles to profl. jours. Recipient Louis Dienes award Internat. Orgn. Mycoplasmology, Vienna, Austria, 1988. Mem. Gideons (zone leader 1990-93). Baptist. Office: U NC Chapel Hill Dept Pediatrics 5135 Bioinformatics Cb 7220 Chapel Hill NC 27599-0001 E-mail: uncacl@med.unc.edu.

COLLIER, BOYD DEAN, finance educator, management consultant; b. Waco, Tex., Jan. 16, 1938; s. Denis Lee and Anne Alice (Berry) C.; m. Barbara Nell Joseph, June 20, 1966; children: Diedra Michelle, Christopher Boyd. BBA, Baylor U., 1963, MS, 1965; PhD, U. Tex., 1970. Diplomate Am. Bd. Forensic Acctg.; CPA, Tex. Asst. prof. Univ. of NC, Greensboro, NC, 1969-72, asst. dean, 1970-72; assoc. prof. U. Houston, Tex., 1972-73; chief ops. auditor Glastron Boat Co., Austin, Tex., 1973; prof. bus. econs., dean Ctr. for Bus. Adminstrn. St. Edward's U., Austin, Tex., 1974-83; prof. fin., head dept. acctg. and fin. Tarleton State U., Stephenville, Tex., 1983-96, exec. dir. office planning, evaluation and instrnl. rsch., accreditation liaison officer, 1996—. Co-owner Vranich, Collier Co., CPA's, Austin, 1974-83; v.p. fin. Execucom Sys., Austin, 1979; sr. lectr. U. Tex., Austin, 1980-83; compliance officer Tex. A&M U.; bd. dirs. Acctg. Info. Sys., Houston, 1974-78; advisor Office of Atty. Gen., State of Tex., Austin, 1986, Office of Comptr., State of Tex., Austin, 1986. Author: Measurement and Environmental Deterioration, 1971; editl. advisor Jour. Accountancy, NYC, 1982—; contbr. articles to profl. jours. Faculty advisor Coll. Reps. of Tex., Stephenville, 1984-1988. With USN, 1955-59. Fellow Earhart Found., Ann Arbor, Mich., 1963, 68, NSF, Washington, 1966. Mem. AICPA, Nat. Acctg. Assn. (v.p. 1978-83, Outstanding Svc. award 1983, Sargent Americanism award 1989), Am. Acctg. Assn., Tex. Soc. CP's, Southwestern Fin. Assn., U. Tex. Austin Ex-Students Assn. (life), Sigma Xi. Liberterian. Avocations: tennis, hiking, collecting coins and walking canes. Home: 930 N Charlotte Ave Stephenville TX 76401-2004 Office: Tarleton State U 1603 W Washington PO Box 505T Stephenville TX 76401-0505 E-mail: collier@tarleton.edu.

COLLIER, DAVID ALAN, management educator; b. Lexington, Ky., Aug. 3, 1947; s. J. Hamlet Jr. and Dorothy (Gifford) C.; m. Cindy Eddins, June 5, 1983; children: Christopher David, Thomas Andrew. BSME, U. Ky., 1970, MBA, 1972; PhD, Ohio State U., 1978. Materials mgr. Babcock & Wilcox Co., Barberton, Ohio, 1972-74; asst. prof. mgmt. Duke U., Durham, N.C., 1978-81; assoc. prof. U. Va., Charlottesville, 1981-86; prof. Ohio State U., Columbus, 1986—. Cons. numerous corp. exec. programs, 1980—; mem. bd. examiners Malcolm Baldrige Nat. Quality Award, 1991, 92. Author: Service Management: Automation of Services, 1985 (Freedom Found. for Econ. Excellence award 1985), Service Management: Operating Decisions, 1987, The Service/Quality Solution, 1994; contbr. articles to profl. jours. (recipient numerous awards). Ameritech Faculty fellow, 1989, U. Warwick Vis. Faculty fellow, 1995. Mem. Am. Soc. Quality Control, Decision Scis. Inst., Sigma Alpha Epsilon. Home: 1354 Hickory Ridge Ln Columbus OH 43235-1131 Office: Ohio State U 1775 S College Rd # 303 Columbus OH 43210-1309

COLLIER, EVELYN MYRTLE, elementary school educator; b. Newton, Ala., Dec. 11, 1942; d. Palmer Lee and Jessie Beryl (Williams) C. BA, Samford U., 1965; M Religious Edn., Southwestern Sem., 1967; MS, Troy State U., 1977. Youth dir. Calvary Bapt. Temple, Savannah, Ga., 1967-69; tchr. Newton Elem. Sch., 1969-77, prin., 1977-94; asst. prof. elem. edn. Fla. Bapt. Theol. Coll., Graceville, Fla., 1994—. Mem. ASCD, Ala. Assn. Elem. Sch. Prins. (exec. bd. 1984-94, sec. 1985, dist. IX pres. 1983, dist. IX Disting. Prin. award 1986, 89, 92), Ala. Coun. Sch. Adminstrs. and Suprs. (bd. dirs. 1991-94), Nat. Assn. Elem. Sch. Prins., Delta Kappa Gamma (Alpha Kappa chpt., Beta state exec. bd. 1987-96, pres. Ala. chpt. 1991-93, 1st v.p. 1989-91, 2d v.p. 1987-89, Golden Gift Fund award 1983, Internat. scholar 1996), Phi Delta Kappa, Kappa Delta Pi. Baptist. Avocations: singing, reading, swimming. Office: Bapt College Fla 5400 College Dr Graceville FL 32440-1831

COLLIER, JUDITH BRANDES, elementary education educator; b. Chgo., June 11, 1941; d. Rico G. and Frances (Miller) Bosca; m. Stanley H. Brandes, June 14, 1964 (div. May 1, 1987); children: Nina Stonebarger, Naomi; m. Neil Adrian Collier, June 11, 1987. BA, U. Calif., Berkeley, 1965. Bilingual tchr., resource tchr., reading recovery tchr. West Contra Costa Unified Sch. Dist., Richmond, Calif., 1978-97, project asst. Title VII, curriculum guide, 1997—. Mem.: Phi Beta Kappa, Phi Delta Kappa. Avocations: gardening, walking, traveling, birding. Home: 1335 Peralta Ave Berkeley CA 94702-1127 Office: Bayview Sch 3001 16th St San Pablo CA 94806 E-mail: jbcnajc@pacbell.net.

COLLIER, LINDA ARLENE, kindergarten educator; b. York, Pa., June 26, 1948; d. Daniel O. Sr. and Teresa M. (Phillips) Bumbaugh; m. George William Collier. BS, Elizabethtown Coll., 1970. Cert. tchr., Pa. Tchr. kindergarten Red Lion (Pa.) Area Sch. Dist., 1969—, elem. computer coord., 1985-86. Mem. tchr. adv. bd. York campus Pa. State U., 1991—. Mem. St. Paul's U.C.C. Ch., Dallastown, 1996—, Fools for Christ clown ministry, 1989—, York Symphony Chorus, 1995—, Jubilate Choral Ensemble, 1996—. Recipient Presdl. award for Excellence in Sci. and Math. Teaching NSF, 1992, 93. Mem. ASCD, Pa. Coun. Tchrs. Math., Nat. Coun. Tchrs. Math., Red Lion Area Math. Com., York Quilters Guild, NEA, Pa. State Edn. Assn., Red Lion Area Edn. Assn. Avocations: quilting, making teddy bears, reading historical fiction, composing music, playing oboe. Home: 290 Chestnut Hill Rd York PA 17402-9562 Office: North Hopewell Winterstown Elem Sch 12165 Winterstown Rd Red Lion PA 17356-8030

COLLIER, RUTH BERINS, political science educator; b. Hartford, Conn., June 20, 1942; d. Maurice and Esther (Meyers) Berins; m. David Collier; children: Stephen, Jennifer. AB, Smith Coll., 1964; MA, U. Chgo., 1966, PhD, 1974. Asst. prof. rsch. Ind. U., Bloomington, 1975-78; asst. to assoc. rsch. polit. scientist U. Calif., Berkeley, 1979-83, lectr., 1983-90, assoc. prof., prof., 1990—. Author: Regimes in Tropical Africa, 1982, The Contradictory Alliance: Labor Politics and the Regime Change in Mexico, 1992 (Hubert Herring award, 1993), Paths Toward Democracy: The Working Class and Elites in Western Europe and South America, 1999; co-author: Shaping the Political Arena: The Labor Movement, Critical Junctures, and Regime Dynamics in Latin America, 1991 (Comparative Politics Sect. award Am. Polit. Sci. Assn., 1993). Fellow Ctr. for Advanced Study in the Behavioral Scis., Stanford, 1994-95.

COLLIER, TOM WARD, musician, educator; b. Puyallup, Wash., June 30, 1948; s. Ward L. and Ethel M. (Turner) C.; m. Cheryl Anne Zilbert, May 31, 1970; children: Cara, Nina. BA, MusB, U. Wash., 1971. Freelance musician Seattle Symphony/Northwest Chamber Orch., 1967-74; drummer, vibraphonist Northwest Jazz Quintet, Seattle, 1972-80; studio musician various artists and shows including Barbra Streisand, Ry Cooder, American Music Awards, Harry O., Los Angeles, 1975-78; timpanist L.A. Repertoire Orch., 1976-77; jazz drummer Howard Roberts Quartet/Bill Smith Trio, Los Angeles, Seattle, 1975-82; freelance percussionist various artists including Johnny Mathis, Paul Williams, Jermaine Jackson, Sammy Davis Jr., Bob Hope, Barbra Streisand, Ry Cooder, Olivia Newton-John, The Beach Boys, Bud Shank, Earl "Fatha" Hines, Diane Schurr, Los Angeles, Seattle, 1976-91; jazz vibraphonist Collier/Dean Duo, Seattle, 1977—; rec. artist, leader band Tom Collier, Seattle, 1987—; faculty, dir. percussion studies U. Wash., Seattle, 1980—, sound prodn. evening degree adv. bd. dirs., 1994-2000. Leader Tom Collier Duo/Trio, Wash. State Arts Commn. Cultural Enrichment Program, 1980-95, Arts In Edn. Program, 1996-2001; owner Mallet Head Music, 1979—, T.C. Records, 1987-91; dir. N.W. Percussion Inst., Seattle, U. Wash. Jazz Inst., 1989—; dir. jazz studies U. Wash., 2001—; bd. dirs. South Ctr. Sch. Dist., Seattle, 1987-91; acad. cons. Experience Music Project, Museum, Seattle, 1990-2000. Rec. artist: (records) Whistling Midgets, 1981, Illusion, 1987, Pacific Aire, 1991; author: History of Jazz, Lecture Notes, Overheads and Listening Examples, 1997, (book/records) Jazz Improvisation and Ear Training, 1983, rev., 2003, Studio Call simulated Recording Sessions, 1984; composer: Quintet for Percussion Ensemble, 1972, Xenolith for Jazz Quartet and String Quartet, 1973, Piece for Electric Bass, Vibraphone and Orch., 1979, Nina's Joy, Busy Body, Tightwad, Subito Sox, 1991; jazz performances with Larry Coryell, Buddy DeFranco, Eddie Daniels, Emil Richards, 1975-2000; various film soundtrack performances with John Williams, Oliver Nelson, Kim Richmond, Henry Mancini; world premier performance of own composition Three Movements for Solo Marimba, 2000; pub. music includes Bar Code, Springtide, Day In, Day Out, Studio 4 Music Pub. Mem. arts adv. bd. Fed. Way Sch. Dist., 1992-94. Rockefeller rsch. grantee U. Wash., 1967-71, Royalty Rsch. Fund grantee, 2003. Mem. ASCAP (Spl. award 1981-97), Percussive Arts Soc., Nat. Assn. Jazz Educators (Outstanding Service award 1980), Music Educators Nat. Conf. (faculty advisor, 1986-88), Musicians Union. Office: U Wash Sch Music 353450 Seattle WA 98195-0001

COLLINS, ALLAN MEAKIN, cognitive scientist, psychologist, educator; b. Orange, N.J., Aug. 7, 1937; s. Clinton and Sarah Amy (Meakin) C.; m. Anne Marjorie Linstead, Aug. 24, 1963; children: Antony, Elizabeth. MA in Communication Scis., U. Michigan, 1962, PhD in Psychology, 1970. Sr. scientist Bolt, Beranek & Newman Inc., Cambridge, 1967-82, prin. scientist, 1982-2000; prof edn. and social policy Northwestern U., Evanston, Ill., 1989—; co-dir. Ctr. for Tech. in Edn., Bank St. Coll. of Edn., N.Y.C., 1991-94; rsch. prof. of edn. Boston Coll., 1998—2002. Lectr. various colls. and univs. Editor: Representation and Understanding, 1975, Cognitive Science, 1976-80, Readings in Cognitive Science, 1988; author: The Cognitive Structure of Emotions, 1988. Guggenheim fellow, 1974, Sloan fellow, 1980. Fellow AAAS; mem. Nat. Acad. Edn., Cognitive Sci. Soc. (chmn. 1979-80, goving. bd. 1979-87), Am. Assn. for Artificial Intelligence (fellow 1990), Am. Ednl. Rsch. Assn. Achievements include launched research on human semantic memory (with R. Quillian); development of first intelligent tutoring system (with J.R. Carbonell); development of cognitive apprenticeship (with J.S. Brown). Home: 135 Cedar St Lexington MA 02421-6516 E-mail: a-collins@northwestern.edu.

COLLINS, ALMA JONES, English educator, writer; d. Walter Melville Jones and Anne Teresa Harrington; m. Daniel Francis Collins, Apr. 9, 1994. BA, Conn. Coll., 1943; MA, Trinity Coll., 1952, U. Conn., 1962. Tchr., counselor W. Hartford (Conn.) Bd. Edn., 1947-72; pres. Arts Universal Rsch. Assocs., 1978—. Interviewed Salvador Dali (CD located in archives Wadsworth Atheneum Mus. Art), 1978, 79; cons. for corp. product devel.; rep. for artists. Contbr. articles and monographs in nat. and internat. publs. Mem. Phi Beta Kappa, Delta Kappa Gamma Internat. Avocation: writing poetry and fiction. Home and Office: 275 Steele Rd A318 West Hartford CT 06117-2763

COLLINS, ANGELO, science educator; b. Chgo., June 15, 1944; d. James Joseph and Mary (Burke) C. BS, Marian Coll., 1966; MS, Mich. State U., 1973; PhD, U. Wis., 1986; hon. degree, Edgewood Coll. High sch. biology tchr. various schs., Wis., 1966-81; rsch. asst. U. Wis., Madison, 1981-86; asst. prof. Kans. State U., Manhattan, 1986-87, Stanford (Calif.) U., 1988-90, Rutgers U., New Brunswick, N.J., 1990-91; assoc. prof. Fla. State U., Tallahassee, 1991-95; prof. Vanderbilt U., 1995—2000; exec. dir. Knowles Sci. Tchg. Found., 2000—. Mem. Working Group on Sci. Stds., Washington, 1992, dir. 1993—; sci. com. Nat. Bd. Profl. Tchg. Stds., Washington, 1991—; chmn. adv. bd. BioQuest, Beloit, Wis., 1988—; bd. dirs. Jour. for Rsch. in Sci. Tchg. Editor Tchr. Edn. Quarterly, 1991; reviewer several books; contbr. articles to profl. jours. Henry Rutgers fellow Rutgers U., 1990; recipient Devel. Scholar award Fla. State U., 1993-94. Fellow AAAS; mem. Nat. Assn. Biology Tchrs. (Outstandng Biology Tchr. Wis. 1977), Nat. Assn. Rsch. Sci. Tchg., Assn. Edn. Tchrs. Sci., Am. Ednl. Rsch. Assn., Sch. Sci. and Math., Assn. Tchr. Educators, Sigma Xi, Phi Delta Kappa. E-mail: angelo.collins@kstf.org.

COLLINS, ARLENE, secondary education educator; b. Mandan, N.D., Sept. 7, 1940; d. John Marcellus and Cecelia Magdalena (Schaaf) Weber; m. Abdul Rahman Rana (dec.); children: Fazale Rahman, Habeeb Rahman; m. Freddie L. Collins. BS in math., N.D. State U., 1962; postgrad., W.Va. Inst. Tech., 1974; M in Edn. Adminstrn., WVCOGS, 1988. Cert. mid. sch. tchr., W.Va. Tchr. physics, math. Montgomery (W.Va.) H.S., 1970; tchr. math., sci. Spencer (W.Va.) Jr. H.S., 1974-80; sci. tchr. Poca (W.Va.) Mid. Sch., 1980—, team leader, 1983-96. W.Va. textbook adoption com., W.Va. Bd. Edn., 1984-90. Leader Girl Scouts U.S.A., Montgomery, 1966-70, 99—, Boy Scouts Am., Montgomery, 1966; bd. dirs. Violet Twp. Womens League, 2002-. Mem.: NOW (bd. dirs. 1986), Am. Fedn. Tchrs., Laurel Soc., Am. Legion Aux. (sec. 2002—), Buckeye Sertoma, Soroptimists Internat. Home: 7292 Fox Den Ct Pickerington OH 43147-9019 E-mail: ac0907@aol.com.

COLLINS, BARBARA LOUISE, retired elementary school educator; b. Pasadena, Nov. 6, 1934; d. Harry Carl and Grace Eleanor (Varnum) Wallerman; m. Wayne G. Collins, July 6, 1961; children: Lisa, Garth. BA in Elem. Edn., Calif. State U., LA, 1956; postgrad., U. Vienna, Austria, 1960; Cert. Art Specialist, Clarke Coll., Dubuque, Iowa, 1980. Tchr. Mt. Diablo Sch., Concord, Calif., 1957—60; prin. asst. Regina Pub. Sch., Canada, 1961—62; tchr. adult basic edn. Dubuque, Iowa, 1966—67; substitute tchr. K-12 Dubuque Pub. Schs., 1967—, substitute art specialist. Tutor trainer Laubach Literacy, Dubuque, Iowa, 1970—90; tchr. pottery, painting, weaving Dubuque Mus. Art, 1985—98; artist-in-residence Cedar Falls (Iowa) Schs., 2000—01. Clay sculpture, pottery, water color paintings, color pencil drawings, exhibitions include Clarke Coll. Gallery, 1985, Dubuque Mus. Art Old Jail Gallery, 1987. Bd. dirs. Dubuque Mus. Art, 1994—97, chair Friends of DUMA, 1995—97. Recipient Best of Show, Grant Wood Art Fest, 1994. United Ch. Of Christ. Avocations: sewing, travel, camping, cooking. Home: 11092 Mound View Rd Dubuque IA 52003

COLLINS, CAROL ANN, primary education educator; b. Manchester, Conn., Aug. 31, 1946; d. John Stanley and Katherine Sophia (Ploszaj) Piela; m. Ronald Joseph Collins, July 5, 1975; 1 child, David Anthony. BS, Ea. Conn. State U., 1968; MEd, Ctrl. Conn. State U., 1975. Profl. tchg. cert. Conn. Elem. tchr. Vernon (Conn.) Pub. Schs., 1968-81; pvt. tutor Windsor, Conn., 1982—; pre-sch. tchr. Windsor (Conn.) Discovery Ctr., 1988; substitute tchr. Town of Windsor, Conn., 1988, head start tchr., 1988-90; pre-sch. tchr. St. Joseph Coll. Sch. for Young Children, West Hartford, Conn., 1990-94; kindergarten tchr. St. Joseph Coll. SYC, West Hartford, 1994—. Head tchr. Sch. for Young Children, St. Joseph Coll., West Hartford, Conn., 1994—; presenter in field. Cub scout leader Boy Scouts Am., Windsor, 1984-85; CCD tchr. St. Joseph Ch., Poquonock, 1985-90. Mem. Nat. Assn. for the Edn. Young Children, Conn. Assn. for the Edn. Young Children, Hartford Assn. for the Edn. Young Children, Capital Region Edn. Coun. (cooperating tchr. mentor program 1992—). Roman Catholic. Avocations: reading, cooking, camping, crafts. Home: 1202 Poquonock Ave Windsor CT 06095-1811 Office: SYC St Joseph Coll 1778 Asylum Ave West Hartford CT 06117-2603

COLLINS, CONNIE WOODS, educational administrator; b. Brewton, Ala., May 24, 1957; d. Wilford S. Woods and Evelyn Marshall Woods Watson; m. Edward L. Collins, Jr., Dec. 23, 1977; children: Candace, Michael. BA in Sociology, U. West Fla., 1977; MEd in Ednl. Leadership, U. Ctrl. Fla., 1993, EdD in Ednl. Leadership, 2002. Tchr. Orange County Pub. Schs., Orlando, Fla., 1984-94; prin. Seminole County Pub. Schs., Sanford, Fla., 1994—. Delores Auzanne fellow State of Fla., 1992-93. Mem. ASCD, Nat. Assn. Secondary Sch. Prins., Seminole Adminstrs. and Suprs., Phi Delta Kappa, Alpha Kappa Alpha. Democrat. Mem. Ch. of Christ. Avocation: travel. Home: 7037 Hiawassee Oak Dr Orlando FL 32818-8355 Office: Crooms Acad Info Tech Magnet HS 2200 W 13th St Sanford FL 32771 E-mail: connie_collins@scps.k12.fl.us.

COLLINS, DELORIS WILLIAMS, secondary school educator; b. Jackson, Miss., Oct. 24, 1959; d. Eddie (Stepfather) and Mary Louise Lewis; m. Bobby Collins, July 18, 1981; children: Garrian V., Bryan L. AA, Hinds Jr. Coll., Jackson, Miss., 1987; BBA in Office Adminstrn., Jackson State U., 2000. Circulation clk. Eudora Welty Libr., Jackson, Miss., 1989—91; tech. specialist/libr. circulation clk. H.T. Sampson Libr. Jackson State U., 1991—93; libr. media tech. specialist Canton Pub. Schs. Dist., 1993—96; with U.S. Postal Svc., Jackson, 1999—2000; substitute tchr. Jackson Pub. Schs. Dist., Jackson, 2000—. Cert. facilitator Family Connections, Jackson, 1999; seminar and workshop condr. Author: They Are Throwing Rocks, 1997, Chasing After the Wind, 1998, Anointed Hyms-Poems, 1999, Treasured Recipes, 1999, Marriage in Yesterday and Today Society: There is Hope, Its All in the Lord, 2000. Nominee Poet of the Yr., 2003; named to Wall of Tolerance, Civil Rights Meml. Ctr., 2003. Mem.: Internat. Soc. of Poets (hon.). Avocations: reading, cooking. Home: 403 Stillwood Dr Jackson MS 39206

COLLINS, DOROTHY CRAIG, retired educational administrator; b. Evansville, Ind., Oct. 11, 1912; d. Edmund Lawrence and Mable Irene (Ross) Craig; m. Ralph Leonard Collins, June 13, 1940; 1 child, David Harrington. BA cum laude, Western Coll. for Women, 1934; MA, U. Chgo., 1937. Rsch. asst. Kinsey Inst., Ind. U., Bloomington, 1951-56; asst. dir. Instnl. Rsch., Ind. U., Bloomington, 1963-64; rsch. asst. Office of Pres., Ind. U., Bloomington, 1965-69; rsch. and editl. assoc. Office of Univ. Chancellor, Ind. U., Bloomington, 1969-92; ret., 1992. Co-author: Pictorial History of Indiana University, 1992. V.p. United Way of Monroe County, Bloomington, 1974; pres. bd. dirs. Bloomington Hosp., 1963; pres. Monroe County Comprehensive Health Planning, Bloomington, 1971-73. Mem. Univ. Women's Club (pres.), Consumers Health Task Force, Theatre Circle (pres.), Friends of Lilly Libr. (bd.), Office of Women's Affairs (adv. bd.), Collins Living-Learning Ctr. (adv. bd.). Democrat. Avocations: reading, travel, theatre attendance, art appreciation. Home: 919 Juniper Pl Bloomington IN 47408-1285

COLLINS, GEORGE EDWIN, computer scientist, mathematician, educator; b. Stuart, Iowa, Jan. 10, 1928; s. Martin Wentworth and Linnie (Fry) C.; m. Dorothy Day Guise, Sept. 4, 1954 (dec. Aug. 1986); children: Cynthia Day, Nancy Helen Rusch, Rebecca Lynne. BA in Math., State U. Iowa, 1951, MS in Math., 1952; PhD in Math., Cornell U., 1955; DrRerNat honoris causa, Tübingen U., 1996. Mathematician IBM Corp., Yorktown Heights, N.Y., 1955-59, rsch. staff, 1959-66; from assoc. prof. to prof. U. Wis., Madison, 1966-86; prof. Ohio State U., Columbus, 1986-91; vis. prof. Johannes Kepler U., Linz, Austria, 1991-96; rsch. prof. U. Del., Newark, 1996—2002, NC State U., 2002—. Chmn. dept. U. Wis., Madison, 1970-72; vis. prof. Stanford (Calif.) U., 1972-73, U. Kaiserslautern, West Germany, 1974-75, U. Karlsruhe, West Germany, 1978. Editor, author: Computer Algebra, 1982; editor: Jour. of Symbolic Computation; contbr. articles to profl. jours. With USN, 1946-47. Rsch. grantee NSF, 1968-91, 97-2001, Austrian Sci. Found., 1992-96. Mem. Math. Assn. Am., Assn. for Computing Machinery. Achievements include pioneering work in computer algebra; invention of method for cylindrical algebraic decomposition and quantifier elimination. Office: NC State Univ Dept Math Asheville NC 28804 Home: 1124 Climbing Rose Turn Cary NC 27511-9650 E-mail: gecollin@nc.rr.com.

COLLINS, HERBERT, JR., retired elementary education educator; b. Washington, Oct. 27, 1931; s. Herbert Sr. and Marie Eleanor (Paris) C. BS, U. D.C., 1955; MA, George Washington U., 1962; postgrad., Cath. U. Am., 1974; diploma paralegal, Barclay Career Sch., 1991. Tchr. kindergarten-6th grade D.C. Pub. Schs., 1955-80; legal asst. Legal Aid Soc. D.C., 1991; libr. asst. D.C. Pub. Libr. System, 1992—; paralegal, 1991—. Instr. Career Blazers Learning Ctr., 1999-2000. Active Columbia Sr. Ctr., Washington, 1992—; active share program Cath. Charities, Washington, 1992—. With U.S. Army, 1956-58, D.C. N.G. 1958-63. Mem.: Francis L. Cardozo Sr. H.S. Alumni Assn., Inc. (v.p. 1975, pres. 1977—79, 1986—, chmn. scholarship com.). Democrat. Unitarian Universalist. Avocations: organ, piano, museums, voice concerts, drama. Home: 1319 Allison St NW Washington DC 20011-4440

COLLINS, JEAN KATHERINE, English educator; b. Norfolk, Va., June 14, 1928; d. Elwood Brantley and Katherine Belle (Lambertson) C. BA in Liberal Arts, James Madison U., Harrisonburg, Va., 1945-49; MA in English, U. Richmond, 1950-51; edn. credits, U. Va., Eastern Shore of Va., 1950, 60; art edn. credits, Millersville State Tchrs. Coll, summer 1970. Continuity writer Radio Station WLEE, Richmond, Va., 1949; English, critic tchr. Farmville H.S., Longwood Coll., Va., 1951-53; English tchr., art tchr. Hermitage H.S., Richmond, Va., 1953-55; prin., art tchr. Cape Charles (Va.) H.S., 1957-59; head English dept., tchr. Northampton H.S., Eastville, Va., 1960-63; art tchr. Pvt. Studio, Cape Charles, Va., 1964-90. Pres. Lambda chpt. Delta Kappa Gamma Soc., Eastern Shore of Va., 1966-68; recording sec. Iota State Delta Kappa Gamma Soc., Headqtrs., Richmond, Va., 1967-69; adv. bd. Eastern Shore Pub. Libr., Accomac, Va., 1981-89; bd. dirs. Eastern Shore of Va. Hist. Soc., Onancock, Va., 1957-60. Author: (poetry) Madison Quarterly, 1948, 49; author, illustrator: An Eastern Shore Sampler, 1975; author: History of Trinity United Methodist Church, 1993. Named Woman of Yr. Young WOmen's Club of Cape Charles, Va., 1958. Mem. Eastern Shore of Va. Hist. Soc., Cape Charles Hist. Soc., Trinity United Meth. Ch., Delta Kappa Gamma Soc.. Republican. Methodist. Avocations: painting, needlework, history, theater, dance, writing.

COLLINS, JOE LENA, retired secondary school educator; b. Mt. Pleasant, Tenn., Nov. 18, 1922; d. Morton Daniel and Rosetta Francis C. BS in English, Tenn. Tech., 1949; MA in English, George Peabody, 1968, EdS in English, 1975. Cert. profl. tchr. Sec. to Dr. G.C. English and Dr. C.D. Walton, Mt. Pleasant, Tenn., 1942-46; tchr. Maury Co. Schs., Mt. Pleasant, Tenn., 1949-51, Tenn. Tech., Cookeville, Tenn., 1951; acct. Cookeville Prodn. Credit, Tenn., 1951-52; tchr. Metro Nashville Schs., 1952-88. Lectr. Ret. Learning Vanderbilt U., 2000—. Mem. Shepherd's Ctr. West End Book Club, 1989—2002, Metro Retired Tchrs. Assn., 1988—; chmn. Shepherd's Ctr. West Book Club; com. work Dem. Party, 1980—2003. Mem. AAUW (pres.), Tenn. Art League, Tenn. Writers Alliance, Tenn. Hist. Soc., Women in the Arts, United Meth. Women (Woman of Purpose award). Avocations: reading, writing, painting, sports. Home: 6212 Henry Ford Dr Nashville TN 37209-1738

COLLINS, MARGARET ELIZABETH, librarian; b. Greenwood, Miss., May 10, 1934; d. Eugene and Sylvia Ann (Holmon) Brown; m. William Collins Jr., Sept. 4, 1952; children: Sylvia Collins Wetzel, Deirdre Collins Wolff, William Collins II. BS, Harris Stowe State Coll., St. Louis, 1960; MLS, U. Mo., 1985; postgrad., U. Mo., St. Louis, 1986, 87, 89, Maryville U., 1988, Tchrs. Acad., 1993, Oxford (Eng.) Coll., 1993. Cert. tchr., libr., Mo. Substitute tchr. St. Louis Pub. Schs., 1976-80, libr., 1981-82, 85—, St. Louis Archdiocese Sch., 1982-85. Adv. bd. Centennial/Delta Sigma Theta Learning Ctr., St. Louis, 1990—; charter participant Community Leadership Program for Tchrs., St. Louis, 1990. Brownie leader Girl Scouts U.S., St. Louis, 1972-80; exec. bd. Peoples Health Ctrs., St. Louis, 1983—, (sec. 1987-89); pres. Waring Sch. Mothers Club, St. Louis, 1972-80; v.p. S.W. High Sch. PTO, St. Louis, 1975-81. Recipient Apple for the Tchr. Iota Phi Lambda, 1990. Mem. AAUW, St. Louis City Libr. Assn. (MASL chair 1987), Mo. Assn. Sch. Librs., Delta Sigma Theta (worship chair 1983, sch. Am. chair 1990-91). Baptist. Avocations: storytelling, sewing. Home: 406 Hampshire Ct Saint Louis MO 63119-4831 Office: Pruitt Mil Acad 1212 N 22nd St Saint Louis MO 63106-2701

COLLINS, MARGERY LOUISE, elementary school educator; b. Manilla, Iowa, Nov. 12, 1932; d. Edward Henry and Theresa Caroline (Nickelsen) Theobald; m. Thomas Joseph Collins, Mar. 11, 1955; 1 child, Ann. BS in Elem. Edn., Butler U., 1964; MA in Early Childhood Edn., San Jose State U., 1975, MA in Adminstrv. Svcs., 1977. Cert. elem. tchr., adminstrv. svcs., early childhood edn., reading specialist, jr. coll. tchr., Calif., Ind. Tchr. Mapleton Iowa) Pub. Schs., 1952-54, Hammond (Ind.) Pub. Schs., 1954-55, Met. Schs. of Lawrence Twp., Indpls., 1964-65; tchr., team leader Palo Alto (Calif.) Unified Schs., 1965—, mentor tchr., 1992-94, literacy mentor, literacy trainer, 1996—. Resident tchr. San Jose State U., San Francisco State U., 1970-80; mentor, mem. rev. team Calif. State Dept. Edn., Sacramento, 1976-78; instr. DeAnza Coll., Cupertino, Calif., 1977—, U. San Diego Ext., 1997—; workshop leader, presenter, spkr. in field, 1977—; grant writer Palo Alto Schs., 1980-97 Co-creator, co-chair Internat. Visitors Ctr., Palo Alto, 1986-92; mem. Sister Cities Internat./Neighbors Abroad, 1973— (pres. 1986-87); mem. adv. bd. Gamble Garden, 1996-98. Lucille Nixon scholar, 1974; grantee Whitney Found., Hewlett-Packard, Palo Alto Found.; recipient Tall Tree award for outstanding profl. Palo Alto C. of C., 1994. Mem. AAUW (pres. 1992-93, mem. state nominating com. 1994), NEA, Calif. Tchr. Assn., Palo Alto Edn. Assn., Calif. Reading Assn., Santa Clara County Reading Assn., ASCD, UN Assn. (bd. dirs. 1994-96), Phi Delta Kappa, Phi Kappa Phi. Democrat. Roman Catholic. Avocations: reading, hiking, travel, gardening. Home: 3950 Duncan Pl Palo Alto CA 94306-4550

COLLINS, MARTHA, English language educator, writer; b. Omaha, Nov. 25, 1940; d. William E. and Katheryn (Essick) C.; m. Theodore M. Space, Apr. 1991. AB, Stanford U., 1962; MA, U. Iowa, 1965, PhD, 1971. Asst. prof. N.E. Mo. U., Kirksville, 1965-66; from instr. to prof. English U. Mass., Boston, 1966—2002, co-dir. creative writing, 1979—2000; Pauline Delaney prof., co-dir. creative writing Oberlin (Ohio) Coll., 1997—. Author (poetry): The Catastrophe of Rainbows, 1985, The Arrangement of Space, 1991, A History of Small Life on a Windy Planet, 1993, Some Things Words Can Do, 1998; translator: The Women Carry River Water, 1997. Fellow Bunting Inst., 1982-83, Ingram Merrill Found., 1988, NEA, 1990; grantee Witter Bynner/Santa Fe Art Inst., 2001, Lannon Found. Residency, 2003; recipient Pushcart prize, 1985, 96, 98, Di Castagnola award, 1990, Lannan residency, 2003. Mem. Poetry Soc. Am., Assoc. Writing Programs. Democrat. Office: Oberlin Coll Rice Hall Oberlin OH 44074

COLLINS, MICHAEL PAUL, secondary school educator, earth science educator, consultant; b. Chula Vista, Calif., Jan. 2, 1959; s. William Henry and Linda Lee (Capron) C.; children: Christopher M., Matthew R., Kyle P., Colby W. A in Gen. Studies, Clatsop Community Coll., Astoria, Oreg., 1983; BS in Sci. Edn., BS in Geology, Oreg. State U., 1987; postgrad., U. Alaska, Anchorage. Cert. tchr., Wash., Alaska. Emergency med. technician II, fireman Sitka (Alaska) Fire Dept., 1978-80; paramedic Medix Ambulance, Astoria, 1980-83; cartographer technician U.S. Geol. Survey, Grants Pass, Oreg., 1985; tchr. earth sci. Lake Oswego (Oreg.) Sch. Dist., 1987-88; tchr. sci. Gladstone (Oreg.) Sch. Dist., 1988-90; radon technician Radon Detection Systems, Portland, Oreg., 1988-90; dir. sales and mktg. Evergreen Helicopters of Alaska, Inc., Anchorage, 1990-91; tchr. math. and sci. Anchorage Sch. Dist., 1991—99; Alaska pharm. ter. bus. mgr. Ventiv Health/Bristol Myers Squibb Co., 1999—2001, Reliant Pharms, 2001—02; acct. mgr. RS Med., Inc., 2003—. Instr. geology Alaska Jr. Coll., Anchorage, 1992—93; cons. earth sci. edn. Project ESTEEM, Ctr. Astrophysics, Harvard U., Cambridge, Mass., 1992—95; field technician Water Quality divsn., City of Anchorage, 1993; cons., atmospheric ednl. resource agt. Project Atmosphere Am. Meteorol. Assn., 1994—99; cons. Ala. State H.S. Scis. Olympics, 1998; cons. Project MicroObs. Ctr. for Astrophysics Harvard U., 1995—98; coord. instr. Project DataStreme Am. Meteorol. Soc., 1996—99; cons. geologist Unocal Alaska, 1997; geologist II Shannon & Wilson, Inc., 1998; Alaska pharm. ter. bus. mgr. Ventiv Health/Bristol Myers Squibb Co., 1999—2001, Reliant Pharms., 2001—02; acct. mgr. RS Med., Inc., 2003—. Co-author: Merrill Earth Science Lab Activities, 1989. With USCG, 1977-81. Mem.: NEA, Alaska Pharm. Assn., Nat. Assn. Geosci. Tchrs. (pres. N.W. sect. 1996—99), Alaska Geol. Soc. Inc., Am. Meteorol. Soc., Am. Geol. Inst., Nat. Sci. Tchrs. Assn., Geol. Soc. Am., Am. Assn. Petroleum Geologists. Avocations: weight training, fishing, hiking, camping, real estate. Home and Office: 2340 Sentry Dr Apt 802 Anchorage AK 99507

COLLINS, RICHARD FRANCIS, microbiologist, educator; b. St. Paul, Minn., Jan. 22, 1938; s. Francis Bernard and Maude Roegene (Night) C.; m. Deanne Margaret Scafati, Dec. 28, 1960 (div. 1970); children: Lisa, Mark, Michael; m. Judy A. Wright, Feb. 15, 1978; children: Kristyn, Todd. AB, Shepherd Coll., 1962; MA, Wake Forest U., 1968; PhD, U. Okla., 1973. Tchr. Alexandria (Va.) Schs., 1962-66; instr. U. Okla., Oklahoma City, 1972-73; lab. dir. Infectious Disease Svc. U. Ill./Rockford Sch. of Medicine, 1974-80; asst. prof. U. Ill., Rockford, 1973-80; assoc. prof. U. Osteo. Medicine and Health Scis., Des Moines, 1980-85, faculty pres., 1990-91, pres.-elect, 1997-98, prof., dept. head, 1985-95; prof., divsn. head Midwestern U., Glendale, 1997—. Cons. U.S. EPA, Washington, 1975-81; mem. Nat. Bd. Podiatry Examiners, Princeton, N.J., 1983-96, Nat. Bd. Osteo. Med. Examiners, Des Plaines, Ill., 1994-97; participant mission project Christian Med. Soc., Dominican Republic, 1977. Mem. editorial bd. African Jour. Clin. Exptl. Immunology, 1979-83; contbr. articles to profl. jours. Vol. Blank Guild, Iowa Meth. Hosp., Des Moines, 1988-91. Recipient awards NSF, 1962-67, fellowship NIH, 1969-70, Gov.'s Vol. awards State of Iowa, 1988, 89. Mem. Am. Soc. for Microbiology, Am. Soc. Tropical Medicine and Hygiene, Sigma Xi (pres. 1987-90, 96-97, treas. 1990-91). Avocations: photography, auto restoration. Home: 4131 W Tierra Buena Ln Phoenix AZ 85053-3717 Office: Midwestern U Ariz Coll Osteo Medicine 19555 N 59th Ave Glendale AZ 85308-6813 E-mail: rcolli@midwestern.edu.

COLLINS, ROBERT ARNOLD, English language educator; b. Miami, Fla., Apr. 25, 1929; s. John William and Edna (Arnold) C.; m. Laura Virginia Roberts, June 3, 1960; 1 child, Judith. BA in English, U. Miami, Coral Gables, Fla., 1951; MA in English, U. Ky., 1960, PhD in English, 1968. Chair English Midway (Ky.) Jr. Coll., 1960-64; assoc. prof. English No. Ill. U., DeKalb, 1964-68, Morehead (Ky.) State U., 1968-69; from assoc. prof. to prof. English Fla. Atlantic U., Boca Raton, 1970—. Founder, dir. Internat. Conf. on the Fantastic in the Arts, Ft. Lauderdale, Fla., 1980—. Author: Thomas Burnett Swann: A Critical Biography, 1980, Science Fiction and Fantasy Book Review Annual, 1987-91; editor: Scope of the Fantastic, 1985, Modes of the Fantastic, 1995; editor Fantasy Rev., 1981-87; mng. editor Jour. of the Fantastic in the Arts, 1995—; contbr. articles to profl. jours. Recipient World Fantasy award World Fantasy Conv., New Haven, 1982, Balrog award Sword and Shield, 1982, 83. Home: 1320 SW 5th St Boca Raton FL 33486-4404 Office: Fla Atlantic U English Dept 777 Glades Rd Boca Raton FL 33431-6424 E-mail: collins@fau.edu.

COLLINS, ROBERT OAKLEY, history educator; b. Waukegan, Ill., Apr. 1, 1933; s. William George and Louise Van Horsen (Jack) C.; m. Janyce Hutchins Monroe, Oct. 6, 1974; children by previous marriage: Catharine Louise, Randolph Ware, Robert William. BA, Dartmouth Coll., 1954; AB (Marshall scholar 1954-55), Balliol Coll., Oxford U., 1956, MA, 1960; MA (Ford fellow), Yale U., 1958, PhD, 1959. Instr. history Williams Coll., Williamstown, Mass., 1959-61; lectr. U. Mass. Extension, Pittsfield, 1960-61; vis. asst. prof. history Columbia U., N.Y.C., 1962-63; asst. prof. history Williams Coll., 1963-65; mem. faculty U. Calif., Santa Barbara, 1965—, prof. history, 1969-94, dir. Ctr. for Study Developing Nations, 1967-69, acting vice chancellor for research and grad. affairs, 1970-71, dean grad. div., 1971-80; prof. emeritus, 1994—; vis. sr. assoc. fellow St. Antony's Coll., Oxford U., Eng., 1980-81; Trevelyan fellow Durham U., 1986—. Dir. Washington Ctr. U. Calif., Santa Barbara, 1992-94; mem. Internat. Adv. Group for the Nile Basin, World Bank, 1997. Author: The Southern Sudan, 1883-1898, 1962, King Leopold, England and the Upper Nile, 1968, Problems in African History, 1968, The Partition of Africa, 1979, Land Beyond the Rivers: The Southern Sudan, 1898-1918, 1971, Europeans in Africa, 1971, An Arabian Diary, 1969, The Southern Sudan in Historical Perspective, 1975, Shadows in the Grass: Britain in the Southern Sudan, 1983, The British in the Sudan, 1898-56, 84, The Waters of the Nile: Hydropolitics and the Jonglei Canal, 1900-1988, 1990, Western African History, Eastern African History, Central and Southern African History, 1990, The Nile Waters: An Annotated Bibliography, 1991, Problems In African History, The Pre-Colonial Centuries, 1993, Requiem for the Sudan, 1994, Historical Problems of Imperial Africa, 1994, Problems in the History of Modern Africa, 1996, Africa's Thirty Years' War: Chad, Libya and the Sudan, 1963-1993, 1999, Historical Dictionary of Pre-Colonial Africa, 2001, Documents from the African Past, 2001, The Nile, 2002, Revolutionary Sudan: Hasan al-Turabi and the Islamist State, 1989-2000, 2003. Recipient Gold class award Order Scis. and Arts Dem. Republic of Sudan, 1980; John Ben Snow Found. prize, 1984; NDEA lang. fellow, 1960-61, Social Sci. Rsch. Coun. fellow, 1962-63; Rockefeller Found. scholar-in-residence Bellagio, Italy, 1979, 87; Ford Found. fellow, 1979-81; Fulbright sr. rsch. fellow, 1982, 90; Woodrow Wilson fellow, 1983; vis. fellow Trevelyan Coll. mem. Soc. Fellows Durham U., 1986, fellow Balliol Coll., Oxford U., 1986-87; fellow Am. Coun. Learned Soc. 1990. Fellow Am. Philos. Soc.; mem. Am. Hist. Assn., African Studies Assn., Western River Guides Assn., Sudan Studies Assn., Explorers Club, Phi Beta Kappa. Home: 735 Calle De Los Amigos Santa Barbara CA 93105-4438 Office: U Calif Dept History Santa Barbara CA 93106-9410

COLLINS, RONALD WILLIAM, psychologist, educator; b. N.Y.C., Jan. 6, 1947; s. Edward H. Collins Jr. and Estelle Lott. BA, Rutgers U., 1969; MS, Nova U., 1987; EdD, Fla. Internat. U., 1990; PhD, Saybrook Inst., 1996. Diplomate Am. Bd. Psychol. Spltys.; lic. profl. counselor, Mont., mental health counselor, Fla., psychologist, Colo. Spl. agt., ret. U.S. Secret Svc., Miami, Fla., 1971-91; adj. prof. St. Thomas U., Miami, 1990-91; asst. prof. Ea. Mont. Coll., Billings, 1991-94, Mont. State U., Billings, 1994-95; psychol. intern Inst. for Psychol. Growth, Ft. Lauderdale, Fla., 1994-95; adj. prof. instrnl. analysis/design Fla. Internat. U., Ft. Lauderdale, 1995-96; psychologist Dept. Corrections, Canon City, Colo., 1998-99, in pvt. practice, Miami, 1999-2000; dept. chair gen. studies U. Phoenix, Ft. Lauderdale, Fla., 2000—00; prof. Am. Inter Continental U., 2001—. Pvt. cons., adj. prof. U. Phoenix, Nova Southeastern U., Ft. Lauderdale, Keiser Coll., 2001—. Author: Kabiroff Papers, 1988, Transfer of Learning, 1990, Psychological Perspectives on Security Issues, 2000; contbr. articles to profl. jours. Mem. Billings Family Violence Task Force, 1992. Mem. APA, Am. Coll. Forensic Examiners, Am. Ednl. Rsch. Assn., Mental Health Assn. Broward County. Episcopalian. Avocations: skiing, horseback riding, flying, fiction writing, jogging. Office: PO Box 2053 Fort Lauderdale FL 33303-2053 Fax: (954) 761-7119. E-mail: r.collins.phd@worldnet.att.net.

COLLINS, SANDRA DEE, physical education educator; b. Herkimer, N.Y., Dec. 18, 1963; d. Leland Daniel Sr. and Elizabeth Hazel (Seamon) C. Student, St. Bonaventure U., 1982-84; BS, Russell Sage Coll., 1987; MEd, Springfield Coll., 1995. Cert. tchr., N.Y. Asst. dir. summer program Town of Stark, Van Hornesville, N.Y., 1982-84; supr. lifeguards Sheraton Airport Inn, Albany, N.Y., 1984-87; coach jr. varsity volleyball Shenendehowa High Sch., Clifton Park, N.Y., 1985; coach volleyball, varsity and jr. varsity Owen D. Young Cen. Sch., Van Hornesville, 1987; asst. camp dir. Kenwood Child Devel. Ctr., Albany, 1988, 89; recreation supr. Glenmont (N.Y.) Job Corps Ctr., 1988-89; personal fitness trainer, 1991—; tchr. phys. edn., coach varsity volleyball Bethlehem Ctrl. Sch. Dist., Delmar, N.Y., 1988—. Camp dir. Troy Jewish Cmty. Ctr., 1990-93; head volleyball coach Russell Sage Coll., 1996—. Mem. AAHPERD, N.Y. State Assn. Health, Phys. Edn., Recreation and Dance, Am. Volleyball Coaches Assn. Democrat. Roman Catholic. Avocations: volleyball, swimming, tennis, rollerblading, cross-country skiing. Office: Bethlehem High Sch 700 Delaware Ave Delmar NY 12054-2436

COLLINS, S(ARAH) RUTH KNIGHT, education educator; b. Northumberland, Pa., May 13, 1939; d. Walter Brown and Alice Marie (Neighbour) Knight; m. Frank Gibson Collins, June 13, 1960; children: James, Pamela Collins Williams. BA, Wheaton Coll., 1960; MA, U. Tex., Austin, 1974; PhD, Vanderbilt U., 1980. Tchr. various levels, Evanston, Ill., 1960-61, Berkeley, Calif., 1961-71; demonatration tchr. for head start and kindergarten U. Tex., Austin, Tex., 1969-74, tchr. in early childhood, 1972-74; tchr. reading Motlow State C.C., Tullahoma, Tenn., 1977-91, coord. of English, 1979-81, prof. edn., 1982-93, coord. social scis., 1986-93. Mem. state-wide adv. coun. for tchr. edn. and cert., 1987-90, state-wide adv. coun. for minorities in tchr. edn., 1990-91; pres. faculty coun. Motlow C.C., 1979-80, tchr. 1978; adj. prof. edn. Mid. Tenn. State U., 1979-89; presenter at profl. confs. Writer and proofreader for religious publ. sci. tech. editor, Tullahoma Telesis, 1980—, columnist, 1996—; writer for HealthWise, 1998—; contbr. articles to profl. jours. Actress Cmty. Playhouse, Tullahoma, 1973-87; storyteller various librs. and pub. schs., 1974—; violinist Mid. Tenn. Symphony Orch., Murfreesboro, 1987-89; presenter programs on grief and loss at various profl. confs. and cmty. orgns., 1973—; bd. mem., yearly speaker Compassionate Friends, 1985—; active Unitarian Universalist Ch., Tullahoma, 1993—; home vol. Hospice Highland Rim.; tchr. competitve swimming, diving, water ballet, program dir., 1949-68; panelist (TV series) How to Combat Juvenile Delinquency, Chgo., 1956; vol. Harton Regional Med. Ctr., 1997—, Hands-On Sci. Ctr., 1999—. Recipient Gov. Ned McWherter's cert. of recognition Tenn. Collaborative Leadership Acad., 1991. Mem. NEA, ASCD, AAUP (v.p. 1986-87, sec. 1990-91), Assn. Tchr. Educators, Bus. and Profl. Women's Club, Tenn. Edn. Assn., Internat. Reading Assn., Nat. Assn. for Edn. of Young Children (pres.-elect local chpt. 1972-73); Phi Delta Kappa, Kappa Delta Pi. Avocations: reading, sewing, playing and teaching violin/fiddle, public speaking. Home and Office: 1703 Country Club Dr Tullahoma TN 37388-4831

COLLINS, WILLIAM JOHN, educational administrator; b. Binghamton, N.Y., May 7, 1944; s. John William and Philomena Alice (Delaney) C.; children: Michael, Kathleen, Meghan. BS, LeMoyne Coll., 1965; MS, Syracuse U., 1971, postgrad., 1971-75. Tchr. math. Smith Jr. H.S., Syracuse, N.Y., 1965-70; math. lab specialist Charles Andrews Sch., Syracuse, 1971; tchr. math. Young Mothers Ednl. Devel. Program, Syracuse, 1971-72; vice-prin. Levy Jr. H.S., Syracuse, 1972-74, acting prin., 1974; adult basic edn. tchr. Syracuse Ednl. Opportunity Center, 1978-79. Adj. prof. Onondaga C.C., 1981-85, Le Moyne Coll., 1985-98; supr. instrn. math K-12, Syracuse Sch. Dist. 1974-82, asst. to dir. rsch. and evaluation, 1982-89, supr. Math. and Computers, 1989-94; math. supr. 1994-98; NSF SSI coord., 1993-98; coord. Profl. Devel. Schs. Le Moyne Coll., 1999--; cons. and lectr. in field. Contbr. articles to profl. jours. Tchr. Upward Bound Summer Program, Le Moyne Coll., Syracuse, 1965-70; parish coun. pres. Ch. of St. Andrew the Apostle, Syracuse, 1976-77, 85-86; bd. dirs. Syracuse Girls Club, 1985-88; regional chmn. Syracuse Roman Cath. Diocesan Pastoral Coun., 1989-90. Mem. Nat. Coun. Tchrs. Math., Assn. Math. Tchrs. N.Y. State (mem. assembly 1979-80), Nat. Coun. Supr. of Math., N.Y. Assn. Math. Suprs. (pres. 1979-80, bd. dirs. 1990), Onondaga County Math. Tchrs. Assn. (pres. 1974-75), Nat. Assn. Secondary Sch. Prins., Sch. Adminstrs., Assn. Internat. Study Group in Ethnomathematics. Office: Edn Dept LeMoyne Coll 1419 Salt Springs Rd Syracuse NY 13214-1302

COLLINSON, VIVIENNE RUTH, education educator, researcher, consultant; b. Kitchener, Ont., Can., July 30, 1949; d. Earl Stanley and Mary Magdalena (Sauder) Feick; m. Charles L. Collinson, May 21, 1983. BA, Wilfrid Laurier U., Waterloo, Ont., 1974; MEd, U. Windsor, Ont., 1989; PhD, Ohio State U., 1993. Cert. administr. Tchr. Waterloo County Bd. Edn., 1969-84, Windsor Bd. Edn., 1984-89; vis. asst. prof. U.Windsor, 1989-90, U. Md., College Park, 1993-94, asst. prof. edn., 1994-98; assoc. prof. Mich. State U., 1999—. Author: Teachers As Learners, 1994, Reaching Students, 1996. Charter mem. Eleanor Roosevelt Found., 1989—; benefactor Stratford (Ont.) Shakespearean Festival Found. Recipient Ont. Silver medal for piano U. We. Ont. Conservatory of Music, 1965, McGraw-Hill awrd, 1969; Ont. scholar, 1968; Wilfrid Laurier U. grad. scholar. Mem. AAUW, Am. Ednl. Rsch. Assn., Fedn. Women Tchrs. Assn. Ont. (provincial resource leader 1988-94), Nat. Soc. for Study of Edn., Delta Kappa Gamma (Doctoral Dissertation award 1994), Phi Kappa Phi. Avocations: music, theatre, travel. Fax: 313-824-2949.

COLLYER, ESTHER RITZ, volunteer, educator; b. Crothersville, Ind., Feb. 25, 1907; d. Volna Ernest and Mamie Audrey (Gallion) Ritz; m. George Stanley Collyer; 1 child, George Stanley Jr. BS in Music, DePaw U., 1928. Tchr. music, art Knightstown (Ind.) Pub. Schs., 1928-31; dir. music, art Allen County Schs., Ft. Wayne, Ind., 1946-63; tchr. Butler U. Sch. Music, Indpls., summer, 1953, Ind. U. Sch. Music, Bloomington, summer, 1954. Editor: The Libretto. Chair Fine Arts Festival, Arts United, Ft. Wayne; asst. dir. Ft. Wayne Mus. Art, interim dir., bd. dirs.; pres., bd. dirs. Ft. Wayne Philharmonic Orch., bd. adv. docent prog. IU Art Mus. Esther Ritz Collyer Award for Lifetime Achievement, Arts United Fort Wayne. Avocations: sculpture, painting, dancing, reading, travel. Home: 1049 Sassafras Cir Bloomington IN 47408-1281

COLMAN, RONALD WILLIAM, computer science educator; b. L.A., Sept. 13, 1930; s. William Maynard Colman and Edna Eliza (Halford) Smith. BA in Math., UCLA, 1957; PhD in Computer Sci., U. Calif., Irvine, 1976. Electronics tech. Lockheed Aircraft Corp., Burbank, Calif., 1952-53; staff specialist Western Electric Co., N.Y.C., 1957-58; assoc. math. Burroughs Corp., Pasadena, Calif., 1958-60; sr. computer analyst Beckman Instruments, Inc., Fullerton, Calif., 1960-62; mgr. L.A. dist. Digital Equipment Corp., L.A., 1962-64; chmn. computer sci. Calif. State U., Fullerton, 1964-80, prof. computer sci. Northridge, 1980-89; ptnr. Windward Ventures, Venice, Calif. Chmn. session on heuristic search Internat. Joint Conf. on Artificial Intelligence, Stanford, 1973; chmn. nat. symposium on computer sci. edn. Assn. Computing Machinery, Anaheim, Calif., 1976; chmn. registration Nat. Computer Conf., Anaheim, 1978, 80. With USN, 1948-52. Avocations: skiing, opera, scuba diving. Home: 850 E Ocean Blvd Unit 1311 Long Beach CA 90802-5456

COLON, ELSIE FLORES, American and English literature educator; b. N.Y.C., Oct. 26; d. Juan and Rosa Catalina (Caban) Flores; m. Daniel Colon, July 16, 1977. BA magna cum laude, Hunter Coll., 1992; postgrad., Grad. Sch. and Univ. Ctr., N.Y.C., 1992—; MA, Queens Coll., 1998; M Philosophy, Grad. Sch. and Univ. Ctr., 1999. Cons. Clairol, Inc. Bristol-Myers Co., N.Y.C., 1983-91; tchr.-counselor Manhattan North Ctr. Assn. for Children with Retarded Mental Devel. Inc., N.Y.C., 1992. Adj. prof. Touro Coll., N.Y.C., 1993—. Scholar Estate of J. Raymond Gerberick, 1992-93, Jewish Found. for Women, 1992-94; rsch. fellow Columbia U., 1991; Mellon assoc. Mellon Found., 1990-92; Dean K. Harrison fellow CUNY Grad. Sch., 1999, 2000. Mem. MLA, AAUW, Nat. Coun. Tchrs. of English, Am. Mus. Natural History (assoc.). Avocations: writing, reading, painting, drawing, travel. Office: Touro Coll 240 E 123d St New York NY 10035

COLONY, PAMELA CAMERON, medical researcher, educator; b. Boston, Apr. 18, 1947; d. Donald Gifford Colony and Priscilla (Adams) Pratley; m. E. Paul Cokely Jr., Apr. 26, 1986 (div. 2000); 1 child, Daniel Patrick Cokely; m. Richard M. Sparling, June 1, 2003; 1 child, John Travis Cokely. BA, Wellesley (Mass.) Coll., 1969; PhD, Boston U., 1976. Rsch. asst. sch. medicine Boston U., 1969-71, U. Hosp., 1971-73, Peter Bent Brigham Hosp., Boston, 1973-75; instr. dept. anatomy Harvard Med. Sch., 1975-77; assoc. staff in medicine Peter Bent Brigham Hosp., Boston, 1976-79; sr. fellow, instr. Harvard Med. Sch., Boston, 1979-81; asst. prof. anatomy and medicine Pa. State Coll. Medicine, Hershey, Pa., 1981-88; assoc. prof. rsch., pre-health advisor Franklin and Marshall Coll., Lancaster, 1988-91; adj. assoc. prof. of surgery Pa. State Coll. Medicine, Hershey, 1988-91, sr. rsch. assoc. dept. surgery, 1991-95; asst. prof. SUNY, Cobleskill, 1995-97, assoc. prof., 1997-99, program dir. histotech., 1995—, prof. biology, 1999—, co-dir. Women in Sci., 1996—. Bd. dirs. N.Y. State Histotechnol. Soc.; ind. assessor Nat. Health and Med. Rsch. Coun., Australia, 1985—; ad-hoc reviewer NIH, Nat. Cancer Inst., Bethesda, Md., 1986; lectr., adj. instr. Harrisburg Area Cmty. Coll., 1991—95. Contbr. articles to profl. jours. Fellow Nat. Found. Ileitis and Colitis, 1979-81; grantee Fed. Republic Germany, 1978, Cancer Rsch. Ctr., 1982-83, NIH, 1982-91. Mem.: AAAS, Nat. Soc. for Histotech., N.Y. Histotechnol. Soc. (bd. dirs. 2001—), Nat. Assn. Advisors Health Profls., Am. Gastroent. Assn., N.Y. Acad. Sci., Am. Soc. Cell Biology. Avocations: endurance and competitive trail riding, breeding and showing horses. Office: SUNY Cobleskill Dept Natural Scis Main St Cobleskill NY 12043 E-mail: colonyp@cobleskill.edu.

COLOSIMO, MARY LYNN SUKURS, psychology educator; b. Chgo., Aug. 14, 1950; d. Charles Paul and Charlotte Pearl (Bartkus) S.; m. Ronald Alfred Colosimo, Nov. 26, 1977; children: Elizabeth Catherine, Victoria Carmella, Christina Charlotte, Diana Clare. BA, Bradley U., 1972, MA, 1974; PhD, U. Chgo., 1981. Cert. tchr., Ill. Tchr. Lincoln (Ill.) High Sch., 1973-75; counselor Lyle Elem. Sch., Bridgeview, Ill., 1975-78; prof. St. Xavier Coll., Chgo., 1984-86; prof. ednl. psychology, tchg. methods, coord. tchr. interns field placements Trinity Christian Coll., Palos Heights, Ill., 1988-99; dir. recruitment and cmty. rels. S.W. Chgo. Christian Schs., Palos Heights, Ill., 1999-2001; adj. prof. Trinity Christian Coll., 2001—. Pvt. practice as counselor, cons., Orland Park, Ill., 1983-90; educator women's ministry, retreat work; rschr. in gifted edn., gender equity, tchg. methods. Contbr. articles to profl. jours. Mem. ACA, ASCD, AAUW, Am. Ednl Rsch. Assn., Assn. Rsch. Value Issues in Counseling,, Assn. Christian Therapists, Am. Assn. Christian Counselors, Nat. Gifted Edn. Assn., Ill. Gifted Edn. Assn., Nat. Assn. Guidance Counselors, Ill. Assn. Guidance Counselors, Phi Kappa Phi. Avocations: tennis, swimming, downhill skiing. E-mail: mlcolosimo@aol.com.

COLPITTS, GAIL ELIZABETH, artist, educator; b. Chgo., Nov. 26, 1954; d. Robert Moore and Mary Lee (Means) C. BA, Greenville Coll., 1976; MA, No. Ill. U., 1984, MFA, 1990. Grad. tchg. asst. No. Ill. U., DeKalb, Ill., 1982-83, tchg. intern, 1990, instr. Office Campus Recreation, 1989-90; artist-tchr. MFA program Vt. Coll., Montpelier, 1993; instr. Harold Washington Coll., Chgo., 1993, Columbia Coll., Chgo., 1995; artist, lectr. Judson Coll., Elgin, Ill., 1995, asst. prof. art, 1996—2000, assoc. prof. art and design, 2000—, chair dept. art and design, 2001—. One-woman shows include Bethel Coll., Arden Hills, Minn., 1995, Greenville (Ill.) Coll., 1993, No. Ill. U., DeKalb, 1990, Wheaton (Ill.) Coll., 1996, Trinity Christian Coll., Palos Heights, 1998, Cliff Dwellers, Chgo., 1999, Northwestern Coll., St. Paul, Minn., 2000, Judson Coll., Elgin, Ill., 2003; assoc. editor: Shoal Dance, 1995-96, contbr. revs. and news; contbr. poetry to mags.; included in Best of New Ceramic Arts, 1997, Making Visible the Invisible, 2003. Dir. Christians in the Visual Arts, 2003. Grad. sch. fellow No. Ill. U., 1987-88. Mem. Coll. Art Assn., Christians in Visual Arts, Chgo. Artists Coalition, Ill. Higher Edn. Art Assn. (bd. dirs.). Wesleyan. Avocations: genealogical research, reading, travel. Office: Art Dept Judson Coll 1151 N State St Elgin IL 60123-1404

COLPOYS-COIA, PATRICIA ANN, elementary school educator; b. Lewiston, N.Y., Sept. 2, 1965; d. Carroll John and Barbara Ann (Williams) C.; m. Daniel Coia, Nov. 11, 2000. BS in Elementary Edn., SUNY, Buffalo, 1988; MS in Elem. Edn., State U. Coll., Buffalo, 1993. Tchr. grade 4 St. Peter's Roman Cath. Sch., Lewiston, 1988-89; kindergarten tchr. North Tonawanda (N.Y.) pub. schs., 1989—; tchr. North Tonawanda City Sch. Dist., 1989—. Roman Catholic. Avocations: boating, camping. Home: 1002 92nd St Niagara Falls NY 14304-2818

COLSTON, FREDDIE CHARLES, political science educator; b. Gretna, Fla., Mar. 28, 1936; s. Henry Bill and Willie Mae (Taylor) C.; m. Doris Marie Suggs, Mar. 13, 1976; 1 child, Deirdre Charisse. BA, Morehouse Coll., 1959; MA, Atlanta U., 1966; PhD, Ohio State U., 1972. Instr. social sci. Ft. Valley (Ga.) State Coll., 1966-68; assoc. prof. polit. sci. So. U., Baton Rouge, 1972-73, U. Detroit, 1973-76; assoc. prof., chmn. div. social sci. Dillard U., New Orleans, 1976-78; asst. prof. polit. sci. Delta Coll., University Center, Mich., 1978-79; assoc. dir. Exec. Seminar Ctr. U.S. Office Pers. Mgmt., Oak Ridge, 1980-87; prof. Inst. of Govt. Tenn. State U., Nashville, 1987-88; prof., dir. pub. adminstrn. program N.C. Ctrl. U., Durham, 1988-91; prof. dept. history and polit. sci. Ga. Southwestern Coll., Americus, 1992-97. Pres. Broward County (Fla.) Social Studies Coun., 1961-62; mem. constn. com. Fla. State Tchrs. Assn., 1963-64; chmn. human rels. coun. Ga. Southwestern State U.., 1997. Contbr. articles to profl. jours. Mem. bd. mgmt. Northwestern Br. YMCA, Detroit, 1976; mem. govt. subcom. Task Force 2000, City of Midland, Mich., 1979. Morehouse Coll. scholar, 1955, Atlanta U. scholar 1965, Nat. Def. Edn. Act scholar, 1964, Ford Found. Internat. Studies Summer fellow, 1967, So. Fellowships Fund fellow, 1968-71; recipient C-Span Faculty Devel. grants, 1994, 95, 96; recipient Mr. Psi award, Omegi Psi Phi, 1959, Outstanding Faculty award, Kappa Delta Sorority, Ga. SW Univ., 1995. Mem. Am. Polit. Sci. Assn. (com. on the status of blacks in the profession 1977-80), Nat. Conf. Black

Polit. Scientists, Ctr. for Study of Presidency, Assn. for Study of Afro-Am. Life, So. Polit. Sci. Assn., Pi Sigma Alpha, Alpha Phi Gamma. Avocations: reading biographies, photography, spectator sports. Home: 126 Hazleton Ln Oak Ridge TN 37830-7929 E-mail: freedie@icx.net.

COLUCCIO, JOSEPHINE CATHERINE, primary and elementary school educator; b. Bklyn., Oct. 21, 1952; d. Dominic Anthony and Catherine (Pomponio) Ferone; m. Frank Anthony Coluccio, June 26, 1976; 1 child, Nancy Marie. BA in Edn. cum laude, Bklyn. Coll., 1974. Cert. nursery, kindergarten, and elem. tchr., N.Y., nursery and elem. tchr., N.J. Elem. math. and sci. tchr.-coord. Our Lady of Perpetual Help Sch., Bklyn., 1974-77; pub. rels. coord. McDonald's Corp., S.I., N.Y., 1977-78; day care group tchr. Congress of Italian Am. Orgns., Bklyn., 1979-80; elem. math. and sci. tchr.-coord. Resurrection Elem. Sch., Bklyn., 1980-83; owner, dir. Little Yellow House, Toms River, N.J., 1984-90, Little Explorers-An Ed U Care Program, Toms River, 1990—. Active Rep. Nat. Com., Washington, 1991—. Mem. ASCD, Nat. Assn. for Edn. Young Children, Am. Family Assn., Nat. Safety Coun., Soc. Children's Book Writers and Illustrators (assoc.), Assn. for Curriculum and Devel. Republican. Roman Catholic. Avocations: piano playing, bowling, arts and crafts, cooking, writing children's stories.

COLWELL, JAMES LEE, humanities educator; b. Brush, Colo., Aug. 31, 1926; s. Francis Joseph and Alice (Bleasdale) C.; m. Claudia Alsleben, Dec. 27, 1957; children: John Francis, Alice Anne. BA, U. Denver, 1949; MA, U. No. Colo., 1951; cert., Sorbonne, Paris, 1956; diploma, U. Heidelberg, Germany, 1957; AM (Univ. fellow), Yale U., 1959, PhD (Hale-Kilborn fellow), 1961. Tchr. H.S., Snyder and Sterling, Colo., 1948-52; civilian edn. adviser USAF, Japan, 1952-56; assoc. dir. Yale Fgn. Student Inst., summers 1959-60; asst. dir. European divsn. U. Md., Heidelberg, 1961-65; dir. Office Internat. Edn., assoc. prof. Am. Lit. U. Colo., Boulder, 1965-72; prof. Am. studies, chmn. lit. U. Tex. Permian Basin, Odessa, 1977-82, dean Coll. Arts and Edn., 1972-77, 82-84, K.C. Dunagan prof. humanities, 1984-87, prof. emeritus, 1988—. Contbr. articles to learned jours. Mem. nat. adv. coun. Inst. Internat. Edn., 1969-75; v.p. Ector County chpt. ARC, 1974-76; mem. Ector County Hist. Commn., 1973-75. Served with USAAF, 1945, brig. gen. USAF Res. Ret. Mem. AAUP, MLA, NEA (life), Am. Studies Assn., Western Social Sci. Assn. (life, pres. 1974-75), Orgn. Am. Historians (life), South Ctrl. MLA, Permian Basin Hist. Soc. (life, pres. 1980-81), Air Force Assn. (life), Air Force Hist. Found. (life), Res. Officers Assn. (life), Ret. Officers Assn. (life), Phi Beta Kappa. Unitarian-Universalist. Home: 4675 Gordon Dr Boulder CO 80305-6747

COMBS, LINDA JONES, management company executive, researcher; b. Jonesboro, Ark., Apr. 12, 1948; d. Dale Jones and Neva Craig; 1 child, Nathan Isaac. BSBA, U. Ark., 1971, MBA, 1972, PhD in Bus. Adminstrn., 1983. Assoc. economist Bur. Bus. and Econ. Rsch., Fayetteville, Ark., 1973-76; pres. Combs Mgmt. Co., Springdale, Ark., 1976-83; asst. prof. fin. U. Ark., Fayetteville, 1983-87; asst. prof. fin. and mktg. Western Ill. U., Macomb, 1987-88; asst. prof. bus. adminstrn. Cen. Mo. State U., Warrensburg, 1988-89; assoc. prof. bus. adminstrn. N.E. State U., Tahlequah, Okla., 1989—. Cons. in credit and polit. rsch. Fayetteville Adv. Coun., 1975-76; cons. in fin. and banking, Fayetteville, 1973-76. Contbr. articles to profl. jours. Mem. Ark. Gov.'s Inaugural Com., Little Rock, 1985; county co-chmn. Clinton for Gov., Washington County, Ark., 1984, 86, 90; bd. dirs. Shiloh Mus., Am. Cancer Soc., South Washington County, North Ark. Symphony Soc.; bd. dirs. Ark. State Hosp. Sys., sec., chmn., 1991-95; active numerous polit. campaigns for candidates and issues. Mem. Am. Mktg. Assn. (health care mktg.), Transp. Rsch. Forum. Avocations: gardening, quilting. Office: Combs Mgmt Co PO Box 1452 Fayetteville AR 72702-1452

COMBS, SANDRA LYNN, state parole board official; b. Lancaster, Pa., Aug. 31, 1946; d. Clyde Robert and Violet (Sensenig) Boose; m. Allen Evans Combs, Aug. 30, 1969; children: Evan McKenzie, Leslie Ann. AAS in Nursing, Thomas Nelson C.C., Hampton, Va., 1980; BS in Psychology, Juniata Coll., 1968. RN, Va. Dir. vols. in probation Yorktown (Va.) Juvenile Ct., 1973-74; emergency nurse assoc. to pvt. practice physician Hampton, Va., 1980-82; chmn. bd. dirs., CEO Hampton Roads Gulls Profl. Hockey Team, Hampton, 1981-82; mem. sch. bd. York County Pub. Schs., Yorktown, 1985-94; vice chmn. Va. Parole Bd., Richmond, 1994—. Mem. supt.'s adv. coun. York County Pub. Schs., 1984-94, mem. long range strategic planning com., 1989-94; trustee New Horizons Tech. Ctr., Gov.'s Sch., Hampton, 1991-94; mem. Va. edn. tech. adv. com. Va. Dept. Edn., 1992-95; mem. Va. Bd. Correctional Edn., 1994—, Va. Adult Basic Edn. and Literacy Adv. Coun., 1994—. Pres. Hampton Med. Soc. Aux, 1977-78, Dare Elem. PTA, York County, 1979-81, York County Coun. PTA, 1983-84; chmn. York County Rep. Com., 1984-90, 1st Dist. Rep. Congl. Com., Va., 1990-94; adviser edn. policy George Allen for Gov., Richmond, 1992-93. Capt. USAF, 1968-73, Vietnam. Decorated Bronze Star medal, Cross of Gallantry (Vietnam), Air Force Commendation medal. Mem. ASCD, VFW, Va. Sch. Bds. Assn. (bd. dirs. 1990-94, award of Excellence 1990, 91, 92), Mil. Order World Wars. Methodist. Avocations: reading, travel, ice hockey. Home: 150 Barn Swallow Rdg Yorktown VA 23692-6167 Office: Va Parole Bd 6900 Atmore Dr Richmond VA 23225-5644

COMEAU, CAROL SMITH, school system administrator; b. Berkeley, Calif., Sept. 4, 1941; d. Floyd Franklin and Bessie Caroline (Campbell) Smith; m. Dennis Rene Comeau, Dec. 27, 1962; children: Christopher, Michael, Karen. BS in Edn., U. Oreg., 1963; M in Pub. Sch. Adminstrn., U. Alaska, 1985. Third grade tchr., Springfield, Oreg., 1963-64; elem. sch. tchr. Ocean View Elem. Sch., Anchorage, 1975-84, 2d-6th grade tchr.; 6th grade tchr. Spring Hill Elem. Sch., Anchorage, 1985-86; adminstrv. intern Tudor Elem. Sch., Anchorage, 1986-87; prin. Orion Elem. Sch., Anchorage, 1987-89; prin. Spring Hill Elem. Sch., 1989-90; exec. dir. elem. edn. Anchorage Sch. Dist., 1990-93; asst. supt. instrn., 1993-2000; supt., 2000—; community activist ednl. issues. Chair Alaska PTA Edn. Commn., 1987-88; sec. bd. Frontier (Alaska) State Credit Union, 1987-91; vice-chair Anchorage United Way, 2002--; bd. dirs. KAKM pub. TV, 1990-92, Alaska Ctr. Performing Arts. Named Tchr. of Yr., Anchorage Sch. Dist. PTA Coun., 1976, Top 25 Most Powerful Alaskans, 2002, Alaska Supt. of Yr., 2003. Mem. NEA, Nat. Assn. Elem. Sch. Prins., Alaska Assn. Elem. Sch. Prins., Anchorage Edn. Assn. (Tchr. of Yr. 1986), Phi Delta Kappa, Kappa Delta Pi. Democrat. Home: 13632 Jarvi Dr Anchorage AK 99515-3934 Office: Anchorage Sch Dist Adminstrn Bldg 4600 Debarr Rd Anchorage AK 99519-6614

COMEAUX, TINA BOISSEY, school board executive, civic worker; b. Groves, Tex., Mar. 21, 1956; d. Robert Oliver and Jim Marie (Glenn) Boissey; m. Charles Allen Comeaux, Jan. 3, 1976; children: Candice Lynn, Christy Ann. Student, Lamar U., 1974-76. Saleswoman Burkett's Jewelry, Port Neches, Tex., 1974-78. Trustee Port Neches Ind. Sch. Dist., 1987—, sec., 1991-92, v.p., 1992-93, pres. 1993—; co-chmn. summer reading program Groves Pub. Libr., 1984-89, founder, tchr. presch. reading program, 1986-89; del. area coun. Van Buren Sch. PTA, Groves, 1984-90, parent. vol., 1990; treas. Grove Elem. Sch. PTA, 1988-92, mem. exec. bd., 1990—; libr. vol. Grove Elem. LOVE Program, 1991-92; mem. exec. bd. Port Neches-Groves Area Coun. PTA, 1993—, Port Neches Mid. Sch. PTA, 1993-95; mem. Port Neches-Groves Parent Tchr. Student Assn., 1993—; vol. computer coord. Woodcrest Elem., 1993-94; treas. Groves Mid. Sch. PTA, 1992-93; pres. Groves Pub. Libr., 1986-89; others. Presdl. scholar Lamar U., 1974. Mem. Am. Heart Assn., Nat. Sch. Bds. Assn., Tex. Computer Edn. Assn., Tex. Assn. Sch. Bds. (rep. 1989-91), Tex. Vols. in Pub. Schs., Sabine-Neches Adminstrs. and Sch. Bd. Mems. Assn. (co-chmn. 1989-91), Van Buren Sch. PTA (life), S.E. Tex. Art Mus. Roman Catholic. Avocations: cooking, reading, yardwork, swimming, piano. Home: 17114 Loblolly Bay Ct Houston TX 77059-3222

COMEFORO, JEAN ELIZABETH, hearing impaired educator; b. Urbana, Ill., June 2, 1947; d. Jay E. and Jean Carolyn (Raff) Comeforo. BS in Biology, Coll. St. Elizabeth, 1969; MEd of Deaf, Smith Coll., 1972; MEd, Cheyney State Coll., 1982. Cert. tchr. of deaf, N.J., Pa., tchr. biol. and comprehensive scis., oral interpreter for deaf. Houseparent Katazenbach Sch. for Deaf, West Trenton, N.J., 1969-70; math. and sci. tchr. Western Pa. Sch. for Deaf, Edgewood, 1971-76; tchr. of deaf Delaware County Intermediate Unit, Media, Pa., 1976-98; tchr. of the deaf Archbishop Ryan Sch. for Children with Deafness, 2001—; tchr. of the deaf, itinerant hearing therapist, oral interpreter. Presenter in field. Leader Girl Scouts U.S.; chaperone Miss Deaf Pa., 1987-89. Recipient citation for inspirational teaching of sci. subjects Buhl Planetarium, Annie Sullivan award; named Best Producer Community Svc. TV Program, Am. Cablevision Pa. Mem. Alexander Graham Bell Assn. (bd. dirs. Marion Quick chpt. 1983-91, pres. 1989-91), Internat. Orgn. Of Hearing Impaired (Tchr. of Yr. award 1990-91), Delaware Valley Assn. Oral Hearing Impaired, Quota Clubs (gov. dist. II 1985-87), Optimists Internat. (sec. 1995-96, pres. 1996-98, chair Pa. Upper Delaware dist. Contest for the Deaf and Hard-of-Hearing 1995-98, lt. gov. zone 2 1998-99), Beta Beta Beta Nat. Biology Honor Soc. Home: 315 Catch Penny Ln Media PA 19063-5420

COMER, BRENDA WARMEE, educator, real estate company executive; b. Lakewood, Ohio, May 14, 1938; d. Walter Byron and Annabelle (Broderick) Warmee; m. Gerald Edmund Comer, June 30, 1962; children: Brian, James, David, Kristen. BS, Kent State U., 1961; postgrad., Bowling Green State U., 1981, 82, 83-84; reading cert., Baldwin Wallace Coll., 1987. Elem. tchr. Lorain (Ohio) Bd. Edn., 1961-63, tchr. aux. svcs. remedial reading and math., 1979-87, tchr. Chpt. I reading program, 1987—. V.p. Warmee, Inc., real estate. Vice pres. Lakeland Woman's Club, Loraine, 1972, scholarship chmn., 1973-76. Mem. NEA, Ohio Edn. Assn., Loraine Edn. Assn., Internat. Reading Assn., Daniel T. Gardner Reading Coun., AAUW (v.p. Lorain 1981-82, scholarship chmn. 1986-90). Home: 1075 Archwood Ave Lorain OH 44052-1248

COMER, DEBRA RUTH, management educator; b. Phila., Apr. 11, 1960; d. Nathan Lawrence and Rita C.; m. James Michael Maloney; children: Rudy Gabriel Malcom and Jacob Eli Malcom (twins). BA, Swarthmore Coll., 1982; MA, Yale U., 1984, MPhil, 1985, PhD, 1986. Instr. Yale U., New Haven, 1983-84; orgnl. devel. cons. Port Authority of N.Y. & N.J., N.Y.C., 1984-87; asst. prof. mgmt. Hofstra U., Hempstead, N.Y., 1987-93, assoc. prof. mgmt., 1993-99, chairperson dept. mgmt. and GB, 1995-97, assoc. dean faculty devel. Sch. of Bus., 1997-98, prof. mgmt., 1999—. Co-author: Instructor's Manual: Developing Management Skills, 2002; contbr. articles to profl. jours. Yale U. fellow, 1982-86, Joshua B. Lippincott fellow Swarthmore Coll., 1982; Hofstra U. grantee, 1988-2000. Mem. APA, Acad. Mgmt., Ea. Acad. Mgmt., Orgnl. Behavior Teaching Soc. Jewish. Avocations: music, fitness, cooking, reading. Office: Hofstra U Dept Mgmt and Gen Bus 228 Weller Hl Hempstead NY 11549-1340

COMER, DOUGLAS EARL, computer science educator, consultant; b. Vineland, N.J., Sept. 9, 1949; BS, Houghton (N.Y.) Coll., 1971; PhD, Pa. State U., 1976. Asst. prof. computer sci. Purdue U., West Lafayette, Ind., 1976-81, assoc. prof. computer sci., 1981-84, prof. computer sci., 1984—; mem. tech. staff Bell Labs., Murray Hill, N.J., 1982-83. Dean Interop Grad. Inst., Foster City, Calif., 1996-98, instr. seminars on Transmission Control Protocol/Internet Protocol and networking, 1989—, cons., 1987—; cons. networking Softbank Corp., 1987—. Author 11 books in networking field and 4 books in operating system design, including: Operating System Design, Vol. 1, 1984, Vol. 2, 1987, Internetworking with TCP/IP, 3 vols. and rev. edits., 1991-2000, The Internet Book, 1994, rev. edit., 2000, Computer Networks and Internets, 1999; contbr. articles to profl. jours. Recipient Lifetime Achievement award Software Tools Users Group USENIX, 1996; rsch. grantee NSF, Sun, Digital Equipment, AT&T, Def. Advanced Rsch. Projects Agy., 1983—. Fellow Assn. for Computing Machinery (Outstanding Tchg. award Purdue chpt. 1995); mem. Sigma Xi, Upsilon Pi Epsilon. Avocation: postscript drawings. Office: Purdue U Dept Computer Sci University St R 156 Lafayette IN 47907-1398

COMER, JAMES PIERPONT, psychiatrist, educator; b. East Chicago, Ind., Sept. 25, 1934; s. Hugh and Maggie (Nichols) C.; m. Shirley Ann Arnold, June 20, 1959 (dec. Apr. 1994); children: Brian Jay, Dawn Renee. AB, Ind. U., 1956; MD, Howard U., 1960; MPH, U. Mich., 1964; DSc (hon.), U. New Haven, 1977; LittD (hon.), Calumet Coll., 1978; LHD (hon.), Bank St. Coll., N.Y.C., 1987, Albertus Magnus Coll., 1989, Quinnipiac Coll., 1990, DePauw U., 1990; DSc (hon.), Ind U., 1991, Wabash Coll., 1991; EdD (hon.), Wheelock Coll., 1991; LLD (hon.), U. Conn., 1991; LHD (hon.), SUNY Buffalo, 1991, New Sch. for Social Rsch., 1991; D Pedagogy (hon.), R.I. Coll., 1991; DSc (hon.), Amherst Coll., 1991; LHD (hon.), John Jay Coll. Criminal Justice, 1991, Wesleyan U., 1991; DH (hon.), Princeton U., 1991; DSc (hon.), Northwestern U., 1991, Worcester Poly. Inst., 1991; LHD (hon.), U. Pa., 1992; DPD (hon.), Niagara U., 1992; LHD (hon.), Hamilton Coll., 1992; DSc (hon.), Brown U., 1992; LHD (hon.), U. Mass. at Lowell, 1992; DSc (hon.), Med. Coll. Ohio, 1992, Howard U., 1993, W.Va. U., 1993; LLD (hon.), Lawrence U., 1993; DSc (hon.), Morehouse Sch. Medicine, 1993; LLD (hon.), Columbia U., 1994, Boston Coll., 1994; LHD (hon.), Briarwood Coll., 1994, Cleve. State U., 1996; DSc (hon.), St. Mary's Coll., Md., 1996, Albion Coll., 1997, Conn. Coll., 1997, So. Conn. State Coll., 1998; D in Pediats., Long Island U., 1999; LHD (hon.), Ea. Mich. U., 2000; LHD (hon.), N.C.State Univ. Served with USPHS, Washington and Chevy Chase, Md., 1961-68; intern St. Catherine's Hosp., East Chicago, 1960-61; resident Yale Sch. Medicine, 1964-67; asst. prof. psychiatry Yale Child Study Center and dept. psychiatry, 1968-70, assoc. prof., 1970-75, prof., 1975-76, Maurice Falk prof. child psychiatry, 1976—; assoc. dean Yale Med. Sch., New Haven, 1969—. Dir. pupil svcs. Baldwin-King Sch. Project, New Haven, 1968-73; dir. sch. devel. program Yale Child Study Ctr., 1973-97, founder sch. devel. program adv. bd., 1997—; dir. Conn. Energy Corp., 1976—, Nat. Acad. Found. N.Y., N.Y.C., 1993—; co-dir. Black Family Roundtable Greater New Haven, 1986—; cons. Joint Commn. on Mental Health of Children, Nat. Commn. on Causes and Prevention of Violence, NIMH; mem. nat. adv. mental health coun. HEW; Henry J. Kaiser Sr. fellow Center for Advanced Study in the Behavioral Scis., Stanford, 1976-77. Author: Beyond Black and White, 1972, Black Child Care, 1975, 2d edit., 1992, School Power, 1980, 2d. edit., 1993, Maggie's American Dream, 1988, Rallying the Whole Village: The Comer Process for Reforming Education, 1996, Waiting For a Miracle: Why Schools Can't Solve Our Problems-And How We Can, 1997, Child by Child: The Comer Process for Change in Education, 1999; mem. editl. bd. Am. Jour. Orthopsychiatry, 1969-76, Youth and Adolescence, 1971-87, Jour. Negro Edn., 1973-83; guest editor Jour. Am. Acad. Child Psychiatry, 1985; columnist Parents mag.; contbr. articles to profl. jours. Bd. dirs. Field Found., 1981-88, Dixwell Soul Sta. and Yale Afro-Am. House; trustee Hazen Found., 1974-78, Wesleyan U., 1978-84, Nat. Coun. for Effective Schs., 1985—, Albertus Magnus Coll., 1989—, Carnegie Corp., 1990, Milton S. Eisenhower Found., Washington, 1991—, Conn. State U., 1991-94; bd. dirs., mem. profl. adv. bd. Children's TV Workshop, 1972-88; mem. profl. adv. coun. Nat. Assn. Mental Health; mem. ad. hoc adv. com. Conn. Rsch. Commn.; mem. adv. coun. Nat. Com. for Citizens in Edn.; mem. nat. adv. coun. Hogg Found. for Mental Health, 1983-86; mem. adv. com. adolescent pregnancy prevention Children's Def. Fund, 1985—; mem. adv. coun. Nat. Com. for Citizens in Edn., 1983—; mem. nat. adv. coun. Hogg Found for Mental Health, 1983-86; mem. edn. adv. bd., bd. dirs. (hon.) Kids Voting USA, 1997—; mem. nat. evaluation adv. coun. Kellogg Youth Initiative Partnerships W.K. Kellogg Found., 1997—. Recipient Child Study Assn.-Wel-Met Family Life book award, 1975, Howard U. Disting. Alumni award, 1976, Rockefeller Public Service award, 1980, Media award NCCJ, 1981, Cmty. Leadership award Greater New Haven C. of C., 1983, Disting. Fellow award Conn. chpt. Phi Delta Kappa, 1984, Elm and Ivy award New Haven Found., 1985, Disting. Svc. award Conn. Assn. Psychologists, 1985, Disting. Educator award Conn. Coalition of 100 Black Women, 1985, Outstanding Leadership award Children's Def. Fund, 1987, Whitney M. Young Jr. Svc. award Boy Scouts Am., 1989, Prudential Leadership award Prudential Found., 1990, Harold W. McGraw Jr. prize in Edn., 1990, James Bryant Conant award Edn. Commn. States, 1991, Charles A. Dana prize in Edn., 1991, Disting. Svc. award Coun. Chief State Sch. Officers, 1991, Family Focus Nat. award, 1991, Charles A. Dana award for pioneering achievement in edn., 1991, Ind. U. Disting. Alumni Svc. award, 1992, Burger King Disting. Svc. to Edn. award, 1992, Conn. Assn. for Human Svcs. Pres. award, 1992, Golden Acorn award Bronx C.C., 1994, Presdl. citation Am. Ednl. Rsch. Assn., 1995, Health Trac Found. prize, 1996, Heinz Family award, 1996, Lehigh U. Outstanding Svc. to Coll. Edn. award, 1996, Ann Vanderbilt Achievement award for ednl. leadership, 1997, Great Friend to Kids award Assn. Youth Mus., 1997, Disting. Svc. medal Tchrs. Coll., 1997, Friends of the Family citation, Working Mother Mag., 1997, World of Children award Judge Baker Children's Ctr., 1997, Michael Bolton Lifetime Achievement award, 1997, Edn. award Inst. Student Achievement, 1999, Disting. Pub. Svc. award Conn. Bar Assn., 1999, Martin Luther Freedom award New Haven Chpt. NAACP; John and Mary Markle Found. scholar, 1969—; James Comer NIMH Minority Fellowship established in his honor, 1991.; Disting. Service Award, Covenant to Care, Inc., 2001. Mem. APA (Disting. Svc. award 1993), Am. Acad. Child Adolescent Psychiatry, Nat. Med. Assn., Nat. Mental Health Assn. (Lela Rowland Prevention award 1989), Am. Psychiat. Assn. (Agnes Purcell McGavin award 1990, Solomon Carter Fuller award 1990, Spl. Presdl. Commendation 1990, Disting. Svc. award 1993), Am. Orthopsychiat. Assn. (Vera S. Paster award 1990), Am. Acad. Child Psychiatry, Black Psychiatrists of Am., NAACP, Black Coalition of New Haven, Greater New Haven Black Family Roundtable (co-dir. 1986—), Alpha Omega Alpha, Alpha Phi Alpha. Avocations: photography, travel, sports fan. Office: Yale U Child Study Ctr PO Box 207900 New Haven CT 06520-7900 E-mail: james.comer@yale.edu.

COMER, NATHAN LAWRENCE, psychiatrist, educator; b. Phila., Nov. 10, 1923; s. Rubin L. and Fannie (Cassover) C.; m. Rita Ellis, June 19, 1949 (dec. Mar. 1978); children: Robert, Susan Comer Kitei, Debra R., Marc J. BA, U. Pa., 1944; MD, Hahnemann Med. Coll., 1949; postgrad., U. Pa. Diplomate Am. Bd. Psychiatry and Neurology, Am. Bd. Profl. Disabiligy Cons., Sr. Disability Analyst of Am. Bd. Disability Analysts, Am. Bd. Forensic Examiners, Am. Bd. Forensic Medicine. Intern Hahnemann Med. Coll., Phila., 1949-50; resident, NIMH fellow Inst. of Pa. Hosp., Phila., 1951-53, sr. attending psychiatrist, 1968—, resident in psychiatry, 1951-53; chief of psychiatry Ford Rd. campus Thomas Jefferson U. Hosp., Phila., 1978-94; clin. assoc. prof. psychiatry and human behavior Jefferson Med. Coll., Thomas Jefferson U., Phila., 1994—; clin. assoc. prof. psychiatry Drexel U. Coll. Medicine, Phila., 1978—; emeritus attending psychiatrist Hosp. Med. Coll. Pa., 2000—. Pres. med. staff Belmont Ctr. Comprehensive Treatment (formerly Phila. Psychiat. Ctr.), 1975—77, emeritus sr. attending physician, 1988—; pres. med. staff Inst. of Pa. Hosp., 1983—85. Contbr. articles to profl. jours. Bd. dirs. Temple Adath Israel of Main Line, Merion, Pa., 1958-78. Fellow Coll. Physicians Phila., Am. Psychiat. Assn. (disting. life); mem. AMA, Am. Soc. for Adolescent Psychiatry, Hahnemann Med. Coll. Alumni Assn. (pres. 1973-74), B'nai B'rith. Republican. Jewish. Home and Office: 1100 Hillcrest Rd Narberth PA 19072-1224 Fax: (610) 668-7417.

COMFORT, PRISCILLA MARIA, retired college official, human resources professional; b. Ft Dix, NJ, Feb. 20, 1947; d. Jennie Rita (Manes) McGuire; children: James, Aimee. BS, Montclair State Coll., 1969; MEd, Trenton State Coll., 1980. Cert. tchr., guidance counselor, NJ. Tchr. Burlington Twp. and City Sch., NJ, 1969-72; employment svc. interviewer NJ Dept. Labor and Industry, 1972-74; career devel. specialist, pers. tech. princ. NJ Dept. Civil Svc., Trenton, 1974—79; dir., asst., assoc. v.p. Human Resources Richard Stockton Coll. NJ, Pomona, 1979—2003, spl. asst. to pres., 2003—. Mem. Pres.'s adv. coun. NJ Gov.'s Task Force on Sexual Harassment, 1993, pers. adv. bd., human resources coun., 2002. Mem.: NJ CUPA-HR (life; life). Roman Catholic. Avocations: reading, travel, collecting bells, books, candles. Office: Richard Stockton Coll NJ Jim Leeds Rd Pomona NJ 08240

COMITAS, LAMBROS, anthropologist, educator; b. N.Y.C., Sept. 29, 1927; s. Dennis and Magdaline (Livanis) C.; m. Irene Mousouris. AB, Columbia U., 1948, PhD in Anthropology, 1962. Instr. anthropology Columbia U., N.Y.C., 1958-61, asst. prof., 1962-64, assoc. prof. anthropology and edn. Tchrs. Coll., 1965-67, prof., 1967-87, Gardner Cowles prof. anthropology and edn., 1988—, dir. div. philosophy, social scis. and edn., 1979-96, dir. Inst. Latin Am. and Iberian studies, 1977-84; dir. Rsch. Inst. study of man, 1985-2001; adminstr. Ruth Landes Meml. Rsch. Fund, 1991—; pres. Comitas Inst. Anthrop. Study, 2003—. Mem. drug abuse, clin., behavioral and psychosocial rsch. rev. com. Nat. Inst. Drug Abuse, 1977-81. Author books and articles in field. With U.S. Army, 1946-47. Office Edn. fellow, 1968-69, Guggenheim fellow, 1971-72; Fulbright grantee, 1957-58, Nat. Inst. Drug Abuse grantee, 1975-79. Mem. Soc. Applied Anthropology (pres. 1970-71), Am. Anthrop. Assn., Am. Ethnol. Soc., Nat. Acad. Edn. (chmn. com. anthropology and edn.), N.Y. Acad. Scis. Home: 1107 5th Ave New York NY 10128-0145 Office: Teachers Coll Columbia U New York NY 10027 E-mail: lc137@columbia.edu.

COMPAGNON, ANTOINE MARCEL, French language educator; b. Brussels, July 20, 1950; came to U.S., 1985; s. Jean and Jacqueline (Terlinden) C. Ecole, Nat. des Ponts et Chaussees, Paris, 1975; D es Lettres, U. Paris VII, 1985. Rsch. attache Centre Nat. de la Recherche Scientifique, Paris, 1975-78; lectr. Ecole Poly., Paris, 1978-85, French Inst., London, 1980-81, U. Rouen, France, 1981-85; prof. Columbia U., N.Y.C., 1985—, Blanche W. Knopf prof., 1991—; vis. prof. U. Pa., Phila., 1986, 90; prof. U. Le Mans, France, 1989-90, U. Paris, Sorbonne, 1994—. Author: La Seconde Main, 1979, Ferragosto, 1985, Proust entre deux Siecles, 1989; editor: Marcel Proust, Sodome et Gomorrhe, 1988. Fellowship Found. Thiers, 1975-78, Guggenheim Found., 1988, All Souls Coll., Oxford U., 1994. Mem. Am. Acad. Arts and Scis. Office: Columbia U 517 Philosophy Hall New York NY 10027 E-mail: amc6@columbia.edu.

COMPTON, NORMA HAYNES, retired university dean, artist; b. Washington, Nov. 16, 1924; d. Thomas N. and Lillian (Laffin) Haynes; m. William Randall Compton, Mar. 27, 1946; children: William Randall, Anne Elizabeth. AB, George Washington U., 1950; MS, U. Md., 1957, PhD, 1962; D of Letters, Purdue U., 1996. Rschr. Julius Garfinckel & Co., Washington, 1955; tchr. Montgomery Blair High Sch., Silver Spring, Md., 1955-57; instr. U. Md., 1957-60, teaching and rsch. fellow Inst. Child Study, 1960-61, assoc. prof., 1962-63; psychology extern St. Elizabeths Hosp., Washington, 1962-63; assoc. prof. Utah State U., 1963-64, prof., 1964-68, head dept. clothing and textiles, 1963-68, dir. Inst. for Rsch. on Man and His Personal Environment, 1967-68; dean Sch. Home Econs. Auburn (Ala.) U., 1968-73; dean Sch. Consumer and Family Scis. Purdue U., 1973-87, prof. family studies, 1987-90; faculty The Edn. Ctr., Longboat Key, Fla., 1991-2000, mem. ednl. adv. bd., 1995-98. Cons. Burgess Pub. Co., Mpls., 1975-81, Nat. Advt. Rev. Bd., N.Y.C., 1978-82; bd. dirs. Armour & Co., Phoenix, 1976-82, Home Hosp., Lafayette, Ind., 1983-89; adv. com. Women's Resource Ctr. of Sarasota, Fla., 1992-96; chair Adv. Commn. Status Women, Sarasota, 1993-96; mem. advocates coun. Family Law Network Sarasota, 1994—; exec. bd. Sarasota-Manatee Phi Beta Kappa Assn., 1996-99; bd. trustees Plymouth Harbor, Inc., 2003—. Author: (with Olive Hall) Foundations of Home Economics Research, 1972, (with John Touliatos) Approaches to Child Study, 1983, Research Methods in Human Ecology/Home Economics, 1988; contbr. articles to profl. jours. Mem. exec. coun. Plymouth Harbor Residents Assn., Sarasota, 2001—, bd. trustees,

2003—. Recipient Woman of Impact Lifetime Achievement award, 1997. Mem.: PEO, AAUW, APA, Nat. League Am. Pen Women (v.p. Sarasota br.), Am. Assn. Family and Consumer Sci., Sigma Xi, Phi Beta Kappa, Psi Chi, Omicron Nu, Phi Kappa Phi. Congregational United Ch. Christ. E-mail: normahc@aol.com.

CONANT, HOWARD SOMERS, artist, educator; b. Beloit, Wis., May 5, 1921; s. Rufus P. and Edith B. (Somers) C.; m. Florence C. Craft, June 18, 1943; children: Judith Lynne Steinbach, Jeffrey Scott; m. Virginia E. Lusk, June 7, 1999. Student, Art Students League of N.Y., 1944-45; BS, U. Wis.-Milw., 1946; MS, U. Wis.-Madison, 1947; Ed.D., U. Buffalo, 1950. Instr. art, asst. head housefellow U. Wis., 1946-47; asst. prof. art SUNY, Buffalo, 1947-50, prof. art, 1950-55; chmn. dept. art and art edn. also chmn. art collection NYU, 1955-76; head dept. art U. Ariz., Tucson, 1976-86, prof. art, 1986-87; profl. artist, 1987—. Art edn. cons. NBC-TV, also Girl Scouts Am. TV series, 1958-60; field reader, also Title III program cons. U.S. Office of Edn.; adviser N.Y. State Council on Arts, 1962-63, Conn. Commn. on Arts, 1967-68; cons. Ford Found., 1973, Children's Theatre Assn., 1973, Getty Trust, 1985; examiner Internat. Baccalaureate Orgn., 1998. Moderator: weekly TV program Fun to Learn About Art, WBEN-TV, Buffalo, 1951-55; numerous one man shows; represented maj. group exhbns. pub. art mus. and coll. art collections; represented by Sol Del Rio Gallery, San Antonio, Art Source Inc., Tulsa, Ideas and Products, Tucson; executed mural Sperry High Sch., Henrietta, N.Y., 1971, Good Samaritan Med. Ctr., Phoenix, 1982, Valley Nat. Bank, Tucson, 1983; one-man retrospectives, Amarillo (Tex.) Art Mus., 1989, Tucson Jewish Cmty. Ctr., 1995, Sun City (Ariz.) Art Mus., Prescott (Ariz.) Fine Arts Assoc., 1996; author: (with Arne Randall) Art in Education, 1959, 63; author, editor: Art Workshop Leaders Planning Guide, 1958, Masterpieces of the Arts, New Wonder World Cultural Library, Vol. 4, 1963, Art Education, 1964, Seminar on Elementary and Secondary School Education in the Visual Arts, 1965, Lincoln Library of the Arts (2 vols.), 1973; art editor: Intellect, 1975-78, USA Today, 1978-85; assoc. editor Arts mag., 1973-75; contbr. articles profl. publs. Dept. State lectr., India, 1964; Dir. Waukesha County (Wis.) YMCA Art Program, 1946-48; pres., dir. Children's Creative Art Found., 1959-60; mem. adv. com. Coll. of Potomac, 1966; mem. cultural exchange mission to Mex., Ptnrs. of the Ams., 1988, 90; Lt. USAAF, 1943-46. Recipient 25th Ann. medal Nat. Gallery Art, 1966, Disting. Alumnus award U. Wis.-Milw., 1968, Purchase award Richard Florsheim Art Fund, 1992; Disting. fellow Nat. Art Edn. Assn., 1985, Nat. Endowment Arts sr. fellow in painting, 1985. Mem. Coll. Art Assn., Nat. Art Edn. Assn., Internat. Art Critics Assn., Alliance for Arts in Edn., Nat. Assn. Schs. Art and Design, AAUP, Nat. Com. Art Edn. (council, chmn. 1962-63), Inst. Study of Art in Edn. (bd. govs. 1965-72, pres. 1965-68) Clubs: Torch (N.Y.C.) (pres. 1965-66). Studio: 6954 E Cicada Ct Tucson AZ 85750-1395

CONANT, KIM UNTIEDT, elementary education educator; b. Del Norte, Colo., July 26, 1944; d. Warren Malvern and Annine (Gredig) Untiedt; m. Spicer Van Allen Conant, July 9, 1966 (div. Mar. 1983); children: Spicer V., Reid F., Lee G. BA in Am. Studies, Scripps Coll., 1966; MA in Secondary Reading, San Diego State U., 1996. Cert. elem. tchr., Calif. Tchr. asst. Greenwich (Conn.) Country Day Sch., 1966-67; tchr. Katherine Delmar Burke Sch., San Francisco, 1969-70, Cupertino (Calif.) Schs., 1968-69, Kachina Country Day Sch., Phoenix, 1980-83, Paterson (N.J.) Schs., 1985, Black Mountain Mid. Sch., San Diego, 1985-89, Bernardo Heights Mid. Sch., San Diego, 1989—, ELD coord., 2000—. Tchr. trainer Poway (Calif.) Unified Schs., 1996—. Fulbright Exch. tchr. Exeter, Eng., 1998-99. Avocations: swimming, reading, gardening. Home: 14735 Poway Mesa Dr Poway CA 92064-2961 Office: Bernardo Heights Mid Sch 12990 Paseo Lucido San Diego CA 92128-4479

CONANT, PATRICIA CAROL, printmaker, educator; b. Boston, Oct. 8, 1939; d. George Bernard and Bernice Jessica (Smith) Madsen; BFA, Mass. Coll. Art, 1961; MFA, Tufts U./Boston Mus. Sch., 1962; m. Ronald Conant, Sept. 2, 1962 (div. 1969); 1 dau., Tara. Art tchr. Boston Pub. Schs., 1962-64, Woburn (Mass.) H.S., 1968-69; mem. faculty Westfield (Mass.) State Coll., 1969—, prof. printmaking, 1977—; group shows include: Mass. Coun. Arts and Humanities, Boston, 1967, 12th-22d Ann. Boston Printmakers Exhbns., 1962-70, 23d Ann. Exhbn., DeCordova Mus., Lincoln, Mass. (Purchase award), 1971, N.Y. Pub. Libr., 1972, Boston Ctr. for Arts, 1972, 76, Conn. Acad. Fine Arts, Hartford, 1976, SUNY, Potsdam, 1976, Silvermine (Conn.) Guild Artists, 1976, Berkshire Art Mus., Pittsfield, Mass. (Graphics award; Cain, Hibbard and Myers Purchase award), 1976, Worcester (Mass.) Art Mus., 1977, Conn. Acad. Fine Arts (prize for Graphics), 1978, Phila. Print Club, 1979, 32d Boston Printmakers Nat. Exhbn., 1980, 4th Miami Internat. Print Exhbn., Coral Gables, Fla., 1980, Silvermine Guild Artists, 1980, Walkey Gallery, Lincoln, Mass., 1982, Wenniger Gallery, Boston, 1982, New Eng. Print and Pot exhbn. Newport Art Mus., 1985, Beth El 63d Exhbn., 1987, Printworks Exhbn., Greenfield, Mass., 1988, Soc. Am. Graphic Artists 63d Nat. Print Exhbn., 1989, U. Mass., Worcester, 1990, Acad. Artist Assn., 1990, G.W.V.S. Mus., Springfield, Mass., 1990, Slater Meml. Mus., Norwich, Conn., 1990, U. Hartford, 1991, Mus. Fine Arts, Springfield, 1991, Springfield Art League, 1992, Schenectady (N.Y.) Mus., 1992, Assoc. Artists Gallery, Winston Salem, N.C., 1992, Conn. Acad. Fine Arts (painting award 1992), Allied Artists of Am., Inc., N.Y.C., 1992, Holyoke (Mass.) Heritage State Park Mus., 1992, Somerstown Gallery, Somers, N.Y., 1992, Acad. Artists Assn., Springfield, 1993, Albany Mus., 1993, Arts Alive Galleries, Springfield, 1993, Chadron State Coll., Ctrl. Coll., Pella, Iowa, 1994, Albany Print Club, 1995, Westfield State Coll., 1995, Art Inst. Permian Basin, 1996, Day Six Gallery, North Adams, Mass., 1997/98; one-woman shows include Westfield Atheneum, 1997; Atlantic Ctr. for the Arts (assoc. artist), 1994, Finalist 1% Arts Wash., DC and Phila., PA, Am. Print Survey, Plainview, TX, 1999, The Boston Printmakers Black and White Exhbn., Boston, Mass., 1999, "Consanguinity", mother/daughter Exhbn. (Tara Conant), Springfield, Mass., 2000, "Small Works", Attleboro Mus., Mass., 2000, "Women Printmakers", Univ. Ctrl. Ark., 2001, New England Watercolor Soc. Exhbn., Marblehead, Mass., 2001, N.E. Juried Exhbn., Springfield Art League, Mass., 2000-02; mural commd. for Charles A. Gallagher Terminal, Lowell, Mass., 1983; mural Westfield Dist. Courthouse, Mass., 1985; mural Baystate Med. Complex, Springfield, 1987, Bench Design "ButtStop ART" SBID & PVTA, Springfield, Mass., 2003; represented in permanent collections: N.Y. Public Library, DeCordova Mus., Library of Congress, U. Pitts., Pine Manor Jr. Coll., Newton, Mass., State St. Bank, Boston. Author (book): Broadsides; (poems) by Robert D'Amato, 1966, Shawmut Bank Baystate Med. Complex. Mem. Boston Printmakers, Springfield Art League, Atlantic Ctr. for the Arts (assoc. 1990), Albany Print Club, Phila. Print Club, Berkshire Art Assn. Home: 13 Heritage Ln Westfield MA 01085-3404 Office: Westfield State Coll Westfield MA 01086

CONARD, ALFRED FLETCHER, legal educator; b. Grinnell, Iowa, Nov. 30, 1911; s. Henry S. and Laetitia (Moon) C.; m. Georgia Murray, Aug. 7, 1939; children— Joy L., Deborah J. AB, Grinnell Coll., 1932, LL.D., 1971; postgrad., U. Iowa, 1932-34; LL.B., U. Pa., 1936; LL.M., Columbia, 1939, J.S.D., 1942. Bar: Pa. 1937, Mich. 1967. Practice in Phila., 1937-38; asst. prof. U. Kansas City (Mo.) Law Sch., 1939-42, acting dean, 1941-42; atty. OPA, 1942-43, Office Alien Property Custodian, 1945-46; asso. prof., then prof. law U. Ill. Law Sch., 1946-54; prof. law U. Mich. Law Sch., 1954-81, prof. emeritus, 1981—. Vis. prof. U. Tex., 1952, U. Colo., 1957, 84, U. Ariz., 1982, U. Calif., Berkeley, 1983, Pepperdine U., 1985-86, U. San Diego, 1989; vis. prof. Stetson U., 1990, vis. scholar, 1991-93; lectr. U. Istanbul, 1958-59, Luxembourg, 1959, Mex., 1963, Brussels, 1965, Salzburg, 1971, Saarbrucken U., 1988, 90; chmn. editorial adv. bd. Bobbs-Merrill Co., 1962-78; exec. com. Am. Assn. Law Schs., 1964-65, chmn. rsch. com., 1968-70, pres. 1971, chmn. bus. assns. sect., 1979. Author: Studies in Easements and Licenses, 1942, Cases on Business Organization, 3d edit., 1965, Automobile Accident Costs and Payments: Studies in the Economics of Injury Reparation, 1964, Corporations in Perspective, 1976, Enterprise Organization, 4th edit., 1987; editor-in-chief Am. Jour. Comparative Law, 1968-71; chief editor bus. and pvt. orgns.: Internat. Ency. Comparative Law, 1965-82; editorial adv. bd. Am. Bar Found. Rsch. Jour., 1976-86. Served OSS AUS, 1943-45. Decorated Purple Heart; Ordre des Chevaliers de la Couronne Belgium; recipient Kulp Meml. award Am. Risk & Ins. Assn., 1965; Guggenheim fellow, 1975 Mem. AAUP (chpt. pres. 1963-64), NRC, Am. Bar Assn. (exec. com. corp. law sect. 1967-71, com. on corp. laws 1974-80, com. on clin. legal edn. 1981-84), Internat. Acad. Comparative Law, State Bar Mich., Am. Law Inst., Law and Soc. Assn. (trustee 1968-75), Council on Law-Related Studies (trustee 1969-74), Phi Beta Kappa, Order of the Coif. Clubs: Rotarian (club pres. 1976-77). Mem. Soc. Of Friends. Address: 80 Kendal Dr Kennett Square PA 19348-2326

CONARD, NORMAN DALE, secondary education educator; Tchr. social studies Uniontown (Kans.) High Sch., 1987—. Recipient State Tchr. of Yr. Social Studies award, Kans., 1992. Office: Uniontown High Sch 601 E 5th St Uniontown KS 66779-0070

CONATY, JOSEPH C. federal agency administrator; PhD in Sociology, U. Wis., 1977. Assoc. prof. U. Utah; joined U.S. Dept. Edn., Washington, 1987—, acting dir. Office of Rsch., dir. Nat. Inst. on Student Achievement, Curriculum and Assessment, dir. acad. improvement and tchr. quality programs. Vis. prof. sociology and stats. U. Chgo. Contbr. articles to profl. jours. Mem.: Nat. Ctr. for Edn. Stats. Office: US Dept Edn FOB-6 Rm 5C141 400 Maryland Ave SW Washington DC 20202*

CONAWAY, MARY ANN, behavioral studies educator; b. Pulaski, Ill., Nov. 3, 1940; d. Harry Sr. and Anna Mary (Walsh) Tolar, m. Larry Kay Conaway, June 25, 1960; children: Mary Kay, Larissa Jean, Stephen Patrick. BS, So. Ill. U., 1962; MEd, U. Mo., 1980; PhD, St. Louis U., 1991. Cert. secondary tchr., Mo.; lic. profl. counselor, Mo. Secondary tchr. Equality (Ill.) H.S., 1962-63; data processor Blue Bell Meat Packing Plant, DuQuoin, Ill., 1963-64; secondary tchr. Dixon (Mo.) High Sch., 1964-66; ednl. cons. St. Louis, 1980-83; marriage, family therapist Christian Psychol. and Family Svcs., St. Louis, 1983-87, Psychologists & Educators, St. Louis, 1987-88; min. single adults and family Fee Fee Bapt. Ch., Bridgeton, Mo., 1988-89; min. edn. Concord Bapt. Ch., St. Louis, 1989-91; assoc. prof. psychology Mo. Bapt. U., St. Louis, 1992-93, dean of students, 1993-96, dir. grad. edn. program, 2000—; guidance counselor Eskridge H.S., St. Louis, 1998—2000; pvt. practice St. Louis, 2000—. Mem. ACA, Am. Assn. Marriage and Family Therapists, So. Bapt. Assn., Family Mins., Pi Lambda Theta, Chi Sigma Iota. Democrat. Avocations: reading, cooking.

CONAWAY, PATRICIA LOUISE, secondary education English educator; b. Ironton, Ohio, June 29, 1940; d. Edward Carl and Venus Virginia (Mann) Hughes; m. Harold R. Conaway, July 6, 1963; children: Susan, Anne, Laura. BA, Olivet Nazarene U., 1963; MA, Marshall U., 1971. Cert. tchr. provisional 5-yr. English, history, Calif.; life lic. English, history, govt., Ind. Tchr. history and English Chesapeake (Ohio) Sch. Dist., 1963-65; tchr. English Fairland Sch. Dist., Proctorville, Ohio, 1966-67, Carmel (Ind.) H.S., 1984-87, Sequoia Jr. H.S., Simi Valley, Calif., 1988-93, Royal H.S., Simi Valley, Calif., 1993—. Dept. chair Sequoia Jr. H.S., Simi Valley, 1990-93, com. mem. high sch. task force, 1993—; program quality rev. com. mem. Program Quality Rev., Ventura County, Calif., 1991-94. sch. improvement coun., 1995—, rsch. team Am. lit. and hist., begining tchr. mentor. Mem. Nat. Coun. Tchrs. English. Home: 1982 Calle Yucca Thousand Oaks CA 91360-2255

CONCANNON, GEORGE ROBERT, business educator; b. Berkeley, Calif., June 2, 1919; s. Robert Lawrence and Hilda (Morgan) C. AB, Stanford U.; MBA, Harvard U.; postgrad., Stanford U., U. Calif., Berkeley, Hudson Inst., U.S. Fgn. Svc. Inst., U.S. Nat. War Coll., U.S. Indsl. Coll. Armed Forces. Sales exec. Marchant Calculators, Inc.; U.S. govt. v.p. Holiday Airlines; corp. v.p. Kaiser Industries; pres., CEO Concannon Wine Co., Concannon Co.; prof. bus. U. Calif., Berkeley. Mem. Dun's Rev. Indsl. Roundtable; vis. prof. Webster U., Austria, Ecole Superieure Commerce de Tours, France, U. Wollongong, Australia, Urals Electromech. Inst., Russia, Estonian Bus. Sch., Estonia, Concordia Internat. U., Estonia. Contbr. articles to profl. jours. Tech. advisor State of Calif. Econ. Devel. Agy.; bd. dirs. Stanford Camp Assn.; mem. Am. Indsl. Devel. Coun., World Affairs Coun. Recipient Service to Country award Internat. Exec. S.C. Mem. Urban Land Inst. Home: 2995 Woodside Rd Ste 400 Woodside CA 94062-2448

CONDE, CESAR AUGUSTO, cardiologist, educator; b. Lima, Peru, Oct. 31, 1942; s. Aurelio Vicente and Mercedes (Portocarrearo) C.; m. Maria C. Perez-Teran, Sept. 8, 1972; children: Cesar R., Jorge C., Enrique A. MD, San Marcos U., Lima, Peru, 1967. Resident Henry Ford Hosp., Detroit, 1969-71; resident in cardiology Mt. Sinai Hosp. and Mt. Sinai Sch. Medicine, 1971-73, asst. prof. medicine and cardiology, 1973-74; asst. clin. prof. medicine and cardiology U. Miami, 1974-78, assoc. clin. prof., 1978-84, clin. prof., 1984—. Chief div. cardiology Parkway Gen. Hosp., Miami, Fla., 1977-84; chief staff Parkway Regional Med. Ctr., Miami, 1984—, bd. dirs.; chief cardiology Cedars Med. Ctr., 1990-92; dir. internat. cardio-vascular program Mt. Sinai Med. Ctr., Miami Beach, 1991—. Pres. Am. Heart Assn. of Greater Miami, 1986-87. Fellow Am. Coll. Cardiology, ACP, Nat. Coun. Clin. Cardiology; mem. Am. Heart Assn. (pres-elect Greater Miami), Miami Heart Assn. (dir.), Big Five (Miami), Fisher Island, Peruando de la Fla. Roman Catholic. Home: 8100 Los Pinos Blvd Miami FL 33143-6457 also: 4302 Alton Rd Ste 100 Miami FL 33140-2891 E-mail: cesarcondemd@aol.com.

CONDON, MARIA DEL CARMEN, retired elementary school educator; b. Laredo, Tex., Aug. 31, 1929; d. Florencio and Carmen (Diaz) Briseno; m. James Robert Condon, July 24, 1967 (dec. Apr. 1978). BA, Tex. Woman's U., 1962. Tchr. Laredo Ind. Sch. Dist., 1963-9. Supervising tchr. Laredo State U., 1984—. Mem. Tex. ASCD, Tex. Ret. Tchrs. Assn., Tex. Classroom Tchrs. Assn., Nat. Alumnae Assn. of Tex. Woman's U. Democrat. Roman Catholic. Avocations: stamp collecting, classical records, walking, travel. Home: 1514 Hibiscus Ln Laredo TX 78041-3325

CONDRON, BARBARA O'GUINN, metaphysics educator, school administrator, publisher; b. New Orleans, May 1, 1953; d. Bill Gene O'Guinn and Marie Gladys (Newbill) Jackson; m. Daniel Ralph Condron, Feb. 29, 1992; 1 child, Hezekiah Daniel. BJ, U. Mo., 1973; MA, Coll. Metaphysics, Springfield, Mo., 1977, DD, D in Metaphysics, 1979. Cert. counselor; ordained min. Interfaith Ch. Metaphysics. Field rep. Sch. Metaphysics, New Orleans, 1978-80; dir. Interfaith Ch. Metaphysics, 1884-89; pres. Nat. Hdqs., Sch. Metaphysics, Windyville, Mo., 1980-84, prof., 1989—, chmn. bd. dirs., 1991-98, mem. coun. elders, bd. govs. internat. edn., 1998—; CEO SOM Pub., Windyville, 1989-98. Guest lectr., instr. Wichita (Kans.) State U., 1977, U. New Orleans, 1979, La. State U., 1981, Am. Bus. Womens Assn., 1982, U. Mo., Kansas City, 1984, Unity Village, 1985, Kans. Dept. Social Svcs. Conf., Topeka, 1986, U. Mo., Columbia and St. Louis, 1986, Mo. Tchrs. Conf., St. Louis, 1991, U. Okla., Norman, 1988—89, Parliament of World's Religions, Chgo., 1993, Mo. Writers Guild Conf., 2001, many others; creator Sch. Metaphysics Assocs., 1992; initiator Universal Hour Peace, 1995; initiator, internat. coord. Nat. Dream Hotline, 1988—; radio and TV guest, 1977—; creator Maker's Dozen-Visionary Schs. Recognition, 1999, Taraka Yoga Psi Counseling Program; initiator Spiritual Focus Sessions, 1997—; internat. coord. Peace Dome dedication, 2003. Author: What will I do Tomorrow?, Probing Depression, 1977, Search for a Satisfying Relationship, 1980, Strangers in My Dreams, 1987, Total Recall: An Introduction to Past Life & Health Readings, 1991, Kundalini Rising, 1992, Dreamers Dictionary, 1994, The Work of the Soul: Past Life Recall & Spiritual Enlightenment, 1996, Uncommon Knowledge, 1996, First Opinion: 21st Century Wholistic Health Care, 1997, Spiritual Renaissance Elevating Your Conciousness for the Common Good, 1999, The Bible Interpreted in Dream Symbols, 2000, Every Dream is About the Dreamer, 2001, Remembering Atlantis: The History of the World Vol. 1, 2002, How to Raise an Indigo Child, 2002; author series When All Else Fails; editor-in-chief Thresholds Jour., 1990-2001; editor Wholistic Health and Healing Guide, 1992-2000; also numerous poems. Mem. Internat. Platform Assn., Am. Bus. Women's Assn., Interfaith Ministries, Kundalini Rsch. Network, Planetary Soc., Heritage Found., Mo. Writers Guild, Sigma Delta Chi. Office: Sch Metaphysics World Hdqs Windyville MO 65783

CONELY, LOIS ANN, elementary education educator; b. Red Banks, N.J., Aug. 22, 1953; d. Kenneth M. and Sherra (Crites) Woolet; m. Robert Lane Conely, Apr. 7, 1979; children: Brandon, Bradley. BS, Murray State U., 1971-75; MEd, U. Louisville, 1986. Tchr. Bullitt County Sch., Shepherdsville, Ky., 1975-79, tchr. chpt. I reading, 1987-91, primary tchr. ungraded, 1991-92; project discovery trainer Ohio Valley Ednl. Coop., 1992-95; tech. assistance cons. Collaborative for Elem. Learning, 1995—2003; program dir. Collaborative for Tchg. and Learning, 1997—; tchr. social studiesgrades 7 and 8 Anchorage Ind. Schs., 2003—. Named Compensatory Edn. Tchr. of Yr. Bullitt County Sch., 1989. Avocations: reading, cooking. Office: Spring River Bus Park 2302 River Rd Ste 100 Louisville KY 40206

CONERLY, EVELYN NETTLES, educational consultant; b. Baton Rouge, Aug. 25, 1940; d. Noel Douglas and Evelyn Elsie (Pratt) Nettles; children from previous marriage: Douglas Wayne, Kelee Lynne. BS, La. State U., 1962, MEd, 1965, PhD, 1973. Tchr. East Baton Rouge Parish Pub. Schs., 1962-67, elem libr., 1967-73, prin., 1973-81, 1983-84, elem. libr. supr., 1981-83; ednl. cons. Baton Rouge, 1984—. Co-owner Acad. Learning Ctr., 1986—92; dir. Libr. Power Project East Baton Rouge Parish, DeWitt Wallace-Reader's Digest Fund, 1992—96; vol. pub. sch.; with Nat. Libr. Power Program Network Cons., 1996—2000; program evaluator La. State Bd. Elem. and Secondary Edn., 1996—2002, program adminstr., 1998—99; supr. office field experiences Southeastern La. U. Coll. Edn., 1997—98. Co-author: (book) Principals' Pointers for Parents, 1985. Mem.: AASL, ALA, Inst. Reality Therapy (cert.), La. Libr. Assn., La. Reading Assn., Internat. Reading Assn., Assn. Tchr. Educators (pres. La. 1981—82), La. Ret. Tchrs. Assn., Delta Kappa Gamma, Phi Delta Kappa, Phi Kappa Phi. Presbyterian. Home and Office: 3727 Woodland Ridge Blvd Baton Rouge LA 70816-2772 E-mail: econerly@att.net.

CONEY, ELAINE MARIE, English and foreign languages educator; b. Magnolia, Miss., Aug. 9, 1952; d. Allen Leroy and Katie Jane (McLeod) C. BA in Spanish, Millsaps Coll., 1974; MA in Spanish, U. Interam. Saltillo Coahuila, Mex., 1975, PhD, 1977; MEd, U. So. Miss., 1979, EdS in Higher Edn. Adminstrn., 1997. Tchr. fgn. langs. South Pike High Sch., Magnolia, Miss., 1977-91; tchr. English Amite County Schs., Liberty, Miss.; instr. Jackson (Miss.) State U.; GED instr. South Pike Schs., Magnolia, Miss.; instr. Spanish, French and English composition S.W. Miss. Community Coll., Summit, 1989—. Mem. NEA (del. conv. 1986, 88), MLA, Am. Coun. Tchrs. Fgn. Langs., Am. Assn. Tchrs. French, Am. Assn. Tchrs. Spanish and Portuguese, Miss. Assn. Educators (instructional profl. devel. com.), Nat. Coun. Tchrs. English, Miss. Fgn. Lang. Assn. (pres. 1991-93, Disting. Svc. award 1998), SPAE (treas.). Home: PO Box 208 Magnolia MS 39652-0208

CONFALONE, PATRICIA CULLEN, language arts and reading specialist; b. New Rochelle, N.Y., May 11, 1950; d. John Francis Lincoln and Catherine Agnes (Hennessy) Cullen; m. Gerard Lewis Confalone, Aug. 9, 1975; children: Bradley Cullen, Tyler Cullen. BS in Anthropology, CUNY H. Lehman Coll., Bronx, 1972; MS in Reading, 1975; reading recovery cert., NYU, 1992. Cert. reading, elem. edn., N.Y. Tchr. Blessed Sacrament Sch., New Rochelle, N.Y., 1972-78; reading specialist Elmsford (N.Y.) Union Free Dist., 1981-85; reading specialist, testing coord. New Rochelle (N.Y.) City Sch. Dist., 1985—. Workshop presenter N.Y. State Reading Assn., 1991; seminar presenter Reading Recovery Conv., Albany, N.Y., 1992. Devel. com., 1987—, Alumnae coord. centenial, 1992, The Ursuline Sch., New Rochelle, N.Y. Recipient Author's Day grant Staff Resource Ctr., New Rochelle, N.Y., 1989. Mem. Westchester Reading Coun., N.Y. State Reading Assn., Internat. Reading Assn. Avocations: tennis, swimming. Office: Davis School New Rochelle City Sch Dist 80 Iselin Dr New Rochelle NY 10804-1030

CONGER, SUE ANN, computer information systems educator; b. Akron, Ohio, Nov. 6, 1947; d. Scott Stanley and Norma Marie (Bauknecht) Summerville; m. David Boyd Conger, July 3, 1971 (dec. June 1997); 1 child, Kathryn Summerville. BS, Ohio State U., 1970; MBA, Rutgers U., 1977; PhD, NYU, 1988. Programmer, analyst USDA, Washington, 1970-72; project leader Ednl. Testing Svc., Princeton, N.J., 1972-73; 2d v.p. Chase Manhattan Bank, N.Y.C., 1973-77; tech. dir. Lambda Technology, Inc., N.Y.C., 1977-80; sr. cons. Mobil Corp., N.Y.C., 1980-83; asst. prof. computer info. systems Ga. State U., Atlanta, 1988-90; asst. prof. Baruch Coll. CUNY, 1990-94; assoc. prof. So. Meth. U., Dallas, 1994-99; dir. electronic commerce Sewell Automotive Cos., Dallas, 1999—2001; assoc. prof., dir. IT program U. Dallas, Irving, 2001—. Freelance cons., educator, 1970—. Author: The New Software Engineering, 1994, Planning and Designing Effective Web Sites, 1998; contbr. articles to profl. jours. Grantee, U.S. Army Info. Systems Engrng. Command, 1989, The CMI Group, 2002. Mem. IEEE, AIS, Assn. for Computing Machinery, Acad. of Mgmt. Avocations: reading, sports, cooking. Office: Univ of Dallas 1845 W Northgate Dr Irving TX 75062 E-mail: sconger@aol.com.

CONIGILARO, PHYLLIS ANN, retired elementary education educator; b. Ilion, N.Y., Nov. 27, 1932; d. Gus Carl and Jennie Margaret (Marine) Denapole; m. Paul Anthony Conigilaro, July 16, 1983. BS cum laude, SUNY, Cortland, 1955; MA in Edn., Psychology, Cornell U., 1961. Cert. tchr., N.Y. Elem. classroom tchr. Mohawk (N.Y.) Central Sch., 1955-88. Contbr. articles to profl. jours. Bd. dirs. United Fund of Ilion, Herkimer, Mohawk and Frankfort, 1984-86, pres., 1986; pres. bd. edn. St. Mary's Parochial Sch., 1978; mem. Herkimer County Hist. Soc., 1988—, trustee, 1994-97; bd. dirs. local Federal Emergency Mgmt. Agy., 1987-96. Recipient Outstanding Elem. Tchrs. of Am. award, 1974, Outstanding Elem. Tchrs. of Am, 1974. Mem. N.Y. State United Tchrs., Mohawk Tchrs. Assn. (past pres.), AAUW (pres. Herkimer chpt. 1981-82), N.Y. State Ret. Tchrs. Assn. (past legis. chmn. Herkimer County chpt.), Rep. Women's Club, Kappa Delta Pi. Republican. Roman Catholic. Avocations: golf, travel, reading, music. Home: 137 7th Ave Frankfort NY 13340-3612 E-mail: pconigil@twcny.rr.com.

CONIGLIO, CHARLES, JR., secondary education educator; b. Buffalo, N.Y., Nov. 16, 1935; s. Charles Frank and Frances Caroline (Mogavero) C.; m. Rosalind Jeanne Andreozzi Coniglio, Dec. 27, 1958; children: David Michael (dec.), Rebecca Jeanne. BS, SUNY Coll. Edn., Buffalo, 1960; MS, 1964. Tchr. 5th grade Williamsville (N.Y.) Ctrl. Schs., 1960-62, Amherst (N.Y.) Ctrl. Schs., 1962-64, tchr. English, Social Studies, Reading, 1964-91; tchr. Effective Speed Reading Niagara U., Niagara Falls, N.Y., 1970-80; tchr. English Methods, Secondary Reading Canisius Coll., Buffalo, N.Y., 1991—. Pvt. teaching, cons. Harris Hill Reading Clinic, Amherst, N.Y., 1966-75; lang. arts. cons. Home Office, Williamsville, N.Y., 1975—. Advisor: Ventures, 1989, 90, 91 (3 nat. awards). Recipient Spl. Svcs. for Teaching award Amherst (N.Y.) PTA, 1991. Mem. Nat. Coun. Tchrs. English, Internat. Reading Assn. Roman Catholic. Avocations: reading, movies, theater, puzzles, cooking, travel. Home: 37 Hunters Ln Williamsville NY 14221-4541

CONKLIN, D(ONALD) DAVID, academic administrator; b. Waynesburg, Pa., Oct. 29, 1944; s. Donald David and Esther Louise (McCracken) C.; children: Donald David III, Elizabeth Ann. BA, Pa. State U., 1966, MEd, 1967; EdD, NYU, 1975. Asst. dean. instrn. SUNY, Farmingdale, 1970-72, exec. asst. to pres., 1972-78; spl. asst. N.J. Dept. Higher Edn., Trenton, 1978-80; dean for planning and devel. Mercer County Community Coll., Trenton, 1980-83, dean for adminstrn., 1983-86, dean for acad. affairs, 1986-92; pres. Dutchess Community Coll., Poughkeepsie, N.Y., 1992—. Cons. AAA of No. N.J., Morristown, 1984, Harrisburg Area C.C., 1983, Ednl. Testing Svc., Princeton, N.J., 1990, Educom Cons. Svcs., Princeton, 1985-90, Md. Higher Edn. Commn., 1992-95. Contbr. articles to profl. jours., chpts. to books. Chair Dutchess County Empire Zone Bd.; chmn. bd. dirs. United Way of Dutchess County; vice chmn., bd. dirs. St. Francis Hosp., Cmty. Fund of Dutchess County, Hudson Valley Philharm., Hudson Valley coun. Boy Scouts Am., Dutchess County Econ. Devel. Corp.; mem. SUNY Coun. of Pres.; chmn. Coll. Bd. CC Adv. Com. Recipient Adminstrs. award for excellence in aviation edn. FAA, 1989. Mem. Poughkeepsie C. of C., Rotary, Phi Theta Kappa, Alpha Mu Gamma, Phi Delta Kappa, The Club. Presbyterian. Avocations: tennis, golf, reading. Home: 57 Pendell Rd Poughkeepsie NY 12601-1512 Office: Dutchess CC Pendell Rd Poughkeepsie NY 12601 E-mail: conklin@sunydutchess.edu.

CONKLIN, HAROLD COLYER, anthropologist, educator; b. Easton, Pa., Apr. 27, 1926; s. Howard S. and May W. (Colyer) C.; m. Jean M. Morisuye, June 11, 1954; children: Bruce Robert, Mark William. AB, U. Calif.-Berkeley, 1950; PhD, Yale U., 1955. From instr. to assoc. prof. anthropology Columbia U., 1954-62; lectr. anthropology Rockefeller Inst., 1961-62; prof. anthropology Yale U., 1962-96, chmn. dept., 1964-68, Crosby prof. anthropology, 1990-96; curator of anthropology Yale Peabody Mus. Natural History, 1974-96, dir. divsn. anthropology, 1994-96, Crosby prof. emeritus, curator emeritus, 1996—. Mem. Inst. for Advanced Study, Princeton, N.J., 1972; fellow Ctr. for Advanced Study in Behavioral Scis., Stanford, Calif., 1978-79; field rsch. in Philippines, 1945-48, 52-54, 55, 57-58, 61, 62-63, 64, 65, 68-69, 70, 73, 80-81, 82-85, 90-91, 95, 2000-01, Malaya, Malaysia and Indonesia, 1948, 57, 83, Melanesia, 1987, N.Y., 1942, 48, 52, Calif., 1943, 48, 51, Guatemala, 1959, Peru, 1987; dir., com. problems and policy Social Sci. Rsch. Coun., 1963-70; bd. dirs. Survival Internat. USA, 1985-90; spl. cons. Internat. Rice Rsch. Inst., Los Baños, Philippines, 1962—; book rev. editor Am. Anthropologist, 1960-62; mem. Pacific sci. bd. Nat. Acad. Scis.-NRC, 1962-66. Author: Hanunóo Agriculture, 1957, Folk Classification, 1972, Ethnographic Atlas of Ifugao, 1980; other publs. on ethnol., linguistic and ecol. topics. Served with AUS, 1944-46. Guggenheim fellow, 1973; recipient Internat. Sci. prize Fyssen Foundation, 1983 Mem. NAS; Fellow Am. Acad. Arts and Scis., Am. Anthrop. Assn. (exec. bd. 1965-68), Royal Anthrop. Inst., N.Y. Acad. Scis. (sec. sect. anthropology 1956); mem. Am. Ethnol. Soc. (councilor 1960-62, pres. 1978-79), Koninklijk Inst. voor Taal- Land- en Volkenkunde, Conn. Acad. Arts and Scis., Linguistic Soc. Am., Kroeber Anthrop. Soc., Phila. Anthrop. Soc., Am. Geog. Soc., Am. Oriental Soc., Assn. Asian Studies, Classification Soc., Linguistic Soc. Philippines, Indo-Pacific Prehistory Assn., Soc. Econ. Botany, Internat. Assn. Plant Taxonomy, AAAS, Phi Beta Kappa, Sigma Xi. Home: 106 York Sq New Haven CT 06511-3625 Address: Yale Univ Dept of Anthropology PO Box 208277 New Haven CT 06520-8277

CONKLIN, JOHN EVAN, sociology educator; b. Oswego, NY, Oct. 2, 1943; s. Evan Nelson and Susan Estelle (Brenner) C.; m. Ruth Tiffany Edmonds, July 10, 1965 (div. Oct. 1974); children: Christopher Perry, Anne Tiffany; m. Sarah Hubbard Belcher, Jan .2, 1982; children: Lydia Catherine, Gillian Jane. AB, Cornell U., 1965; PhD, Harvard U., 1969. Research assoc. Harvard U. Law Sch., Cambridge, Mass., 1969-70; asst. prof. sociology Tufts U., Medford, Mass., 1970-76, assoc. prof. sociology, 1976-81, prof. sociology, 1981—, chmn. dept. sociology, 1981-86, 90-91. Author: Robbery and the Criminal Justice System, 1972, The Impact of Crime, 1975, Illegal But Not Criminal, 1977, Criminology, 1981, 8th edit., 2004, Sociology: An Introduction, 1984, 2d edit., 1987, Art Crime, 1994, Why Crime Rates Fell, 2003; editor: The Crime Establishment, 1973, New Perspectives in Criminology, 1996. Mem. Am. Sociol. Assn., Am. Soc. Criminology. Avocations: collecting books, movie memorabilia. Office: Tufts U Dept of Sociology Eaton Hall Medford MA 02155 E-mail: john.conklin@tufts.edu.

CONKLIN, SUSAN JOAN, psychotherapist, educator, corporate staff developer, TV talk show host; b. Bklyn., Feb. 7, 1950; d. Joseph Thomas Hallek and Stella Joan (Kubis) Kuceluk; m. John Lariviere Conklin, July 25, 1981; children: Genevieve Therese, Michelle Therese. BA, CCNY, 1972; MSW, CUNY, 1975. Lic. ind. clin. social worker; cert. diplomat. Shop counselor Assn. for Help of Retarded Citizens, N.Y.C., 1971-75; dir. social svcs., acting exec. dir. North Berkshire Assn. for Retarded Citizens, North Adams, Mass., 1975-77; project dir. Title XX tng. grant State of Mass., North Adams, 1978-79; pvt. practice psychotherapy, Williamstown, Mass., 1979—. Adj. asst. prof. Mass. Coll. Liberal Art, 1977—2000, Berkshire C.C., Pittsfield, Mass., 1985—86, Pittsfield, 1995; docent Clark Art Inst., 1995—2003; Therapeutic Touch practitioner, 1978—; talk show host Pub. Access TV, 1998—; bd. dirs. Willinet TV Channel 17, 1999—2003; vol. Salvation Army. WTC Disaster Relief Family Assistance Ctr., 2001, 9/11 United Svcs. Group, 2002; adj. faculty Springfield Coll. Sch. Social Work, 2002. Pres. Williamstown PTO, 1989-91; bd. dirs., edn. com., spl. events coord. Hospice No. Berkshire, Inc., 1989—. Named Berkshire County Social Worker of Yr., 1999, Mass. Social Worker of Yr., 2002. Mem. NASW (bd. dirs. 1981-83, regional coun. mem. 1980-83, 93-2003), LWV, Nurse Healers-Profl. Assn., Inc. (trustee 1981-83, rec. sec., editor-in-chief Coop. Connection newsletter 1983-88), Women of Vision Action. Democrat. Episcopalian. Office: 85 Hawthorne Rd Williamstown MA 01267-2700 Home: 5 Fallingwater Dr Linwood NJ 08221

CONLEY, BOBBIE JEAN, English educator; b. Crystal Springs, Miss., Oct. 13, 1946; d. Eunice Marie (Jackson) Headspeth; m. Eugene Weathersby, Dec. 18, 1966 (div. Oct. 1970); m. Willie Lee Conley, Jan. 1972 (dec. Nov. 1978); children: Eunice Willette, Sherrie Elaine. BS, Jackson (Miss.) State U., 1967. Cert. tchr., Miss. English tchr. Starksville (Miss.) Pub. Schs., 1967-68, Hinds High Sch., Utica, Miss., 1968-70, Waterloo (Iowa) Community Schs., 1974-77, Hazlehurst (Miss.) HIgh Sch., 1978-81, Crystal Springs Mid. Sch., 1986—; tchr., reading supr. Grenada (Miss.) Pub. Schs., 1970-73; reading tchr. Utica High Sch., 1977-78; reading and lang. arts tchr. Miss. Job Corp Ctr., Crystal Springs, 1985-86. Chair English dept., mem. spelling and essay coms. Crystal Springs Mid. Sch., 1986—, chair dramatic contest, 1988—; mem. sch. evaluation com. So. Assn. Accreditation of Schs.; Job Tng. Partnership Act tchr. Copiah County Schs., Crystal Springs Schs., 1988-91; mem. textbook adoption com. Copiah County Schs., 1991-92. Local coord. oratorical contest Optimst Club, Crystal Springs Mid. Sch., 1988—; dir. bd. Christian edn. St. Paul C.M.E. Ch., Crystal Springs, 1992. Mem. NEA, Miss. Edn. Assn., Miss. ASCD Avocations: public speaking, piano, singing, writing, youth activities. Home: 3068 Old Highway 27 # 2 Crystal Springs MS 39059-9155

CONLEY, PATSY GAIL, retired elementary education educator; b. Oceana, W.Va., Mar. 10, 1943; d. Ruble and Ruth (Hatfield) C.; m. Jose L. Abelleira (div. Feb. 1978); 1 child, Joseph L. Abelleira. BA, Glenville State Coll., 1965; MS, Nova Southeastern U., 1983, EdD, 1987. Tchr. kindergarten Head Start, Miami, Fla., 1965-67, facilitator, 1967-68; tchr. kindergarten Dade County, Miami, 1969-75, tchr. 1st grade, 1975-84, tchr. kindergarten, 1984—2002, ret., 2003. Mem. faculty coun. Schoolsite, Miami, sch. adv. com., writing com., dept. chair; mem. clin. tchr. program U. Miami Dade County Pub. Schs., U. Miami; adj. prof. Nova Southeastern. Author: (rsch.) ERIC Listening A Program for First Grade, 1987. Avocations: painting, reading, crafts.

CONLEY, RAYMOND LESLIE, English language educator; b. Manhattan, Kans., Feb. 25, 1923; s. Orville Ray and Goldie Gladys (Wallack) C. AB with honors, Park Coll., 1947; postgrad., Nebr. U., 1948-50; MA, Northwestern U., Evanston, Ill., 1958; postgrad., Ol Dominion U., 1968. Cert. tchr. speech, English, social scis. Dep. county clk. Nemaha County, Auburn, Nebr., 1942-45; tchr., English, speech St. Edward (Nebr.) High Sch., 1948-50, Oakland (Nebr.) High Sch., 1950-52, Nebraska City (Nebr.) High Sch., 1952-56, Galesburg (Ill.) High Sch., 1956-58, Maine Twp. High Sch. East, Park Ridge, Ill., 1958-65; asst. prof. English, speech Meth. Coll., Fayetteville, N.C., 1966-77; English prof. Campbell U., Buies Creek, N.C., 1980-83, aux. faculty Fort Bragg, NC, 1978—2001. Coach Nebr. State Debate Champs, 1951, 52; judge Iowa State Speech Contest, 1952, 53; mem. Coun. Status of Women, Fayetteville, 1965-68; aux. faculty Campbell U., Pope AFB, N.C., 1985-2001; speech coach, judge local and sectional contests Toastmistress Club. Actor Fort Bragg Vietnam War Tng. Films. Precinct officer Dem. party, Fayetteville, 1964-68; coord. Congrl. Dist. Common Cause, 1978, mem. state program action com., state and gov. bd. 1976-78, 95-2000; dir. state governance bd. Common Cause, N.C., 1995-2000; mem. Congress Watch/Pub. Citizen, People for the Am. Way, ACLU, N.C. ACLU; conservation coord. Sierra Club, 1978; mem. Amnesty Internat.; vol. Fayetteville Mus. Art. Recipient Am. Legion Citizenship award, 1938. Mem. NOW, AAUP, Internat. Platform Assn., Fayetteville Fgn. Film Soc. (co-founder 1967), Inst. for So. Studies, World Future Soc., Found. For Nat. Progress, N.C. Alliance For Democracy, Amnesty Internat., Ams. United for Separation Ch. and State, Lambda Chi Alpha. Presbyterian. Home: 1076 Stamper Rd Fayetteville NC 28303-4191

CONLEY, SUSAN BERNICE, medical school faculty pediatrician; b. Coldwater, Mich., Feb. 3, 1948; d. Kenneth D. and Mary F. (Spence) C. MD, U. Mich., 1973. Instr. Washington U. Med. Sch., St. Louis, 1977-78; asst. prof. pediatrics U. Tex. Med. Sch., Houston, 1978-84, dir. pediatric nephrology, 1983-91, assoc. prof. pediatrics, 1984-91; dir. pediatric renal ctr. Calif. Pacific Med. Ctr., San Francisco, 1991-94; prof. pediatrics sch. medicine Stanford (Calif.) U., 1994-97; med. dir. dialysis and renal transplantation, chief clin. nephrology Packard Children's Hosp. at Stanford, Calif., 1994-97; prof. pediatrics St. Christopher's Hosp. Children, Phila., 1997—, chief sect. nephrology; prof. pediatrics Drexel U., Phila., 1997—. Exec. com. No. Calif. affiliate Nat. Kidney Found., pres. region V western states. Mem. exec. com. Nat. Kidney Found. No. Calif., 1991-97, pres. we. states, 1994-96; mem. kidney/pancreas com. United Network Organ Sharing, 1994-96. Fellow Am. Acad. Pediatrics; mem. Am. Soc. Nephrology, Am. Soc. Pediatric Nephrology, Soc. for Pediatric Rsch., Women in Nephrology (exec. com. 1997-2000).

CONLEY, TOM CLARK, literature educator; b. New Haven, Dec. 7, 1943; s. Walter Frederick and Hazel Mason (Hatch) C.; m. Verena Andermatt; children: David, Francine. BA, Lawrence U., 1965; MA, Columbia U., 1966; PhD, U. Wis., 1971. Prof. U. Minn., Mpls., 1971-95; prof. renaissance lit., cinema Harvard U., Cambridge, Mass., 1995—, dir. grad. studies in French. Vis. prof. U. Calif., Berkeley, 1978-79, CUNY Grad. Ctr., 1985-87, Miami U., Ohio, 1989, UCLA, 1995; instr. Folger Inst., 1998; summer seminar leader NEH, 1998; seminar leader Sch. Critical Theory, 2003. Author: Lectura de Bunuel, 1988, Film Hieroglyphs, 1991, Graphic Unconscious, 1992, Self-Made Map, 1995; translator 5 books, editor 2 books; editor jour. Lendemains, 1985—, Diacritics, 2000—; corr. jour. Litterature, 1988—; contbr. articles to profl. jours. Woodrow Wilson fellow, 1965-66, Fulbright fellow, 1968-69, study fellow Am. Coun. Learned Socs., 1975-76, summer fellow NEH, 1974, 89, Inst. for Rsch. in Humanities fellow, 1990, Newberry Libr. fellow, 1992, Soc. Humanities fellow, 1998, Harvard Cabot fellow, 2002, Guggenheim fellow, 2003—. Mem. MLA, Renaissance Soc. Am., Assn. Study Dada/Surrealism, Midwest MLA (mem. exec. com. 1977-80), Sixteenth Century Studies Soc. (exec. com. 1994—), Alpha Omega Alpha. Avocations: handball, fishing, mycology. Office: Harvard U Romance Langs 201 Boylston Hall Cambridge MA 02138 E-mail: tconley@fas.harvard.edu.

CONN, PHILIP WESLEY, academic administrator; b. Decatur, Ala., Jan. 4, 1942; s. Charles William and Edna Louise (Minor) C.; m. Donna Kay Taylor, Dec. 18, 1971; children: Chadwick Austin, Philip Cason, Cynthia Louise, Christina Anne. BA, Berea (Ky.) Coll., 1963; Diploma in Social Policy, Inst. Social Studies, The Hague, Netherlands, 1966; MA, U. Tenn., 1972; MPA, U. So. Calif., 1982, DPA, 1991. Tchr. West Coast Christian Coll., Fresno, Calif., 1963; field rep. Vols. in Svc. to Am., Washington, 1965; asst. exec. dir. Bradley/Cleveland Community Action Corp., Cleveland, Tenn., 1967; dir. alumni affairs Berea Coll., 1968-70; pub. rels. advance dir. Combs/Carroll Campaign Staff, Louisville, 1971; exec. dir. Legis. Rsch. Commn., Frankfort, Ky., 1972-77; assoc. prof. sociology, v.p. univ. and regional svcs. Morehead (Ky.) State U., 1977-84; assoc. prof. mgmt., v.p. for univ. advancement Cen. Mo. State U., Warrensburg, 1985-94; prof. bus., pres. Dickinson (N.D.) State U., 1994—. Mem. exec. com. Gov's. Adv. Commn. on Tourism, Frankfort, 1977-79; bd. chmn. Stas. KMOS-TV and KCMW-FM, Warrensburg, 1985-94. Contbr. articles to profl. publs.; editor The Berea Alumnus, 1968-70. Trustee City of Lakeview Heights, Ky., 1980; chmn. Morehead/Rowan County Indsl. Devel. Authority, 1982; vice chmn. Gateway Area Devel. Dist., Owingsville, Ky., 1984; bd. dirs. Ky. Humanities Coun., Inc., Lexington, 1977-82, Ky. Archives and Records Commn., Frankfort, 1973-77; assoc. dir. Appalachian Vols., Berea., 1964. Named Outstanding Young Man of Ky. Jaycees, 1977, Outstanding Young Man of Yr. Frankfort Jaycees, 1976. Mem. Am. Soc. Pub. Adminstrn., Coun. for Advancement and Support of Edn., Am. Assn. for Higher Edn., Am. Assn. of State Colls. and Univs. (N.D. state rep. 1994—), Nat. Assn. of Intercollegiate Athletics (mem. coun. of pres. 1996—), Warrensburg (Mo.) C. of C. (bd. dirs. 1990-93), Berea Coll. Alumni Assn. (pres. 1976-77, spl. merit 1977), Rotary (fellow The Hague 1965-66), Phi Kappa Phi. Democrat. Methodist. Avocation: internat. travel, Appalachian folklore. Office: Dickinson State U Office of Pres Dickinson ND 58601-4896

CONNALLY, SANDRA JANE OPPY, retired art educator, artist; b. Crawfordsville, Ind., Feb. 10, 1941; d. Thomas Jay and Helen Louise (Lane) Oppy; m. Thomas Maurice Connally, Nov. 9, 1962; children: Leslie Erin Connally Hosier, Tyler Maurice. BS, Ball State U., 1963, MA, 1981. Freelance writer, Muncie, Ind., 1971-76; art/freelance, 1964-81; substitute tchr. Muncie (Ind.) Cmty. Schs., 1980—81, art tchr., 1981—2003; ret., 2003. Two women shows include Emens Auditorium, Ball State U., 1983; exhibited in group shows at Ball State U., 1964, Alford House/Anderson (Ind.) Fine Arts Ctr., 1979-81, Historic 8th St. Exhbn., 1981, Patrons Watercolor Gala, Oklahoma City, 1983, Whitewater Valley Annual Drawing, Painting and Printmaking Competition, Richmond, Ind., 1983; represented in pvt. collections; contbr. short stories to profl. pubis. Grantee Container Corp. Am., 1981, Ball State U. Mus. Art/Margaret Ball Meml. Fund, 1992, Robert B. Bell, 1993-95; recipient Achievement award Ind. Dept. Edn., 1992-94, Nat. Gallery Videodisc Competition, 1993; named disting. UniverCitizen Ball State U., 1992, Tchr. Intergalactic Art First Place Ind. State winner, 1998. Mem. NEA, Ind. State Tchr. Assn., Muncie Tchrs. Assn., Nat. Art Edn. Assn. (del. nat. convention 1998, 2000-03), Art Edn. Assn. Ind. Republican. Methodist. Avocations: computer art, watercolor, interior design, arts, antiques and travel. Home: 1932 Bay Pointe Dr E Bloomington IN 47401-8136

CONNELLY, MATTHEW, history educator; BA, Columbia U., 1990; PhD, Yale U., 1997. Assoc. prof. history Columbia U., N.Y.C., 2000—. Author: A Diplomatic Revolution: Algeria's Fight for Independence and the Origins of the Post-Cold War Era, 2002 (George Louis Beer prize for European internat. history since 1895 Am. Hist. Assn., Paul Birdsall prize for European miliatry and strategic history since 1870); contbr. articles. Fellow, John Simon Guggenheim Meml. Found., 2003. Office: Columbia U Dept History Mail Code 2527 611 Fayerweather Hall New York NY 10027*

CONNER, JEANETTE JONES, elementary school educator; b. St. Charles, Va., Nov. 29, 1934; d. Luster and Georgia (Jessee) Jones; m. Samuel Barton Conner, Aug. 3, 1966. BS in Edn., Campbellsville Coll., 1979; MA in Edn., cert. sch. psychometrist, Western Ky. U., 1980, cert. in exceptional edn. K-12, 1981, cert. reading specialist, 1984, cert. elem. sch. supr., 1985, Edn. Specialist degree, 1986. Cert. tchr., Ky. Factory worker Lee Co. Garment Factory, Pennington Gap, Va., 1956-58; receptionist Harlan (Ky.) Appalachian Hosp., 1959-67; sec. Kemper & Assoc., Louisville, 1967-69, Murray (Ky.) State U., 1970-71, Greer & Assoc., Louisville, 1971-73, Campbellsville (Ky.) Coll., 1974-76; tchr. Taylor Co. Bd. Edn., Campbellsville, 1980—. Tchr. trainer Ky. Early Learning Profile Assessment System; citizen's ambassador People to People Program Del. to Perth 1994 Early Childhood Conf., People to People Del. to China 1999 Early Childhood Conf., 20th Trienniel Australian Early Childhood Conf.; mem. Campbellsville Woman's Club (beautification com.). Commd. Ky. Col., State of Ky., 1989. Mem. AAUW (pres. 1989-90), NEA, South Cen. Reading Coun. of the Internat. Reading Assn. (Pres. 1989-90, v.p. 1990-91), Ky. State Coun. of the Internat. Reading Assn. (bd. dirs. 1988-91), Taylor County Edn. Assn. (v.p. 1989-90, pres. 1990-91), Ky. State Reading Coun. (chair com. on parents and reading 1990-91, svc. awards for promoting reading 1989-90), Ky. Edn. Assn., Ky. Coun. New Tchr. Performance Standards, Ky. Early Childhood Task Force for Early Childhood Cert. Guidelines, Ky. Dept. Special Edn. Task Force (KEA instructional com.), Ky. Assn. Supervision and Curriculum Devel. (bd. dirs., exec. bd. dirs.), Taylor County Bus. and Profl. Women, Phi Delta Kappa. Republican. Baptist. Avocations: travel, reading, tennis, hiking. Home: 619 Shawnee Dr Campbellsville KY 42718-1643 Office: Taylor County Elem Sch Old Lebanon Rd Campbellsville KY 42718

CONNER, SUSAN, elementary school educator; b. Newburgh, N.Y., Sept. 19, 1952; d. John and Irene (Cruver) DeMarco; m. John A. Conner, June 29, 1975; children: Amy, Stacy. BA, Mount St. Mary Coll., 1974; Reading Recovery Tng., NYU, 1990; MLS, L.I. U., 2002. Cert. nursery, elem. tchr., N.Y.; cert. libr. media specialist. Tchr. Newburgh City Sch. Dist.; owner, dir., tutor The Learning Corner, Newburgh; sch. libr. media specialist Newburgh City Sch. Dist., 1999—. Mem. ALA, NYSUT, Newburgh Tchrs. Assn., Beta Phi Mu. Home: 13 Pat Rd Newburgh NY 12550-7219

CONNOLA, DONALD PASCAL, JR., management consultant; b. New Brunswick, N.J., Sept. 25, 1948; s. Donald Pascal and Josephine (Montalbano) C. AB, Rutgers U., 1970, MBA, 1973; JD, Bklyn. Law Sch., 1977. Mktg. control analyst Gen. Foods Corp., White Plains, N.Y., 1973-74, product analyst, 1974, sr. fin. analyst, 1974-75, fin. assoc., 1975-79, fin. specialist, 1979, internal mgmt. cons., 1979-82, mgmt. cons., 1983—. Prof. mgmt. Fairleigh Dickinson U., Rutherford, N.J., 1983-86, dir. MBA program, dir. undergrad. student svcs., 1986-94; prof. bus. adminstrn. Concordia Coll., Bronxville, N.Y., 1995-97; team leader Verizon Comm., 2000—. Mem. N.J. State Bar Assn., Am. Soc. Tng. and Devel., Assn. MBA Execs., Soc. for Human Resource Mgmt. Home: 1220 Cellar Ave Apt 12 Clark NJ 07066-2044 Office: 1500 Teaneck Rd Teaneck NJ 07666

CONNOLLY, JOHN EARLE, surgeon, educator; b. Omaha, May 21, 1923; s. Earl A. and Gertrude (Eckerman) C.; m. Virginia Hartman, Aug. 12, 1967; children: Peter Hart. John Earle, Sarah. AB, Harvard U., 1945, MD, 1948. Diplomate: Am. Bd. Surgery (bd. dirs. 1976-82), Am. Bd. Thoracic and Cardiovascular Surgery, Am. Bd. Vascular Surgery. Intern. in surgery Stanford U. Hosps., San Francisco, 1948-49, surg. research fellow, 1949-50, asst. resident surgeon, 1950-52, chief resident surgeon, 1953-54, surg. pathology fellow, 1954-55, 1957-60, John and Mary Markle Scholar in med. scis., 1957-62; surg. registrar professional unit St. Bartholomew's Hosp., London, 1952-53; resident in thoracic surgery Bellevue Hosp., N.Y.C., 1955; resident in thoracic and cardiovascular surgery Columbia-Presbyn. Med. Ctr., N.Y.C., 1956; from instr. to assoc. prof. surgery Stanford U., 1957-65; prof. U. Calif., Irvine, 1965—, chmn. dept. surgery, 1965-78; attending surgeon Stanford Med. Ctr., Palo Alto, Calif., 1959-65; chmn. cardiovascular and thoracic surgery Irvine Med. Ctr. U. Calif., 1968—; attending surgeon Children's Hosp., Orange, Calif., 1968—, Anaheim (Calif.) Meml. Hosp., 1970—. Vis. prof. Beijing Heart, Lung, Blood Vessel Inst., 1990, A.H. Duncan vis. prof. U. Edinburgh, 1984; Hunterian prof. Royal Coll. Surgeons Eng., 1985-86, Kinmonth lectr., 1987, Hume Lectr. Soc. for Clin. Vascular Surgery, 1998; King James IV lectr. Royal Coll. Surgeons Edinburgh, 2003; Dist. Prof. Lectr. Uniformed Svcs. U. Health Scis., Bethesda, 1998; adv. coun. Nat. Heart, Lung, and Blood Inst.-NIH, 1981-85; cons. Long Beach VA Hosp., Calif., 1965—. Contbr. articles to profl. jours.; mem. editl. bd.: Jour. Cardiovascular Surgery, 1974—, chief editor, 1985—; mem. editl. bd. Western Jour. Medicine, 1975—, Jour. Stroke, 1979—, Jour. Vascular Surgery, 1983—. Bd. dirs. Audio-Digest Found., 1974—, Franklin Martin Found., 1975-80; regent Uniformed Svcs. U. Health Scis., Bethesda, 1992—. Served with AUS, 1943-44. Recipient Cert. of Merit, Japanese Surg. Soc., 1979, 90. Fellow ACS (gov. 1964-70, regent 1973-82, vice chmn. bd. regents 1980-82, v.p. 1984-85), Royal Coll. Surgeons Eng., 1982 (hon.), Royal Coll. Surgeons Ireland, 1988 (hon.), Royal Coll. Surgeons Edinburgh, 1983 (hon.); mem. Japanese Surg. Soc. (hon.), Am. Surg. Assn., Soc. U. Surgeons, Am. Assn. Thoracic Surgery (coun. 1974-78), Pacific Coast Surg. Assn. (pres. 1985-86), San Francisco Surg. Soc., L.A. Surg. Soc., Soc. Vascular Surgery, Western Surg. Assn., Internat. Cardiovascular Soc. (pres. 1977), Soc. Internat. Chirurgie, Soc. Thoracic Surgeons, Western Thoracic Surg. Soc. (pres. 1978), Orange County Surg. Soc. (pres. 1984-85), James IV Assn. Surgeons (councillor 1983—), San Francisco Golf Club, Pacific Union Club, Bohemian Club (San Francisco), Harvard Club (N.Y.C.), Big Canyon Club (Newport Beach, Calif.), Cypress Point Club (Pebble Beach), Pacific Union Club. Home: 7 Deerwood Ln Newport Beach CA 92660-5108

CONNOLLY, MARY CHRISTINE, parochial school educator; b. Waterbury, Conn., July 26, 1965; d. Joseph Thomas Connolly and Mary Justine Hanlon. BS, St. Joseph Coll., 1987. Tchr. St. Francis Sch., Naugatuck, Conn., 1987—. Dir. skiwee program Mt. Southington (Conn.) Ski Area, 1988—; initiator ski club St. Francis Sch., drama/talent club, coach girls' softball, cantor sch. masses, substitute tchr. music classes. Camp dir. Naugatuck YMCA, 1991—. Recipient Disting. Svc. award Naugatuck Jaycees, 1993. Mem. Nat. Catholic Educators Assn., Profl. Ski Instrs. America. Democrat. Avocations: skiing, music, travel, drama/theatre, sports. Home: 3760 Texas St Apt 31 San Diego CA 92104-8303 Office: Saint Francis Sch 294 Church St Naugatuck CT 06770-2805

CONNOLLY, RUTH ANN, school system administrator; b. N.Y.C., May 15, 1947; d. John Wilford and Helen Louise (O'Donoghue) C. BS, Marywood Coll., 1970, MS, 1980; EdD, Fordham U., 1995. Cert. tchr., adminstr., supr., supt., N.Y. Tchr., v.p. Diocese of Bklyn., Wilmington and Rockville Ctr., N.Y., 1970-85, Archdiocese of N.Y., 1970-85; vice prin. St. Mary's Sch., Manhasset, N.Y., 1980-85; prin. Our Lady Queen of Martyrs, 1986-91; dir. master's degree program Fordham U., Bronx, N.Y., 1991-94; supt. schs. Diocese of Scranton, Pa., 1994—. Bd. dirs. Forest Hills Cmty. Ctr., Rego Park, N.Y., 1986-91. Doctoral fellow Fordham U. Grad. Sch. Edn. Adminstrs. and Suprs., 1990-91. Mem. AAUW, ASCD, NEA, Nat. Cath. Edn. Assn., Am. Ednl. Pers. Assn., Pa. Cath. Conf. Avocations: refinishing furniture, cooking. Home: 162 Columbine Ln Milford PA 18337-7128 Office: Cath Schs Office 300 Wyoming Ave Scranton PA 18503-1285

CONNOR, CATHERINE BROOKS, educational media specialist; b. Dothan, Ala., Oct. 29, 1955; d. James Bolling and Margaret Elizabeth (Jones) Brooks; m. Joseph Yauger Whealdon, Jr., June 12, 1983 (div. Aug. 1990); 1 child, Joseph Yauger III; m. William Christopher Connor, Dec. 28, 1991. BS, Fla. State U., 1980, MS in Libr. Sci., 1990. Cert. profl. media specialist, Fla., nat. cert. libr. media specialist. Asst. br. mgr. City Fed. Savs.

and Loan, Birmingham, Ala., 1976-77; elem. tchr. Louise S. McGehee Sch., New Orleans, 1981-85; kindergarten tchr. Lafayette Elem. Sch., New Orleans, 1986; grad. asst. Fla. State U. Sch. Libr. Sci., Tallahassee, 1990; media specialist Lely H.S., Naples, Fla., 1990-91, Frank M. Golson Elem. Sch., Marianna, Fla., 1991—, chmn. sch. adv. coun., 1995-98, leadership team, 1994—. Bd. dirs. Jackson County Pub. Libr.-Friends of Libr., Marianna, 1992-94, mem. adv. bd. 1998—, sec. 1998—; bd. dirs. Jackson County unit Am. Cancer Soc., 1998-2000, novinatina com. chair, 1998-99; charter mem. Libr. of Congress, Washington, 1994—; mem. Panhandle Pub. Libr. Coop. Sys. Bd., 1998—, mem. pers. com., 2000—. Mem. DAR (libr. 2000—), Colonial Dames, Descendants of the Knights of the Garter. Democrat. Episcopalian. Avocations: geneology, travel. Home: PO Box 507 Marianna FL 32447-0507 Office: Frank M Golson Elem Sch 4258 2d Ave Marianna FL 32446-1905

CONNOR, FRANCES PARTRIDGE, retired education educator; b. Bklyn., May 4, 1919; d. Horace K. and Sybil V. (Rafters) P.; m. Leo E. Connor, June 7, 1952. BA, St. Joseph's Coll., 1940; MA, Columbia U., 1948, EdD, 1953; LLD (hon.), Coll. New Rochelle, 1976. Cert. history, social studies tchr., spl. edn. tchr., N.Y. Tchr. history/econs. Haverstraw (N.Y.) Schs., 1940-42; tchr. N.Y. State Rehab. Hosp., West Haverstraw, 1942-49; lectr. Hunter Coll., CCNY, N.Y.C., 1946-54; tchr. spl. edn. Ramapo Ctrl. Schs., Suffern, N.Y., 1949-53; coord. spl. edn. U. Ga., Athens, summers 1952-53; rsch. assoc. U.S. Office of Edn., Washington, 1954-58; survey assoc. Tchrs. Coll., Columbia U., N.Y.C., 1953-54, prof., dir. Rsch. and Demonstration Ctr./Inst. for LD, 1955-87, dept. chair, 1962-85, Richard March Hoe prof. emeritus, 1989—. Mem. profl. adv. bd. Willowbrook Consent Decree, N.Y. State Dept. of Mental Retardation/Devel. Disabilities, Albany, 1977—; mem. bd. dirs. Family Resource Assocs., Shrewsbury, N.J. Author: Education of Homebound and Hospitalized Children, 1964, Experimental Curriculum for Young Mentally Retard Children, 1964; editor: Critical Issues for Low Incidence Populations, 1987. Mem. bd. trustees Mt. Saint Mary Coll., Newburgh, N.Y., 1970—, Human Resources Schs., Albertson, N.Y., 1984—; mem. Pres.'s Com. on Employment of Handicapped, Washington, 1972-89; del., mem. steering com. White House Conf. on the Handicapped, Washington, 1975-78; mem. Coalition of Disabled Women and Their Advocates, Ocean County, N.J., 1990—. Recipient Behavioral Sci. award Nat. Hemophilia Found., 1968, Pioneer in Spl. Edn. award Hofstra U., 1986. Fellow Am. Assn. on Mental Retardation; mem. Coun. for Exceptional Children (pres. 1964-65, Wallin award 1982, Outstanding Contbr. award 1992, R.P. MacKie award 1998), Com. Rehab. Internat. Roman Catholic. Avocations: choral/choir singing, swimming, writing. Home: 23343 Blue Water Cir Apt B113 Boca Raton FL 33433-7074 also: 200 4th Ave Spring Lake NJ 07762 E-mail: franleo@att.net.

CONNOR, JOHN MURRAY, agricultural economics educator; b. Attleboro, Mass., July 7, 1943; s. John Murray Sr. and Victoria Rose (Moro) C.; m. Ulla Maija Niemelä, Apr. 3, 1972; 1 child, Timo. BA cum laude, Boston Coll., 1965; MA, U. Fla., 1974; MS, U. Wis., 1974, PhD, 1976. Vol. U.S. Peace Corps, Nigeria, Uganda, 1966-68; agrl. economist Econ. Rsch. Svc. USDA, Madison, 1976-79, head food mfg. rsch. Washington, 1979-83; assoc. prof. agrl. econs. Purdue U., West Lafayette, Ind., 1983-89, prof., 1989—, asst. dept. head, 1985-88. Adj. prof. Cath. U. Sacred Heart, Piacenza, Italy, 1991—; vis. prof. Åbo (Finland) Akademi U., 1994; cons. subcom. on multinats. U.S. Senate, Washington, 1974-76, select com. on nutrition, 1977-78, UN Ctr. on Transnats., 1981-82, U.S. Dept. Justice, 1999, Nat. Assn. Attys. Gen., 2000-03; chair Orgn. and Performance World Food Systems, 1988-93. Author: Market Power of Multinationals, 1977, Food Processing: An Industrial Powerhouse in Transition, 1988, 2d edit., 1997, Global Price Fixing, 2001; (with others) Food Manufacturing Industries, 1985; contbr. articles to profl. jours., chpts. to books. Grantee US Office Tech. Assessment, 1984-85, Inst. Food Technologists, 1986-88, 94-95, Ind. Dept. Commerce, 1987-91, Econ. Rsch. Svc., USDA, 1988-89, Coop. State Rsch. Svc., USDA, 1989—; recipient Antitrust Writing award Jerry S. Cohen Meml. Trust, 2003. Mem. AAUP (pres. Purdue U. chpt. 1988-90, exec. bd. ind. conf. 1990-94, nat. coun. 1991-92), Am. Agrl. Econs. Assn. (Policy award 1980, Quality of Comm. award 1985, 2002, Disting. Extension Program award 1993), Indsl. Orgn. Soc., Am. Econs. Assn., ACLU. Home: 4355 Creekside Pass Zionsville IN 46077-9292 Office: Purdue U Dept Agrl Econs West Lafayette IN 47907-1445

CONNOR, NANCY KING, elementary school educator; b. Henderson, Tenn., Jan. 16, 1956; d. Lloyd Houston and Lee Nell Lurlene (Stanfill) King; m. Tommy Glen Connor, Aug. 16, 1974; children: Randall Tommy, Emily Nancy. Student, Jackson State U., 1974-75; BS, Lambuth Coll., 1977; MEd, Memphis State U., 1987. Cert. tchr., Tenn. Jackson C.C.; tchr. Chester County Schs., Henderson, 1977—. Mem. nominating com. PTA, Henderson, 1982-83, chmn. budget com., 1990-92; pres.-elect Tchr. Edn. Assn., Henderson, 1990-91, coun. rep., 1991-92, ann. staff, East Chester, 1992—; Sunday sch. tchr. Holly Springs Meth. Ch., 1988—, youth leader Meth. Youth Forum, 1990—. Avocations: reading, collecting musicals, spending time with family, church activities. Home: 540 Smith Rd Luray TN 38352-1785

CONNORS, WILLIAM FRANCIS, JR., dean; b. Mar. 31, 1945; s. William Francis and Ethel Lucille (Sester) C.; m. Susan Edwards, Nov. 20, 1971; children: Terence Michael, Corinne Elizabeth, Kristin Michelle, Jessica Marie. AB, St. Anselm Coll., 1966; MEd, Springfield Coll, 1967; MPA, L.I. U., 1980. Counselor Suffolk C.C., Selden, N.Y., 1967-72, asst. prof. psychology, 1972-73, assoc. prof., 1974-79, prof., 1979—, asst. dean instrn., 1973-87, assoc. dean instrn., 1987-97, dean of faculty, 1997-2000, exec. dean, 2000—, acting dean students, 1987, acting dean instrn., 1993-94. Trustee, v.p. Emma S. Clark Meml. Libr., 1984-92; mem. pres. sch. bd. Sts. Philip and James Sch., St. James, N.Y., 1984-93; mem., pres. Three Village Bd. Edn., 1994—. Roman Catholic. Home: 39 Cinderella Ln East Setauket NY 11733-1708 Office: Suffolk County CC Riverhead NY 11901-3499

CONOVER, ANNELLE ELIZABETH, music educator, educator; b. Plymouth, Pa., Oct. 17, 1949; d. Harold Joseph and Florence Elizabeth (Payne) Thompson; m. Kenneth Alfred Conover, Oct. 29, 1988; children: Ron Thomas Cahill, Tiffany Charisse Cahill. BS, Moravian Coll., 1976; MA, Trenton State U., 1981; MEd, Gratz Coll. Cert. tchr., Pa. Music tchr. Kingwood (N.J.) Twp. Sch., 1979-81, Lopatcong Twp. Sch., Phillipsburg, N.J., 1981-83, Saucon Valley Middle Sch., Hellertown, Pa., 1989—. Chair Middle Sch. Hand Bell Choir Fund, Hellertown, 1994-95, choral dir., 1990—; choral dir. Cambiata Singers, Hellertown, 1994— (invited to White House 1998); dir. Saucon Ringers, Hellertown, 1994—. Active Music Coalition, Allentown, Pa., 1992-93, Northampton County Comty. Singers, Bethlehem, Pa., 1993—; founder, mem. Two Hands singing group. Saucon Valley grantee, 1994. Mem. Christian Women for Am., Gospel Mus. Assn., Music Edn. Assn., Saucon Valley Edn. Assn. Republican. Avocations: playing saxophone, composition, computers, education, singing. Home: 2251 Freemansburg Ave Easton PA 18042-5313 Office: Saucon Valley Middle Sch 2095 Polk Valley Rd Hellertown PA 18055-1538

CONOVER, MONA LEE, retired adult education educator; b. Lincoln, Nebr., Nov. 9, 1929; d. William Cyril and Susan Ferne (Floyd) C.; m. Elmer Kenneth Johnson, June 14, 1953 (div. 1975); children: Michael David, Susan Amy, Sharon Ann, Jennifer Lynne. AB, Nebr. Wesleyan U., 1952; student, Ariz. State U., 1973-75; MA in Edn., No. Ariz. U., 1985. Cert. tchr., Colo., Ariz. Tchr. Jefferson County R-1 Sch., Wheat Ridge, Colo., 1952-56, Glendale (Ariz.) Elem. Sch. 40, 1972-92; dir. Glendale Adult Edn., 1987-92; ret., 1992. Author: ABC's of Naturalization, 1989. Mem. FOGG, Garden of Gods volunterr Information Ctr.,, NIA (Nat. Assn for Interpretation), NEA Ret. Life, Heard Mus., Cheyenne Mountain Zoo, Order of Ea. Star. Republican. Methodist. Avocations: music, travel, photography, history.

CONOVER, NANCY ANDERSON, retired secondary school counselor; b. Manhattan, Kans., July 8, 1943; d. Howard Julius and Wilma June (Katz) Anderson; m. Gary Hites Conover, Aug. 10, 1968; children: Chad Anderson, Cary Hites. BS in Edn., Kans. State U., 1965; MEd, Wichita State U., 1991. Cert. sch. counselor, tchr., Kans.; lic. profl. counselor, Kans. Tchr. Flint (Mich.) Sch. Dist., 1965-66, Unified Sch. Dist. 259, Wichita, Kans., 1967-68, Overland Park (Kans.) Sch. Dist., 1968-70; bus. mgr., sec.-treas. Gary Conover, D.D.S., Wichita, 1985-94; sch. counselor Unified Sch. Dist. 259, Wichita, 1991-94; secondary sch. counselor Unified Sch. Dist. 385, Andover, Kans., 1994—2002; ret., 2002. Mem. Am. Counselors Assn., Kans. Sch. Counselors Assn., Kans. Assn. Counselors, Mental Health Counselors Assn., Kans. Dental Aux. (sec. 1970-74), Wichita Dist. Dental Aux. (pres. 1970-75), Jr. League Wichita (adminstrv. v.p. 1978-82), Gamma Phi Beta, Phi Kappa Phi. Republican. Lutheran. Avocations: golf, reading. E-mail: gcon810000@aol.com.

CONOVER, THOMAS ELLSWORTH, biochemistry educator; b. Plainfield, N.J., Nov. 20, 1931; s. Elmer G. and May (Vincent) C.; m. Prudence Fox; 1 child, Kevin; m. Virginia M. Scherer; children: Martha, Susan. BA, Oberlin Coll., 1953; PhD, U. Rochester, 1958. Rsch. assoc. Johnson Found., Phila., 1963-64; asst. mem. Inst. Muscle Disease, N.Y.C., 1964-69; assoc. prof. Hahnemann U., Phila., 1970-82, prof., 1982-94, Allegheny U., Phila., 1994-98, MCP Hahnemann U., Phila., 1998—2002, Drexel U. Coll. Medicine, Phila., 2002—. Mem. AAAS, Am. Soc. Biochemistry and Molecular Biology. Office: Allegheny U 230 N Broad St Philadelphia PA 19102-1121

CONRAD, CHARLES A. neurologist, neuro-oncologist; b. San Antonio, Tex., June 12, 1961; BS, Tex. A&M U., 1984; MD, U. Tex. Med. Sch., 1988. Cert. bd. cert. Am. Bd. Psychiatry and Neurology, 1995, lic. Tex., Mo., Kans. Intern in internal medicine U. Tex. Med. Sch., Houston, 1988—89, resident in neurology, 1989—92; fellow in neuro-oncology U. Tex. MD Anderson Cancer Ctr., Houston, 1992—94, faculty assoc. dept. neuro-oncology, 1994—95; pvt. practice Cons. in Neurology, P.C., Kans. City, Mo., 1995—2000; assoc. prof. dept. neuro-oncology, ctr. med. dir. M.D. Anderson Cancer Ctr., Houston, 2000—. Rschr. in field. Contbr. articles to profl. med. jours., chapters to books. Recipient Fellowship award, Am. Cancer Soc., 1992—93, 1993—94. Mem.: AMA, Am. Assn. for Cancer Rsch., N.Am. Brain Tumor Consortium, Kans. City Round Table of Hematology/Oncology, Kans. City Neurology and Neurosurgery Soc., Am. Acad. Neurology, Soc. for Neuro-Oncology. Office: Univ Tex MD Anderson Cancer Ctr 1515 Holcombe Blvd Houston TX 77030

CONRAD, KERRY S. language educator; b. Ashland, Ky., Nov. 30, 1964; d. Larry Wayne and Kay Frances (Wheeler) Stephenson; children: Brandon Ray, Megan Kathleen. BA, Morehead State U., 1987, MA, 1993. Tchr. elem. sch. Martin County Bd. Edn., Inez, Ky., 1988-90, Nicholas County Bd. Edn., Carlisle, Ky., 1990—97, tchr. home bound, 1990—97; tchr. Lang. Arts Pendleton County Schs., Falmouth, Ky., 1997—. Tchr. intern program Ky. Dept. Edn., Frankfort, 1994-95; leader Writing Portfolio Cluster, 1998—; mem. Ky. Content Adv. Com.; head Lang. Arts dept., Pendleton County Schs., 1998—; co-dir. No. Ky. Writing Project, 2002—; mem. adv. bd., publicity chair No. Ky. region Scholastic Writing Awards; presenter in field. Contbr. articles to mags. Asst. cubmaster Boys Scouts Am., Carlisle, 1994-95. Writing grantee Ky. Arts Coun., Frankfort, 1993-94, 94-95, Ky. Writing Program, 1994-95. Mem. Nat. Coun. Tchrs. English, Nat. Assn. Gifted Children, Ky. Reading Assn., Ky. Mid. Sch. Assn., Ky. Coun. Tchrs. English/Lang. Arts (publicity chair 2003-2005). Democrat. Avocations: reading, needlework, family, scrapbooks. Home: 2940 Hayes Station Rd Falmouth KY 41040

CONRAD, SISTER LINDA, elementary school educator; b. Lorain, Ohio, Apr. 26, 1951; d. Chester Clifford and Virginia Ann (Smith) C. BA, Notre Dame Coll., Cleve., 1987; MEd, Notre Dame Coll., South Euclid, Ohio, 1996. Cert. tchr., Ohio; mem. Sisters of Notre Dame. Tchr. Julie Billiart Sch., Lyndhurst, Ohio, 1977-85, St. Francis Sch., Cleve., 1987-92, Gesu Sch., Cleve., 1992-94; dir. ctr. for excellence in edn. Notre Dame Coll. Ohio, South Euclid, 1994—. Dir. Project Stars Grant, Cleve., 1991-92, Tchr. Thinking in Art Curriculum Grant, Cleve., 1993-94; moderator Student Coun., Cleve., 1988-92. Roman Catholic. Avocations: reading, sewing, crafts. Office: Notre Dame Coll 4545 College Rd South Euclid OH 44121-4228

CONRAD, MARCEL EDWARD, hematologist, educator; b. N.Y.C., Aug. 15, 1928; s. Marcel Edward and Lulu Marie (Geraghty) C.; m. Marcia Louise Grove; children: Marcel Edward, III, Mark E., Carol J., Erin E., Julia P. BS, Georgetown U., 1949, MD, 1953. Diplomate Am. Bd. Internal Medicine, Am. Bd. Hematology. Commd. 1st lt. M.C. U.S. Army, 1953, advanced through grades to col., 1968; intern Walter Reed Gen. Hosp., Washington, 1953-54, resident, then chief resident in internal medicine, 1955-60; mem. staff Walter Reed Army Inst. Rsch., 1961-74, chief dept. hematology, 1965-74; chief clin. investigation svc. Walter Reed Army Med. Ctr., 1971-74; clin. asst. prof., then clin. assoc. prof. medicine Georgetown U. Med. Sch., 1964-74; prof. medicine U. Ala. Med. Sch., Birmingham, 1974-83, also dir. div. hematology and oncology, 1974-83; prof. medicine, pathology, dir. divsn. hematology, oncology U. South Ala., Mobile, 1983-2001, dir. USA Cancer Ctr., 1985-2001, disting. prof. medicine, 2001. Contbr. numerous articles to med. publs. Decorated Legion of Merit with oak leaf cluster; recipient Skinner medal U.S. Army, 1955, Hoff medal, 1962, John Shaw Billings award, 1967, William Beaumont award, 1972, Walter Reed award, 1974. Fellow Internat. Soc. Hematology, ACP (Laureate award 1989, named Disting. Prof. of Medicine, 2001); mem. AAAS, Assn. Am. Physicians, Internat. Soc. Hematology, Am. Soc. Clin. Investigation, Am. Physiol. Soc., Internat. Soc. Blood Transfusion, Am. Soc. Hematology, Am. Soc. Clin. Oncology, Am. Chem. Soc., Soc. Exptl. Biology and Medicine, So. Soc. Clin. Investigation, Am. Fedn. Clin. Rsch. Roman Catholic. Home: 28451 Perdido Pass Dr Orange Beach AL 36561-3602

CONRAD, MARIAN SUE (SUSAN CONRAD), special education educator; b. Columbus, Ohio, May 3, 1946; d. Harold Marion Griffith and Susie Belle (House) Goheen; m. Richard Lee Conrad, Jan. 23 1971. BS, Ohio State U., 1967. Tchr. spl. edn. West High Sch., Columbus, Ohio, 1967-70; spl. edn. work study coord. North High Sch., Columbus, 1974-79, Whetstone High Sch., Columbus, 1979-80, Briggs High Sch., Columbus, 1980-97, West High Sch., Columbus, 1970-97; ret., 1997. Bd. dirs. Jr. Div., The Columbus Symphony Club, 1972-79; vice chmn. Zoofari, Columbus, 1978-97; bd. dirs., life mem. Wazoo, Columbus, 1974-87; bd. dirs., chair coms. Jr. League, Columbus, 1982-99; vice chmn. devel. com. Dublin (Ohio) Counseling Ctr., 1987-97; trustee Columbus Zoo, 1991—. Recipient Mayors Award for Vol. Svc., Columbus, 1988. Mem. Am. Bus. Women's Assn. (v.p. 1979-80, bd. dirs., Woman of Yr. 1980), Coun. Exceptional Children (pres. 1988-89, Educator of Yr. 1989), Ohio Assn. Suprs. and Work Study Coords., Dublin Women in Bus. and Professions, Country Club at Muirfield, Dublin Women's Club, Iota Lambda Sigma. Republican. Methodist. Avocations: golf, gardening, travel, family, cooking. Home: 8039 Crossgate Ct S Dublin OH 43017-8432

CONRAD, STEVEN ALLEN, critical care and emergency physician, biomedical engineer, educator; b. St. Martinville, La., Aug. 23, 1953; s. Karl Donovan and Dolores Beatrice (Bienvenu) C.; m. Mona Theresa Hollier, Aug. 9, 1974; children: David, Lesley, Taylor. BS, U. S.W. La., 1974; MD, La. State U., Shreveport, 1978; MS, Case Western Reserve, Cleve., 1980, PhD, 1985; MS in Engring., La. Tech. U., 1981; MBA, La. State U., 2001, MS in Info. Sys. Tech., 2003. Diplomate Am. Bd. Internal Medicine, Critical Care Medicine, Am. Bd. Emergency Medicine; cert. nutritional support physician. Postdoctoral trainee in biomed. computing Case Western Res., 1979—80; resident internal medicine La. State U., Shreveport, 1981-84; fellow in critical care medicine Mayo Grad. Sch. Medicine, Rochester, 1984-86; from asst. prof. medicine to prof. bioinformatics and computational biology La. State U. Med. Ctr., Shreveport, La., 1986—2003, prof. bioinformatics and computational biology, 2003—, dir. critical care medicine tng. program, 1987—. Instr. computer sci. Winona State U., 1985—86; adj. prof. biomed. engring. La. Tech. U., Ruston, 1989—, adj. prof. human ecology, 1996—, prof. anesthesiology, 2002—, prof. bioinformatics and computational biology, 2003—; adj. prof. mech. engring. Inst. for Micromanufacturing, 1994—; cons. physician critical care VA Med. Ctr., 1986—, dir. extracorporeal life support program, 1993—, co-dir. nutritional support svc., 1994—, transplant intensivist Willis Knighton Regional Heart Transplant Program, 1994—, attending physician in pediat. ICU, 1994—; mem. emergency med. svcs. task force Shreveport Fire Dept., 1992—; prin. investigator in multiple device and drug trials. Editor: Pulmonary Function Testing: Principles and Practice, 1984; mem. editl. bd. Internat. Jour. Electronic Healthcare, 2003—; manuscript reviewer ASAIO Jour., Artificial Organs, Intensive Care Medicine, Critical Care Chest Medicine, Chest; abstract reviewer Critical Care Medicine; contbr. chpts. to books and articles to profl. jours. Grantee, Am. Heart Assn., NHLBI. Fellow ACP, Am. Coll. Crit. Care Med., Am. Coll. Chest Physicians, Am. Coll. Emergency Physicians; mem. IEEE (sr.), Biomed. Engring. Soc., Shock Soc., Am. Soc. Artificial Internal Organs, Internat. Soc. for Artificial Organs, Soc. for Acad. Emergency Medicine, Am. Soc. for Parenteral and Enteral Nutrition, Alpha Omega Alpha, Sigma Xi, Phi Kappa Phi, Beta Gamma Sigma, Sigma Iota Epsilon. Office: La State U Health Scis Ctr 1501 Kings Hwy Shreveport LA 71103-4228

CONRAN, LISA ANN, special education educator; b. Lawrence, Mass., Oct. 19, 1965; d. Salvatore Frank and Barbara Louise (Boutin) Moschetto; children: Hunter Catherine, Taylor McKenzie, Dalton Justice. BA in Psychology, U. Lowell, 1987, MEd, 1988. Instr. basic skills Timmony Middle Sch., Methuen, Mass., 1989; spl. edn. aide Marsh Sch., Methuen, 1989-90; bilingual develmentally delayed tchr. Tarbox Sch., Lawrence, Mass., 1989-90; instr. head start Greater Lawrence Community Action Coun., 1990-92; program therapy Mediplex Rehab. Facility, Lynn, Mass., 1992-94; ednl. therapist Greenery of North Andover, Worcester, Mass., 1994—95, 1997—99; spl. edn. tchr. Greater Lawrence Ednl. Collaborative, 1999—2001, Lawrence Family Devel. Charter Sch., 2001—. Instr. aerobics. Mem. ASCD. Home: 3 Russell St Methuen MA 01844-7607

CONROW, MARY FRANCES, retired elementary education educator, real estate broker; b. Memphis, Feb. 19, 1926; d. Robert Emmett and Nina Orene (Barber) Enright; m. Job Atkinson Conrow, June 2, 1951 (div.); 1 child, Donna Lynn Conrow Maddox. BS, Memphis State Coll., Tenn., 1950. Tchr. Turrell Schs., Ark., 1950—51, Shelby County Schs., Tenn., 1951—52, Albuquerque Schs., N.Mex., 1952-53, Memphis (Tenn.) City Schs., 1952—88; real estate broker Crye-Leike, Memphis, 1990—95. Mem. Memphis Bd. Realtors. Democratic. Roman Catholic. Home: 8708 Oak Trail Ln Cordova TN 38018-7387

CONSTANTINE, GUS, physical education educator, coach; b. N.Y.C., Nov. 28, 1939; s. Asomatos and Mersina (Almiros) Constantinopoulos; children: Angela, Michael, Valerie. BS, NYU, 1961, MA, 1963. Soccer and baseball coach, athletic dir. CUNY, Bronx, N.Y., 1969-98; soccer coach NYU, N.Y.C., 1986-96, N.Y. Inst. Tech., 1996—2000. CEO Summit Soccer, Inc., Mamaroneck, N.Y.; basketball specialist U.S. Dept. State, 1965—; internat. soccer referee N.Am. Soccer League, N.Y.C., 1967-84, Internat. Futbol Fedn., Zurich, 1982-86; referee Fedn. Internat. Futbol Assn.; bd. dirs. HTC Sports Found., New Rochelle, N.Y. Contbr. articles to sports jours. Bd. dirs. Holy Trinity Ch., New Rochelle, N.Y., St. Michael's Home, Quality Care for Elderly, Yonkers, N.Y. With U.S. Army, 1961-63. Named Hall of Fame, Bronx C.C., 2003; named to, Nat. Soccer Hall of Fame, 2002. Mem. AAHPERD, Nat. Soccer Coaches Assn. (life; nat. assessor 1993—, nat. instr. 1962—), Nat. Intercollegiate Soccer Ofcls. Assn. (charter, nat. instr., nat. assessor, Recognition award 1996, mem. Hall of Fame 2002), Nat. Collegiate Athletic Assn. (dir. nat. youth sports program 1972-86, ea. coll. athletic conf. soccer referee assigner 2003—), U.S. Soccer Fedn. (life), N.Y. Soccer Referee Assn. (life), Am. Collegiate Baseball Coaches, U.S. Soccer Fedn. (nat. instr., nat. assessor 1966—), Ea. N.Y. State Referee Adminstrn., Westchester Flames USISL (dir. opers. 1998—), Am. Hellenic Ednl. Progressive Assn. Greek Orthodox. Avocations: traveling, camping. Home: 191 Woodbrook Rd White Plains NY 10605 Address: PO Box 231 New Rochelle NY 10804 E-mail: guscons@aol.com.

CONSTANTINO-BANA, ROSE EVA, nursing educator, researcher, lawyer; b. Labangan Zamboanga delSur, Philippines, Dec. 25, 1940; came to U.S., 1964; naturalized, 1982; d. Norberto C. and Rosalia (Torres) Bana; m. Abraham Antonio Constantino, Jr., Dec. 13, 1964; children: Charles Edward, Kenneth Richard, Abraham Anthony III. BS in Nursing, Philippine Union Coll., Manila, 1962; MNursing, U. Pitts., 1971, PhD, 1979; JD, Duquesne U., Pitts., 1984. Lic. clin. specialist in psychiatric-mental health nursing; RN. Instr. Philippine Union Coll., 1963-65, Spring Grove State Hosp., Balt., 1965-67, Montefiore Sch. Nursing, Pitts., 1967-70, U. Pitts., 1971-74, asst. prof., 1974-83, assoc. prof., 1983—, chmn. Senate Athletic Com., 1985-86, 89-90, sec. univ. senate, 1991-92, v.p., 1993-95. Project dir. grant divsn. of nursing HHS, Washington, 1983-85; bd. dirs. Am. Jour. Nursing; prin. investigator NIH NINR, 1991-94; bd. dirs. Internat. Coun. on Women's Health Issues, 1986—. Author: (with others) Principles and Practice of Psychiatric Nursing, 1982; contbr. chpts. to books and articles to profl. jours. Mem. Presdl. Task Force, Washington, 1980, Rep. Senatorial Com., Washington, 1980. Fellow Am. Acad. Nursing, Am. Coll. Forensic Examiners; mem. ABA, ATLA, Allegheny County Bar Assn. (bd. cert. forensic examiner), Pa. Bar Assn., Women's Bar Assn., Am. Assn. Nurse Attys., Am. Nurses Assn., Pa. Nurses Assn. (sec. 1994-98), Nat. League Nursing, Pa. League Nursing (chairperson area 6), Allegheny County Bar Assn., U. Pitts. Sch. Nursing Alumni Assn., U. Duquesne Law Alumni Assn., Sigma Theta Tau, Phi Alpha Delta. Seventh Day Adventist. Avocations: cooking, piano. Home: 6 Carmel Ct Pittsburgh PA 15221-3618 Office: U Pitts Sch Nursing 4500 Victoria St Rm 415 Pittsburgh PA 15261-0001

CONTE, SUSAN, secondary school counselor; b. N.Y. d. Anthony Robert and Laura Marie (Di Bartolomeo) C. MA, Fordham, 1974, M in Social Work, 1990; postgrad., NYU. Cert. social worker. Tchr. Archbishop Williams H.S., Braintree, Mass., 1974-76, Ursuline Sch., New Rochelle, N.Y., 1976-87; dir. Ursuline Companions in Mission, Bronx, 1987-92; dir. counseling Ursuline Sch., New Rochelle, 1992—. Bd. trustees Coll. New Rochelle, 1993-99. Mem. Order of St. Ursula Roman Union. Democrat. Roman Catholic. Home: 44 Liberty Ave New Rochelle NY 10801-7143

CONTI, INDALICIO PALOMAR, accountancy educator; b. Dinas, Phillippines, Dec. 22, 1953; s. Ismael Hernandez Conti and Irenea Demit Palomar.. BS in Mgmt., Philippine Coll. of Commerce, Manila, 1976, BSC in Acctg., 1977; LLB, U. of the East, Manila, 1985; MBA, Polytechnic U. of Philippines. CPA. Jr. acct. Gen. Textile Mills, Inc., Libis, Quezon City, Philippines, 1978; dir., acct. Supreme Traders, Inc., Manila, 1978-79; auditor PUP Credit Union, Manila, 1978-83; legal rschr. Polytechnic U. Philippines, Manila, 1992; prof. Coll. Accountancy, Polytechnic U. Philippines, Manila, 1993—; mgng. ptnr. Conti & Assoc. CPA's, Quezon City, Philippines. Fin. cons., bd. trustees Fieldridge Learning Ctr., Brgy. San

Felipe, Batangas, 11999; tax cons., legal rschr. V.C. Ramirez Law Office, Quezon City, 1997—; external auditor N.F.K. Constrn., Merto Manila, 1998—, Vincent Mark Security Agy., Quezon City, 1998—, Psychol. Ext. Evaluation Rsch. Svcs., Quezon City, 1999—; assoc. prof. CBIBE Philippine Women's U., Manila, 1999; mem. faculty Colegio San Lorenzo Project 6, Quezon City, 2000—; CPA, tax practitioner, chief legal rschr., Fabella & Assocs. Law Office, Quezon City, 2002; profl. lectr., Trinity Grad. Sch. (Cmty. Outreach), 2000 Author: (textbooks) Income Taxation Law, 1984, Transfer and Business Taxes, 1986, Fundamentals of Transfer and Business Taxes, 1987, Fundamentals of Income Tax, 1988. Mem. PICPA, GACPA, CALFCI. Roman Catholic. Avocations: martial arts, dancing, playing chess, bowling, reading.

CONTI, JAMES JOSEPH, chemical engineer, educator; b. Coraopolis, Pa., Nov. 2, 1930; s. James Joseph and Mary (Smrekar) Conti; m. Concetta Razziano, May 13, 1961; children: Lori Ann, James Robert. B.Chem. Engring. summa cum laude, Poly. Inst. Bklyn., 1954, M.Chem. Engring., 1956, D. Chem. Engring., 1959. Sr. engr. Bettis atomic power divsn. Westinghouse Electric Corp., 1958—59; mem. faculty Polytech. U. N.Y., 1959—90, prof. chem. engring., 1965—90, chmn. dept., 1964—70, provost, 1970—78, v.p. ednl. devel., 1978—90; pres. Webb Inst. Naval Architecture, Glen Cove, NY, 1990—99, ret., 1999. Cons. in field. Contbr. articles to profl. jours.; patentee in field. Trustee Webb Inst. Naval Architecture, 1974—99. Fellow: AAAS, Am. Inst. Chemists; mem.: AIChE, Am. Soc. Engring. Edn., Omega Chi Epsilon, Phi Lambda Upsilon, Tau Beta Pi, Sigma Xi. Home: 26 Miami Rd Bethpage NY 11714-2229

CONTIE, MARY MARGARITA, primary education educator, consultant; b. Salamanca, N.Y., Oct. 2, 1946; d. Francis Joseph and Mary Glades (Weller) Frost; m. Robert C. Contie, Feb. 14, 1969; children: Nicholas Alan, Paul Anthoney, Douglas Jeffery, Timothy Patrick, Brittany Contie. Secondary sch., Oaxaca, Mex., 1963; BA in Psychology, Incarnate Word Coll., 1971; MA in Human Svcs., St. Edwards U., 1980. Founder, dir., tchr. San Antonio Learning Tree, 1972-83; edn. cons. Intercultural Devel., San Antonio, 1983—; edn. cons., trainer Linguametrects, San Rafael, Calif., 1983-84, Internat. Trainer and Ednl. Cons., San Antonio, 1984—; sr. cons. Creative Beginnings in Early Childhood, San Antonio, 1989—. Ednl. coord. Head Start Region XX, San Antonio, 1991-92; ednl. cons., trainer Scholastic Inc., N.Y.C., 1993—; cons. Kaplan Ind. NC, 1996—; adj. prof. San Antonio Coll., 1991—, Wheelock Coll., Boston; bd. dirs. St. Anthony's Day Care Ctr., San Antonio, 1988-93; mem. licensing adv. bd. Tex. Dept. Human Svcs., 1973; a founder Alamo Coalition Child Care, 1993—. Mem. working group Nat. Latino Children Agenda, San Antonio, 1994; co-coord. children literacy St. Matthew Sch., San Antonio, 1989-93. Grantee State of Tex., 1992. Mem. Nat. Assn. for Edn. Young Children, Nat. Assn. Bilingual Edn. (co-chair 1993-99), Assn. for Childhood Edn. Internat. Roman Catholic. Avocations: family activities, creative puppetry, dancing, camping, sewing. Office: 7715 Mainland Ste 103 San Antonio TX 78250 E-mail: creativebeginnings@msn.com.

CONTINO, ROSALIE HELENE, historian, playwright; b. Bklyn., Apr. 1, 1938; d. Nicholas and Domenica Helen (Nostro) C. EdB, Fordham U., 1959; MA in Ednl. Theater, NYU, 1980, PhD in Ednl. Theater, 1997. Tchg. fellow NYU Ednl. Theater Dept., N.Y.C., 1980-83. Resident costume designer TRG Prodn., N.Y.C., 1979-89, B.F.R. Prodn., N.Y.C., 1980-82, Studio Theatre, 1985-88, Unity Theatre Prodns., 1985-88; co-host Internat. Arts Festival, NYU. Assoc. prodr. : Art for All, Art for the Disabled, Channel 25/58 Cablevision; Telegram, My Grandmother's Garden; playwright: Ricky, Transitions, Kids, Kids, Kids, Twixt 'n' Tween; author: (creative non-fiction) Born to Create; playwright Three One Act Plays (Tree Talk, Is That All There Is?, The Reunion); author (poetry): The Day the Sun Forgot to Shine; author: (short stories) The Telegram, My Grandmother's Garden, Is That All There Is?; author: (poetry) Trees, Days of Future's Past, 1989, Life, The World of Poetry Anthology, 1991, (TV program) Sixteen Hours, Junior High Madness. Former mem. Ladies' Aux. Victory Meml. Hosp., Bklyn., 1964-74. N.Y. Times and N.Y. Sch. Continuing Edn. scholar, 1987; USITT grantee. Mem.: Theatre Libr. Assn., Costume Soc. Am. (region I rec. sec. 1999—2001), NYU Grad. Student Orgn. (treas. 1984—92), Dramatists Guild, U.S. Inst. Theater Tech. (grantee 2000), United Fedn. Tchrs., Am. Alliance for Theatre and Edn., Pi Lambda Theta (Rho chpt., exec. bd. 1987—2001, region I editor 1992—2000, treas. 2000—02). Roman Catholic. Avocations: tennis, bike riding, reading. Home: 74 Bay 10th St Brooklyn NY 11228-3412 E-mail: rhcphd@worldnet.att.net.

CONTRACTOR, FAROK, business and management educator; b. Bombay, Dec. 24, 1946; came to U.S., 1967; s. Jamshed Phirozshaw and Hilla C. Contractor; children: Cyrus, Sahm, Eric. BSME, U. Bombay, 1967; MS in Indsl. Engring., U. Mich., 1968; MBA, U. Pa., 1977, PhD in Managerial Sci. and Applied Econs., 1980. Staff indsl. engr. Max Factor, Inc., L.A., 1969; rsch. fellow U. Mich., Ann Arbor, 1969-70; exec. officer, asst. to mng. dir. TATA Group subs. TATA Adminstrv. Svcs., India, 1970-74; asst. instr. bus. and mgmt. Wharton Sch. Bus., U. Pa., Phila., 1975-77, instr., 1977-80; assoc. prof. Grad. Sch. Mgmt., Rutgers U., Newark and Piscataway, N.J., 1980-90, prof. internat. bus., 1991—, chmn. internat. bus. dept., 1986-88, 90-93. Lectr. Wharton Sch. Bus., U. Pa., 1985-86; vis. scholar UN Ctr. on Transnat. Corps., N.Y., fall 1988; mem. Internat. Bus. Inst., Rutgers U., 1986—, rsch. dir. CIBER, 1997-99, com. mem., 1980-90; NSF reviewer, 1980, 84, 94; organizer, co-chmn. joint conf. on coop. ventures in internat. bus. Rutgers U. and Wharton Sch. Bus., U. Pa., 1986, co-chmn. conf. on coop. strategies and alliances, Lausanne, Switzerland, 2001; licensing and tech. transfer agreements cons.; Unilever Group vis. fellow, vis. prof. Indian Inst. Fgn. Trade, New Delhi, spring 1994; vis. prof. Copenhagen Bus. Sch., 1995, Lubin Sch. Pace U., 1997, Fletcher Sch. Law and Diplomacy, Tufts U., 2000; presenter in field. Author: International Technology Licensing: Compensation, Costs and Negotitation, 1981, Licensing In International Strategy: A Guide for Planning and Negotiation, 1985, Government Policies And Foreign Direct Investment, 1991, Cooperative Strategies in International Business, 1988, Economic Transformation in Emerging Countries: The Role of Investment, Trade and Finance, 1998, the Valuation of Intangible Assets in Global Operations, 2001, Cooperative Strategies and Alliances, 2003, others; co-author: Introduction to International Business, 1986. Esmee Fairbairn fellow U. Reading, Eng., 1982, Fulbright fellow, 1991-92; grantee The German Marshall Fund of U.S., 1986, Carnegie Bosch Found., 1996-98. Fellow Acad. Internat. Bus. (bd. dirs., sec.-treas. 1992-94); mem. Licensing Execs. Soc., Acad. Mgmt. (exec. bd. 1997—2002, pre-conf. workshop chair San Diego meeting 1998, program chmn. Chgo. meeting 1999, pres. internat. mgmt. divsn. 2000—), European Internat. Bus. Assn., Zoroastrian Assn. Greater N.Y., Internat. Trade and Fin. Assn. (bd. dirs. 1995-97). Avocations: antique restoration, skiing, trekking, canoeing, interior design. Office: Rutgers Univ Sch Mgmt 81 New St Newark NJ 07102

CONTRERAS, DEE (DOROTHEA CONTRERAS), municipal official, educator; b. Kansas City, Mo., Nov. 13, 1945; d. Robert MacGregor Hubsch and Dorothea Ann (Bauer) Wilson; m. Michael Raul Contreras, May 1969 (div. Nov. 1979); 1 child, Jason Michael Raul. BA in Anthropology, UCLA, 1967; JD with honors, Western State U., 1979. Bar: Calif. 1979. Sr. social worker San Diego County, 1968-80; sr. field rep. Svc. Employees Internat. Union Local 535, San Diego, 1980-88; bus. rep. Stationary Engrs. Local 39, Sacramento, 1988-90; sr. employee rels. rep. City of Sacramento, 1990-95, dir. labor rels., 1995—. Mem. exec. bd. San Diego Imperial County Labor Coun., 1985-88; tchr. labor history U. Calif. Davis Ext., Sacramento, 1989—. Recipient Bread and Roses award Coalition of Labor Union Women, San Diego, 1981, Outstanding Tchr. award U. Calif. Davis Extension, 1993. Mem. Indsl. Rels. Assn. No. Calif. (exec. bd. 1988-94, pres. exec. bd. 1994-96). Democrat. Avocations: reading, writing. Office: City of Sacramento Ste 601 921 10th St Sacramento CA 95814-2711

CONVERSE, JAMES CLARENCE, agricultural engineering educator; b. Brainerd, Minn., Apr. 2, 1942; s. James L. and Doris E. (Beck) C.; m. Marjorie A. Swanson, Aug. 6, 1965; children— James, Julie, Mark, Katherine AA, Brainerd Jr. Coll, 1962; BS in Agrl. Engring., N.D. State U., 1964, MS in Agrl. Engring., 1966; PhD in Agrl. Engring., U. Ill., 1970. Asst. prof. agrl. engring. U. Wis., Madison, 1970-75, assoc. prof., 1975-80, prof., 1980—, chmn. dept., 1988-96. Fellow Am. Soc. Agrl. Engring. (Gunlogson countryside engring. award 1984). Roman Catholic. Avocations: scouts, soccer. Office: U Wis Dept Agrl Engring 460 Henry Mall Madison WI 53706-1533

CONWAY, EDWARD GERALD, JR., university educational technology administrator; b. Bklyn., Aug. 10, 1948; s. Edward Gerald and Louise (McNamara) C.; m. E. Regina Harris, Nov. 8, 1998. AA, Valley Forge Mil. Acad. Coll., 1969; postgrad., Georgetown Coll., 1969, Bloomfield Coll., 1970, Rutgers U., 1971, Muhlenberg Coll., 1973, Marywood Coll., 1977; BS in Media, Comms. and Tech. cum laude, E. Stroudsburg U., 1983; MS in Instructional Tech., Marywood Coll., 1994. Various acctg. and fin. positions in large cos. in eastern U.S., 1970-77; fin. aid officer Valley Forge Mil. Acad., Wayne, Pa., 1977-80; pers. recruiting, cons. Va., Tex., 1980-87; media technician U. Scranton, Pa., 1987-89, coord. media broadcast, 1989-92, dir. office of instructional techs., prodn. & broadcasting, 1992-95; coord. ednl. affairs Media Svc., Ga. Perimeter Coll., 1995—. Mem. comm. adv. bd. Diocese of Scranton, Pa. 1993-96. Presenter, lectr. at profl. meetings. Mem. Consortium of Coll. and Univ. Media Ctrs., Assn. for Ednl. Comm. and Tech. Avocation: travel. E-mail: egconway@harris-conway.com.

CONWAY, JOHN BELL, biologist, educator; b. Madison, Wis., Apr. 5, 1936; s. John Edward and Barbara (Bell) C.; m. Susan Jane Hawley, Sept. 1, 1961; children: Julie Anne, Steven Douglas. BS in Biology, San Diego State U., 1964, MS in Biology, 1967; MPH in Pub. Health, U. Minn., 1970, PhD in Environ. Biology, 1973. Asst. prof. bio. scis. Wright State U., Dayton, Ohio, 1972—76; asst. prof. bacteria and pub. health Wash. State U., Pullman, 1976—78, assoc. prof., 1978—81; prof. divsn. occupl. and environ. health Grad Sch. Pub. Health, San Diego State U., 1981—92, head divsn. occupl. and environ. health, 1984—87, assoc. dir., prof., 1987—92; assoc. dean, dir. profl. edn. program, prof. SUNY Sch. Pub. Health, Albany, 1993—97, prof. dept. environ. health and toxicology, 1993—2000, interim dean, 1998—2000; prof. allied health U. Tex., El Paso, 2001—, dean Coll. Health Scis., 2001—03, Charles H. & Shirley T. Leavell endowed chair in nursing and health scis., 2001—. Cons. NBS/Lowry Engrs. and Planners, San Diego, 1984-95, Congressman Duncan Hunter, San Diego, 1991-92, Compliance Consultants, N.Y.C., 1993-95; pub. health officer Grand Teton Nat. Park, Moose, Wyo., summers, 1996, 97. Editl. reviewer Jour. Environ. Health, 1978— (Harry Bliss award 1985), Cancer Prevention Internat., 1994—. Recipient Outstanding Faculty award San Diego State U. Alumni, 1986. Mem. Nat. Environ. Health Assn. (chair air and water sect. 1979-80), Nat. Environ. Health Sci. and Protection Accreditation Coun. (chair 1994-96), Am. Pub. Health Assn. (Disting. Svc. award sect. on environ. 1997). Office: U Tex Coll Health Scis Rm 202 Burges CERM El Paso TX 79968-0645 E-mail: jconway@utep.edu., sjanecon@cs.com.

CONWAY, LOIS LORRAINE, piano teacher; b. Caldwell, Idaho, Oct. 20, 1913; d. William Henry and Auttie Arrola (Bierd) Crawford; m. Edward Owen Conway, June 23, 1934; children: Michael David, Judith Ann, Steven Edward, Kathleen Jean. Degree, Albertson Coll. of Idaho, 1960's; student, Shorwood Music Sch., Chgo., Coll. of Notre Dame, San Francisco. Pvt. piano tchr., Ontario, Oreg., 1940-74, Pendleton, Oreg., 19774-92; ret., 1992. Nat. Guild Piano Tchrs. adjudicator spring auditions Am. Coll. Musicians, Austin, Tex., 1972-96. Author: (poetry) Pacifica-The Voice Within (Semi-finalist 1995). Chmn. Nat. Guild Auditions, Ontario, Oreg., 1959-72, Pendleton, Oreg., 1972-80; v.p., publicity Community Concerts Assn., Ontario, 1960-72, membership work, 1972-75. Democrat. Avocations: gardening, playing piano, bridge, duplicate bridge, motor home travel. Home: 114 Shamrock Cir Santa Rosa CA 95403-1156

CONWAY, MARY PATRICIA, speech educator; b. Springfield, Mass., May 11, 1953; d. George Martin and Mary Josephine (Sweeney) C. BA, Boston Coll., 1975; MS, Worcester State Coll., 1984. Cert. elem. edn. and speech, Mass., speech pathologist, Mass. Speech-lang. pathologist Springfield (Mass.) Sch. Dept., 1975—. Corporator Springfield Libr. and Mus., 1980—; divsn. leader Quadrangle Quest, Springfield, 1988—; active Dem. Com., 1980—. Grantee Mass. State Dept., 1986; named Outstanding Young Woman Am., 1984. Mem. Am. Speech-Lang.-Hearing Assn. (cert.), Coun. Exceptional Children, Assn. for Children with Learning Disabilities, Delta Kappa Gamma (Alpha chpt. officer 1989-93). Roman Catholic. Avocations: reading, golf, crafts, cooking, swimming. Home: 82 Pilgrim Rd Springfield MA 01118-1414

CONWAY, THOMAS WILLIAM, biochemist, educator; b. Aberdeen, S.D., June 6, 1931; s. James L. and Agnes (Mullen) C.; m. Mary Patricia Leadon, July 6, 1957; children: Catherine A., James M. BS, Coll. St. Thomas, St. Paul, 1953; MA, U. Tex., 1955, PhD, 1962. Postdoctoral fellow Rockefeller U., N.Y.C., 1962-64; asst. prof. U. Iowa, Iowa City, 1964-68, assoc. prof., 1968-73, prof. biochemistry, 1973-96, prof. emeritus, 1996—. Mem. NIH Physiol. Chem. Study Sect., 1975-79, chmn., 1976-78; Am. Cancer Soc. vis. scholar ICRF Labs., London, 1980-81, vis. prof. U. Chile, 1968. Co-author: Biochemistry: A Case-Oriented Approach, 1974, 6th rev. edit., 1996. 1st Lt. USAF, 1953-58. Named Rosalie B. Hite fellow, U. Tex. Austin, 1958-62, NSF fellow Rockefeller U., N.Y.C., 1962-64, vis. scholar Am. Cancer Soc., London, 1980-81. Mem. Am. Soc. Biol. Chemists, Am. Chem. Soc., Soc. de Biologia de Chile (hon.), Sigma Xi (pres. U. Iowa chpt. 1978-79). Roman Catholic. Home: 1 Wellesley Way Iowa City IA 52245-3830 E-mail: thomas-conway@uiowa.edu.

CONWAY-GERVAIS, KATHLEEN MARIE, reading specialist, educational consultant; b. Bklyn., Apr. 18, 1942; d. John Joseph and Mary Josephine Conway; m. Stephen Paul Gervais, July 10, 1976; 1 child, John Joseph. BA, Coll. Mt. St. Vincent, 1970; MS, Hunter Coll. of N.Y.C., 1973, Reading Specialization, 1974. Cert. reading and social studies tchr., nursery and elem. ecuator, N.Y., N.J. Elem. tchr. Archdiocese of N.Y., N.Y.C., 1963-74; reading specialist Malverne (N.Y.) Union Free Sch. Dist., 1974-86, dist. reading, testing coord., 1986-91, reading specialist, 1992-95, East Meadow (N.Y.) Union Free Sch. Dist., 1995-96; reading cons., tchr. trainer, staff devel. team Uniondale (N.Y.) Union Free Sch. Dist., 1996—. Adv. bd. mem. Newsday in Edn., Melville, 1982—; adj. prof. Nassau C.C., Garden City, N.Y., 1995—, L.I. U. Grad. Sch., 2003. Active Getting Out the vote presdl. election, N.Y., 1992. Recipient Ambassador in Edn. award Newsday, Melville, 1982, Congruence Model Project award N.Y. State Dept. Edn., Albany, 1988, Elizabeth Ann Seton award Office of Cathechesis and Worship, Long Island, 1991. Mem. ASCD, Internat. Reading Assn., N.Y. State Reading Assn., Orton Dyslexia Soc. (del.), Nassau Reading Coun. (bd. dirs., treas., exec. bd.). Democrat. Roman Catholic. Avocations: travel, reading, theater, swimming, computer. Home and Office: 174 Nassau Blvd West Hempstead NY 11552-2218 E-mail: watcher@optonline.net.

CONYARD, SHIRLEY JEAN, college dean; b. Mebane, N.C., Feb. 17, 1940; d. William N. and Thelma (Holt) C. BA, St. John's U., Jamaica, N.Y., 1968; MSW, Fordham U., 1971; MPA, NYU, 1978; DSW, Adelphi U., 1981. Lic. social worker. Rsch. technologist Downstate Med. Ctr., Bklyn., 1959-65; supr. community svcs. Angel Guardian Home, Bklyn., 1968-73; researcher, psychotherapist Jewish Hosp. and Med. Ctr., Bklyn., 1973-79; acad. dean Audrey Cohen Coll., N.Y.C., 1981—; asst. prof. N.Y.C. Tech. Coll., 1982—. Cons. Fordham-Tremont Community Mental Health Ctr., Bronx, 1982-90, Dept. HHS, Washington, 1979—, Bklyn. Councilman-at-Large, 1979-82, Peer Rev. for Social Workers, N.Y.C., 1980—. Contbr. articles to profl. jours. Bd. dirs., exec. sec. Bklyn. Haitian Ralph Good Shepherd, 1981—; bd. dirs., pres., chmn. fundraising William Hodson Cmty. Ctr., Bronx, N.Y., 1989—; bd. dirs., trustee program com. United Bronx Parents, Inc., 1990—. Recipient award of courage Samuel J. Tilden High Sch., Bklyn., 1958; grantee Angel Guardian Home, 1969, Adelphi U., 1979, others. Mem. Nat. Assn. Social Workers, Nat. Assn. for Health Svcs. Execs., Assn. for Black Bus. and Profl. Women. Avocations: travel, gardening, whitewater rafting, stamp collection. Address: Audrey Cohen College 75 Varick St Rm 1401 New York NY 10013-1917

COOEY, WILLIAM RANDOLPH, economics educator; b. Wheeling, W.Va., Feb. 23, 1942; s. William Earl and Marguerite Ruth (Potts) C.; m. Linda Faye Whiteman, Aug. 11, 1973; children: William Justin, Crissa Kaye. BA, Bethany Coll., 1964; MS, W.Va. U., 1966; postgrad., Miss. State U., 1973-74. Prof. Bethany (W.Va.) Coll., 1966—, adminstrv. chair econs. dept., 2002—, John F. and Evelyn Cassey Steen chair in econs., 2002—. V.p., bd. dirs. Cooey-Bentz Co., Wheeling, 1986-90; part-time assoc. prof. Ohio U., St. Clairsville, 1967-86, W.Va. U., West Liberty, 1976-84; pvt. practice legal cons., Bethany, 1975—. Contbr. articles to publs. West Va. Commn. Higher Edn. Advisor Boy Scouts Am., Bethany, 1986-90; asst. coach Little League Baseball, Bethany, 1986-90. Mem. Midwestern Econs. Assn., Beta Beta Beta, Omicron Delta Epsilon, Gamma Sigma Kappa. Avocations: woodworking, making videos, computers. Home: 102 Pt Breeze Dr Bethany WV 26032 Office: Bethany Coll Morlan Hall Bethany WV 26032

COOGAN, MELINDA ANN STRANK, chemistry and biology educator; b. Davenport, Iowa, Mar. 29, 1955; d. Gale Benjamin and Margie Delene (Admire) Strank; children: James Benjamin, Jessica Ann. AA, Stephens Coll., Columbia, Mo., 1975; BS, E. Carolina U., Greenville, N.C., 1978. Biology and phys. sci. educator York (Pa.) Catholic H.S., 1989-90; sci. advisor Bettendorf (Iowa) Children's Mus., 1993; gifted, chemistry and physics educator St. Katherine' Coll. Prep. Sch., Bettendorf, 1994; biology educator Lewisville (Tex.) H.S., 1996-99, chemistry educator, 1996-99; ALS rsch. asst. U. Tex. Southwestern Med. Ctr., Dallas, 1998; chemistry, biology and human anatomy educator Milford HS, Ill., 2000—. Violinist Augustana Symphony Orch., Rock Island, Ill., 1993-94; pres. bd. dirs. Flower Mound (Tex.) Cmty. Orch., 1994-95; founder, instr. Northlakes Violin Acad., Flower Mound, 1994-99; violinist Waterforde Women's String Ensemble, Lewisville, 1995-98, Clinton Symphony, 1999-2001, Country Theater, Cissna Park, Ill., 2002—; bd. dirs. Family Mus. Art and Sci., Bettendorf, 2000-01. student mentor, Earthwatch Prog., We. Ill. U. 2003— . Student mentor Earthwatch, 2003. Mem. Roanoke Art Mus. (docent 1983-86), Jr. Bd. of Quad City Symphony (chair promotion 1987-88), Jr. Svc. League Moline (Ill.) (chair Riverfest 1987-88), Jr. League of York (Pa.) (chair thrift shop spl. sales 1989-92), Jr. League of Quad Cities (nom./placement 1993-94), Jr. League of Dallas (sustaining 1995-96), Gamma Beta Phi, Chi Beta Phi, Phi Kappa Phi. Democrat. Roman Catholic. Home: 2167 E 1170 N Rd Milford IL 60953

COOK, ANN JENNALIE, English language educator; b. Wewoka, Okla., Oct. 19, 1934; d. Arthur Holly and Bertha Mable (Stafford) C.; children: Lee Ann Merrick, Amy Ceil Leonard; m. Gerald George Calhoun, Apr. 1994. BA, U. Okla., 1956, MA, 1959; PhD, Vanderbilt U., 1972. Instr. English, U. Okla., 1956-57; tchr. English, N.C. and Conn., 1958-61; instr. So. Conn. State Coll., 1962-64; asst. prof. U. S.C., 1972-74; adj. asst. prof. Vanderbilt U., Nashville, 1977-82, assoc. prof., 1982-89, prof., 1990-98, prof. emeritus, 1999—. Exec. sec. Shakespeare Assn. Am., 1975-87; chmn. Internat. Shakespeare Assn., 1988-96, v.p. 1996—. Author: Privileged Playgoers of Shakespeare's London, 1981, Making a Match: Courtship in Shakespeare and His Society, 1991; assoc. editor Shakespeare Studies, 1973-80; contbr. articles to profl. jours. Trustee Folger Shakespeare Libr., 1985—90, Shakespeare Birthplace Trust (life); bd. mem. Friends of the Shakespeare Birthplace Trust, 2000—, patron, Nashville Symphony, 2000—, U. Sch. Nashville, 2000—, Nashville Opera Guild, 2000—, Nashville Shakespeare Festival, 2002—, Shakespeare on the Cumberland; pres. English-Speaking Union, 2003—. Recipient Letseizer award, 1956, Nat. Leadership award Delta Delta Delta, 1956; Danforth fellow, 1968-72, Folger summer fellow, 1973, Donelson fellow, 1974-75, fellow Rockefeller Found., 1984, Guggenheim Found., 1984-85; grantee Folger seminar NEH, 1992-93 Mem. Shakespeare Assn. Am., MLA, AAUP, Shakespeare Inst., Deutsche Shakespeare Gesellschaft, Renaissance Soc. Am. (bd. dirs.), Phi Beta Kappa. Episcopalian. Home: 114 Prospect Hl Nashville TN 37205-4721 Office: Vanderbilt U Dept English Nashville TN 37235

COOK, BRUCE LAWRENCE, research analyst; b. Chgo., Dec. 12, 1942; s. David Charles III and Anna Mae (Lawrence) C.; m. Carolyn Winslow Smith Hammock (div. Dec. 1972); 1 child, Steven Winslow; m. Eileen Clare McPeak, Jan. 3, 1973; children: Christopher David, Helen Clare, Bruce Michael. BA in Radio-TV, Ohio Wesleyan U., 1965; MA in Speech Arts, San Diego State U., 1967; PhD in Comm., Temple U., 1979. Trustee comm. rsch. David C. Cook Found., Elgin, Ill., 1972-83; dir. Ill. Mcpl. Inst., Dundee, 1983-88; mng. editor Sr. Am. Newspapers, Dundee, 1988-90; dir. Cook Comm., Dundee, 1990—; rsch. analyst Copley Chgo. Newspapers, Plainfield, 1995-2000; sr. rsch. analyst Reach Chgo., Hollinger Inc. Chgo. (Ill.) Sun-Times, Plainfield, Ill., 2000—. Instr. Columbia Coll., Chgo., 1989—, DeVry U./Keller Grad. Sch. Mgmt., Oak Brook, Ill., 1991—. Author: (monograph) Understanding Pictures in Papua, 1981, (booklet) Serving Mentally Impaired People, 1983; founder, editor website: author-me.com Trustee Village of Sleepy Hollow, Ill., 1983-87; alt. bd. rev. Kane County, Batavia, Ill., 1993-95; v.p. gen. edn. adv. bd. De Vry Inst. Tech., 1997—. Capt. USAF, 1967-72. Mem. Am. Legion. Republican. Home: 1211 Carol Crest Dr Sleepy Hollow IL 60118-2643 Office: Fox Valley Pubs 3101 N Us Highway 30 Plainfield IL 60544-9604 E-mail: cookcomm@gte.net.

COOK, CHRISTINE, elementary education educator; b. Phila., Jan. 24, 1964; d. James Joseph and Ann (Kolankiewicz) B.; m. Kenneth Mark Cook, June 9, 1990; children: Jennifer Lynn, Megan. B in elem. edn., West Chester U., 1985; M in elem. edn., Millersville U., 1992. Nat. bd. cert. tchr. Kindergarten tchr. Somerton Nursery Sch. and Kindergarten, Phila., 1985-86, Milton Hershey Sch., Hershey, Pa., 1986—. Field hockey coach Milton Hershey Sch., 1986-92, softball coach, 1986-92, driver edn. instr., 1989-91. Mem. Assn. for Edn. of Young Children, Assn. for Childhood Edn. Internat. Democrat. Roman Catholic. Office: Milton Hershey Sch PO Box 830 Hershey PA 17033-0830

COOK, CHRISTINE L. endocrinologist, gynecologist, educator; b. Eugene, Oreg., Feb. 8, 1946; d. Wayne Vincent and Grace Louise (DuBois) Burt; m. Larry N. Cook, June 17, 1973; children: Brian D., Amelia L. BA in Microbiology, Oreg. State U., 1967; MD, U. Louisville, 1971. Cert. OB/GYN 1979. Instr. dept. ob-gyn., women's health U. Louisville, 1976-78, asst. prof., 1978-83, fellow reproductive endocrinology, 1980-82, assoc. prof., 1984—2001, prof., 2001—, vice chmn. dept. ob-gyn., women's health, dir. residency program; intern to resident U. of Louisville Hosps., 1971—76. Dir ob/gyn. residency program U. Louisville, 1984—89, 2003—; pres. U. OB/Gyn Assoc., 1998—2001. Author: (chpt.) Clinical Obstetrics & Gynecology, 1991, Dysmenorrhea & Premenstrual Tension, 1985. Fellow Am. Coll. Ob-Gyns; mem. Am. Soc. Reproductive Medicine, Am. Soc. Reproductive Surgeons, Soc. Asst. Reproductive Tech., Am. Andrology Soc., Assn. Profs. Ob-Gyn., Am. Assn. Gynecologic Laparoscopists, Am. Med. Women's Assn. Democrat. Methodist. Home: 2011 Woodford Pl Louisville KY 40205-1929 Office: Univ Louisville Deot Ob-gyn Women's Health Louisville KY 40292

COOK, DANIEL WALTER, rehabilitation education educator; b. Urbana, Ill., Dec. 31, 1945; s. Arthur and Mary Kay Cook; m. Becky Rae Childers, Aug. 10, 1968; 1 child, Carrie. BA, So. Ill. U., Carbondale, 1967; MEd, U. Mo., 1969, PhD, 1974. Lic. psychologist, Ark.; cert. rehab. counselor. Rehab. counselor Fulton (Mo.) State Hosp., 1969-71; sr. rsch. scientist Ark. Rehab. Rsch. and Tng. Ctr., U. Ark., Fayetteville, 1974-83; prof., coord. rehab. edn. Rehab. Edn. and Rsch. U. Ark., Fayetteville, 1983—. Author books, book chpts., articles to profl. jours.; co-editor Rehab. Edn., 1997-2002. Fellow APA; mem. Am. Rehab. Counseling Assn. (mem. exec. coun. 1989-92, rsch. award 1977, 80, 83, svc. award 1980, 93, James Garrett Career Rehab. rsch. award 1998), Nat. Coun. Rehab. Edn. (mem. exec. bd. 1990-92, 92-94, chair exam and rsch. com. 1993-97, commr. commn. rehab. counselor cert. 1992-97, Rehab. Educator of Yr. 1994) Office: U Ark 153 Grad Ed Fayetteville AR 72701

COOK, DAVID MARSDEN, physics educator; b. Troy, N.Y., Apr. 3, 1938; s. Marsden Alfred and Ethel Margaret (Minkwitz) C.; m. Cynthia Ann Gray, July 10, 1965; children: Brian David, Nathan James. BS in Physics, Rensselaer Poly. Inst., 1959; AM in Physics, Harvard U., 1960, PhD in Physics, 1965. Asst. prof. physics Lawrence U., Appleton, Wis., 1965-71, assoc. prof. physics, 1971-79, prof. physics, 1979—, Philetus E. Sawyer prof. sci., 1989—. Manuscript reviewer Am. Jour. Physics, 1974-94, 97—. Author: Theory of the Electromagnetic Field, 1975; editor conf. procs.; assoc. editor Computers in Physics, 1994-98. Grantee NSF, 1988, 93, 97, 2000, Keck Found., 1988, 93, 2002. Mem. Am. Assn. Physics Tchrs., Am. Phys. Soc., Sigma Xi. Avocations: church organist, gardening. Office: Lawrence U PO Box 599 Appleton WI 54912-0599 E-mail: david.m.cook@lawrence.edu.

COOK, DESMOND C. physicist, educator, consultant; b. Geelong, Victoria, Australia, Oct. 19, 1949; came to U.S., 1981; s. C.V. Cook and E.R. (Bartlett) Hall; m. Patricia S. Via, May 16, 1987, children: Rachel Lyn, Daniel John. BSc with honors, Monash U., Melbourne, Australia, 1972, PhD in Physics, 1978. Asst. prof. physics Old Dominion U., Norfolk, Va., 1981-87, assoc. prof., 1987-96, prof., 1996—, rsch. physicist, 1981—. Cons. Bethlehem (Pa.) Steel Corp., 1989—; mem. U.S. High Performance Steel Corrosion Adv. Panel, 2000—. Commodore, So. Chesapeake Bay NACRA Fleet, Virginia Beach, Va., 1988. Recipient Ayrton premium award Inst. Elec. Engrs., London, 1985. Mem. ASTM, Am. Inst. Physics (life), Nat. Assn. Corrosion Engrs., Australian Inst. Physics, Va. Acad. Scis., Sigma Xi. Avocation: sailing.

COOK, DORIS MARIE, accountant, educator; b. Fayetteville, Ark., June 11, 1924; d. Ira and Mettie Jewel (Dorman) C. BSBA, U. Ark., 1946, MS, 1949; PhD, U. Tex., 1968. CPA, Okla., Ark. Jr. acct. Haskins & Sells, Tulsa, 1946-47; instr. acctg. U. Ark., Fayetteville, 1947-52, asst. prof., 1952-62, assoc. prof., 1962-69, prof., 1969-88, Univ. prof. and Nolan E. Williams lectr. in acctg., 1988-97, emeritus disting. prof., 1997—. Mem. Ark. State Bd. Pub. Accountancy, 1987-92, treas., 1989-91, vice chmn. 1991-92; mem. Nat. Assn. State Bds. of Accountancy, 1987-92; appointed Nolan E. Williams lectureship in acctg., 1988-97; Doris M. Cook chair in acctg. U. Ark., Fayetteville, 2000. Mem. rev. bd. Ark. Bus. Rev., Jour. Managerial Issues; contbr. articles to profl. jours. Recipient Bus. Faculty of Month award Alpha Kappa Psi, 1997, Outstanding Faculty award Ark. Tchg. Acad., 1997, Charles and Nadine Baum Outstanding Tchr. award, 1997, Outstanding Leadership and Svc. award from several women's orgns. for Women's History Month, 1999, AAUW, others. Mem. AICPA, Ark. Bus. Assn. (editor newsletter 1982-85), Am. Acctg. Assn. (chmn. nat. membership 1982-83, Arthur Carter scholarship com. 1984-85, membership Ark. 1985-87), Am. Women's Soc. CPAs., Ark. Soc. CPA's (life, v.p. 1975-76, pres. N.W. Ark. chpt. 1980-81, sec. Student Loan Found. 1981-84, treas. 1984-92, pres. 1992-97, chmn. pub. rels. 1984-88, 93-95, Outstanding Acctg. Educator award 1991, Outstanding Com. Svc. award 1995, Student Loan Found. Bd. award 2001, 21 Yrs. Outstanding Svc. award 2001), Acad. Acctg. Historians (life, trustee 1985-87, rev. bd. of Working Papers Series 1984-92, sec. 1992-95, pres.-elect 1995, pres. 1996), Ark. Fedn. Bus. and Profl. Women's Clubs (treas. 1979-80), Fayetteville Bus. and Profl. Women's Clubs (pres. 1973-74, 75-76, Woman of Yr. award 1977) Mortar Bd., Beta Gamma Sigma, Beta Alpha Psi (editor nat. newsletter 1973-77, nat. pres. 1977-78, Outstanding Alumni in Edn. Iota chpt. 1999, Outstanding Svc. award 1999), Phi Gamma Nu, Alpha Lambda Delta, Delta Kappa Gamma (sec. 1976-78, pres. 1978-80, treas. 1989-2000), Phi Kappa Phi. Home: 1115 N Leverett Ave Fayetteville AR 72703-1622 Office: U Ark Dept Acctg Fayetteville AR 72701

COOK, DOUGLAS NEILSON, theater educator, producer, artistic director; b. Phoenix, Sept. 22, 1929; s. Neil Estes and Louise Y. (Wood) C.; m. Joan Stafford Buechner, Aug. 11, 1956; children: John Richard, Peter Neilson, Stephen Barton. Student, Phoenix Coll., 1948-49, U. Chgo., 1949-50, UCLA, 1950-51, Los Angeles Art Inst., 1948; B.F.A., U. Ariz., 1953; MA, Stanford U., 1955; postgrad., Lester Polakov Studio Stage Design, 1966-67. Instr. San Mateo (Calif.) Coll., 1955-57, Nat. Music Camp, Interlochen, Mich., 1961; asst. prof. drama U. Calif., Riverside, 1957-66, assoc. prof., chair theatre dept., 1967-70; head dept. Pa. State U., University Park, 1970-88, sr. prof. theatre arts, 1970—92, disting. prof. emeritus, 1992—; prodr., artistic dir. Utah Shakespearean Festival, Cedar City. Actor Corral Theatre, Tucson, 1952-53, Orleans (Mass.) Arena Theatre, 1953; dir., designer Palo Alto (Calif.) Community Theatre, 1954, Peninsula Children's Theatre, 1956-57; assoc. producer Utah Shakespearean Festival, Cedar City, 1964-90, producing artistic dir., 1990-2002, dir. emeritus, 2003—; producer Pa. State Festival Theatre, State College, 1970-85, The Nat. Wagon Train Show, 1975-76. Instl. rep. Juniata Valley council Boy Scouts Am., 1973-77; bd. dirs. Central Pa. Festival Arts, 1970-75, 84-87, v.p., 1984-86; bd. dirs. Nat. theatre Conf., 1980-90, v.p. 1983-85, pres. 1987-88. Recipient disting. alumni award U. Ariz., 1990; named to Coll. of Fellows of the Am. Theatre, 1994. Mem. AAUP, Shakespeare Theatre Assn. Am. (v.p. 1990-92, pres. 1993-94), Nat. Assn. Schs. Theatre, Am. Theatre Assn. (bd. dirs. 1977-86, exec. com. 1979-80, pres. 1984-85), U.S. Inst. Theatre Tech., Am. Soc. Theatre Rsch., Univ. Resident Theatre Assn. (bd. dirs. 1970-88, v.p. 1975-79, pres. 1979-83), Theatre Assn. Pa. (bd. dirs. 1972-76). Home: PO Box 10194 Phoenix AZ 85064-0194

COOK, GARY DENNIS, music educator; b. Jackson, Mich., Jan. 20, 1951; s. Jerome D. and Mary Jane (Read) Cook; m. Kirsten M. Odmark, June 3, 1972; children: Tekla M., Tamara K. MusB, U. Mich., 1972, MusM, 1975. Instr. music La. Tech. U., Ruston, 1972-75; timpanist/prin. percussion Tucson Symphony Orch., 1976-96; asst. dir. bands U. Ariz., Tucson, 1975-77, from asst. prof. to assoc. prof. music, 1975—90, prof., 1990—, interim dir. Sch. Music and Dance, 1994-96, dir. Sch. Music and Dance, 1996—99. Author: (book) Teaching Percussion, 1988, 2d edit., 1996; co-author: The Encyclopedia for Percussion; contbr. articles to profl. jours. and ency. Recipient Charles and Irene Putnam award for excellence in tchg., Coll. Fine Arts. Mem.: Am. Fedn. Musicians, Music Tchrs. Nat. Assn., Coll. Music Soc., Percussive Arts Soc., Phi Mu Alpha, Kappa Kappa Psi, Pi Kappa Lambda. Avocations: reconditioning instruments and antiques, reading, swimming, skiing, scuba diving. Office: U Ariz Sch Music And Dance Tucson AZ 85721-0001

COOK, GARY RAYMOND, university president, clergyman; b. Little Rock, Ark., Sept. 27, 1950; s. Raymond C. and Vada (James) C.; m. Sheila Gayle Raymer, Dec. 28, 1974; children: David Daniel, Mark Andrew. BA, Baylor U., 1972; MDiv, So. Sem., Louisville, 1975; MA, U. North Tex., 1977; D in Ministry, Southwestern Sem., 1977. Pastor 1st Bapt. Ch., McGregor, Tex., 1976-78; dir. denomination and community rels. Baylor U., Waco, Tex., 1978-88; pres. Dallas Bapt. U., 1988—. Author: Retirees in Mission, 1977; co-editor: Abner McCall: One Man's Journey, 1981. Mayor pro tem City of Waco, 1983-84, mem. city coun., 1981-84; past bd. dirs. Tex. Dept. on Aging; past internat. bd. dirs. Habitat for Humanity. Recipient Humanitarian award Waco Conf. Christians and Jews, 1986, Disting. Alumnus award Southwestern Sem., 2000, Baylor U., 2003. Mem. Rotary (sustaining). Home and Office: 3000 Mountain Creek Pkwy Dallas TX 75211-6700

COOK, JANICE ELEANOR NOLAN, retired elementary school educator; b. Middletown, Ohio, Nov. 22, 1936; d. Lloyd and Eleanor Lee (Caudill) Nolan; m. Kenneth J. Cook, May 16, 1980 (dec.); children: Gerald W. Fultz Jr., Jana Linn Perkins, Jennylee Heard. BSEd, Miami U., 1971; MEd, reading specialist cert., Xavier U., 1982, rank 1 cert., 1987, spl. edn. cert., 1988. Tchr. pre-sch. and elem. Middletown (Ohio) Pub. Schs., 1957-58, 71-80; tchr. Boone County Schs., Florence, Ky., 1980-99; ret., 1999. Resource tchr. Ky. Internship Program, 1985—95; substitute tchr. Lebanon City Schs. Fellow ABI Rsch. Assn. (life); mem. NEA, Nat. Assn. Edn. Young Children, Internat. Reading Assn., Nat. Coun. Tchrs. English, Ky. Edn. Assn., Boone County Edn. Assn., Assn. Childhood Edn. Internat., Nat. Coun. Tchrs. Math. Home: 926 Pineneedle Pl Maineville OH 45039-7019

COOK, KARLA JOAN, elementary education educator; b. L.A., June 24, 1939; d. Charles Paul and Helen Barbara (Hamel) Belanger; m. John Rencoret, Aug. 1962 (div. 1964); 1 child, Renee; m. John Cook, Mar. 15, 1973 (div., 1983); children: Michael Donovan, Melody Marie. AB, Compton Jr. Coll., 1963; BA, Calif. State U., L.A., 1970. Cert. life tchr., Calif. Bookkeeper, asst. 1st Nat. Bank, N.Y.C., 1957-58; bookkeeper, vault teller 1st Western Bank, L.A., 1958-61; Blue-line operator County Sanitation, L.A., 1963-66; tchr. Long Beach (Calif.) Unified Sch. Dist., 1971-72, L.A. Unified Sch. Dist., Calif., 1974-94, 96—, Anaheim (Calif.) Sch. Dist., 1994-96; film background artist many casting cos., 1994—. Founder, dir. Crisis Intervention Resource and Referral Agy., South Gate, Calif., 1991-95; dir. Sunday sch. program Lynwood Ch. of God, 1995. Mem. Christian Blue Collar Workers (pres. 1990-91), United Tchrs. L.A. (chpt. chair 1990-91). Democrat. Avocations: painting, dancing, acting, poetry writing, sculpture. Home: 1602 E Harding St Long Beach CA 90805

COOK, KAY ELLEN, remedial programs coordinator; b. Wenatchee, Wash., Sept. 13, 1942; d. Leonard Melius and Ardys Darlene (McMillan) Erickson; m. Terry Joseph Cook, June 15, 1963; children: Paul Erickson, Joseph Douglas. BA in Edn. and Social Studies, Wash. State U., 1964; MA in Reading, Ctrl. Wash. U., 1975, prin. cert., 1985. Tchr. Selah (Wash.) Schs., 1960-62, West Valley Schs., Yakima, Wash., 1970-79, remedial programs coord., 1979—. Mem. ASCD, Wash. Orgn. Reading Devel., Internat. Reading Assn., Alpha Delta Kappa. Avocations: golf, gardening, handicrafts. Office: West Valley Schs Wide Hollow Elem 1000 S 72nd Ave Yakima WA 98908-1857

COOK, MARCY LYNN, mathematics educator, consultant; b. Culver City, Calif., Mar. 5, 1943; d. Lloyd Everett and Theresa J. (Matusek) Rude; m. Robert Lee Cook, Aug. 26, 1968; children: Bob, Jim. BA, U. Calif., Santa Barbara, 1964; MA, Stanford U., 1968. Tchr. 5th and 6th grades Sunnyvale (Calif.) Sch. Dist., 1964-67; tchr. Thessaloniki (Greece) Internat. H.S., 1968-70; tchr. primary grades Carmel (Calif.) Unified Sch. Dist., 1970-72; faculty of edn. Calif. State U., Fullerton, 1973-80; tchr. gifted and talented Newport Mesa Unified Sch. Dist., Calif., 1980-85; math. cons. Newport Beach, Calif., 1985—. Lectr. in field nationally and internationally. Author over 100 books including Act It Out, Assessing Math Understanding, Basic Games, Book A, Book B, Clues and Cues, Communicating with Tiles, Contrasting Facts, Coop Thinking, Crack The Code Book A, Book B, Do Math, Do Talk It Over, Duo Do Dominoes, Follow the Clues, I Have, Justify Your Thinking, Numbers Please! Questions Please!, Positive Math at Home and School, I, II, Primary Today is the Day, Reason Together, Show Me and Stump Me, Talk It Over, Think in Color, Tile Awhile, many others. Stanford U. fellow, 1968. Mem. Calif. Assn. Gifted, Calif. Math. Coun., Nat. Coun. Tchrs. Math., Assn. for Advancement of Internat. Edn., Nat. Coun. Suprs. of Math. Avocation: travel. Home and Office: PO Box 5840 Newport Beach CA 92662-5840

COOK, MARILYN JANE, elementary school educator; b. Covington, Ky., Jan. 27, 1948; d. Ralph Benjamin and Jane Elizabeth (Doddy) C.; 1 child, Elisabeth Anne Brundrett-Cook. BA, St. Andrews Presbyn. Coll., 1970; MDiv, Austin Presbyn. Theol. Sem., 1974; MS in Curriculum and Instrn., Corpus Christi State U., 1992; MS in Ednl. Adminstrn., Tex. A&M, Corpus Christi, 1996. Cert. tchr., Tex.; master tchr. Nat. Tchr. Tng. Inst.; cert. Irlen screener. Edn. dir. Northwood Presbyn. Ch., San Antonio, 1976-77; mgr. Summer Place, Port Aransas, Tex., 1977-78; adminstrv. asst. Crisis Intervention Svc., Corpus Christi, 1978-79; mgr. Nueces County Mental Health/Mental Retardation, Corpus Christi, 1979-81; educator Sacred Heart Sch., Rockport, Tex., 1982-83, Port Aransas Sch. Dist., 1983—. Mem. leadership team Project 2061, Tex., 1989-95, Tex. Ctr. Sci., Math. and Tech., 1995-98; mem. manuscript and rev. panel and resources reviewer Sci. and Children jour., Arlington, Va., 1991—; mem. dist. and campus site based decision making teams; insvc. facilitator Tex. Elem. Sci. program; Title I sch. support team ESC region 2; adj. Tex. Essential Knowledge and Skills English/Lang. Arts; mem. editl. rev. bd. The State of Reading, 1995—; mem. Tex. Sch. Improvement Iniatitive, 1998—; adj. prof. Tex. A&M U., Corpus Christi, 1997-98. Contbr. articles to profl. jours. Troop leader Girl Scouts USA, Port Aransas, 1992—; bd. dirs. Keep Port Aransas Ceautiful, 1990—93, Dewey Dreyer Cmty. Day Care, Port Aransas, 1988—90; sec. exec. bd. Corpus Christi Ballet, 1996—99, bd. dirs., 1995—; del. Paisano coun. Girl Scouts USA, 2002—; elder Cmty. Presbyn. Ch., Port Aransas. Recipient Sadie Ray Gaff award of merit Keep Tex. Beautiful, 1990, 92, Mini-grant award Tex. State Reading Assn.; Leadership Devel. fellow Edn. Svc. Ctr., Region 2. Mem.: NSTA (presch./elem. program rep. area conv. 1995), Tex. Irlen Assn. (founding mem.), Dyslexia Soc. South Tex. (bd. dirs. 1999—, pres. 2001—02), Nat. Project Wet Crew, Tex. Reading Assn. (pres. manuscript rev. bd. The State of Reading 2001—), Sci. Tchrs. Assn. Tex., Coun. Elem. Sci. Internat., Tex. Coun. Elem. Sci. (area dir. 1993—94, bd. dirs. 1993—, Dillo Press editor jour. 1995—, Dorothy Lohman award 1994), Assn. Environ. Edn. (bd. dirs. 1991—93), Internat. Reading Assn. (book awards com.), Phi Delta Kappa, Kappa Delta Pi. Avocations: reading, writing, traveling, art work, gardening. Office: Port Aransas Ind Sch Dist 100 S Station St Port Aransas TX 78373-5233

COOK, MARTHA JANE, educator, counselor; b. Canton, Ohio, Feb. 23, 1926; d. Harry Alfred and Flossie Faye (Haynam) Barber; m. Marvin Lester Cook, June 5, 1949; 1 child, Mark Dennis. BS in Edn., Ohio State U., 1947; MEd, Kent State U., 1962; EdD, U. Akron, 1978. Cert. high sch. English and sci. tchr., high sch and elem. music tchr., prin.; lic. high sch. and elem. profl. counselor; nat. cert. counselor. Tchr. Fairhope Sch., Louisville, Ohio, 1947-49, Sandyville (Ohio) Elem. Sch., 1949-50, East Sparta (Ohio) Elem. Sch., 1950-54; comptometer operator Hoover Co., North Canton, Ohio, 1949-50; tchr., counselor Sandy Valley H.S., Magnolia, Ohio, 1958-62; counselor Canton South H.S., 1962-80; prof. grad. sch. profl. counseling Malone Coll., Canton, 1980—. Author: Bibliotherapy, 1978, Grammar for Professionals, 1981. Treas., tchr., dir. choir East Sparta Christian Ch., 1954-74; mem. Pike Twp. Zoning Bd. Appeals, 1985—; mem. Canton Loan Fund, 1988—; vice chmn. bd. dirs. Canton Christian Home, 1989—. Named Counselor of Yr., Ohio Sch. Counselors Assn., 1974, Citizen of Yr., KC, 1981, Outstanding Acad. Advisor, Am. Coll. Testing Svc., 1984, Outstanding Educator, Canton YWCA, 1990, Outstanding Educator Malone Coll., 1995. Mem. ACA, Stark County Counselors Assn. (founder, pres.), Kappa Delta Pi, Phi Delta Kappa (McKinley chpt. Outstanding Educator 2001). Republican. Avocations: tennis, reading, table tennis, volleyball, crocheting. Home: 8395 Maplehurst Ave SE East Sparta OH 44626-9320

COOK, MARY GOOCH, elementary school educator; b. Columbus, Ga., May 1, 1943; d. Joe Lee and Ella Mae (Crimes) Gooch; m. Robert James Cook Sr.; children: Robert James Jr., Kevin Scott. BS, Ala. State Coll., 1965, M in Edn., reading spl., 1973; cert. in elem. edn., Tuskegee U., summer 1968; cert. reading specialist, Ga. State U., 1973; cert. edn. specialist, Troy State U., 1991. Cert. tchr., Ga. Tchr. Fox Elem. Sch., Columbus, Ga., 1973-94, Gentian Elem. Sch., Columbus, Ga., 1994—. Arbitrator BBB, Columbus, 1989-95; cmty. leader tchr. Combined Cmty. South Columbus, 1988-91; mem. voter registration com. Bd. Registration, Columbus, 1990-95; mem. support youth activities com. Columbus Cmty. Ctr., 1994. Mem. AAUW, Nat. Coun. Tchrs. Math., Internat. Reading Assn., Muscogee Assn. Educators (faculty rep. Fox Elem. Sch. 1973-94, Gentian Elem. Sch. 1994-96), Sigma Rho Sigma (pres. Montgomery, Ala. chpt. 1964—), Kappa Delta Pi. Home: 4655 Illini Dr Columbus GA 31907-6613 Office: Cusseta Rd Elem Sch 4150 Cusseta Rd Columbus GA 31903-4499

COOK, MARY SHEPARD, education educator; b. Mobile, Ala., June 24, 1948; d. James Warren and Mary Kate (Shepard) C. BS, Auburn U., 1969, MA in Coll. Teaching, 1970. Cert. elem. edn., mental retardation, early childhood edn. Fla. Dept. Edn.; cert. child care trainer; cert. children with spl. needs trainer Fla./Health and Rehab. Svcs.; cert. tech. edn. Fla. C.C. Jacksonville. Grad. teaching asst. Auburn (Ala.) U., Sch. Home Econs./Child Study Ctr., 1969-70; cons., instr., short term tchr. adult home econs. Atlanta (Ga.) Pub. Schs., 1970-72; ednl. supr. Sheltering Arms Assn. of Day Nurseries, Inc., Atlanta, 1972-73; child care instr., adult home econs. City Ctr. for Learning, Sch. Bd. Pinellas County, St. Petersburg, Fla., 1973-74; prof. child care instrnl. svcs. Fla. C.C., Jacksonville, 1974—. Validator Nat. Acad. Early Childhood Programs; mem. Duval County Interagency Coordinating Coun. on Early Childhood Programs, Fla. Community Coll. Early Childhood Educators' Network, HRS-Dist. IV Child Care Tng. Adv. Task Force. Mem. Am. Assn. Family and Consumer Scis. (cert.), Am. Vocat. Assn., Early Childhood Assn. Fla. (life, pres. 1990-91), Fla. Vocat. Assn., Fla. Assn. Family and Consumer Scis., Fla. Family Child Care Home Assn., Fla. Vocat. Home Econs. Assn., Jacksonville Area Caring for Kids (advisor), Nat. Assn. Family Child Care, Nat. Assn. for the Edn. of Young Children (life), So. Early Childhood Assn. (life), Phi Delta Kappa, others. Episcopal. Avocations: pvt. pilot. Home: 4109 Peachtree Cir E Jacksonville FL 32207-6409 Office: FCCJ N Campus A-215 4501 Capper Rd Jacksonville FL 32218-4436

COOK, MYRTLE, special education educator; b. New Orleans, June 15, 1936; d. John Henry and Angeline (Gray) C.; m. Marshall Butler, Dec. 22, 1979 (dec. July 1981). Student, So. U., 1954-55; BA, Southeastern La. U., 1960, MEd, 1971, postgrad., 1975. Cert. elem. tchr., tchr. mentally retarded, student tchr. supr., prin., La. Elem. tchr. Tangipahoa Parish Sch. System, Hammond, La., 1960-61, Ponchatoula, La., 1961-62, 65-67, Kentwood, La., 1963-65, tchr. Headstart Ponchatoula, 1965-65, prin. Headstart, 1965, tchr. spl. edn., 1967-72, Hammond, 1972—, mem. spl. edn. adv. coun. Amite, La., 1987—. Participant and presenter workshops in field. Vol., coach La. Spl. Olympics; active Girl Scouts U.S.A., United Way Tangipahoa Parish, La. Heart Fund; music dir., pianist children's choir Greenfield Bapt. Ch., 1961—, sec. sr. women's aux., 1961—; music dir., organist choirs Little Bethel Bapt. Ch., Amite, 1961—; organist, chmn. music La. Home and Fgn. Mission Bapt. Sr. Women's Aux., 1961—; also others. Named Tangipahoa Parish Tchr. of Yr., La. Edn. Assn., 1974, Educator of Yr. award, Amite, 1975; Spl. Edn. Tchr. of Yr, Tangipahoa Parish Sch. System, 1987; T.H. Harris scholar So. U., 1954-55. Mem. Tangipahoa Parish Edn. Assn., Tangipahoa Fedn. Tchrs. Democrat. Avocations: reading and studying the bible, playing organ and piano, singing in church choir, aerobics, music. Home: 105 Kansas St Hammond LA 70403-3943

COOK, PAUL FABYAN, chemistry educator; b. Ware, Mass., Aug. 2, 1946; s. Fabyan Henry and Almina Carrie (Dragon) C.; m. Sandra Joanne Urban, May 17, 1969; 1 child, Karen Michelle. BA, Our Lady of the Lake, San Antonio, 1972; PhD, U. Calif., Riverside, 1976. Postdoctoral fellow U. Wis., Madison, 1976-80; asst. prof. biochemistry La. State U. Med. Ctr., New Orleans, 1980-82; asst. prof. Tex. Coll. Osteo. Med., Ft. Worth, 1982-84; assoc. prof. U. North Tex. Health Sci. Ctr., Ft. Worth, 1984-86, prof., 1986-88, prof. and chair dept. microbiology and immunology, 1988-94; Grayce B. Kerr prof. biochemistry, prof. chem./biochem. Okla. U., 1996—. Vis. prof. U. Wurzburg, Germany, 1987, 95; mem. adv. bd. Life Sci. Advances, 1986-95; mem. biochemistry study sect. NIH, Bethesda, Md., 1987-92; co-chair Gordon Conf. on Enzymes, Coenzymes and Metabolic Pathways, 1993. Contbr. chpts. to Heavy Atom Isotope Effect in Enzyme-Catalyzed Reactions, 1991, Kinetic and Regulatory Mechanisms from Isotope Effects, 1991, Isotope Effects in Transferase Reactions, 1991, pH Dependence of Isotope Effects, 1991, Isotopes in Organic Chemistry, 1992, Molecular Oncology and Clinical Applications, 1993, Enzymes Dependent on Pyridoxal Phosphate and Other Carbonyl Compounds, 1994, 99, Steenbock Symposium on Enzymatic Mechanisms, 1999, Advances in Enzymology, 2000, Methods in Enzymology, 2003; editor: Enzyme Mechanism from Isotope Effects, 1991; mem. editl. bd.: Jour. Biol. Chemistry, 1984-90, 2001—, Jour. Theoretical Biology, 1988-89, Protein and Peptide Letters, 1994—, Biochimica Biophysica Acta, 1997—; contbr. articles to Biochemistry, Jour. Biol. Chemistry, others. With USAF, 1966-70. Recipient Rsch. Career Devel. award NIH, 1983-88; grantee Robert A. Welch Found., 1985-96, NIH, 1981-99, NSF, 1989—, NATO Sci. Affairs, 1990-97; NIH fellow, 1977-79, Alexander von Humboldt rsch. fellow, 1987, 95. Mem. Am. Chem. Soc. (mem. nominating com. 1991-92, sec. 1992-94 divsn. biol. chemistry, councilor 1996-2000), Biophys. Soc., Am. Soc. Biol. Chemists, N.Y. Acad. Scis. Achievements include development of theory on isotope effects applied to enzyme-catalyzed reactions and determination of enzyme mechanisms. Office: U Okla Dept Chemistry/Biochemistry 620 Parrington Oval Rm 208 Norman OK 73019-3050 Fax: 405-325-7182. E-mail: pcook@chemdept.chem.ou.dept.

COOK, PERRY RAYMOND, computer science educator; BA in Music, U. Mo., 1985, BSEE magna cum laude, 1986; MSEE, Stanford U., 1987, PhD in Elec. Engring., 1991. Cert. engr. in tng., Mo., 1986. Rsch. asst. Ctr. Computer Rsch. in Music and Acoustics, 1987—90, rsch. assoc., 1991—94, sr. rsch. assoc., tech. dir.; cons. Media Vision Inc., 1991—93, sr. rsch. scientist, 1993—94; acting dir. Ctr. Computer Rsch. in Music and Acoustics, 1995; assoc. prof. dept. computer sci. affil. with Princeton music dept. Princeton U., 1996—; dir. Princeton Computer Sci. indsl. affil.'s program, 1996—. Bd. dirs. Internat.Cmty. for Auditory Display; stage mgr. Forum Amphitheater Worlds of Fun, Kansas City, Mo., 1977—78; electronics technician 3M Electornic Bus. Equipment, Kansas City, Mo., 1978; sound technician Worlds/Oceans of Fun, Kansas City, 1978—83, audio cons., 1985. Singer, editor: A Stanford Christmas, 1994; singer (soloist, chorister with Calif. Bach.Soc.): Musica Barocca, 1994; editor, engr., singer varius recordings. Recipient U. Mo. Kansas City Alumni Achievement award in engring., 1992, Swets and Zeitlinger Disting. Paper award, ICMC, 1999; grant, AT&T Lucent Spl. Purpose Grants Program in Sci. and Engring., 1996, Hewlett Packard Philanthropy Program for Ednl. Instns., 1997, Intel Tech. for Edn. 2000 Grant, Princeton SEAS Dean's Grant for Grad. Course Devel., 1999, Career grant, NSF, 2000, grant, N.J. Commn. on Sci. and Tech., fellow, John Simon Guggenheim Meml. Found., 2003. Mem.: IEEE (program/chair signal processing application to audio and acoustics 2001, mem. Internal Conf. on Auditory Display 2000, Internat. Computer Music Conf. 1997, 1st Place Student Paper Competition 1986—87), Computer Music Assn., Acoustical Soc. Am., Assn. Computing Machinery, Internat. Computer Music Assn. (v.p. mem. 2000—), Eta Kappa Nu, Phi Kappa Phi,

Tau Beta Pi. Achievements include patents for Digital Waveguide Speech Synthesis Sys. and Method, 1996; Residual Excited Waveguide, 19967; Economical Generation of Exponential and Pseudo-Exponential Decay Functions in Digital Hardware, 1996; System and Method for Real Time Sinusoidal Signal Generation Using waveguide Resonance Oscillators, 1997; Music Synthesis Controller and Method, 2000. Office: Princeton U Dept Computer Sci 35 Olden St Princeton NJ 08544*

COOK, STANLEY JOSEPH, retired language educator; b. Spicer, Minn., June 9, 1935; s. William Joseph and Lillie Esther (Feeland) Cook; m. Janet Lucille Terry Cook, Oct. 9, 1964 (div. June 1988); children: John Hildon, Laurel Erin; m. Michaela Dianne Higuera, Dec. 18, 1989; 1 stepchild, Richard Scott. BA, U. Minn., 1957; MA, U. Utah, 1966, PhD, 1969. Project specialist in English U. Wis., Madison, 1967; instr. English U. Utah, Salt Lake City, 1968—69; prof. English and fgn. langs. Calif. State Poly. U., Pomona, 1969—. Fieldworker Dictionary of Am. Regional English, 1986—; cons. in field. Editor: Language and Human Behavior, 1973, Man Unwept: Visions from the Inner Eye, 1974; author (with others): The Scope of Grammar: A Study of Modern English, 1980, Cal Poly through 2001: A Continuing Commitment to Excellence, 1987. With res. USMC. Fellow, NDEA, 1969; grantee, NSF, 1966, Calif. State U. and Colls., 1973—74. Mem.: NEA, AAUP, SUBUD, Phi Beta Kappa. Democrat. Roman Catholic. Home: 1744 N Corona Ave Ontario CA 91764-1236

COOK, SUSAN FARWELL, associate director planned giving; b. Boston, Apr. 28, 1953; d. Benjamin and Beverly (Brooks) Conant; m. James Samuel Cook Jr., Aug. 17, 1985; children: Emily Farwell, David McKendree. AB, Colby Coll., 1975; MBA, Thomas Coll., 2002. Bank teller Boston 5 Cent Savs. Bank, 1975-76; asst. technician plan cost John Hancock Mut. Life Ins. Co., Boston, 1976-77, technician plan cost, 1977-78, sr. technician plan cost, 1978-79, asst. mgr. group pension plan cost, 1979-81; assoc. dir. alumni rels. Colby Coll., Waterville, Maine, 1981-86, dir. alumni rels., 1986-97, assoc. dir. planned giving, 1997—. Co-dir. adv. bd. women's studies Colby Coll., 1987-89, adv. women's group, 1987-89; bd. dirs. Maine Planned Giving Coun., 2001—, treas., 2002--. Bd. dirs., newsletter sec. Literacy Vols. Am., Waterville, 1986—89, 1991—92, v.p., 1995—97, pres., 1997—99; treas. Pitcher Pond Improvement Assn., 1988—95, Gagnon/100 Campaign, 1996, 1998; coach Waterville Area Youth Hockey Assn., 1997—2001; bd. dirs. Youth Hockey Assn., 2001—; treas. Gagnon for Senate, 2000, 2002; trustee Universalist-Unitarian Ch., Waterville, 2001—, v.p., 2003—; bd. dirs. Congress Lake Assns., Yarmouth, Maine, 1988—92, Waterville Youth Soccer Assn., 2001—, Kennebec Montessori Sch., 1999—2001; pres. Waterville Youth Soccer Assn., 2002—. Mem. AAUW (sec. Waterville br. 1989-91, pres. 1991-93, co-pres. 1993-95), Coun. Advancement and Support of Edn., CASE Dist. I (exec. bd. dirs. 1994-97, sec. 1996-97, nominating com. 1997-99). Avocations: skiing, sewing, golf. Home: 6 Pray Ave Waterville ME 04901-5339 Office: Colby Coll 4372 Mayflower Hl Waterville ME 04901-8843

COOK, TIMOTHY EDWIN, political science educator; b. Van Nuys, Calif., Aug. 16, 1954; s. Thomas Edwin and Audrey Eloise (Jackson) C. BA, Pomona Coll., 1976; PhD, U. Wis., 1982. Asst. prof. Williams Coll., Williamstown, Mass., 1981-88, assoc. prof., 1988-92, prof., 1992—94, chair dept. polit. sci., 1991-94, Fairleigh Dickinson Jr. prof., 1994—2002. Guest scholar Brookings Instn., Washington, 1984-85; vis. assoc. prof. in the Lombard chair Kennedy Sch. Govt., Harvard U., Cambridge, Mass., 1989-90; vis. prof. Yale U., New Haven, spring 1995, prof. of Man Comm. and Polit. Sci. in the Kevin P. Reilly, Sr. chair, Manship Sch. of Mass Comm., La. State Univ., 2002-. Author: Making Laws and Making News, 1989 (Benjamin Franklin award Am. Book Seller's Assn. 1990), Citizen, Candidate and the Media in a Presdl. Campaign, 1996, Don Eraber award, Am. Polit. Sci. Assn., 2003, Governing With The News, 1998. Grantee NSF, 1991. Mem. Am. Polit. Sci. Assn. (exec. coun., Congl. fellowship 1984-85), Lesbian and Gay Polit. Sci. Caucus (founding mem.). Avocation: classical music. Office: Manship Sch of Music Johnston Hall Baton Rouge LA 70806 E-mail: tec@lsu.edn.

COOK, VICTOR JOSEPH, JR., marketing educator, consultant; b. Durant, Okla., June 25, 1938; s. Victor Joseph and Athelene Ann (Arduser) C.; m. Linda Lee Potter, June 6, 1960 (div. 1971); children: Victor Joseph III, William Randall, Christopher Phelps; m. barbara Brainard, Dec. 29, 1989 (div. 1997). BA, Fla. State U., 1960; MS, La. State U., 1962; PhD, U. Mich., 1965. Rsch. assoc. Mktg. Sci. Inst., Phila., 1965-68; assoc. rsch. dir. Boston, 1968-69; asst. prof. U. Chgo., 1969-75; pres., dir. Mgmt. & Design, New Orleans, 1975-78; prof. Freeman Sch. Bus. Tulane U., 1978—. Pres. The Styjl Furniture, 1998—; cons. Ford Motor Co., Dearborn, Mich., 1964-67, IBM, N.Y.C., 1968-72, Sears, Roebuck & Co., Chgo., 1975-77, Internat. Computers Ltd., ICL, London, 1982-91, The DuPont Co., Wilmington, 1986—, The Bases Group, Cin., 1986-89. Author: Brand Policy Determination, 1967, Readings in Marketing Strategy, 1989; designer, patentee furniture, frameworks, 1976—. Mem. Am. Mktg. Assn., Am. Econ. Assn., Inst. for Ops. Rsch. and The Mgmt. Scis., Beta Gamma Sigma, Phi Beta Kappa. Republican. Office: Tulane U AB Freeman Sch Bus New Orleans LA 70118 E-mail: victor.cook@tulane.edu., vcook@thestyle.com.

COOK, WILLIE CHUNN, retired elementary school educator; b. Uriah, Ala., Feb. 3, 1935; d. Thompson Ann and Minnie Lee (Jay) Chunn; m. Clifford Thomas Cook, Feb. 3, 1974; children: Wendelin Martin Boothe, Melanie Martin. BS, Livingston U., 1956, MEd, 1972. Elem. tchr. Jefferson County Pub. Sch. System, Birmingham, Ala., 1956-58, Mobile County Pub. Sch. System, Mobile, Ala., 1958-60, Norfolk (Va.) City Pub. Sch. System, 1960-61, Mobile County Pub. Sch. System, 1961-66, Pinellas County Pub. Sch. System, Clearwater, Fla., 1966-73; mid. sch. sci. tchr. St. Bernard Pub. Sch. System, Chalmette, La., 1973-76; elem. tchr. Jefferson Parish Pub. Sch. System, Gretna, La., 1976-98, ret., 1998. Mem. system textbook adoption com. Pinellas County pub. Sch. System, Clearwater, 1970, Jefferson Parish Pub. Sch. System, Gretna, 1978-79; coordinating tchr. Yearly Sch. Sci. Fairs, Pinellas County, Fla., 1969-72, Jefferson Parish, La., 1981-92, yearly extended class field trips, Jefferson Parish, 1984-92; sponsor Jefferson Parish Nat. Acad. Games teams, 1981-85; workshop presenter. Treas. Caddo Presbytery Cumberland Presbyn. Women, Marshall, Tex., 1982-83; chmn. Faith Ch. Cumberland Presbyn. Women, Kenner, La., 1980; mem. Christian edn. com. Faith Cumberland Presbyn. Ch., Metairie, La., 1988—; com. on polit. effectiveness Jefferson Fedn. Tchrs., coun. mem. 1987-89, chmn. Ednl. Issues Com. 1987-89, mem. Govs. Edn. Adv. Com. 1987-88, lobbyist in state legis., Jefferosn Parish, and Baton Rouge, 1985-88. Mem. Am. Fedn. Tchrs., La. Fedn. Tchrs., Jefferson Fedn. Tchrs., Nat. Sci. Tchrs. Assn., La. Sci. Tchrs. Assn. Democrat. Avocations: travel, sewing, cooking, camping, reading. Home: 25 Trinidad Dr Kenner LA 70065-3112

COOKE, HERBERT BASIL SUTTON, geologist, educator; b. Johannesburg, Union of South Africa, Oct. 17, 1915; s. Herbert Sutton and Edith Mary (Sutton) C.; m. Dorothea Winifred Hughes, Oct. 23, 1943; children: Christopher, Patrick. BA, Cambridge (Eng.) U., 1936, MA, 1940; MSc, U. Witwatersrand, 1940, DSc, 1947, DSc (hon.), 1998; LLD (hon.), Dalhousie U., 1982. Geologist Central Mining & Investment Corp., Johannesburg, 1936-38; lectr. geology U. Witwatersrand, 1938-47, sr. lectr., 1953-57, reader, 1957-61; pvt. cons. geologist Johannesburg, 1947-53; assoc. prof. geology Dalhousie U., Halifax, N.S., Can., 1961-63, prof., dean arts and sci., 1963-68, Carnegie prof. geology, 1968-81, prof. emeritus, 1981—; geol. cons., 1981-89. Vis. lectr. Inst. Vertebrate Paleontology, Beijing, 1984, U. Calif., Berkeley, 1957-58; chmn. Bernard Price Inst. for Palaeontol. Rsch., Johannesburg, 1958-61. Co-author: (with G.N.G. Hamilton) Geology for South African Students, 1939, rev. edits., 1948, 54, 60, 65, Science in South Africa, 1949; editor: (with V.J. Maglio) Evolution of African Mammals, 1978; contbr. numerous articles to profl. jours. Served with S.African Air Force, 1941-45. Named Royal Soc. Nuffield Found. bursary, 1956-57; recipient Can. Centennial medal, 1967, Queen's Golden Jubilee medal, 2003. Fellow Royal Soc. South Africa (life), Geol. Soc. London, Royal Meteorol. Soc., Geol. Soc. Am., Geol. Soc. South Africa (du Toit Meml. lectr. 1957); mem. Can. Assn. for Physical Anthropology (hon. life), Palaentol. Soc. South Africa (hon. life), Soc. Africanist Archeologists (hon. life), South African Geog. Soc. (pres. 1949-50), Royal Commonwealth Soc. Mainland of B.C. (pres. 1985-91, hon. pres. 1991-94), South African Archaeol. Soc. (pres. 1950-51), South African Assn. for Advancement Sci. (v.p. 1959-60, sect. pres. 1952-54), N.S. Inst. Sci. (pres. 1967-68), Inst. for Study of Man in Africa (Raymond Dart lectr. 1983) Home: 2133 154th St White Rock BC Canada V4A 4S5

COOKE, SARA MULLIN GRAFF, daycare provider, kindergarten educator, medical assistant; b. Phila., Dec. 29, 1935; d. Charles Henry and Elizabeth (Mullin) Brandt Graff; m. Peter Fischer Cooke, June 29, 1963 (div. July 1994); children: Anna Cooke Smith, Peter Fischer Jr., Elizabeth Cooke Haskins, Sara Cooke Lowe; m. Laina Cooke Driscoll, Dec. 18, 1999. AA, Bennett Coll., 1955; BE in Child Edn., Westchester State Tchrs. Coll., 1956. Asst. to tchr. 1st grade The Woodlyn Sch., 1956-58; tchr. Sara Bircher's Kindergarten, Germantown, Pa., 1958-62, Chestnut Hill (Pa.) Acad., 1962-63, Tarleton Sch., Devon, Pa., 1963-64; with F.C.I. Mktg. Co-ordinators Inc., N.Y.C., New Canaan, Conn., 1980-86; fundraiser Children's Hosp., Phila., 1989-92, pres. women's com., 1987-88; coord., master of ednl. ceremonies Phila. Soc. for Preservation Landmarks, 1991-93; coord. Elderhostel Program Landmarks Soc., 1992-93. Pvt. day caretaker Spl. Care, Inc., 1988—; pvt. daycare and doctor's asst., 1994—. Bd. aux. Children's Hosp. Phila., 1970-76, women's bd., 1977—, pres., 1987-88; commonwealth bd. Med. Coll. Pa., 1984-99, Gimbel award com., 1994; alt. del. Rep. Nat. Conv., 1992; co-chmn. benefit St. Martin in the Field, London, 1997; vol. with parents of very sick children Connelly Family Resource Ctr./Children's Hosp. of Phila., 1999—, chmn., 2003; vol. Rep. Nat. Conv., 2000; press vol. Polit. Fest in Laura Bush Libr., 2000. Recipient Silver Cup award, Children's Hosp. Phila., 2002. Mem. Pa. Assn. Hosp. Auxs. (health rep.) Nat. Soc. Colonial Dames (garden com. 1988—), Ch. Women's Assn. (past pres.), Alumnae Assn. Madeira Sch. (class sec., class agt., Vol. Svc. award 1997), Phila. Cricket Club, Jr. League Garden Club (co-chmn. Daisy Day Children's Hosp. 2001). Republican. Episcopalian. Home and Office: 3421 Warden Dr Philadelphia PA 19129-1417

COOK-IOANNIDIS, LESLIE PAMELA, mathematician, educator; b. Kingston, Ont., Can., Aug. 23, 1946; came to U.S., 1956; m. George Ioannidis, Nov. 1972; children: Alexander, James. BA, U. Rochester, 1967; PhD, Cornell U., 1971. NATO postdoctoral fellow U. Utrecht, Netherlands, 1971-72; instr. and rsch. assoc. Cornell U., Ithaca, N.Y., 1972-73; asst. to assoc. prof. UCLA, 1973-83; assoc. prof. math. U. Del., Newark, 1983-89, prof. math., 1989—, interim chair dept. math., 1991-92, chair dept. math., 1992—2000, assoc. dean arts sci., 2000—01; editor-in-chief Soc. Indsl. Applied Math. Jour. Applied Math., 2002—. Co-author: Transonic Aerodynamics, 1986; editor: Transonic Aerodynamics: Problems in Asymptotic Theory, 1993; contbr. articles to profl. jours. NDEA fellow, 1967-70, NSF fellow, 1970-71, 87-88. Mem. Am. Phys. Soc., Assn. Women in Math., Soc. Rheology, Soc. for Indsl. and Applied Math. (coun. mem. 1984-86), Sigma Xi, Phi Beta Kappa, Phi Kappa Phi. Office: Univ Del Dept Math Newark DE 19716

COOKSON, LINDA MARIE, retired elementary education educator; b. Emporia, Kans., Feb. 15, 1944; d. Fred Rolum and Mary Lavern (Bennett) C. BS, Emporia State U., 1966, MS, 1970. Cert. tchr., Kans. Tchr. 2d grade Howard Wilson Sch., Leavenworth, Kans., 1966-67; tchr. 5th and intermediate Unified Sch. Dist. 253, Emporia, 1967-74; youth advisor Lyon County Youth Ctr., Emporia, summer 1975; lectr. in edn. Emporia State U., 1975-80; art tchr. K-8 Unified Sch. Dist. 251, Admire and Americus, Kans., 1980-81, art and title I tchr. K-8 Americus, 1981-82, tchr. 6th grade, 1982-84, art tchr. K-8, 1984-94, comms. tchr. mid. sch., 1994-99. Field editor Country Discoveries. Mem. PTO, 1980—; pres., life mem. PTA, 1966-80. Mem. NEA, Kans. Nat. Edn. Assn. (Sunflower Uniserv region 1 adminstrv. bd. 1995-99), Americus Site Based Coun. (sec. 1994-96). Republican. Methodist. Avocations: travel, photography, antiques. Home: 645 Wilson St Emporia KS 66801-2452

COOL, MARY L. education specialist; b. Buffalo, Dec. 7, 1954; d. Paul G. and Dorothy R. (O'Brien) Wailand; m. Ronald J. Cool, June 23, 1979; children: Logan Elizabeth, Colin Jeffery. BS in Elem. Edn. cum laude, SUNY, Fredonia, 1976; MS in Ednl. Leadership, Nova Southeastern U., 1996. Cert. tchr., N.Y., Fla. Tchr. grade 1, Buffalo, N.Y., 1976-77; tchr. grade 5 Orange County, Orlando, Fla., 1979-85; tchr. grade 1, ESEA Title I head tchr. Manatee County, Myakka City, Fla., 1977-79; tchr. grade 5, media specialist Volusia County, Osteen, Fla., 1985-89; intermediate resource tchr. S.W. Volusia County, Fla., 1989-91; dist. elem. resource tchr., elem. tchr. specialist Volusia County Schs., Fla., 1991-97, staff devel. specialist, 1997-98, sch. improvement coord., 1998—2002; sch. improvement coord. initiative implementation Charter Sch. Dist., 2002—, elem. edn. coord., 2003—. Grade level chair, sci. chair, reading chair, facilitative leader, coop. learning trainer, tchr. coach, tech. edn. coach, tchr. asst. coord., student success team coord., tchr. induction coord. Volusia County Schs.; ednl. cons. Scholastic, Inc., Sports Illus. for Kids, Kids Discover, Marvel Comics, Time for Kids, UNICEF, Miami Mus. Arts and Scis. Mem. ASCD, AAUW, Nat. Coalition for Sex Equity in Edn., Nat. Staff Devel. Coun., Fla. Coun. Elem. Edn., Kappa Delta Pi. Home: 1566 Gregory Dr Deltona FL 32738-6159 Office: PO Box 2410 Daytona Beach FL 32115-2410

COOLEY, FANNIE RICHARDSON, counselor, educator; b. Tunnel Springs, Ala., July 4, 1924; d. Willie C. Richardson and Emma Jean (McCorvey) Stallworth. BS, Tuskegee (Ala.) Inst., 1947, MS, 1951; PhD, U. Wis., 1969. Cert. counselor. Asst. inst. Tuskegee Inst., 1947-48, prof. counseling, 1969-2000, prof. emeritus, 2000—. Instr. Alcorn A&M Coll., Lorman, Miss., 1948-51; asst. prof. Ala. A&M Coll., Normal, 1951-62, assoc. prof., 1964-65; grad. fellow Purdue U., West Lafayette, Ind., 1962-64; house fellow U. Wis., Madison, 1965-69; cons. VA Med. Ctr. Tuskegee, 1969— . Mem. AAUW, AAUP, ASCD (bd. dirs., Disting. Svc. award 1985), Ala. Assn. Counseling and Devel. (pres. 1976-77, Svc. award 1978-79), Ala. Assn. for Counselor Edn. (pres. 1985-86), Aassn. Specialists in Group Work (pres. 1989-90, Career award 1998), Internat. Platford Assn., Chi Sigma Iota. Episcopalian. Home: 802-C Avenue A Tuskegee Institute AL 36088-2402 Office: Tuskegee Inst Dept Counseling and Student Devel Thrasher Hall Tuskegee Institute AL 36088

COOLEY-PARKER, SHEILA LEANNE, psychologist, consultant, educator; b. Oakland, Calif., July 25, 1956; d. Philips Theadore and Helen Ellene (Newbill) Cooley; m. Kenneth Louise Parker. BA, St. Leo Coll., 1979; MS, U. So. Miss., 1986; PhD, Miss. State U., 1990. Lic. psychologist Ky. Counselor Charter Counseling Ctr., Jackson, Miss., 1988—89; staff psychologist Rivendell Psychiat. Ctr., Bowling Green, Ky., 1989—90; program dir. MidSouth Hosp., Memphis, 1990—91; resource ctr. dir. MidSouth Resource Ctr., Ridgeland, Miss., 1991—92; partial hosp. dir. Pathways Partial Hospitalization, Ridgeland, 1991—92; edn. specialist, sr. position Miss. Dept. of Edn., Bur. Spl. Svcs., Jackson, Miss., 1993—94; psychologist Western State Hosp., Hopkinsville, Ky., 1994—99, Caring Connections, Hopkinsville, Ky., 1995; pvt. practice Hopkinsville, Ky., 1996—; chief psychology Ky. State Penitentiary, Eddyville, Ky., 1999—. Adj. prof. Hopkinsville C.C., 2001—, Murray State U., 2003—. Campaign organizer Dem. Mayor, Jackson, Miss., 1992. Mem.: APA, Ky. Psychol. Assn., Theta Pi Sigma, Psi Chi, Phi Delta Kappa. Baptist. Home: 4081 Singletree Dr Hopkinsville KY 42240-9191 Office: PO Box 5128 Eddyville KY 42038-5128

COOMBER, JAMES ELWOOD, English language educator; b. Freeport, Ill., Jan. 17, 1942; s. Elwood Lowell and Vi Anna Margaret (Schoonhoven) C.; m. Eleanor Ruth McKinnon, June 11, 1966; children: Sarah Ellen Suomala Coomber, Matthew James. BS, U. Wis., Platteville, 1964; MA, U. Wis., Madison, 1966, PhD, 1972; student, U. Ariz., 1989, student, 2003. Prof. English Concordia Coll., Moorhead, Minn., 1966—, chair dept. English, 1984—88, 1996—2001. Vis. prof. U. Calgary, Alta., Can., 1979, 81; adj. faculty Hamline U., St. Paul, 1982-98, ND State U., Fargo, 1972—; faculty mem. Prairie Writing Project, Moorhead, 1977-82; dir. Concordia Conf. on Reading and Writing, 1983-99; cons. to pub. sch., Minn., N.D. Co-author: The English Book, 1981, Macmillan Spelling, 1983, Vocabulary for College Reading and Writing, 1984, Words for Success, 1996, Magnificent Chruches on the Prairie: A Story of Immigrant Priests, Builders and Homesteaders, 1997, Teaching Vocabulary: An Internet Course for Teachers, 1998, Wordskills, 1990, 2000, Unwanted Bread: The Struggle of Farmers and Ranchers in North Dakota, 2000, Spelling for Writing: Instructional Strategies, 2001; contbr. articles to profl. jours. Active Bread for the World, Washington, 1988—. Nat. Teaching fellow U.S. Dept. Edn., 1969. Mem. Sierra Club. Democrat. Episcopalian. Avocations: canoeing, hiking, gardening, reading. Office: Concordia Coll Dept Of English Moorhead MN 56562-0001

COOMBS, CASSANDRA RUNYON, geologist, educator; b. Elmira, N.Y., Jan. 19, 1960; d. John Marquis and Dorothy Jane (Hessenius) Runyon; m. Gregory Alton Coombs, June 21, 1985; children: Zoe, Zachary, Zane. AS, Corning (N.Y.) C.C., 1980; BS, SUNY, Fredonia, 1982; MS, So. Ill. U., Carbondale, 1984; PhD, U. Hawaii, 1989. Grad. rsch. asst. So. Ill. U., Carbondale, 1982-84, U. Hawaii, Honolulu, 1985-89; postdoctoral rsch. fellow NRC/NASA Johnson Space Ctr., Houston, 1989-91; staff scientist, program mgr. POD Assocs., Inc., Albuquerque, 1991-93; rsch. asoc. U. Hawaii, Honolulu, 1993-95; asst. prof. Coll. Charleston, S.C., 1995—. Coord. NEAR-C, Albuquerque, 1992-93; mem. NASA adv. bd., Washington, 1992—; cons. Enrichment in Sci. Program, Honolulu, 1987-89; campus dir. NASA Space Grant Consortium, 1995—; summer faculty fellow NASA Johnson Space Ctr., 1995, 96. Author rsch. papers and rev. articles. Harold T. Stearns fellow U. Hawaii, 1989, Mary Manhoff Meml. Sci. Fund scholar, 1987; named Disting. Alumni Corning C.C., 1995. Mem. Geol. Soc. Am. (sec. 1993—), Assn. for Women Geoscientists, Am. Geophys. Union, Am. Assn. Petroleum Geologists, N.Mex. Hazardous Waste Soc. Avocations: swimming, hiking, volleyball, canoeing, camping. Home: 1948 Falling Creek Cir Mount Pleasant SC 29464-7417 Office: Dept of Geology College of Charleston 66 George St Charleston SC 29424-1407

COOMBS, VANESSA MOODY, journalism educator, lawyer; b. Petersburg, Va., May 2, 1955; d. Theodore Washington Moody and Doretha Winifred (Edwards) Moody Raines; m. Cyril Francis Coombs, Mar. 14, 1992; 1 child, Taylor Lindsey. BA, Hampton U., 1977; MA, U. Mich., 1978; JD, Georgetown U., 1983. Bar: D.C., 1983. Reporter, rschr. Money Mag., N.Y.C., 1979-80; comm. atty Schwartz, Woods & Miller, Washington, D.C., 1982-84; gen. assignment reporter WSET-TV, Lynchburg, Roanoke, Va., 1984-85, WGHP-TV, High Point, Greensboro, N.C., 1985-86, WKRN-TV, Nashville, Tenn., 1986-87; reporter, anchor WTVT-TV, Tampa, Fla., 1987-89; nat. correspondent Inside Edition, N.Y.C., 1989-91; gen. assignment reporter WDIV-TV, Detroit, 1991-92; chair and assoc. prof. dept. mass media arts Hampton (Va.) U., 1992—. Bd. dirs. Black Coll. Comm. Assn. Grantee: Freedom Forum, 1993, 95. Mem. Assn. for Edn. in Journalism and Mass Comm. (task force on alliances 1993, 96), Assn. of Schs. Journalism and Mass Comm., (secondary edn. com. 1995, 96). Office: Hampton U Dept Mass Media Arts Hampton VA 23668

COON, THOMAS GARY, alcohol and substance abuse counselor; b. Schenectady, N.Y., Oct. 23, 1957; s. Gary Martin and Lois Mae (Singleton) C. AS, Am. Acad. Dramatic Arts, 1980. Aide to pvt. family, N.Y.C., 1977-78; dir. childrens theatre Town of Colonie Recreation, Latham, N.Y., 1978-80; child care worker Northampton (Mass.) Ctr. for Children and Families, 1987-88, Berkshire Farms, Ctr. for Youth, Canaan, N.Y., 1988-90. Substance abuse counselor Crossroads Drug & Alcohol Awareness Program for Teenage Boys, Canaan, 1989—. Food coord. for participants Jerry Lewis Telethon, N.Y.C., 1982; fellow mem. Matt Talbot Group 20, 1990—, North Shore Animal League, 1990—, Legionaries of Christ, 1991—. Republican. Avocations: animals, children, sports, writing about americans and equality. Address: PO Box 63 Canaan NY 12029-0063

COONROD, DELBERTA HOLLAWAY (DEBBIE COONROD), retired elementary education educator, consultant, freelance writer; b. Eldon, Mo., Oct. 21, 1937; d. Delbert Leland and Zealoth (Stevens) Hollaway; m. Charles Ralph Coonrod, Aug. 26, 1961; children: Charles Leland, Marcia Renee. BS in Edn., U. Kans., 1961; MS in Edn., Ind. U., 1972, EdD in Edn., 1977; postgrad., U. Tex., Tex. Women's U. Cert. elem. tchr., Kans. Classroom tchr. Hood Sch. & Heizer Elem., Barton County, Kans., 1957-60, Emporia (Kans.) Pub. Schs., 1961-62, Lincoln (Nebr.) Pub. Schs., 1964-66, South Bend (Ind.) Sch. Corp., 1967-72; assoc. instr., vis. asst. prof. Ind. U., Bloomington, 1972-79; asst. prof. Ind. State U., Terre Haute, 1975-76; pres. Debcon, Inc., Bloomington, 1979-81; pvt. practice cons. Bloomington, 1981-85; classroom tchr. Ft. Worth Ind. Sch. Dist., 1985—2001; assoc. prof., dir. tchr. edn. Culver-Stockton Coll., Canton, Mo., 2001—02; ret., 2002. Cons. Ft. Hays State U., Kans., 1990, Edison Cmty. Coll., Piqua, Ohio, 1994; instr. Tarrant County (Tex.) Jr. Coll., 1992-94; adj. asst. prof. Tex. Woman's U., Denton, 1987-2000; adj. prof. Tex. Christian U., Ft. Worth, 1991-92; adminstrv. project dir. Monroe County Sch. Corp., Bloomington, 1983-85; instr. Weatherford Coll., 1996-97; kindergarten cons. Penn-Harris-Madison Sch. Corp., Mishawaka, Ind., 1970-71; head adminstr. Hoosier Cts. Nursery Sch., Ind. U., 1978-79; nat. approved trainer Head Start, 1982-85; chair emeritus Who's Who in Am. Edn. adv. bd.; mem. FWISD Dist. adv. com., 1996-98. Contbr. articles to profl. jours. Bd. dirs. 4C's of Monroe County, 1979—85; mem. Greater Ft. Worth Lit. Coun., 1990—99; mem. Hist. Commn. City of Bedford, Tex., 1993—97; chmn. early literacy com. Tex. State Reading Assn., 1993—96; com. co-chair Campaign for Children, 1st Tex. coun. Camp Fire, 1992—94; educator Ft. Worth Sister Cities, 1991—2001; Harashin Educator scholar Nagaoka, Japan, 1992; bd. dirs. Ft. Worth Assn. Edn. Young Children, 1986—87; chmn. spkrs. bur. Ind. Gov.'s Com. for Internat. Yr. of the Child, 1979—80; mem. Shelby County Outreach and Ext. Coun. U. Mo., 2003—; others. Recipient Excellence in English Edn. award Tex. Joint Coun. Tchrs. English, 1990, Ethel M. Leach award Tex. Woman's U., 1990, Outstanding Tchr. award Fort Worth Bus. Cmty./Adopt-A-Sch. Adv. Com., 1991; named Woman of Yr., Monroe County (Ind.) Girls Club, 1985, Yellow Rose of Tex., 1989, Dillard Tchr. of Week, 1992-93; named to Hon. Order Ky. Cols., 1987; Joe E. Mitchell Disting. Educator honoree Tex. Wesleyan U., 1991; honored Tex. Edn. Agy. Early Childhood Promising Practices (inclusion model), 1993-94, NYL Care Health Plans Chair for Tchg. Excellence in Early Childhood Edn., 1997-98. Mem. Ind. Assn. Edn. Young Children (bd. dirs. 1974-80, pres. 1979-80), Pi Lambda Theta (nat. v.p. 1985-89, pres. 1982-84, pres. Great Lakes Region II 1993-97, internat. 1st v.p. 2003—, Greater Ft. Worth area chpt. Internat. Recognition award region VII Outstanding Pi Lambda Thetan 1992, pub. adv. bd. 1995-97, Edn. Endowment bd. 1996-2002), Delta Theta Tau, Delta Kappa Gamma. Republican. Baptist. Avocations: poetry, piano, photography, public speaking. Home: 1362 J Spur Bethel MO 63434-2312

COONS, RONALD EDWARD, historian, educator; b. Elmhurst, Ill., July 24, 1936; s. William A. and Madeline Louise (Theisen) C. BA, DePauw U., Greencastle, Ind., 1958; A.M., Harvard U., 1959, PhD, 1966. Teaching fellow history Harvard U., 1961-62, 63-66; research fellow Inst. Europäische Geschichte, Mainz, Germany, 1962-63; mem. faculty U. Conn., Storrs, 1966—2002, prof. history, 1979—2002, prof. emeritus, 2002—, dir. grad. studies, dept. history, 1983-87, 90-98, assoc. chmn., 1993—94,

2000—02, interim chmn., summer 1994. Author: Steamships, Statesmen and Bureaucrats: Austrian Policy Towards the Steam Navigation Company of the Austrian Lloyd, 1836-1848, 1975, I primi anni del Lloyd Austriaco, 1983; editor: Over Land and Sea. Memoir of an Austrian Rear Admiral's Life in Europe and Africa, 1857-1909 (Ludwig Ritter von Höhnel), 2000; mem. editl. bd. Austrian History Yearbook, 1992-94, 96-97, mem. adv. bd., 1994-96, also articles and revs. Mem. exec. com. St. Mark's Episcopal Ch., Storrs, 1976-82, 83-85, asst. organist, 1980-87; mem. exec. com. U. Conn. Friends of Soccer, 1989-98, v.p., 1993-95, pres. 1995-97; mem. exec. com. New Eng. Hosta Soc., 1989-92; co-chair interim com. St. Paul's Episcopal Ch., Willimantic, 1998-2001, mem. vestry, 2001—, archivist, 2003—. Nat. Endowment Humanities summer fellow, 1969; Am. Council Learned Socs. grantee, 1974, Am. Philos. Soc. grantee, 1974; NIH grantee, 1979; Gladys K. Delmas Found. grantee, 1983-84; Am. Council Learned Socs. grantee, 1985 Mem. AAUP, Am. Hist. Assn., Conf. Group Cen. European History, German Studies Assn., Soc. for Austrian and Habsburg History (exec. com. 1992-97, exec. sec. 1994-96), New Eng. Hist. Assn., Vienna Hist. Soc., Conn. Acad. Arts and Scis., Conn. Hort. Soc., Phi Beta Kappa (chpt. sec. 1976-86, v.p. 1987-88, 99-2000, pres. 1988-89, 2000-2001), Phi Alpha Theta, Phi Mu Alpha. Democrat. Office: U Conn Dept History 241 Glenbrook Rd Storrs Mansfield CT 06269-2103 Home: 1 Gin Still Ln West Hartford CT 06107-2647 E-mail: recoons@hotmail.com.

COONTS, JANET RODMAN, education educator; b. Salem, Oreg., Feb. 17, 1942; d. Bruce E. Rodman and Margaret Louise (Mansfield) Samsel; m. Douglas M. Smith, Sept. 5, 1964 (div. Sept. 1986); 1 child, Christopher; m. Thomas E. Coonts, July 17, 1987. BA, Lewis and Clark Coll., Portland Oreg., 1960; postgrad., Ea. Wash. U., 1984—87. Cert. secondary edn. tchr., Idaho, Wash. G.E.D. instr. Columbia Basin Coll., 1978-86; tchr. English, chmn. dept. Kimberly (Idaho) H.S., 1987—. Recipient Tchr. of Yr. award U. Idaho, 1990, 93. Mem. Nat. Coun. Tchrs. English, Idaho Coun. Tchrs. English (bd. dirs. 1994). Republican. Avocations: running, reading, landscaping, antiques. Home: PO Box 125 Kimberly ID 83341-0125 E-mail: jtcoon@iglide.net.

COOPER, ANGELA B. elementary education educator; b. Pitts., May 30, 1955; d. Elio Joseph and Angeline Rose (Manzione) B. AA, C.C. Allegheny County, 1975; BS, California U. Pa., 1977, postgrad., 1984. Cert. tchr., Pa. Tchr. Clairton (Pa.) Edn. Ctr., 1978—; assoc. in data capture Mellon Bank, Pitts., 1992—. Mem. NEA, Pa. State Edn. Assn., Clairton Edn. Assn. (exec. bd. 1991—), Internat. Reading Assn., Kappa Delta Phi. Democrat. Roman Catholic. Avocation: reading. Home: 1410 Bailey Ave Mc Keesport PA 15132-4605 Office: Clairton Edn Ctr 501 Waddell Ave Clairton PA 15025-1559 E-mail: abcoop@comcast.net.

COOPER, CAROLINE ANN, hospitality faculty dean; b. Gardner, Mass., Oct. 16, 1943; d. Frank D. and Florence M. (O'Neil) Toohey; m. Paul Geoffrey Cooper, Apr. 16, 1972; children: Geoffrey Paul, Heather Ann. BS, Russell Sage Coll., 1966; MBA, Bryant Coll., 1983; EdD, U. Mass., Boston, 2002. Adminstrv. dietitian Mass. Gen. Hosp., Boston, 1967-68; with rsch., devel., mktg. Mkt. Forge Co., Everett, Mass., 1968-71; food svc. administr. Jane Brown R.I. Hosp., Providence, 1971-74; self-employed pres., cons. pvt. practice, Attleboro, Mass.; from instr. to assoc. prof. Johnson & Wales U., Providence, 1978-86, acad. coord., 1984-86, dept. chair HRI, Hospitality, Food Svc. mgmt. and tourism, 1986-91; asst. dean Hospitality Coll., Providence, 1991-94, dean, 1995—2001; exec. dir. bus. and hospitality rels., 2001—. Del. White House Conf. on Travel and Tourism, 1995, mem. implementation team, 1995-96; mem. adv. bd. Ednl. Found. of the Nat. Restaurant Assn., 1998—; mem. bd. advisors Acad. Travel and Tourism, 1997—; mem. product evaluation panel Restaurant Instn., 2000—; trustee Am. Hotel Found., 1998-2000, Am. Hotel Ednl. Found., 2002-, Coun. on Hotel, Restaurant and Instnl. Edn. Vol. Parent Orgn. for Sch., 1978-91, Pub. Sch. System, 1981-84, Cmty. Sports Program, 1989-95. Recipient Hon. Doctorate medallion N.Am. Foodsvc. Assn. Mfrs.; named Pacesetter Nat. Roundtable for Women, 1989. Mem. Am. Dietetic Assn., Am. Hotel Motel Assn. (trustee Ednl. Inst. 1990—, nominating com. 1996-99, chmn. 1999, exec. com. 1998-2000, chmn. certification commn., 1998—, Outstanding Educator 1990), Am. Hotel and Motel Industry, Computer Application Food Svc. Edn. (pres. 1987-89), Internat. Coun. on Hotel Restaurant Inst. Edn. (bd. dirs., pres. N.E. chpt. 1992-93, pres. 1994-95, chmn. bd. 1995-96), R.I. Hospitality and Tourism Assn. (bd. dirs. 1996—, treas. 1998—). Office: Johnson and Wales U Abbott Park Pl Providence RI 02903

COOPER, CHARLEEN FRANCES, special and elementary education educator; b. Jamaica, N.Y., Oct. 23, 1948; d. Charles and Dolly (Oakes) Fells; m. Chris M. Cooper, June 23, 1969 (div.); children: Chris A., Scott F. BS in Spl. Edn. cum laude, Coll. of St. Joseph, Rutland, Vt., 1985; postgrad., The Provider; MA in Edn., Castleton State Coll., 1994. Cert. spl. and elem. edn. tchr., Vt.; cert. learning specialist/consulting tchr. spl. edn. Spl. edn. and resource rm. tchr. Rutland City Pub. Sch., 1985-88; tchr. spl. edn., multi-handicapped Rutland Cen. Supervisory Union, 1988-91; spl. edn. and resource rm. tchr. Addison-Rutland Supervisory Union, 1991-92; mktg. instr. Stafford Tech. Ctr., Rutland City Pub. Schs., 1992-93; vocat. rehab. employment facilitator State of Vt., 1995-96; chpt. 1 title 1 head instr. Bennington Sch., Inc., 1996-97; title 1 head instr. Catamount Elem., Bennington, Vt., 1997—2002, resource rm. tchr., 1998; tchr. resource rm. Poultney Elem. Sch., Poultney, Vt., 2002—. Coord. program, instr. Integration of Proctor High Sch. Students with Spl. Needs, 1989-91. Coll. of St. Joseph scholar. Avocations: gardening, motorcycling, flying. Home: PO Box 40 North Clarendon VT 05759-0040 Office: Pooultney Elem Sch Circle Poultney VT

COOPER, EDWARD HAYES, lawyer, educator; b. Highland Park, Mich., Oct. 13, 1941; s. Frank Edward and Margaret Ellen (Hayes) C.; m. Nancy Carol Wybo, June 29, 1963; children: Lisa, Chandra. AB, Dartmouth Coll., 1961; LL.B., Harvard U., 1964. Bar: Mich. 1965. Law clk. Hon. Clifford O'Sullivan, U.S. Ct. of Appeals, 1964-65; practice law, Detroit, 1965-67; adj. prof. Wayne State U. Law Sch., 1965-67; assoc. prof. U. Minn. Law Sch., 1967-72; prof. law U. Mich. Law Sch., Ann Arbor, 1972-88, assoc. dean for acad. affairs, 1981-94; Thomas M. Cooley prof. of law, 1988—. Advisor Restatement of the Law, 2d Judgments, 1976-80, Complex Litigation Project, Restatement of the Law, 3d Torts-Apportionment, Fed. Jud. Code Project, Transnational Procedure Project, Internat. Jurisdiction Judgment; reporter fed. state jurisdiction com. Jud. Conf. U.S., 1985-91; mem. civil rules adv. com., 1991-92, reporter, 1992—; reporter Uniform Transfer of Litigation Act, 1989-91. Author: (with C.A. Wright and A.R. Miller) Federal Practice and Procedure: Jurisdiction, Vols. 13-19, 1975-81, 2d edit., 1984-2002, 3d edit., 1999—; contbr. articles to law revs. Mem. ABA, Mich. Bar Assn., Am. Law Inst. (council). Office: U Mich 330 Hutchins Law Sch Ann Arbor MI 48109-1215 E-mail: coopere@umich.edu.

COOPER, EDWARD SAWYER, cardiologist, internist, educator; b. Columbia, S.C., Dec. 11, 1926; s. Henry Howard and Ada Crosland (Sawyer) Cooper; m. Jean Marie Wilder, Dec. 2, 1951; children: Lisa Marie Cooper Hudgins, Edward Sawyer Jr.(dec.), Jan Ada, Charles Wilder. AB, Lincoln U., Pa., 1946; MD, Meharry Med. Coll., Nashville, 1949; MS (hon.), U. Pa., 1972. Diplomate Nat. Bd. Med. Examiners, Am. Bd. Internal Medicine. Intern Phila. Gen. Hosp., 1949-51, resident in medicine, 1951-54, NIH fellow in cardiology, 1956-57, pres. med. staff, 1969-71, co-dir. Stroke Rsch. Ctr., 1968-74, chief med. svc., 1973-76; prof. emeritus medicine U. Pa., Phila., 1996—. Bd. dirs. Independence Blue Cross. Trustee Am. Found. Negro Affairs, 1969—, Rockefeller U., 1992—. Served to capt. USAF, 1954—56. Master: ACP; fellow: Phila. Coll. Physicians (coun.); mem.: Am. Heart Assn. (chmn., bd. dirs., past nat. pres.), Alpha Omega Alpha. Democrat. Methodist. Achievements include research in stroke and hypertension. Home: 6710 Lincoln Dr Philadelphia PA 19119-3155 Office: University of Pa Hosp 3400 Spruce St Philadelphia PA 19104-4206 E-mail: ecoopmdphila@aol.com.

COOPER, EUGENE BRUCE, speech, language pathologist, educator; b. Utica, N.Y., Dec. 20, 1933; s. Clements Everett and Beulah (Wetzel) C.; m. Crystal Silverman, Sept. 12, 1965; children: Philip Adam, Ivan Bruce. BS, SUNY, Geneseo, 1955; MEd, Pa. State U., 1957, DEd, 1962. Pathologist speech and lang. Franklin County Schs., Chambersburg, Pa., 1957-59; asst. prof. Ohio U., 1962-64, Pa. State U., 1964-66; program specialist U.S. Office Edn., 1966; exec. sec. sensory study sect., rsch. and demonstrations Rehab. Services Adminstrn., HEW, Washington, 1966-67; faculty U. Ala., Tuscaloosa, 1967-96, prof. speech-lang. pathology, 1969-96, chmn. dept. communicative disorders, dir. Speech and Hearing Ctr., 1967-96, prof., chair emeritus, 1996—; Disting. prof. comm. scis. and disorders Nova Southeastern U., 1997—. Chmn. Ala. Bd. Examiners Speech Pathology and Audiology, 1979; cons.-at-large Nat. Student Speech-Lang.-Hearing Assn., 1983-88. Author: Personalized Fluency Control Therapy, 1976, Understanding Stuttering: Information for Parents, 1979, revised edit., 1990; (with Crystal Cooper) The Cooper Personalized Fluency Control Therapy Program, 1985, 2d edit., 2003, Cooper Assessment for Stuttering Syndromes, 1995; contbr. articles to profl. jours. Fellow Am. Speech, Lang. and Hearing Assn. (legis. coun. 1971-72, 85-97), Divsn. Fluency and Fluency Disorders (steering com. 1993-99, divsn. coord. 1994-99), Am. Speech, Lang. and Hearing Found. (chmn. adv. and devel. bd. 1988-89, trustee 1989-94); mem. Coun. Exceptional Children (pres. divsn. children comm. disorders 1975-76), Nat. Coun. Grad. Programs in Speech, Lang. Pathology and Audiology (pres. 1978-80), Nat. Coun. State Bds. Examiners Speech-Lang. Pathology and Audiology (pres. 1980, 91, mem. exec. bd. 1988-91), Nat. Coun. Comm. Disorders (chmn. 1982), Nat. Alliance Prevention and Treatment on Stuttering (pres. 1985-86), Internat. Fluency Assn. (bd. dirs. 1991-96, pres. 2d world congress on fluency disorders 1997, chmn. specialty commn. on fluency disorders 1997-99).

COOPER, IVA JEAN, special education educator; b. Newark, Mar. 6, 1950; d. William Brady McClintock and Aleata Margaret Locke-McClintock; m. Jeffrey Lamont Cooper, Oct. 18, 1986; children: Brianna, Jasmine. BS Comms., Howard U., 1973; MA Comms., Mich. State U., 1976. Intern Crippled Children's Soc., Hollywood, Calif., 1979—80; speech & lang. therapist pediats. Sierra Permanente Med. Grp., Fontana, Calif., 1980—81; supr. speech & lang. pathology Head Start Devel. Coun., Stockton, Calif., 1981; spl. edn. educator Manteca Unified Sch. Dist., Calif., 1981—. Mem.: Internat. Soc. Poets, AAUW, Am. Speech Hearing & Lang. Assn. Home: 1928 W Bristol Ave Stockton CA 95204

COOPER, JACK ROSS, pharmacology educator, researcher; b. Ottawa, Ont., Can., July 26, 1924; came to U.S., 1948; s. Harry and Jean (Levine) C.; m. Helen Achbar, Aug. 14, 1951; children: Marilyn, Sheila, Nancy. BA, Queen's U. Kingston, Ont., 1948; MA, George Washington U., 1952, PhD, 1954; MA (hon.), Yale U., 1971. Instr. Yale U., New Haven, 1956—58, asst. prof. pharmacology, 1958—63, assoc. prof., 1963-71, prof., 1971—. Author: The Biochemical Basis of Neuropharmacology, 8th edit., 2003. Served with RCAF, 1944. Smith, Kline and French rsch. fellow, 1950-52; USPHS predoctoral fellow, 1952-54; postdoctoral fellow USPHS, 1954-56; spl. fellow USPHS, London, 1965-66. Mem. Am. Soc. Neurochemistry, Internat. Soc. Neurochemistry, Am. Soc. Pharmacology and Exptl. Therapeutics, Soc. Neurosci. Democrat. Jewish. Home: 11 Jenick Ln Woodbridge CT 06525-1935 Office: Yale U Sch Medicine 333 Cedar St New Haven CT 06510-3289

COOPER, JAMES MICHAEL, education educator; b. Steubenville, Ohio, July 29, 1939; s. James Stanley and Regina Marie (Coen) C.; m. Susan Callaway, Sept. 1, 1962 (div. June 1978); children: Jeffrey, Craig, Cynthia; m. Shamim Sisson, June 13, 1987. AB in History with distinction, Stanford U., 1961, AM in Edn., 1962, AM in History, 1966, PhD in Edn., 1967. Tchr. Jordan Jr. High Sch. of Palo Alto (Calif.) Unified Sch. Sys., 1961-63, Palo Alto High Sch., 1963-65; lectr. Stanford U. Sch. Edn., 1967; asst. prof. edn. U. Mass., Amherst, 1968-71; assoc. prof. U. Houston, 1971-74, prof., 1974-84; Commonwealth prof. U. Va. Curry Sch. Edn., Charlottesville, 1984—, dean, 1984-94. Chmn. U. Houston faculty senate, 1982; mem. exec. bd. dirs. Holmes Group, East Lansing, Mich., 1985-94; mem. unit accreditation bd. Nat. Coun. Accreditation of Tchr. Edn., Washington, 1986-90. Co-author: Those Who Can, Teach, 9th edit., 2001; editor: Developing Skills for Instructional Supervision, 1984, Classroom Teaching Skills, 7th rev. edit., 2003; co-editor: Kaleidoscope: Readings in Education, 10th edit., 2001. Recipient Florence B. Stratemeyer award Assn. for Student Teaching, Washington, 1967, Fulbright-Hays award Portugal Coun. Internat. Exch. Scholars, Washington, 1980, Outstanding Leader in Tchr. Edn. award Assn. Tchr. Educators, 1990. Mem.: ASCD, Raven Soc. (The Raven award 2001), Am. Assn. Colls. for Tchr. Edn. (bd. dirs. 1990—93), Am. Ednl. Rsch. Assn., Omicron Delta Kappa, Phi Delta Kappa. Democrat. Roman Catholic. Avocations: golf, traveling.

COOPER, JANELLE LUNETTE, neurologist, educator; b. Ann Arbor, Mich., Dec. 11, 1955; d. Robert Marion and Madelyn (Leonard) C.; children: Lena Christine, Nicholas Dominic. BA in Chemistry, Reed Coll., 1978; MD, Vanderbilt U., 1986. Diplomate Nat. Bd. Med. Examiners; diplomate in neurology Am. Bd. Psychiatry and Neurology; registered med. technologist Am. Soc. Clin. Pathologists. Med. technologist Swedish Hosp. Med. Ctr., Seattle, 1978-80, U. Wash. Clin. Chemistry, Seattle, 1980-82, Vanderbilt U. Hosp., Nashville, 1983-84; intern medicine Vanderbilt U. Med. Ctr., Nashville, 1986-87, resident neurology, 1987-90; instr. neurology Med. Coll. Pa., Phila., 1990-91, asst. prof., clerkship dir., 1991—, mem. curriculum com., 1990-91, vis. asst. prof., 1991-95; neurologist Greater Ann Arbor Neurology Assocs., 1991-93; dir. neurol. svcs., med. dir. Indsl. Rehab. Program St. Francis Hosp., Escanaba, Mich., 1993-98; founder, dir. No. Neuroscis., Escanaba, 1993-98; pres. HolderLady, Ltd., 1996—; chmn. dept. medicine St. Francis Hosp., Escanaba, Mich., 1998-99; dir. Affinity Health Sys., Oshkosh, Wis., 1998—; med. dir. Memory Clinic of the Upper Peninsula, Escanaba, Mich., 1998—. Neurologist Affinity Med. Group, Oshkosh, Wis., 1998—; physician MCP Neurology Assocs., Phila., 1990-91; emergency rm. physician Tenn. Christian Med. Ctr., 1989-90. Contbr. articles to Annals of Ophthalmology, Ophthalmic Surgery. Vol. Rape and Sexual Abuse Ctr., Nashville, 1988-90; mem. adminstrv. bd. Edgehill United Meth. Ch., Nashville, 1989-90; mem. editorial bd. Nashville Women's Alliance, 1989-90; bd. dirs. Upper Peninsula Physicians Network, 1995-98; mem. adv. bd. Perspective Adult Daycare Ctr., 1996-99; founding dir. Memory Clinic of Upper Peninsula, 1998-00; profl. adv. com. NE Wis. Alzheimer's Assn., 1999—. Recipient Svc. award for outstanding contbns. Rape and Sexual Abuse Ctr., 1990; epilepsy minifellow Bowman Gray U., 1995. Mem. AMA (physician's Recognition award 1989—), AAAS, Am. Med. Women's Assn., Am. Acad. Neurology, Am. Psychol. Soc., Wis. State Med. Soc., N.Y. Acad. Scis., Upper Peninsula Neuro Assn. (v.p. 1998-99, trustee 1998-99), Upper Peninsula Physician Network (bd. dirs. 1995-98), Aircraft Owners and Pilots Assn., Women in Aviation Internat. (charter), Air Force Assn. (life patron). Methodist. Achievements include first synthesis of Difluoromethanedisulfonic Acid; research on neurobehavioral disorders; on neuroendocrinology of sexual development, identity and orientation; on the history of women in medicine on effects of dietary lipids on the etiology of Alzheimer's disease; clinical investigation trials for new medications for dementias and epilepsy. Home: 108 Country Club Ln Oshkosh WI 54902-7459 Office: Affinity Med Group Dept Neurology 2725 Jackson St Oshkosh WI 54901-1513 E-mail: jcooper@affinityhealth.org.

COOPER, JO MARIE, elementary school principal; b. L.A., Oct. 13, 1947; d. Joseph M. Langham and Christina (Burton) Lister; m. Leonard Cooper Jr., May 13, 1967; children: Leonard Joseph, Jo-Lynne Louise, Layton Bishop. Grad., Chgo. State Coll., 1967; MA, Governor State U., University Park, Ill., 1975; MA in Ednl. Adminstrn., Gov. State U., University Park, Ill., 1997. Postal worker, mail handler Chgo. Post Office, 1966-67; tchr. Chgo. Bd. Edn., 1968-75, resource tchr., 1975-93, instrnl. adminstrv. asst., 1993—, dean of girls; interim prin. Oglesby Elem. Sch., 1998, prin., 1998—. Advisor Homewood (Ill.) Full Gospel Ch., 1992-94, Homewood Christian Acad., 1994—. Pres. South Ctrl. Women's Aglow, Chgo., 1983-85; chair women's ministries Homewood Full Gospel Ch., 1990-94; South Chicago area leader Marriage Ministries Internat., University Park, 1994—; advisor Human Rels. Commn., University Park, 1987-89. Mem. ASCD. Pentecostal. Avocations: reading, walking, hooklatching, bowling. Office: Oglesby Elem Sch 7646 S Green St Chicago IL 60620-2854

COOPER, JOHN MADISON, philosophy educator; b. Memphis, Nov. 29, 1939; s. Marion Armon and Bernardine (Sheehan) C.; m. Marcia Louise Coleman, Aug. 21, 1965; children: Stephanie Coleman, Katherine Alexander. AB magna cum laude, Harvard U., 1961, PhD, 1967; BPhil, Corpus Christi Coll., Oxford, Eng., 1963. Asst. prof. philosophy and the classics Harvard U., Cambridge, Mass., 1966-71; assoc. prof. U. Pitts., 1971-76, prof., 1976-81, chmn. philosophy dept., 1977-81; prof. Princeton U., N.J., 1981—, chmn. philosophy dept., 1984-92, Stuart prof., 1998—. Author: Reason and Human Good in Aristotle, Seneca: Moral and Political Essays, Plato: Complete Works, Reason and Emotion; mem. editl. bd. Am. Philos. Quar., 1977-80, History of Philosophy Quar., 1983-86, The Monist, 1987—, Ratio, 1988, Archiv für Ges. d. Phil., 1994—; contbr. articles to profl. jours. Recipient Ctr. for Advanced Studies fellow U. Ill., 1969-70, NEH fellow, 1982-83, John Simon Guggenheim fellow, 1987-88, Ctr. for Advanced Study in the Behavioral Scis. fellow, 1992-93, Am. Coun. Learned Socs. fellow, 2002-03. Fellow Am. Acad. Arts and Scis.; mem. Am. Philos. Assn. (ea. divsn. exec. com. 1984-87, chmn. com. def. profl. rights 1983-88, ea. divsn. nominating com. 1991-94, chmn. ea. divsn. program com. 1980, v.p. 1998-99, pres. 1999-2000). Home: 182 Western Way Princeton NJ 08540-7208 Office: Princeton Univ Dept of Philosophy 1879 Hall Princeton NJ 08544-1006 E-mail: johncoop@princeton.edu.

COOPER, JON CHARLES, environmentalist, educator, lawyer; b. N.Y.C., Sept. 28, 1948; s. Joseph Irving and Fay Phylis (Rubin) C.; m. Nancy Louise Hoffman, July 17, 1986; 1 child, Emily Maxwell. BA cum laude, Lawrence U., 1969; MS, U. Wis., 1971, PhD, 1974; JD, Pace U., 1993. Bar: N.Y. 1993, N.J. 1994, Conn. 1994, U.S. Supreme Ct. 1997. Tech. dir. Tex. Instruments, Buchanan, N.Y., 1976-79; staff biologist EPA, Washington, N.Y., 1979-83; sci. dir. Hudson River Found., N.Y.C., 1983-87; pres. Internat. Sch. Environ. Studies Found., New Haven, 1986—; prin. scientist TAMS, N.Y.C., 1987-90; sci. policy dir. Louis Berger & Assocs. Inc., East Orange, N.J., 1990-99; assoc. prof. environ. sci. SUNY, Purchase, 1990—2001; v.p. natural resources and environment Marasco Newton Group Ltd, Arlington, Va., 1999—2000; affiliate prof. dept. environ. sci. and policy George Mason U., 2000—. Contbr. numerous articles to profl. jours. Mem. tree subcom. Town of Greenwich (Conn.), 1990-93. Mem. Am. Chem. Soc., N.Y. Bar Assn., Am. Soc. Limnology, Sigma Xi. Avocations: horseback riding, tennis. Fax: 202-232-1407. E-mail: jccooper10@aol.com.

COOPER, JOSEPH, political scientist, educator; b. Boston, Sept. 10, 1933; s. Charles and Esther (Balder) Cooper; m. Frances Lorna Wollin, Aug. 24, 1965; children: Samuel Wollin, Meryl Charlotte. AB summa cum laude, Harvard U., 1955, AM, 1959, PhD, 1961. Asst. prof. govt. Harvard U., 1963-67; mem. faculty Rice U., Houston, 1967-91, prof. polit. sci., 1970-91, chmn. dept., 1967-72, Lena Gohlman Fox prof., 1978-89, dean Sch. Social Scis., 1979-88, Herbert S. Autrey prof. social scis., 1989-91, pres. Rice Inst. for Policy Analysis Sch. Social Scis., 1989-91; provost, v.p. for acad. affairs Johns Hopkins U., Balt., 1991-96, prof. dept. polit. sci., 1991—. Vis. Olin prof. polit. sci. Stanford U., 1988—89; staff dir. commn. adminstrv. rev. U.S. Ho. Reps., 1976—78; vis. prof. govt. Harvard U., 1984—85; mem. acad. adv. coun. Ctr. Congress Ind. U.; mem. editl. adv. bd. Ctr. Legis. Archives; bd. dirs. Dirksen Congl. Ctr., 1994—2000, 2002—, Consortium Social Sci. Orgns., 1994—97, Pub. Campaign, 1997—. Author: (book) The Origins of the Standing Committes and the Development of the Modern House, 1970, Congress and Its Committees, 1988; contbr. articles to profl. jours.; co-editor: (book) Sage Yearbook on Electoral Studies, 1975—82; mem. bd. editors: Congress and the Presidency, Ency. of U.S. Congress, Legis. Studies Quar., 1987—90, 2001—, assoc. editor: Ency. of Am. Legis. Sys., Congress of U.S. 1789-1989. Mem. adv. com. Records of Congress U.S. Congress and Nat. Archives, 1995—; bd. dirs. Balt. Hebrew U., 1994—2001. Recipient Press award, Congl. Quar., 1989; fellow Brookings Rsch., Harvard U., 1959—60, Sr., NEH, 1973. Mem.: D.C. Area Polit Sci. Assn. (mem. coun. 1993—94, v.p. 1994, pres. 1996), Midwest Polit. Sci. Assn., So. Polit. Sci. Assn., Southwestern Polit. Sci. Assn. (pres. 1977), Am. Polit. Sci. Assn. (sec. 1979, program chmn. 1985, nominations chmn. 1992, exec. com. legis. studies sect. 1999—), Asia Soc. (bd. dirs. 1990—92), Jefferson Davis Assn. (dir. 1980—91), Phi Beta Kappa, Sigma Xi. Office: Dept Polit Sci Johns Hopkins Univ Baltimore MD 21218-2685 E-mail: jcooper@jhu.edu.

COOPER, JUDITH KASE, retired theater educator, playwright; b. Wilmington, Del., Dec. 13, 1932; d. Charles Robert and Elizabeth Edna (Baker) Kase; stepchildren: James, Elizabeth, John, Katherine, Ann, Patty, Doreen, Jeff. BA, U. Del., 1955; MA, Case Western Res. U., 1956. Tchr., dir. children's theatre Agnes Scott Coll., 1956, U. Tenn., 1957, U. Md., Germany, 1958-60, Denver Civic Theatre, Denver U., Kent Sch., 1960-61; dir. children's theatre U. N.H., Durham, 1962-69; dir. theatre resources for youth Somersworth, N.H., 1966-69; assoc. prof. theatre U. South Fla., Tampa, 1969-74, assoc. prof. edn., 1975-83, prof., 1984—99, artistic dir. ednl. theatre, 1976—99, ret., 1999. Project dir. Hillsborough County Artists-in-Schs. Evaluation and Inservice Project, 1980-82; dir. Internat. Ctr. for Studies in Theatre Edn.; mem. Nat. Theatre Conf., Coll. Fellows Am. Theatre. Author: The Creative Drama Book: Three Approaches, other books; editor: Creative Drama in a Developmental Context; Children's Theatre, Creative Drama and Learning, Drama as a Meaning Maker, Introduction to Drama Teacher Resource Guide, Interconnecting Pathways to Human Experience, Teaching the Arts Across the Disciplines; contbr. articles to profl. jours.; pub. (plays) Snow White and The Seven Dwarfs, 1960, The Emperor's New Clothes, 1966, Southern Fried Cracker Tales, 1995. Bd. dirs. Fla. Alliance for Arts Edn., sec., 1976-77, vice-chmn., 1979-82, chmn., 1982-84; chmn. Wingspread Conf. on Theatre Edn., 1977; drama adjudicator Nat. Arts Festival, Ministry of Edn., Bahamas, 1975, 76, 79, 80; regional chmn. Alliance for Arts Edn., chmn. nat. adv. coun., mem. edn. adv. com., 1986—; trustee Children's Theatre Found.; bd. dirs. Coll. Fellows Am. Theatre of J.F. Kennedy Ctr. for Performing Arts, 1991-93, Fla. Assoc. Theatre Ed., exec. dir. 1995-99, Coll. Bus., 1993—; cons. S.E. Ctr. for Edn. in Theatre, 1995, Fla. Dept. Edn., 1994-96; cons. theatre edn. and prodn.; steering com. Arts for a Complete Edn., 1991-92; mem. curriculum writing com. Fla. Dept. Edn., 1994-96. Recipient Disting. Book of Yr. award, 1989, Arts Recognition award Arts Coun. Hillsborough County, 1995. Mem. Children's Theatre Assn. Am. (pres.-elect 1975-77, pres. 1977-79, chmn. symposia 1981-85, spl. recognition citation 1984), Am. Theatre Assn. (chief divsn. pres.'s coordinating coun. 1977-78, commn. on theatre edn. 1982—, elected), Am. Alliance for Theatre and Edn. (dir. & project dir. theatre literacy collaborative study Internat. Ctr. for Studies in Theatre Edn., Presdl. award 1992), Speech Comm. Assn. (membership dir. 1961), Southeastern Theatre Confs. (Sara Spencer award 1980), Fla. Theatre Confs. (Disting. Career award), Nat. Theatre Conf., Internat. Assn. Theatres for Children and Youth, Internat. Amateur Theatre

Assn. (N.Am. bd. dirs.), Fla. Assn. for Theater Edn. (Theatre Edn. of Yr. award 1986, exec. dir. 1994-99), Children's Theatre Found. Am.(bd. trustees 1977-), Tampa Mus. Republican. Episcopalian.

COOPER, KEN ERROL, retired management educator; b. Bryan, Ohio, Mar. 10, 1939; s. George Wayne and Agnes Anibel (Fisher) C.; m. Karen Cremean, June 17, 1961; children: Kristin, Andrew. BS, Bowling Green State U., 1961; MBA, Miami U., Oxford, Ohio, 1962; PhD, U. Minn., 1984. Instr. Miami U., 1962-63; lectr. U. Minn., 1965-67, 84-86; group v.p. Land O'Lakes, Inc., Mpls., 1967-82; v.p. fin. and adminstrn. Hamline U., 1982-84; dean Coll. Bus., Ohio No. U., Ada, 1986-90, prof., 1990-2000; prof., post chair for ethics and professions Am. Coll., Bryn Mawr, Pa., 1994-95, retired, 1995. Vis. prof. (on leave) Coll. of St. Thomas, St. Paul, 1981-82, vis. prof. of mgmt. U. San Diego, 2001-02, U. Evansville, 2002—. Trustee Westmar Coll., 1980-86; bd. dirs., sec.-treas. Acad. Mgmt., 1989-95; mem. Iowa Supreme Ct. Adv. Coun., 1972-75, North Ctrl. Devel. Found. Republican. Methodist. Office: Ohio No U Coll Bus Adminstrn Ada OH 45810

COOPER, KENNETH STANLEY, principal, educator, finance company executive; b. Oxford, N.C., May 17, 1948; s. Stephen and Helen (Norman) Cooper; m. Nancy Robinson, June 26, 1971; children: Danielle Jamilla, Janine Kandyce. AS, Miami Dade CC, 1971; BS in Criminal Justice, Fla. Internat. U., 1973, MS in Adult Edn., 1974; postgrad., Fla. Atlantic U., 1976, Ind. U., 1978. Police officer City of Miami (Fla.) Police Dept., 1971-72; tchr. Dade County Pub. Schs., Miami, 1974-76, 80-83, adminstr., asst. prin., 1983-89, prin. intern exec. tng. program, 1987-88, asst. prin., 1983-90; grad. asst. dept. social studies U. Ind., Bloomington, 1976-78; pres. Cooper Williamson Auto Brokerage, Miami, 1978-80; prin. Jan Mann Opportunity Sch., Miami, 1990-92, Robert Renick Ednl. Ctr., Opa Locka, Fla., 1992-96, Pine Villa Elem. Sch., Goulds, Fla., 1996-97, Mays Mid. Cmty. Sch., Goulds, 1997—; pres. Cooper Fin. Group, Inc., 1999—. Guest columnist: Miami Times, 1988; contbr. articles to profl. jours. Mem. United Tchrs. Dade County, Miami, 1974—76, 1980—83; sec. bd. dirs. Cmty. Crusade Against Drugs, Miami, 1995—96; organizer, activist Young Dems. S. Fla., 1967—68. With U.S. Army, 1969—70. Named Adminstr. of the Yr., Dade County Assn. Counseling and Devel., 1993. Mem.: NAACP. Home: 12840 SW 187th St Miami FL 33177-3000 Office: Arthur and Polly Mays Mid Cmty Sch 11700 SW 216th St Goulds FL 33170-2935 Personal E-mail: kscooper35@hotmail.com.

COOPER, MARK FREDERICK, artist, sculptor, art educator; b. Evansville, Ind., Oct. 5, 1950; s. I. Phillip and J. Janice (Crystal) C.; m. Danette English, Aug. 22, 1987; children: Alexandra Carrey, Jack English. BS, Ind. U., 1972; MFA, Tufts U., 1980. Asst. prof. art Boston Coll., Chestnut Hill, Mass., 1978—; mem. permanent faculty Sch. Mus. Fine Arts, Boston, 1978—. One-man shows include Howard Yezerski Gallery, Boston, 1990, 1995, 1999, New England Bio-Tech Gallery, 1990—91, Ctr. St. Studio Gallery, Boston, 1995, NAO Project Gallery, 2002, NAU Project Gallery, Boston, 2002, Miller-Geisler Gallery, NYC, 2003, exhibited in group shows at Northwest Mo. State U., Maryville, 1996, Bernard Toale Gallery, Boston, 1996, U. Hawaii, Honolulu, 1996, Cambridge Mulicultural Arts Ctr., 1996, 1999, Baum Fine Arts Galleries, U. Ctrl. Ark., Conway, 1997, Whitney Mus. Am. Art, 2000, Davis Mus., 2000, Peabody Essex Mus., 2000, New Bedford Mus., 2002, Butler Inst. Am. Art, 2002, Attelboro Mus., 2002, Mus. Fine Arts, Boston, 2002—03, others; artist (mus. exhbns.) Inst. Contemporary Art, Boston, 1994, Fuller Mus., Brockton, Mass., 1994, Kuntsmuseum, Cologne, Germany, 1992, 1996, Capital Children's Mus., Washington, 1995, 1996, Corcoran Mus. Art, 1995, N.D. Mus. Art, Grand Forks, 1996, Revolving Mus., Boston, 1997, Newhouse Ctr. Gallery, Snug Harbor Cultural Ctr., 2000, numerous others, (commns. include) First Night Boston, 1992—94, House of Blues Corp., 1994, Lyons Group, 1995, Cambridge Hosp., 2000, Pracies Pharmaceutical, 2001. Dir. Project Against Violence, Boston, Washington, N.Y.C., 1991—; bd. dirs. Creativity in the 21st Century. Grantee Ruth Mott Fund, 1995-96, Cafritz Found., 1994, NEA, 1993; recipient pub. svc. award Mayor of Boston, 1995; fellowship Open Soc. Inst., 1998-00, Mass Cultural Coun. sculpture award, 1999. Home: 52 Saint James Ave Somerville MA 02144-2930 Office: c/o Miller Geisler Gallery New York NY 10001

COOPER, PENNY MCEWEN, special education professional; b. Monongahela, Pa., Aug. 16, 1952; d. William Ellis McEwen and Tillie (Dudro) Harrison; m. Lawrence S. Cooper, Aug. 4, 1974; 1 child, Jared K. BS, Duquesne U., 1972, MS, 1974; cert. in paralegal assisting, Pa. State U., 1981; EdD, Pacific Western U., 1992. Cert. tchr., Pa., Fla. Ednl. specialist Intermediate Unit I, California, Pa., 1972-85; program dir. North Broward Sch./Lighthouse Point (Fla.) Acad., 1985—; ednl. cons. Med. Ctr. Delray, Delray Beach, Fla., 1987—; program cons. Excel, Inc., Barrington, Ill., 1989—. Coach Spl. Olympics, California, 1972-74. Mem. ASCD, Coun. Exceptional Children, Phi Delta Kappa. Democrat. Jewish. Avocations: sailing, gourmet cooking, bicycling, reading. Office: North Broward Sch Lighthouse Point Acad 3701 NE 22nd Ave Lighthouse Point FL 33064-3934

COOPER, SHARON KAY, school media specialist; b. Junction City, Kans., Jan. 9, 1952; d. Duane Harvey and Helen Lucille Gugler; m. Stevan Frank Cooper, Aug. 3, 1974; children: Susan Kay, Shelley Kay. BS in Home Econs., Ft. Hays State U., 1974; postgrad., Wichita State U., 1979, Kans. State U., 1983, Emporia State U., 1988; MS in Edn. Adminstrn., Ft. Hays State U., 1996. Home econs. tchr., libr. Brewster (Kans.) H.S., 1974—75; lang. arts tchr., libr. West Smith County Jr. and Sr. H.S., Kensington, Kans., 1975-77; home econs., vocational tchr. Little River (Kans.)-Windom H.S., 1977-80; home econs. tchr. Chase (Kans.)-Raymond Schs., 1980-88; library media specialist Quivira Heights H.S., Bushton, Kans., 1988-95, Quivira Heights K-12 Schs., Holyrood and Bushton, Kans., 1995—. Sch. library rep., vice chairperson Kans. Interlibrary Loan Bd. Dirs., Topeka, 1999—; chmn. Reading Is Fun, Quivira Hts. Elem./Jr. High, 1995—; chmn. Red Ribbon Week Quivira Hts. Pre K-12, 1995—. Troop leader Wheatbelt coun. Girl Scouts U.S., Chase, 1989-96, svc. unit mgr., 1995-97; mem. Smoky Hills Drug-Free Schs. Adv. Coun. Mem. NEA, Kans. Assn. Sch. Librs., Kans. Edn. Assn. (pres. local chpt. 1999-2000), Phi Delta Kappa. Methodist. Avocations: reading, cooking, sewing, snow skiing, travel. Home: 213 Cedar Chase KS 67524 Office: Quivira Heights Pre K-12 Schs 500 S Main St Bushton KS 67427-9749

COOPER, SIGNE SKOTT, retired nurse educator; b. Clinton County, Iowa, Jan. 29, 1921; d. Hans Edward and Clara Belle (Steen) Skott. BS, U. Wis., 1948; MEd, U. Minn., 1955. Head nurse U. Wis. Hosp., Madison, 1946-48; instr. U. Wis. Sch. Nursing, Madison, 1948-51, asst. prof., 1952-57, assoc. prof., 1957-62, prof., assoc. dean, 1948-83, prof. emeritus, 1983—. Prof. U. Wis. Extension, 1955-83. Contbg. author: American Nursing: A Biographical Dictionary, Vol. 1, 1988, Vol. 2, 1992, Vol. 3, 2000; contbr. articles to profl. jours. 1st Lt. U.S. Army Nurse Corps, 1943-46. Recipient NLN Linda Richards award, ANA Honorary Recognition award, Adult Edn. Assn. Pioneer award; named to Nursing Hall of Fame, 2000. Fellow Am. Acad. Nursing (named Living Legend 2003); mem. Am. Assn. for History Nursing (Pres.'s award 2003), Wis. Nurses Assn. (pres.).

COOPER, WILLIAM ALLEN, JR., audiologist, educator; b. Detroit, Aug. 16, 1932; s. William Allen and Ida Louise (Ford) C.; m. Auguste Ingrid Schneider, Oct. 5, 1958; children: Ingrid Louise, Robert William, James Allen. Student, Adrian Coll., 1950-52; BS, Wayne State U., 1958; PhD, Okla. U., 1964. Chief audiology VA Hosp., Oklahoma City, 1963-71; asst. prof. U. Okla., Oklahoma City, 1964-71; assoc. prof. Purdue U., West Lafayette, Ind., 1971-81; prof. U. S.C., Columbia, 1981-98, disting. prof. emeritus, 1998—, chmn. dept. speech pathology and audiology, 1981-83, 96-98. Vis. fellow Inst. Sound & Vibration Rsch., Southampton, U.K., 1979. Contbr. articles to profl. jours. Chmn. bd. dirs. Unitarian Fellowship, Lafayette, Ind., 1975; bd. dirs. Unitarian Ch., Oklahoma City, 1969-70, Columbia, S.C., 1990-91. With U.S. Army, 1954-56, Germany. Am. Speech and Hearing Assn. fellow, 1978; recipient Honors of Assn. award S.C. Speech and Hearing Assn., 1989, Elizabeth P. Wade Meml. award S.C. Acad. Audiology, 1999. Fellow Am. Acad. Audiology; mem. AAAS, Internat. Soc. Audiology, Am. Auditory Soc. Unitarian Universalist. Home: PO Box 765 1002 Jungle Rd Edisto Island SC 29438-0765 E-mail: wac2@bellsouth.net., cooper_william@sc.edu.

COOPER, WYLOLA, retired special education educator; b. Cleve., Feb. 12, 1926; d. William Wilkins and Leola Anderson; m. Henry J. Cooper, Apr. 4, 1948 (dec. May 1992); children: Henry J. Jr., Wylola Jr., Antigone, Yolanda Lee. BE, Chgo. State U., 1967; MA, Roosevelt U., 1974. Itinerant tchr. Dist. 117 Elem. Level, Hickory Hills, Ill., 1968-71; tchr. learning disabled, emotionally and behaviorally handicapped Conrady Jr. High Sch. Dist. 117, Hickory Hills, 1971-86, behavior disorders tchr., 1986-91, dept. chairperson spl. edn. dept., 1988-94, tchr. emotionally disturbed and behaviorally handicapped, 1988-94; ret., 1994. Staff S.W. Coop. of Cook County for Spl. Edn., Oak Forest; mem. organizing com. Ill. Spl. Edn. Program, Springfield, 1971-72. Min. of care U. Children's Hosp.; vol. Midwest Workers in Chgo. Mem. Coun. Exceptional Children, Am. Fedn. Tchrs. Union, S.W. Coop. for Spl. Edn. Democrat. Roman Catholic. Avocations: swimming, counseling. Home: 1451 E 55th St Chicago IL 60615-5429

COOR, LATTIE FINCH, university president; b. Phoenix, Sept. 26, 1936; s. Lattie F. and Elnora (Witten) C.; m. Ina Fitzhenry, Jan. 18, 1964 (div. 1988); children: William Kendall, Colin Fitzhenry, Farryl MacKenna Witten; m. Elva Wingfield, Dec. 27, 1994. AB with high honors (Phelps Dodge scholar), No. Ariz. U., 1958; MA with honors (Univ. scholar, Universal Match Found. fellow, Carnegie Corp. fellow), Washington U., St. Louis, 1960, PhD, 1964; LLD (hon.), Marlboro Coll., 1977, Am. Coll. Greece, 1982, U. Vt., 1991, No. Ariz. U., 2002. Adminstrv. asst. to Gov. Mich., 1961-62; asst. to chancellor Washington U., St. Louis, 1963-67, asst. dean Grad. Sch. Arts and Scis., 1967-69, dir. internat. studies, 1967-69, asst. prof. polit. sci., 1967-76, vice chancellor, 1969-74, univ. vice chancellor, 1974-76; pres. U. Vt., Burlington, 1976-89, Ariz. State U., Tempe, Ariz., 1990—2002, prof. pub. affairs, pres. emeritus, 2002—; chmn., CEO Ctr. for Future of Ariz., 2002—. Cons. HEW; spl. cons. to commr. U.S. Commn. on Edn., 1971-74; chmn. Commn. on Govtl. Rels., Am. Coun. on Edn., 1976-80; dir. New Eng. Bd. Higher Edn., 1976-89; co-chmn. joint com. on health policy Assn. Am. Univs. and Nat. Assn. State Univs. and Land Grant Colls., 1976-89; mem. pres. commn. NCAA, 1984-90, chmn. div. I, 1989; mem. Ariz. State Bd. Edn., 1993-98; chmn. Pacific 10 Conf., 1995-96. Trustee emeritus Am. Coll. Greece. Mem. Nat. Assn. Stae Univs. and Land Grant Colls. (chmn. bd. dirs. 1991-92), New Eng. Assn. Schs. and Colls. (pres. 1981-82), Am. Coun. on Edn. (bd. dirs. 1991-93, 2000-02), Kellogg Commn. on Future of State and Land-Grant Univs. Office: Ctr for Future of Ariz 541 E Van Buren Ave Ste B-5 Phoenix AZ 85004 E-mail: Lattie.Coor@asu.edu.

COPE, KATHLEEN ADELAIDE, critical care and parish nurse, educator; b. Bethlehem, Pa., Sept. 12, 1926; d. Harry Raymond and Mabel Eva (Newhard) Stine; m. Robert Clayton Cope, Aug. 9, 1951; children: Debra Kathleen Howard, Terry Faye Cicero. BA in Psychology summa cum laude, Bellevue (Nebr.) Coll., 1972; diploma, St. Luke's Hosp., Bethlehem, 1951; student, Whitworth Coll., Spokane, 1989, Wash. State U., 1989. RN, Pa., Wash.; cert. nutrition support nurse; cert. critical care nurse, quality improvement, health promotion specialist. Pvt. duty nurse Exeter (N.H.) Hosp., 1957-60; nurse Red Cross Blood Mobile, Portsmouth area, N.H., 1961-65; staff nurse Clarkson Hosp., Omaha, 1966, asst. head nurse, 1966-67, head nurse, 1967-68, supr., organizer coronary care ctr., 1968-70; staff nurse ICU/critical care Sacred Heart Med. ctr., Spokane, 1973—; founder, dir. nutritional risk/identification network Health Improvement Partnership, Spokane, Wash., 1997—. Mem. adv. coun. edn. com. Nutrition Screening Initiative, Washington, 1992—, Nutrition Inst. La., New Orleans, 1993—; apptd. del. by U.S. Senate to White House Conf. on Aging, 1995; developer Body Mass Index awareness cmty. action project through Leadership Spokane Class, 1999; presenter Spokane's body mass index project U.S. Surgeon Gen.'s Inaugural Session on Obesity, 2001. Author: (manual) Malnutrition in the Elderly: A National Crisis, (resolution) Ensuring the Future of the Medicare Program presented to White House and Congress; contbr. articles to profl. jours. Apptd. Silver Senator by U.S. Senate for Wash. in Nat. Silver Haired Congress, 1997. Recipient Cmty. Leadership Recognition award, YWCA, Spokane, 1993, commendation for developing a model for nation from former U.S. Surgeon Gen., 1999, Spl. Recognition award for contrbn. to malnutrition awareness, U.S. Adminstrn. on Aging, 2000. Mem. ANA, Wash. State Nursing Assn., Nat. Coun. on Aging, Am. Soc. for Critical Care Nursing (founding), Am. Soc. for Parenteral and Enteral Nutrition, U.S. apptd. Silver Senator for Wash. State in Nat. Silver Haired Congress, Sigma Theta Tau. Avocations: reading, walking, hiking, bicycle, cooking, crafts. Home: 8315 N Lucia Ct Spokane WA 99208-9654 Fax: (509) 468-1026. E-mail: kcope@mindspring.com.

COPELAND, CAROLYN ABIGAIL, retired university dean; b. White Plains, N.Y., May 5, 1931; d. Robert Erford and Mary Terwillinger; m. William E. Copeland, Aug. 16, 1964; children: Rob Cameron, Diana Elizabeth Bosworth. BA, U. Mich., 1973, MA, 1979, postgrad., 1992—. With dean's office Coll. Lit., Sci. and Arts U. Mich, Ann Arbor, 1967-91, asst. dean, 1980-84, assoc. dean, 1984-91. Rschr. in Buddhist art history. Author: Tankas from the Koelz Collection, 1980. CEW scholar, Rackham grad. student scholar. Mem. Phi Beta Kappa (mortar bd., v.p. Alpha chpt. 1984-86, pres. Alpha chpt. 1986-88). Home: 1867 Morley St Simi Valley CA 93065 Office: U Mich Ann Arbor MI 48109 E-mail: cabby1867@aol.com.

COPELAND, JEAN PARRISH, school system administrator, school board executive; b. Petersburg, Va., June 17, 1936; d. Earl Beckwith and Louise Laverne (Carter) Parrish; m. Kenneth Edward Copeland, June 1, 1957; children: Kenneth Edward Jr., Timothy Scott, Robert Mark, Randall Patrick, Steven Christopher. BS in Elem. Edn., James Madison U., 1965; MEd in Elem. Edn., Va. Commonwealth U., 1970. Postgrad. profl. cert., Va. Tchr. Chesterfield County Pub. Schs., Chesterfield, Va., 1959-68, supr. elem. edn. and reading and lang. arts, 1968-84, mem. sch. bd., 1988-92, chmn., 1990-92; pres. The Copeland Schs., Inc., Chesterfield, 1982—. Bd. dirs. John Tyler C.C., Chester, 1986-88; mem. alumni bd. James Madison U., Harrisonburg, Va., 1989-92, 94-2000; com. mem. Chesterfield County Rep. Com., 1988-92; mem. Chesterfield Bus. Coun., 1988-92; mem. steering com. Metro Richmond (Va.) 2000, 1991—. Mem. Nat. Assn. for Edn. Young Children, Va. Assn. for Early Childhood Edn., Va. Assn. for Edn. Gifted, Proprietary Child Care Assn. Va. (bd. dirs. 1989-91), Va. Child Care Assn. (bd. dirs. 1992), Nat. Assn. Chjild Care Profls., Nat. Child Care Assn. Methodist. Avocations: snow skiing, gourmet cooking, water sports, dickens village collection, travel. Home and Office: PO Box 1076 Chesterfield VA 23832-9101

COPELAND, LEWIS, principal; Prin. W.P. Davidson H.S., Mobile, Ala., 1982—. Recipient Blue Ribbon Sch. award U.S. Dept. Edn., 1990-91, 95-96; named Secondary Prin. of Yr., Ala. State PTA, 1993-94, Outstanding Sch. Adminstr., Ala. Music Educators Assn., 1997. Office: WP Davidson HS 3900 Pleasant Valley Rd Mobile AL 36609-2022

COPES, MARVIN LEE, college president; b. Connersville, Ind., Sept. 19, 1938; s. Kenneth Edward and Frances Gertrude (Bean) C.; m. Luretta Ann Gerand, Aug. 26, 1961; children: Bradley Alan, Brian Keith, Brent Lee. BS, Purdue U., 1961, MS, 1962, PhD, 1975; postgrad., Ind. State U., 1967-68, Ind. U.Southeast, 1967-68. Cert. pub. mgr., Ky. Grad. asst. agrl. edn. Purdue U., 1961-62, grad. instr., 1968-69; tchr. vocat. agriculture Tri-County Sch. Corp., Walcott, Ind., 1964-65; vocat. dir. Met. Sch. Dist. Vernon Twp., Crothersville, Ind., 1965-68; also dir. Ind. Vocat. Agriculture Demonstration Ctr., 1965-68; asst. exec. sec. Kappa Delta Pi Hdqrs., West Lafayette, Ind., 1969-70; dir. Blue River Vocat.-Tech. Ctr., Shelbyville, Ind., 1970-79; nat. curriculum devel. coord. ITT Ednl. Svcs., Indpls., 1979-80, nat. dir. edn., 1980-82; dir. ITT Tech. Inst., Ft. Wayne, Ind., 1982-83, Indpls., 1983-86, Am. Coll., Mobile, Ala., 1986-89; nat. dir. edn. Am. Career Educators, Charlotte, N.C., 1989, v.p. ednl. resources, 1989-91; pres. Treasure Wheel, Inc., Mobile, Ala., 1991-93; dean acad. affairs Phillips Jr. Coll., Mobile, Ala., 1992-96; v.p. acad. affairs Am. Inst. Commerce, Davenport, Iowa, 1993-96; dir. Ky. Tech. Jefferson State Campus, Louisville, 1996-98; pres. Jefferson Cmty. & Tech. Coll., 1998-2000, exec. dir. of occupl., tech. and apprenticeship programs, 2000—02, ceo, Special Programs, 2001—02; dir. Heritage Inst., Falls Ch., Va., 2002—. Chmn. profl. devel. com. Ky. Postsecondary Tchr. Credentialing Adv. Bd.; mem. Welfare Reform Task Force, Ky.; bd. dirs. Pvt. Ind. Coun., Future Connections Sch. to Work; organizer Advanced Tech. Skills Acad., Advanced Welding Tech. Ctr., Heritage Coll., Falls Ch., Va.; pres. CopeSkills Cons., Power Ptnrs. cons. Author: A Curriculum Guide for Training in Agricultural Supply, 1968, Student Handbook for Cooperative Progress in Agricultural Occupations, 1968, A Predictability of Career Choices of High School Seniors, 1975, Personal Awareness Handbook, 1989, Retention Handbook, 1989, Placement Handbook, 1990, Vocational Adjustment Handbook, 1990, Train The Trainer Handbook, 1990, Instructor Certification Handbook, 1990, Administrative Certification Handbook, 1990, Master Teacher, 1990, Wheel of Fortune Enterprise Training Manual, 1991, Instructor Training Manual, 1993, Faculty Inservice Training Manual, 1993, Disaster Plan, 1993, Contract Training, 1994, School-to-Work Training, 1994, Assessment Planning, 1995, Welfare Reform, 1996, Guidelines for Apprenticeship Training, 2002, Guidelines for Corporate College, 2002. Mem. ops. coun. Met. Coll.; pres. Loper PTO, 1974-76; leader 4-H, 1964-68; advisor Future Farmers Am., 1964-70; cubmaster Boy Scouts Am., 1976-80, commr., bd. dirs. Shelbyville coun., 1978-92; mem. vocat. gng. com. Futuring Project, N.Y. State Dept. Edn.; bd. dirs. N.E. India Christian Mission, 1974, Kentuckiana Works; chmn. Shelby County Youth for Christ; mem. Nat. Curriculum Focus Group, 1993-96; bd. dirs., treas. Accrediting Coun. for Ind. Colls. and Schs., 1994; deacon area So. Bapt. Ch., 1995; mem. Kentuckiana Edn. and Workforce Inst., Louisville Area Workforce Devel. Coun., School-to-Work Partnership Coun., Louisville/Jefferson County Redevel. Authority; bd. dirs. Career Resources One Stop Shop/Job Link, Pvt. Ind. Coun.; Louisville/Jefferson County Workforce investment bd., N. Cen. Ky. Workforce Investment Bd.; mem. Louisville/Jefferson County Youth Coun., N. Cen. Ky. Youth Coun., chmn.; mem. Immigrant/Refugee Task Force, Kentuckiana Works Skilled Trades Roundtable. 1st lt. U.S. Army, 1962-64. Mem. ASCD, Am. Vocat. Assn., Ind. Vocat. Assn., Nat. Coun. Local Adminstrs., Ind. Coun. Local Adminstrs., Bus. Profls. Am., Nat. Bus. Edn. Assn., Soc. Mfg. Engrs., Ky. Vocat. Assn. (pres. region 13), Robotics Internat., Network Iowa Svc. Learning, Ind. Assn. Pvt. Career Schs. (bd. dirs.), Future Farmers Am. Alumni Assn., Shelby County C. of C., Prichard C. of C. (bd. dirs.), Pershing Rifles, Gideons Internat., Metro Scholars, Davenport C. of C., Masons, Kiwanis, Order Ea. Star, Alpha Tau Alpha, Kappa Delta Pi, Phi Delta Kappa, Delta Pi Epsilon. Home: 20147 Hardwood Terrace Ashburn VA 20147 Office: Heritage Institute 350 South Washington Falls Church VA 22046 E-mail: mlcopes@msn.com.

COPPENBARGER, CECELIA MARIE, special education educator; b. Kansas City, Mo., Nov. 3, 1961; d. Theodore Francis Bowman, Jr., Betty Marie Bowman; m. Charles Loren Coppenbarger, Jr.; children: Charles Loren Coppenbarger, III, Craig James, Cliff Robert, Joshua Richard, Elena Marie. A in Liberal Arts, Longview C.C., 1983; BA in Secondary Edn., BA in Eng., U. Missouri, 1998; postgrad., Ctrl. Mo. State U. Cert. cross categorical spl. edn. tchr. K-12, secondary Eng.tchr. 9-12. Cross-categorical spl. edn. tchr. Raytown C-2 Sch. Dist., Raytown, Mo., 1998—. Sponsor Raytown Chpt. Mo. State Tchrs. Assn.-Future Tchrs. Am., 2000—. Active James Lewis Elem. PTA, 2002—; mem. Plaza Heights Bapt. Ch. Choir, Blue Springs, 1998—; tchr. Plaza Heights Bapt. Ch. Sunday Sch. and Spl. Needs Ministry, Blue Springs, 1999—; mem. Lucy Franklin Elem. Sch. PTA, Blue Springs, 1998—2001, Blue Springs H.S. Parent Tchr. Student Assn., 1998—2001, Brittany Hills Mid. Sch. Parent Tchr. Student Assn., 1998—2003; educator Raytown South H.S. Parent Tchr. Student Assn., Raytown, 1998—2001. Recipient Outstanding Scholastic Achievment and Excellence award, Golden Key Nat. Honor Soc., 1997, Outstanding Omer award, Odyssey of the Mind Program, 1997; scholar, U. Mo., Kansas City, 1997—98. Mem.: Mo. State Tchrs. Assn., Raytown Cmty. Tchrs. Assn., Coun. Exceptional Children, Pi Lambda Theta. Baptist. Home: 2114 NE 3rd St Blue Springs MO 64014 Office: Raytown South High Sch 8211 Sterling Raytown MO 64138 Personal E-mail: Coppen@DiscoveryNet.com. Business E-Mail: cecelia.coppenbarger@mail.raytown.k12.mo.us.

COPPENS, LAURA KATHRYN, special education educator; b. Hoddesdon, England, Jan. 12, 1948; d. Tomas Adriaan and Sylvia Helen Coppens; m. G. Lawrence McQueen (div. 1985); children: Isaac David, Sean Little Hawk. BA in Edn., John F. Kennedy Coll., Wahoo, Nebr., 1970; MEd in Spl. Edn., William Paterson U., 1976. Spl. edn. tchr. Bellmar (N.J.) Schs., 1970—71, N.J. Commn. for Blind, Teaneck, 1972—76; dir. Randolph County Learning Ctr., Roanoke, Ala., 1976—80; spl. edn. tchr. Lineville (Ala.) H.S., 1980—89, BOCES Alternative Program, Apalachin, NY, 1989—93, Owego (N.Y.) Apalachin Middle Sch., 1993—98, Owego Free Acad., 1998—. Dir. Youth Group, Owego, 2000—; co-coord. Inst. of Arts in Edn., Owego, 1996—; mentor tchr. Owego Apalachin Ctrl. Schs., 1999—. Pres. Randolph County Assn. for Retarded Citizens, Roanoke, 1980—83; lay reader St. Paul's Episc. Ch., Owego, 1998—. Recipient Outstanding Tchr. award, So. Tier Inst. of Arts, Binghamton, N.Y., 1998. Mem.: Broome Tioga Autism Soc. Am., Owego Apalachin Tchrs. Assn. (sec. 1998—), Coun. for Exceptional Children. Episcopalian. Achievements include creation of school for the handicapped in Roanoke; creation of first high school program for the multihandicapped in Lineville. Avocations: tenor recorder, reading, singing in church choir. Home: 412 Forest Hill Rd Apalachin NY 13732 Office: Owego Apalachin Ctrl Schs Talcott St Owego NY 13827 E-mail: lcoppens@oagw.stier.org.

COPPERMAN, STUART MORTON, pediatrician, educator; b. Bklyn., June 5, 1935; s. Irving and Anne (Reisfield) C.; m. Renee Stein, Aug. 17, 1958; children: Beth, Alan, Cara. BA cum laude, Bklyn. Coll., 1956; MD, SUNY-Bklyn., 1960. Diplomate Am. Bd. Pediat. Rotating intern. L.I. Jewish Hosp., New Hyde Park, N.Y., 1960-61, resident in pediat., 1961-63; practice medicine specializing in pediat. Merrick, N.Y., 1965-2000; sr. med. cons. Med. Advisers, P.C., 2001—; mem. staff L.I. Jewish Hillside Med. Ctr., Schneider Children's Hosp., New Hyde Park, Nassau County Med. Ctr., East Meadow, Winthrop U. Hosp., Mineola, North Shore Univ. Hosp., Manhasset; clin. assoc. prof. pediat. SUNY Med. Sch., Stony Brook, 1972-2000; asst. prof. clin. health studies SUNY Sch. Allied Health, Stony Brook, 1977-2000; clin. instr. physicians asst. program Stony Brook Med. Ctr., 1972-2000; prof. pediat. St. George's Med. Coll., St. Vincent, W.I., acting chmn. pediat., 1979-80; healthcare security analyst, healthcare cons., 2000—; medico-legal expert, 2000—; physician exec. Health and Info. Svcs., 2001—02. Med. advisor Assn. Children with Downs Syndrome, 1971-98; mem. com. for handicapped Bellmore Sch. Dist., 1976-86; mem. ad hoc com. on cmty. as sch. Merrick-Bellmore Schs., 1976-90; bd. dirs. North Shore-L.I. Jewish I.P.O., L.I. Sch. Health Edn. Coalition, North Shore Physicians Orgn., North Shore - L.I. Jewish PHO; mem. Nassau County Sch. Health Edn. Commn., 1990-93; mem. ad hoc com. on prevention of birth defects March of Dimes; preceptor in pediat. Physicians Asst. Program, Cath. Med. Ctr.; mem. doctor's adv. com. Shaare Zedek Hosp., Jerusalem, 1974-98; med. cons. Matchbox Toys, 1985-88, Proctor &

Gamble, 1988, Carnation Co., 1989-90, Disney Ednl. Svcs., 1990-95, vaccine divsn. Merck Corp., 1997—, Sepracor, 1999—; cons., mem. spkrs. bur. N.Y. State Med. Soc., N.Y. State Senate Com. Mental Hygiene, 1988—, Lederle Labs., 1989-95, Merck Labs., 1996—, Wallace Labs., 1996—, ucb Pharma, 1999—, Connaught, 1999—, Abbott Labs., 1996—, Pfizer, 1998—, Sepracor, 1999—; author, co-founder, pres., bd. dirs. Child Health Imagery Prodns., 1997—. Appearance TV shows on Downs Syndrome, learning disabilities, CPR, first aid, infant exercise programs, TV's effects on children, infectious disease, parent-infant bonding, immunizations, enuresis, toilet training, prevention of cigarette smoking among children, 1972—, also on HealthLinks (Life Time TV), 1990-93; mem. editl. adv. bd. Jour. Assn. for Physician Assts., 1987—; editl. cons. Jour. Pediat. Mgmt., 1991—; contbr. chpt. to Textbook Pediat. Sports Medicine; developer Babycise (infant parent interactive program in video tape and book form), 1985; rschr. on hetacillin, 1966, pyridoxine effect on serotonin level and performance in children with Down's Syndrome, 1970-75, Alice in Wonderland syndrome as presenting sympton of infectious mononucleosis, 1966-77, on transmission of group A Beta hemolytic strep infection from pet reservoirs to children, 1963-81; med. editor Air Fair Mag., 1991-93, L.I. Parent Mag., 1985-93, L.I. Family Mag., 1994-95; contbr. articles to profl. jours. Mem. sch. bd. Temple Beth Am., Merrick, 1972-78, mem. exec. com., 1973-74, chmn. com. Israel and World Affairs, 1976-78, mem. sch. com., 1976-78, mem. ritual com., 1976-93; mem. N.Y. State Senate com. on mental hygiene, 1990—; mem. profl. adv. bd. So. Shore divsn. YM-YWHA; benefactor Merrick Libr., 1992—. With U.S. Army, 1963-65. Recipient Physician Recognition award AMA, 1966—, testimonial dinner and plaque Assn. Children with Down Syndrome, 1972, Best Clin. Tchrs. of Pediat. award Nassau County Med. Ctr., 1981-82; named Merrick Profl. of Yr., 1994. Fellow Am. Acad. Pediat. (chmn. com. TV effects on children 1976—, mem. nat. com. comm. and pub. info. 1984-85, mem. nat. com. on substance abuse 1998-2001, media spokesperson 1988—, tobacco, alcohol and drug-free generation coord. 1988-98, chmn. substance abuse com. 1992—, N.Y. state chmn. substance abuse com. 1992-94, managed care com. chpt. 2 1993-95), Internat. Coll. Pediat.; mem. AMA, N.Y. State Med. Soc. (com. on alcohol 1997—), Nassau County Med. Soc. (com. on mental health 1980—, project assist 1992—, Nassau Acad. Medicine Pub. Health com. 1991—, libr. com. 1993—, chmn. pediat. sect. 1995—), Nassau Pediat. Soc. (mem. exec. bd. 1972—, chmn. com. on mental health 1972-88, v.p. 1994-95, pres. 1996-97). A Non-Smoking Generation Internat. (organizer, med. dir. Am. divsn.), Am. Lung Assn., Nassau-Suffolk Lung Assn. (life mem., dir. 1982-84), Am. Physicians Fellowship for Israel Med. Assn., Assn. Children with Learning Disabilities (mem. profl. adv. bd.), La Leche League, Latin Am. Parents Assn., L.I. Sch. Health Edn. Coun. (bd. dirs. 1989-92), Alpha Epsilon Pi (chancellor Phi Theta chpt. 1955-56), Phi Delta Epsilon (consul Zeta chpt. 1960), B'nai Brith. Office: 676 Balfour Pl Melville NY 11747 E-mail: smcmd@aol.com.

COPPOLA, JEAN FRANCES, university program administrator; b. Flushing, N.Y., Sept. 11, 1964; d. Ronald and Jean (DiPietrantonio) C. BS in Computer Sci., Hofstra U., 1986; MS in Computer Sci., Pace U., 1990, MS in Telecommunications, 1992. Owner Computer World, Queens Village, N.Y., 1982-85; undergrad. asst. tchr. Hofstra U., Hempstead, N.Y., 1982-85; computer operator Chargit, Inc., Garden City, N.Y., 1985-86; coord. acad. computing Pace U., N.Y.C., 1986-88, small sys. analyst/technician Pleasantville, N.Y., 1988-90, adj. prof. computer sci./tech. sys. N.Y.C., 1989—, univ. microcomputing support analyst, acad. computing Pleasantville, N.Y., 1990-95, univ. mgr. microcomputing sys., 1995-97, mgr. client support office info. tech., 1997-2000, adminstr. major info. tech. initiatives and grants, 2000—. Rsch. asst. Pace U. Computer Graphics, N.Y.C., 1988-93, senator, 1988-96, mem. exec. com., 1988-89, 91-94, mem. adminstrv. coun., Pleasantville, 1988—, mem. faculty affairs, 1988-89, mem. acad. programs and policies com., 1990-91, 94-95, chairperson acad. programs and policies com., 1991-94, mem. instnl. budget and planning com., 1989-91, mem. univ. rels. com., 1994-95. Co-creator computer animation Mandel pot; contbr. articles to profl. jours. Mem. Queens Village Youth Marching Band, Inc., 1984-99, advisor, 1989-90, asst. dir., 1990-91, assoc. dir., 1991-93, dir., 1993-99; chpt. mem. Muscular Dystrophy Assn., Forest Hills, N.Y., 1989-93, vol., 1981—; post advisor Explorer Post 2301, Queens Village, 1989-91; vol. N.Y. Cares, 1995—; parade marshall Radio City Music Hall Prodns., N.Y.C., 1989. Scholar, Astoria (N.Y.) Civic Assn., 1982, N.Y. Regents, 1982-86, Hofstra U., 1982-84; recipient Citizens award for Outstanding Personal Achievement and Dedication to N.Y. Youth, N.Y. State Assembly, 1994, Mayor's Vol. Action award for Youth Svcs., N.Y.C., 1995. Mem. AIAA, IEEE Computer Soc., IEEE Edn. Soc., Assn. Computing Machinery (mem. spl. interest groups on graphics, individual computing environments, univ. and coll. computing svcs., computer sci. edn. and office info. sys.), Upsilon Pi Epsilon. Roman Catholic. Avocations: church choirs, flute, technology management, computer viruses, smart e-classrooms. Home: 151-28 22nd Ave Whitestone NY 11357-3719 Office: Pace U Westhall 100 235 Elm Rd Briarcliff Manor NY 10510 E-mail: coppola@pace.edu.

COPPOLA, JOSEPH ANGELO, computer professional, educator; b. Rome, Dec. 2, 1947; s. Frank and Barbara (Tombasco) C.; m. Elaine Marie Hruby, Aug. 15, 1981; 1 child, Richard McCoy. BT in Indsl. Engring., SUNY, 1985; MS in Computer Engring., Syracuse U., 1990, postgrad., 1992—. Mgr. audio/visual svcs. SUNY, Stony Brook, 1968-77; owner, operator Enchanted Frog Prodns., Port Jefferson, N.Y., 1977-79; customer svc. rep. Xerox Corp., Syracuse, 1979-85; software engr. Rome (N.Y.) Rsch. Corp., 1985-88; sr. adminstr. ops. Syracuse U., 1988-97; asst. prof. elec. tech. SUNY, Morrisville, 1997—, mem. faculty congress, 1998—. Mem. budget com. Vernon-Verona-Sherrill Sch. Bd., 1986-87; mem. engring. tech. adv. com. SUNY, Utica, 1987-88; treas. Fayette Manor Homeowners Assn., 1992-93. Innovation fund grant Syracuse U., 1993-95. Mem. N.Y. State Engring. Tech. Assn., Fayetteville/Manlius Sch. Bd. Com. on Gifted Edn., Order of the Engr., Mycroft Holmes Soc. of Syracuse (pub.), Baker St. Irregulars, Tech. Club. of Syracuse, Hounds of the Internet. Avocations: sherlock holmes, woodworking, radio drama, blacksmithing. Home: 103 Kenny St Fayetteville NY 13066-1230 Office: SUNY Sch of Sci & Tech Morrisville NY 13408 E-mail: coppolja@morrisville.edu.

COPPOLA, PATRICIA L. (SCHEFFEL), elementary school educator; b. Kingston, N.Y., Apr. 27, 1966; d. John J. and Barbara (Brennan) Scheffel; m. Paul A. Coppola, July 11, 1992. BS cum laude, SUNY, Brockport, 1989; MS, SUNY, New Paltz, 1993. Tchr. 1st grade Gov. George Clinton Elem. Sch., Poughkeepsie, N.Y., 1989-91, pre-kindergarten and kindergarten tchr., 1991—, tchr. gifted and talented C.O.M.E.T. program, 1990-96. Mem. Jr. League of Kingston, 1996—. Mem. N.Y. State Reading Assn. (mid-Hudson reading com. 1995—), Kappa Delta Pi. Home: 20 Regent Dr Hopewell Junction NY 12533-5502

COPPOLA, PHYLLIS GLORIA CECIRE, retired special education educator; b. Bklyn., Apr. 20, 1930; d. Marie Corigliano Cecire Manley; m. Ben J. Coppola, Nov. 4, 1950; children: Robert, Joseph, John, Karen. AAS, Nassau C.C., 1972; BA, St. Joseph's Coll., 1974; MS, L.I. Univ., 1978. Cert. tchr., spl. edn. tchr. Head bookkeeper Babylon (N.Y.) Nat. Bank (now Chase Bank), 1948-54; homemaker, 1955-74; tchr. North Babylon (N.Y.) Schs., 1975-78; spl. edn. educator West Islip (N.Y.) Schs., 1978-96. Advisor Udall Rd. Student Coun., West Islip, Beautification, West Islip; mem. sch. adv. bd. Udall Rd. Sch., West Islip; mem. advisory homeroom com. West Islip Sch. Dist.; spl. edn. cons., 1995-96; advisor lit. mag. West Islip Schs., 1994-96, tchr. cons. L.D. specialist, 1978-96. Life mem. Lindenhurst (NY) PTA, 1971, West Islip (NY) PTA, 1984. Recipient commendation United Cerebral Palsy Assn. Mem. AAUW, Orton Soc., Coun. for Exceptional Children, Lions, Coun. for Exceptional Students. Roman Catholic. Avocations: crewel work, cooking, gardening. Home: 333 No Atlantic Ave #312 Cocoa Beach FL 32931

COPPOLA, SARAH JANE, special education educator; b. Alton, Ill., Apr. 20, 1957; d. Howard Earl and Dorothy Elizabeth (Eads) Cox; m. Daniel Joseph Coppola Jr., June 26, 1977; children: Daniel Joseph III, Shawn Marie. BS, Trenton State Coll., 1979; M Counseling Edn., Kean Coll. of N.J., 1995. Cert. guidance counselor, substance abuse counselor, N.J., early childhood cert., CIE coop. coord. cert. 1998, WECEP cert. Substitute tchr. Dunellen (N.J.) Bd. Edn., 1979-87, Greenbrook (N.J.) Bd. Edn., 1979-87, Middlesex (N.J.) Bd. Edn., 1979-87, Bound Brook (N.J.) Bd. Edn., 1983-84; tchr. of handicapped Piscataway (N.J.) Bd. Edn., 1987—, prin. adv. bd., 1990-91, editl. yearbook advisor, 1998—. Youth group advisor Trinity Reformed Ch., North Plainfield, N.J., 1983-91, deacon, 1985-87, 2001—, elder, 1997-2001, head Christian Edn., 1997—, v.p. consistory, 2000. Mem. NEA, N.J. Edn. Assn., Piscataway Edn. Assn., Kean Coll. Alumni Assn. (vol. Fish Hospitality program). Avocations: reading, needlework, church choir. Home: 200 Barclay Ct Piscataway NJ 08854 Office: Piscataway Bd Edn 100 Behmer Rd Piscataway NJ 08854-4161

COQUILLETTE, DANIEL ROBERT, lawyer, educator; b. Boston, May 23, 1944; s. Robert McTavish and Dagmar Alvida (Bistrup) C.; m. Judith Courtney Rogers, July 5, 1969; children: Anna, Sophia, Julia. AB, Williams Coll., 1966; MA Juris., U. Coll., Oxford U., Eng., 1969; JD, Harvard U., 1971. Bar: Mass. 1974, U.S. Dist. Ct. Mass. 1974, U.S. Ct. Appeals (1st cir.) 1974. Law clk. Mass. Supreme Ct., 1971-72; to chief justice Warren E. Burger U.S. Supreme Ct., 1972-73; assoc. Palmer & Dodge, Boston, 1973-75, ptnr., 1980-85; assoc. prof. law Boston U., 1975-78; dean, prof. Boston Coll. Law, 1985-93, prof., 1993-96, J. Donald Monan prof. law, 1996—. Vis. assoc. prof. law Cornell U., Ithaca, N.Y., 1977-78, 84; vis. prof. law Harvard U., 1978-79, 84-85, 94-2001, overseers com., Lester Kissel vis. prof., 2001—; reporter com. rules and procedures Jud. Conf. U.S.; mem. task force on rules of atty. conduct Supreme Jud. Ct. of Mass., 1996-97. Author: The Civilian Writers of Doctors Commons, London, 1988, Francis Bacon, 1993, Lawyers and Fundamental Moral Responsibility, 1995, Working Papers on Rules Governing Attorney Conduct, 1997, (with Basile, Beston, Donahue) Lex Mercatoria and Legal Pluralism, 1999, The Anglo-American Legal Heritage, 1999, (with McMorrow) Federal Law of Attorney Conduct, 2001; editor: Law in Colonial Massachusetts, 1985, Moore's Federal Practice, 3d edit., 1997; bd. dirs. New Eng. Quar., 1986—; contbr. articles to profl. jours. Trustee, sec.-treas. Ames Found; bd. overseers vis. com. Harvard Law Sch.; treas. Byron Meml. Fund; propr., trustee Boston Athenaeum. Recipient Kaufman prize in English Williams Coll., 1966, Sentinel of the Republic prize in polit. sci. Williams Coll., 1965; Hutchins scholar, 1966-67, Fulbright scholar, 1966-68 Mem. ABA (com. on profl. ethics 1990-93), Am. Law Inst., Mass. Bar Assn. (task force on model rules of profl. conduct), Boston Bar Assn., Am. Soc. Legal History (bd. dirs. 1985-89), Mass. Soc. Continuing Legal Edn. (bd. dirs. 1985-89), Selden Soc. (state corr.), Colonial Soc. Mass. (v.p., mem. coun.), Anglo-Am. Cathedral Soc. (bd. dirs.), Mass. Hist. Soc., Am. Antiquarian Soc., Phi Beta Kappa. Democrat. Mem. Soc. Of Friends. Home: 12 Rutland St Cambridge MA 02138-2503 Office: Boston Coll Sch Law 885 Centre St Newton MA 02459-1148 E-mail: coquill@bc.edu.

CORA, SPIRO PETE, retired secondary education educator; b. Greenville, Miss., Jan. 7, 1935; s. Pete George and Nina (Papaspiridon) C.; m. Virginia Lee Brothers, July 9, 1961; children: Michael S., Cathrine Ann, Christopher S. BA in History, Miss. Coll., Clinton, 1963, MA in History, 1969. Cert. tchr. social studies, Miss. Restaurant mgr. Shamrock Drive Inn, Jackson, Miss., 1958-61; tchr. social studies Collier County Schs., Immokalee, Fla., 1963-66; tchr. social studies Enochs Jr. H.S. Jackson Pub. Schs., 1966-69, tchr. social studies Wingfield H.S., 1969-96, ret., 1996. Mem. social studies Miss. Textbook Selection Com., Jackson, 1979-80; mem. Miss. evaluation team Close Up Found., Washington, 1981-82; chmn. dist. social studies dept. Jackson Pub. Schs., 1975-77, 79-80, 91-92. Reviewer of textbooks. Apptd. mem. Miss. Commn. for Nat. and Cmty. Svc., Jackson, 1994—. Mem. Nat. Coun. for Social Studies, Miss. Coun. for the Social Studies (dir. 1982-84), Nat. Coun. for History Edn., World History Assn. Greek Orthodox. Avocations: reading, camping, boating, birding (eagle watching). Home: 230 Swan Lake Dr Jackson MS 39212-5336

CORAY, JEFFREY WARREN, assistant principal, instructor; b. Chgo., July 16, 1958; s. Warren George and Rose (Paul) C. Student, U. Calif., Berkeley, 1976-77; BA, Occidental Coll., 1980; MA, Calif. State U., San Bernardino, 1996. Instr. Damien High Sch., La Verne, Calif., 1982-98, dir. student activities, 1983-87, chair social sci. dept., 1986-88, asst. prin. student activities, 1987-88, asst. prin. acad. affairs, instr. social sci., 1988-98; mgr. tech. support and tng., project mgr. Netel Ednl. Systems, Inc., Claremont, Calif., 1998-99; project mgr., tng. supr. SICORP, Inc., Rockville, Md., 1999—2000; project mgr., mgr. support C-Innovations, Inc., Claremont, 2000—; instr. U. Phoenix, 2000—, Columbia Coll., 1997—. Cons. advanced placement program N.J. Coll. Bd., 1987-98, exam reader, 1988-98. Mem. Omicron Delta Epsilon, Phi Kappa Phi. Republican. Roman Catholic. Avocations: music, theatre, opera. Home: PO Box 116 La Verne CA 91750-0116

CORBATO, FERNANDO JOSE, electrical engineer and computer science educator; b. Oakland, Calif., July 1, 1926; s. Hermenegildo and Charlotte (Jensen) C.; m. Isabel Blandford, Nov. 24, 1962 (dec. July 7, 1973); children: Carolyn Suzanne, Nancy Patricia; m. Emily Susan Fish, Dec. 6, 1975; stepchildren: David Lawrence Gish, Jason Charles Gish. Student, UCLA, 1943-44; BS, Calif. Inst. Tech., 1950; PhD, MIT, 1956. With Computation Ctr. MIT, Cambridge, Mass., 1955-66, dep. dir., 1963-66, head computer sys. rsch. group of project MAC, 1963-72, co-head sys. rsch. divsn., 1972-74, co-head automatic programming divsn., 1972-74, faculty mem., 1962—, prof. elec. engring. and computer sci., 1965-96, prof. emeritus, 1996—, assoc. dept. head computer sci. and engring., 1974-78, 8393, Cecil H. Green prof. computer sci. and engring., 1978-80, dir. computing and telecomm. resources, 1980-83, Ford prof. engring., 1993-96. Co-author: The Compatible Time Sharing System, 1963, Advanced Computer Programming, 1963, With USNR, 1944-46. Recipient Harry Goode Meml. award Am. Fedn. Info. Processing Socs., 1980, Computer & Comms. prize Found. for Computer & Comms. Promotion, Japan, 1998. Fellow IEEE (W.W. McDowell award 1966, Computer Pioneer award IEEE Computer Soc. 1982), AAAS, Assn. Computing Machinery (coun. 1964-66, A.M. Turing award 1990); mem. NAE, Am. Acad. Arts and Scis., Am. Phys. Soc., Sierra Club, Sigma Xi. Home: 88 Temple St Newton MA 02465-2307 Office: 545 Technology Sq Rm 613 Cambridge MA 02139-3539

CORBETT, LENORA MEADE, mathematician, community college educator; b. Reidsville, N.C., Aug. 1, 1950; children: Kenneth Russell Johnson, Ralph Nathaniel Brown. AAS in Electromechanics, Tech. Coll. of Alamance, 1985, AAS in Electronics, 1986; BS in Indsl. Tech., Electronics, N.C. A&T State U., 1996. Cloth insp. Burlington (N.C.) Industries, 1971-74; electrician's helper Williams Electric, Greensboro, NC, 1978, Nobility Mobile Homes, Reidsville, NC, 1979; instr. math. and physics Alamance C.C., Graham, NC, 1985—2002, chmn. learning resources, 1993. Contbr. poems to profl. publs. (Golden Poet award 1991, Merit award 1990, 92). Mem. sr. choir Jones Cross Rd. Ch., Reidsville, 1988-94, pastor's aide mem., 1988-90, jr. Sunday sch. tchr., 1989-91, asst. choir sec., 1988-94; bd. dirs. Nu Generation Enrichment Program; mem. bd. Nu Generation Enrichment Ctr., Teach Tolerance Nat. Campaign Tolerance, 2002, 03. Recipient Famous Poet, 1996, 2000, Editor's Choice Award, 1997, Famous Poets So. Recognition award, 1998. Mem. AAUP, AAUW, Alamance C.C. Alumni Assn., Golden Key, N.C. A&T State U. Alumni Assn. Baptist. Avocations: cooking, reading, writing poetry, drawing, singing.

CORBETT, SUZANNE ELAINE, food writer, marketing executive, food historian; b. St. Louis, Jan. 23, 1953; d. George Edward and Opal Laverne (Duncan) Traxel; m. James Joseph Corbett, Jr., July 17, 1970 (div. 2000); 1 child, James J. III. BA, Webster U., 1994, MA in Media Comm., 1995. Cert. culinary profl., Internat. Assn. Culinary Profls. Tchr. Inst. Continuing Edn. St. Louis C.C., 1976—; tchr. cmty. edn. Lindbergh Sch. Dist. Pub. Schs., St. Louis, 1983-89; confectioner/caterer Suzanne Corbett Seasonal Confections, St. Louis, 1977-84; test baker Fleishman's Yeast, St. Louis, 1983; food stylist St. Louis, 1980—; rsch. cons./food mktg. and rsch. food/product history, 1994; rsch. cons. media prodn. PanCor Prodns., 1994—. Food historian, folklorist Jefferson Nat. Parks Assn., St. Louis County Parks and Recreation, Mo. Hist. Soc., St. Louis Art Mus., Colonial Dames of Am.; food media trainer Internat. Assn. Culinary Profls., 1990; ALFHM lectr. in field. Author: Cowpuncher's Provision, 1988, River Fare, 1990, Pharoh's Pheast-Food from the Nile, 1991, Tips from Missouri Win Country, 1993, Pushcarts & Stalls: The Souland Market History Cookbook, 1999; food writer, cookbook editor St. Louis Bugle food editor, 1991-96, columnist, 1991-96; columnist Sr. Circuit Newspaper; food writer, columnist News Weekly, Connoisseur; contbg. food editor St. Louis Home & Lifestyles, Achieve Mag. Bd. dirs. St. Louis South sect. Am. Heart Assn., Historyonics Theatre Co.; mem. Mo. Grape and Wine Adv. Bd. Recipient Folklife Greentree grant award Ralston Purina, 1989, grant award Commerce Bank, 1990, grant award Wetterau Foods, 1991. Mem. Women in Communications (pres. St. Louis chpt. 1996, Communication awards 1989, 90, 91, 92, 93, 94, 95, 96, 97, 98, 99), Nat. Fedn. Press Women (v.p. Mo. chpt.), Mo. Press Women (past pres., Communication award 1989, 96, 97, Communicator of Yr. 1993), Victorian Soc. Am. (past pres. St. Louis chpt.), James Beard Found. (charter), Am. Inst. Wine and Food, Internat. Assn. Culinary Profls. (cert., culinary historian Boston and Ann Arbor, internat. conf. com. 1990), Assn. Ind. Video and Filmmakers, St. Louis Press Club (former co-editor Courier, interim dir., Pres.' award, Press Club Charitable Fund pres. 1993-94), Nat. Fedn. Press Women (Communication and Writing awards), Nat. Trust for Hist. Preservation, St. Louis Culinary Soc. (sec., bd. dirs.), Order Eastern Star. Roman Catholic. Avocations: folklife crafts, gardening, travel, historic preservation. Home and Office: Apt B 12150 Queens Charter Ct Saint Louis MO 63146-5250 E-mail: corbettsuzanne@aol.com.

CORBITT, EUMILLER MATTIE, elementary and secondary education educator, special education educator; b. Detroit, Jan. 07; d. Harrison and Arnetha (Tatum) Jones; m. Luther Corbitt (div. Dec. 1976); children: Tonya, Stephen. BS, Wayne State U., 1969, MEd, 1976, EdS, 1995. Cert. elem. and secondary sch. tchr., cert. tchr. spl. edn. emotionally and mentally impaired, grades K-12, elem. secondary sch. and central office administration. Tchr. mentally impaired Detroit Pub. Schs., 1969-72, tchr. emotionally impaired, 1972-75, spl. edn. tchr. cons., 1975—, Title I tchr. math. and sci., summers 1993-96; mediator Spl. Edn. Mediation Svcs., Lansing, Mich., 1986-96, Spl. Edn. Mediation Svcs. State Project PL 94-142, Lansing, Mich., 1985—; spl. edn. hearing officer Mich. Dept. Edn., Lansing, 1985—. Developer at-risk program for emotionally impaired, socially maladjusted and ADHD students 12-17 yrs. Wolverine Human Svcs., Detroit, Mich. 1998—; mem. U.S. del. educators and attys. to South Africa for evaluation of schs. and govtl. agys. under leadership of Nelson Mandella Citizen Amb. program People to People, Spokane, Wash., 1996; mem. citizens alliance to uphold spl. edn. study adv. com. Emotionally Impaired Children in Mich./Lansing, 1986; mem. North Ctrl. Assn. accreditation com. Grand Rapids (Mich.) Pub. Schs., 1981; presenter profl. devel. conf. Detroit Fedn. Tchrs. and Det. Pub. Sch. Adminstrs., 1996. Chairperson Met. Detroit chpt. March of Dimes, 1987; chairperson Women Who Dare to Care com. United Negro Coll. Fund, Detroit, 1987-89; gen. coord. Mus. African Am. History, Detroit, 1987; tutor, usher, chairperson Hartford Meml. Bapt. Ch., Detroit, 1979—. Recipient Mayor's award of merit for Cmty. Svc., City of Detroit, 1987, plaque and cert. March of Dimes, 1987; recognized as outstanding educator Detroit Tchr., Detroit Fedn. Tchrs., 1987, 94. Mem. Coun. for Exceptional Children (presenter nat. conv. 1983, cert. 1983), Soc. Profls. in Dispute Resolution, Wayne State U. Alumni Assn., Delta Sigma Theta (chairperson 1965—), Phi Delta Kappa (chairperson). Avocations: golf, writing poetry, racquetball, painting, reading. Home: 1249 Navarre Pl Detroit MI 48207-3014 Office: Martin Luther King Jr Sr HS 3200 E Lafayette Detroit MI 48207 E-mail: eumillercorbitt@aol.com.

CORBRIDGE, JAMES NOEL, JR., law educator, educator; b. Mineola, N.Y., May 27, 1934; s. James Noel Sr. and Edna (Springer) C.; children: Loren, Stuart. AB, Brown U., 1955; LLB, Yale U., 1963. Assoc. Lord, Day & Lord, N.Y.C., 1963-65; asst. prof. law U. Colo., Boulder, 1965-67, assoc. prof., 1967-73, prof., 1973—, v.p. student affairs, 1970-72, v.p. student and minority affairs, 1972-74, vice chancellor acad. affairs, 1974-77, interim vice chancellor acad. services, 1979-81, acting vice chancellor acad. affairs, 1986, chancellor, 1986—. Vis. scholar Inst. for Advanced Legal Studies U. London, 1977, 85, Univ. Linkoping, Sweden, 1985, 1997. Contbr. articles to profl. jours. Served to lt. (j.g.) USNR, 1957-60. Mem. Colo. Bar Assn., Boulder County Bar Assn., Internat. Assn. Water Lawyers, Internat. Water Resources Assn. Clubs: Boulder Country. Episcopalian. Avocations: golf, bird carving, birding. Home: 1635 Dilar Dr Grove OK 74344-5500 Office: U Colo PO Box 401 Boulder CO 80309-0401

CORBY, JOY E(LIZABETH), psychotherapist, educator, marriage and family therapist; b. Mouila, Gabon, Mar. 21, 1955; (parents U.S. citizens); d. J. Albert and Elizabeth H. (Mason) C. BA in Psychology, Nyack Coll., 1977; M Profl. Studies Theology and Missions, Alliance Theol. Sem., Nyack, N.Y., 1980; MA in Clin. Psychology, Wheaton (Ill.) Coll., 1993; PhD in Marriage and Family Therapy, Syracuse U., 2003. Licensed marriage and family therapist, Ill.; supr. in tng. for marriage and family therapy. Youth pastor Long Hill Chapel, Chatham, N.J., 1979-82; missionary Christian and Missionary Alliance, Gabon, Africa, 1982-93; therapist, crisis intervention worker Outreach Cmty. Ministries, Wheaton and Warrenville, Ill., 1993-97; therapist Goldberg Marriage & Family Theapy Ctr., Syracuse, N.Y., 1997-99, Onondaga Pastoral Counseling Ctr., Syracuse, N.Y., 1999-2000; assoc. prof. psychology Crown Coll., St. Bonifacius, Minn., 2000—03; assoc. prof. marriage and family therapy Evang. Sch. Theology, Myerstown, Pa., 2003—. Adj. prof. Syracuse U., 1999-2000; ofcl. worker Christian and Missionary Alliance, 1979—; reviewer new books tyndale House Pubs., Wheaton, 1997—. Contbg. author: Missionary Voices, 1996. Mem. Am. Assn. for Marriage and Family Therapy (clin.), Am. Assn. Christian Counselors, Kappa Omicron Nu. Avocations: tennis, biking, music, sports. Home: 706 Reo Rd Watertown MN 55388 Office: 121 S Coll St Myerstown PA 17067-1299 E-mail: jcorby@evangelical.edu.

CORCORAN, JANET PATRICIA, elementary school educator; b. St. Louis, Feb. 9, 1949; d. Oliver Albert Schuh and Eleanor Louise Schottel; m. Gregory Edward Corcoran, Aug. 29, 1970; children: Kelly, Bryan, Terence, Jason. BS in Secondary Edn., U. Ill., 1971; MA in Specific Learning Disabilities, Marycrest Coll., 1983. Nat. bd. cert. tchr. Tchr. Antioch (Ill.) Schs., 1971—72, Belvidere (Ill.) Schs., 1974—75, Davenport (Iowa) Schs., 1980—. Bd. dirs., sec. Scott County Hist. Preservation Soc., Davenport, 1995—2003; del. Nat. Dem. Conv., N.Y.C., 1992. Mem.: AAUW (scholarship chmn. 1993—2001), NEA (conv. del. 1990—2003), Davenport Edn. Assn. (local rep. 1983—2003). Democrat. Roman Catholic. Home: 4407 N Linwood Davenport IA 52806 Office: JB Young Mid Sch Davenport IA 52806

CORDARO, JOSEPH FRANK, school principal; b. Des Moines, Iowa, Feb. 17, 1949; s. George Santo and Angela Lucie (Sposeto) C.; m. Rose Marie Coury, June 17, 1971; children: Georgina, Mitzi. BS, Drake U., 1971, MA, 1988, Doctor, 1996. Cert. tchr. Tchr., coach Assumption High Sch., Davenport, Iowa, 1971-75; tchr. Visitation Sch., Des Moines, 1975-76; tchr., coach Dowling High Sch., West Des Moines, 1976-88; prin. St.

Anthony Sch., Des Moines, 1988—. Mem. Area Need Com., Des Moines, 1994—. Mem. ASCD, Nat. Cath. Edn. Assn. (Elem. Prin. Acad. award 1994), Iowa High Sch. Athletic Assn. Roman Catholic. Avocations: sports, woodwork, contruction. Office: St Anthony Sch 16 Columbus Ave Des Moines IA 50315-7113 E-mail: jcordaro@dowling.pvt.k12.ia.us.

CORDEIRO, ELIZABETH DALEIN, law enforcement training educator; b. New Bedford, Mass., Oct. 18, 1958; children: Vincent, Lisa. AS in Criminal Justice, Bristol C.C., 1979; BS in Adminstrn. of Criminal Justice, Roger Williams Coll., 1982. Court transp. officer New Bedford 3rd Dist. Ct., 1980-81; police officer U.S. Dept. Defense Police, Mass. and R.I., 1981-86; corrections officer S.E. Correctional Ctr., Bridgewater, Mass., 1986-87; police instr. Police Survival Def. Tactics Tng., New Bedford, 1987—. Specialized training include Training Rsch. Validation, 1989, Use of Force Reporting Systems, 1989, Monadnock PR-24 Police Baton instr., 1988, Court Room Survival, 1989, Edges Weapon Defense, 1989, Street Survival, 1982-87 and others. Author: Who's Who in Law Enforcement Collecting and Police Trainers, 1988; editor, pub.: Who's Who in Law Enforcement Institutes and Schools, Trainers, and Training Organizations, 1995, 2d edit., 1999—, Who's Who in Law Enforcement Trainers, 2d edit., 1999-2000. Office: Police Survival Def Tactics PO Box 6454 New Bedford MA 02742-6454

COREA, LUIGI, cardiologist, educator; b. Taverna, Italy, Apr. 6, 1939; s. Ulisse and Antonia (Garcea) C.; M.D., U. Perugia, 1964; postgrad. U. Pisa, 1969-71; m. Maria Federica Tei, Oct. 7, 1972; children— Francesco, Pierluigi. Intern, resident U. Pisa, 1964-71; house physician Patologie Medica, U. Perugia, Italy, 1964-69, asst. at semeiotica medica, 1969—, registrar, 1972—, sr. registrar, 1974—, assoc. prof. semeiotica medica and cardiology, 1981-83, prof. cardiology Sch. Medicine, 1983—; faculty cardiology Nat. Heart Hosp. and St. Mary's Hosp., London, 1967. Decorated commendatore of St. Gregorio Magno of Vaticano (Rome). Fellow Internat. Coll. Angiology, European Soc. Cardiology, Am. Coll. Cardiology; mem. Italian Soc. Cardiology (council 1970-80, 86—), Italian Soc. Hypertension, Italian Soc. Vascular Pathology, Italian Fedn. Medicine of Sport, Internat. Soc. Hypertension, Italian Soc. Internal Medicine, European Soc. Clin. Investigation. Democrat. Roman Catholic. Author: The Pheocromocytoma, 1980; L'ipertrofia cardiaca; contbg. author: Trattato di Patologia Medica, Trattato Italiano di Cardiologia; contbr. articles on cardiovascular pathology to profl. jours. Home: 8 Degli Olivetani 06100 Perugia Italy Office: Policlinico Universitario Cattedra di Cardiologia 06100 Perugia Italy

CORELLI, JOHN CHARLES, physicist, educator; b. Providence, Aug. 6, 1930; s. John Dominic Corelli and Immacolata (Caldarelli) C.; separated; children: Carolyn Margaret, John Joseph. BS in Physics, Providence Coll., 1952; MS in Physics, Brown U., 1954; PhD in Physics, Purdue U., 1958. Physicist Knolls Atomic Power Lab. GE, Schenectady, N.Y., 1958-61, cons., 1979-81; prof. nuclear engring. and engring. physics Rensselaer Poly. Inst., Troy, N.Y., 1962-96, prof. emeritus, 1997—. Contbr. more than 100 articles to Jour. Applied Physics, Jour. Nuclear Materials, Phys. Rev., Jour. Vacuum Sci. and Tech. Spl. fellow NIH, Rochester Univ., N.Y., 1971., 1971. Mem. Am. Phys. Soc., Am. Nuclear Soc. Home: 1A Salem Ct Albany NY 12203-5932 Business E-Mail: corelj@rpi.edu.

COREY, DONALD EDWARD, elementary education educator; b. Terre Haute, Ind., Nov. 5, 1950; s. Paul Edward and Norma Ruth (Stufflebean) C.; m. Carole Elaine Lee Hos, July 10, 1977 (div. July 1981); 1 child, Andrew Joseph. BS, Ind. State U., 1980, MS, 1986. 6th grade tchr. North Vermillion Elem., Cayuga, Ind., 1981-97; tchr. English North Vermillion H.S./Jr. H.S., 1997—. Sgt. U.S. Army, 1973-75. Baptist. Home: 410 S 34th St Terre Haute IN 47803-2352 Office: North Vermillion Elem RR # 191 Cayuga IN 47928 E-mail: dcorey@nvc.k12.in.us.

COREY, SUSAN HORN, elementary school educator, special education educator; b. Greenwich, Conn., Apr. 5, 1952; d. John Dakin and Edith (Keeney) Horn; m. Kevin Michael Corey, May 19, 1979. AA in Liberal Arts, Bradford Jr. Coll., 1972; BS in Early Childhood Edn., Wheelock Coll., 1974; MA in Spl. Edn., Fairfield U., 1992. Cert. tchr., Conn., spl. edn. tchr., Conn. Tchr. aide Darien (Conn.) Pub. Schs., 1975-76; telex operator Pepperidge Farm, Inc., Norwalk, Conn., 1976-77, payroll clk., 1977-79, sec. human rels., 1979-81, cashier specialist, 1981-86, acct. gen. acctg., 1986-91; tchr. grade 1 Norwalk Pub. Schs., 1991-93, tchr. kindergarten, 1993—. Mem. Citizens Com. Against the Jail, Newtown, Conn., 1989. Mem. Conn. Assn. for Children with Learning Disabilities, Coun. of Exceptional Children, Internat. Reading Assn. Avocations: counted cross stitch, cats, crafts, music. Home: 10 Carol Ann Dr Newtown CT 06470-2317

CORKERY, MARTHA GALLAGHER, elementary education educator; b. Portland, Maine, Apr. 21, 1956; d. Martin Patrick and Laurette (Lauzon) Gallagher; m. David Robert Corkery, Aug. 12, 1989. BA in English & Theatre, U. Maine, 1978; MS in Edn., U. So. Maine, 1989; EdD, Nova S.E. U., 2002. Tchr. English Massabesic High Sch., Waterboro, Maine, 1978-81, Gorham (Maine) High Sch., 1981-94, U. So. Maine, Gorham, 1989-92; assoc. cons. So. Maine Partnership, Gorham, 1992-94; tchr. 6th grade Gorham Village Sch., 1994-97; asst. prin. Bonny Eagle Mid. Sch., 1997—2002; prin. Wescott Jr. HS, 2002—. Speaker in field. Trustee Old Red Ch., Standish, Maine, 1983-86; chair common ground planning com. Maine Leadership Consortium, Augusta, 1993-94. Blaine House scholar, 1988-89. Mem. Nat. Coun. Tchrs. English, Maine Edn. Assn. (bd. dirs. 1992-97), Maine. Coun. Tchrs. English/Lang. Arts, Maine Reading Assn., Gorham Tchrs. Assn. (pres. 1989-95), Internat. Reading Assn. Avocations: sailing, powerboating, cross country skiing, handicrafts, reading. Home: 54 Oak Ridge Dr Standish ME 04084-6019 Office: Wescott Jr HS 426 Bridge St Westbrook ME 04092

CORLESS, DOROTHY ALICE, nurse educator; b. Reno, Nev., May 28, 1943; d. John Ludwig and Vera Leach (Wilson) Adams; children: James Lawrence Jr., Dorothy Adele Carroll. RN, St. Luke's Sch. Nursing, 1964. Clinician, cons., educator, grant author, adminstr. Fresno County Mental Health Dept., 1991—94; instr. police sci. State Ctr. Tng. Facility, 1991-94; pvt. practice, mental health cons., educator, 1970—; sr. assoc. guidance distbn. disaster svcs. ARC, 2003—. Res. asst. officer ARC, Disaster Mental Health Svcs., 1993-2003. Maj. USAFR, 1972-94. Mem. NAFE, Forensic Mental Health Assn. Calif., Calif. Peace Officer's Assn., Critical Incident Stress Found. Office: 3401 38th St NW # 304 Washington DC 20016 E-mail: dorothydmh@aol.com.

CORLEY, DONNA JEAN, education educator, language arts educator; b. LaGrande, Oreg., May 23, 1950; d. Donald D. and Aria Jean (Tufford) Wattenbarger; m. Bill H. Corley, June 12, 1970; children: Jason Andrew, Seth David. AA, Tulsa Jr. Coll., 1983; BS in Elem. Edn., Northeastern State U., Tahlequah, Okla., 1985, MEd in Elem. Edn., 1987; PhD, Tex. A&M U., 1990. Cert. tchr. grades K-8, gifted and talented, Tex. Substitute tchr. Broken Arrow (Okla.) Ind. Sch. Dist., 1983-85; tchr. 5th grade Southside Elem. Sch., Broken Arrow, Okla., 1985-87; coord. microteaching Tex. A&M U., College Station, lectr., 1987-90, tchr. lang. arts methods for the elem. tchr., 1990—; with gifted programs resource div. Conroe (Tex.) Independent Sch. Dist., 1993-94; adj. prof. human growth and devel. Sam Houston State U., Huntsville, Tex., 1994—. Dir. Region VI Tex. Assn. for the Gifted and Talented, 1997—; adj. prof. Sam Huston State U., Huntsville, Tex.; apptd. task force by Tex. Edn. Agy. to devel. guidelines for edn. of gifted learners in Tex., 1996; numerous presentations and insvcs. in field. Contbr. to profl. publs. Delta Kappa Gamma scholar, 1983, 84. Mem. NEA, ASCD, Broken Arrow Edn. Assn., Okla. Edn. Assn., Okla. Reading Coun., Tex. Assn. for the Gifted and Talented (exec. bd.), Kappa Delta Pi, Phi Theta Kappa, Rho Theta Sigma, Alpha Chi. Home: 639 S Rivershire Dr Conroe TX 77304-4903

CORLEY, JENNY LYND WERTHEIM, elementary education educator; b. Lincoln, Ill., June 18, 1937; d. Robert Glenn and Nancy Lynd (Hoblit) Wertheim; m. William Gene Corley, Aug. 9, 1959; children: Anne Lynd Corley Baum, Robert William, Scott Elson. BS in Music Edn., U. Ill., 1959, MS in Music Edn., 1961; postgrad., U. Ill., Loyola U., 1985—. Tchr. choral music Mahomet (Ill.)/Seymour K-12, 1959-61; supr. music Fairfax County (Va.), 1961-63; tchr. music Highland Park (Ill.) 107, 1969, dir. gifted edn., 1969-70; tchr. music Glenview (Ill.) 34, 1981—2003. V.p. Corley Agroleum Properties, 1993—2003; water safety instr./trainer ARC; lifeguard instr./trainer Cmty. First Aid & Safety, 1995. Dir. mid-Am. bd. ARC, Chgo., 1980-86; mem. Chgo. Symhony Orch. Chorus, 1965-75. Recipient Heart of Gold United Way, 1992, Cmty. Svc. award Ill. Park & Recreation Assn./Ill. Assn. Park Dists., 1994, Disting. Svc. award Boys and Girls Swimming Ofcl., Ill. High Sch. Assn., 1994, also 25 yr. recognitiuon as swimming ofcl. Mem. Music Edn. Nat. Conf., North Shore Music Tchrs. Assn. (treas. 1987-90), Jr. League Chgo. (treas. 1978-81), Sigma Alpha Iota, Phi Delta Kappa (found. chmn. 1994—), U. Ill. Music Alumnae (pres. bd. dirs. 1995-97). Presbyterian. Home: 744 Glenayre Dr Glenview IL 60025-4411 E-mail: corley@corleywg.com.

CORLEY, MYRNA LOY, school system administrator; b. Cleve., June 28, 1959; d. James Arthur and Verna Samone (Gaddis) Patton; m. Travis Corley, May 17, 1980; 1 child, Eméus Arthur. BEd, U. Akron, 1980; MEd, Cleve. State U., 1989. Cert. elem. and spl. edn. tchr., elem. and secondary prin., Ohio. Spl. edn. tchr East Cleveland (Ohio) City Schs., 1981-85, work study coord., 1985-90, asst. prin., 1990—. Author: Personal Prose, 1991. Facilitator, trainer System Tng. for Effective Parenting, Cleveland Heights, Ohio, 1991—, Bldg. Family Strenghts, Cleveland Heights, 1991—. Mem. ASCD, Sigma Gamm Rho (pres. 1978-80), Omicron Delta Kappa. Democrat. Baptist. Avocations: writing, fishing, bowling, exercise. Office: Kirk Middle Sch 14410 Terrace Rd East Cleveland OH 44112-3928 Home: 23126 Hardwick Rd Beachwood OH 44122-3158

CORMICAN, M. ALMA, elementary education educator; b. N.Y.C., May 20, 1940; d. Patrick John and Kathleen Teresa (Coleman) C. BS, Fordham U., 1962; MA, CCNY, 1965; MS, Columbia U., 1974. Cert. tchr., N.Y. Tchr. N.Y.C. Bd. Edn., 1962-65, White Plains (N.Y.) Pub. Schs., 1965—. Lobbyist N.Y. State United Tchrs., Albany, 1972, 75, 78-87, 90, 91, 93—. Mem. White Plains Tchrs. Assn. (pres. 1971-72, 79-87, 95—, chief negotiator 1971—), Phi Delta Kappa. Democrat. Avocations: music, chorale music.

CORMICK, ALBINA, foreign language educator; b. Yonkers, N.Y., May 7, 1920; d. Gaston and Albina (Hofbauer) Barre; m. Jean F. Cormick, Aug. 1, 1942; 1 child, Jacqueline. BA, U. Grenoble, France, 1939; MA, Assumption Coll., 1969. Cert. tchr. English, Latin and French. French-English sec. UN, Paris; payroll clk., bookkeeper Worcester (Mass.) Poly. Inst.; sec. to pres. Assumption Coll., Worcester; tchr. French and Latin Worcester Pub. Schs.; prof. French Assumption Coll., Worcester. Recipient awards MaFLA, City of Worcester; named Chevalier dans L'Ordre des Palmes Academiques by Ministere de l'Edn. Francaise; Recipient Benefactor's medal Can. 78th Fraser Highlanders Can., cert. of recognition Gov. of Mass. Mem. NEA, Mass. Tchrs. Assn., EAW, Am. Assn. Tchrs. of French, Mass. Fgn. Lang. Assn., Assn. Francaise, Worcester Profl. Women's Club. Address: 119 Main St # 215 Rutland MA 01543-1316

CORMIER-THOMAS, MARY IRMA, speech and language pathologist; b. New Iberia, La., Mar. 30, 1949; d. Nicholas James and Irma (Jones) C.; m. Maxine Thomas, Aug. 19, 1989; 1 child, Joy Marie. BS, So. U. A&M, Baton Rouge, 1971; MS, So. Ill. U., 1977; postgrad., So. U. A&M, 1987. Speech/lang. therapist Clarksdale (Miss.) Pub. Schs., 1971-75, Dist. 189 Pub. Schs., East St. Louis, Ill., 1975-84; chtp. I lang. therapist E. Baton Rouge (La.) Parish Pub. Schs., 1984—. Planner E. Baton Rouge Parish Strategic Team, 1991; organizer Adopt-A-Sch. program, Baton Rouge, 1989-91. Contbr. articles to profl. jurs. Organizer, leader Girl Scouts U.S.A., E. Baton Rouge, 1985—; commr. Election Bd., Baton Rouge, 1985—. Named Tchr. of the Yr. E. Baton Rouge Parish Pub. Schs., 1990-91. Mem. NEA, La. Speech/Hearing Assn., La. Edn. Assn., Coun. for Exceptional Children, Assn. Tchr. Educators, Internat. Reading Assn., Nat. Social Sci. Assn. (presenter 1989). Democrat. Baptist. Avocations: reading, travel, dancing, volleyball, sports. Home: 4691 Sugarland Dr Baton Rouge LA 70814-8069 Office: Baton Rouge Talent Den Inc 5700 Florida Blvd Baton Rouge LA 70806-4274

CORNBLEET, AILEEN GAIL HIRSCH, English language and social studies educator; b. Chgo., Nov. 8, 1946; d. Irving Carlton and Anne (Ditlov) Hirsch; m. David H. Cornbleet, Aug. 18, 1968; children: Jonathan M., Jocelyn F. BS summa cum laude, U. Wis., 1968; interpreter's degree in German/History, U. Heidelberg, Fed. Republic Germany, 1970; MA in Secondary Edn. summa cum laude, Boston U., 1972. Instr. Heidelberg Am. High Sch., 1968-75, Temple Sholom, Chgo., 1976-88; instr. ESL Oakton Community Coll., Skokie, Ill., 1986-87; supervising tchr. MA students, insr. philosophy and history edn., social studies methods instr. Nat. Coll. Edn., 1987-92; tchr. lit. Armstrong Sch., Chgo., 1993—. Sec. Orgn. Rehab. Tng., Lincolnwood, Ill., 1980; mem. Lincolnwood Sch. Bd. Dist. 74, 1982-87. Recipient Master Tchr. award Bd. Jewish Edn., 1986, Loyola U. 2001 award Tchrs. Applying Whole Lang., 1993, 3d place award McDonald's Ednl. Contest, 1992. Fellow ASCD; mem. Stock Market Club, Phi Alpha Theta, Pi Lambda Phi. Avocations: art, classical music, opera, antique dolls, porcelain.

CORNELIUS, WAYNE ANDERSON, electrical and computer engineering consultant; b. Russellville, Ky., Nov. 8, 1923; s. Eldon and Mabel Ruth (Gentle) C.; m. Elizabeth Grider (dec. Sept. 1946); children: Johanna Vastola, Keith, John(dec.); m. Linda Brady, Apr. 27, 1985; stepchildren: Pam Gondzur, Mark Smith, Todd Smith, Allison Stines. BS, U. Ky., 1953, EE, 1966; MS, U. Louisville, 1962; ABD, U. Cin., 1972. Elec. engr. U.S. Naval Ordnance Sta., Louisville, 1953-66, dir. engring. electronics lab., 1973-85; rsch. assoc. Pa. State U., State College, 1966-67; prof. engring. tech. Miami U., Oxford, Ohio, 1967-72; elec. engr. System Devel. Corp., Dayton, Ohio, 1972-73; chmn. dept. electronics tech. Ivy Tech. Coll., Sellersburg, Ind., 1985-90. Adj. prof. elec. engring. tech. Purdue U., New Albany, 1992-95, U. Louisville, 1976-84; adj. prof. math. Bellarmine Coll., Louisville, 1964-66, Ind. U., New Albany, 1990-91. With USN, 1942-45. Named to Honorable Order of Ky. Cols., 1963. Mem. NSPE, Am. Soc. for Engring. Edn., Phi Delta Kappa. Democrat. Presbyterian. Office: 9005 Lethborough Dr Louisville KY 40299-1437 E-mail: lbcwac@prodigy.net.

CORNELL, DEWEY GENE, psychologist; b. Louisville, ., June 22, 1956; m. Nancy Emily Trinka, Aug. 19, 1978; children: Cristina, Allison, Erin. AB, Transylvania U., 1977; MA, U. Mich., 1979, PhD, 1981. Lic. clinical psychologist. Intern U. Mich. Psychol. Clinic, Ann Arbor, 1979-81; postdoctoral scholar dept. psychiatry U. Mich., Ann Arbor, 1981-83; clin. psychologist Ctr. Forensic Psychiatry, Ann Arbor, 1983-86; asst. prof. Sch. Edn., U. Va., Charlottesville, 1986-91, assoc. prof., 1991-99, prof., 1999—, faculty assoc. Inst. Law, Psychiatry and Pub. Policy, 1986—. Dir. Va. Youth Violence Project, 1996—; asst. prof. psychology Mich. State U., East Lansing, 1985-86; pvt. practice, Charlottesville, 1986—. Author: Families of Gifted Children, 1984, Designing Safer Schools for Virginia, 1998; co-editor Juvenile Homicide, 1989; co-author: Recommended Practices in Gifted Education, 1991; contbr. articles to profl. jours. Fellow Internat. Soc. Rsch. Aggression; mem. APA, Am. Psychology Law Soc., Am. Ednl. Rsch. Assn., Va. Psychol. Assn. Avocations: Go, basketball, tennis. Office: U Va Sch Edn 405 Emmet St Charlottesville VA 22903

CORNELL, MARSHA R. elementary education educator; b. Apr. 1, 1952; m. Robert J. Cornell, June 14, 1987. BS, Pa. State U., 1974; postgrad., Carnegie Mellon U., 1991—. Cert. elem. tchr., environ. edn., Pa. Environ. educator Elizabeth Forward Sch. Dist., Elizabeth, Pa., 1974-81, elem. classroom tchr., 1981-91, middle sch. program devel. coord., 1991-92, middle sch. English tchr., 1992—. Mem. Sch. Restructuring Design Team, Monegehala Valley Edn. Consortium, McKeesport, Pa., 1989—, editorial bd. Pa. Jour. of Teacher Leadership, 1990—; tchr. rep. to Pa. Lead Tchr. Adv. Bd., 1991—; co-chair EF Strategic Plan Sch. Identity Com., 1992—. Recipient Gift of Time tribute Am. Family Inst. at Valley Forge, 1988, Thanks to Tchrs. Excellence recognition, KDKA TV amd Univ. Pitts., 1990; grantee Monogehela Valley Edn. Consortium, McKeesport, 1988. Mem. NEA, ASCD, McKeesport Coll. Club, Pa. State U. Alumni Assn. Avocations: golf, travel. Office: Elizabeth Forward Sch Dist 401 Rock Run Rd Elizabeth PA 15037-2416

CORNFIELD, MELVIN, lawyer, university institute director; b. Chgo., June 5, 1927; s. Harry and Annabelle (Maltz) C.; m. Edith Pauline Haas, June 24, 1951; children: Daniel Benjamin, Deborah S. Cornfield Alexander. AB, U. Chgo., 1948, JD, 1951. Bar: D.C. 1951, N.Y. 1958. Atty. durable goods divsn. Office Price Stblzn., Washington, 1951-53; atty., advisor Chief Counsel's Office IRS, Washington, 1953-58; assoc. Willkie, Farr, Gallagher, Walton & FitzGibbon, N.Y.C., 1958-63; dir. taxes NBC, Inc., 1963-66; staff v.p. tax affairs RCA Corp., N.Y.C., 1966-76, v.p., treas., 1976-82, v.p. tax affairs, 1982-85; dir. NYU Tax Inst., 1985-94. With USAAF, 1946-47. Home: 4703 Iselin Ave Bronx NY 10471-3323

CORNICK, MICHAEL F(REDERICK), accounting educator; b. Evansville, Ind., Apr. 15, 1940; s. Isadore John and Belle (Wigdor) C.; m. Charlotte Bozovich, Mar. 2, 1985; children; Elizabeth Ann, Ann Elliott. BS in Indsl. Mgmt., Purdue U., 1963; MBA, U.N.C., Chapel Hill, 1970, PhD, 1980. CPA, N.C. Stockbro. Thomson and McKinnon, Winston-Salem, N.C., 1965-68; bank officer 1 st. Nat. Atlanta, 1970-72; assoc. prof. acctg. U. N.C., Charlotte, 1985—2002, Winthrop U., 2002—. Adv. Internat. Bus. Club, Charlotte, 1987— ; leader Internat. Acctg. Overseas, Fed. Rep. Germany, London, 1988—. Author: Bank Accounting, 1984: contbr. articles to profl. jours. Mem. British Am. Bus. Coun. 1st lt. U.S. Army, 1963-65. Recipient cert. appreciation, Retarted Citizens Greensboro, 1983. Mem. AICPA, Inst. Mgmt. Accts. (dir. 1985-88), Am. Acctg. Assn., N.C. Soc. CPAs, Charlotte World Trade Assn. Avocations: reading, tennis, basketball. Home: 1409 Biltmore Dr Charlotte NC 28207-2556 Office: Winthrop Univ Rock Hill SC 29733

CORNUEJOLS, GERARD PIERRE, operations research educator; b. Meknes, Morocco, Nov. 16, 1950; came to U.S., 1974; s. Jean and Renee (Floch) C.; m. Chantal Fourgeaud, June 18, 1983 (dec. June 1994). Cert. civil engr., Nat. Sch. Bridges and Roads, Paris, 1974; PhD in Ops. Rsch., Cornell U., 1978. Asst. prof. ops. rsch. Carnegie Mellon U., Pitts., 1978-81, assoc. prof., 1981-87, prof., 1987—, IBM chair, 2000—, u. chair, 2002—. Author: Combinatorial Optimization, 2001; contbr. articles to profl. jours., including Math. of Ops. Rsch., Jour. Combinatorial Theory, Ops. Rsch. Mem. Inst. for Ops. Rsch. and Mgmt. Sci. (chmn. optimization sect. 1999-2000), Math. Programming Soc. Avocation: painting. Office: Carnegie Mellon U GSIA 5000 Forbes Ave Pittsburgh PA 15213 E-mail: gc0v@andrew.cmu.edu.

CORNWELL, CHARLES DANIEL, physical chemist, educator; b. Williamsport, Pa., Dec. 27, 1924; s. John G. and Anna (Moul) C.; m. Blanche M. Haskins, Sept. 1, 1951. AB with distinction, Cornell U., 1947; PhD in Chem. Physics, Harvard, 1951. Research asso. State U. Iowa, 1950-52; mem. faculty U. Wis., 1952—, prof. chemistry, 1958-95, prof. emeritus, 1995—. Served with USNR, 1944-46. Mem. Am. Phys. Soc., Am. Chem. Soc., Phi Beta Kappa, Phi Kappa Phi. Spl. research nuclear magnetic resonance, microwave spectroscopy. Home: 601 N Segoe Rd Madison WI 53705-3174

COROMINAS, JUAN M. language educator, priest; b. Banyoles, Spain, Dec. 7, 1920; s. Sebastian Corominas and Magdalena Pujolàs. MA in Philosophy, U. So. Calif., 1975, PhD in Spanish, 1977. Prof. Calif. State U., Dominguez Hills, 1976—83, Compton (Calif.) C.C., 1984—. Author: books and monographs in Spanish, Catalan and Portuguese on lit. Recipient La Gran Cruz de Isabel la Catolica, Spanish Govt., Premi Batista Roca, Catalan govt. Mem.: Sr. Citizens League, Ret. Pub. Employees Assn. of Calif., Calif. Faculty Assn. Home: Dominguez Sem 18127 S Alameda St Rancho Dominguez CA 90220

COROTIS, ROSS BARRY, civil engineering educator, academic administrator; b. Woodbury, N.J., Jan. 15, 1945; s. A. Charles and Hazel Laura (McCloskey) C.; m. Stephanie Michal Fuchs, Mar. 19, 1972; children: Benjamin Randall, Lindsay Sarah. SB, MIT, Cambridge, 1967, SM, 1968, PhD, 1971. Lic. profl. engr., Ill., Md., Colo., structural engr., Ill. Asst. prof. dept. civil engring. Northwestern U., Evanston, Ill., 1971-74, assoc. prof. dept. civil engring., 1975-79, prof. dept. civil engring., 1979-81, Johns Hopkins U., Balt., 1981-82, Hackerman prof., 1982-83, Hackerman prof., chmn. dept. civil engring., 1983-90, Hackerman prof., assoc. dean engring., 1990-94; dean Coll. Engring. and Applied Sci. U. Colo., Boulder, 1994-2001, Denver Bus. Challenge prof., 2001—. Mem. bldg. rsch. bd. Nat. Rsch. Coun., Washington, 1985-88; mem. steering com. Natural Disasters Roundtable, NRC, 2002—; lectr. profl. confs. Editor in chief Internat. Jour. Structural Safety, 1991-2000; contbr. articles to profl. jours. Mem. Mayor's task force City of Balt. Constrn. Mgmt., 1985. Recipient Engring. Tchg. award Northwestern U., 1977, Disting. Engring. Alumnus award U. Colo. Coll. Engring. and Applied Scis., 2000; named Md. Engr. of Yr., Balt. Engrs. Week Coun., 1989; rsch. grantee NSF, Nat. Bur. Stds., U.S. Dept. Energy, 1973-96. Fellow ASCE (chmn. safety bldgs. com. 1985-89, chmn. tech. adminstrv. com. structural safety and reliability 1988-92, chmn. probabilistic methods com. 1996-98, v.p. Md. chpt. 1987-88, pres. 1988-89, Walter L. Huber rsch. prize 1984, Civil Engr. of Yr. award Md. chpt. 1987, Outstanding Educator award Md. chpt. 1992); mem. Internat. Assn. for Structural Safety and Reliability (chair exec. bd. 1998-2001), NAE, Am. Soc. for Engring. Edn. (mem. pub. policy com. 1998-2001, mem. deans exec. bd. 1998-2001), Am. Concrete Inst. (chmn. structural safety com. 1986-88), Am. Nat. Stds. Inst. (chmn. live loads com. 1978-84), Nat. Inst. Stds. and Tech. (panel on assessment 1999—, vice chair panel on bldg. and fire rsch. lab. 2002—), Nat. Inst. Bldg. Scis. (affiliate, mem. multihazard mitigation coun. 2002—). Office: U Colo Coll Engring & Applied Sci PO Box 428 Boulder CO 80309-0428

CORRAL, JEANIE BELEYN, journalist, school board administrator; b. Wichita, Kans., Aug. 31, 1943; d. George Rush Holloway and Helen Elizabeth (Eberly) Holloway-Jamison; m. Raymond Corral, Sept. 1, 1962; children: Camella, Nena, Cheyminne, Cwennen, Channing. AA, Palo Verde Jr. Coll., 1964; BA in History, Calif. State U., Fullerton, 1983, MA in History, 1989. Writer, cartoonist Lake Elsinore (Calif.) Sun, 1974-83; writer, columnist Lake Elsinore Sun-Tribune, 1983-85, Community News Network, Temecula, Calif., 1990-92; mem. Lake Elsinore Unified Sch. Dist., 1988—, pres., 1991-92; staff writer, columnist Sun Tribune, 1992—98; columnist Californian, 1998—2003; feature writer Canyon Lake Friday Flyer, 1999—2003. Presenter workshops in field. Author: If These Walls Could Speak: Elsmore Union High School 1891-1991, 1996, Scruffy 'n Me, 1993, (ch. history) Growing of a Mustard Seed, 1987; asst. editor Pacific Oral History Rev., 1984. Liaison Mt. San Jacinto Jr. Coll. Dist., Lake

Elsinore, 1988—90; mem. Riverside Centennial Com., 1992—93; mem. city police task force, Lake Elsinore, 1991; mem. bilingual adv. com. Lake Elsinore Unified Sch. Dist., 1984—, mem. curriculum adv. coun., 1988—; coord. Unity parade, Lake Elsinore, 1997—; sec. Riverside County Dem. Ctrl. Com., 1988—91; lay/master catechist St. Frances of Rome Parish Sch., Lake Elsinore, 1963—78; mem. parish coun. St. Frances of Rome Ch., 1987—90; mem. religious life commn. Second Synod of San Diego, 1972—76. Recipient 1st Place Environ. award Twin Counties Press Club, 1982, 2d Place Collaborative Coverage award Twin Counties Press Club, 1983, 4th Place Humor award Woman's Day mag., 1974; McNeal Pearce grantee, 1988. Mem. Calif. Fedn. Women's Club (De Anza Dist. 23 dist. history 1st place 1989, 90, 92, 2d place 1991), Lake Elsinore Women's Club (pres. 1974-76), Rotary, S.W. Oral History Assn., Phi Kappa Phi, Delta Gamma Omega, Phi Alpha Theta. Home: 18014 Heidi Lisa Ln Lake Elsinore CA 92532-1963

CORREA-VILLASEÑOR, ADOLFO, epidemiologist, physician; b. Mazatlán, Sinaloa, Mex., Mar. 2, 1946; arrived in U.S., 1961; s. Adolfo and Estela (Villaseñor) Correa; m. Ana Isabel Alfaro, June 2, 1978. MS, U. Calif., San Diego, 1970, MD, 1974; MPH, Johns Hopkins U., 1981, PhD, 1987. Diplomate Am. Bd. Pediatrics, Am. Bd. Preventive Medicine. Intern San Francisco Gen. Hosp., San Francisco, 1974—75; resident in pediatrics U. Calif., San Francisco, 1975—77, chief resident in pediatrics, 1977—78; epidemic intelligence service officer Ctr. for Disease Control, Atlanta, 1978—80; resident in preventive medicine Johns Hopkins Sch. Hygiene and Pub. Health, Balt., 1980—83, asst. prof. epidemiology, 1987—95, assoc. prof. epidemiology, 1995—98, asst. prof. pediatrics, 1988—92, asst. prof. population dynamics, 1990—95, assoc. prof. population dynamic, 1995—98; chief epidemiology and surveillance sect. Birth Defects and Pediat. Genetics/Nat. Ctr. Environ. Health, Atlanta, 1998—2001; med. officer Nat. Ctr. Birth Defects and Devel. Disabilities, Atlanta, 2001—. Vis. rsch. prof. Sch. of Pub. Health of Mex., 1993. Mem. Soc. for Epidemiologic Rsch., Teratology Soc., Internat. Soc. Environ. Epidemiology. Home: 840 Starlight Dr NE Atlanta GA 30342-2832 Office: Nat Ctr on Birth Defects & Devel Disabilities CDC MS-E 86 1600 Clifton Rd Atlanta GA 30333 E-mail: acorrea@cdc.gov.

CORREU, SANDRA KAY, special education educator; b. Crowley, La., Aug. 24, 1938; d. Edward Dorsey and Elizabeth Mays (Wiggins) Peckham; m. Donald Audrey Correu, Sept. 5, 1959; children: Lisa G., Donald Andrew. BS in Edn., Mo. Western State Coll., 1976; postgrad., N.W. Mo. State Coll., 1980-86. Cert. in learning disabilities, behavior disordered, educable mentally handicapped, trainable mentally handicapped. Tchr. Autistic children Helen Davis State Sch., St. Joseph, Mo., 1976-78; tchr. behavior disordered St. Joseph (Mo.) Sch. Dist., 1978—. Pres., v.p., mem. Assn. for Retarded Citizens, St. Joseph, 1976-86; bd. mem. United Cerebral Palsy, St. Joseph, 1980-86; devel. dir. summer program for MRDD youth in cooperation with Mo. Western State Coll.; presenter in field. Elder Presbyn. Ch. Mem. Nat. Dem., Coun. for Exceptional Citizens, Assn. for Retarded Citizens, Mo. State Tchrs. Assn., Greenpeace, Gorilla Found., World Wildlife Fund, Humane Soc. U.S., Common Cause, People for Ethical Treatment of Animals, Habitat for Humanity, Assn. Handicapped Artists. Avocations: reading, sewing, crafts. Home: 500 NE 44th St Kansas City MO 64116 Office: St Joseph Sch Dist 10th and Edmond Saint Joseph MO 64507 E-mail: skcorreu@aol.com.

CORRIERE, JOSEPH N., JR., urologist, educator; b. Apr. 3, 1937; m. Evelyn Pavia Mossey, June 25, 1960 (div. July 1984); children: Joseph N., Christopher John, Gregory James, Evelyn Anne; m. Eileen Doyle Brewer, Oct. 17, 1987. BA, U. Pa., 1959; MD, Seton Hall Coll. Medicine, 1963. Diplomate Am. Bd. Urology (trustee). Intern Pa. Hosp., Phila., 1963—64; asst. instr. surgery, fellow Harrison Dept. Surgery Rsch. Hosp. U. Pa., Phila., 1964—65, asst. instr. urology, 1965—68, USPHS urol. rsch. trainee, 1967—68, instr. urology, 1968—69, assoc. in urology, 1969—71, asst. prof. urology, 1971—74; veneral disease trainee Phila. Dept. Pub. Health, 1965; radioisotope trainee William H. Donner Ctr. for Radiology, Phila., 1965—66; prof., dir. divsn. urology, dept. surgery U. Tex. Med. Sch., Houston, 0974—1993, interim chmn. dept. surgery, 1980—82, assoc. chmn. dept. surgery, 1984—86; chief urology svc. Hermann Hosp., 1974—93, Tex. Med. Ctr., Houston. Cons. residency rev. com. in urology Lyndon Baines Johnson Hosp., 1993—99, M.D. Anderson Cancer Ctr.; cons. NASA. Contbr. numerous articles to profl. jours. Maj. USAF, 1969—71. Mem.: ACS, Am. Assn. for Surgery of Trauma, Am. Assn. Genitourol. Surgery, Soc. Univ. Urologists, Soc. Univ. Surgeons (sec.-treas. 1984—86, pres. 1987—88, 1987—88), Am. Urol. Assn. (dir. edn. 1993—2002). Roman Catholic. Home: 7511 Morningside Dr Houston TX 77030-3619 Office: MD Anderson Cancer Ctr Box 333 1515 Holcombe Blvd Houston TX 77030-4009

CORRIGAN, FAITH, journalist, educator, historian; b. Cleve., Oct. 16, 1926; d. William John and Marjorie (Wilson) C.; m. Sigvald Matias Refsnes, Sept. 18, 1957 (dec. Feb. 1994); children: Marjorie Refsnes, Sunniva Collins, Stephen Refsnes. BA, Ohio State U., 1948; MAT, Kent State U., 1987. Cert. tchr. English, reading, Ohio. Staff writer women's news N.Y. Times, N.Y.C., 1953-57; investigative reporter Cleve. Plain Dealer, 1962-66; dir. pub. info. Cuyahoga County Bd. Commrs., Cleve., 1966-69; dir. news, publs. Huron Rd. Hosp., East Cleveland, Ohio, 1970-73; lectr. II U. Akron, Ohio, 1990-91; adj. prof. Kent State U., North Canton, Ohio, 1996-97, Kent State U., Ashtabula br., Geauga/Twinsburg, Ohio, 1999—. Lectr. Fordham U., N.Y.C., 1956; expert witness U.S. Senate Medicare Hearings, Cleve., 1965; mgr. Cuyahoga County Welfare Levy Campaign, Cleve., 1966. Author: First Generation, 2002, Bread Glass and History, 2003; contbr. articles to newspapers. TESOL, Lit. Vols. Am.; mem. bd. mgrs. Eleanor B. Rainey Meml. Inst., Cleve., 1966-78; officer, trustee Lake County Cmty. Svcs. Coun., 1984-90; mem. adv. bd. Lake Geauga Legal Aid Soc., Painesville, Lake County, 1984-87; chair Initiative Petition Campaign on Environ. Waste Plant Issue, Willoughby, Ohio, 1991; officer, founder Ohio State U. chpt. Am. Newspaper Guild, 1947-48; del. rep. assembly N.Y. Newspaper Guild, 1954-57; poll judge Lake County Bd. Elections, 1984-98; field rep. U.S. Census Bur., 1989—; recruiter, crew leader U.S. Census 2000. Recipient award of achievement Press Club of Cleve., 1964, Pulitzer nominee Cleve. Plain Dealer, 1964, 1st in state Ohio Newspaper Women's Assn., 1964, 1st in state Pub. Contest of Am. Heart Assn., 1972, 1st pl. publs. award Internat. Assn. Bus. Communicators, 1971-72. Mem. VFW (Ladies Aux.), Willoughby Hist. Soc. (trustee, v.p. 1997-2002, Heritage chmn. 2003-), Ohio Bicentennial Hist. Markers Rsch., Early Am. Pattern Glass Soc. Democrat. Roman Catholic. Avocations: expert on american china, glass, american labor history. Home: 37550 Euclid Ave Willoughby OH 44094-5622

CORRIGAN, JAMES JOHN, JR., pediatrician, dean; b. Pitts., Aug. 28, 1935; s. James John and Rita Mary (Grimes) C.; m. Carolyn Virginia Long, July 2, 1960; children: Jeffrey James, Nancy Carolyn. BS, Juniata Coll., Huntingdon, Pa., 1957; MD (hon.), U. Pitts., 1961. Diplomate Am. Bd. Pediats. (hematology-oncology). Intern, then resident in pediat. U. Colo. Med. Ctr., 1961-64; trainee in pediat. hematology-oncology U. Ill. Med. Center, 1964-66; assoc. in pediat. Emory U. Med. Sch., 1966-67, asst. prof., 1967-71; mem. faculty U. Ariz. Coll. Medicine, Tucson, 1971-90, prof. pediat., 1974-90; chief sect. pediat. hematology-ongology, also dir. Mountain States Regional Hemophilia Ctr., U. Ariz., Tucson, 1978-90; chief of staff U. Med. Ctr. U. Ariz., Tucson, 1984-86; prof. pediat., vice dean for acad. affairs Tulane U. Sch. Medicine, New Orleans, 1990-93, interim dean, 1993-94, dean, 1994-2000, v.p., 2000—02, prof. emeritus pediat., 2002—. Assoc. editor Am. Jour. Diseases of Children, 1981-89, 90-93, interim editor, 1993; contbr. numerous papers to med. jours. Grantee NIH, Mountain States Regional Hemophilia Ctr., Ga. Heart Assn., GE, Am. Cancer Soc. Mem. Am. Acad. Pediatrics, Am. Soc. Hematology, Soc. Pediatric Rsch., Western Soc. Pediatric Rsch., Am. Heart Assn. (coun. thrombosis), Internat. Soc. Thrombosis and Haemostasis, Am. Pediatric Soc., World Fedn. Hemophilia, Pima County Med. Assn. (v.p., 1986—, pres. 1988—), Alpha Omega Alpha. Republican. Roman Catholic. Office: Tulane U Health Scis Ctr Dept Pediat 1430 Tulane Ave New Orleans LA 70112-2699 E-mail: jcorrig@tulane.edu.

CORRIGAN, ROBERT ANTHONY, academic administrator; b. New London, Conn., Apr. 21, 1935; s. Anthony John and Rose Mary (Jengo) C.; m. Joyce D. Mobley, Jan. 12, 1975; children by previous marriage: Kathleen Marie, Anthony John, Robert Anthony; 1 stepdau., Erika Mobley. AB, Brown U., 1957; MA, U. Pa., 1959, PhD, 1967; LHD (hon.), 1995. Researcher Phila. Hist. Commn., 1957-59; lectr. Am. civilization U. Gothenburg, Sweden, 1959-62, Bryn Mawr Coll., 1962-63, U. Pa., 1963-64; prof. U. Iowa, 1964-73; dean U. Mo., Kansas City, 1973-74; provost U. Md., 1974-79; chancellor U. Mass., Boston, 1979-88; pres. San Francisco State U., 1988—. Author: American Fiction and Verse, 1962, 2d edit., 1970, also articles, revs.; editor: Uncle Tom's Cabin, 1968. Vice chmn. Iowa City Human Rels. Commn., 1970-72, Gov.'s Commn. on Water Quality, 1983-84; mem. Iowa City Charter Commn., 1972-73; chmn. Md. Com. Humanities, 1976-78, Assn. Urban Univs., 1988-92; mem. Howard County Commn. Arts, Md., 1976-79; bd. dirs. John F. Kennedy Libr.; trustee San Francisco Econ. Devel. Corp., 1989-92, Adv. Coun. of Calif. Acad. Scis., Calif. Hist. Soc., 1989-92; chmn., bd. dirs. Calif. Compact, 1990—; mem. exec. com. Campus Compact, 1991—, chmn., 1995—; Mayor's Blue Ribbon Commn. on Fiscal Stability, 1994-95; chmn. Pres. Clinton's Steering Com. of Coll. Pres. for Am. Reads and Am. Counts, 1996—. Smith-Mundt prof., 1959-60; Fulbright lectr., 1960-62; grantee Std. Oil Co. Found., 1968, NEH, 1969-74, Ford Found., 1969, Rockefeller Found., 72-75, Dept. State, 1977; recipient Clarkson Able Collins Jr. Maritime History award, 1956, Pa. Colonial Soc. Essay award, 1958, 59, William Lloyd Garrison award Mass. Ednl. Opportunity Assn., 1987; Disting. Urban Fellow Assn. Urban U., 1992. Mem. San Francisco C. of C. (bd. dirs.), San Francisco World Affairs Coun. (bd. dirs.), Pvt. Industry Coun. (bd. dirs.), Boston World Affairs Coun. (1983-88), Greater Boston C. of C. (v.p. 1987-89), Fulbright Alumni Assn. (bd. dirs. 1978-80), Univ. Club, World Trade Club, Commonwealth Club (bd. dirs. 1995-99), Phi Beta Kappa. Democrat. Office: San Francisco State U 1600 Holloway Ave San Francisco CA 94132-1722

CORRIVEAU, ARLENE JOSEPHINE, educational specialist; b. Imlay City, Mich., May 24, 1938; d. Harold and Hazel (Hibbler) Muir; m. Albert Corriveau. BS, Ea. Mich. U., 1959, MA, 1961. Cert. tchr., Mich. Tchr. Utica (Mich.) Community Schs., 1959-61, Van Buren Pub. Schs., Belleville, Mich., 1961-62; asst. prof. Ea. Mich. U., Ypsilanti and Lincoln, 1962-69; tchr. Wayne-Westland (Mich.) Community Schs., 1969-73, learning cons., 1973-92; dir. Dynamic Tutoring Svc., Ypsilanti, 1979—. Author: Pupils Tutoring Pupils, 1973. Mem. ASCD, NEA, CHADD, Mich. Reading Assn., Ann Arbor C. of C. Avocations: reading, game making, music, writing, nature. Home: 5891 W Michigan Ave Ypsilanti MI 48197-9006 Office: Dynamic Tutoring Svc 5891 W Michigan Ave Ypsilanti MI 48197-9006

CORTÉS, CARLOS ELISEO, historian, educator; b. Oakland, Calif., Apr. 6, 1934; s. Carlos Federico and Florence Frieda (Hoffman) C.; m. Laurel Vermilyea, Apr. 26, 1978; 1 child, Alana Madrugada. BA in Comm. and Pub. Policy, U. Calif., Berkeley, 1956; MS in Journalism, Columbia U., 1957; B in Fgn. Trade, Am. Inst. for Fgn. Trade, 1962; MA in Portuguese and Spanish, U. N.Mex., 1965, PhD in History, 1969. Lab. asst. Jensen-Salsbery Chem. Co., Kansas City, Mo., 1952; cable splicer Whitaker Cable Corp., North Kansas City, Mo., 1953-54; editor Univ. Calif. yearbook Blue and Gold, Berkeley, 1955-56; gen. asst. Boxoffice Mag., Kansas City, Mo., 1956; asst. to dir. of pub. relations Am. Shakespeare Festival, Stratford, Conn., 1957; exec. editor Phoenix Sunpapers, 1959-61; proofreader Am. Men of Sci., Tempe, Ariz., 1961; reporter AP, Phoenix, 1961; asst. to dir. area studies Am. Inst. Fgn. Trade, Phoenix, 1961-62; teaching machine programmer Learning Inc., Tempe, 1961-62; acting asst. prof. history U. Calif., Riverside, 1968-69, asst. prof. history, 1969-72, chmn. Latin Am. Studies, 1969-71, asst. to vice chancellor for acad. affairs, 1970-72, assoc. prof. history, 1972-76, 1972-76, chmn. Chicano Studies Program, 1972-79, prof. history, 1976-94, prof. emeritus, 1994—, chmn. dept. history, 1982-86. Intergroup rels. cons. in field to govt. agys., sch. systems, univs., mass media and pvt. bus.; lectr. Smothsonian Inst., 1993-2001. Author: The Children are Watching: How the Media Teach About Diversity, 2000, The Making--and Remaking--of a Multiculturalist, 2002; numerous books and articles to profl. jours. Served with U.S. Army, 1957-59. Kraft scholar; recipient numerous grants and fellowships, Vernon J. Scott award, Hubert Herring Meml. award, Pacific Coast Council on Latin Am. Studies, 1974, Disting. Teaching award, U. Calif.-Riverside, 1976, Eleanor Fishburn award, Washington EdPress Assn., 1977 Disting. Calif. Humanist award, Calif. Council for Humanities, 1980, Keys to the City, Kansas City, Mo. and Kansas City, Kans., 1982, Nat. Multicultural Trainer of Yr. award Am. Soc. for Tng. and Devel., 1989, Hilda Toba award Calif. Coun. Social Studies, 1995, Outstanding Contrbn. to Higher Edn. award Nat. Assn. Student Personnel Adminstrs., 2001; named Bildner Fellow, Assn. Am. Schs. in South Am.; fellow Japan Found., 1986, Rockefeller Found., 1986-87. Mem. Calif. Coun. for Social Studies, Historians Film Com., Immigration History Soc., Internat. Assn. Audio-Visual Media in Hist. Rsch. and Edn., Nat. Assn. Chicano Studies, Nat. Coun. Social Studies, Soc. for Study of Multi-Ethnic Lit. of the U.S., So. Calif. Social Sci. Assn., Phi Beta Kappa, Phi Alpha Theta, Phi Kappa Phi. Home: 3088 Pine St Riverside CA 92501-2364 Office: U Calif Dept History Riverside CA 92521-0001

CORTES, CAROL SOLIS, school system administrator; b. N.Y.C., N.Y., Aug. 16, 1944; d. Jesus and Dora Solis; m. Fernando Miranda, June 25, 1964 (div. Apr. 1978); children: Christopher, Christina Guerra; m. Jose Cortes (div. Nov. 1, 1983). BEd with hon., U. Miami, 1970; MSc, Fla. Internat. U., 1974. Cert. in Social Sci. & Adminstrn. Supr. From tchr. to dep. supt. Miami-Dade County Pub. Sch., Miami, Fla., 1970—96, dep. supt., 1996—. Exec. bd. Gender Equity Network. Exec. bd. Women's C. of C., Miami, Fla., 2000—01. Recipient Hispanic Educator award, Nova U., 1999, Cervantes Outstanding Educator award, 1999, Educator of Yr. award, 1999. Mem.: Phi Delta Kappa. Avocations: travel, dominoes. Home: 2105 SW 123rd Court Miami FL 33175 Office: Miami Dade Pub Schs 1450 NE 2nd Ave Miami FL 33132-1308

CORTÉS-HWANG, ADRIANA, Spanish language educator; b. Valaraíso, Chile, Nov. 9, 1928; came to U.S., 1962; d. Luis Alberto Cortès and Sofía Garcès; m. Arturo Peralta-Vila; 1 child, Verónica Peralta. Lic. English, Inst. Chileno, 1963; BA in English, Portland State U., 1964; MA in Spanish Lit., U. Oreg., 1967; postgrad., U. N.C., 1970, U. Madrid, 1971, Duke U. Cert. secondary edn., Pa., Oreg. Liaison officer Chilean Inst. Culture and U. Chile, 1961-63; instr. Spanish Portland (Oreg.) State U., 1963-64, Grants Pass (Oreg.) Sr. H.S., 1964-65, U. Oreg., Eugene, 1965-67, Wilson Coll., Chambersburg, Pa., 1967-68; asst. prof. Shippensburg (Pa.) State Coll., 1968, coord. Latin Am. studies, 1970, chair com. internat. edn., 1971, fgn. student advisor, 1972; asst. prof. Bloomsburg (Pa.) State Coll., 1980, Kutztown (Pa.) U., 1981—. Vis. instr. summer sch. U. Madrid, 1968; Fulbright rep. Shippensburg State Coll., 1972; spkr. on current polit. issues of Latin Am.; guest spkr. Inst. Pedagógico, U. Chile, Valparaíso, Sch. of Engring, U. Buenos Aires. Mem. MLA, AAUP, Latin Am. Studies Assn., Sigma Delta Pi. Democrat. Roman Catholic. Avocations: swimming, traveling, exploring nature. Home: 337 E Main St Kutztown PA 19530-1518 Office: Kutztown U De Francesco # 204 Kutztown PA 19530

CORTINEZ, VERONICA, literature educator; b. Santiago, Chile, Aug. 27, 1958; came to U.S. 1979; d. Carlos Cortinez and Matilde Romo. Licenciatura en Letras, U. Chile, 1979; MA, U. Ill., Champaign, Ill., 1981, Harvard U., 1983, PhD, 1990. Tchg. asst. U. Chile, Santiago, 1977-79, U. Ill., Champaign, 1979-80; tchg. fellow Harvard U., 1982-86, instr., 1986-89; assoc. prof. colonial and contemporary Latin Am. lit. UCLA, 1989—. Fgn. corres. Caras, Santiago, 1987—. Author: Memoria Original de Bernal Diaz del Castillo, 2000, Cine a la chilena: Las peripecias de Sergio Castilla, 2001; editor: Albricia: La novela chilena del fin de siglo, 2000; mem. editl. bd. Mester/Dept. Spanish and Portuguese of UCLA, 1989—; editor Plaza mag., 1981-89, Harvard Rev., 1983-89; contbr. articles to profl. jours. Recipient award for Tchg. Excellence Derek Bok Ctr., Harvard U., 1982, 83, 84, 85, 86, Tchg. prize Romance Lang. Dept., Harvard U., 1986, Disting. Tchg. award UCLA, 1998; Whiting fellow. Mem. Cabot House, Phi Beta Phi. Avocations: reading, classical films, writing. Office: UCLA Dept Spanish & Portuguese 5310 Rolfe Hl Los Angeles CA 90095-0001

CORTRIGHT, JANE BRIGID MOYNAHAN, educational administrator; b. N.Y.C., Apr. 17, 1934; d. James Henry Seymour and Ethel Velora (Armstrong) Moynahan; m. Richard L. McVity, Sept. 18, 1955 (div. 1974); children: Jonathan, Sarah, Sean Brigid, Eliza; m. Richard Watkins Cortright, May 8, 1974; 1 child, Amy Ethel Marie. BA, Harvard/Radcliffe, 1955; MA, Cath. U. America, 1972. Civics tchr. Iolani High Sch., Honolulu, 1956; tchr. Dover (Mass.) Pub. Schs., 1957-59; remedial reading tchr. Kingsbury Ctr., Washington, 1972-73; work-study coord. Georgetown U., Washington, 1974-77, adminstrv. officer, 1977-81, personnel officer, 1981-82; dir. fin. aid Benjamin Franklin U., Washington, 1984; adminstrv. officer Am. U., Washington, 1985-88; infant coord. FTC, Washington, 1989; dir. Children's Edn. Ctr., Cath. U. Am., Washington, 1990—. Mem. Nat. Assn. for Edn. Young Children, Nat. Coalition Campus Child Care, Harvard Club Washington (v.p. 1973-74). Democrat. Episcopalian. Office: Children's Edn Ctr Cath U Am Washington DC 20064-0001

CORTS, THOMAS EDWARD, university president; b. Terre Haute, Ind., Oct. 7, 1941; s. Charles Harold and Hazel Louise (Vernon) C.; m. Marla Ruth Haas, Feb. 15, 1964; children: Jennifer Ruth Corts Fuller, Rachel Anne Corts Wachter, Christian Haas BA, Georgetown (Ky.) Coll., 1963; MA, Ind. U., 1968, PhD, 1972; DLitt (hon.), Georgetown Coll., 1991; DHL (hon.), Campbell U., 1995, U. Ala., 2002. Asst. to pres. Georgetown Coll., 1963-64, 67-69, asst. prof., 1967-69, exec. dean, 1969-73, exec. v.p., 1973; coord. Higher Edn. Consortium, Lexington, Ky., 1973-74; pres. Wingate (N.C.) Coll., 1974-83, Samford U., Birmingham, Ala., 1983—. Bd. dirs. Samford U. Found., 1990—, Found. Ind. Higher Edn., 1988-92; chmn. Ala. Commn. on Sch. Performance and Accountability, 1993-94. Contbr. articles to profl. jours. Bd. dirs. Birmingham chpt. ARC, 1983-89, Ala. Citizens for Constl. Reform, 2000--; mem. adv. bd. Salvation Army, 1987—; mem. exec. coun. Boy Scouts Am., Birmingham, 1984—; bd. dirs. Leadership Birmingham, 1984-95, Exec. Com. Birmingham Better Bus. Bur., 1996—, Birmingham Summerfest, 1984—, Birmingham Area Consortium on Higher Edn., Ala. Poverty Project, Inc. Recipient Outstanding Alumnus award Georgetown Coll., 1987, Jefferson award Downtown Action Com., Birmingham, 1988, Outstanding Educator award Ala. Assn. Coll. and Univs.-Ala. Assn. Women, Birmingham, 1989, Good Shepherd award Assn. Bapt. for Scouting, 1990, Citizen of Yr., 1990, Most Supportive Pres. award Am. Assn. of Colls. for Tchr. Edn., 1991. Mem. Am. Assn. Pres. of Ind. Colls. and Univs. (v.p. 1990-92, pres. 1992-95, bd. dirs. 1989-2002), Coun. for Advancement of Pvt. Colls. in Ala. (past pres.), Ala. Assn. Ind. Colls., Nat. Fellowship Bapt. Educators (pres. 1988-89), Assn. So. Bapt. Colls. and Schs. (v.p. 1988-89, pres. 1990-91), So. Assn. Colls. and Schs. (trustee 1991-98, mem. commn. on colls., vice chmn. 1991, chmn. exec. coun. 1992-94, pres. 1996), Coun. Higher Edn. Accreditation (bd. dirs. 1995-97), Assn. Governing Bds. (pres.'s commn., chmn. 2001--), Birmingham Area C. of C. (bd. dirs.)Ala. Acad. Honor, Country Club Birmingham, The Club, The Summit Club, Rotary. Democrat. Office: Samford U 800 Lakeshore Dr Birmingham AL 35229-0002 E-mail: tecorts@samford.edu.

CORUM, JANET MAUPIN, child development specialist, child care administrator; b. Pasco, Wash., Jan. 9, 1947; d. James Corbett and Mabel Ruth (Lewis) Maupin; m. Dallas Smith Corum, July 6, 1968; children: Dayana Smith, Mary Katherine. BS in Edn., Mo. State U., 1969; MEd, Baylor U., 1974. Cert. tchr., Mo., Tex.; cert. counselor Tex.; cert. spl. ednl. counselor, Tex. Tchr. Consol. Sch. Dist. # 1, Hickman Mills, Mo., 1970-71, Waco (Tex.) Ind. Sch. Dist., 1971-79; profl. counselor Family Abuse Ctr., Waco, 1982-84; exec. dir. Lakewood Christian Ch. Day Care Ctr., Waco, 1987—. Substitute tchr., vol. 1st United Meth. Presch., St. Paul's Episc. Sch., Waco Ind. Sch. Dist., 1982-87, profl. in-svc. ednl. speaker, 1973; profl. ednl. cons. Region XII Svc. Ctr., Waco, 1978; adv. bd. McLennan Community Coll., Waco, 1989—. Chmn. comm. com. alumni bd. dirs., 1990-91, program devel. com., 1991—, bd. dirs. Leadership Waco, 1990—, Earle-Napier-Kinnard House Hist. Waco Found., 1986—, chmn. Brazos River Festival, 1987-88; selected for 1st inaugural class Lonestar Leadership sponsored by Assn. of Tex. Leadership Programs, bd. dirs., 1996—; elder, edn. com. bd. dirs. Lakewood Christian Ch., 1987—; bd. dirs. St. Paul's Episc. Ch. Parents and Friends Orgn., 1990-91, treas., 1990-91; bd. dirs. Waco-McLennan County Teen Pregnancy Coun., edn. com., 1987—; bd. dirs. McLennan County Mental Health Assn., 1991—; mem. early childhood adv. com. McLennan C.C., 1992-96; mem. McLennan County Youth Collaboration Task Force, 1994—; bd. dirs. YWCA, 1986—. Recipient Pathfinders award YMCA, 1995. Mem. AAUW (pres. 1984-86, chmn. bd. 1982-84, Woman of Yr. 1984, Gift Honoree 1985), Waco Assn. Edn. Young Children (v.p. 1991—, bd. dirs. 1990—, chmn. week of young children 1990), Leadership Waco Alumni Assn. (pres. 1995, Outstanding Alumna 1995), N.W. Waco Rotary Club (bd. dirs. 1994—, v.p. 1994-95, sec. 1996). Republican. Avocations: silk painting, creative writing, crewel, calligraphy, poetry, reading. Home: 10015 Shadowcrest Dr Waco TX 76712-3122 Office: Lakewood Christian Ch Day 6509 Bosque Blvd Waco TX 76710-4162

CORWIN, THOMAS MICHAEL, federal agency administrator; b. Newark, May 16, 1952; s. Edward Stanley and Patricia H. (Goldman) C.; m. Carol A. Cichowski, Mar. 31, 1984; 1 child, Sarah Jessamine. BA, New Coll., Sarasota, Fla., 1974; M Pub. Policy, Harvard U., 1976. Policy analyst, staff assoc. Am. Council on Edn., Washington, 1977-80; program analyst U.S. Dept. Edn., Washington, 1980-86, supv. program analyst, 1986-87, dir. div. elem., secondary and vocat. analysis, Budget Svc., 1987—, acting dep. asst. sec. for elem. and secondary edn., 1999—2001, assoc. dep. undersec. for innovation and improvement, 2001—. U.S. del. OECD edn. com. meeting, Paris, 2000. Consulting editor The Clearing House, 1987—; contbr. articles, reports to profl. jours. Chmn. Fed. Coord. Coun. on Sci., Engring. and Tech.; chmn. com. on Edn. and Human Resources, Working Group on Budget, 1992, 93. Adminstrv. fellow Kennedy Sch. Govt., Harvard U., 1974-76; recipient Presdl. Meritorious Exec. award, 1991, 97, Presdl. Disting. Exec. award, 2002. Home: 5121 Baltimore Ave Bethesda MD 20816-1609 Office: US Dept of Edn 400 Maryland Ave SW Washington DC 20202-0001 E-mail: thomas_corwin@ed.gov.

CORY, LESTER WARREN, electrical engineering educator; b. Tiverton, R.I., July 25, 1939; s. Harold R. and Margaret (Grant) C.; m. Patricia L. Barrett, May 23, 1981; children from previous marriage: Stephen, Dyan, Michael, Ann. MSEE, Northeastern U., 1970; MEd, Bridgewater State Coll., 1974; DSc (hon.), U. R.I., 1996. Prof. elec. engring. U. Mass.-Dartmouth, North Dartmouth, 1963—, dir. Ctr. for Rehab. Engring., 1988—. Co-author: Electrical Measurements for Engineers, 1970. Col. (ret.) R.I. Air NG, 1957-92. Decorated Legion of Merit; recipient Pres. Vol. Action award Pres. Ronald Reagan, 1985, Meritorious Achievement award Johns Hopkins U., 1985, Others award Nat. Salvation Army, 1985, R.I. Star, Gov. of R.I., 1992, citation R.I. State Legis., 1992, Mass. State Legis., 1992, Jefferson award Am. Inst. Pub. Svc., 1995. Mem. IEEE (sr.), Soc. for

Human Advancement through Rehab. Engring. (Share Found. Inc.) (pres. 1982—, founder). Home: 45 Summit Ave Tiverton RI 02878-4632 Office: U Mass Dartmouth Dept Elec Engring North Dartmouth MA 02747

CORY, MIRIAM ELAINE, speech and language pathologist, retired; b. South Bend, Ind., Sept. 4, 1935; d. Paul Wilson Sr. and Helen Marina (White) Bradfield; m. Delbert Jason Cory, June 23, 1956; children: Stephen, Nadine, Catherine, Karen. BS in Edn., Ball State U., 1957. Cert. speech and lang. pathologist. Speech and lang. pathologist Midview Sch. Dist., Elyria, Ohio, 1960-64, Beaufort (S.C.) Schs., 1969-70, N.E. Met. Intermediate Sch. Dist., White Bear Lake, Minn., 1973-2000, ret. Group leader, bd. dirs., day camp dir., and other vol. adminstrv. offices Camp Fire Boys & Girls, Inc., St. Paul, Minn., 1971— (Luther Halsey Gulick award 1983); youth camping com. Minn. Dist. Reorganized Ch. of Jesus Christ of Latter Day Saints, 1981— (World Community Youth Svc. award 1981); bd. dirs., camp standards vis. Northland sect. Am Camping Assn., 1990—. Recipient Good Neighbor award WCCO Radio, St. Paul, 1981, Disting. Svc. award S. Communities Youth and Family Counseling Svcs., Cottage Grove, Minn., 1988. Mem. Am. Speech, Lang. and Hearing Assn., Minn. Speech, Lang. and Hearing Assn. Avocations: special olympics, environmental education, workshops for state dept. of natural resources, hiking, camping.

COSCIA, ROBERT LINGUA, surgeon, educator; b. Memphis, Feb. 16, 1937; s. Louis and Anne (Lingua) C.; m. Joan K. Kingsbury, Dec. 27, 1964 (div. Jan. 1981); children: Paul, Matthew, Lori; m. Karen Kaye Kennedy, June 1, 1989. BS, Tex. A&M U., 1959; MD, U. Tenn., 1962. Intern Parkland Meml. Hosp., Dallas, 1963-64, resident, 1965-69; rsch. fellow dept. surgery U. Tex. Southwestern Med. Sch., Dallas, 1964-65; pvt. practice, Bryan, Tex., 1971-73, Springfield, Mo., 1973-99; asst. clin. prof. U. Mo., Kansas City, 1986-99; trauma med. dir. Brackenridge Hosp., Austin, Tex., 1999—. Bd. dirs. Mo. chpt. Am. Cancer Soc., Springfield, 1975-83; instr. advanced trauma life support, 1982—; del. Mo. State Med. Assn., Jefferson City, 1984; chmn. sub-com. adv. coun. Pediatric EMS, Jefferson City, 1991-94; mem. state adv. coun. EMS, Jefferson City, 1991-94; cons. Mo. Patient Rev. Found., Jefferson City, 1986—. Maj. USAF, 1969-71. Recipient EMS Leadership award Mo. Dept. Health, Jefferson City, 1994, Trauma Achievement award ACOS, Chgo., 1994. Mem. ACS (chmn. Mo. dist. 3 com. on applicants 1987-94, mem. 1978-94, chmn. com. on trauma Chgo. 1989—, chmn. Mo. com. on trauma 1989-95, chmn. region VII com. on trauma 1995—, site visitor 1993—), N.Am. Limousin Found. (bd. dirs. 1986-92, pres. 1990), Internat. Limousin Coun. (pres. 1990-92). Baptist. Avocation: farming. Home: 3801 W Quail HOllow Dr Fort Hall ID 83203 Office: 999 N Curtis Rd Ste 515 Branson MO 83706 E-mail: Roblc44@aol.com.

COSENTINE, SHERRY LEE, elementary education educator; b. Moline, Ill., June 16, 1949; d. Martin and Kitty Lee (Kohler) C. BS in Elem. Edn., We. Ill. U., 1971, MS in Elem. Edn., 1978; postgrad., Drake U., 1991. Cert. tchr., Ill., tchr., prin., Iowa. Classroom instr. 3d grade Colona (Ill.) Grade Sch., 1971—. Membership chair Blackhawk Reading Coun., Rock Island, Ill., 1975-76; co-owner Cosy Connection, 1979—. Co-author: Bishop Hill Children's Activity Book, 1980; newsletter editor Quad-City Ostomy Assn., Rock Island, 1987-88. Treas. Indian Bluff Water Corp., Coal Valley, Ill., 1983-84; co-chair fundraiser Niabi Zool. Soc., Coal Valley; 4-H leader U. Ill. Coop. Extension Svc., Urbana-Champaign, 1978-81. Home: 8406 55th St Coal Valley IL 61240-9670

COSENTINO, PATRICIA BYRNE, English educator, poet; b. Boston, June 6, 1927; d. Charles E. and Patricia (McDermott) Byrne; m. E. McDonough (div. 1953); 1 child, Peter E. McDonough; m. Kenneth Rosenfield, Aug. 29, 1954 (div. 1968); 1 child, R. Noah Rosenfield; m. David Cosentino, June 28, 1990. AS, Newton (Mass.) Jr. Coll., 1967; BS, Boston U., 1972; MA, Regis Coll., 1984. Dir. learning lab. Newton (Mass.) Jr. Coll., 1965-70; asst. to dir. MAT Sch. Edn. Harvard U., Cambridge, Mass., 1970-72; tchr. Wellesley (Mass.) High Sch., 1972-90. Cons. East-West Nexus/Prota, 1987—; writing tchr. Mt. Wachusett C.C., Gardner, Mass., 1999, instr., chair adv. bd. LIFE program, writing and poetry. Author: Cat in the Mirror, 1970, Whetstone, 1990, (poetry) Always Being Born, 2002, 03; editor: Tapestries, An Anthology, 2002; translator Arabic Poetry. Sec., treas. North Ctrl. (Mass.) Assn. Small Bus., 1991—; sec. Gardner-Athol (Mass.) Area Mental Health Assn., 1994—; chair gala Gardner Area League Artists. Recipient Mary F. Lindsley award N.Y. Poetry Forum, 1972. Mem. Am. Acad. Poets, Poetry Soc. Am., Gardner Cultural Coun., New Eng. Poetry Club (treas.). Avocations: golf, music, travel, education, theater. Home: 33 Leo Dr Gardner MA 01440-1211 Office: Reliable Fin & Antiques 177 West St Gardner MA 01440-2121 E-mail: alanahb@earthlink.net.

COSGRIFF, STUART WORCESTER, internist, consultant, medical educator; b. Pittsfield, Mass., May 8, 1917; s. Thomas F. and Frances Deford (Worcester) C.; m. Mary Shaw, Jan. 23, 1943; children: Mary, Thomas, Stuart, Richard, Robert. BA cum laude, Holy Cross Coll., 1938; MD, Columbia U., 1942, D Med. Sci., 1948. Diplomate Am. Bd. Internal Medicine. Intern Presbyterian Hosp., N.Y.C., 1942-43; asst. resident in medicine, 1943, 46-47; chief resident, 1947-48; instr. in medicine Columbia U., N.Y.C., 1948-50, clin. asst. prof. medicine, 1951-63, clin. assoc. prof., 1963-73, clin. prof. medicine, 1973-83, clin. prof. emeritus, 1983—; attending physician Presbyn. Hosp., N.Y.C., 1948-83, cons. emeritus, 1984—; individual practice medicine, specializing in internal medicine and vascular diseases, 1948—. Cons. in medicine to dir. Selective Svc., N.Y.C., 1957-73, N.Y. Giants Baseball Club, 1951-57, San Francisco Baseball Club, 1958-61; dir. thrombo-embolic clinic Vanderbilt Clinic, N.Y.C., 1948-83. Contbr. articles to med. jours. Served to capt. M.C., U.S. Army, 1943-45, ETO. Fellow ACP, Pan Am. Med. Assn.; mem. Am. Heart Assn., N.Y. Heart Assn., Alpha Omega Alpha Clubs: Knickerbocker Country (Tenafly, N.J.). Roman Catholic. Home and Office: 11 Park St Tenafly NJ 07670-2217 Office: 161 Ft Washington Ave New York NY 10032-3713

COSMAN, BARD CLIFFORD, surgeon, educator; b. N.Y.C., Mar. 1, 1963; s. Bard and Madeleine (Pelner) C.; m. Pamela Caren Feldman, Mar. 26, 1989; children: Benjamin, Rafael, Gilead, Ilan. AB magna cum laude, Harvard U., 1983; MPH, MD, Columbia U., 1987. Diplomate Nat. Bd. Med. Examiners, Am. Bd. Surgery, Am. Bd. Colon and Rectal Surgery. Resident in surgery Stanford (Calif.) U., 1987-89, postdoctoral fellow, 1989-91; fellow spinal cord injury svc. Palo Alto (Calif.) VA Med. Ctr., 1989-91; resident in surgery Stanford U. Hosp., 1991-94; resident in colon and rectal surgery U. Minn., 1994-95; asst. clin. prof. surgery U. Calif., San Diego, 1995—2001, assoc. prof. clin. surgery, 2001—; sect. chief Halasz gen. surgery sect., surg. svc. VA San Diego Healthcare Sys., 2000—. Contbr. articles to profl. jours. NRSA Tng. grantee Nat. Cancer Inst., Bethesda, 1990; Giannini Found. Postdoctoral Rsch. fellow Bank of Am., San Francisco, 1990. Home: 8708 Nottingham Pl La Jolla CA 92037-2128 Office: VA Med Ctr Surgical Svc 112E 3350 La Jolla Village Dr San Diego CA 92161-0002

COSMAS, STELLA ANATOLITOU, principal; b. Famagusta, Cyprus, Jan. 31, 1952; came to U.S., 1975; d. Kyriacos and Athina (Hadjikipri) A.; m. Steven C. Cosmas, July 31, 1974; children: Corinna, Alex. BA in Edn., Psychology, U. Athens, Greece, 1974; MA in Ednl. Adminstrn., Montclair State Coll., 1991. Tchr. parochial sch. St. Demetrios Parish, Queens, NY, St. Constantine Parish, Orange, NJ; tchr. pub. schs. Mt. Arlington, NJ, Allamuchy, NJ, Chatham, NJ, Livingston, NJ, 1989—96; prin. Wayne (NJ) Pub. Schs., 1996—. Chair, adviser critical thinking com., Allamuchy, 1986-88, ednl. com., Orange, N.J., 1988—; pres. Greek Coral, Inc. Ednl. Assn., Livingston, N.J.; curriculum presenter, guest speaker N.J. Bds. Assn., Atlantic City, N.J., 1986; coord. Gifted and Talented program Livingston Pub. Schs., 1989-96; mem. selection com. for A+ grants N.J. Bd. Edn., 1993. Author, editor ednl. materials; contbr. articles to profl. publs. Active ednl. com. St. Constantine & St. Helen Ch., Orange, N.J., 1990—. Grantee A+ for Kids Tchrs. Network, 1990, Metacognition grantee Livingston Bd. of Edn., 1991; recipient Gov.'s Recognition award, N.J., 1991; named Tchr. of Yr. N.J. Bd. Edn., 1991. Mem. NEA, Tchrs.' Assn. St. Constantine (v.p. 1977-79), N.J. Assn. Edn. Gifted Children, Prometheas Greek Edn. Assn., Nat. Assn. Gifted Children, Kappa Delta Pi. Eastern Orthodox. Avocations: reading, cooking, travel, viewing classic movies. Home: 5 Bonnyview Dr Livingston NJ 07039-2016

COST, RICHARD WILLARD, university administrator, educator; b. New Brunswick, N.J., June 23, 1942; s. John and Dorothy Mae (Quackenboss) C.; m. Ellen Elizabeth Conner, July 22, 1977; children: Richard Scott, Catherine Anne, Matthew Brian. AB, Syracuse U., 1964; MBA, Old Dominion U., 1970; EdD, Rutgers U., 1977; postgrad., Naval War Coll., 1992; student, Harvard U. Inst. Ednl. Mgmt., 1995. Asst. dean of students Rutgers U., Newark, 1970-71, asst. coordinator of aid New Brunswick, N.J., 1971-72; instr. Bloomfield (N.J.) Coll., 1975-81; exec. assoc. Assn. Ind. Colls., East Orange, N.J., 1972-79; exec. asst. to pres. N.J. Inst. Tech., Newark, 1979-83; v.p. Ind. Coll. Fund N.J., Summit, 1983-89; v.p. instl. advancement Moravian Coll., Bethlehem, Pa., 1989-94; v.p. Bridgewater (Mass.) Coll., 1994—2002; pres. U. Maine, Ft. Kent, 2002—. Chmn. Commonwealth Rev. Team, Harrisburg, Pa., 1987; mem. Mid. State Accreditating Teams, 1983—; mem. mil. acad. selection com., adv. bd. for vets. U.S. Congressman Paul McHale, 1993-94. Contbr. chpts. to books; Editor: Ten Year Compendium, 1973. Dir. Fuller Mus. Art. Capt. USNR ret. Decorated Meritorious Svc. medal USNR, 1997. Mem. Am. Assn. Higher Edn., U.S. Naval Inst. Republican. Avocations: sailing, watercolor painting, stained glass. Office: Univ Maine at Ft Kent 23 University Dr Fort Kent ME 04743 E-mail: RCOST@Maine.edu.

COSTA, DONNA MARIE, secondary education educator; b. Peabody, Mass., Dec. 5, 1955; d. Antonio Sariva Costa and Lulu Rose (Silva) Costa-Smith; children: Dawne Marie Phelan, Brian Michael Phelan II. AS, N. Shore Community Coll., Beverly, Mass., 1982; BA, U. Mass. at Boston, 1986; MEd in Sch. Adminstrn., Salem (Mass.) State Coll., 1988; cert. advanced studies, Harvard U., 1991; EdD candidate, 1992—. Cert. acad. and occpl. tchr., Mass. Instr./dept. head Peabody Sch. Dept., 1981—, sch.-to-work coord., 1998—; tech. prep. site facilitator, 1993—. Instr. North Shore C.C., Mass., 1994—; mem. H.S. Coun. Faculty Adv., Vocat. Adv., Electronics Adv., Ednl. Tech., Extended After Sch. Program bds., Peabody Sch. Dept., ednl. tech. com.; coun. mem. Peabody H.S. Vol. ARC, 1984—. Recipient Horace Mann grants, 1988, 89. Mem. ASCD, NAFE, Phi Delta Kappa (bd. dirs. Harvard chpt.). Roman Catholic. Avocations: softball, Karate, skiing, racquetball, volleyball. Home: 8 Munroe St Peabody MA 01960-4468

COSTA, ROSANN, research associate; b. Bklyn., Sept. 1, 1967; d. Frank Anthony and Diane Grace (Lagiovani) C. BA, CUNY, Flushing, N.Y., 1990; MA, NYU, 1994. Cert. elem. educator, N.Y. Pvt. tutor, 1987—; rsch. asst., data analyst Helen Keller Ctr., Sands Point, N.Y., 1990, 91; edn. evaluator N.Y.C. Bd. Edn., Bklyn., 1991-95; sr. rsch. assoc. Columbia U., N.Y.C., 1995—. Mem. Com. of Hundreds, Futures in Edn. Found., Douglaston, N.Y., 1993, 94; exec. bd. mem. Am. Cancer Soc., N.Y.C., 1993—, CORE team mem., 1994—. Contbr. articles to profl. jours. Dean's list Queen's Coll., 1988-90. Mem. Am. Ednl. Rsch. Assn., Am. Sociol. Assn., Soc. for Study of Social Problems, Assn. Tchr. Edn., Eastern Sociol. Soc. Roman Catholic. Avocations: reading, writing, hiking. Home: 42 W 72d St Apt 7B New York NY 10023 Office: Columbia U Sergievsky Ctr 630 W 168th St New York NY 10032-3795

COSTA, TERRY ANN, principal; b. Huntington, W.Va., Jan. 9, 1951; d. Hobart G. and Beatrice (Chaput) Owens; m. Joseph M. Costa, June 5, 1970; children: Carrie Lynn, Anthony Martin. BA, Marshall U., 1972, MA, 1979; EdS, Nova U., 1988. Cert. specific learning disabilities, mentally and emotionally handicapped, varying exceptionalities, ESOL, speech tchr., coach, ednl. leadership, Fla. Tchr. spl. edn. Cabell County Sch. System, Huntington, 1973-77, 80-86, coach, 1980-86; adj. instr. Marshall U., Huntington, 1979-80; tchr. spl. edn., dept. chmn. Palm Beach County Sch. Sys., West Palm Beach, Fla., 1986-94, coord. exceptional student edn., dept. chairperson, coach, 1989-94; chmn. tng. and devel. Palm Beach County Sch. System, West Palm Beach, Fla., 1988-89; asst. prin. Loggers' Run Cmty. Mid. Sch., Boca Raton, Fla., 1994-98; prin. Christa McAuliffe Cmty. Mid. Sch., Boynton Beach, Fla., 1998—. Chmn. exceptional student edn. instructional materials coun. for math. and sci. Fla. Dept. Edn., West Palm Beach, 1988, clin. educator, 1986-91. Coord., vol. Spl. Olympics, Cabell County, 1974-76; religious tchr., coord. Diocese of Wheeling-Charleston, W.Va., 1980-86; leader Girl Scouts U.S.A., W.Va., 1984-86; sch. campaign chmn. United Way, Palm Beach County, 1988-89. Mem. ASCD, Nat. Assn. Secondary Sch. Prins., Coun. for Exceptional Children (sec. W.Va. 1973-74, corr. sec. 1992-93, Palm Beach County Tchr. of Yr. award chpt. 200, 1989, grantee 1988-90, 92), Fla. Assn. Sch. Adminstrs., Palm Beach County Sch. Adminstrs. Assn. (exec. bd. sec. 1996-2000), Palm Beach County Prins. Assn. (sec., chair tech. com.), Boynton Beach C. of C., Boynton Beach Kiwanis Internat. (treas. 1999-2001, pres. 2003—), Phi Delta Kappa (v.p. membership, Kappan of Yr. 1999-2001). Democrat. Roman Catholic. Avocations: tennis, water skiing, running, fishing, needlecrafts. Home: 880 SE Degan Dr Port Saint Lucie FL 34983- Office: Christa McAuliffe Cmty Mid Sch 6500 Le Chalet Blvd Boynton Beach FL 33437-2304 E-mail: costa@palmbeach.k12.fl.us.

COSTANTINI, WILLIAM JOSEPH, secondary school educator, computer consultant; b. Steubenville, Ohio, Aug. 8, 1945; s. William Joseph and Mary Angela (Carfagna) C.; m. Mary Ann Colsh, Nov. 17, 1990; children: Thomas, Susan Michelle. BS in Music Edn., St. Vincent Coll., Latrobe, Pa., 1967; postgrad., Robert Morris Coll., 1993—. Cert. prof. music and data processing tchr., Ohio. Asst. dir. band Edison Local Sch. Dist., Hammondsville, Ohio, 1967-70, dir. band, 1970-84, tchr. computer applications, 1984—, tech. coord., 1995—. Freelance computer cons., 1986—; workshops on computer use in schs. Jefferson County Sch. Dist., Steubenville, 1989—, mem. tech. com., 1990—; computer cons. Bellofram Corp., Chester, W.Va., 1994—. Compiler: Desktop Reference to MS Works, 1989. Grantee Jefferson County Sch. Dist., 1992. Mem. Edison Local Edn. Assn. (treas., v.p., pres. 1972-94), Lions (past treas. and pres. Richmond, Ohio). Roman Catholic. Avocation: model railroads.

COSTANZO, FRANK DENNIS, music educator; b. Bklyn., Mar. 18, 1949; s. Salvatore and Mary Delores (Fichera) C.; m. Eileen Marie Saviello, June 30, 1973; children: Jennifer, Christopher. BS, NYU, 1971, MA, 1975. Cert. music tchr. Vocal music tchr. Westhampton Beach (N.Y.) Pub. Schs., 1971—. Group specialist Westhampton Beach Summer Recreational Program, 1973-82; camp dir. Red Robin East Day Camp, Center Moriches, N.Y., 1983—; mus. dir. Eastport (N.Y.) PTA, 1990— (appreciation placque 1992); treas. Eastport Athletic Booster Club, 1991—. Mem. Music Educators Nat. Conf., N.Y. State Sch. Music Assn., Suffolk County Music Educators Assn., Hampton Music Educators Assn. (pres. 1981-85, appreciation placque 1985), L.I. Assn. Pvt. Schs. and Day Camps. Republican. Roman Catholic. Avocations: golf, reading, gardening, little league umpire. Home: PO Box 181 Eastport NY 11941-0181 Office: Westhampton Beach Pub Schs Mill Rd Westhampton Beach NY 11978

COSTANZO, NANCI JOY, art educator; b. New Britain, Conn., June 2, 1947; d. Edward Francis and Vivian Evelyn (Allen) Sarisley; m. Joseph Paul Costanzo, Apr. 10, 1974; 1 child, Ashley Allen Bailey. BA, Cen. Conn. State U., New Britain, 1973; MAE, R.I. Sch. Design, 1979; cert. advanced grad. study in Expressive Art Therapy, European Grad. Sch., Leuk, Switzerland, 1999. Assoc. prof. art Elms Coll., Chicopee, Mass., 1985—, also chair dept. visual arts. Exhibited at Western New Eng. Coll., 1977, Springfield Art League Show, 1978, Zone Gallery, 1981, Westfield State Coll., 1985, Valley Women Arts Show, 1980, 83, 85-89, New Britain Mus. Am. Art, 1987-90, Borgia Gallery Elms Coll., 1989-92, Hampden Gallery at U. Mass., 1990, Sino-Am. Women's Conf., Beijing, People's Republic of China, 1990, Monson Arts Coun., 1995, Elms Coll., 1997, European Grad. Sch., Switzerland, 1998-99, Dane Gallery, 2001-02, NY Am. Mus. Illustrators, 2002, Yorktown Mus., NY, 2002, others; one woman shows include Thronja Art Gallery, 1979-80, Elms Coll., 1992, 2002, Dane Gallery, 2001-02; represented in pvt. collections in Mass., RI, Wash., NY, Italy, corp. collections in RI and Conn.; creator Cmty. Art Exhibit for 9-11; contbr. articles to profl. jours.; lectr. Greece, Mex. and China. Recipient Outstanding Arts Educator in Mass. award Mass. Alliance for Arts Edn., 1985, New Britain Mus. Am. Art, 1987, 88; Nat. Endowment for Humanities grantee, 1987, 88; Faculty Devel. grantee, Beijing, 1989, 90. Mem. Nat. Art Edn. Assn., Valley Women Artists, Mass. Art Edn. Assn. (mem. coun. 1984-86, v.p. 1986-88), Nat. Mus. of Women in the Arts, Coll. Art Assn., Nat. Women's Studies Assn., Internat. Soc. for Edn. through Art, Women's Caucus for Art. Avocations: painting, reading, gardening, skiing, sailing. Office: Elms Coll 291 Springfield St Chicopee MA 01013-2837

COSTA-ZALESSOW, NATALIA, foreign language educator; b. Kumanovo, Macedonia, Dec. 5, 1936; came to the U.S., 1951; d. Alexander P. and Katarina (Duric) Z.; m. Gustavo Costa, June 8, 1963; 1 child, Dora. BA in Italian, U. Calif., Berkeley, 1959, MA in Italian, 1961, PhD in Romance Langs. and Lits., 1967. Tchg. asst. U. Calif., Berkeley, 1959-63; instr. Mills Coll., Oakland, Calif., 1963; asst. prof. San Francisco State U., 1968-74, assoc. prof., 1974-79, prof., 1979-98, coord. Italian program, 1992-98, prof. emerita, 1998—. Author: Scrittrici italiane dal XIII al XX secolo, Testi e critica, 1982; editor: Anima, 1997; transl.: Her Soul, 1996; contbr. articles to profl. publs. Sidney M. Ehrman scholar U. Calif., Berkeley, 1957-58, Gamma Phi Beta scholar U. Calif., Berkeley, 1958, Herbert H. Vaughan scholar U. Calif., Berkeley, 1959-60, Advanced Grad. Traveling fellow in romance lang. and lit. U. Calif., Berkeley, 1964-65. Mem. MLA, Am. Assn. Tchrs. Italian, Renaissance Soc. Am., Dante Soc. Am., Croatian Acad. Am. Roman Catholic. Avocations: swimming, hiking, opera, symphony, gastronomy. Office: San Francisco State U Dept Fgn Lang and Lit San Francisco CA 94132

COSTELLO, JOHN ROBERT, linguistics educator; b. N.Y.C., Sept. 12, 1942; s. John and Helen (May) C. BA, Wagner Coll., 1964; MA, NYU, 1966, PhD, 1968. Instr. linguistics NYU, 1967, asst. prof., 1968-72, assoc. prof., 1973-85, prof., 1986—, chmn. dept. linguistics, 1986-93. Cons. Universe Pubs., N.Y.C., 1979-81, Lexik House Pubs., Cold Springs, N.Y., 1980—, NYU Press, 1982, Geers Gross Advt., N.Y.C., 1988, Toyota Corp., 1989, FCB/Leber Katz Ptnrs. (Advt. Agy.), N.Y.C., 1990, Avon Products, Inc., 1991, Doubleday Pub., Soc. for Germanic Philology, Workman's Pub., 1994, SUNY, Albany, 1995. Author: A Generative Grammar of Old Frisian, 1977, Syntactic Change and Syntactic Reconstruction, 1983; editor: Pole Poppenspaeler, 1970, Word, 1977—, Studies Presented to Robert A. Fowkes, 1980, Papers in Honor of 50th Anniversary of Linguistic Circle of N.Y., 1994, Aspects of the History of Linguistics, 1995; assoc. editor: Lang. Scis., 1984-94; contbr. articles to profl. jours. Research grantee NYU, 1978, NEH grantee, 1981. Mem. Internat. Soc. for Hist. Linguistics, Internat. Linguistic Assn. (v.p. 1979-81, pres. 1981-82), Linguistic Assn. of Can. and U.S., Am. Soc. of Geolinguistics, Linguistic Soc. Am., Soc. for German-Am. Studies, Soc. for Germanic Philology, Phi Beta Kappa (pres. Beta chpt. 1984). Mem. Christian Ch. Avocations: writing, computer programming. Office: NYU Dept Linguistics 719 Broadway Dept New York NY 10003-6860

COSTILOW, SUSAN LYNN, education and conference coordinator; b. Morgantown, W.Va., Dec. 31, 1963; d. John Barton Costilow and Rita Irene (Dunn) Towns. BA, W.Va. U., 1986, MA, 1991. Staff writer W.Va. U., Morgantown, 1986-88, program mgr., 1988-93; instr. Fairmont (W.Va.) State Coll., 1992-93; coord. edn. and conf. ctr. Harbor Br. Oceanographic Instn., Ft. Pierce, Fla., 1993—. Contbr. articles to profl. jours. Coord., vol. W.Va. Pub. TV, 1992-93; facilitator, tchr. Learn to Read, Fla., 1996. Mem. MLA, Assn. Conf. and Event Dirs. Internat., Meeting Profls. Internat. Avocations: reading, fitness, theater, movies.

COTE-BEAUPRE, CAMILLE YVETTE, artist, educator; b. Worcester, Mass., May 21, 1926; d. Harvey and Blanche (Trahan) Cote. BA cum laude, Am. Internat. Coll., 1949; cert. in fine arts, Walker Studio Group, 1952; MS, U. Bridgeport, 1967. Dir. arts and crafts South End Cmty. Ctr., Springfield, Mass., 1955-58; art tchr. YWCA, Springfield, 1958-61; dir. workshops Hall Neighborhood House, Bridgeport, Conn., 1961-64, Jewish Cmty. Ctr., Bridgeport, 1964-69; tchr., chmn. art dept. Notre Dame H.S., Fairfield, Conn., 1970-95; chmn. art dept. Kolbe Cathedral H.S., 1995-98, Discovery Mus., 1998—. One-woman shows: Bridgeport Cath. Center, 1978, Creative Mind Gallery, Stratford, Conn., 1978, Burroughs Library, Bridgeport, 1979, Trumbull (Conn.) Library, 1981, St. Vincent's Hosp., Bridgeport, 1981, St. Joseph Manor, Trumbull, 1981, Kellogg Environ. Ctr., Derby, Conn., 1999, Derby Environ. Ctr., 2001; group shows include: Stamford (Conn.) Mus., 1977, Slade Mus., Norwich, Conn., 1975, Mus. Sci. and Industry, Bridgeport, 1974, Sacred Heart U., Bridgeport, 1979, Fairfield (Conn.) U., 1979, 56th Grand Nat. Am. Artists Profl. League, Ho. of Reps., Washington, 1993, Nat. Arts Club, 1996, Creative Graphics Internat. Competition, 1997, others; represented in permanent collections: Eastern Conn. State Coll., Trumbull Libr. Assn., St. Vincent's Hosp., St. Joseph's Manor. Mem. Am. Artists Profl. League, Conn. Classic Arts, Am. Portrait Soc., Acad. Artists Assn., Nat. Arts Club, Conn. Pastel Soc. Home: 12 Melon Patch Ln Monroe CT 06468-1120

COTHERMAN, AUDREY MATHEWS, management and policy consultant, administrator; b. St. Paul, May 20, 1930; d. Anthony Joseph and Nina Grace (Harmon) Mathews; m. Richard Louis Cotherman, Dec. 30, 1950 (div. 1973); children: Steven, Michael, Bruce, Gen Elizabeth. BA, Hamline U., 1952; MA, U. Wyo., 1973, EdD, 1977. Communications coord. Natrona Sch. Dist., Casper, Wyo., 1968-69; hostess TV program KTWO-TV, Casper, 1970-71; exec. dir. United Way, Casper, 1971-73, Wyo. Coun. Humanities, Laramie, 1973-79; dep. state supt. Wyo. Dept. Edn., Cheyenne, 1979-90; devel. officer Coll. Edn. U. Wyo., Laramie, 1990-91; pres. Connections: Mgmt. and Policy Cons., Casper, 1991—; spl. asst. U.S. Dept. Edn. Region VIII, 1996-99; asst. dir. U. Wis. Comprehensive Ctr., 1999—2000; dir. U. Wis. Comprehensive Ctr., 2001—. Exec. sec. Wyo. Bd. Edn., 1979-90; dir. comty. programs HSS, Cheyenne, 1986-90; cons. Wyo. Atty. Gen., Cheyenne, 1990; dealer Profiles, Internat. Dem. precinct chair, Laramie, 1986-90. State exec. policy fellow U.S. Dept. Edn., 1985. Mem. LWV (past pres. local chpts., Wyo. chpt.), Am. Assn. Pub. Adminstrs. (pres. 1987-88), Wyo. Assn. Pub. Adminstrs. (Pub. Adminstr. of Yr. 1982), Phi Delta Kappa. Presbyterian. Avocations: writing, spending time with grandchildren, reading, antique hunting. Home: 8530 Greenway Blvd Apt 214 Middleton WI 53562-4605

COTHRUN, THOMAS KEITH, secondary education educator; b. Miami, Ariz., Mar. 9, 1959; s. Milton James and Nadine L. (Thomas) Cothrun. BA in Edn., U. Ariz., 1982; MA in German Studies, U. N.Mex., 1993. Tchr. German, Alamogordo (N.Mex.) H.S., 1983-86, Las Cruces (N.Mex.) H.S., 1986—. Dir. German Weekend, N.Mex., 1985-89, 99-01; mem. task force Nat. Stds. in Fgn. Lang., Yonkers, N.Y., 1993-96; cons. Coll. Bd., Princeton, N.J., 1993—. Co-author: German-American Partnership Program Handbook, 1993; also articles. Named Tchr. of Yr., Las Cruces Pub. Schs., 1995, Walt Disney Am. Tchr. award honoree, 1995; recipient fellowship U.S. Holocaust Meml. Mus. Mandel, 1999-2000, award for excellence in tchg., Am. Couns. for Internat. Edn., 1999. Mem. ASCD, NEA, Am. Assn. Tchrs. German (v.p., pres.-elect 1994-95, pres. 1996-97, cert. of merit 1993, Outstanding German Educator 2001), Am. Coun. on Tchg. Fgn. Langs. (pres.-elect 2003), S.W. Conf. on Lang. Tchg., N.Mex. Orgn. Lang.

Educators (Creativity in Tchg. award 1993, Tchr. of Yr. 2002), Nat. Bd. for Profl. Tchg. Stds. (fgn. lang. stds. chair 1998-01, bd. dirs. 2002—). Office: Las Cruces Pub Schs 1755 El Paseo St Las Cruces NM 88001-6011

COTTAM, GENE LARRY, biochemistry educator; b. Coffeeville, Kans., Nov. 3, 1940; s. Paul Clifford and Juanita Serene (Carver) C.; m. Melanie Lou Poor, June 8, 1963; children: Laura Ann, Janell Sue, Melinda Kay. BA in Chemistry, U. Kans., 1962; MS in Organic Chemistry, U. Mich., 1963, MA in Biochemistry, 1965, PhD in Biochemistry, 1967. Postdoctoral fellow Southwestern Med. Ctr./U. Tex., Dallas, 1967-68, asst. prof. biochemistry, 1968-73, assoc. prof. biochemistry, 1973-79, prof. biochemistry, 1979-99. Office: U Tex Southwestern Med Ctr 5323 Harry Hines Blvd Dallas TX 75390-7208

COTTEN, ANNIE LAURA, psychologist, educator; b. Oxford, N.C., Nov. 18, 1923; d. Leonard F. and Laura Estelle (Spencer) Cotten; children: Hollis W., Rebecca Ann, Laura Cotten. Diploma, Hardbarger Bus. Coll., 1944; AB, Duke U., 1945; MEd, U. Hartford, 1965; PhD, The Union Inst., 1979. Diplomate Am. Bd. Sexology, lic. Am. Assn. Marriage & Family Therapists, 87. Asst. to pres. So. Meth. U., 1953; rsch. asst. Duke U., 1947-49; exec. sec. Ohio Wesleyan U., 1955-56, Conn. Coun. Chs., 1958-60; adj. prof. U. Hartford, 1976-78, 1976-78; clin. pastoral counselor Hartford Hosp., 1962-65; asst., then assoc. dir. social svcs. Hartford Conf. Chs., 1965-67; tchg. fellow U. N.C., 1970-71; assoc. prof. Ctrl. Conn. State U., New Britain, 1967-93, adj. prof., 1994—2002. Adj. prof. St. Joseph Coll., 1986-96; clin. intern Montefiore Med. Ctr., 1995; dir. elderhostel programs Ctrl. Conn. State U., 1989-93, organizer ctr. adult learners, 1991-93; cons. Somers Correctional Ctr., Conn., 1980-81, instr./rschr., 1980-81; cons. Conn. Life Ins. Mktg. Rsch., 1981-1982; amb. to China, spring, 1986; presenter 3d Internat. Interdisciplinary Cong. on Women, 1987; vis. prof., scholar Duke U., 1989; adj. prof. health and human svcs. Ctrl. Ch. St. U., 1995-2002; vis. prof. Conn. Coll., New London, 1990; mem. clin. faculty, Am. Bd. Sexology, 1994; land developer N.C. Triangle, 1995—. Cons. editor: Jour. Feminist Family Therapy, 2000—. Fellow: Am. Acad. Clin. Sexologists (clin. faculty 1994—, founder), Nat. Coun. Family Rels.; mem.: APA (chair divsn. 1987—91), AAUW, Am. Assn. Sex Educators, Counselors and Therapists, Conn. Assn. Marital & Family Therapists (bd. dirs. 2000—02), Sex Info. & Edn. Coun. of Conn. (bd. dirs. 1994—2002, human sexuality leader of yr. 1997), Conn. Psychol. Assn., Am. Assn. Sex Educators Counselors & Therapists (cert. outstanding svc. 1996, disting. svc. award 1998), Am. Assn. Marriage & Family Therapists, Hartford Women's Network.

COTTER, VINCENT F. assistant principal; b. Phila., Sept. 9, 1950; s. John R. and Matilda (Tyska) C.; m. Christine A. Graeff, Nov. 17, 1973; children: Steven V., Lauren M. MEd, Millersville (Pa.) U., 1979; EdD, Temple U., 1992. Tchr., coach Southeastern Sch. Dist., Fawn Grove, Pa., 1972-76; asst. prin., dept. head, tchr. Sch. Dist. Phila., 1976-91; prin. Colonial, Plymouth Meeting, Pa., 1991—. Mem. ASCD, Nat. Assn. Secondary Sch. Prins., Pa. Sch. Bds. Assn., Montgomery County Prins. and Suprs. Assn. Avocation: vacationing on cape cod. Home: 909 Tennis Way Lansdale PA 19446-4368

COTTINGHAM, MARY PATRICIA, vocational rehabilitation counselor; b. Seattle, May 9, 1930; d. Carl Frank and Frances Mary (Keon) Fox; m. Ken Cottingham, Sept. 15, 1951 (div. Sept. 1982); children: Cathy Ann, David Carl, Susan Mary, Keith Bryan, Patricia Frances. BA, U. Wash., 1974, MEd in Psychology, 1977. Diplomate Am. Bd. Vocat. Experts; cert. mental health counselor, Wash.; cert. vocat. rehab. counselor. Counselor Mental Health North, Seattle, 1974-77; vocat. rehab. counselor Counseling Svcs. Northwest, Lynnwood, Wash., 1977-79; owner, cons. People Systems Inc., Seattle, 1979—. Bd. dirs. King County Mental Health Bd., Seattle, 1982-84; guardian ad litem King County Juvenile Ct., Seattle, 1981-84. Mem. AACD, Am. Mental Health Counselors Assn., Nat. Rehab. Assn., Pvt. Rehab. Orgns. Wash. (sec. 1986-89), Wash. Mental Health Counselors Assn. (sec. 1983-85). Office: People Systems Inc 155 NE 100th St Ste 406 Seattle WA 98125-8010 Address: PO Box 123 Lakewood WA 98259-0123

COTTINGHAM, STEPHEN KENT, real estate development executive, researcher, minister, educator; b. Denver, Dec. 28, 1951; s. Miles Dixon and Ruth (Skeen) C. Student, So. Oreg. Coll., 1970-71; BBA, So. Meth. U., 1974; ThM, Dallas Theol. Sem., 1984; postgrad., So. Meth. U. V.p. Cottingham Constrn. Co., Dallas, 1974-79; project mgmt. Avery Mays Constrn. Co., Dallas, 1981-82; asst. v.p. Pacific Realty Corp., Dallas, 1983-85, v.p., 1985-86, exec. v.p., 1986-88; v.p. Paragon Group, Dallas, 1988-91; regional v.p. The Prime Group Inc., San Antonio, 1991-93; pres. Brock Investment Group, Inc., San Antonio, 1993-95; chairman, pres. SKCI, Inc., San Antonio, 1995—; founder, chmn., pres. Theol. Edn. Found., Internat., 1996—; pres. Princeton Resources, Inc., 1992—; founder, chmn., pres. Cottingham Devel. Corp., San Antonio, 1997—; with planning and devel. divsn. San Antonio River Authority, 2000—; pastor, tchr. Univ. United Meth. Ch., San Antonio, 2002—. Adj. tchr. N.W. Bible Ch. Coll. Class, Dallas, 1981-83; student leader, counselor Young Life Internat., Dallas, 1974-76; chmn. Boyd Ministries, Norfolk, Va., 1996—; bd. dirs. Harvester Ministries, Plano, Tex. Charter mem. Rep. Nat. Com., Washington, 1985—; tchr. Christ Episcopal Ch., San Antonio, chmn. adult edn., exec. com.; founder, pres. Theol. Edn. Foun., Internat., San Antonio, 1996—. Named one of Outstanding Young Men of Am., Montgomery, Ala., 1986; So. Meth. U. Scholar, 1972-74. Mem. Internat. Right of Way Assn., Urban Land Inst. (assoc.), Evang. Theol. Soc., Phi Gamma Delta (treas.), Phi Beta Lamda. Avocations: skiing, antique restoration, cycling, writing, travel, missionary work. Office: Univ United Meth Ch 5084 De Zavala Rd San Antonio TX 78249

COTTON, JOHN PIERCE, principal; b. Winchester, Mass., Nov. 25, 1937; s. Dana Meserve and Geraldine (Pierce) C.; children: John E., Sarah P., Nathaniel C. H., Ethan S.; m. Tami Pleasanton, 1991. AB, Harvard U., 1960; MA, Colo. U., 1968. Trust asst. Old Colony Trust Co., Boston, 1962-64; head upper sch. Colo. Acad., Denver, 1964-68; headmaster Kimball Union Acad., Meriden, N.H., 1968-74, St. Andrew's Sch., Boca Raton, Fla., 1974-86; interim headmaster St. Stephen's Sch., Bradenton, Fla., 1986-87; prin. Francis W. Parker Sch., Chgo., 1987-93; headmaster Ransom Everglades Sch., Miami, Fla., 1993-98; v.p. chancellor beacon Academies, Inc., 1999—. Trustee Gulfstream (Fla.) Sch., 1980-86. Trustee St. Joseph's Episcopal Sch., Fla., 1999, Acad. at the Lakes, 2003—. Mem. Fla. Coun. Ind. Schs. (pres., bd. dirs. 1976-86), Coun. Religion in Ind. Schs. (trustee 1980-87), Ind. Schs. Assn. Greater Chgo. (v.p. 1989-90, pres. 1990-93), Ind. Schs. Assn. Ctrl. States (bd. dirs. 1990-93). Home: 633 Castilla Ln Boynton Beach FL 33435-6103 E-mail: jcotton@chancelloracademies.com.

COUGHLIN, BERNARD JOHN, university chancellor; b. Galveston, Tex., Dec. 7, 1922; s. Eugene J. and Celeste M. (Ott) C. AB, St. Louis U., 1946, Ph.L., 1949, S.T.L., 1956; MSW., U. So. Calif., 1959; PhD, Brandeis U., 1963; DHL (hon.), Seattle U., 1994. Joined S.J., Roman Cath. Ch., 1942, ordained priest, 1955; tchr., counselor chs. in Wis. and Kans., 1949-54; research asst. Los Angeles Juvenile Probation Project, 1959; social work cons. Guatemala City, summer 1960; mem. faculty St. Louis U., 1961-74; social work cons. Peru, Chile, 1967; Fulbright lectr., 1970-71; prof. Sch. Social Service, 1970-74, dean, 1964-74; pres. Gonzaga U., Spokane, Wash., 1974-96, chancellor, 1996—. Mem. program com. Nat. Conf. Cath. Charities, 1964-68, mem. com. legislation social justice, 1973-80, bd. dirs., 1973-80, mem. com. study and study cadre, 1970-72; mem. adv. com. social welfare service Model Cities, St. Louis, 1967-68; council social work edn. Commn. Internat. Social Work Edn., 1968-81, adv. com. project on integrative teaching and learning, 1968-69, adv. com. population dynamics and family planning, 1969-71, structure rev. com., 1970-71; bd. dirs. Health and Welfare Council Met. St. Louis, 1968-74, Shearson Fundamental Value Fund, Inc.; chmn. task force community planning Child Welfare League Am., 1967-69; chmn. Conf. Deans Schs. Social Work, 1972-73; chmn. nominating com. U.S. com. Internat. Council Social Work, 1973-79; cons. in field, del. internat. confs.; mem. Assn. Governing Bds., 1980-81, Council for Postsecondary Edn., 1979-85; mem. gov's. commn. on ethics in govt. and campaign practices. Author: Church and State in Social Welfare, 1965, also articles, revs., chpts. in books. Bd. dirs. United Way Spokane County, 1982-87; mem. Inland Empire council Boy Scouts Am., 1982—; mem. Nat. Conf. Cath. Charities, Washington Citizens' Commn. on Salaries for Elected Officials, 1987—; chmn. Northwest Citizens Forum Def. Waste, 1986-88; trustee St. Louis U., 1988—, Spokane Area Econ. Devel. Coun., 1991—; U.S. rep. to Internat. Coun. on Social Welfare, Study Commn. on Human Rights, Helsinki, Finland, 1968; mem. coun. on social work edn., Task Force on Structure and Quality in Social Work Edn., 1973-74; chmn. Northwest Citizens Forum on Nuclear Waste, 1986-88. Fulbright lectr. Colombia, 1970, 71; Grantee NIMH, 1963-68 Mem. Nat. Assn. Social Workers (chmn. cabinet div. profl. standards 1970-73), Internat. Assn. Schs. Social Work, Internat. Coun. Social Welfare, Nat. Conf. Social Welfare, Internat. Assn. Univ. Presidents (vice chmn. U.S. western regional coun. 1982—, mem. steering com. 1982—), Coun. Social Work Edn., Mo. Assn. for Social Welfare, Assn. Wash. Bus. (bd. dirs. 1991—), Spokane Area C. of C. (trustee 1979-81, vice chmn. 1987-88, chmn. 1988-89). Address: Gonzaga U 502 E Boone Ave Spokane WA 99258-1774

COULDWELL, WILLIAM TUPPER, neurosurgeon, educator; b. Vancouver, B.C., Can., Dec. 15, 1955; s. William John and Janet Mary (Tupper) C.; m. Marie Francoise Simard; children: Sandrine, Mitchell, Genevieve. MD, McGill U., 1984, PhD, 1991. Resident in neurosurgery U. So. Calif., L.A., 1984-89; fellow neuroimmunology Montreal Neurol. Inst., 1989-91, fellow epilepsy surgery, 1990; fellow neurosurgery CHUV, Lausanne, Switzerland, 1990-91; asst. prof. dept. neurol. surgery U. So. Calif., L.A., 1991-95, assoc. clin. prof., 1995-97, U. N.D., Minot, 1995-97; prof., chmn. dept. neurol. surgery N.Y. Med. Coll., Valhalla, 1997—. Contbr. articles to profl. jours. Recipient Preuss award Am. Assn. Neurol. Surgeons, 1991, Clinician Investigator award, 1993; Med. Rsch. Coun. Can. Centennial fellow, 1990; McGill U. scholar, 1984, Wood Gold medal. Fellow ACS; mem. Am. Assn. Neurol. Surgeons (joint sect. on tumors, joint sect. on cerebrovasc. disease 1991—), Congress of Neurol. Surgeons, N.Am. Skull Base Soc., Soc. Neurol. Surgeons, Neurol. Soc. Am. Office: NY Med Coll Munger Pavilion Dept Neurol Surgery Valhalla NY 10595

COULSON, ELIZABETH ANNE, physical therapy educator, state representative; b. Hastings, Nebr., Sept. 8, 1954; d. Alexander and Marilyn (Marvel) Shafernich; m. William Coulson, Feb. 14, 1986. Student, Wellesley Coll., 1972-73; BS in Edn., U. Kans., 1976; cert. in phys. therapy, Northwestern U., Chgo., 1977; MBA, Keller Grad. Sch. Mgmt., 1985; postgrad., U. Ill., 1991. Lic. phys. therapist, Ill. Assoc. prof. dept. phys. therapy Chgo. Med. Sch., North Chicago, Ill., chmn. dept. phys. therapy, 1993-96. Contbr. articles to profl. jours. Trustee Northfield Twp., Ill., 1993-97; Ill. state rep. 17th dist., 1997—. Mem. APHA, Am. Phys. Therapy Assn. (Ill. del. 1986-93, chief del. 1991-93), Ill. Phys. Therapy Assn. (chmn. jud. com. 1989-91). Home: 1701 Sequoia Trl Glenview IL 60025-2022

COULTER, CYNTHIA JEAN, artist, educator; b. Lincoln, Nebr., Jan. 16, 1951; d. George Wallace and Arlene Jean (Winzenburg) C. Student, U. Tex., 1971; BFA in Sculpture, U. Colo., 1975; postgrad., U. Iowa, 1976-77; MFA in Sculpture, U. Okla., 1980. Instr. Arts Annex, Oklahoma City, 1977-78, Firehouse Art Ctr., Norman, Okla., 1979-80, U. Chgo. Lab. Sch., 1984—85, Francis Parker Sch., Chgo., 1986-87, Express-Ways Children's Mus. Art, Chgo., 1987, Wai Sch., Hong Kong, 1987, Field Mus. Natural History, Chgo., 1987-88, Oklahoma City Pub. Schs., 1988-90, Fine Arts Inst. of Edmond, Okla., 1990-91, U. Okla. Mus. Art, 1991, Okla. Sch. Sci. and Math., Oklahoma City, 1992, St. Michael's Presch., Amagansett, L.I., 1994—, Country Sch., Amagansett, 1994—, Guild Hall, East Hampton, N.Y., 1994—. Instr. SPARK Program for Inner City Children, Oklahoma City, 1989; instr., artist-in-residence State Arts Coun., Oklahoma City, 1989-92, City Arts Coun., Oklahoma City, 1977, 89-92, State Arts Coun. Colo., Denver, 1990-95, BOCES Program, Suffolk County, N.Y., 1994-2003; art dir. Hampton Day Sch. Summer Camp, Bridgehampton, N.Y., 1993; set designer Okla. Children's Theater, 1992; instr. adult art edn. City Coll., Chgo., 1982-84; vis. artist Sch. of Art Inst. Chgo., 1980; instr. art fundamentals program U. Okla., 1979-80; NYFA grantee Children's Art Workshop, Libr., Livingston, N.Y., 1999. One-woman shows include Ctrl. Innovative Gallery, Oklahoma City, 1979, Alternative Space, Norman, Okla., 1979, U. Nev. Sheppard Fine Arts Gallery, Reno, 1981, Lenore Gray Gallery, Providence, 1981, Sch. of Art Inst. Chgo. Sculpture Gallery, 1981, ABC No Rio, N.Y.C., 1984, Gas Sta./Performance Space, N.Y.C., 1987, 1997 Gallery with Alvin Gallery, Hong Kong, 1988, Kirkpatrick Ctr., Mus., Oklahoma City, 1989, Helio Gallery, N.Y.C., 1989, Okla. State U. Gardiner Art Gallery, Stillwater, 1990, Oklahoma City Art Mus., 1991, City Arts Ctr., Oklahoma City, 1992, Brickhouse Gallery, Tulsa, 1992, Conscience Point Yacht Club, Southampton, N.Y., 1993, Ashawagh Hall, East Hampton, N.Y., 1994, TSL Warehouse, Hudson, N.Y., 1996, Leslie Urbach Gallery, 1998, Albright Coll., 1999, Upstate Art, Phoenicia, N.Y., 2001, Saratoga Springs Art Ctr., 2004, others; exhibited in group shows at M.A. Doran Gallery, Tulsa, 1991, Individual Artists of Okla. Gallery, Oklahoma City, 1992 (award), U. Ctrl. Okla. Mus. Art, Edmond, 1989-93, Brickhouse Gallery, Tulsa, 1992, Ea. N.Mex. U., Portales, 1992 (award 1992), Spazi Fine Art, Housatonic, Mass., 1992-95, Ashawagh Hall, 1994-95, Gallery North, Setauket, N.Y., 1994 (award), Danette Koke Fine Art/Ramscale Art Assocs., N.Y.C., 1995, Kendall Art & Design, Hudson, N.Y., 1998, Albany (N.Y.) Ctr. Galleries, 1998, N.Y. State Mus., Albany, 1998, Rentschler/Law Gallery, Hudson, N.Y., 1998-1999, Schenectady Mus., 1998, Kendall Art & Design, Hudson, 1999, Upstate Art, 1999, SUNY Albany Art Mus., 2000, Firehouse Gallery, Bainbridge, Ga., 2000, Upstate Art, 2000, Carrie Haddad Gallery, Hudson, 2000-2001, Albany Inst. History and Art, 2002, Arts Ctr. Capital Region, Troy, N.Y., 2002, Upstate Art, Phoenicia, NY, 2003, Columbia Country Coun. Arts, Hudson, NY, 2003, BCB ARt, Hudson, N.Y., 2003, others; represented in permanent collections at Oklahoma City Art Mus., U. Okla. Mus. Art, also pvt. collections; represented in catalog Exhibition by Artists of the Mohawk/Hudson Region, 2002. Bd. dirs. Renaissance Arts Found., Oklahoma City, 1977. Grantee Inst. for Art and Urban Resources, N.Y.C., 1980-81, Ill. Arts Coun., Chgo., 1983-84, Artists Space Exhbn., N.Y.C., 1987, Columbia Coll., Chgo., 1988, Okla. Visual Arts Coalition, 1990, Pollack-Krasner Found., Inc., 1991, Eben Demarest Trust, 1995, N.Y. Found. for the Arts, N.Y.C., 1998, 2003.

COULTER, ELIZABETH JACKSON, biostatistician, educator; b. Balt., Nov. 2, 1919; d. Waddie Pennington and Bessie (Gills) Jackson; m. Norman Arthur Coulter Jr., June 23, 1951; 1 child, Robert Jackson. AB, Swarthmore Coll., 1941; A.M., Radcliffe Coll., 1946, PhD, 1948. Asst. dir. health study Bur. Labor Stats., San Juan, P.R., 1946; research asst. Milbank Meml. Fund, N.Y.C., 1948-51; economist Office Def. Prodn., 1951-52; research analyst Children's Bur.-HEW, 1952-53; from statistician to chief statistician Ohio Dept. Health, 1954-65; lectr. econs., then clin. asst. prof. preventive medicine Ohio State U., 1954-65; asst. clin. prof. biostats. U. Pitts. Sch. Pub. Health, 1958-62; assoc. prof. biostats. U. N.C., Chapel Hill, 1965-72, assoc. prof. econs., 1965-78, biostats. prof., 1972-90; adj. assoc. prof., hosp. adminstr. Duke U., 1972-79; assoc. dean undergrad. pub. health studies U. N.C., Chapel Hill, 1979-86, prof. biostats. emerita, 1990—. Contbr. articles to profl. jours. Mem. AAAS, AAUP, APHA (governing coun. 1970-72), Am. Econ. Assn., Am. Statis. Assn., Am. Acad. Polit. and Social Sci., Biometric Soc., Am. Evaluation Assn., Assn. for Health Svcs. Rsch., Sigma Xi, Delta Omega. Methodist. Home: 1825 N Lakeshore Dr Chapel Hill NC 27514-6734

COULTER, JOHN BREITLING, III, biochemist, educator; b. Stamford, Tex., Nov. 28, 1941; s. John Breitling and Sue Madeline (Morrow) C.; m. Brenda Kay Norman, May 27, 1966; children: Grace Kathleen, John Paul, Peter Stephen. BS, U. Tex., Arlington, 1966; PhD, Baylor U., 1970. Dir. rsch. and diagnostic labs. Scott and White Meml. Hosp. and Clinic, Temple, Tex., 1971—; assoc. prof. pathology and biochemistry Coll. Medicine Tex. A&M U., Temple, 1978—. Adj. asst. prof. chemistry Baylor U., Waco, Tex., 1975-81; cons. chemist Lab. Svc., VA Ctr., Temple, 1973-90. Founder, pres. Christian Info. Coun., Inc., 1981—. With U.S. Army, 1960-63. HEW rsch. grantee, 1971-81; NDEA Title IV fellow Baylor U., 1970. Mem. AAAS, Am. Chem. Soc., Assn. for Rsch. in Vision and Ophthalmology, Am. Assn. Clin. Chemists, Sigma Xi (pres. Temple chpt. 1975). Baptist. Office: Scott & White Hosp and Clinic 2401 S 31st St Temple TX 76508-0001

COULTER, MYRON LEE, retired academic administrator; b. Albany, Ind., Mar. 21, 1929; s. Mark Earl and Thelma Violet (Marks) C.; m. Barbara Bolinger, July 21, 1951; children: Nan and Benjamin (twins). BS, Ind. State Tchrs. Coll., 1951; MS, Ind. U., 1956, EdD, 1959; HLD (hon.), Coll. Idaho, 1982. Tchr. English Reading (Mich.) Pub. Schs., 1951-52; tchr. elem. grades Bloomington (Ind.) Pub. Schs., 1954-56; instr. edn. Ind. U., Bloomington, 1958-59; asst. prof. Pa. State U., 1959-64, asso. prof., 1964-66; vis. prof. U. Alaska, Fairbanks, 1965; asso. dean edn., prof. edn. Western Mich. U., Kalamazoo, 1966-68, v.p. for adminstrn., prof. edn., 1968-76, interim pres., 1974; pres. Idaho State U., Pocatello, 1976-84; chancellor Western Carolina U., Cullowhee, N.C., 1984-94, chancellor emeritus, 1994—. Del. Israeli Univs., 1976, Am. Assn. State Colls. and Univs. to People's Republic of China, 1981, Swaziland Coll. Tech., 1985, People's Republic China, 1985, 87, 88, 90, Jamaica, 1986, 89, 91, 94, Thailand, 1987, 90, The Netherlands, 1991; mem. U.S. Panama Canal Treaty Com., 1977-79 Author school textbooks. Bd. dirs. Kalamazoo C. of C., 1975-76, Pocatello Jr. Achievement; bd. dirs., chair N.C. Arboretum, 1994—; bd. dirs. WNC Pub. Radio, WNC Devel. Assn., WNC Tomorrow, Joint PVO/Univ. Rural Devel. Ctr., WNC Commn. Found., Friends of Great Smoky Mountain Nat. Park, 1994—, Inter-Regional Ctr., 2001—; lay leader Kalamazoo Meth. Ch., 1971-74; mem. Gov.'s Task Force on Aquaculture, 1988, N.C. Bd. Sci. and Tech., 1993—, Commn. for Competitive N.C., 1993—; chair N.C. Indian Gaming Cert. Commn., 1994—; trustee Bronson Hosp., Kalamazoo, 1975-76, N.C. Ctr. Advancement Tchg., C.J. Harris Cmty. Hosp.; chmn. Cherokee Preservation Found., 2001—. With U.S. Army, 1952-54. Named Disting. Alumnus, Ind. State U., 1975, Ind. U., 1994; recipient award Western Mich. U. Alumni Assn., 1974, resolution of tribute Mich. State Legislature, 1976, N.C. Order of the Long Leaf Pine, 1994. Mem. Internat. Reading Assn., Am. Assn. State Colls. and Univs. (bd. dirs. 1981-84, exec. com. 1981-84, sec.-treas. 1984-87, found. bd. dirs. 1987—, chmn. 1988-89), Nat. Soc. Study of Edn., N.C. Assn. Colls. and Univs. (bd. dirs.), Western Coll. Assn., Pocatello C. of C. (bd. dirs. 1977-80), Asheville C. of C. (bd. dirs. 1985-86), Cherokee Hist. Assn., Ind. U. Coll. Edn. Alumni Assn. (Disting. Alumnus award 1994), Phi Delta Kappa, Omicron Delta Kappa, Phi Kappa Phi, Beta Gamma Sigma. Office: Western Carolina Univ Office Chancellor Emeritus 61 Hunter Cullowhee NC 28723 E-mail: mcoulter@wcu.edu.

COULTER, SHERRY PARKS, secondary education educator; b. Milw., May 11, 1950; d. Elizabeth (Humphrey) Parks; divorced; children: Thomas Lloyd, William Lloyd. BS in Edn., Framingham State Coll., 1972—; postgrad., Firchburg State Coll., 1994—. Head family & consumer scis. Gardner H.S., Gardner, Mass., 1972—. Mem. adv. bd. Gardner H.S., 1990-95, mem. peer edn. adv. bd., 1991—; cons. Pampered Chef. Pres. G.G. Jaycees, Gardner, 1979-80; incorporater Cath. of the Pines, Ringe, N.H., 1983-88; hosp. aid Heywood Hosp., Gardner, 1995; mem. Teen Pregnancy Task Force, 1993—; chair Friendly Rememberabces Com., 1980. Named Tchr. of Yr. Family Circle, 1980, Mass. Tchr. of Yr. Mem. Mass. Home Econs. Assn. (v.p. 1992-94), Gardner Edn. Assn. (bldg. rep. 1993-95, 96—), Worcester County Family and Consumer Scis. (pres. 1994-96, v.p. Worcester County 1996-99), Mass. Family & Consumer Sci. (v.p. 1992-94, Spirit of Advising award 1999), Domestic Violence Roundtable. Avocations: skiing, camping, fishing, travel. Home: PO Box 465 51 Baldwinville Rd Templeton MA 01468-1442 Office: Gardner High Sch 200 Catherine St Gardner MA 01440-2098

COUNIHAN, DARLYN JOYCE, mathematics educator; b. Cumberland, Md., May 1, 1948; d. Joseph Paul and Clara Kathryn (Miller) C.; m. Mark W. Chambré, Jan. 20, 1979. AB, Hood Coll., 1970, MA, 1982; postgrad., U. Md., 1971-73. Tchr. math. Cabin John Jr. High Sch., Montgomery County, Md., 1970-75, coach girls volleyball team, 1975; math. resource tchr. Takoma Park (Md.) Jr. High Sch., 1975-77, Ridgeview Jr. High Sch., Gaithersburg, Md., 1977-81; math. tchr. Kennedy High Sch., Silver Spring, Md., 1982-84; magnet math. tchr. Takoma Park Mid. Sch., 1984—, also math. team coach. Mem. area 3 adv. coun. Montgomery County Pub. Schs., 1972-73; coach boys basketball team Montgomery County Recreation Assn., 1971; mem. Mathcounts Adv. Group, Md. Mathalon Com. Co-author geometry textbook. Recipient various acad. athletic award in high sch., coll., Presdl. award for Excellence in Sci. and Math. Teaching, 1990, Women in Edn. award, 1986, David W. Taylor award Sigma Xi, 1993, Albert Shanker award, 1993; NSF grantee, 1971-72, 90, 92. Mem. Am. Fedn. Tchrs., Montgomery County Math. Tchrs. Assn., Nat. Coun. Tchrs. Math., Math. Assn. Am. (Edyth May Sliffe award 1996), Mil. Order of the Cooties Aux., Capts. Cove Golf and Yacht Club, Lake Holiday County Club, VFW Aux., Phi Kappa Phi. Home: 13900 Zeigler Way Silver Spring MD 20904-1160 Office: Takoma Park Mid Sch 6300 Tilden Ln Rockville MD 20852-3741

COUNSELMAN, ANNE, librarian; b. Silas, Ala., Oct. 5, 1940; d. Chester Arthur and Elva (Daniels) Martin; m. Terry J. Counselman; children: Daphne, Bruce, Phillip. BS, U. Montevallo, Ala., 1961; MA, U. Ala., Birmingham, 1979; EdS, U. Ala., Tuscaloosa, 1988. Tchr. Clarke County Bd. Edn., Grove Hill, Ala., 1966-69; libr. asst. Birmingham Pub. Libr., 1971-72, head bookmobile, 1972-73; project dir. Appalachian Adult Edn. Ctr., Birmingham, 1974-75; libr. Birmingham City Bd. Edn., 1975-76, Wallace State C.C., Selma, Ala., 1980-83, Marengo County Bd. Edn., Linden, Ala., 1984—. Reader rsch. and rev. team Libr. Rsch. and Demonstration Div. Libr. Programs, Washington, 1974. Mem. Thomaston (Ala.) Planning and Zoning Bd., 1992, 93; active Thomaston Bapt. Ch. Linly Heflin scholar, 1958-61, scholar Columbus Sch. Speech Correction, 1960, Pacers scholar Program for Rural Svcs. and Rsch., 1987; fellow Coun. for Basic Edn., 1992. Mem. NEA, Am. Edn. Assn., Ala. Edn. Assn., Thomaston Study Club. Home: 122 Lake Cir Thomaston AL 36783-3030 Office: AL Johnson High Sch 500 Lake Cir Thomaston AL 36783

COUNTRYMAN, L. LYNN FLIEGER, fine arts educator; b. Loveland, Colo., Mar. 16, 1954; d. Gordon Wentworth and Barbara Lee (Fuller) Flieger; m. Stanley Ray Countryman, April 31, 1981. AA, Arapahoe Community Coll., 1974; BFA with distinction, U. Colo., 1976; cert., Omaha Art Sch., 1977; MA in Art Edn., U. Colo., 1984; studied with Dr. I.K. Arenberg, Colo., 1981-84. Apprentice Paul Kontny, Colo., 1976-87; tchr. Littleton Pub. High Sch., Colo., 1978-82; prof. comml. art Arapahoe Community Coll., Littleton, Colo., 1983—; artist in residence Colo., 1985-87; tchr. comml. art vocat. program Cherry Creek Sr. High Sch., Denver, 1987-88; gifted art cons. Aurora Pub. Schs., Cherry Creek Pub. Schs., Denver, 1988-89; dir. admissions Colo. Training Inst., 1989; art tchr. grade 6-8 Cherry Creek Pub. Schs., Denver, 1990—. Contbr. to JAMA Mag.; Artist: exhibited at Baehler Gallery, Evans-Lewis Galleries, The Emily Ingram Gallery, Valhalla Gallery, 1978—, Bristot Gallery, Jun Gallery, Phila., Blue Heron Gallery, Chgo., Boca Raton, San Antonio, Dallas, numerous other exhibitions across the U.S.; medical illustrator for Dr. I.K. Arenberg documenting surgical procedures with her drawings. Cons. Arts Advocacy Colo. Dept. of Edn., Denver, 1992—, Students at Risk

Gifted and Talented, Englewood, Colo., 1992—. Grantee Colo. Art Edn. Assn., 1989. Mem. Colo. Art Edn. Assn. (middle sch. rep. 1993), Nat. Art Edn. Assn., Nat. Edn. Assn., Studies in Rsch. Art Edn., Womens Bus. Owners Assn., Phi Beta Kappa. Roman Catholic. Home: 7996 E Phillips Cir Englewood CO 80112-3231 Office: Prairie Middle Sch 12600 E Jewell Ave Aurora CO 80012-5325

COURANT, PAUL NOAH, economist, educator, academic administrator; b. Ithaca, N.Y., Jan. 5, 1948; s. Ernest David and Sara (Paul) Courant; m. Katherine Olive Johnson, Sept. 21, 1969 (dissolved 1984); children: Ernest Mendel, Noah Albert; m. Marta Anne Manildi, Jan. 30, 1988; 1 child, Samuel Robinson Manildi. BA, Swarthmore Coll., 1968; MA, Princeton U., 1972, PhD, 1973. Jr. economist Coun. Econ. Advisers, Washington, 1969—70, sr. economist, 1979—80; asst. prof. econs., pub. policy U. Mich., Ann Arbor, 1973—78, assoc. prof., 1978—84, prof. econs. and pub. policy, 1984—, dir. Inst. Pub. Policy Studies, 1983—87, 1989—90, chmn. econs. dept., 1995—97, assoc. provost, 1997—2001, provost, exec. v.p. acad. affairs, 2002—. Mem. task force long-term econ. growth State of Mich., 1983—84; cons. Mich. Dept. Commerce, Lansing, 1984—85, Congl. Budget Office, Washington, 1988—89; bd. dirs. Mich. Future. Author: (book) America's Great Consumption Binge, 1986; co-author: Economics, 12th edit., 1999; contbr. articles to profl. jours. Bd. dirs. Ctr. Watershed and Cmty. Health, Eugene, Oreg., 1997—. Grantee, NSF, 1976—77, 1979—81, 1994—97, Rockefeller Found., 1985—87, Nat. Cancer Inst., 1992—95. Mem.: Nat. Tax Assn., Assn. Pub. Policy Analysis and Mgmt. (mem. policy coun. 1994—98), Am. Econ. Assn. Avocations: sailing, skiing, tennis, hiking, clarinet. Office: Univ Mich 3074 Fleming Bldg Ann Arbor MI 48109-1340 E-mail: pncourant@netscape.net.

COUREY, MICHAEL HERBERT, health physicist; b. Roanoke, Va., Dec. 8, 1947; s. Herbert Peter and Catherine Pauline (Simon) C.; m. Betty Deal, Mar. 8, 1969; children: Marc Bennett, Emily Leighann. AA, AS, Hillsborough Community Coll., Tampa, Fla., 1973; BA, U. South Fla., Tampa, Fla., 1976; MA, U. South Fla., 1983. Cert. in nuc. medicine. Fla.; lic. lab. supr., Radioassy, Fla.; cert. radiologic tech., Fla.; lic. profl. nuc. medicine cons; lic. med. nuc. physicist, Fla. Radiol. tech. Roanoke Meml. Hosp., Va., 1967; nuclear medicine technologist VA Hosp., Tampa, 1973-80, chief technologist nuclear medicine, 1978-91, mgr. nuclear medicine, 1989-91, radiation safety officer, health physics, 1991—; clin. instr. nuc. medicine Hillsborough Cmty. Coll., 1976-91. Pres. MBR. & Assoc., Inc., Tampa, 1986-2001. Contbr. articles to profl. jour. Legis. chmn. Fla. Nucl. Med. Tech., 1987-89; bd. advisors nucl. medicine Hillsborough C.C., 1974-1996; mem. Gov. Adv. Coun. on Radiation, Fla., 1986-90; pres. Fla. Clin. Ligand Assay Soc., 1993-94; chmn. Clin. Ligand Assay Cert. Bd.; pres. Armistead Manor Civic Assn., 1998-2003; guardian ad litem 13th Jud. Cir. Ct. Fla., 1998—. With USAF, 1967-71. Mem. Am. Registry Radiologic Tech., Fla. Clin. Ligand Assay Soc. (pres. 1988-91), Soc. Nuc. Medicine, Fla. Nuc. Medicine Tech. (pres. 1985-86). Democrat. Roman Catholic. Avocations: chess, woodworking, tennis, cycling, hiking. Home: 16135 Armistead Ln Odessa FL 33556-3304 Office: VA Hosp Chief of Staff Office 13000 Bruce B Downs Blvd Tampa FL 33612-4745

COURNIOTES, HARRY JAMES, academic administrator; b. Chicopee Falls, Mass., Aug. 13, 1921; s. James Harry and Chrisanthe (Gardekas) C.; m. Annette R. Giguere, Sept. 4, 1945; children: James H., Gregory H. BS, Boston U., 1942; Indsl. Adminstr. with high distinction, Harvard U., 1943, MBA with high distinction, 1947; DCS, Western New Eng. Coll., 1976. CPA, Mass. Asst. prof. Am. Internat. Coll., Springfield, Mass., 1946-52, assoc. prof., 1952-58, prof., 1958—, dean Sch. Bus. Adminstrn., 1960-69, v.p., 1964-69, pres., 1969—. Trustee, mem. investment com. Springfield Inst. Savs., 1974-95, vice chmn. bd.,mem. exec. com., 1993-95; trustee Springfield Neighborhood Housing Svc., 1988-92; corporator Springfield Libr. and Mus. Assn., 1997—, former corporator, Springfield Boys Club, 1972-76. Mem. adv. bd. World Affairs Coun., 1970; corporator Springfield Girls Club, 1970—, Wing Meml. Hosp., 1976—; trustee Econ. Edn. Coun. Mass., 1971—; com. mem. United Negro Coll. Fund, 1971; mem. exec. com. Springfield Adult Edn. Coun., 1972-74; mem. exec. com., bd. dirs. Jr. Achievement Western Mass., 1975-76; bd. dirs. Springfield Ctrl. Bus. Dist., 1976-79; mem. bd. adv., N.E. Congl. Inst., 1980; trustee Econ. sponsor Laughing Brook project Mass. Audubon Soc. Lt. AUS, 1943-46. Named Acct. of Yr., Nat. Assn. Cost Accts., 1970; recipient Nat. Human Rels. award NCCJ, 1984, Henry A. Butova Meml. award Western Mass. chpt. Football Found. and Hall of Fame, 1989, Tree of Life award Jewish Nat. Fund, 1993, Disting. Citizen award Pioneer Valley Boy Scouts Am., 1998. Mem. AICPA, Mass. Soc. CPAs (Outstanding Educator for 1991), Fin. Exec. Inst. (chmn. edn. com. 1964-65), Assn. Ind. Colls. and Univs. Mass. (mem. exec. com. 1972-74, 81-84), Greater Springfield C. of C. (dir. 1974-77), Colony Club (Springfield), Harvard Club (Boston), Longmeadow Country Club (Mass.). Home: Cote Rd Monson MA 01057 Office: 1000 State St Springfield MA 01109-3151

COURTNEY, CAROLYN ANN, school librarian; b. Plainview, Tex., Aug. 1, 1937; d. John Blanton and Geneva Louise (Stovall) Ross; m. Moyland Henry Courtney, Aug. 17, 1957; 1 child, Constance Elaine. BA summa cum laude, Wayland Bapt. Coll., 1969; MEd, W. Tex. State Coll., 1976; MLS, U. North Tex., 1990. Cert. elem., secondary, libr. tchr. 5th grade tchr. Hale Ctr. (Tex.) Ind. Sch. Dist., 1970-77, libr., 1977—. Bd. dirs. Plainview Cmty. Concerts, 2000—. Mem. LWV (bd. dirs. 1970-75), DAR (Good Citizen chair 1981-85), Tex. State Tchs. Assn. (life), Tex. Classroom Tchrs. Assn. (sec. 1983-85), Tex. Libr. Assn., Delta Kappa Gamma (rsch. chair 1975-77, pubs. chair 1984-86, pres. 2002–, scholarship 1975). Methodist. Avocations: genealogy, travel. Home: 209 S Floydada St Plainview TX 79072-6665 Office: Hale Center Ind Sch Dist PO Box 1210 Hale Center TX 79041 E-mail: ccourtlibr@hotmail.com.

COURTNEY, DIANE TROSSELLO, library consultant; b. N.Y.C., June 29, 1951; d. Frank and Louise Trossello; m. Patrick K. Courtney, Sept. 2, 1972; 1 child, Heather. BA, NYU, 1972; MLS, Rutgers U., 1973; MPA, CUNY, 1995. Cert. profl. librarian, N.Y. Outreach librarian Yonkers (N.Y.) Pub. Library, 1972-75, youth svcs. librarian, 1975-77, reference librarian, 1977-82, head librarian info. svcs., 1983-87; adult/young adult/media cons. Westchester Libr Sys., 1987—95; dir. Larchmont (N.Y.) Pub. Libr., 1995—. Author (jour.) Bookmark, 1988, Nat. Video Resource Report #12, 1993. Founder, chair N.Y. State Pub. Libr. Systems Video Consortium, 1989-96. Mem. ALA, N.Y. Libr. Assn. (chmn. ref. and adult svcs. sect. consumer health com. 1988-91, dir. membership 1993—, v.p. 1995, pres. 2002-03), Westchester Libr. Assn. (pres. 1991, v.p. 1990), Pi Alpha Alpha. Office: Larchmont Pub Libr 121 Larchmont Ave Larchmont NY 10538-3793 E-mail: courtney@wlsmail.org.

COURVILLE, SUSAN KAY, secondary education educator; b. Port Arthur, Tex., Apr. 27, 1948; d. Robert Owen and Hazel Fae (McCardell) Barnard; children: Kenneth C., Amy Caroline. BS, Tex. Technol. U., 1969; postgrad., U. Houston, 1990. Vocat. Edn. for the Handicapped cert., Tex. Educator Stephen F. Austin H.S., Port Arthur, 1969-70, Sheldon Ind. Sch. Dist., Houston, 1980-84, exec. H. & W. Petroleum, 1985-90; educator C.E. King-Sheldon Ind. Sch. Dist., 1990—. Mem. adv. bd. Vocat. Edn. for the Handicapped, Sheldon Ind. Sch. Dist., Houston, 1991-96. Mem. United Meth. Women, 1st Meth. Ch., Houston, 1971—; mem. Woodforest Women's Club, Houston, 1972-80, sec., 1976; pilot mem. Pilot Internat., Houston, 1989-91. Mem. Alpha Delta Kappa. Avocations: photography, needle arts, travel, reading. Office: Channelview Ind Sch Dist 1100 Sheldon Rd Channelview TX 77530-3518

COUSINS, ROBERT JOHN, nutritional biochemist, educator; b. N.Y.C., Apr. 5, 1941; s. Charles Robert and Doris Elizabeth (Sifferlen) C.; m. Elizabeth Anne Ward, Jan. 25, 1969; children: Sarah, Jonathan, Allison. BA, U. Vt., 1963; PhD, U. Conn., 1968. NIH postdoctoral fellow biochemistry U. Wis., 1968-70; asst. prof. nutrition Rutgers U., 1971-74, assoc. prof., 1974-77, prof. nutritional biochemistry, 1977-79, prof. II (disting. Prof.), 1979-82, dir. grad. program in nutrition, 1976-82, mem. grad. programs in biochemistry, nutrition and toxicology; Boston family prof. human nutrition and biochemistry U. Fla., Gainesville, 1982—, eminent scholar chair, 1982—; dir. Nutritional Sci. Ctr., U. Fla., 1987—, grad. coun., 1990-93. Mem. nutrition study sect. NIH, 1980-84; mem. USDA Expt. Sta., dir. subcom. on human nutrition, 1987-2001; J.L. Pratt vis. prof. Va. Poly. Inst. and State U., 1980; Wellcome vis. prof. Auburn U., 1986; C. Malcolm Trout vis. scholar Mich. State U., 2003; mem. NAS, Inst. of Med. Commn. on opportunites in nutrition and food scis., 1991-93, Food & Nutrition Bd., 1997-2002, Dietary Reference Intakes Sci. Evaluation Commn., 1999—2001, Ad Hoc Bionutrition Commn., NIH, 1993; lectr. in field.. Assoc. editor Jour. Nutrition, 1990-96; mem. editl. com. Ann. Revs. Nutrition, 1985-90, 96-99, assoc. editor, 1999—; contbg. editor Nutrition Revs., 1980-88; mem. editl. bd. FASEB Jour., 1994-99, Biol. Trace Element Rsch.. 1982-2003; contbr. articles in nutritional biochemistry to profl. jours., chpts. to books. Recipient Mead Johnson award in nutrition, 1979, Osborne and Mendel award for basic rsch. in nutrition, 1989, U. Conn. Disting. Alumnus award, 1991, Merit award NIH, 1992, USDA Sec.'s Honor award, 2000, Am. Coll. Nutrition Rsch. award, 2003, Bristol-Myers Squibb/Mead Johnson award for disting. achievement in nutrition rsch., 2003; Future Leader grantee Nutrition Found., Inc., 1973, NIH grantee, 1972—, Am. Coll. Nutrition Rsch. award, 2003. Mem. AAAS, NAS (elected mem. 2000), Am. Soc. Biochem. and Molecular Biology, Am. Soc. Nutrition Sci. (chmn. nominating com. elected officers 1983, coun. 1986-89, pres.-elect 1995-96, pres. 1996-97), Biochem. Soc. U.K., Soc. Exptl. Biology and Medicine (edit. bd. Proc. 1980-86), Am. Chem. Soc., Soc. Toxicology, Fedn. Am. Socs. Exptl. Biology (vice chmn. summer conf. 1985, chmn. summer conf. 1989, bd. dirs. 1989—, v.p. 1990-92, pres., chmn. bd. 1991-92, chmn. subcom. consensus conf. biomed. funding 1991-94, chmn. pub. affairs exec. com. 1992-93), Sigma Xi, Phi Kappa Phi, Gamma Sigma Delta (U. Conn. Disting. Alumni). Home: 4510 NW 20th Pl Gainesville FL 32605-3441 Office: U Fla Ctr for Nutritional Sciences 201 Food Sci & Human Nutr Bldg Gainesville FL 32611 E-mail: cousins@ufl.edu.

COUTURIER, GORDON WAYNE, computer information systems educator, consultant; b. Sparta, Mich., Sept. 14, 1942; s. Clifford Charles and Edith (Reyburn) C.; m. Sylvia Jean Hatch, Mar. 21, 1964; children: Andrew Scott, Laura Couturier Shepard. BSEE, Mich. State U., 1964, MSEE, 1965; PhD, Northwestern U., 1971. Tech. staff Bell Telephone Labs., Naperville, Ill., 1965—72; engr. project leader ITT, Des Plaines, Ill., 1972-80; dir. engr. GTE Subscriber Equipment Group, St. Petersburg, Fla., 1980-82, Paradyne, Largo, Fla., 1982-87; cons. C & C Cons., Tarpon Springs, Fla., 1987—; prof. U. Tampa, 1988—2000. Engr. adv. coun., guest U. Fla. engr. dept., 1985-2001; v.p. prof. devel. ASTD, Clearwater, 1987-90. Contbr. articles to profl. jours.; inventor. Councilman City of St. Charles, Ill., 1971-75; fin. chair Heritage Meth. Ch., Clearwater, Fla., 1982-88; mem., tng. and pub. staff officer USCG Aux., Palm Harbor, Fla., 1993-97. Recipient Men of Achievement award, 1989. Mem.: AIS, Decision Sci. Inst., Lake Tarpon Sail and Tennis Club (sec. 1999—2002, pres. 2003—, treas. 2002—). Avocations: travel, coin collection, philately, tennis. Home: 90 S Highland Ave Apt 2 Tarpon Springs FL 34689-5368 Office: U Tampa UT Box 131F 401 W Kennedy Blvd Tampa FL 33606-1490 E-mail: gcouturier@ut.edu.

COUZENS, JULIA, artist, educator; b. Auburn, Calif., July 9, 1949; d. John Richard and Jean (Little) C.; m. Jay-Allen Eisen, Mar. 22, 1975. BA, Calif. State U., Chico, 1970; MA, Calif. State U., Sacramento, 1987; MFA, U. Calif., Davis, 1990. Vis. lectr. Scripps Coll., Claremont, Calif., 1990-91, U. Calif., Davis, 1993, 95, 98, U. Calif., Santa Cruz, 1995; guest artist Coll. Creative Studies, U. Calif., Santa Barbara, 1995, Claremont Grad. Sch., 1995; vis. artist San Francisco Art Inst., 1997-98; guest curator Armory Ctr. for Arts, Pasadena, 1995-96; artist-in-residence U. Nev., Las Vegas, 1997. One-person shows include Christopher Grimes Gallery, Santa Monica, Calif., 1991, 93, 95, 96, 97, Calif. State U., Sacramento, 1997, Donna Beam Fine Art Gallery, U. Nev., Las Vegas, 1993; exhibited in group shows Am. Cultural Ctr., Brussels, 1992, Crocker Art Mus., Sacramento, 1995, 97, L.A. Mcpl. Gallery, 1995, San Francisco Art Inst., 1995, P.P.O.W., N.Y.C., 1995, Ten in One Gallery, Chgo., 1996, Weatherspoon Art Gallery, U. N.C., Greensboro, 1996, Armand Hammer Mus., L.A., 1997, Nev. Inst. Contemporary Art, Las Vegas, 1997, Palace of the Legion of Honor, San Francisco, 1997, Orange County Mus. of Art, Newport Beach, Calif., 1997; represented in pub. collections M.H. de Young Mus., San Francisco, Oakland Mus. Calif., Univ. Art Mus., Berkeley, Yale U., New Haven. Art-in-pub. places project grantee Sacramento Met. Arts Commn., 1986, artist-in-residence grantee Roswell Mus. and Art Ctr., 1994-95, grantee Louis Comfort Tiffany Found., 1995; grad. rsch. fellow U. Calif., Davis, 1989, fellow Art Matters, Inc., 1995. Mem. Coll. Art Assn. Home: PO Box 450 Clarksburg CA 95612-0450

COVELL, RUTH MARIE, medical educator, medical school administrator; b. San Francisco, Aug. 12, 1936; d. John Joseph and Mary Carolyn (Coles) Collins; m. James Wachob Covell, 1963 (div. 1972); 1 child, Stephen; m. Harold Joachim Simon, Jan. 4, 1973; 1 child, David. Student, U. Vienna, Austria, 1955-56; BA, Stanford U., 1958; MD, U. Chgo., 1962. Clin. prof. and assoc. dean sch. medicine U. Calif. San Diego, La Jolla, 1969—; dir. Acad. Geriatric Resource Ctr. Bd. dirs. Calif. Coun. Geriatrics and Gerontology, Beverly Found., Pasadena, Alzheimer's Family Ctr., San Diego, San Diego Epilepsy Soc., Devel. Svcs. Inc., San Ysidro Health Ctr., NIH SBIR Stude Sect. Geriatrics; cons. Agy. Health Care Po licy and Rsch.; chair Calif. Ctr. Access to Care Adv. Bd. Contbr. articles on health planning and quality of med. care to profl. jours. Mem. AMA (sect. on med. schs. governing coun.), Am. Health Svcs. Rsch., Assn. Tchrs. Preventive Medicine, Am. Pub. Health Assn., Assn. Am. Med. Colls. Group on Instl. Planning (chair 1973-74, sec. 1983-84), Phi Beta Kappa, Alpha Omega Alpha. Home: 164 El Camino Del Teatro La Jolla CA 92037-6338 Office: U Calif San Diego Sch Medicine La Jolla CA 92093-0602

COVER, THOMAS M. statistician, electrical engineer, educator; b. San Bernardino, Calif., Aug. 7, 1938; s. William Llewellyn and Carolyn (Merrill) C.; 1 child, William. BS in Physics, MIT, 1960; MS in EE, Stanford U., 1961, PhD in EE, 1964. Asst. prof. elec. engring. Stanford (Calif.) U., 1964-67, assoc. prof., 1967-71, assoc. prof. elec. engring. and statistics, 1972-73, prof., 1973—, lab. dir. info. systems elec. engring., 1989-96, Kwoh-Ting Li Prof. Engring., 1994. Vis. assoc. prof. elec. engring. MIT, Cambridge, 1971-72. Author: Elements of Information Theory, 1991; editor: Open Problems in Communication and Computation, 1987; contbr. over 100 articles to profl. jours. Vinton Hayes fellow Harvard U., 1971-72. Fellow AAAS, IEEE (pres. info. theory soc. 1972, Claude E. Shannon award 1990, Outstanding Paper prize 1972, Jubilee Paper award 1998, Richard W. Hamming medal 1997), Inst. Math. Stats.; mem. Soc. for Indsl. and Applied Math., Nat. Acad. Engring.

COVERT, EUGENE EDZARDS, aerospace engineer, physics educator; b. Rapid City, SD, Feb. 6, 1926; s. Perry and Eda (Edzards) C.; m. Mary Solveig Rutford, Feb. 22, 1946; children: David H., Christine J., Pamela M., Steven P. BS, U. Minn., 1946, MS, 1948; ScD, MIT, 1958. Registered profl. engr., Mass.; chartered engr., U.K. Preliminary design group USNADC, Johnsville, Pa., 1948-52; mem. staff MIT Aerophysics Lab., 1952-63, assoc. dir., 1963-75, assoc. prof. aeronautics and astronautics, 1963-68, prof., 1968—97, T. Wilson prof. aeronautics, 1993-96, head dept. aeronautics and astronaut., 1985-90; T. Wilson prof. of aeronautics emeritus, 1997—. Cons. Bolt, Beranek & Newman, Inc., Boeing Co., CACI, Inc., Govt. Israel, Pratt and Whitney Aircraft divsn. United Tech., Hercules, Inc., MIT Lincoln Lab., Sverdrup Tech., U.S. Army Rsch. Office, Rand Corp.; chief scientist USAF, 1972—73; mem. panel Naval Aeroballistic Adv. Com., 1965—75; mem. NASA Aeronautical Adv. Com., 1985—89, Aeronautics and Space Engrng. Bd., 1986—92, chmn., 1992; mem., chmn. USAF Sci. Adv. Bd., 1975—86, 1990—94; chmn. Power, Energet. and Propulsion panel Adv. Group for Aerospace R&D NATO, 1982—86; aero. policy com. Office Sci. and Tech. Policy, 1976—92; mem. Pres. Commn. for Investigation of Space Shuttle Accident. Mem. Blue Ribbon Com. on the Osprey, 2001. Served with USNR, 1943—47. Recipient Exceptional Civilian Sci. award USAF, 1973, 86, 94, Univ. Educator of Yr. award, Am. Soc. Aerospace Edn., 1980, Tech. Leadership award U. Minn. Alumni Assocs., 1993, Pub. Svc. award NASA, 1991, von Karman medal Adv. Group for Aerospace R & D, 1980, Wright Brothers Lectureship Aeronautics AIAA, 1997. Fellow AAAS, Royal Aero. Soc., fellow AIAA (hon.; bd. dirs., Ground Testing award 1990, W.F. Durand lectureship for pub. svc. 1992, Wright Bros. lectr. 1997); mem. NAE, N.Y. Acad. Scis., Sigma Xi. Office: MIT 77 Massachusetts Ave Rm 9-466 Cambridge MA 02139-4307

COVINGTON, EILEEN QUEEN, secondary education educator; b. Washington, May 25, 1946; d. Louis Edward and Evelyn (Travers) Q.; m. Norman Francis Covington; children: Norman, Marina, Deanna, Trena. BS, D.C. Tchrs. Coll., 1971; postgrad., George Washington U., 1978-81. Tchr., coach Evan Jr. High Sch., D.C. Pub. Schs., Washington, 1971, Woodrow Wilson H.S., Washington, 1971-95, chmn. phys. edn. dept., 1971-75, 77-81, 1984-87, athletic dir., 1988-95, Anacostia Sr. H.S., Washington, 1995—, chmn. dept. health and phys. edn., tchr. health/phys. edn., 1995—, swim coach, 1996, softball coach, 1996—, student activities dir., 1995. Cons. Coaches Assn., Washington, 1973-76; athletic dir. Woodrow Wilson H.S., 1988-95; pres. DCAA Athletic Dir. Assn., 1997—; sports chmn. in field. Named Coach of Yr., Ea. Bd. Ofcls., 1977, Nat. Coaches Assn. 2d Region, 1982, 86, Nat. Fedn. State H.S. Assns., 2000, Winningest Coach Washington Coaches Assn., 1982, Coach of Yr. U.S., 1986, Coach of Yr. Washington Post, 1987, Athletic Dir. of Yr., 1989, Volleyball All-Interhigh Coach, 1989; recipient Billie Jean King award Women Sports and Am. Fedn. Coaches, 1980-81, Disting. Women award D.C. Polit. Women Com., 1996, D.C. Women's Bd. Affiliated Chs., 1996; inducted into Nat. High Sch. Athletic Coaches Assn. Hall of Fame, 2000. Mem. NAFE, Nat. High Sch. Athletic Coaches Assn. (bd. dirs., named to Hall of Fame 2000, regional dir. region II), D.C. Coaches Assn. (3rd v.p., v.p. volleyball 1981-83, softball coach 1990, Athletic Dir. of Yr. 1992, pres. 1993-96, chmn. crew coun. 1994, Regional Softball Coach of the Yr. 1993, Coach of the Yr. in Volleyball and Softball 1993, Softball Coach of Yr. 1994, 95, Coach/Athletic Dir. of Yr. 1988), NIAAA and D.C. Coaches Assn. (named Athletic Dir. of Yr. 1998, mem. dir.), Assn. Health, Phys. Edn. Athletics, D.C. High Sch. Coaches Club, Women's Sports Found., DCIAA (pres. athletic dir. 1997—). Home: 7601 Ingrid Pl Hyattsville MD 20785-4624 Office: Anacostia Sr HS 16 & R Sts SE Washington DC 20020

COVINGTON, LYNN NORRIS, special education educator; b. Whiteville, N.C., Mar. 10, 1957; d. Carlston Rudolph and Patricia Ann (Wilson) Norris; m. H. Marshall Brown, Aug. 4, 1979 (div. Apr. 1990); m. Richard J. Covington, Nov. 20, 1994. BS in Spl. Edn., East Carolina U., 1979; MEd in Elem. Edn., Francis Marion U., Florence, S.C., 1988. Cert. tchr. in educable mental retardation and trainable mental retardation. Ednl. specialist Murdoch Ctr., Butner, N.C., 1980-81; resource tchr. Chatham County Schs., Pittsboro, N.C., 1979-80, tchr. trainable mentally handicapped, 1981-82, Richmond County Schs., Hamlet, N.C., 1982-85, Marlboro County Schs., Bennettsville, S.C., 1985-92, Sch. Dist. 5 of Lexington and Richland Counties, Ballentine, S.C., 1992-95, Hartsville (S.C.) H.S./Darlington County Schs., 1995—. Mem. adv. bd. Parents and Profls. Active for Spl. Svcs./Dist. 5, 1992—; bd. dirs., sec. Cmty. Based Alternatives, Inc., Rockingham, N.C., 1985-91. Area 2 dir. S.C. Spl. Olympics, Bennettsville, 1985-90; pres. Marlboro County Assn. for Retarded Citizens, Bennettsville, 1988-90; advisor Hamlet N.C.) Juniorettes, 1990-91. Recipient Individual Incentive award Marlboro County Schs., 1989; Dist. Tchr. of Yr. award, 1994; Pee Dee Ednl. Found. grantee, 1990. Mem. Coun. for Exceptional Children, S.C. Edn. Assn., Am. Vocat. Assn., S.C. Vocat. Assn., Delta Kappa Gamma. Methodist. Avocations: reading mysteries, needlecrafts, gardening, tap dancing, antiques. Home: 2026 Hebron Dunbar Rd Clio SC 29525-3415 Office: Hartsville High School 701 Lewellyn Dr Hartsville SC 29550-5235

COVINGTON, PATRICIA ANN, university administrator; b. Mt. Vernon, Ill., June 21, 1946; d. Charles J. and Lois Ellen (Combs) C.; m. Burl Vance Beene, Aug. 10, 1968 (div. 1981). BA, U. N.Mex., 1968; MS in Ed., So. Ill. U., 1974, PhD, 1981. Tchg. asst. So. Ill. U., Carbondale, 1971-74, prof. art, asst. dir. Sch. Art, 1974-88, asst. dir. in admissions and records, 1988-95, assoc. dir. in admissions and records, 1995—2003, emerita assoc. dir., 2003—; cons. records/registration & academic affairs, 2003—. Mem. Am. Coun. on Edn., Nat. Com. for Army, Registry Transcript, AARTS SMART (Sailor, Marines Registry Transcript); mem. tech. com. Ill. Atriculation Initiative, Ill. Bd. Higher Edn.; vis. curator Mitchell Mus., Mt. Vernon, 1977-83, judge dept. conservation; mem. panel Ill. Arts Coun., Chgo., 1982; faculty advisor European Bus. Seminar, London, 1983; edn. cons. Ill. Dept. Aging, Springfield, 1978-81, Apple Computer, Cupertino, Calif., 1982-83; mem. adminstrv. profl. coun. Soc. Ill. U., 1989-93; presenter in field. Exhibited papercastings in nat. and internat. shows in Chgo., Fla., Calif., Tenn., N.Y. and others, 1974—; author: Diary of a Workshop, 1979, History of the School of Art at Southern Illinois University at Carbondale, 1981, Guidelines of Transcripts & Records, 2003; co-author: Transcript and Reel Guide, AACRAO Transcript and Record Guide, 2003; reviewer Mayfield Pub., Random House, William C. Brown, Holt, Reinhart & Winston. Bd. dirs. Humanities Couns. John A. Logan Coll., Carterville, Ill., 1982-88; mem. Ill. Higher Edn. Art Assn., chmn. bd. dirs., 1978-88; mem. Post-Doctoral Acad., 1981-95; sec. adminstrv. profl. coun., 1989-90; lifetime mem. Girl Scouts U.S.A., 1988—, del. 1992-93, 97—, bd. dirs., mgmt. com., fin. com., bldg. com., devel. com., nominating com., Shagbark Coun., treas., 2003, chair assessment com., 2003—. Grantee Kresge Found., 1978, Nat. Endowment for the Arts, 1977, 81, Ill. Bd. Higher Edn. HECA grantee, 1994, 95; named Outstanding Young Woman of Yr. for Ill., 1981, Woman of Distinction Girl Scouts U.S.A. Fellow Ill. Ozarks Craft Guild (bd. dirs. 1976-83); mem. Am. Assn. Coll. Registrars and Admissions Officers (task force on transcript guidelines 2001-03), Ill. Assn. Coll. Registrars and Admissions Officers (chair so. dist., exec. com. 1992-93, nominating com. 1993-94), Spinx (hon.), Rhen Soc., Chancellor's Coun., Phi Kappa Phi. Presbyterian. Home: 389 Lake Dr Murphysboro IL 62966-5955 Office: So Ill U Carbondale IL 62901 E-mail: mmouse@siu.edu.

COVINGTON, STEPHANIE STEWART, psychotherapist, writer, educator; b. Whittier, Calif., Nov. 5, 1942; d. William and Bette (Robertson) Stewart; children: Richard, Kim. BA cum laude, U. So. Calif., 1963; MSW, Columbia U., 1970; PhD, Union Inst., 1982. Diplomate Am. Bd. Sexology, Am. Bd. Med. Psychotherapists. Pvt. practice Inst. for Relational Devel., La Jolla, Calif., 1981—; co-dir. Ctr. for Gender and Justice, La Jolla, Calif., 1981—. Instr. U. Calif., San Diego, 1981—, Calif. Sch. Profl. Psychology, San Diego, 1982-88, San Diego State U., 1982-84, Southwestern Sch. Behavioral Health Studies, 1982-84, Profl. Sch. Humanistic Psychology, San Diego, 1983-84, U.S. Internat. U., San Diego, 1983-84, UCLA, 1983-84, U. So. Calif., L.A., 1983-84, U. Utah, Salt Lake City, 1983-84; co-dir. Inst. Relational Devel.; cons. L.A. County Sch. Dist., N.C. Dept. Mental Health, Nat. Ctrs. Substance Abuse Treatment and Prevention, Nat. Inst. Corrections, others; designer women's treatment, cons. Betty Ford Ctr.; presenter and lectr. in field; addiction cons. criminal justice sys. Author: Leaving the Enchanted Forest: The Path from Relationship Addiction to Intimacy, 1988, Awakening Your Sexuality: A Guide for Recovering Women, 2000, A Woman's Way Through the Twelve Steps, 1994, Helping Women Recover: A Program for Treating Addiction (with spl. edit. for criminal justice sys.), 1999, A Womans Way Through the Twelve Steps

Workbook, 2000, Beyond Trauma: A Healing Journey for Women, 2003; contbr. articles to profl. jours. Mem. NASW (diplomate), Am. Assn. Sex Educators, Counselors and Therapists, Am. Pub. Health Assn., Am. Assn. Marriage and Family Therapy, Assn. Women in Psychology, Calif. Women's Commn. on Alcoholism (Achievement award), Am. Soc. Criminology, Western Soc. Criminology, Internat. Coun. on Alcoholism and Addictions (past chair women's com.), Kettil Brun Soc. (Finland), San Diego Soc. Sex Therapy and Edn., Soc. for Study of Addiction (Eng.). Avocations: reading, theater, raising orchids. Office: 7946 Ivanhoe Ave Ste 201B La Jolla CA 92037-4517 E-mail: sscird@aol.com.

COVINGTON, TAMMIE WARREN, elementary education educator; b. Columbia, S.C., Dec. 20, 1960; d. Charles Larry and Betty Joyce (Collum) Warren; m. Terry Lee Covington, Dec. 22, 1979; 1 child, Matthew Lee. BA in Elem. Edn., U. S.C., 1982, M in Elem. Edn., 1989; M in Ednl. Adminstrn., Troy State U., 2001. Tchr. Ridge Spring (S.C.)-Monetta Elem. Sch., 1982-90, W. Wyman King Acad., Batesburg, S.C., 1991-92, North (S.C.) Elem. Sch., 1992-94, Batesburg (S.C.) Leesville Mid. Sch., 1994—. Mem. Lexington Sch. Dist. 3 Tchr. Forum. Mem. S.C. Edn. Assn., S.C. Mid. Sch. Assn., S.C. Coun. Tchrs. Math., Delta Kappa Gamma. Office: Batesburg-Leesville Mid Sch 425 Shealy Rd Leesville SC 29070

COVINGTON, VERONICA PRO, librarian, educator; b. Laredo, Tex., Nov. 14, 1949; d. Gilberto and Herminia (Esquivel) Pro; m. Billy C. Covington, Jan. 3, 1980; children: Christina, Jennifer, Elizabeth. BS in Edn., Tex. A&I U., 1971; MEd, Sam Houston State U., 1986; PhD in Curriculum and Instruction, Tex. A&M U., 1996. English tchr. Martin H.S., Laredo, Tex., 1970-73; English tchr., chair Dunbar H.S., Lubbock, Tex., 1973-75; asst. dir. Upward Bound Tex. Tech. U., Lubbock, 1975-77; English tchr. Matthews Jr. High, Lubbock, 1977-80; English tchr., chair Mance Park Jr. High, Huntsville, Tex., 1980-90; head libr. Huntsville H.S., 1990-95; coord., testing and program evaluation Huntsville Ind. Sch. Dist., 1995-98; libr. Austin Ind. Sch. Dist., 1998—. Cert. translator Tex. Dept. Criminal Justice, Huntsville, 1989—; adj. prof. children's lit. U. Tex., Austin, 2000-. Contbr. articles to profl. jours. Active Huntsville Leadership Inst., 1996-97; ambassador Huntsville-Walker County C. of C., 1997-98; mentor at-risk students Huntsville Ind. Sch. Dist., 1985-97. Elected del. The White House Conf. on Libr. and Info. Svcs., Washington, 1991. Mem. Nat. Assn. for Bilingual Edn., Tex. Assn. for Bilingual Edn., Tex. Assn. of Sch. Adminstrs., Coun. for Exceptional Children, Nat. Assn. for Gifted Children, Tex. State Tchrs. Assn. (pres. 1986-89), Delta Kappa Gamma (bd. dirs. com. chair 1985). Avocations: reading, travel, writing. Office: Austin Ind Sch Dist Baily Mid Sch 4020 Lost Oasis Holw Austin TX 78739-5501

COWAN, DALE HARVEY, internist, lawyer; b. Cleve., Jan. 25, 1938; s. Milton Jerome and Clara (Umans) jC.; m. Deborah Wolowitz, Jan. 28, 1967; children: Rachel, Morris Benjamin, William Ezra. AB, Harvard U., 1959, MD, 1963; JD, Case Western Res. U., 1981. Diplomate Am. Bd. Internal Medicine with subspecialty cert. in hematology and med. oncology. Bar: Ohio 1981. Intern Cleve. Met. Gen. Hosp., 1963-64, resident, 1964-65, 67-70; practice medicine specializing in internal medicine, hematology and oncology; dir. hematology and oncology Marymount Hosp., Cleve., 1982-2001; asst. prof. medicine Case Western Res. U., Cleve., 1970-75, assoc. prof., 1975-84, clin. prof. environ. health scis., 1985—; assoc. Health Sys. Mgmt. Ctr., 1982-90; of counsel Burke, Haber & Berick, 1984-86; pres. med. staff Parma (Ohio) Cmty. Gen. Hosp., 1997-98; med. dir. Cmty. Oncology Group Cleve. Clinic Found., Cleve., 1999—. Spl. cons. President's Commn. on Bioethics, Washington, 1981-82; mem. nat. adv. coun. Nat. Heart Lung and Blood Inst., Bethesda, Md., 1982-85. Author: Preferred Provider Organizations, 1984; co-editor: Human Organ Transplantation, 1987; contbr. articles to profl. jours. Bd. dirs. Bur. Jewish Edn., 1977-87, Northeast Ohio affiliate Am. Heart Assn., 1982-86; pres. Ohio/W.Va. Oncology Soc., 1990-94; trustee No. Ohio Cancer Resource Ctr., 1998-2001, chmn. 1999-2001. Lt. comdr. USPHS, 1965-67. Fellow ACP, Am. Coll. Legal Medicine (bd. govs. 2001—); mem. AMA, Am. Soc. Hematology, Am. Soc. Clin. Oncology, Am. Assn. for Cancer Rsch., Am. Health Lawyers Assn. (bd. dirs. 1988-94), Am. Soc. Law and Medicine, Acad. Medicine Cleve. (pres. 1997-98), Cleve. Med. Libr. Assn. (pres.-elect 2003—), Ohio State Bar Assn., Greater Cleve. Bar Assn. Home: 19600 Shaker Blvd Cleveland OH 44122-1830 Office: 6100 W Creek Rd Ste 15 Cleveland OH 44131-2133 E-mail: cowand@ccf.org.

COWAN, DENNIS LLOYD, educational administrator; b. N.Y.C., Nov. 26, 1951; s. Lloyd K. and Lillian V. (Langon) C.; m. Anne Vitale, June 17, 1979; children: Christina Anne, Sean Dennis, Jane Lillian. BA, St. John's U., Jamaica, N.Y., 1973, MS, 1977, Profl. Diploma, 1981; Doctoral fellow, Hofstra U., 1994—. Cert. in spl. edn., social studies, reading, adminstrn, elem. edn., N.Y. Per diem tchr. Mineola H.S., Garden City Park, N.Y., 1973-74; tchr. social studies and lang. arts St. Mary Star of the Sea Sch., Far Rockaway, N.Y., 1974-77; tchr. spl. edn. N.Y. Med. Coll., Valhalla, N.Y., 1977-80; socialization program dir. West Nassau Counseling Ctr., Elmont, N.Y., 1988—; summer sch. prin., asst. to prin., dir. adult edn., resource rm. tchr. Elmont Sch. Dist., 1980—. Contbr. numerous articles to profl. jours. Bd. dirs., v.p. West Nassau Mental Health Ctr., Franklin Square and Elmont, 1980-87, L.I. Counselling Ctr. Recipient Nat. Citizenship Edn. Tchr. award, 2002—03. Mem. N.Y. State Congress of Parents and Tchrs. (hon.). Avocations: collecting oriental art, writing, world travel. Office: Elmont Sch Dist 16 Gotham Ave Sch 181 Gotham Ave Elmont NY 11003

COWAN, GEORGE SHEPPARD MARSHALL, JR., surgeon, educator, research administrator; b., June 6, 1938; m. Anne Cowan; children: Scot Peter George, Katherine Beatrice, George Sheppard Marshall III. BA, Columbia Coll., 1959; MD equivalent with honors, MB, ChB, U. Aberdeen, Scotland, 1964. Diplomate Am. Bd. Surgery, Cert. Bd. Nutrition Specialists. Intern Aberdeen Royal Infirmary, 1964—65; resident in surgery Thomas Jefferson Med. U. Hosp., Phila., 1965—68, chief resident in surgery, 1968—70; commd. 1st lt. U.S. Army Med. Corps, 1966; advanced through grades to col. U.S. Army, 1982, resigned with honorable discharge, 1982; from assoc. prof. to prof. of surgery U. Tenn., Memphis, mem. staff Wm. F. Bowld Med. Ctr., 1982—2002; mem. staff City of Memphis Hosp., 1982—2002; mem. active staff Bapt. Meml. Hosp., Memphis, 1982—2002; jr. staff Meth. Hosp., Memphis, 1982—2001. Cons. VA Med. Ctr., 1982—83, 2000—02, surg. staff, 1983—2000; secretariat, sci. com. Internat. Bariatric Surgery Symposium, London, 1989, Japan, 90; mem. organizing com. Annual Obesity Surgery Symposium, L.A., 1988—91; chief obesity wellness ctr. and surg. endoscopy tchg. svc. U. Tenn. Sch. Medicine, 1982—2002; mem. U. Tenn. Memphis Planning Com., 1993—96; exec. U. Tenn. Faculty Senate, pres., 1994—95; faculty advisor to pres. U. Tenn., 1993—96; bd. dirs. Am. Coll. Nutrition, pres.-elect, 2002—03, pres., 2003—, chair program com., 2003; founder, chair TennSens, 1994—95; bd. dirs. Cert. Bd. Nutrition Specialists, 2000—; mem. adv. panel Medscape Endrocrinology, 2000—; co-chair Nat. Nutrition Alliance, 2000—. Editor: Intravenous Hyperalimentation, 1972, (chpt.) The Essence of General Surgery, 1975; co-editor: Bariatric Surgical Stapling, 1987, Update: Surgery for the Morbidly Obese Patient, 2000, Surgical Stapling, 1987; co-founder, co-editor-in-chief: Obesity Surgery Jour., 1990—; bd. editors: The am. Surgeon, 1977-87, Jour. Nutritional Support Svcs., 1984-87, assoc. editor, 1987-88; reviewer Jour. Parenteral and Enteral Nutrition, 1987—; contbr. more than 250 articles to profl. jours.; inventor of surg. instruments, developer surg. products. Mem. Pub. Edn. com. Am. Cancer Soc., Mo., 1980-82. Capt. M.C., USNR, 1983-98, ret. Recipient Shepherd Gold medal in surgery, 1964; Surgeon Gen.'s rsch. fellow Cardiovasc. Rsch. Inst., U. Calif., San Francisco, 1971-73. Fellow: Am. Coll. Nutrition (bd. editors Jour. Am. Coll. Nutrition 1995—, chair program com. 2003, pres. 2003—, bd. dirs., chair exec. dir. search com.); mem.: AAUP (Claxton award 1996), N.Am. Fedn. for the Surgery of Obesity (sci. rev. com. 2001—), Memphis Surg. Soc. (sec.-treas. 1992—94, v.p. 1994—95, pres. 1995—96), Internat. Fedn. for the Surgery of Obesity (sec.-treas. 1995—97, pres. 1997—99, chair bd. trustees 1999—, Gold medal 2000), Am. Fedn. Clin. Rsch., Am. Heart Assn. (bd. dirs. 1974—80), Am. Trauma Soc., Memphis-Shelby County Med. Soc. (comms. com., legis. com.), Tenn. Med. Assn. (del., alt. del. 1990—, comms. com. 1999—), S.E. Surg. Congress, Am. Soc. Parenteral and Enteral Nutrition (membership com. 1994—96), Soc. Am. Gastro-Enterologic Surgeons, Am. Soc. Bariatric Surgery (pres. 1990—91, del. to Svcs. and Splty. Soc. of AMA 1991—, sec.-treas. 1993—96, allied health scis. sect. 2000, Golden Circle award), Memphis Econs. Club, Bachelor's Barge Club (Phila.), Sigma Xi. Office: U Tenn 956 Court Ave Ste A310 Memphis TN 38103-2814 E-mail: owcinc@mindspring.com.

COWAN, JAMES HOWARD, JR., fishery scientist, biological oceanographer; b. Fayetteville, N.C., Mar. 9, 1955; s. James Howard and Imelda Lee C.; m. Jean-Louise Watts, Dec. 30, 1989. BS in Biology, Old Dominion U., 1978, MS in Biol. Oceanography, 1981; PhD in Marine Sci., La. State U., 1985, MS in Exptl. Stats., 1988. Field coord. Atlantic Bluefin Tuna Rsch. Program Nat. Marine Fisheries Svc., 1979-81; rsch. asst. dept. marine sci. and coastal ecology lab. La. State U., 1981-82; fellow La. State U. Marine and Coastal Fisheries, Baton Rouge, 1983-85; rsch. assoc. La. State U. Coastal Ecology Inst., Baton Rouge, 1985-88; postdoctoral rsch. assoc. U. Md. Chesapeake Biol. Lab., Solomons, 1988-90, asst. rsch. scientist, 1990-92; rsch. assoc. Oak Ridge (Tenn.) Nat. Lab., 1990-92; sr. marine scientist Dauphin Island (Ala.) Sea Lab., 1992—; assoc. prof. U. South Ala., Mobile, 1992—. U.S. Del. Internat. Coun. for Exploration of Sea, 1991; reef fish stock assessment panel mem. Gulf Mex. Fish Mgmt. Coun., 1992—, chair, 1995—; mackerel stock assessment panel mem., 1992-96; std. sci. stats. com., 1995—; ctrl. sub-sect. mem. Gulf Mex. Regional Marine Rsch. Bd., 1992—; U.S. del. Pacific Marine Sci. Orgn., 1997, Nat. Acad. Sci., Nat. Rsch. coun., 1997-98; mem. acad. rev. bd. admissions dept. marine sci. La. State U., 1984-85, rsch. and edn. program rev. com. Ctr. for Wetland Resources dept. marine sci., 1985-86; acad. coun. Ctr. for Environ. and Estuarine Studies, U. Md. Sys., 1988-91; recruitment com. dept. marine scis. U. South Ala., 1992—, chair policy and procedures com. dept. marine scis., 1992—; mem. student adv. coms. Old Dominion U., Va. Inst. Marine Scis., U. South Ala., U. Ga., U. Calif., Davis; cons. in field. Contbr. numerous articles to profl. jours. Lyle St. Amant scholar Am. Shrimp Canners Assn., 1982-83, Joseph Lipsey Meml. scholar, 1983-84, scholar Rockefeller Wildlife Refuge, 1982-85, 94, Tech. Commun. Am. Soc. Tech. Commun., Miss-Ala. Sea Grant, 1993—; La. Sea grantee, 1987, La. Fisheries Initiative grantee, 1984-85, grantee Nat. Marine Fisheries Svc., 1987-88, Va. Marine Resources Commn., 1990, Electric Power Rsch. Inst.-Oak Ridge Nat. Lab., 1990—, NSF, 1992—, Calif. Dept. Water Resources, 1991—. Mem. Am. Fisheries Soc. (pres. early life history sect. 1996—, outstanding chpt. award com. Tidewater, La. and Ala. chpt. 1995—), Am. Soc. Limnologists and Oceanographers, Estuarine Rsch. Fedn. (editl. bd. Estuaries 1994-98, Gulf of Mex. Sci. 1996—). Democrat. Avocations: fishing, reading, music. Office: U South Ala Dauphin Island Sea Lab PO Box 369-370 Dauphin Island AL 36528

COWAN, MARIE JEANETTE, nurse, pathology and cardiology educator; b. Albuquerque, July 20, 1938; d. Adrian Joseph and Leila Bernice (Finley) Johnson; m. Samuel Joseph Cowan, Aug. 14, 1961; children: Samuel Joseph, Kathryn Anne, Michelle Dionne. Diploma, Mary's Help Coll., 1961; BS, U. Wash., 1964, MS, 1972, PhD, 1979. Charge nurse Herrick Meml. Hosp., Berkeley, Calif., 1961-62; staff nurse ICU Univ. Hosp., Seattle, 1966-68; asst. prof. Seattle U., 1972-75; from asst. prof. to prof. nursing U. Wash., Seattle, 1979-97, assoc. dean rsch., 1985-96; dean UCLA Sch. Nursing, 1997—. Rsch. grant reviewer Am. Heart Assn. Wash., Seattle, 1977-82, divsn. rsch. grants reviewer nursing study sect., 1987-90; chair CVN AHA, 1989-91. Mem. editl. bd. Am. Rev. Nursing Rsch., Rsch. in Nursing and Health, Nursing Rsch.; contbr. articles to profl. jours. NIH grantee, 1977, 81, 84, 85, 91, 96, 2000. Fellow Am. Acad. Nursing; mem. ANA, AACN, Wash. State Nurses Assn., Calif. State Nurses Assn. Roman Catholic. Office: UCLA Sch Nursing PO Box 951702 Los Angeles CA 90095-1702

COWARDIN, DANA SUE, physical education educator, consultant, coach; b. Dover, Ohio, Oct. 26, 1952; d. William John and Mildred Toomey (Little) Obermiller; m. James Henry Cowardin, June 18, 1983; children: Mary Beth, Claire Marie. BS in Edn., Ohio State U., 1975, health cert., 1976, MA in Spl. Edn., 1981, adapted phys. edn. cert., 2000. Cert. health edn., phys. edn., handicapped (K-12). Recreation leader Columbus (Ohio) Pks. and Recreation, 1975-79; substitute tchr. Columbus Pub. Sch., South-Western City Schs., Whitehall Sch., 1975-79; learning disabilities tutor South-Western City Schs., 1979-80, phys. edn. tchr., 1981—. Saturday family workshop cons. Drug-Free Schs. Consortium and Grove City Police Dept., Columbus, 1991—; coord. core team Finland Mid. Sch., Columbus, 1990—, chmn. advisor/advisee program, 1991—, volleyball coach 1984—; mem. com. Phys. Edn. Course of Study, Columbus, 1988-90, Ohio Mid. Sch. State Conf., Columbus, 1992-93; instr. high ropes course Initiatives and Accessible Challenge, Camp Mary Orton, Columbus, 1985-93; cooperating tchr. Ohio State U., Columbus, 1986—. Recipient Cert. of Recognition, Drug-Free Schs. Consortium, 1992, Educator of Yr. award Ohio Mid. Sch., 1997, Career Tchr. award Ohio State U., 1997. Mem. Nat. Mid. Sch. Assn., Am. Alliance Health, Phys. Edn. and Dance, Ohio Mid. Sch. Assn. (bd. dirs., ctrl. region assoc. rep. 1991—), Ohio Assn. Health, Phys. Edn. and Dance, Greater Columbus Tennis Assn., Franklin County Acad. Phys. Educators. Home: 2812 Pickwick Dr Columbus OH 43221-2924 Office: Finland Mid Sch 1825 Finland Ave Columbus OH 43223-3798

COWART, VERONICA, education administrator; b. Millen, Ga., Dec. 5, 1948; d. Neely Kent and Tommie Lee (Covington) K.; m. James Carlton Cowart, June 16, 1973; children: William Todd, Jodi Michele. BS, Ga. Southern U., 1973, MEd, 1981, EdS. Tchr. Emanuel Co. Inst., Twin City, Ga., 1973-77, Buckhead Academy, Millen, Ga., 1977-80, Jenkins County Elem., Millen, 1980-90; ednl. cons. CS/RA Regional Svc. Agy., Dearing, Ga., 1990-95. Dir. instructional svcs. Jenkins County PAGE, 1986, 95—; mem. Ga. Staff Devel. Coun., Atlanta, 1990—. Mem. DAR, Ga. Mothers Assn., Beta Zeta (past pres., pres-elect, sec., rep), Camellia Garden Club (pres. 1988-89). Baptist. Avocations: singing, piano, gardening, decorating. Home: 4291 Hwy 121 Millen GA 30442-9804 Office: Jenkins County Bd 527 E Barney Ave Millen GA 30442 E-mail: veronica@jchs.com.

COWDEN, JOHN WILLIAMS, eye physician, educator; b. Lafayette, Ind., Aug. 1, 1939; s. Thomas Kyle and Clara B (Williams) C.; m. Patricia Rakestraw, Sept. 3, 1960; children: Catherine, William, Thomas, David, Michael, Daniel, Christine. BA, Mich. State U., 1960; MD, U. Mich., 1964. Diplomate Am. Bd. Ophthalmology. Fellow corneal and external ocular disease U. Fla., 1972-73; asst. prof. Wayne State U., Detroit, 1973-79, ophthalmologist, 1973-93, vice chmn. dept. ophthalmology, 1990-93, assoc. prof., 1979—89, prof., 1989—93, Roy E. Mason Disting. prof. ophthalmology, 1993; med. dir. Mich. Eye Bank and Transplantation Ctr., Detroit, 1973-93; dir. residency program Kresge Eye Inst. Wayne U., Detroit, 1974-90, assoc. prof., 1979-89, prof., 1989—; chmn. dept. ophthalmology U. Mo., Columbia, 1993—. Active staff Univ. Hosps. and Clinics, Truman Meml. VA Hosp., Columbia, Mo.; med. dir. Heartland Eyebanks, 1993—. Contbr. articles to profl. jours. Maj. U.S. Army, 1964-72. Fellow ACS, Am. Acad. Ophthalmology; mem. AMA, Am. Coll. Surgeons, Internat. Soc. Refractive Surgery, Assn. for Rsch. in Vision and Ophthalmology, Eye Bank Assn. of Am., Castroviejo Corneal Soc., ACS, Mich. Ophthalmology Soc. (pres.), Detroit Ophthal. Club., Ocular Microbiology Group, Midwest Corneal Assn., Pan-Am. Assn. Ophthalmology, Soc. Mil. Ophthalmologists, Mo. Soc. Eye Physicians and Surgeons (pres.), Mo. State Med. Assn., Boone County Med. Soc. (pres.), Country Club Mo., Orchard Lake Country Club. Republican. Roman Catholic. Avocation: fgn. travel, skiing, tennis. Home: 1316 Westview Ter Columbia MO 65203-5200 Office: U Mo Mason Eye Inst Dept Ophthalmology One Hospital Dr Columbia MO 65212

COWELL, ROBERT SAMUEL, school principal; b. St. Louis, Apr. 1, 1945; s. Samuel A. and Marcella L. (Zimmerman) C.; m. Karen Ann Gerling, July 8, 1967; children: Robert S., Karen Ann, Kimberly, Keri. BA in Elem. Edn., Harris Stowe State Coll., St. Louis, 1973; MA in Elem. Ednl. Adminstrn., U. Mo., St. Louis, 1984. Tchr. Athena Pub. Sch., Desoto, Mo., 1968-69, St. Joseph Sch., Imperial, Mo., 1969-72, St. Thomas Moore Sch., St. Louis, 1972-73, St. Simon Sch., St. Louis, 1973-83; prin. St. Anthony's Sch., High Ridge, Mo., 1983—. Mem., chair self evaluation teams Archdiocese of St. Louis, 1987-93; mem. drug abuse team R-1 Sch. Dist., High Ridge, 1985—; chair region 10 prins. Archdiocese of St. Louis, Jefferson County, 1989. Chair South County Campfire, St. Louis, 1977-78; mem. St. David's Sch. Bd., Arnold, Mo., 1982; Eucharistic min. St. David's Parish, Arnold, 1981—. Recipient award for energy innovation Dept. Natural Resources, Jefferson City, Mo., 1992, award for charity work St. Jude's Hosp., Memphis, 1993, Svc. award Archdiocese of St. Louis, 1994. Mem. Nat. Cath. Edn. Assn., KC. Avocations: travel, camping. Home: 1000 Utility Dr Arnold MO 63010-5504 Office: St Anthony's Sch 3005 High Ridge Blvd High Ridge MO 63049-2216

COWEN, BARRETT STICKNEY, microbiology educator; b. Lebanon, N.H., May 23, 1939; s. Frank Young and Elsie (Stickney) C.; m. Ruth Maria Consuegra, Sept. 3, 1966; children: Marcella Lucia, Matthew Alfredo. BS, U. Vt., 1963; MS, U. N.H., 1968; PhD, Cornell U., 1973. Lab. asst. Hubbard Farms, Inc., Walpole, N.H., 1963-65; grad. asst. U. N.H., Durham, 1965-67; rsch. specialist Cornell U., Ithaca, N.Y., 1967-73, rsch. assoc., 1973-78; lab. dir. Cobb, Inc., Concord, Mass., 1978-82; assoc. prof. vet. sci. Pa. State U., University Park, 1982-97; dir. rsch. Biomune Co., Lenexa, Kans., 1997—2001. Cons. microbiology dept., 1983; cons. Cobb, Inc., 1983, Pilch, Inc., Troutmen, N.C., 1984, Croton Egg Farms, Ohio, 1985; tech. advisor Pa. Egg Producers, Lancaster, 1984, Biomune, Inc., Lenexa, Kans., 1989-96, Super Pollo, Rancaqua, Chile, 1993—, Incubator Anhalzer, Quito, Ecuador, 1994, Grandparents Poultry (PVT) Ltd., Lahore, Pakistan, 1995. Contbr. articles to profl. jours. Served with U.S. Army, 1960. Pa. Dept. Agr. grantee, 1984-97; J. William Fulbright Fgn. scholar, 1994. Mem. Am. Assn. Avian Pathologists, Am. Soc. Microbiology, Conf. Rsch. Workers in Animal Diseases, Am. Assn. Vet. Lab. Diagnosticians, World Vet. Poultry Assn., Masons, St. John's Lodge, Sigma Xi, Phi Kappa Phi. Republican. Methodist. Avocations: hunting and fishing, tennis, skiing, stamp collecting. Home: 621 Benjamin Ct State College PA 16803-2666

COWEN, SCOTT S. academic administrator; m. Marjorie Cowen; 4 children. BS, U. Conn., 1968; MBA, George Washington U., 1972, DBA in Fin., 1975. Asst. prof. mgmt. Bucknell U., 1974—76; faculty Case Western Res. U., Cleve., 1976—98, dean, Albert J. Weatherhead III prof. mgmt., 1984—98; pres. Tulane U., New Orleans, 1998—, Seymour S Goodman Meml. prof. bus. A.B. Freeman Sch. Bus., 1998—, prof. econs. Faculty of Liberal Arts and Scis., 1998—. Eleanor F. and Philip G. Rust vis. prof. Colgate Darden Grad. Sch. Bus. Adminstrn., U. Va., 1982—83; bd. dirs. Newell Rubbermaid, Inc., Am. Greetings Corp., Jo-Ann Stores, Inc., Forest City Ent., Inc.; cons. in field. Co-author: Introduction to Business: Concepts and Applications, 1981, Information Requirements of Corporate Boards of Directors, 1983, Accounting Today: Principles and Applications, Innovation in Professional Education: Steps on a Journey From Teaching to Learning, 1995; contbr. articles to profl. jours. Bd. dirs. New Orleans Bus. Coun., Com. for a Better New Orleans, New Orleans Regional C. of C., United Way Greater New Orleans. With U.S. Army, 1968—71. Co-recipient award of Achievement in Edn., No. Ohio Live Mag., 1991; named Disting. Alumni, George Washington U., 1998—99; named to, Sch. Bus. Adminstrn. Hall of Fame U. Conn.; recipient Torch of Learning, Hebrew U., Torch of Liberty, Anti-Defamation League, Leadership Cleve. award, Greater Cleve. Growth Assn., 1987—88; fellow, Ernst & Whitney, Cleve., 1978, 1979. Mem.: Nat. Assn. Ind. Colls. and Univs. (bd. dirs.), Am. Coun. Edn. (bd. dirs.), Am. Assembly of Collegiate Schs. Bus. Office: Tulane University 218 Gibson 6823 Saint Charles Ave New Orleans LA 70118-5698 Fax: 504-865-5202. E-mail: scowen@tulane.edu.

COX, ALMA TENNEY, retired English language and science educator; b. Sand Run, W.Va., Apr. 6, 1919; d. Albert Law and Viola Columbia (Gooden) Tenney; m. James Carl Cox Jr., Sept. 8, 1945; children: James Carl III, Joseph Merrils II, Alma Lee, Elizabeth Susan, Albert John. BA, W.Va. Wesleyan Coll., 1946; MEd, West Tex. State U., 1975. Elem. sch. tchr. Floyd (Va.) County Schs., 1940-42, Nicholas County Schs., Summersville, W.Va., 1942-43; high sch. English tchr. Harrison County Schs., Lewisburg, W.Va., 1943-45; English tchr. am. Embassy, Baghdad, 1956-58; high sch. English and Sci. tchr. Tulsa Sch. System, 1965-68, Plainview (Tex.) Ind. Sch. System, 1969-86, ret., 1986. Author: Birds in Plainview, 1998. Pres. Plainview Federated Women's Club, 1988-90, Hale County Retired Tchrs., 1990-91, Hale County Hist. Com., 1985-91, United Meth. Women; sec. Disable Am. Vet. Aux., 1990. Named Woman of Yr. Plainview Federated Women's Club, 1991, Hale County Retired Tchrs., 1990-91, Disable Am. Vet. Aux., 1991, Hale County Hist. Com., 1991; recipient Woman of Distinction AAUW, 1997, disting. youth educator award, Coprock Dist. Federated Womens Club & Texas State Federated womens club, 1997, Delta Kappa Gamma Soc. Internat. Pres. Achievement award, 2000. Mem. Delta Kappa Gamma (pres. Gamma Iota chpt. 1990-92, pres. Epsilon Alpha chpt. 1998-2001). Republican. Avocations: oil painting, reading, travel, tatting, crocheting, flower gardening. Home: 5105 Stacey Ave Fort Worth TX 76132-1628

COX, CATHY A, elementary school educator; b. Marquette, Mich., Nov. 4, 1962; d. Leslie C. and Patricia (Miller) Barnett. BS, Auburn U., 1984. Cert. elem. tchr., Ala. Tchr. Morningview Elem. Sch., Montgomery, Ala., 1992—. Active Educationally Disadvantaged Children; presenter in field. Home: 501 N Panama St Montgomery AL 36107-1717

COX, DONALD CLYDE, electrical engineering educator; b. Lincoln, Nebr., Nov. 22, 1937; s. Elvin Clyde and C. Gertrude (Thomas) C.; m. Mary Dale Alexander, Aug. 27, 1961; children: Bruce Dale, Earl Clyde. BS, U. Nebr., 1959, MS, 1960, DSc (hon.), 1983; PhD, Stanford U., 1968. Registered profl. engr., Ohio, Nebr. With Bell Tel. Labs., Holmdel, N.J., 1968-84, head radio and satellite systems rsch. dept., 1983-84; mgr. radio and satellite systems rsch. divsn. Bell Comm. Rsch., Red Bank, NJ, 1984-91, exec. dir. radio rsch. dept., 1991-93; prof. elec. engring. Stanford (Calif.) U., 1993—, Harald Trap Friis Prof. Engring., 1994—, dir. telecomms., 1993-99. Em. commns. U.S. nat. com. Internat. Union of Radio Sci.; participant enbanc hearing on Personal Comm. Sys., FCC, 1991; mem. rsch. visionary bd. Motorola Labs., 2002. Contbr. articles to profl. jours.; patentee in field. 1st lt. USAF, 1960-63. Recipient Guglielmo Marconi prize in Electromagnetic Waves Propagation, Inst. Internat. Comm., 1983, Alumni Achievement award U. Nebr., 2002; Johnson fellow, 1959-60. Fellow IEEE (Morris E. Leeds award 1985, Alexander Graham Bell medal 1993, Millenium medal 2000), AAAS, Bellcore 1991, Radio Club Am.; mem. NAE, Comm. Soc. of IEEE (Leonard G. Abraham Prize Paper award 1992, Comms. Mag. Prize Paper award 1990), Vehicular Tech. Soc. of IEEE (Paper of Yr. award 1983), Antennas and Propagation Soc. of IEEE (elected mem. adminstrn. com. 1986-88), Sigma Xi. Achievements include rsch. in wireless communication systems, cellular radio systems, radio propagation. Home: 924 Mears Ct Stanford CA 94305-1029 Office: Stanford U Dept Elec Engring Packard 361 Stanford CA 94305-9515

COX, GEORGE SHERWOOD, computer science educator; b. McAllen, Tex., Jan. 12, 1963; s. Jerry Alton and Eldora (Chrismier) C. BA in Comm., U. Tex., Pan American, 1985; MA in Religious Edn., Southwestern Bapt.

Theol. Sem., Ft. Worth, 1988. Lic. to ministry So. Bapt. Conv., 1985, ordained, 1990. Assoc. min. edn. South Hills Bapt. Ch., Ft. Worth, 1987-88; min. youth, assoc. pastor Trinity Bapt. Ch., McAllen, 1989-91; account exec. radio Sta. KVTY, McAllen, 1991; mgr. Tex. Valley Computer, Weslaco, 1991-93; instr. computers South Tex. Vocat. Tech. Inst., McAllen, 1993—. Dir. Bapt. Student Union, U. Tex., Brownsville, Bapt. Gen. Conv. Tex., Dallas, 1988-93. Republican. Home: 320 S Peking St Mcallen TX 78501-8926 E-mail: gcox@rgu.rr.com.

COX, GERARD ANTHONY, academic director; b. N.Y.C. s. Anthony Vincent and Margaret Agnes (Horan) C.; m. Margaret Mary Bellino, Dec. 26, 1970; children: Stephen Anthony, Anthony James, Anne Marie. BA, Marist Coll., 1956; MA, CUNY, Hunter Coll., 1960; newspaper fund fellow, Columbia U.; cert., RCA Inst. Lic. tchr., N.Y., Fla. Tchr. Scanlon High Sch., N.Y.C., 1956-62; dept. head English Christopher Columbus High Sch., Miami, Fla., 1962-67; asst. prof. Marist Coll., Poughkeepsie, N.Y., 1967—, assoc. acad. dean, 1969-79, v.p., dean for student affairs, 1979—2001, assoc. prof., theatre dir., 2001—. Pres. N.Y. Archdiocesan Cath. Forensic League, N.Y.C., 1958-62, Miami (Fla.) Archdiocesan Cath. Forensic League, 1963-67, Nat. Cath. Forensic League, 1964-68. Pub. plays: (short plays) For Second Springs, 1989, (full length plays) The Angel's Share, 1991, The Penny Stealers, 1992, Lead Me Home, 1993. Pres. bd. Community Exptl. Repertory Theatre, Poughkeepsie, 1975-85. Recipient 1st Prize one act playwriting City Lights Inc., Poughkeepsie, 1986. Mem. Am. Assn. for Higher Edn., Assn. for Theatre in Higher Edn., Dramatists Guild. Avocations: reading, writing, gardening, theatre going, spectator sportsman. Office: Marist Coll 82 North Rd Poughkeepsie NY 12603-4321

COX, GLENDA JEWELL, retired elementary school educator; b. Caruthersville, Mo., Mar. 6, 1938; d. Gladys Lee and Vera Lee (Malugen) Malone; m. Samuel Joseph Cox, Sept. 3, 1958; children: Cassandra Ann, Leslie Alexandria, Jonathan Paul, Peter Matthew. BS in Elem. Edn., Charleston (S.C.) So. U., 1975; MA, Maryville U., St. Louis, 1990; prin. cert., U. Mo., St. Louis, 1995. Cert. tchr., gifted, elem. edn. K-12, principal Mo., 1995. Tchr, 2nd/3rd grade combination Midland Park Elem., Charleston, 1975-76; tchr. 2nd grade Summerville (S.C.) Sch. Dist. II, 1978; tchr. 2nd grade, 5th grade math. Mascoutah (Ill.) Dist. 19, 1980-82; 6th grade tchr. Francis Howell Sch. Dist., St. Charles, Mo., 1985-91, gifted facilitator, 1991-97, asst. prin. Ctrl. Elem. Sch., 1997-98, prin., 1998-2000; ret. Mem. curriculum com. Francis Howell Sch. Dist., St. Charles, 1989-90, pilot mentor/mentor, 1988-95, dist. site support team, 1993-96; cooperating tchr. Becky-David Elem., St. Charles, 1986-88; site based team chmn./co-chmn., 1992-96, Odyssey of the Mind coord., 1991-96, tech. com., 1993—, cluster tchr. instr., 1993-97, prins. selection com., 1993. English conversation tchr. Bapt. Ch., Fuchu, Japan, 1969-71, vacation Bible sch. dir., 1970-71; PTA parent vol. chmn. Newington Elem., Summerville, 1977-78; chmn. Cystic Fibrosis Found., Summerville, 1977. Mem. NEA, Gifted Assn. Mo. (dist. A 1994-96, co-dir. 1994-96, dist. A registration chmn. 1992-94, state conf. registration chmn. 1995, 96), St. Louis Assn. Gifted Edn. Baptist. Avocations: bridge, bowling, learning. Home: 14344 Rainey Lake Dr Chesterfield MO 63017-2933 E-mail: gmcox6@hotmail.com.

COX, HILLERY LEE, retired primary school educator; b. Akron, Ohio, Nov. 2, 1946; d. Ellwood Lester Jr. and Leonide Juanita (Williams) Cosper; m. William R. Cox Jr., Apr. 2, 1966; 1 child, Geoffrey William. Student, Ohio U., 1964-65; BS in Edn., U. Akron, 1967, MS in Edn., 1980. Cert. tchr., Ohio; cert. reading specialist, Ohio. Tchr. Copley (Ohio) Fairlawn Schs., 1967-69; presch. tchr. Northminster Coop. Nursery Sch., Cuyahoga Falls, Ohio, 1974-75; ednl. math. aide Stow (Ohio) City Schs., 1975-76; grad. tchg. asst. U. Akron, 1976-77; tchr. Cloverleaf Local Schs., Lodi, Ohio, 1977—2002. Adj. prof. workshop presenter Ashland (Ohio) U., 1992-98; cons. The ABC's of Whole Lang., Copley, 1988—; insvc. presenter various sch. sys. in Ohio, 1988-2002. Contbr. articles to profl. jours. Vol. Doggie Brigade, Children's Med. Ctr. of Akron, 1992-98; driver substitute Mobile Meals, Copley, 1981-84; sec. Copley All Sports Boosters, 1984-88. Named Medina County Tchr. of Yr., 1993; grantee Ohio Dept. Edn., 1978-79, 79-80, Martha Holden Jennings grants, 2001-02.; Martha Holden Jennings Found. scholar, 1994 Mem. NEA, ASCD, Ohio Edn. Assn., Internat. Reading Assn. (pres. Lizotte coun. 1994-95, 97-97, spkr. Great Lakes conf. 1993), Ohio Coun. Tchrs. English and Lang. Arts (presenter 1987, 88, 89), Cloverleaf Edn. Assn. (bldg. rep. 1977—), Nat. Campers and Hikers and Family RVers (pres. local chpt.), Order Eastern Star (acdre officer Ellsworth chpt. 1991—, Worthy Matron 1996), Delta Kappa Gamma. Avocations: camping, crafts, traveling, quilting. Home: 649 S Medina Line Rd Copley OH 44321-1162

COX, JAMES D. law educator; b. 1943; JD, U. Calif. Hastings Sch. Law, 1969; LL.M., Harvard U., 1971; D in Mercature (hon.), U. South Denmark, 2001. Bar: Calif. 1970. Atty.-adv. Office Gen. Counsel FTC, Washington, 1969-70; teaching fellow Boston U., 1970-71; asst. prof. U. San Francisco, 1971-74; assoc. prof. U. Calif. Hastings Sch. Law, 1974-75; vis. assoc. prof. Stanford U., 1976-77; prof. U. Calif. Hastings Sch. Law, 1977-79; vis. prof. Duke U. Sch. Law, spring 1979, prof., 1979-2000, Brainerd Currie prof. law, 2000—. Mem. com. on corps. State Bar Calif., N.C. bus. corp. act. draft com., N.C. nonprofit corp. draft com.; E.T. Bost rsch. prof., fall 1980, 96; mem. legal adv. com. N.Y. Stock Exch., 1995—; mem. legal adv. bd. NASD, 1999—. Author: Financial Information, Accounting and the Law, 1980, Sum and Substance of Corporations, 5th edit., 1988, (with Hillman and Langevoort) Securities Regulation: Cases and Materials, 3d edit., 2001, (with Hazen) Corporations, 2d edit., 2003. Sr. Fulbright Rsch. fellow, Australia, 1989. Mem. Am. Law Inst., Order of Coif, Phi Kappa Phi Office: Duke U Sch Law Durham NC 27706

COX, JOANNE FURTEK, secondary school educator; b. Santa Ana, Calif., Oct. 10, 1947; d. Joseph Stanley and Angela Marie (Palmieri) Furtek; m. Curtis Neel Cox, June 23, 1983. BA in History, Dominican Coll., 1973; MA in History, Trinity U., 1978; ArtsD in History, Carnegie-Mellon U., 1983. Cert. tchr., Tex. Tchr. Queen of Peace Sch., Houston, 1968-69, St. Thomas More Sch., Houston, 1969-73, Alamo Heights High Sch., San Antonio, 1973-79, 81—. Cons. Region XX Service Ctr., com. for Ednl. Testing Service Am. History Achievement Test; tchr. fellow McNay Art Mus., 2002. Contbr. articles to profl. jours. Bd. dirs. Hospice San Antonio, 1987-92; mem. Tchr. Resource Ctr. adv. com. Marion Koogler McNay Art Mus., 1998—. Recipient Trinity prize for Excellence in Teaching, 1987-88; grantee NEH, Carnegie-Mellon U., 1979-81. Mem. AAUW (treas. San Antonio chpt. 1986-87), NEA, Am. Hist. Assn., Nat. Coun. Social Studies, Coll. Bd., Bexar County Social Studies Coun. (treas., 1975-76), Alamo Heights Tchrs. Assn. (v.p. 1984-85), Delta Kappa Gamma (named Key Woman Educator Beta Tau chpt., 1987). Presbyterian. Avocations: swimming, guitar playing, gardening. Office: Alamo Heights High Sch 6900 Broadway St San Antonio TX 78209-3799 E-mail: jfcox@satx.rr.com.

COX, JOSEPH WILLIAM, former academic administrator, education educator; b. Hagerstown, Md., May 26, 1937; s. Joseph F. and Ruth E. C.; m. Regina M. Bollinger, Aug. 17, 1963; children: Andrew, Matthew, Abigail. BA, U. Md., 1959, PhD, 1967; Doctor (hon.), Towson State U., 1990. Prof. dept. engring. & tech. mgmt. Portland State U.; successively instr., asst. prof., assoc. prof., prof. history Towson (Md.) State U., 1964-81, dean evening and summer programs, 1972-75, acting pres., 1978-79, v.p. acad. affairs and dean of univ., 1979-81; prof. history, v.p. acad. affairs. No. Ariz. U., Flagstaff, 1981-87; pres. So. Oregon U., Ashland, 1987-94; chancellor Oreg. Univ. Sys., Eugene, 1994—2002, Disting. Pub. Svc. prof. Author: Champion of Southern Federalism: Robert Goodloe Harper of South Carolina, 1972, The Early National Experience: The Army Corps of Engineers, 1783-1812, 1979; mem. bd. editors Md. Hist. Mag., 1979-89; columnist So. Oreg. Hist. Mag., 1989-94; contbr. articles to profl. jours. Bd. dirs. Oreg. Hist. Soc., Oreg. Shakespearean Festival, 1989-95, So. Oreg. Econ. Devel. Bd., 1988-94, Jackson/Josephine Co., Western Bank, 1993-97, Portland Ctr. Stage, 1999. Mem. AAUP, Am. Assn. Higher Edn., Am. Assn. State Colls. and Univs., Phi Kappa Phi, Omicron Delta Kappa. Episcopalian. Home: 3845 Spring Blvd Eugene OR 97405 Office: Portland State U PO Box 751 Portland OR 97207-0751

COX, KATHY, education commissioner; m. John Hamilton Cox Jr.; children: John, Alex. BA in polit. sci., MA in Polit. Sci., Emory U., Atlanta. Tchr. social studies McIntosh H.S., Fayette County Bd. Edn., Atlanta, 1987—2002; rep Ga. Ho. of Reps., Atlanta, 1998—2002; sch. superintendent State of Ga., Atlanta, 2002—. Supporter Boy Scouts Am. Cub Scout Pack 201, Boy Scout Troop 275. Mem.: Kiwanis, Phi Beta Kappa. Meth. Office: Ga Dept Edn Jesse Hill Dr SE Atlanta GA 30334

COX, MYRON KEITH, business educator; b. Akron, May 6, 1926; s. Carney F. and Nina Castilla (Kenny) C.; B.S., Va. Poly. Inst., 1949; B.S., Pa. State Coll., 1952; M.S., M.I.T., 1957; D.Sc., London Coll., Eng., 1964; m. Emma A. Edwards, July 2, 1950; children: Carney K., Myron D., Eric L., Brett W. Commd. staff sgt. U.S. Air Force, 1950, advanced through grades maj., 1964; radar meteorology staff Hanscom AFB, Mass., 1964-66; electronic countermeasures Wright Patterson AFB, Ohio, 1966-69; ret., 1969; faculty Wright State U., Dayton, Ohio, 1969—, prof. mgmt. sci., quantitative bus. analysis, 1981—, chmn. dept. mgmt. scis., 1989—. Bd. govs. Fairborn (Ohio) YMCA, 1972-73. Served with USN, 1944-46. Registered profl. engr., Mass. Fellow Acad. Mktg. Sci.; mem. Inst. Mgmt. Sci., Am. Statis. Assn., Assn. Inst. Decision Sci., So. Mktg. Assn., Phi Kappa Phi, Tau Beta Pi, Sigma Xi, Eta Kappa Nu, Beta Gamma Sigma, Alpha Iota Delta. Club: Lions, Masons, Shriners. Patentee surface friction tester; contbr. mktg., mgmt., forecast modeling and simulation. Home: 4522 Bellflower Blvd Lakewood CA 90713-2501 Office: Wright State U Dayton OH 45435

COX, PAULYN MAE, retired elementary school educator; b. Oberlin, Ohio, Apr. 19, 1930; d. Lafayette Clinton and Magdalene Elizabeth Cox. AAS, SUNY, 1953; BA, Ithaca Coll., 1958. Cert. tchr., N.Y. Elem. tchr. Bd. Edn., Elyria, Ohio, 1964-65, reading tchr. Grafton, Ohio, 1966-67, St. Colombas Sch., Schenectady, N.Y., 1967-68; elem. tchr. Bd. Edn., Fonda, N.Y., 1968-94. Mem. YWCA, Schenectady; mem. Deaf Ctr., Schenectady. Recipient Sister Rachel award Schenectady Inner City Ministries, 1998. Mem. AAUW, Amnesty Internat., Am. Fedn. Tchrs., N.Y. State United Tchrs., Upper Montgomery County Ret. Tchrs. Avocations: reading, music, walking, mentoring, gardening. Home: 1561 Main St Rotterdam Junction NY 12150-9759

COX, PIERRE NAPOLEON, health education consultant; b. Bethesda, Md., June 12, 1967; s. Raymond Lee and Susie (Vines) C. BS in Leisure Studies, U. D.C., 1990, MEd in Adminstrn. and Supervision, 1992; MA in Orgnl. Comm., Bowie State U., 1994. Spl. cons. D.C. Dept. Recreation Therapeutics Svcs. Bur., Washington, 1986-89; elem. health and phys. edn. tchr. Fletcher-Johnson Edn. Ctr., Washington, 1990-91; program dir. YMCA Urban Program Ctr., Washington, 1991-92, Vet.'s Meml. YMCA, Alexandria, Va., 1991-92; dir. therapeutic aftersch. program for at-risk youth Family Svc. Agy., Inc., Gaithersburg, Md., 1993; cons. Assoc. Cmty. Svcs., Inc., Washington, 1993-94; spl. counsel Healthtrends Cons. Svcs. Inc., 1995—. Mem. D.C. Coalition to Improve Therapeutic Recreation Svcs., 1993, 94; dir. fitness and health enhancement, Arlington Br. YMCA, 1995—. Mem. AAHPERD, Am. Coun. on Exercise (cert. personal fitness trainer), D.C. Assn. for Health, Phys. Edn., Recreation and Dance (mem. host com. for conv. 1993, Merit award 1993), Nat. Strength and Conditioning Assn., Omega Psi Phi. Baptist. Avocations: fitness, music, reading, travel, go-cart racing. Home: 4333 Shell St Capitol Heights MD 20743

COX, SANDY GAIL, elementary education educator; b. Clarksville, Tex., Oct. 18, 1954; d. Marion Frank and Ruth M. (Dodd) Whitten; m. Perry Wayne Cox, June 12, 1976; 1 child, Clinton Wayne. BS in Elem. Edn., East Tex. State U., 1977. Cert. elem. tchr., kindergarten endorsement, Tex. Tchr. Talco-Bogata (Tex.) Consol. Ind. Sch. Dist., 1977-78, Roxton (Tex.) Ind. Sch. Dist., 1978-80; tchr. math. Paris (Tex.) Ind. Sch. Dist., 1980—, leader acad. team, 1992-94. Workshop presenter on math. activities and acad. teaming. Mem. Tex. Classroom Tchrs. Assn. (faculty rep. 1993-95, pres. local chpt., 1995—), Paris Bus. and Profl. Women (chmn. young careerists 1993-95, 1st v.p. 1994-95). Democrat. Baptist. Avocations: reading, crafts, tennis, swimming. Office: Crockett Mid Sch 655 S Collegiate Dr Paris TX 75460-6399 Home: PO Box 6552 Paris TX 75461-6552

COX, SHIRLEY ROSE, elementary education educator; b. Belleplain, Iowa, Nov. 18, 1946; d. George John and Wilma Rae (Morton) Mareda; m. Ronald Wayne Cox, June 17, 1972; children: Jennifer, Christopher. BS in Elem. Edn., Wichita State U., 1969; MS in Psychology, Emporia State Coll., 1973. Tchr. 3d grade St. Mary's Sch., Derby, Kans., 1966-68; tchr. behavior disorders spl. edn. Wineteer Sch., Derby, 1968-70, Larned (Kans.) State Hosp., 1970-73, Wichita (Kans.) Pleasant Valley, 1973-75, Price Sch., Wichita, 1975-77; tchr. 3rd grade Magdalen Sch., Wichita, 1977—, substance abuse coord., 1986-91. Com. mem. Task Force Inclusion Spl. Edn., Wichita, 1990-92. Southwestern Bell grantee, Wichita, 1992-93. Mem. Nat. Jr. Honor Soc. (bd. dirs.). Democrat. Roman Catholic. Avocations: reading, art, music. Home: 1839 S Battin St Wichita KS 67218-4415

COX-BEAIRD, DIAN SANDERS, middle school educator; b. Murchison, Tex., Dec. 18, 1946; d. Jessie Jackson and Lola Mae (Burton) Sanders; m. Richard Lewis Cox, May 24, 1969 (div. Nov. 1993); 1 child, Stuart Scott; m. Charles A. Beaird, Dec. 1994. AA, Kilgore Jr. Coll., 1967; BA, Stephen F. Austin State U., 1969, MEd, 1983. Cert. provisional gen. elem. edn., provisional h.s. history, govt. and polit. sci. Tchr. 8th grade Am. history and 7th grade Tex. history Chapel Hill Ind. Sch. Dist., Tyler, Tex., 1970-79; tchr. 6th-7th grade regular, advanced, remedial reading Sabine Ind. Sch. Dist., Gladewater, Tex., 1981—. Mem., tutor East Tex. Literacy Coun., Longview, 1992—; sec. Sabine Jr. High PTO, Gladewater, 1990-91; faculty sponsor cheerleaders Chapel Hill Ind. Sch. Dist., Tyler, 1970-73, rep. curriculum com., 1976, historian PTO, 1974; mem. anthology com. N.J. Writing Project in Tex., Kilgore, 1991; selected hostess Internat. Reading Conf., Tucson, 1992. Presenter: The Toothpaste Millionaire, 1992; contbr.: (short story) Vocies from the Heart, 1991. Leader Girl Scouts Am., Tyler, 1973; counselor Camp Natowa-Campfire Girls, Big Sandy, Tex., 1970; dir. Bible Sch., 1st Meth. Ch., Overton, Tex., 1980; sec. Young Dems., Kilgore, 1965-67; actress Gallery Theater, Jefferson, Tex.; mem. Opera House Theater and Galley Theater, 1992—, bd. dirs., 1996—; bd. dirs. Opera House, 1996. Named Outstanding Tchr. in Tex., Macmillan/McGraw Hill, 1991; Free Enterprise Forum scholar East Tex. Bapt. U., 1991. Mem. Internat. Reading Assn. (presenter 1992), Tex. Mid. Sch. Assn., Piney Woods Reading Coun., Tex. State Tchrs. Assn. (campus rep. 1990—, sec. Chapel Hill Ind. Sch. Dist. 1971-72), Laubach Literacy Action, Delta Kappa Gamma. Avocations: reading, travel, camping, acting. Home: PO Box 1146 Hallsville TX 75650-1146 Office: Sabine Jr H S RR 1 Box 189 Gladewater TX 75647-9723

COX-KLACZAK, KAREN MICHELLE, marketing educator, computer company official; b. Drexel Hill, Pa., Oct. 16, 1963; d. Robert Harold and Margaret Ellen (O'Brien) Cox; m. Robert John Klaczak, June 4, 1994; children: Joshua Robert, Philip Christopher. BSBA, Drexel U., 1985; MBA, Villanova U., 1994. Fin. analyst Spectacor, Wynnewood, Pa., 1987-89; project mgmt. analyst Wyeth Ayerst Labs., Radnor, Pa., 1990-95; prof. mktg. Villanova (Pa.) U., 1995—. Cons. on advt. Mercia Grassi Assocs., Phila., 1984; cons. on strategy Villa St. John Hosp., Downingtown, Pa., 1992; cons. on new bus. devel. IBM, Wayne, Pa., 1995—. Mem. NAFE, Am. Mktg. Assn., Beta Gamma Sigma. Avocations: photography, collecting sea shells, travel, hiking, design. Home: 612 Thorncroft Dr West Chester PA 19380-6442 Office: Villanova U Mktg Dept 800 Lancaster Ave Villanova PA 19085-1603

COXSON, BETTY JANE, retired secondary school and humanities educator; b. Chgo., July 5, 1926; d. Emmett Massina Coxson and Alma Alvilda (Emmerson) Coxson Martin. BA, Luther Coll., 1948; MA, Long Beach State U., 1961; diploma, Inst. Children's Lit., Conn., 1997. Cert. lifetime secondary sch. tchr., cmty. coll. educator, Calif. Tchr. Peterson (Minn.) H.S., 1948-49, Stockton (Ill.) H.S., 1949-50; editor N.W. Newspapers, Chgo., 1950-51; sec. Delta Star Electric, Chgo., 1951-52; editor, sec. Calif. Taxpayers Assn., L.A., 1952-53; parish worker St. Timothy Luth. Ch., Lakewood, Calif., 1953-56; tchr. Rancho Alamitos H.S., Garden Grove, Calif., 1958-61, Lowell H.S., Whittier, Calif., 1961-63, U.S. Peace Corps, Aba, Nigeria, 1963-66, Sunny Hills H.S., Fullerton, Calif., 1966, U.S. AID, Uganda, 1966-70, Morongo Unified Sch. Dist., Twenty-Nine Palms, Calif., 1971-85, ret., 1985; mem. adj. faculty dept. English and humanities Copper Mountain Coll., Joshua Tree, Calif., 1986-97, ret., 1997. Tchr. English lang. Ednl. Svcs. Exch. with China, Jiading, summer 1990, Changchun, summer 1993. Wall St. Jour. journalism workshop scholar U. So. Calif. Mem. Nat. Coun. Tchrs. of English (judge h.s. writing), Calif. Ret. Tchrs. editor newsletter chpt. 62), Morongo Tchrs. Assn. (editor newsletter), Calif. Assn. Tchrs. of English, Delta Kappa Gamma (treas. 1981-82), Iota Iota chpt., Lambda chpt. Minn., Calif. Tchrs. Assn. Republican. Avocations: travel, writing, collecting stamps. Home: 217 4th St NW Buffalo Center IA 50424-1056 E-mail: b.j.coxson@wctatel.net.

COY, DORIS RHEA, counselor, educator; b. Portsmouth, Ohio, Sept. 7, 1938; d. Haldor Ellsworth and Dorothy Evelyn (Weese) Rhea. BS, U. Rio Grande, Ohio, 1963; MA, Ohio State U., 1966, PhD, 1996. Nat. cert. counselor, nat. cert. career counselor, nat. cert. sch. counselor; lic. prof. counselor; cert. elem. prin., supr., pupil pers., sch. counselor, elem. tchr., Ohio. Sales clk. Morris 5&10, Jackson, Ohio, 1954-58; tchr. Jackson County Schs., Jackson, 1958-59, Whitehall (Ohio) City Schs., 1959-66, sch. counselor, 1966-92, chair dept., 1982-92; pres. Am. Sch. Counselor Assn., Alexandria, Va., 1989-90, ACA, Alexandria, 1994-95; pvt. practice Doris Rhea Coy & Assocs., Pickerington, Ohio, 1979—; lectr. U. North Tex., Denton, 1996-97, asst. prof. counselor edn., 1997—. Co-dir. ERIC/CASS Ctr. for Sch. Counseling, 1998—. Editor: Toward the Transformation of Secondary School Counseling; author booklet, articles and book chpts.; author conflict mgmt. and crisis mgmt. programs. Recipient numerous awards, honors and grants. Mem. ASCD, ACA, Am. Sch. Counselor Assn., Ohio Counseling Assn. (pres. 1992-93), Ohio Sch. Counselor Assn. (pres. 1984-85), Tex. Counseling Assn. (chair profl. devel. com. 1997—), Tex. Career Guidnce assn. (sec./newsletter editor 1997-98, pres.-elect 1998—), Tex. Sch. Counselor Assn., Tex. Assn. for Counselor Educators and Suprs., League for Profl. Women, AAUW, Nat. Career Devel. Assn., Assn. for Counselor Educators and Suprs., Delta Kappa Gamma, others. Office: U North Tex Dept Counseling PO Box 311337 Denton TX 76203-1337

COY, PATRICIA ANN, special education director, consultant; b. Beardstown, Ill., Apr. 2, 1952; d. Ben L. and Dorothy Lee (Hubbell) C. BS in Elem. and Spl. Edn., No. Ill. U., 1974; MS in Spl. Edn., Northeastern Ill. U., 1976, MA in Spl. Edn., 1978; MEd in Spl. Edn., Northeastern U., 1984; postgrad., No. Ill. U., 1988—. Cert. elem. and spl. edn. tchr.; cert. counselor. Mental health supr. Waukegan (Ill.) Devel. Ctr., 1974-77; ednl. therapist Grove Sch. and Residential Program, Lake Forest, Ill., 1977-78; dir. residential svcs. N.W. Suburban Aid for the Retarded, Park Ridge, Ill., 1978-83; exec. dir. The Learning Tree, Des Plaines, Ill., 1983—; dir. residential svcs. Augustanan Ctr. Luth. Social Svcs. of Ill., Chgo., 1984-86, dir. planning and evaluation, 1986-93, dir. cmty. svc., 1993-95; CEO Visions Network (formerly Blare House Inc.), Des Plaines, Ill., 1995—. Behavior advisor Habilitative Systems, Inc., Chgo., 1985-88; program coord. Human Resource Devel. Inst., Chgo., 1986-89; project dir. Support Svcs. Ill., Inc., Chgo., 1987-91; dir. TranSteps Inc. Steps for Success for Adults with Learning Differences, 1991—. Contbr. articles to profl. jours. Mem. Coun. for Exceptional Children, Am. Assn. Mental Deficiency, Chgo. Assn. Behavioral Analysis, Behavior Analysis Soc. Ill., Assn. for Supervision and Curriculum Devel., Nat. Rehab. Assn., Coun. for Disability Rights, Assn. for Learning Disability, Profls. in Learning Disabilities, Cwens, Echoes, Mortar Bd., Kappa Delta Pi. Democrat. Mem. United Ch. of Christ. Home: 8936 N Parkside Ave Apt 118 Des Plaines IL 60016-5517 Office: 7144 N Harlem Ave Ste 344 Chicago IL 60631-1005 also: The Visions Network 960 Rand Rd Ste 214 Des Plaines IL 60016-2355 E-mail: coycondo@aol.com.

COYAN, MICHAEL LEE, art and performing arts educator; b. Dayton, Ohio, Dec. 31, 1954; s. Eugene and Wilma Arlene (Surface) C. BA, Miami U., Oxford, Ohio, 1982, MA, 1985; postgrad., Ohio U., Athens, 1989-92. Asst. to producer, dir. pub. rels. Miami U. Summer Theatre, 1974-78; asst. to pub. rels. dir., box office and house mgr. Cin. Playhouse in the Park, 1977-80; drama dir., tchr. Lebanon (Ohio) H.S., 1980-83; dir., instr., advisor Miami U., 1984-86, vis. instr. interdisciplinary studies, 1993—94; instr., tchg. assoc. Ohio U., Athens, 1989—92; dir. pub. rels. Cin. Commn. on the Arts, 1986-88; grant writer, cons. M.L. Coyan & Assocs., Cin., 1986—; instr. art Sinclair C.C., Dayton, Ohio, 1992—; assoc. prof. theatre Wright State U., Dayton, 1997—2000. Artistic dir. Actors Repertory Theatre, Middletown, Ohio, 1999-2001; exec. dir. Lebanon Regional Arts Coun., 1977-79; chmn. mini-festivals Cin. Symphony Orch., 1977-83; allocations com.-project pool Cin. Fine Arts Fund, 1983-93; lectr. Pratt Inst. Venice Program, 1996; adj. prof. theatre Wright State U., Dayton, Ohio, 1998-2000. Author: The Lebanon Opera House, 1877-82, 1984; playwright: To Touch The Hem of Heaven, 2001, The Gentle Art: An Evening with Mr. Whistler, 2002; contbr. articles to profl. jours. Mem. City Coun., City of Lebanon, 1993-99; theatre dir. Bicentennial Commn., Lebanon, 1975-76; trustee, treas. Friends of the Libr., Lebanon, 1978-83. Recipient Svc. award Miami U., 1984; Hazen Trust Fund grantee, 1973, 77. Fellow Inst. for Edwardian Studies (co-founder), Soc. for a Brit. Theatre Inst.; mem. Coll. Art Assn., Theatre Comms. Group, Ohio Theatre Alliance, Integrative Studies Inst., Phi Kappa Phi. Democrat. Episcopalian. Avocations: antique collecting, gardening, painting, classical piano, travel. Home: 318 N Broadway Lebanon OH 45036-1717

COYLE, CHARLES A. marketing educator; b. Phila., June 13, 1931; s. Charles A. and Roseanne (McPeake) C.; m. Suzanne B. McCann, Sept. 28, 1963; children: Suzanne, Christopher, Kevin, Timothy. BSBA, LaSalle U., 1955; postgrad., US Army Intelligence Ctr., Md., 1956; MBA, Drexel U., 1967; EdD with distinction, Temple U., 1974; postgrad., Mary Immaculate Sem., 1990-95. Sales rep. IBM, SCM, Diebold, Inc., R.E. Lamb, 1958-67; spl. agt. U.S. Dept. Treasury; asst. prof. mktg. and mgmt., curriculum supr. Phila. C.C., 1967-70; asst. prof. mktg. Phila. U., 1970-74; tchr., coord. distributive edn. Middle Bucks (Pa.) AVTS, 1974-76; prof., chmn. mktg. Kutztown (Pa.) U., 1976-2000; prof. emeritus Kutztown Coll. Bus. Chmn. mktg. adv. com. Lehigh Valley Vocat. Tech. Sch., 1984-94; adj. prof. Temple U., La Salle U., St. Josephs U., DeSales U.; presenter in field. Contbr. articles to profl. jours. Mgr., soccer and baseball coach Warminster Little League, 1973—79, Grandlawn Baseball Assn., 1987—88; founder, treas. Deerfield Cmty. Assn., 1983; pres., treas. LaSalle U. Student Congress, 1954—55; prefect min. St. Francis Third Order; ordained permanent deacon Allentown Diocese, 1995—; resource leader Nat. Conf. on New Strategies for Learning, 1969. Sgt. counter-intelligence corps U.S. Army, 1956—58, Tokyo. Recipient award Dale Carnegie Found., Phila., 1967, Outstanding Svc. award Distributive Edn. Clubs Am., 1975, 86, 88, 91, award Lehigh Valley Vocat.-Tech. Sch. Adv. Com., 1993; Direct Mktg. fellow, 1989. Mem. AAUP, Am. Acad. Advt., Sales and Mktgs. Execs., Am. Mktg. Assn., Direct Mktg. Assn., Assn. Pa. Univ. Bus. and Econ. Faculty (bd. dirs. 1989-91), Sales and Mktg. Execs., Am. Mgmt. Assn., Cross Keys, KC (4th degree), Faculty and Adminstrn. Club (pres. Kutztown U. 1988-90, v.p. 1986-88), Sons Union Vets. of the Civil War, CrossKeys Honor Soc., Phi Delta Kappa, Phi Kappa Phi, Alpha Epsilon, Epsilon Delta Epsilon. Home: 1236 Buck Trail Rd Allentown PA 18104-2019

COYLE, MARIE BRIDGET, retired microbiology educator, laboratory director; b. Chgo., May 13, 1935; d. John and Bridget Veronica (Fitzpatrick) C.; m. Zheng Chen, Oct. 30, 1995 (div. Aug. 2000). BA, Mundelein Coll., 1957; MS, St. Louis U., 1963; PhD, Kans. State U., 1965. Diplomate Am. Bd. Med. Microbiology. Sci. instr. Sch. Nursing Columbus Hosp., Chgo., 1957-59; research assoc. U. Chgo., 1967-70; instr. U. Ill., Chgo., 1970-71; asst. prof. microbiology U. Wash., Seattle, 1973-80, assoc. prof., 1980-94, prof., 1994-2000; ret., 2000. Assoc. dir. microbiology labs Univ. Hosp., Seattle, 1973-76; dir. microbiology labs Harborview Med. Ctr., Univ. Wash., 1976—; co-dir. Postdoc Training Clinic Microbiology, Univ. Wash., 1978-96; dir. postdoctoral tng. clin. microbiology, 1996-2000. Contbr. articles to profl. jours. Recipient Pasteur award, Ill. Soc. Microbiology, 1997, Profl. Recognition awards, Am. Bd. Med. Microbiology, Am. Bd. Med. Lab. Immunology, 2000. Fellow Am. Acad. Microbiology; mem. Acd. Clin. Lab. Physicians and Scientists (sec.-treas. 1980-83, exec. com. 1985-90), Am. Soc. Microbiology (chmn. clin. microbiology divsn. 1984-85, coun. policy com. 1996-99, bd. govs. 2000—, recipient bioMerieux Vitek Sonnenwirth Meml. award 1994), Kappa Gamma Pi. Avocations: hiking, skiing, cycling.

COZZOLINO, JOHN MICHAEL, JR., management educator; b. New Haven, Dec. 17, 1940; s. John M. and Lucile (Violante) C.; m. Carol Ann Lombardi, Sept. 7, 1963; children: William John, Stephen Michael. BS, MIT, 1962, MS, 1964, PhD, 1967; MA (hon.), U. Pa., Phila., 1972. Assoc. prof. The Wharton Sch., Phila., 1967-82; prof. decision scis. Coll. Ins., N.Y.C., 1985-86; rsch. dir. Ins. Svcs. Office, N.Y.C., 1986-89; assoc. prof. mgmt. Pace U., N.Y.C., 1989—, dir. Underwriting Edn. Inst. Pleasantville, N.Y., 1992—. Author: Operations Research for Management, 1975, Management of Oil and Gas Exploration Risk, 1977. Office: Lubin Sch Pace U 861 Bedford Rd Pleasantville NY 10570-2700

CRABTREE, JOHN MICHAEL, college administrator, consultant; b. Fostoria, Ohio, Nov. 11, 1949; s. John Dwight and Opal Marie (Tate) C.; m. Cheryl Lynn Wallace, July 6, 1974. AA in Music Edn., Mt. Vernon Nazarene Coll., 1970; B of Music Edn., So. Nazarene U., 1972, MA in Edn., 1976; postgrad., U. Okla., 1976. Sports info. dir. So. Nazarene U., Okla., 1971-80, dir. pub. rels., 1974-80, assoc. dean student devel., 1974-78, dir. alumni and media rels., 1980-89, adminstrv. asst. to pres., 1989-90, dir. univ. advancement, 1989, exec. dir., 1990-91, v.p., 1991-98, asst. to pres., 1998—. Adj. prof. mktg. So. Nazarene U., 1979-82; bd. rsch. advisors Governing Bd. Editors and Pub. Bd. The Am. Biographical Inst. Editor The Perspective, 1981-89. Chmn. United Fund Drive, Bethany, 1983; pub. rels. dir. B.U.I.L.D. (Bethany United Improvement League Downtown); mem. exec. bd. Bethany Main St.; exec. sec. Nazerene Officers Instl. Advancement, 1989-90; pres. Nazarine Officers Instl. Adv., 1996-2000; bd. dirs. Mabel Fry Meml. Libr., Yukon,. Okla., 1990-94, So. Nazerene U. Found., 1993—; mem. Okla. Friends of Libr., Okla Civic Music Assn., exec. bd. dirs.; mem. Oklahoma City Friends Eng., exec. bd. dirs.; mem. Real Effective Action Leadership. Mem.: Oklahoma City Orch. League, Okla. Ind. Coll. Found., Okla. City C. of C. (pub. rels. and econ. devel. bds.), Sports Info. Dirs. Am. (ethics com. 1978—80, job attrition bd. 1980), Okla. Civic Music Assn. (bd. dirs.), Coun. Advancement and Support of Edn., Okla. Coll. Pub. Rels. Assn., Bethany C. of C., Assn. Fundraising Profls., Bethany Hist. Soc. (life), Oklahoma City Audubon Soc. (pub. rels. dir. wildlife film series 1974—93), Oklahoma City N. Rotary, Kiwanis, Sigma Delta Tau. Republican. Avocations: photography, philately, antique book collector. Office: So Nazarene U 6729 NW 39th Expy Bethany OK 73008-2605 E-mail: mcrabtre@snu.edu.

CRABTREE, ROBERT ALLEN, elementary education educator; b. Syracuse, N.Y., June 29, 1949; s. Donald John and Blossom (Allen) C. BA, SUNY, Fredonia, 1971; MS, SUNY, Cortland, 1975, cert. advanced study, 1990. Elem. tchr. North Syracuse (N.Y.) Cen. Schs., 1971—. Instr. West Genesee-Syracuse U. Tchg. Ctr., 1986, 1993—99, 2003. Pres. Dollars for Scholars, North Syracuse, 1989-; vol. We Care Telephone Suicide Prevention Program, North Syracuse, 1988-; Dem. committeeman Town of Clay. Recipient Outstanding Tchr. award Tech. Club of Syracuse, 1990, Syracuse Newspapers Golden Apple award, 1991, North Syracuse Tchr. of Yr. award, 1988. Mem. ASCD, NSTA, Assn. Math. Tchrs. of N.Y. State, Nat. Coun. Tchrs. Math., Sci. Tchrs. Assn. N.Y. State (chmn. ctrl. sect. 1992-96), Optimist Club (v.p. 1991-92, bd. dirs. 1992, 2002—, pres. 1999-2000, lt. gov 2003—). Democrat. Baptist. Avocations: swimming, bowling, jogging. Home: 102 Baxton St North Syracuse NY 13212-2002 Office: Cicero Elem Sch 5979 Rte 31 Cicero NY 13039-8890

CRABTREE, ROBERT HOWARD, chemistry educator; b. Apr. 17, 1948; came to U.S., 1977, naturalized, 1985; s. Arthur and Marguerite (Vaniere) C. BA, Oxford U., 1970; PhD, Sussex U., Eng., 1973, DSc (hon.), 1985. Attache of rsch. Nat. Ctr. Sci. Rsch., Paris, 1975-77; asst. prof. chemistry Yale U., New Haven, Conn., 1977-83, assoc. prof., 1983-85, prof., 1985—. E-mail: robert.crabtree@yale.edu.

CRACROFT, RICHARD HOLTON, English literature educator; b. Salt Lake City, June 28, 1936; s. Ralph and Grace Darling (White) C.; m. Janice Marie Alger, Sept. 17, 1959; children: Richard Alger, Jeffrey Ralph, Jennifer Cracroft Lewis. BA, U. Utah, 1961, MA, 1963; PhD in English and Am. Lit., U. Wis., 1969. Student instr. U. Utah, Salt Lake City, 1961-63; instr. English Brigham Young U., Provo, Utah, 1963-66; grad. instr. U. Wis., Madison, 1966-69; from asst. prof. English to assoc. prof. English Brigham Young U., Provo, 1969-74, prof. English, 1974-2001, prof. emeritus English, 2001—, dept. chair English, 1975-80, dean Coll. Humanities, 1981-86, Nan Osmond Grass Prof. English, 1999-2001. Dir. Ctr. for Study of Christian Values in Lit., Brigham Young U., Provo, 1993-2001; bd. judges David Evans Biography Prize, Logan, Utah, 1983-2001, Orton Prize for Mormon Letters, Salt Lake City, 1991-2001. Author: Washington Irving: The Western Works, 1974; co-editor: A Believing People: The Literature of the Latter-day Saints, 1974, 1979, 22 Young Mormon Writers, 1975, Voices From the Past: (LDS) Journals, Diaries, Autobiographies, 1980, My Soul Delighteth in the Scriptures, 1999; editor: Dictionary of Literary Biography: 20th Century American Western Writers, vols. 206, 212, 256, 1999—2002, (jour.) Lit. and Belief, 1993—2002; founding assoc. editor: The Carpenter, 1966—70, assoc. editor: Dialogue, 1969—73, We. Am. Lit., 1973—86, mem. editl. bd.: BYU Studies, 1981—86, This People, 1996—2000; contbr. articles to profl. jours., chpts. to books. Bishop, stake pres., mission pres. LDS Ch. Democrat. Avocations: reading, writing, gardening, leading tours of western europe. Home: 43 N 550 E Orem UT 84097-4800 Office: Brigham Young U Dept English 3146 Jesse Knight Hum Bldg Provo UT 84602-2724 E-mail: cracroftr@emstar2.net.

CRAFF-MENDEZ, KATHERINE, systems analyst, college official; b. Lima, Peru, Jan. 5, 1966; came to U.S., 1981; d. Antonio and Catalina (Bedoya) Craff; m. Henry Mendez, Aug. 31, 1990; 1 child, Corey Craff-Mendez. BS, Ill. Benedictine Coll., 1989. Tutor, asst. Ill. Benedictine Coll., Lisle, 1985-89; systems mgr., mem. rsch. adv. bd. St. Augustine Coll., Chgo., 1989—. Mem. Assn. for Computer Machinery. Republican. Roman Catholic. Avocations: sports, reading, camping, swimming.

CRAFT DAVIS, AUDREY ELLEN, writer, educator; b. Vanceburg, Ky., June 9, 1926; d. James Elmer and Lula Alice (Vance) Gilkison; m. Vernon Titus Craft, Nov. 5, 1943 (dec. Aug. 1979); children: James Vernon Craft, Alice Ann Craft Schuler; m. Louis Amzie Davis, Oct. 22, 1986. PhD, Ohio U., 1964; Dr. of Metaphysics, Coll. Divine Metaphysics, 1968; DD, Ohio U., 1971; postgrad., St. Petersburg Jr. Coll., 1975; DD (hon.), Assoc. Minister, Coll. Metephysical Studies, 1998. Owner beauty salon Audrey Craft Enterprises, Tampa Bay, Fla., 1970-83, owner cosmetic co. Portsmouth, Ohio, 1958-70; owner, distbr. Nightingale Motivation, Tampa Bay, 1960—; tchr., counselor Bus. Coll. U., Tampa Bay, 1965—; ins. staff Investors Heritage & Wabash, Portsmouth, 1967-70; ins. broker Jackson Nat. & Wabash, Tampa Bay, 1971-91; pres. The Gardens 107, Inc., Tampa Bay, 1987—. Travel writer, counselor Cruises/Travel & Etc., Fla., 1981—. Author: (poetry) Pathways, 1990, Metaphysical Techniques That Really Work, 1994, (Spanish translation), 2nd edit., 2002, Metaphysical Encounters, 1992, How to Stay Secure in a Chaotic World, 1993, Metaphysics Encounters of a Fourth Kind, 1995, How to Safeguard Your World and Avoid Becoming a Target, 1996, Angel Trails, 2002, Hidden Truths and Unusual Events of the Bible, 2002; contbr. articles to profl. jours. Bd. dirs. The Gardens Domicurculums, Cmty. Coun., 1987—; bd. dirs. State Bd. Cosmetology, Columbus, Ohio, 1962-63, Bus. and Profl. Women, Portsmouth, 1967-69, Sci. Rsch., Portsmouth, 1965-69, Tampa Bay, 1972-74. Recipient Key to Miami, Office of Mayor Claude Kirk, 1969, Million Dollar trophy Lt. Gov. John Brown Ohio; commd. Ky. Col. by Gov. Edward T. Breathitt, 1968, Gov. Wendell Ford, 1969. Mem. AARP, S.E. Writers Assn., Christian Writers Guild, Writers Digest Book Club, Nat. Assn. Retired Fed. Employees (assoc.), Am. Heart Assn. (chmn. Seminole area 1994). Democrat. Avocations: writing, lectures, counseling, travel, meditation. Home and Office: 102 Saint Petersburg Dr W Oldsmar FL 34677-3620

CRAIG, ALBERT MORTON, Asian studies educator; b. Chgo., Dec. 9, 1927; s. Albert Morton and Adda (Clendenin) C.; m. Teruko Ugaya, July 10, 1953; children— John, Paul. BS, Northwestern U., 1949; postgrad., Universite de Strasbourg, 1949-50, Kyoto U., 1951-53, Tokyo U., 1955-56; PhD, Harvard, 1959. Instr. U. Mass., 1957-59; instr. Harvard U., Cambridge, Mass., 1959-60, asst. prof., 1960-63, assoc. prof., 1963-67, prof., 1967-89, Harvard-Yenching prof. history, 1989—99, rsch. prof. history, 1999—; dir. Harvard-Yenching Inst., 1976-87. Author: Choshu in the Meiji Restoration, 1961, The Heritage of Chinese Civilization, 2001, The Heritage of Japanese Civilization, 2003, (with others) East Asia: The Modern Transformation, 1965, East Asia: Tradition and Transformation, 1973, 3d edit., 1989, The Heritage of World Civilizations, 1986, 6th edit., 2003; editor: Japan, A Comparative View, 1979; co-editor: Personality in Japanese History, 1970. Served with AUS, 1946-47. Mem. Assn. Asian Studies. Home: 172 Goden St Belmont MA 02478-2951 Office: Kirkland Pl Cambridge MA 02138-2020

CRAIG, CHARLES SAMUEL, marketing educator; b. Atlantic City, May 6, 1943; s. Charles Hays and Catherine Sara (McMullen) C.; m. Elizabeth Anne Coyne, Aug. 10, 1985; children: Mary Catherine, Caroline Elizabeth. BA, Westminster Coll., 1965; MS, U. R.I., 1967; PhD, Ohio State U., 1971. Mktg. rep. IBM, Providence, 1966—68; asst. dir. Mechanized Info. Ctr., Columbus, 1971—73; asst. prof. lib. adminstrn. Ohio State U., Columbus, 1971—73, asst. prof. mktg., 1972—74; asst. prof. mktg. Grad. Sch. Bus. and Pub. Adminstrn. Cornell U., Ithaca, NY, 1974—77, assoc. prof., 1977—79; from assoc. prof. mktg. Stern Sch. of Bus. to prof. NYU, 1979—, dir. entertainment, media and tech. program, 1999—, Catherine and Peter Kellner prof., 2001—. Bd. dirs. P&R Pub. Co., Phillipsburg, NJ; mem. exec. bd. Jour. Retailing, 1985—. Co-author: Consumer Behavior: An Information Processing Perspective, 1982; International Marketing Research, 1983, 2d edit., 2000, Global Marketing Strategy, 1995; co-editor: Personal Selling: Theory, Research and Practice, 1984, The Development of Media Models in Advertising, Repetition Effects over the Years, The Relationship of Advertising Expenditures to Sales, 1986; mem. editl. bd. Jour. Mktg. Rsch., 1978-85, Jour. Retailing, 1980-85, Jour. Advt. Rsch., 1994—, Internat. Jour. of Advt., 1997—; contbr. articles to profl. jours. NDEA fellow, 1969-71. Mem. Am. Mktg. Assn., Assn. Consumer Rsch., Acad. Internat. Bus., Phi Kappa Phi, Omicron Delta Epsilon, Psi Chi. Presbyterian. Home: 100 Bleecker St Apt 28D New York NY 10012-2207 Office: NYU 44 W 4th St New York NY 10012-1106

CRAIG, GEORGE DENNIS, economics educator, consultant; b. Sept. 14, 1936; s. George S. and Alice H. (Childs) C.; m. Lelah Price, Aug. 21, 1984; children: R. Price Coyle, R. Nolan Coyle, Deborah L. Craig, W. Sean Coyle. BA, Wheaton Coll., 1960; MS, U. Ill., 1962, PhD, 1968. Asst. prof. econs. La. State U., Baton Rouge, 1965-69; assoc. prof. sch. bus. No. Ill. U., DeKalb, 1969-82; prof. econs., chmn. Oklahoma City U., 1982—. Cons. AT&T, Oklahoma City, 1984—. Contbr. articles to profl. jours. Mem. Am. Econs. Assn., So. Econs. Assn., Nat. Assn. Bus. Economists, Internat. Inst. Forecasting. Avocations: duplicate bridge, tennis. Home: 6915 Avondale Ct Oklahoma City OK 73116-5008 Office: 6421 Avondale Dr Ste 208 Oklahoma City OK 73116-6429 E-mail: craigg784@aol.com.

CRAIG, JERRY WALKER, engineering graphics educator; b. Kirksville, Mo., Dec. 2, 1934; s. Orval Breckenridge and Edith Yardley (McGlashon) C.; m. Armynta Joyce Stover; children: Jeffrey, Peggy. BS in Edn., N.E. Mo. State U., 1957; MS in Edn., Kans. State U., 1972. Instr. Washington U., St. Louis, 1957-62; design engr. McDonnell-Douglass, St. Louis, 1962-68; dept. chmn. St. Louis C.C., 1968-92; affiliate prof. Washington U., 1992—. Computer cons. Comtek, St. Louis, 1977—. Author: Engineering Graphics Workbook, 1993, An Introduction to Engineering Design, 1994, Engineering and Technical Drawing with Silverscreen, 1995, Engineering and Technical Drawing with AutoCAD, 1996. Dir. Carlyle (Ill.) Sailing Assn., 1980-90. Mem. Am. Soc. Engring. Edn., 1990—. Avocations: sailing, sports car racing. Home: 1009 Carole Ln Ballwin MO 63021-4727 Office: Washington U 1 Brookings Dr Saint Louis MO 63130-4899

CRAIG, JOAN CARMEN, secondary school educator, drama teacher; b. Sacramento, Calif., July 13, 1932; d. Frank Hurtado and Enid Pearl (Hogan) Alcalde; m. Elmer Lee Craig, Aug. 14, 1955 (dec. Jan. 1981); children: Shelley, Wendy, Cathleen, Scott; m. Donald E. Peterson, 1997. BA, San Jose State U., 1954, gen. secondary cert., 1955; postgrad. studies, various univs., 1956—. Cert. tchr. (life), Calif. Drama tchr. Willow Glen High Sch. San Jose (Calif.) Unified Sch. Dist., 1955-58, Kennedy Jr. High Sch. Cupertino (Calif.) Sch. Dist., 1968-93. Cons. Cupertino Unified Sch. Dist., 1990—; coord. program activiy Growth Leadership Ctr., Mountain View, Calif., 1993; presenter Computer Use in Edn., 1990-93. Author, coord.: Drama Curriculum, 1971-93, Musical Comedy Curriculum, 1985-93, (Golden Bell, Calif. 1992). Dir. Nat. Multiple Sclerosis Soc., Santa Clara County, 1983-86. Recipient Spl. Svc. award Nat. Multiple Sclerosis Soc., Santa Clara, Calif., 1986, Hon. Membership award Nat. Jr. Honor Soc., 1990, Hon. Svc. award Calif. Congress Parents, Tchrs. and Students, Inc., 1992; named Tchr. of Year, Kennedy Jr. High, Cupertino Union Sch. Dist., 1993. Mem. AAUW, NEA, Calif. Tchrs. Assn., Cupertino Edn. Assn. (rep. 1982). Avocations: theater, hiking, biking, writing, swimming. Home: 3381 Brower Ave Mountain View CA 94040-4512

CRAIG, JOHN CHARLES, educational researcher, consultant; b. Belvidere, Ill., Dec. 28, 1946; s. John George and Ruth Effie (Coan) C.; m. Mary Louise Loftus, Feb. 16, 1974; children: David Thomas, Jesse Lindsey. BS, No. Ill. U., 1969; PhD, Northwestern U., 1984. Cert. edn. adminstr., tchr. Tchr. Rockford (Ill.) Pub. Sch., 1969-71; rschr., cons. Ill. State Bd. of Edn., Springfield, 1971—. Bd. dirs., v.p. Ill. Fedn. Tchrs., 1987-93, pres. Ctrl. Ill. Area Coun., 1983-91, Ill. Fedn. of State Office Educators, Springfield, 1992-96; cons. nat. ednl. std. setting activities, nat. geographic std. and assessment, nat. assessment; mem. design team Ill. Goal Assessment Program; designer Ill. Prairie State Achievement Test, 1996-99. Editor: Alternate Assessment, Social Sciences, Alternate Assessment, Geography; contbr. articles to profl. jours. Prodr., broadcaster Sta. WSSR Radio, Springfield, 1976-87; leader Boy Scouts Am., Springfield, 1987—. Mem. Am. Acad. Polit. Sci., Nat. Assn. Geographic Edn., Am. Hist. Assn. Mem. Nat. Coun. Social Studies, Nat. Assn. Geog. Edn., Am. Hist. Soc. Avocations: model railroads, woodworking. Office: Ill State Bd Edn 100 N 1st St Springfield IL 62702-5042

CRAIG, JOHN ROBERT, broadcast and cinematic arts educator, researcher; b. New Kensington, Pa., Dec. 21, 1947; s. Raymond R. and Ann (Facemyer) C.; m. Linda Kay Raybuck, Dec. 26, 1971; children: Shea, Tyson, Daedre. BS inEdn., Clarion U. of Pa., 1969, MS, 1971; PhD, U. Mo., 1981. Sports dir. WWCH Radio, Clarion, 1966-69; mem. faculty N.W. Mo. State U., Maryville, 1971-80, Ctrl. Mich. U., Mt. Pleasant, 1980—, chair dept. broadcast and cinematic arts, 1993-96, grad. dir., 1986—94, 1996—2002. Contbr. articles to Lit./Film Quar., Jour. Evolutionary Psychology, Popular Culture Rev., Comm. and Law, Jour. Fantastic in the Arts, Jour. Popular Film and Television, Edn., Feedback, Journalism Educator, Assoc. Ed., Jour. Evolutionary Psychology; reviewer Jour. Fantastic in the Arts. Mem. percussion crew Mt. Pleasant High Marching Band, 1995-98. Mem. NEA, Internat. Assn. on the Fantastic in the Arts (divsn. head film and media 1999—), Assn. for Evolutionary Psychology, Midwest Pop Culture Assn., Far West Pop Culture Assn. Avocations: golf, hockey, tennis. Home: 6033 E Broadway Rd Mount Pleasant MI 48858-8939 Office: Ctrl Mich U 340 Moore Hl Mount Pleasant MI 48859-0001 E-mail: craig1jr@cmich.edu.

CRAIG, LARRY VERNON, secondary school educator; b. Cin., July 30, 1948; s. Vernon Francis and Opal Jewell (Davis) C.; m. Gwendolyn Gale Watson, July 24, 1967; children: Kimberly, David, Jonathan. BS, BA, Tenn. Temple U., 1972; MA in Bible, Ind. Bapt. Coll., Dallas, 1975; MEd, U. North Tex., 1976, PhD, 1979. Cert. tchr. English, math., spl. edn., adminstrn., supervision, Tex. Tchr. Ind. Bapt. Coll., Dallas, 1973-82; pastor First Orthodox Bapt. Ch., Ardmore, Okla., 1982-86; tchr. Irving (Tex.) Ind. Sch. Dist., 1986-91; cons. Region 10 Edn. Svc. Ctr., Richardson, Tex., 1991-92; tchr. math. and computer sci. Grand Prairie (Tex.) Ind. Sch. Dist., 1992—, computer sci. tchr., computer sci. team coach, 1994—. Mem. Assn. Tex. Profl. Educators (regional treas., membership chmn. 1991—, pres. region 10, 1993-95, pres. Grand Prairie 1994-95)j, Nat. Coun. Tchrs. Math. Republican. Baptist. Avocations: exercising, chess, computer programming. Home: 804 S Story Rd Irving TX 75060-3644 Office: South Grand Prairie High 301 W Warrior Trl Grand Prairie TX 75052-5718

CRAIG, ROBERT GEORGE, dental science educator; b. Charlevoix, Mich., Sept. 8, 1923; s. Harry Allen and Marion Ione (Swinton) C.; m. Luella Georgine Dean, Sept. 29, 1945; children: Susan Georgine, Barbara Dean, Katherine Ann. BS, U. Mich., 1944, MS, 1951, PhD in Phys. Chemistry, 1955; MD (hon.), U. Geneva, Switzerland, 1989. Rsch. chemist Linde Air Products Co., Tonawanda, N.Y., 1944-50, Texaco, Inc., Beacon, N.Y., 1954-55; rsch. assoc. U. Mich. Engring. Rsch. Inst., 1955-57; faculty dept. dental materials Sch. Dentistry, U. Mich., Ann Arbor, 1957-87, asst. prof., 1957-60, assoc. prof., 1960-64, prof., 1964-87, chmn. dept., 1969-87, prof. biologic and material sci., 1987-93, Marcus Ward prof. dentistry, 1990-93, prof. emeritus, 1993—; dir. Specialized Materials Sci. Ctr. Nat. Inst. Dental Rsch., Ann Arbor, 1989-93; exec. com. Sch. Dentistry, U. Mich., Ann Arbor, 1972-75; budget priorities com. U. Mich., Ann Arbor, 1978-81, chmn. budget priorities com., 1979-81. Sci. adv. com. Dental Rsch. Inst., U. Mich., Ann Arbor, 1980-89, chmn., 1984-89; cons. Walter Reed Army Hosp., 1969-75; assessor for Nat. Health and Med. Rsch. Coun., Commonwealth Australia; mem. adv. bd. Dental Advisor, 1984—. Co-author (with K.A. Easlick, S.I. Seger and A.L. Russell): Communicating in Dentistry, 1973; co-author: (with W.J. O'Brien, J.M. Powers) Dental Materials-Properties and Manipulation, 6th edit., 1966; co-author: (with J.M. Powers, J.C. Wataha) Dental Materials-Properties and Manipulation, 8th edit., 2004; co-author: (with J.M. Powers) Workbook for Dental Materials, 1979; contbr. articles to profl. jours.; editor (with J.M. Powers): Restorative Dental Materials, 11th edit., 2002; mem. editl. bd.: Mich. State Dental Jour., 1973—77, Oral Implantology Jour., 1988—, editl. assoc.: Jour. Oral Rehab., 1999—. Prin. investigator specialized material Scis. Rsch. Ctr. (funded by Nat. Inst. Dental Rsch. 1989-94). Rsch. grantee Nat. Inst. Dental Rsch., 1965-76, 84-94, Nat. Scis. Res. Svc. Tng., 1976-93; Rsch. fellow E.I. du Pont, 1952-53. Mem. ADA (cons. coun. on dental materials and devices 1983-95), Am. Nat. Stds. Inst. (chmn. spl. com. 1968-77, subcom. with ADA on mouth protectors and materials 1996—), Internat. Assn. Dental Rsch. (pres. dental materials group 1973-74, Wilmer Souder award in dental materials 1975), Am. Assn. Dental Schs. (chmn. biomaterials sect. 1977-79), Am. Chem. Soc. (life), Soc. Biomaterials (Clemson award for basic rsch. in biomaterials 1978, program chmn. 1983, fellow 1994, 96), Acad. Operative Dentistry (George Hollenbach Meml. prize 1991), Sigma Xi (sec. U. Mich chpt. 1978-81), Phi Kappa Phi, Phi Lambda Upsilon, Omicron Kappa Upsilon. Home: 1503 Wells St Ann Arbor MI 48104-3914 Office: U Mich Sch Dentistry 1011 N University Ave Ann Arbor MI 48109-1078

CRAIG, SUSAN LYONS, library director; b. Barksdale Air Force Base, La., Feb. 23, 1948; BA, Trinity Coll., Washington, 1971; MSLS, Fla. State U., 1976; MBA, Rosary Coll., 1989. Pub. svcs. libr. St. Mary's Coll., Moraga, Calif., 1976-79; head pub. svcs. Hood Coll., Frederick, Md., 1979-85, Dominican U. (formerly Rosary Coll.), River Forest, Ill., 1985-87; dir. libr. Aurora (Ill.) U., 1987-97; dir. libr. and acad. info. svcs. Trinity Coll. Libr., Washington, 1997—. Adj. assoc. prof Rosary Coll. Grad. Sch. Libr. and Info. Sci., 1990-97. Mem. ALA, Assn. Coll. and Rsch. Librs. (nat. adv. com., rep. Ill. chpt. 1991-95), Pvt. Acad. Librs. of Ill. (pres. 1994-96), Ill. Libr. Assn. (del. pre-White House Conf., Chgo., 1989-90), Beta Phi Mu, Phi Eta Sigma (hon.). Office: Trinity Coll Libr 125 Michigan Ave NE Washington DC 20017-1091

CRAIG, VIKI PETTIJOHN, English and Spanish languages educator; b. Ft. Worth, Nov. 1, 1947; d. James Newton Jr. and Annie Marie (Spivey) Spencer; m. Carl H. Pettijohn, Feb. 14, 1969 (div. Dec. 1987); m. Richard L. Craig, Apr. 19, 1997 (dec. 2002). BA in English, Tex. Wesleyan U., 1969; MAT in English, Jacksonville U., 1972; PhD in 20th Century Brit. and Am. Lit., Fla. State U., 1994. Tchr. O.D. Wyatt High Sch., Ft. Worth, 1969-70; tchr. English, Spanish Virginia Beach (Va.) Jr. High Sch., 1972-77, Englewood High Sch., Jacksonville, Fla., 1977-84; teaching asst. Fla. State U., Tallahassee, 1985-89, instr. English, 1989-90; instr. English and Spanish Southwestern Okla. State U., Weatherford, 1990-94, asst. prof., 1994-98, assoc. prof., 1999—. Dir. freshman English, 1995-96; presenter in field. Contbr. papers to pubs. Trustee Okla. Found. for Humanities, 1997—; mem. exec. bd. Okla. Humanities Coun., 1998—, vice chair, sec.; pub. outreach task force Nebr. Consortium Regl. Humanities Ctr.. Okla. Found. Humanities grantee, 1991, Okla. Regents grantee, 1992, 93, 98, NEH grantee, 2000; Chautauqua scholar, 1997; listed in Nat. Chautauqua Tour Roster. Mem. AAUW, MLA, South Ctrl. Modern Lang. Assn., Pop Culture Assn., Western Lit. Assn. Independent. Presbyterian. Avocations: acting, vocal music, cooking, writing, cats. Office: Southwestern Okla State U Lang Arts Dept Weatherford OK 73096 Home: 1316 Linwood St Weatherford OK 73096-2416

CRAIN, JOHN KIP, school system administrator; b. Urbana, Ohio, June 14, 1956; s. William Frederick and Patricia Ann (Bumgardner) C.; m. Rebecca Ann Ireland, July 11, 1980; children: Amanda Ann, Tiffany Kay, Kelly Jo. BS in Edn. summa cum laude, Ohio State U., 1985, MA, 1987; postgrad., Bowling Green State U., 1992—. Cert. tchr., supr. dir., prin., asst. supt., supt., Ohio. Drafter, office mgr. Crain Bldgs., Mechanicsburg, Ohio, 1974-82; tchr. drafting Springfield (Ohio)-Clark County Joint Vocat. Sch., 1982-86; supr. Eastland Vocat. Schs., Groveport, Ohio, 1986-91; dir. Oregon (Ohio) City Schs., 1991—. Bd. dirs. Ohio Indsl. Tng. Program, Toledo; co-chair skill olympics Ohio Vocat./Indsl. Clubs Am., Columbus, 1987-89; presenter in field. Author and editor catalog Eastland Vocat. Schs.,

1987. Vol. St. Charles Hosp. Emergency Rm., 1991—; Ohio dist. chair Young Children Priority One, 2002-2003; bd. dirs. Ea. Comty. YMCA, Toledo, 1992-94. Pres.'s sr. scholar Ohio State U., 1984. Mem. Assn. Career Tech. Edn. (life), Ohio Career Tech. Adminstrs. (exec. bd. 1996-99, pres. 1999-2000), Ohio Assn. Career-Tech. Educators (exec. bd. 2000-2001, adminstrv. divsn. pres. 2000-2001), Ohio Assn. Secondary Sch. Adminstrs., Bay Area Jr. C. of C. (state dir. 1991-94), Oregon Area C. of C., Kiwanis (bd. dirs. 1991-95, pres. 1995-96, 98-99, East Toledo chpt., Disting. Svc. award 1996, Divsn. 1N lt. gov. 2001—), Ohio Vocat. Indsl. Club Am. (regional advisor 1984-86, asst. dir. summer leadership camp 1985-86, chmn. state skill olympics 1986-87, author and editor program guidelines 1985, local advisor notebook 1986), Phi Delta Kappa, Pi Lambda Theta, Omicron Tau Theta. United Methodist. Home: 2036 Coe Ct Perrysburg OH 43551-5600 Office: Oregon City Schs 5721 Seaman St Oregon OH 43616-2631

CRAIN, MARY ANN, elementary school educator; b. Dallas, Tex, Sept. 5, 1951; d. Robert Lee and Mary Ann (T.) Crain. MusB education, Fla. State U., 1973; MusM, Ohio State U., 1974; EdS, U. Ga., 1998. Cert. Ga. Profl. Std. Commn., Tchg. T-6, Music P-12, Early Childhood P-5, Mid. Grades 4-8, Ednl. Leadership P-12 Univ. Ga., 2001. First clarinet Vienna Kursalon Orch., Vienna, 1975—77; band dir. Sch. Bd. of Broward County, Ft. Lauderdale, Fla., 1977—78; teller Fla. Coast Bank, Coral Springs, Fla., 1978—79; strings tchr., grades 6-7 DeKalb County Bd. of Edn., Decatur, Ga., 1979—82, band tchr., grades 6-7, 1982—86, classroom tchr., grades 4-7, 1986—96, math specialist, grades 2-5, 1996—2000, early intervention math and reading specialist, grades 2-5, 2000—02; math. specialist, grades 1-5 Bethesda Elem. Sch., Lawrenceville, Ga., 2002—. Office: Bethesda Elem Sch 525 Bethesda Sch Rd NW Lawrenceville GA 30044

CRAINE, THOMAS KNOWLTON, non-profit administrator; b. Utica, N.Y., Apr. 19, 1942; s. Donald Holmes and Marjorie (Knowlton) C.; m. Susan Lynda Moseley, Dec. 21, 1966; children: Matthew Moseley, Tish Marjorie. BA, U. Rochester, 1964; MEd, SUNY, Buffalo, 1966, EdD, 1972. Dir. architecture and planning SUNY, Buffalo, 1968-72, asst. to pres., 1972-76, clin. assoc. prof., 1975-83, asst. v.p. acad. affairs, 1976-79; exec. v.p., assoc. prof. D'Youville Coll., Buffalo, 1979-83; pres. Loretto Heights Coll., Denver, 1983-88; v.p. instl. advancement and planning Iliff Sch. Theology, Denver, 1988-98; pres./CEO YMCA Met. Denver, 1998—2002, pres. emeritus, 2002—03; dir. N. Am. Urban Group of YMCA, 2003—. Evaluator North Cen. Assn. Instns. Higher Edn., 1984—. Assn. Theol. Schs., 1993—; cons. in strategic planning, bd. devel., fund raising. Mailing: YMCA of the USA 101 N Wacker Dr Chicago IL 60606 E-mail: tom.craine@ymca.net.

CRALEY, CAROL RUTH, art educator, academic administrator; b. Phila., Nov. 28, 1949; d. Amos B. and Ruth L. (Ehrig) C. BS, Pa. State U., 1972, MEd, 1975, prin. cert., 1993; postgrad. studies, Lehigh U., U. Mass., Dartmouth, 1990. Cert. tchr., elem. and secondary prin., Pa. Art tchr. Bensalem (Pa.) Twp. Sch. Dist., 1972-98, internal facilitator strategic planning, 1995—, visual art coord., 1990-94; art workshop and activities leader Activities Therapy Dept. Inst. of Pa. Hosp., Phila., 1986-87; curriculum coord. Sch. Dist. Haverford (Pa.) Twp., 1998—. Cons., project leader Bucks County Schs., Doylestown, Pa., 1989-90, 92; v.p. arts edn. trust 1991—, visual art curriculum counsel, 1989-94. Bucks County Commr. Women's Adv. Coun., 1989-91, workshop leader adv. coun. for women, 1990-93; workshop leader Friends Gen. Conf., Boone, N.C., 1991. Recipient Artist in Edn. grant Pa. Coun. Arts, Harrisburg, 1985; George Bartol Arts in Edn. fellowship honoree, 1993, The Nat. Faculty Acad. fellowship, 1994. Mem. ACSD, NEA, Pa. Art Edn. Assn. (Outstanding Art Educator in Pa. 1983, bd. dirs, 1984-87, workshop leader 1983, 87, 91), Nat. Art Edn. Assn. (workshop leader 1981, 89-93), Pa. State Edn. Assn., Robert K. Greenleaf Ctr., Pi Lambda Theta (membership chair). Avocation: photography. Office: Haverford Middle Sch 1701 Darby Rd Havertown PA 19083-3797 Home: 121 Charles Ave Brookhaven PA 19015-2704

CRAMER, CAROLYN MARIE, special education educator; b. Ilion, N.Y., Feb. 5, 1951; d. Lawrence M. and Catherine M. (Cesario) Pumilio; m. Mark C. Cramer, Aug. 25, 1973; children: Caira C., Andrew M., Audra E. BS in Spl. Edn., BS in Elem. Edn., SUNY, Geneseo, 1973; MS in Edn., SUNY, Cortland, 1978. Tchr. spl. edn. Bd. Coop. Ednl. Svcs., Verona, N.Y., 1973—. Team leader Excellence & Accountability Program, Sherrill, 1988-92; cons. in field. Tch. religious edn. St. Helena's Ch., Sherrill, N.Y., 1980—, parish coun. mem., 1991—; parent mem. Fgn. Lang. Com. Vernon-Verona Sherrill Sch. Dist., 1992; pub. rels. com. mem. Madison County Spl. Olympics, 1985-88. Recipient Excellence in Teaching award Madison-Oneida Bd. Coop. Ednl. Svcs., 1991. Mem. Bus. & Profl. Women's Orgn. (corr. sec. 1979-81), Parten-Tchr.-Student Orgn., Women of Rotary. Roman Catholic. Avocations: travel, gardening, cooking. Home: 405 Primo Ave Sherrill NY 13461-1202

CRAMER, JANIS R. educational art specialist, artist; b. Tiffin, Ohio, Oct. 26, 1963; d. Walter Cletus and Regina Marie (Hartzell) Beat; m. Thomas A. Cramer, Oct. 30, 1987; children: Nicholas David. BS in Art Edn., Bowling Green State U., 1986. Cert. tchr., Mich., Ohio. Freelance artist, Battle Creek, Mich., 1986—; gallery mgr. Decor Corp., Kalamazoo, 1987-90; art specialist Crestline (Ohio) Exempted Village Schs., 1986-87, Art Ctr. Battle Creek, 1988—, Battle Creek Pub. Schs., 1990—, mem. sch. improvement core team, 1991—; mem. dist. sch. improvement team, 1994-97; team leader Battle Creek Pub. Schs., 1996—. Seminar coord. W.K. Kellogg Corp., Battle Creek, 1991; participant Koyo Corp. Japanese Tchr. Exch., 1995; mentor Student Expo, 1995, 97. One-woman shows include Sam & Diane's (photography, hon. mention), 1990, B.C. Focus Photography, 1990, Pen Dragon's Calligraphy Show, Kalamazoo, 1991, Mich. Artists Competition, Battle Creek Art Ctr., 1993; student artwork published in book, Peace Ribbon, 1985. Active Battle Creek Hist. Soc., 1992; mem. Battle Creek Hist. Commn., 1996-97; vol. Food Bank South Ctrl. Mich., 1990—; founding, fundraiser mem. Empty Bowls. Recipient Gallery Art Video Disc, Nat. Gallery Art, 1993; W.K. Kellogg expert-in-residence program grantee, 1995. Mem. Nat. Art Edn. (Mich. Art Edn. Assn. region 4 liaison), Mich. Art Edn. Assn., Mich. Alliance for Arts, United Arts Coun. Calhoun County (grantee 1991, 92, 94-97), Leila Arboretum Soc. Roman Catholic. Home: 24 Garrison Ave Battle Creek MI 49017-4730

CRAMER, PHEBE, psychologist; b. San Francisco, Dec. 30, 1935; children: Mara, Julia. BA, U. Calif., Berkeley, 1957; PhD, NYU, 1962. Clin. psychologist Malmonides Hosp., Bklyn., 1962-63; asst. prof. Psychology Barnard Coll., N.Y.C., 1963-65; vis. asst. prof. Psychology U. Calif., Berkeley, 1965-70; assoc. prof. Psychology Williams Coll., Williamstown, Mass., 1970-73, prof. Psychology, 1973—. Pvt. practice in clin. psychology, Williamstown, 1970—; chief psychologist Berkshire Mental Health Ctr., Pittsfield, Mass., 1978-86. Author: (books) Word Association, 1968, Understanding Intellectual Development, 1972, The Development of Defense Mechanisms, 1991, Story-telling, Narrative, and the Thematic Apperception Test, 1996; mem. editl. bd. Jour. of Personality, 1987-96, assoc. editor, 1991-96; mem. editl. bd. Jour. of Personality Assessment, 1989—, European Jour. Personality, 2000—, Jour. Rsch. Personality, 2003—. Judge U.S. Figure Skating Assn., 1989—. Mem.: APA, Soc. Personality and Social Psychology, Soc. for Personality Assessment. Office: Williams Coll Dept Psychology Bronfman Sci Ctr Williamstown MA 01267 Home: 20 Forest Rd Williamstown MA 01267-2029 E-mail: phebe.cramer@williams.edu.

CRAMER, ROXANNE HERRICK, retired gifted and talented education educator; b. Albion, Mich., Apr. 24; d. Donald F. and Kathryn L. (Beery) Herrick; m. James Loveday Hofford, Jan. 29, 1955 (div.); children: William Herrick, Dana Webster, Paul Christopher; m. Harold Leslie Cramer, Apr. 20, 1967. Student, U. Mich., 1952-55; BA, U. Toledo, 1956; EdM, Harvard U., 1967; EdD, Va. Poly. Inst. and State U., 1990. Tchr. Wayland (Mass.) Pub. Schs., 1966-70, Fairfax County (Va.) Pub. Schs., 1970—; tchr./team leader Gifted and Talented program, 1975—; coordinating instr. Trinity Coll., Washington, 1978; nat. coord. gifted children programs Am. Mensa, Ltd., 1981-84; ret. Editor newletter Va. Assn. for the Edn. of Gifted, 1989-90; contbr. articles to profl. jours. Mem. NEA, Nat. Assn. Gifted Children, Fairfax County Assn. for the Gifted, Coalition for Advancement Gifted Edn. (bd. dirs. 1982-84), World Coun. Gifted and Talented Children, Intertel Found., Inc. (bd. dirs. 1986—), chmn. Hollingworth award com. 1984—, Fairfax County Assn. Gifted, Nat. Assn. Gifted Children, Va. Edn. Assn., Fairfax Edn. Assn., Mensa, Harvard Club, Phi Delta Kappa. Home: 4300 Sideburn Rd Fairfax VA 22030-3507 Office: Louise Archer Gifted Ctr 324 Nutley St NW Vienna VA 22180-4213

CRAMER, STANLEY HOWARD, psychology educator, author; b. NYC, Oct. 1, 1933; s. Louis and Sophie (Zimmerman) C.; m. Rosalind Faber, Nov. 26, 1959; children: Elizabeth, Lauren, Matthew. BA, U. Mass., 1955; MA, SUNY, Albany, 1957; EdD, Columbia U., 1963. Prof. counseling psychology SUNY at Buffalo, Amherst, 1965-2000. Author: (with E.L. Herr) Critical Issues in the Helping Professions, 1987, Career Guidance and Counseling Through the Lifespan, 1972, 5th edit., 1996, (with J.C. Hansen and R.H. Rossberg) Counseling: Theory and Process, 1994. Home: 1676 Starling Dr Sarasota FL 34231

CRAMTON, ROGER CONANT, law educator, lawyer; b. Pittsfield, Mass., May 18, 1929; s. Edward Allen and Dorothy Stewart (Conant) C.; m. Harriet Cutter Haseltine, June 29, 1952; children: Ann, Charles, Peter, Cutter. AB, Harvard U., 1950; JD, U. Chgo., 1955; LLD, Nova U., 1980; MA (hon.), Oxford U., 1987. Bar: Vt. 1956, Mich. 1964, N.Y. State 1979. Law clk. to Hon. S.R. Waterman U.S. Ct. of Appeals (2d cir.), 1955-56; law clk. to assoc. justice Harold H. Burton U.S. Supreme Ct., 1956-57; asst. prof. U. Chgo., 1957-61; assoc. prof. U. Mich. Law Sch., 1961-64, prof., 1964-70; chmn. Adminstrv. Conf. of U.S., 1970-72; asst. atty. gen. Justice Dept., 1972-73; dean Cornell U. Law Sch., Ithaca, N.Y., 1973-80, Robert S. Stevens prof. emeritus, 1982—. Mem. U.S. Commn. on Revision Fed. Ct. Appellate Sys., 1973-75; bd. dirs. U.S. Legal Svcs. Corp., 1975-79, chmn. bd., 1975-78; mem. U.S. Commn. on Jud. Discipline and Removal, 1991-93. Co-author: Conflict of Laws, 5th rev. edition, 1993, Law and Ethics of Lawyering, 3d rev. edit., 1999; editor Jour. Legal Edn., 1981-87; contbr. articles to profl. jours. Guggenheim fellow, 1987-88; recipient Rsch. award Am. Bar Found., 2000. Mem. ABA, Am. Law Inst. (council mem.), Assn. Am. Law Schs. (pres. 1985), Am. Acad. Arts and Scis., Order of Coif, Phi Beta Kappa. Congregationalist. Home: 49 Highgate Cir Ithaca NY 14850-1486 Office: Cornell Law Sch Myron Taylor Hall Ithaca NY 14853-4901

CRANDALL, KEITH ALAN, science educator; b. Oceanside, Calif., Apr. 29, 1965; AB, Kalamazoo Coll., 1987; AM, PhD, Washington U., St. Louis, 1993. Alfred P. Sloan postdoctoral fellow U. Tex., Austin, 1993-96; asst. prof. Brigham Young U., Provo, Utah, 1996—2002, assoc. prof., 2002—. Recipient Alfred P. Sloan Young Investigator award, 1996, James A. Shannon NIH Dir.'s award, 1997, Burrough Wellcome Fund Rsch. Travel award, 2000; Fulbright scholar, 2000; Young investigator Am. Soc. Naturalists, 1994; NSF fellow, 1993. Mem. Internat. Assn. Astacologists (sec. 1998—). Office: Brigham Young U 675 Widtsoe Provo UT 84602-5255 Fax: 801-422-0090. E-mail: keith_crandall@buy.edu.

CRANDELL, DEBORAH LYNNE KASKINEN, art educator; b. Manistee, Mich., Sept. 26, 1955; d. Norman Ferdinand and Martha Agnes (Harju) Kaskinen; m. Wayne Buell Crandell, May 23, 1981; children: Kimberley Aliina, Lauren Elizabeth. BFA, BS, Ctrl. Mich. U., 1978, MA, 1987. Cert. tchr., Mich. Tchr. visual arts Harbor Springs (Mich.) Com. Edn., 1976-77; tchr. elem. art Kaleva Norman Dickson Schs., Brethren, Mich., 1978-82, tchr. lang. arts, 1983-88, tchr. high sch. art, 1989—. Artist, owner, operator Artworks affiliate Village Gallery, Traverse City, Mich., 1992-93; coach, coord. Odyssey of the Mind program Traverse City Schs., 1992-93; coach, coord. Odyssey of the Mind program Kaleva Norman Dickson Schs., 1984—, advisor drama club, 1985-87, advisor art club, 1988—. Exhibited in group shows at Finnish Am. Art, Duluth, Minn., 1992, Electronic Gallery, Dearborn, Mich., 1992, No. Ill. U., DeKalb, 1994. Instr. Very Spl. Arts, Manistee, 1979-81; co-instr. pilot program Walk About, 1996—; mem. Traverse City Arts Coun. Recipient Art Educator Robert Rauschenberg Power of Art award. Mem. NEA, Nat. Art Edn. Assn., Northwoods League of Creative Artists, Inland Seas Edn. Assn., Traverse City Arts Coun. Lutheran. Avocations: music, dancing, theater. Home: 5980 Dover Ln Traverse City MI 49684-8012 Office: Kaleva Norman Dickson Schs 4350 Highbridge Rd Brethren MI 49619-9605

CRANE, BEVERLEY DORIS, special education educator; b. Oak Park, Ill., Oct. 19, 1954; d. Robert Earl and Barbara Jule (Lindberg) C. AAS, William Rainey Harper Coll., 1974; BS, No. Ill. U., 1978. Cert. tchr., Ill. Tchr. Early Learners Nursery Sch., Hoffman Estates, Ill., 1974-75; asst. tchr. spl. edn. Hoffman Estates High Sch., 1978—; instr. vocal music, dance Elgin (Ill.) C.C., 1991—. Child care tchr. NOW Orgn., Chgo., 1985-86; sponsor Dance Club, 1980-81. Choreographer musical prodns. Hoffman Estates High Sch., 1981-92, asst. dir. dance troup Variety Show, 1984-91; choreographer Elgin Community Theater, 1990—. Republican. Methodist. Avocations: collecting dolls, church choir. Home: 660 Ashland St Hoffman Estates IL 60194-1944 Office: Hoffman Estates High Sch 1100 W Higgins Rd Hoffman Estates IL 60195-3050

CRANE, CHARLOTTE, law educator; b. Hanover, N.H., Aug. 30, 1951; d. Henry D. and Emily (Townsend) C.; m. Eric R. Fox, July 5, 1975; children: Hillary, Teresa. AB, Harvard U., 1973; JD, U. Mich., 1976. Bar: N.H. 1976, Ill. 1978. Law clk. to presiding judge U.S. Ct. Appeals (6th cir.), Detroit, 1976-77; law clk. to presiding justice U.S. Supreme Ct., Washington, 1977-78; assoc. Hopkins & Sutter, Chgo., 1978-82; asst. prof. Northwestern U., Chgo., 1982-86, assoc. prof., 1986-90, prof., 1990—. Contbr. articles to profl. jours. Mem. U.S. Women's Nat. Crew Team, 1976. Mem. ABA, Chgo. Tax Forum. Office: Northwestern U Sch Law 357 E Chicago Ave Chicago IL 60611-3059

CRANG, RICHARD FRANCIS EARL, plant and cell biologist, research center administrator; b. Clinton, Ill., Dec. 2, 1936; s. Richard Francis and Clara Esther (Cummins) Crang; m. Linda L. Crang, Aug. 10, 1958 (div.). BS, Eastern Ill. U., 1958; MS, U. S.D., 1962; PhD, U. Iowa, 1965. Asst. prof. biology Wittenberg U., 1965-69; assoc. prof. biol. sci. Bowling Green State U., 1969-74, prof., 1974-80; prof. plant biology U. Ill., Urbana-Champaign, 1980—2002, assoc. head dept. plant biology, 1995-97, faculty fellow in acad. adminstrn., 1997-99, dir. Ctr. Elec. Microsci., 1980-92, prof. emeritus, 2002—. Adj. prof. anatomy Med. Coll. Ohio, 1974—80; summer rsch. prof. Lehman Coll., CUNY, Bronx, vis. prof. biol. sci., 1999—2003; vis. scientist in botany Cambridge U., England, 1978—79, Komarov Bot. Inst., Warsaw U., Poland, 1993; rschr., collaborator in fungal adhesion Kaohsiung Med. Coll., Taiwan, China, 1988—90; lectr., China, 1990. Author: (with A. Vassilyev) CD-ROM Text on Plant Anatomy, 2003; rschr., contbr. numerous publs. in field of air pollution effects on plant, fungal, and lichen ultrastructure, 1967—; early developer asynchronous learning techs. by means of networked computers on World-Wide Web, 1995—. Mem. Statewide Democratic Support Group, Ill. Recipient Outstanding Faculty Rsch. Recognition awards Bowling Green State U., 1973, 75; grantee Paint Rsch. Inst., 1976-83, NSF, 1981-83, EPA, 1984-86, USDA, 1986-89, Internat. Plant and Pollution Lab., 1993-98; lifetime assoc. fellow Clare Hall, Cambridge, Eng. Mem. AAAS, Bot. Soc. Am., Internat. Soc. Environ. Botanists (advisor, life mem., inaugurated 1st internat. meeting, Lucknow, India, 1996), Microscopy Soc. Am. (nat. chmn. cert. bd. 1982-89, dir. USA local affiliates 1990-93, Disting. Svc. award 1994, Cecil Hall award for outstanding rsch. in biology with analytical microscopy 1994), Sigma Xi. Mem. Christian Ch. (Disciples Of Christ). Home: 1095 Baytowne Dr # 25 Champaign IL 61822-7971 Office: U Ill Plant Biology 505 S Goodwin Ave 665 Morrill Hall Urbana IL 61801-3707 E-mail: r-crang@life.uiuc.edu.

CRANSTON, JOHN WELCH, historian, educator; b. Utica, N.Y., Dec. 21, 1931; s. Earl and Mildred (Welch) C. BA, Pomona Coll., 1953; MA, Columbia U., 1964; PhD, U. Wis., 1970. Asst. prof. history West Tex. State U., 1970-74, U. Mo., Kansas City, 1974, Rust Coll., Holly Springs, Miss., 1974-80, assoc. prof., 1980-83; historian U.S. Army Armor Ctr., Ft. Knox, Ky., 1983-95; ret., 1995. Adj. prof. history and govt. Elizabethtown C.C., Ft. Knox, 1988-2002. Contbr. history articles to profl. lit. With U.S. Army, 1953-55. NEH fellow, summers 1976, 81. Mem. Am. Hist. Assn., Orgn. Am. Historians. Democrat. Episcopalian. Home: 900 E Harrison Ave Apt D-61 Pomona CA 91767

CRAPOL, EDWARD P. history educator; b. Buffalo, N.Y., Sept. 29, 1936; s. Paul H. and Emmi H. (klinger) C.; m. Jeanne Zeidler, Aug. 1, 1973; children: Heidi, Jennifer, Paul, Andrew. BA, SUNY, Buffalo, 1960; MS, Univ. Wis., 1964, PhD, 1968. Tchr. Amherst Ctrl. Jr. High Sch., Amherst, N.Y., 1961-63; instr. history Wis. State Univ., Eau Claire, Wis., 1966-67; asst. prof. history Coll. William and Mary, Williamsburg, Va., 1967-71, assoc. prof. history, 1971-77; exchange prof. history Univ. Exeter, Exeter, England, 1976-77; prof. history dept. Coll. William and Mary, Williamsburg, Va., 1978—, chmn. history dept., 1981-84, acting chmn. history dept., 1986-87; chancellor prof. history, 1994-99; William E. Pullen prof. Am. history, 1999—. Vis. faculty Utah State U., summer, 1972; reviewer grant proposals NEH, 1983-95; lectr. in field. Author: James G. Blaine: Architect of Empire, 1999; editor: Women and American Foreign Policy: Lobbyists, Critics, and Insiders, 1987, 1992, America for Americans: Economic Nationalism and Anglophobia in the Late Nineteenth Century, 1973; reviewer manuscripts for Diplomatic History, Journal of the Early Republic, Alfred A. Knopf, Scholary Recources, Greenwood Press, Kent State Univ. Press, D.C. Health, Univ. N.C. Press. Va. Found. for Humanities and Pub. Policy grant, 1983, NEH grant, 1984, 1986, Internat. Studies Curriculum Devel. grant Coll of William and Mary, 1987; Univ. Humanities fellow Coll. William and Mary, 1988; Thomas A. Graves Jr. award for Sustained Excellence in Teaching William and Mary Coll., 1991, Thomas Jefferson award Coll. William and Mary, 1992. Mem. Soc. Historians Am. Fgn. Rels., Orgn. Am. Historians, Am. Hist. Assn., Soc. Historians Early Am. Republic. Home: 148 Mimosa Dr Williamsburg VA 23185-4004

CRAVEN, JAMES MICHAEL, economist, educator; b. Seattle, Mar. 10, 1946; s. Homer Henry and Mary Kathleen Craven; 1 child, Christina Kathleen Florindo-Craven. Student, U. Minn., 1966-68; BA in Sociology, BA in Econs., U. Manitoba, Winnipeg, Can., 1971, MA in Econs., 1974. Lic. pilot; cert. ground instr. Instr. econ. and bus. Red River C.C., Winnipeg, 1974-76; lectr. rsch. methods of stats. U. Manitoba, Winnipeg, 1977-78; instr. econ. and bus. Big Bend C.C., Moses Lake, Wash., 1980-81; planning analyst Govt. P.R., San Juan, 1984; prof. econs. and bus. Interam. U. P.R., Bayamon, 1984-85; instr. econs., lectr. history Green River C.C., Auburn, Wash., 1988-92; prof. dept. chair econs. Clark Coll., Vancouver, Wash., 1992—. Vis. prof. St. Berchman's U., Kerala, India, 1981, 83, 86, 91; instr. econs. Bellevue (Wash.) C.C., 1988-92; cons. Bellevue, 1988—, Irwin Pubs., 1995—. Inventor in field; contbr, articles to profl. jours. Platform com. mem. Wash. State Dem., Seattle, 1992; cons. Lowry for Gov. Campaign, Seattle, 1992; mem. (assoc.) Dem. Party Nat. Com., 1994-99; mem. Nat. Steering Com. for Re-election of Pres. Clinton, 1995-96; mem. Pres.'s Second Term Com., 1996-99; tribunal judge Inter-Tribal Tribunal on Residential Schs. in Can., Vancouver, 1998; mem. Blackfoot Nation. With U.S. Army, 1963-66. Recipient pilot wings FAA, 1988-92; Govt. Can. fellow, 1973-74. Mem. Assn. Northwest Econ. Educators, Wash. Edn. Assn., Assn. Nat. Security Alumni, Blackfoot Confederacy. Syrian Orthodox. Avocations: flying, languages, tennis, hiking. Home: 904 NE Minnehaha St Apt C9 Vancouver WA 98665-8732 Office: Clark Coll Dept Econs 1800 E Mcloughlin Blvd Vancouver WA 98663-3598 E-mail: jcraven@clark.edu., blkfoot5@earthlink.net.

CRAVEN, ROBERTA JILL, literature and film educator; b. White Plains, N.Y., Feb. 4, 1962; d. Robert James and Norma Eleanor (Page) Craven; m. Keith M. Stinchcomb, Sept. 16, 2000; 1 child, Sara Page Stinchcomb. BS in Math., U. N.C., 1984, PhD in Comparative Lit., 1999. Account systems engr. IBM Nat. Fed. Mktg., Bethesda, Md., 1984-86, account mktg. rep., 1986-89; telecomm. mktg. support rep. IBM, Research Triangle Park, N.C., 1990; instr. U. N.C., Chapel Hill, 1990-99; asst. prof. film Millersville U. of Pa., 1999—, asst. chair dept. English, 2003—. T.J. Watson Nat. Merit scholar IBM, Armonk, N.Y., 1980, Hon. Regents scholar N.Y. Bd. Regents, 1980, Frank Porter Graham Grad. Hon. Soc., 1993, Dissertation fellow U. N.C., 1997, Sr. fellow, 1998; grantee Commn. on Cultural Diversity, 2002; recipient Women's Issue Endowment award, 2002, Acad. Climate and Cultural Enrichment award, 2002. Mem. MLA, Southern Comparative Lit. Assn., Soc. Cinema & Media Studies, Phi Beta Kappa, Phi Eta Sigma. Avocations: skiing, film, writing. Office: Dept English Chryst Hall PO Box 1002 Millersville U Pa Millersville PA 17551-0302

CRAWFORD, CONNIE ALLENE, elementary education educator; b. Tuscaloosa, Ala., Nov. 5, 1952; d. Allen Cornelius and Elizabeth (Jackson) Wilkerson; m. William Norris Crawford, July 2, 1976; children: William Norris Jr., Meredith Lynn. BS in Elem. Edn., Livingston U., 1975; MA in Elem. Edn., Reading Concentration, U. Ala., 1978. Cert. tchr., Ala. Tchr. Greensboro (Ala.) Pub. Sch. - East, 1975-78, Greensboro Pub. Sch. - West, 1978—. Grantee Livingston U., 1973, 74. Home: RR 1 Box 730 Greensboro AL 36744-9150

CRAWFORD, GENIE ZORN, elementary school educator; b. Annapolis, Md., May 1, 1945; d. Marion Lee and Sidney Ellen (Simpson) Zorn; m. Quincy M. Crawford, Jan. 28, 1967; children: Monty, Sandy, Steve. BS, Frostburg State Coll., 1967; postgrad., Balt. Coll. Cert. tchr., Md. Tchr. St. James' Acad., Monkton, Md., 1980-86, Hawthorne Elem. Sch., Middle River, Md., 1986-90, Oakleigh Elem. Sch., Parkville, Md., 1990-94, Lutherville (Md.) Elem. Sch., 1994—. Spkr. Somirac Sci., Balt., 1992, Md. Coun. Tchrs. Math. Conf., Balt., 1994, Eisenhower Conf., Balt., 1994. Mem. Nat. Coun. Tchrs. Math. (Outstanding Educator of Yr. Md. chpt. 1992), Tchrs. Assn. Baltimore County. Avocation: painting. Home: 1166 Clarendon Dr Annapolis MD 21403-4369

CRAWFORD, KATHRINE NELSON, special education educator; b. Springfield, Mass., June 5, 1954; d. Merrill William and Elizabeth (Hanor) Nelson; m. Michael David Crawford, June 19, 1993; 1 child, Cody M. BS in Phys. Edn. cum laude, U. N.C., Greensboro, 1979. Cert. tchr. phys. edn. K-12, learning disabled K-12, emotionally mentally handicapped K-12, Behavior emotionally handicapped K-12, N.C. Day care dir. Assn. for Retarded Citizens and United Way, Greensboro, 1979-82; behavioral self-contained instr. Guilford County Schs., Greensboro, 1982-88, EMH self-contained instr., 1988—, spl. olympic coach, 1988—. Advisor Action Mag., Scholastic, Inc., N.Y.C., 1999-2002. United Way campaign coord. Guilford County Schs., 1994-98. Recipient Cert. of Recognition for outstanding svc. BEH/Willie M., Guilford County Schs., 1987; named Tchr. of Yr., Eastern Guilford Mid. Sch., 2001-02; Guilford County Schs. grantee, 1990, 96. Mem. Assn. for Retarded Citizens of Greensboro. Republican. Lutheran. Avocations: bowling, camping, cross-stitch, folk guitar, fishing. Home: 3257 Saw Mill Dr Elon NC 27244-9576 Office: Eastern Guilford Middle Sch 435 Peeden Dr Gibsonville NC 27249-8724 E-mail: crawfok@guilford.k12.nc.us.

CRAWFORD, MURIEL LAURA, lawyer, author, educator; d. Mason Leland and Pauline Marie (DesIlets) Henderson; m. Barrett Matson Crawford, May 10, 1959; children: Laura Joanne, Janet Muriel, Barbara Elizabeth. BA with honors, U. Ill., 1973; JD with honors, Ill. Inst. Tech., 1977; cert. employee benefit splst., U. Pa., 1989. Bar: Ill. 1977, Calif. 1991, U.S. Dist. Ct. (no. dist.) Ill. 1977, U.S. Dist. Ct. (no. dist.) Calif. 1991, U.S. Ct. Appeals (7th cir.) 1977, U.S. Ct. Appeals (9th cir.) 1991; CLU; chartered fin. cons. Atty. Washington Nat. Ins. Co., Evanston, Ill., 1977-80; sr. atty., 1980-81; asst. counsel, 1982-83; asst. gen. counsel, 1984-87; assoc. gen. counsel, sec., 1987-89; cons. employee benefit splst., 1989-91; assoc. Hancock, Rothert & Bushoft, San Francisco, 1991-92. Author: (with Beadles) Law and the Life Insurance Contract, 1989, (sole author) 7th edit., 1994, Life and Health Insurance Law, 8th edit., 1998; co-author: Legal Aspects of AIDS, 1990; contbr. articles to profl. jours. Recipient Am. Jurisprudence award Lawyer's Coop. Pub. Co., 1975, 2nd prize Internat. LeTourneau Student Med.-Legal Article Contest, 1976, LOMA FLMI Ins. Edn. award, 1999. Fellow Life Mgmt. Inst.; mem. Ill. Inst. Tech./Chgo.-Kent Alumni Assn. (bd. dirs. 1983-89, Bar and Gavel Soc. award 1977). Democrat.

CRAWFORD, PEGGY SMITH, design educator; b. Christiansburg, Va., Dec. 27, 1943; d. Andrew Morgan Smith and Margie Smith (Hill) Blakeslee; m. John Linnie Crawford, Jan. 12, 1963 (div. May 1979); children: John Christopher, James Andrew. Sec. Draper's Meadow EGA, Blacksburg, Va., 1983-85, 1999—, 2nd v.p., 1989-90; com. mem. Smithfield Needlework Exhibit, Blacksburg, 1986-87, com. chairperson, 1987-88; pres. Blue Ridge Embroiderer's Guild, Roanoke, Va., 1989-90; regional rep. Brazilian Dimensional Embroidery Internat. Guild, Washington, 1991—, sec., 1996-97. Tchr. Nat. Embroiderer's Guild Am., Inc. seminar, Greensboro, N.C., 1991, Reynolds Homestead, Critz, Va., 1993, Nat. Embroiderer's Guild Nat. Seminar, Williamsburg, Va., 1994, Brazilian Dimensional Embroidery Internat. Guild, Inc. seminars, 1994—, Oreg., 1999. Author: Stitching the Wildflowers of Virginia., 1992. Mem. Am. Needlepoint Guild, Blue Ridge Embroiderer's Guild, Drapers' Meadow Embroiderer's Guild Am., Inc., Brazilian Dimensional Embroidery Internat. Guild. Avocations: needlework, sports, reading, hiking, music. Home: 206 Upland Rd Blacksburg VA 24060-5351 Office: Va Polytech and State U 1700 Pratt Dr Blacksburg VA 24060-6361

CRAWFORD, RONALD MERRITT, history and geography educator; b. San Diego, Apr. 21, 1949; s. Leslie Merritt and Annie Louise (Briden) C. BA in History and Geography, UCLA, 1971, MA in History, 1972. Cert. standard secondary tchr. Tchr. social scis. divsn. Anchorage C.C., 1972-87; prof. Coll. Arts and Scis. U. Alaska Anchorage, 1987—, chmn. history/geography dept., 1988—. V.p. Anchorage C.C. Campus Assembly, 1985-87; 1st v.p. Faculty Senate U. Alaska Anchorage, 1987-89, 2d v.p., 1990-91; mem. Univ. Assembly, 1988-89; mem. Bartlett lectr. com. U. Alaska Anchorage, 1987-90, audio-visual adv. bd., 1989—, promotion and tenure appeals com., 1989-90; mem. exec. bd. Alaska C.C.s Fedn. Tchrs., 1984—, Harry S. Truman scholarship com. Anchorage C.C., 1978-82; advisor Golden Key Honor Soc., 1993—, Campus Cinema Film Series, 1972—, Anchorage C.C. Student Assn., 1983-85; coord. history/geography discipline Anchorage C.C., 1979-87; columnist Anchorage Daily News, 1984-87; host Alaska Home and Gardens Program Sta. KAKM-TV, 1990. Host fund drives Sta. KAKM-TV, 1983—; guest speaker Anchorage Sch. Dist. Community Resource Ctr., 1972—, McLaughlin Youth Ctr., 1975—; advisor Friends of Libr. Film Program Loussac Libr., 1985—; presenter geography awareness programs Alaska Staff Devel. Network Summer Acad., 1990, 91, Alaska Geog. Alliance Inst., 1992, 93. Recipient Disting. Teaching Achievement award Alaska State Legislature, 1992, Disting. Teaching Achievement award Nat. Coun. Geog. Edn., 1992. Mem. Am. Fedn. Tchrs., Am. Film Inst., Nat. Coun. Geographic Edn., Alaska Geography Alliance, Assn. Pacific Coast Geographers, Univ. Film and Video Assn., Phi Alpha Theta. Avocations: travel, movie history, hiking, photography, videography. Home: PO Box 670572 Chugiak AK 99567-0572 Office: U Alaska Dept History & Geography 3211 Providence Dr Anchorage AK 99508-4614

CRAWFORD, SHEILA JANE, elementary education librarian, reading consultant; b. Beckley, W.Va., Mar. 1, 1943; d. Roger and Ruth (Ashworth) Crawford; m. Lloyd E. Johnston, June 4, 1966 (dec.); 1 child, Jacqueline; m. Troy Thomason, June 28, 2000. BA, Tenn. Tech. U., 1963; MA in Christian Edn., Seabury Western Theol. Sem., 1965; MS in Curriculum and Instrn., U. Tenn., Martin, 1989; EdD in Instrn. and Curriculum Leadership, U. Memphis, 1994; postgrad., San Jose State U., U. Calif., Berkeley, U. Utah, Tex. Woman's U. Cert. tchr. Tenn. Dir. Christian edn. St. Luke's Episcopal Ch., Rochester, Minn., 1965-66; elem. tchr. Santa Catalina Sch. Girls, 1967-69, Rowland-Hall St. Mark's Sch., Salt Lake City, 1968-69, Union City (Tenn.) Christian Sch., 1984-87; libr. Dept. Edn. U. Tenn. at Martin, 1987-89; rsch. asst. U. Memphis, 1989-92, adj. prof., 1996; prof., edn. dept. chair Lane Coll., Jackson, Tenn., 1992-94; reading tchr., drama club sponsor Ashland (Miss.) Mid. Sch., 1994-95; workshop presenter Jackson, Tenn., 1989-96; ednl. cons. Delta Faucet of Tenn. divsn. Masco Corp., Jackson, 1995—; homebound tchr. Jackson-Madison County Schs., 1996-97; instr., libr. LaGrange-Moscow (Tenn.) Sch., 1997-99; libr. Lauderdale Sch., Memphis. Mem. campus All Stars, Honda, Jackson, Tenn., 1992—93; cons. in field. Contbr. articles to profl. jours. Mem. AAUW, DAR, Nat. Libr. Assn., Ch. and Synagogue Libr. Assn., Order Eastern Star (worthy matron 1980-81), Sch. Libr. Assn., Sigma Tau Delta, Kappa Delta Pi. Anglican. Achievements include research in the effect of chess on predicting and summarizing skills. Home: 3207 Thirteen Colony Mall Apt 1 Memphis TN 38115-2972 E-mail: sheil101@cs.com.

CRAWFORD, WILLIAM ARTHUR, geologist, educator; b. Norman, Okla., Mar. 25, 1935; s. Francis Weldon and Mildred Eva (Crall) C.; m. Maria Luisa Buse, Aug. 29, 1963. BS, Kans. State U., 1957; MS, U. Kans., 1960; PhD, U. Calif., Berkeley, 1965. Cert. and registered profl. geologist. Advanced through grades to capt. USAR, 1957-68; instr. geology U. Calif., Berkeley, 1965; asst. prof. geology Bryn Mawr Coll., 1965-72, assoc. prof., 1972-81, prof., 1981-98, prof. emeritus, 1998—, dept. chmn., 1995-98. Contbr. articles to profl. jours. Fellow Geol. Soc. Am.; mem. Mineral. Soc. Am., Nat. Assn. Geology Tchrs., Phila. Geol. Soc. (pres. 1981-82), Assn. Geologists in Developing Countries, Am. Inst. Profl. Geologists, Assn. Women Geoscientists, Mineral. Assn. Can. Democrat. Episcopalian. Avocations: fishing, woodworking. Home: 131 Pennsylvania Ave Bryn Mawr PA 19010-3110 Office: Bryn Mawr Coll Geology Dept Bryn Mawr PA 19010-2899

CREAMER, GERMAN GONZALO, bank executive, educator; b. Caracas, Venezuela, Oct. 31, 1960; arrived in Ecuador, 1978; s. Claudio Creamer and Maria Del Carmen Guillen; m. Maria Consuelo Botero, June 19, 1992; children: Mateo, Carolina. BA in psychology, Cath. U. Ecuador, 1985, BA in Sociology, 1986; MA, U. Notre Dame, 1989, PhD in Econs., 1993; MSc in Fin. Engring., Columbia U., 2002. Dir. human resource dept. Constructora Elepeve, Quito, Ecuador, 1985-86; econ. advisor President of Ecuador, Quito, 1990-91; econs. program officer UN, Quito, 1992-93; assoc. prof., econs. coord. FLACSO, Quito, 1993-95; mgr. planning and econ. studies Banco del Pacifico, Guayaquil, 1996-97; prof. Catholic U, Guayaquil and Espol, 1995-97; vis. assoc. prof. fin. Bus. Sch., Tulane U., New Orleans, 1998—2002; adj. prof. bus. Tulane U., 2002—. Cons. UN, Equatorial Guinea, 1991, USAID, Quito, 1991, 94; Komex 1995, Urbana-World Bank, 2000; instr. Columbia U., 2002—. Author: Redistribution, Inflation, and Adjustment Policies, 1992; co-author: La desarticulacion del Mundo Andino, 1986, Las economias Andinas, 1993, The Ecuadorean Participation in the Andean Pact, 1996, Ecuador en la Economía Mundial, 1997, The Cost of Hospital Cholera Treatment in Ecuador, 1999, Open Regionalism, Trade, Liberalization and the Role of Small Producers, 1999; contbr. articles to profl. jours. Fulbright scholar, N.Y., 1986, Inst. for Study of World Policies scholar, N.Y., 1988, MacArthur Found. scholar, U. Notre Dame, 1990, Kellogg Inst., 1989; grantee Bd. Regents, State of La., 1999. Mem. Am. Econ. Assn., Am. Fin. Assn., Bus. Assn. of Latin Am. Studies, Am. Assn. Artificial Intelligence. Home: 150 Claremont Ave Apt 5D New York NY 10027 Office: 520 W 120th St #450 New York NY 10027 E-mail: gcreame@hotmail.com.

CREDE, CAROL ANN JOHNSON, principal; BA, Immaculate Heart Coll., 1979; MEd, Loyola Marymount U., 1989, MA in Counseling, 1993. Cert. tchr., adminstrn. svcs., pupil personnel svcs. and counseling credential, Calif. Tchr. Visitation Sch., L.A., 1972-80, prin., 1980—. Tchr. credentialing adv. bd. Loyola Marymount Univ., 1990-93; sch. adminstr. adv. bd. mem. Loyola Marymount Univ., 1993. Mem. AACD, ASCD, Am. Assn. Sch. Adminstrs., Nat. Assn. Elem. Sch. Prins., Nat. Coun. Tchrs. of Math., Nat. Cath. Edn. Assn., Am. Sch. Counselor Assn., Assn. Counselor Edn. and Supervision, Calif. Assn. Supervision and Curriculum Devel., Calif. Assn. Sch. Psychologists, Assn. Calif. Sch. Adminstrs., Westchester-L.A. C. of C. (edn. affairs com.). Office: Visitation Sch 8740 Emerson Ave Los Angeles CA 90045-3723

CREEKMORE, VERITY VEIRS, media specialist; b. Cin., May 13; d. Noble L. and Maxine (Wright) Veirs; m. Kenneth L. Creekmore, Nov. 23, 1961; 1 child, Kenneth L. Jr. BS in Edn. magna cum laude, S.C. State U., 1975; MLS, U. S.C., 1978. Cert. libr. media specialist, S.C. Media specialist John Ford High Sch., St. Matthews, S.C., 1976-77, St. John High Sch., Cameron, S.C., 1977-82, St. John Elem./Mid. Sch., Cameron, 1982-86, Sheridan Elem. Sch., Orangeburg, S.C., 1986—. Directed libr. U. S.C., Columbia, 1997—; adj. tech. instr. S.C. State Dept. Edn., 1997—. Rep. S.C. Sci. Hub. Sys. Operator Sheridan Sch. Local Area Computer Network: Trainer Laubach Literacy Program, Orangeburg, 1990—. Recipient IMAGEMAKER award SCASL, 1999. Mem. NEA, ALA, S.C. Assn. Sch. Librs., Nat. Assn. Storytelling, S.C. State Coun. Internat. Reading Assn., So. Assn. Colls. and Schs. (evaluator), S.C. Edn. Assn. (dist. rep. 1991-93, IPD rep. 1993-97), Hon. Order Ky. Cols., Order Ea. Star, Alpha Kappa Mu. Avocations: reading, church work, travel. Home: 1172 Caw Caw Hwy Saint Matthews SC 29135-8300 Office: Sheridan Elem Sch 1139 Hillsboro St NE Orangeburg SC 29115

CREGER, JOHN HOLMES, secondary school educator, writer; b. San Francisco, Oct. 10, 1951; s. William Philip and Nancy Christine (Smith) C.; m. Meilan Ho Creger, June 25, 1988; children: Rebecca, Hana. BA, U. Calif., Berkeley, 1986, cert. tchg., 1987; MA, San Francisco State U., 1997. Cert. tchr., Calif. Carpenter foreman Pat Pellilo Constrn., Concord, N.H., 1975-77, Cmty. Builders, Canterbury, N.H., 1977-79; staff writing tutor U. Calif., Berkeley, 1985-86; English and ESL tchr. Am. H.S., Fremont, Calif., 1987—; freelance writer, guitarist, 1980—. Mentor tchr., Calif. Dept. Edn., Fremont, 1993-95; presenter Universe Wired workshop series for tchrs. on making learning more personal, 1998—. Composer 6 cassette albums of original solo guitar and song lyrics; author published poetry and non-fiction. Organizer Citizens Party, 1980; fin. support, activist So. Poverty Law Ctr., 1990—; precinct leader Clinton/Dem. Campaign, 1992. Recipient James Moffett Meml. Award for Tchr. Rsch., NCTE, 2001; fellow, U. Calif., 1985—86. Mem. NEA, ASCD, Calif. Assn. for the Gifted, Nat. Coun. Tchrs. English, Calif. Assn. Tchrs. English, Calif. Tchrs. Assn., Alpha Gamma Sigma. Democrat. Jewish. Avocations: swimming, hiking, biking, writing, composing on the guitar and piano. Office: Am HS 36300 Fremont Blvd Fremont CA 94536-3511 E-mail: jcreger@jps.net.

CREGIER, DON MESICK, historian, educator, researcher, consultant; b. Schenectady, N.Y., Mar. 28, 1930; s. Harry Mesick and Marion (Shovea) C.; m. Sharon Kathleen Ellis, June 29, 1965. BA, Union Coll., 1951; MA, U. Mich., 1952; PhD, Columbia Pacific U., 1999. Instr. history U. Tenn., Knoxville, 1956-57; asst. prof. history Baker U., Baldwin City, Kans., 1958-61, Keuka Coll., Keuka Park, N.Y., 1962-64, St. John's U., Collegeville, Minn., 1964-65, St. Dunstan's U., Can., 1966-69; assoc. prof. history U.P.E.I., Charlottetown, 1969-85, prof., 1985-96, adj. prof., 1996—2002. Salvage editor, rsch. cons., 1996—. Author: Bounder from Wales: Lloyd George's Career before the First World War, 1976, Novel Exposures: Victorian Studies Featuring Contemporary Novels, 1979, Chiefs Without Indians: Asquith, Lloyd George and the Liberal Remnant (1916-1935), 1982, The Decline of the British Liberal Party: Why and How?, 1985, Freedom and Order: The Evolution of Liberalism and the Liberal Party in Great Britain Before 1868, 1988; co-author: The Rise of the Global Village, 1988; editor Quest for Edn., 1966-67; fgn. book rev. editor Can. Rev. Studies in Nationalism, 1996-98; abstracter ABC-Clio Info. Svcs., 1978—; assessor Internat. Rev. Periodical Lit., 1988-89; contbr. articles to profl. jours. Social Scis. and Humanities Rsch. Coun. Can. grantee, 1984-86; Mark Hopkins fellow, 1965-66, Can. Coun. fellow, 1972-73. Mem.: Soc. Acad. Freedom and Scholarship, Nat. Assn. Scholars, Nat. Coalition Ind. Scholars, Can. Assn. Univ. Tchrs., Am. Hist. Assn., Assn. Contemporary Historians, The Hist. Soc. N.Am. Conf. on Brit. Studies, Mark Twain Soc., Internat. Churchill Soc., Oxford Club, Pi Gamma Mu, Phi Kappa Phi, Phi Beta Kappa, Phi Sigma Kappa. Office: PO Box 1100 Montague PE Canada COA 1RO E-mail: dcregier@upei.ca.

CREGIER, SHARON ELLIS, ethologist, information skills educator; b. Malone, N.Y., May 5, 1942; d. Reginald Drew and Juanita (Webster) Ellis; m. Don M. Cregier, June, 29, 1965. BA, Keuka Coll., 1964; MA, Antioch U., 1969; PhD, Walden U., 1980; FIASH (hon.), Edinburgh U., 1981. Tchr. social studies Harrison Jr. H.S., Malone, N.Y., 1964-66; tchr. world history Charlottetown (P.E.I.) Regional H.S., 1966-70; freelance hist. rschr., 1967-73; editor The Cruiser Courier, Charlottetown, 1975-80; equine journalist and columnist, 1973—; N.Am. editor Equine Behaviour Jour., Over Darwen, England, 1983—. Lectr. libr. skills U. P.E.I., Charlottetown, 1991-95; cons. ethologist, expert witness. Author: Alleviating Surface Transit Stress on Horses, 1981, Road Transport of the Horse: An Annotated Bibliography, 1984, Farm Animal Ethology: A Guide to Sources, 1989; contbr. articles to profl. jours. Advisor Royal Can. Mounted Police Venturer Scouts, Montague, 1994—99; vol. Habitat for Humanity, 2003—. Mem.: World Farrier Assn., Assn. for Equine Sports Medicine, Animal Transp. Assn. (Animal Welfare award 2003), Animal Behaviour Soc., Internat. Soc. Applied Ethology. Avocations: archaeology, travel, C.S. Lewis studies, gardening. Office: Cheiron's Ct Valleyfield PE Canada Mailing: PO Box 1100 Montague PE Canada C0A 1R0 E-mail: scregier@pei.sympatico.ca.

CREIGHTON, JOANNE VANISH, academic administrator; b. Marinette, Wis., Feb. 21, 1942; d. William J. and Bernice Vanish; m. Thomas F. Creighton, Nov. 9, 1968; 1 child, William. BA with honors, U. Wis., 1964; MA, Harvard U., 1965; PhD, U. Mich., 1969. From instr. to prof. English Wayne State U., Detroit, 1968—85, assoc. dean liberal arts, 1983—85; dean arts and scis., prof. English U. N.C., Greensboro, 1985—90; v.p. acad. affairs, provost, prof. English Wesleyan U., Middletown, Conn., 1990—94, interim pres., 1994—95; prof. English, pres. Mt. Holyoke Coll., South Hadley, Mass., 1995—. Author: William Faulkner's Craft of Revision, 1977, Joyce Carol Oates, 1979, Margaret Dabble, 1985, Joyce Carol Oates: Novels of the Middle Years, 1992. Grantee, Am. Coun. Learned Socs. Mem.: Phi Kappa Phi, Phi Beta Kappa. Home: 45 College St South Hadley MA 01075-1403 Office: Mount Holyoke Coll Office of Pres 50 College St South Hadley MA 01075-1423

CREIGHTON, JOHN WALLIS, JR., novelist, publisher, former management educator, consultant; b. Yeung Kong, China, Apr. 7, 1916; s. John Wallis and Lois (Jameson) C.; m. Harriet Harrington, June 30, 1940; childrn: Carol (Mrs. Brian LeNeve), Joan (Mrs. Robert Nielsen). Student, Wooster Coll., 1933-36; BS in Forestry, U. Mich., 1938; AB, Hastings Coll., 1939; PhD in Wood Tech. and Indsl. Engring., U. Mich., 1954. Operator, sawmill, Cuyahoga Falls, Ohio, 1939—41; mem. staff U.S. Bd. Econ. Warfare, Ecuador, 1941—44; asst. gen. mgr. R.S. Bacon Veneer Co., Chgo., 1944—45; gen. mgr., v.p. Bacon Lumber Co., Sunman, Ind., 1944—45; faculty Mich. State U., Lansing, 1945—54, prof. wood tech., 1945—54; asst. to gen. mgr., v.p. Baker Furniture Inc., Grand Rapids, Mich., 1954—58; pres. Creighton Bldg. Co., Santa Barbara, Calif., 1958—65; prof. mgmt. Colo. State U., Ft. Collins, 1965—67, U.S. Naval Post grad. Sch., Monterey, Calif., 1967—86, chmn. dept., 1967—71, dir. fed. exec. mgmt. program, 1974—82, emeritus prof., 1986. Cons. in field. Assoc. editor, co-founder Jour. Tech. Transfer, 1975-88; fiction writer, 1986--; author: Waring's War, 2001, Aira in Red, 2002; contbr. articles to profl. jours. Former mem. Forestry Commn., Carmel, Calif., 1986-95. Recipient numerous Rsch. grants. Mem. Tech. Transfer Soc., Writer's Internat. Network, Calif. Writer's Club. Presbyterian. Home: 8065 Lake Pl Carmel CA 93923-9514

CRENSHAW, CORINNE BURROWES, kindergarten educator; b. Houston, Nov. 15, 1941; d. H. Clark and Corinne (Rue) Burrowes; m. James Leon Crenshaw Jr., June 2, 1963; children: Terri Lynn, James Alan. BS in Edn., Sam Houston State U., 1963; MEd, U. St. Thomas, Houston, 1991. Cert. tchr., Tex. 1st grade tchr. Lakeview Elem. Sch., Sugarland, Tex., 1963-64; kindergarten tchr. Calvery Episcopal Ch., Richmond, Tex., 1966-67, Holy Ghost Cath. Sch., Houston, 1978—. Co-author, prodr. sch. newsletter, 1984-87. Rep. Parish Coun., Holy Ghost Ch., Houston, 1981-84, 85-88; leader/co-leader Girl Scouts U.S., Houston, 1971-81, neighborhood jr. rep., 1982-84. Dyslexia awareness grantee Neuhaus Sch., 1990. Mem. Nat. Assn. for Edn. of Young Children, Tex. Assn. for Edn. of Young Children, Houston Area Assn. for Edn. of the Young Child (Educator of Young Children award 1993), Galveston-Houston Early Childhood Assn. (mem. evaluating achievment tests com. 1990-91, sec. 1992-95, kindergarten report card com. 1995, Galveston-Houston diocese accreditation com. 1992-93), Kindergarten Tchrs. of Tex., Kappa Delta Pi. Roman Catholic. Avocations: refinishing furniture, arts and crafts, crocheting. Office: Holy Ghost Cath Sch 6920 Chimney Rock Rd Houston TX 77081-5614

CRENSHAW, JAMES L(EE), theology educator; b. Sunset, S.C., Dec. 19, 1934; s. B. D. and Bessie (Aiken) C.; m. Juanita Rhodes, June 10, 1956; children: James Timothy, David Lee. AA, North Greenville Coll., 1954; BA, Furman U., 1956, DD, 1993; BD, So. Bapt. Theol. Sem., 1960; PhD, Vanderbilt U., 1964. Asst. prof. religion Atlantic Christian Coll., Wilson, N.C., 1964-65; assoc. prof. Mercer U., Macon, Ga., 1965-69; prof. Old Testament Vanderbilt Div. Sch., Nashville, 1970-87, Duke U., Durham, N.C., 1987-93, Robert L. Flowers Disting. prof., 1993—. Author 14 books; editor/contbg. author 60 books; series editor 15 books contbr. articles to profl. jours. Grantee NEH, 1974, Am. Coun. Learned Socs., 1981; fellow Soc. Values in Higher Edn., 1972-73, Assn. Theol. Schs., 1978-79, 90-91, Guggenheim Found. 1984-85, NEH, 1990-91, Pew Evangel. scholar, 1996-97. Mem. Soc. Bibl. Lit. (editor 1978-84), Cath. Bibl. Assn. (editor 1991-99), Soc. Values in Higher Edn., Colloquium Bibl. Rsch., Internat. Orgn. Study of Old Testament, The Soc. for Old Testament Study, Phi Beta Kappa. Democrat. Home: 8 Beckford Pl Durham NC 27705-1856 Office: Duke U The Div Sch PO Box 90967 Durham NC 27708-0967

CRENSHAW, LORETTA ANN, retired elementary education educator; b. Youngstown, Ohio, Mar. 27, 1947; d. Thomas Lenzia and Ruth (Daniels) Hallman; m. Paul Leslie Crenshaw, June 17, 1972; 1 child, Paul Leslie II. BS in Edn., Youngstown State U., 1970. Cert. tchr. elem. edn. Tchr. Hubbard (Ohio) Exempted Village, 1970—2000, ret., 2000—. Faculty adv. bd. mem. Roosevelt Elem. Sch., Hubbard, 1993-95. Mem. no. 2 Usher Bd. Triedstone Missionary Bapt. Ch., Youngstown, 1979—. Recipient Class Act award WFMJ-TV 21, 1991. Mem. NEA, Ohio Edn. Assn., Hubbard Edn. Assn. (exec. com. 1993-95). Avocations: crossword puzzles, shopping, decorating. Home: 2730 Wardle Ave Youngstown OH 44505-4067

CREPAGE, RICHARD ANTHONY, school system administrator; b. Youngstown, Ohio, May 1, 1948; s. Edward Joseph and Mary Lucille (Maskulka) C.; m. Ruth Anne Schneider Fife-Crepage, June 15, 1991; children: Lori, Teri. BA, Youngstown State U., 1970, MS in Edn., 1978. Math. tchr. East Jr. High-Warren (Ohio) City Schs., 1972-78, Warren G. Harding High, Warren, 1978-81, asst. prin., 1981-88; prin. Harry B. Turner Middle Sch., Warren, 1988-94; supr. pers./grants Ashtabula County Bd. Edn., Jefferson, Ohio, 1994—. Treas., bd. mem. Trumbull Art Gallery, Warren, 1985—. Scholar Martha Holden Jennings Found., Cleve., 1978. Mem. ASCD, Ohio ASCD, Nat. Mid. Sch. Assn., Ohio Mid. Sch. Assn., Buckeye Assn. Sch. Adminstrs., Phi Delta Kappa. Roman Catholic. Office: Ashtabula County Bd Edn PO Box 186 Jefferson OH 44047-0186

CREPET, WILLIAM LOUIS, botanist, educator; b. N.Y.C., Aug. 10, 1946; s. Louis Henry and Adaire Elaine (Richardson) C.; m. Laura Marie Stewart, July 29, 1972 (div. 1978); m. Ruth Chadab, July 27, 1980. BA, Harpur Coll., SUNY, Binghamton, 1969; MPh (Wadsworth fellow), Yale U., 1972, PhD (Cullman fellow), 1973. Cons. to Grad. Sch. U. Tex., Austin, 1972-73; lectr. Ind. U., 1973-75; asst. prof. U. Conn., 1975-78, assoc. prof., 1979-84, prof., 1985—, head dept., 1985-90; chmn., prof. Bailey Hortorium Cornell U., 1990—. N.Y. State Regents scholar SUNY, 1969. Fellow Explorers Club; mem. Bot. Soc. Am. (chmn. paleobotany sect. 1979-80, Paleobot. award 1972), Am. Inst. Biol. Scis., Beta Chi Sigma. Achievements include research in Mesozoic and Tertiary genera. Office: Cornell U LH Bailey Hortorium 467 Mann Library Ithaca NY 14853-4301

CREQUE, LINDA ANN, non-profit educational and research executive, former education commissioner; b. N.Y.C. d. Noel and Enid Louise (Schloss) DePass; m. Leonard J. Creque, July 29, 1967; children: Leah Michelle, Michael Gregory. BS, CUNY-Queens, 1963, MS, 1969; PhD, U. Ill., 1986. Tchr. 2d grade Bd. Edn., N.Y.C., 1963, tchr. demonstrations, team tchr., 1964-65, master tchr., 1965-66; elem. tchr. P.S. 69, Jackson Hgts., N.Y., 1963-67; tchr. English Cath. U., Ponce, P.R., 1967; cmty. exch. elem. tchr. grades K-6 Ponce, 1966-67; tchr. 4th grade Dept. Edn., V.I., 1967-69, tchr. remedial reading, master tchr., 1968-69; program coord. Project HeadStart, V.I., 1969-73, coord. Inst. Developmental Studies, 1970-71, acting dir., 1972-73; prin. Thomas Jefferson Annex Primary Sch., St. Thomas, V.I., 1973-80, Joseph Sibilly Elem. Sch., St. Thomas, 1980-87; commr. edn. Dept. Edn., St. Thomas, 1987-94; founder, pres. V.I. Inst. for Tchg. and Learning, St. Thomas, 1995—. Cons. Edn. Devel. Ctr., Mass. Nat. SSI Project, 1992-93, Coll. V.I., 1978; mem. exec. com., bd. overseers Regional Lab. Ednl. Improvement NE and Islands, Andover, Mass., 1988-92; bd. dirs. V.I. Pub. TV; mem. exec. bd. Leadership in Edn. Adminstrv. Devel., V.I., 1989—; presenter, keynote spkr. confs. in field. Contbr. articles to profl. publs. Trustee U. V.I., 1989—; mem. V.I. Residential Task Force for Human Svcs., 1989-94, V.I. Labor Coun.; bd. dirs. Nat. Urban Alliance for Effective Edn. Tchrs. Coll. Columbia U., N.Y.C., 1993—, Cultural Inst. V.I., 1989-94; mem. cultural endowment bd., V.I., 1989-94; mem. governing bd. East End Health Ctr., 1979-80; mem. Gov.'s Conf. Librs., 1978. Grantee V.I. Coun. on Arts Ceramics for Primary Children, 1974-78, Comprehensive Employment and Tng. Act, 1977, NSF, 1989-93, Carnegie Found., 1988-90; recipient award NASA, award St. Thomas-St. John Counselors Assn., 1988, Ednl. Excellence award Harvard U. Prins. Ctr., Ill. Edn. Svc. Ctr., 1975, Outstanding Leadership award FEMA, 1990, Disting. Svc. award Edn. Commn. of U.S., 1991, Outstanding Svc. award Coun. of Chief State Sch. Officers, 1995. Mem. LWV, St. Thomas Reading Coun., Nat. Assn. Tchrs. Math., Edn. Commn. of States (commr. 1987-93, steering com. 1988-92, internal audit com. 1988, policies priority com. 1991, exec. com. 1992, alt. steering com. 1991-94), Coun. Chief of State Sch. Officers (chair extra jurisdictions com., bd. dirs., task force early childhood edn., ednl. equity com., restructuring edn. com.), Phi Kappa Phi, Kappa Delta Pi, Phi Delta Kappa. Office: VI Inst for Tchg and Learning PO Box 301954 St Thomas VI 00803-1954

CRESCENZ, VALERIE J. music educator; b. Bethlehem, Pa., Mar. 8, 1956; d. George Henry and Florence Showers; m. Joseph Martin Crescenz, July 26, 1980; children: Monica Lynn, Melanie Jane. BS in Music Edn., West Chester (Pa.) State Coll., 1978, MusM in Piano Performance, 1980. Music instr. West Chester State Coll., 1979—80, Delaware County C.C., Media, Pa., 1990—95; composer Hinshaw Music, Inc., Chapel Hill, NC, 1994—; music tchr., dir. Downingtown (Pa.) Sch. Dist., 1995—. Composer (choral music): various titles, including 3 written with composer James Green of Durham, N.C. ; composer: (commd. works) Durham Sch. Arts, 2002. Mem.: Music Educators Nat. Conf., ASCAP, NEA, Pa. State Edn. Assn., Pa. Music Educators Assn. (commn. 2001, 2002). Home: 10 Juniata Dr Coatesville PA 19320 Office: West Bradford Elem Sch 1475 Broad Run Rd Downingtown PA 19335

CREW, ANDREW JACKSON, retired secondary school educator, band director; b. Whigham, Ga., Mar. 16, 1937; s. Andrew Jackson and Lucy Hull Crew; m. Shirley Wallace, Aug. 4, 1959; children: Sharon Metcalf, Sheryl Copeland, Shelly Jackson. MusB Edn., Fla. State U., Tallahassee, 1959, MusM Edn., 1972. Cert. tchr. Fla., 1959. Instrumental music tchr. Plant City (Fla.) Elem. Schools, 1960—64; dir. of bands Plant City H.S., 1964—68, Riverview H.S., Sarasota, Fla., 1968—83, Mosley H.S., Panama City, Fla., 1983—85, Lakeland (Fla.) H.S., 1985—94, Lincoln H.S., Tallahassee, 1994—2001; ret., 2002. Named Man of the Yr., VFW, Sarasota, FL, 1980, Mac Award to the Outstanding Bandmaster in Fla., A.R. McAllister Found., 1976, Outstanding Music Educator Sect. 3, Nat. Fedn. Interscholastic Music Assn., 1995; recipient Sudler Flag of Honor, John Philip Sousa Found., 1993, Legion of Honor award, 1990. Mem.: NEA, Music Educators Nat. Conf., Fla. Music Educators Assn. (Outstanding Music Educator 1991), Am. Bandmasters Assn. (bd. dirs. 1989—91), Nat. Band Assn., Fla. Bandmasters Assn. (pres. 1983—84), Phi Beta Mu (Outstanding Bandmaster 1986). Methodist. Avocation: tennis. Home: 3312 Clifden Dr Tallahassee FL 32309 Personal E-mail: acrew5@comcast.net.

CREWS, CINDA MELANE, assistant principal; b. Kansas City, Mo., Mar. 22, 1949; d. Roy Thomas and Charlotte (Browning) Barnes; m. Gibbs Eakens, Mar. 29, 1969 (div. May 1975); m. Rockey McNeal Crews, Dec. 27, 1975; children: Scott, Stephanie. BS, U. Tex., 1971; MS, Tex. A&I U., 1988. Cert. tchr., mid-mgmt. adminstr., bilingual/ESL edn., Tex. Tchr. San Antonio Ind. Sch. Dist., 1971-77, Judson Ind. Sch. Dist., Converse, Tex., 1977-79, N.E. Ind. Sch. Dist., San Antonio, 1979-89, asst. prin. Jackson Keller Elem. Sch., 1989-91, asst. prin. Oak Meadow Elem. Sch., 1991—. Bd. dirs. Alamo Metro Chorus, San Antonio, 1991-93, mem. Sweet Adelines Internat., 1972—. Recipient Gov.'s Ednl. Excellence award Gov. Ann Richards, 1990. Mem. ASCD, Tex. Elem. Prin. and Supervisors Assn., North Ctrl. Optimist (chair Help Them See program), Delta Kappa Gamma. Republican. Mem. Christian Ch. (Disciples Of Christ). Avocations: singing, dancing, aerobics, walking. Home: 1727 Whitehaven San Antonio TX 78232-4871

CRIBBS, MAUREEN ANN, artist, educator; b. Marinette, Wis., Feb. 17, 1927; d. Roy Cecil Hubbard and Lillian Worner (Hubbard) Yeoman; m. James Milton Cribbs, Apr. 22, 1950; children: Cynthia, Valerie. BA, DePauw U., 1949; student, Sch. of Art Inst., Chgo., 1971-72, 79-81; MA, Govs. State U., 1973. Cert. secondary sch. tchr., Ill. Tchr. art Sch. Dist. 163, Park Forest, Ill., 1960-78; instr. humanities Sch. Dist. 227, Park Forest, Ill., 1978-79; artist, painter, printmaker Park Forest, 1979—; instr. painting Village Artists, Flossmoor, Ill., 1980-87. Lectr. Chgo. State U., 1980—81; chair study group Homewood-Flossmoor cmty. assocs. of woman's bd. Art Inst. Chgo., 1989—95, sec., 1995—96; adj. prof. Govs. State U., University Park, 1995; artist-in-residence Ox Bow Sch. of Art, 1993; outreach presenter Art Insights, Art Inst. of Chgo., 1995—; docent Nathan Manilow Sculpture Park, Govs. State U., 1996—; instr. art, art history Robert Morris Coll., Orland Park, Ill., 1996—2001; woodcut printing and presenter Sr. Celebrations, Art Inst. Chgo., 1998—2002; participant printmaking Santa Reparata Graphic Art Ctr., Florence, Italy, 1999; mem. faculty Tall Grass Arts Assn. Sch., Park Forest, Ill., 2000, Tall Grass Arts Assn., 2001—. Exhibitions include Union St. Gallery, Chicago Heights, 2001, Recent Work South Suburban C.C., Thornton, Ill., 2001, Farnsworth House Gallery, Plano, Ill., 2001—, Art de Chgo. Gallery, Highland Park, Ill., 2001, Union St. Gallery, Chicago Heights, 2002, Creative Experience Gallery, Frankfort, Ill., 2002—03, Mid Am. Print Coun., Denver (Colo.) Airport, 2002, Ox Bow Benefits, 2002, 2003, A Portrait of Music, Ill. Philharm. Orch., 2003, numerous others, one-woman shows include S. Suburban Coll., 2001, Moraine Valley Cmty. Coll., 2001, Tall Grass Arts Assn. Gallery, Park Forest, 2002, Prairie State Coll., 2002, No. Ind. Arts Assn., 2002, Denver Internat. Airport, 2002, Lessedra Gallery, Sofia, Bulgaria, 2003, World Art Print Ann., Palace of Culture, Sofia, Represented in permanent collections Amity Found., Woodbridge, Conn., Lessedra Gallery. Bd. dirs. Ill. Philharm. Orch., Park Forest, 1981-83, Grace Migrant Day Care, Park Forest, 1981-85, LWV, Park Forest chpt., 2003-; adminstrv. chair Grace United Protestant Ch., Park Forest, 1984-94, v.p. Women's Christian Assn., 1999—; lay mem. No. Ill. Ann. Conf. of United Meth. Ch., 1996—, mem. commn. on christian unity and interreligious concerns, 1996—. Monetary grantee to produce 15 works Freedom Hall, 1982, Ill. Arts Coun. and Park Forest Cmty. Arts Coun.; Artist-in-Residence Cmty. Arts Coun. Park Forest, 1983, Sch. of Art Inst. of Chgo. at Ox Bow, 1993; recipient Russia Peace ribbon, 1987—. Mem. LWV, Mid-Am. Print Coun., Am. Print Alliance, Chgo. Artists Coalition, Chgo. Southland Visual Arts Coalition. Methodist. Avocations: reiki master, studying herbs & wildflowers, reading, travel, swimming. Home: 74 Blackhawk Dr Park Forest IL 60466-2146 Studio: 266 Somonauk St Park Forest IL 60466-2241

CRIDER, ANDREW BLAKE, psychologist; b. Cleve., June 11, 1936; s. Blake and Doris (Towne) C.; m. Anne Horrocks, Apr. 25, 1964; children: Juliet Gage, Jonathan Andrew. BA, Colgate U., 1958; MS, U. Wis., 1960; PhD, Harvard U., 1964. Lic. psychologist, Mass. Rsch. assoc. Harvard Med. Sch., Boston, 1964-68; asst., then assoc. prof. psychology Williams Coll., Williamstown, Mass., 1968-77, prof., 1977-84, Warren prof. psychology, 1984-94, chmn. dept., 1986-91, dir. Oxford program, 1991-93, prof. emeritus, 1994—. Cons. Berkshire Med. Ctr. Psychiatry Dept., Pittsfield, Mass., 1979-85, Harvard Med. Sch. Dept. Psychiatry, Boston, 1996—; bd. dirs. Biofeedback Certification Inst. Am., 1994—. Author: Schizophrenia, 1979; (with others) Psychology, 1983; contbr. articles to profl. jours. Bd. dirs. No. Berkshire Mental Health Assn., 1982-91. Fulbright scholar U. Brussels, 1958-59; NIH rsch. grantee, 1964-74. Mem. APA, Soc. Psychophysiol. Rsch., Assn. for Applied Psychophysiol. and Biofeedback. Home: 770 Hancock Rd Williamstown MA 01267-3016 Office: Williams Coll Dept Psychology Williamstown MA 01267

CRIDER, IRENE PERRITT, education educator, small business owner, consultant; b. Chatfield, Ark., Apr. 29, 1921; d. Dolphus France and Eula Allan (Springer) Perritt; m. Willis Jewel Crider, Aug. 3, 1945; 1 child, Larry Willis. BA, Bethel Coll., 1944; MA, Memphis State U., 1957; EdD, Fla. Atlantic U., 1977. Cert. elem., secondary tchr., administr., Tenn. Tchr. various schs., Tenn., 1941-57; dean girls Lake Worth (Fla.) Jr. High, 1957-65; dean women Lake Worth High Sch., 1965-73; gen. instructional supr. Palm Beach (Fla.) County Pub. Schs., 1973-75; asst. prin. Jupiter (Fla.) High Sch., 1975-76; supr. interns Fla. Atlantic U., Boca Raton, 1977-83, Palm Beach Atlantic Coll., West Palm Beach, Fla., 1982-84; cons. Paris, Tenn., 1984-87; owner, beauty sys. cons. Irene's Acad. Individual Image Improvement, from 1991. Instr. edn. Bethel Coll., McKenzie, Tenn., 1987, prof. MEd Grad. Program; cons. in field. Contbr. articles to profl. jours. Founder, bd. dirs., charter mem. Palm Beach County Kidney Assn., 1973-93; chmn. citizens action com. Fla. Ch. Women United, 1982-84. Mem. Tallahassee Theatre Guild, Women's Club Tallahassee, Tallahassee Area C. of C., Zonta (Lake Worth, pres. 1969-70), Order Ea. Star, Delta Kappa Gamma (charter pres. Beta Xi-Mu 1968-70, chmn. state com., scholarship), Phi Delta Kappa, Beta Phi Mu. Democrat. Methodist. Avocations: gardening, reading, spectator sports, color analysis, Amera Natural nails cons. and beauty systems cons. Died Apr. 4, 2000.

CRIGLER, SAMMIE MAE, secondary school English language educator; b. Sunflower, Miss., Aug. 20, 1953; s. Sam and Algena (Jenkins) Wash; m. Mosie Crigler, Jan. 4, 1974; 1 child, LaKisha Antoinette. BA in English, Mississippi Valley State U., Itta Bena, Miss., 1975; MEd, Miss. State U., Starkville, 1981; Edn. Specialist, Delta State U., 1993. Tchr. English Indianola (Miss.) Sch. Dist., 1974—; adj. prof. English Miss. Delta C.C., Moorhead, 1991-94. Mem. supt. adv. coun. Indianola Sch. Dist., 1994—; tchr./cons. Delta Area Writing Project, Cleveland, Miss., 1987—, co-chairperson adv. com., 1992-94; mem. textbook com. Miss. State Dept. Edn., Jackson, 1990. Contbr. articles to profl. publs. Tchr. Sunday sch. Travelers Rest, Moorhead, 1987—. Recipient Impact II award Miss. Effective Sch. Consortium, 1988, Golden Apple award Miss. Com. on Educating Black Children, Jackson, 1990, Good Apple award Indianola Sch. Bd., 1993. Mem. Nat. Assn. Educators, Miss. Assn. Educators, Nat. Coun. Tchrs. of English (state judge achievement writing contest 1993), Miss. Coun. Tchrs. of English (sec. 1988-90, treas. 1988—, Leadership award 1991, 93), Indianola Assn. Educators (pres. 1992-94). Democrat. Baptist. Avocations: reading, writing, decorating, organizing church youth activities. Home: PO Box 308 Moorhead MS 38761-0308 Office: Gentry H S 801 Bb King Rd Indianola MS 38751-3300

CRIPE, JULIANN WOODS, education educator; b. Waterloo, Iowa, Sept. 6, 1952; d. Francis J. and Evelyn M. (Youngman) Woods; children: Corey, Jeanna, Katrina. BA, U. No. IOwa, 1973, MA, 1974; PhD, U. Oreg., 1990. Speech-lang. pathologist Keystone Area Edn. Agy., Elkader, Iowa, 1975-82; rsch. asst. Bur. Child Rsch. U. Kans., Parsons, 1983-85, asst. scientist Life Span Inst., 1991—, courtesy asst. prof. speech-lang.-hearing dept., 1992—; unit dir. Parsons State Hosp. and Tng. Ctr., 1985-86; rsch. asst. infant monitoring project U. Oreg., Eugene, 1986-87, early intervention cons. Western Regionl Resource Ctr., 1990-91, rsch. assoc. linked systems outreach tng., 1991—; co-dir. linked assessment Intervention and Evaluation Outreach Project, Eugene, 1988-91. Assoc. prof. spl. ed. comm. disorders dept. Valdosta State U. Grantee U.S. Dept. Edn./Divsn. Pers. Preparation, 1988-91, 89-90, U.S. Dept. Edn./Handicapped Children Early Edn. Program, 1988-91, 90-93, U.S. Dept. Edn./Early Edn. Programs for Children with Disabilities, 1991-94. Mem. Am. Speech-Lang.-Hearing Assn., Coun. for Exceptional Children (v.p. Oreg. chpt. 1990-91, pres. Kans. div. 1992-96), Nat. Assn. Edn. Young Children, Kans. Div. Early Childhood. Office: Valdosta State U Coll Ed Valdosta GA 31602 Home: 3481 Welwyn Way Tallahassee FL 32309-8204

CRISAFULLI, FREDERICK SALVATORE, internist, educator; b. N.Y.C., Apr. 16, 1943; s. Santo and Pauline (Birretella) Crisafulli; m. Bettina Patricia Miraglia, Dec. 18, 1965; children: Laura, Marc, Christopher, Rachel. AB in Natural Sci., St. Peter's Coll., 1965; MD, NYU, 1969. Diplomate Am. Bd. Internal Medicine. Resident, chief resident in medicine SUNY Downstate, N.Y.C., 1969—72; clin. instr. medicine Brown U., Providence, 1973—77, asst. clin. prof. 1977—; fellow in cardiology Miriam Hosp., Providence, 1972—73; practice medicine specializing in internal medicine and primary care Medicine Assocs., Ltd., Providence, 1973—. V.p., med. dir. Health Care Rev. Inc., Providence, 1984—, pres., 1985—87, chmn. bd., 1987—97. Maj. USAR, 1972—78. Fellow: ACP (gov.'s coun.); mem.: Am. Soc. Internal Medicine (gov.'s coun.). Republican. Roman Catholic. Home: 43 Scott St Pawtucket RI 02860-6107 Office: Medicine Assocs Ltd 9 Pleasant St Providence RI 02906-1715 E-mail: fscrisafulli@yahoo.com.

CRISMORE, AVON GERMAINE, English language educator, researcher; b. Chgo., Oct. 7, 1929; d. Rupert Paul and Alice Leona (Miller) Wellendorf; m. Edward Noel Crismore, July 30, 1949; children: Sheryl, Jill, Debra, Ryan, Randy, Noel. Student, Carthage Coll., 1947-49; BA, St. Francis Coll., 1965, MEd, 1967; PhD, U. Ill., 1985. English tchr. Norwell High Sch., Ossian, Ind., 1964-80; communications instr. Ind. Tech. Coll., Ft. Wayne, 1973-80; rsch. asst. Ctr. for the Study of Reading U. Ill., Champaign, 1980-84; assoc. faculty English Ind. U.-Purdue U., Ft. Wayne, 1979-80, assoc. prof. English, 1985-98, prof. English, 1999—. Vis. dir. Ednl. Opportunity Program, U. Ill., Champaign, 1983-84; vis. prof., asst. dir. Learning Ctr., Ind. U., Bloomington, 1984-85; item writer Nat. Assessment Ednl. Program, 1983-84, Ill. State Edn. Dept., Springfield, 1983-84; textbook reviewer Ginn Pubs., 1984, Harper Collins Pub., 1992, St. Martins Pub., 1993—; writing, English, ESL tchr., Inst. Tech. Mara, Malaysia, 1991, Polytechnic Tng. Ctr., Malaysia, 1995; del. to China, Linguistic Educators U.S., 1991. Author: How to Write Well in College, 1984, Talking with Readers, 1990; editor: Reading Comprehension Research, 1984; contbr. articles to profl. jours. Grantee Nat. Coun. Rschrs. English, 1986—, Nat. Coun. Tchrs. English, 1990—, U.S. Info. Svc., 1992. Mem. MLA, Nat. Coun. Tchrs. English (lang. commn. 1992-94, reviewer nat. tchr. assessment early adoles. and middle sch. English tchrs. draft, 1993), Soc. for Lit. and Sci., Rhetoric Soc. Am., Internat. Reading Assn., Coll. Composition and Communications Conf., Nat. Reading Conf., Am. Edn. Rsch. Assn., Phi Delta Kappa (grantee 1986—), Kappa Delta Pi, Phi Kappa Phi (mentor fgn. students, 2000—). Democrat. Lutheran. Avocations: photography, reading, traveling. Home: PO Box 96 Uniondale IN 46791-0096 Office: Ind U Purdue U 2101 E Coliseum Blvd Fort Wayne IN 46805-1445 E-mail: crismore@ipfw.edu.

CRISP, JOHN N. engineering educator, former dean; b. Hiawassee, Ga. BSME, Ga. Inst. Tech., 1958; MS in Engring., U. Akron, 1964; PhD in Mech. Engring., Carnegie-Mellon U., 1968. Dean engring. U. New Orleans; mech. engr. Timken Roller Bearing Co., 1958-64, rsch. engr., 1964-66, rsch. assoc., 1968-69; asst. engr. mech. engr. Tri-State Coll., 1969-71, assoc. prof., chmn. mech. engr., aero. engr. dept., 1971-73; assoc. prof., sr. rsch. engr. mech. engr. dept. U. Dayton, 1973-79; prof., chmn. mech. engr. dept. U. Kans., 1979-83; Jess H. Davis prof. of mech. engr., dept. head Stevens Inst. Tech., 1983-86, dep. provost, dean of engr., 1986-88, acting dean fac., 1988; dean engring., prof. mech. engr. U. New Orleans, 1988—2003, exec. dir. Gulf Coast Region Maritime Tech. Ctr., 1994—. Recipient Fellow Mems. award Am. Soc. Engring. Educators, 1992, A.B. Paterson medal La. Engring. Soc., 2003. Fellow ASME. Office: Gulf Coast Region Maritime Tech Ctr Cerm Bldg Rsch and Tech Pk 2000 Lakeshore Dr New Orleans LA 70148*

CRIST, WILLIAM GARY, artist, retired educator; b. Pocatello, Idaho, Jan. 17, 1937; s. Margaret Alice (Zimmerman) C.; 1 child, Julie Anne. BA in Art Edn., U. Wash., 1966, postgrad., 1966-69; MFA in Sculpture, Cranbrook Acad. Art, Detroit, 1971; student, Staatliche Kunstakademie, Dusseldorf, West Germany, 1981, 83. Tchr. Mt. Si High Sch., Snoqualmie, Wash., 1966-69; instr. Bellevue (Wash.) C.C., 1967-69; asst. prof. Wesleyan Coll., Macon, Ga., 1971-72; instr. Cameron U., Lawton, Okla, 1972-74; asst. prof. art U. Mo., Kansas City, 1974-78, assoc. prof., 1978-88, prof., 1988-2000, prof. emeritus, 2000—. Vol. art tchr. St. Helens (Oreg.) Sch. Dist., 2003—; cons. Wayne (Nebr.) State Coll., 1987, Ctrl. Mo. State U., Warrensburg, 1985, Spelman Coll., Atlanta, 1984, U. Akron, Ohio, 1984; part-time art instr. Portland (Oreg.) C.C., 2003—. Creator computer art, exhibited in shows at Pleiades Gallery, N.Y.C., 1992, 3d Nat., Phoenix, 1992, 31st Nat., Ft. Collins, Colo., 1992, Images '92, Highland, Kans., 1992, Columbia Ctr., St. Helens, Oreg., 2000. Served as sgt. U.S. Army, 1959-62, Korea. Rockefeller/Nat. Endowment Arts interdisciplinary arts fellow, 1986; U. Mo. grantee, 1981, 82, 92, 99. Avocations: outdoor activities, boating, hiking. Office: U Mo Kansas City Dept Art 51st and Holmes Kansas City MO 64110

CRITES, GAYLE, artist, educator; b. Denver, June 23, 1949; d. Melvin V. and Mary E. Crites; children: Mychael Moe, Travis Moe. BA, Colo. State U., 1971. Artist-image Dairy Ctr. for the Arts, Boulder, Colo., 1999. Exhibitions include Colo. Gov.'s Invitational Exhibit, 1993—99, Rocky Mtn. Nat. Pk., Estes Pk., Co., 2002—03, Represented in permanent collections Art in Embassies, U.S. Dept. State, commd., City of Boulder, 2002, Silver Canyon Coffee, Boulder C. of C. Home: 4280 Peach Way Boulder CO 80301-1737

CRITTENDEN, MARY LYNNE, science educator; b. Detroit, Oct. 27, 1951; d. William and Marie (Ryall) C. BS, Wayne State U., 1974; MS, U. Detroit, 1984; postgrad., Wayne State U., 1991—,, 1997—. Tchr. sci. Detroit Bd. Edn., 1974-77, Highland Park (Mich.) C.C., 1980—. Faculty rschr. Air Force program Wright Patterson AFB, Dayton, Ohio, 1991; speaker Mich. Ednl. Occupational Assn., 1989, Liberal Arts Network Devel., Lansing, Mich., 1990, 95; presider Qualities Edn. Minorities, Math., Sci. Engring. Conf., Detroit, 1996; adj. prof. U. Detroit, 1996-97. Author ednl. materials; contbr. to profl. publs. Mem. AAAS, Am. Chem. Soc. (outreach program 1992—), Civic Ctr. Optimist Club (bd. dirs. 1991-94, coord. scis. 1990-94), Mich. C.C. Biologists, Human Anatomy and Physiology Soc. Achievements include development of successful paradigm and teaching methods to make science palatable to urban community college students, modeling normal values in humans and some rodents applicable to physiologically-based pharmacokinetics. Home: 15386 Alden St Detroit MI 48238-2104 Office: Highland Park Schs 20 Bartlett St Highland Park MI 48203-3720

CRITTENDEN, MARY RITA, clinical psychology educator; b. Binghamton, N.Y., Apr. 6, 1928; d. John Patrick and Anna Elizabeth (Griffin) Saxton; m. Rodney Whitman Crittenden, Aug. 6, 1955; children: John Whitman, Anne Catherine, Jean Patricia. BA, Cornell U., 1950; MA, Mills Coll., Oakland, Calif., 1952; PhD, Calif. Sch. Profl. Psychology, San Francisco, 1977. Cert. Nat. Sch. Psychologist; lic. clin. psychologist, ednl. psychologist, Calif. Psychologist numerous schs., N.Y., Calif., 1953-67; chief psychologist, asst. prof. dept. pediatrics U. Calif., San Francisco, 1967-93, clin. prof. dept. pediatrics, 1993—. Lectr. Coll. Notre Dame, Belmont, Calif., 1963-66; coord. Child Assessment Svc., San Francisco Mental Health Svcs., 1993—. Contbg. editor Jour. Soc. Pediatric psychology, 1974-80; contbr. articles to profl. jours. Mem. bd. dirs. San Francisco Assn. for Gifted and Talented, 1972-81. Mills Coll. fellow, 1950-52; grantee U. Calif. San Francisco Acad. Senate, 1981. Mem. APA, NASP, Nat. Acad. Neuropsychology, Western Psychology Assn., Calif. Assn. Sch. Psychologists, Calif. Psychology Assn., Soc. Behavioral Pediatrics. Roman Catholic. Avocation: child advocacy. Office: U Calif Dept Pediatrics A-203 Box 0314 400 Parnassus San Francisco CA 94143-0001

CROCETTI, GINO, elementary and secondary education educator; b. N.Y.C., Oct. 18, 1945; s. Guido M. and Annemarie F. Crocetti. AB in Philosophy, Columbia Coll., N.Y.C., 1970; BS in Psychology, SUNY, 1989; MA in Pub. Policy, PhD in Edn., Columbia Pacific U., 1989. V.p., gen. mgr. Douglas Books and Douglas Record, N.Y.C., 1971-73; one of organizers No. Manhattan Health Planning Project, N.Y.C., 1972-81; dir. Project on New Food Devel.-INFORM, N.Y.C., 1978-80; program dir. Sexton Edn. Programs (now Thinking Skills Ctr.) Fairleigh Dickinson U., NJ, 1977—96; sci. tchr., math. tchr. City and Country Sch., N.Y.C., 1980—. Assoc. fellow Inst. Policy Studies, Washington, 1971; editl. cons. dept. psychiatry Johns Hopkins U., Balt., 1972-73; cons. survey data Coll. Medicine and Dentistry N.J., New Brunswick, 1974-75; instr. occupl. and environ. health N.Y. State Sch. Ind. and Labor Rels., N.Y.C., 1979; instr. computer use Learning Annex, N.Y.C., 1984-88. Co-author: What's for Dinner Tomorrow: Corporate Views on New Food Product Development, 1980, Preparing for the LSAT, 1982, Preparing for GMAT, 1983, Preparing for the GRE, 1984; contbr. articles on health planning, computer use and mental hygiene to profl. jours. Mem. N.Y. County Dem. Com., N.Y.C., 1974, 2000, N.Y. County Dem. Jud. Com., N.Y.C., 1974, 99; instr. health and safety ARC Greater N.Y., 2001—. Mem. AAAS, ASCD, Assn. Computers in Math. and Sci. Edn., Nat. Sci. Tchrs. Assn., Nat. Coun. Tchrs. Math., Am. Pub. Health Assn., CEDAM Internat. Avocations: diving, fish collecting, skiing, water sports. Office: City and Country Sch 146 W 13th St New York NY 10011-7802

CROCKER, BETTY CHARLOTTE, education educator; b. Jackson, Miss., Sept. 2, 1948; d. William Charlie and Virginia Frances (Cayson) C. BS, U. Tex., 1970; EdD, U. Ga., 1985. Cert. sci. edn., earth-life sci., elem. edn. Tchr. 5th grade Harlingen (Tex.) Ind. Schs., 1970-71, Am. Sch. Found., Monterrey, Mexico, 1971-74; tchr. grades 6-8, sci. chair Clear Creek Ind. Schs., Webster, Tex., 1974-83; asst. prof. edn. So. Oreg. State U., Ashland, 1985-88; asst. to assoc. prof. edn. U. North Tex., Denton, 1988—. Adv. com. to state bd. edn. Tex. Environ. Edn. Adv. Com., Austin, 1991—; sci. spkr. The Edn. Ctr., Torrance, Calif., 1994-95; spkr. in field. Author: Food for Thought, 1992, 93, 94, 95; editl. bd. mem. Jour. Elem. Sci. Edn., 1989-95; contbr. articles to profl. jours. Bd. dirs. hands-on mus. Science-Land, Denton's (Tex.) Discovery Mus., 1994-95; mem. sci. writing team Tex. Essential Knowledge and Skills, 1995-97, mem. tool kit writing team, 1996-98; trainer TEKS Teams, 1998—; coord. Hall of Excellence, Assn. Childhood Edn. Internat., 1998. Sci. tchg. grantee Exxon Corp., 1997, 98, 99. Mem. S.W. Assn. Educators of Tchrs. of Sci. (sec.-treas. 1994-95, dir. elect 1995, dir. 1996-98), Sci. Tchrs. Assn. Tex. (v.p. 1990-91, pres. 1991-92, past pres. 1992-93, 94-95, Lawrence Buford award 1991), Phi Delta Kappa (sec.-treas. 1987-88, v.p. for programs 1989-90, pres. 1990-91). Avocations: underwater photography, folk dancing, needlework, color analysis. Office: Univ North Tex Coll Edn PO Box 13857 Denton TX 76203

CROCKER, EVELYNE MARIE, retired physical education educator; b. Hollis, Okla., Mar. 13, 1936; d. Horace Norton Crocker and Maezell Elizabeth Tarr; m. Kenneth D. Burgess-Bean, May 6, 1956 (div. 1980); children: R. N. Burgess-Bean, K.R. Burgess-Bean, W. R. Burgess-Bean. Student, Cisco Jr. Coll., N.Mex. State U. Cert. Medical Specialist 1956. Governess Brown Family, Snyder, Tx, 1954—55, The Burgess-Bean Family, Maryville, Tn, 1956—68; instr. phys. edn. Bishop Bryan Cath. H.S., Port Arthur, Tex., 1968—69; governess The Hitch Family, Albany, Tex., 1981—82; owner, operator Bean's Lawn and Landscape Co., 1982—; proprietor King Crocker Am. Boers, Abilene, Tex., 1997—2001, Crocker Scouting Svc., Abilene, Tex., 2000—01. Author (web sites): Texann Prairie Land Country, 1996. Vol. state coord., owner Tex. Am. Local History Net; webmaster, author A.M. Crocker -1720 rootsweb.com project; vol. county coord., webmaster TXGenWeb projects; den leader, coach Scouting, Maryville, Tenn., 1977—79. Pfc WAC, 1955—57. Recipient Cold War Cert., Sec. War, 2000. Mem.: Founding Families of the State of S.C. Before Statehood, Tex. Sheriff Assn. (assoc. Appreciation award 1999, 2000, 2001). Spiritualist. Avocations: historical re-enactment, genealogy, photography, preservation. Business E-Mail: ecrocoil@camalott.com.

CROCKETT, GEORGE EPHRIAM, secondary education educator; b. Chgo., July 5, 1940; s. Edmund and Ethel Teva (Cowan) C.; m. Ethelene Standifer, Nov. 25, 1968; children: Patricia Johnson, Ronald O'Neal, Michael O'Neal. BS, Ill. State U., 1964; MA in History, Northeastern Ill. U., 1981; postgrad., U. Ill., Champaign. Cert. tchr., Ill. History tchr. John Marshall Metro High Sch., Chgo., 1964—, chmn. social studies dept., 1992—. Tng. specialist John Marshall Metro Evening High Sch., 1966-69, counselor, 1980-83; cons. curriculum guide Chgo. Bd. Edn., 1970. Active Cen. Meml. Bapt. Ch., Chgo., 1957—; mem. com. explorer scouts Boy Scouts Am., 1977-79; mem. Citi-Educators Team Project, DePaul U., 1989. Recipient Tchr. of Yr. award Chgo. Bd. Edn., 1974, Black Educator award Push Found., 1977, Blum-Kovler Ednl. Found. award, 1984, merit award N. Eastern Ill. Alumni, 1985, Midwest Community award, 1990—. Mem. Ill. Coun. Social Studies, Chgo. Social Studies, Chgo. Afro-Am. Tchrs. Assn.,

Chgo. Area Alliance Black Sch. Educators, NAACP, Nat. Urban League, Midwest Community Coun., Operation Push, So. Christian Leadership Conf. Avocations: reading, sports, public speaking, gardening. Home: 3130 W Fulton St Chicago IL 60612-1728 Office: John Marshall Met High Sch 3250 W Adams St Chicago IL 60624-2901

CROFT, JANET BRENNAN, academic librarian; b. Pitts., May 5, 1961; d. Earl David and Marian (Maxwell) Brennan; m. Duane Shiffler, Aug. 11, 1984; 1 child, Sarah Gail. BA in English & Classical Civilization, Ind. U., 1982, MLS, 1983. Libr. Jenner and Block Law Firm, Chgo., 1983-84, Carnegie Libr. Pitts., 1985, Sewickley (Pa.) Pub. Libr., 1985-88, Moon Twp. Pub. Libr., Coraopolis, Pa., 1988-89, 90; libr. dir. Martin Meth. Coll., Pulaski, Tenn., 1993-2000, costume designer, 1997-2000; head access svcs. U. Okla. Libr., 2001—. Contbr. articles to profl. jours. Mem.: ALA, Popular Culture Assn., Mythopoeic Soc. Avocations: quilting, wearable art. Office: U Okla Bizzell 104NW 401 W Brooks St Norman OK 73019-6030 E-mail: jbcroft@ou.edu.

CRON, JUANITA MARLENE, elementary education educator; b. Blossburg, Pa., Jan. 9, 1948; d. William B. and Berea L. Reppard; m. Gerald A. Cron, July 10, 1971; children: Rebecca, Laura. BS, Mansfield (Pa.) U., 1969; postgrad., Pa. State U., 1969, Mansfield U., 1970. Cert. in elem. edn., Pa. Tchr. 2d grade Athens (Pa.) Area Schs., 1969-71; elem. sch. tchr. Pennridge Schs., Perkasie, Pa., 1971-72, So. Tioga Schs., Blossburg, 1972-74, Athens Area Schs., 1983—. Active Sayre (Pa.) Christian Ch. Recipient Gift of Time Tribute, 1994. Mem. NEA, Pa. State Edn. Assn., Athens Area Edn. Assn. Avocations: family activities, reading, sewing. Home: 110 Roosevelt St Sayre PA 18840-1132

CRON, MICHAEL THOMAS, pediatric optometry educator; b. Celina, Ohio, Apr. 28, 1949; s. Thomas Henry and Evelyn Louise (Reichard) C.; m. Connie Jean Hall, June 22, 1974; children: Cara Michelle, Andrew Charles. OD, Ill. Coll. Optometry, 1973. Optometrist, Spring Lake, Mich., 1974-82; clin. assoc. Ferris State U. Coll. of Optometry, Big Rapids, Mich., 1977-79, asst. prof., 1980-84, assoc. prof., 1984-88, chief pediat. optometry svcs., 1984-92, prof., 1988—, assoc. dean, 1992-99. Optometric cons. Presch. Multicap Program, Muskegon, Mich., 1980-92. Author: (chpt.) Optometric Management of Learning-Related Vision Disorders, 1994; referee Jour. Am. Optometry Assn., 1985—; mem. editl. bd. Jour. Vision Devel., 1992—. Mem., officer Grand Haven (Mich.) Area Jaycees, 1976-82, Citizens Curriculum Adv. Coun., Big Rapids, 1984-94. Fellow Am. Acad. Optometry; mem. APHA, Am. Optometric Assn., Mich. Optometric Assn., Coll. Optometrists in Vision Devel., Mich. Pub. Health Assn. (v.p. 1993-94). Avocations: camping, fishing, photography, bridge. Home: 9217 Elmwood Ct Stanwood MI 49346-9305 Office: Mich Coll Optometry 1310 Cramer Cir Big Rapids MI 49307-2738 E-mail: cronm@ferris.edu.

CRONE, EUGENE N. addictions counselor, retired educator; b. Newton Falls, Ohio., Apr. 17, 1929; s. Clarence Bennet and Violet Richards Crone. BM, Youngstown U., 1954; MA, Columbia U., 1958; PhD, Nat. U. Grad. Studies, Dallas, 1974. Cert. addiction profl., MAC-master addiction counselor, nat. cert. addiction counselor II, internat. cert. alcohol and drug counselor. Tchr., prof. various pub. schs. and colls., 1952—78; dir. addictions Horizon Psychiatric Hosp., Clearwater, Fla., 1978—95, Nat. Deaf Acad., Mt. Dora, Fla., 1995—, La Amistad Health Svcs., Maitland, Fla., 1999—2003; with Nat. Deaf Acad., Mt. Dora, Fla., 2003—. Presenter in field. Author: They Hear Through Their Eyes, 2003; contbr. articles to profl. jours. PFC U.S. Army, 1950—52. Recipient Profl. of Yr. Nat. award, NAADAC Nat. Conv., 1997, Profl. of Yr. award, Fla. NAADAC, 1996. Mem.: NAADAC, Addiction Profls. of Fla., Internat. Cert. Alcohol & Drug Counselors. Methodist. Home: 1001 Bristol Lake Rd #212 Mount Dora FL 32757 Office: Nat Deaf Acad 19650 US Hwy 441 Mount Dora FL 32757

CRONEN, MICHAEL JAMES, lawyer, educator; b. Montery Park, Calif., Feb. 8, 1958; s. James Leslie and Katherine Mary C.; m. Nelle P. Vereecke, Sept. 19, 1987; children: Kennan, Julian. BA in Polit. Sci. with honors, Calif. State U., L.A., 1983; JD, Hastings Coll. of Law, 1987. Bar: Calif. 1987, U.S. Ct. Appeals (9th cir.) 1987, U.S. Ct. Appeals (fed. cir.) 1989. Crew supr. Calif. Conservation Corps., Sacramento, 1978-80; asst. dir. Binlingual Edn. Ctr., L.A., 1980-83; law clk. Law Offices of William K. Obrien, San Francisco, 1984-85; extern clk. hon. Jerome Smith Calif. Ct. Appeals, San Francisco, 1986; lawyer Law Offices of Harris Zimmerman, Oakland, Calif., 1987—. Assoc. prof. intellectual property law Calif. State U., Hayward, 1994—; instr. intellectual property law St. Mary's Coll. Calif., 1996-97; guest lectr. Haas Sch. Bus., U. Calif., Berkeley. Mem. ABA (intellectual property sect., copyright legis. com.), Am. Intellectual Property Law Assn., San Francisco Intellectual Property Law Assn. Democrat. Avocations: trumpet playing, golfing.

CRONENWETT, WILLIAM TREADWELL, electrical engineering educator, consultant; b. Texarkana, Tex., Jan. 3, 1932; s. John E. and Frances P. (Treadwell) C.; m. Carolyn E. Somers, June 8, 1963 (div. Oct. 1976); children: Will J., Carrie. BS, Tex. A&I U., 1954; MS, U. Tex., 1960, PhD, 1966. Registered profl. engr., Tex., Okla. Rsch. engr. Electro Mechanics Co., Austin, Tex., 1959-62; Welch Found. fellow U. Tex., Austin, 1964-66; rsch. fellow U. Leicester, Eng., 1966-68; prof. U. Okla., Norman, 1968-97. Cons., 1981—; expert in field of electrical accidents, equipment malfunctions, investigations. Contbr. articles and reports to profl. publs. Recipient Dist. 1st prize AIEE, Dist. 15, 1952, Wonders of Engring. award Ctrl. Okla. Soc. Profl. Engrs., Tulsa, 1972. Mem. IEEE (sr. mem.), Am. Welding Soc., Sigma Xi. Achievements include patents and research grants. Office: Univ of Okla Elec Engring 202 W Boyd St Norman OK 73019-1020

CRONHOLM, LOIS S. center administrator; b. St. Louis, Aug. 15, 1930; d. Fred and Emma (Tobias) Kisslinger; m. James Cronholm, Sept. 15, 1965 (div. 1974); children: Judith Frances, Peter Foster; m. Stuart E. Neff, Apr. 11, 1975. BA, U. Louisville, 1962, PhD, 1966. Asst. prof. biology dept. U. Louisville, 1973-76, assoc. prof., 1976-80, dean arts and scis., 1979-85, prof., 1980-85; dean arts and scis., prof. Temple U., Phila., 1985-92; sr. v.p. acad. affairs, prof. Baruch Coll., CUNY, 1992-98, interim pres., 1998-99; CEO Ctr. for Jewish History, N.Y.C., 1999—2001; sr. v.p., chief operating officer CCNY, 2001—. Bd. dirs. J. History Ideas, 1987-93. Contbr. articles to profl. jours. Chmn. Human Relations Commn., Louisville, 1976-79; group capt. Dems., Valley Station, Ky., 1975-78; sec. Grass Roots Dem. Club, Valley Station, 1975; chmn. Southwestern Jefferson County Econ. Devel. Com., Valley Station, 1983-84; pres. Hampden-Booth Theater Libr., 1997-99. Recipient Pre-Doctoral fellowship NIH, 1963-66, Post-Doctoral fellowship NIH, 1967-70. Mem. Nat. Assn. Land Grant and Urban Univs. (chmn. com. arts and scis. 1987-89, bd. dirs. divsn. urban affairs 1988-90, sec. bd. dirs. internat. divsn. 1991-92), Coun. Colls. Arts and Scis. (bd. dirs. 1987-90, pres.-elect 1989-90, pres. 1990-91, chair commn. on faculty recruitment ethics 1991-93), Players Club N.Y.C. (sec. bd. 1994). Democrat. Jewish. Avocations: gardening, cooking.

CRONIN, RICHARD JAMES, university official, educator; b. Needham, Mass., Dec. 2, 1958; s. John Joseph and Margaret Mary (Healy) C. BS in Fgn. Svc., Georgetown U., 1980, JD, 1984. Bar: Mass. 1985. Asst. to dean Sch. Langs. and Linguistics, Georgetown U., Washington, 1980-84, asst. dean, 1984-92, assoc. dean, 1992-95, assoc. dean Georgetown Coll., 1995—, lectr. divsn. interpretation and translation, 1986-98. Roman Catholic. Office: Georgetown U Coll Dean's Office Washington DC 20057

CRONIN, THOMAS EDWARD, academic administrator; b. Milton, Mass., Mar. 18, 1940; s. Joseph M. and Mary Jane Cronin; m. Tania Zaroodny, Nov. 26, 1966; 1 child, Alexander. AB, Holy Cross Coll., 1961; MA, Stanford U., 1964, PhD, 1968; LLD (hon.), Marietta Coll., 1987, Franklin Coll., 1993. Tchg. fellow Stanford U., Calif., 1962—64; staff mem. The White House, Washington, 1966—67; faculty mem. U. N.C., 1967—70; staff fellow Brookings Instn., 1970—72; faculty mem. Brandeis U., Waltham, Mass., 1975—77, U. Del., Newark, 1977—79; McHugh prof. of Am. instns. The Colo. Coll., Colorado Springs, 1985—93, acting pres., 1991; pres. Whitman Coll., Walla Walla, Wash., 1993—. Bd. dirs. Cascade Natural Gas Co.; moderator Aspen Inst. Exec. Sems., 1975—; pres. CRC, Inc., 1980—, Presidency Rsch. Group, 1981—82; cons. in field; guest polit. analyst various tv programs; mem. Wash. Com. Humanities. Author: The State of the Presidency, 1980, Direct Democracy, 1989, Colorado Politics and Government, 1993, The Paradoxes of the American Presidency, 1998, 2004. Dir. IES Chgo., Jr. Statesmmman Found.; bd. dirs. Inst. Am. Univs.; trustee Jr. Statesman Am., 2002—. Mem.: Inst. Edn. Internat. Students, Western Polit. Sci. Assn. (pres. 1993—94), Am. Polit. Sci. Assn. (exec. com. 1990—92), C. of C., Pi Sigma Alpha. Avocations: tennis, hiking. Office: Whitman Coll Pres Ofc Memorial 303 345 Boyer Ave Walla Walla WA 99362-2067

CRONK, MILDRED SCHIEFELBEIN (MILI CRONK), special education consultant; b. Waverly, Iowa, May 29, 1909; d. Emil August and Nettie Marie (Berger) Schiefelbein; m. Dale Cronk, July 20, 1930; children: Barbara Cronk Burress, Bruce, Margaret, Michael. Student, Wartburg Coll., Waverly, 1927, Tampa (Fla.) U., 1944-45, Los Angeles City Coll., 1957; BA in Psychology, Calif. State U., 1960, MA in Spl. Edn. Supervision, 1971. Aircraft communicator, weather observer CAA, Fla. and Calif., 1942-49; dir. Parkview Nursery Sch., L.A., 1956-57; tchr. trainable mentally retarded Hacienda-LaPuente United Sch. Dist., LaPuente, Calif., 1961-74; cons. spl. edn. La Mirada, Calif., 1975—. In-svc. trainer for tchrs.; mem. Spl. Olympics S.E. L.A. County com., 1977—; mem. Internat. Very Spl. Arts Festival Com., 1981; mem. adv. com. Very Spl. Arts Festival, Orange County, 1976—, chmn., 1986-87; treas. Very Spl. Arts Calif., 1986-87, bd. dirs., 1986—. Author: Create with Clay, 1976, Vocational Skills Taught through Creative Arts, 1978, Attitude Change toward Trainable Mentally Retarded Students—Mainstreaming in Reverse, 1978, Career Education for Trainable Mentally Retarded Students—It's for Life!, 1982, also others. Mem. Am. Assn. on Mental Deficiency (bd. dirs. region II, editor Newsette, 1975-77, chmn. publicity com., 1977-79, presenter ann. confs.), Coun. for Exceptional Children (bd. dirs. Calif., editor Calif. State Fedn./Coun. for Exceptional Children Jour., 1977-80, past pres. San Gabriel Valley chpt. 538, mem.-at-large So. Calif. div. mental retardation 1976-79, pres. Calif. div. mental retardation 1980-81, sec. 1988-89, chmn. com. on officers' handbook, nat. coun., div. mental retardation, 1977-78, mem. Orange County chpt. 188, bd. dirs. 1987—, presentation coord. internat. conf. coun. for exceptional children 1989, liason to Very Spl. Arts., 1987—, coun. for exceptional children, spl. recognition awards, 1976, 77, 78, 79, 89), Nat. Assn. for Retarded Citizens (rec. sec. 1980-81), Nat. Soc. Autistic Children (nat., state, local orgns.), Nat. Ret. Tchrs. Assn. (nat., state, local orgns.), Am. Ceramic Soc. (design div.), Smithsonian Instn., Wilderness Soc., Psi Chi. Democrat. Home and Office: 13116 Clearwood Ave La Mirada CA 90638-1814

CRONSHAW, STEVEN FRANK, psychology educator; b. London, Ont., Can., Oct. 24, 1951; s. Frank and Gudny Thorunn (Johnson) C.; m. Kayla Elaine Dawn Jiricka, Aug. 12, 1972; children: Kristjan, Kenton. BA, U. Saskatchewan, 1974, B of Commerce, 1979; MA, U. Akron, 1983, PhD, 1984. Asst. prof. U. Waterloo, Ont., Can., 1984-86; assoc. prof. U. Guelph, Ont., Can., 1986-99, prof., 1999—. Exec. dir. Guelph Ctr. for Occupl. Rsch. Inc., 1992-95, chmn., bd. dirsl; human resource mgmt. cons., 1984—; dir. Joint Waterloo PhD Program in Indsl. and Orgnl. Psychology, Guelph, 1992-94. Author: Industrial Psychology in Canada, 1991, Recruitment and Selection in Canada, 1996, Functional Job Analysis: A Foundation for Human Resources Management, 1999; contbr. articles to profl. jours. Coord. Iceland-Guelph Exch. Program, U. Guelph, 1994—. Rsch. grant Social Scis. and Humanities Rsch. Coun. of Can., 1980-90s. Fellow: Can. Psychol. Assn.; mem.: Can. Soc. for Indsl. and Orgnl. Psychology. Avocation: study of icelandic language and literature. Home: 30 Pacific Pl Guelph ON Canada N1G 4R6 Office: U Guelph Dept of Psychology Guelph ON Canada N1G 2W1 E-mail: cronshaw@psy.uoguelph.ca.

CROOKE, PHILIP SCHUYLER, mathematics educator; b. Summit, N.J., Mar. 10, 1944; s. Philip Schuyler Jr. and Emma T. C.; m. Barbara E. Carey, Aug. 31, 1968; children: Philip Alexander, Cornelia Elizabeth. BS, Stevens Inst. Tech., 1966; PhD, Cornell U., 1970. Asst. prof. math. Vanderbilt U., Nashville, 1970-76, assoc. prof., 1976-86, prof., 1986—, prof. edn. secondary, 1995—. Vis. fellow Cornell U., Ithaca, N.Y., 1982. vice dir., Biomath Study Group, 2001— .vice chmn. Dept. Math., 2003— . Contbr. articles to profl. pubs. Mem. Am. Math. Soc. Home: 611 Cantrell Ave Nashville TN 37215-1020 Office: Vanderbilt U Dept Math Nashville TN 37240-0001

CROOKS, LISA ZAHN, elementary education educator; b. Kansas City, Mo., Oct. 1, 1958; d. F. George and Sue (Scott) Z.; children: Whitney, Rebecca. BA, Kansas City U., 1980; MS, U. Kans., 1982. Mid. sch. tchr. Kansas State Sch. for Deaf, Olathe, Kans., 1981-88; tchr. Kansas State Sch. for the Deaf, 1983-88; 4th grade tchr. Briarwood Elem. Sch., Olathe, 1988—97, Black Bob Elem. Sch., 1998—. Portfolio cons. Emporia State U., 1994—; instr. U. Kans., 1992-94; ednl. cons. Soc. Devel. Edn., 2000—. Author: Coloring Your World With Learning, 1995, The Best of Good Apple, 1995, Munchable Math, 2000, Connecting Math and Literature, 2002; contbr. articles to profl. jours. Bd. dirs. Paul Mesner Puppets, Kansas City, Mo., 1993—, com. chmn., exec. com. BOTAR, Kansas City., 1980—; chmn. Am. Royal BBQ Contest; bd. dirs. Midwest Ear Inst., Kansas City, 1988—. Recipient Presdl. award for Excellence in Tchg. Math. Office of Pres. U.S., 1994, Excellence in Tchg. Math. award Kans. Med. Soc., 1993; Christa McAuliffe fallow, 2002; named to Nat. Tchr. Hall of Fame, 2002, Mid-Am. Edn. Hall of Fame, 2003. Mem. Nat. Sci. Tchr. Assn., Nat. Supervisors of Tchrs. of Math., Nat. Coun. of Tchrs. of Math., Soc. Presdl. Awardees, Coun. Presdl. Awards for Math., Delta Kappa. Presbyterian. Avocations: cycling, hiking, needlepoint, backpacking. Home: 5213 W 84th Ter Shawnee Mission KS 66207-1716

CROOKS, W. SPENCER, artist, educator; b. Belfast, Ireland, July 26, 1917; came to U.S., 1927; s. James and Margaret (Coulter) C.; m. Ruth Davis Crandall, Oct. 21, 1950; 1 child, Nadine Jennifer Crooks Corona. Student, RISD, 1933-37, Graphic Design, 1950-52; cert., Shrivenham U., Eng., 1945; DFA (hon.), Roger Williams U., 1987. Graphic artist Boston Symphony, 1947-49, Halladay, Inc., East Providence, 1953-59, Noyes Advt. Agy., Providence, 1959-60; designer and graphic creator Hassenfeld Toy Co., Pawtucket, R.I., 1960-61; art dir. Cardono Advt., Pawtucket, 1961-63; creative artist Paramount Greeting Card Co., Pawtucket, 1963-70; graphic artist, tchr. R.I. Coll., Providence, 1973-83. Bd. dirs. R.I. Heritage Hall of Fame, Providence; dir. workshop Newport-Wickford Watercolor, R.I., 1974-89; instr. art Brown U., Providence, 1968-75, also Narragansett Bay Campus Watercolor Workshop, U. R.I. Exhibited in group shows Royal Acad., London, 1944, Am. Watercolor Soc., RISD, Art Students Group, Brussels, 1945, R.I. Arts Festival, 1960, Samuel Beckett Theatre, Trinity Coll., Dublin, Ireland, 1982, Ireland Nat. Art Gallery, Dublin, 1983, Rockport Art Assn., Symphony Hall Gallery, DeCordova Gallery; represented in numerous pub. and pvt. collections. Govs. Art Com., Providence, 1972-74; chmn. Garden City Art Festival, Cranston, R.I., 1963; v.p. East Greenwich Art Club, 1960. With U.S. Army, 1942-46. Inducted R.I. Heritage Hall of Fame, 1987, bd. dirs. 1988—; recipient Eliza Radeke Meml. award RISD, 1938. Mem. Phila. Watercolor Club, Providence Art Club (Florence Kane award 1961), Rockport Art Assn. (James G. Geddes award 1974), R.I. Watercolor Soc. (numerous awards including Grumbacher gold medal, 1991), Cape Cod Art Assn., Wickford Art Assn. Avocations: phys. culture, opera, collecting paintings. Home: 84 Davis Ave Cranston RI 02910-5706

CROOKSTON, R. KENT, agronomy educator; b. Magrath, Alta., Can., Mar. 8, 1943; s. Bryan Grant and Lisadore (Brown) C.; m. Gayle Loraine Jones, June 22, 1966; children: Rebecca, Casey, Polly, Daniel, Elizabeth, Emily, Sadie. BS, Brigham Young U., 1968; MS, U. Minn., 1970, PhD, 1972. Postdoctoral fellow Agr. Can., Lethbridge, Alta., 1972; rsch. assoc. Cornell U., Ithaca, N.Y., 1972-74; from asst. prof. to prof. U. Minn., St. Paul, 1974—82, dir. sustainable agr. program Coll. Agr., 1988-92, head dept. agronomy, 1990-98. Adj. prof. Inst. Agronomique Et Veterinaire Hassan II, Rabat, Morocco, 1984—; dean Coll. Biology and Agr., Brigham Young U., Provo, Utah, 1998—. Author rsch. manuscripts. With Can. armed forces, 1962. Fellow Am. Soc. Agronomy, Crop Sci. Soc. Am.; mem. Coun. Agrl. Sci. and Tech. Avocations: oil painting, woodworking, writing, photography. Home: 1055 N 1100 E Orem UT 84097-4390 Address: College of Biology and Agriculture 301 WIDB Brigham Young Univ Provo UT 84602-5250 E-mail: kent_crookston@byu.edu.

CROOM, BEVERLY JO, social science educator, retired; b. Coweta County, Ga., Jan. 31, 1937; d. Millard Houston and Grace Maureen (Watson) Eldson; m. Robert Edward Croom, Feb. 2, 1957; 1 child, Yashi Malenka Warner. BA, Ga. State U., Atlanta, 1964, MEd, 1974; M in EdS, Ga. State U., 1991. Social studies tchr. Clayton County Bd. Edn., Jonesboro, Ga., 1965-87, instructional lead tchr., 1987-91; asst. prin. North Clayton High Sch., Jonesboro, 1991-94, prin., 1994-97; retired. Rsch. in field. Contbr. articles to profl. jours. Vis. scholar to China, PRC, 1987; Asian Studies fellow U. Mich., 1986. Mem. ASCD, NEA, Nat. Coun. Social Studies, US-China People's Friendship Assn. (nat. coord. Teach-in-China program), Ga. Assn. Educators, Ga. Coun. Social Studies, Clayton County Assn. Educators. Home: PO Box 387 Union City GA 30291-0387

CROOM, FREDERICK HAILEY, academic administrator, mathematician, educator; b. Lumberton, N.C., Aug. 6, 1941; s. Robert DeVane and Anna Roslyn (Currie) Croom; m. Henrietta Brown, Aug. 17, 1963 (div. May 2000); children: Elizabeth Bonner, Frederick Hailey; m. Nancy Mishoe Brennecke, June 1, 2002. BS, U. N.C., 1963, PhD, 1967. Asst. prof. math. U. Ky., Lexington, 1967-71, U. of the South, Sewanee, Tenn., 1971-74, assoc. prof., 1974-81, prof., 1981—, dir. Summer Sch., 1980-88, assoc. dean, 1984-88, provost, 1989-2001. Author: (book) Basic Concepts of Algebraic Topology, 1978, Principles of Topology, 1989. Pres. Tenn. Coll. Assn., 1999—2000; bd. dirs. St. Andrews-Sewanee Sch., 1981—86, Tenn. Found. Ind. Colls., 1996—99; trustee U. of the South, 1983—85. Fellow Woodrow Wilson, 1963, NSF, 1963—67. Mem.: AAUP, Mat. Assn. Am., Am. Math. Soc., Sigma Xi. Episcopalian. Office: U South University Ave Sewanee TN 37383-0001 E-mail: fcroom@sewanee.edu.

CROSIER, HAZEL JANE, primary education educator; b. Indpls., Jan. 7, 1939; d. Fred Abraham and Mabel Iva (Thomas) Stickle; m. Eugene Delano Crosier, Apr. 6, 1963; children: Robert Eugene, Deborah Jane. BS in Spl. Early Childhood Edn., Butler U., 1960; MA in Spl. Early Childhood Edn., Ball State U., 1975. Cert. elem. edn., spl. early childhood edn. Tchr. grade 3 Indpls. (Ind.) Sch. #3, 1960-61; kindergarten tchr. Grassy Creek Elem.-Met. Sch. Dist. Warren Twp., Indpls., 1961-65; tchr. grade 3 Eastridge Elem.-M.S.D. Warren Twp., Indpls., 1977-82, tchr. grade 4, 1982-92; kindergarten tchr. Eastridge Elem. and Warren Kindergarten Ctr.-M.S.D. Warren Twp, Indpls., 1992—99. Mem. Warren Math. Curriculum Com., 1981-82, 86-87, 91-92, Warren Computer Curriculum Com., 1982, Warren Lang. Arts Com., 1987-88, Warren Ad Hoc Curriculum Com., 1987-88; mem. curriculum adv. bd. M.S.D. Warren Twp., Indpls., 1991-94; prof. U. Indpls., 2000, 02; presenter in field. City chmn. vision screening Ind. Soc. for Prevention Blindness, Indpls., 1966-70; v.p. Eastridge PTA, Indpls., 1974-76; pres. ho. corp. Alpha Tau of Delta Gamma, Indpls., 1986-92, Zeta Pi of Delta Gamma, Indpls., 1992—; sec. United Christian Coun., 1999-2000, 01-02. Recipient Cable award Delta Gamma Fraternity, Columbus, Ohio, 1992. Mem. Nat. Assn. Profl. Educators, Ind. Assn. Profl. Educators, Nat. Reading Assn., Nat. Assn. Edn. Young Children, Am. Edn. Children Internat., Ind. Assn. Edn. Young Children (adv. com. mem. 1993-95), Ind. Reading Coun. (sec. 1992-95), Sigma Delta Pi (sec. 1985-86, v.p. 1986-87, 91-92, pres. 1987-88). Methodist. Avocations: gardening, reading. Office: MSD Warren Twp Eastridge Elem Indianapolis IN 46229 Home: 1042 S Daisy Ln New Palestine IN 46163-9631

CROSKERY, BEVERLY ANN, education consultant; b. Oklahoma City, Okla., Oct. 19, 1934; d. Clarence Glenn and Mildred Estelle (Bell) Fulkerson; m. Robert William Croskery, Aug. 14, 1954; children: Richard W., Robert F., Kathryn Croskery Jones, Virginia. BA, U. Wichita, 1963; MEd, U. Toledo, 1973, PhD, 1978. Cert. provisional supt., elem. prin. Elem. tchr. Hamden (Conn.) Hall Country Day Sch., 1955-56; ROMPER ROOM tchr. Sta. KAKE-TV, Wichita, Kans., 1960-65; elem. tchr. Kenosha (Wis.) Unified Sch., 1966-68, Toledo (Ohio) Pub. Schs., 1969-75, adminstr., 1975-76; instr. U. Toledo, 1977; intermediate supr. N.W. Local Schs., Cin., 1977-79, elem. prin., 1979-84, dir. elem. edn., 1984-95. Trainer, multiple intelligences, 1993—; adj. prof. Wright State U., Dayton, Ohio, 1990—, Coll. of Mount St. Joseph, Cin., 1984—86, Miami U., Oxford, Ohio, 1979, Oxford, 98; writer, cons. WCPO-TV, Cin., 1977—79. Exec. producer (videotape) Children, Community, Challenge, 1994, (writer, producer) The Gifted Child, 1980 (motion picture) Everyone is Special: The Story of the Toledo Public Schools, 1971; author: Attitudes...Toward Death Education, 1979, Shamir the White Elephant: A Rain Forest Adventure, 1997. Mem. Ohio Dept. Edn. Missing Child Task Force, 1988—89; chmn. com., author book on religious curriculum Westwood First Presbyn. CH., Cin., 1994; mem. adv. bd. Classics for Kids Classics for Kids; mem. Supts. Adv. Com., 1982—84. Recipient Award of Honor Am. Cancer Soc., 1994. Mem. Ohio Community Edn. Assn. (pres. 1983-84), Ohio Assn. of Supervision and Curriculum Devel. (bd. dirs. 1980-83), Nat. Staff Devel. Assn. (Ohio affiliate 1992—), Ohio Valley Elem. Prins. Assn. (sec. 1982-83). Avocations: tennis, storytelling. Home: 5300 Hamilton Ave Ste 1000 Cincinnati OH 45224-3153 Office: 5300 Hamilton Ave Ste 1001 Cincinnati OH 45224-3153

CROSS, DENNIS WAYNE, academic administrator; b. Bristol, Va., Apr. 18, 1955; s. Brainard C. and Genevieve Cross; m. Susan Sydney Haire, Aug. 7, 1982; children: Walker Gray, Grier Gordon, Sydney Sullivan. BA, Vanderbilt U., 1976; MDiv, Harvard U., 1979, ThM, 1982; postgrad., Vanderbilt U., 1986, Williamsburg Devel. Inst., 1987. Banking officer 1st Am. Nat. Bank, Nashville, 1982-86; dir. alumni and devel. Coll. Arts and Sci. Vanderbilt U., Nashville, 1986-92; exec. dir. Arts and Scis. Found., Inc., assoc. dean for program devel. Coll. Arts and Scis. U. N.C., Chapel Hill, 1992-2000; v.p. for univ. devel. Coll. William and Mary, Williamsburg, Va., 2000—. Bd. dirs. mid. Tenn. chpt. ACLU, Nashville, 1991-92, Christopher Wren Assn., Williamsburg, Ash Lawn Music Festival, Charlottesville, Va.; exec. com. Friends of Music, Inc., Nashville, 1987-89; mem. membership com. U. Club of Nashville, 1991-92; former head edn. com. Chapel of the Cross, Chapel Hill, N.C., mem. campus ministry; mem. comm. commn. St. Martin's Episcopal Ch., Williamsburg, Va.; vol. bicentennial campaign Coll. of Arts and Scis. U. N.C., 1992-95; bd. dirs., sec.-treas. U. N.C.-Chapel Hill Arts and Scis. Found., Inc., 1992-2000; mem. Thomas Wolfe Centennial Com., 1997-99; advisor Ctr. for the Study of the Am. South, 1998-2000; bd. dirs., asst. sec. Endowment Assn. of Coll. William and Mary; mem. steering com. Campaign for William and Mary, 2000—; mem. exec. com. Arts and Scis. Advancement Profls., 1995-2000; bd. dirs. Chapel Hill-Carrboro Pub. Sch. Found., 1998-2000. Mem. Coun. for Advancement of Secondary Edn., Country Music Found., Coun. of Friends-Tryon Palace, N.C. Triangle Vanderbilt Club (organizer), Kingsmill Golf Club, Phi Beta Kappa (exec. com. U.N.C., chpt. officer 1997-2000), Delta Phi Alpha. Episcopalian. Avocations: reading, baseball, golf, studying southern folk art and material culture of the south. Home: 324 Yorkshire Dr Williamsburg VA 23185-3913 Office: Coll William and Mary Office of Univ Devel PO Box 8795 Williamsburg VA 23187-8795

CROSS, DOLORES EVELYN, former university administrator, educator; b. Newark, Aug. 29, 1938; d. Charles and Ozie (Johnson) Tucker; children: Thomas E., Jane E. BA in Elem. Edn., Seton Hall U., 1963; MS, Hofstra U., 1968; PhD in Higher Edn. Adminstrn., U. Mich., 1971; hon. doctorates, Marymount Coll., Skidmore Coll., Hofstra U., Elmhurst Coll. Asst. prof. edn. Northwestern U., Evanston, Ill., 1971-74; assoc. prof. Claremont Grad. Sch., Calif., 1974-78; vice chancellor CUNY, 1978-81; prof. Bklyn. Coll., 1978-81; pres. N.Y. State Higher Edn. Svc. Corp., Albany, 1981-88; assoc. provost, assoc. v.p. acad. affairs U. Minn., Mpls., 1988-90; pres. Chgo. State U., 1990—97, Gen. Electric Fund, 1996-99, Morris Brown Coll., Atlanta, 1999—2002. Pres. Gen. Electric Fund, 1996-99; bd. dirs. Coll. Bd., Campus Compact, 1997—, Assn. Black Women in Higher Edn., No. Trust Co.; sr. cons. South Africa's Historically Black Colls.; bd. dirs. Inst. Internat. Edn., No. Trust Corp. Editor: Teaching in a Multicultural Society, 1978. Bd. dirs. Field Mus., Chgo. Urban League, Leadership for Quality Edn., Chgo. Area Fulbright Scholars Program. Recipient Tosney award Am. Assn. of Univ. Adminstrs., 1995. Mem. NAACP (life), Am. Edn. Rsch. Assn., Am. Assn. Higher Edn. (chair-elect 1997—), Am. Coun. on Edn. (bd. dirs.) Women Execs. in State Govt. (adv. bd.), Comml. Club (Chgo.). Avocations: running, hiking, bicycling, theatre, writing. Office: IIE Bd of Dirs 155 N Wacker Dr Chicago IL 60606-1787*

CROSS, HAROLD ZANE, agronomist, educator; b. Portales, N.Mex., Dec. 25, 1941; s. Guy Edner and Hagabelle (Lawson) C.; m. Glenda Faye Wilhoit, Nov. 24, 1961; children: Carter Dale, Carson Lee, Curtis Don, Cathryn Faye. BS with honors, N.Mex. State U., 1965, MS, 1967; PhD, U. Mo., 1971. Rancher, Elida, N.Mex., 1965-67; grad. rsch. asst. N.Mex. State U., Las Cruces, 1965-67; NDEA fellow U. Mo., Columbia, 1967-71; asst. prof. N.D. State U., Fargo, 1971-77, assoc. prof., 1977-82, prof., 1982-98, prof. emeritus, 1998—. Cons. Agrl. Inst. Osijek, Yugoslavia, 1984, CIMMYT, Mexico City, 1984, Eli Lilly Co., Indpls., 1987, N.D. State U., Fargo, 1998—. Author: Descendents of Sir Robert Crosse, 2000; contbr. numerous articles to profl. jours. Crops judge N.D. Winter show, Valley City, 1973-98. Santa Fe Rwy. scholar, 1961-62; NDEA fellow, 1967-71; recipient Outstanding Sr. Rsch. award N.D. State U. Coll. Agr., 1992. Mem. Crop Sci. Soc. Am. (editor for maize germplasm 1989-92), Am. Soc. Agronomy, Sigma Xi, Phi Kappa Phi, Gamma Sigma Delta, Alpha Zeta. Achievements include development and release of 51 inbred parental lines of maize and 39 synthetic varieties of maize; 12 plant variety patents; development of maize breeding procedures to genetically improve grain drying rates, procedures to improve leaf growth rates, kernel growth. E-mail: hzcross@earthlink.net.

CROSS, JAMES MILLARD, assistant principal; b. Oneida, Tenn., Nov. 2, 1945; s. Millard and Edna (Posey) C.; student Cumberland Coll., 1961; B.S., East Tenn. State U., 1965; M.A.T., E. Tenn. State U., 1970; Educ. specialist, 1975; Ed.D., U. So. Miss., 1983. Tchr. intern Bristol City (Tenn.) City Sch., 1970; spl. educ. tchr. Elizabethton (Tenn.) City Schs., 1970-71; Washington County (Tenn.) work study coordinator Crockett High Sch., Jonesboro, Tenn., 1972-77; supr. spl. services Washington County Dept. Edn., Jonesboro, 1978-85; spl. assignment U.S. Army, 1985-86, Operation Desert Storm/Shield, 1990-91; asst. prin. David Crockett High Sch., 1986—. Mem. Washington County Republican Exec. Com., 1977— . Col. U.S. Army, 1966-69. Decorated Army Commendation medal, Vietnam Campaign medal, Vietnam Svc. medal, Res. Components Svc. medal, Res. component Achievement medal, Army Achievement medal, Nat. Def. Svc. medal, others; recipient ROA medal Assn. Mil. Surgeons U.S. Mem. Am. Assn. Sch. Adminstrs., Council for Exceptional Children, Nat. Rehab. Assn., Res. Officers Assn., Assn. Supervision and Curriculum Devel., Alpha Phi Omega, Kappa Delta Phi, Phi Delta Kappa. Baptist. Lodge: Masons (32 degree). Office: Washington County Dept Edn David Crockett High Sch 1904 E Myrtle Ave Johnson City TN 37601-2862

CROSS, JOHN WILLIAM, foreign language educator; b. Franklin, Pa., June 1, 1943; s. William Robert and Madaline Ann (Maurin) C.; m. Beverly Jean Boor (div. 2000); 1 child, Catherine Elizabeth. BA, W.Va. U., 1965, MA, 1967; PhD, U. Conn., 1974. Instr. French U. N.C., Asheville, 1967-68; asst. Lycee Louis-Le-Grand, Paris, 1972-73; instr., asst. prof. French SUNY, Geneseo, N.Y., 1969-75; asst. prof. SUNY-Potsdam Coll., 1976-84, chair modern langs., 1985-86, 90-91, 93—, assoc. prof., 1984-91, prof. modern langs., 1991; dir. for lang. programs MLA of Am., N.Y.C., 1991-93. Advanced placement reader Ednl. Testing Svc., Princeton, N.J., 1983-87; cons. in field. Editor Assn. Depts. of Fgn. Langs. Bull.; contbr. articles and revs. to profl. jours. Recipient French Govt. scholarship, Svcs. Culturels Francais, 1990; grantee, NEH, 1977, 1985, 1988, 2001, Office des Universites, 1972—73. Mem. MLA of Am., Am. Assn. Tchrs. French, N.Y. State Assn. Fgn. Lang. Tchrs., Societe d'Analyse de la Topique du Roman, Internat. Courtly Lit. Soc. Avocations: music appreciation, performance, recreational sports, poetry translation. Home: 36 Pierrepont Ave Potsdam NY 13676-2111 Office: SUNY Dept Modern Langs Potsdam NY 13676 E-mail: crossjw@potsdam.edu.

CROSS, JUNE CREWS, retired music educator; b. Creedmoor, N.C., Oct. 7, 1935; d. David Reid and Virginia Frances (Bullock) Crews; m. Joel Allen Cross, June 26, 1965; children: Dhedra Frances, Allen Reid. BS in Music, Reading, East Carolina U., 1957; MS in Recreation Adminstrn., U. N.C., Chapel Hill, 1964. Cert. tchr., N.C. Tchr. music Mecklenburg County Schs., Charlotte, N.C., 1957-58, Granville County Schs., Oxford, N.C., 1958-60, 65-66, tchr. reading, music, 1977-97, lead tchr., 1989-90; asst. dir. recreation John Elmstead Hosp., 1960—65. Pvt. tchr. piano, voice, Creedmoor, 1966-74. Choir dir. Creedmoor United Meth. Ch., 1988-2000; asst. dir. Sparkle, Granville County Show Choir, 1975-2003; accompanist The King and I prodn. Granville Little Theatre, Oxford, 1997; dir. Evening of Entertainment, Creedmoor United Meth. Ch., 2000—. Named Tchr. of Yr. Butner (N.C.) -Stem Elem. Sch., 1993-94. Mem. DAR (treas. John Penn chpt.), Delta Kappa Gamma, Sigma Alpha Iota. Methodist. Avocation: reading. Home: 701 Forest Ln Creedmoor NC 27522-8196

CROSS, KATHRYN PATRICIA, education educator; b. Normal, Ill., Mar. 17, 1926; d. Clarence L. and Katherine (Dague) C. BS, Ill. State U., 1948; MA, U. Ill., 1951, PhD, 1958; LLD (hon.), SUNY, 1988; DS (hon.), Loyola U., 1980, Northeastern U., 1975; DHL (hon.), De Paul U., 1986, Open U., The Netherlands, 1989. Math. tchr. Harvard (Ill.) Community High Sch., 1948-49; rsch. asst. dept. psychology U. Ill., Urbana, 1949-53, asst. dean of women, 1953-59; dean of women then dean of students Cornell U., Ithaca, N.Y., 1959-63; dir. coll. and univ. programs Ednl. Testing Svc., Princeton, N.J., 1963-66; rsch. educator Ctr. R&D in Higher Edn. U. Calif., Berkeley, 1966-77; rsch. scientist, sr. rsch. psychologist, dir. univ. programs Ednl. Testing Svc., Berkeley, 1966-80; prof. edn., chair dept. adminstrn., planning & social policy Harvard U., Cambridge, Mass., 1980-88; Elizabeth and Edward Conner prof. edn. U. Calif., Berkeley, 1988-94, David Pierpont Gardner prof. higher edn., 1994-96. Mem. sec. adv. com. on automated personal data sys. Dept. HEW, 1972-73; del. to Soviet Union, Seminar on Problems in Higher Edn., 1975; vis. prof. U. Nebr., 1975-76; vis. scholar Miami-Dade C.C., 1987; trustee Carnegie Found., 1999—, Berkeley Pub. Libr., 1998—; spkr., cons. in field; bd. dirs. Elderhostel. Author: Beyond the Open Door: New Students to Higher Education, 1971, (with S. B. Gould) Explorations in Non-Traditional Study, 1972, (with J. R. Valley and Assocs.) Planning Non-Traditional Programs: An Analysis of the Issues for Postsecondary Education, 1974, Accent on Learning, 1976, Adults as Learners, 1981, (with Thomas A. Angelo) Classroom Assessment Techniques, 1993, (with Mimi Harris Steadman) Classroom Research, 1996; contbr. articles, monographs to profl. publs., chpts. to books; mem. editl. bd. to several ednl. jours.; cons. editor ednl. mag. Change, 1980—. Active Nat. Acad. Edn., 1975—, Coun. for Advancement of Exptl. Learning, 1982-85; trustee Bradford Coll., Mass., 1986-88, Antioch Coll., Yellow Springs, Ohio, 1976-78; mem. nat. adv. bd. Nat. Ctr. of Study of Adult Learning, Empire State Coll.; mem. nat. adv. bd. Okla. Bd. Regents; mem. higher edn. rsch. program Pew Charitable Trusts; mem. vis. com. Harvard Grad. Sch. Edn., 1998—; bd. dirs. Elderhostel, 1999—; trustee Berkeley Pub. Libr., 1999—, Carnegie Found., 1999—. Mem. Am. Assn. Higher Edn. (bd. dirs. 1987—, pres. 1975, chair 1989-90), Am. Assn. Comty. and Jr. Colls. (vice chair commn. of future comty. colls.), Carnegie Found. Advancement of Tchg. (adv. com. on classification of colls. and univs.), Nat. Ctr. for Devel. Edn. (adv. bd.), New Eng. Assn. Schs. and Colls. (commn. on instns. higher edn. 1982-86), Am. Coun. Edn. (commn. on higher edn. and adult learner 1986-88). E-mail: patcross@socrates.berkeley.edu.

CROSS, RITA FAYE, librarian, early childhood educator, writer; b. Franklin, Va., Apr. 4, 1957; d. Alonza Riddick and Earleen (Smith) C.; m. Cameron Michael Moody. BS in Early Childhood Edn., Elizabeth City State U., 1979; MA in Libr. Sci., U. D.C., 1993. Tchr. kindergarten Great Mt. Zion Day Care, Washington, 1979-86, Woodridge Elem. Sch., Washington, 1986-92; libr. Ea. Sr. H.S., Washington, 1992—. Avocations: writing poetry, horseback riding, boating, concerts, theater. Home: 10207 Fort Hills Ct Fort Washington MD 20744-3913

CROSS, STEVEN JASPER, finance educator; b. Hohenwald, Tenn., Apr. 19, 1954; s. Thomas Edward and Eula Mae Cross; m. Patricia Aldas, Jan. 6, 1995. BS, Mid. Tenn. State U., 1976, MAT, 1980, DA, 1984. Sales rep. U. Ford Inc., Murfreesboro, Tenn., 1976; ins. underwriter Continental Ins., Inc., Nashville, 1976—77; credit rep. SunAm, Inc., Murfreesboro, 1977—78; instr. mgmt. Dyersburg (Tenn.) State C.C., 1980—81; instr. econs. Motlow State C.C., Tullahoma, Tenn., 1981—83, asst. prof. econs., 1983—85; assoc. prof. fin. Delta State U., Cleveland, Miss., 1985—88, prof. fin., chmn. divsn. econs. and fin., 1988—91; dean Sch. Bus., prof. bus. Troy State U., Dothan, Ala., 1991—97, prof. fin., 1997—. Contbr. articles to profl. jours. Mem. AAUP, NEA, Am. Fin. Assn., Am. Econ. Assn., Delta Mu Delta. Home: 112 Wentworth Dr Dothan AL 36305-6906 Office: Troy State U Coll Bus Adminstrn PO Box 8368 Dothan AL 36304-0368

CROSS, VIVIAN ALICIA, university educator; b. New Britain, Conn., Apr. 17, 1944; d. Robert Everett and Gussie (Lampkin) Post; m. William Sherman Cross, Aug. 31, 1968; children: Carla Marie, William Sherman Jr. BS in Elem. Edn., Ctrl. Conn. State U., 1968, MS in Spl. Edn., 1979; tchr. trainer diploma, Hadassah-Wizo-Can. Rsch. Inst., Jerusalem, 1987; EdD in Ednl. Adminstrn., Columbia U., 1991. Cert. preK-8 tchr., K-12 spl. edn. tchr., adminstrn., mentor tchr., Conn. Tchr. lang. arts and enrichment Kingswood-Oxford Pvt. Sch., West Hartford, Conn., 1970; chmn. sci. Rawson Elem. Sch., Hartford, 1976-78; tchr. spl. edn., team leader Quirk Mid. Sch., Hartford, 1983; dir. ednl. support svc. Lighthouse Ministries, Manchester, Conn., 1981—; elem. tchr. Hartford (Conn.) Pub. Schs., 1970-78; ednl. diagnostician Hartford Pub. Schs., 1987-88, curriculum and staff developer, 1987-91, out of dist. placement spl. edn. resource specialist, 1991-92, coord. student svcs., 1992—2001; exec. dir. Found. Ednl. Advancement, Inc., 1996—. Staff insvc. workshop presenter, 1983—; lectr. ednl. opportunity program Ctrl. Conn. State U., New Britain, 1984-87; pres. Found. for Ednl. Advancement, Inc., Simsbury, Conn., 1992-96, v.p., 1996—; forensic ednl. cons. Thompson & Jacobson P.C., Springfield, Mass., 1994, Grenier Cons. Assocs., Inc., Canton, Conn., 1992—, New Britain Pub. Schs., 1993, Pa. Dept. Edn., Harrisburg, 1988; lectr., pres. Conn. Assn. Pvt. Schs., Meriden, 1989, New Eng. Thinking Skills Conf., Storrs, Conn., 1988; developer, initiator, mgr., dir. HPS Symposium Series, 1993—; mem. adv. com. Tchrs. Acad., U. Hartford, 1990—; facilitator, co-implementor grants Aetna Life and Casualty Found., 1990, Nat. Rsch. Ctr. for Gifted, 1993, Conn. Dept. Edn., 1994-95; designer, developer, implementer numerous ednl. initiatives; prof. Ctrl. Conn. State U., 2001-; commnr. Conn. State, 2000-; mem. adv. coun. State Dept. Children & Families. Bd. dirs. San Juan Tutorial Program, Hartford, 1993—; com. mem. Ednl. Reform Com., Hartford, 1994; advisor Youth Congress, 1991-92; rep. Conn. State-Wide Coalition for Ednl. Equity, 1993—; mem. Environ. Justice Cmty. Adv. Bd., Gov's. Office and DEP State of Conn. Mem. ASCD, Hartford Prins. and Suprs. Assn. (ednl. rep. 1993—), Phi Delta Kappa. Avocations: travel, humanitarian service projects, church service activities, interior decorating. Office: Hartford Pub Schs 153 Market St Hartford CT 06103-1300

CROTEAU, GERALD A., JR., retired school system administrator; b. Millbury, Mass., Aug. 6, 1937; s. Gerald A. Sr. and Flora Ann (Nash) C.; m. Eleanore Majewski, Sept. 5, 1959; children: Gerald A. III, Catherine Macone, Robert, André. AB, Assumption Coll., 1959; MEd, U. Mass., 1966, CAGS, 1968, EdD, 1979. Cert. supt. of schs. History tchr. The Arnold Sch., East Pembroke, Mass., 1961-64; French tchr. Hopkins Acad., Hadley, Mass., 1964-66; asst. pers. mgr. Kowlmorgen Corp., Northampton, Mass., 1966-68; adminstrv. intern Eastchester (N.Y.) H.S., 1968-69; supervising prin. Marlborough (N.H.) Pub. Schs., 1969-72; asst. supt. Supervisory Union 53, Suncook, N.H., 1972-74, supt. of schs., 1974-81, Taunton (Mass.) Sch. Dept., 1981—2002. Ptnr. J.W. & Assocs., North Dartmouth, Mass., 1994—; developer curriculum Instrumental Enrichment. Exec. bd. mem. Boy Scouts Am., Taunton, 1984-95, ARC, Taunton, 1986-94; trustee Morton Hosp., Taunton, 1987-95. Recipient Leadership for Learning award Am. Assn. Sch. Adminstrs., 1995. Mem. Taunton C. of C. (dir. 1984-91, v.p. 1987-89), Taunton (Mass.) Rotary Club (dir. 1986-90, pres. 1989-90). Avocations: family activities, reading, sailing, traveling, probability and stats. Home: 157 Fremont St Taunton MA 02780*

CROTEAU, KEVAN HOWARD, computer science educator; b. Keene, N.H., June 25, 1956; s. Howard Ernest and Jeanne (Arsenault) C.; m. Vickie Lynn Fay, Sept. 29, 1984; 1 child, Joshua K. Student, Coll. William & Mary, 1976; ScB, Keene State Coll., 1978; MS in Computer Sci., SUNY, Stony Brook, 1980. Asst. prof. Ill. State U., Normal, 1980-84; dir. acad. computing, asst. prof. U. Dubuque (Iowa), 1984-87; asst. prof., network mgr., dept. tech. resource coord. Francis Marion U., Florence, SC, 1987—. Cons. United Way, Florence, 1988—96. Author: 6 books; contbr. articles to profl. jours. Bd. dirs. Florence Masterworks Choir, 1994-96, Florence Soccer Assn., 1990-92, coach, 1987-91. Mem.: IEEE, Internat. Cryptological Rsch. Assn., Assn. Computing Machinery. Lutheran. Avocations: running, soccer, chess, recreational computing. Office: Francis Marion U Dept Computer Sci Hwy 301 N Florence SC 29501-0547 E-mail: kcroteau@fmarion.edu.

CROTTI, ROSE MARIE, special education educator; b. Scranton, Pa., Aug. 29, 1952; d. Frank Joseph and Cecelia Ann (Bossi) Leitza; m. John Anthony Crotti, Sept. 26, 1975; children: Annette Michelle, Joseph Francis, John Michael. BA, Marywood U., 1974, MS, 1984; student, U. Scranton, 1979-80. Cert. elem. and secondary prin., Pa.; cert. supt., Pa. Program dir. St. Joseph's Ctr., Dunmore, Pa., 1974-75; instr. Northeastern Ednl. Intermediate Unit #19, Scranton, 1976-80, 1980-83, tchr. Learning Disabilities Montdale, Pa., 1983-86, cons. Learning Disabilities Carbondale, Pa., 1988-89; cons., state validator Instrnl. Support Pa. Dept. Edn., Harrisburg, Pa., 1990—; instr. spl. edn. undergrad. and grad. dept. Marywood U., 1994—; asst. sec. prin. Lakeland Sch. Dist., Jermyn, Pa., 1998—2001, guidance dept. coord., 1999—, gifted coord., spl. edn. liaison, 1998—; secondary prin. Lakeland Jr./Sr. H.S., 2001—. Presenter Northeastern Ednl. Intermediate Unit #19, Scranton, 1988—; appeared on PBS, An Apple a Day, 1991, 92; coord., trainer peer tutors Carbondale Sch. Dist., 1992-93, peer mediators, 1993-94; mem. Oxford (England) Round Table, Lincoln Coll., U. Oxford. Co-author: Parent-to-Parent Handbook on Drugs and Alcohol Abuse Among Teenagers, 1993. Active Parent Tchrs. Guild, Clarks Summit, Pa.; chmn. Lackawanna County Handicapped Awareness Day, 1990; co-chmn. Children Without a Conscience Sch. Conf., 1990; coord. Students Against Driving Drunk, 1992-94; chair family festival Marywood Coll., 1993; chair reorgn. PTA Lakeland Elem. Sch., 1993; chairperson Bus. Cmty.-Non-Alcoholic Mix-Off, 1993; bd. govs. Scranton Prep. Sch., v.p., 1992; mem. lead tchr. governing bd., lead tchr. adv. coun., adv. bd. Bishop O'Hara H.S., 1994, pres. PTO, 1996—. Named N.E. Woman of Pa. Scranton Times Newspaper, 1989. Mem. CEC(local chpt. bd. dirs. 1989—), Platform Spkrs. Assn. Roman Catholic. Avocations: cooking, reading, crafts, Broadway shows, shopping. Home: 24 Grove Olyphant PA 18447 Office: Lakeland Sch Dist 1593 Lakeland Dr Jermyn PA 18433-3140 E-mail: rmlhsap@aol.com.

CROUCH, ALTHA MARIE, health educator, consultant; b. Belton, Tex., Aug. 23, 1933; d. Walter Loy and Nancy Elizabeth (Harrison) C. BS in Health, Phys. Edn. and Recreation, Sul Ross State U., 1966, MA in Health, Phys. Edn. and Recreation, 1967; EdD in Curriculum and Instrn., U. N.Mex., 1977; MA in Counseling Edn., Western N.Mex. U., 1992. Bookkeeper Midland (Tex.) Reporter Telegram, 1954-63; instr. physical edn. and health Our Lady of Peace Cath. Elem. Sch., Alpine, Tex., 1964-65; asst. prof., coord. Womens' Programs Wayland Baptist Coll., Palinview, Tex., 1966-71; vis. instr. Tex. Tech. U., Lubbock, 1971-72; teaching assoc., grad. rsch. asst. U. N.Mex., Albuquerque, 1972-75, asst. prof. health edn. and recreation Gallup, 1975-80, asst. prof., co-coord. health edn. program Alburquerque, 1980-83, coord. community edn., part-time tchr. Valencia, 1983-88, asst. prof., coord. health edn. program Gallup, 1988-93, assoc. prof., 1993—. V.p. Faculty Senate, U. N.Mex., Gallup, 1989, 90; exec. dir. Crouch and Assoc. Health Cons., Gallup, 1979—; presenter in field. Assoc. editor N.Mex. Jour. HPERD, 1993; contrb. articles to profl. jours. Bd. mem. Am. Lung Assn., Albuquerque, 1981-87, Am. Heart Assn., Valencia County, 1967-94, Nat. Inst. on Alcoholism, 1980-92, Optimist Club, Gallup, 1990—; cert. ARC, Albuquerque, 1967. Recipient Cert. of Appreciation Svc. award ARC, 1980, 1500 Hours Vol. Svc. in CPR and First Aid award, 1984, Ten Year Svc. Recognition award, 1987, Five Year Disting. Svc. award Wayland Bapt. Coll, 1971, Ella May Small award N.Mex. Sch. Health Assn., 1981, Disting. Svc. award Am. Sch. Health Assn., 1983, Six Yrs. Dist. Svc. Bd. Dirs. award Am. Lung Assn., 1987. Fellow Am. Sch. Health Assn. (internat. health coun. 1989—, rsch. coun. 1981—, budget and fin. com. 1983-85, sec. to study com. 1982, chair 2 coms. 1981-83, conducted surveys 1981, state constituents constitution and by-laws ad hoc com. chair 1981, acting chair resolutions com. 1981); mem. AAHPERD (S.W. dist. asst. resgistrar 1981, presenter 1981, 92-94, N.Mex. chpt. v.p. health sect. 1981-82, 92-94, tchr. accountability task force; developed AS degree in Cmty. Health 1994; developed AA degree in Sch. Health Edn. 1995), Am. Assn. Counseling and Devel., Am. Assn. Advancement Health Edn., N.Mex. Assn. Counseling & Devel., Coalition for Indian Edn. Avocation: dance. Office: U N Mex 220 College Rd Gallup NM 87301-5603

CROUCH, ARLINE PARKS, librarian; b. Corbin, Ky., Jan. 13, 1947; d. Elijah and Edna (Gibbs) Parks; m. Robert Louis Crouch, Aug. 25, 1968; children: Cara Lynn, Carlin Robert. BS, Cumberland Coll., 1967; MA, Union Coll., 1970; postgrad., U. Ky., 1973. Tchr. 3d grade Boone County Bd. of Edn., Florence, Ky., 1967-68, tchr. 2d grade, 1968-69, tchr. 3d grade, 1969-74, libr., 1975-95. Libr. Crescent Springs (Ky.) Bapt. Ch., 1987-90; food svc. rep. Heavenly Ham. Mem. exec. coun. Ky. Educators Pub. Affairs Coun., Florence, 1975-78. Mem. NEA, Ky. Edn. Assn., Boone County Edn. Assn. (treas. Florence chpt. 1975-78), KRTA, AARP. Democrat. Baptist. Avocations: reading, sewing, travel. Home: PO Box 47 Burlington KY 41005-0047

CROUCH, DIANNE KAY, secondary school guidance counselor; b. Campbellsville, Ky., Apr. 28, 1954; d. James Edgar and Imogene (Bailey) Gabbert; m. Thomas Frederick Crouch, June 6, 1987. BA, Campbellsville Coll., 1976; MS, U. Ky., 1984, EdS, 1991. Cert. tchr. English, psychology, counselor, secondary schs., Ky. Tchr. English Grayson County High Sch., Leitchfield, Ky., 1976-78, Jessamine County Jr. High Sch., Nicholasville, Ky., 1978-83, Jessamine County High Sch., Nicholasville, 1983-89, Tates Creek Jr. High Sch., Lexington, Ky., 1989-90; guidance counselor Tates Creek High Sch., Lexington, 1990—. Mem. pub. rels. com. Tates Creek H.S.; selected Inst. Women in Sch. Adminstrn. Ky. Active Calvary Bapt. Ch., Lexington, 1991—; bd. dirs. Lexington C.C. Nursing Program; mem. undergrad. adv. bd. U. Ky. Named Jessamine County Tchr. of Yr., Jessamine County Bd. Edn., Nicholasville, Ky., 1986-87, Outstanding Tchr. 5th Dist., Campbellsville Coll., 1988; sponsor of Jr. High newspaper Tates Creek Clarion named 1 of top 5 in U.S Nat. Jr. Beta Club; recipient Ginny Rollins Leadership award, 2000-01. Mem. Ky. Assn. Secondary and Coll. Admission Counselors, Ky. Counseling Assn. (Ky. H.S. Counselor of Yr.), Ctrl. Ky. Counseling Assn. (past pres., named H.S. Counselor of Yr. 1999-2000, 01-02), Ky. Sch. Counselors Assn. (pres.), Kappa Delta Pi. Avocations: piano, dog training, walking, exercising, travel. Home: 1240 Litchfield Ln Lexington KY 40513 E-mail: dcrouch@fayette.k12.ky.us.

CROUCH, MERCEDES CAIN, special education educator; b. London, Ohio, Mar. 17, 1928; d. William Louis and Wanda (Holloway) Cain; m. Ernest Silver Crouch, Mar. 27, 1965; 1 child, Mara Angela. BS, Howard U., 1961; BS summa cum laude, Cen. State U., 1977, postgrad., 1978-79, 86-87, U. Dayton, 1980, Wright State U., Dayton, Ohio, 1994-95. Cert. tchr., spl. edn. tchr., Ohio. Libr., bibliographer Libr. Congress, Washington, 1955-61; tchr. St. Brigid Sch., Xenia, Ohio, 1961-66, Pope John XXIII Sch., Columbus, Ohio, 1979-80, Springfield (Ohio) City Schs., 1987-88, Buckeye Youth Ctr./Ohio Dept. Youth Svcs., Columbus, 1988-94, Columbus (Ohio) City Schs., 1994—. Mem. NEA, Ohio Edn. Assn., Coun. Exceptional Children, Coun. Children with Behavioral Disorders (divsn. learning disabilities), Ctrl. Ohio Tchrs. Assn., Alpha Kappa Mu. Roman Catholic. Home: 88 W 2nd St London OH 43140-1004

CROUSE, CAROL K. MAVROMATIS, elementary education educator; b. Phila., Nov. 27, 1950; d. George and Helen (Captis) Mavromatis; m. David Crouse (dec. 1998). BS in Edn., Temple U., 1972, MEd in Curriculum and Instrn., 1981. Elem. tchr. grades 1, 3, 4, 5, Upper Darby (Pa.) Sch. Dist., 1974—, mem. Sci. Curriculum Writing Commn., 1974—99. Mem. Excellence in Edn. Team, Hillcrest Elem. Sch., Pa., 1987; cert. NASA Lunar Rock and Meteorite Edn. Program, 1993—; tchr. adv. bd. Phila. Zoo, 1995—; mem. writing and evaluation team Schuylkill Valley Nature Ctr., 1993-94; coord. cmty. svc. Highland Park Elem. Sch. Learn and Serve com., Kids Care Club, 2000-2002, Safety Patrol Advisor, 2002—. Recipient Howard W. McComb award Temple U. Phi Delta Kappa, 1981. Mem.: NSTA, ASCD, Upper Darby Recreation Tennis Players (tournament co-dir. 1983—92).

CROW, JO ANN, secondary education educator; b. Gadsden, Ala., Aug. 28, 1952; d. William Earl and Annie Bell (Pitts) Garrett; m. Jimmie Lee Flanagan Jr., Nov. 1, 1970 (div.); children: Patrick Dale, Kathryn Anne, Kelly Coleen; m. James M. Crow, Dec. 26, 1996. AS, Gadsden (Ala.) State C.C., 1987; BS, Jacksonville State U., 1989; MS, U. Ala., 1994. Cert. secondary math. edn. tchr. Math. tchr. Gadsden (Ala.) City Bd. Edn., 1990—. Sponsor varsity cheerleaders Gadsden H.S., 1995-03. Mem. pers. com. Paden Bapt. Ch., Gadsden, 1986—, chmn. youth com., 1993—. Mem. NEA, Ala. Edn. Assn., Profl. Assn. Gadsden Educators, Gadsden City Coun. PTA's (treas. 1991-93). Home: 108 Paden Rd Gadsden AL 35903-3667 Office: Gadsden High Sch 607 S 12th St Gadsden AL 35901-3802 E-mail: jcrow@gcs.k12.al.us.

CROW, MARY JO ANN, retired elementary education educator; b. Blytheville, Ark., July 13, 1935; d. Clarence and Myrtle Evelyn (Johnson) Williamson; m. Ernest W. Crow, June 4, 1960; children: Jennifer Evelyn, Steven Ernest. BA, Ctrl. Coll., 1957; postgrad., U. Nebr., 1957-60; tchr. cert., Eureka Coll., 1978-81; MS in Edn., Ill. State U., 1993. Cert. tchr. grades K-9, Ill. Lab. tch. U. Nebr. Coll. Medicine, Omaha, 1960-61, VA Hosp., Omaha, 1962-65; chem. tech. USDA Lab., Peoria, Ill., 1965-68; tchr. jr. high sci. Metamora (Ill.) Grade Sch., 1981—2003, ret., 2003. Presenter in field. Contbg. author: Celebrating Science, 1991; contbr. articles to profl.

jours. Active Groundwater Protection Com., Lakeview Mus., Sun Found. Named one of Ill. Outstanding Sci. Tchrs., Ill. State U./NSF, 1988-91, Tchr. of Yr., Peoria area Sigma Chi., Excel--Ill. Tchr. of Yr., 2001. Mem. NEA, Nat. Sci. Tchrs. Assn., Ill. Sci. Tchrs. Assn., Ctrl. Mo. Amateur Astronomers, Metamora Woman's Club. Avocations: astronomy, science fiction, crafts, reading. Office: Metamora Grade School 815 E Chatham St Metamora IL 61548-8745

CROWDER, DOROTHY SHOLES, nursing educator; b. Colonial Heights, Va., June 15, 1926; d. Wilbur Irwin and Dorothy (Townsend) Sholes; m. George Willard Crowder, Nov. 2, 1949; 1 child, Carol Elizabeth Crowder Johnson. BSN, Va. Commonwealth U., Richmond, 1974; MS, Va. Commonwealth U. Med. Sch. Nursing, Richmond, 1976. RN Va.; cert. childbirth educator Va. Night supr. Petersburg (Va.) Gen. Hosp., 1946—49; office nurse Dr. Thomas B. Pope, Petersburg, 1950—60; staff nurse Petersburg Gen. Hosp., 1960—64; instr. Petersburg Gen. Hosp. Sch. of Nursing, 1964—72; asst. prof. nursing Med. Coll. Va. Sch. of Nursing, Richmond, 1976—78, assoc. prof. nursing, 1978—93, assoc. prof. nursing emeritus, 1994—. Author Workbook on Electrolyte Balance; contbr. articles to mursing jours. Ward capt. Civic Assn., Petersburg, Va., 1952—60; Sunday Sch. tchr.; Ch. health and welfare nurse; Bd. dirs. Am. Cancer Soc., Richmond, 1999—, March of Dimes, Richmond, 1999—. Mem.: ANA, Med. Coll. Va. Nursing Alumni Assn., Assn. Women's Health, Obstetric and Neo-natal Nurses (chpt. pres. 1984—86), Va. Nurses Assn. (dist. pres. 1978—92, Maternal and Child Nurse of Yr. 1984), Sigma Tau. Methodist. Avocations: jogging, travel, reading, biking. Home: 205 Honeycreek Ct Colonial Heights VA 23834

CROWDER, ELIZABETH See WADDINGTON, BETTE

CROWDER, LENA BELLE, retired special education educator; b. Winston-Salem, N.C., Apr. 4, 1931; d. Henry Lee and Janie (Woods) Thomas; m. Raymond Crowder, June 12, 1954; 1 child, Rayonette Janease. BS in Edn., Winston Salem State U., 1952; MS in Edn., Agrl. and Tech. Coll., 1959. Cert. elem. edn. tchr., N.C. Tchr. 1st grade Early County Sch. Sys., Blakely, Ga., 1953-56; tchr. kindergarten Thomas-Anderson Kindergarten, Winston-Salem, 1956-57, 58-60, 61-62; tchr. 1st grade Beaufort (S.C.) County Schs., 1957-58; tchr. Chapel Hill (N.C.) City Sch. System, 1960-61, Forsyth County Sch. System, Winston-Salem, 1961-62, 1962-67, Winston-Salem/Forsyth County Schs., 1967-93, ret., 1993. Precinct election recorder Winston-Salem/Forsyth County Election Bd., 1961; fin. sec. Mt. Zion Bapt. Ch. Sunday Sch., Winston Salem, 1977—; supporter Crisis Control Ministry, Winston-Salem, 1982—; participant neighborhood watch system Winston-Salem Police Dept.; chair sch. involvement projects ARC, 1991-92. Mem. NEA, Nat. Assn. Univ. Women, Coun. Exceptional Children, Nat. Women of Achievement (rec. sec. S.E. region 2000, S.E. bd. dirs., Winston-Salem bd. dirs.), Assn. Classroom Tchrs. Democrat. Home: 1140 Rich Ave Winston Salem NC 27101-3432

CROWDER, REBECCA BYRUM, music educator, elementary school educator; b. Suffolk, Va., Apr. 27, 1951; d. Joseph Etheridge and Jane Carroll Byrum; m. Melvin Linnwood Crowder, July 19, 1997. BS in Music Edn., Radford U., 1973, MS in Music Edn., 1976. Cert. music tchr. grades K-12, tchr. grades 4-7. Profl. musician, 1973—; music tchr. East Salem Elem., Salem, Va., 1973—78; music dir. Colonial Ave. Bapt., Roanoke, Va., 1973—79; music tchr. Andrew Lewis Jr. High, Salem, 1979—83, Salem High and Glenvar High, Salem, 1983—84, Glenvar High, Salem, 1984—90, Oak Grove Elem., Roanoke, 1990—. Music tchr. Hollins U., Roanoke, 2000; pianist, accompanist Colonial Ave. Bapt., Roanoke, 1963—79, Shady Grove Bapt., Thaxton, 1979—92, First Bapt., Roanoke, 1992—97, Salem Ch. of Christ, 1997—. Mem.: Music Educators Nat. Conf., Va. Congress Parents and Tchrs., Phi Kappa Phi. Avocations: ballroom dancing, reading, playing piano, crossword puzzles, singing. Home: 1606 Mountain Hgts Dr Salem VA 24153

CROWE, SHELBY, educational specialist, consultant; b. Irvine, Ky., July 5, 1935; s. Claude and Lena (Clem) C.; m. Ina House, May 22, 1961 (div. 1977); children: Craig, Cara; m. Bonnie Wohlslagel, Aug. 6, 1977; children: Tyler, Trisha, Matthew. BA in Edn., Ea. Ky. U., 1958; MEd, Miami U., Oxford, Ohio, 1961; PhD in Ednl. Founds., Ohio State U., 1980. Cert. permanent spl. K-12 art edn. tchr., Ohio. Tchr. Cin. Pub. Schs., 1958-66; tchr. McGuffey Lab. Sch. Miami U., Oxford, Ohio, 1966-70; prof. edn. Wright State U., Dayton, Ohio, 1970-88, U. Dayton, 1988-90; ednl. specialist Dorothy Lane Markets, Dayton, 1990—. Cooperating tchr. U. Cin., 1960-66; instr. Ohio U., 1966; instr. Morehead (Ky.) State U., summers 1964-65; adj. prof. Union for Experimenting Colls. and Univs., Cin., 1982; condr. insvc. workshops, presenter in field local, regional, state and nat. level. Contbr. book revs. to various publs. Recipient Tchg. Excellence award Wright State U. Coll. Edn., 1981, 82, Wright State U. Alumni Assn., 1982, Faculty Mem. of Yr. award Wright State U. Student Govt., 1985, Mem. NEA, ASCD, AAUP, Nat. Coun. for Scoial Studies Edn., Ohio Confedn. Tchr. Edn. Orgns., Ohio Edn. Assn., Nat. Art Edn. Assn. (Students Best Educator award 1973), Ohio Art Edn. Assn., Phi Delta Kappa. Home: 412 Corona Ave Dayton OH 45419-2605

CROWELL, KENNETH LELAND, biology educator; b. Glen Ridge, NJ, July 19, 1933; s. Thomas Irving Jr. and Pauline (Whittlesey) C.; m. Marilyn Nancy Reed, Jan. 12, 1939; children: David, Thomas. BS, Yale U., 1955; PhD, U. Pa., 1961. Instr. Duke U., Durham, N.C., 1961-62; faculty Marlboro Coll., Marlboro, Vt., 1962-66; rsch. assoc. U. Alberta, Calgary, Alberta, Can., 1966-67; prof. biology St. Lawrence U., Canton, N.Y., 1967-95, ret., 1995—. Stewardship com. Nature Conservancy, Deer Isle, Maine, 1970—; trustee Island Heritage Trust, 1994—, pres., 2003. Regional editor Federated Bird Clubs N.Y., 1984-95; contbr. articles to profl. jours. Grantee Rsch. grant, NSF, 1962—73. Fellow Linnean Soc. London, AAAS; mem. Am. Ornithologists Union (elective). Universalist-Unitarian. Achievements include research in populations of landbirds of Bermuda; insular mammals of Gulf of Maine; range expansion and effects of introduced species.

CROWLEY, CYNTHIA JOHNSON, secondary school educator; b. Summit, N.J., June 28, 1930; d. Theodore Eames and Frances Lysett (Wetmore) J.; m. Robert J. Crowley, Sept. 6, 1952 (dec.); children: David Cochrane II, Cynthia Wetmore. BA, U. Pa., 1952; MA, Fairleigh-Dickinson U., Rutherford, N.J. Cert. English tchr., N.J. Tchr. econs. and reading St. Mary's Sch., Peekskill, N.Y., 1952-53; tchr. humanities Henry Hudson Regional Sch., Highlands, N.J., 1969-92, coord. gifted program, 1983-92. Pres. Associated Ednl. Svcs.; with N.J. Curriculum Revision Project; adv. bd. mem. Women's Athletics U. Pa., N.J. Coun. U.S. Congl. Awards Program; ednl. cons.; cons., lectr. creative writing workshops; mem. secondary sch. admissions com. U. Pa. Prodr. TV Tutor Series for Home and Schs. Former mem. Atlantic Highlands (N.J.) Bd. Edn., also past pres.; mem. adv. bd. Women's Athletic bd. U. Pa., 1992—, chair, 1999—; former mem. exec. com. Monmouth County Sch. Bds. Assn. Team Room named in her honor U. Pa., 1997; elected U. Pa. Hall of Fame, 1998. Mem. ASCD, Nat. Coun. Tchrs. English, Nat. Acad. TV Arts and Scis. (N.Y. chpt.), Gifted Educators (exec. com. 1986—), Alumni Pres.'s Coun. Ind. Secondary Schs. (life, past pres.), Phi Delta Kappa. Home and Office: 245 Shore Rd Westerly RI 02891-3707

CROWLEY, JAMES PATRICK, hematologist, medical educator, immunologist; b. Birmingham, Eng., Oct. 13, 1943; came to U.S., 1947; s. Francis Michael and Rose Ann (Donaghy) C.; m. Carol Ann Crowley, Dec. 6, 1943; children: Jason W.F., James M. AB, Providence Coll., 1965; MD, Georgetown U., 1969; MA, Brown U., 1981. Intern Boston City Hosp./Harvard Med. Sch., 1969, resident, 1970, Mass. Gen. Hosp., Boston, 1971, Peter Bent Brigham Hosp., Boston, 1974; instr. medicine Harvard Med. Sch., Boston, 1974; asst. prof. medicine Brown U., Providence, 1975-81, assoc. prof., 1981-92, prof., 1992—; dir. hematology R.I. Hosp./Brown U., Providence, 1992-2000; chief hematology/oncology Meml. Hosp. of R.I., Pawtucket, 2000—; dir. Cancer Ctr. Meml. Hosp. of R.I., 2003—. Bd. dirs. Providence Ambulatory Health Care Found., Inc.; cons. Naval Blood Rsch. Program, USN, 1977—; adj. prof. medicine Tufts U. Sch. Vet. Medicine, 1986—1996. Author: Principles of Transfusion Medicine, 2nd edit., 1995; contbr. articles to profl. jours. Mem. Retirement Bd. City of Providence, 1993—; physician Camp Yawgoog Boy Scouts Am., 1992—. Capt. USNR, 1971-95, ret. Recipient Transfusion Medicine Acad. award NIH, 1984-89, award R.I. Blood Banking Soc., 1986. Mem. Am. Soc. Hematology, R.I. Med. Soc. (pres. 1992-93), Providence Med. Assn., (pres. 1992-92), Mt. Tom Club (v.p. 1994). Democrat. Roman Catholic. Achievements include important contbns. to the devel. of successful system for freezing blood and deglycerolizing blood for transfusion on Navy hosp. ships, successful demonstration that erythropoeitin could enhance autologous pre-donation prior to orthopedic surgery and the immunosuppressive effects of passenger leukocytes during allogeneic transfusion. Office: Cancer Ctr Meml Hosp RI 111 Brewster St Pawtucket RI 02860 E-mail: james_crowley@mhri.org.

CROWLEY, JOSEPH NEIL, university president, political science educator; b. Oelwein, Iowa, July 9, 1933; . James Bernard and Nina Mary (Neil) C.; m. Johanna Lois Reitz, Sept. 9, 1961; children: Theresa, Neil, Margaret, Timothy. BA, U. Iowa, 1959; MA, Calif. State U., Fresno, 1963; PhD (Univ. fellow), U. Wash., 1967. Reporter Fresno Bee, 1961-62; asst. prof. polit. sci. U. Nev., Reno, 1966-71, asso. prof., 1971-79, prof., 1979—, chmn. dept. polit. sci., 1976-78, pres., 1978-2000, pres. emeriyus, regents prof., 2000—. Bd. dirs. Citibank Nev.; policy formulation officer EPA, Washington, 1973-74; dir. instl. studies Nat. Commn. on Water Quality, Washington, 1974-75. Author: Democrats, Delegates and Politics in Nevada: A Grassroots Chronicle of 1972, 1976, Notes From the President's Chair, 1988, No Equal in the World; An Interpretation of the Academic Presidency, 1994, The Constant Conversation: A Chronicle of Campus Life, 2000; editor: (with R. Roelofs and D. Hardesty) Environment and Society, 1973. Mem. coun. NCAA, 1987—92, mem. pres.' commn., 1991—92, pres., 1993—95; bd. dirs. Nat. Consortium for Acads. and Sports., 1992—; Honda Awards Program Adv. Bd., 1994—; bd. dirs. campaign chmn. No. Nev. United Way, 1985; bd. dirs. campaing chmn., 1997—2002; mem. Commn. on Colls., 1980—87; mem. adv. commn. on mining and minerals rsch. U.S. Dept. Interior, 1985—91. Recipient Thornton Peace Prize U. Nev., 1971, Humanitarian of Yr. award NCCJ, 1986, Alumnus of Yr. award Calif. State U., 1989, ADL Champion of Liberty award, 1993, Disting. Alumni award U. Iowa, 1994, Giant Step award Ctr. for Study of Sport in Soc., 1994, William Anderson award AAHPERD, 1998, Lifetime Achievement award Nat. Consortium for Acads. and Sports, 2001; Nat. Assn. Schs. Pub. Affairs and Adminstrn. fellow, 1973-74. Mem. Nat. Assn. State Univs. and Land Grant Colls. (bd. dirs. 1999-2000). Roman Catholic. Home: 1265 Muir Dr Reno NV 89503-2629 Office: U Nev Mail Stop 310 Reno NV 89557 E-mail: crowley@unr.edu.

CROWLEY, JUDITH DIANE, secondary educator; b. Glendale, Calif., Apr. 3, 1941; d. Roy Robert and Omarita (Weldon) Griffee; divorced; 1 child, Timothy Dan. BS in Edn., Kansas State Coll., Pittsburg, 1963. Cert. tchr., Colo. Tchr. Jefferson County Schs., Denver, 1963-65, Adams County Schs., Northglenn, Colo., 1965-66, 68—, Overseas Edn., Fed. Republic Germany, 1966-67. Curriculum writer Adams County Five Star Schs., Northglenn, 1979—. Paintings, pottery and silver exhibited at group art shows, 1964, 79, 81, 84; Exhibited in Denver Mus. of Art, Georgetown Galleries, Minorco Inc., Metro Brokers, Gusterman's. Mem. NEA, Colo. Educators Assn., Nat. Art Educators Assn., Colo. Art Educators Assn., Dist. 12 Tchrs. Assn. Republican. Presbyterian. Avocations: oil painting, watercolor, travel. Home: 6407 N Ponderosa Way Parker CO 80134-5618

CROWSON, HENRY LAWRENCE, mathematician, educator; b. Okeechobee, Fla., Apr. 16, 1927; s. Ernest Hubbard and Mary Elizabeth Crowson; m. Betty Mae George, June 16, 1951; children: Lawrence George, James Maxwell, Timothy David. BChemE, U. Fla., Gainesville, 1953, MS in Math., 1955, PhD in Math., 1959. Cert. engr. in tng., Fla. Asst. prof. U. Fla., Gainesville, 1958-60; advisory mathematician IBM Corp., Gaithersburg, Md., 1960-72; sr. mathematician CACI Corp., Arlington, Va., 1975-77; assoc. prof. U. P.M., Saudi Arabia, 1977-79, U. Houston, 1982-86, TIEC/MUCIA, Shah Alam, Malaysia, 1986-89, Tex. A&M Internat. U., Laredo, 1990-98. Cons. Bell Labs., CACI, Vitro Labs., Cornell U., others, 1955—. Reviewer books and math. texts, 1965-68. Mem. Am. Math. Soc., Sigma Xi, Pi Mu Epsilon. Republican. Avocations: reading, music, composing poetry. Home: 10127 Falls Rd Potomac MD 20854-4107

CROWTHER, ANN ROLLINS, academic administrator, political science educator; b. Zanesville, Ohio, Aug. 29, 1950; d. Walter Edmund and Norma Lucille (Rollins) C. BA in English, Rollins Coll., 1972; M, EdS, U. Fla., 1975; D in Pub. Adminstrn., U. Ga., 1988. Dir. residence hall Ga. Southern U., Statesboro, 1975-78; asst. to head personnel and staff devel. dept. coop. ext. svc. U. Ga., 1978-80, acad. advisor Franklin Coll. Arts & Scis., 1980-81, grad. teaching asst. dept. polit. sci., 1981-84, instr. evening classes program, 1982-85, coord. acad. advising Franklin Coll. Arts & Scis., 1984-89, asst. dean, adj. asst. prof. polit. sci. Franklin Coll. Arts & Scis., 1989-93, assoc. dean, adj. asst. prof. polit. sci. Franklin Coll. Arts & Scis., 1993-99, asst. v.p. for instrn., adj. asst. prof. polit. sci., 1999—2001, assoc. v.p. for instrn., adj. asst. prof. polit. sci., 2001—. Mem. ASPA, Am. Polit. Sci. Assn., Ga. Assn. Women in Edn., Nat. Acad. Advising Assn., Nat. Assn. Women in Edn., Nat. Assn. Acad. Affairs Afminstrs. Avocations: travel, theatre, golf. Home: 375 Ponderosa Dr Athens GA 30605-3321 Office: Univ Ga 210 Old College Athens GA 30602 E-mail: acrowthe@arches.uga.edu.

CRUCE, CAROL ANN, retired principal; b. St. Louis, June 14, 1950; d. Albert M. and Eleanor A. (Lesch) Hofer; m. Robert L. Cruce, Apr. 26, 1980; 1 child, Rebecca A.; stepchildren: Douglas B., Diane L. BS, U. Mo., 1972, MEd, 1981. Cert. elem. prin., elem. tchr., spl. edn. tchr. Tchr. spl. edn. State Sch. for Severely Handicapped, Rolla, Mo., 1972-80; tchr. spl. edn. Hearnes Youth Ctr. Fulton (Mo.) State Hosp., 1980-83; tchr. spl. edn. Bush Sch. Fulton Pub. Schs., 1983-91, elem. prin. Bush Sch., 1991-97. Steering com. mem. Mo. Accelerated Schs. Project, Jefferson City, 1994-97, prin. tng. coord. com., 1994-97. Named Bus. Assoc. of Yr. Fulton Am. Bus. Women's Assn., 1994, Outstanding Young Woman Am., 1982. Mem. Mo. Assn. Elem. Sch. Prins. (life), Mo. State Tchrs. Assn. (life), Mo. Ret. Tchrs. Assn. (life). Roman Catholic. Avocations: golf, boating, reading, counted cross-stitch. E-mail: carol_cruce@fulton.k12.mo.us.

CRUMBLEY, ESTHER HELEN KENDRICK, retired real estate agent, retired secondary school educator, former councilwoman; b. Okeechobee, Fla., Oct. 3, 1928; d. James A. and Corrine (Burney) Kendrick; m. Chandler Jackson, Oct. 24, 1949 (dec.); children: Pamela E., Chandler A., William J. BS in Math. Edn., Ga. So. Coll., 1966; M in Math., Jacksonville (Fla.) U., 1979. Cert. secondary edn. tchr., Ga. Secondary edn. tchr. Camden County Bd. Edn., St. Mary's, Ga., 1958-92, ret.; realtor Watson Realty, St. Mary's, 1985-98, ret., 1998. Dept. chairperson Camden H.S., St. Mary's, 1966-72. Reporter: for hometown newspaper. Councilwoman City of St. Mary's, 1979-86, mayor pro tem, 1981-86. Mem. Camden Ga. Assn. Educators (pres. 1976, sec.-treas. 1977-78, star tchr. 1972), PAGE (biog. com. rep. 1984-92, 1992 retired, named outstanding 8th dist. bldg. rep.), Camden Gen. Mcpl. Assn. (pres., sec.-treas. 1979-88), fin. and budget coms.), Math. Assn., Internat. Platform Assn. Internat. Dictionary Ctr., ABI. Republican. Baptist. Avocations: reading, art. Home: RR 3 Box 810 Folkston GA 31537-9729

CRUMP, CLAUDIA, geography educator; BS in elem. edn., Western Ky. State U., 1952; MS in elem. edn., Ind. U., 1957, EdD in elem. edn., 1952. Co-author: Teaching for Social Values in Social Studies, 1974, Indiana Map Studies, 1983, Indiana Yesterday and Today, 1985, Teaching History in the Elementary School, 1988, People in Time and Place: Indiana Hoosier Heritage, 1992. Home: 309 Whippoorwill Hts New Albany IN 47150-4255 Office: Ind U Southeast Divsn of Edn New Albany IN 47150

CRUMPTON, EVELYN, psychologist, educator; b. Ashland, Ala., Dec. 23, 1924; d. Alpheus Leland and Bernice (Fordham) Crumpton. AB, Birmingham So. Coll., 1944; MA, UCLA, 1953, PhD in Psychology, 1955. Lic. psychologist, Calif.; diplomate Am. Bd. Profl. Psychology. Rsch. psychologist VA Hosp., Brentwood, L.A., 1955-77; asst. chief psychology svc., dir. clin. tng. VA Adminstrn. Med. Ctr. West Los Angeles, 1977-88; clin. prof. dept. psychology UCLA, assoc. rsch. psychologist dept. psychiatry, UCLA Sch. Med., 1957—; cons. chief of staff Brentwood div., VA Adminstrn. Med. Ctr. Contbr. numerous articles to profl. jours. Recipient Profl. Svc. award, Assn. Chief Psychologists VA, 1979. Fellow Soc. Personality Assessment; mem. APA, Western Psychol. Assn., Sigma Xi.

CRUSE, ALLAN BAIRD, mathematician, computer scientist, educator; b. Aug. 28, 1941; s. J. Clyde and Irma R. Cruse. Postgrad. (Woodrow Wilson fellow), U. Calif., Berkeley, 1962-63; MA, 1965. Fellow Dartmouth Coll., 1963-64; instr. U. San Francisco, 1966-73; asst. prof. math., 1973-76; assoc. prof., 1976-79; prof., 1979—. Chmn. math. dept. 1988-91; vis. instr. Stilman Coll., summer 1967; vis. assoc. prof. Emory U., spring 1978; prof. computer sci. Sonoma State U., 1983-85; cons. math edn. NSF fellow, 1972-73. Author: (with Millianne Granberg) Lectures on Freshman Calculus, 1971; rsch. publs. in field. Mem. Am. Math. Soc., Math. Am. Math. Soc., Math. Assn. Am. (chmn. No. Calif. sedt. 1995-96), Assn. Computing Machinery, U. San Francisco Faculty Assn., Sigma Xi (dissertation award 1974). Office: U San Francisco Harney Sci Ctr San Francisco CA 94117

CRUSE, JULIUS MAJOR, JR., pathologist, educator; b. New Albany, Miss., Feb. 15, 1937; s. Julius Major and Effie (Davis) C. BA, BS with honors, U. Miss., 1958; DMS with honors, U. Graz, Austria, 1960; MD, U. Tenn., 1964, PhD in Pathology (USPHS fellow), 1966, USPHS postdoctoral fellow, 1964-67; DD (hon.), Gen. Theol. Sem., N.Y., 1999. Prof. immunology and biology Grad. Sch. U. Miss., 1967—74, prof. pathology, 1974—, assoc. prof. microbiology, 1974—, dir. grad. studies program in pathology, 1974—, dir. clin. immunopathology, 1978—, dir. immunopathology sect., 1978—, dir. tissue typing lab., 1980—, assoc. prof. medicine, 1989—, disting. prof. history medicine Med. Sch., 2003—. Lectr. pathology U. Tenn. Coll. Medicine, 1967-74; adj. prof. immunology Miss. Coll., 1977-1992; mem. NIH study section on transplantation immunology, 1992; mem. sci. adv. bd. Immuno Tech. Corp., L.A.; active FDA Expert Panel on Alternatives to Silicone Breast Implants, 1994—. Author: Immunology Examination Review Book, 1971, rev. edit., 1975, Introduction to Immunology, 1977, Principles of Immuno-pathology, 1979; editor-in-chief Immunologic Rsch., 1981—, Pathology and Immunopathology Rsch., 1982-90, Concepts in Immunopathology, 1985—, The Year in Immunology, 1984—, Pathobiology: Jour. Immunopathology, Molecular and Cellular Biology, 1990-98, Exptl. & Molecular Pathology, 1999—, Transgenics: Biological Analysis Through DNA Transfer, 1992-; immunology cons.: Dorland's Illustrated Medical Dictionary, 1967-1994; contbns. to Microbiology and Immunology; editor Immunomodulation of Neoplasia, Antigenic Variation: Molecular and Genetic Mechanisms of Relapsing Disease, 1987, Autoimmunoregulation and Autoimmune Disease, 1987; The Year in Immunology, vol. 1, 1984-85, vol. 2, 1985-86, The Year in Immunology, vol. 3, 1987, The Year in Immunology, vols. 4, 5, 1988, vol. 6, 1989-90, Genetic Basis of Autoimmune Disease, 1988, Cellular Aspects of Autoimmunity, 1988, Therapy of Autoimmune Diseases, 1989, B Lymphocytes: Function and Regulation, Conjugate Vaccines, 1989, Molecules and Cells of Immunity, 1990, Immunoregulation and Autoimmunity, 1986, Organ-Based Autoimmune Diseases, 1985, Autoimmunity: Basic Concepts, Systemic and Selected Organ-Specific Diseases, 1985, Clinical and Molecular Aspects of Autoimmune Diseases, 1990, Immunoregulatory Cytokines and Cell Growth, 1989, Complement Profiles, 1992; co-editor: Self-Nonself Discrimination in the Immune System, 1992, Complement Profiles, vol. 1, 1992, Illustrated Dictionary of Immunology, 1995, 2d edit., 2003, Atlas of Immunology, 1998, 2d edit., 2003, Immunology Guidebook, 2003, T.S. Eliot Bibliography, 2003; contbr. chpts. to books and articles to profl. jours; editor-in-chief: Experimental and Molecular Pathology, 1999—. Recipient Pathologists award in continuing edn. Coll. Am. Pathologists-Am. Soc. Clin. Pathologists, 1976; Julius M. Cruse collection in immunology established in his honor Middleton Med. Libr., U. Wis., Madison, 1979, Julius M. Cruse collection of T.S. Eliot's works, St. Mark's Libr., Gen. Theol. Sem. (Episcopal), N.Y.C.; Wilson Found. grantee, 1990-95, 93-94, 95-98, 99-2003; B.S. Guyton lectr. on history of medicine, 1998; Fulbright scholar, Univ. Graz, Austria, 1958-60. Fellow AAAS, Royal Soc. Medicine, Royal Soc. Promotion Health, Am. Acad. Microbiology, Am. Soc. for Histocompatibility and Immunogenetics (chmn. publs. com. 1987-95, councillor 1997-99, historian 2000—), Intercontinental Biog. Assn.; mem. AMA (Physicians Recognition award 196-75), Clin. Immunology Soc., Am. Inst. Biol. Scis., Am. Soc. Clin. Pathologists, Can. Soc. Microbiologists, N.Y. Acad. Scis. Exptl. Biology and Medicine, Am. Diabetes Assn., Soc. Francaise d'Immunologie, Reticuloendothelial Soc., Transplantation Soc., Electron Microscopy Soc. Am., Am. Assn. History Medicine, The Paul Ehrlich Soc., Am. Soc. Investigative Pathology, Am. Assn. Pathologists, Am. Chem. Soc., Brit. Soc. Immunology, Can. Soc. Immunology, Am. Soc. Microbiology, Internat. Acad. Pathology, Am. Assn. Immunologists (historian 1990—), T.S. Eliot Soc., Sigma Xi, Phi Kappa Phi, Phi Eta Sigma, Alpha Epsilon Delta, Gamma Sigma Epsilon, Beta Beta Beta. Anglo-Catholic. Office: U Miss Med Ctr Dept Pathology 2500 N State St Jackson MS 39216-4500

CRUSTO, MITCHELL FERDINAND, lawyer, educator, consultant; b. New Orleans, Apr. 22, 1953; BA magna cum laude, Yale U., 1975; BA, Oxford U., Eng., 1980, MA, 1985; JD, Yale U., 1981. Bar: La. 1982, Mo. 1984, Ill. 1985. Law clk. to Hon. John M. Wisdom U.S. Ct. Appeals (5th cir.), New Orleans, 1981-82; assoc. Jones, Walker, Waechter, Pointevent, Carrere & Denegre, New Orleans, 1982-84; sr. v.p., gen. counsel, asst. corp. sec. Stifel, Nicolaus & Co., Inc., St. Louis, 1984-88; CEO Crusto Capital Resources, Inc., St. Louis, 1988-89; assoc. dep. adminstr. for fin., investment and procurement U.S. Small Bus. Adminstrn., Washington, 1989-91; dir. corp. environ. policy Monsanto Co., St. Louis, 1991-93; sr. mgr. Arthur Andersen Environ. Svcs., Chgo., 1993-95; prof. Loyola Sch. Law, New Orleans, 1995—. Vis. prof. Vt. Law Sch., summers 2000-2003, Washington U. Sch. Law, summer 1999; mem. faculty Washington U., St. Louis, 1985-89, St. Louis U. Law Sch., 1987-88, Webster U., St. Louis, 1986; securities advisor to sec. of state State of Mo., 1986-89; lectr. legal divsn. Securities Industry Assn., 1986-88; mem. Pres. Clinton transition team natural resource cluster EPA, 1992; owner Angelic Asset Mgmt., 1998—. Contbr. articles in newspapers, mags., jours. Mem. ABA, La. Bar Assn., Mo. Bar Assn., Ill. Bar Assn., Middle Temple (London). Home: PO Box 791719 New Orleans LA 70179-1719 Office: Loyola U Sch Law 7214 Saint Charles Ave # 901 New Orleans LA 70118-3538 Business E-Mail: mfcrusto@loyno.edu.

CRUZ, JOSE BEJAR, JR., engineering educator; b. Bacolod City, The Philippines, Sept. 17, 1932; came to U.S., 1954, naturalized, 1969; s. Jose P. and Felicidad (Bejar) C.; m. Stella E. Rubia; children by previous marriage: Fe E. Cruz Langdon, Ricardo A., Rene L., Sylvia C. Cruz Loebach, Loretta C. Cruz Spray. BSEE summa cum laude, U. Philippines, 1953; MS, MIT, 1956; PhD, U. Ill., 1959. Lic. prof. engr., Ill., Ohio. Instr. elec. engring. U. Philippines, Quezon City, 1953-54; rsch. asst. MIT, Cambridge, 1954-56, vis. prof., 1973; from instr. to assoc. prof. U. Ill.,

Urbana-Champaign, 1956-65, prof. elec. engring., 1965-86, assoc. mem. Ctr. Advanced Study, 1967-68; rsch. prof. Coordinated Sci. Lab., 1965-86; prof. dept. elec. and computer engring. U. Calif., Irvine, 1986-92, chmn. dept., 1986-90; prof. elec. engring. Ohio State U., Columbus, 1992—, dean Coll. Engring., 1992-97, Howard D. Winbigler chair in engring., 1997—. Vis. assoc. prof. U. Calif., Berkeley, 1964-65; vis. prof. Harvard U., 1973; pres. Dynamic Sys.; mem. theory com. Am. Automatic Control Coun., 1967; gen. chmn. Conf. on Decision and Control, 1975; mem. profl. engring. exam. com. State of Ill., 1984-86; mem. Nat. Coun. Engring. Examiners, 1985-86; mem. project adv. group on engring. and sci. edn. project Dept. Sci. and Tech., Republic of The Philippines, 1993-98. Author: (with M.E. Van Valkenburg) Introductory Signals and Circuits, 1967, (with W.R. Perkins) Engineering of Dynamic Systems, 1969, Feedback Systems, 1972, translated into Chinese, 1976, Polish, 1977, System Sensitivity Analysis, 1973, (with M.E. Van Valkenburg) Signals in Linear Circuits, 1974, translated into Spanish, 1978; Assoc. editor: Jour. Franklin Inst, 1976-82, Jour. Optimization Theory and Applications, 1980—; series editor Advances in Large Scale Systems Theory and Applications; contbr. articles on network theory, automatic control systems, system theory, sensitivity theory of dynamical systems, large scale systems, dynamic games and dynamic scheduling in mfg. systems to sci., tech. jours. Recipient Purple Tower award Beta Epsilon U., Philippines, 1969, Diamond award, 1999, Curtis W. McGraw Rsch. award Am. Soc. for Engring. Edn., 1972, Halliburton Engring. Edn. Leadership award, 1981, Most Outstanding Alumnus award U. of the Philippines Alumni Assn. Am., 1989, Most Outstanding Overseas Alumnus Coll. Engring., U. of the Philippines Alumni Assn., 1990, Richard E. Bellman Control Heritage award Am. Automatic Control Coun., 1994, various alumni awards. Fellow AAAS (sect. com. for sect. on engring. 1991-94, sec. 1998-2003, chair-elect, 2003—), IEEE (chmn. linear sys. com., group on automatic control 1966-68, assoc. editor Trans. on Circuit Theory 1962-64); mem. Control Sys. Soc. (adminstrv. com. 1966-75, 78-80, v.p. fin. and adminstrv. activities 1976-77, pres. 1979, chmn. awards com. 1973-75, ednl. activities bd. 1973-75, editor Trans. on Automatic Control 1971-73, mem. tech. activities bd. 1979-83, chmn. 1982-83, v.p. tech. activities 1982-83, edn. med. com. 1977-79, dir. 1980-85, vice-chmn. publs. bd. 1981, chmn. 1984-85, chmn. panel of tech. editors 1981, chmn. TAB periodicals com. 1981, chmn. PUB. Soc. publs. com. 1981, v.p. publ. activities 1984-85, exec. com. 1982-85, Richard M. Emberson award 1989), Philippine Engrs. and Scientists Orgn., Am. Soc. Engring Edn. (awards policy com.), U.S. Nat. Acad. Engring. (mem. peer com. for electronics engring. 1982, 2000—, vice chair 2002-03, chair 2003-, com. on nat. agenda for career-long edn. for engrs. 1986-88, membership com. 1987-90, 2003—, acad. adv. bd. 1994-97, com. on diversity in engring. workforce 1999-2001), Philippine-Am. Acad. Sci. and Engring. (founding mem. 1980, pres. 1982, chmn. bd. dirs. 1998-2000, Founders Lecture award 2001), Internat. Fedn. Automatic Control (chmn. theory com. 1981-84, vice-chmn. tech. bd. 1984-87, policy com. 1987-93, vice-chmn. 1993, 99, chmn. 1996, congress internat. program com.), Philippine Engrs. and Scientists Orgn., Sigma Xi, Phi Kappa Phi, Eta Kappa Nu. Achievements include introduction of concept of comparison sensitivity in dynamical feedback systems, of leader-follower strategies in hierarchical engineering systems; development of synthesis methods for time-varying systems. Office: Ohio State U Dept Elec Engring Columbus OH 43210-1272 E-mail: jbcruz@ieee.org.

CRYER, PHILIP EUGENE, medical educator, scientist, endocrinologist; b. El Paso, Ill., Jan. 5, 1940; s. Clifford Eugene and Carol Ruth (Cherry) C.; m. Susan Odette Shipman, Dec. 23, 1963 (div. May 1990); children: Philip Clifford, Justine Laurel; m. Carolyn Elizabeth Havlin, Sept. 16, 1994. BA, Northwestern U., 1962, MD, 1965; MD (hon.), U. Copenhagen, 2000. Diplomate Am. Bd. Internal Medicine, diplomate Am. Bd. Endocrinology and Metabolism. Intern Barnes Hosp., St. Louis, 1965-67; fellow in endocrinology Barnes Hosp./Washington U., 1967-68, resident in medicine, 1968-69, 71-72; investigator Naval Med. Rsch. Inst., Bethesda, Md., 1969-71; from instr. to assoc. prof. Washington U. Sch. Medicine, St. Louis, 1971-80, prof., 1981—, Irene E. and Michael M. Karl prof. endocrinology/metabolism, 1995—, dir. gen. clin. rsch. ctr., 1978—, dir. div. endocrinology, diabetes and metabolism, 1985—2002. Connaught-Novo lectr. Can. Diabetes Assn., 1987; Pimstone lectr. Soc. Endocrinology, Metabolism and Diabetes, South Africa, 1989; Kellion lectr. Australian Diabetes Soc., 1992; Plenary lectr. Japan Diabetes Soc., 1994, plenary lectr. Argentine Diabetes Assn., 1998, plenary lectr. Asean Fed. Endocrine Socs., 1999. Author: Diagnostic Endocrinology, 1976, Diagnostic Endocrinology, 2d edit., 1979, Hypoglycemia, 1997, also 74 book chpts.; editor: Diabetes; mem. editl. bd.: Jour. Clin. Investigation, Am. Jour. Physiology; contbr. over 300 articles to profl. jours. Recipient Rorer Clin. Investigator award Endocrine Soc., 1988, Rumbaugh Sci. award Juvenile Diabetes Found., 1989, Banting medal Am. Diabetes Assn., 1994, Excellence in Clin. Rsch. award NIH, 1994, Claude Bernard medal European Assn. Study Diabetes, 2001; Am. Diabetes Clin. Rsch. grantee, 1988-96, NIH Rsch. grantee, 1980—. Fellow ACP; mem. Am. Fedn. Clin. Rsch. (councilor 1979-80), Am. Soc. Clin. Investigation (v.p. 1985-86), Assn. Am. Physicians, Am. Diabetes Assn. (pres. 1996-97), Phi Beta Kappa, Alpha Omega Alpha. Office: Washington U Sch Medicine 660 South Euclid Ave PO Box 8127 Saint Louis MO 63156-8127 E-mail: pcryer@im.wustl.edu.

CRYER, RODGER EARL, educational administrator; b. Detroit, Apr. 2, 1940; AB in Fine Arts, San Diego State U., 1965; MA in Edn. Adminstrn., Stanford U., 1972; PhD in Psychol. Svcs. Counseling, Columbia-Pacific U., 1985; Cert. Credit Union Dir., London Sch. of Bus., U.K., 2000. Cert. tchr., N.J., Calif.; cert. gen. adminstrn., Calif. Spl. asst. to commr. N.J. State Dept. Edn., Trenton, 1967-68; cons. N.J. Urban Sch. Devel., Trenton, 1969-70; mgmt. cons. Rodger E. Cryer, Co., Pinole, Calif., 1970-73; adminstrv. asst. Franklin McKinley Sch. Dist., San Jose, Calif.; pres. Chief Exec. Tng. Corp., San Jose, 1981-82; prin. McKinley Sch., 1986-91, Hellyer Sch., 1991-96. Bd. instl. rev. Calif. State Dept. Edn. Accreditation Commn., 1996—; adj. prof. Nat. U., San Jose, 1996—; ptnr. Guided Learning Enterprises, treas.; bd. dirs. Commonwealth Cen. Credit Union, Our City Forest, Inc., 1994-98. Contbr. articles to profl. jours. Bd. dirs., pres. Friends of San Jose Beautiful, Inc., 1994-95; adv. com. City of San Jose Bicycle, 1994-95; pres. Friends of Evergreen Libr., 2000-01. Mem.: Calif. Sch. Pub. Rels. Assn. (pres.), Nat. Sch. Pub. Rels. Assn. (sec. 1975—86), The Villages Golf and Country Club (rules com. 2002—). Home: 6328 Whaley Dr San Jose CA 95135-1447 E-mail: rodcryer@aol.com.

CRYMES, MARY COOPER, secondary school educator; b. Abilene, Tex., Oct. 27, 1950; d. James Travis and Mary Francis (Chapple) Cooper; m. David Stuart Crymes, Dec. 25, 1970. BS, U. Tex., 1974. Tchr. govt. Midland (Tex.) Ind. Sch. Dist., 1974-80, Abilene (Tex.) Ind. Sch. Dist., 1980—. Author: (poem) Young America Sings, 1970; co-author: County Records Inventory, 1974. Mem. Big Country Tchr. Ctr. Recipient Tchg. Excellence in Free Enterprise 1st prize award West Tex. C. of C., 1980, Martha Washington medal SAR, 1990; named Taft Sr. fellow Taft Inst., 1993. Mem. NEA, Tex. State Tchrs. Assn., Abilene Educators Assn., Nat. Coun. for Social Studies, Tex. Coun. for Social Studies, Abilene Coun. for Social Studies (pres. 1984-86), Daus. of Republic of Tex. (treas. 1990-95, v.p. 1995-2000), West Tex. Geneal. Soc., Big Country Masters Gardeners Assn., Big Country Emmaus Cmty., Big Country Tchr. Ctr., Taylor County Dem. Club, Tex. Exes. Avocation: genealogical research. Office: Abilene High Sch 2800 N 6th St Abilene TX 79603-7190

CRYSTAL, JONATHAN ANDREW, executive recruiter; b. New Rochelle, N.Y., May 18, 1943; s. Robert Garrison and Luella (Peters) C.; m. Pamela Paterson, July 31, 1965; children: Alexandra, Laura, Elizabeth, Matthew. BSBA, Northwestern U., 1965; MBA in Fin., Columbia U., 1971. Mktg. rep. Texaco, Inc., 1965-66; trainee Chase Manhattan Bank, 1971; assoc. corp. fin. Drexel Burnham & Lambert, Inc., 1971-73; acct. officer Citicorp, N.Y.C., 1973-77, asst. v.p., 1975-77, v.p., regional treas. mgr. Houston, 1977-80; prin. Russell Reynolds & Assocs., Houston, 1980-88, SpencerStuart, Houston, 1988—, chmn. audit com., 1997-98. Guest lectr. bus. schs. of Rice U., U. Houston, U. St. Thomas; spkr. in field. Contbr. articles to profl. jours. Adv. bd. Ctr. for Bus. Ethics U. St. Thomas, 1998—. Lt. (j.g.) USN, 1966-69. Named one of Top 200 Recruiters in the U.S. The Career Makers, 1990. Mem. Houston Forum (bd. govs. 1992-2000, exec. com. 1995-2000), Spring Branch Edn. Found. (bd. dirs. 1993-2001, exec. com. 1994-2000, vice-chmn., 1999-2000), Univ. Club, Galveston (Tex.) Country Club. Home: 14419 Broadgreen Dr Houston TX 77079-6635 E-mail: jcrystal@spencerstuart.com.

CSIKSZENTMIHALYI, MIHALY, psychology educator; b. Fiume, Italy, Sept. 29, 1934; came to U.S., 1956; s. Alfred and Edith (Jankovich) C.; m. Isabella Selega, Dec. 30, 1961; children: Mark, Christopher. BA, U. Chgo., 1960, PhD, 1965. Reporter European News Service, Rome, 1952-56; free-lance artist Rome, 1954-56; translator U.S.A. Pubs., Chgo., 1958-64; prof. sociology Lake Forest (Ill.) Coll., 1965-70; prof. psychology human devel., edn. U. Chgo., 1971—. Adv. bd. Ency. Britannica, Chgo., 1985—, J.P. Getty Mus., Malibu, Calif., 1985—. Author: Beyond Boredom and Anxiety, 1975, Flow: The Psychology of Optimal Experience, 1990, The Evolving Self, 1993, Creativity, 1996, Finding Flow in Everyday Life, 1997; (with others) The Creative Vision, 1976, The Meaning of Things, 1981, Being Adolescent, 1984, Optimal Experience, 1988, Television and the Quality of Life, 1990, The Art of Seeing, 1990, Talented Teenagers, 1993, Creating Worlds, 1994. Fulbright Sr. scholar, 1984, 1990, Fellow Ctr. for Advanced Studies in the Behavioral Sci., 1994-95. Fellow Am. Acad. Edn., Am. Acad. Leisure Scis. Clubs: Quadrangle (Chgo.). Avocations: mountain climbing, reading, art, chess. Home: 700 Alamosa Dr Claremont CA 91711 Office: 1021 N Dartmouth Ave Claremont CA 91711

CSÖRGÖ, MIKLOS, mathematics and statistics educator; b. Egerfarmos, Hungary, Mar. 12, 1932; arrived in Can., 1957, naturalized, 1962; s. Miklos and Ilona (Veres) Csörgö; m. Anna Eszter Toth, Aug. 10, 1957; children: Adria, Lilla. BA, Karl Marx U. Econs., Budapest, Hungary, 1955; MA, McGill U., 1961, PhD, 1963. Instr., postdoctoral fellow Princeton U., NJ, 1963—65; asst. prof. McGill U., Montreal, Canada, 1965—68, assoc. prof., 1968—71; vis. prof. U. Vienna, 1969—70; assoc. prof. math. and stats. Carleton U., Ottawa, Canada, 1971—72, prof., 1972—, co-dir. Lab. for Rsch. in Stats. and Probability, 1983—. Vis. prof. U. Utah, 1991—92. Author (with P. Révész): Strong Approximations in Probability and Statistics, 1981; author: Quantile Processes with Statistical Applications, 1983; author: (with others) An Asymptotic Theory for Empirical Reliability and Concentration Processes, 1986; author: (with L. Horváth) Weighted Approximations in Probability and Statistics, 1993; author: (with L. Horvath) Limit Theorems in Change-Point Analysis, 1997; assoc. editor The Annals of Probability, 1979—81, mem. editl. bd. Stats. and Decisions, 1981—2002, Jour. Multivariate Analysis, 1986—87. Fellow, Can. Coun., 1969—70, 1976—77, Killam sr. rsch. fellow, 1978—79, 1979—80. Fellow: Inst. Math. Stats., Royal Soc. Can.; mem.: Hungarian Acad. Sci. (external mem.), Internat. Statis. Inst., Bernoulli Soc., Statis. Soc. Can., Can. Math. Soc., Am. Math. Soc. Office: Carleton U Lab Rsch in Stats 1125 Colonel By Dr Ottawa ON Canada K1S 5B6 E-mail: mcsorgo@math.carleton.ca.

CUBAN, LARRY, education educator, researcher; b. Passaic, N.J., Oct. 31, 1934; s. Morris and Fanny (Janofsky) C.; m. Barbara Joan Smith, June 15, 1958; children: Sondra, Janice. BA in History, U. Pitts., 1955; MA in History, Case-Western Res. U., 1958; PhD, Stanford U., 1974. Cert. tchr., Calif., D.C., Pa. Biology tchr. McKeesport (Pa.) Pub. Schs., 1955-56; social studies tchr. Cleve. Pub. Schs., 1956-63; master tchr. history Washington D.C. Pub. Schs., 1963-65, dir.Cardozo project in urban tchg., 1965-67, social studies tchr., 1967-68, 70-72, dir. staff devel., 1968-70; supt. Arlington (Va.) Pub. Schs., 1974-81; prof. Stanford U. Sch. Edn., 1981—2001. Cons. in field. Author: To Make a Difference: Teaching in the Inner City, 1970, Teachers & Machines, 1986, How Teachers Taught, 2d edit., 1993, Why Is It So Hard to Get Good Schools?, 2003; co-author: (with David Tyack) Tinkering Toward Utopia, 1995, How Scholars Trumped Teachers, 1999, Oversold and Underused: Computers in Schools, 2001. John Hay Whitney Found. fellow, 1960-61; fellow Ctr. for Advanced Studies in Behavioral Scis., 1999-2000; Rsch. grantee Nat. Inst. Edn., 1980, Spencer Found., 1988. Mem. Am. Ednl. Rsch. Assn. (pres. 1990-91), History Edn. Soc., Phi Delta Kappa. Avocation: bicycling. Home: 2846 Kipling St Palo Alto CA 94306-2429 Office: Stanford Univ Sch of Edn Stanford CA 94305

CUBBAGE, ELINOR PHILLIPS, English language educator; b. Milford, Del., Apr. 4, 1948; d. Thomas Allen and Katheryn Augusta (Schaeffer) Phillips; m. James Stephenson, July 11, 1970; children: Kate Allen, Benjamin David. BA, U. Del., Newark, 1970; MS, Ea. Conn. State Coll., 1975; EdD, U. Md., 1993. Tchr. English Vernon (Conn.) H.S., 1971-75; prof. English Wor-Wic C.C., Salisbury, Md., 1977—, chairperson honors program, 1997—, chief writer Middle States Report, 1994-95, 99—. Adj. prof. Salisbury State U., 1975, 99—; rsch. coord. Nat. Ctr. for Devel. Edn., 1990-91. Editor-in-chief Student Creative Arts Mag., 1987—; contbr. articles, poetry to profl. jours. Mem. praise and worship team Rockawalkin United Meth. Ch., Hebron, Md., 2001—. NEH grantee, 1994-95. Mem. Nat. Coun. Tchrs. English, Tchrs. of English in the Two-Yr. Coll. (sec. of exec. bd. 1985-97). Avocation: creative writing. Home: 7180 Rockawalkin Rd Hebron MD 21830-1177 Office: Wor-Wic Cmty Coll 32000 Campus Dr Salisbury MD 21804-1485

CUCCINIELLO, DAWN GRACE, elementary and secondary school educator; b. Bklyn., Aug. 11; d. Vito Jack and Evelyn Anita (Simonetti) Cucciniello. BS in Edn., CUNY, 1969, MS in Edn., 1973, postgrad., 1975; 6th yr. cert. in adminstrn.-supervision, Wagner Coll., 1986. Cert. tchr. N.Y., lic. asst. prin., prin. N.Y.C. Tchr., reading Bd. of Edn., Bklyn, 1969-70, tchr., social studies, 1970-72, tchr., 2nd grade, 1972-84, tchr., 5th grade, 1984—96; tchr., 1st, 3rd, 4th, 5th grade dist. 31 Staten Island, 1996—. Chmn. comprehensive svc. program, Bklyn., 1987—90; sch. liaison Gifted and Talented Network, Bklyn., 1987—90; jr. high and HS tutor, SAT, GED program, 1990—; developed creative writing program for upper grade children; tchr. rep. NY State bd. regents, Albany, 2003. Writer, dir., choreographer children's plays, 1985—. Bd. dirs. Staten Island Coun. Animal Welfare. Finalist NY State Teacher of the Year, 2001; named N.Y.C. Educator of the Year - Staten Island, 2001. Mem.: ASCD, Am. Fedn. Tchrs., United Fedn. Tchrs., Am. com. Italian migration (exec. bd. mem.), Sacred Heart League, UFT Italian-Am. Studies com. (chpt. chair), Am. Cancer Soc. (comprehensive health com.), Pet Lovers United As One (PLUTO), Cat Lovers Am., Worldwide Wildlife Fedn., Humane Soc., Animal Welfare League, Bklyn. Lit. Club, Phi Delta Kappa. Democrat. Roman Catholic. Avocations: animal rights activist, reading, antiquing, theatre, singing.

CUDKOWICZ, LEON, medical educator; b. Lodz, Poland, Jan. 18, 1923; came to U.S., 1956; s. Mauryce and Masza (Malynski) C.;m. Margaret Chandler, Mar. 14, 1950 (div. July 1981); children: Alexander, Penelope; m. Teresa Cuiza de Alfaro, Jan. 18, 1986. BS, U. London, 1946, MD, 1951. James Hudson Brown fellow Yale U. Sch. Medicine, 1956-58; registrar St. Thomas Hosp., U. London, 1958-59; asst. prof. then assoc. prof. medicine Dalhousie U., Halifax, N.S., Can., 1960-69; prof. medicine Thomas Jefferson U., Phila., 1970-74; prof., chmn. Wright State U., Dayton, 1974-79, King Faisal U., Dammam, Saudi Arabia, 1979-81; prof. medicine U. Cin., 1981-95, prof. emeritus, 1995—. Author: Human Bronchial Circulation, 1970; contbr. 107 articles to profl. jours. Capt. RAMC, 1946-49. Fellow RCP, Nat. Pediat. Soc. Bolivia (hon.), NIH (sr.). Avocations: writing, mountaineering, gardening, travel. Home: Yonder Hill Farm Highland OH 45132 Office: U Cin Sch Medicine 253 Bethesda Ave Cincinnati OH 45229-2827

CUE, LOUELLA WASHINGTON, elementary education educator; b. Daytona Beach, Fla., Jan. 22, 1955; d. Evelyn (Washington) Hill. BS, Fla. State U., 1977, MS, 1978, postgrad., 1982-84. Cert. tchr., Fla. Tchr. Heights Elem. Sch., Ft. Myers, Fla., 1978-81, Riley Elem. Sch., Tallahassee, 1981-86, Sabal Palm Elem. Sch., Tallahassee, 1986—. Coord. Westcoast Day Camp and After Sch., Tallahassee, 1991—. Recipient Disting. Black Educator Recognition award Leon County Sch. Bd., 1991; named Mainstream Tchr. of Yr., 1990, 93. Mem. NEA, Fla. Tchrs. Assn. Democrat. Home: 2020 S Magnolia Dr Tallahassee FL 32301-5761 Office: Sabal Palm Elem Sch 2813 Ridgeway St Tallahassee FL 32310-5099

CUFFE, ROBIN JEAN, nursing educator; b. Frankfurt, Sept. 8, 1951; d. Russell Bates and Jean May (Clark) Preuit; m. Ronald Frederick Cuffe, Mar. 9, 1974; 1 child, Matthew David. Diploma, Richmond Meml. Hosp., 1973; BSN, Marymount U., 1982; MS in Edn., Va. Technol. and State U., 1990. RNC; cert. in cardiac rehab. nursing AACN; cert. health edn. specialist. Staff nurse Fairfax Hosp., Falls Church, Va., 1973-75; asst. head nurse, staff nurse, supr. ICU Arlington (Va.) Hosp., 1975-78, asst. coord. cardiac rehab., 1978-81, coord. cardiopulmonary rehab., 1981—. Bd. dirs. Am. Heart Assn., Northern, Va., 1982-91; jr. high youth group leader Ch. of the Holy Comforter, Vienna, Va., 1988-90, mem. adult edn. commn., 1990—. Fellow Am. Assn. Cardiovasc. and Pulmonary Rehab. (chmn. stds. and reimbursement com. 1991—, pres.-elect 1994-95, pres. 1995-96, treas. 1996-98), Va. Assn. Cardiovasc. and Pulmonary Rehab., Sigma Theta Tau (pres. chpt. 1984-86). Episcopalian. Home: 1804 Cloverlawn Ct Mc Lean VA 22101-4299 E-mail: rcuffe@mindspring.com.

CULBERSON, JAMES O. retired rehabilitation educator; b. Floyd County, Ga., Apr. 5, 1932; s. John T. and Willie Mae (Colston) C.; m. Janice May Jaquith, Jan. 11, 1958; children: Pamela, John, Sarah, James Jr. BS, Bob Jones U., 1953; MEd, U. S.C., 1960; EdD, U. Ga., 1970. Prin., tchr. Bur. Ind. Affairs, Juneau, Alaska, 1960-62; English tchr. Floyd County, Rome, Ga., 1962-67; high sch. counselor Gordon County, Calhoun, Ga., 1967-68; prof. counseling psychology U. So. Miss., Hattiesburg, 1970-95, dir. undergrad. rehab. svcs. edn., 1972-95, prof. emeritus of psychology, 1996—. Mem. editorial bd. Rehab. Counseling Bull., 1980-83; contbr. articles to profl. jours. Mem. Nat. Coun. Rehab. Edn., S.E. Coun. Rehab. Edn., Am. Rehab. Counseling Assn. (cert. recognition outstanding svc. 1987). Office: PO Box 17377 Hattiesburg MS 39404-7377

CULBERTSON, JACK ARTHUR, education educator; b. Nickelsville, Va., July 16, 1918; s. Otto Cecil and Lola Kate (Fuller) C.; m. Mary Virginia Pond, Aug. 12, 1952; children: Karen Anne Hasselo, Margaret Lynn. AB in Edn., Emory and Henry Coll., 1943; MA in German, Duke U., 1946; PhD in Ednl. Adminstrn., U. Calif., Berkeley, 1955. Cert. tchr., sch. adminstr., Va., Calif. Tchg. prin. Scott County Sch. Sys., Gate City, Va., 1937—41, Jewell Ridge (Va.) Sch. Sys., 1941—42, Tazewell (Va.) County Sch. Sys., 1947—49; H.S. tchr. Mineral Springs (N.C.) Sch. Sys., 1943—44; tchr. jr. H.S. El Centro (Calif.) Sch. Sys., 1949—51; sch. supt. Ellwood Sch. Dist., Goleta, Calif., 1951—53; prof. U. Oreg., Eugene, 1955—59; exec. dir. Univ. Coun. for Ednl. Adminstrn., Columbus, 1959—81; prof. Ohio State U., Columbus, 1981—86, emeritus prof., 1986—. Cons. W.K. Kellogg Found., Battle Creek, Mich., 1968, Ford Found., N.Y.C., 1967; advisor Edn. Commn. States, Denver, 1967, Pan Am. Union, Washington, 1968; founder 1st Internat. Intervisitation Program in Ednl. Adminstrn., 1966; spkr. OAS, Brasilia, Brazil, 1968, Australian Coun. for Ednl. Rsch., Sydney, 1967, German Assn. for Tng. Sch. Adminstrs., 1975. Author: Building Bridges, 1995; co-author: Administrative Relationships, 1960, Preparing Educational Leaders for the Seventies, 1969. Recipient Commonwealth Fellow award Commonwealth Coun. for Ednl. Adminstrn., 1978, Roald F. Campbell Lifetime Achievement award Univ. Coun. for Ednl. Adminstrn., 1993. Mem. Am. Ednl. Rsch. Assn. (v.p. 1964-66), Am. Assn. Sch. Adminstrs. (adv. commn. 1974-76), Nat. Coun. for Profs. of Ednl. Adminstrn. (exec. com. 1957-60, Living Legends award 1999-2000), Nat. Soc. for Study of Edn. (co-editor yearbook 1986). Avocations: reading, television, card playing. Home: 145 Montrose Way Columbus OH 43214-3634

CULBERTSON-STARK, MARY, art educator; b. Plainfield, N.J., June 2, 1953; d. Robert Warren and Betty Love (MacFarlane) Culbertson; m. Gary Stephen Stark, Dec. 10, 1977. BFA, U. S.C., 1975; MEd in Art Edn., U. Pitts., 1979. Art instr. K-12 Bethel Park (Pa.) Sch. Dist., 1975—, chmn. art dept., 1992—; art instr. K-12 Peters Twp. Mid. Sch., 1987; team leader apprenticeship program Associated Artists of Pitts., Bethel Park, 1994—; painting and drawing fellow Skidmore Coll., Saratoga Springs, NY, 1998, 2000, 2003; assoc. instr. Carnegie Mellon U., Pitts., 2001—02. Cons. Pitts. Fund for Art Edn., 1990—, The Carnegie Mus., Pitts., 1994—; artist liaison Pitts. Cultural Trust, 1993—; edn. cons. Master Visual Artists of Pitts., 1995—; vis. artist Slippery Rock U., 1997; artist-in-residence City of Pitts., 1999. One woman shows, Pitts., 1984—, Carson St. Gallery, 1986-93, Studio Z, Pitts., 1996, Gallery 937, Pitts., 1996, Martha Gault Gallery, Slippery Rock, Pa., 1996, Halan Gallery, Greensburg, Pa., 1998, Gallery Chiz, Pitts., 1998, 99, 2000, 01, 02, Watercolors Gallery, Pitts, 2000, Westmoreland Mus. Am. Art, Greensburg, Pa., 2003; exhibited in numerous group shows, 1984—; (paintings) Ascension of Lisa Steinberg, 1989 (1st pl. award), (illustration work) Theos Foundation Publications, 1991, (sculpture) Hoyt Inst. of Art Regional Exbhn. (Award of Distinction 1995); illus. (children's book) The Princess, The Person and the Fly, 2001; billboard proect Celebration of Women, City of Pitts. Art dir. Art Rm. Gallery, 1986, Nat. Student Coun. Conf., 1985; art cons. Pitts. Commn. for Women Exhbn., 1989-90; cons., speaker Hugh O'Brien Leadership Found., 1993; cons. Mid. States Evaluation, 1993; tchr./mentor Pa. Gov.'s Inst. for Arts Excellence, 2001, 03. Recipient Distinctive Svc. award Nat. Student Coun., 1985, Thanks to Tchrs. award Sta. KDKA-TV, Giant Eagle, 1991, 3 Commendations for Excellence in Art Edn., Pa. House and Senate, award of Distinction Associated Artists Pitts., 1998, Juror's award of excellence Pitts. Watercolor Soc., 2002. Mem. Nat. Art Edn. Assn., Associated Artists of Pitts. (assoc. bd. mem., com. mem. 1992-98, com. chair 1986-94, Svc. award 1988, Distinction award 1988, workshop presenter 1993—), Exec. Women's Coun. Pitts. (com. chair 1992—), South Hills Art League, Pitts. Watercolor Soc. (selection com. 1989—), Pitts. Print Group, Pa. Art Edn. Assn. (workshop presenter interdisciplinary studies). Avocations: reading, golf, sailing. Office: Bethel Park Sr H S 309 Church Rd Bethel Park PA 15102-1607

CULICK, FRED ELLSWORTH CLOW, physics and engineering educator; b. Wolfeboro, N.H., Oct. 25, 1933; s. Joseph Frank and Mildred Beliss (Clow) C.; m. Frederica Mills, June 11, 1960; children: Liza Hall, Alexander Joseph, Mariette Huxham. Student, U. Glasgow, Scotland, 1957-58; SB, MIT, 1957, PhD, 1961. Rsch. fellow Calif. Inst. Tech., Pasadena, 1961-63, asst. prof., 1963-66, assoc. prof., 1966-70, prof. mech. engring. and jet propulsion, 1970-97, Richard L. and Dorothy M. Hayman prof. mech. engring., 1997—, prof. jet propulsion, 1997—. Cons. to govt. agys. and indsl. orgns. Fellow AIAA; mem. Internat. Acad. Astronautics, Internat. Fedn. Astronautics, Am. Phys. Soc. Home: 1375 Hull Ln Altadena CA 91001-2620 Office: Calif Inst Tech Caltech 205-45 207 Guggenheim Pasadena CA 91125

CULLEN, LAWRENCE DAVID, elementary education educator; b. Newark, Apr. 4, 1946; s. Lawrence David and M. Frances (Freiwald) C.; m. Helle Kjersgaard Olsen, Sept. 25, 1971; 1 child, Kurt. BA, Kean Coll., 1968; MA, William Patersen COll., 1975. Tchr. math. Roselle Park (.N.J.) Bd. Edn., 1968-70, Am. Sch. of The Hague, Den Haag, Netherlands, 1970-72; tchr. sci. Whippany Park Mid. Sch., East Hanover, N.J., 1972-73; tchr. elem. sch. Hopatcong (N.J.) Bd. Edn., 1973-75, 86-99, counselor, 1975-86; retired, 1999. Author of poems. Mem. NEA, N.J. Edn. Assn.,

Sussex County Edn. Assn., Hopatcong Edn. Assn. (treas., exec. bd. 1974-77), Sussex County Guidance Assn., Nat. Geog. Soc. Office: Hopatcong Mid Sch PO Box 1029 Hopatcong NJ 07843-0829

CULLEN, RUTH ENCK, reading specialist, elementary education educator; b. Freeport, NY, Mar. 13, 1937; d. Frederick Harold and Grace Bell (Morrow) Enck; m. Thomas J. Cullen, Aug. 22, 1959; children: Randall R., Lauren Cullen Radick, Amy Cullen Linardic. BS, Coll. N.J., 1959; MA, Montclair State U., 1966; PhD, Fordham U., 1977. Cert. elem. edn., reading tchr., reading specialist, pupil pers. svcs., adminstr., supr., N.J. Tchr. Bergenfield (N.J.) Pub. Schs., 1959-61, Tenafly (N.J.) Pub. Schs., 1961-63; reading specialist Westwood (N.J.) Regional Schs., 1967—; adj. prof. Montclair U., N.J., 1967-83, 92, Fordham U., N.Y.C., 1990; Ramapo (N.J.) Coll., 1987. Rschr., conf. Rockaway Twp. (N.J.) Schs., 1978; spkr. N.Y. Reading Assn., 1980, N.J. Edn. Assn., Atlantic City, 1979, Fordham U., Lincoln Ctr., 1976, Monclair State Coll., 1974, Westwood (N.J.) Schs.; instr. summer spl. edn. program Westwood Regional Schs., 1980-2000; rschr., coord. childhood early excellence in reading program, 1994—; mem. Pupil Assistance Coun. Westwood Regional Schs., portfolio assessment com., 1995-98; mem. Curriculum Mapping, 1997—. Assessment com. Westwood Regional Schs., 1992-94, pupil assistance commn., 1985—, coord. Fast Forward program, 1998-99, computer club adv., 1998—. Mem. ASCD, NEA (editorial adv. com. 1980), Internat. Reading Assn., Reading Recovery Coun. N.Am., NJ Edn. Assn., Kappa Delta Pi, Phi Delta Kappa. Avocations: skiing, painting, landscape designing, historic travel, antiques. Home: 12 Shadow Rd Upper Saddle River NJ 07458-1918 Office: Westwood Regional Schs School St Westwood NJ 07675

CULLEN, VALERIE ADELIA, secondary education educator; b. Northampton, Mass., May 28, 1948; d. Stanley Walter and Wanda Mary (Rup) Helstowski; m. Lawrence Joseph Cullen, June 26, 1982; 1 child, Shanna Valerie. BA, Westfield (Mass.) State Coll., 1970; MALS, SUNY, Stony Brook, 1975. Cert. secondary math. tchr., N.Y., Mass. Tchr. math. Brentwood (N.Y.) Pub. Schs., 1970-71, Center Moriches (N.Y.) Jr.-Sr. High Sch., 1971-88, BOCES I, Alternative High Sch. and Adolescent Pregnancy Program, Riverhead, N.Y., 1988-90, Ctr. Moriches (N.Y.) Jr.-Sr. High Sch., 1990—2002. Mem. Nat. Com. to Preserve Social Security and Medicare. Mem.: N.Y. State Ret. Tchrs., N.Y. Math. Tchrs. Assn., N.Y. State United Tchrs., Nat. Coun. Tchrs. Math., Smithsonian Assocs. Home: 4 Keswick Dr East Islip NY 11730-2808

CULLINAN, BERNICE E(LLINGER), education educator; b. Hamilton, Ohio, Oct. 12, 1926; d. Lee Alexander and Hazel (Berry) Dees; m. George W. Ellinger, June 5, 1948 (div. 1966); children: Susan Jane, James Webb; m. Paul Anthony Cullinan, June 9, 1967 (div. 1994); m. Kenneth Seeman Giniger, Apr. 13, 2002.. BS, Ohio State U., 1948, MA, 1951, PhD, 1964. Cert. elem. educator, Ohio, N.Y. Tchr. Maple Pk. Elem. Sch., Middletown, Ohio, 1944-46, Trotwood (Ohio) Elem. Sch., 1946-47, Columbus (Ohio) Pub. Schs., 1948-50, Upper Arlington (Ohio) Pub. Schs., 1950-52; instr. Ohio State U., Columbus, 1959-64, asst. prof., 1964-67, Ohio State U./Charlotte Huck prof. children's lit., 1997; assoc. prof. NYU, N.Y.C., 1967-72, prof. reading, 1972-97, prof. emeritus, 1998—; editor-in-chief Wordsong Books, Honesdale, Pa., 1990—. Adv. bd. The Reading Rainbow, 1979—, WGBH-TV, 1989—; chair selection com. Ezra Jack Keats New Writer award, 1984-2000; exec. sec. English Standards Project, 1993-94. Author (Lee Galda): Lit. and the Child, 1989, 5th edit., 2002; author: Children's Lit. in the Classroom: Weaving Charlotte's Web, 1989, 2nd edit., 1994, Read to Me: Raising Kids Who Love to Read, 1992, 2nd edit., 2000, Let's Read About: Finding Books They'll Love to Read, 1993; author: (with Brod Bagert) Helping Your Child Learn to Read, 1993; author: (with Diane G. Person) The Continuum Ency. of Children's Lit., 2002; author: (with Dorothy Strickland and Lee Galda) Lang. Arts: Learning and Tchg., 2003; author: (with L. Galda and D. Strickland) Lang., Literacy and the Child, 1993; author:, 2002; author: (with Marilyn Scala and Virginia Schroder) Three Voices: Invitation to Poetry Across the Curriculum, 1995; author: 75 Authors and Illustrators Everyone Should Know, 1994; author: (with David Harrison) Poetry Lessons That Dazzle and Delight, 1999; editor: Children's Lit. in the Reading Program, 1987, Invitation to Read: More Children's Lit. in the Reading Program, 1992, Black Dialects and Reading, 1974, Fact and Fiction: Lit. Across the Curriculum, 1993, Children's Voices, 1993, Pen in Hand, 1993, A Jar of Tiny Stars, 1996; editor: (with Diane Person) The Continuum Ency. of Children's Lit., 2001—03; mem. editl. bd. The New Adv., 1987—99, mem. adv. bd. Ranger Rick Mag., 1992—; contbr. articles; author, editor, with M. Jerry Weiss: Books I Read When I Was Young, 1980, Lit. and Young Children, 1977, Children's Lit. in the Classroom: Extending Charlotte's Web, 1993; author (with Bonnie Kunzel): Ency. of Children's Lit., 2003; editor: The Continuum Ency. of Young Adult Lit., 2005. Editorial bd. Nat. Coun. Tchrs. English, Champaign, Ill., 1973-76; selection com. Caldecott Award Am. Libr. Assn., Chgo., 1982-83; trustee Highlights for Children Found., 1993—. Named Outstanding Educator in Lang. Arts, Nat. Coun. Tchrs. English, 2003; named to Ohio State U. Coll. Edn. Hall of Fame, 1995; recipient Ind. U. Citation for outstanding contbn. to literacy, 1995. Mem.: Reading Hall of Fame (pres. 1998—99, inducted 1989), Internat. Reading Found. (trustee 1984—91, Jeremiah Ludington award 1992), Internat. Reading Assn. (bd. dirs. 1979—84, chair Tchrs. Choices 1988—91, Arbuthnot award for outstanding tchr. children's lit. 1989). Avocations: tennis, reading for pleasure, poetry. Home: 1045 Park Ave Apt 6A New York NY 10028 Office: 3 Tudor Ln Sands Point NY 11050-1104 E-mail: BerniceCullinan@Worldnet.att.net.

CULLINEY, JOHN JAMES, radiologist, educator; b. N.Y.C., Oct. 17, 1955; s. Michael and Marion (Dakowski) C.; m. Margaret Mary Steinhardt, Oct. 11, 1986. BS, Rutgers U., 1977, MS, 1981; MD, U Medicine and Dentistry N.J., 1984. Diplomate Am. Bd. Radiology, Nat. Bd. Med. Examiners. Intern physician Med. Coll. of Pa. Hosp., Phila., 1984-85; resident physician U. Medicine & Dentistry N.J., Newark, 1985-89; fellow body imaging, instr. diagnostic radiology Hahnemann U. Hosp., Phila., 1989-90, asst. prof. clin. diagnostic radiology, 1990-92; asst. prof. clin. diagnostic radiology, chief uroradiology U. Med. and Dentistry N.J., Newark, Pa., 1990-92; clin. instr. diagnostic radiology, chief cross-sect. imaging Mercy & Moses Taylor Hosps. affiliates Temple Med. Sch., Scranton, Pa., 1992-2001; pres. Radiol. Cons. Inc., 1999-2001; radiologist and radiation safety officer Kauai Med. Ctr, Hawaii, 2001—, vice-chmn. dept. radiology, 2003—, also bd. dirs. Chief uroradiology U. Med. and Dentistry N.J., Newark, 1990-92; bd. dirs. Radiol. Cons., Inc., Dunmore, Pa., 1994-2001; co-dir. Phoenix Vascular Lab.; dir. radiology Mercy Hosp. Scranton, Clin. Vascular Lab. Mem. AMA, AAUP, Am. Coll. Radiology, Am. Soc. Breast Imagers, Roentgen Soc. N.Am., KC. Roman Catholic. Avocations: amateur radio technician class, skiing. Home: 2940 Kanani St Lihue HI 96766 Office: Kauai Med Clinic 3-3420 Kuhio Hwy Ste B Lihue HI 96766 E-mail: culliney@aol.com.

CULNON, SHARON DARLENE, reading specialist, special education educator; b. Balt., Apr. 20, 1947; d. Clayton Claude and Ann (McIntyre) Legg; m. Allen William Culnon, July 9, 1975. BA in Elem. Edn., U. Mich., 1972; MAT in Reading Edn., Oakland U., 1980; Learning Disabilities Cert., Ariz. State U., 1983. Cert. K-8 edn., K-12 reading specialist, K-12 learning disabilities specialist. Tchr. Mt. Morris (Mich.) Consolidated Schs., 1972-77; reading specialist Paradise Valley Schs., Phoenix, 1978-87, learning disabilities specialist, 1987-90, tchr., 1990-2000. Mem. Kachina Jr. Women's Club, Phoenix, 1980-83, sec., 1981-82. Recipient Learning Leader/dist. award Paradise Valley Bd. of Edn., Phoenix, 1986. Mem. Phi Delta Kappa (historian 1987-88). Presbyterian. Avocations: travel, wildlife viewing and study, reading, pets, photography. Home: 9035 N Concho Ln Phoenix AZ 85028-5318

CULPEPPER, JO LONG, librarian; b. Franklin, Va., Mar. 10, 1945; d. Sidney Earl and Fannie Lou (Flythe) Long; m. Britton Barclay Culpepper, Jr., Aug. 19, 1967; children: Britton B. III, Edmond Scott, Lou Ann. BS, Radford (Va.) U., 1967; MS, Old Dominion U., 1983. Min. of activities Westmoreland Bapt. Ch., Huntington, W.Va., 1967-70; libr. Walter Cecil Rawls Libr. and Mus., Courtland, Va., 1971-79, Hunterdale Elem. Sch., Franklin, Va., 1979—. Dir. Sunday sch. Franklin Bapt. Ch., 1988-98, bd. deacons, 1994-97; trustee Walter Cecil Rawls Libr. and Mus., 1985-89; troop leader Boy Scouts Am. Mem. Va. Ednl. Media Assn., Franklin/Southampton Reading Coun., Va. Reading Coun. Avocations: scouting, reading, bowling, camping. Home: 401 Trail Rd Franklin VA 23851-2909 Office: Hunterdale Elem Sch 23190 Sedley Rd Franklin VA 23851-3848 E-mail: britt_jo_culpepper@hotmail.com.

CULTON, PAUL MELVIN, retired counselor, educator, interpreter; b. Council Bluffs, Iowa, Feb. 12, 1932; s. Paul Roland and Hallie Ethel Emma (Paschal) C. AB, Minn. Bible Coll., 1955; BS, U. Nebr., Omaha, 1965; MA, Calif. State U., Northridge, 1970; EdD, Brigham Young U., 1981. Cert. tchr., Iowa. Tchr. Iowa Sch. for Deaf, Council Bluffs, 1956-70; ednl. specialist Golden West Coll., Huntington Beach, Calif., 1970-71, dir. disabled students, 1971-82, instr., 1982-88; counselor El Camino Coll., Via Torrance, Calif., 1990-93, acting assoc. dean, 1993-94, counselor, 1994-97. Interpreter various state and fed. cts., Iowa, Calif., 1960-90; asst. prof. Calif. State U., Northridge, Fresno, Dominguez Hills, 1973, 76, 80, 87-91, L.A., 1999—; vis. prof. U. Guam, Agana, 1977; mem. allocations task force, task force on deafness, trainer handicapped students Calif. C.C.s, 1971-81. Editor: Region IX Conf. for Coordinating Rehab. and Edn. Svcs. for Deaf proceedings, 1970, Toward Rehab. Involvement by Parents of Deaf conf. proceedings, 1971; composer Carry the Light, 1986. Bd. dirs. Iowa NAACP, 1966-68, Gay and Lesbian Cmty. Svcs. Ctr., Orange County, Calif., 1975-77; founding sec. Dayle McIntosh Ctr. for Disabled, Anaheim and Garden Grove, Calif., 1974-80; active Dem. Cent. Com. Pottawattamie County, Council Bluffs, 1960-70; del. People to People N.Am. Educators Deaf Vis. Russian Schs. & Programs for Deaf, 1993. League for Innovation in Community Coll. fellow, 1974. Mem. Registry of Interpreters for Deaf, Am. Fedn. Tchrs., Am. Sign Lang. Tchrs. Assn., Nat. Assn. Deaf. Mem. Am. Humanist Assn. Avocations: vocal music, languages, community activism, travel, politics. Home: 3939 N Virginia Rd 110 Long Beach CA 90807

CULVERWELL, ROSEMARY JEAN, principal, elementary education educator; b. Chgo., Jan. 15, 1934; d. August John and Marie Josephine (Westermeyer) Flashing; m. Paul Jerome Culverwell, Apr. 26, 1958; children: Joanne, Mary Frances, Janet, Nancy, Amy. BEd, Chgo. State U., 1955, MEd in Libr. Sci., 1958; postgrad., DePaul U., 1973. Cert. supr., tchr. Tchr. Otis Sch., Chgo., 1955-59; tchr., libr. Yates Sch., Chgo., 1960-61, Nash Sch., Chgo., 1962-63, Boys Chgo. Parental, 1969-72, Edgebrook and Reilly Schs., Chgo., 1965-67; counselor, libr. Reilly Sch., Chgo., 1968, tchr., libr., asst. prin., 1973, prin., 1974—. Reviewer Ill. State Bd. Edn. Quality Review Team. Pres. Infant Jesus Guild, Park Ridge, Ill., 1969-70; troop leader Girl Scouts U.S., Park Ridge, 1967-69; sec. Home Sch. Assn., Park Ridge, 1969, v.p. spl. projects, 1970; mem. Ill. Svc. Ctr. Six Governing Bd., 1994; vol. Ctr. of Concern, Park Ridge, Ill., 1997; quality reviewer Ill. State Bd. Edn., 1998; mem. Ill. Quality Edn. Rev. Team, 1998; v.p. Renaissance Art Club, 1999—. Recipient Outstanding Prin. award Citizens Schs. Com., Chgo., 1987, For Character award, 1984-85, Whitman award for Excellence in Edn. Mgmt., 1990, Local Sch. Coun. award Ill. Bell Ameritech, 1991, Ill. Disting. Educator award Milken Family Found. Nat. Educators, 1991, Ill. Edn./Bus. Partnership award, 1994, 96. Mem. AAUW, LWV (chmn. speakers bur. 1969), Delta Kappa Gamma, Phi Delta Kappa. Avocations: acrylic painting, reading, swimming, making doll houses and furniture. Home: 1929 S Ashland Ave Park Ridge IL 60068-5460 Office: FW Reilly Sch 3650 W School St Chicago IL 60618-5358 E-mail: rosemary.culverwell@mciworldcom.net.

CUMMERTON, JOAN MARIE, social work educator; b. Batavia, N.Y., Jan. 11, 1931; d. John J. and Loretta E. (Geissler) C. BS in Social Sci., Carnegie Mellon U., 1953; MS in Social Adminstrn., Case-Western Reserve U., 1956; D in Social Work, Washington U., St. Louis, 1970. Cert. Acad. Cert. Social Workers. Group worker Ferry Rd. Playground, Phila., 1953-54; dist. dir. Girl Scouts, St. Louis, 1956-58, field staff supr., 1958-60; asst. prof. U. Iowa, Iowa City, 1963-70; assoc. prof. San Francisco State U., 1970-80, prof. social work edn., 1980—. Cons. Family Svc. Assn., Des Moines, 1966-67, Women, Inc., San Francisco, 1988-89. Mem. NASW, Coun. on Social Work Edn., Women in Psychology, Nat. Women's Studies Assn. Avocations: sports, gardening, camping. Office: San Francisco State U 1600 Holloway Ave San Francisco CA 94132-1722

CUMMINGS, CAROLE EDWARDS, retired special education educator; b. Dover, Ohio, June 17, 1942; d. John T. and Dorothy M. (Plotts) Edwards; children: Kimberly Cummings Wood, Rebecca Cummings. BS, Kent State U., 1964; MA, Ohio State U., 1986. Cert. elem. tchr., learning disabilities tchr., spl. edn. supervision., Ohio. Elem. tchr. Dover Pub. Schs., 1965-66, 70-71; mid. sch. tchr. South-Western City Schs., Grove City, Ohio, 1971-74, tutor, 1974-76; elem. and high sch. tutor Hamilton Local Sch., Columbus, Ohio, 1976-77, elem. tchr. learning disabilities, 1978-85; high sch. tchr. learning disabilities Southwest Licking Local Schs., Kirkersville, Ohio, 1985-86; cons. Cen. Ohio Spl. Edn. Regional Resource Ctr., Columbus, 1987-91, Lincoln Way Spl. Edn. Regional Resource Ctr., Louisville, Ohio, 1991-93; supr. Stark County Sch. Dist., Canton, Ohio, 1993—2000; prof. Kent State U., 2001—. Mem. Coun. for Exceptional Children, Coun. for Adminstrs. Spl. Edn., DAR, Order Ea. Star, Phi Delta Kappa.

CUMMINGS, CRYSTAL SNEED, special education educator; b. Dublin, Ga., Feb. 7, 1967; d. Willie Gene Thomas and Bernice (Haynes) Barnes; m. Reginald Keith Cummings, Aug. 18, 990; 1 child, Reginald Keith II. BS in Edn., Valdosta State Coll., 1991. Cert. tchr., Ga. Tchr. Bibb County Bd. Edn., Macon, Ga., 1991—. Mem. Coun. for Exceptional Children. Baptist. Home: 607 Woolfolk St Macon GA 31217-3739

CUMMINGS, JUDY ANNETTE, retired secondary education educator; b. Denver, May 27, 1943; d. John Joseph and Garnett Edwana (Ferry) Leuthard; m. Ernest LeRoy Cummings, Aug. 6, 1965; 1 child, Scott Joseph. BS in Edn., Black Hills State U., Spearfish, S.D., 1971. Cert. tchr., Wyo. Clk. Workmen's Compensation, Denver, 1961-62, Woodo Product Co., Berkeley, Calif., 1962, Denver Pub. Sch. Sys., 1964-65; clk.-typist Martin Marietta Corp., Waterton, Colo., 1962-64; sec. Yardney Electric Corp., Pawcatuck, Conn., 1965; substitute tchr. Campbell County Sch. Dist., Gillette, Wyo., 1970-73, tchr. bus. edn., 1973-97, ret., 1997. Dir. drug free sch. program Campbell County H.S., 1993—, quality sch. team, 1995-96, sch. improvement com., 1995-96; sec. CAMPCO Credit Union Bd.; alt. mem. Liaison Com. for Salaries and Benefits; mem. Elem. Sch. Keyboarding Task Force. Mem. adv. com. Juvenile Detention-Treatment Ctr., Gilette, 1993. Recipient plaque as outstanding bus. educator Campbell County H.S., 1991, named Tchr. of Yr., 1994, 96-97. Mem. NEA, Am. Vocat. Assn. (life), Wyo. Edn. Assn., Wyo. Bus. Edn. Assn. (membership chmn. 1985), Wyo. Vocat. Assn. (membership chmn. 1985), Campbell County Edn. Assn. (membership chmn.), Nat. Bus. Edn. Assn., Campbell County Vocat. Assn. (sec.), Campbell County C. of C. (adv. bd. 1982-84), Wyo. Coaches Assn., Future Farmers Am. (hon., cert. of appreciation), Alpha Delta Kappa (past pres.). Republican. Methodist. Avocations: reading, crocheting, embroidery, cross-stitching, travel. Home: 1183 Country Club Rd Gillette WY 82718-5512 Office: Campbell County HS 1000 Camel Dr Gillette WY 82716-4950 E-mail: jcummings@vcn.com.

CUMMINGS, MAXINE GIBSON, elementary school educator; b. Tupelo, Miss., Oct. 7, 1940; d. T. Ruben and Maggie (Ruff) Gibson; m. Willie B. Cummings, Aug. 15, 1964; 1 child, Stanley. BS, Barber-Scotia Coll., Concord, N.C., 1962; MA, Northeastern Ill. U., Chgo., 1974. Cert. tchr., N.C., Ill. Tchr. Walter Reed Elem. Sch., Chgo., 1963-75, reading tchr., 1975-82, social studies tchr., 1982-85; reading resource tchr. Arna Bontemps Sch., Chgo., 1985-91, ESEA lab. tchr., 1991—; Title I reading/math tchr. St. Sabina Acad., Chgo. Mentor tchr. Tchrs. for Chgo. Program, Arna W. Bontemps Sch. Site, 1996—; counselor Westside YWCA, Chgo., 1963-68; chmn. reading com. Bontemps Sch., 1986-92, chmn. activity com., 1992-93; mentor tchr. Bontemps Tchrs. for Chgo. Program; mem. staff devel. team Reading Tchrs. Acad. for Profl. Growth, Chgo. Bd. Edn.; Title I tchr., presenter in field. Contbr. articles to profl. jours. Mem. Vol. Edna White Century Garden; sec. S.W. Morgan Park Civic Assn., Chgo., 1990-92; block rep. Neighborhood Watch Program, Chgo., 1989-90; trustee Morgan Park Presbyn. Ch., peace and justice com., mem. choir; Great Books Discussion leader Walker Br. Libr., ordination elder Morgan Park Presbyn., 1999; race rels. com. Beverly/Morgan Park Neighborhood-Task Force; coord. garden site Metra Train Sta. Grantee Chgo.-Incentive, 1987, NEH, 1984, Northeastern Ill. U., 1980; recipient Regional Cmty. Gardening award, Morgan Park Neighborhood, Chgo., 1998, Mayor Daley's Landscpae Improvement Program award, 1999, 2d place award City Scape Gardening Corner, Chgo., 1999. Mem. Minority Students of Chgo. Area (recruiter), Barber-Scotia Alumni Club (sec. 1989-92), Pi Lambda Theta. Avocations: biking, walking, reading, travel, gardening. Home: 11116 S Longwood Dr Chicago IL 60643-4043 Office: St Sabina Acad 7801 S Throop St Chicago IL 60620-

CUMMINGS, PENELOPE DIRRIG, special education educator; b. Akron, Ohio, Sept. 16, 1944; d. Raymond Joseph and Pearl Penelope (Pantages) Dirrig; m. Ray Cummings, Jn. 21, 1967; children: Michael R., James E. BA in English, U. Akron, 1966; MS in Spl. Edn., U. Kans., 1992. Tchr. English Akron Pub. Schs., 1966-69; tutor learning disabled Delaware (Ohio) Pub. Schs., 1980-82; tutor homebound Trumbull (Conn.) Pub. Schs., 1982-87; tutor homebound, student support svcs. program Olathe (Kans.) Pub. Schs., 1987-91; tchr. English and learning disabled Penn Valley C.C., Kansas City, Mo., 1988-91; tchr. learning disabled Turner Pub. Schs. United Sch. Dist. # 202, Kansas City, Kansas, 1991—. Editor sorority mag. The Compass, 1976-78. Pres., sec. Officer's Wives' Club, Rickenbacher AFB, Columbus, Ohio, 1973-74; active Mortar Bd., Akron, 1965-66, PTA, 1976—. Scholar United Steelworkers Am., 1962-66, U. Akron, 1962-66, Theta Phi Alpha, 1992. Mem. NEA, Coun. for Learning Disabilities, (v.p. Mo.-Kans. chpt. 1992-93, pres. 1994-95), Coun. for Exceptional Children (pres. elect N.E. Kans. coun. 436), Kappa Delta Pi, Phi Sigma Alpha. Democrat. Roman Catholic. Avocations: book discussion, traveling, crafts. Home: 12520 Knox St Overland Park KS 66213-1831 Office: Highland Middle Sch 3101 S 51st St Kansas City KS 66106-3437

CUMMINGS, RUSSELL MARK, aerospace engineer, educator; b. Santa Cruz, Calif., Oct. 3, 1955; s. Gilbert Warren and Anna Mae (Phillips) C. BS, Calif. Poly. State U., 1977, MS, 1985, BA, 1999; Engr. Aerospace Engring., 1982; PhD, U. So. Calif., 1988. Tech. staff Hughes Aircraft Co., Canoga Park, Calif., 1979-86; rsch. assoc. Nat. Rsch. Coun. at NASA Ames Rsch. Ctr., Moffett Field, Calif., 1988-90; prof. aerospace engring. Calif. Poly. State U., San Luis Obispo, Calif., 1986—. Dept. chmn. aero. engring. dept. Calif. Poly. State U., 1992-96; vis. acad. computing lab. Oxford U., 1995-97; Disting. vis. prof. aeronautics U.S. Air Force Acad., 2001-03; presenter in field. Assoc. editor: Jour. Spacecraft and Rockets, 1994—2003; contbr. chapters to books, over 25 articles to profl. jours. Hughes Engring. fellow 1980-84, Howard Hughes Doctoral fellow 1984-86, Boeing faculty summer fellow, 2000; NASA grantee, 1986-2000, Office Naval Rsch. grantee, 2002, NSF Panel Rev., 2002; recipient AIAA Nat. Faculty Advisor award, 1994, Northrop Grumman Excellence in Teaching and Applied Rsch. award, 1995, Undergraduate Faculty Advisor award BF Goodrich Nat. Collegiate Inventors Program, 1998, Excellence in Tchg. award TRW, 1999, Litton Excellence in Rsch. award, 2000, Sci. and Engring. award USAF, 2003. Fellow: AIAA (assoc.; missile sys. tech. com. 1988—91, student activities com. 1991—2002, chair 1999—2002); mem.: Aircraft Owners and Pilots Assn., Royal Aero Soc., Am. Soc. Engring. Educators, Sigma Gamma Tau, Sigma Xi. Republican. Mem. Evangelical Christian Ch. Avocations: piano, tennis, skiing, volleyball, baseball. Office: Calif Poly State U Dept Aero Engring San Luis Obispo CA 93407 E-mail: rcumming@calpoly.edu.

CUMMINGS, SHARON SUE, state extension service youth specialist; b. Trinidad, Colo., Aug. 26, 1945; d. James H. and Mima (McDonald) C. BS, Colo. State U., 1967, MEd, 1974; PhD, Ohio State U., 1991. Summer agt. Colo. State Coop. Extension, Canon City, 1966, extension home agt. Colo. Springs, 1967-68; county dir. Leadville, 1968-70; area extension home economist San Luis Valley, 1970-74; agt., home economist Castle Rock, 1974-80; specialist 4H youth Ft. Collins, 1980-89, '91—; grad. assoc. Ohio State U. Coop. Extension, Columbus, 1989-91. Co-author: National Ambassador Handbook, 1984; (curriculum for youth) over 20 pubs.; assoc. editor (newsletter) Youthoughts, 1990, '91. Com. mem. United Meth. Ch., Colo., 1975—. Recipient Agrl. Extension scholarship Ohio State U., 1991; spotlighted alumna Dept. Human Resources Colo. State U., 1985-86; 1 of 50 in U.S chosen for Exec. Devel. Inst. USDA Extension Svc., 1987-89. Mem. Nat. Assn. Extension 4-H Youth Agts. (pres. Colo. 1981-82), Colo. Home Econs. Assn. (treas. 1983-85), Colo. State U. Extension Specialist Assn. (pres. 1982-84), CERES (assoc., chpt. advisor 1983-85), Phi Kappa Phi, Gamma Sigma Delta (pres. 1999-2000), Epsilon Sigma Phi (pres. Colo. 1996-97). Avocations: reading, walking, working out, yard care S.W. history and lore. Office: Colo State U Coop Extension 127 Aylesworth NW Fort Collins CO 80523-0001

CUMMINGS-SAXTON, JAMES, chemical engineer, consultant, educator; b. Pitts., Dec. 5, 1936; s. James Allen and Margaret Mary (Helsel) Saxton; m. Carolyn Cummings, Aug. 22, 1959; children: Megan Caitlin Cummings-Krueger, James, Jennifer Aine. B Engring. Sci. in Chem. Engring., Johns Hopkins U., 1959; PhD in Chem. Engring., U. Calif., Berkeley, 1966. Registered profl. engr., D.C. Supr. Bellcomm, Washington, 1964-71; sr. v.p. Internat. Rsch. & Tech., Washington, 1971-79; dep. tech. dir. internat. energy program Argonne (Ill.) Nat. Lab., 1979-83; prin. Indsl. Econs., Inc., Cambridge, Mass., 1983—. Instr. chem. engring. Cath. U. Am., Washington, 1974—75, Ill. Inst. Tech., Chgo., 1979—80; rsch. assoc. prof. Clark U., Worcester, Mass., 1994—. Mem.: AIChE (pres. Boston sect. 1993—94), Lions (pres. Nahant, Mass. chpt. 1993—95). Unitarian Universalist. Avocations: hiking, bicycling, reading. Home: 40 Summer St Nahant MA 01908 Office: Indsl Econs Inc 2067 Massachusetts Ave Cambridge MA 02140-1340 E-mail: sax@indecon.com.

CUMMINS, BONNIE NORVELL, gifted and talented education educator; b. Harrodsburg, Ky., Apr. 7, 1938; d. James Herbert Norvell and Pauline (Brown) Boyles; m. Paul Harlan Cummins; children: Carol Anne, Gregory Todd, John-Paul. BA, Centre Coll., 1965; MEd, Ea. Ky. U., 1985, cert. rank I, 1986. acad. coach Mercer Elem. Sch., Harrodsburg, 1986-92; co-founder Mercer Invitational Acad. Tournament. Tchr. Danville (Ky.) City Schs., 1966-68, Duval County Schs., Jacksonville, Fla., 1968-69, Univ. Christian Sch., Jacksonville, 1969-73, Mercer County Schs., Harrodsburg, 1975—. Acad. coach Mercer Elem. Sch., Harrodsburg, 1986-92. Recipient Mercer County Parent Tchr. award for outstanding contbn. to academics, 1988, others. Republican. Baptist. Home: 621 Elizabeth Ct Harrodsburg KY 40330-2143

CUMMINS, DELMER DUANE, academic administrator, historian; b. Dawson, Nebr., June 4, 1935; s. Delmer H. and Ina Z. (Arnold) C.; m. Darla Sue Beard, Oct. 6, 1957; children: Stephen Duane, Cristi Sue, Caroline Renee. BS, Phillips U., Enid, Okla., 1957; MA, U. Denver, 1965; PhD, U. Okla., 1974; LLD, Williams Woods Coll., 1979; HHD (hon.), Phillips U., 1983; DLitt (hon.), Chapman U., 1996. Tchr., Jefferson County Pub. Schs.,

Denver, 1956-67; mem. faculty Oklahoma City U., 1967-77, Darbeth-Whitten prof. history, 1974-77, curator George Shirk Collection, 1977. Chmn. dept. history Oklahoma City U., 1969—72; dir. Robert A. Taft Inst. Govt., 1972—77; pres. Bethany (W.Va.) Coll., 1988—2002, pres. emeritus, 2002—; pres. Brite Div. Sch., 2002—03; vis. scholar in history Johns Hopkins U., 2002—. Author: The American Frontier, 1968, Origins of the Civil War, 1971; : 2d edit., 1978, The American Revolution, 1968, Contrasting Decades, 1920's and 1930's, 1972; : 2d edit., 1978, Consensus and Turmoil, 1972, William R. Leigh: Biography of a Western Artist, 1980, A Handbook for Today's Disciples, 1981, 3d edit., 2003; author: (with D. Hohweller) An Enlisted Soldier's View of the Civil War, 1981, 3d edit., 2003; author: (with others) Seeking God's Peace in a Nuclear Age, 1985; author: The Disciples Colleges: A History, 1987, The Search for Identity, Disciples of Christ-The Restructure Years, 1987, Dale Fiers: Twentieth Century Disciple, 2003; editor: The Disciples Theol. Digest, 1986—88; contbr. articles to profl. jours. Mem. Pitts. Opera Bd., 1996—2001; moderator, active multiple nat. bds. and task forces Christian Ch., 1993—95, pres. higher edn., 1978—88; trustee Culver-Stockton Coll., 1978—88, Tougaloo Coll., 1978—88, vice chmn., 1985—88; bd. dirs. Disciples of Christ Hist. Soc.; Danforth assoc., 1976—78. Mem. Okla. Coun. Humanities (grantee 1974), Phillips U. Alumni Assn. (pres. 1975-76), Nat. Assn. Ind. Colls. and Univs. (secretariat, policy commn. 1990-94), chair pres.'s athletic conf. 1990-92), W.Va. Assn. Ind. Colls. (chair 1994-97, chair east ctrl. coll. consortium 1997-98), Co. of Ind. Colls. (bd. dirs. 1998-2001). Home: 255 Sears Ln Swanton MD 21561 E-mail: d.cummins@mail.bethanywv.edu.

CUMMINS, KATHLEEN K. retired elementary school educator; b. Fountain County, Ind., June 20, 1919; d. Homer Elston Krout and Edith Zerilda Allen; m. Robert E. Cummins, Oct. 4, 1940 (dec. Mar. 1984); 1 child, Robert E. Jr. BS in Edn., Ind. State U., 1952. Elem. tchr. East Allen Cmty. Schs., New Haven and Ft. Wayne, Ind., 1940—76; ret., 1976. Deaconess Trinity English Luth. Ch., Ft. Wayne, 1982—. Recipient Ret. Tchr. of Yr. award, Instant Copy, Ft. Wayne, 1993. Mem.: AAUW (grantee 1984), Allen County Ret. Educators Assn. (pres. 1986—88), Ft. Wayne Hist. Mus. (past pres. Barr St. Irregulars), Ft. Wayne Women's Club (bd. dirs. 1988—, chmn. fine arts dept.), Fortnightly Club (pres. 1994—96), Delta Kappa Gamma (chpt. pres. 1964—66). Democrat. Lutheran. Avocations: painting, reading, bridge, knitting, gardening. Home: 3808 Oak Park Dr Fort Wayne IN 46815

CUMMINS, PATRICIA WILLETT, academic administrator; b. Worcester, Mass., Oct. 16, 1948; d. Warren Joseph and Mary (Shannon) Willett; m. Christopher J. Cummins, Oct. 4, 1975; children: John, Mary. BA cum laude, Smith Coll., 1970; MA, U. Rochester, 1971; PhD, U. N.C., 1974. Asst. prof. Lafayette Coll., Easton, Pa., 1973-74; from asst. prof. to prof. W.Va. U., Morgantown, 1974-84; prof., dept. chairperson No. Ariz. U., Flagstaff, 1984-89; dean Arts and Humanities SUNY, Buffalo, 1989-95; dean Arts and Scis. U. Toledo, Ohio, 1995—99, prof. French, 1995-2000; vice provost acad. affairs. Va. Commonwealth U., Richmond, 2000—01, prof. French, 2000—. Author: Commercial French, 1982; author, editor: Literary and Historical Perspectives of the Middle Ages, 1982, Le Regime Tresultile, 1976, Issues and Methods in French for Business and Economic Purposes, 1995; mem. editl. bd. Ars Lyrica 1980-86, Global Bus. Langs., 1995-2003, Jour. Lang. for Internat. Bus., 1995-2003; editor-in-chief Fgn. Lang. Ann., 1983-85. Bd. dirs. Arts in Edn. Inst. Western N.Y., 1990-95, Buffalo-Lille Sister Cities,Pick of the Crop Dance Ensemble, 1992-95. Recipient Young Scholars award Mediaeval Acad. Am., 1977; NEH fellow, 1976-77, Fulbright fellow 2003; grantee French Govt. Bus., 1983, U.S. Dept. Edn., 1986, 87-89, Que. (Can.) Govt., 1979. Mem. MLA (del. assembly 1979-81), Internat. Courtly Lit. Soc. (chief bibliographer 1979, bibliographer 1974-83), Soc. for Text and Music, Am. Assn. Tchrs. French (v.p. 1985-91, chair pedagogical commn. 1985-91, co-chair proficiency commn. 1990-92, chair French Bus. commn. 1993—96, chair commn. on univs. 2003—), Southeastern Medieval Assn. (v.p. 1981-83, pres. 1983-85), Am. Coun. Tchg. Fgn. Langs., Coun. Colls. Arts and Scis. (chair commn. on comprehensive instns. 1994-96, mem. com. on long term planning 1995-96, chair com. on metro. univs. 1996-98, mem. exec. bd. 1996-98). Democrat. Roman Catholic. Avocations: tennis, squash, softball, bridge.

CUNINGGIM, WHITTY DANIEL, education educator; b. Oxford, N.C., Aug. 18, 1918; d. Ethrel Jenkins and Annie Penelope (Whitty) Daniel; m. Merrimon Cuninggim, June 10, 1939 (dec.); children: Lee C. Neff, Penny, Terry (dec.). BA, Duke U., 1938. Founder, chmn. Reading Is Fun-damental, St. Louis, 1970-76; bd. of edn. Spl. Sch. Dist. St. Louis County, St. Louis, 1970-75, pres., 1975-76; chmn. Adv. Coun. for Exceptional Children, Winston Salem, N.C., 1976-82. Bd. dirs. Nat. Citizens' Com. for Support of Pub. Schs., 1970-76, Nat. Sch. Vol. Program, Alexandria, Va., 1976-83, White House Conference on Edn. Co-founder Catalyst Assocs., St. Louis, 1974; chmn. Forsyth County N.C. 2000, 1982; pres. Women's Forum, N.C., 1985-86, Art Coun., Winston-Salem, 1982-83; mem. N.C. Pub. Edn. Policy Coun., 1983-84; bd. assocs. N.C. Child Advocacy Inst., 1987-89; mem. Md. Edn. Coalition, Balt., 1989—, mem. exec. bd., 1991-95, Leadership Coun., 1995-99; v.p. Broadmead, 1990-92, trustee, 1998-2001; mem. exec. com. N.C. Dems., 1980-84, co-chmn. edn. com. League of Women Voters of Baltimore County, 1995-99. Recipient Duke U. Alumni award, Duke U. Alumni Assn., Winston Salem, 1982, award for Cmty. Svc., League of Women Voters, N.C., 1989; named Woman of Achievment, St. Louis Globe-Democrat, 1968, Nat. Sch. Vol of Year, Nat. Sch. Vol. Program, 1979. Mem. LWV (edn. com. Baltimore County chpt.), Nat. Women's Dem. Club, Phi Beta Kappa, Phi Delta Kappa. Democrat. Avocations: art history, rug hooking. Home: 13801 York Rd Apt E9 Cockeysville MD 21030-1861

CUNNINGHAM, CLARK EDWARD, anthropology educator; b. Kansas City, Mo., Mar. 13, 1934; s. John Stephen and Mary Elizabeth (Brown) C.; m. Ritva Aulikki Kokko, June 2, 1969; children: Nathalie Noëlle, Eric Stephen. BA, Yale U., 1957; B.Litt. (Rhodes scholar), U. Oxford, Eng., 1959, D.Phil., 1963. Rsch. assoc., vis lectr. anthropology Yale U., New Haven, 1963, 65-68; vis. asst. prof. U. Ill., Urbana, 1963-64, assoc. prof., 1968-72, prof., 1972—95, prof. emeritus, 1995—. Vis. assoc. prof. Chiang Mai U., Thailand, 1968-70; project specialist Ford Found., Ujung Pandang, Indonesia, 1975-76; cons. World Bank, 1982, 84, 87; coord. social scis. MUCIA/2d Indonesian Higher Edn. Project, 1987-91. Author: The Postwar Migration of the Toba-Batak to East Sumatra, 1958; co-editor: Changing Lives, Changing Rites: Ritual and Social Change in Indonesian and Philippine Uplands, 1989; co-editor: Studies of Health Problems and Health Behavior in Saraphi, North Thailand, 1970, Symbolism and Cognition, 1981; contbr. articles to profl. jours. Grantee Am. Coun. Learned Socs., Population Coun., Ford Found., Wenner-Gren Found., Midwest Univs. Consortium Internat. Activities, Smithsonian Instn. Fellow Am. Anthrop. Assn., Koninklijk Inst. voor Taal, Land- en Volkenkunde, Royal Anthrop. Inst.; mem. Assn. Asian Studies. Home: 602 Eliot Dr Urbana IL 61801-6730

CUNNINGHAM, DIANNE, minister of intergovernmental affairs; b. Ontario, Canada; Tchr, Ontario (Can.) Schs.; ednl. cons. Self-employed; elected trustee London (Ont.) Bd. Edn., Canada, 1973—88; elected mem. Ontario (Can.) Parliament, Toronto, 1988—. Minister intergovernmental affairs and minister responsible for women's ssues Ontario Parliament, 1995—; mem. Ontario Com. on Legislation and Regulations; Ontario rep. Nat. Coun. on Social Policy Renewal. Recipient Woman of Distinction award, London (Ont.) YM-WCA, 1993. Office: Min Tng Colls and Univs Mowat Block 900 Bay St Toronto On M7A 1L2 Canada

CUNNINGHAM, JACQUELINE LEMMÉ, psychologist, educator, researcher; b. Biddeford, Maine, Apr. 22, 1941; d. S. James and Alice (Fréchette) Lemmé; m. Seymour Cunningham II, Dec. 16, 1960 (dec. 1987); children: Macklin Todd, Danielle, Alyssa. BA in Psychology cum laude, U. Maine, Orono, 1963; MS in Psychology, U. South Ala., 1983; PhD in Ednl. Psychology, U. Tex., 1994. Tchr. Mobile (Ala.) Pub. Schs., 1976-81; psychology intern Devereux Found., Devon, Pa., 1988-89; fellow in developmental disabilities Children's Hosp. Harvard Med. Sch., Boston, 1990; prof. U. S.D., Vermillion, 1994-95; fellow in pediat. neuropsychology Children's Nat. Med. Ctr., George Washington U. Med. Ctr., Washington, 1995—97; psychologist pvt. practice, Wilmington, Del., 1997—2000, Children's Hosp. of Phila., Phila., 2000—. Cons. in field. Contbr. articles to profl. jours., chapters to books. Mem. Am. Psychol. Assn. (outstanding dissertation of yr. award 1994), Internat. Neuropsychol. Soc., Nat. Acad. Neuropsychology, Soc. History Behavioral Scis., Phila. Neuropsychology Soc. (bd. dirs. 1998-2002), Phi Kappa Phi. Avocations: travel, writing. Office: Children's Hosp of Phila 34th St & Civic Ctr Blvd Philadelphia PA 19104

CUNNINGHAM, JOEL LUTHER, university president, vice-chancellor; b. Mooresville, N.C., Jan. 11, 1944; s. Elbert Claxton and Ruth Morton (Journey) Cunningham; m. Trudy Bender, June 12, 1965; children: Nancy Elizabeth, Susan Ruth. BA, U. Tenn., Chattanooga, 1965; MA, U. Oreg., 1967, PhD, 1969. Asst. prof. math. U. Ky., Lexington, 1969—74; dean continuing edn. U. Tenn., Chattanooga, 1974—79; acad. v.p. Susquehanna U., Selinsgrove, Pa., 1979—84, pres., 1984—2000; vice-chancellor, pres. U. South, Sewanee, Tenn., 2000—. Trustee Assn. of Episcopal Coll., 2000—, chair, 2002—; bd. dirs. Sunbury (Pa.) Hosp., 1984—2000, v.p., 1992—98, pres., 1998—2000; bd. dirs. Pa. Campus Compact, 1987—92, Coll. & U. Anglican Commn., 2001—; treas. Coll. & U. Angelican Commn., 2002—; mem. St. Mary's Conf. Ctr., 2000—. Fellow Woodrow Wilson fellow, 1965, Am. Coun. on Edn. fellow, 1976—77. Mem.: Soc. for Values in Higher Edn. (bd. dirs. 1992—99, v.p. 1994—95, pres. 1995—99), Am. Assn. for Higher Edn., Math. Assn. Am., Am. Math. Soc., Sigma Chi (chmn. bd. leadership tng. 1977—87, treas. 1987—89, v.p. 1989—91, pres. 1991—93, Internat. Balfour award 1965), Sigma Xi. Episcopalian. Home: PO Box 3326 Sewanee TN 37375 Office: U South Office VC & Pres 735 University Ave Sewanee TN 37383 E-mail: jcunning@sewanee.edu.

CUNNINGHAM, JUDY EVALYN, elementary school administrator, educator; b. Rockford, Ill., May 11, 1947; d. James William and June Evalyn (Davis) Geddes; m. Charles Edward Cunningham, June 21, 1969 (div. Oct. 1984); 1 child, Charles Arthur. BS in Edn., No. Ill. U., 1969, MS in Edn., 1972, EdD, 1997. Intervention specialist Rockford Office of Edn., 1985-86; counselor Belvidere (Ill.) Jr. H.S., 1986-90; prin., counselor Tibbets Elem. Sch., Elkhorn, Wis., 1990-92; prin., curriculum coord. Sch. Dist. of Beloit, Wis., 1992-95; therapist Janet Wattes Mental Health Ctr., 1996; counselor Rockford Pub. Schs., 1996—. Cons. Ill. 4-H program, Urbana, 1979-83; presenter regional edn. confs., 1987-90. Author: Colors of Leadership, 1981 (Alumni State award 1981). Youth leader First Free Ch., Rockford, 1985—; active Starlight Cmty. Theatre, Rockford, 1988—. Mem. Nat. Counselors Assn., Ill. Counselors Assn., Sports Car Club of Am. (past bd. dirs. local chpt.), Alpha Chi Omega, Pi Lambda Theta, Kappa Delta pi. Avocations: show horses, cattle, theater. Home: 5983 Yale Bridge Rd Rockton IL 61072-9505

CUNNINGHAM, NANCY SCHIEFFELIN, business educator; b. Mobile, Ala., Sept. 14, 1951; d. William Orville and Burline (Livingston) Schieffelin; m. Donald Frank Cunningham, Aug. 18, 1975; children: Benjamin Grant, Paige Allison. BA magna cum laude, U. North Tex., 1975; MA, Ohio State U., 1982. Cert. Myers Briggs Type Indicator adminstr. Mem. English faculty Franklin U., Columbus, Ohio; English curriculum coord. Ctr. for Unique Learners, Rockville, Mo.; mem. English faculty McClennan C.C., Waco, Tex.; coord. bus. writing Baylor U., Waco. Contbr. articles to profl. jours.; created and administers a writing proficiency exam. for bus. students; sr. editor: The Perryman Report, 1991—, The Perryman Texas Letter, 1992—. Baylor U. summer rsch. grantee. Mem. MLA, Assn. for Bus. Communication (rep.), Nat. Coun. Tchrs. English, Soc. for Tech. Comm., Perryman Tex. Editors (editor newsletters). E-mail: nancysc@perrymangroup.com., ncunningham@perrymangroup.com.

CUNNINGHAM, RAYMOND CAROL, JR., elementary school educator; b. Blackshear, Ga., Jan. 10, 1962; s. Raymond Carol Cunningham Sr. and Irma Lucille (Anderson) Cunningham; m. Elizabeth Laura Jones, July 11, 1998; children: Brett Christian, Reason Chandler, Emmaline Lois. AA in Psychology, Waycross Jr. Coll., Waycross, Ga., 1983; BSED in Health/Phys. Edn., U. Ga., 1984; postgrad., Valdosta State U. Cert. Tchg. cert. Ga. Tchr. Grady St. Elem. Sch., Blackshear, 1984—87, Patterson Elem. Sch., Ga., 1987—. Ch. pianist Patterson Bapt. Ch., 1985—. Named Tchr. of Yr., Pierce County Bd. Edn., 1990; recipient Cmty. Svc. award, Patterson Lions Club, 1996. Mem.: Ga. Assn. Educators, Profl. Assn. Ga. Educators. Office: Patterson Elem Sch 3444 Drawdy St Patterson GA 31557-2439 Home: PO Box 531 Patterson GA 31557

CUNNINGHAM, WILLIAM HUGHES, former academic administrator, marketing educator; b. Detroit, Jan. 5, 1944; married; 1 child BA, Mich. State U., 1966, MBA, 1967, PhD, 1971, LLD (hon.), 1993. Mem. faculty U. Tex., Austin, 1971—, assoc. prof. mktg., 1973-79, prof., 1979—, assoc. dean grad. programs, 1976-82, Foley/Sanger Harris prof. retail merchandising, 1982-83, acting dean Coll. Bus. Adminstrn. and Grad. Sch. Bus., 1982-83, dean, 1983-85, pres., 1985-92, Centennial Chair Bus. Edn. Leadership, 1983-85, Regents Chair Higher Edn. Leadership, 1985-92, Lee Hage and Joseph D. Jamail Regents Chair Higher Edn. Leadership, 1992-2000, James L. Bayless Chair for Free Enterprise, 1988—; chancellor U. Tex. Sys., Austin, 1992-2000. Bd. dirs. Jefferson-Pilot Corp., John Hancock Funds, S.W. Airlines Co., Introgen Therapeutics, Hayes Lemmerz Internat., LIN TV; mem. corp. Conf. Bd. Author: (with W.J.E. Crissy and I.C.M. Cunningham) Selling: The Personal Force in Marketing, 1977, 2d edit. (with D.W. Jackson and Cunningham), 1988, Effective Selling, 1977, Spanish edit., 1980, (with S. Lopreato) Consumers' Energy Attitudes and Behavior, 1977, (with Cunningham) Marketing: A Managerial Approach, 1981, 2d edit. (with Cunningham and C. Swift), 1988, (with R. Aldag and C. Swift) Introduction to Business, 1984, 3d edit. (with R. Aldag and S. Block), 1992, 4th edit. (with R. Aldag and M. Stone), 1995, (with B. Verhage and Cunningham) Grondslagen van het Marketing Management, 1984, (with R. Aldag and S. Block) Business in a Changing World, 1992, also monographs and articles; editor Jour. Mktg., 1981-84. Bd. dirs. Houston Area Rsch. Coun., 1984; mem. Mental Health/Mental Retardation Legis. Oversight Com., 1984; mem. adv. bd. Found. for Cultural Exch./The Netherlands-U.S.A.; bd. dirs. Lyndon Baines Johnson Found. Recipient Tchg. Excellence award U. Tex. Coll. Bus. Adminstrn., 1972, Alpha Kappa Psi, 1975, Hank and Mary Harkins Found., 1978, Disting. Scholastic Contbn. award Coll. Bus. Adminstrn. Found. Adv. Council, 1982, Disting. Alumnus award Coll. and Grad. Sch. Bus., Mich. State U., 1983, 93, Tree of Life award Jewish Nat. Fund, 1992; named among top 20 profs. Utmost Mag., 1982; Rsch. grant Univ. Rsch. Inst., 1971-73, Latin Am. Inst., 1972, So. Union Gas Energy, 1975-76, ERDA, 1976 Mem. Am. Inst. for Decision Scis., Am. Mktg. Assn., Assn. Consumer Rsch., So. Mktg. Assn., S.W. Social Sci. Assn., Phi Kappa Phi, Omicron Delta Kappa Office: U Tex PO Box E Austin TX 78713 E-mail: wcunningham@mail.utexas.edu.

CUNO, JAMES, art museum director; b. St. Louis, Apr. 6, 1951; married; 2 children. BA in History, Willamette U., 1973; MA in History of Art, U. Oreg., 1978; AM in Fine Arts, Harvard U., 1980, PhD in Fine Arts, 1985. Asst. curator prints Fogg Art Mus., Harvard U., Cambridge, Mass., 1980-83, dir. Univ. Art Mus., 1991—; asst. prof. dept. art Vassar Coll., Poughkeepsie, N.Y., 1983-86; dir. Grunwald Ctr. for Graphic Arts, UCLA, 1986-89; dir. Hood Mus. Art, Dartmouth Coll., Hanover, N.H., 1989-91. Trustee Wadsworth Atheneum; panelist NEH, NEA; mem. pub. grant adv. com. Getty Grant Program, 1991-96; mem. vis. com. J. Paul Getty Mus. Author, editor exhbn. catalogues (with others) Foirades/Fizzles: Echo and Allusion in the Art of Jasper Johns, 1987, Politics and Polemics: French Caricature and the Revolution, 1789-1799, 1988, Scenes and Sequences: Recent Monotypes by Eric Fischl, 1990, Jonathan Borofsky: Prints and Multiples, 1982-91, 1991, The Popularization of Images: Visual Culture Under the July Monarchy, 1994; contbr. articles to profl. jours. Mem. Assn. Art Mus. Dirs. (trustee, pres.). Office: Harvard U Art Mus 32 Quincy St Cambridge MA 02138-3845

CUNTZ, MANFRED, astrophysicist, researcher, educator; b. Landau, Rheinland-Pfalz, Federal Republic of Germany, Apr. 21, 1958; arrived in U.S., 1988; s. Gerhard Hermann and Irene Emma (Messerschmitt) C.; m. Anne-Gret Vera Friedrich, Sept. 19, 1988; 1 child, Heiko Benjamin. Diplom in Physics, U. Heidelberg, Fed. Republic of Germany, 1985, PhD in Astronomy, 1988. Postdoctoral, rsch. assoc. Joint Inst. Lab. Astrophysics-U. Colo., Boulder, 1989-91; postdoc. rsch. assoc. High Altitude Obs. divsn. Nat. Ctr. Atmospheric Rsch., Boulder, 1992-94; habilitation in astronomy U. Heidelberg, Germany, 1995; sr. rsch. assoc., lectr. mech. engring. Ctr. Space Plasma, Aeronomy and Astrophysics Rsch., U. Ala., Huntsville, 1996-99, adj. assoc. prof. dept. mech. engring., 1999-2000. Vis. prof. dept. physics U. Tex., Arlington, 2000-01, asst. prof. dept. physics, 2001—; guest observer Internat. Ultraviolet Explorer, Hubble Space Telescope, ROSAT, Chandra Newton XMM. Contbr. articles to profl. jours. Grantee German Rsch. Found., NASA, NSF, Dutch Nat. Sci. Orgn. Mem.: AAAS, Astron. Soc. of the Pacific, N.Y. Acad. Scis., German Phys. Soc., German Astron. Soc., Am. Astron Soc., Internat. Astron. Union. Achievements include research in theoretical astrophysics, solar physics, extra-solar planets, astrobiology, magnetohydrodynamics, thermal bifurcation and physics of stellar atmospheres and winds. Office: Dept Physics U Tex Arlington Arlington TX 76019 E-mail: cuntz@uta.edu.

CUPINI, MARIELLEN LOUISE, school district administrator; b. Bethlehem, Pa., Dec. 30, 1952; d. John Joseph and Verna Louise (Rhoads) Mikatavage; children: Alison, Kimberly, John. BS, Nazareth Coll., Rochester, N.Y., 1974, MS, 1977; Cert. Advanced Study, Brockport U., 1993. Cert. sch. dist. adminstr.; lic. speech pathology tchr., tchr. speech and hearing handicapped, N.Y. Lang. coord. Conv. Hosp. for Child, Rochester, 1974-79; speech pathologist Rochester City Sch. Dist., 1988-90; pvt. practice speech pathology Rochester, 1979-90; dir. presch. spl. edn. program Rochester Childrens Nursery, 1990-94; founder, dir. spl. edn./nursery sch. Stepping Stones Learning Ctr., Rochester, 1994—. Speech pathology cons., Lifetime Assistance, Rochester, 1988; nursery sch. adv. bd. Fairport Montessori, Fairport, N.Y., 1982-86. Developer Innovative Inclusion Nursery Sch. Program, 1994. Founding task force mem. ECICMC, Rochester, 1992—. Mem. Preschool Providers, Genesee Valley Speech and Hearing Assn. (ethical practice chmn. 1988-92), Am. Speech, Lang. and Hearing Assn., Rochester Area Early Childhood Assn. Avocations: children, boating, reading. Home: 729 Admiralty Way Webster NY 14580

CUPPO CSAKI, LUCIANA, foreign language educator, writer; b. Trieste, Italy, May 30, 1941; came to U.S., 1965; d. Bruno Cuppo and Nerina Dimini. BA in German, U. Heidelberg, Germany, 1962; MA in German, U. Kans., 1970; PhD in Latin, Fordham U., 1995. Adj. prof. Manhattanville Coll., Purchase, N.Y., 1989-92, CUNY, 1991-95, SUNY, Westchester, 1996—, Albany, 1997-98. Author: The Vivarium Monastery of Cassiodorus After the Year 575 A.D., 1998, The Year 680 as Caput Saeculi in Cas 641, 1998, De schematibus et tropis in Italian Garb, 2002. NEH scholar Summer Seminar, Anglo-Saxon Manuscripts and Texts, 2001. E-mail: dcsakio@yahoo.com.

CURBOW, DEBORAH ELIZABETH, secondary education educator; b. Louisville, Jan. 22, 1950; d. Clarence Herman and Betty Ann (Keeling) C. BS in Elem. Edn., Ind. U., New Albany, 1972; MEd in Supervision and Adminstrn., U. South Fla., 1980. Cert. in elem. edn., mid. sch. sci., social studies and adminstrn., Fla. Tchr. Sch. Bd. Pasco County, Land O'Lakes, Fla., 1974—. Instr. Performance Learning Sys., 1983—; cons. to Dr. Don Peterson, U. South Fla., Tampa, 1988—; participant, instr. Project W.I.Z.E., Bronx (N.Y.) Zoo, 1993-94; presenter mini-conv. Pasco County Schs.; dir. Pasco County Regional Sci. Fair, 1985-87. Sunday sch. tchr. 1st Presbyn. Ch., Port Richey, Fla., 1990—, deacon, 1991—. Named Energy Educator of Yr., Fla. Assn. Women's Clubs, 1985. Mem. Fla. Assn. Sci. Tchrs., Pasco County Assn. Sci. Tchrs., Pi Lambda Theta, Kappa Delta Pi. Avocations: making porcelain dolls, collecting shells. Office: Pine View Mid Sch 5334 Parkway Blvd Land O Lakes FL 34639-3801

CURETON, CLAUDETTE HAZEL CHAPMAN, biology educator; b. Greenville, S.C., May 3, 1932; d. John H. and Beatrice (Washington) Chapman; m. Stewart Cleveland, Dec. 27, 1954; children: Ruthye, Stewart II, S. Charles, Samuel. AB, Spelman Coll., 1951; MA, Fisk U., 1966; DHum (hon.), Morris Coll., Sumter, S.C., 1996. Tchr. North Warren High Sch., Wise, N.C., 1952-60; tchr. Sterling High Sch., Greenville, 1960-66, Wade Hampton High Sch., Greenville, 1967-73; instr. Greenville Tech. Coll., 1973-95, ret., 1995. Bd. dirs. State Heritage Trust, 1978-91; commr. Basic Skills Adv. Program, Columbia, 1990—; mem. adv. bd. Am. Fed. Bank, NCNB Bank, Greenville, 1991—. Mem. Greenville Urban League, NAACP, S.C. Curriculum Congress; v.p. Woman's Bapt. E.& M. Conv. of S.C.; mem. S.C. Commn. on Higher Edn. Com. for Selection of the 1995 Gov.'s Prof. of the Yr.; mem. Gov.'s Task Force on Juvenile Crime, S.C., Gov.'s Juvenile Justice Task Force, 1997, S.C., Gov.'s Juvenile Justice Youth Coun., S.C., 1996—, Best Chance Network Task Force of Am. Cancer Soc., 1995—; bd. dirs. Sisters Saving Sisters, Roper Mountain Sci. Ctr., 2003—. Recipient Presdl. award Morris Coll., 1987, 91, Svc. award S.C. Wildlife and Marine Dept., 1986, Outstanding Jack and Jill of Am. citation, 1986, Excellence in Tchg. award Nat. Inst. for Staff and Orgnl. Devel., U. Tex., Austin, 1992-93, Educator of Yr. award Greenville chpt. Am. Cancer Soc., 1994, Outstanding Svc. award Best Chance Network/Am. Cancer Soc., 1994, Citation S.C. House of Reps., 1995; named Unsung Hero of the Cmty. for Outstanding Svc. to Humankind Greenville Tech. Coll., 1999. Mem. AAAS, AAUW, Nat. Assn. Biology Tchrs., S.C. Curriculum Congress, Nat. Coun. Negro Women, Inc., Higher Edn. S.C. Com. for Selection Prof. of Yr. 1995, Delta Sigma Theta (past v.p. Greenville chpt. alumnae). Home: 501 Mary Knob Greenville SC 29607-5242

CURFMAN, DAVID RALPH, neurosurgeon, educator, civic leader, musician; b. Bucyrus, Ohio, Jan. 2, 1942; s. Ralph Oliver and Agnes Mozelle (Schreck) C.; m. Blanche Lee Anderson, June 6, 1970. Student, Capital U., 1960-62; AB, Columbia Union Coll., 1965; MS, George Washington U., 1967, MD, 1973. Diplomate Nat. Bd. Med. Examiners. Asst. organist, choirmaster Peace Luth. Ch., Galion, Ohio, 1956-62; bus. mgr. Mansfield/Galion Ambulance Svc., Galion, Ohio, 1962-66; with news divsn. Sta. WTOP-TV, Washington, 1965; choirmaster, assoc. organist Grace Luth. Ch., Washington, 1966-73, historian, curator, 1969—; tchg. fellow in anatomy George Washington U., Washington, 1966-67, gen. surgery intern, 1973-74, resident in neurol. surgery, 1974-78, clin. instr. neurol. surgery, 2000—; resident in neuropathology Armed Forces Inst. Pathology, Washington, 1975; resident in pediatric neurol. surgery Children's Hosp. Nat. Med. Ctr., Washington, 1976; teaching fellow in anatomy Georgetown U., Washington, 1967-69, clin. instr. neurol. surgery, nuerol. surgeon, 1978—; neurosurgery faculty George Washington U., Washington, 2001—, asst. clin. prof. neurol. surgery. Chief divsn. neurol. surgery Jefferson Hosp., Alexandria, Va., 1989-93, Wash. Hosp. Ctr. Soc., 1992—, operating room com. 1998—; vice-chmn. bylaws com. Providence Hosp., 1987-95, chief of neorosurgery divsn.; panelist ann. meeting ethical issues in neurol. surgery Am. Assn. Neurol. Surgery; guest spkr. Nat. Youth Leadership Forum, 1996—. Chmn., chief author: Physician's Reference Guide for Medicolegal Matters, 1982, Nat. Capital Astronomers' Association, 1986-87. Elected mem. D.C. Rep. Com., 1988-94; bd. dirs., historian The Christmas Pageant of Peace, Inc., Washington, The Leo Sowerby Found.; pres., bd. govs. Nat. Columbus Celebration Assn. Hon. mem. Quiz Kid Show, 1953; recipient Found. award Cathedral Choral Soc., 1997. Mem.: SAR (bd., D.C. Soc. 1997—), AMA (Phys. Recognition award 1983—), D.C. Soc. (3d v.p.), Order of the Crown in Am., Assn. Mil. Surgeons U.S. (Continuing Edn. Neurosurgery award 1993—), Washington Acad. Neurosurgery (pres.-elect 2003—), Am. Coll. Legal Medicine, Congress Neurol. Surgeons (joint sect. neuro-trauma and critical care), Pan Am. Med. Soc. (mem. exec. bd. 1993—97, pres. 1997—), Med. Soc. D.C. (chmn. medicine and religion com. 1981—83, chmn. medico-legal com. 1986—88), Am. Soc. Law, Medicine and Ethics, Assn. Am. Med. Colls. (nat. student chmn. rules and regulations com. 1971—73), Nat. Gavel Soc., Soc. War 1812 (surgeon gen., Md. chpt., 1st v.p. D.C. chpt., dist. dep. pres. gen.), Pilgrim Soc. (Plymouth chpt.), Hymn Soc. Am., St. Andrew's Soc. (Washington D.C.), Mil. Order of the Crusades, Sovereign Mil. Order Temple of Jerusalem (grand chirurgeon emeritus, Order of Merit), The Baronial Order of Magna Carta, Mil. Hospitaller Order Saint Lazarus Jerusalem (knight), U.S. Capitol Hist. Soc. (founding supporting mem., trust mem.), Nat. Cathedral Assn., Cathedral Choral Soc. (repertoire chmn. 1981—82, v.p. bd. trustees 1981—83, pres. 1984—86, found. award 1977), Am. Guild Organists (dean D.C. chpt. 1974—76, publicity chmn. nat. conv. 1982, state chmn. 1984—91, nat. com. long-range devel. 1990—96), Internat. Congress Organists (Washington program chmn. 1977), Royal Sch. Ch. Music (Eng.), Order of the Crown of Charlemagne (surgeon gen.), Nat. Soc. Ams. Royal Descent (councillor), Order of Ams. of Armorial Ancestry (chaplain), Children Am. Revolution (pres. Ohio 1963—64, hon. sr. nat. v.p. 2001—, hon. Ohio pres.), Gen. Soc. Sons of the Revolution (chmn. bicentennial commemorative com. death of Gen. George Washington 1999, N.Y. and D.C. bd. 2002—), Hereditary Order Descendants of the Loyalists and Patriots of the Am. Revolution, Baronial Order of Magna Charta, Sons & Daughters of Colonial & Antebellum Bench & Bar, Samuel Victor Constant Soc., Order of Wash., Osler Soc., Galion Hist. Soc. (charter), Continental Soc. Sons Indian Wars, Ordo Sancti Constantini Magni, Colonial Order of the Acorn N.Y., Vet. Corps Artillery State N.Y., Am. Revolution Soc., Soc. of 1812, Nat. Soc. Children Am. Colonists (pres. gen. 2003—), Mil. Order Loyal Legion U.S. (Aide-de-Camp to comdr.-in-chief), Sons Am. Colonists (surgeon gen. 1997—), Soc. Colonial Wars (surgeon 1997—), Order of Indian Wars in the U.S. (historian 1999—), Am. Polit. Items Collectors Assn., Sons/Daus. of the Pilgrims (historian gen. 1999—2001, first dep. gov. gen. 2003—), Hospitaller Order of St. John (knight), Lincoln Birthday Nat. Commemorative Com (master of ceremonies 1995—99, vice chmn.), Sons of Union Vets. Civil War (chmn. historic Memorial Day observances), Order Three Crusades (1096-1192), Columbus Philatelic Soc., Crawford County Coin Club (charter mem.), George Washington U. Club, Sr. Nat. Officer's Club (hon. sr. nat. v.p. 2001—, historian 2003—), Elks (Galion Lodge No. 1191), Sigma Xi (pres. George Washington U. chpt. 1981—82), Phi Delta Epsilon (life). Home: 4201 Massachusetts Ave NW Washington DC 20016-4701 Office: 3301 New Mexico Ave NW Ste 210 Washington DC 20016-3622

CURFMAN, FLOYD EDWIN, engineering educator, retired; b. Gorin, Mo., Nov. 16, 1929; s. Charles Robert and Cleo Lucille (Sweeney) C.; m. Eleanor Elaine Fehl, Aug. 5, 1950; children: Gary Floyd, Karen Elaine. BSCE, U. Mo., 1958; BA in Math. Edn., Mt. Mary Coll., 1988. Registered profl. engr., Wis., Mo.; cert. tchr., Wis. Forest engr. U.S. Forest Svc., Rolla and Harrisburg, Mo., Ill., 1958-70, engring. dir. Milw., 1970-84, chief tech. engr. Washington, 1984-86; tchr. Wauwatosa (Wis.) High Sch., 1987-89, Our Lady of Rosary, Milw., 1989-96; retired, 1996. Author: (booklet) Forest Roads-R-9, 1973; co-author: (tng. manual) Transportation Roads, 1966. Co-leader Boy Scouts Am., Harrisburg, 1958-62; activities coord. Cmty. Action Com., Brookfield, 1970-76; bike and hiking trails com. City of Brookfield (Wis.), 1982-83; program chair Math Counts, 1982. With U.S. Army, 1952-54. Mem. ASCE (program chair, Letter Nat. award 1970), NSPE (coms. 1970-86), Nat. Coun. Tchrs. Math., Wis. Soc. Profl. Engrs. (pres. Milw. chpt. 1982-83, State Recognition award 1983). Avocations: travel, auto trips, reading. Home: 1755 N 166th St Brookfield WI 53005-5114

CURIEL, LAURA TAYLOR, special education educator; b. Cynthiana, Ky., Apr. 16, 1951; d. Harry Turner and Geneva Catherine (House) Taylor; m. Julian Eduardo Curiel, Nov. 4, 1978; children: Julia, Catherine. BA, U. Ky., 1989, MS in Speech Pathology, 1991. Cert. speech-lang. pathologist. Speech-lang. pathologist VA Med. Ctr., Lexington, Ky., 1990, Hillhaven Rehab. Ctr., Lexington, Ky., 1991-92, Fayette County Pub. Schs., Lexington, 1991—. Speech-lang. pathologist Hillhaven Rehab. Ctr., Winchester, Ky., 1993-98. Mem. Am. Speech-Lang.-Hearing Assn., Ky. Speech-Lang.-Hearing Assn. (liaison adv. bd. 1992-95). Democrat. Roman Catholic. Avocations: reading, swimming, beachcombing, travel. Office: 701 E Main St Lexington KY 40502

CURLEE, ROBERT GLEN, JR., special education educator; b. Wetumpka, Ala., July 19, 1951; s. Robert Glen and Betty Jean (Poston) C.; m. Cherie Bowick, Apr. 3, 1981; children: Emily, Amy, Christian. BEd in Elem. and Spl. Edn., Auburn U., Montgomery, Ala., 1974; MEd in Adminstrn. and Supervision, Troy State U., Montgomery, 1976. Cert. tchr., Ala. Tchr. Elmore County Headstart, Wetumpka, 1978, supr. of ctr., 1979; elem., jr. and sr. high sch. spl. edn. tchr. of homebound Elmore County Bd. Edn., Wetumpka, 1974—. Mem. Wetumpka Civitan Club (v.p. 1989-91). Democrat. Methodist. Home: PO Box 165 Elmore AL 36025-0165 Office: Elmore County Spl Edn Annex Broad St Wetumpka AL 36092

CURLER, (MARY) BERNICE (MRS. ALBERT ELMER CURLER), writer, educator; b. L.A., Dec. 4, 1915; d. Charles Ether and Josephine Babetta (Meier) Davis; m. Albert Elmer Curler, Apr. 10, 1938; children: Daniel Jay, Dawna Dee. Freelance writer short stories and articles for vairous nat. mags. including McCalls, Parents Mag., Modern Maturity, Success Unltd., Progressive Women, Christian Sci. Monitor, Small World, Ladies Circle, Chevron USA, Writer's Digest, Nat. Enquirer, Westways Mag. Instr. article writing Cosumnes River Evening Coll., Sacramento, 1971—82; staff dir. Sierra Writing Camp; condr. writing seminars. Author (hist. novels): The Visionaries, 2000, Glory Road, 2002; author: (play) Mazie's Red Garter, 1997. Recipient Achievement award, Sacramento Regional Arts Coun. Mem.: Am. Soc. Journalists and Authors, Authors Guild, Calif. Writers Club (pres. 1960—61, dir. 1960—, Jack London award 1981). Home and Office: 555 Freeman Rd Unit 173 Central Point OR 97502-2558

CURLEY, ELMER FRANK, librarian; b. Florence, Pa., Jan. 13, 1929; s. Augustus Wolfe and Bessie (Andrews) C. BA, U. Pitts., 1961; MLS, Carnegie Mellon U., Pitts., 1962; Adv. Cert., U. Pitts., 1964. Ref. libr. U. Pitts., 1962-64; head ref. dept. SUNY-Stony Brook, 1964-67; head pub. svcs. U. Nev.-Las Vegas, 1967-76, asst. dir. libr. svcs., 1976-81, ref. bibliographer, 1981-94, ret., 1994.

CURLEY, MICHAEL JOSEPH, English language educator; b. N.Y.C., Dec. 23, 1942; s. William Paul and Theresa Helen Curley; m. Sandra Jean Plann; children: Austin, Brendan. BA, Fairfield U., 1964; MA in Teaching, Harvard U., 1965; PhD, U. Chgo., 1973. Prof. English U. Puget Sound, Tacoma, 1971—, dir. honors program, 1984—. Vis. prof. U. Wash., Seattle, 1988. Author: Physiologus, 1979, Marie de France: Purgator of Saint Patrick, 1993, Geoffrey of Monmouth, 1994, Alessandro Manzoni: Two Plays, 2002. Recipient Graves award Graves Found., 1982-83; NEH fellow, 1977-78, Am. Coun. Learned Soc. fellow, 1979-80; NEH grantee, 1974, 87. Mem. Medieval Acad. Am., Celtic Soc. N.Am., Internat. Arthurian Soc., Medieval Assn. The Pacific. Office: U Puget Sound N Lawrence St Tacoma WA 98416-0001 E-mail: curley@ups.edu.

CURNAN, SUSAN P. social policy and management educator; b. Hyde Park, N.Y., Mar. 7, 1949; d. Charles Agustus and Mildred (Kron) C. BA cum laude, Stony Brook U., 1971; MS, SUNY, New Paltz, 1972; MFS, Yale U., 1978. Cert. tchr. K-12. Rsch. assoc. Yale U., New Haven, 1976-78; dir. New England Non-Profit Corp., Vt., 1978-82; dep. dir., sr. rsch. assoc. Ctr. Human Resources Brandeis U., Waltham, Mass., 1989-94, dir. Ctr. Human Resources, assoc. prof. Heller Grad. Sch. Advanced Studies in Social Welfare, 1989—, prof. social olicy and mgmt. Heller Sch., dir. Ctr. for Youth and Cmty. Co-founder, pres. ER's Kitchen Cabinet, spec. food co., 2001. Contbr. articles to profl. jours. Trustee Taconic Found., N.Y.C., 1987—93; co-founder, chmn. Inst. for Just Cmtys., 2001. Fellow Berkley Coll. Yale U., 1985, 88; Grad. fellow Yale U., 1976-78; recipient Key to City and Cert. Hon. Citizenship, New Orleans Mayor and City Council, 1991, Outstanding Young Woman in Am. award, 1982; Rsch. grantee Yale U., 1977-78. Mem. Am. Edn. and Rsch. Assn., Yale U. Sch. Forestry and Environ. Studies Alumni Assn. (class sec. 1988—), Assn. Yale Alumni (bd. govs. 1983-86). Home: 174 Boston Post Rd Sudbury MA 01776-3102 Office: Brandeis U 60 Turner St Waltham MA 02453-8923

CURNYN, KATHLEEN MARIE, elementary school educator; b. N.Y.C., July 20, 1943; d. James Aloysius and Sarah Marie (Wamsganz) C. BA, Georgian Ct. Coll., 1970; MA, Seton Hall U., 1973; MPS, Loyola U., 1987. Cert. elem. tchr., N.J., media specialist, adminstr. Tchr. 4th grade St. James Sch., Red Bank, N.J., 1964-65; tchr. 4th-8th grades St. Mary Sch., South Amboy, N.J., 1965-69; tchr. 7th grade St. John Sch., Lambertville, N.J., 1969-71; tchr. 8th grade O. L of Victories Sch., Sayreville, N.J., 1971-72; prin. 1-8 grades St. Ann Sch., Keansburg, N.J., 1972-80; tchr. 8th grade Sacred Heart Sch., South Plainfield, N.J., 1980-83; tchr. 7th grade Holy Spirit Sch., Perth Amboy, N.J., 1983-84; asst. supt. Diocese of Newark, 1984-86; regional supr. Diocese of Bklyn., 1986-90; prin. St. Matthew Sch., Edison, N.J., 1990—. Mem. ASCD, Nat. Cath. Educators. Roman Catholic.

CUROL, HELEN RUTH, librarian, English language educator; b. Grayson, La., May 30, 1944; d. Alfred John and Ethel Lea (McDaniel) Broussard; m. Kenneth Arthur Curol, June 25, 1967 (div. 1988); children: Edward, Bryan. BA, McNeese State U., 1966; postgrad., L.I. U., 1969-70; MLS, La. State U., 1987. Tchr., libr. Cameron Parish Schs., Grand Lake, La., 1966-67; media specialist Brentwood (N.Y.) Sch. Dist., 1967-69; sch. libr. Patchogue (N.Y.) H.S., 1969-70;, 1976-95; reference libr., mgr. circulation dept. McNeese State U., Lake Charles, La., 1976-96; test adminstr. Edn. Testing Svc., Princeton, N.J., 1987-95; asst. prof. McNeese U., 1989-95; owner Curol Consulting, Lake Charles, 1995—; head adult svcs. Laman Pub. Libr., North Little Rock, Ark., 1996. Rschr. Boise Cascade, DeRidder, La., 1987-88, Vidtron, Dallas, 1990-92, Nat. Archives, Washington, 1989; cons. Cmty. Housing Resource Bd., Lake Charles, 1988-93, Boyce Internat. Engrs., Houston, 1988-89, La. Pub. Broadcasting, Baton Rouge, 1989; devel. cons. Calcasieu Women's Shelter, 1988-92; reference cons. Calcasieu Parish Pub. Libr., 1990-95; presenter conf. at Tulane U., South Ctrl. Women's Assn., 1994, La. Conf. for Edn. Technology, Baton Rouge, 2000. Sr. arbitrator Better Bus. Bur., Lake Charles, 1986-95; local facilitator La. Com. for Fiscal Reform, Lake Charles, 1988; state bd. dirs. PTA, Baton Rouge, 1981-83, LWV La., Baton Rouge, 1983-85; chairperson budget panel com. United Way S.W. La., Lake Charles, 1992-94, bd. dirs., 1995-96; judge La. region IV Social Studies Fair, 1979-89; program spkr. region IV tng. conf. HUD, El Paso, 1992. Named Citizen of the Day, Sta. KLOU, 1978; grantee La. Endowment for Humanities, 1987, La. Divsn. Arts, 1989, Fair Housing Initiative Program, 1990, HUD, 1992, La. Ctr. Women and Govt. of Nicholls State U., 1993. Mem. ALA (sec. coun. 1988-90, chairperson coun. 1990-91), AAUW (chairperson intellectual freedom com. 1988-89), La. Libr. Assn. (chairperson reference group 1988-90), La. Assn. Coll. and Rsch. Librs. (chairperson 1995-96), Ark. Libr. Assn., McNeese U. Alumni Assn., S.W. La. C. of C. (mem. legis. com. 1992), Krewe du Feteurs (Mardi Gras Ct. Duchess 1992), Beta Sigma Phi (pres. Lake Charles chpt. 1983-84), Beta Phi Mu. Democrat. Lutheran. Office: La Grange Media Ctr 3420 Louisiana Ave Lake Charles LA 70607-1842 Address: 1005 Cherryhill St Lake Charles LA 70607-4911

CUROTT, DAVID RICHARD, physics educator; b. Passaic, N.J., June 3, 1937; s. Frank L. and Mathilda (Esser) C.; m. Janice F. Warren, July 31, 1982; children: Lisa-Anne, Michael Williams. BS, Stevens Tech., Hoboken, N.J., 1959; MA, Princeton U., 1962, PhD, 1965. Teaching asst. Princeton (N.J.) U., 1965-67; asst. prof. Wesleyan U., Middletown, Conn., 1967-75; assoc. prof. U. North Ala., Florence, 1975-79, prof. physics, 1979-99, planetarium dir., 1980-99, prof. emeritus, 1999—. Contbr. articles to profl. jours. Recipient NASA traineeship, 1962. Mem. Am. Assn. Variable Star Observers (pep adv. com. 1991-94), S.E. Physics Assn. Avocations: astronomy, playing recorder and oboe, genealogy.

CURRAN, DARRYL JOSEPH, photographer, educator; b. Santa Barbara, Calif., Oct. 19, 1935; s. Joseph Harold and Irma Marie (Schlagel) C.; m. Doris Jean Smith, July 12, 1968. AA, Ventura Coll., 1958; BA, UCLA, 1960, MA, 1964. Designer, installer UCLA Art Galleries, 1963-65; mem. faculty Los Angeles Harbor Coll., 1968-69, UCLA Ext., 1972-79, Sch. Art Inst. Chgo., 1975; prof. art Calif. State U., Fullerton, 1967-2001, chmn. art dept., 1989-99; curator various shows, 1971—. Bd. dirs. Los Angeles Center Photog. Studies, 1973-77, pres., 1980-83; juror Los Angeles Olympics Photog. Commns. Project, 1983 One-man shows include U. Chgo., 1975, U. R.I., 1975, Art Space, L.A., 1978, Photoworks Gallery, Richmond, Va., 1979, Alan Hancock Coll., Santa Maria, Calif., 1979, G. Ray Hawkins Gallery, L.A., 1981, Portland (Maine) Sch. Art, 1983, Grossmont Coll., San Diego, 1982, (retrospective) Chaffey Coll., Alta Loma, Calif., L. A. Ctr. for Photographic Studies, 1984, U. Calif. Ext. Ctr., San Francisco, 1986, Cuesta Coll., San Luis Obispo, Calif., 1992, Cypress Coll., 1993, Tex. Woman's U., Denton, 1997, Irvine Valley Coll., 1997, Ellen Kim Murphy Gallery, Santa Monica, 2000, William Marten Gallery, Rochester, N.Y., 2001; two-person show No. Ky. U., 1995; group exhbns. include Laguna Mus. Art, San Francisco, 1992, Friends of Photography, San Francisco, 1993, U.S. Info. Agy. Empowered Images, 1994—, USIA, Jan Abrams Gallery, L.A., 1995; group exhibns. include Mt. St. Mary's Coll., 1997, Ranch Santiago Coll., 1997; represented in permanent collections Mus. Modern Art, Royal Photog. Soc., London, Nat. Gallery Can., Ottawa, Mpls. Inst. Art, Oakland Mus., U. N.Mex., UCLA, Seagram's Collection, N.Y.C., Mus. Photog. Arts, San Diego, Phila. Mus. Art, J. Paul Getty Mus., Phila. Mus. Art, San Francisco Mus. Art. Bd. dirs. Cheviot Hills Home Owners Assn., 1973. Served with U.S. Army, 1954-56. Recipient Career Achievement award Calif. Mus. Photography, 1986; NEA Photographers fellow, 1980; Honored Educator award Soc. Photographic Edn., 1996. Mem. Soc. Photog. Edn. (dir. 1975-79, honored educator 1996). Home: 10537 Dunleer Dr Los Angeles CA 90064-4317 E-mail: localdj@mindspring.com.

CURRENCE, GLENNDA KAY, elementary education educator; b. Davenport, Iowa, Feb. 4, 1954; d. Glenn Elston and Ethel Lucille (Watts) C. BME, Augustana Coll., 1976; M in Counseling, We. Ill. U., 1995. Tchr. elem. vocal music Clinton (Iowa) Cmty. Sch. Dist., 1976-77, Davenport (Iowa) Cmty. Sch. Dist., 1977-95, elem. counselor, 1995—. Organist, pianist Faith United Meth.Ch., Davenport, 1968-77. Mem. NEA, ACA, Am. Sch. Counselors Assn., Internat. Assn. for Addictions and Offender Counselors, Iowa Music Educators Assn. Methodist. Avocations: reading, listening to music, playing piano, exercising. Home: 2032 N Ohio Ave Davenport IA 52804-2838 Office: Davenport Cmty Schs Davenport IA 52803-5025

CURRIE, CONSTANCE MERSHON, investment services professional; b. Missoula, Mont., June 22, 1950; d. Alan Clark Van Horn and Saralee (Neumann) Visscher; m. R. Hector Currie, Aug. 14, 1986 (div. 1997). BA in Art with highest hons., Mont. State U., 1977; MFA in Painting, U. Cin., 1981, MA in Arts Adminstrn., 1988; grad., Tsukuba Daigaku, Ibariki, Japan, 1977-78. Bus. mgr. Fort Peck Summer Theatre, Glasgow, Mont., 1983; asst. telemarketing mgr. Cin. Symphony Orchestra, 1984, telemarketing mgr., 1985; mem. coord. Cin. Mus. of Natural History, 1986-88; mktg. cons. Currie Consulting, Cin., 1988-98; investor info. rep. The Vanguard Group, Scottsdale, Ariz., 1998—. Lectr. fine art Raymond Walters Coll. U., Cin., 1988-96, instr., 1996-97, asst. prof., 1997-98. Exhbns. include SUNY, Binghamton, 1983, Tangeman Gallery/U. Cin., 1981, Miami U., 1981, No. Rockies Regional Exhbn./Sheridan (Wyo.) Coll., 1981, Bell Art Competition, Cin., 1981 (Purchase award. 1981), Willmington Coll., 1979, Mont. State U., 1976, 77 (Printmaking Purchase award 1976, 77), Yellowstone Ehbn., Billings, Mont., 1977 (Printmaking Purchase award 1977), others. Trustee Good Harvest Cooperative, Middletown, Conn., 1974-75, Methuen & Gertrude Currie Found., 1986—; bd. dirs. Bozeman (Mont.) Film Festival, 1982-83; vol. Cin. Chamber Orchestra, 1985-87, Cin. Mus. Natural History, 1988-90; capt. Green-Up Day, Rawson Woods Bird Preserve, 1996, 97. Mem. Beta Gamma Sigma, Tau Pi Phi, Phi Kappa Phi. Address: 21824 N 48th Pl Phoenix AZ 85054-6702

CURRIE, LEAH RAE, special education educator, retired; b. Chgo., Feb. 14, 1942; d. Raymond Carl and Esther Dorthea (Hansen) Strahl; m. William W. Currie, June 15, 1963; children: Raymond, Robert (dec.), Christopher. BS, Nat. Coll. Edn., 1979, MEd, 1989. Cert. elem., spl. edn. tchr., Ill. Learning disabilities tchr. Sch. Dist. 81, Schiller Park, Ill., 1979-80; resource tchr. Sch. Dist. 5, Fox River Grove, Ill., 1980-85; learning disabilities, behavior disorders tchr. Sch. Dist. 84, Franklin Park, Ill., 1985-2000, ret., 2000. Cons., interdistrict learning disabilities guide Leyden Area Spl. Edn. Coop., 1987. Mem. ASCD, Coun. for Exceptional Children, Ill. Divsn. for Learning Disabilities, Ill. Reading Coun., Learning Disabilities Assn. Ill. Avocation: fashion design. Home: 33632 N Christa Dr Ingleside IL 60041-9320 E-mail: leachc14@aol.com.

CURRIE, STEPHEN, educator, writer; b. Chgo., Sept. 29, 1960; s. David Park and Barbara (Flynn) C.; m. Amity Elizabeth Smith, July 3, 1983; children: Irene Elizabeth, Nicholas David. BA, Williams Coll., 1982. Primary tchr. Poughkeepsie (N.Y.) Day Sch., 1982—2001, math specialists lower sch., 2002—; Saturday enrichment tchr. various schs. and orgns., Poughkeepsie, 1988—92; freelance ednl. writer, 1992—. Pvt. tutor, Poughkeepsie, 1982—; workshop leader/presenter, 1986—; materials reviewer Nat. Coun. Tchrs. Math. Author: Music in the Civil War, 1992, Birthday a Day, 1996, We Have Marched Together, 1997, Life in a Wild West Show, 1998, Thar She Blows, 2001, numerous others. Bd. dirs., performer Hudson Valley Gilbert and Sullivan Soc., Poughkeepsie, 1983-92; youth soccer coach Town of Poughkeepsie Soccer Club, 1993-94. Mem. Nat. Assn. for Edn. of Young Children, Nat. Coun. Tchrs. Math. Avocations: singing, swimming, reading, kayaking, snowshoeing. Home: 32 S Grand Ave Poughkeepsie NY 12603-4112 Office: Poughkeepsie Day Sch 140 Boardman Rd Poughkeepsie NY 12603-4831

CURRIS, CONSTANTINE WILLIAM, university president; b. Lexington, Ky., Nov. 13, 1940; s. William C. and Mary (Kalpakis) C.; m. Roberta Jo Hern, Aug. 9, 1974. BA, U. Ky., 1962, EdD, 1967; MA, U. Ill., 1965. Vice pres., dean of faculty Midway (Ky.) Coll., 1965-68; dir. ednl. programs W.Va. Bd. Edn., Charleston, 1968-69; dean student pres. programs Marshall U., Huntington, W.Va., 1969-71; v.p., dean of faculty W.Va. Inst. Tech., Montgomery, 1971-73; pres. Murray (Ky.) State U., 1973-83, U. No. Iowa, 1983-95, Clemson U., 1995-99, Am. Assn. State Colls. and Univs., 1999—. Chmn. emeritus Am. Humanics Inc. Trustee Midway Coll., Allen Coll. Nursing; charter mem. adv. coun. Nat. Small Bus. Devel. Ctr. Recipient Algernon S. Sullivan medallion U. Ky., 1962; named outstanding young man in Ky., Jaycees, 1974, U. Ky. Alumni Hall of Fame, 2000. Mem. Phi Beta Kappa, Omicron Delta Kappa, Sigma Chi. Greek Orthodox. Office: Am Assn State Colls and Univs 5610 Wisconsin Ave Apt 307 Chevy Chase MD 20815-4429

CURRY, CATHARINE TERRILL, health care and marketing executive; b. Mobile, Ala., Sept. 27, 1950; d. Edward Chapin Jr. and Danie (Convey) Terrill; m. Wiliam Thomas Curry Jr., June 27, 1988. BS in Social Sci., Eastern Mich. U., 1974; MA in Counseling, La. State U., 1986. Mgr. Terrill Realty Co., Mobile, 1975-84; dir. community rels. ARC, Mobile, 1981-83; mktg. rep. Ochsner Found. Hosp., New Orleans, 1986-87; dir. mktg. HCA Coliseum Med. Ctrs., Macon, Ga., 1987-88; dir. coop. edn. Mercer U., Macon, 1988-90; sr. med. sales specialist Mead Johnson Labs., Bristol-Myers Squibb, Macon, 1990—; reg. sales coord. Hearthstone/Carestone Assisted Living, 2002—. Mem. NAFE, Internat. Assn. Female Execs., Ga. Coll. Placement Assn., Am. Coll. Placement Assn., Nat. Disting. Svc. Regtistry (chartered), Nat. Coop. Edn. Assn., Art Patrons League, Am. Hosp. Assn., Soc. for Healthcare Pub. Rels./Mktg. and Healthcare Strategic Planning. Republican. Avocations: oil painting, cooking, scuba diving. Home and Office: 2997 Bear Oak Ct Mobile AL 36608-8719

CURRY, DAVID, guidance staff developer; b. Bklyn., Feb. 12, 1940; s. David and Ella (Washington) C.; m. Mary Elaine Cuthrell, Nov. 17, 1962; 1 child, Anjorin Sebastian. BA in Polit. Sci./Econs., CCNY, 1972; MS in Edn., adv. cert. in guidance and counseling, Bklyn. Coll., 1990. Cert. elem. tchr., N.Y. Asst. office mgr. Elmo Roper & Assocs., N.Y.C., 1964-70; accounts investigator Citibank, N.Y.C., 1970-72; rsch. assoc. Nat. Urban League, N.Y.C., 1972-76; adminstrv. dir. Edn. Unltd., Bklyn., 1978-82; guidance counselor N.Y.C. Bd. of Edn., Bklyn., from 1982. County com. Polit. Club; area policy bd. #3 Cmty. Devel. Agy. City of N.Y.; mem. Unity Dem. Club; mem. block assn. With USAF, 1963. Impact II grantee N.Y.C. Bd. Edn., 1984, 86; N.Y. State Dept. Labor fellow, 1995; recipient Cmty. Svc. award HPD of N.Y.C., 1992, William F. Boyland Edn. award, 1996; named Father of Yr. Sisterhood of Single Black Mothers, 1984. Mem. ASCD, ACA, ASCA, Alpha Phi Alpha. Yoruba. Avocations: trombone, baritone horn, camping, writing. Home: Brooklyn, NY. Died Jan. 29, 2002.

CURRY, EMMA BEATRICE, secondary education and college educator; b. Commerce, Ga., July 7, 1927; d. John Henry and Annie Bell (Wilkins) Thomas; m. Harvey Curry, Aug. 4, 1946; children: Gloria Dawn, Harvey Nathaniel, Norbert. BA in Psychology, U. Hawaii, 1971; MEd, counseling degree, Boston U., 1973; postgrad., U. So. Calif., Heidelberg, 1981; postgrad. in fine arts, City Coll., Heidelberg, 1986; postgrad., U. Md., Woxton Coll., Eng., U. Calif., Berkeley. Cert. tchr. social studies, N.J., English, cosmetology, psychology, social studies, DOD. Substitute tchr. Waupahu (Hawaii) H.S. and Leilehua (Hawaii) H.S., 1961-67, DOD, Augsberg, Germany, 1967-69; tchr. Mannheim Am. H.S., Germany, 1971-73, 1977-99; substitute tchr. Pennsauken (N.J.) Ctrl. Elem. Sch., 2000—. Author: (poetry) Feelings: Contemporary Verse, 1999. Bd. dirs. PTA, Mannheim Am. H.S., 1985-86, multicultural chairperson, 1971-73, 77-99; choir condr., soloist Meth. Ch., Wahiwai, 1964, Augsberg, Germany, 1968-69; Sunday sch. tchr. arts and crafts ch., Dachau, Germany, 1955-59. Mem. Nick Virgilio Haiku Assn. Democrat. Methodist. Avocations: poet, artist, sculpturing, piano, guitar. Home: 2251 Merchantville Ave Pennsauken NJ 08110

CURRY, JAMES LINTON, JR., school administrator; b. Rome, Ga., May 11, 1951; m. Penelope A. Roberts; children: Chris, Beth, Brian, Nathan, Ben. BA, Berry Coll., Mt. Berry, Ga., 1973, MEd, 1974; EdS, West Ga. Coll., Carrollton, 1976. Cert. tchr., Ga. Tchr. Garden Lakes Elem. Sch., Rome, 1973-81, asst. prin., tchr., 1981-86; adminstrv. asst., tchr. Glenwood Elem. Sch., Rome, 1986-87; asst. prin. for adminstrn. Adairsville (Ga.) Elem. Sch., 1987-89, Adairsville Middle Sch., 1989-90; asst. prin. for instrn. South Ctrl. Middle Sch., Emerson, Ga., 1990-91; prin. White (Ga.) Elem. Sch., 1991—. JTPA-STEP coord. Bartow County Bd. Edn., Cartersville, Ga., summers 1988-89, summer sch. prin., 1990. Mem. Ga. Assn. Elem. Sch. Prins., Profl. Assn. Ga. Educators, Ga. Assn. Ednl. Leaders.

Methodist. Avocations: music, raising chickens. Home: 62 Harris Rd NE Rome GA 30161-9158 Office: White Elem Sch 1395 Cass White Rd NE White GA 30184-2600

CURRY, JOHN WESLEY, secondary school educator; b. Canton, Ill., Nov. 13, 1948; s. Wesley LeRoy and Clara Mae (Hysler) C.; m. Francene Elizabeth Anderson, July 12, 1970; children: Jennifer, Robert, Rachel. BS, Ill. State U., 1970; MA, Sangamon State U., 1980. Tchr. math., coach Athens (Ill.) H.S., 1970-77, tchr. math., athletic dir., 1978—95, tchr. math., coach, 1983—94. Asst. mgr. Illini Sporting Goods, Springfield, Ill., 1977-78; evening instr. Lincoln Land Community Coll. Sunday sch. tchr. Athens United Meth. Ch., 1973—, bd. dirs., 1973—, chmn. bd., 1978-81, 99-2003, lay leader, 1972-78, 81-2000, 2002—, chmn. bd. trustees, 1982-83. Mem. ASCD, NEA (life), Nat. Coun. Tchrs. Math., Ill. Coun. Tchrs. Math., Ill. Edn. Assn., Ill. Basketball Coaches Hall of Fame. Methodist. Home: 67 Prairie Trl Athens IL 62613-9016 Office: 1 Warrior Way Athens IL 62613-9795

CURRY, LINDA CAROLYN, nursing educator; b. Miami, Fla., Dec. 8, 1943; d. Eddie L. and Lois M. Cox; m. Richard Curry, May 25, 1980 (dec. May 1988); 1 child, Melanie Diane. BSN, U. Fla., 1965, MSN, 1966; PhD, U. North Tex., 1984. RN, Tex., Fla. Part-time staff nurse various hosps. San Angelo, Ft. Worth (Tex.) and Gainesville (Fla.), 1965-87; instr. St. Margaret's Sch. Nursing, Montgomery, Ala., 1967-69; asst. prof. Angelo State U., San Angelo, Tex., 1967-76; prof. Tex. Christian U., Ft. Worth, 1976—. Author: (video) Physical Assessment; Co-Author: (with others) Care of the Older Adult, 1993, Practical Guide to Health Assessment Through the Life Span (book), 2001; contbr. articles to profl. jours. Recipient Ruth Sperry Tchg. Excellence award Harris Coll. of Nursing Alumni, mortar board top prof. 1985; Tex. Christian U., 1992, 1997 Fellow Am. Soc. for Prophylaxis in Obstet. (childbirth educator Ft. Worth 1980—); mem. Am. Coll. Childbirth Educators (cert.), ANA, Assn. Women's Health, Obstetric, and Neonatal Nurses, Tex. Nurses Assn., Sigma Theta Tau (various offices 1965—), Phi Kappa Phi. Methodist. Avocations: handcrafts, reading, swimming, enjoying animals. Office: Tex Christian U Harris Sch Nursing 2800 W Bowie St Fort Worth TX 76129-1738

CURRY, LINDA JEAN, social studies educator; b. Logan, W.Va., Aug. 12, 1947; d. Jack Curry and Jean (Chafin) Hunt; children: Celeste Holley Henderson, Martin McTyeire Holley. BA, U. S.C., 1969; MA, Appalachian State U., 1983; PhD, Tex. A&M U., 1990. Cert. tchr., S.C., Tex. Instr. Tex. A&M U., College Station, 1988-90; asst. prof. social studies, supr. student tchrs. Clemson (S.C.) U., 1990—; Montessori tchr. Dallas Ind. Sch. Sys., 1993—. Editor The Clemson Kappan, 1993—; contbr. articles to profl. jours. Advisor Head Start, Anderson, S.C., 1994—; mem. adv. bd. L.L. Hotchkiss Montessori Acad., Dallas, 1997-98. Mem. Internat. Reading Assn. (Foothills chpt. membership chmn. 1991-92), Phi Delta Kappa (Clemson chpt. v.p. 1991-93, pres. 1993—, Outstanding Achievement award in higher edn. 1993). Democrat. Avocations: gardening, reading, history. Home: Lake Hartwell Anderson SC 29625 Office: Clemson Univ 405 Tillman Hl Clemson SC 29634-0001

CURRY, MARY GRACE, environmental executive; b. New Orleans, June 16, 1947; d. Clyde Lalio and Gladys Ruth (Ehret) C. BS in Biology, U. New Orleans, 1969, MS in Biology, 1971; PhD in Botany, La. State U., 1973. Cert. environ. profl. La. Environ. scientist VTN La., Inc., Metairie, 1974-79; environ. impact officer The Parish of Jefferson, Harahan, La., 1979-97, dir. solid waste and environ. impact, 1997-2000, archives mgr., 2000—. Cons. La., 1979—. Author: Gretna-A Sesquicen, 1986; editor jour. The Louisiana Environmental Professional, 1984—; contbr. articles to hist. and profl. jours. Chmn. City of Gretna (La.) Sesquicentennial, 1985-86; pres. Gretna Hist. Soc., 1986-88; founder Friends of the La. State Fire Mus., 1987; charter mem. Jefferson Hist. Soc. La.; mem. Jefferson Parish Hist. Commn.; founder, pres. La. Marine Fisheries Mus., 1998, 99. Recipient Coll. Scis. Disting. Alumni award, 1993. Mem. DAR (historian), La. Acad. Scis. (chmn. environ. scis. sect.), Daughters of 1812, Colonial Dames of XVII Cent. (chpt. pres.), Friends of German Am. Cultural (bd. dirs., v.p.), La. Environ. Profls. Assn. (founder, pres. 1979, 88, 89, 92, 93, 95—, v.p. 1990), UDC (pres. New Orleans 1984-2000, founder, pres. Crockett chpt. 2001, Jefferson Davis award 1986), German Heritage, Cultural and Geneal. Soc. La. (charter, v.p. 1987-89, pres. 1999—), U. New Orleans Alumni (bd. dirs.). Democrat. Roman Catholic. Avocations: local history, genealogy, interior design, writing. Home: 3404 Tolmas Dr Metairie LA 70002-3818 E-mail: mgcurry1@juno.com.

CURRY, ROBERT RICHARD, health facility administrator; b. Pitts. s. Richard Lee and Mary Louise (Schnuth) Curry; life ptnr. Douglas D. Jasinske, Dec. 2, 1999. BA, U. Dayton, 1985, MSEd, 1989. Asst. exec. dir. Sigma Nu Found., Lexington, Va., 1985—87; asst. dean of students U. Dayton, Ohio, 1987—89; dean of students Rider U., Lawrenceville, NJ, 1989—94; program coord. NENY AIDS Coun., Albany, NY, 1994—95; dir. edn. and tng. Upper Hudson Planned Parenthood, Albany, 1995—. Cons. Cicatelli and Assocs., N.Y.C., 1998—; faculty mem. Albany Med. Coll., 2000—; prin. investigator Ctrs. Disease Control, Atlanta, 2000—01; corp. trainer, Albany, 2000—; mem. rev. com. best practices in reproductive health care and male med. svcs. NY State Dept. Health, 2002. Contbr. articles to profl. jours. Assoc. Planned Parenthood Fedn. Am. Leadership Inst., 2000, 2002—03; co-chmn. N.Y. State AIDS Prevention Planning Group, 2002—03; founder, pres. bd. dirs. Names Project AIDS Meml. Quilt, Albany, 1997; adv. bd. Albany Med. Coll. AIDS Program, 2001; Albany Cmty. Author; ward leader Dem. Com.; bd. dirs. Lark St. Bus. Improvement Dist., Albany, 2000—. Named one of Outstanding Young Man of Am., 1987, 1989; recipient Leadership award, N.Y. State AIDS Inst., 2002, Excellence in Edn. and Tng. award, Planned Parenthood Fedn. Am., 2002, Excellence in Tng. award, Hudson Valley CC Physician's Assts. Program, 2002; grantee, Ctrs. Disease Control; CDC scholar, U. S.C., Columbia, 2001. Mem.: APHA, U. Dayton Alumni Assn. (new student recruiter 2003). Democrat. Avocations: travel, gourmet cooking, wines, music, acting. Home: 75 Willett St Apt 4-F Albany NY 12210

CURRY, SADYE BEATRYCE, gastroenterologist, educator; b. Reidsville, N.C., Oct. 17, 1941; BS cum laude, Johnson C. Smith U., 1963; MD, Howard U., 1967. Intern Duke U. Med. Ctr., Durham, N.C., 1967-68, fellow in gastroenterology, 1969-72; instr. dept. medicine Duke U., Durham, 1969-72; resident medicine VA Hosp., Washington, 1968-69; asst. prof. medicine divsn. gastroenterology Howard U. Coll. Medicine, Washington, 1972-78, assoc. prof. medicine divsn. gastroenterology, 1978—; asst. chief med. officer Howard U. Med. Svc., D.C. Gen. Hosp., Washington, 1973-74; asst. chief medicine in-charge of undergrad. med. edn. Howard U., Washington, 1974-77. Contbr. articles to profl. jours. Mem. bd. trustees Lake Land 'Or Property Owners Assn., Ladysmith, Va., 1989-90. Recipient Howard U. Coll. Medicine Student Coun. Faculty award for Teaching Excellence, 1975, Kaiser-Permanente Faculty award for excellence in teaching, Howard U. Coll. Medicine, 1978, Howard U. Coll. Med. Student/Am. Med. Women's Assn. woman of yr., 1990; named U.S. Friendship Force amb. to West Berlin, 1980. Mem. AAUW, AMA, Nat. Med. Assn., Am. Soc. Internal Medicine, Medico-Chirurgical Soc. D.C., Med. Soc. D.C., Am. Digestive Diseases Soc., Leonidas Berry Soc. for Digestive Diseases, Nat. Coun. of Negro Women, Alpha Kappa Alpha, Beta Kappa Chi, Alpha Kappa Mu. Office: Howard U Hosp 2041 Georgia Ave NW Washington DC 20060-0001

CURRY, THOMAS JOHN, academic administrator; b. Fall River, Mass., July 27, 1942; s. Raymond Francis and Olympia Marie (Conforti) C.; m. Carolyn Elizabeth Sullivan, Aug. 22, 1964; children: Kathleen Curry-Beaulieu, Kelly Curry DiGiammo, Kristin. BSEE, U. Mass.-Dartmouth, Fall River, 1964; MSEE, Worcester Poly. Inst., 1966; PhD in Elec. Engring., U. R.I., 1975. Elec. engr. Naval Underwater System Ctr., Newport, R.I., 1966-71, head sci. and tech. divsn., 1978-81, supr. elec. engring., 1971-77; sci. advisor Comdr. Sub. Force Pacific, Pearl Harbor, Hawaii, 1977-78; dir. rsch. and engring. Gould Ocean System, Inc., Cleve., 1981-83; prof. elec. engring. U. Mass.-Dartmouth, 1983-93, dean coll. engring., 1993—, provost, vice-chancellor acad. affairs, dir. advanced tech. and mfg. ctr. Pres., founder Tech. Applications, Inc., Somerset, Mass., 1983-90; bd. dirs. Southeastern Mass. Mfg. Partnership. Contbr. 44 articles to profl. jour. Treas. Citizens Scholarship Found., Somerset, 1984-86; bd. dirs. Share Found., Dartmouth, 1986-90, Rehab. Engring. Ctr., Dartmouth, 1987-90. Mem. IEEE (sr.), Am. Soc. Engring. Edn., U. Mass. Alumni Assn. (Pers. Achievement award 1992). Achievements include research in management and engineering. Home: 4 Bay Point Rd Swansea MA 02777-1402

CURRY, TONI GRIFFIN, counseling center executive, consultant; b. Langdale, Ala., June 23, 1938; d. Robert Alton and Elsie (Dodson) Griffin; m. Ronald William Curry, June 13, 1959 (div. 1972); children: Christopher, Catherine, Angela. BA, Ga. State U., 1962; MSW, U. Ga., 1981. Lic. clin. therapist; cert. addictions counselor. Tchr. DeKalb County Bd. Edn., Atlanta, 1962-63; counselor Charter Peachford Hosp., Atlanta, 1974-79; dir. aftercare, 1976-79; dir. aftercare and occupational svcs. Ridgeview Inst., Atlanta, 1979-82; owner, dir., adminstr., counselor Toni Cury and Assocs., Inc., Atlanta, 1982—. Cons., lectr. to numerous cos. and orgns.; mem. adv. bd. Peachford Hosp., Atlanta, 1982-87, Rockdale House, Conyers, Ga., 1981—, Outpatient Addictions Clinics Am., 1983-85; bd. dirs. Employee Assistance Programs Inst.; lectr. local, nat. and internat. confs. Cloud's House, Wilshire, Eng., 1986; founder Internat. Recovery Ctr., Cannes, France, 1990; founder, bd. dirs. Anchor Hosp., 1985-93; seminars on addiction in Italy and Switzerland; pres., mem. exec. bd. Ga. Employee Assistance Programs Forum, Atlanta, 1981-86; appointed to Gov.'s Advisory Coun. on Mental Health, Mental Retardation and Substance Abuse, 1984, Gov.'s Commn. Drug Awareness and Prevention, 1986; chairperson Ga. Gov.'s Driving Under Influence of Alcohol Assessment Task Force; adv. bd. Hawthorne House; presenter European Conf. Drugs and Alcohol, Edinburgh, Scotland; faculty Southeastern Conf. Alcohol and Drugs, 1996; annual presenter So. Coastal Conf., Jekyll Is., Ga., 1996—; mem. steering com. personnel programs Delta Air Lines, 1992—. Vol. My Sister's Ho. Mem. Nat. Assn. Social Workers, Ga. Addiction Counselors Assn. (dir. 1982-86), Ga. Citizens Coun. Alcoholism, Employee Assistance Programs Assn., Assn. Behavioral Therapists, Nat. Assn. Alcoholism and Drug Abuse Counselors, Mems. Guild of High Mus. Art, Kappa Alpha Theta. Home: 7245 Chattahoochee Bluff Dr Atlanta GA 30350-1071 Office: 4546 Barclay Dr Atlanta GA 30338-5802

CURRY-CARLBURG, JOANNE JEANNE, elementary education educator; b. Cleve., Oct. 11, 1947; d. James Michael and Joan Marie (Bukky) Curry; m. Stan R. Carlburg. BS, Villa Maria Coll., Erie, Pa., 1973; MEd, Edinboro U. Pa., 1975; EdD, SUNY, Buffalo, 1987. Cert. tchr., reading specialist, Pa. Tchr. Erie Diocese, 1966-76; reading specialist N.W. Tri-County Intermediate Unit 5, Edinboro, Pa., 1976—. Cons. Erie Diocese Cath. Schs., 1990—; adj. faculty Gannon U., Erie, 1991—. Author: Pseudoword Phonics Test, 1986. Active Flagship Niagara League, Erie, Erie Zool. Soc.; pres. bd. trustees Villa Maria Acad., 1999-2001. Recipient Friends of Edn. award Gannon U., 1993; finalist Elem. Sch. Tchr. of Yr. 1995, Commonwealth of Pa., Disting. Alumni award Gannon U., 1998. Mem. ASCD, AAUW, NEA, Pa. State Edn. Assn., Internat. Reading Assn. (Celebrate March 1998 Literacy award, with Erie Reading Coun.), Erie Reading Coun. (pres.-elect), Keystone Reading Assn., U. Buffalo Alumni Assn., Grad. Sch. Edn. Alumni Assn. U. Buffalo, Gannon U. Alumni Assn. Avocations: outdoor activities, golf, walking, photography, reading. Office: Northwest Tri-County Intermediate Unit 5 252 Waterford St Edinboro PA 16412-2373

CURTIS, GAYLE LYNNE, elementary school educator, coach; b. South Bend, Ind., June 4, 1955; d. Everett Philip and Patricia Anne (Landen) Strycker; m. Larry Warren Curtis, June 7, 1975; children: Matthew Philip, Andrew Michael. BA in Elem. Edn., Purdue U., 1977, MS in Edn., 1981. Cert. tchr., Ind. Tchr. LaPorte (Ind.) Community Sch. Corp., 1978—; coach 6th grade girls' volleyball La Porte (Ind.) Community Sch. Corp., 1983, coach elem. girls' basketball, 1990-91, 97—, coach elem. boys' basketball, 1992, 97—. Bd. dirs. Lincoln Sch. PTA, La Porte, 1987-88. Mem. AAUW, Purdue U. Alumni Assn., John Purdue Club, Delta Kappa Gamma. Republican. Methodist. Avocations: sewing, counted cross-stitch, boating. Home: 2441 Pepperidge Ct La Porte IN 46350-9451 Office: LaPorte Community Sch Corp 1921 A St La Porte IN 46350-6639

CURTIS, JAMES MALCOLM, language educator; b. Florence, Ala., Apr. 16, 1940; s. Malcolm C. and Earsel (Smith) C.; m. Victoria Oswald, Sept. 3, 1962 (div. June 1973); 1 child, Elizabeth Helen; m. Donna M. Elvey, Apr. 2, 1983. BA, Vanderbilt U., 1962; MA, Columbia U., 1964, PhD, 1968. Vis. asst. prof. U. Calif., Berkeley, 1966-68; asst. prof. Russian U. Mo., Columbia, 1968-72, assoc. prof., 1972-79, prof., 1979—. Author: Culture as Polyphony, 1978, Solzhenitsyn's Traditional Imagination, 1984, Rock Eras, 1987. Democrat. Buddhist. Avocation: cooking. Address: 127 N Village Ln Chadds Ford PA 19317-9328

CURTIS, JANET LYNN, elementary education educator; b. San Diego, Sept. 24, 1945; d. Kenneth E. and Jean L. (Lain) Brasier; m. Steven C. Curtis, Jan. 21, 1967; 1 child, Christopher. BS in Edn., SE Mo. State U., 1967, MEd, 1984. Nat. cert. tchr.; middle childhood generalist. Elem. tchr. Ferguson-Florissant (Mo.) Pub. Schs., 1967-68, 69-74; 3d grade tchr. Rockwood Pub. Schs., Ellisville, 1968-69; tchr., dir. 1st Presbyn. Ch. Presch., Cape Girardeau, Mo., 1975-76; elem. tchr. Cape Girardeau Pub. Schs., 1976-77, 78-83; math. aide, tchr., gifted resource coord. Norman (Okla.) Pub. Schs., 1977-78, 85-96, tchr. 3d grade, 1996—; learning disabilities tchr. Moore (Okla.) Pub. Schs., 1984-85. Gifted adv. bd. Norman Pub. Schs., 1992-96, computer adv. bd., 1990-96, staff devel. com., 1994-2002, lang. arts adv. bd., 1985-92; mem. Norman Staff Devel. Com., 1993-2002. Choir 1st Christian Ch., Norman, 1985—; chmn. Christian Women's Fellowship, Norman; bell ringer Salvation Army, Norman, 1989—; vol. ARC, Norman, 1985—. Mem. NEA, Okla. Educators Assn., Profl. Educators Norman (bldg. rep., treas., staff devel. com.), Nat. Staff Devel. Coun., Nat. Coun. Tchrs. Math., Okla. Math. Tchrs., Delta Kappa Gamma. Democrat. Avocations: reading, sewing, crafts, travel, photo albums. Office: Truman Elem Sch 600 Parkside Rd Norman OK 73072-4200 E-mail: jcurtis@norman.k12.ok.us.

CURTIS, JOYCE MAE, physical education educator; b. Cleburne, Tex., Aug. 27, 1937; d. Robert Joyce and Maudie Mae C. BS, North Tex. State U., 1959, MS in Phys. Edn., 1960; D of Phys. Edn., Ind. U., 1970. Prof. Abilene (Tex.) Christian U., 1959—; grad. asst. Ind. U., 1967-70. Treas. Tex. Assn. Intercollegiate Athletics for Women, 1971-79. Co-editor: (book) Physical Education Activities Handbook, 1971; author: (manual) Manual for Bowling Teachers at Abilene Christian University, 1982, Manual for Badminton Teachers at Abilene Christian University, 1985; author: (text) Pickle-Ball for Player and Teacher, 3d edit., 1999, Intermediate Bowling Notebook, 1993;contbr. articles to profl. jours. Named Bowler of Yr. Abilene Women's Bowling Assn., 1967, Outstanding Educator of Am., 1975; recipient Disting. Svc. award Tex. Assn. for Intercollegiate Athletics for Women, 1982, Faculty Devel. award Abilene Christian U., 1991; inducted into ACU Sports Hall of Fame, 2003. Mem. AAHPERD (life), Tex. Assn. for Health, Phys. Edn., Recreation and Dance, Delta Psi Kappa (life), Phi Lambda Theta. Mem. Ch. of Christ. Avocations: travel, golf, gardening. Office: Abilene Christian U PO Box 28084 Abilene TX 79699-0001

CURTIS, MARCIA, university dean; b. Boston, Aug. 8, 1931; d. Arthur Bicknell and Ethel Beatrice (Fraser) C. AB in Biology, Colby Coll., 1954; M in Nursing, Yale U., 1957; EdD, Boston U., 1969; HHD (hon.), Francis Marion Univ., 1990. Staff nurse Grace-New Haven Hosp., 1959; instr. Boston U. Sch. Nursing, 1959-65; staff nurse Carney Hosp., Dorchester, Mass., 1961-62, Univ. Hosp., Boston, 1965; instr., cons. Quincy City Hosp. Sch. Nursing, 1966; Human Relations Ctr. teaching fellow in ednl. founds. Boston U. Sch. Edn., 1966-67; assoc. dean Med. U. S.C. Coll. Nursing, Charleston, 1968-84, dean, prof., 1968-84, ret., 1985, dean and prof. emerita, 1987—. Organizer nursing program Winthrop Univ., Rock Hill, S.C., 1977, Francis Marion Univ., Florence, S.C., 1982; cons. Jersey City Med. Center, 1967, S.C. Nurses Assn., 1985, S.C. Regional Med. Program, 1972; ednl. cons. Morris Coll., Sumter, S.C., 1973-74; cons. Lander Coll., Greenwood, S.C., 1981-83, numerous other schs. nursing, hosps.; participant numerous workshops; mem. adv. coun. for comprehensive health planning S.C. Bd. Health; mem. Charleston Area Comprehensive Health Planning Com., Health Edn. Authority, State Task Force on Health Resources; charter mem. Statewide Master Planning Com. on Nursing Edn.; mem. adminstrv. adv. group sub com. for cancer S.C. Regional Med. Program; assoc. Boston U. Human Rels. Ctr.; apptd. by U.S. Sec. of Def. to Def. Adv. Com. on Women in the Svc., 1975-77; cons. nursing edn. programs Lander Coll., Greenwood, Francis Marion Coll., Winthrop Coll.; bd. dirs. Mason Preparatory Sch., Charleston, S.C., 1992-95. Patron Charleston Symphony Orch., Charleston Mus., Smithsonian Assos. Served to lt. Nurse Corps, USNR, 1957-59. Recipient Disting. Alumna award Colby Coll., 1993. Mem. AAUW, APHA, LWV, S.C. Nurses Assn. (bd. dirs., joint commn. on practice, coun. on edn.), NLN, Am. Assn. Colls. Nursing (charter mem., emeritus), Am. Assn. Higher Edn., Nat. Wildlife Assn., Audubon Soc., Concord Coalition, Nature Conservancy, S.C. Nature Conservancy, ACE Basin Project, Nat. Assn. Hist. Preservation, Pi Lamda Theta, Sigma Theta Tau. Home: 18 Charlestowne Ct Charleston SC 29401-1906

CURTIS, MARK ALLEN, engineering educator, author, consultant; b. Battle Creek, Mich., Aug. 2, 1951; s. Lawrence Arthur and Marlene Fay (Furlott) C.; m. Margaret Elizabeth Hustwick, Aug. 14, 1971; children: Aaron, Leah. AAS, Kellogg C.C., 1971; BS, Western Mich. U., 1977, MA, 1982, EdD, 1992. Cert. vocat. tchr., Mich. Tool designer Eaton Corp., Marshall, Mich., 1971-75, prodn. supr., 1977-78, process engr., 1975-77, 78-80, design supr. Galesburg, Mich., 1980-81; asst. prof. Ferris State U., Big Rapids, Mich., 1981-85, assoc. prof., 1985-92, prof., 1992-96, interim dean Coll. Tech., 1996-98; v.p. engring. Millennium Plastics Technologies LLC, El Paso, Tex., 1998-99; dean Coll. Tech. and Applied Scis., asst. provost No. Mich. U., Marquette, 1999—. Author: Tool Design for Manufacturing, 1986, Process Planning, 1988, Handbook of Dimensional Measurement, 3d edit., 1994, Dimensional Management, 2002. Recipient Disting. Faculty award Mich. Assn. Governing Bd. of State Univs., 1993. Mem.: Soc. Mfg. Engrs. (sr.). Episcopalian. Avocations: stained glass, golf, fishing. Home: 1540 W Ridge #4 Marquette MI 49855 Office: No Mich U 101A Jacobetti Ctr 1401 Presque Isle Marquette MI 49855 E-mail: mcurtis@nmu.edu.

CURTIS, MARTHA LOUISE, parochial school social studies educator, administrator; b. Selma, N.C., July 23, 1944; d. Willie Jackson and Dorothy Mae (Reid) C. BS, N.C. A&T State U., 1966; postgrad., Howard U., 1970; MA, U. D.C., 1993. Tchr. Johnston County Bd.Edn., Smithfield, N.C., 1966-69, 71-72, substitute tchr., 1971; grad. counselor Howard U., Washington, 1969-70; tchr. Brook-Wein Bus. Inst., Ltd., Washington, 1974-75; substitute tchr. D.C. Pub. Schs., Washington, 1975-79, tchr., 1979-80, Archdiocese of Washington, 1982—. Mem. search com. for provost-v.p. acad. affairs U. D.C., 1992. Campaign worker Nat. Hdqrs. Dem. party, Washington, 1976, 80; panelist candidates forum D.C. Bd. Edn., 1992; active Selma's Housing Authority, Selma's Human Rels. Coun. Mem. NEA, Nat. Cath. Edn. Assn., Nat. Assn. Devel. Edn., Amles Profl. Women Club, Nat. Fedn. Women's Clubs, Grad. Student Govt. Assn. (mem. at-large 1992), Ea. Star. Roman Catholic. Avocations: reading, dancing, decorating. Home: 3811 Suitland Rd SE Washington DC 20020-1253

CURTIS, MARY LOUISE, artist, educator; b. Houston, Mar. 20, 1928; d. Frank Tracy and Louise (White) Burtle; m. Robert Allen Curtis, June 26, 1946; 1 child, William Allen. BLS magna cum laude, St. Edward's U., 1979; postgrad., Austin (Tex.) Community Coll., 1979-80. Adminstrv. asst. State Bd. Ins., Austin, 1967-80; freelance tchr. drawing, watercolor Austin, 1980—; owner, artist Curtis Art, Austin, 1980—. Spkr. various charities and art groups, Tex., 1980—; tchr. watercolor and drawing classes on radio, Austin, 1989-90; comml. artist, fabric designer clothing; tchr. adult art edn. Lady Bird Johnson Wildflower Ctr., 1995—; tchr. watercolor and pastels Largo Vista (Tex.) Arts Assn., 2001—; tchr. pub. and pvt. classes in pastels and watermedia, Wildlife Refuge, 2002-03; freelance art materials factory rep., tchr., demonstrator. Exhibited in gallery and one-person shows, internat. art sales, pvt. and corp. collections, 1981—; rsch., design cover, illustrator for hist. novels; illustrator Grasses and Plants; represented in permanant collection at City of Austin History Ctr., Camp Mabry Armed Forces Mil. History Mus., Austin, Tex., Unity Ch. of the Hills, Austin, U.S. Dept. Interior Fish and Wildlife Svc., Balcones Canyonlands Nat. Wildlife Ctr.; bird and landscape artist Nat. Wildlife Refuge; contbr. articles to profl. jours. Bd. dirs. Hancock Recreation Ctr., Austin, 1982-83, Austin Artist Harvest, Austin C. of C., 1984-8. Native Plant Soc. Tex., 1984-85; artist State Tex. Sesquicentennial, Austin, 1984-86, Sonora Hist. Mus. (contbr. 2 original water colors); vol. artist Nat. Wildflower Rsch. Ctr., Austin, 1985—, Keep Austin Beautiful artist, 1994—; sec. Balcones Canyonlands Nat. Wildlife Refuge, 2001-02, bd. dirs., 2003, vol. artist March Fed. Refuges Centennial Celebration; vol. artist, songbird festival Lago Vista C. of C., 2003; vol. facilitator mktg. and activities Brookdale-The Island on Lake Travis Retirement Resort, Largo Vista. Mem. Nat. Mus. Women in the Arts (charter), Capital Arts Soc. (pres. 1990-91), Waterloo Watercolor Group (chmn. art show 1982), San Antonio Watercolor Group, Lake Travis Art League (Bluebonnet Bash com. 1995), Heritage Soc. Austin (hist. archtl. illustrations 1996), Am. History Club Austin (artist-officer). Avocations: public speaking, brochure illustration, posters for charity, historical research, flower gardening. Home: Apt 1323 3404 American Dr Lago Vista TX 78645-6546

CURTIS, PAULA ANNETTE, elementary and secondary education educator; b. Natrona Heights, Pa., Apr. 16, 1953; d. Stephen John and Josephine Kathleen (Killian) C. BS In Edn., Geneva Coll., 1974; postgrad., U. Vt., 1975, Pa. State U., New Kensington, 1978. Cert. religious edn. tchr., Pitts. Diocese. Tchr. Transfiguration Sch., Russellton, Pa., 1979—, dir. religious edn., 1995-98; tchr. continuing edn. C.C. of Allegheny County, Pitts., 1992—, Pa. State U., New Kensington, 1988—; tchr. O'Mara Driving Sch., Lower Burrell, Pa., 1976—, Lenape Votech., 1990—; CCD tchr. Transfiguration Sch., Russellton, 1995-97, head tchr., head fine arts dept., 1995-97. Chmn. vision and values in Pitts. Diocese, Transfiguration Sch., 1980-97; CCD tchr. St. Clement Parish, Tarentum, Pa., 1986-92, dir. religious edn., 1987-92; dir. religious edn. St. Joseph Parish, Natrona, Pa., 1992-93; product tester Nat. Family Opinion Poll, 1987—; model Van Enterprises, Cranberry, Pa., 1989-92; tchr. driver edn. Plum (Pa.) Sr. H.S., 1996-98; Act 48 presenter for Penn Hills Sch. Dist. and Pitts. Diocesan Schs., 2002—; freelance model, Fashion Bug, 1998—. Vol. Help Beautify the Cmty. with Art, Russellton. Mem. Nat. Cath. Educators Assn., Nat. English Tchrs. Assn. Democrat. Roman Catholic. Avocations: craft designs, needle work, collecting reptiles, collecting and breeding tropical birds, breeding shih-tzus. Home: 211 W 9th Ave Tarentum PA 15084-1241 Office: Transfiguration Sch CCD Office 100 Mckrell Rd Russellton PA 15076-1100

CURTIS, ROBERT KERN, lawyer, physics educator; b. N.Y.C., June 11, 1940; s. Sargent Jackson and Phyllis (Kern) C.; m. Beverley Meadows, Dec. 26, 1971; 1 child, Phyllis. AB in Physics, Fordham U., 1964, MS in Edn., 1970; Lic. in Philosophy, Woodstock Coll., 1965; JD, Seton Hall U., 1985. Tchr. Bklyn. Prep. Sch., 1965-67; dir. Jesuit Sem. and Mission Bur., N.Y.C., 1967; tchr. Xavier High Sch., N.Y.C., 1967-69, Hackensack (N.J.) High Sch., 1969—; sole practice Hackensack, 1985—. Tchr. law Hackensack Evening Sch., 1980, law for tchrs. Hackensack Pub. Schs., 1986. Mem. Am. Phys. Soc., Assn. Trial Lawyers Am., ACLU, N.Y. Acad. Scis., Am. Assn. Physics Tchrs., Math. Assn. Am., Hackensack Edn. Assn. (pres. 1979-81, 97—). Home and Office: 287 Hamilton Pl Hackensack NJ 07601-3614 E-mail: rkc@rcurtis.com.

CURTIS, TIMOTHY JACK, science educator; b. Chillicothe, Ohio, July 21, 1952; s. Bertsel Eugene and Gladys Maxine (Cuckler) C.; m. Jan Elise Shanks, Apr. 9, 1971; 1 child, Kerri Denise. BS in Edn., Ohio U., 1980; MEd, U. Cin., 1998. Cert. tchr., Ohio. Instr. physics, chemistry Sheffield Lake (Ohio) Schs., 1980-81; tchr. sci. Union-Scioto Local Schs., Chillicothe, 1981-86; instr. physics, chemistry, environment, biology Huntington Local Schs., Chillicothe, 1986—. Tchr., leader physics Ohio's Project Discovery, Oxford, 1993-96; adj. faculty Shawnee State U. Natural Scis., 2000—. With U.S. Army, 1972-75. Recipient Charles Allen Smart award Chillicothe/Ross C. of C., 1991, 92; named Chillicothe Gazette Tchr. Feature, 2000; Martha Holden Jennings scholar, 2000-01. Mem. ASCD, Am. Chem. Soc., Am. Assn. Physics Tchrs., Huntington Local Edn. Assn. (rep., pres. 1986—). Democrat. Home: 1833 Rozelle Creek Rd Chillicothe OH 45601-8942 Office: Huntington Local Schs 188 Huntsman Rd Chillicothe OH 45601-9378 E-mail: tcurtis@eurekanet.com.

CURTIS, VERNA POLK, reading educator; b. Jackson, Miss., Mar. 20, 1940; d. William Grady Polk and Mary Ann Gray; m. Edward L. Curtis, Apr. 12, 1968; 1 child, Vera. BS cum laude, Jackson State U., 1962; MEd, Boston U., 1968; EdS, Jackson State U., 1987; postgrad., Cornell U.; EdD, Jackson State U., 1991. Reading specialist/reading facilitator Jackson Pub. Schs., tchr.; reading instr. Jackson State U. Instr., adj. prof. edn., advisor for second chance careers program Tougaloo Coll. Recipient fellowship. Mem. ASCD, Jackson Area Reading, IRA, MSCD, Miss. Reading Assn. Home: 114 Waylawn Ct Jackson MS 39206-2305

CURTISS, HOWARD CROSBY, JR., mechanical engineer, educator; b. Chgo., Mar. 17, 1930; s. Howard Crosby and Susan (Stephenson) C.; m. Betty Ruth Cloke, Mar. 24, 1956 (dec. June 1985); children: Lisa Crosby, Jonathan Cloke; m. Elizabeth M. Fenton, May 22, 1988. B in Aero.Engring., Rensselaer Poly. Inst., 1952; PhD, Princeton U., 1965. Mem. rsch. staff dept. aerospace and mech. scis. Princeton U., 1956-65, mem. faculty, 1965—, prof., 1970-98; mem. Army. Sci. Bd., 1978-82; prof. emeritus Princeton U., 1998—; mem. Army Sci. Adv. Panel, 1972-77. Mem. Naval Rsch. Adv. Com., 1978-80; hon. prof. Nanjing Aero. Inst., Nanjing, China, 1985—. Author: (with others) A Modern Course in Aeroelasticity, 1978; Editor: (with others) Jour. of Am. Helicopter Soc, 1972-76. Served with USN, 1952-54. Mem. Am. Helicopter Soc. (dir. 1978-79), AIAA, Sigma Xi, Tau Beta Pi. Clubs: Metedeconk River Yacht, Princeton of N.Y. Home: 24 Chestnut St Princeton NJ 08542-3806 Office: Princeton Univ Dept Mech and Aerospace Engring Princeton NJ 08544-0001

CURTISS, ROY, III, biology educator; b. May 27, 1934; m. Josephine Clark, Dec. 28, 1976; children: Brian, Wayne, Roy IV, Lynn, Gregory Clark, Eric Garth, Megan Kimberly. BS in Agr., Cornell U., 1956; PhD in Microbiology, U. Chgo., 1962. Instr., research asst. Cornell U., 1955-56; jr. tech. specialist Brookhaven Nat. Lab., 1956-58; fellow microbiology U. Chgo., 1958-60, USPHS fellow, 1960-62; biologist Oak Ridge Nat. Lab., 1963-72; lectr. microbiology U. Tenn., 1965-72, lectr. Grad. Sch. Biomed. Scis., 1967-69; prof. U. Tenn. (Grad. Sch. Biomed. Scis.), 1969-72, assoc. dir., 1970-71, interim dir., 1971-72; Charles H. McCauley prof. microbiology U. Ala., Birmingham, 1972-83; sr. scientist Inst. Dental Rsch., 1972-83, Comprehensive Cancer Ctr., 1972-83; dir. molecular cell biology grad. program, 1973-82; dir., sr. scientist Cystic Fibrosis Rsch. Ctr., 1981-83; prof. cellular and molecular biology Sch. Dental Medicine Washington U., St. Louis, 1983-91; George William and Irene Koechig Freiberg prof. biology Wash. U., St. Louis, 1984—, chmn. dept. biology, 1983-93, dir. Ctr. Plant Sci. and Biotech., 1991-94. Mem. Ctr. for Infectious Disease, Wash. U., St. Louis; vis. prof. Instituto Venezolana de Investigaciones Científicas, 1969, U. P.R., 1972, U. Católica de Chile, 1973, U. Okla., 1982; recombinant DNA molecule program adv. com. NIH, 1974-77, genetic basis disease rev. com., 1979-83, chmn., 1981-83, vaccine study panel, 2001—; genetic biology com. NSF, 1975-78. Editor: Jour. Bacteriology, 1970-76, Infection and Immunity, 1985-92, Escherichia coli and Salmonella: Cellular and Molecular Biology, 1993-96, exec. editor-in-chief, 2000—. Active Oak Ridge City Coun., 1969-72, Cystic Fibrosis Found. (rsch. devel. program rev. com. 1984-89), Conf. Rsch. Workers on Animal Diseases, Heiser Found. Scientific Adv. Bd., 1996—; bd. dirs. Am. Type Culture Collection, 1989-99, presdl. adv., 2003—; bd. dirs. Whitfield Sch., 1997—, exec. com., 2002—; founder, dir. and sci. adv. MEGAN Health, Inc., 1992-2000, v.p. rsch., 1998-99; mem. Mo. Seed Capital Investment Bd., 2000—. Named Mo. Inventor of Yr., 1997. Fellow: AAAS, Acad. Sci. St. Louis, Am. Acad. Microbiology; mem.: NAS, Internat. Soc. Vaccines, World Health Orgn. (steering com. immunology of TB 1982—85), Coun. Advancement Sci. Writing (dir. 1976—82, v.p. 1978—82), N.Y. Acad. Scis., Am. Soc. Microbiology (parliamentarian 1970—75, dir. 1977—80, editl. bd. ASM News 1987—99, dir. 1989—94, 1999—), Soc. Gen. Microbiology, Internat. Soc. Mucosal Immunology, Am. Assn. Avian Pathologists, Genetics Soc. Am. (chmn. genetics stock ctrs. com. 1987—89), Gateway Strikers Soccer Club (pres. 1995—2001, chmn. bd. dirs. 2001—, founder), Sigma Xi. Home: 6065 Lindell Blvd Saint Louis MO 63112-1009 Office: Washington U Dept Biology Saint Louis MO 63130

CURTLER, HUGH MERCER, JR., philosophy educator; b. Charlottesville, Va., Dec. 31, 1937; s. Hugh Mercer and Nancy Dangerfield (Elsroad) C.; m. Linda Edith Lockwood, June 15, 1962; children: Hugh Mercer III, Rudolph Hirsch. BA, St. John's Coll., 1959; MA, Northwestern U., 1962, PhD, 1964. Instr., asst. prof. U. R.I., Kingston, 1964-66; asst. prof. Midwestern Coll., Denison, Iowa, 1966-68; from asst. prof. to prof. S.W. State U., Marshall, Minn., 1968—. Author: A Theory of Art, 1981, Vivas as Critic, 1982, What is Art?, 1984, Ethical Argument, 1993, Rediscovering Values, 1997, Recalling Education, 2001. Md. State scholar, State of Md., 1955-59; Northwestern U. fellow, Evanston, Ill., 1961-64, Younger Humanist fellow, NEH, 1971-72. Avocations: sports, music, reading. Home: PO Box 102 Cottonwood MN 56229-0102

CURTNER-SMITH, MATTHEW DAVID, sport pedagogy educator; b. Norwich, Eng., Feb. 22, 1961; came to U.S., 1987; s. Peter David and Josephine Marina (Hurley) Smith; m. Mary Elizabeth Curtner, Aug. 13, 1994; children: Lauren, Emma. BEd with Honors, U. Exeter, Eng., 1983; MS, Colo. State U., 1988; EdD, U. No. Colo., 1991. Tchr. Ladymead Sch., Taunton, Somerset, Eng., 1983-87; teaching and rsch. asst. Colo. State U., Ft. Collins, 1987-88, U. No. Colo., Greeley, 1988-91; asst. prof. sport pedagogy U. Ala., Tuscaloosa, 1991-97, assoc. prof., 1997—. Co-author: Progressive Soccer Coaching, 2003; contbr. articles to profl. jours.; mem. editl. bd. Phys. Educator, 1994-97, Jour. Sport Pedagogy, 1995-99, assoc. editor, 1999-2003. Mem. AAHPERD, Phys. Edn. Assn. of Gt. Britain and No. Ireland. Avocations: playing amateur cricket, road racing. Home: 3317 Paddlecreek Ln Northport AL 35473-1965 Office: U Ala Dept Kinesiology PO Box 870312 Tuscaloosa AL 35487-0154 E-mail: msmith@bamaed.ua.edu.

CUSHING, STEVEN, linguist, educator, writer, researcher, consultant; b. Brookline, Mass., June 25, 1948; s. Alfred Edward and Evelyn Cushing. SB, MIT, 1970; MA, UCLA, 1972, PhD, 1976. Rsch. asst. MIT, 1967-70, UCLA, 1973-74; instr. U. Mass., Boston, 1974-75, Roxbury C.C., Boston, 1975-77; rsch. staff Higher Order Software Inc., Cambridge, Mass., 1976-82; rsch. assoc. Rockefeller U., N.Y.C., 1979; from master lectr. to assoc. prof. Boston U., 1986-94; rsch. fellow NASA-Ames Rsch. Ctr., Mountain View, Calif., 1987-88, Stanford U., Palo Alto, Calif., 1987-88, NASA-Langley Rsch. Ctr., Hampton, Va., 1989; asst. prof. St. Anselm Coll., Manchester, N.H., 1983-85, Stonehill Coll., North Easton, Mass., 1985-89; adj. prof. Union Inst. Grad. Sch., Cin., 1994—; lectr. Boston U., 2002—, Northeastern U., Boston, 2003—; instr. Mass. Sch. Law, 2002—. Mem. bd. editl. commentators The Behavioral and Brain Scis., 1978—; chmn. software design Internat. Conf. Sys. Scis., Honolulu, 1978; mem. 1st fgn. del. USSR Acad. of Scis., 1989; session chmn. session on internat. comm. Internat. Pragmatics Conf., Kobe, Japan, 1993; invited spkr. Internat. Conf. on Maritime Edn. and Tng., Rijeka, Croatia, 1999. Author: Quantifier Meanings: A Study in the Dimensions of Semantic Competence, 1982, Fatal Words: Communication Clashes and Aircraft Crashes, 1994, Japanese edit., 2001; assoc. editor Language, 1998-2000; contbr. articles to profl. jours. and mags. Mem. nat. exec. coun. Nat. Ethical Youth Orgn., 1965-66; fiddler Strathspey and Reel Soc. N.H. Recipient New Eng. Regional award Future Scientists of Am., 1965, 1st pl. award U.S. Nat. Scottish Fiddle Composition Competition, 1996; NSF grantee, 1965, 70-71, NIMH grantee, 1970-71, NDEA grantee, 1970-73; Woodrow Wilson Found. fellow, 1970-71, NASA Summer Faculty fellow, 1987-89; rsch. affiliate MIT, 1978-79, Boston U., 1986-88. Mem. Linguistic Soc. Am., Nat. Ctr. for Sci. Edn., Internat. Pragmatics Assn. Home: 20 Parks Dr Sherborn MA 01770 E-mail: stevencushing@alum.mit.edu.

CUSTER, SHARON LYNNETTE, secondary school educator; b. Kansas City, Mo., July 20, 1942; d. William Henry and Gladys Mary Yontz; m. Ronald Eugene Custer; children: Lori Woodfine, Julie Conner, Melanie, Michelle. BSBA, Lincoln U., 1965. Rsch. analyst Divsn. Employment Security, Jefferson City, Mo., 1966—76; daycare provider Tipton, Mo., 1976—79; tchr. Princeton (Mo.) Sch. Dist., 1981—83, Ruskin H.S., Kansas City, Mo., 1983—2002; owner Sha-Ron's Homemade Pizza, Tipton, Mo., 1978—80; SAFE coord. Ruskin H.S., Kansas City, Mo., 1997—, conflict mediator adv., 1994—, chair bus. dept., 1997—. Mem.: Mo. Vocat. Assn., Assn. Career and Tech. Edn., Am. Fedn. Tchrs., Ruskin High PTSA, Gtr. Kansas City Bus. Educators, Young Dems., Tiger Club of Kansas City, Ruskin H.S. Booster Club, Raymore-Peculiar Booster Club. Roman Catholic. Avocations: football, basketball, softball, sprint car racing, reading. Home: 1244 Granada Dr Raymore MO 64083 Office: Ruskin High Sch 7000 E 111th St Kansas City MO 64134 Personal E-mail: scuster42@aol.com. Business E-Mail: sharonc@hickmanmills.org.

CUSTIS, DIANE CAMILLE, special education educator; b. Bluefield, W.Va., Sept. 27, 1948; d. Irving H. and Mary Alice (Perdue) C. BFA, Moore Coll. Art, 1970; MEd, Temple U., 1978. Cert. tchr., Pa. Tchr. spl. edn. Sch. Dist. Phila., 1979—. Mem. Penguin Pl., Phila., 1990. Mem. Delta Sigma Theta. Home: 2 Jackson Dr Tobyhanna PA 18466-3933

CUTHBERTSON, GILBERT MORRIS, political science educator; b. Warrensburg, Mo., Nov. 20, 1937; s. Gilbert and Marion Darlington (Morris) C. BA, U. Kans., 1959; PhD, Harvard U., 1963. Asst. prof. Rice U., Houston, 1963-68, assoc. prof., 1968-77, prof., 1977—. Resident assoc. Will Rice Coll., Houston, 1964—. Author: (book) Political Myth and Epic, 1975, (monographs) Political Power, 1968, Myth, Power, Value, 1982; co-author: Teacher Immortal, 1984. Mem. curator's bd. Mus. of Printing History. Recipient George R. Brown lifetime award for excellence in teaching, 1993; Summerfield scholar U. Kans., 1955-59; Woodrow Wilson fellow Harvard U., 1959-63; Wilson C. Morris fellow. Mem. Am. Polit. Sci. Assn., Scottish Heritage Found. (bd. dirs. Great Scot award), River Oaks Rotary (bd. dirs., Paul Harris fellow), Knife and Fork Club, Phi Beta Kappa (past pres. chpt.), Pi Sigma Alpha, Sigma Tau Gamma, Delta Phi Alpha. Democrat. Presbyterian. Avocation: bridge. Office: Rice U Dept Polit Sci Houston TX 77251-1892 E-mail: poli@rice.edu.

CUTIÉ, DAVID ALAN, school principal; b. Chgo., Mar. 2, 1946; s. David and Mary (Rivera) C.; m. Betty Perez, Aug. 19, 1978; 1 child, Nina. BS in Edn., Fordham U., 1967; MA, Columbia U., 1968; postgrad., Pace U., 1973-74. Cert. tchr., sch. adminstr., N.Y. Tchr. Jr. High Sch. 99, N.Y.C., 1968-72, asst. prin., 1972-76; prin. Pub. Sch. 108, N.Y.C., 1976-84, Community Elem. Sch. 114, Bronx, N.Y., 1986—; pvt. practive, 1984-85; dir. bilingual edn. Community Sch. Dist. 9, Bronx, 1985-86. Cons. Tomorrow's Schs. Today, Rockland, N.Y., 1990—. Mem. ASCD, Am. Assn. Sch. Adminstrs., Am. Assn. Elem. Sch. Prins. Democrat. Roman Catholic. Avocation: t'ai chi. Office: Community Elem Sch 114 1155 Cromwell Ave Bronx NY 10452-8702

CUTLER, EVERETTE WAYNE, history educator; b. Beaumont, Tex., Nov. 29, 1938; s. Homer Everette and Mary Abbie (Osborne) C.; m. Leta Harriet Rush; 1 child, Lori Catherine. BA, Lamar U., 1959; BD, So. Meth. U., 1964; MA, U. Tex., 1967, PhD, 1971. Rsch. assoc. U. Tex., Austin, 1965-67, U. Ky., Lexington, 1970-75; assoc. prof. history Vanderbilt U., Nashville, 1975-87; rsch. prof. history U. Tenn., Knoxville, 1987—. Dir. Polk Project, Vanderbilt U., Nashville, 1975-87, Polk Project, U. Tenn., 1987—. Asst. editor Southwestern Hist. Quar., 1965-67; asst. editor: Papers of Henry Clay, vols. 4 and 5, 1970-75; editor: Correspondence of James K. Polk, vols. 5-10, 1975—, North for Union, 1986. Pres. Nashville Symphony Chorus, 1982-83; vestry St. George's Episc. Ch., Nashville, 1984-87; dir. Tenn. Pres. Trust, 1991—; commodore Concord Yacht Club, 2000-02. Grantee NEH, 1984, 88-96, 2002-03, Nat. Hist. Publs. and Records Commn., 1975—, Tenn. Hist. Commn., 1975—. Mem. Am. Hist. Assn., Orgn. Am. Historians, So. Hist. Assn., Assn. for Documentary Editing, Phi Kappa Phi, Alpha Tau Omega. Democrat. Episcopalian. Avocations: choral music, sailing, fiction writing. Home: 7901 High Heath Knoxville TN 37919-4410 Office: U Tenn Hoskins Libr 216 Knoxville TN 37996-0001 E-mail: wcutler@utk.edu.

CUTLER, MARY JANE VENGER, nursing administrator, educator; b. New Kensington, Pa., Dec. 24, 1917; d. Benjamin H. and Pearl (Yanofsky) Venger; m. Milton Cutler, July 29, 1967 (dec. 1971). Grad. in nursing, Presbyn. Univ. Hosp., 1959; EdD, Columbia U., 1976. Dir. Sch. Nursing Mt. Sinai Hosp., N.Y.C., 1960-67; dir. nursing svcs., dir. sch. nursing Michael Reese Hosp. Med. Ctr., Chgo., Louisville Gen. Hosp., Albert Einstein Med. Ctr., Phila., Huntington Hosp. Mem. rsch. day com. Isabel Stewart Tchrs. Coll., Columbia U., N.Y.C., 1992-98, vol. devel. dept., 1995—; guest spkr. for staff edn., 1995; faculty Tchrs. Coll., Columbia U., Hunter Coll., N.Y.C.; mem. tchrs. coll. coun. Tchrs. Coll., Columbia U., 1997—. Contbr. numerous articles to profl. jours. Recipient Cert. of achievement for vol. svc. Mt. Sinai Med. Ctr., 1994, Outstanding Grad. award Presbyn. Univ. Hosp. Nurses Alumnae Assn., 1999; named to Hall of Fame Nursing Edn. Celebrity Century of Influence, 1989-99. Avocations: cooking, reading, opera, studying italian. Home: 500 E 77th St Apt 1711 New York NY 10162-0017

CUTLIP, RANDALL BROWER, retired psychologist, university president emeritus; b. Clarksburg, W.Va., Oct. 1, 1916; s. M.N. and Mildred (Brower) C.; m. Virginia White, Apr. 21, 1951; children: Raymond Bennett, Catherine Baumgarten. AB, Bethany Coll., 1940; cert. indsl. pers. mgmt., So. Meth. U., 1944; MA, East Tex. U., 1949; EdD, U. Houston, 1953; LLD, Bethany Coll., 1965, Columbia Coll., 1980; LHD, Drury Coll., 1975; ScD, S.W. Bapt. U., 1978; LittD, William Woods U., 1981. Tchr. adminstr. Tex. pub. sch., 1947-50; dir. tchr. placement U. Houston, 1950-51, supr. counselling, 1951-53; dean students Atlantic Christian Coll., Wilson, NC, 1953-56, dean, 1956-58; dean personnel, dir. grad. divsn. Chapman U., Orange, Calif., 1958-60; pres. William Woods Coll., Fulton, Mo., 1960-81, pres. emeritus, 1981—; trustee William Woods U., Fulton, Mo., 1981-85, 92—. Chmn. bd. dirs. Mo. Colls. Fund, 1973-75; chmn. Mid-Mo. Assn. Coll., 1972-76; bd. dir. Marina del Sol, bd. pres., 1985-90, 92-95. Mem. visitors' bd. Mo. Mil. Acad., 1966-70, chmn., 1968-72; trustee Schreiner Coll., Kerrville, Tex., 1983-92, Amy Shelton McNutt Charitable Trust, 1983—. Permanent Endowment Fund, 1987-96, Scholarship Found. and Res. Fund of Christian Ch., 1992-96, Christian Found., 1990—; bd. dir. Univ. of the Americas, 1984-96, exec. v.p., 1985-96; bd. dirs. Tex. State Aquarium, 1994, exec. com., 1994—, pres. 1998; elder emeritus Christian Ch., bd. dir., exec. com. Recipient McCubbin award, 1968, Delta Beta Xi award, 1959 Mem. Am. Pers. and Guidance Assn., Alpha Sigma Phi, Phi Delta Kappa, Kappa Delta Pi, Alpha Chi. Address: 1400 Ocean Dr Corpus Christi TX 78404-2109

CUTNAW, MARY-FRANCES, emeritus communications educator, writer, editor, publisher; b. Dickinson, N.D., June 15, 1931; d. Delbert A. and Edith (Calhoun-Pritchard) C. BS, U. Wis., 1953, MS, 1957, postgrad., to 1968. Life tchg. license in speech, English and French, Wis. Vol. tchr. Vocat. Sch. for World War II Displaced Persons, Stevens Point, Wis., 1951-52; speech tchr. Pulaski H.S., Milw., 1953-55; tchg. asst. dept. speech U. Wis., Madison, 1956-57, spl. asst. Sch. Edn., summer 1957; instr. speech U. Wis.-Stout, Menomonie, 1957-58, dean of women, 1958-59, asst. prof. speech, 1959-64, assoc. prof. speech, 1964-74, prof. emeritus, 1974—. Comm. and pers. cons., St. Paul, 1974—; writer, editor, pub. New Legal Press, 1995—. Author: How to Settle a Living Trust, 1996, 4th edit., 2003. Organizer, past advisor Young Dems., Menomonie, 1959—; founder Edith and Kent Cutnaw Scholarship, U. Wis., Stevens Point, 1960—; bd. dirs. Blaisdell Place, Mpls., 1980-85. Hon. scholar U. Wis., Madison, 1959-60, 67-68. Mem. ACLU, NOW, Internat. Platform Assn., Wis. Acad. Arts and Scis., Wis. Women's Network, Progressive Roundtable (Mpls.), Calhoun Beach Club (Mpls.), Amnesty Internat., World Jewish Congress (charter), U. Club St. Paul, Greenpeace, Dunn County Humane Soc., Sierra Club, Soc. for Prevention of Cruelty to Animals, Humane Soc. U.S., Gamma Phi Beta, Phi Beta, Sigma Tau Delta, Pi Lambda Theta. Roman Catholic. Avocations: ecology, civil rights, animal rights, consumer protection, health and wellness. Office: New Legal Press PO Box 282 Menomonie WI 54751-0282 E-mail: cutnawm@uwstout.edu.

CUTRONE, DEE T. retired elementary education educator; b. Islip, N.Y., Jan. 7, 1942; d. Joseph August and Victoria Harriet (Scepaniak) Boesel; m. Nick J. Cutrone, July 11, 1996; children: Kevin McAllister, Brian J. McAllister, Victoria R. McAllister. BS in Elem. Edn. and Spl. Edn., Marywood Coll., Scranton, Pa., 1963; MA, L.I.U., 1975. Cert. elem. tchr., N.Y., lic. real estate. Tchr. Our Lady of Good Counsel Parochial Sch., Inwood, N.Y., 1963-64, Elmont (N.Y.) Sch. Dist., 1964, Middle County Sch. Dist., Centereach, N.Y., 1968-97, ret., 1997. Union rep. MCTA, Centereach, 1969-70. Recipient Jenkins award N.Y. Congress of Parents and Tchrs., 1997. Mem. Audubon Soc., Mus. Nat. History, Nat. Geographic Soc., NCTM, Internat. Platform Assn., N.Y. State United Tchrs. Avocations: traveling, playing piano, reading, photography, bird watching. Home: PO Box 370757 Las Vegas NV 89137-0757

CUTSHALL, REX RALPH, operations manager, educator, administrator; b. Washington, Ind., June 3, 1962; s. Ralph L. and Virginia M. (O'Dell) C.; m. Michelle A. Driver, May 16, 1992. AS in Bus., Vincennes (Ind.) U., 1982; BS in Bus., Ind. State U., 1984; MBA, U. Evansville (Ind.), 1988; PhD, Kennedy-Western U., 1997. Cert. consumer arbitrator, cert. purchasing mgr. Purchasing agt. Aristokraft, Inc., Jasper, Ind., 1984-86; sr. buyer Johnson Controls, Inc., Vincennes, 1986-87; asst. prof. bus. Vincennes U., 1987-92, chmn. dept. mgmt. and acctg., 1992—2001; lectr. Ind. Univ., 2001—. Author: Business Statistics: Microcomputer Experiences Using Minitab, 1989. Mem. Am. Soc. for Quality Control, Decision Scis. Inst., Inst. for Supply Mgmt., Phi Delta Kappa. Office: Ind Univ Kelley Sch of Bus Vincennes IN 47591

CUTSHALL-HAYES, DIANE MARION, elementary education educator; b. Pitts., Jan. 15, 1954; d. William Edward and Irma Delores (Marion) Snowden; m. John Steven Baran, Jan. 11, 1975 (div. 1982); 1 child, Allison Rae; m. Dean F. Cutshall, Dec. 17, 1989. BA, Eureka Coll., 1975; BS, Ind. U., Ft. Wayne, 1986. First grade tchr. Hoover Elem. Sch., Schaumburg, Ill., 1976-79, Indian Meadows Elem. Sch., Ft. Wayne, Ind., 1979-80, 82-86, Perry Hill Elem. Sch., Ft. Wayne, 1981-82; second grade tchr. Indian Meadows Elem. Sch., Ft. Wayne, 1986—. Tchr. rep. State Ill. Rsch. Adv. Coun., 1991; active ISTEP Blue Ribbon Commn., Ill., 1989, State Ill. Lang. Arts Adv. Commn., 1988, Project REAP Adv. Bd., 1988. Spl. events chair Greater Ft. Wayne (Ind.) Crime Stoppers, 1992-95; active YMCA Camp Potawotami, Ft. Wayne, 1993—, Eureka Coll. Alumni Assn., 1992—, pres., 1995—. Christa McAuliffe fellow State of Ind., 1987; recipient Excellence in Edn. award Inst. Copy Corp., 1988, Outstanding Young Alumna award Eureka Coll., 1990, Armstrong Tchr. Educator award, 1998; named Ind. State Elem. Tchr. of Yr., 1993. Mem. Nat. Coun. Tchrs. Math., Internat. Reading Assn., Tchrs. Applying Whole Langs. Lutheran. Avocations: inline skating, racquetball, reading, walking. Home: 5809 Eagle Creek Dr Fort Wayne IN 46814-3207 Office: Indian Meadows Elem Sch 4810 Homestead Rd Fort Wayne IN 46814-5461

CUTTER, JEFFREY S. secondary education educator, music educator; b. Royal Oak, Mich., July 20, 1956; s. George E. and Joy G. (Dolby) C. MusB with distinction, Wayne State U., 1978, MEd, M in Ednl. Leadership/Administrn., 1994. Cert. tchr., Mich. Performing arts facilitator Warren (Mich.) Consol. Cmty. Edn., 1980—; curriculum cons. Warren Consol. Schs., 2000—. Dir. entertainment The Detroit Lions, Inc. Chmn. Warren Cultural Commn., Warren-Ctr.-Line Thanksgiving Parade Com., Inc. Mem. Am. Sch. Band Dirs. Assn. (chmn. Mich. chpt., nat. treas.), Mich. Sch. Band and Orch. Assn., Optimist (pres., treas. Warren chpt.). Home: 32774 McConnell Ct Warren MI 48092-3111 Office: Frost Curriculum Ctr 14301 Parkside Warren MI 48088 E-mail: cutter@attglobal.net.

CUTTING, EDITH ELSIE, retired secondary education educator, writer; b. Lewis, NY, Mar. 31, 1918; d. Leon Oakley and Amy Gertrude (White) C. BS in LS signum laudis, N.Y. State Coll. Tchrs., 1938; MA, Cornell U., 1946. Cert. English tchr., libr. English tchr., libr. Ellenburg (N.Y) Ctrl. Sch., 1938-41; libr. Larson Jr. Coll., New Haven, 1941-43; English tchr., libr. DeRuyter (N.Y.) Ctrl. Sch., 1943-47; libr. Dryden (N.Y.) Ctrl. Sch., 1947-49; English tchr. Johnson City (N.Y.) Ctrl. Sch., 1949-75. Author: Lore of an Adirondack County, 1944, Whistling Girls and Jumping Sheep, 1951, A Quilt for Bermuda, 1978, Deborah of Nazareth, 1991, Elizabeth of Capernaum, 1991, Three-Minute Bible Stories, 1994, Celebrate Creation, 2000. Mem. N.Y. State Retired Tchrs. Assn., N.Y. Folklore Soc., Delta Kappa Gamma (Alice Pierce award 1967). Methodist. Avocations: reading, travel.

CUTTNER, JANET, hematologist, educator; b. N.Y.C. d. William Robert and Ida Edith C. BA, NYU, 1953; MD, Med. Coll. of Pa., 1957. Diplomate Am. Bd. Internal Medicine, Am. Bd. Hematology. Intern, resident King's County Hosp., Bklyn., 1957-61; hematology fellow Mt. Sinai Med. Ctr., N.Y.C., 1961-63, rsch. assoc. hematology, 1963-65, asst. prof. medicine, 1965-72, assoc. prof. medicine, 1972-86, prof. medicine, 1986—. Recipient Jacobi Medallion Alumni Mt. Sinai Med. Ctr., 1999. Fellow N.Y. Acad. Scis.; mem. Am. Soc. Hematology, Am. Soc. Clin. Oncology, Am. Assn. for Cancer Rsch. Office: 1735 York Ave Ste P2 New York NY 10128

CUZZETTO, CHARLES EDWARD, accountant, financial analyst, educator; b. Tacoma, Wash., Nov. 1, 1954; s. Edward Ralph and Bernice Almira (Schmidt) C.; m. Susan Lynne Race, June 15, 1991; 1 child, Shandey Race Cuzzetto. AA, Tacoma Community Coll., 1975; BA in Acctg., U. Wash.,

1977; MBA, City U., Bellevue, Wash., 1982. CPA, Wash.; cert. internal auditor; cert. mgmt. acct.; cert. fraud examiner; cert. govtl. fin. mgr. Auditor Chevron Corp., San Francisco, 1977-79, Union Oil Corp., Seattle, 1980-83; owner, operator Cuzzetto Enterprises Restaurant, Tacoma, 1981-83; auditor Alaska Airlines, Seattle, 1983-85; dir. auditing Tacoma Pub. Schs., 1985-99; mgmt./fiscal analyst Pierce County Coun., Tacoma, 1991; dir. human resources Peninsula Sch. Dist., 1999—. Instr. bus. and acctg. City U., 1985—; adj. faculty U. Puget Sound, 1995—. Author: Internal Auditing in School Districts, 1993; contbr. articles to profl. jours. Hon. mem. Seattle Ind. Comedy Co-Op, 1983—; chmn. supervisory com. Ednl. Employees Credit Union, 1987-93; vice chmn. bd. dirs. Rainier Pacific Credit Union, 1996—. Mem. Inst. Internal Auditors (Internat. Gold medal 1986), Christopher Columbus Soc. (treas. 1983-92). Avocations: genealogy, wine making, boating. Home: 2614 88th Street Ct NW Gig Harbor WA 98332

CWEKLINSKY, JUDITH ANN, elementary education educator; b. Derby, Conn., Apr. 2, 1944; d. Alexander Joseph and Florence Josephine (Stanis) Nikituk; m. Victor Joseph Cweklinsky, Jr., Dec. 1, 1963; children: Donna, Karen, Christine. BA in Liberal Arts/Fgn. Lang., So. Conn. State U., 1966, MS in Elem. Edn., 1972. 3d grade tchr. Anna Lo Presti Sch., Seymour, Conn., 1972-82, 5th grade tchr., 1982—2003; tchr. 6th grade Seymour Mid. Sch., 2003—. Mem. Seymour Libr. Bd., 1977-79; religious edn. tchr. St. Augustine's Ch., Seymour, 1977-80; housing dir. Little League Tournament, George J. Hummel Little League, Seymour, 1977, 83. Named Seymour Tchr. of Yr., 1989. Mem. Seymour Edn. Assn. (sch. rep. 1975-76), Conn. Edn. Assn., Conn. Geog. Alliance. Avocations: quilting, crafts. Home: 625 S Main St Seymour CT 06483-3229

CWERENZ-MAXIME, VIRGINIA MARGARET, primary and secondary education educator; b. Chgo., Aug. 30, 1937; d. John B. and Bessie (Mayworm) Cwerenz; m. Daniel S. Maxime, June 19, 1988; stepchildren: Lisa, Brian, Mark. BS, Alverno Coll., 1968; MS, No. Ill. U., 1974. Cert. tchr., Ill., Nev. Tchr. grades 1st thru 6th St. Joseph Catholic Sch., Richmond, Ill., 1959-66; tchr. grades 6th thru 8th St. Matthew Sch., Glendale Heights, Ill., 1966-69, St. Teresa Sch., Kankakee, Ill., 1969-70; tchr. art Edison Jr. High Sch., Wheaton, Ill., 1971-78, Wheaton Crtl. High Sch., 1979-83, Edison Jr. High Sch., Wheaton, 1980-83, Edison Mid. sch., Wheaton, Ill., 1983-94; chair dept. fine and applied art Edison Mid. Sch., Wheaton, Ill., 1981-92. Adult educator Wheaton Warrenville Dist. 200, 1973-78, 91-94; art tchr. various elem. schs., 1993-94; co-author art program; art tchr. Gwendolyn Woolley and Cox Elem., Las Vegas, 1994—, G. Woolley & Cox Elem., 1994-96, G. Woolley & L. Creig, 1996-97, G. Woolley, 1997-98, Edith Gareheim, 1998—; exhibitor Educators as Artists of Southern Nevada, 1997, 98; A Plus tchr. Las Vegas Channel 13, 1995; grant participant Getty Found. Discipline Base Art Edn., Cin., 1992. One-woman show includes Hawthorn Bank, Wheaton, 1984; exhibited in group shows at No. Ill. U., DeKalb, 1970-71, various places, Wheaton, 1973-94; tile mural designer, installer Ganechime Elem. Sch., 1999; multicultural mural designer, dir., 1994-95. Mem. art gallery coun. Coll. DuPage, Glen Ellyn, Ill., 1975-76; fund raiser 10M-Fund, Jerry's Kids, ERA Realtors, Wheaton, 1979-83; mem. Las Vegas Art Mus., 1994—; judge various art shows, DuPage. Recipient blue and gold ribbons Ill. State Town and Country, 1970; study grants to Eng., France, Holland, Belgium, Greece and Austria. Mem. NEA, Ill. Edn. Assn., Nat. Art Edn. Assn., Ill. Art Edn. Assn. (v.p. student chpt. 1970-71), Wheaton Warrenville Edn. Assn., DuPage Art League, Clark County Classroom Tchrs. Assn., Nev. State Edn. Assn. and Southern Nevada Art educators. Roman Catholic. Avocations: water colors, choir. Home: 10532 Riva Grande Ct Las Vegas NV 89135-2454

CWIKLA, RICH I. secondary education educator; Secondary tchr. West Fargo (N.D.) High Sch. Recipient Tchr. Excellence for N.D. award Internat. Tech. Edn. Assn., 1992. Office: West Fargo High Sch 801 9th St E West Fargo ND 58078-3100

CYGANOWSKI, CAROL KLIMICK, educator, writer; b. Chgo., Apr. 12, 1949; d. John Nick Sr. and Olga (Kushta) Klimick; m. Daniel Robert Cyganowski, June 20, 1970; 1 child, Claudia Jane. BA, Knox Coll., 1969; MA, U. Chgo., 1970, PhD, 1980. Instr. Roosevelt U., Chgo., 1975-79, vis. asst. prof., 1979; lectr. DePaul U., Chgo., 1981-84, instr., 1984-86, asst. prof., 1986-90, assoc. prof., 1990—, dir. women's studies program, 1990-95, dir. Am. Studies program, 1996—2002. Adj. assoc. prof. George Williams Coll., Downers Grove, Ill., 1983-84; cons. editor Women's Studies Ency., Westport, Conn., 1986-89. Author: Magazine Editors, 1988; asst. editor: Handbook of American Women's History, 1985-89; contbr. numerous articles to profl. jours. Ford Found. fellow U. Chgo., 1969-73, Woodrow Wilson Found. fellow, 1969; DePaul U. grantee, 1986-87, 88, 91, 93-94, 2002. Mem. Midwest MLA (co-chair women's caucus Midwest chpt. 1989-91, exec. com. 1993-96), Nat. Women's Studies Assn., Nat. Mus. of Women in the Arts (founding mem.), Women's Caucus for Modern Langs. (treas. 1991-93), Chgo. Area Women's Studies Assn. (sec. 1991-93, exec. com.). Office: DePaul U 802 W Belden Ave Chicago IL 60614-3214

CYMET, DAVID, secondary education educator; b. Mexico City, Mar. 30, 1931; came to U.S., 1986; s. Israel and Teme (Lerer) C.; m. Elisa Dickter, Oct. 27, 1963; children: Sara Rachel, Ely, Arie, Teme. Grad., Nat. Poly. Inst., Mex. City, 1948-55; M in City Planning, MIT, 1983; PhD in Urban Affairs and Pub. Policy, U. Del., 1991. Prof. planning and architecture Nat. Poly. Inst., 1953-58, dean grad. sch., 1968-70; prof. planning and architecture Nat. U. Mex., Mex. City, 1968-86; tchr. bilingual math. Martin Luther King H.S. of Art and Design, NYC, 1992—. Head planning Bay of Banderas Trusteeship, Mexico City, 1973-76; vice dir. Ministry of Human Settlements, Mexico City, 1977-86; mem. gov. bd. Inst. Geography, Nat. U. Mex., 1979-82. Author: Urban Planning: Its Methodology, 1961, A Systems Approach in Architectures, 1974, From Ejido to Metropoli, Another Path, 1992, Journal of Genocide Rsch.: Study-Polish State Antisemitism and the Holocaust. Cons. city planning Sepanal, Inst. Nat. Vivienda, Mexico City, 1963-86. Recipient Hon. award Soc. Architects, Mex., 1987; Spurs fellow, 1981. Home: 1601 E 21st St Brooklyn NY 11210-5049 Office: Martin Luther King H S of Art and Design 1075 2d Ave New York NY 10022

CYR, KATHLEEN KIRLEY, special education educator; b. Cin., Jan. 5, 1950; d. Owen Francis and Florence Jane (Nees) Kirley; divorced; 1 child, Brian Richard. BS in Spl. Edn. summa cum laude, U. Cin., 1972, MEd in Spl. Edn., 1980. Cert. tchr. and supr., Ohio. Tchr. South Bend (Ind.) Community Sch. Corp., 1972-74, Hamilton County Bd. Mental Retardation and Devel. Disabilities, Cin., 1978—. Speaker in field, 1989-91. Vol. parent's group water polo and swim team Princeton High Sch., Cin., 1991-92. Avocations: antiques, reading. Office: Breyer Sch 2675 Civic Center Dr Cincinnati OH 45231-1398

CZAJKOWSKI, EVA ANNA, aerospace engineer, educator; b. New Britain, Conn., Sept. 4, 1961; Student, Yale U., 1978; BS in Aero. Engring. cum laude, M in Aero. Engring., Rensselaer Poly. Inst., 1983; SM in Aeronautics and Astronautics, MIT, 1985; PhD in Aerospace Engring., Va. Poly. Inst. and State U., 1988. Registered profl engr, NY. Student trainee U.S. Govt., Washington, 1981-82; intern N.Y. State Assembly, Albany, 1983; teaching asst. Rensselaer Poly. Inst., Troy, N.Y., 1983, rsch. asst. U.S. Army Rsch. Office Ctr. Excellence, 1982-83; engring. analyst Pratt & Whitney Aircraft, West Palm Beach, Fla., 1984; rsch. asst. Gas Turbine and Plasma Dynamics Lab., Cambridge, 1984-85; rsch. asst., tchg. asst. dept. aerospace & ocean engring. Va. Poly. Inst. and State U., Blacksburg, 1985-88, aerospace engr., 1988-91, sr. aerospace engr., 1991-94, prin. aerospace engr., 1994-2001, aerospace engring. and tech. mgr., 2001—. Participant U.S. dels. to nine European nations, 1991—2003. Author: (book) Russian Aeronautical Test Facilities, 1994; contbr. scientific papers confs, articles profl jours and ency. Assoc mem Nat Air and Space Mus, Am Mus Natural History; vol. New Britain Gen Hosp, 1977—79. Recipient Medal Hon. Sci. Award, Bausch & Lomb, 1978, Joseph B. Platt Award, 1997, Int. Sci. Medal, 2001, Internat. Woman of Yr., 1991—92, 1996—97, Scientist of Yr., 2001; fellow Amelia Earhart, Zonta Int., 1983—85, Prat Presdl. Eng. Program, 1985—88; scholar, Unico Nat., 1979—80, Am. Helicopter Soc. Vertical Flight Found., 1983. Mem.: NAFE, AIAA, London Diplomatic Acad, NY Acad Scis, Confederation Chivalry (dame, named Dame), Nat Space Soc, World Found Successful Women, Int Platform Asn, Planetary Soc, Polish Rotorcraft Asn, Am Helicopter Soc, Am Astronaut Soc, World Order Sci.-Edn.-Culture (dame, named Dame), Gamma Beta Phi, Phi Kappa Phi, Tau Beta Pi, Sigma Gamma Tau, Sigma Xi. Avocations: art, horseback riding, piano, flying private plane, sailing. Home: 170 Carlton St New Britain CT 06053-3106

CZEKAI, LYNNETTE MARIE, special education educator; b. Midland, Mich., Sept. 27, 1956; d. Donald Andrew and Helen (Katsarelas) Zondlak; m. Richard Dale Czekai, July 7, 1984. BS in Edn., Cen. Mich. U., 1978; MA in Spl. Edn., Mich. State U., 1984, MA in Counseling, 1991. Spl. edn. tchr. Owosso (Mich.) Pub. Schs., 1978-86, elem. tchr., 1986-87; spl. edn. tchr. Carman-Ainsworth Community Schs., Flint, Mich., 1987—, mem. sch. improvement bd., instnl. program com., chmn. strategic planning for staff devel., facilitator sch. improvement instnl. devel., chmn. instnl. program com. Mem. ASCD, ACA, Coun. for Exceptional Children, Carman-Ainsworth Edn. Assn. (exec. com., bd. dirs.), Total Quality Leadership. Office: Carman-Ainsworth Comm Schs 1409 W Maple Ave Flint MI 48507-5613

CZERNIK, JOANNE, elementary and secondary education educator; b. Phila., Apr. 12, 1948; d. Chester Joseph and Bertha (Los). BS, East Stroudsburg U., 1970; MEd, U. Del., 1974; PhD in Psychology of Reading, Temple U., 1989. Middle sch. humanities tchr. Capital Sch. Dist., Dover, Del., 1970-77; reading instr. and supr. Temple U. Reading Clinic Lab. Sch., Phila., 1977-88; reading specialist Delmar (Del.) Sch. Dist., 1988—. Pvt. tutor, Jenkintown, Pa., 1977-88; cons. adult literacy Del. Tech. and C.C., Georgetown, 1992; presenter workshops in field. Author, editor jour. articles in field. Mem. ASCD, Diamond State Reading Assn., Internat. Reading Assn. (chair clinic visits), Coun. for Exceptional Children, Phila. Coun. Internat. Reading Assn. (pres. 1984-89, 94—, Svc. award 1988), Tri Sussex County Reading Coun. (officer 1988—), Diamond State Reading Assn. (mem. bd. 1988—, officer 1995-97). Avocations: reading, writing, research, music. Office: Delmar Sch Dist 200 N 8th St Delmar DE 19940-1374

CZERWIEC, IRENE THERESA, gifted education educator; b. Holyoke, Mass., Dec. 1, 1948; d. Stanley John and Pauline Martha (Zerek) Matuszek; m. Stanley Joseph Czerwiec, Jan. 24, 1970; children: Keith John, Daniel Paul. BS, U. Mass., 1969, MEd, 1987, EdD, 1992. Cert. secondary math. tchr., Mass. Math., physics tchr. Holyoke Cath. High Sch., 1969-71; substitute tchr. Chicopee (Mass.) Pub. Schs., 1979-85; gifted tchr. Bellamy Mid. Sch., Chicopee, 1985-90, math., gifted tchr., 1990-92, tchr. computer, gifted, 1992—. Coach Future Problem Solving Program, Chicopee, 1985—; evaluator State of Mass., 1986—, cons., 1988—; presenter World Future Soc. Conf., Cambridge, 1994, Mass. Future Problem Solving Conf., Harvard, 1994, Worcester, 1996, NSTA conv., Boston, 1992, 2d Ann. Conf. on Gifted and Talented Edn., Worcester, Mass., 1996, New Eng. Future Problem Solving Fall Tng. Conf., Sturbridge, Mass., 1998-99; presenter New Eng. League of Middle Schs.-Unified Arts Conf., Sturbridge, Mass., 1997; participant current students, future scientists, and engrs. workshop, Smith Coll., 1993; bd. dirs. Mass. Future Problem Solving Program. Co-author. Coord. looking forward program Chicopee Centennial, 1990. Recipient Merit award Chicopee Coun. Parents and Tchrs., 1990, cert. of recognition for excellence in coaching a team Internat. Future Problem Solving Conf., Ann Arbor, Mich., 1987, 88, Ednl. Leaders in Math., 1987, 88, Cert. of Merit Mass. Bar Assn., 1988, 89; SpaceMet fellow NSF, 1990-91. Mem. NEA, AAUW, ASCD, World Future Soc., Coun. Exceptional Children, Mass. Tchrs. Assn., Nat. Space Soc., Hampden County Tchrs. Assn., Chicopee Edn. Assn. Roman Catholic. Avocations: reading, gardening. Home: 4 Plainville Cir South Hadley MA 01075-2664 Office: Bellamy Mid Sch 314 Pendleton Ave Chicopee MA 01020-2135

CZIN, FELICIA TEDESCHI, Italian language and literature educator, small business owner; b. Vallata, Avellino, Italy, Jan. 20, 1950; came to U.S., 1958; d. Pasquale Aurelio and Maria (Branca) Tedeschi; m. Peter Czin, Oct. 19, 1972; children: Jonathan, Michael. BA, Douglass Coll., Rutgers U., 1972; MA, NYU, 1978, ABD, 1981, postgrad. Prodr. RAI Corp. Italian TV, N.Y.C., 1973-84; tchg. asst. dept. Italian NYU, 1977-79, adj. instr. dept. English, 1979-81; asst. prof. Vassar Coll., Poughkeepsie, N.Y., 1981-84; co-owner Czin Opticians, Teaneck, N.J., 1984—. Coord. Symposium on Italian Poetry, N.Y.C., 1978; adj. prof. SUNY at the Fashion Inst. Tech., N.Y.C., 2000—. Editor Out of London Press, N.Y.C., 1977-82, dir. pub. rels., 1977-82; editor jour. Yale Italian Studies, 1979-82; translator for jours. Avocations: hiking, swimming, knitting, cooking, sewing. Home and Office: 489 Cedar Ln Teaneck NJ 07666-1710

CZNARTY, DONNA MAE, secondary education educator; b. Bridgeport, Conn., Aug. 17, 1950; d. Richard W. and Dorothy Mae (Kosturko) Oefinger; m. Wiliam C. Cole, Jr., July 11, 1970; 1 child, Michael William Cole; m. Thomas Robert Cznarty, Apr. 29, 1983. BS in Edn., So. Conn. State U., 1973, MS in Edn., 1977. English and reading tchr. Shelton Bd. Edn., Conn., 1973-82; English tchr. Millbrook Bd. Edn., N.Y., 1985-86; sec., bd. dirs. Hopewell Precision, Inc., Hopewell Junction, N.Y., 1986—, CEO, 1999—, 1999. Bd. dirs. Dutchess Arts Coun. Mem. NAFE. Republican. Avocations: interior design, antiques and collectibles, woodworking, boating. Home: Field Haven Stanfordville NY 12581 Office: Hopewell Precision Inc Ryan Rd Hopewell Junction NY 12533

DADMARZ, KEWMARS EBRAHIM, physician, educator; b. Tehran, Iran, Mar. 13, 1928; s. Ebrahim and Nosrat (Hooshyar) D.; m. Lili Azmoudeh; children: Mitra, Ali. MD, U. Tehran, 1955. Diplomate Am. Bd. Surgery, Am. Bd. Disability Analysts. Intern Nashville Gen. Hosp., 1955—56, resident in surgery, 1956—57; resident in gen. surgery Meharry Med. Coll., Nashville, 1957—62; resident in cancer surgery Meml. Ctr. Cancer and Allied Diseases, N.Y.C., 1960-61; resident in thoracic and cardiovascular surgery U. Alta., Edmonton, Canada, 1962-64, fellow in surg. pathology, 1964-65; staff surgeon Wilmington (Del.) VA Med. Ctr.; ret.; assoc. prof. surgery, former chief dept. thoracic surgery U. Tehran; instr. surgery Thomas Jefferson U. Fellow ACS; mem. Assn. Iranian Surgeons, Matthew Walker Surg. Soc. Office: 300 Benham Ct Newark DE 19711-6009 E-mail: kewdadmarz@hotmail.com., kewmars@comcast.net.

DADURIAN, MEDINA DIANA, pediatric dentist, educator; b. Landstuhl, Germany, Apr. 12, 1964; came to U.S., 1964; d. John Gulbenc Jr. and Alice Nartouhi (Vosgeritchian) D.; m. Gregory Sarkis Kinoian, July 3, 1993; children: Melissa Marie, Natalie Anoush. BS, Allegheny Coll., Meadville, Pa., 1986; DMD, U. Medicine and Dentistry N.J., Newark, 1991. Resident in hosp. gen. practice dentistry Hackensack (N.J.) Med. Ctr., 1991-92; tng. in pediatric dentistry Columbia U. Sch. Dental and Oral Surgery, N.Y.C., 1994-96; assoc. dentist pvt. practices, 1992-93, Assocs. for Dental Care, Hackensack, 1993-95; assoc. dental specialist Denville (N.J.) Dental Assocs., 1997—99; owner, pediatric dentist in pvt. practice, Rochelle Park, N.J., 1996—, Fair Lawn, N.J., 1999—; pvt. practice Fair Lawn, N.J., 1999—. Assoc. clin. prof. Hackensack U. Med. Ctr., 1993—; dental adminstr. Hackensack Bd. Edn., 1993—95; dental cons. Hovnanian Sch., New Milford, NJ, 2000; pediatric dental cons. Howard Karaghensian Med. Benevolent Social Orgn. Children's Dental Clinics of Am., 2000—, Howard Karaghusian Commemorative Found., 2001—. Author in field. Dental dir. Bergen County Head Start, Englewood, N.J., 1993-95. Cerebral Palsy fellow United Cerebral Palsy Found., 1995-96; Gulbenkian Found. grantee, 1983-86. Fellow Acad. Gen. Dentistry; mem. ADA, Am. Acad. Pediatric Dentistry, Am. Armenian Dental Soc. Mem. Armenian Apostolic Ch. Avocations: reading, cooking, horseback riding, martial arts, needlework. Home: 377 Elliot Pl Paramus NJ 07652-4647 Office: 18-00 Fair Lawn Ave Fair Lawn NJ 07410-2330 also: 315 Rochelle Ave Rochelle Park NJ 07662-3916 E-mail: mdadurian@aol.com.

DADYBURJOR, DADY B. chemical engineering educator, researcher; b. Bombay, Mar. 16, 1949; arrived in US, 1970; s. Burjor S. and Soona P. (Khambatta) D.; m. Lou E. Crago, Sept. 1, 1973. BTech., Indian Inst. Tech., Bombay, 1970; MSChemE, U. Del., 1972, PhD, 1976. Asst. prof. chem. engring. Rensselaer Polytech. Inst., Troy, N.Y., 1977-83, assoc. prof. chem. engring., 1983, W.Va. U., Morgantown, 1983-87, interim assoc. dean for acad. affairs and rsch., 1991-92, prof. chem. engring., 1987—, chair chem. engring., 1999—. Cons. Schenectady Chems., 1978, Exxon Rsch. and Engring. Co., Florham Park, N.Y., 1987, Union Carbide Corp., South Charleston, W.Va., 1988, Catalytica, 1992, UN Devel. Program, 1992; examiner N.Y. State Civil Svc., Albany, 1980; H&M Stern lectr. Technion, Israel Inst. Tech., 1988; vis. prof. EPFL, Switzerland, 1985, U. Calif., Berkeley, 1989, Kitami Inst. Tech., Japan, 1995; guest prof. State Key Lab. for Coal Conversion, Inst. of Coal Conversion, Taiyuan, China, 1997—2000. Guest editor: Jour. Chem. Engring. Communications, 1987, Catalysis Today, 1993; mem. editl. bd. Jour. Fuel Chemistry and Technology; contbr. articles to profl. jours. Recipient Disting. Alumnus award Indian Inst. Tech., 1983, Disting. Rschr. award W.Va. Coll. Engring., 1985, 95. Mem. AAAS, AIChE (chmn. N.E. N.Y. local sect. 1983, chmn. area 1b nat. program com. 1985-87), Am. Soc. for Engring. Edn., Am. Chem. Soc. (sec. petroleum divsn. 2003—), N.Am. Catalysis Soc. (dir.), Pitts.-Cleve. Catalysis Soc. (pres. 2000-01), Sigma Xi, Tau Beta Pi. Office: WVa U Dept Chem Engring Morgantown WV 26506-6102

DAEMMRICH, HORST SIGMUND, German language and literature educator; b. Pausa, Germany, Jan. 5, 1930; s. Arthur M. and Gertrud A. (Orlamunde) D.; m. Ingrid H. Guenther, June 10, 1962; children: JoAnn, Arthur. AB, Wayne State U., 1958, MA, 1959; PhD, U. Chgo., 1964. Instr. U. Chgo., 1961-62; asst. prof. Germanic langs. and lits. Wayne State U., Detroit, 1962-66, assoc. prof., 1967-70, prof., 1971-80; prof., chair U. Pa., 1981-98. Resident dir. Jr. Year Inst. at U. Freiburg, Germany, 1972-73 Author: The Shattered Self, 1973, Literaturkritik in Theorie und Praxis, 1974 (with Ingrid Daemmrich) Wiederholte Spiegelungen, Themen und Motive in der Literatur, 1978, Karl Krolow, 1980, Wilhelm Raabe, 1981, Themes and Motifs in Western Literature: A Handbook, 1987, Themen und Motive in der abendländischen Literatur, 1987, Spirals and Circles: A Key to Thematic Patterns in Classicism and Realism, 2 vols., 1994, Themen and Motive in der Literatur, Handbuch, 1995; editor: The Challenge of German Literature, 1971, Studies on Themes and Motifs in Literature, 1990; contbr. articles to profl. jours. Mem. Am. Soc. Aesthetics, Acad. Lit. Studies, Am. Lessing Soc., Am. Assn. Tchrs. German (mem. commn. on higher edn. 1974—), Am. Comparative Lit. Assn., MLA (sec. and chmn. 19th century lit. 1972-73), Midwest MLA (sec., chmn. modern Germanic lit. 1966-67), Phi Beta Kappa Home: 307 Suffolk Rd Flourtown PA 19031-2119 Office: U Pa Dept Germanic Langs Philadelphia PA 19104-6305

DAFERMOS, CONSTANTINE MICHAEL, applied mathematics educator; b. Athens, Greece, May 26, 1941; came to U.S., 1964; s. Michael Constantine and Sophia (Raptarchis) D.; m. Stella Theodoracopoulos, Sept. 6, 1964; children: Thalia, Michael. Diploma, Athens Nat. Tech. U., 1964; PhD, Johns Hopkins U., 1967. Fellow Johns Hopkins U., 1967-68; asst. prof. Cornell U., 1968-71; assoc. prof. Brown U., 1971-76, prof. applied math., 1976—, Univ. prof., 1988—, dir. Lefschetz Ctr. for Dynamical Systems, 1988-94. Author: Hyperbolic Conservation Laws in Continuum Physics, 2000; mem. editl. bd. Archive for Rational Mechanics and Analysis, 1972—, Jour. of Thermal Stresses, 1978-2000, Quar. Applied Math., 1985—, Math. Modeling and Numerical Analysis, 1986-96, Proc. Royal Soc. Edinburgh, 1987—, Advances Math. Applied Sci., 1989—, Math. Models and Methods, 1990-97, Comm. on Applied Nonlinear Analysis, 1995—, Ricerche di Matematica, 1997—, Jour. Am. Math. Soc., 1999—, Revista Matematica Complutense, 2000, Jour. Dynamics and Differential Equations, 2002--; contbr. articles to profl. jours. NSF grantee, 1970—, Office Naval Rsch. grantee, 1972-80, 92—, USAF grantee, 1972-73, U.S. Army grantee, 1973-96. Mem. Soc. Natural Philosophy (treas. 1975-76, chmn. 1977-78), Am. Math. Soc., Acad. of Athens, Am. Acad. Arts and Scis. Office: Brown U Lefschetz Ctr Dynamical Sys 182 George St Providence RI 02912-9056 E-mail: dafermos@cfm.brown.edu.

DAFFRON, MARTHA, retired education educator; b. Fairburn, Ga., Apr. 10, 1919; d. William D. and Sarah Jane (Cochran) Duggan; children: Patricia Ruth Daffron Kelly, Doris Vesta Daffron Dodson, Billy Wayne. B in Edn., Miss. State U., 1963, MEd, 1966, PhD, 1971. Lang. arts cons. Office of Dr. Joe Owens, Lincolnton, Ga., 1971-72; lab. asst. Midlands Tech., Columbia, S.C., 1975-76, speed reading tchr., 1976-78; prof. Morris Coll., Sumter, S.C., 1972-91, ret. Rschr. in field; presenter at various reading confs. Contbr. articles to profl. jours. Mem. Internat. Reading Assn., NEA, S.C. Edn. Assn., SEAOPP, SCCSP, Delta Kappa Gamma, Phi Kappa Phi, Kappa Delta Pi. Home: 508 N Lehmberg Rd Lot 2 Columbus MS 39702-4434

DAGENHART, BETTY JANE MAHAFFEY, nursing educator, administrator; b. Welch, W.Va. d. Charley F. and Edith L. (Lucas) Mahaffey; divorced; 1 child, Cynthia Leigh. BA in Health Care Adminstrn., Mary Baldwin, Staunton, Va., 1991; postgrad., St. Joseph's Coll. RN, Va.; cert. nursing adminstr., ANA. Nurse mgr. ortho. and emergency svcs. Cmty. Hosp. of Roanoke (Va.) Valley, Va., 1967-77; asst. dir. nursing svc. Cmty. Hosp. of Roanoke Valley, Va., 1977-83, coord. quality mgmt., dir. occupl. health svcs., dir. emergency svc., 1983-92, dir. med./surg. nursing, 1992-94; dir. nursing edn. City of Salem Sch. Sys., Va., 1994—; dir. med. office asst. program Dominion Coll., Roanoke, 1997. Mem. disaster planning coun. City of Roanoke, 1980-90, pre-hosp. care providers, 1982-88, chmn. pers. com.; organized free standing clinic Cmty. Hosp. Roanoke, 1986. Bd. dirs. Emergency Med. Svcs. Western Va., 1979-92; mem. pers. com. Cave Spring Bapt. Ch., Roanoke, 1991-92. Mem. ANA, Va. Orgn. Nurse Execs., Exec. Females, Health Occupation Educators, Accrediting Coun. Ind. Colls. and Univs. (accreditation team). Avocations: golf, walking, cooking. Home: 139 Ferrum Drive Salem VA 24153 Office: ecpi Technical Coll Dean of Allied Health Sciences 5234 Airport Rd Roanoke VA 24012

DAGGETT, BARBARA DALICANDRO, secondary education director; b. Chgo., Aug. 10, 1949; d. Robert Patrick and Mary Camille (Moreschi) Dalicandro; m. Michael Thomas Daggett, July 21, 1984; children: Samantha, Anthony. BA, U. No. Colo., 1971; MEd, Nat. Lewis U., Evanston, Ill., 1974, CAS, 1980. Cert. tchr. English, reading, psychology; cert. in supervision, adminstrn., superintendency; cert. prin. Instr. lang. arts Manheim Jr. H.S., Melrose Park, Ill., 1971-81, dept. coord., 1978-81; summer sch. dir. Deer Valley Sch. Dist., Phoenix, 1983-86, tchr. English/reading, 1981-86, asst. prin., 1986-87; prin. Vocat. Tech. Ctr., Phoenix, 1987-89; dir. Deer Valley Sch. Dist., Phoenix, 1989—. Bd. dirs. Jobs for Am. Grad.'s, Phoenix, 1992-94, The Ariz. Partnership, Phoenix, 1992. Named Outstanding Prin., Chase Bank, 1991; recipient Pride award Deer Valley Sch. Dist., 1990, Adminstr. award Health Occupations, 1989. Mem. ASCD, Deer Valley Adminstrs. Assn. (pres. 1991-93), Ariz. Coun. Occupational Vocat. Adminstrs. (pres. 1991-92, Outstanding Contbn. award 1992, 93), Am. Vocat. Assn., Ariz. Vocat. Assn. (bd. dirs. 1991-92), Manheim Tchrs. Assn. (v.p. 1978-79), Ariz. Sch. Adminstrs., Nat. Assn. Secondary Sch. Prins., Phi Delta Kappa. Avocations: travel, theater. Home: 13630 N Coral Gables Dr Phoenix AZ 85023-6270 Office: Deer Valley Sch Dist 97 20402 N 15th Ave Phoenix AZ 85027-3636

DAGNA, JEANNE MARIE, special education educator; b. Flushing, N.Y., July 28, 1959; d. Renato Lawrence and Norma Jeanne (Leuchtman) D. BS in Elem. and Spl. Edn., L.I. U., 1982, MS in Spl. Edn., 1984. Cert. spl. edn. tchr., N.Y., Pa. Adminstrv. asst. N.Y. State Dept. Edn., Greenvale, 1983-85; spl. edn. tchr. Baldwin (N.Y.) Sch. Dist., 1985-87, Advances of Wiley House, Reading, Pa., 1989-90; master tchr. Centennial Sch./Lehigh U., Bethlehem, Pa., 1990-92; student assistance liaison Alcohol & Adddictions Dept. of Delaware County, Media, Pa., 1992-93; spl. edn. tchr. children and adolescent units Horsham Psychiat. Clinic, Ambler, Pa., 1993-95; spl. edn. tchr. learning and emotional support Lower Merion H.S., Ardmore, Pa., 1994-2000, spl. edn. liaison in pupil svcs., 2000—. Sec. Main Line Youth Alliance, Wayne, Pa., 1996-99. Contbr. articles to profl. jours. Mem. Crohn's and Colitis Assn., United Ostomy Assn., Coun. for Exceptional Children, Pa. Coun. for Exceptional Children (conf. presenter 1998, 99, Gay, Lesbian, Straight Educators Network. Avocations: reading, flute/oboe, drawing, bicycling. Office: Lower Merion HS 245 E Montgomery Ave Ardmore PA 19003-3339 E-mail: dognaj@lmsd.org.

DAGOGO-JACK, SAMUEL E. medical educator, physician scientist, endocrinologist; b. Abonnema, Rivers, Nigeria, Mar. 17, 1954; came to U.S., 1990; s. Karibi Jim and Titty (Biribota) D.-J.; m. Agbani Ibinabo Iyalla, May 28, 1983; children: Karibi, Ibi, Alali, Tari. MBBS, U. Ibadan (Nigeria), 1978, MD, 1994; MSc, U. Newcastle Upon Tyne (U.K.), 1988. Diplomate Am. Bd. Internal Medicine, Am. Bd. Endocrinology, Am. Bd. Diabetes and Metabolism. Rsch. assoc. U. Newcastle Upon Tyne (U.K.), 1983—85; cons. physician U. Port Harcourt (Nigeria), 1985—89; chief resident endocrinologist King Faisal Specialist Hosp., Riyadh, Saudi Arabia, 1989—90; from rsch. fellow to assoc. prof. medicine Washington U. Sch. Medicine, St. Louis, 1990—2000; assoc. chief internal medicine svc. Barnes-Jewish Hosp., St. Louis, 1996—2000; prof. medicine, endocrinology, diabetes and metabolism, prof. physiology and biophysics, dir. diabetes programs U. Miss. Med. Ctr., Jackson, 2000—01; dir. minority health rsch. Montgomery VAMC, Jackson, 2000—01; prof. medicine, endocrinology, diabetes and metabolism U. Tenn. Coll. Medicine, Memphis, 2001—; assoc. dir. Gen. Clin. Rsch. Ctr., 2001—; prin. investigator DCCT/EDIC NIH Diabetes Rsch. Study, 2001—. Endocrinology and diabetes grant rev. study sect. NIH, 2000—; Todd Brown Disting. Heritage lectr. Meharry Med. Sch., Nashville, Tenn., 2003; Charles Drew vis. prof. Charles Drew U. Sci. and Medicine, 2000; extra-mural rschr. diabetes drugs devel. programs for pharm. cos.; chair Excellence Diabetes Mgmt. Symposium, 1998-99; dir. sophomore endocrine pathophysiology course U. Tenn., 2002—; ad-hoc reviewer in field; lectr. in field. Author: The Diabetes Guide, 1992; (with others) The Washington Manual, 2002, The Uncomplicated Guide to Diabetes Complications, 1999; mem. editl. bd. Kuwait Med. Jour., 1995-98, Current Drug Targets, Cardiology Spl. Edit., 2001—; contbr. over 100 articles to profl. jours. Diabetes Rsch. & Tng. Ctr. grantee, 1999—; recipient Young Investigator Travel award Internat. Soc. Endocrinology, 1987. Fellow ACP (co-dir. workshop urban health 1998), Royal Coll. Physicians (London), Am. Coll. Endocrinology; mem. AAAS, Am. Diabetes Assn. (sec. St. Louis chpt. 1997-98, pres. 1998-00, sci. and med. adv. group, rsch. fellow 1990-91, Clin. Rsch. award 1997-2000), Endocrine Soc., Am. Fedn. for Med. Rsch., Ctrl. Soc. for Clin. Rsch. (chmn. endocrinology sect. 2000-02), Am. Assn. Clin. Endocrinologists. Achievements include rsch. in diabetes edn. and rsch. programs. Office: U Tenn Coll Medicine Dept Med Endocrinology 951 Court Ave Memphis TN 38163 Business E-Mail: sdagogojack@utmem.edu.

D'AGOSTINO, GLORIA M. secondary school educator; b. Ossining, N.Y., Mar. 13, 1950; d. Anthony and Sarah (Leary) D'Agostino. BA, SUNY, New Paltz, 1973, MA, 1977. Sci. tchr. Binghamton (N.Y.) Sch. Dist., 1974—76; tchg. fellow, biology St. Bonaventure U., Olean, NY, 1977—81; instr. biology Westchester County Coll., White Plains, NY, 1981—82; tchr. chemistry Middletown (N.Y.) Sch. Dist., 1982—. Contbr. articles to bulls. Office: Middletown High Sch Gardner Ave Ext Middletown NY 10940

D'AGOSTINO, RALPH BENEDICT, mathematician, statistician, educator, consultant; b. Somerville, Mass., Aug. 16, 1940; s. Bennedetto and Carmela (Piemonte) D'A.; m. Lei Lanie Carta, Aug. 28, 1965; children: Ralph Benedict, Lei Lanie Maria. AB, Boston U., 1962, MA, 1964; PhD, Harvard U., 1968. Lectr. math. Boston U., 1964-68, asst. prof., 1968-71, assoc. prof., 1971-76, lectr. law, 1975-91, assoc. dean Grad. Sch., 1976-78, prof. math. and stats., 1976—, prof. pub. health, 1982—, dir. data analysis and stats. Framingham Heart Study, 1985—, chmn. dept. math., 1986-91, dir. stats. cons. unit, 1986—, dir. Biostats MA/PhD Program, 1988—, prof. law, 1991—. Exec. dir. data mgmt. and biostats. Harvard Clin. Rsch. Inst., 2002—; vis. lectr. Am. Statis. Assn., 1975-86, 88-92; vis. prof. biostats. clin. epidiology unit Univ. Hosp., Geneva, 1993; Rankin vis. prof. U. Wis., 1995; spl. lectr. clin. trials symposium U. Fla., 1995; vis. scientist NHLBI, 1993; Lowell Reed lectr. APHA, 1996; spl. scientist Boston City Hosp., 1981-95, Boston Med. Ctr., 1996—, New Eng. Med. Ctr., 1990—; mem. Health Inst. New Eng. Med. Ctr., 1990—; cons. stats. United Brands, 1968-76, Diabetes and Arthritis Control Unit, Boston, 1971-75, City of Somerville, Mass., 1972, ednl. Harvard U. Dental Sch., 1969, Lahey Clinic Found., 1973-85, Walden Rsch., 1974-79, FDA Biometrics Divsn. and Over-the-Counter Divsn., 1975—, Cardio and Renal Divsn. FDA, 1987—, Gastrointestinal Drug Divsn., FDA, 1994-96, Medical Devine Divsn., Arnold & Porter, 1980, Bedford Rsch. Assn., 1976-81, Corneal Scis., 1976, Biotek, 1979-88, GCA, 1979-87, Lever Bros., 1982-87, Conrail, 1981, FBI, 1984, Ctr. Psychiat. Rehab., Boston U., 1985—, NIMH, 1985, Dade Clin. Assays, 1986-90, Millipore, 1983-92, VLI Corp., 1985-90, New Eng. Coll. Optometry, 1985-93, Dupont Corp., 1985, Bristol Myers, 1986, 93, Cheeseborough Ponds, 1987-96, med. decision making divsn. and health svcs. rsch. unit Tufts New Eng. Med. Ctr., 1986—, Am. Inst. Rsch. in Social Scis., 1983-88, New Eng. Rsch. Insts., 1987-92, Thompson Med., 1987-96, Merck, Sharpe and Dohme, 1988-94, Carter Ctr., Emory U., 1969-75, Unilever, 1991-96, Miles, 1991-95, Ultra Fem., 1991-93, Health Effects Inst., 1992—, Forsyth Dental Clinic, 1992-93, 95—, Bard Vascular, 1990-95, Ultra Slim Fast, 1990-95, Block Med., 1993-95, Bayer Pharm., 1993-98, Astra Pharm., 1993-97, Cytyc, 1993-97, Regua, 1994-96, Smith-Kline Beechman, 1994-95, Proctor and Gamble, 1994-96, 2000—, Sandoz, 1994-96, R W Johnson Pharms., 1997, Mass. Med. Assistance, 1995-97, Cambridge Heart, 1996—, Merck/ Johnson & Johnson, 1999—, Aventis, 2000—, Ajinomoto, 2000, Discovery Lab, 2000—; mem. various FDA coms. including fertility and maternal health drugs adv. com, 1978-81, life support subcom., 1979-81, drug abuse adv. com., 1987-90, gastrointestinal drugs adv. com., 1990-94, nonprescriptive drug adv. com., 1995—, chair, 1996-98; mem. task force on design and analysis of dental and oral rsch., 1979—, Harvard U. health tech. com., 1986-90; mem. Honolulu Heart Study Adv. Com., NIH, 1989-96, Balt. Longitudinal Study of Aging Adv. Com., 1990, NIH Consensus Panel on Liver Transplantation, 1983, Consensus Panel on Fresh Frozen Plasma, 1984, Consensus Panel on Geriatric Assessment Methods for Clin. Decision Making, 1987; mem. task force Office Tech. Assessment, 1980; mem. consensus panel on intraoral techniques ADA, 1990; mem. study sect. Agy. for Health Care Policy and Rsch., 1990-94; mem. Bethesda Conf. on Matching Intensity of Risk Factor Mgmt. With the Hazard for Coronary Disease Events, 1996; prin., co-prin. investigator or sr. statistician on grants Nat. Ctr. Health Svcs. Rsch., 1976-82, NHLBI, 1982—, USAF, 1980-85, Nat. Cancer Inst., 1985—, Nat. Inst. Criminal Justice, 1982-85, Nat. Ctr. Child Abuse and Neglect, 1982-85, Robert Wood Johnson Found., 1981-85, Social Security Adminstrn., 1982-86, 90-93, Motor Vehicles Mem. Assn., 1987, NIOSH, 1985, Nat. Insts. Aging, 1986—, Agency for Health Care Policy and Rsch., 1989—; grant and contract reviewer NAS, 1979—, Nat. Ctr. Health Svcs. Rsch., 1976, 89, NIH, 1983, NSF, 1987-95, AHCPR, 1990; co-prin. investigator Framingham Heart Study, 1993-; chair spl. emphasis panel reviewing small bus. grant proposal Nat. Inst. Dental Rsch., 1996. Author: (with E.E. Cureton) Factor Analysis, An Applied Approach, 1983, (with Shuman and Wolf) Mathematical Modeling, Applications in Emergency Health Services, 1984, (with Stephens) Goodness of Fit Techniques, 1986, (with D. Schiff) Practical Engineering Statistics, 1996; assoc. editor Am. Statistician, 1972-76, Jour. Am. Statis. Assn., 1993-96; editor Emergency Health Svc. Rev., 1981-88, Stats. in Medicine (biostat. tutorials), 1993—, Stats. in Medicine, 1997—; mem. editl. bd. Biostatistica, 1990-99; book reviewer Houghton-Mifflin, Holden, Day, Duxbury Press, Prentice Hall, 1969; contbr. articles to profl. jours.; co-developer instrument for predicting acute ischemic health disease, stroke health risk appraisal function and coronary heart disease risk assessment function. Recipient Spl. citation FDA Commr., 1981, 95, Metcalf awrd for excellence in teaching Boston U., 1985; Am. Heart Assn. fellow, 1991; pre-doctoral fellow NIH, 1962-68. Fellow Am. Statis. Assn. (pres. Boston chpt. 1972, v.p. 1971, mem. nat. coun. 1973-75, vis. lectr. 1976-78, 80—, Statistician of Yr. Boston chpt. 1993, chmn. sect. Health Policy Stats. 1996chmn. sect. 2003); mem. APHA (Lowell Reed lectr. 1996, chmn. sect. emergency health svcs. 1982-83, governing coun. 1983-85), Am. Heart Assn. (mem. cardiovasc. epidemiology coun.), Inst. Math. Stats., Am. Soc. Quality Control, Biometrics Soc. (mem. regional adv. com. 1989-94), Phi Beta Kappa, Sigma Xi. Home: 5 Everett Ave Winchester MA 01890-3523 Office: Boston U Statistics & Cons Unit 111 Cummington St Boston MA 02215-2411 E-mail: ralph@bu.edu.

DAGUM, CAMILO, economist, educator; b. Argentina, Aug. 11, 1925; arrived in Can., 1972, naturalized, 1978; s. Alexander and Nazira (Hakim) D.; m. Estela Bee, Dec. 22, 1958; children: Alexander, Paul, Leonardo. PhD (gold medal summa cum laude), Nat. U. Cordoba, 1949, degree (hon.), 1988, U. Bologna, 1988, U. Montpelier, France, 1995. Mem. faculty Nat. U. Cordoba, 1950-66, prof. econs., 1956-66, dean Faculty Econ. Scis., 1962-66; sr. rsch. economist Princeton U., 1966-68; prof. Nat. U. Mex., 1968-70; vis. prof. Inst. d'Etudes du Devel. Econ. and Social U. Paris, 1967-69, U. Iowa, 1970-72; prof. econs. U. Ottawa, Ont., Can., 1972-91, chmn. dept., 1973-75, mem. acad. senate, 1981-84, bd. govs., 1983-84, prof. emeritus, 1992—. Prof. stats. and econs. U. Milan, 1990-94, chmn. Inst. Quantitative Methods, 1993-94; prof. econs. and stats. U. Bologna, Italy, 1994-02; pres. Cordoba Inst. Social Security, 1962-63; cons. to govt. and industry, 1956—; rsch. prof. U. Rome, 1956-57, London Sch. Econs., 1960-62, Inst. Sci. Econmique Appliquèe, Coll. France, 1965; vis. fellow Birkbeck Coll., U. London, 1960-61, Australian Nat. U., 1985; guest scholar Brookings Instn., 1978-79; vis. prof. U. Siena, Italy, 1987, 88, U. Rome, 1989; spkr. in field. Author books on eocn. theory; editor econ. and statis. jours.; contbr. articles to profl. jours. Mem. Acad. Coun. Rsch. Ctr. on Income Distbn., U. Siena, 1986—, Sci. Com. on Econ. Rsch. and Analysis Program, U. Montreal, 1992-96, Sci. Adv. Com. U. Bologna, Buenos Aires. Res. officer Argentina Army, 1948. Decorated Pro-Patria Gold medal, 1948; hon. prof. Inst. Advanced Studies, Salta, Argentina, 1972; extraordinary prof. Cath. U. Salta, 1981; elected mem. Accademia di Scienze e Lettere, Istituto Lombardo, 1992—. Mem. Internat. Inst. Sociology, Internat. Statis. Inst., Statis. Soc., Econ. Soc., Econ. History Soc. Argentina, U.S. Eastern Econ. Assn., Econometric Soc., Am. Statis. Assn., Am. Econ. Assn., Can. Econ. Assn., Can. Statis. Soc., Assn. Social Econs., N.Y. Acad. Scis., Acad. Scis. of Bologna. Roman Catholic. Home: PO Box 74080 5 Beechwood Ave Ottawa ON Canada Office: U Ottawa Faculty Social Scis Dept Econs 550 Cumberland St POB 450 Station A Ottawa ON Canada K1N 6N5 also: U Bologna Dept Statis Scis Via delle Belle Arti 41 40126 Bologna Italy E-mail: dagum@stat.unibo.it.

DAHIYA, RAJBIR SINGH, mathematics educator, researcher; b. Rattangarh, Haryana, India, Dec. 3, 1940; came to U.S., 1968; s. Ram S. and Kesar (Devi) D.; m. Krishna Tavathia, Dec. 11, 1966; children: Madhu, Ranjan. PhD, Birla Inst. Sci. and Tech., Pilani, India, 1967. Lectr. Birla Inst. Sci. and Tech., 1967-68; asst. prof. math. Iowa State U., Ames, 1968-72, assoc. prof., 1972-78, prof., 1978—. Reviewer math. revs. Zentrallblat; referee applied math. jours. Contbr. over 150 rsch. papers on delay and advanced differential equations, transform theory and spl. functions to U.S., European and Australian profl. jours. Mem. Am. Math. Soc., Soc. Indsl. and Applied Math. Democrat. Hindu. Home: 3144 Sycamore Rd Ames IA 50014-4510 Office: Iowa State U Dept Math Ames IA 50011-0001

DAHL, CATHY DAVENPORT, elementary educator; b. Port Arthur, Tex., Mar. 3, 1958; d. Lawrence Henry and Francis (Louise) Davenport; m. Gregory Raymond Dahl, June 10, 1989; children: Cody Ray, Kyle James, Taylor Kristen. BS in Edn., Murray (Ky.) State U., 1979. Cert. K-8 tchr., Ky., Tex. Elem. tchr. Edgewood Ind. Sch. Dist., San Antonio, 1980-88, tchr. math. and sci., 1988-89; elem. tchr. Northside Ind. Sch. Dist., San Antonio, 1989—, curriculum writer in math., 1991—, Title I math. tchr., 1995—. Tchr.-trainer math. Region 20 Edn. Svc. Ctr., San Antonio, 1987-89; family math. trainer Valley-Hi Elem. Sch., San Antonio, 1990—; text book reviewer Addison Wesley Math., 1991; curriculum writer kinder math. sci., Northside Ind. Sch. Dist., 1992—. Sec. Valley Hi PTA, 1995-96. Named Tchr. of Yr., Burleston Sch. PTA, 1984, Burleson Sch., 1989, Valley Hi Elem. Math. Tchr. of Yr., 1996. Mem. NEA, Edgewood Classroom Tchrs. Assn. (elem. rep. 1988-89). Avocations: counted cross-stitch, reading, camping, spending time with son. Office: Valley-Hi Elem Sch 8503 Ray Ellison Blvd San Antonio TX 78227-4599 Address: 1006 Post Ct Clarksville TN 37043-5051

DAHL, GERALD LUVERN, psychotherapist, educator; b. Nov. 10, 1938; s. Lloyd F. and Leola J. (Painter) Dahl; m. Judith Lee Brown, June 24, 1960; children: Peter, Stephen, Leah. BA, Wheaton Coll., 1960; MSW, U. Nebr., 1962; PhD in Psychotherapy (hon.), Internat. U. Found., 1987. Diplomate Am. Psychotherapy Assn. Juvenile probation officer Hennepin County Ct. Svcs., 1962—65; cons. Citizens Coun. on Delinquency and Crime, Mpls., 1965—67; dir. patient svcs. Mt. Sinai Hosp., Mpls., 1967—69; clin. social worker Mpls. Clinic of Psychiatry, 1969—82, G.L. Dahl & Assocs., Inc., Mpls., 1983—. Assoc. prof. social work Bethel Coll., St. Paul, 1964—83; spl. instr. sociology Golden Valley Luth. Coll., 1974—83; pres. Strategic Team-Makers, Inc., 1985—; adj. prof. U. Wis., River Falls, 1988—90. Author: Why Christian Marriages Are Breaking Up, 1979, Everybody Needs Somebody Sometime, 1980, How Can We Keep Christian Marriages from Falling Apart, 1988, The Sandwich Generation, 1995; contbr. articles to profl. jours. Founder, bd. stewards Family Counseling Svc., Minn. Bapt. Conf., 1994—; bd. dirs. Edgewater Bapt. Ch., 1972—75, chmn., 1974—75; vice chmn. bd. stewards Minnetonka Bapt. Ch., 1995. Mem.: AAUP, Am. Assn. Behavioral Therapists, Pi Gamma Mu. Office: 4825 Highway 55 Ste 140 Minneapolis MN 55422-5155 E-mail: jerryd@stmi.biz., stmi@stmi.biz.

DAHL, JOHN CLARENCE, JR., academic administrator; b. Indpls., Jan. 10, 1948; s. John C. and Dorothy L. (Reed) D.; m. Vickie E. Eckert, Oct. 18, 1980; children: Jennifer, Bradley. BS in Bus., Ind. U., 1970, MS in Edn., 1972, EdD, 1982. Asst. univ. registrar, dir. admissions Ind. U., Bloomington, 1971-80; assoc. vice chancellor, registrar Ind. U.-Purdue U. Ft. Wayne, 1980—. Mem. adv. com. Ind. Commn. for Higher Edn., Indpls., 1982; presenter workshops in field. Mem. Am. Assn. Collegiate Registrars and Admissions Officers (various coms. 1975-87), Assn. for Instnl. Rsch., Soc. for Coll. and Univ. Planning. Office: Ind-Purdue U Ft Wayne 2101 E Coliseum Blvd Fort Wayne IN 46805-1445 E-mail: dahl@ipfw.edu.

DAHL, LAUREL JEAN, human services administrator; b. Chgo. d. James Edward and Gladys Uarda (Boquist) Findlay; m. Philip Nels Dahl, Aug. 29, 1970; children: Eric Nels, John Philip. BA, Trinity Coll., 1970; MS in Human Svcs., Nat. Louis U., 1992. Cert. sr. alcohol and other drug preventionist. Tchr. Grove Sch., Lake Forest, Ill., 1971, Little Bear Child Care Ctr., Waukegan, Ill., 1975-77; sec. to dir. Strang Funeral Home, Antioch, Ill., 1981-87; comptroller, office mgr. Village of Antioch, 1987-92; prevention specialist Lake County Dept. of Health: Mental Health Div., 1992; community coord. Fighting Back Project of Lake County, Round Lake, Ill., 1992-94; dir. prevention svcs. Nicasa, Lake, 1994—. Adj. faculty Nat. Louis U., 1994—; adv. bd. U. Ill. Extension, 1999; dir. Lake County Gang Prevention Alliance, 2000—03; mem. Character Matters in Lake County Found., 1999—, treas., 2001—03, pres., 2003—. Mem. editl. adv. bd. Family Times. Mem. Antioch Cmty. H.S. Bd. Edn., 1987—95, pres., 1991—95, sec., 1989—91; mem. Antioch Cmty. H.S. Drug Task Force, MADD; past pres. PTO; vice chair Human Svc. Coun., 1994—96, chmn., 1996—98, 1999—2003; mem. peer rev. com. Ill. Alcohol and Other Drug Abuse Profl. Cert. Assn., 1996—; mem. women's bd. No. Ill. Coun. on Alcoholism and Substance Abuse, 1996—2003, v.p. for programs, 1997—2003; mem. Cmty. Partnership Bd., 2003—. Recipient commendation for Gt. Lakes Naval Tng. Ctr. for Drug Edn. for Youth, 1994-95, Disting. Svc. award Ill. chpt. Nat. Sch. Pub. Rels. Assn., Enrique Camarena "One Person Can" award, 1995, State Prevention Leadership award Ill. Alcoholism and Drug Dependence Assn., 1996, Individuals in the Forefront for Lake County award, 1998; Paul Harris fellow. Mem.: Ill. Assn. for Prevention, Ill. Student Assistance Profls., Alliance Against Intoxicated Motorists, Round Lake Exch. Club (charter mem. 1999). Home: PO Box 613 Antioch IL 60002-0613

DAHL, MERLIN HUGH, school system administrator; b. Bismarck, N.D., Oct. 15, 1951; s. Merlin P. and Dorothy Y. (Dettmann) D.; m. Carolyn K. Domnanish, June 12, 1981; children: Benjamin H., Cassandra K. AA in Liberal Arts, Bismarck Jr. Coll., 1971; BS in Edn., Moorhead State Coll., 1973; MS in Ednl. Adminstrn., Tri-Coll. U., 1984, postgrad., 1991. Instrumental music tchr. Turtle Mountain Community Sch., Belcourt, N.D., 1973-75; gen. and vocal music tchr. Fergus Falls (Minn.) Jr. High Sch., 1975-77; secondary sch. prin. Mandaree (N.D.) Pub. Sch., 1977-78; elem. and secondary sch. prin. Solen (N.D.) Pub. Sch., 1978-85; supt., prin. Upham (N.D.) Pub. Sch., 1985-91; supt. Walhalla (N.D.) Pub. Schs., 1991—. Cert. tchr., prin., supt., N.D., Minn.; bd. dirs. No. Ctrl. Coun. Sch. TV. Bd. dirs. Peace Garden Spl. Svcs., Bottineau, N.D., 1988-92, Pembina Spl. Svcs., Cavalier, N.D., 1991—; com. chair Walhalla Cub Scout pack Boy Scouts Am., 1991—. Mem. Nat. Assn. Sch. Adminstrs., Nat. Assn. Secondary Sch. Adminstrs., N.D. Assn. Sch. Adminstrs. (pub. rels. com. 1986-87, fin. com. 1987-91), N.D. Coun. Sch. Adminstrs., N.D. Assn. Secondary Sch. Prins., Ducks Unltd., Greater Walhalla Civic Club, Walhalla Country Club (bd. dirs.), Elks, Phi Delta Kappa, Pembina County Wildlife Club, Langdon Eagles Aerie 3454, Pemblier Wildlife Club, Nat. Eagle Scout Assn. (life). Lutheran. Avocations: hunting, fishing, golf, reading, team sports. Home: 912 Emmerling Ave # 39 Walhalla ND 58282-4419 Office: Walhalla Pub Sch 605 10th St # 558 Walhalla ND 58282-4033

DAHL, SHIRLEY ANN WISE, education educator; b. Oklahoma City, Apr. 30, 1941; d. T.W. and Edith F. Wise; m. Ralph L. Dahl, Oct. 7, 1983; children: Chandler S. Fulton, Stephane R. Ready. BA, So. Ark. U., 1968; MEd in Reading, East Tex. State U., 1975, PhD in Elem. Edn. and Reading, 1977; cert., Stephen F. Austin State U., 1987; cert. ESL, Tex. A&M. Cert. diagnostician, Tex., reading specialist, English/Spanish, elem., secondary tchr., profl. supr.; cert. ESL. Cons. Region VII Edn. Svc. Ctr., Kilgore, Tex.; adj. prof. Kilgore Coll., East Tex. State U., Texarkana; prof. East Tex. Bapt. U., Marshall. Exch. lectr. Guandong (China) Fgn. Lang. Normal Sch., summer 1991; mem. task force write outcomes tchr. prepration Tex.'s Instns. Tchr. Edn., 1992-93; tex. tchr. appraiser; cons. in field; pres. Faculty Assembly, 1987. Author: The Teaching of High School Reading, 1918-1972: Objectives as Stated in eriodical Literature, 1977, The Childcare professional Training Program, Semester I and II, Applied Learning Experiences in Child Care (APP-L-E), 1991; contbr. article Ednl. Resources and Techniques, 1980, Centerpoint, 1991, Forum, 1993; co-editor: Tex. Tchr. Educator Forum, 1995-96; mem. editl. bd. Reading To, 1997-98, 98—. Bd. dirs. Tex. Coop. Tchr. Ctr., 1980—. Recipient Pres. Svc. award Tex. Coop. Tchr. Ctr., 1989-90; Piper Prof. award, 1996, Ted Booker award, 1996. Mem. Tex. Assn. Tchr. Educators, Tex. Tchrs. Educators, Assn. Tchr. Educators, Consortium State Orgns. Tchr. Edn. (bd. dirs.), Tex. Soc. Coll. Tchrs. Edn. (pres. 1991-93, Svc. award 1993), Internat. Reading Assn., Tex. Reading Assn., Optimist (Marshall chpt. pres. 1995-96, lt. gov. Zone 15, 1996-97), Piney Woods Reading Coun., Phi Delta Kappa (historian found. rep. 1995—, pres. 1983-84, Svc. award 1984), Alpha Upsilon Alpha, Sigma Tau Delta, Delta Kappa Gamma. Home: 114 Caddo St Marshall TX 75672-2704 Office: East Tex Bapt U 1209 N Grove St Marshall TX 75670-1423

DAHLBEN, SALIN ABRAHAM, neuropsychiatrist; b. Rio de Janeiro, Nov. 2, 1945; came to U.S., 1973; s. Abraham and Emilia D.; m. Sonia Sapolnik, July 8, 1971 (div. 1975); m. Jean Annette Leupold, Nov. 7, 1982 (div. 1996); children: Deborah, Rachael Emily, Lindsay Johanna, Joshua Robert, Brian Andre. BS, Hebrew Coll., Rio de Janeiro, 1963; MD, Fed. U., Rio de Janeiro, 1969. Cert. Bd. Med. Quality Assurance, Calif.; diplomate Am. Bd. Psychiatry and Neurology in gen. psychiatry with added cert. in geriatric psychiatry. Mem. med. staff Naval Hosp., Rio de Janeiro, 1970-71; intern Mt. Sinai Hosp. Svcs., N.Y.C., 1973-74; resident Boston City Hosp., 1974-75; fellow in neurosurgery Lahey Clinic, Boston, 1975-76; resident in neurosurgery U. Iowa Hosps., Iowa City, 1976-78, resident in psychiatry, 1979-80; chief resident Mt. Sinai Hosp. Med. Ctr., Chgo., 1981; med. unit dir. Bridgewater State Hosp., 1983-85; med. dir. Dorchester Mental Health Ctr., Mass., 1985-87; asst. psychiatrist McLean Hosp., Belmont, Mass., 1983—. Clin. instr. psychiatry Harvard Med. Sch., Boston, 1983—; clin. assoc. Mass. Gen. Hosp., 1988—98, Mass. Mental Health Ctr., 1999—; assoc. Cambridge Hosp., 1990—; unit med. dir. psychiatry Metro Boston Lemuel Shattuck Hosp., Boston, 2001—. 1st lt. M.D. Brazilian Navy, 1970-71. Recipient prize Assn. Med. Students, Rio de Janeiro, 1968, 69, Abbey Norman Prince award Mt. Sinai Hosp. Med. Ctr., Chgo., 1981; named one of Am.'s Top Psychiatrists in Neuropsychiatry, Consumers Rsch. Coun. Am., 2003; scholar Nat. Coun. for Rsch., 1969-70. Mem. Mass. Med. Soc., N.Y. Acad. Scis., Am. Mensa, Harvard Faculty Club, Sigma Xi (MIT chpt.). Office: 25 Mount Alvernia Rd Chestnut Hill MA 02467-1057 E-mail: sdahlben@hms.harvard.edu.

DAHLBERG, PATRICIA LEE, parochial school educator; b. Blue Island, Ill., Nov. 13, 1950; d. Frank George and Linda Frances (Burmeister) Toczek; m. Robert James Dahlberg, May 5, 1973. BA in English, Rosary Coll., River Forest, Ill., 1972, MS in Learning Disabilities, 1981. Cert. secondary school tchr., Ill., spl. K-12 tchr. social/emotional disorders, Ill. Tchr. lang. arts St. Nicholas/St. Louis Sch., Chgo., 1972-73; substitute tchr. St. John, St. Charles and St. Bernardine Schs., 1973; tchr. lang arts grades 7 and 8 St. Bernardine Sch., Forest Park, Ill., 1974-77; reading/English tchrs. grades 6-8 Our Lady of the Ridge, Chicago Ridge, Ill., 1977-79, tchr. reading grades 6-8, 1980-94, tchr. reading grades 5-8, 1994-99; grades 7-8 lit.-spelling tchr. St. Michael Sch., Orland Park, Ill., 1999—. Mem. Internat. Reading Assn., West Suburban Reading Coun. Roman Catholic. Avocations: country music, counted cross stitch, reading, cooking, cake decorating. Office: St Michael Sch 14355 Highland Ave Orland Park IL 60462

DAHLE, JOHANNES UPTON, retired academic administrator; b. Ada, Minn., Nov. 28, 1933; s. Upton Emmanuel and Marte (Goli) D.; m. Arlene Isabel Powell, Dec. 27, 1956; children: Randall Douglas, Lisa Johanna. BS, U. Minn., 1956, MA, 1966. Choral dir. U. Minn., Mpls., 1960-62-63-66; dir. choirs Macalester Coll., St. Paul, 1962-63; dir. student activities and univ. programs U. Wis., Eau Claire, 1966-71, dir. univ. ctrs., 1971-84, dir. devel., 1984-95, ret., 1995. Pres., dir. Eau Claire Conv. Tourism Bur., 1979-84; v.p., dir. Eau Claire Regional Arts Coun., 1982-84; bd. dirs. United Way of Eau Claire; mem. Plymouth Congrl. Ch., Mpls. Capt. USAF, 1956-60. Mem. Internat. Assn. Coll. Unions, Coun. for Advancement and Support Edn., Kiwanis (pres. Eau Claire chpt. 1975-76), Phi Kappa Phi (sec. 1982-84), Omicron Delta Kappa (sec. 1981-84), Phi Mu Alpha Sinfonia. Home: 1929 Hunter Hill Rd Hudson WI 54016-5818

DAHLGREN, DENIS ANDREW, elementary education educator; b. Wellsville, N.Y., Aug. 21, 1953; s. Willis Andrew and Della Dean (Hurd) D.; m. Colleen Record Searles, Mar. 19, 1985; children: Jonathan, Christopher, Erin. BA in Edn., SUNY, Geneseo, 1975. Tchr. elem. Wellsville (N.Y.) Schs., 1977—, dept. chair, 1995—, tchr. on spl. assignment, 2002—. Mem. bldg. project com. Wellsville Ctrl. Schs., 1999—, elem. tech. coord., dist. leadership team, 1999—. Bd. dirs. United Way, Allegheny County, N.Y. Mem. Wellsville Educators Assn. (pres. 1993-94, 99-01), Wellsville Kiwanis Club (youth advisor), Wellsville Key Club (advisor 1985-92). Republican. Avocations: sports, computers. Home: 358 E Dyke St Wellsville NY 14895-1641 Office: Wellsville Ctrl Schs 126 W State St Wellsville NY 14895-1399

DAHME, MAUD, educational association administrator; b. The Netherlands; arrived in U.S., 1954; married; 4 children. Mem. N.J. State Bd. Edn., Trenton, 1983—, pres., 1998—. Mem. North Hunterdon Regional H.S. Bd. Edn., 1976—83; chair Interstate Migrant Edn. Coun., 1998; former v.p., pres. Hunterdon County Sch. Bds. Assn. Mem.: Nat. Assn. State Bds. Edn. (pres. 1995). Office: NJ Dept Edn State Bd Office PO Box 500 Trenton NJ 08625-0500*

DAILEY, IRENE, actress, educator; b. New York, Sept. 12, 1920; d. Daniel James and Helen Therese (Ryan) D. Student attended, Uta Hagen, N.Y.C., 1951-61, Herbert Berghof, 1951-61. Cons. Am. Nat. Theatre and Acad., 1965-68; cons., coach for various theatre groups and individual artists., 1956—. Guest artist and tchr. various univ. in U.S., 1965— ; founder Sch. of the Actors Co., N.Y.C., 1961, artistic dir., 1961-72, mem. faculty, 1961-72. Appeared in: (films) Daring Game, 1967, No Way to Treat A Lady, 1968, Five Easy Pieces, 1970, The Grissom Gang, 1970, The Last Two Weeks, 1977, The Amityville Horror, 1978, Stacking, 1986; Broadway plays Andorra, 1962, The Subject Was Roses, 1964-65 (Drama Critics Cir. award), Rooms, 1966-67, (Drama Desk Award), You Know I Can't Hear You When the Water's Running, 1968, (off-Broadway) The Loves of Cass Maguire, 1982; appeared as Jasmin Adair in Tomorrow With Pictures (London Mag. Critics Award), Duke of York's, London, 1960; appeared in The Effect of Gamma Rays on Man-In-the-Moon Marigolds, Chgo., 1970 (Sarah Siddons Award), The House of Blue Leaves, Chgo., 1972 (Joseph Jefferson nomination), Lost in Yonkers, 1993, If We Are Women, Syracuse, 1993, (off-Broadway) Edith Stein, 1993-94, The Last Adam, Syracuse, 1994-95, (Broadway) The Father, 1995-96; appeared in Another World, NBC-TV, 1973-92 (Emmy Award 1980); appeared in (plays) Desire Under the Elms, Princeton, N.J., 1961; The Sea Gull, 1973; author: (play) Waiting for Mickey and Ava, 1978. Mem. Actors Equity Assn., Screen Actors Guild, Nat. Acad. TV Arts and Sci., Am. Ednl. Theatre Assn., AFTRA. Unitarian Universalist.

DAILEY, MARILYN, elementary education educator; b. Lucedale, Miss., Apr. 30, 1957; d. Jesse Lee and Vera Mae Chambers; m. William Harry Dailey, July 27, 1985. BS, William Carey Coll., Hattiesburg, Miss., 1982; MS, Ala. State U., 1995, EdS, 2001. Tchr. spl. edn. New Augusta (Miss.) H.S., 1982-83, Richton (Miss.) H.S., 1983-85; tchr. 1st grade Frisco City (Ala.) Elem. Schs., 1985-86; tchr. 4th grade Southside Elem. Sch., Evergreen, Ala., 1987-89, Thurgood Marshall Elem. Sch., Evergreen, 1989—. Named Tchr. of Yr., Conecuh County Bd. Edn., 1997-98. Mem. Internat. Reading Assn., Ala. Edn. Assn., Assn. Supervision and Curriculum, Nat. Assn. Elem. Sch. Prins., Nat. Coun. Tchrs. English, Sigma Gamma Rho, Kappa Delta Pi, Phi Delta Kappa. Avocations: singing, art. Home: PO Box 917 Evergreen AL 36401-0917

DAILEY, MICHAEL PATRICK, music educator; b. Miller, S.D., Oct. 21, 1957; s. Warren Elmo and Magdalen Theresa (Kluthe) D.; m. Suzanne Marie Dickes, June 7, 1986; children: Michael Francis, John Warren. MusB, Concordia Coll., Moorhead, Minn., 1979; MusM, U. S.D., 1985. Music educator Spencer (S.D.) Pub. Sch., 1980-81, Jefferson (S.D.) Pub. Schs., 1981-83; tchg. asst. U. S.D., Vermillion, 1983-85; music educator Auburn (Nebr.) Pub. Schs., 1985-86, St. Paul (Minn.) Acad., 1987-88, Robbinsdale Pub. Schs., New Hope, Minn., 1988-91, Farmington (Minn.) Pub. Schs., 1991-92, South Sioux City (Nebr.) City Cmty. Schs., 1993—. Faculty advisor Music Educator Nat. Conf., U. S.D., Vermillion, 1984-85; curriculum writing com. Robbinsdale Pub. Schs., New Hope, 1988-91; comprehensive arts planning program Farmington (Minn.) Pub. Schs., 1991-92; Nebr. K-12 visual and performing arts curriculum framework South Sioux City Schs./State Nebr., 1993—. Campaign vol. George McGovern Senate Campaign, Miller, S.D., 1974; contbr. Toy for Tots, South Sioux City, 1994. Alliss Found. scholar Concordia Coll., Moorhead, 1978. Mem. NEA, Am. Choral Dirs. Assn., Music Educators Nat. Conf. (faculty advisor 1984-85), Voice Care Network. Avocations: reading, listening to classical music, golfing. Home: 501 E 32nd St South Sioux City NE 68776-3351 Office: South Sioux City Cmty Schs 820 E 29th St South Sioux City NE 68776-3344

DAJANY, INNAM, academic administrator; b. American Fork, Utah, Oct. 9, 1951; d. Fuad Wafa and Doris Dean (Ault) Dajany; divorced; 1 child, Nadia Marina Fenton. BS, SUNY, Cortland, 1973; MEd, U. Idaho, 1985. Cert. elem. and secondary English tchr., Idaho, Wyo., N.Y. Tchr. Converse County Sch. Dist., Douglas, Wyo., 1973-75; newspaper reporter Casper (Wyo.) Star Tribune, 1974-76; rsch. asst. edn. dept. U. Idaho, Moscow, 1978-81, asst. dir. Early Childhood Learning Ctr., 1980-84, dir. Early Childhood Learning Ctr., 1984-90, cons., coord. Early Childhood Inst., 1989-91; mktg. and sales dir. Golden Arrow Hotel, Lake Placid, N.Y., 1990-92; continuing edn. asst. SUNY, Clinton C. C., 1992-94; coord. Riverview Acad., 1993-95; owner An Original Idea, Crown Point, N.Y., 1996. Cons. Gov.'s Commn. Children and Youth, Boise, Idaho, 1988-90, child devel. specialist region II coun., 1986-90; conf. coord. U.S. Agy. Internat. Devel., 1988-90; independent grant writer, 1993—; ind. real estate agent, patent writer, invention marketer; speaker in field; instr. English, writing SUNY-North County C.C., 1998—. Author: Building Your Child's Self Esteem During Home Reading, 1985, (booklet) You, Your Child, and Reading, 1986, (brochure) Help Arrest Child Abuse, 1982. Tchr., project coord. North Country Women at Work, 1993-95; advisor child care licensing laws City of Moscow, advisor HUD grant; coord. Parents in Action, Moscow, 1989, 90; co-pres. Moscow Swim Team, 1989, 90; leader Bluebirds, Moscow; active N.W. Found. grant, Ford Found. grant with KAID-TV. Mem. Nat. Assn. for Edn. Young Children (state pres. 1989-90, conf. chair 1985-87, leadership trainer and presenter 1981—), Internat. Reading Assn. (state pres. 1987-88, nat. com. literacy devel. 1987-89, nat. com. reading and arts 1985-87, leadership trainer and presenter 1981—), Phi Delta Kappa, Kappa Delta Phi. Avocations: hiking, reading, travel, learning, writing children's and young adult books. Home: PO Box 277 Crown Point NY 12928-0277 Office: Noteco Inc PO Box 533 Crown Point NY 12928-0533 also: SUNY-North County CC Saranac Lake NY 12983

DAKOFSKY, LADONNA JUNG, radiation oncologist, educator; b. N.Y.C., Oct. 30, 1960; d. George S. and Kay (Han) Chung. BA magna cum laude, Columbia U., N.Y.C., 1982; MD, NYU, 1987. Bd. cert. radiation oncologist. Rsch. asst. dept. neurology UCLA, 1980-81, Harvard U., Boston, 1982; tchr. chemistry St. Ann's Sch., Brooklyn Heights, N.Y., 1982-83; resident in internal medicine Lenox Hill Hosp., N.Y.C., 1987-88; resident in radiation oncology Hosp. of U. Pa., Phila., 1988-91; instr. in radiation oncology New Eng. Med. Ctr., Boston, 1991-92; attending physician Norwalk (Conn.) Hosp., 1992—. Clin. asst. prof. radiation oncology Yale U., 1994—; prin. investigator RTOG cancer rsch. Norwalk Hosp., exec. com. hosp. staff, IPA chair of quality improvement subcom.; physician adminstr. Norwalk Radiology Cons. Mem. jr. com. Boys Club N.Y.; sponsor Mus. City of N.Y.; mem. com. Vocat. Found., N.Y.C.; mem. Jr. League of Stamford-Norwalk. Marine Biol. Lab. scholar, 1981. Mem. AMA, Assn. Therapeutic Radiology and Oncology, Fairfield County Med. Assn. (Melville Magida award 1998, Best Younger Physician in Fairfield County 1998), New Eng. Cancer Soc., Met. Breast Cancer Group. Presbyterian. Avocations: writing, sailing, voice. Home: 14 Lamplight Ln Westport CT 06880-6106

DALE, BRENDA STEPHENS, gifted and talented educator; b. Hickory, N.C., Sept. 24, 1942; d. John Doyle and Bertha (Barger) Stephens; m. James Darrell Dale, June 13, 1964; children: Ginger Leigh Rizoti, Jami Lynne Price. BS in English, Appalachian State U., 1964, MA in Reading Edn., 1977; cert. edn. academically gifted, Lenoir Rhyne, Hickory, N.C., 1982. H.S. tchr. Moore County Schs., Carthage, N.C., 1964, Asheboro (N.C.) City Schs., 1964-65; 8th grade tchr. Davidson County Schs., Thomasville, N.C., 1967-68; reading specialist Randolph County Schs., Trinity, N.C., 1970-72, Wilkes N.C. Schs., Wilkesboro, 1972-82, tchr. acad. gifted, 1982—. Tchr. Davidson County C.C., Lexington, N.C., 1965-68, Wilkes C.C., Wilkesboro, 1982-87, 97—; adult literary tutor, 1995 Edn. chair, bd. dirs. Am. Cancer Soc., North Wilkesboro, N.C., 1985-90; mem. Wilkes Regional Med. Ctr. Aux., 1992—; adminstrv. coun. Wilkesboro Meth. Ch., 1997-1999; vol. Samaritan's Purse, 1997-99. Tchr. scholar fellow N.C. Ctr. for Advancement of Teaching, Western Carolina U., 1990; recipient C. B. Eller Teaching award C.B. Eller Found., 1991, N.W. NC Tchr. of Gifted of Yr., NC Assn. Gifted, 2003. Mem. AAUW (charter, fundraiser 1977-78, bd. dirs., chmn. edn. found. 1992-96), NEA, N.C. Assn. Educators (state del. 2002, intellectual profl. devel. com.), Internat. Reading Assn. (sec. 1985-86), Mary Hemphill Svc. Group, So. Appalachian Leadership on Cancer, Lynnwoode Recreation Club, United Meth. Women (dist. membership chair Western N.C. conf. 1996-97, nominating com. 1997-98), NC Assn. Edn. Com. Intellectual Profl. Devel. Com., 2003-2005, Alpha Delta Kappa. Methodist. Avocations: writing, reading, piano. Home: 187 Laurel Mountain Rd North Wilkesboro NC 28659-8122 Office: Wilkes County Schs Main St Wilkesboro NC 28697

DALE, CYNTHIA LYNN ARPKE, educational administrator, retired; b. Plymouth, Wis., Jan. 11, 1942; sd.; children: robert S., Peter D., Kimberly A. (Dale) Keaveny. BS, Wis. State U., Oshkosh, 1964; M degree, U. Ctrl. Fla. Cert. tchr., Wis., Fla. Tchr. Omro (Wis.) Sch. Sys., 1964, West Allis (Wis.) Sch. Sys., 1965-68; substitute tchr. Brevard County Sch. Sys., Melbourne, Fla., 1972-68; early edn. tchr. various schs. Melbourne, Fla., 1980-88; supr. site coord. for S. Brevard County Sch. Sys. Child Care Assn., Melbourne, Fla., 1988-93. Contbg. author: (poetry) A Far Out Place, 1994 (merit award), Forgetfulness, 1995 (merit award), Ickey Poo, A Special Birthday and Beth, 1996, Eh?, Beein' Around, Bad Habits, Memories, Ever Have One of Those Nights?, 1997. Mem. PTA various schs. sys.; mem. choir, Christian edn. com., Sunday sch. tchr. Palmdale Presbyn. Ch., Melbourne; cub scout den mother Boy Scouts Am., Melbourne; soccer mother, coach, asst. Little League, Melbourne, swimming instr.; mem. homeowner's assn. Groveland Mobile Home Park, Melbourne. Mem. AARP, ASCD, Audubon Soc., Internat. Soc. Poets. Republican. Avocations: writing, reading, swimming, hand sewing, dachsunds. Home: 523 Wavecrest Ct Melbourne FL 32934-8043

DALE, DAVID WILSON, English educator, poet; b. Helena, Mont., May 24, 1937; s. Arbie Myron and Dona Wilson Dale; m. Donna Jean Smatlan, Feb. 13, 1960; children: David Matthew, Erich Arbie, James Wilson. BA, Mont. State U., 1962; MA in English, U. Mont., 1969, MFA in Creative Writing, 1991. Cert. tchr. Tchr. English-Spanish Granger (Wash.) H.S., 1964-68; tchr. English Dawson Coll., 1969-70; tchr. English-Spanish Ronan (Mont.) H.S., 1970—75, 1976—99. Mem. exec. coun. Mont. Fedn. of Tchrs., Butte, 1978-82. Author: What We Call Our Own, 1991, The Way on Bear Is, 1994, Montanta Primer, 1996, Skating Backwards, 1999, Stumbling Over Stones, 2002. With USMC, USN, 1954-59. Mem. Mont. Edn. Assn. Democrat. Avocations: fishing, reading, music. Home: PO Box 257 Big Arm MT 59910-0257

DALE, DEBRA EILEEN, elementary school educator; b. Schurz, Nev., Dec. 1, 1953; d. William Winston and Marlene Coffey; m. Kee Dale Jr., Oct. 11, 1970; 1 child, Eileen Frances. AA, Truckee Meadows C.C., 1980; BS in Elem. Edn., U. Nev., 1982; M in Curriculum Instrn., Lesley Coll., Cambridge, Mass., 1992. Cert. tchr. K-8, Nev. Tchr. aide Reno/Sparks Headstart Program, Reno, 1972-73; tchr. aide summer sch. Washoe County Sch. Dist., Reno, 1972-81; community rels. tchr. aide Libby Booth Elem. Sch., Reno, 1973-78; tutor Reno/Sparks Colony, Reno, 1979-82; tchr. summer sch. Washoe County Sch. Dist., 1982; community rels. counselor Wooster/Reed High Schs., Reno, 1982-83; tchr. Roger Corbett Elem. Sch., Reno, 1983—97, Esther Bennett Elem. Sch., Sun Valley, Nev., 1997—2000, Natchez Elem. Sch., Wadsworth, Nev., 2000—. Mem. multi-cultural com. Washoe County Sch. Dist., 1992-93, mentor and lead tchr.; tchr. rep. Title V Indian Edn. Program, 1991—. Co-author: Celebrating Nevada Indians, 1992. Res. police officer Reno/Sparks Indian Colony Tribal Police, Reno, 1989-94. Recipient Outstanding Student Tchr. award U. Nev., 1982. Mem. NEA, Nev. State Edn. Assn., Nev. Native Am. Edn. Assn., Nev. Indian Rodeo Assn., Washoe Edn. Assn., Delta Kappa Gamma (nat. and internat.), Nev. Literacy Coalition, Nev. State Libr. Archives. Avocations: sewing, arts and crafts, drawing and painting. Office: Washoe County Sch Dist 425 E 9th St Reno NV 89512-2800

DALE, LEON ANDREW, economist, educator; b. Paris; m. Arlene R. Dale, Mar. 18, 1975; children: Melinda Jennifer, David Benjamin. BA, Tulane U., 1946; MA, U. Wis., 1947, PhD, 1949. Grad. asst. in econs. U. Wis., 1946-48; Asst. prof. labor econs. U. Fla., 1949-50; internat. economist AFL, Paris, 1950-53; AFL rep. at nat. labor convs. Greece, 1951, 1951, 1950-53; cons. U.S. Govt., 1954-56; internat. economist U.S. Dept. Labor, Washington, 1956-59; prof., chmn. dept. mgmt. and indsl. rels., dir. internat. ctr., coord. courses for fgn. students U. Bridgeport, Conn., 1960-69; chief union task force Coll. Bus. Admstrn. Calif. State Poly. U., Pomona, 1980, coord. internat. activities Sch. Bus. Adminstrn., 1969-77, prof. mgmt. and human resources, 1969-91, prof. emeritus, 1991—, also, acting chmn. bus. mgmt. dept., summer 1973; chief Coll. Bus. Adminstrn. Calif. State U., Pomona, 1981. Lectr. Internat. Conf. Tree Trade Unions Summer Sch., Wörgl, Austria, 1951; lectr. on Am. labor UN, Stockholm, 1952; lectr. U. Wis., Milw., 1960; asst. rschr., asst. moderator Labor Mgmt. Roundtable, 1961; participant televised ednl. programs Sta. WNHC-TV, New Haven, Conn., 1963; seminar leader Mgmt. Ctr, Cambridge, 1962-63, Rey area Police Dept.; Columbia U., 1966, 67, Bernard Baruch Sch. Bus. and Pub. Adminstrn., 1966-69; corrd. adminstrv. ops. and pub. rels. Rey Area Police Pers., 1966; instr. Perkins-Elmer Corp., Wilton, Conn., 1966; cons., arbitrator, fact-finder State of Conn., 1964-69; Am. del., speaker 3d Internat. Symposium on Small Bus., Washington, 1976, 4th Internat. Symposium on Small Bus., Seoul, Korea, 1977, 5th Internat. Symposium on Small Bus., Anaheim, Calif., 1978, 6th Internat. Symposium on Small Bus., Berlin, 1979; also mem. U.S. steering com. Internat. Symposium on Small Bus.; chief union task force Coll. Bus. Adminstrn. Calif. State Poly. U., Pomona, 1980; sr. cons. Am. Grad. U., Covina, Calif., 1981-82; adj. prof. econs. Nat. U., San Diego, 1981-90, Pepperdine U., 1986; discussion leader Calif. Inst. Tech. Internat. Conf. on Combining Best of Japanese and U.S. Mgmt., Anaheim, 1981; lectr. on indsl. rels. to execs. Miller Brewing Co., Irwindale, Calif., 1983; cons. Agy. Internat. Devel., N'Djamena, Republic of Chad, 1987; cons. to Minister for Planning, Republic of Chad; cons., instr. behavior courses U. Chad.; instr. mgmt. French-speaking African Students internat. ctr. Calif. State Poly. U., 1988; participant Ea. Europe and the West: Implication for Africa, So. Calif. Consortium on Internat. Studies conf., Pomona, 1990; lectr. confs. on leadership in French, Dakar, Senegal, 1990; seminar tchr. on leadership and mgmt. Citibank of N.Y., Dakar, Senegal, 1991; presenter, speaker numerous seminars in field; adj. prof. mgmt. Chapman U., Orange, Calif., 1994; adj. prof. econs. Saddleback Coll., Mission Viejo, Calif., 1996, Irvine (Calif.) Valley Coll., 1997, prof. French and econs., 2001. Author: Marxism and French Labor, 1956, A Bibliography of French Labor, 1969; (video tape) Industrial Relations and Human Resources, 1982, Labor Relations in Crisis, 1989; originator Liberté (first French newspaper published in liberated France, 1944); French news announcer to occupied France, BBC London; contbr. articles to profl. jours. Served with U.S. Army, 1942-45. Recipient U. Bridgeport Faculty rsch. grantee, 1962; U. Wis. fellow, 1949; named one of Outstanding Educators of Am., 1972, 73. Mem. Am. Arbitration Assn. (nat. labor panel 1967—), N.Y. Acad. Scis. Avocations: tennis, swimming, ancient and modern art, horticulture, numismatics, philately. Home and Office: 30 S La Senda Dr Laguna Beach CA 92651-6733

DALE, SAM E., JR., retired educational administrator; b. Harmon, La., July 10, 1921; s. Sam E. and Willie Edith (Parr) D.; m. Cathleen Trichel; 1 child: Cathy Sue. BS in Vocat. Agr., La. State U., Baton Rouge, 1947, MS in Vocat. Agr., 1954, PhD in Vocat. Agr., 1972. With Catahoula Parish Sch. Bd., Jonesville, La., 1948-85, supervising prin., 1969-72, dir. career and vocat. edn., 1973-79, supt., 1979-85. Mem. adv. coun. La. State U.; mem. supts. coun. La. Bd. Elem. and Secondary Edn. Chmn. bd. trustees Catahoula Hosp. Dist. #2; mem. County agrl. stabilization and conservation com. Mem. La. Ret. Supts. Assn., La. Ret. Tchrs. Assn., Gideons, Am. Legion. Baptist. Home: PO Box 56 Sicily Island LA 71368-0056

D'ALEO, PENNY FREW, special education educator, consultant; b. Willimantic, Conn., Jan. 15, 1961; d. Hurlburt Harrison and Bettie Jane (Bovee) Frew; m. John Francis D'Aleo, June 25, 1983; children: Gregory, Shelly. BS, So. Conn. State U., 1983; MEd, Westfield State Coll., 1987. Cert. comprehensive K-12 spl. edn. tchr. pre-K and kindergarten, adult edn. tchr., Conn. Learning disabilities specialist Suffield (Conn.) Bd. Edn., 1983-92, 94—, Enfield (Conn.) Adult Edn., 1992-94. Sch. liaison Greater Suffield Learning Disabilities Assn., 1988-89; trained mentor for Conn. BEST program, 1988; conducted pvt. self-esteem workshops for exceptional children, 1992; presenter in field. Mem. adminstrv. bd., fin. bd., Here Wee Grow pre-sch. bd. United Meth. Ch., Hazardville, Conn., 1984-87, 95—. Paul Harris fellow Rotary Internat., 1988. Mem. NEA, Coun. Exceptional Children, KC Aux. (pres. 1987-88, KC Woman of Yr. 1987), Johnson Meml. Hosp. Aux. Republican. Avocations: water skiing, reading, writing, tennis, golf. Home: 41 Grant Rd Enfield CT 06082-5738 Office: Spaulding Elem Sch Mountain Rd Suffield CT 06078

DALESIO, WESLEY CHARLES, former aerospace educator; b. Paterson, N.J., Mar. 26, 1930; s. William James and Sarah (Sheets) Delison; m. Dorothy May Zellers, Nov. 17, 1951; children: Michael Kerry, Debra Kaye Dalesio Weber. Student, Tex. Christian U., 1950, U. Tex., Arlington, 1957. Enlisted USAF, 1948, advanced through grades to sr. master sgt., 1968, aircraft engine mech., mgmt. analyst, 1948-70; ins. agt. John Hancock Ins., Denver, 1970-71; office mgr. Comml. Builder, Denver, 1972-73; aerospace educator Sch. Dist. 50, Westminster, Colo., 1973-93. Dir. aerospace edn. CAP, Denver, 1982—86, Denver, 1994—2000. Mem. Crimestoppers, Westminster, 1988-91, Police and Citizens Teamed Against Crime, Westminster, 1992-93. Lt. col. CAP, 1981—. Mem. Nat. Assn. Ret. Mil. Instrs. (charter mem.), Westminster Edn. Assn., 7th Bomb Wing B-36 Assn. (life), Internat. Platform Assn., Nat. Aeronautic Assn., Acad. Model Aeronautics, Arvada Associated Modelers (life). Episcopalian. Avocations: antique collecting, leatherwork, flying miniature aircraft, model car collecting. Home: 2537 W 104th Cir Westminster CO 80234-3507

DALESSANDRI, KATHIE MARIE, surgeon, educator; b. Stambaugh, Michigan, May 4, 1947; d. Paris H. and Kathryn (Macuga) D.; m. Gordon William Frost, 1986. BS, Mich. Technol. U., 1969; MS, Purdue U., 1971; MD, U. Mich., 1976. diplomate, Am. Bd. Surgery. Intern. Martinez VA Hosp., Calif., 1976-77; resident U. Calif., Davis, Calif., 1977-81; gen. surgeon Martinez VA Hosp., Calif., 1982-92; asst. prof. surgery U. Calif., Davis, Calif., 1983-93; staff surgeon Palo Alto VA Hosp., Palo Alto, Calif., 1992—, Palo Alto VA Hosp., Palo Alto, Calif., 1992—98; assoc. clin. prof. Stanford U., Calif., 1993—; assoc. rsch. sci. U. Calif., Berkeley, Calif., 2003—. Gen. surgeon, Project Hope, Grenada, 1984, 89; Hosp. Albert Sweitzer, Haiti, 1986. Contbr. articles to med. jours. VA grantee, 1983. Fellow ACS, ; mem. Am. Med. Women's Assn., Nat. Coun. Internat. Health, S.W. Surg. Soc. Avocations: water sports, hiking, nature walks.

DALESSIO, DONALD JOHN, internist, neurologist, educator; b. Jersey City, Mar. 2, 1931; s. John Andrea and Susan Dorothy (Minotta) Dalessio; m. Jane Catherine Schneider, Sept. 4, 1954 (dec. Mar. 1998); children: Catherine Leah, James John, Susan Jane. BA, Wesleyan U., 1952; MD, Yale U., 1956. Diplomate Am. Bd. Internal Medicine. Intern N.Y.C. Hosp., 1956-57, asst. resident in medicine and neurology, 1959-61; resident in medicine Yale Med. Ctr., 1961-62; pres. med. staff Scripps Clinic, La Jolla, Calif., 1974-78; chmn. dept. medicine Scripps Clin., La Jolla, Calif., 1974-89, chmn. emeritus, 1989—, cons., 1982—, pres. med. group, 1980-81; clin. prof. neurology U. Calif., San Diego, 1973—. Physician in chief Green Hosp., La Jolla, 1974—89; pres. Am. Assn. Study Headache, Chgo., 1974—76; chmn. Fedn. Western Soc. Neurology, Santa Barbar, Calif., 1976—77; Musser-Burch lectr. Tulane U., 1979; Kash lectr. U. Ky., 1979. Author: (book) Wolff's Headache, 7th edit., 2001, Approach to Headache, 1973, Approach to Headache, 6th edit., 1999; editor: Headache jour., 1965—75, 1979—84, Scripps Clinic Personal Health Letter; mem. editl. bd. Jour. AMA, 1977—87; columnist: San Diego Tribune. Pres. Nat. Migraine Found., Chgo., 1977—79. Capt. U.S. Army, 1957—59. Recipient Disting. Alumnus award, Wesleyan U., 1982. Fellow: ACP; mem.: World Fedn. Neurology (Am. sec. 1980—90, mem. rsch. group migraine), Am. Acad. Neurology (assoc.), La Jolla Beach/Tennis Club, La Jolla Country Club. Avocations: tennis, squash, piano. Home: 8891 Nottingham Pl La Jolla CA 92037-2131 Office: Scripps Clinic & Rsch Found 10666 N Torrey Pines Rd La Jolla CA 92037-1092

D'ALESSIO, JACQUELINE ANN, English educator; b. Morristown, N.J., Jan. 26, 1943; d. Clifford Corbet and Helen Ann (Chrenko) Compton; m. Harold F. D'Alessio, Oct. 28, 1967. BA in English, Coll. New Rochelle, 1964; MA in English, Seton Hall U., 1969. Tchr. Bridgewater (N.J.)-Raritan Regional Sch. Dist., 1964—. Advisor dramatics Bridgewater-Raritan Mid. Sch., Bridgewater, N.J., 1983—. Chmn. pub. rels. Mt. St. Mary Devel. Office, 1985-2000; bd. dirs. N.J. Legis Agenda for Women, Inc., 1993-94. Recipient Gov. Tchr. Recognition, N.J. Dept. Edn., Trenton, 1989, Disting. Svc. award Bridgewater-Raritan Regional Sch. Dist., 2001; named Outstanding Elem. Tchr. in U.S., 1971. Mem. AAUW (N.J. pres. 1990-94, program v.p. 1988-90, rep. Women's Agenda 1989-94, dir. pub. policy 1997-99, treas. 1999—, mid-Atlantic region dir. 2001—). Roman Catholic. Avocations: travel, golf, biking, gardening. Home: 30 Putnam St Somerville NJ 08876-2737

DALEY, VETA ADASSA, educational administrator; b. St. Elizabeth, Jamaica, Jan. 14, 1953; came to U.S., 1981; d. Waldemar and Princess (Bartley) Solomon; m. Vincent Daley, Jan. 27, 1973; children: Yuland, Angelo. Cert. in edn., U. W.I., Jamaica, 1978; BS, Westfield (Mass.) State Coll., 1987, MEd in Adminstrn., 1991. Tchr. Ministry Edn., Jamaica, 1972-81, Forest Park Jr.-Mid. Sch., Springfield, Mass., 1987-92; grad. asst. Westfield State Coll., 1988-90; asst. prin. Duggan Mid. Sch., Springfield, 1992-94; prin. John F. Kennedy Mid. Sch., Springfield, 1994—. Mem. Mass. Curriculum Adv. Commn., Malden, 1992—. Advisor Jamaica Festival Commn., Mandeville, 1973-80, Jamaica 4-H Clubs, 1970-76; vice chmn. adminstrv. bd. Wesley United Meth. Ch., Springfield, 1988—, pres. Meth. Women, 1991-93; chmn. Liberian Christian Fund, Springfield, 1990, New Eng. Conf. United Meth. Women, 1994; mem. African Task Force-R.I., 1991—. Recipient Outstanding Achievement award Jamaica 4-H Clubs, 1975, Outstanding Achievement in Edn. award Jamaican Cmty., Springfield, 1992, citation Mass. Ho. of Reps., 1992. Mem. New Eng. League Mid. Schs., Springfield Adminstrv. Assn., Jack and Jill Am. (pres.

Springfield chpt. 1992—, Disting. Mother of Yr. award ea. region 1994). Home: 81 Embury St Springfield MA 01109-1847 Office: John F Kennedy Mid Sch 1385 Berkshire Ave Indian Orchard MA 01151-1819

DALGARNO, ALEXANDER, astronomy educator; b. London, Jan. 5, 1928; s. William and Margaret (Murray) D.; m. Barbara W.F. Kane, Oct. 31, 1957 (div.); children: Penelope, Rebecca, Piers, Fergus; m. Emily K. Izsak, June 23, 1972 (div.). BSc, U. London, 1947, PhD, 1951; MA (hon.), Harvard U., 1967; DSc (hon.), Queen's U. Belfast, 1980, York U., Can., 2000. Lectr. Queen's U., Belfast, Northern Ireland, 1951-56, reader, 1956-61, prof. math. physics, 1961-67, dir. computation lab., 1961-66; prof. astronomy Harvard U., Cambridge, Mass., 1967—, Phillips prof., 1977—, chmn. dept., 1971-76; dir. Inst. for Theoretical Atomic and Molecular Physics, 1989-93. Assoc. dir. Ctr. for Astrophysics Harvard U., 1973-80; acting dir. Harvard Coll. Obs., 1971-73; rsch. scientist Smithsonian Astrophys. Obs., Cambridge, Mass., 1967—; Vikram A. Sarabhai prof. Phys. Rsch. Lab., Ahmedebad, 2002; Jan Hendrik Oort prof. U. Leiden, 2003; Charles M. and Martha Hitchcock prof. U. Calif., Berkeley, 2003. Editor: Astrophys. Jour. Letters, 1973—2002; contbr. articles to profl. jours. Recipient Hodgkins medal Smithsonian Instn., 1977, Spiers Medal, Royal Soc. Chemistry, 1992; fellow UMIST, 1992, Univ. Coll. London, 1976. Fellow: Internat. Acad. Quantum Molecular Sci. (ann. prize 1967), Internat. Acad. Astronautics, Royal Astron. Soc. (Gold medal 1986), Am. Acad. Arts and Scis., Am. Geophys. Union (Fleming medal 1995), Optical Soc. Am. (Meggers award 1986), Am. Phys. Soc. (Davisson-Germer award 1980), Phys. Soc. (London), Royal Soc. (Hughes medal 2002), Royal Irish Acad. (hon.); mem.: NAS. Home: 27 Robinson St Cambridge MA 02138-1403 Office: Harvard-Smithsonian Ctr Astrophysics 60 Garden St Cambridge MA 02138 E-mail: adalgarno@cfa.harvard.edu.

DALGLISH, MEREDITH RENNELS, artist, educator; b. Bryn Mawr, Pa., Apr. 15, 1941; d. James Garven and Esther Jane (Parsons) D.; m. Thorsten Horton, July 27, 1970 (div. June 1976); m. William G. Beebe, Mar. 23, 1985 (div. 1997). BA, Goddard Coll., 1967; postgrad., U. Wis., 1970-72; MFA, Claremont (Calif.) Grad. Sch., 1983. Dir. Ormond Art Mus., Ormond Beach, Fla., 1986-87; adj. prof. Daytona Beach C.C., 1988-90; art specialist Volusia County Schs., Daytona, Fla., 1990-91; adj. prof. Miami (Fla.) Dade C.C., 1991-93; founder, dir. Women's Inst. for Creativity, Inc., Miami, 1992—; adj. prof. Fla. Internat. U., Miami, 1993—. Adv. bd. Volusia County Arts Commn., Daytona, 1990-91, Women's Caucus for Art, Miami, 1993-95; founder, pres., dir. Women's Inst. for Creativity, Inc., Miami, 1992—; vis. artist Volksogschool, Bergen, Holland, China, Japan, 1976-77, Isle of Eigg, Scotland, 1977; guest artist U. So. Calif., Idyllwild, 1982, Orange County (Calif.) Arts Festival, 1985, Stetson U., DeLand, Fla., 1986, Orlando (Fla.) Mus. Art, 1987; artist in residence Project Leap, Palm Beach County, Fla., 1996—, Arts in Medicine Program, U. Miami, 1996, 2001, Mendocino (Calif.) Art Ctr., 2002-03; artist in edn. State of Fla., 1997—; lectr. in field. One-woman shows include MIEL Ctr., Miami, 1994, 1st Union Bank, Ft. Lauderdale, Fla., 1995; exhibited in group shows at Polk C.C., Winter Haven, Fla., 1987, Zanesville (Ohio) Mus., 1987, Stetson U., 1988, Nat. Assn. Women Artists Centennial Anniversary Exhibit, N.Y.C., 1989, Fla. Ctr. for Contemporary Art, Tampa, 1989, Ceramic League of Miami, 1990 (award), St. Thomas U., Miami, 1995, juried exhbn., 1995, others; represented in permanent collections Ralph Rudin Designs, L.A.,Hyatt-Regency Hotel, Orlando, Sheraton Hotel, Naples, Fla., Marriott Hotel, Washington, Ramada Inn Hotel, Beverly Hills, Calif., Sheraton-Scottsdale (Ariz.) Hotel, Gallery Contemporanea, Jacksonville, Fla., Exec. Suites Holiday Inn, Schenectady, N.Y., IBM Corp., Miami, Adminstrv. Suites Omni Internat. Hotel, Miami, Hilton Hotel, Atlanta, also pvt. collections; prin. works include San Francisco Mus. Art, Barnsdall Mcpl. Art Mus., L.A., Claremont Grad. Sch., U. So. Calif., Idyllwild, Orlando Mus. Art, DeLand Mus., Stetson U., DeLand, Francis Lewis Collection, Dayton Beach C.C.; documented in book The Dinner Party (Judy Chicago), 1979; featured artist Internat. Ceramics Festival, Sao Paulo, Brazil, 1997; documented in film Right Out of History-The Making of The Dinner Party, 1979; prodr.: (video) Earthwing, 1988; TV appearances, live performances. Vol. The Dinner Party Feminist Art Installation, 1977; pres.-elect Women's Caucus for Art, Miami, 1994. Grantee Ruth Chenven Found., N.Y.C., 1990; recipient Elizabeth Kittrell award Kittrell Found., 1969, award Dade Cmty. Found., Miami, 1993. Mem. Layerist Soc., Transformative Art, Nat. Assn. Women Artists, Coll. Art Assn. Avocations: writing, snorkeling, boating, swimming. Office: PO Box 765 45200 Little Lake St Mendocino CA 95460 Business E-Mail: merart@bigplanet.com.

DALINKA, MURRAY KENNETH, radiologist, educator; b. Bklyn., May 13, 1938; s. Joseph and Gertrude (Cohen) D.; m. Janice L. Kolber, Feb. 28, 1982; 1 son, Bradford Gordon; children by previous marriage: Ilene, Ian Scott. BS, U. Mich., 1960, MD, 1964. Diplomate Am. Bd. Radiology. Intern Pa. Hosp., Phila., 1964-65; resident in radiology Montefiore Hosp., N.Y.C., 1965-68; instr. radiology Harvard Med. Sch., 1970-71; from asst. prof. to assoc. prof. radiology Thomas Jefferson U. Hosp., Phila., 1971-76, prof., 1976—; chief orthop. radiology Hosp. U. Pa., 1976—. Chief diagnostic radiology Thomas Jefferson U. Hosp., Phila., 1974-76; . cons.hila. Naval Hosp., 1974-79, Walson Hosp., Ft. Dix Army Base, 1972-77. Author: Arthography, 1980, Symposium on Orthopedic Radiology, 1983; mem. editorial bd. Bone Syllabus IV, 1982—, Skeletal Radiology, 1982—, Conversations in Radiology, 1977-79; guest editor Emergency Medicine Clinics of North America, Vol. 3, 1985; editor: (with J.J. Kaye) Radiology in Emergency Medicine Clinics in Emergency, Vol. 3, 1984, (with J. Edeiken and D. Karasick) Edeiken's Roentgen Diagnosis of Diseases of Bone, 4th edit. Served to capt. USAF, 1968-70. James Picker research fellow, 1972-73 Mem. Internat. Skeletal Soc. (past pres.), Radiol. Soc. N.Am., Am. Coll. Radiology (chmn. panel on musculoskeletal imaging, mem. task force on appropriateness criteria/diagnostic patient care guidelines), Phila. Roentgen Ray Soc. (past pres.). Home: 318 S 21st St Philadelphia PA 19103-6531 Office: U Pa Hosp Dept Radiology 3400 Spruce St Philadelphia PA 19104-4206 E-mail: dalinka@oasis.rad.upenn.edu.

DALMAS-BROWN, CARMELLA JEAN, special education educator; b. Dec. 31, 1959; d. Bruno L. and Mary S. (Pashinski) Dalmas; m. Charles T. Brown; 1 child, Kathlina. AS in Edn., Luzerne County C.C., 1979; BS in Spl. and Elem. Edn., Coll. of Misericordia, 1981; MS in Elem. Edn., Wilkes Coll., 1989. Cert. mentally/physically handicapped tchr., Pa. Substitute tchr. Luzerne Intermediate Unit 18, Kingston, Pa., 1983-84, Pope John Paul II Sch., Nanticoke, Pa., 1983-84, Genesis Sch./First Hosp. Wyo. Valley, Wilkes-Barr, Pa., 1983-84, tchr., 1984-88, head tchr., 1988-94; dir. edn. Genesis Sch., 1995—2000; tchr. spl. edn. Greater Nanticoke Area Sch. Dist., 2000—. Presenter in field; spl. edn. advisor Best Buddies chpt., cheerleader advisor Greater Nanticoke HS. Tchr. Diocese of Scranton, St. Mary's Parish, Nanticoke; former leader brownie troop Girl Scouts USA, now junior leader. Mem. Coun. of Exceptional Children. Democrat. Roman Catholic. Avocations: reading, sports, arts and crafts, photography. Home: 124 W Broad St Nanticoke PA 18634-2205 Office: Greater Nanticoke Area Sch Dist Nanticoke PA 18634-

DALPINO, IDA JANE, retired secondary education educator; b. Newhall, Calif., Oct. 20, 1936; d. Bernhardt Arthur and Wahneta May (Blyler) Melby; m. Gilbert Augustus, June 14, 1963 (div. 1976); 1 child, Nicolette Jane. BA, Calif. State U., Chico, 1960; postgrad., Sacramento State, 1961-65, Sonoma State, 1970-71; MA, U. San Francisco, 1978. Cert. cmty. counselor, learning handicapped, c.c. instr., exceptional children, pupil pers. specialist, secondary tchr., resource specialist. Tchr. Chico High Sch., 1959-60; counselor Mira Loma High Sch., Sacramento, 1960-66; tchr. ESL Phoenix Ind. High Sch., 1968-69; resource specialist Yuba City (Calif.) High Sch., 1971-2000; ret., 2000. English tchr. Rough Rock Demonstration Sch., summers, 1975, 76. Office sec. Job's Daus., North Bend, Oreg., 1953—; active Environ. Def. Fund, Centerville Hist. Assn., Chico, 1991—. Mem. NEA, Calif. Tchrs. Assn., Chico State Alumni Assn., Sierra Club, Nature Conservancy, Audubon, Greenpeace, Sigma Kappa Alumni. Democrat. Mem. Science of the Mind Church. Avocations: reading, ecology, genealogy. Home: 6 Navajo Ln Corte Madera CA 94925 E-mail: idajane@comcast.net.

DALSIMER, ANTHONY STEARNS, retired foreign service officer, educator; b. N.Y.C., July 30, 1935; s. Allan Furth Dalsimer and Helen Stearns; m. Isabel Ann Price (div.); m. Marilyn Nowak (div.); children: Allyn Ann, Melanie, Heather. BA, Grinnell Coll., 1957; MA, Fletcher Sch. Law & Diplomacy, 1958; postgrad., Stanford U., 1971-72, Howard U., 1973-75; MS, U. D.C., 1991. Staff econ. office Dept. of State, Washington, 1960, officer in charge Guinea and Dahomey, 1971-73, divsn. chief Exch. North and West Africa, 1973-75, divsn. chief Cultural Exch. So. and East Africa, 1975-77, dir. rsch. for Africa, 1985-88, dir. Office Ctrl. African Affairs, 1988-91, dir. Office Hist. Document Rev., 1994-97; vice consul/econ. officer Am. Embassy, Ouagadougou, Upper Volta, 1961-63, vice consul Bamako, Mali, 1965, comml. attache Kinshasa, Zaire, 1967-69, dep. chief of mission Ndjamena, Chad, 1977-79, counselor polit. affairs Kinshasa, Zaire, 1979-81, dep. chief of mission Ouagadougou, Burkina Faso, 1981-84, counselor for labor affairs Paris, 1991-94; gen. mgr. Dalsimer Florist, Cedarhurst, N.Y., 1963-64; vice consul Am. Consulate, Hargeisa, Somalia, 1966-67, consul Bukavu, Congo, 1969-70; adj. faculty African history, internat. rels., govt. and politics U. South Fla., Sarasota, 1997—. Lectr. Elder Hostels Eckerd Coll., 2001—. Vol. ARC, Helen Payne Sch. Mem.: Fgn. Svc. Ret. Assn. Fla. (bd. dirs.), Diplomats and Consular Officers, Am. Fgn. Svc. Assn., Greencroft Condo Assn. (pres. 2001—). Democrat. Unitarian Universalist.

DALTON, ALICE L. GORGEN, nursing educator, consultant; b. Glenwood Springs, Col., June 13, 1950; m. Forrest Dean Dalton, Sept. 10, 1993; 1 child, Matthew. Diploma, Immanuel Hosp. Sch. Nursing, 1974; BSN, Midland Coll., 1990; MS, Creighton U., 1998. RN, Nebr.; ACLS, paramedic. Staff nurse emergency dept. Immanuel Med. Ctr., Omaha, 1974-82; mem. faculty Creighton U., Omaha, 1982-95; paramedic nurse coord. Omaha Fire Dept., 1989-93; trauma nurse coord. St. Joseph Hosp., Omaha, 1995-97; EMS edn. coord. Omaha Fire Dept., 1998—2002; clin. educator Pridemark Paramedic Svcs., Boulder, 2002—. Author: Pocket Guide for EMT Prehospital Care, 1994, Advanced Medical Life Support, 1998, Paramedic Refresher: A Case Based Approach, 1999; contbr. articles to profl. jours. Mem. Nat. Assn. Emergency Med. Technicians (prehosp. trauma life support award 1994), Emergency Nurses Assn. (cert.), Nebr. Emergency Med. Technicians Assn. (Ken Kimball award 1992, Maggie award 1986). Office: Pridemark PAramedic Svcs 3297 Walnut St Boulder CO 80301

DALTON, CARYL, school psychologist; b. Mineral Wells, Tex., Aug. 8, 1949; d. Pat Francis Dalton and Yvonne (Ridings) Erwin. BA, U. Tex., 1970, MEd, 1977, PhD, 1987. Tchr. Brown Schs., Austin, San Marcos, Tex., 1971-73; homebound tchr. Rochester (N.Y.) City Schs., 1974-75; asst. dir. Big Buddies, Austin, Tex., 1975-77; ednl. cons. Edn. Svc. Ctr. XIII, Austin, Tex., 1978-79, pvt. practice, Austin, Tex., 1979-84; asst. instr. U. Tex., Austin, Tex., 1983-86; from doctoral intern to sch. psychologist Balcones Special Svcs. Coop., Austin, Tex., 1986-93; psychologist pvt. practice Austin, Tex., 1989—. Cons. Edn. Svc. Ctr. XIII, Austin; adj. prof. U. Tex., Austin, 1990. Mem. YMCA, Austin, Tex., bd. dirs. Austin (Tex.) Rape Crisis Ctr. Mem. APA, Tex. Psychol. Assn. (pub. info. chmn. 1995-96), Audubon Soc. Office: 5750 Balcones Dr Ste 201 Austin TX 78731-4269

DALTON, CLAUDETTE ELLIS HARLOE, anesthesiologist, educator, university official; b. Roanoke, Va., Jan. 18, 1947; d. John Pinckney and Dorothy Anne (Ellis) Harloe; m. Henry Tucker Dalton, May 17, 1973 (div. 1979); 1 child, Gordon Tucker; m. H. Christopher Alexander, III, April 29, 2000. BA, Sweet Briar Coll., 1969; MD, U. Va., 1974. Resident in anesthesiology U. N.C., Chapel Hill, 1974—77; med. edn. Lenoir County Meml Hosp./East Carolina U., Kinston, 1978—80; med. edn. in intensive care Presbyn Hosp., Charlotte, NC, 1981—82; practice anesthesiology Charlotte Eye, Ear, Nose and Throat Hosp., 1982—85, Medivision of Charlotte and Orthopedic Hosp. of Charlotte, 1985—89; asst. prof. U. Va. Health Scis. Ctr., Charlottesville, Va., 1992—; dir. Office of Cmty. Based Med. Edn., Charlottesville, 1994—; asst. dean for cmty. based med. edn. U. Va., Charlottesville, 1996—, med. dir. Pre-Anesthesia Clinic, 1996—, asst. prof. anesthesiology and med. edn., 1996—. Author developer patient edn. materials for illiterate patients, 1979—, emergency med. svc. tng. program, 1981. Bd. dirs. Charlottesville Family Svcs., Family Svcs. Albemarle County, 1992-93, U. Va. Women's Ctr., 1996—, Coun. on Aging, Lenoir County C.C., Am. Cancer Soc.; exec. dir. Cmty. Involvement Coun. Lenoir County, Kinston, 1979; county coord. Internat. Yr. of Child, Kinston, 1979; mem. sch. medicine com. on women U. Va. Med. Sch.; also others. Named Commencement spkr., U. Va. Sch. Medicine Graduation, 1993; recipient Gov.'s award, State of N.C., 1980, cert. of merit for svc. to children, N.C. Dept. Human Resources, Outstanding Tchg. award, U. Va. Sch. Medicine, 1993, Sharon L. Hostler U. Va. Outstanding Woman in Medicine award, 2002. Mem.: Va. Soc. Anesthesiology, Albemarle County Med. Soc., Va. Med. Soc. (bd. dirs. Va. Health Quality Coun. 1995—97, chair ad hoc com. on telemedicine 1996—99, 2d v.p. 1998—99, chair scope of practice com. 1999—2002, dist. dir. 1999—, Med. Sch. Va. alt. del. 2001—, coun. on med. edn. AMA 2003, editor med. news Va. Med. Quar., mem. legis. com., mem. health access com., del. to ann. meeting, reference com., mem. strategic planning and implementation com., mem. women's com., mem. med. affairs com., mem. bd. medicine adv. com.), Alpha Omega Alpha, U. Va. Med. Alumni Assn. (assoc. bd. dirs. 1989—92, chair women in medicine leadership conf. 1998—99). Avocations: natural history, environment, dancing, writing, gardening. Office: U Va Med Sch PO Box 800325 Charlottesville VA 22908-0325 E-mail: ced2t@virginia.edu.

DALTON, LARRY RAYMOND, chemistry educator, researcher, consultant; b. Belpre, Ohio, Apr. 25, 1945; s. Leonard William Henry and Virginia (Maylee) D.; m. Nicole A. Boand. BS with honors, Mich. State U., 1965, MS, 1966; AM, PhD, Harvard U., 1971. Asst. prof. chemistry Vanderbilt U., Nashville, 1971-73, assoc. prof., 1973-77, research prof. biochemistry, 1977-98; assoc. prof. SUNY-Stony Brook, 1976-81, prof., 1981-82, U. So. Calif., Los Angeles, 1982-94, Harold Moulton prof. chemistry, 1994-98, sci. co-dir. Loker hydrocarbon rsch. inst., 1994-98, prof. materials sci. and engring., 1994-98; prof. chemistry U. Wash., 1998—. Dir. NSF Sci. and Tech. Ctr. for Info. Tech. Rsch., 2002—; cons., IBM Corp., Yorktown, N.Y., IBM Instruments Co., Danbury, Conn., 1977-85, Celanese Rsch. Corp., 1987-90, Lockheed Missiles and Space Co., 1988-90, Maxdem Inc., 1990; cons. rev. of NIH sickle cell ctrs. USPHS, 1981-82; mem. parent com. for rev. of comprehensive sickle cell ctrs. Nat. Heart, Lung, Blood Inst.-NIH, 1987, 92; panelist for presdl. young investigator awards NSF, Washington, 1983, 89, panelist for presdl. faculty fellow awards, 1986, mem. materials rsch. adv. com., 1984-90, mem. high magnetic field panel, 1987, info. tech. rsch. panel, 2000; bd. dirs. Key Mgmt., Inc., Bomans, Inc.; mem. NAS-NRC panel for selection of NSF predoctoral fellows, 1989—; mem. panel for selection DOD predoctoral fellows. Editor-author: EPR and Advanced EPR Studies of Biological Systems, 1985 Recipient Burlington No. Found. Faculty Achievement award, 1986, U. So. Calif. Assocs. award, 1990, Profl. Achievement award Spring Arbor Coll., 1993, Disting. Alumni award Mich. State U., 2000; Camille and Henry Dreyfus tchr./scholar, 1975-77; rsch. career devel. grantee NIH, 1976-81; Alfred P. Sloan Found. fellow, 1974-77. Mem. Am. Chem. Soc. (Richard C. Tolman medal 1996, Chemistry of Materials award 2003), Sigma Xi. Avocations: skiing, hiking. Office: U Wash Dept Chemistry PO Box 351700 Seattle WA 98195-1700 E-mail: dalton@chem.washington.edu.

DALY, JOHN AUGUSTINE, communications management researcher and educator; b. Camp Adebury, Ind., June 30, 1952; s. John Augustine and Edith Winslow (Elliott) D.; m. Christine Walaity, Aug. 17, 1974 (div. 1988); 2 children: m. Anita Vangelisti, May 27, 1994. BA, U. Md., 1973; MA, W.Va. U., 1974; PhD, Purdue U., 1977. Vis. lectr. W.Va. U., Morgantown, 1974-90; asst. prof. communication U. Tex., Austin, 1977-82, assoc. prof., 1982-88, Blunk Meml. prof., 1987-88, prof., 1988-94, Amon Carter prof. comm. and mgmt., 1994-98, Liddell prof. comm., 1998—, Univ. Disting. Tchg. prof., 1998—, TCB prof. mgmt., 1999—. Cons. numerous cos. and govt. agys. including the White House 1993. Author: Personality and Interpersonal Communication, 1986, Teaching Communications: Methods, Theory and Research, 1991, 2d edit., 1999, Strategic Communication, 1994, Avoiding Communication: Shyness, Reticence and Communication Apprehension, 1997, Personality: Communication Perspective, 1998, Handbook of Interpersonal Communication, 2003, Presentations in Everyday Life, 2004; editor: Written Comm., 1983-90; Comm. Edn., 1985-87; mem. editl. bd. Human Comm. Rsch., 1977—, Comm. Edn., 1987—, Comm. Monographs, 1983—, Jour. Personal and Social Rels., 1987-90; mem. adv. bd. Orgnl. Comm. Abstracts, 1980-85; contbr. articles to profl. jours. Grantee Fund for Improvement of Postsecondary Edn., 1980-82; Allan Shivers fellow, 1986-87. Mem. APA, Internat. Communication Assn. (v.p. 1979-81, bd. dirs. 1987-90), Am. Ednl. Rsch. Assn., Nat. Communication Assn. (chmn. commn.on communication avoidance 1984-86, chmn. publs. bd. 1989-91, chmn. interpersonal com. divsn. 1993-95, pres. 1997-98). Roman Catholic. Office: U Tex Coll Communication Austin TX 78712

DALY, JOSEPH LEO, law educator; b. Phila., July 31, 1942; s. Leo Vincent and Genevieve Delores (McGinnis) D.; m. Kathleen Ann Dolan, July 24, 1965; children: Michael, Colleen. BA, U. Minn., 1964; JD, William Mitchell Coll. Law, 1969. Bar: Minn. 1969, U.S. Dist. Ct. Minn. 1970, U.S. Supreme Ct. 1972, U.S. Ct. Appeals (8th cir.) 1973, U.S. Ct. Appeals (D.C. cir.) 1974; cert. mediator and arbitrator alternative dispute rev. bd. Minn. Supreme Ct. Ptnr. Franke & Daly, Mpls., 1969-74; prof. law Hamline U. Sch. Law, St. Paul, 1974—. Arbitrator Am. Arbitration Assn., N.Y.C., 1980—, U.S. Fed. Mediation and Conciliation Svc., Washington, 1988—, for the states of Minn., Hawaii, Idaho, Ind., Mass., Mich., N.D., Pa., Oreg., Wisc., V.I and City of L.A.; arbitrator Bur. Mediation Svcs., St. Paul, 1978—; vis. scholar Ctr. for Dispute Resolution, Willamette U., Salem, Oreg., 1985; facilitator Minn. Internat. Health Vols., Kenya, 1985; observer Philippine Constl. Conv., Manila, 1986; participant European Arab Arbitration Congress, Bahrain, 1987; human rights investigator in the Philippines, 1989; vis. scholar U. Oslo, 1990, 91, 92, 96, 97; lectr. on trial skills for human rights lawyers, The Philippines, 1989; lectr. to leaders at Site 2 Cambodian Refugee Camp, Thai/Cambodian border, 1989; lectr. U. Cluj-NAPACA, Romania, 1991; vis. lectr. for developing countries Internat. Bar Assn., 1991-92; lectr. U. Tirana, Albania, 1992, London, 1993, Nat. Econs. U., Hanoi, Vietnam, 1993, 94, Danang (Vietnam) Poly. U., 1993, Ho Chi Minh Econs. U., Saigon, Vietnam, 1993, U. Hanoi Law Sch., 1994, U. Modena, Italy, 1994, Hanoi, Danang and Saigon, 1995, Phnom Penh, Cambodia, 1995, Hong Kong, 1996, Shenzhen, China, 1996, Oslo, Norway, 1996, Karolinska Inst., Stockholm, 1997; vis. prof. So. Cross U., Lismore, Australia, 1998, 99, U. Bergen, Norway, 1999, Tongji U., Shanghai, China, 1999, U. Saigon, Vietnam, 1999, 2000; cons. Chua U., Tokyo, 2001; team leader UN Devel. Programme mid-term evaluation of UN project, Vietnam, Hanoi, 2001; vis. prof. U. Queensland, Brisbane, Australia, 2001, 02; Fulbright scholar U. Montevideo, Uruguay, 2002, 03. Co-author: The Law, the Student and the Catholic School, 1981; co-author, editor: The Student Lawyer: A High School Handbook of Minnesota Law, 1981, rev. edit., 1986, Strategies and Exercises in Law Related Education, 1981, International Law, 1993, The American Trial System, 1994; contbr. more than 50 articles to profl. jours. Mem. Minn. Legislature Task Force on Sexual Exploitation by Counselors and Therapists, St. Paul, 1984-85, Nat. Adv. Com. on Citizen Edn. in Law, 1982-85; bd. dirs. Scenic Am., Washington, 1989-92. Recipient Spurgeon award Mayor and Citizens of St. Paul and Indianhead Scouting, 1983; named a Leading Am. Atty. in Alternative Dispute Resolution: Employment Law; fellow U. Miss. Law Sch. Mem. ABA (contbg. editor Preview of U.S. Supreme Ct. Cases mag. 1984—), Internat. Bar Assn. (London, vis. lectr. for devel. countries 1991—), Minn. State Bar Assn., Minn. Lawyers Internat. (human rights com., rep. to Philippine Constl. Conv. 1986), St. Paul Athletic Club, Phi Alpha Delta. Avocations: jogging, sailing. Office: Hamline U Sch Law 1536 Hewitt Ave Saint Paul MN 55104-1205 E-mail: jdaly@gw.hamline.edu.

DALY, MARY, college administrator; b. Erie, Pa., Dec. 29, 1943; d. Damian John and Letitia (Lawson) D. BS, Mercyhurst Coll., 1966; MA, Fairfield U., 1987; student, Pitts. Inst. Mortuary Sci., 2002. Dir. found. rsch. Mercyhurst Coll., Erie, 1966-67, dir. pub. rels., 1967-78, dir. publs., 1978-80, dir. spl. events and presdl. functions, 1980—, asst. dir. devel., 1972-80, asst. to the pres. for external affairs, 1980-89, sr. asst. to the pres., 1989-91, v.p. pub. rels., 1991—, website developer, content resource mgr., 1997-98, sr. asst. to pres. bd. trustees, 2002—. Comm. cons. Sisters of Mercy of Erie County, Erie, 1970—; polit. cons. Rep. Joseph Giles, Erie, 1980-90, Mayor Joyce Savocchio, Erie, 1986, 89, 93, 97; editor women's studies, Erie Roundtable. Creative dir. for publs. Bd. dirs. Gannondale, Erie, 1990-92, Internat. Inst., Erie, 1988-90, Zonta club Erie, 1980-83, March of Dimes, Erie, 1981-82, Muscular Dystrophy, Erie, 1981-82, Florence Crittendon Home, Erie, 1983-87, Millcreek Hall of Fame, 1995—, Multiple Sclerosis Soc., 2000-, Cath. Daughters Am., 2002-; mem. pub. rels. com. Libr. 21-Erie County Libr.; mem. merchandising, pub. rels. and mktg. com. Greater Erie Bicentennial; mem. pub. rels. com. Warner Theatre Restoration. Fulbright scholar for summer study in Egypt, 1977. Mem. Coun. for Advancement and Support of Edn. (Silver Medal Recognition awards 1986), Pub. Rels. Soc. Am., Am. Coun. on Edn. (regional rep.), Internat. Assn. Bus. Comms. (award of excellence Mercyhurst mag. 1996, 97), Coun. on Pa. Coll. Pub Rels. Execs., Nat. Identification Program for Advancement of Women in Higher Edn., Erie Ad Club (past pres., George Mead Disting. Career award 1984). Democrat. Roman Catholic. Avocations: piano, reading, travel, web-site developer. Home: 1142 W 33rd St Erie PA 16508-2432 Office: Mercyhurst Coll Glenwood Hills 501 E 38th St Erie PA 16546-0002

DAM, KENNETH W. lawyer, law educator, federal agency administrator; b. Marysville, Kans., Aug. 10, 1932; s. Oliver W. and Ida L. (Huepelsheuser) D.; m. Marcia Wachs, June 9, 1962; children: Eliot, Charlotte. BS, U. Kans., 1954; JD, U. Chgo., 1957; LLD (hon.), New Sch. Social Rsch., 1983. Bar: N.Y. State 1959. Law clk. to justice U.S. Supreme Ct., 1957-58; assoc. Cravath, Swaine & Moore, N.Y.C., 1958-60; faculty U. Chgo. Law Sch., 1960-82, prof., 1964-71, 74-82, Harold J. and Marion F. Green prof., 1976-82, provost, 1980-82; dep. sec. of state Dept. State, 1982-85; v.p. law and external rels. IBM Corp., 1985-92; pres., CEO United Way Am., 1992; Max Pam prof. of Am. and fgn. law U. Chgo. Law Sch., 1992—2001; dep. sec. Dept. Treasury, Washington, 2001—. Asst. dir. nat. security and internat. affairs Office Mgmt. and Budget, 1971-73; exec. dir. Coun. Econ. Policy, 1973; vis. prof. U. Freiburg, Germany, 1964; adv. bd. BMW of N.Am., 1990-95. Author: The GATT: Law and International Economic Organization, 1970, Oil Resources: Who Gets What How?, 1976, The Rules of the Game: Reform and Evolution in the International Monetary System, 1982, The Rules of the Global Game: A New Look at U.S. International Economic Policymaking, 2001; co-author: Federal Tax Treatment of Foreign Income, 1964, Economic Policy Beyond the Headlines, 1977, 2d edit., 1998; co-editor: Crytography's Role in Securing the Information Society, 1996; chair bd. advisors Fgn. Affairs jour., 1997-2001. Bd. dirs. Am. Coun. on Germany, 1986-95, Am.-China Soc., 1989-99, Coun. on Fgn. Rels., 1992-2001, Chgo. Coun. on Fgn. Rels., 1992-2001; trustee Brookings Inst., 1989-2001; co-chmn. Aspen Strategy Group,

1991-2001. Mem. Am. Acad. Arts and Scis., Am. Acad. Diplomacy, Am. Law Inst., Met. Club (Washington), Quadrangle Club. Office: Dept Treasury Office of the Secy 1500 Pennsylvania Ave NW Washington DC 20220

DAMASIO, ANTONIO R. physician, neurologist; b. Lisbon, Portugal, Feb. 25, 1944; came to U.S., 1975; m. Hanna Damasio. MD, U. Lisbon, 1969, DMS, 1974. Intern U. Hosp., Lisbon, 1969-72; prof. auxiliar in neurology Med. Sch., U. Lisbon, 1971; assoc. prof. dept. neurology U. Iowa, Iowa City, 1976-80, prof. neurology, 1980-86, prof. neurology, head dept., 1986—, M.W. Van Allen Disting. prof., 1989—, chief divsn. behavioral neurology and cognitive neurosci., 1977—. Adj. prof. Salk Inst., San Diego, 1989—; mem. planning subcom. Nat. Adv. Neurol. Disorders Stroke Coun. Author: Lesion Analysis in Neuropsychgology, 1989 (award Assn. Am. Pubs. 1990); mem. editorial bd. Trends in Neuroscis., 1986-91, Behavioral Brain Rsch., 1988—, Cerebral Cortex, 1990—, Jour. Neurosci., 1990, Cognitive Brain Rsch., Learning and Memory, spl. brain issue Sci. Am, 1992, Descartes' Error: Emotion, Reason, and the Human Brain, 1994, The Feeling of What Happens: Body and Emotion in the Making of Consciousness, 1999. Recipient Disting. prof. award U. So. Calif., Prix Plasticite' Neuronale, Ispen Found., 1997, Golden Brain award, 1995, The Reenpää prize, Finland, 2000, Dr. William Beaumont award AMA, 1990, Pessoa prize Portuguese govt., 1992. Fellow Am. Acad. Neurology, Am. Neurol. Assns.; mem. NAS Inst. Medicine, Soc. for Neurosci., Acad. Aphasia (pres. 1983), Behavioral Neurology Soc., (pres. 1985), Royal Soc. Medicine Belgium (elected), European Acad. Arts and Scis. (elected), Am. Acad. Arts and Scis. Office: U Iowa Hosp & Clinic Dept Neurology 200 Hawkins Dr Iowa City IA 52242-1009

DAMASKA, MIRJAN RADOVAN, law educator; b. Brezice, Slovenia, Oct. 8, 1931; came to U.S., 1972; s. Radovan and Ljerka (Tkalcic) D.; m. Marija Brkoevic, Aug. 10, 1960. LL.M., U. Zagreb, Croatia, 1956; D.Jurisprudence, Ljubljana Law Sch., 1960; LL.M., U. Zagreb, Croatia, 1956. Prof. law U. Zagreb, 1960-72, acting dean Law Sch., 1970-71; prof. law U. Pa. Law Sch., Phila., 1972-76; Ford Found. prof. law Yale U. Law Sch., New Haven, 1976-95, Sterling prof. law, 1996—; cons. Author: Position of the Criminal Defendant, 1962, Faces of Justice and State Authority, 1986, (with Schlesinger, Baade & Herzog) Comparative Law, 1988, Evidence Law Adrift, 1997; contbr. articles to profl. jours. Nat. Found. for Study of Humanities fellow, 1978-79 Fellow Am. Acad. Arts and Scis.; mem. Am. Assn. for Comparative Study of Law, Internat. Acad. Comparative Law.

D'AMATO, ANTHONY, law educator; b. N.Y.C., Jan. 10, 1937; s. Anthony A. and Mary (DiNicholas) D'A.; m. Barbara W. Steketee, Sept. 4, 1958; children: Brian, Paul. BA, Cornell U., 1958; JD, Harvard U., 1961; PhD, Columbia U., 1968. Bar: N.Y. 1963, U.S. Supreme Ct. 1963, U.S. Tax Ct. 1987. Instr. Wellesley Coll., 1963-66; of counsel S.W. Africa Cases, N.Y.C., 1965-66; Woodrow Wilson fellow U. Mich., Ann Arbor, 1966-67; Leighton prof. law Northwestern U. Law Sch., Chgo., 1968—. Author: The Concept of Custom in International Law, 1971, (with O'Neil) The Judiciary and Vietnam, 1972, (with Hargrove) Environment and the Law of the Sea, 1976 (with Wasby and Metrailer) Desegregation from Brown to Alexander, 1977, (with Weston and Falk) International Law and World Order, 1980, 2d edit., 1990, Jurisprudence: A Descriptive and Normative Analysis of Law, 1984, International Law: Process and Prospect, 1987, 2d edit., 1995, How to Understand the Law, 1989, (with Jacobson) Justice and the Legal System, 1992, International Law Anthology, 1994, International Law Coursebook, 1994, International Environmental Law Anthology, 1995, International Law and Political Reality, 1995, Analytic Jurisprudence Anthology, 1995, International Intellectual Property Anthology, 1996, Introduction to Law and Legal Thinking, 1996, International Law Studies, 1996, International Law Studies, 1997, International Intellectual Property Law, 1997; bd. editors Am. Jour. Internat. Law, 1981-95. Recipient Annual Book award Am. Soc. Internat. Law., 1981, Carl L. Fulda award for Outstanding Contbn. to Internat. Law, 1988. Mem. Internat. Law Assn., Am. Soc. Legal and Polit. Philosophy (chair inter-bar study group on ind. of lawyers and judges), ABA (coun. internat. law and practice), Am. Soc. Internat. Law (chair human rights interest group). Home: 5807 Lakeshore Dr N Holland MI 49424-1019 Office: Northwestern U Sch Law 357 E Chicago Ave Chicago IL 60611-3059

D'AMATO, FRANCES LOUISE, art and psychology educator; b. N.Y.C., Mar. 30, 1943; d. Louis and Frances Anna (O'Resto) D'Amato; m. Lewis M. Smoley, Sept. 17, 1977 (div. Mar. 1988). BS in Edn., SUNY, Oswego, 1964; MEd, Hofstra U., Hempstead, N.Y., 1969; MA in Orgnl. Psychology, Columbia U., 1986, MA in Art Edn., 1991. Cert. tchr. K-6, N.Y. Tchr. 5th grade Farmingdale (N.Y.) Pub. Schs., 1965-67; reading supr. Lynbrook (N.Y.) Pub. Schs., 1967-69; reading coord. Am. Cmty. Sch., Beirut, 1969-71; internat tng. cons. Chase Manhattan Bank, N.Y.C., 1971-73; asst. v.p. CIT Fin. Corp., N.Y.C., 1973-78; v.p. human resources Am. Mgmt. Assn., N.Y.C., 1978-81; cons. Tree Group, N.Y.C., 1981—; prof. art Caldwell C.C., Hudson/Boone, N.C., 1988-95; prof. art and psychology Catawba Valley C.C., Hickory, N.C., 1991-95; tchr. printmaking Spirit Square, Charlotte, 1998—. Cons., spkr. Women's Resource Ctr., Hickory, 1990-96; cons. exec. program Columbia U. Bus. Sch., 1981-82; cons. Frye Regional Hosp., Seminar on Assertiveness Tng., 1994; organizer Advent Retreat Cath. Conf. Ctr., Hickory, 1993-96; spkr. various seminars, 1994, 96; conf. leader Dreams Visions of the Night seminar Belmont Abbey Coll. Conf. Ctr., 1995, 96, Stress Reduction seminar, 1996. Author: Benjaman and the Tent, 1986; editor OD Network Newsletter, 1983-87, EIC Intelligence, 1987-90; contbr. articles to profl. publs. Grassroots grant participant N.C. Arts Coun., Boone, 1988-90; participant Blue Ridge Leadership Challenge, Boone, 1990-91; organizer Visual Art Tchrs., Valle Crusis, N.C., 1991; alumni bd. dirs. SUNY-Oswego, 1974-84; coord. bereavement coun. St. Gabriels Ch., Charlotte, 2001—; counselor chs., schs. and orgns; personal trainer, 1999-2003. Recipient Printmaking award Caldwell Arts Coun., Lenoir, N.C., 1989. Mem. ASTD (bd. dirs. 1975-77, mem. awards com. 1980-81), Nat. Art Edn. Assn. (conf. organizer 1991), OD Network (steering com. 1972-84), Kappa Delta Pi. Avocations: printmaking, writing, reading, swimming, sports. Home: 2214-C E 7th St Charlotte NC 28204 Office: 2214 E 7th St Apt C Charlotte NC 28204-3387 E-mail: fldamato@yahoo.com.

DAMATO, KATHRYN LEATHEM, dental hygienist, educator; b. Troy, N.Y., Nov. 30, 1948; d. James J. and Margurite (Judge) Leathem; m. Kenneth James Damato, May 7, 1977; children: Meaghan Leathem Damato, Kaitlyn Leathem Damato; 1 stepchild, Kenneth J. Damato. AS, Hudson Valley C.C.; BS, U. Bridgeport, 1972; MS, So. Conn. State U., 1976. Registered dental hygienist. Clin. dental hygienist pvt. practice, New Haven, Conn., 1975-85; instr. dept. dental hygiene Sch. Dental Medicine and Tunxis Coll. U. Conn., Farmington, 1985-89, asst. prof. Sch. Dental Medicine and Tunxis Coll., 1989—, program developer, rschr. dept. oral diagnosis Sch. Dental Medicine, 1996—. Course leader for clin. component of dental hygiene curriculum, U. Conn., Farminton, 1989—, dir. clin. affairs, 1992—, dental hygiene clin. affairs, 1992-95. Co-editor: Clinical Dental Hygiene Handbook. Adviser Student Am. Dental Hygienist Assn., Conn., 1985-90; cons. infection control and task force AIDS, 1988—; pres., founder Women and Children First, Inc.; oral health coord. spl. skills-spl. athletes Conn. State Olympics. Grantee AIDS Found. participation in Grant Edn., 1991, 92; recipient Conn. Higher Edn. Cmty. Svc. award, 1995. Mem. AAUP, Am. Dental Hygienist Assn., Internat. Assn. Dental Rsch., Am. Assn. Dental Rsch., Nat. Cancer Insts. Info. Assocs., Sigma Phi Alpha. Roman Catholic. Avocations: entertaining, cooking. Home: 1280 Durham Rd Wallingford CT 06492-2667 Office: U Conn Sch Dental Medicine Dept Dental Hygiene Mail Code 2105 Farmington CT 06509 also: Tunxis Coll RR 6 Woodbridge CT 06525-9806

D'AMBRA, EVE, art historian; b. N.Y., Oct. 6, 1956; d. John and Rosalie D'Ambra; m. Franc Dominic Palaia, June 3, 1986. BA, U. Ariz., 1978; MA, UCLA, 1981; PhD, Yale U., 1987. Lectr. Kean Coll. N.J., 1988; asst. prof. U. R.I., 1989-90, Vassar Coll., Poughkeepsie, N.Y., 1990—. Vis. lectr. U. Pa., 1987, Rutgers U., Newark, 1987-88; vis. asst. prof. Boston U., 1989; lectr. Am. Acad. in Rome, 1986, Archaeol. Inst. Am., San Antonio, 1986, N.Y.C., 1987, Balt., 1989, Boston, 1989, New Orleans, 1992, Coll. Art Assn., N.Y.C., 1990, Barnard Coll., 1990, Brown U., 1991, NYU, 1991, Middlebury Coll., 1993, Gardner Mus. Symposium, 1994. Author: Private Lives, Imperial Virtues: The Frieze of the Forum Transitorium in Rome, 1993; editor: Roman Art in Context, 1993; contbr. articles to profl. jours. Recipient Rome prize, 1984-86; fellow Yale U., 1982-86, Fulbright, 1984-85; NEH travel grantee, 1991, rsch. grantee Vassar Coll., 1991, 93. Office: 371 4th St Jersey City NJ 07302-2224

DAME, LAUREEN EVA, nursing administrator, educator; b. Framingham, Mass., Mar. 15, 1947; d. Irving Lawrence Jr. and Cora Justina (Wells) Dame; children: Daryl Lawrence, Jeffrey Lee. Diploma, Dartmouth-Hickock Med. Ctr., Hanover N.H., 1968; BSN, Clayton State Coll., Morrow, Ga., 1996; MSN, Emory U., 1997. RN, Ga., Fla.; cert. profl. in healthcare quality. Staff nurse, charge nurse, team leader maternity and surgical nursing various hosps., N.H., Boston, St. Louis, 1968-69, 80-83; sch. nurse practitioner Dept. Pub. Health, Bedford, Mass., 1983-85; perioperative nurse, 1st asst. South Fulton Hosp., East Point, Ga., 1985-86; nurse, first asst., plastic surgery John Munna M.D., Atlanta, 1986-90; resource nurse, intake coord. Shallowford Hosp., Atlanta, 1989-91, staff educator, quality assurance coord. dept. surg. svcs., 1991-92; quality improvement coord., nursing South Fulton Med. Ctr., East Point, Ga., 1992; nurse coord. quality assurance Kaiser Permanente, Atlanta, 1992-93, dir. quality assurance, 1993-95; mgr. coord. care Egleston Children's Hosp., Emory U., Atlanta, 1995-96; mgr. quality mgmt. Egleston Pediat. Group, Decatur, Ga., 1996-97; dir. dept. surgery Emory U. Hosp., Atlanta, 1997-98; dir. regulatory and quality mgmt. MATRIA Healthcare, Inc., 1998—99; clin. instr. Ga. State U., Atlanta, 2000; adminstr. Midtown Urology Surg. Ctr., 2000—. Mem. NAACOG (charter; chmn. steering com. 1972), AORN (chmn. hospitality com. 1992, mem. workshop and publicity coms. 1983), NAFE, Am. Soc. Plastic and Reconstructive Surg. Nurses, Nat. Assn. Quality Profls., Ga. Assn. Quality Profls., Ga. North Ctrl. Dist. Quality Profls., Am. Acad. Disting. Students, Am. Needlepoint Guild (life), Embroiderers Guild Am. (life), Sigma Theta Tau. Lutheran. Avocations: needlepoint, embroidery, fiber artist (nat. cert. judge). Home: 8726 Twin Oaks Dr Jonesboro GA 30236-5152 Fax: 404-881-6398. E-mail: nedlptprincess@msn.com.

DAMERON, BETTY COFFEY, secondary education educator; b. Washington, June 3, 1935; d. James Wilson Coffey and Elizabeth Neva Swindell; m. Willard N. Dameron, Mar. 23, 1956; children: Bambi Lynne Dameron Payne, Debra Ann Dameron Slingerland, Clifton Willard, George Wilson. BA, Mary Washington Coll., Fredericksburg, Va., 1968, MALS, 1991. Cert. French and English tchr., Va. Tchr. French, Stafford H.S., Falmouth, Va., 1969—. Presenter in field. Mem. NEA, Stafford Edn. Assn., Fredericksburg Runners, Potomac Valley Track Club (Long Distance Runner of Yr. 1989, Runner of Yr. 50+ 1994), Tidewater Striders. Democrat. Roman Catholic. Avocations: long distance track and road racing, showing horses (numerous championships). Home: 11223 Trisler Dr Fredericksburg VA 22407-6475 Office: Stafford HS 33 Stafford Indians Ln Fredericksburg VA 22405-5803

DAMERST, WILLIAM, English and humanities educator; b. Pelham, Mass., Aug. 21, 1923; s. Steven M. and Clara (Peterson) Damerst; m. Dorothy Blackburn, Feb. 16, 1946 (dec. 2001); children: Jeffrey W., Laura Barron, Gail Pashek. Student, Amherst Coll., 1941—43, student, 1945—46, Mich. State U., 1943; BS, U. Ill., 1946; MA, U. Mass., 1955. Officer family bus., 1946—55; instr. English Pa. State U., University Park, 1955—60, asst. prof., 1960—65, assoc. prof., 1965—72, prof., 1972—85, prof. emeritus, 1985—. Cons. Gulf Oil Corp., Phila., Gulf R&D Co., Phila., GE Co., Erie, Pa., St. Joseph Lead Co., Monaca, Pa. Author: (text) Good Gulf Letters and Reports, 1959, Resourceful Business Communication, 1965, Clear Tech. Reports, 1972, Clear Tech. Comm. 3d edit., 1990, (novel) Joey, Joe, and Joseph, 2001. 1st lt. USAF, 1943—45. Decorated Air medal with 5 oak leaf clusters; grantee, Gulf Aid to Edn., 1959, 1960. Address: 705 Jerdon Cir North Myrtle Beach SC 29582

D'AMICO, BEVERLY ANN, elementary education educator; b. Newark, N.J., Sept. 9, 1961; d. James Anthony and Mary Ann (Belluso) D'A. BS magna cum laude, Seton Hall U., 1983, postgrad. Tchr. 2d grade St. Bonaventure Sch., Paterson, N.J., 1983; tchr. supplemental instrn. Belleville (N.J.) Pub. Schs., 1984, tchr. pre-sch. handicapped and transitional kindergarten, 1984-85; tchr. 4th grade Madison Pub. Sch. System, Madison, N.J., 1985—. Mem. adv. com., com. for policy making Senator Robert Martin of Morris County, N.J., 1994—. Mem. NEA, N.J. Edn. Assn. (leadership com. 1994—), Assn. for Supervision and Curriculum Devel., Madison Edn. Assn. (chairperson legis. com. 1994-95, Rudolph Rsch. award for Sci. Excellence in Tchg., 1992). Republican. Roman Catholic. Avocations: arts, travel, tennis, cross country skiing, photography. Home: 15 Madison Ave Apt 4 Madison NJ 07940-1471

D'AMICO, CAROL, educational administrator; MS in Adult Edn., EdD in Leadership and Policy Studies, Ind. U. Sr. program analyst Ind. Gen. Assembly; policy and planning specialist Ind. Dept. Edn.; dean workforce devel. Ivy Tech. C.C. Ind.; asst. sec. vocat. and adult edn. Dept. Edn., Washington, 2001—03; chancellor-elect Ivy Tech. State College's Ctrl. Ind. region, 2004—. Expert workforce devel. and edn. issues; testified before Congress and several state legislatures; sr. fellow Hudson Inst.; spkr. in field. Co-author: (book) Workforce 2020: Work and Workers in the 21st Century; contbr. articles to newspapers and profl. jours. Office: One W 26th St Indianapolis IN 46206-1763

DAMICO, DEBRA LYNN, college official, English and French educator; b. Passaic, N.J., Apr. 15, 1956; d. Nicholas Biagio and Eleanore Lorraine (Hugle) D. BA, Montclair State U., 1978, MA, 1989. Cert. tchr., N.J, reading specialist. Tchr. St. Francis Sch., Hackensack, NJ, 1978—79, Saddle Brook (N.J.) H.S., 1979-80, St. Dominic Acad., Jersey City, 1980-84; tchr. adult basic edn., gen. edn devel. and ESL, Montclair State U., 1974—2001, coord. EXCEL program, 1993—2001; internat. student advisor Manhattan Coll., Bronx, N.Y., 1984—, ESL instr., 1986—, instr. French, 1998—. Instr. Writing Inst. Adult Edn. Resource Ctr., Jersey City State Coll., 1987—; Outstanding Internat. Student advisor, 1989—. Mem. Dist. Wide Curriculum Council, Lodi, N.J., 1977-78; ch. cantor and musician. Named Outstanding Young Woman Am., 1986; grantee, Assn. Internat. Educators, 1985—86. Mem. Nat. Assn. Tchrs. of English as a Fgn. Lang., N.Y. Tchrs. of ESL, Assn. of Internat. Educators, Metro-Internat., Am. Assn. Tchrs. French, YMCA Internat. Student Svc., Kappa Delta Pi, Pi Delta Phi. Democrat. Roman Catholic. Avocations: singing, playing and teaching guitar, cantor and musician at church. Office: Manhattan Coll 4513 Manhattan College Pkwy Bronx NY 10471-4998 Fax: 718-862-8016. E-mail: debra.damico@manhattan.edu.

D'AMICO, THOMAS F. economist, educator; b. N.Y.C., Aug. 20, 1948; s. Lawrence J. and Anita (Mingione) D'A.; m. Franca Paola Paniccia, Sept. 1970; children: Diana Christina, Gina Maria. BA, Fordham Coll., 1970; MA, NYU, 1979, MPhil, 1981, PhD, 1983. Econ. analyst Con Edison, N.Y.C., 1970-72; program dir. East Harlem Community Corp., N.Y.C., 1972-75; instr. St. Peter's Coll., Jersey City, N.J., 1975-78, from assoc. prof. to prof. econs., 1981—, chair dept. econs., 1989—; asst. prof. Manhattan Coll., Riverdale, N.Y., 1978-81. Cons. various pvt. firms and non-profit agys., N.Y. Met. area, 1975—. Author: The Economics of Market and Non-Market Racial Discrimination, 1983; contbr. articles to scholarly jours.; referee various scholarly jours. Mem. AAUP, Am. Econ. Assn., Ea. Econ. Assn., Assn. Social Econs. Roman Catholic. Office: St Peter's Coll Dept Econs Jersey City NJ 07306 E-mail: damico_t@spc.edu.

DAMON, WILLIAM VAN BUREN, developmental psychologist, educator, writer; b. Brockton, Mass., Nov. 10, 1944; s. Philip Arthur and Helen (Meyers) D.; m. Wendy Obernauer (div. 1982); children: Jesse Louis, Maria; m. Anne Colby, Sept. 24, 1983, 1 child, Caroline. BA, Harvard U., 1967; PhD, U. Calif., Berkeley, 1973. Social worker N.Y.C. Dept. Social Svcs., 1968-70; prof. psychology Clark U., Worcester, Mass., 1973-89, dean Grad Sch., 1983-87, chmn. dept. edn., 1988-89; Disting. vis. prof. U. P.R., 1988; prof., chair edn. dept. Brown U., Providence, 1989-92, prof., Mittlemann Family dir. Ctr. for Study of Human Devel., 1993-98; univ. prof., 1997-98; fellow Ctr. for Advanced Study in the Behavioral Scis., 1994-95; prof., dir. Ctr. on Adolescence Stanford (Calif.) U., 1997—. Sr. fellow Hoover Instn., 1999—; mem. study sect. NIMH, Bethesda, Md., 1981-84; cons. State of Mass., 1976, State of Calif., 1978, Allegheny County, Pa., 1979, Pinellas County, Fla., 1990, Com. of Va., 1993, Hawaii, 1995, Children's TV Workshop, 1991-09, Annenberg Adv. Coun. on Excellence in Children's TV, 1996-99, Project for Excellence in Journalism, 2000—; mem. nat. adv. bd. Fox Family TV Network, 1998-2001. Author: Social World of the Child, 1977, Social and Personality Development, 1983, Self-Understanding in Childhood and Adolescence, 1988, The Moral Child, 1988, Child Development Today and Tomorrow, 1989, Some Do Care, 1992, Greater Expectations, 1995 (Parent's Choice Book award, 1995), The Youth Charter, 1997, Handbook of Child Psychology, 1998; : Good Work, 2001, Bringing in a New Era in Character Education, 2002, A Noble Purpose, 2003; editor: New Directions for Child Devel., 1978—. Trustee Bancroft Sch., Worcester, Mass., 1982-84; mem. adv. bd. Ednl. Alliance, 1991—. Grantee Carnegie Corp., N.Y.C., 1975-79, 97—, Spencer Found., 1980, 92-96, 98-2001, N.Y. comty. Trust, 1984-88, Inst. Noetic Scis., 1988-90, MacArthur Found., 1990-95, Pew Charitable Trusts, 1990-95, 98-2000, Ross Inst., 1996—, Hewlett Found., 1997—, The Templeton Found., 1998—, Atlantic Philanthropies, 2003—. Mem. APA, Jean Piaget Soc. (bd. dirs. 1983-87), Am. Ednl. Rsch. Assn., Soc. for Rsch. in Child Devel., Nat. Acad. Edn. Republican. Episcopalian. Office: Stanford U Ctr on Adolescence Cypress Bldg C Stanford CA 94305-4145 E-mail: wdamon@stanford.edu.

DAMPIER, FRANCES MAY, secondary school educator; b. Winona, Miss., Oct. 22, 1947; d. James Sidney Purnell and Hazel (Hobbs) Walker; m. Charles Wayne Dampier, Oct. 3, 1948 (div.); children Charles Wayne Jr., Trevis, Desmond. BS in Speech Edn., Jackson State U., 1970; M in Sch. Mgmt., U. Laverne, 1985. Tchr. Sunnyvale (Calif.) Sch. Dist., 1970-85, San Jose (Calif.) Eastside Sch. Dist., 1986-87; eng. tchr. Sunnyvale Sch. Dist., Sunnyvale, CA, 1987-89, asst. prin., 1989-95; eng. tchr. Sunnyvale Middle Sch., Sunnyvale, CA, 1995-97; prin. Bishop Elementary Sch., 1997—. Dir. WASC accrediation com. Sunnyvale (Calif.) Sch. Dist, 1984-85, activities dir., 1983-85, multicultural dir./coord., 1975-85, stud. counc. adv., presenter, Young Writer's Conf. Outreach leader, group leader, sec., Emmanuel Bapt. Ch., San Jose, Calif., 1983-87; advisor Black Student Union, San Jose, 1986-87; rep. Desegregation com., San Jose, 1986-87. Named tchr. of the year Sunnyvale Sch. Dist., 1985. Mem. NAACP, Nat. Coalition Negro Women, Calif. Teachers Assn. (liason 1975-76), Black Educators of Eastside Sch Dist., GATE Adv. Com., Blue Ribbon Com., Desegregation Task Force, Dist. Lang. Arts Com., Eastside Edn. Assn., Natl. Edn. Assn., Delta Sigma Theta. Democrat. Avocations: reading, jazz dancing, cooking, aerobics. Office: Piedmont Hills High Sch 1377 Piedmont Rd San Jose CA 95132-2497

DAMROSCH, LEO, English educator; b. Manila, Sept. 14, 1941; s. Leopold and Elizabeth (Hammond) D.; m. Sheila Raymond (div.); children: John, Christopher; m. Joyce Van Dyke; children: Luke, Nicholas. BA, Yale U., 1963; MA, Cambridge U., 1966; PhD, Princeton U., 1968. From asst. prof. to prof. U. Va., 1968-83; prof. English U. Md., 1983-89, Harvard U., Cambridge, Mass., 1989—. Author: Samuel Johnson and the Tragic Sense, 1972, The Uses of Johnson's Criticism, 1976, Symbol and Truth in Blake's Myth, 1980, God's Plot and Man's Stories, 1985, The Imaginative World of Alexander Pope, 1987, Fictions of Reality in the Age of Hume and Johnson, 1989, The Sorrows of the Quaker Jesus, 1996. Office: Harvard Univ Dept English Cambridge MA 02138

DANA-DAVIDSON, LAOMA COOK, English language educator; b. Herndon, W.Va., Nov. 23, 1925; d. Virgil A. and Latha (Shrewsbury) Cook; m. William J. Davidson, Apr. 1946 (div. 1971); 1 child, Deborah Davidson Bollom. BE, Marshall U., 1946; MA in Adminstrn., Azusa U., 1981. Cert. tchr., Calif. Tchr. Cajon Valley Union Sch. Dist., El Cajon, Calif., 1958—, San Diego Diocese. Master tchr. to 50 student tchrs. Author: Reading series used in dist., 1968. Former pres. El Cajon Rep. Women Federated; chaplin San Diego County Rep. Women; mem. El Cajon Hist. Assn.; v.p. Cajon Valley Union Sch. Bd.; active literacy program Rolling Readers; mem. Spa-Wars Edn. Com. for Navy Relocation; mem. Alcohol and Drug Prevention Task Force; recent candidate Calif. State Assembly; apptd. hon. chmn. reflectice com. promoting art, music, dance and phys. edn. PTA Coun., 2000. Recipient sabbatical to study British Schs. Cajon Valley Union Sch. Dist., 1977-78. Mem. AAUW (pres. 1964-66, edn. com. 1993-94, policy com., women's issuees com., Chris Lynn Downey rsch. and projects award 1996), League of Women Voters, Grossmont Concert Assn., La Mesa C. of C. (edn. rep. Cajon Valley Sch. Dist.), Delta Kappa Gamma, Phi Delta Kappa. Avocations: travel, writing, reading, tennis, theatre. Office: 609 Ecken Rd El Cajon CA 92020-7312 Fax: (619) 447-4512.

DANAHAR, DAVID C. academic administrator, historian, educator; b. Dobbs Ferry, N.Y., Sept. 29, 1941; s. Walter Vincent and Catherine Marie (Charles) Danahar; m. Cecelia Upritchard, Aug. 24, 1985; children: Deirdre, Rebecca, Michael. BA, Manhattan Coll., Bronx, N.Y., 1963; MA, U. Mass., 1965, PhD, 1970. Instr. U. Mass., Amherst, 1969-70; asst. prof. SUNY, Oswego, 1970-73, assoc. prof., 1973-84, prof., 1984-85; dean Coll. Arts and Scis., prof. history Fairfield (Conn.) U., 1985-92; provost, acad. v.p. Loyola U., New Orleans, 1992-2001; pres. S.W. Minn. State U., 2001—. Vis. prof. U. Pisa, Italy, 1971—72. Contbr. articles to profl. jours. Mem. Fairfield 2000, 1983—88; bd. dirs. New Orleans Mus. Art, 1993—95. Grantee, SUNY Rsch. Found., 1971—73, NEH, 1983—88, others, 1985—; Univ. fellow, U. Mass., 1966—69, Rsch. fellow, Am. Coun. Learned Socs., 1975—76. Mem.: Am. Assn. Higher Edn., Conf. Ctrl. European History, Coun. Colls. Arts and Scis., Am. Conf. Acad. Deans, Am. Hist. Assn. Avocations: travel, sailing. Office: Southwest State U 1501 State St Marshall MN 56258

DANAHY, MARCIA KAREN, gifted education resource educator; b. Mpls., Oct. 16, 1948; d. Russell Gottfried and Minerva Hazel (Chailquist) Blixt; m. Paul Aloysius Danahy Jr., Nov. 27, 1982; 1 child, Sean-Paul Russell. BA with distinction, U. Minn., 1970, MA, 1977; EdS, St. Thomas U., 1981; elem. and kindergarten lic., Hamline U., 1986. Lic. elem. tchr. K-6, secondary tchr. English, speech, theater and communications, Minn. English tchr., drama dir. Golden Valley Pub. Schs., Mpls., 1970-80; English tchr., dept. chair Hopkins Schs., Mpls., 1980-85; adj. prof. edn. Augustana Coll., Sioux Falls, S.D., 1989-90; gifted edn. resource tchr. Hopkins Schs., Mpls., 1990—. Mem. steering com. Bus. Edn. Partnership, Hopkins, 1990—. Vol. fundraiser Children's Home Soc., St. Paul, 1990—, Immaculate Heart of Mary Sch., Minnetonka, 1990—. Recipient Block grant State of Minn., Hopkins Schs., 1991-92, 92-93. Mem. Nat. Coun. Gifted Tchrs., Minn. Coun. Gifted Tchrs., Mpls. Inst. Arts. Office: Hopkins North Jr High 10700 Cedar Lake Rd Minnetonka MN 55305-3361

D'ANCA, JOHN ARTHUR, psychotherapist, educator; b. Chgo., Apr. 19, 1950; s. John Joseph and Josephine Rose (Bartolotta) D.; m. Carol

Amendola; 1 son, Matthew John; stepdaughters, Ingrid, Heidi. BA, DePaul U., 1972; MA, Governors State U., 1975; CAS, No. Ill. U., 1978, EdD, 1982; PsyD, Chgo. Sch. Profl. Psychology, 1996; studied, Harvard U., 1994-95. Cert. eye movement desensitization and reprocessing; lic. clinician, Ill. Mem. counseling faculty Fenwick H.S., Oak Park, Ill., 1973-75; instr. psychology, counselor Triton Coll., River Grove, Ill., 1975-78; assoc. dir. Ball Found., Glen Ellyn, Ill., 1978-79; prof. student devel. Oakton Coll., Des Plaines, Ill., 1979—; pvt. practice psychology Park Ridge, Ill., 1975—. Extern John J. Madden Mental Health Ctr., Dept. of Psychiatry Chgo. Osteo. Hosp.; intern in psychology svc. Edward Hines Jr. VA Hosp., Hines, Ill., 1990—; mem. staff Bayside Clinic, Kenosha, Wis., 1993-97, mem. staff, psychiat. svcs., 1998—; cons. Molex Internat., 1986; lectr. in field; cons. Ill. Dept. Edn., Am. Med. Technologists, Goodwill Industries Internat.; cons., expert witness Ill. Dept. Profl. Regulation. Contbr. articles to profl. jours. Bd. dirs. Chgo. Bd. of Mental Health, Northwest, 1974-75; mem. Oakton Coll. Crusade of Mercy Appeal, 1982; eucharistic min. Roman Cath. Ch. Sears grantee, 1986—; recipient NISOD award for Coll. Tchg. Excellence, U. Tex., Austin, 2003. Mem. NEA, APA, Internat. Soc. Traumatic Stress Studies (presenter 1996), Ill. Edn. Assn., Am. Soc. Clin. Hypnosis, Soc. Clin. and Experimental Hypnosis, Joint Civic Commn. Italian Americans, Midwest Psychol. Assn., N.Am. Assn. Adlerian Psychology, Ill. Guidance and Pers. Assn., Ill. Coll. Pers. Assn., Phi Delta Kappa. Home: 935 Evergreen Way Highland Park IL 60035-3739 Office: 1600 E Golf Rd Des Plaines IL 60016-1234

DANCE, FRANCIS ESBURN XAVIER, communication educator; b. Bklyn., Nov. 9, 1929; s. Clifton Louis and Catherine (Tester) D.; m. Nora Alice Rush, May 1, 1954 (div. 1974); children: Clifton Louis III, Charles Daniel, Alison Catherine, Andrea Frances, Frances Sue, Brendan Rush; m. Carol Camille Zak, July 4, 1974; children: Zachary Esburn, Gabriel Joseph, Caleb Michael, Catherine Emily BS, Fordham U., 1951; MS, Northwestern U., 1953, PhD, 1959. Instr. speech Bklyn. Adult Labor Schs., 1951; instr. humanities, coord. radio and TV U. Ill. at Chgo., 1953—54; instr. Univ. Coll. U. Chgo., 1958; asst. prof. St. Joseph's (Ind.) Coll., Ind., 1958—60; asst. prof., then assoc. prof. U. Kans., 1960—63; mem. faculty U. Wis., Milw., 1963—71, prof. comm., 1965—71, dir. Speech Comm. Ctr., 1963—70; prof. U. Denver, 1971—, John Evans prof., 1995—; prof. homiletics St. John Vianney Theol. Sem., 2002—. Content expert and mem. faculty adv. bd. to Internat. U. on Knowledge Channel, 1993-95; cons. in field. Author: The Citizen Speaks, 1962, (with Harold P. Zelko) Business and Professional Speech Communication, 1965, 2d edit., 1978, Human Communication Theory, 1967, (with Carl E. Larson) Perspectives on Communication, 1970, Speech Communication: Concepts and Behavior, 1972, The Functions of Speech Communication: A Theoretical Approach, 1976, Human Communication Theory, 1982, (with Carol C. Zak-Dance) Public Speaking, 1986, Speaking Your Mind, 1994, 2d edit., 1996; editor Jour. Comm., 1962-64, Speech Tchr., 1970-72; adv. bd. Jour. Black Studies; editl. bd. Jour. Psycholinguistic Rsch; contbr. articles to profl. jours. Bd. dirs. Milw. Mental Health Assn., 1966-67. 2d lt. AUS, 1954-56. Knapp Univ. scholar in comm., 1967-68; recipient Outstanding Prof. award Std. Oil Found., 1967; Master Tchr. award U. Denver, 1985, Univ. Lectr. award U. Denver, 1986. Fellow Internat. Comm. Assn. (pres. 1967); mem. Nat. Comm. Assn. (pres. 1982), Psi Upsilon. Office: U Denver Dept Human Comm Studies Denver CO 80208-0001 E-mail: fdance@du.edu.

DANDO, WILLIAM ARTHUR, academic administrator, geography and geology educator; b. Newell, Pa., June 13, 1934; s. Carl Frederick and Myrtle Jane (Foster) D.; m. Caroline Zaporowsky, July 19, 1958; children: Christina Elizabeth, Lara Margaret, William Arthur II. BS, Calif. U. Pa., 1959; MA, U. Minn., 1962, PhD, 1969. Vis. instr. U. Manitoba, Winnepeg, Can., 1961; instr. U. Md., College Park, 1965-66, lectr., 1967-69, asst. prof., 1970-75; assoc. prof. U. N.D., Grand Forks, 1975-80, prof., 1980-89, chair geography, 1977-82; prof. Ind. State U., Terre Haute, 1989—2002, chair geography, geology and anthropology, 1989—2002, dir. Sr. Scholar Acad., 2002—. Prin. investigator NSF Meteorology-Climatology Project, 1985-92, NIH Multiple Sclerosis Project, 1988-91, NSF Phys. Geography Inst., 1992-96, Dept. Edn. Project GEO, 1992-97, Geo-Technology-GIS Project, 1995-2000. Author: Introduction to Maryland, 1970, The Geography of Famine, 1980, Food and Famine, A Reference, 1991, Russia and the Independent Nations of the Former USSR: Geofacts and Maps, 1995; editor: Innovations in Land Use Management, 1977, World Hunger and Famine, 1995, Russia, 2003. Pres. Univ. Luth. Ch., Grand Forks, 1979, Christus Rex Luth. Campus Ministry, 1979-87, N.D. Luth. Campus Ministry Com. 1986-88; chairperson fin. com. Trinity Luth. Ch., Terre Haute, 1992-97, v.p., 1996-97. Recipient Disting. Tchg. Achievement award Nat. Coun. for Geographic Edn., 1986, 98, Burlington Northern Found. Faculty Achievement award, 1988, Illustrious Alumni Calif. State U. award, 1976, Ind. State U. Pres. award, 1997, Ind. State U. Disting. Prof. award, 2000. Mem. Assn. Am. Geography (chair Mid. Atlantic divsn. 1973-74, chair Great Plains-Rocky Mt. divsn. 1978-80, chair West Lakes divsn. 1994-95, regional councillor 1997-2000, West Lakes divsn. Disting. Svc. award 2002), Nat. Coun. for Geog. Edn. (annual meeting chair 1998), Assn. N.D. Geographers (pres. 1976-80), Geography Educators Network Ind. (dir. devel. 1991-2000), Sigma Xi (U. N.D. chpt. pres. 1986-87, Ind. State U. chpt. v.p. 1991-92, pres. 1992-93, Individual Excellence in Scientific Rsch. award 1983). Lutheran. Avocations: trout fishing, hiking, automobile restoration. Home: 7785 S Carlisle Rd Terre Haute IN 47802-9343 Office: Ind State U Sr Scholar Acad Terre Haute IN 47809-0001

DANFORTH, WILLIAM HENRY, retired academic administrator, physician; b. St. Louis, Apr. 10, 1926; s. Donald and Dorothy (Claggett) D.; m. Elizabeth Anne Gray, Sept. 1, 1950; children: Cynthia Danforth Prather, David Gray, Maebelle Reed, Elizabeth D. Sankey. AB, Princeton U., 1947; MD, Harvard U., 1951. Intern Barnes Hosp., St. Louis, 1951—52, resident, 1954—57; now mem. staff; asst. prof. medicine Washington U., St. Louis, 1960—65, assoc. prof., 1965—67, prof., 1967—, vice chancellor for med. affairs, 1965—71, chancellor, 1971—95, chmn., bd. trustees, 1995—99, vice-chmn. bd. trustees, chancellor emeritus, 1999—. Pres. Washington U. Med. Sch. and Assoc. Hosps., 1965-71; program coord. Bi-State Regional Med. Program, 1967-68; dir. Energizing Holdings; chmn. bd. dirs. Donald Danforth Plant Sci. Ctr. Trustee Danforth Found.; trustee Am. Youth Found., 1963—, Princeton U., 1970-74; pres. St. Louis Christmas Carols Assn., 1958-74, chmn., 1975—; co-chair Barnes/Jewish Hosp., 1996-2002; bd. dirs. BJC Health Systems, 1996-2002. Named Man of Yr., St. Louis Globe-Democrat, 1978. Fellow: AAAS, Am. Acad. Arts and Scis.; mem.: Inst. Medicine. Home: 10 Glenview Rd Saint Louis MO 63124-1308 Office: Washington U West Campus Campus Box 1044 7425 Forsyth Blvd Ste 262 Saint Louis MO 63105-2161

DANG, CHI VAN, hematology and oncology educator; b. Saigon, Vietnam, Nov. 2, 1954; came to U.S., 1967; s. Chieu Van and Nga Ngoc (Nguyen) D.; m. Mary Doreen Seeley, May 18, 1985; children: Eric Van, Vanessa Marie. BS in Chemistry, U. Mich., 1975; PhD in Chemistry, Georgetown U., 1978; MD, Johns Hopkins U., 1982. Diplomate Am. Bd. Internal Medicine, Am. Bd. Med. Oncology. Resident in internal medicine Johns Hopkins Hosp., Balt., 1982-85; fellow in hematology and oncology U. Calif., San Francisco, 1985-87; asst. prof. medicine Johns Hopkins U., 1987-91, assoc. prof., 1991-97, assoc. prof. oncol., pathology, molecular biology & genetics, 1995-97, dir. hematology, 1993—2003, prof. medicine, oncology, and pathology, 1997—, prof. cell biology, 2001—, dep. dir. basic rsch., dept. medicine, 1996-99, co-dir. immunology and hematopoiesis, oncology, 1998-2000; vice dean rsch. Johns Hopkins Sch. Medicine, 2000—. Mem. oncological scis. path B NIH, Bethesda, Md., 1993-97; cons. Abbott Lab., 2002, Novartis, East Hanover, N.J., 1993-98, Genentech, South San Francisco, Calif., 1995; sci. adv. bd. Lion Pharm. Corp., Balt. Contbr. articles to Nature, Molecular and Cellular Biology, Genes and Devel.; mem. editl. bd. Jour. Clin. Invest., 1998—, Neoplasia, 1999—; mem. editl. bd. Cancer Rsch., 2000—, sr. editor, 2003—. Scholar Leukemia Soc. Am., 1992-97, Stohlman scholar award Leukemia Soc. Am., 1996, Merit award NIH/NCI, 1999. Mem. Assn. Am. Physicians, Am. Soc. for Clin. Investigation (pres. 2002), Phi Beta Kappa, Alpha Omega Alpha, Phi Lambda Upsilon. Avocations: india ink sketching, poetry. Home: 217 Upnor Rd Baltimore MD 21212-3425 Office: Johns Hopkins U Sch Med Ross 1025 720 Rutland Ave Baltimore MD 21205-2109 E-mail: cvdang@jhmi.edu.

DANG, JAMES BAC, business planner, educator; b. Bac Ninh, Vietnam, Jan. 10, 1953; came to U.S., 1979; s. Chinh Van and Ut Thi Dang; m. Nguyen Luong, Oct. 17, 1978; children: Tien, Tiffany, Tina, Theresa, Tracy. BS in Agrl. Engring., Saigon (Vietnam) U., 1978; BS in Computer Sci., U. Ctrl. Okla., 1983, MEd in Math., 1985, MS in Applied Physics, 1989; BSEE, Okla. Christian U., 1988; MS in Applied Maths., Oklahoma City U., 1995, MBA in MIS, 1994; BSEE, Okla. U., 1989; postgrad., Walden U., 1993—. Planner mgmt. specialist AT&T Tech. Co., Oklahoma City, 1983—. Adj. instr. Okla. State U., Oklahoma City, 1987-91, Langston (Okla.) U., 1988—, Oklahoma City U., 1990—, Park Coll., Oklahoma City, 1992—, Oklahoma City C.C., 1995—. V.p. Vietnamese Cath. Cmty., Oklahoma City, 1993-96. Mem. Sigma Pi Sigma. Avocations: travel, study. Address: PO Box 6172 Huntington Beach CA 92615-6172

DANIEL, BARBARA ANN, retired elementary school educator; b. LaCrosse, Wis., Mar. 22, 1938; d. Rudolph J. and Dorothy M. (Farnham) Beranek; m. David Daniel; children: Raychelle, Clarence, Bernadette, Brenda. BS in Edn. cum laude, Midwestern U., Wichita Falls, Tex., 1967; postgrad., U. Alaska, Fairbanks, Anchorage, Juneau, U. Alaska, Bethel. Cert. tchr., Alaska. Primary tchr. Bur. Indian Affairs, Nunapitchuk and Tuntutuliak, Alaska, 1967-70; tchr. Lower Kuskokwim Sch. Dist., Tuntutuliak, 1981—2003, English lang. leader grades k-12, 1995—2002, ret., 2003. Mem. lang. arts curriculum revision task force Lower Kuskokwim Sch. Dist., 1990; past mem. state bd. Academic Pentathlon, Alaska; past acad. decathlon, pentathlon coach, 1980's. Rsch. video rec. of elders in Alaskan village. Mem.: NEA, Alaska Coun. Tchrs. English. Home: 25 West Circle PO Box Wtl-8048 Tuntutuliak AK 99680

DANIEL, COLDWELL, III, economist, educator; b. New Orleans; s. Coldwell Jr. and Josephine Agnes (Weick) D.; children: Anne Alexis, Coldwell IV. BBA, Tulane U., 1949; MBA, Ind. U., 1950; PhD, U. Va., 1959; postdoctoral, U. Chgo., 1964-65. Instr. stats. U. Va., 1955-56; instr. econs. Pomona Coll., 1956-57; prof. econs., dept. chmn. U. So. Miss., 1958-65; prof. econs. U. Houston, 1965-70, U. Memphis, 1970—. Rsch. coord. So. Calif. Rsch. Coun., 1956-57; vis. prof. La. State U., 1959; sr. Fulbright prof. econs. Dacca U., Bangladesh, 1961-62; Disting. Fulbright lectr. Shanghai Jiao Tong U., 2001; project dir. Miss. Test Facility Econ. Impact Study NASA, 1963; prin. The Anwell Co., Memphis, 1974—; disting. Fulbright lectr. Shanghai Jiao Tong U., 2001; candidate Fulbright Sr. Specialist Roster, 2002-2005. Author: Mathematical Models in Microeconomics, 1970; reader Jour. Econ. and Bus., 1991—, Social Sci. Jour., 1988—, Am. Jour. Econs. and Sociology, 1990—, Jour. Econ. Edn., 1997—, Internat. Econ. Jour., 1999—, Am. Econ. Rev., 2000; founder, chmn. bd. editors, The So. Quar., 1962-64; co-founder and manuscript rev. editor Jour. Econs. and Fin., 1977-91; mem. editl. bd. Jour. Econs. and Fin., 1991-94, Jour. Econs. and Fin. Edn., 2002—; assoc. editor for econs. Social Sci. Quar., 1968-70, mem. editl. bd., 1972-84; contbr. articles to profl. jours. Trustee Christ United Meth. Ch. With USAF, 1945-46; 1st lt. U.S. Army, 1951-53. Decorated Bronze Star; NSF Sci. Faculty fellow, 1964-66. Fellow Acad. Econs. and Fin.; mem. Am. Econ. Assn., Pakistan Econ. Assn. (life), Southwestern Econs. Assn., Acad. Econs. and Fin. (co-founder, pres. 1977-78, area coord. Indsl. Orgn. and pub. Policy, 1990-94, Disting. Svc. award 1979, Cert. Appreciation 1981), Mo. Valley Econs. Assn. (pres. 1984-85, Meritorious Svc. award 1986), So. Econ. Assn., Atlantic Econ. Soc. (exec. com. 1991-94, area coord. Indsl. Orgn. and Pub. Policy 1989-94), The Raven Soc., Sigma Xi, Beta Gamma Sigma, Omicron Delta Kappa, Pi Kappa Pi, Omicron Delta Epsilon, Pi Gamma Mu, Delta Tau Kappa, Pi Sigma Epsilon, Delta Sigma Pi. Office: U Memphis Dept Econs Memphis TN 38152-0001

DANIEL, DANIELE MALLISON, elementary school educator; b. Portsmouth, Va., Aug. 16, 1962; d. Howard Danford and Norma Mae (Gibbs) Mallison; m. Edward W. Daniel; 1 child, Benjamin W. BFA in Art Edn., Va. Commonwealth U., 1984. Cert. tchr. K-12, Va.; cert. therapeutic recreation asst. Activity dir. Eldercare Gardens Nursing Home, Charlotteville, Va., 1985-86; itinerant art tchr. Henry County Pub. Schs., Collinsville, Va., 1986-87; contract substitute Louisa County (Va.) Pub. Schs., 1988; middle/h.s. art tchr. Grayson County Pub. Schs., Independence, Va., 1988-90; elem. art resource tchr. Orange County (Va.) Pub. Schs., 1990-99, elem. gifted edn. tchr., 1999—. Upward Bound art tchr. Wytheville (Va.) C.C., summer 1990; tchr./cons. Henry County Pub. Schs. in conjunction with Va. Dept. Edn., Collinsville, 1987. Lifetime mem. Va. 4-H All Stars; chmn. young adults Gordonsville United Meth. Ch., 1994-2000, choir, 1994—. Folk Artist grantee Va. Commn. for the Arts, 1992-93, 93-94, Video Arts grantee, 1995-96. Mem. NEA, Va. Edn. Assn., Nat. Art Edn. Assn., Va. Art Edn. Assn., Nat. Therapeutic Recreation Assn., Gordonsville Jaycees (sec. 1992, 94, state dir. 1993). Avocations: arts and crafts, reading, travel, horses, researching native american heritage. Home: 11445 Knolls Rd Orange VA 22960-4554 Office: Orange County Pub Schs PO Waugh Rd Orange VA 22960-0204 E-mail: searchclass@yahoo.com.

DANIEL, ISAAC MORDOCHAI, mechanical engineering educator; b. Salonica, Greece, Oct. 7, 1933; came to U.S., 1955; s. Mordochai Aaron and Bella (Modiano) D.; m. Elaine Rochelle Krule, Feb. 15, 1987; children: Belinda Emily, Rebecca Stefanie, Max Ethan. BS, Ill. Inst. Tech., 1957, MS, 1959, PhD, 1964. Asst. rsch. engr. IIT Rsch. Inst., Chgo., 1959-61, assoc. rsch. engr., 1961-62, rsch. engr., 1962-64, sr. rsch. engr., 1964-75, mgr., 1965-75, sci. advisor, 1975-82; prof., dir. Ill. Inst. Tech., Chgo., 1982-86; prof. Northwestern U., Evanston, Ill., 1986—, Walter P. Murphy prof., 1998—. Dir. Ctr. for Intelligent Processing of Composites, 1997—. Author: Experimental Mechanics of Composite Materials, 1982, Engineering Mechanics of Composite Materials, 1994; editor: Composite Materials: Testing and Design, 1982. Pres. Sephardic Congregation, Chgo., 1980-82. Recipient Disting. Alumni award Ill. Inst. Tech., 1999. Fellow ASME, Am. Acad. Mechanics, Soc. Exptl. Mechanics (Hetenyi awards 1970, 76, B. J. Lazan award 1984, William M. Murray medal 1998); mem. ASTM, AIAA, Soc. Advanced Material Process Engring., Am. Soc. Nondestructive Testing, Am. Soc. Composites (Disting. Rsch. award 1996). Home: 9338 Neenah Ave Morton Grove IL 60053-1457 Office: Northwestern U 2137 Tech Dr Evanston IL 60208-0001

DANIEL, THOMAS MALLON, medical educator, researcher; b. Oct. 27, 1928; s. Lewis Morgan and Hannah Neil (Mallon) D.; m. Janet Ewing, June 27, 1953; children: Virginia, Stephen, Laura, Bruce. BS, Yale U., 1951; MD, Harvard U., 1955. Diplomate Am. Bd. Internal Medicine, Am. Bd. Pulmonary Disease. Intern, resident in medicine Univ. Hosps., Cleve., 1955—59; fellow in microbiology Case Western Res. U., Cleve., 1961—63, instr., asst. prof., 1963—69, prof. medicine, 1977—93, prof. internat. health, 1991—93, prof. emeritus, 1994—, dir. Ctr. Internat. Health, 1991—96. Cons. TB Control Internat. Child Care Program, Port-au-Prince, Haiti, 1974—95. Contbr. numerous articles to sci. jours. and books, chpts. to scholarly texts. Bd. dirs., past pres. Am. Lung Assn. of No. Ohio, Cleve., 1974—85. Capt. U.S. Army, 1959—61. Recipient Markle scholarship, 1967, Fogarty fellowship, Bolivia, 1980; grantee, NIH, NSF. Fellow: AAS, Am. Coll. Chest Physicians, Infectious Diseases Soc. of Am., Am. Acad. Microbiology; mem.: Am. Soc. Microbiology, Cen. Soc. Clin. Rsch., Am. Thoracic Soc. United Church Of Christ. Office: Case Western Res U Sch Medicine Ctr Global Health and Diseases Cleveland OH 44106

DANIELL, JERE ROGERS, II, retired history educator, consultant, public lecturer; b. Millinocket, Maine, Nov. 28, 1932; s. Warren Fisher and Mary (Holway) D.; m. Sally Ann Wellborn, Dec. 1955 (div. 1969); children: Douglas, Alexander, Matthew; m. 2d Elena Lillie, July 19, 1969; stepchildren: Breena Daniell, Clifford Brodsky. AB, Dartmouth Coll., 1955; MA, Harvard U., 1962, PhD, 1964. Asst. prof. history Dartmouth Coll., 1964-69, assoc. prof., 1969-74, prof., 1974—2003, chmn. dept., 1979-83; class of 1925 prof., 1984—; head tutor Heritage Found., Old Deerfield, Mass., 1960-64; ret., 2003. Author: Experiment in Republicanism: N.H. Politics and the American Revolution, 1970, Colonial N.H.: A History, 1981; bd. editors: Univ. Press of New England, 1978-86. Served to lt (j.g.) USN, 1955-58. Mem. Colonial Soc. Mass., N.H. Hist. Soc. (bd. trustee 1979-86, 1999—), Vt. Hist. Soc., Maine Hist. Soc., Mass. Hist. Soc. Home: 11 Barrymore Rd Hanover NH 03755-2401 Office: Dartmouth Coll Dept History Hanover NH 03755 E-mail: jere.r.daniell@dartmouth.edu.

DANIELS, BRUCE EUGENE, school system administrator; b. Blytheville, Ark., Feb. 8, 1946; s. Leonard Doil and Hazle (Hoffsteter) D.; m. Rebecca Sue Starnes, Aug. 26, 1967; children: Bruce E. Jr., Bryce Edward. BA, Hendrix Coll., 1968; MS in Edn., Ark. State U., 1984; PhD, Iowa State U., 1989. Cert. sch. adminstr., Ark., Iowa, Miss. Tchr. math. Camden (Ark.) High Sch., 1968-71; tchr. math., basketball coach Blytheville Pub. Schs., 1971-81; asst. prin. Blytheville High Sch., 1983-87; rsch. assoc. Iowa State U., Ames, 1987-89; asst. supt. Jefferson (Iowa) Community Schs., 1988-89, Tupelo (Miss.) Pub. Schs., 1989—. Pres. Blytheville Optimist Club, 1986. Mem. ASCD, Am. Assn. Sch. Adminstrs., Assn. Quality and Participation, Phi Delta Kappa. Avocations: woodworking, baseball memorabilia. Home: 1108 Dixie St Blytheville AR 72315-1921 Office: Tupelo Pub Schs PO Box 557 Tupelo MS 38802-0557

DANIELS, IRISH C. principal; b. Miami, Fla. children: Irisha, Jessica. BS, Fla. A&M U., 1964, MEd, 1974; postgrad., Fla. State U., 1978. cert. adminstrn., supervision, early childhood, elem. edn., reading gifted edn., health. Tchr. Gadsden County Sch. Bd., Quincy, Fla., Leon County Sch. Bd., Tallahassee, asst. prin.; instr. reality edn. program Leon Co. Elem. Schs., 2000—. Grade level chmn.; sch. SACS chmn.; originator, coord. vocat. incentive program Hartsfield Sch., 1988-90; establisher, coord. Help Ctr. for grades 3-5, 1991; organizer, coord. Parent Tutorial Program, 1993-94; presenter Am. Assn. Colls. tchr. Edn. Conv., 1994, Assn. Tchr. Edn. Conv., 1996; coord. sch. renewal process Pineview Elem., 1997-98. Named Disting. Black Educator from Hartsfield, 1991, Disting. Educator of Minorities, 1992. Mem. Asst. Prins. Facilitator of Sch. Improvement (chair), Phi Delta Kappa, Kappa Delta Pi. Home: 2605 Vence Dr Tallahassee FL 32308-0539

DANIELS, KURT R. speech and language pathologist; b. Chgo., Oct. 22, 1954; s. Donald R. and Phyllis D. (Lenz) D.; m. Renee Perry, July 5, 1980. BS, Ea. Ill. U., 1976, MS, 1977. Cert. clin. competence speech/lang. pathology; lic. speech/lang. pathologist, nursing home adminstr; tchr's. cert. spl. K-12th grades. Hearing and speech specialist Shapiro Devel. Ctr., Kankakee, Ill., 1977-80; dysphagia specialist lead prof. W.A. Howe Ctr., Tinley Pk., Ill., 1980—. Mem. adv. bd. program in comm. disorders Govs. State U., clin. adj. prof.; cons. in field; presenter in field of dysphagia and developmental disabilities. Recipient Editor's Choice award Nat. Libr. Poetry, 1994, 95. Mem. Am. Speech, Lang. and Hearing Assn., Ill. Speech, Lang. and Hearing Assn., Ill. Network for Augmentative and Alternative Commn., Internat. Soc. Poets, Chicagoland Dysphagia Forum (sec.), So. Cook County Speech, Hearing, and Lang. Assn., Chgo. Audiology-Speech-Lang. Assn. Office: Howe Clinic Howe Ctr 7600 W 183d St Tinley Park IL 60477

DANIELS, MARK LEE, secondary education educator; b. Terre Haute, Ind., Nov. 13, 1948; s. Doral Lee and Frances Elizabeth (Hyslop) D.; m. Ofelia Cisneros, June 14, 1986; children: Christopher James, Tyler Lee. BS, Purdue U., 1971, M, 1986. Automotive tchr. Twin Lakes High Sch., Monticello, Ind., 1971; tchr. of indsl. arts Kekionga Jr. High Sch., Fort Wayne, Ind., 1974-78; tchr. of power South Side High Sch., Fort Wayne, 1978-79; tchr. of electricity, graphic arts, and reading Northrop High Sch., Fort Wayne, 1979-89; tchr. of indsl. arts, video coms., and social studies Blackhawk Mid. Sch., Fort Wayne, 1989-93, tech. coord., gifted and talented coord., 1993—. Dir. Fort Wayne Pk. Dept., 1974-78. With U.S. Army, 1971-74. Mem. NEA, Ind. Indsl. Tech. Edn. Assn. (Outstanding State Chmn. 1993), Tech. Educator Ind. (Meritorious Tchr. 1993), Fort Wayne Edn. Assn., Masons, Shriners, Disabled Am. Vets. Methodist. Avocations: videotaping, woodworking, camping, gardening, computers. Home: 2934 Wilderness Rd Fort Wayne IN 46845-1699 Office: Blackhawk Mid Sch 7200 E State Blvd Fort Wayne IN 46815-6499

DANIELS, RICHARD ALAN, retired internist, educator; b. Newark, May 8, 1930; s. Helen Frances (Cooper) D.; m. Norma M. Kasoff, Nov. 16, 1956; children: Steven, Jeffrey, Cathy, Barrie. BA in Chemistry magna cum laude, Syracuse U., 1951; MD summa cum laude, SUNY, Bklyn., 1955. Diplomate Am. Bd. Internal Medicine, Am. Bd. Geriatric Medicine, 1992. Rotating intern Mt. Sinai Hosp., N.Y.C., 1955-56, resident in internal medicine, 1957-59, chief resident in medicine, 1958-59; resident in internal medicine VA Hosp., Bronx, N.Y., 1956-57; practice internal medicine Oakhurst, NJ, 1961—99; assoc. clin. prof. medicine Drexel Coll. Medicine, Phila., 1977—. Sr. attending physician Monmouth Med. Ctr., Long Branch, 1977—, chief internal medicine sect., 1981-88; instr. phys. diagnosis U. Medicine and Dentistry of N.J., New Brunswick, 1980-96. Contbr. articles to profl. jours. Trustee, pres. Monmouth County (N.J.) Heart Assn., 1968-69. Served to maj. USAF, 1959-61. Fellow ACP, N.J. Acad. Medicine; mem. Am. Coll. Cardiology (assoc.), Am. Soc. Internal Medicine, Soc. Tchrs. of Family Practice, N.J. State Med. Soc., Monmouth County Med. Soc., Phi Beta Kappa, Alpha Omega Alpha. Republican. Jewish. Avocations: sailing, hiking, skiing, gardening, bicycling. Office: 16 Waterview Long Branch NJ 07740-9101

DANIELSON, JOHN M. federal official; b. Houston, Tex. Grad., U. Tex., Austin. Spl. asst. to sec. of education U.S. Dept. Education, Washington, 1991—93; nat. comty dir. AMERICA 2000, 1993—94; founder, prin. Comty. Edn. Ptnrs., 1994—2002; chief of staff to U.S. Sec. Edn. U.S. Dept. Edn., Washington, 2002—. Office: US Dept Edn 400 Maryland Ave SW Washington DC 20202

DANIELSON, NEIL DAVID, chemistry educator; b. Ames, Iowa, July 25, 1950; s. Gordon Charles and Dorothy Elisabeth (Thompson) D.; m. Elizabeth Moore, Aug. 4, 1979 (dec. July 28, 1986); 1 child, Glenn James; m. Kami Lee Park, Oct. 7, 1990; children: Kenneth Park, Alex Paul, Ryan Christopher, Evan Phillip. BS, Iowa State U., 1972; MS, Nebr. U., 1974; PhD, Ga. U., 1978. Asst. prof. Miami U., Oxford, Ohio, 1978-83, assoc. prof., 1983-91, prof., 1991—. Vis. scientist E.I. DuPont Co., Wilmington, Del., 1985-86; cons. Interaction Chems., Inc., Mountain View, Calif., 1983-91; sec. Ohio Valley Chromatography Symposium, 1988-96. Contbr. articles to Analytical Chemistry, Jour. Chromatography, Jour. Chromatographic Sci., Ency. Sci. & Tech., others. Achievements include research in high performance liquid chromatography, capillary electrophoresis and chemiluminescence. Office: Miami U Dept Chemistry and Biochem Oxford OH 45056 E-mail: danielnd@muohio.edu.

DANIELSON, WAYNE ALLEN, journalism and computer science educator; b. Burlington, Iowa, Dec. 6, 1929; s. Arthur Leroy and Bessie Ann (Bonar) D.; m. Beverly Grace Kinsell, Mar. 19, 1955 (dec. Oct. 1988); children: Matthew Henry, Benjamin Wayne, Grace Frances, Paul Arthur; m. LaVonne Walker Caffey, July 10, 1993; stepchildren: Kristin Marie, Bradley Neal. BA, State U. Iowa, 1952; MA, Stanford U., 1953, PhD, 1957.

Reporter, research mgr. San Jose (Calif.) Mercury-News, 1953-54; acting asst. prof. Stanford U., 1956-57; asst. prof. journalism U. Wis., 1957-59; mem. faculty U. N.C., 1959-69, prof. journalism, 1963-69; rsch. prof. Inst. Rsch. Social Sci., 1963-69; dean Sch. Journalism, 1964-69; dean Sch. Comm., U. Tex., Austin, 1969-79, prof. journalism and computer sci., 1969—2003, Jesse H. Jones prof. journalism, 1982-89, Dewitt C. Reddick chair, 1989, chmn. dept. journalism, 1991-93, prof. emeritus, 2003—. Mem. steering com. News Rsch. Ctr., Am. Newspaper Pubs. Assn., 1964-73; mem. rsch. com. AP Mng. Editors Assn., 1963-69. Author: (with G. C. Wilhoit, Jr.) A Computerized Bibliography of Mass Communication Research, 1944-64, (with Blanche Prejean) Programed News Style, 1977, 2d edit., 1988; contbr. articles to profl. jours.; founding editor: Journalism Abstracts, 1963-68, 71; mem. editl. bd. Journalism Quar, 1964-72; author, editor instrnl. computer program series. Mem. pub. rels. com. N.C. Heart Assn., 1963-67; chmn. faculty senate U. Tex., 1989-90. Recipient Civitatis award, U. Tex., 2000. Mem. Assn. Edn. Journalism and Mass Comm. (chmn. publs. com. 1968-72, rsch. com. 1980-83, pres. 1970-71, Paul J. Deutschmann award 1993), Am. Assn. Schs. and Depts. Journalism (v.p. 1966-67, pres. 1967-68), Tex. Journalism Edn. Coun. (chmn. 1970-71), Phi Beta Kappa, Kappa Tau Alpha, Phi Kappa Phi. Office: U Tex Sch Journalism Austin TX 78712 E-mail: wayne@mail.utexas.edu.

DANKE, VIRGINIA, educational administrator, travel consultant; b. Spokane, Wash., Mar. 9, 1925; d. William Ernest and Daisy May (Norton) Danke. BS, Wash. State U., 1947; MEd, Whitworth Coll., 1950; postgrad., LaSalle U., 1973. Cert. tchr. Counselor Clarkston (Wash.) Sch. Dist., 1948—48; head phys. edn. dept. LCHS Spokane Sch. Dist., 1948—77; travel cons. Viking Travel, Spokane, 1982—, Empire Tours, Spokane, 1982—. Co-author (editor): Marching Together, 1955. Treas. Fedn. Western Outdoor Clubs, 1980—; com. mem. Future Spokane, 1981—, bd. dirs., Pacific Crest Trail Conf., Santa Ana, Calif., 1984; mem. Friends Centennial Trial, 1992—, bd. dirs., 1994—96; mem. Am. Red Cross Disaster Unit. Named to Wash. State Officials Hall of Fame, 2003; recipient Scroll of Honor-Hall of Fame, Spokane C. of C., 1983, Greater Spokane Sports Assn., 1973, Wash. Interscholastic Activites Assn., 1990, State Officiating, 1992. Mem.: Spokane Ret. Tchrs. Assn. (pres. 1981—82), Wash. State Officials Assn. (Meritorious Svc. award 2002, Hall of Fame 2003), Wash. State Ret. Tchrs. Assn. (bd. dirs. 1987—), Nat. Ret. Tchrs. Assn., Wash. Edn. Assn., Spokane Edn. Assn. (com. chmn. 1960—70), Soroptimist (pres. 1970), Hangman Golf Club (Spokane pres. 1997), Hobnailers Club (pres. 1966—67, 1986—87). Home: 1103 E 14th Ave Spokane WA 99202-2541

DANKER, MERVYN KENNETH, director of education; b. Cape Town, South Africa, Mar. 27, 1944; came to U.S., 1989; s. David Barry and Nina (Selbo) D.; m. Rochelle Gould, Dec. 16, 1969; children: Dionne Bonita, David Jonathan, Gareth Saul. BA, U. Cape Town, 1965, BEd, 1974. Cert. secondary edn. tchr., South Africa, Australia. Tchr. Camps Bay High Sch., Cape Town, 1967-76; vice prin. Herzlia High Sch., Cape Town, 1977; headmaster Theodor Herzl Sch., Port Elizabeth, Republic of South Africa, 1978-86, Carmel Sch., Perth, West Australia, 1986-89; dir. of edn. Solomon Schechter Day Sch., West Hartford, Conn., 1989-97; prin. Jewish Day Sch. of the North Peninsula, 1997—. Author: History of Theodor Herzl School, 1986. Jewish. Avocations: running, tennis, rugby, cycling, reading. Home: 22 Goldenridge Ct San Mateo CA 94402-3718 Office: Jewish Day Sch 800 Foster City Blvd Foster City CA 94404 E-mail: mdanker@juno.com.

DANKO, GEORGE, engineering educator; b. Budapest, Hungary, Apr. 3, 1944; came to U.S., 1986; s. Gyorgy and Ilona (Mihaly) D.; m. Eva Arvay, Dec. 14, 1976; 1 child, Reka. BSME, Tech. U. Budapest, 1968, PhD, 1976; MS in Applied Math., Eotovs U. of Scis., Budapest, 1975; PhD, Hungarian Acad. Scis., Budapest, 1985. Cert. Profl. Ski Instrs. Am. Assn. Asst. prof. Tech. U. Budapest, 1968-75, assoc. prof., 1979-86; fellow Hungarian Acad. Scis., Budapest, 1975-79; rsch. assoc. U. Nev., Reno, 1986-90, assoc. prof., 1990-95, prof. mining engring., 1995—. Cons. Sierra Sci., Reno, 1990—; chmn. High-Level Radioactive Waste Mgmt. Conf., 1991, 92; portrait artist, Reno, 1987-92. Co-author: Methods for the Calculation of Pipeline Transients, 1976, Warming-up and Cooling of Electrical Machinery, 1982; contbr. articles to profl. jours. Com. rep. Truckee River Steering Com., Reno, 1993-94. Grantee U.S. Bur. Mines, 1986-97, U.S. Dept. Energy, 1991—, Clarkson Co., 1992-98. Mem. ASME, ISES (internat. organizing com. 1993-94), IFAC (internat. program com. 1995—), Soc. Mining Engrs., Am. Nuclear Soc. Achievements include patents for methods and apparatus for the determination of the heat transfer coefficient, process and apparatus for the determination of thermophysical properties, underground cooling enhancement for nuclear waste repository, method and apparatus for underground nuclear waste repository, others. Office: U Nev Reno Mining Engring Dept 173 Reno NV 89557-0001

DANNER, CHARLES L. elementary education educator; b. Camden, N.J., May 25, 1940; s. Frank and Jean (Santangelo) D.; m. Ruth E. Bohlman, July 7, 1963 (div. Sept. 1983); children: Bradford, Jane. BA, Glassboro State Coll., 1963; MA, Trenton State Coll., 1970; postgrad., Temple U., 1978-81. Elem. tchr. Rush Sch., Cinnaminson, N.J., 1963-67, Grant Demonstration Ctr. for Urban Edn., Trenton, N.J., 1967-70, Eldridge Park Elem. Sch., Lawrence Twp., N.J., 1970-76, Lawrence Intermediate Sch., Lawrence Twp., 1976-86; coord. Lawrence Twp. Instrnl. Effectiveness Project, 1986-92. Asst. prof. Trenton State Coll., 1967-76; clin. prof. Rider Coll., N.J., 1986-92. Recipient Gov.'s Tchr. Recognition award 1976-86, Outstanding Practitioner award N.J. Assn. Tchr. Educators 1990. Avocations: cooking, music. Home: 71 Park Ct Westmont NJ 08108-1816

D'ANNOLFO, SUZANNE CORDIER, educational administrator, educator; b. Akron, Ohio, Oct. 20, 1946; d. Albert Tennyson and Luella Dorothy Cordier; m. Frank Joseph D'Annolfo, Feb. 12, 1982; children: Casey Cordier, Matthew Scott. BS, Boston U., 1970; student, Slippery Rock (Pa.) State U., 1964-67; MS, Cen. Conn. State U., 1973; EdD, Boston U., 1980. Tchr. West Hartford (Conn.) Pub. Schs., 1970-78, adminstr. health and phys. edn., dir. athletics, 1979-87; asst. prin. Farmington High Sch., 1988—93; prin. Litchfield (Conn.) High Sch., 1993-98, Nat. Sch. of Excellence; dir. curriculum and instrn. grades 9-12 Newington (Conn.) Pub. Schs., 1998-01; CREC prin. Met. Learning Ctr. Nat. Sch. Distinction, A Magnet Sch. for Global & Internat. Studies, 2001—. Coach U.S. Olympic Track and Field Team Learn-by-Doing Clinics, 1977—80; mem. Conn. Gov.'s Coun. on Phys. Fitness and Sport, 1978—87; drug. cons. Nutmeg State Games; mem. edn. coun. U.S. Olympic Com.; dean U.S. Olympic Acad., First World-Scholar Athlete Games, Newport, RI; Ethics Fellow Internat. Inst. of Sport, 1993; adj. prof. Ctrl. Conn. State U. Author: Secondary Physical Education, Stress Management, Ideas II, Drugs and AIDS Education for Elementary Students. Bd. dirs. Spl. Olympics, West Hartford, 1979-87; co-founder Pvt. Victories health newsletter for high sch. students, 1991-98. Named to N.E. Women's Hall of Fame, 1994; recipient Nat. Educator award Milken Found., 1995. Mem. ASCD, NASSP, AAHPERD (com., spkr. nat. conv.), NEA, Conn. Assn. Health, Phys. Edn., Recreation and Dance (pres. 1981-82, Profl. Honor award 1986), Ctrl. Conn. Conf. (life, treas. 1984-87, Leadership award 1987), Nat. H.S. Coaches Assn. (track v.p. 1978-80, Conn. Cross Country Coach of Yr. award 1976, Track Coach of Yr. award), Conn. Prins. Acad., Blue Ribbon Human Resource Bank, Phi Delta Kappa. Avocations: family, writing, swimming, biking, walking. Home: 30 Shadow Ln West Hartford CT 06110-1640 Office: Met Learning Ctr 1551 Blue Hills Ave Bloomfield CT 06002

DANS, PETER EMANUEL, medical educator; b. N.Y.C., June 17, 1937; s. Emanuel and Filomena (Lisanti) D.; m. Colette Lumina Lizotte, May 28, 1966; children: Maria Cristina, Paul Edouard, Thomas Emanuel, Suzanne Elise. BS in Chemistry, Manhattan Coll., 1957; MD, Columbia U., 1961. Intern, resident medicine Johns Hopkins Hosp., Balt., 1961-63; resident medicine Presbyn. Hosp., N.Y.C., 1963-64; fellow rsch. NIH, Bethesda, Md., 1964-67; infectious diseases fellow Harvard U., Boston, 1967-69; asst. prof. medicine U. Colo., Denver, 1969-74, assoc. prof., 1974-78; Robert Wood Johnson health policy fellow Inst. Medicine, Washington, 1976-77, sr. prof. assoc., 1977-78; assoc. prof. medicine Johns Hopkins U. Sch. Medicine and Health Policy and Mgmt., Balt., 1978—, Johns Hopkins U. Sch. Hygiene and Pub. Health, Balt., 1978—; clin. prof. Marshall U. Sch. Medicine, 1995—. Mem. Md. Physician Bd. Quality Assurance, sec. 1988-92; ind. cons. disease mgmt., outcomes, ethics, 1996—; med. cons. Advance PCS, 1996—. Author: Doctors in the Movies: Boil the Water & Just Say Aah!, 2000, Perry's Baltimore Adventure: A Bird's Eye View of Charm City, 2003; co-author: New Medical Market Place: A Physician's Guide to the Health Care Revolution, 1988; dep. editor: Annals of Internal Medicine, 1991—94, assoc. med. dir.: GMIS, Inc., 1994—95, mem. editl. bd.: Pharos, 1988—; contbr. articles to profl. jours., chpts. to books; film reviewer Physician at the Movies, Pharos, 1990—. Pres. Falls Rd. Cmty. Assn., 1980—84, 1987—90; mem. adv. com. on gifted talented program Baltimore County, 1981—90, mem. zoning adv. com., 1985—86, mem. commn. on aging, 1996—98; pres. parish coun. Shrine of Sacred Heart, Balt., 1981—83; lector St. Francis Xavier, Balt., 1997—; bd. dirs. Ctr. Profl. Ethics U. Balt., 1999—2001. Fellow ACP; mem. Epsilon Sigma Pi, Alpha Omega Alpha. Roman Catholic. Avocations: film, birdwatching. Home and Office: 11 Hickory Hill Rd Cockeysville Hunt Valley MD 21030-1624

DANSAK, DANIEL ALBERT, medical educator, consultant; b. McKeesport, Pa., Apr. 27, 1943; s. Henry Daniel and Mary (Francis) D.; m. Judith Lynn Rogers, May 9, 1981 (div. Apr. 1987); m. Melissa Ann Pickett, May 31, 1989. BS, Drexel U., 1966; MD, Georgetown U., 1970. Diplomate Am. Bd. Psychiatry and Neurology. Asst. chief pyschiatry svc. VA, Washington, 1975-77; asst. prof. dept. psychiatry U. N.Mex., Albuquerque, 1977-84; assoc. prof. dept. psychiatry U. South Ala., Mobile, 1984-2000; clin. prof. U. Soth Ala., Mobile, 2002—; chief mental health svc. VA Gulf Coast Veteran's Healht Care Sys., Gulfport, Miss., 2000—, staff psychiatrist, 2002—. Cons. U.S. Dept. Labor, Albuquerque, 1981-84; cons. Ala. Dept. Edn., Mobile, 1986-90; med. dir. Bradford Health Svcs., Mobile, 1989—. Contbr. articles to profl. jours. Mem. bd. trustees Mobile Bay Area Partnership for Youth, 1989-2000. Lt. comdr. USNR, 1973-75. Fellow Am. Coll. Clin. Pharmacology; mem. AAAS. Republican. Roman Catholic. Avocation: fishing. Home: 4012 Dawson Dr Mobile AL 36619-9224 Office: U South Ala Dept Psychiatry 3421 Medical Park Dr Ste 2 Mobile AL 36693-3330

DANSBY-GILES, GLORIA F. counselor, educator; b. Detroit; m. Frank Lee Giles. BA, S.W. Tex. State U., 1974; MA, U. Tex., San Antonio, 1976; EdD, Tex. Tex. U., 1979. Cert. counselor and tchr., Tex.; cert. counselor, Miss., Tex. Dir. student activities St. Phillip's Coll., San Antonio, 1979-84; tchr. San Antoio Ind. Sch. Dist., 1985-89; coord. testing S.W. Tex. State U., San Marcos, 1989-91; asst. prof. Sam Houston State U., Huntsville, Tex., 1990, 91, Jackson (Miss.) State U., 1991—. Mem. editorial bd. Coll. Student Pers. jour., 1991—; contbr. articles to profl. jours. Bd. dirs. Jr. Coll. Student Pers. Assn. Tex., 1981-84;' pres. C.C. Student Activities Assn., 1981-83, Tex. Coll. Pers. Assn., 1983-84. Mem. Am. Counseling Assn. (sec. Capitol area chpt. 1993—), Am. Coll. Pers. Assn. (mem. commn. IX), Miss. Counseling Assn., Miss. Sch. Counselor Assn. (v.p. post secondary rels., newsletter editor 1993—), Phi Delta Kappa, Delta Kappa Gamma, Pi Lambda Theta. Methodist. Office: Jackson State U PO Box 17122 1400 J R Lynch St Jackson MS 39217

DANSO, DANIEL Y. physician, educator; b. Accra, Ghana, Dec. 31, 1957; came to U.S., 1986; s. John K. and Elizabeth Ama (Afrakoma) D.; m. Comfort Adwoa Asiedu, July 31, 1986; children: Maxine, Danielle. MD, U. Ghana, 1985; PhD, U. Fla., 1991. Diplomate in internal medicine, hematology and med. oncology Am. Bd. Internal Medicine. Med. officer Korle-Bu Tchg. Hosp., Accra, 1985-86; grad. rsch. asst. dept. pharmacology/therapeutics U. Fla., Gainesville, 1987-91; resident physician St. Lukes Hosp. Ctr., N.Y.C., 1991-94; clin. and rsch. fellow Meml. Sloan-Kettering Cancer Ctr., N.Y.C., 1994-97; attending physician Muskogee (Okla.) Regional Med. Ctr., 1997-99; staff physician CCOM Med. Group, Muskogee, 1997-99; asst. prof. med., dir. clinical trials Med. Coll. Ohio, Toledo, 1999—. Recipient Merit award Am. Soc. Clin. Oncology, 1997; Dept. fellow U. Fla., 1987-91, NIH grantee, 1995-97. Mem. ACP, Am. Assn. Cancer Rsch., Am. Soc. Clin. Oncologists. Avocations: dancing, truck driving, soccer. Office: Med Coll Ohio Rupert Health Ctr Dept Medicine 3120 Glendale Ave Toledo OH 43614-5811 E-mail: ddanso@mco.edu.

DANTO, ARTHUR COLEMAN, author, philosopher, art critic; b. Ann Arbor, Mich., Jan. 1, 1924; s. Samuel Budd and Sylvia (Gittleman) D.; m. Shirley Rovetch, Aug. 9, 1946 (dec. July 1978); children: Elizabeth, Jane; m. Barbara Westman, Feb. 15, 1980. BA, Wayne State U., 1948; MA, Columbia U., 1949, PhD, 1952; postgrad., U. Paris, 1949-50. Instr. U. Colo., Colo., 1950-51; mem. faculty Columbia U., 1952—, Johnsonian prof. philosophy, 1975-92, chmn. dept., 1979-87, co-dir. Ctr. for Study of Human Rights, 1978-92; prof. emeritus, 1992. Andrew W. Mellon Fine Arts lectr., 1995. Author: Analytical Philosophy of Knowledge, 1968, What Philosophy Is, 1968, Analytical Philosophy of Hist., 1965, Nietzsche as Philosopher, 1965, Analytical Philosophy of Action, 1973, Mysticism and Morality, 1972, Jean-Paul Sartre, 1975, The Transfiguration of the Commonplace, 1981 (Lionel Trilling Book prize 1982), Narration and Knowledge, 1985, The Philosophical Disenfranchisement of Art, 1986, The State of the Art, 1987, Connections to the World, 1989, Encounters and Reflections: Art in the Hist. Present, 1990, Beyond the Brillo Box: Art in the Post Hist. Period, 1992, Mark Tansey: Visions and Revisions, 1992, Robert Mapplethorpe, 1992, Embodied Meanings: Critical Essays and Aesthetic Meditations, 1994, Playing with the Edge: The Photographic Achievement of Robert Mapplethorpe, After the End of Art: Contemporary Art and the Pale of Hist., 1997 (Eugene Kayden prize 1997), The Body/Body Problem, 1999, Philosophizing Art, 1999, The Madonna of the Future, 2000, The Abuse of Beauty: Aesthetics and the Concept of Art, 2003; editor Jour. Philosophy, 1965—, pres., 1987—; art critic The Nation, 1984—; contbg. editor ARTFORUM. Bd. dirs. Amnesty Internat., 1970-75, gen. sec., 1973. Served with AUS, 1942-45. Recipient prize for disting. criticism Mfr.-Hanover/Art World, 1985, George S. Polk award for criticism, 1985, Nat. Book Critics Circle prize for criticism, 1990, ICP Infinity prize for writing in photography, 1993; fellow Fulbright Found., 1949, Guggenheim Found., 1969, 82, Am. Coun. Learned Socs., 1961, 70; Fulbright disting. prof. Yugoslavia, 1976; Phi Beta Kappa prof. Arts and Scis.; mem. Am. Philos. Assn. (v.p. 1969, pres. 1983), Am. Soc. Aesthetics (v.p. 1987, pres. 1989). Fellow AAAS; mem. Am. Philos. Assn. (v.p. 1969, pres. 1983), Am. Soc. Aesthetics (v.p. 1987, pres. 1989), Coll. Art Assn. (Frank Jewett Mather prize for criticism). Office: 420 Riverside Dr New York NY 10025-7773 E-mail: acdi@columbia.edu.

DANTZIC, CYNTHIA MARIS, artist, educator; b. NYC, Jan. 4, 1933; d. Howard Arthur and Sylvia Hazel (Wiener) Gross; m. Jerry Dantzic, June 15, 1958; 1 son, Grayson Ross. Student, Brooklyn Mus. Art Sch., Bklyn., 1947—50, Bard Coll., 1950—52; BFA, Yale U., 1955; MFA, Pratt Inst., 1963. Tchr. art Baldwin Sch., Bryn Mawr, Pa., 1955-58; head art dept. Bentley Sch., N.Y.C., 1958-62; coord. art prog., instr. North Shore Cmty. Arts Ctr., Roslyn, NY, 1962-64; instr. art CUNY-Bronx, N.Y.C., 1963-64; faculty L.I. U., Bklyn., 1964—, prof., 1975—, chair art dept., 1980-86. Adj. assoc. prof. art Cooper Union, 1992—99, adj. prof. art, 1999—2002; lectr., presenter in field. One-woman shows include Resnick Gallery, L.I. U., Bklyn., 1983, 89, 95, 2000, East Hampton Gallery, N.Y.C., 1965-66, St. John's U. Gallery, 1995; exhibited in group shows at Blue Mountain Gallery, N.Y.C., 1984-85, 94-98, 2001, 2002, Hillwood Gallery, Greenvale, N.Y., 1985; commd. artist edit. of photo collages Bklyn. Arts and Culture Assn., 1983; represented in permanent collections Bklyn. Mus., N.Y., Rose Art Mus., Mass., Bard Coll., N.Y.; author, illustrator: Stop Dropping BreAdcrumBs on my YaCht, 1974, Sounds of Silents, 1976, Design Dimensions: An Introduction to the Visual Surface, 1990, Drawing Dimensions: A Comprehensive Introduction, 1999, Antique Pocket Mirrors: Pictorial & Advertising Minatures, 2002; contbr. articles to profl. jours. Trustee Park Slope Civic Coun., 1991—. Mellon grantee, 1984, L.I. Univ. faculty rsch. grantee, 1985—; recipient Newton Teaching Excellence award, 1988, Trustees award single work, 1990, Trustees lifetime award for Scholarly Achievement in art and art edn. L.I. Univ., 1999. Mem. AAUP, Internat. Soc. Copier Artists, L.I. U. Faculty Fedn. (exec. com. 1975—), Coll. Art Assn., Soc. Scribes (bd. govs. 2003—). Avocations: piano, travel, collecting americana and tribal and folk art. Home: 910 President St Brooklyn NY 11215-1604 Office: LI U Art Dept University Pla Brooklyn NY 11201

DANTZLER, JOYCE ELSTON, school system administrator, educator; b. Bluffton, Ind., Aug. 26, 1949; d. Henry and Mary Jane (Cowens) E.; m. Marshall L. Dantzler, Apr. 8, 1972; children: Mark, Brian. BS with distinction, Ind. U., 1972; MEd, Auburn U., 1975, EdS, 1985. Cert. tchr., supr., administrn., prin., Ala., Va. Head tchr. First United Meth. Presch., Honolulu, 1971-72; tchr. Montgomery County (Ala.) Pub. Schs., Montgomery, 1972-76, Fairfax County (Va.) Pub. Schs., Fairfax, 1976-81, 88-90, asst. prin., 1991-92, coord. elem. programs, 1992—; supr. student tchrs. Dept. Edn. Auburn U., Montgomery, 1985-88. Team participant So. Assn. Accreditation, 1974-75, 88; instr. aerobics YMCA, Montgomery, 1984-85; adj. instr. Auburn U., 1985-88; facilitator Mentor Program State of Va., Old Dominion U., Norfolk, 1990-91. Recipient Outstanding Vol. Svc. award Fairfax County, Fairfax, 1982. Mem. Nat. Assn. Elem. Sch. Prins., Va. Assn. Elem. Sch. Prins., Fairfax County Assn. Elem. Sch. Prins., Greater Washington Reading Assn., Ind. U. Alumni Assn., Auburn U. Alumni Assn., Delat Kappa Gamma, Phi Delta Kappa. Methodist. Avocations: aerobics, gardening. Home: 13502 Quiet Stream Ct Fairfax VA 20151-2419 Office: Fairfax County Pub Schs Area IV Administrv Office 10515 School St Fairfax VA 22030-4206

D'ANZA, LAWRENCE MARTIN, management consultant; b. Hindsdale, Ill., June 20, 1953; s. Joseph James and Evelyn (Martinek) D'Anza; m. Teresa D'Anza, June 14, 1980 (div. Sept. 2003). BBEd, Ea. N.Mex. U., 1975; MA, U. N.Mex., 1984. Instr. cashiering Albuquerque Tech. Vocat. Inst., 1975-85; mktg. edn. tchr. coord. Eldorado HS, 1975-2000; enrollment program coord. Del Norte HS, 1983-93; tchr. bus. mktg. Albuquerque Pub. Schs., 1984-85; cons., acct. mgr., ops./sales mgr. N.Mex. ops. DeLaPorte & Assoc., 2000—. Conf. cons. N.Mex DECA, 1978—, chmn., 1983—84, 1989—91, bd. govs., 1988—90, 1996—97; secondary adv. coun. Nat. DECA, 1992—93, 1997—99, chairperson, 1998—99, nat. bd. dirs., 1993—96, conf. coord. western region, 1992, 96, 98, 2000, 02, western region bd. dirs., 1993—98. Mem. N.Mex Gov.'s Workforce Devel. Bd., 1996—99; trustee Youth Opportunities in Retailing, 1996—2001. Recipient Nat. Educator award, Milken Family Found., 1995. Mem.: N.Mex Vocat. Assn. (pres. 1995—96, N.Mex Mktg. Tchr. of the Yr. 1981—82, 1987—88, 1992—93, 1993—94), Am. Vocat. Assn. (Region Iv Mktg. Edn. Tchr. of the Yr. 1994—95, Vocat. Tchr. of the Yr. 1994—95), N.Mex Mktg. Edn. Assn. Avocations: golf, sports, travel. Home: 11005 Costa Del Sol NE Albuquerque NM 87111-1891 E-mail: ldanzadeca@aol.com.

DARBY, JOANNE TYNDALE (JAYE DARBY), arts and humanities educator; b. Tucson, Sept. 22, 1948; d. Robert Porter Smith and Joanne Inloes Snow-Smith; stepchildren: Margaret Loutrel, David Michael. BA, U. Ariz., 1972; MEd, U. Calif., L.A., 1986, PhD, 1996. Cert. secondary tchr., gifted and talented tchr., Calif. Tchr. English, chmn. dept. Las Virgenes Unified Sch. Dist., Calabasas, Calif., 1979-82; tchr. English and gifted and talented edn. Las Virgenes Unified Sch.Dist., Calabasas, Calif., 1983-84; sch. improvement coord./lang. arts/social studies/drama tchr Las Virgenes Unified Sch. Dist., Calabasas, Calif., 1991-92; tchr. English and gifted and talented edn. Beverly Hills (Calif.) Unified Sch. Dist., 1982-83, 84-89, English and drama tchr., 1994; tchr., cons. Calif. Lit. Project, San Diego, 1985-87; cons., free lance editor L.A., 1977—; dir. Shakespeare edn. and festivals project Folger Libr., Washington, 1990-91; field work supr. tchr. edn. program Ctr. X, Grad. Sch. Edn. and Info. Studies, UCLA, 1992-96, Ctr. X postdoctoral scholar, tchr. edn. program, 1996-97; asst. rschr., founding co-dir. Project HOOP, Am. Indian Studies Ctr., UCLA, 1997—2000; asst. prof. Coll. Edn. San Diego State U., 2000—. Cons. arts and edn., L.A., 1991—. Co-editor (with Hanay Geiogamah) Stories of Our Way: An Anthology of American Indian Plays, 1999, American Indian Theater in Performance: A Reader, 2000, (with Stephanie Fitzgerald) Keepers of the Morning Star: An Anthology of Native Women's Theater, 2003; contbr. articles to profl. publs. Mem.: MLA, Assn. for Theatre in Higher Edn., Nat. Coun. Tchrs. English, Am. Ednl. Rsch. Assn., Phi Beta Kappa, Alpha Lambda Delta, Phi Beta Phi. Home: 7350 Golfcrest Pl Apt 2001 San Diego CA 92119-2486

DARBY, KAREN SUE, legal education administrator; b. Columbus, Ohio, Sept. 15, 1947; d. Emerson Curtis and Kathryn Elizabeth (Bowers) Dum; m. R. Russell Darby, Dec. 21, 1974; children: David Randolph, Michael Emerson. BA magna cum laude, Capital U., Columbus, 1969; JD, Ohio State U., 1980. Bar: Ohio 1980, Pa. 1998, U.S. Dist. Ct. (so. dist.) Ohio 1981. High sch. English tchr. Columbus Pub. Schs., 1969-72; employee rels. specialist GE, Circleville, Ohio, 1972-74, mgr. EEO and manpower programs chem. met. div. Worthington, Ohio, 1974-77; atty. Ohio Legal Rights Svc., Columbus, 1980-81; pvt. practice Columbus, 1981-90; assoc. dir. Ohio Continuing Legal Edn. Inst., Columbus, 1989-95; dir. Phila. Bar Edn. Ctr., 1995-97; assoc. dir. Pa. Bar Inst., Phila., 1997—2002; exec. dir. Ill. Inst. for Continuing Legal Edn., 2002—. Mem. rules adv. com. Supreme Ct. Ohio, Columbus, 1989-94. Author, editor: Civil Commitment in Ohio - A Manual for Respondents' Attorneys, 1980. Mem. divorce mediation panel Ohio State U. Commn. on Interprofl. Edn., Columbus, 1988-91; vol. Boy Scouts Am., Columbus, 1988-92, Columbus Pub. Schs., 1984-95. Mem.: ABA, Assn. Continuing Legal Edn., Ill. State Bar Assn., Univ. Club of Chgo. Democrat. Lutheran. Avocations: organ, piano, gardening. Office: IICLE 2395 W Jefferson St Springfield IL 62702

DARBY, LEWIS RANDAL, special education educator; b. Quinwood, W.Va., Mar. 24, 1929; s. Robert B. and Loraine (Richards) D.; m. Christa L. Lachmann, Aug. 30; 1 child, Stephen. BS, W.Va. State Coll., 1960; MA, Mich. State U., 1967; EdS, Oakland U., 1983. Cert. tchr. cons. emotionally impaired, Mich., supr. spl. edn., Mich. Tchr. Macomb Reading Ptnrs., Mt. Clemens, Mich., 1989-91; tchr. cons. Macomb County Youth Home; tchr. Oakland U. Summer Inst., Anshun, China, 1994, Summer Inst., Oakland U., Guiyang, China, 1996. Affiliate Consumer's Union, Yonkers, N.Y., 1992; active ACLU, N.Y., 1992, Children's Def. Fund, Washington, 1991-92. Fellow Mich. State U., 1966. Mem. Nat. Assn. for Edn. of Young Children, Mich. Assn. for Edn. of Young Children (exec. bd. dirs., pub. policy com.). Avocations: swimming, folk guitar, golf, writing short stories, reading. Home: 20930 Riverbend Dr S Clinton Township MI 48038-2487

DARBY, MARIANNE TALLEY, elementary school educator; b. Adel, Ga., Nov. 8, 1937; d. William Giles and Mary (McGlamry) Talley; m. Roy Copeland Darby, Apr. 2, 1958; children: Susan, Leslie Darby Galifianakis, Allison Darby Davis. Student, Emory U., 1955-57; BS in Early Childhood Edn., Valdosta (Ga.) State Coll., 1973. Cert. early childhood and elem. edn. tchr., Ga. Tchr. 2d grade Adel Elem. Sch., spring 1973, tchr. 1st grade, 1973-98, ret., 1998. Pres. Cook County Jaycettes, Adel, 1962. Teacher of Year, Cook Elem. Sch., 1998—. Mem. Internat. Reading Assn. (South Cen. Ga. coun.), Profl. Assn. Ga. Educators, Adel Garden Club, Alpha Epsilon Upsilon, Alpha Delta Kappa (sec. 1980-82), Sigma Alpha Chi, Alpha Chi, Kappa Alpha Theta. Republican. Methodist. Avocations: sewing, piano, reading, african violets. Home: 710 S Forrest Ave Adel GA 31620-3523

DARBY, SAMUEL EDWARD, guidance counselor; b. Cuba, N.Y., June 15, 1952; s. Samuel E. and Jayne (Doswell) D.; m. Diane Miller, July 21, 1952; children: Kelly, Krystal. BA, Columbia Union Coll., 1974; MEd, Trenton State Coll., 1981; EdD, Nova U., 1990. Cert. sch. superintendent, Del., secondary prin., Del., Pa., sch. counselor, Del., Pa., speech instr., Del., sch. psychologist, Pa. Instr. Columbia Union Coll., Takoma Park, Md., 1974-75; tchr., prin. Allegheny East Conf., Pine Forge, Pa., 1975-84; asst. headmaster Pine Forge (Pa.) Acad., 1984-89; instr. Performance Learning Systems, Emerson, N.J., 1989—; guidance counselor Caesar Rodney Sch. Dist., Camden, Del., 1989-90, Great Valley Sch. Dist., DeVault, Pa., 1990—. Mem. adv. bd. for Minority Recruiting and Retention, Dover, Del., 1989-90; program dir. Edutech Cons., Douglassville, Pa., 1991—; coord. for alternative edn. program Pottsgrove (Pa.) Sch. Dist., 1994-96; counselor Ctr. for Self-Esteem, Reading, Pa., 1995—. Bd. chair Pine Forge (Pa.) S.D.A. Elem. Sch., 1990-91. Mem. AACD, NEA, Nat. Assn. for Sch. Psychologists, Pa. Assn. for Counseling and Devel., Great Valley Edn. Assn., Chi Sigma Iota. Avocations: computers, nautilus, travel, fresh water fishing. Office: Gen Wayne Mid Sch 20 Devon Rd Malvern PA 19355-3071

DARCY, KEITH THOMAS, finance company executive, educator; b. N.Y.C., June 18, 1948; s. Donald and Geraldine (Kindermann) D.; m. Lynne Alison Cumming, June 17, 1972; children: Erin Lyn, Timothy James. BS in Econs., Fordham U., 1970; MBA, Iona Coll., New Rochelle, N.Y., 1974; postgrad., N.Y. Theol. Sem., 1988-89. With Bankers Trust Co., N.Y.C., 1970—77; v.p. Marine Midland Bank N.A., N.Y.C., 1977—82; CEO, IGM divsn. Gen. Reins. Corp., Stamford, Conn., 1982—83; dir. human resource divsn. Marine Midland Bank, N.Y.C., 1984—89; pres., CEO, The Leadership Group, Inc., N.Y.C., 1989—94; v.p., assoc. ethics officer Prudential Securities Inc., N.Y.C., 1994—96, sr. ethics advisor, 1996—97; assoc. dean, disting. prof. bus. Georgetown U., Washington, 1995—96; exec. v.p. office of the pres. IBJ Whitehall Bank and Trust Co., N.Y.C., 1997—2002; pres., CEO Ctr. Integrity, Pound Ridge, NY, 2002—. Mem. adj. faculty Marymount Coll., 1978-96, Mercy Coll., 1975-96; mem. faculty advanced exec. edn. at Wharton, U. Pa., 1994—; mem. faculty grad. mgmt. program Antioch U., Seattle, 1989-96; exec.-in-residence grad. program in human resources and orgnl. devel. and grad. program in orgnl. leadership Manhattanville Coll., Purchase, N.Y., mem. corp. adv. bd., 1989—; exec. fellow Ctr. for Bus. Ethics, Bentley Coll., Waltham, Mass., 1993—, mem. exec. com.; tchg. fellow Smith Sch. Bus., U. Md., College Park, 2002—; bd. dirs. Barat House, Purchase, N.Y., 1989—; dir. emeritus Ethics Officer Assn.; mem. steering com. Caux (Switzerland) Round Table, 1996—; nat. adv. bd. Worktalk, 1999—; vice chmn. Ctr. for Values-Based Leadership, 1999—, chmn., bd. trustees BBB Found., 2001—. Co-author: Change Management, 1993, The Ethics Companion, 1999, The Crisis in Corporate Governance-HR's Role, 2003; mem. editl. bd., contbr.: At Work: Stories of Tomorrow's Workplace, 1992—; featured in The Ethical Edge, The Portable Executive, Merchants of Vision, Career Crossroads, Winning the People Wars, Survival Skills in the Fin. Svcs. Industry. Treas. Westchester County Rep. Com., White Plains, N.Y., 1979-89; asst. treas. N.Y. State Friends for Jim Buckley, 1976; dir. NCCJ, 1977-85; trustee Bedford Presbyn. Ch., N.Y., 1982-87, Better Bus. Bur. Found., N.Y., 2001—; mem. Westchester Blue Ribbon Commn. to Formulate County Housing Policy, 1979; trustee March of Dimes, Westchester, 1978-84, chmn. Exec. Walkathon, 1978-81. Mem. Ethics Officers Assn. (dir. emeritus), Caux (Switzerland) Round Table (affil.). Clubs: Soc. Friendly Sons of St. Patrick (pres. 1985). Home: Horseshoe Hl W Pound Ridge NY 10576 Office: 27 Horseshoe Hill W Pound Ridge NY 10576 E-mail: keith.darcy@ethicsinleadership.com.

DARDEN, ALVERTA ELEANOR, elementary educator; b. Balt., Aug. 30, 1940; d. Mark Abraham and Alice Alverta (Anderson) D. BS, Bowie State Coll., 1967; MEd, Towson State U., 1983. Cert. tchr., Md. Tchr. Arnold (Md.) Elem. Sch., 1967—. Author: (newletter) The Wave. Founder Mark Darden/Verdella scholarships, 1989. Mem. NEA, NAACP, Md. State Tchrs. Assn., Women of Color (chair Annapolis unit 1992), Nat. Ch. Ushers Am. (parliamentarian edn. dept.), Tchrs. Assn. Anne Arundel County, Delta Kappa Gamma (v.p. Omega chpt.). Methodist. Avocations: singing, reading, cooking, travel, church activities. Home: 904 Country Ter Severna Park MD 21146-4713

DARDEN, DONNA BERNICE, special education educator; b. Portsmouth, Va., Sept. 15, 1956; d. Howard John and Joyce Bernice Jackson; m. John Holland Darden, June 20, 1975; children: Christopher John, Jamison Marie. AA, Piedmont Va. C.C., Charlottesville, Va., 1987; BA, M of Teaching, U. Va., 1990. Cert. tchr. spl. edn., learning disabilities, emotionally disturbed. Customer svc. rep. Landmark Comm., Inc., Norfolk, Va., 1976-79; computer operator Curtis Mathes Corp., Houston, 1979-80; chief fin. officer Darden, Inc./(div. ColorTyme TV), Charlottesville, 1980-87; learning disabilities tchr. Oakland Sch., Boyd Tavern, Va., 1990—; clin. instr. Curry Sch. of Edn. U. Va., 1995—. Mem. Albermarle County Rep. Com., Va., 1982—; area capt. Key West-Cedar Hills Community Assn., Albermarle County, 1985, 86, mem. chmn., 1987, 2000—; swim meet assoc., Key West Swim Team, 1986-93; co-chmn. Rivanna Scenic River Adv. Bd., 1997—; active Cornerstone Cmty. Ch.; sec. Cornerstone Wesleyan Women, 1998-99, asst. dir. 1999, dir, 2001-2003. Mem. Coun. Exceptional Children, Golden Key, Kappa Delta Pi. Avocations: music, tennis, gardening, nature. Home: 344 Key West Dr Charlottesville VA 22911-8426 Office: Oakland Sch Boyd Tavern VA 22947

DARDEN, JOSEPH SAMUEL, JR., health educator; b. Pleasantville, N.J., July 25, 1925; s. Joseph Samuel and Blanche Catherine (Paige) D.; m. Barbara Cassandra Sellers, Dec. 30, 1955 (div. July 1979); 1 child, Michele Irene. AB, Lincoln U., 1948; MA, NYU, 1952, EdD (Danforth Found. fellow), 1963. Instr. biol. scis. Clark Coll., Atlanta, 1952-55; asst. prof. Albany (Ga.) State Coll., 1955-58, prof., 1959-64; asst. prof. Kean U. of N.J., Union, 1964-67, prof. health edn., 1970—, coord. health, 1977-79, chmn. dept. health and recreation, 1979-84, coord. health, 1984—2002, dir. minority enrollment, 1988-94, prof. emeritus, 2002—. Adj. prof. health Wagner Coll., S.I., N.Y., 1965-88; cons. N.J. Dept. Edn., 1968-73, 76-88. Author: (with others) Growth Pattern and Sex Education, 1967, Updated Supplement to Growth Pattern and Sex Education, 1972, Toward a Healthier Sexuality: A Book of Readings, 1997; editor, co-author: Critical Health Issues Reader, 2002. Bd. advisors Marylawn of Oranges, 1971-73; bd. dirs. N.J. Coun. Family Relations, 1981-83; trustee Planned Parenthood of Essex County, N.J., 1985—; trustee Planned Parenthood of Met. N.J. 1985—. With AUS, 1944-46. Recipient Alumni Achievement award, Lincoln U., 1993, Presdl. Excellence award, Kean U., 2002. Fellow Am. Assn. Health Edn. (charter); mem. AAHPERD (Eastern dist. v.p. for health edn. 1971-72, dist. pres. 1974-75, Eastern dist. rep. 1979-82, honor award Eastern dist. 1976, nat. honor award 1985, Outstanding Tchr. award Eastern dist. 1983, Charles D. Henry award 1988, Edwin B. Henderson award 1991), Am. Sch. Health Assn. (governing coun. 1970-73, Disting. Svc. award 1971), Assn. Advancement Health Edn. (dir. 1975-78, Profl. Svc. award 1990, presdl. citation 1996), N.J. Health Edn. Coun. (founder 1967, honor award 1975), N.J. Assn. Health, Phys. Edn. and Recreation (v.p. health edn. 1967-68, Honor fellow award 1972, Disting. Leadership award 1975), Alpha Phi Alpha. Home: 1416 Thelma Dr Union NJ 07083-6220 Office: Kean U NJ Union NJ 07083 E-mail: jdarden@kean.edu.

DARENSBOURG, CYNTHIA PEPIN, educator; b. New Orleans, Jan. 29; d. Wendell E. and Mercedes A. (Marrero) Pepin; m. Ulysses J. Darensbourg; children: Christopher Joseph, Maria Angele. B.A., Xavier U., 1971, MA, 1986. Mem. sales staff Sears, Roebuck and Co.; clerical and office worker; tchr. elem., kindergarten, and nursery sch., New Orleans. Mem. Am. Fedn. Tchrs., La. Fedn. Tchrs., Nat. Assn. Workshop Way Educators, United Tchrs. New Orleans, La. AFL-CIO, New Orleans AFL-CIO, Council Cath. Women, Knights of Peter Claver Ladies Auxillary.

DARIUS, FRANKLIN ALEXANDER, JR., (CHIP DARIUS), safety consultant, educator; b. New Haven, Apr. 12, 1962; s. Franklin Alexander and Nancy Darius; m. Marla Joyce Borio, July 30, 1988. BS in Human Devel., U. Conn., 1985, MA in Organizational Communication, 1988. Cert. EMT. Account exec. Consultants & Designers, Inc., Hartford, Conn., 1988-89; dir. R&D Powerphone Inc., Madison, Conn., 1989-91; dir. tng. and devel. Holdsworth & Assocs., East Berlin, Conn., 1991-93, v.p., 1993-2000, COO, 1995-2000; pres. Safety Priority Cons., LLC, New Britain, Conn., 2000—. Adj. faculty U. Conn. Storrs, 1986—, Teikyo Post U., Waterbury, Conn., 2000—; cons. Nat. Emergency Number Assn., 1989—, office emergency med. svcs. State of Conn., 1993—, State of W.Va., 1993—, State of Minn., 1994—, State of N.D., 1994—, State of Colo., 1994—; mem. task force pub. info. and edn. Conn. Health Dept., 1992-97, chair, 1997-98; officer Mid-State Regional Emergency Med. Svcs. Coun., 1992-94; mem. Conn. Dept. Environ. Protection, 2001—. Editor: Dispatcher's Guide to Fires & Incidents, 1990; contbr. articles to profl. jours. Asst. scoutmaster Boy Scouts Am., Cheshire, Conn., 1980—86; trustee Multiple Sclerosis Soc., Hartford, 1984—86; pres. The Navigators, U. Conn., 1987; tng. officer Cromwell Fire Dept. EMS, Conn., 1990—91, v.p., 1992—98, dir., 1998—2002; co-founder Fellowship of Internat. Grad. Students, U. Conn., Storrs, 1985—88. Recipient Good Citizen award DAR, 1981, commendation Multiple Sclerosis Soc., 1984, 85, award Outstanding Young Men of Am., 1989. Mem.: ASTD, AACC, NFPA, ASSE, ASTM, Hartford Christian Bus. and Profl. Assn., Promisekeepers, Alpha Phi Omega. Baptist. Home: 7 Fennwood Dr Cromwell CT 06416 Office: Safety Priority LLC 185 Main St Ste 204 New Britain CT 06051 E-mail: cdarius@safetypriority.com.

DARKE, CHARLES BRUCE, academic administrator, dentist; b. Chgo., Sept. 22, 1937; s. Paul Olden and Annie Waulene (Tennin) D.; m. Annetta McRae-Darke, Aug. 15, 1965 (div. 1982); 1 child, Charles B. II; m. Judith Anne Chew, Dec. 15, 1990. AA, Wilson Jr. Coll., Chgo., 1960; DDS, Meharry Med. Coll., 1964; MPH, U. Calif., Berkeley, 1972. Staff dentist Children's Hosp., Oakland, Calif., 1967-68, Mt. Zion Hosp., San Francisco, 1967-71; pvt. practice in dentistry San Francisco, 1967—; dir. dental svcs. San Francisco Gen. Hosp., 1973-88; asst. adminstr. outpatient svcs. San Francisco Med. Ctr., 1980-88; ops. officer primary care network San Francisco Dept. Health, 1988-89; exec. dir. Student Health and Counseling Ctr. Calif. State U., Fullerton, 1989-99; sr. cons. Kaiser Found. Hosps., 1999—. Dental cons. Dept. Labor Job Corps, Washington, 1973-88; chief examiner state dental bd. Calif. State Bd. Dental Examiners, Sacramento, 1976-89; surveyor ambulatory care and network Joint Commn. on Accreditation of Health, Oakbrook, Ill., 1986—; bd. dirs. Yorba Hills Med. Ctr., Yorba Linda, Calif., 1993-96. Found Tooth Trip-Free Dental Care, San Francisco, 1969. Capt. USAF, 1965-67. Mem. ADA, Am. Endodontic Soc., Nat. Dental Assn., Am. Coll. Health Assn., Pacific Coast Coll. Health Assn. (bd. dirs. 1993), Nat. Dental Soc. Bay Area (past pres.). Avocations: scuba diving, photography, magic.

DARLING, JOHN ROTHBURN, JR., business educator; b. Holton, Kans., Mar. 30, 1937; s. John Rothburn and Beatrice Noel (Deaver) D.; m. Melva Jean Fears, Aug. 20, 1958; children: Stephen, Cynthia, Gregory. BS, U. Ala., 1959, MS, 1960; PhD, U. Ill., 1967; PhD (hon.), Chung Yuan Christian U., Taiwan, 1998. Divisional mgr. J.C. Penney Co., 1960-63; grad. teaching asst. U. Ill., Urbana, 1965-66; asst. prof. mktg. U. Ala., Tuscaloosa, 1966-68; assoc. prof. mktg. U. Mo., Columbia, 1968-71; prof. adminstrn., coord. mktg. Wichita State U., 1971-76; dean, prof. mktg. Coll. Bus. Adminstrn. So. Ill. U., Carbondale, 1976-81; v.p. acad. affairs and rsch., prof. internat. bus. Tex. Tech U., Lubbock, 1981-86; provost, v.p. acad. affairs, prof. mktg. and internat. bus. Miss. State U., Mississippi State, 1986-90; chancellor, disting. prof. internat. bus. La. State U., Shreveport, 1990-95; pres. Pittsburg (Kans.) State U., 1995-99, prof. mktg. and internat. bus., 1995-2000; vis. disting. prof. mktg. Rockhurst U., 2000—. Mktg. rsch. cons. Southwestern Bell, 1970; sr. v.p. Boothe Advt. Wichita, 1972; pres. Bus. Rsch. Assocs., 1972-76; cons. Bus. Rsch. Assocs., 1976-82; spl. cons. FTC, Washington, 1972-75, U.S. Dept. Justice, 1973-74, Atty. Gen., State of Kans., 1972-76, Dist. Atty. 18th Jud. Dist., Wichita, 1972-76, Maya Internat. Inc., Houston, 1995—, Morrison and Assocs., Inc., Shreveport, 1995-97; vis. disting. prof. internat. mktg. Helsinki Sch. Econs. and Bus. Adminstrn., 1993—. Author: (with Harry A. Lipson) Marketing Fundamentals, Text and Cases, 1980, (with Raimo Nurmi) International Management Leadership: The Primary Competitive Advantage, 1997; mem. bd. cons. editors Jour. Advt., 1984—; mem. editl. rev. bd. Jour. Internat. Bus. Studies, 1991—, Jour. Entrepreneurship, 1997—; contbr. articles to profl. jours. Bd. dirs. Outreach Found., 1973-79, v.p., 1975-77; trustee Graceland Coll., Lamoni, Iowa, 1976-82; mem. mgmt. com. Park Coll., Kansas City, 1976-79. Dist. Eagle Scout Awd., Boy Scouts Amer., 1998. Mem. Internat. Coun. Small Bus., Am. Mktg. Assn., Am. Mgmt. Assn., Acad. Internat. Bus., Am. Econs. Assn., Am. Arbitration Assn., (mem. nat. panel arbitrators and mediators 1993—), Nat. Assn. Intercollegiate Athletics (mem. governing bd. 1994-95), So. Bus. Adminstrn. Assn., So. Mktg. Assn., So. Econs. Assn., So. Assn. Colls. and Schs. (chair reaccreditation com. 1982-95, chair faculty qualifications criteria com. 1989-90, com. to rev. criteria for accreditation 1990-92, commr. 1992-95, Nat. Assn. State Univs. and Land-Grant Colls. (chair regional accreditation rev. com. 1989-90), Sales and Mktg. Execs. Internat., Beta Gamma Sigma, Phi Kappa Phi, Omicron Delta Kappa, Phi Delta Kappa, Kappa Delta Phi, Mu Kappa Tau, Pi Sigma Epsilon, Alpha Kappa Psi, Chi Alpha Phi, Alpha Phi Omega, Phi Eta Sigma, Delta Mu Delta, Alpha Mu Gamma. Home: 12705 E 37th Terr Ct Independence MO 64055-3179 Office: Office of the President Pittsburg State Univ 1701 S Broadway St Pittsburg KS 66762-5856

DARLING, LYNDA KAREN, secondary education educator; b. Portland, Oreg., Oct. 25, 1949; d. Howard Wayne and Ruth Eileen (Russell) D.; m. Scott Reagen Hannigan, Feb. 14, 1975. BS, Portland State U., 1971, MS, 1976. Cert. basic integrated sci., std. extreme learning problems, std. reading. Reading tchr. Vocat. Village H.S.-Portland (Oreg.) Pub. Schs., 1972—. Mem. Vocat. Village H.S. Citizen Adv. Com., Portland, 1980—; co-founder Read-Rite Assocs., Portland, 1982—. Coach Jr. Bowlers, Portland, 1993—. Recipient Outstanding Support to Spl. Needs Students award Nat. Assn. Vocat. Edn. Spl. Needs Pers., Portland, 1982; named Secondary Alternative Educator of Yr., Oreg. Assn. for Alternatives in Edn., 1990. Mem. Internat. Reading Assn., Oreg. Assn. Learning Disabilities, Portland Assn. Tchrs. (mem. legis. com. 1983-86, bd. mem. tchrs. voice in politics bd. 1984-86), Phi Kappa Phi. Avocations: bowling, golfing, reading. Office: Vocat Village HS 8020 NE Tillamook St Portland OR 97213-6655

DARLING-HAMMOND, LINDA, education educator; BA, Yale U., 1973; EdD in Urban Edn., Temple U., 1978. Dir., sr. social scientist Edn. and Human Resources Program RAND, 1985—89; prof. Columbia U., 1989—98, co-dir. Nat. Ctr. for Restructuring Edn., Schs. and Tchg., Tchrs. Coll., 1989—98, William F. Russell prof. in Founds. of Edn., 1993—98; prof. edn. Stanford U., 1998—. Chair stds. drafting panel Coun. Chief State Sch. Officers, Interstate New Tchr. Assessment and Support Consortium, 1991—; mem. Nat. Adv. Commn., The Coll. Bd., Equity 2000, 1993—, Carnegie Corp. Task Force on Learing in the Primary Grades, 1994—; exec. dir. Nat. Commn. on Tchg. and Ams. Future, 1994—; mem. adv. bd. Ctr. for Policy Rsch. in Edn., 1996—; mem. tech. rev. panel for the schs. an staffing survey U.S. Dept. Edn., 1997—; mem. Internat. Adv. Coun., San Francisco Exploratorium, 1998—; co-chair Calif. Profl. Devel. Task Force, 2000; bd. dirs. Recruiting New Tchrs. Author (with J. Ancess and B. Falk): Authentic Assessment in Action: Studies of Schools and Students at Work, 1995; author: The Right to Learn: A Blueprint for Creating Schools that Work, 1997; editor: Professional Development Schools: Schools for Developing a Profession, 1994; editor: (with Gary Sykes) Teaching as the Learning Profession: A Handbook of Policy and Practice, 1999; contbr. articles to profl. jours. Mem.: Nat. Acad. Edn. (chair com. on tchr. edn. 2000—). Office: Stanford Univ Sch Edn 485 Lasuen Mall Stanford CA 94305-3096*

DARMAN, RICHARD, investor, educator; b. Charlotte, N.C., May 10, 1943; m. Kathleen Emmet, Sept. 1, 1967; children: William Temple Emmet, Jonathan Warren Emmet, Christopher Temple Emmet. BA cum laude, Harvard U., 1964, MBA, 1967, DSc (hon.); DLaw (hon.). Dep. asst. sec. HEW, Washington, 1971-72; asst. to sec. Dept. Def., Washington, 1973; spl. asst. to atty. gen. Washington, 1973; fellow Woodrow Wilson Internat. Center for Scholars, Washington, 1974; prin., dir. ICF, Inc., Washington, 1975, 77-80; asst. sec. Dept. Commerce, 1976-77; lectr. public policy and mgmt. Harvard U., 1977-80; asst. to Pres. Reagan, The White House, Washington, 1981-85; dep. sec. Dept. Treasury, 1985-87; mng. dir. Shearson Lehman Hutton Inc., N.Y.C., 1987-88; dir. office mgmt. and budget, mem. Pres. Cabinet The White House, Washington, 1989-93; prof. JFK Sch. Govt. Harvard U., 1998—2002; ptnr. The Carlyle Group, 1993—. Bd. dirs. Frontier Ventures Corp., 1993—, AES Corp., 2002—, vice chmn., 2002, chmn., 2003—. Editor: Harvard Ednl. Rev, 1970; contbg. editor U.S. News & World Report, 1987-88; author: Who's in Control?, 1996; contbr. articles to profl. jours. Trustee Bennington Coll., Vt., 1974—75, The Brookings Inst., 1987—88; bd. dirs. Smithsonian Nat. Mus. Am. History, 2000—, vice chmn. bd., 2003—; trustee Coun. for Excellence in Govt., 1995—2002, CDC Nvest Funds, 1996—, Loomis Sayles Funds, 2003—; mem. overseers com. to visit Kennedy Sch. Govt. Harvard U., 1988—98, 2003—, Harvard Med. Sch., 1994—99, to visit Kennedy Sch. Govt. Harvard U., 2003—. Office: The Carlyle Group 1001 Pennsylvania Ave NW Washington DC 20004-2505

DARNTON, ROBERT CHOATE, history educator; b. N.Y.C., May 10, 1939; s. Byron and Eleanor (Choate) D.; m. Susan Lee Glover, June 29, 1963; children: Nicholas Campbell, Catherine Choate, Margaret Townsend. BA, Harvard U., 1960; BPhil, Oxford U., Eng., 1962, DPhil, 1964. Reporter N.Y. Times, N.Y.C., 1964; jr. fellow Harvard U., 1964-68; asst. prof. history Princeton U., N.J., 1968-71, assoc. prof., 1971-72, prof., 1972—. Author: Mesmerism and the End of the Enlightenment in France, 1968, The Business of Enlightenment: A Publishing History of the Encyclopédie, 1775-1800, 1979 (Am. Hist. Assn. Leo Gershoy prize 1979), The Literary Underground of the Old Regime, 1982, The Great Cat Massacre and Other Episodes in French Cultural History, 1984 (L.A. Times book prize), The Kiss of Lamourette: Reflections in Cultural History, 1989, Edition et Sédition, L'univers de la littérature clandestine au XVIII e siècle, 1991 (Prix Chateaubriand), Berlin Journal, 1989-90, 1991, Gens de lettres, gens du livre, 1992, The Forbidden Best-Sellers of Pre-Revolutionary France, 1995 (Nat. Book Critics Circle award 1996), The Corpus of Clandestine Literature in France, 1995, Jacques-Pierre Brissot, His Career and Correspondence, 1779-1787, 2001, George Washington's False Teeth. An Unconventional Guide to the Eighteenth Century, 2003. Decorated officer Ordre des Arts et des Lettres, chevalier Légion d'Honneur, 1999; recipient Koren prize Soc. French Hist. Studies, 1973, MacArthur Found. prize, 1982. Fellow Am. Acad. Arts and Scis., Am. Philos. Soc., Brit. Acad. (corr. 2001); mem. Am. Hist. Assn. (pres.-elect 1998, pres. 1999-2000), Am. Soc. 18th-Century Studies (Clifford prize 1971, 73), Internat. Soc. 18th-Century Studies (pres. 1987-1992), Academia Europaea, Belgian Royal Acad. French Lang. and Lit. Office: Princeton U Dept History Princeton NJ 08540

DARST, MARY LOU, secondary school educator; b. Houston, Aug. 12, 1943; d. Carl Kennedy and Sara Catharine (Emmott) Hughes; m. William Maury Darst, Apr. 20, 1963 (dec. May 1990); children: Robert Maury, Catharine Fontaine Darst Knight. Student, Stephen F. Austin State Coll., 1961—63, Galveston Coll., 1970-72, 76-77, U. Tex. Med. Br., 1983—84; BA, U. Houston, Clear Lake, 1989, MS, 1993, BA, 2001; postgrad., U. St. Thomas, 1999—2002, Rice U., 2003. Cert. tchr. elem. edn., secondary English, ESL, gifted and talented, Advanced placement. Sec. William Temple Found., Galveston, 1979-80; new accounts Tex. First Bank, Galveston, 1981-84; med. sec. U. Tex. Med. Br., Galveston, 1984-87; tchr. Galveston (Tex.) Ind. Sch. Dist., 1990—2002, Galveston Coll., 1995-96; ESL tchr. Clear Lake H.S., 2002—. Mem. Jr. League of Galveston, 1966-69; bd. dirs. YWCA, 1972-73. Recipient Title VII grantee, U. Houston at Clear Lake, Houston, 1991—93. Mem.: Galveston Art League, Rock Art, Tex. Neurofibromatosis Found. (sec. 1987—89, pres. 1989—91), Assn. Tex. Profl. Educators, Mus. Fine Arts Houston, Scenic Galveston, U. Houston Alumni Assn., Sierra Club, Theta Zeta, Alpha Chi Omega, Delta Kappa Gamma (v.p. Omicron chpt. 1995—96). Democrat. Episcopalian. Avocations: travel, music, swimming, walking, writing, artist. Home: 1431 San Sebastian Ln Houston TX 77058-3451 E-mail: mldarst@juno.com.

DARVENNES, CORINNE MARCELLE, mechanical engineering educator, researcher; b. Algiers, Algeria, Jan. 19, 1961; came to U.S., 1985, naturalized, 1994; d. René Joseph and Solange Marie (Rosso) D.; m. Glenn B. Focht, Jan. 24, 1989; children: Angeline S., Cyril J. Engring. Degree, Université Technologie de Compiègne, France, 1984; MSc, Inst. Sound and Vibrations Rsch., Southampton, Eng., 1985; PhD, U. Tex., 1989. Rsch. asst. U. Tex., Austin, 1985-89, rsch. engr., 1989-90; asst. prof. mech. engring. Tenn. Technol. U., Cookeville, 1990-95, assoc. prof. mech. engring., 1995—2002, prof. mech. engring., 2002—. Contbr. articles to profl. jours. Recipient Outstanding Faculty award in tchg., Tenn. Tech. U., 2001—02. Mem. ASME, Acoustical Soc. Am., Am. Soc. for Engring. Edn., Soc. Women Engrs., Ins. Noise Control Engrs. (bd. cert.), Sigma Xi, Tau Beta Pi. Office: Tenn Tech U PO Box 5014 Cookeville TN 38505-0001

DARWIN, DAVID, civil engineering educator, researcher, consultant; b. NYC, Apr. 17, 1946; s. Samuel David and Earle (Rives) D.; m. Diane Marie Mayer, June 29, 1968; children: Samuel David, Lorraine Marie. BS, Cornell U., 1967, MS, 1968; PhD, U. Ill., 1974. Registered profl. engr., Kans. Asst. prof. civil engring. U. Kans., Lawrence, 1974-77, assoc. prof., 1977-82, prof., 1982—, Deane E. Ackers disting. prof. civil engring., 1990—, dir. Structural Engring. and Materials Lab., 1982—; dir. Infrastructure Rsch. Inst., 1998-2001. Cons. David Darwin, Lawrence, 1976—. Author: Steel and Composite Beams with Web Openings, 1990; co-author: Concrete, 2d edit., 2003; contbr. articles to profl. jours. Mem. Uniform Bldg. Code Bd. Appeals, Lawrence, 1978-84. Capt. U.S. Army, 1967-72, Vietnam. Grantee NSF, 1976—, Kans. Dept. Transp., 1980-82, 90—, Air Force Office Sci. Rsch., 1985-92, Civil Engring. Rsch. Found., 1991-95, Fed. Hwy. Adminstrn., 1994-98, 2001—, SD Dept. Transp., 2001—, Nat. Coop. Hwy. Rsch. Program, 1994-95; Bellows scholar U. Kans., 2001-02; recipient Miller award U. Kans., 1986, Irvin Youngberg Rsch. Achievement award, 1992, Civil and Environ. Engring. Alumni Assn.'s Disting. Alumnus award U. Ill., 2003. Fellow ASCE (editor Jour. Structural Engring. 1994-2000, bd. govs. Structural Engring. Inst. 2000—, Kans. sect. v.p., pres.-elect 2001-02, pres. 2002-03, Huber Rsch. prize 1985, Moisseiff award 1991, state-of-the-art of civil engring. award 1996, 2000, Richard R. Torrens award 1997), Am. Concrete Inst. (pres. Kans. chpt. 1975, bd. dirs. 1988-91, Bloem Disting. Svc. award 1986, Arthur R. Anderson award for disting. rsch. 1992, Structural Rsch. award 1996); mem. AAAS, ASTM (award of appreciation 2003), Am. Soc. Engring. Edn., Am. Inst. Steel Constrn. (profl.), Prestressed Concrete Inst. (profl.), Post-Tensioning Inst. (profl.), Concrete Rsch. Coun. (chmn. 1990-96), Structural Engring. Inst. (bd. govs. 2000—), Phi Kappa Phi (pres. U. Kans. chpt. 1976-78). Democrat. Unitarian Universalist. Avocations: swimming, walking. Office: U Kans Civil Environ and Archtl Engring Dept 2142 Learned Hall 1530 W 15th St Lawrence KS 66045-7609 E-mail: daved@ku.edu.

DAS, T. K. management educator, consultant; b. Calcutta, India, July 8, 1938; BS with honors, U. Calcutta, 1957; MS, Jadavpur U., Calcutta, 1959; M in Mgmt., Asian Inst. Mgmt., Manila, 1977; PhD, UCLA, 1984. Cert. Assoc. of the Indian Inst. of Bankers. Various exec. positions State Bank of

India, 1960-76; part-time asst. prof. mgmt. Calif. State U., L.A., 1980-83; asst. prof. strategic mgmt. Tex. Tech U., Lubbock, 1984-86; mem. doctoral faculty CUNY, 1987—; asst. prof. strategic mgmt. Baruch Coll., CUNY, 1987-89, assoc. prof., 1990-96, prof., 1997—; area coord. Strategic Mgmt. and Bus. & Soc., 1997—. Author: Human Resource Management and Productivity: State of the Art and Future Prospects, Vol. I: Focus on the United States, 1984, Vol. II: International Perspectives, 1985, The Subjective Side of Strategy Making: Future Orientations and Perceptions of Executives, 1986, The Time Dimension: An Interdisciplinary Guide, 1990; assoc. editor Rev. of Business Studies, 1992-94, Internat. Jour. Orgnl. Analysis, 1993-96; mem. editorial bd. Jour. Managerial Issues, 1991-94, Internat. Jour. Commerce & Mgmt., 1997—, Jour. of Internat. Mgmt., 2000—; contbr. more than 120 articles to scholarly and profl. jours. Recipient 1st prize Indian Inst. Bankers Prize Essay Competition, 1964, Charat Ram Found. award All India Mgmt. Assn., 1968; grantee CUNY Rsch. Found., 1993-94, 97-98, 98-99, 99-2000, 2001-02. Mem. Strategic Mgmt. Soc., Acad. of Mgmt., Inst. for Ops. Rsch. and the Mgmt. Scis., Soc. for Bus. Ethics, World Future Soc., Internat. Soc. for the Study of Time, Indian Inst. Bankers (life), Beta Gamma Sigma. Office: CUNY Baruch Coll Zicklin Sch Bus Dept Mgmt One Bernard Baruch Way Box B9-240 New York NY 10010-5585 E-mail: TK_Das@baruch.cuny.edu.

DASGUPTA, AMITAVA, chemist, educator; b. Calcutta, India, May 6, 1958; came to U.S., 1980; naturalized U.S. citizen, 1996; s. Anil Kumar and Hasi Dasgupta. BS with honors, U. Calcutta, India, 1978; MS in Chemistry, U. Ga., 1981; PhD in Chemistry, Stanford U., 1986. Diplomate Am. Bd. Clin. Chemistry. Fellow in clin. chemistry U. Wash., Seattle, 1986-88; asst. dir. clin. chemistry U. Chgo., 1988-93; dir. clin. chemistry lab. U. N.Mex. Hosp., Albuquerque, 1993-97; assoc. prof. pathology and biochemistry U. N.Mex., Albuquerque, 1993-97; prof. pathology U. Tex.-Houston Med. Sch., 1998—. Lectr in field. Reviewer jours. Clin. Chemistry, Nephron, Jour. Liquid Chromatography; contbr. articles to Clin. Chemistry, Am. Jour. Clin. Pathology, Jour. Am. Soc. Nephrology, SYVA, 1990-91, Home Health Care, 1992-93. Fellow Nat. Acad. Clin. Biochemistry (Grannis award 1993); mem. Am. Assn. Clin. Chemistry, Acad. Clin. Labs. Physicians and Scientists. Hindu. Achievements include research in role of lipids and lipid peroxidation in the pathophysiology of disease; characterization of digoxin-like immunoreactive substance; drug-drug interaction and advantages of monitoring free drug concentrations. Office: U Texas Med School Dept Pathology 6431 Fannin St # Msb2292 Houston TX 77030-1501

DASGUPTA, INDRANIL, physician, educator; b. Barielly, India, May 24, 1960; came to the U.S., 1961; s. Sunil Pryia and Krishna Dasgupta. BA in Philosophy, Duke U., 1982; MPH in Internat. Health, Loma Linda U., 1987; cert. epidemiology, Johns Hopkins U., 1987; MBA in Fin., George Washington U., 1989; MD, St. George's (Grenada) U., 1994. Diplomate Am. Bd. Internal Medicine. Congl. intern U.S. Ho. of Reps., Washington, 1983; rsch. asst. Harvard Med. Sch., Boston, 1983-84, Dartmouth U. Med. Sch., Hanover, N.H., 1985-86; rsch. assoc. Loma Linda (Calif.) Sch. Pub. Health, 1986-87; congl. intern U.S. Senator Ed Kennedy, Washington, 1988-89; med. resident Med. Coll. Pa.-Hahnemann U. Hosps., Phila., 1995-98, rsch. assoc., 1998-99, geriatric fellow, 1998-99; cardiology fellow Robert Wood Johnson Med. Sch. U. Medicine and Dentistry N.J., Camden, 1999—2002, rsch. assoc., 1999—2002; clin. asst. prof. divsn. cardiology Jefferson Med. Coll., Phila., 2002—; attending cardiologist Thomas Jefferson U. Hosp., Phila., 2002—. Contbr.: U.S. House Select Committee on Aging, 1983. Vol. Muscular Dystrophy Assn., Winston-Salem, N.C., 1981, U.S. Spl. Olympics, Wilmington, Del., 1985, Dem. Fund Raising, Washington, 1988. Fellow: Soc. Geriatric Cardiology; mem.: ACP, Am. Soc. Nuclear Cardiology, Internat. Soc. Heart and Lung Transplantation, NY Acad. Scis., NJ Acad. Sci., Nat. Assn. Advancement Sci., Am. Heart Assn., Am. Coll. Cardiology, Delta Omega, Sigma Alpha Epsilon. Democrat. Avocations: traveling, sailing, snorkling, soccer. Home: 2528 Tigani Dr Wilmington DE 19808 Office: Thomas Jefferson U Hosp Jefferson Heart Inst 925 Chestnut St Mezzanine Level Philadelphia PA 19107 E-mail: indranildasgupta@aol.com.

DASH, ALEKHA K. pharmaceutical scientist, educator; b. Gobindapur, Orissa, India, Aug. 1, 1954; came to the U.S., 1984; s. Jagannath Dash and Flurence Panda; m. Kanchanbala Mohapatra, May 9, 1984; children: Debleena, Rohan Dipak. B in Pharmacy, Jadavpur U., Calcutta, 1981, M in Pharmacy, 1983; PhD, U. Minn., 1990. Registered pharmacist, Orissa, India, 1975-77; pharmacy technician U. Minn. Med. Ctr., Mpls., 1984-90; tchg. and rsch. asst. U. Minn., Mpls., 1984-90; asst. prof. Creighton U., Omaha, 1990-95, assoc. prof., 1995—2003, prof., 2003—; adj. asst. prof. U. Nebr., Omaha, 1994—. Editor-in-chief Orissa Soc. of Ams., 1993-95; contbr. chpts. to books. Recipient John C. Kenific awards Health Future Found., Omaha, 1991, 93, Pharmaceutics award Pharm. Mfrs. Assn., Washington, 1993. Mem. AAAS, Am. Assn. Pharm. Scientists (award and publ. com. 1994—), Am. Assn. Colls. Pharmacy. Achievements include development of implantable delivery system for bone infections; use of microdialysis in implantable dosage form design; solid state characterization of tobramycin. Home: 13518 Sahler St Omaha NE 68164-6025 Office: Creighton Univ 2500 California Plz Omaha NE 68178-0001

DASKIN, MARK STEPHEN, civil engineering educator; b. Balt., Dec. 3, 1952; s. Walter and Betty Jane (Fax) D.; m. Babette Reva Levy, July 2, 1978; children: Tamar, Keren. BSCE, MIT, 1974; postgrad. study in Engring., Cambridge, England, 1975; PhD in Civil Engring., MIT, 1978. Tchg. asst. trans. sys. divsn. civil engring. MIT, Cambridge, 1976-77; asst. prof. civil engring. Univ. Tex., Austin, 1978-79, Northwestern U., Evanston, Ill., 1980-83, assoc. prof. civil engring., 1983-89, prof., 1989—, chair dept. indsl. engring. and mgmt. scis., 1995—2001. Author: Network and Discrete Location: Models, Algorithms and Applications, 1995; editor-in-chief Transp. Sci., 1991-94; assoc. editor Location Sci., 1991-2000; contbr. articles to profl. jours. Bd. dirs. North Suburban Synagogue Beth El, Highland Park, Ill., 1991-94. Univ. Tex. Bur. Engring. Rsch. grant, 1978-79, Northwestern Univ. Transp. Ctr. grant, 1980, 81, NSF grant, 1980-82, 84-90, 93-97, 96-99, 1998-. Urban Mass Transp. Adminstr. grant, 1982-84, 84-85, United Parcel Svc. grant, 1983-86, 91-92, Thermo-King Corp. grant, 1990-91, 92-94, Heartland Blood Ctr. grant, 1992, 96; recipient Fulbright Rsch. award, 1989-90, Burlington Northern Found. Faculty Achievement award, 1985, NSF Presdl. Young Investigator award, 1984, Scott Paper Leadership award, 1973-75, IIE Tech. Innovation award in indusl. engring. Mem. ASCE, Inst. Indsl. Engrs. (editor-in-chief IEE Transactions 2001—), INFORMS (v.p. publs. 1996-99), Ops. Rsch. Soc. Am. (jour. editor 1991-94), Inst. Mgmt. Sci., Sigma Xi, Tau Beta Pi, Chi Epsilon. Avocations: swimming, photography. Office: Northwestern U Dept Indsl Engring Mgmt Sci Evanston IL 60208-0001 E-mail: daskin@iems.nwu.edu.

DASS, CHHABIL, chemistry educator; b. Hasalpur, Multan, India, Nov. 5, 1941; came to U.S., 1979; s. Jhanda Ram and Ram Devi (Sardana) Midha; m. Asha Rani Gheyi Midha, Sept. 8, 1969; children: Hemesh, Yatesh. BSc, U. Rajasthan, Jaipur, India, 1962, MSc, 1964; PhD, U. Nebr., 1984. Sci. officer Bhabha Atomic Rsch. Ctr., Bombay, India, 1964-79; rsch. asst. U. Nebr., Lincoln, 1979-84; rsch. assoc. U. Tenn., Memphis, 1984-86, asst. prof., 1986-94, U. Memphis, 1994-96, assoc. prof. chemistry, 1996—. Vis. scientist Ctrl. Bur. Nuclear Measurement, Geel, Belgium, 1969-70; assoc. adj. prof. U. Tenn., Memphis, 1994—. Author: Principles and Practice of Biological Mass Spectrometry, 2001; contbr. articles to profl. jours., chpts. to books. Mem. Am. Soc. Mass Spectrometry (Best Poster award 1986), Am. Soc. Biochemistry and Microbiology, Am. Chem. Soc., Indian Soc. Mass Spectrometry (life). Achievements include research in mass spectrometry, protein and peptide chemistry, gas-phase ion chemistry, chromatography and pharmaceutical drugs. Avocations: bridge, tennis, photography, travel. Office: U Memphis PO Box 526060 Memphis TN 38152-0001 E-mail: cdass@memphis.edu.

DASS, DEAN A. artist, educator; b. Hampton, Iowa, Nov. 16, 1955; s. Marland and Oleta (Liittschwager) D.; m. Patsy A. Maroney, Aug. 26, 1978; children— Erich, Adrienne. B.A., U. No. Iowa, 1978; M.F.A., Temple U., 1980. Instr., Kutztown U., Pa., 1983-84; prof. art U. Va., Charlottesville, 1985—. One-man exbhn. Schmidt/Dean Gallery, Phila., 1992, 96, 99, 2001, U. AAkron, 2003, U. Wyo. Art Mus., 1998; exhibited in group shows Bklyn. Mus., 1981, 83, 85, 89, Assoc. Am. Artists, Phila., 1982, 83; Phila. Print Club, 1979-81, 83-84, Inst. Contemporary Art, Richmond, Va., 1983, Noyes Mus., Oceanville, N.J., 1984, San Diego Print Club, 1984, U. Hawaii, 1984, Dolan-Maxwell Gallery, Phila., 1984-90, Fleisher Art Meml., Phila., 1984, Sonoma State U., Rohnert Park, Calif., 1984, Pa. Acad. Fine Arts, Morris Gallery, Phila., 1985; represented in permanent collections Phila. Mus. Art, Nat. Collection of Poland, Bklyn. Mus.; Smith, Kline & French, Phila., Phila. Savs. Fund Soc., Temple U., N.C. Print and Drawing Soc., Kans. State U., U. Dallas, State of Iowa, U. No. Iowa, U. S.D., Walker Art Mus., Minn., Free Library of Phila., numerous others. Merchant scholar U. No. Iowa, 1979-80; Tyler Sch. Art fellow, Phila., 1979-80, Pa. Council Arts fellow, 1985, Va. State Arts Coun., 1988. Home: 990 Allendale Dr Charlottesville VA 22901-9228 Office: U Va McIntire Dept Art Fayerweather Hall Charlottesville VA 22903

DASSO, JEROME JOSEPH, real estate educator; b. Neillsville, Wis., Jan. 12, 1929; s. Henry J. and Frances (Schweickert) D.; m. Patricia Mary Conger, June 13, 1959 (div. 1978); children: James Daniel, Mary Cecilia, Nancy Ann, Wendy Jo. BS, Purdue U., 1951; MBA, U. Mich., 1952; MS, U. Wis., 1960, PhD, 1964. Ptnr. Dasso Constrn. Co., Dubuque, Iowa, 1956-58; planner Franklin County, Columbus, Ohio, 1960-61; asst. prof. U. Ill., Urbana, 1964-66; vis. chairholder U. Hawaii, Honolulu, 1982-83; mem. faculty U. Oreg., Eugene, 1966-95, H.T. Miner chair in real estate, 1978-95, H.T. Miner chair emeritus, 1995—. Vis. prof. U. Wis., Madison, 1984; cons. Internat. Assn. Assessing Officers, Chgo., 1972-75; ednl. cons. Hawaii Real Estate Commn., Honolulu, 1982-83. Co-author: (S. Kahn, R. Nesslinger et a)l Principle of Right of Way Acquisition, 1972, (with G. Kuhn) Real Estate Finance, 1983, (with A.A. Ring) Real Estate Principles and Practices, 8th edit., 1977, 9th edit., 1981, 10th edit., 1985, 11th edit., 1989, (with Jim Shilling) 12th edit., 1995, Computerized Assessment Adminstration, 1973; contbr. numerous articles to various publs. Lt. USNR, 1952—60. Vivian Stewart vis. fellow Cambridge U., spring, 1987. Fellow Am. Inst. Corp. Asset Mgmt. (bd. govs. 1988-91), Homer Hoyt Inst. Adv. Studies Real Estate & Urban Land Econs.; mem. Real Estate Educators Assn. (pres. 1980-81, Outstanding Svc. award 1981, Disting. Career award 1989), Am. Real Estate and Urban Econs. Assn. (bd. dirs. 1974-77, 80-83), Real Estate Ctr. Dirs. Chairholders Assn. (pres. 1987-88), Am. Real Estate Soc. (life, bd. dirs. 1985-86, v.p. 1988-89, pres. elect 1989-90, pres. 1990-91), Am. Fin. Assn. (life), Nat. Assn. Realtors (edn. com. 1970-76), Internat. Real Estate Soc. (pres. 1994-95), VFW. Roman Catholic. Avocations: golf, skiing, hiking, photography.

D'ASTOLFO, FRANK JOSEPH, graphic designer, educator; b. Charleroi, Pa., July 19, 1943; s. Galderino Joseph and Gustina Evlyn (Petaccia) D'A. BA, Pa. State U., 1966; MA, U. Pitts., 1973. Graphic designer The United Fund, Pitts., 1968-69, Fisher Sci. Co., Pitts., 1969-73; instr. U. Pitts., 1972-76; graphic designer Pitt Studios, Pitts., 1973-74; design cons. Frank D'Astolfo Design, Pitts., 1974-77; instr. Tyler Sch. Art, Phila., 1977-80; design cons. Infield & D'Astolfo, N.Y.C., 1980-88; prof. Rutgers U., Newark, 1980—; design cons. Frank D'Astolfo Design, N.Y.C., 1988—. Cons. in field; chmn. dept. art and design Rutgers U., Newark, 1989-92, dep. chmn. dept. visual and performing arts, 1992-00; bd. dirs. Ringside Inc., N.Y.C., 198 7—; mem. Newark Arts Coun., 1993-96. Graphic designer Print Mag., 1992, 93 (Fifty Best Ann. Reports 1984, 86, Best Logos and Symbols vol. II, III and IV), Graphis Diagram I, 1988, Am. Corporate Identity 5-12, 15, 1989-96, 99 (awards of excellence), Metropolis The Architecture and Design Mag., New York, 1985. Design cons. Architects, Designers and Planners for Social Responsibility, N.Y.C., 1985, ICIS Internat. Ctr. for Integrating Studies, N.Y.C., 1983; dir. Com. for Cultural Awareness and Discussion, Pitts., 1977; cons. Shelly Friedman for Judge Com., Pitts., 1977. Recipient Gold award Art Dir. Club Phila., 1981, Distinctive award Merit Soc. Pub. Designers NY, 1983, Cert. of Distinction Creativity, 19, 22, 29, 1989, Silver award Case Coun. for Advancement and Support of Edn., 1985, Desi award Graphic Design USA, 1982, 83, 85, 87, 88, 92, 94 (Am. Graphic Design award, 1994, 96), Typography 3, 4, 21, TDC, 28, TOC, 28, 29, 46, Cert. of Typo Excellence, Print mag. Regional Design Ann., 1982, 84, 89, 92, 96, 98, 2000; Cert. of Merit Art Dir. Club NY, 1978, 81, 85, 93, Cert. of Excellence Art Dirs. Club NJ, 1981, 82, 83, 85, 98, 2000, Inter Type Design 2 Award of Excellence, 1994, Graphis Letterhead 2 Award of Excellence, 1993, Cert. of Excellence Inter Logos and Trademarks II, V, 1992, 2000, Univ. and Coll. Designers Assn. award of Excellence, 1995, 99), Charles Pine Outstanding Tchr. of Yr. award and Warren I. Susman award for Excellence in Tchg., 1995, Faculty Scholar Tchr. award, 1999, Am. Corp. Identity 2000 and 2001 award, 1998, Cert. of Recognition for Logo Design, Graphis Logo Design 4 award of excellence, 1998., How Mag. Merit award, 2000. Mem. Am. Inst. Graphic Arts (Cert. Excellence 1977, 83), Coll. Art Assn., Graphic Design Edn. Assn., Woodstock Artist Assn., Woodstock Guild. Democrat. Roman Catholic. Home: PO Box 62 Willow NY 12495 Office: Rutgers U Dept Visual and Performing Arts Newark NJ 07102

DATAR, RAM HEMANT, pathologist, educator; b. Nasik, India, Mar. 26, 1959; arrived in U.S., 1996; s. Hemant Madhusudan and Mrinalini Hemant Datar; m. Bharati Gajanan Deshpande, June 15, 1982; 1 child, Nakul R. BSc, Pune (India) U., 1979, MSc, 1981, MPhil, 1984; PhD, Bombay U., 1996. Jr. rsch. fellow Pune U., 1981—82, sr. rsch. fellow, 1983—84; sci. asst. Cancer Rsch. Inst., Bombay, 1983—84, sci. officer, 1991—96; vis. rsch. scholar U. So. Calif., L.A., 1996—98, asst. prof. clin. pathology, 1998—. Cons. spl. emphasis panel NIH, 2001—. Editor: Current Issues in Molecular Biology, 2000—; reviewer: Lancet, 2000—02, Internat. Jour. Cancer, 2000—02, Cancer Rsch., 2000—02. Grantee, NIH, 2000—01, 2001—02, Dept. Def., 2001. Mem.: Am. Assn. Cancer Rsch. (assoc.), Indian Assn. Cell Biology (life). Achievements include patent pending for protein display protocol. Avocations: reading, poetry, travel, writing. Office: U So Calif 2011 Zonal Ave #312C Los Angeles CA 90033

DATTA, SYAMAL KUMAR, medical scientist, educator, researcher; b. Cuttack, Orissa, India, Sept. 21, 1943; came to U.S., 1967; s. Jitendra Nath and Kalyani (Hazra) D.; m. Tapati Chaudhury, 1976; 1 child, Ronjon. BS, U. Calcutta, India, 1960, MB, BS, 1966. Diplomate Am. Bd. Internal Medicine. Resident in medicine Cook County Hosp., Chgo., 1969-71, fellow in hematology, 1971-72; rsch. assoc. Tufts U./New England Med. Ctr., Boston, 1972-74, instr. medicine, 1974-76, asst. prof., 1976-79, assoc. prof., 1979-85, prof., 1985-93; Solovy Arthritis-Rsch. Soc. prof., prof. medicine Northwestern U. Med. Sch., Chgo., 1993—, dir. biomed. rsch. component Multi Purpose Arthritis Ctr., 1996—. Sr. faculty mem. grad. program immunology Sackler Sch., Boston, 1975-93; mem. study sects. NIH, Bethesda, 1987—. Assoc. editor Jour. Immunology, 1984-93; mem. editl. bd. Clin. Immunology, Arthritis and Rheumatism. Recipient Merit award NIH, Faculty Rsch. award Am. Cancer Soc., 1978-83; Leukemia Soc. Am. fellow, 1972-74; Am. Cancer Soc. scholar, 1975-78. Mem. AAAS, Am. Assn. Immunologists, N.Y. Acad. Scis., Am. Coll. Rheumatology, Assn. Am. Physicians. Achievements include development of mouse model for human systemic autoimmune disease; identification of retroviral genes and definition of their relationship to autoimmune disease; identification of pathogenic anti-DNA autoantibodies and their genes; identification T cell receptor genes and co-stimultaory signaling molecules expressed by the pathogenic T helper cells that allow specific therapy designs; devised a method to isolate T helper cell clones that are pathogenic in lupus and identified the peptides that trigger such T cells; identified new subset of T cells in man that play an important role in autoimmune disease; developed specific immunotherapy for lupus. Office: Northwestern Univ Med Sch Rheumatol Divsn Ward 3-315 303 E Chicago Ave Chicago IL 60611-3093

DATTILO, LINDA KATHLEEN, elementary education educator; b. Alton, Ill., Sept. 22, 1948; d. Clayton Kenneth and Jeraldine Marie (Tindall) Ford; m. James Robert Dattilo, Apr. 30, 1969; children: Joseph Anthony, John Peter. BS in Edn., U. Mo., St. Louis, 1993, MEd, 1999. Cert. tchr. elem. edn. 1-8, mid. sch. social studies, lang. arts. Tchr. St. Patrick Parochial Sch., Wentzville, Mo., 1981-95; tchr. Coll. for Kids St. Charles C.C., St. Peters, Mo., 1991-95; tchr. math. Wright City (Mo.) Middle Sch., Wright City, Mo., 1995-96; tchr. grade sci., math. and lang. arts Lincoln County Sch. Dist., 1996—. Sponsor math. team St. Patrick Sch., Wentzville, 1994-95, chmn. curriculum evaluation, 1993-94, coord. sci. curriculum, 1994-95, mentor new tchrs., 1994-95; sponsor Troy (Mo.) Mid. Sch.; mem. 6th grade math. team, 1996—. Panel mem. Citicorp Excellence in Edn. Awards, St. Louis, 1990; program head elem. student-h.s. mentor program St. Patrick-St. Dominic, Wentzville and O'Fallon, 1992. Mem. Mo. Tchrs. Assn., Phi Kappa Phil. Avocations: reading, writing, cooking.

DAUB, MATTHEW FORREST, artist, educator; b. N.Y.C., Aug. 29, 1951; s. Alan J. and Sara Ann (Goldman) D.; m. Barbara Crawford, Aug. 1, 1971; children: Joshua, Sarah. Student, Pratt Inst., 1969-70; BA, So. Ill. U., 1981, MFA, 1984. From asst. prof. to assoc. prof. Kutztown (Pa.) U., 1987-95, prof., 1995—. Author: A Charmed Vision: The Art of Carolyn Plochmann, 1990; one-man shows include Sherry French Gallery, 1984, 86, 88, 91, 93, Jan Cicero Gallery, 1987-89, Evansville (Ind.) Museum Arts and Sci., 1994, Am. Acad. Arts and Letters, 1996, MB Modern Gallery, N.Y., 1998, Demuth Mus., Lancaster, Pa., 2000, Reading (Pa.) Pub. Mus., 2001; contbr. art to calendar Met. Mus. Art, 1991. Home: 920 N Richmond St Fleetwood PA 19522-1905 Office: Kutztown U Sharadin Art Bldg Kutztown PA 19530

DAUER, EDWARD ARNOLD, law educator; b. Providence, Sept. 28, 1944; s. Marshall and Shirley (Moverman) Dauer; m. Carol Jean Egglestone, June 16, 1966; children: E. Craig, Rachel P. AB, Brown U., 1966; LLB cum laude, Yale U., 1969; MPH, Harvard U., 2001. Bar: Conn. 1978, Colo. 1986. Asst. prof. law sch. U. Toledo, 1969-72; assoc. prof. law U. So. Calif., L.A., 1972-74; assoc. prof. Yale U., New Haven, 1975-85, assoc. dean, 1978-83, dep. dean Law Sch., 1983-85; dean, prof. U. Denver, 1985-90, dean emeritus, prof., 1991—. Of counsel Popham, Haik, Schnobrich and Kaufman, 1990—97; vis. scholar Harvard U. Sch. Pub. Health, 1996—2003; pres. CAEJAD Aviation Corp.; assoc. Health Care Negotiations Assocs., Inc. Author: (book) Materials on a Nonadversarial Legal Process, 1978, Conflict Resolution Strategies in Health Care, 1993, Manual of Dispute Resolution: ADR Law and Practice, 1994 (CPR Book award, 1994), Health Care Dispute Resolution, 2000; contbr. articles to profl. jours. Founder, pres. Nat. Ctr. Preventive Law; bd. dirs. New Haven Cmty. Action Agy., 1978—81; mem. Colo. Commn. Higher Edn., 1987—91; bd. dirs. Cerebral Palsy Found., Denver, 1989—, pres., 1992—95; commr. Colo. Advanced Tech. Inst., 1989—91. Recipient W. Quinn Jordan award, Nat. Blood Found., 1994, Paelia award, Harvard Sch. Pub. Health, 1996, Sanbar award, Am. Coll. Legal Medicine, 1999. Mem.: Am. Law Inst. (life), Met. Club, Cherry Creek Athletic Club, Order of Coif. Republican. Home: 127 S Garfield St Denver CO 80209 Office: U Denver Coll Law 1900 Olive St Denver CO 80220 E-mail: edauer@du.edu., edauer@hcna.net.

DAUGHDRILL, JAMES HAROLD, JR., academic administrator; b. LaGrange, Ga., Apr. 25, 1934; s. James Harold and Louisa Coffee (Dozier) D.; m. Elizabeth Anne Gay, June 26, 1954; children: James Harold III, Louisa Rish Daughdrill Hoover, Elizabeth Gay Daughdrill Boyd. Student, Davidson Coll., 1952-54, D.D., 1974; AB, Emory U., 1956; B.D., Columbia Theol. Sem., 1967, M.Div., 1969. Ordained to ministry Presbyn. Ch., 1967. Pres. Kingston Mills, Inc., Cartersville, Ga., 1956-64; minister St. Andrews Presbyn. Ch., Little Rock, 1967-70; sec. of stewardship Presbyn. Ch. in U.S., Atlanta, 1970-73; pres. Rhodes Coll., 1973-99. Past chmn. Nat. Adv. Com. on Instl. Quality and Interity, Dept. Edn.; past chair Assn. Am. Colls.; past dir. Am. Coun. on Edn.; mem. Blue Ribbon adv. com. Memphis Pub. Schs.; dir. So. Univ. Conf., pres., 1998—; bd. dirs. Bulab Holdings, Inc., Union Planters Nat. Bank, Buckman Labs. Author: Man Talk, 1972; co-author: New Directions for Higher Education Source Book. Past chmn. Tenn. Coun. Pvt. Colls.; past pres. Coll. Athletic Conf.; past chmn. bd. So. Coll. Univ. Union; past trustee Memphis-Brooks Art Gallery, Hutchinson Sch.; past bd. dirs. Tenn. Ind. Colls., Liberty Bowl, Chickasaw coun. Boy Scouts Am., Memphis U. Sch., Memphis Ptnrs.; mem. exec. bd. Dixon Gallery and Gardens; trustee The Frank E. Seidman Award in Polit. Economy; mem. blue ribbon adv. com. to the supt. Memphis Pub. Schs. Named Educator of Yr. Greater Memphis State, Memphis Planner of Yr., Pillar of Memphis Jewish Nat. Fund; recipient Spirit of Life award City of Hope, Svc. award Rotary Club Memphis Community, 1987, McCallie Sch. Alumnus of Yr. award 1978, Disting. Nat. Eagle Scout award, 1991; honored by Tenn. Legislature for disting. svc. to higher edn. and to State of Tenn., 1998. Mem. NCJJ (nat. trustee), Assn. Presbyn. Colls. and Univs. (bd. dirs.), World Bus. Coun. (young pres.' orgn., Young Man of Yr. 1961), Chief Execs. Orgn. (past), Memphis C. of C. (past bd. dir.), Univ. Club (N.Y.C.), Phi Delta Theta, Omicron Delta Kappa, Kappa Delta Epsilon (nat. hon.). Home: 4035 Dumaine Way Memphis TN 38117-2909 Office: Rhodes Coll 2000 N Parkway Office Pres Memphis TN 38112-1690

DAUGHERTY, LINDA HAGAMAN, private school executive; b. Denver, Jan. 25, 1940; d. Charles B. and Agnes May (Wall) Hagaman; m. Thomas Daniel Daugherty, Nov. 20, 1965; children: Patrick, Christina Marie. BS in Bus., U. Colo., 1961; postgrad., Tulane U., 1963-64, U. St. Thomas, 1990-91. Sr. systems analyst Lockheed Electronics NASA, Houston, 1966-73; sr. systems cons. TRW Systems Internat., Caracas, Venezuela, 1973-74; sy. systems cons. TRW Systems, L.A., 1974-75; sr. systems analyst Intercomp, Houston, 1979-80; cons. Daugherty Fin. Svcs., Inc., Katy, Tex., 1980-82, pres., 1979-91; mng. ptnr. Motivated Child Learning Ctrs., Katy, 1976—; pres. Williamsburg Country Day Sch., Katy, 1983—, Nottingham Country Day Sch., Katy, 1977—. Pres. Mason Creek Women Reps. Club, Katy, 1980; treas. Nottingham Country Civic Club, Katy, 1979; mem. adv. bd. Nottingham Country Club, 1982-85; co-founder Friends of Archaeology U. St. Thomas, pres., 1991-93; mem. Epiphany Ch. Social Works Commn.; asst. curator Archaeology Gallery, U. St. Thomas; mem., pres. Friends of Boerne Pub. Libr., 1997—; San Antonio World Affair Coun. Mem. Houston Archeology Soc., Tex. Archeology Soc., Archaeology Inst. of Am., Boerne Women's Club. Roman Catholic. Avocations: archaeology, bridge. Office: Nottingham Country Day Sch PO Box 489 Boerne TX 78006-0489

DAUGHTRY, SYLVIA, journalist, educator; b. Nov. 8, 1934; d. Horace T. and Clara Mae Jacobs; m. Frank Daughtry (dec.); children: William H. and Robert B.; m. Joseph B. Brown, 2002. BA, U. S.C., 1957; MEd, U. Ga., 1976. Tchr. Druid Hills High Sch., Atlanta, 1957-59, 1960-62, Dreher High Sch., Columbia, S.C., 1959-60, Briarcliff High Sch., Atlanta, 1962-66; tchr. English, adv. Journalism Tucker (Ga.) High Sch., 1969-92, part time tchr., 1992—95. Treas. PTA Tucker High Sch., 1973-76; pres.-elect Chi Psi Parents Club, DeKalb Assocs. of Educators, 1989-90, pres. 1990-91, parliamentarian 1991-92, legis. chmn., 1994—; mem. state exec. com. Ga. Rep. Party; sec. DeKalb County Exec. Com., 5th Dist. Rep. Party, 1984-89; Sunday sch. tchr. for Bus. and Profl. Women's Class at Briarlake Baptist Ch., pres., 1994—. Recipient Lifetime Achievement award Journalism Edn. Assn., 1992. Mem. Ga. Assn. of Journalism Dirs. (pres. 1983-85), Journalism Edn. Assn. (life mem., Ga. state dir. 1985—), So. Interscholastic Press Assn. (adv. coun. 1983-87, 1989—, exec. com. 1991—), DeKalb County County Classroom Tchrs. (pres. 1965-66). Phi Kappa Phi, Delta Kappa

Gamma (Alpha Rho chpt., pres. 1984-86, com. chmn. 1987—, Psi state dist. dir. 1987-89, Psi state editor 1989—, mem. internat. comm. com. 1994—). Home: 2038 Zelda Dr NE Atlanta GA 30345-3742

DAUKANTAS, GEORGE VYTAUTAS, counseling practitioner, educator; b. Stolzenau, Germany, Dec. 20, 1946; arrived in US, 1949; s. Chester and Alexandra Daukantas. AA magna cum laude, Wesley U., 1973; BA in Psychology, U. Mass., 1976; cert. computer programming/ops., Control Data Inst., 1980; MA in Counseling Psychology, U. No. Colo., 1982; MEd in Psychol. Studies, Cambridge Coll., 2000; postgrad., 2001—. Cert. Coun. for Accreditation for Counseling and Related Ednl. Programs. Asst. tchr. severely challenged boys and girls Boston Pub. Sch., 1997—; tchr.'s asst. spl. needs Richard J. Murphy Elem. Sch., 2000—. Mem. Nat. Campaign for Tolerance, So. Poverty Law Program. Sgt. E-5 U.S. Army, 1964—67 USNG, 1975—82. Recipient Cold War Recognition Cert., US Army, 1999. Mem.: ACLU, ACA, VFW, Assn. Counselor Edn. and Supervision, Mass. Mental Health Counselors Assn., Sierra Club, Amnesty Internat., Am. Legion. Democrat. Roman Catholic. Avocations: yoga, chess, ocean swimming. Home: # 3 135 Eutaw St Boston MA 02128-2546 E-mail: daukantas@hotmail.com.

DAUMAS LADOUCE, PABLO, engineer, educator, consultant; b. Asunción, Paraguay, Feb. 8, 1908; s. Felix and Jeanne (Bourgdelin) D.L.; m. Maria Elena Masi, Jan. 10, 1940 (dec. May, 1987); children: Jorge, Ricardo, Margarita. Topographer, U. Asunción, 1927; B in Engring. cum laude, Breguet, Paris, 1932. Head elec. dept. Cen. Arsenal Chaco War, Asunción, 1932-34, tech. dir. Minas Cué Km 180, Paraguay, 1934-35; exec. several indsl. comml. socs., Asunción, 1935-79; adj. tech. dir. Itaipu-Binacional, Asunción-Itaipu, 1979-89; sec. Paraguayan br. World Energy Coun., Asunción, 1983-89. Prof. physics U. Asunción, 1942-47; founder v.p. Centro Paraguayo de Ingenieros, Asunción, 1939-91; founder, counselor Soc. Paraguay de Fisica, Asunción, 1989-91. Inventor: patents for several inventions in 14 countries; contbr. articles to sci. jours. Founder Found. La France, Asunción, 1977; bd. dirs. paraguayan Red Cross, 1967, Faculty of Philosphy, Asunción U., 1969; plenipotentiary Paraguay to Puerto Rico, 1960, Uruguay, 1961, Washington, 1968. Mem. Am. Phys. Soc. (sr.), N.Y. Acad. Scis., Club Centenario (life), Centro Cultural Paraguayo-Am. (life) Touring Club (life). Avocations: chess, camping, music, education, physics. Address: 8221 SW 164 St Miami FL 33157

DAUPHIN, SHERYL LYNN, elementary school educator; b. Battle Creek, Mich., Jan. 3, 1957; d. Maynard Ray and Laura Agnes (Morgan) Stanton; m. William Francis Dauphin, Nov. 4, 1988; stepson, Brian Dauphin. AA, Kellogg C.C., Battle Creek, Mich., 1977; B in Elem. Edn., Ctrl. Mich. U., 1979; MEd, Gov.'s State U., 1985. Cert. tchr., Mich. Day care worker Red Brick Day Care Ctr., Battle Creek, 1979; asst. sales mgr. K-Mart, Battle Creek, 1975-79; 5th grade tchr. Momence (Ill.) Cmty. Sch. Dist. # 1, 1979—, track coach, 1980-90; volleyball coach Momence Jr. H.S., 1981-91; varsity volleyball coach Momence H.S., 1986-90. Recipient scholarship State of Mich., 1975-79. Mem. Two River Reading Coun., Momence Jaycees (treas., sec., v.p., pres. 1982-91), Ill. Jaycees (lifetime senator, senator dist. dir. 1990—), Kankakee Jaycees. Lutheran. Avocations: reading, camping, swimming, shopping. Home: 1274 N Erickson Dr Kankakee IL 60901

DAUT, ELEANOR GILMORE, vocational education educator; b. Paterson, N.J. d. Edward William and Mary (Ritchie) Gilmore; m. Victor Daniel Daut, Aug. 21, 1943. Grad., Pratt Inst., 1939; BA in Edn., Paterson State Tchrs. Coll., 1962; BS in Home Econs., Montclair State Tchrs. Coll., 1964; postgrad., Rutgers U., 1964-67. Cert. home econs. tchr., N.J. Past tchr. Ringwood (N.J.) Bd. Edn., Paterson Bd. Edn.; tchr. ind. living Bergen County Vocat. Tech. Bd. Edn., Hackensack, N.J., 1970-92, ret., 1992. Chair Drug Abuse Commn., Lincoln Park, N.J., 1970-94; non-voting mem. Boonton (N.J.) Bd. Edn., 1989-93; mem. Lincoln Park Bd. Edn., 1970-93, v.p., pres., 1980-93; apptd. Morris County Mcpl. Cmty. Dispute Resolution Com., Lincoln Park. Named Tchr. of Yr., State of N.J., 1987. Mem. NEA, N.J. Edn. Assn., Edn. Assn. Bergen County (pres., v.p. 1973-94), Morris County Schs. Bds. Assn. (bd. dirs. 1986-93), Lincoln Park Women's Club, Lincoln Park Hist. Assn., Am. Legion, Order Ea. Star, Am. Dietetic Assn. Home: 125 Main St Lincoln Park NJ 07035-1637 Office: Bergen County Vocat Tech Bd Edn 200 Hackensack Ave Hackensack NJ 07601-6110

DAVENPORT, ANN ADELE MAYFIELD, retired home care agency administrator; b. New Orleans, Nov. 12, 1941; d. Henry Louis and Myrtie Iola (Cason) Mayfield; m. John Wayne Davenport, June 18, 1966; children: Steven Lyle, Daniel Ryan, Elaine Adele. BA, Southeastern La. Coll., 1963; MA in Edn., George Peabody C., 1965; MA in Sociology, Tex. Tech. U., 1971. Tchr. various schs., 1963-70; instr. of sociology Tex. Tech. U., Lubbock, 1970-74, James Madison U., Harrisonburg, Va., 1981-82, Ga. So. Coll., Statesboro, 1982-84; 5th grade tchr. Bulloch county Schs., Statesboro, Ga., 1985-87; gerontology project coord. Dept. of Nursing Ga. So. Coll., 1987-88; project dir. Sr. Companion Program Ctr. for Rural Health and Rsch., Ga. So. U., Statesboro, 1988-93; instr. dept. health sci. edn. Ga. So. Coll., Statesboro, 1993-95; exec. dir. Ogeechee Home Health Agy., Statesboro, 1995-96, Homebound Svcs., Statesboro, 1996—2002; ret., 2002. Editor various newsletters, 1987-2002. Bd. dirs. Citizens Against Violence, Statesboro, 1987-88, Habitat for Humanity, 1990-2002; pres. Coun. on Children and Parents, Statesboro, 1988-89, 93-94; mem. steering com. Bulloch County Commn. on Human Svcs., 1989-2002; mem. adminstrv. bd. dirs., coun. on ministries, nominating com. Pittman Park United Meth. Ch.; pres. Ogeechee Wellness Coun., 1992-2002; bd. dirs. Ogeechee Home Health Agy., 1989-93. Mem. Ga. Rural Health Assn. (sec. 1988-89, editor state newsletter 1989-96), So. Sociol. Soc., Ga. Gerontol. Assn., Ga. Sociol. Assn., AAUW (newsletter editor Statesboro 1987-89), Am. Soc. on Aging, Nat. Coun. on the Aging, Am. Rural Health Assn. Avocations: tennis, reading. Home: 1920 Hampton Way Ada OK 74820

DAVENPORT, WILLIAM BRUCE, JR., special education educator; b. Bardstown, Ky., May 14, 1958; s. William Bruce and Mary Ann (Mulligan) D.; m. Cathie Marie Maskey, Oct. 17, 1986; 1 child, Christopher. BS in Elem. Edn., Campbellsville Coll., 1984; postgrad., U. Louisville, 1988. Cert. tchr., Ky. Tchr. Archdiocese of Louisville, 1984-89; tchr. of learning disabled and mentally handicapped students Cox's Creek (Ky.) Elem. Sch., 1989—. Adv. bd. Nelson G. Family Resource Ctr., bardstown, 1992—. Asst. scoutmaster Louisville area Boy Scouts Am. Fellow NEA. Democrat. Roman Catholic. Avocations: camping, hiking, hot air balloons, skiing, swimming. Home: 9416 Plumwood Rd Louisville KY 40291-1312 Office: Coxs Creek Elem Sch Louisville Rd Coxs Creek KY 40013

DAVES, GLENN DOYLE, JR., science educator, chemist, researcher; b. Clayton, N.Mex., Feb. 12, 1936; s. Glenn Doyle and Billye (Parker) D.; m. Pamela Gannarelli, Sept. 5, 1959; children: Laura Lee Daves Schantz, Anne Kathryn, Glenn Graham. BS, Ariz. State U., 1959; PhD, MIT, 1964; PharmD (hon.), U. Uppsala, Sweden, 1987. Rsch. chemist Midwest Rsch. Inst., Kansas City, Mo., 1959-61, Stanford Rsch. Inst., Palo Alto, Calif., 1964-67; asst. prof. chemistry Oreg. Grad. Ctr., Beaverton, 1967-72, assoc. prof., 1972-74, prof., 1974-81, chmn. dept., 1972-79; prof., chmn. dept. chemistry Lehigh U., Bethlehem, Pa., 1981-88; dean provost Rensselaer Poly. Inst., Troy, 1989—2000, dean Project Kaleidoscope, Summer Insts., 2000—, dean provost, 2002—03. Vis. scientist NIH, Bethesda, Md., 1988. Co-editor: Advances in Polyamine Research, Vols. 1-2, 1978, Biologically Active Principals of Natural Products, 1984; contbr. numerous articles to profl. jours. Recipient numerous grants NIH, Am. Cancer Soc., U.S. Forest Svc., 1971—. Mem. Am. Chem. Soc., Internat. Soc. Heterocyclic Chemistry, Coun. for Chem. Rsch. (governing bd. 1985-86, chair manpower and resource com. 1984-87, mem. membership com. 1991). Democrat. E-mail: davesgs@yahoo.com.

DAVEY, CHARLES BINGHAM, soil science educator; b. Bklyn., Apr. 7, 1928; s. Francis Joseph and Mary Elizabeth (Bingham) D.; m. Elizabeth Anne Thompson, July 11, 1952; children: Douglas Alan, Barbara Lynn, Andrew Martin. BS, Syracuse U., 1950; MS, U. Wis., 1952, PhD, 1955. Soil scientist Research Service, Dept. Agr., Beltsville, Md., 1957-62; assoc. prof. N.C. State U., Raleigh, 1962-65, prof., 1965—, head dept., 1970-78, Carl Alwin Schenck Disting. prof., 1978—, Alumni Disting. prof., 1989. Editor: Tree Growth and Forest Soils, 1970; asso. editor: Soil Sci. Soc. Am. proc, 1967-72; contbr. articles to profl. jours. Served with AUS, 1955-57. Fellow AAAS, Am. Soc. Agronomy, Soil Sci. Soc. Am. (pres. 1975-76, Disting. Svc. award); mem. Soc. Am. Foresters (Barrington Moore Rsch. award), Internat. Soil Sci. Soc., Internat. Soc. Tropical Foresters, Sigma Xi (Rsch. award), Phi Kappa Phi, Gamma Sigma Delta, Xi Sigma Pi. Achievements include patents in field. Home: 5219 Melbourne Rd Raleigh NC 27606-1619 Office: Forestry Dept 3113 Faucette Dr Raleigh NC 27695-8008 E-mail: cdavey@unity.ncsu.edu., char1168@bellsouth.net.

DAVEY, ELEANOR ELLEN, science educator; b. Colorado Springs, Colo., Aug. 28, 1910; d. Stanly James and Elizabeth (Bays) Britton; m. Herbert Merritt, Aug. 9, 1932; children: Ted H. Davey, Ronald B. Davey, Betty Nell Davey Ferraro. AB, U. No. Colo., 1934; MS, Ariz. State U., 1967. Cert. tchr., Wyo., Ariz. Credit advisor Montgomery Ward, Denver, 1936-38; swimming instr. Colo. State U., Ft. Collins, 1938; English tchr., swimming tchr. East H.S., Cheyenne, Wyo., 1939-40; dir. phys. edn. Xavier H.S., Phoenix, 1957-63, biology tchr., sci. dept. chair, 1963-76; sci. awards dir. Ariz. State U., Tempe, 1974-88; biology prof. U. Ariz., Tucson, 1980; Ariz. dir. presdl. awards program NSF, Arlington, Va., 1983—2000. Author: (with others) Air Pollution: Man and the Environment, 1971, Mothers of Achievement in American History 1776-1976, 1976; co-author: Strength Through Leadership, 1963. Foster care bd. dirs. Ariz. Dept. Econ. Security, Phoenix, 1978-84. Named Outstanding Secondary Educator of Am., 1974; named to Hall of Fame, Palmer Alumni Assn, 1987; recipient Am. Soc. Microbiology award, 1973—75, Cert. of Recognition, Sigma Xi, 1986, Disting. Svc. award, Ariz. Alliance for Math., Sci. & Tech. Edn., 2000. Fellow Ariz. Nev. Acad. Sci. (Ariz. Outstanding Sci. Tchr. Yr. 1965, dir. Ctrl. Ariz. chpt. 1971-82, chair outstanding sci. tchr. com. 1982-86, chair scholarship com. 1990-95, exec. bd. dirs. 1980-90, Outstanding Svc. award 1997); mem. NSTA (mem. at large, exec. bd. dirs. 1974-76, chair awards com. 1976-77, chair S.W. area conv. 1976, internat. com. h.s. com. nominations 1976, Ariz. contact 1972-99, 2003—, Disting. Svc. to Sci. Edn. award 1975), Nat. Assn. Biology Tchrs. (Ariz. state rep. 1975-80, coord. Region VII 1980-86, 89-91, exec. bd. dirs. 1984-86, chair nominating com. 1987-89, Outstanding Biology Tchr. Ariz. 1973), Ariz. Sci. Tchrs. Assn. (membership sec. 1973-88, pres. 1973-74, exec. bd. dirs. 1973-98, chair nomination/election com. 1990-97, hon. life mem., contact 1973-98, 2003—, Cmty. Svc. award 35+ Yrs., 2000). Avocations: volunteer education programs, reading, swimming, watching basketball and football games. Home and Office: 242 E McLellan Blvd Phoenix AZ 85012-1141

DAVID, CHRISTINE A. artist, educator; b. Buffalo, N.Y., July 15, 1969; AS, Jamestown (N.Y.) C.C., 1986; BFA, Fredonia (N.Y.) State, 1989; MFA, RIT, Rochester, N.Y., 1991; MBA, St. Bonaventure, 1995. Art therapist The Resource Ctr., Jamestown, N.Y., 1989-90; visual arts dir. The Art Coun. for C.C., Jamestown, 1991-93; owner Emanon Gallery, Jamestown, 1992-94; creative dir. Artemis Design Group, Coral Springs, Fla., 1994—; prof. Art Inst. Ft. Lauderdale, Fla., 1997—. Pres. bd. dirs. Grad. Sch. Bd. St. Bonaventure, 1995—. Designer: (illustration) People Mag., 1995-2000 (Pro Com award 1995-97), Esquire Mag., 1995-2000 (Am. Advtg. award 1996, 99), Rolling Stone Mag., 1996-2000; TV comml. for Zippo Mfg.; exhbns. include Horizon Internat. Art Gallery, 1990, Mayor's Pick Show City of Jamestown, 1990, 92, Art Inst. Faculty exhbn., 1997-99. Vol. N.Y. AIDS Col., Am. Assn. for Retarded Children. Art scholar Nat. Honor Soc., 1989.; recipient ADDY award 1997-2002, Clio award 1996-97, Gold Pencil One Show, 1996. Mem. Nat. Assn. Women Artists, Delta Mu Delta. Democrat. Avocations: bike riding, running, painting.

DAVID, DON RAYMOND, artist, educator; b. Springbrook, Oreg., May 2, 1906; s. Melvin Henry and Clara Alice (Heater) D.; m. Margaret Alma Wanamaker, July 10, 1930 (div. 1947); children: Doris Lee, Diane Elizabeth; m. Ruth Andree Golbin, Jan. 6, 1952. Student, Fresno State U., 1927-29, Art Ctr. Sch., L.A., 1941-43, Chouinards, 1943-44, Hans Hofmann Sch., N.Y.C., 1952-56. Artist Weinstocks Dept. Store, Sacramento, 1931-41; designer Dozier, Graham, Eastman Advt., L.A., 1941-43, Helena Rubinstein, N.Y.C., 1952-57; art dir. Robinson Dept. Stores, L.A., 1943-48, Filenes Dept. Stores, Boston, 1949-50; freelance designer Nestle Co., N.Y.C., 1957-61, Burlington Mills, N.Y.C., 1961-78; art instr. Parsons Sch. Design, N.Y.C., 1984—; chmn. illustration Newark Sch. Fine and Indsl. Art, 1969—. Chmn. Camino Artists Coop. Gallery, N.Y.C., 1956-61. One-man shows include Baruch Coll., CUNY, 1968, New Sch., N.Y.C., 1969, Alonzo Gallery, 1970, 74, 76, 79, Parsons Sch. Design, 1987, Gallery Bai, N.Y.C., 1998; exhibited in group show Atlantic Gallery, N.Y.C., 1990, Gallery Bai, N.Y.C., 1998. Mem. Coll. Artists Assn. Democrat. Avocation: photography. Home and Office: Apt 9B 521 E 14th St New York NY 10009-2925

DAVID, GLORIA ELAINE, secondary school educator; b. Niles, Mich., Oct. 27, 1968; d. Dewey A. and R. Ellen (Beardsley) Murdick; m. Kelwyn S. David, June 16, 1991. BA in Spanish, Andrews U., 1990, MA in English, 1997. Cert. secondary tchr. Spanish tchr. Lake Mich. Cath. HS, St. Joseph, Mich., 1991-96, Pine River HS, Le Roy, Mich., 1996—. Leader/organizer yearly tour to Mexico City Spanish club Lake Mich. Cath HS, St. Joseph, 1991—96; leader/organizer bi-yearly tours to Mex. Pine River HS, Le Roy, 2000—. Violinist Michiana Symphony Orch., 1987—95. Home: 17429 Meceola Rd Hersey MI 49639-9622 Office: Pine River HS Pine River School Rd Leroy MI 49655

DAVID, HERBERT ARON, statistician, educator; b. Berlin, Dec. 19, 1925; arrived in U.S., 1957, naturalized, 1964; s. Max and Betty (Goldmann) David; m. Vera Reiss, May 13, 1950 (dec.); 1 child, Alexander John; m. Ruth Finch, Dec. 1, 1992. BSc, Sydney (Australia) U., 1947; PhD, London U., 1953. Rsch. officer Commonwealth Sci. and Indsl. Rsch. Orgn., Sydney, 1953-55; sr. lectr. dept. stats. U. Melbourne, Melbourne, Australia, 1955-57; prof. stats. Va. Poly. Inst., 1957-64; prof. U. N.C., Chapel Hill, 1964-72, Iowa State U., Ames, 1972-96, Disting. prof. liberal arts and scis., 1980-96, disting. prof. emeritus, 1996—, dir. stat. lab., head dept. stats., 1972-84. Author: (book) The Method of Paired Comparisons, 1963, 2d edit., 1988, Order Statistics, 1970; co-author: 3d edit., 2003, Annotated Readings in the History of Statistics, 2001; co-editor: Advanced in Biometry, 1996. Recipient J. Shelton Horsley award, Va. Acad. Scis., 1963, Wilks award, Army Rsch., 1983. Fellow: AAAS, Inst. Math. Stats., Am. Statis. Assn.; mem.: Internat. Statis. Inst., Biometric Soc. (editor Biometrics 1967—72, pres. 1982—83). Jewish. Home: 2334 Hamilton Dr Ames IA 50014-8201 E-mail: hadavid@iastate.edu.

DAVID, JOHN DEWOOD, biology educator; b. Alton, Ill., Dec. 1, 1942; s. Wade Dewood and Mary (Kemper) David; m. Nancy M. Rock, Feb. 6, 1972; children: Henry Wade, Katherine Leslie. BA in Chemistry and Biology, Wabash Coll., 1964; PhD in Molecular Biology, Vanderbilt U., 1969. Postdoctoral fellow U. Calif., San Francisco, 1969-72; asst. prof. U. Mo., Columbia, 1972-78, assoc. prof., 1978—, chair divsn. biol. scis., 1989—. Mem. task force on tchg. of sci. and math. in secondary schs. U. Mo. Columbia, 1983—85; mem. sci., math. engring. and tech. task force U. Mo. Columbia, Mo. State Dept. Edn., 1997—99; chair Chancellor's Strategic Planning and Resource Allocation Coun. U. Mo. Columbia, 2002—, mem. task force on restructuring tchg. preparation, 1994—97. Contbr. articles to profl. jours. Bd. dirs. Columbia Soccer Club, 1989—92. Recipient Recognition award for Integration of Rsch. and Edn., NSF, 1997—2002; grantee, Howard Hughes Med. Inst., 1989—99; Med. rsch. fellow, Giannini Found., 1970—72. Mem.: AAAS, Soc. for Cell Biology, Soc. for Devel. Biology, Beta Beta Beta (hon.). Democrat. Presbyterian. Avocations: soccer refereeing, gardening. Office: U Mo 105 Tucker Hall Columbia MO 65211-7400 E-mail: davidj@missouri.edu.

DAVID, MARTHA LENA HUFFAKER, educator; b. Susie, Ky., Feb. 7, 1925; d. Andrew Michael and Nora Marie (Cook) Huffaker; m. William Edward David, June 24, 1952 (div. Jan. 1986); children: Edward Garry, William Andrew, Carolyn Ann, Robert Cook. AB in Music magna cum laude, Georgetown (Ky.) Coll., 1947; postgrad., Vanderbilt U., 1957-58; Spanish cert., Lang. Sch., Costa Rica, 1959; MEd, U. Ga., 1972. Elem. tchr. Wayne County Bd. Edn., Spann, Ky., 1944-45; music tchr. Mason County, Mayslick, Ky., 1947-49, Hikes Grade Sch., Buechel, Ky., 1949-53; English and Spanish tchr. Jefferson (Ga.) High Sch., 1961-63; music and English tchr. Athens (Ga.) Acad., 1967-71; music tchr. Barrow County Bd. Edn., Winder, Ga., 1971-88; real estate agt. South Best Realty, Athens, 1986-90; ret., 1988. Data collector Regional Ednl. Svcs. Agy., Athens and Winder, 19176-78; tchr. music Union Theol. Sem., Buenos Aires, 1957-60. Author: (poems) Parcels of Love, Book I, 1984, Book II, 1999, Poems and Reflections; composer (music plays) The B.B.'s, The Missing Tune, A Dream Come True, The Stars Who Creep Out of Orbit, 1976-86. Active cultural affairs orgns., Athens, 1962—, Athens Area Porcelain Artists, YWCO; entertainer nursing homes and civic orgns., Athens, 1962; chmn. cancer drives, heart fund drive United Way, March of Dimes, Athens, 1962—; historian, elder, pianist Christian Ch. Winner regional piano competition Ky. Philharm. Orch., 1946; nominated Tchrs. Hall of Fame, Barrow County, 1981. Mem. Ret. Tchrs. Assn., Writer's Group, Ga. Music Tchrs., Nat. Music Tchrs. Assn., Athens Music Tchrs. Assn. (pres. recital chmn.), Ga. World Orgn. China Painters, Athens Area Porcelain Artists, Women's Mus. Arts (assoc.), Women's Mus. Art (Washington), Touchdown Club, Band Boosters, Alpha Delta Kappa (Fidelis Nu chpt., historian), Delta Omicron (life, scholar 1944). Democrat. Mem. Christian Ch. Avocations: porcelain art, oil and acrylic painting, swimming, square dancing, round dancing. Home: 105 Nassau Ln Athens GA 30607-1456

DAVID, YADIN B. biomedical engineer, health care technology consultant; b. Haifa, Israel, Nov. 25, 1946; came to U.S., 1972, naturalized, 1982; s. Bezalel and Ziona (Kovalsky) D.; m. Becky Lask, Jan. 23, 1968; children: Tal, Daniel. BS, W.Va. U., 1974, MS, 1975, PhD, 1983. Registered profl. engr., cert. clin. engr., Tex. Dir. biomed engring. W.Va. U. Hosp., Morgantown, 1976-82, asst. prof., 1979-82; pres. TALDAN Cons., Houston, 1976—; dir. Ctr. for TeleHealth, dir. biomed. engring. St. Lukes Epis. Hosp., Tex. Childrens Hosp., Tex. Heart Inst, Houston, 1982—; adj. assoc. prof. dept. anesthesia U. Tex. Med. Sci. Ctr., Houston, 1984—. Adj. assoc. prof. anesthesia dept. U. Tex. Med. Sci. Ctr., Houston, 1984—; adj. assoc. prof. Baylor Coll. Medicine, 1987—; tech. dir. TeleHealth Ctr., 1988—; pres. Ctr. Telemedicine Law, 1995—; chmn. NFPA com. on LASER Safety and Gas Delivery in Health Care; program chmn. Clin. Engring. Symposium ann. confs., 1983-87. Contbr. chpts. to books, articles to tech. jours. Advisor B'nai B'rith Youth Orgn., Morgantown, 1981-82 W.Va. U. grantee, 1976; recipient FDA Spl. Commr. award, 2002. Mem. IEEE (rep. to standards com. 1978-94, health care engring. policy com. 1984-95), Am. Inst. Med. and Biol. Engring. (founding fellow), Am. Coll. Clin. Engring. (pres 1993), Engring. in Medicine and Biology (chmn. clin. engring. com. 1983-86), Assn. Advancement Med. Instrumentation (mem. edn. com. 1985-87), Eta Kappa Nu. Office: Tex Childrens Hosp Biomed Engring Dept 6621 Fannin St Houston TX 77030-2303

DAVIDSHOFER, CLAIRE H. college instructor; b. Bouake, Cote d'Ivoire, Oct. 1, 1946; BA in English, U. d' Aix-en-Provence, France, 1968; MA in Am. Lit., U. d'Aix-en-Provence, France, 1969. H.s. tchr. MSAD #1/Presque Isle High, Presque Isle, Maine, 1969—73, 1974—78, 1979—80; coll. instr. U. Maine at Presque Isle, 1980—. Office: Univ of Maine at Preque Isle 181 Main St Presque Isle ME 04769

DAVIDSON, ARNOLD I. philosophy educator; MA in Philosophy with distinction, Georgetown U.; PhD in Philosophy, Harvard U., 1981. Asst. prof. dept. philosophy, program in history of sic., program in comparative lit. Stanford U., 1981—84, 1985—86; prin. instr. seminar on epistemology and the liberal arts NEH, Kalamazoo, 1990; prof. dept. philosophy U. Chgo. Staff cons. nat. commn. proteciton of human subjects of biomed. and behavioral rsch. NIH, 1977; vis. asst. prof. philosophy Princeton (N.J.) U., 1984—85; vis. prof. humanities U. Calif., Davis, 1996; vis. prof. Coll. de France, 1997—98, dept. history of sci., Harvard U., 1999, Coll. Internat. Philosophie, 2001. Referee Nous, Ethics, mem. adv. editl. bd. Jour. History of Sexuality, Medicina e Storia. Recipient Whiting fellow in the humanities, Harvard U.; fellow, Inst. Advanced Study, Berlin, hon. fellow, U. Calif. Inst. Humanities, Marta Sutton Weeks fellow, Stanford Humanities Ctr., fellow, Calif. Humanities Inst., John Simon Guggenheim Meml. Found., 2003, grant, Pew Found. Office: U Chgo Dept Philosophy 1050 E 59th St Chicago IL 60637*

DAVIDSON, BONNIE JEAN, gymnastics educator, sports management consultant; b. Rockford, Ill., Nov. 19, 1941; d. Edward V. and Pauline Mae (Dubbs) Welliver; m. Glenn Duane Davidson, June 4, 1960 (dec. Oct. 1993); children: Lori Davidson Aamodt, Wendy Davidson Seerup; m. James A. Johnson, Sept. 15, 2001. Student, Rockford Coll., 1965, Rock Valley Coll., Rockford, 1969-77. Founder, owner, dir. Gymnastic Acad. Rockford, 1977-95; pres., dir., owner Springbrook, Ltd., swim and tennis club, Rockford, 1986-95. Rep. trampoline and tumbling com. AAU, 1989-99—; coach nat. and world champion athetes; mgr., judge, head del. U.S.A. gymnastics teams, 1980—; speaker, lectr., clinician in field.; mem. organizing coms. world championships, also others, 1982-99 Contbr. World Book Ency. Bd. dirs. U.S. Olympic Com., 1995—, U.S.A. Gymnastics, 1991—; instr. ARC. Named one of Most Interesting People, Rockford mag., 1987; named to USA Gymnastics Hall of Fame, 2003; recipient YWCA Janet Lynn Sports award, 1996. Mem. Internat. Fedn. Trampoline and Tumbling (internat. judge, mem. tech. com. 1986-99—, del. to congress 1976-86, hon. lifetime mem. 1998), Internat. Fedn. Sport Acrobats (internat. judge), U.S.A. Trampoline and Tumbling Assn. (hon. life; nat. tumbling chairperson 1980-88, advisor 1988-99—, Coach of Yr. award 1980, Outsanding Contbn. to the Sport award 1987, 96, Master of Sport award 1989), U.S. Sports Acrobatics Fedn. (hon. life; v.p. 1984-95), Nat. Judges Assn. (exec. dir.). Republican. Avocations: skiing, boating, bicycling, birdwatching. E-mail: davidsonbj@aol.com., davidsonbj@insightbb.com.

DAVIDSON, CHANDLER, sociologist, educator; b. May 13, 1936; m. Sharon Lavonne Plummer, Nov. 1, 1986. BA, U. Tex., 1961; PhD, Princeton U., 1969. Rsch. prof. sociology Rice U., Houston, 1966—, prof. polit. sci., 1997—2003, prof. emeritus, 2003—, Radoslav Tsanoff prof. pub. affairs, 2000—03, chair dept. sociology, 1979-83, 86-89, 1995—2003, prof. emeritus, 2003—. Co-prin. investigator NSF, 1988-92, Rockefeller Found., 1990. Author: Biracial Politics, 1972, Race and Class in Texas Politics, 1990; editor: Minority Vote Dilution, 1984, (with Bernard Grofman) Controversies in Minority Voting, 1992, (with Grofman) Quiet Revolution in the South, 1994. Fulbright scholar, 1961-62; Woodrow Wilson fellow, 1963-64, rsch. fellow Nat. Endowment for Humanities, 1976-77; recipient Gustavus Myers Ctr. Human Rights award for outstanding book on human rights, 1993, Ally award Ctr. for the Healing of Racism, 1996, Brown award for superior tchg., Rice U., 1997, 99, 2000, 2002, Brown award for excellence in tchg. Rice U., 1998. Mem. Am. Sociol. Assn., Am. Polit. Sci. Assn. (Fenno prize 1995), Philos. Soc. Tex., Phi Beta Kappa. Office: Rice U Dept Sociology 6100 S Main St Houston TX 77005-1892 E-mail: fcd@rice.edu.

DAVIDSON, CYNTHIA ANN, elementary school educator; b. Neosho, Mo., Nov. 21, 1953; d. Richard Thomas and Cora Nadine (Mitchell)

Morrison; m. Charles Richard Davidson, Aug. 3, 1985; children: Tony, Daniel. AA, Crowder Coll., Neosho, Mo., 1973; BS in Edn., Mo. So. State Coll., 1975; MS in Edn., S.W. Mo. State U., 1977. Tchr. 1st grade Exeter (Mo.) R 6, 1975-76; tchr. 3rd grade East Newto R 6, Stella, Mo., 1976—. Mem. prin.'s adv. com. Triway Elem. Sch., Stella, 1986—. Mem. East Newton CTA (mem. exec. com., bldg. rep.), Internat. Reading Assn., Mo. State Tchrs. Assn. Mem. Ch. of Christ. Avocations: yardwork, 4 h club, horses. Home: 18755 Nettle Dr Neosho MO 64850-8796 Office: Triway Elem Sch Third Grade Stella MO 64867

DAVIDSON, DAN EUGENE, Russian language and area scholar, academic administrator; b. Wichita, Kans., Sept. 18, 1944; s. Clerin D. and Fay E. (Scott) D.; m. Maria D. Lekic, Apr. 20, 1976; children: Michael Scott, Paul Eugene. BA, U. Kans., 1966; MA, Harvard U., 1971, PhD, 1972; DSc (hon.), Russian Acad. Scis., 1995, Almaty State U., Kazakhstan, 1996, U. World Langs., Uzbekistan, 1997. Asst. prof., then assoc. prof. Amherst (Mass.) Coll., 1971-76; from assoc. prof. to prof. Russian Bryn Mawr (Pa.) Coll., 1976—; exec. dir. Am. Coun. Tchrs. of Russian, Washington, 1980—; pres. Am. Couns. for Internat. Edn. ACTR/ACCELS, 1998—. Adj. faculty U. Pa., Columbia U., Harvard U., 1975; cons. UN, N.Y.C., 1987, 88, 91, U.S. Dept. Edn., NEH, Washington; co-chair Internat. Task Force on Ednl. Reform in Russia, Ukraine, Belarus, Kyrgyzstan, Kazakhstan, 1992-94 (Soros Founds.); chmn. Alliance for Internat. Ednl. and Cultural Exch., 1997-99; chmn. U.S.-Uzbekistan Coun., 1997-99; pres. Am. Couns. Internat. Edn., 1998—. Series editor: Soviet-American Textbook Series of Russian, 1974—; author, co-author, editor univ. and high sch.-level textbooks on English and Russian; editor, co-editor scholarly collections, jours.; contbr. articles to scholarly publs. Bd. dirs. numerous non-profit ednl. orgns.; mem. leadership com. co-chmn. ann. fund and major gifts, Barrie Sch., 1995-96, trustee, 1997-2000; mem. Fair Share Campaign Sidwell Friends Sch., 1992-97. Recipient Pushkin medal, 1982, Order Internat. Friendship, USSR, 1990; inducted into Russian Acad. Edn., 1995; recipient Disting. Svc. to Profession award, Am. Assn. Tchrs. Slavic Langs., 1995, Disting. Svc. award Assn. Depts. Fgn. Langs./MLA, 1997; hon. fellow Woodrow Wilson Found., 1966. Mem. MLA, Am. Assn. Advancement Slavic Studies, Am. Coun. Tchrs. of Russian (pres. 1975-79), Internat. Assn. Tchrs. Russian Lang. and Lit. (v.p. 1975-80, 91—), Harvard Club, Phi Beta Kappa, Delta Phi Alpha. Democrat. Episcopalian. Avocations: travel, music, swimming. Office: Am Couns Ste 700 1776 Massachusetts Ave NW Washington DC 20036-1904 E-mail: ceo@americancouncils.org.

DAVIDSON, ERIC HARRIS, molecular and developmental biologist, educator; b. NYC, Apr. 13, 1937; s. Morris and Anne D. BA, U. Pa., 1958; PhD, Rockefeller U., 1963. Research asso. Rockefeller U., 1963-65, asst. prof., 1965-71; asso. prof. devel. molecular biology Calif. Inst. Tech., Pasadena, Calif., 1971-74, prof., 1974—, Norman Chandler prof. cell biology, 1981—. Author: Gene Activity in Early Development, 3d edit, 1986, Genomic Regulatory Systems, 2001. NIH grantee, 1965— ; NSF grantee, 1972— Mem. Nat. Acad. Scis. Achievements include research, numerous publs. on DNA sequence orgn., gene expression during embryonic devel., gene regulation, evolutionary mechanisms, gene networks. Office: Calif Inst Tech Div Biology Mail Code 156 29 Pasadena CA 91125-0001

DAVIDSON, FLORENCE HICKMAN, clinical psychologist, education consultant; b. Merion Station, Pa., Apr. 2, 1928; d. Alfred Marriner and Marjory Letitia (Bunting) Hickman; m. William D. Davidson, Aug. 31, 1949 (div. 1968); children: Christopher, John, Peter, Ben, Bernard, Miriam; m. Leonard Kreidermacher, Jan. 1, 1983. BA, Duke U., 1950; MEd, St. Cloud State U., 1965; EdD, Harvard U., 1974. Lic. psychologist, Mass. Rsch. assoc. Ctr. for Moral Devel., Harvard U., 1974-76; pvt. practice clin. psychology Falmouth, Mass., 1976—; co-founder Mass. Sch. Profl. Psychology. Exec. dir. Mass. Psychol. Ctr., Boston, 1972-78; Bd. mem. and psychol. Cape Cod Free Clin. in Falmouth, 1998-pres. Author: (with Miriam Davidson) Changing Childhood Prejudice: The Caring Work of the Schools, 1994. Bd. dirs. Cambridge (Mass.) Friends Sch., 1972, Tandem Friends Sch., Charlottesville, Va., 1997-99. Bunting Inst. fellow Radcliffe Coll., 1970-72; Milton fellow Harvard U., 1974-76. Democrat. Mem. Soc. Of Friends. Home and Office: 457 Elm Rd Falmouth MA 02540-2414

DAVIDSON, FRED, education educator; b. Chgo., Dec. 10, 1954; s. Harry Vincent and Thalia (Heim) D. BA, U. Ill., 1976, MA, 1981; PhD, UCLA, 1988. Cert. secondary tchr., speech and English, Ill. Vol. Peace Corps, Liberia, West Africa, 1976-78; rsch., teaching asst. U. Ill., Urbana-Champaign, Ill., 1979-81; intern, lectr. ESL Ohio U., Athens, 1981-83; rsch., teaching asst. UCLA, 1983-88; rsch. advisor U. Cambridge Local Examinations Syndicate, Cambridge, U.K., 1988-89; program evaluator Ill. State Bd. Edn., Springfield, Des Plaines, Ill., 1989-90; asst. prof. English as internat. lang. U. Ill., Urbana-Champaign, 1990-96, assoc. prof., 1996—. Author: Principles of Statistical Data Handling, 1996; contbr. articles to profl. jours. Recipient Cert. of Appreciation, Ministry of Edn., Republic of Liberia, 1978, Teaching Excellence awards UCLA, 1983-88, U. Ill., 1979-81, 90—. Mem. TESOL, Nat. Peace Corps Assn., Am. Ednl. Rsch. Assn., Internat. Assn. World Englishes, Lang. Testing Rsch. Colloquim (archivist), Phi Kappa Phi (chair internat. lang. testing assn. task force on testing stds.). Avocations: bicycling, jogging, billiards. Home: 208 E Dodson Dr Urbana IL 61802-2213 Office: U Ill Urbana Champaign Divsn English as Internat Lang 707 S Mathews Ave Urbana IL 61801-3625

DAVIDSON, HUGH MACCULLOUGH, French language and literature educator; b. West Point, Ga., Jan. 21, 1918; s. Robert Calvin Davidson Sr. and Anne Della Stripling; m. Loretta Jane Miller, June 15, 1951; 1 child, Anne Stripling Davidson. AB in Romance Langs., U. Chgo., 1938, PhD in Romance Langs., 1946; MA (hon.), Yale U., 1967. Instr. French U. Chgo., 1946-48, asst. prof. French, 1948-53, asst. dean coll., 1951-53; asst. prof. romance langs. Dartmouth Coll., 1953-56, prof. romance langs., 1956-62, chmn. dept. romance langs., 1957-59; prof. romance langs. Ohio State U., 1962-67, 68-73; prof. French lit. U. Va., 1973-78, commonwealth prof. French lit., 1978, 1978-90, commonwealth prof. French lit. emeritus, 1990—. Vis. prof. French U. Mich., 1967; univ. examiner French and gen. linguistics, humanities U. Chgo., 1946-48; chmn. Coll. French staff U. Chgo., 1948-53; Thomas Jefferson fellow Downing Coll., Cambridge U., Eng., 1979-80; vis. prof. U. Paris Sorbonne, 1982-83; vis. com. humanities and arts Case We. Res. U., 1967; cons. div. edn. programs NEH, 1977; conducts seminars in field. Author: Audience, Words, and Art, 1965, The Origins of Certainty: Means and Meanings in Pascal's Pensées, 1979, Blaise Pascal, 1983, Pascal and the Arts of the Mind, 1993; co-author: A Concordance to the Pensées of Pascal, 1975, A Concordance to Pascal's Les Provinciales, 1980; asst. editor: The Idea and Practice of General Education, 1948; mem. editl. bd. Continuum: Problems in French Literature from the Late Renaissance to the Early Enlightenment, EMF: Studies in Early Modern France; contbr. articles to profl. jours. Capt. USAF, 1942-46. Gen. Edn. fellow Carnegie Found., 1948-49; Fulbright Sr. fellow for rsch. in France, 1959-60; Sr. Rsch. fellow Nat. Found. Arts and Humanities, 1967-68. Mem. MLA (mem. editl. com. publs. 1968-73), Am. Assn. Tchrs. French, Am. Soc. Eighteenth-Century Studies, N. Am. Soc. Seventeenth-Century French Lit., Assn. internat. des études françaises, Soc. internat. d'étude du XVIIe siècle, Soc. internat. d'étude du XVIIIe siècle, Soc. des amis de l'Inst. de littérature française de l'Univ. de Paris Sorbonne, Soc. des amis de Port-Royal, Phi Beta Kappa (mem. nat. Senate 1982-88). Episcopalian. Avocations: history of painting, sculpture, and architecture, history of the liberal arts of grammar, rhetoric, logic, dialectic and their applications in art, science, and philosophy, music. Address: 250 Pantops Mountain Rd Apt 319 Charlottesville VA 22911 Office: U Va Dept French Lit 302 Cabell Hl Charlottesville VA 22908-0001

DAVIDSON, JOHN KENNETH, SR., sociologist, educator, researcher, writer, consultant; b. Augusta, Ga., Oct. 25, 1939; s. Larcie Charles and Betty (Corley) D.; m. Josephine Frazier, Apr. 11, 1964; children: John Kenneth Jr., Stephen Wood. Student, Augusta Coll., 1956-58; BS in Edn., U. Ga., 1961, MA, 1963; PhD, U. Fla., 1974. Asst. prof. dept. psychology and sociology Armstrong State Coll., Savannah, Ga., 1963-67; asst. prof. sociology Augusta Coll., 1967-74; acting chmn., asst. prof. dept. sociology Ind. U., South Bend, 1974-76; assoc. prof. sociology U. Wis., Eau Claire, Wis., 1976-78, prof., 1978—, chmn. dept. sociology, 1976-80, asst. spl. projects to dean grad. studies and univ. rsch., 1987-91, coord. family studies, 1990—. Cons. family life edn.; rsch. cons. dept. ob-gyn. Med. Coll. Ga., Augusta, 1969-74, pediatrics, 1972-73, assoc. dir. health care project, 1971-73, rsch. instr., 1971, rsch. assoc., 1972-73, rsch. cons. dept. community dentistry, 1974-79; program coord. Community Devel. in Process Phase II and III, Title I Higher Edn. Act of, 1965, 1970; sociology and anthropology com. Univ. System Ga., 1970-74, chmn. curriculum sub-com., 1970-72; dir. Sex Edn., The Pub. Schs. and You project Ind. Com. on Humanities, 1975 Author: Marriage and Family, 1992, Speaking of Sexuality: Interdisciplinary Readings, 2001; co-author: Cultural Diversity and Families, 1992; editor: Marriage and Family: Change and Continuity, 1996, Speaking of Sexuality, 2001; editor: (assoc.) Jour. Marriage and the Family, 1975—85, Sociol. Inquiry, 1986—92, Sociol. Imagination, 1993—; editor: (cons.) Jour. Sex Rsch., 1991—95; editor: (cons) Sociol. Inquiry, 2001—; reviewer: Jour. Deviant Behavior, 1979—90, Sociol. Spectrum, 1985—, Jour. Family Issues, 1995—, Jour. Sex Rsch., 1996—; contbr. articles to profl. jours. Past state chmn. pub. affairs Ind. Assn. Planned Parenthood Affiliates, 1975-76; past bd. dirs. Planned Parenthood North Cen. Ind., chmn. pub. affairs com., 1975-76; past bd. dirs., 1st v.p., resources allocation com. Wis. Family Planning Coordinating Council; past bd. dirs., exec., info., internat. and edn. coms., chmn. social sci. rsch. com. Assn. for Vol. Sterilization; past pres. citizens adv. bd. Eau Claire and Chippewa Falls Planned Parenthood Clinics; past mem. dirs. Planned Parenthood of Wis., Inc.; past mem. Eau Claire Coord. Coun., Eau Claire County Adv. Health Forum, Eau Claire County Task Force on Family Planning, Eau Claire Task Force on Teen Pregnancy. Mem. Am. Sociol. Assn., Wis. Sociol. Assn., So. Sociol. Soc., Mid-South Sociol. Assn. (pres.-elect 1998-99, pres. 1999-2000, past pres. 2000-01, hotel negotiator, 2003—), Midwest Sociol. Soc., Groves Conf., Nat. Coun. Family Rels. (past chmn. com. stds. and criteria for cert., former mem. devel. com. and cert. com.), Wis. Coun. Family Rels. (bd. dirs., exec. com., past pres.), Soc. Sci. Study Sex., Tex. Coun. Family Rels., Augusta Coll. Alumni Soc., U. Fla. Alumni Soc., U. Ga. Alumni Soc., Pres. Club. U. Wis.-Eau Claire, Kappa Delta Pi, Phi Kappa Phi (chpt. pres. 1991-92, Nat. Forum editl. com. 1992-99), Phi Theta Kappa, Alpha Kappa Delta (editor nat. newsletter 1979-83, nat. v.p. 1992-94, nat. pres.-elect 1994-96, nat. pres. 1996-98, nat. past pres. 1998-2000, exec. coun. 1992-2000). Episcopalian. Home: 1305 Nixon Ave Eau Claire WI 54701-6574 Office: U Wis Dept Sociology Eau Claire WI 54702

DAVIDSON, MARK, writer, educator; b. N.Y.C., Sept. 25, 1928; BA in Polit. Sci., UCLA, 1948; MS in Journalism, Columbia U., 1950. Sci. writer U. So. Calif., L.A., 1980-90; prof. comm. Calif. State U., Dominguez Hills, Carson, 1985-99; freelance mag. writer. Faculty adviser Soc. Profl. Journalists, 1993-96; writer for Steve Allen Show, 1964, Dinah Shore Show, 1978, CBS Mag. Series with Connie Chung, 1980; sci. conf. spkr. Vienna Tech., 2001, U. Maribor, Slovenia, 2002. Author: Uncommon Sense (About Systems Science), 1984, Japanese transl., 2000, Invisible Chains of Thought Control, 1999, Watchwords: A Dictionary of American English Usage, 2001. Sackett scholar Columbia U.; recipient Nat. Emmy for writing hist. satires NATAS, 1978, Best Paper rating Conf. on Info. Sci., Pori, Finland, 2003. Mem.: PEN, Soc. Advancement of Edn. (assoc. mass media editor 1997—2001), Calif. Faculty Assn. (v.p. Dominguez Hills chpt. 1992—96), Nat. Writers Union (L.A. steering com. 2002—03), Writers Guild Am., Authors Guild, Am. Med. Writers Assn., Nat. Assn. Sci. Writers, Am. Soc. Journalists and Authors. E-mail: wordwatcher@earthlink.net.

DAVIDSON, NORMA LEWIS, concert violinist, composer, music educator, psychologist; b. Provo, Utah, Oct. 12, 1929; d. Arthur and Mary (Mortimer) Lewis; m. William James Davidson, Dec. 29, 1949; children: Kevin James, Nathanael Arthur. Artist's diploma, Juilliard Sch., N.Y.C., 1950; BS, North Tex. State U., 1962, MS, 1965; MusM, So. Meth. U., 1970. Prof. violin and chamber music Mannes Coll. Music, N.Y.C., 1950-54; prof., artist-in-residence Tex. Womans U., Denton, 1961—. Vis. prof. North Tex. State U., Denton, 1968-69; violinist Dallas Symphony Orch., 1955—; violinist, soloist Utah Symphony, Salt Lake City, Ft. Worth Symphony Orch., New Symphony Orch. of N.Y., Richardson Symphony, Wichita Falls Symphony, San Antonio Symphony; assoc. concertmaster Graz (Austria) Symphony, 1990—; soloist movie documentary, Eng., 1987. Numerous concert tours in U.S., Europe, Asia, Mex., Can., 1945—; composer numerous works for voice, violin, viola, string quartet, and chamber music; contbr. articles to profl. jours. Rsch. grantee Tex. Womans U., 1979; recipient cert. of merit Federated Music Clubs, 1978, 1st prize for composition, 1984, 1st prize for composition Tex. Composers Guild, 1980, Emmy award (for PBS series Wishbone), 1996. Mem. APA (assoc.), Am. String Tchrs. Assn., Phi Kappa Phi (internat. rep. for arts, pres. Tex. Womans U. chpt. 1991-93), Sigma Alpha Iota (arts assoc. 1980—), Phi Kappa Phi (nat. rep. for arts 1989-91, editorial bd. Nat. Forum 1994—). Avocations: reading, outdoor activities. Office: Tex Womans U Dept Performing Arts Denton TX 76204

DAVIDSON, RHONDA ELIZABETH, preschool educator; b. Phila., Nov. 26, 1954; d. Charles and Thelma Viola (Porter) Ash.; m. John Carl Davidson, June 10, 1975 (div. Aug. 1977). AAS, C.C. Phila., 1984; student, Chestnut Hill Coll., 1990—. Market rsch. intern WUSL Radio, Phila., 1983-84; telemarketing rschr. Sears Roebuck Inc., Phila., 1984-86; presch. tchr. Sch. Dist. of Phila., 1986—. Bus. cons. M & G Enterprises, Phila., 1984—. Active Girl Scouts U.S., Phila., 1994; majority inspector Dem. Party, Phila., 1993. Mem. ASCD, Assn. for Childhood Edn. Internat. Lutheran. Home: 5934 N Franklin Philadelphia PA 19120-1313 Office: M & G Enterprises 4534 N Smedley St Philadelphia PA 19140-1145

DAVIDSON, ROGER H(ARRY), political scientist, educator; b. Washington, July 31, 1936; s. Ross Wallace and Mildred (Younger) D.; m. Nancy Elizabeth Dixon, Sept. 29, 1961; children: Douglas Ross, Christopher Reed. AB magna cum laude, U. Colo., 1958; PhD, Columbia U., 1963. Asst. prof. govt. Dartmouth Coll., Hanover, N.H., 1962-68; assoc. prof. polit. sci. U. Calif., Santa Barbara, 1968-71, prof., 1971-83, assoc. dean letters and sci., 1978-80, vis. prof., 1994, 1999—; sr. specialist Congl. Rsch. Svc., Washington, 1980-88; prof. govt., politics U. Md., College Pk., 1981-99. Profl. staff mem. U.S. Ho. of Reps., Washington, 1973—74; rsch. dir. U.S. Senate, Washington, 1976—77; cons. White House, 1970—71, U.S. Com. on Violence, Washington, 1968—69, Ctr. for Civic Edn., 2002—; Leon Sachs vis. scholar Johns Hopkins U., Balt., 1997; John Marshall Disting. Fulbright prof. Debrecen U., Hungary, 2002. Author: The Role of the Congressman, 1969; co-author: A More Perfect Union, 4th edit., 1989, Congress and Its Members, 9th edit., 2003; editor: The Postreform Congress, 1992; co-editor: Remaking Congress, 1995, Masters of the House, 1998; contbr. articles to profl. jours. Co-chmn. Upper Valley Human Rights Coun., Hanover, N.H., 1966-68; chmn. Goleta Valley Citizens Planning Group, Santa Barbara, 1974-76; rsch. com. of legis. specialists Internat. Polit. Sci. Assn.; adv. commn. on records of Congress Nat. Archives and Records Adminstrn., 1995-99; bd. dirs. Governance Inst., Archtl. Found. of Santa Barbara, 2003—. Woodrow Wilson Nat. Found. fellow, 1958, Gilder fellow Columbia U., 1960, Faculty fellow Dartmouth Coll., 1965-66. Fellow Nat. Acad. Pub. Adminstrn.; mem. Nat.'Capital Area Polit. Sci. Assn. (pres. 1985-86), Legis. Studies Group (charter, nat. chmn. 1980-81), Am. Polit. Sci. Assn. (joint com. Project 87-Am. Hist. Assn./Am. Polit. Sci. Assn., chmn. congl. fellowship com. 1990, 93, endowed programs com. 1994-95, chmn. 1995-96, co-chmn. exec. com. Centennial Campaign 1997-2003), Western Polit. Sci. Assn. (bd. editors 1977-78). Baptist. Avocations: music, history. Home: Villa L 400 E Pedregosa St Santa Barbara CA 93103-1970 Office: Dept Polit Sci U Calif Santa Barbara CA 93106

DAVIDSON-SHEPARD, GAY, secondary education educator; b. Long Beach, Calif., Dec. 15, 1951; d. Leyton Paul and Ruth Leona (Gritzmaker) Davidson; m. Daniel A. Shepard, June 24, 1983. BA, U. Calif., Irvine, 1972; MA, Columbia Pacific U., 1986. Cert. elem. and secondary edn. tchr. Tchr. mid. sch. Ocean View Sch. Dist., Huntington Beach, Calif., 1973—; team mem. Calif. learning assessment system State Dept. of Edn., Sacramento, 1987—; chief reader Orange County pentathlon and decathlon Orange County Dept. Edn., Costa Mesa, Calif., 1980—; sr. reader new standards State Dept. Edn., Sacramento, 1995—. Lang. arts cons. various sch. dists., Calif., 1976—; chief reader Calif. Learning Assessment System, Sacramento, 1993—; sr. reader New Stds., 1995—; chief reader, asst. chief reader, table leader Golden State Exams, 1997—; item writer Calif. H.S. Exit Exam, 2000—. Author/cons.: Teacher's Guide for Direct Assessment Writing, 1990; test writer Acad. Pentathlon Test, 1984—, Dist. Lang. Art Proficiency Test, 1980—. Mem. NEA, AAUS, AAUW, Nat. Assn. Tchrs. of English, Calif. Reading Assn., Mensa, Calif. Tchrs. Assn., Ocean View Tchrs. Assn. Democrat. Avocations: reading, camping, travel, cooking. Home: 6782 Rook Dr Huntington Beach CA 92647-5641 Office: Mesa View Sch 17601 Avilla Ln Huntington Beach CA 92647-6612

DAVIES, JO ANN, retired secondary school educator; b. Holland, Mich., Sept. 12, 1948; d. Fred and Helen (Doevieno) Gauthier; m. Donald R. Davies, Oct. 18, 1969; 1 child, Brian. BS, SUNY, Albany, 1970, MS, 1975. Lic. sch. dist. adminstr., coord. diversified coop. edn. Dir. career & tech. edn. Bethlehem Cen. Sch. Dist., Delmar, NY, 1979—2003; evaluator prior coll.-level learning Empire State Coll., Albany, NY, 1991—2003; supr. student tchrs. and in-field placements Coll. of St. Rose, Albany, NY, 2003—. Vis. com. chmn. Mid States Assn. Colls. and Schs., Commn. on Secondary Schs., Phila., 1989—; mem. N.Y. state adv. com. Mid. States Assn. Colls. and Secondary Schs., Phila., 1993-98. Weekly columnist Area Auto Racing News, 1986—. Treas. Village Stage, Inc., Delmar, N.Y., 1984-86. Mem. NEA (chmn. 1983-88), Internat. Tech. Edn. Assn., Nat. Bus. Edn. Assn., Am. Vocat. Assn., Suprs. Assn. (v.p., treas. Capital dist. region 1987-92, pres. 1999—), Capital Region Career and Tech. Edn. Supr.'s Assn., N.Y. State Tech. Edn. Assn., N.Y. State Family and Consumer Sci. Edn. Assn., Bethlehem C. of C. Methodist. Avocations: reading, travel, automobile racing. Home: 31 Morningstar Ln Feura Bush NY 12067-9799 Office: Bethlehem Cen Sch Dist 700 Delaware Ave Delmar NY 12054-2436 E-mail: davijhs@bcsd.neric.org.

DAVIES, KELVIN JAMES ANTHONY, research scientist, educator, consultant, author; b. London, Oct. 15, 1951; came to U.S., 1975, dual citizenship, 1993; s. Alfred B. and Phyllis (Garcia) D.; m. Joanna Davies, Sept. 14, 1980; children: Sebastian, Alexander. BEd, Liverpool/Lancaster (Eng.) U., 1974; BS summa cum laude, MS, U. Wis., 1976, 77; CPhil, U. Calif., Berkeley, 1979, PhD, 1981; DSc (hon.), U. Moscow, Russia, 1993; MD (hon.), U. Gdansk, Poland, 1995; D of Univ. (hon.), U. Buenos Aires, 1998. Instr. Beal Sch. for Boys, London, 1974-75; rsch. asst. U. Wis., Madison, 1975-77, U. Calif., Berkeley, 1977-80, lectr. physiology dept. physiology and anatomy, 1980-81; rsch. assoc. dept. biochemistry, inst. toxicology U. So. Calif., L.A., 1981-82, asst. prof. biochemistry, toxicology, 1983-86, assoc. prof. biochemistry, toxicology, 1986-90, prof. biochemistry, toxicology, 1990; instr., sr. rsch. assoc. dept. physiology and biophysics med. sch. Harvard U., 1982-83; prof. biochemistry and molecular biology Albany (N.Y.) Med. Coll., 1991-96, John A. Muntz Univ. prof., 1991-96, chmn. dept. biochemistry and molecular biology, 1991-96, prof. molecular medicine dept. medicine, 1993-96; prof., assoc. dean rsch. Andrus Gerontology Ctr. U. So. Calif., L.A., 1996—; James E. Birren chair gerontology, dir. Andrus Rsch. Inst., 1996—2002. Dir. Nat. Parkinson's Found. Lab., 1996—; founder, dir. STAR program U. So. Calif./L.A. County Schs. Dist., 1984-90; dir. grad. studies inst. toxicology U. So. Calif., 1985-90, mem. cell biology program, 1986-91, fellow inst. molecular medicine, 1988-91; hon. dist. prof. Russian State Med. U., Moscow, 1989; coun. mem. Gordon Rsch. Confs. Frontiers of Sci., 1995-96. Author: Oxidative Damage and Repair: Chemical, Biological and Medical Aspects, 1992, Oxygen '93, 1994, The Oxygen Paradox, 1995; editor in chief: (jour.) Free Radical Biology and Medicine, 1981—, Biochemistry and Molecular Biology Internat., 1999; editor-in-chief IUBMB-LIFE, 1999-2000, mem. editl. bd., 2000—; assoc. editor: Mitochondrion; mem. editl. bd. Advances in Free Radical Biology and Medicine, 1985-87, The Biochem. Jour., 1989-95, Amino Acids, 1991—, Methods in Enzymology, 1991—, Molecular Aspects of Medicine, 1993—; assoc. editor: Jours. Gerontology, 1996—, Cell and Molecular Life Scis., 1999-; contbr. over 200 articles to profl. jours. and books. Active Arts Coun., Pasadena, Calif., 1988-90; pres. Calif. Philharm. Orch. Found., 1996—; bd. govs. The Albany Acad. for Boys, 1994-96. Recipient Chancellors award for Rsch., U. Calif., Berkeley, 1981, Young Investigator award NIH, 1984, 50th Anniversary medal U. Gdansk, 1995; rsch., program project grantee NIH, 1983—; fellow Hoffman-La Roche, 1981, Arco, 1981, Am. Heart Assn., 1982, NIH, 1983. Fellow AAAS, CNR (Italy), Russian Acad. Scis., Gerontol. Soc. Am.; mem. Am. Coll. Sports Medicine, Am. Physiol. Soc. (Harwood S. Belding award 1982), Am. Soc. for Biochemistry and Molecular Biology, Internat. Union Biochemistry and Molecular Biology (coun. mem. 1995—), Biochem. Soc., Biophys. Soc., European Soc. Free Radical Rsch., Internat. Soc. Free Radical Rsch. (coun. 1988—, pres. 2001—), Internat. Cell Rsch. Orgn., N.Y. Acad. Sci., Rsch. Coun. New Zealand, The Oxygen Soc. (fellow, sec. gen. 1987-90, pres. 1992-95, Disting. Achievement award 1997), Osyben Club of Calif. (pres. 2002-), Sigma Xi, Phi Beta Kappa, Kappa Delta Pi. Avocations: opera, symphony, cricket, soccer, food and wines. Office: Univ So Calif Andrus Gerontology Ctr 3715 Mcclintock Ave Rm 306 Los Angeles CA 90089-0001 E-mail: kelvin@usc.edu.

DAVILA, ELISA, language educator, literature educator; b. Libano, Tolima, Colombia, May 29, 1944; arrived in U.S., 1974; d. Rafael Antonio Davilla and Amalia Parra; m. Bruce Roger Smith, Oct. 17, 1973 (div. 1981). BA, U. Pedagogica Nat., Bogota, Colombia, 1966; MA, U. Pacific, 1972; PhD, U. Calif., Santa Barbara, 1983. Asst. prof. U. Valle, Cali, Colombia, 1968-73; rschr. Inst. Colombiano de Pedagogia, Bogota, Colombia, 1973-73; assoc. U. Calif., Santa Barbara, 1974-78, 78-80; instr. W. Tex. State U., Canyon, Tex., 1978-80, Def. Lang. Inst., Calif., 1981-82; prof. SUNY, New Paltz, 1999—, chair fgn. langs., 1990-94, 96—, dir. Latin Am. studies, 1991—. Vis. lectr. U. Calif., Santa Cruz, 1982—; reader, evaluator N.J. Dept. Higher Edn., Princeton, 1987—89; reader Ednl. Testing Svc., Princeton, 1987—89; acad. dir. Spanish Immersion Inst. Bd. Edn. and Office Mental Health, N.Y.C., Albany, 1987—90; project dir. title VI grant undergraduate internat. and fgn. lang. program U.S. Dept. Edn., 2000—. Recipient Disting. Tchr. award, Alumni Assn., 1996; scholar Heloise Brainer, 1964, LASPAU, 1968. Mem.: MLA, Latin-Am. Studies Assn., Am. Assn. Tcrh. Spanish and Portuguese. Avocations: creative writing, poetry. Home: PO Box 423 Hurley NY 12443-0423 Fax: (845) 257-3512. E-mail: davilae@newpaltz.edu.

DAVILA, REBECCA TOBER, health and physical education educator; b. Dallas, Apr. 10, 1942; d. Antonio M. and Aurora Tober (Benavides) D. BS, Tex. Woman's U., 1964, MA, 1969; Cert. in Mgmt. and Adminstrn., North Tex. State U., 1983. Cert. health edn. specialist. Camp counselor Heart O the Hills, Kerrville, Tex., 1962-67; tchr. San Antonio Ind. Sch. Dist., 1964-67; grad. asst. Tex. Woman's U., Denton, 1967-68; tchr., dept. chair Lewisville (Tex.) Ind. Sch. Dist., 1968—. Vol. Am. Heart Assn., Lewisville, 1980s, 90s, Kidney Found., Lewisville, 1980s, Christian Comty. Action, Lewisville, 1980s, 90s. Mem. Tex. Assn. for Health, Phys. Edn., Recreation and Dance (v.p. health divsn. 1994, workshop dir. region XI 1990, 91, 92, membership chair 1992-93, pres. 1999, Health Tchr. of Yr. 1991), Tex. State Tchrs. Assn. (pres. local chpt. 1984-85), Delta Kappa Gamma (pres. local chpt. 1988-90, Achievement award 1989). Democrat. Roman Catholic. Avocations: gardening, reading, fishing, golf, refinishing antique furnisher.

DAVILLA, DONNA ELAINE, school system administrator; b. Galesburg, Ill., Aug. 14, 1948; d. Robert Harold and Melba Anne (Richmond) D. BFA, Drake U., 1970, MFA, 1972. Cert. art administr., Iowa. Grad. asst. Drake U., Des Moines, 1971, substitute tchr., 1971-78; secondary art tchr. Des Moines Pub. Schs., 1972-93, curriculum specialist for arts, 1988-93, art facilitator, 1992-99, art cons., 1999—, dir. gifted and talented program, K-12, 2002—. Facilitator Heartland AEA II, Johnston, Iowa, 1991-93, 2000; bd. dirs. Iowa Designer Crafts, Des Moines, 1978-79; chair art adv. coun. Des Moines Pub. Schs., 1990—, chair textbook selection, 1991—; Middle East Arts Edn. del. People to People, 1994; mem. art adv. bd. Grand View Coll., 1996—. Asst. to campaign mgr. Dole for Pres., Des Moines, 1990; active Greater Des Moines Leadership Inst., 1994, mem.'s coun. Des Moines Art Ctr., 1989—, Print Club, Des Moines Art Ctr. Bd., 1997-99, 2000-01; active Mayor's Task Force for Beautification Des Moines, 2000-01, Alliance Francaise Bd., 2002—. Recipient Take Pride in Des Moines Tchr. award Des Moines City Coun., 1993; Connie Belin fellow U. Iowa, 1985, 92, Fallingwater Conservancy fellow, 1992; named Iowa Disting. Tchr., U. Iowa, 1993, Outstanding Art Supr. of Iowa, Art Educators of Iowa, 1995; recipient Metro Arts Contbn. to Cultural Cmty. award, 1998. Mem. Nat. Art Edn. Assn (presenter 1988, 90-93, 2003), Art Educators Iowa (conf. com. 1994, 95), Nat. Assn. Gifted Children (conf. presenter 2002), Alliance for Arts (co-chair 1992—). Avocations: art collecting, watercolor painting, photography, travel. Home: 1441 Beaver Ave Des Moines IA 50311-2640 Office: Des Moines Pub Schs 1800 Grand Ave Des Moines IA 50309-3382 E-mail: donna.davilla@dmsp.k12.ia.us.

DAVIS, ADA ROMAINE, nursing educator; b. Cumberland, Md., June 7, 1929; d. Louis Berge and Ethel Lucy (Johnson) Romaine; m. John Francis Davis, Aug. 1, 1953; children: Kevin Murray, Karen Evans-Romaine, William Romaine. Diploma in nursing, Kings County Hosp., Bklyn., 1949; BSN, U. Md., Balt., 1973, MS, 1974; PhD, U. Md., College Park, 1979, postdoctoral student, 1985-89. Cert. editor in life scis. Asst. prof. grad. program U. Md., Balt., 1974-79; chmn. dept. nursing Coll. of Notre Dame, Balt., 1979-82; assoc. dean grad. program Georgetown U. Sch. Nursing, Washington, 1982-87; nurse cons. Health Resources and Svcs. Adminstrn., Rockville, Md., 1987-93, HHS, USPHS, Bur. Health Profls., Rockville, 1987-93; assoc. prof. and dir. undergrad. program Johns Hopkins U. Sch. of Nursing, Balt., 1993-98, prof. emeritus, 1998—. Reviewer Choice, ALA; evaluator methodology and findings for rsch. studies; hist./med. biographer. Author: John Gibbon and His Heart-Lung Machine, 1992, Advanced Practice Nurses: Education, Roles and Trends, 1997; editor: Ency. of Home Care for the Elderly, 1995; contbr. articles to nursing jours.; assoc. editor Hopkins InteliHealth, Johns Hopkins Family Health Guide, 1999, Johns Hopkins Insider, 1998; sr. editor Am. Nurses Credentialing Ctr., Washington, 2001—. Recipient excellent performance award HRSA; rsch. grantee U. Md. Grad. Sch. Mem. AAAS, ANA (cert. adult nurse practitioner), Soc. for Neoplatonic Studies, Nat. Orgn. Nurse Practitioner Faculties, Am. Acad. Nurse Practitioners, Am. Pub. Health Assn., Gerontol. Soc. Am., Nat. Trust for Hist. Preservation, Am. Geriat. Soc., Md. History of Medicine Soc., Soc. for the Social History of Medicine (Oxford U.), N.Y. Acad. Scis., Coun. Sci. Editors, Sigma Theta Tau. E-mail: adarom@earthlink.net.

DAVIS, ANN CALDWELL, history educator; b. Alliance, Ohio, June 3, 1925; d. Arthur Trescott and Jane Caldwell D. BA, Western Reserve U., 1947; MA, Columbia U., 1955; PhD, Columbia Pacific U., 1987. Cert. tchr., Ill., Ohio. Pres. The Clio Found. Inc., Gulfport, Fla., 1955—; tchr. Supr. Child Enterprise, Evanston, Ill., 1956-60; human rels. coun. U. Chgo., 1957-58, asst., 1961; tchr., dept. chair Evanston Pub. Schs., 1961-85; project English Northwestern U., Evanston, 1963-64. Cons. Dist. #65 Sch., Evanston, 1985-90. Presenter, author: (speech) Do-it-Yourself Help For The Top 10%, 1964, The Non-Graded School, 1976, Social Studies Reading & Reference Skills, 1979; author: (video) U.S. & Ill. Constn., 1986. Vol. Meals ON Wheels, Treasure Island, Fla., 1990-94, Pinellas County Schs., Fla., 1991, steering com. St. Petersburg, Fla., 1995, health care chair Older Women's League, St. Petersburg, 1995. Mem. Am. Assn. of U. Women, Orgn. of Am. Historians, Ill. & Nat. Edn. Assn. Office: The Clio Found Inc PO Box 5110 Gulfport FL 33737-5110 E-mail: cliofdn@aol.com.

DAVIS, ANN KATHERINE, special education educator; b. Sioux City, Iowa, Jan. 26, 1949; d. Aage Ernest and A. Jeanne (Besser) Neldeberg; m. Ronald Gene Davis, Aug. 30, 1970; children: Krystine, Julie. BA in Elem. and Spl. Edn., Augustana Coll., Sioux Falls, S.D., 1986; MEd, U. Sioux Falls, 2002. Parent advisor for new spl. edn. programs State of Iowa, Sioux City, 1977-80; presch. tchr. Sugar 'N Spice, Omaha, 1980-81; tchr. elem. spl. edn./jr. high English Lennox (S.D.) Sch. Dist., 1986-88; tchr. high sch. spl. edn. Tri-Valley High Sch., Lyons, SD, 1988—99, Lincoln H.S., Sioux Falls, SD, 1999—. Recert. mem. for spl. edn. Tri-Valley High Sch., Lyons, 1989-90. Treas. PTA, Jefferson Elem., Sioux Falls, 1985; pres. Washington High Band Boosters, Sioux Falls, 1989-91. Mem. S.D. Edn. Assn., Sioux Falls Edn. Assn. Lutheran. Home: 1800 Remington Cir Sioux Falls SD 57106-5309 Office: LIncoln HS 2900 S Cliff Ave Sioux Falls SD 57105

DAVIS, ANNA JANE RIPLEY, elementary education educator; b. Uhrichsville, Ohio, Sept. 7, 1931; d. Emmet Frank and Lillie Hazel (Kinsey) Ripley; m. H. Joe Davis, Mar. 16, 1951; children: Alan Joe, Kendal Jay. Assoc., Asbury Coll., 1953; BS with honors, Kent State U., 1962, MEd with honors, 1978, postgrad., 1980—94; student, Richmond Coll., London U., St. Andrews U., Dundee U., Cambridge U., U. Paris, U. Rome, Ohio U. Cert. elem. tchr., Ohio. Tchr. Kenston Schs., Chagrin Falls, Ohio, 1953-55, 58-62, Firestone Rubber Plantation, Harbel, Liberia, West Africa, 1962-64, Newbury (Ohio) Schs., 1964-65, Orange Schs., Pepper Pike, Ohio, 1965-99. Chaperone, counselor Am. Inst. for Fgn. Study, British Isles and Europe, summers 1968-81. Author children's books. Active Kenston PTA, Chagrin Falls and Pepper Pike PTA, Am. Field Svc., Chagrin Falls; bd. dirs. Friends Geauga County Pub. Libr.; book project vol. traveling libr. Geauga County Pub. Libr. for Amish Schs., traveling libr., 1994—; vol. ARC, 1955—; elem. sch. tutor, 1998—; vol. Food Pantry and Clothing for Needy, Kiwanis; mem. edn. com., libr., home care, Sunday sch. com., Sunday Sch., membership com. Prayer Chain, Garfield Meml. United Meth. Ch. Mem. NEA (life), ASCD, Ohio Edn. Assn., N.E. Ohio Tchrs. Assn., Orange Tchrs. Assn. Avocations: family, travel, cycling, hiking, reading, writing.

DAVIS, ANTHONY MAURICE, elementary education educator; b. Lakeland, Fla., Dec. 24, 1956; s. Fred and Vivian (Lawson) D. MusB, U. Miami, 1979. Cert. music tchr., Fla. Music tchr. Shenandoah Elem. Sch., Miami, Fla., mem. adv. bd., 1990—. Mem. field experience adv. com. U. Miami, Coral Gables, Fla., 1991—; chmn. Sch. Based Mgmt., Miami, 1990-91. Mem. United Tchrs. of Dade (rep. shared decision making 1990—, designated bldg. steward). Democrat. Avocations: singing, swimming, dancing, listening, opera. Office: Shenandoah Elem Sch 1023 NW 21st Ave Miami FL 33125-2733

DAVIS, BARBARA SNELL, college educator; b. Painesville, Ohio, Feb. 21, 1929; d. Roy Addison and Mabelle Irene (Denning) Snell; children: Beth Ann Davis Schnorf, James L., Polly Denning Davis Spaeth. BS, Kent State U., 1951; MA, Lake Erie Coll., 1981; postgrad., Cleve. State U., 1982-83. Cert. reading speicalist, elem. prin., Ohio. Dir. publicity Lake Erie Coll., Painesville, 1954-59; tchr. Mentor (Ohio) Exempted Village Sch. Dist., 1972-86, prin., 1986-97; prof. Lake Erie Coll., 1997—. Contbr. articles to profl. jours. Former trustee Mentor United Meth. Ch. Mem. Delta Kappa Gamma (pres. 1982-84), Phi Delta Kappa (pres. 1992-93), Theta Sigma Phi (charter). Home: 7293 Beechwood Dr Mentor OH 44060-6305 Office: 326 College Hall Lake Erie Coll Painesville OH 44077 E-mail: beachbumbarb@aol.com.

DAVIS, BEATRICE ANNA KIMSEY, educator, civic worker; b. Oklahoma City, June 23, 1917; d. Carl Cleveland and Beatrice Mary (Rudersdorf) Kimsey; m. Bruce A. Davis, Jan. 22, 1942; children: Belinda Anne Davis Pillow, Beatrice Annette Davis Orynawka, Beverly Anna Davis Steckler. Grad., Ward-Belmont Jr. Coll., 1938; BA, Vanderbilt U., 1940; MEd, Lamar U., 1973. Pers. interviewer Ft. Sam Houston, San Antonio, 1942; advisor Jr. Achievement, 1974-80; asst. instr. drama Watkins Night Sch., Nashville, 1939-40; substitute tchr. Port Arthur (Tex.) Ind. Sch. Dist., 1950-64; high sch. English tchr. South Park Ind. Sch. Dist., 1964—, head English dept., 1982-85. Tchr. Nederland (Tex.) Ind. Sch. Dist., 1948-50. Co-author: Curriculum Guides for Reading, 1973, 2d edit., 1981, Curriculum Guides for English, 1980; contbr. articles to mags. Adv. bd. Profl. Resource Group, Houston, 1990; pres. Port Arthur Family Svcs. Am., 1979-81, Women's Orgn. Presbyn. Ch. of Covenant, 1989; v.p. Jefferson H.S. PTA; bd. dirs. Hughen Sch. for Crippled Children, Gates Meml. Libr., Tyrell Elem. Sch. PTA, Port Arthur, Parliamentarians of Port Arthur, Story league of Port Arthur, Jr. League, Jefferson County Hist. Commn., 1990-03; docent SE Tex. Mus. Art, Beaumont, 1987-90, McFaddin-Ward House Mus., Beaumont, 1990—, pres. vol. orgn., 1990; mem. Cmty. Concert Assn. Port Arthur; pres. Vol. Svc. Coun.; mem. Women's Commn. S.E. Tex., 1985-00; ensign Head Shore Establishment divsn., Women-Vols. Svc. USNR, Washington, 1943-46; bd. dirs. S.E. Tex. Hist. Commn., 1986—, Tyrell Restoration Geneal. Soc., Beaumont, 1987-98, 2000-02, Tyrell Libr. Hist. and Geneal. Bd., hist. and genealogical bd., 1988—; sec. chpt. CP of P.E.O. Sisterhood, Port Arthur, 1987—, pres., 1993-94, also chaplin; mem. Beaumont Opera Buffs, v.p., 1998-99; trustee, membership com., tchr. Presbyn. Ch. of Covenant, past pres. Women's Orgn.; vol., book reviewer and reader for civic, social orgns.; chair Tex. sub-courthouse Hist. Preservation Port Arthur, 1989—. With USNR, 1942-43, ensign, 1943-46. Recipient awards for outstanding civic svc., ednl. stipends and grants; named Tchr. of Yr., South Park H.S., Tex. Agrl. and Mech. U., 1981-82. Mem. NEA, AAUW (past pres. Port Arthur chpt.), All Tchrs. Assn. Beaumont, Nat. Coun. Reading Tchrs., S.E. Tex. Coun. Reading Tchrs., Tex. Assn. for Specialists in Group Work, Sabine-Neches Pers. and Guidance Assn., Federated Women's Club (past pres. bd. Port Arthur chpt.), Rosehill Bd. (past pres.), Panhellenic Assn. (past pres. Port Arthur chpt.), Women's Orgn. Symphony Club (past pres.), Choral Club (past pres.), Thalian Drama Group (past v.p.), Heritage Soc., Hist. Soc., Knights of Neches Aux., Naval Res. Assn., DAR (chair Nat. Def. 1985-95, regent Col. George Moffett chpt. 1996-98, regent Beaumont chpt. 1996-98, scholar chair 1998-2000), United Daus. Confederacy (chair nat. def., 2d v.p.), Houston English Speaking Union, Houston Wellington Soc., Port Arthur Hist. Assn. (life), Port Arthur Club, Beaumont Own a Book Club (sec. 1999-2000), Beaumont Reading Club, Port Arthur Antique Study Club (pres.), Key Club, Reading Club, Port Arthur Country Club Women's Aux. (past pres.), Civic Opera Buffs (v.p. 1998-99), Lamar Univ. Alumni Assn. (life), Port Arthur Hibiscus Club (pres. 1999-2000), DAR (Captain William Sanders Chpt.), Sigma Kappa Alumni, Phi Lambda Phi, Phi Delta Kappa. Republican. Home: 2816 35th St Port Arthur TX 77640-2650

DAVIS, BILLIE JOHNSTON, school counselor; b. Charleston, W.Va., Sept. 24, 1933; d. William Andrew Jr. and Garnet Macil (Johnston) D. BS, Morris Harvey Coll., 1954; MA, W.Va. U., 1959. Nat. bd. cert. counselor; W.Va. lic. profl. counselor. Tchr. math. Kanawha County Schs., Charleston, 1954-59, counselor, 1959-98. Mem. pub. edn. study commn. W.Va. Legislature, 1980. Mem. W.Va. Commn. on Juvenile Law, 1982-97; bd. dirs. W.Va. Com. for Prevention Child Abuse, W.Va. Sch. Health Adv. Com.; apptd. W.Va. rep. at Tchr.'s Inaugural Experience for Inauguration of Pres. George Bush by Gov. of W.Va., 1989; mem. subcom. W.Va. Health Care Task Force, 1992; trustee W.Va. Youth Advocate Program, 1993-95, Nat. Youth Adv. Program, 1994-95; mem. oversite com. W.Va. Juvenile Predisposition Plan, 1993-97. Mem. adv. bd. W.Va. Divsn. Juvenile Svcs., 2001—. Recipient Anne Maynard award W.Va. Sch. Counselor Assn., 1986; named Am. mid./jr. high Sch. Counselor of Yr. Am. Sch. Counselors Assn., 1987, Citizen of Yr., Dunbar Lions Club, 1987. Mem. Am. Assn. Counseling and Devel. (Spl. Recognition award 1991), W.Va. Assn. Counseling and Devel. (pres. 1964-66, legis. chmn. 1974-98, spl. award legis. svcs. 1981), W.Va. Edn. Assn. (past legis. chmn.), Kanawha County Sch. Counselors Assn. (pres., legis. chmn. 1974-98), W.Va. Sch. Counselors Assn. (chmn. gov. rels., parliamentarian), Alpha Delta Kappa (past chpt. pres.), Phi Delta Kappa. Democrat. Baptist. Home: 12 Warren Pl Charleston WV 25302-3613 E-mail: bjdavis222@aol.com.

DAVIS, BRUCE GORDON, retired principal; b. Fulton, Tex., Sept. 2, 1922; s. Arthur Lee and Clara Katherine (Rouquette) D.; B.A., U. Tex., 1950; M.Ed., U. Houston, 1965; m. Mary Virginia Jackson, Aug. 31, 1946; children— Ford Rouquette, Barton Bolling, Katherine Norvell Davis McLendon. Tchr., Edison Jr. High Sch., Houston, 1951; tchr. Sidney Lanier Jr. High Sch., Houston, 1957-60, asst. prin., 1966-74, prin., 1974-83; tchr. Johnston Jr. High Sch., Houston, 1960-66; prin. Sidney Lanier Vanguard Sch., Houston, 1974-82; ret., 1983. Served with USMC, 1942-45; with U.S. Army, 1951-57. Mem. Nat. Assn. Secondary Sch. Prins., Tex. Assn. Secondary Sch. Prins., Houston Profl. Adminstrs., U.S. Army Officers Res. Assn., Tex. Retired Tchrs. Assn., Am. Legion. Republican. Presbyterian. Club: Masons. Home: 6614 Sharpview Dr Houston TX 77074-6338

DAVIS, CALVIN DE ARMOND, historian, educator; b. Westport, Ind., Dec. 3, 1927; s. Harry Russell and Abbie Jane (Moncrief) Davis. AB, Franklin Coll., Ind., 1949; MA, Ind. U., 1956, PhD, 1961. Tchr. Wilson Sch., Columbus, Ind., 1949-51, 53-54; asst. prof. history Ind. Central Coll., Indpls., 1956-57; teaching assoc. Ind. U., 1958-59; asst. prof. history U. Denver, 1959-62, Duke U., Durham, N.C., 1962-64, assoc. prof., 1964-76, prof., 1976-96, prof. emeritus, 1996—. Cons. NEH, 1974. Contbr. articles to profl. jours.; author: (essays) Ency. U.S. Fgn. Rels., 1997, Oxford Companion to American Military History, 1999, Scribner's Ency. Am. Fgn. Policy, 2002, The United States and the First Hague Peace Conference, 1962 (Albert J. Beveridge award, 1961), The United States and the Second Hague Peace Conference, 1976. With U.S. Army, 1951—53. Mem.: Soc. Historians Am. Fgn. Rels., Orgn. Am. Historians, Am. Hist. Assn. Home: 511 E Nightingale Dr Greensburg IN 47240-8589 Office: Duke U Dept History Durham NC 27708

DAVIS, CAROL ANDERSON, school counselor; b. Wilburton, Okla., Feb. 15, 1947; d. Winfrey and Billy J. (Haynes) Turner; ;m. Paul E. Davis, Sept. 4, 1993; 1 child, Tara Lee Edwards. AA, Northeastern State U., 1966, BA in Edn., 1968, MA in English, 1973, MA in Reading, 1981, MA in Sch. Counseling, 1977. English and speech tchr. Claremore (Okla.) H.S., 1968-70, honors English tchr., 1981-90; lang. arts tchr., libr., counselor Justus Sch., Claremore, 1970-81; counselor Ctrl. Upper Elem. Sch., Claremore, 1990—. Mem. adv. com. on speech edn., mem. state com. for reading excellence Okla. State Reading Coun., Oklahoma City, 1980-81. Mem. NEA, Okla. Edn. Assn. (Rogers County Tchr. of Yr. 1978), Nat. Coun. Tchrs. English, Delta Kappa Gamma. Democrat. Baptist. Avocations: reading, dancing, music, decorating, movies. Home: 2966 W Berwick St Claremore OK 74017-4852 Office: Ctrl Upper Elem Sch 101 W 11th St Claremore OK 74017-5821

DAVIS, CHRISTINE DALE, physical education educator; b. Brookville, Pa., Oct. 4, 1948; d. Harry Dale and Leona Cathrine (Knapp) D. BS, SUNY, Brockport, 1970; MS, SUNY, Buffalo, 1987. Cert. tchr., N.Y. Recreation dir. Town of Hamlin (N.Y.), 1968-70; phys. edn. tchr. Frontier Cen. Sch. Dist., Hamburg, N.Y., 1970—. Soccer, basketball and volleyball coach Amsdell Heights Jr. High Sch., Hamburg, 1970-80; intramural coach Cloverbank Elem. Sch., Hamburg, 1981—; softball coach Town of Hamburg, 1970-75; U.S. fitness del. to People's Republic of China, 1991. Author poetry in nat. Poetry Press Anthology, 1968; inventor phys. edn. equip.; contbr. articles to profl. jours. Com. mem. Frontier Cen. Bond Issue Referendum, Hamburg, 1990. Mem. AAHPERD, Am. Fedn. Tchrs., Frontier Cen. Tchrs. Assn. (v.p. 1986-92, bldg. rep. 1982—), N.Y. State United Tchrs., Women's Sports Found., Soc. for Prevention of Cruelty to Animals, Smithsonian Instn. Avocations: gardening, antiques, dogs, golf. Home: 270 N Main St Angola NY 14006-1032 Office: Cloverbank Elem Sch Cloverbank Rd Hamburg NY 14075

DAVIS, CLAUDE-LEONARD, lawyer, university official; s. James and Mary Davis; m. Margaret Earle Crowley, 1965; 1 child, Margaret Michelle. BA in Journalism, U. Ga., 1966, JD, 1974. Bar: Ga. 1974. Broadcaster Sta. WKLE Radio, Washington, Ga., 1958-62; realtor Assocs. Realty, Athens, Ga., 1963-66; bus. cons. Palm Beach, Fla., 1970-71; asst. to dir. Ga. Coop. Extension Svc., Athens, 1974-81; atty. Office of Pres. U. Ga., Athens, 1981—; mem. faculty, regent Ga. Athletics Inst., 1988-98; broadcaster Leonard's Losers.com, Athens, Ga., 2000—. Cons. numerous agrl. chem. industry groups nationwide, 1977—, Congl. Office Tech. Assessment, Washington, 1978-79, USDA, Washington, 1979-80; del. Kellogg Nat. Leadership Conf., Pullman, Wash., 1980. Editor and contbr. Ga. Jour. of Internat. and Comparative Law, 1972-74; contbr. articles on agr. and fin. planning to profl. jours.; author and editor: DAWGFOOD: The Bulldog Cookbook, 1981, Touchdown Tailgates, 1986. Del. So. Leader Forum, Rock Eagle Ctr., Ga., 1976-99; trainer Ga. 4-H Vol. Leader Assn., 1979—; coordinator U. Ga. Equestrian Team, Athens, 1985-87; mem. Clarke County Sheriff's Posse, 1985-2000. Capt. U.S. Army, 1966-70. Chi Psi Scholar, 1965; Recipient Outstanding Alumnus award Chi Psi, 1972, Service to World Community award Chi Psi, 1975. Mem. Nat. Assn. Coll. and Univ. Attys., DAV, Poets Soc., Am. Legion, Rotary, The President's Club (Athens), Gridiron Secret Soc., Chi Psi (advisor 1974). Baptist. Avocations: martial arts, creative writing, music. Home: 365 Westview Dr Athens GA 30606-4635 Office: U Ga Peabody Hall Ste 3 Athens GA 30602

DAVIS, COLLEEN TERESA, elementary education educator, reading educator; b. Monroe, Wis., Aug. 28, 1946; d. Francis Benedict and Norma Irene Doherty; m. John Oswin Davis, Aug. 25, 1973; children: John Francis, Christine Elizabeth. BS in Elem. Edn., Marian Coll., Fond Du Lac, Wis., 1967; MS in Edn.-Reading, U. Wis., Whitewater, 1975; MS in Ednl. Adminstrn., Ariz. State U., Phoenix, 1994. Cert. K-12 adminstr., K-12 curriculum supr., K-12 reading specialist. Elem. tchr. Holy Trinity Sch., Kewaskum, Wis., 1967-69; reading tchr. Friendship Mid. Sch., Adams, Wis., 1970-71, Ozaukee Mid. Sch., Fredonia, Wis., 1971-73, Johnson Creek (Wis.) Schs., 1973-75, 78-84, reading specialist, 1978-84; adult reading tchr. Waukesha County Tech. Inst., Pewaukee, Wis., 1976-79; reading tchr.-specialist Royal Palm Mid. Sch., Phoenix, 1984-93, chpt. 1 coord./curriculum, 1993-95, tchr. gifted, 1995-96, team tchr. mid. sch., 1996-97, active drug prevention program, 1994-97, mem. adminstrv. discipline resource team, 1997—. Presenter Wis. State Reading, Oconomowoc, 1981-82, Ariz. Reading Assn., Tucson, 1988, Washington Sch. Dist., Phoenix Mid. Sch. Conf., 1995, 6-7-8 Grade Acad., 1996; instr. reading Glendale (Ariz.) C.C., 1995—. Author: (programs) Arizona Quality Programs and Practices, 1987, WSD Promising Practices, 1988. Lit. Days vol. Phoenix West Reading Coun., 1992-93. Recipient Golden Apple award Washington Sch. Dist., 1989, Tchr. of Excellence Royal Palm, PTO, Phoenix, 1989, 92, Lit. award-Leadership in Profession, Internat. Reading Assn./Phoenix West Reading Coun., 1990, Recognition award for drug prevention program, U.S. Dept. Edn., 1995. Mem. ASCD, Internat. Reading Assn., Ariz. Reading Assn. (conf. com. 1984—), Phoenix West Reading Coun. (rec. sec., v.p., pres., membership chair), Ariz. Assn. Sch. Adminstrs. Avocations: travel, reading, camping. Office: Royal Palm Mid Sch 8520 N 19th Ave Phoenix AZ 85021-4201

DAVIS, CYNTHIA ALMARINEZ, nursing educator; b. Manila, Philippines, Dec. 25, 1949; d. Rosauro and Virginia (Alconcher) Almarinez; children: Christopher, Christina, Dean, Robert. Student, Troy State U., 1984-85, Auburn U., 1987-88, Coll. Sequoias, Visalia, Calif., 1988-89; BSN, Fresno State U., 1993. RN, Calif. Staff clk. Pacific Telephone Co., San Francisco, 1970-79, Bechtel Corp., San Francisco, 1980-82; acctg. clk. Pepsi-Cola/7-Up Bottling Co., Montgomery, Ala., 1982-85; staff clk. Montgomery Police Dept., 1986-88; nurse apprentice II St. Agnes Med. Ctr., Fresno, 1991-93; student nurse trainer Valley med. Ctr., Fresno, 1991—; grad. nurse VA Med. Ctr., Fresno, 1993-94, pub. health nurse, 1994—. Author/editor Newsbeat, 1991-92. Attendee Leadership Conf., seattle, 1992, Intercollegiate Leadership Conf., Fresno, 1992. Recipient Univ. and Comty. award Kings County Health Dept. Spirit of Nursing, 1993; pre-RN Rev. Course scholar, 1992. Mem. Calif. Nursing Students Assn. (pres. 1991-92), Sigma Theta Tau. Roman Catholic. Avocations: playing piano, crocheting, reading, movies/mysterie stories. Home: 1463 Belinda Dr Lemoore CA 93245-3975

DAVIS, DAISY SIDNEY, history educator; b. Matagorda County, Tex., Nov. 7, 1944; d. Alex C. and Alice M. (Edison) Sidney; m. John Dee Davis, Apr. 17, 1968; children: Anaca Michelle, Lowell Kent. BS, Bishop Coll., 1966; MS, East Tex. State U., 1971; MEd, Prairie View A&M, 1980; postgrad., U. Tex., Tex. A&M U. Cert. profl. lifetime secondary tchr., Tex.; mid-mgmt. adminstr. Tchr. Dallas pub. schs., 1966—, history dept chairperson, 1998—. Instr. Am. History El Centro Coll., 1991-98; adv. Am. history telecourse Dallas County C.C. dist. Coord. Get Out the Vote campaign, Dallas, 1972, 80, 84, 88, 92, 94, 96, 98, 2000, 02; sec., bd. trustees St. John Bapt. Ch., 1995-98; pres. The Amazons. Recipient Outstanding Tchr. award Dallas pub. schs., 1980, Jack Lowe award for ednl. excellence, 1982; Free Enterprise scholar So. Meth. U., 1987; Constl. fellow U. Dallas, 1988; named to Hall of Fame, Holmes Acad., 1979. Mem. NEA, Tex. State Tchrs. Assn., Classroom Tchrs. Dallas (faculty rep. 1971-77, 95—), Dallas County History Tchrs., Afro-Am. Daus. Republic of Tex. (founder), Top Ladies of Distinction, Zeta Phi Beta. Clubs: Jack & Jill Assocs., (Dallas) (rec. sec., v.p., chair Beautillion Ball, pres., Disting. Mother award, Nat. Committment award 1997). Democrat. Baptist. Home: 1302 Mill Stream Dr Dallas TX 75232-4604 Office: 3000 Martin Luther King Jr Blv Dallas TX 75215-2470

DAVIS, DAVID HOWARD, political science educator; b. Washington, Sept. 14, 1941; s. Dorland J. and Caroline (Baker) D.; m. Laura F. Davis (div.); children: Gregory, Jillian. AB, Cornell U., 1969; MA, Johns Hopkins U., PhD, 1971. Asst. prof. Rutgers U., New Brunswick, N.J., 1971-77; assoc. prof. Cornell U., Ithaca, N.Y., 1977-78; analyst Congl. Rsch. Svc., Libr. Congress, Washington, 1979-80; spl. asst., acting dep. asst. sec. energy and minerals U.S. Dept. Interior, Washington, 1980-81; sr. assoc. cons. Internat. Energy Assocs. Ltd., Washington, 1981-84; assoc. prof. U. Wyo., Laramie, 1984-89; prof. U. Toledo, 1989—, dir. MPA program, 1989-92. Author: How the Bureaucracy Makes Foreign Policy, 1972, Energy Politics, 1992. American Environmental Politics, 1998; editor: Social Sci. Jour., 1986-89. Served to capt. U.S. Army, 1964-67, Vietnam, Korea. Mem. Am. Polit. Sci. Assn., Am. Soc. Pub. Adminstrn. Episcopalian. Office: U Toledo Dept Polit Sci and Pub Adminstrn Toledo OH 43606 E-mail: David.Davis@UToledo.edu.

DAVIS, DIANN HOLMES, elementary school educator; b. N.Y.C., July 5, 1949; d. Henry F. and Pearl B. Holmes; m. Milton Davis, July 24, 1973; children: Milton, Keith, Madelyn. AA, N.Y. Tech. Coll., 1971; BS cum laude, Medgar Evers Coll., 1981; MA, Columbia U., 1994. Lic. reading and early childhood. Sci. tchr. JHS 166, IS 302 Future Day Care, Bklyn.; tchr. N.Y. Bd. Edn., Bklyn. Dance tchr. Faith Hope and Charity Day Care Ctrs.;

parent rep. Start Smart; mem. Bklyn. (N.Y.) Reading Coun. Common Brs. Mem. Hall of Sci., Bklyn. Children's Museum, Assn. for Study of Curriculum Devel. Avocations: bicycle riding, ice skating, roller skating, dancing, sewing.

DAVIS, DONALD GORDON, JR., librarian, educator, historian; b. San Marcos, Tex., Aug. 15, 1939; s. Donald Gordon and Ethel Dorothy (Henning) D.; m. Avis Jane Higdon, Dec. 6, 1969; children: Lucinda Ellen, Samuel Higdon, Caroline Louise. BA, UCLA, 1961; MA, U. Calif., Berkeley, 1963, MLS, 1964; PhD, U. Ill., 1972; MA in Theol. Studies, Austin Presbyn. Theol. Sem., 1996. Adminstrv. asst. Biola Coll. Libr., La Mirada, Calif., 1961-62; sr. libr. asst. U. Calif., Berkeley, 1961-64; sr. reference libr. Fresno State Coll. Libr., 1964-68, head dept. spl. collections, 1966-68; asst. prof. libr. sci. U. Tex., Austin, 1971-77, assoc. prof., 1977-86, prof., 1986—98, assoc. dean Grad. Sch. Libr. and Info. Sci., 2000—02, prof. dept. history, 1998—. Bd. dirs., v.p. Logos Bookstore, Austin, 1974-80; vis. prin. lectr. Birmingham (Eng.) Poly., 1980-81; coord. Libr. History Seminars VI, Austin, 1980, VII, Chapel Hill, N.C., 1985, VIII, Bloomington, Ind., 1990; coord. Ann. Tex. Libr. History Colloquium, 1982-97, Tex. Group for the Study of Books and Print Culture, 1995—; mem. planning com. Libr. History Seminar IX, 1995, Libr. History Seminar X, 2000. Author: The Association of American Library Schools, 1915-68, 1974, Reference Books in the Social Sciences and Humanities, 1977, American Library History: A Bibliography, 1978, ARBA Guide to Library Science Literature, 1970-83, 1987, American Library History: A Comprehensive Guide to the Literature, 1989, Encyclopedia of Library History, 1994, Librarianship and Library Science in India: An Outline of Historical Perspectives, 1994, Library History Research in America, 2000; editor: Libraraies and Culture: Proc. of Library History Seminar VI, 1981, Libraries, Books and Culture: Proc. of Library History Seminar VII, 1986, History of Library and Information Science Education: Library Trends, 1986, Reading and Libraries, proc. of Library History Seminar VIII, 1991, Libraries and Philanthropy, Proc. of Libr. History Seminar IX, 1996, Libraries and Culture jour., 1976—, Handbooks of Texas Libraries, 2000, Winsor, Dewey and Putnam: The Boston Experience, 2002, A Bibliography of Texas Library History, 1695-2000, 2002, A Chronology of Texas Library History, 1685-2000, 2002, Dictionary of American Library Biography, 2d edit., 2003; mem. editl. bd. America: History and Life, 1979—, Annual Bibliography of the History of the Printed Book and Libraries, 1994—, Library History (UK), 1998—; contbr. articles to profl. jours. Pres. PTA Robert E. Lee Sch., Austin, 1979-80; mem. adv. bd. Am. History and Life, 1979—, Heritage Soc. Austin, 1987-92; v.p. Hyde Park Neighborhood Assn., 1983-84; asst. scoutmaster local troop Boy Scouts Am., 1987-91; active USA-USSR Citizens Dialogue, Austin, 1985-93. Recipient Tex. Excellence Tchg. award, 1991-92; Am. Inst. Indian Studies fellow, 1988, Newberry Libr. fellow, 1974, John P. Commons Tchg. fellow, 1986-87, 95, 1998-2000, Alumni Tchg. fellow GSLIS, 2002-03. Mem. Am. Hist. Assn., ALA (chmn. libr. history round table 1978-79, internat. rels. com. 1988-92, exec. com. internat. rels. roundtable 1990-92, Lifetime Achievement award 2003), Internat. Fedn. Libr. Assns., Roundtable of Editors of Libr. Jours. (exec. com. 1987—), Round Table on Library History (exec. com. 1978—), Am. Printing History Assn., Assn. Libr. Info. and Sci. Edn., Assn. Bibliography History (exec. bd. 1982-85), Fellowship Christian Librs. and Info. Specialists (exec. com. 1978-87, 97-2001), Tex. Ctr. for Book (adv. coun. 1987—), Am. Antiquarian Soc. (adv. bd. program in history of book 1987-93), Conf. Faith and History, Hymn Soc. (U.S. and Can.), Libr. Assn. U.K., Tex. Libr. Assn. (program com. archives and local history round table 1997—), Orgn. Am. Historians, InterVarsity Christian Fellowship (nat. faculty and grad. student adv. bds. 1990—), Librarians Christian Fellowship (U.K., v.p. 1990—), Book Club Tex., Soc. Promoting Christian Knowledge/USA (bd. trustees 1999—), Presbyn. Hist. Soc., Presbyn. Hist. Soc. S.W., Tex. State Hist. Assn. (program com. for 1992), World History Assn., Beta Phi Mu (Golden Ann. Disting. award 1999), Phi Kappa Phi. Presbyterian. Home: 706 Harris Ave Austin TX 78705-2518 Office: U Tex Sch of Info 1 University Station D7000 Austin TX 78712-0390 E-mail: dgdavis@ischool.utexas.edu.

DAVIS, EARL JAMES, chemical engineering educator; b. St. Paul, July 22, 1934; s. Leo Ernest and Mary (Steiner) D.; children: Molly Kathleen, David Leo. BS cum laude, Gonzaga U., 1956; PhD, U. Wash., 1960. Design engr. Union Carbide Chems. Co., South Charleston, W.Va., 1956; from asst. prof. chem. engring. to assoc. prof Gonzaga U., Spokane, Wash., 1960-68, dir. computing ctr., 1967-68; rsch. fellow Imperial Coll., London U., 1964-65; assoc. prof. chem. engring. Clarkson U., 1968-73, head socio-environ. program, 1972-74, prof., 1973-78, chmn. chem. engring. dept., 1973-74, assoc. dir. Inst. Colloid and Surface Sci., 1974-78; prof., chmn. chem. and nuclear engring. dept. U. N.Mex., 1978-80; dir. engring. divsn., prof. Inst. Paper Chemistry, Appleton, Wis., 1980-83; rsch. fellow in chem. engring. U. Wash., Seattle, 1957-60, prof. chem. engring., 1983—, assoc. vice provost for rsch., 2001—03. Guest prof. Tech. U. of Vienna, Austria, 2000; sr. scientist, cons. Unilever Rsch. Lab., Port Sunlight, Eng., 1974-75; vis. scholar NAS/Chinese Acad. Scis., China, 1989; adj. prof. Sichuan U., Chengdu, China, 2001-03. Assoc. editor Aerosol Sci. and Tech., 1993-97; mem. editl. bd. Jour. Colloid and Interface Sci., 1984-86; mem. editl. bd. Jour. Aerosol Sci., 1992-98, editor-in-chief, 1999—; mem. adv. bd. Surface and Colloid Sci., 2000—; regional editor (N.Am. and S.Am.) Colloid and Polymer Sci., 1994-99; contbr. articles to sci. publs. NSF fellow, 1964-65, grantee, 1963-89, 92—; recipient Burlington No. award for rsch., 1988; Leeds and Northrup fellow U. Wash., 1960. Fellow AAAS, mem. AIChE (adminstr. Design Inst. Multiphase Processing 1979-87), Am. Chem. Soc., Am. Assn. Aerosol Rsch. (treas. 1990-92, David Sinclair award 1991, v.p. 1996-97, pres. 1997-98), Soc. Applied Spectroscopy, Gesellschaft für Aerosolforschung, Sigma Xi, Phi Lambda Upsilon. Achievements include research on air pollution control, aerosol physical chemistry and colloid science. Office: U Wash Dept Chem Engring PO Box 351750 Seattle WA 98195-1750 E-mail: davis@cheme.washington.edu.

DAVIS, ELEANOR LAURIA, biology educator, volunteer, lecturer; b. Pitts., Aug. 29, 1923; d. Anthony Francis and Antonia Jennie (Bove) Lauria; m. Earle Richard Davis, May 7, 1946; children: Susan Davis Hickerson, Janice Davis Johnston, Lisa Davis Kulp, Elena Davis Smoulder, Amy Davis Gordon, Kent Earle, Eric J. BS, U. Pitts., 1944, M Letters in Biology, 1950. Grad. teaching asst. in physiology dept. biology U. Pitts., 1944-46; instr. in biology Pa. Coll. for Women (now Chatham Coll.), Pitts., 1946-53; libr. Carnegie Libr., Pitts., 1947-50. Instr. Acad. Life Long Learning, Pitts., 1995-96. Co-author: Lab. Manual for Biology, 1948; contbr. editorials to profl. newsletter. Pres. St. Joseph's Hosp. Aux., Pitts., 1977-78, Allegheny County Med. Soc. Aux., 1981-83, chmn. legis. com., 1984—; mem. Coun. on Govt. Rels. and Pa. Med. Polit. Action Com., Harrisburg, 1987-94, Pa. Atty. Gens. Task Force Drugs, 1989-90, Pa. Task Force on Aging, 1988-90, Pa. Task Force on AIDS, 1988-90, Pa. Task Force on the Impaired Physician, 1988-90; committeewoman Dem. Party of O'Hara Twp., 1983—, by-laws com. Allegheny County Dems., 1986-88, chmn. Dem. Party of O'Hara Twp., 1990-95; bd. dirs. Parental Stress Ctr., 1977-94, Bright Beginnings, 1979-94, Am. Cancer Soc. Aux., 1984-86, Vocat. Rehab. Ctr., 1986-88, Injury Prevention Works; bd. dirs., 1992-95, mem. program devel. and pub. rels. coms. Self Help Group Network, 1989-95; chmn. pub. rels. Rx Coun., 1986-92, program com., 1993-97, mem. adv. bd., 1997—; mem. S.W. region Pa. Assn. Hosp. Auxs., 1990—, bd. dirs., 2d v.p., 1995, legis. chmn., 1992-94, health chmn., 1992-94; pub. policy chmn. Alzheimers Disease and Related Disorders, 1987-94, pres.-elect, 1998-99; mem. parish coun. St. Scholastica Ch., 1988-90, Grass Roots Intelligence Team, South Hills Health System, 1989-94, aux. chmn. legis. and health, 1986—, chmn. pub. rels., 1999; mem. adv. bd. Allegheny County Safe Kids Coalition, 1990—, mem. bylaws com., mem. legis. com.; elected del. AMA Aux. Conv., 1979-93; mem. Allegheny County Health Dept. Smoke Detector Task Force, 1983-95, Task Force on Scald and Burn Prevention, 1994-95, task force on health care reform Pa. Med. Soc. Alliance, 1993—. Recipient honor scholarship U. Pitts., 1941-44, Benjamin Rush award Allegheny County Med. Soc., 1987, Person of Yr. award South Hills Health System and Found., Pitts., 1989. Mem. AAUW (Women's Agenda), Nat. Inst. Adult Day Care (stds. com.), Nat. Coun. Aging (task force for day care stds. 1989-90), Allegheny County Fedn. Women's Clubs (RX coun. bd. dirs. 1986—), Stanton Heights Garden Club (pres. 1974-89, program chmn. 1989—), Herb Soc. Am. (program com. western unit), Piccadilly Herb Club (pres. 1994-95, by laws com. 1996, 99, gourmet chmn. 1999—), Hosp. Assn. Pa. (grass roots intelligence team), Pa. Med. Soc. (legis. key contact), Pa. Med. Soc. Alliance (PAMPAC rep. western dist. 1991-95, bylaws com. 1990-94, pres. 1988-89, 92-93, pres. Past Pres.'s Gavel Club 1992-93), Pa. Assn. Hosp. Auxs. (spring conf. planning com. 1995-96), Acad. Lifelong Learning, Theta Phi Alpha, Nu Sigma Nu. Avocations: herbs, gardening, silver jewelry, flower arranging, needlework, painting. Home: 109 Woodshire Rd Pittsburgh PA 15215-1713

DAVIS, ELISE MILLER (MRS. LEO M. DAVIS), writer, educator; b. Corsicana, Tex., Oct. 12, 1915; d. Moses Myre and Rachelle (Daniels) Miller; m. Jay Albert Davis, June 27, 1937 (dec. June 1973); 1 child, Rayna Miller Davis Loeb; m. Leo M. Davis, Aug. 23, 1974. Student, U. Tex., 1930-31. Freelance writer, 1945—. Merchandiser and dir. Jay Davis, Inc., Amarillo, Tex., 1956-73; instr. mag. writing U. Tex., Dallas, 1978; lectr. creative writing Baylor U., Waco, Tex., 1980, 81, 83. Author: The Answer Is God: The Personal Story of Dale Evans and Roy Rogers, 1955; contbr. articles to periodicals, including Reader's Digest, Woman's Day, Nation's Bus., also others. Mem. Am. Soc. Journalists and Authors (bd. dirs. 1985-91). Home: 7838 Caruth Ct Dallas TX 75225-8123

DAVIS, ELLA DELORES, special education educator, elementary school educator; b. Quitman, La., July 19, 1957; d. Gencie Lee and Bessie (J.) D. BA, La. Tech. U., 1979; MS, Grambling State U., 1989. Tchr. lang. arts, social studies and leisure time activities Jackson Parish Sch. Bd., Jonesboro, La., 1982—. Mem. Spl. Edn. Coun. Jonesboro, 1991-93. Author: The Power of Jesus--An Enlightening Story of Incidences That Happened in My Life and How Jesus Interceded, 1989, Behavior Booklet, 1992, A Complete Guide to Setting Up a Special Education Program, 1992, Special Education Lesson Plan Booklet, 1992, My Math Fact Booklet, 1992, My Word Booklet, 1993, Pictorial of Life Photo Album Inserts to Girls and Boys, 2000, Be A Success, 2001; inventor health and beauty aid products, variety other products. Mem. exec. bd. NAACP, Jonesboro, 1992—; mem. 5th Dist. Black Caucus, Monroe, La., 1990—, Jonesboro Beautification Bd., 1993—. Mem. La. Assn. Educators. Democrat. Baptist. Avocations: volleyball, basketball, cooking, travel, reading. Home: 271 Sugar Creek Rd Quitman LA 71268-1313

DAVIS, ELLEN MARIE, business educator; b. Boston, Oct. 9, 1958; d. Charles F. and Ellen (Fahy) Sargent; m. Jack C. Davis, Oct. 13, 1982; children: Elaine, Melissa. BS in Bus. Edn., Salem (Mass.) State Coll., 1981; postgrad., Cameron U., Lawton, Okla., 1988, 89, 91. Cert. K-12 tchr., Okla., Mass. Instr. Big Bend C.C., Friedberg, Germany, 1983-88, Fischer Ednl. Svcs., Lawton, 1989-91; tchr. bus. Am. Coll., Lawton, 1992-93; owner Checker Wrecker and Auto Salvage and E&M Car Ctr., Lawton, 1993—. Pres. Howell Elem. Sch. PTA, 1994-95. Named Tchr. of Month (2), Am. Coll., 1992. Mem. ASCD, Nat. Coun. for Social Studies, Okla. Alliance for Geog. Edn., Smithsonian Assocs. Avocations: reading, crafts. Home: 6109 SW Park Ave Lawton OK 73505-7718 Office: 520 S Sheridan Lawton OK 73501

DAVIS, ERIC LYLE, political scientist, educator, college administrator; b. Boston, Aug. 12, 1952; s. Samuel Joseph and Esther Pearl (Litman) D.; m. Kathleen Louise Jesseman, June 29, 1985. BA, Brown U., 1973; MA, Stanford U., 1975, PhD, 1978. Asst. prof. Middlebury (Vt.) Coll., 1980-84, assoc. prof., 1984-89, prof., 1989—, dean acad. programs, 1991-93, dean acad. planning, 1993-95, v.p. info. tech., 1995-97, sec., 1997—. Mem. Phi Beta Kappa. Office: Middlebury Coll Old Chapel Middlebury VT 05753 E-mail: ericd@middlebury.edu.

DAVIS, ERLYNNE P. social work educator; b. Cleve., Oct. 16, 1925; d. Earle Vernon and Margaret Ruth (Sanders) Poindexter; m. Charles E. Davis Sr. (dec.); 1 child, Charles E. Jr. AB, Oberlin Coll., 1947; MS in Social Adminstrn., Western Res. U., 1950. Case worker Cuyahoga County Welfare Dept., Cleve., 1947-48, Family Svc. Assn., Cleve., 1950-54; supr. Cuyahoga County Welfare Dept., Cleve., 1956-63; instr. Sch. Applied Social Scis. Case Western Res. U., Cleve., 1963-66, asst. prof., 1966-69, assoc. prof. Sch. Applied Social Scis., 1969-87, assoc. prof. emerita Mandel Sch. Applied Social Scis., 1987—. Cons., staff devel. trainer, continuing edn. instr., spkr. in field, 1957-99. Bd. trustees Project Friendship, Cleve., 1986—91, pres., 1987, Youth Visions, 1991—95; bd. dirs. Met. YWCA, Cleve., 1987—92; vol. Ret. Srs. Vol. Program, 1989—2002; mem. adv. coun. Coun. Ret. Srs. Col. Program, Cleve., 1991—94, 1995—2001; active Cmty. Coun., 1993—95, Fairhhill Exec. Coun. Fairhill Ctr. for Aging, 1996—97; vol. Intergenerational Resource Ctr., 1994—99; mem. adv. coun. on sr. and adult svcs. Cuyahoga County, 1996—2000; coun. on older persons Fedn. Cmty. Planning, 1995—2001; mem. IRC Adv. Team, 1997—99; mem. African Am. adv. coun. Cleve. Alzheimer Assn., 1999—2002; mem. St. James African Meth. Episcopal Ch. Recipient 20th Ann. Founders Recognition, Ctr. for Human Svcs., Cleve., 1990, Ebony Rose Edn. award, Murtis Taylor Multi-Svc. Ctr., Cleve., 1990, Ebony Rose Honored award, 1995, Disting. Alumni award, Sch. Applied Social Scis. Case Western Res. U., 1987, Women of Distinction award, Women's Missionary Soc. African Meth. Episcopal Ch., 1983. Mem.: NAACP (life), Alpha Kappa Alpha (Gold mem., Achievement award Alpha Omega chpt. 1963, 1974, 1999, Anna V. Brown award for Cmty. Svc. 1999).

DAVIS, FREDERICK BENJAMIN, retired law educator; b. Bklyn., Aug. 21, 1926; s. Clifford Howard and Anne Frances (Forbes) D.; m. Mary Ellen Saecker, Apr. 21, 1956; children: Judith, Robert, James, Mary. AB, Yale U., 1948; JD, Cornell U., 1953; LLM with honors, Victoria U. of Wellington, New Zealand, 1955. Bar: N.Y. 1953, Mo. 1970, Ohio 1981. Assoc. Engel Judge & Miller, N.Y.C., 1953-54; instr. U. Pa. Law Sch., 1955-56; asst. prof. NYU, 1956-57, U. S.D., 1957-60, assoc. prof., 1960-62, Emory U., 1962-63, prof., 1963-66, U. Mo.-Columbia, 1966-70, Edward W. Hinton prof. law, 1970-81, Edward W. Hinton prof. emeritus, 1981—; dean, prof. law U. Dayton Sch. Law, 1981-86; dean, prof. Memphis State U., 1987-92, prof., 1992-98, prof., dean emeritus, 1998—. Cons. adminstrv. procedure Mo. Senate, 1974-77; vis. prof. Wake Forest U. Sch. Law, 1980, 86-87, U. Wis., 1960, George Washington U., 1965, Tulane U., 1966, U. Mo.-Kansas City, 1973, U. Ky., 1977. Contbr. numerous articles, comments, revs., notes to profl. jours. Served with USNR, 1944-46. Mem. ABA (coun. sect. adminstrv. law 1969-75), Am. Law Inst., Rotary Club (Memphis Ctrl. chpt.), Summit Club. Republican. Episcopalian. E-mail: freddyandmary@aol.com.

DAVIS, GERALDINE SAMPSON, special education educator; b. Tacoma, Wash., Aug. 18, 1919; d. Philip and Merta M. (Thomas) Sampson; m. John Allen Davis, Nov. 26 1942 (div. 1971); children: Denise, Karin, Glen (dec.), Grant (dec.), Page, Gail (dec.). BS with distinction, U. Minn., 1941; MEd, San Francisco State U., 1971. Cert. tchr., Calif., cert. adminstr., Calif. Art and English instr. White Bear Lake (Minn.) Jr. and Sr. High Sch., 1941-43; Am. club mobile operator ARC, Eng. and Europe, 1944-45, exec. dir. Lincoln County chpt., 1947-48; substitute tchr. Santa Cruz (Calif.) County Dept. Edn., 1964-67; learning disabled instr. Live Oak Dist. Schs., Santa Cruz, 1967-89. Peer tutor developer Live Oak Schs., 1970-73, reading program mgr., 1973-76; evaluation team mem. County of Santa Cruz, 1980-84. Exhibited paintings in numerous galleries shows including Los Gatos Art Cooperative, 1961-65, Santa Cruz Art Festival, 1962, San Juan Bautista Art Fair, 1963, Santa Cruz County Fair, 1965; paintings represented in several pvt. collections. Chpt. sec. March of Dimes, Lincoln County, 1949-51, Santa Cruz County; vol. tutor Vols. of Santa Cruz, 1978-83; fundraiser Boulder Creek (Calif.) Schs., 1963; scenic and prop designer Santa Cruz County Schs., 1964, Boulder Creek Theater Group, 1965. Mem. Calif. Assn. Neurol. Handicapped Children (chair 1964-66, scholarships 1968-71), Women's Dem. Club, AAUW (com. chair for women's issues 1990—), Reproductive Rights Network, Santa Cruz Reading Assn. (sec. 1980, rep. Asilomar reading conf. bd. 1981-82, Chpt. and Internat. Reading Assns. award 1985), Calif. Ret. Tchrs. Assn. (nominating com. 1985—), Assn. Ret. Persons, Sr. Citizens Santa Cruz County, Pub. Citizens, Pub. Broadcasting Network, Conservation of Am, Amnesty, Delta Phi Delta (life, pres. Mpls. chpt. 1939-41), Pi Lambda Theta (life). Avocations: swimming, travel, animals, politics, cross generational communication. Home: 319 35th Ave Santa Cruz CA 95062-5514

DAVIS, GLADYS MARIA, early childhood educator; b. Washington, Oct. 26, 1952; d. Henry Halvor and Gladys Virginia (Keyes) Jones; m. Kirkland J. Davis, Oct. 9, 1971 (div. 1989); children: Kirkland J. Jr., Joseph L., LaTora M. AA, Washington Tech. Inst., 1976; BS, U. D.C., 1979, MA, 1990. Cert. tchr., D.C. Tchr. D.C. Pub. Schs., Washington, 1979—. Sch. treas., chpt. adv. chair, Comer sec., fundraising chair Weatherless Elem. Sch., 1991—, chair parental involvement, 1992. Recipient Pub. Educator Excellence award Scottish Rite-32d Degree Masons, Washington, 1992. Mem. ASCD, Washington Tchrs.' Union, Blacks in Govt. Roman Catholic. Avocations: sewing, bowling, collecting bells. Home: 816 Lamberton Dr Silver Spring MD 20902-3037 Office: Weatherless Sch Burns And C St SE Washington DC 20011

DAVIS, GWENDOLYN LOUISE, air force officer, English educator; b. Toledo, Dec. 8, 1951; d. Robert Louis and Marietta Beatrice (Sautter) Davis; m. Barry Dennis Fayne, Jan. 6, 1979 (div. Feb. 2001); children: Ashleigh Elizabeth, Zachary Alexandur-John. BFA, So. Meth. U., 1972; MEd, U. North Tex., 1978; MA, U. Denver, 1987. Cert. tchr., Tex., Ala.; cert. secondary tchg. Am. Montessori Soc. Substitute tchr., Toledo and Dallas, 1972-73; film dir. Channel 39 Christian Broadcasting Network, Dallas, 1973-75; engr., air operator Channel 40 Trinity Broadcasting Network, Tustin, Calif., 1978; commd. 2d lt. USAF, 1978, advanced through grades to maj., 1989, ret., 1995; mgr. western area Hdqrs. USAFR Officers Tng. Corp., Norton AFB, Calif., 1979-81; chief tng. systems support Hdqrs. Air Force Manpower Pers. Pentagon, Washington, 1981-84; pers. policies officer J1, Orgn. of Joint Chiefs of Staff Pentagon, Washington, 1984-85; asst. prof. English, dir. forensics USAF Acad., Colorado Springs, Colo., 1987-92; adj. faculty mem. dept. English Auburn U., Montgomery, Ala., 1994-95; adj. faculty mem. dept. arts and scis. Troy State U., Montgomery, 1994-96; dir. Bullock County HS Learning Ctr., Union Springs, Ala., 1995-96; tech. and acad. tchr. Ctr. for Advanced Tech. Booker T. Washington Magnet H.S., Montgomery, 1996; tchr. speech and English Mountain Brook H.S., Birmingham, Ala., 1997-98; tchr. humanities Joseph Bruno Montessori Acad., Birmingham, 1998-2000; upperschool director Sacred Heart Church Sch., 2000-2001, ednl. cons., 2001—02; founder, dir. Shiloh Village Montessori H.S., 2002—. Assoc. editor Airpower Jour., Maxwell AFB, Ala., 1992-94, mil. doctrine analyst, 1994-95; chmn. mil. affairs Jr. Officer's Coun., Norton AFB, 1981; invited spkr. in field; chmn. program devel. com. for nat. orgn. Cross Exam. Debate Assn., 1990-91. Contbr. articles to profl. jours. Teacher, mem. choir, soloist various chs., 1973; chair publicity com. Birthright, Inc., Woodbridge, Va., 1983. Named Command Jr. Officer of Yr., Hdqrs. USAFR Officers Tng. Corps, 1979. Mem. Nat. Parliamentary Debate Assn. (co-founder, editor Parliamentary Debate jour. 1992-95), Am. Montessori Soc., Phi Upsilon Omicron. Avocations: reading, antiques, sight-seeing, family. Home: 4978 Overton Rd Birmingham AL 35210 E-mail: gwendavis1@aol.com.

DAVIS, HARRISON RANSOM SAMUEL, JR., English language educator; b. Norton, Kans., June 14, 1917; s. Harrison Ransom Samuel and Grace Russell (Powell) D.; m. Doris Kathryn Wagner, July 24, 1947; children: David H., Paul D., Stephen C., Carol L. Davis Herth. BA, Pasadena Coll., 1945, MA, 1947, DD, 1969; postgrad., U. Calif., Berkeley, 1956-57; MA, U. So. Calif., 1963. Ordained minister Church of the Nazarene, 1950. Asst. prof. English and Greek Pasadena (Calif.) Coll., 1947-50; curriculum, instr. Japan Nazarene Bible Coll., Tokyo, 1950-59; pres., prof. Japan Christian Jr. Coll., Chiba City, Japan, 1959-85; ESL instr. Meikei Gakuen, Tsukuba City, Japan, 1985-90; adj. prof. English, ESL So. Nazarene U., Bethany, Okla., 1990-94. Lectr. tchr. edn. Japan Pub. Schs., Chiba Refecture, 1965-85. Author: Bible Doctrines of Salvation, 1959; contbr. articles to profl. jours. Sec. Evangelical Publ. Assn., Tokyo, 1952; treas. Evangelical Missionary Assn. Japan, Tokyo, 1951-52. Named Alumnus of Yr. Point Loma Nazarene Coll., 1983; recipient Significant Contbn. to Edn. award Japan Pvt. Colls. Assn., 1985. Fellow Reed Leadership Found.; mem. Okla. Tchrs. English to Spkrs. Other Langs., Order the Rising Sun. Republican. Mem. Church of the Nazarene. Avocations: memorizing poetry, writing letters, backpacking, horseback riding. Home: 5824 Springburn Dr Dublin OH 43017-9410

DAVIS, HELEN R. elementary and middle school educator; b. Colorado Springs, Sept. 30, 1941; d. Carl Michael and Sarah Anna Pearl (Joe) D. BA cum laude, U. Denver, 1963, MA, 1966; postgrad., Mich. State U., 1968, other univs. Cert. elem. and secondary adminstrn. Campus supr., grad. teaching asst. U. Denver; tchr. Arapahoe County Sch. Dist. 6, Littleton, Colo., retired, 1994. Mem. Dist. Assessment Adv. Coun., Math. Curriculum Rev. Com., North Cen. Evaluation Teams, Jefferson County Sci. Audit Team. Mem. ASCD, Nat. Coun. Tchrs. Math., Nat. Coun. Tchrs. English, Nat. Coun. for Social Studies, Littleton Edn. Assn. (sec., treas 1991-93), Kappa Delta Pi, Delta Kappa Gamma (chpt. pres. 1988-90).

DAVIS, HIRAM JOE, public school administrator; b. Spartanburg, S.C., Feb. 13, 1930; s. Flake Revere and Dolorus Jane (Haigler) D.; m. Anna Jane Ripley, Mar. 16, 1951; children: Alan Joe, Kendal Jay. AB, Asbury Coll., 1951; MEd, Kent State U., 1957. Cert. supt., prin., supervisor, tchr. Elem. sch. tchr., Antrim, Ohio, 1951-52; tchr. Auburn Elem. Sch., Chagrin Falls, Ohio, 1952-57; prin. Kenston Elem. Schs., Chagrin Falls, Ohio, 1957-62; prin., dir. of 16 schs. Firestone Rubber Plantation, Harbel, Liberia, West Africa, 1962-64; asst. high sch. prin. Orange Schs., Pepper Pike, Ohio, 1964-66, prin. Brady Mid. Sch., 1966-84; interim prin. Kenston Schs., Chagrin Falls, Ohio, 1984-98. Past bd. mem. Am. Inst. Fgn. Study, Greenwich, Conn., 1968-84, prin. summer sch. groups to Europe, 1968-82; attendee White House Conf. on Edn.; owner JD Mailboxes. Chmn. trustees Garfield Meml. United Meth. Ch., Pepper Pike, mem. p.p.r. com., mission com.; vol. traveling libr. for Geauga County Pub. Libr. to Amish schs.; scoutmaster troop 1 Liberian Boy Scouts and Boy Scouts Am., Harbel, Liberia, 1962-64; summer session missionary svc. Liberia, 1985, Kenya, 1987; founder Chagrin Valley Jr. Athletic Conf. Mid. Schs. Recipient Dedicated Svc. award Chagrin Valley Jr. Athletic Conf., Garfield Meml. award for dedicated svc. in all areas of churchmanship, Harry Denman Evangelism award for lay leader United Meth. Ch. Conf., Cmty. Svc. award Fedn. Orange Cmties. Mem. NEA (life dept. Nat. Elem. Sch. Prin.), Kiwanis (George F. Hixson award 1964; pres. Lander Cir. 1969-70). Avocation: raising registered belgians.

DAVIS, HOWARD TED, engineering educator; b. Hendersonville, N.C., Aug. 2, 1937; s. William Howard and Gladys Isabel (Rhodes) D.; m. Eugenia Asimakopoulos, Sept. 15, 1960 (dec. July 1996); children: William Howard II, Maria Katherine; m. Catherine Asimkopoulos, Mar. 9, 2000. BS in Chemistry, Furman U., 1959; PhD in Chem. Physics, U. Chgo., 1962. Postdoctoral fellow Free U. of Brussels, 1962-63; asst. prof. U. Minn., Mpls., 1963-66, assoc. prof., 1966-69, prof., 1969-80, prof., head chem. engring. and materials sci., 1980-95, dean Inst. Tech., 1995—, Regent's prof., 1997—. Editor: Springs of Creativity, 1981; author: Statistical Mechanics of Phases, Interfaces and Thin Films, 1995, (with K. Thomson) Linear Algebra and Linear Operators in Engineering, 2000; contbr. over 500 articles to sci. and engring. jours. Fellow Sloan Found., 1967-69, Guggenheim Found., 1969-70. Mem. AAAS, AIChE (Walker award for excellence in publs. 1990), NAE, Am. Chem. Soc., Soc. Petroleum Engrs., Minn. Fedn. Engring. Socs. (Disting. Engr. 1998). Democrat. Methodist. Avocations: tennis, golf, reading, movies. Home: 1822 Mount Curve Ave Minneapolis MN 55403-1018 Office: U Minn 421 Washington Ave SE Minneapolis MN 55455-0373 E-mail: davis@itdean.umn.edu.

DAVIS, JACQUELYN DELORES, elementary education educator; b. St. Thomas, V.I., Mar. 27, 1966; d. Lawrence M. and Ida Aletha (Wattley) Dawson; 1 child, Ashley Chante Davis. BA, U. V.I., 1990. Student worker U. V.I., St. Thomas, 1986-90; adminstrv. asst. LEAD-U. V.I., St. Thomas, summer 1989; tchr. grade 4 Ulla F. Muller Elem. Sch., St. Thomas, 1990—. Chairperson sch. improvement team Ulla F. Muller Elem. Sch., 1992-93; math leader St. Thomas/St. John Dist., 1992—. Recipient Generation-at-Risk mini grant Office of Student Svcs., St. Thomas, 1992. Mem. ASCD, Nat. Coun. Tchrs. Math. (dist. math. textbook com. 1992-93, territorial math curriculum task force com., St. Thomas/St. John Coun. Tchrs. Math., Virgin Islands Tchr. Enhancement Math. Sci. Avocations: swimming, traveling, meeting people, reading, dancing. Office: Ulla F Muller Elem 41-44 Kongens Gade St Thomas VI 00802

DAVIS, JACQUETTA ANDERSON, English language educator; b. Phila., Jan. 16, 1958; d. Jacob Jenkins and Mary Geneva Anderson Brown; m. Eddie Bennie Davis, Jan. 15, 1990; children: Mary Wehma, Decontee Johanna. B in Bible, Phila. Coll. of Bible, 1979; B in Elem. Edn., Trenton (N.J.) State Coll., 1981, MEd, 1985. Cert. elem. edn. tchr., English as second lang. tchr., N.J. Fgn. missionary Fiji Islands United Missionary Fellowship, Inc., Sacramento, Calif., 1978; missionary, evangelist various chs. in Pa. and N.J., 1975-90; curriculum writer in ESL East Windsor Regional Schs., Hightstown, N.J., 1981—. Workshop presenter Nat. TESOL Conf. Miami & Chgo., 1985, 86, N.J. TESOL, 1986, 94, 95, Ctrl. Jersey Network of Black Women for Edn., 1993, 94. Co-author: (with other colls.) ESL Curriculum Management Manual--"English As A Second Language Management Program K-12", 1986. Sun. sch. tchr. various chs. in Trenton, N.J., 1991—; guest spkr. to women and children in various chs. in Pa. and N.J., 1978—. Action grant: software and material for Schoolwide Reading Program in English and Spanish, East Windsor Regional Sch. Dist., 1995. Mem. N.J. TESOL and Bilingual Edn., N.J. Edn. Assn., Kappa Delta Pi (hon. mention for disting. educator award Trenton State Coll. chpt. 1991). Avocations: bible study reading, writing, poetry, visiting hospital and nursing home patients, assisting friends with home computer maintenance and set-up. Office: E Windsor Regional Sch Dist 384 Stockton St Hightstown NJ 08520-4228

DAVIS, JAMES ALLAN, gerontologist, educator; b. Portland, Oreg., May 20, 1953; s. Alfred Jack and Anne (Dickson) D.; m. Lois Carol Lindsay, Dec. 17, 1978; children: Sarah Elizabeth, Matthew Simon. BS, U. Oreg., 1975, MS, 1976, EdD, 1980. State mental health gerontologist Oreg. Mental Health Div., Salem, 1978-80; project dir. Oreg. Long Term Care Tng. Project, Salem, 1979-80; tng. specialist Nat. Assn. Area Agys. on Aging., Washington, 1981; asst. dir. for internships and vol. svc. exptl. learning programs U. Md., 1981-86, mem. rsch. and instructional faculty, 1982-86; com. adminstr. Oreg. State Human Resources Com., Salem, 1987; exec. dir., legis. dir. Oreg. State Coun. Sr. Citizens, Salem, 1987—2002; program coord. for sr. mental health care Oreg. Sr. and Disabled Svc. Div., Salem, 1989—2001; pres. James A. Davis and Assocs. Inc., Portland, 1991—; state project dir. Oreg. Assn. RSVPs, 1995—. Vis. asst. prof. Ctr. for Gerontology, U. Oreg., 1990-92; co-chair Audio-Visual Program, Internat. Congress Gerontology, 1985; nat. gerontology acad. adv. panel, Nat. Hosp. Satellite Network, 1983-85; presenter nat. confs. on aging, health care, exptl. edn., age stereotyping; lobbyist United Srs. Oreg., Oreg. State Coun. Sr. Citizens, Oreg. State Denturist Assn., Oreg. State Pharmacist Assn., Oreg. Soc. Physician Assts., Oreg. Legal Techs. Assn., Oreg. Dental Lab. Assn., Wash. Denturist Assn., Nat. Denturist Assn.; adj. asst. prof. Urban Studies Inst. on Aging, Portland State U., 2003—. Co-author: TV's Image of the Elderly, 1985; contbg. editor Retirement Life News, 1988-92; sr. issues editor Sr. News, 1989-96; contbr. articles to profl. jours.; producer, host approximately 400 TV and radio programs. Founding pres. Oreg. Alliance for Progressive Policy, 1988-89; co-chair mental health com., vice chair legis. com., Gov.'s Commn. on Sr. Svcs., 1988-89; exec. coun., media chair Human Svcs. Coalition Oreg., 1988-89; bd. dirs. Oreg. Health Action Campaign, 1988-92; 2d v.p., bd. dirs. Oreg. State Coun. for Sr. Citizens, 1977-80, 90-92, Oreg. Medicaid Com., 1996—; co-chair Oreg. Medicare/Medicaid Coalition, 1995—, Oreg. Long Term Care Campaign, 1996-98; mem. Gov.'s Task Force for Volunteerism, State of Md., 1983-84, State Legis. Income Tax Task Force, 1990; vice chair Oreg. State Bd. Denture Technology, 1991-96; mem. com. for assessment on needs for volunteerism, Gov.'s Vol. Coun., State of Md., 1984-86; project dir. Oreg. Assn. Ret. and Sr. Vol. Programs, 1995—; mem. exec. bd. dirs. Oreg. Advocacy Coalition of Srs. and People with Disabilities, 1997—; chmn., bd. dirs. Oreg. Campaign for Patient Rights, 1997—. Recipient Disting. Svc. award City of Salem, 1980, Spl. Human Rights award, 1981, Svc. award U. Md., 1984, Hometown U.S.A. award Community Cable TV Producers, 1988, Disting. Svc. award Oreg. State Coun. Sr. Citizens, 1991. Mem.: Oreg. State Coun. of Sr. Citizens (Disting. Svc. of Sr. award 2000), Alzheimers Assn. of Oreg. (Pub. Policy award 2000), Nat. Denturist Assn. (exec. dir. 1982—89), Gerontol. Soc. Am. (mental health task force 1982—84, co-chmn. 1983—84), Nat. Assn. State Mental Health Dir. (nat. exec. com. 1978—80, vice chmn. 1979—80, spl. cons.81 1981—82, mem. aging div., co-chmn. nat. program com. 1984—87, nat. media chair 1985—92), Nat. Gray Panthers (nat. exec. com. 1984—87, nat. bd. dirs. 1984—92, program co-chmn. nat. biennial conv. 1986, nat. health task force 1981—, co-chmn. 1983—84, chmn. mental health subcom. 1981—86, editor Health Watch 1982—84, state program developer Oreg. chpt. 1979—80, 1989, lobbyist 1987—, gov.'s patient protection work group 2000—01). Democrat. Office: James A Davis and Assocs Inc 1020 SW Taylor St Ste 610 Portland OR 97205-2506 E-mail: davisjasr@aol.com.

DAVIS, JANET HOLMES, special education educator; b. Jasper, Ga., July 31, 1959; d. Guin and June Lee (Henderson) Holmes; m. Bobby James DAvis, July 17, 1986. BS in Spl. Edn., West Ga. Coll., 1980; MEd in Interrelated Edn., North Ga. Coll., 1983; diversified tng. coord. endorsement, U. Ga., 1991. Cert. tchr., Ga. Spl. edn. tchr., facilitator to dir. Pickens County Bd. Edn., Jasper, Ga., 1980-87, spl. edn. tchr., coop. coord. secondary edn., 1987-90, diversified coop. tng. coord., 1990—. Coord. Ga. Spl. Olympics, Pickens County, 1981-87. Bd. dirs. Apple Valley Rehab. Ctr., Ellijay, Ga., 1991—. Mem. Am. Fedn. Tchrs., Am. Vocat. Assn., Ga. Vocat. Assn., Lioness Club. Avocations: interior decorating, crafts, reading, investment properties.

DAVIS, JANET MARIE GORDEN, secondary education educator; b. Springfield, Mo., Jan. 6, 1938; d. Ura Arlond and Evelyn Ruby (Nickols) Gorden; m. Benjamin George Davis, June 21, 1980; children: Leslie Anne, John Nathan. BS, S.W. Mo. U., 1960, MA, 1969; PhD, U. Md., 1992. Tchr. Springfield Schs., 1960-64; instr. USAFE-U. Md., Germany, 1965-67, S.W. Mo. U., Springfield, 1969-70; tchr., dept. chair Baltimore County, 1977—. Cons. in internat. edn. World Relief Corp., Wheaton, Ill., 1984; asst. prof. Balt. Internat. Coll., 1993-95. Author: For the Love of Literature: A Survey of Fiction, 1989, For the Love of Literature: Reading and Writing Nonfiction, 1989. Fulbright fellow, Eng., 1980-81. Mem. Dickens Fellowship, Fulbright Assn., Phi Kappa Phi. Baptist. Avocations: piano, animal rights, victorian poetry, hymnology. Home: 6580 Madrigal Ter Columbia MD 21045-4628

DAVIS, JOHN MIHRAN, surgeon, educator; b. N.Y.C., Aug. 13, 1946; s. Drought Delaney and Ruth Radcliff (Kalaidjian) D.; m. Marlene Morgan, Oct. 13, 1973; children— Nicholas Mihran, Elisabeth Whitfield. B.A., Columbia Coll., 1968; M.D., Wayne State U., 1972. Diplomate Am. Bd. Surgery. Intern, then resident N.Y. Hosp., N.Y.C., 1972-77; asst. attending surgeon N.Y. Hosp.-Cornell U. Med. Ctr., N.Y.C., 1977—, Jamaica Hosp., N.Y., 1980— ; asst. prof. surgery Cornell U. Med. Coll., 1977-84, assoc. prof., 1984-97, prof. surgery Robert Wood Johnson Med. Sch., 1997; program dir. Jersey Shore Med. Ctr.; also assoc. dir. trauma, 1984-97 . Author: Andrew W. Mellon, Teacher-Scientist, 1983. Fellow ACS; mem. Am. Burn Assn., Surg. Infection Soc. (charter), N.Y. County-State Med. Soc., N.Y. Surg. Soc., Soc. Univ. Surgeons. Home: 31 Pitman Ave Ocean Grove NJ 07756-1656 E-mail: jmdavis@meridianhealth.com.

DAVIS, JOSEPH LLOYD, educational administrator, consultant; b. Crawfordsville, Iowa, May 4, 1927; s. Whitfield and Jane (Lloyd) D.; m. Margaret Florence Cooper, Dec. 28, 1949; children: Stephen Joseph, Thomas Whitfield, Jane Ellen. BSc, Ohio State U., 1949, MA, 1955, PhD, 1967. Reporter Ohio State Jour., 1943-49, 52-53; tchr. Morey Jr. H.S., Denver, 1949-52, Central H.S., Columbus, Ohio, 1953-54; asst. dir. adminstrv. rsch. Columbus Public Schs., 1954-56, dir. publs. and public info., 1956-60, exec. asst. to supt., 1960-64, asst. supt. spl. svcs., 1964-77, supt. of schs., 1977-82; exec. dir. Ohio Coun. Vocat. Edn., 1985-96. Past pres. Columbus Rotary; adj. prof. Ohio State U., 1983—; founder, dir. emeritus Ohio State U. Nat. Acad. for Supt.; cons. and author in field. Mem., bd. trustees Interprofl. Commn. Ohio, 1999—, Kids Voting/Ctrl. Ohio Region, 1999—; mem., past pres. Friends Bd. WOSU AM, FM and TV, Ohio State U., Columbus, 1986—98, 2000—. With USN, 1945—46, with USN, 1950—51. Recipient award for civic leadership Columbus Area C. of C., 1980, Liberty Bell award Columbus Bar Assn., 1980; named to Pub. Schs. Hall of Fame, Columbus, Ohio, 1993. Mem. Am. Assn. Sch. Adminstrs. (disting. svc. award 1989). Nat. Sch. Pub. Rels. Assn. (pres.'s award 1980), Assn. for Career and Tech. Edn., Ohio Assn. for Career and Tech. Edn., Buckeye Assn. Sch. Adminstrs., Nat. Soc. Study Edn., Horace Mann League, Ohio State U. Alumni Assn. (leadership consortium 2003—), Rotary (Rotarian of Yr. award 1994), Torch Club Columbus, Phi Delta Kappa, Epsilon Pi Tau (laureate 1994, Disting. Svc. award 2000), Kappa Delta Pi, Omicron Tau Theta. Presbyterian. E-mail: jdavis59@columbus.rr.com.

DAVIS, JOY LEE, English language educator; b. N.Y.C., Apr. 3, 1931; d. William Henry and Genevieve (Rhein) Belknap; m. Peter John King, Aug. 26, 1955 (div. Feb. 1985); children: William Belknap King, Russell Stuart King; m. John Bradford Davis, Jr., July 5, 1986. AB, Wellesley Coll., 1952, AM, 1953; PhD, Rutgers U., 1968; postgrad., Oxford (Eng.) U., 1978. Tchr. English Dana Hall Sch. for Girls, Wellesley, Mass., 1953-54; instr. English U. Mo., Columbia, 1954-55, Boston U., 1955-56; tchr. English Brookline (Mass.) High Sch., Spartanburg (S.C.) High Sch., 1956-60; prof. English Ohio Wesleyan U., Delaware, 1966-71, Hamline U., St. Paul, 1972-74, U. Minn., Mpls., 1974-77, Coll. St. Thomas, St. Paul, 1977-88; lectr., dir. Joy Davis Seminars, St. Paul, 1988—. Author: Everything But: An Education Memoir, 1999, The Hero in Literature: Prometheus to Prufrock, 2003; pub. poetry in New World Writing and Crisp Pine Anthology; lit. criticism in Midwest Quar., 1993, Jour. Grad. Liberal Studies, 1996. Wellesley Coll. scholar, 1952. Mem. AAUW (bd. dirs., v.p. ways & means, 2003—, Svc. awrd St. Paul br. 1983), Midwest MLA, Mpls. Inst. Fine Arts, Minn. Club (bd. dirs. 1982-88), New Century Club (bd. dirs., spl. subjects chmn.) Schubert Club (bd. dirs., chmn. mus. com.), Wellesley Coll. Club (regional campaign com.), Delta Kappa Gamma. Republican. Presbyterian. Avocations: reading, travel, creative cuisine. Home and Office: 4312 Pond View Dr Saint Paul MN 55110-4155

DAVIS, JULIE LYNDA, adult and secondary education educator; b. Fresno, Calif., Nov. 5, 1964; d. Richard Arthur and Judith Karen (Haertling) Lang; children: Colton Trevor, Weston Anthony. AA, Modesto (Calif.) Jr. Coll., 1984; BS in Bus., Fresno State Coll., 1986; cert. in teaching, Chapman Coll., 1989, MAwith honors, 1992. Cert. secondary edn. tchr., Calif. Cons. J.C. Penney Co., Modesto, 1986-89; tchr. bus. Modesto High Sch., 1989, Elliott Edn. Ctr., Modesto, 1989-91, tchr. adult edn., 1990—; tchr. bus. Grace M. Davis High Sch., Modesto, 1991—; bus. tech. and profl. devel. instr. Valley Comml. Coll., 1995—. Site facilitator coop. learning Modesto City Schs., 1990—; advisor Future Bus. Leaders of Am., Modesto, 1991—; tech. prep. consortium Curriculum Improvement and Approval Com., 1993; fellow, contbg. author Great Valley Writing Project at Stanislaus State U., 1994. Author: Modesto City Schools Freshman Core Computer Literacy Curriculum, 1994. Campaign worker Wilson for Gov., Modesto, 1990, Lang for Assembly, Modesto, 1990; mem. Rep. Women, 1983—, LWV, Modesto, 1989. Mem. NEA, Calif. Tchrs. Assn., Modesto Tchrs. Assn., Alpha Kappa Psi, Phi Mu. Methodist. Avocations: writing, interior design, family, hunting. Office: Modesto City Schs 426 Locust St Modesto CA 95351-2631

DAVIS, K. JEAN, elementary school educator; b. Sulphur, Okla., Apr. 14, 1964; d. Bobby Joe and Shannon Lee (Hambleton) D. BSE, Okla. Christian Coll., 1986; MEd in Instrl. Media, U. Cen. Okla., 1992. Tchr. Choctaw (Okla.) Sch., Nicoma Park (Okla.) Sch. Named Tchr. of Yr., 1992. Mem. Alpha Chi. Home: 10533 Tumilty Terr Midwest City OK 73130-2111

DAVIS, KAREN ANN (KAREN ANN FALCONER), special education educator; b. Rockford, Ill., Sept. 24, 1948; d. Duane Fay and Vivian Marie (Milani) Falconer. BS in Edn., Ill. State U., 1971; MBA in Mgmt., Kennedy-Western U., 1994; MA in Tchg., Rockford Coll., 1996. Cert. Ill. assessing ofcl. Spl. edn. tchr. Winnebago Co-op, Rockton, Ill., 1971-76; assessor Winnebago Twp., Ill., 1977-85; program coord. Ill. Growth Enterprises, Rockford, Ill., 1977-87; substitute tchr. Rockford Pub. Schs., 1987-89, 92—; estate planner Bradford and Assocs., Rockford, 1988-89, A. Bergners, Rockford, 1989-91; spl. edn. tchr. Eisenhower Middle Sch., Rockford, 1992—. Pub. ofcl. Assessor-Winnebago Twp., 1977-85. Mem. Twp. Assessor's Assn. (treas. 1985), Nat. Audubon Soc. Roman Catholic. Avocations: photgraphy, bird watching, gardening, traveling, antiquing.

DAVIS, KIMBERLY JANE, physical education educator; b. Champaign, Ill., June 7, 1950; d. Thomas Richard and Bernadette (Baude) Davis; m. H.R. Williamson, Sept. 6, 1992. BA, MacMurray Coll., Jacksonville, Ill., 1972; MS, Ind. U., 1977. Cert. tchr., Ind., Ill. Phys. edn. tchr., coach Balyiki Community Schs., Bath, Ill., 1972-77; adapted phys. edn. specialist Ind. U. Inst. for Study of Developmental Disabilities, Bloomington, 1977—. Bd. dirs. Options for Better Living, Bloomington, 1991—; mem. planning com. Gov.'s Child Devel. Ctr., Indpls., 1990—. Author: Adapted Physical Education for Students with Autism, 1990. Mem. Hoosier Hills Child Care Adv. Bd., Bloomington, 1989—; mem. Ind. U. Diversity Anti Harassment Team, 1991-92; mem. Gay-Lesbian-Bisexual Task Force, Bloomington, 1991-92. Mem. AAHPERD, Nat. Assn. for Edn. of Young Children, Coun. for Exceptional Children (div. early childhood), Ind. Phys. Edn. Assn. (adapted phys. edn. chairperson 1980-81, mem. adapted phys. edn. task force 1990—). Avocations: hiking, travel, animals, softball, movies. Office: Ind U Inst Study Devel Disability 2853 E 10th St Bloomington IN 47408-2601

DAVIS, LAURIE LEE, special education educator; b. Evanston, Ill., Oct. 16, 1965; d. Richard Aubrey and Sue Ann (Wheelock) Hunt; m. John Glen Davis, July 29, 1989; 1 child, Julia Marie. BS, Iowa State U., 1987; student, Nat. Louis U., 1988-90. Cert. tchr., Ill. Spl. edn. asst. Lake Forest (Ill.) Sch. Dist. 67, 1987-88; tchr. spl. edn. Palatine Community Consolidated Dist. 15, Palatine, Ill., 1988-89, Arlington Heights (Ill.) Sch. Dist. 25, 1989-93, team leader spl. edn., 1992-93; ret. Home: 4406 Meadowlark Ln La Crosse WI 54601-2989

DAVIS, LYNN HAMBRIGHT, culinary arts educator; b. Gaffney, S.C., Aug. 7, 1950; d. Samuel Anderson and Elizabeth (Nolen) Hambright; m. Ronnie Dale Davis, Aug. 10, 1969; children: Marty, Jennifer. BS in Home Econs. Edn., Winthrop Coll., 1972, MS in Home Econs. Edn., 1982, EDS, 1996. Cert. secondary home econs. edn. tchr., early childhood edn., N.C., S.C. Tchr. Crest Sr. High, Shelby, N.C., 1975-76; dietitian Cleveland Meml. Hosp., Shelby, 1977-78; tchr. culinary arts and food sci. tech. Cherokee Tech. Ctr., Gaffney, 1978—. Chairperson Staff Devel. Com. and Culinary Arts Craft Coun., Gaffney, 1978—; advisor Future Homemakers Am., Gaffney, 1978—. Mem. NEA, Am. Vocat. Assn. (region II policy com. 1992-95, state rep. region II 1992-95), S.C. Edn. Assn., S.C. Vocat. Assn. (v.p. 1991-92, Tchr. of the Yr. 1997), Nat. Assn. Tchrs. Family & Consumer Sci., S.C. Assn. Tchrs. Family & Consumer Sci. (pres. 1991-92, advisor 1992-93, Tchr. of Yr. 1995, 97), Am. Home Econs. Assn., S.C. Assn. Family & Consumer Sci. (sec. food svc. adminstrs. com. 1991-92, Tchr. of Yr. 1993), Home Econs. Edn. Assn., Kappa Delta Phi. Democrat. Baptist. Avocations: reading, computers. Home: 2100 Albert Blanton Rd Shelby NC 28152-8151 Office: Cherokee Tech Ctr 3206 Cherokee Ave Gaffney SC 29340-3500

DAVIS, LYNN HARRY, secondary education educator; b. Jamestown, N.Y., Mar. 6, 1949; s. Harry Lynn and Marjorie Ellen (Greenwood) D.; m. Patricia Ann Carapella; 1 child, Matthew Michael. BS, SUNY, Fredonia, 1971. Cert. tchr., N.Y. Sci. tchr. West Genesee Sch. Dist., Camillus, N.Y., 1972—, adult edn. computer tchr., 1985-91, sci. curriculum coord., 1988—; tech. support specialist Teaching Ctr. Syracuse U., 1991—98; adult edn. computer tchr. Syracuse U. Teaching Ctr., 1984—86. Chmn. Sci. Bldg., West Genessee Sch. Dist., 1983-88, coord. sci. curriculum, 1988—. Contbr. numerous articles to profl. jours. Strategic planning com. mem. West Genesee Cen. Schs.; fundraiser United Way, Syracuse, 1978-81, YMCA, Syracuse, 1981; mem. Friends of Zoo, 1987-98. Mem. ASCD, N.Y. State United Tchrs. (del. 1980-85, 97-2000), Am. Fed. of Tchrs., Nat. Sci. Tchrs. Assn., West Genesee Tchrs. Assn. (v.p. for negotiations 1979-85, sec. 1986—, newsletter editor 1986—, webmaster 1997— (numerous awards)). Avocations: golf, photography, computers. Home: 14 Blackwood Dr Liverpool NY 13090-3764 Office: West Genesee Cen Sch Dist Ike Dixon Rd Camillus NY 13031-9619 Personal E-mail: davis@twcny.rr.com.

DAVIS, MAGGIE L. elementary teacher; b. Bastrop, La., July 13, 1939; m. Killion C. Davis II, May 1, 1961. BA, U. Calif, 1982, postgrad.; PhD, Grambling State U., 1961. Cert. elem. tchr. Tchr. Berkeley (Calif.) Unified Sch. Dist., 1987—. Head supr. Willie Youth Field O.E.S., 1983—. Mem. Alpha Kappa Alpha (sec. 1959), NCNW. Lodges: Pride Alameda, O.E.S. (worth matron 1983—), Queen Sheba L.K.T. (fin. sec. 1982—), Queen Adah Grand Chpt. (grand recorder 1984—, fin. sec. 1983—). Democrat. Baptist. Avocations: sewing, reading, solving puzzles, swimming, tennis. Office: 1501 Harmon St Berkeley CA 94703-2619

DAVIS, MARGARET DINAN, assistant principal, educator; b. Richmond, Va., July 5, 1946; d. Raymond A. and Mary Emily (Carroll) Dinan; m. Glenn Price Davis, Nov. 26, 1966; 1 child, Emily Carey. BA, Coll. William and Mary, 1968, MA, 1974; CAS, Old Dominion U., 1987, PhD, 1995. Cert. tchr., Va. 1st grade tchr. Williamsburg (Va.) Schs., 1968-69, York County Schs., Yorktown, Va., 1970-71, 74-75, demonstration tchr. Title III demonstration project, 1971-74, 6th grade tchr., 1975-77, reading specialist, 1975-91, instrnl. team leader, 1979-91, intern rsch. dept., 1991, asst. prin., 1991—. Participant Tidewater Regional Assessment Ctr., Norfolk, Va., 1990, Springfield Devel. Project, Richmond, Va., 1991; adj. faculty Mary Baldwin Coll. Contbr. articles to profl. publs.; author: (play) Spirit of Yorktown; rec. artist albums of Celtic music (with Joe Healey): '90 Earthtones, '92 Rosebower, '94 Winter Carols. Mem. York County Hist. Bicentennial Com., 1979-81; pianist St. Bede's Cath. Ch. Grantee Va. Commn. of Arts, 1986; recipient Disting. Svc. award Grafton Bethel PTA, 1980, 92; named Tchr. of Yr., Newport News Reading Coun., 1991. Mem. Va. Assn. for Supervision and Curriculum Devel., Va. State Reading Assn., Internat. Reading Assn., Va. Ednl. Rsch. Assn. (grantee 1993), Delta Kappa Gamma (pres.-elect Gamma Phi chpt.), Phi Kappa Phi. Avocations: liturgical music, hammered dulcimer, appalachian music, christian clowning, celtic music. Office: Coventry Elem Sch 200 Owen Davis Blvd Yorktown VA 23693-4521

DAVIS, MARIAN BLOODWORTH, secondary school educator; b. Decatur, Ala., Apr. 7, 1933; d. Benjamin McGowan and Marguerite Maud (Nelson) Bloodworth; m. Judson Ervill Davis, Jr., June 6, 1958; children: Katheryne, Judson Ervill III, James Alexander Bloodworth. BA, U. Ala., Tuscaloosa, 1957; MA, U. North Ala., 1989. Cert. tchr., Ala. Social worker State of Ala., Decatur, 1957-58; tchr. Decatur City Schs., 1979—. Treas., bd. dirs. Jr. League Morgan County, Decatur, 1966-72; area coord. The Close Up Found., Washington, 1990—; mem. Morgan County Reps., 1990—. Mem. NEA, Ala. Edn. Assn., Decatur Edn. Assn., Nat. Coun. Social Studies, Ala. Coun. Social Studies (dist. dir. 1990-94, 99—, pres. 1994-95), Nat. Trust Historic Preservation, Ala. Hist. Soc., Nat. Alumni Assn. U. Ala., Delta Kappa Gamma (sec. 1996—), Kappa Delta. Republican. Baptist. Avocations: reading, travel, counted cross stitch. Home: 2326 Quince Dr SE Decatur AL 35601-6138 Office: Decatur High Sch 1011 Prospect Dr SE Decatur AL 35601-3290

DAVIS, MARY ELLEN K. library director; MLS, U. Ill.; MA, Ctrl. Mich. U. Sr. assoc. exec. dir. Assn. Coll. and Rsch. Librs., 1993—2001, exec. dir., 2001—, dir. comm. and systems, publs. program officer; ref. libr., bibliographer Ctrl. Mich. U. Recipient Girl Scouts Outstanding Vol. award. Mem.: ALA, Am. Soc. Assn. Execs., Soc. Scholarly Publishing, Profl. Conv. and Meeting Planners Assn., Phi Kappa Phi, Beta Phi Mu. Office: 50 East Huron St Chicago IL 60611

DAVIS, MARY HORTMAN, elementary school educator; b. Columbus, Ga., Feb. 21, 1948; d. Madison Henry and Mary Julia (Fields) Hortman; m. Charles Rockwell Davis; children: Clayton, Travis, Meghan. BS in Elem. Edn., Ga. So. Coll., 1970; M in Early Childhood Edn., Ga. Coll., 1981; specialist in edn. cert., Ga. Southwestern Coll., 1994. Cert. elem. sch. tchr., Ga.; cert. counselor. Tchr. grade 4 Gould Elem. Sch., Savannah, Ga., 1969-72; tchr. grade 3 Hartley Elem. Sch., Macon, Ga., 1972, Windsor Acad., Macon, 1973; tchr. grade 2 Barden Elem. Sch., Macon, 1985-87; tchr. grade 4 Bonaire (Ga.) Elem. Sch., 1987-93, Perdue Elem. Sch., Warner Robins, Ga., 1993—, counselor, 2002—. Mem. Ga. Reading Assn. (v.p. Hope chpt. 1991-94), Internat. Reading Assn., Ga. Sch. Counselors Assn. Home: 201 Mount Zion Rd Bonaire GA 31005-4426

DAVIS, MAUREEN FLYNN, nursing educator, administrator; b. Syracuse, N.Y., Oct. 8, 1943; d. Paul V. and Laura C. (Fath) Flynn; m. Charles E. Davis, Jan. 6, 1978 (dec.); children: Michael Briggs, Megan Fath. BSN, Creighton U., 1965; MSN, U. Nebr., 1976. RN, cert. rehab. nurse, cert. legal nurse cons. Staff nurse Gen. Rose Meml. Hosp., Denver, 1965-69; clin. instr. Methodist Hosp. Sch. Nursing, Omaha, 1969-70; asst. instr. U. Nebr., Omaha, 1970-74; staff nurse Clarkson Hosp., Omaha, 1974-75; instr. Coll. St. Mary, Omaha, 1976-77; asst. prof. Clemson (S.C.) U., 1977-85; staff nurse Roger C. Peace Inst. Rehabilitative Medicine, Greenville, S.C., 1981-86, admissions coordinator, program evaluator, 1986-91; staff devel. coord. Hillhaven Healthcare, Greenville, 1991-92; case mgr. Crawford & Co., Greenville, 1992-93; quality assurance cons. Liberty Mut. Ins. Co., Spartanburg, S.C., 1993-96; nurse case mgr. Hew H. Coleman & Assocs., Greenville, 1996—; owner Upstate Legal Nurse Consultants, LLP, 2002—. Resource reviewer: Jour. of Rehab. Nursing, 1987—. Vol. ARC, 1981—, Am. Cancer Soc., 1980 (both Greenville). Mem. ANA, Assn. Rehab. Nurses (bd. dirs. S.C. chpt. 1986), Oncology Nurses Soc., S.C. Assn. Rehabilitation

Profls. (v.p. 2002-03), Sigma Theta Tau (chpt. counselor 1981-83, chmn. nominating com. 1980-81). Republican. Roman Catholic. Home: 14 Keowee Ave Greenville SC 29605-2917

DAVIS, MICHAEL J. public instruction superintendent; m. Karen Davis; 2 children. BBA, Ea. Ill. U.; MA in Bilingual Elem. Edn., N.Mex. State U.; Edn. Specialist in Sch. Adminstrn., U. N.Mex. Vol. Peace Corps, Colombia; tchr. corps intern Las Cruces Pub. Schs., N.Mex.; from tchr. to prin. Chama Valley Ind. Schs., 1974—84; accreditation cons. N. Mex. State Dept Edn., Santa Fe, 1984—87, divsn. supt., 1886—1990, assoc. supt. for sch. mgmt. and accountability, 1990—97, supt., 1997—. Mem.: Coun. Chief State Edn. Officers, Pub. Sch. Capital Outlay Coun., S.W. Ednl. Devel. Lab., Ednl. Retirement Bd. Office: N Mex Dept Edn Edn Bldg 300 Dan Gaspar Santa Fe NM 87501-8786

DAVIS, MICHELLE MARIE, elementary education educator; b. Cleve., Jan. 7, 1956; d. Frank Charles and Rita Theresa (Zdrojewski) Koran; m. Gary Wayne Davis, Sept. 24, 1976; children: Benjamin, Zachary. BA, Ball State U., 1978, MA in Edn., 1989; postgrad., U. S.C., 2003—. Substitute tchr. Baugo Cmty. Schs., Elkhart, Ind., 1982-83, Middlebury (Ind.) Schs., 1982-84, Goshen (Ind.) Cmty. Schs., 1982-84, Elkhart (Ind.) Cmty. Schs., 1984-87; elem. tchr. Ft. Wayne Diocese, Elkhart at St. Thomas, 1987-91, Williamsburg County Schs., Kingstree, S.C., 1991—. Lead tchr. homework ctr. Kingstree Elem. Sch., 1992—93; chair S.C. grammar and composition textbook rev. com., 1996; presenter, lectr. in field. Adminstr. food bank St. Ann's Ch., Kingstree, 1992—94, mem. pastoral coun., 1992—2002, sec., 1992—94, pres., 1995—96, vol. outreach ctr., 1992—. Grantee S.C. Dept. Edn., 1994. Mem.: ASCD, S.C. Coun. Tchrs. Math. (grant), St. Ann's Women's Club. Home: 106 Gourdin St Kingstree SC 29556-2736 Office: Kingstree Elem Sch 500 N Academy St Kingstree SC 29556-3499

DAVIS, NATHANIEL, humanities educator; b. Boston, Apr. 12, 1925; s. Harvey Nathaniel and Alice Marion (Rohde) D.; m. Elizabeth Kirkbride Creese, Nov. 24, 1956; children: Margaret Morton Davis Mainardi, Helen Miller Davis Presley, James Creese, Thomas Rohde. Grad., Phillips Exeter Acad., 1942; AB, Brown U., 1944, LLD, 1970; MA, Fletcher Sch. Law and Diplomacy, 1947, PhD, 1960; postgrad. Russian lang. and area, Columbia, Cornell U., Middlebury Coll., 1953-54, U. Central de Venezuela, 1961-62, Norwich U., 1989. Asst. history Tufts Coll., 1947; joined U.S. Fgn. Service, 1947; 3d sec. Prague, Czechoslovakia, 1947-49; vice consul Florence, Italy, 1949-52; 2d sec. Rome, 1952-53, Moscow, USSR, 1954-56; Soviet desk officer State Dept., 1956-60; 1st sec. Caracas, Venezuela, 1960-62; acting Peace Corps dir., Chile, 1962; spl. asst. to dir. Peace Corps, 1962-63, dept. assoc. dir., 1963-65; U.S. minister to Bulgaria, 1965-66; sr. staff Nat. Security Coun. (White House), 1966-68; U.S. amb. Guatemala, 1968-71, Chile, 1971-73; dir. gen. Fgn. Service, 1973-75, asst. sec. of state for African affairs, 1975; U.S. amb. Switzerland, 1975-77; State Dept advisor and Chester Nimitz prof. Naval War Coll., 1977-83, lectr., 1991—; Alexander and Adelaide Hixon prof. humanities Harvey Mudd Coll., Claremont, Calif., 1983—2002, faculty exec. com., 1986-89, acting dean of faculty, 1990, emeritus prof., 2002—. Lectr. in field. Author: The Last Two Years of Salvador Allende, 1985, Equality and Equal Security in Soviet Foreign Policy, 1986, A Long Walk to Church: A Contemporary History of Russian Orthodoxy, 1995, 2d edit., 2003. Mem. ctrl. com. Calif. Dem. Party, 1987—90, 1991—, mem. exec. bd., 1993—, mem. bus. and profl. caucus, 1992—; mem. L.A. County Dem. Ctrl. Com., 1988—90, 1992—, regional vice chmn., 1994—96; del. Dem. Nat. Conv., 1988, 1992, 1996, 2000; del. So. Calif. conf. United Ch. of Christ, 1986—87. Lt. (j.g.) USNR, 1944—46. Recipient Cinco Aguilas Blancas Alpinism award, Venezuelan Andean Club, 1962, Disting. pub. Svc. award, USN, 1983, Elvira Roberti award for outstanding leadership, Los Angeles County Dem. Com., 1995, spl. merit award (as author), So. Calif. Motion Picture Coun., 1998, Prism award for nat., state, county and local svcs., Jerry Voorhis Claremont Dem. Club, 1999; Fulbright scholar, Moscow, 1996—97. Mem.: AAUP (pres. Claremont Coll. chpt. 1992—96, 1998), Am. Acad. Diplomacy, Coun. on Fgn. Rels., Am. Fgn. Svc. Assn. (bd. dirs., vice chmn. 1964), Cosmos Club, Phi Beta Kappa. Home: 1783 Longwood Ave Claremont CA 91711-3129 Office: Harvey Mudd Coll 301 E 12th St Claremont CA 91711-5901

DAVIS, O. L., JR., education educator, researcher; b. Amarillo, Tex., Nov. 20, 1928; s. O.L. and Viola Mae (Maxwell) D.; m. Joan Elizabeth King, May 29, 1953; children: Luke III, Matthew Donald. BA with honors, U. North Tex., 1949, MEd, 1950; PhD, George Peabody Coll. Tchrs., 1958. Assoc. sec. Assn. Supervision and Curriculum Devel., Washington; lectr. in edn. U. N.C., Chapel Hill; assoc. prof. edn. Kent (Ohio) State U.; assoc. prof. curriculum and instrn. U. Tex., Austin, 1966-70, prof., 1970—2001, Catherine Mae Parker Centennial prof., 2001—. Author (with others): Religion in the Curriculum, 1987, Schools of the Past, 1976, Perspectives on Curriculum Development: 1776-1976, 1976, Oral History, 1983, Looking at History, 1986, The Social Studies, 1981, Learning from Student Teaching, 1985, Basic Teaching Tasks, 1970, 79, Empathy and Perspective Taking in the Social Studies, 2001, Bending the Future to Their Will; Civic Women, Social Education and Democracy, 1999, Building a Legacy: Women in Social Education, 1784-1984, 2002; (sr. author) textbook series Exploring the Social Sciences, 1970, 73, 75; contbr. articles to profl. jours; editor: Jour. of Curriculum and Supervision, 1993—. Capt. USNR, 1948-88. Named Distinguished Alumnus Coll. Edn. U. North Tex., 1983, 1999 ; recipient Mary Anne Raywid award, Soc. Profs. Edn., 2003. Mem. NEA, ASCD (pres. 1982-83), Am. Ednl. Rsch. Assn. (v.p. 1971-73, Lifetime Achievement award 1996), Soc. Study of Curriculum History (pres. 1979-80), Nat. Coun. for Social Studies (Exemplary Rsch. in Social Studies Edn. citation 1974, Disting. Career Rsch. in Social Studies Edn. award 1996), Midwest History Edn. Soc. (pres. 2003—), Kappa Delta Pi (internat. pres. 1980-82, Laureate chpt. 1994), Am. Assn. for Teaching and Curriculum (pres. 1994-95), Midwest History of Edn. Soc.(pres. 2003-04). Home: 6014 Tonkawa Trl Georgetown TX 78628-1224

DAVIS, PATRICIA ANN, school system administrator; b. Indpls., Feb. 16, 1949; d. Henry Daniel and Freddie Bea (Davis) D.; m. Clarence Cuzette Davis Jr., Dec. 27, 1969; children: Clarence C. III, Chad Davis. BS, Bishop Coll., 1971; M in Ednl. Adminstrn., Dallas Bapt. U., 1994; postgrad., Tex. Women's U. Tchr. fourth grade Arlington (Tex.) Ind. Sch. Dist., 1971-92, asst. prin., 1993—. Author Black History curriculum for Arlington Ind. Sch. Dist., 1989, lang. art curriculum, Arlington Ind. Sch. Dist., 1988; mem. Partners of Excellence AISD, 1992-94. Mem. NAACP, Assn. Tex. Profl. Educators, Tex. Alliance Black Sch. Educators, Alpha Kappa Alpha (Silver Star award 1993, Woman of Yr. 1997). Democrat. Baptist. Avocations: reading, skating, sending cards to the bereaved. Home: PO Box 764896 Dallas TX 75376-4896

DAVIS, ROBERT EDGAR, elementary school educator; b. Heidelberg, Germany, Apr. 20, 1955; s. Robert Devere Davis and Barbara Louise (Bryant) Bowen. BA in Teaching, Sam Houston State U., 1977. Cert. tchr., Tex. Tchr. phys. edn. Texas City (Tex.) Ind. Sch. Dist., 1978—, 7th-grade football coach, 1978. Co-chmn. Quest com., Kohfeldt Elem. Sch., Texas City, 1992—. Mem. Tex. Classroom Tchrs. Assn., Sports Card Club for Children. Democrat. Avocations: collecting sports cards, reading, bible research, drawing. Home: PO Box 2583 Texas City TX 77592-2583 Office: Kohfeldt Elem Sch 701 14th St N Texas City TX 77590-5400

DAVIS, RUSSELL HADEN, consultant; b. Washington, Nov. 26, 1940; s. Walter Haden Davis and Virginia (Russell) Edge; m. Iva Lee Crocker, 1964; children: Brandon Denise, Haden Arnold. BA, U. Va., 1962; MDiv, Union Theol. Sem., N.Y.C., 1965; ThM, So. Bapt. Theol. Sem., Louisville, 1966; STM, Union Theol. Sem., N.Y.C., 1978, PhD, 1986. Ordained to ministry So. Bapt. Ch., 1961, endorsed to chaplaincy Alliance of Baptists in the USA, 2000. Clin. chaplain Ky. State Reformatory, LaGrange, 1966-71, Ctrl. State Hosp., Milledgeville, Ga., 1971-77; assoc. minister The Riverside Ch., N.Y.C., 1977-86; asst. prof. psychiatry and religion Union Theol. Sem., N.Y.C., 1986-91; mem. faculty Blanton-Peale Grad. Inst. Pastoral Psychotherapy, N.Y.C., 1989-91; dir. Psy-Law, N.Y.C., 1989-91; asst. prof. U. Va., 1994, assoc. prof., 1994-95; pvt. practice pastoral psychotherapy, 1974-98; exec. dir. Assn. for Clin. Pastoral Edn., Inc., Decatur, Ga., 1995-98; pres. Legacy Group Internat., 1998—; founder sch. clin. pastoral edn. Sentara Norfolk (Va.) Gen. Hosp., 2001—. Author: Freud's Concept of Passivity, 1993; also articles. Founder Sch. of Clin. Pastoral Edn., Sentara Hosps., Norfolk, Va., 2001; bd. dirs. Tidewater Pastoral Counseling Svcs., Norfolk, Va., 2001—, Inst. for Relationship Therapy, NY, 1981—88, Counseling Ctr., Riverside Ch., NY, 1978—82. Named Ky. Col., State of Ky., 1970; fellow Union Theol. Sem., 1979-81, rsch. grantee, 1987-90; fellow Oaklawn Found., 1980. Mem.: Assn. of Profl. Chaplains (bd. cert. chaplain 1974—99), Assn. Clin. Pastoral Edn. (cert. supr.). Office: Sch Clin Pastoral Edn Sentara Norfolk Gen Hosp 600 Gresham Dr Norfolk VA 23507 E-mail: legacy@5pillars.com.

DAVIS, RUTH CAROL, pharmacy educator; b. Wilkes-Barre, Pa., Oct. 27, 1943; d. Morris David Davis and Helen Jane Gillis. BS, Phila. Coll. Pharmacy and Sci., 1967; PharmD, Ohio State U., 1970; AA in Elec. Engring., ITT Tech. Inst., 1999. Cert. pharmacist, Pa., Md. Mgr. pharmacist Fairview Pharmacy, Etters, Pa.; mgr., pharmacist Neighborcare Pharmacy, Balt.; dir. ambulatory svcs. Rombro Health Svcs., Balt.; tchr., pharmacist Boothwyn Pharmacy, Phila.; pharm. cons. Nat. Rx Svcs. of Pa.; Eagle Managed Care, 1996; pharmacist Pharmastat Inc., 1996—; pharmacy supr. Johns Hopkins Hospice Pharmacy, 2000—; asst. prof. pharmacy Anne Arundel C.C., 2001—. Adj. prof. Essex C.C., 1999, Balt. City C.C., 2000. Republican. Baptist. Avocations: music, reading. Home and Office: 75 Lion Dr Hanover PA 17331-3849

DAVIS, SARAH IRWIN, retired English language educator; b. Louisburg, N.C., Nov. 17, 1923; d. M. Stuart and May Amanda (Holmes) D.; m. Charles B. Goodrich, Nov. 18, 1949 (div. 1953). AB, U. N.C., 1944, AM, 1945; PhD, NYU, 1953. Teaching asst. English dept. NYU, 1948-51; tchr. English Elizabeth Irwin High Sch., N.Y.C., 1951-53; editor coll. texts Henry Holt, N.Y.C., 1953-55; editor coll. texts, enclopedias McGraw-Hill, N.Y.C., Rome, 1953-60; asst. prof. English Louisburg (N.C.) Coll., 1960-63, Randolph-Macon Woman's Coll., Lynchburg, Va., 1963-70, assoc. prof. English, 1970-75, chairperson Am. studies, 1971-87, prof. English and Am. studies, 1975-87, ret., 1987. Contbr. articles to profl. jours. Mem. MLA, Am. Studies Assn., N.C.-Va. Coll. English Assn. (various coms.), Franklin County Hist. Soc. (pres. 1989-94). Address: Carol Woods 139 750 Weaver Dairy Rd Chapel Hill NC 27514

DAVIS, SHERIE KAY, special education educator; b. Cin., Dec. 2, 1956; d. Earl Myron and and Irene (Alexander) Huffman; m. Dana Allen, June 18, 1985; 1 child, Lauren Nicole. BS in Edn. and Home Econs., U. Cin., 1979, MEd in Spl. Edn., 1980. Tchr. mid. sch. developmentally handicapped Ross Local Sch. Dist., Hamilton, Ohio, 1980-85, substitute tchr., 1985-87, Three Rivers Local Sch. Dist., Cleve., 1985-87; tchr. high sch. developmentally handicapped New Miami Local Schs., Hamilton, 1987-92; tchr. to developementally handicapped Talawanda City Schs., 1992—. Facilitator leadership conf. New Miami Care Team, Hamilton, 1989—; presenter Coun. for Exceptional Children-State Conv., Dayton, Ohio, 1990; coach varsity volleyball, jr. varsity basketball. Coach Three Rivers Knothole Baseball Assn., Cleve., 1991—. Recipient Quality Initiatives award Southwestern Ohio Spl. Edn. Regional Resource Ctr., Ohio, 1988. Mem. Coun. for Exceptional Children. Avocations: women's competitive softball, recreational volleyball and basketball, weight training. Home: 608 N Miami Ave Cleves OH 45002-1029 Office: Talawanda High Sch 101 W Chestnut St Oxford OH 45056-2698

DAVIS, SHIRLEY STANCIL, retired elementary education educator; b. Selma, NC, Mar. 11, 1945; d. Needham and Betty (Watson) Stancil; m. Wiliam Louis Davis, Nov. 9, 1968; children: Jacqueline, Dana, William Louis Jr. BS, Elizabeth City State U., NC, 1967; EdM, Va. State U., 1983. 4th grade tchr. Surry Elem., Va., 1967-72, 2nd grade, 1983—; 3rd and 7th grade tchr. Lebanon Elem., Surry, 1972-83; media specialist Luther Porter Jackson Mid. Sch., Dendron, Va., 1995-98, ret., 1998. Mem. Surry County Planning Coun., 1988-89; chairperson Self-Study, Surry, 1976; mem. CADRE Adv. Bd., Surry, 1989-97; pres. Bacon's Castle Woman's Club, Surry, 1990-92; bd. dirs. Am. Heart Assn., Surry, 1978, 89; sponsor Saint Jude Bike-A-Thon, Surry, 1991-92; youth dir. Lebanon Bapt. Ch., Surry, 1989-1999, trustee, 1993-2000, chmn. bd. trustees, 1997-2000, appointed to Chippokes Plantation Farm Found. Bd. of Trustee, 2002. HoneyWell grant Honeywell Edn. Found., 1992; recipient Tchr. of Yr. Daily Press and Hampton Automobile Assn., 1994. Mem. NEA, Va. Edn. Assn., Surry County Edn. Assn., Order of Ea. Stars Grace Union #56. Democrat. Avocations: reading, cooking, sewing, dancing. Home: 650 Lebanon Rd Spring Grove VA 23881-7748

DAVIS, STEPHEN HOWARD, applied mathematics educator; b. N.Y.C., Sept. 7, 1939; s. Harry Carl and Eva Leah (Axelrod) D.; m. Suellen Lewis, Jan. 15, 1966. BEE, Rensselaer Poly. Inst., 1960, MS in Math, 1962, PhD in Math., 1964; BSc honoris causa, U. Western Ont., 2001. Research mathematician Rand Corp., Santa Monica, Calif., 1964-66; lectr. in math. Imperial Coll., London U., 1966-68; asst. prof. mechanics and materials sci. Johns Hopkins U., 1968-70, assoc. prof., 1970-75, prof., 1975-78; prof. engring. sci. and applied math. Northwestern U., 1979—, Walter P. Murphy prof., 1987—, McCormick Sch. prof., 2000—. Dir. Ctr. for Multiphase Fluid Flow and Transport, 1986-88; cons. in field; vis. prof. math. Monash U., Australia, 1973; vis. prof. chem. engring. U. Ariz., 1977; vis. prof. aerospace and mech. engring., 1981; vis. scientist Institut für Aerodynamik-ETH, Zurich, Switzerland, 1971; vis. scientist Dept. Math. Ecole Polytechnique Federale, Lausanne, Switzerland, 1984, 85, vis. prof. 1987, 88, 91; mem. U.S. Nat. Com. for Theoretical and Applied Mechanics, 1978-87. Asst. editor Jour. Fluid Mechanics, 1969-75, assoc. editor, 1975-89, editor-in-chief, 2000—; contbr. articles to profl. jours. Recipient Alexander von Humboldt award, 1994, Fluid Dynamics prize Am. Phys. Soc., 1994, G.I. Taylor medal Soc. for Engring. Sci., 2001. Fellow Am. Phys. Soc. (chmn. divsn. fluid dynamics 1978-79, 87-88, councillor divsn. fluid dynamics 1980-82); mem. NAE, Am. Acad. Arts and Scis., Soc. Indsl. and Applied Math. (coun. 1983-87), Sigma Xi, Pi Mu Epsilon. Home: 1199 Edgewood Rd Lake Forest IL 60045-1308 Office: Northwestern U McCormick Sch Engring/Applied Scis Sheridan Rd Evanston IL 60208-0001

DAVIS, SUE ELLEN H. elementary and secondary music educator; b. Girard, Ohio, May 26, 1952; d. Edgar J. and Jane A. (O'Brien) Harris; 1 child, Heidi Elizabeth. BM, Youngstown (Ohio) State U., 1975, MS in Edn./Sch. Counseling, 1985. Cert. counselor, music tchr. K-12, sch. counselor. Tchr. vocal music, kindergarten-12th grade Girard City Schs. Grant coord. Tng. Ohio Parents for Success, Girard City Schs. Active in ch. and community orgns.; co-founder Cmty. Band, 2002. Mem. NEA, Ohio Edn. Assn., Girard Edn. Assn., Nat. Assn. Tchrs. Singing (high sch. div. competition judge), Music Educators Nat. Conf., ASCD, Ohio Sch. Counselor Assn., Ohio Career Devel. Assn., Ohio Assn. Counseling and Devel., Eastern Ohio Counselor's Assn., Ohio Assn. Counselor Educators and Suprs., Ohio Coll. Pers. Assn., Ohio Mental Health Counselors Assn., Ohio Assn. for Specialists in Group Work, Phi Delta Kappa, Delta Kappa Gamma, Sigma Alpha Iota.

DAVIS, SUSAN WELLS, special education educator; b. Fayetteville, N.C., Sept. 25, 1955; d. Darius Lathan and Virginia Rose (Raguse) Wells; m. Gregg Allen Davis, July 27, 2002. BS, East Carolina U., 1978; MEd, N.C. State U., 1987. Spl. edn. educator Johnson County Schs., Smithfield, N.C., 1978-79, Wake County Schs., Raleigh, N.C., 1979-82, 85-89, diagnostic-prescriptive specialist, 1989—92, program specialist, 1992—97; program dir. spl. edn. NC Dept. Correction, 1997—2000; dir. spl. edn. NC Dept. Juvenile Justice Delinquency Prevention, 2000—. Mem. Coun. for Exceptional Children, Coun. Adminstrs. Spl. Edn., Coun. Children with Behavior Disorders. Home: 7901 Oak Orchard Ct Raleigh NC 27613 Office: Dept Juvenile Justice 410 S Salisbury St Raleigh NC 27613

DAVIS, SYLVESTER, JR., secondary education educator; b. Memphis, Apr. 24, 1945; s. Sylvester Sr. and Alma (Williams) D.; m. Laureen Brown, July 23, 1989; 1 child, Sara Jennifer. BS in Indsl. Edn., Chgo. Teachers Coll., 1968; MS in Indsl. Edn., Chgo. State Coll., 1986; LLD, Thurgood Marshall Law Sch., 1984. Drafting tchr. Chgo. Bd. Edn., 1968-70, 74-81, woodshop tchr., 1973-74, architecture tchr., 1984-86, machine shop tchr., 1986--; credentials analysis U. Ill. at Chgo., 1970-72; with admissions and records Malcolm X City Coll., Chgo., 1972-73. Tech. prep. coord. Washburne Trade Sch., Chgo., 1991--. Mem. Am. Vocat. Assn., Phi Beta Sigma. Methodist. Home: 5427 S Blackstone Ave Chicago IL 60615-5406 Office: Washburne Trade Sch 3233 W 31st St Chicago IL 60623-5087

DAVIS, TAMMIE LYNETTE, assistant principal; b. Kingsport, Tenn., Jan. 17, 1961; d. James T. and Gertrude (Bridges) D. BS in Music Edn., Tenn. Technol. U., 1983; MEd in Ednl. Leadership, East Tenn. State U., 1992. Cert. tchr., Tenn. Chorus and orchestra director John Sevier Mid. Sch., Kingsport, 1983—2001; asst. prin. Jefferson Elem. Sch., Kingsport, 2001—. Chmn. dept. fine arts John Sevier Mid. Sch., 1987, 91-93, 98-2000, chmn. adv. bd., 1991-93; participant Music Educators Nat. Conf., 1981—, Tenn. Arts Acad., 1993. Violist Kingsport Symphony Orch., 1979-89, 92-94, bd. dirs., 1987-89; violist Johnson City Symphony Orch., 1995—; mem. (hammered dulcimer folk group) Wire Kwire, Kingsport, 1986—. Designated Career Ladder Tchr. III, State of Tenn., 1992; named one of Outstanding Music Educators, Gov.'s Sch. for Arts, Tenn., 1990. Mem. NEA, ASCD, Tenn. Edn. Assn., Am. String Tchrs. Assn., Kingsport Edn. Assn. (treas. 1992-94, pres.-elect 1994-95, pres. 1995-96), Nat. Assn. for Preservation and Perpetuation of Storytelling, Tenn. Assn. for Preservation and Perpetuation of Storytelling, Bays Mountain Dulcimer Soc. (pres. 1988-90). Avocations: collecting figurines, reading, writing, performing folk music, flea marketing. Home: 2021 Pendragon Rd Kingsport TN 37660-3432 Office: Jefferson Elem Sch 2216 Westmoreland Kingsport TN 37660

DAVIS, TERI CECILIA, elementary education educator; b. Abilene, Tex., Aug. 16, 1963; d. Guy Lewis and Janice Alene (Richardson) Weaver; m. Glen Everett Hackler, June 9, 1984. BS, Tex. Tech. U., 1984, MEd, 1987; EdD in Ednl. Adminstrn. and Leadership, Kans. State U. Cert. mid. mgmt., 1987. 5th and 6th grade tchr. Lubbock (Tex.) Ind. Sch. Dist., 1984—88; transitional 1st grade tchr. Pampa (Tex.) Ind. Sch. Dist., 1988—93; asst. prin. Midland Ind. Sch. Dist./Sam Houston Elem. Sch., Midland, Tex., 1996—97; asst. prof. edn., dir. early childhood edn. program Southwestern Coll., Winfield, Kans., 1997—2000; dir. tchr. preparation and cert. program Tulane U., New Orleans, 2000—. Team mem. strategic planning team Pampa Ind. Sch. Dist., 1989, communication com. rep., 1990. Activities dir. Sunday Sch., 1st Bapt. Ch., Pampa, 1987-90; bd. dirs. Jr. Svc. League, Pampa, 1988-93, Latchkey, Pampa, 1989-92; vol. Big Bros./Big Sisters, 1991; com. mem. Keep Tex. Beautiful, 1993, bd. dirs., 1995—; vice chmn. bd. dirs. Clean Pampa, Inc., 1988-92; bd. dirs. Keep Midland Beautiful, 1992—; mem. sch. leadership team com. Dist. Readiness com., 1992-93. Impact II grantee Lubbock Ind. Sch. Dist., 1987. Mem. ASCD, Internat. Reading Assn., PTA (membership chmn. 1985-86), Future Homemakers Am. (alumni mem.), Kindergarten Tchrs. Tex. (N.W. area dir. 1990-92, state bd. mem., regional conf. coord.), Tex. Classroom Tchrs. Assn. (dist. 16 coord. coun. pres. 1991), Tex. Elem. Prins. & Suprs. Assn., Pampa Classroom Tchrs. Assn. (pres. 1990-91), Delta Kappa Gamma Phi Delta Kappa (bd. dirs., v.p., newsletter editor). Baptist. Avocations: skiing, aerobics, travel. Home: 4017 Georgetown Dr Metairie LA 70001-1565

DAVIS, THOMAS PAUL, music educator, choral director; b. Wellsboro, Pa., Aug. 2, 1953; s. Waldo Ray and Jane Kathryn (Foley) D. B of Music Edn., Nyack Coll., 1976; postgrad. studies, Pa. State U., 1976. Band dir. Juniata Valley H.S., Alexandria, Pa., 1976-79; choral dir. Westmont-Hilltop H.S., Johnstown, Pa., 1979-81, Titusville (Fla.) H.S., 1981—. So. divsn. chmn. for male choirs Am. Choral Dirs. Assn., 1991-97; cast choir dir. Walt Disney World Co., 1988-93. Music dir. St. Luke's Prebyn. Ch. Titusville, 1983-87, Merritt Island (Fla.) Presbyn. Ch., 1991—. Mem. Fla. Music Educators Assn. (mentor program 2001), Fla. Vocal Assn. (bd. mem. 1986-89, 99—, superior Choral Ratings 1984-85, 87-2002), Nat. Choral Dirs. Assn. (divsn. chmn. 1991-97), Music Educators Nat. Conf., Phi Delta Kappa. Democrat. Avocation: travel. Office: Titusville HS 150 Terrier Trl Titusville FL 32780 E-mail: davist2@brevard.k12.fl.us.

DAVIS, THOMAS PINKNEY, secondary school educator; b. Seminole, Okla., Oct. 10, 1956; s. George Pinkney and Flora Elizabeth (Bollinger) D.; m. Leslie Anne Workman, Jan. 26, 1990; children: Brianna Elizabeth, Mary Katherine, James Pinkney, Robert McKenzie, Victoria Anne; stepchildren: Christopher Lee, Jennifer Dawn, Matthew Joseph, Daniel Jacob, Joshua Issiac Beene. BS with Honors, BA with Honors, East Cen. U., Ada, Okla., 1979. Dir. math. lab. East Cen. U., 1991-92; tchr., chair math. dept. Roosevelt (Okla.) High Sch., 1992-93; tchr. math., chair math. dept. Keota (Okla.) High Sch., 1993-2000; tchr., chair math. dept. Spade (Tex.) Ind. Sch. Dist., 2000—. Book reviewer Jour. Assn. of Lunar and Planetary Observers/The Strolling Astronomer; adj. instr. Connors State Coll., 1998-99; rsch. assoc. Fermi Nat. Accelerator Lab., 1999. Reviewer Sci. Books and Films, 1986—. Fellow Brit. Interplanetary Soc., Soc. Antiquaries of Scotland; mem. AIAA, Am. Astronautical Soc., Assn. Lunar and Planetary Observers, Nat. Coun. Tchrs. Math., Okla. Coun. Tchrs. Math., Okla. Acad. Sci., Alpha Chi, Pi Gamma Mu. Republican. Episcopalian. Home: Glazner House PO Box 10 Spade TX 79369-0010 Office: Spade Ind Sch Dist PO Box 69 Spade TX 79369-0069 E-mail: tp_davis@yahoo.com.

DAVIS, VERA, elementary school educator; b. Cornish, N.H., Sept. 16, 1940; d. Francis Edward and Alice Cone (Parkhurst) Williams; m. John T. Davis, July 3, 1968; 1 child, William Guy. BS, Castleton (Vt.) State Coll., 1962; M in Reading, Coll. St. Joseph, Rutland, Vt., 1992. Cert. tchr. Tchr. 2d grade Town of Cavendish, Proctorsville, Vt., Title I tchr., 1996—. Mem. NEA, Vt. Edn. Assn. Home: 66 Main St Ludlow VT 05149-1113

DAVIS, VERDA MERLYN, nursing educator, educator; b. Alexandria, La., Mar. 8, 1936; d. David Huel and Vera Josephine (Tenette) D.; m. Joseph Francis Gray, Aug. 21, 1957 (div. 1965); children: Cornell Francis, Anthony Stephen. BS in Nursing, Dillard U., 1957; MPH, Tulane U., 1964, postgrad., 1979-83. Cert. AIDS educator, trainer of trainers Nat. Inst. Drug Abuse. Instr. practical nursing Orleans Parish Sch. System, New Orleans, 1957-58; pub. health nurse Visiting Nurses Assn., New Orleans, 1958-63; rsch. assoc. Tulane U., New Orleans, 1964-65; asst. prof. health So. U., New Orleans, 1965-90, univ. health officer, 1989-90; asst. prof. health Dillard U., 1990—. Activity dir. Nat. Youth Sports Program, New Orleans, 1972-90; community health educator Family Svcs. Soc. Greater New Orleans, 1981-90; health edn. cons. Headstart Program, New Orleans, 1985-91; edn. cons. Dept. Family Life/AIDS Edn. Orleans Parish Sch. Bd., 1988—; supts. com. infusion of African-Am. Hist.Orleans Parish Sch. Bd., 1990. Contbr. to profl. publs. Vice pres. Love One Another Polit. Orgn., New Orleans, 1980-85; mem. Coun. for Young Children in Need, New Orleans, 1987-88, Mayor's Coalition Against Drugs, New Orleans, 1989; sec. East New Orleans Voters Edn. League, 1988-89; exec. bd. Com. on Alcohol and Drug Abuse, 1991—. Grantee, NCAA, 1972-90; recipient numerous appreciation awards, Headstart Program, New Orleans, 1987-91. Mem. AAHPER, Am. Pub. Health Assn., La. Alliance for Health, Phys. Edn., Recreation and Dance, Nat. Minority Health Affairs Assn., Just Us Gals. Democrat. Roman

Catholic. Avocations: black history, reading, dancing. Home: 14310 Nacogdoches Rd Apt 2503 San Antonio TX 78247-1981 Office: Dillard U 2601 Gentilly Blvd New Orleans LA 70122-3097

DAVIS, VIVIAN, English language educator; Tchr. Spanish Prairie View Coll., Tex.; secondary sch. tchr. English; prof. English Eastfield Coll., Mesquite, Tex. Mem. Nat. Coun. Tchrs. English (exec. com., dir. Comm. on Lang., mem. Achievements Awards in Writing adv. com., adv. com. People of Color, com. Status and Role of Women in the Profession, leadership roles Conf. Coll. Compsition and Comm. Office: Eastfield Coll Dept English 3737 Motley Dr Mesquite TX 75150-2033*

DAVIS, W. ALAN, education educator; b. Evansville, Ind., Nov. 27, 1946; s. William Albert and Mary Lee (Miedreich) D.; m. Elizabeth Van R. Stanwood, June 12, 1971; children: Allison R., Laura M. BA, Pomona Coll., 1968; MA in Tchg., Harvard U., 1970; PhD, U. Colo., 1985. Tchr. Jefferson County Schs., Lakewood, Colo., 1971-79; sr. rschr. N.W. Regional Edn. Lab., Portland, Oreg., 1982-85; sr. assoc. RMC Rsch., Denver, 1985-89; prof. U. Colo., Denver, 1989—. Contbr. articles to profl. jours. Pres., bd. trustees Boulder Unitarian Ch., 1993. Named Outstanding Rschr. U. Colo. at Denver Sch. of Edn., 1993, Outstanding Tchr., 2000. Mem. Assn. of Endl. Evaluators, Am. Edn. Rsch. Assn., Nat. Coun. of Measurement in Edn. Unitarian Universalist. Office: U Colo Box 106 PO Box 173364 Denver CO 80217-3364

DAVIS, WALLACE EDMOND, JR., former university administrator, educator; b. Olney, Tex., Jan. 20, 1932; s. Wallace Edmond and Sara Mildred (Douglas) D.; m. Helen Janis Smith, Aug. 20, 1955; children: Scott, Melanie Williams. BA, Baylor U., 1951, MS, 1955; PhD, U. Tex., 1971. Tchr. Iowa Park (Tex.) Ind. Sch. Dist., 1952-53; high sch. tchr. Corpus Christi (Tex.) Ind. Sch. Dist., 1953-55, elem. tchr., 1955-59, prin., 1959-64, asst. dir. elem. edn., 1964-66, dir. elem. edn., 1966-67, asst. supt. instr., 1967-73; dean of edn. Corpus Christi (Tex.) State U., 1973-89; v.p. acad. affairs Tex. A&M U. at Corpus Christi, 1989-91; pres. Wayland Bapt. U., Plainview, Tex., 1991—2000, chancellor, 2000—02. Mem. incentive and initiative formula study com. Tex. Higher Edn., coord. bd., 1989-95; tchr. edn. Contbr. articles to profl. jours. With U.S. Army, 1952-54, Korea. Mem. Tex. Tchr. Ctr. Network (induction yr. com.). Home: 1307 W 6th St Plainview TX 79072-7811*

DAVIS, WAYNE KAY, medical educator; b. Findlay, Ohio, Mar. 23, 1946; s. Albert Wayne and Freida Evelyn (Winkle) D.; m. Patricia Ann Krimmer, May 26, 1967; 1 child, J Brandon. BA, Central Bible Coll., 1967; MA, U. Mich., 1969, PhD, 1971. Research scientist Ctr. Research Learning and Teaching, Ann Arbor, Mich., 1971-73; asst. prof. U. Mich. Med. Sch., Ann Arbor, 1973-77, assoc. dir. edn. resources and research, 1976-78, assoc. prof., 1977-82, dir. edn. resources and rsch., 1978-98, prof., 1982—, asst. dean, 1982-86, assoc. dean, 1991-98. Adv. mem. ad hoc study sect. Nat. Heart, Lung and Blood Inst., NIH, Bethesda, Md., mem. site visit team Nat. Inst. Arthritis, Metabolic and Digestive Diseases, NIH, Bethesda, 1978-91; cons. Multipurpose Arthritis Ctr., NIH, Bethesda, 1981-83; vis. scholar U. Calif. Med. Sch., San Diego, 1984-85. Author: A Guide to MTS and Remote Terminal Operation, 1972, Moving Medical Education from the Hospital to the Community, 1997; mem. edit. bd. Diabetes Care, 1983-86; assoc. editor Acad. Medicine, 1988-89; contbr. chpts. and articles to med. jours. Bd. dirs. Washtenaw County unit Mich. Hearth Assn., 1977-79. Recipient Best Article award Assn. Diabetes Educators, 1982; Med. Informatics fellow Nat. Libr. Medicine, 2000. Mem. Am. Ednl. Research Assn. (program chmn. div. I, v.p. 1985-87), Assn. Am. Med. Colls. (nat. chair group on ednl. affairs 1994-95), Am. Diabetes Assn., Soc. Dirs. Rsch. in med. Edn. (pres. 1990-91, 93-94), Phi Delta kappa, Gt.Lakes Cruising Club, Seven Seas Cruising Assn. Office: U Mich Dept Med Edn G1215 Towsley Centre 1515 Hospital Dr Ann Arbor MI 48109-0201 E-mail: wkdavis@umich.edu.

DAVISH, NOREEN ROWLAND, elementary education educator, music educator; b. Wilmington, Del., Oct. 20, 1967; d. Fred William and Jewel (Zaleski) R. BS in Music Edn., West Chester U., 1990, MM in Music Edn., 1995. Cert. elem. tchr., Md., Pa. Student tchr. Kennett Consol. Schs., Kennett Square, Pa., 1989; pre-sch. music specialist Darlington Ctr. Performing Arts, Media, Pa., 1989-90, Suburban Music Sch., Chester, Pa., 1990; elem. music specialist Prince George's County Schs., East Marlboro, Md., 1990-91, Gen. Music Programs, Wilmington, 1991-92, Coatesville (Pa.) Area Schs., 1992—2003. Accompanist Kennett Symphony Children's Choir, Kennett Square, 1992-94; pvt. piano tchr., 1990-93. Editor Pa. Collegiate Music Educators Assn. Newsletter, 1989-90. Cherub choir dir. Westminster Presbyn. Ch., West Chester, 1989-90, music dir. vacation Bible sch., 1990; music dir. Hockessin (Del.) United Meth. Ch., 1991-93, Swope Found. scholar, 1989, Hewlett-Packard scholar, 1986. Mem. Nat. Edn. Assn., Pa. Music Educators Assn. (collegiate state sec. 1985-86), Music Educators Nat. Conf., Am. Orff-Schulwerk Assn. (chair nat. conf. com.), Phila. Area Orff-Schulwerk Assn. (sec. and historian 1993-95), Pi Kappa Lambda. Home: 1438 Street Rd Chester Springs PA 19425-1608

DAVIS-JEROME, EILEEN GEORGE, principal, educational consultant; b. N.Y.C., Nov. 10, 1946; d. Rennie and Flora May (Compton) George; m. Bruce Davis, Aug. 8, 1970 (div. 1978); m. Frantz Jerome, Sept. 7, 1982; 1 child, Thais Davis. BFA, Pratt Inst., 1968; MA, CUNY, 1971, PD, 1990; EdD, Nova Southeastern U., 1998. Lic. ednl. adminstr., prin., instrn. specialist, N.Y. Tchr. fine arts Herbert Lehman High Sch., Bronx, N.Y., 1971-75; tchr. English/fine arts Jr. High Sch. 131, Bronx, 1975-76; tchr. English Jr. High Sch. 22, Bronx, 1976-79; tchr. fine arts Andrew Jackson High Sch., Cambria Heights, N.Y., 1979-83, coord. art dept., 1986-92; admissions counselor Fashion Inst. Tech., SUNY, N.Y.C., 1983-85; coord. Queensborough Coll. Project Prize, Bayside, N.Y., 1991-92; project dir. Andrew Jackson Magnet High Sch., Cambria Heights, N.Y., 1993—, project dir. Humanities and the Arts, 1994—; ednl. adminstr. Queens High Sch. Office, N.Y.C. Pub. High Schs., Corona, N.Y., 1993-94; prin. Humanities and the Arts Magnet H.S., Cambria Heights, NY, 1994—2003. Coord. internat. studies Friends of Jackson High Sch., Cambria Heights, 1986-93, equal opportunity coord., 1989-92; exam asst. N.Y. C. Bd. Edn., Bd. Examiners, Bklyn., 1983-87; curriculum/career cons. Fashion Inst., SUNY, Detroit, Washington, Phila., 1983-86. Curriculum writer N.Y. State Project ot Implement Career Edn., 1975, N.Y. State Futuring, 1984; proposal writer Magnet Sch. Funding, 1993; author: Resource Book, 1989. Mem., speaker Cambria Heights Civic Assn., 1983; mem. N.Y. Urban League, N.Y.C.; vol. Mayor's Vol. Action/Alpha Sr. Cr., Cambria Heights, 1984; vol. Black Spectrum Theatre Co., 1983-86; mem. coord. coun. h.s. divsn. N.Y.C. Bd. Edn., 1997—; v.p. for edn. Madam C.J. Walker Found., 2001—. Named Educator of Yr., NAACP/ACT-S0, N.Y.C., 1992; recipient Recognition award, Black Spectrum Theatre Co., 1983, Speakers award, N.Y.C. Bd. Edn. Open Doors, 1983—84, Black Exec. Exch. Program Nat. Urban League, N.Y.C., 1984, Developer Grant award, Impact II Grant, N.Y.C., 1989, Laurelton Club Prol. award, 1996, Disting. Educator award, L.I. br. Nat. Assn. Univ. Women, 2001, Life Membership award, NAACP, N.Y.C., 2001, Excellence in Edn. award, Omega Psi Phi, 2002, Disting. Educator award, Newsday, 2003, Outstanding Citizen citation, N.Y.C. Coun., 2003. Mem. ASCD, N.Y. State Art Tchrs. Assn., N.Y.C. Art Tchrs. Assn. (v.p., sec. 1983-85, cert. 1983-86), Cultural Heritage Alliance (assoc., Recognition award 1986), Greater Queens Chpt. The Links, Inc., Delta Sigma Theta (chair arts and letters 1991-97, Golden Life award 1991), Phi Delta Kappa (Disting. Cert. 1994). Democrat. Episcopalian. Avocations: painting, travel, dance, writing, theater. Office: Magnet HS Humanities and the Arts 20701 116th Ave Jamaica NY 11411-1038

DAVIS-LEWIS, BETTYE, nursing educator; b. Egypt, Tex., Sept. 19, 1939; d. Henry Sr. and Eliza (Baylock) Davis; divorced; children: Kim Michelle, Roderick Trevor. BS, Prarie View A&M U., 1959; BA in Psychology, U. Houston, 1972; MEd, Tex. Southern U., 1974, EdD, 1982. Dir. edn. Houston Internat. Hosp., 1987—; dir. nurses Mental Health & Mental Retardation Auth. Harris County, Houston, 1982-87, Riverside Gen. Hosp., Houston; CEO, owner Diversified Health Care Systems, Inc., Houston, 1985—; asst. clin. prof. psychiat. nursing U. Tex., 1987-88; asst. prof. allied health sci. Tex. So. U., Houton, 1989—. Adj. prof. Coll. Nursing, Prairie View (Tex.) A&M U., 1986—; lectr. in field; leadership extern. Mem. Harris County Coun. Orgns., 1987—; mem. polit. action com. Coalition 100 Black Women, 1988—; founder, mem. Hattie White Aux. br. NAACP, 1988; mem. grievance com. State Bar Tex., 1988—; chmn. S.W. Regional Nat. Black Leadership Initiative on Cancer, 1988—; grad. Leadership Tex.; bd. dirs. Theatre Under the Stars. Recipient Disting. Rsch. award Internat. Soc. Hypertension, Disting. Crystal award, Impact award Wheeler Ave. Bapt. Ch.; fellow Internat. Leadership Forum, Am. Leadership Forum. Fellow Internat. Soc. Hypertension in Blacks; mem. ANA, Nat. Black Nurses Assn. (bd. dirs.), Sigma Theta Tau, Chi Eta Phi. Home: 9114 Mcafee Dr Houston TX 77031-1104

DAVISON, ELIZABETH JANE LINTON, education educator; b. Las Cruces, N.Mex., Mar. 9, 1931; d. Melvy Edgar Linton and Clara Virginia Hale; m. Curwood Lyman Davison, Jan. 29, 1954; 1 child, Lawrence. BS, N.Mex. State U., 1957; postgrad., U. N.Mex.; Grad., Norris Sch. Real Estate, Albuquerque, 1984. Cert. tchr., N.Mex., Oreg.; cert. real estate agt., N.Mex., appraiser. Sec., treas. C.L. Davison, Md., Pa., 1975-88, 1975-88; ind. real estate contractor Century 21, Las Cruces, 1984-85; ret. Albuquerque Pub. Schs., 1957-60, 64-68; pres. Sun Dial Enterprises, 1984-95; tchr. Beaverton Pub. Schs., 1960-64. Mem. NEA, Legis. Coun., N.Mex. Albuquerque Classroom Tchrs. Inter-City Coun. (v.p.), AAUW, Phi Delta Kappa (Svc. key). Home: 3013 Cumberland Dr San Angelo TX 76904-6108

DAVISON, HELEN IRENE, secondary education educator, counselor; b. Oskaloosa, Iowa, Dec. 19, 1926; d. Grover C. and Beulah (Williams) Hawk; m. Walter Francis Davison, June 20, 1953 (div.); 1 child, Linda Ellen. BS in Zoology, Iowa State U., 1948; MS in Biol. Sci., U. Chgo., 1951; MA in Ednl. Psychology and Counseling, Calif. State U., Northridge, 1985. Med. rsch. technician U. Chgo. Med. Sch., 1951-53; tchr. sci. Lane High Sch., Charlottesville, Va., 1953-55; med. rsch. asst. U. Va. Med. Sch., Charlottesville, 1955-56, U. Mich., Ann Arbor, 1956-60; tchr. sci. Monroe High Sch., North Hills, Calif., 1966-98, chmn. sci. dept., 1990-91, sch. site coun., 1993-94, ret., 1998. Rsch. technician Los Alamos Sci. Labs., summer 1954; part-time counselor psychotherapy Forte Found., Encino, Calif., 1987-92, Tarzana, Calif., 1993-2000, Northridge, Calif., 2000—. V.p. San Fernando Valley chpt. Am. Field Svc., 1980-81; vol. counselor Planned Parenthood Am., L.A., 1982-88. NSF fellow, 1985-86. Mem. Calif. Tchrs. Assn., Calif. Assn. Marriage and Family Therapists, Iowa Acad. Sci. (assoc.), AAUW. Avocations: traveling, history, cooking.

DAVIS-TOWNSEND, HELEN IRENE, retired art educator; b. North Adams, Mich., July 25, 1910; d. Bert and Jennie Louisa (Martin) Smith; m. Donald Hicks Davis, Mar. 21, 1931 (dec. Nov. 1944); children: Donald H. Jr., Bernard S., Bruce M., William J.; m. Loal Wendell Townsend, Dec. 27, 1971. BA, Mich. State U., 1952, MA, 1959. Permanent tchg. cert., Mich. Typist, sec. Buermann-Marshall Co., Lansing, Mich., 1928-30; pvt. sec. Frank L. Young, Jr., LLD, Lansing, 1930-31; typist Buermann-Marshall Co., Lansing, 1932-36, Olds Motor Co., Lansing, 1936-37; art tchr. Okemos (Mich.) Pub. Schs., 1952-72. Art club dir. Okemos H.S., 1952-72, tchr. adult edn. classes, 1962-70; supervising tchr. tchr. edn. program Mich. State U., East Lansing, 1960-72; region 8 rep., liaison officer Mich. Art Edn. Assn. State Bd., East Lansing, 1962-70; vis. artist John Wesley Coll., Owosso, Mich., 1979. Author, composer: (children's mus.) That Star Is Shaking Up Our Town, 1974, (song and music) Life Is a Road, 1974; artist numerous paintings. Sec.-typist Mich. Rep. Party, Lansing, 1932; children and youth choir dir. Wesleyan Meth. Ch., Lansing, 1939-72, choir mem., 1929-72; choir mem. Stockbridge (Mich.) United Meth. Ch., 1972-80. Recipient Bonderenco award, 1987; Hinman scholar Mich. State U., 1950, Alumni scholar, 1951-52. Mem. NEA (life), Mich. Edn. Assn. (life), Nat. Mus. of Women in Arts (charter), Art League of Manatee County, Lansing Art Gallery (charter). Methodist. Avocations: painting, playing piano and organ, bowling, theater, traveling.

DAWES, SHARON KAY, elementary school educator; b. Roaring Spring, Pa., Nov. 27, 1951; d. Harold W. and Cora Christine (Baker) Albright; m. Edward L. Dawes; children: Christy Alice, Aaron Russell. BS in Health and Phys. Edn., Slippery Rock State Coll., 1973; Masters Equivalent, Edinboro (Pa.) U., 1977; postgrad., Pa. State U., Harrisburg, U. Pitts., 2002—03. Cert. instructional I health, phys. edn., elem. edn. Elem. tchr. phys. edn. Tyrone (Pa.) Area Sch. Dist., 1973-77; dir. youth and phys. programing Titusville (Pa.) YWCA, 1979-85; substitute tchr. Titusville Area Sch. Dist., 1985-86; phys. edn. specialist St. Titus Elem. Sch., Titusville, 1986-88; asst. tchr. Crawford County Head Start-YWCA, Meadville, Pa., 1988-89; child/family educator Warren Forest Econ. Opportunity Coun., 1989-90; family svc. worker YWCA Twin Creeks Head Start, 1990—. Coach Titusville Youth Soccer League 1990-1996, coach of PA West U18 Soccer Team 1996-1998,Titusville Girls Softball program, 1984-92; asst. leader Girl Scouts U.S., 2002—. Mem. Pa. Assn. for Children and Adults with Learning Disabilities; mem. Ct. Appointed Spl. Adv., 2000-2002. Office: Head Start Titusvill ECLC 330 E Spruce St Titusville PA 16354

DAWICKI, DOLORETTA DIANE, analytical chemist, research biochemist, educator; b. Fall River, Mass., Sept. 13, 1956; d. Walter and Stella Ann (Olszewski) D. BS, S.E. Mass. U., 1978; PhD, Brown U., 1986. Rsch. assoc. Meml. Hosp. R.I., Pawtucket, 1986-92; asst. prof. Brown U., Providence, 1986-96; rsch. assoc. VA Med. Ctr., Providence, 1992-96; quality control tech. svcs. prin. scientist Genzyme Corp., Framingham, Mass., 1996—. Contbr. articles to profl. jours. Mem. AAAS, Am. Soc. for Biochemistry and Molecular Biology, Parenteral Drug Assn. Achievements include research on in vivo antiplatelet mechanism of action of the clinical agent dipyridamole, endothelial cell injury, effects of nucleotides on leukocyte-endothelial cell interaction, assay development, optimization, and validation to monitor drug identity, safety, and efficacy; product testing and quality control release of commercial therapeutic finished drug products. Home: 3 Odyssey Ln Franklin MA 02038-2460 Office: Genzyme Corp PO Box 9322 Framingham MA 01701-9322 E-mail: dale.dawicki@genzyme.com.

DAWKINS, DEBRA, elementary school educator; b. Miami, Fla., Apr. 16, 1950; d. Edmond Rollins and Utha Felts White; m. William Dawkins, Apr. 5, 1975 (div. Nov. 1978); 1 child, Caleb Avery. AA, Miami-Dade Jr. Coll., 1970; BA, Fla. Atlantic U., 1972. Tchr. grade 6 J.W. Johnson Elem. Sch., Hialeah, Fla., 1973-75; tchr. grade 4 J.H. Bright Elem. Sch., Hialeah, 1975-77, tchr. grade 3, 1977-78, compensatory edn. tchr., 1978-80, tchr. grade 5, 1980-85, 89-90, chpt. I facilitator, 1985-89, chpt. I resource tchr., 1990—, dept. chmn., 1993-94. Team writer sch. improvement plan, 1990—; contact person Parent Outreach Program, Hialeah, 1992—; mem. Sch. Adv. Coun., Hialeah, 1992—. Mem. Sch.-Based Mgmt. Shared Decision-Making Cadre, Hialeah, 1990-92; mem. and sec. matron's dept. Nat. Primitive Bapt. Conv. Inc., 1992—; sec. East Fla. Ch. Sch. Conv., 1986—, East Fla. Dist. Primitive Bapt. Assn., 1992—; active Nat. Coalition Title I/Chpt. I Parents. Recipient Appreciation award Dade County Pub. Sch. Chpt. I Program, 1992, Black History Com. of J.H. Bright Elem. Sch., 1991; named Tchr. of Yr., Bright/Johnson Elem. Schs., 1996. Mem. NAACP, Women in the NAACP, United Tchrs. of Dade, Nat. Coalition of Title I/Chpt. I Parents, Zeta Phi Beta. Democrat. Avocations: singing, walking, travel, shopping. Home: 1840 NW 49th St Miami FL 33142-4011

DAWSON, BRUCE ALAN, elementary school educator, software designer; b. Great Falls, Mont., Feb. 3, 1943; s. Frederick Clayton and Helen Marie (Hodges) D.; m. Juleanne Haskey, Aug. 22, 1964 (div. Sept. 1979); children: David Bruce, Michelle Marie; m. Michelle Moore, Nov. 24, 1984. BS, Mont. State U., 1966; MEd, U. Wyo., 1974; PhD, U. Ill., 1989. Math. tchr. Morgan Jr. High Sch., Casper, Wyo., 1968-69; landman Bolex Petroleum Broker, Casper, 1969-70; math. tchr. East Jr. High Sch., Casper, 1970-78; field rep. U. Wyo., Rock Springs, 1979-83; teaching supr., lab. dir. U. Ill., Urbana, 1983-85; computer lab. dir. Eastern Ill. U., Charleston, 1985-86; mgr. multimedia design Maritz Communications Co., St. Louis, 1987-93; systems cons. Systems Svc. Enterprises, Inc., St. Louis, 1993; pres. Dawson Training Svcs., St. Louis, 1994—; 8th grade math. tchr. Hollenbeck Mid. Sch., St. Charles, Mo., 1995—. Lt. U.S. Army, 1966-68. Democrat. Avocations: woodworking, model railroading, camping, travel. Home: 85 Cinnamon Tree Ct Saint Charles MO 63304-7265 E-mail: bruce_dawson@fhsd.k12.mo.us.

DAWSON, CATHY JAYNE, elementary school educator; b. Corpus Christi, Tex., Apr. 2, 1959; d. Richard C. and Esther J. (Zinn) Nieman; m. George H. Dawson Jr., Aug. 14, 1982; 1 child, George Henry III. A degree, Del Mar Jr. Coll., Corpus Christi, 1979; B degree, U. North Tex., 1981. Cert. elem. tchr. Tex., spl. edn. tchr. Tex., gifted and talented tchr. Tex. Elem. spl. edn. tchr. Gregory (Tex.) Portland Ind. Sch. Dist., 1981-85; 3d grade tchr. Lewisville (Tex.) Ind. Sch. Dist., 1985-87; elem. spl. edn. tchr. Woodsboro (Tex.) Ind. Sch. Dist., 1987-89; mid. sch. spl. edn. tchr. Refugio (Tex.) Ind. Sch. Dist., 1989-96, mem. dist. improvement team, 1992-95, mem. supts. adv. coun., 1991-92, sponsor student coun., 1991-95; content mastery tchr. Holleman Elem. Sch., Waller (Tex.) Ind. Sch. Dist., 1996—, chair sci. com., 1997-98. Campus and dist. based decision making team Holleman Elem. Sch., 1998—, drug awareness com., 2000-01, campus vol. coord., 1999-2003, ROPES course facilitator, 2003—, tchr. gifted/talented, 1999—. Vol. ARC, Refugio, 1988-95, summer reading program Nancy Carol Roberts Meml. Libr., Brenham, Tex.; chmn. bd. Good Samaritan Ministries, Refugio, 1993-94; mem. choir 1st United Meth. Ch., Refugio, 1989-95, St. Peter's Episc. Ch., 1996—, EYC sponsor, 1996-97, lay eucharistic min., 1996-2002; mem. vestry St. Peter's Episc. Ch., 2000-03; vol. dir. summer reading program Refugio County Libr., 1988-94; chmn. ptnrs. in ministry com. Ch. of Ascension Episcopal Ch., Refugio; mem. Refugio Cmty. Choir, 1994-95; mem. Leaping Libr. Lizards Band. Mem. Tex. State Tchrs. Assn. (pres. Refugio county chpt. 1988-93; v.p. dist. III chpt. 1988-90, pres. dist. III chpt. 1990-92), Pilot Club, Refugio Woman's Club, Alpha Delta Kappa, Delta Kappa Gamma. Episcopalian. Avocations: reading, needlework, collecting teddy bears, strawberries, santa clauses. Home: 800 S Chappell Hill St Brenham TX 77833-4220

DAWSON, EARL BLISS, obstetrics and gynecology educator; b. Perry, Fla., Feb. 1, 1930; s. Bliss and Linnie (Calliham) D.; m. Winnie Ruth Isbell, Apr. 10, 1951; children: Barbara Gail, Patricia Ann, Robert Earl, Diana Lynn. BA, U. Kans., 1955; postgrad., Bowman Gray Sch. Medicine, 1957-59; MA, U. Mo., 1960; PhD, Tex. A&M U., 1964. Rsch. instr. dept. ob-gyn. U. Tex. Med. Br., Galveston, 1963-65, rsch. asst. prof., 1965-68, rsch. assoc. prof., 1968-89, assoc. prof., 1989—. Cons. Interdeptl. Com. on Nutrition for Nat. Def., 1965-68, Nat. Nutrition Survey, 1968-69. Author: Effect of Water Borne Nitrites on the Environment of Man; contbr. numerous articles to profl. jours., chpts. to books. Scoutmaster Boy Scouts Am., 1969—. With USNR, 1947-52. Nutrition rsch. fellow, 1960-61; scholar NSF, 1961-62; rsch. fellow NIH, 1962-63. Mem. Am. Inst. Nutrition, Am. Soc. Clin. Nutrition, Am. Coll. Nutrition, Am. Fertility Soc., Soc. Exptl. Biology and Medicine, Soc. Environ. Geochemistry and Health, Tex. Acad. Scis., N.Y. Acad. Scis., Mic-O-Say Club (Kansas City, Mo.), Sigma Xi, Phi Rho Sigma. Baptist. Achievements include research on prenatal nutrition, male fertility, epidemiology of lithium in Texas, biochemical changes associated with pre-menstrual syndrome. Home: Apt 8 3431 S Peach Hollow Cir $D Pearland TX 77584-8006 Office: U Tex Med Br Dept Ob-Gyn Galveston TX 77550

DAWSON, KAREN OLTMANNS, nursing educator; b. El Centro, Calif., Mar. 14, 1947; d. Victor Roy and Lois Louise Oltmanns; m. Arthur B. Dawson, Sept. 13, 1970; children: David, Jonathan, Stephen, Matthew, Anna-Lisa. BSN, UCLA, 1969; postgrad., U. Calif., Irvine, 1980; MA, U. Colo., Denver, 1992. Cert. instr. nursing Calif., Colo., pub. health nurse, early childhood spl. edn. instr. Staff nurse, maternal-child Swedish Med. Ctr., Englewood, Colo., 1986-92, parent educator, 1983—; nurse, spl. edn. tchr. Cherry Creek Acad., 1995-97—; adminstr. early intervention ctr. for children with spl. needs, 1997-98; dir., v.p. A. Dawson Tutoring, Inc., 1998—; dir. Children's World ARAMARK Ednl. Svcs. Clin. instr. Aurora Pub. Schs. Vocat. Ctr., C.C. of Denver, Arapahoe C.C., Littleton, Colo.; spl. edn. tchr. Hope Ctr., Denver, 1992-93. Spl. edn. tchr. United Cerebral Palsy Assn., Denver, 1993-95. Mem. Neonatal ICU Connections Task Force, Swedish Med. Ctr. Colo. Consortium for Preterm Infant Devel.

DAWSON-THOMPSON, MARY MARQUETTA, guidance counselor; b. Norwalk, Conn., July 13, 1960; d. John E. and Darlyn F. (Bonner) Dawson; m. Allen Cornelius Thompson, July 7, 1984; children: Joshua Allen Thompson, Jeremy Ashton Thompson. BS, U. Conn., 1983; MS, U. Bridgeport, 1986, 93, 6th yr. cert., 1995. Cert. sch. guidance. Family counseling dir. MDT Counseling, Belrin, Conn., 1991—; guidance counselor Berlin Bd. Edn., 1994; intensive guidance counselor Farmington (Conn.) Bd. Edn., 1995—. Chair, program com. YMCA, 1993—, bd. dirs. sr. programming Shiloh Bapt. Ch. Mem. Am. Counseling Assn., Conn. Counseling Assn., Alpha Kappa Alpha. Baptist. Avocations: reading, aerobics, weight lifting, jogging. Office: Farmington HS 10 Montieth Dr Farmington CT 06032-1041

DAY, ADRIENNE CAROL, artist, art educator; b. Jackson, Miss., Dec. 13, 1955; d. Robert Maxwell and Phyllis Mary (Roberts) D. BFA, U. Okla., 1986; MFA, Ariz. State U., 1990. Adj. instr. Mesa (Ariz.) C.C., 1990; artist-in-residence Arts Coun. Okla., Okla. City, 1991—; vis. lectr. dept. art U. Ctrl. Okla., Edmond, 1993-98; adj. prof. art Okla. City U., 1996—; adj. asst. prof. U. Okla. Coll. Liberal Studies, Norman, 1997—2001; art specialist Western Village Acad., Oklahoma City, 2001—. Coord., organizer Suite Okla. exchange portfolio, 1997. One-woman shows include Ariz. State U., Tempe, 1990, Individual Artists of Okla. exhbn., Okla. City, 1993, ARC Gallery, Chgo., 1995, Leslie Powell Gallery, Lawton, Okla., 1996, U. Southeastern Okla., Durant, 1998; exhibited in group shows at Ariz. State U., Tempe, 1989 (purchase award), Guadalupe Cultural Arts, Ctr., San Antonio, 1989 (cash award), Greenville (N.C.) Mus. Art, 1989, Ind. U., 1989, Shemer Art Ctr. and Mus., Phoenix, 1990, Kirkpatric Ctr. Gallery, Okla. City, 1991, Okla. City Art Mus., 1992, Fla. State U. Mus., Tallahassee, 1993, Corcoran Sch. Art, Washington, 1994-97, U. Ctrl. Okla. Faculty Exhibit, Edmond, 1994-97, Austin Peay U., Clarksville, Tenn., 1994, I.A.O/M.A.R.S. Exchange Exhibit, Phoenix, 1995, Alexander Hogue Gallery, U. Tulsa, Okla., 1997, Truman State U., 1998, Columbia (Mo.) Coll., 1998, Morgan Gallery, Kansas City, 2000, Wichita, Kans., 2001; represented in permanent collections Haarmann and Reimer Corp., Germany, Corcoran Mus., Washington, U. Ctrl. Okla., Fred Jones Mus., Carol Reese Mus., East Tenn. State, U. Tenn., Knoxville, Miss. State U., U. Texas, Tyler, Fellers & Co., Okla. City, U. Fla., Gainsville, Bradley U., Peoria, Ariz. State U., Ohio U., Athens, Brigham Young U., U. Utah, U. Alberta. Recipient Letzeiser Gold medal U. Okla. Sch. Art, Norman, 1987, Abraham and Bessie Lehrer Meml. award Ariz. State U., 1989, faculty purchase award Presdl. Ptrns. U. Ctrl. Olka., Edmond, 1995; first alt. Fourth Annual Nathan Cummings Travel fellow Ariz. State U., 1989; Artist Project grantee Ariz. Commn. on the Arts, 1991, Sudden Opportunity grantee Okla. Visual Arts Coalition, Okla. City, 1992. Democrat. Home and Office: PO Box 6354 Norman OK 73070-6354

DAY, AFTON J. elementary school educator, administrator; b. Murray, Utah, Feb. 11, 1938; d. Hans C. and Eunice (Greenwood) Jensen; m. Sherman R. Day, Dec. 28, 1960; children: Kristin Day Lester, Brad, Sandra Day Barnes. BS, Brigham Young U., 1960; MEd, U. Ga., 1966; EdS, Ga. State U., 1994. Instr. U. Ga., Athens, 1967; instr., supr. Ga. State U., Atlanta, 1968-69; founder The Day Sch. Pre-Sch. and Kindergarten, 1970; tchr., student support coord. King Springs Elem., Smyrna, Ga., 1975-86, adminstrv. asst., 1986-93; learner support strategist Bryant Elem. Sch., Mableton, Ga., 1993-94; tchr. Brumby Elem. Sch., 1994-98. Co-founder Smart Kids; led Brumby teachers in creation of Literacy Suitcases, 1997-98. Author four books; contbr. articles to profl. publs.; developer ednl. program for children Eliminate Your Self Defeating Behaviors. Missionary, Ch. of Jesus Christ of Latter-Day Saints, 1999-2000. Named Reader's Digest Am. Hero in Edn., 1993.

DAY, DONALD LEE, retired engineering educator, researcher; b. Leedey, Okla., Aug. 14, 1931; m. Sarah F. Day; children: Cheryl, Keith, Dennis. BS in Agrl. Engring., Okla. State U., 1954, PhD in Agrl. Engring., 1962; MS in Agrl. Engring., U. Mo., 1958. Registered profl. engr., Ill. Engr. Allis Chalmers Mfg. Co., Milw., 1954; instr. Tex. Tech U., Lubbock, 1957-58; asst. prof. U. Ill., Urbana, 1962-67, assoc. prof., 1967-71, prof., 1971-97; ret., 1994. Adviser UN/WHO, Romania, 1972-75, U.S. Food Grain Coun., USSR, Poland and Czechoslovakia, 1975; cons. Internat. Exec. Svc. Corps., Mex., summer 1978; leader structures and environ. divsn. agrl. engring. dept. U. Ill., 1989-94. Author: Livestock Manure Management, 1983; inventor elec. conversion of organic matter; contbr. articles to profl. jours. Recipient fellowship Japan Soc. for Promotion of Sci., 1992, USDA, Office Internat. Coop. and Devel., 1993, numerous grants. Fellow: Am. Soc. Agrl. Engrs. (Rsch. Paper award 1966); mem.: Aircraft Owners and Pilots Assn., Ill. Pilots Assn., Coun. Agrl. Sci. and Tech., Agrl. Honor Orgns. E-mail: dld@age.uiuc.edu.

DAY, HOWARD WILMAN, geology educator; b. Burlington, Vt., Nov. 17, 1942; s. Wilman Forrest and Virginia Louise (Morton) D.; children: Kristina, Sarah, Susan; m. Judy Lynn Blevins. AB, Dartmouth Coll., 1964; MS, Brown U., 1968, PhD, 1971. From asst. prof. to assoc. prof. geology U. Okla., Norman, 1970-76; from asst. prof. to prof. geology U. Calif., Davis, 1976—, chmn. dept., 1990-96. Co-editor Jour. Metamorphic Geology, 1985-92; contbr. articles to profl. jours. Fulbright fellow, Norway, 1964, Alexander von Humboldt fellow, Fed. Republic Germany, 1977. Fellow Geol. Soc. Am., Mineral Soc. Am.; mem. Am. Geophys. Union. Office: U Calif Dept Geology Davis CA 95616 E-mail: hwday@ucdavis.edu.

DAY, MICHAEL GORDON, information technology executive, educator; b. Madison, Wis., July 30, 1951; s. Lee Monroe and Joan (Meredith) D.; m. Donna Kay Corl, May 26, 1979 (div. Apr. 1986); children: Thomas Lee, Anne Elizabeth; m. Carol Ann Stefanko, Apr. 12, 1997. BA, Pa. State U., 1973; JD, George Washington U., 1976. Bar: Pa. 1976. Assoc. Alan Ellis, Esq., State College, Pa., 1976-77; pvt. practice State College, Pa., 1977-85; with Profl. Planning Cons., State College, Pa., 1985-86, Century Fin. Svcs., State College, Pa., 1986-96; solutions expert Netscape, 1996-99; dir. Info. Tech. Inst./Shepherd Coll., Shepherdstown, W.Va., 1999—. Instr. bus. law Pa. State U., University Park, 1978-79, instr. continuing legal edn., 2002; counsel Boccardo Law Firm, San Jose, Calif., 1983, Rees Law Firm, Washington, 1983; sr. v.p. Century Mortage Corp., 1991-96. Chmn. Com. to Elect Mel Hodes Senator, Pa., 1982, Dem. Com., State College, 1982-84; active Exec. Com. Centre County, 1982-84, United Pennsylvanians, 1982-83; gen. counsel CLEAN, 1982-85; v.p. Mt. Nittany Conservancy, 2000-02; candidate for Pa. Ho. Reps., 1980; candidate for dist. justice 49th Dist. Pa., 1977. Mem. Lions Paw Alumni Assn. (pres. 1999-2001), Parmi Nous, Omicron Delta Kappa, Delta Sigma Rho. United Ch. Of Christ. Office: 400 W Stephen St Martinsburg WV 25401 E-mail: michael@michaelday.org.

DAY, PETER RODNEY, geneticist, educator; b. Chingford, Essex, Eng., Dec. 27, 1928; came to U.S., 1963; m. Lois Elizabeth Rhodes, May 26, 1951; children: Susan Catherine, Rupert Peter, William Rodney. BS in Botany, Birkbeck Coll., Eng., 1950; PhD, U. London, 1954. Sr. scientific officer John Innes Inst., Hertford, Eng., 1957-63; assoc. prof. Ohio State U., Columbus, 1963-64; chief, genetics dept. Conn. Agrl. Expt. Sta., New Haven, 1964-79; dir. Plant Breeding Inst., Cambridge, Eng., 1979-87; prof. genetics, dir. Rutgers U., New Brunswick, NJ, 1987—2002, prof. emeritus, 2002—. Sec. Internat. Genetics Fedn., 1984-93; trustee Internat. Ctr. for Maize and Wheat Improvement, Mexico City, 1986-92; chmn. Mng. Global Genetic Resources Bd. on Agrl., NAS, Washington, 1986-93. Author: Genetics of Host-Parasite Interaction, 1974; co-author: (with J.R.S. Fincham) Fungal Genetics, 1963, (with H.H. Prell) Plant-Fungal Pathogen Interaction, 2001. Commonwealth Fund fellow U. Wis., 1954-56; Guggenheim Meml. fellow U. Queensland, 1972. Home: 394 Franklin Rd New Brunswick NJ 08902 E-mail: day@aesop.rutgers.edu.

DAY, ROBERT ANDROUS, English language educator, former library director, editor, publisher; b. Belvidere, Ill., Jan. 18, 1924; s. Floyd Androus and Mabel May (Dorn) D.; m. Betty Lucy Johnson, Aug. 27, 1949; children— Nancy, Barton, Robin BA, U. Ill., 1949; MS, Columbia U., 1951. Librarian, Sci. and Tech. div. Newark Pub. Library, 1951-53; librarian, editor Inst. Microbiology Rutgers U., 1953-60, dir. Coll. of South Jersey Library, 1960-61; mng. editor Am. Soc. Microbiology, Washington, 1961-80; dir. ISI Press, Phila., 1980-86; v.p. Inst. for Sci. Info., Phila., 1984-86; prof. English, U. Del., Newark, 1986-2000, prof. emeritus, 2000—. Tchr. sci. writing; pub. cons. NSF, NIH, others Author: How to Write and Publish a Scientific Paper, 1979, 5th edit., 1998, Scientific English: A Guide for Scientists and Other Professionals, 1992, 2d edit., 1995. With USAAF, 1943-46. Mem. AAAS, Coun. Science Editors (chmn. 1977-78), Soc. Scholarly Pub. (pres. 1982-84), Am. Med. Writers Assn., Soc. Tech. Comm., European Assn. Sci. Editors, Assn. Tchrs. Tech. Writing. Home: 77 Ritter Ln Newark DE 19711-5174 E-mail: bday@udel.edu.

DAY, ROBERT WINSOR, preventive medicine physician, researcher; b. Framingham, Mass., Oct. 22, 1930; s. Raymond Albert and Mildred (Doty) Day; m. Jane Alice Boynton, Sept. 6, 1957 (div. Sept. 1977); m. Cynthia Taylor, Dec. 16, 1977; children: Christopher, Nathalia, Natalia, Julia. Student, Harvard U., 1949—51; MD, U. Chgo., 1956; MPH, U. Calif., Berkeley, 1958, PhD, 1962. With USPHS, 1956-57; resident U. Calif., Berkeley, 1958-60; research specialist Calif. Dept. Mental Hygiene, 1960-64; asst. prof. Sch. Pub. Health and Sch. Medicine UCLA, 1962-64; dep. dir. Calif. Dept. Pub. Health, Berkeley, 1965-67; prof., chmn. dept. health services Sch. Pub. Health and Community Medicine, U. Wash., Seattle, 1968-72, dean, 1972-82, prof., 1982—; pres., dir. Fred Hutchinson Cancer Rsch. Ctr., Seattle, 1981-97, pres., dir. emeritus, 1997—, mem. pub. health scis., 1997—. Mem. Nat. Cancer Adv. Bd., 1992—98, Nat. Cancer Policy Bd., 1996—2000; chief med. officer Epigenomics, Inc.; sci. dir. Internat. Consortium Rsch. Health Effects Radiation; cons. in field. Fellow: APHA, AAAS, Am. Coll. Preventive Medicine; mem.: Am. Assn. Cancer Insts. (bd. dirs. 1983—87, v.p. 1984—85, pres., chmn. bd. dirs.), Assn. Schs. Pub. Health (pres. 1981—82), Am. Assn. Cancer Rsch., Am. Soc. Preventive Oncology, Am. Soc. Clin. Oncology. Office: 1872 E Hamlin St Seattle WA 98112 E-mail: dlcllc@comcast.net.

DAY, STACEY BISWAS, medical educator; b. London, Dec. 31, 1927; came to U.S. 1955, naturalized 1977. s. Satis B. and Emma L. (Camp) D.; m. Ivana Podvalova, Oct. 18, 1973; 2 children. MD, Royal Coll. Surgeons, Dublin, Ireland, 1955; PhD, McGill U., 1964; DSc, Cin. U., 1971. Intern King's County Hosp., SUNY Downstate Ctr., 1955-56; resident fellow in surgery U. Minn. Hosp., 1956-60; hon. registrar St. George's Hosp., London, Eng., 1960-61; lectr. exptl. surgery McGill U., Montreal, Que., Can., 1964; asst. prof. exptl. surgery U. Cin. Med. Sch., 1968-70; assoc. dir. basic med. rsch. Shriner's Burn Inst., Cin., 1969-71; from asst. to assoc. prof. pathology, head Bell Mus. Pathobiology U. Minn., Mpls., 1970-74; dir. biomed. comm. and med. edn. Sloan-Kettering Inst., N.Y.C., 1974-80; mem. Sloan-Kettering Inst. for Cancer Rsch., 1974-80; mem. adminstrv. coun., field coordinator, 1974-75; prof. biology Sloan Kettering divsn. Grad. Sch. Med. Sci. Cornell U., 1974-80; clin. prof. medicine divsn. behavioral medicine N.Y. Med. Coll., 1980-92; prof. biopsychosocial medicine, chmn. dept. community health U. Calabar (Nigeria) Sch. Medicine, 1982-85; prof. internat. health, dir. Internat. Ctr. for Health Scis. Meharry Med. Coll., Nashville, 1985-89, dir. WHO Collaborating Ctr. ICHS, 1987-89; founding dir. WHO Collaborating Ctr., Nashville, 1987-89, emeritus dir., 1989; adj. prof. family and cmty. medicine U. Ariz. Coll. Med. Scis., Tucson, 1985-89; univ. prof. internat. health U. Calabar, Nigeria, 1989—; permanent vis. prof. med. edn. Oita Med. Univ., Japan, 1992-99. Arris and Gale lectr. Royal Coll. Surgeons, England, 1972; vis. lectr., Ireland, 72; vis. prof. U. Bologna, 1977, Kyushu, Japan, 90, U. Mauritius, 1991, Bratislava U., 1991, U. Tokyo, Japan, 1992—93, U. Nagasaki, Japan, 1992—93, Beijing, 1993; vis. prof. health comm. U. Santiago, Chile, 1979—80, Colombo, Sri Lanka, 1996; vis. prof. Oncologic Rsch. Inst., Tallinn, Estonia, 1976, All India Insts. Health, 1976, U. Maidugari, 1982, Veclore U., India, 1996, De Quito, Ecuador, 1996; vis. acad. Oxford (Eng.) U., 1993—95; moderator med. cartography and computer health Harvard U., 1978, Acad. Scis., Czech Republic, 1987, Australia, 88; Fulbright prof. Charles U., Czech Republic, 1989; prof. (hon.) Coll. Health Scis. U. San Francisco de Quito (Ecuador), 1996; cons. Pam Am. Health Assn., 1974—90, U.S.-USSR Agreement for Health Cooperation, 1976, WHO Collaborating Ctr. Meharry Med. Coll., Nashville, 1985, NAFEO/USAID, 1986—89; mem. expert com. for health, manpower devel. WHO, 1986—90, cons. divsn. strengthening health care resources, 1987—90, UN-FSSTD, 1987, AID/Joint Memorandum of Understanding W. Africa, Kenya, 1987—89, South Africa, 1987—89, Sudan, 1985—89; cons. to dean med. coll. faculty med. and health scis. ABHA, Asir, Saudi Arabia, 1981; cons. to dir. High Tatras symposia Post Grad. Med. Inst., Bratislava, 1990—; cons. to rector U. Autónoma Agraria Antonio Narro, Saltillo, Mexico, 1987—89; pres., chmn. Pub. Cultural and Ednl. Prodns., Montreal, Canada, 1966—85; bd. dirs., v.p. Am. Sci. Activities Mario Negri Found., 1975—80; bd. dirs. Internat. Health, African Health Consultancy Svc., Nigeria, Ekologia & Zivot, Slovakia; founding chmn. (hon.), bd. dirs. Lambo Found. U.S.; v.p., trustee Cancer Relief Found., Calabar; pres., exec. dir. Internat. Found. Biosocial Devel. and Human Health, 1978—86, chmn., 1986—; mem. Medzinárodny Poradny Vybor Nadácie Ekológia Zivot, Slovakia, 1995—; cons. Inst. Health, Lyfford Cay, Bahamas, 1981, Govt. Cross River State, Nigeria, Itreto State and H.H. Obong of Calabar, Nat. Bd. Advisors, Am. Biog. Inst., 1982—; cons. cmty. health and health comms. Navaho Nation, Sage Meml. Hosp., Ganado, Ariz., 1984; founder, cons. Primary Self-Health Clinics, Oban, Ikot Oku Okono and Ikot Imo, Nigeria, 1982—84; cons. High Tatras Internat. Health Symposia, Slovakia, 1990—; apptd. ab. Gov. State of Tenn., 1986—; adj. clin. prof. medicine N.Y. Med. Coll.; prof. (hon.) Colegio Ciencias Salud U. San Francisco, Quito, 1965—; vis. prof. U. San Francisco, 1996. Author: (verse) Collected Lines, 1966, (plays) By the Waters of Babylon, 1966, (verse) American Lines, 1967, (plays) The Music Box, 1967, Three Folk Songs Set to Music, 1967, Poems and Etudes, 1968, (novels) Rosalita, 1968, The Idle Thoughts of a Surgical Fellow, 1968, Edward Stevens-Gastric Physiologist, Physician and American Statesman, 1969, Letters to Ivana from Calabar, 2001, (novella) Bellechasse, 1970, A Leaf of the Chaatim, 1970, Ten Poems and a Letter from America for Mr. Sinha, 1971, Curling's Ulcer: An Experiment of Nature, 1972, Tuluak and Amaulik: Dialogues on Death and Mourning with the Innuit Eskimo of Point Barrow and Wainwright, Alaska, 1974, East of the Navel and Afterbirth: Reflections from Rapa Nui, 1976, Health Communications, 1979, The Biopsychosocial Imperative, 1981, What Is Survival: The Physician's Way and the Biologos, 1981, Developing Health in the West African Bush, 1995; author: (in Czech) Moudrost Samuraju, 1998; author: Selected Poems and Embers of a Medical Life, 1999, In the Shadow of the Bush - Letters from Calabar, 1999-2000, 2000, Vitaesophia of Integral Humanism, 2001, The Klacelka in a Slavic Woodland, 2003; editor: Death and Attitudes Toward Death, 1972, Membranes, Viruses and Immune Mechanisms in Experimental and Clinical Disease, 1972, Ethics in Medicine in a Changing Society, 1973, Communication of Scientific Information, 1975, Trauma: Clinical and Biological Aspects, 1975, Molecular Pathology, 1975; editor: (with Robert A. Good) (series) Comprehensive Immunology, 9 vols., 1976—80; editor: Cancer Invasion and Metastasis-Biologic Mechanisms and Therapy, 1977, Some Systems of Biological Communication, 1977, Image of Science and Society, 1977, What Is A Scientist?, 1978, Sloan Kettering Inst. Cancer Series, 1974—80; editor: (with K. Inokouchi) Selections from the Chronicle of the Hagakure as Wisdom Literature: The Way of The Samurai of Saga Domain, 1993; editor-in-chief, mem. editl. bd. Health Communications and Informatics, 1974—80, editor in chief The American Biomedical Network: Health Care System in America Present and Past, 1978, A Companion to the Life Sciences, Vol. 1, 1979, A Companion to the Life Sciences, Vol. 2, Integrated Medicine, 1980, A Companion to the Life Sciences, Vol. 3, Life Stress, 1981, Advance to Biopsychosocial Health, 1984, editor in chief, mem. editorial bd. Health Communications and Biopsychosocial Health; editor (with others): Cancer, Stress and Death, 1979, 2nd edit., 1986; editor: Computers for Medical Office and Patient Management, 1981, Readings in Oncology, 1980, Biopsychosocial Health, 1981, Primary Health Care Guidelines: A Training Manual for Community Health, 2nd edit., 1986; editor: (with T.A. Lambo) Contemporary Issues in International Health, 1989; sr. editor, with Salat and others Health and Quality of Life in Changing Europe in the Year 2000, 1992, sr. editor, with H. Koga Hagakure-Spirit of Bushido, 1993, sr. editor, with K. Inokuchi Selections from the Chronicles of the Hagakure as Wisdom Literature: The Way of the Samurai of Saga Domain, 1993, sr. editor, with Salát Health Management, Organization, and Planning in Changing Eastern Europe, 1993, sr. editor, with M. Kobayashi and K. Inokuchi, in Japanese The Medical Student and the Mission of Medicine in the Twenty First Century, 1995, sr. editor The Wisdom of Hagakure, 1996, Developing Health in the West African Bush, 2 parts, 1995, Letters of Owen Wagensteen to a Surgical Fellow: with a memoir, 1996, Man and Mu: The Cradle of Becoming and Unbecoming, 1997, Czech Caesura: Golden Prague and the Black Years (Notes from Diaries 1970-1990), 1998, Moudrost Samuraju Trigon (in Czech), 1998, Poems and Embers of a Medical Life, 1998, The Surgical Treatment of Ischaemic Heart Disease with An Account of the Coronary and Intercoronary Circulation in Man and Animals, 1999, Introduction-Comprehensive Medicine (Oriental-Occidental Overview), 2000, Letters to Ivana from Calabar, 2001, Purkynje Address and Other Health Care Lectures Czechoslovakia 1989-1999, 2002, Pliskova's Butterflies-When God Says Enough, 2003, mem. editl. bd. Annual Reviews on Stress, Jour. Stress, cons. editl. bd. Comprehensive Medicine (Japan), Wilhelm Von Humboldt Über Die Unter Dem Namen Bhagavad Gita with commentary, 2001, Purkyne Address and Other Healthcare Lectures, 1989-1999; co-editor: various publs.; contbr. articles; prodr.: TV and health edn. programs, 1982—85, (TV film) Onchocerciasis - River Blindness in Africa, 1988. Served with Brit. Army, 1946-49. Recipient Moynihan medal Assn. Surgeons Gt. Britain and Ireland, 1960, Reuben Harvey triennial prize Royal Coll. Physicians, Ireland, 1957, Arris and Gale award Royal Coll. Surgeons, Eng., 1972, disting. scholar award Internat. Communication Assn., 1980, Sama Found. medal, 1982, disting. citation Hagakure Soc., 1992, Nat. Svc. medal Royal Brit. Legion, 1993; named to Hon. Order Ky. Cols., 1968; named Chieftan Ntufam Ajan of Oban Ejagham People, Cross River State, Nigeria, 1983; hon. prof. Del Colegio De Ciencas De La Salud De La Universidad San Francisco De Quito, 1996; recipient Chieftan Obong Nsong Idem Ibibio Nigeria, 1983, Mgbe (Ekpe) honor Nigeria, commendation WHO address Fed. Govt. Nigeria, Calabar, 1983, Leadership in Internat. Med. Health citation Pres. U.S., 1987, WHO medal, 1987, Agromedicine citation Commr. of Agr., State of Tenn., 1987, Assembly citation State of N.Y., 1987, Citation Congl. Record., 1987; Maestro Honorifo, U. Autonoma Agraria, Coahuila, Mex., 1987; presented Key to the City of Nashville, 1987; recipient Vice-Chancellor's Citation and Presentation for Primary Health Care Teaching in Nigeria, U. Calabar, 1988; Pamétni medal Postgrad. Med. Coll., Prague, 1991, Gold medal U. of Bratislava, 1991, Disting. Citation Hagakure Rsch. Soc., Japan, 1992, Nat. Svc. medal Royal Brit. Legion, 1993, Citation Commendation from Pres. Kyoto Prefectural U. Medicine, Japan, 1993, Citation Commendation on Contbn. to Med. Edn. from Pres. Oita Med. U., Japan, 1997; addresses presented by people of Ikot Imo, Nsit Anyang, Oban, 1982-84, Commendation from King of Calabar, 1984; Ciba fellow Can., 1965; Stacey Day Ward named in his honor by Fed. Min. and Gov. of Cross River State, Calabar Med. Ctr., Nigeria, 1986; charter mem. U.S. Normandy Com., 1988; 1st fgn. hon. mem. Hagakure Res. Soc. (Samurai), Kyushu, Japan, 1991. Fellow: African Acad. Med. Scis. (founder), African Acad. Sci., World Acad. Arts and Scis., Japanese Found. for Biopsychosocial Health (internat. hon. fellow and most disting. mem.), Zool. Soc. London Royal Micros. Soc., Royal Soc. Health; mem.: APHA, AMA, AAS, Adelaide Hosp. Soc. (Ireland), Soc. Med. Geographers USSR, Am. Rural Health Assn. (v.p. internat. sci. affairs, bd. dirs.), Am. Anthrop. Assn., Am. Inst. Stress (bd. dirs.), Am. Assn. History Medicine, N.Y. Acad. Scis., Can. Authors Assn., Internat. Burn Assn., Am. Burn Assn. Home: 6 Lomond Ave Chestnut Ridge NY 10977 E-mail: biosocmed@aol.com.

DAYAL, VIJAY SHANKER, medical educator, physician; b. Ranchi, Bihar, India, Sept. 20, 1936; came to U.S., 1986; s. Ram Shanker Dayal and Vindhyachal (Devi) Devi; m. Susheela Sadhu, Oct. 10, 1961; children: Aneeta, Anjali, Amit. MBBS, Patna (India) Med. Coll., 1959; MSc, McGill U., Montreal, Can., 1966. Resident in otolaryngology McGill U., Montreal, 1960-61, 62-64, resident in surgery, 1961-62; clin. tchr. U. Toronto (Can.), 1967-68, asst. prof., 1968-75, assoc. prof., 1975-81, prof., 1981-86, U. Chgo., 1986—. Mem. editl. bd. Am. Jour. Otolaryngology, 1989—, Otolaryngology Head and Neck Surgery, 1990; author: Clinical Otolaryngology, 1981; contbr. over 70 articles to profl. jours. V.p. Am. Neurotology Soc., 1983-84. Fellow Am. Acad. Otolaryngology, Am. Otological Soc., Am. Trilogical Soc., Barany Soc. Achievements include patent (with others) for Artificial Replacement for Larynx. Office: U Chgo Dept Surgery 5841 S Maryland Ave # 412 Chicago IL 60637-1463

DAYHARSH, VIRGINIA FIENGO, secondary school educator; b. New Haven, Dec. 2, 1942; d. Edward Arthur and Rose (Giaquinto) Fiengo; m. George R. Dayharsh, Dec. 31, 1966 (div. Nov. 1983; children: Regina Lynn Santanello, Jennifer Allison Mullen. BA, Coll. of New Rochelle, N.Y., 1964; MA, So. Conn. State U., 1974, cert. advanced study, 1985. Cert. social studies tchr., Conn. Tchr. Troup Jr. High Sch., New Haven, 1964-65, East Haven (Conn.) Jr. High Sch., 1965-69; tchr., dept. chairperson Lauralton Hall, Milford, Conn., 1979-81; tchr. Nathan Hale Ray High Sch., East Haddam, Conn., 1981-85, Naugatuck (Conn.) High Sch., 1985—2002. Mem. Rep. Town Com., East Haven, 1968-72, Library Bd., East Haven, 1968-81, Bd. of Edn., East Haven, 1986-87. Mem., Conn. Coun. Social Studies, Conn. Social Studies Coun., Coun. Cath. Women, New Eng. Assn. Schs. and Colls. (evaluation com. 1990, 91, 93, 94), New Eng. Assn. History Tchrs., East Haven Hist. Assn. Home: 1360 N High St East Haven CT 06512-1156

DAY-LEBLANC, MARIA ANNE, special education educator, reading specialist; b. Granite City, Ill., Dec. 12, 1962; d. Leon LeBlanc and Marjorie Anne (Whitener) LeBlanc; m. Dennis Alan Day, Mar. 20, 1982. BS in Spl.Edn., So. Ill. U., 1984; MS in Secondary Edn., 1993. Cert. in spl. edn., reading, Ill. Tchr. Beverly Farm, Godfrey, Ill., 1983-84; preschool tchr. Headstart Program, Alton, Ill., 1984-85; spl. edn. tchr. ARC Madison County, Wood River, Ill., 1985-86; habilitation specialist Bellefontaine Habilitation Ctr., St. Louis, 1986-87; spl. end. tchr. Cath. Children's Home, Alton, 1987-90, ednl. coord., 1990-94, asst. ednl. dir., 1994—. GED isntr. LCCC, Godfrey, 1989-93. Jr. League grantee, 1992—. Mem. Internat. Reading Assn., Kappa Delta Pi. Avocations: antiques, reading, aerobics. Home: 4054 E Pelot Ln Alton IL 62002-7923 Office: Cath Children's Home 1400 State St Alton IL 62002-3410

DAYMON, JOY JONES, school psychology specialist; b. Prescott, Ark. d. Coy A. and Alma E. (Honea) Jones; m. Jack C. Daymon, May 3, 1947; children: Jim, Michael, David, Deborah. BA, Long Beach State Coll.; MS in Ednl. Psychology, U. So. Calif., 1974; student, UCLA. Cert. elem. tchr., sch. psychologist specialist, Ark.; lic. profl. counselor, Ark. Tchr. Redondo Beach (Calif.) Sch. Dist.; ednl. examiner El Dorado (Ark.) Schs. Adj. instr. So. Ark. U., Magnolia; presenter workshop on assessment of severe and multi-handicapped various state and nat. convs. Author: Rabbit Pancakes, 1995, Princess Diana the Lamb to the Slaughter, 2002. Mem. NASP (state del., 1984-86), APA, Ark. Psychol. Assn. (treas. 1978-80), Ark. Sch. Psychologists Assn. (state del.), Ark. Counseling Assn., Nat. Bd. Cert. Counselors, Ark. Assessment in Counseling (pres., 1980-81), Delta Kappa Gamma (pres. 1986-87), Phi Delta Kappa. Home: 2202 N Wyatt Dr El Dorado AR 71730-9262 Office: 108 Randolph El Dorado AR 71730

D'CRUZ, OSMOND JEROME, research scientist, educator; b. Mangalore, Karnataka, India, Sept. 27, 1953; s. Francis Salvadore and Juliana Angelina (Pinto) D'C.; m. Ruby Lynne Waters, Jan. 4, 1985; 1 child, Lauren Allison. BSc, U. Mysore, India, 1973, MSc, 1975; PhD, Indian Inst. Sci., 1982. Faculty instr. U. Okla. Health Sci. Ctr., Oklahoma City, 1990-92, asst. prof., 1992-96; dir. fertility rsch. program Hughes Inst., St. Paul, 1996—, dir. reproductive biology dept., 1997—. Author: Iwanami Immunology Series, 1985, Insect Immunity, 1992; co-author: Antisperm Antibodies, 1995; contbr. articles to profl. jours. including Immunology, Orgyn-Internat. Prin. investigator Rockefeller Found., 1993—; NIH grantee. Mem. AAAS, Am. Soc. for Reproductive Medicine (Gen. Program prize 16th World Congress of Fertility and Sterility 1998), Am. Soc. for Reproductive Immunology (New Investigator award 1990), Soc. for Biology of Reproduction, Internat. Soc. Assisted Reproductive Tech./Andrology (Young Investigator award 1996). Roman Catholic. Achievements include 6 patents for the development of novel microbicides and contraceptives. Home: PO Box 270338 Saint Paul MN 55127-0338 Office: Parker Hughes Inst Reproductive Biology Dept 2657 Patton Rd Saint Paul MN 55113 E-mail: odcruz@ih.org.

DEAK, ISTVAN, historian, educator; b. Szekesfehervar, Hungary, May 11, 1926; came to U.S., 1956, naturalized, 1962; s. Istvan and Anna (Timar) D.; m. Gloria Gilda Alfano, July 4, 1959; 1 dau., Eva., U. Budapest, 1945-48; student, Sorbonne, 1950-51, U. Md., Munich, W. Ger., 1953-55; MA, Columbia U., 1958, PhD, 1964. Journalist, librarian and bookseller, Budapest, Paris and Munich, 1945-56; instr. history Smith Coll., 1962-63; mem. faculty Columbia U., 1963—, prof. history, 1973-93, Seth Low prof. History, 1993-97, emeritus prof., 1997—. Mem. Inst. Advanced Study, Princeton, N.J., fall 1981; pres. Conf. on Slavic and East European History, 1985. Author: Weimar Germany's Left-Wing Intellectuals: A Political History of the Weltbühne and Its Circle, 1968, The Lawful Revolution: Louis Kossuth and the Hungarians, 1848-1849, 1979, Hungarian edit., 1983, 2d edit., 1994, German edit., 1989, Beyond Nationalism: A Social and Political History of the Habsburg Officer Corps, 1848-1918, 1990, German edit., 1991, 2d edit., 1995, Hungarian edit., 1993, Italian edit., 1994, Essays on Hitler's Europe, 2001, Hungarian edit., 2003; co-editor: Eastern Europe in the 1970's, 1972, Everyman in Europe: Essays in Social History, 2 vols., 2d edit., 1981, 3d edit., 1989, The Politics of Retribution in Europe: World War II and its Aftermath, 2000. Recipient Lionel Trilling Book award Columbia U., 1979 George Washington award Hungarian-Am. Assn., 1999; German Acad. exch. fellow, 1960-61; Guggenheim fellow, 1970-71; Fulbright-Hays travel fellow, 1973, 84-85; fellow Woodrow Wilson Ctr. for Scholars, Washington, 1985 Mem. Hungarian Acad. Scis., Am. Hist. Assn.,

Am. Assn. Advancement Slavic Studies (Wayne S. Vuchinich Book prize). Home: 410 Riverside Dr New York NY 10025-7974 Office: Columbia U 1209 B Internat Affairs Bldg New York NY 10027

DEAL, BARBARA PICKEL, mathematics educator; b. Bristol, Tenn., May 25, 1936; d. Robert Roger and Willa McCarter Pickel; m. W. Ed Deal; children: Sara Inscho Johnson, Paula Inscho Trentham. AA, BS, Tenn. Wesleyan Coll., 1957; MS, U. Tenn., Knoxville, 1977; postgrad., U. of the South, 1962-66. Cert. tchr., Tenn. Tchr. math. Sevier County H.S., Sevierville, Tenn., 1957-58, Cocoa (Fla.) H.S., 1958-62, Princeton (N.J.) H.S., 1963-65; assoc. prof. math. Hiwassee Coll., Madisonville, Tenn., 1966-69, 85-88; tchr. math. Madisonville H.S., 1972-83, Maryville (Tenn.) H.S., 1983-85, 88-96; instr. math. Maryville Coll., 1996-2000, Maryville Christian Sch., 1998—. Adj. prof. math. Tenn. Wesleyan Coll., Athens, 1983-85; part-time math. tchr. Maryville Christian Sch., 1998—. Co-author: Basic Skills Practice Book, 1986. V.p. Monroe County Dem. Women, Madisonville, 1990-92; mem. Maryville Coll. Cmty. Choir, 1992-93, 94-95; tchr. Sunday sch. 1st Bapt. Ch., Madisonville, 1990-92; mem. Blount County (Tenn.) Juvenile Ct. Foster Care Rev. Bd., 1995—; mem. Broadway United Meth. Ch. Choir, 1997—; vol. music program Asbury Acres Retirement Home. Recipient Tandy Tech. Scholars award of excellence in math., sci. and computer sci. Tandy Found., 1994, Friend of Wesleyan award Tenn. Wesleyan Coll., 2002; NSF grantee, 1962-66; named Tchr. of Yr., Hiwassee Coll., 1986-87. Mem. East Tenn. Edn. Assn. (pres. 1982-83, exec. com. 1976-84), Maryville Edn. Assn. (pres. 1991-92), Tenn. Math Tchrs. Assn., Smoky Mountain Math. Educators Assn., Nat. Ret. Tchrs. Assn., Tenn. Ret. Tchrs. Assn., Blount County Ret. Tchrs. Assn. Methodist. Home: 6812 Resolute Rd Knoxville TN 37918-9762 Office: Maryville Christian Sch 2525 Morganton Rd Maryville TN 37801

DEAL, THERRY NASH, college dean; b. Iredell County, N.C., Apr. 21, 1935; d. Stephen W. and Betty (Sherrill) Nash; m. J.B. Deal, July 10, 1954 (dec. 1990); children: Melaney Dawne, J. Bradley. BS in Home Econs., U. N.C., 1957, MS, 1961, PhD in Child Devel., 1965; postgrad., Harvard U., 1964, 87. Instr. pub. schs., Iredell County, N.C., 1959-61; instr. U. N.C., Greensboro, 1961-65; prof. U. Ga., Athens, 1965-72; dept. chair Ga. Coll., Milledgeville, 1972-82, dir. continuing edn. and pub. svcs., 1982-84, dean continuing edn. and pub. svcs., 1984-95, dean emeritus, 1996—. Bd. dirs. Pvt. Industry Coun., Baldwin Co.; vis. prof. Lanzhou Comml. Coll., China, 1993; participant World Conf. on Women, Beijing, 1995; appointed mem. Ga. Child Coun. Author numerous poems; contbr. articles to profl. jours. Mem. Am. Home Econs. Assn., Nat. Coun. Adminstrs. of Home Econs., Nat. Assn. Edn. of Young Children, Milledgeville/Baldwin County C. of C., DAR., Phi Kappa Phi, Omicron Nu, Delta Kappa Gamma. Democrat. Methodist. Office: Ga Coll Clark St Milledgeville GA 31061

DEAL, WILLIAM BROWN, physician, educator, author, medical school dean; b. Durham, N.C., Oct. 4, 1936; s. Harold Albert and Louise (Brown) D.; m. April Autrey, May 2, 1998; children: Kimberly Deal Wolpert, Kathleen Louise. AA, Mars Hill Coll., 1956; AB, U. N.C., 1958, MD, 1963. Intern in medicine U. Fla. Hosp., Gainesville, 1963-64, asst. resident, 1966-68, fellow in infectious diseases Gainsville, 1968—69, chief resident, instr. dept. medicine Gainesville, 1969-70; asst. prof. dept. medicine U. Fla., 1970-73, assoc. dean Coll. of Medicine, 1973-77, assoc. prof. dept. cmty. health and family medicine, 1973-75, assoc. prof. dept. medicine, 1973-75, prof., 1975-88, acting dean Coll. of Medicine, 1977-78, dean Coll. of Medicine, v.p. clin. affairs, 1978-88, clin. prof. medicine, 1988—; assoc. dean, prof. medicine U. Ala. Sch. of Medicine, 1991-96, sr. assoc. dean, prof. medicine, 1996-97, dean, 1997—; interim CEO UAB Health Sys., 1998-99; v.p. medicine U. Ala., Birmingham, 2000—. Pres. Maine Med. Ctr. Found., Portland, Maine, 1988—90; asst. to sr. v.p. AMA, 1980; lectr. Northwestern U., 1980; vis. clin. tutor City Hosp. U. Edinburgh, Scotland, 1967; bd. dirs. U. Ala. Health Sys., UAB Health Svcs. Found., Callahan Eye Found. Hosp., UAB Med. West, Children's-Women's Health Sys. Contbr. articles to numerous profl. jours. Fellow: ACP, Royal Soc. Medicine; mem.: AMA (chmn. governing coun. sect. on med. schs. 1986—87, liaison com. on med. edn. 1982—87, exec. com. AAMC 1986—88), Nat. Com. Fgn. Med. Edn./Accreditation, Med. Assn. of the State of Ala., Jefferson County Med. Soc., Nat. Rural Health Assn., Ala. Rural Health Assn., Zool. Soc. of Ala., Noble Order of the Flea, Alpha Omega Alpha (bd. dirs. 1986—95, pres. 1993—95), Beta Theta Pi, Phi Chi. Office: Sch of Med FOT 1203, UAB Birmingham AL 35294-0001

DEAN, CHARLES THOMAS, industrial arts educator, academic administrator; b. Humboldt, Nebraska, Feb. 11, 1918; s. Asa Franklin and Carrie Myrtle (Mort) D.; m. Marjorie Ellen (Kennedy), Apr. 11, 1941; children: Carolyn Kay, Thomas Alan, Nancy Ann. BA(hon.), Peru State Tchrs. Coll., Nebr., 1942; MS, Iowa State U., 1948, PhD, 1951. mem. Calif. State Bd. Vocat. Examiners, 1965—. Tchr. sci. and indsl. arts Indianola H.S., Iowa, 1946-47; asst. prof. indsl. edn. Iowa State U., Ames, Iowa, 1947-51; prof. indsl. arts Calif. State Coll., Long Beach, Calif., 1952—, chmn. div. applied arts and scis., 1962—; dean Sch. Applied Arts and Sci. Calif. State U., Long Beach, Calif., 1967-80, dean emeritus, 1980—, dir. aerospace program, 1956-76, dir. Cambodian Contract, 1963-68; v.p. Overseas Constrn. Svc. Co., 1980-87. Mem. tech. adv. coms. Compton (Calif.) Coll., Harbor Jr. Coll., L.A., Orange Coast Coll., Costa Mesa, Calif., El Camino (Calif.) Coll., Calif. Curriculum Com. Indsl. Arts Edn.; membership com. Am. Council Indsl. Arts Tchr. Educators, 1957-86; cons. tech. edn., Cambodia, 1962-69; cons. AID, Swaziland, 1979; dir. rsch. project NASA, 1962-64, 66; cons. tech. and vocat. edn. U.S. Office Edn. Co-author: Principles of Electricity, 1950; Editor: Wade Reynolds, The Man and His Art, 1968; Contbg. chapters to yearbooks. Mem. bd. mgmt. Armed Svc. YMCA, Long Beach, 1968-74, Long Beach coun. United Way, 1969; bd. dirs. Long Beach Pacific Hosp., chmn., 1978-80, mem. corp. bd. 1998-; bd. dirs. 49'er Athletic Found., Long Beach Pacific Hosp. Found., ARC, Molina Med. Group, 1995—, Long Beach Pvt. Industry Coun., 1995—, Long Beach Health Sys., 1984—; mem. Calif. Student Aid Commn., 1969-78, Long Beach Cmty. Devel. Coun., 1996—; trustee Long Beach C.C., 1979-92, pres., bd. trustees, 1981-83, 88-90, mem. exec. com., 1990-93; cons. Samoa C.C., 1978; chmn. Calif. Post secondary Edn. Commn., 1986-88, Calif. Coun. for Pvt. Post secondary and Vocat. Edn., 1990—; mem. com. of 18 Long Beach NCCJ, 1982-85, Calif. Commn. for Tech. Edn., 1990-91; vice-chmn. Long Beach Mayor's Task Force for Edn., 2000, 1985; bd. dirs. New Sch. Arch., 1985-89. lt.(j.g.) USNR, 1943-45, 51-52; capt. Res. ret. Recipient Louise Mears Geog. Award Peru State Tchrs. Coll., 1941; Air Power Award 1st Res. Squadron, Air Force Assn., 1960; named Outstanding Aviation Educator for Calif., 1961; recipient Aero. Space citation Calif. Aero. Commn., 1962, Merit Award citation aviation edn. FAA, 1958, 64, 69, Aerospace Edn. Leadership Award CAP, 1966, 69, 72, Golden Eagle Award Long Beach Pacific Hosp. Found., 1990, many others; named to Hall of Honor Nat. Aerospace Congress, 1976 Mem. Am. Indsl. Arts Assn. (co-chmn. nat. conv. 1959), Calif. Indsl. Edn. Assn. (pres. So. sect. 1958, co-chmn. conv. 1958, 88, chmn. conv. 1982, pres. 1965-66), Calif. Aviation Edn. Assn. (v.p. 1960), Am. Vocat. Assn., Nat. Assn. Indsl. and Tech. Tchr. Educators (hon. mem.), Internat. Platform Assn., Calif. Coast U. Alumni Assn. (pres. 1981-87), Long Beach Exch. Club (Citizen of Yr. award 1988), Blue Key, Masons, Epsilon Pi Tau (hon. life), bd. dirs. 1979-2002, pres. bd. dirs. 1983-85, 90-92), Sigma Alpha Epsilon, Beta Beta Beta, Phi Delta Kappa, Psi Chi, Phi Kappa Phi (lectr. of year 1970), Kappa Delta Pi, Gamma Sigma Delta. Presbyterian (elder, trustee). Home: 9641 Sundune Rd Sun Lakes AZ 85248

DEAN, JOHN F. retired school system administrator; b. Bridgeport, Conn., Nov. 15, 1926; s. James Henry and Mary McKay Dean; m. Katherine Nisbet, Aug. 28, 1949; children: Karol M. Hicks, Brian R. BS in Edn., U. So. Calif., 1950; MA, Calif. State U., 1955; EdD, U. So. Calif., 1966. Tchr. Newport Beach (Calif.) Sch. Dist., 1950-56, elem. sch. prin., 1956-61, dir. curriculum, 1961-69; dean Orange Coast C.C., Costa Mesa, Calif., 1969-70; prof. edn. Whittier (Calif.) Coll., 1970-91; supt. of schs. Orange County Dept. Edn., Costa Mesa, 1991-2001, emeritus, 2001—. Author: Teaching in America, 1978. Bd. dirs. Hoag Meml. Hosp., Newport Beach, Calif., 1972—2003. With USN, 1944—46. Republican. Presbyterian. Avocation: professional writing. Home: 1136 Highland Dr Newport Beach CA 92660-5618

DEAN, NAT, artist, educator; b. Redwood City, Calif., Jan. 13, 1956; d. Richard William and Marianne Ridley (Smith) D.; m. Paul Singdahlsen, May 24, 1987. Student, Calif. Inst. of Arts, 1972-76, Cooper Union Coll., 1975; BFA, San Francisco Art Inst., 1977. Freelance artist, educator, Fla./Calif, 1978-95; annual workshop leader, lectr. Calif. Inst. of Arts, Valencia, 1985—; dir. career planning Calif. Inst. Arts, Valencia, 1986-89; dir. of career ctr. Ringling Sch. of Art and Design, Sarasota, Fla., 1989-92; conf. co-organizer Arts Placment Profls. Groups, 1989, 91, 92, 93; pres., owner Ruta Zinc Fine Arts Agy., San Francisco, NY and L.A., 1980-89; freelance artist, educator N.Mex./Calif., 1995—; owner Ruta Zinc Handmade, San francisco and New Mex., 1999—. Guest lectr. Iowa State U., Ames, 1992; adj. faculty Md. Inst., Balt.; lectr. L.A. Internat. Art Fair, 1988-94; dir., organizer annual Dialogue Among Peers, Santa Fe, 1997—, numerous others. One-person shows and group exhbns. include Valencia C.C., Orlando, Fla., 1995, Durango (Colo.) Art Ctr., 1995, Manatee C.C., Bradenton, Fla., 1994, Ormond Beach (Fla.) Meml. Art Mus., 1994, Oreg. Sch. of Arts & Crafts, Portland, 1993, The Edn. Ctr. Gallery, Longboat Key, Fla., 1993, Nutaalite, Buena Park, Calif., 1993, Sarasota County (Fla.) Arts Coun., 1993, ARTarget, Sarasota, Fla., 1993, Selby Gallery, Sarasota, Fla., 1992, Ctr. Gallaery, Miami-Dade C.C., 1991, NCCA Gallery/New Ctr. for Creative Awareness, Sarasota, 1990, Scottsdale (Ariz.) Ctr. for Arts, 1992, 95, Boca Raton (Fla.) Mus. Art, 1991, Coll. Creative Studies, U. Calif., Santa Barbara, 1990, San Francisco Mus. Modern Art Rental Gallery, 1986, 89, Galerie Anton Meir, Geneva, 1988, Orange County Ctr. Contemporary Art, Santa Ana, Calif., 1990, The Fukuoka Mcpl. Mus., Japan, 1987, Berlin Transit, 2001, San Francisco Ctr. for the Book, 2002, others; co-author: The Visual Artist's Business and Legal Guide, 1995; contbr. Artmaker Mag., 2002. Chmn. visual artists task force Sarasota County Arts Coun., 1991-92; AIDS subcom. Planned Approach to Community Health, Sarasota, 1991-92; visual aids com., Visual Aids: Day Without Art, 1989—; program adv. Regional Occupational Program, Contra Costa Bd. Edn., 1986, numerous others; mem. Mayor's Com. for Concerns of Persons with Disabilities, Santa Fe, 2000-2003. Recipient Residency award The Bemis Project, Omaha, 1986, Profl. Devel. grant Ringling Sch. of Art and Design, Sarasota, 1990, Merit award Calif. Inst. of Arts, Valencia, 1976, others. Mem. Coll. Art Assn. (speaker 1992, 93), Nat. Artists Equity (speaker 1992), Women's Caucus for Art (speaker 1993), Nat. Soc. Exptl. Learning (speaker 1988, 89, 92, 93), Nat. Art Edn. Assn. (speaker 1992), Nat. Assn. Artists Orgns., Coll. Placement Coun., others. Office: 110 Sierra Azul Santa Fe NM 87507-0188

DEAN, ODELL JOSEPH, JR., urologist, educator; b. Nashville, Mar. 9, 1958; s. Odell Joseph and Barbara Jean Dean. BS, Howard U., 1979; MD, La. State U., New Orleans, 1983. Diplomate Am. Bd. Urology. Resident in surgery and urology Howard U. Hosp., Washington, 1984-86; resident in urology Tulane U. Med. Ctr., New Orleans, 1986-89, fellow in renal transplantation, 1989-91; asst. prof. surgery and urology U. Mo., Columbia, 1991-93; asst. prof. urology Tulane U., 1993-95; attending urologist Columbia Healthcare Sys., Tex., 1996—. Cons. Ellis Fischel Cancer Ctr., Columbia, 1991-93, Tulane Cancer Ctr., 1993-95; med. edn. adv. com. Tulane Med. Sch., 1994-95; residency program dir. Tulane dept. urology, 1994-95; assoc. rsch. fellow NIH, Bethesda, 1979-80; mem. prostate cancer adv. com. Tex. Dept. Health, 1996-2002. Contbr. articles to profl. jours. Advisor Neighborhood Youth Corps, New Orleans, 1980-91; sr. cons. Total Cmty. Action, New Orleans, 1993-95; pres. Am. Cancer Soc., Angelina County, Tex., 1998—. Grantee Atrium Med., 1989, Medtronic, 1989, Searle Pharms., Chgo., 1992, Pfizer Pharms., 1994. Fellow ACS; mem. Am. Urol. Assn., Soc. Univ. Urologists, S.W. Oncology Group, Angelina County Med. Soc., Assn. Acad. Minority Physicians. Roman Catholic. Avocations: computer scis., tennis. Office: Ste 104 302 Medical Park Dr Lufkin TX 75904 E-mail: ojdean@cox-internet.com.

DEANGELIS, LISA MARIE, neurologist, educator; b. New Haven, Mar. 5, 1955; d. Daniel and Antoneta (Cocca) DeA. BA, Wellesley Coll., 1977; MD, Columbia U., 1980. Diplomate Am. Bd. Psychiatry and Neurology. Intern in medicine Presbyn. Hosp., N.Y.C., 1980-81; resident in neurology Neurologic Inst. Presbyn. Hosp., N.Y.C., 1981-84, fellow clin. neuro-oncology, 1984-85; fellow neuro-oncology Meml. Sloan-Kettering Cancer Ctr., N.Y.C., 1985-86, clin. asst., 1986-89, asst. mem., 1989-93, assoc. mem., 1993—97, mem., 1997—, chmn. dept. neurology, 1997—, Jerome B. Posner chair in neurology, 1997—; asst. prof. neurology Cornell U., N.Y.C., 1986-92, assoc. prof. neurology, 1992—97, prof. clin. neurology, 1997—98, prof. neurology, 1998—. Contbr. articles to profl. jours. Recipient Clin. Oncology Career Devel. award Am. Cancer Soc., 1986-89, Boyer Young Investigator award Meml. Sloan-Kettering Cancer Ctr., 1992. Fellow Am. Acad. Neurology, Am. Neurol. Assn. Office: Meml Sloan Kettering 1275 York Ave New York NY 10021-6094

DEANGELIS, MICHELE F. school system administrator; b. Boston; d. Carmine and Maria C. Parziale; m. Arthur DeAngelis, Feb. 27, 1971 (dec. Sept. 1987). BS in Edn., U. Mass., Boston, 1960; MEd, Boston U., 1964; cert. advanced grad. study edn. adminstrn., Northeastern U., 1976, EdD in Ednl. Adminstrn., 1986; cert. nat. supt.'s acad., George Washington U., Am. Assn. Sch. Adminstrs., 1992; postgrad., Harvard U., 1993—. Cert. supt. schs., asst. supt. schs., adminstr. spl. edn., reading supr. and specialist, prin. Classroom tchr. Somerville (Mass.) Pub. Schs., 1960-64; reading specialist Dept. Def. Schs., Germany, 1964-67; reading supr. Prince George's County Schs., Bowie, Md., 1967-69; sch. adminstr. cen. office Tewksbury (Mass.) Pub. Schs., 1969—; owner, operator Candelabra Restaurant, Malden, Mass., 1970-72; chief exec. officer Mish Art Diamond Tool Co., Inc., Woburn, Mass., Paterson, N.J., 1973-84; cons. Ednl. Enhancement Assn., Inc., Woburn, 1986—. Adv. bd. mem. Merrimack Edn. Collaborative, Chelmsford, Mass., 1979—, Camp Paul for Handicapped Children, Chelmsford, 1988-90, Harvard U. Prins. Ctr., Cambridge, Mass., 1991—; mem. Mass. Bar Assn. Juvenile Justice Conf. Task Force, 1991—, Blue Ribbon Sch. Task Force, 1991—, high sch. accreditation team New Eng. Assn. Schs. and Colls., 1991, 93, 97; bd. dirs. Juvenile Justice Task Force, Greater Lowell Area, Mass., 1990—; steering com. mem. Merrimack Valley Coalition for Children, Lawrence, Mass., 1990—; ctrl. office rep. Harvard U. Prins. Ctr., 1991-93, adv. counil; mem. Harvard Supts. Round Table, 1999—. Cand. Sch. Com., Somerville, 1969: mem. Ward 2 Civic Assn., Somerville, 1969-80; campaign worker Reelect Mary Tomeo Campaign, Somerville, 1971-75, Elect George Spartichino Campaign, Cambridge, 1990; fnds Sturbridge Village, 1987—; mem. community svc. com. Mass. Bar Assn., 1992—. Recipient commendation Mass. State Dept. Edn., 1985, cert. Appreciation Lowell Task Force Recognition Support Attendant Day Care Program, 1990, cert. Appreciation Mass. Commr. Office Children., letter Appreciation Mass. Bar Assn., 1991, cert. Appreciation, Tewksbury Pub. Schs., 1991, 92, 93. Mem. ASCD, Internat. Reading Assn., Coun. Exceptional Children, N.E. Coalition of Ednl. Leaders, Mass. Adminstrs. for Spl. Edn., Am. Assn. Sch. Adminstrs., Hamilton Reservoir Assn, Kappa Delta Pi, Pi Lambda Theta. Avocations: pianist, drama prodn., travel. Home: 255 Lexington St Woburn MA 01801-5925 Office: Tewksbury Pub Schs 139 Pleasant St Tewksbury MA 01876-2789 Fax: 978-640-7878. E-mail: mdeagelis@tewksbury.mec.edu.

DEAR, RONALD BRUCE, social work educator; b. Phila., Sept. 23, 1933; s. John David and Margaret (McDade) D.; 1 child, Bruce. BA, Bucknell U., 1955; honors cert., U. Aberdeen, Scotland, 1955; MSW, U. Pitts., 1957; PhD in Social Work, Columbia U., 1972. Cert. social worker, N.Y., Wash. Chief social worker Mental Hygiene Cons. Svc., Aberdeen Proving Ground, Md., 1958-60; chief Neuropsychiat. Clinic, 7th Inf. Divsn., Korea, 1960-61; residence dir. Horizon House, Inc., Phila., 1961-64; prof. U. Wash., Seattle, 1970—. Vis. prof. U. Bergen, Norway, 1984, U. Trondheim, Norway, 1996; faculty lobbyist U. Wash., 1983-85, 88-91, faculty pres., 1993-95; master tchr. Coun. on Social Work Edn., 1991, 93, 94, 97; mem. adv. bd. Internat. Population and Family Assocs. Author: Social Welfare Policy: Trends and Issues, 6th edit., 2001; editor: Poverty in Perspective, 1973; mem. editl. bd. Columns, 2001—, The Social Policy Jour., 1992—; mem. editl. adv. com. Columns, 2001—; contbr. articles to profl. jours. and encys. Apptd. by gov. to income assistance adv. com., 1987-93, to adv. com. for Dept. S ocial and Health Svcs., 1980-83, Human Svcs. Policy Ctr., 1996—, adv. com. Wash. State Econ. Svcs., 1996—; mem. nat. adv. bd. Influencing State Policy, 1997—; appeared in centennial program of Columbia U. Sch. of Social Work, 1998. 1st lt. U.S. Army, 1957-61. Mem. NASW (Social Worker of Yr. Wash. chpt. 1981, mem. staff legis. N.Y.C. chpt. 1968-69), Acad. Cert. Social Workers, Coun. on Social Work Edn. Avocations: travel in over 45 countries, photography, hiking. Home: 7328 16th Ave NE Seattle WA 98115-5737 Office: U Wash Sch Social Work 4101 15th Ave NE Seattle WA 98105-6250

DE ARTEAGA-MORGAN, IVETTE, school administrator; b. Santurce, P.R., Aug. 28, 1931; d. Julio Carlos and Irma (Ortiz) de Arteaga; m. Robert H. Morgan, June 13, 1959; children: Robert, Joseph, Elizabeth, Michael. BA in Liberal Arts, Polit. Sci., Spanish and Edn., Coll. Mt. St. Vincent, 1954; MA, Hofstra U., 1957; postgrad., Hunter Coll., 1959, Fla. Atlantic U., 1970; DA in Higher Edn. and Reading, U. Miami, 1976. Cert. elem. tchr., adminstrn. and supervision, reading clinician, lang. tchr., vis. tchr./social worker. Elem. tchr. 3rd, 5th and 6th grades Merrick (N.Y.) Schs., 1954-57; caseworker Cath. Foster Care Svcs., N.Y.C., 1957-58; adminstr. Lennox Hill Settlement House, N.Y.C., 1958-60; elem. tchr. disadvantaged students Roseville (Mich.) Sch. Bd., 1960-61; instr. modern lang. dept. U. Wis., Eau Claire, 1966-68; vis. tchr., social worker inner-city blacks and hispanics Miami, Fla., 1968-70; coord. Spanish Curriculum Devel. Ctr., Miami, 1970-73; assoc. prof. edn., chairperson edn., supr. student teaching Biscayne Coll., Miami, 1975-78; project mgr. Bilingual Alternative for Secondary Edn., Miami, 1978-82; asst. prin. Citrus Grove Mid. Sch., Miami, 1982-84, McMillan Mid. Sch., Miami, 1984-86; coord. Dept. Community Participation, Miami, 1986-88, Project Stay in Sch., Miami, 1988-89; asst. prin. Palmetto Adult and Community Edn. Ctr., Miami, 1989—. Adj. prof. edn. Fla. Internat. U., 1976—; cons. Lau Desegration Ctr., Miami, 1973-89, Key West Sch. (Fla.) Bd., 1976-86, Pub. Sch. 25, Bronx, N.Y., 1970, Miccosukee (Fla.) Adult Edn., 1978, Del. Sch. Bd., numerous others; coord. Bilingual Tng. Classroom Tchrs., Hartford, Conn., Reading Bilingual Classroom, New Haven, Bilingual Curriculum, Phila.; field reader U.S. Dept. Edn., U.S. HHS; presenter, proposal writer in field; chair bd. dirs. League United Latin Am. Citizens Nat. Ednl. Svc. Ctr., Inc. Fla. Contbr. articles to profl. jours. Vol. social worker Cath. Welfare, 1961-66; bd. dirs. Coalition of Hispanic Mental Health and Human Svcs. Orgn., Fla. Cares, La Raza Fla., treas., Dade County's Youth and Family Devel., 1981—; mem. Community Rels. Bd., 1983—, Dem. Exec. Com., Fla., 1988—; past treas. Orgn. P.R. Dems., Fla., 1985; past sec. Coalition Hispanic Women, Fla., 1982; mem. adv. bd. South Fla. Employment and Tng. Consortium; vice chair Gov.'s Commn. Hispanic Affairs, 1984-89; active Women's Polit. Caucus. Recipient Cert. of Merit, Yeshiva U., Dept. Human Resources award Office Neighborhood Svc. Ctrs.; St. Vincent Coll. scholar, 1950-54, N.Y. State scholar, 1959, U. Miami fellow, 1973-77, W.K. Kellogg Found. fellow, 1980, 81. Mem. AAUW, ASCD, ASPIRA (v.p. personnel 1981-87), ASPIRA Fla. (founder, chair 1980—), Nat. Assn. Tchrs. English Speakers Other Langs., Nat. Mental Health Assn., Nat. Assn. for Bilingual Edn. (presentor nat. confs.), Nat. Assn. Latino Elected and Apptd. Ofcls. (founding mem.), Nat. Assn. Tchrs. English, Nat. Conf. Puerto Rican Women (nat. 1st v.p., founder, pres. Miami chpt., Educator of Yr. 1980), Fla. Tchrs. English to Speakers Other Langs. (minority com.), Bilingual Assn. Fla. (sec. 1978, v.p. 1980), Fla. Fgn. Lang. Assn., Am. Coun. on Learning Disabilities, Am. Pers. and Guidance Assn., Fla. Pers. and Guidance Assn. (bd. dirs.), Fla. Assn. for Supervision and Curriculum Devel., Internat. Reading Assn., Fla. Coun. Reading Assn., Bilingual Multicultural Consortium (bd. dirs.), Dade County Sch. Adminstrs. Assn. (legis. com.), Nat. P.R. Coalition, Inc. (bd. dirs.), Am. Hispanic Educators Assn. Dade, Miami Hispanic Club (sec. 1985-87, scholarship chair), Phi Delta Kappa, Epsilon Tau Lambda. Roman Catholic. Office: Miami Palmetto Adult and Community Edn Ctr 7460 SW 118th St Miami FL 33156-4572

DEATON, CHARLES MILTON, lawyer; b. Hattiesburg, Miss., Jan. 19, 1931; s. Ivanes Dean Deaton and Martha Sarah Elizabeth Fortenberry; m. Mary Dent Dickerson, Aug. 15, 1951; children: Diane Rossi, Dara Rogers, Charles M., Jr. BA, Millsaps Coll., 1949-51, 55-56; JD, U. Miss., 1959. Legis. asst. U.S. Ho. of Reps., Washington, 1957; assoc. Brewer, Deaton & Bowman, Greenwood, Miss., 1958—; mem. Miss. Ho. of Reps., Jackson, 1960—80, appropriations chmn., 1976—80; city atty. City of Greenwood, Miss., 1970-84; adminstrv. asst. to Govs. Wm. Winter, B. Allain State of Miss., Jackson, 1980—88; bd. dirs. Bank of Commerce, Greenwood; mem. Miss. State Bd. of Edn., 2003—. Recipient Miss Conservationist of Yr. award The Nature Conservancy, Jackson, 1991, Nat. Oak Leaf award, Arlington, Va., 1992, Sports Hall of Fame award Millsaps Coll., Jackson, Alumnus of Yr. award, 1995, others. Mem. ABA, The Nature Conservancy, Miss. Wildlife Heritage Commn., others. Avocations: cooking, hunting, fishing, conservation, gardening. Office: Brewer Deaton & Bowman 107 W Market St PO Drawer B Greenwood MS 38935

DE BACKER, DAVID PIERRE, educational administrator; b. Erie, Pa., June 17, 1946; s. Pierre and Alice De Backer; m. Bonnie Benjamin; 1 child, Leighan. BA in Gen. Sci. Edn., U. Guam, Agana, 1970, MEd, 1973; MA in Edn., U. Akron, 1991, postgrad. Cert. tchr., Ga. Classroom tchr. Govt. Guam Dept. Edn., Agana, 1968-73, fed. programs coord., 1973-75, Bibb County Bd. of Edn., Macon, Ga., 1975-77; exec. dir. N.W. Pa. Profl. Stds. Rev. Orgn., Erie, 1977-85; asst. dir. continuing edn. Erie Bus. Ctr., 1985-89; asst. unit dir. Greater Erie Comty. Action Com., 1989—. S.E.-regional assoc. Ctr. for Edn. & Mgmt., Macon, 1975-83; computer cons., Erie, 1988—. Treas. North Coast Ballet, Erie; past bd. dirs. Boys and Girls Club of N.W. Pa., Erie. Grad. scholar U. Akron. Mem. Am. Assn. Higher Edn., Am. Edn. Rsch. Assn., Phi Delta Kappa. Home: 5426 Mill St Erie PA 16509-2920 Office: 18 W 9th St Erie PA 16501-1343

DEBAKEY, MICHAEL ELLIS, cardiovascular surgeon, educator, scientist; b. Lake Charles, La., Sept. 7, 1908; s. Shaker Morris and Raheeja (Zorba) DeBakey; m. Diana Cooper, Oct. 15, 1936; children: Michael Maurice, Ernest Ochsner, Barry Edward, Denis Alton; m. Katrin Fehlhaber, July 1975; 1 child, Olga Katarina. BS, Tulane U., 1930, MD, 1932, MS, 1935; more than 50 hon. degrees from prestigious univ. throughout the world. Diplomate Nat. Bd. Med. Examiners, Am. Bd. Surgery, Am. Bd. Thoracic Surgery. Intern Charity Hosp., New Orleans, 1932—33, asst. surgery, 1933—35, U. Strasbourg, France, 1935—36, U. Heidelberg, Germany, 1936; instr. surgery Tulane U., New Orleans, 1937—40, asst. prof., 1940—46, assoc. prof., 1946—48; prof., chmn. dept. surgery Baylor Coll. Medicine, 1948—93, Disting. svc. prof., 1968—, v.p. med. affairs, 1968—69, CEO, 1968—69, pres., 1969—79, Olga Keith Wiess prof. of surgery, 1981—, chancellor, 1978—96, chancellor emeritus, 1996—; pres. The DeBakey Med. Found., 1961—; dir. Nat. Heart Blood Vessel Rsch. Demonstration Ctr., Baylor Coll. Medicine, 1974—84; dir. DeBakey Heart Ctr., Baylor Coll. Medicine, 1985—. Surgeon-in-chief Ben Taub Gen. Hosp., 1963—93; sr. attending surgeon Meth. Hosp.; clin. prof. surgery U. Tex. Dental Br.; cons. surgery VA Hosp., U. Tex. M.D. Anderson Cancer Ctr., St. Luke's Hosp., Tex. Children's Hosp., Tex. Inst. Rehab. and Rsch., Houston, Brooke Gen. Hosp., Brooke Army Med. Ctr., Ft. Sam Houston,

Tex., Walter Reed Army Hosp., Washington, D.C.; mem. med. adv. com. Office Sec. Def., 1948—50; mem. task force med. svcs. Hoover Commn., 1949; founding bd. dirs. Friends of Nat. Libr. of Medicine, 1985—; mem. bd. regents Nat. Libr. of Medicine, 1956—60, 1994—98, chmn., 1959, 98; past mem. nat. adv. heart coun. NIH; mem. Nat. Adv. Health Coun., 1961—65, Nat. Adv. Coun. Regional Med. Programs, 1965—, Nat. Adv. Gen. Med. Scis. Coun., 1965, Program Planning Com., Com. Tng., Nat. Heart Inst., 1961—; mem. civilian health and med. adv. coun. Office Asst. Sec. Def.; chmn. Pres.'s Commn. Heart Disease, Cancer and Stroke, 1964; mem. adv. coun. Nat. Heart Lung and Blood Inst., 1982—87; chmn. Found. Biomedical Rsch., 1988; trustee, v.p. Baylor Med. Found.; adv. Dag Hammarskjöld Med. Sci. Prize Com.; trustee Baylor Coll. Medicine, 1996; fgn. adj. prof. Karolinska Inst., 1997. Author (with Robert A. Kilduffe): Blood Transfusion, 1942; author: (with Gilbert W. Beebe) Battle Casualties, 1952; author: (with Alton Ochsner) Textbook of Minor Surgery, 1955; author: (with T. Whayne) Cold Injury, Ground Type, 1958; author: A Surgeon's Visit to China, 1974, The Living Heart, 1977, The Living Heart Diet, 1985, The Living Heart Brand Name Shopper's Guide, 1992, The Living Heart Guide to Eating Out, 1993, The New Living Heart Diet, 1996, The New Living Heart, 1997; editor: Yearbook of surgery, 1958—70; chmn. adv. editl. bd.: Medical History of World War II, founding editor: Jour. Vascular Surgery, 1984—88; contbr. over 1600 articles to med. jours. Disting. mem. U.S. Army Med. Dept. Rgt., 1989; cons. to Surgeon Gen., 1946—. Col. Office Surgeon Gen. U.S. Army, 1942—46, now Col. Res. U.S. Army. Decorated Legion of Merit, 1945; named in his honor Michael E. DeBakey Dept. Surgery, Baylor Coll. Medicine, 1999, in his honor Michael E. Debakey Heart Inst. Kan., Hays Med. Ctr., 1999, in his honor Michael E. DeBakey Internat. Surgery Chair, Uniformed Svc. Univ. Health Sci., 2000, in his honor Michael E. DeBakey Inst. Comparative Cardiovascular Sci. and Biomedical Devices, Tex. A&M Univ., 2000, innumerable honors and awards including Leader in Medicine, AMA, 1997, charter mem., Tex. Sci. Hall Fame, 2001; named an inductee Space Tech. Hall Fame, 1999; named one of 200 Most Influential People in Telemedicine, Ctr. Pub. Svc. Comm., 1996, Top Ten Heroes, Millenium Soc., 1996; named to Health Care Hall of Fame, Modern Healthcare, 1996, Houston Hall Fame, 1999, Sci. in Tex. Hall Fame, 2000; recipient Rudolph Matas award, 1954, Disting. Svc. award, Internat. Soc. Surgery, 1958, Modern Medicine award, 1957, Leriche award, Internat. Soc. Surgery, 1959, Great medallion, U. Ghent, 1961, Grand Cross, Order Leopold, Belgium, 1962, Albert Lasker award for clin. rsch., 1963, Order of Merit Chile, 1964, St. Vincent prize med. scis., U. Turin, 1965, Centennial medal, Albert Einstein Med. Ctr., 1966, Gold Scalpel award, Internat. Cardiology Found., 1966, Eleanor Roosevelt Humanities award, 1969, Meritorious Civilian Svc. medal, Office Sec. Def., 1970, Medal of Freedom with Distinction Presdl. award, 1969, Inst. Med. Nat. Acad. Sci., 1981, Theodore E. Cummings award, 1987, Nat. Med. of Sci. award, 1987, First Issue Michael DeBakey medal, ASME, 1989, Inaugural award, Scripps Clinic and Rsch. Found., 1989, DeBakey-Bard Chair in Surgery, Baylor Coll. of Medicine, 1990, Disting. Svc. award, Am. Legion, 1990, Lifetime Achievement award, Found. for Biomed. Rsch., 1991, Maxwell Finland award, Nat. Found. for Infectious Diseases, 1992, Acad. of Athens award, 1992, Pres. Disting. Svc. award, Baylor Coll. Medicine, 1992, Gibbon award, Am. Soc. Extracorporeal Tech., 1993, named in his honor Michael E. DeBakey Libr. Svc. Outreach award, Friends of the Nat. Libr. Medicine, 1993, Alton Ochsner award relating smoking to health, 1993, Thomas Jefferson award, AIA, 1993, Lifetime Achievement award, Am. Heart Assn., 1994, prize for basic biomed. rsch., Giovanni Lorenzini Med. Fedn., 1994, Disting. Svc. award, Tex. Soc. Biomed. Rsch., 1994, Heart Saver award, Save A Heart Found., Cedars-Sinai Med. Ctr., 1994, Honor award, United Meth. Assn. Health & Welfare Ministries, 1995, Michael E. DeBakey chair in Pharm., Baylor Coll. Medicine, 1995, Nat. Order of Medicine Vasco Nunez de Balboa, Panama, 1995, Pub. Svc. award, AIAA, 1997, Boris Petrovsky Internat. Surgeons award, 1997, Premio Giuseppe Corradi award, Bevagna, Italy, 1997, Rotary Nat. award, 1997, Sesquicentennial medal, Tulane Coll., 1997, Fire of Genius award, So. Utah U., 1997, Commonwealth Trust award for invention and sci., 1997, Michael E. DeBakey Heart Inst. Wis. named in his honor, Kenosha Hosp. and Med. Ctr., 1992, Michael E. DeBakey, M.D. award for Excellence in Visual Edn. named in his honor, 1993, DeBakey Scholar in Cardiovasc. Scis. MD-PhD Program named in his honor, Baylor Coll. Medicine, 1994, Michael E. DeBakey, MD Excellence in Rsch. award named in his honor, 1994, dedication of Northwestern U. Med. Sch. book, 1995, Michael E. DeBakey H.S. Health Professions named in his honor, 1996, Med. Ctr. of LA Found. Inaugural Spirit of Charity award, 1998, Leader in Medicine honor, AMA, 1997, John P. McGovern Lecture award, Cosmos Club Found., 1998, Lifetime Achivement award, Rsch. Am., 1998, Michael E. DeBakey Presdl. Excellence award named in his honor, 1998, Mus. Health and Med. Sci. Lifetime Membership award, 1999, Disting. Svc. award, Soc. Vascular Surgery, 1999, Sci. Achievement award, Am. Assn. Thoracic Surgery, 1999, inaugural Michael E. DeBakey award contbns. to Am.'s Health, AIA, 1999, Bicentennial Living Legends award, Libr. Congress, 2000, Lifetime Achievement Outstanding Alumnus award, Tulane Med. Alumni Assn., 2000, Tall Texan award, Muscular Dystrophy Assn., 2001, Invention Yr., DeBakey Ventricular Assist Device, NASA, 2001, Mendal Medal award, Villanova U., Pa., 2001, Living Legend award, World Artificial-Organ, Immunology, Transplant Soc., Ottawa, Can., 2001, Inspired Leadership award, Am. Bible Soc., 2001, Wall of Honor tribute for lifetime contributions, 2002, Lifetime Achievement award, Internat. Health and Med. Film Festival, 2002, Golden Hippocrates Internat. Prize for Excellence in Medicine, Horev Med. Ctr., Haifa, Israel and Iraeli Minister Health, 2003, Ben Taub Humanitarian award, Harris County Hosp. District Found., 2003. Fellow: Internat. Acad. Cardiovascular Scis. (hon.), Am. Coll. Cardiology (hon.), Royal Coll. Physicians and Surgeons of U.S. (hon. disting. fellow 1992), Inst. of Medicine Chgo. (hon.); mem.: AMA (Hektoen Gold medal 1954, Disting. Svc. award 1959, Hektoen Gold medal 1970), AAAS, Uniformed Svc. Alumni Assn. (life hon.), Internat. Soc. Surgery, Soc. Univ. Surgeons, Assn. Internat. Vascular Surgeons (pres. 1983), Internat. Cardiovascular Soc. (pres. 1958, pres. N.Am. chpt. 1964), Am. Assn. Thoracic Surgery (pres. 1959), So. Surg. Assn. (pres. 1989—90, chmn. coun. 1995—), Am. Surg. Assn. (pres. 1989, Disting. Svc. award 1981), Soc. Vascular Surgery Lifeline Found. (pres. 1989), Soc. Vascular Surgery (pres. 1954), Am. Heart Assn., Royal Soc. Medicine, Assn. Française de Chirurgie (hon.), Med. Libr. Assn. (hon.), Hellenic Surg. Soc. (hon.), Mex. Acad. Surgery (hon.), Telemedicine 200 Ctr. for Pub. Svcs., Acad. of Athens, University Club (Washington), Houston Club (hon.), Alpha Omega Alpha, Sigma Xi (William Procter prize for sci. achievement 1995). Episcopalian. Achievements include development of roller pump universally used in heart-lung machine; Dacron artificial arteries and Dacron-velour arteries as surgical replacement of diseased arteries; first successful patch-graft angioplasty; fundamental concept of therapy in arterial disease; left ventricular bypass pump for cardiac assistance and first successful clinical application; first successful resection and graft replacement of fusiform aneurysm; establishment of Meth. DeBakey Heart Ctr., Meth. Hosp., Houston, 2001; establishment of DeBakey USU Brigade, 2001; establishment of Michael E. DeBakey award for Long-life Well-lived in Svc. to Mankind, Huffington Ctr. on Aging, 2001; establishment of Michael E. DeBakey Scholarship in Grad. Sch. Biomedical Sci., Baylor Coll. Medicine, 2001; establishment of Michael E. DeBakey Journalism award, Found. Biomedical Rsch., 2002. Office: Baylor Coll Medicine 1 Baylor Plz Houston TX 77030-3411

DEBAKEY, SELMA, science communications educator, writer, editor, lecturer; b. Lake Charles, La. BA, postgrad., Newcomb Coll., Tulane U., New Orleans. Dir. dept. med. communication Ochsner Clinic and Alton Ochsner Med. Found., New Orleans, 1942-68; prof. sci. communication Baylor Coll. Medicine, Houston, 1968—; editor Cardiovascular Research Ctr. Bull., 1970-84. Mem. panel judges Internat. Health and Med. Film Festival, 1992. Author: (with A. Segaloff and K. Meyer) Current Concepts in Breast Cancer, 1967; past editor Ochsner Clinic Reports, Selected Writings from the Ochsner Clinic; contbr. numerous articles to sci. jours., chpts. to books. Named to Tex. Hall of Fame. Mem. AAAS, Soc. Tech. Communication, Assn. Tchrs. Tech. Writing, Am. Med. Writers Assn. (past bd. dirs.; publ., nominating, fellowship, constn., bylaws, awards, and edn. coms.), Council Biol. Editors (past mem. trn. in sci. writing com.), Soc. Health and Human Values, Modern Med. Monograph Awards Com., Nat. Assn. Standard Med. Vocabulary (former cons.). Office: Baylor Coll Medicine 1 Baylor Plz Houston TX 77030-3411

DE BARCZA, GLADYS MARY, art administrator; b. Englewood, N.J., Sept. 4, 1939; d. Stephen Bela and Alice (Mayerberg), de Bence; m. George De Barcza, July 1959; 1 child, Monica. BA, CUNY, 1962, MS, 1966; PhD, U. Ga., 1988. Chair dept. art Am. Sch. Kuwait, 1983-86; instr. U. Ga., Athens, 1986-87; dir. art edn. Modern Mus. Art, Santa Ana, Calif., 1990-91; instr. Coastline C.C., Fountain Valley, Calif., 1991-93, Pasadena City Coll., Calif., 1993-95, L.A. City Coll., The Learning Tree U., Costa Mesa, Calif., Westwood Coll. Tech., 1997—2003; art rschr., cons. Expdn. Oceania, Fiji, 1995-97. Bd. dirs. Internat. Surfing Mus., Huntington Beach, Calif. Art tour dir. "Italian Art Adventureto Rome and Tuscany, Costa Mesa", 1993; One-woman shows include Fili's Fancy, Vuda Point, Fifi, 1997, Ras Tanura, Saudi Arabia; exhibited in group shows at Hist. Lyndon House, Athens, Ga., San Diego Convention Ctr., 1991, Sheraton Fiji Resort Art Gallery, 1996, Dado Art Gallery, Nadi, Fiji, 1996-97; Exhibits: Robert Hondavi Ctr. Juried Mem. Show, 2002-03; Centered at the Ctr., Hunington Beach Art Ctr.; represented in permenant collections Chevron Shipping Corp., Arabian Am. Oil Co.; author: Colour Me Fiji: An Educational Art Gallery, 1989, Color Me Old Town San Diego, 1991, Huntington Beach Educational Coloring Book, 1998; contbg. articles to profl. jour.; So. Calif. Plein Air Painters Assn. Mem. curatorial com. Pasadena Hist. Soc., 1991-92. Fulbright grantee, 1986. Mem. Western Arts and Crafts Soc., Coll. Art Assn., Internat. Soc. for Edn. Through Art, Pacific Arts Assn., Royal Suva Club, Huntington Harbor Yacht Club. Roman Catholic. Avocations: drawing and painting, broken china mosaics, theatre, tennis, sailing.

DEBARI, VINCENT ANTHONY, medical researcher, educator; b. Jersey City, Feb. 1, 1946; s. Vincent and Josephine C. (Buzzanco) DeB.; m. Margaret A. Danning, Feb. 28, 1970; children: Michele, Christopher V., Jillanne. BS, Fordham U., Bronx, N.Y., 1967; MS, Newark Coll. Engring., 1970; PhD, Rutgers U., 1981. Rsch. and devel. chemist Witco Chem. Corp., Oakland, N.J., 1967-73; rsch. chemist St. Joseph's Hosp. & Med. Ctr., Paterson, N.J., 1973-81, dir. renal lab., 1981-89, dir. rheumatol lab., 1989—, dir. rsch., 1988-95; assoc. prof. medicine Seton Hall U. Sch. Grad. Med. Edn., South Orange, N.J., 1988-95, prof., 1995—, dir. rsch. internal medicine, 1989—. Cons. Rutgers U., 1981, Biomed. Clin. Labs., Wayne, N.J., 1985, Micro-Membranes Inc., Newark, 1986-89, GenCare Biomed. Rsch. Corp., Mountainside, N.J., 1989—; med. staff affiliate St. Joseph's Hosp. & Med. Ctr., St. Michael's Med. Ctr., Newark. Edtl. bd. Clin. & Lab. Sci. annuals; contbr. numerous articles to profl. jours. Bd. dirs. Lupus Erythematosus Found. N.J., Elmwood Park, 1983-91; trustee Paquannock Twp. (N.J.) Bd. Edn., 1986-91, Bay Head Shores Club, Point Pleasant, N.J., 1993. Grantee Lupus Found., Elmwood Park, N.J., 1978—, Lions Found., 1981-85; recipient Boston Biomedica award Clin. Ligand Assay Soc., 1989. Fellow Nat. Acad. Clin. Biochemistry, Am. Inst. Chemists; mem. Am. Assn. Clin. Chemistry (chmn. N.J. 1990-92, chair clin. and diagnostic immunology div. 1991-93, Disting. Svc. award 1989, Clin. Chem. Recognition award 1984, 87, 90, 92, Bernard F. Gerulat award 1990), Nat. Coun. Univ. Rsch. Adminstrn., Am. Fedn. Clin. Rsch., Am. Coll. Rheumatology. Roman Catholic. Achievements include recognition of neutrophil defects in chronic hemodialysis patients, studies of autoantibodies in systemic autoimmune diseases and in AIDS, investigation of pathophysiologic effects of endotoxins, studies of relationship between surface electrochemistry and phagocytosis; rsch. on electrophoretic methods to study clonotype restrictions; developed first international standards for antibodies to beta-2-glycoprotein I for patients with antiphospholipid syndrome; developed first standards for antibodies to B2glycoproteinI. Office: St Josephs Hosp & Med Ctr 703 Main St Paterson NJ 07503-2621 E-mail: debariv@sjhme.org.

DEBARLING, ANA MARIA, language educator; b. Del Rio, Tex., Apr. 30, 1938; d. Octauiano and Guadalupe Dominguez; m. Peter Wesley Barling, June 4, 1968 (div. Oct. 1988); children: Laura Blanche, Wesley Peter. BA, San Jose State U., 1968, M in Hispanic Lit., 1970; DEd, U. Pacific, 2001. Cert. sch. administrn. Calif. Secondary tchr. Fremount Union H.S. Dist., Sunnyvale, Calif., 1968—94, dir. gifted edn., 1980—83; lang. prof. West Valley Coll., Saratoga, Calif., 1994—. Cons. Edn. Testing Svcs., San Antonio, 1992—; bilingual proficiency testing City of Morgan Hill and Campbell, Calif., 1995—. Editor: (booklet) Gifted & Talented Education, 1991. Mem. Latina Leadership, San Jose, 1988—, Immigration Edn. Task Force, Santa Clara, Calif., 1999—. Mem.: Am. Tchrs. Fgn. Lang., Faculty Assn. C.C. Democrat. Roman Catholic. Home: 373 Redwood Ave Santa Clara CA 95051 Office: West Valley Coll 14000 Fruitvale Ave Saratoga CA 95070 E-mail: and_maria_de_baring@wuv.edu.

DEBEAR, RICHARD STEPHEN, library planning consultant; b. N.Y.C., Jan. 18, 1933; s. Arthur A. and Sarah (Morrison) deB.; m. Estelle Carmel Grandon, Apr. 27, 1951; children: Richard, Jr., Diana deBear Fortson, Patricia deBear Talkington, Robert, Christopher, Nancy deBear Naski. BS, Queens Coll., CUNY, 1953. Sales rep. Sperry Rand Corp., Blue Bell, Pa., 1954-76; pres. Libr. Design Assocs., Plymouth, Mich., 1976-97, Am. Libr. Ctr., Plymouth, 1981—. Bldg. cons. to numerous librs., 1965—; mem. interior design program profl. adv. com. Wayne State U. Mem. ALA, Mich. Libr. Assn. (oversight com. Leadership Acad. 1990—). Office: Am Libr Ctr Inc 1149 S Main St Plymouth MI 48170-2213 E-mail: ddebear@americanlibrary.com.

DEBELLIS, FRANCINE DARNEL, elementary education educator; b. Honesdale, Pa., June 12, 1951; d. Raymond Louis and Stephanie (DiVinitz) Miller; m. Frank DeBellis, Oct. 5, 1974; children: Christopher, Michael. BA, Fairleigh Dickinson U., 1973; postgrad., William Paterson Coll., 1992-95, St. Peter's Coll., 1993-94, Jersey City State Coll., 1994-95; MAT, Marygrove Coll., 1998. Head tchr. pvt. nursery sch., Union City, N.J., 1973; compensatory tchr. Lyndhurst (N.J.) Bd. Edn., 1974-77, elem. tchr., 1977—, mem. ednl. specifications task force, 1990-91. Faculty liaison Lyndhurst Bd. Edn., 1991-93, mem. instrnl. coun., mem. faculty adv. bd., 1991-93; mem. Lyndhurst Task Force on Youth Violence, 1995; mem. Mayor's Substance Abuse Coun., 1991-92; devel. and implemented All Day Kindergarten Program, Pre-Kindergarten Program, Lyndhurst Bd. Edn., 1992-93. Recipient Gov.'s Tchr. Recognition award, 1990; Lyndhurst Bd. Edn. grantee, 1989, 92. Mem. ASCD, Lyndhurst Edn. Assn. (pres. 1989-90). Methodist. Avocations: reading, horseback riding, relaxing in the country. Home: 824 Pennsylvania Ave Lyndhurst NJ 07071-1323 Office: Roosevelt Sch Lyndhurst Bd Edn 530 Stuyvesant Ave Lyndhurst NJ 07071-2697

DEBENEDETTI, P(ATRICK) J(OHN), director; b. San Francisco, Mar. 4, 1952; s. John Joseph and Ellen Patricia (Hession) DeB.; m. Camille Buckley, Apr. 21, 1979; children: John, Nick. BA in Sociology, Gonzaga U., 1984; BA in Recreation Adminstrn., East Wash. U., 1985. Dir. sch. community Moses Lake (Wash.) Sch. Dist., 1979-88, community sch. coordinator, 1976-79, dir. community affairs, 1988—98, spl. asst. to supt., 1998—. Pres. Community Svcs., Moses Lakes, 1987—, asst. to Pregnant and Parenting Teens, Moses Lake, 1987-88; cons. Washington Spl. Olympics, 1982—. Named Outstanding Young Am., Washington Jaycees, 1990, Citizen of Yr., Moses Lake-Othello Bd. Realtors, 1990. Mem. Wash. State Community Edn. Assn. (bd. dirs. 1978-81, pres. 1982-83, treas. 1986-88, C.S. Mott award 1981, 87), Kiwanis Club. Roman Catholic. Avocations: golf, basketball, softball, travel, sportscards and collectibles. Office: Moses Lake Sch Dist 920 W Ivy Ave Moses Lake WA 98837-2047 E-mail: pjdeben@mlsd.wednet.edu.

DEBENEDICTIS, JOANNE, elementary school educator; b. Jersey City, Nov. 26, 1949; m. Anthony DeBenedictis, Nov. 16, 1973; children: Nicole, Joseph. BA in Early Childhood Edn., Jersey City State Coll., 1974, MA Reading Specialist, 1993. Cert. elem. and early childhood tchr., cert. K-12, N.J. Tchr. Jersey City Head Start Program, 1974-75, Our Lady of Victories Sch., Jersey City, 1983—, tchr. 2nd grade, 1991—. Mem. ASCD, Internat. Reading Assn., N.J. Reading Assn., Nat. Coun. Tchrs. English, Cath. Tchrs. Sodality, Hudson Reading Coun. (sec.), Alpha Upsilon Alpha (pres.). Roman Catholic. Avocations: reading, dancing, sports. Home: 42 Williams Ave Jersey City NJ 07304-1127

DEBERNARDIS, BRUCE, secondary education educator; b. Phila., Oct. 14, 1950; s. Joseph Alexander and Anne Jacqueline (Cooperstein) DeB. BS, Pa. State U., 1972. Tchr. Phila. Sch. Dist., 1972-74, Upper Dublin (Pa.) Sch. Dist., 1974-80, Downingtown (Pa.) Area Sch. Dist., 1980—. Baseball coach Am. Legion, Ft. Washington, Pa. 1980—. Mem. Am. Legion., Am. Baseball Coaches Assn., Nat. High Sch. Baseball Assn. Home: 701 Vance Dr Glenside PA 19038-1319 Office: Lionville Jr High Sch 550 W Uwchlan Ave Exton PA 19341-1562

DEBERRY, PATRICIA YVONNE, education educator; b. Columbus, Ohio, Jan. 10, 1945; d. Arnett Keith Sr. and Alberta Helen (Betts) Lyman. Cert. elem. and secondary sch. tchr., prin., supr., supt., Ohio. Elem. tchr. Columbus Bd. Edn., 1966-67, D.C. Bd. Edn., 1966-73; mid. sch. tchr. Randallwood Sch., Warrensville Heights, Ohio, 1973-80; mid. sch. prin. Warrensville Sch. Dist., Warrensville Heights, 1980-83; mid. sch. and H.S. prin. Beachwood (Ohio) Bd. Edn., 1983-87; program coord. staff devel. Greater Cleve. (Ohio) Ednl. Devel. Ctr., 1988-90; project coord. EQUALS gender project Kent (Ohio) State U., 1990—; K-4th grade dir. Sci., Engring., Aerospace Acad., Cleve., 1993—; regional dir. Famiy Sci., Kent and Portland, Oreg., 1993—. Councilwoman Village of Highland Hills, Ohio, 1990—; co-chair levy campaign Warrensville Heights City Schs., 1994-95. Holmes scholar, 1993—; grantee NASA and Cuyahoga C.C., 1993—, Ohio Bd. Regents, 1980; recipient Martha Jennings Leadership award M. Jennings Found., 1980. Mem. ASCD, Nat. Alliance Black Sch. Educators, Nat. Mid. Sch. Asn. (mem. rsch. com. 1994—), Am. Edn. Rsch. Assn., Nat. Coun. Tchrs. Math., Phi Delta Kappa. Democrat. Lutheran. Avocations: reading, travel. Office: Kent State U 405 White Hall PO Box 5190 Kent OH 44242-0001

DEBICKI, ANDREW PETER, foreign language educator; b. Warsaw, June 28, 1934; came to U.S., 1948, naturalized, 1955; s. Roman and Jadwiga (Dunin) D.; m. Mary Jo Tidmarsh, Dec. 29, 1959 (dec. 1975); children: Mary Beth, Margaret; m. Mary Elizabeth Gwin, May 16, 1987. BA, Yale U., 1955, PhD, 1960. Instr. Trinity Coll., Hartford, Conn., 1957—60; asst. prof. Grinnell Coll., Iowa, 1960—62, assoc. prof., 1962—66, prof., 1966—68; prof. Spanish U. Kans., Lawrence, 1968—76, Univ. Disting. prof., 1976—. Dir. Hall Ctr., 1989-93; dean Grad. Sch. and Internat. Programs, 1993-2000; dir. NEH summer seminars 1976, 78, 89, 2003. Author: La poesia de Jose Gorostiza, 1962, Estudios sobre poesia espanola contemporanea, 1968, 81, Damaso Alonso, 1970, 74, La poesia de Jorge Guillen, 1973, Poetas hispanoamericanos contemporaneos: Punto de vista, perspectiva, experiencia, 1976, Poetry of Discovery, 1982, 87, Angel Gonzalez, 1989, Spanish Poetry of the Twentieth Century, 1994, 97; contbr. articles to various publs. Guggenheim fellow, 1970-71, 80, Nat. Humanities Ctr. fellow, 1980, 92-93, Am. Coun. Learned Socs. fellow, 1966-67, NEH sr. rsch. fellow, 1992-93; ADFL Career award 1999. Mem. MLA (exec. coun. 1989-93), Am. Assn. Tchrs. Spanish and Portuguese. Home: 1445 Applegate Ct Lawrence KS 66049-2937 Office: U Kans Dept of Spanish/Portuguese Lawrence KS 66045-0001 E-mail: adebicki@ukans.edu.

DE BLIJ, HARM JAN, geography educator, editor; b. Schiedam, The Netherlands, Oct. 9, 1935; came to U.S., 1956; s. Hendrik and Nelly (Erwich) de B.; m. Katherine Ruth Powers, Dec. 27, 1964 (div. 1972); children: Tanya Powers, Hugh James; m. Bonnie Helen Doughty, Dec. 15, 1977. BS, U. Witwatersrand, Johannesburg, Republic South Africa, 1955; MA, Northwestern U., 1957, PhD, 1959; DSc (hon.), Marshall U., 1991; HHD (hon.), R.I. Coll., 1995; DSc (hon.), Mich. State U., 1999, Grand Valley State U., 2001, N.C. State U., 2001. Lectr. U. Natal Pietermaritzburg, Republic South Africa, 1959-60; asst. prof. Northwestern U., Evanston, Ill., 1960-61; from asst. prof. to prof. and assoc. dir. African Studies Ctr. Mich. State U., East Lansing, 1961-68; prof., chmn. dept. geography U. Miami, Coral Gables, Fla., 1968, prof., 1968-95, assoc. dean Coll. Arts and Scis., 1976-78; editor Nat. Geographic Rsch. mag. Nat. Geographic Soc., 1984-90; Disting. prof. Sch. Fgn. Svc., Georgetown U., 1990-95; univ. scientist U. South Fla., St. Petersburg, 1995-97; John Deaver Drinko Disting. Prof. Marshall U., Huntington, W.Va., 1998-2000; Disting. prof. Mich. State U., 2000—. Geography editor Good Morning Am., ABC-TV, 1990-96; geography analyst NBC News, 1996-98; cons. pubs., govt. agys. Author 30 books; contbr. numerous articles to profl. jours.; editor: Jour. Geography, 1970-75, National Geographic Research, 1984-90; writer TV series on Africa, 1962-67. Fellow Northwestern U. African Studies program, 1958-59. Fellow African Studies Assn., Am. Geog. Soc. (hon.); mem. Orgn. for Tropical Studies (bd.dirs. 1971-74), Assn. Am. Geographers (councillor 1970-72, sec. 1972-75, steering com. Southeastern div. 1971-73), Phi Beta Kappa, Sigma Xi, Phi Kappa Phi.

DEBO, GERALDINE VIRGINIA, social studies educator; b. St. Louis, July 7, 1937; d. Wendell John and Dorothy (Gebhardt) Leber; m. Anthony Paul Debo, Oct. 18, 1958; children: Tony, Michael, Lisa. BS in Secondary Ed. Social Sci., N.E. Mo. State U., 1958; MAT in Secondary Ed. Social Sci., Webster U., 1978; cert. in elem. edn., U. Mo., St. Louis, 1974. Tchr. phys. edn. Hancock Sch. Dist., Lemay, Mo., 1958-59; tchr. elem. edn. Hazelwood Sch. Dist., Florissant, Mo., 1969-75, tchr. social studies Hazelwood Cen. H.S., 1975—. Mem. numerous curriculum coms. Councilwoman City of Florissant, 1987—. Mem. NEA (bd. dirs., conv. del.), Mo. Edn. Assn. (bd. dirs. 1980-85), Hazelwood Edn. Assn. (pres. 1979-81), Florissant Hist. Soc. (bd. dirs.), Soroptomists (bd. dirs.), Florissant C. of C., Kiwanis. Home: 415 Humes Ln Florissant MO 63031-3020

DEBOER, ANNABEL, English language educator; b. Toledo, Feb. 7, 1948; d. Stanley Arthur and Shirley Mae (Ackerman) Dolgin; m. Bruce Anthony DeBoer, Aug. 22, 1970; children: Allison Beth DeBoer, Tiffiny Lynn DeBoer. BA, U. Mich., 1970; MA, U. Toledo, 1973, specialist cert., 1976. Summer sch. tchr. Toledo Pub. Schs., 1969-70; tchr. Mt. Clemens (Mich.) Pub. Schs., 1970-71, Bedford Pub. Schs., Temperance, Mich., 1971-96. Lang. arts chairperson, Bedford Pub. Schs., 1976-83, 93-96; dir. Young Authors Conf., U. Toledo, 1974-84. Mem. Toledo Jr. League, Kappa Delta Pi. Avocations: skiing, golf, exercising. Home: 6839 Ridgewood Trail Toledo OH 43617-1181 Office: Bedford Pub Schs 8405 Jackman Rd Temperance MI 48182-9459

DEBOLD, JOSEPH FRANCIS, psychology educator; b. Boston, Nov. 3, 1947; s. Joseph Francis and Patricia (Miltimore) DeB.; m. Carol Lynn Hook, Dec. 20, 1969. AB, UCLA, 1969; PhD, U. Calif., Irvine, 1976. Trainee U. Calif. NICHD Devel. & Reproductive Biology, Irvine, 1971-75; instr., rsch. assoc. Mich. State U., East Lansing, 1975-77; asst. prof. Carnegie-Mellon U., Pitts., 1977-79, Tufts U., Medford, Mass., 1979-83, assoc. prof., 1983-91, chmn. dept. psychology, 1990-93, prof., 1991—, chmn. dept. psychology, 2002—; vis. rsch. assoc. Children's Hosp. Med. Ctr., Boston, 1981-85. Advisor NSF, Washington, 1989-92. Mem. editorial bd. Hormones and Behavior, 1987-92; contbr. articles to profl. jours., chpts. to books. Grantee NSF, 1986-99, Nat. Inst. Alcoholism and Alcohol Abuse, 1980-2002, Biomed Rsch. Support Program, 1990-91. Mem. AAAS, Soc.

for Neurosci., Nat. Assn. Advisors for Health Professions, N.Y. Acad. Scis., Rsch. Soc. on Alcholism, Sigma Xi, Psi Chi. Avocations: motorcycling, tennis, volleyball. Office: Tufts U Dept Psychology 490 Boston Ave Medford MA 02155

DEBORD, MARILYN ANNE, retired secondary school educator; b. Nampa, Idaho, Dec. 14, 1936; d. Stanley Bryce and Pauline (Shirk) Keim; m. Robert Franklin DeBord, July 16, 1959; children: Christopher James, Eric Richard. BS, McPherson Coll., 1958. Cert. secondary tchr. Tchr. Boise Independent Dist., Boise, Idaho, 1958-62; tchr. Bishop Kelly High Sch., Boise, 1965, Payette High Sch., Payette, Idaho, 1968—96, ret., 1996. Reporter CBS, NBC, Payette, 1985-89. Mem. NEA, AAUW (pres. Payette chpt. 1987-89), Idaho Coun. Tchrs. English, Payette Edn. Assn. (past pres.), Idaho Edn. Assn. (past regional rep.), Idaho Journalism Advisers Assn., Lower Snake River Ret. Educators (sec., publicity, 1997-2003), Little Country Village Townhouse Owners. Republican. Methodist. Avocations: golf, bridge, walking, swimming.

DE BREMAECKER, JEAN-CLAUDE, geophysics educator; b. Antwerp, Belgium, Sept. 2, 1923; came to U.S., 1948, naturalized, 1963; s. Paul J.C. and Berthe (Bouché) De B.; m. Arlene Ann Parker, Nov. 29, 1952, (dec.); m. Ruth F. Baer, July 6, 1998; children— Christine, Suzanne. MS in Mining Engring, U. Louvain, Belgium, 1948; MS in Geology, La. State U., 1950; PhD in Geophysics, U. Cal. at Berkeley, 1952. Research scientist, sr. research scientist Inst. pour la Recherche Sci. en Afrique Centrale, Bukavu, Congo, 1952-58; Boese postdoctoral fellow Columbia, 1955-56; postdoctoral fellow Harvard, 1958-59; faculty Rice U., Houston, 1959—, prof. geophysics, 1965-94, prof. emeritus, 1994. Research asso. U. Calif., Berkeley, 1966; vis. mem. Tex. Inst. for Computational Mechanics, U. Tex., Austin, 1977; vis. prof. U. Paris, 1980-81 Author: Geophysics, the Earth's Interior, 1985. Chmn. Citizens for McCarthy, Houston, 1968. Served with Belgian Army, 1944-45. Mem. AAUP, Am. Geophys. Union, Fedn. Am. Scientists, Internat. Assn. Seismology and Physics of Earth's Interior (assoc. sec. gen. 1963-71, sec. gen. 1971-79). Home: 3115 Broadmead Dr Houston TX 77025-3819 Office: Rice U Dept Earth Sci Box 1892 Houston TX 77251

DEBS, BARBARA KNOWLES, former college president, consultant; b. Eastham, Mass., Dec. 24, 1931; d. Stanley F. and Arline (Eugley) Knowles; m. Richard A. Debs, July 19, 1958; children: Elizabeth, Nicholas. BA, Vassar Coll., 1953; PhD, Harvard U., 1967; LLD, N.Y. Law Sch., 1979; LHD, Manhattanville Coll., 1985. Freelance translator editor Ency. of World Art divsn. McGraw-Hill Pub., N.Y.C., 1959-62; from asst. prof. to prof. Manhattanville Coll., Purchase, N.Y., 1968-86, pres., 1975-85; trustee, chmn. collections com. N.Y. Hist. Soc., 1985-87, pres., CEO, 1988-92; cons. non-profit orgns. pvt. practice, 1992—. Contbr. articles on Renaissance and contemporary art to profl. publs. Mem. N.Y. Coun. Humanities, 1978-85; mem. Westchester County Bd. Ethics, 1979-84; trustee N.Y. Law Sch., 1979-89; trustee Geraldine R. Dodge Found., 1985—; bd. dirs. Internat. Found. for Art Rsch., 1985-92; trustee Com. Econ. Devel., 1985-94, Bklyn. Mus. Art, 1996—; mem. Coun. Fgn. Rels., 1983—; mem. exec. bd. Bard Ctr. for Decorative Arts, 1995—; bd. govs. Fgn. Policy Assn., 1996-2002; hon. trustee Manhattanville Coll., 1996—, Midori Found., 1998—. AAUW Nat. fellow and Ann Radcliffe fellow, 1958-59; Am. Council Learned Socs. grantee, 1973; Fulbright fellow, Pisa, Italy, 1953, U. Rome, 1954. Mem. Am. Coun. on Edn. (chmn. commn. acad. affairs 1977-79), Young Audiences (nat. dir. 1977-80), Renaissance Soc. Am., Coll. Art Assn., Phi Beta Kappa. Clubs: Cosmopolitan, Century Assn.

DE CELLES, CHARLES EDOUARD, theologian, educator; b. Holyoke, Mass., May 17, 1942; s. Fernand Pierre and Stella Marie (Shooner) De C. BA, U. Windsor, Ont., Can., 1964; MA in Theology, Marquette U., Milw., 1966; PhD, Fordham U., 1970; MA in Religion, Temple U., Phila., 1979. m. Mildred Manzano Valdez, July 17, 1978; children: Christopher Emanuel, Mark Joshua, Salvador Isaiah. Mem. faculty Dunbarton Coll. of Holy Cross, Washington, 1969-70, Marywood Coll. (became Marywood U., 1997), Scranton, Pa., 1970—, prof. religious studies, 1980—. Mem. bd. examiners U. Calicut, Kerala, India, 1985—86; subject specialist Accrediting Commn. of Distance Edn. and Tng. Coun., 1995; moderator Students Organized to Uphold Life, Marywood Coll., 1982—, co-chmn. Task Force Social Justice and Environment, 1992—93, corrector off-campus degree program, 1977—, dept. scribe, 1995—. Author: Paths of Belief, Vol. 2, 1977, prin. co-author rev. edit., 1987; The Unbound Spirit: God's Universal Sanctifying Work, 1985, Jesus: The Eternally Begotten of the Father as Human Being, 1993; editor Biographical Directory Cath. Acad. Scis. in U.S.A., 1994, Science and Religion in Dialogue, 1999; also pamphlets, articles, book revs., guest editorials, columns, letters, occasional columnist Nat. Cath. Register, 1983-87, The Dunmorean, 1996-97; regular columnist The Catholic Observer, 1996—; contbr. articles to profl. jours., mags. and newspapers. Mem. Ecumenism and Inter-faith Commn., Diocese of Scranton, 1992—, Ecumenical Leadership Com., 1999—; bd. dirs. Scranton UN Assn., 1974-75, chmn. UN Day, 1974; mem. ProLife prep. Commn. Scranton Diocesan Synod, 1984-85; mem. Filipino-Am. Assn. N.E. Pa., 1984-91, pub. rels. officer, 1985-91, editor newsletter, 1988-91; bd. dirs. Scranton chpt. Pennsylvanians for Human Life, 1983—, v.p., 1994—; leader Cath. Charismatic Prayer Group, Scranton, 1970-76; mem. pack com. Boy Scouts, Scranton, 1990-95, Cath. religious emblems counselor, 1993-96; chmn. prolife com. Immaculate Conception parish, 1994—. Recipient cert. of appreciation, U.S. Cath. Conf., 1976, Disting. Svc. award, UN Assn. U.S., 1974, Svc. award, Filipino-Am. Assn. N.E. Pa., 1990, cert. appreciation, Boy Scouts Am., 1991, 1992, 1993, 1994, 1995, Defender of Life cert. of appreciation, Susan B. Anthony List, 2003, several athletic awards for rd. running yearly, 1987—96, multiple awards for speed walking, 1990—96, 2000—02, admitted to the Order Cor Mariae, Marywood Coll., 1990, invested knight, Equestrian Order of the Holy Sepulchre of Jerusalem, 1994; Fordham U. Presdl. scholar, 1966—68. Mem. Cath. Acad. Sci. U.S.A. (pub. com. 1991—, chmn. program com. 1993-96, chmn. pub. com. 1997-2001, v.p. 1997—), Coll. Theology Soc. Am., Men of the Sacred Heart (Scranton chpt.), Scranton Organized Area Runners, Wyoming Valley Striders, Theta Alpha Kappa (chpt. moderator 1982—). Roman Catholic. Home: 923 E Drinker St Dunmore PA 18512-2644 Office: Marywood U Dept Religious Studies Scranton PA 18509-1598 E-mail: decelles@es.marywood.edu.

DE CHAMPLAIN, ANDRE FERNAND, educational researcher; b. Ottawa, Ontario, Can., May 9, 1963; came to U.S., 1992; s. Neil and Therese (Larocque) De C.; m. Judy Ellen Bodnarchuk, June 18, 1994. BA in Psychology, U. Ottawa, Ontario, Can., 1986, MA in Edn., 1989, PhD in Edn., 1992. Assoc. measurement statistician Ednl. Testing Svc., Princeton, N.J., 1992-93; rsch. scientist Law Sch. Admission Coun., Newtown, Pa., 1993—. Recipient Master's fellowship Ontario Grad. Studies Coun., 1988-89, Doctoral fellowship Social Scis. Rsch. Coun. of Can., 1989-92. Mem. Am. Ednl. Rsch. Assn., Nat. Coun. on Measurement in Edn., Am. Stats. Assn. Avocation: music. Office: Law Sch Admission Coun 661 Penn St # 40 Newtown PA 18940-1801

DE CHERNEY, ALAN HERSH, obstetrics and gynecology educator; b. Phila., Feb. 13, 1942; s. William Aaron and Ruth (Hersh) DeC.; m. Deanna Faith Saver, June 26, 1966; children: Peter, Alexander. BS in Natural Scis., Muhlenberg Coll., 1963; MD, Temple U., 1967; MA (hon.), Yale U., 1985. Diplomate Am. Bd. Ob.-Gyn. (examiner 1984—, bd. dirs. 1995—), Am.Bd. Reproductive Endocrinology (bd. dirs. 1988-94), Nat. Bd. Med. Examiners (examiner 1987-90). Intern in gen. medicine U. Pitts., 1967-68; resident in ob-gyn. U. Pa., Phila., 1968-72, instr. dept. ob-gyn, 1970-72; asst. prof. ob-gyn. Yale U. Sch. Medicine, New Haven, 1974-78, assoc. prof., 1979-84, prof., 1984-91, John Slade Ely prof. ob-gyn, 1987-92, dir. div. reproductive endocrinology, dept. ob-gyn, 1982-92, lectr. dept. biology, 1985-92; Louis E. Phaneuf prof., chmn. dept. ob-gyn. Tufts U. Sch. Medicine, 1992-96; prof. dept. ob-gyn. UCLA, 1996—. Editor (in chief): Fertility and Sterility, 1996—. Maj. U.S. Army, 1972—74. Recipient Disting. Alumni award Temple U., 1989, 2002, Muhlenberg Coll., 1994. Fellow ACOG, Am. Fertility Soc. (pres. 1994-95), Am. Assn. History of Medicine, Soc. for Assisted Reproductive Tech. (pres. 1987-88), Soc. Reproductive Endocrinologists (pres. 1988), Soc. Reproductive Surgeons (charter, pres. 1991), Endocrine Soc., European Soc. Human Reproductions and Embryology, Soc. Gynecologic Surgeons, Soc. for Study of Reproduction, Soc. Gynecologic Investigation (pres. 1994-95). Office: UCLA Sch Medicine Dept Ob/Gyn 27-177 CHS Mail Code 174017 10833 Le Conte Ave Los Angeles CA 90095-3075

DECICCO, JAMES JOSEPH, media and technology supervisor; children: Mickey, Chuck, Jane. AA in Edn., Atlantic C.C., 1971; BS in Edn., Temple U., 1973, MED, 1978. Cert. media specialist, tchr. N.J. State Dept. Edn. Tchr. Hammonton (N.J.) H.S., 1973-84; media specialist Pinelands Regional Mid. Sch., Tuckerton, 1985-2000; supr. media and tech. Pleasantville (N.J.) Sch. Dist., 2000—. Former vice chmn. Town Planning Bd.; former mem. Hammonton Bd. Edn., Home/Sch. Assn., Hammonton; instr. 1st United Meth. Ch. Pres.'s scholar, 1973. Mem. NEA, ASCD, N.J. Edn. Assn., N.J. Sch. Bds. Assn., Ednl. Media Assn. N.J. Avocations: fishing, mountain biking. Home: 568 Radio Rd Tuckerton NJ 08087 Office: Pleasantville Mid Sch 801 Mill Rd Pleasantville NJ 08232

DECK, JUDITH THERESE, elementary school educator; b. Chgo., Feb. 1, 1947; d. Jerry S. and Rose Christine (Bartik) Pojeta; m. H.H. Skipp Gergory (dec.); children: Kurt, Kevin, Kristina; m. Donald Paul Deck (div.); 1 child, Jennifer. BS in Elem. Edn., Ind. U., Ft. Wayne, 1988, MS in Elem. Edn., 1992, postgrad., 1994—. Cert. mid. sch. tchr. math., lang. arts, social studies, Ind. 6th grade tchr. Smith Green Cmty. Shcs., Churubusco, Ind., 1988—, mem. strategic planning com., tech. plan grant com., staff devel. com., home tutor, 1996—. Sec. Whitley County Youth Improvement Adv. Bd., 1997—. Grantee Ind. and Mich. Power, 1993-94. Mem. Internat. Reading Assn., Sch. Improvement Planning Coun. (curriculm writing/textbook adoption com., student handbook com. 1988-94), Classroom Tchrs. Assn. (co-pres. 1993-94), Kappa Delta Pi. Roman Catholic. Avocations: golfing, reading. Office: Smith Green Cmty Schs 2 Eagle Dr Churubusco IN 46723-1400

DECKER, BEVERLY ANNE, art educator, museum arts program director; b. Dayton, Ohio, Oct. 21, 1945; d. Richard Thomas and Janet (Browning) Dungan; m. Larry Raymond Decker, Aug. 27, 1965; children: Shawn Dungan, Josh Dungan. BA, Calif. State U., Long Beach, 1968; MFA, U. Ariz., 1972. Cert. coll. tchr., Calif. Tchr.'s aid Tucson Sch. Dist., 1970-71; tchr. U. Ariz., Tucson, 1968-72; substitute tchr. various secondary schs. Anaheim and Orange, Calif., 1972-73; art tchr. Orange Coast Coll., Costa Mesa, Calif., 1973-78, Coastline C.C., Costa Mesa, 1973-78, Valdez C.C., Santa Fe, 1980-83, Valdez Mid. Sch., Santa Barbara, Calif., 1989; art tchr. adult edn. Santa Barbara City Coll., 1985—; adminstr. Santa Barbara Mus. Art-Ridley-Tree Edn. Ctr., 1989—. Bd. dirs. Santa Barbara Art Assn., 1987-89; mem. edn. com. Santa Barbara Mus. Art, 1988—; bd. dirs. Art Affiliates U. Calif. Santa Barbara, 1992—; mem. Santa Barbara Arts Commn., 1992—. Exhibited throughout Calif., Ariz., N.M., Can. and Australia. Mem. AIDS Awareness Quilting Bee, Santa Fe, 1979-83. Home: PO Box 1048 Summerland CA 93067-1048 Office: Santa Barbara Mus Art Ridley-Tree Edn Ctr 1600 Santa Barbara St Santa Barbara CA 93101-1912

DECKER, PETER WILLIAM, academic administrator; b. Grand Rapids, Mich., Mar. 20, 1919; s. Charles B. and Ruth E. (Thorndill) D.; m. Margaret I. Stainthorpe, June 10, 1944; children: Peter, Marilyn, Christine, Charles. BS, Wheaton Coll., 1941; postgrad., Northwestern U., 1942-43, U. Mich., 1958-60; DSc, London Inst. Applied Rsch., 1973; LLD, 1975; DSTh, Midwestern Baptist Bible Sem., 1995. Withadvtg. dept. Hotels Windermere, Chgo., 1942; with Princess Pat Cosmetics, Chgo., 1943; market rsch. investigator A.C. Nielson Co., Chgo., 1944-48; pres. Peter Decker Constrn. Co., Detroit, 1948-60; sales mgr. Century Chem. Products Co., Detroit, 1961-62, vice pres., 1962-63, pres., 1963-75; sr. ptnr. G & D Advtg. Assocs., 1967-78; vice pres., treas., exec. dir. Christian Edn. Advancement, Inc., 1975-95; registrar, instr. N.T. Greek Missions and Theology Birmingham Bible Inst., MI, 1973-86; prof. Midwestern Baptist Coll., 1984—, dir. student fin. aid, 1984—. Trustee Midwestern Baptist Coll., 1985—, mem. exec. com., 1984—, asst. to pres. 1985-90, treas. 1991-95; bd. dirs., prof., trusteeMidwestern Bapt. Bible Sem., 1995—, vice pres. Midewestern Bapt. Bible Seminary Grad. Sch., 1998—. Author: Gettin to Know New Testament Greek, Christology, The Pauline Epistles. Scoutmaster, Boy Scouts of Am., 1956-61, neighborhood commr., 1961-66, merit badge counselor, emeritus, 1979—; mem. Bd. Rev. Beverly Hills, Mich., 1957-63; chmn. Bd. Rev. Southfield Twp., Mich., 1964-67; past pres., Beverly Hills Civic Assn., 1956, bd. dirs., 1953-57, pres., 1958-59; trustee, deacon, Birmingham Mich. Bible Inst., instr. Bible Inst.; bd. dirs. Mich. Epilepsy Ctr. and Assn., 1957-71, exec. com., 1962-67. Recipient Arrowhead Honor awd. Boy Scouts Am., 1965. Mem. AAAS, ASTM, Mich. Edn. Assocs., Inc. (exec. com. 1994—, treas. 1994-95), Detroit Soc. Model Engrs. (pres. 1958, 62, bd. dirs. 1955-71), Chem. Splty. Mfg. Assn., Nat. Geog. Soc., Internat. Platform Assn., The Heritage Found., Smithsonian Instn. Assocs., Archaeol. Inst. Am., Bibl. Archaeol. Soc., Bible-Sci. Assn., Creation Rsch. Soc., Mich. Student Fin. Aid Assn., Midwest Assn. Student Fin. Aid Adminstrs. Republican. Avocations: biographies, writings of great christians. Home: 32210 Rosevear St Beverly Hills MI 48025-3921 Office: Midwestern Baptist Coll 825 Golf Dr Pontiac MI 48341-2379

DECKER, ROBERT OWEN, history educator, clergyman; b. Lafayette, Ind., Nov. 6, 1927; s. Samuel Owen and Helen Dale (Noble) D.; m. Margaret Ann Harris, May 30, 1948; 1 child, Terry Lynn Decker DeJulis. AB, Butler U., 1953; AM, Ind. U., 1958; PhD, U. Conn., 1970. Ordained to ministry Congregational Ch., 1990. Instr. City of LaPorte (Ind.) Schs., 1956—59, Ctrl. Conn. State U., New Britain, 1959-63, asst. prof., 1963-73, assoc. prof., 1973-77, prof. history, 1977-89, prof. emeritus, 1989—. Editor manuscripts Wesleyan U. Press, 1977-89; advisor NEH, 1977-89, Connecticut River Found. Author: Whaling Industry of New London, 1973, The Whaling City: A History of New London, 1976, A Student Guidebook to American History, 1983, Hartford Immigrants, 1987, The New London Merchants, 1986, Cromwell, Connecticut 1650-1990: The History of A River Port Town, 1991; contbr. articles and book revs. to profl. jours. Mem. Christian Activities Coun., Hartford, 1965—, pres., 1972-74, 76-78, historian, 1983—, life mem., 1996—; bd. dirs. Hartford Inner City Exch., 1971-81, chmn. bd., 1977-80; chmn. state legis. adv. com. Conn. Devel. Disabilities Coun., 1973-75; evaluator programs Conn. Humanities Coun.; historian Rocky Hill (Conn.) Congl. Ch., 1985-89, Conn. 350th Com., 1985-89; justice of peace, Rocky Hill, 1985-89, 2000—, constable, 1986-89, 2002—, apptd. town historian, 1988—; mem. Assn. Conn. Mcpl. Historians, 1988—, membership sec., 1994—, pres., 1996-97; pastor Eagle Rock Congl. Ch., 1989-93, Bozrah Centre Congl. Ch., 1994-95, supply pastor, 1995-2001; mem. exec. bd. Conn. Congl. Christian Chs., 1995-2001; pastor Barkhamstead Ctr. Congl. Ch., 2001—; mem. UCC Hist. Com., 1989-92, Rep. Town Comm., Rocky Hill, 2000—; dir. Old Towne Tourism Dist. Conn., 1989-90; justice of peace, 1998—. Served with U.S. Army, 1946-52. Asian Studies grantee, 1959; Am. Studies grantee, 1959; Danforth grantee, 1962; Munson Maritime grantee, 1961; Smithsonian Inst. grantee, 1963; recipient Pierport Edwards award, 2003. Mem. AAUP, Orgn. Am. Historians, Am. Hist. Assn., New Eng. Hist. Assn., Conn. Hist. Assn., Assn. for Study of Conn. History, New London County Hist. Soc., Am. Waldensian Aid Soc. (pres. Hartford chpt. 1986-89), Masons (Master Stepney Lodge 1990, 92, Master's award 1992, Arthur E. Warner award 1996, Master Silas Deans Lodge 2001—02, Grand Chaplain 1997-2003, High Priest Delta chpt. 1998-99, Knight Mason 1998—, master Philosophic Lodge Rsch., worshipful master 2000-01, Master's award 2001, 2002, eminent comdr. 2001—02, thrice illustrious master Walcott Coun. I 2000-01, high priest 2001—02, assoc. grand prelate, 2002-), Royal Arch Masons, Phi Alpha Delta. Republican. Congregationalist (life deacon). Home: 2623 Main St Rocky Hill CT 06067-2507 Office: Fellowship Conn Congl Chs 277 Main St Hartford CT 06106-1818 E-mail: robertowendecker@world.net.att.net.

DECOTIS, RUTH JANICE, career planning administrator, educator; b. Lebanon, N.H., July 3, 1949; d. David Gilman Fowler and Olive Leonie Greenwood; m. Terry L. DeCotis, Sept. 2, 1967; children: Gregory, Curtis, Erin. AS magna cum laude in Sec. Sci., Plymouth State Coll., 1989, BS magna cum laude in Adminstrn. Mgmt. & Comm., 1995, MEd magna cum laude in Counselor Edn. & Human Rels., 1998. Sec. Equity Pub., Orford, NH, 1969—79; sec. social sci. dept. Plymouth State Coll., Plymouth, NH, 1980—86, from program asst. to academic & career adv. ctr., 1986—. Travel agt. Plymouth Travel, Plymouth, 1991—. Co-author: Great Jobs for Math Majors, 1998. Mem.: Assn. for Psychol. Type, Nat. Academic Adv. Assn., Nat. Soc. Experiential Edn., Am. Counseling Assn. Avocations: travel, antiques, restoration of old homes. Office: Plymouth State Coll Academic & Career Adv Ctr 17 High St MSC 44 Plymouth NH 03264 Fax: 603-535-2528. E-mail: rdecotis@mail.plymouth.edu.

DE CUBA, MARJORIE HERRMANN, retired bilingual educator; b. Newark, July 21, 1926; d. Ellsworth James and Grace M. Wyre; m. Arthur Herrmann Aug. 1, 1947 (div. 1962); children: Aleta Kennedy, Ralph, Aprylle Desrosiers; m. Aloysius Marcos de Cuba, May 18, 1985. BA, Montclair State U., 1948; MA, Fairfield U., 1969; Maitrise en Lettres Modernes, U. Dijon, France, 1971; PhD, U. Tex., 1975. Cert. French, Spanish, English tchr., N.J., Conn., N.H., Iowa. Bilingual cons. Tex. Edn. Agy. - Region X, Richardson, 1975-76; dir. bilingual tchr. edn. Tex. Christian U., 1976-79; asst. prof., bilingual cons. Boston U., 1979-80; dir. Spanish & Greek bilingual programs, ESOL program Norwalk Pub. Schs., Norwalk, Conn., 1980-81; cons. ESL tchr. training N.H. State Dept. Edn., Concord, N.H., 1980-82; ESL specialist Ind. Vocat. Tech. Coll., 1991-94. Lectr. Tex. Assn. Bilingual Edn., Beaumont, Tex., 1976, Nat. Assn. Bilingual Edn., Boston, 1979. Author: (instrnl. bilingual series) El Pájaro Cú, Pérez y Martina, Las Manchas del Sapo, 1979. Rsch., Lecturing grantee Fulbright Commn., Japan, 1984. Avocations: oil painting, acrylics. Home: 9913 Erinsbrook Dr Raleigh NC 27617-8333

DEDE, BONNIE AILEEN, librarian, educator; b. Racine, Wis., Mar. 21, 1942; d. Edward Charles and Gracebelle Roeber; children: Suzan A., Ercan M. BA, U. Mich., 1963, MA, 1966, AM in Libr. Sci., 1968; cert., U. Ill., 1970. Various positions U. Mich. Libr., Ann Arbor, 1967—88, head spl. formats cataloging, 1988—99, adj. lectr. sch. info., 1989—, head monograph cataloging prodn., 1999—. Mem. part-time faculty libr. and info. sci. program Wayne State U., Detroit, 1993—; vis. lectr. Grad. Sch. Libr. and Info. Sci. U. Ill., Urbana-Champaign, 2003—; cons. Gale Rsch., Detroit, 1993; reviewer Am. Reference Books Ann., 1992—; cons. grant projects OCLC, 1991—92, 1994—96. Mem. editl. bd. MC, Jour. Acad. Media Librarianship, 1992-2002. Grantee Title II-B, U.S. Office Edn., 1970, faculty-libr. coop. rsch. grantee Coun. on Libr. Resources, 1986-88, access grantee NEH, 1990-93. Mem. ALA, Alpha Lambda Delta, Beta Phi Mu (pres. Mu chpt. 1991-96). Office: U Mich 100 Hatcher Libr North Ann Arbor MI 48109-1205

DEEDS, BARBARA CATHERINE, special education vocational educator; b. Johnstown, Pa., May 25, 1947; d. Hubert Bernard and Angeline (B.) Nagle; m. Gary Wayne Deeds, Dec. 5, 1969; children; Adria, Alison, Austin. BA in Edn., U. South Fla., 1969, MA in Edn., 1973. Cert. tchr., vocat. evaluator, Fla. Tchr. Pasco County Schs., Dade City, Fla., 1970-74; cons. Fla. Learning Resource Ctr., Chipley, Fla., 1974-76; tchr., job developer Bay County Schs., Panama City, 1976-80, vocat. specialist, 1980-93; cons., pvt. vocat. evaluation svcs. Panama City, 1990—. State adv. bd. Fla. Network, Gainesville, 1992-94; sch. bd. mem. St. Dominic's Sch., Panama City, 1992-94; state adv. bd. Career Blueprint for ESE, 1990-93; state trainer for curriculum assessment. Mem. Gulf Coast Women's Club, Panama City, 1991-92. Regional dir. Fla. Spl. Olympics, 1980-85; pres. Bay County 4C Coun. Bd., 1982-85; bd. dirs. St. John's Sch., 1986-88; vocat. assessment provider State Dvsn. Worker's Compensation. Recipient Master Tchr. award State of Fla., 1985-87. Mem. Fla. Vocat. Evaluation Assn. (regional dir. 1989-93), Fla. Rehab. Assn., Fla. Spl. Needs Assn. (pres. 1990), Fla. Vocat. Assn., Phi Delta Kappa. Democrat. Roman Catholic. Home: 321 Massalina Dr Panama City FL 32401-3708

DEEDS, ZOE ANN, special education educator, department chairman; b. Bethpage, N.Y., Dec. 20, 1956; d. Douglas Alan and Elinor June (Mills) Deeds; 1 child, Stephanie. AAS, SUNY, Farmingdale, 1977; BS in Elem. Edn., SUNY, Geneseo, 1979; MA in Spl. Edn., Hofstra U., Uniondale, N.Y., 1981; PD in Sch. Adminstrn., L.I. U., 1992. Cert. sch. adminstr., elem., spl. and hearing impaired educator. Evaluator/tchr. Helen Keller Nat. Ctr., Sandspoint, N.Y., 1979-82; spl. edn. tchr. Nassau Ctr. for Developmentally Disabled, Woodbury, N.Y., 1982-85; asst. prin. Lake Grove (N.Y.) Sch., 1985-92; chairperson spl. edn. Lindenhurst (N.Y.) Pub. Schs., 1992—. Adj. prof./tchr. Adelphi U., Garden City, N.Y., 1987-94; cons. and lectr. in field. Com. mem. L.I. Resource Com., 1989, Newsday, Lake Grove, 1987; leader Career Awareness, Boy Scouts Am., Lake Grove, 1987-92; trainer East Farmingdale Fire Dept., 1992. Mem. Coun. Exceptional Children, L.I. Assn. Supervision and Curriculum Devel., Spl. Edn. Parent Assn. (scholarship chair 1992—). Mem. Council for Exceptional Children, L.I. Assn. Supervision and Curriculum Devel., Spl. Edn. Parent Assn. (scholarship chair 1992—). Avocations: skiing, painting, gardening. Avocations: skiing, painting, gardening. Office: Lindenhurst High Sch 350 Charles St Lindenhurst NY 11757-3902

DEEGAN, JOHN, JR., academic administrator, researcher; b. Elizabeth, N.J., Nov. 18, 1944; s. John and Margaret (Pignataro) D.; m. Anita Hope Rochelle, Dec. 19, 1964; children: Michael J.. Matthew B. Student, Monmouth Coll., West Long Branch, N.J., 1962-64; BS, Evangel Coll., Springfield, Mo., 1967; MA, U. Mich., 1969, PhD, 1972. Asst. prof. Rice U., Houston, 1972-75, U. Rochester, N.Y., 1975-80, assoc. prof., 1980; spl. asst. to dep. adminstr. EPA, Washington, 1980; dir. Love Canal Project, 1980-82; assoc. dean Sch. Pub. Health U. Ill., Chgo., 1982-86, acting dean, 1983-85; prof. U. No. Iowa, Cedar Falls, 1986-89, dean Coll. Social and Behavioral Scis., 1986-89; provost, v.p. acad. affairs, prof. U. So. Maine, Portland, 1989-94; dean coll., v.p. acad. affairs, prof. Westminster Coll., New Wilmington, Pa., 1994—2002; pres., prof. St. Andrews Presbyn. Coll., Laurinburg, NC, 2002—. Cons. EPA, 1983-86; trustee Ill. Cancer Coun., 1983-86; bd. dirs. Leopold Ctr. for Sustainable Agr. State of Iowa, 1987-89. Contbr. articles to sci. jours. Recipient EPA Bronze medal award, 1982; U. Rochester fellow in preventive medicine, 1979, Acad. Adminstrn. fellow Am. Coun. on Edn., 1986-87. Mem. AAAS, APHA, Am. Chem. Soc., Sigma Xi, Delta Omega. Democrat. Presbyterian. Avocations: fishing, golfing. Office: Office of the President St Andrews Presbyn Coll Laurinburg NC 28352

DEEGAN, MARY JO, sociology educator; b. Chgo., Nov. 27, 1946; d. William James and Ida May (Scott) Deegan; life ptnr. Michael Ray Hill. AS, Lake Mich. Coll., 1966; BS, Western Mich. U., 1969, MA, 1973; PhD, U. Chgo., 1975. Asst. prof. U. Nebr., Lincoln, 1975-80, assoc. prof., 1980-89, prof., 1989—. Med. trainee U. Chgo. Ctr. for Health Adminstrn., 1972-75; grad. asst. Western Mich. U., 1969-71.; del. Conf. on Directions in Health Econs., New Orleans, 1972. Author: Jane Addams and Men of the Chicago School, 1892-1918, 1988 (Choice award, 1989), American Ritual Dramas, 1989, Race, Hull House, and the University of Chicago, 2002; editor: Women in Sociology, 1991, American Ritual Tapestry, 1998, Play, School and Society, 1999, Essays on Social Psychology, 2001, The New Woman of Color, 2002, Women at the Hague, 2003; co-editor: Women and Disability, 1985, Women and Symbolic Interaction, 1987, Feminist Ethics in Social Research, 1989, With Her in Ourland, 1997; co-editor: (with C.P. Gilman) The Dress of Women, 2002; co-editor: On Art, Labor, and Religion, 2003; series editor Women & Sociological Theory, 2001; contbr. articles to profl. jours. Mem.: Harriet Martineau Sociol. Soc., Internat. Sociol. Assn., Am. Sociol. Assn. (Disting. Scholarly Career award in history of sociology 2002). Office: Dept Sociology 711 Oldfather Hall U Nebraska Lincoln NE 68588-0324

DEEL, GEORGE MOSES, elementary school educator; b. Haysi, Va., Apr. 9, 1938; s. Emory Floyd and Nancy Jane Deel. BS, Emory (Va.) & Henry Coll., 1961; MEd, Radford (Va.) U., 1965. Cert. tchr. Tchr. math. and gen. sci. Grundy (Va.) Jr. High Sch., 1961-79; resource tchr. gifted and academically talented Vansant (Va.) Elem. Sch., 1979-91; ret., 1991; cons. on gifted and talented Vansant (Va.) Elem. Sch., 1991—. Mem. NEA, Assn. Supervision and Curriculum Devel., Va. Edn. Assn., Buchanan Edn. Assn. Avocations: reading, working with computers, listening to music, football spectator. Home and Office: RR 2 Box 168 Haysi VA 24256-9503

DEEL, REBECCA LYNNE, business educator; b. Nashville, Sept. 3, 1964; d. Jack L. and Janis June (Wilcox) Williams; m. Levia Ricardo Deel, Mar. 9, 1990. BS, Free Will Bapt. Bible Coll., Tenn., 1986; MBA, Middle Tenn. State U., Murfreesboro, Tenn., 1989, ArtsD, 1995. Sec. Spanish dept. Randall House Publ., Nashville, 1986-87; grad. asst. internat. student svc. Mid. Tenn. State U., Murfreesboro, Tenn., 1987-88; tchr. Free Will Bapt. Bible Coll., Nashville, 1988—, acting chair bus. dept., 2001—02. Mem. Christian Bus. Faculty Assn.(cert.), Beta Gamma Sigma. Republican. Office: Free Will Bapt Coll 3606 W End Ave Nashville TN 37205-2498 E-mail: rdeel@fwbbc.edu.

DEER, ADA E. former federal agency official, social worker, educator; b. Menominee Indian Reservation, Wis., Aug. 7, 1935; d. Joe and Constance (Wood) D. BA in Social Work, U. Wis., 1957, LDH (hon.), 1974; MSW, Columbia U., 1961; postgrad., U. N.Mex., 1971, U. Wis., 1971-72; D in Pub. Svc. (hon.), Northland Coll., 1974. Group worker Protestant Coun. N.Y., N.Y.C. Youth Bd., 1958-60; program dir. Edward F. Waite Neighborhood House, Mpls., 1961-64; community svc. coord. bur. Indian affairs Dept. of Interior, Mpls., 1964-67; coord. Indian affairs Tng. Ctr. Cmty. Programs U. Minn., Mpls., 1967-68; trainer Project Peace Pipe Peace Corps., Arecibo, P.R., 1968; sch. social worker Mpls. Pub. Schs., 1968-69; dir. Upward Bound U. Wis., Stevens Point, 1969-70, dir. Program Recognizing Individual Determination through Edn., 1970-71; v.p., lobbyist Nat. Com. Save Menominee People and Forest, Inc., Washington and State of Wis., 1972-73; chair Menominee Restoration Com., Wis., 1974-76; lectr. Sch. Social Work, Am. Indians Studies Program U. Wis., Madison, 1977—93, 1997—, dir. Am. Indian Studies program, 2000—; asst. sec. Indian Affairs U.S. Dept. Interior, Washington, 1993—97. Legis. liaison Native Am. Rights Fund, Washington, 1979-81; cons., trainer Nat. Women's Edn. Fund, Washington, 1979-85; founding mem. Am. Indian Scholarships, Inc., Albuquerque, 1973-85; apptd. Joint Commn. on Mental Health of Children, Inc., Washington, 1967-68, Youth for Understanding, Wis., 1985-90; mem. adv. panel Office Technology Assessment, Washington, 1984-86; mem. Nat. Indian Adv. Com., Washington, 1989-91, Milw., 1990—, numerous other coms.; spkr. in field. Vice chair Nat. Mondale/Ferraro Presdl. Campaign, Washington, 1984; del.-at-large Dem. Nat. Conv., San Francisco, 1984; mem. spl. com. minority presence Girls Scouts U.S.A., N.Y.C., 1975-77, mem., 1969-75; bd. dirs. Planned Parenthood, Mpls., 1965-66, Indian Cmty. Sch., Milw., 1989—, Native Am. Rights Fund, Boulder, 1984-90, chmn., 1989-90, chair nat. support com., 1990—; mem. bd. improving health Native Ams. Robert Wood Johnson Found., Princeton, N.J., 1988—; bd. dirs. Quincentenary Com. Smithsonian Instn., Washington, 1989—, Hunt Commn. Dem. Nat. Com., Washington, 1981-82, Ind. Sector, Washington, 1980-84, Rural Am., Washington, 1978-85, Ams. for Indian Oppty., 1970-83; apptd. Pres. Commn. White House Fellowships, 1977-83; active Common Cause, Washington, 1974-78, Wis. Women's Coun., Madison, 1983-84, Camp Miniwanca, Stony Lake, Mich., 1953-57, Coun. Founds., Washington, 1977-83, Madison Urban League; Dem. candidate Wis. Sec. State, 1982; chair Menominee Nation, Wis., 1974-76. Recipient White Buffalo Coun. Achievement award, 1974, Politzer award Ethical Culture Soc., 1975, Wonder Woman Found. award, 1982, Indian Coun. Fire Achievement award, 1984, Nat. Disting. Achievement award Am. Indian Resources Inst., 1991; named Woman of Yr. by Girl Scouts Am., 1982; honoree Nat. Women's History Month Poster, 1987, Heroine Calendar Nat. Women's Studies Assn., 1987; Harvard U. fellow, 1977-78, Delta Gamma Found. Meml. fellow, 1960, John Hay Whitney Found. Meml. fellow, 1960; Menominee Tribal scholar, 1953-55. Mem. ACLU, NOW, Nat. Women's Polit. Caucus, Nat. Congress Am. Indians, Nat. Assn. Social Workers (pres. Wis. chpt. 1988-90, nat. com. women's issues 1988-90, decision making task force 1988-90, minorities com. 1977-81), Assn. Am. Indians and Alaska Native Social Workers (pres. Wis. 1978-80), Common Cause, Nature Conservancy. Avocations: reading, traveling. Office: Ethnic Studies Coll Letters and Sci 318 Ingraham Hall M 1155 Observatory Dr Madison WI 53706*

DEERING, BRENDA FLORINE, secondary education educator; b. Porterville, Calif., July 25, 1953; d. Kenneth Henry Rogers and Barbara Oleta (Herron) Ledbetter; m. Robert Edward Deering, Feb. 14, 1975; children: David James, Duane Jason. BS in Psychology, Tex. Wesleyan U., 1989, MS in Edn., 1993. Lic. alcohol and drug abuse counselor; bd. cert. alcohol & drug abuse, alcohol & drug counselor. Substitute tchr. Birdville Ind. Sch. Dist., Haltom City, Tex., 1984-94; pvt. practice counselor pvt. practice, Bedford, Tex., 1991—; counselor Residential Treatment Ctr., Bedford, Tex., 1990-91; tchr. secondary sch. Birdville Ind. Sch. Dist., 1994—; First Hurst Enrichment Ctr., 1995—. Counseling affiliate Tarrant Bapt. Assn., Ft. Worth, 1992-94; tchr. ESOL Bedford Pub. Libr., 1993-94. Named Vol. of Yr. City of Bedford, 1993. Mem. NEA, Nat. Coun. Tchrs. English, Tex. Assn. Alcohol and Drug Abuse Counselors (edn. com. 1990—), Internat. Reading Assn., Sigma Tau Delta (Creative Writing award 1992), Pi Lambda Theta (corr. sec. 1993-96), Kappa Delta Pi. Avocation: reading. Home: 109 Brush Creek Dr Azle TX 76020-1580 Office: Haltom Mid Sch 5000 Hires Ln Haltom City TX 76117-3615

DEETHS, LENORE CLAIR, retired secondary education educator; b. Omaha, Oct. 27, 1940; d. Edward James and Bess Helen (Sabatka) Baburek; m. Harry Jeoffrey Deeths, June 15, 1963; children: Lisa Marie, Matthew Jeoffrey, Maria Lenore. BA in English, Coll. St. Mary, Omaha, 1962. Tchr. English Holy Name High Sch., Omaha, 1962-64, Berlitz Lang. Sch., Tokyo, 1969-72; substitute tchr. Tachikawa (Japan) USAF High Sch., 1969-72. Chair Coll. St. Mary Alumnae Assn., Omaha, 1979-80, chmn. breakfast series, 1990-92. Editor: (newsletter) Pulse Beat, 1965-69; author/producer (TV show) Health Topics, 1985-91. Chaired Officers' Wives Scholarship Com., 1971; br. chmn. Am. Assn. of Univ. Women Quality of Life Study, 1976-78; chaired fundraiser St. Joseph Hosp. and Creighton Med. Sch., 1979; publicity chmn. Emergency Pregnancy Svc. Omaha, 1980-85. Mem. AAUW (pres. 1991-92, 1st v.p. 1981-83, 3d v.p. 1983-84, br. chmn. 1978-80, br. del. chmn. nat. conv. 1991, br. del. chmn. Nat. Centennial Conv. 1981), LWV, Omaha Symphony Guild, Omaha Comty. Playhouse (box office vol.), Omaha News Bull., Met. Omaha Med. Alliance (Merit award 1991, bd. dirs. 1989-91, pub. rels. com. 1985-90, pres. 1993-94, advisor 1994-95, past editor and co-prodr. health topics for Cox Cable), Nebr. Med. Assn. Alliance (bd. dirs. 1994-96, parliamentarian 1994-97), Friends of Children's Hosp., Girls Inc. (vice chair career devel. 1992-93, chair 1993-94). Avocations: internat. travel, cooking, reading, writing. Home: 402 N 97th Ct Omaha NE 68114-2395

DE FABO, EDWARD CHARLES, photobiology and photoimmunology, research scientist, educator; b. Wilkes-Barre, Pa., June 10, 1937; s. Giovanni and Anna (Marconi) De F.; m. Athena Macris, Aug. 17, 1967 (dec. June 1985); m. Frances Patricia Noonan. BS, Kings Coll., 1958; PhD, George Washington U., 1974. Rsch. scientist USDA, Beltsville, Md., 1974-75, NCI-Frederick (Md.) Cancer Rsch. Ctr., 1978-81; scientist, adminstr. U.S. EPA, Washington, 1975-78; asst. rsch. prof. dept. dermatology George Washington U., Washington, 1981-86, assoc. rsch. prof. dept. dermatology, 1986-92, rsch. prof. dept. dermatology, 1992—. Chmn. project Sci. Com. on Problems of Environ. SCOPE ozone depletion and UV radiation, Paris, 1989-92; cons. U.S. EPA, 1984-85; chmn. project Internat. Arctic Sci. Com., Oslo, 1993—. Editor, organizer publ. Sci. Com. on Problems of Environment, 1992; contbr. articles to rsch. jours.; author: Immunology Today, 1992. Dir. congl. sci. fellowship program Am. Soc. Photobiology, Bethesda, 1981-85. Grantee Internat. Union Against Cancer, 1983, Am. Cancer Soc., 1987-89, U.S. EPA, 1987—, NIH, 1989—; fellow Smithsonian Inst., 1970-74, NSF, 1963-64; recipient Global Ozone award UN Environment Program, 1997, Elaine H. Snyder Cancer Rsch. award George Washington U., 1998. Mem. AAAS, Am. Soc. Photobiology (councilor 1980-83, dir. congl. sci. fellowship program 1981-85). Achievements include discovery (with F.P. Noonan)of a sunlight-activated immune-regulating photoreceptor on skin-urocanic acid; co-designer of unique UV monochromator for in vivo action spectrum studies. Office: George Washington U Med Ctr Ross Hall Rm 101-B 2300 I St NW Washington DC 20037-2336

DE FAZIO, JACK JOSEPH, school system administrator, coach; b. Long Branch, N.J., Aug. 12, 1952; s. Joseph Peter and Josephine Ann (Rubino) De F.; m. Susan De Fazio, Aug. 14, 1976. BA, Marshall U., 1974, MA, 1976. Cert. tchr. K-12 phys. edn., 1-8 elem. edn., 7-12 health edn., K-12 spl. edn., elem. prin., secondary prin., W.Va. Dir. project Y-not YMCA/Cabell County Schs., Huntington, W.Va., 1976-79; elem. phys. edn. tchr. Cabell County Schs., Huntington, W.Va., 1979-86, adapted phys. edn. coord., 1987-92, job developer, 1993—; soccer coach Huntington East H.S., 1979-80, Marshall U., Huntington, 1981-89, Huntington H.S., 1992—, Cabell Midland H.S., 1997—. Cons. U.S. Youth Soccer Assn. Nat. Top Soccer, 1999—. Bd. dirs. W.Va. Spl. Olympics, Parkersburg, 1992—, dir. soccer, 1986—, dir. summers games, 1987-91; pres. Cabell County Spl. Olympics, Huntington, 1985—; co-dir. Mountain State Games, Huntington, 1992. Named one of Outstanding Young Educators Huntington Jaycees, 1976, Coach of Yr. So. Conf., 1982. Mem. W.Va. Soccer Assn. (dir. coaching 1981-85), NAt. Soccer Coaches Assn., Coun. for Exceptional Children (pres. 1976), H.S. Soccer Ofcls. Assn. (pres. 1977-79), H.S. Coaches Assn. (pres. 1979-80, Coach of Yr. 1979, 80). Office: Cabell County Schs 620 20th St Huntington WV 25703-1513 E-mail: jdefazio@access.k12,wu/us.

DEFAZIO, LYNETTE STEVENS, dancer, educator, choreographer, writer, actress; b. Berkeley, Calif., Sept. 29, 1930; d. Honore and Mabel J. (Estavan) Stevens; children: J.H. Panganiban, Joanna Pang. Student, U. Calif., Berkeley, 1950-55, San Francisco State Coll., 1950-51; studied classical dance teaching techniques and vocabulary with Gisella Caccialanza and Harold and Lew Christensen, San Francisco Ballet, 1952-56; D in Chiropractic, Life-West Chiropractic Coll., San Lorenzo, Calif., 1983; cert. techniques of tchg., U. Calif., 1985; BA in Humanities, New Coll. Calif., 1986. Lic. chiropractor, Mich.; diplomate Nat. sci. Bd.; eminence in dance edn., Calif. C.C. dance specialist, std. svcs., childrens ctrs. credentials Calif. Dept. Edn., 1986. Contract child dancer Monogram Movie Studio, Hollywood, Calif., 1938-40; dance instr. San Francisco Ballet, 1953-65; performer San Francisco Opera Ring, 1960-67; performer, choreographer Oakland (Calif.) Civic Light Opera, 1963-70; dir. Ballet Arts Studio, Oakland, 1960; tchg. specialist Oakland Unified Sch. Dist., 1965-80; fgn. exch. dance dir. Academie de Danses-Salle Pleyel, Paris, 1966; instr. Peralta C.C. Dist., Oakland, 1971—, chmn. dance dept., 1985—. Cons., instr. ext. courses UCLA, Dirs. and Suprs. Assn., Pitts. Unified Sch. Dist., 1971-73, Tulare (Calif.) Sch. Dist., 1971-73; rschr. Ednl. Testing Svcs., HEW, Berkeley, 1974; resident choreographer San Francisco Childrens Opera, 1970—, Oakland Civic Theater; ballet mistress Dimensions Dance Theater, Oakland, 1977-80; cons. Gianchetta Sch. Dance, San Francisco, Robicheau Boston Ballet, TV series Patchwork Family, CBS, N.Y.C.; choreographer Ravel's Valses Nobles et Sentimentales, 1976. Author: Basic Music Outlines for Dance Classes, 1960, Basic Music Outlines for Dance Classes, rev., 1968, Teaching Techniques and Choreography for Advanced Dancers, 1965, Basic Music Outlines for Dance Classes, 1965, Goals and Objectives in Improving Physical Capabilities, 1970, A Teacher's Guide for Ballet Techniques, 1970, Principle Procedures in Basic Curriculum, 1974, Objectives and Standards of Performance for Physical Development, 1975, Techniques of the Ballet School, 1970, Techniques of the Ballet School, rev., 1974, The Opera Ballets: A Choreographic Manual Vols. I-V, 1986; assoc. music arranger: Le Ballet du Cirque, 1964, assoc. composer, lyricist: The Ballet of Mother Goose, 1968; choreographer Valses Nobles Et Sentimentales (Ravel), Transitions (Kashevaroff), 1991, The New Wizard of Oz, 1991, San Francisco Children's Opera (Gingold), Canon in D for Strings and Continuo (Pachelbel), 1979, Oakland Cmty. Orch. excerpts from Swan Lake, Faust, Sleeping Beauty, 1998, Rodeo, Alameda Coll. Cultural Affairs Program, 2000, dancer solo dancer Three Stravinsky Etudes, Alameda Coll. Cultural Affairs Program, 1999, appeared in Flower Drum Song, 1993, Gigi, 1994, Fiddler on the Roof, 1996, The Music Man, 1996, Sayonara, 1997, Bye Bye Birdie, 2000, Barnum, the Circus Musical, 2001; musician (violinist): Oakland Cmty. Concert Orch., 1995—; condr. Gil Gleason:. Bd. dirs. Prodrs. Assocs., Inc., Oakland, 1999—. Recipient Foremost Women of 20th Century, 1985, Merit award San Francisco Children's Opera, 1985, 90. Mem. Calif. State Tchrs. Assn., Bay Area Chiropractic Rsch. Soc., Profl. Dance Tchrs. Assn. Home and Office: 4923 Harbord Dr Oakland CA 94618-2506 E-mail: balletarts@bigplanet.com.

DEFEVER, SUSANNA ETHEL, English language educator; b. Manistee, Mich., May 11, 1934; d. Arthur Theodore and Florence Marie Christine (Larson) Mason; m. Charles J. Defever, Aug. 1, 1959; children: Keith S., Kristin E. AB, Cen. Mich. U., 1956; MA, Wayne State U., 1963; postgrad., Mich. State U., 1957, 58. Cert. secondary education tchr. 1959. Tchr. English, journalism, drama Lakeview High Sch., St. Clair Shores, Mich., 1956-65; tchr. English, composition St. Clair County C.C., Port Huron, 1965-70, part time tchr., 1971-77, prof. English, composition, 1977-95. Conf. planning Liberal Arts Network Devel. (LAND) for Consortium of Mich. Cmty. Coll., 1990—93, v.p., conf. chmn., 1994—95, pres., 1995—96, chair LAND millennium award for innovative team tchg., 1999—; dir. writing workshops for K-12 tchrs. Sanilac County Intermediate Sch. dist., 1987, 88, writing workshops for K-12 tchrs. Sanilac County Intermediate Sch. Dist., 1992, Cheboygan Otsego Presque Isle Intermediate Sch. Dist., 1989, 90, Port Huron Area Schs., 1991; mem. adv. com. Mich. Proficiency Exam, 1992—96; exec. com. Mich. Writing Projects, 1987—93; reviewer English Edn., 1993—2001. Editor: The Heritage of Ira, 1990, An Enduring Heritage, 1992; scholar, lectr. Let's Talk About It series, Mich. Libr. Assn., 1987-93, NEH/Modern Poetry series, St. Clair County Libr., 1994, spkr. Whitehills Book Club, East Lansing, 1987—; contbr. articles to profl. jours.; presenter workshops; pub. poet. Founding mem. Marge Boal Drama Festival; newsletter editor, SC4 Retirees 2000-, pres. 2003—; bd. dirs. SC4 Friends of the Arts, Marine City Concert Series, St. Clair County Cmty. Mental Health Authority, 2000—, Devel. Disabled Adv. Coun., 2002—; Anderson music com. St. Clair Cmty. Found., 2001—. Recipient Disting. Faculty award, 1983, Disting. faculty award, 1989, Nat. Inst. Staff Orgn. Devel. Excellence Award for Tchg., U. Austin, 1992, LAND Leadership award, 2000, Beacon grant, 1991—92, Sperry grant, 1994. Mem.: NEA, Cmty. Coll. Humanities Assn., Mich. Coun. Tchrs. English (regional coord. 1979—85, v.p. 1986—87), Mich. Coll. English Assn. (newsletter chmn., editor 1989—91, v.p. 1992), Nat. Coun. Tchrs. English (judge 1983—2002, assoc. chmn. local conv. arrangements 1984, local arrangements com. 1997), SC4 Retirees (pres. 2003—), Delta Kappa Gamma (sec. 1992—94, scholarship chair 2000—02), Phi Theta Kappa (hon.).

DEFFENBAUGH, KAY ANNE, secondary education art educator; b. Kennewick, Wash., Aug. 9, 1956; d. Robert Zwanzig and Frances Carma (Sloan) D.; m. David Roger Thiede, Oct. 22, 1988; 1 child, Shannon. AA, Columbia Basin Coll., 1976; BA in Fine Arts, Washington State U., 1980; cert. in edn., Ea. Wash. U., 1986, MEd, 1991. Cert. tchr., Wash. Wholesale rep. Armstrongs Gallery, Pomona, Calif., 1981-84; tchr. art Prosser (Wash.) Sch. Dist., 1986—. Mem. arts adv. com. Comm. on Student Learning, 1994; fellow Summer Rsch. Internship Program for Tchrs., Battelle, Richland, 1994-96. Mem. Wash. Art Edn. Assn., Nat. Art Edn. Assn., Southeast Wash. Amiga Users Group (pres. 1989-92, fair publicity coord. 1989-90), Arts Coun. Mid-Columbia (bd. dirs. 1992-95). Avocations: photography, stained glass, travel, reading. Home: 1412 Cimarron Ave Richland WA 99352-9441 Office: Prosser Sch Dist PO Box 430 Prosser WA 99350-0430

DEFILIPPO, LINDA KELLOGG, preschool educator; b. Troy, N.Y., Jan. 21, 1947; d. John E. and Dorothy A. (Knapp) Kellogg; children: Elizabeth, Mark. AS, Hudson Valley C.C., Troy, 1966; BS, Russell Sage Coll., 1968, MS, 1980. Substitute tchr. Capital Dist. Schs., 1968-72; dir./owner The Plaza Nursery Sch., Schenectady, N.Y., 1973—; tchr. Albany Sch., Schenectady, N.Y., 1980-81; life skills educator Washington Irving Sch., Schenectady, N.Y., 1981-82; mgr. Family Rental Property, Troy, 1982-84; dir./owner The Plaza Day Care Ctr., Niskayuna, N.Y., 1984—. Tchr. adult basic edn. Schenectady County Jail, 1981-82. Vol. Am. Cancer Soc., Schenectady, 1968—, Am. Heart Assn., Schenectady, 1970—. Mem. AAUW, Soroptimist Internat. Episcopalian. Avocations: skiing, swimming, travel, reading. Home: 1154 Palmer Ave Niskayuna NY 12309-5813 Office: The Plaza Day Care Ctr 1335 Balltown Rd Schenectady NY 12309-5334

DEFLEUR, LOIS B. university president, sociology educator; b. Aurora, Ill., June 25, 1936; d. Ralph Edward and Isabel Anna (Cornils) Begitske; m. Melvin L. DeFleur (div.) AB, Blackburn Coll., 1958; MA, Ind. U., 1961; PhD in Sociology, U. Ill., 1965; HHD (hon.), U. Alaska, 1999. Asst. prof. sociology Transylvania Coll., Lexington, Ky., 1963-67; assoc. prof. Wash. State U., Pullman, 1967-74, prof., 1975-86, dean Coll. Liberal Arts, 1981-86; provost U. Mo., Columbia, 1986-90; pres. Binghamton U., SUNY, 1990—. Disting. vis. prof. USAF Acad., 1976-77; vis. prof. U. Chgo., 1980-81; bd. dirs. Energy East Corp., HealthNow, N.Y. Author: Delinquency in Argentina, 1965; (with others) Sociology: Human Society, 3d edit. 1981, 4th edit., 1984, The Integration of Women into All Male Air Force Units, 1982, The Edward R. Murrow Heritage: A Challenge for the Future, 1986; contbr. articles to profl. jours. Mem. Wash. State Bd. on Correctional Svcs. and Edn., 1974-77, State of N.Y. Edn. Dept. Curriculum and Assessment Coun., 1991-94, Trilateral Task for N.Am. Edn!. Collaboration, USIA, 1993-95. Recipient Disting. Alumni award Blackburn Coll., 1991, Chief Exec. Leadership awrd Coun. for Advancement and Support of Edn., 1999, Civic Leadership award Greater Binghamton C. of C., 2003, Woman of Distinction award Girl Scout Coun., 2002; grantee NIMH, 1969-79, NSF, 1972-75, Air Force Office, 1978-81. Mem. NCAA (pres. commn. 1996, exec. com. 1997-98), Am. Sociol. Assn. (publs. com. 1979-82, nominations com. 1984-86, coun. mem. 1987-90), Pacific Sociol. Assn. (pres. 1980-82), Coun. Colls. of Arts and Scis. (bd. dirs. 1982-84, pres. 1985-87), Aircraft Owners and Pilots Assn., Internat. Comanche Soc., Nat. Assn. State U. and Land-grant Colls. (exec. com. 1990-93, chair coun. of pres. 1994-95, chmn. bd. dirs. 1996-97), Am. Coun. Edn. (bd. dirs. 1994-2000, v.p. chair-elect 1997-98, chair bd. dirs. 1998-99), Consortium Social Sci. Assns. (bd. dirs. 1993-96). Office: Binghamton U Office of Pres PO Box 6000 Binghamton NY 13902-6000

DEFORGE, KATHERINE ANN, secondary education educator; b. Syracuse, N.Y., Nov. 2, 1950; d. Edward Carroll and Genevieve (Pretko) Miles; m. Timothy Edward DeForge, June 26, 1976; 1 child, Tanya Emily. AA, Maria Regina Coll., Syracuse, 1969; BA, LeMoyne Coll., Syracuse, 1972; MS in Edn., SUNY, Cortland, 1978. Tchr., supr. social studies Assumption Cath. Acad., Syracuse, 1972-81, Bishop Grimes H.S., East Syracuse, N.Y., 1981-88, Marcellus (N.Y.) Ctrl. Schs., 1988—. Test cons. N.Y. State Edn. Dept., Albany, 1984—; mem. testing and assessment com. N.Y. State Edn. Dept.; social studies cons. Onondaga-Cortland-Madison BOCES. NEH grantee, 1986, 94. Mem. ASCD, Nat. Coun. for Social Studies, N.Y. State Coun. for Social Studies, N.Y. State Social Studies Suprs. Assn. (sec. 1997-99, v.p. 1999, pres. 2001—), Ctrl. N.Y. Coun. for Social Studies (sec. 1986-88, treas. 1989-91, v.p. 1993-95, pres. 1995-97, Outstanding Social Studies Supr. award 1992). Republican. Roman Catholic. Avocations: travel, reading, theatre, crafts. Home: 230 Malverne Dr Syracuse NY 13208-1841 Office: Marcellus Ctrl Schs Reed Pky Marcellus NY 13108

DE FRANCESCO, JOHN KENNETH, foreign language educator; b. Phila., July 26, 1932; s. John and Anna (Giove) de F. BA, LaSalle Coll., 1955; AM, Middlebury Coll., 1956; postgrad., U. Wis., 1957-58, U. Florence, Italy, 1961, U. Rome, 1962; ABD, Rutgers U., 1963; postgrad., U. Rome, 1964, U. Perugia, Italy, 1990. Tchr. Phila. Pub. Sch., 1955-56; grad. asst. U. Wis., Madison, 1957-58; dir. lang. lab LaSalle U., Phila., 1958-60, asst. prof., 1959-67; assoc. prof. Camden County Coll., Phila., 1967-69, prof., 1969—2001, chmn. Fgn. Lang., 1968—2001, prof. emeritus, 2002; lectr. Cabrini Coll., Radnor, Pa., 1965-68. Lectr. Rutgers U., New Brunswick, NJ, 1962-63; prof. Emeritus, 2001. Recipient Tchg. Excellence award, U. Tex. Austin, 1989; fellow, Rutgers U., 1962—63; scholar, Middlebury Coll., 1952, 1953, 1955, 1956, U. Wis., 1957—58; Fulbright grantee, Rome and Florence, 1961—62, Fulbright-Hays grantee, U. Rome, 1964, study grantee, Govt. Italy, U. Perugia, 1990. Mem. MLA (bd. dir. Phila. sect. 1979-83, 90-94, 1996-2000), Am. Commn. Tchr. Fgn. Langs., Am. Assn. Tchr. Spanish and Portuguese (pres. Phila. and Vicinity chpt. 1979-83, spl. award 1983), Am Assn. Tchr. Italian (pres. Del. Valley chpt. 1990-94, 96-2000, spl. award 1994, 99, 2000, award of excellence 2001), Camden Co. Coll. Faculty Assn. (pres. 1969-71, Spl. award 1971, commencement spkr. 1991, Pres. medal 2000), Fulbright Alumni Assn. (bd. dir. Phila. area 1998—), Sons of Italy (trustee Benvenuto lodge 1995-2002, hist. 1998-2000, state del. 1997-01, v.p. 2001—, trustee dist. 5 1999-2001), Commn. Italians in Fgn. Countries (bd. counselors 1998—, historian 2003-), KC, Overbrook Farms Club, Overbrook Italian-Am. Club, Phila. Area Spanish Educators (charter), Nat. Italian Am. Found., Unione Regionale Abruzzese (bd. dir. 1997-), Smithsonian Assn., Pi Delta Phi. Roman Catholic. Avocations: travel, classical music, dancing. Home: 6491 Sherwood Rd Philadelphia PA 19151-2416

DEFRINO, ANTHONY M. middle school administrator; b. Hartford, Conn., Sept. 4, 1950; s. Jeanette (Thibaudeau) DeFrino; m. Gail Trani, Aug. 3, 1973; children: Carrie, Beth, Jeffrey. BA, Assumption Coll., 1973, MA, 1978, C.A.G.S., 1980. Cert. tchr., Mass. Spl. edn. resource tchr. Assabet Valley Collaborative, Marlboro, Mass., 1976-79; guidance counselor Marlboro High Sch., 1979-81; guidance dir. Shepherd Hill Regional High Sch., Dudley, Mass., 1981-88; asst. prin. Auburn (Mass.) Mid. Sch., 1989—. Tchr. Framingham (Mass.) State Coll., 1989, North Brookfield (Mass.) Sch. Dist., 1992; presenter in field. Bd. dirs. Auburn Youth and Family Svcs., 1984-87; mem. Auburn Youth Commn., 1987-92. Insvc. Devel. grantee Mass. Dept. Edn., 1984. Mem. ASCD, Nat. Assn. Secondary Sch. Prins., New England League Middle Schs., Mass. Middle Level Adminstrs. Assn. Home: 10 Carriage Dr Auburn MA 01501-2714 Office: Auburn Mid Sch Swanson Rd Auburn MA 01501

DEGANN, SONA IRENE, obstetrician, gynecologist, educator; b. Homs, Syria, 1952; d. Papken Stephan and Helen Irene (Wadsworth) Mugrditchian; m. A. David Degann, May 11, 1983; children: Alexander, Seta. BSc,

Am. U. Beirut, Lebanon, 1975; MS, U. Mich., 1976; MD, Johns Hopkins U., 1983. Diplomate Am. Bd. Ob-Gyn. Resident in ob-gyn. N.Y. Hosp., N.Y.C., 1983-87, staff. Clin. instr. Cornell U. Sch. Medicine, N.Y.C., attending Ob-Gyn New York Presbyn. Hosp., N.Y.C. Fellow Am. Coll. Ob-Gyn.; mem. AMA, Med. Soc. State N.Y., N.Y. County Med. Soc.

DEGATANO, ANTHONY THOMAS, educational association administrator; b. Elizabeth, N.J., Apr. 2, 1950; s. Anthony James and Leonora (Malta) D.; m. Jeanne Marie Stevens, Apr. 15, 1972; 1 child, David. BA, Rider Coll., 1971; MA, Kean Coll., 1975. Cert. tchr., supr., prin., chief sch. adminstr. Elem. tchr. Elizabeth Bd. Edn., 1971-77, adult edn. instr., 1972-74, cons., 1977-81; dir. Union County Edn. Svc. Commn., Westfield, N.J., 1981-86, Ind. Child Study Teams, Inc., Jersey City, 1986—. Bd. dirs. Ednl. In-Roads, Jersey City, 1997—; regional v.p. Sylvan Learning Systems, Inc., 1988—. Author: (curriculum guide) Alternate Math Program, 1980, (guide books) Teacher Handbook, 1982, Teacher Resource Book, 1983; editor: Mathematics Series, 1992. 1st pres., founder Union County Commn. Adminstrs. Assn., 1983-86; pres. Herbert Hoover PTO, 1991-92; chmn. edn.-budget subcom. Citizen Adv. Com., Edison, N.J.,m 1992; mem. N.J. Edn. Commr.'s Adv. Com., Trenton, 1988—, PTA/PTO Adv. Coun., Edison, 1991-92; chmn. local edn. agy. Data Rev. Collection and Approval Com., 1992—. Named Outstanding Young Man of Am., U.S. Jaycees, 1983; recipient Recognition for Svc., N.J. Commr. of Edn., 1990, Union County Edn. Svc. Commn. Adminstrs. Assn., 1986. Mem. N.J. Assn. Fed. Program Adminstrs., ASCD, N.J. Coun. Am. Pvt. Edn. Avocations: reading, fishing, scuba diving, gardening, skiing. Home: 148 Howard Ave Edison NJ 08837-3030 Office: ICST Inc 377 Danforth Ave Jersey City NJ 07305-1904

DEGIOIA, JOHN J. university president; b. Orange, Conn. m. Theresa Miller DeGioia; 1 child, John Thomas. BA in English, Georgetown U., 1979, PhD in Philosophy, 1995. Asst. to the pres. Georgetown U., Washington, 1982—85, dean of student affairs, 1985—92, assoc. v.p., chief adminstrv. officer, 1992—95, v.p., 1995—98, lectr., mem. faculty, 1995—, sr. v.p., 1998—2001, pres., 2001—. Mem. adv. group COFHE Quality Mgmt.; mem. com. for presdl. responsibilities in student life Assn. Cath. Colls. and Univs.; participant Forum for Higher Edn.; bd. dirs. Fund for Edn. in South Africa, Washington Found. for Psychiatry. Named one of Young Leaders of the Acad., Change mag., 1998; recipient Chmn.'s award, Georgetown Alumni Admissions Program, 1997. Office: Georgetown U Office of the Pres 204 Healy Hall Box 571789, 37th and O Streets, NW Washington DC 20057

DE GOGORZA, PATRICIA, sculptor, educator; b. Detroit, Mar. 17, 1936; d. Maitland and Julia Harlow (Brodt) de G.; m. Dadi Wirz, Aug. 7, 1958 (div. Dec. 1962); 1 child, Paulo; m. James Edward Gahagan, Apr. 18, 1963 (dec. July 1999); 1 child, Sharon. BA, Smith Coll., 1958; MA, Goddard Coll., 1975. Cert. justice of the peace Vt., 2002. Asst. prof. art Bard Coll., Annandale, N.Y., 1966-69; drawing instr. U. Vt., Burlington, 1980-81; instr. Vt. Studio Ctr., Johnson, 1984—; sculpture instr. The Carving Studio, West Rutland, Vt., 1987—, Johnson State Coll., 1996, Arts Workshop, Akaroa, New Zealand, 1999—. Chair sculpture dept. Goddard Coll., Plainfield, Vt., 1973-74, 78-79; faculty MFA program Vt. Coll., Montpelier, 1992-93; instr. Vt. Clay Studio, Montpelier, 1994-97, Arts Workshop, Alkaroa, New Zealand, 1999—, Sculpture Workshop, Alcaroa, 200—, Clay Figure Study Workshop, Barre, Vt., 2002-03. One-woman shows include Sculpin Gallery, Martha's Vineyard, 1973, Bundy Mus., Waitsfield, Vt., 1982, Dibden Gallery, Johnson (Vt.) State Coll., 1984, Moonbrook Gallery, Rutland, Vt., 1984, A.V.A. Gallery, Hanover, N.H., 1985, Wood Art Gallery, Montpelier, 1988, Hillyer Gallery, Smith Coll., Northampton, Mass., 1989, Brown Libr., Craftsbury, Vt., 1999, exhibited in group shows at Carving Studio Sculptors in Vt., 1988—97, Helen Day Art Ctr., Stowe, Vt., 1986—98, So. Vt. Art Ctr., Manchester, 1993—97, West Branch Sculpture Gardens, Stowe, 1994—98, Akaroa Mus., New Zealand, 1999, Wood Art Gallery, Montpelier, 2000—03, Studio Place Arts, Barre, Vt., 2001—, Represented in permanent collections Sun/Moon Cycle granite sculpture Johnson State Coll., Riverbirds marble sculpture Marble St. Sculpture Pk., West Rutland, Pegasus marble sculpture Burlington City Bike Path, Mermaid, Merman and Dolphin 2 marble sculptures, Tree of Life, State of Vt. Pavilion Bldg., Montpelier, numerous pvt. collections and pvt. sculpture commns. Bd. dirs., pres. Art Resource Assn., Montpelier, 1976-84; chair Dem. Party, Woodbury, Vt., 1982—; art organizer, tchr. Rural Sch. Devel. Program, Woodbury, 1972-74; violinist I Vt. Philharm. Orch., 1979—, Montpelier Chamber Orch., 1997—, Contra Dance Band, 1998—. Mem. Internat. Sculpture Ctr., Art Resource Assn., Carving Studio. Democrat. Avocations: violin, gardening. Home and Office: 1580 Dog Pond Rd East Calais VT 05650-8134

DE GRASSI, LEONARD, art historian, educator; b. East Orange, N.J., Mar. 2, 1928; s. Romulus-William and Anna Sophia (Sannicolo) DeG.; m. Dolores Marie Welgoss, June 24, 1961; children: Maria Christina, Paul. BA, U. So. Calif., 1950, BFA, 1951, MA, 1956; postgrad., Harvard U., 1953, Istituto Centrale del Restauro di Roma, 1959-60, U. Rome, 1959-60, UCLA, 1970-73. Tchr. art Redlands (Calif.) Jr. High Sch., 1951-53, Toll Jr. High Sch., Glendale, Calif., 1953-61, Wilson Jr. High Sch., Glendale, 1961; mem. faculty Glendale Coll., 1962—, prof. art history, 1974-92, chmn. dept., 1972, 89, prof. emeritus, 1992—. Tchr. Cite U., Paris, 1992, Istituto /Schuola Leonardo da Vinci, Florence, Italy, 1992. Prin. works include: (paintings) high altar at Ch. St. Mary, Cook, Minn., altar screen at Ch. St. Andrew, El Segundo, Calif., 1965-71, 14 Stas. of the Cross Ch. St. Mary, Cook, Minn., altar screen at Ch. of the Descent of the Holy Spirit, Glendale, 14 Stas. of the Cross at Ch. of St. Benedict, Duluth, Minn; also research, artwork and dramatic work for Spaceship Earth exhbn. at Disney World, Orlando, Fla., 1980. Decorated Knight Grand Cross Holy Sepluchre, 1974, knight St. John of Jerusalem, 1976, knight Order of Merit of Republic of Italy, 1973 Cross of Merit, 1984, 89; recipient J. Walter Smith Svc. award, 2001, numerous commendations; named First Disting. Faculty, 1987, Outstanding Educator of Am., 1971. Mem. Art Educators Assn., Am. Rsch. Ct. Egypt, Tau Kappa Alpha, Kappa Pi, Delta Sigma Rho. Office: 1500 N Verdugo Rd Glendale CA 91208-2809

DE HAAN, HENRY JOHN, research psychologist; b. St. Clair County, Ill., Nov. 23, 1920; s. Henry J. and Fanny (Haislip) de H.; m. Mary J. Farrell, Oct. 22, 1943. AB, Washington U., St. Louis, 1942, AM, 1949; PhD, U. Pitts., 1960. Postdoctoral Coatesville (Pa.) VA Hosp., 1960-62; rsch. scientist George Washington U., Washington, 1962-64; rsch. psychologist Armed Forces Radiobiol. Rsch. Inst., Bethesda, Md., 1965-69, U.S. Army Rsch. Inst., Alexandria, Va., 1969-86; external rsch. prof. Krasnow Inst. for Advanced Study, George Mason U., Fairfax, Va., 2001—. Mem. faculty U.S. Dept. Agr. Grad. Sch., Washington, 1967-77. Author 10 U.S. govt. sci. and tech. reports, 1954-82; contbr. articles to Perception and Psychophysics, Jour. Comparative and Physiol. Psychology and other jours. With USN, 1944-46, PTO. Mem. AAAS (emeritus), APA (life), Am. Psychol. Soc., N.Y. Acad. Scis. (emeritus), Ea. Psychol. Assn. (life), Internat. Neuropsychol. Soc. (emeritus), Soc. Neurosci. (emeritus), U.S. Tennis Assn. (life), Internat. Primatological Soc. (life), Psychonomic Soc. (life), Sigma Xi (emeritus). Achievements include research on perceptual and cognitive capacities of retarded children and adult psychotics, on effects of temperature on food intake and brain stimulation (in the rat), on effects of ionizing radiation on primate perceptual and cognitive capacities, and research on speech technology and speech compression, including a speech-rate intelligibility threshold. Home: 5403 Yorkshire St Springfield VA 22151-1203

DE HART, FLORA BALLOWE, education educator; b. Lancaster, Pa., Feb. 12, 1931; d. Benjamin Franklin and Beatrice (Cope) B.; m. Sheppard Allen de Hart, Sept. 4, 1955 (div. 1973). BA in Secondary Edn., Longwood Coll., 1952; MA in History, U. Va., 1958; PhD in Edn. Adminstrn., U. Tex., 1976. Tchr. Va. pub. schs., 1952-55; prof. Louisburg (N.C.) Coll., 1956-72; adj. cons. Regional Edn. Lab., Durham, N.C., 1969-72; dean of students Hendrix Coll., Conway, Ark., 1974-75; acad. specialist migrant program St. Edwards U., Austin, Tex., 1977-79, assoc. prof., 1979—, dir. student tchg., certification officer, 1979-97, ret., 1997. Proposal reader U.S. Dept. Edn., 1986, 87; mem. program evaluation com. Tex. Edn. Agy., 1982-83; presenter on integration of tech. in curriculum Soc. for Tech. and Tchr. Edn. Conf., 1992; St. Edward's U. rep. Nat. Tchr. Tng. Inst., 1994—. Campaign vol. Democrats for Pickle, Austin, 1988-89. EPDA grantee, 1971. Mem. Assn. Tchr. Educators (presider, program presenter 1982—), Tex. Assn. Tchr. Educators, Austin Coop. Tchr. Edn. Ctr. (pres. 1986-87), So. Assn. Colls. and Univs. (mem. com. 1990), Phi Delta Kappa, Kappa Delta Pi, Pi Lambda Theta. Methodist. Avocations: travel, writing, reading. Home: 11715 Rydalwater Ln Austin TX 78754-5722

DEHAYES, DANIEL WESLEY, management executive, educator; b. Columbus, Ohio, Sept. 23, 1941; s. Daniel Wesley and June Rosiland (Page) DeH.; married Lisa A. Gregoline; children: Sarah Baxter, Benjamin Wesley. BA in Math. and Computer Sci., Ohio State U., 1963, MBA, 1964, PhD in Bus. Adminstrn., 1968. Asst. prof. systems analysis Naval Postgrad. Sch., Monterey, Calif., 1967-69; asst. prof. sch. bus. Ind. U., Bloomington, Ind., 1969-72, assoc. prof.sch. bus., 1972-79, prof. sch. bus., 1979—, dean of acad. computing, 1981-86, asst. v.p. info. tech., 1987-88; dir. Ctr. For Entrepreneurship and Innovation, Ind. U., Bloomington, 1989-98. Exec. dir. Inst. Rsch. on the MIS, 1989-92, chmn. exec. edn., 1992-93; cons. in field. Textbook author; contbr. articles to profl. jours. Served to capt. U.S. Army, 1967-69 Recipient fellowships and grants Mem. Decision Scis. Inst., Acad. Mgmt. Republican. Methodist. Office: Indiana University Kelley School of Business Bloomington IN 47405

DEHLI-YOUNG, GREGORY LAWRENCE, educational administrator; b. Wauwatosa, Wis., Jan. 21, 1959; s. Victor L. and Dianne M. (Korsmo) Young; m. Sharon A. Dehli, Mar. 26, 1984; children: Kathryn, David. BA, Marquette U., 1981, MEd, 1994. Cert. tchr., secondary adminstrn., Wis. Tchr. Dominican HS, Milw., 1981-82; religious studies tchr., dept. chmn. Thomas More HS, Milw., 1982-95; prin. St. Matthew's Grade Sch., Oak Creek, Wis., 1995—99. Mem. Women's Commn., Archdiocese of Milw., 1983-88. Mem. ASCD, Wis. Educators for Social Responsibility. Roman Catholic. Avocation: milwaukee kickers soccer club. Office: Holy Apostles Sch 3875 S 159 St New Berlin WI 53151-7331

DE HON, RENÉ AUREL, geology educator; b. Wichita, Kans., Nov. 11, 1938; s. Harold Maurice and Margaret Electra (Eaton) De H.; m. Jacqueline Nell Dobyns, Aug. 13, 1960; children: André Maurice, Antoine Elic. BS in Geology, U. Tex., El Paso, 1962; MS in Geology, Tex. Tech U., 1965, PhD in Geology, 1970. Asst. prof. Northwestern State Coll., Natchitoches, La., 1967-72; from asst. to assoc. prof. U. Ark., Monticello, Ark., 1972-77; from assoc. to full prof. Northeast La. U. (now U. La.), Monroe, 1977—. Contbr. over 40 articles to profl. jours. NASA grantee, 1970—. Fellow Geol. Soc. Am.; mem. Sigma Xi, Sigma Gamma Epsilon. Achievements include development of technique for determining thickness of lunar mare lavas; early arguments for martian lakes and calculations of flow history of channels; six published geologic maps on Mars, Mercury, Ganymede. Office: U La at Monroe Dept Geoscis Monroe LA 71209-0001 E-mail: rdehon@ulm.edu.

DEHOUSKE, ELLEN JANE, early childhood education educator, consultant; b. Cleve., Aug. 17, 1945; d. Joseph and Elsie (Eberling) D. BS in Edn., Duquesne U., 1967, MS in Edn., 1973; postgrad., California U. Pa., 1973; PhD, U. Pitts., 1981. High sch. English tchr. Boyle High Sch., Homestead, Pa., 1968-72; spl. edn. tchr. Allegheny Intermediate Unit, Pitts., 1972-79; grad. asst. U. Pitts., 1979-81; mental health cons. Psychiat. Assn. for Consultation and Therapy, Pitts., 1981-82; head tchr., pre-sch. tchr., play therapist Arsenal Family and Children's Ctr., Pitts., 1982-85; spl. edn. tchr. Highland Sch., Pitts., 1988; prof. early childhood edn. Carlow Coll., Pitts., 1988—. Creative writing cons. Arts and Spl. Edn. Project, Harrisburg, Pa., 1980-90; ind. child devel. cons., Pitts., 1979-81; mem. Task Force on Family Resources, Pitts., 1991-92; mem. steering com. Alliance for Early Childhood Edn., Harrisburg, 1991-93. Contbr. articles to profl. jours. Bd. dirs. Shady Ln. Sch., Pitts., 1995—. Mem. Assn. for Childhood Edn. Internat., Nat. Assn. for Edn. Young Children, Coun. for Exceptional Children, Pitts. Assn. for Edn. Young Children (v.p. 1992-96, mem. coun. 1996—), Coun. for Early Childhood Edn. (child advocate), Phi Delta Kappa. Avocations: canoeing, cross-country skiing, reading, art, writing. Home: 710 Copeland St Apt 12 Pittsburgh PA 15232-2259 Office: Carlow Coll Edn Divsn 3333 5th Ave Pittsburgh PA 15213-3109

DEHOVITZ, JACK ALAN, physician, educator, health facility administrator; b. Oceanside, Calif., Aug. 12, 1952; s. Bernard and Ruth (Senturia) DeH. BS, U. Calif., Davis, 1974; MPH, U. Tex., Houston, 1975; MD, U. Tex., Galveston, 1980. Diplomate Am. Bd. Internal Medicine, Am. Bd. Preventive Medicine, Am. Bd. Infectious Disease. Intern medicine St. Vincent's Hosp. and Med. Ctr., N.Y.C., 1980-81; asst. resident medicine N.Y. Hosp.-Cornell Med. Ctr., N.Y.C., 1981-82; Strang fellow in pub. health Cornell U. Med. Coll., N.Y.C., 1983-85; fellow in internat. medicine, infectious diseases N.Y. Hosp., N.Y.C., 1983-85; asst. med. dir. Spellman Ctr. of HIV Disease, N.Y.C., 1985-88; asst. prof. Cornell U. Med. Coll., N.Y.C., 1985—2000, SUNY, Bklyn., 1985-91, assoc. prof., 1991—2000, dir. AIDS Prevention Ctr., 1988-93, dir. HIV Ctr., 1993—, prof., 2000—. Cons. infectious diseases N.Y. State Dept. Health, Albany, 1989-91; cons. Czech Min. Health, Prague, 1990-92. Editor AIDS Manual, 1988, HIV Infection in Women, 1995; contbr. articles to profl. jours. Mem. organizing com. Czech-Am. Med. Com., Prague, 1990. Fellow ACP, N.Y. Acad. Medicine, Infectious Diseases Soc. Am.; mem. APHA, N.Y. Soc. Tropical Medicine, Internat. AIDS Soc. Jewish. Office: SUNY Health Sci Ctr Bklyn 450 Clarkson Ave Box 1240 Brooklyn NY 11203-2056

DEILY, ANN BETH, special education educator, consultant; b. Albany, N.Y., Oct. 16, 1948; d. Ezra Jack and O. Sonya June (Balshan) Sarachan; m. William Edward Deily, Aug. 13, 1972. BA, U. Rochester, 1970; MA, Vanderbilt U., 1971, MS, 1972; PhD, SUNY, Albany, 1977. Speech-lang. therapist Children's Rehab. Ctr., Kingston, N.Y., 1972-73; pvt. practice Chatham, N.Y., 1973-79; teaching fellow SUNY, Albany, 1974-75; dir. dept./developer Speech Hearing Dept. St. Mary's Hosp., Troy, 1974-77; instr. communication disorders Coll. St. Rose, Albany, 1977-78, asst. prof. communication disorders, 1978-82, assoc. prof., 1982-87, prof., 1987-91; pvt. practice speech-lang. pathology Chatham Ctr., NY, 1989—. Dir. rural edn. grant Coll. St. Rose, Albany, 1983-86; cons. State of N.Y. Dept. Edn., State of Conn. Dept. Edn., Wildwood Sch., Schenectady, N.Y., Bd. Coop. Ednl. Svcs. (Renssalaer-Columbia-Greene, Schenectady-Albany, Saratoga), East Greenbush, Albany, Columbia County Spl. Needs Group, A.B. Deily Cons. Assocs., 1990—, early intervention program Columbia County ARC, Ctr. for the Disabled, Regents Coll., Columbia County Early Intervention and Preschool Svcs. Author: Working with Communication Disorders in Rural Settings, 1987; contbr. 30 articles to profl. jours. Founder Capital Area Network for Rural Speech-Lang. Pathologists, 1985; co-founder Capital Dist. Computer Users Group in Speech-Lang. Pathology, 1989, Columbia-Greene Rape Crisis Ctr. (edn. and tng. com., coord. com. 1981). Mem. ASTD (mem. exec. bd. Hudson-Mohawk chpt., membership chair), Am. Speech-Lang.-Hearing Assn. (nat. site visitor, nat. computer tutor, nat. faculty-teleconf.), Am. Coun. Rural Spl. Edn. (editorial rev. bd.), AG Bell Assn. for Deaf (editorial rev. bd.), Computer Users in Speech Hearing (pres.), Coun. Exceptional Children, Ind. Computer Consulting Assn. (cap. region). Home: 128 Merwin Rd Valatie NY 12184-4404

DEISSLER, JANICE KAY, home economics educator; b. Delta, Iowa, Sept. 19, 1940; d. Charles R. and Helen M. (Bitner) Farmer; m. Emil W. Deissler, July 8, 1962; children: Janelle, Jill, Julia. BS in Home Econs., Bradley U., 1962; MS in Home Econs., Ill. State U., 1969; postgrad., U. Ill., 1983-89. Tchr. Sycamore (Ill.) Jr. H.S., 1962-63; substitute tchr. Peoria (Ill.) Pub. Schs., 1964-66, tchr., 1967-70; from instr. to prof. Ill. Ctrl. Coll., East Peoria, 1970-99. Cons. Work/Family Directions, Peoria area, 1982—. Bd. dirs. YWCA; mem. Peoria Pub. Schs. Bd., 1994—; chair nursery sch. bd. Univ. United Meth. Adminstrn. Bd., Peoria, 1995-97, chair, 1997-2000. Mem. Nat. Assn. for Edn. of Young Children, Ill. Assn. for Edn. of Young Children (pres. 1990-93, 2000-02, Charlotte Danstrom award), Family Consumer Econs., Phi Theta Kappa, Kappa Delta Pi, Delta Kappa Gamma. Methodist. Avocations: reading, golf, family and friends. Office: 602 W Glen Peoria IL 61614 E-mail: jdeissler@worldnet.att.net.

DEITERS, SISTER JOAN ADELE, psychoanalyst, nun, chemistry educator; b. Cincinnati, Apr. 28, 1934; d. Alfred Harry and Rose Catherine (Rusche) D. BA, Coll. Mt. St. Joseph, Cin., 1963; PhD, U. Cin., 1967; M in Christian spirituality, Creighton U., Omaha, 1985. Joined Sisters of Charity, Roman Cath. Ch., 1952; cert. psychoanalyst, Westchester Inst. for Tng. in Psychoanalysis and Psychotherapy, 2000. Prof. chemistry Coll. Mt. St. Joseph, Cin., 1969-78; Matthew Vassar Jr. chair Vassar Coll., Poughkeepsie, NY, 1978-96. Contbg. articles to profl. jour. Mem. Am. Chem. Soc., Sisters of Charity, Sigma Xi; Nat. Assn. for Advancement of Psychoanalysis. Home: 73A Raymond Ave Poughkeepsie NY 12603-3117 Office: 39 Collegeview Ave Poughkeepsie NY 12603-2415

DE JONG, DAVID SAMUEL, lawyer, educator; b. Washington, Jan. 8, 1951; s. Samuel and Dorothy (Thomas) De J.; m. Tracy Ann Barger, Sept. 23, 1995; children: Jacob Samuel, Franklin Joseph. BA, U. Md., 1972; JD, Washington and Lee U., 1975; LLM in Taxation, Georgetown U., 1979. Bar: Md. 1975, U.S. Dist. Ct. Md. 1977, U.S. Tax Ct. 1977, U.S. Ct. Appeals (4th cir.) 1978, U.S. Supreme Ct. 1979, D.C. 1980, U.S. Dist. Ct. D.C. 1983, U.S. Ct. Claims, U.S. Ct. Appeals (fed. cir.) 1983; CPA, Md.; cert. valuation analyst. Atty. Gen. Bus. Svcs., Inc., Rockville, Md., 1975-80; ptnr. Stein Sperling Bennett De Jong Driscoll & Greenfeig, PC, Rockville, 1980—. Adj. prof. Southea. U., Washington, 1979-85, Am. U., Washington, 1983-2002; instr. U. Md., College Park, 1986-87, Montgomery Coll., Rockville, 1983; mem. character com. 7th Appeals Cir. Md. Ct. of Appeals. Co-author: (ann. book) J.K. Lasser's Year-Round Tax Strategies, 1989—; editor Notes and Comments, Washington and Lee U. Law Rev., 1974-75. V.p. Seneca Whetstone Homeowners Assn., Gaithersburg, Md., 1981-82, pres. 1982-83. Mem. ABA, AICPA, Am. Assn. Atty.-CPAs (bd. dirs. 1997—, sec. 1998-99, treas. 1999-2000, v.p. 2000-02, pres. elect 2002-2003, pres. 2003—), Md. Bar Assn., Montgomery County Bar Assn. (chmn. tax sect. 1991-92, treas. 1996-97), D.C. Bar Assn., Md. Assn. CPAs, D.C. Inst. CPAs, Nat. Assn. Cert. Valuation Analysts, Inst. Bus. Appraisers, Md. Soc. Accts., Phi Alpha Delta. Office: 25 W Middle Ln Rockville MD 20850-2214

DEJONG, H. WILLIAM, health educator; b. Flagstaff, Ariz., Dec. 19, 1950; s. Henry William and Dorothy Rose (Cooney) DeJ.; m. Maureen Ann Kelley, June 18, 1988; children: Christene A., Margaret M., H. William. AB summa cum laude, Dartmouth Coll., 1973; MA, Stanford U., 1975, PhD, 1977. Dir. evaluation Ctr. for Health Comm., Boston, 1987-90; ind. cons. Wayland, Mass., 1990—; lectr. health comm. Harvard Sch. Pub. Health, Boston, 1995-2001; dir. Higher Edn. Ctr. for Alcohol and Other Drug Prevention, Newton, Mass., 1995—; prof. Boston U. Sch. Pub. Health, 2001—. Author: Preventing Interpersonal Violence Among Youth, 1994, Setting and Improving Policies for Reducing Alcohol and Other Drug Problems on Campus, 1996, The Media and the Message: Lessons Learned from Past Public Service Campaigns, 1998. Bd. dirs. Mothers Against Drunk Driving, Irving, Tex., 1993-96; mem. bd. visitors Rockefeller Ctr., Dartmouth Coll., Hanover, N.H., 1991-95, 96-99; governing mem. Mass. Tobacco Control Oversight Coun., Boston, 1994-98. Recipient Bronze Apple award Nat. Ednl. Media Network, 1997. Mem. APHA, Phi Beta Kappa. Home: 29 Rice Spring Ln Wayland MA 01778-3515 Office: Boston U Sch Pub Health 715 Albany St Boston MA 02118 E-mail: wdejong@bu.edu.

DEJULIO, ELLEN LOUISE, special education administrator; b. Jersey City, June 7, 1946; d. Fred J. and Mary F. (Burns) DeJ. AB in English and Edn., Immaculata (Pa.) Coll., 1968; MEd in Ednl. Therapy, Nat.-Louis U., Evanston, Ill., 1973, CAS in Adminstrn./Supervision, 1982; EdD, Vanderbilt U., 1993. Cert. in ednl. adminstrn., learning disabilities, elem./secondary edn., social-emotional disorders, educable and trainable mentally handicapped. Dir. summer program St. Mary of Providence Ctr., Elverson, Pa., 1967-82; tchr. 2d grade Hillcrest Sch., Downers Grove, Ill., 1968-72; spl. edn. tchr. Longfellow Sch., Downers Grove, 1972-73, Fairmount Sch., Downers Grove, 1973-80; asst. dir. S.E. region Sch. Assn. for Spl. Edn., DuPage County, Ill., 1983-85; dir. spl. svcs. Downers Grove Grad. Sch. Dist. 58, 1980—. Cons. St. Mary of Providence Ctr., 1983-86. Recipient Community Svc. award Ill. Assn. Parks and Recreation/Downers Grove Park Dist. Mem. ASCD, Coun. for Exceptional Children, Assn. for Severely Handicapped, Art Inst. Chgo., Morton Arboretum, Ill. Women Adminstrs., Ill. Adminstrs. of Spl. Edn., Delta Kappa Gamma. Avocations: reading, art appreciation, hiking, theater. Home: 2235 Durand Dr Downers Grove IL 60515-4267 Office: Downers Grove Grade Sch Dist 58 1860 63rd St Downers Grove IL 60516-2471

DE KANTER, ADRIANA ALISON, federal agency administrator; BA in hist., Mount Holyoke Coll., 1977; MPA, U. Tex., Austin, 1980. Dir. policy tech. analysis, support, planning evaluation svc. US Dept Edn., Under Sec. Edn., Wash., 2002—; partnership liaison US Dept. Edn., Elem. Secondary Edn., Academic Improvement Demo. Programs, Wash., 2001—03; spec. adv. afterschool issues US Depte. Edn., Off. of Sec., 1999—2001; dep. dir. US Dept. Edn., Planning Evaluation Svc., 1993—99; dir. State Tex. Off. Gov., Austin, 1993—94, US Dept. Edn., Nat. Assessment Planning Evaluation Svc., Wash., 1991—93; lead program analyst to planning studies br. chief US Army, V Corps, Asst. Chief of Staff for Resources Mgmt., Frankfurt, Germany, 1987—91; regional rep. US Dept. Edn., Kans. City, Mo., 1986—87; program analyst US Dept. Edn. Planning Evaluation Svc., Wash., 1983—86; profl. staff mem. Subcom. Edn., Arts, and Humanities, US Senate, Wash., 1982—83; pres. mgmt. intern US Dept. Edn., Off. Planning and Budget, Wash., 1980—82; sec. Dept. Spanish and other Languages, U. Houston, Houston, 1977—78. Contbr. articles various profl. jours. Recipient Presidential Mgmt Internship award, 1980—82, US Meritorious Civilian Svc. award, 1990, Contribution award, Nat. Cmty. Edn. Assn., 2000, Publ. Svc. Excellence award, Pub. Pvt. Partnerships, 2002. Office: US Dept Edn Under Sec Edn 400 Maryland Ave SW FOB-6 Rm 6W115 Washington DC 20202*

DE KANTER, ELLEN ANN, English and foreign language educator; b. Spokane, Wash., Mar. 10, 1926; d. George L. and Alison P. (Christy) Tharp; m. Scipio de Kanter, Feb. 2, 1949 (dec.); children: Scipio, Georgette, Robert, Adriana. BA, Mexico City Coll.-U. of Ams., 1947; MEd, U. Houston, 1972, MA in Spanish, 1974, EdD, 1979. Dir. bilingual edn., prof. U. St. Thomas, Houston, dir. bilingual edn., 1979—. Contbr. articles to profl. jours. 11 Tchr. Tng. grants undergrad. and grad. students, U. St. Thomas, 1986—. Mem. Nat. Assn. Bilingual Edn. (chmn. 1989 conf., program chair 1993 conf.), Houston Area Assn. Bilingual Edn. (pres. 1987-88), Inst. Hispanic Culture (bd. dirs. 1989-90). Home: 3015 Meadowview Dr Missouri City TX 77459-3308 Office: U St Thomas 3800 Montrose Blvd Houston TX 77006-4626 E-mail: dekanter@stthom.edu.

DEKMEJIAN, RICHARD HRAIR, political science educator; b. Aleppo, Syria, Aug. 3, 1933; came to U.S., 1950, naturalized, 1955; s. Hrant H. and Vahede V. (Matossian) D.; m. Anoush Hagopian, Sept. 19, 1954; children: Gregory, Armen, Haig. BA, U. Conn., 1959; MA, Boston U., 1960; Middle East Inst. cert., Columbia U., 1964, PhD, 1966. Mem. faculty SUNY, Binghamton, 1964-86; prof., chmn. dept. polit. sci. U. So. Calif., Los

Angeles, 1986-90, prof. internat. bus. Marshall Sch. Bus.; also master Hinman Coll., 1971-72. Lectr. Fgn. Svc. Inst., Dept. Def., Dep. State, 1976-87; vis. prof. Columbia U., U. Pa., 1977-78; cons. Dept. State, AID, USIA, UN, Dept. Def. Author: Egypt Under Nasir, 1971, Patterns of Political Leadership, 1975; Islam in Revolution, 1985, 2nd edit., 1995, Ethnic Lobbies in U.S. Foreign Policy, 1997, Troubled Waters: The Geopolitics of the Caspian Region, 2001, The Just Prince: A Manual of Leadership, 2003; contbr. articles to profl. jours. Pres. So. Tier Civic Ballet Co., 1973-76. Served with AUS, 1955-57. Mem. Am. Polit. Sci. Assn., Middle East Inst., Middle East Studies Assn., Internat. Inst. Strategic Studies, Skull and Dagger, Pi Sigma Alpha, Phi Alpha Theta. Office: U So Calif Dept Polit Sci Los Angeles CA 90089-0044 E-mail: dekmejia@usc.edu.

DEKREY, PETRA JEAN HEGSTAD, elementary school educator; b. Oakland, Calif., May 27, 1944; d. Lorentz Reginald and Hazel Dorothy (Danielson) Hegstad; m. Curtis Wayne Martel, Apr. 30, 1966 (div. 1989); children: Christopher W. Martel, Peter L. Martel, Loren R. Martel; m. Donald DeKrey, July 13, 2002. BS in Elem. Edn. and German, Concordia Coll., Moorhead, Minn., 1966; MS in Elem. Edn., Bemidji (Minn.) State U., 1989. Cert. German, elem. edn., reading cons., remedial and devel. reading tchr. K-12, Minn. 2d grade tchr. Rice Creek and Hayes Elem. Schs., Fridley, Minn., 1966-72; chpt. 1 reading tchr. Chief Bug-O-Nay-Ge-Shig Sch., Cass Lake, Minn., 1986-92; tchr. English/reading Rochester (Minn.) Pub. Schs., 1992-93; Chpt. I reading tchr. English/reading Moorhead (Minn.) Jr. H.S., 1993—, student newspaper advisor, 1993—2001. Mem. lic. com. Dist. 152, 2000—02. Vol. den mother Cub Scouts, Bismarck, N.D., 1976-77; vol. com. to establish kindergarten Bismarck Pub. Schs., 1974-75; vol. com. to help refugees relocate Bismarck, 1976; vol. Bemidji Sch. System, 1985. Mem.: NEA, Minn. Edn. Assn., Internat. Reading Assn., Minn. Reading Assn. (sec. 1993—2002), Northland Reading Coun. (pres. 1985—86, honor coun. 1986), Kappa Delta Pi. Avocations: skiing, golf, music, art, travel. Home: 1902 Lakeview Dr Bemidji MN 56601 Business E-Mail: pdekrey@moorhead.k12.mn.us.

DEKSTER, BORIS VENIAMIN, mathematician, educator; b. Leningrad, USSR, Oct. 8, 1938; s. Veniamin Moisey Ziegerman and Faina Aron Dekster; m. Nadezhda Sergey Prokopets, Feb. 7, 1969 (div. May 1985); 1 child, Sonya; m. Monika Bergiel, Dec. 14, 1990 (div. Apr. 1999); children: Lena, Lisa; m. Tatiana Filippova, Feb. 2, 2001. Master's degree, Leningrad U., 1962; PhD, Stelkov Inst., Leningrad, 1971. Research assoc. U. Toronto, Ont., Can., 1974-78, asst. prof., 1981-86, U. Notre Dame, Ind., 1979-81; assoc. prof. Mt. Allison U., Sackville, N.B., Can., 1986-90, prof., 1990—. Contbr. articles on differential geometry and convexity to profl. jours. NSF grantee, 1980-81; Can. Natural Scis. and Engring. Research Council grantee, 1981—. Mem. Am. Math. Soc. Home: 7 Raworth Heights Sackville NB Canada E4L 4H3 Office: Mt Allison U Dept Math 67 York St Sackville NB Canada E4L 1E6

DELACATO, JANICE ELAINE, learning consultant, educator; b. Bklyn., June 6, 1926; d. Frode Siegfried and Vilma (Rils) Fernstrom; m. Carl Henry Delacato, June 20, 1951; children: Elizabeth Delacato Putnam, Carl Henry, David Fernstrom. AB, Bryn Mawr Coll., 1948. Tchr. Rydal Hall, Ogontz Sch., Pa., 1948-49, The Spence Sch., N.Y.C., 1949-50, Chestnut Hill Acad., Phila., 1950-52; co-dir. The Chestnut Hill Reading Clinic, Phila., 1951-65, Delacato & Delacato Cons. in Learning, Phila., 1972-88; mgr. Morton (Pa.) Book Store, 1972-88; co-dir. The Delacato & Delacato Conf. Autism & Learning Disabilities, 1979-82. Editor newsletter Temple U. Med. Ctr. Women's Aux., Phila., 1953-65; class editor Bryn Mawr Coll. Alumnae Bull., 1966-79. Chmn. fund-raising com. Springside Sch., 1969-71; treas. Main St. Fair Antiques Booth, Chestnut Hill Hosp., 1965-77. Recipient Main St. Fair award Chestnut Hill Hosp., 1972. Mem. AAUW, Phila. Cricket Club. Republican. Unitarian Universalist. Home: Apt 1014 Lincoln Woods 9801 Germantown Pike Lafayette Hill PA 19444

DELACOUR, JONELL, music educator; b. St. Joseph, Mo., Jan. 14, 1952; d. John David and Nellie Mae Roberts; m. Michael Gene Delacour, Nov. 8, 1975; 1 child, Jerad William. B in Music Therapy, U. Kans., 1974; MAT, St. Mary Coll., Leavenworth, Kans., 2002. Music therapist Larned (Kans.) State Security Hosp., 1975—83; paraprofl. Larned Sch. Dist., Garfield, 1983—90; vocal music tchr. United Sch. Dist. 447, Cherryvalle (Kans.) Middle/High Sch., 1991—2000; vocal/gen. music tchr. United Sch. Dist. 446, Independence (Kans.) Middle Sch., 2000—. Accompanist children's choir Ind. Area, 2002—. Bd. dirs. Independence Area Childrens' Choir, 2001—03. Mem.: Music Educators Nat. Conf., Kans. Choral Dirs. Assn., Kans. Music Educators Assn. (state tri-m chair 1999—2002, S.E. dist. ms choral chair 2001—03, S.E. dist. pres.-elect 2003—, SE Dist. Middle Sch. Outstanding Tchr. 2000). Office: Independence Middle Sch 300 W Locust Independence KS 67301 E-mail: jdelacour@indyschools.com.

DELAHANTY, REBECCA ANN, school system administrator; b. South Bend, Ind., Oct. 18, 1941; d. Raymond F. and Ann Marie (Batsleer) Paczesny; m. Edward Delahanty, June 22, 1963; children: David, Debbie. BA, Coll. of St. Catherine, Minn., 1977; MA, Coll. St. Thomas, Minn., 1983; PhD, Ga. State U., 1994. Cert. in adminstrn. and supervision Ga. Initiator, tchr. gifted kindergarten Dist. 284 Sch., Wayzata, Minn., 1977-83; gifted kindergarten coord. St. Barts Sch., Wayzata, 1983-85; prin. Dabbs Loomis Sch., Dunwoody, Ga., 1987-91; asst. to supt. Buford (Ga.) City Schs., 1993-98, supt., 1998-99; prof. Ga. State U., 1999-2000; ednl. cons., 2000—; adv. bd. U Saint Thomas, Coll. Edu., 2001—. Staff devel. adv. coun. Ga. Contbr. Mem. adv. bd. Coll. Edn. U. St. Thomas, 2001—. Mem.: ASCD, Minn. Coun. Gifted and Talented, Minn. Assn. Gifted Children, Nat. Assn. Gifted Children, Am. Ednl. Rsch. Assn., Omicron Gamma, Phi Delta Kappa.

DE LANCEY, PATRICIA A. elementary education educator; b. Waukegan, Ill., June 16, 1955; d. Robert A. and Lou Ellen Clark; m. Brian R. DeLancey, Jan. 17, 1976; 1 child,eErin C. BA in Elem. Edn. cum laude, Carthage Coll. Cert. elem. tchr., Wis., Ill. Tchr. Lake Shore Cath. Acad., North Chicago, Ill., 1987-88; kindergarten-8th music tchr. Immaculate Conception Sch., Waukegan, 1987-89, St. Therese Sch., Kenosha, Wis., 1990; k-8th music and computer tchr. St. Bede Elem. Sch., Ingleside, Ill., 1990-94; elem. tchr. St. Casimir Sch., Kenosha, 1994—. Music dir. St. John's United Ch. of Christ, Waukegan, 1993—; pres., citywide pres. Waukegan Pub. Schs. PTO, 1985-86. Mem. ASCD, Phi Lambda Theta. Avocations: geneaolgical research, native american research, research on ill effects of society on today's children.

DELANEY, CORNELIUS FRANCIS, philosophy educator; b. Waterbury, Conn., June 30, 1938; s. Patrick Francis and Margaret (Gavigan) D.; 1 child, Cornelius Francis Jr. MA, Boston Coll., 1961; PhD, St. Louis U., 1967. Prof. philosophy U. Notre Dame, Notre Dame, Ind., 1967—, chmn. philosophy dept., 1972-82, dir. honors program, 1989—. Author: Mind and Nature, 1969m The Synoptic Vision, 1977, Science, Knowledge and Mind, 1993, The Liberalism-Communitarianism Debate, 1994, New Essays on the Philosophy of C.S. Pierce, 2000. Recipient Madden award U. Notre Dame, 1974, Bicentennial award Boston Coll., 1976, Pres.'s award U. Notre Dame, 1984, Sheedy award U. Notre Dame,1987. Mem. Am. Cath. Philos. Assn. (pres. 1985), C.S. Peirce Soc. (pres. 1986), Am. Philos. Assn. (exec. com. 1983-85). Office: U Notre Dame Dept Philosophy 336 O'Shaughnessy Hall Notre Dame IN 46556-5639

DELANEY, ELEANOR CECILIA COUGHLIN, educator; b. Elizabeth, N.J.; d. John C. and Eleanor C. (Fadde) Coughlin; B.S., Sch. Edn. Rutgers U., 1930, M.A., 1939; Ph.D., Columbia U., 1954; 1 son, John. Tchr. public schs., Elizabeth, N.J., 1927; prin. Woodrow Wilson Sch., Elizabeth, 1941-55; prof. Grad. Sch. Edn., Rutgers U., New Brunswick, N.J., 1955-87, prof. emeritus, 1987—, chmn. dept. ednl. adminstrn. and supervision, 1974—; vis. prof. William and Mary Coll., U. Mex., Columbia U.; ednl. cons. sch. systems, N.J., N.Y., Va., 1950—; con. U.S. Dept. State, Health and Edn., coordinator Intern-Am. Affairs. Mem. Elizabeth Charter Commn., 1960-61; chmn. Mayor's Adv. Commn. on Urban Devel., 1962-64, Elizabeth Human Relations Commn., 1968-75; mem. Elizabeth Bd. Edn., 1972-79, pres., 1973-76; mem. exec. bd. Union County chpt. ARC; mem. exec. bd. Vis. Nurse and Health Assn., 1977— ; pres., 1981-85. Mem. AAUW, Nat., N.J. edn. assns., Dept. Elem. Sch. Prins., AAUP, AAAS, Am. Ednl. Research Assn., Kappa Delta Pi (counelor 1970-87, Nat. Honor Key), Pi Lambda Theta, Phi Delta Kappa. Author: Spanish Gold, Lands of Middle America, Our Friends in South America, Science-Life Series, Book 4; Persistent Problems in Education. Contbr. articles to profl. mags. Home: 8411 Forest Hills Dr Apt 102 Coral Springs FL 33065-5404

DELANEY, JANE ELLEN, elementary education educator; b. Chgo., Oct. 7, 1946; d. Francis Xavier and Eileen (Collins) O'Connell; m. Michael Dennis Delaney; children: Collin, Devin. BA, Marian Coll., Fond du Lac, Wis., 1968; MEd in Pub. Policy, Loyola U., Chgo., 1978; postgrad., U. Ill., Chgo. Tchr./jr. h.s. coord. St. Benedict Sch./H.S., Chgo., 1974-78; analyst Mayor's Office of Budget and Mgmt., Chgo., 1978-80; budget dir. Chgo. Fire Dept., 1980, CFO, 1980-82; instr. Gymboree, Lafayette, Calif., 1985, Diablo Valley Montessori, Lafayette, 1985-88; project coord. Family Learning Ctrs./Project Head Start Chgo. United et al, 1992-93; tchr. St. John of the Cross, Western Springs, Ill., 1993—, St. Ignatius Coll. prep., 2001—. Trea. Diablo Valley Montessori Sch., 1983-85. Contbr. to edn. manual Family Learning Centers/Head Start, 1994. Mem. Irish Fellowship Club, Chgo., 1990—. Recipient Merit award disaster svc. ARC, Fond du Lac, 1970, Founder Day award for pub. svc. Marian Coll., 1994, Outstanding Tchr. award St. Ignatius Coll. Prep., 1996, 1998, 2001, Tchrs. Who Make a Difference award Nazareth Acad., 1996. Mem. ASCD, Internat. Reading Assn., Nat. Coun. Tchrs. English,, Nat. Mid. Sch. Assn., Ill. Club for Cath. Women, Phi Delta Kappa. Home: 5241 Harvey Ave Western Springs IL 60558

DELANEY, JEAN MARIE, art educator; b. Jersey City, Nov. 14, 1931; d. John Francis and Genevieve Mary (Boulton) Reilly; m. Donald Kendall Delaney, Dec. 29, 1956; 1 child, Laura Marie. BA in Art Edn., Fairmont (W.Va.) State U., 1954; MA in Clin. Psychology, Loyola Coll., Balt., 1979; PhD in Art Edn., U. Wis., Milw., 1992. Cert. art tchr., prin., supr., Md. Tchr. English and social studies Reedurban Sch., Stark County, Ohio, 1954-56; art tchr. Perry Hall H.S., Stark County, 1956-57, Margaret Brent H.S., St. Mary's County, Md., 1957-59, Middle River Mid. Sch., Baltimore County, Md., 1959-62; home and hosp. tchr. Harford County (Md.) Bd. Edn., 1968-78; lectr. art appreciation U. Md. Extension, Harford County, 1971-76; art educator Baltimore County Bd. Edn., 1979-93; prof. art edn. S.W. Mo. State U., Springfield, 1993-97, asst. head dept. art and design, 1997-98, full prof. art edn., 1998, ret., 1998. Cons. Salisbury (Md.) State Coll., 1987; adj. prof. art edn. Md. Inst. Coll. Art, Balt., 1988-89; cons. bd. examiners and art edn. Nat. Tchr.'s Exam. test devel. com. ETS, Princeton, N.J., 1988-92. Author: Art Image, 6th Grade Units, 1988; co-author, co-editor: Creating Meaning Through Art: Teacher as Choice Maker, 1998; editor: Art Scholarships, 1988; editor videotape Ernest Goldstein: Art Criticism, 1987; author, editor curriculum guide. Recipient Youth Art Month award of excellence Art and Craft Materials Inst., 1989, grant to coordinate Crayola Dreammakers program for Ctrl. Region U.S. and Can., 1994-96; named Mo. Higher Edn. Art Educator of Yr., 1997. Mem. Nat. Art Edn. Assn. (Eastern Region Art Educator award of yr, 1989, Nat. Secondary Art Educator award of yr. 1990), Md. Art Edn. Assn. (state coun. 1985—, v.p. arts advocacy 1988-89, pres.-elect 1992—, Md. Art Educator of Yr. 1988), Internat. Soc. for Edn. Through Art, Mo. Art Edn. Assn. Home: 207 Hillendale Rd Bel Air MD 21014-5119

DELANEY, MARY ANNE, retired theology studies educator; b. Waltham, Mass., Feb. 15, 1926; d. Thomas Joseph and Mary Teresa (Berry) D. BA, Regis Coll., 1953; MEd, U. Mass., Boston, 1973; MDiv, Andover Newton Theol. Sch., Newton Ctr., Mass., 1978. Tchr. various schs., Mass., 1953-73; pastoral counselor Boston City Hosp., 1974-76; dir. pastoral care Cape Breton Hosp., Sydney River, Canada, 1978-81, Nova Scotia Hosp., Dartmouth, 1981-86, Misericordia Hosp., Edmonton, Canada, 1986-91; pastoral counselor Assn. Pastoral Edn., Waltham, Mass., 1992-96, Emmanuel Coll., Boston, 1996—2001; supr. pastoral edn. Leland Retirement Home, Waltham, 1992—2001; ret., 2001. Vice chair bioethics consultative svc. Misericordia Hosp., Edmonton, 1987-91; vis. scholar Andover Newton Theol. Sch., 1991-92. Trustee Pastoral Inst., Halifax, N.S., Can., 1981-86; mem. commn. on ecumenism Archdiocese of Halifax, 1982-86; mem. of the Congregation of Sisters of St. Joseph, Boston, 1945—. Mem. Can. Assn. Pastoral Edn. (cert. com. 1987-91), Assn. for Clin. Pastoral Edn. (cert. supr., accreditation com. 1993-98, cert. com. 1998-2001). Roman Catholic. Avocations: international travel, classical music, international travel, classical music, art, reading. Home and Office: 16 Cutter St Waltham MA 02453-5911 E-mail: sr.marydelaney@mediaone.net.

DELANEY, MATTHEW MICHAEL, school administrator, fine arts educator; b. Boston, Mar. 13, 1948; s. Matthew Michael and Julia Agnes (Perry) D.; m. Patricia Louise Tirrell, Mar. 22, 1970; children: Sara Linde, Elizabeth Kerrin. BS in Art Edn., Mass. Coll. Art, 1970; MEd, Bridgewater State Coll., 1974; MA, Boston Coll., 1981. Nat. bd. cert. in art; cert. fine arts tchr. PK-12, fine arts supervisor/ dir. PK-12, secondary tchr. history, social studies, prin., asst. prin. Instr. fine arts Brockton Pub. Schs., Mass., 1970-74; from instr. fine arts to PK-12 regional curriculum coord., electives program curriculum coord. Whitman-Hanson Regional Sch. Dist., Mass., 1974—. Adj. faculty mem. Mass. Coll. Art, Curriculum in the Visual Arts; facilitator for NBCT candidate support program, U. Mass. at Dartmouth; photographer Brockton Daily Enterprise, 1972-76, Patriot Ledger, 1976-82; instr. fine arts Brockton Art Ctr., 1973-74; cmty. sch. coord. Brockton Pub. Schs., 1971-74; facility Tech. Study Com., Whitman, 1993-94; mem. supt. search com., Abington, Mass., 1991-92; mem. Effective Schs. Com., Whitman-Hanson, 1982-84, instrnl. adv. coun., 1989—, faculty adv. coun., selected for field study Nat. Bd. Cert.. Art; art and music curriculum rep. North River Collaborative; presenter workshops in U.S. and France; peer assessor U.S. Dept. Edn., 1999; scorer Nat. Bd. Profl. Tchg. Standards, 1999. Photographic works in collection Internat. Ctr. for Photography/George Eastman House, Rochester, N.Y.; contbr. art and design to Kiwanis, Spl. Olympics, Shriners, and others; articles to profl. jours. NEH grantee, 1992, Horace Mann grantee, 1988, 89; recipient U.S. Presdl. Recognition, 1997, 99, citation by Mass. State Legislature, 1998, 2000, Mass. Senate 1999, 2000; cert. of honor Commonwealth of Mass., 1999, 2000. Mem. NEA, ASCD, Mass. Tchrs. Assn. (disting. svc. award 1988, recognition achievement award 1997, Whitman-Hanson Regional Sch. Dist. Outstanding Leadership award 1997), Nat. Art Edn. Assn., Abington Cultural Coun., Mass. Art Edn. Assn., Boston Coll. Alumni Assn., Mass. Coll. Art Alumni Assn. Democrat. Episcopalian. Avocations: skiing, sailing, cycling, travel, playing guitar. Office: Whitman-Hanson Regional Sch Dist 600 Franklin St Whitman MA 02382-2599

DELANO, MARILYN ANN, special education educator; b. Boston, Oct. 19, 1945; d. George Witt and Elizabeth (Harrison) D. BEd, Boston U., 1968; MEd, Lesley Coll., 1989. Cert. elem. spl. edn. tchr., Mass. Tchr. spl. class Town of Dracut (Mass.), 1968-70; tchr. work study, spl. edn. City of Peabody (Mass.), 1970-82; sales rep. Met. Ins., Warwick, R.I., 1982-84; resource tchr. Minuteman Tech. Schs., Lexington, Mass., 1983-84; tchr. Town of Methuen, Mass., 1984-94, Town of Londonderry, N.H., 1994—. Off campus liaison Lesley Coll., Cambridge, Mass., 1988—, grad. course instr., 1989—; computer trainer Methuen Spl. Edn., 1987—. Presenter Parent Adv. Spl. Edn. Group, Methuen, 1989. Fellow NEA, ASCD, Coun. Exceptional Children, Mass. Tchrs. Assn., Methuen Edn. Assn. Home: 22 Tanglewood Way Merrimack NH 03054-3116

DELAURA, DAVID JOSEPH, English language educator; b. Worcester, Mass., Nov. 19, 1930; s. Louis and Helen Adeline (Austin) DeL.; m. Ann Beloate, Aug. 19, 1961; children: Michael Louis, Catherine, William Beloate. AB, Boston Coll., 1955, A.M., 1958; PhD, U. Wis., 1960. Mem. faculty U. Tex. at Austin, 1960-74, prof. English, 1968-74; Avalon Found. prof. humanities, prof. English U. Pa., Phila., 1974-99, chmn. dept., 1985-90, univ. ombudsman, 1993-97. Author: Hebrew and Hellene in Victorian England: Newman, Arnold, and Pater, 1969; editor: Victorian Prose: A Guide to Research, 1973; contbr. chpts. to books, articles and revs. to profl. publs. Mem. MLA Assn. (ann. award for outstanding article 1964). Home: 31 Orchard Ln Villanova PA 19085-1133 E-mail: ddelaura@sprynet.com.

DELAY, EUGENE RAYMOND, psychologist, educator, researcher; b. Coeur d'Alene, Idaho, Dec. 24, 1948; s. Raymond Joseph and Fairy Louise (Fisher) D.; m. Rona Jane Moore, Sept. 12, 1971; 1 child, Shawn Patrick. BS in Psychology, U. Idaho, 1972; MS in Biopsychology, U. Ga., 1977, PhD in Biopsychology, 1979. Asst. prof. Regis U., Denver, 1979-84, assoc. prof., 1984-90, prof., 1990—, dir. neurosci. program, 1997—. Provisional clin. cons. Denver VA Hosp., 1981-87; rsch. cons. Brenau Coll., Gainesville, Ga., 1978, Colo. State U., Ft. Collins, 1987-94, rsch. assoc. U. Miami, 1993-94, 97-2003; vis. scientist Brown U., Providence, 1995-96. Contbr. articles to profl. jours. Served with U.S. Army, 1973-75. NSF grantee, 1989, 2000, NIH, 2000, 2003; NIH sr. fellow, 1995. Mem. APA, Southeastern Psychol. Assn., N.Y. Acad. Sci., Rocky Mountain Neurosci. Group, Rocky Mountain Psychol. Assn., Soc. Neurosci., Am. Psychol. Soc., Internat. Behavioral Neurosci. Soc., Assn. for Chemoreception Scis. Achievements include research in cross-modality transfer processes after damage to brain, particularly cortex with emphasis on potential for rehabilitation, recovery of function after brain damage, neuropsychological effects of brain damage and taste transduction of monosodium glutamate and amino acids. Home: 5786 W 81st Pl Arvada CO 80003-1834 Office: Regis U Dept Psychology 3333 Regis Blvd Denver CO 80221-1154 E-mail: edelay@regis.edu.

DEL COLLO, MARY ANNE DEMETRIS, school administrator; b. Norristown, Pa., May 10, 1949; d. John and Julia (Chale) Demetris; m. William Paul Del Collo, July 1, 1973; children: Margaux, Julia, Nicole. BS, West Chester State U., 1971; MEd, Rosemont Coll. Tech., 1995; EdD, Widener U., 2001. Cert. elem. tchr. and sch. adminstr., Pa. Tchr. Phoenixville (Pa.) Area Sch. Dist., 1971-97, adminstr., 1997—, Methacton Sch. Dist., Norristown, Pa., 1998—. Mem. AAUW, Pa. Assn. Elem. and Secondary Sch. Prins., Hellenic Univ. Club, Nat. Middle Sch. Assn., Kappa Delta Pi (v.p. Chi Gamma chpt. 1998-2000, pres. 2000-02, past pres. 2002-). Avocations: technology, walking, reading, antiquing, traveling. Office: Methacton Sch Dist Eagleville Rd Norristown PA 19403

DEL CONTE, L. CATHERINE, special education educator; b. Montour Falls, N.Y., June 8, 1955; d. Leon Clarence and Dorothy Louise May; m. Douglas Kelsey, Aug. 2, 1973; children: Henry Lee Kelsey, Bryon Douglas Kelsey; m. Richard Ralph Del Conte, Apr. 8, 1995. AA in Human Svcs., Genesee C.C., Batavia, N.Y., 1981; BSW, SUNY-Brockport, 1983, MPA in Geriatrics, 1986; M.Spl. Edn., George Mason U., Fairfax, Va., 2000. Case mgr. We Care, Inc., Washington, 1991—92, Brice Warren Corp., Washington, 1992—94, State of Md./Great Oaks MR Ctr., 1994—95, Jewish Social Svcs., Rockville, Md., 1995—97; learning disabilities/ED tchr. Fairfax County Pub. Schs., Annandale, Va., 1998—. Historian Phi Delta Kappa/George Mason U., 1998—2000, rsch. coord., 2000—; ct. apptd. specialist Fairfax County, Fairfax, Va., 1991—93; lead tchr. remediation program Annandale H.S., 1999—2002, mem. attendance adv. com., 2003—. Avocations: hiking, reading, working out, writing poetry. Home: 6006 Scarborough Commons Ln Burke VA 22015 Office: Fairfax County Public Schs 4700 Medford Dr Annandale VA 22003

DEL DUCA, RITA, language educator; b. NYC, Apr. 1, 1933; d. Joseph and Ermelinda (Buonaguro) Ferraro; m. Joseph Anthony Del Duca, Oct. 29, 1955; children: Lynn, Susan, Paul, Andrea. BA, CUNY, 1955. Elem. tchr. Yonkers (N.Y.) Pub. Schs., 1955-57; tchr. kindergarten Sacred Heart Sch., Yonkers, 1962-64; tchr. piano, Scarsdale, N.Y., 1973-79; asst. office mgr. Foot Clinic, Hartsdale, N.Y., 1977-85; tchr. ESL, Linguarama Exec. Sch., White Plains, N.Y., 1985-89; ESL tutor, Scarsdale, 1989—. Dist. leader Greenburgh (N.Y.) Rep. Com., 1991-92. Mem.: ASCAP. Avocations: oil painting, piano teaching, tennis, theatre arts. Home and Office: Unit 79 10 Old Jackson Ave Hastings On Hudson NY 10706

DELFOUR, MICHEL, mathamatics/statistics educator; Prof. math., stats. U. Montreal. Recipient Urgel Archambault prize in Phys. Sci. and Maths., Assn. Canadienne-Francaise pour l'Avancement des Scis., Can., 1995. Office: Dept Mathématiques et statistique U Montreal CP 6128 succ Centre-Ville H3C 3J7 Montreal QC Canada

DELGADO, LISA JAMES, elementary education educator; b. Murfreesboro, Tenn., May 8, 1960; d. J. Butler and JoAnn Ireta (Griswold) James; m. Mark Crawford Delgado, June 28, 1986. BS in Art Edn., U. Ga., 1982, MEd in Ednl. Media, 1984. Cert. media specialist, art tchr., Ga. Media specialist South Jackson Elem. Sch., Athens, Ga., 1984—; sch., system TOTY, 1994-95. Mem. sch. coun., Athens, 1991-94, chairperson, 1992-93. Contbg. author: Exploring Blue Highways: Literacy Reform, School Change and the Creation of Learning Communities; contbr. articles to profl. jours. Mem.: Ga. Coun. of Media Orgns., Profl. Assn. Ga. Educators, Ga. Libr. Media Assn. (dist. chmn. 1998, state treas. 1999—2000). Avocations: reading, scuba diving, genealogy, writing web pages. Office: South Jackson Elem Sch 8144 Jefferson Rd Athens GA 30607-3261

DELGADO, RAMON LOUIS, educator, author, director, playwright, lyricist; b. Dec. 16, 1937; s. Eloy Vincent and Hildegard (Chapman) D. BA, Stetson U., 1959; MA, Baylor U., 1960; MFA, YAle U., 1967; PhD, So. Ill. U., 1976. Tchr. Lyman H.S., Longwood, Fla., 1960-62; mem. faculty Chipola Jr. Coll., Marianna, Fla., 1962-64, Ky. Wesleyan Coll., 1967-72, Hardin-Simmons U., 1972-74, So. Ill. U., 1974-76, St. Cloud (Minn.) State U., 1976-78; prof. speech and theater Montclair State U., Upper Montclair, NJ, 1978—2003. Evaluator N.J. Teen Arts Festival, 1980, 81; judge Am. Theatre Assn. Coll. Theater Festival, 1980, 82, 83, 84, 85, N.J. Teen Galaxy Competition, 1984. Playwright: Waiting for the Bus, 1968, Once Below a Lighthouse, 1972, The Jerusalem Thorn, 1979, A Little Holy Water, 1983, Stones, 1983, The Flight of the Dodo, 1990, Remembering Booth, 1997, The Iron Corset, 1999, Consider the Phoenix, 2000; editor: The Best Short Plays, 1981-89; author: Acting with Both Sides of Your Brain, 1986; contbr. articles to profl. jours. Sec. Forest St. Manor Condo Assn., 1997-99; bd. dirs. 12 Miles West Theatre, 2000-2002. Recipient Samuel French Play award, 1966, U. Mo. Play award, 1971, 75, playwriting awards Am. Coll. Theatre Festival, 1976, 77, 78, Grand prize Music City Song Festival contest, 1988, 7 hon. mentions, 1989; Midwest Profl. Playwrights fellow, 1978; Ford Found. grantee, 1961; playwright-in-residence INTAR, 1980 Mem. Dramatists Guild, Assn. for Theatre in Higher Edn., Nat. Theatre Conf., Theta Alpha Phi, Phi Kappa Phi. Democrat. Home: 16 Forest St Apt 107 Montclair NJ 07042-3519

DELGADO, THERESA MICHELLE, middle school educator; b. Marysville, Calif., Oct. 15, 1965; d. Frank and Cynthia Lee (Navarette) D.; m. Richard Martinez; children: Ricky Delgado-Martinez, Daniel Delgado-Martinez BA, St. Mary's Coll., 1987; tchr. credential, Fresno State U., 1991. Cert. tchr., Calif. Recreation leader City of South San Francisco

(Calif.) Parks and Recreation, 1989; basketball reporter Calif. State U., Fresno, 1989-93; bilingual tchr. Tenaya Mid. Sch., Merced, Calif., 1991—. Cons. Merced Coll. Tchr. Readiness Program, 1992, mentor migrant edn., 1992—; mentor tchr. MCSD; master tchr. Chapman and Nat. Univs. Adviser Club Live/Red Ribbon, Merced, 1992-93; mem. Kops for Kids, Merced, 1992; cheerleading coach Tenaya Mid. Sch., 1992-94. Mem. ASCD, Calif. Reading Assn., Merced Area Reading Assn. Democrat. Roman Catholic. Avocations: basketball, reading, travel, walking, dachsunds. Home: 1976 Fall Brook Ct Merced CA 95340-0758

DELGADO-RODRIGUEZ, MANUEL, secondary school educator; b. Caguas, P.R., Dec. 15, 1932; s. Manuel Delgado-Planas and Angelina Rodriguez-Andaluz. MA in Edn. and History, U. P.R., 1969. Tchr. English Juncos (P.R.) H.S., 1962; social studies/Spanish tchr. Ponce de Leon Jr. H.S., Humacao, P.R., 1962; tchr. history Univ. H.S., Rio Piedras, P.R., 1963-65, 67—. Mem. curriculum com. Univ. H.S., Rio Piedras, coord. presdl. classroom for young Ams., 1970—, personnel com. Scholar Presdl. scholar, 2002. Mem. ASCD, P.R. Assn. Historians, Nat. Coun. for Social Studies. Home: PO Box 461 Humacao PR 00792-0461

DELIA, MARGARET M. elementary education educator; b. Phila., Aug. 24, 1964; d. John and Elsie McLaughlin; m. Christopher C. Delia, Sr., Aug. 16, 1986; children: Christopher, Chad, Curt. BA, Glassboro State Coll., 1986; MA, Rowan Coll. N.J., 1994. Cert. tchr. health/phys. edn., elem. edn., student personnel svcs., supr., N.J., adminstr., dir. student pers. svcs., prin. Tchr. health/phys. edn. Pitman (N.J.) Mid. Sch., 1986-92; elem. tchr. Kindle Sch., Pitman, 1992—; guidance counselor Glassboro (N.J.) High Sch., 1994—, Pitman H.S., 1994—99, Clearview Mid. Sch., Mullica Hill, NJ, 1999—. Writing com. mem. Pitmans Schs., 1992-93. Chairperson Ch. and Soc. FUMC, Glassboro, 1987-89; mem. PTA Glassboro Schs., 1994—, Pitman Schs., 1994; presenter/coord. Am. Heart Assn., N.J., 1987-94, coord. Jum Rope for Heart, 1987-94; scholarship selection com. SJCWS, N.J., 1989-92; mem. United Meth. Women Sunday Sch. Class, 1992-96, chairpersoon C/S, United Meth. Ch., 1987-89. Named N.J.'s New Tchr. of Yr., Sallie Mae, 1987, Delta H.S. Sports Hall of Fame, 2003. Mem. NJAHPERD (cons.), S. Jersey Coaches of Women's Sports (sec./treas. 1989-92, SADD advisor 1997-99). Avocations: family, skiing, crafts, crocheting, golf. Home: 155 Ewan Rd Mullica Hill NJ 08062-2901 Office: Clearview Regional Sch Dist 595 Jefferson Rd Mullica Hill NJ 08062

DELIFORD, MYLAH EAGAN, mathematics educator; b. Chgo., Nov. 7, 1948; d. Charles L.G. Eagan and Shirley R. (Bennett) Lewis; m. Albert Deliford Jr., Nov. 27, 1971 (div. Dec. 1984). BS in Edn., Chgo. State U., 1969; MA in Math., Northea. U., 1977. Tchr. Chgo. Bd. Edn., 1969—. Mem. Math. Assn. Am., Nat. Coun. Tchrs. Math., Nat. Alliance Black Sch. Educators, Chgo. Elem. Tchrs. Math. Club, Met. Math. Club Chgo., Ill. Coun. Tchrs. Math., Benjamin Banneker Assn. Democrat. Roman Catholic. Home: 7467 N Ridge Blvd Chicago IL 60645-1902 Office: Dunbar Vocat Career Acad 3000 S King Dr Chicago IL 60616-3452 E-mail: mdeliford@enc.K12.il.us.

DELIFUS, PATRICIA TUCKER, elementary school educator; b. Jacksonville, Fla., June 25, 1946; d. Lonnie Albert and Arletha Everette Tucker; m. John Adams Flowers, Jr., June 14, 1964 (dec. Jan., 1969); children: Lakesia Ineria Flowers Terry, Patrina Devon Flowers Johnson; m. Daniel Delifus, July 14, 1986. BS in Elem. Edn., Edward Waters Coll., 1974; MEd in Elem. Edn., Fla. A&M U., 1992. Cert. elem. tchr., Fla. Tchr. Biltmore Elem. Sch., Jacksonville, Fla., 1977-78, Gregory Dr. Elem. Sch., Jacksonville, 1978-79, Fla. Comml. Coll., Jacksonville, 1982-83, Macclenny (Fla.) Elem. Sch., 1984—. Sponsor Majorettes, Macclenny Elem. Sch., 1984-87. Recipient Fecognition for Disting. Achievement in Career Edn., Fla. Commendation Meritorius Svc. medal. Mem. Daughters of Sphinx (Vice Grand Matron), Eastern Stars (cert. of adminstrv. degree, assoc. matron). Democrat. Baptist. Avocations: reading, singing, dancing, travel, meeting people. Office: Macclenny Elem Sch 301 South Blvd E Macclenny FL 32063-2539 Home: Apt 1910 1000 Broward Rd Jacksonville FL 32218-5366

DE LISI, JOANNE, media consultant, educator; b. Bklyn. d. Louis Anthony and Maria Anna De Lisi. BA, Hunter Coll., 1972, MA, 1977; postgrad., NYU. Cert. tchr. N.Y. Asst. instr. Hunter Coll., N.Y.C., 1974-75; instr. NYU, N.Y.C., 1974-78; cons. communication N.Y.C., 1976—; instr. Bklyn. Coll., 1978-82, dir. forensics, 1981-82, asst. dir. acad. prep. program, 1980-82; adj. lectr. City U. Sys., N.Y.C., 1983-91. Profl. entertainer, 1953—75; faculty advisor Alpha Tau Omega, Bklyn. Coll., 1980—82. Contbr. articles to profl. jours., poems to anthologies, radio programs, newspapers. Mem. adv. bd. N.Y. State Senator Serphin Maltese. Recipient Nat. award of excellence, POW/MIA, Am. Legion Aux., 1995, Nat. award, USO and Savs. Bonds Jr. Activities Am. Legion Aux., 1996—98, Vets. Affairs, 1998—2000. Mem.: Metro N.Y. Database Internet Users Group, Fencers Am., Hunter Alumni Orgn., Am. Legion (pub. rels. officer Queens County 1991—93, treas. 1991—2001, v.p., girls state chmn. 1993—94, pub. rels. officer, newsletter editor, sec. Leonard unit 1993—94, pres. 1994—95, del. N.Y. state Dept. Conv. 1995, judge Forensics Tournament 1995—2003, pres. unit 104 1996, nat. security chmn., jr. activity chmn., pub. rels. dir. 1996—98, 10th dist. sgt-at-arms, sec., v.p. 2001—), Kappa Delta Pi. Roman Catholic. Avocations: antique collector, travel, jewelry making, fencing dir. Office: Wyckoff Heights Sta PO Box 370029 Brooklyn NY 11237-0029

DELISIO, SHARON KAY, secondary school educator, school administrator; b. Kansas City, Kans., May 7, 1943; d. Bernard James and Bernice Marie (Hansen) Hansen; m. Louis Charles Delisio, 1963; children: Lisa, Annette, Louis. BA summa cum laude, SUNY, Albany, 1974, MS in Reading, 1975, MS in Spl. Edn., 1980; student modified edn. leadership program, Nova U., Melbourne, Fla., 1996. Cert. reading, English, ESOL, varying exceptionalities, ednl. leadership. English tchr. Charlton Sch., Burnt Hills, N.Y., 1975-78, dir. edn., sch. prin., 1978-89; English/reading tchr. Lyndon B. Johnson Jr. High Sch., Melbourne, Fla., 1989-95, tchr., coordinating tchr., 1995-97, asst. prin., 1997-98, Clearlake Mid. Sch., Cocoa, Fla., 1998—. N.Y. del. Internat. Conf. Spl. Edn., Beijing, 1988; bldg. rep., mem. Brevard Fedn. Tchrs., 1993-94; coun. mem. Tchr. Edn. Ctr. Coun., 1994-96; mem. capital planning team Brevard County Schs., 1994, profl. devel. coun., 1995—; tchr. of yr. selection com. and mgmt. plan Devel. Team; chair sch. improvement com. Johnson Jr. H.S., 1997-98. Mem. Melbourne Civic Theatre, 1992-94; supporting mem. Brevard County Zoo, Melbourne, 1993-98; sponsor Youth Crime Watch, Johnson Jr. High, 1996-97. Mem. AAUW (book sale vol. 1992-97), Nat. Coun. of Tchrs. of English (presenter Nat. Conv. at Orlando 1994), Brevard Coun. of Tchrs. of English, Internat. Reading Assn., Brevand Assoc. of Sch. Adminstrs., Secondary Reading Coun. of Fla., Delta Kappa Gamma. Roman Catholic. Avocations: traveling, reading, collecting rare books, exercising. Office: Clearlake Mid Sch 1225 Clearlake Rd Cocoa FL 32922-6403

DELKER, DAVID GLEN, electronic engineering technology educator, consultant; b. Junction City, Kans., Mar. 29, 1952; s. Maurice C. and Marianna (Siebert) D.; m. Shawn Marie Willis, Sept. 29, 1973; children: Ryan, Collin, Kelsey. AT in Electronic Engring. Technology, Kans. Tech. Inst., 1973; BS in Tech. Edn., Okla. State U., 1977, MSEE, 1979. Cert. Engring. Technician. Sr. technician Applied Automation Inc., Bartlesville, Okla., 1973-76; project leader Fluid Power Research Ctr., Okla. State U., Stillwater, 1977-79; head computer tech. dept. Kans. Tech. Inst., Salina, 1979-81, assoc. prof. electronic tech., 1982-84; prof. Kans. State U., 1984—; pres. MicroControl Labs., Inc., Manhattan, 1991-96. Cons. Sias Engring. Inc., Salina, 1982-87; project engr. Inst. for Environ. Rsch., Kans. State U., Manhattan, 1987, head dept. engring. tech., 1998—. Author: Experiments in 8085 Microprocessor Programming and Interfacing, 1989. Cmty. leader 4-H Club, Manhattan and Salina, Kans. 1988-1998; mem. Kans. 4-H Adv. Com., 1988—, Saline County 4-H Found.Salina,Kans., 1996— Mem. IEEE, Am. Soc. Engring. Edn. (DOW Outstanding Young Faculty award 1985). Republican. Avocations: gardening, photography, woodworking. Home: 424 S Country Estates Dr Salina KS 67401-9658 Office: Kans State U Engring Tech Dept Salina KS 67401 E-mail: ddelker@ksu.edu.

DELLA CROCE, NORA LEE, special education educator; b. Summit, N.J., May 24, 1950; d. Bernard and Leanora (Pedecine) De Classis; m. David R. Della Croce, May 31, 1970; 1 child, David R. Jr. BA, Newark State Coll., 1971; MA, Kean Coll. of N.J., 1974, Learning Disabilities Tchr. Cert., 1975. Learning disabilities tchr. cons., N.J. Elem. tchr. Millburn Bd. Edn., Millburn, N.J., 1971-77; exec. dir. Della Croce Ednl. Svcs., Medford, N.J., 1978—. Exec. dir., owner N.J. Dept. Edn. Approved Clinic, Child Study Team Diagnosis and Remediation, Medford, 1988—. Mem. Millburn Bd. of Edn., 1981-83. N.J. State scholar, 1968-71. Mem. Assn. of Ednl. Therapists (profl. mem.), Assn. of Learning Cons., Learning Disabilities Assn. of N.J., Coun. for Learning Disabilities, Learning Disabilities Assn., Children with Attention Deficit Disorder. Republican. Roman Catholic. Avocations: tennis, photography. Office: Della Croce Ednl Svcs 560 Stokes Rd # 23-368 Medford NJ 08055-2905

DELLAGLORIA, JOHN CASTLE, city attorney, educator; b. NYC, June 29, 1952; s. Arthur A. and Marianne Dellagloria; divorced; 1 child, Rebecca; m. Marilyn Castle Dellagloria, Sept. 25, 1988; 1 child, Caitlin. BA in English Lit., SUNY, Binghamton, 1976; JD, U. Miami, 1979. Bar: Fla. 1979, N.Y. 1986, U.S. Ct. Appeals (11th cir.) 1981, U.S. Dist. Ct. (so. dist.) Fla. 1980, U.S. Supreme Ct. Rsch. asst. 3rd Dist. Ct. Appeal, Miami, Fla., 1980-81; assoc. Cassel & Cassel PA, Miami, 1981-82; dep. city atty. City North Miami Beach, Fla., 1983-86; city atty. City South Miami, Fla., 1986-90; chief dep. city atty. City Miami Beach, Fla., 1990-96; city atty. City North Miami, Fla., 1995—; gen. counsel Miami Beach Housing Authority, 1997-2000, South Miami Cmty. Redevel. Agy., 1998—2002. Lectr. Sch. Profl. Devel., U. Miami, 1982-88, dir. paralegal program, 1984-86, lectr. Sch. Bus., 1989—, lectr. real property program; lectr. govt. law sect. Fla. Bar; moderator Rachlin, Cohen & Holtz, Ann. Govt. Law Symposium, 1996—. Com. person Parrot Jungle Com., Pinecrest, Fla., 1998. Mem. Eugene P. Spellman Am. Inn of Ct. (alumnus). Democrat. Jewish. Avocation: long distance running. Office: City North Miami 776 NE 125th St North Miami FL 33161-5654 E-mail: catdel@hotmail.com.

DELLA PENNA, JOAN FRANCES, secondary educator; b. Worcester, Mass., Jan. 23, 1941; d. Howard Frank and Ellen (McKeon) Blodgett; m. Vincent Della Penna Jr., Oct. 5, 1961 (div. 1974); 1 child, Adrienne. BA in Math., U. Mass., 1963; MEd in Ednl. Rsch., Northeastern U., Boston, 1978. Cert. secon. math. tchr., occupational edn. tchr., elem. tchr. Mass. Specialist math., sci., microcomputers and adult high sch. Minuteman Tech., Lexington, Mass., 1974—. Co-chmn. Soviet exch. com. Minuteman Tech., 1989—; cons. Women's Tech. Inst., Boston, 1984, Prindle, Weber & Schmidt, Boston, 1983. Judge sci. fair MIT, Cambridge, Mass., 1990—. Horace Mann grantee, 1987, 86. Mem. Nat. Coun. Tchrs. Math., Assn. Tchrs. Math. in Mass., Princeton Assn. New Eng. (sci. fair del. 1990-92), Princeton Parents Assn. Avocations: interior design, reading, writing, logic puzzles, gardening. Home: 25 Mason St Lexington MA 02421-6327 Office: Minuteman Tech 758 Marrett Rd Lexington MA 02421-7313

DELLER, HARRIS, artist, educator; b. Bklyn., Jan. 28, 1947; s. Joseph Henry and Sarah (Brazilion) D.; m. Jane Emily Berman, July 6, 1970; children: Jenny Elizabeth, Michael Joseph. BA, Calif. State U., Northridge, 1971; MFA, Cranbrook Acad. Art, Bloomfield Hills, Mich., 1973. Instr. Bloomfield Hills Art Assn., Birmingham, Mich., 1971-73, Sch. Art Inst., Chgo., 1973, Ga. So. Coll., Statesboro, 1973-75; prof. art So. Ill. U., Carbondale, 1975—. One-man shows include Garth Clark Gallery, L.A., 1988, 90, Esther Saks Gallery, Chgo., 1988, Mus. SW Tex., Beaumont, 1990, So. Ill. U. Sch. of Med., 1991, Avante Gallery, 1997, Brevard Mus. of Art & Service, 1998, Santa Fe Clay, 1999, Ea. Shore Art Ctr., Fairhope, Ala., 2003; exhibited in group shows, including USIA, Craft Today, 1989, Everson Mus., Syracuse, N.Y., 1990, Ruth Chandler Williamson Gallery, Scripps Coll., Claremont, Calif., 2000, World Ceramic Expo, Korea, 2001, NCECA Belger Art Ctr., Kansas City, Mo., 2002. Dir. Sch. Art and Design, So. Ill. U., Carbondale. Fulbright fellow, Seoul, South Korea, 1981; artist fellow Ill. Arts Coun., 1986, 87, 89, 91, 98, 2000. Mem. Nat. Coun. Edn. Ceramic Arts (bd. dirs. 1987-94).

DELNICK, MARTHA JOYCE, retired elementary education educator; b. Muncie, Ind., July 17, 1939; d. Doyt Randall and Susan (Straley) Whiteman; m. Jerry Spencer, July 6, 1962 (div. 1967); children: Jay Dee, Todd Alan. BA, Ball State U., 1970, MA, 1975; postgrad., Mich. State U., U. Mich. Cert. tchr., Mich. Tchr. Bennett Elem. Sch., Marion, Ind., 1965-67; tchr. elem. sch. Grand Rapids (Mich.) Pub. Schs., 1970-77, reading cons., 1977-87, tchr. compensatory edn., 1987-96, itinerant tchr. Title I, 1996-2001. Tchr. Acad. Summer Success Acad., 1991-95; presenter Compensatory Edn. Parent Orgn., Grand Rapids, 1980-89, Jefferson Sch. Family Math. program, Grand Rapids, 1992; mem. Mich. Math. Insvc. Project K-2, 1991-92, 3-6, 1992-93; math. svc. trainer Compensatory Edn. Tchrs. and Paraprofls., 1991-93; in-svc. MEAP trainer Grand Rapids Pub. Sch. Tchrs., 1995-2001.—. Author curriculum materials. Mem. NEA (life), Mich. Edn. Assn. (life), Grand Rapids Edn. Assn. (rep. 1985-90, sch. bd. contact 1986-88), Mich. Reading Assn., Mich. Coun. Tchrs. Math. Mem. United Ch. of Christ. Avocations: sewing, crafts, cooking. Home: 6211 Woodwater Ave NE Belmont MI 49306-9255

DELONG, DIANE MARGENE, educator resource specialist; b. Vancouver, Wash., June 10, 1949; d. Robert E. and Margie M. DeLong; m. Stan H. Rubinsky, July 13, 1991. Bachelors, Seattle U., 1971; Masters, Nat. U., San Diego, 1991. Life tchg. credential grades K-12 Calif., learning disabled credential Calif., resource specialist credential Calif. Educator St. Catherines Sch., Seattle, 1971—76; retail advt. exec. Desert Sun/Gannet Corp., Palm Springs, Calif., 1976—78; educator St. Theresas Sch., Palm Springs, 1978—80; educator regular/spl. edn. Desert Sands Unified, LaQuinta, Calif., 1981—. Sci. mentor tchr. Desert Sands Unified, La Quinta, 1986—88, program specialist designee, 1988—96. Mem.: Angel View Crippled Childrens Home, Am. Legion Aux., Delta Kappa Gamma, Phi Delta Kappa. Avocations: childrens charity volunteer, golf. Office: La Quinta High Sch 79-255 Westward Ho Dr La Quinta CA 92253

DE LONG, KATHARINE, retired secondary education educator; b. Germantown, Pa., Aug. 31, 1927; d. Melvin Clinton and Katherine Frances (Brunner) Barr; m. Alfred Alvin De Long, June 21, 1947; children: Renée, Claudia, Jane. AA, Mesa Jr. Coll., Grand Junction, Colo., 1962; BA, Western State Coll., Gunnison, Colo., 1964; MA, Colo. State U., 1972. Camp dir. Kannah Creek Girl Scout Camp, 1960-64; tchr. Mesa County Valley Sch. Dist. #51, Grand Junction, 1964-84, dept. chmn., 1970-79; ret., 1984; tour coord., escort Mesa Travel, 1990—2002. Substitute instr. Mesa State Coll., 1986-90; student council sponsor Mesa County Valley Sch., 1976-80; bd. dirs. Am. Red Cross, mem. disaster team, 1996-2000, state svc. coun. rep., 1998-2000. Bd. dirs. Chipeta Girl Scout Coun., Grand Junction, 1960-66; pct. committeewoman Mesa County Dem. Party; mem., vice-chmn. Profl. Rights and Responsibilities Commn. for Dist. #51 Schs., Grand Junction, 1978-84; trustee Western Colo. Ctr. for the Arts, Grand Junction, 1987-88; mem. Mesa County Hist. Soc.; mem. Mesa County Coun. on Aging, 1994—, chmn., 2002—. Mem. AAUW (pres. local chpt. 1979-81, chmn. state cultural interest), AARP (Colo. legis. com. area I, transp. task force, dist. dir. dist. 1, del. to nat. conv., dir. state conv. 1991, legis. com. 1988-90, asst. state dir. 1990-91, dist. dir. 1991-94), LWV (Grand Junction Area, sec. bd. dirs. 1995-2000, Pub. Employees Retirement Assn. (legis. adv. com. 1990-91), Colo. Ret. Sch. Employees Assn. (v.p.), Investment Club (sec. 2001-2003), Wednesday Music Club (treas. 2002-03, pres., 2003—), Phi Theta Kappa. Congregationalist. Avocations: music, theatre, swimming, hiking, travel.

DELONG, MARY ANN, educational administrator; b. Chester, Pa., July 11, 1944; d. Ann (Anthony) Fiduk; m. J. Thomas DeLong, Feb. 13, 1965. BS, West Chester U., 1966; MS, Kutztown U., 1970. Lic. mental health counselor, elem. tchr. adminstr., Fla. Tchr. Exeter Sch. Dist., Pa., 1966-68, Gov. Mifflin Sch. Dist., Shillington, Pa., 1968-71; guidance counselor Wilson Sch. Dist., West Lawn, Pa., 1971-73, Marion County Sch. Bd., Ocala, Fla., 1973-75, coord., testing, 1975-79, supr., guidance, testing and rsch., 1979—. Bd. dirs. Marion Citrus Mental Health Ctr., Ocala, 1982-88, pres. 1987; treas. Marion County Child Advocacy Coalition, 1996-97; chairperson Fla. Statewide Assessment Adv. Com., 1984-85; mem. Fla. Writing Assessment Adv. Com., 1990-93; active Fla. Task Force Counselor Supervision, 1981-83. Named Educator of Yr. Mental Health Assn., Marion County, 1984, Adminstr. of Yr., hon. mention award Fla. Sch. Counselors Assn., 1984. Mem. Fla. Assn. Counselor Educators and Suprs., Fla. Assn. Test Adminstrs. (bd. dirs.), Fla. Ednl. Rsch. Assn. (bd. dirs., membership chmn.), Am. Assn. Suprs. and Adminstrs., Altrusa Internat. Avocations: waterskiing, boating, reading, cats. Office: Marion County Sch Bd PO Box 670 Ocala FL 34478-0670

DE LORCA, LUIS E. public school administrator, educator, speaker; b. L.A., Oct. 18, 1959; children: Nicholus A. and Angelus M. (twins). AA, Rio Hondo Jr. Coll., Whittier, Calif., 1983; BA, Calif. State Poly. U., 1989; MA in Humanities, Calif. State U., Dominguez Hills, 1997; tchg. credential, Nat. U., 1997; adminstrv. credential, U. So. Calif., 1998, D. Football coach various high schs., So. Calif., 1980; pub. rels. dir. Calif. Poly Pomona Music Dept., 1987-89; pres. Exclusive Concepts, L.A., 1987-89; lifeguard L.A. City Recreation Dept., 1980-87; tchr. English Cathedral H.S., L.A., 1989-90; tchr., rsch. specialist Whittier (Calif.) Union H.S., 1990; founder, dir. The Learning Advantage Ctr., Whittier, 1991—; elem. tchr. St. Paul of the Cross Sch., La Mirada, Calif., 1993-95; CEO New Ednl. Wave Inc., Whittier, 1994—; tchr. L.A. County Office Edn., 1995-98; asst. prin. Bassett Unified Sch. Dist., 1998-2000; prin. Franklin Mid. Sch., Long Beach (Calif.) Unified Sch. Dist., 2000—03; con. Urban Edn. Partnership, 2003. Adj. prof. Calif. State U., Dominguez Hills, 2003. Active Big Bros. of Am., Sierra Club Mem. Assn. Calif. Sch. Adminstrs., Whittier C. of C., Cousteau Soc., Phi Delta Kappa (exec. bd. dirs., v.p. projects). Democrat. Avocations: scuba, martial arts, swimming, handball, skiing. Home: 11323 Gradwell St Lakewood CA 90715 E-mail: LDelorca@lbusd.k-12.ca.

DE LORENZO, WILLIAM E. foreign language educator; BA in Spanish and Speech, Montclair State Coll., 1959, MA in Speech and Drama, 1964; PhD in Fgn. Lang. Edn. and Tchr. Edn., Ohio State U., 1971. Tchr. Spanish various locations, N.J.; asst. prof. Spanish, Montclair State Coll.; assoc. prof. emeritus, coord. fgn. lang. edn./2d lang. edn. U. Md., College Park. Organizer, co-dir. symposium for fgn. lang. tchr. candidates. Recipient Florence Steiner award, 1992. Mem. Am. Coun. on Tchg. Fgn. Langs. (charter). Office: U Md Dept Curriculum-Instrn Harold Benjamin Bldg Rm 2311 College Park MD 20742-0001

DELPRETE, AGNES, elementary school educator; b. Brooklyn, Apr. 27, 1952; d. William Ralph and Concetta DelPrete. AA, Kingsborough C.C., 1972; BA, Brooklyn Coll., 1974; MA, Fresno Pacific Coll., 2000. Tchr. Ft. Green Catholic Sch., Brooklyn, NY, 1974—80, Clark Co. Sch. Dist., Las Vegas, Nev., 1980—84, Mt. Pass Elementary, Mt. Pass, Calif., 1984—91, Baker Elementary, 1992—93, Baker Junior High Sch. & High Sch., 1993—94, Baker Elem., 1994—. Home: 3322 Berwyck St Las Vegas NV 89121-3503

DEL ROSARIO, ROSE MARIE, clinical sociologist, educator, consultant; b. Manila, July 20, 1946; d. Vernon Roger and Justina (Lopez) Lemme; married (div. 1989); children: Marjorie Lou Iannella, Tina Marie Bidney. BS in Sociology, Ariz. State U., 1974, MA, 1978, PhD, 1987. Info. specialist U.S. Women's Army Corps, Anniston, Ala., 1966-68; edn. counselor U.S. Armed Forces Edn. Ctr., Clayton, Panama Canal Zone, 1971-73; rsch. co-dir. cmty. needs assessment projects Mesa City Coun., Ariz., 1976-77; instr. U. Phoenix, 1977-78, 81-82; dir. comprehensive manpower ctr. Phoenix Urban League, 1978-82; field underwriter N.Y. Life Inst. Co., Scottsdale, Ariz., 1983-84; instr., grad. assoc. dept. sociology Ariz. State U., Tempe, 1984-87; program assoc., nat. coord. The Nat. Conf. of Christians and Jews, Inc., 1987-91; dir. office of coop. edn. Our Lady of the Lake U., San Antonio, 1991-94; sr. edn. cons. Advanced Edn. Models and Assocs., San Antonio, 1991-94; pres. Genesis Network, Inc., 1994-99; ednl. specialist Appalachia Edn. Lab., Inc., Arlington, Va., 1999—. Instr. dept. sociology Palo Alto Coll. and San Antonio Coll., 1992-94; adj. asst. prof. Dental Diagnostic Ctr., U. Tex. Health Sci. Ctr., San Antonio, 1992-95; mem. resource devel. com. Internat. Folk Culture Ctr., 1992-94; mentor undergrad. and grad. students Sociologists' AIDS Network, Am. Sociol. Assn., 1992—; adj. asst. prof. sociology dept. U. Miami, Fla., Coral Gables, 1995—; vis. scholar Postdoctoral Programs in Geriatrics, Washington, 1993; rschr. HIV/AIDS, U. Mich., Ann Arbor, 1994. Contbr. numerous reports and articles to profl. pubs. Mem. Pres.'s Coun. of the Filipino Club of Ariz., 1982-89; alumna Valley Leadership Program for Phoenix Met. Area, 1981—; dir., choreographer Philippine Performing Arts of Ariz., 1976-84; pres. Filipino club of Ariz., 1982, 84; asst. dir. Southeastern Desegregation Assistance Ctr., Miami, 1996-97. Fellow Am. Sociol. Assn., Doctoral Minority Fellowship Program, 1986-87, Presdl. Svc. award Filipino Club of Ariz., 1982, 84, Humanitarian award Ariz. Affiliate of the League of United Latin Am. Countries, 1982, Spl. Svc. Recognition award Filipino Club of Ariz., 1981; grantee in field. Mem. AAUP, Am. Sociol. Assn., Coop. Edn. Assn., Nat. Assn. for Asian & Pacific Am. Educators, Soc. for Women in Sociology, Sociologists' AIDS Network, Tex. Coop. Edn. Assn., Alpha Kappa Delta, Phi Kappa Phi. Democrat. Avocations: profl. Philippine folk dancing.

DEL ROSSO, JEANA MARIE, literature educator; b. Binghamton, N.Y., Dec. 21, 1970; d. Paul Joseph and Roseann A. Del Rosso; m. David M. Freeman, June 18, 1994. BA in English, Binghamton U., 1992; MA in English, U. Md., 1993, women's studies cert., 1998, PhD in English, 2000. Tchg. asst. U. Md., College Park, 1994—2000; asst. prof. Coll. Notre Dame of Md., Balt., 2001—. Adj. faculty UMBC, Balt., 2000—01, Trinity Coll., Washington, 2000—01. Contbr. articles to jours. Mem.: MLA, Nat. Women's Studies Assn., Nat. Assn. Univ. Women, Golden Key, Phi Kappa Phi, Sigma Tau Delta (sponsor), Phi Beta Kappa. Office: Coll Notre Dame Md Dept English 4701 N Charles St Baltimore MD 21210

DELUCA, ALBERT R., JR., secondary education educator; b. Bklyn., June 27, 1949; s. Albert Renato Sr. and Yolanda M. (Cupo) DeL.; m. Adrienne Chero, Feb. 14, 1992; children: Kristen, Leah, Albert John, Greg. AA in Art, Nassau C.C., Garden City, N.Y., 1969; BS in Edn., Hofstra zU., 1971; MS in Edn., C.W. Post U., 1973, diploma in profl. adminstrn., 1982; PhD in Ednl. Adminstrn., Pacific Western U., 1994; EdD, Berne U., 1995. Vicat. lic. in comm. Instr., team leader Lindenhurst (N.Y.) H.S., 1971—, media instr., coord., 1981—, theatre arts coord., 1983-88, dist. chmn. art, 1986-88. Adj. instr. Suffolk C.C., Selden, N.Y., 1977-89; adj. instr., cons. St. Josephs Coll., Pathogue, N.Y., 1989—; owner, operator DeLuca Photographers, L.I., 1973-83; designer N.Y. State United Tchrs., N.Y.C., 1980-85; freelance artist and photographer; tchr. space program NASA. Contbr. articles to profl. jours. Named Tech. and Learning Tchr. of Yr., 1994; induced into Nat. Tchr. Hall of Fame, 1995. Mem. Nat. Inst. Photography, N.Y. State Art Tchr. Assn., L.I. Art Tchrs. Assn., Media Arts Assn., Profl.

Photographers Am., CW Post Alumni Assn., Hofstra Alumni Assn., Nassau Alumni Assn., Pacific Western Alumni Assn. Avocations: soccer, softball, water sports, theatre, movies. Office: Lindenhurst HS 300 Charles St Lindenhurst NY 11757-3545

DELUCA, JAMES PATRICK, graphic arts and advertising educator, consultant; b. N.Y.C., Aug. 21, 1933; s. Ignazio and Filomena (Romano) D.; m. Teresa Maria Iraggi, Oct. 1, 1960; 1 child, Teresa Maria. AAS, N.Y.C. Community Coll., 1960; BS, NYU, 1963, MA, 1964; EdD, Nova U., 1976. Mem. faculty dept. graphic arts and advt. tech. Ctr. for Advt. Printing & Pub. N.Y.C. Tech. Coll., 1960—; chair dept. N.Y.C. Tech. Coll., 1970-84, prof., chair dept. graphic arts, 1970—; pvt. practice mgmt. cons. to edn. and bus. N.Y. Nat. lectr. on Norman Rockwell, illustrator; asst. examiner N.Y.C. Bd. Edn., 1969, advisor, 1969; ednl. and tech. advisor Graphic Arts, Inc., Pitts., 1967—; co-chair print evaluation sect. Tech. Assn. Pulp and Paper Industry, 1969; mem. ednl. com. The Graphic Arts Tech. Found., 1970—; advisor various pubs. Contbr. articles to profl. jours.; developer grants, 1970—; presenter numerous confs., programs. Trustee Goudy Soc., Am. Printing History Assn.; past pres. Club Printing House Craftsmen. Recipient Gamma Gold Key award GET, 1972, Elmer G. Voigt award Graphic Arts Tech. Found., 1977, Navigators Graphic Arts award Navigators Graphic Arts Assn. N.Y., 1978, James H. Branhey award Printing Mgrs. Assn. Am., 1978, Horace Hart award Graphic Arts Tech. Found., 1982, Soderstrom Soc. Award, 1983, James J. Rudisill award Edn. Council on Graphic Arts, 1978, Van Hanswyk Jasser award Craftsmen, 1978, Man of Year award Lithographic Industries Met. N.Y., 1980, others; named Man of Yr. Printing Tchrs. Guild, 1987. Mem. NEA, Am. Assn. Higher Edn., Am. Assn. Community and Jr. Colls., Am. Tech. Assn., Internat. Graphic Arts Edn. Assn., Printing Industries Am., Nat. Assn. Printers Lithographers (Nat. Key Employee award 1982), Assn. Graphic Arts Assn. N.Y., Am. Vocat. Assn., Am. Mus. Natural History, Smithsonian Hist. Soc., Navigators Graphic Arts Assn. (pres.). Home: 621 8th Ave New Hyde Park NY 11040-5405 Office: CUNY NY Tech Coll 621 8th Ave New Hyde Park NY 11040-5405

DELUCA, ROSE MARIE, special education educator; b. Boston, Feb. 24, 1952; d. Ralph Domenic and Norina (Longo) Colannino; m. Antonio DeLuca, July 14, 1973; children: V. Anthony DeLuca, Christofer R. DeLuca. BS in Elem. Edn./English, Salem (Mass.) State Coll., 1973; MEd in Spl. Edn., Boston State Coll., U. Mass., 1980. Cert. elem. tchr. K-8, spl. edn./moderate spl. needs. Spl. edn. tchr. Revere (Mass.) Pub. Schs., 1973—; also ednl. team leader. Mem. Revere Pub. Schs. PTSA, Suffolk U. Parent Coun., Revere Youth Soccer (bd. dirs., registrar 1985-91, player devel. coord. 1991—). Mem. Salem State Coll. Alumni Assn., Malden Cath. Lancers Assn., Coun. for Spl. Educators, Nat. Assn. Pupil Svcs. Adminstrs., Phi Delta Kappa. Office: Revere Pub Schs/ Paul Revere Sch 395 Revere St Revere MA 02151-4535

DELUIGI, DOMINIC JOSEPH, psychologist, educator; b. Sewickley, Pa., June 9, 1947; s. Oliver Joseph and Sally (Palladini) DeL.; m. Sarah Ann Spinelli, July 5, 1969; children: Kristy, Nicole, Melissa. BA, Coll. of Steubenville, 1969; MEd, Duquesne U., 1971, cert. advanced grad. studies, 1974; PhD, U. Pitts., 1977. Lic. psychologist, Pa.; cert. sch. psychologist, Pa.; nat. cert. sch. psychologist. Tchr. spl. edn. Hancock County Schs., Newell, W.Va., 1969-71; unit supr. St. Peter's Child Devel. Ctr., Sewickley, 1971-73; asst. clin. dir., grad. teaching asst. Duquesne U., Pitts., 1973-74, mem. grad. adj. faculty, 1980-85; sch. psychologist Beaver Valley Intermediate Unit, Monaca, Pa., 1974-83, Hopewell Area Sch. Dist., Aliquippa, Pa., 1983-91, coord. pupil svcs., 1991-93; pvt. practice Monaca, 1986—. Lectr. Beaver Campus, Pa. State U., Monaca, 1980—; mem. adv. bd. Children with Attention Deficit Disorders, Beaver, Pa., Learning Disabilities Assn., Beaver, 1986. Bd. dirs. Assn. for Retarded Citizens, Beaver, 1974-80; pres. bd. dirs. Beaver County Mental Health-Mental Retardation, 1980-82. Named Outstanding Profl. Vol., Assn. for Retarded Citizens, 1977, Partnership in Edn. award Beaver County Edn. Assn., 1986. Mem. APA, NASP, Nat. Assn. Pupil Svcs. Adminstrs., Coun. for Exceptional Children, Pa. Psychol. Assn., Assn. Sch. Psychologists Pa., Pa. Assn. Pupil Svcs. Adminstrs. Home: 1090 Chapel Rd Monaca PA 15061-2753 Office: 337 3rd St Beaver PA 15009-2302

DE LURGIO, STEPHEN ANTHONY, management educator; b. St. Louis, June 27, 1945; s. Louis J. and Amelia Barbara (Machler) De L.; m. Ina C. Kimmel, Nov. 10, 1969; children: Stephen A. II, Patrick M. BSME, U. Mo., 1967; MBA, St. Louis U., 1971, PhD, 1976. Design engr. Emerson Electric, St. Louis, 1967-70; project engr. Coinco Inc., St. Louis, 1970-74; asst. prof. mgmt. U. Ill., Springfield, 1974-76; prof. mgmt. U. Mo., Kansas City, 1976—. Co-author: (books) Quantitative Models for Business Decisions, 1980, Forecasting Systems for Operations Management, 1991, Forecasting Theory, 1998; contbr. articles to profl. jours. Bd. dirs. Animal Health Inst., St. Louis, 1985—. U. Kansas City Faculty fellow U. Kansas City Trustees, 1986. Fellow Am. Prodn. and Inventory Control Soc. (chmn. 1984-89, mem. Cert. Com. 1984-89); mem. The Inst. of Man Sci., Inst. of Indsl. Engrs., Internat. Inst. of Forecasters, Decision Scis. Inst. Avocation: trout/fly fishing. Office: U Mo Bloch Sch Bus Kansas City MO 64110 E-mail: sad@forecast.umkc.edu.

DEL VECCHIO, ELIZABETH ANN, secondary education educator; b. Newark, Feb. 1, 1961; d. Donald Del V. and Dolores (Coppola) PeKaar. BS, Trenton State Coll., 1983; MA in Adminstrn., NYU, 1987. Tchr. spl. edn. Benway Sch., Mahwah, N.J., 1985-87; tchr. dir. athletics Paramus (N.J.) Cath. High Sch., 1987-99; activity/athletic dir., area supr. Cresskill (N.J.) High Sch., 2000—. Home: 798 Saddle River Rd Saddle Brook NJ 07663-4447 Office: Creskill High Sch 1 Lincoln Dr Cresskill NJ 17626 E-mail: bdelvecchio@cresskillboe.k12.nj.us.

DEMAIN, ARNOLD LESTER, microbiologist, educator; b. N.Y.C., Apr. 26, 1927; s. Henry and Gussie (Katz) D.; m. Joanna Kaye, Aug. 2, 1952; children: Pamela Robin Demain McCloskey, Jeffrey Brian. BS, Mich. State U., 1949, MS, 1950; PhD, U. Calif., Berkeley, 1954; Doctorate (hon.), U. Leon, Spain, 1997, Ghent (Belgium) U., 1999, Technion-Israeli Inst. Tech., 2000, Mich. State U., 2000, U. Muenster, Germany, 2003. Rsch. asst. U. Calif., Davis, 1952-54; rsch. microbiologist Merck & Co., Inc., Danville, Pa., 1954-56, Rahway, N.J., 1956-65, founder, head of dept. ferm. microbiology, 1965-69; prof. of ind. microbiology MIT, Cambridge, 1969—2001; fellow Charles A. Dana Rsch. Inst., Drew U., Madison, NJ, 2001—. Author or editor 10 books; contbr. more than 475 articles to profl. jours. With USN, 1945—47. Recipient Hotpack award Can. Soc. Microbiology, 1978, Rubro award Australian Soc. Microbiology, 1978, Indsl. Microbiology award Italian Pharm. Assn., 1989, Hans Knoll meml. award, Germany, 1990, G. Mendel award Czech Acad. Sci., 1998, Andrew Jackson Moyer award USDA, 1998. Mem.: NAS, Am. Chem. Soc. (Marvin Johnson biotech. award), Am. Soc. Microbiology (Waksman award N.J. br. 1975, Biotech. award 1990, Disting. Svc. award 1994, Alice C. Evans award 1998, hon. mem. N.E. br. 1999), Soc. Indsl. Microbiology (pres. 1990, Charles Thom award 1978, Waksman Tchg. award 1995), Hungarian Acad. Sci., Mex. Acad. Sci., Croatian Soc. Biotech. (hon.), Czech Soc. Microbiology (hon.), Soc. Actinomycetes Japan (hon.), French Soc. Microbiology (hon.). Achievements include 21 patents; elucidation of biosynthetic pathway to penicillins and cephalosporins; recognition of phenomenon of biochemical regulation of secondary metabolism; discovery of role of lysine and amino adipic acid in penicillin biosynthesis. Office: Drew Univ RISE HS-330 Madison NJ 07940

DEMAIO, DOROTHY WALTERS, tutorial school administrator, consultant; b. Durham, N.C., Sept. 24, 1944; d. Rudolph Breece and Dorothy L. (Davis) Walters; divorced; 1 child, Mary Margaret Urquhart. BA in Elem. Edn., U. N.C., 1966. Asst. dir. media ctr. Atlanta Speech Sch., 1974-78; dir. nursery St. Patrick's Epis. Ch., 1982-84; adminstr. tutorial sch. for ESOL and spl. edn., 1984-93; educable mentally handicapped mid. sch. tchr., 1993-94; tchr. math. and sci. Dodds Sch., Sicily, Italy, 1994—; Japanese/Am. ESOL cons. Atlanta, 1983-93. Chmn. Lone Troop com. Mem. DAR, Ga. Assn. for Children with Learning Disabilities, Tomadichi Soc., Colonial Dames, Phi Delta Kappa. Avocations: painting, choral music, dance. Office: 78 Saratoga Dr Ceiba PR 00735-2513

DEMAREE, HILMA MARIE, elementary school educator; b. Denmark, Kans., Oct. 20, 1935; d. Frede and Martha Marie (Benson) Skov; m. James L. Demaree, Dec. 27, 1959 (dec. June 1995); 1 child, James André. BS in Home Econs., Ft. Hays State U., 1958; MLS, Emporia State U., 1978. Home econs. tchr. Gypsum (Kans.) H.S., 1958-62; elem. tchr. Lincoln Elem. Sch., Junction City, Kans., 1965-69, Gleniffer Hill Elem. Sch., Salina, Kans., 1969-78; elem. media specialist Sunset Elem. Sch., Salina, 1979—2001; ret. Mem. AAUW (pres.), Kans. Assn. Sch. Librs., Friends of Libr., Delta Kappa Gamma Soc. Internat. (v.p. 1995-97). Rep. Meth. Avocations: reading, travelling. Home: 401 Reed Ave Salina KS 67401-7530

DEMARIE, DARLENE, psychology educator; b. N.Y.C., Oct. 24, 1952; d. Joseph and Elizabeth (Cardella) DeMarie; 1 child, Charles Joseph Dreblow. BA cum laude, Marietta (Ohio) Coll., 1974; MEd, Ohio U., 1978; MS, U. Fla., 1985, PhD, 1988. Tchr. 1st grade Caldwell (Ohio) Exempted Village Schs., 1974-77; grad. asst. Ohio U., 1977-78; tchr. learning disabilities Caldwell (Ohio) Exempted Village Schs., 1978-80; tchr. 2d grade Marietta City Schs., 1980-82; grad. asst. U. Fla., Gainesville, 1982-87; asst. prof. psychology, faculty adminstr. Ctr. for Child Devel., Muskingum Coll., New Concord, Ohio, 1987-93, assoc. prof., faculty administr., 1993-98, co-dir. early childhood summer tng. inst., 1994-97; assoc. prof. ednl. psychology U. South. Fla., 1998—. Rschr. children's attention and memory devel. and children's experiences as reflected in their photography. Contbr. articles to profl. jours. Recipient Cora I. Orr Faculty Svc. award at Muskingum Coll., 1991, Outstanding Educator award, Phi Delta Kappa, Outstanding Undergrad. Tchg. award, 2003. Mem. Am. Psychol. Assn., Am. Psychol. Soc., Am. Ednl. Rsch. Assn., Soc. for Rsch. in Child Devel., Nat. Assn. for Edn. Young Children, Early Childhood Assn. Fla., Hillsborough Early Childhood Assn, Nat. Alliance for Reggio Emelia Educators. Avocations: camping, gardening, canoeing, cooking. Office: U South Fla EDU162 4202 E Fowler Ave Tampa FL 33620-5650

DEMARK, ROBIN KAY, librarian; b. Elmira, N.Y., Oct. 5, 1961; d. John Jr. and Betty E. (Makowiec) DeM. BA in Psychology, East Carolina U., 1984, MLS in Libr. and Info. Sci., 1993. Cert. libr., N.C. Tchr. asst. East Carolina U., Greenville, N.C., 1991-93, reference asst. Joyner Libr., 1992-93; bus./reference libr. Wayne County Pub. Libr., Goldsboro, N.C., 1993-95; reference libr. Pope Air Force Base Libr., 1995—2001, Seymour Johnson AFB, NC, 2001—. Cons., tutor, instr., computer rschr., Goldsboro, 1993—. Author: (manual) An Introduction to Computerized Resources and Database Searching in an Academic Library, 1993. Recipient Festival Event and Mgmt. cert. Strom Thurmond Inst., 1994. Mem. Goldsboro C. of C. (rep. for bus. dept. Wayne County Pub. Libr. 1994—). Democrat. Roman Catholic. Avocation: entertaining. Home: PO Box 592 Goldsboro NC 27533-0592 Office: Seymour Johnson AFB 4 Fighter Wing Pub Affairs Seymour Johnson A F B NC 27531 E-mail: robin.demark@seymourjohnson.af.mil.

DEMARS, JUDITH M. elementary educator; b. Cleve., Mar. 17, 1947; d. Edward C. and Ann J. (Sedivy) Nau; m. Gordon DeMars, Mar. 10, 1973; 1 child, Darren Jay. BS in Edn., Cleve. State U., 1969; MA in Edn., Baldwin Wallace Coll., Berea, Ohio, 1984; PhD, U. Akron, 1990. Cert. tchr. Nat. Bd. Edn., early childhood generalist Nat. Bd. Edn. Tchr. Garfield Heights City Sch., Ohio; tchr. 2nd and 3rd grades Warrensville Heights City Sch., Ohio; tutor developmental reading, 6th-8th grades Medina, Ohio; tutor Chpt. I reading, 1st and 2nd grade, multiage tchr. Highland Local Schs., Medina. Ohio Reads coord. Sharon Elem.; presenter in field. Rsch. on beginning reading methods. Mem. adv. com. Medina County Tchrs. Acad. Martha Holden Jennings grantee. Mem. Internat. Reading Assn. (Ohio coun.), Assn. for Supervision and Curriculum Devel., Assn. for Childhood Edn. Internat. Home: 6704 Kennard Rd Medina OH 44256-8559

DEMARY, JO LYNNE, state official, elementary school educator; BEd, DEd, Coll. of William and Mary; MS in Spl. Edn., U. Va. Commonwealth. Tchr. Fairfax County Schs., Va., Henrico County Schs., Va., from tchr. to asst. supt.; asst. supt. instruction Commonwealth of Va., 1994—99, acting supt. instruction, 1999—2000; supt. of instruction, 2000—. Office: Va Dept Edn PO Box 2120 Richmond VA 23218

DEMBO, DONALD HOWARD, cardiologist, medical administrator, educator; b. Balt., Jan. 27, 1931; s. Sydney Harry and Yetta (Bank) D.; m. Leatrice Cohen, Aug. 10, 1952; children: Steven Jay, Michael Brian Dembo, Susan Ann Weinstein. BA, Johns Hopkins U., 1951; MD, U. Md., 1955. Diplomate Am. Bd. Internal Medicine, Am. Bd. Cardiovascular Disease. Internship Sinai Hosp., Balt., 1955-56; residency in medicine Univ. Hosp., Balt., 1956-58; asst. cardiologist in chief U.S. Army Hosp., Frankfurt, Germany, 1958-60; fellow in cardiology Univ. Hosp., 1960-61; chief of cardiology Md. Gen. Hosp., Balt., 1961-91, Good Samaritan Hosp., Balt., 1975-95; assoc. physician in chief, vice chair of medicine Sinai Hosp., 1995-99; asst. prof. medicine Univ. Md., 1970-91, Johns Hopkins Univ., 1991—; pres. Cen. Md. Cardiology, Balt., 1976-95; med. dir. Johns Hopkins Cardiology, Timonium, Md., 1999—. Contbr. articles to profl. jours. Trustee Cardiopulmonary Resuscitation, Inc., 1975-77; chmn. adv. bd. Easton Waterfowl Festival, Easton, Md., 1990-93. Capt. U.S. Army, 1958-60. Recipient Bronze, Silver & Gold award Am. Heart Assn. (Md. affiliate), Svc. award Md. Gen. Hosp., Svc. award Good Samaritan Hosp., Disting. Physician award Sinai Hosp., AMA Hero in Medicine award, 2001; Cardiology tchg. scholar Hopkins/Sinai Internal Med. Program. Fellow: ACP, Am. Heart Assn. (Md. affiliate pres. 1971—72), Am. Coll. Chest Physicians, Am. Coll. Cardiology (trustee 1990—97, sec./treas. 1997—99, gov. elect Md. chpt. 1999—2000, gov. Md. chpt. 2000—03); mem.: Med. Chi, Md. State Med. Assn. (pres. 1994—95), Balt. City Med. Soc. (pres. 1996—97), Md. Soc. Cardiology (pres. 1976—78). Democrat. Jewish. Avocations: fishing, boating, swimming, tennis, fly fishing, photography. Home: 9430 Bantry Road Easton MD 21601 Office: 110 W Timonium Rd Ste 2C Lutherville Timonium MD 21093-7303 E-mail: ddembo@jhmi.edu., dhdembo@aol.com.

DEMCHIK, VIRGINIA CAROL, secondary education educator; b. Butte, Mont., Apr. 15, 1944; d. Carl A. and Mary V. (Rodriguez) Felosa; m. Michael J. Demchik, Feb. 8, 1969; children: Michael C., Stephanie J. BA in Sci. and Math., Fairmont (W.Va.) State Coll., 1966; MA in Natural Sci. and Math., W.Va. U., 1969, EdD in Tchr. Edn., 1986. Cert. chemistry, physics, math. and gen. sci. tchr., W.Va. Instr., rsch. asst. W.Va. U., Morgantown, 1984-86; tchr. chemistry and physics Jefferson Bd. Edn., Shenandoah Junction, W.Va., 1986—. Instr. math. Shepherd Coll., Shepherdstown, W.Va., 1989-96. Contbr. articles to profl. jours. Fellow U.S. Dept. Energy, 1992, 93, AT&T, 1994. Mem. NSTA (dist. VIII dir. 1998-2000), NEA, Coun. Elem. Sci. Internat. Avocations: reading, cooking, needlework, puzzles. Home: 310 W 5th St Booneville AR 72927 E-mail: vdemchik@access.k12.wv.us.

DEMEGRET, A. JEAN HUGHES, secondary education educator, artist; b. Hancock County, Ind., Oct. 22, 1927; d. Harlin E. and Melva L. Hughes. BAE, Butler U., 1949; student, John Herron Art Inst., Indpls.; MA, Columbia U., 1965; postgrad., No. Ill. U., Europe, 1966. Tchr. art Indpls. Pub. Schs., 1949-51; tchr. art and English Fortville (Ind.) Sch. Sys., 1951-62; supr. art dept. Greenfield (Ind.) Ctrl. H.S., 1962-84; tchr. adult art high schs., Indpls. and Greenfield. Exhibited paintings in Hoosier Art Show, 1960s and 70s, Ind. State Fair, 1960s and 70s, Columbia U. Art Gallery, 1963-66, others. Mem. Indpls. Mus. Art. Mem. Hancock County Ret. Tchrs., Bus. and Profl. Women (past pres.), Order Eastern Star, Ind. Sch. Women's Club, Nat. Art Educators Assn., Nat. Women in Art, Internat. Soc. Educators in Art, Delta Kappa Gamma (past pres.). Methodist. Avocations: painting portraits and horses, music, travel. Home: 411 S Main St Fortville IN 46040-1610

DEMERS, GERALD ZOEL, engineering educator; b. Manchester, N.H., Sept. 25, 1934; s. Henri W. and Laurette A. (Boisvert) D.; m. Maureen E. Lemaire, Dec. 26, 1956; children: Michael, Karen, Brian. BS in Mil. Engrng., U.S. Mil. Acad., 1956; MS in Engrng. Mechanics, U. Ala., Tuscaloosa, 1962. Cert. profl. logistician. Commd. 2d lt. U.S. Army, 1956, advanced through grades to col.; asst. prof. engrng. fundamentals U.S. Mil. Acad., West Point, N.Y., 1965-68; exec. officer dir. logistics Mil. Assistance Command, Saigon, Vietnam, 1969-70; dir. plans and programs XM-1 Tank Sys. Project Office, Warren, Mich., 1970-73; comrd. 81st maintenance batallion 21st Support Command, Mannheim, Fed. Republic Germany, 1973-75; dep. asst. chief of staff logistics V Corps U.S. Army Europe, Frankfurt, Fed. Republic Germany, 1975-77; dir. spl. projects Army Logistics Ctr., Ft. Lee, Va., 1977-80; dep. commandant Army Logistics Mgmt. Coll., Ft. Lee, 1980-83; ret. U.S. Army, 1983; asst. prof. mech. engrng. tech. Va. State U., Petersburg, 1983-94, chmn. engrng. tech. dept., 1994-97; ret., 1997. Editor pamphlet Near-Term Water Resources Doctrine, 1981. V.p. bd. dirs. Petersburg (Va.) Symphony Orch., 1988-94; mem. Colonial Heights Rep. Com., 1994-2000; treas., bd. dirs. Knights of Va. Assistance for Retarded, 1997-2000. Mem. ASME, Soc. Logistics Engrs. (chpt. v.p. edn. 1994-98), Petersburg Area Art League, KC (grand knight 1985, chmn. assistance to retarded campaign 1986-94). Roman Catholic. Avocations: piano, tennis, racquetball. Home: 633 Whispering Pines Ave Tipp City OH 45371

DEMERS, JUDY LEE, former state legislator, university dean; b. Grand Forks, North Dakota, June 27, 1944; d. Robert L. and V. Margaret (Harming) Prosser; m. Donald E. DeMers, Oct. 3, 1964; div. Oct. 1971; 1 child, Robert M.; m. Joseph M. Murphy, Mar. 5, 1977; div. Oct. 1983. BS in nursing, U. N.D., 1966; M in Edn., U. Wash., 1973, post grad., 1973-76. Pub. health nurse Govt., Wash., DC, 1966-68; Combined Nursing Svc., Mpls., 1968-69; instr. pub. health nursing U. N.D., Grand Forks, ND, 1969-71; assoc. dir. Medex program, 1970-72; rsch. assoc. U. Wash., Seattle, 1973-76; dir. family nurse practitioner program, 1977-82; dir. under grad. med. edn., 1982-83; assoc. dir. rural health, 1982-85; mem. N.D. Ho. of Reps., 1982-92; assoc. dean, 1983—; mem. N.D. Senate, 1992-2000. Cons. health manpower devel. staff, Honolulu, 1975-81, Assn. Physician asst. programs, Washington, 1979-82; site visitor cons., AMA Com. Allied Health Edn. Accreditation, Chgo.,1979-81. Author: Educating New Health Practitioners, 1976; mem. editl. bd.: P.A. Jour., 1976-78; contbr. articles to profl. jours. Sec., bd. dirs. Valley Health, Grand Forks, N.D., 1982—; mem. exec. com., bd. dirs. Agassiz Health Systems Agy., Grand Forks, 1982-86; mem. N.D. State Daycare Adv. Com., 1983-93, Mayor's Adv. com. on Police Policy, Grand Forks, 1983-85, N.D. State Foster Care Adv. Com., 1985-87, N.D. State Hypertension Adv. Com., 1983-85, Gov.'s Com. on DUI and Traffic Safety, 1985-91, State wide Adv. Com. on AIDS, 1985-90; bd. dirs. Casey Found., Families First Initiative, 1988-97, Comprehensive Health Assn. N.D., 1993-95, United Health Found., 1990-97, Northern Valley Mental Health Assn., 1994-00, bd. dir., Grand Forks Girl's and Women's Hockey Assn., 1999-2002; bd. dirs., sec.-treas., exec. com., program com., fundraising com., sec.-treas. Devel. Homes, 1999—; adv. bd. Mountainbrooke (formerly Friendship Place), 1992-96; adv. com. Ruth Meiers Adolescent Ctr., Grand Forks, 1988-2002, Altru Health Sys. Corp. Bd., 1997—; mem. Commn. on Future Structure of VA Health Care, 1990-91; bd. dirs. Red River Valley Cmty. action Program, 1991—; mem. Resource and Referral Bd. Dirs., 1990—; caring coun. N.D. Blue Cross and Blue Shield Caring Program for Children, 1995-99; coun. mem. N.D. Health Task Force, 1992-94; healthcare subcom. Northern Gt. Plains Econ. Devel. Commn., 1995-96; adv. com. on telecomms. and healthcare FCC, 1996; mem., chmn. Grand Forks City and County Bd. Health, 2000—. Recipient: Pub. Citizen of Yr. Award, N.D. chpt., Nat. Assn. Social Workers, 1986, Golden Grain Award, N.D. Dietetic Assn., 1988, Person of Yr. Award, U. N.D., Law Women Caucus, 1990, Legislator of Yr. award North Valley Labor Coun., 1990, N.D., Martin Luther King Jr. Award, 1990, Legislator of Yr. Award, Mental Health Assn., N.D., 1993, N.D. Libr. Assn. Legislator of Yr., 1999, Friend of Medicine Award N.D. Med. Assn., 1999, Legislator of Year Award, N.D. Pub. Employees Assn., 1999, Friend of Counseling Award, N.D. State Counseling Assn., 2000, Legislative Svc. Award, ARC of N.D., Friend of Higher Edn. Award, AAUP, 1995. Mem. N.D. Nurses Assn., Alpha Lambda Delta, Sigma Theta Tau, Pi Lampda Theta. Home: Unit 92 N 2200 S 29th St Apt 92N Grand Forks ND 58201-5869 Office: UND Sch Medicine PO Box 9037 501 N Columbia Rd Grand Forks ND 58202-9037 E-mail: jdemers@medicine.nodak.edu.

DEMERS, LAURENCE MAURICE, science educator, biochemist, consultant, editor; b. Lawrence, Mass., May 9, 1938; s. Laurence Onezime and Doris Corrine (Goulet) D.; m. Susan Ruth Bernard, Sept. 29, 1962; children: Laurence H., Michele L., Marc B., Christpher J., Andrew U. AB, Merrimack Coll., 1960; PhD, SUNY Upstate Med. Ctr., Syracuse, 1970. Postdoctoral fellow Med. Sch. Harvard U., Boston, 1970-72, instr., 1972-73; asst. prof. M.S. Hershey Med. Ctr. Pa. State U., Hershey, 1973-76, assoc. prof., 1976-80, prof., 1980—, disting. prof., 1997—. Cons. Robert Wood Johnson Pharm Rsch. Inst., Raritan, N.J., 1978—; bd. dirs. dBi Labs. Inc., Harrisburg, Pa.; vis. prof. U. Oxford, Eng., 1981-82. Editor: Liver Function Testing, 1978, Premenstrual Syndrome, 1985, Premenstrual Syndrome and Menopausal Mood Disorders, 1989; editl. editor Clin. Chemistry Jour., 1990—. Eucharistic min. St. Joan of Arc Cath. Ch., Hershey, 1981—, mem. Knights of Malta, 1990—; trustee Merrimack Coll., 2000. Capt. Med. Svc. Corps, U.S. Army, 1961-65. Recipient Lalor award Lalor Found., 1973, Fogarty Internat. award Fogarty Ctr., NIH, 1981, Pharm. Mfrs. Assn. award, 1974. Fellow Nat. Acad. Clin. Biochemistry (pres. 1984-85, Dubin award 1991); mem. Endocrine Soc., Am. Assn. Clin. Chemistry (pres. 1997, Ames award 1986), Am. Soc. Clin. Pathology, N.Y. Acad. Scis., Assn. Clin. Scientists, Acad. Clin. Lab. Physicians and Scientists, Country Club of Hershey (bd. govs. 2000—). Avocations: golf, tennis. Home: 1175 Stonegate Rd Hummelstown PA 17036-9776 Office: Pa State U MS Hershey Med Ctr University Dr Hershey PA 17033

DEMERS, MARY ADELAIDE, psychotherapist, educator; b. San Mateo, Calif., Sept. 9, 1955; d. Joseph Edward and Patricia Marie (Coughlin) Stanton; m. Paul Jordan, Feb. 15, 1992 (dec. July 1994); children: Jennifer, Philip, Katherine. BS, Santa Clara U., 1983, MA, 1989. Lic. marriage, family and child therapist, Bd. Behavioral Scis. Clin. staff therapist Santa Clara County Children Shelter, San Jose, Calif., 1989-95; clin. dir. Unity Care Group, Inc., San Jose, 1990-96; pvt. cons. Adolescent Clin. Svcs., San Jose, 1992—; instr. grad. divsn. Santa Clara U., 1995—; clin. dir. Gray's Adolescent Group Home, San Jose, 1995—; exec. dir. Adolescent Clin. Svcs., San Jose, 1995—. Featured in books Working Women Today, 1986, Women and Work, 1994. Vol. Kids Vote, San Jose, 1994—. Mem. NAFE, Am. Group Psychotherapy Assn., Calif. Assn. Marriage and Family Therapists. Democrat. Roman Catholic. Avocations: golf, bridge, acoustical guitar, book reviews. Office: Adolescent Clin Svcs 2130 The Alameda Ste 220 San Jose CA 95126-1125

DEMERY, DOROTHY JEAN, secondary school educator; b. Houston, Sept. 5, 1941; d. Floyd Hicks and Irene Elaine Burns Clay; m. Leroy W. Demery, Jan. 16, 1979; children: Steven Bradley, Rodney Bradley, Craig Bradley, Kimberly Bradley. AA, West L.A. Coll., Culver City, Calif., 1976; AS, Harbor Coll., Wilmington, Calif., 1983; BS in Pub. Adminstrn., Calif.

State U., Carson, 1985; MS in Instructional Leadership, Nat. U., San Diego, 1991. Cert. real estate broker, tchr. math. and bus. edn., bilingual tchr., crosscultural lang. and acad. devel.; lang. devel. specialist. Eligibility social worker Dept. Pub. Social Svcs., L.A., 1967-74; real estate broker Dee Bradley & Assocs., Riverside, Calif., 1976—; tchr. math L.A. Unified Sch. Dist., 1985-91; math/computer sci. tchr. Pomona (Calif.) Unified Sch. Dist., 1991—. Adj. lectr. Riverside C.C., 1992—93; mem. Dist. Curriculum Coun./Report Card Task Force, Pomona, 1994—; del. rep. assembly NEA, 1991—2003. Chairperson Human Rights Com., Pomona, 1992—, sec. steering com., 1993—, adv. bd., 1993—; mem. polit. action com. Assoc. Pomona Tchrs., 1993-94. Recipient Outstanding Svc. award Baldwin Hills Little League Assn., L.A., 1972. Mem.: Calif. Tchrs. Assn. (state coun. 2000, chair site base, chair dept. math.), Associated Pomona Tchrs. (site base chairperson, math. chairperson 1994—, nominee to Nat. Coun. Tchrs. of Math. 2001, bd. dirs. 1998—), Aux. Nat. Med. Assn., Nat. Coun. Tchrs. Math., Nat. Bus. Assn. Avocations: hiking, tennis, walking. Office: Simons Middle School 900 E Franklin Ave Pomona CA 91766-5362

DEMES, DENNIS THOMAS, religious studies educator; b. Jersey City, N.J., Apr. 10, 1949; s. Thomas Joseph and Lillian (Harabedian) D. BA, St. John's Coll., Brighton, Mass., 1974; MS in Edn., ThM, Princeton U., 1979. Cert. advanced religious educator. Religious Educator Archdiocese of Boston, 1974-79; dir. religious edn. St. John's the Evangelist Parish, Winthrop, Mass., 1976-81, Holy Rosary Parish, Lawrence, Mass., 1981-83; Prior Soc. St. Benedict of Nursia, Boston, 1984—. Adj. prof. St. Thomas U., Miami, Fla., tchr. history of Christian thought/Western civilization Pope John Paul II H.S., Boca Raton, Fla. Pastoral min. Ascension Cath. Ch., Boca Raton, 1990—, dir. adult edn. Recipient Cath. Campaign for Am. award, 1994. Mem. Nat. Cath. Educators Assn., Soc. St. Benedict. Office: Ascension Cath Ch 7250 N Federal Hwy Boca Raton FL 33487-1606

DEMETRESCU, MIHAI CONSTANTIN, research scientist, educator, computer company executive; b. Bucharest, Romania, May 23, 1929; came to U.S., 1966; s. Dan and Alina (Dragosescu) D.; m. Agnes Halas, May 25, 1969; 1 child, Stefan. M.E.E., Poly. Inst. of U. Bucharest, 1954; PhD, Romanian Acad. Sci., 1957. Prin. investigator Rsch. Inst. Endocrinology Romanian Acad. Sci., Bucharest, 1958-66; rsch. fellow dept. anatomy UCLA, 1966-67; faculty U. Calif.-Irvine, 1967-83, asst. prof. dept. physiology, 1971-78, assoc. rschr., 1978-79, assoc. clin. prof., 1979-83; v.p. Resonance Motors, Inc., Monrovia, Calif., 1972-85; pres. Neurometrics, Inc., Irvine, 1978-82, Lasergraphics Inc., Irvine, 1982-84, chmn., CEO, 1984—. Mem. com. on honor degrees U. Calif.-Irvine, 1970-72. Contbr. articles to profl. jours.; patentee in field. Postdoctoral fellow UCLA, 1966. Mem. IEEE (sr.), Am. Physiol. Soc. Republican. Home: 8 Sunset Hbr Newport Coast CA 92657-1706 Office: 20 Ada Irvine CA 92618-2303 E-mail: Dr.D@lasergraphics.com.

DEMILLE, DIANNE LYNNE, mathematics educator, administrator; b. Dundas, Ontario, Can., Mar. 21, 1948; d. Leslie Benjamin and Helen Isobel (Don) DeMille; m. Tate Stanley Casey, June 16, 1971 (div. June, 1975); 1 child, Marie Anne; m. Thomas John Camacho, Aug. 30, 1980 (div. June, 1999); children: Patricia Suzanne, Tara Lynne. BA in Math., Whittier Coll., 1970, secondary tchg. credential, 1972; PhD, Walden U., 2000. Math. tchr. Mater Dei H.S., Santa Ana, Calif., 1972-79, Santa Ana (Calif.) H.S., 1979; instr. math. Coast C.C., Costa Mesa, Calif., 1979-81; math. tchr., mentor tchr. Downey (Calif.) Unified, 1979-93; specialist Orange County Dept. Edn., Costa Mesa, 1993—2002, coord. math. and assessment NSF CO-PI project, 2002—. Coord. assessment/Golden State exams, devel. algebra/Geometry/h.s. math., 1983—; cons., presenter confs., Orange County Dept. Edn., Costa Mesa, 1986—, Calif. State Dept. of Edn., Sacramento, 1989—; chief math devel. team Calif. Learning Assessment Sys.; chief reader, table leader Golden State Math. Exam.; mem. devel. team, chief reader Calif. State Regional Lead Assessment, coord. devel. team, 1996—; reviewer Am. Coll. Testing. Author: Batch Basic, 1973; author and project specialst (series of books and workshops) So. Calif. Regional Algebra Project Focus on Algebra, Focus on Geometry, 1989—, (units in book) Math A, Investigating Mathematics, 1989. Recipient Wright Bros. Innovative Tchrs. award, Rockwell Co., L.A., 1991; grantee Rockwell Co., 1992. Mem. ASCD, Am. Sch. Counselors Assn., Nat. Coun. Tchrs. Math., Nat. Coun. Suprs. Math., Calif. Math. Coun., Assn. Calif. Sch. Adminstrs., Phi Delta Kappa. Home: #101 1700 W Cerritos Ave Anaheim CA 92804 Office: Orange County Dept Edn 200 Kalmus Dr Costa Mesa CA 92626-5922 E-mail: d.demille@verizon.net.

DEMITCHELL, TERRI ANN, law educator; b. San Diego, Apr. 10, 1953; d. William Edward and Rose Annette (Carreras) Wheeler; m. Todd Allan DeMitchell, Aug. 14, 1982. AB in English with honors, San Diego State U., 1975; JD, U. San Diego, 1984; MA in Edn., U. Calif., Davis, 1990; EdM, Harvard U., 1997. Bar: Calif. 1985, U.S. Dist. Ct. (so. dist.) Calif. 1985; cert. elem. tchr., Calif. Tchr. Fallbrook (Calif.) Union Elem. Sch. Dist., 1976-86; adminstrv. asst. gen. counsel San Diego Unified Sch. Dist., 1984; assoc. Biddle and Hamilton, Sacramento, 1986-88; instr. U. N.H., 1990-93. Teaching asst. U. Calif., Davis, 1987. Author: The California Teacher and the Law, 1985, The Law in Relation to Teacher, Out of School Behavior, 1990, Censorship and the Public School Library: A Bicoastal View, 1991; contbr. chpt. to book. Mem. Calif. Bar Assn., Am. Bar Assn. Office: Apt 2207 10 Chestnut St Exeter NH 03833-1878

DEMITCHELL, TODD ALLAN, education educator; b. Portsmouth, Va., Aug. 9, 1947; s. Wilfred E. and Mary Anna (Hughes) DeM.; m. Terri A. Wheeler, Aug. 14, 1982. BA, U. La Verne, 1969, MA, 1973; EdD, U. So. Calif., 1979; MA, U. Calif., Davis, 1990. Tchr. Pomona (Calif.) Unified Sch. Dist., 1969-71, South Bay Union Elem. Sch. Dist., Imperial Beach, Calif., 1974-75, lead tchr., 1975-78; asst. prin. Fallbrook (Calif.) Union Elem. Sch. Dist., 1978-80, prin., 1980-83; supt., prin. Pauma (Calif.) Sch. Dist., 1983-86; dir. pers. and labor rels. Travis (Calif.) Unified Sch. Dist., 1986-89; postdoctoral vis. scholar, rsch. asst. Nat. Ctr. Ednl. Leadership Harvard U., Cambridge, Mass., 1989-90; asst. prof. U. N.H., Durham, 1990-96, coord. grad. studies, 1993-95, assoc. chair dept. edn., 1995-98, assoc. prof., 1996—99, prof., chair dept. edn., 2001—; assoc. prof., chair dept. ednl. leadership/spl. edn. Sonoma State U. Design team Sch. Leaders Acad., N.H., 1991-93. Co-author: Teacher Unions and TQE: Building Quality Labor Relations, 1994, The Limits of Law-Based School Reform: Vain Hopes and False Promises, 1997; mem. authors com. Education Law Reporter; contbr. more than 90 articles to profl. jours., chpts. to books. Recipient Jim Rubovitz award, New Eng. Ednl. Rsch. Orgn., 2003. Mem. ASCD, Am. Ednl. Rsch. Assn., Edn. Law Assn. Office: U NH Morrill Hall Durham NH 03824

DEMKO, GEORGE JOSEPH, geographer; b. Catasauqua, Pa., Apr. 10, 1933; s. George and Anna (Scarba) D.; m. Jeanette Edwina Small, Aug. 29, 1959; children: Megan, Kerstin. BS, West Chester U., 1958; MS, So. Ill. U., 1959; PhD, Pa. State U., 1964; postgrad., Moscow State U., USSR; DSc (hon.), Shawnee State U. of Ohio, 1995. Instr. Pa. State U, State College, 1963-64; asst. prof. Ind. U., Bloomington, 1964-65; prof. Ohio State U., Columbus, 1965-83; program dir. Geography and Regional Sci., NSF, Washington, 1983-84; The Geographer, dir. Office of The Geographer, State Dept., Washington, 1984-89; dir. Rockefeller Ctr. for Social Scis., Dartmouth Coll., Hanover, N.H., 1989-95, prof. geography, 1989—. Cons. Internat. Research and Exchanges Bd., Princeton, N.J., 1970-95, NASA, 1979-80, Microsoft Corp., 1992—; head subcommn. on geography, US/USSR, Princeton, 1980-91; adj. prof. Charles U., Prague, Czech Republic. Author: The Russian Colonization of Kazakhstan, 1966, Kazakh transl., 1998, Discovery in Geography, 1980, Regional Development in East and West Europe, 1986, Perspectives on Soviet Geography, 1980, Geography in the USSR and U.S.: A Spectrum of Views, 1992, Why In The World: Adventures in Geography, 1993, Populations at Risk in America, 1995, Reordering the World: Geopolitical Perspectives on the 21st Century, 1995; contbr. numerous articles to profl. jours. Sgt. USMC, 1951-54, Korea. Named Outstanding Alumnus, W. Chester (Pa.) U., 1980, University Fellow, Pa. State U., State College, 1986; recipient numerous grants and awards for research and teaching from the Nat. Sci. Found., Rockefeller Found., Gold Medal award for scholarly contbns. Charles U., Prague, Czech Republic, 1998, others. Mem. Assn. Am. Geographers (pres. 1986-88), Am. Assn. for Advancement of Slavic Studies (exec. dir. 1969-74), Kennan Inst. for Advanced Russian Studies (acad. advisor 1982-86), Russian Geog. Soc. (hon.). Avocations: sailing, squash, piano. Office: Dartmouth Coll Dept Geography Hanover NH 03755 E-mail: george.demko@dartmouth.edu.

DEMONG, RICHARD FRANCIS, finance and investments educator; b. Freeport, Ill., May 2, 1944; s. Maurice Dale and Ruth Jane (Kidwell) DeM.; m. Sue Ann Liddle, June 17, 1967 (div. Dec. 1983); children: Cheryl Ann, Lynn Ann; m. Linda H. Krongaard, May 15, 1988. AA, Orange Coast Coll., Costa Mesa, Calif., 1964; BA, Calif. State U., 1966; MBA, Coll. of William & Mary, 1974; PhD, U. Colo., 1977. Cert. cost analyst; chartered fin. analyst. Time keeper Douglas Aircraft Co., Long Beach, Calif., 1966; instr. U. Colo., Boulder, 1974-77; Va. Bankers prof. bank mgmt. U. Va., Charlottesville, 1977—; rsch. dir. Fin. Analyst Rsch. Found., Charlottesville, 1982-85; dir. Ctr. for Fin. Svcs. Studies U. Va., 1991—; registered investment adv. Va., 1996—. Cons. Fin. Forecasting & Svc., 1978—; fin. coord. Dalkon Shield Claimants Trust, 1989-1999. Author: (with others) (monograph) New Financial Instruments: A Descriptive Guide, 1985, 1998 Home Equity Loan Study, 1998, (with others) Principles of Financial Management, 2d edit., 1988; editor (with others) (monograph) Takeovers and Shareholders: The Mounting Controversy, 1985 (monograph, with others) Investing Worldwide III, 1992, The Technology Industry: The Impact of the Internet, 2002. Mem. Va. Small Bus. Coun., Richmond, 1981-82; chmn. U. Va. ROTC com., Charlottesville, 1981-84; co-chmn. Central Va. Score and Ace chpt., Charlottesville, 1981; dir. McIntire Small Bus. Inst., Charlottesville, 1978-82, Innisfree Village, 1995-98, 2002-, Charlottesville Cath. Sch. Bd., 2002-. Capt. USAF, 1966-72, Vietnam, col. USAFR, ret. Decorated DFC; named outstanding Air Force Mobilization Augmentee (reservist), Air Tng. Comman, 1980. Mem. Fin. Mgmt. Assn., Am. Fin. Assn., So. Fin. Assn., Assn. for Investment Mgmtm. and Rsch. Roman Catholic. Avocation: gardening. Office: U Va McIntire Sch Commerce PO Box 400173 Charlottesville VA 22904

DE MORA, JUAN MIGUEL, indologist, educator, writer; b. Mexico City, Oct. 18, 1921; s. Miguel Magdaleno and Emilia Vaquerizo De M.; m. Maria del Carmen Morales, Mar. 16, 1946 (div. Nov. 1978); 1 child, Carlos Miguel; m. Marja Ludwika Jarocka, Aug. 31, 1988. M Letters, U. Nat. Autonoma, Mexico, 1948; PhD, U. Latino-Americana, Havana, Cuba, 1951; PhD honoris causa, Ministerial Tng. Coll., Sheffield, Eng., 1960, Internat. Free Protestant Episcopal U., London, 1962; Spl. Diploma in Sanskrit Studies, U. Paris, 1970. Sr. prof. Oriental Lit. U. Nat. Autonoma, Mexico City, 1965-73, permanent prof. Oriental Lit., 1973—, assoc. rschr. in Sanskrit philology, 1972-78, part-time to full-time rschr. Sanskrit philology, 1978-91, permanent rschr. category C, 1991—; emeritus prof. Jain Vishva Bharati Inst. (deemed Univ.), Ladnun, India. Vis. prof. U. Salamanca, Spain, 1994, U. Delhi, India, 1982, others. Author: approximately 100 books including La Filosofia en la Literatura Sanscrita, 1968, The Principle of Opposites in Sanskrit Texts, 1982, Solo queda el silencio, 2000, El hombre que no habia nacido, 2003, Cota 666, 2003, Ayur Veda, 2003, El concepto de la divinidad en el hinduismo, 2003, Matemáticas y astronomia en la India antigua, 2003; author/translator: (book) El Rig Veda, 1974 (4 edits.); contbr. more than 60 articles to profl. publs. Officer Mexican Red Cross, Mexico, 1943-59. Recipient Merit award Acad. U. Internat., Rome, 1961, Gold medal Mexican Red Cross, 1958. Mem. N.Y. Acad. Scis., Assn. Francaise pour Les Etudes Sanskrites, Kalidasa and Max Muller Internat. Sanskrit Soc., Vishwa Sahitya Sanskriti Sansthan, Internat. Inst. Indian Studies (mem. editl. adv. bd. 1993-98), Internat. Assn. Sanskrit Studies (regional dir. Latin Am. 1994-2000, v.p. 1981-94, cons. com. 2000—), others. Avocations: collecting old and new films on videotape, reading, classical music. E-mail: morajarocka@prodigy.net.mx.

DEMORUELLE, CHARMAINE, music educator; b. New Orleans, Sept. 30, 1952; d. James Ivon and Nell Marie (Porbes) deMoruelle; m. Oren Francis Benedic, Nov. 10, 1973 (div. July 1976); m. John Joseph Brion, Oct. 29, 1989; children: Yvette Jeanne Brion, Jean-Paul deMoruelle Brion. AS, Delgado Jr. Coll., New Orleans, 1973; BA, U. New Orleans, 1979. Tchr. instrumental music Jefferson Parish Sch. Bd., Metairie, La., 1979—. Clarinetist Jefferson Parish Cmty. Band, Am. Legion Post 175 Band; chief of Kickapoo YMCA Indian Guides, Metairie; bd. mem. at large 1st Unitarian Universalist Ch. of New Orleans, 1987. Scholar Seymore Weiss scholar, Delgado Jr. Coll., 1972—73. Mem.: La. Band Masters Assn., La. Music Educators Assn. Unitarian Universalist. Avocations: camping, soccer, karate. Home: 1437 Gardenia Dr Metairie LA 70005 Office: J D Meisler Middle Sch 3700 Cleary Ave Metairie LA 70002

DEMOTT, DEBORAH ANN, lawyer, educator; b. Collingswood, N.J., July 21, 1948; d. Lyle J. and Frances F. (Cummings) DeM. BA, Swarthmore Coll., 1970; JD, NYU, 1973. Bar: N.Y. 1974. Law clk. U.S. Dist. Ct. (so. dist.) N.Y., 1973; assoc. Simpson, Thacher & Bartlett, N.Y.C., 1974-75; from asst. prof. to assoc. prof. Duke U., Durham, N.C., 1975-80, prof. law, 1980—, David F. Cavers prof. law, 2000—. Vis. asst. prof. U. Tex., Austin, 1977-78; Bost rsch. prof. law, 1981; vis. prof. U. Calif. Hastings Coll. Law, 1986, U. Colo., 1989, U. San Diego, 1991; James L. Lewtas vis. prof. law Osgoode Hall Law Sch., Toronto, Ont., Can., 1991; vis. fellow U. Melbourne, 1993, 95, 98; Huber C. Hurst Eminent vis. scholar U. Fla. Coll. Law, 1996; Frances Lewis Scholar-in-Residence Washington & Lee Law Sch., 1998; centennial vis. prof. law dept. London Sch. Econs., 2000-2002. Author: Shareholder Derivative Actions, 1987, Fiduciary Obligation Agency and Partnership, 1991; editor: Corporations at the Crossroads: Governance and Reform; contbr. articles to profl. jours.; bd. advisors Jour. Legal Edn., 1983-86. Trustee Law Sch. Admission Coun., 1984-88; mem. N.C. Gen. Statutes Commn., 1990-98; mem. selection com. Coif Book Award, 1988-90. Recipient Pomeroy prize NYU Sch. Law, 1971-73; AAUW fellow, 1972-73; Fulbright Sr. scholar Sydney U. and Monash (Australia) U., 1986. Mem. ABA, Am. Law Inst. (reporter restatement of agy. 1995—). Office: Duke U Law Sch PO Box 90360 Durham NC 27708-0360

DEMOTT, SARA (SALLY) LOUISE, secondary school educator; b. Granville, N.Y., Oct. 1, 1945; d. Howard E. and Janet A. DeM. BA, Bucknell U., 1967; MS in Edn., U. Pa., 1970. Biology tchr. Upper Darby (Pa.) High Sch., 1967-71; rsch. asst. Nat. Mus. Natural History Smithsonian Inst., Washington, 1971-73; biology tchr., Deborah Loeb Brice endowed chair The Madeira Sch., McLean, Va., 1973—. Cons. advanced placement The Coll. Bd., N.Y.C., 1997-2000; tchr. resident assocs. program Smithsonian Inst., 1980s. Recipient The Tandy Tech. Scholar Tandy prize Radio Shack, 1996. Mem. Nat. Assn. Biology Tchrs. (life, Outstanding Biology Tchr. 1978), Nat. Assn. Sci. Tchrs. Avocations: walking, cycling, reading. Home: 8328 Georgetown Pike Mc Lean VA 22102-1203

DEMPSEY, JACQUELINE LEE, special education director; b. Pitts., Jan. 4, 1951; d. Alexander and Catherine (Rankin) D. BS, Edinboro (Pa.) State Coll., 1972, MEd, 1974; PhD, U. Pitts., 1983. Tchr. Allegheny Intermediate Unit, Pitts., 1975-77, master tchr., 1977-78, instructional advisor, 1978-81, project dir., 1981-86, program adminstr., 1985-86; exec. dir. The Early Learning Inst., Pitts., 1986-95; pres. Early Childhood Internat., Pitts., 1995—. Guest field reviewer Exceptional Children, 1989-95. Chair Pa. Early Intervention Interagy. Coord. Coun., 1992-93; mem. Gov.'s Commn. on Children and Families, 1992-93. Mem. Coun. for Exceptional Children, Early Intervention Providers Assn. Pa. (vice chair 1986-88), Pitts. Area Coun. Adminstrv. Women in Edn. (pres. 1985-86), Phi Delta Kappa. Office: Early Childhood Internat 46 Walnut St Pittsburgh PA 15205-3117

DEMPSEY, RAYMOND LEO, JR., radio and television producer, moderator, writer; b. Providence, June 18, 1949; s. Raymond Leo Sr. and Louise Veronica (Gambuto) D.; m. Patricia Batchelder (div. 1984); children: Joab, Jahdeam, Deezsha, Nathaniel, Talitha. BA in Liberal Arts, R.I. Coll., 1973; cert., Blake Computer Programming Inst., 1977; cert. in Bus., U. R.I., 1979; cert., Billy Graham Sch. Evangelism, Ashville, N.C., 1989; postgrad., Harvard U., Roger Williams U., Bryant Coll., Bristol C.C., C.C. R.I., Providence Coll. Lic. real estate agt., R.I.; lic. radio sta. operator FCC; cert. secondary tchr., videographer, contractor, R.I. Writer local and nat. publs., 1980—88; producer, moderator Chapter & Verse TV, Sta. RICA-TV, Providence, 1983—; tchr. R.I. Pub. High Schs., Providence and Cranston, 1988; producer, moderator radio programs Ch. Focus and People, Sta. WRIB, East Providence, 1989—. Bd. dirs. Blessing, Inc., Providence; spl. corr. Songtime U.S.A. Radio Network, 1988—, spl. reporter, spl. contbr., 1991; host Straight Talk, Sta. WKRI, 1989, dir. World Exch., 1991-93; co-host The Bible Answer Program, Sta. WARV, 1986; judge The Ace Awards, 1992, Cable Ace Awards, 1992; interviewer Gallup Poll, 1987; trainee N.E. Law Enforcement Officers Assn., 1991; elector Radio Hall of Fame, 1993, Stellar Awards, 1993; nursing asst. nursing homes, R.I., 1979; pvt. nurse's asst. R.I. Hosp., 1979; patient attendant R.I. Mental Hosp.; papers placed in permanent reference res. Brit. Libr., London, N.Y.C. Pub. Libr., Libr. Congress, Washington; donated reference libr. U. Steubenville, Ohio, 1995; preliminary judge Audio Pub. Assn. awards, 1996—. Dancer R.I. Coll. Dance Co., 1969; actor: The Wig and Mask Society of La Salle Acad., 1965. Bd. dirs. R.I. Right to Life, Cranston, 1973—; witness R.I. Gen. Assembly, 1973—, R.I. Bd. Health, 1973—; vol. ARC, R.I. Hosp.; registrar voters State of R.I., 1980, 91, 92; del. Rep. Nat. Conv. 1980; sponsor World Vision, Pasadena, Calif., 1981—, Compassion Internat., Colo. Springs, Colo., 1989—; chief boys instr. karate Mattson Acad., Providence, 1968-71; mem. Providence Sci. Outreach of Brown U.; del. Gov.'s Conf. on Libr. and Info. Svcs., 1991; elector White House Conf. on Libr. and Info. Svcs.; Justice of Peace, 1991; regional rep. Students Against Vietnam War, 1971, Taxpayers Action Network, 1991; ptnr. Food for the Hungry, 1984—; del. Ellen McCormack for Pres., 1976; vol. U.S. Fish and Wildlife Svc., R.I. Hosp., Providence, 1975, Providence Amb. Clinic, 1975; elected Rep. City Com. and Rep. State Ctrl. Com.; chmn. Issues and Rsch. Com. Rep. party Providence; numerous collection donations to libraries and Archdiocese of N.Y., 1975—; ret. dir. Ground Zero, Citizens Against Govt. Waste; donator Vt. Hist. Soc., Brattleboro, 1975, Dominican Phillips Meml. Libr., Providence Coll., 1975, reference libr. Brown U., 2001, Cranston (RI) Pub. Libr., 2001, The Master's Sem., Calif., 2001, Joseph Stanton Meml. Libr., NYC, 2001. Named One of Top 4 Local Cable TV Prodrs. in Nation, Nat. Assn. Local Cable Programming, 1987, ofcl. Jerusalem Pilgrim, State of Israel, 1990, Ptnr. in Philanthropy, 1995; recipient 2 Internat. Angel awards for excellence in Cable TV presentations, 1991, cert. U.S. SBA, 1990, Diamond award, 1992, 1st prize for excellence in pub. affairs in R.I. and Mass., 1992, Achievement award Dale Carnegie Orgn., 1992, 1st pl. award Mastermedia: The Spotlight award, 1993; nominated for J.C. Penney Golden Rule award. Mem. AAAS, ASCD, NRA, Am. Math. Soc., Coll. Sci. Tchrs., Sons Union Vets., Nat. Assn. H.S. Tchrs. English, Evangel. Theol. Soc., Soc. for Coll. Tchrs., Nat. Assn. Edn. of Young Children, Nat. Assn. Tchg. Sci., Modern Poetry Assn., Am. Soc. Oriental Rsch., Archaeol. Inst. Am., R.I. Assn. for Edn. Young Children, R.I. Assn. for Supervision and Curriculum Devel., Mental Health Assn. R.I., N.Y. Acad. Scis., Internat. Press Assn. (founding mem.), Nat. Geog. Soc., Nat. Assn. Broadcasters, Modern Poetry Assn., Nat. Assn. Radio Talk Show Hosts, Nat. Acad. Cable Programming, Near East Archaeol. Soc., Internat. Platform Assn., Nat. Assn. Tchrs. Sci., Jewish TV Inst. (charter), Smithsonian Air and Space Mus., Smithsonian Instn. (assoc.), Royal Inst. Pub. Health and Hygiene London (affiliate), Bread for the World, Evangs. for Social Action, Mus. Heritage Soc., Interscholastic Inst., Libr. Co. Phila., John Russell Bartlett Soc. (Brown U.), Intertel, Mensa, USCG Aux., Golden Key, Abraham Lincoln Soc., Internet Soc., Rel. Heritage Am., Providence Athenaeum, Toastmasters Internat., R.I. Pilots Assn., Phi Theta Kappa. Avocations: scuba diving, marksmanship, archaeology. Home and Office: PO Box 41000 Providence RI 02940-1000

DEMSKY, HILDA GREEN, artist, secondary and college art educator; b. Kingston, Pa., July 2, 1936; d. Morris and Sarah (Gelb) Green; m. Sy Demsky, Sept. 6, 1960; children: Bradford, Jordana. BFA, Carnegie Mellon U., 1958; MA, Hunter Coll., 1963. Art tchr. N.Y.C. Bd. Edn., 1959-72, White Plains (N.Y.) City Sch. Dist., 1972—; prof., clin. field supervisor Manhattanville Coll., Purchase, NY, 2001—02. Presenter in field. Contbr. to arts and activities mag.; muralist, 1989. Mem. White Plains Outdoor Art Festival Com., 1985-91. Fulbright fellow, 1992; Nat. Endowment for Arts fellow; Arts fellow Coun. for Basic Edn., Italy, 1992; Christa McAuliffe fellow U.S. Dept. Edn., 1988; N.Y. State Alliance for Arts Edn. grantee, 1986, 88; recipient painting fellowships. Mem. Nat. Art Edn. Assn., N.Y. State Alliance for Art Edn., N.Y. State Art Tchrs. Assn. (chair sect. 7 1992-93, pres. S.E. sect. 1992-93, Raymond C. Henry award 1990), Fulbright Assn. (co-chair Nat. Arts Task Force), Univ. Coun. Art Edn. (bd. dirs. 1997-98), Mamaroneck Artists Guild (sec. 1980-83). Avocations: travel, tennis. Home: 24 Orsini Dr Larchmont NY 10538-1642 Studio: 168 Irving Ave Ste 400A Port Chester NY 10573-4132 E-mail: hilda@demskyart.com.

DEN ADEL, RAYMOND LEE, classics educator; b. Pella, Iowa, Apr. 23, 1932; s. John J. and Nellie (DeGeus) D. BA, Ctrl. Coll., 1954; MA, U. Iowa, 1959; PhD, U. Ill., 1971. Latin tchr. Pella H.S., 1954-55; grad. student Am. Acad., Rome, 1960, Vergilian Sch., Cumae, Italy, 1960, 73; fellow U. Iowa, Iowa City, 1957-58, tchg. asst., 1962-63; Latin and English tchr. Proviso West H.S., Hillside, Ill., 1958-62; v.p. Proviso Ednl. Assn., 1960-61; grad. student Am. Sch. Classical Studies, Athens, 1961, site participant, 1989-90; fellow, asst. and instr. in classics U. Ill., Urbana, 1963-67; dir. Ill. H.S. Latin Conf., 1967; faculty, chair classics dept. Rockford (Ill.) Coll., 1967—97, chair div. lang. and lit., 1971—74, prof., 1975—97, 1997—. Lectr. Ctr. for Learning in Retirement Rock Valley Coll., 2001—03. Bd. dirs. Rockford Cmty. Concert Assn., 1979-85; mem. Burpee Museum of Natural Hist. (life) mem. exec. com. Archaeol. Inst. Am., (life), governing bd., 1990-96, trustee, 1990-94, v.p., 1994-96, Disting. Svc. award, 1997. With CIC, U.S. Army, 1955-57. Fulbright grant, Italy, 1960; named Vol. of Yr., Source Program, Rockford, 1983, Outstanding Coll. Latin Tchr. in Ill., 1987, Outstanding Fgn. Lang. Tchr. in Ill., 1989. Mem.: AAUP (pres. Rockford chpt. 1974—76, Ill. coun. 1977—80, sec. 1984—86, v.p. 1988—89), AIA (Ctrl. Ill. Soc. sec.-treas. 1966—67, coun. 1966—98, Rockford Soc. pres. 1968—70, 1972—74, 1991—93, sec. 1993—94, v.p. 1998—99), Classical Soc. Am. Acad. Rome (sec. 1990—93), Ill. Coun. Tchg. Fgn. Langs., Fulbright Alumni Assn., Biblical Archaeol. Soc., Ill. Classical Conf. (v.p. 1968—69, pres. 1969—70), Am. Assn. Dutch-Am. Studies, Vergilian Soc. Am. (life; sec. 1978—80), Classical Assn. Mid. West and South (life; 1st v.p. 1980—81), Am. Philol. Assn. (life Field Scholarship award 1961), Am. Classical League (life; nat. coun. 1969—82, Scholarship award 1960), Chgo. Classical Club (pres. 1977—79), Rotary (bd. dirs. Rockford chpt. 1987—89, dist. gov. rep. 1989—91, bd. dirs. Rockford chpt. 1991—95, v.p. 1992—93, pres. 1993—94, dist. gov. rep. 1994—97, gov. dist. 6420 1997—98, chair past dist. gov. coun. 1998, Paul Harris 711 Club, bd. dirs. 2002—, Svc. Above Self award Rockford Club and Dist. 6420 1989, Paul Harris fellow, benefactor 1982), Chi Gamma Iota, Phi Sigma Iota, Phi Beta Kappa (v.p.

1988—89, triennial coun. 1988—, pres. Eta Ill. chpt. 1989—92), Eta Sigma Phi (nat. exec. sec. 1974—78), Sigma Tau Delta. Presbyterian. Avocations: photography, travel, reading, philately, music. Home: 701 Broadway St Pella IA 50219

DENCKER, LINDA CRAVEN, secondary school educator; b. Gentry County, Mo., July 15, 1952; d. Duane Fremont Craven and Mildred Kathryn Gregory; m. Robert Luther Dencker, Aug. 15, 1975; children: Lindsay Elizabeth, Drew Craven. BS in Edn., N.W. Mo. State U., 1974; MAT, Webster U., 1990. Tchg./drama sponsor Meramec R-III H.S., Pacific, Mo., 1974—76; tchg./debate coach Francis Howell H.S., St. Charles, Mo., 1976—87, Francis Howell N. H.S., St. Charles, 1987—. Elder St. Charles Presbyn. Ch., 1997—, logos steering com., 1998—, strategic planning com., 2001—. Mem.: AAUW (pres. 1997—99, named gift award 1999), Greater St. Louis Speech Assn. (pres. elect 2000—02, pres. 2002—), Mo. State H.S. Activities Assn. (advisor speech bd. 2001—), Speech and Theatre Assn. Mo. (bd. govs. 1998—2001), Mo. Nat. Edn. Assn., Nat. Forensic League (mem. E. Mo. dist. com. 1993—, Double Diamond award 1996). Avocations: reading, movies, writing, travel. Office: Francis Howell N HS 2549 Hackmann Rd Saint Charles MO 63303

DENDRINOS, DIMITRIOS SPYROS, urban planning educator; b. Argostoli, Kefalonia, Greece, Sept. 2, 1944; came to U.S., 1969; s. Spyros H. and Iris Anninou (Kavalieratou) D. Diploma archtl. engring., U. Thessaloniki (Greece), 1968; M Urban Design, Washington U., St. Louis, 1971; PhD in City and Regional Planning, U. Pa., 1975. Prin. planner Middlesex County Planning Bd., New Brunswick, N.J., 1975; asst. prof. U. Kans., Lawrence, 1975-79, assoc. prof., 1980-83, prof. urban planning, 1983—, dir. urban and transp. dynamics lab., 1989-2001. Vis. rsch. fellow U.S. Dept. Transp., Washington, 1979-80; sr. tech. advisor UN, People's Republic of China, 1988; vis. prof. Chiao-Tung U., Taiwan, 1995, Poly. of Turin, Italy, 1995-96; lectr. numerous univs., U.S. and abroad. Author: Urban Evolution, 1985, Chaos and Socio-Spatial Dynamics, 1990, The Dynamics of Cities, 1992; editor-in-chief Social-Spatial Dynamics, 1989-94; hon. editor, founder Jour. Discrete Dynamics in Nature and Society, 1996—; mem. editl. bd. Geog. Analysis, 1990-95, Sistemi Urbani, 1989—, Annals Regional Sci., 1993-00; reviewer Math. Revs., 1989-95; mem. editl. bd. Nonlinear Dynamics, Psychology and Life Scis., 1995—, Urban Sys., 1995—; contbr. numerous articles to sci. jours. Grantee U.S. Dept. Transp., Washington, 1980, NSF, Washington, 1981, 84, 85, IBM, 1990. Mem. Internat. Geographic Union. Nonlinear Sociospatial Dynamics Soc., Regional Sci. Assn., Soc. Nonlinear Dynamics in Psychology and Life Scis. E-mail: dimitri@ku.edu.

DE NEUFVILLE, RICHARD LAWRENCE, engineering educator; b. N.Y.C., May 6, 1939; s. Lawrence Eustace and Adeline de N.; m. Virginia Lyons; children: Robert, Julie. SB, SM, MIT, 1961, PhD, 1965; Dr. h.c (hon.), Tech U., Delft, 2002. Asst. prof. to assoc. prof. dept. civil engring. MIT, Cambridge, Mass., 1965-75, prof., chmn. Tech. and Policy Program, 1975-2000, prof. engring sys., 2000—. Vis. prof. U. Calif., Berkeley, 1974—76, London Grad. Sch. Bus., 1973, Ecole Centrale de Paris, 1981—82; mem. vis. com. U. Va., Charlottesville, 1987; adj. prof. Ecole Nationale des Ponts et Chausees of Paris, 1988—, U. Bristol, England, 1992—99; vis. prof. Australian Bur. Transport and Comml. Econs., 1995; mem. vis. com. Tech. U., Delft, Eindhoven and Utrecht, The Netherlands, 1996—97; vis. prof. Harvard U., 2000—; advisor Alta. Heritage Fund for Sci. and Engring. Rsch., 2000—, B.C. Leading Edge Found., 2003; adj. prof. Ecole Hassania des Travaux Publics of Casablanca, 2000—01, MBA des Ponts, 2000—; vis. prof. Balliol Coll., Oxford U., 2001; sr. rsch. assoc., life mem. Clare Hall Coll., Cambridge U., 2002—; mem. Netherlands Rev. on Engring. Sys., 2002—; sr. rsch. assoc. Judge Inst. Author: Airport Systems Planning, Design and Management, 2003, Applied Systems Analysis, 1990, Airport Systems Planning, 1976, Systems Planning and Design, 1979, Systems Analysis for Engineers and Managers, 1971; editor Jour. Transp. Rsch., 1975-86, Jour. Air Transport Mgmt., 1993—, Intnerat. Jour. Tech. Policy and Mgmt., 1999—. Bd. dirs. Geographic Data Tech., 1982-90, Urban Data Processing, 1970-80, Ecole Bilingue, French-Am. Internat. Sch. of Boston, 1992-97; trustee Kennedy Meml. Trust (U.K.), 1993-98; Consejo del Rector, Universidad Anahuac del Sur, Mexico, 1999. 1st lt. C.E., U.S. Army, 1961-62. White House fellow, 1964-65, Guggenheim fellow, 1973, U.S.-Japan Leadership fellow, 1990, Class of 1960 fellow, 2000; recipient Sys. Sci. prize NATO, 1974, Risk and Ins. prize Risk and Ins. Soc., 1976, Alpha Kappa Psi award, 1985, Engring. Excellence award Australia Instn. Engrs., 1986, Irwin Sizer award, 1988, FAA prize for tchg. excellence, 1990, Chevalier de l'Ordre des Palmes Academiques, 1999. Mem. ASCE, AAAS, Ops. Rsch. Soc. Am., Brit.-N.Am. Com., Am. Alpine Club, Cambridge Boat Club, Cambridge Skating Club, Cambridge Tennis Club, Internat. House of Japan. Office: MIT Rm E40-245 Cambridge MA 02139 E-mail: ardent@mit.edu.

DENHAM, ELAINE BIRDSONG, business educator; b. Bainbridge, Ga., Jan. 25, 1952; d. John Henry and Eula Renee (Roper) Birdsong; m. Alva Edwin Denham, Sept. 2, 1989. BS in Bus. Edn., Ga. Southwestern, 1975, MS in Edn., 1980; EdS, U. Ga., 1986. Cert. tchr., Ga. Instr. R.E. Lee Inst., Thomaston, Ga., 1975-77, Upson Tehc. Inst., Thomaston, Ga., 1977-92, Macon (Ga.) Tech. Inst., 1992—. Am. Vocat. Assn., Ga. Vocat. Assn. (chmn. pub. com. 1991-93), Southeastern Bus. Edn. Assn., Nat. Bus. Edn. Assn., Nat. Profl. Sec., Phi Beta Lambda (advisor), Phi Kappa Phi (life). Baptist. Avocations: reading, computers. Home: 1873 Pickard Rd Thomaston GA 30286-1627 Office: Macon Tech Inst 3300 Macon Tech Dr Macon GA 31206-3699

DENHAM, ROBIN RICHARDSON, secondary school educator; b. New Haven, Feb. 17, 1946; d. Charles King and Sally Geldart (deFreest) Richardson; m. James Dexter Denham, June 24, 1978; children: Lisa Anne, Jeffrey Scott. BS in Art Edn., U. N.H., 1969. Cert. art educator, N.H. Tchr. art Southside Jr. H.S., Manchester, N.H., 1969-70, Merrimack Valley H.S., Penacook, N.H., 1971—. Chairperson dept. art Merrimack Valley Sch. Dist., 1985-96, chairperson arts curriculum com., 1997—, advisor Nat. Art Honor Soc., 1991—, curator permanent juried art collection, 1993—, yearbook adv. 1996—, active coms.; mem. vis. com. New Eng. Assn. Schs. and Colls., Inc., 1992, 95; mem. adv. bd. Boston Globe Scholastic Art Awards, N.H., 1993—, judge, Mass., 1993—; mem. N.H. Excellence in Edn. Com., 1993—; art educator, coord. children's staff Star Island Conf., Isle of Shoals, N.H., 1993—; panel mem. statewide initiatives N.H. State Coun.'s Arts in Edn., 1994, N.H. Alliance for Arts in Edn., 1995—; mem. steering com. N.H. Alliance in Arts Edn., 1995-96; panel mem. N.H. State Coun.'s Arts in Edn. Educators Panel for Arts in Edn., 1995; lectr. seminar N.H. Assn. Sch. Prins., 1996; co-presenter Block Scheduling Workshop, Milford, Art and Tech. Workshop, Nashua. Writer testimony for inclusion of art edn. Goals 2000: Educator Am. Act, 1993, 94; exhibited in group shows at Manchester Inst. Arts and Scis., 1991—, Star Island Art Exhibit, 1993—, New Eng. Art Edn. Conf., 1993—, Nat. Art Edn. Conv., 1993—; represented in permanent juried art collection Merrimack Valley H.S., 1993—. Com. chair Merrimack Valley Visual Arts Curriculum Sch. Dist., 1997. Recipient resolution in honor of her achievements Concord City Coun., 1993, plaque honoring her achievements Congressman Dick Swett, 1994, award Nat. Scholastic Arts and Writing, 1992, 95, 97-99; "ED"ies (Excellence in Edn.) N.H. Dept Edn., 1994; featured on Front Row cable network TV as favorite educator of major league pitcher Bob Tewksbury, 1997. Mem. NEA, Nat. Art Edn. Assn., N.H. Art Educators Assn. (v.p. region 2 1990-92, pres. elect 1992-93, site coord. fall conf. 1993, chairperson gala and awards ceremony 1994, co-chairperson 1993, pres. 1993-94, past pres. 1994-95, active various coms., long-range planning coms. 1992—, Youth Art Month, 1992—, Excellence in Edn.: Visual Arts Gold Ribbon 1994, chair 1995-96, Art Educator of Month Feb. 1992, Jan. 1994, Art Educator of Yr. 1992, 94, N.H. Outstanding Art Educator of Yr. 1995). Office: Merrimack Valley HS 163 N Main St Concord NH 03303-1106

DENICE, MARCELLA L. counseling administrator; b. 1933; BA in English, Our Lady of the Lake U., 1973, MA in Edn., 1990. English tchr., cross-country track coach Burbank H.S., San Antonio, 1983—90; guidance counselor Highland Park Elem. Sch., San Antonio, 1990—. Named Outstanding Counselor of Yr., Tex. Counseling Assn., 1991; recipient Remarkable Woman award, Our Lady of the Lake, 1995. Office: Highland Park Elem 635 Rigsby San Antonio TX 78210*

DENLINGER, VICKI LEE, secondary school physical education educator; b. Dayton, Ohio, June 13, 1961; d. David Lee and Barbara Ann (Zimmerman) D.; 1 child, David Micheal. Student, Ohio State U., 1979-82; BS in Edn., Wright State U., 1982-85; postgrad. studies, Miami U., Oxford, Ohio, 1986-87, U.S. Sports Acad., Daphne, Ala., 1996-97, U. Dayton, 2001—. Cert. phys. edn. and health tchr., Ohio; lic. athletic trainer, Ohio. Student athletic trainer Wright State U., Dayton, Ohio, 1983-85; asst. athletic trainer Oakwood (Ohio) City Sch., 1984-86; grad. asst. athletic trainer Miami U., Oxford, Ohio, 1986-87; subst. tchr. Oakwood City Sch., Kettering Moraine City Schs., Ohio, 1987-89; athletic trainer Kettering Moraine City Schs., Kettering, Ohio, 1987-96, tchr., 1989—; owner InnerPrize, Kettering, 1996—. Pub. spkr. Greater Dayton Athletic Trainers, 1987—, InnerPrize, 1996—; advisor Kettering Fairmont Student Athletic Trainers Assn., Kettering Moraine City Schs., 1989—96; facilitator Student Assistance Support Group, Kettering-Moraine City Schs., 1994—2000; instr. Kettering Awareness Tobacco Edn. Program, 1997—2001; advisor Students Against Destructive Decisions, 1997—. Mem. PTA Assns. of various Kettering-Moraine Pub. Schs., 1989-00; co-dir. Kettering 24-Hour Relay Challenge, 1999. Named Jaycee of the Month Region E, 1996, Ohio Jaycees, Most Outstanding Write-Up of the First Quarter, 1996, Ohio Jaycees. Mem. NEA, ASCD, Nat. Athletic Trainer's Assn. (cert. athletic trainer), Ohio Athletic Trainers Assn., Greater Dayton Athletic Trainers Assn., Nat. Strength and Conditioning Assn., Internat. Weight Lifting Assn. (cert. weight trainer), Ohio Edn. Assn., Kettering Edn. Assn., Ohio Assn. for Health, Phys. Edn., Recreation and Dance, Am. Coll. Sports Medicine, Nat. Fedn. Interscholastic Coaches Edn. Program/Am. Coaching Effectiveness Program, Sports First Aid Instr. Avocations: Christian studies, fitness, personal devel. and sports, athletics. Home: 3489 Valleywood Dr Kettering OH 45429-4234 Office: Kettering Fairmont HS 3301 Shroyer Rd Kettering OH 45429-2635 E-mail: denlingerv@aol.com.

DENMON, FRANCES, resource specialist educator; b. Detroit, Sept. 11, 1950; d. Andrew Miles Jr. and Loretta (Futch) Jones; m. Lee Andrew Denmon Jr., Mar, 10, 1973; children: Lisa Denise, Lee Andrew III. BA in English, Calif. State U., Northridge, 1972, postgrad., 1975, Calif. State U., Dominguez Hills, 1977-79, 81. Cert. resource specialist, Calif. Tchr. educationally handicapped Hathaway Children's Village, Lakeview Terrace, Calif., 1972-75; spl. edn. tchr. Los Angeles County Office of Edn., Downey, Calif., 1975-87, resource specialist teacher, 1987—. Mem. adv. bd. Children's Enrichment Ctr., Inglewood, Calif., 1977-84; scotopic sensitivity screener Helen Irlen Inst., Long Beach, Calif., 1991—. Patentee Feelings Game, 1986. Recipient Mentor Tchr. award Calif. Supt. Instrn., 1986. Mem. NEA, Calif. Tchrs. Assn. (site rep. 1982-84), Calif. Assn. Resource Specialists (pres. Los Angeles County Ct. Schs. chpt. 1992-94, treas. 1994—, bd. dirs. 1995-97, svc. award 1994, Very Important Person award 1994), Los Angeles County Alliance Black Sch. Educators (founding). Avocations: reading, sewing, crafts. Office: Los Angeles Co Office Edn 9300 Imperial Hwy Downey CA 90242-2813

DENN, MORTON MACE, chemical engineering educator; b. Passaic, N.J., July 7, 1939; s. Herbert Paul and Esther (Taub) D; m. Vivienne Roumani; children: Matthew Philip, Susannah Rachel, Rebekah Leah. BS in Engring., Princeton U., 1961; PhD, U. Minn., 1964, DSc (hon.), 2001. Postdoctoral fellow U. Del., Newark, 1964-65, from asst. prof. to prof. Chem. Engring., 1965-77, Allan P. Colburn prof., 1977-81; prof. U. Calif., Berkeley, 1981-99, chmn. dept. chem. engring., 1991-94. Harry Pierce prof. chem. engring. Technion, Israel Inst. Tech., Haifa, 1979-80; Chevron Energy prof. chem. engring. Calif. Inst. Tech., 1980; vis. prof. chem. engring. U. Melbourne, Australia, 1985; program leader for polymers Ctr. for Advanced Materials Lawrence Berkeley Nat. Labs., 1983-99; vis. Forchheimer prof. Hebrew U., Israel, 1998-99; disting. prof. chem. engring. City Coll. CUNY, 1999—, prof. physics, 2001—, Albert Einstein prof. sci. and engring., 2001—, dir. Benjamin Levich Inst. for Physico-Chem. Hydrodynamics, 2000—. Author: Optimization by Variational Methods, 1969, (co-author) Introduction to Chemical Engineering Analysis, 1972, Stability of Reaction and Transport Processes, 1975, Process Fluid Mechanics, 1980, Process Modeling, 1986; co-editor Chemical Process Control, 1976; contbr. numerous articles to profl. jours., author book chpts. Guggenheim fellow, 1971-72; William M. Lacey lectr. Calif. Inst. Tech., 1979, Fulbright lectr., 1979-80; Peter C. Reilly lectr. Notre Dame U., 1980; Bicentennial Commemoration lectr. La. State U., 1984; Arthur Kelly lectr. Purdue U., 1987; Stanley Katz lectr. CCNY, 1990, other lectureships. Fellow AAAS, AIChE (editor jour. 1985-91, Profl. Progress award 1977, William H. Walker award 1984, Warren K. Lewis award 1998, Inst. lectr. 1999); mem. NAE, Am. Soc. Engring. Edn. (chem. engring. divsn. lectureship award 1993), Soc. Rheology (editor jour. 1995—, Bingham medal 1986), Brit. Soc. Rheology, Polymer Processing Soc., Am. Phys. Soc., Sigma Xi. Office: Levich Inst City Coll CUNY 1M Steinman Hall New York NY 10031 E-mail: denn@ccny.cuny.edu.

DENNING, KAREN CRAFT, finance educator; b. Pitts., Mar. 23, 1952; d. Edward Harvey and Esther Naomi Craft; m. John Thomas Denning; children: Naomi Liza, Chloe, Lacey. AB, Cornell U., 1974; PhD, U. Pitts., 1986. Lectr., asst. prof. Case Western Res. U., Cleve., 1985—88; prof. W.Va. U., Morgantown, 1988—2003, Fairleigh Dickinson U., 2003—. Editor: e-Jour. Social Studies, 2002—; contbr. articles to profl. jours. Bd. dirs. Katz Grad. Sch. Bus. Ph.D. Alumni Bd., Pitts. Grantee Internat. Programs Instrnl. Tech. grantee, W.Va. U., 1998—99. Mem.: Am. Fin. Assn., So. Fin. Assn., Midwestern Fin. Assn., Ea. Fin. Assn., Fin. Mgmt. Assn., 20th Century Club, Beta Gamma Sigma (pres. 1998). Presbyterian. Avocations: travel, piano, reading, skiing.

DENNING, MICHAEL MARION, marketing professional, educator; b. Durant, Okla., Dec. 22, 1943; s. Samuel M. and Lula Mae (Waitman) D.; m. Suzette Karin Wallace, Aug. 10, 1968 (div. 1979); children: Lila Monique, Tanya Kerstin, Charlton Derek; m. Donna Jean Hamel, Sept. 28, 1985; children: Caitlin Shannon, Meghan O'Donnell. Student, USAF Acad., 1963; BS, U. Tex., 1966, Fairleigh Dickinson U., 1971; MS, Columbia U., 1973; PhD, Kingsfield U., 1998. Mgr. systems IBM, White Plains, N.Y., 1978-79, mgr. svc. and mktg. San Jose, Calif., 1979-81; nat. market support mgr. Memorex Corp., Santa Clara, Calif., 1979-81, v.p. mktg., 1981-82; v.p. mktg. and sales Icot Corp., Mountain View, Calif., 1982-83; exec. v.p. Phase Info. Machines Corp., Scottsdale, Ariz., 1983-84, Tricom Automotive Dealer Systems Inc., Hayward, Calif., 1985-87; pres. ADS Computer Svcs., Inc., Toronto, Ont., Can., 1985-87, Denning Investments, Inc., Palo Alto, Calif., 1987, Pers. Solutions Group, Inc., Menlo Park, Calif., 1990-96, Crystal Rsch. Corp., Scottsdale, Ariz., 1997-98; pres., CEO, Landtech Environmental Inc., Scottsdale, Ariz., 1998-99; pres. Impulse Response Group, Inc., Phoenix, 2002—. Adj. prof. Arizona State U. Coll. Bus., Tempe, 1997—; chmn. Exec. Com. Emerging Entrepreneurs, Scottsdale, Az., 1998—. With USAF, 1962-66; Vietnam. Mem. Rotary, Phi Beta Kappa, Lambda Chi Alpha (pres. 1965-66). Republican. Methodist. Office: Impulse Response Group Inc 501 N 44th St Phoenix AZ 85008 E-mail: michael.denning@asu.edu.

DENNIS, DORETHA B. secondary education educator; b. Hazlehurst, Miss., Sept. 16, 1955; d. James Bozeman and Mardies (Smith) Bozeman Coleman; m. Tommie Lee Dennis, Jan. 16, 1978; children: Antrease Lynette, Antawn Carvayatta. B, Jackson State U., 1978; M, Nova U., 1984. Cert. tchr., Fla., Miss. Tchr., Miramar, Fla., 1992—; dept. head, 1992-94; grade level chairperson, 1992-93. Tchr. cons. NSF/USI, 1994. V.p. PTO, Opalocka, Fla., 1983-85. Named Chpt. 1 Tchr. of Yr., 1988-89, Tchr. of Yr. 1992, Sci. Tchr. of Yr., 1993-94. Mem. Nat. Sci. Tchrs. Assn., Fla. Assn. Sci. Tchrs. Avocations: reading, sports, cooking. Home: 2254 SW 81st Ave Miramar FL 33025-2271

DENNIS, GARY C. neurosurgeon, educator; b. Washington, Dec. 27, 1950; s. Creed and Yvonne (Bush) C.; children: Gary Jr., Gina, Gregory. BA, Boston U.; MD, Howard U. Intern Johns Hopkins Hosp., Balt., 1976-77; residency Baylor Coll. of Medicine Affiliated Hosp., Houston, 1977-81; chief of neurosurgery Kern Med. Ctr., Bakersfield, Calif., 1981-83; clin. assoc. prof. U. Calif., San Diego, 1981-85; chief of neurosurgery Howard U., Washington, 1984—, asst. prof surgery, 1984-90, assoc. prof., 1990—; attending physician DC Gen. Hosp., Washington, 1990—. Vis. lectr. neurosurgery Johns Hopkins Sch. Med., 1980-98; surg. cons. D.C. Gen . Hosp., 1986-89; mem. Mayors Commn. to oversee Med. Examiners Office, Washington, 1990, Mayors Transition Team for Health, Washington, 1990; mem. D.C. Commn. on Jud. Disabilities and Tenure, 2000—; mem. Sec.'s Adv. Com. on Regulatory Reform, 2001-02; chmn. bd. Delmarva Found. D.C.; mem. Bd. Med. Edn. for South African Blacks, 2002—. Mem. Practicing Physicians Adv. Coun., Health Care Fin. Agy., Washington, 1991-99, Com. on Health Care Reform, Cong. Black Caucus, Washington, 1994—; bd. dirs. Am. Liver Found., 1999-2002; mem. D.C. Health Care Reform Commn. Named One of Top Drs. S.E. Area, Washingtonian Mag., 1995. Fellow ACS; mem. Med. Soc. D.C. (pres. 1996-98, chmn. bd. dirs. 1998-99, alt. del. to AMA 2001), Nat. Med. Assn. (pres.-elect 1997—, pres. 1998-99), Am. Assn. Neurol. Surgeons (mem. chair 1994-95), Nat. Med. Assn. (trustee 1992-97, 98—, pres. 1998), Howard U. Med. Alumni Assn. (pres. 2002--). Avocations: music, outdoor cooking, fishing. Office: Howard U Hosp 2041 Georgia Ave NW Washington DC 20060-0001 E-mail: gcdennis@pol.net.

DENNIS, PATRICIA LYON, adult education educator; b. Rockford, Tenn., June 13, 1933; d. Howard Stanton and Dora Hester (Maynard) Lyon; m. Norman Bryan Dennis Jr., Jan. 12, 1957 (dec. Jan. 1985); children: Sarah Dennis Banks, Rebecca Dennis Hampton. BS, George Peabody Coll., 1955; MA, U. Mo., 1977; postgrad., Auburn U., 1972-73, U. Kans., 1982-92, U. Mo., Kansas City, 1994, 96. Cert. tchr.; cert. libr. media specialist, Kan; elem. classroom tchr., N.C., Mich., Mo., Ala. 3d grade tchr. Ray Street Elem. Sch., High Point, N.C., 1955-56; kindergarten and 3d grade tchr. Wurtsmith Dependent Sch., Clark AFB, Philippines, 1957-59; spl. reading tchr., 1st grade tchr. McDonald Elem. Sch., K.I. Sawyer AFB, Mich., 1961-63; kindergarten tchr. Gladden Elem. Sch., Richards-Gebaur AFB, Mo., 1964-65; 2d grade tchr., libr. Goose AFB Dependent Sch., Labrador, 1965-67; 2d grade tchr. Edgewood Acad., Wetumpka, Ala., 1969-70; 1st and 4th grade tchr. Trinity Christian Day Sch., Montgomery, Ala., 1970-72; 2d and 3d grade tchr. Fairview Elem. Sch., Olathe, Kans., 1974-77; libr. media specialist Wash. Elem. Sch., Olathe, Kans., 1977-99; instr. continuing edn. Johnson County C. C., Overland Pk., Kans., 1999—. Pres. Pre-Sch. Bd., Gunter AFB, 1968-69; children's choir dir. Leawood (Kans.) Bapt. Ch., 1979-84, Sunday sch. dept. dir., 1987-88, ch. libr., 1990-93; bd. dirs. Scholarship Pageant, Kansas City, 1988-96; chaperone, traveling companion Miss Am.-Kans. Scholarship Pageant, Pratt, Kans., 1989-98; commr., book rev. com. Kans. State Reading Cir. Commn., Topeka, 1985-91, 94-96, 97-99; primary subcom. chairperson Kans. State Reading Circle, 1998-99. Mem.: MLA, NEA, Kans. Reading Assn., Kans. Assn. Sch. Librs. (presenter 1990—97), Olathe Culture Group (v.p. 2002—), Sigma Alpha Iota (treas. 1954), Alpha Delta Kappa (sec. 1999—2002, pres. 2002—, mem. cmty. scholarship bd. 2002—03). Republican. Baptist. Avocations: harp, piano, voice, dance, physical fitness. Home and Office: 10525 Chesney Ln Olathe KS 66061-2775

DENNIS, RUTLEDGE M. sociology educator, researcher; b. Charleston, SC, Aug. 16, 1939; s. David and Ora Jane (Porcher) D.; children: Shay Tchaka, Imaro Marlin Aki, Kimya Nuru, Zuri Sanyika. BS, S.C. State U., 1966; MA, Wash. State U., 1969, PhD, 1975. Dir. Black studies program Va. Commonwealth U., Richmond, 1971-78, assoc. prof. dept. sociology, 1978-89; Commonwealth prof. dept. sociology George Mason U., Fairfax, Va., 1989—, prof. dept. sociology, 1992—. Co-dir. sociology grad. program George Mason U.; coord. Southeastern Regional African Seminar, Richmond-Charlottesville, 1973-76; del. Ea. Va. Internat. Consortium, 1972-77; pres. Assn. Black Sociologists, 1981-83; founder Rutledge Dennis Found. for Human Devel., Ctr. for African Am. Culture and Leadership; co-founder African-Am. Acad. Co-author: The Politics of Annexation, 1982; editor: JAI Press Series in Race and Ethnic Relations, 1990—, Racial and Ethnic Politics, 1994, The Black Middle Class, 1995, W.E.B. Du Bois: The Scholar as Activist, 1996, Black Intellectuals, 1997, Marginality and Society: Issues in Class, Race, and Gender, 2003; series editor: Oliver C. Cox, 2000; co-editor: The Afro-Americans, 1976, Race and Ethnicity in Research Methods, 1993, Race and Ethnicity: Comparative and Theoretical Approaches, 2003. Housing commr. Richmond Redevel. and Housing Authority, 1977-80; bd. dirs. Housing Opportunities Made Equal, Richmond, 1976-80. With U.S. Army, 1960-63. Fellow Fgn. Affairs scholar, 1965; recipient Cmty. Svc. award Boys Clubs Am., 1976; named Outstanding Educator of Am., 1975; recipient Reise-Melton Cultural award, 1980, Disting. Leadership award Afro-Am. Studies Program, 1991, Nat. Black Monitor Family and Cmty. award 1985, Va. Commonwealth U., 1991, Pres.'s award S.C. State U., 1966, Jewish Educators award, 1998, Joseph Himes award for Disting. Scholarship, 2001, Ba'Alay Keriyah Soc., 2003, others; grantee Ford Found., 1970, NEH, 1978, NIMH, 1980-81; 25th Ann. lectr. African-Am. studies program Va. Commonwealth U., 1996, others. Mem. Am. Sociol. Assn., Soc. Study Social Problems, So. Sociol. Soc., Ea. Sociol. Soc. (chmn. minorities com. 1992-96, mem. editl. bd. Race and Soc. 1998--), Assn. Black Sociologists (pres. 1981-82, 82-83, chmn. hist. and archives com., 2002-, Leadership award 1995), African Heritage Soc., Sigma Xi, Omicron Delta Kappa, Alpha Phi Alpha (Acad. Excellence award 1985), Alpha Kappa Mu, Alpha Kappa Delta. Office: George Mason U Dept Sociology Anthrop Fairfax VA 22030

DENNISON, PATRICIA DAVIS, vocational education educator, nurse; b. Russell Springs, Ky., Oct. 12, 1945; d. Harlin and Veda (Gosser) Davis; m. Jerry Lee Dennison, Sept. 19, 1965; children: Sonya Lynette Dennison Kerr, Staci Rena, Jarred Ronald. AS in Nursing, Western Ky. U., 1969, BS in Vocat. Edn., 1991. RN, Ky.; cert. tchr., Ky. Charge nurse obstetrics dept. Bowling Green (Ky.)-Warren County Hosp., 1969-71, Meth. Hosp., Louisville, 1971-72; head nurse Oakwood, Somerset, Ky., 1972-73; tchr. health svcs. Russell County Vocat. Sch., Russell Springs, 1975—. Staff nurse med.-surg. unit Westlake Cumberland Hosp., Columbia, Ky., 1983—; adviser Health Occupational Students Am., 1979—, advisor, 1982-85, 86-87. Chmn. Russell County Blood Donor Program, 1979—; mem. Russell County Health Fest Com., 1988—. Named Outstanding Tchr. Region 14 Vocat. Edn., 1983. Mem. Am. Vocat. Assn., Ky. Vocat. Assn., Med-Cumberland Dist. Vocat. Assn. (v.p. 1979-80, 87-88, pres. 1981-82), Golden Key (charter), Alpha Sigma Lambda (charter). Republican. Mem. Ch. of Christ. Home: 1975 Blair School Rd Russell Springs KY 42642-6423 Office: Russell County Vocat Sch Russell Springs KY 42642

DENNISTON, MARJORIE MCGEORGE, retired elementary school educator; b. Coraopolis, Pa., Mar. 21, 1913; d. Chauncey Kirk and Elsie (George) McGeorge; m. Delbert Dicks Denniston, Dec. 25, 1942 (dec. 1973); 1 child, Robert Bruce. Student, Ohio U., 1931-33; BA, Westminster Coll., 1936; postgrad., U. Kans., 1959, Western Ill. U., 1962, 64. Elem. tchr.

county schs., West Pittsburg, Pa., 1936-42, New Castle Sch. System, Pa., 1942, 51-78. Pres. Newcastle NEA, 1965-67; vol. aid Pa. Assn. Retarded Children, Jameson Hosp., Law County Home, 1984-96; trustee, elder Presbyn. Ch., New Castle, 1986-92, v.p. Ch. Women United, 1990-94. Named First Lady of New Castle, 1989, Outstanding Woman of Yr. for Community Svc. Jr. Woman's Club, 1990, Disting. Alumni Achievement Cmty. Svc. award Westminster Coll., 1990. Mem. AAUW, LWV (sec. New Castle chpt. 1986—), Coll. Club (parliamentarian), Woman's Club (parliamentarian Lawrence County fedn. 1984—, sec. 1986-88), Woman's Club of New Castle (parliamentarian 1990-99), Fedn. Jrs. (v.p. 1994-96), Pa. Assn. State Retirees (v.p. local chpt. 1994—), Cmty. Ch. Women Lawrence County (parliamentarian 1995—), Delta Kappa Gamma. Republican. Avocations: photography, coin and rock collecting, volunteering, book reviewing, travel. Home: 331 Laurel Blvd New Castle PA 16101-2523

DENSLEY, COLLEEN T. principal; b. Provo, Utah, Apr. 12, 1950; d. Floyd and Mary Lou (Dixon) Taylor; m. Steven T. Densley, July 23, 1968; children: Steven, Tiffany, Landon, Marianne, Wendy, Logan. BS in Elem. Edn., Brigham Young U., 1986, MEd in Tchg. and Learning, 1998. Cert. in elem. edn., K-12 adminstrn. Utah. Substitute tchr. Provo Sch. Dist., 1972-85, curriculum specialist, 1999-2001; tchr. 6th grade, mainstreaming program Canyon Crest Elem. Sch., Provo, 1985—94; instructional facilitator Campus Crest Elem., 1994—99; prin. Wasatch Elem. Sch., Provo, 2001—. Tchr. asst., math. tutor Brigham Young U., 1968—69; attendee World Gifted and Talented Conf., Salt Lake City, 1987, Tchr. Expectations and Student Achievement, 1988—89, Space Acad. for Educators, Huntsville, Ala., 1992; supr. coop. tchr. for practicum tchrs., 1987—90; co-chmn. accelerated learning and devel. com.; trainee working with handicapped students in mainstream classroom, 1989; mem. elem. sch. lang. arts curriculum devel. com., 90; mem. task force Thinking Strategies Curriculum, 1990—91; extensions specialist gifted and talented, 1990—91; math, 1991—; master tchr. Nat. Tchr. Tng. Inst., 1993. Co-author: (curricula) Provo Sch. Dist.'s Microorganism Sci. Kit, 1988, Arthropod Sci. Kit, 1988, Tchg. for Thinking, 1990—, PAWS Presents the Internet and the World Wide Web, 1997. Named Utah State Tchr. of the Yr., 1992; recipient Honor Young Mother of Yr. award, State of Utah, 1981. Mem.: NEA, Provo Edn. Assn. (Tchr. of the Yr. 1991—92), Internat. Space Edn. Initiative (adv. bd.), Utah Coun. Tchrs. Math., Utah Edn. Assn., Nat. Coun. Tchrs. Math. Republican. Mem. Lds Ch. Office: Wasatch Elem Sch 1080 N 900 E Provo UT 84604 E-mail: colleend@provo.EDU

DENSLOW, DEBORAH PIERSON, primary education educator; b. Phila., May 2, 1947; d. Merrill Tracy Jr. and Margaret (Aiman) D.; m. James Tracy Grey III, Nov. 24, 1972 (div. Dec. 1980); 1 child, Sarah Elizabeth. BS, Gwynedd Mercy Coll., 1971; MA, Marygrove Coll., Detroit, 2000. Tchr. Willingboro (N.J.) Bd. Edn., 1971—. Union rep. Burlington County Edn. Assn., Willingboro, 1981-82, ednl. adv. Nat. Constitution Ctr., Phila., 2002-.; mem. task force for reoganization Morrisville Sch. Dist., 1991-92. Mem. Borough Coun., Morrisville, 1988—94, pres., 1992—94, rep. candidate, 1986; borough chmn. Am. Cancer Soc., 1986—87; sec. bd. dirs. Morrisville Free Libr., 1988—90, bd. dirs., 1988—2001; mem. Morrisville Mcpl. Authority, chmn., 1994—95, 1996—2000, asst. sec., treas., 1995—96, 2001; judge City Gardens Contest The Pa. Horticultural Soc., Phila., 2002; committeewoman 1st ward Morrisville (Pa.) Rep. Com., 1986—98. Mem. NEA, N.J. Edn. Assn., Willingboro Edn. Assn. (union rep. 1981-82, alt. union rep. 1988-89), Parents without Ptnrs. (bd. dirs. Mercer County chpt. 1981-82, sec. 1982-84), Bucks County Boroughs Assn. (bd. dirs. 1989—, v.p. 1990-92, pres. 1992-93), Pa. Mcpl. Authorities Assn. (profl. devel. com. 2000-2001). Presbyterian. Avocations: swimming, sailing. Home: 1 Garrett Lane Willingboro NJ 08046

DENT, CATHERINE GALE, secondary education educator; b. Salem, Mo., Apr. 20, 1953; d. James Ferguson and Virgina Gale (Martin) Dent; 1 son from previous marriage, M. Cole Schafer; m. Hobart E. Porter, Dec. 29, 1997. Student, U. Mo., 1971-74, 91—, Longview Commun. Coll., Lee's Summit, Mo., 1975, S.W. Bapt. U., Bolivar, Mo., 1985; BA in Liberal Studies, Thomas Edison State Coll.; MS in Ednl. Counseling, PhD in Ednl. Adminstrn., Columbia State U., 1997; MA in Edn., Univ. of Phoenix, 2003. Lic. funeral dir.; cert. secondary tchr., Mo. Feature writer, reporter Dent County Headliner, 1972-74; acctg. clk. Assn. of Unity Chs., Unity Village, Mo., 1974-77; graphic artist The Salem News, 1979; adminstrv. asst. Ozark Lead Co.-Kennecott Corp., Sweetwater, Mo., 1979-82; ch. organist United Meth. Ch., Salem, 1977-97; music tchr. Salem, 1983—; substitute tchr. Salem R-80 Sch. Dist., 1991—99, contracted tchr., 1999—; owner Dent LLC. Bd. dirs. Salem Arts Coun., 1984—; mgr. Salem Community Jazz Band, 1985—; accompanist Salem Community Choir, 1984—, Salem R-80 Sch. Sys. Music Dept., 1990—; dir. Temple Carillons Handbell Choir, Salem, 1985-94; sec. Vocat. Edn. Adv. Com., 1996-99, 2000—. Recipient Children's award Cosmopolitan Club; named to Outstanding Young Women in Am., 1985. Mem. Salem Computer Club, Dent County Hist. Soc., Order Ea. Star, Order of Amaranth, Salem Rebekah Lodge, Fraternal Order of Eagles Ladies Aux., Internat. Order Rainbow for Girls (Grand Cross of Color 1968, supreme dep. 1998), Sorosis Club (pres. 1992-93), Cosmopolitan Club (sec. 1994-98, pres. 1998—), Phi Beta Mu. Democrat. Methodist. Avocations: playing piano, travel. Home: 1300 W Rolla Rd Salem MO 65560-2736

DENT, LEANNA GAIL, secondary art educator; b. Manhattan, Kans., Oct. 21, 1949; d. William Charles and Maxine Madeline Payne; children: Laura Michelle, Jeffery Aaron. BS in Edn., U. Houston, 1973; postgrad., U. Tex., 1975-76; MS in Edn., Okla. State U., 1988. Cert. elementary and secondary art tchr., Okla., Tex. Tchr. art Popham Elem. Sch., Del Valle, Tex., 1973-77; graphic artist Conoco, Inc., Ponca City, Okla., 1987-88; tchr. art Garfield Elem. Sch., Ponca City, Okla., 1988-91, Reed Elem. Sch., Houston, 1991-92, Copeland Elem. Sch., Houston, 1992-94, Campbell Jr. High Sch., Houston, 1994—. Cons. and specialist in field. Author: Using Synectics to Enhance the Evaluation of Works of Art, 1988; group exhibitions in Ala., Kans., Nebr., Okla., Tex. and Pa. Vol. 1st Luth. Day Sch., Ponca City, 1977-91, Ponca City Inds. Sch. Dist., 1987-91; work com. Cy-Fair Ind. Sch. Dist., Houston, 1991-94. Acad. and mem. scholar Okla. State U., 1986-88; named Spotlight Tchr. Yr., 1992-93. Mem. Nat. Art Edn. Assn., Tex. Art Edn. Assn. (judges commendation 1993), Assn. Tex. Profl. Educators, Houston Art Edn. Assn. (v.p. 1992-93, pres.-elect 1993-95, pres. 1995-97, past pres. 1997-99), Phi Delta Kappa, Phi Kappa Phi. Republican. Lutheran. Avocations: riding horses, camping, art, museums, black and white movies. Office: Campbell Jr High Sch 11415 Bobcat Rd Houston TX 77064-3097

DENTON, JOAN CAMERON, reading consultant, former educator; b. Chgo. d. Wallace William and Ruth Elizabeth (Nothof) Cameron; m. Robert Eastman Denton, Aug. 16, 1958; children: Marianne, Lynn, Robert. BS in Edn., Northwestern U., Evanston, Ill., 1954; MS in Spl. Edn. and Reading, U. Nebr., Omaha, 1982. Tchr. English and social studies Berwyn (Ill.) Pub. Schs.; tchr. devel. and advanced secondary reading Omaha Pub. Schs., reading diagnostician; lead tchr. Reading Svcs.; reading cons. Scholastic, Inc. Former mem. external visitation team/reading Boys Town Schs., Omaha Pub. Schs.; supr. summer literacy ctr., instr. U. Nebr., Omaha; mem. instrl. dist. coms.; former mem. rev. bd. Reading Tchr.; co-chair Metro Reading Coun. Lit. Project Listening Libr.; mem. reading leadership team, cons. gifted reading study Omaha Pub. Schs.; coord. OPS/AT&T Reading Pioneers Assisting Literacy in Schs. Program, mem. cons. team. Co-author computer-based reading comprehension course for Ind. Study H.S., U. Nebr. Coll. Continuing Edn. Chmn. Operation Sch. Bell, Assistance League Omaha; bd. dirs. Munro-Meyer Women's Guild, Sacred Hearth Sch. Guild. Recipient Disting. Alumni award U. Nebr. Coll. Edn., Omaha, 1998. Mem. AAUW, NEA, Nebr. Edn. Assn., Omaha Edn. Assn., Internat. Reading Assn., Nebr. Reading Assn., Met. Reading Coun., Phi Delta Kappa, Alpha Xi Delta. E-mail: denton@tconl.com.

DENTON, JUDY HOLLEY, elementary education educator; b. Roanoke, Va., Aug. 2, 1948; d. Dany Paul and Blanche Virginia (Journell) Holley; m. Larry W. Custer, July 24, 1970 (div. 1981); 1 child, Susan Nicole; m. Michael Denton, Nov. 18, 1995. BA in History, Roanoke Coll., 1970; postgrad., U. Va., 1972-74, 78-83, Radford U., 1972, 80, Roanoke Coll., 1985, 86. Cert. tchr.-collegiate profl. Tchr. grade 6 St. Andrews Cath. Elem., Roanoke, 1970-71; substitute tchr. Roanoke County and Roanoke City Schs., Va., 1971-72; tchr. grade 4 Roanoke (Va.) County Schs., 1972-80, 4th grade coord., 1973-80, tchr. grade 6, 1980-86, 87-88, 6th grade coord., 1981-86, 87-88, tchr. grade 5, 5th grade coord., 1986-87, 88—. Sch. rep. Health/Social Studies Tchrs. Roanoke County, 1980-92; mem. Blue Ridge Coun. Math., Roanoke, 1983-84, Va. Assn. Tchrs. English, Roanoke, 1984-85, Profl. Assn. Tchrs. English, Roanoke, 1989-90. Editor: National Excellence Recognition for Mountain View Elementary, 1987-88. Mem. PTA, Mountain View-Roanoke County, 1972—, PTA, Northside Jr./Sr. High, 1987-92; participant, chmn. self study com. Mountain View Sch., Roanoke County, 1972-73, 82-83, 87-88; co-chair Southeastern Assn. of Colls. and Schs. com. on comm. for Mountain View, 1995—, editor report, 1996-97; evaluator Textbook Adoption Com., Roanoke (Va.) County, 1982-83, 86-87; participant Jump Rope for Heart, Am. Heart Assn., Roanoke, 1983-87, 90-92. Mem. NEA, Va. Edn. Assn., Nat. Assn. Tchrs. English, Roanoke Valley Coun. Internat. Reading Assn., Roanoke County Edn. Assn. Brethren. Avocations: reading, gardening, needlework, volleyball, traveling. Home: 1529 Barnett Rd NW Roanoke VA 24017-2309 Office: Mountain View Elem Sch 5901 Plantation Cir Roanoke VA 24019-4937

DENUZZO, RINALDO VINCENT, pharmacy educator; b. Cleve., Oct. 21, 1922; s. Luigi and Domenica Mary (Razzano) DiNuzzo; m. Lucy Bernadine Sneed, June 29, 1946; 1 child, Lisa Ann. BS, Albany Coll. Pharmacy, 1952; MS in Edn., SUNY-Albany, 1956; LHD, Union U., 2003. Registered pharmacist, N.Y., Fla., Vt. Prof. pharmacy N.Y. Coll. Pharmacy, Albany, 1952—, adminstrv. asst., 1963-80. Pharmacist N.Y., Fla., Vt., 1968-95; sr. pharmacist inspector N.Y. State Dept. Health, 1966-95; field dir. Market Measures, Inc.; chmn. tech. pharmacy adv. com., 1977-95; lectr. drug product substitution and generic drugs; notary public. Author: Ann. Albany Coll. Pharmacy Prescription Survey, 1956—84, Substitution, The New York State Experience, 1980, RX Services, XIII Winter Olympic Games, 1980, Ann. DeNuzzo Prescription Survey, 1985—96, Imapct of One-Line Prescription Form on Generic Drug Use, 1987, Cipro, Vasotec, Volatren Post Biggest Gains, 1987, Using the Right Tools to Achieve Personal Success, 1990, Personal Selling, 1991, Annual Survey Tracks Drug Prescribing Trends, 1990, Consumer Prescription Prices Increase, 1991, Changes in Dental Prescribing, 1991, How to Reduce Prescription Medical Costs, 1992, Are Dental Prescriptions a Viable Target for RPhs?, 1992, Financial Success: A Challenge for the Future, 1996, A National Drug Expert Is Needed, 1999, Down Memory Lane, 1999, 2002, What Graduates Need to Know: A Prescription for the Future Financial Success: ACP's Reflection of Progress 1881-2001; A Brief Written and Pictorial History, 2001; editor: Albany Coll. Pharmacy Alumni News, 1961—81; mem. editl. bd. MMM, 1977—80. Instr. first aid, responding to emergencies CPR ARC; mem. East Greenbush Ctrl. Sch. Dist. Bd. Edn., 1974—92, v.p., 1975—76, pres., 1976—78, 1991—92, East Greenbush Edn. Found.; chmn. Albany Coll. Pharmacy Faculty, 1987—89, com. on coms., 1984—87, promotions com., 1989—92, exec. com., grievance com., chair strategic planning steering com., 1995—96; faculty affairs chmn. and rev. Albany Coll. Pharmacy, 1990—94; sr. student status com., faculty ombudsman Albany Coll. Pharmacy Faculty, 1991—2002, mission statement com., 1995; mem. adv. bd. Merrell-Dow Hosp., 1987; sec.-treas. Union U. Pharmacy Coll. Coun., 1970—80; com. on coms. Albany Coll. Pharmacy Faculty, 1996—97; mem. profl. adv. com. Albany Vis. Nurses Assn.; mem. rev. panel on prescription payment rev. commn. Office Tech. Assessment U. S. Congress, 1988; mem. ethics panel Siena Coll., 1992; mem., dir. Rensselaer County Taxpayers Assn.; cons. pharmacist, coord. pharm. svcs. XIII Olympic Winter Games, Lake Placid, NY, 1980; liaison Health Sys. Mgmt. degree Joint MS with Union Coll. With U.S. Army, 1941—46, with USAF, 1946—47, capt. M.C., pharm. officer USAFR, 1948—63, ret. USAFR, 1982. Named Francis J. O'Brien Pharmacy Man of Yr., 1979, 2002; recipient 25 Yr. Svc. citation, ARC, 30 Yr. Svc. citation, Svc. plaque, East Greenbush Ctrl. Sch. Dist., 25 Yr. Svc. award, N.Y. State Dept. Health, Disting. Svc. citation, Rensselaer County Taxpayers Assn., established L. Sneed DeNuzzo Sch., Concord Coll., W.V. Mem.: AAUP (pres. 1978—), AARP, Albany Coll. Pharmacy Alumni Assn. (exec. dir. 1965—86, disting. svc. medal 1975), N.Y. State Pub. Employees Fedn., N.Y. Sch. Bd. Assn., N.Y. State Pharm. Soc., Am. Pharm. Assn., Am. Assn. Colls. Pharmacy (sec.-treas., coun. faculties 1979—80, chmn. elect 1982—83, chmn. 1984—87, dir. 1984—89, roundtable presentation ann. meeting 1996, del. ann. meeting 1997), USA Air Muse, 46th and 72nd Recon. Assn., Nat. Italian-Am. Found. (coun.), Officers Club (West Point, N.Y.), Albany Coll. Pharmacy Pres.'s Club (chmn. bd. 1962—87), Kappa Psi (dep. grand coun. Beta Delta chpt., sec.-treas., Albany grad.), Army Five Star, Beta Delta (ann. Rinaldo V. DeNuzzo lucnheon 1988—). Republican. Roman Catholic. Home: 19 Alva St East Greenbush NY 12061-2027 Office: 106 New Scotland Ave Albany NY 12208-3425 E-mail: reutterd@acp.com.

DENZLER, MARY JOANNE, special education, early childhood educator; b. Tacoma, Apr. 19, 1940; d. Sherman Russ and Mary Lucille (Senour) D. (dec.); divorced; children: Jeanette Deborah Hughes, John Edward Hughes III. B of Univ. Studies with honors, U. N.Mex., 1992, MA in Spl. Edn., 1995. Cert. spl. edn. tchr., N.Mex. Sec. Albuquerque Boy's Acad., 1959; co-owner Alamo Sales, Albuquerque, 1985-86; temp. jobs U. N.Mex., Albuquerque, 1986-95; with Presbyn. Ear Inst. Preschool, Albuquerque, 1995; spl. edn. tchr. Los Lunas (N.Mex.) Sch. Dist., 1995—, extended sch. year spl. edn. tchr., 1995—. Mem. St. Michael and All Angels Episcopal Ch., 1987-94, group facilitator spiritual recovery and healing for female survivors of sexual abuse; lay Eucharist min. St. Michael; lay Eucharist min., lector Cathedral Ch. St. Johns, 1994—, Soc. Mary, Altar Guild, Healing Team; Cursillo candidate Episcopal Diocese of Rio Grande, 1992, Cursillo team, 1994; lay eucharist, min. The Cathedral Ch. of St. John, 1994—; mem. Summer Harvest Healing Team, Episcopal Diocese of Rio Grande; assoc. mem. Internat. Order of St. Luke, 1997—, Friends of Religious Studies, U. N.Mex., AAUW, 1997—. Multicultural tchr. tng. prog. grad. sch. fellow U. N.Mex., 1993-95. Mem. Blue Key Nat. Honor Fraternity (life), Golden Key Nat. Honor Soc. (life). Avocations: painting, drawing, ceramics, listening to chamber music, opera. Home: 1135 1/2 Cinder Ln Los Lunas NM 87031-6510

DEPACKH, MARY FRASER CARTER, artist, retired educator; b. Arlington, Va., May 15, 1914; d. Herbert Pering and Frances Lee (Sickels) Carter; m. David Calvert dePackh, Dec. 1, 1949 (dec. Aug. 1990); 1 child, Selene Naomi. Voice instr. Washington Coll. of Music, 1936-39; pvt. voice, piano, art, theory tchr. Prin. works include bas relief sculpture Margaret Brent Meml., 1983, bas relief bust Mathias de Sousa, 1986, Capt. Sydney Sherby, 1993, statuette horse "Trespasser," 1931, Royal Acad., London, 1932. Founding mem. North End Artists, Leonardtown, Md., 1986-94; conservationist St. Mary's County LWV, So. Md., 1980-95; vol. art tchr. Prince Georges County Pub. Schs., Oxon Hill, Md., 1972-77. Recipient award Prince George's County (Md.) Sch. Bd., 1977, St. Mary's Commn. for Women, 1980's, St. Clement's Island/Potomac River Mus., 1980's, St. Mary's LWV, 1988. Mem. Music Tchrs. Nat. Assn., Pa. Music Tchrs. Assn., Prince Georges Music Tchrs. Assn. Avocation: trying to remain useful. Address: 2221 Spring St Pittsburgh PA 15210-2624

DEPAOLO, ROSEMARY, dean, academic administrator; b. Bklyn., July 17, 1947; d. Nunzio and Edith (Spano) DeP.; m. Dennis B. Smith, 1977 (div. 1983); m. T. Frederick Wharton, 1984. BA, CUNY, Flushing, 1970; MA, Rutgers U., 1974, PhD, 1979. Asst. prof. to prof., dir. Ctr. for Humanities Augusta (Ga.) Coll., 1975-90; asst. dean Coll. Arts and Sci. Ga. So. U., Statesboro, 1990-93; dean Coll. Arts and Scis. Western Carolina U., Cullowhee, N.C., 1993-97; pres. Ga. Coll. and State U., Milledgeville, 1997—2003; chancellor U. North Carolina, Wilington, NC, 2003—. Office: 601 S College Rd Wilmington NC 28403-3297*

DEPEW, MARIE KATHRYN, retired secondary school educator; b. Sterling, Colo., Dec. 1, 1928; d. Amos Carl and Dorothy Emelyn (Whiteley) Mehl; m. Emil Carlton DePew, Aug. 30, 1952 (dec. 1973). BA, U. Colo., 1950, MA, 1953. Post grad. Harvard U., Cambridge, Mass., 1962; tchr. Jefferson County Pub. Schs., Arvada, 1953-73; mgr. Colo. Accountability Program, Denver, 1973-83; sr. cons. Colo. Dept. Edn., Denver, 1973-85, ret., 1985. Author: (pamphlet) History of Hammil, Georgetown, Colorado, 1967; contbr. articles to profl. jours. Chmn. Colo. State Accountability Com., Denver, 1971-75. Fellow IDEA Programs, 1976-77, 79-81. Mem. Colo. Hist. Assn., Jefferson County Edn. Assn. (pres. 1963-64), Colo. Edn. Assn. (bd. dirs. 1965-70), Ky. Colonels (hon. mem.), Phi Beta Kappa. Republican. Methodist. Avocations: historical research, writing, travel, collecting antiques. Home: 920 Pennsylvania St Denver CO 80203-3157

DERE, WILLARD HONGLEN, internist, educator; b. Sacramento, Jan. 8, 1954; s. William Janson and Bessie Lon (Joe) D.; m. Julia Mei Lum, June 18, 1978; children: Melissa Ellen, Kathryn Elizabeth. AB, U. Calif., Davis, 1975, MD, 1980. Intern Health Sci. Ctr., U. Utah, Salt Lake City, 1980-81, resident, 1981-83; instr. internal medicine, geriatrics U. Utah, Salt Lake City, 1985-87, asst. prof., 1987-89; rsch. fellow U. Calif., San Francisco, 1983-85; asst. prof. Ind. U. Sch Medicine, Indpls., 1989-98; clin. assoc. prof. Ind. U. Sch. Medicine, Indpls., 1998—; clin. rsch. physician Lilly Rsch. Labs., Indpls., 1989-91, dir. European regulatory affairs, 1991-94, dir. endocrine rsch., 1994-98, exec. dir. global clin. rsch., 1998-2001, v.p. gen. medicine, 2002—. Dir. emergency rm. VA Med. Ctr., Salt Lake City, 1985-86; cons. U. Utah Student Health Svc., Salt Lake City, 1985-89, acting dir., 1987-88. Editor: Practical Care of the Ambulatory Patient, 1989; Contbr. articles to profl. jour. Hon. assoc. investigator VA, San Francisco, 1984. Mem. ACP, AAAS, Am. Soc. Bone and Mineral Rsch., Assn. Osteobiology. Presbyterian. Achievements include rsch. in adrenocortical function in AIDS, oncogene regulation in thyroid cells, multi-center antibiotic trials, drug safety, health economics, selective estrogen receptor modulators, osteoporosis. Office: Lilly Corp Ctr Lilly Rsch Labs Ctr Indianapolis IN 46285-0001 E-mail: wdere@lilly.com.

DERENZO, STEPHEN E. physics educator, research scientist; b. Chgo., Dec. 31, 1941; married, 1966; 2 children. BS in Physics, U. Chgo., 1963, MS in Physics, 1965, PhD in Physics, 1968. Rsch. asst. Enrico Fermi Inst. U. Chgo., 1964-68; physicist Lawrence Berkeley Lab. U. Calif., Berkeley, 1968-82, lectr. dept. physics, 1969-70, lectr. dept. elec. engring. and computer sci., 1979-87, sr. scientist Lawrence Berkeley Lab., 1982—, prof.-in-residence, 1988—. Grant application reviewer U.S. Dept. Energy, U.S. Nat. Insts. Health; co-chmn. Internat. Workshop on Bismuth Germanate, Princeton U., 1982; active numerous coms. Lawrence Berkeley Lab., U. Calif., mem. recreation adv. panel, 1984-87, mem. computer svc. adv. panel, 1985-88, quality assurance coord. bio-med divsn., 1986-88, asst. dir. rsch. medicine and radiation biophysics divsn., 1990-92, safety coord. rsch. medicine and radiation biophysics divsn., 1991-92, mem. mgmt. integration group, 1990—, authorized reviewer, quality assurance rep., environ. safety and health coord., and asst. dep. life scis. divsn., 1992—. Reviewer Jour. Cerebral Blood Flow and Metabolism, Physics in Medicine and Biology, Jour. Computer Assisted Tomography. Recipient Tech. Brief award NASA, 1973; grantee NIH, 1973—, IBM, 1986, U.S. Nat. Insts. Health, 1989—; ANL fellow Associated Midwest Univs., 1965-66, Shell Found. fellow, 1967-68; Ill. State scholar, 1959-62, U. Chgo. scholar, 1961-63. Mem. IEEE (sr., reviewer Transactions on Nuclear Sci., guest editor 1989, chair med. imaging conf. 1991, fellow award, radiation intrumentation achievement award, 01), Nuclear and Plasma Scis. Soc. of IEEE (mem. tech. com. on nuclear med. sci. 1983—, chair 1988-91, mem. adminstrv. com. 1988-91, Merit award 1992), Am. Phys. Soc., Materials Rsch. Soc. Avocations: long distance running, photography, astronomy. Office: U Calif Lawrence Berkeley Lab Berkeley CA 94720-0001

DERESIEWICZ, HERBERT, mechanical engineering educator; b. Brno, Czechoslovakia, Nov. 5, 1925; s. William and Lotte (Rappaport) D.; m. Evelyn Altman, Mar. 12, 1955; children: Ellen, Robert, William. BME, CCNY, 1946; MS, Columbia U., 1948, PhD, 1952. Sr. staff engr. Applied Physics Lab., Johns Hopkins U., 1950-51; mem. faculty Columbia U., N.Y.C., 1951—, prof. mech. engring., 1962-94, chmn. dept. mech. engring., 1981-87, 90-93, emeritus, 1994—. Cons. stress analysis, vibrations, elastic contact, wave propagation, mechanics of granular and porous media., Fulbright sr. research scholar, Italy, 1960-61, Fulbright lectr., Israel, 1966-67; vis. prof., Israel, 1973-74. Editor Columbia Engring. Rsch., 1975-92; contbr. articles to profl. jours. Served with AUS, 1946-47. Univ. fellow Columbia U., 1949-50. Home: 336 Broad Ave Englewood NJ 07631-4304

DERGALIS, GEORGE, artist, educator; b. Athens, Greece, Aug. 31, 1928; s. Demetrios and Zina Dergalis; m. Margaret Murphey; 1 child by previous marriage, Alexis. MFA, Acad. Belle Arti, Rome, 1951; diploma, Boston Museum Sch., 1956-59. Instr. Boston Mus. Sch., 1961-69, De Cordova Mus., Lincoln, Mass., 1961-94; pvt. instrn. Wayland, Mass., 1969—; chmn., curator Festival Bostonians for Art and Humanity, 1976; chmn. curator prisom art Inst. Contemporary Art Boston, 1975-76; artist-in-residence Ptnrs. of Ams., Colombia, 1979; lectr. Helicon, Harvard U., 1981; juror Once is Not Enough, Cambridge Art Assn., 1994. One-man shows include Woodstock Gallery, London, 1974, Cámera de Comercio de Medellin, Columbia, 1980, Galesburg (Ill) Civic Art Ctr., 1985, Hotel Meridien, Boston, 1987, Wayland Art/Space, 1994; exhibited in group shows Danforth Mus., Framingham, Mass., 1988-90, Mus. Fine Arts, Boston, 1989 (Merit award), Boston Pub. Libr., 1994-95, South Shore Art Ctr., 1994, Boston Corp. Art, 1995—, Indpls. Art Ctr., 2000-01, Mass. State House and Commonwealth Mus., Boston, 2000, Springfield Art Mus., 2002, Foothills Art Ctr., 2003others; represented in permanent collections at Loomis and Sayles, Boston, Scudder, Stevens and Clark, Boston, Novartis, Hale & Dorr, Boston, Decordova Mus. Lincoln, Mass., Alliance Capital Mgmt., N.Y., Museo de Zea, Colombia, U.S. Army Ctr. Mil. History, Washington, also pvt. collections; book It's All in Your Head, 1991, Rocky Mountain NH Watermedia Exhbn., Foothills Art Ctr., Golden Co., 2003, Author, Art of War, 2002. Trustee, Graham Jr. Coll., 1971; hon. dir. Boston Ballet, 1971. With USAF, 1951-54. William Paige scholar, 1959; recipient Prix de Rome, 1951, Civilian merit award U.S. Army Hist. Soc., 1969, Gold medal Accademia Italia delle Arte, 1980, Merit award Mus. of Fine Arts, 1989, Best of Show award Commonwealth of Mass., 2000, Juror's award Watercolor USA, 2002. Mem. Internat. Sculpture Assn., Internat. Sculpture Ctr., Alumni Assn. Boston Mus. Sch. (pres., 1966-67), Copley Soc. Boston (v.p., art chmn. 1978, Excellence in Technique award 1978), DeCordova Mus. Corp. Prgm. Home: 72 Oxbow Rd Wayland MA 01778-1009

DERMAN, CYRUS, mathematical statistician; b. Phila., July 16, 1925; s. Samuel and Bessie (Segal) D.; Martha Winn, Feb. 24, 1961; children: Adam Jason Winn (dec.), Hester Beth Rebecca. AB, U. Penn., 1948, A.M., 1949; PhD, Columbia U., NYC., 1954. Instr. Syracuse U., Syracuse, NY, 1954-55; faculty Columbia U., NYC, 1955—, prof. ops. rsch. NYC., 1965-94; prof. emeritus, 1994. Vis. prof. Israel Inst. Tech., Haifa, 1961-62, Stanford, 1965-66; vis. prof. U. Calf., Davis, 1975-76, U. Calif., Berkeley, 1979 Author: (with Morton Klein) Probability and Statistical Inference for

Engineers, 1959, Finite State Markovian Decision Processes, 1970, (with Leon Gleser and Ingram Olkin) A Guide to Probability Theory and Application, 1973, Probability Models and Applications, 1980, 2d edit., 1994, (with Sheldon Ross) Statistical Aspects of Quality Control, 1996. With U.S. Navy, 1943-46. Recipient John von Neumann Theory prize, INFORMS, 2002. Fellow Inst. Math. Statistics, Am. Statis. Assn. Achievements include research and publs. on theory of Markov chains, Brownian motion, statis. inference, mgmt. sci. and ops. research. Home: 15 Pond Hill Rd Chappaqua NY 10514-2531 Office: Columbia U Mudd Bldg New York NY 10027

DERNOVICH, DONALD FREDERICK, artist, educator; b. Rock Springs, Wyo., Apr. 9, 1942; s. Frank Donald and Francis Irene (Paternel) D.; m. Kathy Joan Fornengo, Aug. 1, 1970; children: Heath, Jessica, Kaitlyn. BA, U. Wyo., 1966, MA, 1967; MFA, Ft. Hays State U., 1983. Artist, illustrator U.S. Army, Ft. George G. Meade, 1967-69; comml. artist Penny Pincher Advtg., Grand Junction, Colo., 1969-70; art tchr. Decatur County Jr. H.S., Oberlin, Kans., 1970-74; tchr., head art dept. McCook (Nebr.) C.C., 1974—. Bd. dirs. Assn. Nebr. Arts Clubs, 1986-90; juror art exhbns., 1980—; guest artist Wyo. Art Assn. annual conv., 1995. Artist: (watercolors) Splash Four, 1996, Splash Five, 1998 (Best of Watercolor, 1997-99); featured in publs. including Am. Artist Mag. Hon. life mem. McCook Arts Coun., 1976—. Work judged in top 100 Arts for the Parks, Jackson Hole, Wyo., 1994, 98, top 200, 1995, 99, 2000, 01, Best Watercolor award Western Spirits Art Show, Cheyenne, Wyo., 1994, 96, 98; 1st Place Oil Painting, Phippen Mus. Western Art Show, 2002; quick draw artist C.M. Russell Art Auction, Great Falls, Mont., 1997, 98, 99, 2000, 01, 03. Mem. Nat. Watercolor Soc., Kans. Watercolor Soc., Assoc. Am. Watercolor Soc. (assoc.), Oil Painters Am. Democrat. Roman Catholic. Avocations: fly fishing, travel, gallery hopping. Home: 210 Taylor PO Box 163 Culbertson NE 69024-0163 Office: McCook Community College 1205 E 3rd St Mc Cook NE 69001-2631

DE ROE DEVON, The Marchioness See GERRINGER, ELIZABETH

DEROO, SALLY ANN, biology, geology and environmental science educator; BS, Eastern Mich. U., 1958; postgrad., 1958-63; MA, U. Mich., 1961, postgrad., 1963—93, Wayne State U., 1964-68, Ohio State U., 1995—, U. So. Calif., Berkley, 1996. Cert. elem. tchr., middle level, all subjects K-8; cert. high sch. level environ. scis., social studies, English, econs. 9-12; cert. tchr. mentally handicapped and emotionally impaired K-12; cert. Master Gardener, Mich. State U., 1997. Asst. prof. sci. Ea. Mich. U., Ypsilanti, 1958-63, asst. prof. biology and geology, 1968—2003, tchr. spl. edn., 1989—2003; tchr. sci. and geology Plymouth-Canton Cmty. Schs., 1963-95; curriculum specialist Ctrl. Mich. U., 1989-90; instr. dept. tchr. edn. Mich. State U., 1994-95; instr. sci. edn. Madonna U., asst. prof., mem. staff student tchr. edn. Dept. Edn., 1992—2003. Asst. prof., mem. staff student tchr. edn. Dept. Edn. Madonna U.; advisor Salem H.S., 1990-95, Wayne State U., Detroit, 1995—, Pitts. State U., Kans. at Greenbush, 1995-97, Oakland U. Sci. Edn., 1997-2003; ednl. cons. Scholastic, Inc., 1996-2000; sci./ednl. cons. DTE Energy, Detroit, 1998-2000; cons. Carolina Biol., 2000—; mem. satellite conf. Tchrs. Making a Difference, 1990; mem. support team Sci. Teaching Edn. STEP adv. bd. Madonna U., Livonia, Mich.; mem. math. and sci. challenge grant design com. Wayne County, 1991; adv. bd. SEMSplus Mich. Envirothon, steering com. Nat. Envirothon, 1996-2003; mem. adv. com., issues author sci. curriculum support guides Mich. Dept. Edn., 1989-90; mem. adv. coun. Mich. Dept. Edn.; mem. Mich. curriculum frameworks joint steering com., 1992-2002, mem. writing com. H.S. proficiency exam., 1993, 94, 95—, mem. adv. com. H.S. sci. proficiency test, 1993, 94, 95-96; dist. commr. Wayne County Soil Dist. USDA, 1996-2000; mem. citizens adv. com. Stockbridge Township, Mich., 2000—; project chair Project Cattail, Tchrs. and Students Making an Environ. Difference, 1992—; project dir. Gt. Lakes-Thunderbay Gt. Lakes Basin Work Shop, Alpena, Mich., 1990-93; cons. Detroit Edison (DTE) Solar Currents curricula, 1997—; Carolina biol. Sci. and Tech. for Children cons., Burlington, N.C.; sci. cons. Houghton Mifflin, Geneva, Ill., 1999—; cons. Carolina-Internat., 1999, Houghton Mifflin, Co., 2000-02; mem. ednl. planning com. Detroit Zool. Inst., 2000; facilitator numerous workshops; presenter in field. Author: (newsletter) Fledgeling, 1990-2003, (tchg. manuals) Exploring Our Environment; contbg. writer Detroit Free Press sci. page; contbr. articles to sci. mags.; writer, dir. 26-week sci. TV series Explore with Me; sci. editor Ann Arbor Pubs., 1968-86; elem. publ. editor Mich. Sci. Tchrs.; adv. (tv waste mgmt. series) Neuton's Apple. Active Rouge River Restoration, 1988—, Friends of Matthaei Bot. Gardens Ann. Flower Show; established Model Adopt-a-Stream Project "River Watch" for Rough River Water Shed, 1994; planning asst. Cobo Ctr. 1st Annual Detroit Bloomfest, 1999—. Recipient Outstanding Educator award Mich. Jaycees, 1963, Best of West Edn. award, 1984, Outstanding Svc. Recognition award Mich. Assn. Mid. Sch. Educators, 1989, 90, Gov.'s citation State of Mich., 1990, 91, Tchr. of Yr. Program award IBM, 1990, Can Doers award Mich. Tech. Coun., 1993, Recognition of Support and Dedication dept. natural resources Builder's Assn. Southeastern Mich., 1990, 91, 92, Land Preservation Recognition award Southeastern Mich. Land Conservancy, 2002; named Outstanding Sci. Educator, Metro Detroit Sci. Tchrs. Assn., 1994; listed in Guinness Book of Records 1990-95 for snail racing. Mem. NEA, Nat. Sci. Tchrs. Assn. (presenter, local leader, chair publicity regional conf. 1999), Mich. Sci. Tchrs. Assn. (dir.-at-large, chair outreach conf., Outstanding Svc. award 1997, Disting. Svc. award 1998), Nat. Mid. Level Sci. Tchrs. Assn. (treas. 1998-2000, dir. publicity-promotions 2001—), Nat. Resource Def. Coun., Mich. Sci. Leaders Assn. (bd. dirs.), Mich. Dept. Edn., Sci. Curriculum Devel. Assn. (mid. sch. goal-based curriculum), Wayne County Task Force (intermediate sch. dist. writing team 1989, bd. dirs.), Mich. Alliance for Outdoor Edn., Detroit Zool. Inst., Internat. Joint Commn. (Gt. Lakes), Mich. Reading Assn. (sci. conf. chairperson 1992—), Citizens Adv. Com., Phi Delta Kappa (editor newsletter U. Mich. chpt.). Address: Wayne State U Dept Edn Gullen Ct Detroit MI 48202

DE ROQUE, BARBARA PENBERTHY, special education educator, consultant; b. Alameda, Calif., July 20, 1927; d. Cecil Albert and Constance (Maimone) Penberthy; m. Earl H. de Roque, June 23, 1950 (dec. Mar. 1989); children: Kathleen Fowler, Michael, Lisa, Richard, Tom, Jim. BA in Speech, U. Calif., Berkeley, 1949; MEd in Spl. Edn., Coll. of the Holy Names, 1979; EdD in Spl. Edn., Lincoln U., 1986. Tchr. Alameda Unified Sch. Dist., 1949-51; tchr. Lafayette (Calif.) Sch. Dist., 1965-66, Sch. of Santa Maria, Orinda, Calif., 1966-74, St. Joseph's Sch., Fremont, Calif., 1974-79; reading cons. Ohlone Coll., Fremont, 1976-77, Coll. of the Holy Names, Oakland, 1979-80; spl. edn. tchr. Fremont Unified Sch. Dist., 1979—; substitute asst. prin., spl. edn. dept. head Horner Jr. H.S., Fremont, 1986—, site coun. cons., student study team. Mentor tchr. Fremont Unified Sch. Dist., 1992—, chmn. spl. edn. curriculum com.; bd. dirs. Holy Rosary Coll., 1974-78; chmn. spl. edn. dept. Horner Jr. H.S., 1981—; peer cons. San Jose State U., 1990-91; mem. Bay Area Writing Project, U. Calif., Berkeley, 1989-91; mem. Spl. Edn. Task Force Program; quality rev. team Fremont Unified Sch. Dist., lead reviewer, 1991-92, site coun. cons., 1992—, state trainer for Alameda County Consortium, 1993—; cons. to Middle Schs. for Program Quality Rev. Team. Commr. Fremont Library, 1975-77; mem., v.p. St. Joseph's Sch. Bd., Fremont, 1979-82; chmn. Cedar Jr. Br. Children's Hosp., Oakland, 1969-71. Mem. NEA, ASCD, Calif. Tchrs. Assn., Coun. Exceptional Children, Assn. of Adults and Children with Learning Disabilities, Assn. Ednl. Therapists, U. Calif. Berkeley Alumni Assn., Alpha Delta Pi Alumni Assn. Avocations: golfing, reading, dancing, walking, computers, music. Home: 5910 Horsemans Canyon Dr Apt 2B Walnut Creek CA 94595-3901 Office: Horner Jr High Sch 41365 Chapel Way Fremont CA 94538-4299

DE ROSE, SANDRA MICHELE, psychotherapist, educator, supervisor, administrator; b. Beacon, N.Y. d. Michael Joseph Borrell and Mabel Adelaide Edic Sloane; m. James Joseph De Rose, June 28, 1964 (div. 1977); children: Stacey Marie, Harrison Marquisa. Diploma in nursing, St. Luke's Hosp., 1964; BA in Child and Cmty. Psychology, Albertus Magnus Coll., 1983; MS in Counseling Psychology with honors, Century U., 1986, PhD in Counseling Psychology with honors, 1987. Gen. duty float nurse St. Luke's Hosp., Newburgh, N.Y., 1964-65; pvt. practice New Haven, 1975—; supr. nurses Craig House Hosp., Beacon, N.Y., 1986-94; dir. staff devel., team dir. divsn. outpatient treatment svc. Conn. Mental Health Ctr., New Haven, 1986-94; dir. edn., 1994-95; clin. instr. Sch. Nursing Yale U., New Haven, 1979-84, clin. instr. dept. psychiatry, 1989-96; dir. edn. outpatient divsn. Conn. Mental Health Ctr., New Haven, 1994-95. Clin. dir. Comprehensive Psychiat. Care, Norwich, Colchester and Willimantic, Conn., 1994-96; group practice Comprehensive Psychiat. Care, Norwich, Conn., 1995-2003, Alternative Paths, Yalesville, Conn., 1995-97. Mem. AAUW, ANA (cert.), Conn. Nurses Assn., Conn. Soc. Nurse Psychotherapists, Assn. for Advancement Philosophy and Psychiatry, New Haven C. of C., Sigma Theta Tau, Delta Mu, Alpha Sigma Lambda. Avocations: music, theater, antiques, interior design/architecture, traveling. Office: 5210 Prospect St New Haven CT 06511-2186

DERR, JEANNIE COMBS, bilingual educator, anthropology educator; b. L.A., May 17, 1954; d. Jack Vincent and Evelyn Mary (Weiss) Combs; m. Dennis Eugene Derr, Aug. 6, 1983; children: Natalie Winona, Jeremy Lloyd. AA in Anthropology, Pasadena City Coll., 1975; BA in Anthropology, Calif. State U., L.A., 1978, MA in Anthropology, 1979. Calif. C.C. credential anthropology; Calif. multiple subjects credential. Textbook adoptions western region corr. Bowmar Noble Pubs., Inc., Glendale, Calif., 1979-80; bilingual tchr. Pasadena (Calif.) Unified Sch. Dist., 1981-82; exch. tchr. bilingual L'ecole Aujourd'hui, Paris, 1982-83; migrant edn., bilingual tchr. Oxnard (Calif.) Sch. Dist., 1983—; instr. anthropology Oxnard Coll., 1989—; instr. humanities St. John's Seminary Coll., Camarillo, Calif., 1990—; instr. ethnic rels. U. LaVerne, Pt. Mugu, Calif., 1995—. Editor (resource booklet) Oxnard Migrant Education, 1987. Violinist Jr. Philharm. Orch. Calif., L.A., 1967—, Opus 1 Chamber Orch., L.A., 1976-79; soprano, officer San Marino (Calif.) Cmty. Ch., 1974-83. Mem. AAUW, Am. Mexican Am. Educators, Am. Soc. Anthropology, Soc. Am. Archeology, Soc. for the Study Evolution. Republican. Presbyterian. Avocations: music, travel, archeology, hiking, bicycling. Home: 1650 Shoreline Dr Camarillo CA 93010-6016

DERRICKSON, DENISE ANN, secondary school educator, educator; b. Seaford, Del., Sept. 20, 1956; d. William Hudson and Patricia Ann (Adkins) D. BS, James Madison U., 1978; MEd in Counseling and Human Devel., George Mason U., 1990, MEd in Curriculum & Instrn., 1994. Social studies instr. Brentsville Dist. High Sch., Nokesville, Va., 1978-91, Woodbridge (Va.) Sr. High Sch., 1991-99. Faculty liaison Parent-Tchr. Action Coun., 1990-91; prin.'s adv. coun., 1994-96. Vol. Childrens Hosp., Washington, 1983-86, Action in the Community through Svc., Inc.-Helpline, Manassas, Va., 1988-92. Recipient Cert. Appreciation Prince William County Sch. Bd., 1989, Outstanding Educator award Va. Govs. Sch., 1990, ACTS-Helpline Outstanding Vol. Svc. award, 1990; presented with U.S. Flag Armed Svcs. Hall of Honor at the dedication of the U.S. Women's Meml., 1998. Mem. NEA, AAUW, ASCD, VFW, Am. Assn. Curriculum Devel., Nat. Soc. for Study of Edn., Va. Edn. Assn., Va. Assn. Supervision and Curriculum Devel., Prince William Edn. Assn., Internat. Platform Assn., Kappa Delta Phi, Phi Delta Kappa. Avocations: sewing, crafts, travel.

DERRICKSON, SHIRLEY JEAN BALDWIN, elementary school educator; b. Balt., Aug. 7, 1943; d. James Francis and Dorothy Elizabeth (Jubb) Baldwin; m. Ernest Hughes Derrickson, Aug. 19, 1978. BA, Knox Coll., 1965; MEd, Goucher Coll., 1969; postgrad., Towson State U., 1970-77. Cert. profl. status elem. tchr., Del. Tchr. Howard Park Elem. Sch., Balt., 1969-70, Lida Lee Tall Learning Resource Ctr., Towson (Md.) State U., 1970-83, Selbyville (Del.) Mid. Sch., 1983-84, East Millsboro (Del.) Elem. Sch., 1984—, lead tchr. in sci., 1995—. Fgn. affairs chmn. Dagsboro (Del.) Century Club, 1990-96, sec., 1986-88; sec. Dagsboro Rep. Club, 1986-88; active Friends of Prince George's Chapel, 1994—, Del. Sr. Olympics, 1998-2002, Nat. Sr. Olympics, 1999. Recipient Washington Regional scholarship, 1961-64. Mem. NEA, Del. State Edn. Assn., Indian River Edn. Assn., PTO, Grace United Meth. Ch. Republican. Methodist. Avocations: canoeing, sailing, golf, tennis, volleyball. Office: East Millsboro Elem Sch 500 E State St Millsboro DE 19966-1199

DERSHOWITZ, ALAN MORTON, lawyer, educator; b. Bklyn., Sept. 1, 1938; s. Harry Dershowitz and Claire Dershowotz; m. Carolyn Cohen; children: Elon Marc, Jamin Seth, Ella Kaille Cohen Dershowitz. BA magna cum laude, Bklyn. Coll., 1959, LLD, 2001; LLB magna cum laude, Yale U., 1962; MA (hon.), Harvard Coll., 1967; LLD (hon.), Yeshiva U., 1989; PhD (hon.), Haifa U., 1993; LLD (hon.), Syracuse U., 1997, Hebrew Union Coll., Monmouth Coll., Bklyn. Coll., 2001. Bar: D.C. 1963, Mass. 1968, U.S. Supreme Ct. 1968. Law clk. to chief judge David L. Bazelon, U.S. Ct. Appeals, 1962—63; to justice Arthur J. Goldberg, U.S. Supreme Ct., 1963—64; mem. faculty Harvard Law Sch., 1964—, prof. law, 1967—, Felix Frankfurter Prof. of Law, 1993—; fellow Ctr. for Advanced Study of Behavioral Scis., 1971—72. Cons. to dir. NIMH, 1967—69, Pres.'s Commn. Civil Disorders, 1967, Pres.'s Com. Causes Violence, 1968, NAACP Legal Def. Fund, 1967—68, NIMH's Pres.'s Commn. Marijuana and Drug Abuse, 1972—73, Coun. on Drug Abuse, 1972—, Ford Found. Study on Law and Justice, 1973—76; rapporteur Twentieth Century Fund Study on Sentencing, 1975—76. Author (with others): Psychoanalysis, Psychiatry and the Law, 1967, Criminal Law: Theory and Process, 1974, The Best Defense, 1982, Reversal of Fortune: Inside the von Bulow Case, 1986, Taking Liberties: a Decade of Hard Cases, Bad Laws and Bum Raps, 1988, Chutzpah, 1991, Contrary to Popular Opinion, 1992, The Abuse Excuse, 1994, The Advocate's Devil, 1994, Reasonable Doubts, The Vanishing American Jew, 1997, Sexual McCarthyism: Clinton, Starr and the Emerging Constitutional Crisis, 1998, Just Revenge, 1999, The Genesis of Justice, 2000, Supreme Injustice, 2001, Letters to a Young Lawyer, 2001, Shouting Fire, 2002; contbr. articles to profl. jours., with others: America Declares Independence, 2003, with others: America Declares Independence, 2003; editor-in-chief: Yale Law Jour., 1961—62. Chmn. civil rights com. New England region Anti-Defamation League, B'nai B'rith, 1980—85; bd. dirs. ACLU, 1968—71, 1972—75, Assembly Behavioral and Social Scis. at NAS, 1973—76. Fellow Guggenheim, 1978—79. Mem.: Order of Coif, Phi Beta Kappa. Jewish. Office: Harvard Law Sch 1575 Massachusetts Ave Cambridge MA 02138-2801

DE SA E SILVA, ELIZABETH ANNE, secondary school educator; b. Edmonds, Wash., Mar. 17, 1931; d. Sven Yngve and Anna Laura Elizabeth (Dahlin) Erlandson; m. Claudio de Sá e Silva, Sept. 12, 1955 (div. July 1977); children: Lydia, Marco, Nelson. BA, U. Oreg., 1953; postgrad., Columbia U., 1954-56, Calif. State U., Fresno, 1990, U. No. Iowa, 1993; MEd, Mont. State U., 1978. Cert. tchr. Oreg., Mont. Med. sec., 1947-49; sec. Merced (Calif.) Sch. Dist., 1950-51; sec., asst. Simon and Schuster, Inc., N.Y.C., 1954-56; tchr. Casa Roosevelt-União Cultural, São Paulo, Brazil, 1957-59, Coquille (Oreg.) Sch. Dist., 1978-96; music tchr. Cartwheels Presch., North Bend, Oreg., 1997—99, 2001. Tchr. piano, 1967—78; instr. Spanish Southwestern Oreg. C.C., Coos Bay, 1991—94; pianist/organist Faith Luth. Ch., North Bend, Oreg., 1995—2002, New Life Luth. Ch., Florence, Oreg., 2002—; vocal soloist, 1996—; voice tchr., 1997—99. Chmn. publicity Music in Our Schs. Month, Oreg. Dist. VII, 1980-85; sec. Newcomer's Club, Bozeman, Mont., 1971. Quincentennial fellow U. Minn. and Found. José Ortega y Gasset, Madrid, 1991. Mem. AAUW (sec., scholarship chmn., co-pres., pres., treas., editor newsletter), Nat. Trust Hist. Preservation, Am. Coun. on Tchg. Fgn. Langs., Am. Assn. Tchrs. Spanish and Portuguese, Nat. Coun. Tchrs. English, Music Educators Nat. Conf., Oreg. Music Educators Assn., Oreg. Coun. Tchrs. English, Confedn. Oreg. Fgn. Lang. Tchrs., VoiceCare Network. Democrat. Avocations: swimming, walking, travel, drama. Home: PO Box 1807 Florence OR 97439

DE SALVO, LORRAINE CONSTANCE, academic administrator; b. June 15, 1950; d. William Joseph and Elizabeth Agnes De S. BS, U. Md., 1972. Cert. paralegal. Personnel officer, classification analyst U. Md., College Park, 1974-75, asst. employment mgr., 1975-76, asst. benefits officer, 1976-77, asst. employment mgr., 1977-78, dir. adminstrv. svcs. dept. physics, 1978—. Mem. space com. Coll. Comuter, Math., and Phys. Scis., 1992—. Mem. Shih Tzu Fanciers Greater Balt., Alumni Assn U. Md., Alpha Xi Delta Alumnae. Office: U Md Dept Physics College Park MD 20742-4111 E-mail: desalvo@physics.umd.edu.

DESANDO, JOHN ANTHONY, retired humanities educator; b. Rochester, N.Y., Sept. 23, 1940; s. Carl James and Marie Louise (Notebaert) DeSando; children: Erik, Courtney, Rachel, Jessica, Thea, Gabrielle. BA, Georgetown U., 1962; MA, PhD, U. Ariz., 1972. Asst. prof. English Norwich U., Northfield, Vt., 1967-74; dir. student activities U. Mass., Boston, 1975-77; dean of students U. Maine, Fort Kent, 1978-79; v.p. acad. affairs Franklin U., Columbus, Ohio, 1980—2002, prof. humanities; ret., 2002. Critic TV program World Film Classics TV series, Columbus, 1990—2003; vice chmn. Film Coun. Greater Columbus, 2000—02; bd. dirs. Spillman Co.; co-host It's Movie Time, WCBE-FM, 2001—. Assoc. editor: Movies on Media Handbook, 1994—; cinema series host Columbus Mus. Art; prodr.: (TV series) World Film Classics, 1998; co-host It's Movie Time, 2001—. Chair humanities divsn. Columbus Internat. Film Festival, 1994—2001; tech. advisor Ohio Humanities Coun., 1995—2001. Recipient Communicator award of Excellence, 2002, Silver Microphone award, 2003. Mem.: MLA, Nat. Coun. Tchrs. English, Nat. Euchre Players Assn. (bd. dirs. 1982—, bd. dirs. literacy coun. 1997—99), Ohio State U. Photography and Cinema Alumni Soc. (bd. dirs. 1997—), Kiwanis (pres. 1994—95). E-mail: desandoj@franklin.edu.

DE SANTIS, VINCENT PAUL, historian, educator; b. Birdsboro, Pa., Dec. 25, 1916; s. Antonio and Martha Mae (Templin) DeS.; m. Helene O'Brien, June 24, 1946; children— Vincent, Edmund, Philip, John; m. Margaret Lois Lambert, May 13, 1978. BS, West Chester U., Pa., 1941; PhD, Johns Hopkins, 1952. Mem. faculty U. Notre Dame, 1949—, prof. history, 1962—, chmn. dept., 1963-71. Vis. prof. Johns Hopkins, 1954, Bklyn. Coll., 1961, Georgetown U., 1962, U. Genoa, 1967-68, U. Queensland, Australia, 1976, 79, 88, U. Victoria, Can., 1986, 88-90. Author: Republicans Face the Southern Question, 1959, The Shaping of Modern America, 1877-1916, 1973, 2nd edit., 1977, Gilded Age Presidents, 1979, President Carter and Human Rights, 1982, The Shaping of Modern America, 1877-1920, 1989, 3rd edit., 2000; co-author: Our Country, 1960, Roman Catholicism and the American Way of Life, 1960, America's Ten Greatest Presidents, 1961, The Democratic Experience, 1963, 68, 73, 76, 81, The Gilded Age, 1968, America Past and Present, 1968, American Foreign Policy in Europe, 1969, America's Eleven Greatest Presidents, 1971, Six Presidents from the Empire State, 1974, The Heritage of 1776, 1976, The Impact of the Cold War, Reconsiderations, 1977, A History of United States Foreign Policy, 4th edit, 1980, Region, Race and Reconstruction, 1982, Popular Images of American Presidents, 1988, The American Presidents, 2000; compiler The Gilded Age, 1973; editor Forum Press Series in American History. Mem. Cath. Commn. on Intellectual and Cultural Affairs. Served to capt. AUS, 1941-45. Recipient R.D.W. Connor award N.C. Lit. and Hist. Assn., 1959, award Am. Philos. Soc., 1955, 62, 63, Disting. Alumni award West Chester State Coll., 1970; Guggenheim fellow, 1960-61; Fulbright lectr., 1967-68, 79, 91-92; Henry E. Huntington grantee, 1973; Radcliffe Coll. grantee, 1982 Mem. Orgn. Am. Historians, Nat. Geog. Soc., Soc. Am. Historians, Am. Cath. Hist. Assn. (pres. 1963-64), Am. Hist. Assn., Soc. for History Edn., Soc. for Historians of Am. Fgn. Rels., So. Hist. Assn., Am. Studies Assn., AAUP, Nat. Audubon Soc., Edward Frederick Sorin Soc., No. Ind. Hist. Soc., Phi Alpha Theta. Home: PO Box 562 Notre Dame IN 46556-0562

DE SANTO, DONALD JAMES, psychologist, educational administrator; b. Bklyn., July 5, 1942; s. Vincent James and Rose Ann (Dowd) DeS.; m. Loretta DePippo, Aug. 25, 1962; children: Dolores, Jennifer, Marisa. BA cum laude, St. Francis Coll., N.Y., 1964; MA in Clin./Child Psychology, St. John's U., 1966; profl. diploma, 1976; hon. degree, Oglala Lakota Coll., 1999. Asst. law libr. rsch. asst. Dewey, Ballantine, Bushby, Palmer & Wood, N.Y.C., 1960-64; rsch. asst. St. John's U., N.Y.C., 1964-65, tchg. fellow, 1965-66; project dir. 2 federally funded grants, 1975-76; dir. The Rugby Sch., Freehold, N.J., 1977—. People to People amb. to Cuba, 2001. Contbg. editor Channels jour. spl. educators, 1986-90, 96—. Mem. Nat. Trust Historic Preservation; mem. Youth Guidance; mem. Youth Guidance Com., Freehold, 1983—, chmn. econ. devel. com., 1984-86; mem. Econ. Devel. Com., Freehold, 1983-87; mem. Zoning Bd Adjustment, Freehold, 1985-86; commr. Lake Topanemus Commn., 1990-94; Rep. campaign chmn., Freehold, 1990, 91; bd. dirs. Monmouth County Transp. Assn., 1990, 91-92; mem. U.S. Selective Svc. Bd., 1991—; apptd. Selective Svc. Commn., 1992; v.p. Freehold Rep. Club, 1991-92; mem. adv. bd. Congl. Awards Com., 1994-98; mcpl. chmn. Freehold Borough Rep. Party, 1995; appt. Rep. Nat. Com., 1995; participant, amb. People to People, Beijing, 1995, Cuba, 2000; mem. exec. bd. Monmouth County Mental Health Assn. Recipient Fire Prevention medal, N.Y.C., 1954, citation for outstanding contbn. to arts in edn. N.J. Commr. Edn., 1981, Pres. award Assn. Schs. and Agys. for the Handicapped, 1995-96, N.J. Very Spl. Arts award, 1996, N.J. Gov.'s Arts in Edn. award, 1996; Title VIb Fed. grantee, 1972-78. Mem. NRA (life), APA (pub. rels. com. div. 16), Nat. Assn. Pvt. Schs. Exceptional Children, Coun. Exceptional Children, N.J. Assn. Schs. and Agys. for Handicapped (sec., conf. chmn. 1983-84, pub. rels. chmn. 1984-86, Pres. award 1995-96, Legacy of Caring award 2002), Nat. Soc. Psychologists in Mgmt., Assn. for Help Retarded Children, Monmouth County Hist. Assn., N.J. Assn. Children With Learning Disabilities, Nat. Assn. Pvt. Schs. Exceptional Children, Optimists, Monmouth County Mental Health Assn. (bd. dirs.), Elks, Nat. Assn. Sch. Psychologists, Psi Chi, Phi Delta Kappa. Roman Catholic. Home: 222 Park Ave Freehold NJ 07728-2006 Office: care Rugby Sch at Woodfield PO Box 1403 Belmar NJ 07719-1403 E-mail: Poppled@aol.com.

DESAULNIERS, PAUL ROGER, physics, marine science, and aquaculture educator, consultant; b. Woonsocket, R.I., June 14, 1956; m. Jane Linn White, April 12, 1985: children: Geneviève Antoinette, Alexandra Elisabeth. BS in Zoology, U. R.I., 1978. Cert. tchr., R.I., N.H., Mass., Maine, asst. prin., Maine. Phys. sci. tchr. Wilton-Lyndeborough Coop. High Sch., Wilton, N.H., 1980-83, Westport (Mass.) Mid. Sch., 1983-86; marine sci. tchr. Dennis-Yarmouth Regional High Sch., South Yarmouth, Mass., 1986-89; physics tchr. Diman Regional Vocat. Tech. Sch., Fall River, Mass., 1989-90; tchr. physics, chemistry Leavitt Area High Sch., Turner, Maine, 1990-96; administrator Maranacook Cmty. Sch., Readfield, Maine, 1996-97; tchr. marine sci./aquaculture, AP Chemistry, Physical Sci. Rockland Dist. H.S., 1997—, head dept. sci., 1999—. Mem. faculty adv. bd. Dennis-Yarmouth Regional H.S., 1987-88, chairmen Sci. Cirriculum CMTE; Scholarship CMTE; Beacon Sch. com., 1992-93; mem. math./sci. curriculum devel. com., 1994-96; steering com. and curriculum sub com. Leavitt Area H.S. Expansion Project, 1995-97. Author: Genesis: An Environmental Series, 1990. Group leader environ. projects, Maine Conservation Corps., 1992-93; tech. curriculm adv. bd. Leavitt Area High Sch. Recipient VIP award Dept. Interior/Nat. Pk. Svc., 1989; Sch. Marine sci. edn. grantee NSF, 1988, Donner Found., 1988, Immunology Edn. grantee NSF, Found. Blood Rsch., Scarborough, Maine, 191, NSF grantee Rivers Project, 1994, Excellence in Edn. grantee for Aquaculture, Md. Bank

N.Am., 1998; merit scholar Maine Math. & Sci. Alliance/Maine Med. Ctr. Rsch. Inst., 1996, 202 Excellence in Edn. Grantee fr Water Quality Monitoring Project in Conguenction with U.S. EPA. Mem. AAAS, NEA, Nat. Sci. Tchrs. Assn., Maine Tchrs. Assn., Nat. Honor Soc. CMTE. Office: Rockland Dist H S Sci Dept Rockland ME 04841

DE SCHRYVER, FRANS CARL, chemistry educator; b. St. Niklaas Waas, Belgium, Sept. 21, 1939; s. Petrus and Lucie (Smet) De S.; m. Suzy Bosteels, June 10, 1962; children: Dominique, Catherine. Lic. in sci., U. Leuven, Belgium, 1961, DSc, 1964. Postdoctoral researcher U. Ariz., Tucson, 1964-65; docent U. Leuven, Belgium, 1969-73, prof., 1973-75, full prof., 1975—; mem. Acad. of Scis., Lit. and Arts, Brussels, 1989—. Vis. prof. U. C. Louvain, Louvain-la-Neuve, Belgium, 1980—; mem. Organische Commn., macro-en supramoleculaire chemie FWO-Vlaanderen, 1997-2002, Commn. Chimie Organique FNRS, 1997-2002, Rsch. Coun. of U. Leuven. Mem. editorial bd. Chem. Phys. Lett., 1998; contbr. numerous articles to profl. jours. Recipient Rsch. award Alexander von Humboldt Found., 1993, Porter medal EPA, Inter Am. Photochemistry Soc., Japan Photochemistry Assn., 1998, Havinga medal, 1999. Fellow AAAS; mem. Am. Chem. Soc., Gesellschaft Deutscher Chemiker, Max-Planck Forschungspreis, 2001. Home: Minnezang 9 B-3210 Linden Belgium Office: KULeuven Celestijnenlaan 200F B-3001 Heverlee Leuven Belgium E-mail: frans.deschryver@chem.kuleuven.ac.be.

DESCHUYTNER, EDWARD ALPHONSE, biochemist, educator; b. Chelsea, Mass., Sept. 3, 1944; s. Alphonso and Josephine Elizabeth (Kiewlicz) D.; m. Carolyn Ann McGraw, Aug. 1, 1971; children: Brian Charles, Matthew Edward. BA, Northeastern U., 1967; PhD, Boston Coll., 1972. Asst. in floriculture Waltham Exptl. Field Sta. U. Mass., 1963-64; lab. technician Mass. Soldiers Home, Chelsea, 1964-65; rsch. asst. New Eng. Med. Ctr. Hosps., Boston, 1965-67; asst. Cancer Rsch. Inst., Boston Coll., 1967-71; from mem. faculty to prof. biology No. Essex C.C., Haverhill, Mass., 1971—2002, prof. biology, 2002—, chmn. dept. natural scis., 1988—95, asst. dean math., sci., and tech., 1995—98, assoc. dean math., sci., techs. and health professions, 1998—2002. Grant rev. panelist NSF, 1976-80; program coord. Eisenhower Title II Math. and Sci. Grant, 1989—; elected Region A dir. Nat. Sci. Edn. Leadership Assn., 1995-98; project dir. Bell Atlantic Ed Link, 1998-99, 2000-01; bd. dirs. Mass. Sci. Educators Hall of Fame, 2002--; project dir. Sci. Adventures for Everyone, 2000--. Author: (software) Biology in Action series, 1983, (with others) Principles of Biology, 2nd. ed., 1986, A Study and Laboratory Guide for Anatomy and Physiology, 2nd. ed., 1990. Recipient citation for Outstanding Performance, Commonwealth of Mass., 1991, Mass. Sci. Educator of Yr. for Essex County, 1996; Named Mass. Assn. Sci. Suprs. Outstanding Sci. Educator of Yr., 1998; Eisenhower Title II Math. and Sci. grantee, 1989-90, 91-92, 92-93, 93-94, 94-95, Nat. Edn. Act fellow Boston Coll., 1968-71, Sci. Educator of Yr. for Essex County, 1996, Outstanding Svc. and Leadership award Nat. Sci. Edn. Leadership Assn., 1998, 99, award for Excellence in Tchg. and Leadership, Nat. Inst. Staff and Orgnl. Devel., 2003; inducted into Mass. Sci. Educators Hall of Fame, 2001. Mem. AAAS, Am. Soc. for Microbiology, N.Y. Acad. Scis., Mass. Assn. Sci. Tchrs., Mass. Assn. Sci. Suprs., Nat. Sci. Tchrs. Assn., North Shore Sci. Suprs. Assn. (pres. 1995-96, 96-97), Nat. Assn. Biology Tchrs. Office: No Essex Community Coll 100 Elliott St Haverhill MA 01830-2306 Business E-Mail: edeschuytner@necc.mass.edu.

DESCY, DON EDMOND, educational technology educator, writer, editor; b. Hartford, Conn., Jan. 11, 1944; s. Henry Julian and Lillian D.V. (Svenson) D. BS in Biology Edn., Ctrl. Conn. State U., 1967, MS in Biology Edn., 1970; cert. in instrnl. media, U. Conn., 1981, PhD in Media and Tech., 1987. Tchg. asst. Ctrl. Conn. State U., New Britain, 1967-68; rsch. asst. Coll. Edn. U. Conn., Storrs, 1985-87; asst. adminstrv. dir. Conn. State Bar Examining Com., Hartford, 1987-89; adj. prof. Ea. Conn. State U., Willimantic, 1987-89, Ctrl. Conn. State U., New Britain, 1988-89; prof. Minn. State U., Mankato, 1989—, tech. coord., 1994—, program dir., 1998—. Numerous presentations in field in 5 countries. Author: Computer as an Educational Tool; mem. editl. bd. Internat. Jour. Instrnl. Media, 1991—, Quar. Jour. Distance Edn., 1999—, Techtrends, 1994—; columnist, editor-in-chief Techtrends, 1993—; contbr. over 80 articles to profl. jours., 4 chpts. to books, 1 textbook. Scholar Conn. Ednl. Media Assn., 1984, rsch. scholar Japan, 1996. Mem. ALA, Internat. Soc. Tech. in Edn., Assn. Ednl. Comm. and Tech. (pres. Twin Cities chpt., Disting. Svc. award 2000), Am. Assn. Sch. Librs., Minn. Ednl. Media Orgn. Office: Minn State U Mankato 313 Armstrong Hall Mankato MN 56001-6042 E-mail: desc4@mnsu.edu.

DESER, STANLEY, physicist, educator; b. Rovno, Poland, Mar. 19, 1931; BS summa cum laude, Bklyn. Coll., 1949; MA, Harvard U., 1950, PhD, 1953; DPhil (hon.), Stockholm U., 1978; DTech (hon.), Chalmers Tech. U., 2001. Mem. Inst. Advanced Study, Princeton, 1953-55, 93-94, Parker fellow, 1953-54; Jewett fellow Inst. for Advanced Study, Princeton, 1954-55; NSF postdoctoral fellow, mem. Inst. Theoretical Physics, Copenhagen, 1955-57; lectr. Harvard U., 1957-58; mem. faculty Brandeis U., Waltham, Mass., 1958—, prof. physics, 1965—, chmn. dept., 1969-71, 76-77, Ancell prof. physics, 1979—; E. Schrödinger prof. U. Vienna, 1996. Vis. scientist European Ctr. Nuclear Rsch., Geneva, 1962-63, 76, 80-81, 94; mem. physics adv. com. NSF, 1982-86; Fulbright and Guggenheim fellow, vis. prof. Sorbonne, Paris, 1966-67, 71-72; Loeb lectr. Harvard U., 1975; S.R.C. sr. fellow Imperial Coll., 1976; vis. prof. College de France, Paris, 1976, 84; vis. fellow All Souls' Coll., Oxford (Eng.) U., 1977; investigator titular ad honorem CIDA (Venezuela); Fulbright prof. U. of the Republic Montevideo Uruguay, 1970. Mem. editl. bd. Jour. Geometry and Physics, Jour. Math Physics, Jour. High Energy Physics, mem. sci. bd. I.H.E.S., France, 1991—97, Inst. Theoretical Physics, Santa Barbara, 1989—93, chmn. sci. bd., 1992—93. Recipient Dannie Heineman prize, Am. Inst. Physics, 1994. Fellow: NAS, Am. Acad. Arts and Scis., Am. Phys. Soc.; mem.: Turin (Italy) Acad. Sci. (hon.; fgn.). Office: Brandeis U Physics Dept MS057 Waltham MA 02454

DESIATO, DONNA JEAN, school system administrator; b. Bridgeport, Conn., Nov. 28, 1949; d. William Joseph and Elvira Rosemarie (Cerreta) Gilberti; 1 child, Danielle DeSiato Creveling. BEd, U. Miami, 1971; MS in Edn., SUNY Cortland, 1977; cert. advanced study, SUNY Oswego, 1983; postgrad., Syracuse U. Cert. permanent tchr. cert. N.Y., 1976, sch. dist. adminstr. N.Y., 1983. Tchr. Syracuse (N.Y.) City Sch. Dist., 1974—79, instrl. specialist, 1979—83, vice prin., 1983—84, prin., 1984—94, dir. elem. edn., 1993—2000, asst. supt., 2000—. Mem. reading and lit. partnership N.Y. State Edn. Dept., Albany, 1999—; mem. lit. collaborative Success By Six, Syracuse, NY, 1999—; mem. edn. adv. bd. Syracuse Newspapers, 1990—95. Mem. Corinthian Club, Syracuse, 2000—. Recipient Outstanding Educator award, Supervisors and Adminstrs. Assn. N.Y. State, 1999, Adminstrs. Excellence award, Supervisors and Adminstrs. Assn. Syracuse, 1996, 1997, 1998, Leadership Recognition award, Commn. on Women in Leadership, 1995, Disting. Alumni award, Onadaga C.C., 2003. Mem.: N.Y. State Assn. Women in Adminstrn. (chair chpt.), Delta Kappa Gamma (Alpha Omega chpt.), Phi Delta Kappa. Office: Syracuse City Sch Dist 725 Harrison St Syracuse NY 13210

DESIDERIO, MIKE FRANCIS, education educator; b. Russellville, Ark., Feb. 8, 1957; s. Frank and Joyce (Johnson) D.; m. Nidia Alicia Farias, Nov. 1, 1986; 1 child, Catherine Inez. BS in Edn., John Brown U., 1985; MEd, Sul Ross State U., 1990; PhD, Tex. A&M U., 1997. Cert. tchr., supt., Tex. Asst. prof. edn. Tex. A & M Internat. U., Laredo, 1998—. Sgt. U.S. Army N.G., 1979-85. Mem. Nat. Mid. Sch. Assn., Nat. Soc. for Study of Edn., Assn. of Tchr. Educators, Kappa Delta Pi. Avocations: golf, woodworking, golf trading cards, making golf clubs. Office: Tex A & M Internat U Coll of Edn 5201 University Blvd Laredo TX 78041-1920

DESILVEY, DENNIS LEE, cardiologist, educator, university administrator; b. May 17, 1942; m. Kathleen Selkirk, Aug. 28, 1965; children: Ethan Selkirk, Caitlin O'Brian, Sarah Candace Shaw. BA in History and Religion magna cum laude, Yale U., 1964; MD, Columbia U., 1968. Lic. Vt., Va.; cert. Advanced Trauma Life Support instr. Intern medicine Cornell Med. Ctr., N.Y.C., 1968-69, resident medicine, 1969-71, resident medicine, cardiology, 1971; chief med. resident medicine North Shore U. Hosp., Manhasset, N.Y., 1972-73, instr. medicine, 1972-73; mem. staff Rancocas Valley Hosp., Willingboro, N.J., 1973-75; cardiologist Brachfeld Med. Assocs., Willingboro, N.J., 1974-75, Castleton (Vt.) Med. Assocs., 1975-77; attending physician Rutland Regional Med. Ctr., Rutland, Vt., 1975-92; pvt. practice Rutland, Vt., 1977-92; adj. asst. prof. clin. medicine Dartmouth Hitchcock Med. Ctr., Hanover, N.H., 1979-92; asst. prof. medicine U. Vt., Burlington, 1983-92; mem. staff Dwight David Eisenhower Med. Ctr., Ft. Gordon, Ga., 1991; dir. ambulatory cardiology, dir. cardiology consult svc., mem. clin. faculty cardiovascular divsn., dept. medicine Health Scis. Ctr. U. Va., Charlottesville, 1992—2001, assoc. prof. medicine Health Scis. Ctr., 1992—. Cons. Southwestern Vt. Med. Ctr., Bennington, 1986—, Keller U.S. Army Hosp., West Point, N.Y., 1985—, internal medicine Veteran Affairs Med. Ctr., Salem, Va., 1993—; mem. critical care com. Rutland Regional Med. Ctr., pharmacy and therapeutics com., investigational review bd., ethics com.; mem. pharmacy and therapeutics com. Health Scis. Ctr. U. Va., nutrition com., health care evaluation com., ambulatory policy com.; bd. dirs., mem. profl. affairs com., mem. bylaws com. Blue Cross/Blue Shield Vt.; bd. dirs., founding mem. Vt. Cardiac Network; presenter New Eng. regional meeting Am. Coll. Physicians, Hanover, N.H., 1976, Advanced Concepts Shock and Trauma, Woodstock (Vt.) Inn, 1982; dir. ACLS Tng. Ctr.; chmn/. Resolution Com. Contbr. articles to profl. jours. Med. advisor skiing svcs. Killington Ski Area, 1975-92, Smokey House Found., 1975-80, Farm and Wilderness Camps, 1975-85; mem. steering com. Vt. Med. Practice Variation Assessment Program, 1988; mem. cardiology study sect. Vt. Program Quality Care, 1988-92, Vt. Gov.'s Coun. Phys. Fitness, 1985-88; vestry Trinity Episcopal Ch., 1986-89; bd. dirs. Vermont Diabetes Assn., 1975-79, Rutland Mental Health Svc., 1975-82, Rutland Area Vis. Nurses Assn., 1975-77, chmn. profl. affairs com., mem. utilization review com.; bd. dirs. Barstow Sch., 1986-90; town health officer Wallingford, Vt., 1975-80. Maj. U.S. Army, 1973-75; col. USAR, 1985—. Decorated Nat. Def. Svc. medal, Reserve Achievement medal, Army Commendation medal; recipient Physician Recognition award Am. Med. Assn., Exceptional Svc. award, Spiritual Aims award Kiwanis Club Am., 1983, U. Va. Pres.'s Report award, 1992. Fellow Am. Coll. Physicians, Am. Coll. Cardiology, N.Am. Soc. Pacing and Electrophysiology; mem. Am. Heart Assn. (ACLS instr., BCLS instr., nat. faculty ACLS Vt., mem. mil. tng. network ACLS, Advanced Trauma Life Support; bd. dirs. 1978-80, bd. dirs., at large appointee 1988-93, agenda planning com. 1986-89, affiliate relations com. 1986-88, sci. pub. com. 1989-93, "heart and stroke" planning com. 1989-90, participant edn. and inf. group heart guide consumer health and info. program, 1989-91, chmn. task force mission to elderly 1989-90; v.p.-elect New Eng. region 1986-87, regional v.p. 1987-88, fellow coun. clin. cardiology, bd. dirs. Charlottesville divsn. 1992—, bd. dirs. Va. affiliate 1992—, bd. dirs. Rutland, Vt. divsn. 1986-92, program coun. 1986-92, bd. dirs. Vt. affiliate 1975-92, exec. com. 1978-92, pres.-elect 1982-83, pres. 1983-85, co-chair capital campaign 1988-90, nominating com. 1984-86, cardiac rehab. com. 1982-85, program coun. 1978-90, ACLS com. 1978-90, cardiac critical care com. 1978-82, hypertension com. 1975-82, chmn. emergency cardiac care com. region V 1976-80, bd. dirs. N.J. affiliate 1973-75, BCLS com. 1973-75, mem. greater N.Y. affiliate 1966-72, BCLS instr. 1968-72, del. N.E. regional heart com. 1985-91, reaffiliation com. 1987-89, nominating com. 1987-88, Pysician of Yr. award 1992), Am. Soc. Echocardiology, N.Y. Acad. Scis., Vt. Cardiac Network (vice chmn. 1982-86), Phi Beta Kappa. Avocations: cycling, running, cross country skiing, hiking, mountain climbing, theology. Home: 2712 Southern Hills Ct North Garden VA 22959 Office: Consultants in Cardiology 108 Houston St Ste B Lexington VA 24450 E-mail: dld3a@virginia.edu.

DESIMONE, RICHARD LOUIS, principal; b. Gilroy, Calif., May 6, 1952; s. Alfred Richard and Robbie Fay (Couch) D.; m. Ida Lee Arellano, July 5, 1975; children: Michael, Basilisa, Carlotta, Raquel. BA in Social Sci., San Jose State U., 1978, MA in Counselor Edn., 1991, adminstrv. credential, 1996. Cert. tchr., lang. devel. specialist, pupil pers. svcs. specialist, Calif. Retreat coord. Mission Trails Search Program, Gilroy, Calif., 1968-88; tchr. Morgan Hill (Calif.) Unified Sch. Dist., 1986-94, counselor, 1994—; English instr. KRATOS, Mexico City, 1991; mem. faculty counselor edn. San Jose State U., 1994—; prin. Rolling Hills Middle Sch., Watsonville, Calif., 1999—. Family counselor Discover Alternatives, Gilroy, 1992-93; exec. dir. Internat. Edn. Specialists, San Jose, 1991-93; mem. Cultural Diversity Task Force, Morgan Hill, 1993—; mem. Calif. Sch. Leadership Team, Morgan Hill, 1993-94. Author: Cross-Cultural Issues in Counseling and Education, 1992; co-author: Child Abuse Reporting Procedures, 1990. Mem. St. Mary Parish Coun., Gilroy, 1984-88; mem. Conflict Resolution Team, Morgan Hill, 1993—; mem. Bilingual Parent Com., Morgan Hill, 1993—. Recipient Mayor's Cmty. Conf. award City of San Jose, 1992, Pope Paul VI Svc. award Archdiocese of San Jose, 1984. Mem. ASCD, Internat. Playback Theater Network, Calif. Continuation Edn. Assn. Avocations: guitar, camping, family. Office: Rolling Hills Middle Sch 130 Herman Ave Watsonville CA 95076 E-mail: Rick_Desimone@prusd.net.

DESJARDINS, CLAUDE, physiologist, dean; b. Fall River, Mass., June 13, 1938; s. Armand Louis and Marguerite Jean (Mercier) D.; m. Jane Elizabeth Campbell, June 30, 1962; children: Douglas, Mark, Anne. BS, U. R.I., 1960; MS, Mich. State U., 1964, PhD, 1967. Asst. prof. dept. physiology Okla. State U., Stillwater, 1968-69, assoc. prof., 1969-72; assoc. prof. physiology U. Tex., Austin, 1970-75; prof. physiology Inst. Reproductive Biology, Patterson Labs., 1975-86, U. Va. Med. Sch., Charlottesville, 1987-96, dir. Ctr. Rsch. Reprodn., 1990-96; prof. physiology & biophysics, sr. assoc. dean med. coll. U. Ill., Chgo., 1996—. Mem. Ctr. for Advanced Studies, 1986; cons. NIH, ASA, VA, FDA. Author: Cell and Molecular Biology of the Testis, 1993, Molecular Physiology of Testicular Cells, 1996; editor-in-chief Am. Jour. physiology: Endocrinology and Metabolism, 1991-95; editor-in-chief Jour. Andrology, 1989-91, Ency. of Reprodn., 1997-98; mem. editl. bd. Biology Reprodn., Endocrinology; contbr. articles to profl. jours.; patentee techs. for male contraception, mechanisms of peptide hormone transport in the microcirculation and ligand-dependent and ligand ind. action of steroid hormones in peripheral vasculature. Fellow The Jackson Lab., Bar Harbor, Maine, 1967, NIH Sr. fellow U. Va. Med. Sch., 1983-84, Danforth Found. fellow, 1960; C.F. Wilcox Found. scholar, 1958. Mem. Am. Physiol. Soc., Soc. Neurosci., Soc. Study Reprodn. (pres. 1982-83), Endocrine Soc., Am. Soc. Cell Biology, The Microcirculatory Soc. Office: U Ill at Chgo Office of Dean M/C 784 1853 W Polk St Chicago IL 60612-4316 E-mail: clauded@uic.edu.

DESKO, BRENDA K. elementary education educator; b. Bloomsburg, Pa., Oct. 13, 1961; d. G. Dane and D. Marilyn (Girton) Keller; m. George Steven Desko, June 21, 1986; children: Joshua, Kayla, Hannah. BS in Bible and Elem. Edn., Johnson Bible Coll., 1983; MEd, Cabrini Coll., 1994. Cert. elem. tchr., Pa. Tchr. Countryside Christian Sch., Cambridge, Md., 1983-86, Washington Elem. Sch., Barto, Pa., 1988—. Avocation: playing piano. Office: Washington Elem Sch 1406 Route 100 Barto PA 19504-8704

DESMOND, MABEL JEANNETTE, state legislator, educator; b. Lower Southampton, N.B., Can., Jan. 30, 1929; d. Charles Edward and Ada Gertrude (Ritchie) Lenentine; m. Jerry Russell Desmond, June 23, 1951; children: Jerry Russell Jr., Ronnee Beth, Jed Carey, Jennifer Shea. BS, Aroostook State Coll., 1964; MEd, U. Maine, 1975. Cert. prin., tchr., Maine. Tchr. Bridgewater (Maine) Elem. Sch., 1949-50, Gouldville Sch., Presque Isle, Maine, 1950-58, Mapleton H.S. and Mapleton Elem. Sch., Maine, 1958-63, 65-67, Gouldville Elem., Presque Isle, Maine, 1964-65, Ashland (Maine) Elem. Sch., 1969-70, Eva Hoyt Zippel Sch., Presque Isle, 1970-91; mem. adj. faculty U. Maine, Presque Isle, 1991—; rep. State of Maine, Augusta, 1995—. Mem. tchr. edn. adv. com. U. Maine Presque Isle, 1995-2003, mem. edn. and cultural affairs com. in legislature. Contbr. editls. to newspapers and articles to profl. jours. Named Legislator of Yr., 2001; recipient Disting. Alumni award, U. Maine, Presque Isle, 1995, Leadership in Edn. award, 2001. Mem.: AAUW, NEA, Aroostook Ret. Tchrs. Assn. (2d v.p. 2001—03, 1st v.p. 2003—), Maine Edn. Assn., U. Maine Presque Isle Alumni Assn. (pres. 1962—63, 1974—75, sec. 1992—96, exec. bd.), Alpha Psi State (parliamentarian 1993—95, 2d v.p. 2001—03, 1st v.p. 2003—), Delta Kappa Gamma (pres. 1984—86). Democrat. Baptist. Avocations: writing, painting, reading. Home: PO Box 207 Mapleton ME 04757-0207 Office: House of Reps 2 State House Sta Augusta ME 04333-0002

DESOTO, CLINTON BURGEL, psychologist, educator; b. Hartford, Conn., Jan. 13, 1931; s. Clinton Burgel and Ruth Esther (Higbie) D.; m. Jane Louise Everhardt, Feb. 4, 1956; children: Brian, William, Stewart; m. Janet Louise Tolbert, Feb. 7, 1975. Student Eau Claire State Coll., Wis., 1948-50; BA, U. Wis., 1952, MA, 1953, PhD, 1956. Instr. Johns Hopkins U., 1956-57, asst. prof., 1957-61, assoc. prof., 1961-69, prof. psychology, 1969—. Contbr. chpts. to books, articles to profl. jours. Mem. Am. Psychol. Assn., Psychonomic Soc., Soc. Exptl. Social Psychology, Eastern Psychol. Assn., AAAS, Sigma Xi Home: 923 Beaverbank Cir Baltimore MD 21286-3314 Office: Johns Hopkins U Dept Psychology Baltimore MD 21218

DESPRES, LEO ARTHUR, sociology and anthropology educator, academic administrator; b. Lebanon, N.H., Mar. 29, 1932; s. Leo Arthur and Madeline (Bedford) D.; m. Loretta A. LaBarre, Aug. 22, 1953; children—Christine, Michelle, Denise, Mary Louise, Renee. BA, U. Notre Dame, 1954, MA, 1956; PhD, Ohio State U., 1960. Research assoc. Columbia Psychiat. Inst. and Hosp., 1957-60; postdoctoral fellow Social Sci. Research Council, Guyana, 1960-61; asst. prof. Ohio Wesleyan U., 1961-63; faculty Case Western Res. U., Cleve., 1963-74, prof. anthropology, 1967-74, chmn. dept., 1968-74; prof. sociology, anthropology U. Notre Dame, Ind., 1974-97, chmn. dept., 1974-80, fellow Kellogg Inst. Internat. Studies, 1982—, prof. emeritus, 1997—. Cons. in field. Author: Cultural Pluralism and Nationalist Politics in British Guyana, 1968; editor: Ethnicity and Resource Competition in Plural Societies, 1975, Manaus: Social Life and Work in Brazil's Free Trade Zone, 1991. Fulbright scholar U. Guyana, 1970-71, Brazil, 1986; research grantee NSF, 1984. Mem. Am. Anthrop. Assn., Am. Ethnol. Soc., Latin Am. Studies Assn., Cen. States Anthrop. Soc. (pres. 1976-77), AAUP. Office: U Notre Dame Dept Anthropology Notre Dame IN 46556 Home: PO Box 6752 South Bend IN 46660-6752 E-mail: hdespres@nd.edu.

DESROSIERS, MURIEL C. music educator, retired nursing consultant; b. Woonsocket, R.I., Jan. 15, 1934; d. Rodolphe J. Desrosiers and Rhea M. Archambault; m. Albert A. Desrosiers; 6 stepchildren. BSN, Boston Coll., 1965; MSN, Boston U., 1967, cert. advanced grad. studies, 1975, EdD, 1977. Instr. St. Anselm's Coll. Sch. Nursing, Manchester, NH, 1968—74; cons. drug abuse prevention N.H. State Dept. Edn., Concord, 1974—75, sch. health cons., 1976—89; instr. piano performance, theory and technique. In-svc. educator N.H. Hosps., 1968—75; instr. leadership workshops, 1968—75; grant writer Sch. Nurse Achievement Program. Vol. Home for Little Wanderers; chair Am. Sch. Health Assn., 1984—87; pres. Nat. Assn. Sch. Health Consultants, 1984—87. Recipient Disting. Svc. award, Am. Sch. Health Assn., 1987, Sch. Nurse Achievement award, 1988. Mem.: N.H. Nurses Assn., Maine Nurses Assn., Maine Music Tchrs. Assn. (chair program 1990—95), Nat. Assn. Music Tchrs. (emeritus). Avocation: writing. Home: RR 4 Box 2350 Waterville ME 04901

DESSASO, DEBORAH ANN, freelance writer, online communications specialist, consultant; b. Washington, Feb. 6, 1952; d. Coleman and Virginia Beatrice (Taylor) D. AS in Bus. Adminstrn., Southeastern U., 1986, BSBA, 1988; MA in English Composition and Rhetoric, U. D.C., 1997. Clk.-stenographer FTC, Washington, 1969—70; sec. NEA, Washington, 1970—72, AARP, Washington, 1972—79, assoc. adminstrv. specialist, 1979—80, adminstrv. specialist, 1979—89, legis. comm. specialist, 1989—2000, mgr. issue response, 2000—01; cons., 2000—; adj. prof. English U. D.C., Washington, 2002—03, dir., The Writing Ctr., 2003—. Adj. prof. English, U. D.C.; founding mem., sec. Andrus Fed. Credit Union, 1980. Mem. Associated Writing Program. Mem. Faith Outreach Cmty. Ch. Home: 3042 Stanton Rd SE Washington DC 20020-7883 E-mail: dessaso749@earthlink.net .

DETERT-MORIARTY, JUDITH ANNE, graphic artist, educator, civic activist; b. Portage, Wis., July 10, 1952; d. Duane Harlan and Anne Jane (Devine) Detert; m. Patrick Edward Moriarty, July 22, 1978; children: Colin Edward, Eleanor Grace, Dylan Joseph. BA, U. Wis., Madison, 1970-73, U. Wis., Green Bay, 1991. Cert. in no-fault grievance mediation, Minn. Legis sec., messenger State of Wis. Assembly, Madison, 1972, 74-76; casualty-property div. clk. Capitol Indemnity Corp., Madison, 1977-78; word processor consumer protection dvsn. Wis. Dept. Agr., Madison, 1978; graphic arts composing specialist Moraine Park Tech. Inst., Fond du Lac, Wis., 1978-79; freelance artist Picas, Pictures and Promotion (formerly Detert Graphics), 1978-90; prodn. asst. West Bend News, 1980-83; devel. asoc. Riveredge Nature Ctr., Inc., Newburg, Wis., 1983-84; exec. dir. Voluntary Action Ctr. Washington County, West Bend, 1984-86; instr. cmty. svcs. Austin (Minn.) C.C., 1988; art and promotional publs. dir. Michael G. and Co., Albert Lea, Minn., 1988-89; corp. art dir. Newco, Inc., Janesville, Wis., 1989-91; owner, artist Art Graphica, 1991-00. Substitute tchr. Janesville Sch. Dist., 1999—. Cartooning instr., contbg. artist Janesville Pub. Schs., 1989-93; contbr. articles to profl. jours.; contbg. artist Spotlight on Kids theatre, 1995-99, Rockport Peace Park Project, 1999-2002. Bd. mem. Montessori Children's House, West Bend, 1983—85; newsletter editor, artist Friends of Battered Women, West Bend, 1983—86; bd. pres. Wash. Co. Rep. Wis. State, 1984—85; bd. mem. Montessori Childrens House, West Bend, Wis., 1984—85; Wis. rep. Planned Parenthood of Wis. Bd., 1984—85; artist LWV Washington County, 1984—86; apptd. Austin Human Rights Commn., 1987—88; fundraiser Victims Crisis Ctr., 1987; cmty. contact, v.p. Caths. for Free Choice Wis., 1990—92; apptd. Janesville Hist. Commn., 1992—95; vol. bd. dirs., chmn. advt. com. Janesville Concert Assn., 1994—97; founder, pres. Parents' Assn., Montessori Childrens House, Janesville, Wis., 1994—97; sec. Janesville Hist. Commn., 1994—95; newsletter editor Roosevelt Elem. Sch. PTA, 1996—2002; vol. newsletter editor Badger coun. Girls Scouts, Inc., 1996—98; founder United Arts Alliance, 1996, pres., 1997—98, sec., 1998—2001, Roosevelt Elem. Sch. PTA, 1999—2001; founder, bd. mem., sec. Bower City Preservation Assn., 1999—; chpt. coord. Project Linus-Janesville, 2000—; editor ArtsRock, 2001—; founder, instr. after-school knitting clubs Roosevelt and Jefferson Elem. Schs. and Boys and Girls Club, Janesville, 2001—; organizer The Lysistrata Project, Janesville, 2003; vol. Austin Pub. Sch. Omnibus Program; newsletter editor, com. chmn. Montessori Childrens House, Janesville, Wis.; bd. mem. Montessori Children's Ho., Janesville, Wis.; student vol. McCarthy for Pres., U. Wis., Madison, 1968; coord. student residences McGovern for Pres., 1972; vol. Udall for Pres., 1976; Washington County Campaign coord. Nat. Unity Campaign for John Anderson for Pres., 1980; publicity coord. Wis. Intellectual Freedom Coalition, 1981; pres., founder People of Washington County United for Choice, 1981—83; bd. dirs., v.p. Wis. Pro-Choice Conf., 1981—82; Washington County ward coord. Earl for Gov., 1982, Mondale/Ferraro, 1984; Washington County campaign chmn. Peg Lautenschlager for Wis. state senate, 1984; sec., newsletter editor Dem. Party of Manitowoc County,

Wis., 1986; precinct ofcr. and affirmative action ofcr. Dem. Party Mower County, Minn., 1986—88; local chair Women's Polit. Caucus1987, 1988; v.p. commn. officer Dem. Party Rock County, Wis., 1988—94, newsletter editor, 1988—; vol. coord. Rock County Dukakis for Pres., 1988; campaign chair Lew Mittness for Wis. State Assembly, 1990; newsletter editor Rock County Voice for Choice, 1990—94; founding exec. bd. dirs., newsletter editor Moral Alternatives, 1990—92; vol. Rock County Clinton for Pres., 1992, 1996; sec., v.p. commn. officer/newsletter editor Rock Co. Dem. Party, Wis., 1998—2001; 1st C.D. 4th vice chair Dem. Party of Wis., 1999—2001; mem. campaign coordinating com. Vote Graf, 2000; Rock County coord. Ralph Nader for Pres., 2000; mem. steering com., bd. mem. Rock County Citizens for Peace, 2001—; v.p. commn. officer Dem. Party Rock County, Wis., 2001—; newsletter editor, mem. coms. Planned Parenthood of Washington County, 1980—85, bd. dirs., 1984—85. Recipient award of Excellence Bd. Report Graphic Artists, 1994, 95, nominee UW-Green Bay Disting. Alumni, 1997, 2000, YWCA Women of Distinction, 1996-98, Governors award in support of the arts, 1997, Comm. Arts Devel. award, 1997. Mem. NOW (newsletter editor Dane County 1977-78, Wis. state 1994-99, coord. Wis. state reproductive rights task force 1982-84, coord. reproductive rights task force North Suburban chpt. 1981-84, Minn. pub. rels. coord. 1987-88), Forward Janesville (steering com. for Celebrate Janesville 1992, 93, 94). Mem. Soc. Of Friends. Avocations: reading, bicycling, gardening, knitting, world wide correspondence, antiques. Office: 23 S Atwood Ave Janesville WI 53545-4003 E-mail: proartist@aol.com.

DETMAR-PINES, GINA LOUISE, business strategy and policy educator; b. S.I., N.Y., May 3, 1949; d. Joseph and Grace Vivian (Brown) Sargente; m. Michael B. Pines, Sept. 11, 1988; 1 child, Drue Joseph Pines. BS in Edn., Wagner Coll., 1971, MS, 1972; MA in Urban Affairs and Policy Analysis, New Sch. for Social Rsch., 1987; MPhil, CUNY, 1995; PhD in Bus./Orgn. and Policy Studies, CUNY-Baruch Coll., 1996. Cert. adminstr. and supr., sch. dist. adminstr. Tchr. pub. schs., N.Y.C., 1971-82; coord. spl. projects, pub. affairs N.Y.C. Bd. Edn., 1982, spl. asst. to exec. dir. pupil svcs., 1983, asst. to chancellor, 1983-84, dir. Tchr. Summer Bus. Industry Program, 1984-93; prof. pub. adminstrn. and mgmt. John Jay Coll. Criminal Justice CUNY, 1992-93; prof. bus. Cen. Conn. State U., 2000—. Vis. prof. Rensselaer at Hartford, 1993—98, Fairfield U., 1998—2000; liaison for the Tech. Industry Program N.Y.C. Partnership, 1985—93. Mem. com. to re-elect Borough pres. Lamberti, S.I., 1985-86; chairperson Crystal Ball event Greater Hartford Easter Seals Rehab. Ctr., 1994, trustee, 1994—; bd. dirs. Hartford Symphony, com. mem. 50th Anniversary Gala, 1993. Mayor's scholar City of N.Y., 1984-96. Mem. ASPA, Fgn. Lang. Instrs. Assn., Strategic Mgmt. Soc., Acad. Mgmt., U.S. Seaplane Pilot's Assn., Internat. Orgn. for Lic. Women Pilots, Jr. League of Hartford, Hartford Task Force on Healthy Families, Chinese-Am. Soc., Am. Mgmt. Soc., Ea. Acad. Mgmt., Acad. of Internat. Bus., Cambridge Flying Group Club. Episcopalian. Avocations: flying, scuba diving, skiing. Office: Ctrl Conn State U 1615 Stanley St New Britain CT 06053-2439

DETOFSKY, LOUIS BENNETT, secondary education educator; b. Phila., Nov. 1, 1944; s. Milton and Fae Minerva (Familant) D. BA, Rutgers U., 1968; MA, Glassboro (N.J.) State Coll., 1976. Cert. secondary edn. tchr., N.J. Instr. geosci., biology and anthropology Washington Twp. H.S., Sewell, NJ, 1968—99. Club advisor Washington Twp. H.S. Geology Club, Sewell, 1968-2000; advisor high adventure geology So. N.J. Coun.; adj. prof. geology Rowan U., Glassboro, N.J., 2000-03. Author: Traversing New Jersey's Geology, 1976, Hawaiian Genesis, 1984, Our Appalachian Heritage, 1985, Jewels of the West Part I: Rocky Mountains, 1987, Jewels of the West Part II: Cascades, 1988. Advisor Explorer Post 8 Boy Scouts Am., 1986-2000; sec. B'nai B'rith, Gloucester County, N.J., 1987-98. Mem. AAAS, Nat. Assn. Geology Tchrs., Nat. Earth Sci. Tchrs. Assn., Geol. Soc. Am., Geol. Assn. of N.J., N.J. Earth Sci. Tchrs. Assn., Nat. Sci. Tchrs. Assn., Delaware Valley Paleontol. Soc., Delaware Valley Earth Sci. Soc. Jewish. Home: 12 Bedford Ter Turnersville NJ 08012-2102 Office: Dept Chemistry/Physics Rowan U 201 Mullica Hill Rd Glassboro NJ 08028

DETWILER, CHRISTINA LEFEVRE, elementary school educator; b. Richmond, Va., July 27, 1968; d. Michael Roy and Linda Harris LeFevre; m. Scott Douglas Detwiler, Aug. 1, 1998; 1 child, Sarah Catherine. Student, Longwood Coll., 1986—88, J. Sargeant Reynolds, Richmond, 1988—90, Va. Commonwealth U., 1990—91, BS in Psychology, MT in Elem. Edn., 1994. Postgrad. profl. lic. in early edn. NK-4. Kindergarten tchr. Elmont Elem., Ashland, Va., 1995—97, 1st grade loop tchr., 1997—98, 1st grade tchr., 1998—99, Acquinton Elem., King William, Va., 1999—2001. Active March of Dimes, Aylett, Va., 1998—, VFW, 1998—, Save the Mattaponi Orgn., King William, 1999—2003, Sept. 11 Fund, 2001. Mem.: NEA, Psi Chi, Sigma Kappa. Baptist.

DEUSCHLE, CONSTANCE JOAN, counselor, educational consultant; b. Indpls., July 16, 1945; d. Delmar Sanford and Mildred Cynthia (Kreis) Gray; m. John Hanlan Deuschle, Nov. 12, 1966; children: Peter John, Thomas Scott, Matthew James. ASN, Southwestern Mich. U., 1976; BS, Ind. U., 1989, MS, 1991, EdD, 1999. Counselor Concord Cmty. Schs., Elkhart, Ind., 1986-92; cons. Ind. Dept. Edn., Indpls., 1992—; counselor Elkhart, 1992—. Cons. C.J. Cons., Goshen, Ind., 1992—; asst. prof. Ind. U., South Bend, 2000—. Co-author: Handbook for School Counselors: Stop the Bus, 2000; contbr. articles to profl. book. Educator drug & Alcohol awareness Concord Schs., 1983-92. Mem. Nat. Student Assistance Assn. (sec. 1995—), Ind. Assn. Student Assistance Programs (bd. dirs. 1994—). Roman Catholic. Avocations: writing, poetry, walking, travel. Home and Office: 58112 Orchard Ln Goshen IN 46528-9078 E-mail: cdeuschl@iusb.edu.

DEUTSCH, JUDITH MARIE, elementary education educator; b. New Prague, Minn., Jan. 28, 1955; d. Edwin and Leona (Giesen) Weiers; m. Ronald Michael Deutsch, June 13, 1975 (dec. July 1994); children: Jessica, Nicholas, Keith, Alyssa, Melanie. BA, Coll. of St. Catherine, St. Paul, 1977; MA in Edn., Coll. of St. Caterine, 2001. Chpt. I tchr. New Prague Pub. Schs., 1979-84; tchr. kindergarten New Prague Elem. Sch., 1984-90, St. Wenceslaus Sch., New Prague, 1990—, mid. sch. tchr. math., 1994-95. Tchr. religious edn. St. Wenceslaus Parish, New Prague, 1984-92, 1999-04, chmn. religious edn. bd., 1994-95; adult leader Scott County 4-H, Jordan, Minn., 1989—. Named Cath. Educator of Yr., Medtronics and Archdioces of Mpls.-St. Paul, 1993. Avocations: reading, baking, sewing. Office: St Wenceslaus Sch 227 Main St E New Prague MN 56071-1800 E-mail: judy.deutsch@saintwenceslaus.org.

DEUTSCH, SID, bioengineer, educator; b. N.Y.C., Sept. 19, 1918; s. Elias and Gussie (Hazen) D.; m. Ruth Appleman, Nov. 15, 1941 (div. June 1969), remarried, 1984; children: Alice, Phyllis, Naomi; m. Jane Arieti, Aug., 1969 (dec. Mar., 1978); m. Annette Page, Apr., 1979 (div. Dec., 1984). BEE, Cooper Union, 1941; MEE, Bklyn. Poly. Inst., 1947, PhD, 1955. Designer Fairchild Camera & Instrument Co., N.Y.C., 1943-44; instr. Madison Inst., Newark, 1946-50; engr. Poly. R & D Co., Bklyn., 1950-54; mem. faculty Bklyn. Poly. Inst., 1954-72, prof. elec. engring., 1962-72; prof. bioengring. Rutgers U. Med. Sch., Piscataway, N.J., 1972-79; vis. prof. U. S.Fla., Tampa, 1983-98. Vis. prof. Tel Aviv U., Israel, 1977, prof. bioengring, 1979-84; cons. Lewyt Mfg. Corp., 1958-60; affiliate Rockefeller Inst., 1961-64. Author: Theory and Design of TV Receivers, 1951, Models of the Nervous System, 1967, Return of the Ether: When Theory and Reality Collide, 1999; co-author: Biomedical Instruments: Theory and Design, 1976, 2d edit., 1992, Neuroelectric Systems, 1987, Understanding the Nervous System: An Engineering Perspective, 1993; assoc. editor: IEEE Transactions on Biomedical Engring., 1991-96; patentee pseudorandom dot scan for TV. Mem. adult edn. com. Roslyn (N.Y.) Pub. Schs., 1955-58. With USNR, 1944-46. Fellow IEEE, Soc. for Info. Display; mem. Sigma Xi, Tau Beta Pi, Eta Kappa Nu. Home: 3967 Oakhurst Blvd Sarasota FL 34233-1447 E-mail: deutsch@eng.usf.edu.

DEVANEY, CYNTHIA ANN, elementary education educator, real estate broker; b. Gary, Ind., Feb. 6, 1947; d. Charles Barnard and Irene Mae (Nelson) Burner; m. Harold Verne DeVaney, Nov. 23, 1974 (dec. 1981). BS, Ball State U., 1970, MS, 1972; postgrad., Ind. U. and Purdue U., 1974-76. Cert. real estate broker, Ind. Real estate broker Century 21 McColly Realtors, Highland, Ind., 1979-86, GMAC McColly Realtors, Merrillville, 1986—, with Pres.' Coun.; tchr. Merkley Elem. Sch., Highland, Ind., 1969—2002; student tchr. supr. Ind. U., Bloomington, 2002—. Supr. student tchrs., Ind. U. Active Schubert Theater Guild, Chgo. Mem. N.W. Ind. Bd. Realtors (Million Dollar Club), Nat. Bd. Realtors, Jr. Ind Hist. Soc., Innsbrook Country Club, Match Point Tennis Club. Democrat. Methodist. Avocations: golf, tennis, traveling, gardening, theater. Home: 607 E 78th Pl Merrillville IN 46410-5624 Office: McColly GMAC 2000 W 45th Ave Highland IN 46322-2504 E-mail: cindevaney@aol.com.

DEVANEY, ROBERT L. mathematician, educator; BA, MA, Holy Cross Coll., 1969; PhD, U. Calif., Berkeley, Calif., 1973. Instr. Northwestern U., Tufts U., U. Md.; prof. Dept. Math. Boston (Mass.) U., 1980—. Dir. Dynamical Sys. and Tech. Project NSF, 1989—, dir. Regional Geometry Inst., 1990—93. Author (or editor): 10 books. Recipient Deborah and Franklin Tepper Haimo award, 1994, Disting. Tchg. award, N.E. Sect. Math. Assn. Am., 1994, Dir.'s award, NSF, 2002, Excellence award, ICTCM, 2002. Office: Dept Math Boston Univ MCS 164 111 Cummington St Boston MA 02215 Office Fax: 617-353-8100. E-mail: bob@bu.edu.*

DEVAUD, JUDITH ANNE See HALVORSON, JUDITH

DEVENS, JOHN SEARLE, natural resources administrator; b. Shickshinny, Pa., Mar. 31, 1940; s. John Ezra and Laura (Bulkley) D.; m. Sharon I. Snyder (div. 1979); children: John, Jerilyn, James, Janis. BS, Belmont Coll., 1964; MEd, Emory U., 1966; PhD, Wichita State U., 1975. Dir. speech and hearing Columbia Coll., Columbia, SC, 1967—70; head dept. audiology Inst. Logopedics, Wichita, Kans., 1970—71; supr. audiology State of Alaska, Fairbanks, 1971—73; asst. prof. U. Houston, Victoria, Tex., 1975—77; pres. Prince William Sound C.C., Valdez, Alaska, 1977—92, Sterling Coll., Craftsbury Common, Vt., 1993—96; dir. Valdez Hearing and Speech Ctr.; exec. dir. Prince William Sound Regional Citizens' Adv. Coun., 1997—; prin., owner The Lake House a Country Inn, Valdez, 2000—. Owner, operator Valdez Hearing and Speech Ctr., 1977—92, Lake House Country Inn, 2000—. Prodr. films on hearing problems; contbr. articles to profl. jours. Mayor City of Valdez, 1985-89, mem. city coun., 1980-89; nat. chmn. adv. com. Horsemanship for Handicapped, 1964-67; mem. Alaska Gov.'s Coun. for Handicapped, 1980-82; pres. Valdez chpt. Alaska Visitors Assn., 1980; mem. small cities adv. coun. Nat. League Cities, 1983-87, mem. internat. econ. devel. task force; mem. Nat. Export Coun., 1982-84; bd. dirs. Resource Devel. Coun.; Dem. nominee U.S. Ho. Reps., 1990, 92; hosted internat. conf. on oil spills for mayors; exec. dir. Prince William Sound Regional Citizens Adv. Coun., 1997—. Mem. Am. Speech-Lang. Hearing Assn. (cert. clin. competence in audiology and speech and lang. pathology), Am. C. of C. in Korea, Valdez C. of C., Alaska Mcpl. League (bd. dirs. 1984-89). Methodist. Avocation: charter boat operator. Home: PO Box 770 Valdez AK 99686-0770 Office: PO Box 3089 Valdez AK 99686-3089 E-mail: jhdvns@aol.com.

DEVER, MERRILL THOMAS, academic administrator, retired police chief; b. Erie, Pa., Oct. 31, 1930; s. Merrill Franklin and Rose Elenore (Miller) D.; m. Barbara Ann Snyder, Sept. 21, 1957; children: Christopher, Lori Ann, Robin Alane, James Joseph, Beth Anne. BS, U. Va., 1973, Kans. State U., 1950. Cert. in firearms. Chief of police Millcreek Twp. Police Dept., Erie, 1980-86; dir. security Mercyhurst Coll., Erie, 1986—97; br. mgr. U.S. Security Assocs., Inc., Erie, Pa., 1998—. Tng. and edn. dir. Northwestern Chiefs of Police, 1978—. Contbr. articles to mags. and newspapers. Dir. FEMA (Millcreek Twp.), Erie County, Pa., 1975-82; pres. Family Crisis Intervention, Erie County, 1979-81; pres. citizens adv. bd. Pa. Bd. Parole, 1984-86; bd. dirs. Times Newsies, 1980—. Lt. U.S. Army, 1952-55. Recipient medal of valor, other medals and awards. Mem. Chiefs of Police (life), Fraternal Order of Police (life mem., pres. 1966- 69). Democrat. Roman Catholic. Avocations: history and civil war roundtables, firearms, hunting, gardening. Office: US Security Assocs Inc 11 W 33rd St Erie PA 16508 Fax: 814-459-2340. E-mail: mdever@greatguards.com.

DEVEREAUX, EVELYN JANINE, librarian, civilian military employee; b. Hamilton Field, Calif., Apr. 4, 1947; d. Ray Wilson and Evelyn Louise (Olin) D.; 1 child, Kenneth Devereaux Black. BS with honors, U. So. Miss., 1976, MLS with honors, 1978. Adminstrv. asst. to dean Sch. Libr. Sci., U. So. Miss., Hattiesburg, 1974-78; mktg. specialist AT&T, 1978-79; aircrew instr. USAFR, Keesler AFB, Miss., 1979-86; base libr. Lajes Field, Azores, Portugal, 1986-89, Rhein-Main Air Base, Fed. Republic of Germany, 1989-91; chief libr. svcs. Charleston AFB, S.C., 1991—; supervisory libr. Air Force Info. Welfare Ctr., San Antonio, 1995—. Vol. literacy tutor. Decorated Air Res. Forces meritorious svc. medal, Air Force Achievement medal, Combat Readiness medal, Air Force Longevity Svc. award, Small Arms Expert Marksmanship ribbon; named Fed. Civilian Woman of Yr., USAF, 1987, Civilian of Yr., 1994, Meritorius Libr., 1994. Mem. ALA, Spl. Librs. Assn., Fed. Librs. Assn., Air Force Libr. Roundtable, Air Force Assn. Home: 4995 Lambs Rd Charleston SC 29418-3561

DEVEREUX, BARBARA L. elementary school educator; b. Portland, Oreg., Oct. 4, 1940; d. Kenneth Bernard and Cecilia Elinor (Zorich) Carlson; m. Emmett L. Devereux, Dec. 26, 1958; children: Michael, Jill, Karen, Brian. BS, U. Oreg., 1973, MEd, 1980. Cert. in curriculum and instrn., reading K-12, Oreg. 1st grade tchr. Laurel Elem. Sch., Junction City, Oreg., 1974-77; 6th grade tchr. Siuslaw Mid. Sch., Florence, Oreg., 1977-81, kindergarten tchr., 1981-84; title I tchr. Rhododendron Primary Sch., Florence, 1984—. Mentor tchr. Florence Sch. Dist., 1987-88. Recipient scholarship to internat. dyslexia conf. Oreg. Dyslexia Soc., 1987. Mem. ASCD, Internat. REading Assn. Avocations: reading, bicycling, computer applications. Office: Rhododendron Primary Sch 2221 Oak St Florence OR 97439-9529

DE VERITCH, NINA, cellist, music educator; b. Montclair, N.J., Aug. 18, 1941; Student, U. So. Calif., 1959-61, Juilliard Sch. Music, 1961-63. Mem. Detroit Symphony Orch., 1968-70; recording artist movies, records, TV, 1971-74; prin. cellist Utah Symphony, 1964-68; mem. faculty U. Utah, 1964-67, Brigham Young U., 1964-68; studio tchr., adjudicator I, master classes, 1980—; freelance cellist, artist tchr., 2002—. Vis. assoc. prof. U. Mich., 1990-91; prin. cellist Ann Arbor Chamber Orchestra, 1988-90. Mem.: Michiana Cello Soc. (past sec., bd. dirs.), Mich. Music Tchrs. Assn., Am. Fedn. Musicians, Am. String Tchrs. Assn. Home: 9800 Adolphus Dr Frisco TX 75035-7073

DEVIGNE, KAREN COOKE, retired amateur athletics executive; b. Phila., July 31, 1943; d. Paul and Matilda (Rich) Cooke; m. Jules Lloyd Devigne, June 26, 1965; children: Jules Paul, Denise Paige, Paul Michael. AA, Centenary Coll., Hackettstown, 1963; student, Northwestern U., 1963-65; BA, Ramapo Coll., Mahwah, 1976; MA, Emory U., Atlanta, 1989. Founder GYMSET, Marietta, Ga., 1981—. Cons. Girls Club Am. Marietta, 1989; vol. Cobb County Gymnastic Ctr., Marietta, 1976-95, Ga. Youth Soccer Assn., Atlanta, 1976-95; fundraiser Scottish Rite Children's Hosp., Atlanta, 1989. Recipient recognition awards from various youth groups, Atlanta, 1976—; named Nominee Woman of Yr. ABC News, Atlanta, 1984. Avocations: skiing, tennis, bridge. Home: 3701 Clubland Dr Marietta GA 30068-4006 also: 445 White Cloud Breckenridge CO 80424

DEVIN, LEE (PHILIP LEE DEVIN), dramaturg, author; b. Glendale, Calif., Apr. 28, 1938; s. Philip Lee Sr. and Bernice Hermoine (Rogers) D.; m. Barbara Kathleen Norton, June 22, 1958 (div. 1986); children: Siobhan Kathleen, Sean Michael. AB, San Jose State Coll., 1958; MA, Ind. U., 1961, PhD, 1967. Lectr. Ind. U. extension, Indpls., 1960-62; instr., tech. dir. U. Va., Charlottesville, 1962-66; instr., assoc. dir. Exptl. Theatre Vassar Coll., Poughkeepsie, N.Y., 1966-67, asst. prof., assoc. dir., 1967-70; assoc. prof., dir. theatre Swarthmore (Pa.) Coll., 1970-79, prof., dir. theatre, 1979-98, prof., 1998—2003, sr. rsch. scholar, 2003—. Electrician, state mgr., prodn. stage mgr. Honey in the Rock, Beckley, W.Va., 1962-64; artist-in-residence Ball State U., Muncie, Ind., 1968, U. Calif. San Diego, La Jolla, 1973; assoc. artist People's Light and Theatre Co., Malvern, Pa., 1977—, dramaturg, 1985—. Author: (with Rob Austin) Artful Making: What Managers Need to Know About How Artists Work, 2003, (radio plays) Elegy for Irish Jack, 1973, When the Time Comes, 1978, Frankenstein, 1981 (WHA, Earplay Purchase awards); (with S. Hodkinson) (drama with music) Lament: for Guitar and Two Lovers, 1963; (active oratorio) Vox Populous, 1973; (opera) St. Carmen of the Main, 1987 actor various roles stage, film, TV; translator (with A. Adams) A Doll House, 1987, Oedipus, 1988. Recipient 1st prize WGBH Radio Drama, Boston, 1968, James S. Helms Playscript award, 1964, Calif. Olympiad of the Arts, 1965; librettist's grantee NEA, Washington, 1974, 75, 77; grantee Mellon Found., 1973, 77; Lang fellow 1990. Mem. Actors' Equity Assn., Assn. for Theatre in Higher Edn., Literary Mgrs. and Dramaturgs of the Ams. Avocation: fly fishing. Home: 603 Hillborn Ave Swarthmore PA 19081-1123 E-mail: ldevin1@swarthmore.edu.

DEVINATZ, VICTOR GARY, industrial relations educator; b. St. Louis, Oct. 19, 1957; s. Allen and Pearl (Moskowitz) D. BSE, Northwestern U., 1979, MA, 1980; MS, U. Mass., 1986; PhD, U. Minn., 1990. Lectr. U. Minn., Mpls., 1990-91; asst. prof. Ill. State U., Normal, 1991-94, assoc. prof., 1994-98, prof., 1998—. Contbr. articles to profl. jours. including Indsl. Rels. Jour. Labor Rsch., Labor Studies Jour., Jour. Collective Negotiations in Pub. Sector, Labor Law Jour. Grantee, Henry J. Kaiser Family Found., Walter P. Reuther Libr., Wayne State U., 1989; Caterpillar scholar, 1999, Merl E. Reed fellow in so. labor history, 2003. Mem. Indsl. Rels. Rsch. Assn., United Assn. Labor Edn. Home: 102 S Oak St Apt 3 Normal IL 61761-3053 Office: Ill State U Dept Mgmt & Quant Methods Normal IL 61790-5580

DEVINE, HAZEL BERNICE, retired secondary school educator; b. Verdigre, Nebr., Oct. 16, 1926; d. Richard and Josephine (Houzvicka) Uhlir; m. Francis Stanley Devine, June 2, 1949. Student, Wayne State Tchrs. Coll., 1943-48; BA, San Diego State Coll., 1959; MA in Ednl. Adminstrn., U. Nebr., 1968. Tchr. Knox County Schs., Niobrara, Nebr., 1943-49, Rock Springs (Wyo.) Sch. Dist., 1953-55, Escondido Union Sch. Dist., San Diego, 1959-61, Rupert (Idaho) County Schs., 1961—65, Louisville (Nebr.) Pub. Schs., 1966-67; team leader, tchr. Cuba (Mo.) Schs., 1972-74. Author: Kids, Taxpayers and Schools, 1982, The Changing Winds, 1999. Mem. Friends of Libr., 1990; v.p. Hastings (Nebr.) YWCA, 1979-81. Mem. AAUW (pres. 1989-93), Ret. Tchrs. Hastings (v.p.), Hastings Area Ret. Tchrs. Assn. (pres. 1988-89), LWV (bd. dirs. 1979-91). Republican. Avocations: writing, politics, painting, dancing, drama. Home: 813 Richmond Ave Hastings NE 68901-3325

DEVINE, KATHERINE, environmental consultant, educator; b. Denver, Oct. 15, 1951; BS, Rutgers U., 1973, MS, 1980; postgrad., U. Md., 1981-82. Lab. technician Princeton (N.J.) U., 1974-76; econ. and regulatory affairs analyst, program mgr. U.S. EPA, Washington, 1979-89, cons., 1989-99; exec. dir. Applied BioTreatment Assn., Washington, 1990-91; pres. DEVO Enterprises, Inc., Washington, 1990-99; sr. editor Scientist, Phila., 2000—01; tchr. Phila. Sch. Dist., 2001—. Chair adv. bd. Applied Bioremediation Conf., 1993; co-chair Environ. Biotech. Conf., 1996, 97, others. Author: N.J. Agricultural Experiment Station of Rutgers Uniersity, 1980, Bioremediation Case Studies: An Analysis of Vendor Supplied Data, 1992, Bioremediation Case Studies: Abstracts, 1992; co-author: Biomediation: Field Experiences, 1994, Bioremediation, 1994; founder, pub., editor (mag.) Biotreatment News, 1990-97; pub. The Gold Book; editor Indsl. Biotech. News, 1998; contbr. articles to profl. jours., chpts. to books; co-sponsor over 20 confs. Mem. Women's Coun. on Energy and the Environment, 1991-93. Recipient numerous fed. govt. and non- govt. awards. Mem. Am. Chem. Soc., Futures for Children, Alpha Zeta. E-mail: devoinc@aol.com.

DEVINE, KATHLEEN ANNE, elementary school educator; b. Phila., Nov. 30, 1963; d. James Raymond and Claire Anne (Merman) D. BFA in Photography, Moore Coll. of Art, 1986; MA in Art Edn., Univ. of Arts, 1992. Cert. art edn. Art instr. St. Dorothy Sch., Drexel Hill, Pa., 1987-90, Radnor (Pa.) Sch. Dist., 1988-89, Moore Coll. of Art/Young People's Art Workshop, Phila., 1988-91, Rose Tree Media (Pa.) Sch. Dist., 1989—. Chandler scholar Moore Coll. of Art, 1988-89; recipient Roberts prize Univ. of Arts, 1993. Mem. Nat. Art Edn. Assn., Pa. Coalition for Arts in Edn., Pa. State Edn. Assn., Phila. Mus. Art. Roman Catholic. Office: Indian Lane Elem Sch 309 S Old Middletown Rd Media PA 19063-4798

DEVINE, LIBBY, art educator, consultant; b. Indpls., Jan. 31, 1952; d. Taylor William and Elizabeth Josephine Jackson; m. Douglas M. Devine, June 12, 1976. BFA, U. Ga., 1974; M of Visual Arts, Ga. State U., 1980. Cert. tchr. Ga., Nat. Bd. Cert. Tchr., 2002, tchr. Early Adolescence through Young Adult. Tchr. art, dept. chair Roswell (Ga.) H.S./Fulton County Schs., 1980—; cons. Ga. Dept. of Edn. Test Devel., Tchr. Cert. Test in Art, 1988—90; sch. arts program coord. Fulton County Dept. of Edn., Fulton County Arts Coun., 1988—, cons. coll. bd., 2002—03; presenter in field. Contbr. articles;, editor curriculum guide. Grantee, Fulton County Arts Coun., 2003—04. Mem.: Profl. Assn. Ga. Educators, Ga. Art Edn. Assn., Nat. Art Edn. Assn. (grant 1991). Office: Roswell HS 11595 King Rd Roswell GA 30075

DEVLIN, BARBARA JO, school district administrator; b. Milw., Oct. 6, 1947; d. Raymond Peter Seeley and Lois Elsa Young; m. John Edward Devlin, June 23, 1973; children: Christine Elizabeth, Kathleen Megan. BA, Gustavus Adolphus Coll., 1969; MA, U. Mass., 1971; PhD, U. Minn., 1978. Cert. tchr., sch. prin., supt., Minn.; cert. supt., Ill., Minn. Tchr. Worthington (Minn.) High Sch., 1971-75; rsch. assoc. Ednl. R & D, Mpls.-St. Paul, 1975-76, 76-77; coord. edn. svcs. Ednl. Coop. Svc., Mpls.-St. Paul, 1977-79; dir. personnel Minnetonka Pub. Schs., Excelsior, Minn., 1979-85, asst. supt., 1985-87; supt. Sch. Dist. 45, Villa Park, Ill., 1987-95, Ind. Sch. Dist. 280, Richfield, Minn., 1995—. Editor working papers Gov.'s Coun. on Fluctuating Enrollments, St. Paul, 1976. Contbr. articles to ednl. jours. Bd. dirs. Richfield Found., 1995—. Ednl. Policy fellow George Washington U., 1977-78; mem. fellow program Bush Found. Pub. Schs., 1984-85; named Ill. Supt. of the Yr., 1994; recipient Disting. Alumni award Gustavus Adolphus Coll., 1994. Mem. Richfield C. of C. (bd. dirs. 1996-99), Rotary Internat. (membership chair Villa Park unit 1989-91, vocat. dir. 1991-92, sec. 1992-93, pres. 1994-95), Optimists Internat. (pres. elect Richfield unit 1998-99, pres. 1999-2000). Methodist. Office: Richfield Pub Schs 7001 Harriet Ave Richfield MN 55423-3061 E-mail: Barbara.Devlin@richfiedl.k12.mn.us.

DEVLIN, JEAN THERESA, educator, storyteller; b. Jamaica, N.Y., Apr. 14, 1947; d. Edward Philip and Frances Margaret (Tillman) Creagh; children: Michael, Bernadette, Patrick. BA magna cum laude, Queens Coll.,

1972, postgrad., 1994—95; MA, St. John's U., Jamaica, 1987; PhD, So. Ill. U., 1991. Substitute tchr. Diocese of Bklyn., 1969-75; tchr. St. Gregory's Sch., Bellerose, N.Y., 1975-82; dist. mgr. Creative Expressions, Robesonia, Pa., 1980-83; asst. to dean, adj. instr. workshop supr. Spl. Univ. Program St. John's U., Jamaica, 1983-87, asst. prof. dept. English, 1992; asst. dean St. John's Coll. Liberal Arts, St. Johns U., 1993-94; owner Tara's Tees and Golden Hands Embroidery, 1984-87; from grad. asst. to doctoral fellow English dept. So. Ill. U., Carbondale, 1987-89, storytelling tchr. Continuing Edn., 1992; adj. asst. prof. St. John's U., Jamaica, 1992-94, Poly. U., N.Y., 1995-96, Bayside Acad., N.Y., 1995-97, St. Anthony's H.S., Huntington, N.Y., 1996-99; tchr. SCOPE (gifted and talented program) South Huntington Dist., N.Y., 1999-2000; tchr., asst. prin., tchr. Rambam Mesivta Maimonides H.S., Lawrence, NY, 1999—2001; tchr. Hicksville H.S., 2002, North Shore Hebrew Acad. H.S., 2002—; asst. prof. L.I. Conservatory, 2002—03. Cons. Family Lit. Project; supr. workshops Popular Culture, 1991-94, Children's Lit. Assn., 1990-92, Midwest Popular Culture, 1991, Wyo. Centennial, 1990; presenter poetry readings, dramatic interpretation, storytelling, including Internat. Rsch. Soc. in Children's Lit., Paris, 1991, Nat. Coun. Tchrs. English Conf., 1992, Ill. Assn. Tchrs. of English, 1990, 91, 92, South Atlantic MLA, 1992, Mid Atlantic Popular/Am. Culture, 1993; speaker Speak Easy Workshop, 1981; showcased Nat. Congress Storytelling, Children's Reading Roundtable, 1990; world-wide storyteller, 1991—; featured spkr. Puppet Guild of L.I., 1997; adj. asst. prof. So. Ill., St. John's U., Polytechnic U., Molloy Coll., 1998—, SUNY, Farmingdale, 2002—. Author: Gabby Diego, 1992, repub. 1994, Rainbows Stories and Customs from Around the World, 1996; contbr. articles to profl. jours. and children's mags.; contbg. photographer Eye of the Beholder, 2000; actress (videotape and audiocassette) Peter Kagan and the Wind, 1990, 91, played at White House, 1992, Sta. WKTS, 1992-94, Excerpts from Shakespeare, 1999, (videotape) Puppets from A to Z, 2000; performed as storyteller on 5 continents, 1991—;singer with North Shore Hebrew Acad. Choir, CD, Shiryla, 2003; mem. editl. bd. Habari Gari: A Newsletter for Catholics of African Ancestry, 1999-2000. Den leader Boy Scouts Am., Bayside, N.Y., 1975-80; troop leader Girl Scouts U.S.A., Flushing, N.Y., 1976-78; vol. Elderwise Day Care, Carbondale, Ill., 1992, Alice Wright Day Care Ctr., Carbondale, 1989-92, ABC Quilts (A Pediatric AIDS group), 1991-2000; mem. The Stage Co., Cill Cais Players. Honored for outstanding svc. Boy Scouts Am., 1978; recipient Outstanding Cmty. Svc. award, named Most Admired Woman of the Decade Sta. WPSD-TV, 1991, Internat. Women of Yr., 1993; grantee So. Ill. Art Coun., 1992; named Educator of Excellence, N.Y. State English Coun., 2000, L.I. Lang. Arts Coun., 2001. Mem.: AAUW, MLA, United Fedn. Tchrs., Am. Fedn. Tchrs., N.Y. State United Tchrs., United Univ. Profs., L.I. Lang. Arts Coun., NY State English Coun., Puppet Guild L.I., Nat. Theatre for Puppet Arts, Children's Lit. Assn., Nat. Assn. Preservation and Perpetuation of Storytelling, Nat. Coun. Tchrs. English, Phi Delta Kappa, Sigma Tau Delta, Alpha Sigma Lambda, Skull and Circle Honor Soc. (St. John's U.). Avocations: needlework, acting, puppetry. Home: 193 W 19th St Huntington Station NY 11746-2118

DEVLIN, THOMAS MCKEOWN, biochemist, educator; b. Phila., June 29, 1929; s. Frank and Ella Mae (McKeown) D.; m. Marjorie Adele Paynter, Aug. 15, 1953; children— Steven James, Mark Thomas. BA, U. Pa., 1953; PhD, Johns Hopkins U., 1957. Rsch. assoc. Merck Inst., Rahway, N.J., 1957-61, sect. head, 1961-66, dir. enzymology, 1966-67; prof., chmn. dept. biochemistry Hahnemann U. Sch. Medicine, 1967-94, prof., 1994-95; prof. emeritus, 1995—; acting dean, Sch. Allied Health Professions Hahnemann U., 1972-74, 80-81. Vis. scientist U. Brussels, 1964-65, Inst. Genetics, Naples, Italy, 1965; mem. NSF rev. panels, 1976-77; mem. coun. acad. soc. Assn. Am. Med. Colls., 1975-79; mem. com. on sci. and arts Franklin Inst., 1977-90; mem. test com. Nat. Bd. Med. Examiners, 1983-85; chair Med. Biochemistry Edn. Bd., 1986-93. Editor: (J. Wiley) Textbook of Biochemistry, 1982, 86, 92, 97, 2002; contbr. numerous articles to profl. jours. Mem. Commn. on Evaluation, Retention and Selection of Judges, Phila. Bar Assn., 1976-79, vice chmn., 1979; vis. com. Lehigh U., 1982-90; mem. selection panel for magistrate judges, 1993, 95; mem. tech. adv. com. Ben Franklin Tech. Ctr., 1991-2000. Mem. Am. Soc. for Biochemistry and Molecular Biology, Am. Assn. Cancer Research, Am. Soc. Cell Biology, Soc. Exptl. Biology and Medicine, Biophys. Soc., Biochem. Soc., Phi Beta Kappa, Sigma Xi. Clubs: Ocean City (N.J.) Yacht, Greate Bay Golf Club. Episcopalian. Home: 159 Greenville Ct Berwyn PA 19312-2071 Office: Drexel U Coll Medicine 159 Greenville Ct Berwyn PA 19312-2071 E-mail: tdevlin@drexel.edu.

DEVNEY, ANNE MARIE, nursing educator; b. Jackson Heights, N.Y., July 31, 1948; d. Edward James and Lillian Hazel (Ryan) D. BSN, U. R.I., 1970; BS, George Washington U., 1978; MSEd, Pepperdine U., 1981; MAEd, San Diego State U., 1985; EdD in Adult Edn., No. Ill. U., 1994. Cert. instructional tech. Commd. ens. Nurse Corps USN, 1968; charge nurse Naval Hosp., St. Albans, Queens, N.Y., 1970-72, Marine Corps Dispensary, Iwakuni, Japan, 1972-74; charge nurse intermediate ICU Naval Regional Med. Ctr., San Diego, 1974-76; advanced through grades to comdr. USN, 1989; nurse anesthetist U.S. Naval Hosp., Long Beach, Calif., 1978-81; ret. USN, 1989; coord. inservice U.S. Naval Hosp., Long Beach, Calif., instr. Naval Sch. Health Scis. San Diego, 1981-84; edn. cons. No. Ill. U., DeKalb; dir. health svcs. Coll. of Lake County, Grayslake, Ill., former coord. allied health svcs.; staff nurse Condell Med. Ctr., Libertyville, Ill. Mem. nursing adv. faculty, dir. Health Ctr., Coll. of Lake County, Grayslake, Ill.; mem. adj. faculty Nat.-Louis U., Wheaton, Ill., Coll. of St. Francis, Joliet, Ill.; cons., pres. Devney Interactive Design. Contbr. articles to profl. jours., chpts. to books; rsch. on The Effectiveness of Interactive Video on Performance of Simple Nursing Procedure, Crisis Learning: Family Members of ICU Trauma Patients. With USN. San Diego Navy League finalist for Mil. Women of the Year award, 1983. Mem. ANA, Ill. State Nurses Assn., Nat. League for Nursing, Am. Ednl. Rsch. Assn., Pi Lambda Theta (pres. Chgo. area chpt.). Home: 18670 W Old Plank Rd Grayslake IL 60030-2250 Office: Coll Lake County 19351 W Washington St Grayslake IL 60030-1148 E-mail: adevney@clcillinois.edu.

DEVOE, DOROTHY S. elementary school educator; b. Dixie, Ga., Jan. 18, 1944; d. Hadley and Rachael (Peeples) Sirmans; m. Allen A. Devoe Jr., Jan. 4, 1965; children: Tonya L., Wrenettia K. BS, Albany (Ga.) State Coll., 1966; MEd, U. No. Fla., 1988; postgrad., Jacksonville U., 1969, Fla. A&M U., 1977-78. Cert. Fla. peer tchr. observer, tchr. rsch. linker in ednl. rsch. and dissemination program, elem. edn. 1-6, reading K-12. Classroom tchr., computer lead tchr. Duval County Pub. Schs., 1986, reading recovery tchr., 1998—. Mem. Duval County Reading Coun. Recipient various awards and certs. Mem. Fla. Reading Assn., Fla. Edn. Assn., Nat. Reading Recovery Coun. N.Am., Nat. Coun. Negro Women, Zeta Phi Beta.

DE VOE, PAMELA ANN, anthropologist, educator; b. Chgo., Ill., Sept. 22, 1946; d. Edward George De Voe and Evelyn Francis De Grave; m. Ronald E. Mertz, Aug. 1971; 1 child, Renée De Voe. BA, U. Wis., 1967; MA, U. Mo., 1971; PhD, U. Ariz., 1979; student, U. Mo., 1980—82. Cons., St. Louis, 1995—99; parent coord. St. Louis Pub. Sch., St. Louis, 1998—99; info. specialist St. Louis C.C., St. Louis, 1999—2001; asst. prof. St. Louis U., St. Louis, 2001—. Adj. faculty Webster U., St. Louis, 2000—, St. Louis C.C., St. Louis, 2000—. Co-prodr.: Refugee Studies Newsletter, 1984—86; editor: Selected Papers in Refugee Issues 1992, 1992; contbr. articles to profl. jours. Fellow Tchg. fellow, U. Ariz., 1976—77, U. Mo., Columbia, 1980—82; grantee HEW Fulbright-Hays grantee, 1977—78, Mo. Humanities Coun., 1989—90. Mem.: Soc. Applied Anthropology, Am. Anthropological. Assn. (com. refugee issues 1986, editor CORI 1988—94, bd. dir. gen. anthropology divsn. 1992—96, com. on refugees & immigrants 1994—96, 2000—), Asian Art Soc. (v.p. 1996—98, pres. 1998—99, bd.dir. 1993—2001). Democrat. Avocations: writing poetry, spinning wool. Home: 165 Bonchateau Dr Saint Louis MO 63141 Office: Internat Inst St Louis 3654 S Grand Blvd Saint Louis MO 63118 Business E-Mail: devoemertz@sbcglobal.net.

DEVONE, DENISE, artist, educator; BFA cum laude, Temple U., 1975; MFA, U. Hawaii, 1978. Instr. Newark Mus., 1990-97; art tchr. Holy Cross Sch., Harrison, N.J., 1995—. Adj. prof. County Coll. of Morris, Randolph, N.J., 1994—; cons. Donald B. Palmer Mus., Springfield, N.J., 1992-95. Executed murals Kaiser Hosp., Honolulu, 1985, Kaiser Pensacola Clinic, Honolulu, 1986, Distinctive Bodies Fitness, Warren, N.J., 1993, Ambulatory Pediatric Clinic, Overlook Hosp., Summit, N.J., 1994; one-woman shows include Contemporary Mus., Honolulu, 1992, ETS, Princeton, 1995, Montclair Kimberly Acad., N.J., 1995, 98, ADP Gallery, Roseland, N.J., 1997, Palmyra Gallery, Bound Brook, N.J., 1999; illustrator: Japanese Pilgramage, 1983, The Art of Featherwork in Old Hawaii, 1985. Recipient Purchase awards Hawaii State Found. on Culture and the Arts, 1976, 78, 80, 86, award of merit City and County of Honolulu, 1988; N.J. State Coun. on Arts/Dept. State fellow, 1994-95. Mem. Nat. Assn. Women Artists, Inc., Studio Montclair, Inc., City Without Walls, Artists Space. Avocation: piano. Home: 33 Kew Dr Springfield NJ 07081-2530

DE VORE, SADIE DAVIDSON, printmaker, art educator, artist; b. Wheaton, Mo., June 12, 1937; d. Noah Fred and Marion Ollie (Jones) Davidson; m. Harry L. De Vore III, Dec. 12, 1959 (dec.); children: Desa De Vore Buffum, H.L. IV, David Christopher. BS, S.W. Mo. State U., 1958, MAT, RIC, 1980; postgrad., U. Kans., 1969, U. Mo., Kansas City, 1970, NYU, 1987, Brooks Inst., 1990, Savannah Coll. Art and Design, 1997. Cert. art K-12 tchr. Art tchr. Springfield (Mo.) Art Mus., 1956-58; comml. artist Springfield Utilities, 1958-59, Springfield, 1959-62; art tchr. Shawnee Mission (Kans.) North H.S., 1963-65; artist, tchr. Stonington Cmty. Ctr., 1971; art tchr. Stonington Pub. Sch., Pawcatuck, Conn., 1972—; art history tchr. Mitchell Coll., New London, Conn., 1989. Art reader Coll. Bd. of N.J., Princeton, N.J., 1996. Exhibited in numerous art shows including Hoxie Gallery, Hat Shop, Conn. Com. of the Arts, Slater Mus., Marcus Gallery, Emporium Gallery, Conn. Coll., Ellison Ctr. Duxbury, Noah's Art, Rockhurst Coll., Weekapaug, Mitchell Coll., Studio 33, James Gallery, Sharon Art Ctr., John Slade Ely House. Skidmore Art fellow, 1989; Margo Rose scholar Eugene O'Neill Theatre Puppetry Workshop, 1998. Mem. Nat. Art Edn. Assn., Nat. Art Honor Soc., Conn. Art Adminstrs. Assn., Conn. Art Edn. Assn., Lyme Art Assn., East Lyme Art Assn., Mystic Art Assn., Vangarde Artists, South County Art Assn., Monotypes Today, Conn. Craftmen, Puppeteers of Conn., Puppeteers of Am., Pawmystonian Puppeteers (founder), Monotype Guild New Eng., Alpha Delta Pi. Democrat. Avocations: gardening, travel, boating, jewelry making. Home: 137 High St Mystic CT 06355-2415 Office: Stonington Pub Schs 176 S Broad St Pawcatuck CT 06379-1924 E-mail: sadiedevore@aol.com.

DEVRIES, BRIGID LARKIN, educational association administrator; b. Lexington, Ky., July 27, 1949; d. Stuart Ralph and Helen Mary (Larkin) D. BA in Phys. Edn., Health and Recreation, U. Ky., 1971, MS in Edn., 1975. Phys. edn. tchr. Nicholas County Elem. Sch., Carlisle, Ky., 1971-73; grad. asst. dept. campus recreation U. Ky., 1973-75; coach women's intercollegiate swimming and track Ohio U., Athens, 1976-79; exec. asst. Ky. High Sch. Athletic Assn., Lexington, 1979—; coach men's and women's diving U. Ky., Lexington, 1980-90. Bd. dirs. Blue Grass State Games, 1984—. Named to Swimming and Diving Hall of Fame U. Ky., 1994. Mem. Citizens for Sports Equity (pres. 1993-96), Nat. Fedn. Rules Com. (gymnastics 1981-84, volleyball 1986-89, swimming and diving 1983-86). Democrat. Avocations: whitewater canoeing, tennis. Office: Ky High Sch Athletic Assn 2280 Executive Dr Lexington KY 40505-4808

DEVRIES, MARVIN FRANK, mechanical engineering educator; b. Grand Rapids, Mich., Oct. 31, 1937; s. Ralph B. and Grace (Buurma) DeV.; m. Martha Lou Kannegieter, Aug. 28, 1959; children: Mark Alan, Michael John, Matthew Dale. BS, Calvin Coll., 1960; BSME, U. Mich., 1960, MSME, 1962; PhD, U. Wis., 1966. Registered profl. engr., Wis. Teaching fellow mech. engring. U. Mich., Ann Arbor, 1960-62; instr. U. Wis., Madison, 1962-66, asst. prof., 1966-70, assoc. prof., 1970-77, prof. mech. engring., 1977—, chmn. dept. mech. engring., 1991-95. Vis. Fulbright prof. Cranfield (Eng.) Inst. Tech., 1979-80; dir Mfg. Systems Engring. Program, Madison, 1983-91; cons in field. Contbr. over 90 articles to profl. jours. Sr. program dir. NSF, Washington, 1987-90. Recipient Ralph Teetor award Soc. Auto. Engrs., 1967, Space Shuttle Tech. award NASA, 1984, Disting. Achievement award L.A. Coun. Engrs. and Scientists, 1985, Internat. Tech. Communications award Calif. Engring. Found., 1985. Fellow ASME, Soc. Mfg. Engrs. (pres. 1985-86, Olin Simpson award 1986, Edn. award 1998), Instn. Prodn. Engrs. (U.K., life); mem. Internat. Instn. Prod. Engring. Rsch. (v.p. 1997-2000). Avocations: travel, sports. Home: 901 Tompkins Dr Madison WI 53716-3267 Office: U Wis 1513 University Ave Madison WI 53706-1539

DEWAN, MANTOSH JAIMANI, psychiatrist, educator; b. Bombay, July 22, 1951; came to U.S., 1975; s. Jaimani and Sheel (Krishen) D.; m. Anita Lall, June 21, 1975; children: Amant, Radhika. MB, BS, Bombay U., 1975. Diplomate Am. Bd. Psychiatry and Neurology. Intern SUNY Health Sci. Ctr., Syracuse, 1975-76, resident in psychiatry, 1976-79, asst. to assoc. prof., 1979-92, prof., 1992—, asst. dir. undergrad. edn., 1982-85, co-dir. undergrad. edn., 1985-88, dir. undergrad. edn., 1988-92, dir. residency tng. in psychiatry, 1992-99, vice chair dept. psychiatry, 1995-99, chmn., 1999—; staff psychiatrist VA Med. Ctr., Syracuse, 1979-85, acting chief, 1985-89. Research cons. Hutchings Psychiat. Ctr., Syracuse, 1984—. Contbr. articles to profl. jours. and author chpts. in books, 1982—. Recipient Sci. award Indo-Am. Psychiatrists Assn., 1998; named exemplary psychiatrist Nat. Alliance for Mentally Ill, 1994. Fellow Am. Psychiat. Assn. (disting., counselor-at-large dist. chpt. 1984-85, sec., treas. 1990-91, pres. 1992-93); mem. Assn. Am. Psychiatrists from India (life), Soc. for Biol. Psychiatry, Am. Assn. Chairs Acad. Depts. Psychiatry. Democrat. Home: 5310 Aquarius Dr Syracuse NY 13224-2146 Office: SUNY Upstate Med Univ Dept Psychiatry 750 E Adams St Syracuse NY 13210-1834

DEWAR, ROBERT EARL, JR., anthropologist, educator; b. Detroit, July 4, 1949; s. Robert Earl and Nancy (Miller) D.; m. Alison F. Richard, Aug. 21, 1976; children: Elizabeth Napier, Charlotte Mary. AB, Brown U., 1971; MPhil, Yale U., 1973, PhD, 1977. Instr. U. Conn., Storrs, 1975-77, asst. prof., 1977-82, assoc. prof., 1982—89, dept. head, 1986—96, prof., 1989—. Bd. dirs. Conn. State Mus. Natural History, Storrs, Liz Clairborne Art Ortenberg Found., N.Y. Editor: Connecticut Archaeology, 1981. Mem. Conn. State Hist. Preservation Rev. Bd., Hartford, 1987-97, Hist. Dist. Commn., Middle Haddam, Conn., 1986—. Recipient rsch. grants NSF, 1984, 86, 88, 92, Nat. Geographic Soc., 1978, 79, McArthur Found., 1998. Fellow Am. Anthropol. Assn.; mem. AAAS, Soc. for Am. Archaeology. Avocation: fly fishing. Home: PO Box 34 Middle Haddam CT 06456-0034 Office: Dept Anthropology Univ Connecticut Dept Anthropology # U-176 Storrs Mansfield CT 06269

DEWEESE, DEVIN A. history educator; b. 1956; PhD in Ctrl. Asian Studies, Ind. U., Bloomington, 1985. Prof. Ctrl. Asian studies Ind. U., Bloomington, 2003—. Author: Islamization and Native Religion in the Golden Horde (Best First Book in the History of Religions Am. Acad. Religion, Albert Hourani Book award Middle East Studies Assn.). Fellow, John Simon Guggenheim Meml. Found., 2003. Office: U Ind Ctrl Asian Studies Goodbody Hall 348 Bloomington IN 47405-7005*

DEWERD, LARRY ALBERT, medical physicist, educator; b. Milw., July 18, 1941; s. Anthony Lawrence and Dorothy M. (Heling) DeW.; m. Vada Mary Anderson, Sept. 14, 1963; children: Scott, Mark, Eric. BS, U. Wis., Milw., 1963; MS, U. Wis., 1965, PhD, 1970. Rsch. assoc. U. Wash., Seattle, 1970-72, rsch. asst. prof., 1973-75; vis. asst. prof. U. Wis., Madison, 1975-76, clin. asst. prof., 1976-79, clin. assoc. prof., 1979-86, prof., 1990—. Mgr. product devel. Radiation Measurements, Middleton, Wis., 1986-90; dir. Radiation Calibration Lab., Madison, 1983-86, 90—; cons. Instrumentarium, Milw., 1990; v.p. Standard Imaging, Madison, 1990—; presenter in field; cons. IAEA. Contbg. author: Brachytherapy, Ionization Chambers and Dosimetry, Thermoluminescence and Mammography; also numerous articles. Science chmn. Am. Cancer Soc. State of Wis., 1986-90. Grantee Nat. Cancer Inst., 1979-86, 94-98. Fellow Am. Assn. Physicists in Medicine (pres. 1990-92), Health Physics Soc., Am. Phys. Soc., Coun. Ionizing Radiation Measurements and Standards (pres. 1995-98), Sigma Xi (bd. dirs. 1984-86). Avocations: golf, fishing, backpacking, hunting. Home: 13 Pilgrim Cir Madison WI 53711-4033 Office: U Wis 1530 Med Sci Ctr 1300 University Ave Madison WI 53706-1510

DEWEY, CLARENCE FORBES, JR., engineering educator; b. Pueblo, Colo., Mar. 27, 1935; s. Clarence F. and Elsie (Hafermalz) D.; m. Carolyn Miller, Aug. 3, 1963; 1 child, Devan Forbes. BE, Yale U., 1956; MS, Stanford U., 1957; PhD, Calif. Inst. Tech., 1963. Aero. rsch. scientist NASA-AMES, Moffet Field, Calif., summer 1956; tech. staff aeronutronic divsn. Ford, Newport Beach, 1957-59; rsch. asst. Calif. Inst. Tech., Pasadena, Calif., 1959-63; asst. prof. mech. engring. U. Colo., Boulder, 1963-68; assoc. prof. MIT, Cambridge, 1968-76, prof., 1976-98, prof. mech. engring. and bioengring., 1998—, head fluid mechanics lab., 1975—83, head microfluids lab., 2001—03; assoc. in pathology Peter Brent Brigham Hosp., Boston, 1978-95. Vis. scientist Inst. Plasma Physics, Garching, Germany, 1966—67; vis. prof. Harvard U. Med. Sch., 1978—79, Hefei Poly. U., China, 1986, Imperial Coll. Ctr. Med. and Biol. Sys., London, 1992, London, 2001; biomed. engr. Mass. Gen. Hosp., Boston, 1975—76, cons. in medicine, 1976—80; founder Mass. Computer Corp., 1981; co-dir. Internat. Consortium for Med. Imaging Tech., 1992—; path. cons. Brigham and Women's Hosp., 1982—96. Patentee in field; contbr. articles to profl. jours. Chmn. MIT United Way, 1996—97; trustee Fidelity Non-Profit Mgmt. Found., 2001—. Grantee NIH, Bethesda, Md., 1971—, Office Naval Rsch., San Diego 1970-75, 1987-89, Air Force Office Sci. Rsch., Washington, 1976-79. Fellow Am. Inst. Med. Biol. Engring. (founding); mem. Am. Phys. Soc., Biomed. Engring. Soc. (sr.). Avocations: trout fishing, skiing. Office: 77 Massachusetts Ave Cambridge MA 02139-4301

DEWEY, DONALD ODELL, dean, academic administrator; b. Portland, Oreg., July 9, 1930; s. Leslie Hamilton and Helen (Odell) D.; m. Charlotte Marion Neuber, Sept. 21, 1952; children: Leslie Helen, Catherine Dawn, Scott Hamilton. Student, Lewis and Clark Coll., 1948-49; BA, U. Oreg., 1952; MS, U. Utah, 1956; PhD, U. Chgo., 1960. Mng. editor Condon (Oreg.) Globe-Times, 1952-53; city editor Ashland (Oreg.) Daily Tidings, 1953-54; asst. editor, assoc. editor The Papers of James Madison, Chgo., 1957-62; instr. U. Chgo., 1960-62; from asst. prof. to prof. Calif. State U., L.A., 1962-96, dean Sch. Letters and Sci., 1970-84, dean Sch. Natural and Social Sci., 1984-96, dean emeritus, prof. emeritus, 1996—; v.p. acad. affairs Trinity Coll. Grad. Studies, Anaheim, Calif., 2000—. Author: The Continuing Dialogue, 2 vols., 1964, Union and Liberty: Documents in American Constitutionalism, 1969, Marshall versus Jefferson: The Political Background of Marbury v. Madison, 1970, Becoming Informed Citizens: Lessons on the Constitution for Junior High School Students, 1988, revised edit., 1995, Invitation to the Dance: An Introduction to Social Dance, 1991, Becoming Informed Citizens: The Bill of Rights and Limited Government, 1995, That's a Good One: Cal State L.A. at 50, 1997, The Federalist and Antifederalist Papers, 1998, Controversial Elections, 2001; contbr. chpts. to books. Recipient Outstanding Prof. award Calif. State U., 1976 Mem. Am. Hist. Assn. (exec. coun. Pacific Coast br. 1971-74), Orgn. Am. Historians, Am. Soc. Legal History (adv. bd. Pacific Coast br. 1972-75), Gold Key, Phi Alpha Theta, Pi Sigma Alpha, Phi Kappa Phi, Sigma Delta Chi. Office: Calif State U Dept History 5151 State University Dr Los Angeles CA 90032-4226 E-mail: ddewey@calstatela.edu.

DEWEY, RALPH JAY, school system administrator; b. N.Y.C., Feb. 8, 1944; s. Ralph Morris and Evelyn Elizabeth (Karle) D.; m. Vivian V. Barone Dewey, Dec. 20, 1970; children: Gabriella Maria, Meredith Elizabeth, Ralph Stephen. BS, Holy Cross Coll., Worcester, Mass.. 1965; MAT, Brown U., Providence, 1968; EdS, Rutgers U., 1985. Teaching Cert., N.Y. Tchr. Moses Brown Sch., Providence, 1965-68; founding head of mid. sch. Portledge Sch., Locust Valley, N.Y., 1968-74; head of lower sch. Rutgers Preparatory Sch., Somerset, N.J., 1974-83; founding headmaster The Winston Sch., Summit, N.J., 1983-87; headmaster St. James Episc. Sch., Corpus Christi, 1987-95; headmaster, bd. dirs. Cape Fear Acad., Wilmington, NC, 1995—2001; dir. Schechter Regional H.S., Bergen County, NJ, 2002—. Regional coord. Southwestern Assn. Episcopal Schs., Corpus Christi, Tex., 1989-93, mem. stds. com. Southwestern Assn. Episcopal Schs., 1994-95, cons., Dallas, 1990-92; workshop presenter Nat. Assn. Ind. Sch., N.Y.C., 1991, Tex. Elem. Prins. and Suprs. Assn., 1991. Author, editor: Winston Newsletter, 1983-87, St. James Episcopal School Newsletter, 1987-95; author: Classical Vocabulary, 1990; contbr. articles to profl. jours. Treas. Coastal Bend Soc. Friends, 1988-95; sec., v.p. Harbor Playhouse, Corpus Christi, Tex., 1989-92; mem. Com. of 100, Wilmington, 1995; mem. exec. coun. Leadership Wilmington, 1996; bd. dirs. Ea. Plains Ind. Conf. Recipient U.S. Dept. Blue Ribbon Sch. Excellence award, Salute to Prins. award Nat. Assn. Elem. Sch. Prins. Mem. N.C. Assn. Ind. Schs. (bd. dirs. 1998-2002, membership chmn. 1998-2001), SAR, ASCD, Assn. Children with Learning Disabilities, Nat. Assn. for Edn. of Young Children, Nat. Coun. for Tchrs. English, Tex. ASCD, Network of Progressive Educators, Wilmington Rotary, Leadership Wilmington, Wilmington Execs. Club, City Club de Rossette. Mem. Soc. Friends. Avocations: russian literature, furniture building. Home: 1010 Primivera Ct Wilmington NC 28409-4869 Office: Solomon Schechter Regional H S 800 Broad St Teaneck NJ 07666

DEWHURST, CHARLES KURT, museum director, cultural administrator, curator, folklorist, English language educator; b. Passaic, N.J., Dec. 21, 1948; s. Charles Allaire and Minn Jule (Hanzl) D.; m. Marsha MacDowell, Dec. 15, 1972; 1 dau., Marit Charlene. BA, Mich. State U., 1970, MA, 1973, PhD, 1983. Editorial asst. Carlton Press, N.Y.C., 1967; computer operator IBM, N.Y.C., 1968; project dir. Mich. State U. Mus., 1975, curator, 1976-83, dir., 1982—. Guest curator Mus. Am. Folk Art, N.Y.C., 1978—83, Artrain, Detroit, 1980—83; dir. Festival of Mich. Folklife, 1987—95, Ctr. for Great Lakes Culture, 2000—. Author: Reflections of Faith, 1983, Artists in Aprons, 1979, Rainbows in the Sky, 1978, Michigan Folk Art, 1976 (Am. Assn. State and Local History award 1977), Art at Work: Folk Pottery of Grand Ledge, Michigan, 1986, Michigan Quilts, 1987, Michigan Folklife Reader, 1988, To Honor and Comfort: Native Quilting Traditions, 1998, MSU Campus: Buildings, Places and Spaces, 2002. Coord. South African-U.S. Partnership Project, 1967—; mem. and chair adv. com. Smithsonian Ctr. for Folklife and Cultural Heritage; vice chair Mich. Humanities Coun., 1995—; chairperson Mich. Coun. for Arts and Cultural Affairs; pres. bd. dirs. Fund for Folk Culture. Recipient Disting. Svc. and Humanities award, 1994. Mem. Am. Folkore Soc., Mich. Folklore Soc., Midwest Soc. Lit., Popular Culture Assn., Mich. Hist. Soc., Mich. Mus. Assn., Am. Assn. Mus., Internat. Coun. Mus. Home: 1804 Cricket Ln East Lansing MI 48823-1225 Office: Mich State U Mus W Circle Dr East Lansing MI 48824

DEXHEIMER, RICHARD JOSEPH, school system administrator; b. Jersey City, Apr. 3, 1945; s. Joseph Aloyisus and Alfreida Kathleen (Sadlowsky) D.; m. Jeanne M. Connolly, Aug. 17, 1968; children: Brent Anthony, Kimberly Anne. BA, Jersey City State, 1967; MA, Seton Hall U.,

1972, EdD, 1993. Tchr. Edgewater (N.J.) Bd. Edn., 1967-75, prin., 1975-82, Island Trees Bd. Edn., Levittown, N.Y., 1983-85; mgr. rsch. and tng. L.I. Lighting Co., Garden City, N.Y., 1986-88; supr. instrn. New Milford (N.J.) Bd. Edn., 1988-94, asst. supt., 1994—. Cons., instr. N.J. D.A.R.E. (Drug Abuse Resistance Edn.) Officers' Assn., 1989-92. Sch. bd. trustee New Milford (N.J.) Bd. Edn., 1984-87; libr. bd. trustee New Milford (N.J.) Pub. Libr., 1988-92. Mem. ASCD, Nat. Assn. Elem. Sch. Prins., Nat. Assn. Secondary Sch. Prins., N.J. Assn. Fed. Program Adminstrs., N.J. Assn. Sch. Adminstrs., N.J. Prin. and Suprs. Assn., Bergen County Assn. Sch. Adminstrs., Kappa Delta Pi. Avocations: computers, videa tape prodns. Home: 309 E Woodland Rd New Milford NJ 07646-2323 Office: New Milford Bd Edn 145 Madison Ave New Milford NJ 07646-2707

DEYETTE, JENNIFER LEE, middle school educator; b. Olympia, Wash., Dec. 17, 1970; d. Jack Dean Barnes and Carol Anne (Robertson) Goodburn; m. Lance Edward Deyette, Aug. 13, 1994. BA in Math., Ctrl. Wash. U., 1993; MEd, Lesley Coll., 1998. Cert. tchr., Wash. Math. tchr., volleyball and track coach Shelton (Wash.) Mid. Sch. Recipient scholarship State of Wash., 1989. Mem. NEA, Shelton Edn. Assn. Avocations: outdoor sports, cross stitch, bowling. Home: 50 E Paisley Way Shelton WA 98584-9631

DEYSHER, PAUL EVANS, training consultant; b. Reading, Pa., Oct. 16, 1923; s. Paul Stauffer and Ida Estelle (Evans) D.; m. Myrtle Constance Stover, June 17, 1950 (dec. Feb. 2003); children: David Paul, Mark Edward. BS, Albright Coll., 1945; M in Ednl. Adminstrn., Temple U., 1949. Math. and sci. tchr. Lebanon City (Pa.) Sch. Dist., 1950-56; asst. h.s. prin. Ocean City Sch. (N.J.) Dist., 1956-57; h.s. prin. Yeadon Sch. (Pa.), Dist., 1957-60; mgr. pers. adminstrn. Philco Corp., Phila., 1960-66; tng. specialist AMP, Inc., Harrisburg, Pa., 1966-80, supr. mgmt. tng., 1980-85, mgr. mgmt. tng. and devel., 1986. Cons. and lectr. in field. Author: (poems) Anthologies of International Library of Poetry, 1999, 00; co-author: Transistor Fundamentals, 1962; contbr. chpts. to books and articles to profl. jours. Pres. Albright Coll., Lebanon County Alumni chpt., 1979—; trustee Albright Coll., Reading, Pa., 1985-89. Mem. NEA (life), Am. Soc. Pers. Adminstrn. (cert., sr. prof. in human resources), ASTD (past pres.), Internat. Soc. Poets (Disting. mem.), Phi Delta Kappa. Republican. Lutheran. Home: 39 S Mill St Lebanon PA 17042-3124

DEZARN, GUY DAVID, English language educator; b. Corona, Calif., Nov. 15, 1956; s. Joseph Gordon and Mary Forbes (Bergman) DeZ.; children: Monique, Zahra. BA in English, George Mason U., 1981; JD cum laude, Am. U., 1995. Tchr. Congrl. Sch. Va., Falls Church, 1981-85, Alexandria City (Va.) Pub. Schs., 1985—; legal intern U.S. Pub. Interest Group, Washington, 1992-95, rschr., 1995—. Adj. prof. Washington Coll. Law, 1996—; prof. legal studies No. Va. C.C., 1996—; commentator Sta. WAMU Radio, 1995—. Mentor tchr. Alexandria Pub. Schs., 1990-91; dir. Early Adolescent Helper Program Ctr. Advanced Studies in Group Edn., 1992-93; founder And Clothing for All, Alexandria, 1988—. Home: 200 N Pickett St Alexandria VA 22304-2120 Office: Alexandria City Pub Schs 5700 Sanger Ave Alexandria VA 22311-5602

DHRYMES, PHOEBUS JAMES, economist, educator; b. Cyprus, Oct. 1, 1932; s. Demetrios and Kyriaki (Neophytou) Dhrymiotis; m. Beatrice Bell Fitch, Dec. 10, 1972; children: Phoebus James, Philip Andrew, Alexander Robert. BA with highest honors, U. Tex., 1957; PhD, MIT, 1961. Asst. prof. econs. Harvard U., 1962-64; assoc. prof. econs. U. Pa., 1964-67, prof., 1967-73; prof. econs. Columbia U., N.Y.C., 1973—. Vis. prof. fin. Wharton Sch. U. Pa., 1984 Author: Econometrics: Statistical Foundations and Applications, 1970, 74, Distributed Lags: Problems of Estimation and Formulation, 1971, 81, Russian edit., 1982, Introductory Econometrics, 1978, Mathematics for Econometrics, 1978, 3d edit., 2000, Topics in Advanced Econometrics: Probability Foundations, 1989, Tropics in Advanced Econometrics: vol. II Linear and Non Linear Simultaneous Equations, 1994, Theoretical and Applied Econometrics: The Selected Papers of Phoebus J. Dhrymes, 1995, Time Series, Unit Roots and Cointegration, 1998; mng. editor, editor Internat. Econ. Rev., 1965-72; co-editor Jour. Econometrics, 1972-77, exec. coun., 1993—. Served with U.S. Army, 1952-54. Fellow Econometric Soc., Am. Statis. Assn.; mem. Am. Econ. Assn. Office: Columbia U Dept Econs New York NY 10027 E-mail: b.pid1@columbia.edu.

DIAL, ELEANORE MAXWELL, foreign language educator; b. Norwich, Conn., Feb. 21, 1929; d. Joseph Walter and Irene (Beetham) Maxwell; m. John E. Dial, Aug. 27, 1959. BA, U. Bridgeport, Conn., 1951; MA in Spanish, Mexico City Coll., 1955; PhD, U. Mo., 1968. Mem. faculty U. Wis.-Milw., 1968-75, Ind. State U., Terre Haute, 1975-78, Bowling Green (Ohio) State U., 1978-79; asst. prof. dept. fgn. langs. and lit. Iowa State U., Ames, 1979-85, assoc. prof., 1985-96, emerita assoc. prof., 1996—. Cons. pub. cos.; participant workshops; del. 1st World Congress Women Journalists and Writers, Mex., 1975, also mem. edn. commn. Contbr. articles, anthologies and revs. to scholarly jours. Active Gov.'s Commn. on Fgn. Langs. and Internat. Studies, 1988-95. NDEA grantee, 1967, Ctr. Latin Am. grantee, 1972, NEH summer seminar UCLA, 1981, U. Calif.-Santa Barbara, 1984. Mem. MLA, Am. Assn. Tchrs. Spanish and Portuguese, Midwest MLA, N. Ctrl. Coun. Latin Americanists, Midwest Assn. Latin Am. Studies, Clermont County Geneal. Soc., Ohio Geneal. Soc., Story County (Iowa) Geneal. Soc., Caribbean Studies Assn., Phi Beta Delta, Phi Sigma Iota, Sigma Delta Pi. Home: 119 9th St Ames IA 50010-6343 Office: Iowa State U Ames IA 50011-0001

DIAMA, BENJAMIN, retired educator, artist, composer, writer; b. Hilo, Hawaii, Sept. 23, 1933; s. Agapito and Catalina (Buscas) D. BFA, Sch. Art Inst. Chgo., 1956. Cert. tchr., Hawaii. Tchr. art, basketball coach Waimea (Kauai, Hawaii) High Sch., 1963-67; tchr. music and art Campbell High Sch., Honolulu, 1967-68; tchr. math. and art Waipahu High Sch., Honolulu, 1968-69; tchr. art and music Palisades Elem. Sch., Honolulu, 1969-70; tchr. typing, history, art and music Honokaa (Hawaii) High Sch., 1970-73; tchr. music Kealakehe Sch., Kailua, 1973-74; ret., 1974. Author, writer, composer: Hawaii, 1983; author: Poems of Faith, 1983-88, School One vs. School Two On The Same School Campus, 1983, The Calendar-Clock Theory of the Universe with Earth-- Above and Beyond, 1984-90, Phonetic Sound-Musical Theory, 1990; contbg. author: Benjamin Diama--The Calendar Clock Theory of the Universe, 1991, 92, (poetry) Celebration of Poets, 1998, Poets Elite, Internat. Soc. of Poets, 2000; prodr., composer (Cassette) Hawaii I Love You, 1986; inventor universal clock, double floater boat, Gardener's Water Box, Full Court Half Court 6 vs. 6, 3 Offense-3 Defense Basketball Game. Recipient Achievement award Waimea Dept. Edn., 1964-67, Purchase award State Found. Arts on Culture and the Arts, 1984, State Found. Arts and Culture Acquisition Painting Art award State of Hawaii Govt. Art Collection. Mem. NEA, Hawaii Tchrs. Assn., Hawaii Edn. Assn., AAAS, Nat. Geog. Soc., Smithsonian Assocs., ASCAP, N.Y. Acad. Scis., Nat. Libr. Poetry (assoc.), Internat. Soc. Poets, Am. Geophysical Union. Mem. Salvation Army. Avocations: singing, writing science, coaching basketball. Home: PO Box 2997 Kailua Kona HI 96745-2997

DIAMANDOPOULOS, PETER, former philosopher, educator; b. Irakleion, Crete, Greece, Sept. 1, 1928; came to U.S., 1948, naturalized, 1964; s. Theodore George and Rita (Mouzenides) D.; m. Maria Stanton, 1980; children: Theodoros, Cybele, Ariadne, Patricia. Diploma with honors, Athens Coll., 1947; AB cum laude, Harvard U., 1951, MA, 1956, PhD, 1957; LHD (hon.), Am. Internat. Coll., 1988. Instr. philosophy Bates Coll., 1958; instr., then asst. prof. philosophy U. Md., 1958-62; mem. faculty Brandeis U., 1962-77, prof. philosophy, 1964-77, dean faculty, 1965-71, chmn. dept. philosophy and history of ideas, 1972-76, faculty mem. bd. trustees, 1974-77; pres. Calif. State U.-Sonoma, Rohnert Park, 1977-83, pres. emeritus, 1983—; univ. trustees' prof. Calif. State U., San Francisco, 1983-85; pres., trustee Adelphi U., Garden City, N.Y., 1985—. Dir. internat. studies Adlai Stevenson Inst., Chgo., 1969-74; cons. history of Sci. Smithsonian Inst., 1959-62; bd. dirs. Atlantic Bank of N.Y.; lectr. to profl., learned socs., acad. instns. Contbr. articles to profl. jours. Trustee Adelphi Acad., Athens Coll., 1987—; chmn., bd. advisers U.S. Command and Gen. Staff Coll., 1987. Recipient Cum Laude Soc. award Am. Internat. Coll., 1988,; named Outstanding Tchr. Confucius Inst. Am., 1983; Teschemacher fellow in classics and philosophy Harvard U., 1954-57; sr. fellow Adlai Stevenson Inst. for Internat. Studies, 1969-74. Mem. AAAS, Am. Philol. Assn., Am. Philos. Assn., MIND Assn. (Oxford, Eng.), Aristotelian Soc., Hellenic Soc., Assn. Am. Colls., Soc. for Promotion Hellenic Studies (London), Coun. for Greek Am. Affairs (dir. 1986—), Assn. Governing Bds. Univs. and Colls., N.Y. Acad. Scis., Nat. Assn. Scholars (bd. Advisors), The Links, Union League Club, Harvard Club of Boston. Avocations: minoan archaeology, art criticism, theater. Home: 530 E 76th St Apt 32G New York NY 10021-3174 Office: Adelphi U Office of Pres South Ave Garden City NY 11530

DIAMENT, PAUL, electrical engineering educator, consultant; b. Paris, Nov. 14, 1938; came to U.S., 1948; s. Zajwel Matys and Rywka (Szmerlowska) D.; m. Carol Goldstein, July 7, 1963; children: Edith Zoe, Theodore Mathis, Benjamin Jay. BS, Columbia U., 1960, MS, 1961, PhD, 1963. Asst. prof. elec. engring. Columbia U., N.Y.C., 1963-69, assoc. prof., 1969-76, prof., 1976—; research assoc. Stanford U. (Calif.), 1966-67; vis. assoc. prof. Tel Aviv U., 1970-71; mem. research staff IBM, Yorktown Heights, N.Y., 1974, 82, 85; cons. in field. Author: Wave Transmission and Fiber Optics, 1990, Dynamic Electromagnetics, 2000; contbr. articles to profl. jours. Mem. Am. Phys. Soc., Optical Soc. Am., IEEE(sr.), Sigma Xi, Tau Beta Pi, Eta Kappa Nu Home: 148 Wellington Ave New Rochelle NY 10804-3729 Office: Columbia U Dept Elec Engring New York NY 10027

DIAMOND, MARIAN CLEEVES, anatomy educator; b. Glendale, Calif., Nov. 11, 1926; d. Montague and Rosa Marian (Wamphler) Cleeves; m. Richard M. Diamond, Dec. 20, 1950 (div.); m. Arnold B. Scheibel, Sept. 14, 1982; children: Catherine, Richard, Jeffrey, Ann. AB, U. Calif., Berkeley, 1948, MA, 1949, PhD, 1953. With Harvard U., Cambridge, 1952-54, Cornell U., Ithaca, N.Y., 1954-58, U. Calif., San Francisco, 1959—62, prof. anatomy Berkeley, 1962—. Asst. dean U. Calif., Berkeley, 1967-70, assoc. dean, 1970-73, dir. The Lawrence Hall of Sci., 1990-95, dir. emeritus, 1995—; vis. scholar Australian Nat. U., 1978, Fudan U., Shanghai, China, 1985, U. Nairobi, Kenya, 1988. Author: (with J. Hopson) Magic Trees of the Mind, 1998; author: Enriching Heredity, 1989; co-author: The Human Brain Coloring, 1985; editor: Contraceptive Hormones Estrogen and Human Welfare, 1978; contbr. over 155 articles to profl. jours. V.p. County Women Dems., Ithaca, 1957; bd. dirs. Unitarian Ch., Berkeley, 1969. Recipient Calif. Gifted award, 1989, C.A.S.E. Calif. Prof. of Yr. award, Nat. Gold medalist, 1990, Woman of Yr. award Zonta Internat., 1991, U. medal La. Universidad Del Zulia, Maricaibo, Venezuela, 1992, Alumna of the Yr. award U. Calif., Berkeley, 1995; Calif. Acad. Scis. fellow, 1991, Calif. Soc. Biomedical Rsch. Dist. Svc. award, 1998, Alumnae Resources-Women of Achievement Vision and Excellence award, 1999, Benjamin Ide Wheeler award 1999, Achievement award Calif. Child Devel. Adminstrs. Assn., 2001; named to Internat. Educators Hall of Fame, 1999. Fellow AAAS, AAUW (sr.; fellowship chair 1970-85, 1st Sr. Scholar award 1997); mem. Am. Assn. Anatomists, Soc. Neurosci., Philos. Soc. Washington, The Faculty Club (Berkeley, v.p. 1979-85, 90-95). Avocations: hiking, sports, painting. Home: 2583 Virginia St Berkeley CA 94709-1108 Office: U Calif Dept Integrative Biology 3060 Valley Life Sciences Bldg Berkeley CA 94720-3116 E-mail: diamond@socrates.berkeley.edu.

DIAMOND, POLLYANN JOYCE KIRK, psychologist; b. Johnstown, Pa., Sept. 24, 1946; d. Edward Arthur and Jane Elizabeth (Woodward) Kirk; m. William F. Diamond, June 6, 1968; children: Gregory Johnathan, Martin Edward. BS in Music Edn., Gettysburg Coll., 1968; MEd in Elem. Edn., Armstrong State Coll., 1978; MEd in Edn. Psychology, Miss. State U., 1986; EdS in Sch. Psychology, Valdosta State Coll., 1990; EdD in Curriculum and Instrn., Valdosta State U., 2001. Cert. tchr., Ga.; cert. sch. psychologist. Tchr. of music Clayton County Schs., Jonesboro, Ga., 1968-69; tchr. of elem. math. Savannah (Ga.) Country Day, 1972-82; tchr. of gifted Lowndes County Schs., Columbus, Miss., 1983-87, Valdosta (Ga.) City Schs., 1987-90, sch. psychologist, 1990—2003, curriculum dir. math. and sci., 2003—. Coord. gifted program Valdosta City Schs., 1990-93. Named Outstanding Grad. Student, Edn. Psychology Dept., Miss. State U., 1986, Elem. Econs. Tchr. of Yr., Ga. Coun. on Econ. Edn., Atlanta, 1989, Nabisco fellow Joint Coun. on Econs., N.Y.C., 1988. Mem. NEA, Ga. Assn. Sch. Psychologists (sec. 1994-95, pres. 1996-97), Nat. Assn. Sch. Psychologists, Ga. Assn. Educators, Coun. of Exceptional Children, Phi Kappa Phi, Sigma Alpha Iota, Phi Delta Kappa. Lutheran. Avocations: music, reading, needlework, tatting, sewing. Office: Valdosta City Schs PO Box 5407 Valdosta GA 31603-5407 E-mail: pdiamond@gocats.org.

DIAMOND, RICHARD, retired secondary education educator; b. N.Y.C., June 23, 1936; s. Oscar and Frieda (Rosenfeld) D.; m. Donna Jean Berkshire Wilson, June 14, 1961 (div. June 1974); m. Betty Ruth Jane Foster, Nov. 17, 1975; children: Thomas, Laura, Rick, Jeff. BA, U. Calif., Berkeley, 1958. Cert. tchr., Calif. Tchr. Riverside (Calif.) Unified Schs., 1959-67, 73-99, coord. social studies, 1967-69, program dir. compensatory edn., 1969-72, attendance officer, 1972-73; project mgr. Biotech. Sch., 1999—2001. Author curriculum programs Afro-Am. history and Chicano studies, 1968; developer law and youth H.S. course, 1978, track coach, 1975-88. Contbr. articles and photographs to profl. jours. Co-creator nationally recognized h.s. vol. program, h.s. svc. learning coord., 1995—; mem. Riverside County Hist. Commn., 1997-2003; Dem. Party worker, 1964-72; Rep. Party worker, 1992—; historic commn. liaison Riverside County Archives Commn., 1998-2002; bd. dirs. Calif. Citrus Hist. State Park, 2000-2002, sec., 2000-2003; pres. Vail Ranch Restoration Assn., Inc., Temecula, Calif., 2000-2002. Named Social Studies Tchr. of Yr., Inland Empire Social Studies Assn., 1980, Tchr. of Yr., Arlington H.S., Riverside, 1992; recipient hon. svc. award Dist. Coun. PTA, Riverside, 1993, Johnny Harris Youth Action award City of Riverside,, 1998. Mem. NEA, Calif. Tchrs. Assn., Riverside County Tchrs. Assn. Presbyterian. Avocations: gardening, travel, reading, woodworking. E-mail: ddiamond@ix.netcom.com.

DIAMOND, ROBERT MACH, higher education administrator; b. Schenectady, N.Y., Mar. 5, 1930; s. Henry Gordon and Ruth Ada (Mach) D.; m. Dolores Lou Jacobs, Apr. 14, 1957; children: Harli Fait, H. Gordon. AB, Union Coll., Schenectady, 1951; MA, NYU, 1953, PhD, 1962. Secondary sch. tchr. math., TV tchr., TV project dir. Schenectady Pub. Schs., 1956-59; assoc. prof. edn., instructional TV prodn. supr. San Jose State U., 1959-63; dir. instructional rsch., vis. prof. U. Miami, Coral Gables, Fla., 1963-66; dir. instructional resources ctr., prof. edn. SUNY, Fredonia, 1966-71; asst. vice chancellor instrnl. devel., dir., prof. edn. Syracuse (N.Y.) U. Ctr. for Instructional Devel., 1971-97, rsch. prof., dir. Inst. Change in Higher Edn., 1998-99; rsch. prof. Syracuse U., 1999—; pres. Nat. Acad. Academic Leadership, St. Petersburg, Fla., 1999—. Nat. adv. bd. Bur. of Handicapped, Office of Edn.; dir. Focus in Tchg. Project, Fund for Improvement of Postsecondary Edn., Washington; Fulbright sr. lectr., 1976; dir. Nat. Project on Instnl. Priorities and Faculty Rewards, Lilly Endowment and Pew Charitable Trusts, Indpls., Phila., 1989-95; cons. NIH, NSF, Office of Edn., various colls., univs. and assns.; lectr. in field. Author: A Guide to Instructional Television, 1964, Designing and Improving Courses and Curricula in Higher Education, 1989, Serving on Promotion and Tenure Committees, A Faculty Guide, 1994, Preparing for Tenure and Promotion Review, 1995; co-author: Instructional Development for Individualized Learning in Higher Education, 1975, National Study of Teaching Assistants, 1987, A National Study of Research Universities on the Perceived Balance Between Research and Undergraduate Teacher, 1991; editor: Field Guide to Academic Leadership, 2002; co-editor: Recognizing Faculty Work: Reward Systems for the Year 2000, 1993, Preparing for Promotion & Tenure Review, 1995, Changing Priorties at Research Universities, 1997, Designing & Assessing Courses and Curriculum, 1998, Aligining Faculty Records With Institution Mission, 1999, The Disciplies Speak, Vol. I, 1995, Vol. II, 2000; mem. editl bd. Jour. Higher Ednl. Rsch. and Devel., South African Jour. Edn.; contbr. chpts. to books and articles to profl. jours. Bd. dirs. Temple Adath, 1990-94, Jewish Family Svcs., Syracuse, 1975-83. With U.S. Army, 1973-75. Recipient award for Outstanding Practice in Instructional Devel., Assn. Ednl. Comm. and Tech., 1989. Mem. Am. Assn. Higher Edn. (cited for innovations in the improvement of higher edn. 1994). E-mail: r.m.diamond@worldnet.att.net.

DIANA, JOANNE MERCEDES, retired medical/surgical nurse, nursing educator; b. Youngstown, Ohio; d. John and Maria Grazia (Marinelli) D. Diploma in Nursing, Youngstown Hosp. Assn., 1961; BS, Youngstown U., 1963; MSN, Med. Coll. Ga., Augusta, 1977; EdD, Walden U., Mpls., 1988. RN, Ohio. Prof. nursing Thiel Coll., Greenville, Pa., 1989—2002, prof. emeritus, 2002—. Mem. Sigma Theta Tau.

DIANGELO, JOSEPH ANTHONY, JR., finance educator, dean; b. Phila., July 5, 1948; s. Joseph Anthony and Lucy (Lazzaro) Diangelo; m. Frances R. Marcelli, Mar. 18, 1972; children: Deana Diangelo, Kristen Diangelo, Joseph Anthony Diangelo III. BS, St. Joseph's U., 1970; MBA, Widener U., 1975; EdD, Temple U., 1985. Tchr. St. Thomas More HS, Phila., 1970-75; archbishop Carroll HS, Radnor, Pa., 1975-78; prof. mgmt. St. Joseph's U., Phila., 1978-80, dean Erivan K. Haub Sch. Bus., 2000—; prof., asst. dean Widener U., Chester, Pa., 1980-87, dean, 1985, asst. provost for grad. studies, 1986-88, dean Sch. mgmt., 1987-2000. Cons. Chespenn Health Svc., Chester, 1984. Contbr. articles to profl. jours. Pres., bd. dirs. Children's Clinic, Chester, 1983—86; gov.'s appointee Trial Ct. Nominating Com. Delaware County, Pa., 1987—; mem. pvt. industry coun. Delaware County, 1990—, workforce investment bd., 1999—; Delaware County Common Pleas Ct. appointee Sch. Dist. Bd. Control; chmn. edn. com., bd. dirs. Columbus Quincentennial Found., 1992—97; mem. Pa. Amb. Team, 1999—. With USNG, 1970—76. Mem.: ASTD, Am. Assn. Colls. Bus. Adminstrn. (bd. dirs. 2003—, internat. chairperson candidacy com. 2003—), Mid-Atlantic Assn. Colls. Bus. Adminstrn. (exec. com. 1994—98, 1st v.p. 1995, pres. 1996—97, sec. 2000—), Am. Arbitration Assn., Acad. Mgmt., Soc. Human Resource Mgmt., Soc. Advancement Mgmt. (Disting. Prof. award 1980—81), Assn. Adv. Coll. Bus. (bus. accreditation com. 1998—2001, bd. dirs. 2003—). Roman Catholic. Avocations: tennis, golf. Office: Widener U 14th Chestnut St Chester PA 19013

DIAS, KATHLEEN R. foreign language educator; b. Phila., Dec. 2, 1950; d. John Joseph and Dorothy; m. Lindolfo C. Dias; 3 children. BA, Immaculata Coll., 1977; cert. acad. excellence, Istituto Italiano di Cultura, Lima, Peru, 1980; MA, Marywood U., 1983; postgrad., Temple U., 1984, U. Pa., 1986-96; cert. proficiency, Berlitz Schs. Langs., 1983. Cert. Spanish K-12 tchr., elem. edn. tchr., 1984, elem./mid. and secondary sch. prin., Pa., 1996. Tchr., program dir. elem. edn., Phila., 1971-74, Chester County, Pa., 1976-78; tutor Fgn. Lang. Affairs, Delaware County, Pa., 1975-76; tchr., dir. Spanish elem. edn. Bucks County, Pa., 1978-79; tchr. ESL Lima, 1979-81; prof. Spanish Immaculata Coll., Pa., 1983, dir. L.Am. studies program, 1983-86; instr. fgn. lang. specialized tutoring program Delaware County, Pa., 1981—; vice-principal Drexel Hill Holy Child Acad., 1997-99, curriculum dir., 1997—. Chmn. VIP dept. U. Pa.; with Am. sect. Mus. Archaeology/Anthropology U. Pa., summers, 1986—, anthropology lab. analysis of Ctrl. and S.Am. artifacts; chmn., tchr. Latin, Spanish and English Holy Child Acad., Drexel Hill, adminstrv. asst., rep. various coms. bd. trustees, 1981-2001; coord. edn. dept. Mus. Anthropology and Archaeology, Univ. Pa., 1995-96, FLES program Haverford Sch. Dist., 2001—; lectr. U. Pa., 1996, Duke U. on Maya studies, 1999. Author 4-yr. lang. program Early Spanish learning for the Elementary School, 1982; Developing a Sensitivity to the Culture and History of Latin America, 1983, Mexico: Land, Culture and People, 1983, The Maya and Aztec Nations, 1984, The Inca Civilization: From Manco Capac to the Spanish Conquest, 1988, Manual for Teachers on Mesoamerican Cultures Grades 7-12, 1997; compilor, editor (study guide) for Hall of Ancient Mex. and Ctrl. Am. at Mus. of Natural History, N.Y.C., 1990; author, editor The Codex, PreColumbian Soc. Pub., 1994-96; contbr. articles to scholarly jours. Mem. citizen's bd. Am. Cancer Rsch.; site mgr./facilitator Maya Quest Interactive Expedition, 1994-95. Nominee Friedel and Otto Eberspacher award for Excellence in Tchg. of a Modern European Lang., Johns Hopkins U., 2001; recipient Disting. Leadership award, Comm. and Tech. award, Pa. State U., 1995; scholar Italian Cultural Attaché scholar, Peru, 1979—81. Mem. MLA, Nat. Coun. Tchrs. English, Assn. Tchrs. Spanish and Portuguese, L.Am. Studies Assn., Pa. Assn. Edn., Pre-Columbian Soc. (bd. dirs. 1993—), Mus. Archaeology and Anthropology of U. Pa.

DIAS, MARI NARDOLILLO, education educator, consultant; b. Providence, July 21, 1952; d. Robert Anthony and Dorothy Ann Nardolillo; m. Raul Dias; children: Lindsay, Adam. BA in Secondary Edn., R.I. Coll., 1974, MA in Vocat. Counseling, 1983; EdD, Johnson & Wales U., 2003—. Cons. Dias & Assocs., N. Kingstown, RI, 1985—; instr. emotional intelligence MotoRing Tech. Tng. Inst., E. Providence, RI, 1995—2000; prof. Johnson & Wales U., Providence, 2000—01; prof. grad. sch. Endicott Coll., Beverly, Maine, 2000—; prof., facilitator Duke U., Durham, NC, 2001. Mentor Feinstein Making a Difference Program, N. Kingstown, 2000—. Actor: (stage play) Talking With, 1996 (Irene Ryan nominee), (musical) The Best Little Whorehouse in Texas, 1996; prodr.: (plays) The Lottery, 1995; dir.: Nicholas Nickelby, 1995, The Monkey's Paw, 1995, James and the Giant Peach, 1997. Patient rep. vol. R.I. Hosp., Providence, 1999—; vol. instr. Odyssey of the Mind; vol. N. Kingstown Sch. Dept. Lights, Camera, Action; vol. performing arts instr. N. Kingstown Recreation Dept.; guest spkr. AIDS Respite Program; vol. cons. R.I. Cambodian Soc.; bd. dirs. St. Mary's Sch., Cranston, RI. Named Outstanding Woman of Yr. in Arts and Edn., Greater Providence YWCA, 2001; recipient Town Hero award, North Kingstown, 1998, Citizen citation, City of Providence, 2001; scholar, Johnson & Wales U., 2000. Mem.: NEA, AAUW (mem. Diversity Task Force, co-author, dir. Reviving the D 1999—, rsch. and projects endowment 2001), Am. Soc. Tng. and Devel., Friends of Oceanography (chair publicity com. 1985—88), Academy Players (bd. dirs. 1992), CCRI Players Club (pres. 1995—96). Avocations: scuba diving, aerobics (cert. instr.), world travel. Personal E-mail: teachdias@home.com. Business E-Mail: MDias@jwu.edu.

DIAZ, SHARON, education administrator; b. Bakersfield, Calif., July 29, 1946; d. Karl C. and Mildred (Lunn) Clark; m. Luis F. Diaz, Oct. 19, 1968; children: Daniel, David. BS, San Jose State U., 1969; MS, U. Calif., San Francisco, 1973; PhD (hon.), St. Mary's Coll. Calif., 1999. Nurse Kaiser Found. Hosp., Redwood City, Calif., 1969-73; lectr. San Jose (Calif.) State Coll., 1969-70; instr. St. Francis Meml. Hosp. Sch. Nursing, San Francisco, 1970—71; pub. health nurse San Mateo County, 1971—72; instr. Samuel Merritt Hosp. Sch. Nursing, Oakland, Calif., 1973—76; asst. dir. Samuel Merritt Hosp. Sch. of Nursing, Oakland, 1976—78, dir., 1978—84; founding pres. Samuel Merritt Coll., Oakland, 1984—; interim pres. Calif. Coll. Podiatric Medicine, 2001. V.p. East Bay Area Health Edn. Ctr., Oakland, 1980-87; mem. adv. com. Calif. Acad. Partnership Program, 1990-92; mem. nat. adv. com. Nursing Outcomes Project; bd. dirs. Calif. Workforce Initiative, U. Calif. San Francisco Ctr. for the Health Professions, 2000--. Bd. dirs. Head Royce Sch., 1990-98, vice chair, 1993-95, chair, 1995-97; bd. dirs. Ladies Home Soc., 1992—, sec. 1994-95, treas., CFO 1995-97, 2nd v.p. 1997-99; bd. dirs. George Mark Children's House, 2001--; mem. adv. bd. Ethnic Health Inst., 1997—; mem. com. minorities higher edn. Am. Coun. Edn., 1998—. Named Woman of Yr., Oakland YWCA, 1996. Mem. Am. Assn. of Pres. Ind. Colls. and Univs., Sigma Theta Tau (Leadership award Nu Xi chpt. 2001). Office: Samuel Merritt Coll 450 30th St Oakland CA 94609-3302 E-mail: sdiaz@samuelmerritt.edu.

DIAZ DE GONZALEZ, ANA MARIA, psychologist, educator; b. San Juan, P.R., July 26, 1945; d. Esteban Díaz-González and Petra (Guadalupe) De Díaz; m. Jorge Gonzalez Monclova, Jan. 7, 1968; children: Ana Teresa, Jorge, Julio Esteban. BS, U. P.R., Río Piedras, 1965, MEd, 1973; MS, Caribbean Ctr. Advanced Study, San Juan, 1982, PhD, 1983. Lic. psychologist, P.R. Home economist U. P.R., Fajardo and San Juan, 1965-82, specialist in human devel. and gerontology San Juan, 1983—. Mem. APA, Assn. Economists Hogar (pres. 1965-92, Disting. Svc. award 1973), Assn. Specialists SEA (pres. 1982-93), Assn. Psychology P.R., Epsilon Sigma Phi (sec. 1970—), Gamma Sigma Delta. Roman Catholic. Avocations: piano, reading, exercise. Home: 1325 Calle 23 San Juan PR 00924-5249 Office: U PR Svc Extension Agr Terrenos Estacion Exptl Río Piedras San Juan PR 00928

DIAZ-GEMMATI, GRISELLE MARITZA, secondary education educator; b. Cabo Rojo, P.R., Apr. 24; d. Nelson Wiscovitch-Diaz and Carmen Leonor (Feliberty) Diaz; m. Oronzo Gemmati, June 15, 1974; children: Vito Antonio, Francesca Katrina. BA in Spanish and Edn., Mundelein Coll., Chgo., 1983; MA in Lang. and Literacy, Nat. Louis U., 1997. Cert. Spanish, bilingual edn., ESL. Sch. and tchr. aide Chgo. Bd. Edn., 1977-82; tchr. bilingual edn. Norwood Park Sch., Chgo., 1983-86, tchr. social studies, 1986—, tchr. rep. local sch. coun., 1989-91. Mem. faculty Chgo. Area Writing Project; mem. writing dept. Roosevelt U.; tchr. rschr. M-class project Ctr. for Study Writing, U. Calif., Berkeley; tchr. rschr. nat. writing project Tufts U., Boston, 1993; part-time faculty Colombia Coll., Chgo. Recipient Excellence in Tchg. award Golden Apple Found., inc., 1993. Mem. Internat. Reading Assn., Nat. Coun. Tchrs. English, Am. Fedn. Tchrs., Nat. Geog. Soc., Kappa Delta Pi. Roman Catholic. Avocations: writing short stories and poetry, languages, crafts, hispanic literature. Office: Norwood Park Sch 5900 N Nina Ave Chicago IL 60631-2408

DIBBLE, DAVID VAN VLACK, visually impaired educator, lawyer; b. San Francisco, Feb. 5, 1928; s. Oliver and Isabelle (Bishop) D.; m. Frances Bauer, May 3, 1984; 1 child, T.C. Clark. AA, San Mateo Jr. Coll., 1948; student, Mexico City Coll., 1950; BA, U. Calif., Berkeley, 1952; JD, U. Calif., San Francisco, 1962; grad. in Edn., Calif. State U., Hayward, 1969; MA, San Francisco State U., 1981. Bar: Calif., 1962; cert. elem. tchr., spl. edn. visually impaired, Calif. Tchr. Marine Corps Inst., Washington, 1953-54; purser Am. Pres. Lines, San Francisco, 1955, passenger agt. Honolulu, 1956-58, San Francisco, 1958-60; trial lawyer Barfield, Barfield & Dryden, San Francisco, 1963-65; ptnr. Thorpe & Dibble, Hayward, Calif., 1966-69; part time tchr. various Calif. sch. dist., 1970-74; lawyer and vision tchr. pvt. practice, San Francisco, 1974-82; sec., dir. Original Sixteen to One Mine, Inc., Alleghany, Calif., 1978-81; vision tchr. Oakland Pub. Sch., Calif., 1982-89; cons. vision edn. pvt. practice, Oakland, 1989—. Contbr. articles on Art of Seeing to various pubs. Pub. defender Legal Aid Soc., San Francisco, 1965-66; bd. dir. Healing Ctr., San Francisco, 1974-78; vol. Multiple Sclerosis Soc. No. Calif., Oakland, 1974-90; bd. dir., v.p. Calif. Heritage Coun., 1970—, Telegraph Hill Dwellers, 1979-88, pres., 1976, San Francisco; bd. dirs., v.p. Diamond Improvement Assn., Oakland, 1987-88; vestry and warden St. Paul's Episcopal Ch., Oakland, 1989-92; dir. Internat. Maritime Ctr., Oakland, 1995—; docent Oakland Mus., 1992, presdl. yacht. U.S.S. Potomac, Jack London Mus.; dir. Fruitvale Cmty. Devel. Dist. Coun., Oakland, 1989-95, Hugenot Soc. Calif., Thomas Jefferson chpt. SAR. Recipient Cert. Appreciation, Calif. Heritage Coun., San Francisco, 1990. Mem. Bar Assn. Calif., Oakland Tchrs. Assn., Calif. Assn. Orientation and Mobility Specialists, Calif. Alumni Assn., Nat. Audubon Soc., Bay Area Assn. Disabled Sailors, San Francisco Bay Wildlife Soc., E.C.V. YB#1, History Soc., Sierra Club, Calif. Mus. History (docent coun.), Calif. Hist. Soc., Alameda County Hist. Soc., Bates-Corbett Tchr. Assn., Phi Gamma Delta. Republican. Episcopalian. Home: 2806 Bellaire Pl Oakland CA 94601-2010

DIBBLE, ELIZABETH JEANE, lawyer, educator; b. Hammond, Ind., May 26, 1958; d. Harold Richard and Janet Deliah (Lane) Elsey; m. John Taylor Dibble, June 7, 1980; children: James Taylor, Katherine Elizabeth. BS in Learning Disabilities cum laude, MacMurray Coll., Jacksonville, Ill., 1979; JD, So. Ill. U., 1983. Bar: Ill. 1983. Tchr. learning disabilities Sedgwick (Kans.) Sch. System, 1979-80; atty. Powless & Brocking, Marion, Ill., 1984-85, Randy Patchett & Assoc., Marion, 1985-86; sole practice Marion, 1987-96. Dir. paralegal studies program Belleville (Ill.) Area Coll., 1996—; part-time lectr. So. Ill. U., Carbondale, 1985—. Fundraiser Rep. Party, Williamson County, Ill, 1986; bd. dirs. So. Ill. Epilepsy Found., Mt. Vernon, 1984-86; mem. Episcopal Ch. Women; religious edn. dir. St. James Episcopal Ch., Marion, 1983-86. Cartwright scholar for women MacMurray Coll., 1976-79. Mem. Williamson County Bar Assn., Ill. State Bar Assn.. Republican. Avocations: racquetball, volleyball, basketball, reading. Home: 6495 Schiermeier Rd Freeburg IL 62243-2035 Office: 400 N Market St Marion IL 62959-2316

DIBBLE, RICHARD EDWARD, academic administrator; b. Elmira, N.Y., Dec. 20, 1946; s. D. Charles and Bernice V. (Brasted) D.; m. Josephine Estrada, June 2, 1973; children: Cristina, Diana. BA in English, SUNY, Buffalo, 1971; MA in Polit. Sci., SUNY, Albany, 1973, PhD in Polit. Sci., 1977; MBA, N.Y. Inst. Technology, 1990. Cert. employment/tng. adminstr., sr. profl. human resources. Legis. intern N.Y. State Assembly, 1972; researcher to dir. rsch. Dept. Employment and Tng. Albany County, N.Y., 1977-80; rsch. and tng. dir. to dean, dir. Ctr. for Labor and Indsl. Rels., N.Y. Inst. Technology, 1980—, prof., 1994—. Labor arbitrator N.Y. State Employment Rels. Bd. panel, 1993—; presenter in field. Author publs./videos in field; editl. bd. mem. Jour. Individual Employee Rights, 1994; contbr. articles and book revs. to profl. jours. Bd. dirs., founding mem. L.I. Health Care Coalition, 1985-91; adv. bd. N.Y. Inst. Technology Transp., 1982-87; mem. task force on chem. dependency in the workplace, N.Y. State Div. Substance Abuse Svcs., 1983-84, N.Y. State Gov.'s Office for Voluntary Svcs., 1990, Addictions Adv. Bd. of L.I., 1993—, Ctr. for Labor and Indsl. Rels. Adv. Coun., 1982—, others; mem. pub. employment rels. bd., Suffolk County, N.Y., 1999—; chmn. youth coun. Town of Hempstead, 2001—. Recipient cert. merit for advancement of legal jurisprudence, Nassau County Acad. Law, 1990, 96, citation for contribution to edn. in dispute resolution, Suffolk County, N.Y., 1989, others; named Vol. of Yr. Adults and Children With Developmental Disabilities, Inc., 1996, MacGregor award L.I. IRRA, 1998. Mem. Am. Arbitration Assn. (comml. arbitrator 1988—), Indsl. Rels. Rsch. Assn. (various officers to pres. local chpt. 1993—, bd. dirs., Pres.'s Spl. Recognition award 1989, 95, MacGregor award 1998), Soc. for Human Resource Mgmt., Soc. Profls. in Dispute Resolution (various offices to pres. local chpt. 1992), Adults and Children with Learning and Devel. Disabilities (bd. dirs. to pres. 1991—, various coms., certs. of appreciation 1990, 91), Delta Mu Delta, also others. Avocation: travel. Office: Ctr Labor and Indsl Rels Rm 517 NY Inst Technology Old Westbury NY 11568 E-mail: rdibble@nyit.edu.

DIBERT, ROSALIE, elementary school educator; Graduate, Calif. U. of Pa., 1964. Tchr. Pitts. Pub. Schs., 1964—2002; coord. Pitts. Initiative, 2002—. Chmn. Exceptional Needs Com.; Gov. at Large for Tchrs. CEC Exec. Bd.; liaison Profl. Standards Com. Finalist Tchr. of Yr., Pa., 1986; named Clarissa Hug Internat. Spec. Educator of Yr., 1990; recipient Bernice Baumgartner Meml. award; Jordan Fundamentals grant, 2000. Mem.: Nat. Coun. for Exceptional Children Com., Pa. Tchrs. Forum, Pa. State Adv. Bd., Western Region Chpt. #104 (pres.), Pa. Fed. Coun. for Exceptional Children, Pa. Chpt. Tchr. of Yr. Chpt. (pres. 1992), Nat. Bd Profl. Tchg. Standards.

DIBIAGGIO, JOHN A. university president; b. San Antonio, Sept. 11, 1932; s. Ciro and Acidalia DiBiaggio; married; children: David John, Dana Elizabeth, Deirdre Joan; m. Nancy Cronemiller, May 27, 1989. AB, Eastern Mich. U., 1954, D (hon.) of Edn., 1985; DDS, U. Detroit, 1958, LHD (hon.), 1985; MA, U. Mich., 1967; DSc (hon.), Fairleigh Dickinson U., 1981; LLD (hon.), Sacred Heart U., Bridgeport, Conn., 1984; LLD (hon.), U. Md., 1985; DHL (hon.), U. New Eng., 1987; DHL (hon.), Tokyo U. Agr., 1991; LLD (hon.), U. Nigeria, Nsukka, 1992; LHD (hon.), Fitchburg State Coll., 1994; LHD (hon.), Amer. Coll. Greece, 1998; LLD (hon.), Tufts U., 2002. Pvt. practice, New Baltimore, Mich., 1958—65; asst. prof., asst. to dean, dept. chmn. sch. dentistry U. Detroit, 1965—67; asst. dean student affairs U. Ky., Lexington, 1967—70; prof., dean sch. dentistry Va. Commonwealth U., Richmond, 1970—76; v.p. for health affairs, exec. dir. health ctr. U. Conn., Farmington, 1976—79, pres. Storrs, 1979—85, Mich. State U., East Lansing, 1985—92, Tufts U., Medford, Mass., 1992—2001, now pres. emeritus, 2001—. Bd. dirs. Kaman Corp.; mem. Knight Found. Commn. on Intercollegiate Athletics, 1990—2001, PEW Health Professions Commn., 1990—93; cons. in field. Author (with others): Applied Practice Management: A Strategy for Stress Control, 1979; contbr. articles to profl. jours. Bd. nominators Am. Inst. Pub. Svc., 1989—92; bd. dirs. Nat. Italian Am. Found., 1988—94; active Bus. Higher Edn. Forum, 1996—, WGBH Ednl. Found., 1992—, chmn. governance com., 1997—; trustee U. Detroit, 1979—86, Am. Film Inst., 1988—, Forsyth Dental Ctr., 1993—, Am. Cancer Soc. Found., 1993—, pres., 1999; trustee Oral Health Am., 1995—97; chmn. adv. com. dental scholars R.W. Johnson Found.; pres. com. Argonne Nat. Lab. 6, 1986—; coun. pres. Univs. Rsch. Assn., 1989—92; bd. dirs. Black Child and Family Inst., 1990, Coun. for Aid to Edn., 1994—96, Mass. Nat. and Cmty. Svc. Commn., 1994—97, Am. Coun. on Edn., 1995—, vice-chmn., 1998, chmn., 1999; exec. com. Mass. Campus Compact, 1995—, exec. dir. search com., 1996, chmn. devel. com., 1996—, governance com., 1996—98, chmn., 1998; bd. assocs. Whitehead Inst. for Biomed. Rsch., 1995—, chmn., 1998. Decorated Order of Merit Italy; named Disting. Profl. of Yr., Mich. Assn. Profls., 1985, Disting. Alumni, Ea. Mich. U., 1986, Man of Yr., City of Detroit, 1985; recipient Leadership award, Sacred Heart U., Pierre Fauchard Gold Medal award, 1989. Fellow: Internat. Coll. Dentists, Am. Coll. Dentist; mem.: NCAA (found. bd. dirs. 1988—2001, found. divsn. III pres.'s coun. 1997—2001), APHA, ADA, Nat. Assn. State Univs. and Land Grant Colls. (chmn. 1986—87), Internat. Assn. Dental Rsch., Am. Assn. Dental Schs., Mass. Automobile Assn. (bd. dirs. 1992—), Am. Automobile Assn. (bd. dirs. 1994—), Am. Film Inst., Golden Key, Alpha Lambda Delta, Alpha Sigma Chi, Alpha Omega Alpha (Achievement award 1993), Beta Gamma Sigma, Omicron Kappa Upsilon, Phi Kappa Phi. Avocations: golf, antique automobiles, skiing. E-mail: john.dibiaggio@tufts.edu.*

DIBLE, ROSE HARPE MCFEE, special education educator; b. Phoenix, Apr. 28, 1927; d. Ambrose Jefferson and Laurel Mabel (Harpe) McFee; m. James Henry Dible, June 23, 1951 (div. Jan. 1965); 1 child, Michael James. BA in Speech Edn., Ariz. State U., Tempe, 1949; MA in Speech and Drama, U. So. Calif., L.A., 1950; fellow, Calif. State U., Fullerton, 1967. Cert. secondary tchr., spl. edn. tchr. English and drama tchr. Lynwood (Calif.) Sr. High Sch., 1950-51, Montebello (Calif.) Sr. High Sch., 1952-58; tchr. English and Social Studies Pioneer High Sch., Whittier, Calif., 1964-65; spl. edn. tchr. Bell Gardens (Calif.) High Sch., 1967-85, spl. edn. cons., 1985-90. Mem. DAR, Daus. Am. Colonists, Whittier Christian Woman Assn., La Habra Womans Club, Eastern Star Lodge, Kappa Delts, Phi Delta Gamma. Republican. Presbyterian. Avocations: church choir, tap dancing, doll collecting, travel. Home: 1201 Russell St La Habra CA 90631-2530 Office: Montebello Unified Sch Dist 123 Montebello Blvd Montebello CA 90640

DI CARLO, ARMANDO, Italian language educator; b. Magliano dei Marsi, Italy, Apr. 2, 1948; came to U.S., 1974; s. Carlo and Costanza (Marini) Di C.; m. Marie A. Morelli, Aug. 29, 1974; children: Carlo, Dino. Doctoral degree, U. Rome, 1972; PhD, U. Mich., 1983. Tchg. asst. U. Mich., Ann Arbor, 1975-79; instr. Miami U., Oxford, Ohio, 1979-82; instr., lang. specialist, dept. chief Def. Lang. Inst., Monterey, Calif., 1982-91, acad. advisor, 1984-87; lectr., dir. Italian lang. program U. Calif., Berkeley, 1991—. Co-author: Italian Basic Course, 1988; contbr. articles to profl. jours. Named Instr. of Yr., Def. Lang. Inst., 1988, recipient exceptional performance award, 1989. Mem. MLA, Dante Soc., Italica, Silarus, Fgn. Lang. Assn. North Calif., Amici dell'Italia (bd. dirs. 1994—). Avocations: travel, gardening, walking, reading, cooking. Office: U Calif 5125 Dwinelle Hl Berkeley CA 94720-0001

DICIOCCIO, GARY FRANCIS, secondary education educator; b. Beaver Falls, Pa., Nov. 28, 1961; s. Americo M. and Rose (D'Ottavio) DiC. BS in Chemistry, Gannon U., 1985. Cert. tchr., Pa. Tchr. chemistry West Mifflin (Pa.) Area Sch. Dist., 1986-88, 90—; instr. chemistry C.C. Allegheny County, Pitts., 1988; lab. asst. INMETCO, Inc. Ellwood City, Pa., 1988; inorganic data control officer Roy F. Weston, Inc., West Chester, Pa., 1989-90; tchr. earth sci. West Shore Sch. Dist., Leymone, Pa., 1990. Fellow Fermi Accelerator Nat. Lab., 1998-99. Proofreader Sci. Tchr. mag,. 1992-94, western Pa. rep., 1994-96. Info. Tech. Edn. scholar Pa. Gen. Assembly, 1988; organic chemistry summer rsch. fellow Bucknell U., 1990, Dept. Energy fellow Argonne Nat. Lab., 1993, 94, ASCI fellow West Pa. Hosp., Pitts., 1993, H.S. Sci. Tchr. Inst. fellow U. Calif., Berkeley, 1995, Sci. and Soc. Inst. fellow U. Miami, Coral Gables, Fla., 1995, NASA Environ. program fellow Jesuit-Wheeling (W.Va.) Coll., 1995, Am. Assn. Immunologists fellow, 1997; grantee Mon Valley Edn. Consortium Great Ideas, 1993-96. Mem. Am. Chem. Soc., Am. Fedn. Tchrs., Am. Film Inst., Natural Sci. Tchrs. Assn., Pa. Sci. Tchrs. Assn., Theater Assn. Pa. Republican. Roman Catholic. Avocations: tennis, swimming, theater, reading. Office: West Mifflin Area H S 91 Commonwealth Ave West Mifflin PA 15122-2396

DICKAU, KEITH MICHAEL (MIKE DICKAU), artist, secondary school educator; b. Monterey Park, Calif., Apr. 20, 1944; s. Keith Robert and Beaula May (Chamness) D.; m. Ramona Sue Wilson, May 6, 1967; children: Robert Michael, Ian Christopher; m. Carolyn Gloria Isaak, Dec. 22, 1973. BA in Zoology, U. Calif., Davis, 1966. Cert. secondary tchr., Calif. Tchr. math. L.A. City Sch. Dist., 1967-70; tchr. sci. and math. Grant Joint Union H.S. Dist., Sacramento and Rio Linda, Calif., 1970-99. Exhibited in numerous shows including Le Sahuc, Sacramento, Candy Store Gallery, Folsom, Calif., A Gallery-Anna Gardner, Stinson Beach, Calif., Artists' Collaborative Gallery, Sacramento, Fla. State U., Tallahassee, Crocker Art Mus. Sculpture Park, Sacramento, Whittier (Calif.) Mus., Gallery 25, Fresno, Calif., L.A. Artist Equity Assn., Mercer Gallery, Rochester, N.Y., The Artery, Davis, Archivio Artistico, Ravenna, Italy, Antic Ajuntament, Terragona, Spain, Santa Barbara (Calif.) Mus., Ecole de Nuces, Valady, France, M.J.C., Saint-Cere, France, 1996, Seulement pour les Fous, Troyes, France, 1996, New Artworks Fine Arts Gallery, Fair Oaks, Calif., 1996, Bur. de Poste, Joigny, France, 1996, The Ink People Ctr. for the Arts, Eureka, Calif., 1996, Mercer Gallery, Monroe C.C., Rochester, N.Y., 1996, L'Inst. Superieur des Arts Appliques, Rennes, France, The Living Room, Santa Monica, Calif., 1997, Design Gallery, U. Calif., Davis, Kawaguchi-Shi, Japan, 1997, Solomon Dubnick Gallery, Sacramento, 1998, Mercer Gallery, Rochester, N.Y., East Sacramento Art Garage, 1999, Artworks/Bookworks, Santa Monica, Calif., Claudia Chapline Gallery, Stinson Beach, L'Ecume du Jour, Bouvais, France, 2000, 621 Gallery, Tallahassee, Fla., La Maison du Livre de L'Image, Villerbanne, France, 2000, Inst. Superiore, Spilimbergo, Italy, 2001, Southern Exposure Gallery, San Francisco, Calif., 2001, Internat. Mus. Postal Image, Ostrense, Italy, 2001, Todd Hughes Fine Art, South Pasadena, Calif., 2001, Shriner Hosps./No. Calif., Sacramento, 2002, Mayakovsky Mus., Moscow, Russia, 2003, others; contbr. poetry and art to mags. Recipient Hon. Sci. award Bausch and Lomb, 1962, Sculpture award Calif. Art League, 1987, Artist of Month award No. Calif. Artists, numerous other awards; NSF grantee, 1972. Mem. No. Calif. Artists, Inc. Democrat. Methodist. Avocations: music, travel. E-mail: mikedickau@aol.com.

DICKEL, HÉLÈNE RAMSEYER, astronomy educator; b. Cambridge, Mass., Mar. 19, 1938; d. Frank Wells and Linda Chapin (Marcus) Ramseyer; m. John Rush Dickel, June 17, 1961; children: Cynthia, Rebecca. AB magna cum laude, Mt. Holyoke Coll., 1959; MA, U. Mich., 1961, PhD, 1964. Rsch. assoc. in astronomy U. Ill., Urbana, 1965-70, 71-77; vis. fellow div. radiophysics Commonwealth Sci. and Indsl. Rsch. Orgn., Epping, N.S.W., Australia, 1970-71; vis. astronomer Sterrewacht te Leiden, The Netherlands, 1977-79; collaborator Los Alamos (N.Mex.) Nat. Lab., 1983-92; rsch. assoc. prof. astronomy U. Ill., Urbana, 1977-92, rsch. prof. astronomy, 1999—2001; vis. astronomer Australia Telescope Nat. Facility, Epping, 1992-93, rsch. prof. emerita, 2001—. Speaker Am. Chem. Soc., Washington, 1986—. Contbr. articles to Astronomy and Astrophysics, Astrophys. Jour., Interstellar Matter Proceedings. Mem. Urbana Park Dist. Adv. Com., 1988-91. Rackham dissertation fellow, 1964; grantee NSF, 1972-80, 91—, NATO, 1980-83, Internat.-NSF, 1985-86. Mem. Am. Astron. Soc. (Harlow Shapley vis. lectr. 1981—, mem. nominating com. 1991—, grantee 1982-85, 90), Internat. Astron. Union (chair working group of commn. 34 1982-91, chair working group on designations of commn. 5 1995-2003, mem. sci. organizing com. commn. 40 1995-2003), Assn. Women in Sci., Astron. Soc. Pacific, Mt. Holyoke Alumnae Club (asst. sec.-treas. 1989-92), Phi Beta Kappa, Sigma Xi. Achievements include co-discovery of first formaldehyde maser found in interstellar space. Office: U Ill Astronomy Dept 103 Astron Bldg 1002 W Green St Urbana IL 61801-3074

DICKENS, SHEILA JEANNE, family preservation educator; b. Cleve., Sept. 15, 1958; d. Joseph David and Stella Maureen (Brown) Cogdell; children: Randy, Laura, Rebecca. AA, Lakeland C.C., Mentor, Ohio, 1985; BA magna cum laude, Walsh U., 1993, MA, 1995. Nat. cert. counselor; lic. profl. clin. counselor; cert. chem. dependency counselor III. Tutor Lakeland Coll., Mentor, 1980-85; mgr. Wohl Shoe Co., St. Louis, 1985-89; merchandise asst. J.C. Penney, Kingsport, Tenn., 1989-91; grad. asst. Walsh U., North Canton, Ohio, 1994-96, instr., counselor-in-residence program coord., 1995-96; nat. cert. counselor Stark County, Ohio Domestic Violence Project, now women's counselor, clin. dir. Vol. Crisis Intervention Ctr., Canton, 1992-94; mem. disaster svc. team ARC, Canton, 1995—. Mem. Am. Acad. Experts in Traumatic Stress, Assn. Nat. Assn. of Alcohol and Drug Addiction Counselors, Chi Sigma Iota/Alpha Mu (liaison 1995-96). Office: PO Box 9432 Canton OH 44711-9432

DICKERSON, CLAIRE MOORE, lawyer, educator; b. Boston, Apr. 1, 1950; d. Roger Cleveland and Ines Idelette (Roullet) Moore; m. Thomas Pasquali Dickerson, May 22, 1976; children: Caroline Anne, Susannah Moore. AB, Wellesley Coll., 1971; JD, Columbia U., 1974; LLM in Taxation, NYU, 1981. Bar: N.Y. 1975, U.S. Dist. Ct. (ea. and so. dists.) N.Y. 1975, U.S. Ct. Appeals (2d cir.) 1975, U.S. Supreme Ct. 1980. Assoc. Coudert Brothers, N.Y., 1974-82, ptnr., 1983-86, Schnader, Harrison, Segal & Lewis, N.Y., 1987-88, of counsel, 1988—; assoc. prof. law St. John's U., Jamaica, N.Y., 1986-88, prof., 1989-2000; prof law Rutgers U., Newark, 2000—. Author: Partnership Law Adviser; contbr. articles to profl. jours. Scholar Arthur L. Dickson scholar. Mem.: ABA, Soc. for Advancement of Socio-Econs., Law and Soc. Assn., Assn. of Bar of City of N.Y., Shenorock Club. Democrat. E-mail: cmdckrsn@rci.rutgers.edu.

DICKERSON, COLLEEN BERNICE PATTON, artist, educator; b. Cleburne, Tex., Sept. 17, 1922; d. Jennings Bryan and Alma Bernice (Clark) Patton; m. Arthur F. Dickerson; children: Sherry M., Chrystal Charmine. BA, Calif. State U., Northridge, 1980; studied with John Pike. Presenter, instr. in field. One-woman shows include Morro Bay Cmty. Bldg., Amandas Interiors, Arroyo Grande, Calif., 1996, Gt. Western Savs., San Luis Obispo, Calif.; exhibited in group shows including Aquarius Show Ctrl. Coast Watercolor Soc., Calif., 2003; represented in permanent collections, including Polk Ins. Co., San Luis Obispo, Med. Ctr. MDM Ins. Co., L.A. Mem. Ctrl. Coast Watercolor Soc. (pres. 1986-87, Svc. award 1998), Art Ctr., Oil Acrylic Pastel Group (chmn., co-chmn. 1989-98, prize Brush Strokes show 1999), Morro Bay Art Assn. (scholarship judge 1998), San Luis Obispo Art Ctr., Valley Watercolor Soc. (co-founder). Avocations: egyptology, chinese painting, art history. Home: 245 Hacienda Ave San Luis Obispo CA 93401-7967

DICKERSON, DENNIS CLARK, history educator; b. McKeesport, Pa., Aug. 12, 1949; s. Carl O'Neal and Oswanna (Wheeler) D.; m. Mary Anne Eubanks, Aug. 6, 1977; children: Nicole Denise, Valerie Anne, Christina Marie, Dennis Clark Jr. BA, Lincoln U., 1971; MA, Washington (Mo.) U., 1974, PhD, 1978; LHD (hon.), Morris Brown Coll., 1990; postgrad., Hartford Sem. Instr. history Forest Park C.C., St. Louis, 1974, Pa. State U. Ogontz, Abington, 1975-76; from asst. to assoc. prof. history Williams Coll., Williamstown, Mass., 1976-85, assoc. prof., 1987-88, prof., 1988-99, Stanfield prof. history, 1992-99; assoc. prof. history Rhodes Coll., Memphis, 1985—87; prof. history and grad. dept. religion Vanderbilt U., Nashville, 1999—. Mem. com. examiners GRE History test Ednl. Testing Svc., Princeton, 1990-96; corporator Williamstown Savs. Bank, 1992-99; vis. prof. Payne Theol. Sem., Wilberforce, Ohio, 1992, 96, 98; vis. prof. Am. religious history Yale Div. Sch., 1995. Author: Out of the Crucible, 1986, Religion, Race and Region: Research Notes on A.M.E. Church History, 1995, Militant Mediator: Whitney M. Young, Jr., 1998; historiographer, exec. dir. rsch. and scholarship, editor A.M.E. Ch. Review; contbr. articles to profl. jours. Historiographer, African Meth. Episcopal Ch., 1988—, min. 1977—; trustee Mass. Coll. Liberal Arts, 1992-95. Rockefeller Found. fellow U. Va., 1987-88. Mem. Am. Bible Soc. (trustee), Am. Soc. Ch. History (pres.-elect 2003), Elks, Alpha Phi Alpha. Office: Vanderbilt U Dept History Nashville TN 37235-0001

DICKERSON, JOE BERNARD, principal, educator; b. Marburg, Hesse, Germany, Mar. 24, 1951; came to U.S., 1954; s. Joseph Bernard and Eva Maria (Heitmann) D.; m. Joylyne Barbara Ginter, June 11, 1972; children: Alia Dawn, Aaron Mitchell. BSc in Edn., Valparaiso (Ind.) U., 1978; MSc in Edn., U. Mich., Dearborn, 1989; EdD, Nova Southeastern U., Ft. Lauderdale, Fla., 1996. Tchr. St. Joseph Sch., Adelaide, South Australia, 1972-74, St. John Bosco Sch., Adelaide, South Australia, 1974-76; prin. Zion Luth. Sch., Detroit, 1978-80, 86-91; tchr. Point Pearce (South Australia) Aboriginal Sch., 1980; prin. Trinity Luth. Sch., Southport, Queensland, Australia, 1980-82, Ceduna (South Australia) Luth. Sch., 1982-86; prof. writing Purdue U., Ft. Wayne, Ind., 1992—; prin. Ctrl. Luth. Sch., New Haven, Ind., 1991-95; supt. Luth. Sch. Foothills, La Crescenta, Calif., 1995-96; prin. Pilgrim Luth. Sch., Santa Monica, Calif., 1996—2002, Grace Luth. Sch., El Centro, Calif., 2002—. Editor: QBD Theatre mag., 1974; author monograph: Into the 80's - Lutheran Education in Australia, 1982. Mem. ASCD, Nat. Assn. Luth. Prins., Nat. Assn. Elem. Prins., Nat. Assn. Tchrs. Math., Nat. Assn. Luth. Dirs. of Devel., Ind. Luth. Prins. Assn. Lutheran. Avocations: outdoor activities, reading, fitness, vegetable gardening. Office: Acension Lutheran School 17910 Prairie Ave Torrance CA 90504-3797 Home: Apt D 250 S Waterman Ave El Centro CA 92243-2256

DICKERSON, NANCY KNEWSTEP, language educator; b. Hampton, Va., Aug. 22, 1943; d. William Edward and Dorothy Marie (Hunt) K.; m. Kenneth J. Stavisky, Sept. 6, 1975 (div. 1996); 1 child, C. Alexandra Stavisky; m. David D. Dickerson, Oct. 11, 1997. BA, Longwood Coll.,

1965; MA, Regent U., 1994. Cert. libr. sci. Tchr. Hampton (Va.) City Schs., 1965-77; libr. Gloria Dei Luth. Sch., Hampton, 1984-91; tchr. English Hampton City Schs., 1991-98. Adj. faculty Old Dominion U., 1995-2000; facilitator, tchr. individual student alternative edn. plan Virginia Beach City Pub. Schs., 2000—. Exec. bd. mem. Longwood Coll. Found. Bd., Farmville, Va., 1990-96; area rep. Episcopal H.S., Alexandria, Va. Mem. ASCD, Nat. Coun. Tchrs. English, Va. Assn. Tchrs. English. Presbyterian. Avocations: rosarian, boating, gardening. Home: 1325 Starling Ct Virginia Beach VA 23451-4953 E-mail: nancyk@whrd.net.

DICKERSON, RUSSELL ROBERT, atmospheric science and chemistry educator; b. Detroit, May 25, 1953; s. Robert Earl and Dorothy Louise (Anderson) D.; m. Pamela Ruth Pehrsson, Sept. 26, 1954; children: Sarah Wren, Nathan Russell. AB in Chemistry, U. Chgo., 1975; MS in Chemistry, U. Mich., 1978, PhD in Chemistry, 1980. Postdoctoral NCAR, Boulder, Colo., 1979-80; vis. scientist Max Planck Inst., Mainz, Germany, 1980-83; asst. prof. meteorology U. Md., College Park, 1983-88, assoc. prof. meteorology, 1988-94, prof. meteorology, 1994—, chmn., 1994—98. Mem. exec. steering com. Ctr. Clouds Chemistry and Climate, U. Calif. San Diego, 1993—, Atmosphere Ocean Chemistry Experiment, 1992—, N.Am. Strategy for Tropospheric Ozone, 1994—. Editor: Glossary of Meteorology, 1995; contbr. reviewed articles to profl. jours., including Science, Nature, and Jour. Geophys. Rsch. Recipient rsch. grants NFS, EPA, NASA, and NOAA, 1980—. Mem. Am. Chem. Soc., Am. Geophys. Union. Achievements include development of several new analytical instruments for measuring the composition and properties of the atmosphere, and use of these instruments to train students to study the interaction of meteorology and atmospheric chemistry to understand better air pollution and global climate change. Office: U Md Dept Meteorology Css Bldg Stadium Dr College Park MD 20742-0001

DICKEY, ELIZABETH BROWN, journalism educator; b. Charleston, S.C., Aug. 18, 1945; d. Joseph Andrew and Nettie Catherine (Bouknight) Brown; m. Gary Clinton Dickey, Jan. 5, 1971; two children. BA, U. S.C., 1967, MA, 1978. Reporter, editor Charleston (S.C.) News, Evening Post and Courier, 1967-71, Columbia Record, 1971-73; from tchg. assoc. to assoc. prof. U. S.C., Columbia, 1973—; exec. dir. Southern Interscholastic Press. Mem. Assn. in Edn. for Journalism & Mass Comms., Scholastic Journalism Divsn., Journalism Edn. Assn., S.C. Soc. Assn. Execs. Lutheran. Office: Coll Mass Comm and Info Studies Journalism U SC Columbia SC 29208-0001

DICKEY, SUSAN B. nursing educator; b. Hamilton, Ohio, Dec. 31, 1952; d. Joseph M., Jr. and Mary (Mauntel) D.; m. Jared Isaacs; 1 child, Elizabeth Carla. BSN cum laude, U. Pa., 1975; MSN, U. Pa., Phila., 1980, PhD, 1992. RN, Pa. Staff nurse Children's Hosp. Phila., 1979-91; instr. nursing Temple U., 1981-84, asst. prof., 1984-91, assoc. prof., 1992—; relief clin. coord. obstetrical-neonatal nursing Hosp. U. Pa., 1986-88. Author: A Guide to the Nursing of Children, 1987, Guide to Patient Evaluation, 1988; co-author (with V. Bowden and C.S. Greenberg): Children and Their Families: The Continuum of Care; contbr. articles to profl. jour., chapters to books. Nurses' Ednl. Fund scholar, 1985, Am. Nurses' Found. scholar, 1989, grantee, 1989. Mem. ANA (cert., chair, PSNA coun. on nursing ethics 2000-03, mem. adv. com. pub. and ethics and human rights 2000—), Pa. Nurses' Assn. (congl. dist. coord., del., Mem. award 1981, 82), Sigma Theta Tau (Kappa Chi chpt. grantee 1989, Outstanding Svc. award 2001). Home: 601 Highland Ave Boyertown PA 19512-2202

DICKIE, ROBERT BENJAMIN, lawyer, consultant, educator; b. Glendale, Calif., Sept. 10, 1941; s. John A. and Dorothy C. Dickie; m. Susan J. Williams, Jan. 28, 1967 (div. 1987); children: Amy, John, Thomas. BA, Yale U., 1963; JD, U. Calif., Berkeley, 1967. Bar: Calif. 1967, N.Y. 1970, Mass. 1971. Assoc. Shearman & Sterling, N.Y.C., 1969-71, Sullivan & Worcester, Boston, 1971-77; asst. prof. mgmt. policy Boston U., 1977-83, tenured assoc. prof., 1983-94; prin The Dickie Group, 1994—. Cons. World Bank, Washington, Fortune 100 Cos., leading law firms in U.S., Europe and Asia. Author: Financial Statement Analysis and Business Valuation for the Practical Lawyer, ABA, 1999; contbr. numerous articles to Nat. Law Jour., Strategic Mgmt. Jour., Columbia Jour. World Bus., others. Mem.: Am. Bar Assn., Calif. Bar Assn., Boston Bar Assn., Longwood Cricket Club, Yale Club Boston. Office: The Dickie Group Reservoir Pl 1601 Trapelo Rd Waltham MA 02451

DICKINSON, BRADLEY WILLIAM, electrical engineering educator; b. St. Marys, Pa., Apr. 28, 1948; s. William Amos and Maxine I. (McDaniel) D.; m. Colette M. Aldrich, Mar. 12, 1983; children: James Aldrich, Betsy Rebecca. BS in Engring., Case Inst. Tech., 1970; MSEE, Stanford U., 1971, PhD in Elec. Engring., 1974. Asst. prof. dept. elec. engring. Princeton U., Princeton, N.J., 1974-80, assoc. prof., 1980-85, prof., 1985—, assoc. dean for acad. affairs Sch. Engring. and Applied Sci., 1991-94. Mng. co-editor: Mathematics of Control, Signals and Systems, 1988-2000; co-editor: Electronic Newsletter (E-Letter) On Systems, Control and Signal Processing, 1987-93, Selected Papers in Multidimensional Signal Processing, 1986, Concurrent Computations, 1988; author: Systems: Analysis, Design and Computation, 1991; contbr. over 60 tech. papers to profl. jours.; 2 patents on video compression. Fellow IEEE; mem. Tau Beta Pi. Office: Princeton U Dept Elec Engring Princeton NJ 08544-5263 E-mail: bradley@princeton.edu.

DICKINSON, ELEANOR CREEKMORE, artist, educator; b. Knoxville, Tenn., Feb. 7, 1931; d. Robert Elmond and Evelyn Louise (Van Gilder) C.; m. Ben Wade Oakes Dickinson, June 12, 1952; children: Mark Wade, Katherine Van Gilder, Peter Somers. BA, U. Tenn., 1952; postgrad., San Francisco Art Inst., 1961-63, Academié de la Grande Chaumière, Paris, 1971; M.F.A., Calif. Coll. Arts and Crafts, 1982, Golden Gate U., 1984. Escrow officer Security Nat. Bank, Santa Monica, Calif., 1953-54; mem. faculty Calif. Coll. Arts and Crafts, Oakland, Calif., 1971-2001, assoc. prof. art, 1974-84, prof., 1984-2001, prof. emerita, 2001—, dir. galleries, 1975-85. Artist-in-residence U. Tenn., 1969, Ark. State U., 1993, Fine Arts Mus. of San Francisco, 2000; faculty U. Calif. Ext., 1967-70; lectr. in field. Co-author, illustrator: Revival, 1974, That Old Time Religion, 1975; also mus. catalogs; illustrator: The Complete Fruit Cookbook, 1972, Human Sexuality: A Search for Understanding, 1984, Days Journey, 1985; commissions: University of San Francisco, 1990-2001; one-woman shows include Corcoran Gallery Art, Washington, 1970, 74, San Francisco Mus. Modern Art, 1965, 68, Fine Arts Mus. San Francisco, 1969, 75, Poindexter Gallery, N.Y., 1972, 74, Smithsonian Inst., 1975-81, U. Tenn., 1976, Galeria de Arte y Libros, Monterrey, Mex., 1978, Oakland Mus., 1979, Interart Ctr., N.Y., 1980, Tenn. State Mus., 1981-82, Hatley Martin Gallery, San Francisco, 1986, 89, Michael Himovitz Gallery, Sacramento, Calif., 1988-89, 91, 93, 97-98, Gallery 10, Washington, 1989, Diverse Works, Houston, 1990, Ewing Gallery, U. Tenn., 1991, G.T.U. Gallery, U. Calif., Berkeley, 1991, Mus. Contemporary Religious Art, St. Louis, 1995, Thacher Gallery, U. San Francisco, 2000; represented in permanent collections Nat. Collection Fine Arts, Corcoran Gallery Art, Libr. of Congress, Smithsonian Instn., San Francisco Mus. Modern Art, Butler Inst. Art, Oakland Mus., Santa Barbara Mus., Nat. Mus. Women in Arts, Washington; prodr. (TV) The Art of the Matter-Professional Practices in Fine Arts, 1986—. Bd. dirs. Calif. Confedn. of the Arts, 1983-88; bd. dirs., v.p. Calif. Lawyers for the Arts, 1986—; mem. coun. bd. San Francisco Art Inst., 1966-91, trustee, 1964-67; sec., bd. dirs. YWCA, 1955-62; treas., bd. Westminster Ctr., 1955-59; bd. dirs. Children's Theater Assn., 1958-60, 93-94, Internat. Child Art Ctr., 1958-68. Recipient Disting. Alumni award San Francisco Art Inst., 1983, Master Drawing award Nat. Soc. Arts and Letters, 1983, Cert. of Recognition, El Consejo Mundial de Artistas Plasticos, 1993, Pres.'s award Nat. Women's Caucus for Art, 1995, Lifetime Achivement award Nat. Women's Caucus for Art, 2003; grantee Zellerbach Family Fund, 1975, Calif. Coll. Arts and Crafts, 1994, NEH, 1978, 80, 82-85, Thomas F. Stanley Found., 1985, Bay Area Video Coalition, 1988-92, PAS Graphics, 1988, San Francisco Cmty. TV Corp., 1990, Skaggs Found., 1991. Mem. AAUP, Coalition Women's Art Orgns. (dir., v.p. 1978-80, 2000—), Coll. Art Assn. (Lifetime Achievement award 2003), Calif. Confederation of Arts (bd. dirs. 1983-89), Calif. Lawyers for Arts (v.p. 1986—), San Francisco Art Assn. (sec., dir. 1964-67), NOW, Artists Equity Assn. (nat. v.p., dir. 1978-92), Arts Advocates, Women's Caucus for Art (nat. Affirmative Action officer 1978-80, nat. bd. dirs. 2000—). Democrat. Episcopalian. Office: Calif Coll Arts and Crafts 1111 8th St San Francisco CA 94107-2247 E-mail: eleanordickinson@mac.com.

DICKINSON, GAIL KREPPS, educator; b. Lewistown, Pa., June 10, 1956; d. Harold and Esther (Bourdess) Krepps; m. Willis H. Dickinson, Dec. 22, 1979 (div. 1998); children: Margaret Lee, Elizabeth Ann. BS, Millersville U. Pa., 1977; MSLS, U. N.C., 1987; PhD, U. Va., 2000. Libr. Cape Charles (Va.) Pub. Sch., 1977-81, Broadwater Acad., Exmore, Va., 1981-85; instrnl. supervisor Union-Endicott Sch. Dist., Endicott, N.Y., 1987-96; asst. prof. U. N.C., Greensboro, 2000—. Adj. prof. James Madison U., Harrisonburg, Va., 1997-99. Mem. AAUW, ASCD, Am. Ednl. Rsch. Assn., Am. Assn. Sch. Librs. (bd. dirs. 1994-97), N.Y. Libr. Assn. (pres. sch. libr. media sect. 1994), Phi Delta Kappa. Avocations: reading, word and video games.

DICKINSON, WADE, physicist, oil and gas company executive, educator; b. Sharon, Pa., Oct. 29, 1926; s. Ben Wade Orr and Gladys Grace (Oakes) D.; m. Eleanor Creekmore, June 12, 1952; children: Mark, Katherine, Peter. Student, Carnegie Inst. Tech., 1944-45; BS, U.S. Mil. Acad., 1949; postgrad., Oak Ridge Sch. Reactor Tech., 1950-51. Commd. 2d lt. USAF, 1949, advanced through grades to capt., 1954, resigned, 1954; cons. physicist Rand Corp., Santa Monica, Calif., 1952-54; engring. cons. Bechtel Group, Inc., San Francisco, 1954-87; tech. advisor U.S. Congress, Washington, 1957-58; pres. Agrophysics, Inc., San Francisco, 1968—, Petrolphysics Inc., San Francisco, 1975—; ptnr. Radialphysics Ltd., San Francisco, 1980—, Robotphysics Ltd., San Francisco, 1983—; mng. mem. The Spark Group, 00—. Lectr. engring. and bus. U. Calif., Berkeley, 1984—; cardiology cons. Mt. Zion Med. Ctr., U. Calif., San Francisco, 1970-95; chmn. bd. Calif. Med. Clin. Psychotherapy. Contbr. articles to profl. jours; patentee in field. Trustee World Affair Coun., 1958-62; mem. San Francisco Com. Fgn. Rels., Young Republicans, Calif. Mem. Am. Phys. Soc., Am. Soc. Petroleum Engrs. Clubs: Bohemian (San Francisco). Lodges: Masons, Guardsmen. Episcopalian. Home: 2125 Broderick St San Francisco CA 94115-1627 Office: Petrolphysics Inc 1388 Sutter St Ste 603 San Francisco CA 94109-5452 E-mail: petrojet@ix.netcom.com.

DICKINSON, ALEXANDER KANE, physical science educator; b. Jamaica, N.Y., Oct. 16, 1943; s. William and Eileen S. (Kane) D.; m. Lois Jean Tansley, Mar. 21, 1967; children: Stephen William, Jonathan Harry. BS, Western Ill. U., 1965; MS, Mont. State U., 1968, EdD, 1972. Instr. U. Wis., Green Bay, 1969-72, Mont. State U., Bozeman, 1972-73, Seminole C.C., Sanford, Fla., 1973—, dept. chmn. phys. scis., 1986—. Adj. prof. U. Ctrl. Fla., Orlando, 1972-83; del. U.S.-Japan-China Confs. on Physics Tchg., 1989, 91, 93; mem. Fla. Statewide Com. on Common Course Numbering, 1981—; reader, table leader Advance Placement Test Readings, 1988-2001; mem. com. on career planning Am. Inst. Physics, 1991-95. Chair Seminole County Hist. Commn., Sanford, 1982—; mem. Citizen com., Expressway Authority, Seminole County, 1989-93; county liason St. John's Water Mgmt. Dist., Seminole County, 1981-91; energy com. East Fla. Regional Planning Com., Seminole county, 1976-82. Mem. NSTA, Am. Physics Soc., Am. Assn. Physics Tchrs. (exec. bd. 1991-95, treas. 1996-2002, Outstanding Physics Tchr. of Yr. award Fla. sect. 1990, Disting. Svc. award 2003), Fla. Assn. Physics Tchrs. (chmn. 1975-76), Fla. Acad. Scis. (exec. sec. 1986-91, Disting. Svc. award 1993), Fla. Assn. Sci. Tchrs., Sigma Pi Sigma. Avocations: history, outdoors, travel, reading, golf. Home: 4851 Hester Ave Sanford FL 32773-9402 Office: Seminole Community Coll 100 Weldon Blvd Sanford FL 32773-6132 E-mail: dickisoa@scc-fl.edu.

DICKMAN, STEVEN RICHARD, geophysicist, educator; b. Bklyn., June 24, 1950; s. Sidney and Eve (Goldberg) D.; m. Barbara L. Alexander, May 16, 1981; 1 child, Jennifer L. AB in Math., Columbia U., 1972; MA in Geophysics, U. Calif., Berkeley, 1974, PhD in Geophysics, 1977. Asst. prof. geophysics SUNY-Binghamton, 1977-84, assoc. prof. geophysics, 1984-91, prof. geophysics, 1991—. Contbr. more than 30 articles to profl. jours. Recipient Chancellor's and Univ. award for excellence in tchr., SUNY-Binghamton, 2001. Master: Am. Geophys. Union; mem.: Internat. Assn. Geodesy, Internat. Astron. Union. Avocations: piano, tennis. Office: SUNY Geology Dept Binghamton NY 13902

DICKSON, KATHARINE HAYLAND, dance educator; b. East Hartford, Conn., Dec. 4, 1904; d. George Wentworth and Marguerite Moore (Stockman) D.; m. Harry Burton Ashenden, June 23, 1928 (dec. 1967); 1 child, David Dickson; m. Theodore Henry Brown, Oct. 26, 1968 (dec. 1973); m. Charles Thomas Alverson, Feb. 18, 1978 (dec. Mar. 1985). BEd, Boston U., 1948. Tchr. Ballroom dance Model Sch. of Modern Dance, Boston, 1923-26; tchr. ballroom, ballet, tap Hazel Boone Sch. Dancing, Boston, 1926-28; tchr. mus. comedy and tap Knickerbocker Sch., Boston, 1928-31; dir. Katharine Dickson Dance Studio, Cambridge, Mass., 1934-68; tchr. ballroom dance Boston Ctr. for Adult Edn., Boston, 1943-74; tchr. ballet and tap Newton Community Ctr., Mass., 1955-74, Hayden Recreation Ctr., Lexington, Mass., 1957-74; ballroom dance tchr. Englewood (Fla.) Recreation Ctr., 1975-88; tchr. ballroom dance Venice, Fla., 1989-94. Tchr. Ramblers Rest Resort, Venice. Author: Stockman-Gallison Ancestral Lines, 1984, Downeast Dicksons, 1987, Burton-Tyler, 1990, The Stockman Story, 1992, My Very Own 20th Century Rag, 1995, Ashenden, the English Background of Harry Burton Ashenden, 1997, A 1998 Sawyer Fickett Update to Downeast Dicksons of 1987; contbr. articles to profl. jours. Mem. Nat. Coun. Dance Tchr. Orgn. (early chmn.), Dance Tchrs. Club Boston (past pres., hon.), N.Y. Soc. Tchrs. Dancing. Unitarian. Avocations: swimming, gardening, growing wildflowers. Home (Winter): 2101 S Pine St Englewood FL 34224

DICKSON, MARJORIE WAGERS THATCHER, secondary school educator; b. Granby, Colo., June 6, 1915; d. Ray W. and Myrtle Lucy (Mitchell) Wagers; m. Harold Leslie Thatcher (div. 1952); children: Terry D., Eileen, Valerie, Maribeth; m. Ned Banks Dickson, 1991. AB, Brigham Young U., 1937; MEd, Utah State U., 1971. Cert. secondary tchr., Utah. English, drama tchr. Alpine Sch. Dist., Orem, Utah, 1937-41; journalism tchr., chmn. English dept. Davis Sch. Dist., Kaysville, Utah, 1953-77; sales assoc. Utah Real Estate Bd., 1977-86; drama, cultural refinement tchr. Latter Day Saint Ward and Stake, Kaysville, Utah, 1953—. Librarian Latter Day Saint Ward, 1980-88, family history counselor, 1989-91. Mem. Utah County Child Guidance Clinic, Provo, 1949=53; active Provo city and schs., 1948-53; officer Rep. Party Precinct, Provo, 1953 mem. Kaysville Planning Commn., 1979-88, Kaysville Bd. Adjustment, 1982—. NDEA scholar, 1965. Mem. AAUW, Utah Women's State Legis. Coun. (state historian 1978—), Kays Creek League Utah Writers (pres. 1987), Lantern Club (pres. 1986-87), Athena Club, Sky-Line Bridge Club, Delta Kappa Gamma (Woman of Yr. 1987). Home: 92 N 100 W Kaysville UT 84037-1935

DICKSON, MAX CHARLES, retired career counselor, coordinator; b. Heber City, Utah, Oct. 15, 1924; s. Albert Douglas and Ruth (Hicken) D.; m. Darlene Newbold, May 22, 1944; children: Michael Kent, Dianne Dickson Smith, Ronald N., Kaylene Dickson Murray. BS, U. Utah, 1950, MS, 1966, M Counseling, 1979. Cert. secondary tchr., adminstr., counselor, Utah. Tchr. Utah pub. schs., 1950-59; tchr., media coord., student govt. adviser Skyline H.S., Salt Lake City, 1960-73; career ctry. coord./counselor, 1973-87; ret., 1987. Former bishop LDS Ch. With A.C., USN, 1943-45, PTO. Decorated Air medal; named Tchr. of Month, Granite Sch. Dist. Edn. Assn., Nov. 1961. Mem. Am. Vocat. Assn., Utah Sch. Counselors Assn., NEA, Utah Edn. Assn., Granite Edn. Assn., Sons of Utah Pioneers, Phi Delta Kappa. Democrat.

DICKSON, NANCY STARR, retired elementary school educator; b. Frankfort, Ind., Apr. 3, 1936; d. Harley Ledger and Geneve (Daugherty) Fickle; m. Sam W. Dickson, Aug. 23, 1959; 1 child, Hal S. BS, Ball State U., 1958, MA, 1964, cert. reading specialist, 1972. Cert. elem. tchr., Ind. Tchr. Edgelea Elem. Sch., Lafayette, Ind., 1958-59, McKinley Elem. Sch., Muncie, Ind., 1959-65; tchr. spl. reading Garfield Elem. Sch., Muncie, 1967-78, reading specialist, 1996-98; tchr. remedial reading and math. various schs., Muncie, 1978-96; ret., 1998. Author (tchr.'s edition textbook): Our Language Today- Grade 3, 1966, Our Language Today- Grade 4, 1966. Mem. NEA (life), Internat. Reading Assn. (literacy award 1986), Ind. Reading Assn. (pres. 1996-97, coord. 6 couns. 1975—, outstanding svc. award 1986, 89), Muncie Area Reading Coun. (membership dir. 1974-96, past pres.), Ind. Tchrs. Assn., Muncie Tchrs. Assn., Ball State U. Women, Pi Lambda Theta (pres. 1988-90), Delta Kappa Gamma (pres. 1990-92), Alpha Sigma Alpha (pres. alumnae 1986-87, advisor 1986-95). Democrat. Methodist. Avocations: reading, sewing, swimming. Home: 3315 W Petty Rd Muncie IN 47304-3271

DICKSON, SUZANNE RATHBONE (SUE DICKSON), educational administrator; b. Dallas, Jan. 21, 1931; d. DeForest Zeller and Fay (Schmitz) Rathbone; m. Robert E. Dickson, Dec. 29, 1954 (div. 1984); children: Dianne Dickson Fix, Robert Jr., Franklin D. BS in Edn., James Madison U., 1952. Cert. tchr., N.J. Tchr. Arlington (Va.) Pub. Schs., 1952-56, Merrydowns Sch., Annandale, Va., 1962-64, Fairfax (Va.) Christian Sch., 1964-66, Mahwah (N.J.) Pub. Schs., 1966-83; cons. Edn. program/TV/CBN, Virginia Beach, Va., 1983-86; author/cons. Kelwynn Effective Schs. Group, 1986-89; pres. Internat. Learning Systems, Inc., Chesapeake, Va., 1988-94, St. Petersburg, Fla., 1994—2000. Workshop provider to schs., 1972—. Author reading/lang. arts program: Sing, Spell, Read and Write, social studies program: Songs of America's Freedoms, Songs that Teach: U.S. Presidents, Winning: The Race to Independent Reading Ability; author play: Pathway to Liberty, Musical Math Facts. Recipient George Washington Tchr's. Medal Freedom Found., Valley Forge, 1968. Mem. Internat. Reading Assn. (pres. North Jersey coun. 1979-80), Soc. Women Educators (past treas., past v.p.), Delta Kappa Gamma (chpt. pres. 1979-80). Avocations: piano, music.

DICOSIMO, PATRICIA SHIELDS, secondary school educator; b. Hartford, Conn., June 27, 1946; d. Richard Nichols and Rose Aimee (Roy) Shields; m. Joseph Anthony DiCosimo, Apr. 18, 1970. BFA in Art Edn. and Printmaking, U. Hartford, 1969; MS in Edn. and Art, Ctrl. Conn. State Coll., 1972; postgrad., Rochester Inst. Tech., 1986-87. Cert. tchr., Conn. Tchr. art Simsbury (Conn.) H.S., 1969—. Tchr. Farmington Valley Art Ctr., Avon, Conn., 1989-95; supr. Nat. Art Honors Soc., Simsbury, 1989—; mem. Conn. regional adv. bd. Scholastic Art Awards, 1991, 93—; mem. Conn. Scholastic Arts Awards Com., 1989—, co-chair exhibit, 1994—, prin.'s faculty adv. com., 1969—; guest lectr. secondary methods in art edn. Ctrl. Conn. State U., 1994; presenter in field; mem. Conn. Curriculum in Arts, 1995-96, writer, 1995. One-woman shows include Farmington Woods, 1972, Ellsworth Gallery Simsbury, 1974, Annhurst Coll., 1976, Canaan Nat. Bank, 1991, Terryvill Libr., 1994; exhibited in group shows at Ctrl. Conn. State Coll., 1969-72 (Best in Show award 1972), Bristol Chrysanthemum Festival Art Show, 1973-84 (Non-objective award 1973, Graphic award 1975, Mixed Media award 1977, Tracy Driscoll Co. Inc. award 1981, Plymouth Spring award 1983, Dick Blick award 1984), Hartford Ins. Co. Art Educators Exhibit, 1990, Simsbury Libr. Gallery Art Educators Exhibit, 1991, 92, 93, Henry James Meml. Gallery, 1992, Riverview Gallery, 1993, Simsbury Dinner Theater, 1994—, Canton Gallery on the Green, 1996, 98 (Best of Conn. Mural Contest 1996), Simsbury Mall Mural, 1999, End Meml. Hall, 2003; author: Design as a Catalyst for Learning, 1997. Sec. Greater Bristol (Conn.) Condo Alliance, 1990-95; mem. Family Life & Marriage Enrichment, New Britain, Conn., 1970-77; vol. painter Boundless Playground for Handicapped, Simsbury, Conn., 2002, W. Hartford Cow Parade, 2003. Named Conn. Art Tchr. of Yr., 1993, Patricia Shields DiCosimo Day in her honor, Town of Simsbury, 1993, Conn. Beginning Educator Support Tchr., Conn. Alliance for Arts Edn. Sch. Dist., 1995—96, Simsbury C. of C. Educator of Yr., 2000; recipient Book award, Hartford Art Sch., 1969, Recycling Cmty. Svc. award, Simsbury, 1999, K-12 Sculpture Tchr. 1st pl., Internat. Sculpture Com., 2001, 1st prize, 2003; grantee, Simsbury Edn. Enhancement Found., 1996—97. Mem. NEA, Nat. Art Edn. Assn., Nat. Art Honor Soc. (advisor 1983—), New Eng. Assn. Schs. and Colls. (evaluator 1998-99, 2001, 03), Conn. Art Edn. Assn. (H.S. rep. 1983-85, sec. 1985—, Conn. Art Educator 1993, Conn. Alliance for Arts Edn. award for Simsbury Art and Music 1995), Conn. Art Alliance Assn., Conn. Edn. Assn. (mem. 3-D curriculum project 1995-96, portfolio rev. com. 1999, Goals 2000 edn. project 1999—), Conn. Craftsman, Farmington Art Guild (tchr. 1992-95), U. Hartford Alumni Assn. Roman Catholic. Avocations: jewelry, painting, golf, travel. Home: 19 Hampton Ct Bristol CT 06010-4738 Office: Simsbury High Sch 34 Farms Village Rd Simsbury CT 06070-2399 E-mail: pat46art@aol.com.

DICOSTANZO, PAMELA S. science and mathematics educator; b. N.Y.C., July 8, 1941; d. William R. and Doris L. (Nigro) Siena; divorced; children: Jennifer Daile, John William. BS, Cen. Conn. State U., 1963; MS, U. Bridgeport, 1969. Cert. tchr. K-8, Conn. Tchr. grade five Columbus-Lincoln Sch., Norwalk, Conn., 1963-66; sci. tchr. Benjamin Franklin Mid. Sch., Norwalk, 1966-71, Brien McMahan H.S., Norwalk, 1972-73, Roton Mid. Sch., Norwalk, 1973—, team leader, 1991—, sci. dept. head, 1989—. Adj. supr. student tchrs. Fla. Inst. Tech., Melbourne, Fla., 1993; workshop presenter in field. Co-author: (curriculum) Project Consntruct, 1994. Publicity chmn. Norwalk Jr. Woman's Club, 1974-75, social chmn., 1973-74; vol. The Maritime Ctr. at Norwalk, 1988-91. Mem. Nat. Sci. Tchrs. Assn. (workshop presenter 1978, workshop evaluator 1977, 79), Nat. Fedn. Tchrs., Maritime Aquarium, Conn. Sci. Tchrs. Assn., Norwalk Fedn. Tchrs. (bldg. steward). Presbyterian. Avocations: reading, travel. Home: 11 Chipmunk Ln Norwalk CT 06850-4309

DIDONATO, DIANE CARMEN, principal; b. Elizabeth, N.J., Aug. 14, 1953; d. Jose Pereira and Augusta (Pimpao) Esteves; m. Stephen Joseph DiDonato, May 25, 1974; children: Nicole Carmen, Lauren Michelle, Anthony Joseph. BS, Newark State Coll., 1974; masters degree, Kean Coll. N.J., 1980. Tchr. Elizabeth Bd. Edn., 1974-77, 80-87, bilingual tchr., 1977-80, vice prin., 1988-89, Howell Twp. Bd. Edn., Farmingdale, N.J., 1989—. Active Washing Rock (N.J.) coun. Girsl Scouts U.S., 1987—. Mem. Prin. Supr. Assn. N.J. (mem. legal aid com. 1989-90), Prin. Supr. Assn. Monmouth County. Democrat. Roman Catholic. Avocations: reading, sewing, cooking, travel. Office: Ardena Elem Sch 535 Adelphia Rd Farmingdale NJ 07727

DIEBOLD, FRANCIS X. economist, educator; b. Nov. 12, 1959; m. Susan S. Diebold; 3 children. BS in Fin. and Econs., U. Pa., 1981, PhD in Econs., 1986. Rsch. economist, mem. bd. govs. FRS, 1986—89; asst. prof. econs., J.M. Cohen term chair U. Pa., 1989—92, assoc. prof., 1992—96, prof., 1996—99, prof. stats. Wharton Sch., 1996—, dir. Inst. Econ. Rsch., Lawrence R. Klein prof. econs., 1999—; faculty rsch. fellow Nat. Bur. Econ. Rsch., 1993—99, rsch. assoc., 1999—; prof. fin. Wharton Sch. U. Pa., 2001—, W.P. Carey prof. econs., 2000—, prof. fin., 2001—. Charter mem. Oliver Wyman Inst., 1996—; vis. prof. fin., econ., stats. Stern Sch. Bus., NYU, 1998-2000; vis. prof. Cambridge U., 1998, Princeton U., 1997, Johns Hopkins U., 1995, U. Chgo., 1993, London Sch. Econs., 1992, U. Minn., 1990; Benedum lectr. W.Va. U., 1992; mem. organizing com. Computational Fin., 1999—; mem. econs. panel NSF, 1998-2000, chmn. forecasting seminar, 1995—. Author: (with G. Rudebusch) Business Cycles: Durations, Dynamics and Forecasting, 1999, Elements of Forecasting, 1998, Empirical Modeling of Exchange Rate Dynamics, 1988; assoc. editor Rev. Econs. and Stats., 1993—, Jour. Bus. and Econ. Stats., 1993—, Jour. Forecasting, 1994—, Stata Tech. Bull., 1994—, Econometrica, 1994-97, Jour. Applied Econometrics, 1991-97, Jour. Empirical Fin., 1992-95, Econometric Revs., 1989-92; mem. adv. bd. Econ. Policy Rev., Fed. Res. Bank N.Y., 1997—, Macroecon. Dynamics, 1996—; co-editor Internat. Econ. Rev., 1993-99, Jour. Forecasting, 1990-94; contbr. articles to econ. and bus. jours.; spkr. at many profl. meetings and confs. Mem. bd. sr. scholars Nat. Ctr. for Ednl. Quality of Workforce, 1993-95. Fellow Wharton Fin. Instns. Ctr., 1997—; Alfred P. Sloan Found. rsch. fellow, 1992-94; grantee NSF, 1989-92, 92-94, 95-98, 98—, Pew Found., 1995-96, NSF and Cornell Super Computer Ctr., 1992-92. Fellow Econometric Soc. (program com. N.Am. winter mtg. 1999, program com. time-series econometrics 1993); mem. Am. Statis. Assn. (mem. editl. selection com. Jour. B sec., Econ. Stats., 1994, 2000, Zellner award selection com. 1995, sec./treas. bus. and econ. stats. sect. 1994, program chair 1991), Am. Econ. Assn., Am. Fin. Assn. Office: Dept Econs U Pa Dept Econs 3718 Locust Walk Philadelphia PA 19104-6297 E-mail: FDiebold@sas.upenn.edu.

DIEBOLT, MONTE SUE, daycare provider; b. St. Louis, June 23, 1939; d. Eldred LaMonte and Mildred Emma (Kirk) Gann; m. John Richard Diebolt, July 24, 1959; children: John David, Michael Joel. BE, Kans. State Tchrs. Coll., Emporia, 1961; MEd in Counseling, Kans. State Tchrs. Coll., 1974; student, Emory U., 1994—. Tchr. Kansas City (Mo.) Pub. Schs., 1961-63; tchr. Oklahoma City Pub. Schs., 1963-65; tchr., counselor, adminstr. Charlotte-Mecklenburg (N.C.) Pub. Schs., 1966-86; dir. preschool and childcare ministries First United Meth. Ch., Statesboro, Ga., 1992—. Part-time local pastor; adv. bd. So. Conf. Ga. So. United Meth. Ch., 1993—, lay speaker, 1992—. Counselor-mentor Genesis-United Meth. Ch., Macon, Ga., 1994—; mem. Symphony Guild, Statesboro, 1992—. Named Tchr. of Yr. Native Ams. of Charlotte-Mecklenburg Schs., 1985. Mem. AAUW. Republican. Methodist. Avocations: reading, travel (Israel, Jan. 1995). Home: 125 Hazelwood Dr Statesboro GA 30458-9141 Office: First United Methodist Ch 101 S Main St Statesboro GA 30458-0921

DIEHL, CAROL LOU, library director, retired, library consultant; b. Milw., Aug. 10, 1929; d. Gilbert Fred and Erna Lou (Braeger) Doepke; m. Russell Phillip Diehl, Aug. 8, 1953; children: Holly Lou Diehl Nelson, Jeffrey Phillip. BS, U. Wis., Madison, 1951; MA, U. Wis., Oshkosh, 1971. Tchr. English, libr. Port Washington (Wis.) High Sch., 1951-54, Minocqua (Wis.) High Sch., 1954-55; libr. Ozaukee High Sch., Fredonia, Wis., 1964-65, Vernon County Tchrs. Coll., Viroqua, Wis., 1965-67; libr. media coord. Manawa (Wis.) Sch. Dist., 1973-77; dir. libr. media svcs. Sch. Dist. of New London, Wis., 1977-95; ret., 1995; lectr. U. Wis., Oshkosh, 1993, 95—. V.p. Coun. on Libr. and Network Devel., Madison, 1979; pres. Lake Forest Bd. Dirs., Eagle River, Wis., 1987-89; libr. cons. Thern Design Ctrs. Inc., 1994. Author: (with others) School Library Media Annual, 1985-87; news corr. Appleton (Wis.) Post Crescent, 1971-81; contbr. articles to profl. jours. Past mem. Fox Valley Symphony League; mem. exec. com. Waupaca County Grand Ole Party, chair, 1994-97, vice chmn., 1991-94; del.-at-large White House Conf. Libr. and Info. Svcs., 1991; trustee Sturm Meml. Libr., 1996-2002, treas., 1998—; mem. bd. edn. Sch. Dist. of Manawa, 1997-2003; mem. Manawa City Appeals Bd., 1999-2002. Named Wis. Sch. Libr. Media Specialist of Yr. Assn. Ednl. Comm. and Tech., 1992. Mem. ALA (councilor-at-large 1998—, legis. com. 1986-91, ALA White House Conf. Libr. and Info. Svcs., 1995—, chair, 1992-95, legis. assembly chair 1989-90, membership com. 1995-99, ALTA legis. com. 1998-99, chair, 1999—, Outstanding Libr. Advocate of 20th Century 2000), AASL (legis. chmn. 1987-95, planning and implementation task force White House Conf. 1990-92, Disting. Sch. Adminstrs. chair 2001-02), Wis. Libr. Assn. (fed. rels. coord. 1990-91), Assn. Wis. Sch. Adminstr., Wis. Edn. Media Assn. (legis. com. 1986-93, Excellence award 1992), Futurae Club of Manawa, Manawa Federated Women's Club, Phi Delta Kappa. Republican. Lutheran. E-mail: diehl@netnet.net.

DIEHM, JAMES WARREN, lawyer, educator; b. Lancaster, Pa., Nov. 6, 1944; s. Warren G. and Verna M. (Hertzler) D.; m. Cathleen M. Hohmeier; children: Elizabeth Ann, Rebecca Jane. BA, Pa. State U., 1966; JD, Georgetown U., 1969. Bar: D.C. 1969, V.I. 1975, Pa. 1988. Asst. U.S. atty., Washington, 1970-74; asst. atty. gen. Atty. Gen.'s Office U.S. V.I., St. Croix, 1974-76; from assoc. to ptnr. Isherwood, Hunter & Diehm, St. Croix, 1976-83; U.S. atty. U.S. V.I., 1983-87; prof. law Widener U., 1987—. Bar examiner U.S. V.I. Bar, 1979-87. Mem. ABA. Republican. Lutheran. Office: Widener U Sch Law 3800 Vartan Way PO Box 69382 Harrisburg PA 17106-9382

DIEM, GORDON NEAL, political science educator, video producer; b. Lancaster, Pa., Oct. 29, 1946; s. Paul F. and Mary (Nolt) D.; m. Tjuana Taylor Shaw, May 8, 1989. BA, Millersville U. of Pa., 1968; MA in Teaching, Miss. State U., 1972; ArtsD, Idaho State U., 1974. Actor Lancaster County Artists Prodns., Lancaster, Pa., 1964-65; news corr. Lancaster Newspapers Inc., 1965-68; asst. prof. of social sci. Mt. Empire C.C., Big Stone Gap, Va., 1974-78; dir. alumni affairs Millersville U. of Pa., 1978-84; asst. prof. of human svcs. adminstrn. Springfield (Mass.) Coll., 1984-88; asst. prof. polit. sci. N.C. Ctrl. U., Durham, 1988-2000; pres., primary assoc. ADVANCE Edn. and Devel. Inst., Durham, 1986—; dir. fund devel. HARB-ADULT, Lancaster, Pa., 2000—01; dir. devel. West Fallowfield Christian Sch., Atglen, Pa., 2001—. Bd. dirs. N.C. Marriage and Family Therapy Certification Bd., Raleigh, 1992-94, Nat. Soc. of Fundraising Execs., Washington, 1983-84, N.C. Soc. for Internat. Devel. (v.p. 1993—), Hampden County Woman's Ctr., Springfield, Mass., 1987-88. Producer, host: (weekly cable TV series) Today's Third World, 1990—(N.C. Cmty. TV award 1994), Counterpoise Durham, 1990— (N.C. Cmty. TV award 1994), Soil and Water Conservation Report, 1992— (N.C. Cmty. TV award 1994), Spotlight, 1990— (N.C. Cmty. TV award 1994). Assoc. supr. Soil and Water Conservation Dist., Durham, 1992-94, supr., 1994—; councilman Marietta (Pa.) Borough Coun., 1982-84; at-large rep. to Durham County Rep. exec. com., 1992—. Lt. col. USAR, 1969—. Recipient 7 Woody awards N.C. Cmty. TV, 1994. Mem. So. Polit. Sci. Assn., N.C. Polit. Sci. Assn., Pa. German Soc., Assn. for Rsch. on Nonprofit Orgns. and Voluntary Action, Phi Kappa Phi, Pi Sigma Alpha. Episcopalian. Avocations: politics, antiques, farming, wildlife advocacy, community research. Home: 1106 Arnette Ave Durham NC 27707-1304 E-mail: AdvanceInstitute@yahoo.com., GordonNeal@netscape.net.

DIEPHOUSE, DAVID JAMES, humanities educator, historian; b. Grand Haven, Mich., June 30, 1947; s. James and Jeannette D.; m. Evelyn De Jong, Aug. 12, 1970; children: Rachel, Amy, Miriam. AB, Calvin Coll., 1969; MA, Princeton U., 1971, PhD, 1974. Instr. Princeton (N.J.) U., 1973-74; asst. prof. Rutgers U., Newark, 1974-76, Calvin Coll., Grand Rapids, Mich., 1976-79, assoc. prof., 1979-84, prof., 1984—, chair dept. history, 1988-94, dean social scis., langs., literature and arts, 1997—2003. Author: Pastors and Pluralism in Wuerttemberg 1918-1933, 1987; translator: (books) The Natural History of the German People, 1990, Early American Railroads: Franz Anton Ritter von Gerstner's Die Innern Communicationen 1842-1843, 1997. Trustee Grand Rapids Christian Sch. Assn., 1987-90, Chamber Music Soc. Grand Rapids, 1988-99; bd. dirs. Interfaith Dialogue Assn., Grand Rapids, 1998; mem. spkrs. bur. Common Cause, Mich., 1977-78. Recipient Rsch. grant Nat. Endowment for the Humanities, fellowship Deutscher Akademischer Austauschdienst, 1982, 91, fellowship Inst. europaeische Geschichte, 1992, Rsch. grant Am. Philosophical Soc., 1992. Mem. Am. Hist. Assn., Am. Soc. Ch. History (mem. conf. onfaith and history, Latourette prize com. 1988-91), German Studies Assn., Conf. Group on Ctrl. European History. Avocations: music, running, hiking, reading, travel. Office: Calvin Coll 3201 Burton SE Grand Rapids MI 49546 E-mail: ddiephou@calvin.edu.

DIERCKS, EILEEN KAY, educational media coordinator, elementary school educator; b. Lima, Ohio, Oct. 31, 1944; d. Robert Wehner and Florence (Huckemeyer) McCarty; m. Dwight Richard Diercks, Dec. 27, 1969; children: Roger, David, Laura. BS in Edn., Bluffton Coll., 1966; MS, U. Ill., 1968. Tchr. elem. grades Kettering City Schs., Ohio, 1966-67; children's libr. St. Charles County, Mo., 1968-69; libr. Rantoul (Ill.) H.S., 1970-71; elem. tchr. Elmhurst (Ill.) Sch. Dist., 1971-72; media coord. Plainfield (Ill.) Sch. Dist., 1980—2001, libr. media cons., 2001—03. Evaluator Rebecca Caudill Young Readers' Book Award, 1990-97; LTA adv. com. Joliet Jr. Coll., 2003. Founder, treas. FISH orgn., Plainfield, 1975-78; pres. Ch. Women United, 1974; sec. Plainfield Cmty. TV Access League, 1987-89; treas. Plainfield Congl. Ch., 1983-88; bd. dirs. Cub Scouts, 1983-86; leader, mem. Girl Scouts USA, Plainfield, 1985—; mem. Bolingbrook (Ill.) Cmty. Chorus, 1986-90, Plainfield Area Cmty. Chorus, 1999—. Mo. State Libr. scholar, 1967, Naperville chpt. Valparaiso U. Guild, treas., 1993-95. Mem.: ALA, Am. Assn. Sch. Librs., Ill. Sch. Libr. Media Assn. (membership chmn. 1992—93, mem. awards com. 1994—96, disaster relief chmn. 1996—97, treas. 2001—03), Plainfield Athletic Club (sec. 1984—86), Rotary (treas. 1994—95, bd. dirs. 1994—, v.p. 1995—96, pres.-elect 1996—97, pres. 1997—98, sec. Plainfield chpt. 2003—), Beta Phi Mu, Pi Delta, Delta Kappa Gamma (Beta Rho) (treas. 1993—97). Home: 13440 S Rivercrest Dr Plainfield IL 60544-8979

DIERKSEN, KATHRYN ZIMMERMAN, secondary education educator; b. Greensboro, N.C., Aug. 9, 1948; d. Bernhard Gus and Anna Mae Zimmerman; m. John Theodore Dierksen, Aug. 10, 1968; children: Elizabeth, David. BS in Edn., U. Tex., 1969; MEd, S.W. Tex. State U., 1984. Tchr. English Shiner (Tex.) Ind. Sch. Dist., 1969-70; spl. edn. tchr. Round Rock (Tex.) Ind. Sch. Dist., 1972-73, New Braunfels (Tex.) Ind. Sch. Dist., 1973-76, 80-85; tchr. history Comal Ind. Sch. Dist., New Braunfels, 1985—2001; social studies dept chair and hist. tchr. San Marcos Ind. Sch. Dist., 2001—02. Active Woodrow Wilson Torch Program, 1993, 94, Nat. Humanities Ctr. Summer Inst., 1994; mem. Holocaust Meml. Mus. Assn. Named Outstanding History Tchr., SAR, 1988, Tchr. of Yr., VFW Aux., 1994; NEH Summer Inst. grantee, 1992, 95. Mem. Tex. Ex-Students Assn., New Braunfels Sophienburg Mus. Assn. Avocations: travel, reading history and historical fiction.

DIERS, CAROL JEAN, psychology educator; b. Bellingham, Wash., July 16, 1933; d. William Donald and Alice H. (West) D.; m. Herbert C. Taylor Jr., Aug. 17, 1973 (dec. 1991). BA, BEd, Western Wash. State Coll., 1956; MA, U. B.C., Vancouver, Can., 1958; PhD, U. Wash., 1961. Tchr. Bellevue (Wash.) Pub. Schs., 1956-57, 58-59; instr. Olympic Community Coll., Bremerton, Wash., 1961-63; asst. prof. psychology Western Wash. U., Bellingham, 1963-65, assoc. prof., 1965-74, prof., 1974-91, prof. emerita, 1991—, dir. honors program, 1970-74. Contbr. articles to profl. jours. Mem. Sigma Xi, Psi Chi. Avocation: travel. Home: 135 Meadow Slope Rd Talent OR 97540-8693

DIERSING, CAROLYN VIRGINIA, educational administrator; b. Rushville, Ohio, Sept. 13; d. Carl Emerson and Wilma Virginia (Neel) Deyo; m. Robert J. Diersing, Dec. 22, 1962; children: Robert, Timothy, Charles, Sheila, Christina. BA, Ohio State U., 1963; state cert., Ohio Dominican, 1985. Cert. tchr., Ohio. Libr. St. Mary's Sch., Delaware, Ohio, 1979-87; tech. svcs. asst. Beeghly Libr. Ohio Wesleyan U., Delaware, 1987-90, dir. curriculum resource dept. edn., 1990-96; libr. assoc. Westerville Pub. Libr., 1997—. Contbr. poetry to Voices. Mem. ALA, Del. Area Recovery Resources (bd. dirs. 1994-96, treas. 1995, sec. 1996), Ohio Libr. Coun. Office: Westerville Pub Libr Adult Svcs Dept 126 S State St Westerville OH 43081-2095 E-mail: cdiersin@wpl.lib.oh.us.

DIETRICH, CAROL ELIZABETH, educator, former dean; b. Pitts., Mar. 19, 1961; d. Herman Karl and Ruby Faye (Mast) D. BA, Carnegie Mellon U., 1983; MA, Ohio State U., 1985, PhD, 1993, MEd, 1994; MTS, Trinity Luth. Sem., 2000. From asst. prof. to prof. DeVry U., Columbus, Ohio, 1988—, dean gen. edn., 1996—98. Mem. MLA, Nat. Coun. Tchrs. English. Avocations: poetry, theology, writing. Home: 276 Pingree Dr Worthington OH 43085-4039 Office: DeVry Univ 1350 Alum Creek Dr Columbus OH 43209-2764

DIETRICH, JOYCE DIANE, librarian; b. Danville, Pa., Aug. 19, 1951; d. LeRoy Charles and Mae Elizabeth (Klinger) Smeltz; m. Lynn Allen, Sept. 2, 1972; children: Sarah Mae, Martha Ferne, David Lynn. BS in Libr. Sci., Millersville (Pa.) U., 1972; MS in Libr. Sci., Shippensburg (Pa.) U., 1974. Cert. in libr. sci., Pa.; cert. decorative artist. Middle sch. libr. Upper Dauphin Area Sch. Dist., 1972-73; high sch. libr. Shippensburg (Pa.) Area Sch. Dist., 1973-80; elem. libr. Greencastle-Antrim (Pa.) Sch. Dist., 1992—. Adj. faculty libr. sci. Shippensburg (Pa.) U., 1982; painting instr. local craft shops, convs., etc., 1985-92. Designer: (painted object) Decorative Painter, 1992, Craftworks, 1992, Homestead Classics Christmas Crafts, 1993. Pianist for children Salem Luth. Ch., Marion, Pa., 1984—, Marion Cmty. Bible Sch., 1984—. Mem. ALA, Pa. Sch. Librs. Assn., Nat. Soc. Decorative Painters, Order of Eastern Star. Democrat. Lutheran. Home: 2798 Warm Spring Rd Chambersburg PA 17201-9269 Office: Greencastle-Antrim Sch Dist 500 E Leitersburg St Greencastle PA 17225-1138

DIETSCHY, JOHN MAURICE, gastroenterologist, educator; b. Alton, Ill., Sept. 23, 1932; s. John C. and Clara A. (Sahner) D.; m. Beverly A. Robertson, Apr. 18, 1959; children: John, Daniel, Michael, Karen. AB, Washington U., St. Louis, 1954; MD, Washington U. Sch. Medicine, St. Louis, 1958. Resident VA Hosp., Denver, 1959-61; asst. prof. internal medicine U. Tex. Southwestern Med. Ctr., Dallas, 1965-69, assoc. prof. internal medicine, 1969-71, prof. internal medicine, 1971—. Mem. adv. bd. Okla. Med. Rsch. Found., Oklahoma City, 1988-92, Children's Hosp. Rsch. Found., Cin., 1990-95; chmn. adv. com. arteriosclerosis hypertension lipid metabolism NIH, 1989-90. Editor: Clinical Gastroenterology Monograph Series, 1976-85, The Science and Practice of Clinical Medicine, 1977-81, Disorders of the Liver, Nutritional Disorders, 1976; contbr. over 200 articles to profl. jours. NIH rsch. grantee, 1964—; Rsch. fellow Boston U., 1961-63, U. Tex. Southwestern Med. Ctr., 1963-65; Markle scholar Acad. Medicine, 1966-71; recipient Heinrich-Wieland prize Lipid Biochemistry, 1983, McKenna medal Can. Assn. Gastroenterology, 1985, Janssen award, 2001. Fellow AAAS (elected); mem. Am. Gastroen. Assn. (pres. 1987-88, Disting. Achievement award 1978), Am. Fedn. Clin. Rsch. (pres. So. sect. 1974-75), So. Soc. Clin. Investigation (pres. 1982). Roman Catholic. Achievements include lipid absorption from intestine, mechanisms regulation of plasma cholesterol concentration, mechanisms prodn. antherosclerosis, mechanisms of neurodegeration. Office: U Tex SW Med Ctr 5323 Harry Hines Blvd Dallas TX 75390-8887

DIETZ, DAVID W. elementary education educator; Tchr. Gainsville (Tex.) Jr. H.S., 1975—. Recipient Tchr. Excellence award Internat. Tech. Edn. Assn., 1992. Office: Gainesville Jr HS 421 N Denton St Gainesville TX 76240-4016

DIETZ, DONALD ARTHUR, vocational education educator; b. Vacaville, Calif., July 11, 1939; s. Arthur H. and Dorothy V. (Donald) D.; widowed, Jan. 1991; children: James, Corine, Loretta. BA in Indsl. Arts, San Francisco State U., 1962, MA in Indsl. Arts and Counseling, 1966; cert. in vocat. edn., U. Calif., Berkeley, 1966; cert. in counseling and adminstrn., U. San Francisco, 1967. Cert. tchr., Calif. Tchr. San Francisco Unified Sch. Dist., 1963-69, Acalanes Union High Sch. Dist., Lafayette, Calif., 1969—, counselor, 1973-76. Guest panelist Internat. Graphic Arts Educator Conf., Calif. State Poly. Coll., 1967; presenter workshop on archtl. model making Calif. Indsl. Edn. Bay Sect., Antioch, 1974; presenter seminar on engring. and drafting orientation Advantage Pers. Svcs., 1991. Contbr. articles to profl. publs. Recipient Outstanding Leadership award Calif. State Dept. Edn., 1990, Program of Excellence award Contra County Sch. Adminstrn., 1992. Mem. Calif. Tchrs. Assn., Calif. Indsl. Tech. Edn. Assn. (past v.p., past bd. dirs. Contra Costa chpt.), Calif. Graphic Arts Educators Assn., Am. Vocalition Assn., Acalanes Edn. Assn. (pres. 1976), Internat. Club Printing House Craftsmen (bd. dirs. Diablo chpt.), Diablo Craftsmens Club (v.p., Outstanding Craftsman award 1992). Avocations: golf, camping, travel. Home: 201 Rainbow Dr # 11393 Livingston TX 77399-2001 Office: Acalanes High Sch 1200 Pleasant Hill Rd Lafayette CA 94549-2623

DIETZ, JANIS CAMILLE, business educator; b. Washington, May 26, 1950; d. Albert and Joan Mildred (MacMullen) Weinstein; m. John William Dietz, Apr. 10, 1981. BA, U. R.I., 1971; MBA, Calif. Poly. U., Pomona, 1984; PhD, Claremont Gard. Sch., 1997. Customer svc. trainer People's Bank, Providence, 1974-76; salesman, food broker Bradshaw Co., L.A., 1976-78; salesman Johnson & Johnson, L.A., 1978-79, GE Co., L.A., 1979-82; regional sales mgr. Leviton Co., L.A., 1982-85; nat. sales mgr. Jensen Gen. divsn. Nortek Co., L.A., 1985-86; retail sales mgr. Norris divsn. Masco, L.A., 1986-88; nat. sales mgr. Thermador Waste King divsn. Masco, L.A., 1988-91; nat. accounts mgr. Universal Flooring divsn. Masco, 1991-92; western regl. mgr. Peerless Faucet divsn. Masco, 1992-95; performance devel. cons. Delta Faucet divsn. Masco, 1995—. Assoc. prof. bus. adminstrn. U. LaVerne, 1995-2002, prof., 2002—; sales trainer, Upland, Calif., 1985—; instr. Calif. Poly. U., 1988-91; lectr. Whittier Coll., 1994. Dir. pub. rels. Jr. Achievement, Providence, 1975-76; trustee Soc. Calif. chpt. Nat. Multiple Sclerosis Soc. Recipient Sector Svc. award GE Co., Fairfield, Conn., 1980, Outstanding Achievement award, 1980. Mem. NAFE, Sales Profls. L.A. (v.p. 1984-86), Toastmasters (adminstrv. v.p. 1985). Unitarian Universalist. E-mail: dietzj@ulv.edu.

DIETZ, MARGARET JANE, retired public information director; b. Omaha, Apr. 15, 1924; d. Lawrence Louis and Jeanette Amalia (Meile) Neumann; m. Richard Henry Dietz, May 30, 1949 (dec. July 1971); children: Henry Louis, Frederick Richard, Susan Margaret, John Lawrence (dec.). BA, U. Nebr., 1946; MS, Columbia U., 1949. Wire editor Kearney (Nebr.) Daily Hub, 1946-47; state soc. editor Omaha World-Herald, 1947-48; libr. aide Akron (Ohio) Pub. Libr., 1963-66, publicity and display dir., 1966-74; editor Owlet, 1966-74; pub. info. officer Northeastern Ohio Univs. Coll. Medicine, Rootstown, 1974-85, dir. Office Commn., 1985-87, ret., 1987. Writer Ravenna (Ohio) Record-Courier, 1988-92; cons. Kent (Ohio) State U. Sch. Music, 1988-91. Author: Akron's Library: Commemorating Twenty Five Years on Main Street, Silver Reflections: A History of the Northeastern Ohio Universities College of Medicine, 1973-98. Mem. culture and entertainment com. Goals for Greater Akron, 1976; pres. bd. Weathervane Cmty. Playhouse, Akron, 1982-85, sec. to the bd., 1988-93, trustee, 1991-93, historian, 1993—, chair 60th anniversary season, 1994-95; trustee Family Svcs. Summit County, Ohio, 1980-84, dist. trustee, 1994—, Am. Heart Assn., Akron dist., 1986-91, Mobile Meals Found., Akron, 1988-91; v.p. Friends of Akron-Summit County Pub. Libr., 1988-94, pres., 1994-95; student tutor LEARN Literacy Coun., 1988-94, trustee, 1988-95. Recipient Trustee award Weathervane Cmty. Playhouse, 1985, Family Svcs. Bernard W. Frazier award, 1994, John S. Knight award Soc. Profl. Journalists, 1995. Mem. Women in Comm. (Mary Kerrigan O'Neill award 1995), LWV (edn. found. 1989-92, newsletter editor Akron 1957-60), Coll. Club, Press Club, Akron Women's City Club. Home: 887 Canyon Trl Akron OH 44303-2401 E-mail: mjd887@earthlink.net.

DIETZE, GOTTFRIED, political science educator; b. Kemberg, Germany, Nov. 11, 1922; came to U.S., 1949; s. Paul and Susanne (Pechstein) D. Dr.Jur., U. Heidelberg, Germany, 1949; PhD, Princeton U., 1952; S.J.D., U. Va., 1961. Instr. polit. sci. Dickinson Coll., 1952-54; mem. faculty Johns Hopkins, 1954—, prof. polit. sci., 1962—. Vis. prof. U. Heidelberg, 1956, 58-60, Brookings Instn., 1960-61, 67 Author: Ueber Formulierung der Menschenrechte, 1956, The Federalist, 1960, In Defense of Property, 1963, Magna Carta and Property, 1965, America's Political Dilemma, 1968, Youth, University and Democracy, 1970, Bedeutungswandel der Menschenrechte, 1971, Academic Truths and Frauds, 1972, Two Concepts of the Rule of Law, 1973, Deutschland-Wo Bist Du?, 1980, Kant und der Rechtsstaat, 1981, Kandidaten, 1982, El Gobierno Constitucional, 1983, Liberalism Proper and Proper Liberalism, 1984, Reiner Liberalismus, 1985, Konservativer Liberalismus in Amerika, 1987, Liberaler Kommentar zur Amerikanischen Verfassung, 1988, Amerikanische Demokratie, 1988, Politik-Wissenschaft, 1989, Der Hitler-Komplex, 1990, Liberale Demokratie, 1992, American Democracy, 1993, Problematik der Menschenrechte, 1995, Briefe aus Amerika, 1995, Begriff des Rechts, 1997, Deutschland, 1999, 1999, Deutschland: besser und schöner, 2001; editor: Essays on the American Constitution, 1964. Lutheran. Office: Johns Hopkins U Dept Polit Sci Baltimore MD 21218

DIFALCO, JOHN PATRICK, lawyer, arbitrator; b. Steubenville, Ohio, Nov. 24, 1943; s. Pat John and Antoinette (Ricci) DiF.; m. Carolyn L. Otten, June 11, 1977; children: Elizabeth Ann, Jennifer Ann, Kevin John. BA, Ohio State U.; MA, U. No. Colo.; JD, Ohio State U. Bar: Ohio 1968, Colo. 1972, U.S. Dist. Colo. 1972, U.S. Ct. Appeals Colo. 1972, U.S. Supreme Ct. 1972, U.S. Ct. Appeals (fed. cir.) 1986, D.C. 1989. Atty., hearing officer, dir. U.S. Postal Svc., Washington, 1970-77; labor rels. specialist City and County of Denver, 1977-80; city atty. City of Greeley, Colo., 1980-87; pvt. practice Greeley, 1987—; prin. John P. DiFalco & Assocs., P.C., Ft. Collins, Colo., 1987—. Instr. Regis U., Denver, U. Phoenix, Denver, Aims Community Coll., Greeley, Arapahoe Community Coll., Littleton, Colo., Pikes Peak Community Coll., Colo. Springs, Tri-State Coll., Angola, Ind.; arbitrator, 1980—; speaker in field. Contbr. Postmaster Advocate mag., also articles to profl. jours. Named an Outstanding City Atty. Colo., 1986. Mem. ABA (com. on pub. employee bargaining), Colo. Bar Assn. (labor law sect., Spl. Achievement award 1987), Fed. Bar Assn. (coms. on pub. sector labor rels., arbitration and office mgmt.), Colo. Trial Lawyers Assn., Indsl. Rels. Rsch. Assn., Nat. Pub. Employer Labor Rels. Assn., Nat. Acad. Arbitrators, Am. Arbitration Assn., Nat. Inst. Mcpl. Law Officers (com. on law office mgmt.), Larimer County Bar Assn., Colo. Mcpl. League (chmn. attys. sect., mcpl. govt. issues and open meeting coms.), Met. Denver City Attys. Assn. (pres.), Ohio State U. Pres.'s Club, Rotary. Republican. Roman Catholic. Avocations: reading, sports, model railroading, historical studies. Office: 5821 Langley Ave Ste 101 Loveland CO 80538-8828

DIFFENDAL, ROBERT FRANCIS, JR., geologist, researcher, educator; b. Hagerstown, Md., June 20, 1940; s. Robert F. and Martha Frances (Martin) D.; m. Anne Elizabeth Polk, June 5, 1967. AB, Franklin & Marshall Coll., 1962; MS, U. Nebr., 1964, PhD, 1971. From instr. to asst. prof. St. Dominic Coll., St. Charles, Ill., 1966-70; from asst. to assoc. prof. Doane Coll., Crete, Nebr., 1970-80; from assoc. to full prof. U. Nebr., Lincoln, 1980—, asst. dir. Sch. Natural Resource Scis., 1997-2000. Mem. geology dept. adv. bd. U. Nebr., Lincoln, 1984-87, pres. faculty senate, 1988-89; exchange prof. Zhongshan U., Guangzhou, China, 1985-86, 90-91, 98, 99; mem. Nebr. Gov.'s Energy Policy Coun., Lincoln, 1990-91. Contbr. articles to profl. jours. Fellow Geol. Soc. Am. (chmn. North Ctrl. sect. 1994-95, exec. sec. 1997—), Ctr. for Great Plains Studies; mem. AAUP (chmn. Nebr. conf. 1978-79), Paleontol. Soc., Nat. Assn. Geology Tchrs., Nebr. Geol. Soc. (pres., treas. 1978-79), Sigma Xi. Home: 3131 S 41st St Lincoln NE 68506-6216 Office: Univ Nebr Lincoln NE 68588-0517 E-mail: rfd@unl.edu.

DIFFILY, DEBORAH LYNN, early childhood education educator; b. San Bernardino, Calif., July 23, 1955; d. J.W. and Bobbye Dale (Funkhouser) Titsworth; m. David Thomas Hawkins, Feb. 1, 1983; 1 child, Michael Spear Hawkins; m. James Patrick Diffily, Aug. 3, 1991. BA, Oral Roberts U., 1976; MA, Tex. Wesleyan U., 1989; PhD, U. North Tex., 1994. Pre-kindergarten tchr. The White Lake Sch., Ft. Worth, 1988-90; kindergarten and 1st grade tchr. Ft. Worth Ind. Sch. Dist., 1990-96; faculty Tex. Wesleyan U., 1996—2000. Co-author: Teaching Young Children, 1998, Implementing Projects with Young Children, 2002; editor: Helping Parents Understand: Newsletter Articles on Early Childhood Issues, 1995; co-editor: Family Friendly Communication in Early Childhood Programs; contbr. articles to profl. jours. Bd. dirs. Tex. Assn. Early Childhood Tchr. Educators, Nat. Assn. Early Childhood Tchr. Educators. Mem. ASCD, Ft. Worth Area Assn. for Edn. of Young Children (pres. 1993-94), Tex. Assn. for Edn. of Young Children, So. Early Childhood Assn., Nat. Assn. for Edn. of Young Children, Phi Delta Kappa. Home: 3905 Sanguinet St Fort Worth TX 76107-7237

DIFFLEY, JUDY HIGH, educator; b. Monticello, Ark., Apr. 19, 1947; d. Horace Eugene and Barbara Lucille (Allison) High; m. Gary Gene Diffley, Dec. 23, 1978. BS in Bus. and Office Edn., N.E. La. U., 1968, MBA in Bus. Adminstrn., 1970; PhD in Bus. Edn., U. Okla., 1982; postgrad., Zhejiang Normal U., Jinhua, China, summer 1992. Cert. profl. sec., cert. adminstrv. profl. Grad. teaching asst. N.E. La. U., Monroe, 1968-70; asst. prof. S.W. Mo. State U., Springfield, 1970-80; grad. teaching asst. U. Okla., Norman, 1976-77; prof. Washburn U., Topeka, 1982—, chair office legal and tech. dept., 1985—96, program dir. office adminstrn., 1982—. Cons. and speaker Colmery-O'Neil VA Med. Ctr., Topeka, 1991—, The Menninger Found., Topeka, 1985; spkr. Payless Shoe Source, Yellow Freight; lectr. in field. Mem. Everywoman's Resource Ctr., Topeka, 1985—. Washburn U. rsch. grantee, 1992. Mem.: Kans. Bus. Edn. Assn., Nat. Bus. Edn. Assn., Adminstrv. Mgmt. Soc., Internat. Assn. Adminstrv. Profls. (dean Inst. for Edn. 2000—), Nat. Assn. Bus. Tchr Edn., N.E. La. U. Alumni Club, Phi Kappa Phi, Phi Delta Kappa, Delta Pi Epsilon, Alpha Lambda Delta. Democrat. Baptist. Avocations: travel, reading, walking. Office: Washburn Univ 1700 SW College Ave Topeka KS 66621-0001

DIFRANZA, VIRGINIA, principal; b. Boston, Apr. 15, 1944; d. John and Vincenza (Long) DiF. BS, Northeastern U., 1966, MEd, 1967, CAGS, 1972; EdD, Boston U., 1979. Cert. supt., prin., guidance counselor, moderate spl. needs tchr., elem. English tchr., Mass. Instr. Coll. of Edn. Northeastern U., Boston, 1966-68; reading specialist Boston Pub. Schs., 1968-73, asst. dir. reading, 1973-78, curriculum coord., 1978-82, asst. headmaster, 1982-91; prin. Perkins Elem. Sch., S. Boston, 1992—. Vis. practitioner Harvard U., Cambridge, Mass., 1991—, adv. bd. Harvard Prins. Ctr., Cambridge, 1992—; bd. dirs. Pentucket Pre-sch., Georgetown, Mass. Author: (newsletter) Harvard Desktop, 1991; editor: (newsletter) Outreach, 1981-82, (jour.) Wisdom in Practice, 1992. Mem. Home and Sch., S. Boston, 1992. Recipient Outstanding Alumnae award Northeastern U., 1989; Edn. Policy fellow George Washington U., 1980-81. Mem. ASCD, Phi Delta Kappa (Harvard chpt.). Avocations: wine tasting, reading mysteries, walking, skiing, political cartooning. Office: Boston Pub Schs 50 Burke St Boston MA 02127-3311

DIGIOVACHINO, JOHN, special education educator; b. Newark, Mar. 20, 1955; s. John and Mary (Trapasso) Di G. BA, William Paterson Coll., l977, MEd, l98l; EdD, Calif. Coast U., 1994. Dir. libr. skills program for mentally handicapped in East Orange (N.J.) Pub. Libr., l978; tchr. handicapped Deron Sch., Livingston, N.J., 1978-80, Dover (N.J.) Pub. Schs., l98l-84, learning disability tchr., cons., 1984-89; dir. child study team Bedminster (N.J.) Pub. Sch., 1989-93; tchr. learning disabilities, cons. Town Dover (N.J.) Bd. Edn.; dir. spl. svcs. Oradell (N.J.) Pub. Sch., 1993-95; v.p., CST coord. Town of Boonton (N.J.) Bd. Edn., 1995-98; prin. Harrison Elem. Sch., Livingston, NJ, 1998—99; dir. curriculum and instrn. Oradell Pub. Sch. Dist., 1999—. Cons. to adv. bd. Bldg. Blocks Learning Child Care Svcs., Randolph, N.J., l985-95. Coord. recreation program for handicapped Friends of East Hanover, N.J., 1977-83; mem. Hanover Park Regional High Sch. Dist. Bd. Edn., East Hanover, 1983-89; mem. East Hanover Twp. Bd. Edn., 1989-95, v.p., 1990-92, pres., 1993-95; chmn. East Hanover Drug Awareness Coun., 1987-96; bd. dirs. Morris County Dept. Human Svcs. CART and CIACC, 1996-97, UNICO, 1998—. Mem. ASCD, N.J. Assn. Pupil Pers. Svcs., N.J. Assn. Learning Cons., Coun. for Exceptional Children, Nat. Assn. of Pupil Svcs. Adminstrs., N.J. Assn. Sch. Adminstrs., N.J. Prins. and Suprs. Assn., North Jersey Spl. Edn. Adminstrs. Assn., K.C., Pi Lambda Theta, Kappa Delta Pi. Home: 26 Goldblatt Ter East Hanover NJ 07936-1416 Office: Oradell Pub Sch 350 Prospect Ave Oradell NJ 07649

DI GIROLAMO, ROSINA ELIZABETH, education educator; b. Monterey, Calif., Aug. 3, 1945; d. Anthony and Frances (Lucido) DiG. AA, Monterey Peninsula Coll., 1965; BA, Calif. State U., Hayward, 1967; MA, Calif. Polytech., San Luis Obispo, 1975. Tchr. Monterey (Calif.) Pub. Unified Sch. Dist., 1968—. Polit. action chairperson Monterey Bay Tchrs. Assn., 1993-94; mem. City's Youth Task Force, 1997. Recipient Outstanding Tchr. award Lori Flagg Found., Monterey, 2002, Outstanding Middle Sch. Tchr. of Yr. Rotary Club, 1998. Mem. Calif. Reading Assn., Calif. Tchrs. of English, Nat. Tchrs. of English, Calif. Leadership Team, Calif. Assn. Student Leaders (advisor). Democrat. Roman Catholic. Avocations: reading, com. work, travel. Home: 77 Via Chualar Monterey CA 93940-2528 Office: Walter Colton Mid Sch 100 Toda Vis Monterey CA 93940-4237

DIGMAN, LESTER ALOYSIUS, management educator; b. Kieler, Wis., Nov. 22, 1938; s. Arthur Louis and Hilda Dorothy (Jansen) D.; m. Ellen Rhomberg Pfohl, Jan. 15, 1966; children: Stephanie, Sarah, Mark. BSME, U. Iowa, 1961, MSIE, 1962, PhD, 1970. Registered profl. engr., Mass. Mgmt. cons. U.S. Ameta, Rock Island, Ill., 1962-67; mgmt. instr. U. Iowa, Iowa City, 1967-69; head applied math. dept. U.S. Ameta, Rock Island, Ill., 1969-74, head managerial tng. dept., 1974-77; assoc. prof. mgt. U. Nebr., Lincoln, 1977-84, dir. grad. studies in mgmt., 1982—, prof. mgmt., 1984-87, Leonard E Whittaker Am. Charter disting. prof. mgmt., 1987-93, Met. Fed. Bank disting. prof. mgmt., 1993-95, First Bank disting. prof. mgmt., 1995-98, U.S. Bank disting. prof. mgmt., 1998—2002, Harold J. Laipply coll. prof., 2002—; dir. Ctr. for Tech. Mgmt. and Decision Scis., 1992-94; interim dir. Gallup Rsch. Ctr., 1994-95; mem. adv. bd. Ctr. for Albanian Studies, 1992—. Cons. various orgns., 1963-72; sec. treas. Mgmt. Svcs. Assocs. Ltd., Davenport, Iowa, 1972-77; owner L.A. Digman and Assocs., Lincoln, 1977—; gen. ptnr. Letna Properties, Madison, Wis., 1978—. Author: Strategic Management: Concepts, Decisions, Cases, 1986, 2d edit., 1990, Strategic Management: Cases, 1995, Strategic Mangement: Concepts, Processes, Decisions, 1995, Network Analysis for Management Decisions, 1982, Strategic Management: Cases for the Global Information Age, 2002; contbr. articles to profl. jours. Recipient Dist. award SBA, 1980, Certs. of Appreciation Dept. of Def., 1972. Fellow Decision Scis. Inst. (charter, program chmn. 1986, pres. 1987-88, coord. doctoral consortium 1989, strategy/policy track chmn. 1991, v.p. 1992-94, strategic mgmt. track chmn. internat. meeting 1993, chair long-range planning com. 1995-96, adv. com. for internat. meeting 1997, chair fellows com., 1999-2000), Pan Pacific Bus. Assn. (bd. adv. 1999—); mem. IEEE, Strategic Mgmt. Soc. (founding), Acad. of Mgmt., Strategic Leadership Forum, Inst. for Ops. Rsch. and Mgmt. Scis. (founding), MBA Roundtable (charter, steering com.), Nebr. Club, Firethorn Country Club, Confrerie de la Chaine Rotisseurs. Roman Catholic. Avocations: gardening, photography, wine tasting. Home: 7520 Lincolnshire Rd Lincoln NE 68506-1635 Office: U Nebr 277 CBA Lincoln NE 68588

DILCHER, DAVID LEONARD, paleobotany educator, research scholar; b. Cedar Falls, Iowa, July 10, 1936; m. Katherine Swanson, 1961; children: Peter, Ann BS in Natural History, U. Minn., 1958, MS in Botany, Geology and Zoology, 1960; postgrad., U. Ill., 1960-62; PhD in Biology, Geology, Yale U., 1964; participant OTS course field dendrology, Costa Rica, 1968. Teaching asst. U. Minn., Mpls., 1958-60, U. Ill., Urbana, 1960-62, Yale U., New Haven, Conn., 1962-63, Cullman-Univ. fellow, 1963-64, instr. biology, 1965-66; NSF postdoctoral fellow Senckenberg Mus., Frankfurt am Main, Fed. Republic of Germany, 1964-65; asst. prof. botany Ind. U., Bloomington, 1966-70, assoc. prof., 1970-76; Guggenheim fellow Imperial Coll., Univ. London, 1972-73; assoc. prof. geology Ind. U., Bloomington, 1975-77, prof. paleobotany, 1977-90, adj. prof. biology, adj. prof. geology, 1990—; grad. rsch. prof. Fla. Mus. Natural History, U. Fla., Gainesville, 1990—. Panel mem. for systematic biology program, NSF, 1977-79, panel mem. for selecting NATO postdoctoral fellow, 1982, mem. adv. com. Earth Sys. History, 1997-2000, bd. mem. on earth scis. and resources NRC, 2001—, minerals, 2001—; vis. lectr. to People's Republic of China Nat. Acad. Sci. com. on scholarly communications with China, 1986; corr. mem. Senckenberg Mus., Frankfurt, Fed. Republic Germany, 1989; hon. prof. Nanjing Inst. Geology and Paleontology, Acad. Sinica, China, 1998—, Jilin U., Changchau, China, 2001—; adj. prof. biology U. Tenn., Martin, 2000—; hon. prof., vice chmn. sci. com. rsch. ctr. paleontoloty and stratigraphy Jilin U., Changchun, China, 2001--; bd. dirs. Smithsonian Inst. Author: (with D. Redmon, M. Tansey and D. Whitehead) Plant Biology Laboratory Manual, 1973, 2d edit., 1975; editor: (with Tom Taylor and Theodore Delevoryas) Plant Reproduction in the Fossil Record, symposium vol., 1979; (with T. Taylor) Biostratigraphy of Fossil Plants: Successional and Paleoecological Analysis, 1980; (with William L. Crepet) Origin and Evolution of Flowering Plants, Symposium Volume, 1984; (with Michael S. Zavada) Phylogeny of the Hamamedidae, symposium vol., 1986; (with Patrick S. Herendeen) Advances in Legume Systematics Part 4, The Fossil Record, 1992; contbr. articles to profl. jours. Mem. utilities bd. City of Bloomington, 1974-76; ruling elder First Presbyn. Ch. Bloomington, 1975-77; bd. dirs. United Campus Ministries, 1971-72, Smithsonian Mus. Natural History, 1998—; mem. coun. Monroe County United Ministries, 1975-77. Dist. Vis. Rsch. scholar U. Adelaide, Australia, 1981, 88; Vis. Rsch. scholar Birbal Sahni Palaeonbot. Inst., Lucknow, India, 1992; grantee Sigma Xi, 1961-62, 66, Ind. U., 1967-68, Orgn. Tropical Studies, 1971, Travel grantee Ind. U., 1968, 71, 77, 80, Rsch. grantee NSF, 1966-89, 96—, Amax Coal Found., 1980-81, NATO Coop, 1991-93; Eaton-Hooker fellow, 1963, Cullman-Univ. fellow, 1963-64, Guggenheim fellow, Giessen, Fed. Republic of Germany, 1972-73, Ind. U., 1972-73, Brit. Mus. Natural History, London, 1988-89; recipient Tracey M. Sonneborn award for disting. rsch. and excellenc in tchg. Ind. U., 1978-88, Bot. Soc. Am. Merit award, 1991, Birbal Sahni Found. award, 1998. Fellow Ind. Acad. Sci.; mem. NAS, AAAS, Bot. Soc. Am. (chmn. paleobot. sect. 1974, sec.-treas. 1975-77, rep. to jour. editl. bd. 1978-79, jour. editl. bd. 1981-82, conservation com. 1978-81, chmn. conservation com. 1981, 82, program dir. 1982-84, exec. bd. 1982-91, sec. 1984-88, pres.-elect 1988-89, pres. 1989-90), Paleontol. Soc., Paleontol. Assn., Internat. Orgn. Paleobotany (N.Am. rep. 1975-81, v.p. 1987-93), Assn. Tropical Biology, Am. Inst. Biol. Scis., Am. Assn. Stratigraphic Palynologists, Internat. Assn. Angiosperm Paleobotany (pres. 1977-80), Geol. Soc. Am. (com. on collection and collecting 1978-85), Ky. Acad. Scis., Senckenberg Natur Mus. und Forschungsgeshellshaft Frankfurt am Main (corr. mem. 1990), Sigma Xi (pres.-elect Ind. chpt. 1985-86, pres. 1986-87). Office: U Fla Dept Natural Sci Fla Mus Natural History PO Box 117800 Gainesville FL 32611-7800 E-mail: dilcher@flmnh.ufl.edu.

DILDY, GARY ANDREW, III, maternal fetal medicine physician, educator; b. New Orleans, May 7, 1959; s. Gary Andrew Jr. and Barbara Mae (Barbier) D. BS, La. State U., 1981; MD, Tulane U., 1985. Diplomate Am. Bd. Ob-gyn, Am. Bd. Maternal-Fetal Medicine. Intern in ob/gyn Baylor Coll. Medicine, Houston, 1985-86, resident in ob/gyn, 1986-89, fellow, 1989-91; dir. Perinatal Ctr., Utah Valley Regional Med. Ctr., Provo, 1991-2000; asst. prof. U. Utah, 1991-97, assoc. prof., 1997-2000; prof. La. State U. Sch. Medicine, New Orleans, 2000—. Contbr. chapters to books Contbr. chpts. to books, articles contbr. articles to profl. jours.; editor: (jours.) editor Obstetrical Emergencies in Contemporary Ob-Gyn., 1993—95; editor-in-chief: textbook Critical Care Obstetrics, 4th edit. Mem. AMA, Soc. for Maternal-Fetal Medicine, Am. Coll. Ob-Gyn., Soc. Gynecologic Investigation. Achievements include orignal work in intrapartum fetal oxygen saturation monitoring. Office: La State U Sch Medicine 1542 Tulane Ave New Orleans LA 70112 E-mail: gdildy3@lsuhsc.edu.

DILL, BONNIE THORNTON, sociology educator; BA in English, U. Rochester, 1965; MA in Human Relations/Edn., PhD in Sociology, NYU, 1979. Trainer and course asst. Ctr. for Human Rels. NYU, 1969-71; adj. lectr. Black and Hispanic Studies Program Bernard M. Baruch Coll., 1972-73; tchg. asst. Sociology Dept. NYU, 1974-75, adj. instr. Sociology Dept., 1976-77; counselor/lectr. Dept. Compensatory Programs Bernard M. Baruch Coll., CUNY, 1970-77; dir. and founder Ctr. for Rsch. on Women Memphis State U., 1982-88, prof. sociology Dept. Sociology and Social Work, 1978-91; prof. dept. women's studies, affiliate prof. sociology U. Md., 1991—, dir. Consortium on Race, Gender & Ethnicity. Mem. adv. bd. on rsch., scholarship and edn. Ms. Mag., 1985-91; mem. editl. bd. Signs: Jour. of Women and Culture in Soc., 1979-89, mem. selection adv. com. U. Chgo. Press; cons. numerous orgns.; presenter and lectr. in field. Co-editor: Women of Color in U.S. Society, 1994, Across the Boundaries of Race and Class: An Exploration of Work and Family Among Black Female Domestic Servants, 1994; contbr. numerous articles to jours. in field. Recipient numerous grants and fellowships including The Ford Found., 1988-89, 1989-91, 1992-94, 1999-2003, Jessie Bernard Disting. Contributions to Teaching, Am. Soc. Assn., Robin Williams Jr. Lectr. Women & Achievement. Mem. Am. Sociol. Assn. (com. on status of women in sociology, com. on noms. 1984-85, task force on minority fellow program 1986-87, Jessie Bernard award com. 1986-89, chair com. on coms. 1995, numerous others), Assn. Black Sociologists (bd. dirs. 1977-79), Nat. Coun. Rsch. on Women (bd. dirs. 1983-86), Nat. Women's Studies Assn., Soc. for the Study of Social Problems (editl. and publs. com. 1986-89, Lee-Founder's award com. 1985, 87, C. Wright Mills award com. 1980-81). Office: U of Md Womens Studies Program 2101 Woods Hall College Park MD 20742-0001

DILL, ELLIS HAROLD, university dean; b. Pittsburg County, Okla., Dec. 31, 1932; s. Harold and Mayme Doris (Ellis) D.; m. Cleone June Granrud, Sept. 12, 1953; children: Michael Harold, Susan Marie. AA, Grant Tech. Jr. Coll., 1951; BS in Civil Engring, U. Calif. at Berkeley, 1954, MS in Civil Engring, 1955, PhD, 1957. Asst. prof. to prof. aeros. and astronautics U. Wash., 1956-77, chmn. dept. aeros. and astronautics, 1976-77; dean engring. Rutgers U., New Brunswick, N.J., 1977-98, univ. prof., 1998—. Mem. Soc. Natural Philosophy. Achievements include research, numerous publications on mechanics of solids. Home: 436 Brentwood Dr Piscataway NJ 08854-3608 Office: Rutgers U Coll Engring 98 Brett Rd Piscataway NJ 08854-8058

DILL, KENNETH AUSTIN, pharmaceutical chemistry educator; b. Oklahoma City, Dec. 11, 1947; s. Austin Glenn and Margaret (Blocker) D. SB, SM, MIT, 1971; PhD, U. Calif., San Diego, 1978. Fellow Damon Runyon-Walter Winchell Stanford (Calif.) U., 1978-81; asst. prof. chemistry U. Fla., Gainesville, 1981-82; asst. prof. pharm. chemistry and pharmacy U. Calif., San Francisco, 1982-85, assoc. prof., 1985-89, prof., 1989—, co-dir. program in quantitative biology, assoc. dean rsch. Sch. Pharmacy, 2001—. Adj. prof. pharmaceutics U. Utah, 1989—. Contbr. numerous sci. articles to profl. publs.; patentee in field. Recipient Hans Neurath award Protein Soc., 1998; PEW Found. scholar. Fellow AAAS, Am. Phys. Soc. (physics policy coun. 2002—), Biophys. Soc. (nat lectr. 1996, pres. 1998); mem. Am. Chem. Soc., Protein Soc. Office: Univ Calif Pharm Chemistry Dept San Francisco CA 94143-0001

DILLARD, DEAN INNES, English language educator, academic administrator; b. Melvern, Kans., Aug. 13, 1947; s. Alva Everett and Dorothy Marie (Whitney) D. BS in Edn., Emporia (Kans.) State U., 1969, MA, 1975, postgrad., 1977, Ft. Hays State U., Hays, Kans., 1980. Tchr. English, Unified Sch. Dist. 379, Clay Center, Kans., 1969-70; tchr. English and social studies Unified Sch. Dist. 208, WaKeeney, Kans., 1972-84; instr. English, Neosho County C.C., Chanute, Kans., 1984—, chair divsn. liberal arts, 1996-99, interim v.p. acad. and student affairs, 1997-98, 99-00. Fine arts task force Neosho County C.C., Chanute, 1990-91. With U.S. Army, 1970-71. Mem.: MLA, VFW (life), Neosho County C.C. Educators Assn., Kans. Assn. Tchrs. English (exec. bd. 1981—84), Midwest Modern Lang. Assn., The Assn. Lit. Scholars and Critics (life), Nat. Coun. Tchrs. English, Kans. Assn. Scholars, Nat. Assn. Scholars, Assembly on Lit. for Adolescents (life), C.C. Humanities Assn., Am. Legion, Chanute Lions Club (zone chmn. 1988—90), Kappa Delta Pi. Republican. Home: 732 S Washington Ave Chanute KS 66720-2713 Office: Neosho County C C 800 W 14th St Chanute KS 66720-2639

DILLARD, LISA REICHERT, assistant superintendent; b. Ironton, Mo., Sept. 27, 1954; d. John Monroe and Darlene Elizabeth (Stirts) Reichert; m. David Warren Dillard, May 22, 1976. AA, Mineral Area Coll., 1975; BS in Elem. Edn., Southeast Mo. State U., 1977, MAT in Art, 1987, EdS, 1992. Cert. (life) elem. edn. tchr., art tchr., elem. prin. 6th grade tchr. South Iron RI, Annapolis, Mo., 1980-81; 2d grade tchr. Arcadia Valley R-2 Schs., Ironton, 1981-86, elem. art tchr., 1986-89, elem. prin., 1989-92, asst. supr., 1992-96, dir. spl. svcs. Mem. Mo. State Tchrs. Assn., Mineral Area Lase Assn., Phi Delta Kappa. Democrat. Roman Catholic. Avocations: drawing, sculpting, walking. Office: Arcadia Valley R-2Sch Dist 750 Park Dr Ironton MO 63650-1480

DILLARD, TERESA MARY, school counselor; b. Columbus, Ga., May 12, 1956; d. Francis Joseph and Sadayo (Takabayashi) Luther; m. David Howard Dillard, July 22, 1978; children: Christine Marie, Justin David. BA, U. Md., 1977, MEd, 1981. Cert. guidance counselor, social studies tchr., modern fgn. lang. tchr., Mass., N.C. Asst. to supr. Bur. Govtl. Rsch., U. Md., College Park, 1977-78; tchr. high sch. Montgomery County Pub. Schs., Rockville, Md., 1978-80; substitute tchr. Anne Arundel Pub. Schs., Annapolis, Md., 1981, Bourne County Pub. Schs., Cape Cod, Mass., 1982-84; guidance counselor Camden County Pub. Schs., Camden, N.C., 1989-95. Counselor, advisor U. Md. Relief Ctr., College Park, 1977, tutor Japanese lang., 1977, vol. substitute instr. Japanese lang. dept., 1977; cons. UCNC Radio Talk Show, Elizabeth City, N.C., 1991; program developer Grandy Primary Sch., Camden, N.C., 1989-95. Designer, creator children's clothing. Religious edn. tchr. Ft. Meade (Md.) Chapel Ctr., 1978, St. Bernadette Ch., Severn, Md., 1979-80; religious edn. tchr. Otis Chapel, Otis Air Nat. Guard Base, Mass., 1982-83, coord., dir. religious edn. program, 1983-84; bd. dirs., tchr. Holy Family Religious Edn. Program, Elizabeth City, N.C., 1989-91; asst. music ministry Holy Family Ch., Elizabeth City, 1991-95. Mem. ACA, Am. Sch. Counselors Assn., U. Md. Alumni Assn., Phi Beta Kappa, Phi Kappa Phi, Alpha Kappa Delta. Roman Catholic. Avocations: sewing, needlework, writing, woodburning, tae kwon do martial arts.

DILLE, ROLAND PAUL, college president; b. Dassel, Minn., Sept. 16, 1924; s. Oliver Valentine and Eleanor (Johnson) D.; m. Beth Hopeman, Sept. 4, 1948; children— Deborah, Martha, Sarah, Benjamin. BA summa cum laude, U. Minn., 1949, PhD, 1962, LHD (hon.), 1995. Instr. English U. Minn., 1953-56; asst. prof. St. Olaf Coll., Northfield, Minn., 1956-61; asst. prof. English Calif. Lutheran Coll., Thousand Oaks, Calif., 1961-63; mem. faculty Moorhead (Minn.) State U., 1964-94, pres., 1968-94; ret., 1994. Author: Four Romantic Poets, 1969; contbr. numerous articles and revs. to profl. jours. Treas. Am. Assn. State Colls. and Univs., 1977-78, bd. dirs., 1978-80, chmn., 1980-81; mem. Nat. Coun. for Humanities, 1980-86; vice-chair Commn. on Higher Edn., North Cen. Assn., 1989-91, chair, 1991-93. With inf. AUS, 1944-46. Disting. Svc. to Humanities award given by Minn. Humanities Commn. named in his honor; named one of 100 most effective Am. coll. pres., 1987. Mem. Phi Beta Kappa. Home: 516 9th St S Moorhead MN 56560-3519 Office: Minn State U Moorhead 11th St S Moorhead MN 56560-9980

DILLEN, WILLIAM C., JR., secondary school educator; b. Freeport, Pa., Mar. 7, 1950; s. William C. and Ann M. (Maradei) D.; m. Sandra K. Swartzlander, Jan. 17, 1972; children: Erik, Brooke, Cari Jo. AS in Applied Sci., Butler (Pa.) Community Coll., 1973; BS in Biology Edn., Slippery Rock (Pa.) U., 1975; postgrad., Pa. State U., 1976-78. Cert. radiology technologist, Pa. Radiol. technologist Alleghney Valley Hosp., Natrona Heights, Pa., 1970-78; tchr. biology, athletic trainer, coach Freeport Area Schs., 1977—. Mem. NEA, Nat. Biology Tchrs. Assn., Pa. Tchrs. Assn., Western Pa. Biology Tchrs. Avocations: fishing, hunting, golf. Home: 2717 Harbison St Natrona Heights PA 15065-1728 Office: Freeport Sr High Sch PO Drawer H Freeport PA 16229 E-mail: dillen@freeport.k12.pa.us.

DILLIN, JAKE THOMAS, JR., healthcare facility executive; b. Jonesboro, Ark., Aug. 19, 1945; s. Jake Thomas and Beatrice B. (Ervin) D.; m. Dec. 26, 1965 (div. Feb. 20, 1992); 1 child, Traci. BS in Chemistry and Biology, Fla. So. Coll.; MBA, Cen. Mich. U., 1982. Cert. Health Care Risk Mgr., Fla. Dir. dept. planned. tng. Busi U. of Tampa, 1968-73; toxicologist, lab. mgr., v.p., bd. dirs. Drs. Lab. Svcs., Inc., Tampa, Fla., 1972-74; pres. Cen. Fla. Biols., Inc., Tampa and Orlando, Fla., 1974-76; dir. lab., pharmacies and mgmt. engring. Orlando Regional Med. Ctr., Inc., 1976-82; sr. v.p., chmn. governing bd. AMI Single Day Surgery, Ameri Med., Internat., 1982-86; pres., chmn. bd. dirs. Ambulatory Health Care Cons., Inc., 1986—; COO The Ophthalmic Group, 1990-95; exec. dir. Eye Surgery Facility Inc., 1993-95, Photorefractive Laser Eye Ctr. West Fla., 1996-97, Kurwa Eye Laser Ctr., Arcadia, Calif., 1997-99; corp. compliance, accreditation officer Cmty. Hosp., Grand Junction, Colo., 1999—2002; chief oper. officer U. Southern Calif., Doheny Refractice Laser Med. Ctr., Los Angeles; ret., 2003. Credentialled cons. field surveyor Joint Commn. Accreditation Healthcare Orgns.; owner Tom Dillin Photography, 1969-72, Spartan Security Sys., Inc., 1989-92; adj. clin. faculty U. Ctrl. Fla. One-man photographic shows at Tampa Photo, Holiday Hosp., Tampa and Orlando. Mem. Orlando Choral Soc. Messiah Chorus, 1977-90, Bach Music Festival, Rollins Coll., U. South Fla. Men's Chorus, 1995-96; pres., bd. dirs., coach gymnastics team Lakemont YMCA, 1975-76; bd. dirs. Riverside Hts. Civic Assn., San Gabriel Valley Choral Co., 1997-99; bd. dirs. fundraising Arcadia Reps. Inc., 1998-99; fundraiser Calif. Philharm. Orch., 1998-99; overseer Sierra Club Angeles Cha Harwood Lodge, 1998-99; bd. dirs. Schumann Singers, Colo., 1999. Mem. Med. Electronics and Data Soc., Soc. Biomed. Equipment Technicians, Hosp. Mgmt. Sys. Soc., Nat. Health Lawyers Assn., Am. Assn. Clin. Chemists (Recognition award 1978), Am. Soc. Law and Medicine, Am. Soc. Quality Control, Internat. Soc. Blood Transfusion (Paris), Clin. Lab. Mgmt. Assn., Assn. Drug Detection Labs., Soc. Human Resource Mgmt., Am. Soc. Ophthalmic Adminstrs., Fla. Soc. Ophthalmic Adminstrs. (founding mem.), Masons (32 deg.), Scottish Rite, Jaguar Club Fla. (founder). Office: Cmty Hosp Adminstrn Grand Junction CO 81501

DILLINGHAM, WILLIAM BYRON, literature educator, author; b. Atlanta, Mar. 7, 1930; s. Cornelius Howard and Emerald (Storey) D.; m. Marion Elizabeth Joiner, July 3, 1952; children: Rebecca Lynn, Judith Ann, Paul Christopher. BA, Emory U., 1955, MA, 1956; PhD, U. Pa., 1961. Instr. Emory U., Atlanta, 1956-62, asst. prof., 1962-66, assoc. prof., 1966-68, prof., 1968-84, chair. dept. English, 1979-82, 85-86, 90-91, Charles Howard Candler prof. Am. lit., 1984-96; prof. emeritus, 1996—. Author: Frank Norris: Instinct and Art, 1969, An Artist in the Rigging, 1972, Melville's Short Fiction, 1977, Melville's Later Novels, 1986, Melville and His Circle: The Last Years, 1996; co-author: Humor of the Old Southwest, 1964, 2d edit., 1975, 3d edit., 1994, Practical English Handbook, 10th edit., 1996;

mem. editl. bd. Nineteenth-Century Lit., 1990-97, South Atlantic Rev., 1986-89, Frank Norris Studies, 1986-94. Served with U.S. Army, 1950-52. Recipient Fulbright award U.S. Govt., 1964-65; Sr. fellow NEH, 1978-79, Guggenheim Found., 1982-83; Heilbrun Disting. Emeritus fellow, 2002-03. Mem. MLA (mem. adv. coun. Am. lit. sect. 1988-90), Nat. Assn. Scholars, Soc. Lit. Scholars and Critics, Frank Norris Soc., Melville Soc. (pres. 1987), Kipling Soc., Phi Beta Kappa, Omicron Delta Kappa. Home: 1416 Vista Leaf Dr Decatur GA 30033-2012 also: 3258 Esperanza Ave Daytona Beach FL 32118-6231

DILLMAN, KRISTIN WICKER, elementary and middle school educator, musician; b. Ft. Dodge, Iowa, Nov. 7, 1953; d. Winford Lee and Helen Caroline (Brown) Egli; m. Kirk Michael Wicker, Jan. 1, 1982 (dec. June 1982); m. David D. Dillman, Apr. 13, 1990; adopted children: Alek Joseph, Andrew Mikhail. AA, Iowa Cen. Coll., 1974; B in Music Edn., Morningside Coll., 1976; M in Mus., U. S.D., 1983. Cert. tchr., Iowa. Tchr. instrumental music Garrigan Affiliated Schs., Algona, Iowa, 1976-77, Sioux City (Iowa) Community Schs., 1977—. Sr. beauty cons. Mary Kay Cosmetics. Asst. prin. bassist Sioux City Symphony, 1974-93, 95—, prin. bassist, 1993-95; freelance bassist Sioux City, 1976—; pianist and accompanist, St. Mark Luth. ch., Sioux City. Named Tchr. of Yr. Sioux City Community Schs., 1988-89. Mem. NEA, Iowa Edn. Assn., Sioux city Edn. Assn., Iowa Bandmasters Assn., Sioux City Musicians Assn., Zeta Sigma, Mu Phi Epsilon. Republican. Lutheran. Avocations: golf, walking, gardening, skiing. Office: Bryant Elem Sch 821 30th St Sioux City IA 51104 E-mail: DunesDave@aol.com.

DILLMAN, MARIE, elementary education educator, music educator; b. Forest, Ohio, July 16, 1939; d. Ralph and Ruth Bear; m. Charles N. Dillman; children: Angie, James. BS, Bluffton Coll., 1967; postgrad., Eastern Mich. U., 1978. Master gardener 2003. Tchr. elem., Galion, Ohio, 1960, Lexington, Ohio, 1960-61, Mt. Gilead, Ohio, 1961-62, Spring Arbor, Mich., 1975—. Tchr. piano, Greenville, Ill., 1970-74, tchr. piano, handbell choir, Spring Arbor; Master Gardener. Supporter Jackson (Mich.) Symphony Orch.; mem. local Rep. party. Recipient award to study Orff instruments Western Mich. U., 1991. Mich. Music Edn. Assn. Republican. Methodist. Avocations: piano, gardening, growing roses, reading. Home: 153 Burr Oak Spring Arbor MI 49283-9728

DILLON, CAROL JEAN, librarian, educator; b. Franklinton, La., Mar. 9, 1954; d. James E. and Carlee (Warren) D. BA in Libr. Sci./Elem. Edn., Southeastern La. U., Hammond, 1976; MS in Instrnl. Leadership, Nat. U., Oakland, Calif., 1990. Tchr. Tandipahoa Parish (La.) Schs., 1977, Washington Parish Schs., Franklinton, 1977-78; tchr., libr. St. Tammany Parish Schs., Bush, La., 1978-80; revenue receipts coder Am. Pres. Co., Oakland, 1981-85; tchr. Shelton Primary Edn. Ctr., Oakland, 1985-86; adolescent counselor Fred Finch Youth Ctr., Oakland, 1986-87; childcare counselor St. Augustine Cath. Sch., Oakland, 1987-88; libr. technician Nat. U., Oakland, 1988-89, Richmond (Calif.) Unified Schs., 1990, Washington Parish Schs., Franklinton, 1990—. Vol. Jesse Jackson Campaign, East Oakland Girls Assn., Teen Pregnancy. Mem. Internat. Reading Assn., Am. Bus. Womens Assn. (San Leandro charter chpt.), Washington Parish Reading Coun. (Libr. of Yr. 1994), La. Fedn. Tchrs. Democrat. Baptist. Avocations: walking, travel, reading, collecting art, playing piano. Home: 43356 Artis Tate Rd Franklinton LA 70438-5266

DILLON, DORIS (DORIS DILLON KENOFER), artist, art historian; b. Kansas City, Mo., Dec. 1, 1929; d. Joseph Patrick and Geraldine Elizabeth (Galligan) D.; m. Calvin Louis Kenofer, Aug. 25, 1950; children: Wendy Annette Kenofer Barnes, Bruce Patrick Kenofer. BA in Art, U. Denver, 1950, MA in Art History, 1965. Stewardess United Air Lines, 1950-51; founder, chmn. fine arts dept. Regis Coll., Denver, 1970-74; cons. Sarkisian's Oriental Imports, Denver, 1975-93; mus. curator Van Vechten-Lineberry Taos Art, Taos, N.Mex., 1995. Coord. Inter-Relationship Between the Fine Arts and Science Seminars, 1970-74, Colo. Coun. on Arts & Humanities, Denver, 1980, adv. panel, 1981; consular rep. United Cultural Conv; dep dir. gen. Internat. Biog. Ctr., Eng., 1997; rsch. bd. advisors Am. Biog. Inst., 1997; lectr. in field. One-woman shows include El Pueblo Art Gallery/Mus., Pueblo, Colo., 1970, Heard Mus., Dallas, 1984, Nelson Rockefeller Collection, N.Y.C., 1984, Amparo Gallery, Denver, 1985, Veerhoff Gallery, Washington, 1986, Colo. Gallery the Arts Mus., Littleton, 1987, Highland Gallery, Atlanta, 1988, The Earth Sci. Mus., Asheville, N.C., 2003, exhibited in group shows at U. Denver, 1970, Denver Art Mus., 1970, Denver Mus. Natural History, 1976, U. Colo., 1986, Denver C. of C., 1987, Cadme Gallery, Phila., 1987, Internat. Platform Assn., Washington, 1998—2001, Nat. League Pen Arts Women, 1999, Lisbon, Portugal, 1999, 26th Congress on Arts and Humanities, Lisbon, Internat. Exhbn. Gallery, 2000, exhibitions include St. Johns Coll., Cambridge, Eng., 2001, Vancouver, Can., 2002, two-person shows, E Margo Gallery, Manhattan N.Y., 2003. Recipient 1st place drawing award, 4 States Conf. Ctr., Colo., 1960, Salute to Women award, AAUW, 1997, Key award, Excellence Arts, Rsch., Tchg., 1997, Best of Show award, Internat. Platform Assn., Washington, 2001, 2002. Mem.: Denver Art Mus., Asian Art assn. (bd. dirs. 1982—84, treas. 1985), Fine Arts Guild (v.p. 1982), Soc. for Arts, Religion and Contemporary Culture, Nat. Mus. for Women in the Arts (assoc.), Mensa (scholarship juror 1993—94). Avocations: piano, travel, bridge, swimming, hiking. Home and Office: 135 Delphia Dr Brevard NC 28712

DILLON, FREDERICK L. secondary education mathematics educator; b. Wadsworth, Ohio, Apr. 2, 1955; s. Frederick O. and Ida Dott D. BS summa cum laude, Kent State U., 1977; MA in Math., Ohio State U., 1985. Cert. math. and English tchr., Ohio; nat. cert. Adolescent Young Adult Math. 7th-9th grade math. tchr. Elyria (Ohio) City Schs., 1977-79, Strongsville (Ohio) City Schs., 1979-84, 10th-12th grade math. tchr., 1985—; grad. asst. in math. Ohio State U., Columbus, 1984-85. Part-time instr. Cleve. State U., 1986, Cuyahoga C.C., Cleve., 1986-87. Chair Ohio Dept. Edn. Glossary for Ohio Model Curriculum, 1994. Mem. Greater Cleve. Coun. Tchrs. Math. (dir. south dist. 1992-95, pres. 1995-97, editor newsletter 1992-2000, v.p. 2000-03), Nat. Coun. Tchrs. Math. (regional conv. program chair 2001, profl. svs. devel. com. 2003-, nat. conv. program com. 2003-), Ohio Coun. Tchrs. Math. (N.E. dist. dir. 1996-98, 2003-, mem. task force, 1995 conv. co-chair, v.p. 1999-2002, award 1993, state award 1997), Ohio Math. Edn. Leadership Coun., Strongsville Edn. Assn. (pres. 1989-90), Nat. Coun. Suprs. Math. Mem. United Ch. of Christ. Home: 15690 Balmoral Ct Strongsville OH 44136-2594 Office: Strongsville HS 22025 Lunn Rd Strongsville OH 44149-4821 E-mail: dillon@strongnet.org.

DILLON, KAREN LEE, secondary school educator; b. Sewickley, Pa., Feb. 5, 1941; d. Norman Wilton and Ruth Elizabeth (Cocanour) Morris; m. Roy Joseph Dillon, Aug. 20, 1966. BS in Edn., Indiana U. of Pa., 1963; MA, Ea. Mich. U., 1990. Tchr. math. Slocum Truax Jr. H.S., Trenton, Mich., 1963-71, Monguagon Middle Sch., Trenton, 1971-81; tchr. math./computer sci. Trenton H.S., 1981—. Mem. dist. sch. improvement team Trenton Pub. Schs., 1990-94, team leader for Trenton H.S., 1990-94; mem. Romulus (Mich.) Environ. Task Force, 1981-94. Named Trenton Tchr. of Yr., 1992-93, Outstanding Educator of Yr., Trenton Jaycees, 1993; recipient Golden Apple Teaching award Wayne County Regional Edn. Svc. Agy., 1993; mini grantee, 1991-93. Mem. Trenton Edn. Assn. (assn. rep.), Delta Kappa Gamma (1st v.p., pres., Woman of Distinction 1993). Methodist. Avocations: fishing, sewing, gardening, reading, travel. Home: 4700 Boutell Ranch Rd West Branch MI 48661-8911 Office: Trenton HS 2601 Charlton Rd Trenton MI 48183-2446

DILLON, MICHAEL EARL, engineering executive, mechanical engineer, educator; b. Lynwood, Calif., Mar. 4, 1946; children: Bryan Douglas, Nicole Marie, Brendon McMichael. BA in Math., Calif. State U., Long Beach, 1978, postgrad. Registered profl. engr., Ala., Alaska, Ariz., Ark., Calif., Colo., Conn., EIT Del., registered Fla., Ga., EIT Hawaii, Idaho, Ill., Ind., registered Iowa, Ky., Md., Mass., Mich., Minn., Mo., Mont., Nebr., Nebr., Nev., NJ, N.Mex., NY, NC, Ohio, Okla., Oreg., Pa., Tenn., Tex., Utah, Va., Wash., Wis., Wyo., chartered engr., U.K. Journeyman plumber Roy E. Dillon & Sons, Long Beach, 1967-69, ptnr., 1969-73; field supr. Dennis Mech., San Marino, 1973-74; chief mech. official City of Long Beach, 1974-79; mgr. engr. Southland Industries, Long Beach, 1979-83; v.p. Syska & Hennessy, L.A. and N.Y., 1983-87; prin. Robert M. Young & Assoc., Pasadena, Calif., 1987-89; pres. Dillon Cons. Engrs., Long Beach, 1989—. Mech. cons. in field; instr. in field; lectr. in field. Contbr. over 160 poems to various publs., contbr. articles to profl. jours. Former chair Mechanical, Plumbing. Elec. and Energy CodeAdv. Commn. of Calif. Bldg. Stds. Commn.; former vice chmn. bd. examiners Appeals and Condemnations, Long Beach; mem. adv. bd. City of LA; mem. bus. adv. bd. City of Long Beach. Recipient Environ. Ozone Protection award U.S. EPA, 1993, John Fies award Internat. Conf. Bldg. Ofcls., 1995. Fellow Chartered Inst. Bldg. Svc. Engrs. Gt. Britain and Ireland, Inst. Refrigeration, Heating, Air Conditioning Engrs. of New Zealand, Inst. Advancement Engring.; mem. ASCE, ASME, Internat. Soc. Fire Safety Sci., Nat. Inst. for Engring. Ethics, Nat. Fire Protection Assn., Internat. Assn. Bldg. Ofcls., Internat. Fire Code Inst., So. Bldg. Code Congress Internat., Bldg. Ofcls. and Code Adminstrn. Internat., Soc. Fire Protection Engrs., Tau Beta Pi, Pi Tau Sigma, Chi Epsilon, others. Avocation: poetry. Home: 669 Quincy Ave Long Beach CA 90814-1818 Office: Dillon Cons Engrs 671 Quincy Ave Long Beach CA 90814-1818 E-mail: medillon@dillon-consulting.com.

DILLY, MARIAN JEANETTE, humanities educator; b. Vining, Minn., Nov. 7, 1921; d. John Fredolph and Mabel Josephine (Haagenson) Linder; m. Robert Lee Dily, June 22, 1946 (dec. Oct. 1987); children: Ronald Lee, Patricia Jeanette Dilly Vero. Studetn, U. Minn., 1944-45; grad., John R. Powers Finishing Sch., N.Y.C., 1957, Zell McC. Fashion Career Sch., Mpls., 1957, Estelle Compton Models Inst., 1966, Nancy Taylor Charm Sch., N.Y.C., 1967, Patricia Stevens Career Sch., Mpls., 1968; BS in English cum laude, Black Hills State U., Spearfish, S.D., 1975. Instr. Nat. Am. U., Rapid City, S.D., 1966-68; instr., dir. Nancy Taylor Charm Sch., 1966-68; hostess TV shows, 1966-74. Lectr. in personality devel., dir., prodr. beauty and talent pageants, freelance coord. in fashion shows, judge beauty and talent pageants of local, state and nat. levels, 1966—. Actress bit parts Nauman Films Inc., 1970. Active ARC; dir., 1st v.p. Black Hills Girl Scout Coun., 1967-72; chmn. bd. dirs., pres. Luth. Social Svc. Aux., Western S.D. and Eastern Wyo., 1960-65; chmn. women's events Dakota Days and Nat. Premiere, 1968; bd. dirs. YMCA, 1976-81; mem. Dallas Symphony Orch. League, 1987-90, Dallas Mus. of Art League, 1987-90, Women's Club. Dallas County, Tex., Inc., 1987-90. Recipient award Rapid City C. of C., 1968, Fashion awards March of Dimes, 1967-72, Svc. award Black Hills Girl Scout Coun., award of appreciation Yellowstone Internat. Toastmistress Club. Mem. AAUW (sec., mem. exec.b d. 1988-90), Nu Tau Sigma (past advisor), Delta Tau Kappa, Singing Tribe of Wahoo. Avocations: golf, bridge, music, skiing. Address: 1607 Woodward St Erie CO 80516-7529

DILWORTH, ROBERT LEXOW, career military officer, educator; b. Chgo., Aug. 19, 1936; s. Robert Oliver and Linda Agnes (Lexow) D.; m. Doris Elthea Smith, Sept. 1, 1981; children by previous marriage: Alexa, Robert. BS in Advt., U. Fla., 1959; MS in Mil. Sci., U.S. Army Command and Gen. Staff Coll., 1971; MA in Pub. Adminstrn., U. Okla., 1975; MEd, EdD, Columbia U., 1993. Commd. 2nd lt. U.S. Army, 1959, advanced through grades to brig. gen., 1986, chief adminstrn. div. office chief of staff, 1968-70, chief mgmt. analysis br. office chief of staff, 1971-75, chief of staff 2nd infantry div., 1975-76, chief mgmt. div. adj. gen. ctr., 1976-77, chief compt. div. Nat. Guard Bur., 1978-81, dep. comdr. 1st pers. command Schwetzingen, Fed. Republic of Germany, 1981-84, dir. resource mgmt. U.S. Mil. Acad. West Point, N.Y., 1984-86, adjutant gen. army Alexandria, Va., 1986-88, dep. chief of staff base ops. support tng./doctrine command Ft. Monroe, Va., 1988-91; assoc. prof. adult edn., human resource devel. Va. Commonwealth U., Richmond, 1993—. Guest lectr. Hungarian Mil. Acad., 1989. Contbr. articles to profl. jours. Mem. ASPA (exec. com. mgmt. sci. and policy analysis sect. 1992-96), ASTD (chair nat. rsch. to practice com. 2000-2002), Acad. Human Resource Devel., Assn. U.S. Army, Mil. Officer Assn., Internat. Soc. Quality Govt. (nat. dir. 1992-93). Methodist. Avocation: writing for publication. Home: PO Box 29 Gum Spring VA 23065-0029 Office: Va Commonwealth U Sch Edn PO Box 842020 1015 W Main St Richmond VA 23284-9061

DI MARCO, BARBARANNE YANUS, special education educator; b. Jersey City, Nov. 16, 1946; d. Stanley Joseph and Anne Barbara (Dalack) Yanus; m. Charles Benjamin DiMarco, Mar. 15, 1986; 1 child, Charles Garrett. BA in Music Edn., Trenton State Coll., 1968; MA in Spl. Edn., Kean Coll., 1971, elem. edn. cert., 1974, adminstrv. cert., 1976. Cert. elem., music, adminstrn., spl. edn., N.J. Vocal music educator Roselle (N.J.) Bd. Edn., 1968-69, tchr. trainable mentally retarded, 1969-76, tchr. multiple handicapped, 1976—. Color guard instr. Roselle Bd. Edn., 1973-88, elem. tutor, 1976-92, adminstrv. asst. to supt., 1980-85; program dir., sec., Expanded Dimensions in Gifted Edn., Westfield, N.J., 1978—. Vestryperson St. Luke's Ch., Roselle, 1989-91. Recipient Govs. Tchr. Recognition award, Gov. Florio, N.J., Trenton, 1992-93. Mem. NEA, N.J. Edn. Assn., Roselle Edn. Assn., N.J. Assn. for Retarded Children, Eastern Star (25-yr award 1991), Delta Omicron. Republican. Episcopalian. Avocations: skiing, flying, oil painting, travel, swimming, music, golf. Home: 13 Gentore Ct Edison NJ 08820-1029 Office: Dr Charles C Polk Sch 1100 Warren St Roselle NJ 07203-2736

DI MARZO, MARINO, engineering researcher, educator; b. Messina, Italy, Feb. 16, 1952; came to U.S., 1978; s. Guido and Maria Pia (Benini) diM.; m. Fulvia Veronese, June 11, 1986; children: Giulia Maria, Marina Antonia. Dr.Ing.Chem.Eng., U. Naples, Italy, 1976; PhD in Mech. Engring., Cath. U., 1982. Registered profl. engr., Italy. Project engr. CTIP, Rome, 1976-78; staff engr. Daedalean & Assocs., Inc., Woodbine, Md., 1978-81; lectr. U. Md., College Park, 1981-82, asst. prof. to assoc. prof., 1982-98, prof., assoc. chair, 1998-2001, prof., chair, 2001—. Vis. scientist Nat. Inst. Standards and Tech., Gaithersburg, Md., 1985-99; cons. U.S. Nuclear Regulatory Commn., 1995—; speaker in field; mem. adv. bd. ECO World, 1992. Contbr. numerous articles to profl. publs. Recipient Excellence in Mfg. award MIPS, 1992, U.S. NRC Spl. Act award, 1995; grantee NRC, 1982-97, U. Md., 1985-86, Nat. Bur. Standards, 1983-85, Md. Indsl. Partnerships, 1989-91, Nat. Inst. Standards and Tech., 1985-2000. Fellow ASME (mem. UIT coordinating com. 1990—, reviewer Jour. Heat Transfer, Nuc. Engrng. and Design, others), Fellow AIChE (chmn. field 7a energy transport rsch. 1991-94, chmn. heat transfer and energy conversion divsn. 1996, mem. various coms., chair various conf. sessions, assoc. editor Heat and Tech.), mem. Internat. Assn. Fire Safety Sci., Soc. Fire Protection Engr., Unione Italiana di Termofluidodinamica. Roman Catholic. Achievements include spray cooling studies applied to fire safety, nuclear power plant behavior during accidents. Home: 8405 Burdette Rd Bethesda MD 20817-2816 also: MS T10G6 Us Nuclear Regulatory Commn Washington DC 20555-0001

DIMICCO, WENDY ANN, nurse educator; b. Newark, Jan. 15, 1948; d. J. Harold and Winifred (O'Connor) Preston; m. Albert Joseph DiMicco, Aug. 23, 1969; 1 child, Michael Albert. BSN summa cum laude, Barry Coll., Miami, Fla., 1969; MSN, U. Ala., Birmingham, 1970, DSN, 2002. Staff nurse Englewood (N.J) Hosp., 1969, St. Vincent's Hosp., Birmingham, Ala., 1970; instr. U. Ala. Sch. Nursing, Birmingham, 1970-72, asst. prof. nursing, 1972—. Cons. in field; lectr. in field. Contbr. articles to profl. jours.; producer videotapes. Mem. AlaCare Home Health Svcs. Adv. Coun., 1983-90; first aid coord. Sonat/Pepsi Vulcan Marathons, Birmingham, 1985, 86; bd. dirs., legis. chmn. Rocky Ridge Elem. Sch. PTA, 1983-85. HEW grantee, 1976-78. Mem. Am. Nurses Assn., Ala. Nurses Assn., ARC, Sigma Theta Tau. Office: U Ala Birmingham AL 35294-1210

DIMINO, SYLVIA THERESA, elementary and secondary educator; b. N.Y.C., June 6, 1955; d. John Anthony and Elena (Berardesca) D. BA, St. John's U., 1977; MPA, NYU, 1980, MA in Elem. and Secondary Edn., 1982, cert. advance studies in ednl. adminstrn., 1986, cert. in advanced studies in mgmt., 1992; MA in Tchg. ESL, Adelphi U., 1984; MA in Libr. Sci., Pratt Inst., 1998; chef, Nat. Gourmet Cooking Sch., 1999. Cert. elem. and secondary tchr., sch. adminstr., in mgmt. practices, social studies, math., N.Y. Traffic coord. Creamer Inc., N.Y.C., 1977-79; tchr. St. Patrick's Sch., N.Y.C., 1979-82, IS 131, Manhattan, N.Y.C., 1984-90, adminstr., coord., 1985-90, asst. prin., 1990-99; tchr. high sch. ESL, N.Y.C. Bd. Edn., 1995-99, libr. sci. tchr., 1999—; chef Natural Gourmet Cookery Sch., 1999—; City Harvest chef for children's programs, 2000—; tchr. Hatha Yoga for Kids, 2000—. Prana yoga tchr., 1998; Thai yoga body massage therapist, 1998. Named to 2000 Most Notable Women. Mem. NAFE, AAUW, Nat. Orgn. Women in Adminstrn., Bus. Cir. N.Y., Nat. Coun. Adminstrv. Women in Edn., Nat. Orgn. Italian-Am. Women (mentoring dir.), Yoga Tchrs. Assn. Roman Catholic. Avocations: walking, hiking, yoga. Address: FH LaGuardia HS Music Arts Performing Arts 100 Amsterdam Ave New York NY 10023-6406

DIMMITT, CORNELIA, psychologist, educator; b. Boston, Mar. 16, 1938; d. Harrison and Martha Fredericka (Read) D.; m. (div.); children: Colin Barclay Church, Jeffrey Harrison Church. BA, Harvard U., 1958; MA, Columbia U., 1966; PhD, Syracuse U., 1970; diplomate, C. G. Jung Inst., Zurich, Switzerland, 1985. Asst. prof. Am. U., Washington, 1970-71; from asst. to assoc. prof. (with tenure) Georgetown U., Washington, 1971-82; pvt. practice Boston, 1985—. Mem. admissions com. Coll. Arts and Scis., Georgetown U., Washington, 1974-76, mem. rank and tenure com., 1977-78; dir. admissions com. C. G. Jung Inst., Boston, 1986-89, pres. tng. bd., 1989-91; pres. NESJA, 1993-97. Author: Classical Hindu Mythology, 1978. NEH fellow, 1979-80. Mem. Am. Oriental Soc., New England Soc. Jungian Analysts, Assn. Grads. in Analytical Psychology (Switzerland), Internat. Assn. for Analytical Psychology. Home and Office: 80 Commonwealth Ave Boston MA 02116-3015

DIMMITT, LAWRENCE ANDREW, retired lawyer, law educator; b. Kansas City, Kans., July 20, 1941; s. Herbert Andrew and Mary (Duncan) Dimmitt; m. Lois Kinney, Dec. 23, 1962; children: Cynthia Susan, Lawrence Michael. BA, Kans. State U., 1963, MA, 1967; JD, Washburn U., 1968. Bar: Kans. 1968, U.S. Dist. Ct. Kans. 1968, U.S. Ct. Appeals (10th cir.) 1969, Mo. 1973, N.Y. 1975, U.S. Supreme Ct. 1986. Atty. Southwestern Bell Tel. Co., Topeka, 1968-73, gen. atty. Kans., 1979-94, atty. St. Louis, 1973-74, gen. atty. regulation, 1979; atty. AT&T, N.Y.C., 1974-79; ret., 1994. Adj. prof. telecom. law Washburn U. Sch. Law, 1996—; mem. polit. sci. adv. coun. Kans State U., 2003—. Mem. master planning com. Hist. Ward-Meade Pk., 1998—; bd. dirs. 1st United Meth. Ch., Topeka, 1979—84, mem. nominating com., 1985—87; bd. dirs. Sunflower Music Festival, 1993—94. Recipient commendation, Legal Aid Soc. Topeka, 1986, 1990, 1993. Mem.: Topeka Bar Assn., Kans. Bar Assn. (pres. adminstrv. law sect. 1985—86, bd. editors newsletter), Jayhawk Lit. Club, Rotary (bd. dirs., 1st v.p. 2000, pres. 2001, asst. gov. 2003—), Phi Alpha Delta (alumni bd. 1986—88, 1993—97). Home: 3123 SW 15th St Topeka KS 66604-2515 E-mail: LLDimmitt@aol.com.

DIMOND, ROBERTA RALSTON, psychology and sociology educator; b. Bakersfield, Calif., Mar. 25, 1940; d. Robert Leroy Vickers and Gail Anderson (Tritch) Ralston; m. James Davis, June 18, 1963 (div. 1970); 1 child, Jamie Amundsen Davis; m. Frederick Henry Dimond, Oct. 20, 1970; children: Frederick Ralston, Robert Vickers (div. 1991). BA in History and English, Stanford U., 1962, MAT in Edn., 1963; MS, U. Pa., 1970, EdD, 1973. Cert. secondary educator, ednl. specialist, counselor, coll. personnel adminstr. Thcr. Kamehameha Sch., Honolulu, 1965-67; asst. to dean of women U. Pa., Phila., 1969-70; asst. prof. Temple U., Ambler, Pa., 1970-87, Montgomery County Coll., Blue Bell, Pa., 1975-80; prof. psychology, speech, sociology Delaware Valley Coll., Doylestown, Pa., 1987—, assoc. prof. liberal arts. Cons. ETS, Princeton, N.J., 1989—; speaker in field; lectr. on sexual responsibilities in the 90s and assertive affirmative action topics; researcher on athletics and aging females syngerism. Author: Gender & RAcial Bias by Vocational Counselors, 1973. Bd. dirs. Concerned Citizens of Upper Dublin, Maple Glen, Pa., 1980-91, Arrowhead Assn., Ambler, Pa., 1990-91. Fellow Newhouse Found., 1960-63; grantee APA, 1969-70. Mem.: MADD, AAUP, APA, Phila. Tennis Assn. (pres.), Stanford Alumni Assn., Phila. Tennis Patrons, U.S. Tennis Assn., Middle States Tennis Assn. (life). Episcopalian. Avocations: tennis (ranked #6 in U.S. in women's 50 and over tennis, # 1 in over 45, # 1 MSTA over 60., duplicate bridge. Home: 236 Amherst Dr Doylestown PA 18901-2381 Office: Delaware Valley Coll Rte 202 Doylestown PA 18901

DINES, DAVID MICHAEL, surgeon, educator; b. N.Y.C., Feb. 4, 1948; s. Aaron and Yuche Yvette Harriet Dines; m. Judith Lori Dines, Jan. 29, 1973; children: Joshua Scott, Alison Kate. BA in Biology, Lehigh U., 1970; MD, N.J. Coll. Medicine, 1974. Diplomate Am. Bd. Surgery. Resident in orthop. surgery N.Y. Hosp. Cornell, N.Y.C., 1974—76, Hosp. Spl. Surgery, N.Y.C., 1976—79, fellow, 1980, Am. Acad. Orthop. Surgery, Chgo., 1981; adj. Cornell U. Med. Coll., N.Y.C., 1983—; clin. prof. orthop. surgery Albert Einstein Coll. Medicine, N.Y.C., 1998—, chmn. dept. orthop. surgery, 1996—. Team physician N.Y. Mets, 1991—97, USTA, 1999—; med. advisor Assn. Tennis Profls., Punte Verde, Fla., 1994—; team physician U.S. Davis Cup Tennis Team, 2000—02. Contbr. articles to profl. jours. Fund raiser Hosp. Spl. Surgery, N.Y.C., 1979—, Rep. Nat. Com., Washington, 1994—. Named one of Best Dr. in N.Y., N.Y. Mag., 1997—, 2002, Best Dr. in Am. 1999-2002; recipient John Chanley Meml. award, U. Liverpool, Eng., 1996. Fellow: Am. Acad. Orthop. Surgeons; mem.: Assn. Team Profl. Med. Soc. (assoc. dir. 1991), Am. Orthop. Assn. (mem. membership com. 1998—), Acad. Orthop. Soc. Am., Am. Shoulder & Elbow Soc. (mem. exec. com. 1999—). Avocations: tennis, golf, politics. Office: Albert Einstein Coll Med 935 Northern Blvd Ste 303 Great Neck NY 11021 E-mail: ddinesmd98@aol.com.

DINGLE, PATRICIA A. education educator, artist; b. Washington, Apr. 19, 1954; d. Asbery and Loretha (Bryant) D. BA, Conn. Coll., 1976; MA in Tchg., RISD, 1977; PhD in Curriculum and Instrn., U. Md., 1996. Cert. art and dance tchr., Md.; ordained to ministry Bapt. Ch., 1998. Instr. dance RISD, Providence, 1976-77; visual artist, dancer R.I. Coun. on Arts, Providence, 1977-78; tchr. art Ctrl. H.S., East Providence, R.I., 1978-79, Friendly H.S., Prince Georges County, Md., 1979-82, Prince George's County Pub. Schs., Upper Marlboro, Md., 1987—; chair dept. fine arts High Point H.S., 2000—02; asst. prof. dept. edn. Clarion U. of Pa., 2002—. Dir. summer playground Md. Nt. Capital Park and Planning Commn., Prince Georges County, 1999; adj. prof. Western Md. Coll., Westminster, 1999; propr. Ding La Gift Studio, Bowie, Md., 1994—; presenter Md. Art Edn. Assn., Towson, 1997, 98, Nat. Coun. Tchrs. Math., Springfield and Phila., Success 2002 Conf., U. Md.; mem. discussion panel Conn. Coll., New London, 1998; vis. minority scholar/artist U. Wis., Eau Claire, 2000; lectr. Cath. U. Am., summer 2000; assoc. min. Amazing Grace Bapt. Ch., 1998-2002; youth min. Village Bapt. Ch., 2002; presenter in field. Exhibited in solo shows at Office of Cmty. Affairs, New London, Conn., 1973, Parkview Bapt. Ch., Landover, Md., 1975, First Bapt. Ch. in Am., Providence, 1978, others; group shows include Marlborough (Conn.) Arts Festival, 1974, Cummings Art Ctr., New London, 1976, Woods-Gerry Gallery, Providence, 1977, Marlboro Gallery/Prince George's C.C., 1981, Montpelier Mansion, Laurel, Md., 1998, Bowie Arts Expo, Allen Pond, 1999, Electronic Exhibit, N.Y., 2001, NAEA Women's Caucus Womens

Artwork, N.Y., 2001, Art Celebrating Women, PA-SSHE Conf., 2002; works represented in permanent collections Carlson Libr. Clarion U.; dir. Young Designers Am. program Ashton-Drake Gallery, 2000. Facilitator youth study circle Prince Georges County Human Rels. Commn., Landover, 1998; mem. grants in comtys. adv. panel Md. State Arts Coun., 2000-01; active In Touch Ministries, 1998—; mem. mission trip Appalachian Outreach Ctr., Jefferson City, Tenn., 2003 Sgt. U.S. Army, 1983-87. Recipient Anna Lord Strauss award for cmty. svc., 1976, awards for art; grad. fellow U. Md., 1989; Md. Tech. fellow, 2000; NEH summer seminar faculty profl. devel. project grantee, 2001, 03; faculty profl. devel. grantee, 2003. Mem.: Nat. Art Edn. Assn. (book reviewer 2002—03). Avocations: research, writing, piano playing, painting. Office: Clarion Univ Pa Dept of Education Clarion PA 16214

DINH, TUNG VAN, obstetrician, gynecologist, pathologist, educator; b. Hoi-An, Vietnam, Aug. 7, 1930; came to U.S., 1975; s. Vinh Van Dinh and Lan Thi Thai; m. Gia D. To, Sept. 1, 1957; children: Tuan, Tue, Tri, Tho. MD, Saigon Med. Sch., Vietnam, 1958. Diplomate Am. Bd. Ob-Gyn., Am. Bd. Pathology. Fellow in ob-gyn. pathology Johns Hopkins Hosp., Balt., 1960-61; resident in ob-gyn. and pathology U. Tex., Galveston, 1976-81; chief of surgery Duy Tan Mil. Hosp., Danang, Vietnam, 1958-60; dir. Danang Gen. Hosp., 1966-75; asst. prof. ob-gyn. Hué (Vietnam) Sch. Medicine, 1970-75; prof. ob-gyn. and pathology U. Tex. Med. Br., Galveston, 1988—. Examiner Am. Bd. Ob-Gyn., Chgo., 1987, 88. Author: Syllabus of Gynecologic Pathology, 1990, 2000, Clinical Gynecologic Oncology Review, 1993, 98, 2000. Pres. Vietnamese Am. Assn., Danang, 1970. Named William Osler scholar, U. Tex. Med. Br., 2001; recipient medal of Health Svcs., Edn. and Social Svcs., Govt. of South Vietnam, 1973, Golden Apple award, U. Tex., Galveston, 1984, 1987. Fellow Am. Coll. Ob-Gyn., Am. Soc. Clin. Pathologists, Internat. Soc. Vulvar Diseases; mem. Assn. Profs. Ob-Gyn., Internat. Soc. Gynecol. Pathologists. Avocations: fishing, gardening, travel, reading. Office: U Tex Med Br Dept Ob-Gyn 301 University Blvd Galveston TX 77555-5302 E-mail: tunginh@utmb.edu.

DINNERSTEIN, SIMON ABRAHAM, artist, educator; b. Bklyn., Feb. 16, 1943; s. Louis and Sarah (Kobilansky) D.; m. Renée Sudler, Aug. 28, 1965; 1 child, Simone. BA, CCNY, 1965; postgrad., Bklyn. Mus. Art Sch., 1964-67, Hochschule für Bildende Kunst, Kassel, Fed. Republic Germany, 1970-71. Instr. in fine arts New Sch. Social Rsch., Parsons Sch. of Design, N.Y.C., 1975—. Adj. lectr. N.Y.C. Tech. Coll., Bklyn., 1979—88; vis. prof. Pratt Inst., Bklyn., 1986—87; vis. artist Calhoun Sch., NY, 1988—89; lectr. Am. Acad. Rome, 1977—78, USIS, Barcelona and Madrid, Spain, 1979, Pa. State U., 1984, Pt. Washington Pub. Libr., 1990, St. Paul's Sch., Concord, N.H., 1991, Nassau County C.C., 1994, NAD, 2000, Walton Arts Ctr., Fayetteville, Ark., 1999, U. Richmond, Va., 2000. One-man shows include Staempfli Gallery, N.Y.C., 1975, 1979, 1988, Inst. Internat. Edn., 1976—77, 1979, Am. Acad. Rome, 1977, Pratt Inst., 1987, New Sch. Social Rsch., 1981, 1993, Martin Luther King, Jr., Labor Ctr., N.Y.C., 1985, St. Paul's Sch., Concord, 1991, N.J. Ctr. for Visual Art, Summit, 1994, ACA Galleries, N.Y., Bread and Roses Gallery, N.Y. and St. Peter's Church, N.Y., 1999, Walton Arts Ctr., Fayetteville, Texarkana Regional Arts Ctr., Tex./Ark., Marsh Art Gallery, U. Richmond, 2000, Arnot Art Mus., 2003; subject of books: The Art of Simon Dinnerstein, 1991, Simon Dinnerstein: Paintings and Drawings, 2000; included in anthology Drawing from Life, 1992, Drawing from Life (Clint Brown), 1997, Centennial Directory, Am. Acad. Rome, 1995, Hooked on Drawing: Illustrated Lessons and Exercises for Grades 4 and up, 1996, Community of Creativity, A Century of MacDowell Colony Artists, 1996, Drawing Dimensions, 1999, Ont. Rev., 1998, St. Ann's Rev., 2000, Rattapallax Jour., 2000, Bklyn. Jews, 2001, Great Am. Writers, 2001, City Secrets, Rome, 2000, City Secrets, Florence, Venice and the Towns of Italy, 2001, City Secrets, New York, 2002, Hanging Loose, 2003; represented, ACA Galleries, N.Y.C. Recipient Rome prize Am. Acad. in Rome, 1976-78, Ingram Merrill Found. award for painting, 1978-79, Cannon prize NAD, 1988, Ralph Fabri prize NAD, 1997, Bertelsen award NAD, 1998; Childe Hassam purchase award Am. Acad. Arts and Letters, 1976-78; fellow Fulbright Found., Germany, 1970-71, Louis Comfort Tiffany Found., 1976, MacDowell Colony, 1969, 79, N.Y. Found. for Arts, 1987; E.D. Found. grantee, 1977-78, 78-79. Mem. NAD, Soc. Fellows Am. Acad. Rome. Democrat. Jewish. Avocations: reading, film, walking, travel, dreaming. Home: 415 1st St Brooklyn NY 11215-2507

DINNIMAN, ANDREW ERIC, county commissioner, history educator, academic program director, international studies educator; b. New Haven, Oct. 10, 1944; s. Harold and Edith (Stephson) D.; m. Margo Portnoy, June 8, 1969; 1 dau., Alexis. BA, U. Conn., 1966; MA, U. Md., 1969; EdD, Pa. State U., 1978. Student pers. worker U. Md., 1969-71, U. Denver, 1971-72; prof. West Chester (Pa.) State U., 1972—, dir. Ctr. for Internat. Programs, 1986-2001; commissioner Chester County, 1992—. Author: Book of Human Relations Readings, 1980, Education for International Competence in Pennsylvania, 1988; contbr. articles to profl. jours. Chmn. Chester County Dem. Com., 1979-85; mem. Pa. Dem. State Com., 1982-89, mem. exec. com., 1984-89; chmn. Eastern Pa. Dem. County Chmn. Assn., 1982-85; mem. Dem. Nat. Com., 1984-89; del. Dem. Nat. Conv., 1984, 88, 92, 96; pres. Pa. Coun. on Internat. Edn., 1989-91; v.p. Downingtown Area (Pa.) Sch. Bd., 1975-79; mem. Ctrl. Chester County Vocat.-Tech. Sch. Bd., 1978-79; mem. Chester County Conservation Dist., 1992—; mem. Pa. State Transp. Adv. Com., 1992-95, mem. Chester County Econ. Devel. Bd., 1992-96; mem. Nat. Assn. Counties Com. on Globalization, 1997-98, Chester County Internat. Trade Coun., 1999—. Recipient Bicentennial award Pa. Sch. Bds. Assn., 1976, Outstanding Acad. Svc. award Commonwealth Pa., 1977, Human Rights award W. Chester State U. chpt. NAACP, 1980, Cmty. Svc. award Coatesville NAACP, 1997, Mil. Order of Purple Heart Nat. citation for outstanding svc., 1998, Excellence in Local Govt. award Commonwealth of Pa., 1998, Grange award for pub. svc., 1999, Regional Leadership award Exton Regional C. of C., 1999, Leadership award Chester County Water Resources Authority, 2003. Mem. Chester County Hist. Soc., Pa. Soc. Jewish. Home: 471 Spruce Dr Exton PA 19341-2025 Office: Courthouse 2 N High St West Chester PA 19380-3025 E-mail: adinniman@chesco.org.

DI NUNZIO, DOMINICK, educational administrator; b. Bristol, Pa., Mar. 7, 1931; s. Anthony and Mary (Minni) Di N.; m. Helen Mae Appleton, Dec. 29, 1953; children: Dominick, Mark, Douglas, Celeste. BS, Millersville (Pa.) U., 1953; MEd, Rutgers U., 1960, postgrad., 1960-63, U. Pa., 1965-68, Temple U., 1969-71, Lehigh U., 1983; PhD, Walden U., 1972. Tchr., basketball coach Bristol H.S., 1955-61; vice prin. Pemberton Twp. (N.J.) H.S., 1961-65, prin., 1965-73, Pemberton Twp. H.S. No. 2, 1973-76, Pemberton Twp. Elem. Schs., 1976-84, Mid. Schs., 1984-91, asst. supt., 1991—. Mem. acad. policy bd. Walden U., 1978-83. With U.S. Army, 1953-55. Recipient Legion of Honor, Chapel of Four Chaplains, 1982, Disting. Alumnus award Walden U., 1982; named Secondary Educator of Am., 1973. Mem. ASCD, NEA, N.J. Edn. Assn., Nat. Assn. Secondary Sch. Prins., N.J. Assn. Secondary Sch. Prins., Am. Assn. Sch. Adminstrs., Nat. Doctorate Assn., N.J. Schoolmasters Club, South Jersey Schoolmens Club, Coun. for Basic Edn., Nat. Soc. for Study Edn., Millersville U. Alumni Assn. (exec. com. 1972—, v.p. 1978-80, pres. 1980-82, Disting. Svc. award 1987, Outstanding Svc. award 1987, Disting. Alumni award 2003), Walden U. Alumni Assn. (pres. 1978-84), Walden U. Mid. States Regional Assn. (pres. 1983-85), Order Sons of Italy in Am., Pemberton Rotary (pres. 1976-77, Paul Harris fellow 1996), Masons (worshipful master 1987, dist. G chmn. Masonic edn. 1988-91, facilitator dist. C Hiram Leadership program 1990—, chmn. dist. C membership devel. and retention 1992—), Phi Delta Kappa. Presbyterian. Home: 37 Underwood Rd Levittown PA 19056-2601 Office: PO Box 98 Browns Mills NJ 08015-0098

DION, SUSAN M. education director, educator; b. L.A., Sept. 15, 1947; d. Alfred H. and Marian B. (Fremont) Johnson; m. Raymond R. Dion, Jr., Feb. 6, 1971 (div. Nov. 1985); children: Scott R., Stacey S., Marian E. BS in Social Sci., Calif. Polytech. Inst., 1971; MA in Edn., U. San Francisco, 1982. Tchr., coach San Gabriel (Calif.) Mission Grammar Schs., 1968-77; prin. St. Dorothy's Sch., Glendale, Calif., 1977-80; study ctr. dir. Walnut (Calif.) H.S., 1980-82; area coord., ctr. dir. Am. Learning Corp./The Reading Game, Covina/Upland, Calif., 1982-84; edn. coord. U. Hosp. Adolescent Unit, Denver, 1986-88; prin. Good Shepherd Sch., Denver, 1987-88; dir. edn. Charter Hosp., Aurora, Colo., 1988-90; tchr. Aurora Pub. Sch., 1990-92, Cherry Creek Sch. Dist., Aurora, 1992-93; transition svcs. dir. Excelsior Youth Ctr., Aurora, 1993-96; dir. edn. Jefferson Hills, Inc., Lakewood, Colo., 1996—2001; ednl. svcs. mgr. Sylvan Lng. Sys., Littleton, Calif., 2001—02, dir. ctr. Thornton, Colo., 2002—. Author: Transition Skills Curriculum, 1994. Mem. adv. bd. for gifted and talented edn. Rowland Sch. Dist., Walnut, Calif., 1981-83. Mem. ASCD. Roman Catholic. Avocations: singing, guitar, choir director. Home: 2991 S Zeno Way Aurora CO 80013-6144 Office: 3750 E 104th Ave Denver CO 80233

DIORIO, EILEEN PATRICIA, retired medical technologist, philosophy educator; b. Pitts., Mar. 17, 1938; d. Charles Frederick and Elizabeth (Maturkanich) Kozlowski; m. David Robert Kaslewicz, June 21, 1958 (div. May 1965); m. Alfred Frank Diorio, June 11, 1983; children: Suzanne C. Kaslewicz Ickes, Fredric C. Kaslewicz, Warren G. Kaslewicz, Jennifer Kaslewicz Dalessandro. Student, Duquesne U., 1956-58. Reg. Med. Technologist, Pa. Microbiology technician Presbyn. U. Hosp., Pitts., 1967-70; supr. virology/immunology lab. Allegheny Gen. Hosp., Pitts., 1970-90. Co-dir. Himalayan Inst. Yoga Science & Philosophy of Pitts., 1977-96. Vol. med. lab. mgr. Himalayan Inst. Hosp., India, 1992-96. Avocations: violin, cooking, meditation.

DIPARDO, ANNE, English language and education educator; BA in English magna cum laude, Calif. State U., Northridge, 1976; MA in English, UCLA, 1977; EdD in Lang. and Literacy, U. Calif., Berkeley, 1991. Assoc. prof. English and edn. U. Iowa, Iowa City, 1991—2002, full prof., 2002—. Author: A Kind of Passport, 1993, Teaching in Common, 1998; co-editor Research in the Teaching of English, 2003—; contbr. articles to profl. jours. Recipient Outstanding Scholarship award Nat. Writing Ctrs. Assn., 1993; NAE/Spencer postdoctoral fellow, 1995—. Mem. MLA, Am. Ednl. Rsch. Assn., Nat. Conf. on Rsch. in English, Nat. Coun. Tchrs. English (Promising Rschr. award 1992, Meade award 2000). Office: U Iowa N246 Linquist Ctr Iowa City IA 52242

DI PASQUALE, PASQUALE, JR., education consultant; b. Boston, Oct. 6, 1928; s. Pasquale and Lucrezia (Caruso) Di P.; m. Charlotte Rose Fasnacht, Aug. 12, 1961; children— Theresa M., Catherine S., Maria E. BA, U. Notre Dame, 1955; MA, Oxford U., 1961; PhD, U. Pitts., 1965; LHD, Assumption Coll., 1979. Head English dept. St. Mary's Sem., Mwanza, Tanganyika, 1957-61; asst. prof. English Seton Hill Coll., 1961-65; assoc. prof. Middle English lang. and lit. U. Oreg., 1965-69; prof. Ill. State U. at Normal, 1969-72; pres. Assumption Coll., Worcester, Mass., 1972-77, Loras Coll., Dubuque, Iowa, 1977-87, St. Thomas U., Miami, Fla., 1987-89, Coll. Misericordia, Dallas, Pa., 1989—92; higher edn. cons., 1992—. Served with USMCR, 1950-52. Fulbright scholar, 1955-56; Fulbright grantee, 1956-57; Office of Sci. and Scholarly Research grantee U. Oreg., 1968. Mem. MLA, Fulbright Assn., Benedictine Acad. Am., Medieval Acad. Am., N.Y. C.S. Lewis Soc. Home: 7761 S Tarbela Ave Tucson AZ 85747-5120 Fax: 520-574-9122. E-mail: dulacaz@aol.com.

DIPIETRO, RALPH ANTHONY, marketing and management consultant, educator; b. N.Y.C., Oct. 27, 1942; s. Joseph and Marie (Borelli) DiP. BBA, CUNY, 1964, MBA, 1966; PhD, NYU, 1972. Chmn., prof. mktg. and internat. bus. dept. Sch. Bus. Montclair State U., Upper Montclair, N.J., 1972—. Adj. prof. mgmt. NYU, 1976-97, mgmt. tng. dir. Inst. Retail Mgmt., 1976-86; cons. Mfrs. Hanover Trust, N.Y.C., 1979-85, Sharp Electronics, N.Y.C., 1980-94, Battus Corp., N.Y.C., 1982-85, AT&T Bell Labs., 1989-91; program dir. Bally of Switzerland, N.Y.C., 1981-93, Fortunoff's, N.Y.C., 1984-86. Author: Managerial Effectiveness: A Review and an Empirical Testing of a Model, 1973; contbr. articles to profl. jours. Mem. Am. Mktg. Assn., Acad. Mktg. Scis., Internat. Assn. Applied Psychology, Omicron Delta Epsilon. Avocations: tennis, swimming, opera. Home: 12 Manor Dr Warren NJ 07059

DIPRETE, JAMES A. educational association administrator; Spanish tchr., Conn., 1960—61; tchr. Cranston High East, RI, 1961; prin. Coventry H.S.; chmn. R.I. Bd. Regents, Providence, 1999—. Named Citizen of the Yr., Coventry C. of C., 1996, Prin. of the Yr., R.I. Assn. Student Couns., 1993; named to, Cranston Hall of Fame, 1996; Fulbright fellow, U. Pisa, Italy, 1965—66. Mem.: New Eng. Assn. schs. and Coll.s. Office: RI Dept Edn 5th Fl 255 Westminster St Providence RI 02903*

DIRECTOR, STEPHEN WILLIAM, electrical and computer engineering educator, academic administrator; b. Bklyn., June 28, 1943; s. Murray and Lillian (Brody) D.; m. Lorraine Schwartz, June 20, 1965; children: Joshua, Kimberly, Cynthia, Deborah. BS, SUNY, Stony Brook, 1965; MS, U. Calif., Berkeley, 1967, PhD, 1968. Prof. elec. engring. U. Fla., Gainesville, 1968-77; vis. scientist IBM Rsch. Labs., Yorktown Heights, N.Y., 1974-75; prof. elec. and computer engring. Carnegie-Mellon U., Pitts., 1977-96, U.A. and Helen Whitaker Univ. prof. electrical and computer engring., 1980-96, prof. computer sci., 1981-96, head dept. elec. and computer engring., 1982-91, univ. prof., 1992-93, dean Carnegie Inst. Tech., 1991-96; Robert J. Vlasic Dean of Engring. U. Mich., Ann Arbor, 1996—, prof. elec. engring. and computer science, 1996—. Advisor info. and comm. tech. Techno Venture Mgmt., 1999—2002; sr. rsch. fellow IC2 Inst., 1996—; sr. cons. editor McGraw-Hill Book Co., N.Y.C., 1976—; dir. Rsch. Ctr. Computer-Aided Design, Pitts., 1982—89; mem. tech. adv. bd. Nextwave, Inc., 1990—95, CAD Framework Initiative, 1991—93, Aspect Devel. Corp., 1991—92, JW2 Inc., 1991—94, LSI Logic, 1994, Autogate Logic, 1994—96, EDF Ventures, 1999—; bd. dirs. Job Gravity, 1999—; hon. prof. Shanghai Jiao Tong U., 2003; mem. adv. coun. Lutron Electronics Inc., 1999—; cons. in field. Author: Introduction to System Theory, 1972, Circuit Theory, 1975, VLSI Design for Manufacturing: Yield Enhancement, 1989, Principles of VLSI System Planning: A Framework for Conceptual Design, 1991; editor: Computer-Aided Design, 1974; co-editor: Advances in Computer-Aided Design for VLSI: vol. 8, Statistical Approach to VLSI, 1994. Chair bd. dirs. Am. Soc. Engring. Edn., Engring. Deans Coun., 1999-2001. Recipient Frederick Emmons Terman award Am. Soc. Engring. Edn., 1976; named Distinguished Alumnus, SUNY, Stony Brook, 1984; Aristotle Award Semicondr. Rsch. Corp., 1996, Outstanding Alumnus award in Elec. Engring. U. Calif., Berkeley, 1996, Berkeley Disting. Engring. Alumnus award U. Calif., 1999. Fellow IEEE (W.R.G. Baker prize 1979, Edn. Soc. Outstanding Achievement award 1995, Edn. medal 1998, Millennium medal 2000); mem. NAE (chair com. on engring. edn.), IEEE Cirs. and Sys. Soc. (pres. 1981, assoc. editor jour. 1973-75, best paper award 1970, 85, 89, 92, Centennial medal 1984, soc. award 1992, Golden Jubilee medal 1999). Office: Univ Michigan Coll Engring Robert H Lurie Engring Ctr Ann Arbor MI 48109 E-mail: director@umich.edu.

DIRKS, KENNETH RAY, pathologist, medical educator, army officer; b. Newton, Kans., Feb. 11, 1925; s. Jacob Kenneth and Ruth Viola (Penner) D.; m. Betty Jean Worsham, June 9, 1946; children: Susan Jan, Jeffrey Mark, Deborah Anne, Timothy David, Melissa Jane. MD, Washington U., St. Louis, 1947. Diplomate: Am. Bd. Pathology. Rotating intern St. Louis City Hosp., 1948, asst. resident in gen. surgery, 1948-49; resident in pathology VA Hosp., Jefferson Barracks, Mo., 1951-53, resident in pathology, asst. chief lab. service Indpls., 1953-54; resident in pathology Letterman Army Hosp., San Francisco, 1956-57; fellow in tropical medicine and parasitology La. State U., Central Am., 1958; asst. in pathology Washington U. Sch. Medicine, 1952-53; asst. chief lab. service VA Hosp., Jefferson Barracks, 1953; instr. pathology U. Ind. Med. Center, Indpls., 1953-54; commd. capt. M.C. U.S. Army, 1954, advanced through grades to maj. gen., 1976; dir. research Med. Research and Devel. Command, Washington, 1968-69, dep. comdr., 1969-71, comdr., 1973-76; asst. surgeon gen., research and devel. U.S. Army, 1973-76; dep. comdr., comdr. Med. Research Inst. Infectious Diseases, Ft. Detrick, Frederick, Md., 1972-73; comdr. Fitzsimons Army Med. Center, Denver, 1976-77; supt. Acad. Health Scis., Ft. Sam Houston, Tex., 1977-80; assoc. prof. to prof. pathology and lab. medicine Coll. Med. Tex. A&M U., College Station, 1980-95; interim head dept. Coll. Medicine, Tex. A&M U., College Station, 1990-91; prof. emeritus pathology, 1995—; asst. dean coll. Coll. Medicine, Tex. A&M U., College Station, 1985-88; dir. dept. student health svcs. and A.P. Beutel Health Ctr. Tex. A&M U., College Station, 1989-95; dir. student health svcs. emeritus, 1995—. Contbr. articles to med. jours. Decorated D.S.M., Legion of Merit with oak leaf cluster, Meritorious Service medal, Army Commendation medal with oak leaf cluster. Fellow Coll. Am. Pathologists, Internat. Acad. Pathology. Address: 2513 Oak Cir Bryan TX 77802-2009 E-mail: kdemeritus@aol.com.

DIRKS, SANDRA L. elementary school educator; b. Libby, Mont., June 5, 1947; d. Ralph C. and Rebecca E. (Webb) Drury; children: Danika Lubinski, Rurik Lubinski; m. Charles Dirks, Nov. 2, 1996. BA, U. No. Colo., 1968; MA, U. Wyo., 1989. Cert. elem. tchr., adminstr., Wyo., Colo.; Montessori-lower elem. tchr. Montessori Edn. Ctr. of Rockies. Elem. and kindergarten tchr., homebound tchr. Mesa County Valley Sch. Dist. 51, Grand Junction, Colo.; elem. tchr. St. Stephens Indian Sch., Wyo.; head tchr., assoc. dir., owner Parker Montessori Edn. Inst., Colo. Mem. ASCD, Am. Montessori Soc., Internat. Reading Assn., Wyo. Assn. Elem. Sch. Prins., Colo. Edn. Assn. (past bldg. rep.), AAUW (br. pres.), PEO, Phi Delta Kappa, Delta Omicron, Pi Lambda Theta.

DIROSA, LINDA MARY, education specialist, diagnostic company executive; b. New Orleans, Mar. 23, 1951; d. Frank Jr. and Emilie Olympe (Ory) DiR. BS, S.W. Tex. State U., 1973; MEd, Lamar U., 1978. Cert. ednl. diagnostician, K-12 prin., mid-mgmt. Tchr. Houston Ind. Sch. Dist., 1974-79, ednl. diagnostician, 1979-83; tchr., prin. designee Fairbanks (Alaska) North Star Borough Sch. Dist., 1983-90, tchr., adminstrv. intern, 1990-92; edn. specialist Tex. Edn. Agy., Austin, 1993-94; pres., CEO Diagnostic/Learning, Austin, 1994—. Mem. state mgmt. team Tex. Edn. Agy., Austin, 1993-94. Fellow World Found. of Successful Women; mem. AAUW, NAFE, Am. Ednl. Rsch. Assn., Nat. Assn. Ednl. Therapists (profl. registry), Tex. Profl. Ednl. Diagnostician (profl. registry), Learning Disabilities Assn. Roman Catholic. Avocations: scuba diving, self improvement, cooking, travel, investing. Address: 97171 Cypresswood #302 Houston TX 77070

DIRST, STEPHANIE LEMKE, special education administrator; b. Chgo., Apr. 10, 1942; d. William Willis and Mildred Katheryn (Murphy) Lemke; children: Gregory D., Douglas L. BA, Blackburn Coll., 1964; MA, U. North Colo., 1968; EdS, Ga. State U., 1988; EdD, Nova Southeastern U., 1996. Cert. tchr., Ga.; cert. dir. of spl. edn., Ga. Instr. Ga. State U., Atlanta; tchr. Am. Sch. for Deaf, Hartford, Conn., 1965-72; dir. Ga. Ctr. for Multihandicapped, Decatur, 1977—99. Chmn. adv. com. Ga. Deaf-Blind Project, 1990—95; instr. Emory U., Atlanta, U. Ga., Atlanta, Kennesaw State U., North Ga. Coll. and State U. Editor: Ga. Learning Resources Sys. Jour., 1991—99. Recipient Vital Svc. award Retarded Citizens of Atlanta. Mem. Ga. Fedn. Exceptional Children (v.p., treas., pres., gov.), Ga. Coun. Tchrs. of Hearing Impaired, Ga. Coun. Adminstrs. Spl. Edn.

DIRUBBO, DANA DAWN, elementary school educator; b. Peekskill, N.Y., Dec. 18, 1969; d. Glynn Albert and Alberta (Tompkins) Fowler; m. Joseph Anthony DiRubbo, Aug. 20, 1994. BS in Edn., SUNY, Fredonia, 1991. Permanent substitute Lakeland Ctrl. Schs., Shrub Oak, N.Y., 1991-93; asst. dir., head tchr. Field Child Care, Yorktown Heights, N.Y., 1993; tchr. 1st grade North Rockland Sch. Dist., Garnerville, N.Y., 1993—. Asst. dir. day camp Town of Cortlandt Recreation Dept., Cortlandt Manor, N.Y., 1991—. Mem. Nat. Assn. for Edn. of Young Children. Office: Thiells Elementary School Rosman Rd Thiells NY 10984

DI RUSSO, TERRY, communications educator, writer; b. Trenton, N.J., Nov. 1, 1947; d. Joy (Urban) Rooy; m. Dennis John, June 23, 1973 (div. July 1985); 1 child, Elaine Marie; m. Robert L. DiRusso, Aug. 17, 2002. BS in Comm., Psychology, Edn., Murray State U., 1970, MS in Comm., 1971; postgrad., Cen. Conn. State U., New Britain, 1972. Tchr., teaching asst. Murray (Ky.) State U., Murray, Ky., 1970-71; instr. adult edn. Wincester Bd. of Edn., Winsted, Conn., 1973-76; special lectr. Central Conn. State U., New Britain, Conn., 1975-85; lectr. comm. dept. Tunxis C.C., Farmington, Conn., 1986—; comm. lectr. U. Conn., Waterbury, 1986, Torrington, 1986—; English educator Wincester Bd. of Edn., Conn., 1971—. Cons., lectr. Vets. Hosp. Nursing Staff, Meridan, 1981, Bus. and Profl. Women, 1982; faculty cons. Conn. State Conf. Emergency Med. Techs., Hartford, 1988-96; cons. Pvt. Individuals Pub. Speaking Coach, 1976—; comms. lectr. gender comms. and sexual harassment United Techs., E. Hartford, Conn., 1995; presenter in field. Author: (mystery novel, as Terry Finello) Absolute Vengeance, 1999; mem. editl. bd. Elements of Speech Comm., 3rd edit., 1995. Mem. AAUP, NEA, Conn. Edn. Assn., Winsted Edn. Assn., Nat. Coun. Tchrs. English, New Eng. League Mid. Schs., Litchfield County Women's Network, Conn. Assn. Pubs. and Authors. Avocations: tennis, writing. Home: 126 Winterbourne Ln Canton CT 06019 Office: Univ Conn University Dr Torrington CT 06790 E-mail: tdirusso@snet.net.

DISALLE, MICHAEL DANNY, secondary education educator; b. Denver, May 16, 1945; s. Michael and Agnes Marie (Kulik) DiS.; m. Marikaye Lucas, June 22, 1968; children: Katharine Marie, Kristin Jean, Michael Charles, Matthew Gregory. BA, Regis Coll., 1967; MEd, Lesley Coll., 1992. Cert. tchr., Colo. Tchr. Assumption Sch., Welby, Colo., 1968-74, Cherry Creek High Sch., Englewood, Colo., 1974-95; poet, writer, 1995—. Author: (computer program/tchr.'s guide) Adventures of Tom Sawyer, 1983, One Day in the Life of Ivan Denisovich, 1984. Asst. den leader Boy Scouts Am., Aurora, Colo., 1988-89. Avocations: fly fishing, gardening, cooking, fly tying.

DISALVO, MELINDA LONG, school system administrator; b. Oxnard, Calif., Oct. 13, 1954; d. John B. Long and Barbara (Gordon) Allan; m. Peter Anthony DiSalvo, Apr. 1, 1989. BS in Edn., Ga. Southwestern Coll., 1976, MEd, 1980; EdD, U. Ga., 1982; postgrad., Harvard U., 1984, 87. Cert. English and elem. edn. tchr., media specialist, adminstr. Media specialist, tchr. Americus (Ga.) City Schs., 1975-81; adminstr. Spl. Edn. Sch. U. Ga., Athens, 1983; cons. IBM, Atlanta, 1984-85; coord. Writing to Read and Writing Express Dekalb County Schs., Decatur, Ga., 1985—. Pub. Design for the Disabled, 1986, Kidney Kids, 1991, Technology in the Primary Grades, 1989—. Mem. Leadership Dekalb, Atlanta Women Who've Made A Difference; chmn. edn. com. Nat. Kidney Found.; active Jr. League, Adolescent Pregnancy Task Force, Battered Women Shelter. Mem. ASCD, Assn. Ednl. Leaders and Tech. Coords., Phi Delta Kappa. Home: 3388 Windsong Ct Roswell GA 30075-5222 Office: Dekalb County Schs Dept Ednl Computing 2652 Lawrenceville Hwy Decatur GA 30033-2520

DISBROW, LYNN MARIE, communication educator; b. Chgo., Sept. 2, 1961; d. Ervin John and Patricia Ann (Grabarek) Lodyga; m. Michael Ray Disbrow, July 14, 1984; children: Matthew Ray, Nicole Marie. BA, Ind. U., South Bend, 1982; MA with distinction, Emerson Coll., Boston, 1986; PhD, Wayne State U., Detroit, 1989. High sch. program mgr. Jr. Achievement of Michiana, Inc., South Bend, 1982-84; account exec. AM The WNDU Stas.,

South Bend, 1984; instr. Emerson Coll., Boston, 1985-86, Wayne State U., Detroit, 1986-87, grad. teaching asst., 1987; lectr. Ind. U., South Bend, 1988; lectr. I Sinclair C.C., Dayton, Ohio, 1989-90, asst. prof., 1993-97, assoc. prof., 1997—2002, prof., 2002—; vis. asst. prof. comm. U. Dayton, 1990-92. Author conv. papers Mass. Comm. Assn., 1985, Nat. Comm. Assn., 1986-91, 94, 96-98, 99-2002, Ctrl. State Comm. Assn., 1989, 91-92, 94-2003, others; mem. editl. bd. Ohio Speech Jour., 1993, 2000-03, Basic Course Annual, 2000-02, N.D. Jour. Speech and Theatre, 1992-2000, Comm. Rsch.eports, 1999, 2000, Ky. Jour. Comm., 1998-2000. Rumble fellow, 1986-87; recipient award for innovative excellence Nat. Ctr. for Tchg., Learning and Tech., 1997, outstanding award Nat. Assn. C.C., 1999, 2000, Disting. Alumni award Ind. U. at South Bend; named Tchr. of Yr., Ohio Assn. 2-Yr. Colls. Mem. Nat. Comm. Assn., Ctrl. States Comm. Assn., Speech Comm. Assn. Ohio (exec. bd. 1995-98). Republican. Roman Catholic.

DISHMAN, ROBERTA CROCKETT, retired elementary education educator; b. Mallory, W.Va., July 6, 1928; d. Ala and Sarah Belle (Cox) Crockett; m. Frank Handy Dishman, July 5, 1946; children: Elva, Kaye, Franklin, James, Aileen. Student, Beckley Coll., Concord Coll., Bluefield State Coll. Notary pub. Clerical asst. to prin. Big Creek High Sch., War, W.Va., 1945-46; gen. clerical aide McDowell County Bd. Edn., Berwind (W.Va.) Jr. High/Elem. Sch, 1967-70, programmed tutor reading, 1970-88, tutor math., 1988-89, tchr. aide math., 1989-91, retired, 1991—. Author: Impy the Salamander, 1985, Bulletin Board Brighteners, 1988; author pub. poems; contbr. articles to profl. jours., newspapers, mags. Mem. Nat. Honor Soc. (sec. 1945-46). Democrat. Baptist. Avocations: gardening, writing, sewing, reading, teaching the bible. Home: RR 1 Box 340 Squire WV 24884-9600

DISMANG, DEBRA CAROLE, special education educator; b. St. Louis, Sept. 22, 1965; d. Robert Lee Sr. and Carole Jean (Kneemiller) Snell; m. Timothy Lee Dismang, Nov. 14, 1992. BS in Edn., Fontbonne Coll., 1989; MA in Edn., Webster U., 1992. Cert. spl. edn. educator, Mo. Tchr. ESL Jefferson Coll., Arnold, 1992-93; tchr. behavior disorders Fox C-6 Sch. Dist., Arnold, Mo., 1990-97, tchr. learning disabilities, 1997—. Mem. Mo. State Tchrs. Assn., Coun. for Exceptional Children. Lutheran. Avocations: reading, bowling, boating. Office: Rockport Heights Elem 3871 Jeffco Blvd Arnold MO 63010-4299

DISMUKES, VALENA GRACE BROUSSARD, photographer, former physical education educator; b. St. Louis, Feb. 22, 1938; d. Clobert Bernard and Mary Henrietta (Jones) Broussard; m. Martin Ramon Dismukes, June 26, 1965; 1 child, Michael Ramon. AA in Edn., Harris Tchrs. Coll., 1956; BS in Phys. Edn., Washington U., St. Louis, 1958; MA in Phys. Edn., Calif. State U., L.A., 1972; BA in TV and Film, Calif. State U., Northridge, 1981. Cert. phys. edn. tchr., standard svc. supr. Phys. edn. tchr., coach St. Louis Pub. Sch., 1958-60, L.A. Unified Sch. Dist., 1960-84; health and sci. tchr., mentor tchr. LA Unified Sch. Dist., 1984-93; coord. gifted and talented program 32d St./U. So. Calif. Magnet Sch., 1993-95, magnet coord., 1995; adminstrv. asst. Ednl. Consortium of Ctrl. LA, Calif., 1993-95; free-lance photographer, 1970—; owner, bus. cons. Grace Enterprises, 1994-95; owner World Class Images, 1997—. Coord. Chpt. I, 1989—93; mem. sch. based mgmt. team, 1990—93; lectr. in field. Author: (photography book) As Seen, 1995; editor: parent newsletter, 1975—80; one-woman shows include The Olympic Spirit, 1984, LA-The Ethnic Pl., 1986, Native Am.: Red Black Connection, 1999, Tibet-Photos from the Roof of the World, 2000, Chocolate Women, 2001, The Tarahamara of Copper Canyon, 2001; photographer (photo montage) Homeless on the Street, 2002, Views from Ghana, 2003; contbr. articles to profl. jour. Mem. adv. coun. Visual Comm., LA, 1980; mem. Cmty. Consortium, LA, 1986—87; mem. adv. com. LA Edn. Partnership, 1986—87; mem. adv. bd. Espo Sports Club, LA, 1994; co-founder Alliance of Native Am. of So. Calif. (ANASCA), 1999; v.p. Alliance of Native Am. of So. Calif., 1999—2003; mem. adv. coun. Ne'ayah, 2001—03; bd. dir. NACHES Found., Inc., LA, 1985—86. Marine Educators fellow, 1992; photography grantee LA Olympic Organizing Com., 1984, See's Candies, 2000, Long Beach Fine Arts, 2001, Teaching grantee L.A. Edn. Partnership, 1987-89; recipient Honor award LA-Calif. Assn. Health, Phys. Edn. and Recreation, 1971. Mem. ACLU, NAACP, Urban League, Sierra Club treepeople. Avocations: travel, collecting dolls and baskets, ethnic art. Home: 3800 Stocker St Apt 1 Los Angeles CA 90008-5119 E-mail: vdismukes@netzero.net.

DITTES, JAMES EDWARD, psychology of religion educator; b. Cleve., Dec. 26, 1926; s. Mercein Edward and Mary (Freeman) D.; children: Lawrence William (dec.), Nancy Eleanor, Carolyn Ann, Joanne Frances; m. Anne Hebert Smith, Nov. 27, 1987. AB, Oberlin Coll., 1949; B.D., Yale U., 1954, MS, 1955, PhD, 1958. Instr. Am. Sch., Talas, Turkey, 1950-52; ordained to ministry United Ch. Christ, 1954; mem. faculty Yale U., 1955—2002, prof. psychology of religion, 1967-84, prof. pastoral theology and psychology, 1984-2001, chmn. dept. religious studies, 1975-82, Squire prof. pastoral counseling, 2001—02. Chmn. Council on Grad. Studies in Religion in U.S. and Can., 1970-71 Author: The Church in the Way, 1967, Minister on the Spot, 1970, Bias and the Pious, 1973, When the People Say No, 1979, The Male Predicament, 1985, When Work Goes Sour, 1987, Men at Work, 1996, Driven by Hope, 1996, Pastoral Counseling, 1999, Re-Calling Ministry, 1999, (with Robert Menges) Psychological Studies of Clergymen, 1965, (with Donald Capps) The Hunger of the Heart, 1990. Served with USNR, 1945-46. Guggenheim fellow, 1965-66; Fulbright Research fellow Rome, 1965-66; sr. fellow NEH, 1972-73 Mem. Soc. Sci. Study of Religion (exec. sec. 1959-63, editor jour. 1966-71, pres. 1971-73) Home and Office: 1157 Whitney Ave Hamden CT 06517-3434

DITTMER, LINDA MAE, elementary school educator; b. Des Moines, Mar. 23, 1948; d. Wayne E. and Mae Elizabeth (Beck) Dillard; m. Daniel Dittmer, July 25, 1970; children: Chad Jason, Jaren Todd, Kyle Garrett. BA in Elem. Edn., Simpson Coll., 1969; MS in Adminstrn., Drake U., 1994. Tchr. grade 1 Pleasantville (Iowa) Cmty. Sch., 1970-71, tchr. grade 6, 1974-86; tchr. grade 6 math. and sci. Indianola (Iowa) Cmty. Sch., 1986-97, dept. head, 1988-97; elem. prin. pre K-6 Twin Cedars Cmty. Sch., Bussey, Iowa, 1997-2000; elem. prin. K-5 Northstar Elem., Knoxville, Iowa, 2000—. Supt. Warren County Fair Bd., Indianola, 1987—; county coun. advisor Warren 4-H, Indianola, 1986-88, leader 4-H, 1988-91. Mem. NAESP, NEA, ASCD, Nat. Coun. Tchrs. of Math., Pleasantville Edn. Assn. (treas. 1976-86), Sch. Adminstrs. Iowa, Iowa State Edn. Assn., Indianola Edn. Assn. (comm. officer 1986-97). Avocations: reading, downhill skiing, antiquing, computers. Home: 20252 240th Ave Lacona IA 50139-9225 Office: Northstar Elem Sch 407 W Larson Knoxville IA 50138 E-mail: dittmli@knoxville.k12.ia.us.

DITTUS, CAROLYN HELEN, special education educator, consultant, realtor; b. Plainfield, N.J., July 6, 1938; d. Joseph William and Catherine Margaret (Donehue) D. BA, Douglass Coll., 1960; EdD, Rutgers U., 1983; MA, Seton Hall U., 1968, Kean Coll., 1970; EdD, Rutgers U., 1983. Cert. K-8 reading tchr., prin., supr., tchr. of handicapped, N.J., cert. paralegal. Tchr. Old Bridge (N.J.) Bd. Edn., 1960-65, reading tchr., 1965-66, supplemental instrn. tchr., 1972-81, learning cons., 1986—; tchr. Siderugica N.Am. Sch., Puerto Ordoz, Venezuela, 1965-66; spl. helps tchr. Dept. Health Edn. & Welfare, Ramey AFB, P.R., 1970-72. Lectr. Inter Am. U., Ramey AFB, 1971-72; adv. bd. Rutgers Mag. Mem. Rutgers U. Alumni Assn. (pres. Grad. Sch. of Edn.), Learning Cons. Assn. (chmn. licensure 1990-95), Old Bridge Edn. Assn. (rep.), Alumni Assn. Grad. Sch. Edn. Rutgers U. (pres., adv. bd. Rutgers mag.), Kappa Delta Pi (past pres., sec. Delta Xi chpt. 1995-96), Alpha Delta Kappa (past pres.), Phi Delta Kappa. Roman Catholic. Avocations: painting, writing, hiking, photography, travel. Office: Dept Spl Svcs Glenn Sch Cindy St Old Bridge NJ 08857

DITTY, MARILYN LOUISE, gerontologist, educator; MS in Psychology, U. San Diego, 1976; postgrad., U. So. Calif., 1977-82; DPA, U. LaVerne, 1990. Lic. health care adminstr., Calif. Exec. dir. San Clemente (Calif.) Srs., Inc., South County Sr. Svcs., 1978—; assoc. prof. dept. continuing edn., coord. emeritus inst. Saddleback Coll., Mission Vievo, Calif., 1979—; dir. San Clemente Sr. Housing, Inc., 1980—; adj. prof. sociology, gerontology Orange Coast Coll., Costa Mesa, Calif., 1987—. Cons. to developers of sr. housing; gov.'s appointee lontg-term care adv. com. Calif. Dept. Aging; past trustee Calif. Human Ins. Trust, bd. dirs. Sr. Housing Coun. Calif. Bldg. Indsutry; accreditation com. Calif. Higher Edn.; invitee White House Conf. on Aging, 1981, Internat. Congress on Gerontology, Eng., 1987. Presenter papers at profl. confs. Grantee Calif. Health Facilities Financing Authority, Calif. Sr. Bond Funds, Calif. Housing Community Devel. Funds, Calif. Dept. Edn., Calif. Dept. Health, Calif. Dept. Aging; recipient Award of Merit Orange County Community Svcs., 1979, Outstanding Svc. award Saddleback Coll., 1980, spl. cert. of merit Orange County Bd. Suprs., 1982, gerontology svc. cert. Nat. Assn. Adult Day Care, 1984, Long-Term Care Svcs. award Area Agy. on Aging. Mem. Calif. Assn. Adult Day Health Care Svcs. (past pres.), Calif. Assn. Nutrition Dirs. (past v.p.), Calif. Assn. Non-Profits. Office: San Clemente Srs Inc PO Box 5887 San Clemente CA 92674-5887

DIVER, COLIN S. academic administrator, educator; b. 1943; BA, Amherst Coll., 1965; LLB, Harvard U., 1968; MA, U. Pa., 1989; LLD, Amherst Coll., 1990. Bar: Mass. 1968. Spl. counsel Office of the Mayor, Boston, 1968-71; asst. sec. consumer affairs Exec. Office Consumer Affairs, Boston, 1971-72; undersec. adminstrn. Exec. Office Adminstrn. and Fin., Boston, 1972-74; assoc. prof. Boston U., 1975-81, prof., 1981-89, from assoc. dean to dean, 1985-89; dean, Bernard G. Segal prof. U. Pa., Phila., 1989—99, Charles A. Heinbold, Jr., prof., 1999—2002; pres. Reed Coll., Portland, Oreg., 2002—. Cons. Adminstrv. Conf. of U.S., 1980-88. Chmn. Mass. State Ethics Com., 1983-89; mem. adv. com. on enforcement policy NRC, 1984-85. Office: Reed Coll 3203 SE Woodstock Blvd Portland OR 97202

DIVIN, NANCY GAIL, gifted and talented student educator; b. Corsicana, Tex., Jan. 8, 1952; d. William Ellis and Mary Magdalene (Dyer) York; m. Norman Owen Divin, Nov. 23, 1973; children: Ryan Christopher, Andrew Owen, Joshua Stuart. BBA, Navarro Coll., 1972; BA, East Tex. State U., 1973; postgrad., Tarleton State U. Cert. tchr., Tex. Tchr. elem. grades Hillsboro (Tex.) Ind. Sch. Dist., 1974-90, coord. gifted/talented program, 1991—. Mem. tchr. adv. bd. to state rep. Pres. Philotechnos Club, Hillsboro, 1990-91; mem. Hillsboro Elem. PTA, Hillsboro Jr. High PTSA; edn. com. Sesame Women's Club, Hillsboro; mem. youth coun. 1st Bapt. Ch., Hillsboro, organist, tchr. Sunday sch. Recipient Sword of Hope award Am. Cancer Soc., 1988. Mem. ASCD, Tex. Assn. Supervision and Curriculum Devel., Tex. Assn. Gifted and Talented (coords. div.), Assn. Tex. Profl. Educators. Avocation: reading. Home: 112 Clyde Dr Hillsboro TX 76645-2365

DIX, ROLLIN C(UMMING), mechanical engineering educator, consultant; b. NYC, Feb. 8, 1936; s. Omer Houston and Ona Mae (Cumming) D.; m. Elaine B. VanNest, June 18, 1960; children: Gregory, Elisabeth, Karen. BSME, Purdue U., 1957, MSME, 1958, PhD, 1963. Registered profl. engr., Ill. Asst. prof. mech. engring. Ill. Inst. Tech., Chgo., 1964-69, assoc. prof., 1969-80, prof., 1980—, assoc. dean for computing, 1980-96; pres. Patpending Mktg., Inc., 1996—. Bd. dirs. USI Romania, Reformteh, Inc., Romania. Patentee road repair vehicle, method for vestibular test. Chmn. bd. dirs. Pilsen affiliate Habitat for Humanity, Chgo. 1st lt. U.S. Army, 1960—61. Fellow: ASME. Home: 10154 S Seeley Ave Chicago IL 60643-2037 Office: Ill Inst Tech 10 W 32d St Chicago IL 60616-3729 Business E-Mail: dix@iit.edu.

DIXON, ALBERT KING, II, retired university administrator; b. Savannah, Ga., Dec. 28, 1936; s. Albert King and Katharine Blanchard (Simmons) D.; m. Augusta Lee Mason, Mar. 27, 1959; children: Albert King III, Augustus Mason, Lee Simmons. BA in Polit. Sci. cum laude, U. S.C., 1959; postgrad., Furman U., 1984, U. Okla., 1985, Am. Inst. Banking, 1984-85. Commd. 2d lt. USMC, 1959, advanced through grades to lt. col., 1975, exec. officer, 1961, Okinawa, Japan, 1961-62, series officer Recruit Depot, athletic officer, head football coach San Diego, 1962-65, commdg. officer, 1966-67, instr., Marine Corps Devel. and Edn. Commd., head platoon tactics sect. Basic Sch., 1967-70, schs. officer, staff sec. to commdg. gen. Pacific Fleet Marine Force Camp Smith, Hawaii, 1970-73; head football coach Quantico Marines, 1968; ops. and ground tng. officer USMC, Okinawa, 1973-74, officer in charge recruiting sta. Oklahoma City, 1974-77, ground support tng. and equipment officer Hdqs. Marine Corps Washington, 1977-81, retired, 1981; exec. dir. Laurens (S.C.) Family YMCA, 1981-83; v.p., city exec. Palmetto Bank, Laurens, 1983-88; assoc. v.p. alumni affairs U. S.C., Columbia, 1988, dir. athletics, 1988-92, spl. asst. to pres. for univ. promotion and leadership devel, 1993-97; ret., 1997. Active Boy Scouts Am.; Sunday Sch. tchr., elder, mem. com. various Presbyn. chs., Hawaii, Okla., S.C., Va.; Chmn. capital campaign Laurens County Libr., 1987-88; past pres. Laurens Dist. H.S. Booster Club, Laurens County Touchdown Club; past bd. visitors Lander Coll.; past mem. U. S.C. Edn. Found.; past mem. found. bd. Piedmont Tech.; bd. dirs. Dixie Youth Baseball, 1987, vice chmn., player agt., bd. dirs., Laurens, 1982-88; bd. dirs. Upper Savannah Coun. Govts., 1988; pres. Laurens 100 Club, 1984, 88; vice chmn. Laurens County Hist. Soc., 1985-87, Laurens County Bicentennial Com., 1985-86, Palmetto Partnership, Found. for Drug Abuse, Columbia, 1989-91; mem. study com. City of Columbia Baseball Stadium, 1989-90; mem. adv. bd. Midlands chpt. Nat. Football Found. and Hall of Fame; mem. steering com. Future Group Richland County; gov. Rotary Dist. 7750, 1987-88. Recipient Dist. award of Merit, Silver Beaver award and Scoutmaster of Yr. award Boy Scouts Am.; named to U. S.C. Athletic Hall of Fame, State of S.C. Athletic Hall of Fame. Mem. S.C. Assn. Regional Couns. (bd. dirs. 1992—, pres. 1995), So. Ind. Collegiate Ofcls. Assn. (athletic dirs. representative 1989-90), Greater Columbia C. of C. (mem. coun. on edn.), Coll. Football Assn. Athletic Dirs. (mem. com. 1989-90), VFW, Am. Legion, Laurens 100 Club (pres. 1984, 88), Masons, Shriners, Rotary Club of Laurens (dist. 7750 gov. 1987-88), Phi Beta Kappa, Sigma Alpha Pi, Omicron Delta Kappa (past pres.), Kappa Sigma Kappa (past pres.), Kappa Alpha. Avocations: reading, jogging, yardwork. Home: 1200 Dixon Rd Laurens SC 29360-6813

DIXON, ARMENDIA PIERCE, school program administrator; b. Laurel, Miss., July 15, 1937; d. L.E. and Denothras (Pickens) Pierce; m. Harrison D. Dixon Jr., Aug. 28, 1971; 1 child, Harrison D. III BS in Edn., Jackson (Miss.) State U., 1960; postgrad., No. Ill. State U., 1965-66; MEd, Edinboro (Pa.) U., 1978; PhD, PhD, Kent State U., 1994. Cert. English and secondary edn., Miss. Tchr. English, libr. Laurel City Schs., 1962-67; tchr. English, dir. summer pre-sch. Erie (Pa.) Pub. Schs., 1967-72; tchr. English, drama, journalism, forensic coach Crawford Cen. Schs., Meadville, Pa., 1972-85, asst. prin., facilitator sch. improvement coun., 1985-89, coord. successful student partnership, 1988—; prin. Meadville Area Sr. High, 1993. Exec. dir. Meadville Latch-Key Program, 1985—; coord. Urban Tchrs. Project, Kent State U., adj. asst. prof., 1989—, dir. Prospective Tchrs. Program for Phi Delta Kappa; charter mem. Results chpt., Kent State U., 1990; dir. high sch. edn. Sch. dist. City of Erie, 1993-2001; instr. English Edinboro U. Pa.; dir. of high sch. edn., The Sch. Dist. of the City of Erie, Pa., 1993—. Fundraiser Cystic Fibrosis Found., Pitts., 1976. 79, 81, Sickle Cell Anemia, Erie, 1978-83; pres. Martin Luther King Jr. Scholarship Fund, Inc., 1979-89; bd. dirs. ARC, Erie, 1996—, Villa Marie Coll., Erie, 1995—, Internat. Inst., 1994—; mem. adv. bd. Am. Enterprise, Erie, 1993—; mem. alumni bd. dirs. Edinboro U. Alumni, 1997—. Mem. NAACP (pres. Meadville chpt. 1984—), Nat. Assn. Secondary Sch. Prins., Pa. Assn. Secondary Sch. Prins., Order Eastern Star (worthy matron), Navy Mothers, Rainbow III, Burres, Phi Delta Kappa, Alpha Kappa Alpha. Methodist. Avocations: collecting dolls, writing, gardening. Home: PO Box 561 Meadville PA 16335-0561 Office: Crawford Ctrl Schs 847 N Main St Meadville PA 16335-2655 E-mail: armendia@alltel.net.

DIXON, BARBARA BRUINEKOOL, provost; b. Sparta, Wis., June 14, 1943; MusB magna cum laude in Applied Piano, Mich. State U., 1966, MusM, 1969; MusD, U. Colo., 1991. Instr. vocal music K-12 Capac (Mich.) Cmty. Schs., 1970-71; tchr. dept. music Ctrl. Mich. U., Mt. Pleasant, 1971-89, assoc. dean coll. arts and scis., 1989-95, interim dean coll. arts and scis., 1995-97; provost, v.p. acad. affairs SUNY, Geneseo, 1997—2003; pres. Truman St. U., Kirksville, Mo., 2003—. Rep. acad. senate exec. bd., acad. senate liaison com., univ. acad. planning coun. Ctrl. Mich. U., 1986-89; dir. tchr. edn. search com., 1990, 95; chair faculty load equity study com., 1988-89, undergrad. curriculum com., 1992-93, formal hearing com. for grievance under senate rules, 1988-89; mem. profl. edn. coun., 1990-95, honors coun., 1989-94, task force on distance learning, 1992-93, piano search com., 1989, 90, 92, 95, music awards policy com., 1980-81, numerous others. One-woman performances include Kirtland C.C., Roscommon, Mich., 1986, Lansing (Mich.) C.C. Artist Series, 1987, Wurlitzer Hdqs., Holly Springs, Miss., 1989, Benefit for Cmty. Arts Coun., Pigeon, Mich., 1991, Beethoven Festival, Lansing, 1993, and others; accompanying performances include Backstage Recital Series, Jasper, Ind., 1984, Bridgeport (Mich.) Voice Symposium, 1986, Manistee (Mich.) Opera House, 1986, Saginaw (Mich.) Choral Soc., 1987, Alma (Mich.) Coll. Faculty, 1995, Black Forest Music Festival (Broadway rev.), Harbor Springs, Mich., 1995, and others. Active Art Reach Mid-Mich. (gallery com. 1995-96, chamber music com. 1995-97, fund drive com. 1996-97, bd. dirs. 1995-97, treas. 1996-97), Lions Club (chair spl. events com., bd. dirs. 1995-97), United Way (liaison to campus campaign); vol. Mich. Spl. Olympics. Mem. Mich. Music Tchrs. Assn. (bd. of certification 1976-79, 84-90, 95-97, chair 1996-97, pres. local chpt. 1991-92; chmn. collegiate activities 1979-81; mem. spkrs. bur. 1974-97, adjudicators bur. 1975-97, exec. bd. 1979-81, 96; rep. Mich. Youth Arts Festival bd. 1976-81, Mich. Alliance for Arts in Edn. 1988-89), Dalcroze Soc. Am., Delta Omicron, AAUW, Am. Assn. Higher Edn., Phi Beta Delta, Pi Kappa Lambda, Phi Kappa Phi Mortar Bd. Office: Truman St U 100 E Normal St MC200 Kirksville MO 63501 E-mail: dixon@truman.edu.*

DIXON, JOANNE ELAINE, music educator; b. Lancaster, Pa., July 3, 1944; d. William Russell and Anna Mary (Allen) D. B Music Edn., Westminster Choir Coll., Princeton, N.J., 1966; MEd, Trenton State Coll., 1982. Cert. music tchr., N.J. Music tchr. Warren (N.J.) Twp. Sch. Dist., 1966-67; vocal music tchr. Branchburg Twp. Sch. Dist., Somerville, N.J., 1967—, handbell dir., 1985—97. Music edn. handbell cons. Somerset County Dept. Edn., 1988-90; handbell dir., cons. Music Educator's Nat. Conf., Washington, 1990; N.J. rep. Com. for Handbells in Music Edn., Dayton, Ohio, 1990—. Handbell ringer First United Meth. Ch., Somerville, 1985—, mem. visions com., 1992-94, substitute handbell dir., 1992-2001; condr. N.J. Schs. Handbell Festival, 1995, 96. Recipient Excellence in Tchg. award State of N.J. Dept. Edn., 1988. Mem. Am. Guild English Handbell Ringers (area II N.J. rep. 1993-96, N.J. state rep. 1993-96, handbell workshop dir. 1993—), Branchburg Fedn. Tchrs. Democrat. Avocations: ringing handbells, painting, reading, stitchery. Office: Old York Sch 580 Old York Rd Somerville NJ 08876-3785 Home: 977 Robin Rd Hillsborough NJ 08844-4440

DIXON, LORI-RENEE, special education diagnostician; b. Chgo., Sept. 6, 1960; d. James Marshall and Alma (Taylor) Dixon. BEd, U. TEnn., 1982; MEd, Ga. State U., 1988. Cert. learning disabilities, interrelated spl. edn., curriculum and supervision, early childhood spl. edn. Behavior therapist Burwell Ctr., Carrollton, Ga., 1982-83; tchr. Atlanta Pub. Schs., 1983-89, diagnostician, 1989—; ednl. coord. Village of St. Joseph, Atlanta, 1994—. Pres., cons. Something Spl. Ctr., Conley, Ga., 1987—; pres. Exceptional Ctr., Conley, 1991—. Author: Inclusion: Metamorphosis or Masquerade?, 1994. Chairperson Commn. on Missions, Ben Hill United Meth. Ch., Atlanta, 1991—; comm. organizer Cynthia McKinney Campaign, Ga., 1992; bd. mem. Genesis Shelter/Atlanta Urban Ministries, Ga., 1990, 94—. Recipient Svc. awards Ga. Fedn. Tchrs., Atlanta, 1994, Ben Hill United Meth. Ch., Atlanta, 1986, 88, 90. Mem. Coun. Exceptional Children (rec. sec. 1989—), Children's Def. Fund, Assn. Child Care Cons., Nat. Alliance Black Sch. Educators, Atlanta Fedn. Tchrs. (exec. com., rec. sec. 1983—, Svc. award 1992), Ben Hill Toastmasters (pres. 1994—). Avocations: writing, cooking, lecturing, travel. Home: 1260 Regency Center Dr SW Atlanta GA 30331-2081

DIXON, MICHEL L. educational administrator; b. Norman, Okla., Oct. 2, 1945; s. Gerald R. and Erma M. (Fischer) D.; m. Mary Dee Brown, July 12, 1970 (div. 1995); children: Terri, Kelly, Kristi, Johanna. BA, Athens Coll., 1968, BE, 1972; MEd, U. Ala., 1976. Ins. adjustor Gen. Adjustment Bur., Birmingham, Ala., 1968-71; tchr. Adamsburg Sch., DeKalb County, Ala., 1971-72, Decatur (Ala.) City Schs., 1972-80; pubs. rep. Economy Pub. Co., Oklahoma City, 1980-82, Jostens Printing & Pub. Div., Mpls., 1982-84; course dir. AS100 Air Force ROTC, Maxwell AFB, Ala., 1984-85; pub. Civil Air Patrol News Aux. USAF, Maxwell AFB, 1985-86; tng. specialist, course mgr. Corps Engrs. Tng. div. U.S. Army, Huntsville, Ala., 1986-89; adminstr. Lawrence County High Sch., Moulton, Ala., 1989-90, Dept. Defense Dependent Sch., Nuernburg, Fed. Repub. Germany, 1990-91; dir. edn. programs in all western states U.S. Army 6th Recruiting BDE, Ft. Baker, Calif., 1991-94; prin. Round Valley H.S., Covelo, Calif., 1994-95; asst. prin. Calexico (Calif.) H.S., 1996-97, Capistrano Adult Sch., 1997-98; dir. cmty. edu. Mt. Brook (Ala.) Schs., Ala., 1998-1999; instrnl. sys. specialist in tech. specialized tng. program Pension Benefit Guaraty Corp., 1999—. With Pension Benefit Guaranty Corp., Washington, 1999—. Author: textbook AS 100, 1984; editor The Air Force Today, 1985; author, editor 3 slide briefings Aircraft and Weapons of AF, Vietnam, Korea, 1984-85; pub. Civil Air Patrol News, 1985-86. Test proctor Am. Mensa Soc. Presbyterian. Avocations: photography, electronics, country dancing, woodworking, bicycling. Home: 631 N Ripley St Alexandria VA 22304-2715 Office: Pension Benefit Guaranty Corp 1200 K St NW Fl 4 Washington DC 20005-4026 E-mail: dixon.mike@pbgc.gov.

DIXON, PAUL WILLIAM, psychology educator; b. N.Y.C., Aug. 1, 1936; s. Edward Everet and Esther (McCracken) D.; children: Michael H., Theodore K., Eleanor T., Aaron T. BA in English, Blackburn Coll., 1960; MA in Gen. Exptl. Psychology, U. Hawaii, 1963, PhD in Gen. Exptl. Psychology, 1966. Cert. tchr., Ill. Prof. psychology Coll. Arts and Scis. U. Hawaii, Hilo, 1965—, chmn. dept. liberal studies Coll. Arts and Scis., 1972-82, chmn. dept. psychology Coll. Arts and Scis., 1972-75. Vis. assoc. prof. psychology internat. divsn. Sophia U., Tokyo, 1971-72; vis. prof. dept. microbiology and immunology, UCLA, 1978-79; all-campus faculty pers. com. U. Hilo, 1967-68, pers. com. social scis. and edn. divsn., 1968-69, faculty senate, 1970-71, libr. com., 1970-71, acad. freedom, privilege and tenure com., 1973-74, dissertation com. dept. polit. sci., 1974-78, Rsch. Coun., 1977-78, chmn. all-coll. faculty pers. com., 1970, libr. com., 1973-74, liberal studies com., 1973-82. Contbr. numerous articles to psychol. and ednl. jours. Presenter, demonstrator Frequency Transfer Hearing Aid to Action Group for the Hearing Impaired, Honolulu, 1980, also to State Hearing and Visual Handicapped Svc., Hilo, Hawaii, 1980; chmn. commn. on anthropology of math. Internat. Union Anthrop. and Ethnol. Scis. Nominee Nobel prize in physics, 1986, 95, 98; NDEA fellow, 1963-66; aid grantee U. Hwaii Rsch. Coun., 1965-70, U. Hawaii Hilo Fund, 1970. Fellow Am. Anthrop. Assn., Soc. for Applied Anthropology; mem. AAAS, APA (travel grantee 1972), Internat. Congress of Anthrop. and Ethnographic Scis. Achievements include pioneering immunotherapy of cancer with levamisole, cancer vaccine, and pyrogen; life extension with immortalized autograft; generation of supernovae via high-energy physics experimentation; solution to Last Theorm of Fermat and Continuum Hypothesis of Gregor Cantor; research in linguistry. Home: PO Box 244 Volcano HI 96785-0244 Office: U Hawaii Coll Arts and Scis 200 W Kawili St Hilo HI 96720-4075

DIXON, RICHARD DEAN, lawyer, educator; b. Columbus, Ohio, Nov. 6, 1944; s. Dean A. and Katherine L. (Currier) D.; m. Kathleen A. Manfrass, June 17, 1967; children: Jennifer, Lindsay. BSEE, Ohio State U., 1967, MSEE, 1968; MBA, Fla. State U., 1972, JD, 1974. Bar: Fla. 1975, Colo. 1985, Mich. 1992, U.S. Dist. Ct. (mid. dist.) Fla., U.S. Dist. Ct. Colo. 1985, U.S. Patent and Trademanrk Office 1975. Telemetry sys. engr. Pan Am. World Airways, Patrick AFB, Fla., 1968-72; sole practice Melbourne and Orlando, Fla., 1975-80; sr. counsel Harris Corp., Melbourne, 1980-85; corp. counsel, dir. strategic and bus. planning Ford Microelectronics, Inc., Colorado Springs, Colo., 1985-89; mgr. strategic alliances electronics divsn. Ford Motor Co., Dearborn, Mich., 1989-90, assoc. counsel intellectual property, 1991-93, dep. chief patent counsel, 1994—2000; with Dixon Mediation Svcs., 2001—. Adj. prof. bus. law U. Cen. Fla., Cocoa, 1977, Fla. Inst. Tech., Melbourne, 1980-84. Cooper Industries Engring. scholar Ohio State U., 1964-67. Mem. ABA, Licensing Execs. Soc., Am. Intellectual Property Law Assn., Am. Corp. Counsel Assn., Sigma Iota Epsilon, Eta Kappa Nu, Phi Eta Sigma. Home and Office: 8162 Old Tramway Dr Melbourne FL 32940-2183

DIXON, ROBERT GENE, retired manufacturing engineering educator, retired mechanical engineering company executive; b. Clatskanie, Oreg., Feb. 15, 1934; s. Hobart Jay and Doris Marie D.; m. Janice Lee Taylor, Sept. 19, 1954; children: Linda Dixon Johnson, Jeffrey, David. AS in Indsl. Tech., Chemeketa C.C., 1978, related spl. courses, 1978-80. Cert. welder, Oreg. Journeyman machinist to asst. mgr. AB McLauchlan Co., Inc., 1956-69; supt. design, rsch., devel. engring. and prodn. Stevens Equipment Co., 1969-70; co-owner, operator Pioneer Machinery, 1970-72; supt. constrn. and repair Stayton Canning Co., 1972-73; mgr. Machinery div. Power Transmission, 1973-75; owner, operator Dixon Engring., Salem, Oreg., 1975-96, ret., 1996; instr., program chair mfg. engring. tech. Chemeketa C.C., 1975-92, tech. project coord. Oreg. Advanced Tech. Ctr., 1992-95; apptd. tech. project coord. Oreg. Advanced Tech. Consortium., 1995-96. With U.S. Navy, 1952-56. Named Tchr. of Yr., Chemeketa Deaf Program, 1978, Outstanding Instr. of Yr., Am. Tech. Edn. Assn., 1983. Mem. ASTD, Am. Prodn. and Inventory Control Soc., Am. Vocat. Assn. (Outstanding Tchr. award 1981), Oreg. Vocat. Assn. (Instr. of Yr. 1980; pres. 1984), Oreg. Vocat. Trade Tech. Assn. (Instr. of Yr. 1979; pres. 1981; Pres.'s Plaque 1982), Soc. Mfg. Engrs. (cert., sr., chmn. Oreg. sect. 1988—, internat. dir. nominating com. 1992, 95, Outstanding Internat. Faculty adv., 1989, 91), Am. Welding Soc., Am. Soc. Metals, Chemeketa Edn. Assn. (pres. 1979), Am Soc. Quality Control, Computer Automated Systems Assn., Phi Theta Kappa. Author: Benchwork, 1980, Procedure Manual for Team Approach for Vocational Education Special Needs Students, 1980, Smart Cam CNC/CAM Curriculum for Point Control Company; tech. reviewer textbook pubs., 1978—; designer, patentee fruit and berry stem remover. Home: 4242 Indigo St NE Salem OR 97305-2134

DIXON, RUTH ANN STOREY, education educator; b. Glen Ellyn, Ill., Dec. 1, 1933; d. Oscar Elmer and Grace Margaret (Raycroft) Storey; m. Richard Dixon, May 12, 1962; children: David Edward, Debra Ann Dixon Burton, Richard Cameron. BA, Wheaton (Ill.) Coll., 1955; MEd, U. Laverne, 1976; EdD, Ball State U., 1989. Tchr. Alliance Acad., Quito, Ecuador, 1957-62; instr. Judson Coll., Elgin, Ill., 1964-67, Ind. Vocat. Tech. Coll., Muncie, 1985-89; tchr., reading specialist Lexington (Ohio) Local Schs., 1971-85; assoc. prof. devel. edn., dir. Learning Ctr., Ind. Wesleyan U., Marion, from 1989. Presenter in field. Contbr. articles to profl. jours. Recipient award for innovative use of tech. in edn. Ameritech Found., 1992. Mem. ASCD, TESOL, Internat. Reading Assn., East Ctrl. Writing Ctr. Assn. (presenter), Midwest Coll. Learning Ctr. Assn. (presenter), North Ctrl. Reading Assn. (presenter), Nat. Assn. for Reading and Study Skills (presenter), Nat. Assn. for Devel. Edn. (presenter). Evangelical. Avocations: travel, reading, walking. Home: Alexandria, Ind. Died Mar. 19, 2001.

DIXON, STEVEN MICHAEL, university administrator; b. McMinnville, Oreg., Apr. 20, 1957; s. Leonard Ray and Margaret Elizabeth Dixon; m. Teresa Sue Mendenhall, Aug. 5, 1980; children: Alexa Michelle, Jason Scott, Kaylene Elizabeth. BA, Graceland Coll., 1979; MA, U. Mo., Kansas City, 1985. Exec. min. RLDS Ch., St. Joseph, Mo., 1983-84; asst. dean, coord. residence life Park Coll., Parkville, Mo., 1984-87; coord. residence life Oreg. Inst. of Tech., Klamath Falls, Oreg., 1987-88; asst. dean, dir. residence life Pacific U., 1988-90; asst. dean of students Simpson Coll., Indianola, Iowa, 1990-92, assoc. dean of students, 1992-97; dir. housing and residence life Eastern N.Mex. U., Portales, 1997—2001, dir. learning cmty., 2001—. Comprehensive tng. com. UMR-ACUHO, 1990-97, profl. devel. com., 1990-92; residential first yr. experience task force ACUHO-I, 1994-97; mem. profl. devel. com. AIMHO. Counselor to pastor RLDS Ch., Clovis, N.Mex., 1997—, ch. youth leader, 1981-84, 95—; adult vol. Boy Scouts Am., Indianola, 1995-97; mem. non-jud. human rels. com., 1994—, chair, 1996-97. Mem. Nat. Assn. of Student Pers. Adminstr. Avocations: travel, camping, photography, cross stitch, reading. Home: 1120 Concord Rd Clovis NM 88101-4402 Office: Enmu Station 34 Portales NM 88130 E-mail: steve.dixon@enmu.edu.

DIXON, VIRGINIA JULIA, parochial school computers educator; b. Pitts., Oct. 21, 1951; d. Julius Frederick and Regina Martha (Müller) Rosentreter; m. Lawrence N. Dixon, Aug. 2, 1975; children: Victoria, Matthew. BA, U. Pitts., 1973. Cert. German and secondary and elem. edn. tchr., Pa. Tchr. German North Allegheny Schs., Pitts., 1973-74, Baldwin-Whitehall Schs., Pitts., 1974-77; computer programmer Mgmt. Sci. Assocs., Pitts., 1977-78; tchr. German Upper Adams Schs., Biglerville, Pa., 1978-82; computer tchr. St. Francis Xavier Sch., Gettysburg, Pa., 1983—. Computer tchr. Annunciation B.V.M. Sch., McSherrystown, Pa., 1983, Immaculate Conception Sch., New Oxford, Pa., 1984-2001, St. Joseph Sch., Hanover, 1984—, Sacred Heart Sch., Hanover, 1988-95, chairperson computer com. Diocese of Harrisburg, Pa., 1985-95; bd. dirs. Lincoln Intermediate Unit 12, New Oxford, mem. adv. com., 1989. Asst. leader Girl Scouts Am., Gettysburg, 1987—91; asst. Cub Scout leader, 1995—99; mem. com. Boy Scout Troop 79, Gettysburg, 2001—. Recipient 3d pl., Computer Learning Contest, 1988. Mem.: AAUW (newsletter editor Gettysburg br.), Delone Cath. H.S. Music Assn. (rec. sec. 2002—03). Home: 41 Pin Oak Ln Gettysburg PA 17325-8523

DIXON-VESTAL, RUTH ELAINE, nurse, educator; b. Casablanca, French Morocco, Sept. 7, 1953; d. Calhoun Hamilton and Blanche Elaine (Lloyd-Jones) Vestal; m. Kenneth Richard Dixon, Oct. 18, 1980; 1 stepchild, Sarah Dixon; 1 child, Drew Morgan Dixon-Vestal. AA, El Camino Coll., 1974; student, San Jose State U., 1975-77; BA in Art History, U. Calif., San Diego, 1981; BSN, Norwich U., 1998. RN, cert. oper. rm. nurse. Oper. rm. staff nurse, mem. open heart team El Camino Hosp., 1974-77; critical care nurse San Jose (Calif.) Registry, 1977-78; clin. nurse ob-gyn, mem. liver transplant team Green Hosp. of Scripps Clinic, 1979-91; clin. edn. supr., clin. instr. nurse intern and extern programs Dartmouth Hitchcock Meml. Hosp., Lebanon, NH, 1991—, dean instrn. sch. surg. tech., 1991—. V.p. edn. Healthcare Enterprises, 1992—; presenter in field. Contbr. articles to med. jours. Vol. Operation Smile, 1994, COAD-3d World Surgery, 1978-81; vol. instr. for adult edn. in reading and ESOL, Hanover; asst. dir. compassion ministry Valley Bible Ch.. Mem. Assn. Oper. Rm. Nurses. Office: Dartmouth-Hitchcock Med Ctr 1 Medical Center Dr Lebanon NH 03756-0002

DIZNEY, ROBERT EDWARD, retired secondary education educator; b. Harlan, Ky., May 22, 1937; s. Robert Edward and E. Beatrice (Rowland) D. BA, Berea (Ky.) Coll., 1961; MEd, Miami U., Oxford, Ohio, 1987, postgrad., 1992—. Cert. tchr., Ohio. Tchr. Lockland (Ohio) City Schs., 1961-62, Deerfield Local Schs., Kings Mills, Ohio, 1962-70; tchr., chmn. dept. English Fairfield (Ohio) City Schs., 1971-94; adj. instr. Miami U., Oxford, Ohio, 1992—. Cons. writing Miami U. Ohio Writing Project, 1984—; co-dir. Miami U. Tchr.-Rsch. Network, 1992—; adj. instr. Miami U., 1992— Contbr. articles to profl. jours. Recipient Ashland Oil Tchr. Achievement award 1993, Hugh Morrison Scholarship Miami U., 1995. Mem. Nat. Coun. Tchrs. English, Internat. Soc. for Philos. Enquiry, Intertel, Mensa, Phi Delta Kappa. Democrat. Roman Catholic. Avocations: travel, photography, philately. Home: 5340 Dellbrook Dr Fairfield OH 45014-3308 Office: Miami U 363 McGuffey Hall Oxford OH 45056

DJERASSI, CARL, writer, retired chemistry educator; b. Vienna, Oct. 29, 1923; s. Samuel and Alice (Friedmann) Djerassi; m. Virginia Jeremiah (div. 1950); m. Norma Lundholm (div. 1976); children: Dale, Pamela(dec.); m. Diane W. Middlebrook, 1985. AB summa cum laude, Kenyon Coll., 1942, DSc (hon.), 1995; PhD, U. Wis., 1945; DSc (hon.), Nat. U. Mex., 1953, Fed. U., Rio de Janeiro, 1969, Worcester Poly. Inst., 1972, Wayne State U., 1974, Columbia U., 1975, Uppsala U., 1977, Coe Coll., 1978, U. Geneva, 1978, U. Ghent, 1985, U. Man., 1985, Adelphi U., 1993, U. S.C., 1995, Swiss Fed. Inst. Tech., 1995, U. Md.- Balt. County, 1997, Bulgarian Acad. Scis., 1998, U. Aberdeen, 2000, Polytechnic U., 2001. Rsch. chemist Ciba Pharm. Products, Inc., Summit, NJ, 1942—43, 1945—49; assoc. dir. rsch. Syntex, Mexico City, 1949—52, rsch. v.p., 1957—60; v.p. Syntex Labs., Palo Alto, Calif., 1960—62, Syntex Rsch., 1962—68, pres., 1968—72, Zoecon Corp., 1968—83, chmn. bd. dirs., 1968—86; prof. chemistry Wayne State U., 1952—59, Stanford (Calif.) U., 1959—2002. Founder Djerassi Resident Artists Program, Woodside, Calif. Author: The Futurist and Other Stories, 1988; author: (novels) Cantor's Dilemma, 1989, The Bourbaki Gambit, 1994, Marx Deceased, 1996, Menachem's Seed, 1997, NO, 1998; author: (poetry) The Clock Runs Backward, 1991; author: (drama) An Immaculate Misconception, 1998, BBC World Svc. Play of Week, 2000; author: (with Roald Hoffmann) (drama) Oxygen, 2001; author: (drama) BBC World Svc. Play of Week, 2001; author: (drama) Calculus, 2002, ICSI--a pedagogic wordplay for 2 voices, 2002; author: (drama) Ego, 2003; author: (with Pierre Laszlo) NO--a pedagogic wordplay for 3 voices, 2003; author: (autobiography) The Pill, Pygmy Chimps and Degas' Horse, 1992; author: (memoir) This Man's Pill, 2001; author: 9 other books; mem. editl. bd. Jour. Organic Chemistry, 1955—59, Tetrahedron, 1958—92, Steroids, 1963—2001, Procs. NAS, 1964—70, Jour. Am. Chem. Soc., 1966—75, Organic Mass Spectrometry, 1968—91, contbr. numerous articles to profl. jours., poems, memoirs and short stories to lit. publs. Named to Nat. Inventors Hall of Fame; recipient Intrasci. Rsch. Found. award, 1969, Freedman Patent award, Am. Inst. chemists, 1970, Chem. Pioneer award, 1973, Nat. medal of Sci. for first synthesis of oral contraceptive, 1973, Wolf prize in Chemistry, 1978, John and Samuel Bard award in Sci. and Medicine, 1983, Roussel prize, Paris, 1988, Discovers award, Pharm. Mfg. Assn., 1988, Nat. medal Tech. for new approaches to insect control, 1991, Nev. medal, 1992, Thomson medal, Internat. Soc. Mass Spectroscopy, 1994, Prince Mahidol award, Thailand, 1995, Sovereign Fund award, 1996, Austrian Cross of Honor First Class, 1999, Othmer Gold medal, Chem. Heritage Found., 2000, Author's prize, German Chem. Soc., 2001, Erasmus medal, Acad. Euopeae, 2003. Mem.: NAS (Indsl. Application of Sci. award 1990), Bulgarian Acad. Scis. (fgn. mem.), Mex. Acad. Scis., Brazilian Acad. Scis., Royal Swedish Acad. Engring. (fgn. mem.), Royal Swedish Acad. Scis. (fgn. mem.), German Acad. Leopoldina, Am. Acad. Arts and Scis., Royal Soc. Chemistry (hon. fellow, Centenary lectr. 1964), Am. Chem. Soc. (award pure chemistry 1958, Baekeland medal 1959, Fritzsche award 1960, award for creative invention 1973, award in chemistry of contemporary tech. problems 1983, Esselen award 1989, Priestley medal 1992, Gibbs medal 1997), NAS Inst. Medicine, Am. Acad. Pharm. Scis. (hon.), Sigma Xi (Proctor prize for sci. achievement 1998), Phi Beta Kappa, Phi Lambda Upsilon (hon.). Office: Stanford U Dept Chemistry Stanford CA 94305-5080 E-mail: djerassi@stanford.edu.

DLAB, VLASTIMIL, mathematics educator, researcher; b. Bzi, Czech Republic, Aug. 5, 1932; came to Can., 1968; s. Vlastimil Dlab and Anna (Stuchlikova) Dlabova; m. Zdenka Dvorakova, Apr. 27, 1959 (div.); children— Dagmar, Daniel Jan; m. Helena Briestenska, Dec. 18, 1985; children: Philip Adam, David Michael. R.N.Dr., Charles U., Prague, Czech Republic, 1956, C.Sc., 1959, Habilitation, 1962, DSc, 1966; PhD, U. Khartoum, Sudan, 1962. Rsch. fellow Czechoslovak Acad. Sci., Prague, 1956-57; lectr., sr. lectr. Charles U., Prague, 1957-59, reader, 1964-65; lectr., sr. lectr. U. Khartoum, Sudan, 1959-64; rsch. fellow, sr. rsch. fellow Inst. Advanced Studies, Australian Nat. U., Canberra, 1965-68; prof. math. Carleton U., Ottawa, Ont., Can., 1968-98; dir. Grad. Inst. Charles U., 1992-94; chmn. dept. Carleton U., Ottawa, Ont., Can., 1971-74, 94-97, disting. rsch. prof., 1998—, prof. emeritus; professorem hospitem Charles U., 1995—. Vis. prof. U. Paris VI, Brandeis U., U. Bonn, Monash U., U. Tsukuba, U. Sao Paulo, U. Stuttgart, U. Poitiers, Nat. U. Mex., U. Essen, U. Bielefeld, Hungarian Acad. Sci., Budapest, U. Warsaw, U. Normal Beijing, U. Vienna, UCLA, U. Va., Czechoslovak Acad. Sci., U. Trondheim, U. Paderborn, U. St. Petersburg, U. Reims, U. Sao Paulo, Osaka U., Yamaneashi U., Shinshu U., Eotvos U., Budapest, Charles U., Prague, U. Murcia, Spain, Erdos Rsch. Ctr., Budapest, Australian Nat. Univ., Canberra, Gadjah Mada U., Jogjakarta; presenter in field. Editor: procs. internat. confs., 1974, 1979; author: Representations of Valued Graphs, 1980, An Introduction to Diagrammatical Methods, 1981; editor: procs. internat. confs., 1984, 1987, 1990, 1992, 1993, 1994; author: Quasi-hereditary Algebras, 1994; editor: procs. internat. confs., 1996, Algebra and Representation Theory, 1998—, procs. internat. confs., 2002; contbr. numerous articles to profl. jours.; editor: Algebra and Discrete Mathematics, 2002—. Recipient Diploma of Honour Union Czechoslovak Mathematicians, 1962; Can. Council fellow, 1974; Japan Soc. Promotion of Sci. sr. rsch. fellow, 1981; sci. exchange grantee Nat. Sci. and Engring. Rsch. Coun. Can., 1978, 81, 83, 85, 88, 91. Fellow Royal Soc. Can. (convenor 1977-78, 80-81, coun. mem. 1980-81, editor-in-chief Comptes rendus mathematiques-Math. Reports 1997—); mem. Am. Math. Soc., Math. Assn. Am., Can. Math. Soc. (coun., chmn. rsch. com. 1973-77, editor Can. Jour. Math. 1988-93), European Math. Soc., London Math. Soc., Czech Math. Union. Roman Catholic. Avocations: sports, music. Home: 277 Sherwood Dr Ottawa ON Canada K1Y 3W3 Office: Carleton U Sch Math & Stat Math Dept Ottawa ON Canada K1S 5B6 E-mail: vdlab@math.carleton.ca.

DLABAL, PAUL WILLIAM, cardiologist, educator; b. Ellsworth, Kans., Dec. 18, 1949; BA summa cum laude, Kans. State U., 1971; MD, Johns Hopkins U., 1975. Diplomate Am. Bd. Internal Medicine, subsplty. in cardiovasc. disease; lic. Calif., Miss., Tex., Md. Intern in internal medicine Wilford Hall USAF Med. Ctr., Lackland AFB, Tex., 1975-76, resident in internal medicine, 1976-78, fellow in cardiology, 1978-80; staff cardiologist USAF Med. Ctr., Keesler AFB, Miss., 1980-82, chmn. pro tempore cardiology dept., 1981, dir. cardiac catheterization lab., 1981-82; staff cardiologist David Grant Med. Ctr., Travis AFB, Calif., 1982-83, chief of cardiology, 1983-84; pres., CEO Interventional Cardiovasc. Cons., PA, Austin, Tex., 1984-95; CEO Cardiovascular Rsch. Assoc. P.A., 1995—. Staff mem. Seton Med. Ctr., Austin, St. David's Comty. Hosp., Austin, Brackenridge Hosp., Austin, South Austin Med. Ctr., Austin, Highland Lakes Med. Ctr., Burnet, Tex.; mem. cons. staff Student Health Ctr., U. Tex., Austin; clin. instr. medicine Health Sci. Ctr. U. Tex., San Antonio, 1979-80; clin. asst. prof. medicine and cardiology Tulane U., New Orleans, 1980-82, U. Calif., San Francisco, 1982-84; mem. quality assurance com. South Austin Med. Ctr., 1986, trustee, 1988-92; mem. adv. com. St. David's Health and Fitness Ctr., 1985-86; mem. critical care com. St. David's Hosp., 1985-86; mem. coronary care unit com. Brackenridge Hosp., 1985-88, spl. procedures com., 1987-90, med. staff sec., 1991; mem. critical care com. South Austin Med. Ctr., 1988-90, chmn. 1990-95; founder Ctr. for Cardiac Rehab, 1992, mgr., 1992-95. Reviewer: Jour. AMA, 1979; contbr. articles to med. jours. Founder, pres. The Dlabal Found., 1995—. Maj. USAF, 1982—84. Recipient Physician's Recognition award AMA, 1979, 81, Best Paper award Am. Coll. Chest Physicians, 1980, Best Paper award ACP/Soc. Air Force Physicians, 1982; Kans. Rhodes scholar, 1970. Fellow ACP, Am. Soc. Coronary Angiography and Intervention, Am. Coll. Cardiology, Am. Fedn. Clin. Rsch., Am. Heart Assn. (fellow coun. on clin. cardiology 1992, bd. dirs. Travis County chpt. 1986-90, pres. Travis County chpt. 1991-92), Am. Soc. Coronary Angiography and Intervention, Am. Coll. Cardiology; mem. Soc. Air Force Physicians, Phi Beta Kappa, Phi Kappa Phi. Avocations: golf, music. Office: Tex Cardiovascular Cons 4007 James Casey St Ste A130 Austin TX 78745-3331

DOBBIN, EDMUND J. university administrator; b. Bklyn., 1935; BA in Philosophy, Villanova U., 1958; MA, Augustinian Coll., 1962; SDT, U. Louvain, Belgium, 1971. ordained priest Roman Cath. Ch., 1962. Tchr. math. and religion, prefect of students Malvern Prep. Sch., 1962-67; tchr. systematic theology Washington Theol. Union, 1971-87, asst. prof., assoc. prof.; assoc. prof. Villanova (Pa.) U., 1987—, pres., 1988—. Trustee Villanova U., 1979-87, Merrimack Coll., North Andover, Mass., 1971-89, chmn. bd., 1986-89; mem. provincial coun. Augustinian Province of St. Thomas of Villanova, 1982-89. Mem. Am. Acad. Religion, Cath. Theol. Soc. Am. Office: Villanova U Office of the President 800 E Lancaster Ave Villanova PA 19085-1603*

DOBBINS, DOLORES PAULINE, education educator, counselor; b. Saltville, Va., Aug. 1, 1943; d. William Ellis and Pauline Goldie (McNew) Farris; m. Ernest Freddrick Dobbins, Aug. 14, 1965; children: Michelle, Christopher. BA, Evangel Coll., 1965; MS, East Tenn. State U., 1971; Specialist Degree in Edn., U. So. Miss., 1979; EdD, Auburn U., 1989. Lic. profl. counselor; cert. sch. counselor, Miss.; nat. cert. counselor. Tchr. Springfield (Mo.) Schs., 1965-66, Bristol (Va.) Schs., 1966-68; sch. counselor Greene County Schs., Leakesville, Miss., 1968-93; adj. prof. U. So. Miss., Hattiesburg, 1990—96. Mem. Ladies Variety Club, Leakesville, !972—. Mem. NEA, Nat. Bd. Cert. Counselors, Am. Assn. Christian Counselors, Miss. Assn. Educators, Greene County Edn. Assn., Phi Kappa Phi. Avocations: sailing, reading, needlework, swimming, travel. Home: 6846 Jernigan Rd Leakesville MS 39451-0579

DOBBS, C. EDWARD, lawyer, educator; b. Richmond, Virginia, July 15, 1949; s. Glenn Wellington and Sarah Catherine (Judy) D.; m. J. Elisabeth (Kuypers), Aug. 29, 1981; children: Elisabeth Peyten, Edward Palmer, Virginia Whitney. BA, Davidson Coll., 1971; JD, Vanderbilt U., 1974. Bar: Ga., 1974, U.S. Dist. Ct. (no., mid. dists.) Ga., 1974, U.S. Ct. Appeals (11th cir. and 5th cir.), 1974, U.S. Supreme Ct., 2001. Ptnr. Kutak Rock, Atlanta, 1974-83, Parker, Hudson, Rainer & Dobbs, LLP, Atlanta, 1983—. Adj. prof., Emory Law Sch., Atlanta, 1987-92; mem. adv. bd., Atlanta Legal Aid Soc., 1980-82. Author: Reorganization Under Chapter 11 of the Bankruptcy Code, 1979, Enforcement of Security Interests in Personal Property, 1978. Bd. dir., trustee Trinity Sch., Inc., Atlanta, 1992-96; chmn. Ga. Fin. Lawyers Conf., 1995—; bd. dir. Comm. Fin. Assn. Edn. Found., 1996—. Fellow Am. Coll. Bankruptcy, Ga. Bar Found., Am. Coll. Comml. Fin. Laws (bd. regents 1990—, pres. 1996-98); mem. ABA (chmn. young lawyers divsn. 1981-82), Am. Arbitration Assn., Southeastern Bankruptcy Law Inst. (bd. dirs., chmn. 1992-93), Order of Coif, Omicron Delta Kappa, Alpha Psi Omega. Presbyterian. Avocations: golf, tennis, fishing, trees. Office: Parker Hudson Rainer and Dobbs LLP 1500 Marquis Two Tower 285 Peachtree Center Ave NE Atlanta GA 30303-1229 E-mail: edobbs@phrd.com.

DOBELLE, EVAN SAMUEL, academic administrator; b. Washington, Apr. 22, 1945; s. Martin and Lillian (Mendelsohn) Dobelle; m. Edith Huntington Kit, June 7, 1970; 1 child, Harry Huntington. BA, U. Mass., 1983, MEd, 1970, EdD, 1987; MPA, Harvard U., 1984. Exec. asst. U.S. Senator Edward Brooke, Boston, 1971—73; mayor City of Pittsfield, 1973—76; commr. environ. mgmt. State of Mass., Boston, 1976—77; chief protocol U.S., Washington, 1977—78; treas. Dem. Nat. Com., 1978—79, dep. chair, 1980—81; chairman Carter-Mondale Presdl. Com., 1979—80; v.p. Bear Stearns and Co., N.Y.C., 1984—87; pres. Middlesex Cmty. Coll., Mass., 1987—90; chancellor City Coll. San Francisco, 1991—; pres. Trinity College, Hartford, Conn., 1995—2001, U. Hawaii, Honolulu, 2002—. Bd. dirs. Jacobs Pillow Dance Festival, Conn. Pub. TV; bd. govs. Jewish Fedn., Hartford, Conn. Jewish. Avocations: golf, swimming, reading, travel, history. Office: Univ Hawaii Office of the President 2444 Dule St Bachman Hall 202 Honolulu HI 96822

DOBERSTEIN, AUDREY K. college president; b. June 12, 1932; m. Stephen C. Doberstein; children: Carole, Stephen, Anne, Curt. BS, East Stroudsburg State Coll., 1953; M.Ed., U. Del., 1957; Ed.D., U. Pa., 1982. Exec. dir. Title I ESEA, Del. Dept. Public Instrn., 1965-69; pres. Ednl. Research and Services, Inc., 1969-79; asso. prof. Cheyney State Coll., 1969-79; pres. Wilmington Coll., New Castle, Del., 1979—. Bd. dirs. Blue Cross Blue Shield Del., Mellon Bank, Conectiv, Inc. Mem. NEA, Am. Assn. Higher Edn., AAUW, Phi Delta Kappa. Office: Wilmington Coll Office of the President 320 Dupont Hwy New Castle DE 19720

DOBIN, HANK (HOWARD), academic administrator, English language and literature educator; b. N.Y.C., Oct. 23, 1952; s. Jerome Dobin and Sydell (Lewis) Marcus; m. Bonnie Bernstein, June 20, 1976; children: Daniel, Noah. BA summa cum laude, Yale U., 1974; PhD, Stanford U., 1982. Tchr. New Rochelle (N.Y.) H.S., 1974-76; asst. prof. dept. English U. Md., College Park, 1983-89, assoc. prof. dept. English, 1989-96, assoc. chair dept. English, 1990-96, acting chair dept. English, 1993; chair College Park (Md.) Senate, 1993-94; assoc. dean of the Coll. Princeton U., 1996—. Cons. MBA Program, U. Md., College Park, 1984-96. Author: Merlin's Disciples, 1990. Mem. MLA, Shakespeare Assn. of Am. Office: Princeton U Office of the Dean of Coll 403 W College Princeton NJ 08544-0001 E-mail: hdobin@princeton.edu.

DOBIS, JOAN PAULINE, education administrator; b. S.I., N.Y., Sept. 11, 1944; d. Victor Raymond and Rosanna Elizabeth (Dandignac) Mazza; m. Robert Joseph Dobis, Dec. 21, 1968. BA in History, Notre Dame Coll., S.I., 1966; MS in Advanced Secondary Edn. and Social Studies, Wagner Coll., 1968; profl. diploma in ednl. adminstrn. supervision, Fordham U., 1979, postgrad. Cert. adminstr. and supr. K-12, social studies and math. tchr. K-12, elem., intermediate and jr. high sch. asst. prin., elem., intermediate and junior high sch. prin., N.Y. Tchr. Prall Intermediate Sch., Staten Island, 1966-98, administrv. asst., 1977-82; coord. social studies Dist. 31, Staten Island, NY, 1998—2003; ret., 2003. Mem. S.I. Hist. Soc., 1968-78, Friends of Down's Syndrome Found., S.I., 1978—, Sister Helen Flynn Scholarship Com., S.I., 1981—, Friends Seaview Hosp. and Home, S.I., 1984—, Friends S.I. Coll., 1979—. Recipient St. John's U. Pietas medal, 1991; scholar N.Y. State Bd. Regents, 1962, Can. Consulate St. Lawrence U., 1987, Internat. Brotherhood Teamsters U. Calif., 1988, Nat. Geog. Soc. Geography Edn. Program SUNY, Binghamton, 1989, Women in History Program, N.Y. State Coun. for the Humanities, Albany, 1992, Immigration Program, Bard Coll., 1999; Impact II grantee N.Y.C. Bd. Edn., 1992, 98. Mem. ASCD, Nat. Coun. Social Studies, N.Y. State Coun. Social Studies, N.Y.C. Coun. Social Studies, S.I. Coun. Social Studies, United Fedn. Tchrs., Am. Fedn. Tchrs., N.Y. State Hist. Soc., Notre Dame Coll. Alumnae Assn. (regent 1978-80, pres. 1982-84), St. John's U. Alumni Fedn. (del. 1980-88, sec. exec. bd. 1988-90, chmn. bd. 1990-94), Phi Delta Kappa (co-founder S.I. chpt., pres. 1985-87, other offices, Tchr. of Yr. award Fordham U. 1993, named Disting. Kappan 1994, Tchr. of Yr. award S.I. chpt. 1998, Kappan of Decade, 1999). Republican. Roman Catholic. Home: 174 Bertha Pl Staten Island NY 10301-3807

DOBOS, SISTER MARION, parochial school educator; b. McKeesport, Pa., Oct. 14, 1940; BS in Edn., Youngstown State U., 1969; MA in Religious Edn., Dayton U., 1981. Tchr. Chgo. Archdiocese Cath. Schs., 1961-64, Queen of Peace Sch., Wichita Falls, Tex., 1964-65, St. Theresa Sch., Pitts., 1975-76, Sts. Peter and Paul Sch., Warren, Ohio, 1965-75, 77-86, St. Anne Ukranian Sch., Austintown, Ohio, 1986-87, Blossom Montessori Sch., Warren, 1987-88, Sts. Peter and Paul Sch., 1988—. Adminstr. Benedictine Early Learning Ctr. Nursing Sch. & Day Care, Warren, 1989-95, Archdiocesan dir. religious edn., 1996—; formation dir. Benedictine Sisters, Warren, 1979-89; dir. religious edn. Sts. Peter and Paul Sch., Byzantine Archdiocese Pitts., 1996. Mem. Nat. Cath. Educators Assn., Ohio Cath. Educators Assn., Assn. for Edn. of Young Children, Greek Cath. Union, Jednota Cath. Lodge, Ohio Cosmetology. Democrat. Avocations: aerobics, crafts, walking. Home: 3605 Perrysville Ave Pittsburgh PA 15214-2229 Office: Office of Religious Edn 3605 Perrysville Ave Pittsburgh PA 15214-2229

DOBRAUC, PATRICIA CECILIA, school board executive; b. Custer, Wis., Mar. 16, 1941; d. Matthew and Clara (Brychel) Schulist; m. Antone John Dobrauc, Mar. 1, 1975; children: Christian, Mary, Joy, Rachel. BS, Wis. State U., Stevens Point, 1971; MS, Pittsburg (Kans.) State U., 1989, EdS, 1994. Cert. tchr. cmty. coll. and higher edn. Tchr. and team leader Rib Mountain Sch., Wausau, Wis., 1970-74; tchr. St. Mary's Sch., Pittsburg, 1975-76; libr./english tchr. St. Mary's Colgan High Sch. Pres. and v.p. St. Mary's Sch. Bd., Pittsburg, 1986-88; mem. sch. bd. St. Mary's/Colgan Schs., Pittsburg, 1992—; sec. St. Mary's Home and Sch., 1991-92; mem. parish coun. Our Lady of Lourdes, Pittsburg, 1987-89; sec. St. Mary's Colgan Fine Arts Com., 1996-99. Recipient outstanding contbn. to Cath. edn. award, 1995. Mem. PEO (chaplain 1993-94), Phi Kappa Phi, Phi Delta Kappa. Home: 3006 Woodgate Dr Pittsburg KS 66762-7002

DOBRIANSKY, LEV EUGENE, economist, educator, diplomat; b. N.Y.C., Nov. 9, 1918; s. John and Eugenia (Greshchuk) D.; m. Julia Kusy, June 29, 1946; children: Larisa Eugenia, Paula Jon. BS (Charles Hayden Meml. scholar), NYU, 1941, MA, 1943, Hirshland polit. sci. fellow, 1943-44, PhD, 1951; LLD, Free Ukrainian U. at U. Munich, Germany, 1952. Faculty NYU, 1942-48; from asst. prof. econs. to prof. Georgetown U., 1948-86; prof. emeritus, 1986—; chmn. dept. Georgetown U., 1953-54; exec. mem. Inst. Ethnic Studies, 1957-65; dir. Inst. Comparative Econ. and Polit. Systems, 1970-86; grad. faculty Nat. War Coll., 1957-58; U.S. ambassador to Bahamas, 1982-86; pres. Global Economic Action Inst., 1987-92; chmn. Victims of Communism Meml. Found., Inc., 1994—. Lectr. on Soviet Union, Communism, U.S. Fgn. Policy; chmn. Nat. Captive Nations Com., Inc., 1959—; pres. Ukrainian Congress Com. Am., 1949-82, Am. Coun. for World Freedom, 1976-79; mem. Economists Nat. Com. on Monetary Policy; strategy staff Am. Security Coun., 1962-70; econs. editor Washington Report; mem. Pres.'s Commn. on Population, 1974-75; cons. Corpus Instrumentation, Kreber Found., Dept. State, 1971-75, USIA, 1971-74; mem. Am. Com. to Aid Katanga Freedom Fighters, Emergency Com. Chinese Refugees; Internat. mem. Pacific Rim Cmty. Inst., 1992-96; hon. pres. Ukrainian Congress com. Am., 1992—. Author: A Philosophico-Economic Critique of Thorstein Veblen, 1943, The Social Philosophical System of Thorstein Veblen, 1950, Free Trade Ideal, 1954, Communist Takeover of Non-Russian Nations in USSR, 1954, Veblenism: A New Critique, 1957, Captive Nations Week Resolution, 1959, Shevchenko Statue Resolution, 1960, Vulnerabilities of USSR, 1963, The Vulnerable Russians, 1967, U.S.A. and the Soviet Myth, 1971; co-author: The Great Pretense, 1956, The Crimes of Khrushchev, 1959, Decisions for a Better America, 1960, Nations, Peoples, and Countries in the USSR, 1964; pub.: Revista Americana, 1977; editor: Europe's Freedom Fighter: Taras Shevchenko, 1960, Tenth Anniversary of the Captive Nations Week Resolution, 1969, The Bicentennial Salute to the Captive Nations, 1977, Twentieth Observance and Anniversary of Captive Nations Week, 1980; assoc. editor: (1946-62) Ukrainian Quar., chmn. editorial bd., 1962-94; contbr.: Peace and Freedom Through Cold War Victory, 1964, Nationalism in the USSR and Eastern Europe, 1977, Ukraine in a Changing World, 1978; contbr. articles to profl. jours. Planning mem. Freedom Studies Center, Boston; asst. sec. Republican Nat. Conv., 1952; adviser Rep. Nat. Com., 1956; mem. Com. on Program and Progress of Rep. Party, 1959; asst. to chmn. Rep. Nat. Conv., 1964; vice chmn. nationalities div. Rep. Nat. Com., 1964; sr. adviser United Citizens for Nixon-Agnew, 1968; exec. mem. ethnic div. Com. to Reelect the Pres., 1972; advisor to Gov. Reagan, 1980; issues dir. Republican Nat. Com., 1980; chmn. Ukrainian Catholic Studies Found., 1970-73; bd. govs. Charles Edison Youth Fund, 1976-87; mem. expert adv. bd. NBC, Washington, 1977-80. chmn. Victims of Communism Meml. Found. Inc. Lt. col. (res.) 352d Mil. Govt. Civil Affairs 1958; col. U.S. Army Res., 1966. Recipient Freedoms Found. award, 1961, 73; Shevchenko Freedom award Shevchenko Meml. Com., 1964; Shevchenko Sci. Soc. medal, 1965; Hungarian Freedom Fighters' Freedom award, 1965; Latvian Pro Merito medal, 1968; Freedom Acad. award Korea, 1969; Wisdom award of honor Calif., 1970; named Outstanding Am. Educator, 1973; decorated M.S.M., 1973; Georgetown U. Centennial medal of honor, 1982; Ellis Island medal of honor, 1986; Thomas C. Corcoran award, 1987. Mem. Free World Forum (exec. com.), Citizens for Democracy, Acad. Polit. Sci., Nat. Acad. Econs. and Polit. Sci., AAUP, Am. Acad. Polit. and Social Sci., Am., Cath. econ. assns., Am. Finance Assn., Nat. Soc. Study Edn., Shevchenko Sci. Soc., U.S. Global Strategy Council, Social List of Washington, Council Am. Ambassadors, NYU Alumni Assn., Georgetown U. Alumni Assn. (hon.), Reagan Alumni Assn., Internat. Cultural Soc. Korea (hon.), Am. Legion, Res. Officers Assn., Nat. War Coll. Alumni Assn., University Club of Washington (hon.), Capitol Hill Club, Internat. Club, Gold Key Soc., Beta Gamma Sigma, Delta Sigma Pi.

DOBSON, ANDREA CAROLE, secondary school educator; b. Spokane, Wash., Sept. 25, 1956; d. Carl Elvin and Neysa Carole Dobson. AA, Spokane Falls C.C., 1977; BA in Edn., Ea. Wash. U., 1979; EdM, Wash. State U., 1990. Cert. tchr. K-12, Wash. Tchr. history and chemistry Grand Coulee (Wash.) Dam Dist., 1979-81, Lind (Wash.) Sch. Dist., 1981-85; tchr. sci. and history Granger (Wash.) Sch. Dist., 1986-87; tchr. sci. Sunnyside (Wash.) Sch. Dist., 1985-94; tchr. sci. and coach Sunnyside Christian H.S., 1994-97, volleyball coach, 1998—; tchr. sci. Kiona-Benton Mid. Sch., 1997—. Homebase coord., food drive coord., drug and alcohol awareness coord. Harrison Mid. Sch. Sunnyside, volleyball coach, 1979—; tchr. history, Reardan, Wash., volleyball, basketball, track and tennis coach. Dir. Evergreen Girls State, Ellensburg, Wash., 1994—, counselor, 1980—; mem. staff Girls Nat. Govt., 1998—2003. Named B-class volleyball Coach of Yr., 1984, winner, volleyball state championship, 1984. Mem. Wash. Edn. Assn., Nat. Fed. High Sch. Coaches, Sci. Tchrs. Wash., wash. Coaches Assn., Am. Legion Aux. (dir. Evergreen Girls State 1994—, exec. com. 1981—), NAFE. Lutheran. Avocations: sports, travel, photography, kite flying. Office: Kiona Benton Sch Dist Benton City WA 99320

DOBSON, JAMES GORDON, JR., cardiovascular physiologist, scientist, educator; b. Waterbury, Conn., Jan. 23, 1942; s. James Gordon and Mildred (Stinson) D.; m. Susan Bentley Jones, Aug. 28, 1971; 1 child, Sarah Bentley. BS in Biology and Chemistry, Cen. Conn. State U., 1965; MA in Biology, Wesleyan U., Middletown, Conn., 1967; PhD in Physiology, U. Va., 1971. NIH postdoctoral fellow U. Calif., San Diego, 1971, asst. rsch. pharmacologist, 1971-73; from asst. prof. to assoc. prof. U. Mass., Worcester, 1974-1985, prof. physiology, 1985—, prof. medicine, 1989—; dir., cellular and molecular physiology grad. program U. Mass. Med. Ctr., Worcester, 1982—. Editl. referee profl. jours., 1975-; cons. NIH, 1978-, Dept. Vet. Affairs merit rev. bd., 1990-94. Mem. editl. bd. Am. Jour. Physiology; contbr. over 10 chpts. to books in field; contbr. over 130 articles to profl. jours.; patentee in field. Active with Citizens Adv. Group, Shrewsbury, Mass.; bd. dirs. Wesley United Meth. Ch., adminstrv. bd., 1975-2000, chmn. fin., 1988-92, chmn. staff-parish rels., 1982-94, Emerging Ministries, 1995-97. Recipient rsch. career devel. award NIH 1980, rsch. merit award Nat. Heart, Lung, and Blood Inst. 1987; numerous rsch. grants. Mem. Am. Heart Assn. (mem. peer rsch. com. 1989-92, mem. rsch. com. 1992-95, vice chmn. peer rev. com. 1994-97, bd. dirs. Mass. affiliate 1995-2001, nat. mem. cell transport and metabolism study com. 1994-97, chair Advocacy for Mass. 1998-), Am. Physiol. Soc. (membership com. 1989-92, awards com. 2002-, editl. bd., 1992-), Biophys. Soc., Internat. Soc. Heart Rsch. Achievements include research involving contractility of the mammalian myocardium, antiadrenergic actions of adenosine, biochemical regulation of performance and metabolism of the healthy, aging and diseased heart. Office: U Mass Med Sch Dept Physiology 55 Lake Ave N Worcester MA 01655-0002

DOBY, JANICE KAY, education educator, science educator; b. Hamlet, N.C., Dec. 4, 1953; d. James Robert and Marguerite (Greene) D. B Music Edn., Lee Coll., Cleveland, Tenn., 1978; MS in Elem. Edn., Nova U., 1992; EdS, Fla. Atlantic U., 1996, EdD, 1997. Elem. tchr. Palm Springs (Fla.) Bapt. Sch., 1981-82; tchr. music, chmn. fine arts Mil. Trail Elem. Sch., West Palm Beach, Fla., 1982-89; tchr. music Seminole Trails Elem. Sch., West Palm Beach, 1989—; sci. tchr. Christa McAuliffe Mid. Sch., 1997; asst. prof. sci. edn. U. S.C., Spartanburg, 1997—. Tchr. music potentially gifted minority student project Palm Beach County Schs., West Palm Beach, summer 1989; mem. adj. faculty elem. and mid. sch. sci. methods Fla. Atlantic U., Boca Raton, 1994-97, rsch. asst. 1995-97; math./sci. specialist West Rivera Math./Sci./Tech. Magnet Sch., 1995-97; dir. music Marantha Ch., Palm Beach Gardens, Fla., Family Worship Ctr., West Palm Beach, Bethel Temple Assembly of God, Lake Worth, Fla.; regional teen talent adjudicator Assemblies of God, Lake Worth, 1982-85; state teen talent adjudicator Ch. of God, Palm Beach Gardens, 1990; judge Local and Dist. Science and Engring. Fairs, 1995-97. Contbg. author, editor: IDEAS Handbook for Teachers, 1995. Recipient citation Palm Beach County Sheriff's Dept., 1989. Mem. ASCD, Fla. Ednl. Rsch. Assn., Fla. Assn. Sci. Tchrs., Nat. Assn. for Rsch. in Sci. Teaching, Higher Edn. Consortium., S.C. Sci. Coun., Kappa Delta Pi. Avocations: reading, research in cognitive science and instructional design, computers.

DOCKHORN, ROBERT JOHN, physician, educator; b. Goodland, Kans., Oct. 9, 1934; s. Charles George and Dorotha Mae (Horton) D.; m. Beverly Ann Wilke, June 15, 1957; children: David, Douglas, Deborah. AB, U. Kans., 1956, MD, 1960. Diplomate Am. Bd. Pediat. Intern Naval Hosp., San Diego, 1960-61, resident in pediat. Oakland, Calif., 1963-65; resident in pediat. allergy and immunology U. Kans. Med. Ctr., 1967-69, adj. asst. prof. pediat., 1969—; resident in pediat. allergy and immunology Children's Mercy Hosp., Kansas City, Mo., 1967-69, chief divsn., 1969-83, practice medicine specializing in allergy and immunology Prairie Village, Kans., 1969-94, U. Mo. Med. Sch., Prairie Village, Kans., 1969-94; pres. Internat. Med. Tech. Cons., Inc., Kansas City, 1979—; with D&B Med. Consulting, LLC, Overland Park, Kans., 1999—. Pres. I.M.T.C.I. (Internat. Med. Tech. Cons., Inc.), Kansas City, 1979-99; founder, CEO Internat. Med. Tech. Cons., Inc., Lenexa, Kans., subs. Immuno-Allergy Tech. Cons., Inc., Clin. Rsch. Cons., Inc. Contbr. articles to med. jours.; co-editor: Allergy and Immunology in Children, 1973. Fellow Am. Acad. Pediatrics, Am. Coll. Allergists (bd. regents 1976—, v.p. 1978-79, pres. 1981-82), Am. Assn. Cert. Allergists (pres. 1991—), Am. Acad. Allergy; mem. AMA, Kans. Med. Soc., Johnson County Med. Soc., Kans. Allergy Soc. (pres. 1976-77), Mo. Allergy Soc. (sec. 1975-76), Joint Coun. Socio-Econs. of Allergy (bd. dirs. 1976—, pres. 1978-79). Home: 8510 Delmar Ln Shawnee Mission KS 66207-1926 Office: D&B Med Consulting LLC 8220 Travis St Ste 101 Overland Park KS 66204-3963 Fax: 913-649-0464.

DOCTORS, SAMUEL ISAAC, management educator, researcher director; b. Phila., July 1, 1936; s. Abraham and Celia (Lakoff) D.; m. Meredith Cahn, 1988; 1 child, Olga; children from previous marriages: Eric, Rachel, Rebecca. BS, U. Miami, 1956, JD, Harvard U., 1967, DBA, 1969. Bar: Mass. 1967. Assoc. engr. Westinghouse Electric Corp., Balt., 1956-58; sr. math. analyst AC Sparkplug div. Gen. Motors, El Segundo, Calif., 1958-59; sr. devel. engr., work dir. aero. div. Honeywell, St. Petersburg, Fla., 1961-64; cons. tech., mgmt., econs. various orgns., 1968-81; project mgr. N. Lawndale Econ. Devel. Corp. & NUGSM, 1971-73; assoc. prof. Northwestern U., Evanston, Ill., 1969-73; faculty advisor, dir. Mgmt. Asst. Clinic, Northwestern U., Chgo., 1969-73; prof. U. Pitts., 1974-84, co-prin. investigator, project monitor, 1977-79; project mgr. Allegheny County Energy Study, 1977; prin. investigator Urban Tech. System Evaluation, NSF, 1978-81, Small Bus. Adminstrn. and Dept. Energy, Washington, 1979-80; prof. adminstrn. Calif. State U., Hayward, 1982—, founder, dir. Ctr. for Bus. & Environ. Studies, 1991—; founder, dir. Calif. Urban Environ. Rsch. and Edn. Ctr., Region IX EPA Environ. Fin. Ctr.; CEO Advancing Calif.'s Emerging Techs., 1995. Lectr. Harvard U. Bus. Sch., 1968-69; chmn. R & D workshop task force on minority bus. edn. and tng. U.S. Office Edn., 1972-73; bus. advisor David Community Devel. Corp., Ky., 1973-76; bd. dirs. Energy Policy Inst., U. Pitts., 1979-81; vis. prof. U. Calif. Sch. Bus., Berkeley, 1980-82; tech. advisor Western Gerontol. Soc., 1984—; prof. bus. adminstrn. Calif. State U. Hayward, 1983—; mem. steering com. Harvard Bus. Sch. Community Ptnrs dir. Ctr. Bus. & Environ. Studies, Calif. State U., Hayward, 1991—, Urban Environ. Rsch. & Edn. Ctr., 1993. Author books (9) and over 40 articles on management. V.p., bd. dirs. Sr. Citizens Service Corp., Pitts.; chairperson Energy Outlook '78, Allegheny County Air Pollution Control Bd. Sponsoring Agy., San Francisco Community Recyclers. Mem. ABA, Am. Polit. Sci. Assn., Am. Econ. Assn., Nat. Assn. Community Devel., AAAS, Nat. Council Small Bus. Devel., Nat. Acad. Mgmt. (sounding bd. manpower div.), Pitts. C. of C. Office: Calif State U Hayward Mgmt Scis Dept Hayward CA 94542

DODD, SYLVIA BLISS, special education educator; b. Ft. Worth, July 21, 1939; d. William Solomon and Sylvia Bliss (Means) Fisher; m. Melvin Joe Dodd, Sept. 4, 1959 (div. 1967); children: Lisa Dawn, Marcus Jay, Chadwick Scott. BA, Tex. Wesleyan Coll., Ft. Worth, 1960; MEd, Tex. Christian U., Ft. Worth, 1976. Tchr. Castleberry Ind. Sch. Dist., Ft. Worth, 1960-62, Hurst-Euless-Bedford (Tex.) Ind. Sch. Dist., 1967-69, dir. spl. edn., 1969-94. Instr. Tex. Wesleyan U., Ft. Worth, 1978, Ft. Worth, 1994—, coord. tchr. cert., 1996—2001; instr. Tex. Christian U., Ft. Worth, 1980. Mem. adminstrv. bd. 1st United Meth. Ch., Ft. Worth, 1990—93, 1995—; lay leader West Ft. Worth Dist. United Meth. Ch., 1992—96, Ctrl. Tex. Conf., United Meth. Ch., 2000—; bd. dirs. Mental Health Assn., Ft. Worth, 1983—88, 1991—95, March of Dimes, Mid Cities, Tex., 1990, United Cmty. Ctrs., 1989—97, pres., 1994—95; bd. dirs. So. Meth. U. Campus Ministry, 1992—97, Tex. Meth. Found., 2000—, Bedford Hist. Found., 2002—. Named Conf. Chairperson of Yr. Nat. Health and Welfare Ministries, 1981; recipient Outstanding Woman award Tex. Wesleyan U., 1991, Disting. Educator award, 1991, Key City, Ft. Worth, 1998. Mem. AAUP, Mental Health Assn. (pres. 1979-80), Nat. Coun. Exceptional Children, Tex. Coun. Adminstrs. Spl. Edn. (Hall of Honor award 1991, pres. 1975-76). Democrat. Methodist. Avocations: music, art, drama, Tex. history, walking. Home: 829 Timberhill Dr Hurst TX 76053-4240

DODDS, LINDA CAROL, special education educator; b. Tucson, June 2, 1957; d. George A. and Bette R. (Bell) D. AA, U. Md., 1979; BA, Tex. Tech U., 1982; MBA, Our Lady of the Lake U., 1986, MEd, 2001. Svc. rep. USAA, San Antonio, 1982-84; portfolio asst. USAA-IMCO, San Antonio, 1984-85; sr. rep. USAA, San Antonio, 1985-86, asst. area mgr. Tampa, Fla., 1986-88, area mgr., 1988-92, dist. mgr., 1992-97, San Antonio, 1997-98; reading resource tchr. Boerne (Tex.) Ind. Sch. Dist., 1999—, head spl. edn. dept., 2000—02; resource tchr. N.E. Ind. Sch. Dist., 2002—. Treas. Forest Hills Homeowners Assn., Tampa, 1992-93; mem. Tex. Fedn. Rep. Women, San Antonio, 1985; co-chair United Way, 1995-96; active USAA Vol. Corp., Tampa, 1989—. Mem. Soc. CPCU, Delta Mu Delta, Sigma Iota Epsilon. E-mail: doddsl@boerne-isd.net.

DODGE, CALVERT RENAUL, education and training executive, author, educator; b. Chgo., Apr. 15, 1921; s. Lawrence Frank and Anna Rose (Manke) D.; m. Mary Irene Dodge, Apr. 2, 1951; children: Lawrence Wesley, Laura Irene, Valarie Le, James Calvert. BS in Agrl. Sci., U. Wyo., 1947, MA in Sociology, 1957; cert., Air U., Montgomery Ala., 1968; PhD in Speech Comm., U. Denver, 1971; BA in Video and Film Prodn., U. Md., 1998. Cert. supr. edn., Calif.; masters lic. 25 ton ships USCG; cert. USAF Parachute Jump Sch., 1969. Dir. youth, edn. activities Standard Oil Ind. AMOCO, Chgo., 1948-51, dir. employee, pub. rels., 1951-55; pres. Western Concrete Products Inc., Laramie, Wyo., 1955-64; dir. state tng. ctr. State of Colo. Youth Svcs., Denver, 1964-71; dir. rsch. Ky. Manpower Devel. Commn., Louisville, 1971-76; instr. U. Ky., 1974-75; assoc. prof. U. D.C., Washington, 1979-82; instr. in Japan, Korea, Turkey, Germany, Spain and U.K. U. Md., 1976-82; exec. v.p. Human Equations, Inc., Balt., 1982-87; pres. Dodge-Marck Assocs., Balt., 1991—. Pres. Seminars at Sea, Balt., 1983-97; dir. pub. affairs Md. Motorcycle Safety Program, Balt., 1990-92, asst. chief tng. and employee devel., dir. videography Md. Transp. Authority, 1992-96. Author: Power Machinery Maintenance, 1955, A World Without Prisons, 1979, Executive Communication Development, 1986, Profit Recovery Management, 1986, Strategic Sales Development System, 1986; editor: A Nation Without Prisons, 1975, New Mind Power, Increasing Your Brain Powers for Lifetime Change with Malcolm E. Bernstein, 1999; producer videos. Sponsors com. Nat. 4H, Nat. FFA, Nat. Jr. Achievement. Grantee U.S. Dept. Justice, 1966, 69; recipient Outstanding Cmty. Svc. award, Am. Assn. Cmty. Resource Devel., 1990, Cmty. Svc. award USAFR, 1968. Mem. ASTD (v.p. 1969-71), Md. Assn. Adult Edn., Inter-Am. Assn., Dodge Family Assn., Annapolis Naval Sailing Assn., Am. Soc. Group Psychotherapy and Psychodrama, Internat. TV Assn., Masons, Alpha Zeta, Omicron Delta Kappa, Tau Kappa Epsilon. Buddhist. Avocations: teaching sailing, oil painting, video and film production. Home: 8 S Broadway Baltimore MD 21231-1713 Office: Dodge-Marck Assocs Baltimore MD 21222 E-mail: granitewyo@aol.com.

DODGE, PAUL CECIL, academic administrator; b. Granville, N.Y., Mar. 25, 1943; s. Cecil John Paul and Elsie Elizabeth Dodge Rogers; m. Margaret Mary Kostyun, June 6, 1964 (div. Sept. 1985); 1 child, Cynthia Ruth; m. Cynthia Dee Bennett, Apr. 26, 1986; children: Michelle Lynn, Jason Paul, Benjamin Charles. BA in Math., U. Vt., 1967. Mgr. data processing Thermal Wire & Electronics, South Hero, Vt., 1967-70, DDSV divsn. Vt. Cos., Burlington, 1970-73, Revere Copper & Brass, Clinton, Ill., 1973-78, Angelica Corp., St. Louis, 1978-81; pres. chief ops. officer Dodge Mgmt., St. Louis, 1981-82; mgr. systems and programming Terra Internat., 1982-87; pres. chief ops. officer Mo. Tech. Sch., 1987—. Mem. Mo. Assn. Pvt. Career Schs. (pres. 1993-94), Nat. Rehab. Assn., Mo. Rehab. Assn. Republican. Presbyterian. Avocations: amatuer radio, chess. Office: Mo Tech Sch 1167 Corporate Lake Dr Saint Louis MO 63132-1716

DODOHARA, JEAN NOTON, music educator; b. Monroe, Wis., Feb. 21, 1934; d. Albert Henry and Eunice Elizabeth (Edgerton) Noton; BA, Monmouth (Ill.) Coll., 1955; MS, U. Ill., 1975, adminstrv. cert., 1980, EdD, 1985; m. Laurence G. Landers, June 7, 1955 (div.); children: Theodore Scott, Thomas Warren, Philip John; m. Edward R. Harris, Nov. 27, 1981 (dec.); stepchildren: Adrianne, Erica; m. Takashi Dodohara, Aug. 7, 1988; 1 stepchild, Eve D. Dodohara. Tchr. music schs. in Ill. and Fla., 1955-76; tchr. ch. music for children, 1957-72; tchr. music Dist. 54, Schaumburg, Ill., 1976-93; teaching asst. U. Ill., 1979. Named Outstanding Young Woman of Yr., Jaycee Wives, St. Charles, Mo., 1968; charter mem. Nat. Mus. Women in Arts. Mem. NEA (life), AAUW, Music Educators Nat. Conf. (life), Ill. Educators Assn. (life), Elgin Area Ret. Tchrs. Assn., U. Ill. Alumni Assn. (life), Mortar Bd., Mensa, Delta Kappa Pi. Mem. United Ch. of Christ. Home: 1068 Hampshire Ln Elgin IL 60120-4905

DODSON, CLAUDIA LANE, athletic administrator; b. Washington, Aug. 31, 1941; d. Claude James and Edna Vera (Lane) D. BS in Phys. Edn., Westhampton Coll., 1963; MS in Phys. Edn., U. Tenn., 1965. Cert. tchr., Va. Tchr., coach Meadowbrook H.S., Chesterfield, Va., 1963-64, 65-71; grad. asst. U. Tenn., Knoxville, 1964-65; asst. dir. Va. H.S. League, Charlottesville, Va., 1971—. Bd. dirs. Coun. on Stds. Internat. Ednl. Travel, 1996—; chmn. USOC Women's Basketball Com., Colorado Springs, Colo., 1976-80; mem. Nat. Basketball Rules Com., Elgin, Ill. and Kansas City, 1976-81; mem. U. Richmond (Va.) Athletic Coun., 1982-85; officials observer Atlantic Coast Conf., Greensboro, N.C., 1989—; spkr. in field. Recipient citation Nat. Fedn. State H.S. Assns., 1997, Disting. Svc. award Va. H.S. Coaches Assn., 1997. Mem. AAHPERD, Va. Assn. Health, Phys. Edn., Recreation and Dance, Nat. Interscholastic Athletic Adminstrs. Assn. (cert. adminstr., Disting. Svc. award), Va. Interscholastic Athletic Adminstrs. Assn. (life), Women's Basketball Coaches' Assn., Westhampton Coll. Alumnae Assn. (chpt. pres. 1977-79), Delta Kappa Gamma (Rho chpt., pres. 1982-84), Phi Delta Kappa (treas. 1986-96). Presbyterian. Avocations: family, sporting events. Home: 2540 Cedar Ridge Ln Charlottesville VA 22901-9412 Office: Va H S League 1642 State Farm Blvd Charlottesville VA 22911-8609

DODSON, DEBORAH ANN, elementary school educator; b. Natrona Heights, Pa., Jan. 29, 1952; d. Kenneth Waid and Betty Ann (Sharon) Ridenour; m. Donald Kenneth Dodson, Aug. 10, 1974; 1 child, Michelle Elizabeth. AD, Allegheny C.C., Monroeville, Pa., 1971; BS, Edinboro State U., 1973. Substitute tchr. Kiski Area Sch. Dist., Vandergrift, Pa., 1973-74, Leechburg (Pa.) Area Sch. Dist., 1973-74; tchr. Middle Twp. Elem. Sch. #1, Cape May Court House, N.J., 1974—. Contbr. poems to profl. publs. Rsch. coord. MADD, Cape May County, N.J., 1992—. Grand Prize winner of Exploration & Discovery Nat. Space Bill of Rights contest McDonalds Corp., Ronald McDonald's Children Charities and Young Astronauts Coun., Washington, 1992. Mem. AAUW, Delta Kappa Gamma. Office: Mid Twp Elem Sch No 1 215 Eldredge Rd Cape May Court House NJ 08210-2280

DODSON, ROBIN POWELL, special education educator; b. South Bend, Ind., Mar. 30, 1962; d. Richard Charles Powell and Helen Mary (Chambers) Johnson; m. Michael Elliott Dodson, June 27, 1985; children: Michael Jr., Benjamin James. BS in Elem. Edn., Manchester Coll., 1984; MS in Spl. Edn., Ind. U., South Bend, 1988. Cert. educable mentally retarded, neurologically impaired. Learning disabilities tchr. Wa-Nee Comty. Schs., Nappanee, Ind., 1984—, ednl. cons., 1988—. Vol. Prison Ministries, North Manchester, Ind., 1983-85; speaker No. Ind. chpt. Jaycees, Mishawaka, Ind., 1988. Mem. Coun. for Exceptional Children, Learning Disabilities Assn. Ind. Avocations: horseback riding, gardening. Office: Nappanee Elem 755 E Van Buren St Nappanee IN 46550-1469

DODSON, W(ILLIAM) EDWIN, child neurology educator; b. Durham, N.C., Dec. 23, 1941; s. Howard William and Mildred (Sorrell) D.; m. Doreen Carol Davis, June 4, 1964 (div. May 1976); children: Anna Elizabeth, William Edwin Jr., Jason David; m. Sandra Schorr (div. Mar. 1993); children: Steven Gage, Matthew Sorrell; m. Karen Leigh Pursel. AB, Duke U., 1963, MD, 1967. Intern Children's Hosp., Boston, 1967-68, resident in pediat., 1970-71; resident, fellow in child neurology Barnes Hosp. and St. Louis Children's Hosp., 1971-75; asst. prof. child neurology Washington U., St. Louis, 1975-80, resident in pediat., 1970-71, assoc. prof., 1980-86, prof. child neurology, 1986—; assoc. dean admissions and fin. aid Washington U. Sch. Medicine, St. Louis, 1990—. Assoc. vice-chancellor for continuing edn., admissions and fin. aid Washington U. Sch. Medicine, St. Louis, 1997—; bd. dirs. Family Resource Ctr., St. Louis, Physicians Corp., Washington U. Alliance Corp., First Tier Health Corp., Grace Hill Health Ctr., Nat. Com. to Prevent Child Abuse, Mo.; pres. bd. dirs. St. Louis Child Abuse Network, v.p. Family Support Network. Mem. editl. bd. Annals of Neurology and Clinical Neuropharmacology; contbr. articles to profl. jours. Bd. dirs. City St. Louis Bd. Children's Welfare, 1984-86; mem. profl. adv. bd. Epilepsy Found. Am., 1987-94, chmn.-elect,

1991-93, pres.-elect, 1993-95, pres. 1995-97, chmn. bd., 1997-98; co-chmn. Blue Ribbon Commn. on Future Svcs. to Children & Families, Mo., 1987-88; chmn. Children's Trust Fund Mo., 1989-91, bd. dirs., 1985-91; bd. dirs. Epilepsy Found. St. Louis, 2000--. Recipient Spl. Recognition award State of Md., 1971, Career Acad. Devel. award NIH, 1975, Disting. Social Svcs. award Mo. Dept. Social Svcs., 1988, Child Adv. award St. Louis Child Abuse Network, 1990, Child Adv. award Family Resource Ctr., 1991, 29th Ann. honoree, 1999; Spl. Recognition award Epilepsy Fedn. St. Louis, 1992, Guardian Angel award St. Louis Family Support Network, 1999, Samuel Clemmens award Epilepsy Found., St. Louis, 1999. Fellow Am. Acad. Neurology, Am. Acad. Pediat.; mem. Child Neurology Soc. (bd. dirs. 1985-87), Am. Neurol. Assn., Soc. Pediat. Rsch., Cen. Soc. Neurol. Rsch. (sec., treas. 1985, pres. 1989), Alpha Omega Alpha. Avocations: fly fishing, water sports, photography. Office: St Louis Childrens Hosp One Childrens Pl Saint Louis MO 63110-1014 E-mail: dodsone@msnotes.wustl.edu.

DOEHR, RUTH NADINE, home economics educator; b. Kingsford, Mich., Nov. 1, 1932; d. Helmuth Herbert and Olga Amanda (Olsen) D.; m. Ray Orentas, July 26, 1957 (div. 1960). BS, Mich. State U., 1961, MA, 1964. Job coord. Lansing (Mich.) Sch. Dist., 1964-68, tchr. sex edn., 1968-69; tchr. personality devel. No. Mich. U., 1969-70; tchr. Engadine (Mich.) Pub. Sch., 1970-72; lectr., supr. student tchrs. Northern Mich. U., Marquette, 1977-78; substitute tchr. Dickinson-Iron Intermediate Sch. Dist., Kingsford, 1988—. Editor: (newsletter) Lansing Ednl. Achievement Programs, 1964-68. Office vol. Crystal Lake Sr. Ctr., Iron Mountain, Mich., 1981-84; election insp. Breitung Twp., East Kingsford, Mich., 1972—; gift shop vol. Dickinson Meml. Hosp., Iron Mountain, 1984—, lifeline program participant, 1984-89, mem. exec. bd. women's league, 1984—, knitting chmn., 1984—. Mem. AAUW. Democrat. Lutheran. Avocations: reading, writing. Home: 229 Hyland St Iron Mountain MI 49802-4904

DOEHR-HODKIEWICZ, DENISE LOUISE, special education educator; b. Milw., Feb. 10, 1963; d. Dennis DeWayne and Mary Lou (Viola) Doehr; m. Jefferey Hodkiewicz, Jul. 22, 1999. BA in Early Childhood Edn., Mt. Mary Coll., 1985; MA in Spl. Edn., Cardinal Stritch Coll., 1989, MS in ednl. leadership, 1998. Tchr. grade 1 St. Jude the Apostle, Wauwatosa, Wis., 1985-89; pvt. practice edn. therapist Wauwatosa, 1986-90; edn. specialist Northbrooke Psychiat. Hosp., Brown Deer, Wis., 1989-91; instr. Waukesha County Tech. Coll., Pewaukee, Wis., 1990-91; edn. therapist Comprehensive Mental Health Svcs., Milw., 1990-92; pvt. practice ednl. therapist West Allis, Wis., 1991-98; spl. edn. tchr. Wis. Conservatory of Lifelong Learning, Milw., 1998—. Spkr., spl. ednl. therapist Northbrooke Hosp., Brown Deer, Wis., 1989-91; spl. edn. jr. h.s. tchr. St. Francis, Milw., 1993-95; acad. coord. St. Francis Children's Ctr., 1994-98. Columnist: Ask the Teacher, Chadd Tiddings, 1994-99. Mem. Friends of the Milw. Symphony Orch.; sec. Zoo Pride, 1995-2002. Theresa Ross scholar Mt. Mary Coll., 1983, 84. Mem. Coun. for Exceptional Children, Internat. Reading Assn., Wis. Reading Assn., Orton Dyslexia Soc. (sec. Wis. br. 1987-88), Learning Disabilities Assn. Wis., Children with Learning Disabilities, Nat. Assn. for Child and Adults with Learning Disabilities, Ch.A.D.D. of S.E. Wis. (sec. 1988-95). Republican. Roman Catholic. Avocations: biking, reading, crocheting, photography, children's literature. Office: WCLL 3120 W Green Ave Milwaukee WI 53221-4178 Address: 5344 W Stack Dr Milwaukee WI 53219-3367

DOERINGER, FRANKLIN M. historian, educator; b. Cleve., Oct. 2, 1940; s. Frank J. and Bertha Ann (Warek) D.; m. Frederica Cagan, Dec. 28, 1975; children: Adam Henry, Andrea Cagan. BA, Columbia Coll., 1962; PhD, Columbia U., 1971. Asst. prof. Chinese Columbia U., N.Y.C., 1970-71; Nathan M. Pusey prof. history and East Asian studies Lawrence U., Appleton, Wis., 1972—, chair East Asian langs. and cultures, 1989-96, chair dept. history, 1997—2000. Author: Discovering the Global Past, 1995; contbr. articles to profl. jours. Curriculum rev. com. mem. Appleton Bd. Edn., 1991—; v.p. bd. dirs. Outagamie County Hist. Soc., 2002—. Grantee 3M Found., 1990, Chiang Ching Kuo Found., 1993, Freeman Found., 2000. Mem. Internat. Soc. Chinese Philosophy, Am. Hist. Assn. Office: Lawrence Univ Dept History Appleton WI 54915

DOERRIE, BOBETTE, secondary education educator; b. Albuquerque, June 22, 1944; d. Neill and Dorothy Madelyn (Jones) Patterson; m. Edward Lewis Horton, Aug. 21, 1966 (div. 1990); children: Leah, James, Carol, Neill; m. Jerome Lee Doerrie, July 28, 1991; children: Jennifer, Elena. BA, McMurry Coll., 1966; MEd, DePaul U., 1977. Cert. sec. broadfield sci. Tchr. physics and phys. sci. G/T coord. Perryton (Tex.) H.S.; tchr. Summit Sch., Dundee, Ill., 1974-77, Lamesa Middle Sch., 1980-85, Lamesa H.S., 1968-69, 85-91, Perryton High Sch., 1991—. Co-dir. Dawson County Sci. Fair, 1981-91; coach Odyssey of the Mind, 1988-91; mem. McMurry U. Ednl. Adv. Bd., 1991-97, engrng. team faculty advisor, 1993—, sci. olympiad coach, 1998-2000, sci. bowl advisor, 2001—; mem. Mus. Bd. Dawson County, 1983-90; mem. Libr. Bd. Ochiltree County, 1993-95, v.p., 1994-95. Recipient Excellence in Teaching award Tex. State Assn. for Physics Tchrs., 1992, Tchr. of Yr., Region XVI Gifted and Talented Tchrs., 1994, Nat. Tchg. award RadioShack, 2001; NSF/Tex. Edn. Assn. Christa McAuliffe grantee, 1993, Outstanding Sci. Educator, Tex. Acad. Sci., 2002, Nat. Tchg. award Health Physics Soc., 2002. Mem.: Sci. Tchrs. of Tex. (treas. 1998—2001, Sci. Bowl Sponsor 2001—03), South Plains Sci. Soc. (pres. 1988, Sharon Christa McAuliffe Tchr. of Yr. 1987), Delta Kamma Gamma (pres.). Avocations: amateur radio, painting, archaeology, reading, writing. Home: 13925 CR B Booker TX 79005-9713 Office: Perryton High Sch 1200 S Jefferson St Perryton TX 79070-3700 E-mail: bdoerrie@yahoo.com.

DOETSCHMAN, DAVID CHARLES, chemistry educator; b. Aurora, Ill., Nov. 24, 1942; s. Charles F. and Mary (Thomas) D.; m. Evelyn Louise Siegel; children: Steven David, Christopher Randall. BS, No. Ill. U., 1963; PhD, U. Chgo., 1969. Rsch. fellow Australian Nat. U., Camberra, Australia, 1969—74, 1998, U. of Leiden, The Netherlands, 1974-75; asst. prof. SUNY, Binghamton, N.Y., 1975-82, assoc. prof., 1982-93, prof., 1993—, chair, 1997, 2003—. Scientist in residence Argonne (Ill.) Nat. Lab., 1982-83; cons. Union Carbide, Parma, Ohio, 1983-85; instrumentation ctr. coord. U. Coll. London, 1988-90; dir. Regional Ctr. for Pulsed EPR and Photochemistry Studies. Contbr. over 50 articles to profl. publs. Named one of Outstanding Young Men of Am. Mem. Am. Chem. Soc., Am. Phys. Soc., Materials Rsch. Soc., Sigma Xi Soc. Office: SUNY at Binghamton Dept of Chemistry Vestal Pky East Binghamton NY 13902-6000

DOHANIAN, DIRAN KAVORK, art historian, educator; b. Somerville, Mass., Mar. 26, 1931; s. Hagop Mardiros and Esther (Babigian) D. B.F.A., Mass. Sch. Art, 1952; A.M. in Teaching, Harvard, 1953, MA, 1955, PhD, 1964. Instr. art Eastern Nazarene Coll., Wollaston, Mass., 1952—55; reader in fine arts Harvard U., Cambridge, Mass., 1954—57, teaching fellow fine arts, 1955—57; vis. asst. prof. history art U. Ala., 1957—58; vis. asst. prof. history Oriental art U. Hawaii, 1959—60; asst. prof. fine arts, dir. course in Oriental humanities U. Rochester, NY, 1960—65, assoc. prof. fine arts, 1965—71, prof., 1971—87, prof. art history, 1988—2001, acting chmn. dept. fine arts, 1977—78, chmn. dept. fine arts, 1980—83, mem. faculty coun. Coll. Arts and Sci., 1991—94, sec. faculty coun., 1992—94, prof. art history emeritus, 2002—. Cons., curator Oriental art The Meml. Art Gallery, Rochester, 1976—88, bd. mgrs., 1977—78, 1980—83; Cooke-Daniels Meml. lectr. Cooke-Daniels Found. and Denver Art Mus., 1965; Louise Weiser lectr. Mt. Holyoke Coll., 1983; cons. in field. Author: The Mahayana Buddhist Sculpture of Ceylon, 1977, also articles in profl. jours. C.R.B. fellow Belgian Art Seminar, Brussels and Antwerp, 1956, Fulbright fellow India, 1958-59, sr. research fellow Am. Inst. Ceylonese Studies, Colombo, 1968, Am. Council Learned Socs. fellow India, 1973; fine arts rsch. scholar, 2002—. Fellow Am. Philos Soc.; mem. Am. Inst. Indian Studies (trustee 1964-65), Am. Com. for History South Asian Art (dir. 1969-71). Home: 269 Payson Rd Belmont MA 02478-3406

DOHERTY, SISTER BARBARA, religious institution administrator; b. Chgo., Dec. 2, 1931; d. Martin James and Margaret Eleanor (Noe) D. Student, Rosary Coll., 1949-51; BA in Latin, English and History, St. Mary-of-the-Woods Coll., 1953; MA in Theology, St. Mary's Coll., 1963; PhD in Theology, Fordham U., 1979; LittD (hon.), Ind. State U., 1990, Dominican U., Ill., 2002. Enter order of the Sisters of Providence. Tchr. Jr. and Sr. High Schs., Ind. and Ill., 1953-63; asst. prof. religion St. Mary-of-the-Woods Coll., Ind., 1963-67, 71-75, pres., 1984-98; provincial supr. Chgo. Province of Sisters of Providence, 1975-83; dir. Inst. of Religious Formation at Cath. Theol. Union, Chgo., 1999—. Summer faculty NCAIS-KCRCHE, Delhi, India, 1970. Author: I Am What I Do: Contemplation and Human Experience, 1981, Make Yourself an Ark: Beyond the Memorized Responses of Our Corporate Adolescence, 1984; editor: Providence: God's Face Towards the World, 1984; contbr. articles to New Cath. Ency. Vol. XVII, 1982, God and Me, 1988, Dictionary of Catholic Spirituality, 1993. Pres. Leadership Terre Haute, Ind., 1985-86; bd. regents Ind. Acad., 1987-98; bd. dirs. 8th Day Cen. for Justice, Chgo., 1978-83, Family Svcs., Swope Art Mus., Terre Haute, Ind., 1988-98. Arthur J. Schmidt Found. grantee, 1967-71. Mem. Women's Coll. Coalition (nat. bd. dirs. 1984-90), Ind. Colls. Ind., Ind. Colls. Found. (exec. bd.), Ind. Conf. Higher Edn. (chair), Leadership Conf. Women Religious of USA (program chairperson nat. assembly 1982-83, chair Neylan commn. 1993-97), Assn. Am. Colls. and Univs. Democrat. Roman Catholic. Avocations: walking, reading, traveling. Office: Cath Theol Union 5401 S Cornell Ave Chicago IL 60615-5664 E-mail: bdoherty@ctu.edu.

DOHMEN, MARY HOLGATE, retired primary school educator; b. Gary, Ind., July 28, 1918; d. Clarence Gibson and Margaret Alexander (Kinnear) Holgate; m. Frederick Hoeger Dohmen, June 27, 1964; children: William Francis, Robert Charles. BS, Milw. State Tchrs. Coll., 1940; M of Philosophy, U. Wis., 1945. Cert. tchr., Wis Tchr. primary grades Baraboo (Wis.) Pub. Schs., 1940-43, Whitefish Bay (Wis.) Pub. Schs., 1943-64. Contbr. articles, story, poems to various pubs. Bd. dirs. Homestead H.S. chpt. Am. Field Svc., Mequon, Wis., 1970-80; mem. Milw. Aux. VNA, 1975—, 2d v.p., 1983-85, Milw. Pub. Mus. Enrichment Club, 1975—, Boys and Girls Club of Greater Milw., 1986—; vol. Reading is Fun program, 1987—, Milw. Symphony Orch. League, 1960—, Ptnrs. in Conservation, World Wildlife Fund, Washington, 1991—, Milw. Art Mus. Garden Club, 1979—, com. chmn., 1981-86; mem. Chancellor's Soc. U. Wis.-Milw., 1991—; travel lectr. various orgns., 1980—. Mem. AAUW, Milw. Coll. Endowment Assn. (v.p. 1987-90, pres. 1991-93), Bascom Hill Soc. (U. Wis.), Woman's Club Wis., Alpha Phi (pres. Milw. alumnae 1962-64), Pi Lambda Theta (pres. Milw. alumnae 1962-64), Delta Kappa Gamma. Republican. Presbyterian. Avocations: writing, travel, nature. Home: 3903 W Mequon Rd Mequon WI 53092-2727

DOHRENWEND, SANDRA BLACKMAN MASTERMAN, superintendent; b. New London, Conn., Oct. 22, 1935; d. Frank Arlington and Dorothy Irene (Danforth) Blackman; m. Robert Masterman, June 22, 1958 (dec. 1976); children: Todd, Drew; m. James Wilckes Dohrenwend, July 1, 1979. BS, Cen. Conn. State U., 1957; MA, Columbia U., 1980. Cert. tchr., prin., supt. Tchr. various schs., Southbury and Fair Lawn, Conn.-N.J., 1957-59, Glen Rock (N.J.) Pub. Schs., 1963-80; coord. physicians insvc. tng. Am. Acad. Pediatrics, Evanston, Ill., 1980-82; prin. Ray Graham Asn. for the Handicapped, Lombard, Ill., 1982-85, dir. edn., 1985-86; prin. Morris Sch. Dist., Morristown, N.J., 1986-89; supt. of schs. Denville (N.J.) Twp. Schs., 1990—. Mem., v.p. bd. edn. Wheaton (Ill.) Pub. Schs., 1983-86; mem. bd. edn. Dupage County Spl. Svcs. Bd., Lombard, 1985-86. Mem. Legis. Ednl. Network DuPage, Ill., 1984-86; mem., sec. bd. trustees Denville (N.J.) Libr., 1990—; mem. Vanguard, Morris County United Way; exec. bd. dirs. Challenge Unltd., Morristown; mem. DuPage County Mental Health Bd., LWV. Named Outstanding Women Leader in Edn., DuPage YWCA, Lombard, 1986. Mem. ASCD, Am. Assn. Sch. Adminstrs., N.E. Coalition of Ednl. Leaders, Morris County Assn. Sch. Administrs., Ill. Large Dist. Schs. (exec. bd.), N.J. Assn. Sch. Adminstrs. (curriculum com.). Presbyterian.

DOI, DOROTHY MITSUE YANO, educator, consultant; b. Honolulu, Feb. 21, 1934; d. Tokuju Yano and Hisayo Kashiwabara; children: Ken Kenichi, Claire Emiko, Garret Seitoku. BS in Edn., Phillips U., Enid, Okla., 1956; postgrad., UCLA, 1958, U. Hawaii, Honolulu, 1966-67, 72-74, Chaminade Coll. Honolulu, 1972-74, 77, LaVerne (Calif.) Coll., 1970-71. Cert. tchr., Hawaii. Tchr. L.A. City Schs., 1957-58, Hawaii, 1956-57, 65, 70-71; account exec. Catering, ind. contractor, Honolulu; skin care, health and beauty cons. Honolulu; travel agt., ind. contractor, dba Triple C Svcs., Honolulu, 1983—. Rschr. Manoa ethnic studies program U. Hawaii; account exec., cons. Royal Banquet, 1988-89. Active Kamuki Y-Teens, 1947-52; fund-raising co-chair Kaimuki HS, Hui O'Hauolani Y-Teens Jesters Ball, 1952; mem. World Wildlife Fund, 1991—, Hawaii Theatre Ctr., 1990—; vol. ARC, 1944-49, Salvation Army, 1945-50, bell ringer, 1989-98; translator Jal Honolulu Marathon Info. Booth Svc., 1995—. Mem. VFW Ladies Aux. (life), Am. Biograph. Rsch. Assn. (rschr., dep. gov.), NAFE, Nature Conservancy Local, Nat., Hawaii Fukuoka Kenjin Kai (gen. chair 35th anniversary and award ceremony 1992, com. chair, editor commemorative booklet, sec. 1988-91, 2d v.p. 1992-93, 1st v.p. 1993-95, pres. 1996, immediate past pres. 1997, vol. mayors and chamber pres. conf. Honolulu 1997, translation svc. registration desk rep Hawaii Fukuoka Kenjn Kai), Smithsonian Instn., Kaimuki HS Alumni Assn. (charter, bd. dirs. 1988-2001, pub. rels. chair 1988-90, writer, rschr., editor, mng. editor Bulldogrowl newsletter), Okla. Sooners Club (Hon. Citizen of Okla. 1985), Japanese Cultural Ctr. Hawaii (hon. lifetime charter), Future Tchrs. Am. (treas. 1955-56), United Japanese Soc. Hawaii (sec. 1991-95, youth com. chair 1992—, gen. chair youth com. picnic Bunka Pikunikku 1994, culture day Bunka-no-Hi 1995, co-chair fundraising com. 1992-93, 95-96, mcee New Year luncheon 1993, 2d v.p. 1994-95, registration, score card analyzer Ganbare Golf Classics 1994-98, Mulligan sales co-chair 1995-97, program com. chair, lei com. chair Japan Festival 1996, chair welfare com. 1999-2001), Internat. Platform Assn., Honolulu Japanese C. of C. (ann. art exhbn. 1997-2000, ann. fundraising 1996-99). Avocations: commemorative postal stamp collecting, spectator sports, cooking and baking. Home: 1628 Kalakaua Ave #405 Honolulu HI 96826-2421

DOIG, JAMESON WALLACE, political science educator; b. Oakland, Calif., June 12, 1933; s. James Rufus and Mary (Jameson) D.; m. Joan Nishimoto, Oct. 8, 1955; children: Rachel, Stephen, Sean. AB, Dartmouth Coll., 1954; M.P.A., Princeton U., 1958, MA, 1959, PhD, 1961. Research asst. N.J. Republican Com., 1957; staff mem. Brookings Instn., 1959-61; from asst. prof. to prof. politics and pub. affairs Princeton U., 1961—; assoc. dean Woodrow Wilson Sch., Princeton U., 1972-73, dir. univ. research program in criminal justice, 1973-93. Dir. grad.studies dept. polit. sci. Princeton U., 1988—90, chair undergrad. studies, 1991—94, chair dept. polit. sci., 1997—2000; dir. Mamdouha S. Bobst Ctr. for Peace and Justice, 2000—, chair Can. studies, 2002—, chair athletics com., 2003—; cons. Fels Fund, 1966—68, Daniel and Florence Guggenheim Found., 1970—, Nat. Prison Overcrowding Project, 1983, Lavenburg Found., 1983—90; vis. prof. John Jay Coll. Criminal Justice, 1967—68, 1970—72; mem. adv. com. Gov. N.J., 1965—71, Vera Inst. Justice, 1986—92; mem. NRC/Trans. Rsch. Bd., 1990—92; mem. adv. coun. N.J. Dept. Corrections, 1974—82, vice-chmn., 1980—82, cons. on parole to gov. of N.J., 1975—78; dir. Guggenheim Summer Intern. Program, 1997—. Author: Metropolitan Transportation Politics and the New York Region, 1966, (with D.E. Mann) The Assistant Secretaries, 1965, (with D.T. Stanley and D.E. Mann) Men Who Govern, 1967, (with M. Danielson) New York: The Politics of Urban Regional Development, 1982, Empire on the Hudson, 2001; co-author, editor: Criminal Corrections: Ideals and Realities, 1983, Leadership and Innovation, 1987, 90, Combating Corruption/Encouraging Ethics, 1990; contbr. Governing the States and Localities, 1969, Agenda for a City, 1970, Metropolitan Politics, 1971, Urban Politics and Policy-Making, 1973, Crime and Criminal Justice, 1975, Public Administration of Law Enforcement Policies, 1979, Politics of Urban Development, 1987, Public Authorities and Public Policy, 1991, Landscape of Modernity, 1992, Studies in American Political Development, 1993, Technology and Culture, 1994, Building the Public City, 1995, Seaport, 2001, Innovation, 2002. Served to lt. (j.g.) USNR, 1954-56. Recipient Herbert Kaufman award, 1989, A.P. Usher prize, 1995, A. Wildavsky award, 1997, Abel Wolman award, 2001, Humanities Honor award, 2002. Mem. Am. Correctional Assn., Am. Polit. Sci. Assn., Am. Soc. Pub. Adminstrn., Law and Soc. Assn., Soc. History of Technology, Policy Studies Orgn., Can. Studies Assn., Phi Beta Kappa. Office: Princeton U Corwin Hall Robertson Hl Princeton NJ 08544-0001

DOLAN, TERRENCE RAYMOND, neurophysiology educator; b. Huron, S.D., May 24, 1940; s. Buell Ellery and Mary Lucille (Engler) D.; m. Mary Ann Mechtenberg, Apr. 23, 1962; children: Katherin, Patrick, Elizabeth, Meaghan. BA, Dakota Wesleyan U., Mitchell, S.D., 1962; MS, Trinity U., San Antonio, 1963; PhD in Psychology and Physiology, U. Tex., Austin, 1966; postdoctoral study, Ctr. Neuroscis., Ind. U., Bloomington, 1966-68. Rsch. assoc. Ctr. Neuroscis., Ind. U., Bloomington, 1968-70; assoc. prof. psychology Loyola U., Chgo., 1970-74, prof. dept. psychology, 1974-76, asst. dean Grad. Sch., 1974-76, dir. Parmly Rsch. Inst., 1970-76; program dir. NSF Neuroscis. Sect., 1976-82; prof. dept. neurophysiology U. Wis., Madison, 1982—, dir. Waisman Ctr. Mental Retardation and Human Devel., prof. dept. neurology, 1997—, prof. dept. psychology, 1997—. NSF rep. to Nat. Inst. Neurol. and Communicative Disease, NIH, 1976-77, liaison rep. to Nat. Eye Coun., NIH, 1976-82; mem. exec. coun. com. on vision NAS-NRC, 1977-82, mem. exec. coun. com. on hearing, acoustics and biomechanics, 1977-84; chmn. NSF task force on Support of Young Investigators-Young Scientists, 1979-80; mem. Fed. Noise Effects Steering Com. EPA, 1977-80; chmn. Assn. Mental Retardation Rsch. Ctr. Dirs., 1984-88; mem. nat. adv. coun. Air Force Office Sci. Rsch., 1984—; pres. Am. Assn. U. Affiliated Programs, 1984-88; pres.-elect Internat. Assn. Sci. Study Mental Deficiency, 1988-92, pres., 1992—; exec. dir. Prince Salman Ctr. for Disability Rsch., Riyadh, Saudi Arabia, 2001—. Contbr. numerous articles to profl. publs. Von Humboldt fellow, Fed. Republic Germany; grantee Nat. Inst. Child Health and Human Devel., 1982-93, Wis., 1984-85, wis. Devel. Disability Coun., 1985-93, others. Mem. Assn. Rsch. in Otolaryngology, Acoustical Soc. Am., Am. Assn. Univ. Affiliated Progs. (pres. 1988-89), Internat. Assn. Sci. Study Mental Deficiency (pres. 1992-96). Office: U Wis-Madison Waisman Ctr Mental Retardation & Human Devel 1500 Highland Ave Madison WI 53705-2274

DOLAN, THOMAS FRANCIS, JR., pediatrician, educator; b. Cambridge, Mass., Mar. 2, 1928; s. Thomas and Agnes (Masterson) D.; m. Margaret Dolan, Jan. 13, 1953; children: Karen, Kevin, Maureen, Evelyn. BA, Harvard U., 1949, MD, 1953; MA, Yale U., 1973. Diplomate Am. Bd. Pediatrics. Intern Children's Med. Ctr., Boston, 1953-59; resident Boston City Hosp., 1956-58; sr. asst. surgeon Nat. Inst. Allergy and Infectious Disease, NIH, Bethesda, Md, 1958-60; staff resident Ellsworth, Maine, 1958-62; attending physician L & M Hosp., New London, 1962-69; instr. Children's Med. Ctr., Boston, 1962-64; asst. prof. pediat. Yale U., New Haven, 1969, assoc. prof., 1970-75, prof., 1975—. Sr. asst. surgeon USPHS, 1956-58. Mem. Am. Pediat. Soc., Am. Thoracic Soc., Conn. Acad. Pediat. (pres. 1976-82). Home: 26 Skytop Dr Madison CT 06443-2539 Office: Yale U Sch Med 333 Cedar St New Haven CT 06510-3289

DOLE, JIM WALTER, biology educator; b. Phoenix, May 28, 1935; s. Harlan Baldwin and Dorothy Lee (Oglesby) D.; m. Betty JoAnn Pickens Patterson, Jan. 15, 1957 (div. 1981); children: Deborah, Phillip, Robert; m. Betty Berryman Rose, Jan. 2, 1987. BA, Ariz. State Coll., 1957; MS, U. Mich., 1959, PhD, 1963. Instr. U. Mich., Ann Arbor, 1961-62; prof. biology Calif. State U., Northridge, 1963—, chair biology dept., 1998—2002. Author: Shrubs and Trees of Southern California Deserts, 1996, Shrubs and Trees of Southern California Coastal Region and Mountains, 1996.

DOLENCE, MICHAEL G. writer, consultant, educator; b. Oct. 18, 1950; m. Maryann Merena, Sept. 24, 1983. BA in Biology, Russel Sage Coll., 1977; postgrad. in Edn. Adminstrn., SUNY, Albany, 1977-79. Founder/CEO Survival One, St. Johnsville, N.Y., 1971-76; co-founder S&D Computer Tech., Albany, 1977-79; dir. rsch. planning The Commn. on Ind. Colls. and Univs., Albany, 1979-85; strategic planning adminstr. Calif. State U., L.A., 1985-94; pres. Michael G. Dolence & Assocs., Claremont, Calif., 1994—. Pres. Sch. Improvement Program, Altadena, Calif., 1989-91. Author: The Survival One Manual of Survival, 1973, Strategic Enrollment Management: A Primer for Campus Administrators, 1993, Transforming Higher Education, 1995, Strategic Enrollment Management: Cases From the Field, 1996, Working Towards Strategic Change: A Step by Step Guide to the Planning Process, 1996, Strategic Change in Colleges and Universities, 1996; syndicated columnist nat. newspapers A Matter of Romance, 1990—; contbr. over 135 articles to profl. jours. Pres. Nine Block Sq. Neighborhood Assn., 1979-83, Baseline Assn. Neighborhoods, Claremont, 1994; chair edn. com. Am. Cancer Soc., Albany, 1980-82; pres. sch. site coun. Elliot Mid. Sch., Altadena, 1989-91. Mem. So. Calif. Planning Forum (v.p. membership, programs, mktg., pres.-elect), Soc. for Coll. and Univ. Planning (seminar faculty 1985—), Am. Assn. Collegiate Registrars and Admissions Officers (seminar faculty 1989—), Poets, Essayists, Novelists, Phi Beta Delta. Office: 848 Decatur Cir Claremont CA 91711-2206

DOLLY, JOHN PATRICK, educational psychologist, educator; b. NYC, May 16, 1942; s. Thomas Joseph and Anna Maria (Barron) D.; m. Carol Ann Dolly, Oct. 23, 1966; children: Sheila, Erin; m. Inez Rovegno, June 2, 2002. BS, Manhattan Coll., 1964; MS, SUNY, 1966; Ed.D., U. Ga., 1973. Area dir. Founds. of Edn. U. S.C., Columbia, 1975-78, asst. dean acad. affairs Coll. Edn., 1978-79, acting dean, 1979-80, asst. dean research and devel., 1980; dean Coll. Edn. U. Wyo., Laramie, 1981-86; dean U. Hawaii, Manoa, 1986-95; dean Coll. Edn. Univ. Ala., Tuscaloosa, 1995—2003. Cons., lectr. in field. Co-author: Learning to Teach: A Decision Making System. Contbr. articles to profl. jours. Served to capt. USAF, 1966-70. Vocat. Rehab. Adminstrn. trainee, 1964-66. Mem. Am. Ednl. Research Assn., Phi Delta Kappa, Phi Kappa Phi, Kappa Delta Pi. Office: Univ Ala Coll Edn PO Box 870231 Tuscaloosa AL 35487-0154

DOMBROSKI, RICHELLE BRAGG, secondary education educator; b. Bloomington, Ill., Nov. 19, 1960; d. Raymond Jack Bragg and Joanne (Phillips) Saravia; m. Ronald E. Dombroski, July 2, 1994. BA in History, U. N.C., 1984. Cert. secondary educator N.C. Interim tchr. John T. Hoggard H.S., Wilmington, N.C., 1984-85; tchr. Williston Jr. H.S., Wilmington, N.C., 1985-88; tchr., dept. chmn. E.A. Laney H.S., Wilmington, N.C., 1986. Chmn. Laney Sch. Improvement Team, Wilmington, 19891997; mem. County Curriculum Com., Wilmington, 1992-93, Laney Sch. Adv. Bd., 1992-93. Vol. Rape Crisis Ctr., Wilmington, 1985-90; mem. Rape Crisis Adv. Bd., Wilmington, 1985-90; tchr. Sunday sch. St. Mary's Cath. Ch., Wilmington, 1992—. Recipient Cram Map award, 1989, Raleigh (N.C.) Gov.'s award, 1991, State Farm Good Neighbor Teaching award, 1995. Mem. Nat. Coun. Social Studies, Nat. Coun. Geographic Edn. (awards com. 1990-94), N.C. Coun. Social Studies (bd. dirs. 1992-95), N.C. Geog. Alliance (steering com. 1987-92, cons. 1987—). Democrat. Avocations: reading, scrapbooks, travel.

DOMBROWSKI, MARK ANTHONY, librarian; b. Oshkosh, Wis., Dec. 13, 1940; s. Alexander Joseph and Veronica Ellen (Gaber) D. BS in English cum laude, U. Wis., Oshkosh, 1966; MSLS, U. Wis., 1968, specialist cert., 1973. Asst. libr. acquisitions Forrest R. Polk Libr. U. Wis., Oshkosh,

1968-74, head libr. acquisitions, 1974-75; libr. dir. Siena Heights Coll., Adrian, Mich., 1975—. Cons. St. Catherine Coll. Libr., Springfield, Ky., 1985. Contbr. articles to profl. jours. Mem. YMCA. With USN and USNR, 1959-66. Legis. scholar State of Wis., 1963-65, scholar Ziegler Found., 1966; Edns. Professions Devel. Act fellow Wis. Dept. Edn., 1972. Mem. ALA, MLA, Am. Culture Assn., Nat. Librs. Assn., Mich. Libr. Assn. (v.p. 1981-82, 87-88), Mich. Libr. Consortium (chmn. bd. 1981-83), Phi Beta Mu, Phi Kappa Delta, Kappa Delta Pi, Phi Beta Sigma. Roman Catholic. Avocations: bridge, antiques, creative writing. Office: Siena Heights Coll 1247 E Siena Heights Dr Adrian MI 49221-1755

DOMEIER, SUE ANN, elementary education educator; b. Ft. Wayne, Ind., Apr. 27, 1955; d. Wilbur Herman and Ruth (Korte) Werling; m. John P. Domeier, May 19, 1979; children: Jennifer, Kathryn, Jessica, John. BA, Concordia U., 1977, postgrad., 1989—. Cert. tchr. grades K-9, 6-12. Coach Oak Park (Ill.) Recreation Dept., 1972-77; tchr. Hope Luth. Sch., Chgo., 1977-81, Christ Our Savior Luth. Ch., Winfield, Ill., 1981-85; coach St. John Luth. Sch., Wheaton, Ill., 1985-88, tchr., 1989—. Chair elect theme com. No. Ill. Dist. Tchrs. Conf., 1994—. Mem. AAHPERD, ASCD, Ill. H.S. Assn. (ofcl. 1991—), Luth. Sports Assn. Inc. (bd. dirs. 1989—, chmn. state basketball tournament 1993-95, pres. 1995—). Lutheran. Avocations: golf, boating, water skiing, family and church activities. Home: 25w689 Macarthur Ave Carol Stream IL 60188-4560 Office: St John Luth Sch 125 E Seminary Ave Wheaton IL 60187-5308

DOMEÑO, EUGENE TIMOTHY, elementary education educator, principal; b. L.A., Oct. 22, 1938; s. Digno and Aurora Mary (Roldan) D. AA, Santa Monica (Calif.) City Coll., 1958; BA, Calif. State U., 1960, MA, 1966. Cert. elem. tchr., gen. sch svcs, special secondary tchr. Elem. tchr. L.A. Unified Sch. Dist., 1960-70; asst. prin. Pomona (Calif.) Unified Sch. Dist., 1970-71, prin., 1971—. Cons. testing and evaluation Pomona Unified Sch. Dist., 1990—. With USNR, 1958-65. Recipient PTA Hon. Svc. award Granada Elem. PTA, Granada Hills, Calif., 1960, Armstrong Sch. PTA, Diamond Bar, Calif., 1990, Calif. Disting. Sch. Calif. Dept. Edn., 1989, Nat. Blue Ribbon Sch. U.S. Dept. Edn., Washington, 1990, Prin. and Leadership award, 1990. Mem. ASCD, Nat. Assn. Elem. Sch. Prins. (Prin. of Leadership award with Nat. Safety Com., 1991), Nat. Assn. Year Round Sch., Assn. Calif. Sch. Administrs., Diamond Bar C. of C. (edn. com.). Avocations: golf, dancing, church, playing the flute. Office: Neil Armstrong Elem Sch 22750 Beaverhead Dr Diamond Bar CA 91765-1566 E-mail: auroratlc@aol.com.

DOMINGUEZ, JORGE IGNACIO, government educator; b. Havana, Cuba, June 2, 1945; came to U.S., 1960; s. Jorge Jose and Lilia Rosa (de la Carrera) D.; m. Mary Alice Kmietek, Dec. 16, 1967; children: Lara Lisa, Leslie Karen. AB, Yale U., 1967; AM, Harvard U., 1968, PhD, 1972. From asst. prof. to prof. govt. Harvard U., Cambridge, Mass., 1972—93, Frank G. Thomson prof. govt., 1993—96, chmn. Latin Am. and Iberian studies, 1979—83, 1990—93, acting dir. ctr. for internat. affairs, 1995, Clarence Dillon prof. internat. affairs, 1996—, dir. Weatherhead Ctr. for Internat. Affairs, 1996—, Harvard Coll. prof., 1998—2003. Active Coun. on Fgn. Rels., Inter-Am. Dialogue, 1982—, sr. fellow, 1993-94, assoc. fellow, 1995—. Author: Cuba: Order and Revolution, 1978, Insurrection or Loyalty, 1980, To Make the World Safe for Revolution: Cuba's Foreign Policy, 1989, Democratic Politics in Latin America and the Caribbean, 1998, Democracy in the Caribbean, 1993, Technopols: Freeing Politics and Markets in Latin America in the 1990s, 1997, Democratic Transitions in Central America, 1997, Toward Mexico's Democratization: Parties, Campaigns, Elections, and Public Opinion, 1999, The Future of Inter-American Relations, 2000, Mexico, Central and South America: New Perceptions, 5 vols., 2001, Constructing Democratic Governance in Latin America, 2003; co-author: Democratizing Mexico: Public Opinion and Electoral Choices, 1996, The United States and Mexico: Between Partnership and Conflict, 2001; mem. editl. bd. Am. Polit. Sci. Rev., 1979—81, Foreign Affairs en español, Polit. Sci. Quar., 1984—, Cuban Studies, 1991—, Latin Am. Rsch. Rev., 2003—, series editor Crisis in Central America: A Four-Part Special Report, Frontline, PBS (Peabody award), 1985—, chief editl. adv. 3-part spl. report Mexico, 1988. Chmn. bd. trustees Latin Am. Scholarship Program of Am. Univs., Cambridge, Mass., 1981-82. Recipient Joseph Levenson Meml. Teaching award Harvard U., 1991; mem. Antilles Rsch. Program Yale U., New Haven, 1974-75; jr. fellow Harvard U., 1969-72, Fulbright-Hays fellow, 1983, 88. Mem. Latin Am. Studies Assn. (pres. 1982-83), New Eng. Coun. Latin Am. Studies (pres. 1980), Inst. Cuban Studies (pres. 1990-94). Clubs: Elihu (New Haven). Office: Harvard U Ctr Weatherband Internat Affairs 1033 Mass Ave Cambridge MA 02138-3016

DOMINGUEZ, PATRICIA BROWN, nursing educator; b. Charleston, W.Va., Feb. 13, 1950; d. Leonard Russell Brown and Coral Lee (Fisher) Craig; children: Pedro Aniceto, Patrick Fisher. BSN, U. Tex. Health Sci. Ctr., 1987, MSN, 1992. CNOR, Tex. RN, OR/PACU West Houston Med. Ctr., Houston, 1992—; asst. prof. Houston Bapt. U., Houston, 1991—. Recipient Opal Goolsby Tchr. of Yr. award Houston Bapt. U., 1991-92. Mem. Assn. Perioperative Nurses, Tex. Nurses Assn. (Outstanding Nurse 2002-2003), Sigma Theta Tau (counselor 1992-98). Republican. Lutheran. Avocations: reading, skiing, sailing, genealogy. Office: Houston Bapt Univ 7502 Fondren Rd Houston TX 77074-3204

DOMOWITZ, IAN, economics educator; b. N.Y.C., Nov. 29, 1951; s. Jacob and Marilyn (Raffer) D.; m. Marguerite Morton, Sept. 25, 1984. BA, U. Conn., 1977; PhD, U. Calif., San Diego, 1982. Asst. prof., assoc. prof., prof. econs. Northwestern U., Evanston, Ill., 1982-98, mem. rsch. faculty Inst. for Policy Rsch., 1987-98; Mary Jean and Frank P. Smeal chaired prof. fin. Pa. State U., University Park, 1998—2002; mng. dir. analytical products and rsch. ITG, Inc., 2001—; bd. mgrs. Ingerence Group, LLC, 2002—. Rsch. dir. K2 Capital Mgmt., 1992-94; cons. IMF, 1992, World Bank, 1993-96, 98-99, to various internat. fin. markets with respect to automated exch. structures, 1991-97; cons. U.S. Commodity Futures Trading Commn., 1991, 95-96; mem. sci. adv. bd. ITG, Inc., 1997-, mem. sci. adv. bd. ITG Europe, 2003—; bd. mgrs. Inference Group LLC, 2002—. Contbr. over 75 articles to profl. jours., chpts. to books. Sgt. U.S. Army, 1972-75, Germany. NSF grantee, 1984, 85, 87, 90. Mem. Am. Fin. Assn., Fin. Mgmt. Assn., Nat. Assn. Securities Dealers (econ. adv. bd. 1998-2000, chair 1998-2000, bond market transparency com. 1998-99). Home: 27 Mercer St Apt 2C New York NY 10013-2517 E-mail: idomowitz@itginc.com.

DONAHUE, DONALD FRANCIS, media specialist; b. Miami, Fla., June 1, 1953; s. Charles Francis and Emma ALetta (Solan). BA, Trenton (N.J.) State U., 1975; Rider Army ROTC, Trenton, N.J., 1971-75. Cert. Tchr. of History, N.J. Sch. bd. mem. Twp. Hamilton, 1973-80, democratic com., 1976—; tchr. St. James Sch., Trenton, N.J., 1985—, coach, athletic dir., 1985-2000; media splst. P.J. Hill, Trenton, 2000—. Drug abuse coord. St. James PTA, Trenton, N.J., 1988-93. Sch. bd. mem., pres. Hamilton Bd. Edn., 1973-80, 1978, 80, 81; basketball coach, softball coach Cath. Youth Orgn. Trenton, N.J., 1986—; P.J. Hill basketball coach, 1998-2000; mem. Mercer County Consortium, 1999. 1st Lt. U.S. Army, 1971-75. Grantee Ptnrs. in Learning, N.J. Dept. Edn., 1987-80, 88-89, George Ahr Endowment Diocese of Trenton, 1988, 91. Mem. Hamilton Democratic Club, N.J. State Democratic Com., Cath. Youth Orgn., Mercer County Young Democratics, Hamilton Twp. Young Democrats. Democrat. Roman Catholic. Avocations: basketball, politics, football. Office: P J Hill Sch 1010 E State St Trenton NJ 08609-1506 Home: # 2 1009 Hamilton Ave Trenton NJ 08629-1908

DONAHUE, JOAN ELIZABETH, elementary school educator; b. Middlesboro, Ky., Oct. 9, 1954; d. Calvin Coolidge and Cassie Marie (Harville) Whitaker; m. Andrew Lewis Donahue, Aug. 13, 1977; children: Timothy, Laura, Christopher. BS in Home Econs., U. Tenn., 1977; MS Edn., Ouachita Bapt., 1987. Cert. tchr., Ark. Home econs. tchr. Claiborne County Schs., Tazewell, Tenn., 1977-81; 2d grade tchr. Sparkman Schs., Arkadelphia, Sparkman, Ark., 1985, Arkadelphia Schs., 1985-87, Shelby County Schs., Memphis, 1987-89; 3d grade tchr. Mobile (Ala.) County Schs., 1989-91, 4th grade tchr., 1991-92, 3rd grade tchr., 1992-94; 4th grade tchr. Knox County Schs., Knoxville, Tenn., 1994-95, Green Magnet Math and Sci. Acad., Knoxville, 1995-96; 3d grade tchr. Shelby County Schs., Memphis, 1996—. Textbook cons. Walsworth Pub. Co., Marceline, Mo., 1991—; mem. supt. adv. bd. Mobile County Schs., 1991—. Active Woman's Club Am., New Tazewell, Tenn., 1977-81, v.p., 1981, Shelby County Govt. Bd. Commrs. (hon. commr. 1986), Memphis City Coun. (hon. commr. 1986). Classroom Econ. grantee Mobile Jr. League, 1989-90. Fellow Beta Sigma Phi (pres. 1986-878, Woman of Yr. 1987); mem. Joint Coun. on Econ. Edn. (2d place award 1987, 3d place award 1990), Ala. coun. on Econ. Edn. (1st place award 1990, 91, named Ala. Elem. Econs. Tchr. Yr. 1992). Republican. Methodist. Avocations: travel, crafts, basket-making, antiques, needlework. Home: 625 Kenrose St Collierville TN 38017-3704 Office: Highland Oaks Elem 5252 Annandale Dr Memphis TN 38125-4263 also: Highland Oaks Elem Sch 5252 Annandale Dr Memphis TN 38125-4263

DONAHUE, LINDA WHEELER, retired English educator, writer; b. Derby, Conn., Nov. 21, 1941; d. Wilson Chatfield and Beatrice (Smith) Wheeler; m. Raymond Maurice Farrell, July 17, 1965 (div. 1977); 1 child, Sarah Elizabeth; m. James John Donahue Jr., Dec. 30, 1977; 1 child, James John III. BS, Nasson Coll., 1963; MS, U. Bridgeport, 1967. Assoc. prof. Mattatuck C.C., Waterbury, Conn., 1968-80; prof. English and humanities Naugatuck Valley C.C., Waterbury, 1980-84, prof. emeritus humanities, 1997—, divsn. dir. arts and humanities, 1988-92. Contbr. articles to profl. jours. Mem. Roosevelt Warm Springs (Ga.) Found., 1960—, Gazette Internat. Polio Newworking Inst., St. Louis, 1975—, Polio Survivors Found., Downey, Calif., 1977—, pres. Polio Outreach of Conn., 2000—, Conn. Coalition Citizens with Disabilities; active in disability movement; chairperson N.W. Activists for Disability Rights; pres. Conn. Union Disability Action Groups, 1998—. Mem. Conn. Heads of English Depts., Nat. Coun. Tchrs. English, NAFE, Assn. Exec. Educators, AAUW, Congress Conn. Cmty. Colls. (pres. 1985), Nat. Orgn. on disability, Am. Rose Soc., Phi Theta Kappa. Congregationalist. Avocations: opera, theatre, design, symphony, persian cats. Home: 75 Tallwood Rd Southbury CT 06488-2751 Office: Naugatuck Valley CC Tech Coll Div Arts-Hums 750 Chase Pkwy Waterbury CT 06708-3089

DONAHUE, RICHARD JAMES, secondary school educator; b. New Rochelle, N.Y., Dec. 11, 1950; s. Raymond Douglas and Helen Andrea (Garibaldi) Silva. BS in Math., SUNY, Oneonta, 1972; MS (spl.), Coll. New Rochelle, 1977; MS in Ednl. Computing, Iona Coll., 1986. Cert. spl. edn. tchr., N.Y., tchr. secondary math., N.Y. Tchr. spl. edn. Adams Sch., N.Y.C., 1973-75, curriculum coord., 1976-77; tchr. math. and computer literacy Eastchester (N.Y.) Jr. H.S., 1975-76, 77—; tchr. math. SAT preparation New Rochelle H.S., 1981-83, tchr. Gen. Ednl. Devel. math., 1981—. Tchr. computers Coll. New Rochelle, 1988, adj. asst. prof., 1988-92; tchr. computers Manhattanville Coll., Purchase, N.Y., 1983-85; mem. challenge gifted and talented program Concordia Coll., Bronxville, N.Y., 1988-89; tchr. tng. courses in computer applications Eastchester Union Free Sch. Dist., 1993-94; tchr. mentor on use of telecom. Am. Online's Scholastic Network, 1994; adv. bd. world wide web Scholastic Network; participant Waikoloa Sci. Project, Hawaii, 1997; ednl. cons. and web designer Nat. Optical Astronomy Observatories and Kitt Peak Nat. Observatory, 1999. Author: BASIC Number Theory Programs, 1985-86, PASCAL Number Theory Programs, 1987, also computer software series in math. edn., 1982-83; also articles and internet column. Recipient N.Y. State Model Schs. Tchr. Integration award Madison-Oneida Bd. Coop. Edn. Svcs., 1998, N.Y. Wired Applied Tech. award The N.Y. Jour. News, 1999; NSF Math. Devel. Program grantee, 1981, NEWMAST grantee Ednl. Workshop NASA, 1994, Tchr. Resource Agt. grantee Am. Astron. Soc., 1996, Reader's Digest Found. Interdisciplinary Learning Project grantee, 1998, BEPT mini grantee, 1998, Impact II grantee BOCES N.Y. State Edn. Dept., Westcherter/Rockland Impact II Developer award, So. Westchester BOCES, 1999, N.Y. Wired Applied Tech. award, N.Y. Jour. News, 1999. Mem. Nat. Coun. Tchr. Math. (reviewer and referee for Math. Tchr. publ.), Assn. Math. Tchrs. N.Y. State, Math. Assn. Am., Eastchester Tchrs. Assn. (treas. 1983-97), N.Y. State Congress of Parents and Tchrs. (life, Jenkins award 1994), Eastchester Tchrs. Inst. (treas. 1983-85), Nat. Sci. Tchrs. Assn., N.Y. State Assn. for Computers and Tech. in Edn., N.Y. State Tech. Edn. Assn., Film Soc. Lincoln Ctr., Am. Film Inst., Bronxville, Eastchester, Pelham and Tuckahoe Consortium, Westchester Amateur Astronomers, Internat. Tech. Edn. Assn. Home: 60 Locust Ave Apt A201 New Rochelle NY 10801-7360

DONALD, ALEXANDER GRANT, psychiatrist, educator; b. Darlington, S.C., Jan. 24, 1928; s. Raymond George and Chesnut Evans (McIntosh) D.; m. Emma Louise Coggeshall, Oct. 25, 1958; children: Sandy, Mary Chesnut, Marion Lide. BS, Davidson Coll., 1948; MD, Med. U. S.C., 1952. Diplomate: Am. Bd. Psychiatry and Neurology. Intern Jefferson Med. Coll., 1952-53; resident in psychiatry Walter Reed Hosp., 1956-59; dir. Mental Health Clinic, Florence, S.C., 1962-66; dept. commr. S.C. Dept. Mental Health, 1966-67; dir. William S Hall Psychiat. Inst., Columbia, 1967-90; prof., chmn. dept. neuropsychiatry and behavioral scis. Sch. Medicine, U. S.C., Columbia, 1975-90, Disting. prof. neuropsychiatry, assoc. dean ednl. planning, 1990-91, Disting. prof. emeritus, 1991—. Bd. dirs. Health Resource Found. Trustee Richland Meml. Hosp., 1993—2002, vice-chmn., 1997, chmn., 1999; bd. dirs. S.C. Inst. Med. Edn. and Rsch., pres., 1992—96; trustee Palmetto Health Alliance, 1999—, vice-chmn., 2003. Fellow Am. Coll. Psychiatrists, Am. Psychiat. Assn. (pres. S.C. chpt. 1967), So. Psychiat. Assn. (v.p.); mem. AMA, Columbia Med. Soc. (v.p. 1981, del. 1981, pres. 1989-90), Evening Music Club (pres. 1989-90), Alpha Omega Alpha. Presbyterian. Office: U SC Sch Medicine 3555 Harden Street Ext Ste 104 Columbia SC 29203-6894 E-mail: grantd@aol.com.

DONALD, DAVID HERBERT, author, history educator; b. Goodman, Miss., Oct. 1, 1920; s. Ira Unger and Sue Ella (Belford) D.; m. Aida DiPace, 1955; 1 son, Bruce Randall. Student, Holmes Jr. Coll., 1937-39; AB, Millsaps Coll., 1941, LHD, 1976; AM, U. Ill., 1942, PhD, 1946, LHD (hon.), 1992; MA (hon.), U. Oxford, 1959, Harvard U., 1973; LittD (hon.), Coll. Charleston, 1985; D in History, Lincoln U., 1996; LHD, U. Calgary, 2000; LLD, Ill. Coll., 2002; LittD, Middlebury Coll., 2003. Teaching fellow U. N.C., 1942; research asst. history U. Ill., 1943-45, research assoc., 1946-47; fellow Social Sci. Research Council, 1945-46; instr. history Columbia U., 1947-49; assoc. prof. history Smith Coll., 1949-51; asst. prof. history Columbia U. Grad. Faculty, 1951-52, assoc. prof., 1952-57, prof. history, 1957-59, Princeton U., 1959-62; prof. Am. history Johns Hopkins U., Balt., 1962-73, Harry C. Black prof., 1963-73, dir. Inst. So. History, 1966-72; Charles Warren prof. Am. history and prof. Am. civilization Harvard U., 1973-91, prof. emeritus, 1991—, chmn. grad. program in Am. civilization, 1979-85. Vis. assoc. prof. Amherst Coll., 1950; Fulbright lectr. Am. history U. Coll. North Wales, 1953-54; mem. Inst. Advanced Study, 1957-58; Harmsworth prof. Am. history Oxford U., 1959-60; John P. Young lectr. Memphis State U., 1963; Walter Lynwood Fleming lectr. La. State U., 1965; Benjamin Rush lectr. Am. Psychiat. Assn., 1972; Commonwealth lectr. Univ. Coll., London, 1975; Samuel Paley lectr. Hebrew Univ. of Jerusalem, 1991. Author: Lincoln's Herndon, 1948, Divided We Fought, A Pictorial History of the War, 1861-65, 1952, Inside Lincoln's Cabinet: The Civil War Diaries of Salmon P. Chase, 1954, Lincoln Reconsidered: Essays on the Civil War Era, 1956, rev. 3d edit., 2001, A Rebel's Recollections, (G.C. Eggleston), 1959, Charles Sumner and the Coming of the Civil War, 1960 (Pulitzer prize in biography), Why the North Won the Civil War, 1960, rev. edit., 1996, (with J.G. Randall) The Civil War and Reconstruction, 2d edit., 1961, rev., enlarged edit., 1969, (with Jean H. Baker and Michael F. Holt) rev. edit., 2001, The Divided Union, 1961, The Politics of Reconstruction, 1863-67, 1965, The Nation in Crisis, 1861-1877, 1969, Charles Sumner and the Rights of Man, 1970, (with Sidney Andrews) The South Since the War, 1970, Gone for a Soldier, 1975, (with others) The Great Republic, 1977, rev. edit., 1981, 3rd edit., 1985, 4th edit., 1992, Liberty and Union, 1978, Look Homeward: A Life of Thomas Wolfe, 1987 (Pulitzer prize 1988), Lincoln, 1995 rev. edit., 1996, Charles Sumner, 1997, Lincoln at Home: Two Glimpses of Abraham Lincoln's Domestic Life, 1999, We Are Lincoln Men: Abraham Lincoln and His Friends, 2003; editor: War Diary and Letters of Stephen Minot Weld, 1979; gen. editor: Documentary History of American Life, The Making of America Series, 6 vols.; co-editor: (with wife) Diary of Charles Francis Adams, 2 vols., 1964; contbr. articles to periodicals. Recipient Abraham Lincoln Lit. award Union League Club N.Y.C., 1977, C. Hugh Holman prize MLA, 1988, Benjamin L.C. Wailes award Miss. Hist. Soc., 1994, Barondess-Lincoln prize, 1996, Christopher award, 1996, Lincoln prize Gettysburg Coll., 1996, Jefferson Davis award Mus. of Confederacy, 1996, Nevins/Freeman award Chgo. Civil War Round Table, 1999, Joseph R. Levenson award Harvard U. 1993; Guggenheim fellow, 1964-65, 85-86, fellow Am. Coun. Learned Socs., 1969-70, Ctr. for Advanced Study Behavioral Scis., 1969-70, George A. and Eliza G. Howard fellow, 1957-58, sr. fellow NEH, 1971-72. Fellow Am. Acad. Arts and Scis.; mem. Orgn. Am. Historians, Am. Hist. Assn., So. Hist. Assn. (v.p. 1968, pres. 1969), Soc. Am. Historians, Mass. Hist. Soc., Am. Antiquarian Soc., Phi Beta Kappa, Phi Kappa Phi, Pi Kappa Delta, Pi Kappa Alpha, Omicron Delta Kappa. Clubs: Harvard (N.Y.C.); Cosmos, Signet, Fox. Episcopalian. Home: 41 Lincoln Rd PO Box 6158 Lincoln MA 01773-6158 E-mail: donald@fas.harvard.edu.

DONALDSON, ROBERT CHARLES, history educator; b. San Francisco, Jan. 28, 1924; s. Donald and Cora Priscilla (Donaldson) Wood; m. Persis Chapple, Jan. 4, 1975. Student, U. Ariz., 1942; BA, U. So. Calif., 1950, MA, 1951; PhD, U. Mich., 1954; Fulbright scholar, U. Brussels, 1953-54. Asst. prof. Eastern Ky. State Coll., 1954-57; asst. prof. history Calif. State U., Sacramento, 1957-62, assoc. prof., 1962-67, prof., 1967-94, chmn. dept., 1969-75, chmn. acad. senate, 1968-69, coll. ombudsman, 1969-70, presiding officer faculty, 1975-77, faculty emeritus, 1995—. Senator Acad. Senate of Calif. State Univs. and Colls., 1970-76; real estate broker, 1990—. Pres. Gold Country Chamber Orch., 2000-2001. Served with AUS, 1943-46. Recipient Meritorious Performance award for outstanding svc. to univ. community, 1988. Mem. Am. Hist. Assn., Faculty Emeritus Assn. (pres. 1995-97), Town and Gown (dir. 1989—), Phi Kappa Phi (pres. campus chpt. 1963-64, 74-76, 92-94, 2003-), Phi Alpha Theta, Blue Key, Phi Beta Delta. Democrat. Home: 1516 Little Ct Carmichael CA 95608-5915

DONALDSON, ROBERT HERSCHEL, university administrator, educator; b. Houston, June 14, 1943; s. Herschel Arthur and Vera Edith (True) D.; m. Judy Carol Johnston, June 27, 1964 (div. Apr. 30, 1984); children: Jennifer Gwynne, John Andrew; m. Sally S. Abravanel, Mar. 31, 1985; children: Mark Elliot, Ryan Scott. AB, Harvard U., 1964, A.M., 1966, PhD, 1969. Prof. polit. sci. Vanderbilt U., 1968-81, assoc. dean Coll. Arts and Sci., 1975-81; provost, v.p. acad. affairs, prof. polit. sci. Herbert H. Lehman Coll. CUNY, 1981-84; pres. Fairleigh Dickinson U., Rutherford, N.J., 1984-90, U. Tulsa, 1990-96, trustees prof. polit. sci., 1996—. Vis. research prof. U.S. Army War Coll., 1978-79; pres. Am. coms. fgn. rels., 2002-. Author: Stasis and Change in Revolutionary Elites, 1971, Soviet Policy toward India, 1974, The Soviet-Indian Alliance: Quest for Influence, 1979, The Soviet Union in the Third World: Successes and Failures, 1981, Soviet Foreign Policy since World War II, 1981, 85, 88, 92, The Foreign Policy of Russia: Changing Systems, Enduring Interests, 1998, 2002. Council Fgn. Relations fellow, 1973-74 Mem. Coun. on Fgn. Rels., Phi Beta Kappa. Republican. Methodist. Home: 6449 S Richmond Ave Tulsa OK 74136-1669 Office: Univ Tulsa 600 S College Ave Tulsa OK 74104-3126 E-mail: robert-donaldson@utulsa.edu.

DONALDSON, THOMAS, ethicist, educator; b. Wichita, Kans., July 23, 1945; s. Paul J. and Louisene (Sadler) D.; m. Sally Leisure, May, 1970 (div. 1973); m. Jean Shephard, Sept. 3, 1977; children: Paul, Keith, Paige. Student, U.S. Naval Acad., 1963-65; BS, U. Kans., 1967, PhD, 1976. Asst. prof. Loyola U., Chgo., 1976-81, assoc. prof., 1981-84, Henry J. Wirtenberger prof. ethics, 1984-88; C. Stewart Sheppard vis. prof. bus. adminstrn. U. Va., Charlottesville, 1988-89; John Carroll prof. bus. ethics Georgetown U., Washington, 1989-92, John F. Connelly prof. bus. ethics, 1992-96; Mark O. Winkelman endowed prof. Wharton Sch., U. Pa., Phila., 1996—. Testified in U.S. Congress (Senate Judiciary Com.) on Sarbanes-Oxley legis., 2002; participant World Econ. Forum, Davos, Switzerland, 2003. Editor: Issues in Moral Philosophy, 1986, Case Studies in Business Ethics, 1987,Ethical Issues in Business, 1979, 83, 87, 92; author: The Ethics of International Business, 1989, Corporations and Morality, 1982, (with Thomas W. Dunfee) Ties That Bind: A Social Contracts Approach to Business Ethics, 1999; assoc. editor Acad. of Mgmt. Rev., 2002—, mem. editl. bd., 1996-2002; contbr. articles to profl. jours.; mem. editl. bd. Bus. Ethics Quar., 1990—. Mem. Haverford Friends Meeting, 1998—. With USN, 1963-65. Fellow Bus. Enterprise Trust; mem. Ctr. for Advanced Study Ethics (coun. scholars 1990—), Phila. Country Club. Avocations: music, skiing. Home: 214 N Roberts Rd Bryn Mawr PA 19010-2818 Office: U Pa Wharton Sch Philadelphia PA 19104

DONALDSON, WILMA CRANKSHAW, elementary education educator; b. Havre de Grace, Md., Aug. 28, 1942; d. John Hamilton and Wilma Chaffee (Thurlow) Crankshaw; m. James Neill Donaldson, Aug. 5, 1967. BA in Edn. cum laude, Westminster Coll., 1964; MA in Edn., Fairfield U., 1976. Educator Hurlbutt Elem. Sch., Weston, Conn., 1964-78, 92—, Weston Mid. Sch., 1979-91; tchr. Greek Mythology Elem. Sch., 1999—. Team leader Hurlbutt Elem. Sch., 1967—68, 1976—78, sci. rep., 1992—99, developer of curriculum; judge Odyssey of the Mind, Conn., 1995—2001; tchr. photography and Greek myth courses elem. sch., 2002—; tchr. pvt. student art courses; tchr. Music/Lit./Theater Workshop, 1997—; presenter in field. Author: (filmstrip script) Science Series, 1972, Metric Math Series, 1973. Chairperson fine arts New England Sch. Accreditation Com., Weston, 1990-91; trainer Project CHEM, Exxon Corp., 1991—; state planning com., program/site chmn. Conn. Elem. Sci. Day Conf., 1994—; organizer, advisor Student Elem. Sch. Environ. Orgn., 1992—; co-organizer, co-founder Elem. Family Sci. Night, Weston, 2000; dir./tchr. Camp Invention, Weston, 2002—. Recipient Faculty Mem. Presdl. Recognition Sch. award U.S. Dept. Edn., 1987-88, Celebration of Excellence award State of Conn., 1989, 92, 95, 98. Mem. NEA, Nat. Sci. Tchrs. Assn. (workshop presenter Moscow 1991, NASA-NEWEST awardee 1997), ASCD, Conn. Edn. Assn., Conn. Alliance Arts Edn. (Weston Tchr. of Yr. 1994-95, Conn. Alliance for Art Edn. Disting. Tchr. of Yr. 1995), Coun. Elem. Sci. Internat. (com. chmn. 1991-98), Delta Zeta. Avocations: art, theater, photography, travel.

DONALSON, MALCOLM DREW, classics educator; b. Albany, Ga., July 24, 1951; s. William Levon Donalson and Julia Janet King; m. Deborah Ellen Hoffman, June 25, 1988; children: Christopher Damian, Sabina Anuradha, Zoë Simone, Simon Zachary. BA in Latin and History, Fla. State U., 1974, MA in Classics, 1985, PhD in Humanities, 1991. Ordained clergy F.O.I., 2000; cert. tchr. Latin and history Fla. Tchr. Latin, Greek, and history Marianna (Fla.) H.S., 1974-84; tchg. asst. dept. classics Fla. State U., Tallahassee, 1984-89; tchr. Latin, Episcopal H.S., Baton Rouge, 1989-90, McKinley Mid. Magnet Sch., Baton Rouge, 1990-91, Istrouma Med. Magnet Sch., Baton Rouge, 1990-91; prof. fgn. langs. Ala. Sch. Math. and Sci., Mobile, 1991—. Author: St. Jerome's Chronicon, 1996, The Domestic Cat in Roman Civilization, 1999, The Cult of Isis in the Roman Empire. Isis Invicta, 2003; contbr. articles. Mem. Am. Classical League, Classical Assn.

Midwest and South, Classical Assn. Ala., Women's Classical Caucus. Hindu. Avocation: classical coinage. Office: Ala Sch Math & Sci 1255 Dauphin St Mobile AL 36604-2519 E-mail: malcolmdonalson@aol.com.

DONDALSKI, LINDA, elementary education educator; b. Williams, Ariz., Sept. 27, 1948; d. Myldon L. and Blanche E. (Claude) Grisey; m. Steven L. Dondalski, Apr. 17, 1971; children: Jennifer N. Dondalski, Jason J. Dondalski. BS, No. Ariz. U., Flagstaff, 1971. Computer asst. San Bernardino (Calif.) Sch. Dist., 1980-90; tchr. computers St. Adelaide Sch., Highland, Calif., 1990—. Roman Catholic. Avocation: travel. Home: 6690 Seine Ave Highland CA 92346-2680 Office: St Adelaide Sch 27487 Baseline St Highland CA 92346-3206

DONEGAN, CHARLES EDWARD, lawyer, educator; b. Chgo., Apr. 10, 1933; s. Arthur C. and Odessa (Arnold) D.; m. Patty Lou Harris, June 15, 1963; 1 son, Carter Edward. BSC., Roosevelt U., 1954; MS, Loyola U., 1959; JD, Howard U., 1967; LL.M., Columbia, 1970. Bar: N.Y. 1968, D.C. 1968, Ill. 1979. Pub. sch. tchr., Chgo., 1956-59; with Office Internal Revenue, Chgo., 1959-62; labor economist U.S. Dept. Labor, Washington, 1962-65; legal intern U.S. Commn. Civil Rights, Washington, summer 1966; asst. counsel NAACP Legal Def. Fund, N.Y.C., 1967-69; lectr. law Baruch Coll., N.Y.C., 1969-70; asst. prof. law State U. N.Y. at Buffalo, 1970-73; assoc. prof. law Howard U., 1973-77; vis. assoc. prof. Ohio State U., Columbus, 1977-78; asst. regional counsel U.S. EPA, 1978-80; prof. law So. U., Baton Rouge, 1980—; sole practice law Chgo. and Washington, 1984—. Arbitrator steel industry, 1972, U.S. Postal Svc., New Orleans, D.C. Superior Ct., 1987—, Fed. Mediation and Conciliation Svc., 1985—, N.Y. Stock Exch.; vis. prof. law La. State U., 1981, N.C. Cen. U., Durham, 1988—, So. U., Baton Rouge, spring 1992; real estate broker; mem. bd. consumer claims Dist. D.C., 1988—; mem. Mayor's Transition Task Force, Washington, 1995; moot ct. judge Georgetown U. Law Sch., Washington, 1987—, Howard U. Law Sch., Washington, 1987—, Balsa, 1987—; spkr. in field. Author: Discrimination in Public Employment, 1975; editor Bat. Bar Assn. Arbitration Section newsletter. 1997-; contbr. articles to profl. jours. Active Ams. for Dem. Action; me. adv. com. D.C. Bd. of Edn. Named one of Top 42 Lawyers in Washington Area, Washington Afro-Am. Newspaper, 1993, 94, 95, 96' Ford Found. scholar, 1965-67. Columbia U., 1972-73, NEH Postdoctoral fellow in Afro-Am. studies Yale U., 1972-73. Mem. ABA (vice-chmn. edn. and curriculum com. local govt. law sect. 1972-80, pub. edn. com. sect. local govt. 1974-84, chmn. liaison com. AALS, 1984, chair arbitration sect.), Nat. Bar Assn. (labor and employment law sect., steering com., editor arbitration sect. newsletter 1997—), D.C. Bar Assn., Washington Bar Assn. (chmn. legal edn. com.), Chgo. Bar Assn., Fed. Bar Assn., Cook County Bar Assn., Am. Arbitration Assn. (arbitrator), D.C. Fee Arbitration Bd. (bd. govs. 1990—), Nat. Conf. Black Lawyers (bd. organizers), Nat. Futures Assn. (arbitrator), Nat. Assn. Securities Dealers (arbitrator), Assn. Henri Capitant, Roosevelt U. Alumni Assn. (rep. at George Washington U. 175th anniversary charter day convocation 1996), Loyola U. Alumni Assn. (v.p. Washington), Howard U. Alumni Assn. (rep. at Hunter Coll. Centennial 1970), Columbia U. Alumni Assn. (v.p. law Washington), Alpha Phi Alpha, Phi Alpha Kappa, Phi Alpha Delta. Home: 4315 Argyle Ter NW Washington DC 20011-4243 Office: 601 Pennsylvania Ave NW Ste 900 Washington DC 20004-3615 also: 311 S Wacker Dr Ste 4550 Chicago IL 60606-6622

DONEHEW, PAMELA K. reading specialist; b. Fairmont, W.Va., Sept. 24, 1949; d. Walter Hal Donehew and Eldora Jean (Eddy) Van Tol; m. E. William Ball, Sr., June 1, 1968 (div. Oct. 1993); children: E. William, Jr., Jennifer Catena, Geoffrey J.; m. Lawrence L. Lambert, Feb. 14, 1999; stepchildren: Leslie L., Laura M. AA, Ocean County Coll., Toms River, N.J., 1986; BA in English and Psychology, Monmouth U., 1989, MA, 1991, MSEd, 1992. Cert. reading specialist, tchr. psychology, English tchr., tchr. grades K-12, N.J. Dir. reading ctr. Monmouth U., West Long Branch, N.J., 1989-92; tchr. psychology Manasquan H.S., N.J., 1992-95; reading specialist West Ga. Tech., LaGrange, 1995—, SAT and ACT supr., 1996—. Learning cons. Georgian Ct. Coll., Lakewood, N.J., 1995; reader coll. bds. AP Psychology Exam, 1996—; GRE, GMAT test administr., 1990-94. Author: Library Handbook, 1996; co-author: Learn to Tutor, 1990. Mem. APA, NEA, Nat. Coun. English Tchrs., Internat. Reading Assn., Phi Delta Kappa. Office: West Ga Tech 303 Fort Dr Lagrange GA 30240-5957 E-mail: pdonehew@westgatec.ga.tec.us.

DONELIAN, ARMEN, pianist, composer, author; b. N.Y.C., Dec. 1, 1950; s. Khatchik Ohannes and Lillian (Sarkisian) D. Artists cert., Westchester Conservatory Music, 1968; BA in Music, Columbia U., 1972; studies with, Carl Bamberger, Ludmila Ulehla, Harold Seletsky, Richard Beirach. Jazz pianist, composer, 1972—; pvt. tchr. piano and theory, 1965—. Instr. piano Westchester Conservatory Music, White Plains, N.Y., 1972-75, 83-87, instr. theory, 1974-75; instr. piano, ear tng., jazz ensemble New Sch. Jazz Program, N.Y.C., 1986—, William Paterson U., N.J., 1993—; founder Jazz in Armenia Project in cooperation with Yerevan State Cons., 1998—. Composer: (albums) Wave, Mystic Heights, The Wayfarer, Stargazer, Secrets, Trio 87, Sofrito, A Reverie, Hurricane, Positively Armenian 2, others; (film) Passion City (Best Film Score, 1988, Tisch Sch. of Arts, N.Y.U.); performer numerous worldwide tours, TV, radio and film appearances, 1976—; pianist with many jazz artists including Sonny Rollins, Mongo Santamaria, Billy Harper, Lionel Hampton, Chet Baker, Dave Liebman, Paquito D'Rivera, Anne-Marie Moss, Night Ark; author: Training the Ear: For the Improvising Musician, 1992; contbr. articles to Jazz World mag. and Op mag., Downbeat mag., Keyboard mag., Rutgers Ann. Rev. of Jazz Studies. Recipient Cert. of Appreciation, New Sch. U., 1998, Internat. Ptnr./Artslink Collaborative award, CEC, 1999, Fulbright Sr. Specialist award, 2003; fellow Nat. Endowment for Arts Jazz Performance, 1983, 1994, 1996, in composition N.J. State Coun. on Arts, 2000; grantee Meet the Composer, 1979, 1983, 1987, 1999, 2000, Faculty Devel. at New Sch., 1995, Nat. Endowment for Arts Jazz Performance, 1986, 1990, 1992; scholar Fulbright Scholar award, 2002. Mem. Am. Fedn. Musicians (local 802), Steinway Affiliated Artist. Office: New Sch Jazz Program 55 W 13th St Fl 5 New York NY 10011-7958 E-mail: info@armenjazz.com.

DONHAM, JEAN, library and information science educator; b. Iowa City, Aug. 9, 1946; d. Edward Patrick and Edith (Reilly) Organ; m. Kelley Jon Donham, Aug. 10, 1968 (div. Dec. 1988); children: Andrew, Joel; m. Robert Moon van Deusen, July 1, 1989 (div. Oct. 1997). BA, U. Iowa, 1967, PhD, 1991; MLS, U. Md., 1972. Cert. secondary tchr., cert. libr. and dir. media grades kindergarten through 12, Iowa. Tchr. Ames (Iowa) Community Schs., 1967-71; adminstrv. intern Iowa City Community Schs., 1978-79, libr. media specialist, 1974-80, dist. coord., 1980-93; asst. prof. Sch. Libr. and Info. Sci. U. Iowa, Iowa City, 1993—2000; coll. libr. Cornell Coll., Mt. Vernon, Iowa, 2000—. Author: Teaching with Computers, 1989, Enhancing Teaching and Learning; a Leadership Guide for Library Media Specialists, 1998, Inquiry-Based Learning: Lessons from Library Power, 2001; contbr. articles to profl. jours. Mem. Iowa Ednl. Media Assn. (bd. dirs. 1978-81, pres. 1990-91, Profl. of Yr. award 1988), Am. Assn. Sch. Librs. (bd. dirs.). Home: 32 High Circle Dr NE Iowa City IA 52240-7935 Office: Cole Libr Cornell Coll Mount Vernon IA 52314

DONICA, CHERYL MARIE, elementary education educator; b. Greensburg, Ind., Aug. 26, 1953; d. Thurman Lloyd and Kathryn Lucille (Chadwell) D. BS in Edn., Ind. U., 1975, MS in Edn., 1979. Tchr. Decatur County Schs., Greensburg, Ind., 1975-81, Escola Americana de Brasilia, Brazil, 1981-85, Fontana (Calif.) Unified Schs., 1986—. Mentor tchr. Fontana Unified Schs., 1989-92, 93-94, program specialist, 1990-92, 96-99, reading recovery tchr., 1993-98. Reading and Literacy Merit award Arrowhead Reading Coun., San Bernardino, Calif., 1989. Mem. NEA, Calif. Tchrs. Assn., Internat. Reading Assn., Assn. Childhood Edn. Internat. Calif. Kindergarten Assn., Nat. Assn. Edn. of Young Children. Republican. Methodist. Avocations: reading, travel. Home: 1823 Brookstone St Redlands CA 92374-1770 Office: Oak Park Elem 14200 Live Oak Ave Fontana CA 92337-8389 E-mail: cmdca@msn.com.

DONKLE, PRISCILLA P. secondary school educator; d. Dr. Raymond Leon and Madeline Margaret Porter; m. Lucius B. Donkle III, Mar. 29, 1980; children: Luke, Alex. BS, Ball State U., Muncie, Ind., 1974; MS, Ind. U., 1980. Cert. Tchr. in Residence Ind. Prof. Standards Bd., 2000. Tchr. math. South Ctrl. Jr.-Sr. H.S., Union Mills, Ind., 1974-85, 90—, Harford Cmty. Schs., Bel Air, Md., 1985-86; adult edn. instr. Harford C.C., Bel Air, 1987-88. Guest lectr. Purdue North Ctrl., Westville, Ind., 1982-83, 84-85, adj. guest lectr., 1988-90; mem. profl. stds. math. adv. com. State of Ind. Profl. Stds. Bd., Indpls., 1994-95; mem. math. adv. com. Ind. Dept. Edn., Indpls., 1990-94, mem. Core 40 math. writing team, 1994-95. Pres. Welcome Wagon Newcomers, Valparaiso, Ind., 1988-89, v.p. alumni club, 1991-92. Recipient Presdl. Award for Excellence in Secondary Math. Teaching, NSF, 1993; named Tchr. of the Yr., South Ctrl. HS, 1994, Nat. Tandy Tech. Award 1997 for Ed. Pres. SC Classroom Tchr. Assoc., Speaker-Nat. and Ind. Coun. of Tchr. of Math. Conferences, Mem. Nat. Coun. Tchrs. Math., Ind. Coun. Tchrs. Math., Coun. of Presdl. Awardees, Alpha Delta Kappa (v.p., pres. 1991—).

DONLEY, DENNIS LEE, school librarian; b. Port Hueneme, Calif., July 19, 1950; s. Mickey Holt and Joan Elizabeth (Smith) D.; m. Ruth Ann Shank, June 10, 1972; children: Eric Holt, Evan Scott. AA, Ventura Coll., 1970; BA with honors, U. Calif., Santa Barbara, 1973; MLS, San Jose State U., 1976. Cert. secondary tchr., Calif. Libr. media tchr. San Diego Unified Sch. Dist., 1975—. Lectr. Calif. State U., L.A., 1987-89; libr. cons. San Diego C.C. Dist., 1990; chmn. sch. adv. com. Point Loma H.S., San Diego, 1986-87; coop. book rev. bd. San Diego County, 1984-86; creator adult sch. curriculum, 1984-86; contbr. Deadbase X, Deadbase 94, The Deadhead's Taping Compendium, Vols. 1-3, The Deadhead's Taping Addendum. Mem. ALA, Calif. Libr. Media Educators Assn. Avocations: reading, music, fitness. Office: Hoover HS 4474 El Cajon Blvd San Diego CA 92115-4312 E-mail: ddonley@mail.sandi.net.

DONLEY, DONALD CHARLES, educational administrator; b. Columbia, Pa., Apr. 7, 1953; s. Ralph Emerson Donley II and Vivian Mary Margaret (Smuck) Gingerich; m. Darla Jo Innerst, Feb. 7, 1993; children: Amanda Laura, Chase Can Preston. BA in Indsl. Edn., Millersville U., 1974, MA in Indsl. Edn., 1982; MA in Ednl. Adminstrn., Western Md., 1992; postgrad., U. Md., 1989—. cert. superintendant, Pa., vocational dir., administration, program specialist, wrestling coach, sports medicine. Tchr. indsl. arts. Susquehannock H.S., Glen Rock, Pa., 1974-79; tchr. power tech. William Penn H.S., York, Pa., 1979-81; dir. alternative edn. York City Sch. Dist., 1981-87; asst. prin. York County Area Vo-Tech., 1987-95; prin. York County Summer Sch, 1987—; vocat. supr York County Area Vo-Tech., 1995—. Legis. chmn. York County Security and Attendance, 1992—; recruiter, interviewer York County Tchr. Consortium, 1992—; cert. assessor NASSP, Arlington, Va., 1992—; com. mem. York County Health Edn. Ctr., 1992—; group seven mem. Charles Kettering Idea Principals Devel. Program, New Oxford, Pa., 1988-90; head coach U.S. Jr. World Wrestling Team, 1982, York High Wrestling Team, 1979-87, Susquehannock Jr. High Wrestling Team, Glen Rock, Pa., 1974-79. Mem. ASCD, Nat. Assn. Sec. Sch. Prins., Am. Assn. Sch. Adminstrs., Pa. Assn. Sec. Prins., Epsilon Pi Tau, Phi Delta Kappa (rsch. chmn., pres. elect). Home: 1496 Stonemill Dr Elizabethtown PA 17022-9422 Office: York County Area Vocational-Tech 2179 S Queen St York PA 17402-4628

DONLON, JOSEPHINE A. diagnostic and evaluation counseling therapist, educator; b. N.Y.C., Apr. 3, 1921; d. Henry R. and Josephine V. (Klarer) Janssen; m. William James Donlon; children: William James, Gregory A., Michele L., DruAnn. R.N., Englewood (N.J.) Hosp., 1941; BA in Psychology, Colo. Coll., Colorado Springs, 1945; MEd, Nat. Coll. Edn., Evanston, Ill., 1975. Cert. in nursing, spl. edn., Ill., Colo.; specialist in social maladjusted, learning disabled, educable mentally handicapped. Pediatric psychiat. nurse N.Y. State Psychiat. Inst., N.Y.C., 1941-42; supr. psychiat. nursing Colo. U. Psychiat. Inst., 1945-47; pub. health nurse Denver Sch., 1947-48; diagnostic educator Schaumburg (Ill.) Sch. Dist. 54, 1969-78; pvt. practice diagnostic evaluation and counseling Brookeville, Md., 1979-87, Pineland, Fla., 1987—. Leader Girl Scouts U.S.A., 1958-62; previously active PTAs in Colo. and Ill. Mem. Council Exceptional Children, Council for Children with Behavioral Disorders, Council for Ednl. Diagnostic Services. Research in genetic endocrine diseases of pancreas and thyroid and relation to learning and behavior. Home: PO Box 2212 Pineland FL 33945-2212

DONNELLY, BARBARA, artist, educator; b. Somerville, Mass. d. Russell Winfield and Pearl Marie (Cameron) Chick; m. Robert Boag Donnelly, May 29, 1954; children: Kathleen, Sharon, Robert Jr., Patricia, Michael, Brian. AA, Boston U., 1954. Tchr. oil painting, watercolors Beverly (Mass.) Adult Edn., 1969-80, 83-90, tchr. basic drawing, 1970-90; tchr. Lakes Region Outdoor Painting, N.H., 1977-85; tchr. pen, ink No. Essex C. C., Newburyport, Mass., 1986-88; court rm. artist Channel 56, Boston, 1987—; tchr. watercolor Gloucester, Mass., 1993—. Presenter Holiday Hill Painting Workshops, N.H., 1998-99. Illustrator: The Little Book Shop, 1989; cover artist: Palette Talk, 1990; one-woman shows include French Embassy, Washington, 1998; contbr. articles to profl. jours. Asst. chmn. Beverly Bicentennial Arts Festival, 1975, chmn. 1976. Named Internat. Artist-in-Residence, Dinan, France, "Les Amis de La Grande Vigne" Mus., 1996. Mem. Am. Artists Profl. League, Acad. Artists Assn., North Shore Arts Assn., Rockport Art Assn., New England Watercolor Soc. (Paul Strisik Meml. award 1998), Guild of Beverly Artists, Copley Soc. of Boston. Roman Catholic. Avocations: photography, computer art, architecture. Office: Barbara Donnelly Art Gallery 19 Harbor Loop Gloucester MA 01930-5003

DONNELLY, CAROL BURNS, education educator; b. Worcester, Mass., Sept. 15, 1946; d. Francis A. and Loretta (Chisholm) Burns; m. James C. Donnelly Jr., June 28, 1968; children: James C. IV, Sarah Y. BA, Wellesley Coll., 1968; MA, U. Miami, 1970; MEd, Harvard U., 1980; EdD, Boston U., 1988. High sch. tchr., guidance counselor Auburn (Mass.) Pub. Schs., 1971-74; parent liaison Cambridge (Mass.) Pub. Schs., 1980; kindergarten tchr. Newton (Mass.) Pub. Schs., 1982-84; early childhood coord. Auburn (Mass.) Pub. Schs., 1984-92, dir. spl. edn., 1992-97; asst. prof. edn. Worcester State Coll., 1997—2002, assoc. prof. edn., 2002—. Adj. instr. Bridgewater (Mass.) State Coll., 1978-79, Quincy (Mass.) Jr. Coll., 1974-79, Curry Coll., Milton, Mass., 1980-81, Boston U., 1979-80; mem. adv. bd. PEAK Program, Worcester Pub. Schs., 1985-87. Co-author: Streams and Puddles: A Comparison of Two Young Writers, 1980. Trustee Elm Park Ctr. for Early Childhood Edn., Worcester, 1988-91, 98—, pres., 1991; trustee Worcester Children's Theatre, 1986-88, Worcester Ctr. for Crafts, 1994—; pres., mem. coun. Worcester Art Mus., 1990-91; v.p. Preservation Worcester, 1990-92; trustee, incorporator Worcester Park Spirit Inc., 1987-90; treas. Shakespeare Club of Worcester, 1999-2000. Mem. ASCD, Mass. Tchrs. Assn., Mass. Assn. Early Childhood Tchr. Educators, Nat. Assn. Edn. Young Children, Pi Lambda Theta, Kappa Delta Pi. Office: Worcester State Coll Dept Edn 486 Chandler St Worcester MA 01602-2832 E-mail: cdonnelly@worcester.edu.

DONNELLY, JOAN MARY, college program director; b. Manchester, N.H., Nov. 8, 1945; d. Edward John and Eva Cecile (Whittemore) D. BS, N.H. Coll., 1967; MEd, U. So. Maine, 1981; PhD, Boston Coll., Chestnut Hill, Mass., 1988; postgrad., Bryn Mawr Coll., 1991. Bus. educator various secondary schs., N.J., N.H., —1972; office occupations dir. Project Second Start, Concord, N.H., 1972-79; adult edn. dir. Concord Sch. Dist., 1979-81; bus. dept. chairperson Notre Dame Coll., Manchester, 1982-87; ednl. coord. U. N.H., Manchester, 1987-88; dir. continuing edn. Keene (N.H.) State Coll., 1988-99, mem. comm. faculty, 1999—. Vis. lectr. Belgorod (USSR) State Pedagogical Inst., 1990; panelist North Am. Assn. Summer Session, Tucson, 1991. Active Environ. Def. Fund, Greenpeace, World Wildlife Fund, Washington. Mem. Nat. U. Continuing Edn. Assn. (instl. rep. 1991—, workshop leader 1991), North Am. Assn. Summer Sessions (instl. rep.), Greater Keene C. of C., Phi Delta Kappa. Avocations: canoeing, gardening, maintaining greenhouse. Office: Keene State Coll 229 Main St Keene NH 03435-0001

D'ONOFRIO, PETER JOSEPH, protective services official, educator; b. Bronx, N.Y., Sept. 20, 1947; s. Elia Danato and Chella Concetta (Diorio) D'O.; m. Sharon Warner, Oct. 17, 1971 (div. 1976); m. Barbara Ann Jefferson, Dec. 10, 1977; children; Randyll Thomas, Robyn Margaret Smith. AAS, Sinclair C.C., Dayton, Ohio, 1973; BSBA, U. Dayton, 1974, MBA, BS in Edn., 1975; AAS in Fire Sci., Columbus State C.C., 1988; grad. exec. fire officer program, Nat. Fire Acad., Emmitsburg, Md., 1993; PhD in Am. History, LaSalle U., 1998. Registered paramedic, fire, EMS instr., fire safety inspector, Ohio. Fire tng. officer, emergency med. svcs. tng. coord. Ohio Fire Acad., Reynoldsburg, 1984—. Mem. faculty paramedic edn. Grant Med. Ctr., Columbus, 1987—; mem. adj. faculty Nat. Fire Acad., 1989—; firefighter, paramedic, insp., investigator Miami Twp. Fire Divsn., Miamisburg, Ohio, 1980-84; emergency rm. technician Kettering (Ohio) Med. Ctr., 1978-79; firefighter, paramedic Huber Heights (Ohio) Fire Divsn., 1976-78; instr. Sinclair C.C., 1977-84; lectr. Bowling Green (Ohio) Fire Sch., Ohio State Firefighters Conf., Am. Med. Writers Assn., Fire Dept. Instrs. Conf., others. Editor, pub. newsletter North South Med. Times, 1984-96; editor, pub. Jour. of Civil War Medicine, 1996—. Vol. firefighter Kettering Fire Dept., 1974-80; vol. paramedic Minerva park (Ohio) Fire Dept., 1992-95, Truro Twp. (Ohio) Fire Dept., 1995-97. Mem. Internat. Rescue and Emergency Care Assn. (conf. lectr.), Internat. Assn. Fire Fighters (charter, hon.), Nat. Registry EMT's, Ohio Soc. Fire Svc. Instrs. (bd. dirs. 1985-87), Ohio EMT Instrs. Assn., Mil. Order Loyal Legion of U.S., Hon. Order Ky. Cols., VFW (Meritorious Svc. award 1977), Soc. Civil War Surgeons (pres., CEO 1988—). Avocations: civil war medical reenactments, fire and ems patch collecting, stamp collecting. Home: 539 Bristol Dr SW Reynoldsburg OH 43068 Office: Ohio Fire Acad 8895 E Main St Reynoldsburg OH 43068-3340

DONOGHUE, MILDRED RANSDORF, education educator; b. Cleve. d. James and Caroline (Sychra) Ransdorf; m. Charles K. Donoghue (dec. 1982); children: Kathleen, James. EdD, UCLA, 1962; JD, Western State U., 1979. Asst. prof. edn. and reading Calif. State U., Fullerton, 1962-66, assoc. prof., 1966-71, prof., 1971—. Founder, dir. Donoghue Children's Lit. Ctr., Calif. State U., Fullerton, Calif., 2001—. Author: Foreign Languages and the Schools, 1967, Foreign Languages and the Elementary School Child, 1968, The Child and the English Language Arts, 1971, 75, 79, 85, 90, Using Literature Activities to Teach Content Areas to Emergent Readers, 2001; co-author: Second Languages in Primary Education, 1979; contbr. articles to profl. jours. and Ednl. Resources Info. Ctr. U.S. Dept. Edn. Mem. AAUP, AAUW, Nat. Network for Early Lang. Learning, Nat. Coun. Tchrs. English, Nat. Coun. Tchrs. Math., Nat. Coun. Social Studies, Nat. Sci. Tchrs. Assn., Am. Ednl. Rsch. Assn., Nat. Soc. for Study of Edn., Am. Assn. Tchrs. Spanish and Portuguese, Internat. Reading Assn., Nat. Assn. Edn. Young Children, Orange County Med. Assn. Women's Aux., Assn. for Childhood Edn. Internat., Phi Beta Kappa, Phi Kappa Phi, Pi Lambda Theta, Alpha Upsilon Alpha. Address: 800 State College Blvd Fullerton CA 92831

DONOHUE, EDITH M. human resources specialist, educator; b. Nov. 10, 1938; d. Edward Anthony and Beatrice (Jones) McParland; m. Salvatore R. Donohue, Aug. 23, 1960; children: Kathleen, Deborah. BA, Coll. Notre Dame, Balt., 1960; MS, Johns Hopkins U., 1981; postgrad., CASE (cert. of adv. study in edn.), 1985; PhD in Human Resources, CASE, 1990. Cert. counselor, national, sr. profl. human resources. Dir. pub. rels. Coll. Notre Dame, Balt., 1970—71, dir. continuing edn., 1981—86; program coord. bus. and industry Catonsville C.C., Balt. County, Md., 1986—88; mgr. tng. and devel. Sheppard Pratt Hosp., Balt., 1988—90; assoc. prof., Sch. Edn. Barry U., 1993—98; cons. in human resources Stuart, Fla., 1985—. Adj. faculty Loyola Coll. Grad. Studies Program, Fla. Inst. Tech., Indian River C. of C. Co-author: Communicate Like a Manager, 1989, Life After Layoff, 2003; contbg. author career devel. workshop manual, 1985; contbr. articles to profl. jours. Pres. Cathedral Sch. Parents Assn., 1972-74; asst. treas., treas. Md. Gen. Hosp. Aux., 1975-78; dir. sect. Exec. Women's Network, Balt., 1983-85; adv. bd. Mayor's Commn. on Aging, 1981-86; dir. Md. Assn. Higher Edn., 1985-88; vol. trainer United Way Martin County, co-chair campaign, 1994—, strategic planning com., 1998—; mem. steering com. Chautaugua South. Recipient Mayor's Citation, City of Balt. Council, 1985, Woman of Distinction, Martin County, 1999. Mem. AAUW (dir., v.p. 1980-83),, Am. Assn. Tng. and Devel. (bd. dirs.), Am. Counseling Assn., Soc. Human Resources Mgmt., Martin County Personnel Mgt. Assn. (edn. chmn. 1991-94), Martin County Libr. Assn. Inc. (pres. 2001-2003), Martin County C. of C. (edn. com. 1991-94), Friends of Lyric (bd. dirs. chmn., strategic planning, pres.), Soroptimist Internat. of Stuart, Chi Sigma Iota (pres.), Phi Delta Kappa. Republican. Roman Cath. Avocations: tennis, performing arts, reading, wellness. Home: Apt 3103 144 NE Edgewater Dr Stuart FL 34996-4477 E-mail: edonohue@gate.net.

DONOHUE, MARC DAVID, chemical engineering educator; b. Watertown, N.Y., Sept. 10, 1951; s. Paul Francis and Beverly Gertrude (Hodge) D.; m. Mary Ann Chamberlain, July 20, 1974; children: Paul, Megan, Ian. BS, Clarkson Coll. Tech., 1973; PhD, U. Calif., Berkeley, 1977. Asst. prof. chem. engrng. Clarkson Coll. Tech., Potsdam, N.Y., 1977-79; asst. prof. Johns Hopkins U., Balt., 1979-83, assoc. prof., 1983-87, prof., 1987—, chmn. dept., 1984-95, assoc. dean, 1999—. Recipient Adminstr.'s Pollution Prevention award for Region III, U.S. EPA, 1992, Md. sect. Outstanding Engring. Achievement award NSPE, 1989. Mem. Am. Inst. Chem. Engrs., Am. Chem. Soc. (Md. chemist 1999), Am. Soc. Engring. Edn. (Outstanding Young Engr. award 1984), Tau Beta Pi. E-mail: mdd@jhu.edu.

DONOHUE, NICHOLAS C. education commissioner; m. Mariane DiMascio; children: Jennifer, Dorothy. BA, Wesleyan U., 1981; MEd, Harvard Bus. Sch., 1990. Elem. sch. tchr. and program adminstr. Pub Schs., Mass.; dir. learning innovations Stoneham, Mass.; dep. commr. N.H. Dept. Edn., Concord, NH, 1997—2000; commr. NH Dept Edn., Concord, NH, 2000—. Office: NH Dept Edn State Office Park S 101 Pleaseant St Concord NH 03301

DONOHUE, PATRICIA CAROL, academic administrator; b. St. Louis, Jan. 11, 1946; d. Carroll and Juanita Donohue; m. James H. Stevens Jr., Aug. 27, 1966 (div. Mar. 1984); children: James H. Stevens III, Carol Janet Stevens. AB, Duke U., 1966; MA, U. Mo., 1974, PhD, 1982. Tchr. math. in secondary schs., Balt., St. Louis and Shawnee Mission, Kans., 1966-71; lectr. U. Mo., Kansas City, 1975-76, rsch. asst. affirmative action, 1976-79, coord. affirmative action, 1979-82, instl. rsch. assoc., 1982-84, acting dir. affirmative action and acad. pers., 1984; dir. instl. rsch. Lakeland C.C., 1984-86; asst. dean acad. affairs, math., engrng. and tech. Harrisburg Area C.C., 1986-89, dean sch. bus., engrng., and tech., 1989-93, dean Lebanon campus, v.p. cmty. devel. and external affairs, 1993; vice chancellor edn. St. Louis C.C., 1993—2002, acting pres. Florissant Valley campus, 1998-99; pres. Luzerne County C.C., 2002—. Active Pa. Coun. on Vocat. Edn., 1989—93; v.p. St. Louis Sch. to Work, Inc., 1994—96, pres., 1996—2002; chairperson Pa. Occupl. Deans, 1988—93; bd. dirs., chmn. edn. com. Humane Soc. Mo., 1997—2002; cons. evaluator North Ctrl. Assn., 2000—; bd. dirs. Diamond City Partnership. Leader Hemlock coun. Girl Scouts U.S.A.; bd. dirs., v.p. Am. Cancer Soc. Jackson County, 1975—84; mem. adv. coun. Ben Franklin Partnership, 1988—93; sec. Ctrl. Pa. Tech. Coun., 1992—93; mem. steering com. New Baldwin Corridor Coalition,

1991—93, chair edn. task force, 1992—93; mem. Leadership St. Louis, 1996—97, Exec. Leadership Wilkes-Barre, 2003; bd. dirs. Hemlock coun. Girl Scouts U.S.A., 1986—93, PTA, 1975—77, Cmty. Lebanon Assocs., Ctrl. Pa. Tech. Coun., 1989—93, Mantec, 1988—93, Delta Gamma Ctr. for Children with Visual Impairments, 2001—02, Osterhout Libr., 2003—. Recipient Outstanding Service and Achievement award U. Mo. Kansas City, 1976, Outstanding Svc. award Ctrl. Pa. Tech. Coun., 1993; Jack C. Coffey grantee, 1978; named Outstanding Woman AAUW, 1989, one of Outstanding Leaders Nat. Inst. Leadership Devel., 1986, Exec. Leadership Inst., 1990. Mem.: Assn. Inst. Rsch., Women's Network, Nat. Assn. Student Pers. Adminstrs., Women's Equity Project, Soc. Mfg. Engrs. (chmn. 1989—90), Am. Assn. Women in Cmty. and Jr. Colls. (Pa. state coord. 1988, bd. dirs. Region 3 1989—91), Nat. Coun. for Occupl. Edn. (chairperson diversity task force 1991, chairperson job tng. 2000 task force 1992, v.p. programs 1992—93, bd. dirs. 1992—2000, v.p. membership 1993—94, pres. 1995—96, past pres. 1996—97), Am. Assn. Cmty. Colls. (coun. affiliated chairpersons 1994—2000, commn. on cmty. and workforce devel. 1995—97, chairperson coun. 1996—2000, commn. on cmty. and workforce devel. 1998—2001, acad. pres. 2003), Am. Vocat. Assn., Math. Assn. Am., Nat. Coun. Tchrs. of Math., ASCD, Delta Gamma (v.p., del. nat. conv. 1988, pres. 1989-91, bd. dirs. Delta Gamma Ctr. for Children with Visual Impairment 2001-) (del. nat. conv. 1988, pres. 1989—91, v.p., Cream Rose Outstanding Svc. award 1970), Pi Lambda Theta, Phi Kappa Phi, Phi Delta Kappa (pres. 1975, Read fellow 1989). Home: 40 Elmcrest Dr Dallas PA 18612 Office: Luzerne County C C 1333 S Prospect St Nanticoke PA 18634

DONOVAN, BRUCE ELLIOT, classics educator, university dean; b. Lawrence, Mass., Mar. 8, 1937; s. Harry Albert and Ruth Hannah (Kent) D.; m. Doris Louise Stearn, Sept. 7, 1959; children: Gregory Stearn, Erika Ruth. AB, Brown U., 1959; postgrad., U. Bristol, Eng., 1959-60; MA, Yale U., 1961, PhD, 1965; postgrad., Rutgers Center for Alcohol Studies, 1976. Instr. Yale U., 1962-65; from instr. to prof. classics Brown U., Providence, 1965—, assoc. dean for chem. dependency, 1977—2003, dean freshmen and sophomores, 1981-87, assoc. dean coll., 1977—2003. Instr. summer sch. alcohol studies Rutgers U.; cons. on collegiate alcoholism and other drug abuse. Author: Euripides Papyri from Oxyrhynchus, 1969; author articles and revs. on ancient Greek lit. and alcohol and other drug issues. Bd. dirs. Vols. in Action, 1975-90, R.I. Coun. on Alcoholism and Other Drug Dependence, 1973-94, New Eng. Inst. Alcohol Studies, 1978-91; founding mem. New Eng. Coll. Alcohol Network, Academics Recovering Together; steering com. Network Colls. and Univs. Committed to the Elimination of Substance Abuse, 1988-93. Fulbright fellow, 1959-60; Woodrow Wilson fellow, 1960-61; fellow Center for Hellenic Studies, Washington, 1971-72 Mem. Am. Philol. Assn., Employee Assistance Profl. Assn. Home: 261 President Ave Providence RI 02906-5537 Office: Brown U PO Box 1865 Providence RI 02912-1865

DONOVAN, MARGARET, educational association administrator; b. Boston, Sept. 4, 1946; d. George Henry and Margaret Mary (Gilligan) Donovan; m. Marvin Lee Manheim, July 20, 1974 (div. Jan. 1997); children: Susannah Leigh, Marisa Kara. BA, Boston U., 1969; MEd, Boston State Coll., 1971. Cert. tchr. English, history, social studies, Mass. Homebound tchr. Somerville (Mass.) Pub. Schs., 1971-73, English tchr., 1973-75; program dir. Rochelle Lee Fund, Chgo., 1996—. Mem. Evanston Sch. Dist. 202 Cmty. Task Force, 1995—. Bd. dirs. Invest Evanston, 1994—; mem. parents' coun. Shady Hill Sch., Cambridge, Mass., 1981-83; mem. parents' assn. North Shore Country Day Sch., Winnetka, Ill., 1984-86, v.p., 19877-88; v.p. PTA, King Lab. Sch., Evanston, Ill., 1990-91; sec. PTA Coun., Evanston/Skokie County ot PTAs, 1991-92, pres., 1992-94; v.p. Dist. 202 Parent/Tchr./Student Assn., Evanston Twp. H.S., 1994—, mem. curriculum forum, 1994—, writer sch.-based health clinic com., 1994—; mem. curriculum adv. coun. Sch. Dist. 65, Evanston, 1992-94; co-founder, co-chair, sec. Mothers Against Gangs, Evanston, 1992—; founder HIV Edn. Task Force, PTA Coun., Evanston, 1992—; observer Dist. 65 Sch. Bd., LWV, 1992—; bd. dirs. Youth Orgns. Umbrella, Evanston, 1993—; mem. violence prevention curriculum task force Ill. Coun. for Prevention of Violence, Chgo., 1994—; bd. dirs. Evanston Symphony Orch., 1987-92. Recipient State PTA HIV Edn. award Ill. PTA, 1993, Those Who Excel award of recognition Ill. State Bd. Edn., 1996-97. Mem. North End Mothers Club. Democrat. Roman Catholic. Avocations: reading, travel. Home: 2757 Marcy Ave Evanston IL 60201-1139 Office: Rochelle Lee Fund 5153 N Clark St Chicago IL 60640-6823

DONOVAN, MAUREEN HILDEGARDE, librarian, educator; b. Boston, Dec. 13, 1948; d. Alfred Michael and Maureen Hildegarde (Murphy) D.; m. James Richard Bartholomew, Sept. 9, 1978; 1 child, Thomas Alfred Bartholomew. BA, Manhattanville Coll., 1970; MA in East Asian Langs. and Cultures, Columbia U., 1973, MS in Libr. Svc., 1974. Asst. editor R.R. Bowker Co., N.Y.C., 1973; librarian I Gest Oriental Libr. Princeton (N.J.) U., 1974-77, libr. II, 1977-78; instr., Japanese studies libr. Ohio State U., Columbus, 1978-88, asst. prof., Japanese studies libr., 1988-94, assoc. prof., Japanese studies libr., 1994—. Vis. lectr. Sch. Libr. and Info. Sci. Keio U., Tokyo, 1995-96; cons. U. Wis., Madison, 1991, McGill U., Montreal, Que., 1993, RMG, Inc., Chgo., 1993; webmaster East Asian Librs. Cooper WWW, 1994—; vis. rsch. scholar Internat. Rsch. Ctr. for Japanese Studies, Kyoto, 2003—; Japan specialist Digital Asia Libr., 1999-2002, Portal to Asian Internet Resources, 2002—. Editor mailing list Asian Database Online Cmty., 1993-97, editor electronic newsletter, 1998—. Fellow Japan Found., Tokyo, 1995-96; grantee U.S. Dept. Edn., 1994-96, Japan-U.S. Friendship Commn., 1994-96, Sun Microsystems, Inc., 1995; inductee Matignon H.S. (Cambridge, Mass.) Achievement Hall of Fame, 1999. Mem. ALA, Assn. for Asian Studies (chair com. on East Asian librs. 1991-94), Internat. Assn. Orientalist Librs. Home: 2372 Lytham Rd Columbus OH 43220-4640 Office: 328 Main Libr 1858 Neil Ave Columbus OH 43210-1225 E-mail: donovan.1@osu.edu.

DONOVAN, RITA R. nurse anesthetist, trauma and critical care nurse, educator; b. Bklyn., May 19, 1957; d. Joseph and Antoinette (Burdo) Nigro. Student, Bklyn. Coll., 1975-77; BSN, SUNY, Bklyn., 1979. RN, N.Y. Sr. staff nurse med. surg. unit Maimonides Med. Ctr., Bklyn., 1979—81, staff nurse med. ICU, 1981—84, asst. head nurse pulmonary ICU, 1985—86; grad. nurse anesthetist Kings County Hosp., Bklyn., 1988—89, clin. and acad. instr., 1989—90; clin. specialist surg. ICU Maimonides Med. Ctr., Bklyn., 1990—91; performance improvement coord. dept. anesthesia Kings County Hosp., Bklyn., 1991—, clin., acad. instr., 1991—. Contbr. rsch. articles to profl. jours. and texts. Anesthetist, ICU Desert Storm Task Force, 1991; mem. Healing the Children, Tunja, Columbia, 1998. Recipient 5-Yr. Outstanding award Maimonides Med. Ctr., 1985, Agatha Hodgins Meml. award Outstanding Nurse Anesthetist, 1988, Cert. award Cardiac Anesthesia, Kings County Hosp., 1988, others; named Best All Around Student, 1988. Mem. ACN, Am. Assn. Nurse Anesthetists, Soc. Critical Care Medicine, Soc. Trauma Nurses. Office: Kings County Hosp Ctr Dept Anesthesia 451 Clarkson Ave Rm B2175 Brooklyn NY 11203-2097

DONOVAN, WILLARD PATRICK, retired elementary education educator; b. Grand Rapids, Mich., Sept. 1, 1930; s. Willard Andrew and Thelma Alfreda (Davis) D.; m. Dorothy Jane Nester, Nov. 27, 1954 (dec. May 1981); children: Cindy Jane, Kimberly Sue. BS, Ea. Mich. U., 1965, MA, 1969. Cert. grades K-8, Mich. Enlisted U.S. Army, 1947, advanced through grades to master sgt., 1953; platoon sgt. U.S. Army of Occupation, Korea, 1947-48, 1948-50, U.S. Army Korean War Svc., 1950-51; ret. U.S. Army, 1964; pharm. sales Nat. Drug Co., Detroit, 1964-66; tchr. Cromie Elem. Sch. Warren (Mich.) Consol. Schs., 1966—, ret., 1995. Reading textbook and curriculum devel. com. Warren (Mich.) Consol. Schs., 1969-73, sci. com., 1970-95; curriculum and textbook com. Macomb County Christian Schs., Warren, 1982-95. Decorated Combat Infantry badge U.S. Army, Korea, 1947-50, Purple heart with three clusters, Korea-Japan Svc. medal, 1951, Presdl. citation, 1951, Korean medal with three campaign clusters, 1951, Nat. Def. Svc. medal, 1951, Bronze star, Silver star; Chosin few Army and Marines Assn. 31st Inf. Assn. Mem. NRA, Am. Quarterhouse Assn., Assn. U.S. Army, Detroit Area Coun. Tchrs. Math., Met. Detroit Sci. Tchrs. Assn., The Chosin Few (U.S. Army), Nat. Edn. Assn., Mich. Edn. Assn., Warren (Mich.) Edn. Assn., U.S. Army Assn. Avocations: theatre, arts, horsemanship, traveling, pistol shooting. Home: PO Box 563 8440 Mission Hills Arizona City AZ 85223

DOODY, AGNES G. communications educator, management and communication consultant; b. New Haven; d. Daniel M. and Carrie Mae (Goodrich) D.; m. Arthur D. Jeffrey, Dec. 22, 1962 (dec. Sept. 1985); children: Andrew N., Jill; m. Ellis H. Maris, Jr., June 28, 1991. BA, Emerson Coll., l952; MA, Pa. State U., l954, PhD, l96l; cert. program on negotiation, Harvard U. Prof. communications U. R.I., Kingston, l958—; pres. Arthur Assocs. Bd. dirs., co-chairperson PierBank, Narragansett, R.I., 1994. Mem. Soc. Profls. in Dispute Resolution, Internat. Comm. Assn., Nat. Comm. Assn., Ea. Comm. Assn. (pres. l967-68), Rotary (newsletter editor Wakefield l989-90). Avocations: photography, travel, gardening. Home: One Post Rd Wakefield RI 02879

DOODY, MARGARET ANNE, English language educator; b. St. John, N.B., Can., Sept. 21, 1939; came to U.S., 1976; d. Hubert and Anne Ruth (Cornwall) D. BA, Dalhousie U., Can., 1960; BA with 1st class hons., Lady Margaret Hall-Oxford U., Eng., 1962, MA, 1965, D.Phil., 1968; LLD (hon.), Dalhousie U., 1985. Instr. English U. Victoria (B.C., Can.), 1962-64, asst. prof. English, 1968-69; lectr. Univ. Coll. Swansea, Wales, 1969-76; assoc. prof. English U. Calif.-Berkeley, 1976-80; prof. English dept. Princeton U., N.J., 1980-89; Andrew W. Mellon prof. humanities, prof. English Vanderbilt U., Nashville, 1989-99, dir. comparative lit. program, 1992-99; John and Barbara Glyn Family prof. lit. U. Notre Dame, 2000—, dir. PhD in Lit. program, 2001—. Author: (non-fiction) A Natural Passion: A Study of the Novels of Samuel Richardson, 1974, The Daring Muse: Augustan Poetry Reconsidered, 1985, Frances Burney: The Life in the Works, 1988, The True Story of the Novel, 1996, (novels) Aristotle Detective, 1978, The Alchemists, 1980, Aristotle e la giustizia poetica, 2000, Aristotle and Poetic Justice, 2002; author: (with F. Stuber) (play) Clarissa, 1984; editor (with Peter Sabor): Samuel Richardson Tercentenary Essays, 1989; co-editor (with Douglas Murray): Catharine and Other Writings by Jane Austen, 1993; co-editor: (with Wendy Barry and Mary Doody Jones) Anne of Green Gables, 1997; author: (novels) Aristotle and the Secrets of Life, 2003. Guggenheim postdoctoral fellow, 1979; recipient Rose Mary Crawshay award Brit. Acad., 1986. Episcopalian. Office: U Notre Dame PhD in Literature Program Notre Dame IN 46556 E-mail: mdoody@nd.edu.

DOOLEY, JENNIE LEE, art educator; b. Wolbach, Nebr., Mar. 7, 1933; d. John William and Inez Margaret (McKelvey) McIntyre; m. Leonard Wayne, May 24, 1953; children: Stanley Lewis, Deborah Marlaine, Diana Lynne, Jennie LaVonne, Jane Inez. BS, U. So. Colo., 1983; MA, Adams State Coll., 1988. Elem. educator, Wolbach, Nebr., 1951-53, Belgrade, Nebr., 1957-58; art educator Wiley, Colo., 1979—; adult educator Lamar (Colo.) Community Coll., 1974-80, Lamar Community Coll., 1984—. Art show judge, 1988-92; North Ctrl. Evaluation Team, Colo. Dept. Edn., Holyoke, Colo., 1988, Idaho Springs, Colo., 1990—, Cripple Creek, Colo., 1993. One-person show includes Picetwire Players, 1986, Prowers Co. Mus., 1991. Nominated for Colo. State award for Excellence in Art, 1993, Colo. High Sch. Art Educator of the Yr., 1994-95. Mem. NEA, Colo. Artist Assn. (pres. 1990-91, conv. chairperson 1992, 1st v.p. 1993), Colo. Art Educator Assn. (area rep. 1991-92, exec. bd. sec. 1992-94), Colo. Edn. Assn., Colo. State China Painters (1st v.p. 1992-94), Southeastern Colo. China Painters, Southeastern Colo. Art Guild, Fine Arts League, Wiley Edn. Assn. (pres. 1989-90), Lamar Daubers Club, Brush and Palette Club, Phi Delta Kappa. Methodist. Avocations: travel, doll collecting, painting, sculpting, silversmithing, reading. Home: 3001 Memorial Dr Lamar CO 81052-4341 Office: Wiley Consol Schs Wiley CO 81092

DOOLEY-HANSON, BARBARA ANN, special education educator; b. Vici, Okla., Feb. 16, 1948; d. Loitz Eldon and Cora Lee (Morgan) Myers; m. Donald R. Hanson, Sept. 25, 1993; children: Lisa M. White, James B. Dooley. BS in Spl. Edn., Ctrl. State U., 1989, MEd in Spl. Edn., 1992. Cert. tchr., Okla. Tchr. Ctrl. City Bapt. Acad., Oklahoma City, 1975-76; spl. edn. tchr. Seminole (Okla.) Pub. Schs., 1977-78; tchr. Jones (Okla.) Pub. Schs., 1978-79; spl. edn. tchr. Midwest City-Del City Pub. Schs., 1979-95; spl. edn. coord. II State Dept. Edn., 1995—. Adj. prof. U. Ctrl. Okla., fall 1995. Co-author: Doorway-Transition to the Real World, 1993. Mem. Citizens for a Safe Environ., Edmond, Okla., 1994; soccer coach Edmond Soccer Assn., 1985, 88. Mem. Learning Disabilities Assn., Kappa Delta Pi (v.p., pres., exec. bd. dirs. 1989—), Spl. Edn. Vocat. Edn. Assn. (mem. adv. bd. 1993, 95). Baptist. Avocations: reading, golfing, playing the piano, spending time with my children, gardening. Home: 13205 Golden Eagle Dr Edmond OK 73013-7406 Office: State Dept Edn Spl Edn Sect 2500 N Lincoln Blvd Oklahoma City OK 73105-4503

DORAN, ROBERT STUART, mathematician, educator; b. Winthrop, Iowa, Dec. 21, 1937; s. Carl Arthur D. and Imogene (Ownby) Doran Nodurft; m. Shirley Ann Lange, June 27, 1959; children: Bruce Robert, Brad Christopher. BA with hons., U. Iowa, 1962, MA, 1964; MS, U. Washington, 1967, PhD, 1968. Instr. U. Wash., 1968; asst. prof. U. No. Iowa, Cedar Falls, 1968-69; asst. to prof. math. Tex. Christian U., Ft. Worth, 1969—, chmn. dept. math., 1990—, John William and Helen Stubbs Potter prof. math., 1995—. Vis. prof. U. Tex., Austin, 1979; cons. in field. Author: Approximate Identities and Factorization in Banach Modules, 1979, Characterizations of C*-Algebras: The Gelfand-Naimark Theorems, 1986, Representations of Locally Compact Groups and Banach *-Algebraic Bundles, 1988; editor: Selfadjoint and Nonselfadjoint Operator Algebras and Operator Theory, 1991, C*-Algebras: A Fifty Year Celebration, 1994, Automorphic Forms, Automorphic Representations and Arithmetic, 1999, The Mathematical Legacy of Harish-Chandra, 2000; editor Cambridge U. Press, 1987; contbr. articles to profl. jours. Chmn. bd. deacons Birchman Bapt. Ch., Ft. Worth, 1987; vol. Van Cliburn Internat. Piano Competition, 1994—, Am. Cancer Soc., 1987—. Recipient Burlington No. award for Disting. Teaching, 1988, Top Ten Prof. award Ho. of Reps., 1986, 87, 91, Mortar Bd. Preferred Prof. award, 1983, 87, 91, 93, 95, Gold medal for Prof. of Yr. Coun. for Advancement and Support of Edn., 1989, Honors Prof. of Yr. award, 1993; vis. scholar MIT, 1981, Oxford U., 1988; Minnie Stevens Piper prof., 1989. Mem. Inst. Advanced Study (chmn. we. U.S. 1984—), Assn. Mems. Inst. for Advanced Study (pres. bd. trustees 1990-99), Am. Math. Soc., Math. Assn. Am. (vis. lectr. 1990—, Beckenbach Book award prize com. 1990-94), Phi Beta Kappa, Sigma Xi, Pi Mu Epsilon. Republican. Avocations: chess, running, swimming. Home: 4204 Ridglea Country Club Dr Fort Worth TX 76126-2224 Office: Tex Christian U Dept Math Fort Worth TX 76129-0001

DORAN, TIMOTHY PATRICK, educational administrator; b. N.Y.C., July 1, 1949; s. Joseph Anthony and Claire (Griffin) D.; m. Kathleen Matava, Aug. 1, 1981; children: Claire Marie, Bridget Anne. BA in Econs., Le Moyne Coll., 1971; MA in Tchg., U. Alaska, Fairbanks, 1984; Edn. Specialist, U. Alaska, 1990. Cert. type A secondary, econs., type B K-12 prin., supt. Svc. rep. Emigrant Savings Bank, N.Y.C., 1971-72; exec., dir. Project Equality Northwest, Seattle, 1972-73, Jesuit Vol. Corps., Portland, Oreg., 1973-75, adminstv. advisor Kaltag City (Alaska) coun., 1975-77; program developer Diocese Fairbanks, Alaska, 1978-81, adminstr., supt. St. Mary's Cath. High Sch., 1981-83; prin. intern U. Alaska, Fairbanks, 1984, vis. instr., 1990-94; tchr. Anthony A. Andrews Sch., St. Michael, Alaska, 1984-86; prin., tchr. James C. Isabell Sch, Teller, Alaska, 1986-88; prin. Unalakleet (Alaska) Schs., 1988-90, Denali Elem. Sch., Fairbanks, 1992—. Acad. coord. U. Alaska summers, Fairbanks, 1984—86; instr. Elderhostel, 1991—; docent U. Alaska Mus., 1991—; sch. edn. adv. bd. U. Alaska, 1998—, adj. instr., Anchorage, 2001—. Active nat. com. Campaign for Human Devel., 1980-83; mem. manpower planning coun. Tanana Chiefs Conf., 1976-77, parish coun. Sacred Heart Cathedral, 1979-81; Sunday Sch. tchr. St. Mark's Univ. Parish, 1990-97, adv. coun., 1998-2001; mem. com. chair Fairbanks Arts and Culture in Edn., 1995—; bd. dirs., v.p., pres. Literacy Coun. Alaska, 1997-2002. Recipient Merit awards Alaska Dept. Edn., 1986-90; named Alaska Disting. Prin., 1998, Fairbanks Elem. Prin. of Yr., 2003. Mem. ASCD, Nat. Assn. Elem. Sch. Prins., Alaska Assn. Elem. Sch. Prins. (v.p., pres.-elect, pres. 2000-2002, past pres.), Fairbanks Prins. Assn. (v.p., pres. 1999-2000), Alaska Math. Consortium (bd. dirs. 1992-99). Home: 512 Windsor Dr Fairbanks AK 99709-3439 Office: Denali Elem Sch 1042 Lathrop St Fairbanks AK 99701-4124 E-mail: tdoran@northstar.k12,ak.us.

DORATO, PETER, electrical and computer engineering educator; b. N.Y.C., Dec. 17, 1932; s. Fioretto and Rosina (Lachello) D.; m. Marie Madeleine Turlan, June 2, 1956; children: Christopher, Alexander, Sylvia, Veronica. BEE, CCNY, 1955; MSEE, Columbia U., 1956; DEE, Poly. Inst. N.Y., 1961. Registered profl. engr., Colo. Lectr. elec. engring. dept. CCNY, 1956-57; instr. elec. engring. Poly. Inst. N.Y., Bklyn., 1957-61, prof., 1961-72; prof. elec. engring., dir. Resource System Analysis U. Colo., Colorado Springs, 1972-76; Gardner-Zemke prof. elec. and computer engring. U. N.Mex., Albuquerque, 1984—, chmn. dept., 1976-84. Hon. chaired prof. Nanjing Aero. Inst., 1989; vis. prof. Politecnico di Torino, Italy, 1991-92l dir. Ctr. for Intelligent Systems Engring. U. N.Mex., 2001. Author: Analytic Feedback Systems Design, 2000; co-author Linear Quadratic Control, 1995, Robust Control for Unstructured Perturbations, 1992, Robust Control-System Design, 1996, Italian Culture—A View from America, 2001; editor: Robust Control, Recent Results in Robust Control and Advances in Adaptive Control, reprint vols., 1987, 90, 91, IEEE Press Reprint Vol. Series, 1989-90; assoc. editor Automatica Jour., 1969-83, 89-92, editor rapid publs., 1994-98; assoc. editor IEEE Trans on Edn., 1989-91; contbr. articles on control systems theory to profl. jours. Recipient John R. Ragazzini edn. award Am. Automatic Control Coun., 1998 Fellow IEEE (3rd Millenium medal); mem. IEEE Control Systems Soc. (Disting. Mem. award)., World Automation Congress (Life Achievement award 2002). Democrat. Home: 1514 Roma Ave NE Albuquerque NM 87106-4513 Office: U NMex Dept Elec Computer Eng Albuquerque NM 87131-1356 E-mail: peter@eece.unm.edu.

DORE, ANITA WILKES, English language educator; b. N.Y.C., Dec. 16, 1914; d. Abraham P. and Rose (Hirsch) Wilkes; m. Robert M. Dore, June 26, 1938; children: Marjorie Dore Allen, Elizabeth. BA, Vassar Coll., 1935; MA with honors, Columbia U., 1937. Cert. English tchr., N.Y. Tchr. H.S. English, Bd. Edn., N.Y.C., 1937-41, 56-59, TV broadcaster, producer, 1961-65, coordinator English jr. high sch. div., 1959-61, chair English dept., 1965-67, asst. dir. English, 1967-73, dir. English, N.Y.C. schs., 1973-83, cons., 1983—; cons. Young Playwrights Dramatists Guild, N.Y.C., 1983-87. Author: Premier Book of Major Poets, 1970, Emerging Woman, 1974; co-author: Distrust of Authority, 1981; also articles. Pres., bd. dirs. Sch. Settlement House, Bklyn., 1951-53; mem. edn. com. NOW, N.Y.C., 1972-75; chair Child Study Children's Book Com. Bank St. Coll., 1983-98; sec., bd. dirs. Westport-Westport Arts Ctr., Conn., 1983-93; trustee Westport Libr., Conn.; 1985-92; chair adv. com. young poets and playwrights festivals of Conn. Westport Arts Ctr., 1983—. Recipient Elizabeth Dana prize in English, Vassar Coll., 1934; named Honoree Salute to Women YWCA, 1991. Fellow N.Y. State English Council (v.p. 1970-75); mem. Nat. Council Tchrs. English Lit. Commn., N.Y.C. Assn. Tchrs. English (v.p. 1962-70), Alumnae Assn. Vassar (class 1935 pres. 1996—). Democrat. Avocations: theatre, traveling, politics. Home: 36 E 36th St New York NY 10016-3463

DORFMAN, CYNTHIA HEARN, government agency administrator; BA in English with honors, Skidmore Coll., 1970; M in English, Middlebury Coll. Sr. exec. fellow Kennedy Sch. Govt., Harvard U.; dir. OCRI Found.; mgr. Dept. Publs. and Outreach Programs and Projects U.S. Dept. Edn., Washington, dir. media and info. svcs. Office Ednl. Rsch. and Improvement, dir. comm. Office Innovation and Improvement. Office: US Dept Edn IES Capital Place 555 New Jersey Ave NW Washington DC 20208*

DORMAN, B(RUCE) HUGH, anesthesiologist, educator; b. Columbus, Ohio, May 6, 1953; m. René Mott, June 26, 1976; children: Justin B., Tyler H. PhD, U. N.C., 1982; MD, Duke U., 1986. Cert. in anesthesiology. Intern U. Wash., Seattle, 1986-87, resident in anesthesiology, 1987-90. Dir. of rsch. dept. anesthesiology Med. U. S.C., Charleston, 1994—, dir. cardiothoracic anesthesiology, 1994—, prof. anesthesiology. Editor: (book) Anesthesia for Orthopedic Surgery, 1995; contbr. articles to profl. jours. Mem. AMA, Am. Soc. Anesthesiology, Soc. Cardiovasc. Anesthesiology, N.Y. Acad. Scis. Office: Med U S C Dept Anesthesiology 171 Ashley Ave Dept Charleston SC 29425-0001

DORMAN, CRAIG EMERY, oceanographer, academic administrator; b. Cambridge, Mass., Aug. 27, 1940; s. Carlton Earl and Sarah Elizabeth (Emery) D.; m. Cynthia Eileen Larson, Aug. 25, 1962; children: Clifford Ellery, Clark Evans, Curt Emerson. BA, Dartmouth Coll., 1962; MS, Navy Post Grad. Sch., 1969; PhD, MIT/WHOI Joint Prog. Oceanog., 1972. Commd. ensign USN, 1962, advanced through grades to rear adm., 1987, ret., 1989; CEO Woods Hole (Mass.) Oceanographic Instn., 1989-93; dep. dir. Def. Rsch. and Engring. for Lab. mgmt., Washington, 1993-95; sr. scientist Applied Rsch. Lab. Pa. State U., 1995—2002; chief scientist, tech. dir. internat. field office Office Naval Rsch., 1995-98, ONR01D, 1998-99; chief scientist ONR, 1999—2001; govt. coord., GSC chair Medea, 2000—02; chief scientist CH Internat. Assts., 2001—; v.p. rsch. U. AUSEA, 2002—. Dir. Maritrans, Tampa; vis. prof. Imperial Coll., London, 1996-97. Corp. mem. WHOI, Bermuda Biol. Sta. for Rsch.; trustee Naval Undersea Mus. Found. Decorated Legion of Merit (2). Mem. Russian Acad. Natural Sci. Home: 4107 27th Rd N Arlington VA 22207-5116 Office: 800 N Quincy St Arlington VA 22217-0001 E-mail: dormanc@onr.navy.mil.

DORMAN, JO-ANNE, elementary school educator; b. Greenville, Miss. d. Joe Edward and Constance Bonita (Parks) D. BS, Delta State U., 1963. Cert. tchr., Fla. Tchr. Oakcrest Elem. Sch., Pensacola, Fla., 1963-93; ret., 1993; substitute tchr. Sch. Dist. Escambia County, Pensacola, Fla., 1993—. Traffic sch. instr., 1997—. Sunday sch. tchr. Methodist Ch., Pensacola, Fla., 1963, 65, 68; voter precinct clk. Escambia County, 1997—; vol. Sr. Friends, 2000—. Mem.: U. West Fla. Leisure Learners Soc., Pensacola Dog Fanciers Assn., Papillon Club Am., Five Flags Dog Tng. Club. Democrat. Methodist. Avocations: travel, reading, photography, theater, dogs. Home: 188 Talladega Trl Pensacola FL 32506-3202

DORMAN, PATRICIA M. sociologist, educator; b. Salt Lake City; d. Charles C. McLain and Phyllis C. (Rees) DeBois; m. Lynn C. Dorman, May 4, 1963; 1 child, Terrance Lynn. BS, U. Utah, 1960, MS, 1961, PhD, 1971. Project dir. Idaho Office on Aging, Boise, 1969-70; co-dir. Idaho State Exec. Inst., Boise, 1978-82; rsch. analyst Idaho Dept. Health, Boise, 1961-64, asst. project dir., 1965-67; prof. sociology Boise State U., 1967—2002, sociology dept. chair, 1972-77, 86-90, 1998—2002, dir. women's studies, 1997—2002, ret., prof. emeritus, 2002—. Bd. dirs. Instnl. Rev., Boise; cons./trainer U.S. Soil Conservation Svc., Northwest Region, Calif., 1975-86; faculty senate Boise State U., 1988-92; reviewer for several pubs. of sociology texts, 1990—. Assoc. editor: Social Sci. jour., 1993—; contbr. articles to profl. jours. Pres. bd. dirs. Idaho Lung Assn., Boise, 1975-76, mem., 1970-77; chair Ada County Democrats, 1976-78. Grantee Idaho State

Bd. Edn, 1993, 97, GTE, NSF, U.S. Soil Conservation Svc., 1980s. Mem.: AAUP, AAUW, NOW, Am. Soc. Pub. Adminstrs., We. Social Sci. Assn. (exec. coun. 1995—98, v.p. 2001—02). Democrat. Avocations: golf, bowling, gardening, reading.

DORN, CHARLES MEEKER, art education educator; b. Mpls., Jan. 17, 1927; s. Melville Wilkinson and Margaret (Meeker) D.; m. Virginia Josephine Coble, July 11, 1947; children: Mary Jan, Charles Meeker. BA, MA, George Peabody Coll. Tchrs., 1950; Ed.D., U. Tex., 1959. Asst. prof. art Union U., Jackson, Tenn., 1950-54; instr. art and edn. Memphis State U., 1954-57; lectr. edn. U. Tex., 1957-59; head art dept. Nat. Coll. Edn., Evanston, Ill., 1959-61; assoc. prof. art No. Ill. State U., 1961-62; exec. sec. Nat. Art Edn. Assn., Washington, 1962-70; prof., chmn. dept. art Calif. State U., Northridge, 1970-72; prof. creative arts Purdue U., Lafayette, Ind., 1972-86, head dept., 1972-76; prof., dir. Ctr. for Arts Adminstrn. Fla. State U., Tallahassee, 1986—, chmn. dept. art edn., 1986-90. Served with AUS, 1945-46. Recipient 25th Anniversary award for disting. service Nat. Gallery Art, 1966. Mem.: Internat. Soc. Edn. Through Art, Nat Art Edn. Assn. (pres. 1975—77, Disting. Svc. award 1979, Disting. fellow 1982, Southeastern Higher Edn. Art Educator award 1990, Higher Edn. award 1990, 1999, Nat. Art Educator of the Yr. 2003), Fla. Art Edn. Assn., Kappa Phi Kappa, Phi Delta Kappa. Home: 377 Castleton Cir Tallahassee FL 32312 Office: Fla State U Dept Art Edn Tallahassee FL 32306 E-mail: dornetal@aol.com., cdorm@mailer.fsu.edu.

DORNAN, JOHN NEILL, public policy center professional; b. Canonsburg, Pa., July 20, 1944; s. Carl Edward and Kathryn (Neill) D.; m. Jacquelin Riggs (div. 1971); children: Jodie Lynn, John Neill; m. Carol Michaels (div. 1976); m. Anne Marie Deegan (div. 1993). BA, Indiana U. of Pa., 1966; postgrad., U. Pitts., 1966-68. English tchr. Moon Twp., Coraopolis, Pa., 1966-69; field rep. NEA, Harrisburg, Pa., 1969-70, media rep. San Francisco, 1970-71; asst. exec. dir. Ill. Edn. Assn., Springfield, Ill., 1970-74; asst. to pres. AFSCME, Washington, 1974-75; assoc. exec. dir. Coalition of Am. Pub. Employees, Washington, 1975-76, N.Y. Edn. Assn., Albany, 1976-82; exec. sec. N.C. Assn. Educators, Raleigh, 1982-86; pres. Pub. Sch. Forum, Raleigh, 1986—. Cons. in field; adj. faculty Cornell U., Albany, 1981-82, Appalachian U., Boone, N.C., 1987-88, N.C. Prin's. Exec. Program, 1986-90. Contbr. numerous articles to profl. jours. Nat. bd. dirs. Parents for Pub. Schs., The Columbia Group; bd. dirs. N.C. Ctr. Internat. Inderstanding, Wake Edn. Ptnrship; treas. S.E. Ctr. Tchg. Quality Found. Mem.: Raleigh C. of C. Democrat. Presbyterian. Avocations: reading, collecting antique posters. Home: 1409 Granada Dr Raleigh NC 27612-5109 Office: Koger Ctr Cumberland Bldg 3739 National Dr Ste 210 Raleigh NC 27612-4844

DORNBURG, RALPH CHRISTOPH, biology educator; b. Nuernberg, Federal Republic of Germany, Aug. 12, 1952; came to U.S., 1986; s. Robert and Freia (Puchtler) Dornburg; m. Ute Peitrass, Aug. 12, 1980 (div. Apr. 7, 1999); children: Alex, Rebecca. Diploma, Ludwig-Maximilians U., Munich, 1982; postgrad., Max-Planck Inst. Biochemistry, Martinsried, Fed. Republic Germany, 1982-86; PhD, U. Munich, 1986. Deutsche Forschungs-Gemeinschaft postdoctoral fellow McArdle Lab. for Cancer Rsch., Madison, Wis., 1986-89; asst. prof. U. Medicine and Dentistry of N.J., Piscataway, 1989-96; assoc. prof. Thomas Jefferson U., Phila., 1996—. Author: Encyclopedia of Human Biology, 1991, 97, Encyclopedia of Microbiology, 1999; contbr. articles to Nature Biotechnology, Molecular and Cellular Biology, Jour. Virology, Human Gene Therapy, others. Achievements include patents for cell-type specific gene transfer, recombination activating sequences, and retroviral vectors capable of infecting quiescent cells. Office: Thomas Jefferson Univ Divsn Infectious Diseases 1020 Locust St Philadelphia PA 19107-6731 E-mail: ralph.dornburg@mail.tju.edu.

DORNEMAN, PENNY LEE HARDING, educational products developer; b. Greensburg, Pa., May 10, 1957; d. William R. Jr. and Amelia (Streif) Harding; m. Stephen H. Dorneman, Dec. 29, 1979. BSBA summa cum laude, Northeastern U., 1988; MBA with honors, Simmons Coll., 1991. Head buyer Boston Mus. Sci., 1982-88; purchasing agt BKM, Inc., Charlestown, Mass., 1988-90; dir. learning products WGBH Learningsmith, Cambridge, Mass., 1991—95, Netmarket Group, Inc., Trumbull, Mass., 1997—2001, Trilegian Corp., Norwalk, Conn., 2001—. Mem. Boston Mus. Sci., Sigma Epsilon Rho. Avocation: needlework. Home: 44 Bristol Ter Milford CT 06460-3427

DORNETTE, W(ILLIAM) STUART, lawyer, educator; b. Washington, Mar. 2, 1951; s. William Henry Lueders and Frances Roberta (Hester) D.; m. Martha Louise Mehl, Nov. 19, 1983; children: Marjorie Francès, Anna Christine, David Paul. AB, Williams Coll., 1972; JD, U. Va., 1975. Bar: Va. 1975, Ohio 1975, U.S. Dist. Ct. (so. dist.) Ohio 1975, D.C. 1976, U.S. Ct. Appeals (6th cir.) 1977, U.S. Supreme Ct. 1980. Assoc. Taft, Stettinius & Hollister, Cin., 1975-83, ptnr., 1983—. Instr. law U. Cin., 1980-87, adj. prof., 1988-91. Co-author: Federal Judiciary Almanac, 1984-87. Mem. Ohio Bd. Bar Examiners, 1991-93, Hamilton County Rep. Exec. Com., 1982—; bd. dirs. Zool. Soc. Cin., 1983-94, Cin. Parks Found., 1995—; bd. visitors U. Cin. Law Sch., 2002—. Mem. FBA, Ohio State Bar Assn., Cin. Bar Assn., Am. Phys. Soc., Nat. Assn. Coll. and Univ. Attys. Methodist. Home: 329 Bishopsbridge Dr Cincinnati OH 45255-3948 Office: 1800 US Bank Tower 425 Walnut St Cincinnati OH 45202-3923 E-mail: dornette@taftlaw.com.

DORNFELD, DAVID ALAN, engineering educator; b. Horicon, Wis., Aug. 3, 1949; s. Harlan Edgar and Cleopatra D.; Barbara Ruth Dornfeld, Sept. 18, 1976. BS in Mech. Engrng. with honors, U. Wis., 1972, MS in Mech. Engrng., 1973, PhD in Mech. Engrng., 1976. Asst. prof. dept. sys. design U. Wis., Milw., 1976-77; asst. prof. mfg. engrng. U. Calif., Berkeley, 1977-83, assoc. prof. mfg. engrng., 1983-89, vice-chmn. instrn. dept. mech. engrng., 1987-88, dir. Engrng. Sys. Rsch. Ctr., 1989-98, prof. mfg. engrng., 1989—, Will C. Hall Family prof. engrng., 1999—, assoc. dean interdisciplinary studies Coll. Engrng., 2001—; assoc. dir. rsch. Ecole Nationale Superieure des Mines de Paris, Berkeley, 1983-84. Invited prof. Ecole Nationale Superieure D'Arts et Metiers, Paris, 1992-93; cons., expert witness for intellectual property issues, sensor systems, mfg. automation. Contbr. articles to profl. jours., chpts. in books; presenter numerous seminars, confs.; patentee in field. Recipient Dist. Svc. citation U. Wis. Coll. Engrng, Madison, 2000. Fellow ASME (past editor, mem. editl. bd. Mfg. Rev. Jour., pres advisory com., Blackall Machine Tool and Gage Award 1990), Soc. Mfg. Engrs. (fellow editl. bd. Jour. Mfg. Systems, Outstanding Young Engr. award 1982); mem. Am. Soc. Precision Engrng., Acoustic Emission Working Group, N.Am. Mfg. Rsch. Inst. (past pres., scientific com.), Japan Soc. Precision Engrng., Coll. Internat. pour l'Etude Scientifique des Techniques de Production Mechanique (CIRP). Avocations: hiking, travelling, reading. Office: U Calif Dept Mech Engring Berkeley CA 94720-1740 E-mail: dornfeld@me.berkeley.edu.

DOROBEK, CARROLL FRANCES, retired secondary school educator; b. LA, Sept. 30, 1939; d. Joseph Stanley and Gretchen Frances (Frock) D. BA, Immaculate Heart Coll., 1961; MS, Calif. Luth. Coll., 1981. Tchr. elem. LA Unified Sch. Dist., 1961—63, tchr. secondary, 1964—2001; ret., 2001. Therapist pvt. practice, L.A., 1981—. Mem. Coun. Exceptional Children, Assn. Ednl. Therapist (bd. dirs. 1989-91, treas. 1991-97), Delta Kappa Gamma. Avocations: reading, horseback riding. Home: 821 N Catalina St Burbank CA 91505-3020

DORPAT, THEODORE LORENZ, psychoanalyst; b. Miles City, Mont., Mar. 25, 1925; s. Theodore Ertman and Eda (Christiansen) D.; married; 1 child, Joanne Katherine. BS, Whitworth Coll., 1948; MD, U. Wash., 1952; grad., Seattle Psychoanalytic Inst., 1964. Resident in psychiatry Seattle VA Hosp., 1953-55, Cin. Gen. Hosp., 1955-56; instr. in psychiatry U. Wash., 1956-58, asst. prof. psychiatry, 1958-59, asso. prof., 1969-75, prof., 1976—; practice medicine specializing in psychiatry Seattle, 1958-64; practice psychoanalysis, 1964; instr. Seattle Psychoanalytic Inst., 1966-71, tng. psychoanalyt, 1971—, dir., 1984. Chmn. Wash. Gov.'s Task Force for Commitment Law Reform; trustee Seattle Community Psychiat. Clinic; pres., trustee Seattle Psychoanalytic Inst. Contbr. numerous articles, books, revs. to profl. jours. Served to ensign USNR, 1943-46. Fellow Am. Psychiat. Assn.; mem. Am. Psychoanalytic Assn., AMA, Seattle Psychoanalytic Soc. (sec.-treas. 1965-67, pres. 1972-73), AAAS, Alpha Omega Alpha, Sigma Xi. Home: 7700 E Green Lake Dr N Seattle WA 98103-4971 Office: Blakely Bldg 2271 NE 51st St Seattle WA 98105-5713

DORRIS, PETER GEORGE, secondary mathematics educator; b. Ottawa, Ill., Feb. 17, 1940; s. George Constantine and Helen (Theodore) D.; m. Lynn Englis Melcher Barrett, Dec. 29, 1963 (div. Aug. 1980); children: Maria, Daphne; m. Gayla Malone, Sept. 6, 1987; children: Carrie, Amy, Wendy. BA, Knox Coll., Galesburg, Ill., 1962; MS, Oreg. State U., Corvallis, 1964; postgrad., Temple U., 1970-72. Cert. tchr., Ill., Fla. Tchr. math. Albany (Oreg.) Union H.S., 1963-66; tchr., head dept. math. Am. Acad., Athens, 1966-69; adminstrv. asst. to supt. Am. Cmty. Schs., Athens, 1970; rsch. assoc. Rsch. for Better Schs., Phila., 1970-72; tchr., head dept. math. ARAMCO Schs., Dhahran, Saudi Arabia, 1972-92; supr. support svcs. unit, loss prevention dept. ARAMCO, Dhahran, 1980-92; tchr. math. Martin County Schs., Stuart, Fla., 1992—; instr. math. Palm Beach C.C., West Palm Beach, Fla., 1994—. Author: School Improvement, 1978. Recipient I Make A Difference Tchr. award Palm Beach Post/Channel 12 TV, 1993-94. Mem. Am. Soc. Safety Engrs., Nat. Coun. Tchrs. Math., Fla. Coun. Tchrs. Math., Phi Gamma Delta (chpt. pres. 1961-62). Home: 342 Fairway N Tequesta FL 33469-1915 Office: Palm Beach Gardens HS 4245 Holly Dr Palm Beach Gardens FL 33410-5503

DORSEN, NORMAN, lawyer, educator; b. N.Y.C., Sept. 4, 1930; s. Arthur and Tanya (Stone) D.; m. Harriette Koffler, Nov. 25, 1965; children: Jennifer, Caroline Gail, Anne. BA, Columbia U., 1950; LLB magna cum laude, Harvard U., 1953; postgrad., London Sch. Econs., 1955-56; LLD (hon.), Ripon Coll., 1981, John Jay Coll. Criminal Justice, 1992. Bar: D.C. 1953, N.Y. 1954. Law clk. to chief judge Calvert Magruder U.S. Ct. Appeals, Boston, 1956-57; law clk. to Justice John Marshall Harlan U.S. Supreme Ct., Washington, 1957-58; assoc. Dewey, Ballantine, Bushby, Palmer & Wood, N.Y.C., 1958-60; prof. law NYU Sch. Law, N.Y.C., 1961-81, Stokes prof., 1981—, dir. Hays civil liberties program, 1961—, dir. global law sch. program, 1994-96, chmn., 1996—2002; counselor to pres. NYU, 2002—. Vis. prof. law London Sch. Econs., 1968, U. Calif., Berkeley, 1974-75, Harvard U., 1980, 83, 84; cons. U.S. Commn. on Violence, 1968-69, Random House, 1969-73, B.B.C., 1969-73, U.S. Commn. on Social Security, 1979-80, Native Am. Rights Fund, 1978-89; exec. dir. spl. com. on courtroom conduct Assn. Bar N.Y.C., 1970-73; chmn. Com. for Pub. Justice, 1972-74; vice chmn. HEW sec.'s rev. panel on new drug regulation, 1975-76, chmn., 1976-77; mem. N.Y.C. Commn. on Status of Women, 1978-80; chmn. Sec. of Treasury's Citizen Rev. Panel on Good O' Boy Round-up, 1995-96. Author (with others): Political and Civil Rights in U.S., 3rd edit., 1967, Political and Civil Rights in U.S., 4th edit., Vol. I, 1976, Political and Civil Rights in U.S., 4th edit., Vol. II, 1979, Frontiers of Civil Liberties, 1968, Discrimination and Civil Rights, 1969, Comparative Constitution, 2003; author: (with L. Friedman) Disorder in the Court, 1973; author: (with S. Gillers) Regulation of Lawyers, 1985, Regulation of Lawyers, 2d edit., 1989; editor: The Rights of Americans, 1971; editor: (with S. Gillers) None of Your Business, 1974; editor: Our Endangered Rights, 1984, The Evolving Constitution, 1987; editor: (with others) Human Rights in Northern Ireland, 1991, The Unpredictable Constitution, 2001, with P. Gifford: Democracy and the Rule of Law, 2001; ; editor: (with others) Constitutionalism Cases and Materials, 2003; editl. dir. Internat. Jour. Constl. Law, 2002—. 1st lt. JAGC, U.S. Army, 1953-55. Recipient medal French Minister of Justice, 1983, Eleanor Roosevelt Human Rights award 2000; Fulbright Disting. Prof., Argentina, 1987, 88. Fellow Am. Acad. Arts and Scis.; mem. ABA (chmn. com. free speech and press 1968-70), ACLU (gen. counsel 1969-76, pres. 1976-91), Am. Law Inst., Coun. on Fgn. Rels., Lawyers Com. Human Rights (chmn. bd. dirs. 1995-2000), Lawyer Com. Civil Rights, Internat. Assn. Constnl. Law (exec. com.), U.S. Assn. Constnl. Law (pres. 1996—), Soc. Am. Law Tchrs. (pres. 1972-74, Tchg. award 1997), Thomas Jefferson Ctr. for Free Expression (trustee). Home: 146 Central Park W New York NY 10023-2005 Office: NYU Sch Law 40 Washington Sq S New York NY 10012-1005 E-mail: norman.dorsen@nyu.edu.

DORSETT, JUDITH A. elementary education educator; b. Tacoma, Oct. 18, 1944; d. Lyall Edgar and Elnora (Hutton) Templin; m. Nick A. Dorsett, Aug. 28, 1965; children: Charles, Drew. BA, Cen. Washington U., 1967. Tutor K-adult edn., Yakima Valley, Wash., 1968—; elem. tchr. and tech. resource tchr., reading specialist Yakima (Wash.) Dist. 7, 1967—. Ednl. seminar leader in Northwest, 1971—. Author: Bulletin Board Activity Centers, Creative Calling and Effective Follow-Up, Handbook of Creativity, Bulletin Board Builders, #2, #3, #4, Creative Bible Games; contbr. articles to children's and tchrs.' mags. Elem. Christian edn. coord. Stone Ch. AG, Yakima, Wash., 2000—. Recipient PTA Golden Acorn award, 1985; named Tchr. of Yr., 1985, Vol. of Yr., 1984. Home: 2606 Draper Rd Yakima WA 98903-9216 Office: Whitney Elem Sch 4411 W Nob Hill Blvd Yakima WA 98908-3740 E-mail: judyd62667@aol.com.

DORSEY, J(ONNIE) NAOMI, vocational education educator, consultant; b. Wrens, Ga., Sept. 3, 1943; d. Rufus Allen and Myrtle Marie (Combs) Lee; m. Oliver Dorsey, Sept. 17, 1971; children: Oliver II, Omar Jermaine. BS, Ft. Valley State Coll., 1965; MEd, Ga. State U., 1981, EdS, 1983. Cert. tchr., Ga. Tchr. Dougherty County Bd. Edn., Albany, Ga., 1965-67, Henry County Bd. Edn., McDonough, Ga., 1967-88; cons. vocat. edn. Ga. Dept. Edn., Atlanta, 1988—. Program mgr. for spl. populations Ga. Dept. Edn., 1992—, mem. quality basic edn. coordinating com., 1991—. Author: (play) Come Into the Stable, Now, 1990; (recitations) Fragmented Memories, 1985. Active Parents, Tchrs., Student Assn., Columbia High Sch., 1992, Glenwood Hills Assn., Decatur, Ga., 1985. Named Tchr. of Yr. Henry County, 1977-78; featured in Women in Action series Henry Herald Newspaper, McDonough, 1978. Mem. NAACP, Am. Vocat. Assn., Nat. Assn. Vocat. Spl. Needs Pers., Ga. Vocat. Assn. (Educators award), Assn. Vocat. Spl. Needs Pers., Ga. Assn. Educators (pres. 1978-79), Vocat. Opportunities Clubs Am. (state advisor/dir. 1988—), Toastmasters Internat. (Best Speaker award 1990-91), Kappa Depta Pi. Baptist. Avocations: public speaking, sewing, writing prose and poetry. Home: 2321 Columbia Woods Ct Decatur GA 30032-6724 Office: Ga Dept Edn 1770 Twin Towers E Atlanta GA 30334-9047

DORSEY, RHODA MARY, retired academic administrator; b. Boston, Sept. 9, 1927; d. Thomas Francis and Hedwig (Hoge) D. BA magna cum laude, Smith Coll., 1949, LLD, 1979; BA, Cambridge (Eng.) U., 1951, MA, 1954; PhD, U. Minn., 1956; LLD, Nazareth Coll. Rochester, 1970, Goucher Coll., 1994; DHL (hon.), Mount St. Mary's Coll., 1976, Mount Vernon Coll., 1979, Coll. St. Catherine, 1983, Johns Hopkins U., 1986, Towson State U., 1987, Coll. Notre Dame of Md., 1995, Coll. of Notre Dame Md., 1995. Mem. faculty Goucher Coll., Balt., Md., 1954-94, prof. history, 1965-68, dean, v.p., 1968-73, acting pres., 1973-74, pres., 1974-94, pres. emeritus, 1994—. Lectr. history Loyola Coll., Balt., 1958-62, Johns Hopkins U., Balt., 1960-61; bd. trustee Roland Park County Sch., 1995—. Bd. dirs. Friends of Cambridge U., 1978—, sec., 1989-93; bd. dirs. Gen. German Aged Peoples Home, Balt., 1984—, Greater Balt. Med. Ctr., 1990—, Md. Humanities Coun., Baltimore County Landmarks Preservation Commn., 1994—; bd. dirs., chair Hist. Hampton, Inc., 1992—; trustee Loyola, Notre Dame Libr., Balt., 1994—, Roland Park Country Sch., 1995—; chair Gov.'s Commn. Svc., 1994—. Named Outstanding Woman Mgr. of 1984 U. Balt. Women's Program in Mgmt. and WMAR-TV, Woman of Yr. Balt. County Commn. for Women, 1993; recipient Outstanding Achievement award U. Minn. Alumni Assn., 1984, Andrew White medal Loyola Coll., Balt., 1985; named in peer survey as one of 100 Most Effective Coll. and Univ. Pres. in U.S., Chronicle of Higher Edn., 1986. Mem. Internat. Women's forum, Smith Club, Hamilton St. Club (Balt.), Cosmopolitan Club (N.Y.C.).

DORTCH, SUSAN MADELINE, elementary education educator; b. Phila., Nov. 5, 1951; d. Ulester L. Mahoney and Flora (Blair) Simmons; m. Eulas C. Dortch, Feb. 10, 1973; children: Candace Alexis, Brandon Edward, Bryan Vincent. BS in Edn. and Infancy magna cum laude, Temple U., 1976; postgrad., U. Md., 1988—, Bowie State U., 1995. Tchr. nursery Phila. Bd. of Edn., 1976-83, tchr. kindergarten, 1983-85, Prince Georges County Bd. of Edn., Upper Marlboro, Md., 1986, tchr. 3d grade, 1987-88; tchr. 2d grade Prince Georges County Bd. Edn., Upper Marlboro, Md., 1989-97, tchr. writing, math., 1994-97, instrnl. coord., 1995—; magnet sch. coord. Phyllis E. Williams Acad. Ctr., Largo, Md., 1997—. Multicultural edn. cluster coord. Prince Georges County Bd. edn., 1996—, tchr. coord. talented and gifted, 1990—, elem. math. coord., 1994—, mentoring task force, mentor tchr., staff devel. adv. coun., 1997, magnet sch. coord., 1998; union rep. Phila. Tchr. Union, 1981-82; instrnl. coord. Highland Park Elem., 1999—. Sec. Largo H.S. PTSA, 1986—; mem. Phila. Zool. Soc., 1983—; sch. vol. O.A.S.I.S., 1995—; treas. Largo H.S. Band Family. Named Educator of Yr., C. of C., 1990-91, Outstanding Educator, Kettering Elem Sch., 1991; grantee Black Male Achievement, Action Rsch., 1997 Mem. Prince George's County Aspiring Prins. Program, Delta Sigma Theta, Prince George's City Alumnae Chpt. Office: Highland Park Elem 6501 Lowland Dr Landover MD 20785-4359

DOSAMANTES-BEAUDRY, IRMA, psychology educator; b. Mexico City; m. Walter A. Beaudry. BS, CUNY, 1959, MA, 1962; PhD, Mich. State U., 1967; postgrad., UCLA, 1972-73; grad. psychoanalyst, L.A. Inst./Soc. Psych. Studies, 1993. Assoc. dir., counselor SUNY, Stonybrook, 1968-71; assoc. prof. U. No. Colo., 1973-74, Calif. State U., L.A., 1974-77; prof. UCLA, 1977—. Dir. dance/movement therapy program UCLA, 1977—. Author: (book) Body-Image: A Cross-Cultural Perspective, 1993; editor-in-chief: (profl. jour.) The Arts in Psychotherapy Jour., 1998—, mem. editl. bd., 1986-87; mem. editl. bd. Am. Dance Therapy Jour., 1988-97. U. Calif. Pacific Rim Rsch. grantee, 1991-92. Mem. APA, Am. Dance Therapy Assn. (bd. dirs. 1974-84, pres. 1980-82, Chace Found. award 1997), Am. Assn. for Study of Mental Imagery (bd. dirs. 1982-86, pres. 1983-84), Internat. Psychoanalytic Assn., L.A. Inst. and Soc. for Psychoanalytic Studies. Avocations: tennis, gardening. Office: UCLA World Arts & Cultures Dept PO Box 951608 Los Angeles CA 90095-1608

DOSS, RICHARD, principal; BS in Edn., Ind. U., 1986; MS in Adminstrn. and Curriculum, Butler U., 1993. Sci. tchr. Fulton Jr. H.S., Indpls., 1986—94; asst. prin. Brownsburg (Ind.) Jr. H.S., 1994—95, prin., 1995—. Presenter in field. Office: Brownsburg Jr HS 1555 S Odell St Brownsburg IN 46112

DOTSON, VICKY LYNN, special education educator; b. Stuttgart, Ark., Feb. 3, 1953; d. William John and Maxine (McDowell) Schott; m. Robert Earl Dotson, May 15, 1976; children: Robert Daniel, Shannon Lynn. B in Music Edn., U. Cen. Ark., 1976; postgrad., Longwood Coll., 1991—. Cert. music tchr., Va.; cert X-Ray technician. Music lab. operator U. Cen. Ark., Conway, 1972-75; computer operator, X-Ray technican Dr. Earl Dotson, Dental Practice, Richmond, Va., 1976-88; music tchr. Fuqua Sch., Farmville, Va., 1989—, daycare coord., 2002—. Bd. dirs. Fuqua Sch., Farmville; fund raising chmn. Parent Tchr. Student Assn. Fuqua Sch. Fund; chmn. after prom party, Fuqua Sch. Choir dir. Oakwood United Meth. Ch., Columbia, Va., 1979—, bd. trustees, 1988—, Sunday sch. treas., 1991—, tone chime dir.; dental asst. Goochland Women's Correctional Inst., 1986-88; pres., treas. Tiny Tots Nursery Bd., Columbia, 1989-92; mem. Band Boosters Fuqua Sch., 1992—. Mem. ASCD, Nat. Assn. Music Educators, Va. Music Educators Assn., Assn. Va. Acads., Am. Choral Dirs. Assn., Lioness Club (pres. Richmond 1979-81), Alpha Chi, Gamma Beta Phi. Republican. Avocations: needlework, swimming, sewing, weekend at the beach, gourmet cooking, catering. Home: 1155 Ampthill Rd Columbia VA 23038-2807 Office: Fuqua Sch PO Box 328 Farmville VA 23901-0328

DOTTIN, ERSKINE S. education educator; b. St. Michael, Barbados, July 21, 1940; s. Grafton Howard and Beryl Dottin; m. Cynthia E. Dottin, Apr. 25, 1970; 1 child, Farrell S. BS, U. West Fla., 1973, MEd, 1974; PhD, Miami U., Oxford, Ohio, 1976; AA, Pensacola (Fla.) Jr. Coll., 1972. Tchr. Pensacola Sch. Liberal Arts; from instructional specialist to assoc. prof. edn. U. West Fla., Pensacola, 1977-92; prof. Fla. Internat. U., 1992—. Author: Thinking About Education, 1989, Teaching as Enchancing Human Effectiveness, 1994, Developing a Conceptual Framework, 2001, Enhancing Effective Thinking and Problem Solving for Preservice Teacher Education Candidates and IN-Service Professionals, 2001. Mem.ASCD, Am. Ednl. Rsch. Assn., Am. Ednl. Studies Assn., Fla. Founds. Edn. Soc. (past pres.), NCATE (unit accreditation bd.), S.E. Philosophy Edn. Soc. (past pres.), Coun. Social Founds. of Edn. (pres. 1998-2001), Phi Kappa Phi, Phi Delta Kappa. Home: 14810 SW 149th Ave Miami FL 33196-2334 Office: Fla Internat Univ Coll Edn Leadership & Polit Studies Univ Park Miami FL 33199-0001 E-mail: dottine@fiu.edu.

DOTY, DUANE HAROLD, business educator; b. Wichita, Kans., July 5, 1960; s. David H. and Martha (Parker) D.; m. Susan Michal Smith, Dec. 30, 1991; children: Lindsey, Michala, Zachary, David. BA with honors, S.W. Tex. State U., San Marcos, Tex., 1982; MBA, U. Tex., Austin, 1986, PhD, 1990. Asst. prof. U. Ark., Fayetteville, 1990—95; chair dept. strategy and human resources Syracuse U. Sch. Mgmt., 1995. Contbr. articles. Mem.: Acad. Mgmt. (mem. editl. bd. Acad. Mgmt. Jour., Best Article award 1993, Scholarly Achievement award human resouces divsn. 1997). Avocations: family, hunting, fishing, horses. Office: Syracuse U Sch Mgmt Syracuse NY 13244 Office Fax: 314.443.5457. Business E-Mail: hdoty@som.syr.edu.

DOTY, RICHARD L. medical researcher; b. Boulder, Colo., Oct. 14, 1944; s. George David and Frances Amelia (Bradley) D. BS, Colo. State U., 1966; MA, Calif. State U., 1968; PhD, Mich. State U., 1971; postgrad., U. Calif., Berkeley, 1973. Instr. dept. psychology Calif. State U., San Francisco, 1971-72, U. San Francisco, 1971-72; asst. mem. Monell Chem. Senses Ctr., Phila., 1974-76, assoc. mem., head human olfaction sect., 1976-78; dir. smell and taste ctr. Hosp. U. Pa., Phila., 1979—, Sch. Medicine, U. Pa., Phila., 1980—, asst. prof. dept. otorhinolaryngology, human communication, 1983-89, assoc. prof., 1989-93; prof. dept. otorhinolaryngology U. Pa., Phila., 1994—. Cons. in field; lectr. in field; editorial cons. for numerous profl. jours.; external adv. bd. Taste and Smell Ctr. U. Conn./Yale U., 1982-84, Rocky Mountain Taste and Smell Ctr., U. Colo. Sch. Medicine, 1985, Mayo Found. Project, 1989; internat. adv. bd. 1st Internat. Congress on Food and Health, Salsomaggiore Terme, Italy, 1985. Author: The Smell Identification Test (TM) Administration Manual, 1983, 2d edit., 1989, 3d edit., 1995; editor: Mammalian Olfaction, Reproductive Processes and Behavior, 1976, Handbook of Olfaction and Gustation, 1995, 2d edit., 2003; co-editor: (with T.V. Getchell, E.P. Koster) Chemical Senses, spl. edit., 1981, (with D.G. Laing, W. Breopohl) Human Olfaction, 1990, (with L.M. Bartoshuk, T.V. Getchell and J.B. Snow) Smell and Taste in Health Disease, 1991, (with D. Muller-Schwartze) Chemical Signals in Vertebrates VI, 1992. NIH postdoctoral rsch. fellow, 1973-75; grantee Nat. Inst. on Aging, 1989-91, Nat. Inst. Deafness and Other Comm. Disorders, 1980—. Mem. European Chemoreception Rsch. Orgn. (mem. organizational com. 1981), Assn. for Chemoreception Scis. (mem. program com. 1985, 87, mem. elections com. 1987), AAAS, N.Y. Acad. Scis., Assn. for

Rsch. in Otolaryngology, Am. Acad. Otolaryngology (head and neck surgery), Am. Psychol. Assn., Internat. Soc. for Chem. Ecology, Phila. Coll. Physicians (mem. adv. com., sect. on geriatrics and gerontology). Home: 125 White Horse Pike Haddon Heights NJ 08035-1909 Office: U Pa Smell & Taste Ctr 5 Ravdin Bldg 3400 Spruce St Philadelphia PA 19104-4206 E-mail: doty@mail.med.upenn.edu.

DOTY, VICTORIA SKOWER, elementary educator; b. Stafford, Conn., Sept. 25, 1946; d. Frank Albert Jr. and Emily Marie (Jedziniak) Skower; m. Edwin Wilfred Doty, Oct. 14, 1978; 1 child, Peter Edwin. BA, Am. Internat. Coll., Springfield, Mass., 1969; MA, Elms Coll., 1991. Cert. elem. tchr., Mass., Conn. Coord. inventory control Hallmark Cards Inc., Enfield, Conn., 1969-89; substitute tchr. Enfield and Longmeadow, Mass., 1991—98; tchr., chair mid. sch. reading and lang. arts St. Gabriels Sch., Windsor, Conn., 1998—. Sec. Thompsonville Little League, 1991-94, fin. sec., 1988-89, 93-94; elected to parish coun. St. Adalbert Ch., 1994-98; coord. local and county dist. Modern Woodmen of Am. Oration Contest, 2000—. Mem. St. Adalbert Home and Sch. Assn. (historian 1991-93, fin. sec. 1988-89, 93-94, treas. 1987-88). Republican. Roman Catholic. Avocations: folk art, crafts, crocheting, reading. Home: 45 Alden Ave Enfield CT 06082-2866

DOUBEK, FAYOLA MARIE, nurse, educator; b. Brainerd, Minn., Mar. 4, 1952; d. Clifford Earl and Irma Irene (Ramsdell) Olson; m. William Jerry Doubek, Feb. 14, 1985; children: Daniel William, Adam Jerome, Elizabeth Fay Jean. Diploma of nursing, Arthur B. Ancker Meml. Sch. Nursing, 1974; BS in Community Service, Bemidji State U., 1980; MS in Nursing, U. Minn., 1984. Mem. staff Bemidji (Minn.) Community Hosp., 1974-76, Ah Gwah Ching (Minn.) State Nursing Home, 1976-77, shift supr., 1977-79, unit supr., 1979-80; edn. coord. St. Croix Valley Meml. Hosp., St. Croix Falls, Wis., 1983-85; clin. nurse specialist Riverside Med. Ctr., Mpls., 1985-90; membership coord. Third Dist. Nurses, Mpls., 1990-98, Ebenezer Soc., Mpls., 2000—. Mem. ANA, Minn. Nurses Assn., 3d Dist. Nurses, Am. Assn. Diabetes Educators, Mpls.-St. Paul Diabetes Educators, Am. Diabetes Assn., Am. Cancer Soc. (honor citation 1985, I Can Cope Svc. award 1986). Lutheran. Avocations: reading, crotcheting, embroidery, bicycling. Home: 4048 86th Ln NE Circle Pines MN 55014-4006 Office: Ebenezer Soc 2545 Portland Ave S Minneapolis MN 55404 E-mail: fdoubekl@fairview.org., fayola@yahoo.com.

DOUD, DENNIS ADAIR, secondary educator; b. Waukegan, Ill., Oct. 10, 1943; s. Webster Hawley and Adrienne (Gaiennie) D.; m. Mary Ann Loesch, July 11, 1970; children: Christopher, Tristan, Tiffany. BS, Loyola U., Chgo., 1965; MA, Loyola U., 1972. Cert. secondary tchr., Ill. Grad. asst. Loyola U., 1966-67; tchr., coach North Chicago (Ill.) H.S., 1967-72; tchr. modern European history, humanities, European hist. AP Evanston (Ill.) H.S., 1972—2002. Jr. varsity sophmore basketball coach Evanston H.S., 1972-81. Basketball coach Waukegan Park Dist., 1985-96; coach Waukegan Baseball Assn., 1990—, Waukegan Soccer Assn.; soccer coach Gurnee (Ill.) Park Dist., 1989-93. Recipient Outstanding Tchr. award U. Chgo., 1986, 87, 89, spl. tchr. recognition Carleton Coll., 1987, influentia. tchr. recognition Wesleyan U., 1991; named One of Top 5 Tchrs., Evanston High Sch., 1989. Mem. IEA-NEA, Newberry Libr. Consortium for History Tchrs. Avocations: model building and railroading, stamp collecting, reading, refereeing basketball, umpiring. Home: 2012 Kingston Rd Waukegan IL 60087-2115 Office: 1600 Dodge Ave Evanston IL 60201-3449

DOUD, GUY R. motivational speaker, former secondary education educator; Degree summa cum laude, Concordia Coll., 1975; LHD (hon.), Judson Coll., 1992. Tchr. lang. arts Brainerd (Minn.) Sr. High Sch. Recipient Nat. Lang. Arts Tchr. of Yr. award, 1986.*

DOUDS, VIRGINIA LEE, elementary education educator; b. Pitts., Jan. 17, 1943; d. Leland Ray and Virginia Helen (Dodds) Frazier; m. William Wallace Douds, June 20, 1964; children: William Stewart Douds, Michael Leland Douds. BA in Elem. Edn., Westminster Coll., New Wilmington, Pa., 1964; MA (Master's Equivalency), Dept. Edn., State of Pa., 1990. Cert. elem. tchr., Pa. Elem. tchr./non-graded Good Hope Elem. Sch., Glendale-Riverhills, Wis., 1964-65; elem. tchr./1st grade Carlisle Elem. Sch., Delaware, Ohio, 1965-66; elem. tchr./3rd grade Meml. Elem. Sch., Bethel Park, Pa., 1973-74; elem. tchr./1st and 3rd grades Logan Elem. Sch., Bethel Park, 1974-91; elem. tchr./3rd grade Neil Armstrong Elem. Sch., Bethel Park, 1991-99, Ben Franklin Elem. Sch., Bethel Park, 1999—. Software cons. Coal Kids, U.S. Dept. Mines, 1993; mem. lang. arts, reading com. Bethel Park Schs., 1989-92, cooperating tchr., 1986—, mentor tchr. 1992-93, 95—, mem. instrnl. support team, 1988-91, integrated lang. arts com., 1999-2000; judge Ben Franklin Scholarship Comm., 2001-03; mem. Mid. States Accreditation com., 1993-94, strategic planning com., 1994-95; SIP scholarship com. Bethel Park Fedn. Tchrs., 1973—. Mem. alumni coun. exec. bd. Westminster Coll., 1979-83; mem. exec. bd. Parents Assn., 1985-89. Recipient mini grant/writing, publishing ctr. Bethel Park Schs., 1989, Gift of Time tribute Am. Family Inst., 1990, 91, All Star Educator award U. Pitts./Pitts. Post Gazette, 1996. Mem. Nat. Coun. Tchrs. of English (lang. arts/reading com. 2000-01), Bethel Park Fedn. Tchrs., PTO. Republican. Presbyterian. Avocations: reading, gardening, golf. Home: 2679 Burnsdale Dr Bethel Park PA 15102-2005

DOUGAL, ARWIN ADELBERT, electrical engineer, educator; b. Dunlap, Iowa, Nov. 22, 1926; s. Adelbert Isaac and Goldya (White) D.; m. Margaret Jane McLennan, Sept. 3, 1951; children: Catherine Ann, Roger Adelbert, Leonard Harley, Laura Beth. BS, Iowa State U., 1952; MS, U. Ill., 1955, PhD, 1957. Registered profl. engr., Tex. Radio engr. Collins Radio Co., Cedar Rapids, Iowa, 1952; research asst., research asso., asst. prof., asso. prof. U. Ill., Urbana, 1952-61; prof., mem. grad. faculty, dir. labs. for electronics and related sci. research U. Tex., Austin, 1961-67, prof., 1969—91; dir. Electronics Research Center, 1971-77, sec. grad. assembly, 1972-74; dir. Austron, Inc., 1977-82; prof. emeritus U. Tex., 1992—. Asst. dir. def. research and engring. for research Office Sec. Def., Washington, 1967-69; cons. Tex. Instruments, Inc., Dallas, Gen. Dynamics Corp., Ft. Worth, U. Calif. Los Alamos Sci. Lab. Contbr. articles to profl. jours. Faculty sponsor U. Tex. Conservative Democrats Club, 1966-67; sr. mem. CAP, 1984—; elder local Presbyn. Ch. With USAF, 1946-49. Recipient Teaching Excellence awards U. Tex. Students Assn., 1962, 63, Spl. award for outstanding service as program chmn. S.W. IEEE Conf. and Exhbn., 1967; Outstanding Grad. Adviser award Grad. Engring. Council, U. Tex., 1971; Disting. Advisor award Grad. Engring. Council, U. Tex., 1977, 84; Teaching Achievement award Grad. Engring. Council, U. Tex., 1977; Profl. Achievement citation in engring. Iowa State U. Alumni Assn., 1975 Fellow Am. Phys. Soc., IEEE (dir. 1980-81, Centennial medal 1984, Student Br. citation 1988, Outstanding Br. Counselor award, 1991, chmn. ctrl. Tex. sect. 1993-94); mem. Am. Soc. Engring. Edn., Rockport Yacht Club, Sigma Xi, Phi Kappa Phi, Tau Beta Pi, Eta Kappa Nu, Pi Mu Epsilon, Phi Eta Sigma. Home: 6115 Rickey Dr Austin TX 78757-4437 E-mail: aadougal@att.net.

DOUGHERTY, DENNIS A. chemistry educator; b. Harrisburg, Pa., Dec. 4, 1952; s. John E. and Colleen (Canning) D.; m. Ellen M. Donnelly, June 3, 1973; children: Meghan, Kayla. BS, MS, Bucknell U., 1974; PhD, Princeton U., 1978. Postdoctoral fellow Yale U., New Haven, 1978-79; from asst. prof. to prof. Calif. Inst. Tech., Pasadena, 1979—2002, George Grant Hoag prof., 2002—. Contbr. articles to sci. jours. Recipient ICI Pharms. award for excellence in chemistry, 1991, Arthur C. Cope Scholar award, 1992; Alfred P. Sloan Found. fellow, 1983; Camille and Henry Dreyfus Tchr. scholar, 1984. Fellow AAAS, Am. Acad. Arts and Scis.; mem. Am. Chem. Soc., Biophys. Soc., Phi Beta Kappa. Home: 1817 Bushnell Ave South Pasadena CA 91030-4905 Office: Calif Inst Tech Div Chemistry & Chem Engring # 164-30 Pasadena CA 91125-0001

DOUGHERTY, JAMES, orthopedic surgeon, educator, author; b. Lawrence, Mass., July 31, 1926; s. James A. and Maude D. (Dillard) D.; m. Marilyn Hays (dec.); m. Rita Buchman; children: James (dec.), Charles, Janice, Jonathan, Christopher. BS, Trinity Coll., Hartford, Conn., 1950; MD, Albany Med. Coll., N.Y., 1951. Diplomate, examiner and monitor Am. Bd. Orthopaedic Surgery, 1965-82; diplomate Am. Bd. Forensic Examiners, Am. Bd. Forensic Medicine. Intern U. Chgo. Clinics, 1951-52, resident, 1951-56, instr., 1955-56; chmn. divsn. orthop. surgery SUNY, Syracuse, 1958-60; prof. clin. surgery Albany Med. Coll., 1960-96, attending surgeon, 1961-94, chief of staff, 1987-89, prof. emeritus, 1996—. Trustee Albany Med. Ctr., 1993-95; cons. Subacute Care Alternative Project, Washington. Author: Ponies in The Window, 1998, (hymns) Life's Narrow Pathways, A Babe Was Born; mem. editl. bd.: Techniques in Orthops.; proponent and architect Fla. state program for pro-bono volunteerism of ret. physicians for medically disadvantaged, 2001; contbr. articles to profl. jours. and Ency. Brittanica. Mem. bd. edn. Ravena-Coeymans-Selkirk Ctrl. Schs., Ravena, NY, 1960—75; med. dir. N.Y. Sr. Games, 1986—89, Catskill Children's Orthop. Clinic, 1960—95; trustee Schaeffer Meml. Libr., 1990—92, Albany Med. Ctr., 1993—95; vol. coord. We Care Program, Lee County, Fla.; bd. dirs. Inst. for Study of Aging, 1990—95. Served with U.S. Army, 1944—46. Recipient Alumni medal Albany Med. Coll., 1951. Fellow: Am. Acad. Orthopaedic Surgeons; mem.: Sr. and Ret. Physicians' Assn. of Lee County Fla. (founder, pres. 1997—98), Albany Med. Coll. Alumni Assn. (trustee 1990—99, pres. 1994—96, Meritorious Svc. award 1996), Northeastern Regional Assn. Sports Medicine (chmn. 1984—89), Asean Orthop. Soc. (hon.), We. Orthop. Soc. (hon. honored guest, Scottsdale, Ariz. 2000), U. Chgo. Surg. Soc., Crawford Campbell Soc. (founder, pres. 1978—88), Sigma Nu, Sigma Psi, Alpha Omega Alpha. Presbyterian. Home: 3510 Pine Fern Ln Bonita Springs FL 34134-1918

DOUGHERTY, JAMES PATRICK, English language educator; b. Wichita, Kans., Mar. 20, 1937; s. James P. and Cora M. Dougherty; m. Jacqueline M. Centunzi, Aug. 18, 1962. BA, St. Louis U., 1959; PhD, U. Pa., 1962. Asst. prof. English U. Calgary, Alta., Can., 1962-66; from assoc. prof. to prof. English U. Notre Dame, Ind., 1966—. Author: The Fivesquare City, 1980, Walt Whitman and the Citizen's Eye, 1993; editor: Religion and Literature, 1984—. Bd. dirs. Renew, Inc., South Bend, Ind., 1984—. Roman Catholic. Office: U Notre Dame Dept English 356 O Shaugnessy Hall Notre Dame IN 46556-5639

DOUGHERTY, JOHN KEVIN, secondary school administrator; b. Jersey City, July 13, 1947; s. Edward Joseph and Florence Elizabeth (Miller) D.; m. Nancy Elizabeth Fassold, June 21, 1969; children: Michael, Brian, Elizabeth, Maryellen. BS, St. Peter's Coll., 1969; MA, Fairleigh Dickinson U., 1972; EdD, Calif. Coast U., 1991. Cert. secondary history and English tchr., prin., supr., sch. bus. adminstr., N.J. Secondary English and history tchr. Lyndhurst (N.J.) H.S., 1969-73, Jackson (N.J.) H.S., 1973-92; prin. Franklin H.S., Somerset, N.J., 1992-96; asst. prin. Princeton (N.J.) H.S., 1996—2001; prin. Winslow Twp. Mid. Sch., 2001—. Adj. instr. history Ocean County Coll., 1984—; mem. devel. team Princeton U. Acad. Program. Author edn. column View From the Classroom for Asbury Park Press, 1991—; contbr. articles to profl. jours. Mem. Gov.'s Juvenile Justice Commn., Trenton, N.J., 1993—; hospitality minister St. Joseph Ch., Toms River, N.J. Named Tchr. of the Yr., Gov.'s Grant Program, 1988. Mem. ASCD, Prin's Ctr. of NJ, Alternative Edn. Assn. of N.J. (bd. dirs., pres. 1988-93), Phi Delta Kappa. Home: 605 Weston Dr Toms River NJ 08755-3249

DOUGHERTY, MICHAEL KEVIN, special education educator; b. Bklyn., Apr. 8, 1951; s. Edwin Matthew and Katherine (Scherzinger) D.; m. June 15, 1974 (div. 1989); children: Shawn Michael, Patricia Mary, Katherine Mary; m. Denise F. Iovino, Sept. 17, 1989; 1 child, Michael Kevin. BS in Human Svcs., SUNY, Old Westbury/Empire State, 1990; MS in Spl. Edn., Dowling Coll., Oakdale, N.Y., 1992. Cert. spl. edn. tchr., N.Y., Fla. Police officer N.Y.C. Police Dept., 1972-80; residential skills instr. to mentally retarded adults Assn. for Adults and Children with Learning Disabilities, Westbury, N.Y., 1986-92; tchrs. aide BOCES-Carmen Rd. Sch. for Physically Handicapped, Massapequa, N.Y., 1986-90, substitute spl. edn. tchr., 1991-92; spl. edn. tchr. for profoundly multiply handicapped Hillcrest Spl. Sch., Ocala, Fla., 1992—. Mem. Coun. for Exceptional Children, N.Y. C. Police Benevolence Soc. Roman Catholic. Avocations: scuba diving, boating, fishing, basketball. Office: Hillcrest Spl Sch 3143 SE 17th St Ocala FL 34471-5510 Home: 188 N Hawthorne St Massapequa NY 11758-3006

DOUGHERTY, NEIL JOSEPH, physical education educator, safety consultant; b. Elizabeth, N.J., Apr. 7, 1943; s. Neil Joseph and Doris Burnett (Lindsay) D.; m. Margaret Ruth Quaranta, July 17, 1965; 1 child, Margaret Elizabeth. BS, Rutgers U., 1964, EdM, 1965; EdD, Temple U., 1970. Tchr. phys. edn. St. Joseph's Sch., Bound Brook, N.J., 1964-65; teaching assoc. Temple U., Phila., 1967-70; prof. Rutgers U., New Brunswick, N.J., 1970—. Mem. adv. bd. Youth Sports Rsch. Coun., New Brunswick, 1987—; nat. faculty mem. U.S. Sports Acad., 1988—. Co-author: Understanding and Assessing Human Movement, 1980, Management Principles in Sport and Leisure Sciences, 1985, Contemporary Approaches to the Teaching of Physical Education, 1979, 87, Sport, Physical Activity and the Law, 1993, 2002; editor: Physical Education and Sport for Secondary School Students, 1983, 93, 2002, Principles of Safety in Physical Education and Sport, 1987, 93, 2002, Outdoor Recreation Safety, 1998, (jour.) The Reporter, 1977-81, (monograph series) Briefings, 1974-75; mem. editl. bd. Leisure Times Focus, 1984-88, Jour. of Tchg. in Phys. Edn., 1981-85, Safety Notebook, 1998—; contbr. to profl. jours. 1st lt. U.S. Army, 1965-67. Recipient Merit award Ea. Assn. for Health, Phys. Edn., Recreation and Dance, 1980, Honor award, 1982, Honor award Soc. for Study of Legal Aspects of Sport and Phys. Activity, 1998. Fellow N.Am. Soc. Health Edn., Phys. Edn, Recreation, Sport and Dance (charter); mem. Am. Assn. Active Lifestyles and Fitness (pres. 2001—03), Nat. Assn. Phys. Edn. Higher Edn. (pres. 1984-86), Sch. and Comty. Safety Soc. Am. (pres. 1996-98, Profl. Svc. award 1991, 97, Scholar award 1994), N.J. Assn. of Dirs. of Health, Phys. Edn. and Recreation (pres. 1976-78), N.J. Assn. for Health, Phys. Edn., Recreation and Dance (pres. 1979-80, Honor fellow award 1983, Disting. Leadership award 1982), Coll. and Univ. Phys. Edn. Coun. (chmn. 1985-88). Avocations: fishing, water sports, golf. Home: 1655 East Dr Point Pleasant NJ 08742-5117 Office: Rutgers U Dept Exercise Sci/Sport Stu New Brunswick NJ 08903 E-mail: njd@rci.rutgers.edu.

DOUGHERTY, PERCY H. geographer, educator, politician, planner; b. Kennett Square, Pa., Feb. 20, 1943; s. Percy H. Sr. and Anna (Cloud) D.; m. Anne Barbara Zinn, July 9, 1966; children: Thomas P., Robert J. BS in Geography, Biology, West Chester U., 1967, MEd in Phys. Geography, 1968; PhD in Phys. Geography, Geology, Boston U., 1980. Tchr. geography and earth sci. Plymouth Meeting (Pa.) Jr. H.S., 1967-68; asst. prof. West Chester (Pa.) U., 1968-70, Trenton (N.J.) State Coll., 1972-77, CUNY, 1977-78, U. Cin., 1978-83; vis. prof. Ohio U., Athens, 1983-84; vis. asst. prof. U. Ky., Lexington, 1984-85; assoc. prof. Kutztown (Pa.) U., 1985-90, prof. geography, 1990—. Editor of 2 books on karst; editor GEO2, 1980-88, Bulletin of the Nat. Speleological Soc., 1984-85; contbr. articles to profl. jours. Chmn. Lower Macungie Twp. Planning Commn., 1991-92; bd. dirs. Sloans Valley Conservation Task Force, Lexington, Ky., Allentown (Pa.) Art Mus., Allentown Symphony, Lehigh Valley Arts Coun., Wildlands Conservancy; past chmn. comprehensive planning com., bd. dirs. Lehigh Valley Planning Commn. Lehigh and Northampton Counties, Pa., 1990-95, past chmn. bd. dirs. 1995-97; Rep. committeeman Lower Macungie Twp. Dist. 2, 1990-96; elected mem. Lehigh County Commn., 1994—, chmn., 2000-03; bd. dirs. County Commn. Assn. Pa., 1998-2000, 02—, chair energy, environ. and land use com., 1998-2000. NSF fellow, 1971, 80, 92, NASA fellow, 1981, NOAA fellow, 1982. Fellow Nat. Speleol. Soc. (life), Miami Valley Grotto (hon. life), Ctrl. Jersey Grotto (hon. life); mem. Assn. Am. Geographers (life, mem. com. c.c.'s 2000-01, nat. councillor 2000-03, past pres., sec., treas., editor, bd. dirs.), Delaware Valley Geog. Assn. (past pres., bd. dirs.), Nat. Coun. Geog. Edn. (life), Am. Water Resources Assn., Am. Soc. Photogrammetry and Remote Sensing, Conf. Latin Am. Geography, Pa. Geog. Soc. (past v.p., bd. dirs.), Am. Wine Soc. (cert. wine judge). Achievements include research on remote sensing, air photo, geomorphology, karst, climatic geomorphology, groundwater diffusion, water resources, geographic education, planning. Office: Kutztown Univ Dept Geography 115 Grim Hall Kutztown PA 19530-9621 also: Lehigh County Courthouse PO Box 1548 Allentown PA 18105-1548 E-mail: percydougherty@lehighcounty.org., doughert@kutztown.edu.

DOUGHERTY, RICHARD MARTIN, library and information science educator; b. East Chicago, Ind., Jan. 17, 1935; s. Floyd C. and Harriet E. (Martin) D.; m. Ann Prescott, Mar. 24, 1974; children— Kathryn E., Emily E.; children by previous marriage— Jill Ann, Jacquelyn A., Douglas M. BS, Purdue U., 1959, LHD honoris causa, 1991; M.L.S., Rutgers U., 1961, PhD, 1963; LHD honoris causa, U. Stellenbosch, South Africa, 1995. Head acquisitions dept. Univ. Library, U. N.C., Chapel Hill, 1963-66; assoc. dir. libraries U. Colo., Boulder, 1966-70; prof. library sci. Syracuse U., N.Y., 1970-72; univ. librarian U. Calif-Berkeley, 1972-78; dir. univ. library U. Mich., Ann Arbor, 1978-88, acting dean. Sch. Library Sci., 1984-85, prof. sch. info., 1978-98, prof. emeritus, 1999—; pres. Dougherty & Assocs., 1994—. Cons., change mgmt. librs.; founder, pres. Mountainside Pub. Corp., 1974—. Author: Scientific Management of Library Organizations, 2d edit., 1982; co-author: Preferred Futures for Libraries II, 1993; editor Coll. and Research Libraries jour., 1969-74, Jour. Acad. Librarianship, 1975-94, Library Issues, 1981—. Trustee Ann Arbor Dist. Libr., 1995—2002, pres. bd. trustees, 1998—2000. Recipient Esther Piercy award, 1968, Disting. Alumnus award Rutgers U., 1980, Acad. Librarian Yr., Assn. Coll. and Research Libraries, 1983, ALA Hugh C. Atkinson Meml. award, 1988, Blackwell Scholarship award, 1992, Joseph Lippincott medal, 1997; fellow Council on Library Resources. Mem. ALA (coun. 1969-76, 89-92, exec. bd. 1972-76, 89-92, endowment trustee 1986-89, pres. 1990-91), Assn. Rsch. Librs. (bd. dirs. 1977-80), Rsch. Librs. Group, Inc. (exec. com. 1984-88, chmn. bd. govs. 1986-87), Soc. Scholarly Pub. (bd. dirs. 1990-92, exec. com. 1991-92), Internat. Fedn. Libr. Assns. (round table of editors of library jours. 1985-87, standing com. univ. libr. sect. 1981-87). Home: 6 Northwick Ct Ann Arbor MI 48105-1408 Office: Dougherty & Assoc PO Box 8330 Ann Arbor MI 48107-8330 E-mail: rmdoughe@umich.edu.

DOUGHTEN, MARY KATHERINE (MOLLY DOUGHTEN), retired secondary education educator; b. Belvidere, Ill., Apr. 26, 1923; d. Edwin Albert and Theora Teresa (Tefft) Loop; m. Philip Tedford Doughten, Oct. 15, 1947; children: Deborah Doughten Hellriegel, Susan Doughten Myers, Ann Doughten Fickenscher, Philip Tedford Jr., David, Sarah Doughten Wiggins. BA, DePauw U., 1945; MS, Western Res. U., 1947. Social worker Children's Svcs., Cleve., 1947, San Antonio, 1948-49; tchr. English Indian Valley High Schs., Gradenhutten, Ohio, 1962-66; tchr. English and sociology New Philadelphia (Ohio) High Sch., 1966-86. Mem. Tuscarawas County Juvenile Judges Citizen's Rev. Bd., 1980—2003, United Way, 1960—67, ARC, PTA, 1955—58, coun. pres., 1960—62, mental health chmn. state bd., 1963—65, libr. chmn., 1966—68; mem. Hospice, 1987—; founding com. Kent State U. Tuscarawas campus, 1961—62; v.p. Tuscarawas County U. Found., 1996—98, pres., 1998—2000; leader Girl Scouts, 1959—68; bd. mem. Tuscarawas County U. Found., 2000—; vol. Ohio Reads, 2000—; vol. reach for recovery Am. Cancer Soc., 2002—; mem. arts coun. Tuscarawas Philharmonic League; vol. Tuscarawas County Work and Family Svcs., 2003—; mem. Dem. Women, 1986—; bd. dir. Tuscarawas Valley Guidance Ctr., 1950—62, Cmty Mental Health Care, Inc., 1974—82, 1984—92, pres., 1979—81; bd. dir. Alcohol, Drug and Mental Health Svcs. bd., Tuscarawas-Carroll County, 1992—2001, v.p., 1996—98; bd. mem. State CC, 1965—68; founder, bd. dir. Ohio Cmty. Mental Health Svcs., Columbus, Ohio, 1970—80; bd. dir. Mobile Meals, 1992—. Recipient Mental Health award Community and Profl. Svcs., 1978; Martha Holden Jennings scholar, 1975-76; named WJER Woman of the Yr., 2002. Mem. AAUW (sec. 1962, v.p. 1996-98), Ohio Ret. Tchrs. (sec. 1987-89), New Philadelphia Edn. Assn., Friends of Libr., Chestnut Soc. (bd. dirs. 1987-89, 2001—), Tuscarawas County Med. Aux. (pres. 1959-60, 86-87, state bd. 1960-64), Union Hosp. Aux. (bd. dirs. 1986-98, editor 1986-98), DAR, Tuscawawas County Ret. Tchrs. Assn. (bd. dirs. 1999—), Coll. Club (scholarship chair 1989-91, 99-2001), Union Country Club, Atwood Yacht Club, Lady Elks, Mortar Bd., Phi Beta Kappa, Alpha Chi Omega, Theta Sigma Phi. Democrat. Presbyterian. Avocations: travel, golf, sailing, reading, photography. Home: 204 Gooding Ave NW New Philadelphia OH 44663-1727 E-mail: philmoll@tusco.net.

DOUGLAS, JEANNE MASSON, academic administrator, education educator; b. Albany, Vt., Oct. 9, 1938; d. Leonard Arnold and Helena Mary (LaRocque) Masson; m. Harlan L. Douglas, Dec. 2, 1960 (dec. Sept. 1978); 1 child, Mason. BS in Edn., Johnson State Coll., Johnson, Vt., 1960; MS Cert. Instrnl. Tech., U. So. Calif., 1968; MEd, U. Mass., 1978, EdD in Tchr. Edn., 1982. Dir. instrnl. devel. ctr. Burlington County Coll., Pemberton, N.J., 1969-72; dir. ednl. resources ctr. Reading (Pa.) C.C., 1972-75; dir. staff devel. ctr. Berks Heim Geriatrics Instn., Reading, 1975-76; measurement design specialist SIGNALS (sch. collaborative), Norton, Mass., 1978-79; dir. gifted edn. program Springfield (Vt.) Sch. Dist., 1981-83; dir. curriculum and instrn. Poultney (Vt.) Sch. Dist., 1983-85; coord. curriculum and instrn. and gifted/talented Orleans-Essex Supervisory, Union, Vt., 1987-90; coord. spl. edn. program for gifted School Adminstrn. Dist. #34, Belfast, Maine, 1990-92; coord. paraprofessional tng. program Kennebec Valley Cmty. Coll., Fairfield, Maine, 1993—. Cons. cmty. colls. in N.Y., Conn., Md., Pa., Ont., Can., 1971-84; evaluator Pub. Sch. Approval vis. team, South Burlington, Vt., 1990; adv. bd. PEDS project, Maine Child Devel. Svcs., 1993—; adv. bd. Rural Spl. Edn. project, U. Maine, 1993—. Author: Learning Environments/Rural Schs., 1982; contbr. articles to profl. jours. Speaker, learning disabled giifted advocate pub. info. meetings, Maine, Vt. sch. dists., 1988-92; mem., extension program advocate U. New Eng., Belfast Acad. Forum, 1990-92; speaker, spl. edn. advocate pub. info. meetings, ctrl. Maine sch. dists., 1993—. Recipient gifted edn. programming grant U.S. Dept. Edn., 1982-83, spl. edn. technician program Maine Dept. Edn., 1994-95. Mem. ASCD, Maine Assn. Dirs. of Svcs. for Children with Exceptionalities, Vt. Network for the Gifted, Maine Educators of the Gifted and Talented, Poetry Soc. Vt. (editor Mountain Troubadour 1993—). Avocations: writing (non-fiction, poetry), collecting antiquarian books, reading, informal debate (history, polit. sci.). Home: PO Box 2901 Waterville ME 04903-2901 Office: Kennebec Valley Tech Coll 92 Western Ave Fairfield ME 04937-1337 E-mail: jdouglas@kvcc.me.edu.

DOUGLAS, KATHLEEN MARY HARRIGAN, retired psychotherapist, educator; b. Boston, Apr. 24, 1950; d. John Joseph and Kathleen Margaret (Connolly) Harrigan; m. Dr. Robert E. Douglas, Feb. 24, 1977; children: David, Pamela, Elizabeth. Student, Uxbridge, England; BA in Psychology, Sophia U., Tokyo, 1972; MA in Counseling Psychology, Chapman U., Orange, Calif., 1983; PhD in Counselor Edn., U. Fla., 1990. Elem tchr. Marymount Prep Sch., Palos Verdes, Calif., 1973-99; pvt. practice Orlando, Fla., 1985-95; psychology prof. Valencia C.C., Orlando, Fla., 1989-93; prof. Fla. Inst. Tech., 1990-94; asst. prof., grad. acad. advisors, clin. internship supr. Troy State U., Orlando, Fla., 1993-97; software developer of clinically oriented software, 1994—; assoc. prof. Barry U., Orlando, 1999—2002; ret., 2002. Drug/alcohol counselor, Ft. Belvoir, Va., 1981—82; counselor Orange County Mental Health Ctr., Winter Park, Fla., 1982—83; victims of child abuse therapist Thee Door, Orlando, 1983—84; presenter in field. Author: The Therapeutic Superhighway, 1995. Counselor Winter Park Towers Nursing Home, 1985; vol. group counselor Hillcrest Halfway House, Orlando, 1985. 1st Lt. U.S. Army, 1976-80. Recipient Marion medal

Cath. Ch., Boston, 1966, Civic award Spouse Abuse, Inc., Orlando, 1984. Mem.: Fla. Assn. Mental Health Counselors (elected counselor edn.), Am. Assn. for Counseling and Devel., Chi Sigma Iota, Pi Lambda Theta, Kappa Delta Phi. Roman Catholic. Home: 1781 Lake Berry Dr Winter Park FL 32789-5911 E-mail: drkathyd@msn.com.

DOUGLAS, MARGARET ANN, special education educator; b. Atlantic City, N.J., Mar. 2, 1952; d. Edward Joseph Sr. and Frances (Coughlin) D. BA, Glassboro State Coll., 1977, MA, 1990. Cert. tchr. of the handicapped, learning disabilities tchr./cons. Resource rm. tchr. Pomona (N.J.) Sch., 1977-79, Arthur Rann Mid. Sch., Absecon, N.J., 1979—, leader spl. edn. unit, 1990—. Tchr. cons. Learing Disabilities Child Study Team, Galloway Twp. Bd. Edn., Absecon, 1991, 92. Recipient Gov.'s Award for Excellence, N.J., 1989; named Tchr. of Yr., Galloway Twp. Edn. Found., 1990. Mem. Coun. Learning Disabilities, Learning Disabilities Assn. Atlantic County and State of N.J. (Tchr. of Yr. 1989), Arthur Rann PTA, Alpha Delta Kappa (historian 1990-92), Phi Delta Kappa. Democrat. Roman Catholic. Avocations: biking, quilting, needlework, reading. Home: 30 Oxford Vlg # B Pleasantville NJ 08232 Office: Arthur Rann Mid Sch 8th Ave Absecon NJ 08201

DOUGLAS, MARY CHRISTINE, artistic director, dance instructor; b. Bronx, N.Y., Apr. 12, 1962; d. Patrick Joseph and Victoria Ann (Barone) O'D.; m. Patrick Kevin Douglas, May 7, 1983; children: Patrick Kevin, Thomas Patrick (twins). Student, Eglevsky Sch. Ballet, Massapequa, N.Y., 1976-80; diploma in dance, Boces Cultural Arts Ctr., Syosset, N.Y., 1980; student, Neubert Ballet Inst., N.Y.C., 1981-84. Cert. dance tchr., N.Y. Artistic dir. South Shore Acad. Ballet, Massapequa, 1980—; tchr. dance Young People's Cultural Arts, Massapequa, 1980—. Tap and jazz dancer Yates Musical Theater, Paramus, N.J., 1981-82, Arvell Shaw All-Stars, L.I., N.Y., 1984; ballet dancer N.Y. Dance Theatre, Huntington, 1982-83; exercise instr. North Shore Health Club, Manhasset, N.Y., 1982-84, Roslyn (N.Y.) Pub. Schs., 1983—. Creator exercise tape The Mary Douglas Workout, 1987. Dir. humane removal and relocation of stray cats Suburbia Owners, Farmingdale, N.Y., 1986. Scholar Greenwich Acad. Ballet, 1980, Adelphi U., 1980, Neubert Ballet Inst., 1981. Mem. Royal Acad. Dancing (cert. dance instr., registered tchr., Worldwide Registration of Tchrs. award 1987,), Dance Educators Am. (cert. tchr.), Arthritis Found. (cert. exercise instr.). Republican. Roman Catholic. Avocations: traveling, gardening, cats, theater. Home and Office: South Shore Acad Dance 850 N Broadway Massapequa NY 11758-2337

DOUGLAS, MARY YOUNGE RILEY, secondary education educator; b. St. Louis, Dec. 4, 1930; d. Walter Archibald and Jerdie Lee (Bibb) Younge; m. John Samuel Riley Jr., Apr. 17, 1954 (dec. July 1973); children: John Samuel Riley III, Jerda Marie Riley, Joel Younge Riley; m. Walter Wadsworth Douglas, Jan. 14, 1989. Student, Fisk U., 1947-49; BS, Fontbonne Coll., 1951; Masters, U. Ill., 1953. Tchr. Sumner High Sch., St. Louis, 1953-55, Hadley Tech. Sch., St. Louis, 1956-57; subs. tchr. St. Louis C.C., 1975; tchr. Soldan High Sch., St. Louis, 1975-90, Roosevelt High Sch., St. Louis, 1990-93, Soldan-Internat. High Sch., 1993—2001. Past bd. dirs. Nursery Found., St. Louis, Met. YWCA, St. Louis, Mo. Assn. Social Welfare.

DOUGLAS, ROXANNE GRACE, secondary school educator; b. Orange, N.J., Dec. 17, 1951; d. Joseph Samuel and Mary (Ferro) Battista; m. Richard Joseph Douglas, June 26, 1982; 1 child, Regina Grace. BA cum laude, Montclair State Coll., 1973; student, Sorbonne U., Paris. Cert. French, social studies and elem. sch. tchr., N.J. Tchr. social studies West Orange (N.J.) Bd. Edn., 1973-74, Orange (N.J.) Bd. Edn., 1974-75; substitute tchr. various schs. N.J., 1975-76; supplemental tchr. Irvington (N.J.) Bd. Edn., 1976-80, tchr. govtl. programs, 1980—. Advisor 7th dist. NJSFWC-JM State Bd., 1991-93, 2002-04, membership chmn., 1994-96, 98—, pub. affairs chmn., 1996—, state membership task force, 1999—, edn. chmn., 2000-01, dist. asst., 2001—, 7th dist. v.p., 2002—. InSchool System, James Caldwell High Sch. Scholarship Fund. 2nd v.p., James Caldwell High Sch. HSA Corresponding sec. West Caldwell town columnist for local newspaper. Mem. West Caldwell Centennial Com., 2002—; cultural arts chmn. Caldwell/West Caldwell HSA League. Recipient Creative Writing awards NJSFWC-JM, Citizenship award Am. Legion. Mem. Victorian Soc., N.J. Edn. Assn., Nat. French Hon. Soc., Nat. Edn. Hon. Soc., Jr. Women's Club of West Essex (co-pres., liaison internat. affairs chmn., pub. affairs chmn.), Coll. Club Orange-Short Hills, West Essex Women's Club (liaison to jr. woman's club, chmn. internat. affairs and pub. affairs dept. 1st night com. mem., pres., parent adv. coun.-bd. edn., pres., 1994—, internat. affairs chmn., centennial chmn., comm. chmn., performing arts chmn. 1996—), Verona Women's Club (membership chmn., v.p. 1998—, recording sec. 2000—, twp. centennial com. mem., first v.p. 2003-04), Willing Hearts and Cultural Arts (chmn.), Caldwell West Caldwell HSA League, NJJFWC (state bd. 2002-04), West Essex League Hist. Soc. (Seventh Dist. v.p., corrs. sec.), JCHSS (v.p. scholarship com. 2003-04), James Caldwell H.S. HSA (corrs. sec. 2003-04). Roman Catholic. Avocations: reading, antiques, walking, writing, travel.

DOUGLAS, WANDA SUE LENARD, middle school educator; b. Downsville, La., May 23, 1940; d. Sherman and Easter Ruby (Jordan) L.; m. Kenneth Wayne Douglas, Apr. 13, 1963; children: Kenneth Wayne, II, Cris Alan. BA, N.E. La. U., 1961; MEd, McNeese State U., 1975, postgrad., 1977-83. Cert. tchr., prin. parish supr., supr. student tchrs., La.. master tchr., La. Sec. N.E. La. U., Monroe, 1958-61; tchr. Calcasieu Parish Sch. Bd., Lake Charles, La., 1961—; master tchr. McNeese State U., Lake Charles, 1971—. Mem. Calcasieu Parish Schs. Com. on Guidebook for Supervision, Lake Charles, 1972; tchr. pilot program La. State Dept. Social Studies Curriculum Devel., 1989, Architect Design in La., 1989; chmn. Workshops on Social Studies; sponsor yearbook staff F.K. White Middle Sch., 1981-92. Editor, author: Social Studies Units, 1992. Mem. NEA, La. Assn. Educators, Caicasieu Assn. Educators, Nat. Coun. Social Studies, La. Coun. Social Studies, Alpha Delta Kappa (pres. 1978-80) Republican. Avocations: travel, taping social studies lessons, embrodery, reading, gardening. Home: 121 Overhill Dr Lake Charles LA 70605-6213 Office: FK White Middle Sch 1000 E Mcneese St Lake Charles LA 70607-5838

DOUGLASS, ENID HART, educational program director; b. L.A., Oct. 23, 1926; d. Frank Roland and Enid Yandell (Lewis) Hart; m. Malcolm P. Douglass, Aug. 28, 1948; children: Malcolm Paul Jr., John Aubrey, Susan Enid. BA, Pomona Coll., 1948; MA, Claremont (Calif.) Grad. Sch., 1959. Research asst. World Book Ency., Palo Alto, Calif., 1953-54; exec. sec., asst. dir. oral history program Claremont Grad. U., 1963-71, dir. oral history program, 1971—, lectr. history, 1977—. Mem. Calif. Heritage Preservation Commn., 1977-85, chmn. 1983-85. Contbr. articles to hist. jours. Mayor pro tem City of Claremont, 1980-82, mayor, 1982-86; mem. planning and rsch. adv. coun. State of Calif.; mem. city coun. City of Claremont, 1978-86; founder Claremont Heritage, Inc., 1977-80; bd. dirs., 1986-95; bd. dirs. Pilgrim Pla., Claremont; founder, steering com., founding bd. Claremont Cmty. Found., 1989-95, pres., 1990-94. Mem. Oral History Assn. (pres. 1979-80), Southwest Oral History Assn. (founding steering com. 1981, J.V. Mink award 1984), Nat. Coun. Pub. History (founding com. 1980), LWV (bd. dirs. 1957-59, Outstanding Svc. to Cmty. award 1986). Democrat. Home: 1195 N Berkeley Ave Claremont CA 91711-3842 Office: Claremont Grad U Oral History Program 710 N College Ave Claremont CA 91711-3921 E-mail: enid.douglass@cgu.edu.

DOVE, DONALD AUGUSTINE, city planner, educator; b. Waco, Tex., Aug. 7, 1930; s. Sebert Constantine and Amy Delmena (Stern) Dove; m. Cecelia Mae White, Feb. 9, 1957; children: Angela, Donald, Monica Gilstrap, Celine, Cathlyn, Dianna, Jennifer. BA, Calif. State U., L.A., 1951; MA in Pub. Adminstrn., U. So. Calif., 1966. Planning & devel. cons. D. Dove Assocs., L.A., 1959-60; supr. demographic rsch. Calif. Dept. Pub. Works, L.A., 1960-66; dir. transp. employment project State of Calif., L.A., 1966-71, chief L.A. Region transp. study, 1975-84; chief environ. planning Calif. Dept. Transp., L.A., 1972-75; dir. U. So. Calif., L.A., 1984-87; panelist, advisor Pres. Conf. Aging, Washington, 1970—; environ. coord. Calif. Dept. Pub. Works, Sacramento, 1971-75; panelist, advisor Internat. Conf. Energy Use Mgmt., 1981. Guest lectr. univs. We. U.S., 1969—. Author: Preserving Urban Environment, 1976, Small Area Population Forecasts, 1966. Chmn. Lynwood City Planning Commn., Calif., 1982—; pres. Area Pastoral Coun., L.A., 1982—83; mem., del. Archdiocesan Pastoral Coun., L.A., 1979—86, Compton Cmty. Devel. Bd., Calif., 1967—71; pres. Neighborhood Esteem/Enrichment Techniques Inst., 1992—93. With U.S. Army, 1952—54. Mem.: Assn. Environ. Profls. (co-founder 1973), Am. Inst. Cert. Planners, Calif. Assn. Mgmt. (pres. 1987—88), Am. Inst. Planners (transp. chmn. 1972—73), Am. Planning Assn., Optimists Club (sec. 1978—79). Democrat. Roman Catholic. Home and Office: 11356 Ernestine Ave Lynwood CA 90262-3711 E-mail: dondve@aol.com.

DOVE, RITA FRANCES, poet, English language educator; b. Akron, Ohio, Aug. 28, 1952; d. Ray A. and Elvira E. (Hord) D.; m. Fred Viebahn, Mar. 23, 1979; 1 child, Aviva Chantal Tamu Dove-Viebahn. BA summa cum laude, Miami U., Oxford, Ohio, 1973; postgrad., Universität Tübingen, Fed. Republic Germany, 1974-75; MFA, U. Iowa, 1977; LLD (hon.), Miami U., Oxford, Ohio, 1988, Knox Coll., 1989, Tuskegee U., 1994, U. Miami, Fla., 1994, Washington U., St. Louis, 1994, Case Western Res. U., 1994, U. Akron, 1994, Ariz. State U., 1995, Boston Coll., 1995, Dartmouth Coll., 1995, Spelman Coll., 1996, U. Pa., 1996, U. N.C., 1997, U. Notre Dame, 1997, Northeastern U., 1997, Columbia U., 1998, Washington & Lee U., 1999, SUNY, Brockport, 1999, Pratt Inst., 2001, Howard U., 2001. Asst. prof. English Ariz. State U., Tempe, 1981-84, assoc. prof., 1984-87, prof., 1987-89, U. Va., Charlottesville, 1989-93, Commonwealth prof. English, 1993—; U.S. poet laureate, cons. in poetry Libr. of Congress, Washington, 1993-95, spl. cons. in poetry, 1999-2000; columnist Washington Post, 2000—02. Writer-in-residence Tuskegee (Ala.) Inst., 1982; lit. panelist Nat. Endowment for Arts, Washington, 1984-86, chmn. poetry grants panel, 1985; judge Walt Whitman award Acad. Am. Poets, 1990, Pulitzer prize in poetry, 1991, Ruth Lilly prize 1991, Nat. Book award in poetry 1991, 98, Anisfield-Wolf Book awards, 1992—, Shelley Meml. award, 1997, Amy Lowell fellowship, 1997; poetry panel chmn. Pulitzer prize, 1997; final judge Brittingham and Pollack prizes, 1997; juror Christopher Columbus Fellowship Found., 1998—, Duke Ellington awards, 1999. Author: (poetry) Ten Poems, 1977, The Only Dark Spot in the Sky, 1980, The Yellow House on the Corner, 1980, Mandolin, 1982, Museum, 1983, Thomas and Beulah, 1986 (Pulitzer Prize in poetry 1987), The Other Side of the House, 1988, Grace Notes, 1989 (Ohioana award 1990), Selected Poems, 1993 (Ohioana award 1994), Lady Freedom Among Us, 1994, Mother Love, 1995, Evening Primrose, 1998, On the Bus with Rosa Parks, 1999 (Ohioana award 2000); (verse drama) The Darker Face of the Earth, 1994 (W. Alton Jones Found. grant 1994, Kennedy Ctr. Fund for New Am. Plays award 1995, Geraldine Dodge Found. grant, 1997), completely rev. 2d edit., 1996 (first performance Oreg. Shakespeare Festival 1996); (novel) Through the Ivory Gate, 1992 (Va. Coll. Stores Book award 1993); (short stories) Fifth Sunday, 1985 (Callaloo award 1986); (essays) The Poet's World, 1995, (song cycle) Seven for Luck (music by John Williams), 1st performance Boston Symphony Orch., Tanglewood, 1998; mem. editl. bd. Nat. Forum, 1984-89, Iris, 1989—; mem. adv. bd. Ploughshares, 1992—, N.C. Writers Network, 1992-99, Civilization, 1994-97; assoc. editor Callaloo, 1986-98; adv. and contbg. editor Gettysburg Rev., 1987—, TriQuarterly, 1988—, Ga. Review, 1994—, Bellingham Rev., 1996—, Internat. Quarterly, 1997—, Callaloo, 1998—, Mid-Am. Rev., 1998—; editor Best Am. Poetry, 2000. Commr. The Schomburg Ctr. for Rsch. in Black Culture, N.Y. Pub. Libr., 1987—; mem. Renaissance Forum Folger Shakespeare Libr., 1993-95, Coun. of Scholars Libr. of Congress, 1994—; mem. nat. launch com. AmeriCorps, 1994; mem. awards coun. Am. Acad. Achievement, 1994—; mem. adv. bd. Thomas Jefferson Ctr. Freedom of Expression, 1994—, U.S. Civil War Ctr., 1995-99, Va. Ctr. Creative Arts, 1995—; The Poets Corner elector Cathedral Ch. St. John the Divine, N.Y.C., 1991—; bd. govs. Humanities Rsch. Inst. U. Calif., 1996-99. Presdl. scholar, 1970, Nat. Achievement scholar, 1970-73; Fulbright/Hays fellow, 1974-75, rsch. fellow U. Iowa, 1975, teaching/writing fellow U. Iowa, 1976-77, Guggenheim Found. fellow, 1983-84, Mellon sr. fellow Nat. Humanities Ctr., 1988-89, fellow Ctr. for Advanced Studies, U. Va., 1989-92, fellow Shannon Ctr. for Advanced Studies, U. Va., 1995—; grantee NEA, 1977, 89; recipient Lavan Younger Poet award Acad. Am. Poets, 1986, GE Found. award, 1987, Bellagio (Italy) residency Rockefeller Found., 1988, Ohio Gov.'s award 1988, Literary Lion citation N.Y. Pub. Libr., 1991, Women of Yr. award Glamour Mag., 1993, NAACP Great Am. Artist award, 1993, Golden Plate award Am. Acad. Achievement, 1994, Disting. Achievement medal Miami U. Alumni Assn., 1994, Renaissance Forum award for leadership in the literary arts Folger Shakespeare Libr., 1994, Carl Sandburg award Internat. Platform Assn., 1994, Heinz award in arts and humanities, 1996, Charles Frankel prize/Nat. Humanities medal Pres. of U.S. and NEH, 1996; inducted Ohio Women's Hall of Fame, 1991, Nat. Assn. of Women in Edn. Disting. Woman award, 1997, Sara Lee Frontrunner award, 1997, Barnes & Noble Writers for Writers award, 1997, Levinson prize Poetry mag., 1998, John Frederick Nims Translation prize, 1999, Libr. Lion award N.Y. Pub. Libr., 2000, Duke Ellington Lifetime Achievement award, 2001, Emily Couric Women's Leadership award, 2003; named Phi Beta Kappa poet Harvard U., 1993. Mem. PEN, ASCAP, Am. Philos. Soc., Poetry Soc. Am., Associated Writing Programs (bd. dirs. 1985-88, pres. 1986-87), Am. Acad. Achievement (mem. golden plate awards coun. 1994—), Phi Beta Kappa (senator 1994-2000), Phi Kappa Phi. Office: U Va Dept English 219 Bryan Hall PO Box 400121 Charlottesville VA 22904-4121

DOVIAK, INGRID ELLINGER, elementary school educator; b. New Britain, Conn., Feb. 10, 1971; d. John Leonard and Marjorie Chain Ellinger; m. Stephen Michael Doviak, June 8, 1996. BS, MA, So. Conn. State U., 1993. Tchr. head dept. enrichment grades k-8 Wntergreen Interdist. Magnet Sch., Hamden, Conn., 1998—. Adj. instr. deptl edn. Sacred Heart U., Fairfield, Conn., 2000—; adj. instr. So. Conn. State U., New Haven, 1998—; presenter Atomic Math Conf., 2001, 02, Conn. Assn. Math. Precocious Youth, 2000, 01, 02, Conn. Assn. Schs.

DOW, TERESA ELMERICK, guidance and special needs professional; b. Jackson, Miss., Oct. 23, 1957; d. Bernard J. and G. Lorraine (Sanders) Elmerick; m. L.W. Dow, May 29, 1982 (dec. Aug. 1990); 1 child, J. Paul. AA, Hinds Jr. Coll., Raymond, Miss., 1977; BS, Miss. State U., 1979, MEd, 1982. Cert. secondary tchr. Ark. Tchr. distributive edn. Horn Lake (Miss.) High Sch., 1979-81; grad. asst., hall dir. Miss. State U., 1981-82; adminstrv. asst. Tulane U., New Orleans, 1982-83; faculty mem. Am. Coll., Fayetteville, Ark., 1984; tchr. asst. Fayetteville Schs., 1983-84; tchr., tutor migrant edn. Prairie Grove (Ark.) Schs., 1984-87; community faculty Flaming Rainbow U., Stilwell, Okla., 1986-91; spl. needs coord. Siloam Springs (Ark.) High Sch., 1989-98; spl. populations program mgr. Ark. Dept. of Workforce Edn., Little Rock, 1998—. Pres. St. Mary's Altar Soc., St. Mary's Cath. Ch., Siloam Springs, 1990-91, sec. parish coun., 1990-91, organist, 1989-91, guitarist, 1992-2000, religious edn. tchr., 1990-94, coord. religious edn., 1994-97; mem. Siloam Springs Sch. Dist. Renewal Com., 1992-98, pers. policy com., 1992-97. Recipient Personal Courage award Nat. Parents Day Coun. Ark., 2002, Commrs. arrowhead Boy Scouts Am., 1997, wood badge, 1998, St. George badge, 2003; named Outstanding New Vocat. Tchr. of Yr. in Ark., 1990-91. Mem. Nat. Assn. Vocat. Edn. Spl. Needs Pers., Ark. Assn. Vocat. Edn. Spl. Needs Pers. (pres.-elect 1992-93, pres. 1993-94), Nat. Assn. Distributive Edn. Tchrs. (Hall of Fame 1980), Miss. Assn. Distributive Edn. Tchrs., Am. Vocat. Assn., Distributive Edn. Clubs Am., Siloam Springs Jaycees (individual devel. v.p. 1992-93, mgmt. devel. v.p. 1993-94), Iota Lambda Sigma. Avocations: crafts, camping, church activities. Home: 108 Melrose Cir North Little Rock AR 72114-4628

DOWBEN, CARLA LURIE, lawyer, educator; b. Chgo., Jan. 22, 1932; d. Harold H. and Gertrude Lurie; m. Robert Dowben, June 20, 1950; children: Peter Arnold, Jonathan Stuart, Susan Laurie. AB, U. Chgo., 1950; JD, Temple U., 1955. Bar: Ill. 1957, Mass. 1963, Tex. 1974, U.S. Surpeme Ct. 1974. Assoc. Conrad and Verges, Chgo., 1957-62; exec. officer MIT, Cambridge, Mass., 1963-64; legal planner Mass. Health Planning Project, Boston, 1964-69; assoc. prof. Life Scis. Inst. Brown U., Providence, 1970-72; asst. prof. health law U. Tex. Health Sci. Ctr., Dallas, 1973-78, assoc. prof., 1978-93; ptnr. Choate & Lilly, Dallas, 1989-92; head health law sect. Looper, Reed, Mark & McGraw, Dallas, 1992-95, of counsel, 1995-99. Adj. assoc. prof. health law U. Tex., 1993-95; cons. to bd. dirs. Mental Health Assn., 1958-86, Ft. Worth Assn. Retarded Citizens, 1980-90, Advocacy, Inc., 1981-85; dir. Nova Health Systems, 1975—, Tockwotton Home, 1994-98. Contbr. articles to profl. jours. Active in drafting helath and mental health legis., agy. regulation in several states and local govts. Mem. ABA, Tex. Bar Assn., Dallas Bar Assn., Am. Health Lawyers Assn., Hastings Inst. Ethics, Tex. Family Planning Assn. Mem. Soc. Of Friends.

DOWD, JANICE LEE, foreign language educator; b. N.Y.C., Jan. 6, 1948; d. Edward H. and Mary A. (Vanek) D. BA, Marietta (Ohio) Coll., 1969; MA, Columbia U., 1971, MEd, 1979, EdD, 1984. Tchr. Teaneck (N.J.) Bd. Edn., 1970-99, supr. world langs., 1999—. Adj. asst. prof. Queens Coll., CUNY, 1984-94, Columbia U., N.Y.C., spring 1988, 93—; N.J. alternate route prof., 1990—; asst. prof. MA TESOL program in China, Changsha, 1986, Shanghai, 1987; SAT program adminstr. Teaneck H.S., 1978-83, yearbook sponsor, 1975-79, newspaper sponsor, 1984-92, co-chair Global/Multicultural Mgmt. Team, 1992-95. Contbr. articles to profl. jours. Mem. program com. PEO, Teaneck, 1966—. Fellow Rockefeller Found., l988. Mem. Am. Assn. Tchrs. of French, Tchrs. English to Speakers Other Langs., N.Y. State Tchrs. English to Speakers Other Langs., N.J. Tchrs. English to Speakers Other Langs., Am. Assn. Applied Linguists, Am. Coun. Tchrs. Fgn. Langs., Fgn. Lang. Educators N.J., Nat. Assn. of Dept. Heads and Suprs. of Fgn. Langs. Home: 56 Boulevard New Milford NJ 07646-1602 Office: Teaneck High Sch 100 Elizabeth Ave Teaneck NJ 07666-4798

DOWER GOLD, CATHERINE ANNE, music history educator; b. South Hadley, Mass., May 19, 1924; d. Lawrence Frederick Dower and Marie (Barbieri) Barber; m. Arthur Gold, Mar. 24, 1994 (dec. Oct. 1998). AB, Hamline U., 1945; MA, Smith Coll., 1948; B in Liturgical Music, U. Mont., Gregorian Inst. Am., 1949; PhD, The Cath. U. Am., 1968. New England rep. Gregorian Inst. Am., Toledo, 1948-49; tchr. music, organist St. Rose Sch., Meriden, Conn., 1949-53; supr. music Holyoke (Mass.) Pub. Schs., 1953-55; instr. music U. Mass., Amherst, 1955-56; prof. music Westfield (Mass.) State Coll., 1956-90, prof. emerita, 1991—; columnist and freelance writer Holyoke Transcript Telegram, 1991-93. Organist St. Theresa's Ch., South Hadley, 1937-41, St. Michael's Ch., N.Y., 1945-46; concert series presenter Westfield State Coll., 1987-91, rschr. tchr.; vis. scholar U. So. Calif., 1969; vis. assoc. prof. music Herbert Lehman Coll. CUNY, 1970-71. Author: Puerto Rican Music Following the Spanish American War, 1898-1910, 1983; (monograph) Yella Pessl, 1986, Alfred Einstein on Music, 1991, Yella Pessl: First Lady of the Harpsichord, 1992, Fifty Years of Marching Together, 2001; editor: (newsletter) Westfield State Coll., 2000—; presenter Irish Concert Springfield Symphony Orch., 1981 (plaque 1982); author numerous poems. Pres. Coun. for Human Understanding Holyoke, 1981-83, Friends of Holyoke Pub. Libr., 1990-91; bd. dirs., chmn. nominating com. Holyoke Pub. Libr., 1987-89; bd. dirs. Holyoke Pub. Libr. Corp., 1991-94, Springfield Symphony Orch., 1992—; bd. dirs. Fla. Philharm. Orch., 2000-03, trustee, 2002-03; presiding officer inauguration Dr. Irving Buchman pres. of Westfield State Coll.; ethics com. Holyoke Hosp., 1988-94; sec. Haiti Mission, 1982-94; bd. overseers Mullen U., 1993; hon. mem. bd. Coun. Human Understanding, 1994-; hon. mem. WSC Found., 1994-; co-chair United Jewish Appeal/Jewish Fedn. Boca Lago Women's Divsn., South Palm Beach County, 1996-97; 1st. v.p. fin. and adminstrn. Temple Beth El Women in Reformed Judaism, Boca Raton, 1997-99; active St. Patrick's Com., 1991—; bd. dirs. Friends of Music of Lynn U. Conservatory Music, 2003—. Recipient citation Academia Inter-Americana de P.R., 1978, plaque Mass. Tchrs. Assn., Boston, 1984, medal Equestrian Order Holy Sepulchre of Jerusalem, Papal Knighthood Soc., Boston, 1984, Performance award Gov. Dukakis, Mass., 1988, award from Puerto Rican Jour. Al. Margens, 1992, Human Rels. award Coun. for Human Understanding, Holyoke, 1994; named Lady Comdr., Equestrian Order of the Holy Sepulche of Jerusalem, 1987, with star, 1990, Career Woman of Yr., Quota Internat. Holyoke, Mass., 1988; Westfield State U. concert series named Catherine A. Dower Performing Arts Series in her honor, 1991; recipient 1st prize in Raddock Eminent Scholar Chair Essay Contest, Fla. Atlantic U., 1996, Internat. Poet of Merit Silver Bowl award Internat. Libr. Poetry, 2002, First prize Essay Contest on World Peace by Broherly Love Press, Mass. 2002, Outstanding Achievement in Poetry award Internat. Sox. Poets, 2003. Mem. Nat. Soc. Arts and Letters, Am. Musicol. Soc., Coll. Mus. Soc., Ch. Music Assn. Am. (journalist), Acad. Arts and Scis. P.R. (medal 1977), Internat. Platform Assn., Friends of the Holyoke Pub. Libr. (pres. 1990-91), Irish Am. Cultural Inst. (chmn. bd. 1981-89), Holyoke Quota (v.p. 1976-79, pres. 1979-81, 90-92, chmn. speech and hearing com. 1987-94), B'nai B'rith of Boca Lago (sec. bd. dirs. 1994-1999, newsletter editor 1999-2000), Lifelong Learning Soc. Fla. Atlantic U. (life, sec. 1994-97, bd. dirs. 2003—), Westfield State Coll. Found., Women's Symphony League (life), Philharm. Assn. Boca (pres. 2002-03), Univ. Club Fla. Atlantic U. (parliamentarian 2003—), Nat. Soc. Art Letters, Phi Beta Kappa. Democrat. Home: 8559 Casa Del Lago Boca Raton FL 33433-2107 E-mail: cathig@juno.com.

DOWLING, DORIS ANDERSON, business owner, educator, consultant; b. Clover Valley, Minn., Sept. 24, 1917; d. Gustaf Axel and Amanda Sophia (Karlsson) Anderson; m. John Joseph Dowling, Jan. 8, 1943 (dec. Feb. 1953); 1 child, Mary Kathryn. Home econs. degree, U. Minn., Virginia, 1937. Fashion coord., lectr. Fair Store/Montgomery Ward, Chgo., 1939-65, Marshall Field's, Chgo., 1967-82; founder, owner Doris Anderson Sewing Schs., 1948—. Cons. colls., textile industry, retail stores, 1948—; lectr. retail stores, 1954-94. Author: Simplified Systems of Sewing and Styling, 1948. Career counselor, trainer, Chgo., 1948-82. Recipient Future Farmers Am. award Duluth C. of C. Coun. Agr., 1934. Mem. Nat. Needlework Assn., Fashion Group Internat. Inc., Assn. Crafts & Creative Industries, Chgo. Apparel Ctr., Merchandise Mart. Avocations: designing, gardening, writing, research. Home and Office: Doris Anderson Sewing Schs 222 E Pearson St Apt 1108 Chicago IL 60611-7356

DOWLING, JOHN CLARKSON, language educator; b. Strawn, Tex., Nov. 14, 1920; s. Albert Clarkson and Georgia Ann (Turrill) Dowling; m. Constance Guinevere Ford, Dec. 26, 1949; 1 child, Robert Clarkson. BA, U. Colo., 1941; MA, U. Wis., 1942, PhD, 1950. Instr. Spanish U. Wis., Madison, 1951-53; prof., head fgn. langs. Tex. Tech. U., Lubbock, 1953-63; prof., chmn. Spanish & Portuguese Ind. U., Bloomington, 1963-72; prof., head romance langs. U. Ga., Athens, 1973-79, dean grad. sch., 1979-89, prof. alumni found., 1980-91, prof. emeritus alumni found., 1992—. Vis. prof. romance langs. U. Tex., Austin, 1957; vis. prof. Spanish U. Iowa, Iowa City, 1993; interim dean arts & humanities Fla. Atlantic U., Boca Raton, 1995. Author: (book) Saavedra Fajardo, 1957, Saavedra Fajardo, 2d edit., 1977, Moratin, 1971, Jose Melchor Gomis, 1974; contbr. articles to profl. jours. Mem. exec. com. grad. deans African-Am. Inst., N.Y.C., 1985—92. Lt. (j.g.) USNR, 1942—46, lt. comdr. USNR, 1946—66. A.C. Markham Travel fellow, U. Wis., 1950—51, J. S. Guggenheim fellow, 1959—60,

Rsch. grantee, Am. Philos. Soc., 1971, 1974. Mem.: Critica Hispanica Diechiocho, Am. Assn. Tchrs. Spanish & Portuguese, Hispanic Soc. Am. (corr.). Episcopalian. Home: 7101 Patriots Colony Drive Williamsburg VA 23188-0131

DOWLING, JOHN ELLIOTT, biology educator; b. Pawtucket, R.I., Aug. 31, 1935; s. Joseph Leo and Ruth W. (Tappan) D.; children by previous marriage: Christopher, Nicholas.; m. Judith Falco, Oct. 18, 1975; 1 dau., Alexandra. AB, Harvard U., 1957, PhD, 1961; MD (hon.), U. Lund (Sweden), Sweden, 1982. Asst. prof. biology Harvard U., Cambridge, 1961—64, prof., 1971—87, Maria Moors Cabot prof. natural sci., 1987—2001, Llura and Gordon Gund prof. neurosci., 2001—; assoc. prof. Johns Hopkins Sch. Medicine, 1964—71. Pres. Marine Biol. Lab., 1998—. Author: The Retina: An Approachable Part of the Brain, 1987, Neurons and Networks: An Introduction to Neuroscience, 1992, 2d edit., 2001, Creating Mind: How the Brain Works, 1998; contbr. numerous articles on vision to profl. jours. Recipient ann. award N.E. Ophthal. Soc., 1979, award of merit Retina Research Found., 1981, Prentice medal Am. Acad. Optometry, 1991, Von Sallman prize, 1992, The Helen Keller prize for vision rsch., 2000, Gund award Found. Fighting Blindness, 2001. Fellow Am. Acad. Arts and Scis., AAAS; mem. Am. Philos. Soc., Assn. Rsch. in Vision and Ophthalmology (Friedenwald medal 1970), Nat. Acad. Sci., Neurosci. Soc., Soc. Gen. Physiologists. Home: 135 Charles St Boston MA 02114-3264 Office: Harvard U Biology Labs Cambridge MA 02138 E-mail: dowling@mcb.harvard.edu.

DOWNEN, THOMAS WILLIAM, retired school system administrator; b. Evansville, Ind., Jan. 24, 1936; s. William Elijah Downen and Elfrieda Mary Fieth Brenner. BS, Ind. U., 1958, MS, 1961; AMD, Fla. State U., Tallahassee, 1969, PhD, 1971. Cert. media specialist, leadership, Ga.; cert. tchr., Ind. Tchr. Dept. Def. Schs., Frankfurt, Germany, 1962-63, Evansville (Ind.)-Vanderburgh County Schs., 1957-62, tchr., media specialist, 1963-67; cons. to sch. librs. Ind. Dept. Pub. Instrn., Indpls., 1967-68; from asst. prof. to assoc. prof. U. Mich., Ann Arbor, 1971-82; assoc. prof. U. Ga., Athens, 1982-87; media specialist Savannah (Ga.) Pub. Schs., 1987-92, adminstrv. coord. media, 1992-94; media specialist Camden County (Ga.) Sch., 1994-96; ret., 1996. Contbr. chpt. to book, articles to profl. jours. HEA Title IIB fellow, 1968-71. Mem. ALA (bd. dirs. young adult svcs. div. 1979-82), Am. Assn. Sch. Librs., Beta Phi Mu. E-mail: dh32034@peoplepc.com.

DOWNEY, MARY ETHEL, elementary school educator; b. Wakefield, Mass., Jan. 5, 1935; d. Thomas Francis and Ethel Marguerite (Hickey) D. BS, Tufts U., 1956; cert. in phys. edn., Bouvé-Boston Sch., 1956; MEd, Salem (Mass.) State U., 1965. Jr. and sr. H.S. phys. edn. instr., coach Woburn (Mass.) City Schs., 1956-57; elem. specialist in phys. edn. Wakefield Sch. Sys., 1957-93; ret., 1993. Swimming instr. Camp Fernwood, Oxford, Maine, 1953-60; adult edn. tchr. YMCA/Town of Wakefield, 1957-65. Mem. AAHPERD (life), Mass. Assn. Health, Phys. Edn., Recreation and Dance (life). Avocations: swimming, gardening, ceramics, travel, dog training. Home: 11 Murray St Wakefield MA 01880-2730

DOWNIE, DAVID LEONARD, political science educator; b. Columbus, Ohio, Mar. 1, 1961; s. Leonard Downie and Barbara (Lindsey) Sims; m. Laura Marriette Whitman, June 6, 1992. BA cum laude, Duke U., 1983; MA in Polit. Sci., U. N.C., 1988, PhD in Polit. Sci., 1996. Asst. prof. dept. polit. sci. and internat. affairs Columbia U., N.Y.C., 1994—, dir. environ. policy studies, Sch. of Internat./Publ. Affair, 1994—; assoc. dir. Ctr. for Sci. Tech. and Environ. Policy. Report writer: UN environ. programme Ozone Layer Negotiations, 1993—. Author newspaper columns, 1992; book reviewer in jour., 1992—; contbr. articles to profl. jours., 1993—. Fellow Inst. for Study of World Politics, 1992-93, U. N.C. fellow, 1993-94; recipient NATO-Berlin Study Tour award Atlantic Coun., 1989. Mem. Internat. Studies Assn., Am. Polit. Sci. Assn., Sierra Club (life). Avocations: hiking, scuba diving. Home: 272 Quincy St Fairfield CT 06430-6621 Office: Columbia U Internat Affairs Bldg 420 W 118th St New York NY 10027-7213 E-mail: dd113@columbia.edu.

DOWNS, FLOYD L. mathematics educator; b. Winchester, Mass., Jan. 21, 1931; s. Floyd L. and Emma M. (Noyes) D.; m. Elizabeth Lenci, Dec. 29, 1955; children: Karla C., John N. AB, Harvard U., 1952; MA, Columbia U., 1955. Lic. math. tchr. Math. tchr. East High Sch., Denver, 1955-60, Kent (Conn.) Sch., 1960-62, Newton High Sch., Newtonville, Mass., 1962-63; math. tchr., dept. chair Hillsdale High Sch., San Mateo, Calif., 1964-89; lectr. Ariz. State U., Tempe, 1988—. Math. scis. adv. com. The Coll. Bd., N.Y., 1979-85; mem. U.S. nat. com. 2d Internat. Math. Study, 1979-86; Golden state math. com. Calif. State Dept. Edn., Sacramento, 1985-91; exec. dir. Ariz. Math. Coalition, 1991-96. Co-author: Geometry, 1964, 91. With U.S. Army, 1952-54, Korea. Mem. Nat. Coun. Tchrs. Math., Nat. Coun. Suprs. Math., Math. Assn. Am., Calif. Math. Coun., Ariz. Assn. Tchrs. Math., Phi Delta Kappa. Office: Ariz State U Math Dept Tempe AZ 85287-1804 Home: PO Box 19206 Fountain Hills AZ 85269-9206

DOWNS, JON FRANKLIN, drama educator, director, writer; b. Bartow, Fla., Sept. 15, 1938; s. Clarence Curtis and Frankie (Morgan) D. Student, Ga. State Coll., 1956-58; BFA, U. Ga., 1960, MFA, 1969. Drama dir. Ga. Perimeter Coll. (formerly DeKalb Coll.), Clarkston, 1969-99. Dir., author The Beastly Purple Forest (marionettes) U. Ga., 1968, Dracula: A Horrible Musical, DeKalb Coll., 1971; dir. A Streetcar Named Desire, DeKalb, 1974, Brigadoon, DeKalb, 1981, West Side Story, 1983, Amadeus, 1984, Noises Off, 1986, The Three Musketeers, 1988, A Midsummer Night's Dream, 1990, A Little Night Music, 1991, Hamlet, 1993, over 200 others; actor Wedding in Japan, N.Y.C., 1960, Dark at the Top of the Stairs, N.Y.C. and on tour, 1961, A Life in the Theatre, DeKalb Coll., 1981, numerous others; designer Sweeney Todd, DeKalb Coll., 1970, Romulus, 1971, Grass Harp, 1972, A Funny Thing Happened on the Way to the Forum, 1998, many others; writer, dir. plays Tokalitta, Gold!, The Vigil; on tour of Ga. summers 1973-76; author: The Illusionist, 1979, Rapunzel, 1997; film reviewer So. Flair mag., 1994—, arts editor, 2000—. Grantee arts sect. Ga Dept. Planning and Budget, 1973, 74, State Bicentennial Commn., 1975, Nat. Bicentennial Commn., 1975. Mem. Southeastern Theater Conf. (state rep. 1971-73), Ga. Theater Conf. (exec. bd. 1970-73, 79-82). Office: Ste 110-11 403 W Ponce De Leon Ave Decatur GA 30030-2445

DOWNS, KEVIN ERNEST, screenwriter, film director, educator; b. Leesburg, Va., Apr. 18, 1955; s. Oswald Clifton and Virginia Florida (Thompson) D. BA, Va. Commonwealth U., 1978; MFA, NYU, 1984. Screenwriter Daughton/Roque Prodns., N.Y.C., 1984-85, Ang Lee/Vol. L-K Prodns., N.Y.C., 1985-86, Chammas Prodns., L.A., 1987; asst. to producer IndieProd Prodns., L.A., 1988; dir. Juna Prodns./CBS Records, L.A., 1989; prof. advanced screenwriting, directing techniques Georgetown U., Washington, 1993—. Freelance dir. McCarthy Prodns., Washington, 1994; guest spkr. in field; mem. adv. bd. Creative Screenwriting. Recipient Louis B. Mayer award, Louis B. Mayer Found., N.Y.C., 1987, Va. Ctr. for the Creative Arts award Cafritz Found., Washington, 1992, Bronze Internat. Telly award, Cin., 1996, Silver award WorldFest-Houston, 1996.

DOWNS, WILLIAM ROBERT, social worker, educator; b. Louisville, Aug. 3, 1951; s. William Randall and Betty Jean (Cannon) D.; m. Carol Ann Arndt, Nov. 1, 1980; children: Erika Pauline, Stephen Robert. BA, U. Minn., 1972; MSW, U. Wis., 1975, PhD, 1982. Social worker Dunn County Dept. Social Svcs., Menomonie, Wis., 1975-77; asst. prof. Iowa State U., Ames, 1982-85, SUNY, Buffalo, 1985-89, assoc. prof., 1989-92; assoc. rsch. scientist Rsch. Inst. on Addictions, Buffalo, 1987—; dir. Ctr. for Study of Adolescence U. No. Iowa, Cedar Falls, 1992—, prof. dept. social work, 1992—; hon. prof. U. Hull, Eng. Cons., bd. dirs. People Against Violence, Pathways Behavioral Svcs., Waterloo, Iowa. Author 3 book chpts.; book reviewer; contbr. articles to profl. jours. Bd. dirs. Story County Sexual Assault Care Ctr. and Battered Women's Project, Ames, Iowa, 1982-85; mem. Erie County Coalition Against Family Violence, Buffalo, 1985-92, Erie County Task Force on Sexual Abuse, Buffalo, 1986-92. Recipient Fulbright Rsch. grant Coun. for Internat. Exch. of Scholars, 1994-95, Rsch. grant Nat. Inst. on Alcohol Abuse and Alcoholism, 1988-92, Rsch. grant Nat. Inst. on Drug Abuse, 1992-97, Nat. Inst. Justice grantee, 1996—. Mem. Am. Soc. Criminology, Nat. Coun. on Family Rels. Democrat. Presbyterian. Achievements include research in fields of family violence and development of alcoholism in women. Office: Univ No Iowa Ctr for Study Adolescence 115 Sabin Hl Cedar Falls IA 50614-0001

DOWTY, ALAN KENT, political scientist, educator; b. Greenville, Ohio, Jan. 15, 1940; s. Paul Willard and Ethel Lovella (Harbaugh) D.; m. Nancy Ellen Gordon, Sept. 8, 1961 (div. 1972); children: Merav Aurli, Tamar Eliea, Gidon Yair; m. Gail Gaynell Schupack, Jan. 1, 1973; children: Rachel Miriam, Rafael Jonathan; 1 stepchild, David Freeman. BA, Shimer Coll., 1959; MA, U. Chgo., 1960, PhD, 1963. Lectr. Hebrew U., Jerusalem, 1965-72, sr. lectr., 1972-75; assoc. prof. U. Notre Dame, Ind., 1975-78, prof. polit. sci., 1978—; Kahanoff chair Israeli studies U. Calgary, 2003—. Exec. dir. Leonard Davis Inst., Jerusalem, 1972-74; editl. bd. Middle East Rev., N.Y.C., 1977-90; project dir. Twentieth Century Fund, N.Y.C., 1983-85; reporter experts meeting Internat. Inst. Human Rights, Strasbourg, France, 1989. Author: The Limits of American Isolation, 1971, Middle East Crisis, 1984 (Quincy Wright award 1985), The Arab-Israel Conflict (with others), 1984, Closed Borders, 1987, The Jewish State, 1998; book reviewer Jerusalem Post, 1964-75; contbr. numerous articles to topical publs. Exec. com. Am. Profs. for Peace in Mid. East, 1976-90; witness U.S. Senate Fgn. Rels. Com., Washington, 1976; nat. adv. com. Union of Couns. for Soviet Jews, Washington, 1980-91. Woodrow Wilson fellow, 1959-60; Rothschild fellow Hebrew U., 1963-64; resident fellow Adlai Stevenson Inst., Chgo., 1971-72; Skirball fellow Oxford Ctr. for Hebrew and Jewish Studies, 2000; recipient Charles W. Ramsdell award So. Hist. Assn., 1966; grantee Twentieth Century Fund, N.Y.C., 1983. Mem. Am. Polit. Sci. Assn., Internat. Polit. Sci. Assn., Internat. Studies Assn. (exec. com. 1977-79, Quincy Wright award 1985), Assn. Israel Studies (v.p. 2003—). Jewish. Avocations: travel, jewish studies. Office: U Notre Dame 313 Hesburgh Ctr Notre Dame IN 46556-5677 E-mail: dowty.1@nd.edu.

DOYLE, CONSTANCE TALCOTT JOHNSTON, physician, educator, medical association administrator; b. Mansfield, Ohio, July 8, 1945; d. Frederick Lyman IV and Nancy Jean Bushnell (Johnston) Talcott; children: Ian Frederick Demsky, Zachary Adam Demsky. BS, Ohio U., 1967; MD, Ohio State U., 1971. Diplomate Am. Bd. Emergency Medicine; bd. cert. in emergency crisis response. Intern Riverside Hosp., Columbus, Ohio, 1971-72; resident in internal medicine Hurley Hosp., U. Mich., Flint, 1972-74; emergency physician Oakwood Hosp., Dearborn, Mich., 1974-76, Jackson County (Mich.) Emergency Svcs., 1975-95; cons. Region II EMS, 1978-79, disaster cons., 1983-95; St. Joseph Mercy Hosp., Ann Arbor, 1995—, med. flight physician helicopter life support svcs., 1996-2000; core faculty St. Joseph Merch Hosp./U. Mich. Emergency Residency, Ann Arbor, 1995—; survival flight physician helicopter rescue svc. U. Mich., 1983-91; course dir. advanced cardiac life support and chmn. advanced life support com. W.A. Foote Meml. Hosp., Jackson, 1979-95; dep. dir. emergency svcs. med. ctrl. bd. Washtenaw Livingston County, 2000—; core faculty St. Joseph Mercy Hosp., Ann Arbor, 1996. Clin. instr. emergency svcs., dept. surgery U. Mich., 1981—; faculty combined emergency medicine residency St. Joseph Mercy Hosp.-U. Mich., Ann Arbor, 1995—; asst. med. dir. Region 2 South Biodef. Network, 2002-03, co-med. dir., 2003—; instr. EMT refresher courses, Jackson County, Jackson C.C.; MedFlight physician, 1996-99; Washtenaw County Subcom. on Bioterrorism, 2000—; Washtenaw County Local Emergency Planning Com., 1998—; dep. med. dir. Washtenaw/Livingston County Med. Control Authority, 2000—. Contbg. author: Clinical Approach to Poisoning and Toxicology, 1983, 89, 97, May's Textbook of Emergency Medicine, 1991, Schwartz Principles and Practice of Emergency Medicine, 1992, Reisdorff Pediatric Emergency Medicine, 1993; contbr. articles to profl. jours. Mem. Disaster Med. Assistance Team, 2000—. Fellow Am. Coll. Emergency Physicians (pres. Mich. disaster com. 1987-88, bd. dirs. Mich. 1979-88, chmn. Mich. disaster com. 1979-85, mem. nat. disaster med. svcs. com. 1983-85, chmn. 1987-88, cons. disaster mgmt. course Fed. Emergency Mgmt. Agy. 1982, treas. 1984-85, emergency med. svcs. com. 1985, pres. 1986-87, councillor 1986-87, chair steering com. policy sect., 1994—, mem. disaster sect., 1995—, exec. com. disaster sect. 1997—, chair policy sect. disaster 1995—, vice chair sect. careers in emergency medicine 1997—, chair, 2000—), Nat. Assn. Coll. Emergency Physicians (vice chair sect. of disaster med. svcs. 1990-92, nat. disaster subcom. 1989-90, chair subsect. psychol. rehab. svcs., disaster med. svcs. 1992-94, chair policy and legis. 1994-96, task force on hazardous materials 1993—, steering com. sect. disaster medicine 1994—, exec. com. sect. disaster medicine 1995); mem. ACP, Am. Med. Women's Assn., Am. Assn. Women Emergency Physicians, Mich. Assn. Emergency Med. Technicians (bd. dirs. 1979-80), Mich. State Med. Soc., Washtenaw County Med. Soc., Sierra Club. Jewish. Office: 1251 King George Blvd Ann Arbor MI 48108 also: St Joseph Mercy Hosp Dept Emergency Medicine Ann Arbor MI 48109

DOYLE, DELORES MARIE, retired principal; b. Madison, S.D., July 24, 1939; d. Martin N. and Pearl M. (Anderson) Berkelo; m. Patrick J. Doyle; children: Kathleen, Shawn, Tamara, Timothy. AS, Dakota State Coll., Madison, 1959; BS, Mid. Tenn. State U., 1966, MEd, 1968, EdS, 1975; PhD, Peabody/Vanderbilt U., 1980. Cert. career ladder III tchr. Tchr. 4th grade Meriden-Cleghorn Schs., Meriden, Iowa, 1960-62; tchr. 1st grade Hanover (Ill.) Sch., 1963-66; tchr. 2d grade Hobgood Sch., Murfreesboro, Tenn., 1969-70; tchr. 1st grade Reeves-Rogers Sch., Murfreesboro, 1972-80, tchr. 2d grade, 1981-97, prin., 1997-2000; ret., 2000. Cooperating tchr. Mid. Tenn. State U. Student Tchrs., Murfreesboro, 1972—97, mem. task force edn., 1992—93; summer sch. dir. Murfreesboro City Schs., 1986—98; lead project tutor Reeves-Rogers Sch., Murfreesboro, 1987—90. Active Edn. 2000 Com., Murfreesboro C. of C., 1993; trustee Mid Tenn State U. Found., 1995—2001; bd. dirs. Grace Luth. Ch., Murfreesboro, 1991—93, 2001—03, mem. choir, 1975—. Named Career Ladder III Tchr., Dept. Edn., Nashville, 1984; named to Tenn. Tchrs. Hall of Fame, 2001; recipient Tenn. Tchr. of the Yr. award, Dept. Edn., Nashville, 1992, Murfreesboro City Tchr. of the Yr. award, Murfreesboro City Schs., 1991, Mid-Cumberland Dist. Tchr. of the Yr. award, Dist. Dept. Edn., 1991, Trailblazer award, 1995; Creative Tchg. grantee, State Dept. Edn., 1992, 1993. Mem.: Murfreesboro Edn. Assn. (pres. 1981—82), Tenn. Edn. Assn. (Disting. Classroom Tchr. award 1992, Disting. Adminstr. award 2000), Tenn. State Tchr. of Yr. Orgn. (v.p. 2000—), Nat. State Tchr. of Yr. Orgn., Kappa Delta Pi, Delta Kappa Gamma. Democrat. Avocations: bridge, travel, reading, bicycling. Home: 1710 Sutton Pl Murfreesboro TN 37129-6513 E-mail: pandddoyle@comcast.net.

DOYLE, DENISE ELAINE, principal; b. Pitts., Oct. 23, 1952; d. Alfonso and Antoinette (Sciullo) Cincione; m. Thomas Michael Doyle, Aug. 16, 1975; 1 child, Jennifer Elaine. BS in Elem. Edn., Duquesne U., 1974; MS in Ednl. Leadership, Nova U., 1990. Tchr. Webster Elem. Sch., Hillsboro, Ohio, 1975-79; kindergarten tchr. Carlow Coll. Campus Sch., Pitts., 1982-84; tchr. Berkshire Elem. Sch., West Palm Beach, Fla., 1984-85, H.L. Johnson Elem. Sch., Royal Palm Beach, Fla., 1985-86; primary resource tchr. Loxahatchee Groves Elem. Sch., 1986-87, Wellington Elem. Sch., West Palm Beach, Fla., 1987-88, New Horizons Elem. Sch., Wellington, 1988-91; asst. prin. Crestwood Mid. Sch., Royal Palm Beach, Fla., 1991-95, Starlight Cove Elem. Sch., West Palm Beach, Fla., 1995-97; prin. S.D. Spady Elem. Sch., Delray Beach, Fla., 1997-2000, Heritage Elem. Sch., Greenacres, Fla., 2000—. Grantee Edn. Found. Palm Beach County, 1990, Fla. Mentor Tchr. Piolot Program, Dept. of Edn., 2000-02. Mem. AAUW, ASCD, Fla. Reading Coun., Palm Beach County Reading Coun. Avocations: tennis, swimming, golf, reading best sellers, dancing. E-mail: doyle@mail.palmbeach.k12.fl.us.

DOYLE, JOELLEN MARY, special education educator; b. N.Y.C., Jan. 19, 1951; d. Daniel Francis and Florence (Ward) D. BA, Wilson Coll., Chambersburg, Pa., 1972; MS in Edn.-Spl. Edn., Coll. New Rochelle (N.Y.), 1974, MS in Edn.-Gifted Edn., 1990; profl. diploma in adminstrn./supervision, Fordham U., N.Y.C., 1984; postgrad., Columbia U. Itinerant tchr. B.O.C.E.S., Port Chester, N.Y., 1974-76; spl. needs tchr., team leader Brookfield (Conn.) Pub. Schs., 1976-81; spl. edn. tchr. Hendrick Hudson Sch. Dist., Montrose, N.Y., 1981-82; spl. edn. tchr., coord. gifted and talented, curriculum coun. mem. Tuckahoe Pub. Schs., Estchester, N.Y., 1982—. Coord. sch./coll./bus. partnership, Coll. New Rochelle/IBM, 1990—; grad. asst. Coll. New Rochelle, 1974-75, rsch. asst., 1990; policy bd. Tchrs. Ctr.; mem. steering com., program chair, local coord. BEPT; bd. dirs. Tuckahoe After Sch. Care Program, chair scholarship com. Saturday Morning Math and Sci. Program. Bd. sec. Fordham U. Sch. of Edn. Alumni Assn.(achievement award, 1995). Recipient Recognition Svc. award Tuckahoe PTA, 1990, 91, nominated for Phoebe Appearson Hearst award and 1993 Tchr. of Yr.; grantee ACES, CEC Found., Meet the Composer Found.; recipient Fordam Sch.. of Edn. Alumni Achievement award, 1995. Mem. AAUW, Tuckahoe Tchrs. Assn. (sec., bd. trustees, Tchr. of Yr. 1993), Coun. Exceptional Children (pres.), Conn. Assn. Children with Disabilities (bd. dirs., sec., Hall of Fame award 1982), Bldg. Compact Team, Westchester Assn. Children with Disabilities, Assn. Women Adminstr. in Westchester, Assn. Edn. Gifted Underachieving Students, Kappa Delta Pi. Office: Tuckahoe Pub Schs 2 Siwanoy Blvd Tuckahoe NY 10707-3734

DOYLE, JOSEPH FRANCIS, III, art educator; b. Boston, Jan. 20, 1960; s. Joseph Francis Jr. and Ellen Mary (Hayes) D.; m. Ginger Leigh Davis, Dec. 18, 1993. BFA, Tex. Tech U., 1983, M of Edn., 1990. Coord. elem. art Round Rock (Tex.) Ind. Sch. Dist., 1983-84; art educator Ctrl. High Sch., San Angelo, Tex., 1985-86; art educator, art dept. chmn. Aldine Jr. High Sch., Houston, 1986-92; art educator MacArthur Sr. High, Houston, 1992-99; art educator, dist. dir. arts program Aldine Ind. Sch. Dist., Houston, 1999—. Tchr. night high sch. continuing edn. Aldine Ind. Sch. Dist., 1988, chmn. dist. youth art month, sponsor nat. jr. art honor soc., 1989-91, chmn. textbook selection com. elem. art, 1989, chmn. textbook selection com. sr. high art, 1995, mem. dist. tchr. of yr. selection com., 1992-93; insvc. trainer Tex. Arts Coun., Austin, 1991-93; presenter in field. Exhibited in group show Tex. Art Edn. Assn., 1988, 89, Tex. Trends Art Edn., 1989, Nat. Art Edn. Assn., 1990. Vol. graphic arts Tex. Spl. Olympics, Houston, 1988-90. Recipient Vol. in People award Sta. K-Lite-FM, 1990; named Houston Post Tchr. of Week, 1992; Disting. Alumnus award Texas Tech. U., 1992. Mem. Nat. Art Edn. Assn. (nat. conv. evaluator jr. high concerns, 1988, Western Region Art Educator of Yr., 1992, Nat. Jr. Art Hon. Soc. Sponcer of the Year, 1993), Tex. Art Edn. Assn. (v.p. youth arts month 1993-95, long range task force com., region VI rep., chmn. reps., insvc. presenter 1985-92, Rising Sun award 1983, Excellence in Art award 1990, Outstanding Art Educator jr. high/mid. sch. divsn. 1991, v.p. youth art month 1992-94, state treas. 1995-98), North Houston Art Edn. Assn. (pres. 1989-92). Roman Catholic. Avocations: swimming, martial arts, music. Home: 8510 Canyon Ridge Dr Spring TX 77379-6329

DOYLE, MICHAEL JAMES, education educator, organist; b. Bell, Calif., Aug. 24, 1939; s. Joseph Edward and Irma Louise (Smith) Doyle; m. Mina Katherine Martensen, Feb. 8, 1964; children: Michael James II, Mary Katherine, Matthew John. BA, Whittier Coll., 1961, MEd, 1971. Tchr. El Rancho Unified Sch. Dist., Pico Rivera, Calif., 1961-79, dept. chmn., 1967-74, acting prin., 1979; tchr., asst. prin. Alta Loma (Calif.) Sch. Dist., 1979-86, summer sch. prin., 1985, prin., 1986-95; assoc. faculty Nat. U., Riverside, Calif., 1995-98; adj. prof. Calif. State U., San Bernardino, 1995—, Nat. U., San Bernardino, Calif., 1998—. Organist, dir. various Luth. chs. in So. Calif., 1955-86; organist St. Paul's Luth. Ch., Pomona, Calif., 1986—; mem. Calif. State Program Rev., 1982-83; assoc. mem. Calif. Sch. Leadership Acad., Ontario, 1986-89; v.p. So. Calif. Luth. Music Clinic, 1978-81. Author: Sent Forth by God's Blessing, 1999 (award Concordia Hist. Inst., 2000), Mother of the Valley, 2001 (award Concordia Hist. Inst., 2002), Life and Times of Hans and Lydia Mertensen, 2003. Clk. Zion Luth. Sch. Bd. Edn., Maywood, Calif., 1962-64, chmn., 1966-67; mem. Downey (Calif.) City Water Bd., 1977-78; mem. Luth. High Personnel Commn., La Verne, Calif., 1988-92; asst. archivist Pacific S.W. Dist. Luth. Ch., Mo. Synod, 1999—. Named Outstanding Tchr. of Yr., Burke Jr. High Sch. PTA, Pico Rivera, 1973; recipient hon. svc. award Jasper Sch. PTA, Alta Loma, 1983, continuing svc. award, 1988, Golden Oak Svc. award, 1996, Written Books award Concordia Hist. Inst., St. Louis, 2000, 02; employee recognition award Alta Loma Sch. Dist., 1985. Mem. Assn. Calif. Sch. Adminstrs., Assn. West End Sch. Adminstrs., Calif. Tchrs. Assn., Am. Guild Organists, Downey Hist. Soc., Cucamonga Hist. Soc., Casa de Rancho (Cucamonga, Calif.), Phi Delta Kappa (pres. Mt. Baldy chpt. 1993-97, 2001—, advisor 1997-2000, found. chmn. 1991-93). Democrat. Lutheran. Home and Office: 2085 N Palm Ave Upland CA 91784-1476 E-mail: mdoyle@adelphia.net.

DOYLE, MICHAEL PATRICK, microbiologist, educator, director; b. Madison, Wis., Oct. 3, 1949; s. Donald Vincent and Evelyn (Bauer) Doyle; m. Annette Marie Ripple, Dec. 27, 1971; children: Michael Patrick, Patrick Matthew, Kristen Anne. BS in Bacteriology, U. Wis., 1973, MS in Food Microbiology, 1975, PhD in Food Microbiology, 1977. Sr. project leader Ralston Purina Co., St. Louis, 1977-80; asst. prof. U. Wis., Madison, 1980-84, assoc. prof., 1984-88, prof., 1988-91; prof., dir. U. Ga., Griffin, 1991—, dept. head Athens, 1993-99; chmn. sci. bd. U.S. Food and Drug Admin., 2003—. Regents prof. Bd. Regents Ga. U. Sys., 1997—; mem. food and nutrition bd. Inst. Medicine, NAS, 1991—97, com. to ensure safe food from prodn. to consumption, 1998, chair rev. com. USDA E. coli 0157:H7 in ground beef risk assessment, 2001—02, chair food forum, 2003—; mem. nat. adv. com. on microbiol. criteria for foods USA, Washington, 1988—90, Washington, 1994—2000; trustee Internat. Life Scis. Inst.-n.Am., Washington, 1992—, sci. advisor, 1987—96; mem. Internat. Commn. on Microbiol. Specifications for Foods, 1989—2000; Wis. Disting. prof. bd. regents U. Wis., Madison, 1988—91; James M. Craig Meml. lectr. Oreg. State U., Corvallis, 1990; sci. lectr. Am. Soc. Microbiology Found., 1991—93, 1999—2001; Peter J. Shields lectr. U. Calif., Davis, 1993; G. Malcolm Trout vis. scholar Mich. State U., Lansing, 1994; mem. sci. adv. coun. Refrigeration Rsch. and Edn. Found., 1997—2002; York Disting. lectr. Auburn U., 1999; chmn. com. rev. USDA, 2001—02; chmn. sci. bd. U.S. Food and Drug Adminstrn., 2003—; chmn. food forum Inst. Medicine Nat. Acad. Scis., 2003—. Editor: Food Microbiology: Fundamentals and Frontiers, 1997, Food Microbiology: Fundamentals and Frontiers, 2d edit., 2001, Foodborne Bacterial Pathogens, 1989; contbr. articles to profl. jours. Named one of Top 100 Most Cited Rschrs. Agrl. Scis., Inst. Sci. Info., 2002; recipient award for Profl. Excellence, Am. Agrl. Econs. Assn., 1992, Silver Plow Honor award, USDA, 1998, Ptnrs. in Pub. Health award, Ctrs. Disease Control and Prevention, 2001. Fellow: Am. Acad. Microbiology, Inst. of Food Technologists (Fred W. Tanner lectr. 1986, sci. lectr. 1987—90, exec. com. 2000—03, Samuel Cate Prescott award for rsch. 1987, Nicholas Appert award for preeminence in and contbns. to field of food tech. 1996), Internat. Assn. Food Protection (pres. 1992—93, Norbert F. Sherman article excellence award 1993, NFPA food safety award for outstanding contbn. to food safety rsch. and edn. 1999); mem.: Am. Soc. for Microbiology (chmn. food microbiology divsn. 1987—89, Found. lectr. 1991—93, 1999—2001, P.R. Edwards award for outstanding career achievements 1994), Internat. Assn. Food Protection, Gamma Sigma Delta, Phi Kappa Phi. Roman Catholic. Achievements include patents for for monoclonal antibody to enterohemorrhagic E. coli; for competitive exclusion bacteria to reduce carriage of enterohemorrhagic E. coli by cattle; development of of methods to control and detect foodborne pathogens. Office: U Ga Ctr Food Safety 1109 Experiment St Griffin GA 30223-1797 E-mail: mdoyle@uga.edu.

DOYLE, ROBERT CHARLES, historian, educator; b. Phila., Jan. 20, 1946; s. Edward James and Arvella Wilhemena (Gaetz) D.; m. Beate Theresa Engel, Aug. 23, 1986. BA, Pa. State U., 1967, MA, 1976; PhD, Bowling Green State U., 1987. Bandleader, mgr. Buffalo Chipkickers, State College, Pa., 1973-77; owner, mgr. Bob Doyle Talent Agy., State College, 1978-86; lectr. in Am. studies Pa. State U., University Park, 1986-94; Fulbright jr. lectr. Westfälische Wilhelms Univ., Münster, Germany, 1994—; assoc. prof. U. Strasbourg II, France, 1995-96, Franciscan U. of Steubenville, Ohio, 2000. Cons. Phila. '76 Inc., 1976, WPSX-TV, University Park, 1981, 83, MGM, Warhart Prodsn. for Hart's War, 2002; manuscript reviewer Univ. Press Kans., Lawrence, 1994, Naval Inst. Press, 1997, 2000, Fordham U. Press, 2002, Tex. A&M U. Press, 2002; guest lectr. Monash U., Melbourne, Australia, 1994. Author: Voices From Captivity, 1994, A Prisoner's Duty, 1997, 99; contbr. Learning the Fiddlers Ways, 1980; contbr. articles, book revs. to profl. publs.; lectr. in field. Lt. USN, 1967-71. Rsch. grantee Pa. Coun. Arts, 1974-75. Mem. Am. Studies Assn., VFW, Am. Fedn. Musicians (mem. exec. bd. local 660 1987-94). Roman Catholic. E-mail: bdoyle@uov.net.

DOYLE, WENDELL E. retired band director, educator; b. Higbee, Mo., July 8, 1940; s. Travis E. and Hattie Erma (Webb) D.; m. Julia Ann Vail, June 23, 1963; children: Dora Michelle, Michael E., Melissa Kae. BS in Edn., Northeast Mo. State U., 1962; MEd in Music, U. Mo., 1967. Cert. lifetime tchr., Mo. Band dir. Braymer (Mo.) C-4, 1962-68, Brookfield (Mo.) R-3, 1968-72, Platte County (Mo.) R-III, 1972-92; ret., 1992. Exchange tchr. Platte County R-III Schs., Warwickshire, Eng., 1984. Pres. Barry Heights Homes Assn., 1986—; minister of music Park Bapt. Ch., Brookfield, 1968-72, Northgate Bapt. Ch., Kansas City, 1972-85. Mem. Mo. State Tchrs. Assn. (pres. Greater Kans. City dist. 1978), Music Educators Nat. Conf., Mo. Music Educators Assn., Mo. Bandmasters Assn. (sec.), Phi Beta Mu (pres. 1990-91, Outstanding Band Dir. award Lambda chpt., 1993), Mo. Bardmasters Assn. (Hall of Fame 1997). Democrat. Avocations: fishing, reading, golfing, travel. Home: 2330 NW Powderhorn Dr Kansas City MO 64154-1311

DOYLE, WILLIAM THOMAS, physicist, retired educator; b. New Britain, Conn., Dec. 5, 1925; s. Thomas William and Kathleen (McConn) D.; m. Barbara May Grant, June 16, 1951; children— Peter, Jeffrey. Sc.B. in Physics, Brown U., 1951; MA, Yale, 1952, PhD, 1955. Mem. faculty Dartmouth, 1955-97, prof. physics, 1964-97, chmn. dept., 1967-71. Served with USNR, 1943-46. NSF predoctoral fellow, 1953-54, 54-55; postdoctoral fellow, 1958-59 Mem. AAAS, Am. Phys. Soc., Sigma Xi. Home: 6 Tyler Rd Hanover NH 03755-2232

DOZIER, HERBERT RANDALL, school system administrator; b. Whiteville, N.C., Dec. 10, 1954; s. Herbert A. and Catherine (Stroud) D.; m. Susan Rogers, Aug. 12, 1978; children: Joseph Andrew, Catherine Claire. BA, Francis Marion U., 1977; MEd, U. S.C., 1980, edn. specialist cert., 1985, PhD, 1997. Tchr., coach Greenville (S.C.) County Schs., 1978-81; asst. prin. Greenville Travelers Rest (S.C.) High Sch., 1981-88; prin. Hillcrest Mid. Sch., Simpsonville, S.C., 1988-90, Travelers Rest High Sch., 1990-95; asst. supt. for middle schs. Sch. Dist. Greenville (S.C.) County, 1995-96, assoc. supt. for adminstrn., 1996—. Pres.-elect High Sch. Prins.' Assn., Greenville County, 1994. Trustee Francis Marion U., Florence, S.C., 1991—; active PTA (lifetime hon. mem.). Recipient Hon. State FFA Degree, Future Farmers Am., 1992. Mem. S.C. Assn. Sch. Adminstrs., Phi Delta Kappa, Pi Gamma Mu, Rotary. Protestant. Avocations: running, jogging, golf, collecting coins and stamps. Home: 4575 Carriage Run Cir Murrells Inlet SC 29576-5867 Office: Office Sch Dist Greenville County PO Box 2848 Greenville SC 29602-2848

DOZIER, THERESE KNECHT, educational association administrator, educator; BA in Social Studies Edn., U. Fla., 1974, MEd in Secondary Social Studies, 1976; EdD in Curriculum and Instrn., U. S.C., 1995; LHD (hon.), Winthrop Coll., 1985, U. S.C., 1985. Tchr. Lincoln Mid. Sch., Gainesville, Fla., 1974—76, Miami Edison Mid. Sch., Fla., 1976—77, Singapore Am. Sch., Singapore, 1986—89, Irmo H.S., Columbia, SC, 1977—85, 1989—90, 1992—93; instr. and coord. profl. devel. schs. U. S.C., Columbia, 1991—92; spl. advisor on tchg. to U.S. Sec. of Edn. Richard W. Riley U.S. Dept. Edn., Washington, 1993—97, sr. advisor on tchg. to U.S. Sec. of Edn. Richard W. Riley, 1997—2001; nat. tchr.-in-residence and assoc. prof., dir. ctr. tchr. leadership Sch. Edn. Va. Commonwealth U., Richmond, 2001—. Mem. Nat. Conf. State Legislatures Taskforce on Sch. Leadership, Nat. Com. on Tchr. Mobility, Com. to Enhance K-12 Tchg. Profession in Va., Va. State Action for Ednl. Leadership Consortium; mem. adv. bd. Nat. Tchr. Recruitment Clearinghouse; mem. adv. panel SRI Internat.'s Study of Alt. Cert. of Tchrs.; mem. meritorious new tchr. com. Mid-Atlantic Regional Tchr. Project; advisor rural initiative Nat. Bd. Profl. Tchg. Stds.; mem. policy and planning coun. Met. Ednl. Rsch. Consortium; advisor DeWitt-Wallace Reader's Digest Found. Tchr. Leadership Initiative; mem. acad. coun. Nat. Inst. Cmty. Innovations Internat. Grad. Ctr.; sr. counsel on tchr. quality issues Widmeyer Comm.; cons. N. Ctrl. Regional Lab. Profl. Devel. Ctr., Asian-Pacific Econ. Coun. Tchr. Devel. Web Portal Project, NBPTS Prin.'s Initiative; presenter in field; bd. dirs. Coun. Basic Edn. Named Nat. Tchr. of Yr., 1985, S. Carolinian of Yr., 1985, Alumna of Outstanding Achievement, U. Fla., 1997; recipient Disting. Alumnus award U. Fla., 1985, Nat. Jefferson award for outstanding pub. svc. benefiting local communities, 1986, Hammer award for helping to make govt. more efficient and effective V.P. Gore, 1995; named to the Order of the Palmetto, 1985; Fulbright-Hays fellow to China, 1985; Holmes scholar U. S.C., 1991-93.*

DRACHMAN, SALLY SPAID, educational foundation administrator; b. Washington, July 3, 1931; d. William and Estelle (Abbott) Spaid; m. Harold D. Adamson, Aug. 23, 1952 (div. 1972); children: David, Douglas, Daniel; m. Roy P. Drachman, Mar. 16, 1978. BS, U. Ariz., 1951, MEd, 1974, PhD in Adminstrn., 1983. Tchr. Vine Grove (Ky.) High Sch., 1952-54; co-counselor Student Counseling Bur. U. Ariz., Tucson, 1973, in-svc. trainer Student Housing, 1978-84, project dir. Student Housing, 1974-84; devel. officer U. Ariz. Found., Tucson, 1983-84, exec. dir. Pres.'s Club, 1984-90, dir. devel. Ariz. Arthritis Ctr., 1986-90, dir. devel. Ariz. Astronomy, 1988-90, assoc. dir. major gifts, 1990—. Chair Nat. Philanthropy Day Conf. and Banquet, Tucson, 1991. Contbr. articles to profl. jours. Bd. dirs. La Jolla (Calif.) Cancer Rsch. Ctr., 1989—, Div. Sch. of Pacific, Berkeley, Calif., 1989—, Tucson Symphony, 1983-91, pres., 1988-90; hon. chair Women on Move Banquet, Tucson, 1990; mem. Ariz. Women's Town Hall, Chandler, 1991, Ariz. Town Hall, Grand Canyon, 1991. Recipient Ann Eve Johnson award Jr. League Tucson, Inc., 1993; named to Order of Omega Greek Hall of Fame, U. Ariz., 1994. Mem. AAUW, Nat. Soc. Exec. Fundraisers (cert., bd. dirs. local chpt. 1989—, pres.-elect 1993, Fund Raising Exec. of the Yr. award 1993), Women Mgrs., Pi Delta Kappa, Pi Lambda Theta. Avocations: hiking, gardening. Office: U Ariz Found 1111 N Cherry Ave Tucson AZ 85719-4516

DRAGO, JOSEPH ROSARIO, urologist, educator; b. Jersey City, N.J., Oct. 28, 1947; m. Diane Lavacca; children: Andrea, Daniella, Denise. BS, U. Ill., 1968, MD, 1972. Diplomate Nat. Bd. Med. Examiners, Am. Bd. Urology; cert. Yag Laser, laparoscopic surgery. Intern Pa. State U. Milton S. Hershey Med. Ctr., 1972-73, resident in urology, 1973-77, instr. urology, 1976-77; asst. prof. urology, dir. urology oncology U. Calif., Davis, 1977-79, Milton S. Hershey (Pa.) Med. Ctr., 1979-80, assoc. prof. to prof. of surgery, dir. urologic oncology, 1980-85; assoc. staff Children's Hosp., Columbus, Ohio, 1985—; interim chief of staff elect, prof., dir. urologic oncology Ohio State U. Arthur G. James Cancer Hosp., Columbus, Ohio, 1990-92; with Easton (Pa.) Warren Urology, Easton, Pa., 1992-95; pvt. practice Washington, N.J., 1995—. Mem. editl. bd. In Vivo Jour.; advisor Internat. Urologic Svcs., Inc., 1987; cons. in field; visiting prof. over 30 univs. and hosps. Author 12 book chpts.; reviewer various profl. jours., 1979—; contbr. articles to profl. jours. Recipient various rsch. grants, 1978-81. Fellow Internat. Coll. Surgeons in Urology; mem. AMA, Am. Coll. Surgeons, Am. Fertility Soc., Am. Inst. Ultrasound in Medicine, Am. Soc. Andrology, Am. Urologic Assn., Assn. Academic Surgery, Assn. Surgical Edn., Hershey Surgical Soc. (sec.-treas. 1983-85), Pa. Med. Soc., Phila. Urologic Soc., others. Home: 4559 Pinehurst Greens Ct Estero FL 33928 Office: 224 Roseberry St Phillipsburg NJ 08865-1632

DRAGONWAGON, CRESCENT (ELLEN ZOLOTOW), writer, educator; b. N.Y.C., Nov. 25, 1952; d. Maurice and Charlotte (Shapiro) Zolotow; m. Mark Parsons, Mar. 20, 1969 (div. 1973); m. Ned Shank, Oct. 1978 (dec. Nov. 2000). Owner, operator, Dairy Hollow House, Eureka Springs., Ark., 1981-99; writing seminars, N.Y., Phila., Phoenix, San Francisco, Providence, Mpls., Chgo., San Diego; co-founder Writers' Colony at Dairy Hollow, 1998—, lectr./seminar leader, Fearless Writing Wkshps.; spokesperson Calif. Almond Bd., 1993; chef du jour TVFN, 1996, Good Morning Am., 1992, Today Weekend, 2002. Author: (adult fiction) The Year It Rained, 1985 (N.Y. Times 100 Notable Books of 1985); (children's books) Rainy Day Together, 1970, Strawberry Dress Escape, 1975, Wind Rose, 1976, When Light Turns Into Night, 1977, Will It Be Okay?, 1977, Your Owl Friend, 1977, If You Call My Name, 1981, (with Paul Zindel) To Take a Dare, 1982, Katie in the Morning, 1983, I Hate My Brother Harry, 1983, Coconut, 1984, Jemima Remembers, 1984 (Nat. Coun. Tchrs. English Choice award 1985), Always, Always, 1984 (Parents' Choice Literary Honor 1984, Social Scis. Book of Yr.), Half a Moon and One Whole Star, 1986 (Coretta Scott King Recognition for 1986-87), Diana, Maybe, 1987, Alligator Arrived with Apples, 1987, Dear Miss Moshki, 1988, Margaret Ziegler Is Horse-Crazy, 1988, I Hate My Sister Maggie, 1989, This Is the Bread I Baked for Ned, 1989, The Itch Book, 1990, Homeplace, 1990 (Golden Kite award Soc. Children's Book Writers), Winter Holding Spring, 1990, Alligators and Others All Year Long, 1993, Annie Flies the Birthday Bike, 1993, Brass Button, 1997, Bat in the Dining Room, 1997, Is this a Sack of Potatoes?, 2002, And Then the Sun Came Out, 2003; (nonfiction) Dairy Hollow House Cookbook, 1986 (World of Cookbooks Best Regional award 1986, L.A. Times 10 Best 1986), Dairy Hollow House Soup and Bread Cookbook (nominated for Julia Child and James Beard awards), 1992, Passionate Vegetarian, 2002; contbr. book revs., articles to mags., newspapers including N.Y. Times, Cosmopolitan, Los Angeles, Lear's, Fine Cooking, Mode, Bon Appetit, Book Page. Recipient Porter Fund award for writing, Ark., 1991, Women on the Move award, Wyndham, 1997, 1st prize profl. category Newman's Own Recipe Contest, 1997; Ossabaw Found. fellow, 1982, Ragdale Found. fellow, 1990. Mem. Authors Guild, Internat. Assn. Culinary Profls. (judge IACP/Julia Child Cookbook Awards 1997), So. Food Writers' Alliance (Judge James Beard award 1999), Soc. Children's Book Writers, Words, Ark. Lit. Soc., Eureka Group, Archimedes Investment Mgmt. (pres. 1999). Avocations: cooking, reading, restoration of older buildings, canoeing. Home: 1 Frisco Eureka Springs AR 72632-9287

DRAGO-SEVERSON, ELEANOR ELIZABETH E. developmental psychologist, educator, researcher; b. N.Y.C., N.Y., Nov. 25, 1961; d. Rosario Philip and Betty Louise (Brisgal) Drago; m. David Irving Severson, Dec. 30, 1989. BA summa cum laude, L.I. U., 1986; EdM, Harvard U., 1989, EdD, 1996. Cert. biology, chemistry tchr., N.Y. Tchr. math. Palm Beach (Fla.) Acad., 1986-87; h.s. tchr. math., basketball coach Hackley Sch., Tarrytown, N.Y., 1987-88; tchr. biology, dir. human devel. Palm Beach Day Sch., 1990-91, dir. human devel., 1990-91; tchg. fellow Harvard U., Cambridge, Mass., 1993-96, assoc. in edn. Grad. Sch. Edn., 1996—2002, postdoctoral fellow Sch. Edn., 1997-2001, instr., rsch. assoc. Sch. Edn., 1997—2002, lectr. edn. Grad. Sch. Edn., 1998—. Co-dir. J.V. Mara C.Y.O. Sports Camp, Putnam Valley, N.Y., summer 1987. Mem. colloquium com. Harvard U., Cambridge, Mass., 1991-92, chair, 1992, mentor to incoming grad. students, 1992-96. Joseph Klingenstein fellow, 1987, tchg. fellow, 1993-96, doctoral fellow, 1994-96; Spencer sm. grant rsch. award, 2000. Mem. ASCD, APA, AAUW, Am. Ednl. Rsch. Assn., Soc. for Rsch. in Adult Devel., Nat. Staff Devel. Coun., Phi Delta Kappa. Roman Catholic. Home: 39 Kirkland St Apt 403 Cambridge MA 02138-2072

DRAHN, PRISCILLA CHARLOTTE, special education educator; b. Postville, Iowa, July 1, 1960; d. Lloyd Carl and Marjorie Charlotte (Otis) D. BA, U. No. Iowa, 1983; MS in Edn., Mo. State U., 1991. Tchr. Essex (Iowa) Community Schs., 1983—. Mem. Spl. Edn. Compliance Rev. Team, 1993; spl. edn. tchr. Spl. Edn. Adv. Com., Shenandoah, Iowa, 1986-93. Mem. S.W. Iowa Theatre Group, Shenandoah, 1992. Mem. NEA, Iowa State Edn. Assn., Essex Edn. Assn. (treas. 1991-93), Coun. for Exceptional Children, Learning Disabilities Assn., Iowa Jaycees. Republican. Avocations: volleyball, riding horses, theatre, vocal music, skiing. Office: Essex Community Schs 111 Forbes St Essex IA 51638-3034 Address: 128 1/2 Story St Boone IA 50036-4239

DRAIN, CECIL B. university dean, nurse anesthetist educator, retired army officer; b. Ft. Worth, Aug. 25, 1943; s. Harry Eugene and F. Colene (McDonald) D.; m. Cynthia M. Pfaff, Aug. 21, 1965; children: Timothy, Stephen, Kathryn. Diploma, St. Joseph Hosp. Sch. Nursing, Ft. Worth, 1967; BSN, U. Ariz., 1976, MS in Med.-Surg. Nursing, NS in Adult Pulmonary Nursing, U. Ariz., 1980; PhD in Ednl. Curriculum and Instrn. in Higher Edn., Tex. A&M U., 1986. RN, Va., Tex.; cert. RN anesthetist. Staff nurse recovery room, head nurse psychiatry St. Joseph Hosp., 1967; commd. 2d lt. U.S. Army, 1968, advanced through grades to col.; chief nurse anesthetist 121st Evacuation Hosp., Seoul, Republic of Korea, 1972—73; staff nurse anesthetist, chief respiratory therapy U.S. Gen. Leonard Wood Army Community Hosp., Ft. Leonard Wood, Mo., 1973-74; staff nurse anesthetist Tucson Med. Ctr., 1974—76, Brooke Army Med. Ctr., Ft. Sam Houston, Tex., 1976—78, spl. project officer, 1986-89; asst. program dir. U.S. Army-SUNY-Buffalo anesthesiology for ANC officers course U.S. Army Acad. Health Sciences, Ft. Sam Houston, 1980-83; program dir. program in anesthesia nursing U.S. Army-Tex. U.S. Army/Tex. Wesleyan U./Acad. of Health Scis., Ft. Sam Houston, 1989-92; dir. program in anesthesia nursing U. Tex. Health Sci. Ctr. Houston/AMEDD Ctr. and Sch., Ft. Sam Houston, 1992-93; prof. clin. nursing U. Tex. Health Sci. Ctr., Houston, 1992-93; prof. Va. Commonwealth U., Med. Coll. Va. Campus, Richmond, 1993—; chmn. dept. nurse anesthesia Med. Coll. Va., Richmond, 1993-96, interim dean Sch. Allied Health Professions, 1996-97, dean Sch. Allied Health Professions, 1997—. Teaching asst. U. Ariz., 1979-80; clin. instr. family medicine U. Okla., 1983; adj. prof. Tex. Wesleyan U., 1989-92; guest lectr. Tex. A&M U., 1986-93; numerous presentations in field; mem. long-term civilian profls. Schooling Selection Bd., Alexandria, Va., 1988; reviewer Clin. Rev. Series in Critical Care Nursing, 1988—. Author: Perianesthesia Nursing: A Critical Care Approach, 4th edit., 2003; mem. editl. bd.: Heart and Lung: Jour. Critical Care, 1977—92, Nurse Anesthesia, 1987—94, Am. Jour. Critical Care, 1992—, Jour. Am. Assn. Nurse Anesthetists, 1980—93, 1992—2000, Jour. Perianesthesia Nursing, 2002—; contbr. articles abstracts and book revs. to profl. jours., chpts. to books. Baseball commr., Ft. Sam Houston, 1980-81; bd. dirs. March of Dimes, San Antonio, 1981-83; umpire USTA, Bryan, Tex., 1985—; trustee Yankton Coll., 2003--. Decorated Legion of Merit, Meritorious Svc. medal with oak leaf cluster. Fellow Am. Acad. Nursing; mem. ANA, AACN (cert. of achievement 1980), Am. Assn. Nurse Anesthetists (jour. faculty 1982-83, bd. dirs. Ednl. and Rsch. Found. 1983-91, cert. of profl. excellence 1976), Am. Soc. Post Anesthesia Nurses (rsch. com. 1986-87), Tex. Assn. Post Anesthesia Nurses (life), 38th Parallel Nurses Soc. (pres. 1971), So. Assn. Allied Health Deans of Acad. Med. Ctrs. (treas. 2002--), Assn. Schs. Allied Health Profls. (treas. 2002--), Ret. Officers Assn. (life), Ret. Army Nurse Corps Assn. (assoc.), Order of Mil. Med. Merit, Downtown Kiwanis, Sigma Theta Tau, Phi Delta Kappa, Sigma Epsilon Chi. Republican. Methodist. Home: 5511 W Bay Rd Midlothian VA 23112-2509 Office: Va Commonwealth U Med Coll Va Campus Sch Allied Health Profs Richmond VA 23298 E-mail: cdrain@hsc.vcu.edu.

DRAKE, ANNE KELLY, social worker, educator; b. Peoria, Ill., Nov. 13, 1951; d. Walter Reuel and Ada Frances (Dixon) Wright; m. Daniel L. Drake; children: James, N. Jason, Justin. AA, Lincoln Land C.C., 1975; BA in Child Family Comty. Svc., U. Ill. Sangamon campus, 1978; MEd, U. Ill., 1990. Cert. child protective investigator, child devel. specialist II, Ill.; lic. State of Ill.; cert. child welfare specialist. Case coord. Jacksonville (Ill.) Area Assn. Retarded Citizens, 1975-76; surrogate parent/ednl. advocate Ill. State Bd. Edn., Vermillion County, 1977-79; child care specialist Parents Anonymous, Champaign, Ill., 1990-91, parent facilitator, 1991-93; child devel. specialist Devel. Svcs. Ctr., Champaign, Ill., 1990-94; child protective investigator Ill. Dept. Children and Family Svcs., Charleston, Ill., 1994-2000, licensing quality assurance, day care cons. Savoy, Ill., 2000—, child protective svcs. worker Charleston, Ill., 2001—. Parent group facilitator, sponsor Parents Anonymous, Champaign, Ill., 1990-92; vol. EMT Midleford Vol. Ambulance, Potomac, Ill., 1986-89; surrogate parent/ednl. advocate Ill. State Bd. Edn., Vermillion County, 1986-89; grad. rsch. asst. dept. spl. edn. U. Ill., Champaign, 1987-90; v.p., rep. dept. spl. edn. Coun. Grad. Students in Edn., U. Ill., Champaign, 1987-90. Sec. Middlefork Twp. Vol. Ambulance, Potomac, Ill., 1987—89. Grantee Kappa Delta Pi, U. Ill., Champaign, 1990; Hilton-Perkins scholar, 1993. Mem.: Nat. Assn. Edn. Young Children, Kappa Delta Pi. Republican. Mem. Lds Ch. Home: 1212 Reynolds Dr Charleston IL 61920

DRAKE, MIRIAM ANNA, librarian, educator, writer; b. Boston, Dec. 20, 1936; d. Max Frederick and Beatrice Celia (Mitnick) Engleman; m. John Warren Drake, Dec. 19, 1960 (div. Dec. 1985); 1 child, Robert Warren. BS, Simmons Coll., Boston, 1958, MLS, 1971; postgrad., Harvard U., 1959-60; LHD (hon.), Ind. U., 1994; DLS (hon.), Simmons Coll., 1997. Assoc. United Rsch., Cambridge, Mass., 1958-61; with mktg. svcs. Kenyon & Eckhardt, Boston, 1963-65; cons. Boston, 1965-72; head rsch. unit libraries Purdue U., West Lafayette, Ind., 1972-76, asst. dir. libraries, prof. library sci., 1976-84; dean, dir. libraries, prof. Ga. Inst. Tech., Atlanta, 1984-2001, prof. emerita, 2001—. Trustee Online Computer Libr. Ctr., Inc., 1978-84, chair, 1980-83; trustee Corp. for Rsch. and Edn. Networking, 1991-94, U.S. Depository Libr. Coun., 1991-94, Simmons Coll., 1999—; trustee, corporator adv. bd. Engring. Info., 1997—. Author: User Fees: A Practical Perspective, 1981, Information Today, 2002; co-author: (with James Matarazzo) Information for Management, 1994; editor: Ency. Libr. Info. Sci., 2nd edit.; mem. editl. bd. Coll. and Rsch. Librs. Jour., 1985-90, Librs. and Microcomputers Jour., 1983-93, Sci. and Tech. Librs., 1989-98, Database, 1989-97; contbr. chpts. to books, articles to profl. jours. Recipient Alumni Achievement award Simmons Coll. Sch. Libr. and Info. Sci., 1985, Kent Meckler Media award U. Pitts., 1994. Fellow: Nat. Fedn. of Abstracting and Indexing Svs. (hon.); mem.: ALA (councilor at large 1985—89, Hugh Atkinson Meml. award 1992), Assn. Info. and Dissemination Ctrs. (pres. 2001—03), Spl. Librs. Assn. (pres.-elect 1992—93, pres. 1993—94, H.W. Wilson award 1983, John Cotton Dana award 2002), Am. Soc. Info. Sci., Am. Mgmt. Assn. Office: Ga Inst Tech Lib Info Ctr Atlanta GA 30332-0900 E-mail: mdrake@library.gatech.edu.

DRAKE, RICHARD PAUL, physicist, educator; b. Washington, Oct. 25, 1954; s. Hugh Hess and Florence Jean (Steele) D.; m. Joyce Elaine Penner, Aug. 30, 1980; children: Katherine Anne, David Alexander. BA in Philosophy and Physics magna cum laude, Vanderbilt U., 1975; PhD in Physics, Johns Hopkins U., 1979. Physicist Lawrence Livermore (Calif.) Lab., 1979-89; assoc. prof. dept. applied sci. U. Calif., Davis, 1989-91, prof., 1991-93; dir. Plasma Physics Rsch. Inst. Lawrence Livermore Nat. Lab., 1990-96; vis. prof. U. Mich., Ann Arbor, 1996-98, prof. space sci., 1998—, dir. Space Physics Rsch. Lab., 1998—2002. Ski instr. Squaw Valley, Calif., 1985-92; referee NSF, Nature, Phys. Rev. Letters, others. Contbr. over 140 articles to profl. jours. Mem. Fellow Am. Phys. Soc. (chmn. topical group on plasma astrophysics 2002); mem. AAAS, Am. Geophys. Union, Am. Astron. Soc., Am. Vacuum Soc., Optical Sci. Am., Phi Beta Kappa. Achievements include rsch. in exptl. astrophysics fundamental experiments and theory on waves, instabilities, and turbulence in plasmas; time-dependent systems. Home: 3204 W Dobson Pl Ann Arbor MI 48105-2580 Office: U Mich Campus 2455 Hayward St Ann Arbor MI 48109-2143 E-mail: rpdrake@umich.edu.

DRAKULICH, MARTHA, retired arts educator; b. Wiesbaden, Germany, Feb. 11, 1931; d. Hans and Martha (Minor) Zwinkau; m. Mike Drakulich, Mar. 1953; 1 child, Starley. BA, Von Teuffel, Wiesbaden. Tchr. Phoenix Parks and Recreation and Librs., Phoenix, Glendale (Ariz.) Community Coll.; ret., 2002. Contbr. articles to profl. jours. Founder, pres. U. Ariz. Coop. Extension Homemaker's Club. Home: 6439 W Willow Ave Glendale AZ 85304-1050

DRANOVE, DAVID, business educator, consultant, economist; b. N.Y.C., July 25, 1956; s. Alfred and Dorothy Dranove; m. Deborah Salgo, Aug. 21, 1983; children: Daniel, Michael. BA, Cornell U., 1977, MBA, 1979; PhD, Stanford U., 1983. Chmn. Dept. Mgmt. and Strategy Northwestern U., Evanston, Ill., 1996—2000, Walter McNerney disting. prof. of health industry mgmt., 2000—, dir. Ctr. Health Industry Mkt. Econ., 2001—. Bd. dirs. Ped. Faculty Found., Chicago. Author: How Hospitals Survived, 1999, Economics of Strategy, 2003, Economic Evolution of American Health Care, 2001, What's Your Life Worth?, 2003; contbr. articles to profl. jours. Recipient John Thompson prize, Assn. U. Programs in Health Adminstrn., 1993. Mem.: Am. Econ. Assn. Avocations: audiophile, sports enthusiast, fine dining enthusiast. Office: Kellogg Sch of Mgmt 2001 Sheridan Rd Evanston IL 60208 Office Fax: 847-467-1777. Business E-Mail: d-dranove@kellogg.northwestern.edu.

DRANTZ, VERONICA ELLEN, science educator and consultant; b. Chgo., Sept. 5, 1943; d. Albert William and Veronica Grace (Crowe) D. BS with high honors, U. Ill., Urbana, 1965, MS, 1969; PhD, De Paul U., Chgo., 1987. Biol. sci. forensic analytical chemist Chgo. Police Dept., Chgo., 1970-72, asst. head forensic analytical chemist, 1972-74; instr. Evanston Hosp. Sch. Anesthesia, Chgo., 1975—, East-West Univ., Chgo., 1982-84, dir. biol. and phys. sciences, 1984—, asst. prof., 1987-88, assoc. prof., 1988-91, prof., 1991—, dir. electroneurodiagnostic technology program, 1988—; asst. prof. in MS of nursing DePaul U., Chgo., 1989—. Spkr. Ill. Assn. Nurse Anesthetists, 1978-80, Ill. Soc. Electroneurodiagnostic Tech., 1986—, Am. Soc. Electroneurodiagnostic Tech., 1994—; sci. cons., spkr. Chgo. Tchrs. Ctr., 1989; instr. Chgo. Heart Assn., 1989—. Co-author: Population Genetics A BSCS Self Instructional Prog., 1969 Recipient Rsch. assistantship NSF, U. Ill., 1965-66, Rsch. Fellowship NSF, U. Ill., 1966-70, Schmidt Acad. fellowship Schmidt Found., DePaul U., 1975-80, Cardiopulmonary Resuscitation award Chgo. Heart Assn., 1990. Mem. Phi Beta Kappa. Avocations: camping, hiking, nature study, photography, computers, gardening. Office: 4942 W School St Chicago IL 60641-4340 E-mail: drdrantz@msn.com.

DRECHNEY, MICHAELENE, secondary education educator; b. Chgo. d. Bill and Pearl (Krupocki) D. BS, Loyola U., Chgo., 1968, MA, 1976. Cert. tchr., Ill., Ohio. Tchr. adult edn. Wright Coll., Chgo., 1983-84; tchr. English, Gordon Tech. High Sch., Chgo., 1977-84; tchr. sci. St. Francis Xavier Sch., Wilmette, Ill., 1973-76; tchr. sci., dir. art St. Monica Sch., Chgo., 1977-93; tchr. Thorp Scholastic Acad., Chgo., 1993—. Grantee Edn. System of People's Republic of China, Woodrow Wilson Found., 1989, Nat.

Sci. Tchr.'s Assn., NSF, 1990, NSF, Inst. for Chem. Edn., 1991, Project W.I.Z.E., 1995, Tchrs. as Scholars, 2000, Project Physics, 2002; recipient presdl. award Assn. Sci. Tchrs., Project Lava award 1998. Mem. ASCD, Nat. Sci. Tchrs. Assn. (cert.), Argon Chemistry Tchrs., Nat. Middle Level Sci. Tchrs., Coun. for Elem. Sci. Internat., Nat. Sci. Suprs. Assn., Ill. Sci. Tchrs. Assn. Home: 6550 W Belmont Ave Chicago IL 60634-3995 Office: 6024 W Warwick Ave Chicago IL 60634-2554

DREES, ELAINE HNATH, artist and educator; b. Orange, N.J., Aug. 20, 1929; d. John Anthony and Helen Louise (Godlesky) Hnath; m. Thomas Clayton Drees, Feb. 9, 1952; children: Danette, Clayton, Barry, Nancy. A.Comml. Art, Parsons Sch. Design, N.Y.C. Colorist and designer Hesse Wallpaper, N.Y.C., 1950-51; designer Lanz Wallpaper, N.Y.C., 1951-52; gallery asst. Longpre Gallery, La Canada, Calif., 1976-78; pvt. art tchr. La Canada, Calif., 1985—; pres. Elly's Originals, La Canada, 1980—. One-woman shows include La Canada, Calif., 1984, Barbara's Gallery, Agoura, Calif., 1989, Pasadena Livery Gallery, 1996, Holly St. Bar and Grill, Pasadena, 1999; group shows include Hasenbein Gallery, Glendale, Calif., 1978, White's Gallery, Montrose, Calif., 1980, Graphic Showcase Gallery, Pas, Calif., 1985, Artistic Endeavors Gallery, Simi Valley, Calif., 1987, Mission West Gallery, South Pasadena, Calif., 1991; commns. include paintings for Alpha Therapeutic, Pasadena, 1980, Shannon Interiors, Pasadena, 1988-92; contbr. reproductions to Cal. Art Rev. 1989. Recipient Cert. of Honor, Centre Internat. D'Art Contemporain, Paris, 1984. Mem. Verdugo Hills Art Assn. (awards 1988-94). Republican. Roman Catholic. Home: 784 Saint Katherine Dr La Canada Flintridge CA 91011-4119

DRENNAN-TAYLOR, JOAN MARIE, director; b. DeQuincy, La., June 4, 1942; d. Cute Ethelbert and Debra (Wincey) Hyatt; m. Troy Comer Drennan, Dec. 19, 1965 (dec. Nov. 1970); 1 child, Lisa Marie; m. Bill D. Taylor, May 8, 1993; 1 child, Thomas D. B in Music Edn., S.W. Tex. State U., 1965, M in Elem. Edn., 1966; postgrad., U. Colo., 1989, U. Wis., 1990. Classroom tchr. Schertz (Tex.)-Cibolo U.C. Ind. Sch. Dist., 1964-71; elem. tchr. San Antonio Ind. Sch. Dist., 1971-91, grade level chairperson, 1971-81, acad. coord., 1981-91, math./sci. specialist, 1991-92, implementation coord. project 2061, 1991-94; dir. project 2061 San Antonio Ind. Sch. Dist., of the AAAS, 1995—; program mgr. San Antonio New Schs. Devel. Found., 1992—, documentation coord., 1993—. Bd. dirs. Rockefeller Grant for San Antonio Ind. Sch. Dist., 1994—; team mem. Project 2061, San Antonio, 1989—; program com. Conf. for Advancement of Math Tchg., San Antonio, 1994—; presenter in field. Author: Texas Elementary Science Inservice Program, 1990-91; author/editor curriculum model/curriculum, 1989—. Bd. dirs. Young Adult Literacy League, San Antonio, 1993—; mem. San Antonio 2000, 1993—. Named Tchr. of Yr. San Antonio Tchrs. Coun., 1984, Friend of Edn. PTA, 1985. Mem. NEA, Tex. State Tchrs. Assn. (del.), San Antonio Tchrs. Coun. (rep. 1984), Nat. Coun. of Supv. of Math., Nat. Coun. of Tchr. of Math., Tex. Aviation Coun., Nat. Coun. of Staff Devel., Tex. Assn. of Supervision and Curriculum Specialists, Assn. of Supervisors and Curriculum Specialists, Sci. Tchrs. of Tex. Assn., Nat. Sci. Tchrs. Assn., Tex. Assn. of Gifted and Talented, Alamo Dist. of Tchrs. of Math., Delta Kappa Gamma. Mem. Ch. of Christ. Avocations: singing, playing organ, fishing, computers. Home: 17330 Lookout Rd Selma TX 78154-9505 Office: Project 2061 San Antonio Ctr 1305 W Durango Blvd San Antonio TX 78207-3935

DRENNON-GALA, DONNEY THOMAS, sociologist, educational consultant, writer; b. Rochester, N.Y., Dec. 20, 1953; s. Donney Lamar and Anna Marie Drennon; m. Katy Rodriguez Gala, May 10, 1980; stepchildren: William G. Bosch, Stephen Bosch, S. Anita Bosch. AAS, Monroe C.C., Rochester, 1974; BS, Rochester Inst. Tech., 1978; MA, U. Ctrl. Okla., 1982; MS in Edn., U. Rochester, 1988, PhD, 1994. Fed. officer Fed. Bur. Prisons, U.S. Dept. Justice, 1983-85, correctional treatment specialist, 1989—; pres. Paragon Homes, Inc., Rochester, N.Y., 1985-88; exec. dir. Fundamental Rsch. and Evaln. in Edn., Inc., Chattanooga, 1999—. Mem. bd. Chattanooga Area Law Enforcement Commn., 1991-2000; assoc. prof. U. N.C., Fayetteville (N.C.) State U., 1995-97; owner, ednl. cons., sociologist practitioner Drennon-Gala & Assocs., Chattanooga, 1995—. Reviewer Free Inquiry in Creative Sociology, 1992—; author: Delinquency and High School Dropouts: Reconsidering Social Correlates, 1995; assoc. editor Free Inquiry in Creative Sociology, 1996—99; contbr. Myth or Fact: The Relationship Between Family Structure and Delinquency - Some Implications, 1997; contbr.: Sociological Abstracts, 1997, Sociol. Practice, 1999—, Tchg. Sociology, 1999—, Social Commentary, 1999—; contbr. Controlling Violence By Defusing An Incident and The Fed. Disciplinary Process, 2001; Corrections: A Comprehensive View, 2001, Educating All Learners: Refocusing on the Comprehensive Support Model, 2002, Free Inquiry in Creative Sociology, 2002—; contbr. Educating All Children: Future Prospects, 2002, Refocusing On the Comprehensive Support Model, 2002. Bd. dirs. Friends of Moccasin Bend Nat. Park, Chattanooga, 1997—. Sgt. USAF, 1976-80, sgt. USAFR, 1980-82. Master: Masons; mem.: Soc. Profl. Journalists, The Authors Guild, Inc., Acad. Criminal Justice Scis., Am. Correctional Assn. (profl. II), Am. Soc. Criminology, Am. Sociol. Assn., Pi Gamma Mu, Kappa Delta Pi, Alpha Phi Sigma. Avocation: writing. Office: PO Box 302 Chattanooga TN 37343-0302 E-mail: ddgala@doctor.com., ddgala1@comcast.net.

DRESBACH, DAVID PHILIP, financial consultant, educator; b. Columbus, Ohio, Feb. 23, 1947; s. Donald Philip and Marilyn Jo (Armstrong) D.; m. Vicki Elaine Smith, Feb. 25, 1966 (div. 1980); children: Chad, Andrew; m. Mary Louise Mathes, Nov. 29, 1980. MA, Ohio U., 1972. Adminstr. Ohio Univ., Athens, 1969-73; regional mgr. State of Ohio, Columbus, 1973-77, adminstr., 1977-79, State of Minn., St. Paul, 1979-82; mgr. Evensen Dodge, Inc., Mpls., 1983-84, v.p., 1985-93, Springsted, Inc., St. Paul, 1993-95, coord. higher edn. group, 1993-95, newsletter editl. bd. mem., 1994; pres. Dresbach & Assocs., Inc., St. Paul, 1995—; sr. v.p. Evensen Dodge Investment Advisors, 2000—03, mgr., 2001—03; sr. mng. cons. Pub. Fin. Mgmt., 2003—. Lectr., adj. prof. Ohio U., Athens, 1969-74, Franklin U., Columbus, 1975, Columbus Tech. Inst., 1976-79, Met. State U., Mpls., 1980, U. Minn., Mpls., 1980-84. Author poetry anthologies, 1970, 90, 91, 93; contbr. articles to profl. jours. Soccer coach, chmn. Grove City Kids Assn., 1977-79; chmn. Dakota County Solid Waste Mgmt. Com., Minn, 1999—. Named Boss of Yr. Am. Businesswomen's Assn., St. Paul, 1980. Mem. Nat. Coun. Higher Edn. Loan Programs, Minn. Soc. Inst. CFPs (bd. dirs.), Am. Assn. Individual Investors, Fin. Planning Assn., Minn. Fin. Planning Assn. (pres. 2000, chair 2001, chair Dakota County Solid Waste Mgmt. adv. com. 2000-), Mpls. Inst. Art, Acad. Am. Poets. Avocations: reading, oil painting, sailing, golf. Office: Dresbach & Assocs Inc 710 Mager Ct Ste 100 Saint Paul MN 55118-4356 E-mail: DPandme@worldnet.att.net.

DRESBACH, MARY LOUISE, state educational administrator; b. St. Paul, Feb. 17, 1950; d. Ernest Joseph and Kathryn Marion (Lauer) Mathes; m. David Philip Dresbach, Nov. 29, 1980. BA, Coll. St. Catherine, 1972; postgrad., U. St. Thomas, 1979-80; MA, Coll. of St. Catherine, 1995. Tchr. St. Paul Pub. Schs., 1974-78; dir. cmty. outreach, human resources and agy. svcs. Minn. Higher Edn. Svcs. Office, St. Paul, 1978—. Speaker Minn. Quality Conf., 1994, chair, 1996. Contbg. author Leading Edge Newsletter. Mem. exec. steering com. Minn. Quality Coll., 1998. Mem.: Assn. for Psychol. Type, Internat. Pers. Mgmt. Assn. (Minn. chpt.), Minn. Coun. Mgrs. (chair 1998), Minn. Ctr. for Women in Govt., Dakota County Quality Initiative, Dakota County Quality Coun., Minn. Quality Initiative, Am. Soc. for Quality, Nat. Assn. Exec. Women, Am. Bus. Womens Assn. (sec. 1979—80), Citizens League-Minn., Met. Mus. Art, Mpls. Inst. Arts, AAUW, Pi Gamma Mu, Phi Beta Kappa.

DRESCHER, SEYMOUR, history educator, writer; b. N.Y.C., Feb. 20, 1934; s. Sidney and Eva Rita (Levine) D.; m. Ruth Lieberman, June 19, 1955; children: Michael, Jonathan, Karen. BA, CCNY, 1955; MS, U. Wis., 1956, PhD, 1960. Instr. history Harvard U., 1960—62; asst. prof. U. Pitts., 1962—65, assoc. prof., 1965—69, prof., 1969—86, Univ. prof., 1986—, chmn., 1980—83; acad. dean. semester-at-sea, 1998, 2002. Vis. disting. prof. CUNY, 1987; Roger T. Anstey Meml. lectr., Canterbury, Eng., 1984; bd. advisors Slavery and Abolition, 1985—; George A. Miller lectr., 1987, Pa. Commonwealth Speakers Program, 1989-91, rsch. fellow Univ. Ctr. Internat. Studies, Pitts., 1992, 00; C-SPAN adv. com., Tocqueville. Author: Toqueville and England, 1964, Dilemmas of Democracy, 1968, Econocide, 1977, Capitalism and Antislavery, 1986, From Slavery to Freedom, 1999, The Mighty Experiment: Free Labor versus Slavery in British Emancipation, 2002; co-author: The Abolition of Slavery and the Aftermath of Emancipation in Brazil, 1988; editor Jour. Contemporary History, 1991-99; editor: Tocqueville and Beaumont on Social Reform, 1968, Anti-Slavery, Religion and Reform, 1980, Political Symbolism in Modern Europe, 1982, The Meaning of Freedom, 1992, A Historical Guide to World Slavery, 1998, Slavery, 2001, Tocqueville's Memoir on Pauperism, 1997; contbr.: Fifty Years Later: Antislavery, Capitalism and Modernity in the Dutch Orbit, 1995, Is the Holocaust Unique?, 1996, Jews and the Expansion of Europe to the West, 2001; creator film: Confrontation, Paris, 1968, 70. Recipient Pres.'s Rsch. award U. Pitts., 1992; Fulbright scholar, 1957-58; NEH fellow, 1973-74, Guggenheim Found. fellow, 1977-78, Resident fellow Bellagio Ctr. for Scholars, 1980, 90, Woodrow Wilson fellow, 1983-84, sec. European program Wilson Ctr., 1984-85. Mem. Am. Hist. Assn., Hist. Soc., Soc. for French Hist. Studies (v.p. 1978-79), N.Am. Conf. on Brit. Studies, Dutch Royal Inst. Linguistics and Anthropology, Fulbright Assn., Commn. Tocqueville (France). Home: 5550 Pocusset St Pittsburgh PA 15217-1913 Office: U Pitts Dept History Pittsburgh PA 15260

DRESSELHAUS, MILDRED SPIEWAK, physics and engineering educator; b. Bklyn., Nov. 11, 1930; d. Meyer and Ethel (Teichteil) Spiewak; m. Gene F. Dresselhaus, Aug. 25, 1958; children: Marianne Dresselhaus Cooper, Carl Eric, Paul David, Eliot Michael. BA, Hunter Coll., 1951; DSc (hon.), CUNY, 1982, Hunter Coll., 1982; Fulbright fellow, Cambridge (Eng.) U., 1951—52; MA, Radcliffe Coll., 1953; PhD in Physics, U. Chgo., 1958; D Engring. (hon.), Worcester Poly. Inst., 1976; DSc (hon.), Smith Coll., 1980, Hunter Coll., 1982, N.J. Inst. Tech., 1984; DHC (hon.), U. Catholique de Louvain, 1988; DSc (hon.), Rutgers U., 1989, U. Conn., 1992, U. Mass., Boston, 1992, Princeton U., 1992; DEngring, Colo. Sch. Mines, 1993; D (hon.), Technion, Israel Inst. Tech., Haifa, 1994; DHC (hon.), Johannes Kepler U., Linz, Austria, 1993; DSc (hon.), Harvard U., 1995, Ohio State U., 1998; PhD (hon.), U. Paris, Sorbonne, 1999; DSc (hon.), Columbia U., 1999; DHC (hon.), Cath. U. Louvain, 2000; DSc (hon.), Northwestern U., 2003. NSF postdoctoral fellow Cornell U., 1958—60; mem. staff Lincoln Lab., MIT, Lexington, 1960—67; prof. elec. engring. MIT, Cambridge, 1968—, assoc. dept. head elec. engring., 1972—74, Abby Rockefeller Mauze chair, 1973—85, dir. Ctr. for Materials Sci. and Engring., 1977—83, prof. physics, 1983—, Inst. prof., 1985—; dir. Office of Science, U.S. Dept. of Energy, Washington, 2000—01. Vis. prof. dept. physics U. Campinas, Brazil, 1971, Technion, Israel, 1972, 90, Nihon and Aoyama Gakuin Univs., Tokyo, 1973, IVIC, Caracas, Venezuela, 1977; vis. prof. dept. elec. engring. U. Calif., Berkeley, 1983; Graffin lectr. Am. Carbon Soc., 1982; chmn. steering com. on evaluation panels Nat. Bur. Stds., 1978—83; mem. Energy Rsch. Adv. Bd., 1984—90; bd. dirs. Rogers Corp. Contbr. articles to profl. jours. Mem. governing bd. NRC, 1984—87, 1989—90, 1992—96; trustee Calif. Inst. Tech., 1993—2000; overseer Harvard U., 1997—2000; chmn. bd. Am. Inst. Physics, 2003—; bd. govs. Argonne Nat. Lab., 1986—89, Weizmann Inst., Rehovot, Israel, 1999—2000, 2001—. Named to Hunter Coll. Hall of Fame, 1972, Women in Tech. Internat. Hall of Fame, 1998; recipient Alumnae medal, Radcliffe Coll., 1973, Killian Faculty Achievement award, 1986—87, Nat. medal of Sci., 1990, Sigri Great Lakes Carbon award, 1997, Profl. Achievement award, Hunter Coll., CUNY, 1998, Nicholson medal, 2000, Karl T. Compton medal, 2001, Weizmann Woman and Sci. Millennial Lifetime Achievement award, 2000, Nat. Materials Advancement award, Fedn. Materials Socs., 2000. Fellow: AAAS (bd. dirs. 1985—89, pres. 1997—98, chair bd. dirs. 1998—99), IEEE, Am. Carbon Soc., Am. Acad. Arts and Scis., Am. Phys. Soc. (pres. 1984); mem.: NAS (coun. 1987—90, chmn. engring. sect. 1987—90, chmn. class III 1990—93, coun. 1992—96, treas. 1992—96), Am. Philos. Soc., Brazilian Acad. Sci. (corr.), Engring. Acad. Japan (fgn. assoc. 1993—), Soc. Women Engrs. (Achievement award 1977), Nat. Acad. Engring. (coun. 1981—87). Office: MIT 77 Massachusetts Ave Rm 13-3005 Dept Elec Engring Cambridge MA 02139

DRESSLER, BRENDA JOYCE, health educator, consultant, book and film reviewer; b. N.Y.C., Jan. 30, 1943; d. Herbert and Betty (Kirshner) Dressler; m. Irving Kaufman, Dec. 30, 1961 (div. Dec. 1979); 1 child, Joshua Ari. BA, CCNY, 1964; MA, CUNY, 1969; PhD, NYU, 1986. Cert. health edn. specialist. (CHES) educator sex and health N.Y.C. Bd. Edn., 1964-75, 1979—; educator sex and health Sex Info. and Edn. Coun. U.S., N.Y.C., 1985-86; assoc. prof. edn. N.Y. Inst. Tech., 1997—. Health cons., 1996—; cons. PTA and curriculum adv. com. Steinway Jr. High Sch., N.Y.C., 1985-87, Bayside High Sch., 1987-90; regional coord. and cons. on family living, Queens, 1990—; comprehensive health coord. high sch. HIV/AIDS Edn., Queens, 1991—; adj. instr. C.W. Post, N.Y. Inst. Tech., 1992—; cons. UFT Tchrs. Ctr. Consortium. Columnist: Women Mean Business; contbr. numerous articles to profl. jours.; curriculum writer HIV/AIDS Edn. K-6; writer instrnl. tng. design on HIV/AIDS; tchr. tng. design HIV/AIDS Edn. 7-9; health counselor, instr. Bayside H.S., HIV/AIDS team leader; adj. instr. NYIT, CW POST. Awards chair Sophe, 1996—. Mem. Am. Bd. Sexology, Soc. Phys. and Health Edn., Kappa Delta Pi. Avocations: physical fitness training, piano, traveling, cycling, ping pong. Home and Office: 16241 Powells Cove Blvd Whitestone NY 11357-1449

DREW, CLIFFORD JAMES, university administrator, special education and educational psychology educator; b. Eugene, Oregon, Mar. 9, 1943; s. Albert C. and Violet M. (Caskey) D. BS magna cum laude, Eastern Oreg. Coll., 1965; EdM, U.Ill., 1966; PhD (hon.), U. Oreg., 1968. Asst. prof. edn. Kent State U., Ohio, 1968-69; asst. prof. dir. rsch. and spl. edn. U. Tex., Austin, Tex., 1969-71; assoc. prof. spl. edn. U. Utah, Salt Lake City, 1971-76, prof., 1977—; asst. dean Grad. Sch. Edn., 1974-77, assoc. dean, 1977-79, 89-95, prof. spl. edn., edn. psychology, 1979—, coord. instrnl. tech., acad. v.p. office, 1995-97, assoc. acad. v.p., 1997—. Cons. HEW, 1969-80; Bd. dir. Far West Lab. Ednl. Rsch. and Devel., San Francisco, 1974-80; mem. exec. bd. Salt Lake County Assn. Retarded Children, 1971-72; mem. adv. com. Mental Retardation Counseling Svc., Tex. Dept. Mental Health Mental Retardation, 1969-70. Co-author (with P. Chinn and D. Logan): Mental Retardation: A Life Cycle Approach, 1975; author: Intro. to Designing Rsch. and Evaluation, 1976; co-author (with M. Hardman and H. Bluhm): Mental Retardation: Social and Ednl. Perspectives, 1977; co-author: (with M. Hardman and W. Egan) Human Exceptionality: Soc., Sch. and Family, 1984; author: Designing and Conducting Behavioral Rsch., 1985; co-author (with M. Hardman and D. Logan): Mental Retardation: A Life Cycle Approach to People with Intellectual Disabilities, 1988; co-author: (with B. Wampold) Theory and Application of Stats., 1990; co-author: (with M. Hardman and D. Logan) Mental Retardation: A Life Cycle Approach, 1992; co-author: (with M. Hardman and A. Hart) Designing and Conducting Rsch.: Inquiry in Edn. and Social Sci., 1996; co-author: (with M. Hardman and D. Logan) Mental Retardation: A Life Cycle Approach, 1996; co-author: (with M. Hardman), 2000; co-author: (with M. Hardman and W. Egan) Human Exceptionality: Soc., Sch. and Family, 2002; co-author: (with D. Gelfand) Understanding Child Behavior Disorders, 2003; contbr. numerous articles to profl. jour. NDEA fellow, 1965-66; U.S. Office Edn. fellow, 1966-68. Fellow Am. Assn. Mental Retardation; mem. Am. Psychol. Assn.; Am. Ednl. Rsch. Assn. Office: U Utah Acad V P Office 201 Presidents Cir Rm 205 Salt Lake City UT 84112-9007

DREW, JODY LYNNE, secondary education educator; b. L.A., Apr. 12, 1959; d. Marvin Wayne and Patricia Ann (Dozier) D. BA in English, Whitworth Coll., 1981; MA in English, U. Washington, 1990. Cert. tchr., Wash. Tchr. Eastside Catholic H.S., Bellevue, Wash., 1982-87, B.E.S.T. Alternative Sch., Kirkland, Wash., 1987-88, White River H.S., Buckley, Wash., 1989-92, Issaquah (Wash.) H.S., 1992-96, restructuring chair, 1992; tchr. Roosevelt H.S., Seattle, 1996—. Commr. Seattle women's commn. City of Seattle, 1998-99; Officer precinct com. Wash. State Dem. Com., Seattle, 1988-95, mem. McDonnell Project, U. Wash. Mem. ASCD, Nat. Coun. Tchrs. English, Wash. Edn. Assn. (pulse rep. 1992), Issaquah Edn. Assn. (bldg. rep. 1992-96, exec. bd. mem., 1994-96, sr. project coord., 1996), So. Poverty Law Ctr. (tchg. project, leadership conf.). Democrat. Avocations: cycling, rock climbing, spanish language and literature, aids prevention education. Office: Roosevelt HS 1410 NE 66th St Seattle WA 98115-6744

DREW, KATHERINE FISCHER, history educator; b. Houston, Sept. 24, 1923; d. Herbert Herman and Martha (Holloway) Fischer; m. Ronald Farinton Drew, July 27, 1951. BA, Rice Inst., 1944, MA, 1945; PhD, Cornell U., 1950. Asst. history Cornell U., 1948-50; instr. history Rice U., 1946-48, mem. faculty, 1950—, prof. history, 1964—, Harris Masterson, Jr. prof. history, 1983-85, Lynette S. Autrey prof. history, 1985-96, prof. emeritus, 1996—, chmn. dept. history, 1970-80; editor Rice U. (Rice U. Studies), 1967-81, acting dean humanities and social scis., 1973, acting chmn. dept. art and art history, 1996-98. Author: The Burgundian Code, 1949, Studies in Lombard Institutions, 1956, The Lombard Laws, 1973, Law and Society in Early Medieval Europe, 1988, The Laws of the Salian Franks, 1991, also articles; editor: Perspective in Medieval History, 1963, The Barbarian Invasions, 1970; mem. bd. editors Am. Hist. Assn. Guide to Hist. Lit., 1987-94, Am. Hist. Rev. 1982-1985; contbr.: Life and Thought in the Middle Ages, 1967. Guggenheim fellow, 1959; Fulbright scholar, 1965; NEH Sr. fellow, 1974-75 Fellow Mediaeval Acad. Am. (coun. 1974-77, 2d v.p. to pres. 1985-87, del. to Am. Coun. Learned Socs. 1977-81); mem. Am. Hist. Assn. (coun. 1983-86), Am. Soc. Legal History, So. Hist. Assn. (vice chair, chair European sect. 1986-88, exec. com. 1989-91), Phi Beta Kappa. Home: 9333 Memorial Dr # 306 Houston TX 77024-5739 Office: Rice U Dept History MS 42 PO Box 1892 Houston TX 77251-1892 E-mail: kdrew@rice.edu.

DREW, NANCY MCLAURIN SHANNON, counselor, consultant; b. Meridian, Miss., Apr. 29, 1934; d Julian Caldwell and Emma Katherine (Sanders) Shannon; m. Thomas Champion III, Feb. 11, 1956; children: Thomas Champion IV, Julian C. Shannon. BA, Furman U., 1956; MEd, N.C. State U., 1968. Cert. sch. counselor; cert. supr. curriculum and instrn., N.C. Rsch. asst. N.C. State U., Raleigh, 1957-59; tchr. English Raleigh City Schs., 1959-60; dir. guidance program Millbrook Sr. High/Wake County Schs., Raleigh, 1969-77; guidance chmn. Daniels Middle Sch./Wake County Schs., Raleigh, 1977-84, guidance info. specialist, 1984-85; guidance supr. Wake County Pub. Schs., Raleigh, 1985-88; coord. model dropout prevention program Wake County Pub. Sch./State Dept. Pub. Inst., Raleigh, 1985-88; counseling chmn. Garner Middle Sch., Raleigh, 1988-96. Presenter, cons. 1st and 2d Nat. Dropout Prevention Confs., Winston-Salem, N.C., 1986-87, Raleigh, 1986-88, N.C. Sch. Counselors Conf., Raleigh, 1986-88, Am. Pers. and Guidance Assn., 1976, N.C. Mid. Sch. Assn., 1987-88; presenter career workshops ParentScope 1996, speakers' staff ParentScope 1995-96. Contbr. articles to profl. jours. Vice chmn. bd. trustees Crossnore (N.C.) Sch., 1977—; mem. adv. bd. Tamassee DAR Sch., 1994—; sec., bd. dirs. Wake Teen Med. Svcs., Raleigh, 1978-88, Garner Edn. Found., 1991-95; mem. Wake County Bus. and Edn. Leadership Coun., 1992-96, L.L. Polk Found. Named Outstanding Sr. Citizen, Raleigh Jaycees, 1999. Mem. AACD, NEA, DAR (area rep. spkrs. staff N.C. 1995-98, chmn. state DAR sch. com. 1985-88, state editor DAR News 1989-91, 94-97, chpt. regent 1992-95, nat. house com. 1992-94, nat. vice chmn. spl. svcs., state officer 1989-91, dir. dist. VI N.C. State DAR 1992-99, N.C. Outstanding Jr. Mem. 1970, nat. vice chmn. membership 1996-98, nat. vice chmn. DAR sch. com. 1986-89, nat. vice chmn. mem. contest 1998-2001), N.C. Edn. Assn., Am. Sch. Counselors Assn., N.C. Sch. Counselors Assn., Phi Delta Kappa, Delta Kappa Gamma (pres. chpt. 1985-88, state chmn. 1991-93, state com. chmn. 1994-96). Republican. Methodist. Home: 6000 Winthrop Dr Raleigh NC 27612-2142

DREXLER, NORA LEE, retired gifted and talented educator, writer, illustrator; b. Bellefonte, Pa., Nov. 17, 1947; d. Bengt Gerdis and Leanore Francis (Bates) Bjalme; m. Raymond George Drexler, June 27, 1970; 1 child, Michelle Ann. BA of Sci., Villa Maria Coll., 1969; MEd, Gannon U., 1974. Tchr. gifted and talented Millcreek Sch. Dist., Erie, Pa., 1969-99; ret., 1999; pres. Drexler Assocs., Inc., 2003—. Founder, nat. program dir. Coalition Pathways, Inc.; computer tech. facilitator World Confs. and Ednl. workshops; vice chair Pennsylvanians Against Underage Drinking; presenter AMA, Parents Resource Inst. for Drug Edn., 2d Comty. Anti Drug Coalition of Am.; cons. White House Office of Nat. Drug Control Policy, Nat. Youth Anti-Drug Media Campaign, Ctr. for Substance Abuse Prevention, Office of Juvenile Justice and Delinquency Prevention, cons., trainer, Ctr for Substance Abuse Prevention, Nat. Guard Northeast Counter Drug Training Ctr. Recipient 1st Pl. Nat. award for outstanding coalition 1997, Comty. Anti Drug Coalitions of Am., 1997, 1st. Pl. Nat. award Nat. Commn. Against Drunk Driving, 1997, DUI Leadership award, citations Pa. Ho. of Reps. and Pa. Senate, Nat. Exemplary Program award Ctr. for Substance Abuse Prevention, 1999, Disting. Alumni award Gannon U., 2000, Nat. award Nat. Hwy. Traffic Safety Adminstrn., 2001. Mem. NEA, Pa. Edn. Assn. Millcreek Edn. Assn. Democrat. Roman Catholic. Avocations: writing, drawing, pet dog. Home: 5639 Mill St Erie PA 16509-2923 E-mail: ndrexler@erie.net.

DREYFUSS, M(AX) PETER, research chemist, educator; b. Frankfurt, Germany, Sept. 24, 1932; came to U.S., 1938; s. Fritz David and Charlotte Pauline Dreyfuss; m. Patricia Marie Gajewski, Jan. 30, 1954; children: David Daniel, Simeon Karl. BS, Union Coll., 1952; PhD, Cornell U., 1957. Postdoctoral fellow U. Liverpool, Eng., 1963-65; sr. rsch. chemist B.F. Goodrich Co., Brecksville, Ohio, 1956-63, rsch. assoc., 1965-73, sr. rsch. assoc., 1973-81, sr. R&D assoc. Avon Lake, Ohio, 1982-84; sr. rsch. scientist, rsch. prof. Mich. Molecular Inst., Midland, 1984-90, adj. prof., 1986-92, Mich. Technol. U., Houghton, 1986-91, Cen. Mich. U., Mt. Pleasant, 1987-96. Vis. prof. Polish Acad. Scis., Poland, 1974; cons. in field. Contbr. over 25 articles to profl. jours., books. Leader Boy Scouts Am., Akron, Ohio, 1965-70, explorer advisor, 1970-81. Mem. Am. Chem. Soc. (treas. Akron ch. 1981, chmn. Midland ch. 1991), Phi Beta Kappa. Achievements include 5 patents in field; development of living oxonium ion polymerization. Home and Office: 3980 Old Pine Trl Midland MI 48642-8891

DREZDZON, WILLIAM LAWRENCE, retired mathematics educator; b. Feb. 19, 1934; Math. and computer sci. Oakton C.C., Des Plaines; paralell programmer FERMI Lab, Batavia, Ill. Home: 1600 Ashland Ave Des Plaines IL 60016-6606

DRIES, COLLEEN PATRICIA, adult education educator; b. Lansing, Mich., Apr. 15, 1948; d. Peter C. and Mary Alice (Campion) D. BA, St. Louis U., 1971; postgrad., U. Ill.; MA, Bradley U., 1996. Cert. elem. edn., secondary edn., ESL edn., gen. adminstrn. Elem., mid. and jr. high sch. tchr. Holy Family Grade Sch., Peoria, Ill., 1973—76; tchr. Peoria Pub. Schs., 1977—, ESL tchr., GED tchr.; prin. Adult Edn. & Family Literacy Ctr. Tchr.

adult basic edn., mem. Peoria Pub. Schs. Adult Edn. Task Force; mem. Commn. on Adult Basic Edn., region 4 rep., 1994-96, nominations and elections com., 1996. Mem. Gov.'s Parent Sch. Initiative Region 12 Adv. Com., 1993; Ill. rep. to Dept. Edn.'s Nat. Forum on Adult Edn. and Literacy, 1998. Named Ill. Adult Edn. Tchr. of Yr., 1989. Mem.: ASCD, Ill. Adult and Continuing Educators Assn. (regional dir. 1987—91, conf. chair 1991—92, conf. com. 1991—2002, pres. 1992—93, nomination and elections chair 1993—94, membership chair 1994—98, legis. chair 1994—, Ill. adult edn. adv. com. 1997—99, com. to advance adult edn. funding 2000—02, legis co-chair 2003—, Pres. award outstanding contbns. to adult edn. in Ill. 1995), Ctrl. Ill. Addv. Edn. Svc. Ctr. (GED adv. com.), Nat. Coun. Tchrs. English, Am. Assn. Adult and Continuing Edn. (nominations and elections com. 1996, mem. adult basic edn.), Internat. Reading Assn. Home: 107 Terrace Ln East Peoria IL 61611-2164 Office: 839 W Moss AVe Peoria IL 61606 E-mail: cpdries@yahoo.com.

DRIGGS, MARGARET, educator; b. Kansas City, Kans., June 30, 1909; d. William Foster and Lillian Edith (Landers) Brazier; m. J.W. Quarrier, Nov. 26, 1933 (div. July 1945); children: John Chilton, Philip Harrington, Camille Elizabeth; m. Howard R. Driggs, Sept. 26, 1948 (dec.). AB, U. Kans., 1930; postgrad., Hofstra Coll., 1960, Grad. Sch. Libr. Sci., Pratt Inst., 1964-65. Adminstrv. asst. to sec., dir. pub. rels. Hofstra Coll., 1956-61, staff adivser Nexus (yrbook.), 1961; mem. faculty Westover Sch., Middlebury, Conn., 1964-65; dir. devel. pub. rels., asst. to dean Cathedral Sch. of St. Mary, Garden City, N.Y., 1965, also yrbook adviser. Nat. dir. pub. rels. Am. Pioneer Trails Assn., 1948; chmn. pub. rels. NYU Faculty Women's Club, 1950-54; nat. 1st v.p. Assn. parents and Friends Kings Point, 1957-58; judge Nat. Svc. Acad. Debate Tournament, 1956; hostess Kings Point Congl. com., 1957; installed Duchess of Richelieu collection St. Mary's Libr., 1973; co-chmn. Guides N.J. Gov.'s Mansion Morven, 1975-82. Contbr. Kansas City Star and Johnson County (Kans.) Herald, 1930-33; editor Am. Trails Series filmstrips; curator Driggs Collection of Americana; represented in Native N. Am. Women Exhbn., Skillman Libr., Lafayette Coll., 1992; editor: New Light on Old Glory, 1950, Pitch Pine Tales, 1951, Nick Wilson, 1951, George, The Handcart Boy, 1952,The Old West Speaks, 1956, When Grandfather was a Boy and Western Cowkid, 1957 (all by Howard R. Driggs); contbg. editor Nat. Assn. Ind. Schs. Archives, Harvard, 1965; editor and photographer Vive Rochambeau, Vive Washington. Chmn. docents N.J. Hist. Soc. at Morven, Princeton, 1982-86; mem. women's coun. Hofstra Coll., 1959-60; mem. U.S. Com. for UN Children's Fund, 1957; mem. Friends of Princeton U. Libr., 1975, Friends of the Winston Churchill Meml. and Libr., Westminster Coll., 1989; mem. Princeton Med. Ctr. Aux.; chmn. Civilian Hostesses 15th Ann. U. S. Army Mus. Conf., Princeton, 1986, Salute to Hall of Fame Ceremony the Voice of Am. Broadcast, Gould Meml. Libr., NYU, 1953; mem. Am. Farm Trust, 1992; mem. Denver Pub. Libr. Friends Found. Recipient Disting. Svc. Citatin Am. Pioneer Trails Assn., 1943, Columbia Scholastic Press Assn. medal, 1970, pin for vol. work in Princeton, 1976, French-Am Alliance medal, cert. and hist. house tile award N.J. Hist. Soc., 1984; Margaret Brazier Driggs Collection of Americana established at U. Kans., 1953, Hofstra Coll., 1961. Mem. Hist. Soc. Gov.'s Mansion Guides, Internat. Platform Assn., Assn. Coll. and Rsch. Librs., Hist. Soc. Princeton, Nat. Trust Hist. Preservation, Smithsonian Assocs., Nat. Parks and Conservatin Assn., Women's Bd. N.J. Hist. Soc., Smithsonian Nat. Mus. of Am. Indian (charter 1999), Met. Mus. Art, Women's Coll. Club Princeton, Woodrow Wilson Internat. Ctr. for Scholars (assoc. 1999), Amiga of Orgn. of Am. States, NYU Faculty Club (hon., life), Libr. of Congress (charter assoc. 1994), Present Day Club (Princeton), Gold Medal Club, Learned Club, Pi Delta Epsilon (grand councilman 1960-61). Home: 2943 W 116th Pl Apt 107 Denver CO 80234-2519

DRISCOLL, BARBARA HAMPTON, special education educator; b. Natchitoches, La., July 25, 1949; d. Rick Hampton and Frances (Lovell) Davis; children: Kelli Anne, Christopher Mark. BS, Northwestern State U., 1970; MEd in Adminstrn., U. Miss., Oxford, 1977; EdS, Northwestern State U., 1988. Prin. Proprietary Bus. Sch., Shreveport, La., 1979-80; curriculum cons. St. John Berchman's Sch., Shreveport, 1987-88; tchr. severely emotionally disturbed adolescents Caddo Parish Pub. Schs., Shreveport, 1983—2001, 1983-87, juvenile delinquency residential facility tchr., 1987-96, tchr. mild/moderately handicapped, 2001—; pvt. cons. for exceptional children, 1987—. Tchr. Boyce (La.) High Sch., 1970-71, John H. Martyn Vocat.-Tech. High Sch., New Orleans, 1971-73, Northwestern State U., Natchitoches, 1977-78; minister to children Kings Hwy. Christian Ch., 2000—. Mem. bd. deaconesses Kings Hwy. Christian Ch., Shreveport, 1987-91; vol. Hospitality House, Shreveport, 1985-88; active local campaigns, Shreveport, 1980; vol., leader Girl Scouts U.S., Shreveport, 1986-89; asst., vol. Boy Scouts Am., Shreveport, leader, 1986—. Mem. ASCD, Coun. for Exceptional Children, Coun. for Children with Behavioral Disorders. Mem. Christian Ch. (Disciples Of Christ). Avocations: reading, crossword puzzles, church activities. Home: 513 Wayne Shreveport LA 71105-3025 Office: Kings Highway Christian Church 806 Kings Hwy Shreveport LA 71104 E-mail: barbarahampton-driscoll@juno.com.

DRISCOLL, CONSTANCE FITZGERALD, education educator, writer, consultant; b. Lawrence, Mass., Mar. 29, 1926; d. John James and Mary Anne (Leecock) Fitzgerald; m. Francis George Driscoll, Aug. 21, 1948; children: Frances Mary, Martha Anne, Sara Helene, Maribeth Lee. AB, Radcliffe Coll., 1946; postgrad., Harvard U., U. Hartford, U. Bridgeport, U. Mass. Secondary sch. tchr., North Andover, Mass., 1946-48; book reviewer N.Y.C. and Boston pubs., 1955-64; asst. conf. edn. dir. U. Hartford, 1964-68; lectr. Pace U., N.Y.C., 1973-74; edn. commentary Radio WVOX, New Rochelle, N.Y., 1974-75; asst. ednl. adv. Nat. Girl Scouts, 1972-74; pres., owner, dir. Open Corridor Schs. Cons., Inc., Bronxville, N.Y., 1972-84; pres., dir. Open Corridor Schs., Inc., Oxford, Mass., 1984—2003, Sarasota and Jacksonville, Fla., 2003—, Bradenton, Fla., 2003—. Dir. assoc. grad. edn. program with U. Hartford, Bronxville, N.Y., 1975-82; dir. grad. edn. program Witt U. Bridgeport, Greenwich, Conn., 1975-82; creator in svc. edn. programs pub. schs., Norwalk, Conn., 1983-88; assoc. Worcester State Coll., 1984-85, Fitchburg State Coll., 1986-87; dir. assoc. grad. edn. for tchrs. Anna Maria Coll., Paxton, Mass., 1990-94; assoc. grad. tchr. edn. courses Fitchburg State Coll., 1995-99; English instr. grades 9-12, Bais Chana H.S. for Girls, Worcester, Mass., 2000—; provider long distance learning grad. edn. courses, Antigua and Anguilla, 1997—, U. Bridgeport, Conn., 1995—, assoc. agy. for grad. edn. courses for tchrs., 1995—; profl. devel. points provider Mass. State Dept. Edn., 1995—; tutor, cons. Worcester County Sch. Dists., 1989-95; CEU mgr. for Conn. Dept. Edn. O.C.S., Inc., Conn., 1989—; bi-lingual instr. for Indian and Vietnamese students in grades 5-12, 1988-91; freelance writer newspapers and small jours., 1991—; dir. grad. edn. courses for tchrs. Mass. Coll. Liberal Arts, North Adams, Mass., 1999—; cons. coll./univ. and grad. sch. placement, admissions procedures, 2000—; adviser, cons. Radcliffe Coll. Admissions Coun., 1946-48; summer dir. swim program ARC, North Andover, Mass., 1942-47; cons. Girl Scouts U.S., health guide multicultural program Greater Lawrence, Mass., 1946-48, holiday radio program, Thanksgiving 1774, Antigua and Barbuda; lectr., series for Girl Guides, Antigua, W.I., Nov., 1974. Author curriculum materials; contbr. poetry to Poetry Corner in The Patriot newspaper, 1994—, others. Recipient Educator award Nat. Coun. ARC, Washington, 1985, Edn. award Nipmuc Am. Indian Coun., Webster, Mass., 1985. Office: Open Corridor Schs Inc 3522 53d Ave W Ste 160 Bradenton FL 34210 also: Open Corridor Schs Inc 1015 Atlanta Blvd Ste 273 Atlantic Beach FL 32233

DRISCOLL, DAVID P. commissioner, educator; BS in Math., Boston Coll.; PhD in Ednl. Adminstrn., Boston Coll; MS in Ednl. Adminstrn., Salem State Coll. Math. tchr. Jr. HS, Somerville, Mass., Sr. H.S., Melrose, Mass.; supt. schs. Melrose, 1984—93; dep. commr. schs. State of Mass., 1993—99; commr. dept. edn. Mass., 1999—. Prin. investigator in Mass. NSF Math. and Sci. Program; co-developer five year master plan Mass. Dept. Edn., 1995; mem. oversight bds. School to Work Initiative, Mass.; chmn. Mass. Tchrs. Retirement Bd., 1998—. Office: Mass Dept Edn 350 Main St Malden MA 02148-5023

DRISCOLL, VIRGILYN MAE (SCHAETZEL), retired art educator, artist, consultant; b. Fond du Lac, Wis., May 14, 1932; d. Edward William and Louise (Heider) Schaetzel; m. Patrick A. Driscoll, Aug. 13, 1955; children: Mark P., Craig A., Chris T. BS in Art Edn., Wis. State Coll., 1954; MS in Art, U. Wis., Milw., 1973. Tchr. elem. art Green Bay (Wis.) Pub. Schs., 1954-55, Elm-Brook Pub. Schs., Elm Grove, Brookfield, Wis., 1955-58, supr. elem. art, 1958-66; tchr. secondary art, dept. chair Greendale (Wis.) Pub. Schs., 1967—93; exec. dir. Wis. Alliance Arts Edn., 1993—2000; dir., co-founder Wis. Champions for Arts Edn. Bus. and Cmty. Advs., Inc., 2002—. Arts Edn. Cons., 2000—; art curriculum task force Wis. Dept. Pub. Instrn., 1981—85; mem. task force Wis. Plan Arts Edn., Arts in Sch.s Basic Edn. Grant, 1986—88; mem. State Supts. Commn. Arts Edn., 1988—89; coord. Student Art Exhibit Wis. Assn. Sch. Bd. Joint Conv., 1988—; mem. steering com. arts edn. Wis. Arts Bd., Wis. Alliance Arts Edn., Dept. Pub. Instrn., 1992—; chmn. Wis. Challenging Content Stds. in Arts, 1994—96; coord., facilitator State Supt.'s Blue Ribbon Commn. Arts Edn., 1999—2000; mem. task force Wis. Dept. Pub. Instrn. Integrated Curriculum Guide, 1999—2000; hon. bd. dirs. Wis. Alliance Arts Edn., 2000—. Mem. editl. bd. Spectrum: Jour. Wis. Art Edn., 1986—87, 1988—90; author: (handbook) National Year of Secondary Art, 1990. Named Educator of the Yr., Beloit (Wis.) Coll., 1986, Wis. Rep. Tchr. Inst., 50th Ann. Nat. Gallery Art, Washington, 1991; recipient Excellence in the Arts award, 2000, cert. of Recognition in the Arts and Art Edn., 2000, Disting. Alumnus award, U. Wis., 2001, Distinction award for Dance Edn., 2002. Mem.: NEA, Milw. Area Tchrs. Art (pres. 1982—83), Wis. Painters and Sculptors, Wis. Alliance Art Edn. (pres. 1991—, bd. dirs.), Wis. Art Edn. Assn. (mem. adv. bd. Young Artists Workshop 1982—99, pres. 1985—87, 1987—89, mem. coun., Wis. Art Educator of the Yr. 1989, Career award 2000—), Nat. Art Edn. Assn. (bd. dirs. 1984—89, secondary divsn. dir., mem. exec. com. 1989—91, We. Region Art Educator of Yr. 1990), U. Wis. Milw. Alumni Assn. (1st v.p. 1966—73, pres. 1968—69, pres., emeritus bd. trustee 1996—2000, emeritus trustee 2000—, co-chair Chancellor's Soc. 2000—03, bd. dirs. womens alumni). Avocation: running. Home: 1161 N Lost Woods Rd Oconomowoc WI 53066-8790

DRISKELL, CHARLES MARK, principal; b. El Paso, Tex., July 22, 1957; s. Charles Patrick and Marylee (Lindsay) D.; m. Vicki Driskell; children: Quentin Patrick, Lisa, Charlotte, Sarah. BS in Animal Sci., Sul Ross State U., 1979, MS in Animal Sci., 1986, MEd, 1989. Cert. vocat. agrl. mid-mgr., Tex. Tchr. agrl. sci. Crosbyton (Tex.) Ind. Sch. Dist., 1980-88; prin. Southland (Tex.) Ind. Sch. Dist., 1988-90; asst. prin. Littlefield (Tex.) Ind. Sch. Dist., 1990-91, prin., 1991—. Dist. chair discipline com. Littlefield Ind. Sch. Dist., 1992-93, textbook com., 1992-93. Mem. ASCD, Nat. Assn. Secondary Sch. Prins., Tex. Assn. Curriculum Devel., Tex. Assn. Secondary Sch. Prins., Rotary. Home: 13307 Bandera Dr Amarillo TX 79111-1416 Office: Littlefield High Sch 1100 Waylon Jennings Blvd Littlefield TX 79339

DRISKELL, CLAUDE EVANS, college director, educator, dentist; b. Chgo., Jan. 13, 1926; s. James Ernest and Helen Elizabeth (Perry) D., Sr.; m. Naomi Roberts, Sept. 30, 1953; 1 child, Yvette Michele; stepchildren: Isaiah, Ruth, Reginald, Elaine. BS, Roosevelt U., 1950; BS in Dentistry, U. Ill., 1952, DDS, 1954. Practice dentistry, Chgo., 1954—; adj. prof. Chgo. State U., 1971—; dean's aide, adviser black students Coll. Dentistry U. Ill., 1972—. Dental cons., supervising dentist, dental hygienists supportive health services Bd. Edn., Chgo., 1974. Author: The Influence of the Halogen Elements Upon the Hydrocarbon, and their Effect on General Anesthesia, 1962; History of Chicago's Black Dental Professionals, 1850-1983; co-author (with Claude Driskell) Essays on Professor Dr. Earl Renfroe-A Man of Firsts, 2001; author, editor and publisher: Original Forty Club's 75th Anniversary Book (1920-1995); author, editor, archivist, historian Forty Club, 1993-2000; mem. editl. bd. Nat. Dental Assn. Quar. Jour., 1977—; contbr. articles to profl. jours. Vice pres. bd. dirs. Jackson Park Highlands Assn., 1971-73. Served with AUS, 1944-46; ETO. Fellow Internat. Biog. Assn., Royal Soc. Health (Gt. Britain), Acad. Gen. Dentistry; mem. Lincoln Dental Soc. (editor), Chgo. Dental Soc., ADA, Nat. Dental Assn. (editor pres.'s newsletter; dir. pub. relations, publicity; recipient pres.'s spl. achievement award 1969) dental assns., Am. Assn. Dental Editors, Acad. Gen. Dentistry, Soc. Med. Writers, Soc. Advancement Anesthesia in Dentistry, Omega Psi Phi. Home: 6727 S Bennett Ave Chicago IL 60649-1031 Office: 11139 S Halsted St Chicago IL 60628-3910

DRIVER, MARTHA WESTCOTT, English language educator, writer, researcher; b. N.Y.C., Oct. 24; d. Albert Westcott and Martha Louise (Miller) D.; m. Thomas Edward Earl Rhodes, Aug. 4, 2001. BA, Vassar Coll., 1974; MA, U. Pa., 1975, PhD, 1980. Lectr. English Vassar Coll., N.Y.C., 1980-81; from asst. prof. to assoc. prof. Pace U., N.Y.C., 1981-95, prof. English, 1995—2003, Disting. prof. English, 2003—, dir. honors program, 1998-2000. Cons. N.Y. Pub. Libr., 1984; seminar participant Folger Inst., Folger Shakespeare Libr., 1994. Editor: Jour. of the Early Book Soc., 1998—2003; guest editor: Film & History: The Middle Ages, 1998—99, Literary and Linguistic Computing, 1999; contbr. 35 articles to profl. jours. Mem., lectr. St. John the Divine, N.Y.C., 1995. Recipient Dyson Achievement award, 2003; grantee Rsch. tools grantee, NEH, 1995, travel grantee, Am. Coun. Learned Socs., 1995, NSF, 2001—;, Houghton Libr. Harvard U. fellow, 1996—97. Mem. Early Book Soc. (chair 1988—), Coll. Art Assn., Medieval Acad. Am., Modern Humanities Rsch. Assn. (U.K.), Medieval Club of N.Y. (conf. coord. 1989-94. pres. 1987-89), Internat. Ctr. Medieval Art, Internat. Arthurian Soc., Medieval Feminist Art History Project, New Chaucer Soc. Episcopalian. Avocations: dancing, museums, theater, concerts. Office: Pace U English Dept 41 Park Row New York NY 10038-1508 E-mail: mdriver@pace.edu.

DRNEVICH, VINCENT PAUL, civil engineering educator; b. Wilkinsburg, Pa., Aug. 6, 1940; s. Louis B. and Mary (Kutcel) D.; m. Roxanne M. Hosier, Pa., Aug. 20, 1966; children: Paul, Julie, Jenny, Marisa. BSCE, U. Notre Dame, 1962, MSCE, 1964; PhD, U. Mich., 1967. Registered profl. engr., Ky., Ind. Asst. prof. civil engring. U. Ky., Lexington, 1967-73, assoc. prof., 1973-78, prof., 1978-91; chmn. civil engring., 1980-84; acting dean engring. U. Ky., Lexington, 1989-90; prof., head Sch. Civil Engring. Purdue U., West Lafayette, Ind., 1991-2000. Dir. joint hwy. rsch. project Purdue U., 1991-95; pres. Soil Dynamics, Instruments, Inc., West Lafayette, 1974—. Inventor in field. Fellow ASCE (chmn. dept. heads coun. exec. com. 1996-2000, vice chmn. com. on edn.-practitioner interface, 1994-98, Norman medal 1973, Huber Rsch. prize 1980), ASTM (exec. com., tech. editor Geotech. Testing Jour. 1985-89, C.A. Hogentogler award 1979, Merit award 1993, Woodland Shockley award 1996); mem. NSPE, Am. Soc. Engring. Edn. (sec./treas. civil engring. divsn. 1995-98, dir. 1999—, vice chair 2002-03, chair 2003—), Transp. Rsch. Bd., Earthquake Engring. Rsch. Inst., Ind. Soc. Profl. Engrs. (pres. A.A. Potter chpt.), Chi Epsilon (Harold T. Larson award 1985, James M. Robbins award 1989). Roman Catholic. Avocations: golf, fishing. Office: Purdue U 550 Stadium Mall Dr West Lafayette IN 47907-2051

DRNJEVIC, JONATHAN MARK, language educator; b. Phoenix, Dec. 20, 1959; s. Mirko and Ruth Drnjevic. PhD, Ariz. State U., 1997. Faculty assoc. English dept. Ariz. State U., Tempe, Ariz., 1998—, libr. specialist. Mem.: MLA. Lutheran. Home: 4032 E St Joseph Way Phoenix AZ 85018-1102 Personal E-mail: jmd@asu.edu.

DROBAC, NIKOLA (NICK DROBAC), education educator, consultant; b. Rochester, Pa., Feb. 11, 1953; s. Stevan Sr. and Madeline Mildred (Resanovich) D. AS, C.C. of Beaver County, 1975; BS, U. Pitts., 1977; MS, U. So. Calif., 1986. Sr. loss control cons. Fireman's Fund Ins. Cos., Fairfax, Va, 1977-87; risk mgmt. cons. Carnegie-Mellon U., Pitts., 1988-89; ins. mgr. Gen. Nutrition, Inc., Pitts., 1989-90; pers. cons. Tricon Tech., Pitts., 1990-92; lectr. bus. dept. C.C. Beaver County, Monaca, Pa., 1992-93; intermittent intake interviewer unemployment compensation Commonwealth Pa. Dept. Labor and Industry Beaver County Job Ctr., 1992-96; instr. C.C. of Allegheny County, 1994-95; tchr. So. Garrett County H.S., Oakland, Md., 1995—2003; head golf coach So.Garrett County H.S., Oakland, Md., 1995-96; head tennis coach So. Garrett County H.S., Oakland, Md., 1997, asst. mock trial advisor, 2000. Adj. instr. bus./computer applications Garrett C.C., McHenry, Md., 1996, 97. Del. Rep. Presdl. Conv., Washtenaw County, Mich., 1980; vol. basketball coach Carnegie-Mellon U., Pitts., 1988-89; vol. football coach and scout Aliquippa (Pa.) H.S., 1991-92; mem. choir St. Elijah Serbian Orthodox. Ch.; instrument player Kumovi Adult Tamuritzan Group, Pitts. Mem. Masons (Monaca Ctr.), Am. Serbian Eastern Rite Brothers (3d v.p. 1997-99, 2d v.p. 1999-2001, 1st v.p. 2002—), Shriners. Serbian Orthodox. Avocations: computers, golf, photography, church choir. Home: 1616 Tyler St Aliquippa PA 15001-2036 E-mail: professor@beer.com., professor@teachers.org.

DROEGEMUELLER, LEE, state education official; Prof. U. Ariz., 1981—87, U. W. Fla.; commr. edn. Kansas, 1987—95. Office: 9701 Shadow Wood Dr Pensacola FL 32514*

DROEGEMUELLER, WILLIAM, gynecologist, obstetrician, medical educator; b. Chgo., Sept. 7, 1934; s. William Herbert and Florence (Schribner) D.; m. Marlene Koehler; children, Susan Droegemueller Fairholm, Karen. Student, Dartmouth Coll., 1952-53; BA, U. Colo., 1956, MD, 1960. Diplomate Am. Bd. Ob-Gyn. (dir. evaluation 1988—). Intern Cleve. Met. Gen. Hosp., 1960-61; resident U. Colo. Med. Ctr., Denver, 1961-62, 64-66; inst. U. Colo. Med. Sch., Denver, 1965-66, asst. prof. dept. ob-gyn., 1966-70, assoc. prof., 1970-76, prof., vice chmn. dept. ob-gyn., 1976-77; prof., assoc. head dept. ob-gyn. Ariz. Health Scis. Ctr., Tucson, 1977-82; prof., chmn. dept. ob-gyn. U. N.C., Chapel Hill, 1982—96, clin. prof., 1999—. Cons. for gynecology VA Hosp., Denver, 1967-77, VA Hosp., Tucson, 1979-82; faculty sponsor Waring Soc., 1967-72; mem. sci. adv. com. Program for Applied Rsch. on Fertility Regulation, AID, 1972-79, 83-88; chmn. Coun. on Resident Edn. in Ob-Gyn., 1985-87; mem. appeals panel Accreditation Coun. for Grand Med. Edn., 1987-93; trustee Berlex Found., 1987—, chmn. 2002—. Author: (with others) Female Sterilization: Prognosis for Simplified Outpatient Procedures, 1972, Outpatient Surgery, 1973, Controversies in Obstetrics and Gynecology, 1974, Female Sterilization Techniques, 1976, Risks, Benefits and Controversies in Fertility Control, 1978, Reversal of Sterilization, 1978, New Developments in Vaginal Contraception, 1979, Obstetrics and Gynecology, 5th edit., 1986 (also assoc. editor), Controversy in Obstetrics and Gynecology - III, 1983, The Problem Oriented Medical Record for High Risk Obstetrics, 1984, Surgical Decision Making, 3d edit., 1991, Current Therapy, 1986, 91, 92, 02, Comprehensive Gynecology, 1987, 2d edit., 1992, 3rd edit., 1997, 4th edit., 2001; assoc. editor Ob-Gyn. Survey, 1984-91, Ob-Gyn., 1986—, Gynecology and Obstetrics, vol.1, 1981-84; adv. com. on policy Am. Jour. Ob-Gyn., 1982-86, 88-89; editorial adv. bd. Jour. Reproductive Medicine, 1982-85; specialists rev. com. Internat. Jour. Gynaecology and Obstetrics, 1980-86; author or co-author numerous articles in jours. Capt. USAF, 1962-63. Recipient Outstanding Prof. award Jr. Fellows Am. Coll. Ob/Gyn, 1986, Silver and Gold Disting. Alumni award U. Colo. Med. Alumni Assn, 1988, Outstanding Teaching award Chief Residents Dept. Ob/Gyn U. N.C., 1988, 90, Disting. Svc.award, Am. Coll. Ob/Gyn, 1999. Fellow Carolina Population Ctr. (policy bd. mem. 1984-86); Am. Assn. Obstetricians and Gynecologists, Am. Assn. Planned Parenthood Physicians, Assn. Planned Parenthood Profls. (progam com. 1983-85, exec. com. 1983-87, chmn. learning resources commn., 1983-85), Am. Fertility Soc., Am. Gynecol. and Obstet. Soc. (asst. sec. 1985-89), Am. Gynecol. Club, Am. Gynecol. Soc., Assn. Profs. Gynecology and Obstetrics (mem. coun. 1980-83, program chmn. 1984, sec.-treas. 1985-87, pres.-elect 1988, pres. 1989), Cen. Assn. Obstetricians and Gynecologists (bd. trustees 1979-81), Cen. Travel Club, Durham-Orange County Med. Soc., Internat. Family Planning Rsch. Assn., N.C. Med. Soc., N.C. Obstet. and Gynecol. Soc., Obstet. and Gynecol. Travel Club, Robert A. Ross Obstet. and Gynecol. Soc., Soc. of Gynecol. Surgeons, So. Atlantic Assn. Obstetricians and Gynecologists (mem. tech. adv. com. Family Health Internat., 1983—), Am. Coll. Obstetricians and Gynecologists, Phi Beta Kappa, Phi Sigma, Alpha Omega Alpha. Home: 1103 Burning Tree Dr Chapel Hill NC 27517-4005 Office: U NC Sch Med Ob/Gyn Macnider Clb # 7570 Chapel Hill NC 27599-0001

DROKE, EDNA FAYE, elementary school educator, retired; b. Sylvester, Tex., Dec. 4, 1932; d. Ira Selle and Faye Emily (Seckinger) Tucker; m. Louis Albert Droke, June 2, 1951; children: Sherman Ray, Lyndon Allen, Lona Faye Droke Cheairs. BEd, Tarleton State U., Stephenville, Tex., 1983. Cert. ESL and 3d-8th lang. arts tchr., Tex. Tchr. ESL and lang. arts Wingate (Tex.) Ind. Sch. Dist., 1983-86; tchr. 2d grade and ESL Collidge (Tex.) Ind. Sch. Dist., 1986-88; tchr. 4th grade and ESL Peaster (Tex.) Ind. Sch. Dist., 1988-89; tchr. Chpt. I in 1st-6th grades, ESL in K-12th grades Ranger (Tex.) Ind. Sch. Dist., 1989-96, tchr. E.S.L. 3d grade, reading recovery tchr., 1996-98, ret., 1998; substitute tchr. I.S.D., Blanket, Tex.; E.S.L. tchr. 220th CSCD, Comanche, Tex. Tutor Hispanic probationers in English for 220th Dist. Ct., Comanche, Tex., Gustine (Tex.) Ind. Sch. Dist. Reading Improvement, 2000-2003. Mem. ASCD, Kappa Delta Pi, Alpha Chi. Baptist. Avocations: reading, quilting, knitting, playing piano, painting. Home: PO Box 44 Comanche TX 76442-0044

DROMS, WILLIAM GEORGE, finance educator, investment advisor; b. Schenectady, Aug. 20, 1944; s. George William and Frances (Maguire) D.; m. JoAnn Gilberti, June 17, 1967; children: Courtney, Justin. AB, Brown U., 1966; MBA, George Washington U., 1971, DBA, 1975. Chartered financial analyst. Prof. Georgetown U., Washington, 1973—, John J. Powers Jr. Chair prof., 1990—, assoc. dean, faculty chair Sch. Bus., 1978-81, 87-89, 92-94, 98-99. Fin. cons., 1975—; pres. Droms Strauss Advisors, Inc., 1994—. Author: Finance and Accounting for Nonfinancial Managers, 1979, 5th edit., 2003, Dow Jones-Irwin No-Load Mutual Funds, 1984, 85, 86; author: (with others) The Dow Jones Irwin Guide to Personal Financial Planning, 1982, 86, Personal Financial Management, 1982, 86, The Life Insurance Investment Advisor, 1988, Investment Fundamentals, 1994; editor: Asset Allocation for Individual Investors, 1987, Managing a Global Investment Program, 1991; contbr. numerous articles to profl. jours. Lt. USN, 1966-70. Mem. Am. Fin. Assn., Eastern Fin. Assn., Assn. for Investment Mgmt. and Rsch., Fin. Mgmt. Assn., D.C. Soc. Investment Analysts, Cosmos Club. Republican. Roman Catholic. Avocations: tennis, golf. Office: Georgetown U Sch Bus Washington DC 20057-0001 E-mail: dromsw@msb.edu.

DRONET, JUDY LYNN, elementary educator, librarian; b. Kaplan, La., Dec. 9, 1946; d. Percy Joseph and Zula Mae (Harrington) D. BA in Elem. Edn., McNeese State U., 1968, MEd, 1971. Cert. tchr., libr., adminstr., La. Tchr. Shady Grove High Sch., Rosedale, La., 1968-69, Lake Arthur (La.) Elem. Sch., 1969-86, 88-90, Lake Arthur High Sch., 1986-88, 91-92, 1994-95; libr. Henry Heights Elem. Sch., Lake Charles, La., 1992-93, Welsh Elem. Sch., 1993-94, West End Elm. Sch., 1995-96, Northside Jr. HS, 1996—; state assessor, 1997—; tchr. mentor, 1998—. Univ. supr. McNeese State U., Lake Charles, 1990-91, student tchr. supr.; dir. sch. musical prodns., Lake Arthur, 1976-85; judge sci. and social studies fairs, Lake Arthur, 1985-90, math fair, Jeff Davis Parish, 1993; parish com. Sch. Improvement Plan, 1999—; presenter workshops. Coach girls' softball Lake Arthur Jaycees, 1974; mem. Jeff Davis Parish Arts Coun., Jennings, La., 1990—; mem., hostess Friends of Zigler Mus., Jennings, 1990—; state 1st v.p. Bea Davis Leadership Devel., state com. mem. Mem. La. Assn.

Educators, Jeff Davis Parish Assn. Educators (rep.), Calcasieu Parish Assn. Educators, Calcasieu Reading Coun., Women's Libr. Club, Cath. Daus. Am. (sec., regent 1968-93, Dau. of Yr. 1979-80, 93-94), La. Songwriters' Assn. (sec.-treas.), A Block Off Broadway Theater Group (actress, state/props mgr., bd. dirs., choreographer), Delta Kappa Gamma (dist. dir., state chmn., state music rep., state 2nd v.p., Alpha Kappa Golden Apple award, 1999, Epsilon State Achievement award, 2002). Democrat. Roman Catholic. Avocations: oil painting, needlepoint, songwriting, creative writing, singing. Home: PO Box 214 203 Pleasant St Lake Arthur LA 70549-4513

DRONET, VIRGIE MAE, educational technology educator; b. Kaplan, La., Mar. 17, 1941; d. Percy Joseph and Zula Mae (Harrington) D. BS, U. Southwestern La., 1963, MEd, 1970; EdS, McNeese State U., 1976; EdD, East Tex. State U., 1979. Tchr. sci.-math, Lake Arthur, La., 1962-89; asst. instr. Center Ednl. Media and Tech., East Tex. State U., 1977-78, with photog. prodn. lab., 1977-78; tchr. physics, chemistry, biology, algebra, computer scis. Lake Arthur High Sch., 1962-88; prof. McNeese State U., 1998—, head dept. ednl. leadership and instructional tech. Vis. lectr. McNeese State U., 1982-88. Author articles in field; editor La. Deltion, 1981-87. Delta Kappa Gamma scholar, 1973, 77; NSF grantee, 1967, La. grantee, 1990, 96, 2000. Mem. NEA, Assn. Ednl. Comms. and Tech., Nat. Coun. Tchrs. Math., Assn. Supervision and Curriculum Devel., Jefferson Davis Assn. Educators, Catholic Daus. Am., Delta Kappa Gamma (participant leadership seminar Baylor U. 1982), Phi Kappa Phi, Phi Delta Kappa, Kappa Delta Pi, Kappa Mu Epsilon, Alpha Omega, Delta Kappa Gamma (state pres. 1989-91, mem. internat. scholarship com., 1980-82; chmn. internat. rsch. com., 1982-84; chmn. internat. nom. com., 1992; mem. internat. leadership devel. com., 1992-94, internat. constitution com., 1996-98, internat. comm. com., 2000-02). Democrat. Home: PO Box 674 Lake Arthur LA 70549-0674 Office: McNeese State U Coll Edn PO Box 91815 Lake Charles LA 70609-1815 E-mail: vdronet@aol.com.

DROOGER, JACQUELYN MARIE, special education educator; b. Waynesboro, Pa., Mar. 29, 1958; d. Roy Melvin and Alva May (Brady) Newcomer; m. Douglas Mark Drooger, June 6, 1981; children: Marah Ann, Haven Kathleen. BA in Behavioral Sci., Messiah Coll., Grantham, Pa., 1979; MEd, Shippensburg (Pa.) U., 1982. Play therapist George Frey Ctr., Harrisburg, Pa., 1980; tchr. spl. edn. Lincoln Intermediate Unit 12, New Oxford, Pa., 1981—. Mem. Coun. for Exceptional Children, Pa. Edn. Assn. Office: Fairview Elem Sch 122 Fairview Ave Waynesboro PA 17268-1406

DROSSMAN, DOUGLAS ARNOLD, medical investigator, educator, gastroenterologist; b. Bklyn., Mar. 20, 1946; s. Murray and Ruth (Cohen) D.; m. Deborah Risa Ducoff, June 3, 1970; children: David, Daniel. BA cum laude, Hofstra U., 1966; MD, Albert Einstein Coll., 1970. Diplomate Am. Bd. Internal Medicine, Gastroenterology. Intern, resident U. N.C., Chapel Hill, 1970-72; resident N.Y.U.-Bellevue Med. Ctr., N.Y.C., 1972-73; fellow in psychosomatic medicine U. Rochester, N.Y., 1975-76; fellow in gastroenterology U. N.C., Chapel Hill, 1976-78, instr. in medicine, 1977-78, asst. prof. medicine and psychiatry, 1978-83, assoc. prof. medicine and psychiatry, 1983-90, prof. medicine and psychiatry, 1990—. Mem. internship selection com. U. N.C., 1977-84, housestaff-faculty com., 1980-84; health promotion/disease prevention steering com., 1983, co-dir. med.-psychiat. liaison program faculty-resident study group in behavioral medicine, 1977-91; vis. prof. over 100 med. ctrs. and univs.; chair Functional Brain-Gut Rsch. Group, 1989-1993, chair multinat. working teams for diagnosis of functional GE disorders, Rome I, II and III, 1990—, internat. sci. com. Editor: The Functional Gastrointestinal Disorders, 1994, 2d edit., 2000; sect. editor: Functional Brain Gut Rsch. Group Newsletter, 1989—, Participate, 1997—, The Merck Manual, 17th edit., 1999; assoc. editor: Gastroenterology, 2001—; mem. editl. bd. Behavioral Medicine Abstracts, 1985-91, Stress Medicine, 1985-92, Current Concepts Gastroenterology, 1986-90, Jour. Clin. Gastroenterology, 1986—, Psychosomatic Medicine, 1998; ad hoc reviewer over 20 profl. jours.; contbr. over 250 articles to profl. jours., chpts. to textbooks; prodr. 8 ednl. videotapes. Maj. Med. Corps, USAF, 1973-75. Grantee S.S. Zlinkoff Found., 1979, Smith, Kline, Beckman, 1982, NIH, 1983-86, 91-2003, Burroughs Wellcome Co. Inc., 1984-85, Core Ctr. for Diarrheal Diseases, U. NC, 1986, Nat. Found. for Ileitis and Colitis, 1987-88, Bristol-Myers Pharm. Group, 1988-90, Procter & Gamble, 1991, Hoffman La Roche Co., 1991-92, NIMH, 1991-95, Glaxo, 1993—, Sandoz, 1995—, SKB, 1996—, Pfizer, 1997—, others. Fellow ACP (med. knowledge self-assessment program XI 1989-91), Am. Coll. Gastroenterology; mem. Am. Psychosomatic Soc. (councillor 1985-88, 90-92, 1986 program com. 1985-86, chmn. membership com. 1988-92, sec.-treas. 1992-96, pres. 1997-98), Am. Acad. on Phys. and Patient (charter fellow), Am. Fedn. for Clin. Rsch., Am. Gastroenterol. Assn. (program selection com. 1985-86, program selection chmn., coun. co-chair 2001-03, chair nerve-gut 2003—), Am. Soc. for Gastrointestinal Endoscopy, So. Soc. for Clin. Investigation (co-dir. Ctr. Functional GE and Motion Disorders, 1993—, Janssen award for clin. rsch. in gastroenterolgy 1999). Avocations: tennis, magic, jogging. Office: U NC Div Digestive Diseases # 7080 1110 Bioinformatics Bldg Chapel Hill NC 27599-7080

DROZDIK SEASOCK, LORA MARIE, elementary education educator; b. Scranton, Pa., May 15, 1967; d. Andrew and Mary Margaret (Weller) D.; m. John P. Seasock, Aug. 8, 1992. BS, Marywood Coll., 1989, postgrad., 1993—. Cert. tchr., Pa. Kindergarten tchr. Magic Yrs. Child Care & Learning Ctr., Scranton, 1989-92, group supr., 1990-92, asst. dir., 1992—. Mem. Assn. Childhood Edn. Internat. Home: 145 Sharpe St Kingston PA 18704-2833 Office: Magic Yrs Child Care & Learning Ctr 511 Morgan Hwy Scranton PA 18508-2606

DRUCKMAN, MARGARET SMITH, consultant, retail executive, administrator; b. Wilkes-Barre, Pa., May 9, 1937; d. Gibson Willard and Mary Louise (Schuster) Smith; m. Clayton Edward Hudnall, 1964 (div. 1976); children: Mary Margaret, Clayton John; m. Harvey Saul Druckman, 1981. BA, Coll. Misericordia, 1958; postgrad., U. Edinburgh, Scotland, 1960; MA, Marquette U., 1960; postgrad., U. Ill., 1962-64. Proposal writer Vanderbilt U., Nashville, 1967-70; tchr. N.W. Cath. High Sch., West Hartford, Conn., 1973-79; dir. communications U. Hartford, West Hartford, 1979-81, dir. found. rels., 1980-81, dir. capital support, 1981-85, dir. capital campaign Springfield, Mass., 1985-86; pres. Windsor (Conn.) Findings, Inc., 1986-91; chief operating officer Golden Apple Jewelers, Windsor, 1986—; exec. dir. devel./alumni rels. U. of Hartford, 1988-91; cons. fund raising Druckman Assocs., Windsor, Conn., 1991—; dir. corp./found. resources U. Conn., Storrs, 1993—. Contbr. articles to mags. Mem. NAFE. Democrat. Roman Catholic. Avocations: writing, travel, reading. Office: 41 Bedford Ave East Hartford CT 06118-3101

DRUHE BRANDT, IRIS CLAIRE, retired elementary school educator; b. New Orleans, Oct. 28, 1935; d. Olivia Catherine Clair and Frederick George Druhe; m. Eugene Maximillian Brandt, June 11, 1960; children: Fred, Brenda, Philip. BA, So. La. U., 1956. Tchr. 2nd and 3rd grades, New Orleans, 1956-59; tchr. 2nd grade Pensacola, Fla., 1961; pre-sch. tchr. Escondido, Calif., 1984-89; clin. rschr. cancer U. Calif., Irvine, Calif., 2002—. Clin. cancer rschr. U. Calif., Irvine, 2002—. Vol. sec. Indian Wells Youth Football League; active Brownie and Cub Scouts Am.; vol. nutritional advisor, counselor Wellness Clinic, Morena Valley, Calif., 1998—2001; mem. Episcopal Women St. Marks. Mem.: AAUW (chair ways and means com.), Humane Soc. U.S., San Diego North County Diabetes County Diabetes Support Group, Women's Assn. Commn. Officers Mess, Navy Relief Soc. (chmn. Lafayette chpt. 1961), Officers Wives Assn. (hospitality chmn., v.p., pres.). Home: 4527 Coronado Dr Oceanside CA 92057-4252

DRUM, ALICE, academic administrator, educator; b. Gettysburg, Pa., June 22, 1935; d. David Wentz and Charlotte Rebecca (Kinzey) McDannell; m. D. Richard Guise, June 15, 1957 (div. Aug. 1975); children: Gregory, Brent, Richard, Robert, Clay; m. Ray Kenneth Drum, Mar. 2, 1979; 1 child, Trevor. BA magna cum laude, Wilson Coll., 1957; PhD, Am. U., 1976. Adj. prof. gen. studies Antioch U., Columbia, Md., 1976-78; adj. asst. prof. English Gettysburg (Pa.) Coll., 1977-80; lectr. gen. studies Georgetown U., Washington, 1980-81; lectr. gen. honors U. Md., College Park, 1980-83; asst. prof. English Hood Coll., Frederick, Md., 1981-85, coord. writing program, 1981-83, assoc. dean acad. affairs, 1983-85; dean freshmen Franklin and Marshall Coll., Lancaster, Pa., 1985-88, v.p., 1988-2001, prof., chair womens studies, 2001—. Team mem. Mid. States Accreditation Assn., 1989-2003; cons. in field. Co-author: Funding A College Education, 1996; contbr. chpts. to books, articles and book revs. to profl. jours. Chair Lancaster County DA Commn., Lancaster, 1990-91; mem. Lancaster County Commn. on Youth Violence, Lancaster, 1990-91; bd. trustees Wilson Coll., 1997—, YWCA, Lancaster, Mellon grant, 1979; Davison Foreman fellow, 1975-76. Mem. MLA, N.E. MLA, Deans (pres. 1988-89), Coll. English Assn., Phi Beta Kappa (pres. chpt. 1990-91), Phi Kappa Phi. Democrat. Episcopalian. Avocations: hiking, reading, visiting art museums. Office: Franklin & Marshall Coll Lancaster PA 17604-3003

DRUM, JOAN MARIE MCFARLAND, federal agency administrator, educator; b. Waseca, Minn., Mar. 31, 1932; d. Leo Joseph and Bergetthe (Anderson) McFarland; m. William Merritt Drum, June 13, 1954; children: Melissa, Eric. BA in Journalism, U. Minn., 1962; MEd, Coll. William and Mary, 1975, postgrad., 1984-85. Govt. ofcl. fgn. claims br. Social Security Adminstrn., Balt., 1962-64; freelance writer Polyndrum Publs., Newport News, Va., 1967-73; tchr. Newport News (Va.) Pub. Schs., 1975-79; writer, cons. Drum Enterprises, Williamsburg, Va., 1980-82; developer, trainer communicative skills U.S. Army Transp. Sch., Ft. Eustis, Va., 1982-86; govt. ofcl. test assistance div. U.S. Army Tng. Ctr., Ft. Eustis, 1986, course devel. coord. distributed tng. office, 1992. Adj. faculty English dept. St. Leo Area Coll., Ft. Eustis, 1975-78; del. Communicative Skills Conf., Ft. Leavenworth, Kans., 1983; mem. Army Self-Devel. Test Task Force, 1991-92; task force mem. U.S. Army Tng. FAA; program developer multi-media electronic delivery prototype; tech. tng. facility trainer. Author: Ghosts of Fort Monroe, 1972, Travel for Children in Tidewater, 1974, Galaxy of Ghosts, 1992, Hampton's Haunted Houses, 1998, How to Feed a Ghost, 1998; editor: army newsletter for families, 1968-73, Social Services Resource Reference, 1970; contbr. articles to profl. jours. Chmn. Girl Scouts U.S., Tokyo, 1964-66, Army Cmty. Svc., Ft. Monroe, Va., 1967-68; chmn. publicity Hist. Home Tours, Ft. Monroe, 1971-73; chmn. adv. bd. James City County Social Svcs., 1989-95, chmn. adult svcs., 1989-90; mem. James City County Leadership Devel. Program Bd. Recipient numerous civic awards including North Shore Cmty. Svc. award, Hialeah, Hawaii, 1966, Home Bur. Svc. award, 1975, Svc. award Girl Scouts U.S., Tokyo, 1965, Comdrs. achievement award for civilian svc., 1995, 98. Mem. N Va. Writers Club, Kappa Delta Pi. Home: 9 Bray Wood Rd Williamsburg VA 23185-5504 E-mail: jdrum@hroads.net.

DRUMMOND, CAROL CRAMER, voice educator, singer, artist, writer; b. Indpls., Mar. 5, 1933; adopted d. Burr Ostin and L. Ruth Welch; m. Roscoe Drummond, 1978 (dec. 1983). Student, Butler U., 1951—53; studied voice with Todd Duncan, Frances Yeend, James Benner, Rosa Ponselle, Dr. Peter Herman Adler and John Bullock; studied drama with Adelaide Bishop, Washington, D.C. Original performer Starlite Musicals, Indpls., 1951; singer Am. Light Opera Co., Washington, Seagle Opera Colony, Schroon Lake, N.Y., 1963, 64; soloist St. John's Episcopal Ch., Lafayette Sq., Washington, 5th Ch. of Christ, Scientist, Washington, 1963-78; performer Concerts in Schs. Program, Washington Performing Arts Soc., 1967-99; soloist with Luke AFB band ofcl. opening Boswell Meml. Hosp, Sun City, Ariz., 1970; painter, artist, 1980—; pvt. tchr. voice, 1986—; voice tchr. Ellsworth H.S., Mt. Desert Island H.S., 1986—. Soloist numerous oratorio socs.; appearances with symphony orchs. including Nat. Symphony Orch., Fairfax (Va.) Symphony Orch., Buffalo Philharm. Orch., Concerts in the Pk., Arlington Opera Co., Lake George Opera Co., Glens Falls, NY, The Nat. Cathedral, Washington, Noye's Flood, Lufkin, Tex., 1965, Washington Opera; voiceover radio and TV commls., 1965—84; U.S. Govt. host The Sounding Bd., Sta. WGTS-FM, Washington, 1972—78; dir. ensembles, music/voice cons. Summer Festival of the Arts, S.W. Harbor, Maine, 1992—95, mem. adv. bd., 1986—; dri. Amahl and the Night Visitors, 1992; vocal solo concert The Smithsonian Instn., 1980. Former columnist: Animal Crackers, writer: newspaper and mag. articles and stories; one-woman shows include, Lemon Tree, Bangor, 1995, 1996, Grand Theater, Ellsworth, Maine, 1995, Southwest Harbor (Maine) Pub. Libr., 1997, U. Maine, 1999, Border's, Bangor, 2002; two-woman shows including, Am. Art League, Washington, 1997, two-woman show Cosmos Club, Wash., 1996, Arts Club, 1994, 1995, 1996, artist, owner Dream Come True Notecards, 1997—. Bd. dirs. Washington Sch. Ballet, 1978; life bd. dirs. Internat. Soundex Reunion Registry, Carson City, Nev. Recipient 1st pl. women's divsn. Internat. Printers Ink Contest, 1951. Mem.: Nat. League Am. Pen Women, Beta Sigma Phi, Kappa Kappa Gamma. Republican. Episcopalian. Avocations: cats, knitting, gardening, reading, travel. Home: PO Box 791 79 Clark Point Rd Southwest Harbor ME 04679 Office: 10802 Tradewind Dr Oakton VA 22124-1800 E-mail: ccdrummond@gwi.net.

DRUMMOND, DOROTHY WEITZ, geography education consultant, educator, author; b. San Diego, Dec. 19, 1928; d. Frederick W. and Dora (Weidenhofer) Weitz; m. Robert R. Drummond, Sept. 5, 1953 (dec. June 1982); children: Kathleen, Gael, Martha. AB, Valparaiso U., 1949; MA, Northwestern U., 1951. Cert. tchr., Ind. Social studies tchr. Woodrow Wilson Jr. High Sch., Oxnard, Calif., 1949-50; editorial asst. Am. Geog. Soc., N.Y.C., 1951-53; substitute tchr. Vigo County Sch. Corp., Terre Haute, Ind., 1960-67; social studies tchr. Ind. State U. Lab. Sch., Terre Haute, 1963-64. Geog. edn. cons., author, workshop presenter, Terre Haute, 1953—; adj. asst. prof. geography Saint Mary-of-the-Woods (Ind.) Coll., 1967-99, Ind. State U., Terre Haute, 1990—; dir. project GEO, Ind. State U., 1992-96; cons. McGraw-Hill, Scott-Foresman, Agy. for Instrnl. Tech., Hudson Inst.; grant developer GIS for the Twenty-First Century, Ind. State u., 1996-98. Co-author: The World Today, 3d edit., 1971, World Geography, 1989; author: People on Earth, 3d edit., 1988, Holy Land, Whose Land?, 2002; contbr. numerous articles to profl. jours. Organizer, leader ednl. tours to China, 1986, 1988, 1998, 2001; organizer, leader ednl. tours to Australia, 1993, 1996, 1997, 1999, 2000, 2002; organizer, leader ednl. tours to New Zealand, 2003; bd. dirs. Mental Health Assn. Wabash Valley, Terre Haute, 1984—93, Coun. on Domestic Abuse, Terre Haute, 1987—92, 1997—99, United Ministries Ctr., Terre Haute, 1991—94, 2003—. Fulbright scholar, Burma, 1957-58; grantee Geography Educators Network Ind., 1988-96, Ind. Commn. Higher Edn., 1990, 92, 94, 96, NSF, 1993, 95, 96, 97, U.S. Dept. Edn., 1992-96. Mem. Ind. Coun. Social Studies, Geography Educators Network Ind. (bd. dirs.), Nat. Coun. Geog. Edn. (pres. 1990), Nat. Coun. Social Studies. E-mail: dd2@indstate.edu.

DRUMMOND, HAROLD DEAN, retired education educator; b. Bettsville, Ohio, June 8, 1916; s. Ray W. and Velma T. D.; m. Erma Catherine Street, Aug. 30, 1939 (dec. Aug. 1986); 1 child, Harold Evan; m. E. Josephine (Stanley) Raths, Nov. 23, 1988. Student, Westminster Coll., 1933-35; AB, Colo. State Coll. Edn., 1937, MA, 1940; EdD, Stanford U., 1948. Prin., tchr. White Deer (Tex.) Ind. Sch. Dist., 1938-42; prof. elem. edn. George Peabody Coll. for Tchrs., Nashville, 1947-60; acting prof. tchr. edn. assigned to U. Philippines, Stanford (Calif.) U., 1954-55; prof. elem. edn. U. N.Mex., Albuquerque, 1960-79, emeritus prof., 1979—. Adv. bd. Childcraft, 1957-60, 67-80. Author: (with Charles R. Spain and John I. Goodlad) Educational Leadership and the Elementary School Principal, 1956; Our World Today series, A Journey Through Many Lands, Journeys Through the Americas, The Eastern Hemisphere, The Western Hemisphere, 1960-83. Lt. USNR, 1942-45, PTO. Laureate mem. Kappa Delta Pi, 1984; laureate counselor, 1984-88, 89-90. Mem. Ednl. Forum (mem. editl. rev. panel 1997-2003), ASCD (pres. 1964-65), NEA, Nat. Assn. Elem. Sch. Prins., Nat. Coun. Social Studies, Nat. Coun. Geog. Edn., Nat. Soc. Study Edn., Profs. Curriculum. Home: 536 Graceland Dr SE Albuquerque NM 87108-3333

DRUMMOND, JULIA ELAINE BUTLER, retired middle school educator; b. Charleston, S.C., Oct. 26, 1943; d. Benjamin Harris and Audrea Mae (Kerr) Butler; m. Darrell Gene Drummond, Mar. 18, 1967 div., remarried Dec. 18, 1999; children: William Brian, Bradley Criswell. BA in English, Winthrop Coll., 1965; Ma in Teaching in English Edn., Converse Coll., 1974; postgrad., Clemson U., Furman U., Coll. Charleston, U. S.C., U. Paris; EdD, Century U., 1999. Cert. K-12 English and French tchr., elem. tchr., mid. sch. English, social studies and sci. tchr., S.C. Tchr. English Wren High Sch., Piedmont, S.C., 1965-66, J.L. Mann High Sch., Greenville, S.C., 1970; tchr. English and French Sans Souci Jr. High Sch., Greenville, 1966-68; tchr. Greenville Mid. Sch., 1970-80, Bryson Mid. Sch., Simpsonville, S.C., 1980-97, ret., 1997. Assoc. prof. English, North Greenville Coll., Tigerville, S.C., 1981-84, 98—, Greenville Tech. Coll., 1986-99, Furman U., Greenville, 1998; great books co-leader Nat. Writing Project, 1988—; S.C. artist-in-residence, 1991—. Grantee S.C. Edn. Improvement Act, 1984, Tchr. Incentive Program, 1986. Mem. DAR, NEA, S.C. Edn. Assn., Greenville County Edn. Assn.-Ret., Sigma Tau Delta, Alpha Delta Kappa. Republican. Baptist. Home: 115 Inglewood Way Greenville SC 29615-3127 E-mail: jdrummond@ngc.edu.

DRUMMOND, MARSHALL EDWARD, business educator, university administrator; b. Stanford, Calif., Sept. 14, 1941; s. Kirk Isaac and Fern Venice (McDeritt) D. BS, San Jose State U., 1964, MBA, 1969; EdD, U. San Francisco, 1979. Adj. prof. bus. and edn. U. San Francisco, 1975-81; adj. prof. bus. and info. systems San Francisco State U., 1981-82; prof. MIS, Ea. Wash. U., Cheney, 1985—, exec. dir. info. resources, 1988, assoc. v.p. adminstrv. svcs., chief info. officer, 1988-89, v.p. adminstrv. svcs., 1989-90, exec. v.p., 1990, pres., 1990-98; chancellor L.A. C.C. Dist., 1999—. Cons. Sch. Bus., Harvard Coll., U. Ariz. Contbg. editor Diebold Series; contbr. articles to profl. jours. Democrat. Avocations: running, water sports, equestrian sports., horse breeding and trainging. Office: LA C C Dist 770 Wilshire Blvd Los Angeles CA 90017-3856

DRUSHAL, MARY ELLEN, educator, former university provost; b. Peru, Ind., Oct. 24, 1945; d. Herrell Lee and Opal Marie (Boone) Waters; m. J. Michael Drushal, June 12, 1966; children: Lori, Jeff. B of Music Edn., Ashland Coll., 1969; MS, Peabody Coll., 1981; PhD, Vanderbilt U., 1986. Dir. music and spl. ednl. projects Smithville (Ohio) Brethren Ch., 1969-74; tchr. music Orrville (Ohio) Pub. Schs., 1969—70; seminar leader Internat. Ctr. for Learning, Glendale, Calif., 1974-76; dir. Christian edn. First Presbyn. and Christ Presbyn. Ch., Nashville, 1976-84; assoc. prof. Ashland (Ohio) Theol. Sem., 1984-91, acad. dean, 1991-95; provost Ashland U., 1995—2001, prof. edn., 2001—, dir. instnl. effectiveness, 2001—03. Cons. in strategic planning for not-for-profit orgns. Author: On Tablets of Human Hearts: Christian Education with Children, 1991; co-author: Spiritual Formation: A Personal Walk Toward Emmaus, 1990; contbr. articles to profl. jours. Trustee Brethren Care Found., Ashland, 1989-99, Ashland Symphony Orch., 1986-87; pres., fundraiser Habitat for Humanity, Ashland, 1990-94; bd. dirs. JOY Day Care Ctr., 1988-90. Grantee Lilly Endowment Inc., 1991, 93, Brethren Ch. Found., 1989, 90. Mem. Assn. Theol. Schs. (com. under-represented constituencies 1994-96), Am. Assn. for Higher Edn., Nat. Assn. Ch. Bus. Adminstrs., N.Am. Assn. Profs. of Christian Edn., Assn. Profs. and Rschrs. in Religious Edn., Nat. Assn. Evangelicals, Nat. Assn. Black Evangelical Assns., Epiphany Assn. (bd. dirs. 1994-98). Republican. Presbyterian. Avocations: reading, needlepoint. Office: Ashland U 401 College Ave Ashland OH 44805-3799 E-mail: medrusha@ashland.edu.

DRVAR, MARGARET ADAMS, vocational education educator; b. Morgantown, W.Va., Dec. 22, 1953; d. Lester Morris and Daun Collette (Benson) Adams; m. Marvin Lynn Drvar, July 29, 1978; children: Jacob Elias, Jared Nathaniel. BS in Family Resources, W.Va. U., 1977, MS in Family Resources, 1982. Cert. tchr., vocat. family and consumer scis. tchr., W.Va. Substitute tchr. Monongalia County Bd. Edn., Morgantown, 1983-86; tchr. vocat. family and consumer sci. Clay Battelle Jr.-Sr. H.S., Blacksville, W.Va., 1986-89, 91-92, South Mid. Sch., Morgantown, 1992—, treas. faculty senate, 1997—. Instr. culinary arts Monongalia County Tech. Edn. Ctr., Morgantown, 1989-91; youth group adv. Family, Career, Cmty. Leaders Am. (formerly Future Homemakers of Am.), 1986—. V.p. United Meth. Women, Brookhaven, W.Va., 1985-92; sec. bd. trustees Brookhaven United Meth. Ch., 1989-97; bd. dirs., sec. Morgantown AES Fed. Credit Union, 1989—; vol. 4-H leader Brookhaven Bulls 4-H Club, 1992—. Recipient Master Advisor award, Future Homemakers Am. Inc., 1996, Golden Apple Achiever award, Ashland Oil, 1996, Outstanding 4-H Leader Monongalia County award, 1996, Tchr. of Yr. award, W.Va. Family and Consumer Sci. Assn., 2002, Top 10 Tchrs. of the Yr., Am. Assn. of Family and Consumer Scis., 2002, All Star award for yrs. of cmty. svc., W.Va. 4-H, 2003. Mem.: NEA, Monongalia County 4-H Leaders Assn. (pres. 1998—99, 2001—03), W.Va. Vocat. Assn. (historian family and consumer sci. divsn. 1995—96), Assn. for Career and Tech. Edn., Monongalia County Assn. of Family and Consumer Scis., W.Va.Assn. Family and Consumer Scis., Monongalia County Edn. Assn., W.Va. Edn. Assn., Am. Assn. Family and Consumer Scis. (cert.) (Top 10 Tchr. of Yr. 2002), Gamma Phi Beta, Alpha Upsilon Omicron. Avocations: travel, camping. Home: 3307 Darrah Ave Morgantown WV 26508-9187 Office: Monongalia County Schs South Mid Sch 500 E Parkway Dr Morgantown WV 26501-6839 E-mail: mdrvar@access.k12.wv.us.

DRYBURG, ANN, secondary education educator; b. Roscoe, Pa., Nov. 8, 1913; d. Walter and Jane V. (Cairns) D. BS in Elem. Edn., BS in Secondary Edn., Waynesburg Coll., 1947. Cert. elem. tchr., secondary history tchr., elem. and secondary religious edn. tchr. Prin., tchr., grades 1-8 Centerville Dist., West Brownsville, Pa.; jr. high sch. math. tchr. Bethlehem-Ctr. Sch. Dist., Fredericktown, Pa. Recipient Am. Nat. Red Cross award, 1942-43, Pres. Harry Truman award, 1948, Am. Legion award, 1983. Mem. NEA, ASCD, Pa. State Edn. Assn., Beth Center Edn. Assn., Centreville Edn. Assn. (teas.), Nat. Coun. and State Coun. Tchrs. Math. Home: Brownsville, Pa. Died Nov. 20, 1997.

DRYSDALE, ESTHER ANN, elementary school educator; b. Bessemer, Ala., Apr. 18, 1952; d. Robert Lee and Marion Roberta (Criss) Coker; m. James Duncan Drysdale IV, Mar. 12, 1974; children: James Robert, Jennifer Ann. BS, U. Montevallo, Ala., 1974; MA, U. Ala., 1982, postgrad., 1994—. Tchr. Thomas Acres Pvt. Sch., Bessemer, 1972-76; tchr. reading and math. C.F. Hard Elem. Sch., Bessemer, 1976-80, Jonesboro Elem. Sch., Bessemer, 1980—. Mentor, persenter to faculty on elem. curriculum documents Ala. Dept. Edn., 1987-88; pilot reading tchr. for system on reading series adoption, 1988-89; curriculum writer. Mem. ASCD, NEA, Ala. Edn. Assn., Alpha Delta Kappa. Democrat. Baptist. Avocations: going to beach, reading, traveling. Office: Jonesboro Elem Sch 125 Owen Ave Bessemer AL 35020-7699

DU, DING-ZHU, mathematician, educator; b. Qigihaer, China, May 21, 1948; s. Jin-Gao and Ai-Hua (Xu) D.;m. Shu-Mei Li, Jan. 20, 1953; 1 child, Hong-Wei. MS, Chinese Acad. Scis., Beijing, 1982; PhD, U. Calif., Santa Barbara, 1985. Asst. prof. Inst. of Applied Math., Beijing, 1981-82; postdoctoral Math. Scis. Rsch. Inst., Berkeley, Calif., 1985-86; asst. prof. MIT, Cambridge, 1986-87; prof. Inst. of Applied Math., Beijing, 1987-90; rsch. assoc. Princeton (N.J.) U., 1990; prof. U. Minn., Mpls., 1991—. Editor: Combinatorial Group Testing and Its Applications, Theory of Computational Complexity: Combinatorial Group Testing and Applications, 2001, Problem Solving in Antamata, Languages and Complexity; editor-in-chief Jour. Combinatorial Optimization, 2001; contbr. over 130 articles to profl. jours. Mem.: Am. Math. Soc. Achievements include proof of Derman, Leiberman and Ross' conjecture on optimal consecutive-2-out-of-n system in 1982, proving Gilbert and Pollak's conjecture on Steiner ratio; solution to open problem on Rosen's method in nonlinear optimization; research on one-way function in complexity theory; proposing quillotine cut in approximation. Office: U Minn Computer Sci Dept Minneapolis MN 55455 E-mail: dzd@cs.umn.edu.

DUARTE, CRISTOBAL G. nephrologist, educator; b. July 17, 1929; s. Cristobal Duarte and Emilia Miltos; m. Norma Aquino, 1984. BS, Colegio de San Josè, Asuncion, 1947; MD, Nat. U. Asuncion, 1953. Intern De Goesbriand Meml. Hosp., Burlington, Vt., 1956; resident in medicine Carney Hosp., St. Elizabeth's Hosp., Boston, 1956-58; fellow in medicine Lahey Clin., Boston, 1959; fellow hypertension and renal medicine Hahnemann Hosp., Phila., 1960; assoc. in medicine U. Vt. Coll. Medicine, 1962-65, clin. investigator VA, 1966-68, staff physician, 1968-73; dir. Renal Function Lab. Mayo Clin. and Found., Rochester, Minn., 1973-77; asst. prof. lab. medicine Mayo Med. Sch., Rochester, Minn., 1973-77; commd. lt. col. U.S. Army, 1977-84; assoc. prof. medicine and physiology Uniformed Svcs. U. Health Scis., Bethesda, Md., 1977-84; attending in medicine Walter Reed Army Med. Ctr., Washington, 1977-84; chief nephrology svc. Bay Pines VA Med. Ctr., 1984-87; assoc. prof. medicine U. So. Fla., Tampa, 1984-87; med. officer cardio-renal drug products FDA, Rockville, Md., 1987—. Editor: Renal Function Tests, 1980; contbr. articles to profl. jours., chpts. to books. Recipient cert. of accomplishment VA, 1969, Physician's Recognition award AMA, 1993; Cordell Hull Found. fellow 1958-59. Fellow Am. Coll. Nutrition; mem. Nat. Kidney Found., Am. Fedn. Clin. Rsch., Am. Physiol. Soc., Am. Soc. Pharmacology and Exptl. Therapeutics, Midwest Salt and Water Club, Am. Soc. for Clin. Rsch., Inter-Am. Soc. Hypertension, Internat. Soc. Nephrology, Central Soc. Clin. Rsch., Am. Soc. Nephrology, Sigma Xi. Roman Catholic. Current work: Radiocontrast-induced renal failure. Subspecialty: Nephrology. E-mail: duarte@cder.fda.gov.

DUATO, ARLENE CHANA LEAH, special education educator, consultant; b. Boston, Apr. 13, 1946; d. Menachem Mendel and Lillian Leiba Greece; 1 child, Yisroel Peter E. BA in Sociology, U. Mass., 1972; MS in Elem. Edn. and Spl. Edn., Adelphi U., 1985. Day care tchr. Headstart, Boston, 1970; social worker Dept. Pub. Welfare, Boston, 1970—78; spl. edn.tchr. Bd. Edn., Bklyn., 1985—97, clinician, evaluator, 1997—. Contbr. articles to profl. jours.:, author poems. Pres. parent group WDCC (Wesley Day Care Ctr.), Boston, 1970—72; co-chairwoman mivtzayim N'shei Chabad, Bklyn., 1985—2001. Avocations: photography, theater, swimming, travel. Office: PS 289 SBST RM 240 900 St Marks Ave Brooklyn NY 11213

DUBIN, MARTIN STEVEN, principal; b. Queens, N.Y., July 1, 1950; s. Herman and Fay Dubin; m. Ellen Marlene Kohn, Aug. 18, 1973; children: Rachel Fay, David Isaac. BA, Hofstra U., 1972, MS in Edn. with univ. honors, 1974; D of Edn., Vanderbilt U., 1981. Cert. nursery, kindergarten, grades 1-6, social studies 7-9, spl. classes for emotionally disturbed K-12, Va.; kindergarten, elem. 1-7, spl. edn. for emotional disturbance and learning disabilities, elem. prin., secondary prin. Tchr. emotionally disturbed Mt. Vernon Ctr., Alexandria, Va., 1974-76; head tchr. emotionally disturbed Riverside Elem., Alexandria, 1976-77; resource tchr. emotionally disturbed Franconia Ctr., Alexandria, 1977-81; dept. chmn. learning disabled Robinson Secondary, Fairfax, Va., 1981-83; prin. Armstrong Ctr., Reston, Va., 1988-90, Franconia Ctr., Alexandria, 1990-97, Crestwood Elem., Springfield, Va., 1997-98; adminstrv. prin. Hayfield Secondary, Alexandria, 1998—. Adj. prof. George Mason U., Fairfax, 1988-93; learning disabilities/mild mental retardation specialist Area IV Adminstrv. Office, Fairfax, 1983-88; grant evaluator U.S. Office of Edn., Washington, spring 1991, 93, 95. Pres. Adat Reyim, Springfield, Va., 1997-99; mem. Springfield Coalition, 1997-98. U.S. Office of Edn. rsch. grantee, 1979. Mem. CEC, Nat. Assn. Elem. Sch. Prins., Phi Delta Kappa. Achievements include study in how attitudes of non-disabled students influence the integration and mainstreaming of emotionally disabled students. Office: Hayfield Secondary Sch 7630 Telegraph Rd Alexandria VA 22315-3898 E-mail: 4dubins@prodigy.net., martin.dubin@fcps.edu.

DUBIN, SUSAN HELEN, private school educator, storyteller; b. L.A., Jan. 12, 1948; d. Hyman Benjamin and RoseAnne (Giser) Klane; m. Marc Jeffrey Dubin, June 5, 1969; children: Victor Matthew, Roseanne Danyelle. BA, UCLA, 1970; postgrad., Trenton State U., 1970-72, Hebrew Union Coll., L.A., 1982—. Cert. tchr., N.J., Calif. Tchr. Valley Campus Pres-Sch., North Hollywood, Calif., 1966-68; tchr., asst. dir. Storyland, North Hollywood, 1968-70; tchr. 2d grade Burlington Twp., N.J., 1970-72; pre-kindergarten tchr., dir. summer program Adat AriEl Pre-Sch., North Hollywood, 1972-75; substitute tchr. pvt. schs., L.A., 1975-78; owner, dir., tchr. Canby Hall, Reseda, Calif., 1978-80; pre-kindergarten tchr. Beth Kodesh Pre-Sch., Canoga Park, Calif., 1980-81; kindergarten tchr. Hillel Acad., L.A., 1981-82; libr. instr. Valley Beth Shalom Day Sch., Encino, Calif., 1982—; owner, dir. Off the Shelf Libr. Svcs., Northridge, Calif., 2000—. Presenter seminars. Author: Teacher's Guide On Line Lesson Plans for Molly's Pilgrim Video, JEET, JEET Gift of Shabbat, Gift of Chanuka Lessons for Early Childhood; contbg. author: Starbright, 1986, Teaching Judaic Values in Literature Using Noah's Ark, 1985; author: (filmstrip and tchr.'s guide) The Tree, 1971. Mem. San Fernando Valley Arts Coun., 1992-93; mem. pers. practices com. Bur. Jewish Edn., Los Angeles County, 1993-99. Recipient Milken Family Found. Outstanding Jewish Educator award, 1998. Mem. Nat. Coun. Tchrs. English, Assn. Jewish Librs. (pres. Sch. Synagogue Ctr. Divsn., 2002-04, co-chair conv. 1990-92, 97-2001, accreditation chair 1993-97, parliamentarian 1994-2000, constitution com. chair 1995, recipient Fanny Goldstein award for Judaic Librarianship), Assn. Jewish Librs. of So. Calif. (program v.p. 1985-89, pres. 1989-93, Dorothy Schroeder award, western regional conv. chair 1996), Internat. Reading Assn., Calif. Assn. Ind. Schs. Libr. Network. Avocations: storytelling, book collecting. Home: 18901 Marilla St Northridge CA 91324-1837 Office: Off the Shelf Libr Svcs 18901 Marilla St Northridge CA 91324-1837 E-mail: sdubin@lausd.k12.ca.us.

DUBLIN, STEPHEN LOUIS, secondary school educator, singer, musician; b. L.A., Aug. 17, 1948; s. Thomas Newton and Carole Louise Dublin. BM, Chapman U., 1970; M in Sch. Adminstrn., U. LaVerne, 1988. Vocal music and English tchr. Leland Stanford Jr. H.S., 1973-74; vocal music and gen. music tchr. Walter B. Hill Jr. H.S., 1974-77, 80-88, Woodrow Wilson H.S., 1977-80; govt. and econs. tchr., mem. various sch. coms., mentor tchr., chmn. history dept. Robert A. Millikan H.S., Long Beach, Calif., 1988—. Mem. campaign com. Harriet Williams Bd. Edn., Long Beach, 1988, 90; Calif. tchr. liason Senate Ralph Dells, Long Beach, 1988-92. Scholar Chapman U., 1966-70, Bougess White scholar, 1998; named Tchr. of Yr. Millikan H.S., 1993; nominee Tchr. of Yr., League of Calif. High Schs., 1999; named 1 of 5 most popular tchrs., sr. class Millikan H.S., 1999, Most Inspirational Tchr., 1998, tchr. who influenced 2 students most in their lives, 1999, Tchr. of Yr., Long Beach PTA, 1999, Svc. award PTA, 1999; honoree work with homeless children Long Beach USD, raising money Long Beach Red Cross. Mem. Calif. Assn. Econs. (charter), Social Studies Coun., Choral Conductors Guild, So. Calif. Vocal Assn., Constnl. Rights Found. (premier tchr.), Phi Delta Kappa. Avocations: singing, conducting. Home: 4045 E 3d St #112 Long Beach CA 90814

DUBOIS, CINDY A. guidance counselor; b. Biddeford, Maine, Aug. 14, 1958; d. Arthur E. and Phyllis L. Dubois. BA in Psychology, Regis Coll., 1980, MA in Spl. Edn., 1983; MA in Counseling Psychology, Tufts U., 1989. Cert. guidance counselor, sch. psychologist, moderate spl. needs tchr., social studies tchr. Spl. edn. tchr. Burlington (Mass.) H.S., 1983-87, Marshall Simonds Middle Sch., Burlington, 1989-91, guidance counselor, 1991—. Summer camp vol. Burlington (Mass.) Recreation Dept., 1974-75; vol. counselor Burlington (Mass.) Cmty. Life Ctr., 1988-89; religious edn. tchr. St. Malachy's Parish, Burlington, 1994-97. Mem. Nat. Assn. Sch. Psychologists, Mass. Assn. Sch. Psychologists. Roman Catholic. Home: 23 Daniel Dr Burlington MA 01803-2701 Office: Marshall Simonds Middle Sch 114 Winn St Burlington MA 01803-3109

DUBOIS, MARY LOU HOWELL, elementary education educator; b. Woodbury, N.J., Mar. 17, 1947; d. Glendon and Rose (Pettit) Howell; m. Robert Carl DuBois, Aug. 2, 1974 BA in Gen. Elem., Galssboro State Coll., 1969, MA, 1981, MA in Student Pers. Svcs., 1990. Cert. elem. tchr. and guidance counselor, N.J. Tchr. Elmer (N.J.) Elem. Sch., 1969—. Mem. Odyssey of Mind, problem capt. N.J. state coun. Recipient DuPont Ptnrs. Sci. award, 1992; grantee state and fed. govt., 1988-92. Mem. N.J. Counselors Assn., N.J. Sch. Women's Club. Presbyterian. Avocations: raising and showing persian cats, clown ministry, collecting antiques. Office: Elmer Elem Sch Front St Elmer NJ 08318

DUBOIS, NANCY Q. elementary school educator; b. St. Petersburg, Fla., June 6, 1960; d. Thomas Malcolm and Barbara Jean (Leitner) Quehl; m. Donald F. Dubois, Nov. 27, 1981; children: Jacquelyn Nicole, Justin Jared. BA, U. South Fla., Tampa, 1983; MEd, U. Fla., 1993; Mid-Mgmt. Cert., Schreiner Coll., 1999. Cert. tchr., Fla., N.Mex., Tex. Tchr. St. Patricks Sch., Fayetteville, N.C., 1984-85, The Most Holy Name Sch., Gulfport, Fla., 1985-88, Kirtland Elem. Sch., Albuquerque, 1988-91; field advisor Coll. Edn., U. Fla., Gainesville, 1991-93; 4th grade tchr. Schulze Elem. Sch., San Antonio, 1993-97; tchr. Bellaire Elem. Sch., San Antonio, 1997-2001; USI peer tchr., 1997-2001. USI peer tchr., 1997—. Named Tchr. of Yr., Bellaire Elem. Sch., 1998-99; recipient grad. asst. Tchg. award U. Fla., 1993; Trinity U. fellow, 1999-2000. Mem. ASCD, Internat. Reading Assn., Fla. Coun. Tchrs. of Math., Kappa Delta Pi. Republican. Roman Catholic. Avocations: reading, cross-stitch, swimming.

DUBOSE, CORNELIUS BATES, educational director; b. Chgo., Feb. 21, 1951; s. Lloyd and Margaret (Collier) DuB.; m. Linda I. Vaccaro, June 13, 1980; 1 child, Cornelius B. Jr. BA, North Park Coll., Chgo., 1972; MS, Nat.-Louis U., Evanston, Ill., 1990. Cert. tchr., Ill. Elem. tchr. Unit Sch. Dist. 187, North Chicago, Ill., 1972-86, computer resource tchr., 1986-91, coord. computer svcs., 1991-93; coord. tech. resource Lake Forest Elem. Sch. Dist. 67, 1993-95, tech. coord., 1995—. Instr. Pascal Ctr. for Talent Devel., Northwestern U., Evanston, summers 1989—; instr.computers in edn. Nat.-Louis U., 1990—; instr. computer programming Barat Coll., Lake Forest, Ill., 1990—. Author: The Martin Luther King Story—A Children's Play, 1976. Mem. ASCD, Internat. Soc. for Tech. in Edn., Ill. Computing Educators. Avocations: photography, basketball. Office: Lake Forest Sch Dist 67 95 W Deerpath Rd Lake Forest IL 60045-2153

DUBOSE, FRANCIS MARQUIS, clergyman; b. Elba, Ala., Feb. 27, 1922; s. Hansford Arthur and Mayde Frances (Owen) DuB.; BA cum laude, Baylor U., 1947; MA, U. Houston, 1958; BD, Southwestern Bapt. Sem., 1957, ThD, 1961; postgrad. Oxford (Eng.) U., 1972; m. Dorothy Anne Sessums, Aug. 28, 1940; children: Elizabeth Anne Parnell, Frances Jeannine Huffman, Jonathan Michael, Celia Danielle. Pastor Bapt. chs., Tex., Ark., 1939-61; supt. missions. So. Bapt. Conv., Detroit, 1961-66; prof. missions Golden Gate Bapt. Sem., 1966—, dir. World Mission Ctr., 1979—, sr. prof., 1992; lectr., cons. in 115 cities outside U.S., 1969-82; v.p. Conf. City Mission Supts., So. Bapt. Conv., 1964-66; trustee Mich. Bapt. Inst., 1963-66; mem. San Francisco Inter-Faith Task Force on Homelessness. Mem. Internat. Assn. Mission Study, Am. Soc. Missiology, Assn. Mission Profs. Co-editor: The Mission of the Church in the Racially Changing Community, 1969; author: How Churches Grow in an Urban World, 1978, Classics of Christian Missions, 1979, God Who Sends: A Fresh Quest for Biblical Mission, 1983, Home Cell Groups and House Churches, 1987, Mystic on Main Street, 1994; contbr. to Toward Creative Urban Strategy; Vol. III Ency. of So. Baptists, also articles to profl. jours. E-mail: fddubose@aol.com. Home: 1062 Fulton St San Francisco CA 94117

DUBOV, SPENCER FLOYD, podiatrist, educator; b. Bklyn., Nov. 26, 1935; s. Simon and Ella D.; children: Valerie Ellen Dubov Tantillo, Coreycott. Student, Bklyn. Coll., 1956; D of Podiatric Medicine, N.Y. Coll. Podiatric Medicine, 1960; BS, Regent Coll, 1992. Diplomate Am. Bd. Ambulatory Foot Surgery (divsn. Am. Bd. Podiatric Surgery). Internship Foot Clinics N.Y., 1959-60; podiatrist out-patient dept. Queens Hosp. Ctr., L.I. Jewish Hosp., 1961-76; podiatrist Queens Foot Care, Flushing, N.Y. Mem. surg. staff St. Joseph's Hosp., Cath. Med. Ctr., North Shore U. Hosp. at Plainview, Massapequa Gen. Hosp., N.Y. Hosp. Med. Ctr. of Queens; mem. attending staff Clearview Nursing Home; mem. peer rev. com. N.Y. State, 1971, 86-89, 90—; chair N.Y. State Bd. Podiatry; mem. faculty foot care confs., 1963-65, 71, N.Y. Coll. Podiatric Med., 1978-79; chmn. N.Y. State Grad. Edn. Program, 1965. Contbr. articles to profl. jours. Fellow Assn. Ambulatory Foot Surgery; mem. Am. Podiatric Med. Assn., Queens County Div. Podiatric Med. Soc. State N.Y. (pres., chmn. medicare liason com., Podiatrist of Yr. award 1976), Aircraft Owners Pilots Assn., Am. Radio Relay League, L.I. Mobile Amateur Radio Club, Lions Club, B'nai Brith, Knights of Pythias. Avocations: jogging, paddle and raquet ball, tennis, golf, hunting. Office: Queens Foot Care 69-20 Main St Flushing NY 11367-1703

DUBUC, MARY ELLEN, educational administrator; b. N.Y.C. July 20, 1950; d. Patrick Joseph and Catherine (McKenna) Reynolds; BA cum laude (scholar), Marymount Manhattan Coll., 1972; MA, Columbia U., 1973; cert. advanced grad. studies R.I. Coll., 1985; m. Leo Dennis Dubuc Jr., Sept. 9, 1978; children: Brian Robert, Kimberly Ann. Spl. edn. tchr. Cardinal Cushing Sch., Hanover, Mass., 1973-76, Ferncliff Manor Sch., Yonkers, N.Y., 1976-77; program coordinator Bronx Devel. Services, 1977-78; dir. edn. R.I. Assn. Retarded, Woonsocket, 1978-84, spl. edn. cons., 1984-92; qualified med. retardation profl. Seacliff, Inc., Cumberland, R.I., 1988-91; tchr. BICO Collaborative Program, North Attleboro, Mass., 1989; acting exec. dir. Seacliff, Inc., 1991-93; dir. quality assurance Avatar, Inc., 1992; dir. specialized svcs. The ARC of No. R.I., Woonsocket, 1992-99, asst. adminstr. habilitative svcs., 1999—. Fed. trainee, 1971, 72. Mem. North Smithfield PTA, 1986—; ednl. evaluator No. R.I. Collaborative, 1992. Recipient FrankBerchman award for Profl. of Yr., ARC of No. R.I. Mem. Assn. Severely Handicapped, R.I. Assn. Retarded Citizens, NAFE, R.I. Assn. Adult and Continuing Edn. (v.p. pub. rels. 1986-89, corr. sec. 1991-93), Alpha Chi. Democrat. Roman Catholic. Office: The ARC of No RI 80 Fabien St Woonsocket RI 02895-6277

DUBUC-SCHINDLER, DEBORAH JO, special education educator; b. Manhattan, Kans., Feb. 7, 1957; d. Philip Louis and Elouise Ann (Vanderbilt) Humbargar; m. Gary Gerard Dubuc, May 31, 1975 (div. July 1976); 1 child, Devin Anthony; m. Joseph Julian Schindler Jr., Mar. 18, 2003. BS Edn. and Psychology magna cum laude, Marymount Coll. Kans., Salina, 1981; MS in Spl. Edn., Kans. State U., 1990. Cert. regular and spl. edn.-learning disabilities tchr. Tchr. 3rd grade Unified Sch. Dist. 475, Geary County Schs., Ft. Riley, Junction City, Kans., 1981-87, self-contained learning disabilities tchr. Junction City, 1987-88, mem. English, reading, math. and sci. task force Ft. Riley, Junction City, 1986-88; learning disabilities itinerant tchr. United Sch. Dist. 305, Salina (Kans.) Pub. Schs., 1989-95, spl. edn. resource tchr. K-12, 1995-97, interrelated spl. edn. instr., 1997—; realtor Broker's Realty, Salina, Kans., 1995—. Univ. supr. on honorarium Kans. State U., 1991; Homebound spl. edn. instr. Unified Sch. Dist. #239, 1992. Co-curriculum guides math., sci., English, reading, 1986-88; contbr. articles to profl. jours. Chair Orgns. Com., Salina, 1979-81, Custer Hill Social Com., Ft. Riley, 1986-87; scout leader Girl Scouts U.S., Salina, 1980-81; asst. leader Cub Scouts, Boy Scouts Am., Manhattan, Kans., 1985-86, comm. officer, 1986-87; mem. choir First Nazarene Ch., Salina, 1989-92; active Salina Area Transition Coun., 1990-97. Mem. Coun. for Exceptional Children (rep. 1988-89, 94-95), Kans. Nat. Ednl. Assn. (alt. del. 1998—), Internat. Reading Assn., Junction City Edn. Assn. (mem. pub. rels. com. 1981, elected mem. profl. devel. com. United Sch. Dist. 305 term 1991-92, 92-93), Assn. Ctrl. Colls. of Kans. (univ. supr. 1991, 93, 94, spl. edn. instr. 1993), Learning Disabilities Assn., Alpha Chi. Avocations: gourmet cooking, travel, vocal music, recreational swimming, writing. Home: 1633 E Beloit Ave Salina KS 67401-8368 Office: Cen Kans Coop in Edn 715 N 9th Salina KS 67401-8038

DUCHANE, KIM ALLEN, health and physical education educator; b. Tawas City, Mich., May 7, 1955; s. Richard John and Doris June (Frechette) D.; m. Rita Ann Willibey, June 24, 1989; 1 child, Jamie Nicole. BS, No. Mich. U., 1978; MA, Sam Houston State U., 1987; PhD, Tex. Woman's U., 1996. Cert. tchr., Tex. Tchr., coach Munising (Mich.) Pub. Schs., 1978-79, Spring Ind. Sch. Dist., Houston, 1981-87; adminstrv. asst., coach Lake Superior State U., Sault Ste. Marie, Mich., 1979-81; rsch. asst. Tex. Woman's U., Denton, 1987-88; tchr. Tomball (Tex.) Ind. Sch. Dist., 1988-90, Aldine Ind. Sch. Dist., Houston, 1990-92; assoc. prof. dept. health and phys. edn. Manchester Coll., North Manchester, Ind., 1992—. Adapted phys. edn. cons. Manchester Coll., Ind., 1992—; mem. adapted phys. edn. team Ind. Dept. Edn., Indpls., 1993—. Contbr. articles to profl. publs., chpt. to book. Bd. dirs. Inter-Collegiate Ministries, North Manchester, 1993—; Sunday sch. tchr., Sweetwater Assembly of God, North Manchester, 1992—; vol. phys. edn. tchr. Laketon Elem. Sch., North Manchester, 1993—. Mem. AAHPERD, Ind. Assn. Health, Phys. Edn., Recreation and Dance, Men's Ministry of Sweetwater Assembly of God. Home: 715 N Sycamore St North Manchester IN 46962-1249 Office: Manchester Coll 604 E College Ave MC Box PERC North Manchester IN 46962-1276 E-mail: kaduchane@manchester.edu.

DUCHARME, ADELE, educational administrator; b. Alexandria, La., Mar. 2, 1943; d. Robert James and Mary Elizabeth (Holly) Ducharme; children— Shannon M. Rutland, Shawn H. Rutland; m. Lack James Watford. BS in Elem. Edn., La. State U.-Baton Rouge, 1964, MEd, 1981, Ed.D., 1984. Tchr., Parkview Elem. Sch., Baton Rouge, 1977, Trinity Episc. Sch., Baton Rouge, 1977-82; grad. teaching asst. La. State U., Baton Rouge, 1982-84; asst. prof. elem. edn. Troy State U., Montgomery, Ala., 1984—, asst-dean edn.; cons. Trafton Acad., Baton Rouge, 1984; dir., cons. Learning Unltd., Baton Rouge, 1983-84; dept. head. middle grades edn. Valdosta State U. Contbr. articles to profl. jours. Mem. Internat. Reading Assn., Nat. Reading Conf., Nat. Middle Grades Assn., Ga. Middle Grades Assn., Assn. for Supervision and Curriculum Devel., Kappa Kappa Iota, Phi Delta Kappa. Avocations: painting; gardening. Home: 103 Worthington Pl Valdosta GA 31602-4236 Office: PO Box 4419 Montgomery AL 36103-4419

DUCHARME, DONALD WALTER, pharmacologist, educator; b. Saginaw, Mich., June 14, 1937; s. Walter Arnold and Marion (Law) DuC.; m. Doris Barbara Rieck, Aug. 30, 1958; children: Michael Kevin, Mark Donald, Daniel Paul. BA in Biology and Chemistry, Cen. Mich. U., 1959; PhD in Pharmacology, U. Mich., 1965. Rsch. scientist cardiovascular disease rsch. The Upjohn Co., Kalamazoo, 1965-78, rsch. head, 1978-84, assoc. dir., 1984-88, sr. scientist, 1988-90, sr. scientist safety pharmacology, 1990-94; owner Lakeside Entertainment Ctr., South Haven, Mich., 1997—. Adj. asst. prof. dept. biology Western Mich. U., Kalamazoo, 1970-73; adj. prof. dept. pharmacology Med. Coll. Ohio, Toledo, 1977-94. Contbr. over 60 articles to profl. jours.; editorial bd. Clinical and Experimental Hypertension, 1979-96, Jour. of Cardiovascular Pharmacology, 1985-96. Bd. dirs. Kalamazoo unit Mich. Heart Assn., 1968—, Am. Heart Assn. Mich., Detroit, 1972-98, pres., 1981-82, Am. Heart Assn., Midwest affiliate, 1998—. USPHS fellow, 1961-65; recipient W.E. Upjohn award, 1977. Fellow Am. Heart Assn. (Coun. for High Blood Pressure Rsch., Harry Goldblatt award 1991, H.E. Dodge award 1993, F.D. Dodrill award 1995); mem. Am. Soc. for Pharmacology and Exptl. Therapeutics. Lutheran. Achievements include 9 patents for medical use of novel chemicals; research on neurogenic and humoral control of the circulatory system, role of the kidney in regulation of vascular capacity, role of prostaglandins in pathophysiologic regulation of cardiovascular system, pathophysiologic role of endogenous ouabain in regulation of the cardiovascular system. Home: 48251 29 1/2 St Paw Paw MI 49079-9408 E-mail: d.ducharme@att.net.

DUCHOWNY, MICHAEL S. physician, educator; b. N.Y.C., Nov. 17, 1945; s. Boris M. and Helen J. Duchowny; children: Alexandria, Catherine, Margot. AB, Cornell U., 1966; MD, Albert Einstein Coll. Medicine, 1970. Cert. Am. Bd. Pediat., Am. Bd. Neurology (spl. competency in child neurology), Am. Bd. Clin. Neurophysiology. Intern in pediat. U. Chgo., 1970—71; resident in pediat. Montefiore Hosp., N.Y.C., 1971—72; rsch. assoc. NIH, 1972—74; resident in neurology Harvard U., Boston, 1974—77, asst. prof., 1979—80; dir. epilepsy program Miami Childrens Hosp., 1987—; clin. prof. neurology & pediat. U. Miami, Fla., 1992—. Academic chair pediatric epilepsy Miami Children's Hosp., 1999. Editor (assoc. editor): Jour. Child Neurology; mem. editl. bd.: Epileptic Disorders Pediatric Neurology, Epilepsy Currents; editor: (book) Intractable Focal Epilepsy, 2000; contbr. articles to profl. jours. Fellow: Am. Acad. Neurologists, Am. Acad. Physicians. Avocations: banjo, racquetball, fly fishing, photography, hiking. Office: Miami Childrens Hosp 3200 SW 60th Ct Miami FL 33155 Business E-Mail: michael.duchowny@mch.com.

DUCKETT, BERNADINE JOHNAL, retired elementary principal; b. Flint, Mich., Aug. 7, 1939; d. John and Bernice (Robinson) Edwards: m. Ellis Duckett Jr., Apr. 15, 1963; children: Bruce Devlon, Janeen Jae; 1 stepchild, Ellis III; m. Charles Teaberry (div. June 1960). BS in Edn., Ctrl. Mich. U., 1962; MA in Ednl. Adminstrn., U. Mich., 1966; Reading Specialist, Mich. State U., 1970; postgrad., Flint (Mich.) C.C., 1989-92. Cert. elem. tchr., Mich. Classroom tchr. Dort Elem. Sch., Flint, 1959-65; reading tchr. Dort & Dewey Elem. Sch., Flint, 1965-67; instrnl. specialist Doyle and Dewey Elem. Sch., Flint, 1967-71; asst. prin. Dewey, Merrill & Cook Elem. Sch., Flint, 1971-74; prin. Garfield & Elem. M.L. King, Flint, 1974-96; ret., 1996. Presenter, mem. Internat. Ednl. Symposium, Rome, 1988-92, Flint Schs. Employee of Month Program, 1985-92. Author: Diet on the Lighter Side, 1988, My Grandparents Said Go 4 It, 1989; author joint books: Bicentennial Sch. Cookbook, 1976, Tapestry, 1988, URA Winner, 1994; presenter Tribute to Georgia Hyche, 2003; contbr. articles to mags. and newspapers. Mem. Faith Tabernacle Choir, 2003; fundraiser walk-a-thons United Negro Coll. Fund, Children's Miracle, Flint, 1991, Crim Race for Spl. Children, Flint, 1989—2003, Riverbend Striders, Flint, 1993—; mem., presenter Consortium to Prevent Child Abuse, 1990; vol. St. Joseph Hosp. Aux., Flint, 1990—98; walker March of Dimes, 2002; walker, medalist marathon Arthritis Found., 2000. Named to Greater Flint Afro-Am. Sports Hall of Fame, 1992—2003; recipient Outstanding Educator plaque, NAACP, Flint Intern Plaque, 1986, Flint OBE Pioneer Plaque, 1993, Ednl. Contbns. as Family award, 1993, Walker medal, Leukeima Soc., 1996, Walker-Prevention of Breast Cancer medal, 2000—01, medal, Nat. Arthritis Hawaii Marathon Walker, 2001; grantee, Flint Cmty. Schs., 1990—93. Mem. Nat. Assn. Elem. Sch. Prins. (dir. founds. 1992-96, cons., student discipline Focus Group on Ethnic Minorities 1981, 92, 94, Outstanding Svc. Plaque 1993), Nat. Assn. Media Women (sec. Flint chpt. 1989-92, Media Woman of Yr. 1990), Mich. Assn. Elem. and Mid. Sch. Prins. (chairperson awards, mem. conf. planning and summer camp com., treas., membership chair, del., presenter 1977-92, certs. 1985, 87, 91, plaque 1990), Nat. Alliance Black Sch. Educators (presenter 1993), Internat. Platform Assn., Flint Assn. Elem. Prins. (sec., election chair, social chair 1980-96), Global Network of Schs., U. Mich. Alumni Assn., Nat. Leukemia Soc. (Alaskan marathon walker, medalist 1996), Quota Club Internat. (mem. com. aiding hard of hearing, 1994-2003, guest speaker "Tribute to Georgia Hyche Day" 2003). Avocations: marathon walking, writing poetry, reading, flower gardening, singing. Home: 3720 Circle Dr Flint MI 48507-1879

DUCKWORTH, GUY, musician, pianist, educator; b. L.A., Dec. 19, 1923; s. Glenn M. and Laura (Lysle) D.; m. Ballerina Maria Farra, May 23, 1948. BA, UCLA, 1951; MusM, Columbia U., 1953, PhD, 1969. Piano soloist Metro Goldwyn Mayer Studios, 1936-41, Warner Bros. Studios, 1936-41, Sta. KFI, L.A., 1938, Sta. KNX, L.A., 1939, Sta. KHJ, L.A., 1940; artist Columbia Artists, 1942-49; asst. prof. music. U. Minn., Mpls., 1955-60, assoc. prof., 1960-62; prof. piano, fellow Northwestern U., Evanston, Ill., 1962-70, chmn. dept. preparatory piano, 1962-70; prof. music U. Colo., Boulder, 1970-88, prof. emeritus, 1988, originator, coordinator masters and doctoral programs in mus. arts. Piano concert tours in U.S., Can., Mexico, 1947-49; condr. various music festivals, U.S., 1956—; dir. Walker Art Children's Concerts, Mpls., 1957-62; nat. piano chmn. Music Educators Nat. Conf., 1965-71; vis. lectr., scholar 96 univs., colls. and conservatories, U.S. and Can., 1964—; cons. to Ill. State Dept. Program Devel. for Gifted Children, 1968-69; vis. prof. U. Colo., 1988-90. Creator, performer: TV series "A New Dimension in Piano Instruction", 1959 (Nat. award for outstanding ednl. TV series from Nat. Ednl. TV); author: Keyboard Explorer, 1963, Keyboard Discoverer, 1963, Keyboard Builder, 1964, Keyboard Musician, 1964, Keyboard Performer, 1966, Keyboard Musicianship, 1970, Guy Duckworth Piano Library, 1974, Guy Duckworth Musicianship Series, 1975, Keyboard Musician: The Symmetrical Keyboard, 2 vols., 1987-88, Keyboard Musician: The Symmetrical Keyboard, 1988, rev. edit., 1990; contbr. to over 6 books, 23 articles on pedagogy of music to various jours.; prodr., performer video tapes on piano tchg.; prodr., writer (film) The Person First: A Different Kind of Teaching, 1984 Nominator Irving S. Gilmore Internat. Keyboard Festival, Gilmore Artist and Young Artist Awards. With U.S. Army, 1943-46. Recipient All-Univ. Teaching award for excellence, U. Colo., 1981, Pedagogy Honors award Nat. Conf. Piano Pedagogy, Chgo., 1994; named Pioneer Pedagogue Nat. Corp. Piano Pedagogy, Princeton U. Retrospective, 1992. Mem. Music Tchrs. Nat. Assn., Colo. State Music Tchrs. Assn., Coll. Music Soc., Music Educators Nat. Conf., Music Teachers Assn. Calif., Phi Mu Alpha, Pi Kappa Lambda. Office: U Colo Coll of Music Boulder CO 80302

DUCKWORTH, MARVIN E. lawyer, educator; b. Aug. 16, 1942; s. Marvin E. and Maryann Duckworth; children: Matthew, Brian, Jennifer, Jeffrey. BS in Indsl. Engring., Iowa State U., 1964; JD, Drake U., 1968. Bar: Iowa 1968, U.S. Dist. Ct. (no. and so. dists.) Iowa 1969. Assoc. Davis, Huebner, Johnson & Burt, Des Moines, 1968-70; asst. prof. Drake U., 1970-71, lectr. law, 1971-85, assoc. dean clin. programs, 1986-87, adj. prof., 1987—; shareholder Hopkins & Huebner, P.C., Des Moines, 1971—. Spkr. in field. Pres. Drake Law Bd. Counselors, 1991-92, Drake Law Endowment Trust, 1995-96. Named Alumnus of Yr. Drake Law Sch., 1997. Fellow Iowa Bar Found.; mem. ABA (chmn. workers compensation and employers liability law 1986-87, vice hmn. toxic and hazardous substances and environ. law com. 1989-93), Iowa Bar Assn. (pres. young lawyers sect. 1977-78, Merit award 1982, chair workers compensation sect. 1992-93), Def. Rsch. Inst., Fedn. Ins. and Corp. Counsel (workers compensation com.), Iowa Assn. Workers Compensation Lawyers (pres. 1988-89), Iowa Acad. Trial Lawyers, Order of Coif. Office: 2700 Grand Ave Ste 111 Des Moines IA 50312-5215

DUCKWORTH, PAULA OLIVER, secondary school educator, freelance artist, writer, photographer; b. Dallas, Aug. 5, 1940; d. Allen Oliver and Minnie Lila (Paul) D. BA, U. Tex., 1963; MA, So. Meth. U., 1968; postgrad., U. London, 1972, R.I. Sch. Design, 1983, U. North Tex., 1985—87. Tchr. English San Antonio Ind. Sch. Dist., 1963-65; tchr. art and English Highland Pk. Ind. Sch. Dist., Dallas, 1965—2001; tchr. art Yarneh Acad., Dallas, 2001—. Tchr. Perkins Sch. of Theology, So. Meth. U., 1995-97. Illustrator: A Cotton Feast, 1982; paintings exhibited in several shows and pvt. collections. Patron, Kimball Art Mus., Dallas Mus. Art, Meadows Mus. at So. Meth. U.; elder Highland Pk. Presbyn Ch. Mem. Nat. Art Edn. Assn., So. Meth. U. Alumni Assn., Highland Pk. Alumni Assn., Kappa Alpha Theta, Delta Kappa Gamma (Sim Green scholar 1973). Democrat. Presbyterian.

DUCOMB, SUZANNE MARIE, health and physical education educator; b. Havertown, Pa., Feb. 17, 1961; d. William Crawford and Arlene Catherine (Riegler) DuC. BS in Health and Phys. Edn., West Chester (Pa.) State Coll., 1983; MEd in Phys. Edn. and Sport Mgmt., East Stroudsburg (Pa.) U., 1994. Cert. tchr. health and phys. edn.; lic. soccer coach. Coach and per diem substitute Rose Tree-Media (Pa.) Sch. Dist., 1983-85; health club supr. Penn Estates Resort Cmty., Analomink, Pa., 1985-87; tchr. health and phys. edn. Phillipsburg (N.J.) Cath. H.S., 1987-90, Ctrl. Dauphin Sch. Dist., Harrisburg, Pa., 1993—. Dir. Goals for Girls Soccer Camp, Pa., 1991—; coaching sch. instr. Ea. Pa. Youth Soccer Assn., 1991—, Olympic Devel. Program coaching staff, 1982-85, 90—. Mem. AAHPERD, Women's Soccer Found., Nat. Soccer Coaches Assn. of Am., U.S. Soccer Coaches Orgn. Avocations: racquetball, reading, photography. Office: Goals For Girls Soccer Camp PO Box 6030 Harrisburg PA 17112-0030

DUCOTE, DEBORAH M. elementary education educator, reading specialist; Elem. tchr. Richardson Mid. Sch., West Monroe, La.; curriculum coord. Richardson H.S., West Monroe. Named La. State Tchr. of Yr., 1993.*

DUDA, PATRICIA MARY, gifted education educator, owner cosmetics company; b. Trenton, N.J., Jan. 19, 1949; d. Frank Donald and Marion Monica (Hollingsworth) Girard; m. Michael L. Duda, July 27, 1974; 1 child: Michael Patrick. BA, Alvernia Coll., 1970; degree, U. Sorbonne, Paris, 1973; postgrad., Trenton State Coll., 1974, 78, 80, St. Mary's Coll., London, 1971. Cert. tchr., N.J. French tchr. Hamilton East High Sch., Trenton, 1970-80; activities dir. Sears, Roebuck and Co., Trenton, 1975-80; tchr. Barbizon Modeling Sch., Princeton, N.J., 1976-78; tchr. of gifted Hamilton West High Sch., Trenton, 1980—. Grant recipient writer area sch. dist., 1979, 88, 89, 90, 91, 92. Sch. union rep. Hamilton Twp. Bd. Edn., 1970—; com. mem., canvasser Am. Cancer Soc., 1989; active Am. Heart Assn., 1989—, Clean Air Assn., 1989—, Police Benevolent Assn., 1989—, Nat. Aquarium Assn., 1989—. Recipient Curriculum award, Hamilton Bd. Edn. Mem. AAUW (co-chair scholarship com., 1987-89), Nat. Storytellers Assn., N.J. Edn. Assn., N.J. Curriculum and Suprs. Assn., Hamilton Twp. Edn. Assn. (tchr.'s union rep. 1975-78, liaison to bd. dirs., tchr.'s bldg. rep. 1978-89), Delta Kappa Gamma (recipient Rose award, 1988). Roman Catholic. Avocations: collecting baseball cards, antique glass, jewelry, perfume bottles and furniture. Office: Hamilton Twp Bd Edn 90 Park Ave Trenton NJ 08690-2024

DUDDEN, ARTHUR POWER, historian, educator; b. Cleve., Oct. 26, 1921; s. Arthur Clifford and Kathleen (Bray) D.; m. Adrianne Churchill Onderdonk, June 5, 1965; 1 child, Alexis Dudden; children by previous marriage: Kathleen Dudden Rowlands, Candace L. Dudden (Schweitzer). AB, Wayne State U., 1942; A.M., U. Mich., 1947, PhD, 1950. Faculty Bryn Mawr Coll., 1950—, prof. history, 1965-92, Fairbank prof. humanities, 1989-92, Katharine E. McBride prof. history, 1992-95, 98-99, prof. emeritus history and Fairbank prof. emeritus humanities, 1992—. Instr. CCNY, summer 1950; vis. asst. prof. Am. civilization U. Pa., 1953-54, edn. coord. spl. program Am. civilization, 1956, mem. faculty Inst. Humanistic Studies for Execs., 1953-59, vis. assoc. prof. history, summers, 1958, 62-65, vis. prof. history, 1965-68; vis. assoc. prof. Princeton (N.J.) U., 1958-59, Haverford Coll., 1962-63; vis. prof. Trinity Coll., summer 1965; cons. Peace Corps, 1962-66; mem. Bicentennial Com. on Internat. Confs. of Americanists, 1973-76; founding pres. Fulbright Assn. of Alumni, 1976—, exec. dir., 1980-84; cons. Nat. Archives, 1993-95; adj. prof. history Lehigh U., 1993-95. Author: Teachers Manual to the American Republic, vols. I and II, 1959, 60, 70, Understanding the American Republic, vols. I and II, 1961, 70, Objective Tests, The American Republic, 1962, The Assault of Laughter, 1962, The United States of America: A Syllabus of American Studies, 2 vols, 1963, The Instructor's Guide to the United States, 3d edit, 1972, The Student's Guide to the United States, 2d edit, 1967, Joseph Fels and the Single Tax Movement, 1971, Pardon Us, Mr. President!, 1975, The Fulbright Experience, 1946-1986, 1987, American Humor, 1987, The American Pacific, 1992, paperback edit., 1993; editor: Woodrow Wilson and the World of Today, 1957, The Logbook of the Captain's Clerk, 1995; compiler: International Directory of Specialists in American Studies, 1975; contbr. Ency. Am. Social History, 1993, Ency. U.S. Fgn. Rels., 1997. Served with USNR, 1942-45. Sr. Fulbright scholar Denmark, 1959-60 and West Europe, 1992. Mem. Fellows Am. Studies (sec.-treas. 1957-59, pres. 1960-61), Am. Studies Assn. (treas. 1968, 72, exec. sec. 1969-72, Bode-Pearson prize 1991), Am. Hist. Assn., Orgn. Am. Historians (local arrangements chmn. Phila. 1969), Harriton Assn. (bd. dirs. 1962—), Hist. Soc. of Pa. (trustee 1993-99). Home: 829 Old Gulph Rd Bryn Mawr PA 19010-2910 E-mail: adudden@brynmawr.edu.

DUDENHOEFFER, FRANCES TOMLIN, physical education educator; b. San Antonio, Aug. 8, 1943; d. Arthur Reader and Annie Beatrice (Everett) Tomlin; m. Arthur Wood Dudenhoeffer, July 17, 1976. BS in Edn., S.W. Tex. State U., San Marcos, 1965; MS in Phys. Edn., U. N.C., Greensboro, 1967; PhD, U. Tex., 1977. Cert. recreational sports specialist; cert. tchr., Tex.; mem. cast My Three Angels prodn. Eastside Ch. of Christ, 2002. Grad. asst. U. N.C., Greensboro, 1965-66; instr. U. Okla., Norman, 1966-70, asst. prof., 1970-72; recreational sports specialist U. Tex., Austin, 1971-72, grad. asst., 1973-74; lectr., women's intramural dir. U. North Tex., Denton, 1974-76; intramural dir. N.Mex. State U., Las Cruces, 1976-97; field staff Kappa Delta Pi Internat., 1998-2000. Mem. intramural task force Las Cruces Pub. Schs., 1987-89; content rev. panel N.Mex. Dept. Edn., Santa Fe, 1984; expert witness Lea County Atty., Lovington, N.Mex., 1988. Author: (manual) Intramural Staff Handbook, 1992; editl. com.: Navigating the Tides of Change, 1994; editor/author: (pamphlet) Guidelines for Intramural Programs, 1992; contbr. articles to profl. jours. Bd. dirs. Los Amigos de Krwg, Las Cruces, 1994-97. Recipient Excellence in Programming Nat. Intramural Sports Coun., Reston, Va., 1989, Disting. Alumnus in Phys. Edn. award S.W. State U., San Marcos, Tex., 1990, Disting. Svc. award Nat. Assn. Sports and Phys. Edn., Reston, Va., 1993, Ft. Bliss Fed. Credit Union Svc. award for N.Mex. State U. Profl. Staff, 1996. Mem. AAHPERD (pres. S.W. dist. 1992-93, Honor award 1994, reviewer Jour. of PERD 1997—), Nat. Intramural Recreational Sports Assn. (state dir. 1994-96, editl. bd. NIRSA Jour. 1996-99), N.Mex. Assn. Health, Phys. Edn., Recreation and Dance (pres. 1988-89, Honor award 1989), Kappa Delta Pi (chpt. counselor 1987-97), Phi Delta Kappa, Alpha Xi Delta Alumnae Assn. (publicity chair Pike's Peak chpt. 1999-2003, pres. 2003—). Avocations: stamp collecting and exhibiting, racquetball, golf, badminton. Home: 4980 Molly Pond Ct Colorado Springs CO 80917-1045 E-mail: f.dudenhoeffer@att.net.

DUDERSTADT, JAMES JOHNSON, academic administrator, engineering educator; b. Ft. Madison, Iowa, Dec. 5, 1942; s. Mack Henry and Katharine Sydney (Johnson) D.; m. Anne Marie, June 24, 1964; children: Susan Kay, Katharine Anne. B in Engring. with highest honors, Yale U., 1964; MS in Engring. Sci, Calif. Inst. Tech., 1965, PhD in Engring. Sci. and Physics, 1967. Asst. prof. nuclear engring. U. Mich., 1969—72, assoc. prof., 1972—76, prof., 1976—81; dean U. Mich. (Coll. Engring.), 1981—86; provost, v.p. acad. affairs U. Mich., 1986—88, pres. univ., 1988—96, pres. emeritus, prof. sci. engring., 1996—. Dir. Millennium Project, 1996—. AEC fellow, 1964-68; recipient E. O. Lawrence award U.S. Dept. Energy, 1986, Nat. medal of Tech., 1991; named Nat. Engr. of Yr., NSPE, 1991. Fellow Am. Nuclear Soc. (Mark Mills award 1968, Arthur Holly Compton award 1985); mem. NAE (coun.), Am. Phys. Soc., Nat. Sci. Bd. (chair 1991-94), Am. Acad. Arts & Scis., Sigma Xi, Tau Beta Pi, Phi Beta Kappa. Office: Millennium Project 2001 Media Union Ann Arbor MI 48109*

DUDLEY, BROOKE FITZHUGH, educational consultant; b. East Orange, NJ, Oct. 22, 1942; s. Benjamin William and Jean (Peeples) D.; m. Elizabeth Slater; 1 child, Catherine Sanford. AB in Econs., Colgate U., 1966. Sales mgr. De La Rue Instruments, Phila., 1968-71; comml. banker Bankers Trust Co., N.Y.C., 1966-68, Provident Nat. Bank, Phila., 1972-74; dir. admissions/fin. aid St. Stephen's Episc. Sch., Austin, Tex., 1974-78; exec. dir. U. Tex. Law Sch. Found., Austin, 1978-85; ednl. cons., 1982—; founding ptnr. The Edn. Group Southwest, Inc., 1989-92; exec. dir. San Antonio Art Inst., 1992-93; founding ptnr. Peninsula Group, 1999—. Chmn. bd. trustees Austin Evaluation Ctr.; trustee Austin Repertory Theater; chmn. bd. dirs. All Saints Episc. Day Sch., Austin; Bishop's com. St. Michael's and All Angels Episcopal Ch., Blanco, Tex.; bd. dirs. Symphony Sq., Austin Child Guidance and Evaluation Ctr.; adv. trustee Winston Sch., San Antonio; Rep. campaign mgr., NYC, 1966-68; trustee Rio Blanco Montessori Sch.; founding chmn. bd. trustees Ind. Ednl. Cons. Found. With U.S. Army, 1962-64. Mem. Ind. Ednl. Cons. Assn. (past chmn. bd. trustees, found. chmn. bd. trustees), Hill Sch. Alumni Assn. (exec. com. 1968-71), Edna Gladney Austin Aux. (past pres.). Episcopalian. Office: PO Box 867 Blanco TX 78606 E-mail: dudley@moment.net.

DUDLEY, KATHRYN MARIE, anthropology and American studies educator; b. Dec. 9, 1958; BA in Psychology, U. Wis., Milw., 1984; MA in Anthropology, Columbia U., 1987, PhD in Anthropology, 1991. Adj. asst. prof. anthropology Columbia U., N.Y.C., 1991—93; from asst. prof. to assoc. prof. anthropology Yale U., New Haven, 1993—2002, prof. anthropology and Am. studies, 2002—. Author: The End of the Line: Lost Jobs, New Lives in Post-Industrial America, 1994, Debt and Dispossession: Farm Loss in America's Heartland, 2000. Recipient Harry Chapin Media award, 1995, Margaret Mead award, 2000. Mem. Phi Beta Kappa. Office: Yale U Dept Anthropology PO Box 208277 New Haven CT 06520-8277

DUDLEY, RICHARD MANSFIELD, mathematician, educator; b. East Cleveland, Ohio, July 28, 1938; s. Winston Mansfield and Charlotte Mae (Wheaton) D.; m. Elizabeth Allen Martin, June 3, 1978. AB, Harvard U., 1959; PhD, Princeton U., 1962. Asst. prof. math. U. Calif., Berkeley, 1963-66; asso. prof. MIT, 1967-72, prof., 1972—. Author: Real Analysis and Probability, 1989, 2d edit., 2002, Uniform Central Limit Theorems, 1999; editor: White Mountain Guide, 1979, Annals of Probability, 1979—81. Alfred P. Sloan Found. fellow, 1966-68, Guggenheim Found. fellow, 1991. Fellow AAAS, Am. Statis. Assn., Inst. Math. Stats.; mem. APHA, Am. Math. Soc., Bernoulli Soc., Internat. Statis. Inst. Democrat. Home: 92 Lewis St Newton MA 02458-1840 Office: MIT 77 Massachusetts Ave Rm 2-245 Cambridge MA 02139-4307

DUDRICK, STANLEY JOHN, surgeon, scientist, educator; b. Nanticoke, Pa., Apr. 9, 1935; s. Stanley Francis and Stephania Mary (Jachimczak) D.; m. Theresa M. Keen, June 14, 1958; children: Susan Marie, Paul Stanley, Carolyn Mary, Stanley Jonathan, Holly Anne, Anne Theresa. BS cum laude, Franklin and Marshall Coll., 1957; MD, U. Pa., 1961; MA (hon.), Yale U., 1999. Diplomate Am. Bd. Surgery. Intern Hosp. of U. Pa., Phila., 1961-62, resident in gen. surgery, 1962-67; acad. practice specializing in surgery Phila., 1967-72, 88-90, Houston, 1972-88, 90-94, Waterbury, New Haven, 1994—, Bridgeport, 2000—; chief surg. svcs. Hermann Hosp., Houston, 1972-80, surgeon in chief, dir. Ctr. Cardiovascular Disease, dir. nutritional support svcs., dir. Nutritional Sci. Ctr., 1990-94; prof. surgery U. Tex. Med. Sch., Houston, 1972-82, clin. prof. surgery, 1982-95, chmn. dept. surgery, 1972-80. Cons. in surgery M.D. Anderson Hosp. and Tumor Inst., 1973-88, clin. prof. surgery, cons. to pres., 1982-88; sr. cons. surgery and medicine Tex. Inst. for Rehab. and Rsch., 1974-88; mem. Anatomical Bd., State of Tex., 1973-78; examiner Am. Bd. Surgery, 1974-78, bd. dirs., 1978-84, sr. mem. 1984-2000, also mem. and chmn. various coms.; chmn. sci. adv. com. Tex. Med. Ctr. Libr., 1974; mem. food and nutrition bd. NRC-Nat. Acad. Scis., 1973-75; mem. sci. adv. com. Nat. Found. for Ileitis and Colitis; mem. surgery, anesthesia and trauma study sect. NIH, 1982-86; chmn. dept. surgery Pa. Hosp., Phila., 1988-90, surgeon in chief, 1988-91, hon. surgery staff, 1991—; clin. prof. surgery U. Pa., 1988-93; assoc. chmn. dept. surgery, 1994-2000, 02--, dir. surgery program, 1994-2000, 02--, dir. Med. Edn., 1995-2000, 02--, St. Mary's Hosp., Waterbury, Conn.; clin. prof. surgery, Yale U., New Haven, Conn., 1995-99, prof. surgery, 1999—; chmn. dept. surgery, dir. surg. edn. Bridgeport Hosp.-Yale U. New Haven Health Sys., 2000-02; adj. prof. surgery Quinippiac U., 1996—. Editor: Manual of Surgical Nutrition, 1975, Manual of Preoperative and Postoperative Care, 1983, Current Strategies in Surgical Nutrition, 1991, Practical Handbook of Nutrition in Clinical Practice, 1994, Surgical Nutrition: Strategies in Critically Ill Patients, 1995; assoc. editor Nutrition in Medicine, 1975—; editorial bd. Annals of Surgery, 1975—, Infusion, 1978—, Nutrition and Cancer, 1980—, Nutrition Support Services, 1980-86, Jour. Clin. Surgery, 1980-83, Nutrition Research, 1981—, Intermed. Communications Nursing Services, 1981—, Postgraduate General Surgery, 1992—; others; contbr. chpts. to books, articles to profl. jours.; inventor of new technique of intravenous feeding and anti-cholesterol therapy. Bd. dirs. Found. for Children, Houston, Harris County unit Am. Cancer Soc., Phila. chpt., 1988-90; trustee Franklin and Marshall Coll., 1985—, mem. student life, art collection, and trusteeship coms., 1986-2002, mem. overseers bd., 1986-2002, exec. com. 1986-2002, alumni programs and devel. com., 1991—, pres. regional adv. coun., 1992—, vice chmn. 1994-2002, John Marshall Soc., 1993—; founder Benjamin Rush Soc., 1987, hon. chmn., 1999—, campaign nat. chmn., 1995-2002, campaign exec. com. chmn., 1995—, mem. bldgs. and grounds com., 2002--. Decorated knight Order St. John of Jerusalem Knights Hopitalier; recipient VA citation for significant contbn. to med. care, 1970; Mead Johnson award for rsch. in hosp. pharmacy, 1972; Seale Harris medal So. Med. Assn., 1973; AMA-Brookdale award in medicine, 1975; Great Texan award Nat. Found. Ileitis and Colitis, 1975; Modern Medicine award, 1977; Disting. Alumnus citation Franklin and Marshall Coll., 1980; WHO, Houston, 1980; Stinchfield award Am. Acad. Orthopedic Surgery, 1981; Bernstein award Med. Soc. State of N.Y., 1986, Alumni Svc. award U. Pa. Med. Sch., 1996, Excellence in Surgical Tchg. Awd., St. Mary's Hosp., 1999, Roswell Park award Buffalo Surgery Soc., 2000, numerous others. Fellow ACS (vice chmn. pre and post operative com. 1975, gov. 1979-85, com. on med. motion pictures 1981-90, SESAP com. 1990-94, co-chmn. multiple choice com. 1993-94, mem. Conn. chpt.), Philippine Coll. Surgeons (hon.), Coll. Medicine and Surgery of Costa Rica (hon.), Am. Coll. Nutrition (Grace A. Goldsmith award 1982), Phi Beta Kappa; mem. AMA (council on food and nutrition 1971-76, exec. com. 1975-76, council on sci. affairs 1976-81, Goldberger award in clin. nutrition 1970), AAAS, AAUP, Am. Surg. Assn. (Flance-Karl award 1997), Am. Acad. Pediatrics (hon., Ladd medal 1988), Am. Pediatric Surg. Assn. (hon.), Am. Soc. Nutritional Support Services (bd. dirs. 1982-87, pres. 1984, Outstanding Humanitarian award 1984) Soc. Univ. Surgeons (exec. council 1974-78), Assn. for Acad. Surgery (founders group), Internat. Soc. Surg., Internat. Fedn. Surg. Colls., Internat. Soc. Parenteral Nutrition (exec. council 1975-81, pres. 1978-81), Internat. Fedn. Surgery Soc., So. Med. Assn. (chmn. surgery sect. 1984-85), Houston Gastroent. Soc., Houston Surg. Soc., Tex. Surg. Soc., Tex. Med. Assn. (com. nutrition and food resources), Tex. Med. Found., Harris County Med. Soc., New Haven (Conn.) County Med. Soc., Conn. Soc. Am. Bd. Surgeons, New England Surg. Soc., Am. Radium Soc., Am. Soc. Clin. Oncology, Am. Soc. Parenteral and Enteral Nutrition (pres. 1977, bd. advs. 1978—, chmn. bd. advisers 1978, Vars award 1982, Rhoads lectr. 1985, Dudrick Rsch. Scholar award named in his honor), Penn. Nutritionists Soc. (pres. 1985), Am. Gastroent. Assn., Soc. Surg. Oncology, James Ewing Soc., Ravdin-Rhoads Surg. Assn., Excelsior Surg. Soc. (Edward D. Churchill lectr. 1981), Soc. Laparoendoscopic Surgery, Soc. Surg. Chairmen, So. Surg. Assn., Southwestern Surg. Congress, Southeastern Surg. Congress, Surg. Biology Club II, Surg. Infection Soc. (chmn. membership com. 1987-90), Western Surg. Soc., Halsted Soc., Allen O. Whipple Surg. Soc., Am. Inst. Nutrition, Soc. Clin. Surgery, Am. Soc. Clin. Investigation, Soc. for Surgery of Alimentary Tract, Am. Trauma Soc. (founders group), Am. Assn. for Surgery of Trauma, Soc. Clin. Surgery, Am. Soc. Clin. Nutrition, Fedn. Am. Soc. Exp. Biology, Am. Burn Assn., Assn. Program Dirs. Surgery (bd. dirs. 1998—), John Marshall Soc., Coll. Physicians Phila., Phila. Acad. Surgeons, George Hermann Soc., Union League Phila., Med. Club Phila., Franklin Club Phila., Houston Doctors Club (gov. 1973-76), Nat. Alumni Coun. U. Pa. Med. Sch. (chmn. 1994-2001), Conn. United for Rsch. Excellence (bd. dirs. 1995-2001), Waterbury Symphony Orch. (bd. dirs. 1999—, chmn. endowment com. 2002—), Cosmos Club, Athenaeum, The Penn Club (charter), Phi Beta Kappa Assocs., Sigma Xi, Alpha Omega Alpha. (sec.-treas. Houston chpt. 1982-83), Home: 40 Beecher St Naugatuck CT 06770-2721 Office: St Mary's Hosp 56 Franklin St Waterbury CT 06706- E-mail: sdudrick@stmh.org.

DUDYCHA, ANNE ELIZABETH, retired special education educator; b. Rockford, Ill., Aug. 15, 1934; d. O. Garfield and Agnes Marie (Anderson) Beckstrand; m. W. Johnson, 1956 (div. Nov. 1978); children: Carole, Deanna, Sheila; m. Lee Dudycha, Feb. 1993. BA, Carthage Coll., 1956; MEd, U. Minn., 1982. Cert. tchr., emotional/behavioral disorders, dir. spl. edn., learning disabilities. Tchr., English Edn. Han. Jr. H.S., Lancaster, Pa., 1956-57; home bound. Hopkins and St. Louis Park (Minn.) Sch. Dists., 1971; tchr., spl. edn., adolescent therapy program Golden Valley (Minn.) Health Ctr., 1972-77, tchr., spl. edn., 1977-80, 82-85; tchr., spl. edn., emotional and behavioral disorders Robbinsdale (Minn.) Jr. H.S., 1977-79, Sandburg Mid. Sch., Golden Valley, 1979-93, spl. edn. adminstrv. liaison, 1990-92, behavior specialist, cons., 1992-93, dist. spl. edn. coord., 1993-96; ret., 1996. Lectr. Carthage Coll., Kenosha, Wis., 1996-2002; program com. mem. Devel. Severely Emotionally Disordered, Robbinsdale, 1985-86, 90-96; com. mem. Program and Curriculum for Implementation of Mid. Sch., Robbinsdale, 1986-87. Mem. design com. Holy Nativity Luth. Ch., New Hope, Minn., 1987-90, co-chmn. fund drive, 1987, mem. coun., 1988-93, pers. com., 1985-96, mem. choir, 1970-96. Mem. Minn. Educators Emotionally Disordered (profl. growth chmn. 1982-83), Minn. Coun. Children-Behavioral Disorders (pres. 1987-88, advocacy com. 1989-96), Minn. Assn. Mid. Level Edn. (bd. dirs. 1991-94), Phi Kappa Phi. Avocations: concerts, plays, reading, walking, hand work.

DUDZIAK, MARY LOUISE, law educator, lecturer; b. Oakland, Calif., June 15, 1956; d. Walter F. Dudziak and Barbara Ann Campbell; 1 child, Alicia. AB in Sociology with highest honors, U. Calif., Berkeley, 1978; JD, Yale Law Sch., 1984; MA, MPhil in Am. Studies, Yale U., 1986, PhD in Am. Studies, 1992. Adminstrv. asst. to dep. dir. Ctr. Ind. Living, Berkeley, 1978-80; law clk., nat. legal staff ACLU, N.Y.C., 1983; law clk. Judge Sam J. Ervin, III Fourth Cir. Ct. Appeals, Morganton, N.C., 1984-85; assoc. prof. coll. law U. Iowa, Iowa City, 1986-90, prof. coll. law, 1990-98. Vis. prof. U. So. Calif., 1997-98, prof. U. So. Calif., 1998-2002, Judge Edward J. and Ruey L. Guirado prof. law and history, 2002-; mem. faculty senate task force on faculty devel. U. Iowa, 1989-90, mem. faculty welfare com., 1990-92, mem. faculty senate task force on faculty spouses and ptnrs., 1991-92, mem. presdl. lecture com., 1992-95; v.p. rsch. adv. com. in social scis., 1992-94; fellow law and pub. affairs program Princeton U., 2002; presenter in field. Author: Cold War Civil Rights: Race and the Image of American Democracy, 2000; editor, co-author: September 11 in History: A Watershed Moment?, 2003; mem. bd. mng. editors Am. Quar., 2003—; contbr. articles to profl. jours. Bd. dirs. Iowa Civil Liberties Union, 1987-88; chairperson office svcs. for persons with disabilities program rev. com., U. Iowa, 1987-88, law sch. ombudsperson, 1991. Charlotte W. Newcombe Doctoral Dissertation fellow Woodrow Wilson Fellowship Found., 1985-86; Old Gold fellow U. Iowa, 1987, 88, 89, Moody Grant Lyndon Baines Johnson Fdn., 1998, Theodore C. Sorenson Fell., JFK Libr.

Fdn., 1997, Orgn. Am. Historians-Japanese Assn. for Am. Studies fellow 2000; travel grantee Eisenhower World Affairs Inst., 1993; recipient Scholars Devel. award Harry S. Truman Libr. Inst., 1990. Mem. Am. Soc. Legal History (mem. com. on documentary preservation 1988-2000, mem. program com. for 1988 conf., mem. exec. com., bd. dirs. 1990-92, 95-97, chairperson program com. 1993, mem. nominating com. 1999-2001, chair nominating com. 2001), Am. Hist. Assn. (Littleton-Griswold rsch. grantee 1987), Am. Studies Assn. (mem. nominating com. 1999-2002, chair nominating com. 2002), Assn. Am. Law Schs. (sec.-treas. legal history sect. 1987, vice chair 1988, chair 1989), Law and Soc. Assn. (mem. Hurst prize com. 1992), Orgn. Am. Historians, Soc. Am. Law Tchrs., Soc. for Historians Am. Fgn. Rels. Democrat. Office: U So Calif Law Sch Los Angeles CA 90089-0001 E-mail: mdudziak@law.usc.edu.

DUENES BROWN, ELENA MARIE, speech/language pathologist; b. Inglewood, Calif., Dec. 8, 1967; d. Edward Manuel and Julia Ellen Duenes. BA, U. Calif., Irvine, 1990; MA, Northwestern U., 1992. Cert. clin. competence; lic. speech/lang. pathology, Calif. Speech pathologist Gardner/Manzella Inc., Sherman Oaks, Calif., 1992-93, Pace Therapy Inc., Cypress, Calif., 1993-94, Beverly Enterprises, Seal Beach, Calif., 1994-2000; speech Lang. hearing assoc. Torrance (Calif.) Unified Sch. Dist., 1999—. Mem. Am. Speech Lang. Hearing Assn. Avocations: reading, running, bicycling, swimming, singing. Home: 2824 W 156th St Gardena CA 90249-4508 E-mail: delightedin@wwdb.org.

DUERKSEN, GEORGE LOUIS, music educator, music therapist; b. St. Joseph, Mo., Oct. 29, 1934; s. George Herbert and Louise May (Dalke) D.; m. Patricia Gay Beers, June 3, 1961; children— Mark Jeffrey, Joseph Scott, Cynthia Elizabeth Student, Tabor Coll, 1951-52; BMusEdn, U. Kans., 1955, MMusEdn, 1956, PhD, 1967. Cert. music educator Kans., Mo., registered music therapist Nat. Assn. Music Therapy, bd. cert. music therapist Bd. for Music Therapists, 1988. Tchr. music Tonganoxie High Sch., Kans., 1955-56, Stafford Jr. and Sr. High Sch., Kans., 1959-60, Labette County High Sch., Altamont, Kans., 1960-62, Shawnee Mission (Kans.) North High Sch., 1962-63; asst. prof., dir. psychology of music lab. Mich. State U., East Lansing, 1965-69; prof., chmn. dept. art and music edn. and music therapy U. Kans., Lawrence, 1969-93, dir. Singing Jayhawks, 1979-83, prof., dir. music edn. and music therapy divsn., 1993—, prof., interim chair dept. music and dance, 2000-01, dir. Ctr. for Rsch. on Music Behavior, 2001—; assoc. dir. Kans. North Ctrl. Assn. Colls. and Schs., 1992-2000. Cons., vis. prof. U. Hawaii, Honolulu, summer 1978; cons., vis. prof. U. Melbourne, Australia, summer 1981; cons., lectr. N.Z. Soc. for Music Therapy, Wellington, 1983, Ctr. for Contemporary Music Rsch., Athens, 1991, U. Thessaloniki, Greece, 1993, Korean Assn. for Music Therapy, 1994, 97, Sook Myung U., Seoul, 1997; cons. functional music applications, 1967—, Deakin U., Geelong, Victoria, Australia, 1990. Author: (monograph) Teaching Instrumental Music, 1973; Music for Exceptional Children, 1981; contbr. articles to profl. jours. Fulbright scholar Inst. for Internat. Edn., Australia, 1956-57; U.Kans. fellow, Lawrence, 1963-64; U.S. Office Edn. grantee, 1966-67, 73-75, 78-81 Mem. AAAS, Music Educators Nat. Conf., Am. Music Therapy Assn.(award of merit, 2000), Music Edn. Rsch. Coun. (chmn. 1980-82), Brit. Soc. for Music Therapy, Coun. for Rsch. in Music Edn., Pi Kappa Lambda, Phi Mu Alpha, Phi Delta Kappa. Avocations: photography, boating, travel. Office: U Kans Music Edn and Music Therapy Div 448 Murphy Hall 1530 Naismith Dr Lawrence KS 66045-3102 E-mail: gduerksen@ku.edu.

DUERR, DIANNE MARIE, physical education educator, sports medicine consultant; b. Buffalo, July 14, 1945; d. Robert John and Aileen Louise D. BS in Health and Phys. Edn., SUNY, Brockport, 1967; cert., SUNY, Oswego, 1982; postgrad., Canisius Coll., 1970-71. Cert. tchr., N.Y. Tchr. North Syracuse (N.Y.) Sch. Dist., 1967—; tchr. dept. orthopedic surgery SUNY Upstate Med. U., Syracuse, 1982—2003; creator Inst. for Human Performance SUNY Health Sci. Ctr., Syracuse, 1988. Coord. scholastic sports injury reporting system project SUNY, 1985-98; mem. com. on scholastic sports-related injuries NIH Inst. Arthritis, Musculoskeletal and Skin Diseases, 1993-96. Author: SSIRS Pilot Study Report, 1987, SSIRS Fall Study Report, 1988, SHASIRS Report, 1991; creator Scholastic Sports Injury Reporting System, 1985, Scholastic Head and Spine Injury Reporting System, 1989. Co-chmn. sports medicine USA Amateur Athletic Union, Nat. Jr. Olympic Games, Syracuse, NY, 1987; vol. sports medicine N.Y. State Sr. Games, 1990—95, sports medicine coord., 1990—95, U.S. Roller Skating Nat. Championships, 1995, N.Y. State Womens Lacrosse Championships, 1995, U.S. Nat. Precision Ice Skating Championships, 1997, Youth Basketball of Am., Northeast Regional Tournament, 1999; co-chmn. health-care, security Empire State Games, Syracuse, 2002; mem. com. sports injury surveillance Ctrs. for Disease Control, 1995; cons. N.Y. Sci., Tech. and Soc. Edn. Project, 1995. Mem. AAUW, N.Y. State AAHPERD (pres. exercise sci. and sports medicine sect., 1994-98), Am. Coll. Sports Medicine, United Univ. Profs., Women's Sports Fedn., Am. Fedn. Tchrs., N.Y. United Tchrs., North Syracuse Tchrs. Assn., Phi Kappa Phi. Avocations: swimming, cycling, ice skating, reading, photography. Office: 418 Buffington Rd Syracuse NY 13224-2208 E-mail: dmduerr@twcny.rr.com.

DUFF, GARY NOLAN, secondary education educator; b. Butte, Mont., Apr. 1, 1939; s. Nolan E. and Frances Zita (Briggeman) D.; m. Bette Larene Kleve, Dec. 19, 1959 (separated 1993); children: Donald, Kimberly, Robyn, Ryan. BA, Carroll Coll., 1973; postgrad., Northern Mont. Coll., 1982-83. Cert. vocat. edn. tchr. 1983. Engrs. aide Milw. St. Paul & Pacific Railroad, Deer Lodge, Mont., 1957-58, Mont. Dept. Hwys., Helena, 1958-61, Utah Dept. Hwys., Salt Lake City, 1962-63; elec. sales Elec. Parts Supply, Missoula, Mont., 1963-65; draftsman Morrison-Maierle Inc., Helena, 1965-73; contractor self employed, Helena, 1973-76; engring. tech. Mont. Dept. Hwys., Helena, 1976-80; instr. drafting Capital High Sch., Helena, 1980—. Bd. dirs. Helena Housing Authority, 1985-87; advisor Vocat. Indsl. Clubs Am., Helena, 1980—. Mem. NEA, Mont. Edn. Assn. Avocations: photography, computer animation, camping, fishing, woodworking. Office: Capital H S 100 Valley Dr Helena MT 59601-0163 Home: 20 Colter Loop Helena MT 59602-7757

DUFF, JOHN BERNARD, college president, former city official; b. Orange, N.J., July 1, 1931; s. John Bernard and Mary Evelyn (Cunningham) D.; m. Helen Mezzanotti, Oct. 8, 1955 (div.); children: Michael, Maureen, Patricia, John, Robert, Emily Anne; m. Estelle M. Shanley, July, 1991. BS, Fordham U., 1953; MA, Seton Hall U., 1958; PhD, Columbia U., 1964; DHL (hon.), Seton Hall U., 1976, Northeastern U., 1982, Emerson Coll., 1983, Lincoln Coll., 1993. Sales rep. Remington-Rand Corp., 1955-57, dist. mgr., 1957-60; mem. faculty Seton Hall U., 1960-70, prof. history, 1968-70, acad. v.p., 1970-71, exec. v.p., acad. v.p., 1971-72, provost, acad. v.p., 1972-76; pres. U. Lowell, Mass., 1976-81; chancellor of higher edn. State of Mass., 1981-86; commr. Chgo. Pub. Libr. System, 1986-92; pres. Columbia Coll., Chgo., 1992-2000, ret., 2000—. Mem. Gov.'s Commn. to Study Capital Punishment, 1972-73; chmn. bd. dirs. Mass. Corp. Ednl. Telecommunications, 1983— ; dir. Mass. Tech. Park Corp. Author: The Irish in the United States, 1971, also articles.; Editor: (with others) The Structure of American History, 1970, (with P.M. Mitchell) The Nat Turner Rebellion: The Historical Event and the Modern Controversy, 1971, (with L. Greene) Slavery: Its Origin and Legacy, 1975. Dem. candidate to U.S. Congress, 1968; mem. State Bd. Edn., 1981-86; chmn. Livingston Town Dem. Com., 1972-76; bd. dirs. Merrimack Regional Theatre, 1981-84, Mass. Higher Edn. Assistance Corp., 1981-86, Chgo. Metro History Fair ; trustee Essex County Coll., 1966-70, Mass. Community Coll. System., St. John's Prep. Sch., Danvers, Mass.; chmn. Lowell Hist. Preservation Commn., 1979-86; mem. adv. bd. Wang Inst., 1979-81; mem. bd. visitors Emerson Coll., 1986-90; pres. Nat. Coun. of Heads of Public Higher Edn. Systems; mem. nat. adv. com. on accreditation and indsl. eligibility U.S. Dept. Edn., 1981-82; mem. Ill. Lit. Coun., 1986-92, adv. com. Ill. State Libr., 1986-92; chmn. Fedn. Ind. Ill. Colls. and Univs., 1996-98. With U.S. Army, 1953-55. Mem. Univ. Club, Tavern Club.

DUFF, SHERYL KAY, parochial school educator; b. Frankenmuth, Mich., May 14, 1961; d. Eldon Earl and Ellen Christine (Rummel) D. BA, Concordia U., 1983; MS in Edn., Nat. Louis U., 2000. Tchr. 6th grade Lutheran Sch. Assn., Decatur, Ill., 1983-87; tchr. science St. John Lutheran, Wheaton, Ill., 1987—; instr. Nat. Louis U., 2001—. Tchr. Solid Waste Edn. Ctr., Wheaton, Ill., 1995. Mem. Lutheran Edn. Assn., Ill. Sci. Tchrs. Assn. Lutheran. Avocations: camping, gardening, canoeing.

DUFFEY, JOSEPH DANIEL, academic administrator; b. Huntington, W.Va., July 1, 1932; s. Joseph I. and Ruth (Wilson) Duffey; m. Anne Wexler, 1974; children: Michael, David, Danny Wexler, David Wexler. BA, Marshall U., 1954; STM, Yale U., 1963; BD, Andover Newton Theol. Sch., 1958; PhD, Hartford Sem. Found., 1969; LHD, CUNY, 1978, U. Cin., 1978, U. Mass., 1991; LittD, Dickinson Coll., Pa., 1978, Centre Coll., Ky., 1977, Gonzaga U., Wash., 1980, Monmouth Coll., 1980, CCNY; LLD, Amherst Coll., Bethany Coll., Austin Coll., Ritsuimaneu U., Kyoto, Japan, 1993; LittD, Alderson-Broadus Coll., Adelphi U., Central Fla. Asst. prof. Hartford (Conn.) Sem., 1960—63; assoc. prof., dir. Ctr. Urban Studies, 1965—70; fellow Harvard U. Kennedy Sch. Govt., 1971; adj. prof. and fellow Calhoun Coll., Yale U., 1971—73; exec. officer AAUP, 1974—77; asst. sec. for edn. and cultural affairs Dept. State, 1977; chmn. NEH, 1978—81; chancellor U. Mass., Amherst, 1982—, pres., 1990—91, Am. U., Washington, 1991—93; dir. U.S. Info. Agy., Washington, 1993—98; sr. exec., chmn. internat. univ. project Sylvan Learning Sys., Washington, 1999—. Mem. U.S. dept. 20th and 21st gen. confs. UNESCO, 1978, 80; mem. exec. com. Nat. Coun. Competitiveness Govt. and Industry Univ. Panel Nat. Acad. Scis.; bd. dirs. Bay Bank, Springfield, Mass. Contbr. articles to profl. jours. Bd. dirs. Woodrow Wilson Internat. Ctr. Scholars, East-West Ctr., Western Mass. Area Devel. Corp., Jewish Theol. Sem. Libr., Springfield Symphony. Decorated Order of Leopold IV Belgium; recipient Tree of Life award, Nat. Jewish Fund, 1987; scholar, Rockefeller Found., 1966—68. Mem.: Century Assn., Coun. Fgn. Rels., Cosmos Club. Office: Sylvan Learning Sys 2801 New Mexico Ave NW Apt 311 Washington DC 20007-3913 E-mail: jdoffey@earthlink.net.

DUFFEY, ROSALIE RUTH, elementary school educator; b. Randolph, Mo., July 4, 1938; d. Joseph Anthony and Katherine Ruth Spruytte; m. Robert Lee Duffey, Oct. 20, 1956; children: Susan, Carolyn, Janice, Maryann, Philip, David, Mark. AS in Early Childhood Edn., Ctrl. Mo. State U., 1973, BS in Edn., 1977, MS in Edn., 1980. Cert. tchr. elem. and spl. edn. Mo. Dir. ednl. ops. Head Start West Ctrl. Mo. Rural Devel. Corp., Appleton City, 1966—79; tchr. spl. edn. Butler (Mo.) Elem. Sch., 1979—87; tchr. Parents as Tchrs. Cass RIX Pub. Sch., Harrisonville, Mo., 1987—98; tchr. Marillac Sch., Kansas City, Mo., 1998—99, Trails West State Schs. for Severely Handicapped, Kansas City, 1999—. Mem. policy coun. Head Start, Appleton City; foster parent Divsn. of Family Svcs., Cass and Henry Counties, Mo., 1977—2000. Mem.: Ctrl. Mo. State U. Alumni Assn., Mo. State Ret. Tchrs. Assn., Assn. of Retarded Citizens, Coun. for Exceptional Children, Alpha Phi Delta, Kappa Delta Pi, Phi Kappa Phi, Alpha Phi Sigma. Roman Catholic. Avocations: quilting, gardening, walking.

DUFFIELD, ELEANOR MCALPIN, secondary education educator; b. Lexington, Va., May 5, 1942; d. Henry F. Jr. and Elizabeth Wilson (Jones) McAlpin; m. Joseph Hood Duffield, Aug. 21, 1971. BS, Madison Coll., 1964; MEd, U. Va., 1972. Tchr. social studies Fairfax (Va.) County Pub. Sch. Bd., 1964—; peer observer for performance evaluation of tchrs. Fairfax County, 1987—; clin. faculty George Mason U., 1989—. Sponsor Students Involved in Volunteering; co-advisor Harvard Model Congress, 1990-92; co-coord. sch. renewal So. Assn. Colls. and Schs., 1994—. Co-author: Fairfax County Government: A Handbook for Teachers, 1975. Pres. Fairfax Com. of 100, 1988-90; bd. dirs. Fairfax-Falls Church United Way, 1986-88; v.p. Faxfair Corp., 1988-89; elder Fairfax Presbyn. Ch., mem. session, 1993-95. Recipient Ptnr. in Edn. award Vienna Optimist Club, 1988, citation of merit Washington Post, 1988; fellow Taft Inst., 1986. Mem. NEA, ASCD, Nat. Coun. Social Studies, Va. Coun. Social Studies (conf. presenter, Tchr. of Yr. award no. region 1983), Va. Edn. Assn., Fairfax Edn. Assn. Home: 909 Frederick St SW Vienna VA 22180-6451 Office: James Madison High Sch 2500 James Madison Dr Vienna VA 22181-5599

DUFFY, BRIAN FRANCIS, immunologist, educator; b. St. Louis, June 20, 1959; s. Francis G. and Eithne (Neville) B.; m. Katharine Tibbs, May 18, 1984. BS in Microbiology, Pub. Health, Mich. State U., 1981; MA in Biotech., Washington U., St. Louis, 1991. Cert. histocompatibility specialist Am. Bd. Histocompatibility and Immunogenetics. Rsch. technician ARC, St. Louis, 1981-87; rsch. devel. technologist Barnes Hosp., St. Louis, 1987-89; technologist specialist Barnes-Jewish Hosp., St. Louis, 1990—. Cons. Washington U. Sch. Medicine, St. Louis, 1991—. Contbr. articles to Jour. Immunol. Methods, Transfusion, Transplantation, Transplantation Proceedings, Hybridoma, Jour. Immunology, Human Immunology. Mem. Am. Soc. Histocompatibility Immunogenetics (lab. inspector 1988—, mem. exam. com. 1989—, chmn. regional edn. com. 1992—), N.Y. Acad. Sci. Achievements include patent for method of ultra-violet irradiation of platelets that are transfusable, non-immunogenic and functional.

DUFFY, JOHN LEWIS, retired Latin, English and reading educator; b. Whittemore, Iowa, Oct. 6, 1934; s. Lewis A. and Dorothy (Bestenlehner) D.; m. Anne O'Brien, July 19, 1958; children: Jane, Paul, Sarah, Steven. BA, Loras Coll., Dubuque, Iowa, 1956; MS Ed, Creighton U., 1961; student, U. Minn., summer 1967. Jr. and sr. H.S. tchr., coach Presentation Acad., Whittemore, Iowa, 1957-58; H.S. tchr. Clear Lake (Iowa) Cmty. Schs., 1958-61; teaching asst. U. Iowa, Iowa City, 1961-62; tchr. Latin Larkin H.S., Elgin, Ill., 1962-96, students' coun. advisor, 1965-71, chmn. English and fgn. langs., 1969-77, chmn. English and reading divsn., 1977-96. Tchr. prep. courses for ACT, PSAT and SAT Elgin YWCA and Larkin H.S., Elgin, 1977-96. Summer chef's asst. The Frugal Gourmet, WTTW-TV, Chgo., 1983. Bd. trustees Elgin C.C., 1975—, chmn., 1980-81, 85-87, 97-2001, vice-chmn., 1981-84, 94-95; bd. dirs. Elgin Area Cath. Social Svcs., 1981-90, pres., 1986-88; mem. St. Laurence Parish Bd., 1974-79, Edn. Commn., 1972-79, chmn. Edn. Commn., 1974-79; state advisor Iowa Jr. Classical League, 1960-61. Named Kane County Distinguished Educator of Yr., 1982, Outstanding Young Men in Am., 1970; recipient Outstanding Young Educator award Elgin Jaycees, 1969. Mem.: Am. Assn. Cmty. and Jr. Colls., Ill. Coun. Tchrs. English, Nat. Coun. Tchrs. English, Ill. Classical League, Am. Classical League, Elgin Assn. Sch. Adminstrs., Elgin Tchrs. Assn. (welfare chmn. and chief negotiator 1963—65, pres. 1966—67), Ill. Edn. Assn. (legis., chmn. northeastern divsn. 1968—71, chmn. ad hoc com. on tchr. tenure 1972—73), Ill. C.C. Trustees Assn. (exec. com. 1981—84, chmn. west suburban region 1981—84, chmn. fed. rels. com. 1982—87, bd. rep. 1986—95, 1997—, exec. com. 1998—2000, chmn. west suburban region 1998—2000, exec. com. 2002—04, chmn. west suburban region 2002—04, Trustee of Yr. award 2002), Am. Assn. C.C. (bd. dirs. 1990—93), Assn. C.C. Trustees (chmn. ctrl. region nominating com. 1981—82, sgt.-at-arms ann. conv. 1982, mem. com. on internat. rels. 1983—84, bd. dirs. 1983—89, chmn. future directions com. 1984—86, fed. rels. commn. 1985—93, chmn. ctrl. region 1987—88, vice-chmn. fed. rels. commn. 1987—88, chmn. fed. rels. commn. 1988—89, chmn. ctrl. region nominating com. 1992—93, Ctrl. Region Trustee of Yr. award 1991, 2002). Home: 192 Kathleen Dr Elgin IL 60123-5914 also: 4840 Heron Run Cir Leesburg FL 34748-7819 Fax: (847) 429-0408.

DUFFY, LAWRENCE KEVIN, biochemist, educator; b. Bklyn., Feb. 1, 1948; s. Michael and Anne (Browne) D.; m. Geraldine Antoinette Sheridan, Nov. 10, 1972; children: Anne Marie, Kevin Michael, Ryan Sheridan. BS, Fordham U., 1969; MS, U. Alaska, 1972, PhD, 1977. Tchg. asst. dept. chemistry U. Alaska, 1969-71, rsch. asst. Inst. Arctic Biology, 1974-77; postdoctoral fellow Boston U., 1977-78, Roche Inst. Molecular Biology, 1978-80; rsch. asst. prof. U. Tex. Med. Br., Galveston, 1980-82; asst. prof. neurology (biol. chemistry) Med. Sch. Harvard U., Boston, 1982-87, adv. biochemistry instr. Med. Sch., 1983-87; instr. gen. and organic chemistry Roxbury C.C., Boston, 1984-87; prof. chemistry and biochemistry U. Alaska, Fairbanks, 1992—, head dept. chemistry and biochemistry, 1994-99; assoc. dean for grad. studies and outreach Coll. Sci. Engring. and Math., U. Alaska, Fairbanks, 2000—. Coord. program biochemistry and molecular biology for summer undergrad. rsch., 1987-96; pres. U. Alaska Fairbanks Faculty Senate, 2000-01. Mem. editl. bd. Sci. of Total Environment. Pres., bd. dirs. Alzheimer Disease Assn. of Alaska, 1994-95; mem. instnl. rev. bd. Fairbanks Meml. Hosp., 1990; sci. adv. bd. Am. Fedn. Aging Rsch, 1994-95. Lt. USNR, 1971-73. NSF trainee, 1971; J.W. McLaughlin fellow, 1981; W.F. Milton scholar, 1983; recipient Alzheimers Disease and Related Disorders Assoc. Faculty Scholar award, 1987; Carol Fiest Outstanding Advisor award, 1994, 97, Nat. Inst. Deafness & Commn. Disorders, NIH Cert. of Merit for mentoring, 1996, North Star Bough Sch. Dist. Svc. award, 1998, Alumni Achievement award for profl. activity U. Alaska-Fairbanks, 1999, Usibelli award for rsch., 2002. Fellow: Am. Inst. Chemists (mem. editl. bd. Sci. of Total Environment 1999, assoc. editor Jour. Alzheimer's Disease 2000, bd. dirs. 2002—, sec. bd. dirs. 2003, cert. profl. chemist); mem.: AAAS (arctic divsn. exec. dir.), Soc. Environ. Toxicologists and Chemists, Am. Soc. Circumpolar Health (bd. dirs. 1999—2001, 2003), Internat. Soc. Toxinologists, Am. Chem. Soc. (Analytical Chemistry award 1969), N.Y. Acad. Scis., Am. Soc. Biol. Chemists, Am. Soc. Neurochemists, Sigma Xi (assoc. regional dir. 2000—02, pres. 1991 Alaska club, nominating com.), Phi Lambda Upsilon. Roman Catholic. Office: U Alaska Fairbanks Dept Chemistry and Biochemistry Box 756160 Fairbanks AK 99775

DUFFY, PATRICIA LYNNE, English language educator; b. N.Y.C., May 8, 1952; d. John Joseph and Estelle V. (Vahlsing) D.; m. Joshua Brett Cohen, Dec. 25, 1986. BA, CUNY, 1975; MA in Tchg. ESOL, Columbia U., 1981. Asst. prof. ESL Am. Lang. Inst., NYU, N.Y.C., 1981-91; tchr., writer lang. program UN, N.Y.C., 1985—. Program prodr. English-lang. tchg. TV series Jiangsu TV, U. Nanjing, People's Republic of China, 1987-88; presenter in field. Author: (textbooks) Variations, 1986, Innovations and Innovators, 1993; freelance journalist for Boston Globe, N.Y. Newsday, Village Voice. Organizer benefit parties City Harvest, N.Y.C., 1992—; vol. tchr. of immigrants Concerned Citizens of Queens, Corona, N.Y., 1983-84. NYU grantee, 1986. Mem. Nat. Assn. Tchrs. ESL. Avocations: travel, writing, studying french and chinese languages, reading literature.

DUFFY, WILLIAM EDWARD, JR., retired education educator; b. Fostoria, Ohio, Aug. 30, 1931; s. William Edward and Margaret Louise (Drew) D.; m. Sally King Wolfe, Nov. 21, 1958 (div. 1978). BS, Wayne State U., 1958, MEd, 1960; PhD, Northwestern U., 1967. Tchr. social studies Detroit Pub. Schs., 1957-61; instr. Northwestern U., Evanston, Ill., 1961-65; asst. prof. gen. edn. U. Iowa, Iowa City, 1965-70, assoc. prof., 1970-94, coord. Soc. Found. Edn. program, 1978-93, chmn. divsn. founds., postsecondary edn., 1981-88; ret., 1994. Lectr. in field. Mem. editl. bd. Ednl. Philosophy Theory, 1969-71; contbr. book revs. and articles to profl. jours. With USAF, 1951-54. Fellow John Dewey Soc., Philosophy Edn. Soc.; mem. Am. Ednl. Rsch. Assn. Home: 376 Samoa Pl Iowa City IA 52246-3632

DUGAN, JOHN VINCENT, JR., legislative affairs specialist, researcher; b. Lost Creek, Pa., Oct. 22, 1936; s. John Vincent and May Ann (Curley) D.; m. Joan Elaine Thomas, Dec. 26, 1964; children: John Edward, Paul Michael, Michael Thomas, Erin Elaine (dec.). BA in Chemistry, Lasalle Coll., 1957; PhD in Phys. Chemistry, U. Notre Dame, 1965. Scientist, adminstr. NASA Lewis Rsch. Ctr., Cleve., 1961—75; dir. Washington ops. Cortana Corp., Falls Church, Va., 1988-92; sr. phys. scientist ozone depletion, atmospheric chemistry Tech. Assessment Systems, Inc., Washington, 1992; v.p. congl. affairs Gen. Dynamics Space Systems Divsn., 1992—94; v.p. govt. affairs Martin Marietta Corp., 1994—95; dir. for energy, environ. and space legis. affairs Lockeed-Martin Co., Arlington, Va., 1995—99, cons. energy, sci. and tech., pub. policy, 1999—. Author: (with John L. Magee) Dynamics of Ion Molecule Collisions, 1971; contbr. more than 50 tech. papers and articles to profl. jours. Head physics judge Fairfax County Sci. Fairs, Va., 1985-92; mem. adv. bd. Fairfax County Com. on Exceptional Children, 1977-79. Named Man of the Yr., Shenandoah (Pa.) C. of C., 1982. Mem. E.F. Sorin Soc. (Founder's Cir. U. Notre Dame), Founders Club (LaSalle Coll.), Sigma Xi. Roman Catholic. Achievements include first analytical and computer studies of directional forces in dynamics of ion-molecule collisions and predicted formation of long-lived collision complexes; development of computer movies of ion-molecule collisions involving orientation dependent forces; advanced research in concept integration, hydrodynamics, advanced materials and automation. Home: 8301 Miss Anne Ln Annandale VA 22003-4619

DUHL, LEONARD, psychiatrist, educator; b. N.Y.C., May 24, 1926; s. Louis and Rose (Josefsberg) D.; m. Lisa Shippee; children: Pamela, Nina, David, Susan, Aurora. BA, Columbia U., 1945; MD, Albany Med. Coll., 1948, postgrad., 1956-64. Diplomate Am. Bd. Psychiatry and Neurology (examiner 1977, 85). With USPHS, 1951-53, 54-72, med. dir., 1954-72; fellow Menninger Sch. Psychiatry Menninger Sch. Psychiatry, Winter VA Hosp., Topeka, 1949-51, resident psychiatry, 1953-54; asst. health officer Contra Costa County (Calif.) Health Dept., 1951-53; with USPHS, 1949-51, 53-54; psychiatrist profl. svcs. br., chief office planning NIMH, 1954-66; spl. asst. to sec. HUD, 1966-68; cons. Peace Corps, 1961-68; assoc. psychiatry George Washington Med. Sch., 1961-63, asst. clin. prof., 1963-68, assoc. prof., 1966-68; prof. public health Sch. Pub. Health U. Calif., Berkeley, 1968—93; prof. city planning Coll. Environ. Design U. Calif., Berkeley, 1968-92; dir. dual degree program in health and med. scis. U. Calif., Berkeley, 1971-77, clin. prof. psychiatry San Francisco, 1969—; pvt. practice psychiatry Berkeley; sr. assoc. Youth Policy Inst., Washington. Mem. sci. adv. coun. Calif. Legis., 1970-73, sr. cons. Assembly Office of Rsch., 1981-85; cons. Health Cities Program, Environ. Health, WHO, UNICEF, ICDC, Florence, Global Forum of Parliamentarians and Spititual Leaders, 1989—, Ctr. for Fgn. Journalists, 1987-90, Am. Hosp. Assn. Health Rsch. and Edn. Trust, 1995—. Author: Approaches to Research in Mental Retardation, 1959, The Urban Condition, 1963, (with R.L. Leopold) Mental Health and Urban Social Policy, 1969, Health Planning and Social Change, 1986, Social Entrepreneurship of Change, 1990, 1995, Health and the City, 1993; bd. editors Jour. Community Psychology, 1974, Jour. Cmty. Mental Health, 1974—, Jour. Mental Health Consultation and Edn., 1978—, Jour. Prevention, 1978—, Nat. Civic Rev., 1991—; contbr. articles to tech. lit. Trustee Robert F. Kennedy Found., 1971-83; bd. dirs. Citizens Policy Ctr., San Francisco, 1975-85, New World Alliance, 1980-84, Calif. Inst. for Integral Studies, 1991-95, Ptnrs. for Dem. Change, 1990—; chair First Internat. Healthy Cities Conf., San Francisco, 1993; exec. trustee Nat. Inst. for Citizen Participation and Negotiation, 1988-90; trustee Menninger Found., Topeka, 1994—, bd. dirs., 1995—; bd. dirs. Louis August Jonas Found. (Camp Rising Sun), 1990—, Ctr. for Transcultural Studies, 1996—; exec. dir. Internat. Healthy Cities Found., 1993—. Recipient World Health Day award, WHO, 1996, Health Cities award for Coalition of Healthier Cities and Cmtys., 1999, A. Horwitz award, 2002. Fellow Am. Psychiat. Assn. (life), Am. Coll. Psychiatry (life), No. Calif. Psychiat. Soc. (life), Group for Advancement in Psychiatry (chmn. com. preventive psychiatry 1962-66), APHA. Home: 639 Cragmont Ave Berkeley CA 94708-1329 Office: U Calif Sch Pub Health 410 Warren Hl Berkeley CA 94720-0001 E-mail: len-duhl@socrates.berkeley.edu.

DUHON, DAVID LESTER, business educator, management consultant; b. Crowley, La., Oct. 21, 1948; s. J. Lester and Winona Faye Duhon; m. Roxanne Istre, Jan. 25, 1970; children: Jonathan, Leah, Sarah. BS in Bus., U. Southwestern La., 1970; MBA, La. State U., 1975, PhD in Mgmt., 1981. Instr. mgmt. La. State U., Baton Rouge, 1978-80; from asst. prof. to assoc. prof. U. Southwestern La., Lafayette, 1980-88, petroleum land mgmt. coord., 1981-88; from asst. prof. to assoc. prof. U. So. Miss., Hattiesburg, 1988—, dir. external rels. Coll. Bus., 1995-99. Ptnr. People Solutions LLC, Hattiesburg, Miss.; cons. Jaws Offshore, Lafayette, 1984-88, Continuing Edn. U. So. Miss., Hattiesburg, 1988—, Miss. Personnel Bd., Jackson, 1990—, Pine Belt Mental Health, Hattiesburg, 1992—; interim chair divsn. bus. U. S. Miss.-Gulf Coast, Long Beach, 1996-97; vis. lectr. Ecole Superieure de Commerce, Fontainbleu, France, 1997, 98; instr. Brit. studies program, London, 2001—. Contbr. articles to profl. jours. Chair fin. com. Ch. of the Nazarene, Hattiesburg, 1992-99, chair lay retreat com., Jackson, 1994-96; pres. faculty senate, U. So. Miss., Hattiesburg, 1997-98, co-chair United Way campaign, 1998-99. Summer Instrn. grantee U. So. Miss., 1992, 95. Fellow E./W. Centre-Honolulu; mem. Area Devel. Partnership, Acad. Mgmt., Allied Acads., So. Mgmt. Assn. Republican. Avocations: reading, traveling, hunting, fishing. Home: 2264 Old Highway 24 Hattiesburg MS 39402-7751 E-mail: duhon@cba.usm.edu.

DUJON, DIANE MARIE, director, activist; b. Boston, Dec. 29, 1946; d. Alfred and Agnes C. (Hall) White; 1 child, Lisa M. Dujon. BA, U. Mass., 1983, MS, 1996. Asst. dir. assessment Coll. Pub. and Cmty. Svc. U. Mass., Boston, 1984-93, co-dir. assessment Coll. Pub. and Cmty. Svc., 1993-97, dir. experiential learning Coll. Pub. and Cmty. Svc., 1997—. Co-editor: For Crying Out Loud: Women's Poverty in U.S., 1996 (Myers Ctr. for the Study of Human Rights in N.Am. Outstanding Book award 1997); prodr. (radio documentary) Workfare: Anatomy of a Policy, 1982 (Alice award 1982), Nat. Commn. on Working Women; alternative radio (NPR) recorded speech, Women, Welfare and Poverty, 1998. V.p. Survivors, Inc., Boston, 1986—. Recipient Earl Douglas award City Mission Soc., 1987; named Unsung Heroine Rosie's Place, 1997. Mem. Nat. Welfare Rights Union, Mass. AFL-CIO (mem. exec. women's com. 1997-2001), U. Mass. Profl. Staff Union (bd. mem. chpt. Svc. Employees Internat. Union, Local 888). Baptist. Office: U Mass/Boston 100 Morrissey Blvd Boston MA 02125-3300

DUKE, PHYLLIS LOUISE KELLOGG HENRY, school administrator, management consultant; b. Mason City, Iowa, May 3, 1932; d. Wilbur Rhode and Dorothy Margaret (Bauer) Kellogg; children— Curtis Dean Henry, Catherine Rose Henry Jones, David Russell Henry. A.A. in Elem. Teaching, U. No. Iowa, 1953; B.A. Calif. State U.-Los Angeles, 1963, M.A., 1968. Cert. elem. tchr., cert. reading specialist, sch. adminstrn. credential. Tchr., Arlington pub. schs., Iowa, 1951-52, St. Louis Park pub. schs., Minn., 1953-55; tchr., supr. ABC Sch. Dist., Cerritos, Calif., 1963-69; cons. in reading State Dept. of Calif., Sacramento, 1969-70; cons. in edn. Orange County Dept. Edn., Santa Ana, Calif., 1970-75; sch. adminstr. Oakwood Acad., Long Beach, Calif., 1975— ; chmn. bd. dirs. New City Bank, Orange, Calif.; cons. in field. Author: Song of Sounds, 1969; (with others) Beginnings for Christian Schools, 1976. Conf. coordinator State Dept. Edn., Calif., Sacramento, Santa Barbara, 1970 (Outstanding Leadership award 1974-75). Mem. Nat. Ind. Pvt. Sch. (v.p. 1982-83, dir. seminars 1983), Pre-Sch. Assn. Calif. (legis. chair 1978-84), Reading Specialists Calif. (pres. 1970-73). Republican. Avocations: skiing; scuba diving; painting; photography; travel. Home: 1208 S Lemon Ave Walnut CA 91789-4822 Office: Oakwood Acad 2951 N Long Beach Blvd Long Beach CA 90806-1532

DUKE, STEVEN BARRY, law educator; b. Mesa, Ariz., July 31, 1934; s. Alton and Elaine (Altman) D.; m. Janet Truax, 1956 (div. 1971); children: Glenn, Warren, Alison, Sally; m. Margaret Munson, 1984 (div. 1999); children: Jennifer, Lauren. BS, Ariz. State U., 1956; JD, U. Ariz., 1959; LL.M., Yale U., 1961. Bar: Ariz. 1959. Law clk. to Supreme Ct. Justice Douglas, 1959; grad. fellow Yale Law Sch., 1960, mem. faculty, 1961—, prof. law, 1966—, Law of Sci. and Tech. prof., 1982—99. Vis. prof. U. Calif.-Berkeley, 1965, Hastings Coll. Law, 1981, Ariz. State U., 1986; Bd. dirs. New Haven Legal Assistance Assn., 1968-70; cons. Commn. to Revise Fed. Criminal Code; mem. Conn. Commn. on Medicolegal Investigations, 1976—; bd. visitors Fordham U. Law Sch., 1986-1999. Author: (with A. Gross) America's Longest War: Rethinking Our Tragic Crusade Against Drugs, 1993; editor-in-chief Ariz. Law Rev.; contbr. articles to profl. jours. Mem. Woodbridge (Conn.) Bd. Edn., 1970-72; mem. Woodbridge Democratic Town Com., 1967-72. Mem. Nat. Assn. Criminal Def. Lawyers, Am. Trial Lawyers, ACLU, Phi Kappa Phi, Alpha Tau Omega. Home: 250 Grandview Ave Hamden CT 06514-3028 Office: Yale Law Sch PO Box 208215 New Haven CT 06520-8215 E-mail: steven.duke@yale.edu.

DUKETTE, ANN MARIE, elementary education educator, reading specialist; b. Bklyn., Oct. 25, 1954; d. William Henry and Gwendolyn (Clower) D.; 1 child, Niambi. BS in Edn., Wheelock Coll., 1976; MA in Reading, Manhattan Coll., 1991. Cert. tchr., N.Y., Mass. Tchr. kindergarten Evelyn M. Williams Sch., U.S. V.I.; sr. exec. Ohrbach's Inc., N.Y.C., 1979-82; tchr. Pub. Sch. 24X, Bronx, N.Y., 1982—. Counselor, troop com. Riverdale (N.Y.) area Boy Scouts Am., 1988—. Mem. ASCD, Internat. Reading Assn., Kappa Delta Pi, Alpha Upsilon Alpha. Democrat. Roman Catholic. Office: Pub Sch 24X 660 W 236th St Bronx NY 10463-1393

DUKORE, BERNARD FRANK, theatre arts and humanities educator, writer; b. N.Y.C., July 11, 1931; s. Herman and Leah Rita (Herman) D.; children: Joan, Samuel Zebadiah, Lucile Leah. BA, Bklyn. Coll., 1952; MA, Ohio State U., 1953; PhD, U. Ill., 1957. Instr. Hunter Coll., Bronx, N.Y., 1957-60; asst. prof. U. So. Calif., L.A., 1960-62; assoc. prof. Calif. State U., L.A., 1962-65; prof. CUNY, 1966-72, U. Hawaii, Honolulu, 1972-86; Univ. disting. prof. theatre arts and humanities Va. Poly. Inst. and State U., Blacksburg, 1986-97, univ. disting. prof. emeritus, 1997—. Vis. assoc. prof. Stanford (Calif.) U., 1965-66; Hoffman Eminent scholar chair Fla. State U., Tallahassee, fall 1997. Author: Bernard Shaw, Director, 1971, Bernard Shaw, Playwright, 1973, Theatre of Peter Barnes, 1980, Harold Pinter, 1982, rev. edit., 1988, Alan Ayckbourn: A Casebook, 1991, Bernard Shaw, the Drama Observed, 4 vols., 1992, Shaw and the Last Hundred Years, 1994, Barnestorm: The Plays of Peter Barnes, 1995, Bernard Shaw and Gabriel Pascal, 1996, Bernard Shaw on Cinema, 1997, Sam Peckinpah's Feature Films, 1999, Shaw's Theater, 2000. Guggenheim Found. fellow, 1969-70, NEH rsch. fellow, 1976-77, 84-85, vis. fellow Humanities Rsch. Ctr., Australia, 1979, Fulbright rsch. fellow, 1991-92. Home: 2510 Plymouth St Blacksburg VA 24060-8256

DULA, ROSA LUCILE NOELL, retired secondary education educator; b. Hillsborough, N.C., May 18, 1914; d. Frederick Young and Mary Rebecca (Lloyd) Noell; m. Thomas Hershaw Dula (dec.); children: Thomas Hunter, Harry Sutton, Frederick Lloyd (dec.). BA, East Carolina U., 1934; MEd, Duke U., 1951. English, history and algebra I tchr. Hillsborough High Sch., 1935-36; English and history tchr. Aberdeen (N.C.) High Sch., 1937, Hillsborough High Sch., 1937-40, Garner (N.C.) High Sch., 1942-43; tchr. Caldwell High Sch., Rougemont, N.C., 1943-44, Elon College (N.C.) High Sch., 1944-45; English and history tchr. Aycock High Sch., Cedar Grove, N.C., 1945-48; English Tchr. Burlington (N.C.) High Sch., 1948-51; English, speech and advanced composition tchr. Walter Williams High Sch., Burlington, 1951-74. Speech events coach Burlington High Sch., Williams High Sch., 1948-74; mem. com. readers N.C. English Tchrs., 1960-84. Author: Pelican Guide to Hillsborough, 1979, rev. edit., 1989, Morsels for Miscellaneous Moments, 1986; contbr. prose, fiction, poems to lit. publs. Editor newsletter St. Matthew's Episcopal Ch., Hillsborough, 1983, lay reader, 1982-85, 95—, 1st woman lay reader 1981; judge local speech events; speaker to schs., civic and religious groups; v.p. Orange County Retired Sch. Pers., 1994-96. Recipient Commendations for high sch. Voice of Democracy participation VFW, 1959-61, Degree of Distinction, Nat. Forensic League, 1957, Honor plaques Freedom's Found. Valley Forge, 1969-72, Extraordinary Woman of N.C. award Lady Stetson div. Coty, 1987, light verse awards Idaho Writers League, 1988, N.C. Poetry Soc., 1989, Valley Forge Tchrs. award, 1974; Nat. Coun. Tchrs. of English grantee English Inst., Duke U., summer 1962, Purdue Speech Workshop, summer, 1969. Mem. Am. Assn. Ret. Persons, Acad. Am. Poets, N.C. Poetry Soc., Hillsborough Hist. Soc., N.C. Ret. Tchrs. Assn., Orange County Rep. Sch. Pers. (v.p. 1994—), Am. Legion Aux., Nat. Soc. of the DAR (cert. award outstanding achievement in history 1997), Nat. Soc. of the SAR (Bronze good citizenship medal, cert. in recognition of notable svcs.), Kappa Delta Pi. Democrat. Avocations: communications, area cultural events, protecting and preserving environment and human and animal rights. Home: PO Box 222 Hillsborough NC 27278-0222

DULATT, LORRAINE EDWINA SIMON, special education educator, reading specialist; b. St. Louis, July 12, 1949; d. Richard Kenneth and Leora B. (Zoleman) Simon; m. Patrick Michael Dulatt, Aug. 4, 1972; children: Joseph William, Christopher Patrick, Edward Matthew. AA, Florissant (Mo.) Valley, 1969; BS in Elem. Edn., BS in Spl. Edn., So. Ill. U., 1971; MAT in Spl. Edn. and Reading, Webster U., Webster Groves, Mo., 1992. Cert. in K-12 learning disabilities, K-12 behavior disorders, K-12 educable mentally handicapped, K-12 trainable mentally handicapped, 1-8 elem., kindergarten, reading specialist, all Mo.; cert. 1-8 elem. edn., trainable mentally handicapped, Tex. Substitute tchr. Spl. Sch. Dist., Town & Country, Mo., 1970-71, tchr. mentally handicapped, 1971-72; tchr. multicategorical El Paso (Tex.) Ind. Schs., 1972-73; tchr. aide early childhood Spl. Sch. Dist., Town & Country, 1983-84, tchr. asst. behavior disorder, 1984-85, tchr. resource learning disabilities/behavioral disorders, 1985—. Religious coord. St. Agatha Parish. Mem. Coun. Exceptional Children, Mo. State Tchrs. Assn., Internat. Soc. for Tech. in Edn., Learning Disability Assn., Attention Deficit Disorder Assn., Regional Consortium for Edn. and Tech., Found. for Applied Rsch. in Edn., Internat. Reading Assn. (Mo. state coun.), Orton Dyslexia Soc., Alumni Assn. Webster U., Alumni Assn. So. Ill. U. Edwardsville, Phi Theta Kappa. Roman Catholic. Avocation: reading. Home: 288 Portwind Pl Ballwin MO 63021-5058 Office: Spl Sch Dist 12110 Clayton Rd Saint Louis MO 63131-2599

DULEY, MARGOT IRIS, historian, educator; b. St. John's, Can., Sept. 15, 1944; d. Cyril Chancey and Florence (Pitcher) Duley; m. Lance Franz Morrow, Aug. 28, 1969 (div. Oct. 1986). BA with 1st class honors, Meml. U. of Newfoundland, 1966; MA, Duke U., 1968; PhD, U. London, 1977. Instr. dept. history St. Andrew's Presbyn. Coll., Laurinburg, N.C., 1970-71, Hiram (Ohio) Coll., 1973-75; dir., lectr. pilot program U. Mich., Ann Arbor, 1975-78, dir. law club, 1978-79, assoc. dir. honors program Coll. Lit. Sci. and the Arts, 1979-84; dir. women's studies program, assoc. prof. history Denison U., Granville, Ohio, 1984-89; dir. univ. honors program, assoc. prof. history U. Toledo, 1989-92; prof. dept. history and philosophy Ea. Mich. U., Ypsilanti, 1989—, head dept. history and philosophy, 1992-97, dir. women's studies program, 2000—02, interim assoc. dean Coll. Arts & Scis., 2002—. Adv. bd. Project on Equal Ednl. Rights, Mich., 1978—82. Editor, chief author: book The Cross Cultural Study of Women, 1986; author: Where Once Our Mothers Stood We Stand, 1993; hist. cons.: films Untold Story, 1999. Mem. Ford Lake Adv. Commn., Ypsilanti, Mich., 1996—, chair, 1998—2001, sec., 2001—02; vice-chair Water Conservation Commn., 2003—. Fellow, Duke U., 1966—67, Lord Rothermere Trust, U. London, 1967—70, Can. Coun., 1971—72, Robert Good, Denison U., 1989; grantee, Nfld. Provincial Adv. Com. on the Status of Women, 1988. Mem.: NOW (chair Mich. ERA task force 1978—80, pres. Mich. conf. 1980—82), Berkshire Conf. Women's History, Can. Hist. Assn., Am. Hist. Assn., Phi Kappa Phi (hon.). Avocations: sailing, hiking, travel, poetry. Office: Dept History and Philosophy Eastern Mich U 701 Pray Harrold Hall Ypsilanti MI 48197-2210

DULIN, TERESA DIANNE, primary school educator; b. Winchester, Ky., Oct. 18, 1955; d. Elmer Noland and Dorothy Jean (Chism) Wall; m. Freddie Mitchell Dulin, Jan. 9, 1975; 1 child, Adam Mitchell. BA, Morehead State U., 1979; MA, Ea. Ky. U., 1987. Kindergarten tchr. Emmanuel Episc. Day Sch., Winchester, Ky., 1979-80; tchr. 4th and 5th grades Clark County Bd. Edn., Winchester, 1980-85, 87-88, kindergarten tchr., 1988-95, tchr. primary (grades 2-3), 1995—. Mem. NEA, Phi Kappa Phi. Home: 134 Monet Blvd Winchester KY 40391-8757 Office: Trapp Elem Sch 11400 Irvine Rd Winchester KY 40391-9334

DULING, GRETCHEN ANNE, music educator; b. Gallipolis, Ohio, Jan. 30, 1940; d. Russell Smith and Halma Grace (Moore) Hoff; m. Dennis Carl Duling, Mar. 26, 1960; two children. BA in Music Edn., Roosevelt U., 1963, 69; MS in Creative Studies, Buffalo State Coll., Buffalo, 1980; PhD in Elem. Edn., Buffalo U., Buffalo, 1993; MS in Ednl. Adminstrn. and Supervision, Canisius Coll., Buffalo, 1986. Cert. elem. and secondary tchr., N.Y.; cert. adminstr. and supr., N.Y. Choral dir., tchr. gen. music Chgo. Pub. Schs., 1963-69; substitute tchr. music various schs., N.Y., Mich., Ohio, Mass., 1969-78; tchr. music jr. high, chorus dir. North Collins (N.Y.) Sch. Dist., 1979; grad. rsch. asst. N.Y. State Rsch. Found. SUNY, Buffalo, 1980-81, 90-92; tchr. gifted, coord. gifted edn. Eden and East Aurora (N.Y.) Sch. Dists., 1981-85; gifted programming specialist Williamsville (N.Y.) Ctrl. Schs., 1985-95; asst. prof. Ctr. for Studies in Creativity Buffalo State Coll., 1995—. Presch. tchr. in alt. high sch. Newton (Mass.) Pub. Schs., 1975; cons. in field.; presenter workshops. Author: (Teddie Books) Going to the Hospital, 1973, Moving to a New Home, 1975; Adopting Joe, Black Vietnamese Child, 1978; (story) Ghosts of Our House Tavern, 1977. Vol. Spl. Olympics, 1988—; elder Westminster Presbyn. Ch., Buffalo, 1991—; participant MS Walk/Annual, Buffalo, 1959—. Grantee Ohio State U. of Music, 1959; grantee Rossevelt U., 1961-62, USOE fellow Buffalo State Coll., 1979-80, fellow SUNY, 1990. Mem. Am. Ednl. Rsch. Assn., Nat. Assn. Gifted Children (John Gowan award 1980), N.Y. Assn. Gifted and Talented Edn., Creative Edn. Found., Oral History Assn., Spl. Edn. Parent/Tchr. Assn., Phi Delta Kappa. Presbyterian. Avocations: collecting antiques, colleting oral history, fast walking, nutrition, golf. Home: PO Box 175 Youngstown NY 14174-0175 Office: Buffalo State Coll Chase Hall/Ctr for Studies in Creativity 1300 Elmwood Ave Buffalo NY 14222-1004

DULLES, JOHN WATSON FOSTER, history educator; b. Auburn, N.Y., May 20, 1913; s. John Foster and Janet Pomeroy (Avery) D.; m. Eleanor Foster Ritter, June 15, 1940; children: Edith, John, Ellen, Avery. AB, Princeton U., 1935; MBA, Harvard U., 1937; BS in Metall. Engring., U. Ariz., 1943, Metall. Engr., 1951. Clk. The Bank of N.Y., N.Y.C., 1937-38; miner Callahan Zinc-Lead Co., Patagonia, Ariz., 1938-41; head ore dept., smelter operator Cia Minera de Peñoles, S.A., Monterrey, Mex., 1943-49, head comml. divsn., 1949-51, asst. gen. mgr., 1951-59, exec. v.p., 1959; v.p. Cia Mineração Novalimense, Belo Horizonte, Brazil, 1959-62; prof. history U. Ariz., Tucson, 1966-91; univ. prof. L.Am. studies U. Tex., Austin, 1962—. Advisor to U.S. delegation to OAS Conf., Vina Del Mar, Chile, 1967; cons. U.S. Dept. State, Bur. Intelligence and Rsch., 1968-72. Author: Yesterday in Mexico, 1961, Vargas of Brazil, 1967, Unrest in Brazil, 1970, Anarchists and Communists in Brazil, 1973, Castello Branco: The Making of a Brazilian President, 1978, President Castello Branco, 1980, Brazilian Communism, 1935-1945, 1983, The São Paulo Law School, 1986, Carlos Lacerda: Brazilian crusader, Vol. 1, 1991, Vol. 2, 1996 (Brazilian Union Writers and Carioca Acad. Leters prize 2000), Sobral Pinto: The Conscience of Brazil, 2002. Pres. exec. bd. Union Ch. Monterrey, Mexico, 1948—49, elder, 1957—59. Recipient Achievement medal U. Ariz., 1960, Ptnrs. of the Alliance Medal, Brazilian Govt., 1966. Fellow Calif. Inst. Internat. Studies; mem. The Am. Soc. of the Most Venerable Order of the Hosp. of St. John of Jerusalem (knight), Am. Hist. Assn., Tex. Inst. of Letters, Theta Tau (Alumni Hall of Fame), Inst. History and Geography Brasil. Avocation: tennis. Office: U Texas PO Box 7934 Austin TX 78713-7934 E-mail: dulles@mail.utexas.edu.

DUMERER, LORRAINE JOANNE LORI, social studies educator, clinician, consultant; b. Providence, July 10, 1946; d. John and Edith (Flippin) Florio; m. James Edward Dumerer, Nov. 23, 1966; children: James, Marc, Jennifer, Matthew, Paul. Student, Seton Hill Coll., 1964-66, St. Louis U., 1966; AB, U. Ill., 1969, MAT, 1972; postgrad., Tex. Women's U., 1987-88, U. Tex., Dallas, 1993, So. Meth. U., 1999-2001. Cert. social studies tchr. talented and gifted Tex., coll. bd. endorsed Advanced Placement cons. Tchr. Dayton (Ohio) Pub. Schs., 1970—71, St. Benedicts Sch., San Antonio, 1979—80, Incarnate World H.S., San Antonio, 1980—81, Diocese of Dallas, 1981—88, Dallas Ind. Sch. Dist., 1988—97; tchr., chmn. social studies dept., dean of faculty Long Trail Sch., Dorset, Vt., 1997—98; tchr. govt. and politics, macro and microecons., law studies Carrollton-Farmer's Branch Ind. Sch. Dist., 1998—. Coach Fed Challenge econs. competition, 1998-2001, North Dallas H.S. CIS-site based team, 1996-97; mem. R.L. Turner H.S. CIC-site based team, 1999—; mem. train the writers program US Dept Edn. Nat. Coun. for Econ. Edn., Romania, 2003; coach model UN teams, 2000—; clinician Acad. Clin. Svc., Dallas, 1985—; coord. nat. history day Diocese of Dallas, 1985-87; coord. Jane Goodall CHIMP project, 1991; chmn. dept. social studies, student coun. advisor North Dallas H.S., 1993-97; ednl. cons., presenter Specialty Limited English Proficient Integration, 1990—. Tex. Coun. Social Studies, Advanced Placement Reading Strategies, Cross-grade Level Curriculum Integration; Creating an Inclusive AP and Pre-AP Program, Integrating State Mandates in Pre-AP and AP Programs, Nat. Coun. for the Social Studies, AP Econ. Strategies, AP Govt., others; participant NEH Inst., 1995, Woodrow Wilson Inst., U. Tex., Dallas, 1993-1995, Congress in the Classroom Dirksen Ctr., Ill., 2003, Econs. for Leaders Found. for Tchg. Econs., So. Meth. U., 2000; reader Coll. Bd. Am. Govt., 2001-03; nat. endorsed Coll. Bd. cons.; selected for Tng. of Writers Project, Nat. Coun. Econ. Edn., U.S. Depts. of State and Edn., Bucharest, Romania, 2003; presenter in field Author: (essays) Economic Forces in American History, Foundation for Teaching Economics, 2001, numerous poems; contbr. chapters to books. Referee coord. N.E. Youth Soccer Assn., 1979-80, coach, 1979-80; coach, referee Mesquite Soccer Assn., 1981-86, referee liaison, 1981-82, sec., 1982-83, commr. of coaches, 1982-83. Mellon grantee, 1994; named Tchr. of Yr. Dallas Coun. for Social Studies, 1996, Outstanding HS Social Studies Tchr. of Yr., Tex. Coun. for Social Studies, 2002; named one of 50 Elite Tchrs., Tex. Coun. Econ. Edn., 2001. Mem. Nat. Coun. Social Studies, Tex. Coun. for Social Studies (sec. Peter's Colony Coun. for social studies 1998-99, v.p. 2000, pres. 2001-03), North Tex. Women's Soccer Assn. (capt. 1989-95), Ctr. for Applied Linguistics (cons. World Culture Project 1996), Nat. Coun. Econ. Edn. Avocations: writing, soccer, travel. Home: 3535 Misty Meadow Dr Dallas TX 75287-6027 E-mail: dumererl@cfbisd.edu., dumererl@earthlink.net.

DUMITRESCU, DOMNITA, Spanish language educator, researcher; b. Bucharest, Romania; came to U.S., 1984; d. Ion and Angela (Barzotescu) D. Diploma, U. Bucharest, 1966; MA, U. So. Calif., 1987, PhD, 1990. Asst. prof. U. Bucharest, 1966-74, assoc. prof., 1974-84; asst. prof. Spanish Calif. State U., L.A., 1987-90, assoc. prof., 1990-94, prof., 1995—. Author: Gramatica Limbii Spaniole, 1976, Indreptar Pentru Traducerea Din Limba Romana in Limba Spaniola, 1980; translator from Spanish lit. to Romanian; assoc. editor: Hispania, 1996—; contbr. articles to profl. jours. Fulbright scholar, 1993—. Mem. MLA, Linguistic Soc. Am., Internat. Assn. Hispanists, Linguistic Assn. S.W., Am. Assn. Tchrs. Spanish and Portuguese (past pres. So. Calif. chpt., Tchr. of Yr. award 2000), Sigma Delta Pi (v.p. West 1996—). Office: Calif State U 5151 State University Dr Los Angeles CA 90032-4226 E-mail: ddumitr@calstatela.edu.

DU MONT, ALLEN ANDRÉ, psychotherapist, educator; b. N.Y.C., Nov. 17, 1942; s. Phillip J. DuMont and Gabrielle Dumas; m. Marilyn Sciacca, May 28, 1983; 1 child, James. BA, CUNY, Queens, 1965; MSW, Adelphi U., 1974; PhD, NYU, 1984. Cert. social worker, clin. social worker; bd. cert. diplomate Am. Bd. Examiners in Clin. Social Work; cert. psychoanalytic psychotherapy L.I. Inst. Mental Health; primary cert. Inst. Rational Emotive Therapy; cert. ojbect rels. couples therapy Met. Ctr. for Objective Relative Therapy. Clin. field instr. office staff devel. N.Y.C. Human Resources Adminstrn., 1985-89, psychotherapy supr., 1986—; dir. Child and Family Therapy Ctr of Bayside, 1983—; sch. social worker N.Y.C. Bd. Edn., 1989—98. Child and family therapist L.I. Consultation Ctr., Rego Park, N.Y., 1985-90, St. Anthony's Guidance Clin., Mineola, N.Y., 1977-82; dir. spl. asst. for tng. office field svcs. Child Welfare Adminstrn., N.Y.C., 1980-84. Recipient Cath. Charities Svc. award, 1982; fellow L.I. Inst. Mental Health, 1979; grad. assistantship Adelphi U., 1973. Fellow Am. Orthopsychiat. Assn.; mem. NASW, N.Y. Soc. Clin. Social Work Psychotherapists (diplomate, 1st v.p., state treas., mem.-at-large Queen's chpt. pres.), NY Soc. Clin. Social Work (pres. 1998-2001, diplomate), Clin. Social Work Fedn. (fin. chmn. 2000-02, pres.-elect 2002—). Home and Office: 39-06 219th St Bayside NY 11361-2344

DU MONT, NICOLAS, psychiatrist, educator; b. San Juan, P.R., Dec. 22, 1954; s. Joseph Henri and Isabel (Solano) Du M. Postgrad. adult psychiatry, Columbia U., 1990; MD, U. P.R., 1986; postgrad. child, adolescent psychiatry, Columbia U., 1992, postgrad. pub. cmty. psychiatry, 1993. Assoc. prof. Polytech. U., San Juan, 1984-88, InterAm. U., San Juan, P.R., 1986-87; med. dir. Holistic Med. Ctr., N.Y.C., 1993-94; asst. prof. Albert Einstein Coll. of Medicine, N.Y.C., 1991-96, Mt. Sinai Sch. of Medicine, N.Y.C., 1993-96, Columbia Physicians and Surgeons Coll. Medicine, N.Y.C., 1997—; asst. attending physician Elmhurst Med. Ctr., N.Y.C., 1993-94; asst. physician Mt. Sinai Med. Ctr., N.Y.C., 1993-96; v.p., CEO Engring. Med. Support, Inc., N.Y.C., 1992—; asst. prof. Columbia Physicians and Surgeons Coll. Medicine, N.Y.C., 1997—. Attending physician Westchester Jewish Med. Svcs., Hartsdale, N.Y., 1990-95, Montefiore Med. Ctr., N.Y.C., 1991-96, Albert Einstein Coll. Medicine, 1991-96, Puerto Rican Family Inst., 1994—; asst. attending physician and med. dir. Tavares Hispanic Mental Health Clin. at Columbia Presbyn. Med. Ctr., 1997—. Assoc. editor: Jour. Pagan Studies (N.Y. edit.), 1990—. Vis. fellow N.Y. State Psychiat. Inst., 1992-93. Mem. Assn. Hispanic Mental Health Profls. (exec. bd. dirs. 1999—, treas.). Office: Engring Med Support Inc 200 W 70th St Ste 8F New York NY 10023-4326 E-mail: info@dumont.org.

DUNAGAN, GWENDOLYN ANN, special education educator; b. Youngstown, Ohio; d. Charles J. and Juanita A. Hicks; 1 child, Byron Keith Miles; m. Kenneth Robert Dunagan, 1972. BS in Edn., Youngstown U., Ohio, 1963; postgrad., Ashland U., 1986-89. Cert. elem. tchr., Ohio, learning disabilities tchr., Ohio, tchr. to severe behavior disorder, Ohio. Elem. tchr. Youngstown Bd. Edn., 1963-67, 1968-72; adminstr., tchr. Free Kindergarten Assn., Youngstown, 1967-68; liaison home-sch. Alliance (Ohio) Bd. Edn., 1972-86, tchr. disadvantaged pupils, 1986-89, intervention tchr. learning disabilities, 1989-90, tchr. specific learning disabilities, 1990-94, spl. edn. tchr., 1994—. Contestant, winner TV show Price is Right; group leader Youngstown Detention Ctr. Contbr. articles to profl. mags., area newspapers. Pres. Domestic Violence Shelter, Alliance, 1990—92, hon. mem., 1992—, D.&E. Kirksey Reunion, Kirksey-Young-Hawkins Reunion; trustee Alliance Domestic Violence Shelter, 1999—; pres. John Slimack Homeless Shelter, Alliance, 1989—93; pres., founder Cmty. Civic Com., Alliance, 1987—; treas. Altrusic Civic Club, Alliance, 1988—91; chair Alliance Area Desert Storm Celebration Com.; mem. Family Counseling Ctr. YWCA; mem. Dr. King Birthday Celebration Com.; mem., v.p. Dr. Martin Luther King Jr. Steering Com., 1995; adv. bd. Salvation Army, 1994—; parade marshal Dr. M.L. King Jr. Hist. Parade, 1998; mem. Cable Task Force (mayoral appointment), 1999, Alliance Area Black Caucus;

assoc. Race Rels. Group; trustee Alliance Neighborhood Ctr.; chair Second Ward Coun. Campaign, 1999, 2001; mem. choir Holy Temple Ch. God in Christ, Alliance, 1972—, mem. usher bd. dirs., fin. sec., sec. Sunday sch., 1989—, deaconess, Aspirant Missionary; tchr. Prayer and Bible Band, 1990—; mem. Union of Missions. Honored for cmty. svc. Stark County Cmty. Action Agy., 1990; named Master Tchr.; included in YWCA Wall of Fame, 2000. Mem. AAUW, Alliance Edn. Assn. (Dowling scholarship com.), NAACP (2d v.p. 1990-93), Alpha Kappa Alpha. Avocations: writing poetry, collecting poetry and readings, collecting antique plates, gospel music, Scrabble. Home: 1115 S Seneca Ave Alliance OH 44601-4068

DUNAGAN, WALTER BENTON, lawyer, educator; b. Midland, Tex., Dec. 11, 1937; s. Clinton McCormick and Allie Mae (Stout) D.; m. Tera Childress, Feb. 1, 1969; children: Elysha, Sandi. BA, U. Tex., 1963, JD, 1965, postgrad., 1965-68. Bar: Tex. 1965, Fla. 1970, U.S. Dist. Ct. (mid. dist.) Fla. 1971, U.S. Ct. Appeals (11th cir.) 1982. Corp. atty. Gulf Oil, New Orleans, 1968-69, Getty Oil Co., L.A., 1969—, Westinghouse/Econocar, Internat., Daytona Beach, Fla., 1969-72; assoc. Becks & Becks, Daytona Beach, 1973-75; prin. Walter B. Dunagan, Daytona Beach, 1975—. Cons. Bermuda Villas Motel, Daytona Beach, Buccanneer Motel, Daytona Beach, Pelican Cove West Homeowners Assn., Edgewater, Fla. Organizer Interfaith Coffee House, New Orleans; tchr., song leader various chs.; chief Indian guide/princess program YMCA, Daytona Beach; bd. dirs. Legal Aid, Daytona Beach. Lance cpl. USMC. Mem. Volusia County Bar Assn., Lawyers Title Guaranty Fund, Phi Delta Phi. Avocations: reading, languages. Home and Office: 714 Egret Ct Edgewater FL 32141-4120 Fax: 386-409-3710. E-mail: wbdunfla@msn.com.

DUNATHAN, HARMON CRAIG, college dean; b. Celina, Ohio, July 25, 1932; s. Harry V. and Mildred B. (Greek) D.; m. Katy Mary Dragati, Mar. 15, 1956 (div. July 1990); children: Christine, Susan, Amy, Andrea; m. Mary Frances Pitts, Sept. 29, 1990. BA, Ohio Wesleyan U., 1954; MS, Yale U., 1956, PhD, 1958. Mem. faculty Haverford (Pa.) Coll., 1957-75, assoc. prof. chemistry, 1964-70, prof., 1970-75; provost, dean faculty Hobart and William Smith Colls., Geneva, N.Y., 1975-84, acting pres., 1978-79; dean faculty Hampshire Coll., 1984-87; dean acad. affairs Rhodes Coll., Memphis, 1987-93; prof. chemistry, dir. rsch. and sponsored programs LeMoyne-Owen Coll., Memphis, 1993-95, prof. chemistry, interim v.p. instl. advancement, 1996-97, 00-01, prof. chemistry, dir. internat. rsch. and planning, 1997—. Home: 2014 Hallwood Dr Memphis TN 38107-4703

DUNAWAY, PHILLIP LEE, JR., secondary school education educator; b. Asher, Okla., Jan. 29, 1936; s. Phillip L. and Jannie (Smith) D.; m. Marlene Ann Dixson, Nov. 19, 1960; children: Russell Phillip, Curtis Lee. MusB, BA, U. Pacific, 1958; postgrad., San Francisco State U., Sonoma State U. Cert. gen. elem., gen. secondary, spl. secondary music, Calif. Tchr. Benicia (Calif.) Unified Sch. Dist., 1958-66, Mt. Diablo Unified Sch. Dist., Concord, Calif., 1966—99; chair social studies dept. Foothill Mid. Sch., 1978-93. Gospel singer, rec. artist, 8 albums, 1966—; min. music various chs., 1961-87; pres. Philmar Ministries, Inc., Benicia, 1971—, active fgn. missions ministry, 1976—; music dir. Celebration of Life TV show, San Francisco, 1975-77; dist. social studies com. Mt. Diablo Unified Sch. Dist., 1978-93; tour dir. 8th grade trip to Washington Foothill Mid. Sch., 1980-99. Arranger, composer: (records) Songweaver on the Move, 1967-68, Paul Weaver Chorale On Stage, Young Life Songs; arranger, composer Sacred Concert Pub., 1965-70, Lillenas Pub. Co., 1971. Counselor Am. Heritage Merit badge Boy Scouts Am., 1986-87. Recipient Nat. Evangel. Film Found. award, 1968; scholar Am. Legion Freedom Found., 1979. Mem. NEA, Mt. Diablo Edn. Assn., No. Calif./Nev. Assemblies of God, Calif. Tchrs. Assn., Phi Mu Alpha Sinfonia. Avocations: photography, gardening. Home: 2257 1st St Benicia CA 94510-2139

DUNAWAY, WILLIAM PRESTON, retired educator; b. Lineville, Ala., June 30, 1936; s. Robert Johnson and Zylpha Mae (Preston) D.; m. Carolyn Bennett, Mar. 3, 1943; 1 child, Robert Bennett. BS, Jacksonville (Ala.) State U., 1959; MEd, Auburn (Ala.) U., 1966; AA, U. Ala., 1972; EdD, U. Miss., 1974. Tchr. math. Clay County High Sch., Ashland, Ala., 1960-61, Benjamin Russell High Sch., Alexander City, Ala., 1961-65; asst. supt. Alexander City Bd. Edn., 1965-67; asst. prin. Erwin High Sch., Birmingham, Ala., 1967-70; headmaster St. James Sch., Montgomery, Ala., 1970-71; prin. Anniston (Ala.) High Sch., 1971-73; prof. Sch. Adminstrn. Jacksonville (Ala.) State U., 1974-91, prof. emeritus, 1993—. Cons. in field; computer edn. dir. Jacksonville State U., 1983-91. Contbr. articles to profl. jours. Boy scout and cub scout master, bd. dirs. coun. Boy Scouts Am., Anniston, contbr. Handicapped Scouting Manual 1980; officer, tchr., First Presbyn. Ch., Jacksonville, 1975—; mem. Jacksonville Housing Authority Commn., 1992—, vice chair, 1993—; founding mem. Nat. Campaign for Tolerance, Wall of Tolerance. Capt. U.S. Army Res. and N.G., 1954-68. Recipient Jacksonville State U. Research award, 1988, Citizen of Yr. award, 1984; grantee Ala. Commn. on Higher Edn., 1986. Mem. Nat. Assn. Secondary Sch. Prins., Am. Assn. Sch. Adminstrs., Coun. for Computer Edn., Assn. Pub. Housing and Devel., Kiwanis, Sierra Club, Kappa Delta Pi, Phi Delta Kappa. Democrat. Avocations: computer enthusiast, landscape gardening, environmental issues, church and civic activities. Home and Office: 902 11th St NE Jacksonville AL 36265-1230

DUNBAR, BURDETT SHERIDAN, anesthesiologist, pediatrician, educator; b. Kewanee, Ill., Dec. 6, 1938; s. C. Marion and Marjorie LaVonne (Sweat) D.; m. Kathleen C. Empsucha, Aug. 12, 1989; children: Michael Eugene, Brian Randal, Alex Seaton, Bradley Hughes. BS cum laude, U. Ill., 1960, MD, 1963. Diplomate Am. Bd. Anesthesiology, Nat. Bd. Med. Examiners; lic. physician, Pa., Ill., D.C., Va., Tex. Intern Springfield (Ohio) City Hosp., 1963-64; resident U. Pa. Hosp., Phila., 1964-66; NIH fellow U. Pa., Phila., 1966-67; clin. asst. prof. anesthesiology U. Tex., San Antonio, 1968-69; asst. prof. U. Chgo., 1969-71; from asst. prof. to assoc. prof. anesthesiology George Washington U. Med. Ctr., Washington, 1974-80, prof., 1980-86; prof. anesthesiology U. Tex., Houston, 1986-89; prof. anesthesiology and pediatrics Baylor Coll. Medicine, Houston, 1989—, interim chmn. dept. anesthesiology, 1999—. Clin. cons. Bexar County Hosp. Dist., San Antonio, 1968-69; assoc. attending physician Michael Reese Hosp. & Med. Ctr., Chgo., 1969-71; assoc. dir. spl. care unit George Washington U. Hosp., Washington, 1971-74, attending staff, 1971-86; assoc. chmn. anesthesiology Children's Hosp. Nat. Med. Ctr., Washington, 1974-83, acting chmn., 1983-85, sr. attending staff, 1974-86; attending staff Hermann Hosp., Houston, 1987-89; chief pediatric anesthesiology svc. Tex. Children's Hosp., Houston, 1989—. Author: (with others) Surgical Diseases of the Chest, 1974, The Practice of Clinical Engineering, 1977, Pediatric Trauma Surgery, 1979; contbr. numerous articles and abstracts to profl. jours. and newsletters. Emergency med. svcs. D.C. Dept. Health and Human Svcs., Washington, 1975-81, transp. safety com. 1981-84, vice-chmn. pub. info. com. 1983-85. Capt. USAF, 1967-69. Fellow Am. Coll. Anesthesiologists, Am. Acad. Pediatrics; mem. AMA, AAAS, AAUP, Am. Soc. Anesthesiologists (del. Ho. of Dels. 1979-85, alt. dir. 1985-86), Am. Bd. Anesthesiology (sr. assoc. examiner 1987—), Am. Soc. Anesthesiolgoists, Md./D.C. Anesthesiology Soc. (pres. 1985-86), Tex. Gulf Coast Anesthesia Soc., Tex. Med. Soc., Internat. Anesthesia Rsch. Soc., Harris County Med. Soc., Soc. Critical Care Medicine, Soc. Edn. Anesthesia, Soc. Ambulatory Anesthesia, Soc. Pediatric Anesthesia. Avocations: history, travel. Office: Tex Childrens Hosp 6621 Fannin St # 1495 Houston TX 77030-2303 E-mail: burdettd@bcm.tmc.edu.

DUNCAN, ADREN LEE, special education educator; b. Perry County, Tenn., Apr. 4, 1946; s. Buford Andrew and Vera Eudora Pearl (Barham) D.; m. Barbara K. Thornberry, Dec. 15, 1978. BS, Austin Peay State U., 1977. Licensed social worker, 1986. Rehab. asst. Lions World Svcs. for Blind, Little Rock, 1978-85, communications instr., 1985—. Mem. Assn. Edn. and Rehab. of Blind and Visually Impaired (bd. dirs. 1993—), Lions Club Internat., Am. Coun. of the Blind Lions (dir. 1989-91, 91-93, 1st v.p. 1991-93, pres. local chpt. 1987, 88, dir. state chpt. 1993—), Toastmasters Internat. (area B-4 gov. 1992-93, dvsn. B gov. 1993—), Cen. Ark. PC Users Assn., Pulaski Heights Lions Club (com. chairperson 1982-92), Sigma Chi (life). Baptist. Avocations: piano, keyboard, voice, fiddle. Home: 2309 S Jackson St Little Rock AR 72204-5254 Office: Lions World Svcs for Blind 2811 Fair Park Blvd Little Rock AR 72204-5044

DUNCAN, CONSTANCE CATHARINE, psychologist, educator, researcher; b. Watertown, Wis, Nov. 2, 1948; d. Howard Burton and Mary Elizabeth (Fagan) Duncan; m. R.E. Johnson, Jr., 1974 (div. 1984); m. Allan Franklin Mirsky, July 4, 1986. BA, Northwestern U., 1970; AM, U. Ill., 1973, PhD, 1978. Sr. rsch. analyst Adolf Meyer Mental Health Ctr., Decatur, Ill., 1971-73; asst. in rsch. and tchg. dept. psychology U. Ill., Champaign, 1974-78; NIMH postdoctoral fellow in neurosis. Stanford U. Sch. Medicine, Palo Alto, Calif., 1978-81; rsch. psychologist VA Med. Ctr., Palo Alto, 1978-81; sr. staff fellow Lab. Psychology and Psychopathology, NIMH, 1981-88; chief unit on psychophysiology NIMH, Bethesda, Md., 1982-89, rsch. psychologist, 1988-89, rsch. specialist, 1989-93; pvt. practice Bethesda, Md., 1981—. Adj. assoc. prof. Johns Hopkins Sch. Hygiene and Pub. Health, Balt., 1987—; guest rschr. Lab. Psychology and Psychopathology NIMH, 1993—97, Sect. on Clin. and Exptl. Neuropsychology NIMH, 1997—; rsch. assoc. prof. Uniformed Svc. Univ. Health Sci., 1993—. Assoc. editor Psychophysiology, 1987-91; mem. editl. bd. Internat. Jour. Psychophysiology, 2002—; cons. editor numerous sci. jour.; contbr. articles to profl. jour., chpt. to books. Found. assoc. Nat. Women's Econ. Alliance; mem. NIMH/NINCDS Assembly of Sci. Coun., 1982-84. Recipient Nat. Rsch. Svc. award, NIMH, 1978-81, Golden Anniversary Scholarship award, AAUW, 1974; NIMH fellow, 1970-74. Fellow: APA, Internat. Orgn. Psychophysiology, Am. Psychol. Soc.; mem.: EEG and Clin. Neurosci. Soc., Am. Psychopathol. Assn., Internat.Neuropsychol. Soc., Soc. for Neurosci., Soc. for Rsch. in Psychopathology (bd. dirs. 1986—88, membership com. 1987—88), Soc. for Psychophysiol. Rsch. (program com. 1979, 1980, nominating com. 1981, chmn. early career award com. 1981—84, program com. 1982, bd. dirs. 1982—85, nominating com. 1983, chmn. conv. com. 1983—87, program com. 1986, chmn. program com. 1987, program com. 1988, nominating com. 1989, Blue Ribbon Panel on state of soc. in Yr. 2000 1990—93, chmn. enhancement com. 1992—93, chmn. early career award com. 1994—96, conv. com., sec.-treas. 1996—99, com. governance and ops. 2000—01, program com. 2001, sr. award com. 2001—, chair sr. award com. 2002—, pres. 2002—, Early Career Contbn. award 1980), Phi Beta Kappa, Pi Mu Epsilon, Alpha Lambda Delta, Phi Kappa Phi, Sigma Xi, Shi-Ai, Mortar Bd. Achievements include electrophysiological and neuropsychological research on normal and disordered attn. and cognition. Office: Uniformed Svc U Health Sci Clin Psychophysiology and Psychopharm Lab 4301 Jones Bridge Rd Bethesda MD 20814-4799

DUNCAN, DEBRA LYNN, elementary education educator; b. Huntingdon, Pa., Oct. 16, 1954; d. Robert L. and Pearle A. (Snyder) Morrow; m. Robert E. Duncan, Aug. 9, 1975; children: Jeremy, Jason. BA summa cum laude, U. Tex., San Antonio, 1989; MA, U. Tex., 1994. Cert. elem. tchr., mid. mgmt. adminstr., Tex. 3rd, 4th grade tchr. N.E. Ind. Sch. Dist., San Antonio, 1990-92; 5th grade tchr. Seguin (Tex.) Ind. Sch. Dist. Dir. Sparks, Awana, Converse, Tex., 1988-93. Mem. New Life Bapt. Ch., Converse, 1987—. Mem. ASCD, Assn. Tex. Profl. Educators, Nat. Coun. Tchrs. of English, Internat. Reading Assn., Kappa Delta Pi, Alpha Chi. Avocations: reading, collecting stamps.

DUNCAN, DONNA FOWLER, secondary school educator; b. Greenville, S.C., July 15, 1957; d. James Robert Fowler and Betty (Worthy) Goodnough; children: William Jennings, Emily Jo. BS, Clemson U., 1979, MEd, 1991. Cert. tchr., S.C. Tchr. math. Wren Mid. Sch., Piedmont, S.C., 1979—. Sch. rep. Supt. Tchr. Com., Piedmont, 1991-92, mem. dist. pub. rels. com., 1991-93; tchr. rep. Sch.-Wide Restructuring Com., Piedmont, 1991-92; rep. Dist.-Wide Math. Curriculum Com., 1991-93, Dist.-Wide Total Quality Edn. Team, 1993. Mem. ASCD, S.C. Edn. Assn., S.C. Coun. Tchrs. Math., Alpha Delta Kappa. Baptist. Avocations: reading, cross-stitch, spectator sports. Home: 307 Cranberry Hill Cir Mauldin SC 29662-2573 Office: Wren Mid Sch 1010 Wren School Rd Piedmont SC 29673-8099

DUNCAN, DOUGLAS ALLEN, education educator; b. Sodus, N.Y., Apr. 2, 1956; s. Allen Lee and Barbara Ann (Payne) D.; m. Jody Ann Cianciotto, June 10, 1978; children: Holly Ann, Kristen Marie. BA, SUNY, Fredonia, 1978; MA, Mary Washington Coll., 1988; postgrad., U. Va., 1991-92. Cert. tchr., prin., Va. Grad. asst. State U. Coll. Fredonia, N.Y., 1978-79; tchr. Geneva (N.Y.) High Sch., 1979-82, Orange (Va.) County Pub. Schs., 1984-90, 92—, peer coach, 1990-92. Adj. instr. Lord Fairfax C.C., Middletown, Va., 1989-90; cons. St. Mary's County Pub. Schs., Loveville, Md., 1990, Whitko Cmty. Sch. Corp., Pierceton, Ind., 1992, Blaine County Pub. Schs., Hailey, Idaho, 1992-95, Tigerton (Wis.) Pub. Schs., 1992-94, Green River (Wyo.) Pub. Schs., 1992-94, Twin Falls (Idaho) Pub. Schs., 1993, Noble (Okla.) Pub. Schs., 1993, Lake Ctrl. Sch. Corp., St. John, Ind., 1993, Ind. Sch. Dist. 748, Sartell, Minn., 1993, Byron (Mich.) Pub. Schs., 1995; presenter in field. Mem. Bethlehem United Meth. Ch., Unionville, Va., Prospect Heights Middle Sch. PTA, Somerset (Va.) Steam and Gas Engine Assn. Coun. for Basic Edn. fellow, 1990; Gov.'s fellow U. Va., Charlottesville, 1991-92. Mem. ASCD, Va. Middle Sch. Assn. (exec., adv. bd. 1989-91), Coun. for Basic Edn., Phi Delta Kappa. Avocations: reading, writing, golf, tennis. Office: Orange County Pub Schs PO Box 349 Orange VA 22960-0204

DUNCAN, ELIZABETH CHARLOTTE, retired marriage and family therapist, educational therapist, educator; b. L.A., Mar. 10, 1919; d. Frederick John de St. Vrain and Nellie Mae (Goucher) Schwankovsky; m. William McConnell Duncan, Oct. 12, 1941 (div. 1949); 1 child, Susan Elizabeth Duncan St. Vrain. BA, Calif. State U., Long Beach, 1953; MA, UCLA, 1962; PhD, Internat. Coll., 1984. Cert. marriage and family therapist; cert. clin. psychopathologist, Wash. Dir. gifted program Palos Verdes (Calif.) Sch. Dist., 1958-64; TV tchr., participant ednl. films Los Angeles County, 1961-64; dir. U. So. Calif. Presch., L.A., 1965-69, Abraham Maslow rsch. assoc., 1962-69; pvt. practice family counseling Malibu, Calif., 1979—2003, Ventura, 1979—2003, Eastsound, 1979—2003, Seattle, 1979—2003; pvt. practice psychotherapy West Seattle, 1994—2003; ret., 2003. Psychotherapist Children's Program North Sound Regional Support Network, 1992; resident psychologist for film series Something Personal, 1987—; mem. Rsch. Inst. of Scripps Cliic, La Jolla, Calif.; charter mem. Inst. Behavioral Medicine, Santa Barbara, Calif.; pub. spkr., lectr. comm.; cons. in field. TV performer in documentary The Other Side, 1985; creator: Persephone's Child, 1988. Active Chrysalis Ctr., L.A., 1984-86; mem. Ventura County Mental Health Adv. Bd., 1985-86, United Way, L.A., 1985-92; mem. Menninger Found. San Juan County, Wash., 1992; mem. adv. bd. North Sound Regional Support Network, 1992, Amb.'s People to People, San Juan County Network, 1998-00. Recipient Emmy award for best documentary Am. Acad. TV Arts and Scis., 1976; named Child Adv. of Yr., Calif. Mental Health Adv. Bd., 1987. Mem. AACD (Disting. Svc. award 1990), Transpersonal Psychol. Assn., Calif. State Orgn. Gifted Edn. (sec. 1962-64), Internat. Platform Assn., Am. Assn. for Marriage and Family Therapy (supr. licenses). Democrat. Avocations: swimming, plays, concerts, boating, political issues, especially women and child abuse. Home: 4455 Providence Point Pl SE Issaquah WA 98029 E-mail: drduncan@foxinternet.com.

DUNCAN, FRANCES MURPHY, retired special education educator; b. Utica, N.Y., June 23, 1920; d. Edward Simon and Elizabeth Myers (Stack) Murphy; m. Lee C. Duncan, June 23, 1947 (div. June 1969); children: Lee C., Edward M., Paul H., Elizabeth B., Nancy R., Frances B.(dec.), Richard L.(dec.). BA, Columbia State U., 1942; MEd, Auburn U., 1963, EdD, 1969. Head sci. dept. Arnold Jr. H.S., Columbus, Ga., 1960-63; tchr. physiology, Spanish Jordan H.S., Columbus, Ga., 1963-64; tchr. spl. edn. mentally retarded Muscogee County Sch. Sys., Columbus, Ga., 1964-65; instr. spl. edn. Auburn (Ala.) U., 1966-69; assoc. dir. Douglas Sch. for Learning Disabilities, Columbus, 1969-70; prof. edn. and spl. edn. Columbus Coll., 1970-85, ret., 1985. Past dir. Columbus Devel. Ctr.; past sec. exec. bd. Muscular Dystrophy Assn., 1968-70; 73-74; mem. Gov.'s Commn. on Disabled Georgians; past trustee Listening Eyes Sch. for Deaf; past mem. Mayor's Com. on Handicapped; mem. team for evaluation and placement of exceptional children Columbus Pub. Schs. Vol. Med. Ctr. Columbus Regional Healthcare Sys., Ga., Achievement Acad., Columbus, Ga., Columbus Hospice, Columbus, Ga. Fellow Am. Assn. Mental Retardation; mem. AAUP, AAUW (pres. 1973-75, divsn. rec. sec. 1975—), Coun. Exceptional Children (legis. chmn. 1973-74), Psi Chi, Phi Delta Kappa. Roman Catholic. Home: 1811 Alta Vista Dr Columbus GA 31907-3210

DUNCAN, GLENDA JULAINE, elementary education educator; b. Castle, Okla., Feb. 18, 1943; d. William Edgar and Joyce Mayree (Branscum) Johnson; m. Jimmie Leon Duncan, June 11, 1960; children: Deborah, Danny, David. BA, Okla. Bapt. U., 1974. Tchr. 1st grade Will Rogers Elem. Sch., Shawnee, Okla., 1974-75, tchr. 3d grade, 1975-77, tchr. 5th and 6th grade, 1977-86; tchr. 5th grade Ctr. Washington Sch., 1986-89, Will Rogers Elem. Sch., 1989—. Sch. rep. Sch. Improvement Com., Shawnee, 1989-93. Mem. NEA, Okla. Edn. Assn., Assn. Classroom Tchrs., Nat. Reading. Assn. Democrat. Baptist. Avocations: reading, gardening, music. Home: RR 1 Box 108B Earlsboro OK 74840-9801

DUNCAN, GWENDOLYN MCCURRY, elementary education educator; b. Walhalla, S.C., Feb. 24, 1943; d. Benjamin Harrison and Lucy Rosa (Quarles) McCurry; m. Harold Edward Duncan, July 29, 1962; children: Gregory Scott, Michael Lane. BA in Elem. Edn., Clemson (S.C.) U., 1984, MA in Elem. Edn., 1999. Cert. tchr. S.C., Nat. Bd. Tchr. Cert., 2002. Tchr. Westminster (S.C.) Elem. Sch., 1984-97, Orchard Park Elem. Sch., Westminster, 1997—. Sunday sch. tchr. Mountain View Bapt. Ch., Walhalla, 1968—; mem. Westminster Elem. PTA, 1984-97, Orchard Park Elem. PTA, 1997—. Mem. NEA, Oconee County Edn. Assn., S.C. Edn. Assn., S.C. Tchrs. of Math., Nat. Coun. of Tchrs. of Math., Kappa Delta Pi. Baptist. Avocations: reading, camping, traveling, growing roses. Home: 389 Fowler Rd West Union SC 29696-3122 Office: Orchard Park Elem Sch 600 Toccoa Hwy Westminster SC 29693-1638

DUNCAN, IRMA WAGNER, retired biochemist, museum educator; b. Buffalo, Jan. 30, 1912; d. Carl R. and Emily (Leue) Wagner; m. David R.L. Duncan, Mar. 21, 1937 (dec. Aug. 1972); children: David L., Paul R. BS, U. Buffalo, 1933; MS, U. Chgo., 1935, PhD, 1950. Prof. sci. Colo. Women's Coll., Denver, 1944-48; assoc. prof. chemistry U. Denver, 1951-59; rsch. chemist Arctic Health Rsch. Ctr., HEW, USPHS, Anchorage, Alaska, 1960-67, Fairbanks, Alaska, 1967-74, Ctrs. for Disease Control, USPHS, Atlanta, 1974-82; docent N.Mex. Mus. Nat. History and Sci., Albuquerque, 1984-93, 98—, Maxwell Mus. Anthropology, U. N.Mex., Albuquerque, 1984—. Editor work books; contbr. articles to profl. jours. Trustee Manzano Day Sch., Albuquerque, 1993-97. Mem. Am. Assn. Ret. Persons, Nature Conservancy, Sigma Xi (emeritus). Avocations: hiking, camping, cooking, natural history, anthropology. Home: 1620 Francisca Rd NW Albuquerque NM 87107-7118

DUNCAN, JOHN WILEY, information professional, retired air force officer; b. San Francisco, Aug. 8, 1947; s. Vernon Alexander and Nellie May (Shaw) D.; m. Trudy Rae Hirsch, Feb. 25, l967; children: Amber Rose, John Anthony. BS in Math. and Physics, N.W. Mo. State U., l969; MBA, So. Ill. U., l973; MS in Computer Sci., U. Tex., San Antonio, l982. Tchr. Savannah (Mo.) High Sch., 1969; enlisted USAF, 1969, advanced through grades to maj., aeromed. officer 9AES, 1978-80; student UTSA, San Antonio, 1981-82; systems implementation team leader Sch. of Health Care Scics., Sheppard AFB, Tex., 1982-83; asst. chief med. systems Hdqrs. Air Tng. Command, Randolph AFB, Tex., 1983-86; chief med. systems Hdqrs. Pacific AF, Hickham AFB, Hawaii, 1986-89, 15 Med. Group, Hickham AFB, Hawaii, 1989; instr. Kapiolani C.C., Honolulu, 1989-94; sys. mgr. Hawaii Correctional Industries, Aiea, 1994-96, Sci. Applications Internat. Corp., Ft. Shafter, Hawaii, 1996—2002. Computer cons., 1977—; instr. Midwestern U., Wichita Falls, 1982-83, Tex. Luth. Coll., Seguin, 1986-86, Hawaii Pacific Coll., Honolulu, 1987-89, Leeward C.C., 1989-1999, Kapiolani C.C., 1989-94. Cons. Ronald McDonald House, San Antonio, l986. Presbyterian. Avocations: computing, tennis, reading, travel. Home and Office: 235 N Chestnut Ave Earlham IA 50072 E-mail: John.Duncan@TheWolfsPaw.com.

DUNCAN, MARGARET A. elementary education educator; Tchr. McGhee Elem. Sch., Lewiston, Idaho. Named Idaho State Elem. Tchr. of Yr., 1992.*

DUNCAN, RICHARD FREDRICK, JR., secondary education educator, travel consultant; b. Millry, Ala., July 12, 1947; s. Richard F. and Claire Louise (Wood) D.; m. Rebecca Susan Davis, July 14, 1973. AA, Okaloosa-Walton Jr. Coll., 1967; BS, Fla. State U., 1969, MS, 1971; postgrad., Ore. State U., 1981-82. Tchr. Gadsden County Sch. Bd., Quincy, Fla., 1970-71, Leon County Sch. Bd., Tallahassee, Fla., 1972-73, Beaverton (Oreg.) Sch. Dist. No. 48, 1973—. Microbiologist Washington County, Hillsboro, Ore., 1971-72; cons. on sci. edn. Northwest Regional Ednl. Lab., Portland, Ore., 1978-79; cons. on marine edn. Ore. Dept. Edn., Salem, 1980-81. Recipient award for excellence in sci. teaching Ore. Mus. Sci. and Industry, Portland, 1984, Psdl. award, 1984. Mem. Assn. Presdl. Awardees in Sci. Teaching (nat. pres. 1987-88), Nat. Assn.Biology Tchrs. (Ore. Biology Tchr. of Year award 1981), Nat. Sci. Tchrs. Assn. (Presdl. award for excellence in sci. teaching, 1983, Sheldon award 1993, Nat. Disting. Svc. to Sci. award 2001), Oreg. Sci. Tchrs. Assn. (pres. 1980-81, Oreg. Jr. High Tchr. of Yr. award 1982), North Assn. Marine Educators (state dir. 1978-80), Masons, Shriners. Democrat. Avocations: sports, photography, sailing, scuba diving, camping. Home: 13240 SW Juanita Pl Beaverton OR 97008-6831 Office: Beaverton Sch Dist # 48 PO Box 200 Beaverton OR 97075-0200

DUNCAN, ROBERT BANNERMAN, strategy and organizations educator; b. Milw., July 4, 1942; s. Robert Lynn and Irene (Hoenig) D.; m. Susan Jean Phillips, June 12, 1965; children: Stephanie Olcott, Christopher Robert. BA, Ind. U., 1964, MA, 1966; PhD, Yale U., 1971. Asst. prof. Northwestern U. Kellogg Grad. Sch. Mgmt., Evanston, Ill., 1970-73, assoc. prof. orgn. behavior, 1973-76, prof., 1976, Earl Dean Howard prof. orgn. behavior, 1980-83, J.L. Kellogg disting. prof. strategy and orgns., 1983-86, 92—, J. Allen disting. prof. strategy and orgns., 1986-89; Richard L. Thomas prof. leadership orgnl. change Northwestern U., Evanston, 1996—2002; assoc. dean acad. affairs Northwestern U. Kellogg Grad. Sch. Mgmt., Evanston, Ill., 1975-76, 80-82, 84-86; provost, chief acad. affairs Northwestern U., Evanston, 1987-92; Eli and Edythe L. Broad dean Eli Broad Coll. Bus. Mich. State U., East Lansing, 2002—. Co-author: Innovations and Organizations, 1973, Strategies for Planned Change, 1977; also numerous articles in profl. jours. Fellow Acad. Mgmt. (chair nat. program 1980-81, pres. 1983-84). Avocation: sailing.

DUNCAN, STEPHEN ROBERT, elementary education educator; b. Lancaster, Pa., June 23, 1950; s. Robert L. Duncan and Joan L. (McLaughlin) Turns; m. Deborah R. Jakubik, June 30, 1973; children: Rhiannon Alissa, Teague Stephen. BS in Edn., California U. of Pa., 1972; MEd, Coll. N.J., 1977, postgrad. Cert. elem. tchr., sch. program specialist, Pa. 5th grade tchr. Council Rock Sch. Dist., Richboro, Pa., 1972-83, 85-90, 2d grade tchr., 1983-85, math./tech. integration specialist, 1990—, staff computer instr.,

1982—, bldg. lead tchr., 2001—; dist. staff math. resource, 1995—. Chmn. Newtown (Pa.) Twp. Youth Aid Panel, 1987-97. Recipient Outstanding Svc. award Bucks County Juvenile Cts., 1991; Council Rock Found. technology grantee, 1998. Mem. NEA, Nat. Coun. Tchrs. Math., Pa. State Edn. Assn., Coun. Rock Edn. Assn. Avocations: golf, tennis, computers. Office: Newtown Elem Sch 1 Wrights Rd Newtown PA 18940-1336 E-mail: sduncan@crsd.org.

DUNCAN, SYLVIA LORENA, gifted education educator; b. Henderson, Tex., Dec. 19, 1949; d. William Presley and Sylvia Lorena (Cherry) Bumpass; m. Barry Patrick Duncan, Apr. 13, 1981. AA, Kilgore (Tex.) Jr. Coll., 1969; BS, North Tex. State U., 1971, MEd, 1975. Cert. tchr. generic spl. edn., elem. edn., elem. English, psychology, tchr. mentally retarded, Tex. Spl. edn. tchr. Henderson Ind. Sch. Dist., 1971-72, Mesquite (Tex.) Ind. Sch. Dist., 1972-85, tchr. 2nd grade, 1985-88, tchr. of gifted/talented, 1988-95. Faculty rep. Mesquite Ind. Sch. Dist., 1974-76, vice chairperson admission, rev. and dismissal com., 1979-85, chairperson spl. edn. referral, 1990—. Contbr. editor (newspaper) News at 10, 1976. Zoo parent Dallas Zool. Soc.; sustaining mem. Dallas Mus. Art, Dallas Symphony Assn.; active Assn. Retarded Citizens, Dallas and Richardson, Tex. Mem. Tex. Assn. for Gifted and Talented, Mesquite Edn. Assn., Smithsonian Assocs., Nat. Mus. Women in Arts (charter). Avocation: foreign and art films.

DUNCAN, VERNE ALLEN, state legislator, dean, education educator; b. McMinnville, Oreg., Apr. 6, 1934; s. Charles Kenneth and S. La Verne (Robbins) D.; m. Donna Rose Nichols, July 11, 1964; children: Annette Marie Kirk, Christine Lauree Didway. BA, Idaho State U., 1960; M.Ed., Univ. Idaho, 1964; PhD, U. Oreg., 1968; MBA, U. Portland, 1976. Tchr. Butte County (Idaho) Pub. Schs., 1954-56, prin., 1958-63, supt. schs., 1963-66; rsch. asst. U. Oreg., 1966-68, asst. prof. ednl. adminstrn., 1968-70; supt. Clackamas County (Oreg.) Intermediate Edn. Dist., 1970-75; elected supt. pub. instrn. State of Oreg., 1975-89, re-elected, 1978, 82, 86; dean, prof. Sch. Edn. U. Portland, 1989-96, prof. emeritis, 1996-, dean, prof. edn. emeritus, 1996—; mem. Idaho Ho. of Reps., Boise, 1963-65, Oreg. Senate, Salem, 1997—2003, asst. majority leader, 2001—03; ret. Mem. Oreg. Youth Conservation Corps, 1997—, chmn. bd., 2002—; mem. Oreg. State Capital Found., 1999—, chmn. bd., 1999—2003; bd. dirs. End of Oreg. Trail, 2003—; chmn. commn. on ednl. credits and credentials Am. Coun. Edn.; commr. Gov.'s Commn. on Futures Rsch.; mem. Edn. Commn. of States. Author numerous articles on ednl. adminstrn. Life trustee Marylhurst U. (life); mem. gov. bd. Fund for Improvement & Reform of Schs. & Teaching U.S. Dept. Edn., 1989-92; mem. Idaho Ho. of Reps., 1962-65, chmn. econ. affairs com.; mem. interim com. Oreg. Legis. Assembly Improvements Com.; mem. Nat. Coun. Chief State Sch. Officers, 1975-89, pres., 1987-89; bd. dirs. Nat. Conf. State Legislators, 1999-2003; bd. Coun. of State Govt's., 199-2003—. Served to col. U.S. Army, 1956-58. Mem. Am. Assn. Sch. Officers (pres. 1987-89), Res. Officers Assn., Nat. Forum Edn. Leaders, Sons and Daus. of Oreg. Pioneers (state pres. 1993—), Oreg. Assn. Colls. Tchr. Edn. (pres. 1994—), Phi Delta Kappa (educator-statesman of yr. award 1977). Presbyterian.

DUNFEE, THOMAS WYLIE, law educator; b. Huntington, W.Va., Nov. 15, 1941; s. Wylie Ray and Chloe Edith (Wylie) D.; m. Dorothy Jane Taylor, Aug. 26, 1967; children: John Wylie, Jennifer Sue, Shannon Elizabeth. AB, Marshall U., 1963; JD, NYU, 1966, LLM, 1969. Instr. N.Y. Inst. Tech., 1965-68; asst. prof. Ill. State U., Normal, 1968-70, Ohio State U., Columbus, 1970-72, assoc. prof., 1972-74; assoc. prof. legal studies Wharton Sch., U. Pa., Phila., 1974-79, prof., 1979—, Kolodny prof. social responsiblity, 1982—, chmn. dept. legal studies, 1980-84, 87-91, dir. Wharton ethics program, 1995-96, dir. Zicklin Ctr. for Bus. Ethics Rsch., 1997-2000, vice dean, 2000—03. Vis. prof. U. Fla., 1989, U. Newcastle, Australia, 1981, 85, Georgetown U., 1994, U. Mich., 2000; cons. United Way of Am., McGraw-Hill, Ind. Stds. Bd., Citibank, GM, Honda, GlaxoSmithKline, AT&T. Author: Business and Its Legal Environment, 1992, Modern Business Law, 1996; co-editor: Business Ethics: Japan and the Global Economy, 1993; co-author: (with Thomas Donaldson) Ethics in Business and Economics, 2 vols., 1997, Ties That Bind: A Social Contracts Approach to Business Ethics, 1999; editor-in-chief Am. Bus. Law Jour., 1976-79; contbr. articles to profl. jours. Grantee Exxon Found., 1985-86, Kemper Found., 1993. Mem. Acad. Legal Studies in Bus. (pres. 1989-90, Disting. Sr. Faculty award for Excellence 1991), Soc. Bus. Ethics (pres. 1995-96). E-mail: dunfeet@wharton.upenn.edu.

DUNGAN, WILLIAM JOSEPH, JR., insurance broker, economics educator; b. New London, Conn., Mar. 19, 1956; s. William Joseph and Alpha (Combs) D.; m. Janet Dudek, May 28, 1983. BS in Biology, Old Dominion U., 1978, postgrad. in Econs., 1978-80; postgrad., U. Pa., 1984-85, Coll. for Fin. Planners, 1983-84; MS in Fin. Svcs., Am. Coll., 1988, MS in Mgmt., 1990. CLU; chartered fin. cons., cert. fund. specialist. Rep. Prudential Ins. Co., Norfolk, Va., 1979-80; assoc. Russ Gills and Assocs., Virginia Beach, Va., 1980-88; instr. Tidewater C.C., Virginia Beach, Va., 1979-86; v.p. life and employee benefits Henderson & Phillips Inc., Norfolk, Va., 1988—; founding prin. First Fin. Resources, 1987—. Instr. employee benefits and econs. Inst. Mgmt., Old Dominion U., 1988—, chmn. cert. employee benefit specialists adv. bd.; instr. employee benefits U. Va., 2000—; instr. CEBS program U. Va., 2000—. Bd. dirs. Epilepsy Assn. Va.; trustee Old Dominion U. Ednl. Found., 1991-99; v.p. Epilepsy Assn. Va.; treas. Hampton Roads Youth Hockey Assn., 1999—. Mem. Internat. Assn. Fin. Planning (pres. Hampton Rds. chpt.), Nat. Assn. Life Underwriters, Assn. for Advanced Life Underwriting, Inst. Cert. Fin. Planners, Inst. Cert. Employee Benefits Specialists, Am. Soc. CLUs, Norfolk Assn. Life Underwriters (bd. dirs.), Monarch Bus. Soc., Old Dominion Univ.'s Ins. and Fin. Svcs. Ctr., Epilepsy Assn. Va. (bd. dirs.), Million Dollar Round Table. Republican. Avocations: tennis, travel, reading. Home: 4201 Mercedes Ct Virginia Beach VA 23455-5649 Office: Henderson & Phillips Inc 235 E Plume St Norfolk VA 23510-1755

DUNHAM, BARBARA JEAN, administrator; b. Brockton, Mass., May 30, 1948; d. Colin Laird Manzer and Beatrice May (Anderson) Manzer-Sweetman; m. Carroll James Dunham, Aug. 6, 1989; children: Richard Howard Cicchetti Jr., Derek Colin Cicchetti. BS, Bridgewater State Coll., 1977; MEd, Bridgewater State U., 1982, CAGS Computers in Edn., 1986; EdD in Ednl. Leadership, Nova Southeastern U., 1998. Reading specialist Sharon HS, Mass., 1978—84; dir. tech. Sharon Sch., Mass., 1987—2000, tchr. computer applications/programming, 1985-95, asst. supt. sch., 2000—. Owner, cons. BJC Software, Sharon, 1980—; instr. Bridgewater (Mass.) State Coll., 1987. Author: (software) Teacher Student Vocabulary, 1982. Horace Man grantee, Mass. Dept. Edn., Sharon, 1988,'89. Mem. ASCD, Internat. Soc. Tech. in Edn., Mass. Tchrs. Assn., Sharon Tchrs. Assn., Mass. Computer-Using Educators, Boston Computer Soc. Avocations: computer-related activities, horses, animals, swimming, motorcycling.

DUNHAM, LUCIA ANN VARANELLI, elementary school educator; b. Waterbury, Conn., Jan. 8, 1962; d. Pasquale A. and Janet (Norton) Varanelli; m. Glen E. Dunham, Oct. 12, 1991; children: Patrick, Catherine, Matthew. BS in Biology, Fairfield (Conn.) U., 1984; student, Ctrl. Conn. State U., New Britain, 1989; MS, So. Conn. State U., New Haven, 1994—. Tchr. h.s. sci. Pub. Schs., Naugatuck, Conn., 1987-88, Middletown, Conn., 1989-90; tchr. mid. sch. sci. Shelton (Conn.) Intermediate Sch., 1990—2003; tchr. chemistry, biology Shelton HS, 2003—. Mem. St. Mary's Hosp. Aux., Bridgeport Hosp. Aux., Humane Soc., Maryknoll Soc. Roman Catholic. Office: Shelton Intermediate Sch N Constitution Blvd Shelton CT 06484-6038

DUNHAM, MARY HELEN, elementary education educator; b. Skiatook, Okla., Dec. 12, 1945; d. Walter and Anna Mae (Escue) Lonsinger; m. Roger Dale Dunham, May 13, 1967; children: Roger Lewis, Carl David. BS in Edn., Northeastern State U., Tahlequah, Okla., 1967. Tchr. elem. sch. Skiatook (Okla.) Marrs Elem. Sch., Vera (Okla.) Sch., Blue Sch., Locust Grove, Okla., St. Paul Sch., Memphis. Mem. Nat. Reading Assn., Okla. Reading Assn., Tulsa Reading Assn., Sigma Epsilon Alpha. Avocations: gardening, outdoor sports, travel. Home: 40301 N 3970 Rd Skiatook OK 74070-4135

DUNHAM, REBECCA BETTY BERES, school administrator; b. Cleve. d. Michael Charles and Veda Mary Beres; m. William Grant Dunham; children: Heidi Rebecca, Aaron William, Amanda Elisabeth (dec.), Meredith Lynne. BA, Kent State U., 1977. Rschr. Phillips Exeter (N.H.) Acad., 1977-84, dir. found. support, 1984-88, assoc. dir. capital giving, 1988-93; assoc. dir. alumni and alumnae affairs and devel. Groton (Mass.) Sch., 1993-95, dir. alumni and alumnae affairs and devel., 1995-98, dir. devel. and parent programs, 1995-98; dir. devel. Spence Sch., N.Y., 1999—. Pres., v.p. Richie McFarland Children's Ctr., Exeter, 1981-89; spkr., mem. Gov. Coun. Volunteerism, Concord, N.H., 1985-86; chair, vice-chair Partnership Philanthropy, N.H., Maine, Vt., 1990-91. Trustee Mary Bartlett Meml. Libr., Brentwood, N.H., 1992-93; vol. Swasey Ctrl. Sch., Brentwood, 1978-85; bd. dirs., sec. bd., Montessori Sch. Creative Learning, North Hampton, 1976-78; active Friday Forum, 1996—, Women in Devel., 1997-98, Boston, 1999—, N.Y.C., Greater Lowell Cmty. Found., 1998-99. Mem. Coun. Advancement and Support Edn., Coun. N.H. Fund Raising (pres. bd. 1989-92), Planned Giving Group New Eng., Assn. Ind. Schs. New Eng. (devel. com., evaluation team 1997), Aisa Soc., N.Y. Hist. Soc. Avocations: historic preservation, perennial gardens, quilting, fishing.

DUNHAM, WILLIAM WADE, mathematics educator; b. Pitts., Dec. 8, 1947; s. Wade Harold and Claramae (Hieber) D.; m. Penelope Higgins, Sept. 26, 1970; children: Brendan H., Shannon S. BS, U. Pitts., 1969; MS, Ohio State U., 1970, PhD, 1974. Lectr. math. Ohio State U., Columbus, 1974-75, vis. assoc. prof., 1987-89; asst. prof. Hanover (Ind.) Coll., 1975-81, assoc. prof., 1981-90, prof., 1990-92; Koehler prof. of math Muhlenberg Coll., 1992—. Seminar dir. NEH, Washington, 1988, 90, 92, 94, 96. Author: Journey through Genius, 1990 The Mathematical Universe, 1994, Euler: The Master of Us All, 1999; also articles. Recipient Baynham award Hanover Coll., 1981, Humanities Achievement award Ind.Humanities Coun., 1990George Polya award (Math Assn. Am.), 1993, Trevor Evans award (Math Assn. Am.), 1997; grantee Lilly Endowment, Inc., 1983. Mem. Math. Assn. Am., Nat. Coun. Tchrs. Math., Phi Beta Kappa. Avocations: civil war history, sherlock holmes, history of art, basketball. Office: Muhlenberg Coll Dept Math 2400 W Chew St Allentown PA 18104-5564 E-mail: wdunham@muhlenberg.edu.

DUNIVENT, JOHN THOMAS, artist, educator; b. Moberly, Mo., Apr. 24, 1928; s. Everett B. and Bertha (Goetze) D. Student, St. Louis U., 1946-47; BFA, Washington U., St. Louis, 1951; postgrad., Berkshire Music Ctr., Lenox, Mass., 1951; MA, N.Mex. Highlands U., 1957. Asst. prof. drama dept. Fontbonne Coll., St. Louis, 1967-71; lectr. photography and society U. Mo., St. Louis, 1984, 90; lectr. history of photography Washington U. Sch. Fine Arts, St. Louis, 1987; art instr. Parkway Sch. Dist., St. Louis County, Mo., 1960-67, 71-94. Vis. prof. art edn. U. Maine, Portland, summers 1971, 72. Illustrator (ink drawings, book) Amerind: Gestural Communication for the Speechless, 1978, (photographs, book) St. Louis Currents, 1986; painter ann. midyear show Butler Inst. Am. Art, Youngstown, Ohio, 1981; solo exhibit of photographs Ctr. for Met. Studies, U. Mo., St. Louis, 1988. Panel mem. master tchr. symposium U. Kans. Sch. Fine Arts, Lawrence, 1985; bd. dirs. Young Audiences, Inc., St. Louis, 1968-74, 80-83. Spl. agt. Counter Intelligence Corps, U.S. Army, 1952-54. Recipient award for pastel painting Chautauqua (N.Y.) Inst., 1959. Avocation: collecting photographs. Home and Office: 607 Forest Ct Saint Louis MO 63105-2759

DUNKEL, JANET L. middle school educator; b. Independence, Ind., July 3, 1945; d. Edward Lester and Lorrayne (Bloom) Lane; married, June 3, 1967; children: Gayle L., Todd E., Trisha, M. BA in Elem. Edn. and English, Upper Iowa U., 1967; MA in Sci. Edn., U. Iowa, 1995. Cert. tchr. grades K-12, Iowa. 3rd grade tchr. Jefferson Elem. Sch., Charles City, Iowa, 1967-68, 6th grade tchr., 1971-93; 2d grade tchr. Paul Revere Elem. Sch., San Francisco, 1968-70; 8th grade tchr. Charles City Mid. Sch., Iowa, 1993—. Sci. cons. U. Iowa, 1988-96. Co-author: Association for Education Rural Science Education Teachers Yearbook, 1995; contbr. articles to profl. jours. Recipient Woman of Yr. award Jaycees, 1977, Gov.'s Leadership award Iowa Cmty. Betterment, 1989, Iowa Gov.'s Sci. award Iowa Alliance, 1990. Mem. NEA, ASCD, AAUW (grant named in her honor 1988, chairperson, pres. Charles City br. 1977-79), Nat. Sci. Tchrs. Assn., Iowa Acad. Sci., Charles City Arts Coun. (chairperson 1991-94), Charles City C. of C. (chairperson edn. com. 1990-93, dir. 1990-93), Charles City Red Hat Soc., Alpha Delta Kappa. Avocations: walking, golfing, gourmet cooking, friends. Home: 2129 Pin Oak Estates Ln Charles City IA 50616-8812 Office: Charles City Mid Sch 500 N Grand Ave Charles City IA 50616-2836

DUNKERLEY, EILEEN TOMLINSON, elementary education educator; b. N.Y.C., Dec. 5, 1936; d. Robert Alexander and Ethel Ermina (Rolph) Tomlinson; m. Donald Austin Dunkerley, June 24, 1961; children: David Austin, Kathleen Elizabeth Idelette. BS, Adelphi U., 1959; MA, NYU, 1961. Cert. tchr., N.Y., N.J., Fla. Elem. tchr. Yonkers (N.Y.) Pub. Schs., 1959-61, Mountainside (N.J.) Pub. Schs., 1961-62; tchr. mid. sch. English, Scarsdale (N.Y.) Pub. Schs., 1962-66; editor African Women, UN, N.Y.C., 1967-69; tchr. So. Assn. Christian Schs., 1971-77, asst. dir., 1977-83; coord. lang. arts Creative Learning Ctr., Pensacola, Fla., 1979—. Vice chmn. Morning Star, Pensacola and Tallahassee, 1991-94; bldg. coord. Fla. Beginning Tchr. Program, Pensacola, 1987—; adj. prof. Jacksonville (Fla.) U., 1990—. Author: Pensacola's Historic Walking Tour for Children, 1994, Pensacola's Bold Adventurers, 1994. Co-chmn. Morning Star Program for retarded children, Pensacola, 1991—. Mem. Fla. Coun. Ind. Schs., Fla. Coun. Social Studies, Pensacola Hist. Soc. Avocations: world travel and teaching, walking, writing, gourmet cooking. Home: 2605 Tambridge Cir Pensacola FL 32503-4256

DUNLAP, PATRICIA PEARL, elementary school educator; b. Chgo., Jan. 16, 1951; d. Henry Law and Lucille Roberta (Singley) D. AA in Elem. Edn., Kennedy-King Coll., 1976; BS in Elem. Edn., Chgo. State U., 1978, MS in Elem. Edn., 1998, MA in Ednl. Leadership, 2001. Cert. intermediate/upper and primary tchr. with endorsements in computer sci., lang. arts, gen. sci. and social sci., Ill. Intermediate tchr. Wentworth Sch., Chgo., 1978-82; kindergarten tchr. Grimes/Fleming Sch., Chgo., 1982-83; intermediate/upper computer tchr. Harvard Sch., Chgo., 1983—. Chorus music dir. Harvard Sch., Chgo., 1984—; computer cons. First Bapt. Ch., Chgo., 1989-93, Workshops R Us, Chgo., 1992—. Author, composer: Start With Me, 1993, Just Have Faith, 1994, Is It Me, 1994, We've Got The Power, 1994. Recipient Ella Flag Young award, Chgo., 1986. Mem. ASCD, Nat. Alliance of Black Sch. Educators, Kappa Delta Pi. Democrat. Avocations: computer technology, videography, photography, reading, sports. Office: Harvard Sch 7525 S Harvard Ave Chicago IL 60620-1670

DUNLOP, MARIANNE, retired English as second language educator; b. Niobrara, Nebr, Mar. 14, 1933; d. Harvey Wesley LaBranche and Karen Sanna Arneson; m. Richard Campbell Dunlop, Apr. 26, 1959; 1 child, Christopher Campbell. BA, Vt. Coll., 1985, MA, 1989. Bd. dir./bd. mem. The Sargent House Mus., Gloucester, Mass., 1992-96; ESL educator Penasquitos Laubach Literacy Ctr., San Diego, 1999—2002; ret., 2002. Author: (book) Judith Sargent Murray: Champion of Social Justice, 1993; editor: (book) Judith Sargent Murray: Her First 100 Letters, 1995; writer, contbr.: (book) Standing Before Us: Unitarian Universalist Women and Social Reform 1776-1936, 1999; spkr., contbr. (documentary) Judith Sargent Murray: 18th Century Feminist. Officer, bd. dirs. Sargent House Mus., Gloucester, Mass., 1992—96, mem. adv. bd., 1996—; ESL educator Penasquitos Laubach Literacy Ctr., San Diego, 1999—2002; mem. Sargent House Mus. Mem. Virginia Woolf's Outsider Soc., Unitarian Universalist Women's Heritage Soc. Unitarian Universalist. Avocation: honoring otherness. Home: 11032 Ipai Ct San Diego CA 92127-1382

DUNN, ANNE EWALD NEFFLEN, elementary education educator; b. Elkins, W.Va., Feb. 9, 1935; d. Edgar Lantz and May (Bradley) Nefflen; m. Delma Douglas Dunn, July 20, 1961; children: Susan Bradley Dunn, Robert Cameron, Richard Tullos. BS in Home Econs., U. Md., 1956; student, U. Miami, 1953-54, San Diego State Coll., 1958-60; MEd, U. Ark., 1985. Cert. elem. tchr., reading specialist, gifted and talented, Ark. Tchr. 2d grade San Diego City Schs., 1958-61, Oak Harbor (Wash.) Schs., 1961-63; tchr. 2d and 3d grades Albuquerque Pub. Schs., 1963-65; tchr. 3d grade Prairie Grove (Ark.) Sch. Dist., 1978-85, tchr. gifted and talented, coord., 1985-88, tchr. remedial reading and math., 1988-92; tchr., coord. At-Risk Alternative Edn. 1st grade, 1992-94; chpt. I reading specialist, reading tchr., 1994—. Interviewer Navy Relief Soc., Whidbey Island, Wash., 1961-63. Leader 4-H Horse Club, Whidbey Island, 1961-63, 4-H Club, Prairie Grove, 1979-81; leader, trainer Girl Scouts U.S., Prairie Grove, 1975-78; mem. Prairie Grove Libr. Bd., 1980-82; show sec. Nat. Arabian Horse Assn. Show, Albuquerque, 1965. Mem. Phi Delta Kappa. Presbyterian. Avocations: sewing, reading, horseback riding. Home: 22530 Cove Crk S Prairie Grove AR 72753-9230 Office: Prairie Grove Elem Sch 824 N Mock St Prairie Grove AR 72753-2610

DUNN, CHARLES DEWITT, academic administrator; b. Magnolia, Ark., Dec. 2, 1945; s. Charles Edward and Nora Lucille (Bailey) D.; m. Donna Jane Parsons, Apr. 9, 1966; children: Aimee, James, Joseph, Mary Elizabeth. BA, So. Ark. U., 1967; MA, North Tex. State U., 1970; PhD, So. Ill. U., 1973; cert. inst. ednl. mgmt., Harvard U., 1991. Instr. polit. sci. U. Ark., Monticello, 1969-72, asst. prof., 1972-75; assoc. prof. U. Ctrl. Ark., Conway, 1975-80, prof., 1980—, chmn. dept. polit. sci., 1976-82, dir. govt. rels., 1982-86; pres. Henderson State U., Arkadelphia, Ark., 1986—. Chmn. Commn. for Ark.'s Future, 1989-93; chmn. Ark. Higher Edn. Coun., 1992-96; chmn. fin. com. Ark. Cmty. Found. Bd. Dirs., v.p., 2000-02, pres., 2002-03; active Blue Ribbon Commn. on Pub. Edn., 2001-02. Mem. Am. Assn. State Coll. and Univs., NCAA (pres.'s commn. 1996-97, pres.' coun. 1997-2001, pres. Gulf South conf. 1998-2000), Ark. Polit. Sci. Assn. (pres. 1976-77), Conway C. of C. (bd. dirs. 1984-85, v.p. 1985-86), Arkadelphia C. of C. (bd. dirs. 1987-91), Rotary. Methodist. Office: Henderson State U PO Box 7532 1100 Henderson St Arkadelphia AR 71999-0001 E-mail: cddunn@hsu.edu.

DUNN, CHARLOTTE VALBORG LUND, elementary education educator; b. Brady, Tex., Mar. 24, 1935; d. Otto Henry and Freda (Young) Lund; m. Thomas N. Dunn, Dec. 25, 1953; children: Lisa D., Keith W., Wade H. BS, S.W. Tex. State Coll., 1956, MEd, 1976; EdD, Tex. A&M U., 1988. Cert. tchr., supr., Tex. Tchr. Comal Ind. Sch. Dist., New Braunfels, Tex., 1957-59, 65-92; dir. week day kindergarten 1st United Meth. Ch., New Braunfels, Tex., 1963-65; vis. asst. prof. dept. edn. Tex. Luth. Coll., Seguin, 1993—. Adj. asst. prof. S.W. Tex. State U., San Marcos, 1986-93; cons. in field. Author: Otto, 1998, Freda, 1999. Mem. NEA, ASCD, Tex. Tchrs. Assn., Tex. Ret. Tchrs. Assn., Kappa Delta Pi, Alpha Chi. Methodist. Avocations: playing piano, knitting, traveling. Home: PO Box 310738 New Braunfels TX 78131-0738

DUNN, DEBORAH DECHELLIS, special education educator; b. Plainfield, N.J., Jan. 16, 1960; d. Anthony and Joan Dora (Brown) DeChellis; m. Paul Michael Dunn, May 13, 1989; children: Joseph Daniel, Brian Jacob. BS in Elem. Spl. Edn., U. Hartford, 1982. Spl. edn. tchr. Hartford (Conn.) Pub. Schs., 1982-83, East Hartford (Conn.) Pub. Schs., 1983-84; individual retirement account ops. supr. Conn. Nat. Bank, Hartford, 1984-87; individual retirement account adminstr. Glastonbury (Conn.) Bank & Trust, 1987, mgr. fin. mgmt. svc. ops., 1987-91; asst. treas., FMS adminstr. Glastonbury (Conn.) Bank & Trust Co., 1988-94, investment rep., trust adminstr., asst. treas.; fin. cons. Mktg. One Inc., 1994-95, Dime Securities N.Y., Inc., 1995-96; tchr. of handicapped Lakeview Sch., Edison, NJ, 1997—. Investment cons., 1994; ind. edn. cons. Democrat. Methodist. Avocations: reading, cooking, needlework, racquetball, softball. Office: Lakeview Sch Edison NJ 08837

DUNN, DONALD JACK, law librarian, law educator, dean, lawyer; b. Tyler, Tex., Nov. 9, 1945; s. Loren Jack and Clara Inez (Milam) Dunn; m. Cheryl Jean Sims, Nov. 24, 1967; 1 child, Kevin. BA., U. Tex.-Austin, 1969, MLS, 1972; JD, Western New Eng. Coll., 1983. Asst. to law libr. U. Tex., 1969-72, supervising libr. Criminal Justice Reference Libr., 1972-73; law libr., prof. law Western New Eng. Coll., Springfield, Mass., 1973-96, interim dean, 1996-98, dean, 1998—2001, assoc. dean for libr. and info. resources, prof. law, 2002—03; dean, prof. law U. La Verne Coll. Law, Ontario, Calif., 2003—. Editor (with Flynn): Immigration and Nationality Law Rev., vols. 3-7, 1979—84; editor: (with Mersky) Fundamentals of Legal Research, 8th edit., 2002. Bd. dirs. Pioneer Valley chpt. ARC; pres. Scribes, 2001—. Fellow: Am. Bar Found.; mem.: ABA (chair law librs. com. 1988—92), ALA, Am. Law Inst., Law Librs. New Eng. (pres. 1982—83), Spl. Libr. Assn., Am. Assn. Law Librs. (chair acad. law librs. spl. interest sect. 1989—90), Scribes (pres. 2001—03). Democrat. Episcopalian. Office: U La Verne Coll Law 320 East D St Ontario CA 91764 E-mail: dunnd@ulv.edu.

DUNN, DORIS MARJORY, retired educator, volunteer; b. Chgo., Jan. 7, 1921; d. William Christian and Mary Esther (Hoffman) Rose; m. Jack Harold Wheeler Dunn, Sept. 19, 1945 (dec. June 1978); children: Randall L., Jon G., Bonham. BS in Edn., Ind. U., 1942; postgrad., Northwestern U., 1943-44; MS, Valparaiso U., 1973. Life lic. in teaching, Ind. Tchr. Crown Point (Ind.) High Sch., 1963-74, Lowell (Ind.) High Sch., 1942-45; sch. tchr., jr. coll. tchr., 1976-78. Asst. to engring.libr. U. Tex., Austin, 1947-49. Pres. LWV, Crown Point, 1974; pres.-elect Good Samaritan Hosp. Aux., v.p., 1988-89, pres., 1989-90; buyer Good Samaritan Gift Shop, 1989—; chmn. ways and means Assistance League, 1988-89, regional coun. rep., 1990-91, mem. resource devel. nat. bd., 1991-98; pres. Luckiamute Water Bd., 1988—; mem. Republican Senatorial Inner Circle, State of Oreg., 1997-98. Mem. P.E.O. (pres. 1989-90), Corvallis Country Club. Ladies Orgn. (pres. 1989-90), Kappa Kappa Kappa (pres. 1975), Delta Kappa Gamma. Methodist. Avocations: wood carving, golf, flying, stained glass creation, travel. Home: 12260 Rolling Hills Rd Monmouth OR 97361-9758

DUNN, FRANCIS MICHAEL, classicist, educator; b. Aberdeen, Scotland, Oct. 15, 1955; came to U.S. 1966; s. Peter Norman and Pamela Delsie (Shakespeare) D.; m. Cynthia Lee Hoffmann, Oct. 18, 1986; children: Andrew Nicholas, Alexander Adrian. BA, Yale U., 1976, MA, 1980, MPhil, 1982, PhD, 1985. Vis. instr. N.C. State U., Raleigh, 1985-86; asst. prof. Northwestern U., Evanston, Ill., 1986-93, U. Calif., Santa Barbara, 1993-96, assoc. prof., 1996—. Acad. dir. Food: Ritual, Metaphor, Politics, Northwestern Alumni Coll., 1992. Author: Tragedy's End, Closure and Innovation in Euripidean Drama, 1996; editor: Yale Classical Studies Beginnings in Classical Literature, 1992, Drama, Sophocles' Electra in Performance, 1995, Classical Closure, Reading the End in Greek and Latin Literature, 1997; assoc. editor Classical Bull.; referee Classical Antiquity, Trans. Am. Philol. Assn., Classical Philology; contbr. articles to profl. jour. Recipient Humanities Rsch. award Northwestern U., 1989-90, Ill. Humanities Coun. major grantee, 1992-93; Am. Coun. Learned Socs. fellowship, 1997-98, Nat. Endowment Humanities sr. fellowship, 1997-98. Mem. Am. Philol. Assn., Classical Assn. Mid. West and South, Calif. Classical Assn. Avocations: gardening, brewing. Office: U Calif Dept Classics Santa Barbara CA 93106

DUNN, HELEN ELIZABETH, retired secondary school educator; b. Peoria, Ill., July 14, 1930; d. Albert Edward and Corinne Ada (Rudel) Joos; m. Harry Christie Dunn, Feb. 4, 1951; children: Pamela Elizabeth Dunn Baumann, Patricia Louise Dunn Marshall. BS in Edn., Bradley U., 1951, MA in Guidance/Counseling, 1969. Tchr. Pub. Schs. of Hawaii, Lanai City, 1951-54, Ulupalakua, 1954-56, Pub. Schs. of Peoria, 1956-69; English LaSalle (Ill.)-Peru H.S., 1970-71; counselor, tchr. Peru (Ill.) Pub. Schs., 1971-89; ret., 1989. Contbr. poems to books: The Best Poems of the '90s, 1992, Distinguished Poets of America, 1993, Best Poems of 1995, 1995. Presenter programs on Hawaii, Peoria. Mem.: PEO, LWV (bd. dirs. 1973—89, treas. 1982—89), NEA (del. 1951—56, rep. 1957—69), Ret. Tchrs. Assn. (legis. com. 1991—98), Peoria Area Ret. Tchrs. Assn. (sec. 2001—02), Peoria Women's Club (corr. sec. 2000—03), Phi Lambda Theta, Sigma Kappa (alumni chpt., pres. 1962, 1991), Delta Kappa Gamma (pres. 1968—70, 1978—80, 1992—94). Methodist. Avocations: writing poetry, tennis, dancing, reading, singing.

DUNN, JUDITH LOUISE, secondary school educator; b. L.A., Jan. 6, 1945; d. Arthur B. and Lillian M. (Eyrich) D. BA, U. Calif., Santa Barbara, 1966; MA Edn., Pepperdine U., 1978; postgrad., U. Calif., Santa Barbara, 1967. Cert. secondary tchr., adminstr., Calif; cert. lay spkr. United Meth. Ch., 1987-95; cert. cross culture and lang. devel. English tchr. Santa Maria (Calif.) Joint Union High Sch. Dist., mentor tchr., chmn. dept. English, 1991-94, lead tchr. Am. Lit., writing action team leader. Adv. coun. Student Age Parenting and Infant Devel. Program; dist. tchr. rep. Impact II Adv. Coun., 1992-94; dist. rep. Ctrl. Coast Literacy Coun., 1992-94; schoolwide assessment team, del. tchrs. of English of People to People Citizen Amb. Program visitation to Gt. Britain, 1995; mem. Sch. Site Coun., Steering Com. for Accreditation, Dist. English Stds. Com. Assoc. lay leader Santa Barbara dist. Calif.-Pacific Annual Conf., 1986-89, United Meth. Ch., bd. Higher Edn. and Campus Ministry, 1982-90; English tchr. del. citizen amb. program People to People to Gt. Britain, 1995. Fellow South Coast Writing Project; Disseminator grantee, 1988, 89, 91, 97, Adaptor grantee, 1991, 92. Mem. CTA, NEA, Nat. Coun. Tchrs. English, Local Faculty Assn. (profl. rels. chair 1986-88), Delta Kappa Gamma (past pres. Eta Lambda chpt.). Office: Santa Maria High Sch 901 S Broadway Santa Maria CA 93454-6613

DUNN, MARY DENISE, reading specialist, freelance editor; b. Brookline, Mass., Sept. 17, 1936; d. William Joseph and Mary Denise (McGillicuddy) O'Brien; m. William F. Dunn, Oct. 8, 1960; 1 child, Mary Denise. BS, Boston Coll., 1958; MEd in Reading and Lang., U. Mass., Lowell, 1981; postgrad., MIT, 1980-82, Simmons Coll., 1988-90. Cert. 7-12 English tchr., K-12 reading specialist, dir. reading, cons. in reading, Mass. Substitute tchr. secondary schs., 1974-78; tchr. English, Parker Jr. H.S. and Chelmsford (Mass.) H.S., 1978-84; tchr. ESL, Bartlett Sch., Lowell, Mass., 1990-91; reading specialist McCarthy Mid. Sch., Chelmsford, 1984-88, 92—. Editor: Life Insurance: Rate of Return (William D. Brownlie), 1993; also others. Vol. local nursing homes for elderly, 1975-92, Citizens for Mitt Romney for U.S. Senate, Boston, 1994; vol. tchr. ESL, S.E. Asia Comm. Ctr., Lowell, 1990-92; vol. driver Mass. Right-To-Life, Lawrence, Lowell, 1973-78; mem. St. John the Evangelist Parish, North Chelmsford, Mass., Cardinal's Guild Archdiocese of Boston, vol. dir. religious edn., 1967-76. Mem. ASCD, Mass. ASCD, Internat. Reading Assn., Nat. Coun. Tchrs. English, Assn. for Childhood Edn. Internat., U. Mass.-Lowell Alumni Assn., Boston Coll. Alumni Assn., Am. Fedn. Tchrs., Mass. Fedn. Tchrs., Chelmsford Fedn. Tchrs., Mass. Citizens for Life, Boston Eire Soc., Phi Lambda Theta (charter Gamma Eta chpt.). Roman Catholic. Avocations: literature, pianoforte, classical music, chorale singing, travel, writing. Office: Chelmsford McCarthy Mid Sch 250 North Rd Chelmsford MA 01824-1409

DUNN, MARY MAPLES, former university dean; b. Sturgeon Bay, Wis., Apr. 6, 1931; d. Frederic Arthur and Eva (Moore) Maples; m. Richard S. Dunn, Sept. 3, 1960; children— Rebecca Cofrin, Cecilia Elizabeth. BA, Coll. William and Mary, 1954, LHD (hon.), 1989, MA, Bryn Mawr Coll., 1956, PhD, 1959; LLD (hon.), Marietta Coll., 1987, Amherst Coll., 1987, Brown U., 1989; LittD (hon.), Lafayette Coll., 1988, Haverford Coll., 1991; LHD (hon.), Transylvania U., 1991, U. Pa., 1995, Mt. Holyok Coll., 1996, Smith Coll., 1998, U. Mass., 1998, U. South, 1999. Faculty Bryn Mawr Coll., 1958-85, prof. history, 1974-85; acting dean Undergrad. Coll. Bryn Mawr (Pa.) Coll., 1978-79, dean, 1980-85; pres. Smith Coll., Northampton, Mass., 1985-95; Carl and Lily Pforzheimer Found. dir. Arthur and Elizabeth Libr. Radcliffe Coll., 1995-99; acting pres., acting dean Inst. for Advanced Study Harvard U., 1999—2000. Author: William Penn: Politics and Conscience, 1967; editor: Political Essay on the Kingdom of New Spain (Alexander von Humboldt), 1972, rev., 1988, (with Richard S. Dunn) Papers of William Penn, vols. I-IV, 1979-87. Trustee The Clark Sch. for the Deaf, 1988-95, Acad. Mus., 1985-95, Hist. Deerfield, Inc., 1986—, Bingham Fund for Teaching Excellence at Transylvania U., 1987—, John Carter Brown Libr., 1994-99, NOW/Legal Def. and Edn. Fund., 1996—, Marlboro Music, 1996—. Recipient Disting. Tchg. award Lindbeck Found., 1969, Radcliffe medal Radcliffe Assn., 2001; fellow Inst. Advanced Study Princeton U., 1974. Mem. Berkshire Conf. Women Historians (pres. 1973-75), Coordinating Com. Women Hist. Profession (pres. 1975-77), Am. Hist. Assn., Am. Philos. Soc. (co-exec. officer), Inst. Early Am. History and Culture (chmn. adv. council 1977-80), Mass. Hist. Soc., Phi Beta Kappa. Office: American Philosophical Society Exec Office 104 S Fifth St Philadelphia PA 19106-3287*

DUNN, PATRICIA ANN, school system administrator, English language educator; b. Englewood, N.J., Mar. 17, 1942; d. Thomas Joseph and Rosanna Valerie (Cummings) D.; m. James Edward Egan, 1963 (div. 1974); 1 child, Deirdre Tracy. BA in English Edn., William Paterson U., 1963, MA in Communication Arts, 1974; postgrad., Montclair (N.J.) State U., 1986—. Cert. tchr., N.J., N.Y.; cert. prin., supr., N.J. Tchr. English, Intermediate Sch. Dist. 218, Bklyn., 1965-66, tchr. English and humanities, 1966-67, co-chmn. dept. humanities, 1967-68; tchr. English Midland Park (N.J.) Schs., 1969-91, staff devel. coord., 1987—, dir. curriculum, instrn., staff devel., 1991—. Coord. bus. workshops Women in Bus., 1983, Stress, 1983. Editor N.J. Staff Devel. Coun. Newsletter, 1988-91; contbr. articles to profl. publs. Co-founder, coord. Ministry for Separated and Divorced Caths., Montclair, 1983-86. Recipient N.J. Woman of Distinction award World of People. Mem. ASCD, AAUW, N.J. Prins. and Suprs. Assn., Nat. Staff Devel. Coun., N.J. Staff Devel. Coun. (co-founder, dir. 1991-94, pres. 1995-96, trustee 1997—, editor Exchange 1996—98), N.J. Ctr. for Achievement of Sch. Excellence, N.J. Coalition Essential Schs. (del. to nat. congress 1996—98, co-chair exec. bd. 1995-2002), Nat. Coun. Tchrs. English, Midland Park Adminstrs. and Suprs. Assn. (pres. 1996—), Dramund Springs Club. Democrat. Roman Catholic. Avocations: dance, reading. Office: Midland Park High Sch 250 Prospect St Midland Park NJ 07432-1398

DUNN, WESLEY JOHN, dental educator; b. Toronto, Ont., Can., May 21, 1924; s. John James and Grace Eleanor (Bryan) D.; m. Jean Mildred Nicholls, Nov. 6, 1948; children: Steven, Brian, Bruce. D.D.S., U. Toronto, 1947. Pvt. practice dentistry, Toronto, 1947-55; registrar, sec.-treas. Royal Coll. Dental Surgeons, Ont., 1956-65; founding dean Faculty Dentistry, U. Western Ont., London, 1965-82, prof. community dentistry, 1965-89; prof. emeritus U. Western Ont., London, 1989—. Chmn. Ont. Council Univ. Health Scis., 1973-75; charter mem. Ont. Council Health, 1966-71; weekly dental columnist Toronto Star, 1972-74; pres. Assn. Can. Faculties of Dentistry, 1976-78 Editor Oral Health, 1950-53, Jour. Can. Dental Assn., 1953-58. Bd. dirs. Women's Coll. Hosp., Toronto, 1960-65, London YM-YWCA, 1966-70, United Cmty. Svcs. London, 1968-71; bd. dirs., chmn. Christmas Seals, Lung Assn. London and Middlesex; exec. sec. Ont. Commn. Interuniv. Athletics, 1990-97; mem. Thames Valley Dist. Health Coun., 1992-98, chmn., 1996-97; chmn. Dist. Health Couns. of S.W. Ont., 1998; bd. dirs. London Health Scis. Ctr.; mem. exec. com. Region # 5 Ont. Hosp. Assn., 2001—. Fellow Am. Coll. Dentists (Inaugural Disting. Svc. award Ont. sect. 1993), Royal Coll. Dentists Can. (hon.), Acad. Dentistry Internat. (hon.), Internat. Coll. Dentists (hon.); mem. London Dist. Dental Soc. (hon.) Ont. Dental Assn. (hon., Barnabus W. Day award 1988), Can. Dental Assn. (hon. mem. 1991), Royal Coll. Dental Surgeons Ont. (bd. dirs. 1966-70, councillor 1985-88, pres. 1989-90), Can. Dental Assn. (chmn. coun. edn. 1967-70), Am. Assn. Dental Editors (pres. 1958), U. West Ont. Alumni Assn. (award of merit 1986), U. Toronto Dental Alumni Assn. (award of merit 1991). Home: 134 Wychwood Pk London ON Canada N6G 1R7

DUNNE, JAMES ROBERT, academic administrator, management consultant, business educator; b. Cleve., July 8, 1929; s. Carroll Joseph and Wilma Agnes (Sutmore) D.; m. Nancy Anne McSween, Oct. 28, 1952; children: James Jr., Stephen. BA, Albion Coll., 1951; MA, SUNY, Albany, 1964, PhD, 1972; postgrad., Nova Southeastern U., Webster U., Nat. Def. U. Sect. mgr. news bur. GE, Schenectady, N.Y., 1955-63; asst. to chancelor SUNY, Albany, 1963-68; dir. pub. affairs N.Y. State Office Gen. Svcs., Albany, 1968-73; v.p. mktg. N.Y. State Higher Edn. Assistance Corp., Albany, 1973-76; exec. on loan N.Y. State U.S. Office Edn., 1976-78; pres. J.R. Dunne, Inc., Orlando, Fla., 1978-94; program mgr. Eagle Tech., Inc., Orlando, 1983-85; asst. prof. mgmt., acad. program chmn. Fla. Inst. Tech., Orlando, 1985-89; sr. mgmt. analyst Star Mountain, Inc., 1989-90; regional dir. Webster U., Orlando, Fla., 1990-98, spl. asst. devel. to exec. v.p., 1998-2000; dir. Sarasota Met. Campus and Bradenton Classrm. Ctr., 1999-2000; assoc. emeritus Webster U., 2000—. Adj. prof. Schenectady C.C., 1968-76, SUNY, Brockport, 1970-72; adj. instr. Valencia C.C., Orlando, 1980-94, Fla. So. Coll., Orlando, 1980-81, Brevard C.C., Titusville, Fla., 1979-80, Columbia Coll., Orlando, 1980-94; mem. nat. faculty Nova U., Ft. Lauderdale, Fla., 1980-91; acad. assoc. Atlantic Coun., 1982-96; advisor doctoral dissertation Nova U., 1988-2001; cons. Am. Schs. Corp., 1998-2000; bd. dirs., tutor K-5 grades Anna Maria Island Cmty. Ctr., 2001-03, tutor, 2003—. Pres. Westbay Point and Moorings Condo Assn., 2003—; mem. steering com. Manatee Visioning Program, 2002—03; dirs. Manatee-Sarasota chpt., United Nations Assn., 2003—; mem. Parks and Beautification Com., City of Holmes Beach; lector, eucharist min. St. Bernard's Roman Cath. Ch., Holmes Beach, Fla.; bd. dirs. South Fla. Mus., 2002—. With USN, 1952—55, capt. USNR, 1955—89. Paul Harris fellow, 1989. Mem.: VFW, Mil. Officers of Am., Rotary (chmn. dist. youth exch. 1981—91, mem. Paul Harris Sch. com. 1988—89, pres. Anna Maria Island chpt. 2001—03, Dist. 6960 Paul Harris Ambassadorial Scholarship com. 2001—, Area 8 dep. dist. gov. 2003—, Rotarian of Yr. Altamonte Springs chpt. 1981, 1983, 1985). Republican. Roman Catholic. Avocations: golf, travel. Home: 6400 Flotilla Dr Apt 31 Holmes Beach FL 34217-1425

DUNNE, JUDITH DOYLE, information scientist, educator; b. Mineola, NY, Dec. 17, 1962; d. James Macdonnel and Lois Hart Doyle; m. Michael John Dunne, May 28, 1989. BS, North Adams State Coll., 1984. Elem. edn., art tchr. Rosary Acad., Watertown, Mass., 1985—86; 3d and 6th gr. math. tchr. St. Patrick's Sch., Watertown, Mass., 1986—91; art tchr. Holy Name, West Roxbury, Mass., 1991—96; Tech. coord. computer, art and math. tchr. Good Shepherd Sch., Perryville, Md., 1997—. Mem.: Nat. Cath. Edn. Assn. Avocations: crafts, skiing, ice skating, in-line skating. Office: Good Shepherd Sch 810 Aiken Ave Perryville MD 21903

DUNNE, THOMAS, geology educator; b. Prestbury, U.K., Apr. 21, 1943; arrived in U.S., 1964; s. Thomas and Monica Mary (Whitter) D. BA with honors, Cambridge (Eng.) U., 1964; PhD, Johns Hopkins U., 1969. Rsch. assoc. USDA-Agrl. Rsch. Svc., Danville, Vt., 1966—68; rsch. hydrologist U.S. Geol. Survey, Washington, 1969; asst. prof. McGill U., Montreal, Canada, 1969—73; from asst. prof. to prof. U. Wash., Seattle, 1973—95, chmn. dept., 1984—89; prof. sch. environ. scis. & mgmt. U. Calif., Santa Barbara, 1995—. Vis. prof. U. Nairobi, Kenya, 1969-71; cons. in field, 1970—. Author (with L.B. Leopold) Water in Environmental Planning; (with L.M. Reid) Rapid Evaluation of Sediment Budgets, 1996. Fulbright scholar 1984; grantee NSF, NASA, Rockefeller Found., 1969—; named to NAS. 1988, Guggenheim fellow, 1989-90. Fellow AAAS, Am. Acad. Arts and Scis., Am. Geophys. Union (Robert E. Horton award 1987, Langbein lectr. 2003), Calif. Acad. Scis.; mem. NAS (G.K. Warren prize in Fluviatile Geology 1998), Geol. Soc. Am. (Easterbrook award 2003), Sigma Xi. Office: U Calif Donald Bren Sch Environ Scis & Mgmt 4670 Physical Sciences N Santa Barbara CA 93106

DUNNIHOO, DALE RUSSELL, physician, medical educator; b. Dayton, Ohio, June 8, 1928; s. John Russell and Hazel Nora (Roth) D.; m. Betty Lu Patterson, Sept. 1, 1950; children: Diana Lynn, John Russell, Dale Russell, Brian Michael, Janet Elizabeth. BS in Biology, Gannon U., 1949; MS in Zoology, U. Mich., 1950; MD cum laude, Washington U., St. Louis, 1956; PhD in Physiology, U. So. Calif., 1972. Diplomate Am. Bd. Obstetrics and Gynecology; lic. in medicine, Mo., Alaska, Calif., Miss., La. Asst. prof. biology Millsaps Coll., Jackson, Miss., 1950-52; intern straight medicine, resident in ob-gyn Washington U./Barnes Hosp., St. Louis, 1956-58, 61-63, fellow in oncology, 1963-64; commd. USAF, 1958, advanced through grades to col., 1978; fellow in maternal-fetal medicine U. So. Calif., L.A., 1969-72; dir. ob.-gyn. E.A. Conway Meml. Hosp., Monroe, La., 1980-88; prof. ob-gyn., prof. family medicine and comprehensive care La. State U., Shreveport, 1980-94, vice chmn. dept. ob-gyn, 1988-92; clin. prof. ob.-gyn. U. La. Med. Sch., Shreveport, 1994—. Cons. to USAF Surgeon Gen., 1973-78; clin. asoc. prof. Tulane U., 1973-78; cons. Am. Jour. Ob-Gyn., 1980, 90-92, 95, 96, Ob-Gyn. Jour., 1990, 98; cons. in Ob-gyn. Risk Mgmt. Divsn. State of La., 1994—; dept. chmn. and residency program dir. Keesler USAF Hosp., Biloxi, Miss., 1972-78, interim dep. commdr., 1975, 78; sec. med. staff E. A. Conway Meml. Hosp., 1984-85, vice chief of staff, 1985-86, chief of staff, 1986-87; adv. panel on ob-gyn. U.S. Pharmacopeial Conv., 1985-90; USAF reg. cons. Keesler USAF Med. Ctr., 1987-91; rep. to Assn. Am. Med. Colls., 1990-94. Author: Fundamentals of Gynecology and Obstetrics, 1990, 2d edit. 1992, translated into Italian, 1995; contbr. numerous articles to profl. jours. Recipient tchr. of family practice award Am. Acad. Family Physicians, 1980-88, disting. alumni award Gannon U., 1990; named hon. citizen New Orleans, 1977, Admiral in L.A. Navy, 1977; decorated meritorious svc. medal USAF, 1978; Jackson-Johnson scholar Washington U., 1955, 56. Fellow Am. Coll. Ob-Gyn. (chmn. Armed Forces dist. 1974-77, Appreciation award 1973, 77, 79, Kermit Krantz Cons. award Armed Forces dist. 1992, exec. bd. 1974-77, Continuing Med. Edn. award 1984-87, 87-90, 90-93, 93-96), ACS, Royal Soc. Medicine (London), Internat. Coll. Surgeons; mem. AMA (Physician's Recognition award 1984-87, 87-90, 90-93, 93-96), AAAS, Assn. Profs. Ob-Gyns., Gulf Coast Ob-Gyn. Soc. (founder, 1st pres.), So. Perinatal Assn., Soc. Air Force Clin. Surgeons, Miss. Ob-Gyn. Soc., Ctrl. Assn. of Ob-Gyns., La. Med. Soc., U.S. Power Squadron, St. Louis Gynecologic Soc., San Antonio Ob-Gyn. Soc., Am. Soc. Psychosomatic Ob-Gyn, Ouachita Parish Med. Soc., Masons, Shreveport Med. Soc., Lambda Chi Alpha (Hall of Fame 1996), Alpha Epsilon Delta, Phi Beta Pi. Episcopalian. Home: 1701 Parks Rd Benton LA 71006-4224

DUNNING, JEREMY DAVID, industrial research director, educator, dean; b. Washington, Feb. 15, 1951; s. John Laurance and Jacquelin (Creamer) D.; m. Deborah Humeler, June 3, 1972; children: Katherine, Nicholas, Abigail. BA in Geology with honors, Colgate U., 1973; MS, Rutgers U., 1975; PhD, U. N.C., 1978. Asst. prof. Oreg. State U., Corvallis, 1978-79, Ind. U., Bloomington, 1979-84, assoc. prof., 1984—, assoc. dean, 1985—, dir. indsl. rsch. liaison program, 1986—. Hearst disting. lectr. U. Calif., Berekely, 1986; advisor Nat. Acad. Sci.; cons. in field. Contbr. articles to profl. jours. Mem. bd. advisors NASA/USRA, nationwide, 1987—; mem. nat. adv. bd. Gov.'s Tech. Assessment, Ind., 1989-90; mem. Gov.'s Modernization Bd., Ind., 1990; dir. Ind. Univ. Res. Park, 1993-96; dean Sch. of Continued Studies, 1996—. Mem. Am. Geophys. Union, Econ. Devel. Assn., NAMTAC. Office: Ind U Sch Continuing Studies Owen Hall Rm 205 Bloomington IN 47401

DUNPHY, EDWARD JAMES, crop science extension specialist; b. Frederick, Md., Nov. 14, 1940; s. Edward John and Marie W. (Barlow) D.; m. Judith Kay Mitchell, Aug. 18, 1962; children: Kevin James, Brian Patrick, Cory Edward. MS, U. Ill., 1964; PhD, Iowa State U., 1972. Rsch. asst. U. Ill., Urbana, 1962-64; agronomist Dunphy's Feed & Fertilizer, Sullivan, Ill., 1964-66; rsch. asst. Iowa State U., Ames, 1969-72, crop prodn. specialist Des Moines, 1972-75; extension specialist soybeans N.C. State U., Raleigh, 1975—, prof. crop sci., 1986—. Instr. soybean prodn. N.C., 1975—; mem. N.C. Land Use Value Adv. Bd., Raleigh, 1987—. Author 4 computer programs; contbr. numerous articles to profl. jours. Cubmaster Boy Scouts Am., Raleigh, 1976-81, troop com. chair, 1979-98; officer Athens Dr. Band Boosters, Raleigh, 1983-90. Sgt. U.S. Army, 1966-69. Recipient Meritorious Svc. award N.C. Soybean Producers. Mem. Am. Soc. Agronomy (com. chair, fellow, Agronomic Extension Edn. award), Crop and Soil Sci. Socs. Am., Am. Soybean Assn. (mem. S.Am. soybean mission), Coun. for Agrl. Sci. and Tech., Alpha Zeta, Epsilon Sigma Phi, Gamma Sigma Delta, Phi Eta Sigma, Phi Kappa Phi, Sigma Xi. Achievements include research on soybean varieties, production, management and econ. Home: 3708 Swift Dr Raleigh NC 27606-2572 Office: NC State U Box 7620 Raleigh NC 27695-7620 E-mail: jim_dunphy@ncsu.edu.

DUNPHY, MAUREEN MILBIER, reading educator; b. Springfield, Mass., Feb. 25, 1949; d. Donald J. and Mary C. Milbier; m. Terrence Michael Dunphy. BS in Edn., Westfield State Coll., 1971, MEd, 1975, Cert. Advanced Grad. Study, 1988; cert. paralegal, 1996. Tchr. Thornton Burgess Intermediate Sch., Hampden, Mass., 1971-75; reading specialist, reading dept. head West Springfield Jr. H.S., 1975—2002; reading supr. K-12 Westfield (Mass.) Pub. Schs., 2002—. Acting asst. prin. W. Springfield Jr. HS, 1989; cons. Nat. Evaluations Systems, Amherst, Mass. Mem. editl. bd.: MRA Primer, 1999—. Mem. Long Range Bldg. Needs Com., Westfield, 1986-87, 2000-02. Mem. Pioneer Valley Reading Coun. (pres. 1977-79), Mass. Reading Assn. (dir. 1977-81), West Springfield Edn. Assn. (negotiations sec.), Mass. Tchrs. Assn., Hampden County Tchrs. Assn. Home: 282 Steiger Dr Westfield MA 01085-4934 Office: North Mid Sch 350 Southampton Rd Westfield MA 01085

DUNSFORD, DEBORAH WILLIAMS, English language, journalism educator; b. Sedalia, Mo., Dec. 17, 1956; d. Clyde Marion and Oleta Jean (Hoard) Williams; m. Bart Roberts Dunsford, May 24, 1980. BS in Agrl., Kans. State U., 1979; MA in English, Tex. A&M U., 1987, PhD, 1993. Asst. editor, reporter Ag Press Publ., Manhattan, Kans., 1978-80; editorial asst. High Plains Jour., Dodge City, Kans., 1980-82; adminstrv. clk., customer svc. rep. Gen. Tele. Co. the S.W., Bryan, Tex., 1982-85; asst. editor Tex. Real Estate Rsch. Ctr., College Station, 1985-86; instr. English, journalism Tex. A&M U., College Station, 1987-91; lectr. English, journalism Old Dominion U., Norfolk, Va., 1991; lectr. English, study skills Mt. St. Clair Coll., Clinton, Iowa, 1992-93; asst. editor, ext. N.C. State U., Raleigh, 1993-94; asst. prof. agrl. journalism Tex. A&M U., College Station, 1994—. Instr. Wake Tech. C.C., Raleigh, 1993, Ctrl. Carolina C.C., Sanford, N.C., 1993, Clinton (Iowa) C.C., 1992-93, Blinn C.C., College Station, 1989-90; tech. writer Computer Data Systems, Inc., Norfolk, Va., 1991; comm. specialist, ext. Tex. A&M U., College Station, summers, 1986-91, grad. teaching asst., 1987, 89-90; freelance writer Fayetteville (N.C.) Observer-Times, 1993, Raleigh News & Observer, 1993. Contbr. articles to local newspapers. Vice-chair Clinton County Dem. Party, 1993; vol. campaign worker Brazos County, 1988; sec.-treas. Internat. Assn. Bus. Communicators, 1986-87, Brazos bravo com. 1987-88; Tex. A&M Conf. on lang. and lit. com. English Grad. Students Assn., 1989-90; dir. Bryan-College Station Jaycees, 1985-86. Recipient Brazos Bravo award Internat. Assn. Bus. Communicators, Bryan, 1986, Future Farmers Am. awards, Kans., 1974-75. Mem. MLA, Nat. Coun. Tchrs. English, Assn. for Edn. in Journalism and Mass Comm., Assn. for Advanced Composition, Eighteenth Century Soc., Gold Key Nat. Honor Soc. Democrat. Avocations: hiking, camping, opera, classical music, cooking. Office: Tex A&M U Dept Journalism Reed Mcdonald Bldg College Station TX 77843-0001

DUNWOODY, SHARON LEE, journalism and communications educator; b. Hamilton, Ohio, Jan. 24, 1947; d. Walter Charles and Fanchon (Kapp) D. MA, Temple U., 1975; PhD, Ind. U., 1978. Asst. prof. journalism Ohio State U., Columbus, 1977-81; from asst. prof. to prof. Sch. Journalism and Mass Comm. U. Wis., Madison, 1981—, dir. Sch. Journalism and Mass Comm., 1998—2003, assoc. dean Grad. Sch., 2003—. Instr. Inst. Environ. Studies U. Wis., Madison, 1985—, head acad. programs, 1995-98. Co-editor: Scientists and Journalists, 1986, Communicating Uncertainty, 1999. Mem. AAAS (chair sect. on gen. interest in sci. and Eng. 1992-93), Soc. for Social Study of Sci., Midwest Assn. for Pub. Opinion Rsch. (pres. 1989-90). Home: 1306 Seminole Hwy Madison WI 53711-3728 Office: Univ Wis Sch Journalism & Mass Comm 821 University Ave Madison WI 53706-1412

DUPEE, PAMELA ANNETTE, fisheries biologist, educator, consultant; b. Lemmon, S.D., Nov. 4, 1957; d. William Morrison and Dorothy Faith (Winkowitsch) D. BS in Fisheries with honors, Oreg. State U., 1982; MS in Zoology, U. Queensland, Brisbane, Australia, 1985. Cert. coxswains powerboat, Queensland; divemaster, rescue diver, advanced diver, open-water diver, Nat. Assn. Underwater Instructors. Fish culture asst. U.S. EPA, Corvallis, Oreg., 1978-80; fish and game cadet Oreg. State Police, Medford, 1981; U.S. fgn. fisheries biologist U. Wash., Seattle, 1979, 80, 82; edn. and rsch. specialist Reef Biosearch Pty. Ltd., Pt. Douglas, Australia, 1986-89; prof. naturalist Daintree (Australia) Reef and Rainforest Ctr., 1989; profl. photographer Pt. Douglas, 1987-90; rsch. fisheries habitat biologist Ea. Oreg. State Coll. Oreg. Dept. Fish and Wildlife, Hines and LaGrande, 1990-95; sales and mktg. rep. MCI Telecom., Inc., Colorado Springs, 1996-99; home equity loan specialist Wells Fargo Home Equity, Colorado Springs, 1999—. Contbr. numerous articles, reports, and presentation to profl. confs. and publs. Recipient 3 photographic awards for color prints and audiovisual, 1984-87, R.E. Chambers Meml. award for outstanding rsch. and writing in environ. and ecol. concerns, 1982, Albany Kiwanis Outstanding Achievement award, 1976; rsch. grantee (2) Gt. Barrier Reef Marine Park Authority, 1983-84; Milwaukie Rod and Gun Club scholar, 1979, Albany Altrusa scholar, 1976, Fulbright scholar U. Queensland, 1982-85. Mem. NAFE, Am. Fisheries Soc. (Oreg. State U. student rep. 1979, Cert. Recognition Oreg. chpt. 1995), Ocean Realm, Mortar Board, Alpha Zeta. Avocations: photography, fishing, hunting, travel, swimming, scuba. Home: Apt 207 9020 Vance St Broomfield CO 80021-6497 E-mail: pdupee@juno.com.

DUPLESSIS, AUDREY JOSEPH, school system administrator; b. New Orleans, June 23, 1920; d. Louis Joseph and Sidonie Josephine (DeLaRose) Boyer; m. Norwood Jerome Duplessis, Sr., June 27, 1984. B in Vocat. Edn., So. U., Baton Rouge, 1942; BA, Calif. State U., 1959, MA, 1966. Tchr., dir. Tri State Coll., New Orleans, 1948-50; from elem. tchr. to dir. Magnet Sch. L.A. Unified Schs., 1954—2002, dir. Magnet Sch., 2002—. Playground L.A. Unified Schs., 1956-59, reading resource tchr., 1965-70, curriculum coord., 1972-78, dir. L.A. Unified Magnet Sch., 1978-02; reading tchr. Calif. Lutheran Coll., Thousand Oaks, 1968-70. Mem. United Tchrs. PAC, L.A., 1980-88. Recipient svc. award Congress of Parents, L.A., 1988, spl. recognition U.S. Congress, 1988. Mem. Internat. Assn. Childhood Edn. (state pres. 1987-89, appreciation award 1989), St. Brigid Edn. Com., Delta Sigma Theta. Democrat. Roman Catholic. Avocations: reading, sewing, traveling, opera, listening to music.

DUPRÉ, LOUIS, retired philosopher, educator; b. Veerle, Belgium; came to U.S., 1958, naturalized, 1966; s. Clement and Francisca (Verlinden) D. PhD, U. Louvain, Belgium; PhD (hon.), Loyola Coll., 1989, Sacred Heart U., 1992, Georgetown U., 1996, Siena Coll., 1997, Regis Coll., U. Toronto, 1998, St. Michael's Coll., 2002. From asst. prof. to prof. philosophy Georgetown U., Washington, 1959-73; T. Lawrason Riggs prof. philosophy of religion Yale U., New Haven, 1973-98. Author: Kierkegaard as Theologian (also in Dutch), 1963, The Philosophical Foundations of Marxism, 1966, Dutch edit., 1970, Korean edit., 1982, The Other Dimension, 1972, French edit., 1977, Chinese edit., 1986, Polish edit., 1990, Dutch edit., 1991, Korean edit., 1995, Spanish edit., 1999, Transcendent Selfhood, 1976, Dutch edit., 1981, A Dubious Heritage, 1979, The Deeper Life, 1981, Polish edit., 1994, German edit., 2002, Marx's Social Critique of Culture, 1983, The Common Life, 1984, Polish edit., 1994, Passage to Modernity, 1993, Metaphysics and Culture, 1994, Religious Mystery and Rational Reflection, 1997, Symbols of the Sacred, 2000; editor: Faith and Reflection, 1968; co-editor: Light from Light, 1987, 2d edit., 2001; contbr. articles to profl. jours. Recipient Phi Beta Kappa medal as Tchr. of Yr. at Yale U., 1996, Aquinas medal, Am. Cath. Philos. Assn., 1997. Mem. Am. Cath. Philos. Assn. (pres. 1971), Hegel Soc. Am. (pres. 1972-73), Am. Acad. Arts and Scis., Belgian Acad. Letters, Arts, & Scis. Roman Catholic. Home: 67 N Racebrook Rd Woodbridge CT 06525-1407 Office: 451 College St New Haven CT 06520 E-mail: louis.dupre@yale.edu.

DUPREE, SHERRY SHERROD, historian, religion consultant, writer; b. Raleigh, N.C., Nov. 25, 1946; d. Matthew Needham and Mary Elouise (Heartley) Sherrod; m. Herbert Clarence DuPree, Jan. 11, 1975; children: Amil, André, Andrew. BS, N.C. Ctrl. U., 1968, MA, 1969; MLS, U. Mich., 1974, EdS, 1978. Media specialist Ann Arbor (Mich.) Pub. Schs., 1970-77; assoc. ref. libr. U. Fla. Librs., Gainesville, 1977-83; ref. libr. Santa Fe C.C. Libr., Gainesville, 1983—. Project dir. Inst. Black Culture U. Fla., Gainesville, 1982—; vis. prof. Ea. Mich. U., Ypsilanti, 1975; prof. edn. Bethume Cookman Coll., Daytona Beach, Fla., 1984-88. Author: Displays for Schools: An Avenue of Communication, 1976, rev. edit., 1979, Busy Bookworm: Good Conduct, 1980, Mini Course in Library Skills, 1983, Bible Lessons for Youth, 1987, What You Always Wanted to Know About the Card Catalog But Were Afraid to Ask, 1988, Biographical Dictionary of African Americn Holiness--Pentacostals: 1880-1990, 1989, African American Pentecostals: Sourcebook, 1992, Exposed! Federal Bureau of Investigation (FBI) Unclassified Reports on Chruchs and Church Leaders, 1993, African-American Goods News (Gospel) Music, 1993, African-American Holiness Pentecostal Movement: An Annotated Bibiography, 1996, The Rosewood Massacre At A Glance, 1997; designer, dir. Gospel Music Travel Exhibit, 1995, Rosewood Traveling Exhibit, 1999. Chair Rosewood Massacre Forum; archivist for Gospel Music Hall of Fame and Mus., Detroit. Vis. fellow Smithsonian Instn., 1987; recipient Gov.'s Achievement award State of Fla., 1986, Black Achievers award in religion Fla. conf. Black State Legislators, 1997; rsch. grants Nat. Coun. Chs., 1983, Gatorade Found., 1987, 88, 90; travel grants NEH, 1983, So. Regional Edn. Bd., 1987, 88, 89, 90; grant-in-aid fellow Bd. Regents, State of Fla., 1980-81, Horace H. Rackham's Opportunity grant, 1975-76, OEG Libr. Sci. grant U. Mich., 1973-74, grad. fellow N.C. Cen. U., 1968-69; recipient Sojourner Truth award, 1995, Resources to Religion award Fla. Libr. Assn., 1997, Alpha Phi Alpha award, 1997, Zeta Phi Beta award, 1998, Humanitarian of Yr. award Marion County Teen Ct., Fla., 1999, others; grantee Fla. Humanities Coun., 1999, others. Mem. ALA, NAACP, Soc. Pentacostal Studies, Soc. Am. Archivists, Alachua Libr. League, Fla. Libr. Assn. (chair resources to religions caucus 1994-96), Fla. C.C. Assn., League Innovations. Democrat. Mem. Ch. of God in Christ. Avocation: reading. Office: Santa Fe C C Libr 3000 NW 83rd St Bldg S Rm 212 Gainesville FL 32606-6210

DUQUET, SUZANNE FRANCES, special education educator; b. Detroit, July 15, 1954; d. Nicholas John and Frances Catherine (Muscat) Calleja; m. Michael Patrick Duquet, Aug. 26, 1978; children: Michael II, James, Michelle, Christopher. AA, Siena Heights Coll., 1974, BA, 1976; continuing edn. & spl. edn. endorsement, Ea. Mich. U., 1980; MAT with LD Specialty, Madonna U., 1996. Sec. to dean of students Siena Heights Coll., Adrian, Mich., 1973-76; tchr. Boysville of Mich., Clinton, 1976-81, asst. prin., 1981-85; tchr. spl. edn., tchr. cons. Pinckney (Mich.) Cmty. Schs., 1985—. Cons. Livingston Pediat. Ctr., Brighton, Mich., 1990-00; mem. adv. com. dept. student tchrs. Siena Heights Coll. Edn., Adrian, 1983-93. Author: (curriculum) Human Sexuality Program, 1983, K-12 Special Education Curriculum, 1991, Transition of Learning Disabled Students from High School to Adult Life: A Survey of Former Students, 1996. Eucharistic min., lector Holy Spirit Cath. Ch., Hamburg, Mich., 1986—, mem. parish leadership coun., 2002-03, mem. ednl. commn., 2003—; mem. MADD, Brighton, 1990—; faculty advisor Students Against Driving Drunk, Pinckney H.S., 1987—; sponsor internat. student travel Pinckney Cmty. Schs., 1998—. Scholar Daus. of Korean Conflict, 1972, Walsh scholar Siena Heights Coll., 1973; tuition grantee State of Mich., 1972-76; named SADD-Mich. advisor of Yr., 1999-2000. Mem.: Coun. for Exceptional Children, Mich. Edn. Assn. Avocations: reading, boating, ceramics, theater, traveling. Home: 9456 Lakecrest Dr Whitmore Lake MI 48189-9388 Office: Pinckney Cmty Schs 10255 Dexter Pinckney Rd Pinckney MI 48169-8918 E-mail: duquet@pcs.k12.mi.us.

DURACK, DAVID TULLOCH, physician, educator; b. Perth, Australia, Dec. 18, 1944; s. Reginald Wyndham and Grace Enid (Tulloch) D.; m. Carmen Elizabeth Prosser, July 25, 1970; children: Jeremy, Kimberley, Sonya, Justin. MB BS, U. Western Australia, 1969; DPhil, Oxford U., Eng., 1973. Diplomate Am. Bd. Internal Medicine, Royal Australasian Coll. Physicians, Royal Coll. Physicians U.K. Chief resident medicine, asst. prof. medicine U. Wash., Seattle, 1975-77; chief div. of infectious diseases and internat. health Duke U., Durham, N.C., 1977-94, prof. medicine, microbiology and immunology, 1982-94, cons. prof. medicine, 1994—; chmn. dept. medicine, chief divsn. infectious diseases Health Care Internat., Clydebank, Scotland, 1994-95; worldwide med. dir. Becton Dickinson Microbiology Systems, Balt., 1995—99, v.p. corp. med. affairs Franklin Lakes, NJ, 1999—. Co-editor: Infections of the Central Nervous System, 1996; contbr. articles to profl. jours. Rhodes scholar, 1969; NIH grantee, 1980, 86-91, grantee R.J. Reynolds Co., 1983-88, Carnegie Corp., 1989-94, grantee Roche Labs., 1991-94. Fellow Royal Coll. Physicians U.K., ACP, Royal Australasian Coll. Physicians, Infectious Diseases Soc. Am., Am. Soc. Clin. Investigation, Am. Fedn. Clin. Research Presbyterian. Avocation: flying (instrument-rated multi-engine pilot). Office: BD Technologies PO Box 12016 Durham NC 27709-2016

DURAN, MATIAS MARTIN, adult education educator; b. Valladolid, Yucatan, Mexico, Feb. 24, 1922; s. Marcelo Duran, Aureliana Martin; m. Faasoa Togiaso Duran, Nov. 15, 1980; children: Mary F., Martin T., Marcelo, Matthias. Aa, Riverside City Coll., Calif., 1970; BA, U. Calif., Riverside, 1974; MA, U. Dominguez Hills, Long Beach, Calif., 1988. Psychiat. technician Met. State Hosp., Norwalk, Calif., 1965; correctional officer Calif. Rehab. Ctr., Norco, 1966—72; probation officer Riverside County Probation, Blythe, Calif., 1975—77; ESL tchr./bilingual crosscultural instr. Compton Unified Sch. Dist., Calif., 1977—93. Mem.: K.C. (warden of coun. 1999—). Home: 140 W Barclay St Long Beach CA 90805-2108

DURAND, HENRY J., JR., academic administrator; b. Griffith, Ga., June 14, 1948; s. Henry James and Mildred C. (Elliott) D.; m. Bonita Ruth Cobb, Nov. 12, 1979; children: Leroy Alan Larkin, Aprille L. Whiting, Kendra N., Anitra R. BA in Sociology, Denison U., 1971; MEd, Xavier U., 1976; EdD, U. Cin., 1988. Classroom tchr., reading specialist Cin. Bd. Edn., 1972-74; instr. reading skills ctr. U. Cin., 1974-78, dir. acctg. reading skills ctr., 1978-80, dir. learning resources coll. medicine, 1980-82; dir. tng. Bushido Tng. Cons., Cin., 1982-86; asst. prof. sociology No. Ky. U., Highland Heights, 1987-90; sr. rsch. assoc., assoc. adj. prof., cons. Ctr. Applied Pub. Affairs Studies SUNY, Buffalo, 1990—, dir. Ctr. Acad. Devel., 1990—. Bd. Dirs. Nile Valley Schule, Buffalo, Adv. bd. Urban Appalachian Coun., Cin., 1986-90; mem. Coalition to Prevent Domestic Violence, Cin., 1986-90; bd. dirs. Housing Opportunities Made Equal, 1988-90; mem. coun. Pres.'s Task Force on Violent Crime, Buffalo, 1992—. Mem. Am. Assn. Univ. Administrs., Am. Assn. Higher Edn., Am. Edn. Rsch. Assn. Baptist. Avocation: martial arts. Home: 153 Winspear Ave Buffalo NY 14215-1033 Office: SUNY Ctr Buffalo 208 Norton Hall Buffalo NY 14260-1800

DURDEN, WILLIAM G. academic administrator; Grad., Dickinson Coll., 1971; MA in German Lit. and Lang., PhD in German Lit. and Lang., Johns Hopkins U.; postgrad., U. Freiburg, Germany, U. Münster, U. Basle, Switzerland. Exec. dir. Inst. for the Acad. Advancement of Youth; faculty mem. German dept. Johns Hopkins U.; pres. Sylvan Acad., Sylvan Learning Sys. Inc., Dickinson Coll., Carlisle, Pa., 1999—. Sr. edn. cons. U.S. Dept. State, chair adv. com. exceptional children and youths. Actor: (books); contbr. articles to prof. jours. Recipient Klingenstein award, Tchrs. Coll., Columbua U.; fellow Klingenstein fellow, Wis. Policy Rsch. Inst.; grantee, Am. Coun. Learned Socs., Volkswagen Found., German Soc. Md.; scholar, Fulbright. Office: Dickinson Coll PO Box 1773 Carlisle PA 17013-2896 Fax: 717-245-1457.

DUREK, DOROTHY MARY, retired English language educator; b. Pitts., Jan. 23, 1926; d. Joseph Adam and Helen Barbara (Ondich) D. BS in Edn., Youngstown State U., 1962; MS in Edn., Westminster Coll., 1969. Cert. English tchr., Ohio, comprehensive English cert., Pa. Tchr. English Brookfield (Ohio) Schs., 1962-64, Sharon (Pa.) City Schs., 1964-88. Mem., pres. Coll. Club Sharon, 1993-94. Charter mem., bd. dirs. LWV Mercer County, Pa., 1993—97; docent Butler Inst. Am. Art, Youngstown, 1988—; mem. Shenango Valley Women's Interfaith Coun., Jewish-Christian Dialogue Group, Sharon; charter mem. Mus. Women's Art, Washington, Nat. Mus. of the Am. Indian, Washington; mem., bd. dirs. Christian Assocs. Shenango Valley. Mem.: AAUW, NEA, Read and Discuss Group, Sharon Lifelong Learning Coun. (bd. dirs. 1995), Cath. Collegiate Assn., Sharon Tchrs. Assn., Pa. State Educators Assn., Prospect Heights Lit. Club. Roman Catholic. Home: 260 S Buhl Farm Dr Apt 236 Hermitage PA 16148-2528

DURGIN, PATRICIA HARTE, college administrator, chemistry educator, counselor; b. Addison, Vt., Mar. 9, 1934; d. Patrick Francis and Helen (Cawley) Harte; m. Francis John Durgin, June 15, 1957; children: Ann Durgin Reese, Mary Durgin Iacocca. BS in Chemistry, Trinity Coll., 1954; MS in Counseling, Syracuse U., 1970. Cert. chemistry, earth sci., math. 7-12 tchr., guidance counselor. Rsch./tchg. asst. U. Vt., Burlington, 1954-58; tchr. chemistry Ctrl. Tech. H.S., Syracuse, N.Y., 1958-60; counselor Syracuse City Sch. Dist., 1972-74, Fayetteville-Manlius (N.Y.) Sch. Dist., 1974-76; dir. Career Ctr. Cazenovia (N.Y.) Coll., 1976—. Convener local chpt. Women's Internat. League for Peace and Freedom, Syracuse, 1969—71; pres. Ctrl. NY chpt. NOW; chair bd. dirs. Syracuse Peace Coun., 1966—71. Recipient Unsung Heroine award NOW, Syracuse, 1995, Outstanding Alumna award for achievement, Trinity Coll., 1996. Mem. Nat. Assn. Women Educators, Ea. Coll. and Employers Network. Avocations: tennis, bridge, travel, gardening. Office: Cazenovia Coll Career Ctr Cazenovia NY 13035 E-mail: pdurgin@cazcollege.edu.

DURGIN, SCOTT BENJAMIN, radio frequency engineer, physics educator, engineering executive; b. Lewiston, Maine, July 9, 1966; s. Walter Brian and Mae Susan (Fenner) D.; m. Lisa Marie Haskell, Sept. 3, 1988; children: Lindsay Rebecca, Brittany Mae, Benjamin Zachary. AA, Ea. Nazarene Coll., Boston, 1990; BSEE, BS in Physics, U. Maine, Orono, 1993. Rsch. asst. high power microwave comm. The Mitre Corp., Lexington, Mass., 1989-90; engrng. tech. high frequency analog/digital circuitry Integrated Tech. Corp., Tempe, Ariz, 1990-92; product design engr. Passive Power Products, Gray, Maine, 1993-97, engrng. sales mgr., 1997-99; product line mgr. Andrew Passive Power Products, Gray, 1999—2001; contr., acct. Kornerstone Kindergarten, Auburn, Maine, 1995—; CFO, bus. mgr. Kornerstone Kindergarten & Presch., Auburn, 1997—2001; engring. mgr. Internat. Mfg. Svcs., Inc., Portsmouth, R.I., 2001—. Tchr. physics Ctrl. Maine Tech. Coll., Auburn, 1997-2001. Sunday sch. tchr. Ch. of the Nazarene, Phoenix, Ariz., 1991-92. Mem. IEEE, Giga Soc., Glia Soc., Pi Mu Epsilon. Libertarian. Avocations: antique collector, amateur historian, biking, hiking, student of freemasonry. Home: 40 Tefft Ridge Ln South Kingstown RI 02879 Office: Internat Mfg Svcs Inc 50 Schoolhouse Ln Portsmouth RI 02871 E-mail: sdurgin@ims-resistors.com.

DURHAM, FLOYD WESLEY, JR., economist, educator; b. Yuma, Ariz., Feb. 9, 1930; s. Floyd Wesley and Inez (Irvin) D.; BA, North Tex. State U., 1951, MA, 1952; PhD, U. Okla., 1963; m. Patricia Keehan, May 24, 1973; children— Mark Kipling, Ronald Chappell. Claimsman, Liberty Mutual Ins. Co., Boston and Ft. Worth, 1955-58; mem. faculty dept. econs. Tex. Christian U., Ft. Worth, 1960—, prof., 1971— ; cons., 1964— . Pres., Suicide Prevention Tarrant County, 1968-69. Bd. dirs. Ft. Worth Literacy Council, 1963-70, Cen. Tax Authority, Parker County, Tex. Served with AUS, 1953-55. Danforth Found. grantee, 1969-70. Mem. AAUP, Am. So. Econ. Assns., Southwestern and Western Social Sci. Assns., Western Writers Am., Beta Gamma Sigma, Omicron Delta Epsilon, Lambda Chi Alpha. Author: A Pilot Methodological Study to Determine Dibilitating Conditions, 1967; The Trinity River Paradox; Flood and Famine, 1976. Contbr. articles to profl. jours. Home: 6025 Wrigley Way Fort Worth TX 76133-3535 E-mail: durham8@charter.net.

DURHAM, GUINEVERE MCCABE, educational administrator, writer, consultant; b. Elmira, N.Y., Apr. 24, 1937; d. John Francis and Carmelita (Fusare) McCabe; divorced; children: Susan Hendricks, John Scheithauer, Judy Velten, Elizabeth Price, Margaret Jarvis; m. H. Sarge Durham, June 20, 1986. AAS, Elmira Coll., 1957, BS, 1968, MS, 1971; EdD, Nova U., 1983. Cert. tchr., adminstr., Fla. Tchr. Horseheads (N.Y.) Cen. Schs., 1968-77, Fla. Youth Detention Home, Titusville, 1978, Brevard County Schs., Cocoa, Fla., 1978-79, primary specialist, 1979-85, asst. prin. Melbourne, Fla., 1985-90; elem. prin. Lafayette Sch. Dist., Mayo, Fla., 1990-92, Gilchrist County Sch. Dist., Bell, Fla., 1992—. Owner Automotive Svc. Ctr., Elmira, 1968-77, Merritt Island, Fla., 1977-83; tax prepared H & R Block, Melbourne, 1989-90; Gesell cadre trainer Brevard Sch. Bd., Melbourne, 1985. Author: (textbook) Test Taking Strategies K-4th Grade, 1985; contbr. articles to mags. Leader Boy Scouts Am., Horseheads, 1968-70, Girl Scouts U.S.A., Horseheads, 1968-72, 77-79. Ednl. grantee State of Fla., 1983-89. Mem. ASCD, Fla. Assn. Sch. Adminstrs., Fla. Reading Assn., Kiwanis. Democrat. Roman Catholic. Avocations: reading, sewing, crafts, fishing. Home: Adams St Bell FL 32619 Office: Bell Elem Sch PO Box 639 Bell FL 32619-0639

DURHAM, HARVEY RALPH, academic administrator; BS, Wake Forest U., 1959; MA, U. Ga., 1962, PhD in Math., 1965. Asst. prof. math. Appalachian State U., Boone, N.C., 1965-67, assoc. prof., chair dept. math., 1967-71, prof. math., 1971-74, assoc. dean faculty, 1971-74, assoc. vice chancellor for acad. affairs, 1974-79, acting vice chancellor for acad. affairs, 1979-80, vice chancellor for acad. affairs, 1980-89, provost, exec. vice chancellor, 1989—. Office: Appalachian State U Office Acad Affairs Boone NC 28608-0001 E-mail: durhamhr@appstate.edu.

DURHAM, J(OSEPH) PORTER, JR., lawyer, educator; b. Nashville, May 11, 1961; AB in Polit. Sci. and History cum laude, Duke U., 1982, JD, 1985. Bar: Tenn. 1985, Md. 1988. Ptnr. Miller & Martin, Chattanooga, 1990-96, Baker, Donelson, Bearman & Caldwell, Chattanooga, 1997—2003, chmn. corp. dept., 1998—2003. Adj. prof. dept. acctg. and fin. U. Tenn., Chattanooga, 1992-98; participant Russian tax code adv. group, 1999; assoc. dir. edn. divsn. and gen. coun. Duke Endowment, 2003—. Editor Duke Law Mag., 1984-85; contbr. articles to profl. jours. Mem. Balt. Citizens Planning and Housing Assn., 1988-90; career edn. spkr. Explorer Scout program Boy Scouts Am., 1985, 88, 90-92; mem., v.p. bd. dirs., chmn. fin. com. Waxter Ctr. Found., 1989-91; mem., sec. bd. dirs. Assn. for Visual Artists, 1993-96; trustee Good Shepherd Sch., 1992-93; chmn. spl. mgmt. com. Nashville Rehab. Hosp., 1995; trail maintenance vol. U.S. Pk. Svc., 1993-95; mem. adv. com. Chattanooga State Tech. C.C.; bd. dirs. Sr. Neighbors, Inc., 2001-03. Recipient Outstanding Svc. award Waxter Ctr. Found., 1991. Mem. ABA, Tenn. Bar Assn., Md. Bar Assn., Duke U. Law Sch. Alumni Assn. (bd. dirs. 1994-97), Duke U. Gen. Alumni Assn. (bd. dirs. 1986-92, exec. com. 1989-92). Office: The Duke Endowment 100 N Tryon St Ste 3500 Charlotte NC 28202-4012

DURHAM, MARTHA L. retired secondary school educator; b. Delhi, La., May 10, 1925; d. George Erwin and Gertrude Vera (Martin) LeFevre; children: Martha Jean, Karen Lynn, Kathy Louise. AA, Santa Ana Coll., 1960; BA, U. Calif., Fullerton, 1962, MA, 1965. Cert. gen. secondary tchr. Tchr. Anaheim H.S., 1963—66, Katilla H.S., 1966—68, Los Alamitos (Calif.) Unified Sch. Dist., 1968—94; ret., 1994. Co-sponsor CSF; mem. NDEA Program Devel. Inst., NDEA Inst. in English Advanced Placement English, CATE Ad hoc Com. on Evaluation of English Tchrs., English Coun. Calif. State Colls. Recipient PTA Hon. Svc. award; named one of Outstanding Secondary Educators of Am., 1974, 75, Orange County Tchr. of Yr., 1979, Calif. Tchr. of Yr. finalist, 1979. Mem. LAEA, Nat. Coun. Tchrs. English, Calif. Assn. Tchrs. English, Calif. Tchrs. Assn., Phi Theta Kappa, Phi Kappa Phi. Home: 10400 Trinity Way Stanton CA 90680-1528

DURIG, JAMES ROBERT, chemistry educator; b. Washington, Pa., Apr. 30, 1935; s. and Roberta Wilda Mounts; m. Kathryn Marlene Sprowls, Sept. 1, 1955; children: Douglas Tybor, Bryan Robert, Stacey Ann. BA, Washington and Jefferson Coll., 1958, D.Sc. (hon.), 1979; PhD, M.I.T., 1962. Asst. prof. chemistry U. S.C., Columbia, 1962-65, assoc. prof., 1965-68, prof., 1968-93, Ednl. Found. prof. chemistry, 1970-73, dean Coll. Sci. and Math., 1973-93; dean Coll. Arts & Scis. U. Mo., Kans. City, 1993—2000, prof. chemistry & geosci., 1993—. Editor: Vibrational Spectra and Structure, 24 vols., 1972—, Jour. Raman Spectroscopy, 1979-94; mem. editl. bd. Jour. Molecular Structure, 1972—; contbr. articles to profl. jours. Served with Chem. Corps U.S. Army, 1963-64. Recipient Russell award U.S.C., 1968; Alexander von Humboldt Sr. Scientist award W. Ger., 1976; award Spectroscopy Soc. of Pitts., 1981; U. S.C. Ednl. Found. award, 1984 Mem. Am. Chem. Soc. (So. Chemist award Memphis sect. 1976, Charles A. Stone award S.E. Piedmont sect. 1975), Am. Phys. Soc., Soc. for Applied Spectroscopy (Pitts. sect. award 1981), Coblentz Soc. (mem. governing bd. 1972-76, pres. 1974-76, award for outstanding research in molecular spectroscopy 1970), Internat. Union Pure and Applied Chemistry (chmn. sub-commn. on infrared and Raman spectroscopy 1975-95, mem. commn. molecular spectra and structure 1978-89, sec. 1981-83, chmn. 1983-89, editor Spectrochimica Acta 1999—), Blue Key Soc., Phi Beta Kappa (pres. Alpha chpt. S.C. 1970), Sigma Xi, Phi Lambda Upsilon. Presbyterian. Home: 1213 W 64th Ter Kansas City MO 64113-1516 Office: Univ Mo 410 RHFH Kansas City MO 64110

DURNIN, RICHARD GERRY, education educator; b. Haverhill, Mass., Mar. 9, 1920; s. William Edward and Ehtel (Millett) Durnin. BS, Columbia U., 1947; MEd, Harvard U., 1950; postgrad. summers, U. Nottingham, 1950, U. Oxford, 1956; EdD, U. Pa., 1968. Tchr. pub. schs. N.J., Mass., 1946-49; instr. State Coll. at Fitchburg (Mass.), 1949-51; dir. Antioch Sch., Yellow Springs, Ohio, 1951-52; asst. prof. SUNY, Buffalo, 1952-58; vis. lectr. edn. Tufts U., spring 1957; dir. Smith Coll. Day Sch., 1958-59; asst. prof. edn. Rutgers U., 1959-65; prof. social and hist. founds. of edn. CCNY, 1965-90, prof. emeritus, 1990—. Instr. U. Nev., U. N.H., Coll. William and Mary, Johns Hopkins U., 1951—68. Author: (book) American Education: A Guide to Information Sources, 1982; contbr. articles to profl. jours. Mem. nat. coun. Travelers Aid Internat. Social Svc., 1972—77; mem. coun. Middlexsex County (N.J.) Cultural and Heritage Commn., 1976—95; mem. adv. commn. Mercer County (N.J.) C.C., 1980—87; Rep. committeeman Middlesex County, 1992—; bd. dirs. Internat. Social Svc.-WAIF; trustee Proprietary Ho. Assn., NJ, 1977—97; mem. adv. com. Old Barracks, Trenton, NJ, 1982—88, trustee, 1992—98. 1st lt. USAF, 1942—46. Mem.: SAR, Soc. Colonial Wars, Jamestowne Soc., Soc. War of 1812, N.J. Hist. Soc., Nat. R.R. Hist. Soc., New Brunswick Hist. Soc. (pres. 1969—71), History Edn. Soc., Mil. Order Fgn. Wars, Essex Inst., English-Speaking Union (pres. New Brunswick br. 1991—93), Joyce Kilmer Centennial Commn. (v.p. 1986—), St. George Soc. N.Y., Soc. Mayflower Descs., Colonial Order Acorn, Phi Delta Kappa, Kappa Delta Pi. Episcopalian. Home: 50 Chester Cir New Brunswick NJ 08901-1526

DURR, MARGUERITE DENISE, school system administrator; b. Wilkes-Barre, Pa., Mar. 27, 1941; d. Francis A. and Mary J. (Mitchell) Dooley; m. Edwin Joseph Durr, July 4, 1964; children: Brian Gerard and Dwayne Joseph. BS in Elem. Edn., Coll. Misericordia, 1963; MEd, The Citadel Charleston, 1977; EdD, Nova U., 1992. Cert. supervision, leadership. Tchr., 5th grade St. Clair St. Elem. Sch., Wilkes-Barre, 1963-64; tchr., 1st, 2d grade Goose Creek (S.C.) Elem. Sch., 1965-70; tchr. 1st-6th grades Newington/Summerville (S.C.) Elem. Schs., 1971-86; chpt. I tchr., reading specialist 6th-8th grades Camden Middle Jr. High Sch., Kingsland, Ga., 1986-89; vice prin. Camden County Bd. Edn., Kingsland, Ga., 1989-93. V.p. exec. bd. PTA, St. Mary's, Ga., 1991-93. Pres. Summerville Edn. Assn., 1984, lector, Eucharistic min. St. Francis and Our Lady of the Sea Chs., St. Mary's, 1989-93. Honor scholar Coll. Misericordia. Mem. Ga. Assn. Elem. Sch. Principals, Profl. Assn. Ga. Educators, Assn. Supervision and Curriculum Devel., Delta Kappa Gamma (sec., fellowship/scholarship chmn.). Roman Catholic. Avocations: reading and leadership research, christian fellowship, snorkeling, cooking, swimming. Home: 2941 Alexander Court Saint Marys GA 31558

DURR, MELISSA ANN, nonprofit executive; b. Lafayette, Ind., July 3, 1952; d. Stephen Frank and Elizabeth Ann (Sullivan) May; m. Gregory Allen Durr, July 22, 1972; children: Kerensa Lea, Alexander Joseph. BS in Secondary Edn., Ind. U., Indpls., 1974, MS in Secondary Edn., 1977; cert. tng. cons., Ball State U., 1991. Social studies tchr. Taylor Cmty. Sch., Kokomo, Ind., 1974-77; co-owner Customer Keepers, Muncie, Ind., 1982-83; dir. religious edn. Unitarian Univarsalist Ch., Muncie, 1985-93; cons., owner Leadership Connection, Muncie, 1993—; edn. and tng. coord. Ind. Assn. of Area Agencies on Aging. Adj. faculty mem. Ind. Inst. Tech., Indpls., 1993—, Ivy Tech. State Coll., Muncie, 1995-97. Contbr. columns to newsletters, articles to profl. publs. Chair religious edn. com. Ohio Valley Unitarian Universalist Dist., Indpls., 1989-92; mem. commn. on lawyer discipline Ind. Bar, Indpls., 1993-95; mem. Citizens' Commn. on Cts., Indpls., 1994—; mem. Hoosier Forums Steering Com., Indpls., 1993-96. Recipient Anne Miller award for excellence in religious edn. Ohio Valley Unitarian Universalist Dist., 1992, Vivian Conley award for civic involvement Muncie Women's Coalition, 1993. Mem. NAFE, LWV (pres. Ind. 1991-95, v.p. Muncie chpt. 1995-96, chair nat. nominating com. 1996-98), Ind. Assn. Nonprofit Orgns. (bd. dirs. 1994—), Muncie-Delaware County C. of C. (mem. Gateways task force 1990-95), Liberal Religious Educators Assn., Optimist Club (pres. Muncie Hometown chpt. 1993-95, Growth award 1994). Avocations: reading, travel, walking. Office: Leadership Connection 8100 N Oak Flat Rd Muncie IN 47303-9310

DURRANCE, JOAN C. library and information science educator; b. Miami, Fla., Apr. 20, 1937; d. Benjamin Aldon and Elizabeth (Burkett) Coachman; m. Raymond E. Durrance, May 4, 1961; children: E. Brian, J. Katharine, Joseph R. BA, U. Fla., 1959; MSLS, U. N.C., 1960; Specialist Cert., U. Wis., 1975; PhD, U. Mich., 1980. Librarian Miami (Fla.) Pub. Library, 1960-62; internat. documents librarian U. N.C., Chapel Hill,

1962-65; community svcs. librarian Cen. Wis. Colony, Madison, Wis., 1972-73; instr. U. Toledo, 1975-76; asst. prof. Sch. Info. & Libr. Studies U. Mich., Ann Arbor, 1980-86, assoc. prof. Sch. Info., 1986-96, prof., 1996—, assoc. dean, 1986-88. Mem. nat. adv. coun. Kellogg Edn. Info. Ctrs., 1987-90. Contbr. articles to profl. jours.; author: Armed for Action, 1984, Serving Job Seekers, 1993, Meeting Community Needs, 1994, Online Community Information, 2002. Grantee, W.K. Kellogg Found., Inst. for Mus. and Libr. Svcs., NEH, Alliance for Cmty. Tech. Mem. ALA (mem. coun. 1978-82, Assn. Libr. Info. Sci. Edn. (bd. dirs. 1984-87, 95—, pres.-elect 1995-96, pres. 1996-97, Bowker-Mudge award 1997), Beta Phi Mu. Democrat. Office: Univ of Mich 550 E University Ave Ann Arbor MI 48109-1092

DURST, CAROL GOLDSMITH, food studies educator; b. Bklyn., Mar. 1, 1952; d. Hyman and Florence (Weisblatt) Goldsmith; m. Marvin Ira Durst, June 18, 1972 (div. Sept. 1977); m. Leslie Mark Wertheim, Apr. 1, 1984; 1 child, William David. BA, Hamilton Kirkland Coll., 1973; MA, Columbia U., 1974; postgrad., Union Inst., 2000—. Career counselor Hofstra U., Hempstead, N.Y., 1974-75, Ocean County C.C., Toms River, N.J., 1975-76; rsch. assoc. Catalyst, N.Y.C., 1975-77; coord. displaced homemakers program N.Y. State Dept. Labor, N.Y.C., 1977-79; dir. N.Y. restaurant sch. New Sch. Social Rsch., N.Y.C., 1979-83; owner New Am. Catering Corp., N.Y.C., 1983-98; tchr., career counselor Peter Kump's N.Y. Cooking Sch., N.Y.C., 1988-98. Adj. prof. food studies dept. NYU, 1997—, Westchester C.C., 2001—, Kingsborough C.C., 2003. Author: I Knew You Were Coming So I Baked a Cake, 1997. Mem. AAUW, N.Y. Women's Culinary Alliance (new mem. chair 1995-96), Women Chefs and Restaurateurs (co-chair mentoring program 2003-2004), Nat. Mus. Women in the Arts, Am. Mus. Natural History, Met. Mus. Art. Avocations: fine arts, piano, opera, ice skating. Home and Office: PO Box 270 Millwood NY 10546-0270

DUSANENKO, THEODORE ROBERT, retired math educator, county official; b. Bronx, N.Y., Jan. 28, 1942; 010s. Teddy B. and Harriet T. Dusanenko; m. Dolores A. James, Aug. 31, 1986; children: Debra Garvey, Roger L. James. BS, SUNY, Albany, 1964, MS, 1967. Cert. secondary math. tchr., N.Y. Tchr. math. Clarkstown North H.S., New City, N.Y., 1964-80, 82-83, 85-96, wrestling coach, 1964-73; ret., 1996; legislator Rockland County, New City, 1970—85, 1989—; real estate salesman ERA Kennedy & Kennedy Real Estate, Piermont, NY, 1986—. Mem. New City Vol. Ambulance Corps, 1964-76, Rockland County Rep. Com., 1964—, O'Grady Brown Scholarship Com., 1981—; supr. Town of Clarkstown, New City, 1980-85, councilman, 1992-95; mem. Hudson River Valley Econ. Devel. Comm.; mem. region III N.Y. State Fish and Wildlife Bd.; initiator Clarkstown Youth Ct., 1981—. Mem. Elks. Roman Catholic. Avocations: gardening, grandparenting. Home: 462 Storms Rd Valley Cottage NY 10989-1213 Office: ERA Kennedy & Kennedy Real Estate 540 Piermont Ave Piermont NY 10968-1035

DUTCHER, SUSAN K. geneticist, educator; b. Denver, Mar. 18, 1953; d. Robert Sprague Dutcher and Wilma Evelyn Wilson McCarthy; m. Gary D. Stormo, Jan. 12, 1985; children: Benjamin M., Adrienne E.D. BA, Colo. Coll., 1974; PhD, U. Wash., 1980. Postdoctoral fellow Rockefeller U., N.Y.C., 1980-83, asst. prof., 1983-84, U. Colo., Boulder, 1983-90, assoc. prof. genetics, 1990-96, prof., 1996—, Wash. U. Sch. Medicine Dept. of Genetics, St. Louis, 1999—. Panel mem. NSF, Washington, 1988-90, Am. Cancer Soc., Atlanta, 1989, Dept. Energy, 1983. Contbr. articles to profl. jours. Searle scholar, Chgo. Community Trust, 1984-87; grantee NIH, 1983—, NSF, 1986—, U. Colo., 1989. Mem. Genetics Soc. Am. (nominating com. 1990), Am. Soc. Microbiology, Am. Soc. Cell Biology. Office: Wash Univ Sch Medicine Box 8232 660 S Euclid Ave Saint Louis MO 63110-1010

DUTILE, FERNAND NEVILLE, law educator; b. Lewiston, Maine, Feb. 15, 1940; s. Wilfred Joseph and Lauretta Blanche (Cote) D.; m. Brigid Dooley, Apr. 4, 1964; children: Daniel, Patricia. AB, Assumption Coll., 1962; JD, U. Notre Dame, 1965. Bar: Maine 1965. Atty. U.S. Dept. Justice, Washington, 1965-66; prof. law Cath. U. Am., Washington, 1966-71, U. Notre Dame Law Sch., Ind., 1971—. Bd. dirs. Ind. Lawyers Commn., Indpls., 1975-85, Legal Svcs. No. Ind., South Bend, 1975-83; dir. South Bend Work Release Ctr., 1973-75, Ind. Criminal Law Study Commn., 1991-99. Editor: Legal Education and Lawyer Competency, 1981; author: Sex, Schools and the Law, 1986; co-editor: Early Childhood Interventiion and Juvenile Delinquency, 1982, The Prediction of Criminal Violence, 1987; co-author: State and Campus, 1984. Democrat. Roman Catholic.

DUTILE, SHELLEY SUE REED, elementary school counselor; b. Lewiston, Maine, Aug. 19, 1950; d. Gerald Jackson and Helen Edith (Thompson) Reed; m. Alan Thomas Jacob, June 19, 1971 (div. 1980); 1 child, Derek Alan; m. Richard Roland Dutile, Apr. 16, 1983; children: Peter Reed, Kathryn Helen. BS in Edn., U. Maine, Farmington, 1972; M Ednl. Counseling, U. So. Maine, 1980. Cert. tchr., guidance counselor, Maine. Tchr. Lake St. Sch. and Merrill High Sch., Auburn, Maine, 1972-85; elem. sch. counselor Lewiston Pub. Schs., 1986—. Intern supr. Lewiston-Auburn Coll., U. So. Maine.; chair truancy dropout alternative edn. adv. com., Augusta, Maine, 1990-92; mem. adv. com. Kids as Planners, Lewiston, 1992—; adv. com. Headstart, Augusta, 1991—; presenter workshops on parenting issues; author, program developer Student-At-Risk program, 1988. Sunday sch. tchr. 1st Ch. Christian Scientist, Auburn-Lewiston; mem. Milhouse Community Com., Lewiston, 1991—. Grantee Maine Dept. Edn., 1992—. Mem. NEA, ACA, Am. Sch. Counselors Assn., Maine Edn. Assn., Maine Sch. Counselors Assn. (pres.-elect 1994—, v.p. elem. sect. 1992—). Democrat. Avocations: reading, hiking, canoeing, music. Address: RR 2 Box 795 Greene ME 04236-9613 Office: Montello Sch East Ave Lewiston ME 04240

DUTKO, CARA MARIE, secondary school educator; b. Homewood, Ill., Sept. 13, 1973; d. David Peter and Barbara (Fidanzi) Dutko. B Music Edn., Ill. Wesleyan U., 1995; M Fine Arts, Roosevelt U., Chgo., 2001. Adminstrv. asst. AON, Chgo., 1996; gen. music tchr. McKinley Elem. Sch., Chicago Heights, Ill., 1996—97; choral dir. Washington Jr. H.S., Chicago Heights, Ill., 1997—98, Lincoln-Way East H.S., Frankfort, Ill., 2001—02. Pvt. voice/piano studio, Homewood, Ill., 1997—. Roman Catholic. Office: Marian Cath HS 700 Ashland Chicago Heights IL 60411

DUTT, KAMLA, medical educator; b. Lahore, Punjab, India; came to U.S., 1969; d. Gulzari Lal and Raj Bansi Dutt. BS with honors, Panjab U., Chandigarh, India, 1961, MS in Zoology with honors, 1962, PhD, 1970. Rsch. assoc. Harvard Med. Sch. Sidney Farber Cancer Ctr., Boston, 1972-76; rsch. assoc. Eye Inst. Retinal Fedn., Boston, 1977-80; sr. rsch. assoc. Yale Med. Ctr., New Haven, 1980-81, Emory U., Atlanta, 1981-82; asst. prof. Morehouse Sch. Medicine, Atlanta, 1983-89, assoc. prof., 1989—2001, prof., 2001—. Sci. adv. bd. Fernbank Sci. Ctr., Atlanta. Contbr. numerous articles to sci. jours.; author short stories (in Hindi); prodr., actor 3 maj. plays, Atlanta; actor 11 maj. plays, India. Bd. dirs. VSEI (vol. fundraising orgn. for edn. in India), 1973-78; v.p. Indian Am. Cultural Assn., 1985; podium spkr., participant King Week, 1990, 91, 93; spkr. Gandhi Day Celebration, 1984, 85; key participant Intercultural Conf., 1990; main participant joint document Women's Perspective; active human rights issues; stake holder Vision 20/20 Collaborative State of Ga., diversity and edn. coms., 1995. Hindu. Achievements include establishment of human ocular cell lines by gene trasfaction, used as model for study of eye diseases and tissue engineering. Office: Morehouse Sch Medicine 720 Westview Dr SW Atlanta GA 30310-1458

DUTTON, JO SARGENT, education educator, researcher, consultant; b. L.A., Calif., Oct. 26, 1940; d. Paul and Jayne (O'Toole) Sargent; m. Ted W. Dutton, Nov. 15, 1979; children: Brooks, Berndan, Mark; step-children: Robert, William, Jeanne, Jerry. BS, U. So. Calif., 1962, MS, 1966; PhD, U. Calif. Riverside, 1996. Cert. elem. tchr., Calif.; corp. paralegal cert.; preliminary adminstrv. svcs. credential. Elem. sch. tchr. 6th grade Lawndale Unified Sch. Dist., 1963-64; reading instr. Culver City (Calif.) Unified Sch. Dist., 1964; prof. edn. U. So. Calif., 1964-65; remedial reading instr. Santa Monica (Calif.) Unified Sch. Dist., 1965-66; dist. remedial reading instr. San Marino Unified Sch. Dist., 1967-70; real estate broker Calif., 1972-96; adj. prof. English Chaffey C. C., Rancho Cucamonga, Calif., 1991-93; rsch. fellowCalif. Ednl. Rsch. Coop. U. Calif., Riverside, 1993-95. Prof. Calif. Bapt. Coll., 1997; dir. rsch. Calif. Virtual U., 1997; dir. devel. U. Calif. Riverside, Sch. Edn., 1997-2000. Contbr. articles to profl. jours. Mem. exec. com. Inland Empire Cultural Found., 1980-83, Sister Cities Internat., Ontario, Calif., 1980-82; chair steering com. San Bernardino County Arts League, 1983-84; commr. San Bernardino County Mus.; mem. bd. Inland Empire Symphony; survey and assessment conductor Calif. Arts Coun. Mem. Am. Ednl. Rsch. Assn., Chaffey Cmty. Arts Assn., Calif. Ednl. Rsch. Assn. Home: PO Box 2960 Blue Jay CA 92317-2960 Office: U Calif Riverside Sch of Edn Riverside CA 92502-9874

DUTTON, SHARON GAIL, retired elementary school educator; b. Greenville, S.C., Jan. 5, 1947; d. Melvin Thornton and Bessie Mae (Whitmire) B. BS in Elem. Edn., E. Tenn. State U., 1969; MA in Early Childhood Edn., Western Carolina U., 1976, EdS in Early Childhood Edn., 1983. Cert. tchr. N.C. elem, secondary, sch. adminstrn., early childhood. Tchr. grade 4 Brevard (N.C.) Elem. Sch., 1970; tchr. grade 3 Rosman (N.C.) Elem. Sch., 1970, tchr. grade 2, 1970-72, tchr. reading, 1972-73, tchr. grades 2, 3, 1973-87, tchr. grade 4, 1987-89; ret. Transylvania Sch. System, 1998. Tchr. Headstart Rosman Elem. Sch. 1971, summer sch., 1972; lead tchr. Teacher Corps Grade 2 Western Carolina U., Cullowhee, N.C., Rosman, 1974-76; clin. practicum and reading conf. Western Carolina U., VA Ctr., Oteen, N.C., summer 1976. Organist, pianist, East Fork Bapt. Ch., Brevard, N.C. Mem. NEA, ASCD, Am. Fedn. Tchrs., N.C. Assn. Edn., Transylvania County Assn. Edn. Democrat. Avocations: art, crafts, reading, piano and organ playing, listening to classical and pipe organ music. Home: Rosman, NC. Deceased.

DUVALL, CATHLEEN ELAINE, elementary school educator, consultant; b. Port Hueneme, Calif., Apr. 19, 1954; d. Joseph Manuel and Mary Kathryn (Gerweck) Morris; m. Edward Mehl Duvall, Aug. 16, 1980; children: Nicolette Mareen, Rebecca Lauren. BS, Longwood Coll., 1976; MEd, Va. Commonwealth U., 1980; postgrad., U. St. Thomas, 1989-92. Cert. reading specialist, supr., early childhood tchr., gifted specialist, elem. tchr., writing project trainer, Tex. Classroom tchr. Chesterfield (Va.) County Pub. Schs., 1976-80, Alief (Tex.) Ind. Sch. Dist., 1980-82, reading specialist, 1982-85, gifted specialist, 1985-86, social studies specialist, 1985-90; English lang. arts coord. Fort Bend Ind. Sch. Dist., Sugar Land, Tex., 1990—2003, reading recovery tchr. leader in tng., 2003—. Instr. U. Houston/Victoria, Tex.; cons. Port Nueces Groves Ind. Sch. Dist., LaMarque Ind. Sch. Dist., Northside Ind. Sch. Dist., Alief Ind. Sch. Dist., Tex., Dauphin Sch. Dist., Pa. Mem. Internat. Reading Assn., Tex. State Reading Assn., Greater Houston Area Reading Coun. (bd. dirs. 1991—, pres. 1997), Nat. Coun. Tchrs. English, Tex. Coun. Tchrs. English (Outstanding Elem. English Lang. Arts Educator award 1996-97), West Houston Area Coun. Tchrs. English (bd. dirs. 1991—, pres. 1995-97), Assn. Tex. Profl. Educators (pres. region IV 1990-93, bd. dirs. 2000—, Christa McAuliffe Tchg. Excellence award 1988), Coalition Reading and English Suprs. Tex. (pres. 2002—). Republican. Avocations: reading, gardening, cooking, traveling. Office: Fort Bend Ind Sch Dist 16431 Lexington Blvd Sugar Land TX 77479-2308 E-mail: 907cd048@fortbend.k12.tx.us.

DUVALL, MARJORIE L. English and foreign language educator; b. Lehighton, Pa., Dec. 2, 1958; d. Charles Jacque and Carole Faye (Eckhart) Lusch; m. Glenn Edward Duvall, July 26, 1954. BA in German, Lafayette Coll., 1980; MA in German, U. Fla., 1998; postgrad., East Stroudsburg U., 1982, Ga. So. U., Middlebury Coll., 1988, Augusta State U., U. Pa., 1994, U. S.C., 1993; degree, Goethe-Inst., Germany, 2003; student, Accord Lang. Sch., Paris, France, 2003. German and French tchr. Evans (Ga.) Mid. Sch., 1987-89, Harlem (Ga.) Mid. Sch., 1989-92; ESOL tchr. Lakeside Mid. and H.S.'s, Evans, Ga., 1992-97; ESL tchr. Davidson & Murphy H.S.'s, Mobile, Ala., 1997-99; German tchr. Brookwood H.S., Snellville, Ga., 1999-00; tchr. ESOL and lang. arts for gifted Freedom Middle Sch., Stone Mountain, Ga., 2000—03; tchr. English, Dunwoody H.S., Ga., 2003—. Contbr. articles to profl. jours. Recipient scholarship Profl. Assn. Ga. Educators, 1994. Mem.: TESOL, Fgn. Lang. Assn. Ga., Ga. Assn. Gifted Children, Nat. Coun. Tchrs. English, Am. Assn. Tchrs. of French, Am. Assn. Tchrs. of German, Friends of Goethe, DeKalb County Supporters of the Gifted, Mensa. Lutheran. Avocations: choral music, piano, swimming, baton twirling, dance. Home: 4452 Beacon Hill Dr SW Lilburn GA 30047 Office: Dunwoody HS 5035 Vermack Rd Dunwoody GA 30338 E-mail: pardette80@aol.com.

DUVALL, PATRICIA ARLENE, secondary education educator; b. Pitts., June 27, 1950; d. William Richard and Willene Alberta (Goode) Addison; 1 child, Tiyonda Aikee. BA in Math., Carnegie-Mellon U., 1972; MEd, U. Pitts., 1981. Long distance telephone operator AT&T, Pitts., 1968-71; switchboard operator Union Nat. Bank, Pitts., 1972; tchr. math. Allegheny Intermediate Unit, Pitts., 1978-79; math. skills program Chatham Coll., Pitts., 1983—; tchr. math. Pitts. Bd. Pub. Edn., 1972—. Math instr. Kids and Teens coll. program Community Coll. Allegheny County, summer 1986, 87; tennis coach Allegheny High Sch., Pitts., 1979-81. Mem. U.S. Tennis Assn., Am. Alliance Health Phys. Edn., Recreation and Dance, Women's Tennis Assn., Nat. Coun. Tchrs. Math. Jehovah'S Witness. Avocations: stamp collecting, tennis, reading, collecting comic books, home computers. E-mail: parelene@netscape.net.

DUVALL, RICK, education educator; b. Bowling Green, Ky., Jan. 30, 1965; BA, U. Ky., 1987; MA, U. S.C., 1992, PhD, 1997. Cert. tchr., S.C. Tchr. English Ctrl. Comprehensive Sch., Grantham, Eng., 1987; tchr. 6th grade S.A. Hull Middle Sch., Jacksonville, Fla., 1988-89; tchr. 5th grade Joseph Keels Elem., Columbia, S.C., 1989, Horrell Hill Elem. Sch., Hopkins, S.C., 1990-91, tchr. spl. edn., 1991-93, curriculum resources coord., 1993-94, with multi-age class, 1994-95; tchr. in residence U. S.C., 1995-96; upper grade tchr. Ctr. for Inquiry, 1996-98; asst. prof. elem. and mid. grades edn. Western Carolina U., 1998—. Counselor Gwynn Valley Camp, Brevard, N.C., 1987-95; trainer The Wright Group, Bothell, Wash., 1992—; instr. U. S.C., S.C. State Dept. Edn., Columbia, 1992-97; mem. writing team S.C. English Lang. Arts Curriculum Framework, S.C. Nat. Goals document Putting Children and Families First, Lt. Govs. Action Coun. for Youth, 1993-94. Author: Building Character and Community in the Classroom, 1997. Youth advisor Eastminster Presbyn. Ch., Columbia, 1989-97; vol. Habitat for Humanity, 1990—. Named Sallie Mae Tchr. of Yr., 1988, Richland I Dist. Tchr. of Yr., 1992-93, S.C. Sci. Educator of Yr., 1994; grantee S.C. Dept. Edn., 1990-91, BellSouth, Columbia, 1992-93. Mem. NEA, Assn. for Childhood Edn. Internat., Nat. Coun. Tchrs. English, Nat. Coun. Tchrs. Math., Nat. Sci. Tchrs. Assn., Internat. Reading Assn., S.C. Tchrs. Forum (leadership coun.), Richland I Tchrs. Forum (chmn.), Whole Lang. Umbrella, S.C. Bus. Edn. Partnership. Avocations: camping, skiing, rafting, tennis, reading. Home: Apt 2303 1700 Woodbury Rd Orlando FL 32828-6025

DUVIC, MADELEINE, dermatologist, educator, scientist; b. New Orleans, June 28, 1951; BA, Rice U., 1973; MD, Duke U., 1977. Intern, resident in medicine Duke U., Durham, N.C., 1978-82, fellow in dermatology, 1979-82, fellow in molecular biology and geriatrics, 1982-84; assoc. medicine Duke U. Med. Sch., Durham, 1982-84; asst. prof. dermatology and medicine U. Tex. Med. Sch./M.D. Anderson Cancer Ctr, Houston, 1984-89, chief sect. dermatology, 1986—, assoc. prof., 1989-95, prof. dermatology and medicine, 1995—. Mem. Grad. Sch. Biol. Scis. U. Tex.-Houston, 1985—; mem. NIH Study Sect., Washington, 1990-94; sci. com., chair Dermatology Found., Evanston, Ill.; mem. adv. bd. dermatology FDA, Washington, 1996. Contbr. numerous articles to profl. jours., chpts. to books. Fundraiser Rice U., Houston, 1986—. Named Outstanding Student, NSF, 1968; Nat. Merit scholar, 1969, Basil O'Conner scholar March of Dimes, 1985; grantee NIH, 1978-2003; recipient Bus. Profl. Woman Rsch. award, 2003. Mem. Soc. Investigative Dermatology (bd. dirs., program chair 1992-97), Am. Acad. Dermatology (bd. dirs. 2004—), Nat. Psoriasis Found. (mem. adv. bd. 1995), Nat. Alopecia Areata Found. (mem. adv. bd. 1995). Episcopalian. Achievements include development of new therapy to CTCL; cloning of epidermal genes; keratinocyte transglutaninase, GST-pi, epidermal surface antigen; studies of pathogenesis of T cell mediated skin diseases with respect to HLA, cytokines, genetics, clinical research; AZT for psoriasis, receptor selective retinoids for psoriasis, CTCL, K Sarcoma; patent for AZT for psoriasis. Office: MD Anderson Cancer Ctr Dept Dermatology Box 434 1515 Holcombe Blvd Houston TX 77030-4009

DUVIVIER, KATHARINE KEYES, lawyer, educator; b. Alton, Ill., Jan. 1, 1953; d. Edward Keyes and Marjorie (Attebery) DuVivier; m. James Wesley Perl, Mar. 30, 1985 (div. Aug. 1997); children: Alice Katharine, Emmett Edward Perl. BA in Geology and English cum laude, Williams Coll., 1975; JD, U. Denver, 1982. Bar: Colo. 1982, U.S. Dist. Ct. Colo. 1982, U.S. Ct. Appeals (10th cir.) 1982. Intern-curator Hudson River Mus., Yonkers, N.Y., 1975; geologist French Am. Metals Corp., Lakewood, Colo., 1976-79; assoc. Sherman & Howard, Denver, 1982-84, Arnold & Porter, Denver, 1984-87; atty. Office of City Atty., Denver, 1987-90; sr. instr. sch. law Univ. Colo., 1990-00; reporter of decisions Colo. Ct. of Appeals, Denver, 2000; asst. prof., dir. Lawyering Process Program U. Denver Coll. Law, 2000—. Chair Appellate Practice Subcom., 1998—2000, vice-chmn., 1996—98, 2000—. Contbr. articles to profl. jours. Mem. Denver Botanic Gardens, 1981—88; vol. Outdoor Colo., Denver, 1985—87, 1998—. Mem.: ABA (vice chmn. subcom. 1985—91), Boulder Women's Bar Assn. (pres. 1991—93), Colo. Bar Assn., Alliance Profl. Women (bd. dirs. 1985—90, pres. 1988—89), Work and Family Consortium (bd. dirs. 1988—90), St. Ives, William Coll. Alumni Assn. (co-pres. Colo. chpt. 1984—86), Phi Beta Kappa. Avocation: Avocations: geology, skiing, dancing, swimming. Home: 4761 McKinley Dr Boulder CO 80303-1142 E-mail: kkduvivier@law.du.edu.

DUZAN, DEE, elementary school principal; b. Terre Haute, Ind., Apr. 25, 1938; d. George Ernest Shick and Helen Lorene (Tuttle) McClafferty; children: David, Christopher, Kimberly. BS, Ind. State Univ., 1959; MA, Western Mich. Univ., 1971. Cert. tchr., Mich. Tchr. Porter Coll., Indpls., 1959, Lawrence (Ind.) Elem. Sch., 1959-60, Martinsville (Ill.) Pub. Schs., 1960-62, Rockford (Mich.) Pub. Schs., 1968-71, reading cons., 1971-74, dir. of reading, 1974-77, elem. prin., 1977—. Pub. speaker on Motivating Students to Read., 1992— Chmn. Children's Lit. Com., Mich. Reading Assn., 1987-88; co-chmn. Summer Lit. Conf., Mich. Reading Assn., 1987-88, chmn. compensatory Edn. Conf., Grand Rapids, Mich., 1987. Recipient Celebrate Literacy award Kent Reading Coun., 1991, Adminstr. of Yr., Mich. Reading Assn., 1987. Mem. ASCD, Internat. Reading Assn., Mich. Reading Assn. (coord. 1991-93), pres. 1991-92), Kent Reading Coun. (pres. 1987-88), Mich. Elem. Middle Sch. Prins. Assn. Avocations: reading, biking. Home: Eastbank Riverfront Towers 4767 6 Mile Rd Marne MI 49435-9503 Office: Rockford Pub Schs 350 N Main St Rockford MI 49341-1092

DUZYJ, DORIS NACHWOSTACH, middle school educator, gifted and talented education consultant; b. Detroit, July 4, 1950; d. Leon John and Olga (Tittiane) Nachwostach; m. Andrey Ivan Duzyj, May 18, 1979; children: Christina, Mykola, Melanie. BA in French, Oakland U., 1971, BA in Pol. Sci., 1973, MA in Tchg., 1991. Cert. tchr., Mich. Substitute tchr. Warren (Mich.) Consolidated Schs., 1986-87; grad. asst. Oakland U., Rochester, Mich., 1987-88; substitute tchr. Warren Con. and Lamphere, Warren and Madison Heights, 1991-92; French instr. Lamphere Schs., Madison Heights, 1992; 3d grade tchr. Immaculate Conception Grade Sch., Warren, 1992-94; 7th grade tchr. Immaculate Conception Schs., Warren, 1994. Gifted cons. Lamphere Schs., Madison Heights, 1992; presenter Mich. Coun. for Social Studies, Southfield, Mich., 1988. Author (poem) Great American Poetry Anthology, 1988. Recipient Grad. assistantship Oakland U., 1987, scholarship Ukrainian-Am. Found., 1988. Mem. ASCD, Coun. for Exceptional Children, Macomb Reading Coun., Warren Consolidated Alliance for Gifted Edn. (pres. 1992-94), Mich. Alliance Gifted Edn., Assn. for the Gifted. Ukrainian Catholic. Avocations: reading, skiing, tennis. Home: 26511 Wexford Dr Warren MI 48091-1032 Office: Immaculate Conception Schs 29500 Westbrook Ave Warren MI 48092-5427

DWINELL, ANN JONES, retired special education educator; b. Lowell, Mass., Oct. 28, 1934; d. George Hubert and Bridget Jones; m. Roland A. Dwinell, Dec. 23, 1956; children: Theresa, Joseph, Richard, John. BA, Framingham State Coll., 1972; MEd, Lesley Coll., 1974; PhD, Boston Coll., 1991. Cert. Eng. tchr., moderate spl. needs instr., Mass., adminstr., supt., spl. edn. adminstr., R.I. Spl. edn. tchr., adminstr. Marlborough (Mass.) Pub. Sch., 1972-78; core chairperson Malden (Mass.) Pub. Schs., 1978-80, spl. edn. specialist, 1980—2001. Contbr. articles to profl. jours. Mem. NEA, Mass. Tchrs. Assn. (rep. 1983-85, liaison 1987—), Phi Delta Kappa. Roman Catholic. Avocations: dancing, music, boating, reading.

DWORKIN, IRMA-THERESA, school system administrator, researcher, secondary school educator; b. Busk, Galacia, Poland, May 1, 1942; d. Moses E. and Hedwig (Rappaport) Auerbach; m. Sidney Leonard Dworkin, Aug. 19, 1975 (dec. June 1984); children: Marc Elazar, Meyer Charles, Rebecca Joy. BS in Edn., CCNY, 1964, MS in Ednl. Psychology, 1966, cert. in clin. sch. psychology, 1968; EdD in Reading and Human Devel., Harvard U., 1971. Cert. tchr., reading cons., sch. psychologist, sch. adminstr. Tchr. N.Y.C. Pub. Schs., 1964-66; rsch. asst., lectr. Bd. Higher Edn., N.Y.C., 1966-69; lectr., prof. Haifa (Israel) U., 1971-74; lectr., sr. investigator CUNY, N.Y.C., 1974-76; adminstr., evaluator, proposal and grant writer Bridgeport (Conn.) Pub. Schs., 1984—. Asst. Edn. Clinic CCNY, N.Y.C., 1964—66; Kunin-Lunefeld Found. endouwed prof. chair Haifa U., 1973. Contbr. articles to profl. jours. Vol. Cmty. Closet, Bridgeport, 1991—98; mem. Rep. Town com., Bridgeport, 1992—; bd. dirs. Jewish Bd. Edn., Bridgeport, Jewish Fedn. Greater Bridgeport, chairperson Holocaust edn. com., 1986—89, sec., 1996. Fellow Grolier, Harvard U., 1969—71; grantee fed. and state project. Mem.: Conn. Fedn. Sch. Adminstrs. (sec. 1997—, newsletter editor, website editor 1997—), Bridgeport Coun. Adminstrs. and Suprs. (editor, exec. bd. dirs. 1992—98, continuing edn. units mgr. 1993—98, v.p. 1994—98), Conn. Assn. Sch. Psychologists, Conn. Testing Network (newsletter editor). Avocations: reading, physical fitness, painting, writing.

DWORKOSKI, ROBERT JOHN, headmaster; b. Hackensack, N.J., July 9, 1946; s. Alexander George and Pauline Mary (Jurgaitis) D.; m. Amy Walsh, Nov. 22, 1975 (div. 1991); 1 child, Kathryn Louise; m. Kristin Okey, Dec. 24, 1991; 1 child, Hillary Anne. BA in Polit. Sci., George Washington U., 1964-68; AM in History, NYU, 1970; MA in History, Columbia U., 1971, PhD, 1978. Adj. instr. history Bklyn. Coll., 1976, N.Y. Inst. Tech., N.Y.C., 1976-78, Essex County Coll., Newark, N.J., 1976-78; tchr. history Woodmere (N.Y.) Acad., 1978-80, chair social studies, 1979-80; head upper sch. Harvard Sch., North Hollywood, Calif., 1980-86; headmaster Viewpoint Sch., Calabasas, Calif., 1986—. Contbr. articles to profl. jours. Bd. dirs. Will Geer Theatrum Botanicum, Topanga, Calif., 1993, Gold Coast Performing Arts Assn., Thousand Oaks, Calif.; mem. com. for satellite mus.

L.A. County Natural History Mus., L.A., 1988. Fulbright scholar, 1983; grantee NEH, 1993. Mem. Nat. Assn. Coll. Admissions Counselors, Calif. Assn. Ind. Schs. Avocations: travel, hiking, gourmet dining, theatre, running. Office: Viewpoint Sch 23620 Mulholland Hwy Calabasas CA 91302-2097

DWORNIK, LYNDA BEBEE, elementary school educator; b. Cripple Creek, Colo., Dec. 21, 1949; d. Alfred Henry and Wilda Louise (McGuffin) Bebee; m. Clarence Dewain Dwornik, Mar. 26, 1977. BS in Vocat. Edn., Colo. State U., 1971; MBA in Learning Disabilities, Ariz. State U., 1976; PhD in Early Childhood Edn., Walden U., 1994. Cert. tchr. grades kindergarten through 8. Tchr. sci. and math. grades 3-6, 1971-72; instr. h.s. vocat. edn., 1972-73; learning disabilities resource tchr. grades kindergarten-6, 1974-79; tchr. grade 2, 1979—. Ind. ednl. cons.; author, presenter (lectures) Conceptual Devel. of Literacy in Young Children, Rsch. on Relationship of Concepts of Print in Reading Level and At-Risk Status. Home: HC 63 Box 5137 Snowflake AZ 85937-9713

DWYER, GERALD PAUL, JR., economist, bank executive; b. Pittsfield, Mass., July 9, 1947; s. Gerald Paul and Mary Frances (Weir) Dwyer; m. Katherine Marie Lepiane, Jan. 15, 1966; children: Tamara K., Gerald P. III, Angela M., Michael J. L., Terence F. BBA, U. Wash., 1969; MA in Econs., U. Tenn., 1973; PhD in Econs., U. Chgo., 1979. Economist Fed. Res. Bank, St. Louis, 1972-74, Chgo., 1976-77, asst. v.p. Atlanta, 1997-98, v.p., 1998—; asst. prof. Tex. A&M U., College Station, 1977-81, Emory U., Atlanta, 1981-84, sr. rsch. assoc. Law and Econ. Ctr., 1982-84; assoc. prof. U. Houston, 1984-89; prof. Clemson (S.C.) U., 1989-99, acting head dept. econ., 1992-93. Cons. Arthur Bros., Corpus Christi, Tex., 1980—81, FTC, Washington, 1983—84, Amerigas, Houston, 1985, We. Container Corp., 1987, Metrica, Inc., Bryan, Tex., 1989—93; vis. scholar Fed. Res. Bank, Atlanta, 1982—84, St. Louis, 1987—89, Atlanta, 1994—97, Mpls., 1995; vis. fin. economist Commodity Futures Trading Commn., Washington, 1990; vis. faculty Ga. State U., 1997, U. Ga., 1999—2000, 2003—, Univ. Rome, 2000—. Contbr. articles to profl. jours. Fellow, Earhart Found., 1975—77; Weaver fellow, Intercollegiate Studies Inst., 1974—75, Rsch. grantee, Earhart Found., NSF. Mem.: Econometric Soc., Am. Stats. Assn., Am. Fin. Assn., Am. Econ. Assn., Phi Kappa Phi, Beta Gamma Sigma. Avocation: sailing.

DWYER, MARY ELIZABETH, nursery school director; b. N.Y.C., Sept. 23, 1928; d. Frank Stanton Burns and Eula Louise Gavin; m. Melvin Charles Christensen, Aug. 13, 1949 (dec. 1980); children: Mark, Alan, Paul; m. William Frederick Dwyer, Dec. 3, 1989. Student, Adelphi U., 1948, San Diego State U., 1949, SUNY, Farmingdale, 1980-86. Clk. Merrill Lynch, N.Y.C., 1946-47; sec. Ace Fence Co., Franklin Square, N.Y., 1949-50; switchboard operator Best & Co., Garden City, N.Y., 1950-51; dir. St. Francis Play Day Sch., Levittown, N.Y., 1978—. Active Levittown Rep. Club, 1960-89; mem. com. Inst. for Learning and Retirement, Farmingdale, N.Y., 1991-93. Recipient Bishop's Cross for Disting. Parochial Svc., Diocese of L.I., 1984. Mem. Amnesty Internat., Levittown Hist. Soc. (exec. dir. 1991—). Republican. Episcopalian. Avocations: bridge, travel, volunteer church work. Home: 39 Old Oak Ln Levittown NY 11756-4614

DYBOWSKI, DOUGLAS EUGENE, education educator, economist; b. Wiesbaden Air Base, Germany, Dec. 7, 1946; s. Eugene L. and Margaret Alma (Hart) D.; m. Deborah Jane Dalpiaz, Dec. 27, 1986; children: Noelle C., Eric W. BA in Govt. and Politics, U. Md., College Park, 1969; grad. edn. econ., Trinity U., San Antonio, 1971; Calif. teaching credential, Calif. State U., San Bernardino, 1975; AS in Computer Sci., San Bernardino Valley Coll., 1982. Stockman J.C. Penny Co., 1965; advtg. asst. Sears & Roebuck, Washington, D.C., 1966; air conditioning and heating asst. J&W Contractors, McLean, Va., 1967; legis. aide to hon. Michael Feighan, U.S. Congress, Washington, 1969; asst. mgr. Mr M Food Store, San Antonio, Tex., 1970-71; econ. Bur. Labor Statistics Dept. Labor, Dallas, 1971-73; fine jewelry salesman May Co., San Bernardino, Calif., 1974-78; tchr. Rialto and San Bernardino Sch. Dists., 1973-85; realtor Gallery of Homes, San Bernardino, Calif., 1979; tchr. Diocese of San Bernardino, Calif., 1985-87; instr. computer sci. San Bernardino Valley Coll., Calif., 1983-84; tchr. Colton (Calif.) Joint Unified Sch. Dist., 1987—; art ctr. San Bernardino, Calif., 1989-95. Cons. Rickert's Art Ctr. Artist (painting) San Bernardino County Mus., 1994, Riverside (Calif.) City Mus., 1997. Recipient Lounsbury Svc. award San Bernardino Valley Coll., 1982. Mem. Sigma Chi. Republican, Presbyterian. Avocations: art collecting, painting, gourmet cooking, letter writing, gardening. Office: Colton Joint Unified Sch Dist 1212 Valencia Dr Colton CA 92324-1798

DYCE, MICKEY, principal; b. Nashville, Jan. 30, 1949; s. John and Lucy (Vann) D.; m. Marsha Gayle Pigg, Oct. 8, 1971; 1 child, Jacob Michael. BS, Mid. Ten.. State U., 1971; Masters, Trevecca, 1987. Cert. tchr., Tenn. Tchr. East Cheatham Elem. Sch., Ashland City, Tenn., 1972-76, Sycamore Jr. High Sch., Pleasant View, Tenn., 1976-87, Cheatham County High Sch., Ashland City, 1976-87, asst. prin., athletic dir., 1987-89; prin. Pleasant View Elem. Sch., 1989—. Bd. dirs. Mid-Cumberland Community Action Agy., Murfreesboro, Tenn. Bd. dirs. United Way Tenn., Ashland City, 1990-91. Recipient Recognition award Dept. Edn. State Tenn., 1988, Outstanding Accomplishments award Servicemaster, 1989; named Tchr. of Yr., Cheatham County Edn. Assn., 1985. Mem. ASCD, Nat. Assn. Sch. Prins., So. Assn. Accredited Schs. and Colls. (com. mem.), Tenn. Assn. Elem. Sch. Prins., Tenn. Assn. for Sch. Supervision and Adminstrn., Ashland City C. of C. (b. dirs. 1992—). Baptist. Avocations: golf, hiking, family activities, hunting, fishing. Office: Pleasant View Elem 2625 Church St Pleasant View TN 37146-8157

DYCHE, KATHIE LOUISE, secondary school educator; b. Waynoka, Okla., Sept. 8, 1949; d. Loren Neil and Bessie Louise (Wait) Callaway; m. Steven Lee Dyche, July 5, 1969; children: Cherilyn Nettie, Bradley Callaway. BA in Edn. in Art, Northwestern Okla. State U., 1972; postgrad., Southwestern Okla. State U., 1975, 78, Phillips U., 1981, 83-85; MEd, U. Cen. Okla., 1993. Cert. art, Am. history and democracy tchr., Okla. Tchr. art Fairview (Okla.) Pub. Schs., 1973-81, cons., 1973-76; asst. to handicapped Glenwood Elem. Sch., Enid, Okla., 1982-83; reading and math. asst. Longfellow Jr. High Sch., Enid, 1983-84; tchr. art Emerson Jr. High Sch., Enid, 1984—; art cons. Endi Pub. Schs., 2000—. Freelance artist Gaslight Theater, Okla. Small Bus. Devel. Ctr., also others; represented by Galery of Fine Arts, Enid, Okla. Exhibited in group shows Amarillo (Tex.) Artists' Studio, 1975, Kallistos Invitational Show, 1985, Dean Lively Gallery, Edmond, Okla., Art Educators as Artists exhibit Philbrook, Tulsa, 1994, 96, Oklahoma Fall Arts Inst. Capitol Exhibit, Oklahoma City State Capitol, 1997. Pres., v.p., sec., historian, reporter Gamma Mother's Club, Fairview, 1973-80; co-chmn. Fairview Show of Arts, 1979, 80; art vol. Glenlwood Elem. Sch., 1981-82; pres., historian, parlimentarian Delta Child Study Club, Enid, 1981-84. Recipient Okla. Fall Arts Inst. Honor award, 1992, 94, 95-2001; Northwestern Okla. State U. scholar, 1968. Mem. NEA, Nat. Art Edn. Assn., Okla. Art Edn. Assn., Okla. Edn. Assn., Cardinal Key, Kappa Delta Pi, Delta Kappa Gamma (sec. 1986-88, scholar 1993, 2d v.p. 1994-96), Phi Delta Kappa (historian 1995-96, v.p. 1998—99). Episcopalian. Avocations: drawing, painting, designing clothes, reading, crafts. Office: Emerson Jr High Sch 700 W Elm Ave Enid OK 73701-3000

DYCK, GEORGE, psychiatry educator; b. Hague, Sask., Can., July 25, 1937; came to U.S., 1965; s. John and Mary (Janzen) D.; m. Edna Margaret Krueger, June 27, 1959; children: Brian Edward, Janine Louise, Stanley George, Jonathan Jay. Student, U. Sask., 1955-56; B of Christian Edn., Can. Mennonite Bible Coll., 1959; MD, U. Man., 1964; postgrad., Menninger Sch. Psychiatry, 1965-68. Diplomte in psychiatry and geriatric psychiatry Am. Bd. Psychiatry and Neurology; cert. psychiatrist Royal Coll. Physicians and Surgeons, Can. Fellow cmty. psychiatry Prairie View Mental Health Center, Newton, Kans., 1968-70; clin. dir. tri-county svcs. Prairie View Mental Health Ctr., 1970-73; prof. dept. of psychiatry U. Kans.-Wichita, Wichita, 1973—2002, chmn. dept. of psychiatry, 1973-80, 98-99; dir. geriatric psychiatry U. Kans., 1993-2001, prof. emeritus, 2002—; med. dir. Prairie View, Inc., 1980-89. Cons. Shenyang Psychiat. Hosp., People's Republic of China, 1990, Palestinian Mental Health Program, West Bank, 1990; mem. Kans. Hosp. Closure Commn., 1995; bd. dirs. Kidron Bethel Retirement Svcs., Newton, Kans., 1994-2002, chmn., 2001-02. Bd. dirs. Mennonite Mut. Aid, Goshen, Ind., 1973-85, Chmn., 1982-85; bd. dirs. Mid-Kans. Cmty. Action Program, 1970-73, Wichita Council Drug Abuse, 1974-76, Kauffman Mus. North Newton, 1995-98. Fellow Am. Psychiat. Assn. (pres. Kans. chpt. 1982-84, dep. rep. 1984-86, rep. 1986—, cert. in adminstrv. psychiatry 1984); mem. AMA, Kans. Med. Soc., Kans.-Paraguay Ptnrs. (treas. 1986-89). Mennonite. Home: 1505 Hillcrest Rd Newton KS 67114-1340 E-mail: gdyck@cox.net.

DYCK, WALTER PETER, gastroenterologist, educator, university official; b. Winkler, Man., Can., 1935; MD, U. Kans., 1961. Diplomate Am. Bd. Internal Medicine, Am. Bd. Gastroenterology. Intern Henry Ford Hosp., Detroit, 1961-62, resident in internal medicine, 1962-63, 65-66; rsch. fellow gastroenterology U. Zurich, Switzerland, 1963-64; fellow enzymology rsch. U. Toronto, Ont., Can., 1964-65; fellow gastroenterology Mt. Sinai Sch. Medicine, N.Y.C., 1966-68; mem. sr. staff Scott and White Clinic, Temple, Tex., 1968—, chmn. dept. rsch., 1969-72, dir. divsn. gastroenterology, 1972-96; prof. medicine, dir. divsn. gastroenterology Tex. A&M Coll. Medicine, 1978-96; adminstrv. dir. rsch. and edn. divsn., chief acad. officer Scott and White Meml. Hosp., Temple, 1996—; sr. assoc. dean Tex. A&M Coll. Medicine, 1996—. Mem. gen. medicine study sect. A NIH, 1973-77. Fellow ACP, Am. Coll. Gastroenterology; mem. AMA, Am. Fedn. Clin. Rsch., Am. Gastroenterology Assn., Am. Physiol. Soc., So. Soc. Clin. Investigation, Soc. for Exptl. Biology and Medicine, Am. Pancreatic Assn., N.Y. Acad. Scis. Office: Scott and White Hosp 2401 S 31st St Temple TX 76508-0002

DYE, LINDA KAYE, elementary school educator; b. Shelbyville, Tenn., Dec. 26, 1962; d. John William Dye and Adeline Stewart Dye Adams. BS, David Lipscomb Univ., Nashville, 1985; postgrad., Middle Tenn. State U. Title I reading tchr. Bedford County Bd. Edn., Shelbyville, Tenn. Mem. NEA, Tenn. Edn. Assn., Nat. Coun. Tchrs. English, Bedford County Edn. Assn.

DYE, NANCY SCHROM, academic administrator, historian, educator; b. Columbia, Mo., Mar. 11, 1947; d. Ned Stuart and Andrea Elizabeth (Ahrens) Schrom; m. Griffith R. Dye, Aug. 21, 1972; children: Molly, Michael. AB, Vassar Coll., 1969; MA, U. Wis., 1971, PhD, 1974. Asst. prof. U. Ky., Lexington, 1974—80, assoc. prof., 1980—88, prof., 1988, assoc. dean arts and scis., 1984—88; dean faculty Vassar Coll., Poughkeepsie, NY, 1988—92, acting pres., 1992—94; pres. Oberlin Coll., Oberlin, Ohio, 1994—. Author: As Equals And As Sisters, 1981; contbr. articles to profl. jours. Bd. mem. Pomona Coll. Mem.: Coun. Colls. of Art and Scis. (bd. dirs. 1980—91). Office: Oberlin Coll Cox Admin Bldg, Room 201 70 N Professor St Oberlin OH 44074-1090 Fax: 440-775-8937.

DYE, SALLY ANN, middle school educator; b. Cleve., June 3, 1947; d. Chester James and Sarah Ellen (Harris) Ullom; children: Tammy Dye Anderson, Terry Dye. BS in Elem. Edn., Ohio State U., 1979, MA in Edn., 1986. Social studies and reading tchr. 6th grade Cardington (Ohio) Lincoln Mid. Sch., 1980—. Sunday sch. tchr. Ctr. United Meth. Ch., 1978—, mem. adminstrv. bd., 1991—, sec. pastor parish rels. com., 1996—, United Meth. Ministries of So. Morrow County Coun., sec., 1996—, Sunday sch. treas., 1997—. Mem. AAUW (pres. Morrow County br. 1991-93, 99-2001, Ohio dist. coord. 1993-98, Ohio v.p. membership 1998-2000, program v.p. 2000-02, diversity chair 2002—), NEA, Ohio Edn. Assn., Internat. Reading Assn. (also Ohio Coun. and Morrow County Coun.), Ohio Coun. Tchrs. English Lang. Arts, Ohio State U. Alumni, Reveille Club (treas., 1998-2000, program v.p. 2001-03, pres. 2003), Delta Kappa Gamma Soc. (pres. chpt. 1996-98, treas. 2003—), Phi Delta Kappa. Avocations: reading, sports. Home: 157 S 3rd St Cardington OH 43315-1046 Office: Cardington Lincoln Mid Sch 349 Chesterville Ave Cardington OH 43315-9217

DYER, JAMES HAROLD, JR., language educator, educator; b. Christiansburg, Va., Mar. 23, 1946; s. James Harold and Dorothy Louise (Bennett) Dyer. BA in English, Augusta Coll., 1970; MEd in English Edn., Ga. State U., 1975, EdS in English Edn., 1978; PhD in Brit. Lit., U. S.C., 1992. Cert. secondary sch. tchr. S.C. English tchr. Aiken (S.C.) HS, 1975-79; prof. English Ga. Mil. Coll., Ft. Gordon, 1979—2000; prof. grad. English, grad. English MEd program coord. Troy State U., Augusta, Ga., 2002—. Grad. tchg. asst. U. S.C., Columbia, 1982—83. Mem.: MLA, Children's Lit. Assn., Dickens Fellowship, Lambda Iota Tau (Saul Bellow hon. pres.). Avocations: book collecting, chess, golf. Office: Troy State U Dept Grad English 2743 Perimeter Pky Ste 201 Augusta GA 30909

DYER, V. JEFFREY, educational administrator; b. Richardson, Tex., July 30, 1967; s. Van E. and Deborah L. Dyer; m. Robin Jane, Dec. 16, 1989; children: Drew Jeffrey, Abigail Marie. BS in Elem. Edn., Henderson St. U., 1989, MS in Elem. Adminstrn., 1995. Elem. tchr. Port Arthur Sch. Dist., Tex., 1989-91; mid. sch. tchr. Bryant Sch. Dist., Ark., 1991-92, elem. tchr., 1992-96; elem. asst. prin. Alma Sch. Dist., Ark., 1996—2001, Booneville Sch. Dist., Ark., 2001—. Area dir. Ark. Spl. Olympics, state tng. clinician, mem. games mgmt. team; coach World Summer Games Spl. Olympics, 1995, 99; Nat. Coach Team USA Special Olympics World Summer Games, Ireland, 2003, mem. Alma Vol. Fire Dept.; mem. Logan County Child Devel. Adv. Bd.; bd. dirs. South Logan County Boys and Girls Club, pres. of BGCSLC bd.; trustee Booneville United Meth. Ch.; apptd. Ark. Legis. Health Adequacy Adv. Com. Mem. NAESP, ASCD, Ark. Assn. Edn. Adminstrs., Henderson St. Alumni Bd., Saline Co. Henderson Alumni (charter, pres. 1993-95), Rotary Internat., Sigam Phi Epsilon. Avocations: golf, softball, reading, movies. Home: 980 E 6th St Booneville AR 72927 Office: 327 W 5th St Booneville AR 72927 E-mail: jdyer@bps.wsc.k12.ar.us.

DYER-COLE, PAULINE, school psychologist, educator; b. Methuen, Mass., Aug. 20, 1935; d. E. Dewey and Rose Alma (Des Jardins) Dyer; m. Richard Grey, Aug. 1, 1964 (dec. 1977); children: Douglas Richard, Christopher Lachlan, Heather Judith; m. Malcolm A. Cole, July 23, 1983. BS in Edn. and Music, Lowell State Coll., 1957; MEd, Boston State Coll., 1961; EdD, Clark U., 1991. Lic. ednl. psychologist, Mass.; cert. sch. psychologist, Mass.; nat. cert. sch. psychologist. Supr. music and art Merrimac and W. Newburg (Mass.) Pub. Schs., 1957-59; music editor textbooks Allyn & Bacon, Inc., Boston, 1959-64; prof. music West Pines Coll., Chester, N.H., 1969-72; sch. psychologist Nashoba Regional H.S., Bolton, Mass., 1979—2001, chair SPED dept., 1995—2001, dir. SPED dept., 1998—2001; child study dept. Worcester (Mass.) Pub. Schs., 2001—. Vis. lectr., then vis. prof. Framingham (Mass.) State Coll., 1980—; dir. psychol. testing Nashoba Regional Sch. Dist., Bolton, Mass., 1980-94. Author: The Play Game Songbook, 1964. V.p., bd. dirs. Timberlane Devel. Ctr., Plaistow, N.H., 1970-73; founder Friends of Kimi Nichols Devel. Ctr., Plaistow, N.H., 1973; chmn. human svcs. St. Ann Parish, Southborough, Mass., 1974-77, active, 1973-85; citizen amb. del. People to People, China, 1995; active The Regional Lab., Andover, Mass., 1993-2001. Recipient Frances L. Hyatt fellow, Clark U., 1977—79. Mem. Nat. Assn. Sch. Psychologists (cert.), Mass. Assn. Sch. Psychologists, Mass. Tchrs. Assn., People to People Internat. Roman Catholic. Avocations: music, boating, swimming, reading, creative writing. Home: 43 Crowningshield Dr Paxton MA 01612-1253 Office: Child Study Dept 24 Chatham St Worcester MA 01609 E-mail: dyercole@charter.net.

DYER-RAFFLER, JOY ANN, special education diagnostician, educator; b. Stiltner, W.Va., Aug. 10, 1935; d. Ralph William and Hazel (Terry) Dyer; m. John William Raffler, Sr., Jan. 1, 1993; 1 child from a previous marriage, Keith Brian DeArmond. BA, U. N.C., 1969; MEd in Secondary Edn., U. Ariz., 1974, MEd in Spl. Edn., 1976. Cert. spl. edn.-learning disabilities, art edn., spl. edn.-emotionally handicapped. Art educator Tucson Unified Sch. Dist., Tucson, 1970-75, spl. edn. educator, 1975-89, spl. edn. diagnostician, 1989—. Den mother Cub Scouts Am., Raleigh, N.C., 1968-69. Recipient grant Tucson Unified Sch. Dist., 1977. Mem. NEA, CEC, Learning Disabilities Assn. Avocations: oil painting, snow skiing, bird watching, weight lifting, jogging. Home: 4081 N Kolb Rd Tucson AZ 85750-6127 Office: Rosemont Svc Ctr 750 N Rosemont Blvd Tucson AZ 85711-1229

DYKES, BILL G. principal, administrator; b. Somerset, Ky., Mar. 21, 1947; s. Lloyd Samuel and Wanda Lee (Taylor) D.; m. Janet Morell, July 29, 1972; children: Heather Lynn, Benjamin Lee, Jennifer Layne, Bethany Leigh. BA, U. Ky., 1969; MEd, Xavier U., 1975. History and govt. tchr. Marion L. Steele High Sch., Amherst, Ohio, 1969-72; history tchr. Mt. Healthy (Ohio) Pub. High Sch., 1972-73, Landmark Christian Sch., Cin., 1973-74, asst. prin., 1974-78, prin., 1978-80, Blue Grass Bapt. Sch., Lexington, Ky., 1980-82; dir. admissions, registrar Lexington Bapt. Coll., 1983-94; prin., adminstr. Landmark Christian Sch., Cin., 1996-2000; assoc. dean acad. affairs, dean of enrollment svc.bd. regents Temple Bapt. Coll., 1998—, assoc. dean acad. affairs, dean enrollment svc., 2003—. Coach football Marion L. Steele High Sch., Amherst, 1969-71, Landmark Christian Sch., Cin., 1977-80; presenter Ky. Ednl. Cons., Lexington, 1989—. Active Dixie Elem. PTA, Lexington, 1983-96, Ashland Ave. Bapt. Ch., Lexington, 1980-96; coach, asst. coach No. Little League, Lexington, 1986-89, Landmark Bapt. Temple, Cin., 1996—. Mem. Ky. Assn. Coll. Registrars and Admissions Officers (exec. com. 1989-91), So. Assn. Coll. Registrars and Admissions Officers, Ky. Assn. Coll. Admissions Counselors. Avocations: baseball, football, reading. Home: 15 Maple St Cincinnati OH 45215

DYKMAN, ROSCOE ARNOLD, psychologist, educator; b. Pocatello, Idaho, Mar. 20, 1920; s. Henry Arnold and Mable (Balderston) D.; m. Virginia June Johnston, Sept. 17, 1941 (div. June 1975); children: Richard Arnold, Thomas Ross, Susan Lane, Laura Jane; m. Kathryn Donita Bowman, May 10, 1980. BS, George Williams Coll., 1946; PhD, U. Chgo., 1949. Instr. Ill. Inst. Tech., Chgo., 1948-50; postdoctoral fellow Johns Hopkins Med. Sch., Balt., 1950-52, instr., 1952-53; asst. dir. studies Assn. Am. Med. Colls., Chgo., 1953-55; assoc. prof. U. Ark. Med for Med. Scis., Little Rock, 1955-58, prof., dir. psychiat. rsch. lab., 1958-75, prof., head div. behavior scis., 1975-90; prof., head psychophysiology lab. Ark. Children's Hosp., Little Rock, 1990—. Grant reveiwer NIMH, Nat. Inst. for Child Health and Devel., 1990—. Contbr. articles to profl. jours., chpts. to books; cons. editor Jour. Learning Disabilities, 1975—. Elder St. Andrews Ch., Little Rock, 1967-70; mem. Ark. State Planning Commn. for Mental Health, Little Rock, 1980-83. Recipient Rsch. award NIMH, 1961-72, Disting. Scientist award Pavlovian Soc. Am., 1970, Pioneer award Learning Disabilities Soc., 1991. Fellow APA; mem. Am. Psychol. Soc., Psychophysiology Soc. (bd. dirs., cons. editor). Democrat. Presbyterian. Achievements include research in autonomic conditioning (heart rate and blood pressure), attentional deficit disorders, learning disabilities and nutrition. Home: 23103 Chandler Dr Little Rock AR 72210-4916 Office: Ark Children's Hosp Dept Pediatrics 1212 Marshall St Dept Little Rock AR 72202-3591

DYM, CLIVE LIONEL, engineering educator; b. Leeds, Eng., July 15, 1942; came to U.S., 1949, naturalized, 1954; s. Isaac and Anna (Hochmann) D.; children: Jordana, Miriam; m. Joan Dym, June 28, 1998. BCE, Cooper Union, 1962; MS, Poly. Inst. Bklyn., 1964; PhD, Stanford U., 1967. Asst. prof. SUNY, Buffalo, 1966-69; assoc. professorial lectr. George Washington U., Washington, 1969; research staff Inst. Def. Analyses, Arlington, Va., 1969-70; assoc. prof. Carnegie-Mellon U., Pitts., 1970-74; vis. assoc. prof. TECHNION, Israel, 1971; sr. scientist Bolt Beranek and Newman, Inc., Cambridge, Mass., 1974-77; prof. U. Mass., Amherst, 1977-91, head dept. civil engring., 1977-85; Fletcher Jones prof. engring. design Harvey Mudd Coll., Claremont, Calif., 1991—, dir. Ctr. Design Edn., 1995—, chair dept. engring., 1999—2002. Vis. sr. rsch. fellow Inst. Sound and Vibration Rsch., U. Southampton, Eng., 1973; vis. scientist Xerox PARC, 1983-84; vis. prof. civil engring. Stanford U., 1983-84, Carnegie Mellon U., 1990; Eshbach vis. prof. Northwestern U., 1997-98; cons. Bell Aerospace Co., 1967-69, Dravo Corp., 1970-71, Salem Corp., 1972, Gen. Analytics Inc., 1972, ORI, Inc., 1979, BBN Inc., 1979, Avco, 1981-83, 85-86, TASC, 1985-86, D.H. Brown Assocs., 1991, Johnson Controls, 1996; vice chmn. adv. bd. Amerinex Artificial Intelligence, 1986-88. Author: (with I.H. Shames) Solid Mechanics: A Variational Approach, 1973, Introduction to the Theory of Shells, rev. edit. 1990, Stability Theory and Its Applications to Structural Mechanics, 1974, 2002, (with E.S. Ivey) Principles of Mathematical Modeling, 1980, (with I.H. Shames) Energy and Finite Element Methods in Structural Mechanics, 1985, (with R.E. Levitt) Knowledge-Based Systems in Engineering, 1990, Engineering Design: A Synthesis of Views, 1994, Structural Modeling and Analysis, 1997, (with P. Little) Engineering Design: A Project-Based Introduction, 1999, 2d edit., 2003, (with P.D. Cha and J.J. Rosenberg), Fundamentals of Modeling and Analyzing Engineering Systems, 2000; editor: (with A. Kalnins) Vibration: Beams, Plates, and Shells, 1977, Applications of Knowledge-Based Systems to Engineering Analysis and Design, 1985, Computing Futures in Engineering Design, 1997, Designing Design Education for the 21st Century, 1999, (with L. Winner) Social Dimensions of Engineering Design, 2001, Artificial Intelligence for Engring. Design Analysis and Mfg., 1986-96; contbr. articles and tech. reports to profl. publs. NATO sr. fellow in sci., 1973; Outstanding Engring. Educator award (first-runnerup), 2001. Fellow Acoustical Soc. Am., ASME, ASCE (Walter L. Huber research prize 1980); mem. Am. Assn. for Artificial Intelligence, Computer Soc. of IEEE, ASEE (Western Electric Fund award 1983, Fred Merryfield Design award 2002). Jewish. Office: Harvey Mudd Coll Engring Dept 301 E 12th St Claremont CA 91711-5901

DYMACEK, BILLY JOE, retired secondary school educator; b. Wichita, Jan. 10, 1943; s. Joseph Edward and Wilma Modd (Law) D.; m. Merilee Sue Neis, June 5, 1971; children: Kristen Maureen, Wendy Lynn. BA, Southwestern Coll., Wingfield, Kans., 1967; MS, No. Ariz. U., 1972. Tchr. sci. and computer sci. Unified Sch. Dist. 231, Gardner, Kans., 1967—2001. Mem. Douglas County Fair Bd., Lawrence, Kans., 1981; mem. coun. St. Paul United Ch. of Christ, 1968-72, 74-76, 78-80, 2002—. Southwestern Bell grantee, 1987; recipient Excellence in Tchg. award Kans. Earth Sci. Tchrs., 2000. Mem. NEA, Kans. Assn. Mid-Level Educators, Nat. Sci. Tchrs. Assn. Democrat. Avocations: fossil collecting, woodworking, shooting sports, painting, antiques. Office: Nike Middle Sch I-35 At Gardner Rd Gardner KS 66030

DYNES, ROBERT C. academic administrator; b. London, Ont., Can., Nov. 8, 1942; m. Frances Hellman. BS of Math. & Physics, U. Western Ont., 1964; MS of Physics, McMaster U., 1965, PhD of Phys., 1968. Postdoctoral fellow AT&T Bell Labs, Murray Hill, NJ, 1968—70, mem., technical staff, 1970—74, dept. head, semiconductor & chem. physics rsch., 1974—81, dept. head, solid state & physics of materials rsch., 1981—83, dir., chem. physics rsch., 1983—90; physics prof. U. Calif., San Diego, 1991—2003; chair, dept. physics U. Calif, San Diego, 1994—95; sr. vice chancellor, acad. affairs U. Calif., 1995—96, Chancellor, 1996—2003, U. Calif. System, Oakland, 2003—. Recipient Fritz London award Low Temp. Physics, 1990. Fellow: Can. Inst. Advances Rsch., Am. Phys. Soc.; mem.: Am. Acad. Arts & Scis., Nat. Acad. Scis. Office: Office of Pres U Calif System 1111 Franklin St Oakland CA 94607-5200*

DYSON, ANNE HAAS, English language educator; BS in Elem. Edn., U. Wis., 1972; MEd in Curriculum and Instrn. (Reading), U. Tex., 1976, PhD in Curriculum and Instrn. (Lang. Arts/Reading), 1981. Elem. tchr. 2d grade El Paso Cath. Diocese, Tex., 1972-73; adult educator Crawford English Acad., El Paso, Tex., 1973; substitute tchr. Austin Ind. Sch. Dist., Tex., 1974-75, presch. tchr. for 4 yr olds, 1975, elem. tchr. 1st grade, 1977-79; dir., staff coord. learning abilities ctr. materials lab., tutoring coord. learning abilities ctr. U. Tex., Austin, 1975-76, teaching asst., 1975-77, instr., 1979-80, rsch. asst., 1981, grad. fellow, 1980-81; head tchr., coord. summer lang. arts/reading program Alamo Heights Ind. Sch. Dist., San Antonio, 1978; asst. prof. dept. lang. edn. U. Ga., 1981-85, grad. faculty, 1984-85; vis. asst. prof. divsn. lang. and literacy sch. of edn. U. Calif., Berkeley, 1984-85, asst. prof. divsn. lang. and literacy sch. of edn., 1985-87, assoc. prof. divsn. lang. and literacy sch. of edn., 1987-91, prof. divsn. lang. and literacy sch. of edn., 1991—2002, co-dir. Ctr. for the Study of Writing and Literacy, 1990—2002; prof. tchr. edn. Mich. State U., 2002—. Author: Multiple Worlds of Child Writers: A Study of Friends Learning to Write, 1989; co-author: Language Assessment in the Early Years, 1984; editor: Collaboration Through Writing and Reading: Exploring Possibilities, 1989; contbr. articles to profl. jours., contbr. chpts. to books; editor, adv. bd. mem. Early Childhood Yearbook, 1990—; mem. editl. bd. Research in the Teaching of English, 1992—, Language and Literacy, 1989—; co-editor rsch. currents dept. Language Arts, 1983-90; editor Newsletter of the Spl. Interest Group in Language Devel. Am. Ednl. Rch. Assn., 1984-86; speaker in field. Recipient Annual Human Rights award Oakland Baha'is, 1991, Lois Gadd Nemec Disting. Alumni award U. Wis., 1990, Promising Rechr. award Nat. Coun. Tchrs. of English, 1982, award for Excellence in Ednl. Journalism Ednl. Press Assn. Am., 1982.*

DYSON, ROBERT HARRIS, museum director emeritus, archaeologist, educator; b. York, Pa., Aug. 2, 1927; s. Robert and Harriet Myrtle (Duck) D. AB, Harvard U., 1950, PhD, 1966; AM (hon.), U. Pa., 1971. Asst. curator, asst. prof. U. Pa. Mus., Phila., 1955-62, assoc. curator, assoc. prof., 1962-67, curator, prof., 1967-95; curator, prof. emeritus, 1995—; dean faculty arts and scis. U. Pa., Phila., 1979-82; dir. mus. U. Pa. Mus., Phila., 1982-94; dir. emeritus, 1995—; field dir. Iran expdn. U. Pa. Mus., Phila., 1956-77. Hon. trustee Am. Inst. Iranian Studies, 1975-78, 79—, pres., 1968, 87-89; mem. Archaeological Inst. Am., pres., 1979-81; mem. Brit. Sch. Archaeology Iraq, Brit. Inst. of Persian Studies. Decorated chevalier de l'Ordre des Artes et des Lettres (France); Order Houmouyan 4th rank (Iran). Mem. Soc. Fellows Harvard U., Am. Philos. Soc., Deutschen Archäologischen Inst., Inst. Italiano per l'Africa e l'Oriente. Office: U Pa Mus Archaeology & Anthropology 33rd & Spruce Sts Philadelphia PA 19104 E-mail: robertd@sas.upenn.edu.

DZIEWANOWSKA, ZOFIA ELIZABETH, neuropsychiatrist, pharmaceutical executive, researcher, educator; b. Warsaw, Nov. 17, 1939; came to U.S., 1972; d. Stanislaw Kazimierz Dziewanowski and Zofia Danuta (Mieczkowska) Rudowska; m. Krzysztof A. Kunert, Sept. 1, 1961 (div. 1971); 1 child, Martin. MD, U. Warsaw, 1963; PhD, Polish Acad. Sci., 1970. MD recert. U.K., 1972, U.S., 1973. Asst. prof. of psychiatry U. Warsaw Med. Sch., 1969-71; sr. house officer St. George's Hosp., U. London, 1971-72; assoc. dir. Merck Sharp & Dohme, Rahway, N.J., 1972-76; vis. assoc. physician Rockefeller U. Hosp., N.Y.C., 1975-76; adj. asst. prof. of psychiatry Cornell U. Med. Ctr., N.Y.C., 1978—; v.p., global med. dir. Hoffmann-La Roche, Inc., Nutley, N.J., 1976-94; sr. v.p. and dir. global med. affairs Genta Inc., San Diego, 1994-97; sr. v.p. drug devel. and regulatory Cypros Pharms. Corp., Carlsbad, Calif., 1997-99; pres., med. dir. New Drug Assocs., La Jolla, Calif., 1999—; sr. v.p. clin. and regulatory Maxia Pharms, San Diego, 2001—02; v.p. clin. rsch. Ligand Pharm, Inc., San Diego, 2002—. Lectr. in field. Contbr. articles to profl. publs. Bd. dirs Royal Soc. Medicine Found.; mem. alumni coun. Cornell U. Med. Ctr. Recipient TWIN Honoree award for Outstanding Women in Mgmt., Ridgewood (N.J.) YWCA, 1984. Mem. AMA, AAAS, Am. Soc. Pharmacology and Therapeutics, Am. Coll. Neuropsychopharmacology, N.Y. Acad. Scis., PhRMA. (vice chmn. steering com. med. sect., chmn. internat. med. affairs com., head biotech. working group), Royal Soc. Medicine (U.K.), Drug Info. Assn. (Woman of Yr. award 1994), Am. Assn. Pharm. Physicians. Roman Catholic. Achievements include original research on the role of the nervous system in the regulation of respiratory functions, research and development and therapeutic uses of many new drugs, pharmaceutical medicine and biotechnology; molecular biology derived as well as conventional products including antisense, interferon efficacy in cancer, virology and AIDS and drugs useful in cardiovascular, immunological, neuropsychiatric, infectious diseases, and others; impact of different cultures on medical practices and clinical research; drug evaluation and development management strategies of pharmaceutical industries; treatments against cardiac and brain ischemia, cytoprotection; speaker in field.

DZIEWANOWSKI, MARIAN KAMIL, history educator; b. Ukraine, Russia, June 27, 1913; came to U.S., 1947, naturalized, 1953; s. Kamil Antoni and Zofia (Kamienska) D.; m. Ada Karczewska, Oct. 4, 1946; children: Barbara, Jan. MLaw, Warsaw U. (Poland), 1937; diploma, Warsaw French Inst., 1937; MA, Harvard U., 1948, PhD, 1951. Commentator BBC, London, 1942-44; rsch. fellow Russian Rsch. Ctr., Harvard U., 1949-52; rsch. assoc. Ctr. Internat. Studies, MIT, 1952-53; prof. history Boston Coll., 1954-65; Ford exchange prof. Poland, 1958; exchange scholar, 1960; vis. prof. Brown U., Providence, 1961-62, 68, NATO, 1972-73; prof. history Boston U., 1965-78, U. Wis., Milw., 1979—. Assoc. Russian Rsch. Ctr., Harvard U., 1960-68; vis. prof. European Inst., Florence, Italy, 1979; lectr. in field. Author: The Communist Party of Poland, 1959, 76, Chinese edit., 1994, Joseph Pilsudski: A European Federalist, 1969, Poland in the 20th Century, 1977, 80, A History of Soviet Russia, 1979, 85, 89, 92, 96, Chinese edit., 1990, War at Any Price: World War II in Europe, 1939-45, 1987, 2d edit., 1990, Alexander I: Russia's Mysterious Tsar, 1990, Polish Edit., 1999, Russian edit., 2003, One Life is Not Enough: Memoirs of an incorrigible optimist, 1995, Wellington Destroyer of Napoleon, 1997, Prince Adam Czartoryski, 1998, Napoleon, 1998, Russia in the 20th Century, 2002; co-author 30 other books.; editor: The Russian Revolution, 1970; co-editor: Documentation the History of European Integration, 1985; contbr. articles to profl. jours. Lt. Polish Army, 1939-46, Polish, French campaigns; asst. to mil. asst. attaché 1944, Washington. Decorated Polish Cross of Valor (two), Polish Order of Merit, British medal WWII. Fellow Polish Inst. Arts and Scis. in Am.; mem. Am. Assn. Advancement Slavic Studies, Polish Acad. Arts and Sci. (corr. mem. Cracow, Poland). Home: 3352 N Hackett Ave Milwaukee WI 53211-2943

DZIUK, PHILIP JOHN, animal scientist educator; b. Foley, Minn., Mar. 24, 1926; s. Edmund William and Ellen Catherine (Carlin) D.; m. Patricia Rosemary Weber, Sept. 29, 1951; children: Corinne, Constance, Rita, Catherine, Kenneth, Ronald, Carl. BS, U. Minn., 1950, MS, 1952, PhD, 1955. From rsch. asst. to rsch. assoc. U. Minn., Mpls., 1950-55; from asst. prof. to prof. U. Ill., Urbana, 1955-88, prof. emeritus, 1988—. Cons. Upjohn, Abbott, Eli Lilly, Am. Cynamid, Schering, Batelle, Advisys; reviewer of grants NIH, Bethesda, Md., 1982-86, USDA, Beltsville, Md., 1983-89. Contbr. peer reviewed publs. in sci. and profl. jours. With USN, 1945-46. Fellow Lalor Found., 1958, 61, Pig Industry Devel. Authority, Eng., 1961; recipient Achievement in Rsch. award Am. Fertility Soc., 1970, Sr. Scientist award Alexander von Humboldt Found., 1981, Pioneer award Internat. Embryo Transfer Soc., 2001, Outstanding Achievement award U. Minn., 2002. Mem. AAAS, KC, Am. Assn. Anatomist, Am. Soc. Animal Scis. (fellow 1987, Rsch. in Physiology award 1971), Soc. Study of Fertility, Soc. Study of Reproduction (dir., pres. 1987-88, Disting. Svc. award 1989), Lions Internat. (pres., sec. 1992-94), Farm House, Sigma Xi, Gamma Alpha, Phi Kappa Phi, Phi Zeta, Gamma Sigma Delta, Alpha Zeta. Avocations: woodworking, gardening, racquetball. Office: U Ill Dept Animal Scis 1207 W Gregory Dr Urbana IL 61801-4733

DZUIBLINSKI, GERARD ARTHUR, theatre educator, artistic director; b. Detroit, Sept. 23, 1954; s. Arthur Harold and Irene (Rogacki) D.; m. Anne Mansfield, Oct. 12, 1991; 1 chld, Illyana. BA in Comms. and Learning Environments, Antioch Coll., 1975; MA in Directing, Antioch U., 1991. Ednl. cons. Project Headline, Detroit, 1976; co-dir. Fantasy Theatre, Detroit, 1977-78; artistic dir. Exptl. Performing Arts Assn., Chira Twp., Mich., 1978—; theatre faculty Wayne County C.C., Detroit, 1979-87; dir. Theatre for Young Audiences, Henry Ford C.C., 1989—; children's theatre instr. Marygrove Coll., Detroit, 1982-96; TV acting faculty Detroit Bd. Edn., 1985-87; adj. theatre faculty Henry Ford C.C., Dearborn, Mich., 1987—, tech. dir., 1996—; drama dir. Crestwood H.S., Dearborn Hts., Mich., 1993-98; TV acting faculty Casablancas Model and Talent, Sterling Hts., Mich., 1996-99. Bd. dirs. Pathway Family Ctr. Author: (play) The Lion Roars, 1996; adaptor: (play) A Christmas Carol, 1995, Pinnochio, 1996; co-author: (handbook) Our New Family: Instructor's Guidebook, 1991, (Cable mini-series) The Gerry the Fool Show, 1986, (mime show) Only Fooling, 1983. Recipient Keystone award, and other awards for best prodn., scenic design, lighting design, tech. dir. and makeup design Dearborn Press and Guide. Mem.: ASCD, Network of Performing and Visual Arts Schs. Office: Henry Ford CC 5101 Evergreen Rd Dearborn MI 48128-2407 Personal E-mail: gdzub@hotmail.com.

EACHO, ESTHER MACLIVELY, special education educator; b. Springfield, Mass., Feb. 28, 1943; d. Charles James and Mary Eileen (May) MacL.; m. Robert Lee Eacho, Sept. 11, 1971; 1 child, Carla Eileen. BS in Edn., Westfield (Mass.) State Coll., 1964; MA in Edn., Am. Internat. Coll., 1969; M in Learning Disabilities, Am. U., 1990; postgrad., Harvard U., 1998. Cert. tchr., Va., Md., Conn. Classroom tchr., Conn., Md., 1964-71; pres. Eileen-Lee Assocs., McLean, Va., 1979-83; v.p. ops. Fabulous Foodstuffs, Ltd., Alexandria, Va., 1983-89; dir. of learning disabilities program Seton Cts., Falls Church, Va., 1989-92; learning disabilities specialist Fairfax County Pub. Schs., Va., 1992—; edn. specialist, cons. Va., 1998—. Bd. dirs. Gourm-E-Co Imports, Sterling, Va. V.p., sec. Jr. Woman's Club, McLean, 1972-79. Mem. ASCD, ASTD, CEC. Avocations: reading, travel, cooking, creative design.

EADS, ALBERT E., JR., school system administrator; b. Chgo., Aug. 30, 1937; s. Albert E. and Pauline (White) E.; m. Margaret Oliver, Dec. 31, 1957; children: Rosemarie, Albert E. III, Randy, David, Ellen. BS, The Citadel, Charleston, S.C., 1959; MEd, Duke U., 1964; advanced cert., U. S.C., 1973, PhD, 1974. Cert. English, social sudies, gen. sci., elem. reading tchr., reading supr., elem. and secondary prin., supt., S.C. Prin. Riverland Terr. Elem. Sch., 1960-63, Stiles Point Elem. Sch., Charleston, S.C., 1963-66, St. John's High Sch., Darlington, S.C., 1976-84, Gaffney (S.C.) High Sch., 1984-86; supt. schs. Hampton Dist. 2, Estill, S.C., 1988-96; exec. dir. S.C. Assn. for Rural Edn., St. George, SC, 1996—2002; pres. Nat. Rural Edn. Assn., 2002—. Contbr. articles to profl. publs. Recipient numerous civic awards; fellow NDEA. Mem. ASCD, Am. Assn. Sch. Adminstrs. (S.C. Supt. Yr. 1994), Nat. Assn. Secondary Sch. Prins., Internat. Reading Assn., S.C. Optimists (past gov.), Phi Delta Kappa, Kappa Delta Pi.

EAGAN, JOHN GAYLE, business educator; b. New Castle, Pa., Aug. 4, 1945; s. J. Gayle and M. Carolyn (Book) E. BSBA, Youngstown U., 1967; MBA, Ohio U., 1968. Instr. Erie Community Coll., Buffalo, 1971-78, asst. prof., 1978-82, assoc. prof., 1982-86, prof. bus., 1986—, chair dept. bus., 1991—. Lectr. Buffalo Urban League, 1992—. Dep. sheriff Erie County Sheriff's Dept. Sci. Staff, Buffalo, 1977—; bd. dirs. West Side Bus. and Taxpayers Assn., 1990—. Mem. NEA, Acad. Mgmt., Judges and Police Conf., K.C., Moose, Kiwanis, Phi Kappa Phi. Republican. Roman Catholic. Home: 770 W Ferry St Apt 21B Buffalo NY 14222-2401 Office: Erie Community Coll 121 Ellicott St Buffalo NY 14203-2601

EAGAN, SUSAN LAJOIE, finance educator, consultant; b. Worcester, Mass., Oct. 31, 1951; d. Alexander George Lajoie, Jr. and Nora Lajoie; m. Patrick L. Eagan; 1 child, Nora Elizabeth. BA summa cum laude, U. Mass., 1973; M Pub. Policy, Harvard U., 1975, PhD Pub. Policy, 1978. Exec. dir. Mardel Ctr. for Nonprofit Orgns. Case Western Reserve U., Cleve., 2001—; Mandel prof. Case Western Reserve U., Cleve., 2001—. Instr. U. Mass., Boston, 1977—78. Exec. v.p. Cleve. Found., 1999—2001, assoc. dir., 1990—99, asst. dir., 1986—90, program officer, 1982—86, program analyst, 1980—82, cons., 1978—80; co-chair Ohi Cts. Futures Commn., Columbus, 1996—2000; mem. Ohio Commn. on the Pub. Svc., 1992—93, Cleve. Bicentennial Legacy Com., 1993—94; trustee Inst. Ednl. Renewal. Recipient Woman of Influence award, Crain's Cleve. Bus., 1997, Carrer Woman of Achievement award, YWCA, Cleve., 2000. Mem.: Inst. Ednl. Renewal, Ohio Assn. Nonprofit Orgns., Women's Cmty. Found., Found. Ctr., Phi Kappa Phi, Phi Beta Kappa. Avocations: reading, hiking, music, gardening. Office: Case Western Reserve U 10900 Euclid Ave Cleveland OH 44106 Fax: 216-368-8592. Business E-Mail: sle7@po.cwru.edu.

EAGLESON, PETER STURGES, civil engineer, environmental engineer, educator; b. Phila., Feb. 27, 1928; s. William Boal and Helen (Sturges) E.; m. Marguerite Anne Partridge, May 28, 1949 (div.); children: Helen Marie, Peter Sturges, Jeffrey Partridge; m. Beverly Grossmann Rich, Dec. 27, 1974. BS in Civil Engring, Lehigh U., 1949, MS, 1952; Sc.D., MIT, 1956; D of Engring. (hon.), Lehigh U., 1998. Jr. engr. George B. Mebus (cons. engr.), Glenside, Pa., 1950-51; teaching asst. Lehigh U., 1951-52; research asst. Mass. Inst. Tech., 1952-54; mem. faculty MIT, 1954-93, prof. civil engring., 1965-93, head dept. civil engring., 1970-75, emeritus prof. civil and environ. engring., 1993—. Vis. asso. Calif. Inst. Tech., 1975-76; Fulbright sr. research scholar Commonwealth Sci. and Indsl. Research Orgn., Canberra, Australia, 1966-67 Author: (with others) Estuary and Coastline Hydrodynamics, 1966, Dynamic Hydrology, 1970, Ecohydrology, 2002. Served to 2d lt. C.E. AUS, 1949-50. Recipient Desmond Fitzgerald medal, 1959, Clemens Herschel prize, 1965 both Boston Soc. Civil Engrs., rsch. prize ASCE, 1963, William Bowie medal Am. Geophysical Union, 1994, Stockholm Water prize Stockholm Water Found., 1997. Fellow AAAS, Am. Meteorol. Soc. (hon.), Am. Geophys. Union (Robert E. Horton award 1979, Robert E. Horton medal 1988, pres. 1986-88, William Bowie medal 1994), Internat. Assn. Hydrological Scis. (Internat. Hydrology prize 1991); mem. NAE, European Geophys. Soc. (John Dalton medal 1999). Office: MIT Dept Civil & Environ Engring Room 48-335 Cambridge MA 02139

EAKIN, RICHARD RONALD, academic educator, mathematics educator; b. New Castle, Pa., Aug. 6, 1938; s. Everett Glenn and Mildred May (Hammerschmidt) E.; m. Jo Ann McGeehan, Aug. 23, 1960; children: Matthew Glenn, Maridy Lynn. AB in Math., Geneva Coll., Beaver Falls, Pa., 1960; MA in Math., Washington State U., 1962, PhD in Math., 1964. Asst. prof. math. Bowling Green (Ohio) State U., 1964-68, assoc. prof. math., 1968-87, asst. dean grad. sch., 1969-72, vice-provost student affairs, 1972-80, vice-provost instl. planning, 1979-80, exec. vice-provost budgeting and planning, 1980-83, v.p. budgeting and planning, 1983-87; chancellor, prof. math. East Carolina U., Greenville, 1987—2001, prof. edl. leadership., 2001—. Editor revs. and evaluations sect. (jour.) The Math. Tchr., 1968-70. V.p. and mem. bd. dirs. Nat. Hemophilia Found., N.Y.C., 1983-84, chmn. bd., v.p. adminstrn. and fin., 1984-87; mem. bd. dirs. Ednl. Commn. for Fgn. Med. Grads., 2002—. NDEA fellow Wash. State U., Pullman, 1960-63, NSF fellow, 1963-64. Mem. Math. Assn. Am., So. Assn. Colls. and Schs. (commn. on colls.), Phi Kappa Phi, Omicron Delta Kappa. Office: East Carolina U Ragsdale Bldg Rm 219 Greenville NC 27858

EAMES, SHERRY DIANE, educational consultant; b. Valparaiso, Ind., June 28, 1948; d. Thomas Andrew and Betty Margaret (Gustafson) Rees; m. Edward Arthur Eames, July 28, 1990. BS, Ind. U., 1970; MS, Ind. State U., 1974, cert. in adminstrn., 1987. Cert. tchr., Ind. Elem. tchr. Sch. City of Hobart, Ind., 1970-74, 75-79, 1990-92, asst. prin., 1989-90; elem. tchr. Dept. Def., Ramstein, Germany, 1974-75; edn. cons. Ind. Dept. Edn., Indpls., 1993—. Mem. Network for Women Adminstrs., Pi Lambda Theta, Phi Delta Kappa. Avocations: sewing, needlework, travel. Home: 1640 Fieldbrook St Henderson NV 89052-6475 Office: Ind Dept Edn State House Rm 229 Indianapolis IN 46204-2728

EARHART, LUCIE BETHEA, volunteer, former secondary school educator; b. Atlanta, July 17, 1954; d. Rufus Hagood and Jacqueline (Harrington) Bethea; m. Philip Charles Earhart, Nov. 27, 1976; 1 child, Carolyn Frances. BA, U. of South, 1976; MEd, U. New Orleans, 1989. Asst. actuary Waters-Parkerson, New Orleans, 1976-80, Franklin H. Jones & Co., Inc., New Orleans, 1980-81; tchr. math. Jefferson Parish Sch. Bd., Metairie, La., 1984, St. Martin's Episcopal Sch., Metairie, 1984-85, Crescent City Bapt. Sch., Metairie, 1987-90, Calcasien Parish Sch. System, Lake Charles, La., 1990-94. Bd. dirs. Lake Charles Symphony. Mem. Jane Austen Soc., Jr. League of Lake Charles. Republican. Episcopalian. Avocations: reading, needlework. Home: 5001 W St Charles St Lake Charles LA 70605-6754

EARLE, ELIZABETH DEUTSCH, biology educator; b. Vienna, Oct. 6, 1937; came to U.S., 1939; d. George F. and Sabina (Edel) Deutsch; m. Clifford J. Earle, Jr., Dec. 27, 1960; children: Rebecca A., Susan D. BA, Swarthmore Coll., 1959; MA, Radcliffe Coll., 1960; PhD, Harvard U., 1964. Rsch. fellow biology Harvard U., Cambridge, Mass., 1968-69; rsch. assoc. floriculture Cornell U., Ithaca, N.Y., 1970-74, rsch. assoc. plant breeding, 1975-78, sr. rsch. assoc. plant breeding, 1978-79, assoc. prof. plant breeding, 1979-86, prof. plant breeding, 1986—; vis. scholar biology Stanford (Calif.) U., 1986, chmn. plant breeding, 1993-2001. Mem. NSF Rev. Panel, Washington, 1979—82, USDA Rev. Panel, Washington, 1983—85; dir. Plant Tissue Culture FacilityC Cornell U., Ithaca, 1983—89; cons. on internat. biotech. issues. Editor Plant Cell Reports, 1986—. Trustee Cornell U., 2002—. Recipient predoctoral fellowship NSF, 1959-63, postdoctoral fellowship NIH, 1964-65; grantee NSF, USDA, Dept. Energy, Industry, 1978—. Mem.: Crucifer Genetics Coop., Am. Soc. Plant Biologists, Internat. Assn. Plant Tissue Culture, Phi Beta Kappa, Sigma Xi. Achievements include development of procedures for tissue culture and genetic manipulation of maize, sorghum, brassica, tomato, potato; development of improved cytoplasmic male-sterile and disease and insect-resistant lines of brassica vegetables. Office: Cornell U Dept Plant Breeding 514 Bradfield Hall Ithaca NY 14853-1901 E-mail: ede3@cornell.edu.

EARLE, JAMES ANTHONY, education consultant; b. St. Louis, Aug. 18, 1945; s. William C. Earle Jr. and Dorothy C. (Kersting) Wieck; m. Portia K. Newport, June 13, 1970; children: James A. Jr., John W. BS in Edn., Cen. Mo. State U., 1968; MS, NE Mo. U., 1973; PhD, U. Ill., 1981; adminstrv. cert., So. Ill. U., 1987. Cert. phys. edn. and health tchr., elem. prin., supt., Mo. Elem. sch. prin. Sch. Dist. Riverview Gardens, St. Louis, 1986-97; exec. dir. Solutions for Edn., 1997—. Adj. prof. NE Mo. State U., Kirksville, 1974-98. Recipient Bravo award St. Louis County, 1991. Mem. ASCD, NAESP, AAHPERD, Mo. Assn. Elem. Sch. Prins., Phi Delta Kappa, Phi Epsilon Kappa. Home and Office: 3905 Sunnyvale Ct Florissant MO 63034-3217

EARLS, IRENE ANNE, art history educator; d. William Thomas and Constance Ellen (Yanalavage) O'Connor; m. Walter Edward Earls, June 21, 1958. BA, U. Miami, Coral Gables, Fla., 1959; MA, U. Colo., 1968; PhD, U. Ga., 1975. Tchr. advanced placement history of art, English lang. and composition, advanced placement English lit. and composition Orlando (Fla.) Pub. Schs.; prof. classics dept. U. Fla., Gainesville, 1994—. Author: Book Renaissance Art, 1987, Napoléon III l'Architecte et l'Urbaniste de Paris, 1991, Baroque Art, 1997, Young Musicians in World History, 2003; contbr. articles to profl. jours. Named Tchr. of Yr., 1987-88, Nat. Honor Soc. Tchr. of Yr., 1987-88, also others. Mem. Western Soc. French History (officer of program com.), Soc. for French Hist. Studies, Consortium on Revolutionary Europe. Avocation: writing. Office: 1625 Beulah Rd Winter Garden FL 34787-4407

EARLY, JOHNNIE L., II, pharmacy educator; b. Macon, Ga. s. Johnnie L. and Florine (Mongeon) E.; m. Diane Seay, Aug. 21, 1971; children: Tiffanie S., Johnnie L. III. Student, Ft. Valley State Coll., 1967-70; BS, Mercer U., 1973; MS, Purdue U., 1976, PhD, 1978. Asst. prof. Fla. A&M U., Tallahassee, 1978-81, program dir. MBRS, 1980-87, assoc. prof., 1981-88, prof., 1988-93, asst. dean rsch., 1980-87, program dir. RCMI, 1985-93, dean Coll. of Pharmacy, 1987-93; dean, prof. Coll. Pharmacy Med. U. S.C., Charleston, 1994-2000; dean, prof. The U. of Toledo/Coll. of Pharmacy, 2000—. Cons. HHS, USPHS, NIH, NIGMS, MARC, Washington, 1989-93; mem. NIH/NCRR, Washington, 1983—. Contbr. articles to profl. jours. Bd. dirs. Fla. Edn. Fund, 1990-93, Pharm. Edn. and Devel. Found., 1994-2000. Mem. Nat. Pharm. Assn. (pres. 1996-98), Soc. Toxicology, Purdue Alumni Assn., Phi Beta Sigma, Sigma Pi Phi. Democrat. Avocations: photography, jogging, fishing. Office: The Univ of Toledo Coll Pharmacy PO Box 250141 2801 W Bancroft St Toledo OH 43606-3328

EARNEST, C. LYNN, art educator, sculptor, artist; b. Welch, W.Va., Oct. 4, 1946; d. Melville McKinney and Irene Delores (Cardea) E. BA, Queens Coll., Charlotte, N.C., 1968; MFA, George Washington U., 1970. Social worker W.Va. Dept. Welfare, Welch, 1964-65; microscopic illustrator NSF Grants Queens Coll., Charlotte, 1966-68; art dept. asst. Queens Coll., Charlotte, 1967-68; biomed. abstractor Tracor, Washington, 1969-70; pvt. practice artist Fine Arts Studio, Chgo., 1970-74; farm owner, operator spl. breeding Arabian horse Old Schoolhouse Hollow Farm, Griffithsville, W.Va., 1974—; prof. fine arts So. W.Va. C.C., Logan, 1974—, lead tchr. humanities dept., 1991-92. Artist-in-residence Huntington (W.Va.) Galleries, 1970-74; guest faculty, lectr. W.Va. State Coll., 1970-74; workshop presenter Cabell County Bd. Edn., Huntington, W.Va., 1970-74; pub. awareness cons. W.Va. Dept. Culture and History, 1976; mem. editl. adv. bd. Collegiate Press, Alta Loma, Calif.; instr. and cons. Talented in Hamlin, W.Va. Sch. Sys.; lectr. Spkrs. Bur. of W.Va. Dept. of Humanities Inst.; resource cons. W.Va. U. Ext. Svc.; environ. design cons. Lincoln Sch. Design, Hamlin, W.Va.; resource cons. State of W.Va. Ednl. TV Networks; spkr./lectr. in field. One-woman shows include Stifel Fine Arts Ctr., Wheeling, W.Va., 2000, exhibited in group shows at Charleston (W.Va.) Town Ctr. Gallery, Nat. Bank Commerce, Charleston, Huntington Gallery, Genesis, Huntington, Mary Washington Coll., Washington, Dimock Gallery, Carol Hall Gallery, Charlotte, Lift Head Gallery, Bluefield, W.Va., others. Mem. AAUW, ACLU, NOW. Avocations: horsewoman, swimming, biking, sport driving. Home: Old Schoolhouse Hollow Farm Star Rt 1 Box 128 Griffithsville WV 25521 Office: SWVCC PO Box 2900 Mount Gay WV 25637-2900

EARNEST, LINDA KAY HART, elementary educator; b. Frankfort, Ind., Jan. 18, 1946; d. Lester Vern and Bessie Karlene (Crail) Hart; m. Martin Leon Earnest, Aug. 19, 1967. BS in Edn., Ind. Wesleyan U., 1968; MA in Edn., Ball State U., 1971; postgrad., U. Indpls., 1990. Cert. K-8 tchr., Ind. Elem. tchr. Oak Hill United Schs., Swayzee, Ind., 1967—99; tchr. Sylvan Learning Ctr., Anderson, Ind., 1999—; dep. assessor Fairmount Twp., 2000—. Sunday sch. tchr., Lakeview Wesleyan Ch., Marion, Ind., 1968, 69, 76-82, mem. choir, sponsor youth group, 1968-83, mem. choir, Fairmount Wesleyan Ch., 2000—; mem. steering com. Youth for Christ, Madison-Grant High Sch., 1980-92, statistician football offense, 1991-2000. Mem. NEA, Ind. Tchrs. Assn., Classroom Tchrs. Assn. (discussion com.), Ind. Reading Assn. Avocations: travel, singing, sewing, camping, hiking. Home: 567 Circle Dr Fairmount IN 46928-1963 Office: Sylvan Learning Ctr Anderson IN 46986

EARTHMAN, JAMES CALVIN, JR., material sciences educator, consultant; b. Tulsa, Okla., Nov. 27, 1957; s. James Calvin and Norma June (Swartz) E.; m. Vivien Ruth Jackson, Apr. 2, 1988; children: James Albert, Jack Calvin. BS, Rice U., 1980; MS, Stanford U., 1982, PhD, 1986. Rsch. assoc. Swiss Fed. Inst. Tech., Lausanne, Switzerland, 1986-88; asst. prof. U. Calif., Irvine, 1988-94, assoc. prof., 1994—2000, prof., 2000—, assoc. dir. biomed. engrng. program, 1994—2000. Dir. rsch. Newport Coast Oral-Facial Inst., Newport Beach, Calif., 1993—; failure analysis cons., Irvine, 1989—; reviewer proposals NSF, U.S. Dept. Energy; mem. organizing com. workshop U. Calif., Irvine, 1993, chair organizing com. 7th internat. conf. creep & fracture engrng. materials & structures, 1997. Reviewer Materials Sci. and Engring. Jour., Metall. Trans. Jour., Scripta Metallurgica et Materialia Jour., Jour. Heat Transfer, Acta Stereologica Jour., Internat. Jour. Fracture; mem. edtl. rev. bd. Metall. and Materials Trans., 1994—. Recipient Augumentation award for sci. and engrng. rsch. tng. Air Force Office of Sci. Rsch., 1992, grants Apple Computer, Inc., U. Tech. Transfer Inc., Air Force Office of Sci. Rsch., U.S. Dept. Energy, NSF, NASA, Office of Naval Rsch., 1988—. Mem. ASTM, Am. Soc. Metals Internat., The Minerals Metals & Materials Soc. (flow and fracture com. 1991—, vice chmn. 1995—, chmn. session 1991, 93), Materials Rsch. Soc., Minerals, Metals and Materials Soc. of AIME (chmn. organizing com. symposium 1994), Am. Soc. for Non-Destructive Testing. Avocations: music, astronomy, golf.

EASTERLING, CHRISTINE DAVIS, educational administrator; b. Blackstone, Va., Dec. 18, 1939; d. Lynwood and Harriet Ann (Bates) Davis; m. William D. Easterling. BS in Bus. Edn., St. Paul's Coll., 1962; MA in Adminstrn. and Counseling, Howard U., 1969; MA in Adult Edn. and Curriculum Devel., U. D.C., 1979; postgrad., George Washington U., 1981-83. Cert. tchr. Washington. Curriculum coord. Howard U./Washington (D.C.) Tchrs. Corps, 1979-82; dir. Computer Tech. Ctr. Burdick Career Ctr., D.C. Pub. Schs., Washington, 1982-86; dir. Careers on the Mall Mktg. Edn. Program Wilson Sr. High Sch., Washington, 1986-88; program coord. Teaching Professions Program Coolidge High Sch., Washington, 1988—. Coord., instr. Computer Literacy Tng. Program, Div. Adult, Continuing Edn. and Staff Devel., D.C. Pub. Schs., 1983; tchr. Neighborhood Youth Corps., D.C. Evaluation Unit, Washington, 1969, Tng., Rsch. and Devel. Corp., Washington, 1968-69, presenter in field. Named Miss Future Bus. Leader of Am., St. Paul's Coll., Lawrenceville, Va., 1963; recipient Outstanding Tchr. of 1977 award NEA, 1977, Outstanding Leadership in Competency-Based Curriculum award Bell Vocat. High Sch., Washington, 1979, Firt Sex Equity in Vocat. Edn. mini-grant, D.C. Pub. Sch. System, 1979, Supts. Spl. Commendation award for secondary schs., Washington, 1985, Pres.' medal for outstanding teaching Trinity Coll., Washington, 1990. Mem. Assn. Tchr. Educators, Am. Assn. Colls. for Tchr. Edn., Future Educators Am. Clubs (supts. task force, outstanding and dedicated svc. award 1990), Alpha Kappa Alpha, Phi Delta Kappa (new mem. of yr. award 1989). Democrat. Office: Coolidge High Sch 5th and Tuckerman Sts NW Washington DC 20011

EASTERN, CYNTHIA RENEE, secondary education educator; b. Milw., Apr. 26, 1957; d. Marion Edsel and Seldon Marie (Jarnagin) E. BA, Marquette U., 1979. Cert. secondary tchr., Wis. Market adminstr. Wis. Bell, Milw., 1979-84; adminstrv. supr. AT&T, Brookfield, Wis., 1984-85, asst. staff mgr. Morristown, N.J., 1985-87; gen. aide Milw. Pub. Schs., 1987-90, intern tchr., 1990, tchr., 1990—. Recipient Bronze Tchr. Recognition award Wis. Bell/Ameritech, 1992, Achievement award Wis. Dept. Pub. Instruction, 1992. Mem. NAACP, Met. Milw. Alliance Black Sch. Educators, Nat. Coun. for Social Studies, Delta Sigma Theta. Avocations: reading, bowling. Home: 4169 N 13th St Milwaukee WI 53209-6903

EASTIN, DELAINE ANDREE, federal agency administrator; b. San Diego, Aug. 20, 1947; d. Daniel Howard and Dorothy Barbara (Robert) Eastin; m. John Stuart Saunders, Sept. 17, 1972. BA in Polit. Sci., U. Calif., Davis, 1969; MA in Polit. Sci., U. Calif., Santa Barbara, 1971. Instr. Calif. Community Colls., various locations, 1971-79; acctg. mgr. Pacific Bell, San Francisco, 1979-84; corp. planner Pacific Telesis Group, San Francisco, 1984-86; assemblywoman Calif. State Legis., Sacramento, 1986-95; supt. of public instruction Calif. Edn. Dept., Sacramento, 1995—2003; exec. dir. Nat. Inst. Sch. Leadership, 2003—. Bd. dirs. CEWAER, Sacramento, 1988-2003; commr. Commn. on Status of Women, Sacramento, 1990—; mem. coun. City of Union City, Calif., 1980-86; chair Alameda County Libr. Commn., Hayward, Calif., 1981-86; planning commr. City of Union City, 1976-80; mem., pres. Alameda County Solid Waste Mgmt. Authority, Oakland, Calif., 1980-86. Named Outstanding Pub. Ofcl. Calif. Tchrs. Assn., 1988, Cert. of Appreciation Calif. Assn. for Edn. of Young Children, 1988-92, Legislator of the Yr. Calif. Media Libr. Educators, 1991, Calif. Sch. Bd. Assn., 1991, Ednl. Excellence award Calif. Assn. Counseling and Devel., 1992. Mem. Am. Bus. Women's Assn. (Outstanding Bus. Woman 1988), The Internat. Alliance (21st Century award 1990), World Affairs Coun., Commonwealth Club. Democrat. Avocations: photography, hiking, reading, theater. Home: 4228 Dogwood Pl Davis CA 95616-6066*

EASTMAN, DONNA KELLY, composer, music educator; b. Denver, Sept. 26, 1945; d. Donald Lewis and Frances Marie (Smith) Kelly; m. John Bernard Eastman, July 1, 1973; children: Jonathan Kelly, James Alan; stepchildren: Barbara Kathleen, Sally Toye. B Music Edn., U. Colo., 1967; MA, U. Md., 1973, D in Mus. Arts, 1992. Pvt. studio tchr., coach, 1960—; choral dir. Dept. Def. Overseas Sch., Okinawa, Japan, 1970-72; dir. Choraleers Choral Ensemble, Stuttgart, Germany, 1974-76, Bangkok Music Soc. Ensemble and Madrigal Singers, Thailand, 1982-84; instr. in music No. Va. C.C., Alexandria, 1986-89. Creator, pianist, vocalist Am. Music Programs for U.S. Mission, Thailand, 1981-84; vis. asst. prof. Ill. Wesleyan U., Bloomington, 1994; vis. composer Sweet Briar (Va.) Coll., 1998, Grinnell (Iowa) Coll., 1999. Composer choral, orchestral, opera, vocal/instrumental solo and chamber, and electronic works; recs. include Capstone Records-Soc. of Composers, Inc. Series CPS 8632, 1996, and New Music for Flute and Piano, CPS 8664, 1999; Living Artist Recs.-Music from the Setting Century Series, Vol. 2, 1996; New Ariel Recordings-Contemporary American Eclectic Music for the Piano Series, AE002, 1996; Columbine Chorale Recs.--European Tour, 1999, Blue House Productions--Alone Into the Crowd, 2002; contbr. to jours. Recipient 6 Internat. Composition awards, Composer Guild, 1991—, Internat. Piano Composition award, Roodeport Internat. Eisteddfod, South Africa, 1991, Glad-Robinson-Youse Composition award, Nat. Fedn. Music Clubs, 1992, Internat. Choral Composition award, Florilège Vocal Tours, France, 1995, Keyboard award, Delius Composition Competition, 1997, Margaret Fairbank Jory Copying Assistance award, Am. Music Ctr., 1999, Nat. Music Composition Competition award, Nat. League of Am. Pen Women, 2000, Miriam Gideon award, Internat. Alliance for Women in Music Search for New Music, 2002; fellow, Charles Ives Ctr. for Am. Music, 1990; grantee, 1993, Ragdale Found., 1991, Va. Ctr. for Creative Arts, 1991—2002. Mem. Soc. for Electro-Acoustic Music in the U.S., Internat. Alliance for Women in Music (Miriam Gideon prize for new music 2002), Soc. of Composers, Inc. (life), Nat. Mus. Women in Arts (charter), Broadcast Music, Inc., Am. Composers Forum, Southeastern Composers League (pres.), Friday Morning Music Club Washington, Phi Kappa Phi, Pi Kappa Lambda, Sigma Alpha Iota. Avocations: travel, handicrafts, photography. Home: 6812 Dina Leigh Ct Springfield VA 22153-1019 E-mail: deastman@erols.com.

EASTMAN, HAROLD DWIGHT, retired social studies educator, journalist; b. Harbor Springs, Mich., Dec. 11, 1915; s. William Raymond and Edith Georgianna (Cross) Eastman; married, June 1, 1943; children: Danite Rae, Bruce Clyde, Jonathan Porter. BA, Sioux Falls Coll., 1941; MA, Coll. William and Mary, 1947; PhD, U. Iowa, 1954. Caseworker ARC, St. Paul, 1946-52; chief divsn. diagnosis and treatment Youth Conservation Commn., St. Paul, 1950-52; asst. prof. sociology Macalester Coll., St. Paul, 1947-50; assoc. prof. sociology Midland Coll., Fremont, Nebr., 1954-57; prof. sociology Carroll Coll., Waukesha, Wis., 1957-63; vis. prof. sociology U. Glasgow, Scotland, 1967-68; vis. lectr. Ottumwa Heights Coll., Ottumwa, Iowa, 1969-70; prof., head dept. sociology Parsons Coll., Fairfield, Iowa, 1963-71; head dept. sociology Truman State U., Kirksville, Mo., 1971-81, prof. emeritus Point Lookout, Mo., 1981—; guest prof. sociology Coll. of the Ozarks, Point Lookout, Mo., 1981-98, ret., 1998. Mem. Mayor's Com. Alcoholism, Mayor's Com. Juvenile Delinquency, Mayor's Com. Drug Abuse, 1963—70, Mayor's Study Com. Housing Needs for Impoverished Sr. Citizens, 1963—70. Author: poems; contbr. articles to profl. jours. Hospice creator, Kirksville, Mo., 1975; transport provider for terminally ill patients Branson, Mo.; pres. Waukesha County Coun. Social Agys., 1957—63; provost marshal 84th Divsn. Tng., Milw., 1957—63; chmn., co-founder N.E. Mo. Hospice Com., 1979—81; vol. Ozark Mountain Hospice, Branson, 1983—; chair com. Election of Hubert Humphrey for U.S. Senate, St. Paul, 1950; elected mem. Waukesha County Bd. Suprs., 1957—63; elder United Presbyn. Ch., 1971—; chmn. scholarship com. UNICO, Waukesha, 1957—63. Lt. col. U.S. Army, 1941—46. Mem.: Mark Twain Mental Health Assn. (bd. dirs. 1976—79), Am. Sociol. Assn., Am. Assn. Univ. and Coll. Profs., Ret. Officers Assn. (pres. 1987), Mo. Hospice Assn., Phi Kappa Phi, Kappa Delta Pi, Alpha Kappa Delta. Home: 15 Fleming Dr Columbia MO 65201-5418

EASTMAN, JOHN ROBERT, education educator; b. San Diego, June 30, 1945; s. John Henry and Theresa (Wimberger) E. BA, Va. Poly. Inst. and State U., 1968; PhD, Julius-Maximilians U., Wuerzburg, 1985. Cert. tchr., Va. Tchr. So. H.S., Harwood, Md., 1968-69; instr. for English Dolmetscher Inst., Wuerzburg, 1976-83; bilingual tourist guide Arbeitsamt, Wuerzburg, 1976-85; summer sch. tchr. Archbishop Spalding H.S., Severn, Md., 1992; substitute tchr. Ft. Meade High Sch., 1990, Old Mill H.S., 1992, Anne Arundel Co., Md., 1987-97, Hampton (Va.) City Schs., 2001—; tchr. Peninsula Cath. H.S., Newport News, Va., 1997—2001; asst. prof. German Old Dominion U., Norfolk, Va., 2002—. Author: Papal Abdication in Later Medieval Thought, 1990; editor: Aegidius Romanus, De Renunciatione Pape, ·1992; contbr. Internat. Medieval Bibliography, 1995—; contbr. articles to profl. jours. Mem. Am. Hist. Assn., Southeastern Medieval Assn., Nat. Coalition Ind. Scholars, Capital Area Ind. Scholars (sec.-treas. 1992-94, newsletter editor 1994-96), Am. Philol. Assn., Am. Cath. Hist. Assn., Am. Assn. Tchrs. German. Avocation: genealogy. Home: 11311 Winston Pl Apt 8 Newport News VA 23601-2238

EASTMAN, TAMARA JANE, private investigator, educator; b. Ft. Lee, Va., Apr. 8, 1961; d. William Charles and Shirley Frances (Auen) E. Assoc. degree, Dominion Bus. Inst., Colonial Heights, Va., 1982; student, John Tyler Coll., Chester, Va., 1992—, Am. Coll., Marylebone, London, 1994. Registered pvt. investigator. Sec. Dept. Corrections, Richmond, Va., 1982-86; pvt. security cons. Richmond, Va., 1986-94; intern criminal rsch. Met. Police, London, 1994; pvt. investigator Dept. Criminal Justice, London, 1994—; tchr. world and maritime history Hopewell (Va.) Pub. Schs. Contbr. articles to profl. publs. Recipient Student Govt. Assn. Jefferson Cup, 1992; Va. C.C. scholar, 1994. Mem. Nat. Assn. Profl. Investigators Internat., Union Students, Profl. Secs. Internat. Democrat. Baptist. Avocations: drawing, cooking, traveling, collecting antiques, classical music. Office: Hopewell City Pub Schs 103 N 11th Ave Hopewell VA 23860-2301

EASTWOOD, PATRICIA J. school system administrator; b. Gloversville, N.Y., Oct. 4, 1946; d. John Connelly Joseph and Della Louisa (Brown) E.; m. Charle A. Neyhart Jr. (div.); children: Kristina Elaine Neyhart, Karl John Neyhart. BA, Pa. State U., 1967. Cert. secondary sch. tchr., diversity trainer, mediator. Exec. dir. Yamhill Co. Displaced Homemaker and Widowed Svcs., McMinnville, Oreg., 1978-79, Cmty. Svcs. Consortium, Corvallis, Oreg., 1980-87, Cmty. Outreach, Inc., Corvallis, 1988-92, Umpqua Cmty. Action Agy., Roseburg, Oreg., 1992-93, Habitat for Humanity Chester County, Coatsville, Pa., 1993; recruitment, tng. mgr. Pa. Assn. Colls. and Univs., Harrisburg, 1993-96; program facilitator Wa. State Office Secondary Edn., Sunnyside, 1996—; faciliation trainer State of Wash., 1997—. Mediator Dispute Resolution Ctr., Yakima, Wash., 1999—. Prin. author: guide Washington State Migrant Counselor Guide, 1999, Leaders in Service Replication Guide, 2000; contbr. to tng. manual, handbook. Vol. UMM Now, Sunnyside, Wash., 1997—; mem. com. Chicano/Latino Mentor Program, Seattle, 1997-99. Mem. AAUW (recording sec. 1998-99), Nat. Assn. Exptl. Educators, Pa. State Alumni Assn., Assn. Supts. and Curriculum Dirs. Home: 124 N 52nd Ave Yakima WA 98908

EATON, DOREL, elementary school educator; b. Atlantic City, N.J., Sept. 08; d. Ethel Donovan Joyce; divorced; 1 child, Melissa Elizabeth Eaton-Midgley. BA in Edn., U. Fla.; MS, Barry U., 1973; Design degree, Sch. for Interior Design, Miami Shores, Fla., 1976. Cert. guidance counseling, elem. educator, Fla. Elem. edn. tchr. Dade County Pub. Sch., Miami. Art displayed in numerous galleries including The Curzon Art Gallery of Boca Raton (Fla.) Country Club, Bill Nessen's Showroom/Design Ctr. of the Americas, Dania, Fla.; contbr. Book Nat. Coalition Against Pornography. Vol. Ctr. Reclaiming Am. Named Outstanding Alumnus Barry U., 1996. Mem. MADD, Am. Family Assn., Nat. Coalition for Protection of Children and Families, U.S. Holocaust Meml. Mus. (charter mem.), Morality in Media, Inc., Prison Fellowship, Design Ctr. of the Ams., Physicians Com. for Responsible Medicine, Fla. Right to Life, Nat. Trust for Hist. Preservation. Avocations: writing, painting, reading, interior design, drama.

EATON, EMMA PARKER, special education educator; b. Conway, N.C., June 21, 1945; BS in Special Edn., Norfolk State Coll., 1978; MA, Norfolk State U., 1995. Spl. edn. eduator Norfolk Pub. Schs., Va.

EATON, GORDON PRYOR, geologist, consultant; b. Dayton, Ohio, Mar. 9, 1929; s. Colman and Dorothy (Pryor) E.; m. Virginia Anne Gregory, June 12, 1951; children: Gretchen Maria, Gregory Mathieu. BA, Wesleyan U., 1951, Doctorate (hon.), 1995; MS, Calif. Inst. Tech., 1953, PhD, 1957; Doctorate (hon.), Colo. Sch. Mines, 2001. From instr. geology to asst. prof. Wesleyan U., Middletown, Conn., 1955-59; from asst. prof. to assoc. prof. U. Calif., Riverside, 1959-67, chmn. dept. geol. sci., 1965-67; with U.S. Geol. Survey, 1963-65, 67-81, 94-97; dep. chief Office Geochemistry and Geophysics, Washington, 1972-74; project chief geothermal geophysics Office Geochemistry Geophysics, Denver, 1974-76; scientist-in-charge Hawaiian Volcano Obs., 1976-78; assoc. chief geologist Reston, Va., 1978-81; dean Tex. A&M U. Coll. Geoscis., 1981-83; provost, v.p. acad. affairs Tex. A&M U., 1983-86; pres. Iowa State U., Ames, 1986-90; dir. Lamont-Doherty Earth Obs. Columbia U., Palisades, N.Y., 1990-94, U.S. Geol. Survey, Reston, Va., 1994-97; prin. Pac NW, SeaMountain Country, Tex., Wash., 1997—. Former mem. Com. on Internat. Edn., Am. Coun. Edn.; mem. bd. earth scis. and resources; ocean studies bd., and com. on formation of nat. biol. survey NRC, also mem. geophysics study com.; bd. dirs. Midwest Resources, Inc., Bankers Trust; mem., chair adv. com. U.S. Army Command and Gen. Staff Coll.; adv. bd. Sandia Nat. Lab. Geoscis. & Environ. Ctr.; adv. bd. Ohio State U. Ctr. Mapping. Mem. editl. bd. Jour. Volcanology and Geothermal Rsch., 1976-78; contbr. articles to profl. jours. Trustee Wesleyan U., 1995-98, Geol. Soc. Am. Found., 1999-2003; pres., bd. dirs. Iowa 4-H Found., 1986-90; mem. adv. bd. Sch. Earth Sci. Stanford (Calif.) U., 1995-2000; mem. U.S. del. sci. and tech. com. Gore-Chernomyrdin Commn., 1996-97; mem. vis. com. Colo. Sch. Mines; mem. water res. adv. com. Island Co., 2001—. Named Gordon P. Eaton Hall in his honor, Iowa State U., 2003; grantee, NSF, 1955—59; Standard Oil fellow, Calif. Inst. Tech., 1953. Fellow: AAAS, Geol. Soc. Am. Home: 201 Pershing Ave College Station TX 77840 Office: Dept Geology and Geophysics Tex A&M U College Station TX

EATON, JANA SACKMAN, secondary school educator; b. Riverton, Wyo., Nov. 5, 1943; d. Kemper Eugene and Lois Barbara (Horn) Sackman; m. Leonard Middleton Eaton; children: Heather Grace, Brook Leonard. BA, Northwestern U., 1966; MEd, West Chester U., 1970; EdD Widener U., 2002. Cert. tchr. social studies, comm. Tchr. social studies Unionville (Pa.) H.S., 1969-73, 80—. Recipient Global Educator award Peace Corps, 2001. 2nd All-USA Tchr. Team award USA Today, 2001, Excellence in Tchg. award, 1999; named Pa. State Tech. Tchr. of Yr., 1992, 98; Study/Travel fellow Keizai Koho, 1997, Fulbright fellow, 1998, Korea Soc. fellow, 2000. Mem. Unionville-Chadds Ford Edn. Assn. (pres. 1971-73, exec. com. 1992-2000), Delta Kappa Gamma, Phi Kappa Phi. Avocations: travel, skiing, walking, reading. Home: 365 Firethorne Dr West Chester PA 19382-8150 Office: Unionville H S 750 Unionville Rd Kennett Square PA 19348-1531

EATON, JOSEPH W. sociology educator; b. Nuremburg, Germany, Sept. 28, 1919; s. Jacob and Flora (Wechsler) E.; m. Helen Goodman, June 8, 1947; children: David, Seth, Debra, Jonathan. BS, Cornell U., 1940; PhD, Columbia U., 1948. Faculty Wayne State U., Detroit, 1947-56; lectr., then vis. prof. Sch. Social Welfare, U. Calif. at Los Angeles, 1956-60; prof. social work rsch. U. Pitts., 1960-70, dir. advanced program, 1966-69, prof. sociology in pub. health and social work research, 1970-73; prof. sociology in pub. health and social work rsch. Sch. Pub. and Internat. Affairs, 1974—, prof., later dir. program in econ. and social devel.; co-dir. U.S. Comparative Mgmt. Survey Title Ins., 1999—. Russell Sage Found. vis. prof. We. Res. U. (Med. Sch.), 1958-59; project dir. Conf. on Social Welfare Consequences of Migration and Residential Movement, 1969; dir. instn. bldg. program Interuniv. Rsch. Consortium, 1966-71; curriculum cons., later dir. social work and social adminstrn. program U. Haifa, Israel, 1970-74 USIA cons., lectr., Africa, 1979, Sweden, Fed. Republic Germany, 1982, 86, Romania, 1982, Abu Dhabi, Pakistan, Egypt, Sudan, Israel, 1986, Nepal, Pakistan, Egypt, Ethiopia, Iraq, 1988, Yugoslavia, USSR, 1989; Fulbright lectr. and cons., 1979, NAS. guest scholar in Poland and German Dem. Republic, 1980; co-dir. Jordan River Basin Water Resources Devel., U.S. Inst. Peace, 1992—; co-investigator search for inherited causes of schizophrenia in a genetically isolated cmty., 1997—; co-prin. investigator A Pub. Policy-Oriented Audit of Title Ins., 1999—. Author: (with Saul M. Katz) Research Guide on Cooperative Group Farming, 1942, Exploring Tomorrow's Agriculture, 1943, (with Albert Mayer) Man's Capacity to Reproduce, 1954, (with Robert J. Weil) Culture and Mental Disorders, 1955, (with Kenneth Polk) Measuring Delinquency, 1961, Stone Walls Not a Prison Make: The Anatomy of Planned Adminstrative Change, 1962, Prisons in Israel, 1964, (with Michael Chen) Influencing the Youth Culture: A Study of Youth Organization in Israel, 1970, The Rurban Village, 1980, Can Business Save South Africa, 1980, Card Carrying Americans: Security, Privacy and the National ID Card Controversy, 1986, (with Yuri Lvov) Capitalist Communism, 1991, The Privacy Card: A Low Cost Strategy to Combat Terrorism, 2003; also contbr. chpts. to books, articles to profl. jours.; editor: Institution Building and Development, 1972. Mem. cable svc. adv. com. City of Pitts. City Coun., 1994—, chmn., mem. cable comm. adv. com., 1996—. With AUS, 1941-46. Faculty Rsch. fellow Social Sci. Rsch. Coun., 1962 Mem. NASW (chmn. rsch. coun. 1968-71), Internat. Assn. Social Psychiatry (coun. 1969-72). Home: 1008 Summerset Dr Pittsburgh PA 15217-2535 Office Fax: 412-421-4288.

EAVES, DOROTHY ANN GREENE, music educator; b. Pinson, Ala., Feb. 27, 1938; d. Albert Anderson Greene and Dorothy Elizabeth McCool; m. Richard Glen Eaves, June 19, 1959; 1 child, Lisa Michelle Eaves Stooksbury. MusB magna cum laude, Miss. State Coll. for Women, 1959; student, Peabody Coll., 1959, U. Ala., 1960-65; MEd, Auburn U., 1970. Tchr. piano and organ Clarke Coll., Newton, Miss., 1959-62; min. of music Bay Springs (Miss.) Bapt. Ch., 1960-62; ind. piano tchr. Clinton, Miss., Tuscaloosa and Auburn, Ala., 1963-86; adj. tchr. music edn. Auburn U., 1971-72; adj. tchr. piano and ch. music Miss. Coll., Clinton, 1984-89; pianist Woodville Heights Bapt. Ch., Jackson, Miss., 1985-86. Music accompanist Auburn U., 1968-70; piano competition judge, recitalist, Ala., Miss., La., 1970—; instr. piano and music history Hinds C.C., Raymond, 1986—. Mem. faculty Miss. Piano Camp, Raymond, 1988, 90, 95—. Faculty devel. grantee Hinds C.C., Raymond, 1995, 98. Mem. Music Tchrs. Nat. Assn. Republican. Baptist. Avocations: travel, reading, walking, church projects. Home: 5 Pheasant Run Clinton MS 39056-3538

EAVES, STEPHEN DOUGLAS, vocational administrator, educator, consultant; b. Honolulu, Aug. 30, 1944; s. Alfred Aldee and Phyllis Clarissa (Esty) E.; m. Sally Ann Winslow, Apr. 27, 1974; children: Trevor Bernard, Lindsay Douglas, Christian Francis. BA in Polit. Sci., U. Hawaii, 1967; MS in Bus. Mgmt., U. Ark., 1974; PhD in Edn. Adminstrn., Colo. State U., 1997. Cert. secondary tchr., prin., vocat. dir., post secondary bus. tchr., Colo. Commd. 2d lt. USAF, 1967, advanced through grades to lt. col., ret., 1989; aerospace sci. tchr. Adams County Sch. Dist. 50, Westminster, Colo., 1989-94, vocat. dir./prin., 1994—. Cons. Dept. of Edn., Colo., 1993—. Eucharistic min. Spirit of Christ Cath. Ch., Arvada, Colo., 1989—. Decorated Silver Star, DFC, Air medals, Commendation medals, Air Force Achievement medal; named Outstanding Tchr. Focus on Excellence Program, 1992, Outstanding Nat. Aerospace Sci. Tchr., 1994. Mem. ASCD, Coun. for Exceptional Children, Am. Vocat. Assn., Colo. Vocat. Assn., Colo. Assn. Vocat. Adminstrs., Colo. Assn. Sch. Execs., Am. Nat. Rose Soc., Royal Nat. Rose Soc., Lions (sec. Adams Centennial chpt. 1991-92, Lion of Yr. 1992), Elks, Phi Delta Kappa, Omicron Tau Delta. Avocations: snow skiing, rose gardening. Home: 8708 Independence Way Arvada CO 80005-1247 Office: Career Enrichment Park 7300 Lowell Blvd Westminster CO 80030-4821

EBBS, GEORGE HEBERLING, JR., university executive; b. Sewickley, Pa., Sept. 20, 1942; s. George Heberling and Mae Isabelle (Miller) E.; m. Agnes Rak, 1989; children: Stacey Kirsten, Cynthia Lynn, George Heberling III, Alexandra Christine. BS in Engring., Purdue U., 1964; MBA, U. Wash., 1966; PhD in Bus., Columbia U., 1970. Sr. engr. Boeing Co., Seattle, 1966; assoc. Booz Allen & Hamilton, N.Y.C., 1969-72, sr. v.p., 1974-86; v.p. Fry Cons., N.Y.C., 1973; chmn., pres. The Canaan Group, Park City, Utah, 1986-98; pres. Embry-Riddle Aeronautical U., Daytona Beach, Fla., 1998—. Bd. dirs. Pinnacle Bank, NBAA-AMAC. Bd. dirs. Daytona Lively Arts; chmn. S.E. SATS Lab Consortium; mem. adv. bd. Aerospace Edn. Found., advisor. Bronfman fellow. Fellow: Royal Aero. Soc.; mem.: AIAA, Air Force Assn., Nat. Bus. Aviation Assn. (assoc. mem. adv. coun.), Purdue Old Masters, Iron Key, Wings Club (bd. govs.), Met. Opera Club, Aero Club of Washington, Oceanside Country Club, Prestwick Country Club, Beta Gamma Sigma, Omicron Delta Kappa. Presbyterian. Office: Embry-Riddle Aeronautical U 600 S Clyde Morris Blvd Daytona Beach FL 32114-3966

EBEDES, ALLAN NORMAN, academic administrator; b. Johannesburg, Dec. 22, 1951; came to Can. 1973, naturalized 1976; s. Harry and Miriam (Laiserowitz) E.; m. Heddy Ebedes, Aug. 4, 1974; children: Mark, Nicole, Gavin, Lauren. BCom, U. Witwatersrand, South Africa, 1971; MBA, U. Toronto, Can., 1976; CA, U. Toronto, 1977. Chartered acct. Acct. Coopers & Lybrand, Toronto, 1973-76; pres. Stuarts Furniture & Appliances, Downsview, Ont., 1976-82, Toronto Sch. Bus., Ont., 1976, dir., 1976; pres. Internat. Bus. Schs., Ont., 1986—. Dir. Compucollege, 1979. Served to 2nd lt. SAF, 1968-69. Mem. Can. Inst. Chartered Accts., Assn. Can. Career Colls., Ont. Assn. Career Colls., Nat. Assn. Career Colls., Career Coll. Assn., Young Pres. Orgn. Home: 29 Lincombe Dr Thornhill ON Canada L3T 2V6 Office: Toronto Sch Bus 5734 Yonge St Ste 400 Toronto ON Canada M2M 4E7

EBENSO, ENO EFFIONG, chemistry educator; b. Ibadan, Nigeria, Nov. 18, 1964; s. Effiong Moses and Affiong Moses Ebenso; m. Glory E. Avoh. BSc in chemistry, U. Calabar, PMB 1115, Nigeria, 1983—86, PhD in physical chemistry, 2002; MSc in physical chemistry, U. Ibadan, Nigeria, 1988—90. Cert. chemist. Tchg. asst. U. Ibadan, 1988—89; asst. lectr. U.

Calabar PMB 1115, 1990—93, lectr. II, 1993—97, lectr. I, 1997—. Cons. chemist Unicalcons/Shell Petroleum Devel. Co., Port Harcourt, Nigeria, 1991—95, Aluminium Smelting Co. (Alscon), Ikotabasi, Nigeria, 1996—98, Globen (Nig) Ltd., Uyo, Nigeria, 2000—01, Agip and Exxon-Mobil Oil Co., Nigeria. Co-author: An Introduction to Physical Chemistry, 1999, (articles) various profl. jours., 1999—2000. Scribe NAS Intern., Calabar, CRS, 1997—98, v.p., 2000—01, 2002—04. Recipient Post Graduate Studies Sch. award, Fed. Govt. Nigeria, U. Ibadan, 1990; fellow Short Term Rsch. fellowship, DAAD (German Acad. Svc.) Universitat des Saarlandes, Germany, 1999—2000; grantee TWAS South-South Travel, TWAS/JNCASR, India, 1999. Mem.: NACE (Nat. Assoc. Corrosion Engrs.), Am. Chem. Soc., Chem. Soc. Nigeria. Achievements include research in contemporary chemistry and physics and materials, solid state chemistry corrosion. Avocations: reading, travel, chess, cricket, scrabble. Office: U Calabar Dept Chemistry PMB 1115 Calabar Nigeria Home: #17 John Eteta-Ita Str Calabar Nigeria E-mail: ebenso@unical.anpa.net.ng., egebenso@hotmail.com.

EBERHARD ASCH, THERESA J. retired assistant principal; b. Danbury, Conn., Aug. 30, 1942; d. Louis Vincent and Marie Stiffen Fiore; m. Daniel Thomas Eberhard, June 26, 1965 (dec. Apr. 1997); children: Suzanne Lynn, Christopher Quinn; m. Richard Asch, 2003. BS, Western Conn. State U., 1964, MS, 1972; 6th yr. cert., So. Conn. State U., 1985. 1st grade tchr. Brookfield (Conn.) Bd. Edn., 1964-68, 4th-6th grade tchr., 1975-85, asst. prin., 1986—2001; ret., 2001. Bd. trustees Conn. State U. Sys., Hartford, 1997—; chair Commn. on Aging, Brookfield, 1994-98. Mem. ASCD, Nat. Assn. Secondary Prins., Women's Club of Brookfield, Phi Delta Kappa. Republican. Roman Catholic. Avocations: reading, travel, exercise. Office: Whisconier Mid Sch 17 W Whisconier Rd Brookfield CT 06804 E-mail: Teber56230@aol.com.

EBERLIN, RICHARD D. education educator; b. Erie, Pa., Sept. 28, 1947; s. Harry M. and Florence F. (Space) E.; m. Deanna A. Barron, Aug. 7, 1971; children: Richard D., Charles A. BS in Edn., Edinboro State Coll., 1969, MS in Edn., 1973. Tchr. Crawford Cen. Sch. Dist., Meadville, Pa., 1969-76, Millcreek Twp. Sch. Dist., Erie, Pa., 1976—, chair dept. sci., 1997—. Bd. dirs. Pa. State Edn. Assn., Harrisburg, 1996—, pres. N.W. region, 1998-2002, pers. com., 1999-2002; asst. scoutmaster Boy Scouts of Am., Erie, 1985-96. Mem.: NEA (bd. dirs. 2002—). Office: McDowell HS 3580 W 38th St Erie PA 16506-4021

EBERLY, CHARLES, counseling and student development educator; b. McComb, Ohio, Sept. 8, 1941; s. George and Herma Elizabeth (Sower) Eberly; m. Sharon Rosalee Newcomer, June 21, 1964; children: Mary Barbara, Judith Elizabeth, Michael Charles. BS in Chemistry, Bowling Green State U., 1963; MS in Edn., Syracuse U., 1966; PhD in Higher Edn., Mich. State U., 1970. Acting asst. dean students Wilmington Coll., Ohio, 1964; instr. student pers. U. Wis., Oshkosh, 1966—69; asst. prof. evaluation svcs. Mich. State U., East Lansing, 1970—74, assoc. prof. undergrad. univ. divsn., 1974—87, asst. to dir. admissions, 1981—87; asst. prof. ednl. psychology, coord. grad. program coll. pers. work Ea. Ill. U., Charleston, 1987—, assoc. prof. counseling and student devel., 1990—, prof., 1994—. Vis. instr. Mie U., Tsu, Japan, 1977—78; mem. nat. adv. bd. Chronicle Guidance Publs., Moravia, NY, 1987—; bd. dirs. Ea. Ill. U., Stockman Inst., 1990—93. Author: Building and Maintaining the Chapter Library, 1970; mem. editl. bd.: Jour. Coll. Student Retention, 1999—. Mem. zoning bd., Mason, Mich., 1970—71; bd. dirs. Ctr. for the Study of Coll. Fraternities, 1999—, pres., 2000—. Named to Hall of Fame, MMOGSISP, 2002, Order of the Golden Heart, 2003; recipient Carter Ashton Jenkens award, Sigma Phi Epsilon, 1964, Sigma Phi Epsilon Disting. Alumnus award, 1995, Spirit of Greek BGSU award, Bowling Green U., 2002. Mem.: ACA (human rights commn. 1991—94), AACD, Ill. Counseling Assn. (senator 1990—91, jour. editl. bd. 1995, 2001—, conv. program com.), Ill. Assn. for Assessment in Counseling (Disting. Svc. award), Assn. for Interdisciplinary Initiatives in Higher Edn., Assn. of Fraternity Advisors (mem. perspectives editl. bd. 1993—95), Am. Assn. Collegiate Registrars and Admissions Officers, Ill. Assn. Measurement and Evaluation in Counseling and Devel. (pres. 1991—92, past pres. 1992—93), Ill. Coll. Pers. Assn. (Dennis Trueblood award 2002), Mich. Coll. Pers. Assn. (mem.-at-large exec. com. 1986—87), Nat. Assn. Student Pers. Adminstrs. (dissertation of yr. award com. 1989—2002), Am. Coll. Pers. Assn. (dir. Commn. IX 1969—72, co-founder Commn. XVI 1979, mem. profl. standards com. 1980—83, chmn. conv. evaluation com. 1991, mem. transition team 1991—92), Mich. Assn. Counseling and Devel. (chmn. adminstrv. asst. evaluation com. 1984—85, editor jour. 1985—87), Mich. Assn. for Measurement and Evaluation in Guidance (pres. 1984—85, Outstanding Profl. Svc. award 1985—86), Mich. ACT Coun. (exec. coun. 1981—86), Assn. for Measurement and Evaluation in Counseling and Devel. (newsletter editor 1979—84, treas. 1984—88, pres.-elect 1988—89, pres. 1989—90, past pres. 1990—91), Order of Omega, Omicron Delta Kappa, Phi Kappa Phi, Alpha Phi Omega, Sigma Phi Epsilon (chpt. counselor Ill. NU 1991—, fraternity advisor award 1992, individual initiative award (renamed Dr. Charles & Mrs. Sharon Eberly Essence of Fraternal Values award by the Ea. Ill. U.'s IFC and PHC in 2003) 1994, fraternity advisor award 1996, 2001), Phi Delta Kappa (Ea. Ill. U. chpt. rsch. award 1994). Republican. Methodist. Avocations: cycling, woodworking, music, early American pattern glass. Home: 2609 6th Street Cir Charleston IL 61920-4113 Office: Ea Ill U Dept Counseling and Student Devel Buzzard Hall Charleston IL 61920-3099 E-mail: cfcge@eiu.edu.

EBERSOLE, HELEN BROWNSBERGER, elementary school educator; b. Glendale, Ariz., Nov. 23, 1916; d. Albert Joseph Brownsberger and Estella Simmons; m. Walter Jennings Ebersole, Aug. 17, 1941; children: Brian, Susan, Joan. BA, LaVerne Coll., 1938; cert., UCLA. Tchr. Azusa Ctr., 1938—42, Bonita Unified Sch. Dist., LaVerne, Calif., 1956—77. Spkr. on traveling. Vol. ministries disaster child care Red Cross & Ch. of Brethren, 1980—90; vol., dir. song leader Camp LaVerne, Ch. Brethren, 1926—60. Mem.: DAR, AAUW, Traveler's Century Club. Republican. Protestent. Avocations: art, travel, reading, sports. Home: 3530 Damien Ave #198 La Verne CA 91750-3214

EBERSOLE, JUDY ANN, special education educator; b. Fulton, Mo., Sept. 17, 1943; d. Russell Edward and Dorothy Agnes (Giboney) Maddox; m. John Randolph Ebersole, Oct. 28, 1961; children: Bryan, Kent, Derek, Nicole. BS in Elem. Edn./Learning Disabilities, William Woods U., 1980, credentials of the deaf, 1982. Sec. Binkley Co., Warrenton, Mo., 1961-66; opthalmic tech. Richard White, O.D., Fulton, 1967-73; tchr.'s aide Mo. Sch. for Deaf, Fulton, 1974-79, tchr., 1980—. Cheerleader sponsor Mo. Sch. for Deaf, 1984-87, student coun. sponsor, 1993-94, jr./sr. class sponsor, 1983-84, chair of football/basketball, 1980-90. Mem. County-wide Profl. Devel. Com., Profl. Devel. Com., Mo. Bar Assn., Nat. Coun. for Social Studies, Theta Chi (pres., v.p., sec., other offices 1973-86). Avocations: home decorating, ballgames, golf, swimming, camping. Home: 1401 Marbrooke Dr Fulton MO 65251-1360

EBERT, JAMES DAVID, research biologist, educator; b. Bentleyville, Pa., Dec. 11, 1921; s. Alva Charles and Anna Frances (Brundege) E.; m. Alma Christine Goodwin, Apr. 19, 1946; children: Frances Diane, David Brian, Rebecca Susan. AB, Washington and Jefferson Coll., 1942, ScD, 1969; PhD, Johns Hopkins U., 1950; ScD (hon.), Yale, 1973, Ind. U., 1975, Duke U., 1992; LLD (hon.), Moravian Coll., 1979. Jr. instr. biology Johns Hopkins U., 1946-49, Adam T. Bruce fellow biology, 1949-50, hon. prof. biology, 1956-86, hon. prof. embryology Sch. Medicine, 1956-86; instr. biology Mass. Inst. Tech., 1950-51; asst. prof. zoology Ind. U., 1951-54, assoc. prof., 1954-56, Patten vis. prof., 1963; dir. dept. embryology Carnegie Instn. of Washington, 1956-76, pres., 1978-87, trustee, from 1987; prof. biology Johns Hopkins U., from 1987, dir. Chesapeake Bay Inst., 1987-92. Vis. scientist med. dept. Brookhaven Nat. Lab., 1953-54; Philips vis. prof. Haverford Coll., 1961; instr. in charge embryology tng. program Marine Biol. Lab., summers 1962-66, trustee, 1964-98, hon. trustee, 1998—, pres., 1970-78, 91-98, dir., 1970-75, 77-78, dir. emeritus, 1999—; mem. Commn. on Undergrad. Edn. in Biol. Scis., 1963-66; vis. com. for biol. and phys. scis. Western Res. U., 1964-68; mem. panels on morphogenesis and biology of neoplasia of com. on growth NRC, 1954-56; adv. panel on genetic and developmental biology NSF, 1955-56, mem. divisional com. for biology and medicine, 1962-66, mem. univ. sci. devel. panel, 1965-70, adv. com. for instl. devel., 1970-72; mem. panel basic biol. rsch. in aging Am. Inst. Biol. Sci., 1957-60; mem. panel on cell biology NIH, USPHS, 1958-62, child health and human devel. tng. com., 1963-66; mem. bd. sci. counselors Nat. Cancer Inst., 1967-71, Nat. Inst. Child Health, 1973-77; mem. Com. on Scholarly Communication with People's Republic of China, 1978-81, chmn., 1989-95; chmn. Nat. Com. on Sci. Edn. Stds. & Assessment, 1992-93, Com. on Transportation and a Sustainable Environment, Transportation Rsch. Bd., 1995-97; vis. com. to dept. biology MIT, 1959-68, Harvard, 1969-75, Princeton, 1970-76; chmn. bd. sci. overseers Jackson Lab., 1976-80; mem. Inst. Medicine; bd. dirs. Baxter Internat., Transcend Therapeutics, Inc. (formerly Free Radical Sci., Inc.). Author: (with others) The Chick Embryo in Biological Research, 1952, Molecular Events in Differentiation Related to Specificity of Cell Type, 1955, Aspects of Synthesis and Order in Growth, 1955, Interacting Systems in Development, 2d edit., 1970, Biology, 1973, Mechanisms of Cell Change, 1979, This Our Golden Age, 1994; mem. editl. bd. (with others) Abstracts of Human Developmental Biology; editor: (with others) Oceanus; contbr. articles to profl. jours. Trustee Worcester Found. Lt. USNR, 1942-46. Decorated Purple Heart. Felow AAAS (v.p. med. scis. 1964), Am. Acad. Arts and Scis., Internat. Soc. Devel. Biology; mem. NAS (chmn. assembly life scis. 1973-77, v.p. 1981-93, chmn. Govt., Univ. and Industry Rsch. Roundtable 1987-92, chmn. on transp. and a sustainable environment 1994-97), Korean Acad. Sci. and Tech. (hon. fgn. mem.), Am. Philos. Soc., Am. Inst. Biol. Scis. (pres. 1964, President's medal 1972), Am. Soc. Naturalists, Am. Soc. Zoologists (pres. 1970), Soc. Study Growth and Devel. (pres. 1957-58), Phi Beta Kappa, Sigma Xi, Phi Sigma. Home: Baltimore, Md. Died May 22, 2001.

EBERT, ROBERT PETER, education educator; b. Mt. Vernon, N.Y., Aug. 5, 1944; s. Robert Frederick and Verna Marion (Lashier) E.; m. Martha Ann Epp, June 9, 1969; children: Peter, Margaret. AB, Union Coll., 1966; MA, U. Wis., 1968, PhD, 1972. Asst. prof. U. Chgo., 1972-79; assoc. prof. Princeton (N.J.) U., 1979-87, prof., 1987—. Vis. asst. prof. U. Calif., Berkeley, 1977-78. Author: Infinitival Complement Constructions in Early New High German, 1976, Historische Syntax des Deutschen, 1978; co-author: Frühneuhochdeutsche Grammatik, 1993. Mem. Linguistic Soc. Am., Phi Beta Kappa. Avocation: musician.

EBERTS, JOHN JACOB, social science educator, department chair; b. July 3, 1949; BS, Pa. State U., 1972, MEd, 1974; MS, St. Johns U., 1990; PhD, Internat. U. Metaphysics, 1998. Tchr. Pinellas County (Fla.) Sch. Dist., 1984—. Adj. prof. St. Petersburg Coll., Clearwater, Fla., 1986—, Pasco-Hernando C.C., 1990—. Recipient Am. Medal of Honor in Edn., 2003. Fellow Royal Anthropol. Inst. Gt. Britain and Ireland; mem. Am. Sociol. Assn., Assn. for the Sociology of Religion, Royal Inst. Philosophy, The Philos. Soc. Eng., N.Y. Acad. Sci. (Tchr. of Yr., 1999, Internat. Man of Yr. Edn. 2001), 21st Century award 2002). Address: 2746 Kavalier Dr Palm Harbor FL 34684-4200

EBIEFUNG, ANIEKAN ASUKWO, mathematics educator and researcher; b. Nto Mbadum, Akwaibom State, Nigeria, Nov. 10, 1958; came to U.S., 1985; s. Asukwo Thomas and Florence Asukwo (Udofa) E.; m. Anne Aniekan Ekon, Jan. 2, 1989; children: Ediobong, Uduak. BS in Math. and Statistics with honors, U. Calabar, Nigeria, 1982; MS in Math., Howard U., 1987; PhD in Math. Scis., Clemson U., 1991. Instr. math. Federal U. of tech., Owerri, Nigeria, 1982-83, U. Cross River State, Uyo, Nigeria, 1983-85, U. D.C. Lorton (Va.) Prison Coll. Program, 1987-88, Howard U., Washington, 1985-88; teaching asst. Clemson U., 1988-91; asst. prof. math. U. Tenn., Chattanooga, 1991-96, U.C. found. assoc. prof., 1996—2001, prof. math., 2001—. Lectr. in field; ctr. chmn. Tenn. Math. tchrs. Assn. state-wide math contest, U. Tenn., Chattanooga, 1992—. Contbr. articles to profl. jours.; editor NASM Bull., 1980-81. Grantee Ctr. of Excellence for Computer Applications, 1993, scholar, 1995-96, 98-99; grantee Oak Ridge Assoc. Univs., 1993, UC Found., 1993, Tenn. Higher Edn. Commn., 1994-95, 97-99. Mem. Math. Assn. Am., Am. Math. Soc., Ops. Rsch. Soc. Am., Chattanooga Area Math. Tchrs. Assn., Internat. Linear Algebra Soc. Avocations: writing, tennis, reading. Office: Univ of Tenn 615 Mccallie Ave Chattanooga TN 37403-2504

EBY, CARL PETER, English educator; PhD, U. Calif., Davis, 1995. Lectr. Mich. State U., East Lansing, 1996-98; asst. prof. English U. S.C., Beaufort, 1998—, assoc. prof. english, 2003—. Author: Hemingway's Fetishism, 1999. Recipient Robert J. Stoller Found. Essay award for Psychoanalytic Rsch., 1996, John F. Kennedy Libr. Hemingway rsch. grant, 1996, S.C. Gov.'s Disting. Prof. award, 2001. E-mail: carlpeby@gwm.sc.edu.

EBY, CECIL DEGROTTE, English language educator, writer; b. Charles Town, W.Va., Aug. 1, 1927; s. Cecil and Ellen (Turner) E.; children: Clare Virginia, Lillian Turner. AB, Shepherd Coll., 1950; MA, Northwestern U., 1951; PhD, U. Pa., 1958. Instr., then asst. prof. English High Point Coll., 1955-57; asst. prof., then asso. prof. Madison Coll., 1957-60; mem. faculty Washington and Lee U., 1960-65; prof. U. Mich., 1965—; prof. English, chmn. dept. U. Miss., University, 1975-76. Fulbright prof. Am. lit. U. Salamanca, Spain, 1962-63; Fulbright prof. Am. studies U. Valencia, 1967-68; Fulbright prof. Am. lit. U. Budapest, 1981; prof. U. Szeged, 1988-89. Author: Porte Crayon: The Life of David H. Strother, 1960, The Siege of the Alcazar, 1965, (translations in Italian, German, Finnish, Dutch, Portuguese) Between the Bullet and the Lie: American Volunteers in the Spanish Civil War, 1969 (transl. in Spanish), That Disgraceful Affair: The Black Hawk War, 1973, The Road to Armageddon: The Martial Spirit in English Popular Literature, 1987, The War in Hungary: Civilians and Soldiers in World War II, 1998; editor: The Old South Illustrated, 1959, A Virginia Yankee in the Civil War, 1961. Served with USNR, 1945-46. Episcopalian. E-mail: cdeby@umich.edu.

EBY, G. NELSON, geoscience educator; b. Bethlehem, Pa., Jan. 6, 1944; s. George Carmany and Annie May (Nelson) E.; m. Susan Jane James, Sept. 7, 1968; children: Stephanie L., Jennifer A. BA, Lehigh U., 1965, MS, 1967; PhD, Boston U., 1971. Asst. prof. Lowell (Mass.) State Coll., Lowell, Mass., 1970-75; assoc. prof. U. Lowell, Lowell, Mass., 1975-86; prof. U. Mass., Lowell, Mass., 1986—. Assoc. editor Canadian Mineralogist, 1995-97; regional editor Jour. of African Earth Scis., 1994-97. Co-editor: Alkaline Rocks: Petrology & Mineralogy, 1996; contbr. articles to profl. jours. Erskine fellow U. Canterbury, 1998; Rsch. grantee NATO, 1996-98, Nat. Rsch. Coun., 1996. Fellow Geological Soc. Am.; mem. Geochemical Soc., Am. Geophysical Union, Sigma Xi. Avocations: photography, hiking. Office: Univ Mass Dept Environ Earth & Atmosph Scis 1 University Ave Lowell MA 01854-2893 E-mail: Nelson_Eby@uml.edu.

ECCLES, JACQUELYNNE S. psychology educator; BA in social psychology, U. Calif. Berkeley, 1966; PhD, U. Calif. Los Angeles, 1974. HS math sci. tchr. US Peace Corps, Ghana, 1966—68; asst. prof. Smith Coll., 1974—76; asst. to assoc. to full prof. U. Mich., 1974—92, asst. v.p. rsch., 1987—88; prof. U. Colo., 1988—92. Chair Internat. Doctorate Program, Life Span Devel. with Max Planck, Berlin, 2002—; mem. Psychology Dept. Exec. Com., U. Mich., 1981—86; Chair U. Mich., Edn., Psychology, 1992—2002; mem. U. Mich., Rackham Exec. Com., 1993—95, Pres. Adv. Com. on Women's Issues, U. Mich., 1993—98; interim chair U. Mich., Dept. Psychology, 1998—99. Mem.: NSF, Nat. Acad. Edn., Pathways to Coll. Network Rsch. Scholars Panel, Adv. Com. for Jossey-Bass Series on new Directions for Youth Devel., Coun. for Soc. for Rsch. Adolescence, Coun. for Soc. for Psycho. Study of Social Issues, Am. Psycho. Assn. Office: U Mich Inst Rsch on Women and Gender 204 S State St Ann Arbor MI 48109 Home: 1109 Pearl St Ypsilanti MI 48197 Office Fax: 734-936-7370. E-mail: jeccles@umich.edu.*

ECHOLS, IVOR TATUM, retired educator, assistant dean; b. Oklahoma City, Dec. 28, 1919; d. Israel E. and Katie (Bingley) Tatum AB, U. Kans., 1942; postgrad., U. Nebr., 1945-46; MS in Social Work, Columbia U., 1952; postgrad., U. So. Calif., 1961-62, DSW, 1968. Tchr. social studies h.s., Holdenville, Okla., 1942-43, Geary, Okla., 1943-45; caseworker ARC, Chgo., 1946-47; resident group worker Dosoris House for Teen-Age Girls Cmty. Svcs. Soc., N.Y.C., 1950-51; supr. group work Walnut Grove Ctr. Neighborhood Clubs, Oklahoma City, 1948-51; program dir. Camp Lookout YWCA, Denver, 1951; dir. program svcs. Presbyn. Neighborhood Svcs., Detroit, summer 1960; supr. group work Merrill-Palmer Inst., Detroit, 1951-70; asst. dir. Merrill-Palmer Camp, Dryden, Mich., 1951-59; prof. Sch. Social Work U. Conn., West Hartford, 1970-89, also asst. dean, ret., 1989. Del. Inter-Univ. Consortium of Social Devel., Nairobi, Kenya, 1974, Hong Kong, 1980; mem. Conn. adv. com. U.S. Commn. Civil Rights. Mem. ad hoc com. Citizens Concerned with Equal Ednl. Opportunity, Detroit, 1964—; cons. to NEA Conf. Family Camping Washington, 1959, ednl. film Scott Paper Co., Phila., 1963, 64; summer study skills project Presbyn. Ch. Bd. Nat. Missions, Knoxville, Tenn., 1965—; nat. sec. United Neighborhood Ctrs. Am., N.Y.C.; pres. Protestant Cmty. Svcs., Detroit, 1969-70; trustee Conn. Energy Found., 1987-92; commr. Conn. Hist. Commn., 1986-96, ret., 1996. ARC scholar; fellow Nat. Urban League, Porter R. Lee fellow, fellow NIMH; recipient Educator Human Rights award UN Assn., 1987, Sojourner Truth award Detroit chpt. Nat. Assn. Negro Bus. and Profl. Women, 1969, UN Assn. award for Edn. and Women's Rights, 1987, Maria R. Stewart Women's Rights award Conn. Women's Ednl. and Legal Found., 1991, Outstanding Women award U. Conn., 1991, Achievement award Assn. Advancement Soc. Groupwork, 1994, 1st Truth award Capitol C.C. Hartford, 1999; named Conn. Social Worker of Year NASW, 1979; Ivor J. Echols Endowment Fund named in her honor U. Conn. Found., 1990. Mem. Nat. Assn. Colored Women's Clubs (participant White House conf. on Children and Youth 1960), A.M.E. Ministers Wives, Acad. Certified Social Workers (hon.), Nat. Assn. Black Social Workers (honored as founding mem. 1968), Nat. Trust for Hist. Preservation, Delta Sigma Theta (Delta Dear recognition 1998). Mem. A.M.E. Ch. Office: U Conn 1798 Asylum Ave Ste 1 West Hartford CT 06117-2603 Home: PO Box 23 Windsor CT 06095-0023

ECK, GAIL ANN, elementary education educator; b. Jacksonville, Ill., May 29, 1948; d. Charles Joseph and Gloria Ann (Bentley) Standley; m. George E. Eck, June 21, 1969. BA, Ill. Coll., 1971; MS in Edn., Western Ill. U., 1981. Cert. elem. tchr., Ill. Asst. phys. therapist Norris Hosp., Jacksonville, 1966-70; tchr. 1st, 2d grades, chpt. I Franklin (Ill.) Cmty. Schs., 1971-90; Reading Recover tchr. leader Springfield (Ill.) Pub. Schs., 1990—. Summer sch. coord., summer libr. program dir., jr. high softball coach Franklin Cmty. Schs.; adj. prof. U. Ill., 1991-97; adj. prof. Nat.-Louis U., 1997—. Mem. NEA, ASCD, Internat. Reading Assn., Nat. Coun. Tchrs. Math., Ill. Edn. Assn., Ill. Reading Coun., Cen. Ill. Reading Coun. (past pres., treas., v.p.), Ill. Assn. Supervision and Curriculum Devel., Ill. Coun. Math. Tchrs., Ill. Assn. Chpt. I Dirs., Franklin/Alexander Classroom Tchrs. (past pres., sec., v.p., mem. negotiations team), Springfield Edn. Assn. Roman Catholic. Avocations: genealogy, reading, calligraphy, swimming, canoeing, travel. Home: RR 1 Box 18 Alexander IL 62601-9801

ECKAUS, RICHARD SAMUEL, economist, educator; b. Kansas City, Mo., Apr. 30, 1926; s. Julius and Bessie (Finklestein) E.; m. Patricia L. Meaney; 1 child, Susan L. BS, Iowa State Coll., 1946; MA, Washington U., St. Louis, 1948; PhD, MIT, 1954. Instr., asst. prof., assoc. prof. Brandeis U., 1951-62; rsch. assoc. Ctr. Internat. Studies MIT, Cambridge, 1954-61, from assoc. prof. to prof., 1962—96, Ford internat. prof., 1977-96, head dept. econs., 1987-90, emeritus prof., 1996—2002. Vis. scholar Roxbury C.C., 1996—2002; nat. adv. coun. for environ. and tech. policy EPA; joint program sci. and policy climate change; mem. Bd. Econ. Advisors to Gov. Mass., 1963—65; cons. ADB, OECD, AID, World Bank, govts. of Jamaica, Portugal, Egypt, Sri Lanka, Chile, China, Mexico; vis. scholar Roxbury C.C., 1996—2002. Author: (with K. Parikh) Planning for Growth, 1968; editor: (with J. Bhagwati) Foreign Aid, 1970, Development and Planning, 1973, Basic Economics, 1972, Estimating the Returns to Education, 1973, Appropriate Technologies for Developing Countries, 1976; contbr. articles to profl. jours. Served with USNR, 1944-46. Guggenheim and Social Sci. Rsch. Coun.fellow, 1962; Ford Found. Faculty fellow, 1965. Mem. Am. Econ. Assn. Home: 131 Sewall Ave Apt 72 Brookline MA 02446-5336 Office: MIT Dept Econs 50 Memorial Dr Cambridge MA 02142-1347

ECKBERG, E. DANIEL, secondary education educator; b. Mpls., June 13, 1936; s. E.B.L. and Alvina H. (Sunde) E.; m. Mary Alice Banke, Dec. 27, 1962 (dec. Oct. 1982); children: David D. (dec.), Paul A. BA, St. Olaf Coll., 1958; BS, U. Minn., 1962, PhD, 1986. cert. tchr. econs., history, social studies, curriculum coord. K-12. Recording engr. WCAL-Radio, Northfield, Minn., 1954-58; recording engr., film editor TALC Divsn. TV, Radio and Film, St. Paul, Minn., 1958-62; tchr. Hopkins (Minn.) H.S., 1962-97, chmn. social studies dept., 1967-68; instr. Coll. Edn. U. Minn., Mpls., 1964-66; asst. dir. Hopkins (Minn.) Modular Curriculum Project, 1968-70; project dir. Demonstration Evaluation Ctr., Hopkins, 1970-73; coord. instr. svcs. Hopkins H.S., 1970-97; coord. dist. TV Hopkins Sch. Dist., 1982-97; ednl. cons., 1997—. Mem. social studies adv. com. Minn. State Bd. Edn., St. Paul, 1966-68; mem. European history and world cultures com. Coll. Entrance Exam. Bd., Princeton, N.J., 1970-81; mem. evaluation teams Nat. Coun. for Accreditation of Tchr. Edn., Va., Colo., Wis., 1974-82; mem. program goals for media arts participation Minn. Sch. and Resource Ctr. of the Arts, 1987; curriculum writer various orgns. Producer: (TV program) All the Difference: Youth Svc. in Minn., 1988, A Gift of Yourself, 1990. Chmn. tng. com. viking coun. Boy Scouts of Am., Mpls., 1960-62, scoutmaster, 1962-74. Recipient Nat. Physics Hon. award Sigma Pi Sigma St. Olaf Coll., 1957, Outstanding Sr. Man award Coll. Edn. U. Minn., 1962, Program of Excellence award Commr. Edn. State of Minn., 1985, Exec. Dept. Commendation award Gov. State of Minn., 1988, 91. Mem. Nat. Coun. Social Studies (nom. com., curriculum com.), Minn. Fedn. Local Cable Programmers, Alliance for Cmty. Media, Phi Kappa Phi Nat. Grad. Student Honor Soc., Phi Delta Kappa. Office: 5211 Kellogg Ave Minneapolis MN 55424-1304

ECKER, ALLISON JOANNA, elementary education educator; b. Smithtown, N.Y., May 31, 1970; d. Barbara Goldstein. BA in Polit. Sci., SUNY, Stony Brook, 1992; MS in Edn., Dowling Coll., 1994. Cert. elem. tchr., math. tchr., social studies tchr., reading tchr., N.Y. Tchr. social studies and math Babylon (N.Y.) Union Free Sch. Dist., 1993-95; elem. tchr. Ctrl. Islip (N.Y.) Union Free Sch. Dist., 1995—; dir. Ctrl. Islip Adult Edn., 1999—. Coord., student liaison N.Y. State Mentoring Program; regional asst. chief test adminstr. Nat. Evaluation Systems, Inc., Amherst, Mass.; tchr. adult edn. Ctrl. Islip Union Free Sch. Dist., 1991-93. Treas. Islandia (N.Y.) Civic Assn.; historian Village of Islandia; vol. St. John of God Food Pantry, Central Islip. Jenkins Meml. scholar PTA. Mem. Nat. Coun. Tchrs. Math., Nat. Coun. Tchrs. Social Studies, Internat. Reading Assn., Pi Sigma Alpha, Psi Chi, Golden Key, Phi Beta Kappa, Phi Delta Kappa. Avocations: computers, swimming, bridge. Home: 16 Cayla Ln Port Jefferson NY 11776

ECKERT, JEAN PATRICIA, elementary education educator; b. Pitts., July 22, 1935; d. Homer Michael and Berdena Leona (Kessler) Canel; m. William L. Eckert, June 13, 1959; 1 child, Suzanne Mary. BS, Indiana U. Pa., 1957; postgrad., U. Pitts., 1958-59, U. San Diego, 1981. Cert. pub. instrn., Pa. Elem. tchr. Pine-Richland Sch. Dist., Gibsonia, Pa., 1957—60, substitute tchr., 1963—65; elem. tchr. Shaler Twp. Sch. Dist., Glenshaw, Pa., 1965—66, St. Scholastica Sch., Diocese of Pitts., Aspinwall, Pa., 1966—91, substitute tchr., 1991—, tutor, 1991—. Judge election 4th dist. Rep. Party, Aspinwall, 1962-65, 91—. Mem.: AAUW, Nat. Cath. Edn. Assn., Literacy Vols. Am., Ind. U. (Pa.) Alumni Assn., Delta Zeta (sec. 1955, pres. 1956). Roman Catholic. Avocations: travel, literature. Home: 210 12th St Pittsburgh PA 15215-1600

ECKERT, NANCY RUSCIO, school system administrator; b. Cortland, N.Y., June 12, 1954; d. Max Alson and Shirley Margaret (Cook) Stoker; m. Joseph John Ruscio, Nov. 20, 1976 (dec. 1999); children: Stephanie Rae, Joey Corin, Kiley Christine, Justin Maxwell; m. Roger P. Eckert, Oct. 11, 2002. BS, SUNY, Oswego, 1976; MS, SUNY, Cortland, 1982, Cert. of Advanced Study, 1985. Grade 2 tchr. Moravia (N.Y.) Ctrl. Sch., 1976-81, staff devel. trainer, 1984-85, asst. H.S. prin., 1984-94; elem. sch. prin. Manchester-Shortsville (N.Y.) Ctrl Sch., 1994-95; dir. instrn. Manchester-Shortsville Ctrl. Sch. Dist., 1995-96; asst. to supt. stds. and regional capacity bldg. Wayne Finger Lakes BOCES, 1996-98; staff devel. specialist Canandaigua City Sch. Dist., 1998-2000, asst. supt. for instrn., 2000—. Facilitator Wayne Finger Lakes, Stanley, N.Y., 1986—. Bd. dirs. Ontario County Youth Mus., Canandaigua, N.Y., 1989; chairperson of pastor's parish com., Farmington (N.Y.) United Ch., 1994—. Republican. Methodist. Avocations: golf, family activities. Office: 143 Pearl St Canandaigua NY 14424 Home: 230 Pickering St Canandaigua NY 14424-1073 E-mail: eckertn@canandaiguaschools.org.

ECKERT, SANDRA LYNN, secondary education art educator; b. Pottstown, Pa., Nov. 2, 1957; d. Edward Eckert and Margareta Theresa (Rennig) Strohm; 1 child Megan Dillon LeVance. BFA, Kutztown (Pa.) U., 1987. Cert. in art edn., Pa. Long term substitute tchr. Allentown (Pa.) Sch. Dist., 1988, Pottstown Sch. Dist., 1988; theatre arts instr. Stage-Door Workshop, Allentown, 1989—; tchr. art East Penn Sch. Dist., Emmaus, Pa., 1988-93, Saucon Valley Sch. Dist., Hellertown, Pa., 1993—. Dir. one-act plays Emmaus (Pa.) Jr. H.S., 1992-93, Saucon Valley H.S., Hellertown, 1993-96; cons. Binney and Smith, Art Skills, Inc. Exhibited photog. works in gallery, 1993. Edn. chair Easton (Pa.) Scarecrow Festival divsn. Easton Pride, 1994; facilitator Anne Frank Workshop, Pa. Stage Co., Allentown, 1994, illustrator, Easton Heritage Alliance Hist. House Tours (3 yrs.) . Chrysler First grantee, 1989, Artist in Edn. grantee Pa. Coun. on Arts, 1993, 94, Saucon Valley Sch. Dist. grantee, 1994;. Mem. Nat. Art Edn. Assn.(regional rep. to Pa. Art Edn. Assn. bd. dirs., 3-time winner Outstanding Regional Rep. award), Saucon Valley Edn. Assn., Am. Whitewater Assn., Lehigh Valley Club, Delta Kappa Gamma. Avocations: painting, reading, theater, gardening. Home: 319 S Fulton St Allentown PA 18102 Office: Saucon Valley Sr HS Polk Valley Rd Hellertown PA 18055

ECKHARDT, KAREN BOYCE, educational consultant; b. Riverside, Calif., June 09; d. Ben Lee and Mary Lu (Bingaman) Boyce; m. Robert Fuess Eckhardt. BA, Angelo State U., 1975; MA, U. Tex., 1984. Sales mgmt. positions, Houston and Austin, Tex., 1975-81; tchr. Leander, Spring and Humble Ind. Sch. Dists., Tex., 1981-88; lectr. Sam Houston State U., Huntsville, Tex., 1989-90; ednl. cons. Nystrom, Houston, 1991—. Speaker, presenter in field. Author: Shots: A Group Performance, 1984. Mem. ASCD, Tex. Coun. for Social Studies, Speech Comm. Assn., Phi Kappa Phi. Avocations: reading, snorkeling, bicycling, volunteer work on drug education. Office: Nystrom PO Box 62101-0420 Houston TX 77205

ECKLUND, CONSTANCE CRYER, French language educator; b. Chgo., Nov. 20, 1938; d. Gilbert and Electra (Papadopoulos) Cryer; m. John E. Ecklund, Mar. 22, 1975. BA magna cum laude, Northwestern U., 1960; PhD, Yale U., 1965. Asst. prof. Ind. U., Bloomington, 1964-66; asst. prof. French Southern Conn. State U., New Haven, 1967-70, assoc. prof., 1970-76, prof., 1976—2002. Speaker in field. Contbr. articles to profl. jours. Named Tchr. of Yr., So. Conn. State U., 2002. Mem. AAUP, Am. Coun. Teaching Fgn. Langs., Am. Assn. Tchrs. French, Modern Lang. Assn., Phi Beta Kappa. Republican. Avocations: piano, gardening, cooking, travel, graphic art. Home: 27 Cedar Rd Woodbridge CT 06525-1642

EDDY, NANCY C. counselor; BS in Elem. Edn., EdM in Sch. Counseling, U. Ark.; JD, U. Ark., Little Rock. Counselor Clinton Elem., Sherwood, Ark., 1984—. Treas., bd. dirs. S.W. Ednl. Lab., 2003—. Chmn. Pulaski Fedn. Tchrs. Cmty. Svcs.; co-chmn. Ctrl. Ark. Jobs With Justice; vol. United Way; pres. Ctrl. Ark. Labor Coun., 1999. Office: Clinton Elem 142 Hollywood Ave Sherwood AR 72120*

EDELHERTZ, HELAINE WOLFSON, mathematics educator; b. Queens, N.Y., June 22, 1953; d. David and Sylvia Guttman Wolfson; m. Melvyn Paul, June 6, 1976; children: Allyson Leigh, Dustin Scott. BS, SUNY, Oneonta, 1977; MS, SUNY, New Paltz, 1985. Cert. tchr., N-6, N.Y. Substitute tchr. Roscoe (N.Y.) Cen. Sch., 1978-82; tchr. Yeshiva Sch., South Fallsburg, N.Y., 1982-83; substitute tchr. Middletown (N.Y.) City Sch. Dist., 1984-86, home tchr., 1984-87, math. specialist, 1987-92. With Math Turnkey, Meml. Elem. Sch., Middletown, 1989-93, Excellence and Accountability Program, 1989-92; math. com. Middletown Schs., 1989-95; bldg. com. Study Math. Portfolios, 1992—, instr. math. manipulations. Bd. dirs. Wallkill Farms Homeowner's Assn., 1986-88, budget com., 1992—; asst. summer coord. Roscoe Free Libr., 1983. Mem. Am. Math. Tchrs. N.Y. State, Nat. Coun. Tchrs. Math., Middletown Tchrs. Assn. (sr. bldg. rep. 1992-95, bldg. rep. 1997—, exec. bd. dirs.). Jewish. Avocations: gardening, sewing, knitting, cooking, dance. Home: 77 Lopresti Rd Middletown NY 10940-8421 Office: Maple Hill Elem Sch 491 County Rte 78 Middletown NY 10940

EDELMAN, NORMAN HERMAN, medical educator, university dean and official; b. N.Y.C., May 21, 1937; s. Irving H. and Pearl Ruth (Solomon) E.; m. Ida Nadel, June 1959; children: David, Ruth, Deborah. AB, Bklyn. Coll., 1957; MD, NYU, 1961. Diplomate Am. Bd. Internal Medicine, Am. Bd. Pulmonary Diseases. Intern NYU Med. Sch., N.Y.C., 1961-62, resident, 1962-63; rsch. fellow NIH, Balt., 1963-65; vis. fellow Columbia U., Presbyn. Med. Ctr., N.Y.C., 1965-67; rsch. assoc. Michael Reese Med. Ctr., Chgo., 1967-69; asst. prof. medicine U. Pa. Sch. Medicine, Phila., 1969-72; prof. medicine, chief pulmonary medicine Robert Wood Johnson Med. Sch., U. Medicine and Dentistry of N.J., New Brunswick, N.J., 1972-95, dean, 1988-95; prof. medicine and physiology and biophysics SUNY, Stony Brook, 1996—, v.p. health sci. ctr., dean Sch. Medicine, 1996—. Cons. for sci. Am. Lung Assn., N.Y.C., 1984—; mem. pulmonary disease adv. com. NIH, 1984-88. Contbr. articles, abstracts to profl. jours., chpts. to med. textbooks; mem. editorial bd. Jour. Applied Physiol., Am. Rev. Respiratory Diseases. Served as surgeon USPHS, 1963-65. Fellow AAAS; mem. Assn. Am. Physicians, Am. Soc. Clin. Investigation, Am. Thoracic Soc., Am. Physiol. Soc.

EDELSTEIN, BRENDA, school administrator; b. Georgia, USSR, June 2, 1945; came to U.S., 1951; d. Moshe and Sima Moses; m. Fred Edelstein, June 19, 1966; children: Marc, David, Steven. BA in Edn., Bklyn. Coll., 1967, MS in Edn., 1982; 6th yr. profl. cert., Coll. S.I., 1989. Tchr. grade 1 P.S. 181, N.Y.C., 1967-68; substitute tchr. Bd. Edn., Bklyn., 1976-78; tchr. creative writing P.S. 27 K, Bklyn., 1978-79; elem. sch. tchr. P.S. 279 K, Bklyn., 1979-86, coord. early childhood, 1986-91, asst. prin., 1991—. Mentor Mentor Program-U.F.T., N.Y.C., 1988. Recipient Nat. Excellence award U.S. Dept. Edn., 1988. Mem. ASCD, Am. Women in Edn., N.Y. Coun. Reading. Avocations: painting, drawing, visiting museums, cooking. Home: 1726 E 7th St Brooklyn NY 11223-2216

EDELSTEIN, DAVID SIMEON, historian, educator; b. NYC, Jan. 19, 1913; s. William and Clara (Brener) E.; m. Frances Fisher, June 4, 1939 (dec. Jan. 1990); children: Helen Freedman, Henry, Daniel Louis; m. Gertrude Bernstein, Jan. 5, 1997. BA, CCNY, 1932; MA, Columbia U., 1933, PhD, 1949. Cert. elem. tchr., N.Y. Tchr., adminstr. various sch., NYC, 1934-67; lectr. in-svc. courses Bd. Edn., NYC, 1946-65; lectr. History CCNY, 1947-67; lectr. Edn. U. Colo., 1960, Yeshiva U. Grad. Sch. Edn., 1960-61, Hunter Coll., 1964-65; prof. Edn. Western Conn. State U., Danbury, 1967-83; adj. assoc. prof. History Fordham U., Bronx, NY, 1967-70; instr. in-svc. course Stamford Bd. Edn., Conn., 1970-71; adj. assoc. prof. History CUNY, 1970-75; adj. prof. History Western Conn. State U., Danbury, 1984-85. Lectr. in field. Author: Joel Munsell, Printer and Antiquarian, 1950; author: (with others) M. Stern: editor: Publishers for Mass. Entertainment in the Nineteenth Century, 1980; contbr. biog. sketches Nat. Am. Biography, 1999; contbr. articles to profl. jours. Mem. AAUP, Am. Assn. Sch. Adminstrs., Am. Hist. Assn., Conn. Edn. Assn., Nat. Assn. of Elem. Sch. Prins., N.Y.C. Elem. Sch. Prins. Assn. (life), Nat. Coun. of Local Adminstrs. of Vocat. Edn., Social Studies Coun., Coun. of Chmn. of Acad. Subjects, Nat. Soc. for the Study of Edn., New Eng. Hist. Assn., New Eng. Assn. of Tchr. Educators, Phi Alpha Theta, Phi Delta Kappa. Democrat. Jewish. Home: 118 Rosedale Rd Yonkers NY 10710-3033 Office: Western Conn State U 181 White St Danbury CT 06810-6826

EDELSTEIN, ROSEMARIE (ROSEMARIE HUBLOU), medical/surgical nurse, educator, medical and legal consultant; b. Drake, N.D., Mar. 3, 1935; d. Francis Jerome and Myrtle Josephine (Merbach); m. Harry George Edelstein, June 22, 1957 (div.); children: Julie, Lori, Lynn, Toni Anne. BSN, St. Teresa of Avila Coll., Winona, Minn., 1956; MA in Edn., Holy Names Coll., Oakland, Calif., 1977; EdD, U. San Francisco, 1982, postgrad., 1987, U. Ariz., 1985—; cert. pub. health nurse, U. Calif., Berkeley, 1972. Dir., clin. supr. San Francisco Sch. for Health Professions, 1971-74, Rancho Arroyo Sch. of Vocat. Nursing, Sacramento, 1974-75; intensive care nurse Kaiser-Permanente Hosp., San Rafael, Calif., 1976-77; dir. insvc. edn. Ross Hosp., Calif., 1977-78; dir. nursing edn. St. Francis Meml. Hosp., San Francisco, 1978-85; med.-legal nursing cons., med.-surg. staff nurse met. hosps., San Francisco, 1985-90, St. Luke's Hosp., Duluth, Minn., 1990-91, St. Charles Hosp., New Orleans, 1992, U. Tex. Med. Br., Galveston, 1992-94; staff nurse family medicine faculty practice, 1995; med.-surg. nurse St. Anthony of Padua Hosp., Oklahoma City, 1994-95; nurse Northgate Conv. Hosp., San Rafael, 1995—. Night charge nurse Creekside Conv. Hosp., Santa Rosa, Calif., 1996; charge nurse medications, treatment and Alzheimer's Unit Fallon Conv. Ctr., Nev., 1996; charge nurse Medicare unit White Pine Conv. Ctr., Ely, Nev., 1997; emergency rm., ICU nurse Battle Mt. Gen. Hosp., Nev., 1997; nurse supr. Medicare-Med. Seaview Care Ctr. Sun Corp., Eureka, Calif., 1997—98; mem. staff Walker Post Manor Oxford, NE Lantis Corp., 1998, The Lincoln Ambassador, 1999, Rapid City (S.D.) Care Ctr. Beverly Enterprises, 2000—01, Houghton County Med. Care Facility, Hancock, Mich., 2000—, Norlite Nursing Ctr., Marquette, Mich., 2001—02, Whidbey Island Manor, Oak Harbor, Wash.; mem. staff Medicare unit Everett (Wash.) Rehab. and Care Ctr., 2002, St. Joseph Care Ctr., Spokane, 2003; invited mem. People to People Nursing Edn. and Adminstrn.; candidate to East Asia Philosophy, 1985; postgrad. candidate U. Zurich, Switzerland, 1988; staff Everett Rehab. and Care Ctr., 2002, Whidbey Island Manor, Oak Harbor, Wash., 2003, St. Joseph's Care Ctr., Spokane, Wash., 2003. Author: The Influence of Motivator and Hygiene Factors in Job Changes by Graduate Registered Nurses, 1977; Effects of Two Educational Methods Upon Retention of Knowledge in Pharmacology, 1981; co-author: (with Jane F. Lee) Acupuncture Atlas, 1974. Candidate U.S. Senate Inner Circle, 1988, 89. Lt. col. USAR Med. Res. Mem. Am. Heart Assn., Calif. Nurses Assn., Sigma Theta Tau. Roman Catholic.

EDEN, BECKY DESPAIN, dental educator; b. Oklahoma City, July 14, 1948; children: Brian Thomas, Meredith Lynn. BS in Dental Hygiene, Baylor U., 1970; MEd, Cen. State U., Okla., 1982. Registered dental hygienist. Pvt. practice clin. dental hygienist, Oklahoma City, 1970-73; instr. Coll. Dentistry, Okla. U. Health Scis. Ctr., Oklahoma City, 1973-82, asst. prof., 1982-85, acting chair dept. dental hygiene, 1984-85, clin. dental hygienist faculty practice, 1977-85; assoc. prof., dir. Caruth Sch. Dental Hygiene Baylor Coll. Dentistry, Dallas, 1985-93, assoc. prof. dept. pub. health scis., 1993—; clin. dental hygienist Drs. Israelson, Plemons & Jaynes, Richardson, Tex., 1995-97. Clin. instr. Rose Jr. Coll., Midwest City, Okla., 1972; mem. affil. staff Okla. Children's Meml. Hosp., Oklahoma City, 1977-85; clin. dental hygienist North Tex. Periodontal and Implant Assn., Richardson, 1988-91; mem. test constrn. com. Nat. Bd. Dental Hygiene, ADA, Chgo., 1987-91, dental hygiene cons. Commn. on Dental Accreditation, 1989-96; investigator grants and contracts HHS, NIH; bd. dirs. Childrens Oral Health Ctr. Dallas. Editorial rev. bd.: Jour. Dental Hygiene, Chgo., 1982-2000, Jour. Practical Hygiene, 2002—; contbr. abstracts and articles to profl. jours. Spkr. sch. vols. program Oklahoma City Pub. Schs., 1976-85; project dir. Oral Healthlink: Dallas-Ft. Worth Coalition for Oral Health 2000; bd. dirs. Dallas chpt. ACLU of North Tex., pres., 1996-97; Tex. coord. nat. spit tobacco edn. program, Oral Health Am., 1996-97; bd. dirs. So. Methodist U. YWCA, 1997-98. Recipient small grant award Rsch. Coun., OUHSC, Oklahoma City, 1985, Dental Hygiene Rsch. grant Oral-B Labs., Redwood City, Calif., 1985. Mem. APHA, Am. Assn. Dental Schs., Am. Assn. Dental Rsch., Am. Dental Hygienists Assn. (del. 1980-84), Am. Assn. Pub. Health Dentistry (editor), Tex. Dental Hygienists Assn., Tex. Dental Hygiene Dirs. Assn. (sec. 1990-92), Dallas Dental Hygienists Soc. (v.p. 1994, pres.-elect 1995, pres. 1996), The Woman's Ctr. of Dallas (chair health care task force, bd. dirs. 1994-96, health com. Women's Coun. of Dallas County 1995-97), Sigma Phi Alpha, Kappa Delta Pi. Office: Baylor Coll Dentistry PO Box 660677 Dallas TX 75266-0677

EDGAR, HAROLD SIMMONS HULL, legal educator; b. 1942; AB, Harvard U., 1964; LLB, Columbia U., 1967. Bar: N.Y. 1968. Law clk. to judge U.S. Ct. Appeals (D.C. cir.), 1967—68; asst. prof. Columbia U., N.Y.C., 1968—73; now Julius Silver prof. law, sci. and tech. Columbia U. Sch. Law, N.Y.C., dir. program in law, sci. and tech., 1985—. Mem. The Hastings Ctr., 1978—; rapporteur UNESCO Internat. Com. on Bioethics, 1992—96. Office: Columbia U Law Sch 435 W 116th St New York NY 10027-7201

EDGAR, RUTH R. retired elementary school educator; b. Great Falls, S.C., Jan. 7, 1930; d. Robert Hamer and Clara Elizabeth (Ellenberg) Rogers. AA, Stephens Coll., Columbia, Mo., 1949; BS, So. Meth. U., 1951; MA, Appalachian State U., Boone, N.C., 1977; postgrad., Limestone Coll., Gaffney, S.C., 1971. Lic. real estate salesman, broker. Home economist Lone Star Gas Co., Dallas, 1951-53, So. Union Gas Co., Austin, Tex., 1953-56, Southwestern Pub. Svc. Co., Amarillo, Tex., 1956-57; with Peeler Real Estate, 1970-71, Burns High Sch., Lawndale, N.C., 1971-73, Cen. Cleveland Mid. Sch., Lawndale, 1973-77, Burns Jr. High Sch., Lawndale, 1977-88; resource tchr. South Cleveland Elem. Sch., Shelby, N.C., 1988-90, Elizabeth Elem. Sch., Shelby, 1990-94, Washington Elem. Sch., Waco, N.C., 1990-92; ret., 1994. Mem. supts. adv. coun., Cleveland County, 1971-75, Cleveland County Art Soc., 1972-73, Cen. United Meth. Ch. Home: 401 Forest Hill Dr Shelby NC 28150-5520

EDGELL, KARIN JANE, reading specialist, special education educator; b. Rockford, Ill., July 17, 1937; d. Donald Rickard and Leona Marquerite (Villard) Williams; m. George Paul Edgell III, May 6, 1960; 1 child, Scott. Student, Rollins Coll., 1955-57; BS, U. Ill., 1960, MEd, 1966; MA, Roosevelt U., 1989; adminstrv. endorsement, U. Va., 2001. Tchr. Alexandria (Va.) City Pub. Schs., 1963-79; asst. to dir. Reading Ctr. George Washington U., Washington, 1979-80; tchr. Winnetka (Ill.) Pub. Schs., 1982-89, Arlington County (Va.) Pub. Schs., 1989—. Mem. NEA, ASCD, Nat. Coun. Tchrs. Eng., Internat. Reading Assn., Va. Edn. Assn., Va. Reading Assn., Greater Washington Reading Coun., Coun. Exceptional Children, Phi Delta Kappa. Presbyterian. Home: Landmark Mews 6275 Chaucer View Cir Alexandria VA 22304-3546 E-mail: Karinedgell@mindspring.com.

EDGELL, STEPHEN EDWARD, psychology educator, statistical consultant; b. Inglewood, Calif., June 20, 1947; s. Stephen F. and Evelyn L. (Humborg) E.; m. Donna M. Grassello, Aug. 17, 1974. AA in Math., El Camino Jr. Coll., Gardena, Calif., 1968; AB in Psychology, Calif. State U., Long Beach, 1970; PhD in Math. Psychology, Ind. U., 1974; MA in Math., U. Louisville, 1987. Tchg. and rsch. asst. Ind. U., Bloomington, 1971-72, rsch. asst., computer sys. programmer, 1972, fellow, 1972-73, assoc. instr., 1973-74; asst. prof. psychology U. Louisville, 1974-80, assoc. prof., 1980-85, prof., 1985—, dir. exptl. psychology program, 1983, 88-91. Mgr. software devel. Shelton Metrology Lab., Paducah, Ky., summer 1979; cons. on statis. analysis and exptl. design, product design, customer profile analysis, discrimination, computer software sys.; presenter in field at confs. and profl. meetings. Contbr. articles to profl. jours. Fellow NIMH, 1970-71. Mem. Soc. for Judgment and Decision Making (sec.-treas. 1986-89, newsletter editor 2000-02), Soc. for Med. Decision Making, Soc. for Math. Psychology, Am. Statis. Assn., Psychometric Soc., Psychonomic Soc., Cognitive Sci. Soc., Sigma Xi. Achievements include research on judgment, decision making and choice with emphasis on using mathematical models, artificial neural network models, artificial intelligence and computer simulation of decision making, including Bayesian methods, development of statistical techniques, medical decision making. Home: 10604 Grassy Ct Louisville KY 40241-2011 Office: U Louisville Dept Psychol and Brain Scis Louisville KY 40292-0001 E-mail: edgell@louisville.edu.

EDGERTON, MILLS FOX, JR., retired foreign language educator; b. Hartford, Conn., June 11, 1931; s. Mills Fox and Miriam (Reynolds) E.; m. Marianne Simonsson, Dec. 27, 1957; children: Michael, Nicholas. BA, U. Conn., 1953; student, Nat. Autonomous U. Mex., Mexico City, 1951; AM, Princeton U., 1955, PhD, 1960. Instr. Romance langs. Princeton (N.J.) U., 1957, Rutgers U., 1957-60; assoc. prof., chmn. dept. Spanish Bucknell U., Lewisburg, Pa., 1960-66, prof., 1966-93, chmn. dept. modern langs., lit. and linguistics, 1968-74. Dir. Univ. Press, 1976-97, assoc. dir., 1997-98; dir. Middlebury Coll. Grad. Sch. Spanish in Spain, Madrid, 1971-72, Middlebury Coll. Intensive Lang. Program, 1973; prof. The Spanish Sch. of Middlebury Coll.; interim dir. The Madrid Ctr. of the Inst. of European Studies, 1993-94; chmn. N.E. Conf. on Tchg. Fgn. Langs., 1972, Spanish Com. for Grad. Record Exams., 1965-69. Author: (poetry) Aquí y allá, 1997, La rosa azul, 1998, Episodios familiares, 1998, Je me souviens, 1999, Una honda copa de tinto, 1999, La ultima gota, 2000, Les Eaux vertes, 2001, El frío viento, 2001, La verdad desnuda, 2002; author: (short story) L'Histoire de Harthur, 1998; writer poems in Spanish, French and Italian; contbr. articles to profl. jours. Recipient Lindback award for disting. tchg., 1971, 1st prize Prix Vitrail Francophone, Soc. Poetes Artistes de France, 1997; Alexander von Humboldt Found. grantee, 1961, Am. Philos. Soc. grantee, 1962 Roman Catholic. Home: 143 Willowbrook Blvd Lewisburg PA 17837-9349

EDIGER, MARLOW, education educator; b. Inman, Kans., Oct. 10, 1927; BS in Edn., Kans. State Tchrs. Coll., 1958, MS in Edn., 1960; EdD, U. Denver, 1963. Tchr. Sandcreek Sch., rural Newton, Kans., 1951-52; English tchr. Mennonite Sch., Jericho, 1952-53; tchr. English and geography Friends Boys Sch., Ramallah, Jordan, 1953-54; tchr. Countryside Sch., Lehigh, Kans., 1955-57; tchr., prin. Lincolnville Grade Sch., Kans., 1957-61; prof. edn. Truman State U., Kirksville, 1962—92. Spkr. in field at over 200 nat., internat. tchr. edn. convs.; evaluator over 135 PhD theses at numerous univs. in India including Kerala U., Mother Theresa U., U. Madras, Utkal U., Sambalpur U., Alagappa U.; mem. editl. bd. Experiments in Edn. Jour., India, Jour. Karnataka Sate Edn. Fedn., India, Reading Improvement, Edn., Jour. English Lang. Tchg. in India, The Progress of Edn. in India, Edutracks (India), Jour. of Rsch. in Edn.; v.p. NMSU-AAUP, 1974—75, pres., 1975—76. Author: Relevancy in the Elem. Curriculum, 1975, Relevancy in the Elem. Curriculum, 2nd edit., 1991, The Elem. Curriculum, A Handbook, 1977, The Elem. Curriculum, A Handbook, 2nd edit., 1988, Social Studies Curriculum in the Elem. Sch., 5th edit., 2000, Lang. Arts Curriculum in the Elem. Sch., 1983, 1992, Lang. Arts Curriculum in the Elem. Sch., 2nd edit., 1988, Lang. Arts Curriculum in the Elem. Sch., rev., 1994, The Modern Elem. Sch., 1997, Tchg. Math in the Elem. Sch., 1997, Improving the Tchg. of Elem. Sch. Math., 1999, The Holy Land, 1998, Tchg. Sci. in the Elem. Sch., 2nd edit., 2000, Tchg. Reading Successfully, 2000, Tchg. Sci. Successfully, 2001, Tchg. Social Studies Successfully, 2001; mem. editl. bd.: The Edn. Rev., The Math Tchr., Jour. English Lang., also Edn., publ.: more than 2,400 manuscripts on six continents; co-author: Tchg. Reading Successfully, 2000, Tchg. Math. Successfully, 2000, Lang. Arts Curriculum, 2003, Improving Sch. Admin., 2003, Elem. Curriculum, 2003; contbr. articles to profl. jours. Treas. Marion County Kans. Tchrs. Assn., 1958-59, pres., 1959-60; mem. adv. coun. Himalayan Jour. Ednl. R&D, India; mem. nat. coun. social studies com. Religion in the Schs.; chmn. Marion County Curriculum Com., 1960-61tchr. Sunday sch., 1950-52, 54-58, 64-99. Mem. ASCD, NSTA (com. tchr. edn.), NEA (life, Mo. chpt., core competencies and key skills com., higher edn. com., com. on pub. rels. 2000-01), Internat. Reading Assn. (sub com. evaluating literacy standards), Nat. Coun. Social Studies (adv. coun. rural schs. and social studies, ethics com., pub. rels. curriculum com., archives com.), Nat. Coun. Tchrs. English (vice chmn. rural lang. arts com., lang. and learning across the curriculum com., tracking in the pub. schs com.), Mo. Coun. Social Studies (bd. control), Sci. Tchrs. Mo. (bd. dirs.), Mo. Geog. Alliance, Phi Delta Kappa. Office: 201 W 22nd PO Box 417 North Newton KS 67117-0417 E-mail: mediger2@cox.net.

EDISON, DIANE, artist, educator, administrator; b. Plainfield, N.J., Sept. 3, 1950; d. Anthony Joseph and Davie Wilhelmina (Johnson) E. BFA, Sch. Visual Arts, N.Y.C., 1976; postgrad., Skowhegan Sch. Painting, 1984; MFA, U. Pa., 1986. Asst. prof. Savannah (Ga.) Coll. Art and Design, 1990-92, U. Ga., Athens, 1992-96, assoc. prof., 1997—, assoc. dir. Lamar Dodd Sch. Art, 1997-99; asst. prof. U. Ga. Studies Abroad, Cortona, Italy, 1993, 99. Panelist Telfair Acad. Arts and Scis., Savannah, 1992, Ga. Mus. Art, Athens, 1993, Ga. Coun. for Arts, 1993—, Womens Caucus for Arts Nat. Conf., Phila., 1997, Ark. Art Ctr., Little Rock, 1996, Mid-Am. S.E. Coll. Art Assn., 1997; mem. gala com. Kwang Ju (Korea) Biennial Korea, 1997, Geffen Contemporary Mus. Art, L.A., 1997, Grand Arts, Kansas City, 1998. Solo exhbn. Macon Mus. Arts and Scis., 1998; exhbns. include Marymount Manhattam Coll. Gallery, N.Y.C., 1989, Islip (N.Y.) Art Mus. Brookward Hall, 1989, The Bertha and Karl Leubsdorf Art Gallery, N.Y.C, 1990, Cork Gallery Lincoln Ctr., N.Y.C., 1990, Salena Gallery L.I. U., Bklyn., 1990, Savannah Coll. Art and Design, 1990, Rotunda Gallery, Bklyn., 1991, St. Louis Artist Guild, 1992, Frumkin/Adams Gallery, N.Y.C., 1992, 94-95, Ark. Arts Ctr., Little Rock, 1992-96, Ga. Mus. Art, Athens, 1993, Ga. Artist Registry, Atlanta, 1994, Charles More Gallery, Phila., 1994, U. Mo., Kansas City, 1994, U. Ga., Athens, 1994, Southeastern Ctr. Contemporary Art, Winston-Salem, N.C., 1994, Chattahoochee Valley Art Mus., Lagrange, Ga., 1995, Nexus Contemporary Art Ctr., Atlanta, 1995, George Adams Gallery, N.Y.C., 1995-97, SFA Gallery, Nacogdoches, Tex., 1996, Sawhill Gallery James Madison U., 1997, Tatischeff & Co., Inc., N.Y.C., 1997, Macon Mus. Arts and Scis., 1998, George Adams Gallery, 1998, Grand Arts, Kansas City, 1998, Berman Mus., Collegeville, Pa., 1998-99, Nexus Biennial, 1999; represented in permanent collections at Ark. Arts Ctr., Am. Embassy, Moscow, Agnes Scott Coll., Decatur, Ga., also pvt. collections. Artist grantee Ga. Coun. for Arts, 1993, Nat. Endowment for Arts, 1994, jr. faculty rsch. grantee U. Ga., 1994; Milton Avery Found fellow, N.Y.C., 1995; artist resident Millay Colony for Arts Inc., Austerlitz, N.Y., 1995, Blue Mountain Ctr., Blue Mountain Lake, N.Y., 1996. Mem. AAUP, Coll. Art Assn. Democrat. Episcopalian. Avocation: guitar. Office: U Ga Visual Arts Bldg Jackson St Athens GA 30602

EDLESON, MICHAEL EDWARD, economist, finance educator, consultant, writer; b. St. Louis, Apr. 25, 1958; s. Edward and Joan Edleson; m. Jan Katherine Taulman, Sept. 6, 1981; 1 child, Christopher. BS with distinction, U.S. Mil. Acad., 1979; MBA with highest honors, Suffolk U., 1986; MS, MIT, 1986, PhD, 1990. Commd. 2d lt. U.S. Army, 1979; with Army Corps Engrs., 1979-84; asst. prof. fin. econs. U.S. Mil. Acad., West Point, N.Y., 1986-90; asst. prof. fin. Harvard Bus. Sch., Boston, 1990-96; vis. assoc. prof. fin. Tuck Sch. Dartmouth Coll., 1995-96; dir. risk mgmt. Infinity fin. Tech., 1996-97; v.p. NASD, 1997-99; sr. v.p., chief economist NASD/Nasdaq, 1999—. Bd. dir. Geodynamics Corp. Author: Value Averaging, 1991, 2d edit., 1993, Armed Forces Guide to Personal Financial Planning, 1991; columnist National Forum, 1994—96; contbr. articles to profl. jours., chpts. to books; creator of the Value Averaging Investment Technique, 1988. Fellow, grantee, Army Rsch. Inst., 1988, 89, 90, Sci. Rsch. Lab., 1988, 89. Mem. Fin. Mgmt. Assn. (1996-2000), Internat. Assn. Fin. Engrs., Fin. Execs. Inst., Phi Kappa Phi.

EDLICH, RICHARD FRENCH, biomedical engineering educator; b. N.Y.C., Jan. 19, 1939; MD, NYU, 1962; PhD, U. Minn., 1973. From instr. to assoc. prof. U. Va. Sch. Medicine, Charlottesville, 1971-76, prof. plastic surgery and biomed. engring., 1976-82, disting. prof. plastic and maxillofacial surgery and biomed. engring., 1983-96, Raymoon F. Morgan prof. plastic surgery and disting. prof. biomed. engring., 1996—2001. Dir. Emergency Med. Svc. and Burn Ctr., 1974-85; physician tech. adviser Bur. Emergency Svc., HEW, 1974-79; cons. Divsn. Health Manpower and Nat. Ctr. Health Svc. Rsch., 1977-79. Editor-in-chief: Jour. Long-Term Effects of Med. Implants. Recipient outstanding teaching award U. Va., 1989, Thomas Jefferson award, 1991, outstanding faculty award Commonwealth of Va. Coun. Higher Edn., 1989, 5th Ann. David Boyd Lectr. in Emergency Medicine, 2001. Mem. ACS, Soc. Univ. Surgeons, Am. Assn. Surg. Trauma, Am. Burn Assn. (Harvey Stuart Allen award 2000), Univ. Assn. Emergency Medicine, Am. Soc. Plastic and Reconstructive Surgeons, Soc. of Acad. Emergency Medicine, Coll. Emergency Physicians, Am. Surg. Assn. Achievements include research in the biology of wound repair and infection. Home and Office: 16155 New Jenne Lake Ct Beaverton OR 97006

EDMONDS, DEAN STOCKETT, JR., physicist, educator, director; b. N.Y.C., Dec. 24, 1924; s. Dean Stockett and Mary Watkins (Arms) Edmonds; m. Mary Louise Wilson, July 28, 1951 (dec. May 1978); children: Dean Stockett III, Louis Round Wilson, Ann Helene Edmonds Mahoney, Elizabeth V. Casey; m. Wendy Nickerson Adams, Nov. 7, 1993. BS, MIT, 1950, PhD, 1958; MA, Princeton U., 1952. Co-founder, v.p., dir. Nuclide Corp., 1958-65; asst. prof. physics Coll. Liberal Arts Boston U., 1961-67, assoc. prof. physics, 1967-83, prof. physics, 1983-91, prof. emeritus, 1991—; co-founder, pres., chmn. Tachisto Laser Sys., Inc., 1971-85; dir., chief sci. adv. bd. Gen. Ionex Inc., 1974-85; regional v.p., dir. Nat. Aeronautic Assn., 1988—. Vis prof physics Univ Western Ont, London, 1972—74; research fellow Harvard Univ, Cambridge, Mass., 1959—61; guest physics dept MIT, Cambridge, Mass., 1959—61. Author: (book) Novel Experiments in Physics II, 1975; author: (with B Cioffari) Experiments in College Physics, 6th ed, 1978, Cioffari's Experiments in College Physics, 7th ed, 1983, Cioffari's Experiments in College Physics, 10th ed, 1997; co-editor: Experiments in Physics for General Physics Courses Without Calculus, 1968, Experiments in Physics for General Physics Courses With Calculus, 1968; contbr. articles to profl jours. Master sgt U.S. Army, 1943—47, ETO, PTO. Mem.: IEEE, Am. Assn. Physics Tchrs. (Spec Merit Award), Am Phys. Soc., Cosmos Club Washington. Achievements include research in molecular beams leading to cesium atomic clock, the present internat. time standard; development of of the racetrack microtron accelerator for cancer therapy. Avocations: amateur radio, restoring antique aircraft and sports cars, sport flying, opera, building high fidelity systems. Home: 1019 Spyglass Ln Naples FL 34102-7734 Office: Boston U Dept Physics 590 Commonwealth Ave Boston MA 02215-2521

EDMONDS, MARIA NIEVES, college administrator; b. Arecibo, P.R., July 7, 1945; came to U.S., 1965; d. Giobel and Cruz Maria (Montes) Nieves; 1 child, Maria Elizabeth Ries; m. David C. Edmonds, Mar. 1, 1997. BA cum laude, U. P.R., 1965; MS, Fla. State U., 1967; Hon. Degree, Baoji Coll. Arts and Scis., China, 1995. Disability adjudicator Vocat. Rehab., Tallahassee, 1968-71; vocat. rehab. counselor State of Fla. Vocat. Rehab. Office, Clearwater, 1971-73; instr. psychology St. Petersburg Jr. Coll., Clearwater, 1973-76, dir. women on the way program, 1980-85, dir. exptl. learning and coop. edn. programs, 1985-88, coord. Ctrl. Am. Scholarship Program, 1988-94, asst. provost internat. edn., 1994—. Co-dir. Fla.-Japan Inst., State of Fla.; bias reviewer for coll. level acad. skills project State of Fla.; mem. adv. bd. Educators in Industry, Pinellas County, Fla.; chair Clearwater Job Svc. Employer's Com.; sponsor, coord. numerous topical seminars and workshops with cmty. colls.; seminar presenter cultural transition P.R., Ecuador, Costa Rica, China, Guatemala, Honduras, Nicaragua, Dominican Republic, 1988—. V.p., pres. Leadership Pinellas, Clearwater; vice-chair Pinellas Assn. Children and Adults with Learning Disabilities, Clearwater; founder, mem. Bay Area Assn. for Women, Tampa; treas., sec. Found. for Quality Pub. Svc., Pinellas County. Recipient Susan B. Anthony award NOW, 1980, Women Honoring Women award Soroptimjist Internat., Pinellas County, 1981, Twin award Tribute to Women in Industry, YWCA, 1988, Disting. Leadership award Nat. Assn. Cmty. Leadership, 1990. Mem. Univ. Women's Assn., Cmty. Colls. for Internat. Devel., Women in Edn. Assn., Fla. Women's Alliance, Pinellas County Assn. Children and Adults with Learning Disabilities (v.p. 1988), Fla. Assn. Cmty. Colls. Avocations: avid walking, travel, antique collecting. Office: St Petersburg Jr Coll 2465 Drew St Clearwater FL 33765-2816

EDMONDS, VELMA MCINNIS, nursing educator; b. NYC, Feb. 17, 1940; d. Walter Lee and Eva Doris (Grant) McInnis; children: Stephen Clay, Michelle Louise. Diploma, Charity Hosp. Sch. Nursing, New Orleans, 1961; BSN, Med. Coll. Ga., 1968; MSN, U. Ala., Birmingham, 1980; D of Nursing Sci., La. State U., 2001. Staff nurse Ochsner Found. Hosp., New Orleans, 1961-63, 1987—, clin. educator, 1987-89; staff nurse Suburban Hosp., Bethesda, Md., 1963-65; asst. DON svc., dir. staff devel. Providence Hosp., Mobile, Ala., 1967-70; staff nurse MICU U. So. Ala. Med. Ctr., Mobile, 1980-82, clin. nurse specialist, nutrition/metabolic support, 1982-84; instr., coord., BSN completion program Northwestern State U. Coll. Nursing, Pineville, La., 1984-86; head nurse So. Bapt. Hosp., New Orleans, 1986-87; instr. nursing La. State U. Health Sci. Ctr., New Orleans, 1989-91, asst. prof. nursing, 1991—; clin. coord. Transitional Hosp. Corp., 1994-95; cons., vis. prof. U. of Guam Coll. of Nursing and Health Scis., 2002—. Gov.-apptd. mem. La. Bd. Examiners in Dietetics and Nutrition, 1990-98, sec.-treas., 1996-97; cons. on internat. health and nursing edn., 1992—; rschr. with recently immigrated Honduran women; cons., faculty U. Guam, 2002—; presenter in field. Advisor Hispanic C. of C., New Orleans; adv. bd. Cmty. Vietnamese Outreach Program, Meth. Hosp., New Orleans; chmn. Silent Auction, New Orleans Dollars for Scholars Found., 2000; founding bd. dirs., edn. coord. Orgn. Health and Med. Profession Women. Recipient Excellence in Nursing group award Ochsner Fedn. Hosp., New Orleans, 1987, cert. Merit Tuberculosis Assn. Greater New Orleans, 1961. Mem. ANA, Nat. Soc. Nutrition Edn., La. State Nurses' Assn. (dist. 7), Am. Soc. Parenteral and Enteral Nutrition, La. State Soc. Parenteral and Enteral Nutrition (program and edn. coms.), Mobile Area Nonvolitional Nutrition Support Assn. (past pres.), Transcultural Nursing Soc., Soc. Nutrition Edn., Orgn. Health & Med. Profl. Women (Guam & We. Pacific region founding bd. dirs., edn. coord.), Sigma Theta Tau. Office: LSU Health Scis Ctr Sch of Nursing 1900 Gravier St New Orleans LA 70112 E-mail: vedmonds@ite.net.

EDMONDSON, MICHAEL HERMAN, secondary school educator; b. Lafayette, Ala., Aug. 9, 1954; s. Herman L. and M. Ruth (Hurley) E. BSEd in Chemistry and, Edn., Columbus (Ga.) Coll., 1978, MS in Gen. Sci., 1986, Specialist in Edn., Sci., 1990; PhD in Sci. Edn., Auburn U., 2001. Cert. tchr. sci. edn. T-7, chemistry, tchr. support, curriculum and adminstrn. L-7. Tchr. sci., chemistry and physics William H. Spencer H.S., 1980-94; tchr. phys. sci., chemistry and physics Hardaway H.S., Columbus, Ga., 1995, 1997—2002; lead tchr. sci. tech., chair dept. Carver H.S.; lead flight dir. Ga. Space Sci. Ctr.; lead sci. tchr., engring. magnet coord. Northside H.S., 2002—. Staff devel. instr. computer course Muscogee County Sch. Dist., 1987-90; part-time lab. instr. Columbus Coll., summers, 1988, 89, organizer, tchr. summer chemistry program for h.s. students, summer 1989, part-time instr., 1990-93, Ext. in LaGrange, 1994; instr. Columbus Coll. Youth Acad., 1993; instr. KIDS Club, Ga. Inst. Tech., 1993, Workshop for Middle Sch. Tchrs., Auburn U., 1993, 94, summer programs for engring. students Ga. Inst. Tech., 2002—; project reviewer chemistry and physics edn. NSF, Washington, 1990; head tchr. sci./tech. Magnet Sch. Program, Carver H.S. Planning Team, 1991; advisor sci., math., integrated tech. magnet sch. program Dimon Elem. Sch., 1993; developer chemistry camp ages 11-14 Columbus Coll. Continuing Edn. Ctr., 1994; tchr. rep. Muscogee County Sch. Dist.; inst. Columbus State U., part-time 1998—; lead flight dir. Coca-Cola Space Sci. Ctr., 1994-97; planner magnet program Carver H.S., 1990-92; planner engring. and architecture magnet program Northside H.S., 2002. Co-author: Atomic Structure and the Periodic Table: A Resource Book for Teachers, 1987, Chemistry for the Health Sciences, Part 1: Inorganic chemistry, 1988, Part 2: Organic Chemistry, 1988; contbr. numerous articles to profl. jours.; writer numerous sci. curriculums; contbr. to America Online Edn. Librs., Compuserve's Education+ and Science/Math+ Forums' Librs., FCClient Bull. Bd. Svc.: Education, Debates and Hypercard Librs., 1994; lectr. in field. Vol. Ft Benning Inf. Mus., 1984; reader's adv. coun. Ledger-Enquirer newspapers, 1989, chmn., 1986-89; bd. dirs. Springer Theater Co., 1986-87, 88-90, Springer Children's Theatre, 1986-89, sec., 1987-89, mailing list organizer, 1986-89, nominating com., 1988; participant Alzheimer's Memory Walk, 1994; originator Christmas Stocking and Coloring Book project for Housing Project Day Care Ctr. Children, Easter Egg project; actor Springer Theatre, 1982—; bd. dirs. Edn. Excellence Found., 2003—. Recipient cert. of excellence NSF Summer Inst., 1985, Page One award, 1987, cert. of appreciation Nat. Honor Soc. Spencer H.S., 1988, 89, 92, Gov.'s tech. award for Muscogee County, 1988, cert. of recognition Key Club Spencer H.S., 1989, Outstanding Southeastern Educator award Optical Soc. Am., 1989, Presdl. award for excellence in sci. and math. tchr., Ga., 1989, Outstanding Physics Tchr. award Am. Assn. Physics Tchrs., 1990, Swift Textiles Outstanding Educator award, 1990, Tchr. of Yr. award Muscogee County Sch. Dist., 1990, 93, Ga. Secondary Schs., 1989; Tandy Tech. scholar, 1990; grantee NSF, Muscogee County Sch. Dist.; sci.-math. fellow Coun. for Basic Edn., 1995; finalist Christa McAuliffe fellowship, 1994. Mem. Nat. Sci. Tchrs. Assn., Ga. Sci. Tchrs. Assn. (Dist. VI Sci. Tchr. Yr. 1989, Ga. Secondary Schs. Sci. Tchr. of Yr. 1989), Am. Chem. Soc., Valley Area Sci. Tchrs. (v.p. 1989, Valley Area Sci. Tchrs. pres. 1993-94, 2000-2001), Optical Soc. Am., Assn. Presdl. Awardees for Excellence in Sci. Teaching, Nat. Sci. Tchrs. Assn., Phi Delta Kappa (Secondary Schs. Tchr. of Yr. 1993), Kappa Delta Pi. Avocations: reading, computers, walking, photography, cooking. Home: 4913 River Rd Columbus GA 31904-5836 Office: Northside HS 2002 American Way Columbus GA 31909

EDMUND, NORMAN WILSON, educational researcher; b. Feb. 27, 1916; Cert., U. Pa., 1939. Founder, pres. Edmund Sci. Co., Barrington, N.J., 1942-75; ednl. rschr. Ft. Lauderdale, Fla., 1989—. Author: The General Pattern of the Scientific Method, 1994, The Scientific Method Today, 2000. Office: 407 NE 3rd Ave Fort Lauderdale FL 33301-3233 E-mail: nwe@scientificmethod.com.

EDMUNDS, LELAND NICHOLAS, biology educator; b. Aiken, S.C., Apr. 21, 1939; s. Leland Nicholas and Elizabeth Hemphill (Grier) E.; children: Sunja Eve, Kira Beth, Alissa Lee. BS, Davidson Coll., 1960; MA, Princeton U., 1965, PhD, 1964. Instr. Princeton (N.J.) U., 1964-65; from asst. prof. to prof. anatomy SUNY, Stony Brook, 1965—, acting provost, head divsn. biol. sci., 1975-76. Vis. investigator Biol. Inst., Carlsberg Found., Copenhagen, 1972, Lab. du Phytotron, CNRS, Gif-sur-Yvette, France, 1978-79, Lab. des Membranes Biologiques, U. Paris VII, 1986; vis. prof. Dept. Human Genetics, Sackler Sch. Med., Tel Aviv U., 1983, Suzhou Med. Coll., People's Rep. China, 1994. Author: Cellular and Molecular Bases of Biological Clocks, 1988; editor: Cell Cycle Clocks (Marcel Dekker), 1984; editor jour. Chronobiology Internat., Biol. Rhythm Rsch.; contbr. articles to profl. jours. Mem. AAAS, Soc. Rsch. Biol. Rhythms, Group d'Etudes des Rythmes Biologiques,Internat. Soc. Chronobiology (bd. dirs. 1987-99, pres. 1993-97). Home: Crystal Brook Park PO Box 390 Mount Sinai NY 11766-0390 Office: SUNY Sch Med Health Scis Ctr Dept Anatom Scis Ctr Stony Brook NY 11794-0001

EDSON, RAY ZACHARIAH, middle school educator; b. Flint, Mich., May 13, 1943; s. Robert Ara and Frances (Lucile) E. BA, Anderson U., 1966; MA, Ea. Mich. U., 1969. Tchr. Bentley Community Sch., Burton, Mich., 1966-68, Flint Community Schs., 1968-92. Rschr. Dow Corning, Midland, Mich., 1988, 91; coach Flint S.W Acad. Sci. Olympiad, 1987-89. Tutor West Court Ch. God, Flint, 1992-93. NSF scholar 1970, 71, 72. Mem. NEA, Nat. Sci. Tchrs. Assn., Mich. Edn. Assn. Home: 3117 Brentwood Dr Flint MI 48503-2339

EDWARDS, DIANNE CAROL, retired secondary school educator; b. San Jose, Calif., July 20, 1945; d. Wallace Robinson and Ethel Louise (Egling) Murray; m. Jack Lee Edwards, Dec. 14, 1968; 1 child, Jennifer Lynn. BA, San Jose State U., 1966; MA, U. San Francisco, 1976. Cert. secondary tchr., Calif. (life). Secondary tchr. Santa Clara (Calif.) Unified Sch. Dist., 1967—2000, mentor tchr., 1989—99, SIP facilitator, 1993-97, dist. coord. new tchr. program; ret., 2000. Cons. Advancement Via Individual Determination program Santa Clara County Office Edn., 2000—02. Author: (with M.L. Luchetti) Wear Comfortable Shoes and Bring a Sack Lunch, 1976. Named Tchr. of Yr., Wilcox High Sch., 1977. Mem.: Calif. Ret. Tchrs. Assn. (publicity chair divsn. 6), Automatic Mus. Instruments Collectors Assn. (founding chpt.), Delta Kappa Gamma. Democrat. Lutheran. Avocation: automatic musical instruments. Home: 1681 Mt Vernon Dr San Jose CA 95125-5551

EDWARDS, ELWOOD GENE, mathematician, educator; b. New Bern, N.C., Jan. 5, 1944; s. Calvin and Blanche Ethel (Edwards) E.; m. Lucretia Walker; children: Ronnie, Glenn, Myrei Chrysti. BA, CCNY, 1966; MA, NYU, 1969; MS, PhD, Columbia Pacific U., 1982; DD (hon.), Am. Bapt. U., 1980. Cert. math. tchr., N.Y. Ins. cons. Met. Life Ins. Co., N.Y.C., 1966-68; tchr., math. specialist-tchr. N.Y.C. Bd. Edn., 1968—2001. Lectr., adj. prof. CUNY, 1969-78; tax preparer Bklyn., 1973—; tutor math., Spanish, English, Bklyn., 1969—. Contbr. articles to profl. jours. V.p. 89th St./Ave. B Block Assn., Bklyn., 1987-89. Mem. AAAS, Soc. for Indsl. and Applied Math., Am. Statis. Assn., The Planetarium Soc., Nat. Coun. Tchrs. Math., Math. Assn. Am., Am. Math. Soc., N.Y. Acad. Sci., Phi Theta Kappa. Democrat. Unitarian Universalist. Avocations: reading, walking, bowling, golf, creating recreational math puzzles.

EDWARDS, GRACE COLEMAN, librarian; b. Charlotte, N.C., Dec. 30, 1935; d. Winson Ralph and Theodora (Dugas) Coleman; m. Bobby L. Edwards, Sept. 3, 1960; children: Annette E. Edwards Grasty, Marcia, Brian. BA, Bennett Coll., 1957; MA, Ind. U., 1962. Elem. libr., Lynchburg, Va., 1957-59; libr. Marie Davis Elem. Sch., Charlotte, 1959-61; English tchr. Cen. High Sch., Louisville, 1964-65, libr., 1965-87, Waggener High Sch., Louisville, 1987—. Vol. Hospice of Louisville. Mem. NEA, Jefferson County Media Assn., Jefferson County Tchrs. Assn., Ky. Edn. Assn., Delta Sigma Theta. Presbyterian. Home: 7600 Upper River Rd Prospect KY 40059-9601 Office: Waggener High Sch 330 S Hubbards Ln Louisville KY 40207-4099

EDWARDS, JACK LEE, retired secondary school educator; b. Raton, N.Mex., July 22, 1943; s. Jack and Pauline (Lee) E.; m. Dianne Carol Murray, Dec. 14, 1968; 1 child, Jennifer Lynn. Student, Fullerton Coll., 1963; grad., San Jose State U., 1966; MA, U. San Francisco, 1976; postgrad., U. Calif., Santa Cruz. Cert. tchr., Calif. Tchr. Lincoln H.S., San José, Calif., 1968-83, Willow Glen H.S., San José, 1983—2002, chmn. English dept., 1998—2002; ret., 2002. Mem.: Calif. Ret. Tchrs. Assn. (transp. chmn. area 6), Automatic Musical Instrument Collector's Assn. (founding chpt.), Sierra Club. Democrat. Lutheran. Avocations: music, photography, theatre.

EDWARDS, JAMES LEE, university president; Pres. Anderson U. Office: Anderson U Office of President Anderson IN 46012-3495

EDWARDS, JAMES LYNN, college dean; b. Yates Center, Kans., Jan. 1, 1952; s. Raymond P. and Evelyn I. (Patterson) E.; m. Nioma R. Lemke, Apr. 4, 1973 (div. Mar. 1992); 1 child, Jessica; m. G. Susie Butler, May 29, 1993; 1 child, Taylor. AS, Butler County Community Coll., 1971; BS, Emporia State U., 1973, MS, 1979. Mktg. instr. Shawnee Mission West High Sch., Overland Park, Kans., 1973-74; mem. mgmt. staff SS Kresge Co., Joplin, Mo., 1974-75, K-Mart, St. Louis, 1975-76; tchr. Wichita Heights (Kans.) High Sch., 1976-78; instr. mktg. Butler County Community Coll., El Dorado, Kans., 1978-83, outreach coord., 1983-87, dir. Western Ctr. Andover, Kans., 1987-90; dean adult and cmty. edn. Butler County C.C., El Dorado, Kans., 1990-97, dean corp. tng. and workforce devel., 1997—. Author: Display Topics, 1980, How To Build an Off Campus Center on a Shoestring, 1988, Adjunct Advisors-A Means To Grow By, 1989, Adjunct Evaluation System, 1992, Student Service Quality Assurance: A Model the Works, 1993, Reaching Students Where They Live-At-Home-Through Technology, Adult Learning, 1994. Mem. ASTD, El Dorado C. of C., Phi Delta Kappa. Democrat. Mem. Christian Ch. (Disciples Of Christ). Avocations: woodworking, lawn work, gardening. Home: 914 Rim Rock Rd El Dorado KS 67042-4163 Office: Butler County C C 901 S Haverhill Rd El Dorado KS 67042-3225

EDWARDS, JOHN DUNCAN, law educator, librarian; b. Louisiana, Mo., Sept. 15, 1953; s. Harold Wenkle and Mary Elizabeth (Duncan) E.; m. Beth Ann Rahm, May 21, 1977; children: Craig, Martha, Brooks. BA, Southeast Mo. State U., 1975; JD, U. Mo., Kansas City, 1977; MALS, U. Mo., Columbia, 1979. Bar: Mo. 1978, U.S. Dist. Ct. (we. dist.) Mo. 1978. Instr. legal research and writing U. Mo., Columbia, 1978, dir. legal research and writing, librarian, 1979-80; pub. svcs. librarian Law Sch., U. Okla., Norman, 1980-81, assoc. librarian, 1981-84, adj. instr. sch. library sci., 1983-84; prof. law, dir. law library law sch. Drake U., Des Moines, 1984—. Adj. instr. Columbia Coll., 1979-80; cons. Cleveland County Bar Assn., 1984. Editor: Emerging Solutions in Reference Services: Implications for Libraries in the New Millennium, 2001, Iowa Legal Research Guide, 2003; contbr. articles to profl. jours. Cons. Friends Drake U. Libr., 1985—; coach, mgr. Westminster Softball Team. Des Moines, 1987-94; pres. Crestview Parent-Tchr. Coun., Des Moines, 1988-90; trustee Westminster Presbyn. Ch., Des Moines, 1988-89, treas., 1990, pres., 1991; mem. Clive City Coun., 1995—, mayor pro tem, 1998—; trustee Des Moines Metro Transit Authority, 1996—, chmn. bd. dirs., 1997-98, 2003—, sec.-treas., 1996, 2001-02. Recipient Presdl. award Drake U. Student Bar Assn., 1987; named Outstanding Vol., Crestview Elem. Sch., 1989-90. Mem. Am. Assn. Law Librs. (chmn. awards com. 1987-88, chmn. grants com. 1996-97, chmn. scholarship com. 1998-99), Mid-Am. Assn. Law Librs. (chmn. resource sharing 1986-93, v.p. 1994-95, pres. 1995-96), Mid-Am. Law Sch. Librs. Consortium (pres. 1986-88), Delta Theta Phi, Beta Phi Mu. Avocations: softball, tennis. Office: Drake U Libr Law Sch 27th & Carpenter Sts Des Moines IA 50311

EDWARDS, JOHN STUART, zoology educator, researcher; b. Auckland, N.Z., Nov. 25, 1931; came to U.S., 1962; s. Charles Stuart Marten and Mavis Margaret (Wells) E.; m. Ola Margery Shreeves, June 21, 1957; children— Richard Charles, Duncan Roy, Marten John, Andrew Zachary B.Sc., U. Auckland, 1954, M.Sc. with 1st class honors, 1956; PhD, U. Cambridge, Eng., 1960. Asst. prof. biology Western Res. U., 1963-67, assoc. prof., 1967; assoc. prof. zoology U. Wash., Seattle, 1967-70, prof., 1970—, dir. biology program, 1982-88, dir. univ. honors program, 1994—, prof. emeritus, 2001—. Recipient Alexander von Humboldt award, 1981; Guggenheim fellow, 1972-73; vis. fellow Gonville and Caius Coll., Cambridge U., Eng., 1989-90. Fellow Royal Entomol. Soc., AAAS; mem. Soc. Neurosci., Am. Soc. Zoologists, Western Apicultural Soc. (v.p. 1983) Home: 5747 60th Ave NE Seattle WA 98105-2035 Office: U Wash Dept Biology box 351800 Seattle WA 98195-0001

EDWARDS, JOHN W. school superintendent; b. Schenectady, May 27, 1944; s. William T. and Dorothy (Wells) E. BA, SUNY, New Platz, 1966, MS, 1968, cert. advanced study, 1973; postgrad., NYU. Cert. dist. supt., R.I., N.J., N.Y.; sch. psychologist, N.Y., N.J.; elem. tchr., N.Y. Dir. spl. svcs. Marlboro (N.J.) Bd. Edn., 1980-83; dir. region V. New Milford (N.J.) Bd. Edn., 1983-84; dir. pupil pers. svcs. Middletown (N.J.) Bd. Edn., 1984-88; supt. schs. Bridgehampton (N.Y.) Union Free Sch. Dist., 1990—; supt. Tiverton (R.I.) Sch. Dept., 1988-90. Recipient community svc. resolution N.J. Senate; grad. fellow SUNY. Mem. ASCD, Am. Assn. Sch. Adminstrs. (Nat. Supt.'s Acad. 1988), Nat. Assn. Secondary Sch. Prins., N.Y. ASCD, R.I. ASCD. Home: PO Box 313 Bridgehampton NY 11932-0313 Office: Bridgehampton Sch PO Box 3021 Bridgehampton NY 11932-3021

EDWARDS, JOYCE ANN, principal; b. Independence, La., July 5, 1953; d. Willie and Leona (Scott) Collier; m. King Edwards, Aug. 7, 1990; 1 child, Shanta Denise Taylor. BS in Elem. Edn., La. State U., 1978, MEd, 1982. Lic. elem. edn. tchr., 1st-8th grades, supr. student tchrs., elem. sch. prin. Elem. tchr. East Baton Rouge (La.) Parish Schs., 1978-85, dean students, 1993-94, asst. pring. adminstrn., 1994—; instr. La. State U., Baton Rouge, 1985-89; elem. tchr.-supr. West Feliciana Parish Schs., St. Fancisville, La., 1989-93; prin. Bains (La.) Lower Elem. Sch., 1993—. Tchr., trainer K-1 D.A.S.H. Project, U. Hawaii, Honolulu, 1989—. Dir. Destiny's Children, Zachary, La., 1991—; dean children's ministry United Ministries Fellowship, Zachary, 1994; mem., communicator Christians for Polit. Action, Zachary, 1993—. Recipient Motherhood-Sisterhood award Nat. Coun. Christians and Jews, 1994. Mem. Capitol Area Reading Coun., La. Assn. Sch. Execs., Nat. Assn. Elem. Sch. Prins., La. Assn. Principals. Avocations: reading, travel, drama, choreography. Home: 337 E Plains Port Hudson Rd Zachary LA 70791-6021 Office: Bains Lower Elem 9974 Bains Rd Saint Francisville LA 70775-4630

EDWARDS, JULIE ANN, science researcher; b. Berea, Ohio, Jan. 31, 1945; d. Ralph Frederick and Elsie Marie (Koch) Schmiedlin; m. O. James Edwards; children: J. Patrick, Tommie, Jami. BA in Biology, U. Detroit-Mercy, 1967; postgrad., Murray (Ky.) State U., 1985, Ea. Mich. U., Ypsilanti, 1988-89. Rschr. VA Hosp., Ann Arbor, Mich., 1969-72, U. Mich., Ann Arbor, 1987—2003; ret., 2003. Contbr. articles to profl. jours. Mem. Sci. Rsch. Club of U. Mich. (sec.), Sigma Xi. Avocations: gardening, sewing, arts and crafts.

EDWARDS, JUNE CAROLINE, retired education educator; b. Oklahoma City, Okla., Mar. 5, 1934; d. Ralph Eldon and Katharine Louetta (Rose) Kirkhuff; m. Richard Alan Edwards, Sept. 3, 1958 (div. Oct. 1992); children: Jennifer, Emily, Jonathan. BA, U. Okla., 1955; MEd, Va. Poly. Inst. and State U., 1974, EdD, 1977. Jr. high sch. tchr. Markham (Ill.) Sch. Dist., 1960-62, 66-68; mid. sch. tchr. Greenville (Pa.) Sch. Dist., 1968-72; lectr., Sch. of Edn. Va. Polytechnic Inst. and State U., 1974-77; asst. prof. dept. of English Marquette U., Milw., 1985-87; asst. prof. dept. of edn. Nat.-Louis Univ., Evanston, Ill., 1987-89; assoc. prof. dept. of edn. SUNY, Oneonta, 1992—2000, prof., 2000—02, prof. emerita, 2003—. Author: Opposing Censorship in Public Schools: Religion, Morality and Literature, 1998, Women in American Education, 1820-1955: The Female Force and Educational Reform, 2002; contbr. articles to profl. jours. Bd. dirs. ACLU, Milw., 1990-92, Catskill Choral Soc., Oneonta, 1994—. Mem. Phi Delta Kappa (pres. Catskill area 1994-96, Marquette U. chpt. 1988-89, v.p. 1987-88, G. Read travel fellowship). Democrat. Unitarian Universalist. Avocations: singing, travel, writing.

EDWARDS, KAMALA DORIS, humanities educator; b. Hoshangabad, India, July 11, 1942; d. Seth Jason and Doris Mary (Bernard) E.; m. Vinod Ghildiyal; 1 child, Jaya Ghildiyal. BA summa cum laude, U. Jabalpur, 1962, MA summa cum laude, 1965; postgrad., Haggai Inst., Singapore, Delhi U., India, Cairo U., Edinburg U., Scotland; PhD, U. South Fla., 1975; postgrad., Harvard U.; A (Mus) T.L.C. I, Trinity Coll. Music, London; vocal student, Madame Anne Roselle Studios. Lectr. Women's Christian Coll., Madras, India, 1966-67; assoc. prof., dir. honors program, advisor internat.-intercultural studies & fgn. students Bethune-Cookman Coll., Daytona Beach, Fla., 1974-79; pres. Isabella Thoburn Coll., Lucknow, India, 1979-87; asst. prof. dept. English George Washington U., Washington, 1987; prof. humanities, social sci., edn. divsn. Montgomery Coll., Germantown, Md., 1989—. Vis. prof. dept. English Houghton (N.Y.) Coll., 1967-68, Fla. So. Coll., Lakeland, 1968-72; adj. prof. dept. English U. South Fla., 1972-74; cons. The World Bank, Washington, 1988—, Ctr. Skills Devel., Washington, 1988—, Aqua Safe Internat. Health Systems, Vienna, Va., 1989—; commr. Commn. Humanities Rockville County, Md., 1990, vice chair, 1991—, program, devel., liaison coms.; presenter numerous seminars. Appeared internationally in various recitals, guest solos and benefit concerts; mem. editorial bd. Collegiate English Handbook, 1994; contbr. articles to profl. jours. Exec. bd. India Literacy House, New Delhi; chairperson triennia conf. Asian Women's Inst., Manila, Phillipines; nat bd. govs. YWCA India, New Delhi; panelist, moderator The Round House Theater, Montgomery County, Md. Recipient Citation as Youngest Pres. Asia's Oldest Women's Coll United Meth. Bd. Higher Edn., 1979, Citation as First Major Coll. Pres. U. So. Fla. Alumni Assn., 1979, Amb. Goodwill Cert. Disting. Accomplishment Hon. Gov. State of Ark., 1976, Disting. Educator award U.P. Govt., Lucknow, India, 1981, Lilly Endowment; grantee Ford Found., Mellon Found., United Meth. Ch., Govt. India, Ch. Aux. Social Action. Mem. AAUW, MLA, Nat. League of Pen Women (judge nat. poetry and fiction contests), Nat. Fedn. Indian-Am. Assns. (devel. com.), Internat. Platform Assn., Assn. Colls. and Univs. for Internat.-Intercultural Studies (exec. bd., bd. dirs., Cert. Excellence Disting. Svc., 1975-78), All India Assn. Christian Higher Edn. (exec. bd.), C. C. Humanities Assn. (moderator workshop), Inst. Svc. Edn. (task force), Phi Kappa Phi, Sigma Tau Delta, Alpha Chi. Democrat. Methodist. Home: 13106 Collingwood Ter Silver Spring MD 20904-1416

EDWARDS, KATHRYN INEZ, educational technology consultant; b. L.A., Aug. 26, 1947; d. Lloyd and Geraldine E. (Smith) Price; 1 child, Bryan. BA in English, Calif. State U., L.A., 1969; supervision credential, 1974, adminstrn. credential, 1975; MEd in Curriculum, UCLA, 1971; PhD, Claremont Grad. Sch., 1979. Tchr. L.A. Pub. Schs., 1969—78, adv. specially funded programs, 1978—80, advisor librs. and learning-resources program, 1980—81, instructional specialist, 1981—84; cons. instructional media L.A. County Office of Edn., Downey, Calif., 1984-90; coord. ednl. media and tech. Pomona (Calif.) Unified Sch. Dist., 1990-92; cons. edn. tech. Apple Computer, Inc., 1992-96; client mktg. rep. IBM; sales devel. mgr. SUN Microsys., 1999—2000; dir. mktg. Vinendi Universal Interactive Pub., 2000—02; mgr. strategic urban initiatives Apple Computer, 2002—. Cons. Walt Disney Prodns., Alfred Higging Prodns., others; mem. distance lng. think tank U.S. Office Edn., 1997. Author guides and curriculum kits. Apptd. by assembly spkr. Willie Brown to Calif. Ednl. Tech. Com., 1990-92, Calif. State Assembly Resolution from Gwen Moore, 1988, Edn. Coun. for Tech. in Learning, 1993-96; mem. spl. com. Cable Access Corp. co-owners, 1991-92. Recipient cert. commendation Senator Diane Watson, 1988, Mabel Wilson Richards scholar, 1968, Calif. Congress Parents and Tchrs. scholar, 1968, UCLA fellow, 1968; named Outstanding Woman of Yr. L.A. Sentinel, 1987. Mem. ASCD, Nat. Assn. Minority Polit. Women, Internat. Reading Assn. (spkr. nat. conv. 1988), L.A. Reading Assn. (pres.), Calif. Assn. Tchrs. of English (conf. del. 1982), Calif. Media and Libr. Educators Assn. (state conf. co-chair 1989, v.p. legal divsn. 1992—), Nat. Assn. Media Women (Media Woman of Yr. 1987), Alpha Kappa Alpha. Democrat. Roman Catholic. Avocations: reading, gardening, travel. Office: IBM Corp 400 N Brand Blvd Glendale CA 91203-2311 E-mail: Kathryne1@attbi.com.

EDWARDS, KEITH DAVID, special education educator; b. West Mifflin, Pa., June 3, 1954; s. John Willis and Mildred (Oliver) E. AA, Community Coll. Allegheny Co., 1975; BS in Edn., Calif. State Coll. of Pa., 1977; MS in Edn., Duquesne U., 1981. Cert. spl. edn. tchr., elem. edn. tchr., reading specialist, Pa. EMH tchr. (10-12) East Liverpool (Ohio) High Sch., 1977-78; learning support tchr. Bairdford Sch., West Deer, Pa., 1978-81, Swissvale (Pa.) High Sch., 1981-82, Rankin (Pa.) Sch., 1982-86, Swissvale High Sch., 1986-87, West Mifflin (Pa.) Intermediate Sch., 1987-88, West Mifflin Area High Sch., 1988—. Mem. Allegheny Intermediate Unit Learning Disabilities Curriculum Writing, Pitts., summer 1979; mem. elem. rev. com. Duquesne U., Pitts., 1982-83, curriculum com. West Mifflin High Sch., 1990-91; co-advisor West Mifflin Area High Sch. Student Coun. and Homecoming, 1991—, Future Educators, 1989—, Gift of Time Tribute, 1991. Mem. West Mifflin Area High Sch. PTA, 1988—, Neighborhood Crime Watch, Edgewood, Pa., 1990—; canvasser Mothers March of Dimes, Edgewood, 1992—. Great Ideas grantee Mon Valley Edn. Consortium, 1990-91, 92-93. Mem. ASCD, NEA (del. 1987-89), Coun. for Exceptional Children, Allegheny Intermediate Unit Edn. Assn. (sec., negotiation team mem., rep. to coun., grievance officer, unification com.), Kappa Delta Pi. Democrat. Methodist. Avocations: film, walking, collecting steins, theatre, music. Home: 112 Harlow St Pittsburgh PA 15218-1616 Office: West Mifflin Area High Sch 91 Commonwealth Ave West Mifflin PA 15122-2310

EDWARDS, LARRY DAVID, internist, educator; b. Macomb, Ill., June 20, 1937; s. Richard Marshall and Anna Louise (Hare) Edwards; m. Ann Leanor Will, Mar. 31, 1959; children: Elliott, Sharon, Beth. Pre-Med, U. Ill., 1961, MD, 1965. Diplomate Am. Bd. Internal Medicine, Am. Bd. Infectious Disease, Am. Bd. Geriatric Medicine, Nat. Bd. Med. Examiners, Am. Bd. Med. Mgmt., Am. Coll. Healthcare Execs; cert. physician exec., healthcare exec. Rotating intern USPHS Hosp., Staten Island, N.Y., 1965-66, resident in internal medicine, 1966-68; fellow in infectious diseases Rush-Presbyn.-St. Luke's Med. Ctr., Chgo., 1968-70; instr. dept. internal medicine U. Ill. Coll. Medicine, Chgo., 1968-70; asst. prof. depts. internal medicine, preventive medicine, microbiology Rush Med. Coll., Chgo., 1972-74; assoc. prof. internal medicine U. Ill. Coll. Medicine, Rockford, 1974-80, prof., 1980-81; prof. internal medicine Oral Roberts U. Sch. Medicine, Tulsa, 1981-90; dir. div. infectious diseases Rockford Sch. Medicine, 1974-81, dep. head dept. biomed. scis., 1980-81; prof. internal medicine U. Va., Charlottesville, 1991-92; chief of staff VA Med. Ctr., Salem, Va., 1990-92; assoc. dean for acad. affairs VA, U. Va., Charlottesville, 1991-92. Adj. assoc. prof. epidemiology U. Ill. Sch. Pub. Health, 1977—81; affiliate dept. medicine Abraham Lincoln Sch. Medicine, U. Ill., Chgo., 1977—81; dir. divsn. infectious diseases Oral Roberts U., 1981—84; assoc. dean clin. affairs Oral Roberts Sch. Medicine, 1981, 84, vice chmn. dept. internal medicine, 1981—83, chmn., 1983—86, chmn. preventive and internat. medicine, 1987—88, dean, 1984—90, v.p. for health affairs, 1987—90; COO City of Faith Med. & Rsch. Ctr., 1989—90; med. dir. Cen. Bapt. Home for Aged, Norridge, Ill., 1968—74, Columbia County Homes, Wyocena, Wis., 1974—80; asst. dir. infectious diseases, hosp. epidemiologist, dir. infectious disease research Rush-Presbyn.-St. Luke's Hosp., Chgo., 1972—74, asst. sci. dept. microbiology, 1970—74; asst. med. dir. Mcpl. Contagious Disease Hosp., Chgo., 1970—74; cons. infectious diseases numerous other hosps. and med. ctrs.; med. dir. City of Faith Hosp., Tulsa, 1984—87, chmn. bd., 1989—90; bd. dirs. City of Faith Clinic, Tulsa, 1985—87; pres. Infectious Diseases Cons. Svcs., Inc., Barnhart, Mo., 1993—2001; med. dir., missionary Bible Basics Internat. Contbr. numerous articles to med. jours. Advisor resource com. Sch. Health Coalition of N.W. Ill., 1979-81; med. adv. com. State of Ill. Refugee Health Services Program, 1980-81; Ill. health svcs. task force State Ill. Dept. Pub. Health, 1980-81; infectious disease adv. com. Tulsa City-County Health Dept., 1981-88; physician manpower adv. com. Okla. Bd. Regents, 1984-88; Titan scholarship bd. Oral Roberts U., 1985-87; v.p. World-Wide Med. Missions, Oral Roberts Evangelistic Assn., 1986-88, pres. 1989-90; active Leadership Roanoke Valley, 1991-92; dir. Strategic Tchg. and Reaping; med. dir. Bible Basics Internat.; Bible tchr., missionary in Russia, Dominican Republic, Chile, Honduras. With U.S. Army, 1955-58, with USPHS, 1965-70, lt. col. USAR, 1985, col. 1990-97, ret., 1997. Smith, Kline and French fellow for study in Ethiopia, 1964; named Outstanding Faculty Mem. of Yr. Oral Roberts U. Sch. Medicine, 1982-83. Fellow: ACP, Am. Coll. Healthcare Execs. (ret.), Am. Coll. Physician Execs., Infectious Diseases Soc. Am. (emeritus). Avocations: reading, writing.

EDWARDS, LILLIE JOHNSON, history educator; b. Columbus, Ga., Dec. 11, 1952; d. Allen and Laverna (Williams) Johnson; m. Paul Bryant Edwards; Sept. 20, 1982; children: Paul Johnson, Nia Molliene. BA, Oberlin Coll., 1975; MA, U. Chgo., 1976, PhD, 1981. Asst. prof., coord. African-Am. studies Earlham Coll., Richmond, Ind., 1981-83; asst. prof. U. N.C., Chapel Hill, 1983-87, DePaul U., Chgo., 1987-89, assoc. prof., 1989—, dir. Am. studies, 1990-92; prof., dir. African-Am. studies Drew U., Madison, N.J., 1992—. Cons., lectr. NEH Summer Inst., Trenton, N.J., 1987, N.J. State Grants, Trenton, 1986; cons. N.J. Higher Edn., Trenton, 1985-87, Exxon Found., N.Y.C., 1983. Mem. exec. bd. Oberlin Coll. Alumni Coun., Ohio, 1987-88; music dir. St. Matthews Ch., Chgo., 1987—; v.p. Oberlin Coll. Class of 1975, 1986-89. Rockefeller fellow, 1986-87. Mem. Orgn. Am. Historians, Am. Hist. Soc., Am. Studies Assn., Assn. Black Women Historians (nominating com. 1986-87, 89-90, nat. dir. 2000-01), Assn. for Study Afro-Am. Life and History (program com. 1987, 90), NJ Amistad Comm., 2002-. Democrat. Methodist. Office: Drew U Dept History Madison NJ 07940 E-mail: ledwards@drew.edu.

EDWARDS, LINDA L. former elementary education educator; Tchr. Highland Park Elem. Sch., Lewistown, Mont.; ret., 1999. Named Mont. State Elem. Tchr. of Yr., 1993. Office: Highland Park Elem Sch 1312 7th Ave N Lewistown MT 59457-2112

EDWARDS, LOUISE WISEMAN, career counselor, educator; b. Greeley, Colo., Feb. 20, 1932; d. Hunter R. and Sarah L. (Spencer) Wiseman; m. Jasin W. Edwards (div. 1975); children: Mark Hunter, Kathleen Margaret. BA, U. Colo., 1953; MA, U. N.Mex., 1983. Lic. profl. clin. counselor. Asst. dir. pub. info. Mills Coll., Oakland, Calif., 1956-57; ESL tchr. Peace Corps, Santiago, Chile, 1963-64; career counselor U. N.Mex. Career Svcs., Albuquerque, 1980-84, supr. career counseling, 1984-87, asst. dir., 1987-98, interim dir., 1992-93; pvt. counselor, 1998—. Presenter U. N.Mex. Law Sch., 1982-95, Nat. Assn. Med. Schs. Admissions and Registrations Conv., 1993; instr. Anderson Sch. Mgmt. U. N.Mex., 1983-95. Active Dem. Women of N.Mex., 1970-80. Mem. N.Mex. Career Devel. Assn. (bd. dirs., George Keppens award 2002), Rocky Mt. Placement Assn. (co-chair conf. 1980—). Avocations: singing with univ. chorus, hiking, cross country skiing, docent. Home: 2821 Tennessee St NE Albuquerque NM 87110-3707

EDWARDS, LYNN A. retired school system administrator; b. Cicero, IL, Apr. 1, 1923; d. Calvin S. Yakley and Linda Olson; m. Edward M. Edwards; children: Dean, Dyke, Elizabeth. BA, U. Ill., 1944; MEd, U. Toledo, 1975. Secondary tchr. Sylvania Schs., Sylvania, Ohio, 1968—70, media specialist, 1971—83, sch. adminstr., 1984—86. Named Ironman Triathlon World Champion, 1992—93; recipient Olympic Distance World Triathlon Champion, Can., 2001, Long Course World Champion, Ind., 1997, numerous championships in marathons and running events.; fellow Fulbright scholar to India, U.S. Congress, 1980 and, 1984. Avocation: Participating in numerous running events..

EDWARDS, MARGARET H. English as second language instructor; b. Falkirk, Scotland, Jan. 28, 1940; came to U.S., 1967; d. John Hobbs and J. Catherine Muir (Rankine) Erskine; m. W. Peter Edwards, Dec. 24, 1964; 1 child, Gemma Rhiain. Diploma, U. Grenoble, France, 1960, U. Santander, Spain, 1962; BA, U. Durham, Eng., 1961, MA, U. Wash., 1970; grad. diploma in edn., U. Leicester, 1962. Head dept. French Chester-le-Street H.S., England, 1962-64; tchr. English, French, Spanish Maple Ridge Sr. H.S., Haney, B.C., Can., 1964-66; tchg. asst. U. Wash., Seattle, 1968-69; instr. Sullivan lang. sch. Behavioral Rsch. Labs., Palo Alto, Calif., 1970-71; field researcher DIME Project, Denver, 1971-72; instr. French Evergreen State Coll., Olympia, Wash., 1986-91; ESL, French, Spanish instr. No. Thurston H.S., Lacey, Wash., 1976—. Mem. Wash. Assn. Educators of Spkrs. of Other Langs., TESOL (Tchr. of Yr. 1977, Dick Williams award 1998). Avocations: travel, language learning, tennis. Office: No Thurston HS 600 Sleater Kinney Rd NE Lacey WA 98506-5241

EDWARDS, MARGARET SALLY, retired educational administrator; b. Jones Fork, Ky., Mar. 1, 1937; d. Manis Casebolt and Mary (Slone) Layne; m. Cecil Edwards, Nov. 13, 1953; children: David, James. BS in Elem. Edn., Miami U., Oxford, Ohio, 1966, MEd in Ednl. Adminstrn., 1979, PhD in Ednl. Adminstrn. and Curriculum, 1991. Cert. supt., supr., prin., edn. specialist, tchr., Ohio. Tchr. elem. edn. Middletown (Ohio) City Schs., 1965-81, asst. prin., 1981-83, coord. elem. edn., 1983-85, coord. state and fed. programs, 1985-96. Adj. prof. Miami U., Oxford, 1991-93; turnkey trainer Exemplary Ctr. for Reading Instrn., Salt Lake City, 1984-90. Bd. dirs. Sorg Opera Co., Middletown, 1991-93, Madison Twp. Life Squad, Middletown, 1993-94. Mem. Nat. Assn. for Edn. Young Children, Ohio Coun. Internat. Reading Assn. (membership dir. 1990-93), Ohio Assn. for Supervision and Curriculum Devel. (pres. 1993-94, Leadership Devel. award 1994), Middletown Artist-in-Residency (pres. 1987-91), Delta Kappa Gamma (legis. chair 1994-96), Phi Delta Kappa (pres. 1991-93, Svc. key 1994, Disting. award 1987, 92). Avocations: reading, sewing, crafts, gardening.

EDWARDS, MARGERY FAYE, alternative elementary/middle school educator, real estate investor; b. Mount Vernon, Wash., Jan. 22, 1947; d. Victor Worth and Erdice Gertrude Cain; children: Jacob Ali, Wren Marie. BA in Edn., U. Wash., 1970; MA in Psychology, Antioch U., 1989; postgrad. in Drama, North Seattle C.C., 1994-95. Cert. tchr., Wash. Alternative educator New Sch. for Children, Seattle, 1971, Alternative Sch. # 1, Seattle, 1971-79, 85—. Family planning counselor Seattle King County Family Planning, 1971; alternative prin. Alternative Sch. # 1, 1977-79, site coun. mem., 1971-79, 85-; alternative educator Orca Sch., Seattle, 1972-78; founder, dir. Whole Brain Learning, Seattle, 1985—. Prodr.: (TV show) Meet Your Local Artist, 1994; actress, playwright, dir., theatrical presentations, 1988—; designer, implementor Basic Skills Through Drama Program at Alternative Sch. # 1, 1995—. Bd. dirs. Unity Ch. of Truth, Seattle, 1989, N.W. Inst. Restorative Justice, 2002—, sec., 2003-. Office: Alternative Sch # 1 11530 12th Ave NE Seattle WA 98125-6310

EDWARDS, MARY ANN, special education educator; b. Bay City, Mich., Jan. 6, 1955; d. Thomas Daniel and Sophie Marie (Rosek) Brown; m. Roger Dean Edwards, Nov. 11, 1978; children: Melissa Lynn, Jessica Rae. BS in Edn. cum laude, Ctrl. Mich. U., Mt. Pleasant, 1978, MA, 1987. Cert. in mental impairment, psychology, Mich. Tchr. Tuscola Intermediate Sch. Dist., Caro, Mich., 1978—, tchr. severely mentally impaired spl. needs/behavioral, 1992-93, intermediate TMI spl. needs/behavioral, 1993—96; chair SMI/SCI dept. Highland Pines Sch., Caro, 2000—02. Mem. sch. improvement com. and 3 to 5 yr. planning com. for Highland Pines Sch., Caro, 1994-98. Contbr. articles to profl. jours. Vol. Mitten Bay coun. Girl Scouts U.S.A., 1992—; trained vol. Skywarn spotter, Tuscola County, Mich., 1991—. Mem. Mich. Edn. Assn. (E. Dale Kennedy award 1992, 93), Mich. Edn. Assn.-Retirement, Tuscola Intermediate Edn. Assn. (treas. 1984-86, 88-89, 90-91, 92—), Tuscola Assn. Retarded Citizens (bd. dirs. 1988-98). Roman Catholic. Avocations: arts and crafts, reading. Home: 709 S Almer St Caro MI 48723-1812

EDWARDS, MAUREEN SUSAN, elementary school educator; b. N.Y.C., Apr. 17, 1970; d. George David and Susan Mary (Nelson) E. BA, Cath. U. of Am., 1992; MA in Devel. Psychology, Columbia U. Tchrs. Coll., 1995, Columbia U., 1995. Tchr. 4-yr.-olds Ivy League Sch., Edgewater, N.J., 1992-93; head tchr. 7th grade, basic skills tchr., SRA instr. Palisades Park (N.J.) Jr./Sr. H.S., 1993—. CCD 7th grade tchr. St. Lawrence Parish, Weehawken, N.J., 1992-95; asst. cheerleading coach Palisades Park Jr./Sr. H.S., 1993—. Mem. N.J. Tchrs. Assn. Roman Catholic. Home: 1 Bellevue Ter Weehawken NJ 07086-6901

EDWARDS, PAUL BEVERLY, retired science and engineering educator; b. Ridge Spring, S.C., Nov. 12, 1915; s. Paul Bee and Chloe Agnes (Watson) E.; m. Sarah Dee Barnes, Apr. 10, 1943 (dec. July 1999); 1 child, Susan Dee Edwards Von Suskil. BS, U. Tampa, 1937; EdM, Harvard U., 1958; EdD, George Washington U., 1972. Owner, operator Edwards' Hobbies, Tampa, Fla., 1938-54; tchr. math. Hillsborough High Sch., Tampa, 1955-60; head dept. math. King High Sch., Tampa, 1960-63; coord. Grad. Ctr., supr. edn. and tng. Johns Hopkins U. and Applied Physics Lab., Balt. and Laurel, Md., 1963-75, dir. Grad. Ctr., supr. edn. and tng., 1975-81. Contbr. articles to profl. jours. Mem. Sun City Ctr. Voters League, 1989—, Community Assn., Sun City Ctr., 1987—; mem. Greenbriar Property Owners Assn., Sun City Ctr., 1987—. Lt. comdr. USNR, 1942-46. Named Meritorious Tchr., State of Fla., 1962; recipient various fellowships. Mem. Ret. Officers Assn., Naval Res. Assn., Golf and Racquet Club. Avocations: swimming, computing, photography. Home: 1843 Wolf Laurel Dr Sun City Center FL 33573-6422

EDWARDS, PETER, education educator, writer; b. Kalgoorlie, Australia; m. Susan Christine Maslowski, Feb. 1, 1985; children: Lance, Michael, Diana, Tania, Dean, Monique. BA, U. West Australia, Perth, 1964, BEd, 1968; MA, U. B.C., Vancouver, Can., 1972, EdD, 1974. Cert. tchr., West Australia, B.C., VA. Tchr. Edn. Dept. West Australia, Perth, 1957-68, Edn. Dept. B.C., Vancouver, 1968-71; lectr. edn. U. B.C., 1974-75; sr. lectr. Monash U., Melbourne, Victoria, Australia, 1976-89; adj. instr. Saginaw (Mich.) Valley State U., 1989-90; assoc. prof. Clarion (Pa.) U. Pa., 1990-92; prof. SUNY, Plattsburgh, 1992-98, VA Edn. Dept., 1998-2001, SUNY, New Paltz, 2001—. Cons. Tchrs.' Resource Ctr., Canberra, Australia, 1976, Aboriginal Affairs, Melbourne, 1977, 80, Commonwealth of Australia, Canberra, 1980-83. Author: Reading Problems, 1981, Edwards Diagnostic Reading Test, 1981, Seven Keys to Successful Study, 1991, 2d edit., 1996, Literacy Techniques, 1995, 2nd edit., 2002; (with others) Reading Education, 1981, Special Education, 1981; (simulation game) Successful Negotiation, 1984; (computer program) Reading and Study Skills, 1988; (video) Creative Responses to Reading, 1991, Reading Showcase, 1992; contbr. articles to ednl. publs. Mem.: Am. Fedn. Tchrs., United Univ. Professions, Internat. Reading Assn., Ulster County Reading Coun., Kappa Delta Phi. Avocations: creative writing, traveling. Office: OMB 223 SUNY New Paltz NY 12561

EDWARDS, SARAH ALEXANDER, minister, educator; b. N.Y.C., Feb. 17, 1921; d. James S. and Hortense Clapp (Heywood) Alexander; m. Robert L. Edwards, Sept. 6, 1947; children: Edith Heywood, James Deane. AB cum laude, Bryn Mawr (Pa.) Coll., 1943; MDiv, Union Theol. Sem., 1950; STM, Hartford Sem., 1966, PhD, 1974. Ordained to ministry Congregational Ch., 1951. Interim pastor various chs., 1951-61; v.p. Ct. Fellowship of Congrl. Christian Women; adj. prof. bibl. studies Hartford Sem., 1976—. Coauthor: Christological Perspectives, 1984, Christology in Dialogue, 1993. Bd. dirs. Union Theol. Sem., N.Y.C., 1962-77. Democrat. Avocations: skiing, hiking, swimming, canoeing. Home: 275 Steele Rd West Hartford CT 06117-2716

EDWARDS, SUSAN FREDA, history educator; b. Roslyn, N.Y., Jan. 29, 1956; d. Thomas Joseph and Rosemary (Arthur) Freda; m. Allan Richard Hult, Nov. 18, 1978 (div. 1982); m. Jefferson Dudley Edwards, Oct. 13, 2001. BA in Polit. Sci., Fla. So. Coll., 1977; MA in History, Clemson U., 1985; postgrad., Rice U., 1985-89, U. Houston, 1989—. Read-a-thon coord. Multiple Sclerosis Soc., Tampa, Fla., 1977-78; divsnl. sales mgr., asst. buyer Ivey's Fla., Winter Park, 1978-81; pres. dir. Tampa Hilton Hotel, 1981-82; grad. asst. Clemson (S.C.) U., 1984-85; prof. history Ctrl. Coll., Houston, 1986—2002; mem. staff Houston C.C., 1988—2002; dept. chair history/philosophy/geography Ctrl. Coll., Houston, 1996—2001; mem. staff Cy-Fair Coll., 2002—, prof. history, 2001—. Vis. asst. prof. history U. Alaska Southeast, Sitka, 1993-94; adj. instr. Sheldon Jackson Coll., Sitka, 1994; archivist Liberty Life Ins. Co., Greenville, S.C., 1985; pres. faculty assn. coun. Houston C.C. Sys., 1995-96, pres.-elect, 1994-95, sec., chair, 1992-93, treas., chair fundraising com., 1991-92, chair salary com., 1992-94, chair governance com., 1990-91; lectr. Houston C.C., 1988-2002, Cy-Fair Coll., 2002—; presenter in field. Editl. asst.: Papers of Jefferson Davis, Rice U., 1987—88, Jour. So. History, 1985—87; editor: Teaching the Civil Rights Movement: Freedom's Bittersweet Song, 2002. Active, docent Mus. Fine Arts Houston Guild; bd. dirs.. Houston Fedn. Profl. Women, 1999-2000; campaign worker various Dem. candidates, Houston, 1987—vol. Project Nicaragua, 1994-95, 98-99. NEH grant, 1994, 95, 98, 2000, Houston C.C. Sys. grant, 1991-95, Fulbright-Hays grant, 1994, 99, East-West Ctr. grant, 1998; Illabelle Shanahan Morrisin fellow Alpha Chi Omega Found., 1985. Mem.: Assn. Women Adminstrs., C.C. Humanities Assn. (editor rev. 1999—2001), Tex. Assn. Women C.C.s, Tex. C.C. Tchrs. Assn. (pres.), Am. Assn. Women in C.C.s (nat. bd. dirs. 1999—2002, region VI dir.), Fulbright Assn., Phi Theta Kappa (seminar leader 1995—96, Tex. adv. bd. 1996—99, internat. honors com., seminar leader 1999, 2001, 2003, mem. honors com. 2001—, Horizon award 1996, Robert Giles award 2000, Mosal Scholar award 2002), Kappa Delta Pi, Omicron Delta Kappa, Phi Alpha Theta. Avocations: reading, singing, the arts, photography, tennis. Home: 4006 Julian St Houston TX 77009-5243 Office: Cy-Fair Coll 14955 NW Freeway Houston TX 77040 E-mail: susan.h.edwards@nhmccd.edu.

EDWARDS-TATE, LAURIE ELLEN, human services administrator, educator; b. San Diego, June 3, 1951; d. Donald Morgan and Doral (Erickson) Hurd; m. William James Tate Jr., Jan. 1, 1995. Student, Calif. Poly. State U., 1977; BA, Nat. U., San Diego, 1978; MS, Chapman Coll., 1986. Instr. bus. local C.C., 1979—91; founder, owner Am. Med. Claims, La Jolla, Calif., 1981-86; pres., founder At Your Home Svcs., San Diego, 1985—, Familycare, 1996—; founder The Learning Acad. Mem. Rancho Bernardo Chamber; edn. co-chair San Diego Coun. Aging, North County Providers Coun., South Bay Providers Coun. Mem.: NAFE, Nat. Assn. Homecare, San Diego Regional Home Care Coun. (edn. com.), North County Inland Providers, East County Providers Coun. (health com., aging and indp. svcs.), Calif. Assn. Health Svcs. at Home (past bd. dirs., steering com., providers co-chair Long Term Care Integration Project, adv. bd., governance com.), Soft-Coated Wheaten Club So. Calif. Avocations: photography, travel, dog fancier. Office: At Your Home Familycare 6540 Lusk BlvdSte C-266 San Diego CA 92121 E-mail: familycare@ayhs.cncdsl.com.

EDZERZA, JOHN, legislator; b. Lower Post, Brit. Columbia, Aug. 14, 1948; m. Jennifer Edzerza; 4 children. Attended H.S., Yukon; student, Coll. Journeyman welder Various Orgns., 1965—80; healer, counselor Self employed, 1980—2000; elected min. Legis. Assembly Yukon, Canada, 2002—. Mem. Kwanlin Dun Justice Com., Kwanlin Dun Hiring com.; main table negotiator Separation Kwanlin Dun and Ta'an First Nations; elected mem. First Nation chief and Coun, 1996—. Office: Yukon Legis Assembly Box 2703 Whitehorse Yukon Y1A 2C8 Canada

EFFLER, WILMA JEAN, elementary education educator; b. Knoxville, TN, Nov. 15, 1953; d. Ralph Coy and Barbara Jean (Berry) Kear; m. Robert Paul Effler, Jr., June 8, 1973; children: William Charles, Neil Robertson. BSBA, U. Tenn., 1975; MEd, Lincoln Meml. U., 1993. Cert. supervisor and adminstr., elem. and secondary tchr. Bus. tchr. Knox State Area Vocat. Tech. Sch., Knoxville, 1975-89; tchr. Alcoa (Tenn.) City Schs., 1989-90, Maryville (Tenn.) City Schs., 1990—. Articulation com. mem. Tenn. State Bd. Edn., 1987-88. Extended session Sunday tchr. Maryville First Bapt. Ch., 1984-88, Sunday sch. youth tchr., 1988-92, youth bd. mem., 1988-92. Mem. ASCD. Republican. Baptist. Avocations: reading, cross stitching, music. Home: 351 Vernie Lee Rd Friendsville TN 37737-3109 Office: Sam Houston Elem Sch 330 Melrose St Maryville TN 37803-4814

EFFROS, RICHARD MATTHEW, medical educator, physician; b. N.Y.C., Dec. 10, 1935; BA, Columbia U., 1957; MD, NYU, 1961. Intern, then resident NYU Sch. Medicine, 1961-64, fellow in nephrology, 1964-66, fellow in cardiopulmonary, 1966-68; instr. medicine Goldwater Meml. Hosp., N.Y.C., 1967-68; asst. prof. N.J. Coll. Medicine, 1968-71, assoc. prof., 1971-74, Harbor-UCLA Med. Ctr., Torrance, Calif., 1974-80, prof., 1980-89, Med. Coll. Wis., Milw., 1989—, chief pulmonary & critical care, 1989—91. Mem. adv. com. Nat. Heart, Blood, Lung Inst., 1975-93, Am. Heart Assn., 1977-89, Am. Lung Assn., 1986-90, VA Merit Rev., 1989-92. Contbr. articles to Sci., Jour. Applied Physiology, Jour. Clin. Investigations, Circulation Rsch. Recipient Career Devel. award NIH, 1973-78; grantee pulmonary edema NIH, 1974—. Mem. ACP, Am. Physiol. Soc., am. Thoracic Soc., Am. Coll. Chest Physicians. Achievements include research in the documentation of carbonic anhydrase activity on endothelium of lungs and other organs, in vivo measurements of intracellular pH in organs, active Na+ transport in lungs, detection of lung injury with scanning procedure, urea transporters in liver, cystic fibrosis exhaled breath condensates. Home: 9360 N Broadmoor Rd Bayside WI 53217-1307 Office: Med Coll Wis 9200 W Wisconsin Ave Milwaukee WI 53226-3522

EGAN, MARTHA AVALEEN, history educator, archivist, consultant; b. Kingsport, Tenn., Feb. 26, 1956; d. Jack E. and Opal (Pugh) E. BS in Comm., U. Tenn., 1978; MA in History, East Tenn. State U., 1986; postgrad., U. Ky., 1986-89, Milligan Coll., 1990. Cert. tchr., Tenn.; cert. Am. Acad. Cert. Archivists. News reporter, anchor WJCW-AM/WQUT-FM, Johnson City, Tenn., 1980-82; staff asst. 1st Dist. Office U.S. Senator Jim Sasser, Blountville, Tenn., 1982-84; instr. history East Tenn. State U., Johnson City, 1984-86; tchg. asst. dept. history U. Ky., Lexington, 1986-89; rschr./writer history project Eastman Chem. Co., Kingsport, 1991; adj. faculty history and humanities N.E. State Tech. C.C., Blountville, 1992—93, adj. faculty history, 2000—03; archivist Kingsport Pub. Libr. and Archives, 1993—2002; adj. asst. prof. history King Coll., Bristol, Tenn., 1994-99; adj. faculty history Emory and Henry Coll., Emory, Va., 2002—. Author: Images of America: Kingsport, 1998; rschr., writer: Eastman Chemical Company: Years of Glory, Times of Change, 1991; contbr. Ency. of Appalachia, Tenn. Ency. History and Culture, Ency. of the Harlem Renaissance, Ency. of Am. Indsl. History, Dictionary of Am. History, Ency. of History and Culture. Vice chair Sullivan County Dem. Party, 1992-93; rec. sec. Sullivan County Dem. Women's Club, 1992, corr. sec., 1994; mem. Kingsport Symphony Chorus, sec.-treas., 1994-95; mem. East Tenn. Camerata, Johnson City Civic Chorale; mem. flute choir First Broad St. Meth. Ch.; mem. St. Christopher's Episcopal Ch. Mem. AAUW (Kingsport chpt.), Orgn. Am. Historians, Appalachian Studies Assoc., Soc. Am. Archivists, Tenn. Archivists, Kingsport Music Club (corr. sec. 1995-97), Sullivan County Hist. Soc. (bd. dirs.), Nat. Flute Assn., Phi Alpha Theta, Pi Gamma Mu, Sigma Delta Chi. Avocations: flute, photography. Home: 544 Rambling Rd Kingsport TN 37663

EGAN, PATRICIA JANE, foundation executive, former university development director, writer; b. San Francisco, Aug. 7, 1951; 1 child, Kathryn Michele. AB, U. Calif., Berkeley, 1978; postgrad., N.J. Inst. Tech., 1996—. Cert. fund raising exec. Grants officer The Mus. Modern Art, N.Y.C., 1979-81; assoc. devel. officer grants Whitney Mus. Am. Art, N.Y.C., 1981-84; assoc. dir. devel. Columbia Bus. Sch., Columbia U., N.Y.C., 1984-86; mgr. major gifts New York Bot. Garden, N.Y.C., 1987-88; dir. devel. N.Y.C. Partnership, 1989-91; dir. devel. Cal Performances U. Calif., Berkeley, 1991-92; cons., 1992—. Cons. to various cultural and environ. orgns., N.Y., N.J., Calif., 1983—; co-prodr. distance learning course proposal writing N.J. Inst. Tech., 1997—. Prodr., program host including Terpsichore, KUSF-FM, 1978-79. Bd. dirs. Universala Esperanto Asocio/N.Y., 1980-83, Dance Perspectives Found., N.Y.C., 1985-2002, treas. 1987-91, found. officer, treas.; trustee Riverside Ch., N.Y.C., 1986-87. Fellow Nat. Endowment Arts, 1977. Mem. Soc. for Tech. Comm. (Bernard J. Goodman Meml. award N.Y. Metro chpt. 1998), Women in Comm., Internat. Assn. Bus. Communicators, Esperanto League of N.Am., Jr. League of San Francisco, Churchill Club, Alpha Epsilon Lambda. Avocations: art and technology, ballet, modern dance, martial arts. Office: PO Box 194391 San Francisco CA 94119-4391

EGASHIRA, SUSAN LEA, elementary education educator; b. Spokane, Wash. d. Masao Murphy and Ruby Kumi (Bunya) Iga; m. Jerry Egashira, June 21, 1970; children: Alicia, Scott, Derek. BA, Nat. Coll. Edn., 1970; MA, San Francisco State U., 1978. Cert. elem. and secondary edn., Wash. Human rels. aide San Mateo (Calif.) City Sch. Dist., 1971-73; tchr., prin. Woodland Sch., Redwood City, Calif., 1981-82; tchr. St. Thomas Sch., Medina, Wash., 1984-87; tchr., dir. Rainbow Sch., Issaquah, Wash., 1987-91; asst. dir. early childhood svcs. Jewish Cmty. Ctr., Mercer Island, Wash., 1991-93; tchr. North Creek Country Day Sch., Bothell, Wash., 1993-96, Keystone Sch., Lynnwood, Wash., 1996—, Dartmoor Learning, Bellevue, Wash., 1996-97, Spiritridge Elem. Sch., Bellevue, Wash., 1999—. Office: Spiritridge Elem Sch 16401 SE 24th St Bellevue WA 98008 E-mail: egashiras@bsd405.org., siegashira@hotmail.com.

EGELSON, POLLY SELIGER, artist, educator; b. Balt., Aug. 6, 1928; d. Robert Victor Seliger and Beatrice Regina (Gordon) Summers; m. Louis I. Egelson, June 6, 1949; children: Robert, Betsy, David, Jane. BA, Radcliffe Coll., 1950. Sculptor, instr. Fuller Mus. Art, Brockton, Mass., 1976-93, Danforth Mus. Art, Framingham, Mass., 1976-79, Cape Mus. Art, Dennis, Mass., 1976-79, Falmouth (Mass.) Artists Guild, 1976—. Bd. govs. Copley Soc., Boston, 1970-73; pres. New Eng. Sculptors Assn., Boston, 1972-74; chair Newton (Mass.) Cultural Com., 1974-76. Sculpture exhibits include Boston City Hall, 1976, Boston Art Festival, 1978, Ward-Nasse Gallery, N.Y.C., Lincoln Ctr., N.Y.C., 1977, Grand Prix Internat. Art Show, Monaco, 1977-78, Cahoon Mus. Am. Art., Cotuit, Mass.; represented in permanent collections Towson (Md.) State Coll., Cape Mus. Fine Arts, Dennis, Mass., Duxbury (Mass.) Mus. Complex; contbg. artist: (books) Falmouth, A Timeless Legacy, Women Artists in America. Assoc. mem. Nat. Mus. Women, Washington, 1995; panel mem., invited artist Cape Cod Women, Yarmouth, Mass., 1995-96. Recipient Best Sculpture award Attleboro Mus. Art, 1975, Cape Cod Art Assn., 1979, Curators Choice award. Mem. New Eng. Sculptors Assn., New Eng. Monotype Guild (bd. dirs. 1994-96), Falmouth Artists Guild (v.p. 1995), Crazy Quilters Guild (sec. 1990-96). Avocations: swimming, reading.

EGELSTON, ROBERTA RIETHMILLER, writer; b. Pitts., Nov. 20, 1946; d. Robert E. and Doris (Bauer) Riethmiller; m. David Michael Egelston, Oct. 10, 1975; 1 child, Brian David. BA in Bus. Administrn., Thiel Coll., 1968; MLS, U. Pitts., 1974. Bus. mgr. Pitts. Pastoral Inst., 1968-70; administrv. asst. Coun. Alcoholism and Drug Abuse, Lancaster, Pa., 1970-72; dir. career planning libr. U. Pitts., 1974-78; writer, 1978—; libr. Pitts. Inst. Mortuary Sci., 1991—2001, instr. bus. English, 1992-98; mem. site-based mgmt. team Fox Chapel Area H.S., 1999-2001. Instr. beginning genealogy, 1991-98; book reviewer Coll. Placement Coun., Bethlehem, Pa., 1977-78; cons. State Affiliated Colls. and Univs., 1976; group leader Johns-Norris Assocs., Pitts., 1975-76. Author: Career Planning Materials, 1981, Credits and Careers for Adult Learners, 1985. Bd. dirs. Lauri Ann West Libr., Pitts., 1983-84; active PTA, 1985-88; mem. peace and justice com. Fox Chapel Presbyn. Ch., 1994-2000, deacon, 1995-98, mem. libr. com., 2000-02; mem. spiritual life com. East Liberty Presbyn. Ch., 2002-. Mem. AAUW (bd. dirs. Fox Chapel Area br. 1980-91, 2001-03), Les Lauriers (sr. women's hon. at Thiel Coll.), Western Pa. Geneal. Soc. (libr. rsch. com. 1990-94, edn. com. 1992—), Beta Phi Mu. Avocations: hiking, reading, gourmet cooking.

EGERTON, CHARLES PICKFORD, anatomy and physiology educator; b. Toronto, Ont., Can., Mar. 17, 1939; (parents Am. citizens); s. Matthew Davis and Margaret Swain (Pickford) E.; m. Carol Anne Carlson, Dec. 16, 1976; children: Matthew, Andrew, Victoria. BA in Zoology, Duke U., 1962; BS in Medicine, U. Okla., Oklahoma City, 1978; MS in Sci. Edn., U. So. Miss., 1981, PhD in Sci. Edn., 1991, MPH in Health Edn., 1994. Cert. physician asst. Nat. Commn. on Cert. Physician Assts. Commd. 2d lt. USAF, 1962, advanced through grades to maj., 1980, ops. officer, 1962-76, primary care med. officer, 1978-88; ret., 1988; instr. anatomy and physiology Miss. Gulf Coast C.C., Gautier, 1992—. Mem. Miss. Health Adv. Coun., Jackson, 1990—; guest lectr. dept. physician asst. studies U. South Ala. Author: Student Study Guide for Anatomy and Physiology; editor: Physician Assistant Handbook, 1995, Principles of Anatomy and Physiology, 9th edit., 2000; contbr. articles to profl. jours. Lectr. Miss. Inst. Drug-Free Sch., Hattiesburg, 1992; lectr. single parent-displaced spouse, Guatier, 1994-97; dir. smoking cessation Keesler AFB Med. Ctr., 1986-88; lay reader St. Luke's Anglican Ch., Gulfport, Miss., 1986-94. Mem. Am. Assn. Anatomists, Am. Acad. Physician Assts., Human Anatomy and Physiology Soc., Miss. Acad. Scis., Miss. Sci. Tchrs. Assn., Phi Delta Kappa, Eta Sigma Gamma. Democrat. Avocation: boating. Home: 6008 E Moreton Pl Ocean Springs MS 39564-2725 Office: Miss Gulf Coast CC PO Box 100 Gautier MS 39553-0100 E-mail: charles.egerton@mgccc.edu., egerton@cableone.net.

EGGERS, GEORGE WILLIAM NORDHOLTZ, JR., anesthesiologist, educator; b. Galveston, Texas, Feb. 22, 1929; s. George William Nordholtz and Edith (Sykes) E.; m. Mary Futrell, Dec. 30, 1955; children: Carol Ann, George William. BA, Rice U., Tex., 1949; MD, U. Tex., Galveston, Tex., 1953. Diplomate Am. Bd. Anesthesiology. Instr. dept. anesthesiology, U. Tex., Galveston, Tex., 1956-59; asst. prof. dept. anesthesiology, U. Tex., Galveston, Tex., 1959-61; assoc. prof. dept. anesthesiology, U. Mo., 1961-67; prof. dept anesthesiology U. Mo., 1967—94, acting chmn. dept. anesthesiology, 1969, chmn. dept. anesthesiology, 1970-94, prof. emeritus, 1994—2001. Vis. instr. USAF Hosp., Lackland AFB, San Antonio, 1956-61; vis. rsch. prof. dept. anesthesiology Northwestern U. Med. Sch., Chgo., 1968-69; rsch. assoc. Space Sci. Rsch. Ctr., U. Mo., 1965-66. Contbr. over 50 articles to profl. jours. Recipient Ashbel Smith Disting. Alumnus Award U. Tex., 1993. Mem. Am. Soc. Anesthesiology (bd. dirs. 1979-86, v.p. 1986-89, 1st v.p. 1990, pres. elect 1991, pres. 1992), Am. Coll. Anesthesiology (bd. govs., 1965-74, chmn. bd. govs., 1973), Soc. Acad. Anesthesiology Chmn. (pres. 1971), Assn. Am. Med. Colls. (adminstrv. bd. coun. acad. socs. 1976-79), Mo. Soc. Anesthesiologists (pres. 1970, Disting. Svc. Award 2001), Tex. Gulf Coast Anesthesiology Soc. (v.p. 1960), Boone County Med. Soc. (pres. 1988), Am. Bd. Anesthesiology (assoc. examiner 1968, joint coun. with Am. Soc. Anesthesiology on in-tng. exams.), Acad. Anesthesiology (pres. 1994, Citation of Merit 1997), Accreditation Coun. Grad. Med. Edn. (mem. residency rev. com. for anesthesiology 1989-94), Anesthesia Found. (trustee 1993-2003), Alpha Omega Alpha, Mu Delta, Sigma Xi. Republican. Roman Catholic. Avocations: hunting, astronomy, magic, photography, shooting. Home: 1509 Woodrail Ave Columbia MO 65203-0931 Office: U Mo Dept Anesthesiology 1 Hospital Dr Dept Columbia MO 65201-5276

EGGERS, WALTER FREDERICK, academic administrator; b. Mt. Vernon, N.Y., May 31, 1943; s. Walter F. and Catherine Elaine (Carney) E.; m. Sue Mac Hatcher, Aug. 21, 1967 (div. 1981); m. Kelly Ann Houston, Dec. 26, 1986; children: Walter F. III, Jane Branson, Robert Houston, Sam Houston, Max Brand. AB in English with honors, Duke U., 1964; PhD, U. N.C., 1971. Vis. asst. prof. St. Andrews Coll., Laurinburg, N.C., 1967-68; lectr. U. N.C., Chapel Hill, 1968-69; from asst. prof. to full prof. U. Wyo., Laramie, 1969-89; dean Coll. ARts and Scis. Arts and Scis., Laramie, 1985-89; prof., provost, v.p. acad. affairs U. N.H., Durham, 1989-2000. Commr. Commn. on Higher Edn. New Eng. Assn. Schs. and Colls. Author: (with Sigrid Mayer) Ernst Cassirer: An Annotated Bibliography, 1988; co-d-editor: Teaching Shakespeare, 1977; contbr. articles to profl. jours. Recipient Teaching award Amoco found., 1975, Program award Assn. Am. Colls., Program award NEH, 1983-85; faculty fellow Sch. of Criticism and Theory U. Calif., Irvine, 1977. Mem. MLA, Am. Assn. Higher Edn., Academic Roundtable. Home and Office: Univ NH Office Academic Affairs Durham NH 03824-4724

EGINTON, CHARLES THEODORE, surgeon, educator; b. Staples, Minn., 1914; m. Sally Eginton; children— William C., Julie Ann, Mark Theodore, C. William, Nancy Elizabeth. BA, Macalester Coll., 1935; BS, U. Minn., 1937, M.B. with distinction, 1938, MD, 1939, MS in Surgery, 1942. Diplomate: Am. Bd. Surgery. Intern Ancker Hosp., St. Paul, 1938-39; fellow in surgery Mayo Found., Rochester, Minn., 1939-42; asst. in surgery Mayo Clinic, 1941-42; practice medicine specializing in surgery St. Paul, 1946-67; chief surg. svc. VA Hosp., Fargo, N.D., 1967-71, chief of staff, 1971-78, chief surg. svcs., 1978-87, ret. surg. svcs., 1987—. Clin. prof. surgery U. N.D., 1970— ; adj. prof. pharmacy N.D. State U., 1970— Served to maj., M.C. AUS, 1942-46. Fellow ACS, Internat. Coll. Surgeons; mem. AMA, Phi Beta Kappa, Alpha Omega Alpha. Home: 509 1/2 N Shore Dr Detroit Lakes MN 56501-4411

EGINTON, MARGARET L. movement educator, dancer, theater director; b. Iowa City, June 9, 1955; d. William Leonard and Kay Ruth (Boehnke) E.; m. John Alden Howell, June 16, 1979 (div. 1985); 1 child, Robert Burr. BA, Sarah Lawrence Coll., 1977. Registered movement therapist. Prin. dancer Merce Cunningham Dance Co., N.Y.C., 1977-80, Stephen Petronio Co., N.Y.C., 1984-88, Bill Irwin & Friends, N.Y.C., 1988-90; artistic dir. Meg Eginton & Dances, N.Y.C., 1980-87; movement educator Yale U., New Haven, 1988, NYU, 1988-94, Practical Aesthetics Workshop, Burlington, Vt., 1994; theatre fellow U. Iowa, Iowa City, 1994—97; assoc. prof. movement Fla. State U., 2002—. Movement coach Atlantic Theatre Co., N.Y.C., 1988-94, Am. Repertory Theatre, 1998-02; head movement inst. advanced theatre tng. Harvard U., 1998-02. Mem. edtl. bd. Dance Ink, N.Y.C., 1988-89. With workshops with retarded adults Kennedy Ctr. Spl. Arts, N.Y.C., 1987; with workshops with homeless children Children's Aid Soc., N.Y.C., 1988. Young Profl. Artist fellow Am. Dance Festival, 1975, Iowa Arts fellow U. Iowa, 1994-97; choreography grantee JCT Found., 1985; recipient N.Y. Dance and Performance award BESSIE Com., 1987. Mem. AFTRA, NAFE, SAG, AEA, Am. Guild Mus. Artists, Internal Somatic Movement Therapy and Edn. Assn. Democrat. Episcopalian. Home: 1010 Villagio Cir Sarasota FL 34237

EGLI, JACQUELINE RAE, special education educator; b. Columbus, Ohio, June 20, 1957; d. Larry Dale and Roberta (Raney) Adams; m. Richard C. Egli, June 5, 1982; children: Jason Albert, Kelli Ann. Grad., U. South Fla., 1978, U. Cen. Fla., 1983. Cert. profl. tchr., Fla., specific learning disabilities mentally handicapped. Tchr. spl. edn. Pace Pvt. Sch., Longwood, Fla., 1978-88, Forest City Elem. Sch., Altamonte Springs, Fla., 1988—. Cons. Cen. Fla. Community Sch., Winter Garden, 1990—; chairperson Forest City Invent Am. Com., 1990-92; mem. sch. adv. com. Forest City Elem. Sch., 1992-93; mem. Seminole County Tchr. Adv. Com., 1991—. Leader Citrus coun. Girl Scouts U.S., Altamonte Springs, 1979; instr. Pacesetter Cloggers, Orlando, Fla., 1978-85, Forest City Stompers, Altamonte Springs, 1991-92; treas. Spl. Edn. PTA, 1992-93. Grantee, Seminole County Assn. Children with Learning Disabilities, Longwood, Fla., 1990, Chpt. II Funds, Seminole County, 1991, Found. Advancement of Community Through Schs. Found., Sanford, Fla., 1991. Mem. Coun. for Exceptional Children, Fla. Assn. for Children with Learning Disabilities. Presbyterian. Avocations: clogging, scouting activities, bowling, stained glass, collecting antiques. Home: 540 Walnut St Altamonte Springs FL 32714-2329 Office: Forest City Elem Sch 1010 Sand Lake Rd Altamonte Springs FL 32714-7043

EHDE, AVA LOUISE, librarian, educator; b. Buffalo, Feb. 11, 1963; d. Louise and Robert Andrew Kinn(Stepfather), Henry Emil Nonnenberg. BA in History and German, SUNY, Buffalo, 1995, MLS, 1997. Cert. pub. libr. N.Y. Intern libr. Niagara Falls (N.Y.) Pub. Libr., 1996—97, local history libr., 1997—98; reference libr. Trocaire Coll., Buffalo, 1998—99, libr. dir., 1999; libr. Buffalo & Erie County Pub. Libr., 1999—2002; head reference, sys. coord. D'Youville Coll. Libr., Buffalo, 1999—2002; adj. faculty SUNY Sch. Informatics, Buffalo, 2001—; adult svcs. reference libr. Manatee County Pub. Libr. Sys., Bradenton, Fla., 2002—. Co-chair Western N.Y. Reference Discussion Group, Buffalo, 2000—02; mem. Regional Automation Com., Buffalo, 2000—02. Co-author (workshop): Networking and Operating Systems for Librarians, 2001—. Reader Niagara Frontier Radio Reading Svc., Cheektowaga, NY, 1999—2002. Named Alberta Riggs Meml. scholar, Sch. Info. and Libr. Studies, 1997; recipient Dr. Marie Ross Wolcott Meml. award, 1997; grantee, NYLA Reference and Adult Svcs. Sect. Continuing Edn., 2002; Profl. Devel. grant, Western N.Y. Libr. Resources Coun., 2001—02. Mem.: AAUP (v.p., exec. com. 2001—02), ALA, Assn. Coll. and Rsch. Librs., Libr. and Info. Tech. Assn., Beta Phi Mu. Avocations: bicycling, hiking, reading, scuba diving, cooking. Home: 401 Clark Lane Holmes Beach FL 34217 Office: Manatee County Libr Sys Ctrl Libr 1301 Barcarrota Blvd W Bradenton FL 34205 Fax: 941-749-7155. E-mail: librarianava@hotmail.com., ava.ehde@co.manatee.fl.us.

EHLINGER, JANET ANN DOWLING, elementary school educator; b. Des Moines, Mar. 1, 1955; d. Joseph Patrick and Sadie Agnes (Klein) Dowling; m. Steven Mark Ehlinger, July 22, 1989; children: Bridget Ann, Brian Mark. BS, Benedictine Coll., Atchison, Kans., 1977; MEd, U. St. Thomas, Houston, 1985. Cert. tchr., Tex. Tchr. English, sci. Our Lady Mt. Carmel, Houston, 1977-78; tchr. social studies, history, religion St. Michael's Sch., Houston, 1978-82; tchr. social studies and history Kinkaid Sch., Houston, 1982-90; tchr. lit., English and vocabulary The Tenney Sch., Houston, 2000—. Substitute tchr. St. Thomas More Sch., Houston, 1998—99. Active Mus. Fine Arts, Houston, 1992, Children's Mus. of Houston, 1993-96; bd. dirs. St. Cyril of Alexandria Ladies Guild, Houston, 1992; leader Girl Scouts Am., 1996—. Mem. Nat. Coun. Social Studies, Tex. State Hist. Assn., Houston Zool. Soc., Kappa Delta Pi (rep.-at-large Pi Lambda chpt. 1985-86, sec. 1987-89). Avocations: reading, sewing, piano, travel. Home: 6111 Cheena Dr Houston TX 77096-4614

EHLMANN, BRYON KURT, computer science educator; b. St. Charles, Mo., Sept. 11, 1948; s. Kurt Gustav Alvin and Anna Marie (Soenker) E.; m. Judith Pauline List, Nov. 18, 1973; children: Bethany List, Jonathan List; m. Barbara Kay Mossman, June 17, 2000. BS in Computer Sci., U. Mo., Rolla, 1970; MS in Computer Sci., U. Mo., 1971; PhD in Computer Sci., Fla. State U., 1992. From sys. analyst to project mgr. Burroughs Corp., Detroit, Irvine, Calif., 1971-80; asst. prof. Chapman Coll., Orange, Calif., 1980-85; project sys. programmer Unisys Corp., Mission Viejo, Calif., 1985-87; instr. Fla. State U., Tallahassee, 1987-88; from asst. prof. to prof. computer sci. Fla. A&M U., Tallahassee, 1988-2000; assoc. prof. computer sci. So. Ill. U., Edwardsville, Ill., 2000—. Vis. researcher Supercomputer Computations Rsch. Inst., 1992; courtesy faculty mem. Fla. State U., 1993. NSF fellow, 1970. Mem. IEEE Computer Soc., Assn. Computing Machinery, Upsilon Pi Epsilon, Phi Kappa Phi. Avocations: running, reading, politics. Home: 1602 Terrace Cove Ct Edwardsville IL 62025 Office: So Ill U Dept Computer Sci Edwardsville IL 62026

EHMANN, WILLIAM DONALD, chemistry educator; b. Madison, Wis., Feb. 7, 1931; s. William F. and Victoria V. (Koperski) E.; m. Nancy M. Gallagher, July 16, 1955; children: William J., John M., James T., Kathleen E. BS, U. Wis., 1952, MS, 1954; PhD, Carnegie Inst. Tech., 1957. NRC-NSF rsch. assoc. Argonne Nat. Lab., Ill., 1957-58; mem. faculty U. Ky., Lexington, 1958—, asst. prof., 1958-63, assoc. prof. chemistry, 1963-66, prof., 1966-95, chmn. dept., dir. grad. studies, 1972-76, Coll. Arts and Scis. Disting. prof., 1968-69, univ. rsch. prof., 1977-78, assoc. dean for rsch. Grad. Sch., 1980-84, prof. emeritus, 1995—. Vis. prof. Ariz. State U., Tempe, 1969, Fla. State U., Tallahassee, 1972; cons. Argonne Nat. Lab., 1958-67; rsch. dir. project AEC, 1960-71, Agr. Dept., 1968-70, NASA, 1968-77, NIH, 1977-80, 84-98, DOE, 1983-85, NSF EPSCOR, 1986-91, NIST, 1993-94; rsch. in chemistry of meteorites, moon, human brain and activation analysis. Author: Radiochemistry and Nuclear Methods of Analysis, 1991; contbr. articles to profl. jours. Hon. assoc. Sanders-Brown Ctr. on Aging, 1988-95; bd. dirs. U. Ky. Rsch. Found., 1991-93; bd. dirs., mem. exec. com. Alzheimer's Disease Rsch. Ctr., U. Ky., 1990. Recipient William D. Ehmann award in radioanalytical chemistry Am. Nuclear Soc., 1996, Sturgill award U. Ky., 1987; Fulbright scholar; hon. fellow Australian Nat. U. Inst. Advanced Studies, Canberra, 1964-65. Fellow AAAS, Meteoritical Soc.; mem. Am. Chem. Soc. (chmn. Lexington sect. 1963-64, Herty medal for career achievements 1994, nat. award in nuclear chemistry 1996), Ky. Acad. Scis. (bd. dirs. 1964-67, Disting. Ky. Scientist award 1982), Sigma Xi, Phi Lambda Upsilon, Phi Eta Sigma, Phi Theta Kappa. Roman Catholic. Achievements include first analysis (with others) of Apollo Mission lunar samples; research on the chemistry of meteorites, lunar samples and trace elements involvement in neurological diseases; on the etiology of Alzheimer's Disease. Home: 769 Zandale Dr Lexington KY 40502-3371 Office: U Ky 312 Chem Physics Bldg Lexington KY 40506-0055 E-mail: wdehmann@att.net.

EHMEN, JAMES EDWARD, elementary education educator; b. Storm Lake, Iowa, Mar. 30, 1945; s. Henry Frank and Rose Laura (Ackerman) E. BA, U. No. Iowa, 1967, MA, 1992. Cert. tchr., Iowa. 5th grade tchr. Janesville (Iowa) Consol. Sch., 1967-68, 6th grade tchr., 1970—2002; adj. instr. U. No. Iowa, Cedar Falls, 2002—. Sub-unit rep. N.E. Iowa Edn. Unit, Fayette, Iowa, 1987-93, v.p., pres.-elect, 1993-97; mem. Bd. Ednl. Examiners, 1995-2002. Recipient Nat. Edn. award Milken Family Found., 1996. Scoutmaster Boy Scouts Am., Janesville, 1988-2003. With U.S. Army, 1968-70. Recipient Dist. award of merit Winnebago coun. Boy Scouts Am., 1992. Mem. NEA, Nat. Sci. Tchrs. Assn., Acad. Sci., Nat. Coun. for Social Studies, Nat. Coun. for Social Studies, Iowa State Edn. Assn. Democrat. Avocations: camping, biking, coin collecting, cooking. Office: U No Iowa SEC 618 Cedar Falls IA 50614

EHRENBERG, RONALD GORDON, economist, educator; b. N.Y.C., Apr. 20, 1946; s. Seymour and Judith G. E.; m. Randy Ann Birch, June 29, 1967; children: Eric L., Jason H. BA in Math. cum laude, SUNY, Binghamton, 1966; MA, PhD, Northwestern U., 1970. Instr. econs. Northwestern U., Evanston, Ill., 1970; asst. prof. econs. Loyola U., Chgo., 1970-71, U. Mass., Amherst, 1971-72, assoc. prof. econs., 1972-75; assoc. prof. econs. and labor econs. Cornell U., 1975-77, chmn. dept. labor econs., 1976-81, prof. econs. and labor econs., 1977-85; dir. rsch. N.Y. State Sch. Indsl. and Labor Rels., 1979-95; Irving M. Ives prof. indsl. and labor rels. and econs. Cornell U., 1985—, v.p. for acad. programs, planning and budgeting, 1995-98. Rsch. assoc. Nat. Bur. Econ. Rsch., 1981—; dir. Cornell Inst. Labor Mktg. Policies, 1990-98, dir. Cornell Higher Edn. Rsch. Inst., 1998—; staff Coun. Econ. Advisors, 1970; cons. in field. Author: Fringe Benefits and Overtime Behavior: Theory and Econometric Analysis, 1971, The Demand for State and Local Government Employees: An Economic Analysis, 1975, The Regulatory Process and Labor Earnings, 1979, (with R. Smith) Modern Labor Economics: Theory and Public Policy, 1982, 8th edit., 2003, (with others) Economic Challenges in Higher Education, 1991, Labor Markets and Integrating National Economics, 1994, Contemporary Policy Issues in Education, 1995, The American University: National Treasure of Endangered Species, 1997, Gender and Family Issues in the Workplace, 1997, Tuition Rising: Why College Costs So Much, 2000; contbr. articles to profl. jours. Endowment study advisors bd. Nat. Assn. Coll. and Univ. Bus. Officers, 2001—. Rsch. grantee NSF, U.S. Dept. Labor, various pvt. founds.; NDEA fellow, 1969; Woodrow Wilson Nat. Fellowship Found. Dissertation Yr. fellow, 1970. Mem. AAUP (chmn. com. on econ. status of the profession 2002—), Am. Econ. Assn. (exec. com. 1996-98), Indsl. Rels. Rsch. Assn., Am. Edn. Fin. Assn., Soc. Labor Economists (pres. 2002), Nat. Acads. (assoc.), Nat. Acad. Edn. Office: Cornell Higher Edn Rsch Inst 256 Ives Hall Ithaca NY 14853-3901 E-mail: rge2@cornell.edu.

EHRENFELD, DAVID WILLIAM, biology educator, writer; b. N.Y.C., Jan. 15, 1938; s. Irving and Anne Ehrenfeld; m. Joan Gardner, June 28, 1970; children: Kate, Jane, Jonathan, Samuel. BA, Harvard Coll., 1959; MD, Harvard Med. Sch., 1963; PhD, U. Fla., 1966. From asst. prof. biology to assoc. prof. biology Barnard Coll. Columbia U., N.Y.C., 1967-74; prof. biology Cook Coll. Rutgers U., New Brunswick, N.J., 1974—. Author: Biological Conservation, 1970, Conserving Life on Earth, 1972, The Arrogance of Humanism, 1978, Beginning Again: People and Nature in the New Millennium, 1993, 1995, Swimming Lessons: Keeping Afloat in the Age of Technology, 2002; founder, editor Conservation Biology, 1987—93, consulting editor, 1994—, bd. editors Ecosys. Health, 1994—, columnist (mag.) Orion, 1989—2002; contbg. editor: (mag.) Orion, 2003—; contbr. articles to profl. and popular publs.; co-author (with C.K. Mack): (novels) The Chameleon Variant, 1980. Trustee E.F. Schumacher Soc., Great Barrington, Mass., 1979-2002, bd. founders, 2003—; bd. trustees Caribbean Conservation Corp., Gainesville, Fla., 1980—, Ednl. Found. Am., Westport, Conn., 1987-93, 98-2002. Fellow AAAS; mem. Ecol. Soc. Am., Internat. Union for the Conservation of Nature, Marine Turtle Specialist Group. Jewish. Home: 44 N 7th Ave Highland Park NJ 08904-2931 Office: Rutgers U Cook Coll New Brunswick NJ 08901-8551

EHRENREICH, HENRY, physicist, educator; b. Frankfurt, Germany, May 11, 1928; came to U.S., 1940, naturalized, 1945; s. Nathan and Frieda (Rosenstein) E.; m. Tema P. Hasnas, Feb. 1, 1953; children: Paul, Beth Herst, Robert. Student, Columbia U., 1950-51; BA, Cornell U., 1950, PhD, 1955; MA (hon.), Harvard U., 1963. Theoretical physicist Gen. Electric Research Lab., Schenectady, N.Y., 1955-63; vis. lectr. Harvard U., 1960-61, Gordon McKay prof. applied physics, 1963-82, Clowes prof. sci., 1982—2001, Clowes rsch. prof., 2001—02; vis. prof. Brandeis U., 1969, U. Paris, 1969, U. Pa., 1976; univ. ombudsman Harvard Univ., Cambridge, Mass., 2002—. Mem. def. scis. rsch. coun. Advanced Rsch. Projects Agy., U.S. Dept. Def., 1972-2002; sec. solid state commn. Internat. Union Pure and Applied Physics, 1978-81; mem. solar photovoltaic energy adv. com. Dept. Energy, 1980-83; dir. Harvard Materials Rsch. Lab., 1982-90; cons. White House Office Sci. and Tech., 1991. Contbr. articles to profl. jours.; bd. editors Phys. Rev. 1965-67; co-editor: Solid State Physics, 1966—; asst. editor Annals of Phys., 1984-2002. Trustee Dibner Inst. for History of Sci. and Tech., 1992-98; cons. Wolf Found., 1997-99. Fellow AAAS, Am. Acad. Arts and Scis., Am. Phys. Soc. (chmn. div. solid state physics 1969, chmn. study group on solar energy 1977-81, chmn. panel on pub. affairs 1990-91); mem. Phi Beta Kappa, Sigma Xi. Office: Harvard U Divsn Engring and Applied Scis and Physics Dept Cambridge MA 02138 E-mail: ehrenreich@deas.harvard.edu.

EHRLICH, PAUL RALPH, biology educator; b. Phila., May 29, 1932; s. William and Ruth (Rosenberg) E.; m. Anne Fitzhugh Howland, Dec. 18, 1954; 1 child, Lisa Marie. AB, U. Pa., 1953; AM, U. Kans., 1955, PhD, 1957. Research assoc. U. Kans., Lawrence, 1958—59; asst. prof. biol. scis. Stanford U., 1959—62, assoc. prof., 1962—66, prof., 1966—, Bing prof. population studies, 1976—, dir. grad. study dept. biol. scis., 1966—69, pres. Ctr. for Conservation Biology, 1988—, dir. grad. study dept. biol. scis., 1974—76. Cons. Behavioral Rsch. Labs., 1963—67; corr. NBC News, 1989—92. Author: How to Know the Butterflies, 1961, Process of Evolution, 1963, Principles of Modern Biology, 1968, Population Bomb, 1968, Population Bomb, 2d edit., 1971, Population, Resources, Environment: Issues in Human Ecology, 1970, Population, Resources, Environment: Issues in Human Ecology, 2d edit, 1972, How to Be a Survivor, 1971, Global Ecology: Readings Toward a Rational Strategy for Man, 1971, Man and the Ecosphere, 1971, Introductory Biology, 1973, Human Ecology: Problems and Solutions, 1973, Ark II: Social Response to Environmental Imperatives, 1974, The End of Affluence: A Blueprint for the Future, 1974, Biology and Society, 1976, Race Bomb, 1977, Ecoscience: Population, Resources, Environment, 1977, Insect Biology, 1978, The Golden Door: International Migration, Mexico, and the U.S., 1979, Extinction: The Causes and Consequences of the Disappearance of Species, 1981, The Machinery of Nature, 1986, Earth, 1987, The Science of Ecology, 1987, The Birder's Handbook, 1988, New World/New Mind, 1989, The Population Explosion, 1990, Healing the Planet, 1991, Birds in Jeopardy, 1992, The Birdwatchers Handbook, 1994, The Stork & the Plow, 1995, Betrayal of Science and Reason, 1996, World of Wounds, 1997, Human Natures, 2000, Wild Solutions, 2001; contbr. articles to profl. jours. Co-recipient Crafoord prize in population biology and conservation biol. diversity, 1990; recipient World Wildlife Fedn. medal, 1987, Volvo Environ. prize, 1993, World Ecology medal, Internat. Ctr. Tropical Ecology, 1993, UN Sasakawa Environ. prize, 1994, Heinz prize for the environment, 1995, Tyler Environ. prize, 1998, Heineken prize for environ. sci., 1998, Blue Plant prize, 1999; fellow MacArthur Prize fellow, 1990—95. Fellow: AAAS, Entomology Soc. Am., Am. Philos. Soc., Am. Acad. Arts and Scis., Calif. Acad. Scis.; mem.: NAS, Lepidopterists Soc., Am. Mus. Natural History (hon.), Am. Mus. Natural History (life), Brit. Ecol. Soc. (hon.), Am. Soc. Naturalists, Soc. Systematic Biology, Soc. for Study of Evolution, Ecol. Soc. Am. (Eminent Ecologist award 2001). Office: Stanford U Dept Biol Scis Stanford CA 94305

EHRLICH, THOMAS, law educator; b. Cambridge, Massachusetts, Mar. 4, 1934; s. William and Evelyn (Seltzer) E.; m. Ellen (Rome), June 18, 1957; children, David, Elizabeth, Paul. AB, Harvard U., Cambridge, Mass., 1956, LLB, 1959; LLD (hon.), Villanova U., 1979, Notre Dame U., 1980, Pa. State U., 1987. Bar: Wis., 1959. Law clk. Judge Learned Hand U.S. Ct. Appeals 2d. Cir., 1959-60; spl. asst. to legal adviser U.S. State Dept., 1962-64, spl. asst. to under-sec., 1964-65; assoc. prof. law Stanford U., Stanford, Calif., 1965-68; prof. Stanford U., Stanford, Calif., 1968-75; dean Stanford U., Stanford, Calif., 1971-75, Richard E. Lang dean and prof., 1973-75; pres. Legal Services Corp., Washington, 1976-79; dir. Internat. Devel. Coop. Agy., Washington, 1979-81; provost, prof. law U. Penn., Phila., 1981-87; pres., prof. law Ind. U., Bloomington and Indpls., Ind., 1987-94; vis. prof. Duke U., Durham, NC, 1994; disting. Univ. scholar U. Calif., San Francisco, 1995-2000. Vis. prof. Stanford Law Sch., 1994-99; sr. scholar, Carnegie Found. for Advancement of Tchg., 1997—. Author: (with Abram Chayes and Andreas F. Lowenfeld) The Internat. Legal Process, 3 vols., 1968; (with Herbert L. Packer) New Directions in Legal Edn., 1972, Internat. Crises and the Role of Law, Cyprus, 1958-67, 1974; editor: (with Geoffrey C. Hazard Jr.) Going to Law School?, 1975; (with Mary Ellen O'Connell) Internat. Law and the Use of Force, 1993, The Courage to Inquire, 1995, Philanthropy and the Nonprofit Sector in a Changing Am., 1998, Civic Responsibility and Higher Edn., 2000; (with Jane V. Wellman) How the Student Hour Shapes Higher Education: The Tie that Binds, 2003; (with others) Educating Citizens: Preparing America's Undergraduates for Lives of Moral and Civic Responsibility, 2003. Office: Carnegie Found Advancement Tech 555 Middlefield Rd Menlo Park CA 94025-3443

EHRMANN, SUSANNA, foreign language educator, writer, photographer; b. Detroit, Oct. 17, 1944; d. Frederick Michael and Stephanie (Fiala) Ehrmann. Student, Universite Laval, summer 1965; BA, Antioch Coll., 1966; MAT, U. Chgo., 1968. Cert. tchr., Ill., Tex. Tchr. fgn. lang. U. Chgo. Lab. Schs., 1967-74, Maimonides Sch., Brookline, Mass., 1975-76, North Shore Country Day Sch., Winnetka, Ill., 1977-78, Copenhagen Internat. Jr. Sch., 1978-79, Houston C.C., 1979-81, 84, Kinkaid Sch., Houston, 1980-82, Alief Ind. Sch. Dist., Houston, 1982-85, Houston Ind. Sch. Dist., 1990-91; pvt. instr., 1986—; freelance rschr., editor, 1986—; writer, photographer, 1993—. Mem. North Cen. evaluating teams, Chgo., Rockford, 1971; mem. MAT coordinating com. on Romance langs., U. Chgo., 1971-74. Creator German Grammar Game, 1982. Reader for the blind, Chgo., 1972-74. NDEA fellow, 1966-68; Goethe Inst. grantee, summer 1983. Mem. MLA, Am. Assn. Tchrs. of French, Am. Assn. Tchrs. of German. Home: 3001 Landwehr Rd Northbrook IL 60062-7517 E-mail: fiala3@juno.com.

EI, SUSAN M(ICHELLE), English language educator; b. Detroit, Apr. 3, 1952; d. Raymond Denis Ei and Eileen Winifred Willson; m. Paul S. Zalon, Sept. 22, 1990. BA in Art History, U. Mich., 1974, MA in Linguistics, 1985. Sales rep. Typographic Insight, Ann Arbor, Mich., 1980-86; theater mgr. Fifth Forum Theater, Ann Arbor, Mich., 1972-78; photographer's asst. Stan Ries Studios, N.Y.C., 1987-89; lectr. in ESL LaGuardia Coll., N.Y.C., 1986-90; pvt. instr. to corp. execs. in ESL N.Y.C., 1986—. Mem. libr. staff Pequot Libr., Southport, Conn. Mem. Foote Family Assn. Am. (historian 1988-94). Democrat. Unitarian Universalist. Avocations: photography, running, skating. Home and Office: 51B Spruce St Southport CT 06890-1442

EICHMAN, CHARLES MELVIN, school counselor, career assessment educator; b. Ft. Hays, Kans., June 16, 1950; s. Melvin Joseph and Barbara Ann (Bennett) E. BA, U. No. Colo., 1972; MA, Fuller Theol. Sem., 1974; grad., U. Mo., 1991; cert. K-12 sch. adminstr., Idaho State U., 2002. Cert. vocat. evaluator, career guidance specialist, sch. counselor, job devel. specialist, secondary sch. tchr, sch. admin. K-12, vocational admin. Youth activity coord. YMCA, Glendale, Calif., 1972-74; counselor U. Colo., Colorado Springs, 1975-76; resident hall advisor U. No. Colo., Greeley, 1976-77; secondary tchr., coach Jefferson County Dist. R-1, Lakewood, Colo., 1978-80; pres., owner Big Sky C.F.M. and Mgmt. Resources, Rock Springs, Wyo., 1980-85; secondary tchr. Boulder (Colo.) Valley Dist. RE-2, 1986-88; vocat. evaluator and dir. Platte County Dist. RE-111 Vocat. Evaluation Ctr., Platte City, Mo., 1988-92; pres., owner Career Assessment Svcs., Arvada, Colo., 1992-94; sch. counselor, head dist. elem. at-risk student program Albany Schs. Re-1, Laramie, Wyo., 1993-94; sch. counselor, dir. dist. model Kids at Risk program Franklin Jr. H.S. and New Horizons Alt. H.S., Pocatello, 1994—; developer counseling program New Horizons Alt. H.S., Pocatello, 1994—. Affiliate faculty and site supr. Idaho State U., 2001—. Contbr. articles to profl. jours. Mem. ACA (one of 25 nat. legis. inst. participants 2000), Am. Vocat. Assn., NEA, Nat. Assn. Vocat. Edn. Spl. Needs Pers. (region III com. chair 1989-90, cert. of recognition 1990), Am. Sch. Counselors Assn., Am. Assn. Marriage and Family Therapy, Vocat. Evaluation and Work Adjustment Assn. (Wyo. rep. 1993-94, conf. presenter 1991), Mo. Vocat. Spl. Needs Assn. (exec. v.p. 1990-92, spkr. 1989-92, Outstanding Achievement award 1990-91, certs. of appreciation 1988-91), Mo. Sch. Counselors Assn. (spkr. 1989-91), Mo. Vocat. Assn. (spkr. 1992), Idaho Edn. Assn. (assembly del. 2001-03, state legis. del. 2002), Idaho Sch. Counseling Assn., Idaho Counseling Assn. (chair pub. policy and legislation com. 1999-2002, conf. presentor, exec. bd. dirs. legislative bill writing), Idaho Assn. Marriage and Family Therapy, Idaho Vocat. Guidance Assn. (com. chair 1997), Idaho Assn. Career Devel., Kiwanis. Avocations: handball, skiing, outdoor adventure trips, creative arts activities, swimming. Office: PO Box 4931 Pocatello ID 83205-4931 E-mail: CMEichman@aol.com.

EIDELHOCH, LESTER PHILIP, physician, educator, surgeon; b. N.Y.C., Jan. 7, 1932; s. Abraham David Eidelhoch and Ella (Sarah) Lovinger; m. Cecily Ruth Rosenberg, Apr. 28, 1963; children: Alison Marc, Arthur Mark, Meredith Marc. BA, Columbia U., 1952; MD, NYU, 1956. Diplomate Am. Bd. Med. Examiners. Intern Strong Meml. Hosp., Rochester, N.Y.; resident Harvard Surg. div. Boston City Hosp., 1958-62; pvt. practice New Hartford, N.Y., 1965—. Med. dir. Walsh Med. Ctr., Rome, N.Y., 1991—; mem. faculty SUNY. Bd. dirs. Jewish Fedn., Utica (N.Y.) Symphony, Charles T. Sitrin Home. Lt. comdr. USN, 1962-64. Recipient Lindner Surg. award NYU. Fellow ACS, Royal Coll. Medicine; mem. N.Y. Cen. Soc. Surgeons, Cen. N.Y. Acad. Medicine, Oneida County Med. Soc. Republican. Avocations: skiing, sailing. Home and Office: 6 Old Willow Rd New Hartford NY 13413-2419

EIDSON, COLLEEN (KELLY) FRANCES, elementary counselor; b. Auburn, N.Y., Apr. 9, 1958; d. Francis Charles and Valencia Alice (Nervina) Bellnier; m. Thomas Allen Eidson, Aug. 7, 1981; 1 child, Tyler James. AA, Cayuga County C.C., Auburn, N.Y., 1978; BS, Kent (Ohio) State U., 1981; MS, Canisius Coll., Buffalo, 1989. Cert. tchr. spl. edn. K-12, learning disabilities and behavior disorders, elem. edn. 1-8, counseling k-12. Specific learning disabilities tchr. Rootstown (Ohio) Mid. Sch., 1981-84; adapted phys. edn. instr./cons. Greenville (Tenn.) Sch. Dist., 1984-85; specific learning disabilities tchr. Build Acad., Buffalo, 1985-86, Mill Mid. Sch., Williamsville, N.Y., 1986-88, Rootstown Elem. and H.S., 1988-95; elem. sch. counselor East Woods Sch., Hudson Sch. Dist., Hudson, Ohio, 1995—. Girls' track coach Rootstown Local Schs., 1981-83, dir. internat. book project, 1983-84. Contbr. articles to profl. jours.; co-editor RTA Front Page News, 1992-94. Grantee Mid-Eastern Ohio Spl. Edn. Regional Coun., 1981,, 2000, 03, Buffalo Tchrs. Ctr., 1986, Maplewood Career Edn. Program, 1991, Kiwanis, 1991, Martha Holden Jennings, 1995, MEO/SERRC, 2000. Mem. Rootstown Tchrs. Assn. (union rep. 1991-95), Kappa Delta Phi. Roman Catholic. Avocations: antiques, soccer, gardening, crafts. Home: 721 Fairchild Ave Kent OH 44240-2131 Office: East Woods Sch 120 N Hayden Pkwy Hudson OH 44236-3199 E-mail: eidsonc@hudson.edu.

EIGEL, EDWIN GEORGE, JR., mathematics educator, retired university president; b. St. Louis, June 4, 1932; s. Edwin George and Catherine (Rohan) E.; m. Marcia Jeanne Duffy, May 30, 1959; children: Edwin George III, Mary Marcia. BS, MIT, 1954; postgrad., U. Marburg, Germany, 1954-55; PhD, St. Louis U., 1961; DHL (hon.), U. Bridgeport, 1999. Lectr. math. George Washington U., 1961; asst. prof. math. St. Louis U., 1961-64, assoc. prof., 1964-69, asst. to dean Grad. Sch., 1965-67, prof., 1969-79, dean Grad. Sch., 1967-71, assoc. acad. v.p., 1971-72, acad. v.p., 1972-79, exec. v.p., 1973; assoc. prof. math. U. Bridgeport, Conn., 1979-82, prof., 1982—2002, Univ. prof., 1995—, v.p. acad. affairs, 1979-91, provost, 1981-91; pres., 1991-95; pres. emeritus U. Bridgeport, Conn., 1995—. Mem. adv. com. on accreditation Conn. Dept. Higher Edn., 1989—92. Commr. McDonnell Planetarium, St. Louis, 1972-79; mem. Conn. Disting. Citizens Task Force on Quality Tchg., 1982-83; acting exec. dir. Bridgeport Area Consortium Colls. and Univs., 1989; bd. dirs. Bridgeport Pub. Edn. Fund, 1993-97, Bridgeport Regional Bus. Coun., 1994-95, United Way Ea. Fairfield County, 1994-98, Univ. Bridgeport, 1995—. Mem. Am. Math. Soc., Math. Assn. Am., Rotary (bd. dirs. Bridgeport 1994-97), Phi Beta Kappa, Phi Beta Kappa Fellows, Sigma Xi, Pi Mu Epsilon, Phi Kappa Phi, Beta Gamma Sigma, Upsilon Pi Epsilon, Sigma Beta Delta. Achievements include: research in math. applications of computers. Home: 33 Pepperbush Ln Fairfield CT 06824-4036 E-mail: egeorgee@optonline.net.

EIKENBERRY, KEVIN LEON, training consultant; b. Ludington, Mich., May 26, 1962; s. Phillip L. Eikenberry and Janet M. (Lindamood) Wallis; m. Lori A. West, Aug. 30, 1986; children: Parker, Kelsey. BS in Agriculture, Purdue U., 1984. Sales rep. Chevron Chem. Co., Evansville, Ind., 1986, mktg. coord. San Francisco, 1986-88, tng. coord. San Ramon, Calif., 1988, telemarketing mgr., 1988-90; tng. cons. Chevron Corp., San Francisco, 1990-93; pres., tng. cons. Performance Ptnrs., Indpls., 1993-95; pres., tng.cons. The Discian Group, Indpls., 1995—. Contbg. author: Active Training Designs, 1995, McGraw Hill Training and Development Yearbook, 1995-2003, Walking with the Wise, 2003. Named an Outstanding Alumnus, Purdue U., 2002. Mem. ASTD, N.Am. Simulation and Gaming Assn. (bd. dirs. 1993—, chmn. 1996-97, pres. 1997-98, chair 1998-99, contbg. editor TechRepublican), Internat. Soc. for Permance Improvement, Internat. Alliance for Learning, Purdue Agrl. Alumni Assn. (bd. dirs. 1993—, pres.-elect 2003). Office: The Discian Group 7035 Bluffridge Way Indianapolis IN 46278-2812

EINODER, CAMILLE ELIZABETH, retired secondary education educator; b. Chgo., June 15, 1937; d. Isadore and Elizabeth T. (Czerwinski) Popowski; m. Joseph X. Einoder, Aug. 5, 1978; children: Carl Frank, Mark Frank, Vivian Einoder, Joe Einoder, Tim Einoder, Sheila Einoder, Jude Eindoer. Student, Fox Bus. Coll., 1954; BEd in Biology, Chgo. Tchrs. Coll., 1964; MA in Analytical Chemistry, Gov.'s State U., 1977; MA in Adminstrn. and Supervision, Roosevelt U., 1986; postgrad., 1992—. Sec., Chgo., 1955-64; tchr. biology Chgo. Bd. Edn., 1964-1975, tchr. biology and agr., 1975-81, tchr. biology, agr. and chemistry, 1981-2000, ret., 2000. Human rels. coord. Morgan Park High Sch., Chgo., 1980—, tchr. biology Internat. Studies Sch., 1983—, adv. bd., 1989—; owner Einoder Masonry, 1997—, Einoder Antiques, 1996—; career devel. cons. for agr. related curriculum; internat. baccalaureate tchr., Chgo. pub. schs. consulting tchr., 1997; edn. cons. Neighborhood Coun., 1974; rep. Chgo. Tchrs. Union, 1969; exec. bd. dir. The Lira Ensemble, 1996—; mem. Renaissance Circle, DePaul U.; edn. com. Polish-Am. Initiative of Chgo. Cmty. Trust, 1999—; owner Einoder Masonry, 1998—; antique dealer, 1995—. Bd. dirs., founding mem., author constn. Cmty. Coun., 1970—; bd. dirs., edn. cons. Neighborhood Coun., 1974; rep. Chgo. Tchrs. Union, 1969; exec. bd. dirs. The Lira Ensemble, 1996—. Mem. AAAS, NSTA, Polish Inst. for Arts and Sci., Am. Chem. Soc., Am. Biology Tchrs. Assn., Nat. Assn. Women Bus. Owners, Found. Women Contractors, Copernicus Found., Kosciuszko Soc., Polish Arts Club, Phi Delta Kappa, Iota Sigma Pi. Home: 10637 S Claremont Ave Chicago IL 60643-3101 E-mail: camilleein@aol.com.

EINSPRUCH, NORMAN GERALD, physicist, engineering educator; b. N.Y.C., June 27, 1932; s. Adolph and Mala (Goldblatt) E.; m. Edith Melnick, Dec. 20, 1953; children— Eric, Andrew, Franklin. BA in Physics, Rice U., 1953; MS in Physics, U. Colo., 1955; PhD in Applied Math, Brown U., 1959. Mem. tech. staff, central research labs. Tex. Instruments, Inc., Dallas, 1959-62, mgr. electron transport physics br., central research labs., 1962-68, dir. advanced tech. lab., central research labs., 1968-69, dir. tech., chem. materials div., 1969-72, dir. central research labs., 1972-75, asst. v.p., 1975-77, mgr. corp. devel., 1975-76, mgr. tech. and planning consumer products, 1976-77; prof. dept. elec. and computer engring. Coll. Engring. U. Miami, Coral Gables, Fla., 1977—, dean Coll. Engring., 1977-90, sr. fellow in sci. and tech., 1990—, chmn. dept. indsl. engring., 1994-99. Vis. prof. Rensselaer Poly. Inst., 2001-02; chmn. panel on thin film microstructure sci. and tech. NRC, 1978-79, mem. panel on impact of Dod bery high speed integrated crcts. program, 1980-81, panel on edn. and utilization of the engr., 1981-82; bd. dirs. Covanta Energy Corp, Zinc Matrix Power, Inc. Author: Electronic Genie: The Tangled History of Silicon, 1998 editor: (series) VLSI Electronics: Microstructure Science, 24 vols., VLSI Handbook, 1985; contbr. articles to profl. jours. Recipient George Washington Honor medal Freedoms Found. Valley Forge. Fellow Am. Phys. Soc., Acoustical Soc. Am., IEEE, AAAS; mem. Golden Key, Iron Arrow, Sigma Xi, Omicron Delta Kappa, Tau Beta Pi, Eta Kappa Nu, Phi Kappa Phi, Alpha Pi Mu, Tau Sigma Delta. Home: 1415 Trillo Ave Miami FL 33146-2312 Office: U Miami Coll Engring PO Box 248581 Coral Gables FL 33124-8581 E-mail: neinspruch@miami.edu.

EIRICH (STEIN), GENEVIEVE THERESA, reading specialist, elementary school educator; b. Sheboygan, Wis., Oct. 26, 1945; d. Alfred A. and Irene E. (Bonde) Stein; m. Stephen E. Eirich, Dec. 23, 1967; children: Michelle Ann, Sharon Marie. BA, U. Wis., 1975; MA, Carthage Coll., 1981; MA adminstrn. dir. of instr., Alverno Coll., Milw., 2003. Cert. tchr. elem. edn. 1-8, reading K-12, reading specialist K-12. Elem. tchr. Milw. Archdiocese, Sheboygan, Wis., 1965-72, Kenosha (Wis.) Unified Schs., 1975-88, reading specialist, 1988—, coord. beginning tchrs. and mentors, 1994-95; instr. Carthage Coll., 1996—; reading recovery tchr. Kenosha (Wis.) Unified Schs., 1997—; literacy collaborative trainer Ohio State Univ., 2001—. Mem. site-based village partnership, dimensions of learning action team, task force for dist. implementation of inclusion, staff devel. coun., mem. core com. Mem. parish coun. St. Mary's Catholic Ch., Kenosha, 1990-93, 96-99, liturgy com., 1989—. Recipient Herb Kohl award Herb Kohl Edn. Found., 1994. Mem. ASCD, NEA, Internat. Reading Assn., Nat. Staff Devel. Coun., Assn. for Early Childhood, Wis. Reading Assn., Nat. Coun. Tchrs. English, Racine-Kenosha Reading Coun., Staff Devel. Coun., Kenosha Edn. Assn. (bd. dirs. 1980—), Phi Delta Kappa. Avocations: exercise, reading.

EIS, LORYANN MALVINA, secondary education educator; b. Muscatine, Iowa, Apr. 3, 1938; d. Chester N. and Anna M. (Lenz) E. AB, Augustana Coll., 1960; MEd, U. Ill., 1963; postgrad., Montclair State Coll., 1965-67, Indiana U. of Pa., 1968, U. Iowa, 1970, Western Ill. U., 1978-80. Cir. analysis engr. Automatic Electric Co., Northlake, Ill., 1960-61; math. tchr. Orion (Ill.) Community Sch. Dist., 1961-63; math. tchr., chmn. div. math. and sci. United Twp. High Sch., East Moline, Ill., 1963—; lectr. Augustana Coll., Rock Island, Ill., 1982—. Cons. General Mathematics Textbook, 1978-79. Chmn. math. task force Edn. Svc. Ctr. #8, 1986-89; bd. sec. Citizens to Preserve Black Hawk Park Found., 1977—. Muscatine C.C. Alumni, vice chmn.; Am. Scandanavian Assn. Bd.; v.p. coun. Salem Luth. Ch.; sec. Salem Luth. Endowmen Com.; treas. Augustana Coll. Hist. Soc. Bd. Mem. NEA, Ill. Edn. Assn., Nat. Coun. of Math. Suprs., Nat. Sci. Tchrs. Assn., Nat. Coun. Tchrs. of Math., Assn. of Math. Tchrs. Educators, Ill. Sci. Tchrs. Assn., Ill. Coun. Tchrs. of Math., Classroom Tchrs. Assn., Assn. Supervision and Curriculum Devel., Rock Island Scott Counties Sci. and Math. Tchrs. Assn., AAUW (past state pres., past regional dir. Great Lakes chpt., grantee 1975-76), Delta Kappa Gamma (state pres. 1995—, past state treas., past chair internat. fin. com.), Am. Philatelic Soc., TransMiss. Philatelic Soc., Quad City Stamp Club. Republican. Home: 2037 15th St Moline IL 61265-3966 Office: 1275 42nd Ave East Moline IL 61244-4145

EISEMAN, TIMOTHY WILLIAM, art and history educator; b. Ann Arbor, Mich., Feb. 5, 1950; s. Alfred F. and Marian J. (Fischer) E.; m. Irene A. Pengrin, Dec. 30, 1978. Assoc. Architecture, Washtenaw C.C., 1970; B Art Edn., Ea. Mich. U., 1974, MA, 1978, MA, 1998. Cert. elem. and secondary art tchr., Mich. High sch. art tchr. Chelsea (Mich.) Pub. Schs., 1975; art tchr. Ann Arbor Pub. Schs., 1975-87, 88, art coord., 1988, mem.

visual arts curriculum team, 1978-95. Mem. curriculum arts and editorial panel Mich. State Bd. Edn., Lansing, 1987-88. Recipient Tech. in Edn., Gov. of Mich., 1990. Mem. NEA, Mich. Edn. Assn., Mich. Alliance for Arts in Edn., Nat. Art Edn. Assn., Mich. Art Edn. Assn. Avocations: fine arts, architecture, outdoor recreation, motorcycle touring and travel. Office: Slauson Mid Sch 1019 W Washington St Ann Arbor MI 48103-4241

EISEN, GLENN PHILIP, management consultant, teacher; b. Chgo., Feb. 8, 1940; s. Sol Eisen and Lorraine (Winsberg) Lukinsky; m. Devera Arne Chiz, May 7, 1961 (div. 1974); children: Julia, Steven; m. Barbara Baxter McNear, June 7, 1987. BS in Indsl. Mgmt., Ill. Inst. Tech., 1972. Cert. mgmt. cons.; registered EMT, Conn., Calif. Prodn. supr. Intercraft Industries, Chgo., 1961-64; sr. buyer Simoniz Co., Chgo., 1964-65; purchasing/packaging mgr. Paper Mate div. Gillette, La Grange Park, Ill., 1965-69; assoc. The Packaging House Inc., Chgo., 1969-73; cons. Israel Inst. of Packaging, Tel Aviv, 1973-74; prin. The Emerson Cons., N.Y.C., 1975-80, Arthur Andersen & Co., Chgo., 1980-87; chief exec. officer The Eisen Group, Wilton, Conn., 1987-96; prin. The Omega Cons., LLC, 1996-2000. Internat. comml. arbitrator Am. Arbitration Assn., N.Y.C., 1985—2003; bd. fin. Wilton, Conn., 2001-02; lectr., mgr. mfg. industry edn. Arthur Andersen Ctr. for Profl. Edn., 1980-83; lectr., seminar leader Am. Mgmt. Assn., 1967-99; clin. instr. UCLA Ctr. Prehospital Care, 2003—; counselor Svc. Corps. Ret. Execs., 2003—. Author: Purchasing Negotiations, 1983, Group Buying in Health Care, 1985, Supply Market Management, 1989, Maximizing Your Value When Using Management Consultants, 1992, Ethical Practices and Conflicts of Interest Benchmark Study, 1994, Procurement Best Practices, 1997, Maintenance Planning and Management Best Practices, 1998; mem. editl. bd.: In Bound Logistics Mag., 1990. Active Westport Emergency Med. Svc. 2000-02; disaster med. assistance team Los Angeles County, 2002—; CPR and 1st aid instr. ARC, 1999—, Am. Heart Assn.; mem. western nat. med. response team U.S. Dept. Homeland Security, 2003—. With U.S. Army, 1958-61. Mem. Kiwanis Internat. Jewish. Home and Office: 1860 Homewood Dr Altadena CA 91001

EISENBERG, HOWARD EDWARD, physician, psychotherapist, consultant, educator, writer; b. Montreal, Que, Can, Aug. 5, 1946; s. Harold and Elsie (Goldbloom) Eisenberg; m. Susan Doelman; children: Taryn Noelle, Jory Michael, Meredith Kate, Tessa Chloe. BS Psychology(hon.), McGill U., Montreal, 1967, MS in Psychology, 1971; internship, Sunnybrook Med. Ctr., U of Toronto, Toronto, Can., 1972—73; MD, McGill U., Montreal, 1972. Lic. LMCC Med. Coun. Can., cert. Province of Ont., 1973, Province of Brit. Columbia, 1980, State of Vt., 1988. Rsch. asst. psychology dept. McGill U., 1966-69, rsch. asst. gerontology unit Alan Meml. Inst. Psychiatry, 1968; intern Sunnybrook Med. Ctr. U. Toronto, Canada, 1972—73; lectr. Ctr. Continuing Edn. York U., 1973-78, supr. individual directed study Faculty Environ. Studies, 1975; clin. fellow Clarke Inst. Psychiatry U. Toronto, 1973, lectr. dept. interdisciplinary studies, 1975, instr. ind. studies program Innis Coll., 1975-78, lectr., 1976-81, spl. conf. coord., 1977-79, 88-89, lectr. Sch. Continuing Studies, 1977-89; pvt. practice Mind/Body Med., Toronto, 1973—91; lectr. Sheridan Coll., Oakville, 1974-76; lectr. Sch. Adult Edn. McMaster U., 1980—89; assoc. staff dept. family practice Drs. Hosp., Toronto, 1987—92; cons. staff dept. med.-psychiatry Copley Hosp., Morrisville, Vt., 1990—96; lectr. continuing edn. U. Vt., 1990—92; pvt. practice Mind/Body Med., Stowe Wellness Ctr., Vt., 1991—98; clin. assoc. prof. dept. family practice Coll. Medicine, U. Vt., 1993—99; pvt. practice Mind/Body Med., Toronto, 1999—. Assoc. dir. edn. and growth opportunities program York U., 1975—76, dir. E.G.O. program, 1976—78; lectr. Sch. Adult Edn. McMaster U., 1980—89; instr. profl. and mgmt. devel. Humber Coll., 1982—85; pvt. practice psychotherapy and behavioral medicine, Toronto, 1973—91, Toronto, 1999—, Stowe, Vt., 1991—98; assoc. prof. dept. family practice Coll. Medicine U. Vt., 1993—99; cons. staff dept. medicine Copley Hosp., Vt., 1990—96; pres. Synectia Cons., Inc., Toronto, 1980—84, Syntrek, Inc., Montpelier, Vt., 1989—2000, Toronto, 1974—; co-founder Healthcare Knowledge Mgmt. Consortium, 1998. Author: (book) Inner Spaces, 1977, The Tranquility Experience, 1987, Stress Mastery for the Real World, 2d edit., 1995, Fundamentals of High Performance Teamwork, 1995, Creative Thinking Tools for Innovation, 2d edit., 1997; contbr. articles to profl. jours.; prodr.: (presentation) VI World Congress of Psychiatry, Max Planck Inst. of Psychiatry, Langley-Porter Neuropsychiatric Inst., UCLA Neuropsychriatric Inst., Sci. Coun. of Can., Allan Mem. Inst. of Psychiatry, Acad. of Organ. & Occupl. Psychiatry. Fellow McGill Scholar, 1966—67, Earle C. Anthony, 1967—68; scholar Que., 1967—68, Med. Rsch. Coun. Can., 1977. Mem.: Ont. Med. Assn. (former chmn. sect. ind. physicians). Achievements include co-founder of Health Care Knowledge Mgmt. Consortium, 1998-2000. Office: Syntrek Inc 7 B Pleasant Blvd Ste 1008 Toronto ON Canada M4T 1K2 E-mail: howard@syntrek.com.

EISENBERG, ROBIN LEDGIN, religious education administrator; b. Passaic, N.J., Jan. 10, 1951; d. Morris and Ruth (Miller) Ledgin. BS, West Chester State U., 1973; M Edn., Kutztown State U., 1977. Administrv. asst. Keneseth Israel, Allentown, Pa., 1973-77; dir. edn. Cong. Schaarai Zedek, Tampa, Fla., 1977-79, Kehilath Israel, Pacific Palisades, Calif., 1979-80, Temple Beth El, Boca Raton, Fla., 1980-99, 2003—, Levis Jewish Cmty. Cen., Boca Raton, 1999—2003. Contbr. Learning Together, 1987, Bar/Bat Mizvah Education: A Sourcebook, 1993, The New Jewish Teachers Handbook, 1994. Chmn. edn. info., Planned Parenthood, Boca Raton Fla. 1989. Recipient Kamiker Camp award Nat. Assn. Temple Educators, Pres.'s award for adminstrn., 1990; Mandel fellow in Jewish Edn., Levis Jewish Cmty. Ctr., 2001-2003. Mem. Nat. Assn. Temple Educators (pres. 1990-92, chair UAHC-CCAR-NATE commn. on Jewish edn. 1997-99, accreditation chair 2000—), Coalition Advancement of Jewish Edn. (chair strategic planning com. 2003—), Assn. Jewish Ctr. Profls. (Profl. of Yr. award 2003). Avocation: photography. Home: 2428 NW 35th St Boca Raton FL 33431 Office: Temple Beth El 333 SW 4th Ave Boca Raton FL 33432 E-mail: robledeise@aol.com., robine@bocafed.org.

EISENBERG, THEODORE, law educator; b. Bklyn., Oct. 26, 1947; s. Abraham Louis and Esther (Waldman) E.; m. Lisa Wright, Nov. 27, 1971; children: Katherine Wright, Ann Marie, Thomas Peter. BA, Swarthmore Coll., 1969; JD, U. Pa., 1972. Bar: Pa. 1972, N.Y. 1974, U.S. Ct. Appeals (2d cir.) 1974, Calif. 1977. Law clk. U.S. Ct. Appeals, D.C. Cir., 1972-73; law clk. to U.S. Supreme Ct. Justice Earl Warren, 1973; assoc. Debevoise & Plimpton, N.Y.C., 1974-77; prof. law UCLA Law Sch., 1977-81, Cornell U. Law Sch., Ithaca, N.Y., 1981-96, Henry Allen Mark prof. law, 1996—. Vis. prof. law Harvard U. Law Sch., 1984-85; vis. prof. Law, Stanford U. Law Sch., 1987. Author: Civil Rights Legislation, 1981, 4th edit., 1996, Bankruptcy and Debtor-Creditor Law, 1984, 2d edit., 1988; editor Jour. Empirical Legal Studies; mem. adv. bd. Law and Soc. Rev., Am. Law and Econ. Rev.; contbr. articles to profl. jours. Am. Bar Found grantee, NSF grantee. Fellow Royal Statis. Soc.; mem. ABA, Assn. Bar City N.Y., Law and Soc. Assn., Am. Law and Econ. Assn., Am. Bankruptcy Inst. Office: Cornell U Law Sch Myron Taylor Hall Ithaca NY 14853 E-mail: te13@cornell.edu.

EISENDRATH, CHARLES RICE, journalism educator, farmer, consultant; b. Chgo., Oct. 9, 1940; s. William Nathan and Erna Sarah (Rice) E.; m. Julia Cardozo, Jan. 28, 1967; children: Benjamin Cardozo, Mark William. BA, Yale U., 1962; MA, U. Mich., 1965. Reporter Post-Dispatch, St. Louis, 1962, 64, Evening Sun, Balt., 1966-68; corr. Time Mag., Washington, London, Paris, bur. chief Buenos Aires, 1968-73; prof. U. Mich., Ann Arbor, 1975—. Propr. Overlook Farm, East Jordan, Mich., 1972—; chmn. Grillworks, Inc., Ann Arbor, 1978—; cons. Midland Bank of London, Pfizer, W.K. Kellogg Found.; mem. Pulitzer Prize Jury, 2002—03. Contbr. articles to profl. jours.; inventor in field. Dir. Knight-Wallace Journalism Fellows, 1986—; founding dir. Livingston Awards, Ann Arbor, 1980—; judge nat. barbecue contest, 1994—; pres. task force journalism Columbia U., 2002-03. NEH Mich. Journalism fellow, 1974-75. Mem. Coun. Fgn. Rels., Century Assn. (N.Y.C.), Soc. Profl. Journalists, Com. of Concerned Journalists (founding), Project on the State of the Am. Newspaper (founding bd. dirs. 1998-2000), Landsdowne Club (London), Phi Kappa Phi. Jewish. Office: Wallace House 620 Oxford Rd Ann Arbor MI 48104-2623 E-mail: drath@umich.edu.

EISENSTEIN, HESTER, sociology educator; b. N.Y.C., Oct. 14, 1940; d. Myron and Ruth (Richards) E.; m. Michael David Tanzer; stepchildren: David, Kenneth J., Charles. BA, Harvard U., 1961; MA, Yale U., 1962, PhD, 1967. Instr., asst. prof. Yale U., New Haven, 1966-70; coord. exptl. studies program Barnard Coll., Columbia U., 1970-80; sr. officer, assoc. dir. Equal Opportunity in Pub. Employment, Sydney, Australia, 1980-86; leader EEO unit Dept. Edn., Sydney, 1986-88; vis. prof. SUNY, Buffalo, 1988-90, prof. Am. studies, 1990-96; prof. Sociology Queens Coll., Grad. Sch. & Univ. Ctr. CUNY, 1996—, dir. women's studies Queens Coll., 1996-2000. Author: Contemporary Feminist Thought, 1983, Gender Shock, 1991, Inside Agitators: Australian Femocrats and the State, 1996. Office: The Grad CtrCUNY PhD Program in Sociology 365 Fifth Ave New York NY 10016

EISNER, ELLIOT W. education educator; MA in art and edn., Roosevelt U., 1954; MS in art edn., Ill. Inst. Tech., 1955; MA in edn., U. Chgo., 1958, PhD in edn., 1962. Prof. Stanford U., Edn., Art Depts., Stanford, Calif., 1970—; HS art tchr. Chgo., 1956—58; art tchr. U. Chgo., 1958—60; instr., art edn. Ohio State U., 1960—61; instr. edn. U. Chgo., 1961—62, asst. prof. edn., 1962—65; assoc. prof. to prof. edn. and art Stanford U., 1965—. Contbr. articles various profl. jours. Mem.: Nat. Acad. of Edn., John Dewey Soc., Just and Caring Edn., J. Paul Getty Ctr. for Edn. in the Arts (pres. 1998—2000). Achievements include research in the rold of artistic thinking in the conduct of social sci. rsch., programs to further arts edn. in Am. schs., the role of artistry in ednl. theory and practice. Office: Stanford U Sch of Edn 485 Lasuen Mall Stanford CA 94305-3096 Office Fax: 650-725-7412. E-mail: eisner@stanford.edu.

EISNER, GAIL ANN, artist, educator; b. Detroit, Oct. 17, 1939; d. Rudolph and Florence (White) Leon; m. Marvin Michael Eisner, June 14, 1959 (dec. Feb. 1993); 1 child, Alan. Student, Art Student League of N.Y.; BFA, Wayne State U. Alan prof. Pace U., N.Y.C. (one-woman shows) The Starkweather Art Cultural Ctr., Romeo, Mich., Shiawassee Arts Ctr., Owosso, Mich., Worthington Art Ctr., Ohio, OK Harris/David Klein Gallery, Birmingham, Mich., Sinclair Coll., LRC Gallery, Dayton, Ohio, U. Mich. Hosps., Ann Arbor, Collin County Coll., Plano, Tex., 1997, Art Ctr. Mt. Clemens, (group shows) Islip Art Mus., East Islip, N.Y., Columbia (Mo.) Coll., Tubac (Ariz.) Ctr. of Arts, Ft. Wayne (Ind.) Mus. of Art, C.W. Post Coll., Brookville, N.Y., NAWA, Jacob K. Kavits Ctr., N.Y.C., Schoharie County Coun. of Arts, Cobbleskill, N.Y., ARC Gallery, Chgo., McPherson (Kans.) Coll., Med. Coll. Ga., Augusta, Heckscher Mus. Art, Huntington, Nassau County Mus. Art, Roslyn, N.Y., Guild Hall, East Hampton, N.Y., Castle Gould, Sands Point, N.Y., Pastel Soc. Am., N.Y.C., Carrier Found., Belle Meade, N.J., Hill Country Arts Found., Ingram, Tex., Cunningham Meml. Art Gallery, Bakersfield, Calif., Henry Hicks Gallery, Bklyn. Hts., U. N.D., Grand Forks, Nassau C.C., Garden City, N.Y., Trenton (N.J.) State Coll., Wenatchee Valley (W.Va.) Coll., Del Mar Coll., Corpus Christi, Tex., Minot (N.D.) State U., Ctrl. Mo. State U., McNeese State U., Lake Charles, La., Worthington Art Ctr., Ohio, Art Ctr., Mt. Clemens, Mich., Oakland C.C., Krasl Art Ctr., St. Joseph, Mich., Fontana Concert Soc., Kalamazoo, Mich., Art Ctr. Battle Creek, Mich., Ctrl. Mich. U., Mt. Pleasant, Birmingham (Mich.) Bloomfield Art Assn., Cmty. House, Birmingham, Sch. Art Inst., Chgo., Cheekwood Mus. Art, Nashville, Grand Rapids (Mich.) Mus. Art, Flint (Mich.) Inst. Arts, Ariana Gallery, Royal Oak, Mich., Judith Paul Gallery, Medford, Oreg., The Art Collector, San Diego, Gwenda Jay Gallery, Chgo., Columbia Greens Coll., Hudson, N.Y., Worthington (Ohio) Art Ctr., Holland Area Arts Coun., Mich., The Art Source, Santa Barbara, Calif., Outside The Line Gallery, Grosse Ile, Mich., (permanent collections) Rabobank, Chgo., Resurrection Hosp., Kanai (Hawaii) Hotel, Jules Joyner Designs, Royal Oak, Mich., The Lumber Store, Chgo., others, (also pvt. collections). Recipient Adriana Zahn award Pastel Soc. Am., Heckscher Mus. award, Our Visions: Women in Art award Oakland C.C., 1995, Beatrice G. Epstein meml. award, 1997. Mem. Nat. Assn. Women Artists (Sara Winston Meml. award 1992), N.Y. Artist Equity Assn., Art Student League N.Y. (Sidney Dickinson Meml. award), Birmingham Bloomfield Art Assn. Studio: Ste 108 27600 Farmington Rd Farmington Hills MI 48334-3365

EJIMOFOR, CORNELIUS OGU, political scientist, educator; b. Owerri, Nigeria, Oct. 10, 1940; came to U.S., 1963; s. Osuji and Helen Domaonu (Atashia) E.; m. Priscilla Loveth Amaugo, Mar. 10, 1966; children: Cornelia, Caroline, Cornelius Jr., Priscilla, Ebere. AA, Warren Wilson Coll., 1965; BA in Polit. Sci., Wilberforce U., 1966; MPA, U. Dayton, 1967; MA, PhD, U. Okla., 1971. Tchr. Cath. Mission Schs., Emekuku, Nigeria, 1959-63; rsch. asst. U. Dayton, Ohio, 1966-67; instr. polit. sci. Edward Waters Coll., Jacksonville, Fla., 1967-68, prof. polit. sci., 1992—, chmn. divsn. arts and scis., 1992-93; grad. asst. U. Okla., Norman, 1968-70; asst. prof. William Paterson Coll., Wayne, N.J., 1970-72; from assoc. prof. to prof. Tuskegee (Ala.) U., 1972-80, dept. head polit. sci., 1972-77; sr. lectr., reader U. Nigeria, Nsukka, 1980-91, prof. polit. sci., 1991-92. Coord., head, prof. sub-dept. pub. adminstrn. and local govt. U. Nigeria, 1990-92, coord. local govt. tng. programs, 1990-92. Author: British Colonia Objectives and Policies in Nigeria, 1987, Management of Human Resources: A Generic Approach, 1992. Mem. AAUP (sec. Fla. chpt., sec. Edward Waters Coll. chpt.), Am. Soc. Pub. Adminstrn., Am. Polit. Sci. Assn., KC. Democrat. Roman Catholic. Avocations: swimming, reading and writing, discussing civics. Home: 157 Lamson St Jacksonville FL 32211-8066 E-mail: cejimofor@ewc.edu.

EKSTROM, KATINA BARTSOKAS, secondary education educator, artist; b. Springfield, Ill., Nov. 8, 1929; d. Tom A. and Elsie (Heinrich) Bartsokas; m. John Warren Ekstrom (div. Feb. 1978); children: John A., Kenneth M., Richard M., Timothy W., Christopher P. BFA, U. Ill., 1955, MAE, 1975. Tchr. art Urbana (Ill.) Jr. H.S., 1974-89, Bronx (N.Y) Sch. Dist., 1990-91, Astoria (N.Y.) Jr. H.S., 1991—2002. Tchr. adult edn., 1975-80, Urbana Pk. Dist., 1977-88; artist Colwell Collection catalog, Champaign, Ill., 1985; juror Chgo. Ann. Met. History Fair, 1985, Cen. Ill. Scholastics High Sch., Springfield, 1988-89, others; Fulbright cultural exch. tchr., 1986; cachet artist 1st edit. stamps, 2003. Exhibited in group shows at Champaign Arts and Humanities Assn., 1983-84, Cen. Park Ranger 1990, Swoope Gallery, Ind., Lincoln Ctr., N.Y.C., 1994, Abney Gallery, N.Y.C., 1995; cachet artist first edition stamps, 2003; designer (children's book) Cacie's NYC Visit, 2003. Artist Peace Coalition Concerts, Champaign, 1985-86, U. Ill. Sinfonia, Champaign, 1986-88. Recipient Merit award 1994 Manhattan Arts Internat. Cover Art Competition, 2d pl. award in painting Ill. Ann. Art Exhbn. Mem. Urbana Educators Assn. (Outstanding Educator award 1986), Ind. Artists Ill., U. Ill. Alumni Assn., Kappa Delta, Phi Delta Kappa. Achievements include design of first edition stamps on envelopes, 2003. Home: 30 W 96th St # 2D New York NY 10025-6555

EKUM, KRISTI ANN, special education educator; b. McPherson, Kans., Dec. 25, 1953; d. Thomas Roy and Osa Gwendolyn (Roth) E. BS in Elem. Edn., Fort Hays State Coll., Hays, Kans., 1976; MS in Spl. Edn., Fort Hays State U., Hays, Kans., 1982. Lic. elem. tchr., Kans. Tchr. mentally retarded High Plains Spl. Edn. Coop., Hugoton, Kans., 1976-80; tchr. behaviorally disordered S.W. Kans. Area Coop. Dist., Dodge City, 1980—. Insvc. coun. S.W. Kans. Area Coop. Dist., Dodge City, 1985—, Mandt trainer, 1992-2000. Treas. PTA, 1992—93; pres. PTO, 2003—. Mem. NEA, Internat. Reading Assn., Coun. Exceptional Children, Kans. Reading Assn. (corr. sec. 1985-86, v.p. 1986-87, pres. 1987-88, historian 1990-93). Lutheran. Home: 3104 Ross Ct Apt 1 Dodge City KS 67801-7400 Office: Linn Elem 1900 Linn St Dodge City KS 67801

EL-BAZ, FAROUK, science administrator, educator; b. Zagazig, Egypt, Jan. 1, 1938; came to U.S., 1967, naturalized, 1970; s. El-Sayed Mohammed and Zahia Abul-Ata (Hammouda) El-B.; m. Catherine Patricia O'Leary, 1963; children: Monira, Soraya, Karima, Fairouz. BSc, Ain Shams U., 1958; MS, U. Mo., 1961; PhD, U. Mo. and MIT, 1964; DSc (hon.), New England Coll., 1989. Demonstrator geology dept. Assiut U., Egypt, 1958-60; lectr. Mineralogy-Petrography Inst., U. Heidelberg, Germany, 1964-65; geologist exploration dept. Pan Am.-UAR Oil Co., Egypt, 1966; supr. lunar exploration Bellcomm and Bell Tel. Labs., Washington, 1967-72; rsch. dir. Center for Earth and Planetary Studies, Nat. Air and Space Mus., Smithsonian Instn., Washington, 1973-82; v.p. sci. and tech. Itek Optical Sys., Litton Industries, Lexington, Mass., 1982-86; cons. geology, prof. geology and geophysics U. Utah, 1975-77; prof. geology Ain Shams U., Egypt, 1976-81, 95—; sci. adviser Pres. Anwar Sadat of Egypt, 1978-81; sr. advisor Nat. Rsch. Inst. for Astronomy and Geophysics, Helwan, Egypt, 1996—; dir. Ctr. for Remote Sensing Boston U., 1986—. Author: Say It in Arabic, 1968, Astronaut Observations from the Apollo-Soyuz Mission, 1977, Egypt as Seen by Landsat, 1979, The Geology of Egypt: An Annotated Bibliography, 1984; co-author: Coprolites: An Annotated Bibliography, 1968, Glossory of Mining Geology, 1970, The Moon as Viewed by Lunar Orbiter, 1970, Apollo Over the Moon: A View from Orbit, 1978; co-editor: Apollo-Soyuz Test Project Summary Science Report: Earth Observations and Photography, 1979, Desert Landforms of Southwest Egypt: A Basis for Comparison with Mars, 1982, Physics of Desertification, 1986, Remote Sensing and Resource Exploration, 1989, Sand Transport and Desertification in Arid Lands, 1990, The Gulf War and the Environment, 1994, Atlas of State of Kuwait from Satellite Images, 2000; editor: Deserts and Arid Lands, 1984; contbr. articles to profl. jours. Decorated Order of Merit 1st class Egypt; recipient certificate merit U.S. Bur. Mines, 1961, Exceptional Sci. Achievement medal NASA, 1971, Alumni Achievement award U. Mo., 1972, Honor citation Assn. Arab-Am. U. Grads., 1973, Outstanding Contbns. to Sci. and Space Tech. award Am.-Arab Anti-Discrimination Com., 1995, Achievement award Egyptian-Am. Profl. Soc., 1995, Human Needs award Am. Assn. Petroleum Geologists, 1996. Fellow: AAAS (Pub. Understanding of Sci. and Tech. award 1992), Geol. Soc. Am. (cert. commendation 1973), Royal Astron.; mem.: Nat. Acad. Engring., Internat. Inst. of Boston (Golden Door award 1992), World Aerospace Edn. Orgn. (Cert. of Merit 1973), Explorers Club, Sigma Xi. Office: Boston U Ctr Remote Sensing 725 Commonwealth Ave Boston MA 02215-1401 E-mail: farouk@bu.edu.

ELDENBURG, MARY JO CORLISS, mathematics educator; b. Tacoma, Wash., Mar. 5, 1942; d. John Ronald and Mary Margaret (Slater) Corliss; m. Paul Garth Eldenburg, Aug. 31, 1963; 1 child, Anthony Corliss. BA with honors, Wash. State U., 1964; MS, SUNY, Buffalo, 1971. Cert. secondary math. tchr. Tchr. math. Colton (Wash.) High Sch., 1964-65, Bellevue (Wash.) Jr. High Sch., 1965-68, Issaquah (Wash.) Jr. High Sch., 1968-75, Issaquah High Sch., 1975-77; tchr. math., dept. chair Liberty High Sch., Issaquah, 1977-93, Holy Names Acad., Seattle, 1994—2001, Forest Ridge Sch. of the Sacred Heart, Bellevue, Wash., 2001—. Co-editor books: Cartesian Cartoons, 1980, Cartesian Cartoons, Holiday, 1990, Lil Gridders, 1977. Treas. Sch. Bd., Kirkland, Wash., 1987-90; pres. Bridle Trails/South Rose Hill Neighborhood Assn., Kirkland, 1987-93; precinct committee woman Issaquah Precinct, 1980-84. Mem. Issaquah Edn. Assn. (sec., negotiator 1969-75, 74-86), Wash. Edn. Assn. (dir. 1970-74), Math. Assn. Am., Oreg. State Coun. Tchrs. Math., Wash. State Coun. Tchrs. Math., Nat. Coun. Tchrs. Math., Phi Kappa Phi. Democrat. Roman Catholic. Avocations: tennis, skiing, reading. Office: Forest Ridge Sch 400 139th Ave SE Bellevue WA 98006

ELDER, JENNIFER HOWARD, accounting educator; b. Morristown, N.J., Jan. 14, 1960; d. Brian Turner and Eunice Alexandra (Roy) Howard; m. Samuel Fletcher Elder III, Oct. 1, 1995. BA, U. Mass., 1981; A of Bus. Sci., McIntosh Coll., 1985; postgrad., Antioch New Eng., Keene, N.H., 1995. CPA, N.H., CMA, CIA. Mgr. James Baker & Co., North Andover, Mass., 1989, Stafford & Assoc., Portland, Maine, 1989; asst. prof. McIntosh Coll., Dover, N.H., 1989-90, dept. chair, acctg., 1990-92, dir. spl. acctg. programs, 1992—; pvt. practice, acct., cons. Portsmouth, N.H., 1990—. Author: (text) CPA Review Program, 1993. Recipient Outstanding Educator award N.H. Soc. of CPA's, Manchester, 1993. Mem. AICPA, Inst. Mgmt. Accts., Inst. Internal Auditors, Fibromyalgia Network. Avocations: sailing, stained glass, travel. Office: McIntosh Coll 23 Cataract Ave Dover NH 03820-3908

ELDRED, THOMAS GILBERT, secondary education educator, historian; b. Rochester, N.Y., Jan. 16, 1933; s. Millard Frederick and Helen Anna (Jenne) E. BA, SUNY, Albany, 1954; MA, Syracuse U., 1965. Cert. social studies tchr., N.Y. Social studies tchr. Union Springs (N.Y.) Ctrl. Sch., 1954-92; county historian Cayuga County, Auburn, NY, 1975—2001. Coord. Nat. History Day, U. Md., College Park, 1990-98. Author: (student textbooks) Citizen in Our Local Environment, 1960, East of Cayuga Bridge, 1987. Chmn. Planning Bd., Union Springs, 1970-75, Bicentennial Commn., Union Springs, 1975-77, Cayuga County Bicentennial, 1997-99; founder Frontenac Hist. Soc., Union Springs, 1975—, Cayuga County Model Senate, Auburn, N.Y., 1976—. Recipient Valley Forge Classroom Tchrs. medal Freedoms Found., 1962, Dewitt Clinton award for community svc. Warren Lodge F.A.M. #147, 1991; named Outstanding Secondary Educators of Am., 1974, Outstanding Tchr. of Am. History, N.Y. State DAR, 1982. Mem. Nat. Coun. for Pub. History, N.Y. State Coun. for Social Studies, Canal Soc. N.Y. State, Nat. Rwy. Hist. Soc., N.Y. State United Tchrs., N.Y. State Hist. Assn. (Yorker advisor 1955-92), County Historians Assn. of N.Y. State (v.p. 1990-93, pres. 1993-97), Assn. Pub. Hist. N.Y. State. Republican. Episcopalian. Avocations: golf, travel, camping, baseball, basketball. Home: 10 Center St Union Springs NY 13160

ELDREDGE, CHARLES CHILD, III, art history educator; b. Boston, Apr. 12, 1944; s. Henry and Priscilla Marion (Bateson) E.; m. Jane Allen MacDougal, June 11, 1966; children: Henry Gifford, Janann Bateson. BA, Amherst Coll., 1966; PhD, U. Minn., 1971. Curator asst. Minn. Hist. Soc., St. Paul, 1966-68; mem. edn. dept. Mpls. Inst. Arts, 1967-69; teaching assoc. art history U. Minn., 1968-70; asst. prof. art history, curator collections Spencer Mus. Art, U. Kans., Lawrence, 1970-71, dir. mus., 1971-82, assoc. prof., 1974-80, prof., 1980-82; dir. Nat. Mus. Am. Art, Washington, 1982-88; Hall disting. prof. of Am. art and culture U. Kans., Lawrence, 1988—. C.H. Hynson vis. prof. U. Tex., Austin, 1985; trustee Watkins Cmty. Mus., Lawrence, 1972-76, Assn. Art Mus. Dirs., 1982, 87, Reynolda House Mus. Am. Art, 1986-88, Amherst Coll., 1987-93, trustee Georgia O'Keeffe Found., 1989-95, Amon Carter Mus., 2003—; rsch. assoc. Smithsonian Instn., 1988—; founder Smithsonian Studies in Am. Art, 1987. Author: Marsden Hartley: Lithographs and Related Works, 1972, Ward Lockwood, 1894-1963, 1974, American Imagination and Symbolist Painting, 1979, Charles Walter Stetson, Color and Fantasy, 1982, Pacific Parallels: Artists and the Landscape in New Zealand, 1991, Georgia O'Keeffe, 1991, Georgia O'Keeffe: American and Modern, 1992, The College on the Hill, 1996, Reflections on Nature: Small Paintings by Arthur Dove, 1997, The Floor of the Sky: Artists and the North American Prairie, 2000; co-author: The Arcadian Landscape: 19th Century American Painters in Italy, 1972, Art in New Mexico, 1900-1945, 1986, Georgia O'Keeffe and The Calla Lily in American Art, 2002; gen. editor: The Register of Mus. Art, 1971—82; mem. editl. bd. Am. Studies, 1974—77, Am. Art, 1996—. Fulbright scholar N.Z., 1983; Smithsonian Instn. fellow Nat. Collection Fine Arts, 1979, Found. Visitor fellow U. Auckland, 1993, Smithsonian fellow Nat. Mus. Am. Art, 1995, Kemper Teaching fellow, U. Kans., 2003; recipient Outstanding Alumnus award U. Minn., 1986, Ctr. for Tchg. Excellence award U. Kans., 2000. Mem. Coll. Art Assn. Am., Am. Studies Assn., Am. Assn. Mus., Assn. Art Mus. Dirs. (hon.). Office: U Kans Dept Art History 209 Spencer Mus Art 1301 Mississippi St Lawrence KS 66045-0001 E-mail: cce@ku.edu.

ELDRIDGE, J. CHARLES, endocrinologist, researcher, medical educator, medical educator; b. Chgo., June 7, 1942; s. John Godfrey Eldridge, Carol Boedeker Eldridge; m. Pat Hudler. BA in Biology, North Cen. Coll., Naperville, Ill., 1965; MS in Physiology, No. Ill. U., 1967; PhD in Endocrinology, Med. Coll. Ga., 1971. Instr. biology Orange County C.C., Middletown, NY, 1967—68; rsch. assoc. I.N.S.E.R.M., Bordeaux, France, 1971-72, Med. Coll. Ga., Augusta, 1973; asst. prof. lab. medicine Med. U. S.C., Charleston, 1974-79; asst. prof. physiology and pharmacology Wake Forest U. Sch. Medicine, Winston-Salem, NC, 1979—87, assoc. prof. physiology and pharmacology, 1987—99, prof. physiology and pharmacology, 1999—. Grant reviewer Nat. Inst. Aging, NIH, Bethesda, Md., 1990—93; rsch. cons. EPA, Washington, 1999—, mem. endocrine disruptors methods validation com., 2001—; cons. Internat. Life Scis. Inst., Washington, 1992—94; med. edn. cons. various schs., 1988—; adj. faculty Harvard Macy Inst. Med. Educators, 2001—. Mng. editor: Basic Sci. Educator, 1999—2002, mem. editl. bd.: Biology of Reproduction, 2000—, Jour. Internat. Assn. Med. Sci. Educators, 2002—; contbr. articles to profl. jours. Coord. United Way, Winston-Salem, 1986—98; elder, deacon, other positions Reynolda Presby. Ch., 1992—. Recipient Disting. Alumni award, Med. Coll. Ga., 2002; grantee, NIH, 1976—97, Nat. Inst. Drug Abuse, 1990—98; Macy fellow in edn., Harvard Med. Sch., 2001. Mem.: Soc. for Study of Reproduction, Internat. Assn. for Med. Sci. Educators, Soc. Neurosci., Endocrine Soc., Shriners (bd. dirs. 1988—91), Masons. Presbyterian. Avocations: music, travel, cuisine. Office: Wake Forest U Sch Medicine Dept Physiology and Pharmacology Winston Salem NC 27157-1083

ELFTMAN, SUSAN NANCY, physician assistant, childbirth-lactation educator, research director; b. Oakland, Calif., Apr. 3, 1951; d. Arthur Gerhardt Samuel and Ella Johanna (Nelson) E. AA summa cum laude, Chabot Coll., 1971; BA in Zoology, U. Calif., Berkeley, 1973; BS in Med. Sci. magna cum laude, Alderson-Broaddus Coll., 1980; MPH, UCLA, 1990. Bd. cert. physician asst., Calif. Physician asst. So. Calif. Permanente Group, San Diego, 1981-82, Mem. Med. Ctr., Long Beach, Calif., 1982-88, Harriman-Jones Med. Group, Long Beach, 1988-90, Pamela Kushner, MD, Long Beach, 1990—. Spkr. Am. Cancer Soc., Long. Beach, Meml. Med. Ctr., Long Beach, March of Dimes. Fellow Am. Acad. Physician Assts., Calif. Acad. Physician Assts.; mem. Am. Soc. for Psychoprophylaxis in Obstetrics (cert. lactation and childbirth educator). Home: 625 Termino Ave Long Beach CA 90814 Office: Pamela Kushner MD 2865 Atlantic Ave Ste 207 Long Beach CA 90806-1730

ELGART, MERVYN L. dermatologist, educator; b. Bklyn., Aug. 12, 1933; s. Jacob and Sally R. E.; m. Sheila Ruth Cliff, June 13, 1954; children— Brian, George, Paul, Adam, James. AB, Bklyn. Coll., 1953; MD, Cornell U., 1957. Intern Buffalo Gen. Hosp., 1957-58; resident in dermatology Walter Reed Gen. Hosp., Washington, 1960-63; chief dermatology Andrews AFB Hosp., Washington, 1964-66; mem. faculty George Washington U. Med. Sch., 1967-97, prof. dermatology, 1974-97, chmn. dept., 1975-97, prof. pediatrics, 1974-97, prof. medicine, 1974-97; clin. prof. dermatology, medicine and pediatrics Univ. Dermatology Assocs., Washington, 1997—2002, emeritus prof. dermatology, 2002—. Mem. med. adv. com. Nat. Orgn. Rare Diseases, 2000—. Served as officer M.C. USAF, 1958-66. Fellow Am. Acad. Dermatology; mem. AMA, So. Med. Assn., Internat. Soc. Dermatology, Washington Dermatol. Soc., Am. Dermatol. Assn., Phi Beta Kappa, Alpha Omega Alpha. Roman Catholic. E-mail: mervynelgart@netscape.net.

ELGAVISH, GABRIEL ANDREAS, physical biochemistry educator; b. Budapest, Hungary, July 29, 1942; arrived in Israel, 1957, came to U.S., 1979; s. László and Katalin Barbara (Szentmiklóssy) Schwarcz; m. Ada Stephanie Simcas, Dec. 28, 1967; children: Rotem László Abraham, Eynav Elgavish. BSc, Hebrew U., Jerusalem, 1967; MSc, Tel-Aviv U., 1972; PhD, Weizmann Inst. of Sci., 1978. Vis. fellow NIH, Balt., 1979-81; asst. prof. U. Ala., Birmingham, 1981-87, assoc. prof., 1987-95, prof., 1995—. Contbr. articles to profl. jours. 1st lt. Israeli Army, 1961-64. Mem. Am. Chem. Soc., Am. Soc. for Biochemistry and Molecular Biology, Am. Heart Assn./Basic Sci., Soc. Magnetic Resonance in Medicine. Jewish. Achievements include patents on Contrast Agents for Nuclear Magnetic Resonance Imaging; research in biomedical nuclear magnetic resonance spectroscopy. Office: U Ala THT 336 1900 University Blvd Birmingham AL 35294-0006 E-mail: gabi@uab.edu.

EL-GHAZALY, SAMIR, electrical engineering educator; b. Luxor, Egypt, July 1, 1959; came to U.S., 1986; s. M. E. El-Ghazaly; m. Siham A. Abdel-Naby, June 27, 1985; children: Sarah, Hada, Amal. BS, Cairo U., Egypt, 1981, MSc, 1984; PhD, U. Tex. at Austin, 1988. Asst. lectr. Faculty of Engring. Cairo (Egypt) U., 1981-84; rschr. U. Lille, France, 1982-83; rschr., teaching asst. U. Ottawa, Ontario, Can., 1984-85; rsch. asst., postdoctoral rsch. assoc. U. Tex., Austin, 1986-88; asst. prof. Ariz. State U., Tempe, 1988-93, assoc. prof., 1993-98, prof., 1998—2002; head elec. and computer engring. dept. U. Tenn., Knoxville, 2002—. Cons. Superconductor Tech., Inc., Santa Barbara, Calif., 1990-92; summer faculty fellow Jet Propulsion Lab., Pasadena, Calif., 1994. Contbr. over 75 articles to profl. jours. Mem. Commn. D, Internat. Union of Radio Scis., Washington, 1988, Commn. A, Geneva, 1994; sec. U.S. Nat. Com. of URSI Commn. A, 1996-99, vice-chmn. 1999-2000, chmn. 2000-02; gen. chair Internat. Microwave Symposium, Phoenix, Ariz., 2001, editor in chief Microwave and wireless components letters, 2001—; chmn. U.S. Nat. Com. of URSI Comm. D, 2003—. Recipient Young Scientist award Internat. Union Radio Sci., 1990, Teaching Excellence award Ariz. State U., 1992. Fellow IEEE (internat. chpt. funding coord. 1993-96, chmn. Phoenix chpt. 1992-93, chmn. chpt. activities 1997), Microwave Theory and Techniques Soc. Avocations: tennis, sight seeing, travel. Office: Dept Electrical and Computer Engring U Tenn 414 Ferris Hall Knoxville TN 37996-2100

ELIAS, JOSEPH, secondary school educator; b. Wilkes-Barre, Pa., Dec. 7, 1948; s. Michael and Marianne (Skaff) E.; m. Mary Susan Pomanek, Dec. 4, 1976; children: Amy, Amber. BA, Wilkes Coll., 1970; MA, U. Md., 1972; Reading Specialist, Scranton U., 1975-77. Cert. tchr., Pa. Reading tchr. Wilkes-Barre Area Sch. Dist., 1975—. Mem. Mid. States Evaluation Teams, 1982-95. Arab.-Am. commr. Pa. Heritage Commn., 1993. Mem. NEA, Wilkes-Barre Area Edn. Assn. (treas. 1994—), Pa. Edn. Assn., Internat. REading assn., Northeastern Pa. Assn. Arab Ams. (pres. 1984-86), Nat. Assn. Arab Ams. (bd. dirs. 1982-84), Arab-Am. Anti-discrimination Com., Arab Am. Inst. Democrat. Antiochian Orthodox Ch. Avocations: reading, travel, chess, book collecting. Home: 302 Poplar St Wilkes Barre PA 18702-4571 Office: Leo E Solomon Jr H S 22 Abbott St Plains PA 18705-1904

ELIAS, MERRILL FRANCIS, behavioral/cardiovascular epidemiology researcher; b. Apr. 17, 1938; m. Penelope K. Elias; children: Susan P., Eric J. and Benjamin J. BA, Allegheny Coll., 1960; MS, Purdue U., 1961, PhD, 1963; MPH, Boston U., 1996. Asst. prof. Allegheny Coll., Meadville, Pa., 1965-68; asst. prof. med. psychology, coordinator aging research tng. program Duke U., Durham, N.C., 1971-72; assoc. prof. psychology W.Va. U., Morgantown, 1972-73, Syracuse (N.Y.) U., 1973-77; prof. psychology U. Maine, Orono, 1977—; adj. rsch. prof. medicine and pub. health Boston U., 1994—95, rsch. prof. math. and stats., 1995—. Dr. clin. tng. U. Maine, Orono, 1986—; vis. rsch. prof. medicine, vis. prof. pub. health Sch. of Medicine, Boston U., 1991-93; allied health scientist Maine Med. Ctr., Bangor, Maine, 1986—; vis. acad. U. Oxford, Eng., 1987, The Jackson Lab., Bar Harbor, Maine, 1968, 70, 74, 75; assoc. med. staff Bangor Mental Health Inst., 1977-79; instr. psychology Syracuse U., Mohawk Valley Community Coll., 1963-64; rsch. assoc. Purdue U., 1960-63; cons. bd. sci. counselors Nat. Inst. on Aging, 1984, mem. animal adv. com., 1982—, evaluation panel animal resources prog., 1981-82, others. Contbr. articles to profl. jours.; speaker in field. Grantee, NSF, 1967-70, NIH, 1970-71, 73-75, 76-80, 82-84, 84—, NATO-Eng.-U.S. Rsch. Collaboration, 1986. Fellow APA, Soc. Behavioral Medicine, Acad. Behavioral Med. Rsch., Am. Heart Assn. (coun. on epidemiology and high blood pressure), Am. Psychosomatic Soc. Home: PO Box 40 Mount Desert ME 04660-0040

ELIASON, NANCY CAROL, education consultant; b. Washington, Feb. 24, 1929; d. Lester Frank Kirchner and Nancy Lee (Rhea) Wiebe; m. William A. Eliason, Jan. 29, 1956 (div. June 1969)(rem. May 30, 1970); children: Charles Henry, William T., Leslie C. AB, Mary Baldwin Coll., 1950; MA, U. Md., 1953. Editor, writer Telenews, Inc., Washington, 1951-53; exec. dir. Blue Ridge Area Girl Scout Coun., Inc., Winchester, Va., 1954-55; asst. registrar Wheaton Coll., Norton, Mass., 1966-68; registrar and instr. Social Scis. Massasoit Community Coll., North Abingdon, Mass., 1968-70; assoc. prof. Social Scis. Lehigh Carbon C.C., Schnecksville, Pa., 1970-76; dir. devel. and spl. projects Am. Assn. of C.C., Washington, 1976-85; edn. policy analyst Nat. Govs. Assn., Washington, 1985-86; dir. devel. Close Up Found., Arlington, Va., 1986-88. Cons., evaluator Fund for Improvement of Post Sec. Edn., Title III and Vocat. Edn. Programs; sch. bd. Charlotte County, Fla., vice-chmn., 1992-94; mem. Fla. Com. on Lang. Arts Textbook Selection, 1994-98; pres. Learning in Retirement, 1997—; sec. New Operation Coop., Inc., 1997—. Contbr. articles and booklets to profl. mags. and jours. on various areas of small bus. Mem. Nat. Adv. Com. on Small Bus. Devel. Ctrs., 1985-89, Univ. Bus. Collaboration/Am. Assn. State Colls. and Univs., 1985-87, Nat. Ctr. for Rsch. in Vocat. Edn., 1978-80, Nat. Adv. Bd. Adult Learning, Coll. Bd., 1979-86, Office Adult Learning Svcs., 1983-87; mem. Nat. Evaluation Com. on Future Funds for Post-Secondary Edn., 1978-79; vice chair Charlotte County Sch. Bd., 1992-96; pres. Learning Ret. at Edison C.C., 1996—. Nominee State award, 1991; named Vol. of Yr. for Ret. Educators of Charlotte County, 1990—91. Mem. AAUP, AAUW, Am. Assn. Cmty. and Jr. Colls. (Woman of Yr. 1977, Nat. Coun Community Svc. and Continuing Edn. Person of Yr. 1983), Charlotte County LW (pres. 1990-92), Alpha Xi Delta, Delta Kappa Gamma. Home: 601 Shreve St Apt 65A Punta Gorda FL 33950-3348 Address: 601 Shreve St Apt 65A Punta Gorda FL 33950-3348 E-mail: beliason@earthlink.net.

ELIEL, ERNEST LUDWIG, chemist, educator; b. Cologne, Germany, Dec. 28, 1921; came to U.S., 1946, naturalized, 1951; s. Oskar and Luise (Tietz) E.; m. Eva Schwarz, Dec. 23, 1949; children: Ruth Louise, Carol Susan. Student, U. Edinburgh, Scotland, 1939-40; degree in phys.-chem. sci., U. Havana, Cuba, 1946; PhD, U. Ill., 1948; DSc (hon.), Duke U., 1983, U. Notre Dame, 1990, Babes-Bolyai U., Cluj, Romania, 1993. Mem. faculty U. Notre Dame, South Bend, Ind., 1948-72, prof. chemistry, 1960-72, head dept., 1964-66; W.R. Kenan Jr. prof. chemistry U. N.C., Chapel Hill, 1972-93, prof. emeritus, 1993—. Le Bel Centennial lectr., Paris, 1974; Sir C.V. Raman vis. prof. U. Madras, India, 1981; Geoffrey Coates lectr. U. Wyo., 1989; Smith, Kline & French lectr. U. Ill., 1990; Richard and Doris Arnold lectr. U. So. Ill., 1997. Author: Stereochemistry of Carbon Compounds, 1962, Elements of Stereochemistry, 1969, From Cologne to Chapel Hill, 1990; co-author: Conformational Analysis, 1965, Stereochemistry of Organic Compounds, 1994, Basic Organic Stereochemistry, 2001; co-editor: Topics in Stereochemistry, vols. I-XXI, 1967-94. Pres. Internat. Rels. Coun., St. Joseph Valley, Ind., 1961-63; chmn. bd. U.S.-Mex. Found. for Sci., 1994-96. Recipient Coll. Chem. Tchrs. award Mfg. Chemists Assn., 1965, Laurent Lavoisier medal French Chem. Soc., 1968, Amoco Teaching award U. N.C., 1975, Thomas Jefferson award U. N.C., 1991, N.C. award in Sci., 1986, Chirality medal Internat. Symposium on Chiral Discrimination, 1996; NSF sr. rsch. fellow Harvard U., 1958, Calif. Inst. Tech., 1958-59, E.T.H. Zurich, Switzerland, 1967-68, Guggenheim fellow Stanford U., Princeton U., 1975-76, Duke U., 1983-84; named One of Top 75 Disting. Contbrs. to Chem. Enterprise, Chem. and Engring. News, 1998. Fellow AAAS (chmn. chemistry sect. 1991-92), Royal Soc. Chems.; mem. NAS (award for chemistry in svc. to society 1997), AAUP (chpt. pres. 1971-72, 78-79), Am. Acad. Arts and Scis., Am. Chem. Soc. (chmn. St. Joseph Valley sect. 1960, councillor 1965-73, 75—, chmn. com. publs. 1972, 76-78, dir. 1985-93, chmn. bd. dirs. 1987-89, pres. 1992, Morley medal Cleve. sect. 1965, Harry and Carol Mosher award Santa Clara Valley sect. 1982, Herty medal Ga. sect. 1991, So. Chemist award Memphis sect. 1991, Madison Marshall award North Ala. sect., 1993, George C. Pimentel award in Chem. Edn. 1995, Priestley medal 1996), Coun. Sci. Soc. Pres.'s (pres. 1996), Royal Spanish Chem. Soc. (hon.), Argentine Chem. Assn. (hon.), Peruvian Chem. Soc. (corr.), Mex. Chem. Soc. (hon.), Mex. Acad. Scis. (corr.), Chilean Chem. Soc. (hon.), Cuban Chem. Soc. (hon.), Sigma Xi (pres. U. Notre Dame chpt. 1968-69), Phi Lambda Upsilon, Phi Kappa Phi. Home: 345 Carolina Meadows Villa Chapel Hill NC 27517-7519 E-mail: eliel@email.unc.edu.

ELIN, RONALD JOHN, pathologist, educator; b. Mpls., Apr. 14, 1939; s. John Matthew and Helen Sophia (Lind) E.; m. Susan May Krogh, June 14, 1969; children: Derek, Justin. BA, U. Minn., 1960, BS, 1962, MD, 1966, PhD, 1969. Diplomate Am. Bd. Pathology, Am. Bd. Clin. Chemistry. Intern U. Hosp. Calif., San Diego, 1969-70; commd. med. officer USPHS, 1970, advanced through grades to med. dir., 1975; staff assoc. Nat. Inst. Allergy and Infectious Diseases NIH, Bethesda, Md., 1970-73, resident clin. pathology dept., 1973-74, chief clin. pathology dept., 1975-97, chief chemistry svc., 1977-97; vice chmn. pathology U. Louisville, Ky., 1997—2001, chmn. dept. pathology and lab. medicine, 2002. Clin. prof. Uniformed Svcs. U. of Health Scis., Bethesda, 1978-97; initiator, first chmn. Gordon Rsch. Conf. on Magnesium in Biomed. Processes and Medicine, 1978. Contbr. more than 200 articles to profl. jours. Decorated Commendation medal USPHS, 1980, Meritorious Svc. medal USPHS, 1984. Fellow Am. Coll. Nutrition, Coll. Am. Pathologists, Am. Soc. Clin. Pathologists; mem. Am. Assn. Pathologists, Am. Assn. Clin. Chemistry (Outstanding Contbns. to Clin. Chemistry in a Selected Area of Rsch. award 1994), Acad. Clin. Lab. Physicians and Scientists (sec.-treas. 1985-87, pres. 1990-91, Gerald T. Evans award 1995). Lutheran. Achievements include research on magnesium metabolism, properties of endotoxin. Office: U Louisville Hosp Dept Pathology and Lab Medicine 512 S Hancock St Rm 203 Louisville KY 40202-1675 E-mail: rjelin01@gwise.louisville.edu.

ELIOT, JOHN, psychologist, educator; b. Washington, Oct. 28, 1933; s. Charles William and Regina (Dodge) E.; m. Sylvia Hewitt, July 3, 1959; children: John Cooper (dec.), Mary Ashley, Catherine Hewitt. AB, Harvard U., 1956, M of Art in Teaching, 1958; EdD, Stanford U., 1966. Asst. prof. Northwestern U., Evanston, Ill., 1967-69; assoc. prof. U. Md., College Park, 1969-77, prof., 1977-99, prof. emeritus, 1999—. Author: (with I. Smith) Spatial Tests, 1983, Models of Psychological Space, 1987; contbr. articles to profl. jours. Trustee Reservations, Milton, Mass., 1960—. Fellow APA; mem. Am. Psychol. Soc., Democrat. Episcopalian. Avocation: swimming. Home: 2705 Silverdale Dr Silver Spring MD 20906-5322

EL KHADEM, HASSAN SAAD, chemistry educator, researcher; b. Cairo, Mar. 24, 1923;, naturalized, 1975; s. Saad S. and Nimet (Zulficar) El K.; m. Nadia M. Said, Sept. 6, 1951 (dec. 2002); children: Samiha, Saad. DSc Tech., ETH Zurich, Switzerland, 1950; PhD, Imperial Coll., London, 1952; DSc, U. London, 1967; BSc with honors, Cairo U., 1946; DSc, U. Alexandria (Arab Republic of Egypt), 1963. Lectr. Alexandria U., 1952-58, asst. prof., 1958-64, prof. organic chemistry, 1964-71; prof. chemistry Michigan Tech. U., Houghton, 1971-74; head dept. chemistry and chem. engring. Mich. Tech. U., Houghton, 1974-80, pres. prof. chemistry, 1980-84; Isbell prof. chemistry The Am. U., Washington, 1984-93, Isbell prof. chemistry emeritus, 1993—. Mem. editorial bd. Carbohydrate Rsch., 1966-92; contbr. over 170 articles on carbohydrates and medicinal chemistry to profl. jours.; author 15 books including Carbohydrate Chemistry: Monosaccharides and their Oligomers, Synthetic Methods for Carbohydrates, Anthracycline Antibiotics; patentee in field. Fulbright scholar U.S. Dept. State, Ohio State U., Columbus, 1963-64; recipient Phys. Sci. award Washington Acad. Sci., 1992. Mem. AAAS, Am. Chem. Soc. (chmn. carbonhydrate div. 1984-85, Melville L. Wolfrom award 1989), Sigma Xi. Achievements include discovery of a lost Greek manuscript by Zosimos (300 A.D.) translated to Arabic in a twelveth century Alchemy book (donated to the Libr. of Congress). Home: 4948 Sentinel Dr Apt 101 Bethesda MD 20816-3586 Office: Am U Dept Chemistry Beeghly Bldg 4400 Massachusetts Ave NW Washington DC 20016-8001

ELKINS-ELLIOTT, KAY, law educator; b. Dallas, Nov. 21, 1938; d. William Hardin and Maxidine (Sadler) E.; m. Michael Gail Hodgson, July 7, 1960 (div. Dec. 1974); children: Michael Brett, Ashley Kim, Samantha; m. Frank Wallace Elliott, Aug. 15, 1983. AA with honors, Stephens Coll., 1958; JD, U. Okla., 1964; LLM, So. Meth. U., 1984; MA, U. Tex., Dallas, 1990. Bar: Okla. 1964, Tex. 1982, U.S. Dist. Ct. (no. dist.) Tex. 1982, U.S. Supreme Ct. 1984, U.S. Dist. Ct. (we. dist.) Okla. 1989. Assoc. Ben Hatcher and Assocs., Oklahoma City, Okla., 1964-65; dir., gen. counsel Take-A-Tour Swaziland, Mbabane, Swaziland, 1966-74; atty. Dept. Health and Human Svcs., Dallas, 1975-80; hearing officer EEOC, Dallas, 1980-84; atty. pvt. practice, Dallas, 1984-92; vis. assoc. prof. Tex. Wesleyan U. Sch. Law, Dallas, 1992-95; arbitrator State Farm Ins., Dallas, 1991-96. Adj. prof. Wesleyan U. Sch. Law, 1995—, coach nat. ABA champion negotiation team, 1998; mediator pvt. practice, Dallas, Granbury, 1991—; coord. cert. in conflict resolution program Tex. Woman's U., 1996—; coach internal champion negotiation team ICOD, 2002-; coach internat. champion online dispute resolution competition; cons. in field. Author: (with others) West Texas Practice, 1995; (with Frank Elliott) State Bar of Texas ADR Handbook, 2003. Dir. diversity tng. State Bar Tex. 9/11 project. Mem. ABA (negotiation and tng. coms., alternative dispute resolution sect.), Tex. Bar Assn. (ADR sect. coun. mem. 1998-2001, chair publs. com.), Tex. Bar Found., Tex. Initiatives for Mediation in Edn. (founder, planning com. 1993-95), Assn. for Conflict Resolution (pres. Dallas region 1995-97), Tex. Assn. Mediators, Dallas Bar Assn. (coun. mem. 1993-94), Inst. for Responsible Dispute Resolution (charter), Granbury C. of C. and Historic Merchants Assn., Toastmasters (v.p. 1993-94, pres. 1996-97), Optimist Internat. Avocations: singing, public speaking. Home: 2120 N Rough Creek Ct Granbury TX 76048-2903 Office: 2401 Turtle Creek Blvd Dallas TX 75219-4712 E-mail: k4mede8@swbell.net.

EL KODSI, BAROUKH, gastroenterologist, educator; b. Cairo, Aug. 24, 1923; arrived in U.S., 1957, naturalized, 1963; s. Moussa and Zohra (Aslan Cohen) El Kodsi; m. Marie Menasha, Mar. 26, 1960; children: Sylvia, Robert, Karen. MD, Cairo U., 1945. Intern Univ. Hosp. Cairo Sch. Medicine, 1946; resident in gen. medicine Jewish Hosp., Cairo, 1947—50, attending physician, 1950—57; intern Miriam Hosp., Providence, 1958; resident in internal medicine Boston City Hosp., 1959—61, chief resident, 1961—62, fellow in gastroenterology, 1962—64; asst. dir. medicine Union Hosp., Framingham, Mass., 1964—65; assoc. dir. medicine Maimonides Med. Ctr., Bklyn., 1965—67, dir. gastroenterology, 1968—; chief gastroenterology Coney Island Hosp., N.Y.C., 1967—68. Instr. Boston City Hosp., 1962—65; instr. Downstate Med. Ctr., SUNY, Bklyn., 1965—69, asst. prof. medicine, 1969—76, assoc. prof., 1976—. Contbr. articles to profl. jours. Named one of Best Drs. N.Y., New Yorker, 1966—67, 1968—89, NY Mag., 1996—2002. Fellow: ACP, Am. Coll. Gastroenterology; mem.: AMA, N.Y. Gastroent. Assn. (pres. 1985—86), Am. Soc. Study of Liver Disease, Am. Soc. Gastrointestinal Endoscopy, Am. Gastroent. Assn., Am. Fedn. Clin. Rsch., Ostomy Club (mem. exec. coun.). Home: 118 Girard St Brooklyn NY 11235-3010 Office: 925 48th St Brooklyn NY 11219-2919

ELLENBECKER, CATHERINE RIEDL, secondary art educator, web developer; b. Milw., July 16, 1950; d. Charles A. and Mary Wendt Riedl; m. Thomas L. Ellenbecker, Aug. 22, 1970; children: Mary Elizabeth, Thomas Jr., Timothy, Margaret, Kathleen, Colleen. BA in Art Edn. cum laude, Mt. Mary Coll., Milw., 1973; MS in Art Edn., U. Wis., Milw., 1982. Cert. tchr. grades K-12, Wis.; cert. web developer-designer. Art specialist Mother of Good Counsel Sch., Milw., 1974-80; substitute tchr. Sch. Dist. Ripon and Green Lakes, Wis., 1982-84; art specialist grades 7-12 Sch. Dist. Montello, Wis., 1984—; CEO Ellenbeelar C.com LLC, 1999—. Pres. com. Arts and Humanities Nat. Report, 1998. Exhibited works at Mt. Mary Coll., 2000. Recipient tchr.'s citation Milw. Jour. Sentinel Student Calendar Art, 1991, 95, 97, 98, honors citation Nat. Scholastic Art Program, 1987, 89, 93, 94, 95, 99, Madonna medal for profl. excellence Mt. Mary Coll., 1999, grand prize Primo Radicchio Art Exhibit, Treviso, Italy, 1999, Congl. Report citation 1998, 2002, Disting. Program award Wis. Alliance for Arts Edn., 1999; nominee Kennedy Ctr. award Wis. Alliance for Arts Edn., 1999. Mem. Nat. Art Edn. Assn., Wis. Art Edn. Assn., Wis. Edn. Assn., Wis. Designer Crafts Coun., Kappa Gamma Pi. Avocations: art, family activities, technology. Office: Sch Dist Montello 222 Forest Ln Montello WI 53949-9390

ELLER, LINDA SADLER, elementary school educator, district administrator, technology specialist; b. Atlanta, Aug. 14, 1952; d. James Emmett and Mary Love (Dempsey) Sadler; m. David Warner Eller, Dec. 21, 1974; 1 child, Laura Marylove. BS in Elem. Edn., Tenn. Tech. U., 1974; MA in Curriculum and Instrn., U. Memphis, 1986; postgrad., Cumberland U. Cert. elem. tchr, 1-9, Tenn., cert. career ladder III. Tchr., tutor Jackson (Miss.) Tutorial Acad., 1974-75; tchr. DeSoto County Acad., Olive Branch, Miss., 1975-76, Glenmore Acad., Memphis, 1976; tchr. grades 1-6 Memphis City Schs., 1976—98, tech. coord. Newberry Elem., 1998—2000, staff devel. coord., Tchg. and Learning Acad., 2001—; instructional cons. Tchr. Ctr., Memphis, 1991-95. Pres. Memphis City Schs. Tchr. Ctr. Adv. Bd., Memphis, 1993-95 Leader Girl Scouts of U.S., Memphis, 1987-97; vol. Arts in the Park, Memphis, 1993, 95. Named amb. to Edn. Ctr. N.C., 1993-94, Apple Disting. Educator, 2003; recipient Top Ten Thanks to Tchr. award, 1997, Tchr. of Excellence award Rotary, 1997, Tchr. of Yr. WalMart, 1997; grantee Memphis City Schs., 1984, Rotary, Memphis, 1987, Tenn. Dept. Edn., 1994; fellow Delta Tchrs. Acad., 1994-97, Nat. Faculty fellow, 1997. Mem.: ASCD, West Tenn. Reading Assn., Internat. Reading Assn. (membership liaison 1994—95), Internat. Soc. Tech. in Edn., Zeta Tau Alpha, Delta Kappa Gamma (parliamentarian 2002—, state webmaster 2001—03, v.p. 1995—97, pres. 1998—2000), Kappa Delta Pi. Episcopalian. Avocations: reading, painting, craftwork, needlework, camping. Office: Tchg and Learning Acad Memphis City Schs 2485 Union Ave Memphis TN 38112 Home: 1641 Durhamshire Cv Cordova TN 38016-2359 E-mail: ellerl@mcsk12.net.

ELLERBEE, DIANE TURNER, elementary school educator; b. Gordon, Ga., Apr. 15, 1948; d. J.C. and Johnie (Pagett) Turner; m. Terrell Stanton Ellerbee, Dec. 20, 1969; 1 child, Amy Diane. AS, Kennesaw (Ga.) Jr. Coll., 1968; BS in Edn., West Ga. Coll., 1969, MEd, 1973. Tchr. Cobb County Bd. Edn., Marietta, Ga., 1969—; tchr. 7th grade sci. McEachern Jr. High Sch., Powder Springs, Ga., 1969-74; Title I edn. tchr. Big Shanty Elem. Sch., Kennesaw, 1975-77; tchr. 3rd grade Due West Elem. Sch., Marietta, 1977—. Active PTA, Powder Springs, 1969-92, Citizens Adv. Coun., Marietta, 1984-85; ch. leader First Meth. Ch., Powder Springs, 1966-89. NEA, Ga. Edn. Assn., Cobb County Edn. Assn., Ga. PTA (hon. life). Democrat. Avocations: needlework, reading, antiquing. Office: Due West Elem Sch 3900 Due West Rd Marietta GA 30064-1020

ELLINGSEN, MICHAEL O. music educator, theater educator; b. Two Harbors, Minn., June 16, 1953; s. Esther L Ellingsen; m. Susan P Amundson, July 2, 1977; children: Andrew, Katherine. BS magna cum laude, Bemidji State U., 1975; MusM, Mankato State U., 1984. Cert. K-12 music tchr. Minn. Vocal and instrumental music East Chain Pub. Schools, Blue Earth, Minn., 1975—80; vocal music and drama tchr. grades 7-12 Blue Earth Area HS, 1980—. Singer: (vocal ensemble) Nova Cantabile, 1990—; actor: (musical theater) The Secret Garden, 1998 (Archibald Craven), You're a Good Man Charlie Brown, 1999 (Charlie Brown), Into the Woods, 1996 (Jack). Treas. Blue Earth Town and Country Players, Blue Earth, Minn., 1984—2002; dir. Trinity Luth. Sr. Choir, Blue Earth, Minn., 1980—2002. Recipient East Chain Pub. Sch. Tchr. of the Yr., 1979—80, Golden Apple Award, Ashland Oil Co., 1984, Blue Earth Area Sch. Tchr. of the Yr., 2001—02. Mem.: NEA, Minn. Music Educators Assn. (choral v.p. 1992—94), Am. Choral Directors Assn. (life). Lutheran. Avocations: quilting, bicycling, music, theater. Home: 312 North Holland Blue Earth MN 56013-1231 Office: Blue Earth Area HS 1125 Highway 169 North Blue Earth MN 56013 Office Fax: 507-526-3260. Personal E-mail: ellingsen@charter.net. E-mail: mellingsen@blueearth.k12.mn.us.

ELLINGTON, CHARLES RONALD, lawyer, educator; b. Cuthbert, Ga., Sept. 3, 1941; s. Charles Bartlett and Annie Claire (Moore) E.; m. Jean Alice Spencer, Apr. 29, 1967; children— Gregory Spencer, Alicia Nicole. AB summa cum laude, Emory U., 1963; LL.B., U. Va., 1966; LL.M., Harvard U., 1978. Bar: Ga. 1967, D.C. 1967. Assoc. firm Sutherland, Asbill and Brennan, Atlanta, 1966-69; mem. law faculty U. Ga. Sch. Law, 1969—, prof. law, 1977—, Thomas R.R. Cobb prof. law, 1983-93, dean, 1987-93, J. Alton Hosch prof. law, 1993-99, A. Gus Cleveland prof. legal ethics and professionalism, 1999—. On leave as scholar in residence U.S. Dept. Justice, Washington, 1979-80; reporter Standards of the Profession Com., State Bar of Ga., mem. formal adv. opinion bd. Harvard U. fellow in law and humanities, 1973-74. Mem. Am. Law Inst. Avocation: hiking. Office: Univ Ga Sch Law Herty Dr Athens GA 30602

ELLINGTON, CYNTHIA HEMPHILL, elementary education educator; b. Winder, Ga., Nov. 30, 1965; d. John Sylvan and Margaret Ann (Shore) Hemphill; m. Jerrel Keith Ellington, July 6, 1966. BS in Edn. cum laude, U. Ga., 1988, MEd, 1990; EdS, Brenau U., 1994. Tchr. South Jackson Elem. Sch., Jackson County, Ga., 1988-89, Kennedy Elem. Sch., Winder, Ga., 1989-90, County Line Elem. Sch., Winder, Ga., 1990-95, Bethlehem Elem., 1995—2001, Kennedy Elem., 2001—. Tech. adv. bd. Brenau U., Gainesville, Ga., 1994—. Named County Line Tchr. of Yr., 1994-95. Mem. Golden Key Honor Soc., Phi Delta Kappa. Avocations: softball, volleyball. Office: Kennedy Elem 200 Matthews Sch Rd Winder GA 30680 Home: 143 Sunningdale Dr Winder GA 30680-4093 E-mail: cellington@barrow.k12.ga.us.

ELLINGTON, KAREN RENAE, secondary education resource specialist; b. Turlock, Calif., Oct. 19, 1965; d. Edward Ray and Barbara Janet (Rafatti) E. BS, Calif. Poly., 1989; postgrad., Chapman U., 1994-96. Tchg. credentials include multiple subject, agr., bus., spl. edn.-learning handicapped; cert. resource specialist; cert. crosscultural, lang. and acad. devel. specialist. Asst. mgr. House of Fabrics, San Luis Obispo, Calif., 1985-88, Macy's, Sacramento, 1988-90; clk. Raley's, Modesto, Calif., 1990-93; substitute tchr. Merced & Stanislaus Counties, Calif., 1993; resource specialist Los Banos (Calif.) H.S., 1994—. Computer instr. ARBOR, Modesto and Merced, 1994-97. Leader 4-H, Merced County, 1990—, dir. 1998—; mem. Calif. State Citizenship Coun., 1999—. Mem. NEA, Calif. Tchrs. Assn., Los Banos Tchrs. Assn., Coun. for Exceptional Children, Calif. Ag. Tchrs. Assn. (assoc.), Internat. Dyslexia Assn. Avocations: traveling, stitchery, photography, athletics. Office: Los Banos HS 1966 S 11th St Los Banos CA 93635-4812 E-mail: karenellington@hotmail.com., kellington@losbanosusd.k12.ca.us.

ELLINGTON, MILDRED L. librarian; b. Marion, Ohio, June 7, 1921; d. Edward J. and Julia Ellen (Oiler) E. BA, Olivet Nazarene Coll., Kankakee, Ill., 1943; MA in French, Ohio State U., 1952; MA in English, Bowling Green (Ohio) U., 1964; MLS, Rosary Coll., River Forest, Ill., 1976. English and French tchr. Morral (Ohio) High Sch., 1944-49, Reddick (Ill.) High Sch., 1949-55; English tchr. Bremen Community High Sch., Midlothian, Ill., 1955-58, Bloom Twp. High Sch., Chicago Heights, Ill., 1958-60, Willowbrook High Sch., Villa Park, Ill., 1960-66; English tchr., then library dir. Addison (Ill.) Trail High Sch., 1966-82; reference librarian Maywood (Ill.) Pub. Library, 1982—. Sunday sch. supt. Elgin (Ill.) Ch. of the Nazarene, 1985-92. Mem. Ill. Library Assn. Democrat. Mem. Ch. of the Nazarene. Avocations: opera, singing, genealogy, travel. Office: Maywood Pub Libr 121 S 5th Ave Maywood IL 60153-1307

ELLINGWOOD, BRUCE RUSSELL, structural engineering researcher, educator; b. Evanston, Ill., Oct. 11, 1944; s. Robert W. and Carolyn L. (Ehmen) E.; m. Lois J. Drager, June 7, 1969; 1 son, Geoffrey D. BSCE, U. Ill., 1968, MSCE, 1969, PhD, 1972. Profl. engr., D.C. Structural engr. Naval Ship Rsch. and Devel. Ctr., Bethesda, Md., 1972—75; rsch. structural engr., leader structural engrng. group Ctr. Bldg. Tech., Nat. Bur. Standards, Washington, 1975—86; prof. civil engring. Johns Hopkins U., Balt., 1986—2000, chmn. dept., 1990—97; chmn. sch. civil and environ. engrng. Ga. Inst. Tech., Atlanta, 2000—02, prof. civil engring., 2002—. Lectr., cons. Editor Jour. Structural Safety; mem. editl. bd. Engring. Structures, Probabilistic Engring. Mechanics; contbr. articles to profl. jours. Recipient Dural Research prize U. Ill., 1968, Nat. Capital award for Engring. Achievement D.C. Joint Council Engring. and Archtl. Socs., 1980, Walter L. Huber prize ASCE, 1980, Silver medal U.S. Dept. Commerce, 1980, Markwardt Rsch. prize Forest Products Rsch. Soc., 1988; named Engr. of Yr. of U.S. Dept. Commerce, Nat. Soc. Profl. Engrs., 1986. Mem. ASCE (pres. Md. sect. 1998-99, State of Art in Civil Engring. award 1983, 88, Norman medal 1983, 98, Moisseiff award 1988, Walter P. Moore award 1999), Am. Concrete Inst., Am. Nat. Stds. Inst., Am. Inst. Steel Constrn. (T.R. Higgins lectureship 1988), Nat. Acad. Engring., Sigma Xi, Chi Epsilon, Tau Beta Pi. Presbyterian. Achievements include administered the secretariat of American National Standard Committee A58 on minimum design loads from 1977-84 and was responsible for coordinating and directing revisions to the A58 Standard that culminated in the publication of ANSI A58.1-1982 (now ASCE Standard 7), the first load standard in the U.S. to contain probability-based load combinations for limit states. Such load combinations now are used in Canada, the U.S. and in the Eurocodes now being developed in the common market. Was instrumental in the move by the steel industry toward limit states design. Office: Ga Inst Tech Sch Civil and Environ Engring Dept Civil Engring Atlanta GA 30332-0355

ELLIOTT, CINDY SUE, academic administrator; b. Ontario, Calif., Jan. 23, 1958; d. Harvey Charles and Mary Alice (Doherty) Wilkin. AS, Richland Community Coll., Dallas, 1982; BA in Psychology, U. Tex., Dallas, 1982, MA in Teaching, 1983. Cert. tchr., Tex. Teaching asst. The Willows Montessori Sch., Dallas, 1979-80; tchr. Richland Childrens Ctr., Richardson, Tex., 1981-82, Palisades Childrens Ctr., Plano, Tex., 1981-82; sec. student govt. U. Tex.-Dallas, Richardson, 1982, rsch. asst. tchr. edn., 1982-87, sec. admissions office, admissions asst., 1987, admissions counselor, 1987-93; instrnl. aide Victor Primary Sch., Victorville, Calif., 1993-96; tutor Sylvan Learning Ctr., Victorville, 1993-96, now dir. edn., ctr. dir., 1999—. Tchr. lang. arts Vista Compana Sch., Apple Valley, Calif., 1999—. Mem. AAUW, Assn. Metroplex Internat. Educators, Nat. Assn. Fgn. Student Affairs, North Tex. Coun. Coll. and Univ. Admissions Officers, Order Eastern Star. Republican. Christian Scientist. Avocations: tennis, reading, walking, ceramics.

ELLIOTT, EDWIN DONALD, JR., law educator, federal administrator, environmental lawyer; b. Chgo., Apr. 4, 1948; s. Edwin Donald and Mary Jane (Bope) E.; m. Geraldine Gennet (div. 1980); m. Mary Ellen Savage, Nov. 22, 1980 (div. 1999); children: Eve Christina, Ian Donald; m. Gail Charnley. BA, Yale U., 1970, JD, 1974. Bar: D.C. 1975, U.S. Dist. Ct. D.C. 1975, U.S. Ct. Appeals (2d cir.) 1982. Law clk. to judge U.S. Dist. Ct. D.C., Washington, 1974-75, U.S. Ct. Appeals, Washington, 1975-76; assoc. Leva, Hawes et al, Washington, 1976-80; assoc. prof. law Yale U., New Haven, 1981-84, prof. law, 1984-89, 91-92; asst. adminstr., gen. counsel U.S. EPA, Washington, 1989-91; Julien & Virginia Cornell chair environ. law and litigation Yale U., New Haven, 1992-94, adj. prof. law, 1994—; cons. Fried, Frank, Harris, Shriver & Jacobson, N.Y.C., Washington, 1991-93, ptnr., head of DC Environ. Practice Washington, 1993-96; ptnr. Paul, Hastings, Janofsky & Walker, Washington, 1996—, co-chair nat. environ. practice group. Adj. prof. law Georgetown U., Washington, 1997—; advisor Fed. Cts. Study Com., UN Environment Programme, 1993; cons. Asian Devel. Bank, 1994, Carnegie Com. Sci., Tech. and Govt., 1989-93, chair Role of Sci. and Risk Assessment; with Nat. Environ. Policy Inst., 1994—, Overseas Pvt. Investment Corp., Washington, 1983-85, Adminstrv. Conf. U.S., 1987-89, Aetna Ins. Co., 1987-89, G.D. Searle Co., 1988-89; spl. litigation counsel GE Co., Fairfield, Conn., 1985-89; gen. series editor Prentice Hall Environ. Series. Co-author: Sustainable Environmental Law, 1993; bd. advisors Environment Law Reporter; mem. editl. bd. Jour. Indsl. Ecology. Resources for the Future fellow, 1989. Mem. ABA (vice chmn. com. on separation of powers 1985-89, jud. rev. 1992—, environ. values 1993—, chair govt. policy liaison), Environ. Law Inst., Gruter Inst. for Law and Behavioral Rsch. (adv. bd. 1986—), Nat. Environ. Policy Inst. (chair sci. and risk assessment), Yale Club N.Y.C., New Haven Lawn Club. Republican. Presbyterian. Home: 826 A St SE Washington DC 20003-1340 also: 56 Beach Ave Milford CT 06460-8156 Office: Paul Hastings Janofsky & Walker 1299 Pennsylvania Ave NW Washington DC 20004-2400 also: Yale Law Sch PO Box 208215 New Haven CT 06520-8215 E-mail: edelliot@phjw.com.

ELLIOTT, EMERSON JOHN, education consultant, policy analyst; b. Ann Arbor, Mich., Nov. 13, 1933; s. Clarence Hyde and Ella Ruth (Kohl) E.; m. Joyce Ann Dodge, Aug. 19, 1956; children— Douglas, Stuart, Susan BA, Albion Coll., Mich., 1955; M.P.A., U. Mich., 1957. Chief edn. br. OMB, Washington, 1967-70, dep. chief human resources programs div., 1970-72; dep. dir. Nat. Inst. Edn., Washington, 1972-77; dir. ednl. staff seminar Inst. for Ednl. Leadership, Washington, 1977-79; dir. sch. fin. study U.S. Dept. Edn., Washington, 1979-81, dir. planning and evaluation, 1981-82, dir. issues analysis, 1982-84; head Nat. Ctr. for Edn. Stats., Washington, 1984-92; com. of edn. stats., 1992-95; dir. spl. projects Nat. Coun. Accreditation Tchr. Edn., Washington, 1995—. Recipient Disting. Alumnus award Albion Coll., 1975; Dirs. Superior Service award Nat. Inst. Edn., 1979; Presdl. Rank awards for Meritorious Service U.S. Govt., 1983, 91. Disting. Service U.S. Govt., 1987. Office: Nat Coun Accred Tchr Edn Ste 500 2010 Massachusetts Ave NW Washington DC 20036-1012

ELLIOTT, GORDON JEFFERSON, retired English language educator; b. Aberdeen, Wash., Nov. 13, 1928; s. Harry Cecil and Helga May (Kennedy) E.; m. Suzanne Tsugiko Urakawa, Apr. 2, 1957; children: Meiko Ann, Kenneth Gordon, Nancy Lee, Matthew Kennedy. AA, Grays Harbor Coll., 1948; BA, U. Wash., 1950; Cert. Russian, Army Lang. Sch., Monterey, Calif., 1952; MA, U. Hawaii, 1968. Lifetime credential, Calif. Community Coll. System. English prof. Buddhist U., Ministry of Cults, The Asia Found., Phnom Penh, Cambodia, 1956-62; English instr. U. Hawaii, Honolulu, 1962-68; dir., orientation English Coll. Petroleum and Minerals, Dhahran, Saudi Arabia, 1968-70; asst. prof., English/linguistics U. Guam, Mangilao, 1970-76; tchr., French/English Medford (Oreg.) Mid High Sch., 1976-77; instr., English Merced (Calif.) Coll., 1977-98, ret., 1998. Cons. on Buddhist Edn., The Asia Found., San Francisco, Phnom Penh, Cambodia, 1956-62; cons. on English Edn., Hawaii State Adult Edn. Dept., Honolulu, 1966-68; conf. on English Edn. in Middle East, Am. U., Cairo, Egypt, 1969; vis. prof. of English, Shandong Tchrs. U., Jinan, China, 1984-85. Co-author: (textbooks, bilingual Cambodian-English) English Composition, 1962, Writing English, 1966, (test) Standard English Recognition Test, 1976; contbr. articles to profl. jours. Mem. Statue of Liberty Centennial Commn., Washington, 1980-86, Heritage Found., Washington, Rep. Presdl. Task Force Founders' Wall, 2001, Lincoln Inst., Am. Near East Refugee Aid, Washington, Rep. Presdl. Task Force, 2001. Sgt. U.S. Army Security Agy., Kyoto, Japan, 1951-55. Tchr. Fellowship, U. Mich., Ann Arbor, 1956; recipient summer seminar stipend, Nat. Endowment For Humanities, U. Wash., Seattle, 1976, travel grants, People's Rep. of China, Beijing, 1984-85. Mem. NRA, Collegiate Press (editorial adv. bd.), Merced Coll. Found., Am. Assn. Woodturners, Elks. Republican. Avocations: swimming, woodturning, classical guitar, stamp/coin collecting, travel. Home: 680 Dennis Ct Merced CA 95340-2410 Office: Merced Coll 3600 M St Merced CA 95348-2806 E-mail: gjelliott@aol.com.

ELLIOTT, HAROLD MARSHALL, geography educator; b. Sebring, Fla., Jan. 4, 1943; s. Vernon G. and Elise Elliott; m. Anna J. Lang, Jan. 24, 1975; children: Dora Louise, Sarah Ariel; 1 child from previous marriage, Laura Diane. BA, San Francisco State U., 1964, MA, 1970; diploma, Infantry OCS, Ft. Benning, Ga., 1965; PhD, U. Okla., 1978. Ticket agt. United Airlines, San Francisco, 1961-64; instr. Coll. San Mateo, Calif., 1969, Cameron U., Lawton, Okla., 1970-72; security agt. Pinkerton's, Inc., Santa Monica, Calif., 1976-77; instr. Fla. Internat. U., Miami, 1977-78; from asst. prof. to assoc. prof. Weber State U., Ogden, Utah, 1979-88, prof., 1988—, chmn. dept. geography, 1994—, ethnic studies coord., 2000—. Cartographer Thomas Bros. Maps, L.A., 1977; asst. planner Coral Gables (Fla.) City Planning Dept., 1978. Assoc. editor: The Scottish-American Patriot, 1999—; contbr. articles to profl. jours. Del. Weber County Dem. Conv., 1980-83 (Geography Prof. of Yr. 1981, 82, Ogden Standard-Examiner "Apple for the Teacher" Teaching award 1992); pres. Utah Geog. Soc., 1993-2002; mem. Utah mil. and vets. affairs com. 1st lt. U.S. Army, 1964-67. Recipient Bronze Citizenship award SAR, 2000. Mem. ACLU, Assn. Am. Geographers, Am. Soc. Planning Ofcls., Assn. Pacific Coast Geographers, Am. Mensa, Am. Geog. Soc., Western Social Sci. Assn., Nat. Coun. for Geog. Edn., Fla. Soc. Geographers, Utah Acad. Arts and Scis., Internat. Geog. Union, Am. Legion (post comdr. 1997-98, post adj. 1999—), SAR (state bd. dirs. 1999—), Scottish-Am. Mil. Soc. (post adj. 1999—), Res. Officers Assn., Vietnam Vets. Am., Mil. Order World Wars, Order Crown of Charlemagne, Sons Union Vets., Okla. Acad. Scis., Burlingame H.S. Alumni Assn., Toastmasters Internat., Nat. Eagle Scout Assn., Am. Planning Assn., Audit Bur. Circulations, Utah Scottish Assn., United Empire Loyalists' Assn. Can., Geneal. Assn. Nova Scotia, First Families Mass., First Families Ohio, Order Fgn. Wars, Gamma Theta Upsilon, Alpha Phi Omega, Alpha Eta Rho. Office: Weber State U Geography Dept Ogden UT 84408

ELLIOTT, JOHN, accountant, educator, dean; b. Sacramento, Calif., Sept. 27, 1945; s. John William and Martha (Arnold) E.; children: Elizabeth Dawn, Jesse John. BS Econs. with high honors, U. Md., 1967, MBA, 1972; PhD Acctg., Cornell U., 1982. CPA, N.Y. Instr. acctg. U. Md., 1970-72; asst. prof. St. Lawrence U., 1972-76, Ctrl. Washington State Coll., 1976-77; vis. prof. U. Chgo., 1983, 88; prof. Johnson Sch. Cornell U., 1982—, assoc. dean, 1997—. Mem. Fin. Policies and Procedures Staff Westinghouse Electric, 1969-70; staff mem. Arthur Andersen & Co., 1967-69. Author (with C. Horngren, G. Sundem) Introduction to Financial Accounting; assoc. editor Contemporary Acctg. Rsch., 1996-97; edit. bd. The Acctg. Review, 1984-87, 89-92, Jour. Acctg. and Pub. Policy, 1983-85, Jour. Fin. Statement Analysis, 1995-98; contbr. articles to profl. jours. Trustee Hangar Theatre, Ithaca, N.Y., 1985-94, Cayuga Med., Ithaca, N.Y., 1992-2001. Mem. AICPA, Am. Acctg. Assn. Home: 220 Prospect Hill Rd Horseheads NY 14845-7979 Office: Johnson Grad Sch Mgmt Cornell U 346 Sage Hall Ithaca NY 14853-6201

ELLIOTT, MARION LOUISE DICK, arts education and management consultant; b. Flagstaff, Ariz., June 24, 1930; d. Joseph B. and Helen M. (Brozovich) Dick; m. Harold L. Elliott, Apr. 19, 1952; children: Diana M., Linda J. BS in Edn., No. Ariz. U., Flagstaff, 1951, MA in Art Edn., 1957; postgrad., Ariz. State U., U. Copenhagen, Denmark. Supr. art Flagstaff Sch. Dist., 1951-52; chair dept. art Mohave County Union H.S., Kingman, Ariz., 1952-54; dir. art dept. Yuma (Ariz.) Sch. Dist. One, 1955-85; cons. arts edn. and mgmt. Yuma, 1985—. Art edn. curriculum devel. Ariz. State Dept. Edn., Phoenix, 1955-90; cons. art acquisition Yuma (Ariz.) Regional Med. Found., 1985-90; governing bd. Ariz. Commn. on the Arts, Phoenix, 1987-93, Arizonans for Cultural Devel., 1993-98. Contbr. articles to profl. jours. Chair Parents Are Tchrs., Too, Yuma County, 1985-90, Image of Yuma art collection City of Yuma, 1986-87; v.p. Found. No. Ariz. U., Flagstaff, 1980—, pres., 1996-2000; bd. dirs. Ariz. Humanities Coun., 1999—. Recipient Gov.'s Art award Ariz. Commn. on Arts, 1991, Alumni Achievement award No. Ariz. U., 1979, Centennial award, 1997, others; named to Hall of Fame, Yuma County Edn. Found., 1995. Mem. Nat. Art Edn. Assn. (M.Q. Dix Leadership award 1984), Ariz. Art Edn. Assn., Ariz. Hist. Soc., Phi Kappa Phi, Delta Phi Kappa.

ELLIOTT, RICHARD L. school administrator; b. Colorado Springs, Colo., Apr. 6, 1943; s. Harry Raymond Elliott and Georgia Louise (McCarty) Coston; m. Erlene Frances Oxtoby, June 11, 1977; children: Shane Maurice, Tiffany Louise. BA, No. Colo. U., 1966; MEd, Ea. N.Mex. U., 1986. Cert. tchr., adminstr., N.Mex., Colo. Tchr., football coach St. Mary's High Sch., Colorado Springs, 1967-69, Palmer High Sch., Colorado Springs, 1969-73, Mitchell High Sch., Colorado Springs, 1973-76, Fruita Monument High Sch., Grand Junction, Colo., 1976-77; custom home builder Bump Elliott Constrn., Colorado Springs, 1977-80; tchr., football coach Air Acad. High Sch., Colorado Springs, 1980-81; asst. athletic dir., football coach N.Mex. Mil. Inst., Roswell, 1981-88; athletic dir. Las Cruces (N.Mex.) Pub. Schs., 1988—. Bd. dirs. Bantam Weight Youth Sports Assn., Las Cruces, 1989—, United Way Dona Ana County, Las Cruces, 1990—, March of Dimes, Las Cruces, 1994—. Named Region 8 Athletic Dir. of Yr., Nat. High Sch. Athletic Coaches Assn., 1992. Mem. AAHPERD, N.Mex. Athletic Dirs. Assn. (pres. 1990-91), Nat. Fedn. Interscholastic Coaches, Nat. Interscholastic Athletic Adminstrs., Nat. Coun. Secondary Schs. Athletic Dirs. (Western Regional Athletic Dir. of Yr. 1992), N.Mex. H.S. Coaches Assn. (Athletic Dir. of Yr. 1990), N.Mex. Activities Assn. (exec. com. 1989—, Adult Sportsman of Yr. 1990), K.C., Lions, Elks. Roman Catholic. Home: 797 Frank Maes Ave Las Cruces NM 88005-1230 Office: Las Cruces Pub Schs Loretto Towne Ctr 505 S Main St Las Cruces NM 88001-1245

ELLIOTT, SALLY ANN, special education educator; b. Wichita, Kans., Aug. 6, 1941; m. Robert Wayne Elliott, June 1, 1963; children: Thomas Robert, Matthew Wayne. BA in Elem. Edn., Wichita State U., 1963; MS in Spl. Edn., Kans. State U., 1979. Cert. tchr., Ala. Tchr. 3rd grade Price Elem. Sch., Wichita, 1963-65, 4th grade tchr. McLean Elem. Sch., 1966-67; primary tchr. gifted, talented and creative edn. Wichita, 1977-81; tchr. spl. programs for acad. and creative excellence Blossomwood Elem. Sch., Huntsville, Ala., 1981—, coord. staff devel., 1988—. Mem. task force Ala. Spl. Edn. Dept., Montgomery, 1990-92. Mem. choir 1st Meth. Ch., Huntsville, 1992; supr. Sunday sch. Huntsville Evang. Free Ch., 1988-91. Mem. Huntsville Edn. Assn. (rep. 1987-89, 92-93, bd. dirs. 1988-90), Delta Kappa Gamma (sec. 1986-88, v.p. 1988-92). Democrat. Avocations: cross country skiing, walking, baking, wild flowers, gardening. Home: 806 Lenlock Dr SE Huntsville AL 35802-1928 Office: Blossomwood Elem Sch 1321 Woodmont Ave SE Huntsville AL 35801-2699

ELLIOTT, THOMAS MICHAEL, retired association executive, educator, consultant; b. Evansville, Ind., Aug. 4, 1942; s. Thomas Ira and Pauline (Dawson) E.; m. Susan M. Spiers, July 8, 1967 (div. Aug. 1975); 1 son, Christopher Michael; m. Loretta S. Glaze, Jan. 28, 1976. AB in Zoology, Ind. U., 1965, MS in Higher Edn., 1967, EdD, 1970. Asst. to pres. Purdue U., West Lafayette, Ind., 1972-73, asst. provost, 1973-74; exec. dir. Nat. Commn. United Meth. Higher Edn., Nashville, 1974-77; ptnr. Planning Mgmt. Services Group, Washington, 1976-82; dep. commr. Mo. Dept. Higher Edn., Jefferson City, 1977-79; exec. dir. Ark. Dept. Higher Edn., Little Rock, 1979-82; exec. dir., CEO IEEE Computer Soc., Washington, 1982-2000; ret., 2001—. Cons. numerous colls. and univs. Author: Computer Simulation System, 1975; contbr. articles to profl. jours. Bd. dirs., mem. exec. com. So. Regional Edn. Bd., Atlanta, 1980-82; mem. Cabinet of Gov. Bill Clinton and Gov. Frank White, State of Ark., 1979-82. Mem. IEEE (sr.), IEEE Computer Soc., State Higher Edn. Exec. Officers Assn., Am. Soc. Assn. Execs., Am. Mgmt. Assn., Assn. Computing Machinery. Home: 1735 Q St NW Washington DC 20009-2407

ELLIOTT, WILLIE LAWRENCE, education educator, department chairman; b. Cin., July 18, 1948; s. Harry and Mary (O'Neal) E.; m. Deloris Ragsdale, June 15, 1979; children: Wymanette, Willye, Courtney. BA in History, Ky. State U., 1971; MSW, U. Ky., 1973; D Ministry in Counseling, Ashland (Ohio) Theol. Sem., 1989. Lic. ind. social worker; diplomate clin. social work. Asst. prof. Ky. State U., Frankfort, 1974-79; mental health counselor Seven Counties Svcs., Louisville, 1979-81; program dir. Ashland U., 1981-86; v.p. Day-Mont West, Dayton, Ohio, 1986-89; assoc. prof. edn., chmn. dept. No. Ky. U., Highland Heights, 1989—. Mem. Acad. Cert. Social Workers.

ELLIS, CYNTHIA BUEKER, musician, educator; b. Santa Monica, Calif., Dec. 3, 1958; d. Robert Arthur and Patricia June Bueker; m. Tony Lyle Ellis, June 18, 1983. B Music, Calif. State U., 1981, M Music, 1983. 2nd flutist Pasadena (Calif.) Chamber Orch., 1981—84; piccoloist Pacific Symphony Orch., Santa Ana, Calif., 1979—; prin. flutist Opera Pacific Orch., Costa Mesa, Calif., 1995—; lectr. Calif. State U., Fullerton, 1985—; applied flute instr. Pomona Coll., Claremont, Calif., 1990—92. Adj. faculty Claremont Grad. Sch., 1996—97; mem. faculty Pacific Symphony Inst., 1993—; flute instr. Pomona Coll., 1990—92. Contbr. articles to profl. jours.; musician: (songs) (for motion pictures) Twilight, 1998, Kissing a Fool, 1998, Pentagon Wars, 1998, She's So Lovely, 1997, First Time Felon, 1997, Campfire Tales, 1996, Breaking Commandments, 1996, Baby's Day Out, 1994, Pochahontas, 1994, Stayed Tuned, 1992, Wind, 1992; numerous others. Family coord. Southern Calif. Labrador Retriever Rescue, 1999—. Mem.: Music Tchrs. Assn. Calif., Nat. Flute Assn. (chamber music competition 1st place award 2000), Mu Phi Epsilon, Phi Kappa Phi, Pi Kappa Lambda. Republican. Methodist. Avocations: fitness, cooking. Home: 1192 Beechwood Dr Brea CA 92821

ELLIS, DONNA LITTON, special education educator; b. Blackwell, Okla., Dec. 23, 1956; d. Keith Gerald and Marcille June (Brown) Litton; m. Denny Ray Ellis Jr., Oct. 24, 1981; 1 child, Ward James. BS in All-Leval Music and Voice, Tex. Woman's U., 1978; cert. in early childhood handicapped, East Tex. State U., 1984. Music and reading tchr. Friendswood (Tex.) Ind. Sch. Dist., 1978-79; music, reading and English tchr. Mansfield (Tex.) Ind. Sch. Dist., 1979-81; sec. III Hunters Engrs., Dallas, 1981-82; 6th grade music tchr. Forney (Tex.) Ind. Sch. Dist., 1982-84, 1st grade tchr., 1985-86, tchr. early childhood-handicapped, 1988—, Royce City (Tex.) Ind. Sch. Dist., 1984-85; 5th and 6th grade music tchr. Kaufman (Tex.) Ind. Sch. Dist., 1986-87, tchr. early childhood-handicapped, 1987-88. Vol. Forney Beautification Program, 1986-88, Kaufman County Rep. Party, 1988, 92, local sch. bd. and city coun. elections, Forney, 1988—. Mem. Nat. Assn. Tchrs. of Singing, Tchrs. of Music Edn. Assn., Tex. Choral Dirs. Assn., Music Educators Nat. Conf., Music Tchrs. Nat. Conf., Early Childhood Inst. Republican. Baptist. Avocations: music, bike riding, walking, horseback riding, tennis. Home: 502 Redbud Dr Forney TX 75126-9653

ELLIS, DORSEY DANIEL, JR., lawyer, educator; b. Cape Girardeau, Mo., May 18, 1938; s. Dorsey D. and Anne (Stanaland) E.; m. Sondra Wagner, Dec. 27, 1962; children: Laura Elizabeth, Geoffrey Earl. BA, Maryville Coll., 1960; JD, U. Chgo., 1963; LLD, Maryville Coll., 1998. Bar: N.Y. 1967, U.S. Ct. Appeals (2d cir.) 1967, Iowa 1976, U.S. Ct. Appeals (8th cir.) 1976. Assoc. Cravath, Swaine & Moore, N.Y.C., 1963-68; assoc. prof. U. Iowa, Iowa City, 1968-71, prof., 1971-87, v.p. fin. and univ. svcs., 1984-87, spl. asst. to pres., 1974-75; dean Washington U. Sch. Law, St. Louis, Mo., 1987-98, prof. law, 1998-99; disting. prof. law, 1999—. Vis. mem. sr. common room Mansfield Coll., Oxford U., Eng., 1972-73, 75; vis. prof. law Emory U., Atlanta, 1981-82, Victoria U., New Zealand, 1999; vis. sr. rsch. fellow Jesus Coll. Oxford U., Eng., 1998; bd. dirs. Maryville Coll., 1989-98, 99—, vis. scholar U. Va., 2003. Contbr. articles to profl. jours. Trustee Mo. Hist. Soc., St. Louis, 1995-2000. Nat. Honor scholar U. Chgo., 1960-63; recipient Joseph Henry Beale prize, 1961, Alumni award Maryville Coll., 1988. Mem. ABA, Am. Law Inst., Bar Assn. Metro St. Louis, Mound City Bar Assn., Iowa Bar Assn., AALS Acad. Resource Corps., Order of Coif. Home: 6901 Kingsbury Blvd Saint Louis MO 63130 Office: Box 1120 1 Brookings Dr Saint Louis MO 63130-4862 E-mail: ellis@wulaw.wustl.edu.

ELLIS, KATHERINE ANN, school administrator; b. Mich., Nov. 3, 1955; d. Raymond Joseph Sr. and Dorothy May Florian; m. Mark Ellis, Aug. 9, 1985. BA, Ea. Mich. U., Ypsilanti, 1978, M Interdisciplinary Tech., 1983; Doctorate Candidate, U. Mich., 1986—. Jr. high art/sci. tchr. Lincoln Consol. Schs., Ypsilanti, 1978-91, jr. high asst. prin., 1991-93, elem. asst. prin., 1993-95, talent devel. dir., 1993—. Dist. testing coord. Lincoln Consol. Schs., Ypsilanti, 1994-95, new tchr. profl. devel. coord., 1994-95, at risk/drug free coord., 1994-95, profl. devel. for dist. wide staff, grants dist. test coord., 1989-95. Active Audubon Soc., Detroit Zool. Soc. U. Mich. fellow, Ann Arbor, 1986-87; named Disting. Adminstr. of yr. Coun. for Black Student Achievement, Belleville, Mich., 1993; recipient Achievement award United Students Orgn., Ypsilanti, 1993. Mem. AAUW, Curriculum, Supervision and Instrn., Assn. Childhood Edn., Mid. and Elem. Sch. Prins. Assn., Nat. Assn. Gifted Children, Detroit Inst. Arts, Phi Delta Kappa. Democrat. Avocations: golf, art. Office: Lincoln Consol Schs 8970 Whittaker Rd Ypsilanti MI 48197-9440

ELLIS, MAXINE ETHEL, social services administrator, educator; b. Kansas City, Apr. 2, 1941; d. Charles Boyd and Ethel Freda (Zeebe) Armstrong; m. Herbert Joseph Ellis, June 15, 1974; children: Carine Elizabeth, Alina Suzanne. BA in Biology, William Jewell Coll., Liberty, Mo., 1963; MS in Biology, Kans. State Coll., Emporia, Kans., 1967; AS, Moraine Parktech Coll., West Bend, Wis., 1982; postgrad., U. Mo., 1968-73. Cert. tchr. Kans., Wis. Sci. tchr. Indian Hills Jr. High, Prarie Village, Kans., 1963-69; Bio. tchr. Shawnee Mission East High Sch., Prairie Village, 1969-74; bus. mgr. Hartford (Wis.) Com. Day Care, Inc., 1978-83; workshop writer CESA Local Watershed Problems, Madison, Wis., 1979-81; substitute tchr. Hartford/West Bend (Wis.) Schs., 1974-83; econ. asst. worker Washington Co. Dept. of Soc. Svcs., West Bend, Wis., 1983—. Writer and presentor, Curriculum Guide, Local Watershed Problems Study Guide, 1981; Contbr.: book, Wis. Women: A Gifted Heritage, 1982. Curriculum Com. & Vol., Lac Lawrann Conservacy, West Bend, Wis., 1987—; mem. Riveredge Nature Club, Newburg, Wis., 1976—. Named Top 5 Finalist, Star Student Award, Moraine Park Tech. Coll., West Bend, 1982. Mem. Am. Assn. of U. Women (treas. 1989-91), Am. Fedn. of State, County & Mcpl. Workers (treas. 1985-89), Nat. Sci. Tchrs. Assn. (life mem.). United Ch. of Christ. Avocations: environ. activities. Home: 5818 Wildlife Dr Allenton WI 53002-9521

ELLIS, NANCY KEMPTON, adult education educator; b. Chgo., Nov. 3, 1943; d. Robert Lawrence and Mildred Elizabeth (Kitcher) Kempton; m. William Grenville Ellis, Dec. 30, 1963; children: William Grenville Jr., Bradford Graham. AA, Endicott Coll., 1963; BA, Castleton State Coll., 1970; MA, Marian Coll., 1989. Tutor remedial reading Waterville (Maine) Pub. Schs., 1975-79, migrant tutor, 1980, tchr. 1st grade, 1980-81; tchr. 4th grade Vassalboro (Maine) Pub. Schs., 1981-82; dir. study skills Wayland Acad., Beaver Dam, Wis., 1983-89, chair ednl. support, 1989-91, dir. spl. programs, 1993-95, co-pres., 1982-95. Chair Wis. Ind. Sch. Educators, 1985-89, conf. co-chair, 1988; active Wis. Fellowship of Poets, 1993-95; wildlife presenter Beaver Dam Pub. Schs., 1994-95; adj. faculty Grad. Sch., Concordia U. Wis., Mequon, 1997—; presenter in field. Editor Marshland Monarch, 1984-88, Spouse News. Bd. dirs., festival dir. Beaver Dam Arts Assn., 1990-93; bd. dirs. AAUW Beaver Dam, 1992-95; coord. Beaver Dam Cmty. Forum on Health Care. Avocations: wildlife rehab. & mgmt., walking, bread baking, personal poetry. Office: 8655 N Regent Rd Fox Point WI 53217-2362

ELLIS, BROTHER PATRICK (H. J. ELLIS), academic administrator; b. Balt., Nov. 17, 1928; s. Harry James and Elizabeth Alida (Evert) E. AB, Cath. U. Am., Washington, 1951; AM, U. Pa., 1954, PhD, 1960; postgrad., Barry Coll., 1963-64, Inst. Catholique, Paris, 1958; LHD (hon.), Assumption Coll., 1982, La Salle U., 1992; HHD (hon.), King's Coll., 1987; LLD (hon.), U. Scranton, 1988, C.C. Phila., 1992, Quincy U., 1993; PdD, Manhattan Coll., 1993; DEd, Anna Maria Coll., 1993, Loyola U., 1997; LHD (hon.), Villa Julie Coll., 2002. Joined Bros. of Christian Schs., Roman Cath. Ch., 1946. Tchr. English dept. West Cath. High Sch. for Boys, Phila., 1951-60, chmn. English dept., 1956-58, guidance dir., 1959-60; dir. practice teaching, sch. prin. St. Gabriel's Hall, Phoenixville, Pa., summers 1960-61, 65-66; asst. prof. English La Salle U., Phila., 1960-62, assoc. prof., 1968-73, prof., 1973—, dir. housing, 1961-62, dir. honors program, 1964-69, dir. devel., v.p., 1969-76, pres., 1977-92; prin. La Salle HS, Miami, Fla., 1962—64; pres. Cath. U. Am., Washington, 1992-98. Author: Called To Teach: Persons Are Forever, 2001; condr.: series for How To Read Gt. Books, U. of the Air, WFIL-TV, Phila., 1961, 65; Contbr. articles to profl. publs. Trustee Manhattan Coll., N.Y.C., Calvert Hall H.S., Balt., to 2001; bd. dirs. Phila. Cath. Charities, 1986-92, Greater Phila. Urban Coalition, Police Athletic League, Phila., Free Libr. Phila., 1991-92, Del. Valley Citizens Crime Commn., Fed. City Coun., D.C. Econ. Club, D.C. Bd. Trade; former trustee Cmty. Leadership Seminars, BBB; mem. recognition com. Coun. for Higher Edn. Accreditation, 1999-2001. Recipient Lindback award for disting. teaching LaSalle Coll., Phila., 1965 Mem. Sunday Breakfast Club (Phila.), Phila. Club, Univ. Club (Washington), Phi Beta Kappa, Knights of Holy Sepulchre. Home and Office: Calvert Hall HS 8102 La Salle Rd Baltimore MD 21286-8022 E-mail: brotherpatrickellis@erols.com.

ELLIS, SYLVIA D. HALL, development and library education consultant; b. Kewanee, Ill., June 21, 1949; d. Martin Orrill and Elizabeth Jean (Boase) Dunn; m. J. Theodore Ellis, Dec. 24, 1990. BA, Rockford Coll., 1971; MLS, U. N. Tex., 1972; MA, U. Tex., San Antonio, 1975; PhD, U. Pitts., 1985. Libr. Holding Inst., Laredo, Tex., 1972-73; dist. coord. San Antonio Pub. Librs., 1973-76; divsn. libr. Corpus Christi Pub. Librs., Tex., 1976-78; asst. dir. So. Tier Libr. System, Corning, N.Y., 1978-81; devel. officer Pitts. Regional Libr. Ctr., 1981-85; dir. librs. Rocky Mountain Coll. of Art and Design, Denver, 1992-93; asst. prof. Sam Houston State U., Huntsville, Tex., 1993-96; devel. officer Region 1 Edn. Svc. Ctr., Edinburg, Tex., 1995-97; dir devel. Mid-Continent Regional Ednl. Lab., Aurora, Colo., 1997-98; mng. ptnr. 886, Inc., 1998—. Dir. Tech. Prep of Rio Grande Valley, Inc., Harlingen, Tex., 1995—; cons. States of Colo., Mont., Iowa, S.D., Tex., Pa., 1981—; prof. U. Denver, 2000—, Emporia (Kans.) State U., 2000—, San Jose State U., 2002—. Author: Grant Writing for Small Libraries and School Library Media Centers, 1999, Grants for School Libraries, 2003; contbr. articles to profl. jours. Democrat. Episcopalian. Mailing: PO Box 61048 Denver CO 80206-1048 Office: 2135 E Wesley Ave Ste 107 Denver CO 80208-4709 E-mail: shellis@bigplanet.com.

ELLIS, VIRGINIA LYNN, gerontology services educator; b. Logan, W.Va., July 28, 1950; d. Ronald Lee and Betty Ann (Claypool) Cook; m. John Michael Knowles, July 31, 1971 (div. Jan. 1997); children: Jennifer Lee Knowles Lewis, Jason Edward Knowles; m. W. Dale Ellis, July 28, 2000. BSN, W.Va. U., 1972. Coord. health occupations Wyo. County Vocat.-Tech. Ctr., Pineville, W.Va., 1974—78; quality assurance coord. Glenwood Park Retirement Village., Princeton, W.Va., 1979-99; DON Royalcare of Pigeon Forge (Tenn.), 2000; Medicare/MDS coord. Mariner Health of Newport, Tenn., 2000—01, Bryan Ctr., Weaverville, NC, 2002—03; regional care mgmt. coord. Mariner Health Care, 2002—03, billing auditor, 2003—. Chmn. vocat. nursing skill competition W.Va. State, 1988; condr. statewide workshops on electronic data submission Health Care Fin. Assn., 1998; Beta-tested computer med. records program for long-term care, 98. Author (first state-approved curriculum): Sch. Practical Nursing. Mem.: Am. Assn. Nurse Assessment Coords. (charter). Home: 105 N Ridge Dr #C Asheville NC 28804-9017 E-mail: ginnyk_37821@yahoo.com.

ELLIS, VOLEEN, education educator, researcher; b. N.Y.C., June 15, 1938; d. Eileen Fanning and Robert Niles; m. Richard Ellis, Oct. 27, 1975. BA, Rutgers U., 1971; MA, Calif. State U., 1992. Cons. Meriks Industries, Denver, 1990—. Office: Meriks Industries 2940 E Colfax Ave #515 Denver CO 80206-1607

ELLIS, WAYNE ENOCH, nursing educator, retired air force officer; b. Reno, Jan. 24, 1945; s. Willard Edward and Thelma Miriam (Patterson) Ellis; m. Robin Marie Mumme, Dec. 25, 1987; children: Wayne II, Sharon, Terri Lynn, Michael W., Melissa D., Rebekah J. Stube, Christopher H. Stube, Marina Noel, Peter E., Yuri Charles, Tatiana Elena, Daniel Albert. Diploma, L.S. Kaufmann Sch. Nursing, 1965; BS, Chapman U., 1982, MS, 1984; PhD in Edn., Tex. A&M U., 1990; DD, St. George's Sch. Theology, Oxford U., 1999; MSN, Canyon Coll., 2003. Commd. 2nd lt. U.S. Army, 1966; trans. U.S. Air Force, 1980, advanced through grades to col., 1992, ret., 1995; asst. operating room supr., instr. regional ctr. U.S. Army, Ft. Bragg, NC, 1987, dir. inhalation therapy regional ctr. Ft. Benning, Ga., 1970—72; chief anesthesia U.S. Air Force Hosp. U.S. Air Force, Edwards AFB, Calif., 1980—83, asst. edn. dir. sch. anesthesia Wilford Hall Med. Ctr. Lackland AFB, Tex., 1983—86, liaison officer Inst. Tech. Wright Patterson AFB, Ohio, 1986—89; instr., coord. paramedical programs Cochise Coll., Sierra Vista, Ariz., 1975—79; pvt. practice Ellis Enterprises, Sierra Vista, 1972—79; chief nurse anesthetist Hobart (Ind.) Anesthesia Assocs., 1979—80; clin. dir. anesthesia program U. Tex. Health Sci. Ctr. Sch. Nursing, San Antonio, 1989—93; advanced through grades to col. U. Tex. Health Sci. Ctr., San Antonio, 1993—95, program dir., facilitator Sch. Nursing/USAF nurse anesthesia, 1990—93; dir. nurse anesthesia clin. tng. USAF David Grant Med. Ctr., Travis AFB, Calif., 1990—93; program dir., facilitator UTHSCSASN/USAF Nurse Anesthesia Major, 1993—95; asst. prof., dir. anesthesia nursing program U. Iowa Coll. Nursing, Iowa City, 1995—97, 1995—97; program coord., asst. prof., dir. grad. nursing program So. Ill. U. Sch. Nursing, Edwardsville, 1997—2003; dir. Trover Found./Murray State U. program in anesthesia, assoc. prof. dept. nursing Murray State U., Madisonville, Ky., 2003—. Chief cons. to USAF surgeon gen., 1992—94; cons., program coord. N.W. Anesthesia Seminars, Pasco, Wash., 1983—; bishop Anglican Diocese of the S.W., Anglican Ch. Author tng. manual for respiratory therapy, emergency medicine; contbg. author Nurse Anesthesia Practice; contbr. articles to profl. jours. Decorated Legion of Merit; Cross of Gallantry with Palms (Vietnam). Mem.: Ill. Nurses Assn., Ill. League of Nursing, Ill. Assn. Nurse Anesthetists, Am. Assn. Adult and Continuing Edn., Am. Assn. Nurse Anesthetists. Republican. Anglican. Avocation: computers. Office: 435 N Kentucky St Ste A Madisonville KY 42431

ELLIS, WILLIAM GENE, neuropathologist; b. Cin., June 12, 1932; s. Richard Karl and Lucile E.; m. Arlene Lois Kaslow, June 12, 1960; children: David Karl, Heidi Beth. BA, Iowa Weslyan Coll., 1953; MD, U. Iowa, 1957. Diplomate Am. Bd. of Neurology, 1965, Am. Bd. of Neuropathology, 1976. Staff neurologist Hines (Ill.) VA Hosp., 1965-66; asst. neuropathologist Langley Porter Neuropsychiat. Inst., San Francisco, 1966-72; prof. U. Calif., Davis, 1972—; dir. neuropath. Cons. Napa (Calif.) State Hosp, Sonoma Devel. Ctr., Eldridge, Calif. Contbr. articles to profl. jours. Capt. U.S. Army, 1961-63. Fellow Am. Acad. Neurology; mem. Am. Assn. Neuropathologists, Royal Soc. Med., U.S. and Can. Acad. Pathology. Office: UC Davis Med Ctr Dept Pathology 2315 Stockton Blvd Sacramento CA 95817

ELLIS, WILLIAM GRENVILLE, academic administrator, management consultant; b. Teaneck, N.J., Nov. 29, 1940; s. Grenville Brigham and Vivian Lilian (Breeze) E.; m. Nancy Elizabeth Kempton, 1963; children: William Grenville, Bradford Graham. BS in Bus. Adminstrn., Babson Coll., 1962; MBA, Suffolk U., 1963; MEd, Westfield State Coll., 1965; EdD, Pa. State U., 1968; MS, Concordia U., 1991; MLE (Sears Roebuck Found. scholar), Harvard U., 1980; postgrad., U. Chgo., 1983, MIT, 1984, Harvard U., 1988, 96. Asst. prof. bus. Rider U., 1968-69; div. dir., assoc. prof. Castleton (Vt.) State Coll., 1969-72; exec. v.p., prof. St. Joseph Coll. in Vt., Rutland, 1972-73; acad. v.p., dean grad. sch. Thomas Coll., Waterville, Maine, 1973-82; pres. Wayland Acad., Beaver Dam, Wis., 1982-95, New Eng. Coll., Henniker, N.H., 1995-97; dean Sch. Bus. and Legal Studies, Concordia U. Wis., Mequon, 1997—. Mem. adv. bd. CFX Bank, 1996-97; corporator 1st Consumers Savs., 1974-81, Maine Savs., 1981-82. Author: The Analysis and Attainment of Economic Stability, 1963, The Relationship of Related Work Experience to the Teaching Success of Beginning Business Teachers, 1968, Marketing for Educational Administrators, 1991, A Gunner's Moon, 1997; contbr. numerous articles and abstracts to profl. jours. Trustee C.C. Vt., 1972-73, Marian Coll., 1988-91, Wayland Acad., 1982-95, New Eng. Coll., 1995-97; auditor Town of Castleton, 1969-71; pres. Kennebee Valley Youth Hockey, Augusta, Maine, 1975-77; pres. Beaver Dam C. of C., 1985, 86, Midwest Classic Athletic Conf., 1989, Wis. Assn. Ind. Schs., 1984-86; chair bd. dirs. Beaver Dam Cmty. Hosp., 1985-95; dir. North Ctrl. Assn. Colls. and Secondary Schs., 1991-94, Ind. Schs. Ctrl. States, 1991-95; dir. N.H. Coll. and Univ. Coun., 1995-97; dir. Ozaukee County Indsl. Devel. Corp., 2003—. Recipient Cmty., Svc. award Rutland C. of C., 1973, Disting. Svc. citation Wayland Acad., 1995, Excellence in Edn. award Pa. State U., 2001; named Cons. of Yr., SBA, 1975, 77, Prof. of Yr. Concordia U. Wis., 1999. Mem. APA, Nat. Assn. Intercollegiate Athletics (cert. of merit 1979), Soc. for Advancement of Mgmt., Cum Laude Soc., Pheasant City Club, Rotary, Alpha Chi, Pi Omega Pi, Alpha Delta Sigma, Delta Pi Epsilon, Phi Delta Kappa. Home: 8655 N Regent Rd Fox Point WI 53217-2362 Office: Concordia U Sch Bus & Legal Studies 12800 N Lake Shore Dr Mequon WI 53097-2418 E-mail: william.ellis@cuw.edu.

ELLISON, BETTY D. retired elementary educator; b. Meriwether County, Ga., Jan. 28, 1950; d. Haywood Sr. and Mary Susan (Green) Daniel; m. Darthus Ellison, Jr., June 25, 1972; children: Darthus III, Keith Brandon. BA, Morris Brown Coll., 1972; MA, Atlanta U., 1975. Cert. tchr. Tchr. Meriwether County Bd. Edn., Greenville, Ga.; reading specialist Talbot County Bd. Edn., Talbotton, Ga. Advisor Nat. Jr. Honor Soc.; owner, operator Ellison's Tutorial Svc. Ga. State Tchrs. scholar; named County Star Tchr., 1991. Mem. NEA, Internat. Reading Assn., Ga. Assn. Educators, Zeta Phi Beta, Pi Delta Phi. Home: 88 Johnson Ave Manchester GA 31816-1602

ELLISON, DAVID CHARLES, special education educator; b. Agana, Guam, Apr. 20, 1957; s. Leo Charles and Joan Ruby (Hendrickson) E.; m. Teresa Josephine Vos, Dec. 20, 1980; children: Johanna Marie, Matthew David. BAA in Social Sci., U. Minn., Duluth, 1980. Tchr. spl. edn. ISD #94, Cloquet, Minn., 1981—; spl. edn. adminstr. ISD # 94, Cloquet, Minn., summers 1991-99. Head coach Cloquet Lumberjacks Spl. Olympics, 1981—; girls varsity hockey asst. coach Cloquet Lumberjacks. Recipient Transition Excellence award Dept. Children, Families and Learning in Minn., 1997. Democrat. Roman Catholic. Avocations: fishing, camping, hunting, family outings. Home: 705 Jasper St Cloquet MN 55720-1212 Office: ISD # 94 Cloquet Sr H S 1000 18th St Cloquet MN 55720-2438

ELLISON, JAMES MORTON, secondary education educator; b. Rocky Mount, N.C., May 26, 1945; s. William Lee and Sallie (Boddie) E. BS, Fla. A&M U., 1968; MEd, Wayne State U., 1980, Ednl. Specialist, 1992. Cert. tchr., Fla., Mich. Tchr. Detroit Bd. Edn., 1967—; dir. of bands Murray Wright High Sch., Detroit, 1981—. Counselor Detroit Police Jr. Cadets, 1987—. Mem. Wayne State U. Coll. Edn. Alumni Assn. (1st v.p. 1992-93, pres. 1993-94), Detroit Renaissance Lions Club (chair all-state band 1992—), Phi Delta Kappa, Pi Lambda Theta. Avocations: jogging, swimming, tennis, trumpet, reading. Home: 8817 Pembroke Ave Detroit MI 48221-1126 Office: Detroit Bd Edn 5057 Woodward Ave Detroit MI 48202-4050

ELLIS-SCRUGGS, JAN, theater arts educator; b. Phila., Apr. 7, 1951; d. Roger C. and Greta M. Ellis; m. William Marquis Scruggs, Aug. 8, 1970; children: William Marcus Jr., Christopher Michael. BA, Cheyney U., 1987; MA, Villanova U., 1991. Lectr., instr. U. Conn., Storrs, 1989-90; theatre arts instr. Delaware County C.C., Media, Pa., 1994-95; asst. prof. theatre arts Cheyney (Pa.) U., 1993-94, 97—; actor, singer, dir., theater educator, adminstr. U.S. and London. Assoc. prodr., Citeaux, Inc., London, 1979-83; dir. Cheyney U., 1997—. Mem. editl. adv. bd., Collegiate Press, San Diego, 1999—. Missionary, Mother Bethel African Meth. Episc. Ch., Phila., 1994—. Mem. AFTRA, SAG (Screen Actors Guild), Actors Equity Assn., Alpha Psi Omega. Home: 7942 Cedarbrook Ave Philadelphia PA 19150 Office: Cheyney U of Pa Marian Anderson Music Ctr Cheyney PA 19319 E-mail: jebs267@aol.com.

ELLIS-VANT, KAREN MCGEE, elementary and special education educator, consultant; b. La Grande, Oreg., May 10, 1950; d. Ellis Eddington and Gladys Vera McGee; m. Lynn F. Ellis, June 14, 1975 (div. Sept. 1983); children: Megan Marie, Matthew David; m. Jack Scott Vant, Sept. 6, 1986; children: Kathleen Erin, Kelli Christine (dec.). BA in Elem. Edn., Boise State U., 1972, MA in Spl. Edn., 1979; postgrad. studies in curriculum/instrn., U. Minn., 1985-86. Tchr. learning disabilities resource rm. New Plymouth Joint Sch. Dist., 1972-73, Payette Joint Sch. Dist., 1973; diagnostician project SELECT, 1974-75; cons. tchr. in spl. edn. Boise Sch. Dist., 1975-90, tchr. 1-2 combination, 1990-91, team tchr. 1st grade, 1991-92, 95—, site based leadership team, 1997-99. Chpt. 1 program cons., 1992-95, mem. Idaho Mgmt. Change Project, 1997-99, Learning for the 21st Century project, 1999—; mem. profl. Stds. Commn., 1983-86. Contbr. articles to profl. jours.; editor, author ednl. texts and comminique; conductor of workshops, leadership tng. coop. learning and frameworks. Bd. dirs. Hotline, Inc., 1979-82; mem. Idaho Coop. Manpower Com., 1984-85; mem. First United Meth. Ch., childcare bd., 1998-2000, mem. diversity com., 2001-02, mem. leadership team Many Hands One Spirit, 2002—03; bd. dirs. Idaho Coun. for History Edn., 2001—02, FUMC, 2002. Recipient Disting. Young Woman of Yr. award Boise Jaycettes, 1982, Idaho Jaycettes, 1983; Coffman Alumni scholar U. Minn., 1985-86. Mem. NEA (mem. civil rights com. 1983-85, state contact for peace caucus 1981-85, del. assembly rep. 1981-85), NSTA, ASCD, Internat. Reading Assn. (v.p. Boise chpt. 1996-97), NCTE, NCHE, Internat. Coop. Learning Assn., Idaho Edn. Assn. (bd. dirs. region VII 1981-85, pres. region VII 1981-82), Boise Edn. Assn. (v.p. 1981-82, 84-85, pres. 1982-83), Nat. Coun. Urban Edn. Assn., World Future Soc., Coun. for Exceptional Children (pres. chpt. 1978-79), Nat. Coun. Tchrs. English, Minn. Coun. for Social Studies, Calif. Assn. for Gifted, Assn. for Grad. Edn. Students, Phi Delta Kappa. Office: Highlands Elem 3434 Bogus Basin Rd Boise ID 83702-1507

ELLNER, JOSEPHINE HELENE, art educator; b. N.Y.C., Apr. 5, 1940; d. Angelo Edward and Ann (Ballentoni) Bilello; m. Michael William Ellner, Aug. 24, 1957; children: Eileen Lorraine, Deborah Lynn, Laurence Steven. AA in Art, San Jose City Coll., 1972; BA with great distinction, San Jose State U., 1974, MA, 1976, postgrad, 1976-77, U. Calif., Santa Cruz, 1980-81, U. Calif., San Francisco, 1985. Cert. secondary art tchr., community coll. art tchr., Calif., learning handicapped life tchr., resource specialist life tchr., administrv. credential. Art and English tchr. John Muir Jr. High Sch., San Jose, 1975-80, tchr. art, humanities, gifted, 1981-82; spl. edn. tchr. Pioneer High Sch., San Jose, 1982-84, chair art dept., 1984-91; visual arts coord., dept. chair A. Lincoln AVPA Magnet High Sch., San Jose, 1991-97; Saturday Acad. San Jose Unified Sch. Dist., 1996—; prof. art San Jose City Coll., 1996—. Mentor tchr. San Jose Unified Sch. Dist., 1984-88; cons. Coll. Bd., San Jose, 1989-97; advisor Nat. Art Honor Soc., San Jose, 1984—; co-convenor Lincoln H.S. Magnet Curriculum Coun., San Jose, 1991-97; intern advisor Casa Program, San Jose, 1991—; guest curator MACLA Gallery, San Jose, Genesis Gallery, San Jose, San Jose Art League; curator Egyptian Mus. Art Gallery, San Jose, San Jose, New World Gallery, San Jose, Visions Gallery, San Jose, 1970—. Paintings included in numerous pub. collections including Coll. Bd., San Jose, Calif., Foot Mus., Long Beach, Calif.; mural grant Rose Garden Assn., San Jose, 1996, exhibited in over 200 group and one-person shows; executed 6 cmty. murals; curator more than 100 art exhbns.; represented inseveral art books on painting, sculpture and poetry. Recipient award San Jose Adminstrn. Assn., 1984; grantee San Jose Found., 1985, Calif. Tchrs. Instrnl. Incentive Program, 1986, Nat. League Am. Pen Women, 1994-99, program awards Nat. Blue Ribbon Sch., 1998, Magnet Sch. Am., 1991-93, Calif. Dist. Sch. award, 1992, 96, Golden Bell award, 1994, Kennedy Ctr. award for the arts, 1995, Excellence in Edn. award City of San Jose, 2000, Youth Focus award, 1999; inductee Calif. State Senate Youth Mentor's Hall of Fame, 1999. Mem. Nat. Art Edn. Assn., Calif. Tchrs. Assn., NEA, San Jose Tchrs. Assn., Artists Alliance Calif., Cmty. Partnership Santa Clara County, San Jose Inst. Contemporary Art (open studios South Bay artists steering com., Anti-Graffit Program, Phi Kappa Phi. Avocations: art, painting, muralist, sculpture, jewelry design. Home: 1429 Scossa Ave San Jose CA 95118-2456

ELLNER, MICHAEL WILLIAM, art educator; b. N.Y.C., Apr. 1, 1938; s. Charles and Sylvia May (Golub) E.; m. Josephine Helene Bilello, Aug. 24, 1957; children: Eileen Lorraine, Deborah Lynn, Laurence Steven. AA in Engring., San Jose City Coll., 1963, AA in Art, 1966; BA, Coll. Notre Dame, 1970; MA, San Jose State U., 1971, postgrad., 1973-74, U. Calif., Santa Cruz, 1980. Cert. secondary art tchr., c.c. art tchr., Calif. Chair art dept. John Muir Jr. High Sch., San Jose, Calif., 1973-80; assoc. prof. art San Jose State U., 1974; chair art dept. Willow Glen Edn. Park, San Jose, 1980-91; visual arts coord. A. Lincoln AVPA Magnet High Sch., San Jose, 1991-96. Cons. Coll. Bd., San Jose, 1989-97, San Jose Unified Sch. Dist., Saturday Acad., San Jose, 1996—; prof. art San Jose City Coll., 1996—; advisor Nat. Art Honor Soc., San Jose, 1991—; intern advisor Casa Program, San Jose, 1991—; co-convenor Lincoln HS Magnet Curriculum Coun., San Jose, 1991-96; mentor tchr. San Jose Unified Sch. Dist., 1985-94. Paintings included in more than 200 collections including San Jose Mus. Art, Calif., De Saisset Mus., Santa Clara, Calif., Foot Mus., Long Beach, Calif., Coll. Notre Dame, Belmont, Calif.; guest curator Egyptian Mus. Art Gallery, San Jose, Calif., New World Gallery, San Jose, Calif., San Jose Art League, Calif.; guest curator Macla Gallery, San Jose, Calif., Genesis Gallery, San Jose, Calif., 1970—; exhibited in more than 300 group and one-person shows; created 21 cmty. murals; curator over 100 art exhbns.; represented in several art books on painting, and murals and poetry. Past pres. San Jose Art League; past treas. Cambrian Art League; mem. Anti-Graffiti Program, San Jose. Recipient Program Stds. award Nat. Art Edn. Assn., 1993, 94, 95, 96, Art grant City of San Jose, 1994, Mural grant Rose Garden Assn., San Jose, 1996, grant Nat. League Am. Pen Women, 1996, 97, 98, 99, Program awards Nat. Blue Ribbon Sch., 1998, Magnet Sch. of Am., 1991, 92, 93, Calif. Disting. Sch. award, 1992, 96,

Golden Bell award, 1994, Kennedy Ctr. award for the arts, 1995, State Farm Good Nieghbor award Nat. Art Edn. Assn., 1996; inductee Calif. State Senate Youth Mentor's Hall of Fame award, 1999, Excellence in Edn. award City of San Jose, 2000, Youth Focus award, 1999; named Tchr. of Yr., Willow Glen Edn. Park PTA, 1985, San Jose Shrine, 1986. Mem. Calif. Tchrs. Assn., NEA, San Jose Tchrs. Assn., San Jose Inst. Contemporary Art, Artists Alliance Calif., South Bay Artists Assn. (adv. com.), Cmty. Partnership Santa Clara County, San Jose Art League (past pres.), Cambrian Art League (past treas.), Phi Kappa Phi. Avocations: painting, poetry, murals. Home: 1429 Scossa Ave San Jose CA 95118-2456

ELMEN, GARY WARREN, educational consultant; b. Chgo., Feb. 13, 1947; s. Warren N. and Oween C. (Michelson) E.; m. ELizabeth Caldwell, Apr. 4, 1980; children: Kathryn, Lindsay, Brittany. BA, U. Ill., 1968, MEd, 1970, EdD, 1995. Cert. tchr., Ill. Tchr. Downers Grove (Ill.) N. H.S., 1968-83, dean of students, 1983-84; asst. prin. Downers Grove S. H.S., 1984-87; prin. Waubonsie Valley H.S., Aurora, Ill., 1987—99, asst. supt., 1999—2002; founder Ednl. Leadership Initiatives, 2003—. Mem. govs. property tax adv. commn. State of Ill., Springfield, 1974; trustee Golden Apple Found. for Excellence in Teaching, Chgo., 1989-96; chmn. Legis. Commn., Ill. H.S. Assn., Bloomington; mem. State Supts. Adv. Com., 1994-96. Elected trustee Ill. Tchrs. Retirement System, Springfield, 1979-91; mem. Samaritan Interfaith Counseling Ctr. Bd., 2003-. Recipient Golden Achievement award Nat. Sch. Pub. Rels. Assn., 1986, Ill. Those Who Excel Merit award, 1995. Mem. ASCD, NEA (life), Am. Assn. Sch. Adminstrs., Nat. Assn. Secondary Sch. Prins., Ill. Prins. Assn. (Herman Graves award, 1999), Kiwanis Internat., Phi Beta Kappa. Presbyterian. Avocations: reading, sports, photography.

ELMES, DAVID GORDON, psychologist, educator; b. Newton, Mass., Feb. 15, 1942; s. Leslie and Ruth (Adams) E.; m. Anne Louise Lawrence, June 7, 1963; children: Matthew David, Jennifer Anne. BA, U. Va., 1964; MA, U.Va., 1966; PhD, U. Va., 1967. Mgmt. trainee C & P of Va., 1963; asst. prof. psychology Washington and Lee U., Lexington, Va., 1967-71, assoc. prof., 1971-74, prof., 1975—, head dept. psychology, 1990-2000, co-dir. cognitive sci., 1987-2000. Rsch. assoc. Human Performance Ctr., U. Mich., 1973-74; vis. fellow Univ. Coll., Oxford (Eng.) U., 1987. Author: Readings in Experimental Psychology, 1978, Experimental Psychology, 2004, Research Methods in Psychology, 2003; contbr. articles to profl. jours. Bd. dirs. Rockbridge Mental Health Clinic, 1968-73. Fellow Am. Psychol. Soc.; mem. Psychonomic Soc., Va. Acad. Sci., Coun. on Undergrad. Rsch. (past pres.), Phi Beta Kappa. Office: Washington and Lee U Dept Psychology Lexington VA 24450-0303 E-mail: elmesd@wlu.edu.

ELMORE, DAVID, physicist, educator; b. Los Alamos, N.Mex., Dec. 19, 1945; s. William Cronk and Barbara (Page) E.; m. Janet Fox, Aug. 24, 1968; children: Andrew, Steven, Amanda, Emily. BS in Physics, Case Inst. Tech., Cleve., 1968; PhD, U. Rochester, 1974. Rsch. scientist U. Rochester, N.Y., 1974-86; sr. rsch. scientist Argonne (Ill.) Nat. Lab., 1986-88; prof. physics Purdue U., West Lafayette, Ind., 1989—. Office: Purdue University Dept Physics 525 Northwestern Ave West Lafayette IN 47907-2036

ELMORE, GARLAND CRAFT, information science educator; b. Bluefield, W.Va., May 3, 1946; s. Garland C. and Helen M. (Sutherland) E.; m. Jean Anne Schans; 1 child, Martha Erin. BA, Concord Coll., 1968; MA, Marshall U., 1971; PhD, Ohio U., 1979. Teaching asst. Marshall U., Huntington, W.Va., 1969-71; instr. So. West Community Coll., Logan, W.Va., 1971-74; teaching asst. Ohio U., Athens, 1974-75; asst. prof. So. W.Va. Community Coll., Logan, 1975-76; assoc. faculty Ind. U., Indpls., 1976—77, resident lectr., 1977—79, from asst. to assoc. prof., dir. telecommunications, 1979—89, assoc. dean faculties, dir. office of learning techs., 1989—92, exec. dir. integrated techs., 1992—94, assoc. vice chancellor for info. techs., 1992—97, assoc. v.p. tchg. and learning info. techs., dean, 1997—, founding faculty mem. New Media Sch. Informatics, 1997. Pres. faculty, chmn. faculty senate So. W.Va. Community Coll.; mem. numerous coms. at Ind. U., also nat. profl. assns. and cmty. orgns. Author: Communication Media in Higher Education: A Directory of Academic Programs and Faculty in Radio-Television-Film and Related Media, 1987, The Communication Disciplines in Higher Education, 1990, 2d edit., 1993, 3rd edit., 1995; contbr. articles to profl. jours. Served to sgt. U.S. Army, 1966-72. Mem. Educause Ctr. for Applied Rsch., Midwestern Higher Edn. Commn., Coalition for Networked Info., Am. Assn. Higher Edn., Nat. Learning Infrastructure Initiative, Assn. Assn. for Computing Machinery, Educause, Assn. for Commn. Adminstrn., Educause. Office: Ind U Office of VP for Info Tech ES 2129 902 W New York St Indianapolis IN 46202-5157

ELMORE, RICHARD F. education educator; B in Polit. Sci., Whitman Coll.; M in Polit. Sci., Claremont U.; EdD in Ednl. Policy, Harvard U. Prof. edn. Harvard U., 1991—. Sr. rsch. fellow Consortium for Policy Rsch. in Edn., co-dir. rsch. project on sch. accountability. Co-author (with B. Fuller and G. Orfield): Who Chooses, Who Loses? Culture, Institutions, and the Unequal Effects of School Choice, 1996; co-author: (with S. Fuhrman) The Governance of Curriculum; co-author: (with P. Peterson and S. McCarthey) Restructuring in the Classroom, 1996; co-author: (with C. Abelmann) Building a New Structure for School Leadership, 2000; contbr. articles to profl. jours. Grantee, OERI/ED. Mem.: NAS, NAE (bd. mem., bd. on testing and assessment), Nat. Rsch. Coun., Am. Ednl. Rsch. Assn. Office: Harvard Grad Sch Edn Gutman 448 Cambridge MA 02138*

ELRICK, BILLY LEE, English language educator; b. Jackson, Miss., May 21, 1941; d. William Robert and Wesley James (Hall) Chambers; m. Donald Lee Elrick, June 29, 1965; children: Laura Katherine, John William. BA, Millsaps Coll., 1963; MA in Edn., U. Phoenix, 1992. Tchr. lang. arts North Arvada (Colo.) Jr. High, 1963-92, dept. chair, 1984-92; dean Wheat Ridge (Colo.) High Sch., 1993; tchr. English Arvada (Colo.) H.S., 1993-94, 95—, asst. prin., 1994-95, Chatfield Sr. H.S., 1995—. Mentor tchr. Jefferson Couty Schs.-North; workshop presenter in field. Mem. ASCD, Nat. Assn. Secondary Sch. Prins., Colo. Assn. Sch. Execs., Phi Delta Kappa, Delta Kappa Gamma (sec. 1990-94, 2d v.p. 1994—), Sigma Lambda, Kappa Delta Epsilon, Colo. Assn. Sch. Execs. Democrat. Methodist. Avocations: Karate, reading. Home: 10615 Irving Ct Westminster CO 80031-2238 Office: Chatfield Sr H S 7227 S Simms St Littleton CO 80127-3245

ELROD, BEN MOODY, academic administrator; b. Rison, Ark., Oct. 13, 1930; s. Benjamin Searcy and Frances Othello (Sadler) E.; m. Betty Lou Warren, Aug. 7, 1951; children: Cynthia Lou, William Searcy. BA, Ouachita Baptist U., 1952; ThD, Southwestern Bapt. Theol. Sem., 1962; EdD, Ind. U., 1975. Ordained to ministry Baptist Ch., 1950; pastor First Bapt. Ch., Atkins, Ark., 1951-53, Tioga, Tex., 1955-57, Marlow, Okla., 1957-60, South Side Bapt. Ch., Pine Bluff, Ark., 1960-63; pres. Oakland City (Ind.) Coll., 1968-70, Georgetown (Ky.) Coll., 1978-83, Ind. Colls. of Ark., 1983-88; v.p. devel. Ouachita Bapt. U., Arkadelphia, Ark., 1963-68, 70-78, pres., 1988-97, chancellor, 1998—. Commr. Ark. Econ. Devel. Commn., 2002—08; vis. lectr. in field; cons. in higher edn. Contbr. articles to religion jours. Page U.S. Ho. of Reps., 1946-47; trustee Clark County (Ark.) Hosp., 1973-77, chmn., 1975-77; trustee Ark. Bapt. Med. System, 1978, 1989-2001. Mem. Nat. Assn. Ind. Colls. and Univs. (chmn. tax policy commn. 1993), Ark. State C. of C. (bd. dirs. 1990-98), Assn. So. Bapt. Colls. and Schs. (pres. 1996-97), Consortium for Global Edn. (chmn. bd. dirs. 1997-99, mem. exec. com. bd. dirs. 1997-2002). Home: 1008 Village Dr Arkadelphia AR 71923-2922 Office: Ouachita Bapt Univ Ouachita Sta Arkadelphia AR 71923-3221

ELSBREE, LANGDON, English language educator; b. Trenton, N.J., June 23, 1929; s. Wayland Hoyt and Miriam (Jenkins) E.; m. Aimee Desiree Wildman, June 9, 1952; 1 child, Anita. BA, Earlham Coll., 1952; MA, Cornell U., 1954; PhD, Claremont Grad. Sch., 1963. Instr. in English Miami U., Oxford, Ohio, 1954-57, Harvey Mudd Coll., Claremont, Calif., 1958-59; instr. humanities Scripps Coll., Claremont, Calif., 1959-60; instr., prof. Claremont McKenna Coll., 1960-94, prof. emeritus, 1994; mem. grad. faculty Claremont Grad. Sch., 1965—. Part-time lectr. Calif. State U., L.A., 1968-70; vis. prof. Carleton Coll., 1987. Author: The Rituals of Life, 1982, Ritual Passages and Narrative Structures, 1991; co-author: Heath College Handbook, 6th-12th edits., 1967-90; guest editor D.H. Lawrence Rev., 1975, 87. Bd. dirs. Claremont Civic Assn., 1964-66; mem. founding com. Quaker Studies in Human Betterment, Greensboro, N.C., 1987. Fulbright Commn. lectr., 1966-67; grantee NEH, 1975, Claremont McKenna Coll., 1980, 82, 87. Mem.: MLA, Sci. Fiction Rsch. Assn., Virginia Woolf Soc., Friends Assn. Higher Edn., D.H. Lawrence Soc. (exec. bd. 1990), Phi Beta Kappa. Democrat. Soc. Of Friends. Avocations: traveling, reading, swimming, films, photography. Office: Claremont McKenna Coll Bauer Ctr 890 Columbia Ave Claremont CA 91711-3901 E-mail: lelsbree@earthlink.net.

EL SHAMI, PATRICIA ANN, elementary school tutor; b. Brockport, N.Y., June 17, 1950; d. Myron Earl and Dorothy Elizabeth (Nichols) Williams; m. Ahmed Said El Shami, May 26, 1973; children: Omar, Amir. AA, Stephens Coll., Columbia, Mo., 1970, BA, 1972. Cert. tchr., Calif. Pvt. tutor Diagnostic Ctr. Calif. Luth. U., Thousand Oaks, 1990-94; pvt. tutor Camarillo, Calif., 1994—, The Learning Clinic, 1997—. Rep. Santa Rosa Homeowners Assn., Camarilla, 1992—, mem. Camelot Estate Arch. Com., 1995-97, Camelot Estate Bd., 1997-98, Santa Rosa Valley Cmty. Assn. Bd., 1999—. Recipient Disting. Svc. award Las Virgenes Unified Sch. Dist. Agoura Hills, Calif., 1989. Mem. Nat. Coun. Tchrs. Math., Internat. Reading Assn., Ventura County Reading Assn., Santa Rosa Valley Cmty. Assn. (bd. dirs. 1999—). Avocations: logic puzzles, cruising, gardening, snorkeling, music, miniature modeling. Home: 11016 Red Barn Rd Camarillo CA 93012-9268

ELSON, CHARLES MYER, law educator; b. Atlanta, Nov. 12, 1959; s. Edward Elliott and Suzanne (Goodman) E.; m. Aimee F. Kemker, Dec. 18, 1993; children: Caroline Kemker, Charles MacKenzie. AB magna cum laude, Harvard U., 1981, postgrad., 1981—82; JD, U. Va., 1985. Bar: N.Y. 1987, D.C. 1988, U.S. Dist. Ct. (so. and ea. dists.) N.Y. 1987, U.S. Ct. Appeals (11th cir.) 1987. Law clk. to judge U.S. Ct. Appeals (11th cir.), Atlanta, 1985-86; assoc. Sullivan & Cromwell, N.Y.C., 1986-90; asst. prof. Stetson U. Coll. Law, St. Petersburg, Fla., 1990-93, assoc. prof., 1993-96, prof., 1996-2001; Edgar S. Woolard Jr. prof. corp. governance U. Del., 2000—, dir. John L. Weinberg Ctr. for Corp. Governance, 2000—. Vis. prof. law U. Ill., Champaign-Urbana, 1995, Cornell U. Law Sch., Ithaca, N.Y., 1996, U. Md. Law Sch., Balt., 1998; cons. Holland & Knight, 1995—, Towers, Perrin, 1998; bd. dirs. Alderwoods Group, Inc., Auto Zone, Inc., Nuevo Energy Co., Investor Responsiblity Rsch. Ctr. Bd. dirs. Big Apple Circus, Ltd., N.Y.C., 1987-93, Circon Corp., 1997-99, Sunbeam Corp., 1996-2002; trustee Talladega Coll., 1994-2001, Tampa Bay Performing Arts Ctr., 2000—, Tampa Mus. Art, 1993-99, Del. Mus. Natural History, 2003—. Salvatori fellow Heritage Found., 1993-94. Mem.: ABA (vice chair com.on corp. governance, mem. com.on corp. laws), Nat. Assn. Corp. Dirs. (commn. dir. compensation 1995, commn.dir. professionalism 1996, com. on securities litig. reform and fraud detection 1997, adv. coun. 1997—, com.on succession planning 1998, com. on audit coms. 1999, com on role of bd. in strategic planning 2000, com. on dir. evaluation 2001, com. on exec. compensation 2003, com. on compensation coms. 2003), Assn. of Bar of City of N.Y., Am. Law Inst., Univ. Club N.Y.C., Down Town Assn., Harvard Club N.Y.C., Chevaliers du Tastevin. Home: 906 Cecil Rd Wilmington DE 19807 Office: U Del Coll Bus and Econs Alfred Lerner Hall Newark DE 19716 E-mail: elson@lerner.udel.edu.

ELSORADY, ALEXA MARIE, secondary education educator; b. San Francisco, Jan. 4, 1946; d. Willard John and Helen Mary (Bardmess) Saunders; m. R.M. Elsorady, Nov. 24, 1972; children: Tarik, Alexander. BA, San Jose State U., 1967, MA, 1976. Cert. secondary and cmty. coll. tchr. Tchr. biology, integrated sci., English, and social studies Fremont Union High Sch. Dist., San Jose, Calif., 1970—. Mem. Workforce Silicon Valley Leadership Inst., summers 1996, 98, 99, 2000, 01; instr. School-Within-a-School sci. team Lynbrook H.S., 1994-2000; mem. task force com. Calif. Health Occupations Resource Ctr. Mission Coll., 1998-99; mem. Lynbrook Leadership Team, 1997—, chmn., 2000-01. Named English Mentor Tchr., State of Calif., 1987-88, Sci. Mentor, 1993-94; grantee Superschs. Found. Sci.-Math.; fellow NSF, 1992, Evolution and Nature of Sci. Inst., San Jose State U., 1993, Mayor Susan Hammer's San Jose Edn. Network Tech. Inst., summer 1994. Mem.: Nat. Sci. Tchrs. Assn., Calif. Acad. Scis. (mem. biology forum 1990—), San Jose State U.alum (life), Calif. Sci. Tchrs. Assn. (life), Phi Alpha Theta (life), Phi Kappa Phi (life), Kappa Alpha Theta (life). Home: 1233 Redmond Ave San Jose CA 95120-2745 Office: Lynbrook High Sch 1280 Johnson Ave San Jose CA 95129-4199

ELSTUN, ESTHER NIES, foreign language educator; b. Berkshire Heights, Pa. d. Frank Emory and Florence Mae (Sweigart) Nies; m. James Palmer Elstun, Sept. 1, 1956; 1 child, John Dudley. BA magna cum laude, The Colo. Coll., 1960; MA, Rice U., 1964, PhD, 1969. Asst. prof. to prof., German George Mason U., Fairfax, Va., 1969—. V.p., faculty senate ov Va., 2001-2003; pres. Va. Coun. for Study Abroad, 1981-82, Va. Humanities Conf., 1989-90; mem. exec. bd. Va. Conf. of the AAUP, 1990-92, 2002—. Author: The Life and work of Richard Beer-Hofmann, 1983; contbr. articles to profl. jours. Vol. Amnesty Internat., 1978—. Recipient Amerika-Kreis Munster scholar, Univ. of Munster, Germany, 1954-55; rsch. grant George Mason Univ. Found., Houghton Libr., Harvard and the Leo Baeck Inst., N.Y., 1974. Mem. AAUP, Am. Assn. Tchrs. of German, Modern Lang. Assn. Am., German Studies Assn., Internat. Arthur Schnitzler Rsch. Assn., Phi Beta Kappa, Delta Phi Alpha. Presbyterian. Avocations: gardening, piano, travel, needlework. Office: George Mason Univ 4400 University Dr Fairfax VA 22030-4444

ELY, DONALD J(EAN), clergyman, secondary school educator; b. Frederick, Md., July 15, 1935; s. George Kline and Jennie Mabel (Boyer) E. m. Lois Jean Kirkpatrick, Aug. 27, 1967; children: Kathleen Rose, Stephen David, Yvonne Elaine. AB, Gettysburg Coll., 1955; BD, Lancaster Sem., 1958; MEd, Bloomsburg State U., 1972. Ordained to ministry Evang. and Reformed Ch., 1958. Pastor St. John Evang. and Reformed Ch., Riegelsville, Pa., 1958-61, Zion's Reformed Ch., Ashland, Pa., 1961-64, Augusta Reformed Parish, Sunbury, Pa., 1964-74, Salem United Meth. Ch., Middleburg, Pa., 1974-79, Salem Ind. Brethren Ch., Middleburg, Pa., 1979-83; tchr. social studies Shikellamy High Sch., Sunbury, Pa., 1966-98; ret., 1998. Bd. dirs. Sunbury Area YMCA, 1966—, sec., 1973-80, 88-2000; bd. dirs. Greater Susquehanna Valley YMCA, 1993—, sec. 1999—; bd. dirs. Northumberland County unit Am. Cancer Soc., 1971-74, Snyder County unit, 1974-84; rep. candidate state legis., 1982; vice chmn. Govt. Study Commn. of City of Sunbury, 1989-91; mem. Northumberland County Rep. com., 1987—, state committeeman, 1992—. Mem.: SAR (chaplain 1971—, chpt. pres. 1981—86, 1992), Greater Susquehanna Valley C. of C., Federalist Soc., Commonwealth Found., Intercollegiate Studies Inst., Am. Conservative Union, Hist. Soc. Evang. and Ref. Ch., Northumberland County Hist. Soc. (life; trustee 1972—83), Snyder County Hist. Soc. (life; pres. 1980—83), Union County Hist. Soc., Hereditary Register of U.S., Rolls Royce Owners' Club, Susquehana Valley Country Club, Antique Auto Club Am., Masons. Home and Office: PO Box 765 Sunbury PA 17801-0765 Fax: 570-286-4444.

ELY, JAMES WALLACE, JR., law educator; b. Rochester, NY, Jan. 20, 1938; s. James Wallace and Edythe (Farnham) E.; m. Ruth Buell MacCameron, Aug. 27, 1960; children: A. Elizabeth, Kimberly Farnham, Suzanne B., James W. AB, Princeton U., 1959; LLB, Harvard U., 1962; PhD, U. Va., 1971. Bar: N.Y. 1962, U.S. Dist. Ct. (we. dist.) N.Y. 1963. Assoc. Harris, Beach and Wilcox, Rochester, 1962-67; instr. U. Va., 1970; from instr. to asst. prof. U. Richmond, Va., 1970-73; asst. prof. law Vanderbilt U., Nashville, 1973-75, assoc. prof., 1975-78, prof., 1978—, Milton R. Underwood prof. law, 1999—. Vis. prof. law. U. Leeds, Eng., 1981-82; Chapman disting. vis. prof. U. Tulsa, 1985. Author: The Crisis of Conservative Virginia: The Byrd Organization and the Politics of Massive Resistance, 1976, The Guardian of Every Other Right: A Constitutional History of Property Rights, 1992, 2d edit., 1998, The Chief Justiceship of Melville W. Fuller 1888-1910, 1995, Railroads and American Law, 2001; co-author (with Bruce): Modern Property Law: Cases and Materials, 1984, 5th edit., 2003, The Law of Easements and Licenses in Land, 1988, rev. edit., 1995, 2001; co-editor (with Bodenhamer): Ambivalent Legacy: A Legal History of the South, 1984, The Bill of Rights in Modern America: After 200 Years, 1993; co-author (with Brown): Legal Papers of Andrew Jackson, 1987; co-author: (with Hall) An Uncertain Tradition: Constitutionalism and the History of the South, 1989; editor: Property Rights in American History, 6 vols., 1997—, A History of the Tennessee Supreme Court, 2002; co-editor (with Hall, Grossman, Wiecek): The Oxford Companion to the Supreme Court, 1992; co-editor: (with Hall, Clark, Grossman, Hull) The Oxford Companion to American Law, 2002; mem. editl. bd.: Am. Jour. Legal History, 1987—99. Mem. Am. Soc. Legal History (treas. 1980-81, 82-83, 84-85), Orgn. Am. Historians, So. History Assn. Office: Vanderbilt U Sch Law 21st Ave S Nashville TN 37240-0001

ELZINGA, KENNETH GERALD, economics educator; b. Coopersville, Mich., Aug. 11, 1941; s. Clarence Albert and Lettie (Albrecht) E.; m. Barbara Ann Brunson, June 17, 1967 (dec. 1978); m. Terry M. Maguire, Aug. 9, 1981. BA, Kalamazoo Coll., 1963; MA, Mich. State U., 1966, PhD, 1967; LHD, Kalamazoo Coll., 2000. Rsch. economist Senate Antitrust and Monopoly Subcom., 1964; asst. instr. Mich. State U., 1965-66; asst. prof. U. Va., Charlottesville, 1967-71, assoc. prof., 1971-73, prof., 1973—; fellow in law and econs. U. Chgo., 1974; vis. prof. econs. Trinity U., 1984; Thomas Jefferson fellow Cambridge U., 1990, Cavaliers Disting. Tchg. Professorship, 1992-97, Robert C. Taylor prof. econ., 2002—. Spl. econ. advisor to asst. atty. gen., antitrust divsn. Dept. Justice, 1970-71; trustee Hope Coll., 1983-90, Inter-Varsity Christian fellowship, 1992-2000; mem. editl. bd. Antitrust Bull., 1977—. Author: (with others) The Antitrust Penalties, 1976, The Fatal Equilibrium, 1985, Murder at the Margin, 1993, A Deadly Indifference, 1995, The Antitrust Casebook, 3rd edit. 1996. Recipient Thomas Jefferson award U. Va., 1992, Commonwealth of Va. Outstanding Faculty award, 1992, Kenan Enterprise award for tchg. econs., William R. Kenan Jr. Charitable Trust, 1996, Templeton Honor Roll award for Edn. in a Free Soc. John Templeton Found., 1997, Disting. Alumni award Mich. State U., 1999; named Tchr. of the Yr. Phi Eta Sigma, 1992. Mem. ABA, Am. Econs. Assn., Mystery Writers of Am., Am. Law and Econs. Assn., So. Econ. Assn. (pres. 1991), Internat. J.A. Shumpeter Soc., Industrial Orgn. Soc. (pres. 1979). Presbyterian. Avocations: water skiing, travel. Office: U VA Dept Econs PO Box 400182 Charlottesville VA 22904-4182

EMANUEL, GLORIA PAGE, secondary school educator; b. Dallas, Apr. 5, 1947; d. Daniel and Leola (Green) Page; m. Lawrence Ray Emanuel, Oct. 2, 1971; children: Lawrence Ray Jr., Kevin Lawrence. Student, Paul Quinn Coll., 1966—67; BS, Ea. Tex. State U., 1970; MEd, Prairie View A & M U., 1975. Cert. tchr. Tex., profl. counselor Tex. Tchr. social studies Waco H.S., Tex., 1971—82, Univ. Mid. Sch., 1982—. Chairperson solcial studies, block leader, 1985—93; assn. rep. UMS, 1985—93, coord. Adopt-a-Sch., 1992—; mem. Campus Action Com., 1985, Campus Adv. Coun., 1990—91, Supt. Adv. Coun. for Social Studies, 1991—92. Mem. North Tex. Min. Wives, Waco-Temple, 1971—; asst. sec. area II Waco-Temple Missionary Soc.; mem. Joshua Chapel AME Ch., Waxahachie, Tex. Mem.: NAFE, NEA, Heart of Tex. Counselors Assn., Tex. State Tchrs. Assn., Order Ea. Star, Sigma Gamma Rho. Avocations: travel, collecting historical stamps, collecting scenic post cards, collecting scenic slides. Home: 2024 King Cole Dr Waco TX 76705-2749

EMANUEL-SMITH, ROBIN LESLEY, special education educator; m. Allen Weston Smith, Apr. 14, 1983; children: David, Ariel, Weston. BS in Engring., U.S. Mil. Acad., 1981; BS in Health-Phys. Edn. summa cum laude, Cameron U., Lawton, Okla., 1992; M Spl. Edn., Coll. of St. Rose, Albany, 1995. Cert. spl. edn., health and phys. edn. tchr., N.Y. Enlisted U.S. Army, 1974-76, commd. 2nd lt., 1981, advanced through grades to capt., 1984, resigned, 1990; tchr. spl. edn. Ulster County Bd. Coop. Ednl. Svcs., Port Ewen, N.Y., 1992—. Roman Catholic. Avocations: weightlifting, coaching and officiating youth soccer, softball and baseball. Office: Ulster County Bd Coop Ednl Svs Rt 32 New Paltz NY 12561

EMBER, MELVIN LAWRENCE, anthropologist, educator; b. NYC, Jan. 13, 1933; s. Martin William and Ida F. (Trebuchovskaya) E.; m. Irma Stalberg, July 11, 1954 (div. Jan. 1970); children: Matthew, Rachel; m. Carol Lee Ruchlis, Mar. 21, 1970; children: Katherine, Julie. BA, Columbia Coll., 1953; PhD, Yale U., 1958. Postdoctoral fellow Yale U., New Haven, 1958-59; rsch. anthropologist NIH, Bethesda, MD, 1959-63; from asst. to assoc. prof. anthropology Antioch Coll., Yellow Springs, Ohio, 1963-67; assoc. prof. Hunter Coll., CUNY, 1967-70, prof., 1971-87; pres. Human Rels. Area Files, Inc., Yale U., New Haven, 1987—. Chmn. dept. anthropology Hunter Coll., CUNY, 1968-73, exec. officer PhD program in anthropology Grad. Sch., 1973-75. Co-author: Anthropology, 1973, Cultural Anthropology, 1973; : 10th edit., 2002, Marriage, Family and Kinship, 1983, Anthropology: A Brief Introduction, 1992, 5th edit., 2003, Sex, Gender and Kinship: A Cross-Cultural Perspective, 1997, Cross-Cultural Research Methods, 2001; co-editor: Portraits of Culture, 1998, Research Frontiers in Anthropology, 1998, Cross-Cultural Research for Social Science, 1998, Encyclopedia of Cultural Anthropology, 1996, American Immigrant Cultures: Builders of a Nation, 1997, Cultures of the World, 1999, Countries and Their Cultures, 2001, Encyclopedia of Prehistory, 2001—02, Encyclopedia of Urban Cultures, 2002, Archaeology: Original Readings in Method and Practice, 2002, Physical Anthropology: Original Readings in Method and Practice, 2002; editor: Cross-Cultural Rsch.: The Jour. of Comparative Social Sci., 1982—. Fellow AAAS, Am. Anthrop. Assn.; mem. Soc. for Cross-Cultural Rsch. (pres. 1981-82). Office: Yale U Human Rels Area Files Inc 755 Prospect St New Haven CT 06511-1225

EMBRY, JULIA EDWARDS, elementary education educator; b. Louisville, Feb. 9, 1951; d. Raymond Theodore and V. Ruth (Davidson) Edwards; m. Lowell Randall Embry Jr., Nov. 12, 1971; children: (Lowell) Randall III, Bradley, Christopher. BS, U. Louisville, 1972, MEd in Early Childhood Edn., 1977, postgrad., 1991; EdD, Nova Southeastern U., Ft. Lauderdale, Fla., 1994. Cert. tchr., cons., Ky. Reading recovery tchr. leader tng. Ohio State U., Columbus, 1988-89; tchr. Jefferson County Pub. Schs., Louisville, 1978—, reading recovery tchr. leader, 1989—, Ctrl. Ky. Edn. Coop., Lexington, 1993—; cons. Bill Martin, Jr. Whole Lang. Workshops, Commerce, Tex., 1989—; instr. U. Ky., Lexington, 1993—. Cons. Internat. Inst. of Commerce, Tex. Literacy Learning, 1989—. Mem. NEA, Ky. Edn. Assn., Jefferson County Tchr. Assn., Internat. Reading Assn., Greater Louisville Reading Assn. (membership chair 1990-92), Ky. Reading Assn., Nat. Coun. Tchrs. English, Phi Delta Kappa. Baptist. Avocations: reading, walking, collecting children's literature. Home: 1309 Tycoon Way Louisville KY 40213-1511 Office: Jefferson County Pub Schs 3300 Newburg Rd Louisville KY 40218-2414

EMBRY, KAREN THOMPSON, elementary education educator; b. Atlanta, Sept. 25, 1958; d. James Newton and Billie Reese (Cleveland) Thompson; m. Sterling Charters Embry, Aug. 14, 1982 (div. Jan. 1994); 1 child, Juliette Reese Embry; stepchildren: Hugh Cooper Embry III, Headen Davidson Embry. BA in Early Childhood Edn., LaGrange Coll., 1980; postgrad., North Ga. Coll., 1989-90, Lanier Tech. Inst., 1996—. Cert. EMT, 1996. Kindergarten tchr. Hall County Bd. Edn., Gainesville, Ga., 1980-81,

1st grade tchr., 1981-90, ESOL tchr., 1990-95, 5th grade tchr., 1995-96, 3d grade tchr., 1996-97, 4th grade tchr., 1997—2001, ESOL tchr., 2001—. Mem. adv. com. on ESOL needs for Hall County, 1993—, curriculum devel. com. ESOL Tchrs. of Hall County, 1993—. Contbr. articles to newspapers. Gateway House for Battered Women, Gainesville, 1992, Meals on Wheels, Gainesville, 1993; vol. interpreter Good News at Noon Med. Clinic, Gainesville, 1994—.; coord. Safe Kids, 1996—. Mem. Ga. Assn. Educators, Hall County Assn. Educators, Jr. League of Gainesville-Hall County. Democrat. Methodist. Avocations: gardening, needlework, artwork, horseback riding, reading. Home: 4588 Buckhorn Rd Gainesville GA 30506-3024 Office: Myers Elem Sch 2676 Candler Rd Gainesville GA 30507-8961

EMCH-DÉRIAZ, ANTOINETTE SUZANNE, historian, educator; b. Geneva, Nov. 9, 1935; came to U.S., 1964; d. Louis Georges and Renée Gabrielle Dériaz; m. Gérard Gustav Emch, July 25, 1959; children: Florence Christiane, René-Didier Guillaume. PhD, U. Rochester, N.Y., 1984. Tech. asst. Am. Inst. of Physics, N.Y.C., 1968-70; vis. scholar U. Pa., Phila., 1981; rsch. assoc. U. Rochester, 1984; asst. prof. U. Miss., Oxford, 1985-92; adj. faculty U. Fla., Gainesville, 1992—. Vis. scholar U. Goettingen, Germany, 1985, Wellcome Inst., London, 1994, U. Vienna, 1994. Author: 18th Century Concept of Health, 1984, Tissot: Physician of the Enlightenment, 1992; contbr. chpt. to books, articles to profl. jours. Mem. Am. Hist. Assn., Am. Assn. for History Medicine, Am. Soc. 18th-Century Studies. Presbyterian. Office: U Fla PO Box 117320 Gainesville FL 32611-7320 E-mail: aedz@history.ufl.edu.

EMEAGWALI, GLORIA THOMAS, humanities educator; b. Trinidad, West Indies, Feb. 6, 1950; came to U.S., 1991; BA, U. W.I., 1973; edn. dipl., London U., 1975; MA, Toronto U., 1976; PhD, Ahmadu Bello U., Zaria, Nigeria, 1986. Asst. prof. Ahmadu Bello U., Zaria, Nigeria, 1979-86; assoc. prof. Nigerian Def. Acad., 1986, Ilorin U., Nigeria, 1986-89; vis. prof. U. W.I., Trinidad, 1989, Oxford U., U.K., 1990-91; assoc. prof. history and African studies Conn. State U., New Britain, 1991-96, tenured prof. history and African studies, 1996—. Vis. prof. Internat. Devel. Ctr., Oxford (Eng.) U., spring 2000; mem. editl. bd. Review of African Political Economy, U.K., chief editor Africa Update, CCSU.; mem. adv. bd. Encyclopedia of the History of Science, Technology and Medicine, Hampshire Coll., Amherst. Keynote speaker, Third World Foundation, Chicago March 2001. Keynote Speaker, Southern cntrl and East African Libr. assn. SCESAL, 2002. Editor: Historical Development of Science and Technology in Nigeria, 1992, Science and Technology in African History, 1992, African Systems of Science Technology and Art, 1993, Women Pay the Price: Structural Adjustment in Africa and the Caribbean, 1995, African Civilization, 1997. Recipient UNESCO award, 1999; Oxford U. fellow, 1990; grantee Old Dominion U., 1986, 88. Mem. AAUP (Conn. state award 1992, 97, 2002), Internat. Soc. for Study of Comp. Civilization (mem. governing body, exec. com. 1992—), World Anthrop. Soc., World Archeaol. Congress, Am. Hist. Assn., African Studies Assn. Avocations: keyboard playing, table tennis. Office: Cen Conn State U History/African Studies Dept New Britain CT 06050

EMERSON, MARION PRESTON, mathematics educator; b. Washburn, Mo., Feb. 24, 1918; s. William Alfred and Alice Maud (Wilson) E.; m. Jane Cornwell Barber, Sept. 20, 1947; children: William David, Anne Ellen, Alice Marie. BS, S.W. Mo. State U., 1938; MS, U. Wis., 1948; PhD, U. Ill., 1952. Cert. pub. sch. tchr. Asst. prof. math. SUNY, Binghamton, 1952-56; assoc. prof. math. S.W. Mo. State U., Springfield, 1956-61; chmn. math. dept. Emporia (Kans.) State U., 1961-79, prof. math., 1979-87, prof. emeritus, 1987—. Co-author: College Albebra, 1955. Capt. USAF, 1942-46. Methodist. Avocation: genealogy. Home and Office: 1425 Luther St Emporia KS 66801-6040

EMERT, GEORGE HENRY, former academic administrator, biochemist; b. Tenn., Dec. 15, 1938; s. Victor K. Emert and Hazel G. (Shultz) Ridley; m. Billie M. Bush, June 10, 1967; children: Debra Lea Lipp, Ann Lanie Taylor, Laurie Elizabeth, Jamie Marie. BA, U. Colo., 1962; MA, Colo. State U., 1970; PhD, Va. Tech. U., 1973. Registered profl. chem. engr. Microbiologist Colo. Dept. Pub. Health, Denver, 1967-70; post doctoral fellow U. Colo., Boulder, 1973-74; dir. biochem. tech. Gulf Oil Corp., Merriam, Kans., 1974-79; prof. biochemistry, dir. biomass rsch. ctr. U. Ark., Fayetteville, 1979-84; exec. v.p. Auburn (Ala.) U., 1984-92; pres. Utah State U., Logan, 1992—2000, pres. emeritus, porf. biochemistry, 2001—. Adj. prof. microbiology U. Kans., Lawrence, 1975-79. Editor, author: Fuels from Biomass and Wastes, 1981; author book chpt.; contbr. articles to profl. jours.; poet. Mem. So. Tech. Coun., Raleigh, N.C., 1985-92; dir. Ala. Supercomputer Authority, Montgomery, 1987-92, Blue Cross Blue Shield Utah, 1996—, Utah Partnership Econ. Devel.; trustee, adv. bd. First Security Bank. Capt. U.S. Army, 1963-66, Vietnam. Named to Educators Hall of Fame, Lincoln Meml. U., 1988. Fellow Am. Inst. Chemists; mem. Rotary (Paul Harris fellow, pres., v.p 1989-90), Phi Kappa Phi, Sigma Xi. Republican. Achievements include patent for method for enzyme reutilization. Office: Utah State U 0300 Old Main Logan UT 84322

EMERY, MARGARET ROSS, elementary school educator; b. Columbus, Ohio, May 21, 1923; d. Galen Starr and Stella May (Albright) Ross; m. Richard Clayton Emery, Oct. 27, 1943 (dec. June 1988); children: Richard C. Jr., Margaret Elizabeth Chapman. BA in Edn., U. Mich., 1944; MS in Elem. Guidance, U. Notre Dame, 1967. Life lic. in edn., Ind. 1st grade tchr. Grosse Ile (Mich.) Schs., 1944-45; 2nd grade tchr. Rumson (N.J.) Pub. Schs., 1945-46; homebound tutor Schenectady (N.Y.) Pub. Schs., 1946-48; tutor Hinsdale (Ill.) Pub. Schs., 1948-50; substitute tchr. South Bend (Ind.) Pub. Schs., 1951-53, 93—; head lower sch., guidance couns., 1st grade tchr. The Stanley Clark Sch., South Bend, 1958-88. Mem. St. Joseph County Rep. Women, South Bend, 1958-96; election day clk. Election Bd., South Bend, 1986-96; docent No. Ind. Hist. Soc., South Bend, 1990—. Mem. AAUW, Panhellenic Assn. (pres. South Bend Mishawaka 1993-95), Zonta Internat. (historian, bd. mem. 1994—), Delta Kappa Gamma (pres. Nu chpt. 1992-94). Republican. Presbyterian. Avocations: reading, needlework, golf, volunteer tutoring, bridge. Home: 322 Rue Flambeau Apt 403 South Bend IN 46615-2827

EMERY, RITA DOROTHY, physical education educator; b. Berkeley, Calif., Sept. 21, 1939; d. Byron Elden and Charlotte Antoinette (Siwinski) E. AA, Contra Costa Coll., 1960; BA, Chico State Coll., 1963; MA, Wash. State U., 1977. Cert. tchr., Calif. Instr. phys. edn., coach Churchill County High Sch., Fallon, Nev., 1963-65; instr. phys. edn., coach, dept. chair Lower Lake (Calif.) High Sch., 1967-76; coach women's volleyball Contra Costa Coll., San Pablo, Calif., 1977; coach women's softball Oreg. State U., Corvallis, 1977-80; instr. phys. edn., coach, athletic dir. St. Leonard Sch., Fremont, Calif., 1985-89; instr. phys. edn. Campbell (Calif.) Unified Sch. Dist., 1989-90; elem. phys. edn. specialist, coach Vacaville (Calif.) Unified Sch. Dist., 1990-95; dir. jr. programming Club Sport of Pleasant, Calif., 1995—. Intramural dir. Contra Costa Coll., 1957-60; coach, coord. recreation Holy Spirit Ch., Fremont, 1980-85; instr. youth sports Fremont Leisure Svcs., 1988-90, teen youth coord., 1988-93; girls basketball coach Wood High Sch., Vacaville, 1993-95. Speaker Alameda County chpt. Am. Heart Assn., 1983-90; vol. coach, officer, ofcl. Fremont Little League, 1983-86; vol. Hall of Health/Kids Safe Program, Berkeley, Calif., 1990—. Named Vol. of Yr. Am. Heart Assn., 1986, 88. Mem. AAHPERD (adv. com. for devel. of athletic tng. coun.), Calif. Assn. Health, Phys. Edn., Recreation and Dance. Avocations: bicycling, walking, cacti, gardening, youth activities. Office: Club Sport of Pleasant 7090 Johnson Dr Pleasanton CA 94588-3328

EMERY, VICKI MORRIS, school library media administrator; b. Kansas City, Mo., Sept. 7, 1948; d. Arthur Paul and Merna Alva (Powell) Morris; m. Harvey William Emery Jr., July 19, 1974. BS in Edn., Emporia (Kans.) State U., 1970; M in Urban Affairs, Va. Poly. Inst. and State U., 1980; MS in Libr. Sci., Cath. U. Am., 1995; postgrad. student in ednl. leadership, U. Va., 1997—. Tchr. St. Pius X Sch., Mission, Kans., 1970-72, Shawnee Mission (Kans.) Pub. Schs., 1973-74; editing supr. CTB/McGraw-Hill, Monterey, Calif., 1975-76; sch. libr. media specialist Fairfax County (Va.) Pub. Schs., 1995-99, sch. libr. adminstr., 1999—. Mem. adv. bd. Fairfax County Sch. Bd., 1996-99. Contbr. revs. and articles to profl. jours. Pres. PTA Sangster Sch., Springfield, Va., 1994-95, 96-98, scholarship chair Fairfax County Coun. PTAs, 1995-99; pres., bd. dirs. Spring-Mar Coop. Presch., Springfield, 1989-90. Recipient Outstanding Svc. award Va. Coop. Presch. Coun., 1991. Mem. ALA, Am. Assn. Sch. Librs. (mem. pres.'s program com. 1998), Assn. Supervision and Curriculum Devel., Va. Ednl. Media Assn., Va. Soc. Tech. Edn., Va. Congress Parents and Tchrs. (hon. life mem.), Beta Phi Mu (local chpt. sec. 2000—). Office: Lake Braddock Secondary Sch 9200 Burke Lake Rd Burke VA 22015-1682

EMILSSON, ELIZABETH MAYKUTH, special education educator; b. Bozeman, Mont., Feb. 23, 1936; d. Frank Leopold and Dolores Muriel (Lawrence) Maykuth; m. Robert Gunnar Emilsson, May 8, 1961 (dec.); children: Gunnar R., Ingrid L., John. BS, Mont. State Coll., 1958; MEd, Mont. State U., 1974; Spl. Edn. Cert., U. Mont., 1976, postgrad., 1978. Tchr. grades 4-8 Virginia City (Mont.) Schs., 1958-59; tchr. grades 7-8 El Camino Jr. H.S., Santa Maria, Calif., 1959-60; tchr. grade 6 Miller St. Sch., Santa Maria, 1960-61; tchr. grades 1-3 Stevenson sch., Ransomville, N.Y., 1967-72; resource tchr. Three Forks (Mont.) Unified Schs., 1974-76; spl. edn. cons. Mont. Reg. Svcs., Glendive, Mont., 1976-79; spl. edn. tchr. cons. Big Country Edn. Coop., Miles City, Mont., 1979-89, spl. edn. dir., 1990—; exec. dir. Big Country Edn./Head Start, 1991-99; ret., 1999; ednl. cons., tech. adv. Mont. State Office of Pub. Instruction, 1999—. Pres. bd. dirs. South Eastern Mont. Adv. Prog., Miles City, 1987-88. Bd. dirs. Miles City Youth Soccer Assn., 1986-88. Mem. Coun. for Exceptional Children (Mont. pres. 1985-86, Nat. Bd. Govs. 1991-94, distinguished svc. award state fedn. 1994), PEO Sisterhood, Delta Kappa Gamma. Democrat. Lutheran. Avocations: hiking, fishing, reading, gardening. Home: 2203 Main St Miles City MT 59301-3801 E-mail: bettye@midrivers.com.

EMMEL, BRUCE HENRY, retired secondary education mathematics educator; b. St. Cloud, Minn., Jan. 8, 1942; s. Henry Joseph and Mary Ann Emily (Kangas) E.; m. Phyllis Wanda Campbell, Aug. 29, 1982; children: Debra Lynn Huber, Kathi Marie, Brent Boyd, Daniel Henry Huber, Brandi Rose, Joseph Skye Olson. BS, St. Cloud State U., 1967; MA in Edn., Ball State U., 1973; PhD, Univ. N.D., 2002. Cert. vocat. tchr., Minn. Tchr. Lincoln Jr. High Sch., Hibbing, Minn., 1967-70, West Concord (Minn.) High Sch., 1970-72; vocat. tchr. Moorhead (Minn.) Tech. Coll., 1972-90; tchr. Moorhead Pub. Schs., 1984-2000, ret. Mem. Dist. Math. Com., Moorhead, 1978-2000. Comdr. Fargo (N.D.) CAP, 1984-86, 89, 94-96; dir. pub. affairs N.D. CAP, Mandan, 1986-89; precinct chmn. Dem. Com., Moorhead, 1968-90. Mem. Phi Delta Kappa, Kappa Delta Pi. Congregationalist. Avocations: flying, aircraft builder, hunting, walking, traveling. Home: 1121 3rd St S Moorhead MN 56560-4015

EMMETT, MICHAEL, physician, educator; b. Linz, Austria, Oct. 29, 1945; arrived in U.S., 1949; s. Issac and Pearl (Gladstone) E.; m. Rachel Kozuch, Aug. 2, 1969; children: Mira, Daniel, Joshua. BS, Pa. State U., 1967; MD, Temple U., 1971. Diplomate Am. Bd. Internal Medicine, Am. Bd. Internal Medicine, Nephrology. Intern, then resident Yale U. Med. Ctr., New Haven, 1971-74; nephrology fellow Hosp. U. of Pa., Phila., 1974-76; clin. asst. prof. medicine U. Tex. Southwestern Med. Sch., Dallas, 1976-80, clin. assoc. prof. medicine, 1980-85, clin. prof. medicine, 1985—; Ralph Tompsett prof. medicine Baylor U. Med. Ctr., Dallas, 1986—, dir., nephrology/metabolism, 1986-96, dir. nephrology endocrinology labs, 1986—, chief of medicine, 1996—. Cons. physician Parkland Hosp., Dallas, 1976—, Presbyn. Hosp., Dallas, 1976—. Contbr. articles to profl. jours. Fellow ACP; mem. Am. Fedn. Clin. Rsch., Dallas County Med. Soc., Tex. Med. Assn., So. Med. Soc., Am. Soc. Nephrology, Internat. Soc. Nephrology. Avocations: tennis, skiing. Office: Baylor U Med Ctr 3500 Gaston Ave Dallas TX 75246-2096 E-mail: m.emmett@baylorhealth.edu.

EMMETT, RITA, professional speaker; b. Chgo., Apr. 12, 1943; d. Thomas Henry Dorney and Helen Fischer; m. Bruce Karder, May 21, 1994; children: Robb Sean, Kerry Shannon. BA in English, Northeastern Ill. U., 1979; MS in Adult and Cont. Edn, Nat. Louis U., Evanston, Ill., 1985. Coord. edn. programs Leyden Family Svc., Franklin Park, Ill., 1977-95; pres. Emmett Enterprises, Inc., Des Plaines, 1994—. Adj. faculty Triton Coll., River Grove, Ill., 1977-99, Wright Coll., Chgo., 1985-99; presenter in field. Author: The Procrastinator's Handbook: Mastering the Art of Doing It Now; The Procrastinating Child: A Handbook for Adults to Help Children Stop Putting Things Off; Great Speakers Anthology; contbr. articles to newspapers and mags. Pres. Parent's Club, River Grove, 1987-88; keynote spkr. Gov.'s Mansion, Springfield, Ill. Mem. Bus. and Profl. Women (Achievement award 1986), Assn. Consultation and Edn. (sec.), Ill. Prevention Network, Century Club, Nat. Spkrs. Assn., Profl. Spkr.'s of Ill. (bd. dirs. 1995-96, 2002-03). Roman Catholic. Avocations: reading, writing, travel, friends. E-mail: rita@ritaemmett.com.

EMMONS, JANET GALBREATH, secondary education educator; b. Columbus, Ohio; d. George Robert and Jean (Evans) G. BA in English, Sam Houston State U., 1972, MEd, 1985; EdD, U. Houston, 2000. English tchr. Conroe (Tex.) H.S., 1973-77, 84-86, English and Creative Writing tchr., 1986-88; tchr. Reaves Intermediate Sch., 1981-84; English/Journalism tchr. The Woodlands (Tex.) High Sch., 1988—; prof. English Montgomery Coll., 1996—. Mem. NCTE, TCTE, AERA, TEA, Phi Delta Kappa, Kappa Delta Pi, Delta Delta Delta . Home: 643 Tallahassee Park Conroe TX 77302-2001 Office: The Woodlands High Sch 6101 Research Forest Dr The Woodlands TX 77381-6028 E-mail: jemmons@worldnet.att.net.

EMSWILLER, ELLA MAE CUSTER, retired secondary school educator; b. Beckley, W.Va., Aug. 2, 1939; d. Lyle Letcher and Ora Lee (Crotty) Hudson; m. Derwood Carlton Custer, June 3, 1962 (dec. Mar. 19); children: Carlton Custer, Adrian Custer; m. Fred R. Emswiller, Jr., June 14, 1980 (dec. Sept. 1999); stepchildren: Mitchel, Martin, Lynn. BS in Ecn., Concord Coll., 1961; MEd, U. Va., 1978. Tchr. home econs. Hillsboro (W.Va.) H.S., 1961—64, Elkton (Va.) H.S., Elkton, 1964—71, tchr. 4th grade, 1978—81, Ashby Lee Primary, Mt. Jackson, Va., 1981—87, New Market Mid. Sch., 1987—91, North Fork Mid. Sch., 1991—2000; ret., 2000. Bd. dirs. Harrisonburg Rockingham Day Care. Mem.: Internat. Reading Assn., Shenandoah Valley Reading Coun., Shenandoah County Edn. Assn., Va. Edn. Assn., United Meth. Women's Club (Elkton). Methodist. Home: 483 Eastover Dr Harrisonburg VA 22801-4409

ENDAHL, ETHELWYN MAE, elementary education educator, consultant; b. Duluth, Minn., May 27, 1922; d. Herman and Florence Jenny (Mattson) Johnson; m. John Charles Endahl Sr., Nov. 27, 1943; children: Merrilee Jean, Marsha Louise, John Charles Jr., Kimberly Ann. BS in Library Science, U. Minn., Mpls., 1943; MA in Edn., Fairfield U., 1978; attended, Elmhurst (Ill.) Coll., 1966-68, U. Bridgeport, Conn., 1981-83, Northeastern U., Martha's Vineyard, Mass., 1982-85, U. Conn., 1971. Cert. Tchr. Conn. Librarian children's hosp. Davenport (Iowa) Pub. Library, 1943-44; librarian Omaha (Nebr.) Pub. Library, 1944; tchr. 4th gr. Center Elem. Sch., New Canaan, Conn., 1968-81, writing coord., 1981-83; staff devel. Dept. Edn. State of Conn., 1986-88; writing coord. East Elem. Sch., New Canaan, 1986-88; instr. Grad. Sch. Edn. Simmons Coll., Boston, 1989. Leader Reminiscence Writing Courtland Gardens Nursing Home, Stamford, Conn., 1985-86; leader adult writing group Charlotte Hobbs Library, Lovell, Maine, 1987-89; leader writing process-children's group Cmty. Ctr., Boca Grande, Fla., 1994; cons. writing process Banyan Elem. Sch., Sunrise, Fla., 1995-96. Mem. AAUW, Nat. League of Pen Women, Older Women's League. Democrat. Presbyterian. Avocations: women's studies, book groups, writing groups, hiking. Home: # Sg-77 630 SW 6th St Pompano Beach FL 33060-7718 E-mail: Ettaend@aol.com.

ENDICOTT, JENNIFER JANE REYNOLDS, education educator; b. Oklahoma City, Oct. 17, 1947; d. M. Ector and Jessie Ruth (Carter) Reynolds; m. William George Endicott, June 2, 1969 (dec. Sept. 1976); 1 child, Andrea A. BA History, U. Okla., 1969, MEd Adminstrn., 1975, PhD, 1987. Cert. secondary edn. tchr.: history, govt., geography, econs., adminstr., Okla. Mid. sch. tchr. Norman (Okla.) Pub. Schs., 1970-77, adminstr. elem. edn., 1977-80; grad. asst. U. Okla., Norman, 1984-88; adj. lectr. U. Ctrl. Okla., Edmond, 1988-90, asst. prof., 1990-94, assoc. prof., 1995-98, prof., 1999—. Mem. adv. bd. The Annual Editions Series, Guilford, Conn., 1994—; editor Okla. Assn. Tchr. Educators Jour., 1997-2001, mem. editl. bd., 2002—; reviewer Action in Teacher Education ATE Jour.; contbr. articles to profl. jours. Bd. dirs. Cleveland County Hist. Soc., Norman, 1980-88, Arts and Humanities Coun., Norman, 1982-88; bd. dirs. Jr. League, Inc., Norman, 1982-90; bd. dirs. Assistance League, Norman, 1982-90, pres. 1988-89. Recipient Harriet Harvey Meml. award U. Okla. Found., 1984; named Norman Cmty. Family of the Yr. Finalist, LDS Ch., Norman, 1985; named to The Educator's Leadership Acad., The Outstanding Profs. Acad., 1999-2000. Mem. ASCD, Okla. Assn. for Supervision and Curriculum Devel., Okla. Assn. Tchr. Educators (bd. dirs. 1994-2003, pres. 1996-97, exec. sec. 2001-03), Am. Assn. Tchr. Educators, Soc. for Philosophy and History of Edn., Nat. Soc. Study of Edn., Am. Ednl. Rsch. Assn., Philosophy of Edn. Soc., Kappa Delta Pi (univ. sponsor 1991-96), Phi Delta Kappa (bd. dirs. Mid. State chpt. 1993-99, v.p. 1997-99, Svc. Key 1998). E-mail: jendicott@ucok.edu.

ENDICOTT, JOHN EDGAR, international relations educator; b. Cin., Aug. 9, 1936; s. Charles Lafayette and Alice Willa (Campbell) E.; m. Mitsuyo Tiffani Kobayashi, Aug. 24, 1959; children: Charlene Nobel, John Edward. BA, Ohio State U., 1958; MA in History, Omaha U., 1968; MA in Internat. Rels., Tufts U., 1972, MALD, PhD, Tufts U., 1973; student, Natl. War Coll., 1982, Air Command Staff Coll., 1978, Air War Coll., 1976, Squadron Officer Sch., 1963. Commd. USAF, advanced through grades to col.; dep. head polit. sci. and philosophy dept. USAF Acad., 1969-71, 73-78; dep. Air Force rep. mil. staff com. UN Security Coun., 1979-81; dir. internat. affairs divsn. Air Force Plans, The Pentagon, 1978-81; assoc. dean Nat. War Coll., 1981-83; dir. rsch. directorate Nat. Def. U., 1983-86; dir. Inst. Nat. Strategic Studies, Dept. Def., 1986-89; prof. Sam Nunn Sch. Internat. Affairs Ga. Inst. Tech., Atlanta, 1989—, founding dir. Ctr. Internat. Strategy Tech. and Policy, 1989—; apptd. Olympic attache Mongolian Olympic Com., Ulaan Bataar, 1995-96. Co-chair Coun. U.S.-Japan Security Rels.; bd. dirs. Nat. Def. U. Found.; cons. Dept. Def., Chmn. Joint Chiefs Staff, Process for Accreditation of Joint Edn. Program, NRC of NAS, Office Internat. Affairs, Def. Task Force, Inst. Def. Analysis, others; chmn. interim secretariat Agy. for Ltd. Nuclear Weapons-Free Zone for N.E. Asia, 1996—; mem. rev. group Funabashi Commn. U.S.-Japan Alliance and Disarmament, 1999—; bd. dirs. UN Assn., Atlanta, 1998-2000; mem. Task Force on U.S. Policy in Korea, 2003; bd. advisors Atlanta Coun. for Internat. Rels., 2003—. Mem. editl. bd. The Japan Digest, Small Wars and Insurgencies, New South Mag.; author: Japan's Nuclear Option, 1975; co-editor, contbr.; American Defense Policy, 1977, Regional Security Issues, 1991; co-author: Politics of East Asia, 1978; contbr. articles to profl. jours. Mem. bd. advisors Atlantic Coun. for Internat. Rels., 2003—. Decorated Def. Superior Svc. medal, Legion of Merit, Bronze Star, Meritorious Svc. medal, Air medal with oak leaf cluster, Air Force Commendation medal with oak leaf cluster; Vietnam Svc. Medal with 2 bronze stars; Natl. Defense Svc. Medal, Rep. of Vietnam gallantry cross with device; Rep. of Vietnam Campaign Medal; Dept. of the Army Exceptional Civilian Svc. Medal; W. Alton Jones rsch. grantee Ploughshares Found.; rsch. grantee Carnegie Corp., 2d Chance Found., MacArthur Found. Nat. Security Seminar Series. Fellow Internat. Inst. Strategic Studies; mem. Internat. Studies Assn., Assn. Asian Studies, Army and Navy Club, Ga. Polit. Sci. Assn., Japan-Am. Soc. Ga. (recipient Mike Mansfield award 1996, exec. com., bd. dirs.), S.E. Korea-Am. Friendship Soc. (charter, bd. dirs., exec. vice chmn. 2000—), Georgian Club, Phi Beta Kappa. Avocations: tennis, French horn, writing, language study. Office: Ga Inst Tech Ctr Internat Strategy Atlanta GA 30332-0001 E-mail: john.endicott@inta.gatech.edu.

ENDRUSICK, ROSE MARIE, educator; b. Creighton, Pa., Feb. 11, 1929; d. Paul Anthony and Ann Catherine Fricioni; m. Stanley Endrusick, June 19, 1950; children— Anne, Scott. B.S., Drexel Inst. Tech., 1950; M.A., Calif. State U.-Los Angeles, 1970; cert. Culinary Inst. Am., 1973. Tchr. home econs., Springdale, Pa., 1950-53, Glendale, Calif., 1953-55, Arcadia (Calif.) Unified Sch. Dist., 1955-83; designer antique doll clothes. Named Outstanding Tchr. in Arcadia, So. Calif. Industry-Edn. Council, 1968. Mem. Am. Home Econs. Assn., Calif. Tchrs. Assn., NEA, Arcadia/San Gabriel PTA (hon. life), Doll Collectors Gallery Calif. (v.p. 1981-83). Republican. Roman Catholic. Office: 301 S 1st Ave Arcadia CA 91006-3802

ENDSLEY, JANE RUTH, nursing educator; b. Harrisburg, Ill., Oct. 14, 1942; d. Clifford B. Bond and Haroldene (Malone) Miller; m. William R. Endsley, June 6, 1964. Grad., Deaconess Hosp. Sch. Nursing, Evansville, Ind., 1963; student, So. Ill. U., 1968; BSN cum laude, U. Evansville, 1978. RN, Ind., Ill. Staff nurse Deaconess Hosp., 1963-64; psychiat. nurse med.-surg. emergency rm. and obstetrics Ferrell Hosp., Eldorado, Ill., 1964-68, DON, 1969-70; DON, Good Shepherd Nursing Home, Eldorado, 1971-72; instr. nursing Southea. Ill. U., Harrisburg, 1973—; pres., sec. Peartree Antiques, Inc., Eldorado, 1995—. Cons. parents too soon Egyptian Pub. Health Dept., Eldorado, 1985. Vice chmn. Pvt. Industry Coun., Harrisburg, 1983-91; precinct committeeperson Harrisburg Dem. Com., 1986-90; donor chmn. ARC, Harrisburg, 1970—; instr. CPR to civic orgns. and students, 1980-87. Mem. AAUW, Ill. Nurses Assn. (nominating com. 1975), Southeastern Ill. Coll. Edn. Assn. (pres. 1988-91), Faculty Wives and Women Southeastern Ill. Coll. (sec.-treas. 1974-75), Assn. Antique Dealers and Collectors, Ill. Preservation Coun., Nat. Hist. Soc., Sigma Theta Tau. Avocations: reading, gardening, travel, interior decorating, antiques. Home: PO Box 345 1075 Shawnee Hills Rd Harrisburg IL 62946-4943

ENFIELD, SUSAN ANN, secondary school educator; b. San Francisco, May 30, 1968; d. D. Michael and Julia Ann (Bettencourt) Enfield. Student, York (Eng.) U., 1988-89; BA in English, U. Calif., Berkeley, 1990; MEd, Stanford U., 1993, Harvard U., 2002. Editl. asst. Jossey-Bass, Inc. Pubs., San Francisco, 1990-92; tchr. Homestead HS, Cupertino, Calif., 1993-97; tchr. English Sir Francis Drake HS, San Anselmo, Calif., 1997-99; HS support provider U. Calif. Berkeley Tchg. and Learning Alliance, 1999—2001; bur. dir. curriculum and academic svcs. Pa. Dept. Edn., Lancaster, 2003—. Co-author: (book) When Tutor Meets Student. Named Outstanding Tchr., Tufts U., 1994, Carleton Coll., 1995, Coll. Wooster, 1996, U. Calif., Santa Barbara, 1997, U. Ariz., 1997. Mem.: Am. Assn. Sch. Adminstrs., Phi Delta Kappa.

ENGBRETSON, GUSTAV ALAN, bioengineering educator, neuroscientist; b. Fargo, N.D., Nov. 28, 1943; s. Gustav Andrew and Leona Mary (Welter) E.; m. Brenda Gaye Mackie, Apr. 23, 1983; children: Andrew Craig, Heather Anne. BA, Calif. State U., Sacramento, 1968, MA, 1971; PhD, U. Okla., 1976. Postdoctoral rsch. fellow dept. anat. sci. SUNY, Stony Brook, 1976-78, rsch. asst. prof. dept. anat. sci., 1978-79; rsch. asst. prof. Inst. Sensory Rsch. Syracuse (N.Y.) U., 1979-84; asst. prof. dept. bioengrng. Syracuse U., 1984-87, assoc. prof. dept. bioengrng., 1987—, chmn., dept. bioengrng. and neurosci., 1992-97; rsch. assoc. prof. cell and development biology, ophthalmol. Health Sci. Ctr. SUNY, Syracuse, 1989—. Mem. Inst. Sensory Rsch. Syracuse U., 1984—; participant Nat. Geog. Soc./ U. Okla. expedition to Lake Titicaca, Bolivia, 1974; cons. Nat.

Adv. Eye Coun. Nat. Eye Inst., 1982; reviewer grants NSF, manuscripts to profl. jours. Co-author: Field Guide to Oklahoma, 1974; contbr. over 60 articles to scholarly and profl. jours. Mem. Onondaga County Environ. Mgmt. Coun., Syracuse, 1986-89. Rsch. grantee Nat. Eye Inst., 1978-90, 2000-03, Whitaker Found., 1997—. Mem. AAAS, Am. Soc. Engring. Edn., Assn. Rsch. in Vision and Ophthalmology, Biomed. Engring. Soc., Soc. for Neurosci., Sigma Xi (pres. Syracuse chpt. 1989). Achievements include advanced research on structure and functioning of parietal eye of lacertilians; development of this simple eye as a model for visual info. processing in vertebrate retina. Office: Dept Bioengring & Neurosci 373 Link Hl Syracuse NY 13244-0001 E-mail: gus_engbretson@isr.syr.edu.

ENGEL, BARBARA ALPERN, history educator; BA in Russian Studies, CCNY, 1965; MA in Russian Studies, Harvard U., 1967; PhD in Rusian History, Columbia U., 1974. Part-time instr. Drew U., Madison, NJ, 1972—73; instr. Columbia U., N.Y.C., 1974; asst. prof. Sarah Lawrence Coll., 1974—76, U. Colo., Boulder, 1976—82, assoc. prof., 1982—92, prof., 1992—, dir. Ctrl. and Ea. European studies, 1993—95, chair dept. history, 1995—98. Author, co-editor: Five Sisters: Women Against the Tsar, 1975; author: Spanish transl., 1980, new edit., 1992, Mothers and Daughters: Women of the Intelligentsia in Nineteenth Century Russia, 1983; author, co-editor: Russia's Women: Accomodation, Resistance, Transformation, 1991; author: Between the Fields and the City: Women, Work and Family in Russia, 1861-1914, 1994, paperback edit., 1996; co-editor: A Revolution of their Own. Voices of Women in Soviet History, 1998; cons. editor Feminist Studies, 1979—98, mem. editl. bd. Frontiers, 1980—86, Slavic Rev., 1996—2001; contbr. articles. Recipient Heldt Article award, 1991, cert. tchg. excellence, Mortar Bd. Sr. Honor Soc., 1994, Heldt prize for Outstanding Achievement in Slavic Studies, AWSS, 1996, numerous other awards, grants; Wallenberg fellow, Rutgers Ctr. Hist. Analysis, 1995, fellow, John Simon Guggenheim Meml. Found., 2003, Sr. Exch. grant with the Soviet Union, IREX, 1985, 1987, 1991, Fulbright-Hays tng. grant, Faculty Rsch. Abroad program, 1987, Woodrow Wilson fellow, 1991, John D. and Catherine T. MacArthur Found. grantee, 1993—95, NEH fellow, 2003—. Mem.: Am. Assn. for Advancement of Slavic Studies, We. Assn. Women Historians (book prize com. 1990), Internat. Fedn. Socs. Rsch. Women's History (mem. U.S. com. 1988—91), Am. Hist. Assn. (com. on women historians 1987—89, mem. profl. divsn. 1990—92, mem. program com. 1994—95), Phi Beta Kappa. Office: U Colo Dept History Boulder CO 80309-0234

ENGEL, EMILY FLACHMEIER, educational consultant; b. Columbus, Tex., Sept. 15, 1938; d. William August and Jeanette D. (Hastedt) Flachmeier; m. Lars N. Engel, Dec. 28, 1957; children: Jan Kristin, Karen Gale. BSEd, U. Tex., 1959, MEd, 1966. Cert. tchr., counselor, adminstr. N.Mex. Sch. counselor, guidance team leader Los Alamos (N.Mex) Pub. Schs., 1967-85, coord., fed. projects, 1985-87; asst. prin. Los Alamos Mid. Sch., 1987-89; prin. Mountain Elem. Sch., Los Alamos, 1989-95; ednl. cons., 1995—. Presenter nat. confs. and convs. Trustee Children's Trust Fund N.Mex, 1999—2002; bd. dirs. Los Alamos Family Coun., 1985—91, Family Strengths Network, 1994—, pres., 1999—2002; bd. dirs. Self-Help, Inc., 1993—2002; adv. com. Sci.-at-Home, 1994—95. Mem.: NDEA (mem. counseling and guidance inst. U. Tex. Austin 1962—63), ASCD, Los Alamos Assn. Sch. Adminstrs. (pres. 1991—92), N.Mex. Assn. Elem. Sch. Prins. (pres.-elect 1992—93, pres. 1993—94), Nat. Assn. Elem. Sch. Prins., Alpha Omnicron Pi, Pi Lambda Theta, Delta Kappa Gamma (Rho chpt. sec.). Methodist. Home and Office: 192 Loma Del Escolar St Los Alamos NM 87544-2525

ENGEL, RICHARD LEE, lawyer, educator; b. Syracuse, NY, Sept. 19, 1936; s. S. Sanford and Eleanor M. (Gallop) E.; m. Karen K. Engel, Dec. 26, 1965; children: Todd Sanford, Gregg Matthew. BA, Yale U., 1958, JD, 1981. Bar: N.Y. 1961. Law asst. justices Appellate Divsn. NY 4th Jud. Dist., 1961-63; law clk. judge NY Supreme Ct., 1963-65; sr. ptnr. Nottingham, Engel, Gordon & Kerr LLP, Syracuse, 1970—. Adj. prof. law Syracuse U. Coll. of Law; law and medicine, equine law trial practice Am. Arbitration Assn.; AP Com. reviewer Prudential Class Action; lectr. in field; mem. various editl. adv. bds. Contbr. articles to profl. jours. Pres. Temple Soc. Concord, 1985-87; bd. dirs. Am. Field Svcs. Intercultural Programs, Inc., 1974-81. Mem. ABA, Am. Coll. Legal Medicine, N.Y. State Bar Assn., Onondaga Bar Asn. (mem. trial lawyers com. 1978-80, chmn. med. legal liaison com. 1976-77, chmn. spl. ins. com. 1988, Bench and Bar com. 1991, found. bd. 1992-98, grievance com. 1998—), N.Y. State Trial Attys. Assn., Upstate Trial Attys. Assn. (pres. 1973-74, chmn. bd. 1974-77), No. Dist. N.Y. Fed. Ct. Bar Assn. Inc. (trustee, program chmn. 2003—), Fed. Bar Coun. No. Dist. N.Y., Thoroughbred Owners and Breeders Assn. (owners coun.), Cavalry Country, Saratoga Reading Rooms, Inc., Yale (pres. Ctrl. N.Y.). Home: 603 Kimry Moor Fayetteville NY 13066-1832 Office: Nottingham Engel Gordon & Kerr LLP One Lincoln Ctr 8th Flr Syracuse NY 13202 E-mail: EquineEsq@aol.com.

ENGEL, THOMAS, chemistry educator; b. Yokohama, Japan, Apr. 2, 1942; came to U.S., 1947; s. George Walter and Juliane (Urban) E.; m. Esther Neeser, Aug. 23, 1979; 1 child, Alex. BS, Johns Hopkins U., 1963, MS, 1964; PhD, U. Chgo., 1969; Dr. rer. nat. habil., U. Munich, Fed. Republic Germany, 1979. Instr. Tech. U. Clausthal, Clausthal-Zellerfeld, Fed. Republic Germany, 1969-75, U. Munich, 1975-78; staff mem. IBM Rsch. Lab., Zurich, Switzerland, 1978-80; assoc. prof. chemistry U. Wash., Seattle, 1979-84, prof., 1984—, chmn. dept. chemistry, 1987-90. Contbr. papers and book chpts. to profl. publs. Recipient numerous grants NSF, Air Force Office Sci. Rsch., Office Naval Rsch, Am. Chem Soc. award in Colloid or Surface Chemistry, 1995. Mem. Am. Chem. Soc. (Surface Chemistry award 1995), Am. Vacuum Soc. Office: U Wash Dept Chemistry Bldg 10 Seattle WA 98195-0001 E-mail: engel@chem.washington.edu.

ENGELHARDT, HUGO TRISTRAM, JR., physician, educator; b. New Orleans, Apr. 27, 1941; s. Hugo Tristram and Beulah (Karbach) E.; m. Susan Gay Malloy, Nov. 25, 1965; children: Elisabeth, Christina, Dorothea. BA, U. Tex., Austin, 1963, PhD, 1969; MD with honors, Tulane U., 1972. Asst. prof. U. Tex. Med. Br., 1972-75, assoc. prof., 1975-77; mem. Inst. Med. Humanities, 1973-77; Rosemary Kennedy prof. philosophy of medicine Georgetown U., 1977-82; sr. research scholar Kennedy Inst. Center for Bioethics, Washington, 1977-82; prof. depts. internal medicine, community medicine and ob-gyn. Baylor Coll. Medicine, Houston, 1983-2001, prof. emeritus, 2001—; mem. Ctr. for Med. Ethics and Health Policy, Houston, 1983-2001; prof. dept. philosophy Rice U., Houston, 1983—. Chmn. adv. panel on infertility prevention and treatment for office of tech. assessment of the U.S. Congress, 1986-87; vis. scholar Internat. Akad. für Philosophie, Liechtenstein, 1997, Liberty Fund, spring, 1998. Author: Mind Body: A Categorial Relation, 1973, The Foundations of Bioethics, 1986, The Foundations of Bioethics, rev. edit., 1996, Bioethics and Secular Humanism, 1991, The Foundations of Christian Bioethics, 2000; co-author: Bioethics: Readings and Cases, 1987; assoc. editor: Ency. of Bioethics, 1978—83; assoc. editor Jour. Medicine and Philosophy, 1974—84; mem. editl. adv. bd.: Ethik in der Medizin, 1988—, Bioetica, 1993—, Teaching Philosophy, 1975; editor: Jour. Medicine and Philosophy, 1984—, (series) Philos. Studies in Contemporary Culture, 1992, Philosophy and Medicine series, 1974—, Clin. Med. Ethics, 1987—2002, Christian Bioethics, 1995—; editor: (with others) Evaluation and Explanation in the Biomedical Sciences, 1975, Philosophical Medical Ethics, 1977, Mental Health, 1978, Clinical Judgment, 1979, Concepts of Health and Disease, 1981, New Knowledge in the Biomedical Sciences, 1982, Scientific Controversies, 1987, The Use of Human Beings in Research, 1988, Sicherheit und Freiheit, 1990, Allocating Scarce Medical Resources, 2002; editor: Hegel Reconsidered, 1994, The Philosophy of Medicine, 2000. Mem. bioethics com. Nat. Found. March of Dimes, 1975—. Fulbright fellow, 1969-70, Woodrow Wilson vis. fellow, 1988; fellow Inst. for Advanced Studies, Berlin, 1988-89. Mem. Am. Philos. Assn., European Acad. Scis. and Arts. Home: 2802 Lafayette Houston TX 77005-3038 Office: Rice U Dept Philosophy PO Box 1892 Houston TX 77251-1892 E-mail: htengelh@rice.edu.

ENGELHARDT-ALVAREZ, MADELINE, retired preschool administrator; b. Cape Girardeau, Mo., Sept. 26, 1927; d. Rudolf and Stella (Thomala) Engelhardt; widow; 1 child, Arden Lynn; m. Robert Switzer, Nov. 24, 1951 (div. June 1958). BS, Mt. Senario Coll., 1969; MS in Tchg., U. Wis., Eau Claire, 1971; postgrad., U. Wis., Madison, 1974. Cert. tchr., Wis. Kindergarten tchr. pub. sch., Internat. Falls, Minn., 1951-54; tchr. pub. sch. Bruce, Wis., 1954-55, Craig, Colo., 1955-58; kindergarten tchr. pub. sch. Columbia Heights, Minn., 1958-65; presch. tchr. pvt. sch. Cocoa Beach, Fla., 1965-67; spl. edn. tchr. pub. sch., Independence, Mo., 1970-73; spl. edn. instr. materials tchr. Fennimore, Mo., 1973-82; dir. spl. edn. Coop. Edn. Svcs. Assn., Janesville, Wis., 1974-82; Headstart dir., coord. Indianhead Cmty. Action Agy., Ladysmith, Wis., 1982-97. Bd. dirs. Green County. Mem. Coun. for Exceptional Children, Wis. Head Start Assn., Wis. Early Childhood Assn., Nat. Assn. for Edn. of Young, Nat. Assn. Head Start Children. Avocations: camping, reading, knitting, indoor plants. Address: 5912 San Bernardo Ave Laredo TX 78041-2506

ENGELL, JAMES THEODORE, English educator; b. Danville, Pa., Sept. 6, 1951; s. Frederick Jacob and Ruth Louise Engell; m. Ainslie Sheridan Brennan, June 2, 1984; children: Marleny Brennan, Alexander E. BA, Harvard Coll., 1973; PhD, Harvard U., 1978. Asst. prof. Harvard U., Cambridge, Mass., 1978-80, assoc. prof., 1980-83, prof. English and comparative lit., 1983—2000, Gurney prof. English, prof. comparative lit., 2000—, chair degree program in history and lit., 1988-93, dir. undergrad. studies in English, 1995-97. Author: The Creative Imagination, 1981 (Thomas Wilson prize 1982), Forming the Critical Mind, 1989, The Committed Word: Literature and Public Values, 1999; editor: Coleridge: The Early Family Letters, 1994; co-editor: Coleridge, Biographia Literaria, 1983; editor, contbr.: Johnson and His Age, 1984, Teaching Literature: What Is Needed Now, 1988; editl. advisor Jour. History of Ideas, 1986—, Coll. Lit., 1990—, 1650-1850 Ideas, Aesthetics, and Inquiries in the Early Modern Era, Eighteenth-Century Thought, Literature and Religion. Corporator Emerson Hosp. and Health System, Concord, Mass., 1989-94. Recipient Levenson Tchg. prize, 1995, Roslyn Abramson Tchg. award, 1997, Coun. for Advancement and Support Edn. Gold award, 1999, Phi Betta Kappa Tchg. award, 2002, John Marquand Advising prize, 2003; Ford Found. grantee, 1978; Cabot fellow, 2001. Mem. MLA, Am. Soc. 18th Century Studies, Johnsonians (chair 1990-91), Assn. Lit. Scholars and Critics (pres. 2001-2002, sec. 2002—), Friends of Coleridge. Avocations: travel, sports, music. Office: Harvard U Barker Ctr Dept English 12 Quincy St Cambridge MA 02138-3804

ENGELMANN, PAUL VICTOR, plastics engineering educator; b. Ann Arbor, Mich., Jan. 15, 1958; s. Manfred David and Patricia (Park) E.; m. Sarah C. Sanford, Oct. 24, 1998; children: Thomas, David. AS in Geology, Lansing (Mich.) C.C., 1980; BS in Indsl. Edn., Western Mich. U., 1982, MA in Vocat. Edn., 1984, EdD in Ednl. Leadership, 1988. Owner H.L. & S. Auto Restoration & Fabrication, Lansing, Mich., 1977-82; from tchg. asst. dept. engrng. tech. to prof. dept. indsl. and mfg. engrng. Western Mich. U., Kalamazoo, 1982—2000, prof. Indsl. and Mfg. Engring. Dept., 2000, asst. chmn. dept., 2001—02, chmn. dept., 2002—. Prin. investigator Rsch. and Tech. Inst., Grand Rapids, Mich., 1988-97; prin. investigator Right Place, Grand Rapids, 1997—; rschr. Robert Morgan & Co., Battle Creek, Mich., 1990-94; prin. investigator Copper Devel. Assn. Inc., 1995—; cons. plastics Parker Hannafin Corp., Ostego, Mich., 1990-97; v.p. Western Mich. SPE Edn. Found., 1994-97. Author: Manufacturing Technology, 1989; contbr. 50 articles to profl. jours.; patentee in field. Pres. Plainwell (Mich.) Hist. Preservation Soc., 1990-91, 97-99; pres. bd. dirs. Pipp Found., 1992—, sec. 1992—; chmn., bd. trustees 1st United Meth. Ch., Plainwell, 1996-97, vice chmn. bldg. com., 1997-00. Presdl. scholar, 1982; recipient Protective Package of the Yr. award Children's Hosp. of Birmingham, 1990, Teaching Excellence award Western Mich. U., 1990. Mem. Soc. Plastics Engrs. (sr., past pres. 1992-93, pres. 1991-92, pres.-elect 1990-91, v.p. Western Mich. sec. 1989-90, sec. 1988-89, edn. chmn. 1985-88, Sectional award 1986, 87, 88, Best Paper award 1993, 99, 2000, Outstanding Mem. award 1994). Methodist. Avocations: antique auto restoration, old house preservation, environmental preservation. Home: 311 E Chart St Plainwell MI 49080-1703 Office: Western Mich U Dept Indsl and Mfg Engring MailStop 5336 Parkview Campus Kalamazoo MI 49008-5336 E-mail: paul.engelmann@wmich.edu.

ENGELMANN, REINHART WOLFGANG HANNS, physics educator; b. Berlin, Aug. 21, 1934; came to U.S., 1961; s. Helmut Julius Toni and Johanna Elise Emma (Rudel) E.; m. Wilhelma Steinmetz, July 15, 1967; children: Robert L., Arnold H., Claudia J.K., Flora E.A. Dipl.phys., Tech. U., Munich, 1958, Dr.rer.nat., 1961. Device physicist CBS Labs., Stamford, Conn., 1961-63; mem. tech. staff Hewlett-Packard Assoc./Labs, Palo Alto, Calif., 1963-66; lab. supr. AEG-Telefunken Rsch. Inst., Ulm, Germany, 1967—73; mem. tech. staff, project mgr. Hewlett-Packard Labs., Palo Alto, 1973-85; instr. U. Santa Clara, Calif., 1984-85; sr. scientific adviser, group leader Siemens Corp. Rsch., Inc., Princeton, N.J., 1985-89; prof. Oreg. Grad. Inst., Beaverton, 1990—97, adj. prof., 1997—. Cons. Siemens A.G., Munich, 1989. Co-author: Gunn-Effect Electronics, 1975; contbr. articles to profl. jours. Mem., chairperson Sch. Site Coun., Mountain View, Calif., 1978-80; chairperson Piaget Parent Group, Mountain View, 1979-80; referee Ayso Soccer League, Los Altos, Calif., 1980; mem. fund raising com. Mountain View Sch. Bd., 1982-83. Fellowship Study Found. of the German People, Bad Godesberg, Fed. Republic Germany, 1954. Mem. IEEE (sr., IEDM subcom. 1981-82), Am. Phys. Soc. Achievements include 6 patents on semiconductor devices; development of reliable high-power semiconductor laser; establishment of feasibility of leaky-mode coupled semiconductor laser arrays; evaluation of conditions for laser oscillation and superradiant amplification in double heterostructure lasers. Home: 17410 SW Augusta Ln Beaverton OR 97006-4321 Office: OGI Sch Sci & Engring OHSU 20000 NW Walker Rd Beaverton OR 97006-8921

ENGERRAND, DORIS DIESKOW, business educator; b. Chgo., Aug. 7, 1925; d. William Jacob and Alma Wilhelmina (Cords) Dieskow; m. Gabriel H. Engerrand,Oct. 26, 1946 (dec. June 1987); children: Steven, Kenneth, Jeannine. BS in Bus. Adminstrn., N. Ga. Coll., 1958, BS in Elementary Edn., 1959; M. Bus. Edn., Ga. State U., 1966, PhD, 1970. Tchr., dept. chmn. Lumpkin County H.S., Dahlonega, Ga., 1960-63, 65-68; tchr. Gainesville, Ga., 1965; asst. prof. Troy (Ala.) State U., 1969-71; asst. prof. bus. Ga. Coll. and State U., Milledgeville, 1971-74, assoc. prof., 1974-78, prof., 1978-90, chmn. dept. info. sys. and comms., 1978-89; retired, 1990. Contbr. articles on bus. edn. to profl. publs. Named Outstanding Tchr. Lumpkin County Pub. Schs., 1963, 66; Outstanding Educator bus. faculty Ga. Coll., 1975, Exec. of Yr. award, 1983. Fellow Assn. for Bus. Communication (v.p. S.E. 1978-80, 81-84, 89-92, bd. dirs.), Nat. Bus. Edn. Assn., Ga. Bus. Edn. Assn. (Postsecondary Tchr. of Yr. award 10th dist. 1983, Postsecondary Tchr. of Yr. award 1984), Am. Vocat. Assn., Ga. Vocat. Assn. (Educator of Yr. award 1984, Parker Liles award 1989), Profl. Secs. Internat. (pres. Milledgeville chpt. 1996-97), Ninety-nines Internat.. (chmn. N. Ga. chpt. 1975-76, named Pilot of Yr. N. Ga. chpt. 1973). Methodist. Home: 1674 Pine Valley Rd Milledgeville GA 31061-2465

ENGERRAND, KENNETH G. lawyer, law educator; b. Atlanta, June 30, 1952; s. Gabriel H. and Doris A. (Dieskow) E.; m. Anne Walts, Mar. 16, 1985; children: Caroline Elizabeth Turner, Catherine Anne Denton. BA, Fla. State U., 1973; JD, U. Tex., 1976. Bar: Tex. 1976, U.S. Dist. Ct. (so. dist.) Tex. 1977, U.S. Ct. Appeals (5th cir.) 1978, U.S. Supreme Ct. 1980, U.S. Ct. Appeals (11th cir.) 1981, U.S. Dist. Ct. (ea. dist.) Tex. 1987. Assoc. Royston, Rayzor, Vickery & Williams, Houston, 1976-80, Brown, Sims & Ayre, Houston, 1980; v.p., gen. counsel Huthnance Offshore Corp., Houston, 1980-86; ptnr. Brown, Sims, Wise & White, Houston, 1986-2000, Brown Sims PC, Houston, 2000—. Adj. prof. law S. Tex. Coll. Law, 1978-93; columnist The Reporter, 1984-87; contbr. articles to profl. jours.; faculty advisor to spl. maritime edits. S. Tex. Law Jour., 1981-86. Fund drive vol. Houston Grand Opera, 1985-93, trustee, 1986-93; trustee Judge John R. Brown Scholarship Found., 1994—. Recipient outstanding contbn. to cmty. award Houston Jaycees, 1983. Mem. ABA (vce chmn. admiralty and maritime law com., tort and ins. practice sect. 1986-89), Def. Rsch. Inst., Maritime Law Assn., Coll. of State Bar Tex., Order of Coif, Phi Beta Kappa, Phi Delta Phi. Republican. Episcopalian. Avocations: legal writing, cultivating roses. Home: 3511 Durness Way Houston TX 77025 Office: Brown Sims PC 1177 West Loop S STE 1000 Houston TX 77027-9083 E-mail: kengerrand@brownsims.com.

ENGGAS, GRACE FALCETTA, university administrator; b. Hartford, Conn., May 25, 1946; d. Giacomo and Frances Catanzaro Falcetta; m. David Hirsh Enggas, Mar. 16, 1974. BA, U. Conn., 1971; MA, Ohio State U., 1973; grad., New Eng. mgmt. Inst., Wellesley, Mass., 1995. Cert. in Myers Briggs Type Inventory, 1987. Contract underwriter Travelers Ins. Cos., Hartford, 1965-71; asst. mgr., Jones Grad. Twr. Ohio State U., Columbus, 1972-73; resident counselor Worcester (Mass.) State Coll., 1974-77; area coord. Ea. Conn. State U., Willimantic, 1977-78, assoc. dir. housing, 1978-87, dir. housing, 1987—2002, coord. scholarship and fin. aid counseling, 2002—. Bd. dirs. and v.p. Literacy Vols. of Conn., 1990—; treas. Charter Cable Adv. Bd., 1989—. Mem. Nat. Assn. Student Pers. Adminstrs., Assn. Coll. and Univ. Housing Officers, State U. Adminstrv. Faculty/Am. Fedn. State, County and Mcpl. Employees local #2836 Collective Bargaining Unit (treas. 1978, sec. 1986-92, v.p. 1992—, del. 1992, sec. Local 2836 1998—). Democrat. Home: 58 Mountain Rd Mansfield Center CT 06250-1211 Office: Ea Conn State Univ 83 Windham St Willimantic CT 06226-2211

ENGHETA, NADER, electrical engineering educator, researcher; b. Tehran, Iran, Oct. 8, 1955; came to U.S. 1978; s. Abdollah and Meymanat (Mesghali) E.; m. Susanne Hoshyar, Oct. 15, 1983; children: Alex Cameron, Sarah Katherine. BSEE, U. Tehran, 1978; MSEE, Calif. Inst. Tech., 1979, PhD in Elec. Engring., 1982. Grad. rsch. asst. Calif. Inst. Tech., Pasadena, 1979-82, postdoctoral rsch. fellow, 1982-83; sr. rsch. scientist Dikewood Divsn. Kaman Scis. Corp., Santa Monica, Calif., 1983-87; asst. prof. elec. engrng. U. Pa., Phila., 1987-90, assoc. prof. elec. engring., 1990-95, prof. elec. engring., 1995—, UPS Found. Disting. Educator chair, 1999-2000. Grad. group chmn. elec. engring. U. Pa., 1993-97; gen. chmn. Benjamin Franklin Symposium, Phila., 1990-91; vis. lectr., UCLA, spring 1986; condr. seminars in field; IEEE Antennas and Propagation Soc. Disting. lectr., 1997-99. Guest editor spl. issue Jour. Electromagnetic Waves and Applications on Wave interaction with chiral and complex media, Vol. 6, No. 5/6, 1992, mem. editl. bd., 1993—, guest editor Jour. Franklin Inst. on Antennas and Microwaves, 13th Ann. Benjamin Franklin Symposium, Vol. 332B, No. 5, 1995, assoc. editor Radio Sci., 1991—96, IEEE Trans. on Antennas and Propagation, 1996—2001; contbr. over 60 articles to profl. jours., chpts. to books; co-guest editor (journal) Wave Motion, on Electrodynamics in Complex Environments, vol. 34, No. 3, 2001. NSF Presdl. Young Investigator, 1989; AT&T Spl. Purpose grantee, 1988; U. Pa. Rsch. Found. grantee, 1988, 90, 93; recipient Engring. Tchg. Excellence award W.M. Keck Found., 1995, Fulbright Naples Chair award for Italy, 1998, Guggenheim Fellowship award 1999. Fellow IEEE (chmn. antennas and propagation/microwave theory and technique Phila. chpt. 1990-91, 3d millennium medal 2000), Optical Soc. Am.; mem. AAAS, Am. Phys. Soc., Internat. Union of Radio Sci. (commn. B and D of USNC), Sigma Xi. Achievements include six patents (with others) for method of measuring chiral parameters of chiral materials, novel electromagnetic shielding reflection and scattering control using chiral materials, waveguides using chiral materials; printed-circuit antenna using material, rodomes using chiral materials, method of using polarization differencing to improve vision; patents pending (with others) for electromagnetically non-reflective material, novel antenna arrays using chiral materials, novel lenses using chiral materials; research on applied and theoretical electromagnetics, optics, complex unconventional electromagnetic materials, electromagnetic chiral materials, microwave, biologically-inspired polarization-difference imaging, waveguide theory, role of fractional calculus and fractiional paradigm in electrodynamics; patentee in field. Office: Univ of Pa 200 S 33rd St Philadelphia PA 19104-6314 E-mail: engheta@ee.upenn.edu.

ENGLAND, ANTHONY WAYNE, electrical engineering and computer science educator, astronaut, geophysicist; b. Indpls., May 15, 1942; s. Herman U. and Betty (Steel) E.; m. Kathleen Ann Kreutz, Aug. 31, 1962. SB, MIT, 1965, PhD, 1970, SM, 1965. With Texaco Co., 1962; field geologist Ind. U., 1963; scientist-astronaut NASA, 1967-72, 79-88; with U.S. Geol. Survey, 1972-79; crewmember on Spacelab 2, July, 1985; adj. prof. Rice U., Houston, 1987-88; prof. elec. engring. and computer sci. U. Mich., Ann Arbor, 1988—, prof. atmospheric, oceanic and space sci., 1989—, assoc. dean Rackham Grad. Sch., 1995-98. Mem. space studies bd. NRC, 1992-98. Assoc. editor Jour. Geophys. Rsch. Recipient Antarctic medal, Spaceflight medal NASA, Spaceflight award Am. Astron. Soc., Outstanding Scientific Achievement medal NASA. Fellow IEEE; mem. Am. Geophys. Union. Home: 7949 Ridgeway Ct Dexter MI 48130-9700 Office: U Mich Dept Elec Engring-Comp Sci Ann Arbor MI 48109-2122

ENGLAND, DIANA WHITTEN, elementary education educator; b. Cleve., June 12, 1951; d. George Herbert Whitten and Evelyn Mixon Herring; m. Henry England Jr., Sept. 26, 1971. BS in Elem. Edn., Kent State U., 1974; MEd, Cleve. State U., 1984, postgrad., 1992. Cert. tchr. gifted and talented, supr. gifted and talented, Ohio. Classrm. tchr. East Cleveland (Ohio) Bd. Edn., 1974—79, tchr. gifted and talented students, 1979—89, math. coach, 1991—2001, supr. curriculum and instrn., 2001—; vis. instr. Cleve. State U., 1989—91, coord. Gov.'s Summer Inst., 1991—. Family math. presenter Kent (Ohio) State U., 1991—; coord. L.E.A.P., East Cleveland Bd. Edn., 1993, 94, 95. Elder, St. Mark's Presbyn. Ch., Cleve., 1990-92; moderator St. Mark-Elizabeth Clarke Scholarship, Cleve., 1983—. Nominee Ohio Tchr. of Yr., East Cleveland Bd. Edn., 1989; named Educator of Yr., East Cleveland PTA, 1988, Eisenhower Exemplary Tchr., Ohio Dept. Edn., 1994; recipient Martha Holden Jennings scholar, 1991. Mem. Nat. Coun. Tchrs. of Math., Ohio Assn. for Gifted Children (Cert. of Merit 1986), Ohio Coun. Tchrs. of Math., Nat. Coun. Suprs. of Math., Met. Cleve. Alliance Black Sch. Educators (1st v.p.), Phi Delta Kappa (pres. 1990-91, Svc. Key 1993). Presbyterian. Avocations: reading, collecting african-american art. Home: 15924 Glynn Rd East Cleveland OH 44112-3533 Office: East Cleveland Bd Edn 15305 Terrace Rd East Cleveland OH 44112-2933

ENGLAND, JOHN DAVID, neurologist, educator; b. Clarksburg, W.Va., Jan. 20, 1954; s. John Draper and Imogene Lucille (Alexander) E.; m. Cathy Ann Drummond, Nov. 22, 1975. BA in Chemistry, W.Va. U., 1976, MD, 1980. Diplomate Nat. Bd. Med. Examiners, Am. Bd. Psychiatry and Neurology, Am. Bd. Electrodiagnostic Medicine; lic. physician, S.C., Pa., Colo., La. Intern Med. U. S.C., Charleston, 1980-81, resident in neurology, 1981-84; clin. neuromuscular fellow dept. neurology Hosp. of U. Pa., Phila., 1984-85, postdoctoral rsch. fellow dept. neurology, 1985-87; asst. prof. neurology U. Colo., Denver, 1987-92; assoc. prof. neurology La. State U., New Orleans, 1992-98, prof. neurology and neurosci., 1998-2001; attending physician U. Colo. Health Scis. Ctr., Denver, 1987-92, dir. electromyography lab., 1987-92; attending physician Med. Ctr. La., New Orleans, 1992-2001; prof. neurology and neurosci. La. State U., New Orleans, 1998-2001, dir. MDA clinic, 1998-2001; chmn. neurology, dir. neurosci. Deaconess Billings Clinic, Billings, Mont., 2001—. Lectr. in field. Contbr. numerous articles to profl. jours.; editl. cons. Muscle and Nerve,

1987—, Ann. Neurol., 1990—, Brain, 1993—; mem. editl. bd. Muscle & Nerve, 2000—. Recipient Koehler award in chemistry, Handbook award Chem. Rubber Co., Whitehall award of dept. chemistry; W.Va. U. Bd. Regents scholar, Masonic scholar, others; grantee Muscular Dystrophy Assn., 1985-87, NIH, 1987-88, Nat. Inst. Neurol. Disorders and Stroke, 1988-93, Nat. Inst. Aging, 1991-94, La. State U. Neurosci. Ctr. for Excellence, 1993-94, Dept. Def., 1993—. Mem. AMA, Am. Neurol. Assn., Am. Assn. Electrodiagnostic Medicine (profl. practice com. 1988-91, liaison rep. 1991-92, spl. interest group com. 1992-93, tng. program com. 1993-96, program com. 1996—, bd. dirs.), Am. Acad. Neurology (21st Century Leader in Neurology 2003), Am. Neurol. Assn., N.Y. Acad. Scis., Am. Soc. Neurol. Investigation, Soc. for Neurosci., Am. Acad. Clin. Neurophysiology (pres. 2002-2003, Disting. Svc. award 2003) 21st century leader in Neurology selected by Am. Acad. of Neurology,2003; Distinguished Serv. award from Am. Acad. of clin. Neurophysiology,2003, W.Va. U. Alumni Assn., Alpha Omega Alpha, Phi Kappa Phi, Phi Lambda Upsilon, Phi Beta Kappa. Democrat. Methodist. Avocations: skiing, running, hiking, reading. Office: Deaconess Billings Clinic Dept Neurology 2825 8th Ave N PO Box 37000 Billings MT 59107-7000

ENGLAND, RICHARD C., JR., special education educator; b. Birmingham, Ala., Mar. 16, 1955; s. Richard C. Sr. and Martha C. (Darnall) E.; m. Barbara L. England, Aug. 25, 1974; children: Richard III, Amy, Micah, Kathryn. Student, Freed-Hardeman U., 1972-74; MusB, Union U., 1976; MusM, Memphis State U., 1982, EdD, 1985. Diplomate Am. Coll. Forensic Examiners. Pub. sch. tchr., 1978-84; mem. staff Ala. Commn. on Higher Edn., Montgomery, 1984-91; prin. Jackson (Tenn.) Christian Sch., 1991-93; headmaster Clifton Ganus Sch., New Orleans, 1993-94; prof. spl. edn. Freed-Hardeman U., Henderson, Tenn., 1994—; asst. supt. dept. mental health/mental retardation State of Tenn. Mental Health Inst. Mem. round table Lincoln Coll. U. Oxford, Oxford, England, 2003. Author: Displaced Children in Crisis: Our Enabling System for High Risk Behavior, 2003; contbr. articles to profl. jours., chpt. to textbooks. Commr. So. Assn. Colls. and Schs., 1994-95, Coun. on Occupl. Edn., 1995-99; vol. Madison County Juveline Ct., Jackson. Mem. ASCD, Nat. Assn. Sch. Psychologists, Tenn. Assn. Sch. Psychologists. Mem. Ch. of Christ. Avocations: ham radio, fly fishing, reading, camping. Office: Freed-Hardeman U Dept Spl Edn Henderson TN 38340

ENGLE, MARY ELIZABETH, dietitian, educator; b. Nowata, Okla., July 28, 1914; d. Charles Levi and Vena Ethel Engle. BS, So. Mo. State U., 1934; MS in Instn. Mgmt., Kans. State U., 1945; postgrad., Iowa State U., 1939, 40, 48, U. Wis., 1965-66. Tchr. home econs. Forsyth (Mo.) H.S., 1934-38; tchr. vocat. home econs. Richland (Mo.) H.S., 1938-43, Aurora (Mo.) H.S., 1943-44; grad. asst. instn. mgmt. Kans. State U., Manhattan, 1944-45, U. Wis., Madison, 1965-66; assoc. prof. Ctrl. Mo. State U., Darrensburg, 1967-80. Mem. NEA, AAUW (pres.), Mo. Tchrs. Assn., Delta Kappa Gamma, Sigma Kappa, Kappa Omicron Phi. Methodist. Avocations: bridge, travel, cooking. Home: 37 Timberline Dr Warrensburg MO 64093-2906

ENGLE, MOLLY, program evaluator, preventive medicine researcher, medical educator; b. Ft. Leavenworth, Kans., Apr. 12, 1947; d. Robert Thomas and Phyllis Adele (Germann) E. BSN, U. Ariz., 1971, MS, 1973, PhD, 1983. RN, Ariz. Rsch. assoc. U. Ariz., Tucson, 1979-82; program assoc. Am. Coll. Testing, Iowa City, 1982-84; instr. Sch. Medicine U. Ala., Birmingham, 1984-87, asst. prof. Sch. Medicine, 1987-94; dir. rsch. and evaluation Health East, Mpls., 1992-93; assoc. prof. dept. medicine Sch. Medicine U. Ala., Birmingham, 1994-98; assoc. prof. extension svc., dept. pub. health Oreg. State U., Corvallis, 1998—. Co-dir. Geriat. Edn. Ctr., U. Ala., Birmingham, 1990-91; evaluation cons. Am. Soc. Aging, San Francisco, 1990-94, USPHS Health Resources and Svcs. Adminstrn., Bur. of Health Professions, Rockville, Md., 1996-98; cons. health svcs. rsch. and evaluation HealthEast, 1993-94. Prodr. (video series) Substance Abuse and the Pregnant Woman: A Series, 1994. Co-chair Adam Elem. Sch. Parent Tchr., Corvallis, 1999—2001. Recipient fellowship NIMH, 1972-73, fellowship Health Scis. Consortium, 1989, Postdoctoral fellowship Gerontol. Soc. Am., 1990. Mem.: Am. Evaluation Assn. (health topical interest group program chair 1986—2001, bd. dirs. 1992—94, pres.-elect 2001, pres. 2002—03, sec. 2003, Svc. Recognition award 1994). Avocations: reading, travel, violin. Office: Oreg State U Extension Svc 307 Ballard Extension Hall Corvallis OR 97331-8538

ENGLEBRETSON, ROSANN CAMILLE, education educator, writer; b. Chgo., July 16, 1950; d. Carl Gustave and Anne Frances (DeMoon) Ohlund; m. Mark Steven Englebretson, June 16, 1973; childern: Eric, Steven, Jennifer. BA, UCLA, 1972; MA, U. Colo., 1989; EdD, Nova U., 1995. Cert. elem. educator Calif. Tchr. Colorado Springs (Colo.) Montessori Sch., 1972-73; tchr. elem. sch. Apple Valley (Calif.) Sch. Dist., 1974-76; tchr. Edwards (Calif.) Presch., 1976-77; ednl. cons., writer Coronado Publishers, San Deigo, 1981-85; edn. cons., author Holt Rinehart & Winston Publishers, Austin, Tex., 1986-89, HBJ, Orlando, Fla., 1986-89; author, cons. Franklin Learning Resources, Mt. Holly, N.J., 1989-91, Simon & Schuster Publishers, Needham Heights, Mass., 1991—; instr. continuing edn. U. Colo., Colorado Springs, 1990—; prof. Colo. Christian U., 2000—; author, cons. Silver Burdett Ginn, 1993—. Co-dir. youth program Nat. Wildlife Fedn., Summit, 1985—; mem. adv. bd. Colo. Presch. Project, Colorado Springs, 1991—; tchr. trainer Sunday Sch. In-Svc. Programs, Colo., Tex., Ariz., Tenn., Okla., 1989—. Author: (textbook) Rainbows, 1989, Language Master Learning Strategies System, 1990, Interactive Phonics, 1993; cons. author: (textbook) World of Reading, 1993; co-author: Silver Burdett Ginn Reading Series Literature Works, 1996, Ready Readers Modern Curriculum Press, 1995. Dir. tchr. tng. 1st Presbyn. ch., Colorado Springs, 1985-88; children's leader Bible study Fellow Bible Ch., Colorado Springs, 1988-91, adminstrv. asst., 1990-2002, Sunday sch. tchr., 1989-93, co-adminstr. Promiseland, 1993—; co-dir. Jr. Naturalist program Nat. Wildlife Fedn. Summits, 1985—. Mem. Nat. Assn. Edn. Young Children, Internat. Reading Assn., Assn. Supervision and Curriculum Devel. Avocation: reading. Home and Office: 5390 Setters Way Colorado Springs CO 80919-7922

ENGLERT, WALTER GEORGE, classics and humanities educator; b. Oakland, Calif., June 30, 1952; s. Walter George and Isobel Ann (O'Hearne) E.; m. Mary Ellen Mecchi; children: Francesca, Molly. BA summa cum laude, St. Mary's Coll. Calif., 1974; MA, U. Calif. Santa Barbara, 1976; postgrad., Am. Sch. Classical Studies, Athens, 1979; PhD, Stanford U., 1981. Teaching asst. U. Calif., Santa Barbara, 1974-76, Stanford U., 1977-78; vis. lectr. U. Mich., Ann Arbor, 1980-81; vis. assoc. prof. U. Calif., Berkeley, 1986, Intercollegiate Ctr. Classical Studies, Rome, 1992-93; Omar and Althea Hoskins prof. Reed Coll., Portland, Oreg., 1981—. Organizer and lectr. Reed Latin Symposium for H.S. Students, 1988-2003; participant TAG Spring Interdisciplinary confs., 1988; tchr. Paideia Class, 1989, 91, 96, 97, Reed MALS Seminar, 1988, 93, 97, 2001, Reed Elderhostel Program, 1989; mem. faculty Reed Alumni Coll., 1989, 95; lectr. Seattle Reed Alumni Group, 1991; guest Town Hall TV show, 1991. Contbr. articles to profl. jours. Grantee NEH, 1983, 95, Mellon Faculty Seminar, 1986-87, Sloan Found., 1987-88. Office: Reed Coll 3203 SE Woodstock Blvd Portland OR 97202-8138 E-mail: walter.englert@reed.edu.

ENGLISH, JOHN RIFE, educational administrator; b. Barney Brooks, Ga., Mar. 22, 1926; s. Andrew James and India Mariah (Williams) E.; AB, U. Ga., 1949, M.Ed., 1950, postgrad., 1957-75; postgrad., Ga. So. Coll., 1972-73; m. Helen Marie Langford, June 7, 1947; children: Julianne, Helen Marie, Kathleen, John Cornelius. Prin., Midville (Ga.) H.S., 1950-56; asso. prin. Comml. H.S., Savannah, Ga., 1956-59, Groves H.S., Savannah, 1959-60; prin. Chatham Jr. H.S., Savannah, 1960-62, Mercer Jr. H.S., Garden City, Ga., 1962-64, Robert W. Groves H.S., 1964-70; purchasing mgr. 1st Dist. Coop. Ednl. Services Agy., Statesboro, Ga., 1970-72; headmaster Bulloch Acad., Statesboro, 1972-74; prin. Appling County Hi.S., Baxley, Ga., 1974-75, Norris Middle Sch., Thomson, Ga., 1975-83; adminstrv. asst. McDuffie County Schs., Thomson, 1983-85; ret., 1985; mem. Ga. Adv. Council Title III ESEA. Bd. dirs. Burke County Library, 1954-56; mem. bd. registrars Garden City, 1961-70. Served with USNR, 1942-45. Mem. Nat. Assn. Secondary Sch. Prins., Assn. Curriculum Devel., Ga. Assn. Educators, NEA, Profl. Assn. Ga. Educators, Burke County Edn. Assn. (pres. 1952-53), Chatham County Edn. Assn. (pres. 1960-61), McDuffie Edn. Assn. (pres. 1978-79), Internat. Platform Assn., Pi Sigma Alpha, Kappa Delta Pi. Methodist. Lodges: Lions (pres. Midville 1952-53, Garden City 1967-68), Kiwanis (pres. Thomson 1978-79). Home: Lawrenceville, Ga. Died Jan. 6, 2002.

ENGLISH, JUJUAN BONDMAN, women's health nurse, educator; b. El Dorado, Ark., Dec. 16, 1947; d. Irvin Raymond and Ida Ruth (Payton) Bondman; m. Frederick J. English, Aug. 28, 1976; children: Michael, Christopher, Meagan. ADN, So. State Coll., Magnolia, Ark., 1970; BSN, U. Ark., 1988; MSN, U. Miss., 1992; PhD in Med. Sci., U. Ark., 2002. Cert. childbirth educator. Charge nurse Union Med. Ctr., El Dorado, Warner Brown Hosp., El Dorado, labor and delivery supr.; instr. nursing U. Ark., Monticello, asst.. prof. nursing, 1993-95; dir. nursing edn. Area Health Edn. Ctr.-South Ark., 1995—2002; coord. off campus BSN program U. Ark., 2002—. Coord. Parenting Coalition of South Ark. Chair teen pregnancy prevention com. TEA Coalition for Union County. Mem. ANA (Ho. Dels. 1997, 98), Nat. Perinatal Assn., Ark. Nursing Assn. Found. (bd. trustees 1999-01), Ark. State Nurses Assn. (strategic planning com., sec. 1994-96, pres.-elect 1996-97, pres. 1997-99, exec. com., Outstanding Dist. Pres. 1994, Ark. Nurse of Yr. 1995, Disting. Svc. award 1995), Ark. Nursing Coalition (steering com., Salute to Nursing com. chair), So. Nursing Rsch. Soc. (rsch. reviewer for D. Jean Wood award 1993), Nat. League Nursing, Ark. League Nursing, So. Regional Heideggerian Hermeneutrical Inst., So. Ark. Breast Feeding Coalition (chair edn. com.), Assn. Women's Health, Obs. & Neonatal Nurses, Sigma Theta Tau.

ENGLUND, PAUL THEODORE, biochemist, educator; b. Worcester, Mass., Mar. 25, 1938; s. Theodore John and Mildred Elizabeth (Anderson) E.; m. Jean Elizabeth Nelson, Aug. 12, 1961 (div. 1987); children: Suzanne Elizabeth, Maria Jean; m. Christine R. Schneyer, Nov. 24, 1990; stepchildren: Jennifer, Peter. BA, Hamilton Coll., 1960; PhD, Rockefeller U., 1966. Postdoctoral fellow Stanford U., 1966-68; asst. prof. Johns Hopkins Sch. Medicine, Balt., 1968-74, asso. prof., 1974-80, prof., 1980—; co-dir. biology of parasitism course Marine Biol. Lab., Woods Hole, Mass., 1985-88. Bd. dirs. Internat. Lab. for Rsch. on Animal Diseases, Nairobi, Kenya, 1987-93. Editorial bd.: Jour. Biol. Chemistry, 1981-87, Molecular and Biochem. Parasitology, 1982—, Nucleic Acids Research, 1986-94, Sci., 1988-99, Eukaryotic Cell, 2002—; contbr. articles to profl. jours. Faculty research grantee Am. Cancer Soc., 1969-74, grantee NIH; Fogarty Sr. Internat. fellow, 1980; Burroughs-Wellcome scholar in molecular parasitology, 1982-87. Mem. Am. Soc. for Biochemistry and Molecular Biology. Home: 105 Longwood Rd Baltimore MD 21210-2119 Office: 725 N Wolfe St Baltimore MD 21205-2105 E-mail: penglund@jhmi.edu.

ENHORNING, GORAN, obstetrician, gynecologist, educator; b. Birkdale, Eng, Mar. 18, 1924; came to US 1986; s. Emil Augustin and Maria Rosina (von Haartman) E.; m. Louise Christina Carlberg, Apr. 16, 1955; children: Ulf, Dag and Peder (twins), Marianne. MD, Karolinska Inst., Stockholm, 1952, PhD in Physiology, 1961. Asst. prof. ob/gyn. Karolinska Inst., Stockholm, 1952-61; Fulbright scholar U. Utah, Salt Lake City, 1961-63, UCLA, 1963-64; assoc. prof. ob/gyn. Karolinska Inst., 1964-71, U. Toronto, Canada, 1971-75, prof. ob/gyn., 1975-86; prof. ob/gyn. and physiology SUNY, Buffalo, 1986—2002. Contbr. articles to profl. jour. initiation of concept that symptoms of asthma and infectious bronchiolitis may be due to a surfactant dysfunction, caused by airway inflammation, an allergic reaction, an inhalation of cold air, or a hydrolysis of surfactant phospholipids, catalyzed by phospholipase A2 (PLA2) and by lysophospholipase (LPL) from eosinophils. The way the surfactant dysfunction causes airway blockage, and thus breathing difficulties is demonstrated with the Capillary Surfactometer, a new instrument developed to simulate surfactant function in terminal airways. Home: 21 Oakland Pl Buffalo NY 14222-2008 E-mail: gee1@acsu.buffalo.edu.

ENLOW, DONNA LEE, elementary school counselor; b. Dodge City, Kans., May 24, 1949; d. Lyle L. and Betty L. (Cox) E. AA, Dodge City Community Jr. Coll., 1969; BEd, Kans. State Tchrs. Coll., 1971; MEd, Emporia (Kans.) State Coll., 1975. Lic. elem. tchr., phys. edn. and health, counselor edn., Kans., Mo. Tex. Tchr., coach Peabody (Kans.) Unified Sch. Dist., 1971-73; grad. asst. Emporia State Coll., 1973-75; instr., coach S.E. Mo. State U., Cape Girardeau, Mo., 1975-78; tchr., coach Pasadena (Tex.) Ind. Sch. Dist., 1978-91, elem. counselor, 1991—. Curriculum writer Pasadena Ind. Sch. Dist., 1979-80, campus improvement team, 1991-93. Mem. AAHPERD, Tex. Assn. Health, Phys. Edn., Recreation and Dance, Local PTA, Tex. Counselor's Assn.

ENNIS, CALVIN JOSEPH, art educator; b. Pasadena, Tex., June 29, 1956; s. Johnnie Wilson and Bernice Margaret (Hoppman) E.; m. Roma Joann Rehmert, June 25, 1957; children: Aaron Christopher, Jenny Christine. BSE in ARt Edn., Ctrl. Mo. State U., Warrensburg, 1978; postgrad., Ctrl. Mo. State U., Pittsburg (Kans.) State U. Cert. in art edn. K-12, Mo., Kans. Art therapist Higginsville (Mo.) State Sch. and Hosp., 1978-85; teaching counselor Jasper County Sheltered Facilities, Joplin, Mo., 1981-85; adminstr. Kingman County Girls Home, Kingman, Kans., 1985, Living Skills Ctr., St. Paul, Kans., 1986; retail mgr. Art World, Kansas City, Mo., 1987; substitute tchr. Kearney (Mo.) R-IV Schs., 1988-90; program mgr. K.R. Alm House, Kansas City, Mo., 1988-90; tchr. art Blue Springs (Mo.) R-IV Schs., 1990—. Instr. art Continuing Edn., Parkhill Sch. Dist., Park Hill, Mo., 1993—, North Kansas City (Mo.) Sch. Dist., 1993—; art dir. Kid Campus, Blue Springs, 1993—. Religion tchr. St. Theresa's Ch., Parkville, Mo., 1993—; cons. Boy Scouts Am., Kansas City, Mo., 1993—. Named Tchr. of Yr. Blue Springs R-IV Sch. Dist., 1994. Mem. Nat. Art Edn. Assn., Mo. State Tchrs. Assn., KC, Kappa Delta Pi. Republican. Roman Catholic. Avocations: fishing, weight lifting, reading, painting and drawing. Home: 2316 NW Powderhorn Dr Kansas City MO 64154-1311 Office: Cordill Mason Elem Sch 4001 SW Christiansen Dr Blue Springs MO 64014-5508

ENNIS, LORI LEE, elementary education educator; b. Ft. Worth, Aug. 2, 1967; d. Charles L. and Julia M. (Austin) Brown; m. Ronald Allen Ennis, May 26, 1990. BS in Elem. Edn., Pensacola Christian, 1989, MS in Ednl. Adminstrn., 1993. Cert. elem. tchr. Ohio. Substitute tchr. Norwood (Ohio) Bapt. Christian Sch., 1987; tchr. day care La Petite Day Sch., Stone Mountain, Ga., 1988; corr. sch. grader Pensacola (Fla.) Christian Coll., 1988-89, student tchr., 1989; tchr. 1st grade, day care supr. Liberty Christian Acad., Columbus, 1990—. Active with children's clubs Pensacola Christian Coll., 1986-87; children's program dir. Madeira Bapt. Ch., Cin., 1984-85; athletic dir. Omega Delta Rho Pensacola Coll., 1988. Adminstrv. clk. Madeira (Ohio) City Hall, 1984-85, 86-87; press rm. clk. Statehouse, Columbus, 1990. Republican. Baptist. Avocations: tennis, swimming, crafts, reading. Home: 3022 Whitlow Rd Columbus OH 43232-5425

ENNIS, WILLIAM LEE, physics educator; b. Houston, Aug. 10, 1949; s. Arthur Lee and Helen Ennis; m. Constance Elizabeth Livsey, July 20, 1991. BS, Auburn (Ala.) U., 1974, BA, 1978. Rsch. tech. Nat. Tillage Lab., Auburn, Ala., 1974-76; tchr. Stanford Jr. H.S., Hillsborough, N.C., 1979-81; physics tchr., chmn. sci. dept. East H.S., Anchorage, 1981—. Chmn. Anchorage Sch. Dist. Physics Tchrs.; curriculum devel. sci. cons. Copper River Schs., Anchorage, 1991. Recipient Nat. Tchr. award Milken Family Found., 1999; named Tandy Tech. Outstanding Tchr., 1989-90, Tchr. of Excellence Brit. Petroleum, 1996, Brit. Petroleum Tchr. of Yr., 1996, Disting. Tchr., White House Commn. on Presdl. Scholars; Fermi Lab. scholar U.S. Dept. Energy, 1991. Mem. AAAS, Am. Assn. Physics Tchrs., Am. Phys. Soc., Nat. Sci. Tchrs. Assn., Alaska Sci. Tchrs. (life), Am. Mountain Guides Assn., Am. Alpine Club. Avocations: mountaineering, outdoor activities, sailing, computers. Office: East HS 4025 E Northern Lights Blvd Anchorage AK 99508-3588

ENNS, ANN WILSON, retired mathematics educator; b. Salem, N.J., Dec. 9, 1928; d. Merritt Bingham and Jennie (Flanegan) Wilson; m. John Frank Enns, June 25, 1983 (dec. June 1995); stepchildren: Susan Kristine, Stephen John. BS, Rutgers U., 1950; MEd, U. Del., 1955. Cert. tchr., supr., prin., N.J. Tchr. Salem City Bd. Edn., 1950-92, chmn. dept. math., 1955-92; ret., 1992. Moderator 1st Bapt. Ch., Salem, 1976-77, 2000-03, clk., 1984-89, pres. Women's Fellowship, 1988-99; pres. Am. Bapt. women's ministries West N.J. Bapt. Assn., 1996-2002. Grantee NSF, 1959-69. Mem. AAUW (pres. Salem County br. 1957-59), NEA, N.J. Edn. Assn., Salem City Tchrs. Assn. (pres. 1973-74), Assn. Math. Tchrs. N.J. (exec. coun. 1984-87), Nat. Coun. Tchrs. Math., Salem Women's Club (3d v.p., chmn. edn. and membership 1992-2002), Delta Kappa Gamma (pres. Beta chpt. 1986-88). Republican. Avocations: travel, stamp collecting, photography, piano, organ. Home: 287 Morrison Ave Salem NJ 08079-2113

ENOKIAN, RALPH AVEDIS, school administrator, retired; b. West Newton, Mass., Nov. 21, 1939; m. Elizabeth Ann Koury, 1964; children: Elizabeth Anne, Thomas Avedis. MusB, Boston U., 1962; MS, Albany State U., 1972. Cert. music educator, sch. adminstr. and supr., sch. dist. adminstr. Music tchr. Mechanicville (N.Y.) Pub. Schs., 1962-65, Shenendehowa Ctrl. Schs., Clifton Park, N.Y., 1965-99; dir. music Shenendehowa Cntrl. Schs., Clifton Park, N.Y., 1991-99, ret., 1999. Conductor All-County Festivals, Captial Dist., 1962—, Monday Musical Club Women's Chorus, Albany, N.Y., 1981-84; choral dir. Eastern U.S. Music Camp, Cortland, N.Y., 1982-84; dir. R.P.I. Men's Glee Club, Troy, N.Y., 1983-86; lt. comdrs. Armenian Knights of Vartan, Latham, N.Y. Recipient Scholars' Recognition award Capital Region Bus. and Edn. Partnership Scholar Recognition Program, 1989, Excellence in Edn. award Shenendehowa Ctrl. Schs., 1993, N.Y. State Disting. PTA award, 1999. Mem. Shenendehowa Tchrs. Assn. (bldg. rep., chmn. 1965—), Am. Chroal Dirs. Assn., Music Educators Nat. Conf., N.Y. State United Tchrs. Assn., N.Y. State Sch. Music Assn., N.Y. State Coun. Adminstrs. Music Edn., Suburban Coun. Music Dirs. (sec. 1991—), Elks. Avocations: performing as a musician, gardening, sports spectator. Home: 111 Wilkens Ave Albany NY 12205-1714

ENRICO, LISA RENEE, music educator; b. St. Louis, Jan. 4, 1968; d. Bobbie Marvin and Sally Ann (Morton) Rush; m. Jon Lambert Enrico, June 23, 1990; 1 child, Hannah Renee. MusB, Culver-Stockton Coll., Canton, Mo., 1990. Cert. tchr. music edn. K-6, vocal/instrumental. Music specialist Discovery Pre-Sch., Coral Springs, Fla., 1990-91; band/chorus dir. Okeechobee (Fla.) H.S., 1991; guidance counselor/music tchr. Okeechobee Ctr., 1991-94; music tchr. North Elem. Sch., Okeechobee, 1994-95; with Hagemann Elem. Sch., St. Louis, 1995—. Mem. Music Educators Nat. Conf., Fla. Music Educators Assn., Fla. Couunselors Assn., Fla. Elem. Music Educators Assn., Fla. Sch. Counselors Assn., Delta Kappa Gamma. Avocation: aerobics instructor. Home: 3954 Thomas Dr Imperial MO 63052-1126

ENRIQUEZ, NORA OLAGUE, artist, educator; b. El Paso, Tex., May 2, 1953; d. Rubén and Gloria (Castillo) Olague; m. Alfonso Enriquez, Dec. 26, 1976; 1 child, Alejandra. Student, Sch. Art and Design, London, 1970, U. de Cd Juarez, Mexico, 1979, U. Pa., Phila., 1988; BA in Art, endorsement bilingual edn., U. Tex., El Paso, 1989. Cert. art tchr., Tex. Lectr. U. Autonoma, Juarez, Mex., 1974-75; asst. editor Masca Jour., Mus. Phila., 1983-84; tchr. Ysleta Sch. Dist., El Paso, 1989-90, Socorro (Tex.) Ind. Sch., 1991-93. Author design Ann. Reunion Bilingual Program, 1991, logo design Socorro Mid. Sch., 1993. Vol. Nuns, Retirement Village, 1990. Recipient 1st pl. painting, 2nd place sculpture Socorro Sch. Dist., 1991, 1st pl. painting, 2nd pl. mixed media, lst pl. sculpture Socorro Sch. Dist., 1992, 1st pl. ceramics, best of show print, 1st pl. print, hon. award painting Socorro Sch. Dist., 1993. Mem. Juntos Art Assn., Mus. Women in Arts. Roman Catholic. Avocations: crafts, music, sewing.

ENSIGN, JERALD C. bacteriology educator; BA, Brigham Young U., 1955; PhD, U. So. Calif., 1963. Postdoc rschr. U. Ill., Urbana, 1963; prof. dept. bacteriology U. Wis., Madison, 1990—94, prof. emeritus, 1994—. Recipient Disting. Tchr. award Carski Found., 1992. Office: Univ Wis Dept Bacteriology 114 E Fred Hall 1550 Linden Dr Madison WI 53706-1521*

ENTHOVEN, ALAIN CHARLES, economist, educator; b. Seattle, Sept. 10, 1930; s. Richard Frederick and Jacqueline E.; m. Rosemary Fenech, July 28, 1956; children: Eleanor, Richard, Andrew, Martha, Nicholas, Daniel. BA in Econs., Stanford U., 1952; M.Phil. (Rhodes scholar), Oxford (Eng.) U., 1954; PhD in Econs, MIT, 1956. Instr. econs. MIT, Cambridge, 1955-56; economist The RAND Corp., Santa Monica, Calif., 1956-60; ops. research analyst Office of Dir. Def. Research and Enging., Dept. Def., Washington, 1960; dep. comptroller, dep. asst. sec. U.S. Dept. Def., Washington, 1961-65, asst. sec. for systems analysis, 1965-69; v.p. for econ. planning Litton Industries, Beverly Hills, Calif., 1969-71; pres. Litton Med. Products, Beverly Hills, 1971-73; Marriner S. Eccles prof. pub. and pvt. mgmt. Grad. Sch. Bus. Stanford (Calif.) U., 1973-2000, prof. health care econs. Sch. Medicine, 1973-2000; sr. fellow Ctr. for Health Policy, Stanford U., 2000—. Cons. The Brookings Instn., 1956-60; vis. assoc. prof. econs. U. Wash., 1958; mem. Stanford Computer Sci. Adv. Com., 1968-73; cons. The RAND Corp., 1969— ; mem. vis. com. in econs. MIT, 1971-78; mem. vis. com. on environ. quality lab. Calif. Inst. Tech., 1972-77; mem. Inst. Medicine, Nat. Acad. Scis., 1972— ; mem. vis. com. Harvard U. Sch. Pub. Health, 1974-80; cons. Kaiser Found. Health Plan, Inc., 1973— ; vis. prof. U. Paris, 1985, London Sch. Hygiene and Tropical Medicine, 1998-99; vis. fellow St. Catherine's Coll., Oxford U., Eng., 1985, New Coll., 1998-99; dir. Hotel Investors Trust, 1986-87, PCS Inc., 1987-90, Caresoft, 1996-2002, Rx Intelligence, 2000—, eBenX Inc, 2001-03. Contbr. numerous articles on def. spending and on econs. and pub. policy in health care to profl. jours.; author: (with K. Wayne Smith) How Much is Enough? Shaping the Defense Program 1961-69, 1971, Health Plan: The Only Practical Solution to the Soaring Cost of Medical Care, 1980; editor: (with A. Myrick Freeman III) Pollution, Resources and the Environment, 1973, Theory and Practice of Managed Competition in Health Care Finance, 1988, In Pursuit of an Improving National Health Service, 1999. Bd. dirs. Georgetown U., Washington, 1968-73, Jackson Hole Group, 1993-96; bd. regents St. John's Hosp., Santa Monica, 1971-73; chmn. Gov's Taskforce Managed Health Care Improvement, 1997-98, vis. com. Harvard U. Kennedy Sch. Govt., 1998-2003. Recipient President's award for disting. fed. civilian svc., 1963, Disting. Pub. Svc. medal Dept. Def., 1968, Baxter prize for health svcs. rsch., 1994, Bd. Dirs.' award Healthcare Fin. Mgmt. Assn., 1995, Ellwood award Found. for Accountability, 1998, Rock Carling fellow, Nuffield Trust, 1999 Mem. Am. Assn. Rhodes Scholars, Am. Acad. Arts and Scis., Integrated Healthcare Assn. (bd. dirs. 1999—), Phi Beta Kappa. Home: 1 McCormick Ln Atherton CA 94027-3033 Office: Stanford Univ Grad Sch Business Stanford CA 94305-5015 E-mail: enthoven@stanford.edu.

ENTMAN, MARK LAWRENCE, cardiologist, biomedical scientist, educator; b. N.Y.C., Dec. 24, 1938; s. Sidney and Rose Ann (Newman) E.; m. Carol Ann Snyder, Mar. 31, 1968; children: Karen M., Susan J. Student, U. Fla., 1956-59; MD, Duke U., 1963, postgrad., 1965-66. Diplomate Am. Bd. Internal Medicine, Am. Bd. Cardiology. Student rsch. fellow in cardiology Duke U. Med. Ctr., Durham, N.C., 1962-63, fellow in cardiology, 1964-65, postdoctoral fellow, 1965-66, asst. resident, 1966-67, assoc. in medicine, 1967-68; intern Johns Hopkins Hosp., Balt., 1963-64; asst. prof. Baylor

Coll. Medicine, Houston, 1970-73, assoc. prof. medicine and cell biophysics, 1973-76, co-dir. med. scientist program, 1976-80, prof. medicine and biochemistry, 1976—. Head sect. cardiovascular scis., dir. divsn. rsch., nat. rsch. and demonstration ctr. Baylor Coll. Medicine, 1977-85, scientific dir. DeBakey Heart Ctr., 1996—; investigator Howard Hughes Med. Inst., 1972-78; adj. prof. dept. psychology U. Houston, 1983—, med. biochemistry Kurume (Japan) U., 1988—; pharmacology study sect. NIH, 1977-81; chmn. Calif. Tobacco Rsch. Rev. Com., 1990; mem. nat. cardiology merit rev. bd. VA, 1987-90; co-chmn. Am. Heart Assn. Cardiovascular B Rsch. Study Com., 1989-91. Assoc. editor Fedn. Procs., 1977-86, FASEB Jour., 1986-92, Circulation, 1992—; mem. editorial bd. Am. Jour. Cardiology, Am. Jour. Physiology, Jour. Cyclic Nucleotide Rsch., New Jour. Am. Coll. Cardiology, Circulation Rsch.; contbr. articles to profl. jours. Bd. dirs. Beth Yeshurun Congretation, Houston, 1988-92, Am. Heart Assn., Houston, 1989—. Maj. USAF, 1968-70. Recipient Merck award, 1963, Roussell award for cardiology, 1985, Duke U. Disting. Alumnus award, 1996. Fellow Am. Coll. Cardiology; mem. Am. Soc. Clin. Investigation, Am. Heart Assn. (numerous coms.), Am. Fedn. Clin. Rsch., So. Soc. for Clin. Investigation, Am. Soc. for Pharmacology and Exptl. Therapeutics, Biophys. Soc., Am. Soc. Biol. Chemists, Cardiac Muscle Soc., Am. Physiol. Soc., Assn. Am. Physicians, Internat. Soc. for Heart Rsch. (Outstanding Rsch. award 1985), Alpha Omega Alpha (pres. 1963). Democrat. Jewish. Home: 4978 Dumfries Dr Houston TX 77096-4230 Office: Baylor Coll Medicine 1 Baylor Plz Houston TX 77030-3411

ENTMAN, ROBERT MATHEW, communications educator, consultant; b. Bklyn., Nov. 7, 1949; s. Bernard and Rose (Jacobson) E.; m. Francie Seymour, June 1, 1979; children: Max, Emily. AB, Duke U., 1971; PhD, Yale U., 1977; M in Pub. Policy, U. Calif., Berkeley, 1980. Asst. prof. Dickinson Coll., Carlisle, Pa., 1975-77, Duke U., Durham, N.C., 1980-89; postdoctoral fellow U. Calif., 1978-80; assoc. prof. comm. Northwestern U., Evanston, Ill., 1989-94; prof. comm. N.C. State U., Raleigh, 1994—, dir. Ctr. for Info. Tech. and Policy, 1999—. Adj. prof. U. N.C., Chapel Hill, 1995-98; Lombard vis. prof. Harvard U., 1997; cons. subcom. on telecom. U.S. Ho. of Reps., Washington, 1982, Nat. Telecom. and Info. Adminstrn., Washington, 1984-85, Aspen Inst., Washington and Aspen, Colo., 1986—; mem. working group Commn. on TV Policy, 1990-96; guest scholar Woodrow Wilson Ctr., Washington, 1989. Author: Democracy without Citizens, 1989, (monograph) Blacks in the News, 1991, Diversifying Broadcast Media, 1998, The Black Image in the White Mind, 2000; co-author: Media Power Politics, 1981; co-editor Mediated Politics: Communication in the Future of Democracy, 2000, (book series) Communication, Society and Politics, 1998—; also articles. Recipient McGannon award for comm. policy rsch., 1993, Mott award, 2000, Lane award, 2000, Goldsmith Book prize, 2002; rsch. grantee Markle Found., 1984, 86, 88, 95, Chgo. Cmty. Trust, 1989-92, 95-97; rsch. fellow Ameritech., 1989-90. Mem. Am. Polit. Sci. Assn. (coun. polit. comm. sec. 1990-91, mem. editl. bd. Polit. Comm. 1992—, mem. editl. bd. Jour. Comm. 1994-98, mem. editl. bd. Comm. Law and Policy 1994-2002, sec.-treas. polit. comm. sec. 1996-99, vice chair 1999-2000, chair 2000-01), Social Sci. Rsch. Coun. (mem. working group on media and fgn. policy 1990-93). Avocations: wine collecting and tasting, tennis. Office: NC State U Dept Comm PO Box 8104 Raleigh NC 27695-8104

ENTWISLE, DORIS ROBERTS, sociology educator; b. Wilbraham, Mass., Sept. 28, 1924; d. Charles Edwin and Helen (McMenigall) Roberts; m. George Entwisle, Aug. 31, 1946; children: Barbara, Beverly, George H.; m. 2d Donald Roberts, Nov. 12, 1993. BS, U. Mass., 1945; MS, Brown U., 1946; PhD, Johns Hopkins U., 1960. Postdoctoral fellow Social Sci. Research Council Johns Hopkins U., Balt., 1960-61, research assoc. edn. and elec. engring., 1961-64, part-time asst. prof., 1964-67, assoc. prof., 1967-71, prof. sociology and engring. sci., 1971-98, prof. emerita, 1998—2003, rsch. prof., 2003—. Mem. com. on child devel. and pub. policy NRC, 1982-87. Harvard vis. com. for sociology dept., 1986-91. Author: (with S.G. Doering) The First Birth, 1981, (with L.A. Hayduk) Early Schooling, 1982, (with K.L. Alexander and Susan Dauber) The Success of Failure, 1984, 2d edit., 2002, (with K.L. Alexander, L.S. Olson) Children, Schools and Inequality, 1997; editor: Sociology of Education, 1975-78; assoc. editor Am. Sociol. Rev., 1972-75, 95-98; co-editor Jour. Rsch. in Adolescence, 1990-94. Guggenheim fellow, 1976-77 Fellow APA, Am. Sociol. Assn. (chair sect. children); mem. Am. Ednl. Rsch. Assn., Soc. Rsch. in Child Devel. (pub. com. 1987-93, chair 1989-91, governing coun. 1993-99). Office: Johns Hopkins U 530 Mergenthaler Baltimore MD 21218 E-mail: entwisle@jhu.edu.

ENZ, DIANE S. rehabilitation services professional, therapist, educator; b. Chgo., Oct. 28, 1937; d. Horst W. and Ann Burkward Ritter; m. Dominic Enz, Jan. 21, 1967; children: Leonard, Catherine, Michael. BS, U. Ill., Chgo., 1959; MEd, U. Mo., 1969. Lic. occupl. therapist, Ill., Iowa. Occupl. therapist, rehab. supr., asst. prof. U. Mo., Columbia, Mo., 1968-70; asst. prof. Univ. Ill., Chgo.; dir. occupl. therapy Waukegan (Ill.) Sch. Dist. 60, 1979-94; psychiat. occupl. therapy dir. Pinel Hosp., Chgo.; asst. prof. occupl. therapy St. Ambrose U., Davenport, Iowa, 1994—. Advisor Severely Physically Handicapped Students, Jr. Achievement; occupational therapist on tech. team, Northeastern Ill. Assistive Tech. Consortium, 1992-94. Author: Use of Computers, Pre-school Through High School, 1987, Facilitating the Use of Computers into the Environment of Special Needs, 1988, Parenting and Use of Computers with Special Needs Children, 1988; contbr. articles to profl. jours. Women's Fedn. Club grantee; Office Vocat. Rehab. grantee (3). Mem. Am. Occupl. Therapy Assn. (lic.), World Fedn. Occupl. Therapy, Occupl. Therapy Assn., Ill. Occupl. Therapy Assn., Iowa Occupl. Therapy Assn. (chair spl. interest tech. sect.), Coun. for Exceptional Children, Ill. Phys. Handicapped Assn., Quad Cities Occupl. Therapy Assn. (co-chair), Spl. Edn. Computer Com. (chair). Home: 18450 W Streamwood Ct Gurnee IL 60031-1364

EOVALDI, KAREN ANN, elementary education educator; b. Cleveland, Ohio, Apr. 10, 1944; d. Richard Dale and Norma Elizabeth (Meyers) Wiese; m. George Robert Eovaldi, Mar. 28, 1970; children: Robert Dale, Georgina Ann. AS, Mt. Vernon (Ill.) C.C., 1964; BA, Western Mich. U., 1966. Tchr. of educable mentally handicapped Franklin Elem. Sch., Mt. Vernon, 1966-67; tchr. remedial reading Farrington Community Consol. Sch., Bluford, Ill., 1967-68, tchr. first/second grades, 1968-69; tchr. remedial reading Webber Twp. High Sch., Bluford, 1967-68; tchr. third grade Peter Hoy Sch., Lombard, Ill., 1969-70; tchr. Christopher (Ill.) Elem. Sch., 1970—. Tchr. Sunday sch. First Bapt. Ch., Sesser, Ill., 1989—96, mem. choir, soloist, 1976—, sec.-treas. Bapt. Women, 1995—97, dir. Bapt. Women's Ministries, 1997—. Mem. Christopher Elem. Edn. Assn., Ill. Fedn. Tchrs. Am. (sec. 1988-90), Fedn. Tchrs. Affiliate (v.p. 1992-94). Republican. Baptist. Avocations: bible reading, gospel singing, clarinet, needle crafts, tole painting. Office: Christopher Elem Sch Christopher Comm Unit Dist 99 501 S Snider St Christopher IL 62822-1360

EPEL, DAVID, biologist, educator; b. Detroit, Mar. 26, 1937; s. Jacob A. and Anna K. E.; m. Lois S. Ambush, Dec. 18, 1960; children: Andrea, Sharon, Elissa. AB, Wayne State U., 1958; PhD, U. Calif.-Berkeley, 1963. Postdoctoral fellow Johnson Research Found., U. Pa., 1963-65; asst. prof. Hopkins Marine Sta., 1965-70; assoc. prof., then prof. Scripps Instn. Oceanography, 1970-77; Jane and Marshall Steel Jr. prof. marine scis. Hopkins Marine Sta., Stanford U., Pacific Grove, Calif., 1977—; acting dir. Hopkins Marine Sta., Pacific Grove, 1984—88. Co-dir. embryology course Marine Biol. Lab, Woods Hole, 1974—77. Mem. editl. bd. Acta Histochemica, Biol. Bull, Zygote. Bd. dirs. Rsch. Inst., Monterey Bay Aquarium, 1987-89, trustee, 1985-88. Guggenheim fellow, 1976-77, Overseas fellow Churchill Coll., Cambridge, Eng., 1976-77; recipient Allen Cox medal for fostering excellence in undergrad. rsch. Stanford U., 1995. Fellow AAAS (mem.-at-large, sect. G 1979-84, chmn. sect. on biol. scis. 1998—), Calif. Acad. Scis.; mem. Am. Soc. Cell Biology (mem. council 1978-80), Soc. Devel. Biology, Internat. Soc. Devel. Biology, Soc. Integrative and Comparative Biology (chairperson devel. and cell biology sect. 1990-92). Home: 25847 Carmel Knolls Dr Carmel CA 93923-8845 E-mail: depel@stanford.edu.

EPLER, GARY ROBERT, physician, author, educator; b. Chico, Calif., Apr. 5, 1944; s. Deane Chandler and Kathryn Louise (McNeil) E.; m. Joan Susan Weidman, Sept. 10, 1983; children: Gregory C., Brett H. MD, Tulane U., 1971; MPH, Harvard U., 1978. Diplomate in internal medicine and pulmonary medicine Am. Bd. Internal Medicine. Intern Harlem Hosp., Columbia U., 1971-72; resident U. Hosp., Boston, 1974-76, pulmonary medicine fellowship, 1975-78; asst. prof. medicine Sch. Medicine Boston U., 1978-85, assoc. clin. prof. medicine, 1985-96, Harvard U., Boston, 1995—; med. dir. respiratory therapy, chmn. dept. medicine New England Bapt. Hosp., Boston, 1983-98, med. dir. rehab. unit, 1983-98. Parasitology rsch. fellow Tulane U., Cali, Colombia, 1969-70, USPHS, Ctrs. Disease Control, 1972-74; tuberculosis cons. CDC Vietnamese Refugee Camps, Eglin AFB, Fla. and Indiantown Gap, Pa., 1975, Cuban Refugee Camp, Indiantown Gap, 1980; med. cons. CDC, Vietnamese Refugee Programs in Hong Kong, Thailand, Philippines, Malaysia, Indonesia; vis. attending physician U. Hosp., Boston City Hops. and Boston VA Hosp., 1978-98, Brigham and Women's Hosp., Boston, 1999—; med. dir. Occupational Health Ctr., Wilmington, Mass; vis. prof. Kyoto (Japan) U., 1990; many others. Author book on diseases of bronchioles, 1994; editor book on occupational lung diseases; editl. reviewer New England Jour. Medicine, Annals of Internal Medicine, Jour. AMA, Am. Rev. Respiratory Diseases, Chest, Jour. Respiratory Medicine, Jour. Western Medicine, Jour. Rheumatology, European Respiratory Jour.; contbr. chpts. to books, more than 85 articles to sci. jours. Lt. comdr. USPHS, 1972-74. Recipient cert. of appreciation Am. Lung Assn. Mass.; named one of Outstanding Med. Specialists in U.S., Town and Country Mag., 1989. Fellow ACP, Am. Coll. Chest Physicians (chmn. com. on occupational and environ. health 1987-88, v.p. New England States chpt. 1989-91, pres. chpt. 1991-93); mem. AMA (alt. del. 1987-93), Am. Soc. Law and Medicine (treas. 1983-85, Disting. Svc. award 1985), Am. Coll. Physician Execs., Mass. Thoracic Soc. (mem. coun. 1980-84, sec.-treas. 1984-85, pres. 1986-88), Mass. Med. Soc. Office: Brigham and Women's Hosp Pulmonary/Critical Care Med 75 Francis St Boston MA 02115-6106

EPLEY, THELMA MAE CHILDERS, retired gifted and talented education educator; b. Ft. Wayne, Ind., Dec. 28, 1918; d. Harley Ellsworth and Bessie Mae (Corathers) Childers; m. Joseph Mendel Epley, Sept. 14, 1946. BS, Ind. U., 1941; MA, Calif. State U., Northridge, 1958; postgrad., U. So. Calif., 1964-65. Cert. elem., secondary tchr., adminstr., Calif. Tchr. Ft. Wayne Pub. Schs., 1941-42, 43-46; tchr., counselor Muncie (Ind.) Pub. Schs., 1942-43; tchr. L.A. Unified Sch. Dist., 1948-56, reserve tchr., 1955-57, specialist gifted program, 1958-70, tchr. adult edn., 1964-69, instrnl. adviser, 1970-75; instr. Occidental Coll., Eagle Rock, Calif., 1952-61, Calif. State U., 1958; newspaper edn. coord. Copley LA Newspapers, Santa Monica, Calif., 1978-93; ret. Mem. adv. bd. gifted parents groups, L.A., 1958-75; ednl. cons. state bds. edn., 1975-86; project affiliate Nat. and State Leadership Tng. Inst. for Gifted and Talented, 1976-87; instr. U. Calif., L.A., 1964-75, Mt. St. Marys Coll., Doheny, 1970-71, U. Tucson, 1983-85, U. Calgary, Can., 1985. Author: Annotated Bibliography on Gifted, 1958, Models For Thinking, 1982, Futuristics, 1985, Promoting Productive Thinking, 1988; contbr. articles to profl. jours. Active Nat. Rep. Com., Washington, 1982-93, Citizen Amb. Program, Washington, 1990-93. Mem. Nat. Assn. for Gifted (Achievement award 1958-75), World Coun. on Gifted, World Future Soc., Calif. Ret. Tchrs. Assn., Calif. Coords. of Newspaper in Edn., Assoc. Adminstrs. of L.A. Unified Sch. Dist., Delta Kappa Gamma (pres. Gamma Lambda chpt. 1963-65, Woman of Yr. award 1990). Republican. Avocations: reading, traveling, painting, decorating, gardening. Home: 5067 Avenida Del Sol Laguna Woods CA 92653-1803

EPP, DIANNE NAOMI, secondary educator; b. Yankton, S.D., Oct. 1, 1939; d. Willard H. and Florence A. (Leigh) Waltner; m. Anthony R. Epp, Aug. 18, 1964; children: Alain-René Epp Weaver, Rachel Epp Buller. BA in Chemistry, Bethel Coll., 1961; MA, U. Mo., 1963; cert. etudes, L'Ecole d'Administration, Brussels, 1965. Chemistry instr. Bethel Coll., North Newton, Kans., 1963-64; sci. tchr. Ecole Secondaire, Sundi-Lutete, Zaire, 1965-67; rsch. chemist FMC Glass Lab., Golden, Colo., 1967-70; vis. instr. Nebr. Wesleyan U., Lincoln, 1973-74, 77-79, 1980-81; chemistry tchr. East High Sch., Lincoln, 1982-93, 94—; vis. scholar Miami U., Oxford, Ohio, 1993-94. Cons. NSF Doing Chemistry Videodisc, 1988; cons. small scale CD ROM Synapse Corp., Lincoln, 1993. Author: Chemical Manfacturing: The Process of Mixing, 2000, Experimental Design: The Chemistry of Adhesives, 1998, Product Testing: The Chemistry of Ice Cream, 1998; cons. editor: Starting at Ground Zero, 1989; author: (monograph series) A Palette of Color, 1995; contbr. articles to profl. jours. Recipient Excellence in Teaching award Cooper Found., 1990, Excellence in High Sch. Chemistry Teaching award Am. Chem. Soc., 1990, 91, Presdl. award for Excellence in Sci. and Math. Teaching NSF, 1994, Kiewit Found. Tchg. award, 1997, 01. Mem. Nat. Sci. Tchrs. Assn. Office: East High Sch 1000 S 70th St Lincoln NE 68510-4297

EPPELHEIMER, LINDA LOUISE, software educator; b. Ames, Iowa, Dec. 10, 1949; d. Allyn Francis and Ada Geraldine (Hough) Van Dyke; m. Donald Mark Eppelheimer, Mar. 10, 1973; children: Matthew Allyn, Carrie Louise. BS, Mich. State U., 1972; AD, We. Wis. Tech. Inst., La Crosse, Wis., 1984. Tchr. jr. high sch., Onalaska, Wis., 1973-74, LaCrescent (Minn.) High Sch., 1974-75; instr. adult edn. WWTI, 1974-84; from programmer mgr. tng. Winnebago Software Co., Caledonia, Minn., 1984—2000, mgr. tng., 2000—; ISO 9001 mgmt. rep., 1994—97. Contbr. chpt. to book and articles to profl. jours. Mem. Sch. Bd., LaCrescent, 1991-98, pres., 1994-97; leader 4-H Clubs, Houston County, Minn., 1985-95. Mem. ALA, Am. Soc. for Quality. Avocations: hiking, camping, gardening, birdwatching. Home: 1230 County Rd # 6 La Crescent MN 55947 Office: Sagebrush Corp 131 Bissen Street Caledonia MN 55921-1356

EPPERSON, KRAETTLI QUYNTON, lawyer, educator; b. Ft. Eustis, Va., May 2, 1949; s. Dimpster Eugene Sr. and Helen Walter (Davidson) E.; m. Kay Lawrence, Aug. 22, 1970; children: Kraettli L., Kristin J., Kevin Q., Keith W. BA in Polit. Sci., U. Okla., 1971; MS in Urban and Policy Scis., SUNY, Stony Brook, 1974; JD, Oklahoma City U., 1978. Bar: Okla. 1979, U.S. Dist. Ct. (we. dist.) Okla. 1984, Fed. Claims Ct. 1997. Urban planner Gov.'s Office of Community Affairs and Planning, Oklahoma City, 1974-75; adminstr. of pub. transp. planning Okla. Dept. of Transp., Oklahoma City, 1975-79; title examiner Lawyers Title of Oklahoma City, Inc., 1979-80; gen. counsel, v.p. Am. First Land Title Ins. Co., Oklahoma City, 1980-82; assoc. Ferguson & Litchfield, Oklahoma City, 1982-85; of counsel Ames & Ashabranner, Oklahoma City, 1986-88, ptnr., 1989-93, Cook & Epperson, Oklahoma City, 1994-97, Oklahoma City, 1997—2002, Rolston, Hamill, Epperson, Myles & Nelson, 2002—. Adj. prof. law Okla. land titles Oklahoma City U., 1982—; instr. real property Okla. Bar Rev., 1998—; instr. real property titles Grad. Realtors Inst., 1998-99. Author: Basye Clearing Land Titles, 1998-2000, contbr., 2001-; contbg. author, editor: Vernon's Oklahoma Forms 2d-Real Estate, 2000—; contbr. articles to profl. jours. Asst. scoutmaster Boy Scouts Am., Oklahoma City, 1984-88, 1993-2000, asst. cubmaster, 1989-90, cubmaster, 1990-91, webelos leader, 1991-95, dist. vice-chair, 2000-01, dist. chair, 2001—. 2d lt. USAR, 1971. Recipient Dist. Svc. award, Boy Scouts Am., 2001. Mem. ABA (vice-chmn. conveyancing com. 1987-88, 93-94, chmn. 1991-93, chmn. state customs and practice subcom. 1987-88, project chmn. title exam. standards nat. survey 1988—), Am. Land Title Assn. (legis. com. 1981-82, jud. com. 1981-82), Okla. Bar Assn. (real property sect. 1979—, dir. 1982-88, 94-95, chmn. 1985-86, project chmn. Okla. Title Exam. Standards Handbook project 1982-85, mem. title exam. standards com. 1980—, chmn. 1992—, legis. liaison com. 1986-92, co-chmn. abstracting standards com. 1982-84), Oklahoma City Real Property Lawyers Assn. (dir. 1985-91, pres. 1990-91), Oklahoma City Commml. Law Attys. Assn. Republican. Episcopalian. Avocations: skeet, storytelling, camping. Home: 3029 Rock Ridge Ct Oklahoma City OK 73120-5731 Office: 4334 NW Expressway St Ste 174 Oklahoma City OK 73116-1574 E-mail: kqelaw@aol.com.

EPPLEY, FRANCES FIELDEN, retired secondary education educator, author; b. Knoxville, Tenn., July 18, 1921; d. Chester Earl and Beulah Magnolia (Wells) Fielden; m. Gordon Talmage Cougle, July 25, 1942; children: Russell Gordon Eppley, Carolyn Eppley Horseman; m. Fred Coan Eppley, Mar. 8, 1953; 1 child, Charlene Eppley Sellers. BA in English, Carson Newman Coll., 1942; MA, Winthrop U., 1963. Tchr. East Corinth (Maine) Acad., 1942-43, pub. schs., Charlotte, N.C., 1950-53, 59-83, Greenville, S.C., 1954-56, Spartanburg, S.C., 1957-58; Head Start tchr., summers 1964-68. Author: First Baptist Church: Its Heritage, 1982, Flint Hill Church, 1984, Religion and Astrology, 1991, Astrology and Prophecy, 1992, Sammy's Song, Jericho, Aunt Lillian's Sea Foam Candy, The First Astrologer, 1993, The Story of William Fielden, 1998, Search for an Ancestor, 1999, Christmas Magnus, Stella and the Sitting Stone, Messiah, An Immediate Family, 1999, The Signs of Your Life, 2000, Another Mary, 2000, The Winter Solstice, 2001, Of Course Your Child Can Read!, 2002, Columbus: The Race Home, 2003; : Canada Trilogy, 2003; : Canada Trilogy, 2003, Wacky Kings and Mystic Things, 2003, The Yellow River, 2003. Mem. hist. com. N.C. Bapt. Conv., 1985-88. Alpha Delta Kappa Grantee, 1970. Mem. NEA, N.C. Social Studies Conf., Writers Assn., Alpha Delta Kappa, Pi Kappa Delta, Alpha Psi Omega. Baptist. Home: 4119 Bannockburn Pl Apt B Charlotte NC 28211 E-mail: ffielden@bellsouth.net.

EPPLING, JACQUELINE QUON, elementary school educator; b. Honolulu, Nov. 10, 1949; d. Bung Yuen and Dorothy Mew-Seong (Yap) Quon; m. John Clarence Eppling, Dec. 28, 1975; children: Natalie Kwai-Ying, Melissa Kwai-Fei. BA, Whitworth Coll., 1971; MEd, U. No. Colo., 1973. Cert. elem. tchr., Hawaii. 1st grade and lang. arts tchr. Monaco Elem. Sch., Commerce City, Colo., 1974, 2d grade tchr., 1975; 3rd grade tchr. Dupont Elem. Sch., Commerce City, Colo., 1976; 1st grade tchr. Kamehameha Schs., Honolulu, 1987-92, math. resource tchr., 1992-95, tchr. 3d grade, 1995—. Site coord. Iolani Speech Festival, 1991; kindergarten admissions tester Kamehameha Schs., 1991—, judge spring festivals, 1993; guest lectr. U. Hawaii, 1991, elem. math. methods lectr., 1994; instr. Family Math. Workshops, Honolulu, 1992, 93, NCTM and math. curriculum Ahuimanu Elem. Sch., Honolulu, 1993-94; conf. presenter Hawaii Assn. for the Edn. of Young Children, Honolulu, 1994, Cath. Schs., 1994, Whole Lang. Umbrella Conf., San Diego, 1994, Hawaii Assn. for Pvt. Schs., Honolulu, 1994, Hawaii Coun. Tchrs. Math., Honolulu, 1994, Maui County Math./Sci. Conf., Kahului, 1994, Nat. Coun. Tchrs. Math., Boston, 1995; workshop presenter integrating math. and lang. arts Hawaii Coun. for Tchrs. of Math., Honolulu, 1993, Kauai and Big Island, Hawaii, 1993, Linapuni Elem. Sch., Honolulu, 1994. Mem. Nat. Coun. Tchrs. Math. Avocations: reading, shopping, children's activities. Home: 45-603 Olakino Pl Kaneohe HI 96744-1754 Office: Kamehameha Schs 225 Bishop Cir Honolulu HI 96817-1568

EPPS, EDWIN CARLYLE, English language educator; b. Columbia, S.C., Aug. 17, 1948; s. Edwin Carlyle and Alice (Fleetwood) E.; m. Helen Carol Edens, Dec. 20, 1975 (div. Aug. 2002); children: Catherine Clair Edens, William Fleetwood Tennyson. BA, Emory U., 1970; MA, U. S.C., 1973, EdD, 1993, NBCT, 2000. Tchr. Union Elem. Sch., Paulding County, Ga., 1970-71; teaching asst. U. S.C., Columbia, 1971-73; tchr., dir. debate Spring Valley High Sch., Columbia, 1973-79; gen. ptnr. Woodspurge Books, Staunton, Va., 1979-81; tchr. McCracken Jr. High Sch., Spartanburg, S.C., 1981-90; tchr.-in-residence Writing Improvement Network U. S.C., Columbia, 1990-94; tchr. McCracken Jr. H.S., Spartanburg, S.C., 1994-2000, Spartanburg H.S., 2000—. Co-dir. Spartanburg Writing Project, 1984-2000; coord. S.C. Writing Project, 1986-2000; presenter in field. Editor newsletter S.C. Writing Tchr., 1990-94; asst. editor jour. Teaching Edn., 1988-93; mem. editorial staff Carolina English Tchr., 1984-89; contbr. articles to profl. jours.; contbr. poetry to magazines and anthologies. Tchr. incentive grantee S.C. Dept. Edn., 1984, dissemination grantee S.C. Dept. Edn., 1985, tchr. incentive grantee S.C. Dept. Edn., 1987, NEH summer grantee, 1986. Mem. NEA, Nat. Coun. Tchrs. English, S.C. Coun. Tchrs. English (secondary dir., v.p., liaison, pres. 1996-97, cert. for profl. tchg. stds. 2000). Democrat. Methodist. Avocations: writing, collecting rare books, traveling. Home: PO Box 18404 Spartanburg SC 29318-8404 Office: Spartanburg High Sch 500 DuPre Dr Spartanburg SC 29307-2615 E-mail: eepps@spart7.k12.sc.us.

EPPS, ROSELYN ELIZABETH PAYNE, pediatrician, educator; b. Little Rock, Dec. 11, 1930; d. William Kenneth and Mattie Elizabeth (Beverly) Payne; m. Charles Harry Epps, Jr., June 25, 1955; children: Charles Harry III (dec.), Kenneth Carter, Roselyn Elizabeth, Howard Robert. BS, Howard U., 1951, MD, 1955; MPH, Johns Hopkins U., 1973; MA, Am. U., 1981. Intern Freedmen's Hosp., Howard U., Washington, 1955-56, pediatric resident, 1956-59, chief resident, 1958-59; practice medicine specializing in pediatrics Washington, 1960; med. officer, pediatrics D.C. Dept. Pub. Health, Washington, 1961-64, dir. Clinic for Retarded Children, 1964-67, chief Infant and Pre-Sch. div., 1967-71, dir. children and youth project, 1970-71, dir. maternal and crippled children services, 1971-75; chief Bur. Clin. Services D.C. Dept. Human Services, Washington, 1975-80, acting commr. pub. health, 1980; instr., asst. research investigator Howard U. Coll. Medicine, Washington, 1960-61, prof. Dept. Pediatrics and Child Health, 1980-98, chief divsn. child devel., dir., 1985-89, dir. Child Devel. Ctr., 1985-89; rsch. assoc., vis. scientist smoking tobacco and cancer program, div. cancer prevention and control Nat. Cancer Inst. NIH, Washington, 1989-91; expert Nat. Cancer Inst. NIH, Pub. Health Applications Br., Bethesda, Md., 1991-97; scientific program adminstr. Nat. Cancer Inst. Pub. Health Applications Branch, Bethesda, Md., 1997-98; med. pub. hlth cons., 1998—; sr. program advisor for women's health programs Women's Health Inst., Howard U., Wash., 1999—. Chmn. task force to prepare comprehensive child care plan for D.C. Dept. Human Services, 1973-74; mem. nat. task force on pediatric hypertension Heart, Lung and Blood Inst., NIH, 1975; chmn. rsch. grants rev. com. maternal and child health and crippled children's svcs. HEW, Rockville, Md., 1978-80; sec. Commn. Licensure to Practice Healing Arts, Washington, 1980; trustee med. svc. D.C. Blue Shield Plan Nat. Capital Area, 1980; chmn. sec.'s adv. com. on rights and responsibilities of women HEW, Washington, 1981; dir. high-risk young people's project Howard U. Hosp., 1981-85; Washington coord. Know Your Body Program Am. Health Found., N.Y.C., 1982-91; mem. bd. advs. Coll. Home Econs. Ohio State U., Columbus, Ohio, 1983-87; adv. com. Nat. Ctr. for Edn. in Maternal and Child Health Georgetown U., Washington, 1983-89; nat. steering com., subcom. chmn. Healthy Mothers, Healthy Babies Coalition, Washington, 1983-90, mem. nominating com., 1991; cons. sickle cell disease NIH, 1984-88, Govt. Liberia and World Bank, 1984, UN Fund for Population Activities, N.Y. and Caribbean, 1984, filmstrip Miriam Berg Varian/Parents Mag. Films, 1978; bd. dirs. Vis. Nurse Assn., Inc., Washington, 1983-89; pres. bd. dirs. Hosp. for Sick Children, Washington, 1986-90, bd. dirs., 1984-94; frequent guest lectr. Weekly columnist Your Child's Health, Afro-Am. Newspaper, Washington, 1960-63; contbr. articles syndicated column Nat. Newspaper Pubs. Assn., 1982, Nat. Newspaper Assn., 1986-87; co-author audiocassettes; exhibitor sci. program; contbr. more than 90 articles to profl. jours. US trustee Children's Internat. Summer Villages, Casstown, Ohio, 1969—76, pres., 1974—75; trustee nat. bd. Palmer Meml. Inst., Sedalia, NC, 1969—71, Ford's Theater, Washington, 1973—79; bd. mgrs. YWCA of DC, 1970—83, vice chmn., 1975—76; v.p. Jack and Jill of Am., Inc., Washington, 1970—71; nat. bd. dir. Ctr. Population Options, Washington, 1980—86, Alexander Graham

Bell Assn. for Deaf, Washington, 1974—78; bd. dir. Washington Performing Arts Soc., DC, 1971—81, v.p., 1979—81, hon. dir., 1981—. Recipient Leadership and Meritorious Service in Medicine award Palmer Meml. Inst., 1968, 14th Ann. Fed. Women's award CSC, Washington, 1974, Superior Performance award D.C. Govt., 1975, Meritorious Community Service award Howard U. Sch. Social Work Alumni Assns. and vis. com., 1980, Cert. Commendation Mayor of D.C., 1981, Roselyn Payne Epps M.D. Recognition Resolution of 1983 Council D.C., 1983, Disting. Vol. Leadership award March of Dimes Birth Defects Found., 1984, Community Svc. award D.C. Hosp. Assn., 1990, Physician of Yr. award Women's Med. Assn. N.Y.C., 1990, 91; named Outstanding Vol. in Leadership category YWCA Nat. Capital Area, 1983; inducted into D.C. Women's Hall of Fame D.C. Commn. for Women, 1990; grantee Robert Wood Johnson Found., Princeton, N.J., 1982, div. maternal and child health HHS, Rockville, Md., 1986; honored Tribute Resolution of 1981 declaring Feb. 14 Dr. Roselyn Payne Epps Day, Council of D.C., 1981; recipient Ophelia Settle Egypt award Planned Parenthood of Met. Washington, 1991, Advocacy award Soc. Advancement Women's Health, 1996, Horizon award Nat. Assn. Negro Bus. and Profl. Women's Clubs, 1999, Dorothy I Height award, Nat. Coun. of Negro Women, 2001, Lifetime Achievement award, Girls Inc., 2003. Fellow Am. Acad. Pediatrics (alt. state chmn. D.C. 1973-75, exec. com. D.C. chpt. 1983-94, pres. D.C. chpt. 1988-91, sec. cmty. pediatrics sect. 1973-75, cert. appreciation 1979, mem. coun. of child and adolescent health, cmty. and internat. health sect., charter mem., exec. com. 1992-94); mem. Acad. Medicine, AMA (alt. del. Nat. Med. Assn. 1983-85), Am. Med. Women's Assn. (chmn. pub. health com. 1973-75, pres. br. 1 1974-76, sec. 1988, v.p. 1989, pres-elect nat. 1990, pres. 1991, found. founding pres. 1992, bd. dirs. 1992-97, chmn. nominating com. 1993, Physician of Yr. award 1991, Cmty. Svc. award 1990, Elizabeth Blackwell award 1992), Women's Forum Washington, Med. Soc. D.C. (exec. bd. 1990, sec. 1990, pres.-elect 1991, pres. 1992, chair exec. bd. 1993, ann. Cmty. Svc. award 1982), Am. Pediatric Soc., D.C. Hosp. Assn. (Cmty. Svc. award 1990), Am. Pub. Health Assn. (action bd. 1977-79, joint policy com. 1978-79, gov. council 1978-81), Met. Washington Pub. Health Assn. (gov. council 1975-78, 81-83, ann. award 1981), Nat. Med. Assn. (chmn. pediatric sect. 1977-79, Ross Labs. award 1979, Outstanding Svcs. to Children during Internat. Yr. of Child award 1979, Meritorious Service Appreciation award 1979, W.M. Cobb co-lectr. 1985, mem. Coun. on Maternal and Child Health, 1974-92, chmn. 1979-89, ann. Roselyn Payne Epps Symposium 1994—, Grace Marilyn James award for Disting svc. Pediatric sect. 1991, Achievement award 1993, ann. Roselyn Payne Epps symposium 1994—), Am. Hosp. Assn. (maternal and child health sect. governing coun. 1989, 1992-94, maternal and child health nominating com. 1991), Soc. for the Advancement of Women's Health Rsch. (award for advocacy 1996), The Women's Forum of Washington, Alpha Omega Alpha, Delta Omega, Alpha Kappa Alpha. Mem. United Ch. of Christ. Clubs: Pearls (pres. 1984-86), Carrousels (corr. sec. 1978-80), Links (pres. Met. chpt. 1986-89) (Washington), Cosmos. Lodge: Zonta, Internat. Women's Forum. Home and Office: 1775 N Portal Dr NW Washington DC 20012-1014

EPSTEIN, DAVID MAYER, composer, conductor, music theorist, educator; b. N.Y.C., Oct. 3, 1930; s. Joshua S. and Elizabeth (Mayer) E.; m. Anne Louise Merrick, June 21, 1953; children: Eve Miriam, Beth Sara. AB, Antioch Coll., 1952; MMus, New England Conservatory Music, 1953; MFA, Brandeis U., 1954, Princeton U., 1956, PhD, 1968. Asst. editor, music critic Musical America, N.Y.C., 1956-57; asst. prof. music Antioch Coll., 1957-61, assoc. prof., 1962; music dir. Ednl. Broadcasting Corp., N.Y.C., 1962-64; assoc. prof. music MIT, Cambridge, 1965-69, prof., 1970-95, prof.emeritus, from 1995. Vis. fellow Max-Planck Inst., Seewiesen, Germany, 1980—81, Neurosci. Inst., La Jolla, Calif., 1996; vis. prof. U. Munich., 1980—82, 1987—89, 1992, U. Lisbon, 1980, U. Iowa Sch. Music, 1989, U. Dusseldorf, 1994, U. Tex., Austin, 2000, U. N. Tex., 2001, Columbia U., 2001; guest condr. Nouvel Orch. Philharm. de Paris, 1982, 84, Haifa Symphony Orch., 1979, 81; participant Salzburg Easter Festival, 1983—87, Herbert von Karajan Music Symposium, Vienna, Austria, 1988, Hannover Congress (Geist und Natur), 1988, Rochester U. Conf. on Time, 1988, Inst. for Advanced Study, Budapest, Hungary, 1996; master classes in conducting Salzburg Mozarteum, 1984—85, 1987, 92, Dresden Hochschule for Music, 1988, 90, 1992—93, Berlin Hochschule for Music, 1992, Weimar Hochschule for Music, 1996, Am. Symphony Orch. League, 1989, 93, Vogtland Philharm., 1994, The Conductors Guild, 2000. Guest condr. Berlin Radio Orch., 1967, Czech Radio Orch., Pilsen, 1966, Cleve. Orch., 1961, N.Y.C. Ctr., 1966, N.J. Symphony, 1961, Bavarian Radio Symphony, 1973, Vienna Tonkuenstlerorchester, 1973, Israel Broadcasting Orch., 1971, Jerusalem Orch., 1982, Royal Philharm. Orch., 1974, Am. Symphony Orch., 1978, Bamberg Symphony Orch., 1978, Orch. de la Suisse Romande, 1981, 88, Symphony Orch. Radio Brussels, 1984, Robert Schumann Philharmonie, Karl-Marx-Stadt, Germany, 1986, 87, 90, Orch. Nat. Lyon, 1986, Danish Radio Orch., 1987, Helsinki Festival, 1987, Nat. Orch. State Mex., 1989, Neubrandenburg Philharmonie, Germany, 1993, Xalapa Symphony Orch., Mex., 1994, Mittelsachsische Philharmonie, 1995, Vogtland Philharmonie 1994, 95, 96; also Antioch Shakespeare Festival, 1957, Jena Philharmonic, 1995, Szeged (Hungary) Philharmonic, 1996, Orquestra Metro. de Lisboa, 1996. Orquestra Sinfonica de Portugal, 1999; music dir. Harrisburg Symphony Orch., 1974-78, Worcester Orch. and Worcester Festival, 1976-80, New Orch. Boston, 1984—; composer documentary films, Nat. Ednl. TV, 1964-65; founder, dir. N.Y. Youth Symphony Orch., 1963-66; recs. on EMI, Everest, Desto, AR/DGG, Vox, Turnabout, Pantheon Internat., Newport Classic labels; author: Beyond Orpheus: Studies in Musical Structure, 1979; Shaping Time: Music, The Brain and Performance, 1995; mem. editl. bd. Music Theory Spectrum, 1995-98; contbr. articles to profl. jours.; editor Beauty and the Brain: Biological Aspects of Aesthetics, 1988. Bd. dirs. New England Lyric Theatre, Adirondack Found. of Arts, Young Audiences Boston, Conductors Guild, 1998—; alumni bd. Antioch Coll., 1996-99, bd. trustees, 1999—. Recipient Louisville Orch. award, Fromm Found. award, BMI award, N.Y. State Coun. for Arts Commn., 1973, Sr. Scientist award Alexander Von Humboldt Found., 1985, Deutsche Forschungsgemeinschaft award, 1980-82, 91, 94, Mass. Arts and Humanities Found. award, 1977, Boston Symphony Orch. Young People's Concerts Commn., 1972, ASCAP Deems Taylor award, 1996; Rockefeller Found. grantee, 1971, Ford Found. rec. grantee, 1971, 76; Kulas Found. fellow, sr. fellow in arts and humanities MIT, 1998. Mem. ASCAP, Am. Soc. Univ. Composers, Am. Symphony Orch. League (chmn. univ. orch. sect. 1960-62), Am. Fedn. Musicians, Am. Music Ctr., Am. Brahms Soc. (bd. dirs. 1983—), Robert Schumann-Gesellschaft, Internat. Soc. for Study of Time (exec. bd. 1979-83), Soc. for Music Theory, Soc. for Music Perception and Cognition. Home: Lexington, Mass. Died Jan. 15, 2002.

EPSTEIN, HERMAN THEODORE, biophysics educator; b. Portland, Maine, Apr. 13, 1920; s. Robert and Rebecca Sue (Govitsky) E.; m. Doris Elaine Wright, May 30, 1947; children: Becky Sue, Karen Ann, Erika Beth, David Alexander. BA, U. Mich., 1941, PhD, 1949. Asst. prof. physics U. Pitts., 1949-53; asst. prof. physics and biophysics Brandeis U., Waltham, Mass., 1953-57, assoc. prof. biophysics, 1957-61, prof. biophysics, 1961—. Author: Elementary Biophysics, 1957, A Strategy for Education, 1970.

EPSTEIN, WILLIAM LOUIS, dermatologist, educator; b. Cleve., Sept. 6, 1925; s. Norman N. and Gertrude (Hirsch) E.; m. Joan Goldman, Jan. 29, 1954; children: Wendy, Steven. AB, U. Calif., Berkeley, 1949, MD, 1952. Mem. faculty U. Calif., San Francisco, 1957—, assoc. prof. div. dermatology, 1963-69, prof. div. dermatology, 1969—, dir. dermatol. rsch., 1957-70, acting chmn. div. dermatology, 1966-69, chmn. dept. dermatology, 1970-85. Cons. dermatology Outpatient Dept.; cons. various hosps. Calif. Dept. Public Health; cons. Food and Drug Adminstrn., Washington, 1972—, Dept. Agriculture, 1979; dir. div. research Nat. Program Dermatology, 1970-73; Dohi lectr., Tokyo, 1982; Beecham lectr., 1988-89; Nippon Boehringer Ingelheim lectr. 18th Hakone Symposium on Respiration, Japan, 1990. Decorated medal of honor Order of the Rising Sun, gold rays with neck ribbon (Japan). Mem. AAAS, AMA, Am. Soc. Cell Biology, Am. Acad. Dermatology and Syphlology (nominating com. 1984), Am. Contact Dermatology Soc. (hon.), Pacific Dermatologic Assn., Am. Fedn. Clin. Rsch., Am. Contact Dermatitis Soc. (hon.), Soc. Investigative Dermatology (bd. dirs., pres. 1985), Am. Dermatol. Assn., Assn. Profs. Dermatology (sr. mem.), Dermatology Found. (pres. 1986-87), Phi Beta Kappa, Sigma Xi. Home: 267 Golden Hinde Psge Corte Madera CA 94925-1953 Fax: 415-681-9165. E-mail: wle@itsa.vcsf.edu.

EPSTEIN-SHEPHERD, BEE, mental skills golf coach, hypnotist, professional speaker; b. Tubingen, Germany, July 14, 1937; came to U.S., 1940; naturalized, 1945; d. Paul and Milly (Stern) Singer; m. Leonard Epstein, June 14, 1959 (div. 1982); children: Bettina, Nicole, Seth; m. Frank Shepherd, 1991 (dec. 1992). Student, Reed Coll., 1954-57; BA, U. Calif., Berkeley, 1958; MA, Goddard Coll., 1976; PhD, Internat. Coll., 1982; DCH, Am. Inst. Hypnotherapy, 1999. Bus. instr. Monterey Peninsula Coll., 1975-85; owner, mgr. Bee Epstein Assocs., 1977—; cons. to mgmt. Carmel, Calif., 1977—; pres. Success Tours Inc., Carmel, 1981—; founder, prin. Monterey Profl. Spkrs., 1982. Instr. Monterey Peninsula Coll., Golden Gate U., U. Calif., Santa Cruz, Am. Inst. Banking, Inst. Ednl. Leadership, Calif. State Fire Acad., U. Calif., Berkeley, Foothill Coll., U. Alaska; pres. Becoming Media Inc., 2002; sr. v.p. TheHoundIsLoose.com Inc. Author: How to Create Balance at Work, at Home, in Your Life, 1988, Stress First Aid for the Working Woman, 1991, Free Yourself From Diets, 1994, Mental Management for Great Golf, 1996, Mental Mastery System, 2001; contbr. articles to newspapers and trade mags. Rsch. grantee, 1976. Mem. NAFE, Nat. Spkrs. Assn., Peninsula Profl. Women's Network Assn. for Advancement Applied Sports Psychology, Nat. Guild of Hypnotists. Democrat. Jewish. Office: PO Box 221383 Carmel CA 93922-1383 E-mail: DrBeeMM@aol.com.

ERB, JAMES BRYAN, music educator, conductor, musicologist; b. La Junta, Colo., Jan. 25, 1926; s. Tillman Harvey and Phebe Ann (King) E.; m. Ruth Hildegard Esther Urbancic, Mar. 1, 1952; children: Martin Georg, Paul David, Christina Elizabeth, Jonathan Tillman. BA, Colo. Coll., 1950; Staatszeugnis (Gesang), Staatsakademie Musik, Vienna, Austria, 1952; MM in Singing, Ind. U., 1954; MA, Harvard U., 1964, PhD, 1978. Tchr. City Schs., Cheyenne, Wyo., 1952-53; from instr. to assoc. prof. music U. Richmond, Va., 1954-78, prof., 1978-94, prof. emeritus, 1994—. Music dir. Cafur, Richmond, 1966-94; chorus master Richmond Symphony Chorus, 1971—. Arranger (choral adaptation) Shenandoah, 1975; editor: O. diLasso Sämtl-Werke, Neue Reihe, vols. 13-17, 1981-88; author: O. diLasso, A Guide to Research, 1990. With U.S. Army, 1944-46. Named Outstanding Educator, Va. Coun. Higher Edn., 1993; Tchr. study grantee Danforth Found., 1962-65, Study grantee Martha Baird Rockefeller Fund Music, 1968-69. Mem. Am. Musicological Soc., Am. Brahms Soc., Am. Renaissance Soc., Gesellschaft Für Bayerische Musikgeschichte. Home: 4703 Patterson Ave Richmond VA 23226-1343

ERBAN, JOHN KALIL, medicine educator, cancer specialist, researcher; b. Boston, Aug. 26, 1955; s. John Kalil and Najla Teresa (Maloof) E.; m. Lisa Ann Benoit, Sept. 4, 1982; children: Laura Elizabeth, John Kalaail IV, Stephen Benoit. AB, Harvard U., 1977; MD, Tufts U., 1981. Diplomate Am. Bd. Internal Medicine. Intern U. Pa., 1981—82, resident, 1982—84, 1986—87; assoc. prof. medicine New Eng. Med. Ctr., Tufts U. Sch. Medicine, Boston, 1990—, dir. med. oncology breast cancer program, 1992—; with Pub. Health Svcs., 1984—86. Med. editor Tufts Medicine, 1991—; contbr. articles to sci. and med. jours. Fellow Tufts U., 1987—90. Office: New Eng Med Ctr 750 Washington St Boston MA 02111-1526

ERBE, YVONNE MARY, music educator, marketing specialist, guidance counselor; b. Wausau, Wis., Nov. 18, 1947; d. Rudolph Anton and Lucille Virginia Karlen; children: Daniel, Heather. BMus Edn., U. Wis., Madison, 1969, postgrad.; MA in Guidance/Counseling Edn Psychology, Eastern Ky. U., Richmond. Lic. music educator, Wis. Music-vocal tchr. Bayport H.S., Greenbay, Wis., 1969-70; tchr. bassoon, oboe U. Wis., Greenbay, 1969-70; jr. high choral dir. Kenosha Unified Schs., Wis., 1970-76; adjudicator, clinician, 1969—. Univ. supr.-edn. U. Wis.-Parkside, Kenosha, 1976-78; mem. parent adv. com. Northern Hills Sch. and Onalaska Mid. Sch., 1987-88; mktg. specialist Metro Prodns., La Crosse, Wis., 1984-85; tchr. music elem., jr. high sch., sr. high, LaCrosse, Wis.; secondary high sch. choral dir., Lexington, Ky., 1988-99, guidance counselor, 1999—. Parent vol. coord. Fauver Hill Sch., 1983-84; sec. exec. bd. Great River Festival of Arts, La Crosse, 1982-83, 1st v.p. exec. bd., chmn. adult choral workshop and performance, chmn. swing choir workshop, 1983-84, pres. bd. dirs., 1984-85; pres. La Crosse Area Newcomers Club, 1982-83; tchr. Confraternity of Christian Doctrine, 1985-88, bd. dirs. La Crosse Boy Choir, 1985-88; condr. Lexington Children's Choir, 1995-96; upward bound instr. Eastern Ky. U., 1994-95; conductor Ctrl. Ky. Youth Choruses, 1995-98. Mem. NEA, Ky. Edn. Assn., Ky. Counseling Assn., Ky. Adminstrs. Assn., Sigma Alpha Iota. Roman Catholic. Avocations: tennis, cross-country skiing, aerobic exercises, needlecrafts, gourmet cooking.

ERBER, THOMAS, physics educator; b. Vienna, Dec. 6, 1930; m. Audrey Burns. BSc, MIT, 1951; MS, U. Chgo., 1953, PhD in Physics, 1957. Asst. prof. physics Ill. Inst. Tech., Chgo., 1957-62, assoc. prof., 1962-69, prof., 1969—, prof. math., 1986—, disting. prof., 1999—. Vis. scientist Stanford Linear Accelerator Ctr., 1970; prof. physics U. Graz, 1971, 82, hon prof., 1971—; prof. physics UCLA, 1978-79, 84-85, 87—, U. Grenoble, 1982; prof. physics U. Chgo., 1998-99; adv. bd. rsch. corp. Mem. editl. bd. Acta Physica Austriaca. Rsch. fellow, Brussels, Belgium, 1963-64. Fellow: Inst. Physics (U.K.), Am. Math. Soc., Am. Phys. Soc.; mem.: IEEE (life sr.), Nuclear, Plasma & Magnetics Soc., Am. Acad. Mechanics, Am. Radio Relay League, Magnetics Soc., Oesterreichische Physikalische Gesellschaft, European Phys. Soc. Office: Ill Inst Tech Dept Physics Chicago IL 60616

EREKSON, LAURIE IDA, school administrator; b. San Jose, Calif., Jan. 10, 1957; d. Harry and Geraldine Anne (Caliri) Copelan; m. Scott Erekson; children: Scott R., Nicholas J., Daniel R. BS in History with honors, Portland State U., 1982; MPA, cert. in ednl. adminstrn., Lewis & Clark Coll., 1993. Math. tchr. Parrish Mid. Sch.-Salem (Oreg.) Sch. Dist., 1984-91, Mountain View Intermediate Sch.-Beaverton (Oreg.) Sch. Dist., 1983-84; sch. adminstr. Richmond Elem. Sch., 1993-94, Waldo Mid. Sch., 1994—. Mem. Expanding Your Horizons Conf., 1987-95. Mem. ASCD, AAUW, N.W. Women in Adminstrn., Confedn. Oreg. Sch. Adminstrs., Oreg. Mid. Level Assn., Nat. Mid. Sch. Assn., Salem Assn. Sch. Adminstrs. (pres. 1996—). Home: 1075 Ridge Rd Mccall ID 83638-4609

ERFANI, SHERVIN, academic administrator, engineering educator; b. Tehran, Iran, Mar. 28, 1948; came to U.S. 1982; s. Ibrahim and Rashedeh (Naraghi) Erfani; m. Janet E. Kovar, Dec. 30, 1982. MSEE, U. Tehran, Iran, 1971; MS, So. Meth. U., 1974, PhD in EE, 1976. Asst. prof. Nat. U. Iran, Eveen, 1978-82; rsch. assoc. So. Meth. U., Dallas, 1982-83; asst. prof. U. Mich., Dearborn, 1983-85; mem. tech. staff Lucent Techs. Bell Labs., Holmdel, NJ, 1985—2002; prof., chmn. dept. elec. and computer engring. U. Windsor, Canada, 2002—. Vis. prof. U. P.R., 1992-93; adj. prof. dept. elec. engring. and computer sci. Stevens Inst. Tech., Hoboken, N.J., 1996-2000; mem. rsch. staff Racal-Datacom, Ft. Lauderdale, Fla., 1997-98. Translator: Elec. Engring. textbook, Circuit Design & Synthesis, 1985; assoc. editor Computers and Elec. Engring.: An Internat. Jour.; sr. editor Jour. of Network and Systems Mgmt.; contbr. articles to profl. jours. 2d lt. Signal Corps. Iranian Army, 1972—73. Mem. IEEE (sr., v.p. S.E. Mich. chpt. 1985), Inst. Elec. Engrs. U.K. (chartered engr.), N.Y. Acad. Scis., Tau Beta Pi, Eta Kappa Nu. Moslem. Avocations: flying, numismatics, antiques, philately. E-mail: erfani@uwindsor.ca.

ERICKSON, DOROTHY LOUISE, counselor, secondary school teacher; d. Knute Emanuel and Agnes Victoria (Bergsten) Swanson; m. Richard Harold Erickson, Aug. 30, 1953; children: Victoria Helen, Richard Edward. BA in Edn., U. Mo., Kansas City, 1967, MA in Edn. Counseling, 1971. Tchr. home econs. Ctr. Jr. High, Kansas City, 1970—86. counselor, 1983—86, Red Bridge Elem. Sch., Kansas City, 1986—94, ret., 1994. Vol. coord., bd. dir. Kimberly Area Libr.; vol., Welcome Wagon. Mem. Nat. Edn. Assn., Mo. Sch. Counseling Assn., Greater Kansas City Sch. Counselors Assn., Mo. Sch. Counselors Assn. (exec. bd. dirs., sec. and chmn. pub. affairs com.), Ctr. Edn. Assn., U. Mo. Kansas City Alumni Assn. (bd. dirs. sch. edn., v.p., v.p. pub. affaris). Home: 454 Nature Trail Blue Eye MO 65611-7117

ERICKSON, ELAINE MAE, composer, poet; b. Des Moines, Iowa, Apr. 22, 1941; d. Iver Carl and Ruth Eloise (Johnson) E. MusB, Wheaton Coll., 1964; MusM, Drake U., 1967. Pvt. piano tchr., Des Moines, 1964—; music libr. Main Pub. Library, Des Moines, 1965-67; composer-in-residence Ford Found. Fellowship, Ft. Lauderdale, Fla., 1967-68; tchr. piano music theory Drake U., Des Moines, 1969-72; pianist Ctr. for New Music State U. Iowa, Iowa City, 1974-76; piano tchr. Waxter Ctr., Balt., 1988-89, Church Lane Elem. Sch., Balt., 1989-90; tchr. music composition Ctrl. Coll., Pella, Iowa, 1993-96; composer-in-residence Charles Ives Ctr. Am. Music, New Milford, Conn., 1981—83, 1993. Guest composer Meet the Composer, Saranac Lake, NY, 1987; touring artist Very Spl. Arts Iowa, 1994—. Author (poetry) Separate Trains, 1988, A Visit Home, 1990, Solo Drive, 1992, Portraits and Selected Poems, 1994, The Cottage, 2001; writer 5 operas, 3 performed at Peabody Conservatory, Balt., 1986-91; contbr. poetry to numerous jours. Pianist various retirement homes, Balt., Des Moines, 1978—, music appreciation tchr., Balt., 1991-93, Des Moines, 1993—; organist Divinity Luth. Ch., Towson, Md., 1987-88. Recipient Pyle Commn. award Iowa Composers Forum, Des Moines, 1997, composition award Nat. League Am. Pen Women, 1992; touring grantee Iowa Arts Coun., 1974-75, 81-82. Democrat. Avocation: photography. Home and Office: 3700 Hillsdale Dr Des Moines IA 50322-3947

ERICKSON, HOWARD HUGH, veterinarian, physiology educator; b. Wahoo, Nebr., Mar. 16, 1936; s. Conrad and Laurene (Swanson) E.; m. Ann E. Nicolay, June 6, 1959; children: James, David. BS, DVM, Kans. State U., 1959; PhD, Iowa State U., 1966. Commd. 1st lt. U.S. Air Force, 1959, advanced through grades to col., 1979; veterinarian U.K., 1960-63; vet. scientist Sch. Aerospace Medicine, Brooks AFB, Tex., 1966-75; dir. rsch. and devel. aerospace med. divsn. Brooks AFB, 1975-81; prof. physiology Kans. State U., Manhattan, 1981—, acting head dept. anatomy and physiology, 1989—90, Roy W. Upham prof. vet. medicine, 2001—. Sci. adv. bd. Morris Animal Found., Englewood, Colo., 1990-93; cons. Tex. Higher Edn. Coordination Bd., Austin, 1990-91; clin. asst. prof. U. Tex. Health Sci. Ctr., San Antonio, 1972-81; vis. mem. grad. faculty Tex. A&M U., College Station, 1967-81; affiliate prof. Colo. State U., Fort Collins, 1970-75. Editor: Animal Pain, 1983; contbr. articles to profl. jours. Trustee Kans. State U. Golf Course Rsch. and Mgmt. Found., Meadowlark Cmty. Found. Recipient Alumni Achievement award Midland Luth. Coll., Fremont, Nebr., 1977, Merck award for Creativity, 1993, Bayer Excellence in Equine Rsch. award Am. Vet. Med. Assn. Coun. on Rsch., 2000. Fellow AAAS, Royal Soc. Health, Aerospace Med. Assn. (assoc.); mem. Am. Vet. Med. Assn. (chmn. coun. on rsch. 1984), Am. Physiol. Soc. (exec. bd.), Optimists Club (trustee). Republican. Lutheran. Home: 1700 Kings Rd Manhattan KS 66503-7550 Office: Kans State U Coll Vet Medicine Dept Anatomy and Physiology Manhattan KS 66506 E-mail: erickson@vet.ksu.edu.

ERICKSON, LARRY EUGENE, chemical engineering educator; b. Wahoo, Nebr., Oct. 8, 1938; s.Conrad Robert Nathaniel and Laurene Hanna (Swanson) E.; m. Laurel L. Livingston, May 31, 1981. BSChemE, Kans. State U., 1960, PhD, 1964. Instr. chem. engring. Kans. State U., Manhattan, 1964-65, asst. prof., 1965-67, assoc. prof., 1968-72, prof., 1972—. NIH spl. rsch. fellow U. Pa., Phila., 1967-68; vis. scientist MIT, Cambridge, 1975, USSR Acad. Scis., Pushchino, 1977-78; dir. Ctr. for Hazardous Substance Rsch., 1989—. Contbr. articles to profl. jours. Pres. Lutheran Help Assn., Manhattan, 1984. Recipient Career Devel. award NIH, 1970-75, Prof. Baehr award Beta Sigma Psi, 1981; Phi Tau Sigma award, 1995. Mem. AIChE, Am. Chem. Soc. (sec.-treas. chpt. 1983), Inst. Food Tech., Sigma Xi. Avocation: square dancing. Home: 408 Wickham Rd Manhattan KS 66502-3751 Office: Kans State U Dept Chem Engring Durland Hall Manhattan KS 66506-5102 E-mail: lerick@ksu.edu.

ERICKSON, LINDA RAE, elementary school educator; b. Huron, S.D., Aug. 17, 1948; d. Robert Emil and Esther (Schorzman) E. BS, U. Nebr., 1966; MA, U. No. Colo., Greeley, 1970; cert., U. Denver, 1990. Cert. elem. tchr., adminstr., prin. Spl. edn. resource tchr., Ignacio, Colo., 1983-85; elem. tchr. Woodland Park, Colo., 1985-86; tutor spl. edn. Am. Sch. London, 1987; elem. tchr. Borough of Brent, London, 1987, Internat. Sch. Hampstead, London, 1987-88; tchr. spl. edn. Carronhill Sch. for Handicapped, Stonehaven, Scotland, 1988-89; elem. tchr. Littleton (Colo.) Pub. Schs., 1970-83, 89-01; staff developer Pub. Edn. Bus. Coalition, 2001—; affiliate faculty Regis U., 2001—. Enrichment program coord. Sandburg Sch., 1991; co-chair Alternative Authentic Assessment Com., 1991—2001, Sandburg Parent Adv. Com., 1993—96; facilitator Littleton Pub. Schs., 1977—83, 1990—2001; workshop presenter Nat. Coun. Tchrs. English, Nat. Coun. Social Studies, WNET-TV Sta.; mem. Littleton Dist. Assessment Com., 1997—2001; chair Mother/Daughter Book Club, 1997—; affiliate faculty, supr. student tchrs. Regis U., 2001—; presenter in field. Active Fawcett Soc., London, 1987-89, NEA-Colo. Edn. Assn. Women's Caucus, 1979-01; mem. Sandburg Sch. mother/daughter book club, 1996—; founder mother/son book club, 1999-2000. Woman of Yr. nominee Littleton Jaycees, 1982; fed. grantee Use of Group Paperbacks in the Elem. Classroom, 1978. Mem. ASCD, NEA (women's leadership tng. cadre 1978-85), NOW, Colo. Edn. Assn., Littleton Edn. Assn. (bd. dirs., chair unit-bargaining team 1976-85), Internat. Reading Assn. (chair Pikes Peak 1986, Colo. coun. children's books award com. 1993-97, workshop presenter, reader meets writer com. co-coun. 1996—, tutor comitis crisis ctr. for homeless 1995-97, conf. presenter), Nat. Coun. Tchrs. English (co-lang. arts soc. exec. bd. dirs. 1995-97, co-chair storytelling contest 1997-98, mem. editl. bd. 1997-2001, presenter state conf. 1997), Planned Parenthood, Sierra Club, Alpha Delta Kappa, Phi Delta Kappa. Democrat. Lutheran. Avocations: skiing, water skiing, scuba diving, mountain biking, gardening. Home: 439 Saddlewood Cir Highlands Ranch CO 80126-2284

ERICKSON, LUTHER EUGENE, chemist, educator; b. Pulaski, Wis., June 30, 1933; s. Elmer and Luella (Thorson) E.; m. Jenny Sue Payne, June 22, 1957; children: Louise Elizabeth, Hans Luther. BA, St. Olaf Coll., 1955; PhD, U. Wis., 1959. Asst. prof. chemistry Dickinson Coll., Carlisle, Pa., 1959-62; mem. faculty Grinnell (Iowa) Coll., 1962—, prof. chemistry, 1968—, Dodge prof., 1974—. Contbr. articles to profl. jours. Recipient Catalyst award Chem. Mfrs. Assn., 1983; sci. faculty fellow NSF, 1968-69; Camille and Henry Dreyfus scholar, 1993-95. Fellow AAAS; mem. Am. Chem. Soc., Iowa Acad. Scis. Home: 3 College Park Rd Grinnell IA 50112-1207

ERIKSSON, BARBARA DUNLAP, secondary education educator; b. Whittier, N.C., Sept. 11, 1939; d. Lee Wilson and Nellie Grey (Denton) Dunlap; m. Edward N. Eriksson, July 29, 1960; 1 child, Michael N. BA, Stetson U., DeLand, Fla., 1961, MA, 1965; MS, Johns Hopkins U., 1986. Cert. tchr. social sci., adminstrn., supervision. Tchr./libr. Volusia County Bd. of Edn., DeLand, Fla., 1961-63; libr. Newport News Bd. of Edn., 1963-67; adminstrv. asst./travel agt. Kentron Hawaii, Ltd., Honolulu, 1968; tchr. Napa Valley Bd. of Edn., Napa, Calif., 1969-71, Anne Arundel County Bd. Edn., Annapolis, Md., 1974—, social studies dept. chair, 1984—. Owner Homestead Crafts, Cherokee, N.C., Barbara's Attic, Md. Pres. Anne

Arundel County Social Studies Coun., Annapolis; sec. faculty coun., interdisciplinary team leader Chesapeake Bay Mid Sch.; active church activities. Ford Found. fellow; Chesapeake Bay Found. Environ. grantee. Mem. AAUW, ASCD, Tchrs. Assn. Anne Arundel County, Ladies of Elks (sec.). Republican. Methodist. Home: 603 Bay Green Dr Arnold MD 21012-2008

ERION, CAROL ELIZABETH, music educator; b. Quincy, Ill., Jan. 16, 1943; d. Alva Eugene and Margaret Althea (Kaempfer) McKenney; m. David F. Erion, June 19, 1965; children: Elizabeth Celia Erion Matthews, Paul Frederick. MusB, Oberlin Coll., 1965; MusM, New England Conservatory Music, 1982; cert., U. Toronto, Ont., Can., 1978, Mozarteum Acad. Music, Salzburg, Austria, 1979. Music tchr. Montessori Sch. No. Va., Annandale, 1972-84, St. Agnes Episcopal Sch., Alexandria, Va., 1984-85, The Sidwell Friends Sch., Washington, 1985-87; music and fine arts tchr. Arlington (Va.) Pub. Schs., 1988-00; supr. arts edn. Arlington Pub. Schs., 2000—. Music dir. All Saints Episcopal Ch., Alexandria, 1983-90; workshop clinician various music edn. orgns. in U.S., 1980—; adj. instr. George Mason U., Fairfax, Va., 1983-2001; cons. WETA-TV, Washington, 1987. Author: Tales to Tell, Tales to Play, 1982; contbr. articles to profl. jours. Humanities fellow Coun. Basic Edn., 1989. Mem. NEA, AAUW, ASCD, Am. Recorder Soc., Am. Orff Schulwerk Assn. (pres. 1993-95), Arlington Edn. Assn. (pres. 1998-2000). Democrat. Episcopalian. Home: 19 W Linden St Alexandria VA 22301-2621 E-mail: cerion@arlington.k12.va.us.

ERLANGER, BERNARD FERDINAND, biochemist, educator; b. N.Y.C., July 13, 1923; s. Leo and Frieda (David) E.; m. Rachel Fenichel, June 23, 1946; children: Laura, Louis, Leon. BS with highest honors, CCNY, 1943; MA, NYU, 1949; PhD, Columbia U., 1951. Chemist U.S. Indsl. Chems. Co., Inc., Newark, 1943-44; tech. adviser Manhattan Project, U.S. Army, Los Alamos, 1944-46; prodn. mgr. Hexagon Labs., Inc., N.Y.C., 1946-48; faculty Columbia, 1951—, prof. microbiology, 1966—; vis. scientist Instituto Superiore di Sanita, Rome, 1961-62, Inst. Cell Biology, Shanghai, People's Republic of China, 1978. Mem. Fulbright-Hays Award Com., 1966-72; invited expert analyst biochem. and molecular biology edit. Chemtracts; mem. study sect. neurol. C, NIH, 1985-88. Recipient 600th Anniversary medal Copernican Med. Acad., Cracow, Poland, 1979,Sigma Alpha/Mu Gamma award N.Y. Heart Assn., Townsend Harris medal CUNY, 1995; Fulbright scholar U. Republic of Uruguay, 1967, Guggenheim fellow Inst. Phys.-Chem. Biology, Paris, 1969, Am. Cancer Soc. scholar Pasteur Inst., Paris, 1979. Recipient Physicians and Surgeons Disting. Svc. award Columbia U., 1996. Mem. Am. Chem. Soc., Am. Soc. Biol. Chemists, Biochem. Soc., N.Y. Acad. Scis. (mem. conf. com. 1978), Soc. Exptl. Biol. Medicine (assoc. editor proceedings 1981-88), Harvey Soc., Am. Soc. Immunologists, N.Y. Heart Assn., Am. Soc. Photobiology, Phi Beta Kappa, Sigma Alpha Mu (Gamma award). Achievements include research in mode of action of antibiotics and on cancer; investigation of mechanisms of enzyme catalysis; investigation of macromolecules concerned with genetics immunology of fullerenes, photoregulation, biological receptors; investigation of immunochemistry of buckminsterfullerenes, nanobiotechnology. Home: 16316 15th Dr Flushing NY 11357-2935 Office: Columbia U 701 W 168th St New York NY 10032-2704 E-mail: bfel@columbia.edu.

ERLENMEYER-KIMLING, L. psychiatrist, researcher; b. Princeton, N.J. d. Floyd M. and Dorothy F. (Dirst) Erlenmeyer; m. Carl F. E. Kimling. BS magna cum laude, Columbia U., 1957, PhD, 1961; DSc (hon.), SUNY, Purchase, 1997. Sr. rsch. scientist N.Y. State Psychiat. Inst., N.Y.C., 1960-69, assoc. rsch. scientist, 1969-75, prin. rsch. scientist, 1975-78, dir. div. devel. behavioral studies, 1978—, chief med. genetics, 1991—; asst. in psychiatry Columbia U., 1962-66, rsch. assoc., 1966-70, from asst. prof. to assoc. prof. psychiatry and genetics, 1970—78, prof., 1978—. Vis. prof. psychology New Sch. Social Rsch., 1971—97; mem. peer rev. group NIH, 1976—80; mem. work group guidance and counseling Congl. Commn. Hungtinton's Disease, 1976—77; mem. task force intervention Pres.'s Commn. Mental Health, 1977—78; mem. initial rev. group NIMH, 1981—85; mem. adv. bd. Croatian Inst. Brain Rsch., 1991—93. Editor: (book) Life-Span Research in Psychopathology, 1986; issue editor: Differential Reproduction, Social Biology, 1971, Genetics and Mental Disorders, Internat. Jour. Mental Health, 1972, Genetics and Gene Expression in Mental Illness, Jour. Psychiat. Rsch., 1992, Measuring Liability to Schizophrenia: Progress Report, 1994; mem. editl. bd. Schizophrenia Bull., 1978—; issue editor: Schizophrenia Bull., 1994; mem. editl. bd. Social Biology, 1970—79, Jour. Preventive Psychiatry, 1980—84, Croatian Med. Jour., 1991—, Neurology/Psychiatry/Brain Rsch., 1991—, Neuropsychiat. Genetics, —, Am. Jour. Med. Genetics, 1992—. Recipient Disting. Investigator award, Merit award, NIMH, 1989—96, William K. Warren Schizophrenia Rsch. award, Internat. Congress Schizophrenia Rsch., 1995, Lifetime Achievement award, Internat. Soc. of Psychiatric Genetics, 2002; grantee, NIMH, 1966—69, 1971—, Scottish Rite Com. Schizophrenia, 1970—74, 1984—87, 1989—94, W. T. Grant Found., 1978—86, MacArthur Found., 1981, Stnaley Found., 1995—, NARSAD, 1996—2000. Fellow: APA, Am. Psychol. Soc., Am. Psychopath. Assn.; mem.: AAAS, Soc. Study Social Biology (bd. dirs. 1969—84, 1992—96, sec. 1972—75, pres. 1975—78), N.Y. Acad. Scis., Internat. Soc. Psychiat. Genetics (Lifetime Achievement award 2002), Behavior Genetics Assn. (mem.-at-large 1972—74, Theodosius Dobzhansky award 1985), Am. Soc. Human Genetics, Sigma Xi, Phi Beta Kappa. Office: NY State Psychiat Inst Dept Med Genetics 1051 Riverside Dr Mail Unit 6 New York NY 10032-2603 E-mail: le4@columbia.edu.

ERLICHSON, HERMAN, physics educator; b. Bklyn., Mar. 22, 1931; m. Barbara H. Erlichson, Apr. 3, 1966; children: J. Peter, Andrew, Mark, Ellen. PhD in Philosophy, Columbia U., 1968; PhD in Physics, Rutgers U., 1980. Asst. prof. to prof. Coll. of S.I., 1960—. Contbr. articles to profl. jours. Mem. History of Sci. Soc., Am. Assn. Physics Tchrs.

ERMOLAEV, HERMAN SERGEI, Slavic languages educator; b. Tomsk, Russia, Nov. 14, 1924; came to U.S., 1949, naturalized, 1956; s. Sergei and Vera (Kozminykh) E.; m. Tatiana Kuzubova, June 8, 1975; children: Michael, Natalia, Katherine. Student, U. Graz, Austria, 1949; BA, Stanford U., 1951; MA, U. Calif.-Berkeley, 1954, PhD, 1959. Mem. faculty Princeton U., 1959—, prof. Slavic langs. and lits., 1970—. Author: Soviet Literary Theories, 1917-1934, The Genesis of Socialist Realism, 1963, 77, Mikhail Sholokhov and His Art, 1982, Censorship in Soviet Literature, 1917-1991, 1997, Mikhail Sholokhov and His Art (in Russian), 2000; co-author: Sholokhov's Tikhii Don, A Commentary, 1997; also articles; translator: Untimely Thoughts (Gorky), 1968, 95. McCosh fellow, 1967-68 Mem. Am. Assn. Advancement Slavic Studies, Am. Assn. Tchrs. Slavic and East European Langs. (pres. 1971-72) Home: 206 Moore St Princeton NJ 08540-3404 E-mail: ermolaev@princeton.edu.

ERNST, KELLI ANNE, special education educator; b. Indpls., Jan. 15, 1970; d. Robert Lee and Nelda Suzanne (Arvin) E. BS in Edn. of Handicapped, U. Dayton, 1991. Cert. tchr., Ohio, also cert. in multi-handicapped and developmentally handicapped. Tchr. devel. handicapped unit Wilson Jr. High Sch., Hamilton, Ohio, 1991-92, Walter Shade Elem. Sch., West Carrollton, Ohio, 1992—. Coach Spl. Olympics, Montgomery County, Ohio, 1992. Mem. Coun. Exceptional Children (mental retardation div.), Chi Omega, Sigma Tau Epsilon, Epsilon Delta Upsilon. Republican. Roman Catholic. Avocations: dancing, working out. Home: 5810 Kingstowne Ctr # 120-746 Alexandria VA 22315-5711 Office: Walter Shade Elem Sch 510 E Pease Ave West Carrollton OH 45449-1359

ERNST, RICHARD DALE, chemistry educator; b. Long Beach, Calif., Oct. 23, 1951; s. Erwin Harry and Martha Miriam (Jircik) E.; m. Chariya Asawaroengchai, Aug. 11, 1973; children: Kenneth, Christopher, Anjulee. BS, U. Calif., Berkeley, 1973; PhD, Northwestern U., 1977. Asst. prof. chemistry U. Utah, Salt Lake City, 1977-84, assoc. prof., 1984-87, prof., 1987—. Cons. Phillips Petroleum Co., Bartlesville, Okla., 1979-94. Mem. AAAS, Am. Chem. Soc. Roman Catholic. Home: 3238 Oakcliff Dr Salt Lake City UT 84124-5660 Office: U Utah Dept Chemistry 315 S 1400 E Salt Lake City UT 84112-0850 E-mail: ernst@chem.utah.edu.

ERNST, RICHARD JAMES, former academic administrator; b. Niagara, Wis., Feb. 3, 1933; s. Seymour and Rose Marie (Berger) E.; m. Elizabeth Lyle McGeachy, Dec. 23, 1959; children: Marie Elizabeth, Theresa Ann, Richard James. BS with high honors, U. Fla., 1956, MEd (univ. fellow), 1959; EdD, Fla. State U., 1965. Tchr. Pinellas and Hillsborough County pub. schs., Fla., 1958-62; adminstrv. intern Pinellas County Pub. Schs., 1962-63; instr., asst. dean instrn. St. Petersburg (Fla.) Jr. Coll., 1963-65, dean acad. affairs, 1965-68; pres. No. Va. C.C., Annandale, 1968-99; ret., 1999. Bd. dirs. Consortium for Continuing Higher Edn. in No. Va., 1972—, chmn. bd., 1978; mem. extension and pub. svc. adv. com. Va. Coun. Higher Edn., 1972-73, mem. gen. profl. adv. coun., 1978—; mem. nat. commn. on acad. affairs Am. Coun. on Edn., 1972-74, mem. commn. on mil.-higher edn. rels., 1978—; mem. adv. com. nat. orgns. Corp. for Pub. Broadcasting, 1972-74; mem. Va. Adv. Coun. Vocat. Edn., 1976—; mem. Va. adv. com. Nat. Identification Program for Advancement of Women in Higher Edn. Aminstrn., 1977—; mem. Va. Forum on Edn., 1978—; chmn. fin. com., chmn. personnel com., mem. exec. com., adv. coun. pres.'s, mem. rsch. and edn. com., acad. and student affairs com., chmn. intellectual property task force on continuing edn. and non-credit instrn. Va. C.C. Sys.; adv. bd. Jr. Svc. League No. Va., 1969-71; v.p. bd. trustees Fairfax Hosp., 1972—, also mem. exec. com., chmn. planning and program devel. com., chmn. joint conf. com.; mem. fin. comn., mem. adv. panel on hosp.-physician contracts Fairfax Hosp. Assn., 1978—; bd. dirs. Interfaith Ctr. on Corp. Responsibility, 1975—; Coop. for Advancement Cmty.-Based C.C. Edn., 1975—; chmn. acad. affairs com., trustee Mary Baldwin Coll., 1976—; mem. exec. com. bd. trustees; mem. gen. assembly mission bd. Presbyn. Ch. in U.S., 1974—, chmn. investment com., 1974—, chmn. long-range planning task force, vice chmn. divsn. ctrl. support svcs., chmn. fiscal and data sub-divsn.; mem. trustees' assembly United Way Nat. Capital. Area; mem. Washington Dulles Taks Force Adv. Com., 1983-84, Gov.'s Task Force Sci. and Tech., 1982-83; founding mem. Congl. award Coun.; bd. dirs. Am. Am. Cancer Soc.. Served with AUS, 1956-58. Fla. Ho. of Reps. scholar, 1952-56. Mem. No. Va. Ednl. TV Assn., So. Assn. Colls. and Schs. (com. on standards and reports, chmn. commn. on colls., chmn. accrediting coms.), Am. Assn. C.C. (nat. commn. on instrn., c.c. satellite network commn.), Nat. Coun. Cmty. Svcs. and Continuing Edn. (Regional Person of Yr. awd. 1992), Am. Coun. on Edn. (commn. on ednl. credit and credentials), Va. Coun. Pres., Assn. Va. Colls. (past pres.), Servicemembers Opportunity Colls. (past chmn. adv. bd. dirs.), George Mason Inst. (indsl. policy bd.), Va. C.C. Assn. (legis. action commn.), Va. C.C. Sys. (exec. com., adv. coun. pres., acad. and student affairs com., adv. coun. pres., chmn., intellectual property task force, chmn. task force on continuing edn. and non-credit instrnl.), Phi Eta Sigma, Phi Kappa Phi, Kappa Delta Pi, Phi Delta Kappa. Home: 8524 Pappas Way Annandale VA 22003-4433

ERNST, WALLACE GARY, geology educator; b. St. Louis, Mo., Dec. 14, 1931; BA, Carleton Coll., 1953; MS, U. Minn., 1955; PhD, Johns Hopkins U., 1959. Geologist U.S. Geol. Survey, Washington, 1955-56; fellow (Geophys. Lab.), Washington, 1956-59; mem. faculty UCLA, 1960-89, prof. geology and geophysics, 1968-89, chmn. geology dept. (now earth and space scis. dept.), 1970-74, 78-82, dir. Inst. Geophysics and Planetary Physics, 1987-89; dean Stanford Sch. of Earth Scis., 1989-94; prof. geol. and environ. scis. Stanford (Calif.) U., 1989—, Benjamin M. Page prof., 1999—, dean Sch. of Earth Scis., 1989-94. Author: Amphiboles, 1968, Earth Materials, 1969, Metamorphism and Plate Tectonic Regimes, 1975, Subduction Zone Metamorphism, 1975, Petrologic Phase Equilibria, 1976, The Geotectonic Development of California, 1981, The Environment of the Deep Sea, 1982, Energy for Ourselves and Our Posterity, 1985, Cenozoic Basin Development of Coastal California, 1987, Metamorphic and Crustal Evolution of the Western Cordillera, 1988, The Dynamic Planet, 1990, Integrated Earth and Environmental Evolution of the Southwestern United States, 1998, Planetary Petrology and Geochemistry, 1999; editor: Earth Systems: Processes and Issues, 2000, (with R.G. Coleman) Tectonic Studies of Asia and the Pacific Rim--A Tribute to Benjamin M. Page, 2000, (with J.G. Liou) Ultrahigh-Pressure Metamorphism and Geodynamics in Collision-Type Orogenic Belts, 2000. Trustee Carnegie Instn. of Washington, 1990—. Recipient Miyashiro medal Geol. Soc. Japan, 1998. Mem. NAS (chmn. geology sect. 1979-82, chair class I 2000—), AAAS, Am. Philos. Soc., Am. Geophys. Union, Am. Geol. Inst., Geol. Soc. Am. (pres. 1985-86), Am. Acad. Arts and Sci., Geochem. Soc., Mineral Soc. Am. (recipient award 1969, pres. 1979-80). Office: Stanford U Dept Earth & Environ Scis Green Earth Sci #209 Palo Alto CA 94303-1823

ERSKINE, WILLIAM CRAWFORD, academic administrator, accountant, health facility administrator; b. Seattle, Feb. 29, 1924; s. Alwin Crawford and Emilie Hildred (Davies) E.; m. Mary Jean Hopkins, Feb. 28, 1946; children: Scott Crawford, Nancy Page. BA in Bus. Adminstrn., U. Wash., 1950. CPA, Wash. Auditor Arthur Andersen & Co., 1950-54; sr. auditor Ansell Johnson & Co., CPAs, Seattle, 1956-59; contr. Food Giant Stores, Seattle, 1959-64; comptr. U. Wash., Seattle, 1964-70; v.p. bus. U. Colo., Boulder, 1970-74; exec. v.p. U. Nebr. system, Lincoln, 1974-80; v.p. bus. affairs U. Tex., El Paso, 1980-88; ret., 1988. Dir. West Tex. Higher Edn. Authority, El Paso, 1982-88, Sunwest Bank El Paso, 1986-96, Providence Hosp. P.H.A., Inc., 1994-96; cons. Educator Cons. Panel GAO, 1978-86. Treas. St. Francis on the Hill Episcopal Ch., 1996-99. With U.S. Air Corps, WWII. Mem.: Coronado Country Club (treas. 1990—93). Home: 6136 Los Robles Dr El Paso TX 79912-1933 E-mail: werskine@elp.rr.com.

ERTAN, ATILLA, medical educator, physician, researcher, health facility administrator; b. Eskisehir, Turkey, June 21, 1940; arrived in US, 1969; s. Rasim and Veliye E.; m. Inci E. Ertan, June 2, 1973; children: Basak, Baris R. MD, Ankara (Turkey) U. Med. Sch., 1963, Internal Medicine, 1967. Intern Ankara U. Med. Sch., 1963—64, resident in internal medicine, 1964—67; instr. medicine U. Pa., Phila., 1969—71, fellow in gastroenterology, 1971; assoc. prof. Ankara U. Med. Sch., 1972—76, prof., 1976—82, Tulane U. Med. Sch., New Orleans, 1982—90, chief GI, 1985—90, interim chair, 1989—90; prof., chief GI BCM/TMH, Houston, 1990—2000; prof., med. dir. dept. digestive diseases Meth. Hosp., Houston, 1990—. Founder Turkish GI Rsch. Fund, Ankara, 1996. Editor: Best Practice of Med. Gastroent., 1998; mem. editl. bd.: Digestive Disease Sci., 1994—, Ann. Med. Sci., 1999—, Med. Sci., 2002—; contbr. over 140 articles to profl. jours., chapters to books. Named Hon. Citizen, City of New Orleans, 1989, Best Physician, CCFA, 1996; named one of Top Drs. in Am., 1997—2003; recipient Med. Sci. award, TUBITAK, 1992. Master: Am. Coll. Gastroenterology; mem.: ASGE, AAAS, Am. Gastroenterol. Assn. (Disting. Clinician award 2003), Turkish GI Soc. (hon. pres. 1996), L'Union Med. Balkanique (hon. Best Rschr. award 1973), So. Soc. Clin. Investigation, Am. Fedn. Med. Rsch. Achievements include research in biliary and pancreatic disorders, Barrett's esophagus and inflammatory bowel diseases. Avocations: travel, reading, exercise. Home: 6337 Mercer St Houston TX 77005 Office: 6560 Fannin St Ste 2208 Houston TX 77030

ERTEL, GRACE ROSCOE, freelance non-fiction writer, educator; b. Santa Monica, Calif., Oct. 10, 1921; d. Thomas Benedict and Grace (Kelly) Roscoe; m. Donald Joseph Ertel, Sept. 28, 1946; children: Eileen Ariel, Adrienne Marie. BA, UCLA, 1943; teaching credential, U. Calif., Sacramento, 1970. Tchr. remedial reading Grant Sch. Dist., RioTierra-Sacramento, Calif., 1965-66; tchr. English as a second lang., other subjects Sacramento City Adult Schs., 1966-86, Grant Adult Schs., North Highlands, Calif., 1986—2002; freelance writer, 1975—. Lectr. on writing Am. River Coll., Sacramento, 1982. Author: (booklet) Plant an Ecology Garden, 1972, 76; contbr. articles to popular mags. Mem. citizens adv. Sacramento County Solid Waste Reclamation, 1975-80. Mem. Am. Soc. Journalists and Authors, Internat. Food, Wine & Travel Writers Assn., Outdoor Writers Calif. Avocations: photography, gardening, international cuisine. Home and Office: 6350 Dorchester Ct Carmichael CA 95608-3442

ERTL, RITA MAE, elementary education educator; b. Appleton, Wis., Dec. 22, 1939; d. Irving John and Bertha Helen (Van Ryte) Petrie; m. Andrew Philip Ertl, June 12, 1971; children: Kristyn Marie, Jessica Lynn. Student, Silver Lake Coll., 1961-71. Religious instr. for mentally handicapped Holy Name Parish, Sheboygan, Wis., 1965-69; tchr. grade 3 Holy Name Sch. (name now Holy Family Sch.), Sheboygan, 1969-72, learning ctr. coord., 1984—2001; tchr. aide Holy Family Sch., 2001—. Tchr. grade 2 St. Mary's Sch., Sheboygan Falls, 1961-69; mem. CCD bd. Holy Name Sch. Co-founder Human Rights Assn., Sheboygan, 1960-69. Avocations: sewing, reading, good music, volunteer work, gardening.

ERWIN, DONALD CARROLL, plant pathology educator; b. Concord, Nebr., Nov. 24, 1920; s. Robert James and Carol (Sexson) E.; m. Veora Marie Endres, Aug. 15, 1948; children: Daniel Erwin, Myriam Erwin Casey. Student, Wayne State (Nebr.) Tchrs.Coll, 1938-39; BSc, U. Nebr., 1949, MA, 1950; PhD, U. Calif.-Davis, 1953. Jr. plant pathologist U. Calif., Riverside, 1953-54, asst. plant pathologist, 1954-60, assoc. plant pathologist, 1960-66, prof. plant pathology, 1966—, emeritus prof., 1991. Sr. author: Phytophthora Diseases Worldwide, 1996; editor: Phytophthora: Its Biology, Taxonomy, Ecology and Pathology, 1983; contbr. articles to profl. jours. With U.S. Army, 1942-46; ETO. Nathan Gold fellow, 1949, Guggenheim fellow, 1959. Mem.: Am. Phytopathol. Soc. (fellow), Sigma Xi. Democrat. Roman Catholic. Office: U Calif Dept Plant Pathology Riverside CA 92521-0001

ERWIN, VICKI CORNELIUS, b. Greensboro, N.C., Sept. 7, 1951; d. George Rankin and Betty Jean (Thompson) C. BS in Edn., Western Carolina U., 1973, MA in Edn., 1975; edn. specialist, U. Miami, 1984; postgrad., U. Ga., 1992-93. Cert. educator K-12 reading, elem. 1-6, math 4-9, lang. arts, ESOL. Loan teller Coconut Grove Bank, Miami, Fla., 1973-74; math tchr. Palm Springs Jr. High, Hialeah, Fla., 1975-76; reading, math tchr. Campbell Drive Jr. High, Homestead, Fla., 1976-79, Homestead H.S., 1979-82, Riviera Mid. Sch., Miami, 1982-95, curriculum coord./facilitator and reading/test chairperson, 1995-98; reading tchr. McDougle Mid. Sch., Chapel Hill, 1998—2001; tchr. Eastridge Elem. Sch., Aurora, Colo., 2001—. Choreographer, assoc. dir. Miami Christmas Pageant, 1984-97. Mem. Internat. Reading Assn. Baptist. Home: 5195 Quitman St Denver CO 80212 Personal E-mail: ricnvic@mindspring.com.

ESCALET, FRANK DIAZ, art gallery owner, artist, educator; b. Ponce, P.R., Mar. 16, 1930; s. Frank Thillet and Concepcion Rodriquez (Diaz) E.; m.Shirley Leslie Fanner, Sept. 29, 1953 (div. Aug., 1955); children: Judith Alicia, Sudan Edith Escalet Barry; m. Marjorie Janet Gaydash-Huebner, July 19, 1964; 1 child, Frank Daniel (dec.). Owner, operator Talent Shop, N.Y.C., 1955-58, House of Escalet, N.Y.C., 1958-71, Pandora's Box, Eastport, Maine, 1971-73, Cobbler's Bench Art Gallery, Pembroke, Maine, 1973-82, House of Escalet Gallery, Kennebunkport, Maine, 1982-84, House of Escalet Studios, Kennebunkport, 1984—. Tchr. leathercraft Pasamaquoddy Reservation, Perry, Maine, 1971-72, Vocat. Sch. for Retarded Children, Calais, Maine, 1972-73. One-man traveling show Czechoslovakia, Russia, Poland, Yugoslavia, Hungary, Ukraine, 1991—; represented in permanent collections at Naprstkovo Mus., Prague, Union of Artists, Moscow, Bratslavia Primitive Mus., Slovakia, Frydek-Mistek Mus. No. Moravia, Museo Chicano, Phoenix, S.E. Tex. Art Mus., Beaumont, Arch. M. Huntington Gallery, Austin, Tex., Housatonic Mus., Bridgeport, Conn., Orgn. of Am. States Art Mus., Washington, Maryknoll (N.Y.) Sisters Ctr., Mus. City N.Y., 1998; featured on pub. TV, 1978, 82, 89; works in permanent collections Mus. City of N.Y., Ellen Noel Mus. Art of Permian Basin, Odessa, Tex., Dowd Fine Arts Mus., Cortland, N.Y., New Britain Mus. Am. Art; artist: Song and Dance Man acrylic, 1996. With US Air Force, 1947-54. Recipient numerous internat. and U.S. awards. Avocations: photography, antiques, gardening, travel, reading. Home and Office: House of Escalet Studios 24 Fletcher St Kennebunk ME 04043-6707 E-mail: escalet@gwi.net.

ESCHNER, JOAN ELIZABETH MICHAEL, elementary education mathematics educator; b. Lackawanna, N.Y., Sept. 14, 1939; d. John Emory and Ethel Pat Elizabeth Michael. BS, SUNY, Buffalo, 1961, MS, 1966. Tchr. West Seneca (N.Y.) Ctrl. Schs., 1961-96; instr. SUNY Coll., Buffalo, 1999—. Editor Bulkhead, U.S. Power Squadron, 1988—. Named Tchr. of Yr. West Seneca Tchrs.' Assn., 1978; recipient Presdl. State award NSF, 1991, Excellence in Teaching award Nat. level, 1994. Mem. AAUW, Nat. Coun. Tchrs. Math. (reviewer articles 1980—, reviewer ednl. materials 1990—, contbr. chpt. to yearbook 1984), Assn. Math. Tchrs. N.Y. State, Tech. Team West Seneca. Avocations: skiing, sailing, camping, fishing, gardening. Home: 30 Meadowbrook Dr Elma NY 14059-9524

ESCOBAR, DEBORAH ANN, gifted and talented education educator; b. Schenectady, NY, Aug. 21, 1952; d. Richard H. and Rose Marie (Denny) Quay; m. Jorge Escobar, Oct. 25, 1975; children: Rosana, Michael, Jorge R. AA, Schenectady County C.C., NY, 1988; BA, Russell Sage Coll., Troy, NY, 1990; MA, State Univ. Albany, NY, 1995. Lic. tchr. social studies, secondary edn., N.Y. Asst. editor, legis. liaison Internat. Assn. Fire Chiefs, Washington, 1972-76; tchr. gifted and talented Guilderland Sch. Dist., NY, 1991—. Author: Answering the Call, 1993, Teaching the History of the Albany Internat. Airport, 2000, Creating Hist. Documentaries, 2001, From Africa to NY: Slavery in NY State, 2001, (website) NYS Archives Legacies, 2003. Named Outstanding New Tchr. Sally Mae and Am. Assn. Sch. Adminstrs., Washington, 1992, NYS Hist. Day Tchr. of the Yr., 2001; Nat. Hist. Day Richard T. Ferrell Tchr. of Merit, 2001. Mem. NY State Hist. Assn. (Yorker advisor 1992-94), NY State Coun. Social Studies, Capital Dist. Coun. Social Studies, Phi Alpha Theta, Phi Kappa Phi, Phi Theta Kappa. Democrat. Avocations: writing, dancing, genealogy. Office: Farnsworth Mid Sch State Farm Rd Guilderland NY 12084

ESENBERG, ROBERT THOMAS, principal; b. Chgo., Sept. 24, 1948; s. Vernon Theodore and Evelyn Martha (Aurich) E.; m. Linda Rose Spitzer, June 18, 1972 (div. 1985); children: Bryan Nathan, Jefferey Steven, Gregory Todd; m. Regina Jay Berg, Dec. 21, 1985; children: Vanessa Tamarah, Robert Joseph. BA, Northeastern Ill. U., Chgo., 1970, MA, 1974, MA, 1988; EdD, Nova Southeastern U., 1994. Cert. tch., Ill.; cert. prin., Ill., Ind. Tchr. spl. edn. Cornell Elem. Sch., Chgo., 1971-80, Tanner Elem. Sch., Chgo., 1981-89; asst. prin. Sullivan Elem. Sch., Chgo., 1989-90, prin., 1990—. Dir. Beaconridge Sch., Bolingbrook, Ill., 1982-85. Sports writer The Times, 1987-92. Pres. Beaconridge Area Reps., Bolingbrook, 1978-82. Mem. Ill. Volleyball Assn. (dir. Region I 1986-88). Lutheran. Avocations: writing, volleyball, softball, travel. Office: Sullivan Elem Sch 8255 S Houston Ave Chicago IL 60617-2195

ESHAM, RICHARD HENRY, internist, educator, geriatrician, educator; b. Maysville, Ky., Oct. 6, 1942; s. Elwood and Ruth (Opfer) E.; m. Tamela Edwards; children: Ashley Ruth, Richard Henry II, Clay Hamlet. MD, U. Louisville, 1967. Resident in internal medicine U. Ala. Hosps. and Clinics, Birmingham, 1968—72, straight med. intern, 1967-68; pvt. practice Mobile, Ala., 1974-90; prof., dir. div. gen. internal medicine and geriatrics U. South Ala., Mobile, 1990-95, chief resident, 1971—72, asst. to v.p. for med. affairs Coll. Medicine, 1994-97, vice-chmn. clin. programs dept. internal medicine, 1994—2000, prof., dir. divsn. gen. internal medicine and geriat., 1997—2000, adminstrv. medicine, 2000—. Instr. medicine U. Ala. Hosps. and Clinics, 1971-72; chmn. Bd. Med. Examiners, Montgomery Ala.,

1992-94, Ala. Bd. Health, Montgomery, 1992-94; adj. prof. allied health, med. dir. PA studies program U. South Ala., 1997—. Contbr. med. articles to profl. jours. Bd. dirs. Arthritis Found., Mobile, 1974-81. Maj. U.S. Army, 1972-74. Fellow ACP; mem. Med. Assn. State of Ala. (officer, counselor, bd. censors 1984-94, vice chmn. 1991-92, chmn. 1992-94), Mobile Area C. of C. (bd. dirs. 1991-92, med. svcs. com. 1991-94), Southern Medical Assn. (assoc. councilor, mem. editl. bd. jour.), Alpha Omega Alpha. Avocations: fishing, hunting. Office: CPSI Med Dir 6600 Wall St Mobile AL 36695 Fax: 251-341-6159. E-mail: eshamrh@pol.net.

ESHOO, BARBARA ANNE RUDOLPH, academic official; b. Worcester, Mass., Sept. 27, 1946; d. Charles Leighton and Irene Isabella (Wheeler) Rudolph; divorced: l child, Melissa Clinton; m. Robert Pius Eshoo, July ll, 198l. Student, Morehead State U., 1964-66, U. N.H., 1974, 75; BA, New England Coll., 1976. Asst. to dir. Currier Gallery Art, Manchester, N.H., 1976-78, coord. pub. rels., 1979-82; dir. pub. rels. Daniel Webster Coll., Nashua, N.H., 1982-87, chief advancement officer, 1988-95; v.p. instnl. advancement Ea. Conn. State U., Willimantic, 1995—. Mem. faculty Currier Art Ctr., Manchester, 1977-79; bd. advisers New Eng. Coll. Art Gallery, Henniker, N.H., 1989-91. Advisor on planned giving United Way, Nashua, 1989-90; com. mem. Manchester Mayor's Task Force on Youth Affairs, 1986-88, Manchester Bd. of Sch. Commn., 1986-90; del. N.H. Sch. Bds. Assn., 1988-90; trustee, bd. sec. Manchester Hist. Assn., 1989-95; mem. Mayor's Com. on Leadership, Manchester, 1988-91; bd. dirs. Swiftwater coun. Girl Scouts U.S., 1990-95; chairperson parents com. Bennington Coll. Mem.: Assn. Fundraising Profls., Coun. for Advancement and Support of Edn., Assn. Governing Bds. of Univs. and Colls. (planning com., facilitator), Conn. Com. on Planned Giving, Nat. Com. on Planned Giving, Am. Coun. on Edn. (state of Conn. rep. Office Women in Higher Edn.), Conn. Women in Higher Edn., Nat. Soc. Fundraising Execs. (bd. dirs., v.p. pub. affairs N.H./Vt. chpt. to 1995), Newcomen Soc. Conn. (treas. 1997—99), Rotary (Nashua West chpt. 1990—95), Advt. Club N.H. (bd. dirs., v.p. 1980—82). Office: Ea Conn State U 83 Windham St Willimantic CT 06226-2211 E-mail: eschoob@easternct.edu.

ESKRIDGE, JUDITH ANN, educator, administrator; b. Tuscola, Ill., July 15, 1941; d. Reed Warren and Marjorie May (Reeder) Blain; m. Donald R. Henderson, July 10, 1966 (div. Dec. 1977); m. Howard Dean Eskridge, June 29, 1986; children: Kendra Eskridge Chriss, Jodi Henderson Samsa. BA, MacMurray Coll., 1963; MEd, U. Ill., 1968. Title I tchr., dir. Arcola (Ill.) Cmty. Unit #306, 1978—. Recipient Cert. of Appreciation Ea. Ill. Area Spl. Edn., 1988. Mem. NEA, Internat. Reading Assn., Ill. Reading Coun., Title I Dirs., Arcola Edn. Assn. Methodist. Avocations: reading, gardening, exercising, traveling. Home: 424E E County Road 1250 N Tuscola IL 61953-7074 Office: Arcola High Sch 351 W Washington St Arcola IL 61910-1120

ESLER, ANTHONY JAMES, historian, novelist, educator; b. New London, Conn., Feb. 20, 1934; s. Jamie Arthur and Helen Wilhelmina (Kreamer) E.; m. Carol Eaton Clemeau, June 17, 1961 (div. 1988); children: Kenneth Campbell, David Douglas; m. Helen Campbell Walker, July 24, 1992. BA, U. Ariz., 1956; MA, Duke U., 1958, PhD, 1961. Mem. faculty Coll. William and Mary, 1962-99, prof. history, 1972-99. Vis. prof. Northwestern U., 1968-69. Author: The Aspiring Mind of the Elizabethan Younger Generation, 1966, Bombs, Beards and Barricades: 150 Years of Youth in Revolt, 1971, The Youth Revolution: The Conflict of Generations in Modern History, 1974, Castlemayne, 1974, Hellbane, 1975, Lord Libertine, 1976, Forbidden City, 1977, The Freebooters, 1979, Babylon, 1980, Bastion, 1980, Generations in History: An Introduction to the Concept, 1982, The Generation Gap in Society and History: A Select Bibliography, 1984, The Human Venture, 5th edit., 2003, The Western World: A Narrative History, 2d edit., 1997; co-author: A Survey of Western Civilization, 1987, World History: Connections to Today, 1997, 2d edit., 2001, 3rd edit., 2003. Fulbright fellow U. London, 1961-62; research fellow Am. Council Learned Socs., 1969-70; Fulbright travel grantee Ivory Coast and Tanzania, 1983 Mem. World Hist. Assn., Am. Hist. Assn., Authors Guild, Amnesty Internat. Home: 416 Harriet Tubman Dr Williamsburg VA 23185 Office: Coll William and Mary Dept History Williamsburg VA 23187-8795 E-mail: anthonyesler@aol.com.

ESMAILZADEH, EBRAHIM, mechanical engineering educator, consultant; b. Mashhad Khorasan, Iran, Apr. 6, 1944; s. Mohammad and Fakhrolsharieh (Riaz) E.;m. Rouhangiz Daei Sadeghi, July 15, 1977; children: Reza, Ali. BSc with honours, U. London, 1967, MPhil, 1969, PhD, 1971. Chartered engr., U.K. Lab. instr. U. London, 1967-71; asst. prof. Arya-Mehr U. Tech., Tehran, 1971-75; vis. assoc. prof. MIT, Cambridge, Mass., 1976-77; prof. Sharif U. Tech., Tehran, 1980-89, univ. disting. prof., 1992-97, v.p., 1979-80; prof. dir. mfg. engring. program U. Ontario, Oshawa, Canada. Vis. prof. U. Victoria, Can., 1990-91, 97—; rsch. advisor Ministry of Heavy Industry, Iran, 1982-84; tech. cons. in field. Author textbooks and jour. articles on mech. engring.; mem. editl. bd. nat. and internat. jours.; spkr. in field. Named Excellent Prof., Iranian Soc. Mech. Engrs., 1994, Exemplar Prof. of Iranian Univs., 1993. Fellow Instn. Mech. Engrs. Eng., ASME; mem. Soc. Automotive Engrs., Iranian Acad. Scis. Tehran (chair mech. engring. dept. 1995-97), Iranian Soc. Control and Instrumentation Engrs. (dir. 1994). Avocations: chess, photography, music, ball games, skiing. Office: U Ontario Inst Tech 2000 Simcoe St N Oshawa ON Canada L1H 7K4

ESMOND, CHERI SUE, secondary school educator; b. Oak Park, Ill., Oct. 16, 1943; d. Fred W. and Shirley C. (Reiser) Wassmundt; m. Jack B. Esmond, Aug. 22, 1964; children: Jill Esmond Letbetter, Heather Esmond Camden. BS in Maths., U. Ill., 1965, MEd in Secondary Edn., 1966. Cert. secondary edn. tchr., Tex., Ill., N.Y., Mich.; lic. real estate broker, Ill. Tchr. Mahomet (Ill.) Seymour H.S., 1965-67, Ottawa (Ill.) H.S., 1972-73, Klein (Tex.) H.S., 1977—2000, Tomball Coll., 2000—02, Montgomery Coll., 2002—. Yearbook judge Nat. Scholastic Press Assn., Mpls., 1967-73. Treas. Jr. Guild Adv. Bd., Houston, 1989-90, provisional coord., 1990-92. Mem. Nat. Coun. Tchrs. of Math., Tex. Assn. Gifted and Talented, Tex. Math. and Sci. Coachess Assn. (Number Sense Coach of Yr. 1997, 99, 2000, Sweepstakes Coach of Yr. 1997-2000), Raveneaux Country Club, U. Ill. Alumni Assn., Cypress Creek Investment Club (treas. 2002—), Chi Omega Alums (pres. 1995-97), Kappa Delta Pi. Avocations: travel, scuba diving, golf. Home: 10835 Clubhouse Cir Magnolia TX 77354-6915 E-mail: esmond@hal-pc.org.

ESP, BARBARA ANN LORRAINE, educational researcher, educator; b. Bklyn., Nov. 10, 1947; d. Lawrence Joseph and Evelyn (Webber) Barbeire; m. Edward J. Esp, Aug. 31, 1968; children: Jacqueline, Michelle. BA, Adelphi U., 1969; PhD, Hofstra U., 1978. Counselor, tchr. U.S. Army Dept. Def., Wildflecken, Fed. Republic of Germany, 1970-73; adj. asst. prof. Hofstra U., Hempstead, N.Y., 1974-81; cons., rsch. program evaluator various sch. dists. N.Y., 1982-86; program rsch. analyst N.Y. State Div. Parole, N.Y.C., 1986-88; dir. pupil pers. svcs. Cleary Sch. for Deaf, Nesconset, NY, 1989—. Adj. prof. St. Joseph's Coll., Patchogue, NY, 2000—. Contbr. articles to profl. jours. Leader Girl Scouts U.S., Farmingville, N.Y., 1976-78; bd. dirs. Nassau-Suffolk Counties Alzheimers Assn., Patchogue, N.Y., 1984-86. Hofstra U. fellow, 1975-76. Republican. Roman Catholic. Home: 2 Jacqueline Dr Manorville NY 11949-2615

ESPARZA, THOMAS, SR., academic athletics administrator; b. Edinburg, Tex., May 21, 1921; s. Greg and T.R. (Tirsa) E.; m. Esther La Madrid, June 1, 1949; children: Tommy Jr., steven, Teylene. BS, Tex. A&I U., 1948; MS, 1951, PhD, 1977. Coach Edinburg (Tex.) Consol. Ind. Sch. Dist., 1963-65; instructional media cons., 1963-65; athletic events mgr., 1957-68; health, phys. edn. cons., 1950-68; dir. intramurals dept. phys. edn. Pan Am. U., Edinburg, from 1968; univ. chmn. steering com. Nat. Phys. Edn. and Sports Week. Mem. steering com. Met. Bank, 1973—; bd. dirs. Ednl. T.V. Channel 60; workshop cons. health and phys. edn. to various schs., 1968—; lectr. phys. edn. and athletic dirs., Mex., 1981—; pres. Edinburg Tchrs. Credit Union, 1958-65, Pan Am. U. Credit Union, 1970 Author: (with others) Humpty Dumpty and Friends in Southwest, 1990, numeropus publs. in field. Cons. edn. City Park bd., 1968—; appted. to Tex. Am. Legion Pub. Rels. Commn., 1989; coord. dist. I, Spl. Olympics, 1968-78; mem. selection com., steering com. Rio Grande Valley All-Acad. Football Team, 1985—; pres. Leo Najo Amateur Baseball League, 1985—; mem. Multi-purpose Sports Complex for Hidalgo County; co-coord. Rio Grande VAlley Leo Najo Baseball Reunion, Edinburg; co-founder, v.p. Rio Grande Valley Sports Hall of Fame, 1985—, pres., 1983—, also governing agt.; founder All Sports Reunion Edinburg, 1991; bd. dirs. Am. Cancer Soc., 1948-73, v.p. Edinburg unit, 1976, ednl. dir. Edinburg unit, 1977—; founder ann. Panocha Bread Cook-Off, 1979; mem. com. to inaugurate softball leagues in Mex.; mem. commissioning com. USS Gonzalez, 1996; bd. dirs. Guardian Paver Vets. War Meml., McAllen, Tex., 1996; mem. spl. com. to bring sports complex to Hidalgo County. With USNR, 1946-48. Named to Alice (Tex.) Baseball Hall of Fame, 1990, South tex. Baseball Hall of Fame, 1984, Recreation (emeritus); honoree Rio Grande Valley East-West All-Star Baseball Game, 1985; recipient Cert. of Appreciation Hidalgo County. Mem. NEA, AAHPER, Tex. High Sch. Coaches Assn., Tex. Assn. Health Phys. Edn., Tex. State Tchrs. Assn., Nat. Intramural Assn., Edinburg C. of C., Hidalgo County Hist. Soc. (bd. dirs.), Tex. A&I Alumni Assn. (bd. dirs. 1989—), Am. Legion (comdr. post 1970-75, 83—, 15th dist. baseball chmn. 1975—, 3rd divsn. baseball chmn. 1975—, state baseball chmn. 1980—, mem. state Americanism, constn. and by-laws, credentials coms. 1976—, nat. exec. com. 1983—, nat. legis. coun. 1982—, Tex. legis. coun. 1988—, award outstanding svc. legion at local state and nat. levels. 1996), DAV (life), Am. Legion (life, Tex. legis. coun., nat. legis. coun. 1980, comdr.'s recruitment team 1990, mem. exec. com. 1994). Home: Edinburg, Tex. Died Aug. 2, 2001.

ESPESETH, ROBERT D. park and recreation planning educator; b. Cameron, Wis., July 11, 1930; s. Robert I. and Mary (Willemssen) E.; m. Mary Ann Krepps, Dec. 30, 1952; children: Robert D. Jr., Steven R., Michael W., Karen S. BS in Landscape Architecture, U. Wis., 1952, MS in Landscape Arch./Regional Planning, 1956. Registered landscape architect, Ill., Neb. Park planner div. state forest and parks Wis. Conservation Dept., Madison, 1955-56; chief park planning bureau state parks and recreation Wis. Dept. Natural Resources, Madison, 1956-67; with Genessee County Park and Recreation Commn., Flint, Mich., 1967-73; asst. prof. dept. leisure studies U. Ill., Champaign, 1973-79, assoc. prof., 1979-95; dir. Ill.-Ind. Sea Grant Program, 1982—94. Expert witness, Champaign, Ill., 1974—. Author monographs, Site Planning of Park Areas, 1987, Developing a Bed and Breakfast Business Plan, 1988, Use of Conservation Easements, 1990, Community Park and Recreation Planning, 1994. Commr. Champaign County Forest Preserve Dist., Mahomet, Ill., 1974-86; bd. dirs. Green Meadows coun. Girl Scouts USA, 1975-83. With USN, 1952-54, capt. USNR, ret. Recipient Disting. Svc. award Am. Inst. Park Execs., 1965, Scroll Honor award Navy League U.S., 1973. Fellow Ill. Park and Recreation Assn. (bd. dirs. 1977); mem. Nat. Soc. Park Resources (Meritorious Svc. award 1985), Nat. Recreation and Park Assn. (trustee 1989-95, Park Profl. of Yr. award 1992), Univ. Club (past pres. U. Ill.). Avocations: golf, gardening, fishing, biking. Office: U Ill 1206 S 4th St Ste 104 Champaign IL 61820-6920 E-mail: respeset@uiuc.edu.

ESPINOZA, DORIS LOIDA, music educator, minister; b. Albuquerque, Oct. 9, 1950; d. Jose Leandro and Abedulia (Martinez) Padilla; m. Bernardino Pedro Espinoza Jr., Aug. 11, 1972; children: Eunice Dina, Eli Jose. Student, L.Am. Bible Inst., El Paso, Tex., 1969-72; BA in Christian Edn., S.W. Assemblies of God U., 1987. Ordained to ministry Assemblies of God Ch., 1986. Sec.-treas. Women's Ministries Gulf L.Am. Dist., 1972-75, 88—, dist. youth choir dir., 1980-85, choir dir., 1988-98; exec. sec. Straus-Frank, San Antonio, 1973-75; sect. missionette coord. Villa Del Sol, Crystal City, Tex., 1985-88; music tchr. Wintergarden Christian Acad., Crystal City, Tex., 1990-96; home sch. tchr. Crystal City, Tex., 1985-91, 97—. Cons., counselor; musical group dir. Composer; author numerous poems. Coord. Missionette Girls Club, Crystal City, 1985-88; mem. drug free com. Crystal City, 1988-94; exec. sec. Assembly God Gulf Latin Am. Dist., 1976-82 Mem. L.Am. Bible Inst. Alumni Assn. (pres. 1982-86), Religious Conf. Mgmt. Assn. Avocations: walking, jogging, handcrafts, singing, playing the piano. Office: Womens Ministries GLAD PO Box 313 Crystal City TX 78839-0313

ESPINOZA, FERNANDO, science education educator; b. Rovira, Tolima, Colombia, Mar. 30, 1951; came to U.S., 1969; s. Alfonso and Melba (Lopez) E.; m. Katherine Mary Shannon, Nov. 17, 1989; children: Victoria, Gabriella, Gerard, Olivia. BA in Physics, CUNY, 1980, MA in Physics, 1983; EdD in Sci. Edn., Columbia U., 1996. Adj. lectr. Queens Coll., CUNY, 1980-88; tchr. sci. Molloy H.S., Jamaica, N.Y., 1983-98; asst. prof. sci. edn. Lehman Coll., CUNY, Bronx, 1998—. Adj. prof. SUNY Coll. Old Westbury, N.Y., 1986-99. Contbr. articles to profl. jours., including Sci. Activities, Sci. Tchr., AVISTA Jour., also chpt. to book. Mem. N.Y. State Tchrs. Assn. (coll. rep. Suffolk chpt. 1998%), Am. Mus. Natural History. Avocation: wine and educational consulting. Office: CUNY Lehman Coll 250 Bedford Park Blvd W Bronx NY 10468 E-mail: espinoza@lehman.cuny.edu.

ESPOSITO, AUDREY MATTHEWS, elementary school educator; b. Englewood, N.J., Mar. 9, 1941; d. Roger F. and Dorothy Alma (Ungerer) Matthews; m. Salvatore A. Esposito, June 27, 1964; children: Carolyn, Jennifer, Kristine. BA, Trenton State Coll., 1963; spl. edn. cert., William Paterson Coll., 1986; M in Gen. Profl. Edn., Seton Hall U., 1993. Cert. elem. edn., N.J., tchr. of the handicapped. Classroom tchr. South Brunswick (N.J.) Bd. Edn., 1964-66, Rockaway (N.J.) Boro Bd. Edn., 1980; title I coord., tchr. Stanhope (N.J.) Bd. Edn., 1976-79; classroom tchr. Mendham Twp. Bd. Edn., Brookside, N.J., 1983—. Freelance writer Ednl. Pubs. Recipient Gov.'s Tchr. Recognition award, 1989. Mem. NEA, N.J. Edn. Assn. (past v.p., mem. profl. devel. com. 2002—), Mendham Twp. Tchrs. Assn. (past pres., mem. negotiations team past and present 2003). Home: 12 Linda Terr PO Box 273 Ironia NJ 07845-0273 Office: W Main St Brookside NJ 07926

ESQUER, DEBORAH ANNE, elementary school educator; b. Omaha, Oct. 28, 1950; d. Thomas Ross and Carolyn Mae (Wright) Woods; m. Mario H. Esquer, Aug. 21, 1971 (div. Apr. 1991); children: Mario, Michael. BA, Ariz. State U., 1972, MA in Edn., 1972, 78; postgrad., Ottawa U., Phoenix, 1990-92. Cert. elem. tchr., spl. edn. Tchr. Paradise Valley Sch. Dist., Phoenix, 1972—. Mem. Valley Leadership Class, 1999-2000; bd. dirs. Wesley Cmty. Ctr., 2000—, bd. pres.; mission team co-chair Paradise Valley United Meth. Ch.; bd. dirs. ASU Coll. Edn. Alumni. Tchr. venture grantee, Phoenix, 1988. Mem. NEA, Ariz. Edn. Assn., Ariz. Reading Coun., Paradise Valley Edn. Assn., Paradise Valley Reading Coun., Phoenix Art Mus., Ariz. Hist. Soc., Paradise Valley Jr. Women's Club (corr. sec. 1991-92), Alpha Delta Kappa (pres. 1986-88, ctrl. dist. treas. 1986-88, corr. sec. 1992-94, treas. 1994—, state com.), Alpha Phi. Democrat. Methodist. Office: Desert Springs 6010 E Acoma Dr Scottsdale AZ 85254-2599

ESSA, LISA BETH, elementary school educator; b. Nov. 19, 1955; d. Mark Newyla and Elizabeth (Warda) Essa. BA, U. Pacific-Stockton, 1977, MA in Curriculum and Instrn. Reading, 1980. Cert. tchr. elem., multiple subject and reading specialist Calif. Libr. media specialist Delhi (Calif.) Elem. Sch. Dist., 1978-80; reading clinic tutor San Joaquin Delta C.C., Stockton, Calif., 1980; libr. media specialist Hayward (Calif.) Unified Sch. Dist., 1980—. Chair curriculum coun. Hayward Unified Sch. Dist., 2000—01; support provider Beginning Tchr. Support Assessment, 2000—01. Supr. San Francisco host com. Dem. Nat. Conv., 1984. Named Master Tchr., Intel Teach to the Future; recipient Hon. Svc. award, 1999. Mem.: Hayward Unified Tchrs. Assn., Calif. Tchrs. Assn., Jr. League San Francisco. Episcopalian. E-mail: chalktalk1@aol.com.

ESSARY-ANDERSON, CATHERINE, elementary education educator; b. San Francisco, Jan. 21, 1947; d. John G. and Margaret H. (Heinisch) Baker; m. Dennis E. Anderson, June 8, 1968 (div. 1991); 1 child, Donald L.; m. John W. Essary, 1995. BA, Calif. State U., Chico, 1968; tchg. cert., St. Mary's Coll., Calif., 1985; MA in Edn., Chapman U., 1993. Cert. tchr. Social worker Social Svcs., Fresno, Calif., 1969-71; ECE aide/resource specialist aide Mt. Diablo Sch. Dist., Concord, Calif., 1983-85; tchr. Antioch (Calif.) Sch. Dist., 1985-87; office mgr. House Master Am., Danville, Calif., 1987-89; tchr. Worldwide Ednl. Svcs., Concord, 1989-90; mentor tchr. Mt. Diablo Sch. Dist., Concord, 1990—. Contbr. articles to math. jours. and fashion mags. Commr. Concord Planning Commn., 1991, Contra Costa County Libr. Commn., Martinez, Calif., 1991; bd. dirs. Concord Hist. Soc., 1991; co-chair Alliance for Better Librs., Concord, 1986. Named Disting. Citizen Salvation Army 1972; Presdl. grantee in edn. for tchr. rsch. U. Calif., 1996-98; Cress Ctr. grantee, 1998; EXXON grantee, 1999; Spencer Found. grantee. Mem. AAUW (past pres. 1979, past state bd. dirs. 1986-88, named gift honoree 1983, Woman of Yr. 1981), LWV, NEA, Calif. Tchrs. Assn., Mt. Diablo Edn. Assn., Delta Kappa Gamma. Democrat. Avocations: travel, quilting, crafts, reading, personal growth. Office: Rio Vista Elem Sch 611 Pacifica Ave Bay Point CA 94565-1359

ESSENBERG, LOUISE MARIE, special education, physical education educator; b. Chgo., June 6, 1957; d. Peter John and Ellen Agnes (Gibbons) Vandenbergh; m. William Allen Essenberg, July 1, 1989. BS, George Williams Coll., 1979; MS, U. Ill., Chgo., 1984. Teaching cert. spl. K-12. Phys. edn. tchr. St. Gertrude Sch., Franklin Park, Ill., 1979-82, Sacred Heart Sch., Melrose Park, Ill., 1980-82, Madonna High Sch., Chgo., 1982-84, Chute Mid. Sch. Dist. # 65, Evanston, 1984-91, Park Sch. Dist. # 65, Evanston, 1991—. Park dist. worker Norridge (Ill.) Park Dist., 1979-82; coach athletic teams Madonna High Sch., Chgo., 1982-84, Chute Middle Sch., Evanston, 1984, 85, 90, Park Sch., Evanston, 1992, 93, 94. Info. collector Maine-Niles Assn. Spl. Recreation, 1991. Mem. AAHPERD, Ill. Assn. Health, Phys. Edn., Recreation and Dance (N.E. dist. rep. 1988-89). Roman Catholic. Avocations: playing tennis, caring for plants.

ESSIEN, FRANCINE B. geneticist, educator; BA in Biology, Temple U.; PhD in Genetics, Yeshiva U.; postgrad., U. Conn. Prof. dept. biol. scis. Rutgers U., New Brunswick, N.J., 1997—. Dir. Minority Undergrad. Sci. Programs, Rutgers U., 1988—, founder, co-founder Success in the Scis., Biomed. Careers Program, Rsch. Apprentice Program, ACCESS-MED, mem. adv. bd. Douglass Project for Rutgers Women in Math, Sci. and Engring.; mem. rev. panel NSF/NIH; cons. CUNY, Atlanta U.; lectr. in field. Contbr. articles to profl. jours. Fulbright scholar; recipient Spina Bifida Assn. Am. award, N.J. Women of Achievement award Woodrow Wilson Found. Instns.; named Black Achiever in Sci., Chgo. Mus. Sci. and Industry, U.S. Prof. of Yr. for Rsch. and Doctoral Univs., Carnegie Found. Advancement of Teaching.; Disting. Black Scholar-in-Residence, U. Cin., 1988; CASE Professor of the Yr. 1994-95; recipient W.E.B. DuBois award for edn. NAACP of Cen. N.J., 1997. Office: Rutgers U Nelson Lab/Busch Campus 604 Allison Rd Piscataway NJ 08854-8000*

ESSIG, KATHLEEN SUSAN, university official, management consultant; b. Denver, July 5, 1956; d. Robert and Ethel Essig. BS in BA, Colo. State U., 1979, MS, 1987. CPA, Colo. Personal fin. planner, v.p. fin. Successful Money Mgmt., Ft. Collins, Colo., 1987-88; accts. payable technician Colo. State U., Ft. Collins, 1980-81, supr. comml. accts. receivable, 1981-83, gen. acct. II, 1983-85, supr. student loans, 1985-87, supr. accts. receivable, acct. II, 1988-89, cost acct. III, 1989-94, univ. ofcl., contr., 1994; univ. mgmt. cons. KPMG Peat Marwick, Denver, 1994-97, 1995-97; mgr. prin. cons. Oracle Corp., Redwood Shores, Calif., 1998—. Mem. Am. Bus. Women's Assn. (v.p. 1985, Woman of Yr. 1985), Nat. Assn. Accts. Avocations: photography, golf, skiing, scuba diving.

ESSINGER, SUSAN JANE, special education educator; b. Paris, Ill., Oct. 7, 1952; d. Rex Milburn and Virginia Ellen (White) E. BS in Edn., Ea. Ill. U., Charleston, 1973; MS in Edn., Ind. State U., 1981, postgrad. Cert. learning disabilities, elem., educationally mentally handicapped with early childhood endorsement. Elem. tchr. Havana (Ill.) Sch. Dist., 1973-74; tchr. early childhood spl. edn. Paris Sch. Dist. 95, 1974—. Mem. APA, NEA, IDEC, CEC, Assn. for Edn. Young Children, Ill. Edn. Assn., Paris Tchrs. Assn. Avocations: dollmaking, gardening, collecting coins and stamps. Home: 1104 S Main St Paris IL 61944-2823 Office: Paris Sch Dist 95 S Main St Paris IL 61944 E-mail: sessinger@comwares.net.

ESTABROOKS, GORDON CHARLES, secondary education educator; b. Cambridge, Mass., Jan. 26, 1927; s. Gordon MacIntosh and Nettie Katherine (McIvor) E.; m. Alice Marian McEwen. AB, Boston U., 1964; MA, Suffolk U., 1971; MEd, Northeastern U., 1976; M in Natural Sci., Worcester Poly., 1980; Cert. Advanced Grad. Studies, Northeastern U., 1990. Chem. tech. Union Past Co., Boston, 1953-60; tchr. math. and sci. Grover Cleveland Jr. Boston (Mass.) Sch. Dept., 1964-67; tchr. sci. Boston (Mass.) Latin Sch., 1967—. Lectr. physics Northeastern U., Boston, 1983—. Editor: Seaweed and Seascape Marine Newsletters, Kelp Inc. Pres. Camp Paul for Exceptional Children, Chelmsford, Mass., 1977-83, Kennebunk Enrichmnet Learning Program, Kelp Inc., Mass., 1981—, Learning Disabilities Mass., Weston, 1989-91. Staff sgt. USAF, 1948-52, Korea. Recipient Disting. Svc. award Assn. for Retarded Citizens, Chelmsford, 1980, State of Mass. citation Com. of Mass. Senate, 1983, fellowship in sci. GTE, Mass., 1985, cert. appreciation Mass. Marine Educators, Woods Hole, Mass., 1989, Spl. award, 1991, Annual award of distinction, 1992, and many others. Mem. Mass. Assn. Sci. Tchrs. (bd. mem., Suffolk County dir., Sci. Educator of Yr. award 1990), Mass. Marine Educators (treas.). Episcopalian. Avocations: sports, reading, birding. Home: 37 Sleigh Rd Chelmsford MA 01824-4223 Office: Boston Latin Sch 78 Avenue Louis Pasteur Boston MA 02115-5791

ESTEBAN, MANUEL ANTONIO, academic administrator, language educator; b. Barcelona, June 20, 1940; arrived in U.S., 1970; s. Manuel and Julia Esteban; m. Gloria Ribas, July 7, 1962; 1 child, Jacqueline. BA in French with 1st class honors, U. Calgary, Can., 1969, MA in Romance Studies, 1970; PhD in French, U. Calif., Santa Barbara, 1976. From asst. prof. to prof. French and Spanish langs. and lit. U. Mich., Dearborn, 1973-87, assoc. dean, 1984-86, acting dean Coll. Arts, Scis., and Letters, 1986-87; dean arts and scis. Calif. State U., Bakersfield, 1987-90; provost, v.p. acad. affairs Humboldt State U., Arcata, Calif., 1990-93; pres., prof. French and Spanish Calif. State U., Chico, 1993—2003, pres. emeritus, prof. emeritus, 2003—. Bd. dirs. Calif. Joint Policy Coun. Agr. and Edn., 1995—. Author: (book) Georges Feydeau, 1983; contbr. to book revs. and articles to profl. publs. Trustee Enloe Hosp. Fellow, U. Mich., 1982—83; Woodrow Wilson fellow, 1969, Doctoral fellow, U. Calif., Santa Barbara, 1970—73, Can. Coun. Doctoral fellow, Govt. of Can., 1970—73, Rackham grantee, U. Mich., 1979. Mem.: Am. Assn. State Colls. and Univs., Am. Coun. Edn., Sierra Health Found. (bd. dirs. 1998—), Greater Chico C. of C. Avocations: golf, woodworking, glass blowing. Office: Calif State Univ O'Connell 407 Chico CA 95929-0003

ESTELL, DORA LUCILE, retired educational administrator; b. Ft. Worth, Mar. 3, 1930; d. Hugh and Hattie Lucile (Poole) E. BA, East Tex. Bapt. U., 1951; MA, U. North Tex., 1959; EdD, East Tex. State U., 1988. Tchr. Mission (Tex.) Ind. Sch. Dist., 1951-53; tchr., adminstr. Marshall (Tex.) Ind. Sch. Dist., 1953-68; dep. dir. Region VII Edn. Svc. Ctr., Kilgore, Tex.,

1968-94, ret., 1994. Contbr. articles to profl. jours. Bd. dir. South Milan County United Way, Richards Meml. Hosp. Named Rockdale Citizen of Yr., 2001. Mem. Rockdale C. of C. (bd. dirs.), Phi Delta Kappa. Baptist. Avocations: photography, gardening. Home: 611 W Bell Ave Rockdale TX 76567-2809

ESTENES, JOSEPH JOHN, JR., academic administrator; b. New Brunswick, N.J., Mar. 11, 1943; s. Joseph John Sr. and Eleanor (Narozanick) E.; children: Joseph John III, Gina. BS, Seton Hall U., 1964, MBA, 1967; postgrad., Rutgers U., 1967, U. Nebr., 1969. Lic. sch. bus. adminstr., N.J. Sheriff's officer Monmouth County Sheriff's Office, Freehold, N.J., 1963-65; maintenance adminstr. Owens-Ill., Lily-Tulip div., Holmdel, N.J., 1965-69; bus. mgr. Monmouth Coll., West Long Branch, N.J., 1969-72; bus. adminstr. Lakewood (N.J.) Pub. Schs., 1972-73; bus. mgr. The Ethical Culture Schs., N.Y.C., 1973-78; v.p. adminstrn., treas. Westminster Choir Coll., Princeton, N.J., 1978-84; CFO, pub. safety dir. Stetson U. Coll. Law, St. Petersburg, Fla., 1984—. Adj. lectr. Ocean County C.C., Toms River, N.J., 1970-73. V.p. Hamilton Vol. Fire Dept., Neptune, N.J., 1972-73; capt. Hamilton First Aid and Rescue Squad, Neptune, 1973-74; coach, mgr. Little League, Neptune, 1973-75; coach Babe Ruth League, Neptune, 1975-78. Mem. Nat. Assn. Coll. and Univ. Bus. Officers, Assn. Phys. Plant Mgrs., Nat. Assn. Edni. Buyers, Ind. Coll. and Univ. Bus. Officers State Fla., Fla. Police Chiefs Assn., Fla. Assn. Campus Safety and Security Adminstrs., Tampa Bay Area Chiefs Police. Republican. Office: Coll Law 1401 61st St S Saint Petersburg FL 33707-3246

ESTERHAMMER, ANGELA, literary theorist, educator; d. Hermann and Marianne E.; married, Feb. 20, 1989. BA, U. Toronto, 1983; postgrad., U. Tübingen, Germany, 1983-84; PhD, Princeton U., 1990. Asst. prof. dept. modern langs. U. Western Ont., London, Canada, 1989—94, assoc. prof., 1994—99, prof., 2000—, chair dept., 2000—. Vis. prof. Free U. Berlin, 1996—98. Author: Creating States: Studies in the Performative Language of John Milton and William Blake, 1994, The Romantic Performative: Language and Action in British and German Romanticism, 2000; editor Romantic Poetry, 2002, translator (and introduction): Two Stories of Prague by R.M. Rilke, 1994; contbr. articles to profl. jours. Recipient Protégé award, Toronto Arts Award Found., 1988, John Charles Polanyi prize, Govt. of Ont., 1990, Hellmuth prize for Achievement in Rsch., 2002; Whiting fellow in Humanities, Princeton U., 1988, Alexander von Humboldt Found. rsch. fellow, Free U. Berlin, 1996—97. Mem. MLA, N.Am. Soc. for Study of Romanticism (founding mem.), Can. Comparative Lit. Assn. (pres. 2003—), Internat. Comparative Lit. Assn. Mem. United Ch. of Can. E-mail: angelae@uwo.ca.

ESTERHAY, JUDITH M. physical education educator; b. Cleve., Jan. 5, 1943; d. Anthony S. and Marcella H. (Petch) E. BS in Edn., Cleve. State U., 1965; MS in Edn., Kent State U., 1975. Instr. Case Western Res. U., Cleve., 1972-73, Baldwin Wallace Coll., Berea, Ohio, 1973-74; assoc. prof. phys. edn. Cuyahoga C.C., Cleve., 1974—; grad. asst. Kent (Ohio) State U., 1971-72. Mem. Am. Coll. Sports Medicine (fitness instr.). Avocations: running, cross-country skiing, cycling, sailing. Office: Cuyahoga CC 11000 W Pleasant Valley Rd Parma OH 44130-5114

ESTERSON, MORTON M. special education educator; b. Balt., June 25, 1926; s. Julius and Celia (Etelson) E.; m. Hinda Feldman, Aug. 21, 1949; children: Rachel, Samuel. BSS, CCNY, 1950, postgrad., 1950-51, Yeshiva U., 1951-52, NYU, 1952, U. Md., 1952-53, Johns Hopkins U., 1953-55; MEd, Loyola Coll., 1966, cert. for advanced study in edn., 1967. Cert. tchr., Md. Tchr. Alicia Crossland Sch. 9, Balt., 1951-56, Clifton Park Jr. H.S. 90, Balt., 1956-60; specialist Divsn. Spl. Edn., Balt., 1960-68, supr., 1968-71, area supt., 1971-73; coord. Office of Program Svcs., Balt., 1973-80, Johns Hopkins U., Balt., 1974-79, Office Mgmt. Svcs., Balt., 1978-81. Adj. prof. Loyola Coll., Balt., 1962—; bd. dirs. The Chimes, Inc., Balt.; bd. trustees St. Elizabeth Sch., Balt.; mem. adv. com./bd. dirs. dept. spl. edn. Loyola Coll., Balt., Impartial Hearing Officers of Md. ; mem. adv. com. Recreation Svcs. for Handicapped, 1978-79; mem. edn. com. Ptach of Balt., Inc., 1980-84; mem. task force on new consultative bd. St. Elizabeth Sch., 1988-89. Co-author: Related Services for Handicapped Children, 1986, (filmstrips) Number Concept Series, 1981, Visual Perception Series, 1981, (video) Education, 1972. Dir. Bais Yaakov Day Camp, Balt., 1951-60; mem. adv. com./bd. dirs. Suburban Orthodox Congregation Toras Chaim; mem. Chevra Ahavas Chesed, Inc., Jewish Hist. Soc., Religious Zionists of Am., Union of Orthodox Jewish Congregations; bd. dirs. Shaarei Zion Congregation, 1958-60, Religious Zionists of Balt., 1970-71; pres. PTA, Bais Yakov Sch. for Girls, 1959-60; chmn. day camp com. Am. Camping Assn., 1959-60; mem. Balt. Jewish Coun., 1985-88. Recipient Appreciation cert. Balt. chpt. ARC, 1957, Vol. Svc. medal Am. Nat. Red Cross, 1960, Appreciation cert. Balt. City Spl. Olympics, 1976-80, plaque, 1982, plaque Coun. for Exceptional Children, 1981, Silver Tray award Suburban Orthodox Congregation, Balt., 1985, Recognition cert. City Coun. Balt., 1989, Mayor's citation for Pub. Svc., Mayor of Balt., 1990, Gov.'s citation, 2001; Morton M. Esterson Media Ctr. dedicated in honor George W.F. McMechen Sch., 1982, Morton M. Esterson Med. Ctr. dedicated in honor William S. Baer Sch., 1986, others. Mem. Coun. for Exceptional Children, Nat. Ret. Tchrs. Assn., Md. Ret. Tchrs. Assn., Pub. Sch. Adminstrs. and Suprs. Assn., Impartial Hearing Officers of Md. (steering com.), Phi Delta Kappa (Alpha Rho chpt.). Democrat. Home and Office: 6607 Park Heights Ave B1 Baltimore MD 21215 E-mail: esterson@loyola.edu.

ESTES, CAROLYN ANN HULL, retired elementary school educator; b. Memphis, June 11, 1933; d. Elmer Franklin and Annie Vernon (Jeter) Hull; m. Robert Marion Estes, June 4, 1955; children: Robert Franklin, David Carlton. BS, Memphis State U., 1955; postgrad., U. Tenn., 1958, Nat. Coll. Edn., 1968, N. Tex. State U., 1970, Tex. Christian U., 1984, U. Tex., Arlington, 1985. Cert. elem. and secondary tchr., Tex. 4th grade tchr. Memphis City Schs., 1955-56, 63-66; 6th grade tchr. Knoxville (Tenn.) City Schs., 1957-58; 3d grade tchr. Elk Grove Village (Ill.) Schs., 1968-69; sci. tchr. Stripling Middle Sch., Ft. Worth Ind. Sch. Dist., 1970-76; 5th grade magnet tchr. Eastern Hills Sch., Ft. Worth Ind. Sch. Dist., 1976-78; 5th grade honors tchr. Westcreek Elem. Sch., Ft. Worth Ind. Sch. Dist., 1978-91, computer instr., technol. coord., 1991-96; ret., 1996. Author: Hull's Heritage, 1986; contbg. author: Hardeman County History, 1979, also curriculum materials. Life mem. Tex. Coun. PTA, program chairperson, 1984-86; mem., bd. dirs. Ft. Worth Geneal. Assn. Named Walt Disney Salutes the Am. Tchr. Alternate, 1994, 2000 Most Memorable Tchrs., Baylor U. Mem. Nat. Edn. Assn., DAR (Outstanding Am. History Tchr. award 1988), Tex. State Tchrs. Assn., Ft. Worth Classroom Tchrs. (faculty liaison 1983-86, chmn. Tchr. Ethics and Profl. Standards 1989, Tchr. of Yr. 1985), Sigma Kappa (alumnae chpt., Significant Sigma award 1990). Home: 141 Club House Dr Weatherford TX 76087-4001

ESTES, NATHAN ANTHONY MARK, III, cardiologist, medical educator; b. Newport, R.I., Aug. 20, 1949; s. Nathan Anthony Jr. and Ione (Lewis) E.; m. Noël Evangeline Thorbecke, June 22, 1974; children: Elise Thorbecke, N.A. Chace, Kathryn Elizabeth. BA cum laude, U. Pa., 1971; MD magna cum laude, U. Cin., 1977. Diplomate Am. Bd. Internal Medicine, Am. Bd. Cardiovascular Disease, Am. Bd. Cardiac Electrophysiology. Intern New Eng. Deaconess Hosp.-Harvard Med. Sch., Boston, 1977-78, resident, 1978-80; fellow in cardiology New Eng. Med. Ctr.-Tufts U., Boston, 1980-82; fellow in electrophysiology Mass. Gen. Hosp.-Harvard Med. Sch., Boston, 1982-83; dir. cardiac arrhythmia New. Eng. Med. Ctr. Svc., Boston, 1983-96, dir. heart station, 1983-91; assoc. prof. medicine Tufts U. Sch. Med., Boston, 1983-90, prof., 1990-96, chief New Eng. Cardiac Arrythmia Ctr., 1996-97; chief New. Eng. Arrhythmia Ctr., Boston, 1996—, Lifespan Cardiac Arrhythmia Consortium, Boston, 1998. Bd. dirs. Lifespan; ednl. cons., 1985-96; mem. internat. safety monitoring bd. 3M Pharms., Mpls., 1990-96; co-chmn. pubs. com. NIH, Bethesda, 1993-96; chmn. instl. rev. bd. Tufts U. Sch. Medicine, 1996-2001. Contbr. over 200 articles to profl. jours.; contbr. over 30 chpts. to books; editor books, 1994-96; mem. editl. bd. Jour. Interventional Electrophysiology, 1995—, Pacing and Cardiac Electrophysiology, 1995—, Jour. Cardiovasc. Electrophysiology, Am. Jour. Sports and Medicine, 1998, Am. Jour. Cardiology. Vestry mem. Trinity Ch., Newton, Mass., 1985-87; coach Baystate Tournament of Champions, Waltham, Mass., 1990-94; judge N.H. Racing Assn., Lincoln, 1993-95; bd. trustees Moses Brown Sch., Providence, R.I., 1997—. Fellow Am. Coll. Cardiology; mem. Am. Heart Assn. (chmn. bd. trustees Boston chpt. 1998, vice-chair New Eng. affiliate 1999, pres.-elect New Eng. affiliate 2000, coun clin. cardiology), N.Am. Soc. Pacing and Electrophysiology (chmn. publs. com., trustee 2001), New Eng. Electrophysiology Soc. (pres. 1994-97), Lifespan (bd. dirs. 2001), N.Am. Soc. Pacing and Electrophysiology (trustee 2001), Alpha Omega Alpha. Episcopalian. Avocations: sailing, skiing, tennis, running. Office: New Eng Med Ctr 750 Washington St Boston MA 02111-1526

ESTEVEZ, ELIA, secondary education mathematics educator; b. Rio de Janeiro, July 2, 1961; came to the U.S., 1981; d. Benito and Maria Tereza (Vidal) Fernandez; m. Jose Estevez, June 3, 1984; children: Adriana, Gabriel, Alexis. BS, Hofstra U., 1988, MA, 1991; BS, Columbia U., 2002. Cert. secondary math tchr. Restaurant hostess La Rioja Restaurant, Island Park, N.Y., 1984-93; math tchr. grades 7-12 Long Beach (N.Y.) Sch. Dist., 1989-91, Hempstead (N.Y.) H.S., 1992—. Rschr. Hofstra U., Hempstead, 1991, summer math. tchr., 1991-93. Avocations: traveling, writing, reading, dancing. Home: 72 Parma Rd Island Park NY 11558-1043

ESTOK, ROSEMARIE DENORSCIO, educational administrator; b. Newark, Apr. 26, 1946; d. John F. and Theresa (Tordilio) DeNorscio; m. Louis G. Estok, July 25, 1981. BA, William Paterson Coll., 1967; MA, Kean Coll., 1974. Elem. tchr. Woodbridge (N.J.) Twp. Sch. Dist., 1967-79, learning disabilities tchr. cons., 1979-90, spl. edn. curriculum specialist, 1990-93, supr. spl. edn., 1993—. Instr. aerobics YMCA, Metuchen, N.J., 1981-94, Middlesex County Coll., 1990. Named Outstanding Elem. Tchr. Am., 1973. Mem. N.J. Assn. Learning Cons. (treas. 1987-89, pres.-elect 1991-92, pres. 1992-93), N.J. Schoolwomen, Alpha Delta Kappa (charter, pres. Alpha Epsilon chpt. 1975-78, state sec. 1989-91, state historian 1991-93, state treas. 1993-96). Avocations: tennis, golf, travel. Office: Woodbridge Twp Sch Dist PO Box 428 School St Woodbridge NJ 07095

ESTREICHER, SAMUEL, lawyer, educator; b. Bergen, Democratic Republic Germany, Sept. 29, 1948; came to U.S., 1951; s. David and Rose (Abramowicz) E.; m. Aleta Glaseroff, Aug. 10, 1969; children: Michael, Hannah. BA, Columbia U., 1970, JD, 1975; MS in Labor Rels., Cornell U., 1974. Bar: N.Y. 1976, D.C. 1978, U.S. Dist. Ct. (so. and ea. dists.) N.Y., U.S. Ct. Appeals (2d and 11th cirs.), U.S. Supreme Ct. Law clk. to assoc. judge Harold Leventhal, U.S. Ct. Appeals (D.C. cir.), 1975-76; assoc. Cohn, Glickstein, Lurie, Ostrin & Lubell, N.Y.C., 1976-77; law clk. to assoc. justice Lewis F. Powell Jr. U.S. Supreme Ct., Washington, 1977-78; prof. law NYU, 1978—; of counsel Cahill, Gordon & Reindel, N.Y.C., 1984-98; labor and employment counsel O'Melveny & Myers LLP, N.Y.C., 1998—2002; spl. counsel Morgan Lewis & Bockius LLP, N.Y.C., 2002—. Vis. prof. law Columbia U., 1984-85; dir. NYU-Inst. Jud. Adminstrn., 1991—, Ctr. for Labor and Employment Law at NYU Sch. Law, 1996—. Author: Redefining the Supreme Court, 1986, Labor Law and Business Change, 1988, The Law Governing the Employment Relationship,1990, 2d edit., 1992, Labor Law: Text and Materials, 5th edit., 2003, Procs. of 49th NYU Annual Conference on Labor, 1997, Employee Representation in the Emerging Workplace: Alternatives/Supplements to Collective Bargaining, 1999, Sexual Harassment in the Workplace, 1999, Foundations of Labor and Employment Law, 2000, Employment Discrimination and Employment Law, 2000, Global Competition and The American Employment Landscape, 2000; contbr. articles to profl. jours.; editor-in-chief Columbia U. Law Rev., 1974-75. Pulitzer Fund scholar, 1966-70; Herbert H. Lehman fellow, 1970-72. Mem. ABA (labor and employment law sect. 1978—, sec.-elect sect. on labor and employment law 2003—), N.Y. State Bar Assn. (labor and employment law sect. 1980—), Assn. Bar City N.Y. (chmn. labor and employment law com. 1984-87), Am. Law Inst. (reporter Restatement of Employment Law 2000—). Office: NYU Sch Law 40 Washington Sq S New York NY 10012 E-mail: samuel.estreicher@nyu.edu.

ETEFIA, FLORENCE VICTORIA, school psychologist; b. Alton, Ill., Feb. 13, 1946; d. Esau and Pearl (Taylor) Anthony. BA, Mich. State U., 1968; MAT, Oakland U., Rochester, Mich., 1972; EdS, Wayne State U., 1977, MA, 1987, postgrad. Cert. tchr. mentally impaired, Mich.; spl. edn. supr., Mich.; cert. tchr. mentally impaired, learning disabled, K-8 gen. edn., psychology, Mich. Special edn. tchr. Sch. Dist. of Pontiac, Mich. Mem. NEA, Mich. Edn. Assn., Pontiac Edn. Assn., Delta Sigma Theta. Home: 3035 Debra Ct Auburn Hills MI 48326-2044

ETHERN, ABERDEEN, music educator; b. LaBelle, Mo., June 1, 1917; d. Richard and Stella Mae Butler Range; m. Luceluits Ethern, July 30, 1938 (dec. Feb. 1986); children: James R., Stella L. BA, Drake U., 1936; M of Music, U. Mo. Kansas City, 1992. Piano accompanist Kansas City Sch. Dist., 1965-76; music tchr. Upbound Rockhurst Coll., Kansas City, 1970-71; pianist, organist Friendship Bapt. Ch., Kansas City, Mo., 1946-86; music tchr. Ethern Sch. of Music, Kansas City, 1975-92. Receipient Spl. Recognition award Friendship Bapt. Ch., 1996. Mem. NAACP, Kansas City Organ Guild (sec. 1991-92), Music Tchrs. Nat. Assn., Kansas City Music Tchrs. Assn. Home: 900 E Armour Blvd Apt 608 Kansas City MO 64109-2366

ETHERTON, BUD, botanist, educator, researcher; b. Wardner, Idaho, Nov. 16, 1930; s. Lewis Washington and Hannah (Sutton) E.; m. Alison Elliott Mann, Sept. 14, 1957; children: Kirk, Laura. BS in Psychology, Wash. State Coll., 1956; PhD in Botany, Washington State U., 1962. Rsch. assoc. biophysics dept. U. Edinburgh, Scotland, 1962-63; lectr. plant sci. dept. Vassar Coll., Poughkeepsie, N.Y., 1963-64, asst. prof. biology dept., 1964-67; vis. scientist biology div. Argonne (Ill.) Nat. Lab., 1967-68; assoc. prof. botany dept. U. Vt., Burlington, 1968-80, prof. botany dept., 1980—99, emeritus prof., 1999—. Mem. editorial bd. Plant Physiology jour., 1979-92; contbr. articles to Sci. and Plant Physiology. Mem. Nat. Resource Commn., South Burlington, Vt., 1973-75. Postdoctoral fellow NSF, 1962-63, rsch. grantee, 1965-67, 73-75, 79-81. Mem. Am. Soc. Plant Physiology (mem. exec. com. N.E. sect. 1991-93). Democrat. Unitarian Universalist. Achievements include discovery of active extrusion of sodium ions by plant cells; potassium gradients do not generate all of pea root membrane potentials; first reliable measurements of membrane potentials in higher plants; first report of auxin hyperpolarizing membrane potentials of plant cells. Home: 42 Elsom Pky South Burlington VT 05403-6609 Office: Univ Vt Botany and Agrl Biochemistry Dept Burlington VT 05405-0001

ETO, HAJIME, information scientist, educator; b. Tokyo, June 16, 1935; s. Yoshio and Kikuko (Tamari) E. BA, U. Tokyo, 1959, MA, 1962; MS, U. Calif., Berkely, 1967; PhD, Tokyo Inst. Tech., 1979. Rschr. Hitachi Ltd., Tokyo, 1962-76; prof. U. Tsukuba, Japan, 1976-99, Chiba Keizai U., Japan, 1999—; prof. emeritus U. Tsukuba, 1999—. Author, editor: R & D Management Systems in Japanese Industry, 1984, R & D Strategies in Japan, 1993; mem. editl. bd. Scientometrics Jour., 1979—, Human Sys. Mgmt., 1980-84, Internat. Jour. of the Sci. of Scis., 1994—, Internat. Jour. Svc. Tech. & Mgmt., 1998—; contbr. sci. articles to profl. jours. Recipient Fulbright scholarship U.S.-Japan Edn. Com., 1966. Mem. AAAS, Internat. Soc. Scientometrics and Informetrics (mem. coun. 1993—, mem. editl. bd. 1995—), Japan Assn. for Philosophy Sci. (mem. coun. 1970-92), Japan Soc. for Sci. Policy (bd. dirs. 1994-96, coun. 1997—), Assn. of France on Cybernetics, Econs. and Tech. (mem. editl. bd. 1985—), N.Y. Acad. Sci. Home: Nakano 3-43-17-305 Nakano-ku Tokyo 164-0001 Japan Business E-Mail: eto@cku.ac.jp.

ETTINGER, JAYNE GOLD, physical education educator; b. N.Y.C., Oct. 18, 1954; d. Benjamin and Joan Louise (Hyman) Gold; m. Brian K. Ettinger, July 10, 1988; 1 child, Bradley Joseph. AA, Green Mountain Coll., Poultney, Vt., 1973; BS, Cortland State Coll., 1975; MS, Western Conn. State Coll., 1981. Lic. phys. edn. tchr., N.Y. Phys. edn. tchr. Lakeland Cen. Schs., Shrub Oak, N.Y., 1975—. Volleyball ofcl. Hudson Valley Bd. of Ofcls., 1984-88, pres., 1987-89. Coord. Jump Rope for Heart, Mohegan Lake, N.Y., 1988—, Basketball Shoot Contest, Easter Seal Soc., 1989—, Hopping-Disability Awareness, 1992-99. Mem. AAHPERD, N.Y. State Assn. Health, Phys. Edn., Recreation and Dance, Lakeland Fedn. Tchrs. (sec. 1985-97), Kappa Delta Pi. Office: George Washington Elem Sch 3634 Lexington Ave Mohegan Lake NY 10547-1244

ETTMAN, PHILIP, business law educator; b. N.Y.C., Mar. 28, 1948; s. Sidney J. and Fay (Brostowsky) E.; m. Marilyn L. Swartz, May 28, 1972; 1 child, Glenn M. BA, SUNY, Buffalo, 1968; JD, Boston U., 1972; MBA, U. Conn., 1981. Bar: Mass. 1972, Conn. 1980, N.Y. 1981, U.S. Ct. Internat. Trade 1981. Prof. Westfield (Mass.) State Coll., 1983—, chair dept. econs. and bus., 1992-96. Pvt. practice, Simsbury, Conn., 1985—; sr. assoc. Serko & Simon, N.Y.C., 1982-83; asst. gen. counsel Security Ins. Group, Hartford, Conn., 1978-82; regional counsel GNY Ins. Cos., Boston, 1974-78; export legal assistance coord. SBA, Dept. Commerce for Conn. and R.I., 1985—. Pres. Farmington Valley Jewish Congregation, Simsbury, 1989-91, bd. dirs., 1981-93; regional bd. dirs. Union Am. Hebrew Congregation, Brookline, Mass., 1989-91; commr. Joseph Eisner Camp, Great Barrington, Mass., 1993—. Mem. Acad. Legal Studies in Bus., Soc. Bus. Ethics. Avocations: photography, jazz, scuba diving. Office: Westfield State Coll Western Ave Westfield MA 01085

EUSDEN, JOHN DYKSTRA, theology educator, minister; b. Holland, Mich., July 20, 1922; s. Ray Anderson and Marie (Dykstra) E.; m. Joanne Reiman, June 14, 1950; children: Andrea Bonner, Alan Tolles, John Dykstra Jr., Sarah Jewell. AB, Harvard U., 1943; postgrad., Harvard Law Sch., 1946; BD cum laude, Yale U., 1949, PhD in Religion, 1954. Ordained to ministry United Ch. of Christ, 1949. Instr. in religion Yale U., 1953-55, asst. prof., 1955-60; assoc. prof. religion, chaplain Williams Coll., Williamstown, Mass., 1960-70, Nathan Jackson prof. Christian theology, 1970-90, vis. prof. environ. studies, 1990-92; vis. prof. religion and asian studies Mt. Holyoke Coll., Mass., 1992-93; min. 1st Congl. Ch., Bennington, Vt., 1991—; cons. Asian programs and environ. studies Williams Coll., Williamstown, Mass., 1992—. Lectr., research fellow Kyoto U., 1963-64, 76, 81-82; theologian-in-residence Am. Ch. in Paris, 1972; lectr. Doshisha U., Kyoto, Japan, 1976, 82; bd. dir. Associated Kyoto Program, Japan. Author: Puritans, Lawyers and Politics in Early 17th Century England, 1958, 68, Zen and Christian: The Journey Between, 1981, The Spiritual Life: Learning East and West, 1982, (with John H. Westerhoff III) Sensing Beauty: Aesthetics, the Human Spirit, and the Church, 1998, Thirsting for Healing and Wholeness, 2003; contbr. articles to profl. jours.; translator, editor, author introduction: The Marrow of Theology (William Ames), 1975, 86; author introduction: Zen Buddhism and Christianity in Y. Takeuchi Festschrift (Japanese edition), 1993, Christology: The Dialogue of East and West in Christology in Dialogue, 1993, Chinese Healing: A Practical Mysticism in John Sahadat Festschrift, 2002. Mem. adv. coun., campus ministry program Danforth Found., 1966-70; bd. dirs. Wellesley Coll. Parents Assn., 1972-75, pres., 1974-75; rsch. fellow Ctr. for Study of Japanese Religion, Kyoto, 1976-94; trustee Lingnan Found., N.Y.C., 1964—, Buxton Sch., Williamstown, Mass., 1970-83, Chewonki Found., Wiscasset, Maine, 2002—; leader trips, People's Republic of China, 1978, 81, 86, 88, 90, 94. 1st lt. USMCR, 1943-45. Scholar Harvard U.; faculty fellow Am. Assn. Theol. Schs., 1958-59, Sterling fellow Yale U., 1950-53, fellow Folger Shakespeare Libr., 1958-59, 71-72; Lilly postdoctoral grantee, 1963-64, Danforth campus ministry grantee, 1963-64; fellow Am. Council Learned Socs., 1967-68; Fulbright rsch. travel grantee, 1967-68; research fellow U. Utrecht, Netherlands, 1968; rsch. grantee Williams Coll., 1976. Mem. AAUP, Am. Acad. Religion, Am. Soc. Ch. History, Am. Soc. Christian Ethics, Nat. Assn. Coll. and Univ. Chaplains, Soc. Values in Higher Edn., Appalachian Mountain Club, Randolph Mountain Club (pres. 1973-75). Home: 75 Forest Rd Williamstown MA 01267-2028 Office: Williams Coll Stetson Hall Williamstown MA 01267

EUSTICE, JAMES SAMUEL, legal educator, lawyer; b. Chgo., June 9, 1932; s. Burt C. and Julia (Bohon) E.; m. LaVaun Schild, Jan. 29, 1956 (dec. 1994); m. Carol Fonda, Nov. 1995; children: Cynthia, James M. BS, U. Ill., 1954, LLB, 1956; LLM in Taxation, NYU, 1958. Bar: Ill. 1956, N.Y. 1958. Assoc. White & Case, N.Y.C., 1958-60; prof. law NYU, 1960—; counsel Kronish Lieb, N.Y.C., 1970—. Author: (with Kuntz) Federal Income Taxation of Subchapter S Corporations, 2001, (with Bittker) Federal Income Taxation of Corporations and Shareholders, 2000. Mem. ABA, N.Y. State Bar Assn., Am. Coll. Tax Counsel, Order of Coif. Club: University (N.Y.C.). Republican. Presbyterian. Office: NYU Sch Law 40 Washington Sq S New York NY 10012-1005

EUSTICE, RUSSELL CLIFFORD, consulting company executive, academic director; b. Hackensack, N.J., July 11, 1919; s. Russell C. and Ethel (Hutchison) E.; m. Veronica B. Dabrowski, Mar. 14, 1946; children: Russell Clifford, David A., Paul M. BA, Colgate U., 1941; MBA, Am. U., 1973. With Vick Chem. Corp., N.Y.C., 1941-42, 46-47, Johnson & Johnson, N.Y.C., 1947-61, divsn. sales mgr., 1954-61; nat. sales mgr. Park & Tilford divsn. Schenley Affiliates, N.Y.C., 1961-62; pres. Mid-Atlantic Assos., Inc., Prospect Harbor, Maine, 1962—. Dir. Small Bus. Inst., Husson Coll., Bangor, Maine, 1979-88, alt. regional rep. New England Region - Svc. Corps. Ret. Execs., SBA, 1991—; asst. prof. bus. adminstrn., 1979-88; part-time instr. mktg. The Am. U., Washington, 1970-74; active VISTA; bus. develop. specialist Washington-Hancock Community Agy., 1989. Capt. AUS, 1942-46. Mem. Assn. Mil. Surgeons, Res. Officers Assn., Assn. Mktg. Educators, SBA, Alpha Tau Omega. Republican. Methodist. Home: 1732 Spring Lilly Ln Hillsborough NC 27278-8492 also: 211 S Gouldsboro Rd Gouldsboro ME 04607

EVANS, ANACLARE FROST, college librarian; b. Feb. 4, 1942; BA, Monmouth Coll., 1963; MSLS, Western Reserve U., 1964; PhD, Wayne State U., 2000. Libr. Wayne State U., Detroit, 1964—.

EVANS, ANTHONY HOWARD, university president; b. Clay County, Ark., Sept. 24, 1936; s. William Raymond and Thelma Fay (Crews) E.; m. Lois Fay Kirkham, Aug. 29, 1959. BA, East Tex. Bapt. Coll., Marshall, 1959; MA, U. Hawaii, 1961; PhD, U. Calif.-Berkeley, 1966. Program officer Peace Corps, Seoul, Korea, 1970-72, chief program planning Washington, 1972-73, dir. planning office, 1973-75; asst. to pres. Eastern Mich. U., Ypsilanti, 1975-76, exec. v.p., 1976-79, acting pres., 1978-79, provost, v.p. acad. affairs, 1979-82; pres. Calif. State U., San Bernardino, 1982-97, trustee prof. San Marcos, 1997—. Mem. Orgn. Am. Historians, Phi Kappa Phi Home: 4228 Olivos Ct Fallbrook CA 92028-9249

EVANS, ARTHUR RICHARD, visual arts educator; s. Arthur and Tena (Rollinson) E. BS, Pa. State U., 1971, MEd in Art Edn., 1972. Cert. art educator, supr., N.J. Grad. teaching asst. Pa. State U., University Park, 1971-72; art educator Fairchance-Georges Jr. Sr. High Sch., Uniontown, Pa., 1972-74; art instr. Pa. State U., Fayette County, Pa., 1973-74; adj. prof. Ocean County Coll., Toms River, N.J., 1974-80, Kean Coll., Union, N.J., 1991—; art educator Lakewood (N.J.) High Sch., 1974-84; counselor

Stockton State Coll., Pomona, N.J., 1984-86; supr. student tchrs. Monmouth Coll., West Long Br., N.J., 1991—; visual arts chairperson Grover Cleveland Middle Sch., Elizabeth, N.J., 1988—. Coun. mem., commr. edn. adv. coun. for arts edn., Trenton, N.J., 1990—, standards panel mem. Fine and Performing Arts, N.J., 1992—; panel mem. Core Course Proficiency Panel for Fine and Performing Arts, Trenton, 1992-93; chairperson Middle States Assn. Colls. and Schs., Trenton, 1980, 81. Profl. solo art exhibits incl.: J and M Madison Art Gallery, Middletown, N.J., 1977, Georgian Ct. Coll., Lakewood, N.J., 1978, C.C. Phila., 1981, Lakehurst (N.J.) Naval Air Engring. Ctr., 1984, Monmouth County Libr., Shrewsbury, N.J., 1984, Ocean County Coll., Toms River, 1986, St. John's Ch., Passaic, N.J., 1988, Univ. of the Arts Phila., Felician Coll., Lodi, N.J., 1988, C.C. of Phila., Consolidated Bank and Trust Co., Richmond, Va.; exhibited in group shows at Atlantic City Boardwalk, 1976 (2d place award), The Painted Bride Arts Ctr., Phila., 1982, The Gallery of the Art Inst., Phila., 1983, C.C. Phila., 1987, Glassboro State Coll. Westby Gallery, 1990; subject of several articles in local newspapers. Grantee Elizabeth Bd. Edn., 1989, 91; recipient First Pl. Art award for Painting, Millburn-Short Hills C. of C., 1987, Third Pl. Art award for Paintings, Hazlet Art Festival, 1988, Dr. Martin Luther King Scholarship Grant award Pa. State U., 1970. Mem. Alliance for Arts Edn. N.J., Art Educators N.J., Polit. Sci. Adv. Coun. of Brookdale, Assn. for Supervision and Curriculum Devel., Pa. State U. Alumni Assn., Phi Delta Kappa. Avocations: piano (classical, ragtime, modern), reading, languages. Home: PO Box 1814 Philadelphia PA 19105-1814 Office: Elizabeth Pub Schs Grover Cleveland Middle Sch 436 1st Ave Elizabeth NJ 07206-1122

EVANS, BERNARD WILLIAM, geologist, educator; b. London, July 16, 1934; came to U.S., 1961, naturalized, 1977; s. Albert Edward and Marjorie (Jordan) E.; m. Sheila Campbell Nolan, Nov. 19, 1962. BSc, U. London, 1955; PhD, Oxford U., Eng., 1959. Asst. U. Glasgow, Scotland, 1958-59; departmental demonstrator U. Oxford, 1959-61; asst. research prof. U. Calif., Berkeley, 1961-65, asst. prof., 1965-66, assoc. prof., 1966-69; prof. geology U. Wash., Seattle, 1969—2001, chmn. dept. geol. scis., 1974-79; emeritus prof. U. Washington, 2001—. Contbr. articles to profl. jours. Recipient U.S. Sr. Scientist award Humboldt Found., Fed. Republic Germany, 1988-89; Fulbright travel award, France, 1995-96. Fellow Geol. Soc. Am., Mineral Soc. Am. (pres. 1993-94, award 1970), Geochem. Soc., Geol. Soc. London, Mineral. Soc. Gt. Britain, Swiss Mineral. Soc. Home: 8001 Sand Point Way NE Apt C55 Seattle WA 98115-6399 Office: U Wash Dept Earth and Space Scis PO Box 351310 Seattle WA 98195-1310 E-mail: bwevans@u.washington.edu.

EVANS, BONITA DIANNE, adult education educator; b. N.Y.C., Jan. 14, 1940; d. Roy Simon and Verna (Ashton) Evans; m. Robert John Watts, Aug. 1981 (div. 1996); 1 child, Helena Watts. BA, U. Canberra, Australia, 1990; MDS, Monash U., Melbourne, Australia, 1992; PhD, Walden U., Minn., 1996. With Dept. of Prime Minister and Cabinet, Australian Dept. Fgn. Affairs, Canberra, 1986—88; devel. rsch. officer Aboriginal Hostels, Canberra, 1986—88; cultural affairs asst. U.S. Embassy, Canberra, 1988—90; mem. Diplomatic Corps UN Mission to Nambia, S.W. Africa, 1978; field officer Israeli/Egyptian border UN Peacekeeping Forces, 1979—80; adj. prof. English Montclair State U., NJ, 1996—2000; vis. prof. Rutgers U., Newark, 1999—2000; mem. internat. adv. bd., literacy; faculty African and African-Am. studies and Women's Studies depts. William Paterson U.; tchr. bilingual dept. Essex County Coll., 2003—. Author: Youth in Foster Care, 1997, Kijani, 2002, New Hope Rising, 2002.

EVANS, CAROLE CLINTON, special education educator; b. Logansport, Ind., Feb. 21, 1946; d. Charles M. and Norma (Collins) Clinton; m. Richard Martin Evans, Feb. 18, 1967; children: Nathaniel C., Ashley E. BS in Edn., U. Tenn., 1969, MS, 1973. Lic. tchr., career ladder III, Tenn.; professionally recognized spl. educator. Tchr. Tenn. Sch. for Deaf, Knoxville, 1969-70; tchr. spl. edn. Bryan (Tex.) Pub. Schs., 1971-72; grad. asst. dept. spl. edn. U. Tenn., Knoxville, 1972-74; tchr. spl. edn. Oak Ridge (Tenn.) Schs., 1980—. Follow-up course facilitator, vol. summer workshop Ctr. for Innovation, Oak Ridge, 1990-97; site coord. Reading Is Fundamental Program, Oak Ridge, 1986-2002. Leader Girl Scouts U.S.A., Oak Ridge, 1985-87, Camp Fire, Oak Ridge, 1986—; vol. Spl. Olympics, Knoxville, 1986-95; vol. Very Spl. Arts Festival, Oak Ridge, 1984-89. Grantee Oak Ridge Tchrs. Ctr., 1985, Tenn. Dept. Edn., 1991, Lifetouch Nat. Sch. Studios, Inc., 1993, Youth Garden, 1997. Mem. NEA, Coun. for Exceptional Children, Tenn. Edn. Assn., Oak Ridge Edn. Assn. (team leader 1995—, sch. rep. 1994-96), Assn. for Retarded Citizens, Learning Disabilities Assn., Ctr. for Innovation in Edn. (life), Phi Delta Kappa. Methodist. Home: 901 S Illinois Ave Oak Ridge TN 37830-8032

EVANS, DARRELL J. higher education educator; b. Pocatello, Idaho, Dec. 3, 1937; s. Cedric Coffin and Elsie Christine (Jensen) E.; m. Laurel Bradley, June 13, 1955 (div. Apr. 1962); children: Mark Bradley, Athena Denice; m. Penny L. Deay, Aug. 1963 (div. June 1980); 1 child, Dana Jacqueline; m. Judith Claire Peterson, Feb. 10, 1984 (div. Apr. 1993); m. Leiola Irene Reeder, Aug. 4, 1995 (div. July 1996). AA, San Diego Jr. Coll., 1967; BA, San Diego State Coll., 1969; MA, UCLA, 1970; PhD, U. Idaho, 1997. Cert. tchr. art advanced secondary, Idaho, advanced secondary vocat. specialist, Idaho, C.C. cert., Calif. Asst. art instr. Chula Vista (Calif.) Sch. Dist., summer 1968; dir. arts and crafts Camp Roosevelt, Mountain Center, Calif., summer 1970; art tchr., intern Blackfoot (Idaho) High Sch., 1971-72; chief illustrator-draftsman USN, 1972-84; tech. and art tchr. McCall (Idaho)-Donnelly High Sch., 1984-97; asst. prof. art edn. U. Tex., El Paso, 1997-98; assoc. prof. art edn. Ala. A&M U., Huntsville, 2000—. Art tchr. Fairfield (Calif.) Suisun Evening Sch., 1973-74; art instr. U. Md.-Naples, Italy, 1975-76; mem. panel Idaho Commn. on Arts, Boise, 1990, 91, 94; owner Evans Design Inc., McCall, Idaho, 1989-2000, Huntsville, 2000—; mem. fine arts framework writing com. Schs. 2000, Idaho State Dept. Edn., 1994; co-chair art 5-12 curriculum writing com. Idaho State Dept. Edn. With USN, 1954-84, ret. 1984. Art Coun. scholar UCLA Art Coun., 1969-70. Mem. Nat. Art Edn. Assn. (chair tech. com. dels. assembly 1995). Avocation: residential archtl. design. Home: 2319 Gallatin St SW Huntsville AL 35801-3825

EVANS, DAVID ALLAN, English educator; b. Sioux City, Iowa, Apr. 11, 1940; s. Arthur Clarence and Ruth (Lyle) E.; m. Janice Kay Johnson, July 4, 1958; children: Shelly Evans Moreau, David Allan Jr., Karlin Evans Bauer. BA, Morningside Coll., 1962; MA, U. Iowa, 1964; MFA, U. Ark., 1973. Asst. U. Iowa, Iowa City, 1965, U. Ark., Fayetteville, 1971-72; asst. prof. English, Adams State Coll., Alamosa, Colo., 1966-68, S.D. State U., Brookings, 1968-78, prof., 1978—, writer-in-residence, 1997—; poet laureate SD, 2002. Faculty exch. prof. Yunnan Normal U., Kunming, China, 1988—89; poet laureate, SD, 2002—. Author: (poetry chapbook) Among Athletes, 1970, (poetry) Train Windows, 1976, Real and False Alarms, 1980, Hanging Out with the Crows, 1990, Decent Dangers, 2001, (essays) Remembering the Soos, 1982; (with Jan Evans) Double Happinesss: Two Lives in China, 1995; co-editor: From Language to Idea, 1970, Statement and Craft, 1972, The Sport of Poetry/The Poetry of Sport, 1979; editor: New Voices in American Poetry, 1973; gen. editor, writer What the Tall Grass Says, 1982. Writing mentor S.D. State Prison, Sioux Falls, 2001—; mem. steering com. Brookings Arts Coun., 2001—; active participant artist in schs. SD Arts Coun. Named S.D. Centennial Poet, 1989; recipient Exemplary Tchr. award Guangdong U. Fgn. Studies, 1999; athletic scholar Augustana Coll., 1958-60, Breadloaf scholar, Vt., 1973, Fulbright scholar, China, 1992-93, 98-99; writing grantee Nat. Endowment for Arts, 1975, 80, grantee S.D. Arts Coun., 1981, artist grantee Bush Found., 1990. Mem. Poetry Soc. Am. Democrat. Avocations: racquetball and other exercise, reading, travel. Home: 1432 2nd St Brookings SD 57006 Office: SD State U Scobey Hall 008 Box 504 Brookings SD 57007 E-mail: evanspl@brookings.net.

EVANS, DAVID CHARLES, retired elementary school educator; b. Cleve., Sept. 23, 1945; s. Howard Robert and Verna Eileen (Stark) E.; m. Nancy Ellen Smith, Aug. 10, 1968; children: Charles Ray, James Neal. BS in Edn., Otterbein Coll., Westerville, Ohio, 1967; MEd, Kent State U., 1970. Cert. tchr., elem. prin., Ohio. Tchr. 6th grade Columbus (Ohio) City Schs., 1967; tchr. grades 4-6, team leader Parma (Ohio) City Schs., 1967-77; tchr. 6th grade Southwestern City Schs., Grove City, Ohio, 1978; tchr. grades 5-8 Upper Arlington (Ohio) City Schs., 1978—2002, also team leader, summer sch. tchr.; supr. student tchrs., interns and field experience students Ashland U., Ohio, 2002—. Coord. Dist. Washington trip Recipient Golden Apple Achiever award Ashland Oil, Inc., 1995, 96, others, Golden Apple award Upper Arlington Civic Assn., 1989, 91; named to Outstanding Young Men in Am., 1974, Over-All Tchr. of Yr. in Upper Arlington Schs., State of Ohio Ho. Representatives, 1995; Jennings scholar, 1972. Mem. NEA, Ohio Edn. Assn., Upper Arlington Edn. Assn. (pres. 1982-83), Nat. Mid. Sch. Assn., Nat. Coun. Tchrs. English. Home: 4323 Stratton Rd Columbus OH 43220-4371

EVANS, DOUGLAS MCCULLOUGH, surgeon, educator; b. Vandergrift, Pa., July 31, 1925; s. Archibald Davis and Helen Irene (McCullough) E.; m. Thelmajean Volkers, Aug. 1, 1959; children: Matthew Kirk, Daniel Scott. MD, Western Res. U., 1952; postgrad., U. Mich., 1956-58. Diplomate Am. Bd. Surgery. Resident in surgery Henry Ford Hosp., 1952-57, chief resident in surgery, 1957-58, mem. surgery staff, 1959-60, Akron (Ohio) Gen. Hosp., 1960-70; chmn. dept. surgery Akron Gen. Med. Ctr., 1971-90, rsch. cons.; prof. and chmn. surgery emeritus Northeastern Ohio U. Coll. Medicine. Served with AUS, 1943-46. Fellow: ACS; mem.: AAAS, AMA, N.Y. Acad. Scis., Ohio Med. Assn., Midwest Surg. Soc., Soc. Critical Care Medicine, Metastasis Rsch. Soc., Am. Assn. Cancer Rsch. Republican. Presbyterian. Office: 400 Wabash Ave Akron OH 44307-2433

EVANS, EDITH TODD, elementary education educator; b. Phila., Oct. 5, 1945; d. Melville and Mary (Johnson) Yancey; m. Wenfra Evans, Nov. 14, 1969; 1 child, Shaun C. Student, Knoxville Coll., 1970; MA in Guidance and Counseling, Trinity Coll., 1985. Tchr. D.C. Pub. Schs., 1970—. Social studies liaison Simon Elem./D.C. Pub. Sch. Bd. dirs. Nannie Helen Burroughs/Covenant Bapt. ch., 1992—; dir. youth svcs. nat. chpt. Jr. Red Cross, Washington, 1994. Named Jr. Red Cross Tchr. of Yr., 1991. Avocations: flower arrangements, reading.

EVANS, ELOISE SWICK, retired educator, writer; b. Capitol Heights, Md., Sept. 27, 1920; d. Clarence Herbert and Hattie May Swick; m. Latimer Richard Evans, Aug. 24. 1942 (dec. Aug. 1991); children: Carol, Beth, Marget, Scott. BA, Am. U., 1941; MS in Organic Chemistry, Purdue U., 1945. Tchr. chemistry and physics Las Cruces (N.Mex.) Pub. Schs., 1961-73, co-founder, coord. San Andres (Alternative) H.S., 1973-86; ret., 1986. Mem. adv. bd. Adolescent Family Life Ctr., Las Cruces, 1986-90, Los Niños, Las Cruces, 1991-95. Contbr. short stories and articles to profl. and lit. publs. Bd. dirs. United Way S.W. N.Mex., Las Cruces, 1997. Mem.: LWV (pres. Greater Las Cruces 1989, 1992—94, bd. dirs. N.Mex. 1992—97, sec. 1995—96), Las Cruces Assn. Ednl. Retirees (pres. 2001), Desert Writers. Avocations: oral historian on Las Cruces retired teachers, writing. Home: 5120 Oriole Rd Las Cruces NM 88011-7598 E-mail: pevans@zianet.com.

EVANS, GARY LEE, communications educator and consultant; b. Davison, Mich., June 26, 1938; s. Joe Howard and Annie Annette (Colden) E.; m. Katherine Strand; children: Gary James, Aimee Lynn; stepchildren: John E. Holkeboer, Maja K. Holkeboer. BA, Wayne State U., 1962; MA, U. Mich., 1965, PhD, 1977. Prof. organizational and intercultural communication Eastern Mich. U., Ypsilanti, 1964—. Pres. Comm. Rsch. and Tng. Assocs.; cons. Volvo Corp., GM Corp., Ford Motor Car Co., Mich. Pub. Schs. and other ednl. instns.; speaker in field; instr., Davos, Switzerland, 1989; internat. program instr., Australia, New Zealand, Switzerland. Mem. Peace Corps Tng. and Teaching. Named Outstanding Continuing Educator of the Yr., Ea. Mich. U., 1994, Disting. Sr. Tchg. Award, 1998, Disting. Faculty Mem., 1998, Disting. Tchg. award Ea. Mich. U. Alumni, 2001. Mem. Internat. Communication Assn., Speech Communication assn., Mich. Acad. Sci., Arts and Letters (communication chmn. 1982), Mich. Speech Communication Assn. (communication chmn. 1978—), Golden Key Nat. Honorary Soc., Phi Kappa Phi (pres. 1998—), Delta Sigma Rho, Pi Kappa Delta. Home: 11353 Pleasant Shore Dr Manchester MI 48158-9739 Office: Ea Mich U 121 Quirk Hall Ypsilanti MI 48197-2220

EVANS, HELEN RUTH, music educator, pianist; b. Grant City, Mo., May 26, 1913; d. John Larkin and Inez (Florea) Hall; m. Donald Maurice Mathias, Oct. 7, 1934 (div.); m. Thomas Claude Evans, Sept. 1. Student, No. Colo. U., 1968-69. Piano tchr., Colo., 1940-50, 1950-96; ret., 1996. Mem. AAUW, N.Mex. Music Tchrs. Assn., Delta Kappa Gamma. Republican. Presbyterian. Avocations: pianist, reading, cooking. Home: 3400 San Medina Ave Farmington NM 87401-2338

EVANS, JAMES HANDEL, university administrator, architect, educator; b. Bolton, Eng., June 14, 1938; came to U.S., 1965. s. Arthur Handel and Ellen Bowen (Ramsden) E.; m. Carol L. Mulligan, Sept. 10, 1966; children: Jonathan, Sarah. Diploma of Architecture, U. Manchester, Eng., 1965; MArch., U. Oreg., 1967; postgrad., Cambridge (Eng.) U., 1969-70. Registered architect, Calif., U.K.; cert. NCARB. Assoc. dean. prof. architecture Calif. Poly. State U., San Luis Obispo, 1967-78; prof. art and design San Jose (Calif.) State U., 1979—, assoc. exec. v.p., 1978-81, interim exec. v.p., 1981-82, exec. v.p., 1982-91, interim pres., 1991-92, pres., 1992-95; vice chancellor Calif. State U System, Long Beach, CA, 1995-96; planning pres. Calif. State U. Channel Islands, Ventura, 1996-2001; pres. HE Cons. Inc., 2001—. Cons. Ibiza Nueva, Ibiza, Spain, 1977-80; vis. prof. Ciudad Universitaria, Madrid, 1977; vis. lectr. Herriott Watt U., Edinburgh, 1970; mem. adv. com. Army Command Staff Coll., Ft. Leavenworth, Kans., 1988. Trustee Good Samaritan Hosp., San Jose, 1987-90; bd. dirs. San Jose Shelter, 1988-90; dir. San Jose C. of C., 1991-94, Ventura County Mus. History and Art. Sci. Rsch. Coun. fellow Cambridge U., 1969-70. Fellow AIA; mem. Royal Inst. Brit. Architects, Assn. Univ. Architects. Avocation: golf. E-mail: jhevans@adelphia.net.

EVANS, JAMES WILLIAM, metallurgical educator; b. Dobcross, Yorkshire, Eng., Aug. 22, 1943; came to U.S., 1970; s. James Hall and Alice Maud (Dransfield) E.; m. Beverley Lynn Connor, July 22, 1967 (div. 1978); 1 child, James; m. Sylvia Marian Johnson, Jan. 5, 1985; children: Hugh Edmund, Claire Meredith. BS, Univ. Coll., London, 1964; PhD, SUNY, Buffalo, 1970. Tech. adviser Internat. Computers Ltd., London, 1964-65; chemist Can. Cyanamid, Niagara Falls, Ont., Can., 1965-67; engr. Ethyl Corp., Baton Rouge, 1970-72; from asst. prof. to prof. U. Calif., Berkeley, 1972—, chmn. dept., 1986-90. Co-author: Gas-Solid Reactions, 1976, Mathematical and Physical Modeling of Primary Metals Processing, 1988, The Production of Inorganic Materials, 1991; contbr. over 280 articles to profl. jours. Mem. Minerals, Metals and Materials Soc. (bd. dirs. 1985-89), Extractive Metallurgy Sci. award, 1973, 83, 2002, Champion H. Mathewson Gold medal 1994, Extractive and Processing Lectr. 1994), Electrochem. Soc., Iron and Steel Inst. Japan. Democrat. Avocations: sailing, skiing, hiking. Office: U Calif Dept Matls Sci & Mineral Eng Berkeley CA 94720-0001

EVANS, JOEL RAYMOND, marketing educator; b. N.Y.C., Sept. 17, 1948; s. Joseph and Betty Evans; m. Linda Ruth, Dec. 19, 1970; children: Jennifer Faith, Stacey Beth. BA, Queens Coll., 1970; MBA, Bernard M. Baruch Coll., 1974; PhD, CUNY, 1975. MBA dir. Hofstra U., Hempstead, N.Y., 1975-77, asst. prof., 1975-79, assoc. prof., 1979-84, prof. mktg., 1984—, assoc. dean, 1981-82, chmn. dept. mktg. and internat. bus., 1978-85, RMI disting. prof. bus., 1989—, co-dir. retail mgmt. inst., 1989-96, co-dir. bus. rsch. inst., 1992-96. Cons. NCR, Pepsico, ARA/Slater Food Svcs., McCrory, Fortunoff, also other orgns. Co-author: Readings in Marketing Management, 1984, Principles of Marketing, 3d edit., 1995, Retail Management, 9th edit., 2004, Marketing, 8th edit., 2002, Can. edit., 2000. Recipient Disting. Service award, Hofstra U., 1982, Hofstra U. Sch. Bus. Dean's award, 1979, 81, 98; named One of Outstanding Young Men of Am., 1979. Mem. Am. Mktg. Assn., Acad. Mktg. Sci., Mktg. Educators Assn., Am. Collegiate Retailing Assn., Southwestern Mktg. Assn., Soc. for Mktg. Advances, Beta Gamma Sigma. Avocations: jogging, tennis. Home: 14 Melrose Ln Commack NY 11725-1615 Office: 134 Hofstra U Dept Mktg & Internat Bus 222 Weller Hall Hempstead NY 11549

EVANS, JOHN JOSEPH, management consultant, executive, educator, writer; b. St. Louis, Mar. 1, 1940; s. Roy Joseph and Henrietta Frances (Schweizer) E.; children: Todd, Karlyn, Jane, Mark. BA, Centenary Coll., 1962; postgrad., Syracuse U., 1969, U. Wis., 1971, Harvard Bus. Sch., 1970—73; MBA, Pepperdine U., 1972, DSc (hon.), 1974. Pres., CEO Evans Distbg. Cos., La., 1962-72, Evans & Co., La., 1966—; v.p., corp. sec. Lee Nat. Life Ins. Co., La., 1973; pres., CEO La. REIT; v.p. mktg. UMB, 1974; divsn. gen. mgr. AgMet, La., 1974-76; gen. mgr. Exxon Ofc Products, L.A., 1976-78; pres., CEO Universal Mfg. Corp., L.A., 1982; corp. dir. tng. & devel. Mitchell Internat., San Diego, 1983-87, Sun Electric Corp., Crystal Lake, Ill., 1988-90; corp. dir. tng. Chilton Publs., Radnor, Pa., 1990-92. Adj. prof. Centenary Coll., Golf Acad. San Diego. Bd. dirs. ARC; trustee Grad. Sch. Sales Mgmt. and Mktg.; chmn. bd. dirs. N. La. Mental Health Hosp.; co-chair United Way, 1965-69. Recipient awards United Way, 1965-69, ITVA awards, 1987-88. Mem. Nat. Beer Wholesalers Assn. (adv. dir.), Sales and Mktg. Execs. of Shreveport (pres.), S.W. Sales and Mktg. Execs. Coun. (pres.), Young Pres. Orgn., Pres.'s Assn., Conf. Bd., Aspen Inst., Sales and Mktg. Execs. Internat., Am. Soc. Tng. and Devel., Am. Soc. Pers. Adminstrn., Syracuse U. Grad. Sch. Sales Mgmt. and Mktg. Alumni Assn. (past pres., past trustee), Westlake Village C. of C. (past v.p., bd. dirs.), Shreveport C. of C. Pers. and Indsl. Rels. Assn. (vice chmn., bd. dirs.), Harvard Club San Diego. Home and Office: 11305 Affinity Ct 131 San Diego CA 92131-2758

EVANS, JUDITH CHRISTIEN LUNBECK, elementary school principal; b. Jackson Hole, Wyo., Aug. 15, 1938; d. Joseph Beal Lunbeck and Augusta Lou Smith; m. Thomas Daniel O'Neil III, Nov. 30, 1957 (div. Nov. 1960); 1 child, Thomas Daniel O'Neil IV; m. Howard Charles Evans, Mar. 1, 1963; children: Morgan Howard, Joseph Heath. BS, U. Wyo., 1962; MS, Ea. Mont. Coll., 1980. Tchr. Granite Sch. Dist., Salt Lake City, 1962-66, State of Hawaii, Honolulu, 1968, Newport (R.I.) Sch. Dist., 1969-74, Billings (Mont.) Sch. Dist. 2, 1977-85, elem. prin., 1986—. Mem. Action Force, Nat. FFA Mentoring Program, Alexandria, Va., 1990—; grant reader Dept. Edn., Washington, 1992; site vis. Pres. Blue Ribbon Schs., 1992; participant China Breakers conf. RJR Nabisco, 1993. Editor Mont. Reading Jour., 1986. Bd. dirs. Jr. Achievement, Billings, 1991-92, Girl Scouts Ea. Mont., 1992. Keizai Koho Ctr. fellow to Japan, 1990; Taft Inst. fellow on Am. Govt., Eugene, Oreg., 1991. Mem. ASCD, NEA, Mont. Edn. Assn., Billings Edn. Assn., Mont. Assn. Elem. Prins., Billings Assn. Elem. Prins. (pres. 1991-92), Nat. Assn. Elem. Sch. Prins., Mont. Reading Coun., Internat. Reading Assn., Phi Delta Kappa. Republican. Episcopalian. Avocations: swimming, skiing, biking, hiking. Office: Billings Sch Dist 2 415 N 30th St Billings MT 59101-1298 Address: 3481 Masterson Cir Billings MT 59106-9651

EVANS, KATHLEEN TARA, special education administrator; b. Easton, Pa., Sept. 6, 1955; d. Richard Eugene and Audrey Rae (Hofschild) Bertsch; m. William Michael Evans, July 29, 1978; children: William Jr., Bryan. BA, West Chester State Coll., 1977; MA in Teaching, Manhattanville Coll., 1986; 6th-yr. degree in adminstrn., So. Conn. U., 1990. CVert. tchr., N.Y. Rehab. counselor Albert Einstein Coll., Bronx, N.Y., 1977-78, Rockland Psychiat. Ctr., Orangeburg, N.Y., 1978, United Cerebral Palsy, Purchase, N.Y., 1978-80; instrnl. asst. Bedford Sch. Dist., Mt. Kisco, N.Y., 1983-85; tchr. spl. edn. Carmel (N.Y.) Sch. Dist., 1985, Pawling (N.Y.) Sch. Dist., 1985-86, Brewster (N.Y.) Cen. Sch. Dist., 1986-90, asst. to dir. spl. edn. svcs., 1990-91, dir. spl. ednl. svcs., 1991—. Presenter workshops Mental Health Assn. Westchester, Tarrytown, N.Y., Spl. Edn. Adminstrs. Leadership Tng. Acad., Tarrytown, 1991, Spl. Edn. Tng. and Resource Ctr., Yorktown, N.Y., 1992. Recipient community svc. award Green Chimneys Sch., 1992. Mem. ASCD, Coun. Exceptional Children, Lower Hudson Assn. Pupil Pers. Adminstrs., Sch. Adminstrs. Assn. N.Y. State. Home: RD 4 Ridge Rd Brewster NY 10509 Office: Brewster Cen Sch Dist Farm to Market Rd Brewster NY 10509

EVANS, LAWRENCE E. lawyer, educator; b. Houston, Mar. 30, 1950; s. Lawrence Edgar and Edith (Kinzy) E.; m. Nancy Campbell, Aug. 20, 1977; children: Christopher, Laura. BA, Washington & Lee U., 1973; JD, South Tex. Coll., 1977. Bar: Tex. 1977, Mo. 1989; registered patent atty. Lawyer Gunn, Lee & Miller, Houston, 1977-88, Herzog, Crebs & McGhee, St. Louis, 1988-2000, Blackwell, Sanders, Peper, Martin LLP, St. Louis, 2000—. Adj. prof. Washington Univ. Sch. of Law, St. Louis. Mem. Metro. Bar Assn. St. Louis (chmn. Patent, Trademark and Copyright sect. 1994), Internat. Trademark Assn., Am. Intellectual Property Law Assn. Office: Blackwell Sanders Peper Martin LLP 720 Olive St Ste 2400 Saint Louis MO 63101 E-mail: levans@blackwellsanders.com.

EVANS, LINDA MARIE, educational diagnostician, secondary education educator; b. Mobile, Ala., Jan. 3, 1960; d. John Ronald and Joe Ann (Terrell) Evans; m. F. Joseph Risser, July 8, 1992. BS, S.W. Tex. State U., 1993; EdM, Tex A&M, Univ. Kingsville, 2000. Tchr. Providence HS, San Antonio, 1993-94, Poth (Tex.) Ind. Sch. Dist., 1994—97, Floresville (Tex.) Ind. Sch. Dist., 1997—2001, Judson HS, Converse, 2001—02; ednl. diagnos. Stockdale (Tex.) Ind. Sch. Dist., 2002—. Mem. Coun. Exceptional Children, Phi Upsilon Omicron (alumni); Alpha Chi (alumni); Kappa Delta Pi (alumni); Golden Key (alumni). Avocations: needle craft, floral crafts. Home: 4810 Chedder Dr San Antonio TX 78229-5304

EVANS, MARIE ANNETTE LISTER, school system administrator; b. Lakeland, Ga., Sept. 20, 1941; d. Lawton C. and Jeffrie (Metts) Lister; m. Marvin Velton Evans, Nov. 28, 1957; children: Marvin, Theresa, Evan, Bruce. AA, North Fla. Jr. Coll., 1970; BS, Valdosta State Coll., 1972, MEd, 1976, EdS, 1984. Tchr. Clyattville (Ga.) Elem. Sch., 1972-81; tchr., team leader Lowndes Mid. Sch., Valdosta, Ga., 1981-89, asst. prin., 1989—. Instr. Valdosta State Coll., 1991; instr. in classroom mgmt. Regional Ednl. Svc. Agy., Valdosta, 1989. Bd. dirs. Mental Health Assn., Valdosta, 1991—, sec., 1992-93; coord. St. Jude's Math-A-Thon, Lowndes Mid. Sch., 1985-91. Recipient Excellence in Teaching Math. award Ga. Math. Coun., 1989; named Tchr. of Yr., Lowndes County, 1988. Mem. Nat. Assn. Educators, Ga. Assn. Educators (uniserv dist. pres. 1988-89), Lowndes Assn. Educators (pres.-elect 1987-88, pres. 1988-89, constitution com. 1991-92), Ga. Mid. Sch. Assn., Ga. Secondary Sch. Prins., Ga. Mid. Sch. Prins. Democrat. Baptist. Avocations: travel, reading, crafts. Home: RR 1 Box 184 Pinetta FL 32350-9850 Office: Lowndes Mid Sch 506 Copeland Rd Valdosta GA 31601-6691

EVANS, MICHAEL DUANE, middle school educator; b. NYC, Jan. 1, 1947; s. Warren Michael and Alma Kay (Williams) E.; m. Piromrak Karnsaway, Oct. 5, 1987; children: Teresa Marie, Katherine Anne. BA, Coll. of Steubenville, 1969; MS in Guidance and Counseling, James Madison U., 1971; PhD in Adult Continuing Edn., Tex. Woman's U., 1986. Cert. tchr., secondary adminstr., in guidance, Va. Tchr., coach St. Mary's Sch., Sandusky, Ohio, 1969-70, Francis C. Hammond Jr. HS, Alexandria, Va., 1972—; guidance dir., coach Northampton Sr. HS, Eastville, Va., 1971-72. Tennis dir. Camp Taconic, Hinsdale, Mass., summers 1974-77,

Camp Mah-Kee-Nac, Lenox, Mass., summers 1979-91; pre-GED adult edn. instr. Alexandria (Va.) City Pub. Sch., 1991—; T-ball coach Fairfax Police Youth Club 1995—; league dir. 10 and under girls basketball Braddock Rd. Youth Club, 1998-1999, 12 and under girls softball coach, Braddock Road Youth Club; 7th grade leader, soc. studies dept. head FC Hammond Mid. Sch., 2001-02, alt. edn. program dir., 2002—; varsity tennis coach T.C. Williams H.S., 1974-80; jr. varsity basketball coach F.C. Hammond Sch., 1972-78, freshman basketball coach, 1978-81. Contbr. articles to profl. jour. Mgr. Little League Baseball, Eastville, 1972, Fairfax, Va., 1989; select girls basketball coach, 2002-. Mem. ASCD, Nat. Assn. for Social Studies. Avocations: family, tennis, basketball, reading.

EVANS, PAULINE D. physicist, educator; b. Bklyn., Mar. 24, 1922; d. John A. and Hannah (Brandt) Davidson; m. Melbourne Griffith Evans, Sept. 6, 1950; children: Lynn Janet Evans Hannemann, Brian Griffith. BA, Hofstra Coll., 1942; postgrad., NYU, 1943, 46-47, Cornell U., 1946, Syracuse U., 1947-50. Jr. physicist Signal Corps Ground Signal Svc., Eatontown, N.J., 1942-43; physicist Kellex Corp. (Manhattan Project), N.Y.C., 1944; faculty dept. physics Queens Coll., N.Y.C., 1944-47; teaching asst. Syracuse U., 1947-50; instr. Wheaton Coll., Norton, Mass., 1952; physicist Nat. Bur. Standards, Washington, 1954-55; instr. physics U. Ala., 1955, U. N.Mex., 1955, 57-58; staff mem. Sandia Corp., Albuquerque, 1956-57; physicist Naval Nuclear Ordnance Evaluation Unit, Kirtland AFB, N.Mex., 1958-60; programmer Teaching Machines, Inc., Albuquerque, 1961; mem. faculty dept. physics Coll. St. Joseph on the Rio Grande (name changed to U. Albuquerque 1966), 1961—, assoc. prof., 1965—, chmn. dept., 1961—. Mem. AAUP, Am. Phys. Soc., Am. Assn. Physics Tchrs., Fedn. Am. Scientists, Sigma Pi Sigma, Sigma Delta Epsilon. Achievements include patents on mechanical method of conical scanning (radar), fluorine trap and primary standard for humidity measurement Home: 730 Loma Alta Ct NW Albuquerque NM 87105-1220

EVANS, ROBERT BYRON, software engineer, educator; b. Winchester, Va., July 8, 1942; s. Quentin Marcellus and Catherine Virginia (Ours) E.; m. Nancy Lee Irwin, Oct. 24, 1964 (div. Sept. 1983); children: Richard Todd, Christine Kay, Danielle René. AB in Math., Ind. U., 1963; M Engring. in Computer Sci., Vanderbilt U., 1991. Customer svc. rep. R.R. Donnelley & Sons, Warsaw, Ind., 1963-68, prodn. planner, 1968-74, Gallatin, Tenn., 1974-81, bindery mgr., 1981-85, sr. software engr., 1985—. Adj. asst. prof. computer sci. Volunteer State C.C., Gallatin, 1991—; frequent speaker on data mining applications including the 1997 Miller Freeman Data Mining Summit in San Francisco. Author numerous articles on applied machine learning. Sgt. Ind. Army N.G., 1963-69. Mem. IEEE, Am. Assn. Artificial Intelligence, Assn. for Computing Machinery, Mensa. Achievements include patent pending for system and method for interactively identifying conditions leading to a particular result in a multi-variant system. Home: 820 Newton Ln Gallatin TN 37066-8750

EVANS, ROSEMARY KING (MRS. HOWELL DEXTER EVANS), librarian, educator; b. Forsyth, Ga., Nov. 16, 1924; d. Wiley Gwin and Mary (Goggans) King; m. Howell Dexter Evans, June 29, 1945; children: Joseph William, Curtis McKenney. BS, Tift Coll., 1957; librarian's certificate, Woman's Coll. of Ga., 1963; M Library Edn., U. Ga., 1972, postgrad. in library edn., 1975. Tchr. elementary sch., Forsyth, Ga., 1946-48, 54-62; librarian Mary Persons High Sch., Forsyth, 1962-73; catalog librarian Tift Coll., Forsyth, 1973-74; head librarian Stratford Acad., Macon, Ga., 1974-77; head librarian, asst. prof. Gordon Jr. Coll., Barnesville, Ga., 1977-87; chmn. regents' acad. com. libraries State Bd. Regents Univ. System of Ga. Librarian, educator; b. Forsyth, Ga., Nov. 16, 1924; d. Wiley Gwin and Mary (Goggans) King; B.S., Tift Coll., 1957; librarian's certificate Woman's Coll. of Ga., 1963; M. Library Edn., U. Ga., 1972, postgrad. in library edn., 1975; m. Howell Dexter Evans, June 29, 1945; children— Joseph William, Curtis McKenney. Tchr. elementary sch., Forsyth, Ga., 1946-48, 54-62; librarian Mary Persons High Sch., Forsyth, 1962-73; catalog librarian Tift Coll., Forsyth, 1973-74; head librarian Stratford Acad., Macon, Ga., 1974-77; head librarian, asst. prof. Gordon Jr. Coll., Barnesville, Ga., 1977-87; chmn. regents' acad. com. libraries State Bd. Regents Univ. System of Ga.: Mem. Ga. State Bd. Certification of Librarians. Author: The Christmas Tree Farm, 1989. Spiritual edn. chmn. PTA, 1960-61; mem. Monroe County Hosp. Authority, 1988—, chmn., 1994-98; mem. Monroe County Libr. Bd., 1990—. Named Star Tchr., 1966. Mem. Nat., Ga., Monroe County (sec. 1959-60, v.p. 1961-62, pres. 1962-63) edn. assns., Ga. (dis. pres. 1965), ALA, Southeastern library assns., Ga. Library Assn. Methodist (chmn. local edn. bd. 1964-65, chmn. commn. on Christian vocation 1965—, exec. com., tchr. adult Bible class). Author: Backhome Cuisine, 1984. Author: Backhome Cuisine, 1984, The Christmas Tree Farm, 1989. Spiritual edn. chmn. PTA, 1960-61; mem. Monroe County Hosp. Authority, 1988—, chmn., 1994-98; mem. Monroe County Libr. Bd., 1990—. Named Star Tchr., 1966. Mem. Ga. State Bd. Certification Librarians, Nat., Ga., Monroe County (sec. 1959-60, v.p. 1961-62, pres. 1962-63) edn. assns., Ga. (dis. pres. 1965), ALA, Southeastern library assns., Ga. Library Assn. Methodist (chmn. local edn. bd. 1964-65, chmn. commn. on Christian vocation 1965—, exec. com., tchr. adult Bible class). Home: Evans Rd Smarr GA 31086

EVANS, SARA MARGARET, history educator; b. McCormick, S.C., Dec. 1, 1943; d. J. Claude and Maxilla (Everett) Evans; m. Harry Chatten Boyte, June 5, 1966 (div. Aug. 1994); children: Craig Evans Boyte, Jae Sook Lee; m. Charles Kelly Dayton, June 21, 2002. BA, Duke U., 1966, MA, 1968; PhD in History, U. N.C., 1976. Instr. history dept. Duke U., Durham, N.C., 1974-75, U. N.C., Chapel Hill, 1975-76; asst. prof., then assoc. prof. history dept. U. Minn., Mpls., 1976-89, dir. ctr. for advanced feminist studies, 1987-90, prof., 1989—, Disting. McKnight U. prof., 1997—, chair history dept., 1991-94. Mem. editl. bd. Feminist Studies, College Park, Md., 1985-96. Author: Personal Politics, 1979, Born for Liberty, 1989, 2d edit., 1997, Tidal Wave, 2003; co-author: Free Spaces, 1986, Wage Justice, 1989; editor: Journeys That Opened Up the World, 2003; cons. editor: Jour. Am. History, 1990-95. Recipient Book award Policy Studies Orgn., 1990; Kellogg Nat. fellow W.K. Kellogg Found., 1982-86; Am. ASsn. Learned Socs. fellow, 2001-02. Mem. AAUP, Orgn. Am. Historians (bd. dirs. 1991-94), Am. Studies Assn. (bd. dirs. 1990-93), Am. Hist. Assn. Methodist. Office: U Minn History Dept 267 19th Ave S Minneapolis MN 55455-0499

EVANS, THOMAS PASSMORE, business and product licensing consultant; b. West Grove, Pa., Aug. 19, 1921; s. John and Linda (Zeuner) E.; m. Lenore Jane Knuth, June 21, 1947; children: Paula S., Christina L., Bruce A., Carol L. BS in Elec. Engring., Swarthmore Coll., 1942; M in Engring., Yale U., 1948. Registered profl. engr., Pa. Engr. atomic power divsn. Westinghouse Electric Corp., Pitts., 1948-51; dir. R&D AMF, Inc., N.Y.C., 1951-60; dir. rsch. O.M. Scott & Sons Co., Marysville, Ohio, 1960-62; v.p. R&D W. A. Sheaffer Pen Co., Fort Madison, Iowa, 1962-67; dir. rsch. Mich. Tech. U., Houghton, 1967-80; dir. rsch., mem. faculty Berry Coll., Mt. Berry, Ga., 1980-88, prof. bus. adminstrn., 1980-86. Lt. USN, 1943-46. Mem. IEEE, AAAS. VFW, Am. Forestry Assn., Nat. Defense Industl. Assn., Am. Phys. Soc., Soc. Plastics Engrs., Yale Sci. and Engring. Assn., Nat. Coun. Univ. Rsch. Adminstrs., Air Force Assn., Am. Legion, Hunter Mus. Art, Nat. Trust Hist. Preservation, Yale Club of Ga., Sigma Xi, Tau Beta Pi. Achievements include patents in field. Home: 1220 Broadrick Dr Apt 1222 Dalton GA 30720-2809

EVANS, VALERIE ELAINE, elementary education educator; b. Winston-Salem, N.C., July 12, 1971; d. Lindsay McRay an Beverly Kaye (Moser) E. BS in Edn., U. Ctrl. Fla., 1993, MEd in Math, Sci. and Tech., 1998. Nat. bd. cert. tchr. Vol. Pershing Elem. Sch., Orlando, Fla., 1991-92; intern Waterford Elem. Sch., Orlando, Fla., 1993; tchr. kindergarten Orange Ctr. Elem. Sch., Orlando, Fla., 1993-94, tchr. 4th grade, 1994-96, Little River Elem. Sch., Orlando, Fla., 1996—. Mem. computer tech. team, 1994, 1996-97, sci. amb. 1996—, childcare team, 1994, mem. curriculum com., 1998-99. Democrat. Methodist. Avocations: reading, computers, swimming, volleyball.

EVANS-O'CONNOR, NORMA LEE, secondary education educator, consultant; b. Vanceburg, Ky., Sept. 4, 1952; d. Herbert Martin and Nellie Irene (Parker) E.; 1 child, Karen. AB, Morehead State U., 1975; MEd, Xavier U., 1982; EdS, Nova Southeastern U., 2001. Cert. tchr. Fla., Ky., Tenn., Ohio. Tchr. Forest Hills Sch. Dist., Cin., 1977-83, Osceola County Schs., Kissimmee, Fla., 1983—2003; asst. prin. Ninth Grade Ctr., Osceola H.S., 2003—. Dean of students, curriculum resource tchr., chair sch. adv. coun. Osceola High Sch., activities dir., 1997—, head social studies dept.; mem. student coun. bd. Nat. Assn. Secondary Sch. Prins., Va., 1990—91; staff mem. Horatio Alger Assn.; cons. Walt Disney World, Lake Buena Vista, Fla., 1991—; retail theft operative Walt Disney World Co., Lake Buena Vista, 1988—; movie checker Theatrical Entertainment Svcs., L.A., 1990—2000. Nominated for Nat. Tchrs. Hall of Fame, 1997-98. Mem. NEA, Nat. Assn. Workshop Dirs., Osceola County Tchrs. Orgn., Phi Delta Kappa. Democrat. Roman Catholic. Avocations: basketball, softball, cheerleading. Office: Osceola County Schs 420 S Thacker Ave Kissimmee FL 34741-5963 E-mail: nleoc@cfl.rr.com.

EVAUL, CHARLEEN MCCLAIN, education educator; b. Huntington, Pa., Dec. 1, 1944; d. Charles Lewis and Eunice C. (Keim) McClain; children: Michael C., Christopher R.; m. Jerome O. Evaul Jr. BS in Edn., Secondary Edn., Math., Millersville U., 1968; cert. in mentally and/or physically handicapped, Kutztown U., 1986; MS in Education, Allentown Coll., 1996; Cert. Supervision of Spl. Edn., Millersville U., 2000. Adult edn. supr. secondary math. Orrville (Ohio) City Schs., 1969-74; substitute tchr. math., sci. Hamburg (Pa.) Area Schs., 1974-76; instructional aide SR/TMR, Reading, Pa., 1976-85; tchr. learning support Conrad Weiser High Sch., Robesonia, Pa., 1985-97; cons. Sci. Rsch. Assocs., Chgo., 1991—; instr. Berks County Intermediate Unit, Reading, 1989—; itinerant tchr., cons. Conrad Weiser S.D., 1997—. Adj. prof. Pa. State U.; instr. Learning Inst. St. Joseph's U. Contbr. articles to profl. jours. Recipient Sam Kirk award Pa. Assn. for Learning Disabilities, Annie Sullivan award Pa. Assn. Intermediate Units, Salute to Teaching award Pa. Acad. for Profession of Teaching, Outstanding Educator award Berks County Learning Disabilities Assn. Mem. ASCD, Internat. Soc. Tech. Edn., Pa. Assn. Ednl. Computing & Tech., Coun. Exceptional Children, Assn. Direct Instrn., Phi Delta Kappa. Avocations: flowers, computer bulletin boards, reading. Office: Conrad Weiser HS 44 Big Spring Rd Robesonia PA 19551-8900 E-mail: charleenh@aol.com.

EVENS, RONALD GENE, radiologist, medical center administrator; b. St. Louis, Sept. 24, 1939; s. Robert and Dorothy (Lupkey) E.; m. Hanna Blunk, Sept. 3, 1960; children: Ronald Jr., Christine, Amanda. BA, Washington U., 1960, MD, 1964, postgrad. in bus. and edn., 1970-71. Intern Barnes Hosp., St. Louis, 1964-65; resident Mallinckrodt Inst. Radiology, St. Louis, 1965-66, 68-70; rsch. assoc. Nat. Heart Inst., 1966-68; asst. prof. radiology, v.p. Washington U. Med. Sch., 1970-71, prof., head dept. radiology, dir., 1971-72, Elizabeth Mallinckrodt prof., head radiology dept., 1972-99, prof. med. econs., 1988—; pres., sr. exec. ofcr. Barnes-Jewish Hosp., St. Louis, 1999—. Radiologist-in-chief Barnes Hosp., St. Louis, 1971-99; radiologist-in-chief Children's Hosp., 1971-99, pres., chief exec. officer, 1985-88; vice chancellor fin. Washington U., St. Louis, 1988-91; mem. adv. com. on splty. and geog. distbn. of physicians Inst. Medicine, Nat. Acad. Scis., 1974-76, Hickey lectr., 1976, Carmen lectr. Calif. U., 1985, Kiewit lectr. Eisenhower Med. Ctr., 1986; Hornick lectr. U. Pitts., 1986; ann. orator Can. Radiol. Soc., 1984; Hodes lectr. Jefferson U., 1991—; Smith lectr. Royal Coll. Physicians, Edinburgh, 1992; Seaman lectr. Columbia Presbyn., 1992; dir. Boatmens Bank Inc., Mallinckrodt Group Inc., Right Choice Inc., Blue Choice, Inc.; chmn. bd. Med. Care Group St. Louis, 1980-86. Contbr. over 210 articles to profl. jours. Active Boy Scouts Am., 1975—; elder Glendale Presbyn. Ch., 1971-74, Kirkwood Presbyn. Ch., 1983-86. Served with USPHS, 1966-68. Advance Acad. fellow James Picker Found, 1970; recipient Disting. Svc. award. St. Louis C. of C., 1972; named Disting. Eagle Scout Nat. Coun., 1983. Fellow Am. Coll. Radiology (chair elect 1995, chair bd. chancellors 1996—); mem. AMA (editl. bd. JAMA), Mo. Radiol. Soc. (pres. 1977-78), Soc. Nuclear Medicine (trustee 1971-75), St. Louis Med. Soc., Mo. State Med. Assn., Soc. Chmn. Acad. Radiology Depts. (pres. 1979), Radiol. Soc. N.Am., Assn. Univ. Radiologists (pres. 1988), Am. Roentgen Ray Soc. (pres. 1989), Phi Beta Kappa, Alpha Omega Alpha (Sheard-Sanford award). Office: Barnes Jewish Hosp Mallinckrodt Inst Radiology Barnes Jewish Plz Saint Louis MO 63110-1016 Address: Barnes-Jewish Hosp One Barnes-Jewish Hospital Plz Saint Louis MO 63110

EVENSON, MERLE ARMIN, chemist, educator; b. LaCrosse, Wis., July 27, 1934; s. Ansel Bernard and Gladys Mabel (Nelson) E.; m. Peggy L. Kovats, Oct. 5, 1957; children— David A., Donna L. BS in Chem. Physics and Math., U. Wis., LaCrosse, 1956; MS in Guidance, MS in Sci. Edn., Madison, 1960, PhD in Analytical Chemistry, 1966. Diplomate Am. Bd. Clin. Chemists, v.p., 1978-81. Tchr. math. and physics St. Croix Falls (Wis.) High Sch., 1956-57; tchr. chemistry Central High Sch., LaCrosse, 1957-59; instr. dept. medicine U. Wis., Madison, 1965-66, asst. prof., 1966-69, asso. prof., 1971-75, prof., 1975—, prof. dept. pathology, 1979—; asst. dir. clin. lab. Univ. Hosps., 1965-66, dir. clin. chemistry lab., 1966-69, dir. toxicology lab., 1971-87. Chmn. Gordon Rsch. Conf. on Analytical Chemistry, 1978; vis. lectr. Harvard Med. Sch., 1969-71; mem. staff Peter Bent Brigham Hosp., Boston, 1969-71; cons. on analytical and clin. chemistry to AEC, 1968-93, Am. Chem. Soc., Nat. Bur. Standards, FDA, NIH, study sect. mem. 1968-72, ad hoc memberships, 1973-87. Bd. editors: Chemical Instrumentation, 1973-87, Analytical Chemistry, 1974-77, Jour. Analytical Toxicology, 1976-79, Selected Methods in Clin. Chemistry, 1977-81; editor: Contemporary Topics in Analytical and Clincal Chemistry, 1974-83; contbr. numerous chpts. to books, articles to profl. jours.; patentee continuous oil hemoperfusion unit. NIH fellow, 1970-71, NSF, 1959-62; recipient Maurice O. Graff Disting. Alumni award U. Wis., LaCrosse, 1981 Mem. AAAS, Acad. Clin. Lab. Physicians and Scientists, Am. Assn. Clin. Chemists (bd. editors Clin. Chemistry 1970-80, nat. chair pub. rels. com. 1973-78, diplomat 1974, v.p. 1978-81), Am. Chem. Soc. (com. on clin. chemistry 1973-93), Sigma Xi, Kappa Delta Pi. Office: U Wis 1300 University Ave Madison WI 53706-1510

EVERDELL, WILLIAM ROMEYN, humanities educator, educator; b. NYC, June 25, 1941; s. William and Eleanore (Darling) E.; m. Barbara Scott, Dec. 21, 1966; children: Joshua William, Christian Romeyn. AB, Princeton U., 1964; MA, Harvard U., 1965; PhD, NYU, 1971. Asst. English Lycee Arago, Paris, 1963-64; chmn. dept. history St. Ann's Sch., Bklyn., 1972-73, head upper shc., 1973-75, co-chmn. dept. history, 1975-84, dean humanities, 1984—. Adj. instr. NYU, N.Y.C., 1984-85, 86, 87, 89; steering com. U.S. history assessment Nat. Assessment Ednl. Progress, 1991-92; rev. panel NEH Tchr. Fellowships, U.S. Dept. Edn. Blue Ribbon Schs., 1992; ednl. testing svc. World History AP Exam. Devel. Com., 1999-2000. Author: The End of Kings, 1983, 2d edit., 2000, Christian Apologetics in France, 1987, The First Moderns, 1997; co-author: Rowboats to Rapid Transit, 1974; contbr. articles and poems to profl. jours. and newspapers. With USMC, 1966-68. Recipient Poetry prize Acad. Am. Poets, 1963; Fullbright travel grantee, Paris, 1963; Woodrow Wilson fellow, 1964, 70, NEH fellow, 1985, 90; NEH/Wallace Found. tchr./scholar, 1990-91. Mem. Internat. Soc. Intellectual History, Nat. Coun. History Edn., Am. Hist. Assn., N.Y. Acad. Sci., Orgn. History Tchrs. (pres. 2002—), East Ctrl. Am. Soc. 18th Century Studies (pres. 1997), Bklyn. Hist. Soc., New Eng. Soc. Bklyn., Rembrandt Club. Democrat. Episcopalian. Avocation: bicycling. Office: St Ann's Sch 129 Pierrepont St Brooklyn NY 11201-2793 E-mail: weverdell@earthlink.com.

EVERETT, CLAUDIA KELLAM, retired special education educator; b. Mobile, Ala., Dec. 28, 1933; d. Claude M. and Minnie L. Kellam; m. Thomas Sherwood Everett Sr., June 18, 1953; children: Thomas Sherwood Jr., Sherilisa Ann. BA magna cum laude, Roberts Wesleyan Coll., 1958; MS summa cum laude, Barry U., 1988. Cert. English, spl. edn. tchr. Fla., N.Y. Tchr. Dade County Pub. Schs., Miami, Fla., 1959-67, Carol City Elem. Sch., Miami, 1967-77; pers. mgr., payroll supr. Harrington Cos., Miami, 1977-81; honors English tchr. Citrus Grove Jr. HS, Miami, 1981-87; spl. edn. tchr. Citrus Grove Mid. Sch., Miami, 1987-90; tchr. severely emotionally disturbed children Hilton (N.Y.) HS, 1990-91; tchr. emotionally disturbed and mentally retarded, learning disabled Hill Elem. Sch., Brockport, NY, 1991-92; tchr. emotionally/learning disabled, mentally retarded Oliver Mid. Sch., Brockport, 1991—2001; ret., 2001. Cons. cmty. benevolent agys., Miami, 1969—83; pvt. tutor, 2001—. Author: numerous poems. Youth dir. Ctrl. Alliance Youth, Miami, 1960—80; cmty. advisor youth affairs Carol City, Miami, 1970—87; founder, pres. Tchr.-Parent Study Group, Miami, 1970—80; 1st v.p., sec., treas. PTA Carol City, 1967—77; pres. Teens to S.Am. Christian Missionary Alliance, Miami, 1978—80, cons. tech. action, 1980—90. Recipient Svc. award, Christian Missionary Alliance Cmty., 1980, Youth in Action award, S.Am. Missions, 1978. Mem.: S.E. Edn. Opportunities Handicapped, Coun. Exceptional Children (mem. divsn. learning disabilities 1989—, mem. divsn. mentally retarded 1989—, mem. divsn. emotionally handicapped 1989—). Republican. Avocations: reading, photography, tutoring, writing for children, visiting elderly in nursing homes. Home: 2355 Westside Dr Rochester NY 14624-1933

EVERETT, GRAHAM, English language educator, poet, publisher; b. Oceanside, N.Y., Dec. 23, 1947; s. James H. and Jacqueline (Vaughn) E.; m. Elyse Arnow, Dec. 27, 1981; 1 child, Logan James. BA in English, Canisius Coll., 1970; MA in English, SUNY, Stony Brook, 1987, PhD in English, 1994. Pub., editor Street Press, Port Jefferson, N.Y., 1972-92; dir. Backstreet Editions, Inc., Port Jefferson, 1980-86; asst. dir. Poetry Ctr. SUNY, Stony Brook, 1988-91. Prof., acad. tutor Adelphi U.; writer in residence N.Y. State Poets in Sch. Program, L.I., 1973-86. Author: (poetry) Strange Coast, 1979, Sunlit Sidewalk, 1985, Minus Green, 1992, Minus Green Plus, 1995, Corps Calleux, 2000; editor: The Doc Fayth Poems, 1998; co-editor: Paumanok Rising, 1980. Mem. MLA, Nat. Coun. Tchrs. English. Office: Street Press PO Box 772 Sound Beach NY 11789-0772

EVERETT, KAREN JOAN, retired librarian, genealogy educator; b. Cin., Dec. 12, 1926; d. Leonard Kelly and Kletis V. (Wade) Wheatley; m. Wilbur Mason Everett, Sept. 25, 1950; children: Karen, Jan, Jeffrey, Jon, Kathleen, Kerry, Kelly, Shannon. BS in Edn. magna cum laude, U. Cin., 1976, postgrad., 1982-85, Coll. Mt. St. Joseph, 1981-86, Xavier U., Cin., 1985-87, U. Cin., 1982-85, Miami U., 1987. Libr. S.W. Local Schs., Harrison, Ohio, 1967-97, dist. media coord., 1980-97, dist. vol. dir., 1980-97, ret., 1997; instr. genealogy U. Cin., 1998—. Tchr. genealogy U. Cin., 1997—; cons. in field; bd. dirs. U. Cin. ILR; lectr. in field. Contbr. articles to profl. jours. Pres. Citizens Adv. Coun., Harrison, Ohio, 1981-84, 88—, Citizens Adv. Coun., 1989; state chmn. supervisory div. Ohio Ednl. Libr./Media Assn.; mem. Ohio Ambulance Licensing Bd., 1991—. Named Woman of the Yr., Cin. Enquirer, 1978, Xi Eta Iota, 1979; named PTA Educator of the Yr., 1981, others. Mem. NEA, Ohio Ednl. Libr./Media Assn. (chair supervisory div. 1990—, bd. dirs. 1993-94), Ohio Edn. Assn., S.W. Local Classroom Tchrs. Assn., Hamilton County Geneal. Soc. (bd. dirs. 1992—). Avocations: flying, travel, genealogy. Office: U Cin PO Box 210146 Cincinnati OH 45221-0146

EVERETT, WOODROW WILSON, electrical engineer, educator; b. Newton, Miss., Oct. 11, 1937; s. Woodrow Wilson and Katherine (Thrash) E.; m. Cherry Donna Sarff, Aug. 23, 1958; children: Woodrow W., Leanne Everett Traver. B.E.E., George Washington U., 1959; MS, Cornell U., 1965, PhD, 1968. Project engr. Scott Paper Co., 1959, Ithaca (N.Y.) Rsch. Labs., Atlantic Rsch. Corp., 1962-64; postdoctoral program dir. Rome (N.Y.) Air Devel. Ctr., 1964-75; chmn. bd. N.E. Consortium for Engring. Edn., St. Cloud, Fla., 1975—. Bd. dirs. Device Assocs. Corp. N.Y., Masonwood, Inc., Sunoric Corp., ITG, Inc., Thrash Homestead Corp., The Cherwood Corp., SCEEE Svc. Corp. Author works in field. Democratic committeeman, Madison County, N.Y., 1976-79; pres. Village of Groton (N.Y.) Appeals Bd., 1966-69; chmn. Groton Planning Bd., 1968-69. Served with USAF, 1959-62. Fellow IEEE (life); mem. Air Force Assn. (life), Res. Officers Assn. (life), Am. Soc. Engring. Edn. Clubs: Rotary. Home: Cherwood-Alligator Lake 1161 Walnut Grove Rd Bridgeport NY 13030 Office: 1101 Massachusetts Ave Saint Cloud FL 34769-3733

EVERETT NOLLKAMPER, PAMELA IRENE, legal management company executive, educator; b. L.A., Dec. 31, 1947; d. Richard Weldon and Alta Irene (Tuttle) Bunnell; m. James E. Everett, Sept. 2, 1967 (div. 1973); 1 child, Richard Earl; m. Milton Nollkamper, Dec. 20, 2000. Cert. Paralegal, Rancho Santago Coll., Santa Ana, Calif., 1977; BA, Calif. State U.-Long Beach, 1985; MA, U. Redlands, 1988. Owner, mgr. Orange County Paralegal Svc., Santa Ana, 1979—; pres. Gem Legal Mgmt. Inc., Fullerton, Calif., 1986—; co-owner Bunnell Publs., Fullerton, Calif., 1992-96. Instr. Rancho Santiago Coll., 1979-96, chmn. adv. bd., 1980-85; instr. Fullerton Coll., 1989-2002, Rio Hondo Coll., Whittier, Calif., 1992-94; advisor Saddleback Coll., 1985—, North Orange County Regional Occupational Program, Fullerton, 1986-99, Fullerton Coll. So. Calif. Coll. Bus. and Law; bd. dirs. Nat. Profl. Legal Assts. Inc., editor PLA News. Author: Legal Secretary Federal Litigation, 1986, Bankruptcy Courts and Procedure, 1987, Going Independent--Business Planning Guide, Fundamentals of Law Office Management, 1994. Republican. Avocation: reading. Office: 940 Manor Way Corona CA 92882 E-mail: 2Pan@attbi.com.

EVERHART, THOMAS EUGENE, retired university president, engineering educator; b. Kansas City, Mo., Feb. 15, 1932; s. William Elliott and Elizabeth Ann (West) E.; m. Doris Arleen Wentz, June 21, 1953; children: Janet Sue, Nancy Jean, David William, John Thomas. AB in Physics magna cum laude, Harvard, 1953; MSc, UCLA, 1955; PhD in Engring., Cambridge U., Eng., 1958. Mem. tech. staff Hughes Research Labs., Culver City, Calif., 1953—55; mem. faculty U. Calif., Berkeley, 1958—78, prof. elec. engring. and computer scis., 1967—78, Miller research prof., 1969—70, chmn. dept., 1972—77; prof. elec. engring., Joseph Silbert dean engring. Cornell U., Ithaca, 1979—84; prof. elec. and computer engring., chancellor U. Ill., Urbana-Champaign, 1984—87; prof. elec. engring. and applied physics, pres. Calif. Inst. Tech., Pasadena, 1987—97, pres. emeritus, 1997—. Fellow scientist Westinghouse Rsch. Labs., Pitts., 1962-63; guest prof. Inst. Applied Physics, U. Tuebingen, Germany, 1966-67, Waseda U., Tokyo, Osaka U., 1974; vis. fellow Clare Hall, Cambridge, U., 1975; chmn. Electron, Ion and Photon Beam Symposium, 1977; cons. in field; mem. sci. and ednl. adv. com. Lawrence Berkeley Lab., 1978-85, chmn., 1980-85; mem. sci. adv. com. GM, 1980-89, chmn., 1984-89; bd. dirs. Saint-Gobain Corp., Raytheon Co.; tech. adv. com. R.R. Donnelly & Sons, 1981-89; sr. sci. advisor W.M. Keck Found., 1997—; pro-vice chancellor Cambridge U., 1998. Chmn. Sec. of Energy Adv. Bd., 1990-93; bd. dirs. KCET, 1989-97, Corp. for Nat. Rsch. Initiatives; trustee Calif. Inst. Tech., 1998—; mem. bd. overseers Harvard U., 1999—. Marshall scholar Cambridge U., 1955-58, NSF sr. fellow, 1966-67, Guggenheim fellow, 1974-75. Fellow IEEE, AAAS, ASEE, Royal Acad. Engring.; mem. NAE (ednl. adv. bd. 1984-88, mem. com. 1984-89, chmn. 1988, coun. 1988-94, 96-2002), Microbeam Analysis Soc. Am., Electron Microscopy Soc. Am. (coun. 1970-72, pres. 1977), Coun. on Competitiveness (vice-chmn. 1990-96), Assn. Marshall Scholars and Alumni (pres. 1965-68), Athenaeum Club, California Club,

Sigma Xi, Eta Kappa Nu. Home: PO Box 1639 Santa Barbara CA 93116-1639 Office: Calif Inst Tech Office Pres Emeritus/202-31 1200 E California Blvd Pasadena CA 91125-0001

EVERLY, DEBRA GOETTSCH, elementary educator; b. DeWitt, Iowa, Nov. 26, 1952; d. Lyle Henry and Mary Kathleen (Green) Goettsch; m. Rocky R. Everly, Oct. 5, 1985. BA, St. Ambrose U., Davenport, Iowa, 1975; MA with highest honors, Marycrest Coll., Davenport, 1988. Permanent lic. profl. tchr., Iowa. Tchr. student lit. corps, comm. arts Kirkwood C.C., Cedar Rapids, Iowa, 1990; tchr. reading/sci. mid. sch. Lisbon (Iowa) Community Sch., 1975-88, tchr. study skills high sch., 1978-80, tchr. self-contained 3rd grade, 1988—. Coord. Iowa Teen Book Awards, Lisbon, 1975-88, World Wise Schs., Lisbon, 1988—, Iowa Children's Choice, Lisbon, 1988—; speaker Young Parents Network, Cedar Rapids, Iowa, 1992. Actress: (play) The Boys Next Door, 1992 (Prodn. of Yr. 1992), Madam Butterfly, 1993. Edn. rep. Mt. Vernon/Liston RARE Recycling, 1991—; vol. ARC, Cedar Rapids, 1973—; vol. Theatre Cedar Rapids, 1991—, Cedar Rapids Mus. of Art-Rural Outreach, 1991—. Recipient Cert. of Recognition ARC; dist. nominee Iowa Disting. Tchr., 1985-86, 86-87. Mem. NEA (pres. 1992—), ASCD, Internat. Reading Assn., Iowa Edn. Assn., Lisbon Edn. Assn. (treas. 1990-91, pres. 1992-93). Lutheran. Avocations: reading, spectator sports, music, swimming, travel. Office: Lisbon Community Sch 235 W School St Lisbon IA 52253 Home: 2937 Ivanhoe Gln Fitchburg WI 53711-5298

EVERLY, JANE, gifted education educator; b. Corona, Calif., Nov. 13, 1964; d. John W. and Esther (Hubberstey) E. BS magna cum laude, Belhaven Coll., 1985; MS, MEd, Miss. Coll., Clinton, 1987, EdS, 1989. Cert. elem. edn., gifted edn., computer edn. and sch. adminstrn., Miss. Tchr. 6th grade Casey Elem., Jackson, Miss., tchr. gifted, Siwell Mid. Sch., Jackson. Coord. Summer Challenge Camp. Author: Cavern's Quest, 1994. Coach 6 state champion teams Odessey of the Mind. Mem. Miss. Profl. Edn. Home: 1821 Linden Pl Jackson MS 39202-1220

EVERSON, JEAN WATKINS DOLORES, librarian media technical assistant, educator; b. Forest City, N.C., Feb. 14, 1938; d. J.D. Watkins and Hermie Roberta (Dizard) Watkins; children: Curtis Bryon, Vincent Keith. BS Elem. Edn., U. Cin., 1971, M Secondary Edn., 1973. Cert. X-ray technician. Educator Cin. Pub. Schs., Cin., 1965—2002, classroom tchr., parent/school coord., 1965—2002; work study coord. Butler County Edn. Ctr., Fairfield, Ohio, 1997—98; long term sub. Brown County -Georgetown Sch. Sys., Gerogetown, Ohio, 1993; sr. staff asst., cpc/alcohol substance abuse, inc. Cin. Pub. Schs., Cin., 1992—93; libr. tech. media; libr. media tech. asst. langsam libr. University of Cin.cinnati-Langsam Library, Cincinnati. Dir. and coord. tutoring program So. Baptist Ch., Cincinnati, 1990—91. Author: (booklet) Gospel Music: Copywrite Laws, 1987 (1987). Prodr./dir./coord. city music festival in music hall Cin. Pub. Schs., 1972—77. Mem.: Ohio Assn. Suprs. and Work Study Coords., Music Educator Nat. Conf. Baptist. Avocations: travel, walking. Home: PO Box 8337 West Chester OH 45069 Office: Cin City Pub Schs-Woodward 7001 Reading Rd Cincinnati OH 45237 Home Fax: 513-858-6880; Office Fax: 513-758-1279. Personal E-mail: jeanwatkinseverson@msn.com. Business E-Mail: eversoj@cpsboe.k12.oh.us.

EVERSON, NINA MARIE BRODE, small business owner, preschool educator; b. Marietta, Ohio, Aug. 21, 1949; d. Edward Van and Mary Isabelle (Moore) Perry; m. Gary Allen Brode, Sept. 1, 1972 (div. June 1980); 1 child, Jonathan Andrew; m. Larry Austin Everson, May 2, 1990; stepchildren: Austin James, Amber Dawn. BA, Glenville (W.Va.) State Coll., 1986; cert. in Montessori pre-primary, Carlow Coll., 1987; MA in Early Childhood Edn., W.Va. U., 1990. Cert. pre-primary tchr. AMS. Owner, artist Art Unltd., Davisville, W.Va., 1978-89; ad layout artist Cox's Dept. Store, Parkersburg, W.Va., 1979-83; preparer bank deposits Montgomery Ward, Parkersburg, 1981-91; ad exec. Sta. WIBZ, Parkersburg, 1983; counselor Open Door Home, Marietta, Ohio, 1984-85, 86; tchr. De Sales Heights Acad., Parkersburg, 1984-91; owner, tchr. Montessori Experience Pre-Sch., Parkersburg, 1991—. Docent Parkersburg Art Ctr., 1978-81; pvt. tutor, Parkersburg, 1989-91; guest speaker in field, 1987-91. C&P Telephone Co. scholar, 1984-85. Mem. Am. Montessori Soc. (tchr.), Field Painter's Assn. (artist), Glenville State Coll. Alumni Assn. Roman Catholic. Avocations: camping, hiking, horseback riding, swimming, concerts. Home: 507 Ellis Ave Parkersburg WV 26101-3818 Office: The Montessori Experience 1701 19th St Parkersburg WV 26101-3503

EVERT, JILL LORENE, elementary special education educator; b. Kansas City, Mo., July 7, 1966; d. Kenneth Dale and Sandra Kay Huey; m. Denny Marker, Aug. 30, 1986 (div. May 1997); children: Jinny, Megan; m. David Alan Evert, Aug. 17, 1997; children, Paige, Madeline. BS, Mo. Valley Coll., 1988; MA, U. Mo., 1996. Tchr. elem. spl. edn. Excelsior Springs (Mo.) Sch. Dist., 1988—. Mentor tchr. Roosevelt Elem., Excelsior Springs, 1998—. Mem. Excelsior Springs Edn. Assn. (bldg. rep. 1997-99), Lambda (pres. 1996-97, Girl of Yr. 1994). Avocations: golf, walking, playing piano.

EVETT, RUSSELL DOUGHERTY, internist, educator; b. Norfolk, Va., Feb. 1, 1932; s. Edward Hall and Elizabeth (Dougherty) E.; m. Mary Gail Kirby, Aug. 18, 1956; children: Stephen, Anne, Gail, John. BS, Randolph-Macon Coll., 1953; MD, Med. Coll. Va., 1957; MS in Medicine, Mayo Clinic and U. Minn., 1963. Diplomate Am. Bd. Internal Medicine. Intern DePaul Hosp., Norfolk, 1957-58; fellow in internal medicine Mayo Clinic, Rochester, Minn., 1960-63; pvt. practice internal medicine Norfolk, 1964—. Pres. med. staff Leigh Meml. Hosp., Norfolk, 1970-72; chmn. dept. internal medicine Norfolk Gen. Hosp., 1972-74; assoc. prof. medicine Eastern Va. Med. Sch., 1974— ; mem. staff Med. Center Hosps., DePaul Hosp., to 1998; mem. Va. Health Info. Bd., 1997—; bd. dirs. Med. Coll. Va. Found., 1998—. Served with USNR, 1958-60. Mem. Va. Health Info. Bd., 1997—, Norfolk Cmty. Svcs. Bd., 2000—. Served with USNR, 1958-60. Fellow ACP (Laureate award 1997); mem. Va. Gastroenterol. Soc. (pres. 1975-77), Norfolk Acad. Medicine (pres. 1976-77), Med. Soc. Va. (pres. 1994-95), AMA (alt. del. 1985-95, del. 1995-99), Norfolk Cmty. Svcs. Bd., So. Med. Assn., Norfolk Yacht and Country Club, Harbor Club, Phi Beta Kappa, Omicron Delta Kappa, Alpha Omega Alpha. Methodist. Home: 6147 Studeley Ave Norfolk VA 23508-1044 E-mail: rdemd@att.net.

EVINS, MARYLOU, retired special education educator; b. Salem, Mo., Nov. 1, 1926; d. Harry Truman and Emma (Davis) Jackson; m. Marvin Calvin Evins, July 30, 1950; children: Mildred Lee, Emma Grannon, Bretta Scott, Franklin. BS in Elem. Edn., S.W. Mo. State U., 1981. Cert. K-12 elem. and spl. edn. tchr., Mo. Tchr. rural schs., Mo., 1944-50; spl. edn. aide Willow Springs (Mo.) R-4 Schs., 1975-77, remedial math. aide, 1977-80, learning disabilities resource tchr., 1980—, tutor, 1989-92. Program chmn. PTA, Willow Springs, 1990-91; asst. sec. youth activities Willow Springs Civic Ctr., 1991-92, treas. youth activities, 1992-94; sec., treas. Lost Camp Assn., 1990-94, treas., 1994-97; bd. dirs. Litaracy Coun., 1994-97. Mem. ASCD, Coun. for Exceptional Children (publicity chmn. chpt. 164, 1990—), Mo. Tchrs. Assn., Willow Springs Bus. and Profl. Women (corr. 1991—), C. of C. (sec. 1993-94). Avocations: sewing, crocheting, embroidery, woodworking, gardening. Home: 2256 Hwy 60-63 Willow Springs MO 65793-9225

EWALD, WENDY TAYLOR, photographer, writer, educator; b. Detroit, June 28, 1951; d. Henry Theodore and Carolyn Davison (Taylor) E.; m. Thomas Joseph McDonough, Oct. 21,1990; 1 child, Michael German. BA, Antioch Coll., 1974. Founder, dir. Camera Work, London, 1971-73, Mountain Photography Workshop, Whitesburg, Ky., 1975-81; tchr. photography Self-Employed Women's Assn., Raquira, Colombia, 1982-84, Gujarat, India, 1988-89; edn. cons. Fotofest, Houston, 1989-91; sr. rsch. assoc. Duke U., Durham, N.C., 1991—; vis. assoc. prof. photography Bard Coll., Annandale, N.Y., 1996. Artist-in-residence Ky. Arts Coun., Whitesburg, 1976-80; asst. dir., scriptwriter Cine-Mujer, Bogota, 1986. Author, editor: Appalachia: A Self-Portrait, 1978; author: Portraits and Dreams, 1985, Magic Eyes, 1992, I Dreamed I Had A Girl In My Pocket, 1996, Secret Games: Collaborations with Children, 1969-99, 2000, I Wanna Take Me a Picture: Teaching Writing and Photography to Children, 2001, The Best Part of Me: Childen Talk About Their Bodies, 2001. Recipient prize Lyndhurst Found., 1986; Fulbright fellow, fellow Nat. Endowment for Arts, 1988, non-fiction fellow N.Y. Found. for Arts, 1990, MacArthur fellow, 1992. Home: PO Box 582 Rhinebeck NY 12572-0582

EWERS, PATRICIA O'DONNELL, university administrator; b. Chgo., July 22, 1935; d. Patrick Brenden and Johanna Marie (Galvin) O'D.; m. John Leonard Ewers, July 26, 1958; children: John P., Michele M. Ewers DeCesare. BA in English summa cum laude, Mundelein Coll., 1957; MA in English, Loyola U., Chgo., 1958, PhD in English, 1966; LHD (hon.), DePaul U., 1998. Instr. English Mundelein Coll., Chgo., 1964-66; asst. prof. English DePaul U., Chgo., 1966-69, assoc. prof. English, 1969-76, dir. humanities divsn. gen. edn. program, 1969-73, chair dept. English, 1973-76, prof. English, 1976-90, dean Coll. Liberal Arts and Scis., 1976-80, v.p., dean faculties, 1980-90; pres. Pace U., N.Y.C., 1990-2000. Ptnr. N.Y.C. Ptnrs., 1990-2000; chmn., mem. North Ctrl. Assn. Accreditation Teams, 1977-90; mem. nat. identification program for women in higher edn. Ill. State Com. for Am. Coun. on Edn., 1983-86; commr.-at-large North Ctrl. Assn. Colls./Schs., 1984-87; mem. com. on study of undergrad. edn. State of Ill. Bd. Higher Edn., 1985-86, 1989-90; mem. Commn. Minorities in Higher Edn., Am. Coun. Edn., 1990-93; mem. N.Y.C. Workforce Devel. Commn., 1993-94; mem. human resources bd. AT&T Corp., Basking Ridge, N.J., 1994-96; mem. adv. coun. on postsecondary edn. State Dept. Edn., 1994-96; mem. adv. com. on telecom., State Edn. Dept., Albany, N.Y., 1995-96. Trustee Riverside (Ill.) Pub. Libr., 1980-86, Cath. Theol. Union, Chgo., 1985-90, sec., 1986-90, NYU Downtown Hosp., 1991-99, Coun. Adult and Exptl. Learning, 1992-95, Our Lady of Mercy Med. Ctr., Bronx, N.Y., 1993-2000, El Museo del Barrio, N.Y.C., 1994—; trustee Commn. Ind. Colls. and Univs./N.Y. State, 1992—, chair, 1995-96; bd. dirs. Cath. Charities, 1984-90, Com. on Social Svc., 1986-90, subcom. on employer assistance programs, 1986-88, Fortune Brands, 1991—, Phoenix Theatre, 1992-96, Drama League, N.Y.C., 1993-96, Richard Tucker Music Found., 1993—, Westchester County Assn., 1993—, Am. Gen. Life Ins. Co. N.Y., 1996—, U.S. Life Ins. Co. in City of N.Y., 1996—; mem. Chgo. Network, 1986-90; steering com. Assn. Colls. and Univs./N.Y. State Commn. Ind. Colls. and Univs., 1992-96; individual investors adv. com. to bd. dirs. N.Y. Stock Exch., 1994-99; mem. commn. on leadership and institutional effectiveness Am. Coun. Edn., Washington; mem. com. econ. devel., N.Y.C., 1996—, citizens budget commn., 1996—. Recipient Outstanding Alumna award Loyola U., Chgo., 1984. Mem. Nat. Assn. Ind. Colls. and Univs. (vice chair bd. dirs. 1997-98, chair bd. dirs. 1998-99), Am. Australian Assn. (bd. dirs. 1994-2000), Regional Plan Assn. (coun. for the region tomorrow 1990-93), Downtown Lower Manhattan Assn., Inc., Westchester Assn. Women Bus. Owners (adv. bd. 1997-2000), Women's Forum, Inc., Fin. Women's Assn., Econ. Club of N.Y., Univ. Club, Met. Club, St. Andrew's Golf Club, Phi Gamma Mu, Beta Gamma Sigma, Alpha Lambda Delta, Delta Epsilon Sigma. Roman Catholic. Office: Pace U One Pace Plz New York NY 10038

EWERSEN, MARY VIRGINIA, educator, poet; b. Van Wert County, Ohio, June 7, 1922; m. Herbert Ewersen (dec.); 2 children. BS in Elem. Edn., Bowling Green, 1966, Toledo and Ohio State U. Cert. tchr. K-12, reading, Ohio. Remedial reading tchr. Port Clinton (Ohio) City Schs., 1966-70, reading tchr. chpt. I/coord., 1970-94; ret. Lyrics writer Hilltop Records. Author: Keepsakes and Celebrations!, 1997, (activity card set)) From Hyperactive to Happy-Active in Limited Spaces, 1979, The Lures of Pan, 2001. Mem. Internat. Reading Assn., Sandusky Choral Soc., Acad. Am. Poets, Internat. Soc. Poets, Kappa Delta Pi. Home: 1786 S Hickory Grove Rd Port Clinton OH 43452-9637 Office: 431 Portage Dr Port Clinton OH 43452-1724

EWING, ALEXANDER COCHRAN, retired chancellor; b. N.Y.C., Feb. 25, 1931; s. Thomas and Lucia (Chase) E.; m. Carol Sonne, Feb. 15, 1958 (dec.); children: Alexander, Eric, Caroline; m. Sheila Cobb, Oct. 31, 1970. BA, Yale U., 1953. Bus. mgr., gen. dir. Joffrey Ballet, N.Y.C., 1963-70, assoc. dir., 1990-91; pres. Hillbright Enterprises Inc., Millbrook, N.Y., 1973-90; chancellor N.C. Sch. of the Arts, Winston Salem, 1990—2000; ret., 2000. Home: 500 S Main St Winston Salem NC 27101-5328*

EWING, RAYMOND PEYTON, educator, author, management consultant; b. Hannibal, Mo., July 31, 1925; s. Larama Angelo and Winona Fern (Adams) E.; m. Audrey Jane Schulze, May 7, 1949; 1 child, Jane Ann. AA, Hannibal La-Grange Coll., 1948; BA, William Jewell Coll., 1949; MA in Humanities, U. Chgo., 1950. Sr. editor Commerce Clearing House, Chgo., 1952-60; dir. corp. communications Allstate Ins. Cos. & Allstate Enterprises, Northbrook, Ill., 1960-85, dir. issues mgmt., 1979-85; pres. Issues Mgmt. Cons. Group, 1985—; assoc. prof., founding dir. grad. corp. pub. rels. program Medill Sch. Journalism Northwestern U., Evanston, Ill., 1986-89, prof., 1989-90; vis. prof., 1990-91. Pub. rels. dir. Chicago Mag., 1966-67, book columnist, 1968-70; staff Book News Commentator, Sta. WRSV, Skokie, Ill., 1962-70. Author: Mark Twain's Steamboat Years, 1981, Managing the New Bottom Line, 1987, Handbook of Communications in Corporate Restructuring and Takeovers, 1992; contbr. articles to mags. Mem. Winnetka (Ill.) Libr. Bd., 1969-70; pres. Skokie Valley United Crusade, 1964-65; bd. dirs. Suburban Community Chest Coun., Onward Neighborhood House, Chgo.; mem. House Commerce Com., Pvt. Sector Foresight Task Force, 1982-83. Served with AUS, 1943-46, ETO. Mem. Pub. Rels. Soc. of Am. (accredited; Silver Anvil awards for pub. affairs, 1970, 72, for fin. rels. 1970, for bus. spl. events 1976, chmn. nat. pub. affairs sect. 1984), Publicity Club of Chgo. (v.p. 1967, bd. dirs. 1966-68; Golden Trumpet award for pub. affairs, 1969, 70, 72, 79, for fin. rels. 1970), Insurers Pub. Rels. Coun. (pres. 1980-81), Issues Mgmt. Assn. (founder, pres. 1981-83, chmn. 1983-84, Disting. Profl. Contbns. award 1994), Internat. Sculpture Ctr., Mensa, World Future Soc., U.S. C. of C. (trends and perspective coun.), Chgo. Poets and Writers Found. (pub. rels. dir. 1966-67), Union League (Chgo.), Internat. Sculpture Ctr. Home: 316 Richmond Rd Kenilworth IL 60043-1139

EXELBERT, MICHAEL MARK, educational administrator; b. Bklyn., Nov. 30, 1948; s. Fred and Eva Vilma (Singer) E.; children— Eric, Janet, Ian, Brian; m. Arlene Wietz Rosenkoff, Sept. 21, 1986. B.Ed., U. Miami (Fla.), 1970, M.Ed., 1975. Tchr., Dade County Public Schs. (Fla.), 1970-75, dist. adminstrv. coordinator exceptional student edn., 1975-77, ednl. planner, 1977-79, dist. budget specialist exceptional student edn., 1979-82; dist. supr. Home Hosp. and Alternative Telecommunication Instrns. Ctr., Dade County Pub. Schs., Miami, 1982-84; prin. Merrick Edn. Ctr., 1984—; coordinator spl. programs Fla. Internat. U., Miami, 1973-75; dir. habilitation program for exceptional adults Miami Dade Community Coll. North, Miami, 1972-74; chmn. Fla. Com. for Home and Hospitalized, 1975— ; mem. nat. adv. bd. United Synagogue Am., 1987—, v.p., southeast region, 1987; pres. Temple Zion Israelite Ctr., 1987; mem. Metro Dade Local Rev. Panel for Services and Demonstration Project for Paratransit Devel.; co-chmn. Occupational Inst. Handicapped, Fla. Internat. U.; mem. adv. bd. Metatherapy Inst., Fla. Diagnostic and Learning Resource Systems; regional commr. Am. Youth Soccer Orgn.; past pres. South Dade Hebrew Acad.; mem. exec. bd. Temple Zion; mem. Pres.'s Com. for Employment Handicapped. Commr. Boy Scouts Am. South Fla. Coun., 1989-91, chmn. scouting for the handicapped, 1991—. Recipient McDonald award Fla. Rehab. Assn., 1973, Silver Beaver award, 1992; citation Fla. Gov.'s Com. for Employing Handicapped, 1975. Mem. Assn. Devel. Exceptional (past pres., chmn. bd.), Assn. Retarded Citizens, Miami U. Alumni Assn., Council Exceptional Children (past pres. state div. physically handicapped, dir.), Fla. Home Hosp. Tchrs. and Adminstrs. Assn. (past pres.), Phi Delta Kappa. Democrat. Lodges: Masons (past master), B'nai B'rith. Author: How to Travel By Bus, 1975. Office: 39 Zamora Ave Miami FL 33134-4121 Home: 11590 S Budd Dr Hollywood FL 33026-3700

EXLEY, WINSTON WALLACE, middle school educator; b. Clyo, Ga., July 1, 1941; s. Miller Franklin and Marie Amanda Exley; m. Marsha Ann Tatum, 1964 (div. 1977); children: Lisa Star Exley Woods, Winston Wallace, Jr.; m. Sarah Dianne Phillips Brown, Mar. 27, 1986; children: Mindy D. Brown Gentry, S. Angela Brown Lord. AB, Newberry Coll., 1963; MEd in Social Sci., Ga. So. U., 1976. Cert. social sci. tchr., supr., Ga., S.C. Social studies tchr. Effingham County High Sch., Springfield, Ga., 1963-83, supervising tchr., 1967-83; staff, student tchr. supr. program Ga. Southern Univ., 1968-83; head dept. social studies Effingham County High Sch., Springfield, Ga., 1980-83; social studies tchr. Hilton Head (S.C.) Middle Sch., 1983—; head dept. social studies McCracken Mid. Sch., Hilton Head, 1988—, team leader 7th grade, 1990—. Mem. individual/campus tchr. dist. com., mem. incentive pay com. Beaufort (S.C.) County Schs., 1984-89; mem. com. Nat. Geography Bee, State of S.C., 1988-91; advisor Allied Med. Careers Club, Springfield, 1968-76; part time instr. Savannah Area Vocat. Tech. Sch., 1970-83; Global Studies program leader McCracken Mid. Sch., 2001-02; mem. Beaufort County Power Standards com., 2002-03; presenter S.C. Mid. Sch. Conf., 2002. Author curriculum guide in field. Sunday sch. tchr. Laurel Hill Luth. Ch., Ga., 1966-73. With USAF, 1958-64. Beaufort County Schs. grantee, 1990-91, 91-92. Mem. ASCD, Salsburger Hist. Sco., Coun. Social Sci., Phi Kappa Phi. Democrat. Luth. Avocations: farming, boating, guitar, naturalist, writing poetry. Home: 4121 Highway 119 N Clyo GA 31303-3629 Office: Hilton Head Mid Sch Wilborn Rd Hilton Head Island SC 29926 E-mail: winstonwallaceexley@yahoo.com.

EXUM, CYNTHIA PHILLIPS, headmaster; b. Phila., July 20, 1951; d. George William and Frankie (Michael) Phillips; m. Frank Emanuel Exum Jr., June 11, 1971 (div. Aug. 1991); children: Christine Karen, Frank Emanuel III. BA in Elem. Edn., Coker Coll., 1988; MEd in Edn. Adminstrn., Winthrop U., 1994. Tchr. 1st United Meth. Ch., Bennettsville, S.C., 1985-87, Marlboro County Schs. Dist., Bennettsville, S.C., 1988-91; headmaster Thomas Hart Acad., Hartsville, S.C., 1991-96; head sch. Patrick Henry Acad., Estell, S.C., 1996—. Co-chair Leadership Hartsville C. of C., 1993-94, chair edn. day, 1993-95; mem. Marlboro County adv. com. S.C. Govs. Early Childhood Devel. Coun., Bennettsville, 1985-86. Mem. ASCD, Nat. Coun. Tchrs. Math., Nat. Assn. Elem. Sch. Prins., Nat. Sci. Tchrs. Assn., S.C. State Headmaster's Assn. (v.p. 1994-95, pres. 1995-96), S.C. Ind. Sch. Assn. (bd. dirs., mem. exec. com. 1991-94), S.C. Assn. Sch. Adminstrs., Rotary, Phi Kappa Phi. Republican. Methodist. Avocations: choirs, theatre, art. Office: Patrick Henry Acad PO Box 788 Hwy 601 Estill SC 29918 Address: 304 3rd St Norway SC 29113-9281

EYSTER, JOHN W. secondary school educator; b. Lake Geneva, Ohio, Oct. 12, 1940; s. Walter C. and Bessie Eva (Adlard) E.; m. Marilyn M. Philpott, June 4, 1965; children: Beth Kari Shore, Mark Erik. BA in Internat. Rels., Am. U., 1962; MDiv in Theology, Wesley Theol. Sem., 1966; MA Teaching in History, U. Wis., Whitewater, 1971; MA in Ednl. Adminstrn., U. Wis., Madison, 1979. Ordained deacon United Ch. of Christ, 1963, minister, 1984. Pastor United Meth. Ch., Wis., 1968-71; social studies tchr. Parker H.S., Janesville, Wis., 1971-2000, chair social studies dept., 1986-2000; legis. liaison Sch. Dist. of Janesville, 2000—. Tentmaker, pastor Emerald Grove Ch., United Ch. of Christ, 1973-95; cons. advanced placement govt. and politics Midwest region Coll. Bd., Evanston, Ill., 1976—; reader advanced placement govt. and politics exam Ednl. Testing Svcs., 1987—; developer ednl. program Washington Seminar; mem. Civics Edn. Task Force, 1998-2000; democracy edn. curriculum com. Wis. Dept. Pub. Instrn., 2000—; spkr. in field. Co-author: Roads to Learning, 1977, (curriculum book) Profiles of Promise #7 - Integrated Social Studies, 1972. Adv. coun. Wis. Advanced Placement. Recipient Valley Forge Tchr.'s medal Freedoms Found., 1978, Outstanding Social Studies Program, Wisc. Coun. for Social Studies, 1990; named Outstanding U.S. History Tchr., Nat. Soc. Daus. Colonial Wars, 1981, Outstanding Tchr., Beloit Coll., 1988; Kohl Ednl. Found. fellow, 1991; profile featured on Salute to Am. Tchr., Disney Channel, 1993. Mem. Wis. Alliance for Excellent Schs., Sons of Norway. Mem. United Ch. of Christ. Avocations: running, cross country skiing, reading, writing. E-mail: jweyster1@msn.com.

EZEKWE, MICHAEL OBI, animal science educator; b. Abatete, Anambra, Nigeria, Nov. 16, 1944; came to U.S., 1972; s. Okudo Ebudike and Ogaobaka (Anyaralu) E.; m. Edith Ifeyinwa Uzodinma, May 18, 1974; children: Obi, Kenechi, Ifemefuna, Chijioke, Nneamaka. BS with honors, U. Nigeria, 1971; MS, Pa. State U., 1974, PhD, 1977. Rsch. scientist Va. State U., Petersburg, 1978—, coord. program, 1993-97; assoc. prof., dir. Swine Devel. Ctr. Alcorn State U., Lorman, Miss., 1997—. Cons. in field. Contbr. articles to Jour. Animal Sci., Growth, Devel. and Aging, Va. Jour. Sci., Nutrition Report Internat., Hormone and Metabolic Rsch., Jour. Am. Oil Chemists Soc., Plant Foods Human Nutrition, Ann. Reciprocal Meats Conf. Eucharistic min. St. Joseph's Ch., Port Gibson, Miss., 1999—. USDA-CSRS grantee, 1986—. Mem. Am. Soc. Animal Sci., Am. Soc. Nutritional Scis., KC, Sigma Xi, Gamma Sigma Delta. Roman Catholic. Achievements include discovery of usefulness of maternal diabetes in developing fetal pigs; patent in demonstrating the beneficial effects of purslane plant in lowering plasma cholesterol and triglycerides. Office: Alcorn State U Box 1374 1000 Alcorn State U Dr Lorman MS 39096-9400 E-mail: ezekwe@lorman.alcorn.edu.

EZELL, MARGARET J. language educator; John Paul Abbott prof. of liberal arts Tex. A&M U., College Sta., 1997—; dir. Rsch. Inst. Inner Asian Studies. Author: The Patriarch's Wife: Literary Evidence and the History of the Family, Writing Women's Literary History, Social Authorship and the Advent of Print; editor: (series) Women Writers in English, 1350-1830. Fellow, John Simon Guggenheim Meml. Found., 2003. Office: Tex A&M U Dept English 243D Blocker Bldg (MS 4227) College Station TX 77843*

EZELL-GRIM, ANNETTE SCHRAM, business management educator, academic administrator; b. West Frankfort, Ill., June 19, 1940; d. Woodrwo C. and Rosa (Franich) Schram; m. John R. Grim III; children: Michael L., Rona Maria. BS, U. Nev., 1962, MS in Physiology, 1967, postgrad., 1969; EdD in Pub. Adminstrn., Brigham Young U., 1977. Mem. staff Washoe Med. Ctr., Reno, Nev., 1962; tchg. asst. U. Nev., Reno, 1962-63, instr., 1963-64, 65-67, asst. prof., 1967-71; curriculum specialist U. Nev. Med. Sch., 1971-72; project mgr. Fed. Grant Intercampus Edn. Project, 1969-71; assoc. prof., curriculum specialist rural practitioner program, 1971-73; staff assoc. Mountain States Regional Med. Program, 1974-75; cons. Nev. Dept. Edn., 1975-77; asst. dean acad. affairs U. Utah, Salt Lake City, 1977-80, acting dean, 1981, dir., prof. doctoral program Edn. Adminstrn.; prof., dept. head Coll. Human Devel. Pa. State U., 1982-85; dean Coll. Profl. Studies, prof. bus. adminstrn. U. So. Colo., Pueblo, 1985-87; sr. asst. to pres. Towson State U., Balt., 1987-94, assoc. prof. mgmt. sch. bus., 1994-95; assoc. dean prof. bus. mgmt. Wor Wic C.C., Salisbury, Md., 1995—. Cons. higher edn., TV edn., research methology; adviser to various research, polit. and ednl. bds. Mem. Am. Edn. Rsch. Assn., AAAS, Am. Acad. Arts and Scis., AAUP, Am. Coun. on Edn., Am. Assn. Higher Edn., Soc. for Coll. & Univ. Planning, Decision Scis. Inst., Sigma Xi, Phi Kappa Phi, Delta Kappa Gamma. Office: Wor Wic CC 32000 Campus Dr Salisbury MD 21804-1485

FABER, KATHERINE THERESA, materials science educator; b. Buffalo, N.Y., June 19, 1953; d. Robert George and Agnes Mary (Mahoney) F.; m. Thomas Felix Rosenbaum, Nov. 7, 1987; children: Daniel, Michael. BS in Ceramic Engring., Alfred U., 1975; MS in Ceramic Sci., Pa. State U., 1978; PhD in Materials Sci. and Engring., U. Calif., Berkeley, 1982. Invited summer employee Lawrence Livermore (Calif.) Lab, 1975, 76; devel. assoc. The Carborundum Co., Niagara Falls, N.Y., 1978-79; asst. prof. ceramic engring. Ohio State U., Columbus, 1982-85, assoc. prof. ceramic engring., 1985-87; assoc. prof. materials sci. and engring. Northwestern U., Evanston, Ill., 1988-92, assoc. dean rsch. and grad. studies, 1992-97, prof. materials sci. and engring., 1992—, chmn. materials sci. and engring., 1998—2003. Mem. rsch. coordination coun. Gas Rsch. Inst., Chgo., 1991-97; bd. trustees Alfred (N.Y.) U., 1989-92; bd. mem. Northwestern U. Evanston Research Park Bd., 1996—. Editor: Semiconductors and Semimetals, vol. 37, 1992; contbr. articles to scientific jours., including Jour. Am. Ceramic Soc., Jour. Applied Physics, Jour. Materials Rsch., Acta Materialia, Jour. Materials Sci., Scripta Metallurgica. Named Presdl. Young Investigator NSF, 1984, Academician Acad. Ceramics, Faenza, Italy, 1996; recipient YWCA Outstanding Achievement award in edn., 1997, Creativity Extension award NSF, 2001-2003. Fellow ASM Internat., Am. Ceramic Soc. (v.p. 1992-93, 94-95); mem. Am. Soc. Engring. Edn. (AT&T Found. award 1986), Soc. Women Engrs. (sr.; Disting. Engring. Educator 1995), Sigma Xi.

FABICK, MARY MARIE, medical and surgical and emergency nurse, educator; b. Mexico, Mo., Oct. 19, 1954; d. Rodney Rockwell and Margaret Helen (Blevins) Wylde; m. Douglas Alan Fabick, June 28, 1980; children: Kimberly Michelle, Kristen Marie. Diploma in nursing, Burge Sch. Nursing, 1979; BSN, S.W. Mo. State U., 1981; MEd, Drury Coll., 1985; MSN, Bellarmine Coll., 1993. Cert. CEN; cert. BCLS instr. Am. Heart Assn., 1982-88, 90-92; cert. ACLS instr. Am. Heart Assn., 1983-88. Staff nurse emergency trauma ctr. St. John's Regional Health Ctr., Springfield, Mo., 1979-81, asst. charge nurse emergency trauma ctr., 1981; faculty Burge Sch. Nursing, Lester E. Cox Med. Ctr., Springfield, 1981-84; staff nurse emergency and trauma ctr. Lester E. Cox Med. Ctr., Springfield, 1984-85, shift supr. emergency and trauma ctr., 1985, 86-87, interium adminstrv. dir. emergency and trauma ctr., 1985-86; staff nurse Humana Hosp. Audubon, Louisville, 1988, nurse mgr., 1988-90; asst. prof. Bellarmine Coll. Lansing Sch., Louisville, 1990-95; asst. prof. dept. nursing Milligan Coll., Tenn., 1996—2001, assoc. prof., 2001—. Asst. instr. emergency med. technicians Emergency Med. Svcs., Springfield, 1983; mem. steering com. S.W. Mo. State U. Nursing Honor Soc., Springfield, 1983, v.p., 1983-84; cons. Oldham County Pub. Sch., Goshen, Ky., 1991-92; ; NCLEX-RN review classes KAPLAN, Louiseville, Ky., 1991-95; faculty advisor Lambda Psi chpt. Sigma Theta Tau Internat. Honor Soc., 1991-95; NCLEX-RN review classes MEDS Pub., 1996—; parish nurse Preston Hills Presbyn. Ch., Kingsport, Tenn., 2000—; presenter in field. Social chmn. Drury Coll. Student Coun., Springfield, 1982-83, v.p., 1983-84; assoc. advisor Med. Explorer Post, Springfield, 1983-87; troop leader Girl Scouts Am., Crestwood, Ky., 1989-95. With USN, 1973-79. Mem. ANA, Ky. Nurses Assn., Emergency Nurses Assn., Sigma Theta Tau. Presbyterian. Avocations: softball, cake decorating, gardening, camping, birdwatching. Home: 4617 Sterling Ln Kingsport TN 37664-4925 Office: Milligan Coll 305 Hardin Hall PO Box 500 Milligan College TN 37682-0500

FABRICANT, MONA, mathematics and computer science educator; b. N.Y.C., Apr. 22, 1946; BA, Queens Coll., N.Y.C., 1966; MA, Queens Coll., 1967; EdD, Rutgers U., 1974. Editor Harcourt Brace Jovanovich, N.Y.C., 1970-72; asst. prof. math. LaGuardia C.C., Long Island City, N.Y., 1972-74; freelance author and editor, 1974-82; asst. prof. dept. math. and computer sci. Queensborough C.C., Bayside, N.Y., 1982-87, assoc. prof., 1987-90, prof., 1990—, chair dept. math. and computer sci., 1993—2002. Author: Algebra 2 with Trigonometry, 1990, Advanced Mathematics: A Precalculus Approach, 1993 (TAA Excellence award 1994); author articles. Mem. Nat. Coun. Tchrs. Math., N.Y. State Math. Assn. Two-Yr. Colls. (award for outstanding contbns. to math. edn. 1992), Math. Assn. Am. (vice chair for two-yr. colls. N.Y. Met. Region 1987-89, Disting. Coll. or Univ. Teaching Math. award 1997), Phi Beta Kappa, Kappa Delta Pi. Office: Queensborough CC 56th Ave & Springfield Blvd Bayside NY 11364 E-mail: mfabricant@qcc.cuny.edu.

FABRIZIO, LOUIS MICHAEL, computer scientist, educator; b. N.Y.C., Feb. 3, 1952; s. Fiore and Concetta (Del Bove) F.; m. Betsy Jo Jackson, Apr. 9, 1977 (div. Aug. 1984); 1 child, Erin; m. Katherine Kilburn, Nov. 21, 1987; children: Clair, Maria. BS in Physics, Georgetown U., 1974; MS in Edn. Adminstrn., N.C. State U., 1979. Tchr. math. and sci. Kalorama Children's Program, Washington, 1974; Head Start edn. dir. Wake County Opportunities, Inc., Raleigh, N.C., 1975, dir. head start, 1975-77; edn. cons. N.C. Dept. of Pub. Instruction, Raleigh, 1978, evaluation cons., 1979-81, CTB McGraw-Hill, Monterey, Calif., 1982-88, sr. evaluation cons., 1990-92; nat. evaluation cons., instr. software cons. CTB Macmillan/McGraw-Hill, Monterey, 1993; nat. assessment cons. CTB/McGraw-Hill, Monterey, Calif., 1994-96; dir. divsn. accountability svcs. N.C. Dept. Pub. Instrn., Raleigh, 1996—. Fellow Edn. Policy Fellowship Program, Washington, 1979. Active Dem. Nat. Com., N.C., 1988—, N.C. Dem. Com., 1990—. Mem. ASCD, Coun. for Basic Edn., Am. Ednl. Rsch. Assn., N.C. Assn. for Rsch. Edn. (sec. 1984-87, pres. 1988), Georgetown U. Alumni Assn. (chmn. admissions com. ea. N.C. 1985-89), Phi Delta Kappa (bd. dirs. 1985-89, historian 1999-01, Svc. Key 1990). Avocations: music, reading, sports, travel. Home: 1719 Park Dr Raleigh NC 27605-1610 Office: 301 N Wilmington St Raleigh NC 27601-2825 E-mail: Lfabrizi@dpi.state.nc.us., Lfabrizio@aol.com.

FACCIANO, PAULINE ROSE, education educator; b. Burbank, California, Aug. 31, 1959; d. Joseph John and Blanca Rosa (Portuguez) F. AB, U. Calif., Berkeley, 1985, MA, 1999. Fellow NEA, Washington, 1987. Adj. prof. English lit., Menlo Coll., Atherton, Calif., 2000—. Democrat. E-mail: pfacciano@juno.com.

FACELLI, JULIO CESAR, physics researcher, university administrator; b. Buenos Aires, Feb. 9, 1953; came to U.S., 1983; s. Julio César and Elva Nelida (Morato) F.; m. Ana Maria Elena Ferreyro, Oct. 18, 1980; children: Julie Anna, Maria Elizabeth. Licenciado in Physics, U. Buenos Aires, 1977, PhD, 1981. Undergrad. asst. dept. physics U. Buenos Aires, 1976, grad. asst. dept. physics, 1977-82; dir. Instituto de Fisica de la Atmósfera Servicio Meteorologico Nacional, Buenos Aires, 1979; rsch. assoc. dept. chemistry U. Ariz., Tucson, 1983, U. Utah, Salt Lake City, 1984-86, rsch. asst. prof. dept. chemistry, 1986-90, assoc. dir. acad. supercomputing Utah Supercomputing Inst., 1989-95, acting dir. Utah Supercomputing Inst., 1992-95, dir. Ctr. for High Performance Computing, 1995—, adj. prof. chemistry, 1996—. Rsch. prof. physics, 1996-2001, adj. prof. physics, 2001—, adj. prof. med. informatics, 2002—; assoc. prof. ad honorem dept. physics, U. Buenos Aires, 1987—, vis. prof., 1992; adj. assoc. prof. dept. chemistry, U. Utah, Salt Lake City, 1990-96; reviewer Jour. Am. Chem. Soc., Jour. Phys. Chemistry, Chem. Revs., Jour. Computational Chemistry, Theoretica Chimica Acta, Magnetic Resonance in Chemistry (mem. editl. bd. Computer Applications in Engring. Edn.); invited spkr. various univs., rsch. ctrs. and confs.; steering com. Supercomputing by Univ. People for Edn. and Rsch., 1989-92, chmn., 1990-91; insts. and confs. adv. bd. U. Utah; mem. steering com. SUP'EUR European user's group, 1990-91, SC 98; libr. and data comm. com., Utah Edn. Network, 1993-2000. Contbr. numerous articles in sci. jours. 1st lt. Argentinian Air Force, 1978-80. Mem. Am. Chem. Soc., IEEE (Computer Soc.). Roman Catholic. Avocations: running, gardening, swimming. Home: 1847 S 2600 E Salt Lake City UT 84108-3369 Office: Ctr for High Performance Computing Univ Utah 155 S 1452 E Rm 405 Salt Lake City UT 84112-0190

FADELEY, ELEANOR ADELINE, secondary education educator; b. Phila., Aug. 30, 1924; d. Nicholas William and Eleonora (Miceli) Battafarano; m. Herbert John Fadeley, Jr., Feb. 8, 1947; children: Herbert John, Brett Duane, Theresa Jane, Scott Lewis. BS, Drexel U., 1946; postgrad. Sch. Law, Temple U., 1949-51. Exec. trainee Lit Bros., Phila., 1946-47; sec. Hyde-Rakestraw, cotton yarn brokers, Phila., 1947-48; lab. asst. pub. rels. rep. Indsl. By Products & Rsch. Corp., Phila., 1948-51; tchr. Atlantic City Friends Sch., 1957-58; subs. tchr. Troy (N.Y.) Pub. Schs., 1970-71, 78-86; curriculum chmn. Friends of W. Kenneth Doyle Mid. Sch., Troy, 1977-78; English and sci. asst. Troy Pub. Schs., 1976-77. Legis. chmn. Samaritan Hosp. Aux., 1975-78, v.p., 1978-79; bd. dirs. Rensselaer County Am. Cancer Soc., 1980-83; chmn. Town of Brunswick Residential Crusade, 1982; vol. Bellevue Maternity Hosp., Niskayuna, N.Y. Mem. AAUW (mem. chmn., sec.-treas. Ea. area interbr. coun. 1981-82, vice-chmn. 1982-83, pres. Troy br. 1979), Home Econs. Legis. Monitors, Drexel Alumnae Assn., St. Johns Altar Guild, N.Y. State Gen. Fedn. Women's Clubs (Rensselaer County chmn. 1980-82, internat. chmn. 3d dist., scholarship chmn. 3rd dist. 1994-2002, 3rd dist. nominating com.), Embroiders' Guild Am. Inc. (N.Y. capital dist. chpt.), Panhellenic Alumnae Assn. Schenectady, Panhellenic Garden Club (pres. 1983-84, sec.-treas. 1990-91, v.p. 1994-95), Troy Woman's Club (pres. 1976-78, v.p. 1982-83, 96-98, bd. dirs. 1993-95, 99-2001, 2003—, vol. Stories Offer Activity Read 1993-95, mem. permanent funds bd. 1995-98, chmn. ann. luncheon 1998-2002, bd. dirs. 1993-95, 99-2001, 2003—), Alpha Sigma Alpha (life). Republican. Episcopalian. Home: 150 Tallmadge Pl Albany NY 12208-1086

FADELY, JAMES PHILIP, public relations executive, educator, writer; b. New Castle, Ind., Jan. 10, 1953; s. Harry Ellison and Viola (Clapp) F.; m. Sally Jane Fehsenfeld, Aug. 16, 1975; children: James Philip Jr., Adele Langsdale. BA, Hanover Coll., 1975; MA, Ind. U., 1977, PhD, 1990. Tchr. Brookstone Sch., Columbus, Ga., 1975-76, Savannah (Ga.) Country Day Sch., 1979-83; lectr. Ind. U., Indpls., 1984—; tchr., asst. headmaster St. Richard's Sch., Indpls., 1988-90, tchr., 1990-91, dir. admission and fin. aid, tchr., 1991-2000; dir. mktg./pub. rels., history tchr., dir. coll. counseling Univ. H.S., 2000—. Nat. bd. dirs. English-Speaking Union, 1997—, exec. com., 1998-2001, pres. Indpls. br., 2002—; v.p. Ind. Libr. and Hist. Bd., 1997—; lectr. Butler U., 1985, U. Indpls., 1995. Author: A Brief History of St. Richard's School, 1960-1995, 1995, Thomas Taggart: Public Servant, Political Boss, 1856-1929, 1997, The Origins of Woodstock Club, 1997; contbr. articles to profl. jours. Dem. nominee 6th Dist. of Ind. for Congress, 1990; friend Woodrow Wilson House. Mem.: Friends of Hist. Deerfield, Hist. Madison, Nat. Assn. Coll. Admission Counseling, Ind. Hist. Soc. (grant 1991—94), Ind. Assn. Historians, Hist. Landmarks Found. Ind., Nat. Coun. for History Edn., Am. Hist. Assn., Lanier Mansion Found., Soc. Ind. Pioneers (bd. govs. 2001—), Hanover Coll. Alumni Assn. (bd. dirs. 1985—88), Marion County Hist. Soc., Nat. Trust for Hist. Preservation, Leelanau Hist. Soc., Woodstock Club, Hanover Club Indpls. (bd. dirs. 1988—96), Indpls. Lit. Club, Leland (Mich.) Yacht Club, Phi Delta Theta. Democrat. Roman Catholic. Avocation: travel. Home: 9146 N Kenwood Dr Indianapolis IN 46260-1400 Office: Univ HS 2825 W 116th St Carmel IN 46032 E-mail: fadely@worldnet.att.net.

FADERMAN, LILLIAN, adult education educator; b. Bronx, N.Y., July 18, 1940; d. Mary Lifton; life ptnr. Phyllis Irwin; 1 child, Avrom. BA, U. Calif., Berkeley, 1962; MA, UCLA, 1964, PhD, 1967. Prof. Calif. State U., Fresno, 1967—. Vis. prof. UCLA, 1989—91. Author: (book) Surpassing the Love of Men, 1981, Scotch Verdict, 1983, Odd Girls and Twilight Lovers, 1991, Chloe Plus Olivia, 1994, To Believe in Women, 1999, Naked in the Promise Land, 2003. Recipient Best Lesbian/Gay Book award, ALA, 1981, 1991, Lambda Lit. award, 1991, 1994, 1999, Paul Monette award, 1999, James Brudner award, Yale U., 2001, Disting. Sr. Scholar award, AAUW, 2002. Office: Calif State U Cedar & Shaw Fresno CA 93740-0001 E-mail: lillian_faderman@csufresno.edu.

FAFOGLIA, BARBARA ANN, school administrator; b. Springfield, Ill., Feb. 16, 1951; d. Robert Frank and Nina Marie (Hashman) Wanless; 1 child, Erin Elizabeth. BA in Edn., So. Ill. U.; MA in Health Edn. Adminstrn., U. Ill. Cert. tchr., Ill.; cert. relapse prevention specialist. Tchr. English/lang. arts Ball-Chatham (Ill.) Unit Dist. #5, 1974-85; ednl. cons. Ctrl. Ill. Day Care Providers Assn., Springfield, 1985-88; communications specialist Ill. Prevention Resource Ctr., Springfield, 1985-90; consulting writer, editor So. Ill. U. Sch. of Medicine, Springfield, 1985-90; drug-free programs coord. Springfield Pub. Schs. Dist. 186, 1990—. Mem. NEA, ACA, ASCD, Ill. Edn. Assn., Nat. Coun. Tchrs. English, Nat. Soc. DAR, Am. Guidance Svc. (book reviewer), Ill. Alcoholism and Drug Dependence Assn., Nat. Prevention Coalition, nat. Prevention Network, Springfield Youth Network, Am. Counseling Assn., Ill. Assn. Student Assistance Profls., Nat. Assn. Leadership for Student Assistance Programs, Am. Guidance Svc.(book reviewer), Kappa Delta Pi Internat. Honor Soc.

FAGER, JENNIFER JEANNE, education educator; b. Lincoln, Nebr., Feb. 4, 1961; d. Howard Dee Fager and Jeanne Lorraine Dobbs Drevo. BA in Polit. Sci., U. Nebr., 1983, MA in Curriculum and Instrn., 1988, PhD in Adminstrn., Curriculum & Instrn., 1992. Asst. prof. S.D. State U., Brookings, 1992-94, U. N.H., Manchester, 1994-95, Western Mich. U., Kalamazoo, 1995—. Cons. in field. Mem. Am. Ednl. Rsch. Assn., Midwestern Ednl. Rsch. Assn. (assn. coun., divsn. chair), Nat. Coun. on Measurement in Edn. Methodist. Office: Coll Edn Dept Edn and Profl Devel Western Mich Univ Kalamazoo MI 49008-5192

FAGERSTEN, BARBARA JEANNE, special education educator; b. San Francisco, Feb. 29, 1924; d. Ernest Mauritz and Louise (Hopkins) F.; m. Harold Gurish, Feb. 7, 1950 (div. 1970); children: Michael, Matthew, Jonathon. BA, San Francisco State U., 1951; MS, Dominican U., 1973, degree in spl. edn., 1975; degree in adminstrn. and supervision, 1976, degree in community coll. instruction, 1981. Personnel sec. Arabian Am. Oil Co., San Francisco, 1944-45; union sec. Jeweler's Union, San Francisco, 1946-48; med. sec. Mt. Zion Hosp., San Francisco, 1949-50; spl. edn. tchr. Marin Office Edn., San Rafael, Calif., 1967-92. Bd. dirs. DeWitt Learning Ctr., San Rafael, 1969. Bd. dirs. Marin Tchrs. Credit Union, San Rafael, 1978-93, Marinwood Cmty. Svcs., San Rafael, 1986-87; commr. Parks and Recreation Marinwood, San Rafael, 1983-86. Mem. Calif. Assn. Neurol. Handicapped Children (trustee 1973-74). Democrat. Avocations: opera, symphony, theater, painting, writing. Home: 272 Blackstone Dr San Rafael CA 94903-1508

FAHERTY, PATRICIA BERNADETTE, secondary education educator; b. N.Y.C., Jan. 8, 1938; d. Michael Francis and Beatrice (McGovern) F. BS in Edn., Fordham U., 1964; MA in English, St. John's U., Jamaica, N.Y., 1978. Cert. tchr. K-6, English and social studies 7-12, N.Y. Elem. sch. tchr. Various Schs. in N.Y.C., 1950-64; tchr. Elem. Jr. High Sch., Houma, New Orleans, La., 1964-69, Hicksville (N.Y.) Jr. High Sch., 1970-86, Hicksville Sr. High Sch., 1986—. Author Curriculums for Drama, 1980's, Gifted and Talented, 1980's, for Aids Edn., 1992. Mem. Hicksville Congress of Tchrs. (negotiatior 1989,'92, conv. del., sec., 1990—). Roman Catholic. Avocations: hiking, nature appreciation, reading.

FAHLBERG, SHEREE LYNN, special education educator; b. Moline, Ill., July 31, 1955; d. Richard Paul and Shirley Rae (Anderson) Rosenberg; m. Mark Randolph Fahlberg, Oct. 11, 1975; children: Zach, Todd. AA, Black Hawk Coll., 1975; BS, So. Ill. U., 1978. Cert. K-12 tchr., Ill., emotional disorders, lng. disabilities, educable mentally handicap K-12, Ill. Phys. edn. tchr., coach Egyptian Unit Sch., Tamms, Ill., 1980; substitute tchr. various schs., Ill., 1978-84; adaptive phys. edn. tchr., coach Tri-County Edn. Ctr., Anna, Ill., 1985-87; tchr. learning disabilities resource, phys. edn., coach Anna-Jonesboro Cmty. H.S., 1988-92; 7-8th grade learning disabilities tchr. Cairo (Ill.) Jr. H.S., 1992-93; spl. edn. tchr. Goreville (Ill.) Unit Sch., 1993-94; spl. edn. resource tchr. Carbondale (Ill.) Cmty. H.S., 1994—. Phys. edn., health, spl. edn. tchr., coach Anna Jr. H.S., 1983-84; GED instr. Shawnee Cmty. Coll., Ullin, Ill., 1984-87; cons. adaptive phys. edn. rehab. svcs. Alton (Ill.) Mental Health and Devel. Ctr., 1987; cooperating tchr. student svcs. So. Ill. U. Coll. Edn., 1996—. Assst. cub scout master Boy Scouts Am., Anna, 1991-92; youth soccer coach, 1997-98. Mem. Phi Theta Kappa. Avocations: travel, hiking, camping, swimming, weight training. Home: 4185 Boyd Rd Anna IL 62906-3750

FAHN, STANLEY, neurologist, educator; b. Sacramento, Nov. 6, 1933; s. Ernest and Sylvia F.; m. Charlotte, June 21, 1958; children: Paul N., James D. BA, U. Calif.-Berkeley, 1955, MD, 1958. Diplomate Am. Bd. Neurology. Resident in neurology Neurol. Inst., N.Y., 1959-62; rsch. assoc. NIH, 1962-65; mem. faculty Columbia U., N.Y.C., 1965-68, prof. neurology, 1973-78, H. Houston Merritt prof., 1978—, dir. Morris K. Udall Parkinson Disease Rsch. Ctr., 1999—2003; mem. faculty U. Pa., Phila., 1968-73. Dir. Dystonia Rsch. Ctr., 1981-97; sci. dir. Parkinson's Disease Found., 1979—; chmn. adv. com. peripheral and ctrl. nervous sys. drugs FDA, 1987-89, 91-96. Editor Movement Disorders, 1985-95; assoc. editor Neurology, 1977-87. With USPHS, 1962-65 Grantee NIH, 1974—77, 1980—82, 1984—91, 1994—. Mem.: Inst. of Medicine, Dystonia Med. Rsch. Found. (hon. life, bd. dirs. 1998—), Movement Disorder Soc. (pres. 1988—91), Am. Neurol. Assn. (v.p. 1987—88, chair jour. oversight com. 1994—96), Am. Acad. Neurology (chair edn. com. 1986—93, v.p. 1993—97, pres.-elect 1999—2001, pres. 2001—03). Home: 155 Edgars Ln Hastings On Hudson NY 10706-1107 Office: 710 W 168th St New York NY 10032-2603

FAHRLANDER, PHILLIP RAYMOND, retired secondary school educator, music educator; b. Brule, Nebr., Dec. 20, 1934; s. Raymond Frank and Freda Louisa (Ulrich) F.; m. Ruth Nadine Adcock, July 26, 1959; children: Eric, Jeff. AB in Edn., Peru State Coll., 1959; MS in Edn., Kearney State Coll., 1968. Dir. music Diller (Nebr.) Pub. Schs., 1959-64, North Loup-Scotia (Nebr.) Schs., 1964-68; dir. bands Minden (Nebr.) Pub. Schs., 1968—97; ret., 1997. Author: (workbook) N. Spires Creativity Machine, 1992; columnist Nebr. Music Educator, 1986—; artist cover design and logos Nebr. State Bandmasters Assn., 1984—, Nebr. Music Educator, 1986—. Dir. bands Minden Pub. Schs., 1968-97; choir master, various coms. Meth. Ch., Minden, 1969—; program coord. Minden Opera House, 1999-2000. Recipient Excellence in Tchg. award Cooper Found., 1987, Outstanding Educator award Minden Area Jaycees, 1968. Mem. NEA, Nebr. Bandmasters Assn. (pres. 1991-93), Minden Edn. Assn. (pres. 1990), Nebr. State Bandmasters Assn. (pres. elect., pres. 1990-93, Don Lentz Outstanding Band Dir. award 1997), Nebr. Music Educators Assn. (chair band affairs 1985-86, Disting. Svc. award 1994), Music Educators Nat. Conf., Minden C. of C. (coord. bandfest marching contest 1990—). Democrat. Avocations: writing, art, antique autos. E-mail: pf80353@navix.net.

FAIGNANT, JOHN PAUL, lawyer, educator; b. Proctor, Vt., Mar. 24, 1953; s. Joseph Paul and Ann (DeBlasio) F.; children: Janelle, Melissa. BA, U. New Haven, 1974; JD, George Mason U., 1978. Bar: Va. 1978, Vt. 1979, U.S. Dist. Ct. Vt. 1979, U.S. Ct. Appeals (4th cir.) 1979, U.S. Supreme Ct. 1992. Assoc. Griffin & Griffin, Rutland, Vt., 1978-79, Miller, Norton & Cleary, Rutland, 1979-84, ptnr., 1984-87, Miller, Cleary and Faignant PC, Rutland, 1988-91, Miller & Faignant, Ltd., Rutland, 1991-97, Miller Faignant & Whelton PC (now Miller Faignant & Behrens), Rutland, 1997—. Adj. prof. Coll. St. Joseph, Rutland, 1982-90. Mem. Rutland Town Fire Dept., 1989—; mem., pres. No. New England Def. Counsel, 1995-96. Mem. Va. Bar Assn., Vt. Bar Assn., Assn. Trial Lawyers Am., Def. Rsch. Inst., Am. Bd. Trial Advocates. Roman Catholic. Avocation: antique trucks. Home: RR 1 Box 3762 Rutland VT 05701-9214 Office: Miller Faignant & Behrens PC 36 Merchants Row PO Box 6688 Rutland VT 05702-6688

FAILINGER, MARIE ANITA, law educator, editor; b. Battle Creek, Mich., June 29, 1952; d. Conard Frederick and Joan Anita (Lang) F.; children: Joanna, Kristina. BA, Valparaiso U., 1973, JD, 1976; LLM, Yale U., 1983; postgrad., U. Chgo., 1990. Bar: Ind. 1976, U.S. Dist. Ct. (no. dist.) Ind. 1976, U.S. Dist. Ct. (so. dist.) Ind. 1977, U.S. Ct. Appeals (7th cir.) 1979, Minn. 1984, U.S. Supreme Ct. 1980. Prof. of law Hamline U., St. Paul, 1983—, assoc. dean, 1990-93. Editor: Jour. of Law and Religion, 1988—; contbr. articles, book revs. to profl. publs. Treas. Am. Indian Policy Ctr., 1993—; sec. Church Innovations Inst.; treas. Luth. Innovations. Mem. Minn. Women Lawyers (bd. dirs. 1989-90), Am. Assn. Law Schs. (chair poverty sect. 1984-88, exec. com. law and religion sect.), Ctrl. Minn. Legal Svcs. Bd., Nat. Equal Justice Libr. (bd. dirs. 1989—). Democrat. Mem. Evang. Luth. Ch. Am. Office: Hamline U Sch Law 1536 Hewitt Ave Saint Paul MN 55104-1284

FAILLA, SOPHIA LYNN, artist, educator; b. Bronx, Oct. 23, 1928; d. Joseph John and Lucy (Iaia) F.; divorced; 1 child, Lynn. Student, Brevard C.C., 1968-75. Asst. designer Vogue Patterns/Conde Nast, Old Greenwich, Conn., 1948-51; owner The Sewing Box, Darien, Conn., 1953-55; draftsman C.B.F., Stamford, Conn., 1957-58; outreach tchr. Brevard (Fla.) C.C., 1969-75; missionary, founder Honduran Christian Crafts, Honduras, 1975-79; owner, founder Fashions of Love, Lompoc, Calif., 1983-89; artist, tchr. Especially for You Gallery, Melbourne, Fla., 1989—. Founder Amigos de Jesus. Recipient Excellence award Manhattan Art Internat., cert. of merit Stockholm Internat. Art Show, 1st prize Internat. Art League, 1998; winner 1998 Internat. Art competition (pub. in Art Times). Mem. AAUW, Nat. Mus. Women in Arts. Avocations: teaching, painting, travel, black choir music. Studio: Especially for You Gallery 909 E New Haven Ave # 5-67 Melbourne FL 32901-5478

FAIN, JOHN NICHOLAS, biochemistry educator; b. Jefferson City, Tenn., Aug. 18, 1934; s. Samuel Clark and Virginia Manson (Hunt) F.; m. Ann Duff, June 7, 1958; children: Margaret Ann, John Nicholas Jr., James Clark. BS magna cum laude, Carson-Newman Coll., 1956; PhD in Biochemistry, Emory U., 1960. Rsch. assoc. Emory U., Atlanta, 1960-61; NSF fellow NIH, Bethesda, Md., 1961-62, postdoctoral fellow USPHS, 1962-63; biochemist NIH and Nat. Inst. Arthritis and Metabolic Diseases, Bethesda, 1963-65; asst. prof. Brown U., Providence, 1965-68, assoc. prof., 1968-71, prof., 1971-85, chmn. biochemistry, 1975-85; Van Vleet prof., dept. chmn. U. Tenn., Memphis, 1985-2000, Van Vleet prof. of molecular scis., 2000—. Contbr. numerous articles to sci. jours. Del. gen. assembly United Presbyn. Ch., Providence, 1972. Recipient Disting. Alumnus award Carson-Newman Coll., 1986; fellow Cambridge U., 1977-78; NIH Fogarty fellow, 1984-85; Macy Faculty scholar, 1977-78. Mem. Am. Soc. Biol. Chemists. Democrat. Office: U Tenn Health Scis Ctr Coll Medicine Dept Mol Scis 858 Madison Ste GO1 Memphis TN 38163 Fax: 901-448-7360. E-mail: jfain@utmem.edu.

FAINSTEIN, NORMAN, college president; m. Susan Fainstein; 2 children. BS with highest honors, MIT, 1966, PhD with highest distinction, 1971. Prof., dep. chair undergrad. programs in gen. studies, dir. summer session dept. sociology Columbia U., N.Y.C., 1971—76; prof., assoc. dean acad. affairs Grad. Sch. Mgmt. and Urban Professions New Sch. for Social Rsch., N.Y.C., 1983—87; prof., dean Sch. Liberal Arts and Scis. Baruch Coll. CUNY, 1987—95; prof., dean of faculty Vassar Coll., Poughkeepsie, NY, 1996—2001; pres. Conn. Coll., New London, 2001—. Author: 4 books; contbr. numerous articles to profl. jours. Active Poughkeepsie Inst., Andrew W. Mellon Found. Fellow Woodrow Wilson, NSF, Stouffer, Harvard-MIT Joint Ctr. for Urban Studies. Office: Conn Coll 270 Mohegan Ave New London CT 06320

FAIR, DARLENE ANN, school system administrator; b. July 11, 1948; Postgrad., Centenary Coll.; BS, Nicholls State U., Thibodeaux, La., 1970; M in Edn., Centenary Coll, Shreveport, La., 1982, M plus 30, 1984. Tchr. 2d grade South Highlands Elem. Sch., Eden Gardens Elem. Sch., Shreveport, 1975-98; reading specialist Centenary Coll., Shreveport, 1982, supr.

student tchrs., 1984, 2001; sch. coord. South Highlands Elem. Magnet Sch., Shreveport, 1999—. Cons. in field. Royalty chair, treas., bd. dirs. Krewe of Centaur, 1994-99, Queen Centaur V, 1996; usher and box officer helper Shreveport Little Theatre, Marjorie Lyons theatre, Gas Light Players, 1980—; co-dir. Artbreak Talent Show, 1996-2000. 8G Block grantee La. Dept. Edn., 1995, 96, 97, 2000, 01, 02, 03. Mem. Krewe Femmes Mystique, Krewe Justinian, Beta Sigma Phi, Alpha Delta Kappa (pres. 1994). Home: 630 Huron St Shreveport LA 71106-1652

FAIR, HARRY DAVID, academic administrator, physicist; b. Indiana, Pa., Dec. 2, 1936; s. Harry Dale and Ruth Roxanne (Crawford) F.; m. Isabelle Cadwallader (div. 1985); children: David Eric, Martin Crawford, Courtney Tyler; m. Nancy Jo Shiro, Dec. 19, 1986; 1 child, Katie Anne. BS, Indiana U. Pa., 1958; MS, U. Del., 1960, PhD, 1966. Rsch. physicist Picatinny Arsenal, Dover, N.J., 1960-67, chief energy conversion sect., 1967-70, chief solid state physics br., 1970-73, chief solid state physics and chemistry br., 1973-75, chief Energetic Materials Lab., 1976-76, chief Propulsion Tech. Lab., 1977-81; dir. land warfare div. Def. Advanced Rsch. Projects Agy., Washington, 1981-85; dir. Joint Program Office Def. Advanced Rsch. Projects Agy., U.S. Army, USMC, Washington, 1985-87; dir. Inst. for Advanced Tech., U. Tex., Austin, 1988—. Vis. prof. U. Paris, 1974, Royal Instn. Gt. Britain, 1975. Editor: Physics and Chemistry of Azides, Vols. 1 and II, 1977; also over 100 articles on solid state physics; patentee in field. 1st lt. U.S. Army, 1960-62. Recipient R and D awards U.S. Army, 1972-75, 1st citation for achievement Indiana U. Pa., 1977, Edison medal IEEE, 1982, Founder's award IEEE Electromagnetic Launch Symposium, 1988; fellow Sec. Army, 1974. Mem. AIAA, AAAS, Am. Phys. Soc., Sigma Xi, Sigma Pi Sigma. Home: PO Box 645 Dripping Springs TX 78620-0645 Office: U Tex Austin Inst Advanced Tech Ste 400 3925 W Braker Ln Austin TX 78759-5316

FAIR, JAMES RUTHERFORD, JR., chemical engineering educator, consultant; b. Charleston, Mo., Oct. 14, 1920; s. James Rutherford and Georgia Irene (Case) F.; m. Merle Innis, Jan. 14, 1950; children: James Rutherford III, Elizabeth, Richard Innis. Student, The Citadel, 1938-40; BS, Ga. Inst. Tech., 1942; MS, U. Mich., 1949; PhD, U. Tex., 1955; DSc (hon.), Wash. U., 1977; HHD (hon.), Clemson U., 1987. Rsch. engr. Shell Devel. Co., Emeryville, Calif., 1954-56; with Monsanto Co., 1942-52, 56-79; engring. dir. corp. engring. dept. Monsanto Co. (World hdqrs.), St. Louis, 1969-79; McKetta chair chem. engring. U. Tex., Austin, 1979—. Dir., v.p. Fractionation Research, Inc., Bartlesville, Okla., 1969-79; pres. James R. Fair Inc., 1981—. Author: North Arkansas Line, 1969, Distillation, 1971, Louisiana and Arkansas, 1997, Distillation, 1998; contbr. numerous articles to profl. publs. Recipient profl. achievement award Chemical Engineering mag., 1968, King award U. Tex., 1987. Fellow AIChE (bd. dirs. 1965-67, Walker award 1973, Practice award 1975, Founders award 1977, Inst. lectr. 1979, Separation Tech. award 1994); mem. NSPE, NAE, Am. Chem. Soc. (Separation Sci. and Tech. award 1993), Am. Soc. Engring. Edn., Faculty Club U. Tex., Headliners Club (Austin), Sigma Nu. Republican. Presbyterian. Home: 2804 Northwood Rd Austin TX 78703-1603 Office: U Tex Dept Chem Engring Separations Rsch Progr Austin TX 78712 E-mail: fair@che.utexas.edu.

FAIR, JERALD DUANE, principal; b. Milw., June 30, 1949; s. J.C. Fair and Linnie (Hadley) Pitchford; m. Patsy Ann Gordon, June 15, 1984 (div. Dec. 1990); 1 child, Codrye Duane Fair. BA, Carthage Coll., 1971; MEd, So. U., 1975, JD, 1981. Tchr. Milw. (Wis.) Pub. Schs., 1971-82, asst. prin., 1982-89, prin., 1989—. Active poll place GOP, Baton Rouge, 1983. Fellow Nat. Acad. for Urban Sch. Leaders; mem. Nat. Assn. Secondary Sch. Prins., Assn. Wis. Sch. Adminstrs., Phi Alpha Delta (vice justice 1979-80, justice 1980-81), Omega Psi Phi, Phi Delta Kappa, Prince Hall Masonic Order (apprentice). Republican. Baptist. Avocations: horseback riding, traveling, fishing, reading. Home: 7010 N 55th St Apt B Milwaukee WI 53223-6349 Office: Milw Pub Schs 5225 W Vliet St Milwaukee WI 53208-2627

FAIR, MARY LOUISE, retired elementary school educator; b. Emporia, Kans., July 16, 1931; d. Dale Franklin Fair and Beulah Fair (Emma) Martin. BA, Marymount Coll., 1953. Bus. edn. tchr. Geneseo (Kans.) High Sch., 1953-55, St. John (Kans.) High Sch., 1955-56; sec. YMCA, Salina, Kans., 1956-57; alumna sec. Marymount Coll., Salina, Kans., 1957-58; bus. edn. tchr. Hayden High Sch., Topeka, Kans., 1958-59; sec. Mental Health Assn., Denver, 1959-60; sec., substitute tchr. Denver Pub. Schs., 1960-62, elem. tchr., 1962-86. 1st v.p. AARP, Heather Gardens, Aurora, Colo., 1988-90, pres. 1991, parliamentarian 1994, publication com. 1994—, Heather Gardens Restaurant Comm., 1995—; tutor Aurora and Cherry Creek elem. schs., 1987—. Mem. AAUW (Aurora br., historian 1993-94), Marymount Coll. Alumnae Assn. (pres. 1956-58), Luncheon Optomist Club, Altrusa Club Aurora, Alpha Delta Kappa (state sgt.-at-arms 1982-84, state pres. 1986-88, S.W. regional sgt.-at-arms 1989-91, internat. chmn. living meml. scholarship com. 1991-93, chpt. pres. 1994-96, chpt. pres. coun. (pres. 1994-96). Republican. Baptist. Avocations: travel, reading, embroidery. Home: 3022 S Wheeling Way Apt 311 Aurora CO 80014-5607

FAIRBANKS, MARY JOANNE, educational administrator; b. Dec. 21, 1939; d. James William and Inez (Cappiello) Phillips. A in Bus. Aminstrn., Ctrl. City Bus. Inst., Syracuse, N.Y., 1959; AS in Acctg., LaSalle Ext. U., 1974. Sec. elec. and computer engring. dept. Syracuse U., 1959-65, asst. to adminstrv. asst., 1965-72, publs. mgr. Assembly Univ. Governance, 1970-72, coord. computer confs., 1972-81, supr. asst. to chmn. dept. elec. and computer engring., 1972-78, mgr. Air Force Post-Doctoral Program Rome Air Devel. Ctr., 1972-78, adminstr. Air Force intrasystem analysis program, 1974-78, adminstrv. asst. to chmn. dept. indsl. engring. & ops. rsch., 1978-82, dir. Engring., Computer Sci. Coop. Edn. Program, 1982—. Coord. workshops computer architecture, 1977-79; mgr. electromagentic compatibitliy analysis techniques advancement program, 1978-82. Editor 7 elec. engring. textbooks, 1960-78; co-author: Career Portfolio for Volunteers, 1980, Patterns of Government in Onondaga County, 1981; author: The Road to the Voting Booth, 2 vols., 1986; editor-in-chief: A Guide to New York State Government, 1989; contbr. articles to profl. jours. Mem. scoring team XIII Olympic Winter Games, Lake Placid, N.Y., 1980; alpine ofcl. U.S. Ski Assn., 1980—; mem. career coun. Syracuse U., 1988—; mem. open ho. com. L. C. Smith Coll., 1990—, mem. awards com., 1992—; ednl. coord. Techreach, 1992—; mgr., editor publs. Onondaga County Bicentennial Celebration, 1976. Mem. Am. Soc. Engring. Edn. (chair membership coop. edn. divsn. 1988-91, exec. bd. 1991-93, ann. meeting program chair coop. edn. divsn. 1991, sec., treas. 1993-95, chair-elect 1996, chair 1997, Alvah K. Borman award 1994), Coop. Edn. Assn., Nat. commn. Coop. Edn., Coop. Edn. Network (mem. steering com. 1996—), N.Y. State Coop. and Exptl. Edn. Assn. Office: Syracuse U 367 Link Hl Syracuse NY 13244-0001

FAIRCHILD, JOSEPH VIRGIL, JR., accounting educator; b. New Orleans, Nov. 26, 1933; s. Joseph Virgil and Georgiana Malone (Bourgeois) F.; m. Judith Champagne, Aug. 12, 1961; children: Georgianna, Joseph, Benjamin. BS in Geology, La. State U., 1956, MBA, 1963, PhD, 1975. CPA, La. Geologist United Core, Inc., Houston, 1956-57; assoc. acct. Humble Oil & Refining Co., New Orleans, 1963-64; ptnr. L.A. Champagne & Co., Baton Rouge, 1964-69; pvt. practice acctg. Thibodaux, La., 1969-2000; ret., 2000; asst. prof. acctg. Nicholls State U., Thibodaux, 1969-75, assoc. prof., 1975-76, prof., 1976-84, disting. prof. acctg., 1984—2000, asst. dean Coll. Bus., 1985-86, dir. grad. bus. studies, 1982-85, disting. prof. emeritus, 2002—; prof. acctg. Henderson State U., Arkadelphia, Ark., 2000—. Rsch. reviewer USAF Bus. Rsch. Mgmt. Ctr., Wright-Patterson AFB, Ohio, 1974-84; cons. Def. Sys. Mgmt. Coll., Ft. Belvoir, Va., 1980-81; faculty senate v.p. govt. com., chmn. dean's search com. Author: (with others) The Acquisition and Distribution of Commercial Products, 1980, 1985-86, 1986-87, 1987-88 and 1988-89 Income Tax Guides for State Legislators; contbr. articles to profl. jours.; actor: (TV, movies) The Kingfish-TNT, Orleans-CBS, Deadman Walking; (plays) South Pacific, Arsenic and Old Lace, Brigadoon, Damn Yankees. Mem. St. Genevieve Sch. Bd., Thibodaux, 1979-83, E.D. White Cath. H.S. Bd., 1985-87, chmn. fin. com., 1985-87; lector St. Genevieve Ch., 1975—, choir, 1989—. 1st lt. USAF, 1957-60, lt. col. USAFR ret. Recipient Acad. Excellence award Henderson State U., 2003; Trueblood Prof. Touche-Ross Found., N.Y.C., 1987. Mem. AICPA, Soc. La. CPA's (lectr. seminars, La.'s Outstanding Acctg. Educator 1994), Am. Acctg. Assn., Nat. Assn. Accts., Nicholls State U. Alumni Assn. (Hon. Alumnus award 1991, Case Educator of Yr. 1994). Roman Catholic. Avocations: flying, skiing, photography, fishing. Home: 412 Plater Dr Thibodaux LA 70301-5616 Office: Nicholls State U Dept Acctg Thibodaux LA 70310-0001

FAIRCHILD, PHYLLIS ELAINE, school counselor; b. Franklin, La., Feb. 23, 1927; d. Joseph Virgil and Georgiana (Bourgeois) F. BS in Chemistry and Biology, U. Southwestern La., 1946; postgrad., La. State U., 1949-50, MEd in Guidance, 1966. Cert. chemistry, biology, gen. sci., Spanish and social studies tchr., counselor, La. Tchr. sci. St. Mary Parish Sch. Bd., Franklin, 1952-58, counselor, 1977-82; tchr. sci. Am. Dependent Schs., Yokohama, Japan, 1958-60, London, Lakenheath, Eng., 1960-61, Ramey AFB, PR, 1961-62, Norfolk (Va.) City Schs., 1962-63, Iberville Parish Sch. Bd., Plaquemine, La., 1963-66; tchr. sci., counselor East Baton Rouge Parish Sch. Bd., Baton Rouge, 1966-77; counselor Hanson Sch. Bd., Franklin, 1982-94, 96-98; ret., 1998. Mem. adv. com. La. Dept. Edn., Baton Rouge, 1976, 78. Mem. DAR (regent Attakapas chpt. 2003—), La. Landmarks Soc., Cath. Daugs. Am. (co-chmn. religious litergy 1992-94), Fortnightly Lit. Club (pres. 1982-83), Sigma Delta Pi, Pi Gamma Mu, Kappa Kappa Gamma, Delta Kappa Gamma (chmn. membership, scholarship, profl. affairs 1971-77, parliamentarian 1996-98). Avocations: reading, walking, piano, writing. Home: 214 Morris St Franklin LA 70538-6127

FAIRFIELD-SONN, JAMES WILLED, management educator and consultant; b. Nashua, N.H., Aug. 21, 1948; s. David Alexander and Christine Mary (Fairfield) Sonn; m. Lynn Groark, July 3, 1982; children: Anne Madeline, James Willed, Jr., John Thomas. MS, Cornell U., 1979; MA, Yale U., 1980, MPhil, 1982, PhD, 1985. Mgr. office adminstrn. Hartford Ins. Group, Indpls., 1972-76; asst. prof. mgmt. U. Hartford, West Hartford, Conn., 1982-88, assoc. prof., 1988—2002, prof., 2002—, chmn. mgmt. dept., 1987-90, dir. exec. MBA, 1993-95. Pres. Fairfield-Sonn Assocs., Centerbrook, Conn., 1981—; v.p. bd. dirs. ENCOMPASS Software. Author: Corporate Culture and the Quality Organization, 2001; contbr. articles and revs. to profl. jours. Named Outstanding Tchr. of Yr., Barney Sch., 1999; Cornell U. indsl. and labor rels. fellow, 1977-78, Yale U. fellow, 1978-82, Olin fellow, 1981. Mem.: Assn. Yale Alumni (chmn. grad. and profl. schs. com. 1982—83), Ea. Acad. Mgmt., Acad. Mgmt. Republican. Congregationalist. Avocations: tennis, travel, gardening. Home and Office: PO Box 1047 Old Lyme CT 06371-0998 E-mail: jimfs@fairfield-sonn.net.

FAIRLEIGH, JAMES PARKINSON, music educator; b. St. Joseph, Mo., Aug. 24, 1938; s. William Macdonald and Mable Emily (Parkinson) F.; m. Marlane Alberta Paxson, June 25, 1960; children: William Paxson, Karen Evelyn. MusB, U. Mich., 1960; MusM, U. So. Calif., 1965; PhD, U. Mich., 1973. Instr., asst. prof. Hanover (Ind.) Coll., 1965-75; assoc. prof. R.I. Coll., Providence, 1975-80; prof., head music dept. Jacksonville (Ala.) State U., 1980—2001, prof. emeritus music, 2001—. Dir. of music First Presbyn. Ch., Anniston, Ala., 1981-2001; presenter, lectr. at meetings of profl. orgns., 1974-. Contbr. articles to profl. jours., mags., 1966—. Served to 1st lt. U.S. Army, 1960-62. Mem. Am. Musicol. Soc., Ala. Music Tchrs. Assn. (cert., treas. 1982-86, 1st v.p. 1986-88, pres. 1988-90), Coll. Music Soc. (southern chpt. exec. bd. 1996-98), Music Tchrs. Nat. Assn. (cert.), Assn. Ala. Coll. Music Adminstrs. (sec., treas. 1985-89, pres. 1989-91), Phi Beta Kappa, Phi Kappa Phi, Pi Kappa Lambda, Phi Eta Sigma, Phi Mu Alpha Sinfonia. Republican. Avocations: water-skiing, swimming, backpacking.

FAKE, INGRID CHRISTINE, middle school educator; b. Ashland, Pa., May 28, 1968; d. Klaus Bernd and Diane Adrian (Robbins) Runge; m. Michael William Fake, Aug. 24, 1991,. Kutztown U., 1990. Asst. mgr. Frugal Frank's Shoes, Media, Pa., 1985-86; cashier Burger King, Brookhaven, Pa., 1987-89; recreator Elwyn (Pa.), Inc., 1988-91; art tchr. elem. Kutztown (Pa.) Area Sch. Dist., 1990-91; art tchr. middle sch. Owen J. Roberts Middle Sch., Pottstown, Pa., 1991—; arts and crafts coord. Muhlenberg Twp., Hyde Park, Pa., 1992. Named to Dean's List, Kutztown U., 1986-90. Mem. AAUW, Nat. Art Edn. Assn., Pa. Art Edn. Assn. Lutheran. Avocations: physical fitness, camping, travel, gardening. Home: 912 Tuckerton Rd Reading PA 19605-1084 Office: Owen J Roberts Sch Dist 881 Ridge Rd Pottstown PA 19465-9801

FALANA-GREEN, ROSEBUD DIXON, elementary school educator; b. Atlanta, Sept. 25, 1955; d. Ernest Leonard and Rosebud (Brown) Dixon; m. Juan F. Green, Nov. 10, 1982 (dec. June 1987); 1 child, Tiffany Cher. BS in Elem. Edn., Clark Atlanta U., 1975; Assoc. Fine Arts, Boston Conservatory, 1977; postgrad., Ga. State U., Atlanta, 1979, West Ga. Coll., 1985-87. Cert. elem. tchr. Asst. tchr. deaf Atlanta Pub. Schs., 1973-75, tchr. hearing impaired, 1975-82, tchr. speech and drama Northside Saturday Sch. for Arts, 1982-83, tchr. middle grades edn. Wiliam J. Scott Elem. Sch., 1982-92, tchr. middle grades edn. West Fulton Middle Sch., 1992—. In school support team chairperson Atlanta Pub. Schs., W.J. Scott, 1985-87, chairperson leadership team, 1987-88, 88—. Appeared in Verne Miller, Unconquered, The Catlins, Freedom Road, Porgy and Bess, The Program. Mem. AFTRA, SAG, NAACP, U.S. Track & Field, Am. Guild Variety Artists, Actors Equity Assn., Ga. Coun. Social Studies Tchrs., Ga. Coun. Exceptional Children, Atlanta Fedn. Tchrs., Atlanta Assn. Educators, Atlanta Coun. Social Studies. Democrat. Baptist. Avocations: writing, lyricist, composing, artistic mgmt., track and field ofcl. Office: West Fulton Mid Sch Bankhead Hwy Atlanta GA 30318

FALB, PETER LAWRENCE, mathematician, educator, investment company executive; b. N.Y.C., July 26, 1936; s. Harry and Bertha (Kirschner) F.; m. Karen Forslund, Oct. 9, 1971; children— Hilary, Alison AB, Harvard U., 1956, MA, 1957, PhD, 1961. Mem. staff Mass. Inst. Tech. Lincoln Lab., Cambridge, 1960-66; asso. prof. applied math. U. Mich., Ann Arbor, 1966; prof. Brown U., Providence, 1967—; prin., treas. Dane, Falb, Stone & Co., Inc., Boston, 1977—. Chmn. Barberry Corp., 1968-85; also bd. dirs.; bd. dirs. FES Computing Co., LTCQ, Inc., Toreador Royalty, Infolenz, LTC Media; mng. dir. F-Co. Holdings Co.; vis. prof. Lund (Sweden) Inst. Tech., summers 1971, 72, 74, 76, 78; cons. NASA, Bolt, Beranek & Newman Co. Author: (with M. Athans) Optimal Control: An Introduction to the Theory and its Applications, 1966, (with R. Kalman and M. Arbib) Topics in Mathematical System Theory, 1969, (with J. deJong) Some Successive Approximation Methods in Control and Oscillation Theory, 1969; Methods of Algebraic Geometry in Control Theory, Part I: Scalar Linear Systems and Affine Algebraic Geometry, 1989, Methods of Algebraic Geometry in Control Theory, Part II: Multivariable Linear systems and Projective Algebraic Geometry, 1999. Home: 245 Brattle St Cambridge MA 02138-4614 Office: Dane Falb Stone & Co Inc 15 Broad St Ste 406 Boston MA 02109-3803 also: Brown U Box F Providence RI 02912 E-mail: plf245@aol.com.

FALBAUM, BERTRAM SEYMOUR, law educator, investigator; b. N.Y.C., July 28, 1934; s. Abraham and Shari (Greenfield) Falbaum; m. Roberta Jessie Oberstone, Sept. 1, 1957; children: Vance Leonard, Stacy Lynn. AA, L.A. City Coll., 1961; BS with honors, Calif. State U., L.A., 1962; postgrad., George Washington U., 1966—68; MPA, Syracuse U., 1972. Lic. pvt. investigator Va., Washington, Ariz. Agt. U.S. Customs Svc., L.A. and Nogales, Ariz., 1961—66, spl. agt. Washington, 1969—73; instr. Treasury Law Enforcement Sch., Washington, 1966—69; dep. chief law enforcement U.S. Fish & Wildlife Svc., Washington, 1973—78, spl. projects officer, 1978—79; sr. criminal investigator U.S. Dept. Justice (office spl. investigations), Washington, 1979—86; v.p. The Investigative Group, Inc., Washington, 1986—92; pres. Investigative Dynamics, Inc., Tucson, 1992—. Adj. prof. Am. U., 1977—78, 1990—91; bd. dirs. Forensic Scis. Corp.; adv. bd. Found. Genetic Medicine, Inc. Chmn. troop com. Nat. Capital Area coun. Boy Scouts Am., Centreville, Va., 1974—77; bd. dirs. 88-CRIME, 1998, pres., 2002. Served with USAF, 1953—57. Recipient commendations, U.S. Customs Svc., U.S. Dept. Justice. Fellow: Am. Bd. Forensic Examiners; mem.: INTELNET (adv. bd. 1997—), Vidocq Soc., Customs Spl. Agt. Assn. (pres. 1994—), Internat. Assn. Law Enforcement Intelligence Analysts, Global Investigators Network, World Investigators Network, Calif. Assn. Licensed Investigators, Pvt. Investigators Assn. of Va., Pvt. Investigators and Security Assn., Nat. Assn. Chief of Police, Fraternal Order of Police, Fraternal Order of Border Agts., Fed. Law Enforcement Officers Assn., Ariz. Assn. Lic. Pvt. Investigators (bd. dirs. 1994—96, pres. 1997, 2000), Nat. Coun. Investigation and Security Svcs. (bd. dirs. 1998), Assn. of Former Intelligence Officers, So. Ariz. Counter Intelligence Corps Assn., Am. Criminal Justice Assn. (life; chpt. pres. 1959—61), Internat. Assn. Chiefs of Police (life), Am. Coll. Forensic Examiners (life; cert.), Internat. Narcotic Enforcement Officers Assn., Nat. Assn. Legal Investigators, World Assn. Detectives, Coun. Internat. Investigators (treas. 2002—, cert.), Nat. Dist. Attys. Assn., Am. Soc. Indsl. Security (cert. protection profl.), Assn. Cert. Fraud Examiners (cert.), Am. Law Enforcement Officers Assn., Am. Fedn. Police, Fed. Criminal Investigators Assn., Am. Judicature Soc., Assn. Fed. Investigators (bd. dirs. 1979—86, cert. profl. investigator), 88-CRIME (bd. dirs. 1998—, pres. 2002—), La Paloma Country Club (golf com. and handicap chmn. 1994—95, vice chmn. 1996—98, chmn. 1999—2000, vice chmn. 2002, bd. dirs. 2003), Chantilly Country Club (v.p. for golf 1978, 1980, 1981, 1983, bd. dirs. 1984, chmn. bd. 1985—89), Lambda Alpha Epsilon (life). Home: 4921 N Fort Verde Trl Tucson AZ 85750-5903 E-mail: bertfalbaum@compuserve.com.

FALCO, CHARLES MAURICE, physicist, educator; b. Fort Dodge, Iowa, Aug. 17, 1948; s. Joe and Mavis Margaret (Mickelson) F.; m. Dale Wendy Miller, May 5, 1973; children: Lia Denise, Amelia Claire. BA, U. Calif., Irvine, 1970, MA, 1971, PhD, 1974. Trainee NSF, 1970-74; asst. physicist Argonne (Ill.) Nat. Lab., 1974-77, physicist, 1977-82, group leader superconductivity and novel materials, 1978-82; prof. physics and optical scis., research prof. U. Ariz., Tucson, 1982-97, prof. optical scis., chair condensed matter physics, 1998—, dir. lab. x-ray optics, 1986—. Vis. prof. U. Paris Sud, 1979, 86, U. Aachen, 1989; lectr., 1974—; mem. panel on artificially structured materials NRC, 1984-85; co-organizer numerous internat. confs. in field, 1978—; mem. spl. rev. panel on high temperature superconductivity Applied Physics Letters, 1987—; mem. panel on superconductivity Inst. Def. Analysis, 1988—; researcher on artificial metallic superlattices, X-ray optics, auperconductivity, condensed matter physics, electronic materials; curatorial advisor Solomon R. Guggenheim Mus., 1997—, co-curator The Art of the Motorcycle exhbn.. Editor: Future Trends in Superconductive Electronics, 1978, Materials for Magneto-Optic Data Storage, 1989; contbr. articles to profl. jours.; patentee in field. Mem. divsn. condensed matter physics Exec. Com. Arts, 1992-94. Alexander von Humboldt Found. sr. disting. grantee, 1989; recipient Art Motorcycle Exbhn. award Internat. Assn. Art Critics, 1999. Fellow Am. Phys. Soc. (counselor 1992-94, exec. com. div. condensed matter physics 1992-94, exec. com. div. internat. physics 1994-98), Optical Soc. Am.; mem. IEEE (sr.), Materials Rsch. Soc., Sigma Xi. Achievements include rsch. on artificial metallic superlattices, X-ray optics, superconductivity, condensed matter physics, electronic materials. Home: 13005 E Cape Horn Dr Tucson AZ 85749-9734 Office: U Ariz Optical Scis Ctr Box 210077 Tucson AZ 85721-0077

FALCONER, KAREN ANN See DAVIS, KAREN ANN

FALEALI'I, LOGOLEO T. V. educational services administrator; b. Onenoa, Am. Samoa, June 25, 1937; s. Falealí'i Maui and Siigavaa Faga; m. Tela T. Itumalo, July 11, 1958; children: Tele'a Jr., Laura, Mika, Paulena, Meritiana, Sepulona, Tautai, Mareta. BS in Edn., N.E. Mo. State U., 1963, MA, 1964; EdD, U. Pacific, 1976. Cert. life teaching, Mo. Tchr. Samoana High Sch., Utulei, Am. Somoa; prin. Leone High Sch., Leone, Am. Somoa; secondary edn. dir. Dept. of Edn., Utulei, Am. Somoa, ednl. svcs. deputy dir. Pago Pago. Adj. faculty U. Hawaii, Am. Somoa; vis. prof. BYU, Provo; chmn. Instl. Team, coord. tchr. cert., tchr. yr. project. Contbr. articles on Pacific Islands problems. Mem. ASCD, Am. Vocat. Assn., Ctr. for Advancement of Pacific Edn., Phi Delta Kappa. Home: PO Box 1667 Pago Pago AS 96799-1667

FALK, BARBARA HIGINBOTHAM, music educator; b. Grindstone, Pa., May 22, 1950; d. Warren Charles and Erma Lou (Randolph) Higinbotham; m. Helmut Falk, July 7, 1973; children: Gregory Brock, Jennifer Arlene. BA in Music Edn., Western Ky. U., 1972; postgrad., Jersey City State Coll., 1974, postgrad., 1997, Montclair State Coll., 1990—91, Yale U., 1993; MA in Creative Arts Edn., Rutgers U., 1994; postgrad., Caldwell Coll., 1996, St. Peter's Coll., Jersey City, 1996—98. Cert. music tchr. N.J., Orff cert. tchr. N.J. Band dir. Bridgeton (N.J.) Jr. H.S., 1972—73; instrumental music tchr. Hopewell Twp. Sch., Bridgeton, 1972—73; gen. music tchr. Marlboro (N.J.) Twp. Schs., 1973—79; music dir. S. Br. Ref. Ch. Nursery Sch., Somerville, NJ, 1987; vocal and gen. music tchr. Washington Twp. Schs., Long Valley, NJ, 1988—. Youth choir dir. First Bapt. Ch., Freehold, NJ, 1981—83, Bridgewater Bapt. Ch., 1987—89; mem. master tchr. governing com. N.J. Symphony Orch., 1993—; cons. to N.J. Dept. Edn. State Arts Curriculum Framework Writer, Trenton, NJ, 1997; mem. Morris County profl. devel. bd. N.J. Dept. Edn., 1999—; chair Morris County Profl. Devel. Bd., 2002—03; presenter in field. Bible sch. music dir. Jackson (N.J.) Bapt. Ch., 1977—79, 1st Bapt. Ch., Bridgeton, 1980—86. Recipient Master Tchr. award, N.J. Symphony Orch. and Dodge Found., 1993; grantee Creating Original Opera grant, N.Y. Met. Opera Guild, 1993. Mem.: N.J. Edn. Assn. (profl. devel. bd. 2001—), Music Educators Nat. Conf., Washington Twp. Edn. Assn. (exec. com. 1993—, pres. 2001—), Kappa Delta Pi. Baptist. Avocations: golf, gardening. Home: 645 Case Rd Neshanic Station NJ 08853 Office: Old Farmers Rd Sch 51 Old Farmers Rd Long Valley NJ 07853 Home (Summer): 30 Garfield Pl Ocean City NJ 08826

FALK, MARSHALL ALLEN, retired university dean, physician; b. Chgo., May 23, 1929; s. Ben and Frances (Kamins) F.; m. Marilyn Joyce Levoff, June 15, 1952; children: Gayle Debra, Ben Scott. BS, Bradley U., 1950; MS, U. Ill., 1952; MD, Chgo. Med. Sch., 1956. Diplomate Am. Bd. Psychiatry. Intern Cook County Hosp., Chgo., 1956-57; resident Mt. Sinai Hosp., Chgo., 1964-67; gen. practice medicine Chgo., 1959-64; resident in psychiatry, faculty dept. psychiatry Chgo. Med. Sch., 1964-67, prof., acting chmn. dept. psychiatry, 1973-74, dean, 1974-92, v.p. med. affairs, 1981-82, exec. v.p., 1982-91, dean emeritus, emeritus prof. psychiatry, 1991—. Med. dir. London Meml. Hosp., 1971-74; mem. cons. com. to commr. health City of Chgo., 1972-82; mem. Ill. Gov.'s Commn. to Revise Mental Health Code, 1973-77, Chgo. Northside Commn. on Health Planning, 1970-74, Ill. Hosp. Licensing Bd., 1981-91. Contbr. articles to profl. jours. Trustee John F. Kennedy Hosp., Antlantis, Fla., 1993-95, cons., 1991-92; trustee Quantum Found. for Health, Palm Beach, Fla., 1995—; vice chmn. grants com. Quantum Found., 1997—; trustee Finch U./Chgo. Med. Sch., 1998—, chmn. bd. trustees, 1998—. Capt. AUS, 1957-59. Recipient Bd. Trustees award for rsch. Chgo. Med. Sch., 1963, Disting. Alumni award Chgo. Med. Sch., 1976, Alumnus of Yr. award Bradley U., 1990. Fellow Am. Psychiat. Assn., Am. Coll. Psychiatrists; mem. Ill. Coun. Deans (pres. 1981-83), Coun. Free Standing Med. Sch. Deans (bd. dirs. 1984-92, pres. 1989-91), Sigma Xi, Alpha Omega Alpha. E-mail: maf/mjf@aol.com.

FALK, ROBERT BARCLAY, JR., anesthesiologist, educator; b. Lancaster, Pa., July 1, 1945; s. Robert Barclay and Miriam (Neff) F.; m. Carol Anne Gundel, May 30, 1970; 1 child, Juliana Gundel. BA, Franklin and Marshall Coll., 1967; MD, Jefferson Med. Coll., 1971. Diplomate Am. Bd. Anesthesiology. Intern Conemaugh Valley Meml. Hosp., Johnstown, Pa., 1971-72; resident in anesthesiology M.H. Hershey Med. Sch. Hosp., 1974-77; ptnr. Anesthesia Assocs., Lancaster, 1977—, sr. v.p., 1993-94, pres., 1994-2000, exec. v.p., 2000—. Staff anesthesiologist Lancaster Gen. Hosp., 1977—, vice chmn. dept. anesthesiology, 1984-85, chmn., 1985-92; clin. asst. prof. dept. anesthesiology Hershey (Pa.) Med. Sch., 1977-2002. Contbr. articles to profl. jours. Participant alumni phonathon Franklin and Marshall Coll., 1978-81, vice chmn., 1981, chmn., 1983, mem. alumni admissions com., 1977-79, chmn., 1980-87, chmn. 20th reunion gift com.; mem. Lancaster Regional Alumni Coun., 19987-91, trustee athletic com., 1988-96, 98; mem. Lancaster Area Arts Coun., 1989-91; Sunday sch. tchr. Trinity Luth. Ch., Lancaster, 1977-80; bd. dirs. Lancaster Summer Arts Festival, 1981—, v.p., 1982-84, pres., 1985-90; bd. dirs. Pa. Acad. Music, 1991—, vice-chmn., 1991-92, chmn., 1993—; bd. mgrs. Lancaster Assembly, 2000—, chmn., 2003—. Lt. M.C., USNR, 1972-74. Mem. Am. Soc. Anesthesiologists, Pa. Soc. Anesthesiologists, Intenat. Anesthesia Rsch. Soc., Pa. Med. Soc., Lancaster Country Club, Hamilton Club (v.p. 1995-97, pres. 1997-99), Masons, Shriners, Chaine des Rotisseurs. Republican. Home: 1025 Marietta Ave Lancaster PA 17603-3106 Office: Anesthesia Assocs 133 E Frederick St Lancaster PA 17602-2222 E-mail: gundelfh@aol.com.

FALKNER, ANN COODY, secondary school educator; b. Shannon, Tex., Sept. 2, 1933; d. Ira Lee and Mildred (Fry) Coody; m. Felix Lee Falkner, July 31, 1954; children: Cynthia Falkner Johns, Angela Heather Steagall. BA in Math., Tex. Women's U., Denton, 1954; MA in Math., U. Tex., 1957; postgrad., U. Wis., 1965-66, U. Ariz., 1966-72. Cert. tchr. appraisor Tex., 1987; cert. supt. Tex., Colo. Pvt. practice fin. planner, Dallas, 1959-65; math. prof. U. Ariz., 1966-71; research assoc. Ariz. State Dept. Edn., 1971-72; instr. math. Corpus Christi (Tex.) Ind. Sch. Dist., 1974—; cons. U.S. Dept. Edn., 1968—. Mem. rev. com. Fulbright Tchr. Exchange, Washington, 1983—; appointed to prin.'s adv. com. Corpus Christi Ind. Sch. Dist., 1989—, Career Ladder Rev. Com., 1990, dist. adv. com., 1992-96; spl. asst. Commr. Edn., Washington, D.C., 1967-68; cons. in field; mem. adv. couns. Internat. Biog. Ctr., Cambridge, Eng., 1990—, rsch. coun., 2003— Author: Management By Objectives v.s. Office of Education, 1968, Arizona Needs Assessment, 1973; composer: I do, I do, 1949, later musical; contbr. articles to profl. jours. Dir. aerospace edn. Tex. Wing CAP, Austin, 1992—; mem. adminstrv. staff Cadet Leadership Sch. Coll. N.Mex., San Antonio, 1985, U.S. Adv. Commn. on Pub./Diplomacy, Washington, 1983, The United Way Coastal Bend Allocations Coun., 1988; dep. comdr. CAP Nat. Staff Coll., 1988, Jefferson award for Volunteers, 1992; invited by Mrs. L.B. Johnson to participate in celebration of 25th Anniversary of L.B. Johnsons's Inauguration, 1990; mem. Civil Air Patrol, 1984—. Fellow NSF, 1965-66, U.S. Dept. Edn., 1967-68, Coastal Bend Cmty. Fund, 1984, Advanced Inst. Princeton, 1984, Advanced Inst., 1985-88, Internat. Biog. Assn., 2003; recipient Fulbright Tchr. Exchange award U.S. Dept. Edn., 1982, 89, Leadership award CAP, 1984-88, Gil Robb Wilson award, 1989, Observer award, rsch. grant Woodrow Wilson Inst. in Math., 1990, Disting. Tchr. award South Tex., 1990, Jefferson award 1998, Leaders Math. Edn. award Corpus Christi Ind. Sch. Dist., 2003. Mem.: Nat. Coun. for Tchrs. of Math., Tex. Assn. Aero. Engrs., Am. Math. Assn., Internat. Platform Assn., Internat. Bulb Soc. Democrat. Methodist. Avocations: gardening, fishing, traveling, gourmet cooking, flying. Home: 830 St Martin St Corpus Christi TX 78418-5701 Office: King High Sch 5225 Gollihar Rd Corpus Christi TX 78412-3317

FALKNER, DAVID A. principal, educator; b. St. Louis, Mar. 2, 1948; s. Virgil W. and Lucille L. (Burroughs) F.; m. Margaret A. Hyder, June 4, 1979; children: Kalissa, Allen. BA, U. Ariz., 1970; MEd, Tex. Christian U., 1975; postgrad., U. Ariz., 1995; PhD, Vision Christian U. Tchr. Tucson Unified Sch. Dist.; prin. Faith Luth. Sch., Tucson, Ariz.; prin., tchr. Luth. Sch. of the Foothills, La Crescenta, Calif.; minister of edn. Ramona (Calif.) Luth. Sch.; prin. St. John Luth. Sch., New Orleans. Lt. col. USAF, 1970-92. Mem. ASCD, Nat. Guard Assn. (Calif. chpt.), Lutheran Educators Assn. Office: Saint John Luth Sch 3937 Canal St New Orleans LA 70119 Home: 172 W Nicholai St Hicksville NY 11801-3828 E-mail: stjluthdd@cs.com.

FALKOW, STANLEY, microbiologist, educator; b. Albany, N.Y., Jan. 24, 1934; s. Jacob and Mollie (Gingold) F.; children from previous marriage: Lynn Beth, Jill Stuart; m. Lucy Stuart Tompkins, Dec. 3, 1983. BS in Bacteriology cum laude, U. Maine, 1955, DSc (hon), 1979; MS in Biology, Brown U., 1960, PhD, 1961; MD (hon.), U. Umea, Sweden, 1989. Asst. chief dept. bacterial immunity Walter Reed Army Inst. Rsch., Washington, 1963-66; prof. microbiology Med. Sch. Georgetown U., 1966-72; prof. microbiology and medicine U. Wash., Seattle, 1972-81; prof., chmn. dept. med. microbiology Stanford (Calif.) U., 1981-85, prof. microbiology, immunology & medicine, 1981—. Karl H. Beyer vis. prof. U. Wis., 1978-79; Sommer lectr. U. Oreg. Sch. Medicine, 1979, Kinyoun lectr. NIH, 1980; Rubbro orator Australian Soc. Microbiology, 1981; Stanhope Bayne-Jones lectr. Johns Hopkins U., 1982; mem. Recombinant DNA Molecule Com, task force on antibiotics in animal feeds FDA, microbiology test com. Nat. Bd. Med. Examiners. Author: Infectious Multiple Drug Resistance, 1975; editor: Jour. Infection and Immunity, Jour. Infectious Agents and Diseases. Recipient Ehrlich prize, 1981, Becton-Dickinson award in Clin. Microbiology, ASM, 1986, Altemeier medal Surg. Infectious Diseases Soc., 1990, Disting. Achievement in Infectious Disease Rsch. award Bristol-Myers Squibb, 1997; Bristol-Myers Squibb unrestricted infectious disease grantee. Fellow Am. Acad. Microbiology; mem. Inst. of Medicine, AAAS, Infectious Disease Soc. Am. (Squibb award 1979), Am. Soc. Microbiology, Genetics Soc. Am., Nat. Acad. Sci., Sigma Xi. Office: Stanford U Dept Microbiology and Immunology Fairchild D309A Stanford CA 94305-5402 E-mail: falkow@stanford.edu.

FALL, DOROTHY ELEANOR, librarian; b. Havre de Grace, Md., Feb. 4, 1945; d. James Huey Jr. and Blanche Cecelia (JOhnson) Fall. BA, Lake Erie Coll., 1967; MEd, Westfield State Coll., 1976; EdD, Nova U., 1995. Cert. tchr. Mass, Va. Tchr. Big Spring (Tex.) Sch. System, 1968; substitute tchr. Dept. Defense Schs., Clark AFB, Philippines, 1969-70; tchr. Fayetteville (N.C.) Sch. System, 1971-72, Granby (Mass.) Pub. Schs., 1973-78; eligibility tech. State of Conn., Danbury, 1980-85; libr. Loudoun Country Day Sch., Leesburg, Va., 1990—. Ednl. liaison Granby Pub. Schs., Granby Pub. Libr., 1973-78; libr. trustee Loudoun County Libr. System, 1990-94; lectr. Shenandoah U., Winchester, Va., 1994—; adj. prof. edn. Mary Baldwin Coll. Contbr. articles to newspapers and jours. Vol. ARC, Ala, Ohio, Philippines, 1960-69, United Way, Conn., Va., 1984-86, Am. Cancer Soc., Va., 1988; pres. P.E.O. sisterhood, 1988-90; bd. dirs. Vol. Svcs., Loudoun County, 2002—; mem. Cmty. of Caring. Named Hidden Heroine Girl Scouts Am., 1976. Mem. ALA, ASCD, Va. Libr. Assn., Va. Edn. Media Assn., P.E.O. Presbyterian. Avocations: herb gardening, catering, decorating, calligraphy, sewing. Office: Loudoun Country Day Sch 237 Fairview St NW Leesburg VA 20176-2009

FALLETTA, JOHN MATTHEW, pediatrician, educator; b. Arma, Kans., Sept. 3, 1940; s. Matthew John and Norma (Luke) F.; m. Carolyn Ontjes, June 22, 1963; children: Elizabeth, Matthew. AB, U. Kans., 1962, MD, 1966. Diplomate Am. Bd. Pediat., Am. Bd. Hematology-Oncology. Intern in mixed medicine Kans. U. Med. Ctr., Kansas City, 1966-67; surgeon Epidemic Intelligence Svc., Tex. Children's Hosp. USPHS, Houston, 1967-69; asst. instr. pediat. Baylor Coll. Medicine, Houston, 1967-69, resident, 1969-71, chief resident Tex. Children's Hosp., 1971, postdoctoral fellow hematology-oncology, 1971-73, asst. prof. pediat., 1973-76; assoc. prof. Duke U., Durham, N.C., 1976-83, prof., 1984—, chief divsn. hematology-oncology, 1976-94, dir. Clin. Pediat. Lab., 1976-95. Chmn. transfusion com. Duke U. Med. Ctr., 1978—, mem. exec. com. med. staff, 1978—, instl. rev. bd. human rsch., 1979—, chmn., 1994—; mem. instl. rev. bd. human rsch. Baylor Coll. Medicine, 1974-76; mem. acad. coun. Duke U., 1982-86, 87-96, 98-2000, exec. com., 1988, faculty compensation com., 1988—, faculty com. on univ. governance, 1988, trustee-faculty com. to rev. pres., 1989, search com. for pres., 1992; cons. pediat. hematologist-oncologist Charlotte (N.C.) Meml. Hosp., 1978-, mem. Copernicus Independant Review Bd., 2002-; mem. med. adv. bd. Children's Cancer Rsch. Fund, 2001-. Contbr. more than 120 articles to Nature, Am. Jour. Ophthalmology, Pediat., New England Jour. Medicine, Clin. Pediat. Oncology, others. Cons. pediat. hematologist-oncologist Project Hope, Pediatric Inst., Krakow, Poland, 1979—; prin. investigator Pediat. Oncology Group, 1981-95, chmn. epidemiology com., mem. prin. investigator's exec. com., new agts. and pharmacology com.; chmn. prophylactic penicillin study I Nat. Heart, Lung and Blood Inst., NIH, 1982-86, chmn. study II, 1987-95; active Cancer Ctr. Support Rev. Com. Nat. Cancer Inst. NIH, 1986-90, NIH Reviewers Res., 1990—, Cancer Clin. Investigation Rev. Com., 1991-96, chmn., 1995-96; trustee Ronald McDonald House Charities, 1986—; mem. med. adv. bd. Children's Cancer Rsch. Fund, 2001—. Mem. Am. Assn. Cancer Rsch., Am. Acad. Pediat., Am. Pediat. Soc., Am. Soc. Clin. Oncology, So. Soc. Pediat. Rsch. (pres. 1981-82), Soc. Pediat. Rsch., N.C. Pediat. Soc., N.C. Med. Soc., Phi Beta Kappa, Alpha Omega Alpha, Children's Rsch. Fund, Nat. Med. Advisory Bd. Office: Duke U Med Ctr PO Box 2991 Durham NC 27710-2991

FALLON, RAE MARY, psychology educator, early childhood consultant; b. N.Y.C., Apr. 13, 1947; d. Frank J. and Santa A. T.; m. John J. Fallon, 1972; children: Sean, Christopher. BA, CUNY, 1968, MA, 1971; PhD, Fordham U., 2001. Cert. N-6 tchr., spl. edn. tchr., N.Y. Elem. tchr. Pub. Sch. 1, Bronx, NY, 1968—72; pre-sch. tchr. Valley Nursery Sch., Walden, NY, 1972—73; tchr. spl. edn. Orange-Ulster Bd. Coop. Edn. Svcs., Goshen, NY, 1973—75, early childhood specialist, 1982—89; instr. edn. Mt. St. Mary Coll., Newburgh, NY, 1989—93, asst. prof., 1993—2001, assoc. prof. psychology, 2001—. Early childhood cons., Montgomery, N.Y., 1989—; mem. early childhood com. Valley Ctrl. Sch. Sys., Montgomery, 1994. Mem. West Street Sch. Cmty. Sch. Bd., Newburgh, 1990—; mem. early intervention com. Orange County Health Dept., Goshen, 1993—; chmn. program com. Montgomery Rep. Club, 1990-94. Mem. ASCD, Coun. for Exceptional Children, Assn. for Edn. Young Children (regional coord. 1991-92), Kiwanis, Delta Kappa Gamma (pres. Alpha chpt. 2002-04), Phi Delta Kappa. Roman Catholic. Office: Mt St Mary Coll 330 Powell Ave Newburgh NY 12550-3412

FALLS, HAROLD BROWN, JR., biomedical sciences educator, physiologist; b. Savannah, Tenn., Dec. 16, 1934; s. Harold Brown Falls Sr. and Alene Maybelle Foster; m. Anita Rose Myers, 1958; children: Karen Knetzer, Brian, Elizabeth Cline. BA, Morehead State U., 1960; MPE, Purdue U., 1961, PhD, 1964. Asst. prof. Ft. Hays Kans. State Coll., 1963-64, U. Ark., Fayetteville, 1964-66, S.W. Mo. State U., Springfield, 1966-68, assoc. prof., 1968-73, prof., 1973-89, disting. scholar, 1989-94, dept. head, prof., 1994—. Mem. adv. coun. FITNESSGRAM, Cooper Inst. for Aerobics Rsch., Dallas, 1985—. Author: Essentials of Fitness, 1980; editor-in-chief Rsch. Quarterly for Exercise and Sport, 1980-83; assoc. editor The Physician and Sportsmedicine, 1987-93; contbr. chpt. to book and articles to profl. jours. Mem. Mo. Gov.'s Coun. on Phys. Fitness and Health, Jefferson City, 1981-85; trustee Mo. Found. for Fitness, Health and Sports, Jefferson City, 1985-87. Cpl. U.S. Army, 1957-58. Fellow Am. Coll. Sports Medicine (pres. Ctrl. States chpt. 1972-73, 90-91, Honor award Ctrl. States chpt. 1998), Am. Acad. Kinesiology and Phys. Edn.; mem. Am. Alliance for Health, Phys. Edn., Recreation and Dance (pres. rsch. consortium, chair task force on youth fitness, mem. task force on Olympic sports devel. 1973-75, 77-80, 77-78, Scholar award 1981, Honor award 1982, Phys. Fitness Coun. Honor award 1988). Avocations: golf, hiking, photography. Home: 3566 S Primrose Ct Springfield MO 65807-4521 Office: Dept Biomed Scis Southwest Mo State Univ Springfield MO 65804 Fax: 417-836-5588. E-mail: hbf931f@smsu.edu.

FALLS, JACQUELINE O'BARR, psychotherapist, educator; b. Birmingham, Ala., June 2, 1947; d. Melvin Hughlett O'Barr and Reba Anna (Kizziah) Dillon; m. Robert Perry Falls Sr., Sept. 11, 1981; children: Kathy Falls Copeland, Robert Perry Jr. BA, U. Ala., Birmingham, 1981, MEd, 1988, postgrad. studies marriage and family, 1988-94. Lic. marriage and family therapist; lic. profl. counselor; cert. counselor supr., Ala. Coord. admissions U. Ala. Sch. Medicine, Birmingham, 1970-83; dir. records Birmingham-So. Coll., 1983-87; registrar U. Montevallo, Ala., 1987-88; pvt. practice cons. Birmingham, 1988-89; counselor, coord. U. Ala., Birmingham, 1989-91; pvt. practice psychotherapist Birmingham, 1991—. Contract counselor Bell South Telecomm. Employees Assistance, Atlanta, 1992—, Ala. Dept. Human Resources, Cullman and Jefferson Counties, 1992—, Concerned Citizens for Youth, Jasper, Ala., 1994-96, Nat. Employee Assistance Svc., Waukesha, Wis., 1995—, Magellan Behavioral Health, Atlanta, 1996—; instr. Jefferson State Coll., 1997—. Co-dir. Lighthouse Youth Ctr., Birmingham, 1971-76; vol. counselor Ptnr. Assistance to Homeless, Birmingham, 1988-89, Rape Crisis Ctr., Birmingham, 1990-92. Scholar dept. sociology U. Ala., 1985. Mem. ACA, Am. Profl. Soc. Child Abuse, Ala. Assn. Marriage and Family, Friends of Jung South, Chi Sigma Iota (pres. 1991-97), Kappa Delta Pi. Avocations: reading, gardening, hiking, crafts, dreams analysis. Office: Rm 2175 ADC 3196 Hwy 280S0 Birmingham AL 35243

FALZANO, COLLEEN, special education educator; b. Glens Falls, NY, Oct. 9, 1962; d. Richard Joseph and Patricia Anne (Sheridan) F. AA, Ulster County C.C.; BA in Psychology, SUNY, New Paltz; MS in Edn., SUNY, Brockport; diploma with honors, St. John's U., 2001, EdD, cert. in instrnl. leadership, St. John's U., 2003. Substitute tchr. Kendall (N.Y.) Ctrl. Sch. Dist., 1986-87, Holley (N.Y.) Ctrl. Sch. Dist., 1986-87, Albion (N.Y.) Sch. Dist., 1986-87; tchr. spl. edn. Children's Home Kingston, N.Y., 1987-90, New Paltz Ctrl. Sch. Dist., 1990-91, Saugerties (N.Y.) Ctrl. Sch. Dist., 1991-93; tchr. resource room, cons. Kingston City Sch. Dist., 1993—. Recipient Gappy Gurrison award, 1981. Mem. ASCD, Internat. Soc. Tech. Edn., NY Mid. Sch. Assn., Nat. Coun. Tchrs. Math., Nat. Sci. Tchrs. Assn., Mid-Hudson Field Hockey Ofcls. Assn. (pres.), Phi Delta Kappa. Avocations: mountain biking, hiking, writing, jogging. Home: 5 Boxwood Ct Saugerties NY 12477-2009 E-mail: ccfalz@yahoo.com.

FAMA, KATHERINE, English and journalism educator, multicultural literature consultant; b. New Brunswick, N.J., Oct. 5, 1946; d. Philip A. and Ethel (Petrich) Cahill; m. Peter A. Fama, Oct. 25, 1980. BA, Coll. Misericordia, 1968; MA, Trenton State Coll., 1973. Cert. tchr. Eng., Journalism, student pers. svcs. English, journalism tchr. Franklin Twp. Bd. Edn., Somerset, N.J., 1968—; tchr. multicultural lit. Coll. Misericordia, 1993—. Participant Econ. Opportunity Office program Rutgers U., New Brunswick, 1990. Co-author, editor series of multicultural source works in lit., 1992; author style manual, 1986. Treas. Milltown (N.J.) Libr. Bd. Trustees, 1985, v.p., 1987, pres., 1988. Named High Sch. Tchr. of Yr., Somerset County div. Internat. Reading Assn. Mem. Nat. Coun. Tchrs. English, Globelink. Office: Franklin Twp Bd Edn Amwell Rd Somerset NJ 08873

FAN, DAVID P. scientist biologist, educator; b. Hong Kong, Jan. 18, 1942; s. Hsu Yun Fan; m. Maryse von der Weid; children: Vincent, Regis, Cedric. BS, Purdue U., 1961; PhD, MIT, 1965. Mem. faculty U. Minn., St. Paul, 1969—; pres. InfoTrend Inc., St. Paul, 1986—. Author: Predictions of Public Opinion from the Mass Media: Computer Content Analysis and Mathematical Modeling, 1988. Mem. Am. Assn. Pub. Opinion Rsch., Internat. Comm. Assn. Achievements include patents on information processing expert system for text analysis and prediction; founded Infotrend, Inc., a high technology, software based company. Home: 2115 Dudley Ave Saint Paul MN 55108-1415 Office: U Minn Dept Genetics Cell Biology and Devel Saint Paul MN 55108

FAN, HUNG Y. virology educator, consultant; b. Beijing, Oct. 30, 1947; s. Hsu Yun and Li Nien (Bien) Fan. BS, Purdue U., 1967; PhD, MIT, 1971. Asst. research prof. Salk Inst., San Diego, 1973-81; asst. prof. U. Calif., Irvine, 1981-83, assoc. prof., 1984-88, prof., 1988—, dir. Cancer Rsch. Inst., 1985—, acting dean Sch. Biol. Scis., 1990-91. Editor: Jour. Virology, 1998—; contbr. more than 140 articles to profl. jours. NIH grantee, 1973—, grant review coms., 1973—; Woodrow Wilson Found. grad. fellow, 1967, Helen Hay Whitney Found. postdoctorate fellow, 1971. Fellow AAAS, Am. Acad. Microbiology; mem. Am. Soc. Microbiology, Am. Soc. Virology, Am. Assn. Cancer Rsch. Avocation: chamber music. E-mail: hyfan@uci.edu.

FAN, LEE SIU, business executive and vocational training program administrator; b. Hong Kong, Aug. 5, 1948; came to U.S., 1974; s. Kwok-Kam and Po-Hang (Law) F. BSc in Bus. Mgmt. and Mktg., U. Wis., Superior, 1975; MSc in Spl. Edn., Portland State U., 1989; DBA in Bus. Mgmt., Pacific Western U., 1997. Cert. foodsvcs. mgmt. profl. Prodn. and sales mng. coord. Castle Peak Garment Factory Co., Ltd., Hong Kong, 1969-70; mng. exec. Wilson Garment Mfg. Co. Ltd., Hong Kong, 1970-74; ops. mgr. Portland State U., 1975-92; CEO Handily Enterprises (U.S.A.) Inc., Portland, 1991—, Happy Heart Foods Inc., Portland, 1992—, Lok Hop, Inc., Portland, 1996—. Vocat. tng. programs coord. Portland Pub. Schs., Lake Oswego Sch. Dist., Clackamas County Employment Tng. and Bus. Svcs., Oreg. Comm. for the Blind, Westside Youth Ctr., 1986-92; adv. bd. Unicorn Fisheries Ltd., Hong Kong, 1990—. Cmty. svc. provider Loaves & Fishes Sr. Cmty. Ctr., Portland, 1991—; coord. Oreg. Gov.'s Ann. Food Dr., Salem, 1991; mem. diversity commn. Portland State U., 1992; mem. delegation on learning disabilities Citizen Ambassador of People to People Internat., Spokane, Wash., 1994. Recipient Exemplary Svc. award Portland State U., 1985, Extraordinary Svc. award, 1987, various svc. awards, 1972-92. Mem. Coun. for Exceptional Children (Beyond the Call of Duty Svc. award 1992), Nat. Assn. of Coll. and Univ. Food Svcs. (Leadership Program rep. 1986-92, named Food Svc. Mgmt. Profl. 1992), Nike Portland Running Club (2d master runner of yr. 1988, 89), Oreg. Rd. Runners Club (Inspirational Runner of Yr. 1990). Democrat. Avocations: running, community services, coin collecting. Office: Handily Enterprises (USA) 6335 SE 82nd Ave Portland OR 97266-5607 Home: 4635 SE 31st Ave Portland OR 97202-3639

FANCHER, EDWIN CRAWFORD, psychologist, educator; b. Middletown, N.Y., Aug. 29, 1923; s. Frank Dane and Elizabeth (McGarr) F.; m. Vivian Kramer, Nov. 8, 1969; children: Bruce Daniel, Emily Jill. BA, The New Sch. U., 1949, MA, 1951. Psychologist Linden (N.J.) Mental Hygiene Clinic, 1955-58; therapist Cmty. Guidance Svc., N.Y.C., 1958-88; pvt. practice psychology, counseling N.Y.C., 1958—; co-founder, dir. Washington Sq. Inst. Psychotherapy and Mental Health, N.Y.C., 1960-70. Co-founder, pub. Village Voice, N.Y.C., 1955-74; dir. Orange County Telephone Co., Middletown, N.Y., 1946-60; cons. Plumsock Fund, Indpls., 1974-96, pres. 1985-96; founding pres. N.Y. Sch. for Psychoanalytic Psychotherapy and Psychoanalysis, 1978—. Founder, past chmn. N.Y. Neighborhoods Coun. on Narcotics Addiction. Served with U.S. Army, 1943-46. Decorated two Bronze stars. Mem. APA, Internat. Psychoanalytical Assn., Am. Inst. Psychotherapy and Psychoanalysis, Am. Orthopsychiat. Assn., N.Y. State Psychol. Assn., N.Y. Sch. for Psychoanalytic Psychotherapy and Psychoanlysis (pres. 1978—), N.Y. Freudian Soc. (mem. faculty tng. analyst 1985—), Gipsy Trail. Democrat. Home: 40 5th Ave New York NY 10011-8843 Office: 33 Greenwich Ave New York NY 10014-2701 E-mail: edwinfancher@earthlink.net.

FANELLI, SEAN A. college president; b. N.Y., Dec. 31, 1937; s. Alphonse and Rose (Siconolfi) F.; m. Marion Ryan, Dec. 27, 1969; children: Elizabeth, Thomas, James. BS, St. Francis Coll., Bklyn., 1966; PhD, Fordham U., 1970. Prof. biology Westchester C.C., Valhalla, N.Y., 1969-72, chmn. dept. biology, sci., 1970-72, assoc. dean health sci., 1972-76, dean acad. affairs, 1976-82; pres. Nassau C.C., Garden City, N.Y., 1982—. Evaluator, chmn. Middle States Assn., Phila., 1977— ; cons. N.J. Dept. Higher Edn., 1977-84. Mem. Westchester County Emergency Med. Svc. Coun., N.Y., 1982-82, Nassau County Criminal Justice Coordinating Coun., N.Y., 1984—; chmn. L.I. Regional coun. High Edn., 1984-86 L.I. Regional Adv. Bd. Higher Edn., 1994-95; chair Museums at Mitchel, 2000—. Recipient Alexander Meiklejohn award for acad. freedom AAUP, 1995, NDEA fellow, 1967-70, William J. Brennan, Kr. award, 2001. Mem. Am. Coun. Edn. (comm. ednl. credit and credentials 1992-96), Assn. Pres.' of Pub. C.C. (pres. 1985-86), AAAS, Order Sons of Italy in Am., Dante Found., Sons of St. Patrick. Avocations: photography, computers. Office: Nassau Community Coll One Education Dr Garden City NY 11530-6793

FANG, JOONG, philosopher, mathematician, educator; b. Piongyang, Korea, Mar. 30, 1923; arrived in U.S., 1948, naturalized, 1962; s. Gabiong and Igab (Kim) Fang; children: Eva Maria, Guido Andreas. Student, Chuo U., Tokyo, 1939-41; BS, Coll. Tech. Seoul, Korea, 1944; MA, Yale U., 1950; PhD, U. Mainz, Germany, 1957. Asst. prof. math. Jinhae Coll., also U. Pusan, Republic of Korea, 1945-48, Valparaiso (Ind.) U., 1958-59, St. John's U., 1959-61, U. Alaska, 1961-62; assoc. prof. No. Ill. U., 1963-67; prof. math. and philosophy Memphis State U., 1967-73; prof. philosophy Old Dominion U., Norfolk, Va., 1974-90, prof. emeritus, 1990—. Vis. prof. U. Münster, Germany, 1971. Author: (book) Das Antinomienproblem, 1957, Abstract Algebra, 1963, Kant-Interpretation, I, 1967, Numbers Racket: The Aftermath of the "New Math", 1968, Towards a Philosophy of Modern Mathematics, I, Bourbaki, 1970, II, Hilbert, 1970, Mathematicians from Antiquity to Today, I, 1972, Sociology of Mathematics and Mathematicians, 1975, The Illusory Infinite: A Theology of Mathematics, 1976, Logic Today, Basics and Beyond, 1979, Linguistic Sense of the Japanese (in Japanese), 1984, Kant and Mathematics Today, 1997, Learning, East and West, 2002, Docta Ignorantia, 2003; editor: Philosophia Mathematica, 1964—92. Mem.: Am. Philos. Assn., Am. Math. Soc. Address: 9745 Oakview Dr North VA 23128-9041

FANNIN, DONALD RAY, elementary school educator; b. Inez, Ky., Oct. 18, 1946; s. Luthor and Ethel (Kirk) F.; m. Juanita Jude, Aug. 19, 1967; children: Sherrie R., Stephanie L. BS, Morehead State U., 1968, MA, 1971, EdS, 1985. Cert. adminstr., supr., Ky. Tchr. Martin County Schs., Inez, Ky., 1968-71, head start dir., 1971-73; v.p. Nu-Look Fashions, Inc., Columbus, Ohio, 1973-74, Bill V. Martin Coal Corp., Bloomington, Ill., 1974-78; equipment operator Mapco Coal Corp., Tulsa, 1978-85; spl. educator Martin County Schs., Inez, 1985-91; prin. Tomahawk (Ky.) Elem. Sch., 1991-93; edn. specialist and cons. pvt. practice, Inez, (Ky.), 1993—. Pastor Rockcastle U. Bapt. Ch., Inez, 1990—. Baptist. Avocation: reading and self-improvement classes. Home: PO Box 1117 Inez KY 41224-1117

FANNIN, JUANITA JUDE, guidance counselor; b. Pilgrim, Ky., May 14, 1949; d. David Stepp and Ethel (Fredrick) Jude; m. Donald Ray Fannin, Aug. 19, 1967; children: Sherrie R., Stephanie L. AA, Prestonsburg C.C., 1985; AB, Morehead State U., 1985, MA, 1988, cert. in spl. edn., 1990. Cert. guidance counselor, Ky. Owner, mgr. RoSan Dress Shoppe, Kermit, W.Va., 1975-80; owner, dir. Inez (Ky.) Med. Clinic, 1980-81; tchr. spl. edn. Martin County Sch. System, Inez, 1986-88; guidance counselor Ky. Tech.-Mayo Campus, Paintsville, 1988—. Mem. ASCD, Am. Vocat. Assn., East Ky. Vocat. Assn. (pres.-elect 1991-92), East Ky. Counselor Assn., Ky. Counselor Assn. Baptist. Avocations: reading, self-improvement classes, painting, cross-stitch. Home: PO Box 1117 Inez KY 41224-1117 Office: Ky Tech Mayo Campus 513 3rd St Paintsville KY 41240-1032

FANNING, WANDA GAIL, retired elementary school educator; b. Chattanooga, Dec. 8, 1947; d. O' Knox and Hazel W. (McClendon) F.; stepmother E. Martha (O'Kelley) F. BEd, U. Ten., 1969; MEd, Trinity U., San Antonio, 1982. Elem. tchr. C.Z. Govt., Balboa, 1969-79, Dept. Def. Dependent Schs., Albrook, Panama, 1979-87, tchr. spl. edn. Panama, 1982-84, ednl. prescriptionist, 1987-95, tchr. trainer, drug edn. trainer Panama City, 1987-96, cooperative learning trainer, 1994-96, case mgr., 1995-96; literacy success tchr. Pinellas County (Fla.) Schs., 1998—. Chmn. fine arts Ishmian Coll. Club, Balboa, 1985, fin. chmn., 1985; mem. Theatre Guild, Ancon, Panama, 1975-96; pres. Diablo Elem. Sch. Adv. Com., 1990-91; mem. orgnl. com. Spl. Games for Spl. People, Panama City, 1983-85. Recipient Just Cause cert. dept. nursing Gorgas Army Hosp., 1990, Spl. Act award Dept. Def. Dependents Sch., 1990. Mem. ASCD, CEC (treas. 1987-88), Nat. Coun. Tchrs. Math., Phi Delta Kappa (pres. 1990-91, Kappan of Yr. 1991, 94, v.p. 1991-92, del. 1992, 93), Kappa Delta Pi. Avocations: reading, travel, theater, music. Address: 2255 Grove Valley Ave Palm Harbor FL 34683-3226

FANNO, DAVE, English composition and speech communications educator; b. Hammond, Ind., Apr. 26, 1959; s. Hubert and Claudette F.. BS, Purdue, 1991; M, Purdue U. Calumet, Hammond, Ind., 2002. News editor Star Newspapers, Tinley Park, Ind., 1990—98; instr. Purdue U. Calumet, Hammond, 1996—; English composition instr. Moraine Valley C.C., Palos Hills, Ill., 2002—. Media advisor Purdue Chronicle, Hammond, 1995—2001. Mem.: Coll. Media Advisers, Soc. Profl. Journalists. Home: 6954 Baring Ave Hammond IN 46324 Office: Purdue U Calumet 2200 169th St Hammond IN 46323 Personal E-mail: dfanno@juno.com.

FANT, GENE CLINTON, JR., English language educator; b. Laurel, Miss., June 30, 1963; s. Gene C. and Ramona Faith (Hankins) F.; m. Lisa Anne Williams, Mar. 25, 1989. BA, James Madison U., 1984; MA, Old Dominion U., 1987; MDiv, New Orleans Bapt. Theol. Sem., 1991; MEd, PhD, U. So. Miss., 1995. Instr. Hampton (Va.) City Schs., 1985-87; instr. of English Gloucester (Va.) County Schs., 1987-89, Phillips Coll., Metairie, La., 1989-90, William Carey Coll., Hattiesburg, Miss., 1991-92; teaching asst. in English U. So. Miss., Hattiesburg, 1992-94, asst. dir. dept. edn., 1994-95, aide to univ. pres., 1995; asst. prof. Miss. Coll., Clinton, 1995—2002; assoc. prof., chair English dept. Union U., Jackson, Tenn., 2002—. Cons. Miss. River Ministry, Jackson, 1992. Author: Petrarchan Hagiography in Wroth, 1995, Expectant Moments, 1999; contbr. articles to profl. jours. Crisis counselor, New Orleans, 1990-92. Linwood Orange fellow U. So. Miss., 1993. Mem. MLA, Conf. on Christianity and Lit. (Daub-Maher prize 1994), Philological Assn. La., Gamma Beta Phi. Avocations: film studies, sports, travel. Office: Union U Box 3142 1050 Union University Dr Jackson TN 38305

FANT, JOSEPH LEWIS, III, academic administrator, retired army officer; b. Columbus, Miss., June 23, 1928; s. Joseph Lewis, Jr. and Julia Elizabeth (Brazeale) F.; m. Carolyn Adeline Watkins, Apr. 30, 1955; children— Carolyn Laura, Julia Lynn, Joseph Lewis, IV A.S., Marion Inst., 1947; BS, U.S. Mil. Acad., 1951; A.M., U. Pa., 1960, PhD, 1984. Commd. 2d lt. U.S. Army, 1951, advanced through grades to maj. gen., 1980; ret., 1985; pres. Fidelity Capital, Inc., Columbus, Miss., 1986-88, Marion (Ala.) Mil. Inst., High Sch. and Jr. Coll., 1990-94. Co-editor: Faulkner at West Point, 1964. Named Disting. Mississippian, 1974. Mem. Masons (32d degree). Methodist. Avocations: hunting; tennis. Home: 1014 College St Columbus MS 39701-5807

FANTON, JONATHAN FOSTER, foundation administrator; b. Mobile, Ala., Apr. 29, 1943; s. Dwight F. F. and Marion (Foster) Fanton Bemer; m. Cynthia Greenleaf, Aug. 2, 1986. BA, Yale U., 1965, M.Phil., 1977, PhD, 1978. Carnegie teaching fellow in history Yale U., 1965-66, lectr. history, 1966-78, spl. asst. to pres., 1970-73, exec. dir. Summer Plans, 1973-76, assoc. provost, 1976-78; v.p. planning U. Chgo., 1978-82; pres., prof. history New Sch. Social Rsch., N.Y.C., 1982—99; pres. John D. and Catherine T. MacArthur Found., Chgo., 1999—. Author: The University and Civil Society, Vol. 1, 1995, Vol. 2, 2002; co-editor: John Brown, The Manhattan Project, 1991. Advisor, trustee Rockefeller Bros. Fund; chmn. Human Rights Watch; co-chmn. Internat. Com. Acad. Freedom; bd. dirs. Chgo. Hist. Soc., Am. Ctr. in Berlin. Mem. Am. Hist. Assn., Coun. on Fgn. Rels., Econ. Club. Home: 4375 Congress St Fairfield CT 06430-1722 Office: 140 S Dearborn St Chicago IL 60601

FARAH, CAESAR ELIE, Middle Eastern and Islamic studies educator; b. Portland, Oreg., Mar. 13, 1929; s. Sam Khalil and Lawrice Farah; m. Irmgard Tenkamp, Dec. 13, 1987; 1 child, Elizabeth;children from previous marriage: Ronald, Christopher, Ramsey, Laurence, Raymond, Alexandra. Student, Internat. Coll. Am. U. Beirut, 1941-46; BA, Stanford U., 1952; MA, Princeton U., 1955, PhD, 1957. Pub. affairs asst., cultural affairs officer ednl. exchanges USIS, New Delhi, 1957-58, Karachi, Pakistan, 1958; asst. to chief Bur. Cultural Affairs, Washington, 1959; asst. prof. history and Semitic langs. Portland State U., 1959-63; asst. prof. history Calif. State U.-Los Angeles, 1963-64; assoc. prof. Near Eastern studies Ind. U., Bloomington, 1964-69; prof. Middle Eastern and Islamic history U. Minn., Mpls., 1969—, chmn. South Asian and Middle Eastern studies, 1988-91. Guest lectr. Fgn. Ministry, Spain, Iraq, Iran, Ministry Higher Edn., Saudi Arabia, Yemen, Turkey, Kuwait, Qatar, Tunisia, Morocco, Syrian Acad. Scis., Acad. Scis., Beijing; vis. scholar Cambridge U., 1974; resource person on Middle East media and svc. group, Minn., 1977—; bd. dirs., chmn. Upper Midwest Consortium for Middle East Outreach, 1980—; vis. prof. Harvard U., 1964, 65, Sanaa U., Yemen, 1984, Karl-Franzens U. Austria, 1990, 91, 1997—98, Ludwig-Maximilian U., Munich, 1992—93; vis. Fulbright-Hays scholar U. Damascus, 1994; vis. lectr. Am. U. Beirut, 2001; exec. sec., editor Am. inst. Yemeni Studies, 1982—86; sec.-gen., exec. bd. dirs. Internat. Com. for Pre-Ottoman & Ottoman Studies, 1988—2000, v.p., 2000—; fellow Rsch. Ctr. Islamic History, Istanbul, 1993, Ctr. Lebanese Studies & St. Anthony Coll., Oxford, England, 1994; vis. cons. Sultan Qaboos U., Oman, 2000. Author: The Addendum in Medieval Arabic Historiography, 1968, Islam: Beliefs and Observances, 7th edit., 2003, Eternal Message of Muhammad, 1964, 3d edit., 1981, Tarikh Baghdad li-Ibn-al-Najjar, 3 vols., 1980—83, 2d edit., 1986, al-Ghazali on Abstinence in Islam, 1992, Decision Making in the Ottoman Empire, 1992, The Road to Intervention: Fiscal Policies in Ottoman Mount Lebanon, 1992, The Politics of Interventionism in Ottoman Lebanon, 2000, The Sultan's Yemen, 2002, Ottomans & Arabs, 2002, First Arab Traveler to Latin America, 2003; contbr. articles to profl. jours.; mem. editl. bd.: Digest of Middle East Studies. Mem. Oreg. Rep. Committeeman, 1960—64. Named Fulbright-Hayes lectr., 1993—94; recipient cert. of merit, Syrian Minstiry Higher Edn.; fellow, Am. Coun. Learned Socs., 1953, Am. Rsch. Ctr. Egypt, 1966—67, Fulbright Tgn. and Rsch., Germany, 1992—93, Ford Found., 1966, Am. Philos. Soc., 1970—71; grantee Participants Program, Dept. State Am., 1981, 1984, 1993, Minn. Humanities Commn., 1981, 1985, 1989, 1995, 1998, 2001, Am. Inst. Yemeni Studies, 1999, Coun. Am. Overseas Rsch. Ctrs., 2000, Travel to Collection, NEH, 1989, others; scholar Fulbright Rsch., 1966—67, 1985—86, 1992—93. Mem.: Turkish Studies Assn., Am. Assn. Tchrs. Arabic (exec. bd.), Mid. East Studies Assn. N.Am., Am. Hist. Assn., Royal Asiatic Soc. Gt. Britain, Am. Oriental Soc., Stanford U. Alumni Assn. (Leadership Recognition award), Princeton Club, Stanford Club Minn. (dir., pres. 1979), Phi Alpha Theta, Pi Sigma Alpha. Greek Orthodox. Home: 5125 Blake Rd S Edina MN 55436-1125 Office: Univ Minn 839 Soc Sci Towers Minneapolis MN 55455 Fax: 612-624-9383. Business E-Mail: farah001@umn.edu.

FARAH, FUAD SALIM, dermatologist, educator; b. Haifa, Palestine, 1929; MD, Am. U., Beirut, 1954. Diplomate Am. Bd. Dermatology. Internship Am. U., Beirut, 1954-55, residency, 1955-56, resident in internal medicine, 1956-57; fellowship Barnes Hosp., 1957-59; dir. immunology rsch. & tng. ctr. WHO, Beruit, Lebanon, 1970-76; prof. medicine SUNY Upstate Med. U., Syracuse, chief sect. dermatology, 1976—; pvt. practice Syracuse. Instr. dept. medicine Am. U., Beirut, 1959-60, asst. prof., 1960-66, assoc. prof., 1966-74, prof., 1976. Fellow Am. Acad. Dermatology; mem. Lebanese Dermatologic Soc. (founding mem. 1962, pres. 1970-72), Lebanese Assn. Pub. Health, Ctrl. N.Y. Dermatol. Soc., Assn. Profs. Dermatology, N.Y. State Dermatology Soc.. Office: The Hill Med Ctr 1000 E Genesee St Syracuse NY 13210-1892 also: Upstate Med U 750 E Adams St Syracuse NY 13210-2306 Fax: 315-422-3129.

FARBER, DONALD CLIFFORD, lawyer, educator; b. Columbus, Nebr., Oct. 19, 1923; s. Charles and Sarah (Epstein) F.; m. Ann Eis, Dec. 28, 1947; children: Seth, Patricia. BS in Law, U. Nebr., 1948, JD, 1950. Bar: N.Y. 1950. Assoc. Newman, Hauser & Teitler, N.Y.C., 1950-58; pvt. practice, N.Y.C., 1958-80; of counsel Conboy, Hewitt, O'Brien & Boardman, N.Y.C., 1980-84; ptnr. Tanner Propp Fersko & Sterner, N.Y.C., 1984-95, Farber & Rich LLP, N.Y.C., 1995-98; of counsel Hartman & Craven LLP, N.Y.C., 1998—2000, Jacob Medinger & Finnegan LLP, N.Y.C., 2000—. Prof. law York U., Toronto, Ont., Can., 1970, 72-73; prof. theatre law Hofstra Law Sch., Hempstead, N.Y., 1974-75; prof. New Sch. for Social Rsch., N.Y.C., 1972—, Hunter Coll., 1978. Author: From Option to Opening, 1968, 4th edit., 1st Limelight edit., 1988, Producing on Broadway, 1969, Actor's Guide: What You Should Know About the Contracts You Sign, 1971, Producing, Financing and Distributing Film, 1973, 2d edit., 1991, The Amazing Story of the Fantasticks: America's Longest Running Play, 1991, Producing Theatre: A Comprehensive Legal and Business Guide, 1981, 3d Limelight edit., 1997, Common Sense Negotiation-The Art of Winning Gracefully, 1996; gen. editor (10 vol. series, author theatre vol.) Entertainment Industry Contracts-Negotiating and Drafting Guide. With AUS, 1941-44, ETO. Mem. Order of Coif. Home: 14 E 75th St New York NY 10021-2657 Office: Jacob Medinger & Finnegan LLP 1270 Ave of Americas New York NY 10020 E-mail: donaldc14@aol.com., dcfarber@jmfnylaw.com.

FARERI, VERONICA HELEN, church musician, liturgist, educator; b. Bklyn., Sept. 11, 1953; d. Gerald Joseph and Irene Helen (Sassano) F. BMus, Westminster Choir Coll., Princeton, N.J., 1976; MMus, Northwestern U., 1983. Cert. tchr. vocal music K-12. Dir. music St. Anne Ch., Bethlehem, Pa., 1976-78; assoc. dir. music, music tchr. St. Barbara Ch., Brookfield, Ill., 1978-81; dir. music St. Elizabeth Ann Seton, Omaha, 1989-94, The Archdiocese of Omaha, Omaha, 1981-95, Sts. Peter & Paul Ch., Omaha, 1995-98; dir. liturgy and music St. Robert Bellarmine Ch., 1998—. Dir., master tchr. Nat. Children's Choir Dir. Sch., 1997—2002; workshop presenter Nat. Assn. Pastoral Musicians, Washington, 1978—. Mem. Am. Guild of Organists, Choristers Guild, Nat. Assn. Pastoral Musicians (nat. coun., nat. chair edn. com.), Music Educators Nat. conf. Home: 707 S 68th St Omaha NE 68106-1121 E-mail: VeronicaF@stroberts.com.

FARIA, ANTHONY JOHN, marketing educator, consultant, researcher; b. Highland Pk, Mich., Dec. 29, 1944; s. Anthony and Barbara Anne (Hemeli) F.; m. Barbara Elaine Oakes, Apr. 28, 1974; children: Lara Maria, Robert Gordon. BSc, Wayne State U., 1967; MBA, Mich. State U., 1969, PhD, 1972. Buyer Davidson Bros., Detroit, 1970-71; instr. Mich. State U., East Lansing, 1971-72; buyer Chrysler Corp., Centerline, Mich., 1972; asst. prof. Wayne State U., Detroit, 1973-74, Ga. So. U., Statesboro, 1974-76; dir. Bus. Resource Ctr., Windsor, Ont., Can., 1976; prof. U. Windsor, Ont., Can., 1977—. Ptnr. Adevco Cons., Belle River, Ont., 1978—; pres. Marcon Mktg., Windsor, Ont., 1979—; dir. Office of Automotive Rsch., Windsor, 1995—. Author: Compete, 1994, Creative Selling, 1995, How to Use the Business Library, 1996, The Sales Management Simulation, 1997, The Marketing Management Simulation, 1998, Principles of Marketing, 2002. Bd. dirs. Essex County Childrens Svcs. Coun., Windsor, Ont., 1985—, BBB, Windsor, 1986—; Victorian Order of Nurses, Windsor, 1991—, Assn. Bus. Simulation and Experimental Learning, Baltimore, 1999-, Mktg. Mgmt. Assn., Chgo., 2003-. Recipient Disting. Svcs. award Victorian Order Nurses, Windsor, 1996. Mem. Internat. Simulation and Gaming Assn., Sales/Mktg. Execs. Internat., Am. Mktg. Assn. (bd. dirs., Disting. Svcs. award 1995), Acad. Mktg. Scis. (Disting. Svcs. award 1993), Assn. for Bus. Simulation and Exptl. Learning (fellow 1994), Decision Scis. Inst. Republican. Avocations: golf, photography. Home: 315 Gary LaSalle ON Canada N9J 1V3 Office: Faculty Bus Adminstrn Univ Windsor Windsor ON Canada N9B 3P4

FARIS, ANNE MARIE, secondary education dean; b. Methuen, Mass., Feb. 1, 1953; d. Anthony F. and Lucille A. (Mignanelli) Bonanno; m. Michael G. Faris, Aug. 9, 1986; 1 child, Andrea M. BA, Merrimack Coll., North Andover, Mass., 1974; MEd, Fitchburg State U., 2001. Cert. secondary tchr. English, French and social studies, vocat. tech., supr./adminstr. coord., Mass. Jr. h.s. tchr. English and French St. Mary's of the Annunciation, Danvers, Mass., 1974-77; Chpt. I reading tchr. Methen (Mass.) H.S., 1977-79; tchr. English Greater Lawrence Tech. Sch., Andover, Mass., 1979-93, dean of discipline, 1993—. Cheerleading coach, tennis coach, softball coach Greater Lawrence Tech. H.S., 1979—. Mem. ASCD, Nat. Assn. Secondary Sch. Prins., U.S. Tennis Assn., Nat. Coun. Tchrs. English, Mass. Coun. Tchrs. English. Avocations: tennis, reading, piano. Office: Greater Lawrence Tech HS 57 River Rd Andover MA 01810-1144 E-mail: afaris@glts.tec.ma.us.

FARISON, JAMES BLAIR, electrical biomedical engineer, educator; b. McClure, Ohio, May 26, 1938; s. Blair Albert and Marie Lucille (Ballard) F.; m. Gail Donahue, Mar. 30, 1961; children: Jeffrey James, Mark Donahue. BS summa cum laude in Elec. Engring, U. Toledo, 1960; MS, Stanford U., 1961, PhD, 1964. Registered profl. engr., Tex., Oh. Asst. prof. elec. engring. U. Toledo, 1964-67, asso. prof., 1967-74, prof., 1974-95; asst. dean engring., 1969-71; dean engring. U. Toledo, 1971-80, prof. elec. engring. and computer sci., 1995-98; prof. bioengring., 1996-98; prof., chmn. dept. engring. Baylor U., Waco, Tex., 1998—. Adj. prof. Med. Coll. Ohio, 1987-98. Contbr. articles on control sys. design and image processing to profl. jours. Recipient Outstanding Young Man of 1971 award Toledo Jr. C. of C., 1972, Boss of Year award Limestone chpt. Am. Bus. Women's Assn., 1973, Toledo's Engr. Yr. award, 1984, Outstanding Tchr. award U. Toledo, 1986; named Disting. Alumnus, U. Toledo, 1983. Fellow Ohio Acad. Sci. (Centennial honoree 1991); mem. IEEE (sr. mem., Toledo Elec. Engr. of Yr. 1972, 74, 76), NSPE, Ohio Soc. Profl. Engrs. (Young Engr. of Yr. 1973, Citation 1983, Outstanding Engring. Educator 1984), Toledo Soc. Profl. Engrs. (Young Engr. of Yr. 1973), ASME, Biomed. Engring. Soc., Am. Soc. Engring. Edn. (Outstanding Campus Rep. 2003), Machine Vision Assn., Soc. Mfg. Engrs. (sr. mem.), Internat. Soc. Optical Engring., Instrumentation, Sys. and Automation Soc. (sr. mem.), Tex. Soc. Profl. Engrs., Soc. Woman Engrs. (sr. mem.), Blue Key, Sigma Xi, Tau Beta Pi, Pi Mu Epsilon, Phi Kappa Phi, Eta Kappa Nu (Outstanding Young Elec. Engr. 1971). Home: 9613 Old Farm Rd Waco TX 76712-6402 Office: Baylor U PO Box 97356 Waco TX 76798-7356 E-mail: Jim_Farison@baylor.edu.

FARK, SANDRA JEAN, preschool, daycare provider/administrator; b. Chgo., Mar. 18, 1953; d. Robert John and Ardis June (Kroening) McDonald; m. Terry G. Fark, July 13, 1974; children: Amanda, Allison. BA in Elem. Edn., Psychol., Concordia Tchrs. Coll., 1975; MEd in Early Chilhood Edn., Curriculum, and Instrn., U. New Orleans, 1981. Preschool tchr. Twin Oaks Early Learning Ctr., Joliet, Ill., 1974-75; first grade tchr. Kinder Castle, New Orleans, 1975-76; kindergarden tchr. St. Paul's-First English Sch., New Orleans, 1976-78, Concordia Sch., Marrero, L.A., 1978-80; dir., tchr. Bethany Lutheran Day Sch., Alexandria, Va., 1981-84, Emmanual Lutheran Nursery Sch., Dearborn, Mich., 1985-86; early childhood specialist, Parent-Child Resource Class, Adult and Community Edn. Dept. Dearborn Pub. Schs., 1986-88, preschool tchr./coord., Adult and Community Edn. Dept., 1986—. Rep. early childhood educators from U.S. at Citizen Ambassador Program, St. Petersburg, Moscow, Warsaw. Mem. Nat. Assn. for the Edn. of Young Children, Metro-Detroit Assn. for the Edn. of Young Children, Assn. for Childhood Edn. Internat. Lutheran. Avocations: reading, crafts, swimming, skiing. Home: RR 4 Box 665 Murphysboro IL 62966-9466

FARKAS, ANDREW, library director emeritus, educator, writer; b. Budapest, Hungary, Apr. 7, 1936; came to U.S., 1956; s. Miklos and Renee (Schwartz) F. Student, Eotvos Loránd U. Law, Budapest, 1954-56; BA, Occidental Coll., Los Angeles, 1959; MLS, U. Calif., Berkeley, 1962. Asst. bibliographer U. Calif., Davis, 1962-63, gift and exchange librarian, 1962-65, asst. head acquisitions dept., 1965-67, chief bibliographer, 1966-67; asst. mgr. Walter J. Johnson, Inc., N.Y.C., 1967-70; dir. libraries, prof. library sci. U. North Fla., Jacksonville, 1970—2003. Dir. Emeritus U. Library, U. North Fla., program com. mem. Fla. Gov.'s Conf. on Librs., Tallahassee, 1978; expert witness IRS, Atlanta, 1981, cons., Washington, 1982; Sharp & Gay, 1995. Author, editor: Titta Ruffo: An Anthology, 1984, (with Enrico Caruso Jr.) Enrico Caruso: My Father & My Family, 1990, (with Anna-Lisa Björling) Jussi, 1996; author: (annotated bibliography) Opera and Concert Singers, 1985; editor: (ann. handbook) Librarians Calendar, 1984—, Opera Biographies Series, Great Voices Series, Lawrence Tibbett, Singing Actor, 1989; contbr. editor: The Opera Quarterly, 1993—. Mem. Coun. Interinstnl. Planning, Jacksonville, 1983-85. With U.S. Army, 1959-61. Mem. ALA. Avocations: research, creative writing, travel, photography, book and record collecting. Office: U North Fla 4567 Saint Johns Bluff Rd S Jacksonville FL 32224-2646 E-mail: afarkas@unf.edu.

FARLEY, CYNTHIA CROCKET, special education educator, consultant; b. North Conway, N.H., June 14, 1955; d. David Scott and Beulah Gaylord (Richardson) C.; m. Robert Michael Farley, June 24, 1978; children: Robert M. Jr., Christopher R. BA, Mount Holyoke Coll., 1977; MA, Rutgers U., 1981; post-masters certification, Montclair State Coll., 1985, 92. Cert. spl. edn., elem., nursery, learning disability, N.J. Tchr. 2d grade Queen of Angels Sch., Newark, N.J., 1980-81; tchr. Comty. Day Nursery, East Orange, N.J., 1981-83, Early Intervention Program Beth Israel Hosp., Newark, 1986--87; resource ctr. tchr. Alpha (N.J.) Bd. Edn., 1989-90, Union Twp. (N.J.) Bd. Edn., 1990-91, Greewich Twp. Bd. Edn., Stewartsville, N.J., 1991-92; learning cons. Harmony Twp. Bd. Edn., Phillipsburg, N.J., 1992-93, Phillipsburg Bd Edn., 1993—. Bd. dirs. First Mountain Day Care Ctr., S. Orange, N.J., 1986-87, edn. com., Coll. Hill Presbyn., Ch., Easton, Pa., 1988-91, 96—; mem. March Sch. PTA, Easton, 1988-98. Mem. NEA, N.J. Edn. Assn., N.J. Assn. Learning Cons., Coun. for Exceptional Children, Mount Holyoke Alumnae Assn. Democrat. Presbyterian. Home: 641 Chestnut Ter Easton PA 18042-1527 Office: Phillipsburg Bd Edn Bd Edn Offices 445 Marshall St Phillipsburg NJ 08865

FARLOW, JOEL WRAY, school system administrator; b. High Point, N.C., Mar. 11, 1947; s. William Howard and Dorothy Elizabeth (Cook) F.; m. Judi Morris, Dec. 18, 1971; 1 child, Jodi. BA, High Point U., 1969; MS, N.C. A&T State U., 1979. Cert. prin. N.C.; cert. tchr. N.C. Tchrs. grade 7-9 High Point Pub. Schs., 1969-76; learning lab specialist Guilford C.C., High Point, 1975-78; chief adminstr. Wesleyan Edn. Ctr., Highpoint, 1976—. Bd. dirs. Guilford C.C. Child Care Adv. Bd.; instr. internat. Sch. Project, 1993. Author: (with others) Handbook for Christian Living, 1991. Bd. dirs. John Wesley Coll. Mem. Assn. of Christian Schs. Internat. (bd. dirs., seminar spkr.), Nat. Assn. Elem. Sch. Prins., N.C. Assn. Ind. Schs. (bd. dirs.), So. Assn. Colls. and Schs. (state com.). Wesleyan. Avocations: camping, back packing, traveling, golfing. Home: PO Box 92 Trinity NC 27370-0092 Office: Wesleyan Edn Ctr 1917 N Centennial St High Point NC 27262-7602

FARMAKIS, GEORGE LEONARD, education educator; b. Clarksburg, W.Va., June 30, 1925; s. Michael and Pipitsa (Roussopoulos) F. BA, Wayne State U., 1949, MEd, 1950, MA, 1966, PhD, 1971; MA, U. Mich., 1978; postgrad., Columbia U., Yale U., Queens Coll. Tchr. audio-visual aids dir. Roseville (Mich.) Pub. Schs., 1951-57; tchr. Birmingham (Mich.) Pub. Schs., 1957-61, Highland Park (Mich.) Pub. Schs., 1961-90; substitute tchr. Grosse Pointe Pub. Schs., 1990—2003. Lectr. Oakland County C.C., 1990-92, Lawrence U., 1990-98, Oakland U., 2000—; instr. Highland Park C.C., 1966-68, Wayne County C.C., 1969-70; assoc. mem. grad. faculty Coll. Edn. Wayne State U., 1988-89; founder Ford Sch. Math. High Intensity Tutoring Program, 1971; chairperson Highland Park Sch. Dist. Curriculum Coun. and Profl. Staff Devel. Governing Bd., 1979-82; pres. Mich. Coun. Social Studies, 1985-86; founder, dir. Mich. Social Studies Olympiad, 1987; founder, editor Mich. Social Studies Jour., 1986; participant ESEA Title I/Nat. Diffusion Network. Author, translator: Letters of Nicholas Gysis, 1842-1901; co-author: Michigan School Finance Curriculum Guide; contbr. poems to books of poetry, articles to Focus jour. Cpl. USNG, 1948-51. Recipient spl. commendation Office of Edn., 1978, Outstanding Svc. award Nat. Coun. Social Studies, 1987, Presdl. award Mich. Coun. Social Studies, 1988, 96. Mem. ASCD (bd. dirs. Mich. chpt. 1983-86), Internat. Reading Assn., Am. History Assn., Nat. Coun. Social Studies (pres. SIG-CASE 1987-88, pres. JESIG 1988-89), Am. Philol. Assn., U. Mich. Alumni Assn., Wayne State U. Coll. Edn. Alumni Assn. (bd. dirs. 1985-86), Mich. Reading Assn., Masons (32 degree), Shriners, Ancient Accepted Scottish Rite, Phi Delta Kappa (Outstanding Educators award 1988). Greek Orthodox. Home: 15215 Windmill Dr Macomb MI 48044-4929

FARMER, ANN DAHLSTROM, English language educator; b. South Gate, Calif., June 18, 1934; d. Merrill Xanthus and Marcia Hazel (Ross) Dahlstrom; m. Roger Lee Chandler, Aug. 19, 1956 (div. 1960); 1 child, Mark Walton Chandler; m. Malcolm French Farmer, Oct. 25, 1963. BA, Whittier Coll., 1956, MA, 1971, Calif. State U., Fullerton, 1976. Prof.'s asst. Whittier (Calif.) Coll., 1960-62, gen. studies instr., 1963-70, English instr., 1970-72, dir. freshman English, 1972-87, dir. English lang. prog. for internat. students, 1978-86, asst. prof. English, 1983-95, assoc. prof. English, 1995—99. Author: Jessamyn West, rev. edit., 1996; co-author: Jessamyn West: A Descriptive and Annotated Bibliography, 1998, Creative Analysis, rev. edit., 1978. Mem.: Linguistic Soc., Western Lit. Assn., AAUW (gift honoree 1995, Las Distinguidas award 2003), Whittier Hist. Soc. (sec. 2000—), Friends of the Shannon Ctr. at Whittier Coll. (Bookfaire co-chair 2000—, v.p. 2002—, Dorothea S. Boyd award 2001), Phi Kappa Phi, Delta Kappa Gamma (Star in Edn. 1990). Democrat. Mem. Soc. Of Friends. Avocations: dollhouse miniatures, rubber stamps, antiques, family history, cats. E-mail: Farmer6146@yahoo.com.

FARMER, HIRAM LEANDER, physical education educator; b. Tallahassee, Fla., Aug. 23, 1958; s. Alton Ernest and Betty Geneva (Gainey) F.; m. Yolanda Lavonne Vines, Jan. 15, 1988; children: Gregory Maurice, Grant Malik. BS, Fla. A&M U., 1981. Phys. edn. tchr. MacIntyre Park, Thomasville, Ga., 1981-82; instructional asst. Program for Adolescence Coop. Edn. Sch., Tallahassee, 1982-88, Bond Elem. Sch., Tallahassee, 1988, Leon County Juvenile Detention Ctr., Tallahassee, 1988; phys. edn. tchr. Charles R. Hadley Elem. Sch., Miami, Fla., 1988—, head dept. phys. edn., 1991—, chmn. health and nutrition, 1993-94; 2d v.p. Christian Plan Support Group, 1994-95. Chmn. sports ministry Covenant Missionary Bapt. Ch., Florida City, Fla., 1994—, youth ministry, 1988—, Christian Plan Support Group 2d v.p., 1994-95, asst. chmn. bd. trustees; coord. Jump Rope for Heart, Am. Heart Assn., Miami, 1991—; mem. spl. events adv. com. City of Homestead, 1999. Mem. ASCD, Fla. A&M U. Nat. Alumni Assn., Kappa Alpha Psi. Avocations: exercising, music, sports. Home: 813 SW 5th St Homestead FL 33030-6977 Office: Charles R Hadley Elem Sch 8400 NW 7th St Miami FL 33126-3802

FARMER, JAMES ALEXANDER, JR., retired education educator; b. N.Y.C., Mar. 12, 1931; s. James A. and Margaret (Belknap) F.; m. Helen Sweeney, Jan. 25, 1955; children: James S., Paul A. BA, Hamilton Coll., 1953; MDiv, Union Theol. Sem., 1956; MA, Columbia U., 1968, EdD, 1969. ordained by United Ch. of Christ, 1956. Pastor Oxford (Conn.) Congl. Ch., 1956-59; founding pastor United Ch. of Hayward, Calif., 1959-63; minister of adult edn. Riverside Ch., N.Y.C., 1963-69; asst. prof. UCLA, 1969-74; assoc. prof. U. Ill., Urbana/Champaign, 1974-93, prof. continuing edn., 1993-98, prof. emer., 1998—. Cons. Am. Acad. Orthopaedic Surgeons, 1970—, Am. Orthopaedic Soc. for Sports Medicine, 1985—. Co-author: Psychomotor Skills in Orthopaedic Surgery, 1981, Instructional Design: Implications From Cognitive Science, 1991. Recipient George D. Rovere Edn. award Am. Orthopaedic Soc. for Sports Medicine, 1994, Career Achievement award U. Ill. Coll. Edn. Mem.: Adult Edn. Assn. of USA (pres. 1975), Am. Osteo. Acad. Orthopedics (hon.). Avocations: fishing, snorkeling, diving. Home: 2204 S Staley Rd Champaign IL 61822-9763 E-mail: jfarmer@uiuc.edu.

FARMER, JANE WARNER, elementary education educator; b. Florence, S.C., Feb. 16, 1956; d. Eugene Lawson and Viola (Warner) F. BS, Francis Marion Coll., 1976, MEd, 1982. cert. elem. tchr., S.C. Tchr. Johnakin Jr. High Sch., Marion, S.C., 1977-78, Southside Elem. Sch., Marion, 1978-79, North Vista Elem. Sch., Florence, 1979-85, Spring Elem. Sch., Darlington,, S.C., 1985-95, Brunson-Dargan Elem.Sch., Darlington, S.C., 1995—. Treas. Pisgah United Meth. Ch., Florence, 1985-89, 90-93. Mem. Nat. Coun. Tchrs. Math., Internat. Reading Assn. (Pee Dee coun.), Palmetto State Tchrs. Assn. Avocations: cross-stitch, cake decorating, reading. Home: 3307 Cherrywood Rd Florence SC 29501-7352 Office: Brunson-Dargan Elem Sch 400 Wells St Darlington SC 29532-3024

FARMER, JANENE ELIZABETH, artist, educator; b. Albuquerque, Oct. 16, 1946; d. Charles John Watt and Regina Mortimere (Brown) Kruger; m. Michael Hugh Bolton, Apr. 1965 (div.); m. Frank Urban Farmer, May 1972 (div.). BA in Art, San Diego State U., 1969; postgrad., U. San Diego, San Diego State U., U. Calif., San Diego, 1983—85. Owner, operator Iron Walrus Pottery, 1972-79. Tchr. Cath. schs., San Diego, 1983—86, Ramona Unified Sch. Dist., 1986—, mentor tchr., 1994—98; tchr. environ. art San Diego Natural History Mus., 1996—97, San Diego Wild Animal Park, 1996; cons. tchr. Ramona Unified Sch. Dist., 2001—03; instr. Extension Dept. U. Calif., San Diego, 2003. Exhibited in group shows at San Diego Mus. Art, San Diego City Adminstrn. Bldg., University City Libr., San Diego, Art Scene Gallery, San Diego, Kauai, Hawaii, Am. Soc. Interior Designers, San Diego, Sierra Club Bookstore, San Diego, Quail Bot. Gardens, Encinitas, Calif. Mem. Coronado Arts and Humanities Coun., 1979-81; edn. adv. com. La Jolla (Calif.) Playhouse, 1996; edn. com. Calif. Wolf Ctr., 1999-2001, U. Calif. San Diego Extension, 2003. Grantee Calif. Arts Coun., 1980-81, resident artist, instr. U. Calif., San Diego; U. San Diego grad. fellow Dept. Edn., 1984. Roman Catholic. Home: # 35 4435 Nobel Dr San Diego CA 92122-1559 E-mail: farmerj4@mac.com.

FARNHAM, ANTHONY EDWARD, English language educator; b. Oakland, Calif., July 2, 1930; s. Willard Edward and Frances Fern (Hicks) F.; m. Frances Anne Larkey, Dec. 28, 1957; children: Allen Nicholas, Timothy John. AB, U. Calif.-Berkeley, 1951; MA, Harvard U., 1957, PhD, 1964. Instr. English Mt. Holyoke Coll., South Hadley, Mass., 1961-64, asst. prof., 1964-69, assoc. prof., 1969-72, prof., 1972-99, dept. chmn., 1979-85, prof. emeritus, 1999—. Editor: A Sourcebook in the History of English, 1969; author: Statement and Search in the Confessio Amantis, Mediaevalia 16, 1993. Served with M.I. U.S. Army, 1953-56. Mem. MLA, Am. Cath. Hist. Assn., Medieval Acad. Am., Assn. Literary Scholars and Critics, Dante Soc., New Chaucer Soc., Phi Beta Kappa. Roman Catholic. Home: 23 Atwood Rd South Hadley MA 01075-1601 Office: Mt Holyoke Coll Dept English 50 Coll St South Hadley MA 01075-6421

FARNHAM, DAWN MARIE, secondary education educator; b. French Camp, Calif., Aug. 16, 1945; d. Frank Page and Claudia Marie (Howard) F. BA in English, Colby Coll., 1975; MA in English, U. Maine, 1990. Cert. profl. tchr. grades 7-12, Maine. Tchr. English Hampton High Sch., Hampton, Victoria, Australia, 1975-77, Dirigo High Sch., Dixfield, Maine, 1979-80, Fryeburg (Maine) Acad., 1980—, chairperson English dept., 1988—. Advisor on tchr. assessment design team Nat. Bd. Profl. Tchg. Stds. at Edn. Devel. Ctr., Newton, Mass., 1994-95. Grantee NEH Inst., 1985, Maine Collaborative Inst., 1993. Mem. ASCD, Nat. Coun. Tchrs. English, New England Assn. Tchrs. English, Maine Coun. for English Lang. Arts. Home: PO Box 344 Conway NH 03818-0344 Office: Fryeburg Acad 152 Main St Fryeburg ME 04037-1329

FARNSWORTH, E(DWARD) ALLAN, lawyer, educator; b. Providence, June 30, 1928; s. Harrison Edward and Gertrude (Romig) F.; m. Patricia Ann Nordstrom, May 30, 1952; children: Jeanne Scott, Karen Ladd, Edward Allan (dec.), Pamela Ann. BS, U. Mich., 1948; MA, Yale U., 1949; JD (Ordronaux prize 1952), Columbia U., 1952; LLD (hon.), Dickinson Law Sch., Pa. State U., 1988; Docteur en Droit (hon.), U. Paris, 1988, U. Louvain, 1989. Bar: D.C 1952, N.Y. 1956. Mem. faculty Columbia U., N.Y.C., 1954—, prof. law, 1959—, Alfred McCormack prof. law, 1970—. Vis. prof. U. Istanbul, U. Dakar, 1964, U. Paris, 1974-75, 90, 93, Harvard Law S ch., 1970-71, Stetson Coll. Law, 1991, 94, U. Mich., 1994; mem. faculty Salzburg Seminar Am. Law, 1963, Columbia-Leyden-Amsterdam program on Am. law, 1964, 69, 73, 85, San Diego Inst. Internat. and Comparative Law, Paris, 1982, 94, Tulane Summer Inst., Paris, 1995, 98, 99, 00, Rhodes, 1996, China Ctr. for Am. Law Study, Beijing, 1986; dir. orientation program on Am. law Assn. Am. Law Schs., 1965-68; U.S. rep. UN Commn. on Internat. Trade Law, 1970-81; reporter Restatement of Contracts 2nd, 1971-80; cons. N.Y. State Law Revision Commn., 1956, 58, 59, 61, P.R. comml. code revision, 1988-91; mem. coms. validity and agy. internat. sales contracts Internat. Inst. Unification Pvt. Law, Rome, 1966-72, mem. governing coun., 1978-98; mem. adv. com. on pvt. internat. law Sec. of State, 1985-89; spl. counsel city reorgn. N.Y.C. Coun., 1966-68; U.S. del. Vienna Conf. on Internat. Sales Law, 1980, Bucharest and Geneva Conf. on Internat. Agy., 1979, 83. Author: Changing Your Mind: The Law of Regretted Decisions, 1998, An Introduction to the Legal System of the United States, 3d edit., 1993; (with J. Honnold, S. Harris, C. Mooney, and C. Reitz) Cases and Materials on Commercial Law, 5th edit., 1993; (with W.F. Young and C. Sanger) Cases and Materials on Contracts, 6th edit., 2001, Cases and Materials on Negotiable Instruments, 4th edit., 1993, Treatise on Contracts, 1982, 3d edit., 1999; (with V. Mozolin) Contract Law in the USSR and the United States, 1987, Farnsworth on Contracts, 3 vols., 1990, 2nd edit., 1998, United States Contract Law, 1992, 2d revised edit, 1999. Capt. USAAF, 1952-54. Fellow British Acad.; mem. ABA (Theberge award for pvt. internat. law 1996), Am. Philos. Soc., Am. Law Inst., Assn. of Bar of City of N.Y. (chmn. com. on fgn. and comparative law 1967-70, chmn. spl. com. on products liability 1979-82), Phi Beta Kappa, Phi Delta Phi. Unitarian Universalist. Home: 201 Lincoln St Englewood NJ 07631-3158 Office: Columbia U 435 W 116th St New York NY 10027-7201 E-mail: allan@law_columbia.edu.

FARNSWORTH, JUDITH MARIE, elementary education educator; b. Lapeer, Mich., May 21, 1942; d. Warren Willard and Florence LaVern (Eckel) Gingell; m. Leon Edwin Farnsworth, June 8, 1963; children: Deborah Lynn, Edwin Lee. BS, Ea. U., 1964; M of Elem. Edn. Adminstrn., Ctrl. Mich. U., 1989. Cert. ITIP tng., teacher effectiveness tng. Subs. tchr. pub. schs., Davison, Lapeer, Mich., 1964-66; tchr. 1st grade Davison Pub. Schs., 1966-67; tchr. 4th grade Fowler (Mich.) Pub. Schs., 1975-77, tchr. 1st grade, 1977—, supervising tchr., 1992, 94. Chair Fowler Lang. Curriculum Team, 1991-92. Leader Girl Scouts, Grand Ledge, Mich., 1971-75; supt. Beginner Dept. Sunday Sch., Bpat. Ch., 1972-75, ch. organist, 1979—; counselor Rainbows, Fowler, 1990-91. Mem. NEA, Mich. Edn. Assn., Mich. Reading Assn., Mich. Accreditation Prrogram for Elem. Schs. (chair 1989—), Fowler Edn. Assn. (chair, bargain team mem. 1981, pres. 1983—), Clinton Reading Assn., Ingham Clinton Edn. Assn. Avocations: crafts, playing piano and organ, reading. Home: 1021 Tulip St Grand Ledge MI 48837-2044

FAROKHI, HELEN ELIZABETH (BETH), university official; b. Augusta, Ga., Feb. 16, 1948; d. Walker Leonard and Helen (Ouzts) Dupree; m. Nasrolah Rashid, Nov. 30, 1974; children: Amir Reza, Arman. BA, LaGrange Coll., 1970; MA in Tchg., Emory U., 1974; EdD, U. Ga., 1978. Tchr. Cobb County Bd. Edn., Marietta, Ga., 1970-76; rsch. asst. Inst. Higher Edn., U. Ga., Athens, 1976-77; higher edn. cons. Clayton Jr. Coll. (now Clayton State Coll.), Morrow, Ga., 1977-78, Ga. Gov.'s Com. on Postsecondary Edn., Atlanta, 1978-82, Profl. Standards Commn., Atlanta, 1979-80; higher edn. cons. Ga. career info. system Ga. State U., Atlanta, 1982-83, asst. coord. spl. projects, 1983, coord. curriculum and scheduling Coll. Edn., 1983-91, adminstrv. specialist, 1991-92, assoc. to dean, 1992—. Contbr. articles to profl. jours. Treas., program chmn., pres.-elect, pres. Galloway Sch. Parent Assn., Atlanta, 1985-98; vice chmn. gen. parent solicitation com. Galloway Sch., 1986, trustee, 1988-89; mem. coun. Atlanta United Way, 1988-91; adminstrv. bd. East Cobb United Meth., 1991-93; mem. curriculum adv. bd. Atlanta Girls Sch., 2000, strategic planning com., 2002; mentor Big Brothers and Big Sisters, 2001-; mem. Leadership North Fulton, 2001. NSF grantee, 1995-99. Mem. AAUW (bull. editor Cobb County bd. 1982-83, v.p. programs 1983-85, pres. 1986-88, named gift honoree 1991, 93, 97, program v.p. Ga. divsn. 1989-91, pres.-elect 1991-92, pres. 1992-94, nat. bd. dirs., South Atlantic regional dir., 1995-99, legal advocacy fund bd. dirs. 1997-99, exec. v.p./sec. 2001-), Internat. Fedn. Univ. Women, Kappa Delta Pi (coll. counselor 1990-95). Avocations: reading, women's and children's issues, sports, walking, travel. Home: 101 Hunting Creek Dr Marietta GA 30068-3417 Office: Ga State U Coll Edn University Plz Atlanta GA 30303 E-mail: bfarokhi@gsu.edu.

FARQUHAR, JOHN WILLIAM, physician, educator; b. Winnipeg, Man., Can., June 13, 1927; arrived in U.S., 1934; s. John Giles and Marjorie Victoria (Roberts) Farquhar; m. Christine Louise Johnson, July 14, 1968; children: Margaret F., John C.M.;children from previous marriage: Bruce E., Douglas G. AB, U. Calif., Berkeley, 1949; MD, U. Calif., San Francisco, 1952. Intern U. Calif. Hosp., San Francisco, 1952—53, resident, 1953—54, 1957—58, postdoctoral fellow, 1955—57; resident U. Minn., Mpls., 1954—55; rsch. assoc. Rockefeller U., N.Y.C., 1958—62; asst. prof. medicine Stanford (Calif.) U., 1962—66, assoc. prof., 1966—73, prof., 1978—, C.F. Rehnborg prof. in disease prevention, 1989—2000; dir. Stanford Ctr. Rsch. in Disease Prevention, 1973—98; dir. collaborating ctr. for chronic disease prevention WHO, 1985—99; prof. health rsch. and policy, 1988—. Mem. staff Stanford U. Hosp.; chair Victoria Declaration Implementation com. Author: The American Way of Life Need Not Be Hazardous to Your Health, 1978, 1987; author: (with Gene Spiller) The Last Puff, 1990; author: The Victoria Declaration for Heart Health, 1992, How to Reduce Your Risk of Heart Disease, 1994, The Catalonia Declaration: Investing in Heart Health, 1996, Worldwide Efforts to Improve Heart Disease, 1997; author: (with Spiller) Diagnosis Heart Disease: Answers to Your Questions about Recovery and Lasting Health, 2001; contbr. articles to profl. jours. Served with U.S. Army, 1944—46. Recipient James D. Bruce award, ACP, 1983, Myrdal prize, 1986, Dana award for Pioneering Achievement in Health, Dana Found., 1990, Nat. Cholesterol award for Pub. Edn., Nat. Cholesterol Edn. Program of NIH, 1991, Rsch. Achievement award, Am. Heart Assn., 1992, Order of St. George for Svc. to Autonomous Govt. of Catalonia, 1996, Joseph Stokes Preventive Cardiology award, Am. Soc. Preventive Cardiology, 1999, Ancel Keys Meml. lectureship, Am. Heart Assn., 2000. Mem.: Internat. Heart Health Soc., Soc. Behavioral Medicine (pres. 1991—92), Am. Heart Assn. (coun. epidemiology and prevention), Am. Soc. Clin. Investigation, Inst. Medicine NAS, Gold Headed Cane Soc., Alpha Omega Alpha, Sigma Xi. Episcopalian. Office: Stanford U Sch of Medicine Prevention Rsch Ctr 211 Quarry Rd Stanford CA 94305-5705 Fax: 650-498-7623. E-mail: JFarquhar@stanford.edu.

FARQUHARSON, PATRICE ELLEN, primary school educator; b. West Haven, Conn., Feb. 10, 1956; d. Robert Douglas and Margaret Ellen (Dietle) Farquharson; children: Julia, Elena. BS in Edn., U. Conn., 1978; MS in Edn., So. Conn. State U., 1984; EdD, Nova Southeastern U., 1995. Cert. tchr., adminstr., Conn. Asst. dir. West Haven (Conn.) Child Devel. Ctr., 1978-82, exec. dir., 1982-96, 97—; edn. cons. dept. pediatrics div. child and family studies U. Conn., 1993-95; mgmt. cons. West Haven Child Devel. Ctr., Inc., 1996—; asst. prof. early childhood, dir. early childhood programs Teikyo-Post U., Waterbury, Conn., 1996—. Adj. prof. U. Conn. Inst. Pub. Policy, 1996; cons. early childhood edn., workshop presenter, internat. and New Eng., 1987—; profl. cheerleader The New Eng. Patriots football team, 1980; dir., ptnr. New Eng. Cheerleading Camp, West Haven, 1982-84; cheerleading coach U. New Haven, 1982-90; textbook webguide developer Thomson Pub., 2001; online course developer Teikyo Post U., Charter Oak State Coll. Conn. Early Childhood Edn. Coun. scholar, 1993-96. Mem. AAUW, Nat. Assn. Edn. Young Children, Conn. Assn. Edn. Young Children, Coalition for Children (Jimmy Fund Cmty. Svc. award 2001), Dirs. Forum, Gov. Adv. Coun. Early Childhood Edn., South Ctrl. Conn. Agy. on Aging (adv. coun.), West Haven Rotary Club. Avocations: ballet, jazz dancing, horseback riding, reading, traveling. Home: 5 Sunflower Cir West Haven CT 06516-6229 Office: West Haven Child Devel Ctr 201 Noble St West Haven CT 06516-6047

FARR, JUDITH BANZER, writer, literature educator; b. N.Y.C., Mar. 13, 1937; d. Russell John and Frances Anna (Wissell) Banzer; m. George F. Farr, Jr., June 30, 1962; 1 child, Alec Winfield. BA, Marymount Manhattan Coll., 1957, LHD, 1992; MA, Yale U., 1959, PhD, 1965. Instr. in English Vassar Coll., Poughkeepsie, N.Y., 1961-63; asst. prof. St. Mary's Coll., Moraga, Calif., 1964-68; assoc. prof. SUNY, New Paltz, 1968-77, Georgetown U., Washington, 1978-90, prof. of English and Am. Lit., 1990-99, prof. emerita, 1999—. Vis. assoc. prof. Georgetown U., 1977-78. Author: The Life and Art of Elinor Wylie, 1983, The Passion of Emily Dickinson, 1992, I Never Came to You in White: A Novel, 1996; editor: Twentieth Century Interpretations of Sons and Lovers, 1970, New Century Views: Emily Dickinson, 1995; contbr. articles, poems, short stories to profl. and comml. publs. Am. Philos. Soc. fellow, 1983, Morgan-Porter fellow Yale U., 1960-61; grantee Am. Coun. Learned Socs., 1984, 86, N.Y. State Rsch. FOund., 1974, Georgetown U. Ctr. German Studies, 1992; recipient Alumnae award for Distinction in Arts and Letters, Marymount Manhattan Coll., N.Y.C., 1976, Alpha Sigma Nu Best Book award, 1993. Mem. AAUP, Modern Lang. Assn., Cosmos Club. Avocations: antiques, especially 18th century china, gardening, american painting. Home: 5064 Lowell St NW Washington DC 20016-2616 Office: Georgetown U 330 New North Hall 37th St and O Washington DC 20057

FARR, REETA RAE, special education administrator; b. Edhube, Tex., Jan. 15, 1926; d. Paul Ray and Verna (Biggerstaff) Wright; m. Gerald Edward Self, June 1, 1946 (dec. Dec. 1977); children: Eddie, Lee; m. Barnie B. Farr Jr., Dec. 28, 1978 (wid. Mar. 1997). BS, Southeastern Okla. State U., 1959, MS. 1963. 1st grade tchr. Sherman (Tex.) Pub. Schs., 1959-61, Denison (Tex.) Pub. Schs., 1961-64, spl. edn. tchr., 1964-72, spl. edn. counselor, 1972-76, spl. edn. diagnostician, 1976-85, dir. spl. edn., 1985-94. Named Educator of Yr. Denison Edn. Assn., 1991. Mem. NEA, AAUW (pres. 1981-83), Tex. State Tchrs. Assn. (local pres. 1971), Tex. Ednl. Diagnostician Assn., Tex. Assn. Counseling and Devel., Phi Delta Kappa (sec.-treas. 1983, del. 1978-99), Delta Kappa Gamma. Mem. Ch. Of Christ. Avocation: reading. Home: 23000 2d Fork Rd Ola ID 83657-5015 E-mail: rfarr@bigskytel.com.

FARRAN, DALE CLARK, education educator; Student, Wesleyan Coll., Macon, Ga., 1961—63; BA in Psychology with highest honors, U. N.C., 1965; PhD in Edn. and Child Devel., Bryn Mawr Coll., 1975. Rsch. assoc., curriculum specialist N.C. Advancement Sch., Winston-Salem, 1965—67; rsch. assoc. Pa. Advancement Sch., Phila., 1967—71; with psychology dept. Children's Aid Soc., Phila., 1971—74; NICHHD postdoctoral fellow Frank Porter Graham Child Devel. Ctr. U. N.C., Chapel Hill, 1974—75, instr. Sch. Edn., 1975—76, clin. asst. prof. divsn. spl. edn., Sch. Edn., 1976—80, rsch. assoc. Health Svcs. Rsch. Ctr., 1980—86, faculty Bush Inst. for Child and Family Policy, Faculty, Rsch. Tng. Program for Rsch. in Mental Retardation, 1979—84, clin. assoc. prof. divsn. spl. edn. Sch. Edn., 1980—84; assoc. prof. psychology dept. U. Hawaii, 1984—87; head child devel. rsch. dept. Ctr. for Devel. Early Edn. Kamehameha Schs./Bishop Estate, 1984—87; prof. dept. human devel. and family studies U. N.C., Greensboro, 1987—96; prof. depts. tchg. and learning, psychology and human devel. dir. Susan Gray Sch. for Children, assoc. dir. John F. Kennedy Ctr. for Rsch. Human Devel Peabody Coll., Vanderbilt U., Nashville, 1996—. Co-author (with D. Cooper): (book) Cooper-Farran Behavioral Rating Scale, 1991; co-editor (with J. D. McKinney): Risk in Intellectual and Psychosocial Development, 1986; co-editor: (with L. Feagans) The Language of Children Reared in Poverty: Implications for Evaluation and Intervention, 1982; contbr. articles to profl. jours. and chpts. to books. Named Profl. of Yr., Mayor's Adv. Coun. on Disabilities, 1999, hon. coach, Vanderbilt U. Women's Basketball Team, 1998, 2000; recipient Peabody Award for Excellence in Rsch., 1984, Outstanding Young Scholar award, Spencer Found., 1978, 1980. Fellow: Am. Psychol. Soc.; mem.: CEC (divsn. early childhood), Nat. Assn. for Edn. of Young Children, Am. Ednl. Rsch. Assn. (early childhood spl. interest group), Internat. Soc. for Study of Behavioral Devel., Soc. for Rsch. in Child Devel., Phi Beta Kappa. Office: Vanderbilt U Peabody Coll Dept Tchg and Learning PO Box 330 Nashville TN 37203*

FARRAND, WILLIAM RICHARD, geology educator; b. Columbus, Ohio, Apr. 27, 1931; s. Harvey Ashley and Esther Evelyn (Bowman) F.; m. Claudine Brickmann, Aug. 17, 1962 (div. 1983); children: Frederic Hervé, Anne Marie; m. Carola Hill Stearns, Dec. 6, 1988; 1 child, Michelle Diane. BS in Geology, Ohio State U., 1955, MS in Geology, 1956; PhD, U. Mich., 1960. Rsch. assoc. Lamont Geol. Obs. Columbia U., N.Y., 1960-61, asst. prof., 1961-64; rsch. assoc. in geology U. Mich., Ann Arbor, 1962; postdoctoral rsch. fellow NAS/NRC, Strasbourg, France, 1963-64; asst. prof. geol. scis. U. Mich., Ann Arbor, 1965-67, assoc. prof. geol scis., 1967-74, prof., 1974-2000, prof. emeritus, 2000—, curator analytical collections Mus. Anthropology, 1975-2000, dir. Exhibit Mus., 1993-2000. Vis. prof. U. Strasbourg, France, 1964-65, Hebrew U., Jerusalem, 1971-72, U. Colo., Boulder, 1983, U. Tex., Austin, 1986; fellow Inst. for Advanced Study, Ind. U., 1985; mem. archaeometry panel NSF, 1989-91; apptd. mem. U.S. Nat. com. Internat. Quaternary Assn., 1989-99, chair, 1995-99; sr. fellow Inst. for Study Earth and Man, So. Meth. U., Dallas, 1991—. Mem. editorial bd. Quaternary Sci. Review, Paleorient, Jour. Archaeological Sci., Review Archaeology, Stratigraphica Archaeologica; contbr. articles and maps to profl jours. With U.S. Army, 1951-53. Fellow AAAS, Geol. Soc. Am. (mem. panel quaternary geology and geomorphology divsn. 1978, vice chmn. archaeological geology divsn, 1979, chmn, 1980, Archaeological Geology award 1986), Ohio Acad. Sci., 1994-96; mem. Am. Quaternary Assn. (sec. 1978-90, program chmn. biennial meeting 1980, pres. 1994-96), Mich. Acad. Sci., Arts and Letters, Internat. Union for Quaternary Rsch. (chmn. working group on Southwest Asia commn. paleoecology early man 1975-83), L'Assn. Francaise pour l'Etude de Quaternaire, Sigma Xi, Phi Beta Kappa. Office: U Mich Mus Anthropology 4009 Ruthven Mus Ann Arbor MI 48109-1079 E-mail: wfarrand@umich.edu.

FARRAR, DAVID CONRAD, secondary school educator, coach; b. Lincoln, R.I., Nov. 26, 1942; s. David Victor and Edith Mae (Conrard) F.; m. Ruth Doris Farrar, May 24, 1980; children: Kenneth L., David L., Jonathan J., Monique J., Daniel C. BS in Edn., U. Maine, 1964; MEd, Salem State Coll., 1968, postgrad., U. N.H. Cert. tchr., Mass. Tchr. history, soc. studies and guidance Beverly (Mass.) H.S., 1964—, cross-country coach, track coach, 1969-90, class advisor, 1984-87, 90—, mem. faculty senate, 1991—. Cons. Commonwealth of Mass., Dept. Edn., 1998—, Boston Globe, 1999; devel. curriculum workshops and consultation U. KwaZulu Natal, Pieter, Maritzburg, Republic of South Africa. Mem. vestry St. Peter's Ch., Beverly, 1988-89; regional rep. Diocese of Mass., 1988-94, mem. congl. resources and devel. commn., 1992-96, mem. diocesan coun., 1999—; campaign worker Dem. Orgn., Beverly, 1992-94. Fellow R.I. Coll., 1992, Salem State Coll., 1989; Tchg. fellow Thomas B. Watson Inst. for Internat. Studies Brown U., Providence, 1995. Mem. NEA, Nat. Coun. Social Studies, Orgn. Am. Historians, New Eng. History Tchrs. Assn., Mass. Tchrs. Assn., Beverly Tchrs. Assn. (gov. bd. 1992-94, rep. 1980-94), Mass. Track and Field Ofcls. Assn., Nat. Honor Soc. (hon.). Episcopalian. Avocations: popular music records, physical fitness, track and field, reading. Home: 16 Herrick St Beverly MA 01915-3126

FARRAR, RICHARD BARTLETT, JR., school system administrator; b. Penn Yan, N.Y., Apr. 25, 1939; s. Richard B. and Margaret M. (Stevenson) F. BS, Houghton Coll., 1960; MEd, Frostburg (Md.) State U., 1990. Cert. wildlife biologist. Sci. tchr. Hinckley (Maine) Sch., 1960-61, Concord (Mass.) High Sch., 1962-64; program dir. Mass. Audubon Soc., Lincoln, 1964-65; instr. U. Ill., Chgo., 1966-68; chair sci. dept. Woodstock Country Sch., 1968-73; exec. dir. Vt. Inst. Natural Sci., Woodstock, 1971-73, N.J. Audubon Soc., Franklin Lakes, 1974-78; field exec. Nat. Wildlife Fedn., Washington, 1979-81; wildlife biology cons. Washington, 1982-86; lead sci. tchr. Garrett County Bd. Edn., Oakland, Md., 1987-97; dir. PPEPTEC High Schs., Tucson, 1997—. Rsch. advisor Coastal Facilities Rev. Act, State of N.J., Trenton, 1977-78; mem. State of N.J. Natural Resources Coun., 1978-79; advisor Savage River State Forest Coun., 1991-92; NASA sci. tchr. amb., 1994—; mem. legisl. subcom. on edn. State of Ariz., 2000—. Author: Birds of East-Central Vermont, 1971, The Hungry Snowbird, 1975, The Birds' Woodland, 1976; editor Vt. Natural History mag., 1970-73, N.J. Audubon mag., 1974-78; contbr. articles to popular and sci. publs. Treas. League for Conservation Legis., N.J., 1978; dir. Mid.-Atlantic Naturalist Soc., Md., 1981-82. Recipient Outstanding Biology Tchr. award Nat. Assn. Biology Tchrs., 1971, Conservation award Connecticut River Watershed Coun., 1971, Children's Sci. Book award Children's Libr. Coun., 1975, NSTA, 1976. Mem. Assn. for Supervision and Curriculum Devel., Nat. Coun. for Tchrs. Math., Internat. Reading Assn., Nat. Sci. Tchrs. Assn., Nat. Coun. for Social Studies, Rotary (treas. Friendsville, Md. 1988). E-mail: rfarrar2@earthlink.net.

FARRAR, RUTH DORIS, reading and literacy educator; b. Freeport, N.Y., June 11, 1943; d. Frederick and Ruth Harriet (Pagington) F.; m. David Conrad Farrar. BA, Ea. Nazarene Coll., 1965; MS in Edn., Hofstra U., 1975, EdD, 1989. Cert. cons. tchr. of reading and supr. reading programs, tchr. English 7-12. Tchr. English Newport (R.I.) Pub. Schs., 1965-66; tchr. reading and English Norwin Pub. Schs., North Huntingdon, Pa., 1966-67; kindergarten tchr. USN Base, Somerset, Bermuda, 1967-68; clin. diagnostician Brookwood Child Care, Bklyn., 1972-76; instr. reading Nassau C.C., Garden City, N.Y., 1974-76; reading specialist Cambridge (Mass.) Sch. Dept., 1976-80; reading coord. Brookwood Sch., Manchester, Mass., 1980-90; asst. prof. Bridgewater (Mass.) State Coll., 1990-92, assoc. prof., 1998—2003, prof., 2003—; asst. prof. Rivier Coll., Nashua, N.H., 1992-93. Dir. The Reading Ctr. Bridgewater State Coll., Am. Reads, Bridgewater State Coll.; vis. lectr. Salem (Mass.) State Coll., 1987—; adj. prof. Hofstra U., Hempstead, NY, 1989—; mem. Mass. Consortium for Media Literacy Edn., 1994—; sponsor summer reading enrichment program Bridgewater-Raynham Regional Pub. Schs., 1994—; coord. grad. programs reading, coord. curriculum leadership ctr. Bridgewater State Coll., co-chair student affairs com., 1998—, convener Resources for Reading Specialists; univ.

rep., mem. Curriculum Team for English Lang. Arts Salem Pub. Schs., Canton, Mass., Pub. Schs. PALMS Leadership Team, LEAD Program; mem., curriculum cons. Brockton Pub. H.S.; grant dir. after-sch. reading enrichment program Brockton Pub. Schs., 1998—, grant dir. Sat. morning reading enrichment program; presenter Assn. Am. Colls. Tchr. Edn., 2000; ptnr., trainer, cons. John F. Kennedy Sch., Brockton, 2000—; lectr. U. Natal at Pietermaritzburg, Kwazulu, South Africa, 2002—; co-sponsor UN Literacy Day, 2003; mem. cmty. coordinating coun. Rockland Regional Adult Learning Ctr.; cons. Houghton-Mifflin Co., McGraw Hill, Allyn & Bacon, Bay State Readers Initiative Tng. Modules, Bay State Readers Initiative Higher Edn. Editor The Massachusetts Primer, 1991-94; reviewer Mass. Dept. of Edn. Baystate Readers Initiative. Sr. warden St. Peter's Episcopal Ch., Beverly, Mass., chair spiritual formation com., 2000—01. Grantee Ctr. for Advancement Rsch. and Tchg., Bridgewater State Coll., 1993-94; fellow reading dept. Hofstra U., Hempstead, N.Y., 1985-86; Continuing Edn. Faculty Award, New England Region of the Univ. Continuing Edn. Assn., 2003. Mem. ASCD, Am. Edn. Rsch. Assn., Internat. Reading Assn. (presenter, chair publs. spl. interest group), Internat. Listening Assn. (presenter), Assn. Tchr. Edn. (presenter, curriculum, assessment com.), Nat. Coun. Tchrs. English (presenter), Mass. Reading Assn. (bd. dirs.), Mass. Assn. Coll./Univ. Reading Educators (bd. dirs. 1993—, pres. 1998-99), Kappa Delta Pi. Home: 16 Herrick Street Ext Beverly MA 01915-2731 Office: Bridgewater State Coll Sch Edn 133 Hart Hl Bridgewater MA 02325-0001 E-mail: rfarrar@bridgew.edu.

FARRAR, SUSAN LEE, special education educator, consultant; b. Princeton, Ind., Sept. 30, 1960; d. William Ellis and Mary Lee (Staley) Hinman; m. Francis Bruce Farrar, Mar. 30, 1985. BS in Edn., Ind. State U., 1982; MS in Edn., Ind. U. S.E., 1990. Tchr. emotionally handicapped New Albany (Ind.)-Floyd County Consol. Schs., 1983-90; tchr. learning disabled Spl. Svcs., Johnson County Schs., Franklin, Ind., 1990-91, cons. emotionally handicapped students, 1991—. Mentor tchr. divsn. spl. edn. Ind. State Dept. of Edn., Indpls., 1992-97. Mem. Coun. for Exceptional Children, Coun. for Children with Behavioral Disorders (Ind. chpt., Tchr. of Yr. award 1989), Ind. State Tchrs. Assn. (negotiations com. 1993, discussions com. 1993—). Avocations: reading, traveling, playing cards. Office: Johnson County Schs Spl Svcs 500 Earlywood Dr Franklin IN 46131-9711

FARRAR, THOMAS C. chemist, educator; b. Independence, Kans., Jan. 14, 1933; s. Otis C. and Agnes K. F.; m. Friedemarie L. Farrar, June 22, 1963; children: Michael, Christian, Gisela. BS in Math., Chemistry, Wichita State U., 1954; PhD in Chemistry, U. Ill., 1959. NSF fellow Cambridge U., Eng., 1959-61; prof. chemistry U. Oregon, Eugene, 1961-63; chief, magnetism sect. Nat. Bur. Standards, Washington, 1963-71; dir. R & D Japan Electron Optics Lab., Cranford, N.J., 1971-75; dir. instr. NSF, Washington, 1975-79; prof. chemistry U. Wis., Madison, 1979—. Chmn. adv. com. MIT Nat. Magnetics Lab., Cambridge, Mass., 1979-84. Author: Introduction to Pulse NMR Spectros, 1989, Density Matrix Theory, 1995; contbr. over 120 articles to profl. jours. Recipient Silver medal Dept. Commerce, Washington, 1971, Silver medal Nat. Science Found., Washington, 1979. Fellow Wash. Acad. Science; mem. Am. Chem. Soc. (sec.-treas. Wis. sect. 1986-89), Am. Physical Soc. Office: Univ Wis Dept Chemistry 1101 University Ave Madison WI 53706-1322 E-mail: tfarrar@chem.wisc.edu.

FARRELL, BRIAN E. special education supervisor; b. Boston, Oct. 19, 1955; s. Robert D. and Eleanor L. (Sheehy) Farrell; m. JoAnne Gulvas, Aug. 21, 1982; children: Caitlin, Sara(dec.). BA, Stonehill Coll., 1980; MA, Fairfield U., 1985. Cert. sch. psychologist Conn., adminstrn. & supervision 2000. Sr. psychology assoc. Southbury (Conn.) Tng. Sch., 1985; sch. psychologist Waterbury (Conn.) Pub. Schs., 1988—. Avocation: computer adaptation for the handicapped. Home: 352 High Ridge Rd Southbury CT 06488-1168 Office: Dept Student Svcs 1488 Woodtick Rd Wolcott CT 06716

FARRELL, DAVID HENRY, biochemistry and molecular biology educator; b. Pasadena, Calif., Oct. 17, 1956; BS, UCLA, 1979; PhD, U. Calif, Irvine, 1986. Postdoctoral fellow U. Calif., Irvine, 1986, Oreg. Health Sci. U., Portland, 1986-88; sr. fellow U. Wash., Seattle, 1988-93; asst. prof. Pa. State U., Hershey, 1993-98; assoc. prof. Oreg. Health Sci. U., Portland, 1998—. Co-chmn. rsch. review Am. Heart Assn. (Pa. affiliate), Camp Hill, 1995-97. Recipient R29 award, NIH, 1997; grantee, Am. Heart Assn., 1996, 1998, 1999, 2002, KO2 award, NIM, 1999; rsch. grantee, W.W. Smith Charitable Trust, 1995. Mem. Am. Assn. for Advancement of Sci., Am. Heart Assn., Am. Soc. Biochemistry and Molecular Biology, Am. Soc. Hematology. Democrat. Lutheran. Office: Oreg Health Sci U Dept Pathology 3181 SW Sam Jackson Park Rd Portland OR 97239-3098

FARRELL, EDMUND JAMES, retired English language educator, writer; b. Butte, Mont., May 17, 1927; s. Bartholomew J. and Lavinia H. (Collins) F.; m. Jo Ann Hayes, Dec. 19, 1964; children: David, Kevin, Sean. AB, Stanford U., 1950, MA, 1951; PhD, U. Calif., Berkeley, 1969. Chmn. English dept. James Lick H.S., San Jose, Calif., 1954-59; supr. secondary English, U. Calif., Berkeley, 1959-70; adj. prof. English, U. Ill., Urbana, 1973-78; prof. English edn. U. Tex., Austin, 1978-92, prof. emeritus, 1992—; pres. Farrell Ednl. Svcs., Inc., Austin, 1981-97; ret., 1997; sr. editl. cons. EMC Paradigm Pub. Co., 1993—. Participant revision lit. objectives Nat. Assessment of Ednl. Progress, Denver, 1972-73, 78; mem. adv. com. Ctr. for the Book, Libr. of Congress, 1980-86; chmn. adv. com. on English, Coll. Bd., N.Y.C., 1974-79, mem. council acad. affairs, 1978-79; guest lectr. local, state and nat. confs. of English tchrs., 1954—; reader compositions for advanced placement program Rider Coll., Princeton, N.J., 1969, 72-77; pres. Calif. Assn. Tchrs. English, 1962-63; sr. cons. EMC Masterpiece Series, 1999—. Author: (with others) Exploring Life Through Literature, 1964, Counterpoint in Literature, 1967, Projection in Literature, 1973, Outlooks Through Literature, 1973, Fantasy: Forms of Things Unknown, 1974, Science Fact/Fiction, 1974, Comment, 1976, Myth, Mind and Moment, 1976, I/You, We/They, 1976, Traits and Topics, 1976, Reality in Conflict, 1976, To Be, 1976, Arrangement in Literature, 1979, Purpose in Literature, 1979, Album U.S.A., 1983, Discoveries in Literature, 1985, classic edit., 1989, Patterns in Literature, 1985, classic edit., 1989, Transactions with Literature, 1990, The Perceptive I, 1997. With USN, 1945-46. Fellow Nat. Conf. Rsch. on Lang. and Literacy; mem. Nat. Coun. Tchrs. English (field rep. 1970-71, asst. exec. sec. 1971-73, assoc. exec. dir. 1973-78, chmn. commn. lit. 1979-83; trustees rsch. found. 1983-85; fund for tchg. of English 1993-96, Disting. Svc. award 1982, James R. Squire award 1999), Tex. Joint Coun. Tchrs. of English (pres. 1986-87, Disting. English Educator award 1989-90, Disting. Lifetime Svc. award 1999). Unitarian Universalist. Home: 6500 Sumac Dr Austin TX 78731-4117 Office: U Tex Dept Curriculum and Instrn Austin TX 78712

FARRELL, FRANCINE ANNETTE, psychotherapist, educator, author; b. Long Beach, Calif., Mar. 26, 1948; d. Thomas and Evelyn Marie (Lucente) F.; m. James Thomas Hanley, Dec. 5, 1968 (div. Dec. 1988); children: Melinda Lee Hanley Flynn, James Thomas Hanley Jr.; m. Robert Erich Haesche, June 3, 1995. BA in Psychology with honors, Calif. State U., Sacramento, 1985, MS in Counseling, 1986. Lic. marriage and family therapist, Calif.; nat. cert. addiction counselor. Marriage, family and child counselor intern Fulton Ct. Counseling, Sacramento, 1987-88; pvt. practice psychotherapy, Sacramento, 1988—. Instr. chem. dependency studies program, Calif. State U., Sacramento, 1985-94, acad. coord. chem. dependency studies program, 1988-90; instr. cert. program in alcohol and drug studies U. Calif.-Davis Extension Programs, 1997-98; trainee Sobriety Brings a Change, Sacramento, 1986-87; assoc. investigator, curriculum coord. Project S.A.F.E., Sacramento, 1990-91; presenter Sacramento Conf., ACA, 1986, 88, 89, 91, 92, Ann. Symposium on Chem. Dependency, 1993. Presenter (cable TV series) Trouble in River City: Charting a Course for Change, 1991, H.O.W. Seminar Series, 1988-2000. Mem. AAUW, Calif. Assn. Marriage and Family Therapists, Calif. Assn. Alcoholism and Drug Abuse Counselors (bd. dirs. region 5, 1988-90), Phi Kappa Phi. Roman Catholic. Avocations: photography, writing, boating. Office: 2740 Fulton Ave Ste 100 Sacramento CA 95821-5184 Fax: 916-971-0388. E-mail: ffarrell@sbcglobal.net.

FARRELL, KAROLYN KAY MCMILLAN, adult education educator; b. Springfield, Mo., June 23, 1938; d. Octa H. and Ruth Marie (Funkhouser) McMillan; m. Donald Paul Farrell, June 19, 1960; children: Shawn McMillan, Beth Melanie. BS in Edn. cum laude, SW Mo. State U., 1960; M Adult Edn., U. Ark., 1983, EdS, 1991; postgrad., U. Mo., 1964. Cert. adult edn. adminstr. Instr. art, sci., vocat. home econs. Indian Head High Sch., Charles County, Md., 1960-62; instr., cons. Kansas City (Mo.) Bd. Edn., 1962-63, cons. enrichment, 1963-68; instr. art Fayetteville (Ark.) Arts Gallery, 1973-77; artist in residence Butterfield Sch., Fayetteville, 1973-77; creator, developer Curriculum Disseminating Ctr., U. Ark., Fayetteville, 1979-82; dir. community and adult edn. Fayetteville Community Schs., 1979—. Dietary asst. Trinity Luth. Hosp., Kansas City, 1962-63;instr. health Fayetteville High Sch., 1976-79; freelance artist, Fayetteville, 1980—. Vol. visual arts com. Walton Arts Ctr., 1980—; vol. Nelson Atkins Mus., Friends of Art, Kansas City, 1988—; co-chmn. N.W. Ark. Project Literacy U.S., 1988—; cmty. trustee Ark. Arts Ctr., 1994—. Levi grantee, Fayetteville, 1983-85; recipient numerous art awards. Mem. Am. Assn. Adult and Continuing Edn., Ark. Assn. Adminstrs. Adult Edn. (pres. 1989-91, sec. 1992—), Nat. Cmty. Edn. Assn., Ark. Assn. Pub. Continuing and Adult Edn. (facilitator), Rotary (fellowship and cmty. devel. coms.), Phi Delta Kapa (found. com. 1988—). Baptist. Avocations: travel, art museums, painting, classical music, opera. Home: 1567 Anson Pl Fayetteville AR 72701-3705

FARRELL, KELLY JEAN, health and physical education educator; b. Mechanicsburg, Pa., Jan. 10, 1953; d. Eugene S. and Arlene M. (Wiley) Cromer; m. Charles F. Farrell, July 15, 1978 (div. Aug. 1983). BS, Lock Haven State Coll., 1974. Cert. health and phys. edn. tchr., Pa. Tchr. health and phys. edn. Ctrl. Dauphin High Sch., Harrisburg, Pa., 1974—, chair health and phys. edn. dept., 1991—2000; instr. tennis for C.D. Acad. Ctrl. Dauphin Sch. Dist., 1992—2000. Varsity softball coach Ctrl. Dauphin High Sch., Harrisburg, 1975—, varsity girls' basketball coach, 1974-93, varsity field hockey coach, 1977, varsity girls' tennis coach, 1994-2002, health and phys. edn. curriculum writing coms., 1987, 93-95; softball coach Keystone State Games, 1984-85. Mem. NEA, AAHPERD, Pa. State Edn. Assn., Ctrl. Dauphin Edn. Assn., Pa. State Assn. Health, Phys. Edn., Recreation and Dance, Pa. State Women's Golf Assn. (bd. dirs. Ctrl. Region 1991-93). Avocations: golf, reading, movies, Penn State football. Home: 210 N 62nd St Harrisburg PA 17111-4327 Office: Central Dauphin High Sch 4600 Locust Ln Harrisburg PA 17109-4498

FARRELL, RODNEY ALAN, management consultant; b. Lewistown, Pa., May 10, 1950; s. Morris Rodney and Betty Jean (Fultz) F.; m. Susan A. Bearly, Mar. 28, 1970; children: Rodney Jr., Erin M., Zachary C. BS in Edn., Ind. U. Pa., 1972; MS in Instructional Systems, Pa. State U., 1989. Tchr. Mifflin County Sch. Dist., Lewistown, Pa., 1975-84, Belleville (Pa.) Mennonite Sch., 1984-85; asst. dir. regional computer resource ctr. Tuscarora Intermediate Unit, McVeytown, Pa., 1985-87; tech. specialist Montgomery County Intermediate Unit, Erdenheim, Pa., 1987-91; instr. Phila. Coll. Textiles & Sci., 1988-91; pres., cons. Farrell Assocs., Reedsville, Pa., 1991-92, curriculum, planning, and tech. specialist ctrl. intermediate unit, 1992—. Pres. Pa. Assn. Ednl. Communications and Tech. With USN, 1972-75. Mem. ASCD, Internat. Soc. Tech. in Edn., Assn. Ednl. Comm. and Tech., Assn. for Devel. of Computer-Based Instructional Sys. Avocation: fishing. Office: Farrell Assocs Pearl St Ste 137 Reedsville PA 17084

FARRELL, WILLIAM JOSEPH, university chancellor; b. Milw., Aug. 17, 1936; s. William John and Rita (Taggart) F.; m. Carol Mary Leeming, Aug. 1, 1959; children: William Jr., Charles, Elizabeth. BS summa cum laude, Marquette U., 1958, MBA, 1976; MA, U. Wis., 1959, PhD, 1961; DHL (hon.), St. Anselm's Coll., 1998. Instr. U. Chgo., 1961-63, asst. prof., 1963-68; assoc. prof. Marquette U., Milw., 1968-75, dir. of Found. Support, 1970-75; assoc. v.p. of research U. Iowa, Iowa City, 1975-84; pres. Plymouth (N.H.) State Coll., 1984-92; chancellor Univ. System of N.H., 1992—. Vis. prof. U. Calif., Berkeley, 1967-68; trustee Univ. Sys. N.H., 1984—, St. Anselm's Coll., 1992—, chair ednl. policy com., 1995—, mem. exec. com., 1995—, state del. New Eng. Bd. Higher Edn., 1984—, chair N.H. del., 1995—. Co-editor English Literature 1600-1800: A Bibliography of Modern Studies, 1972; editor: (jour.) Renascence: Essays on Values in Literature, 1969-72; contbr. numerous articles to profl. jours. Bd. dirs. N.H. Music Festival, Center Harbor, 1984-93, Bus. and Industry Assn. of N.H., 1998—; mem. N.H. Postsecondary Edn. Commn., 1984—, mem. exec. com., 1988-93, chmn., 1990-92. Woodrow Wilson fellow, 1958, Danforth fellow, 1958. Mem. N.H. Coll. and Univ. Coun. (chmn. 1989-91), Am. Assn. State Colls. and Univs., Am. Coun. on Edn., Nat. Assn. Sys. Heads, Nat. Assn. State Univs. & Land Grant Colls., State Higher Edn. Exec. Officers, N.H. Bus. and Industry Assn. (bd. dirs. 1998—). Roman Catholic. Home: PO Box 873 17 Denbow Rd Durham NH 03824-3104 Office: Univ System NH Dunlap Ctr 25 Concord Rd Durham NH 03824-6624

FARRIGAN, JULIA ANN, retired small business owner, educator; b. Albany, N.Y., July 19, 1943; d. Charles Gerald and Julia Tryon (Shepherd) F. BS in Elem. Edn., SUNY, Plattsburgh, 1965; MS in Curriculum Planning and Devel., SUNY, Albany, 1973, U. Manchester, Eng., 1973; postgrad. in adminstrv. svcs., Calif. State U., Fresno, 1976-78. With Monroe-Woodbury Ctrl. Sch. Dist., Monroe, N.Y., 1965-90; dist. coord. gifted programs The Pine Tree Sch., 1979-90; ptnr. Baskets Plain and Fancy, Jackson, Ga., 1994—; owner The Basket House. Adj. prof. Gifted Edn. Contbr. articles to profl. jours. Vol. Jackson United Meth. Ch.; chmn. bd. Butts County Hist. Soc., docent, editor newsletter; coord. blood drive ARC Butts County. Mem. DAR (registrar William McIntosh chpt., state 2d vice regemt 2002—), AFT, ASCD, N.Y. United Fedn. Tchrs., Nat. Assn. for Gifted Children, Coun. Exceptional Children, Monroe-Woodbury Tchr.'s Assn., Hawthorne Garden Club (officer), Kiwanis (officer), Basket Weavers Guild of Ga., Delta Kappa Gamma (officer Upsilon chpt., state editor). Democrat. Methodist.

FARRIMOND, GEORGE FRANCIS, JR., management educator; b. Peerless, Utah, Sept. 23, 1932; s. George Francis and Ruth (Howard) F.; m. Polly Ann Fowler, Mar. 21, 1988; children: George Kenneth, Ronald Kay, Carrie Frances, Holly Jean, Celine Brooke, Karli Elise. BS, U. Utah, 1955; MBA, U. Mo., 1968; PhD, Portland State U., 1989. Cert. profl. contracts mgr. Enlisted USAF, 1955, advanced through grades to lt. col., 1971, master navigator, 1955-71, flight commdr. 360th tactical elec. war squadron Saigon, Socialist Republic of Vietnam, Vietnam, 1971-72, chief procurement ops. Wright-Patterson AFB, Ohio, 1972-73, chief pricing ops. div., 1973-76, ret., 1976; asst. prof. bus. So. Oreg. State Coll., Ashland, 1976-82, assoc. prof., 1982-89, prof., 1989—. Cons. small bus., Jackson County, Oreg., 1976-95; cons. Japanese mgmt., Jackson County, 1981-94; facilitated decision making body for econ. devel. in So. Oreg., 1995. Author: (computer program) Spanish Verb Conjugation, 1980, (workbook) Pricing Techniques, 1983. Chmn. Wright-Patterson AFB div United Fund, 1973-76; little league coach various teams, Ark. and Mo., 1963-71; Sunday Sch. tchr. Ch. of Latter-day Saints, various states. Decorated Disting. Flying Cross, 5 Air medals; Minuteman Ednl. scholar Air Force Inst. Tech., 1964, Education with Industry scholar Air Force Inst. Tech., 1970. Mem. Nat. Assn. Purchasing Mgmt., Air Force Soc., Soc. Japanese Studies, Beta Gamma Sigma. Republican. Avocations: oil painting, grandfather clocks, personal computers, reforestation. Home: 550 Carmen Rd Talent OR 97540-9708 Office: So Oreg Univ Sch Bus 1250 Siskiyou Blvd Ashland OR 97520-5010

FARRINGTON, GREGORY C. university administrator; b. Bronxville, N.Y. B in Chemistry, Clarkson U., 1968; AM in Chemistry, Harvard U., 1970, PhD in Chemistry, 1972; degree (hon.), U. Uppsala, Sweden, 1984. Staff sci. GE, Schenectady, N.Y., 1972-79; assoc. prof. materials sci. and engring. U. Pa., 1979-84, prof., 1984, chair dept. materials sci. and engring., 1984-87, dir. Lab. for Rsch. on Structure of Matter, 1987-90, dean Sch. Engring. and Applied Sci., 1990-98; pres. Lehigh U., 1998—. Office: Lehigh U Office of the Pres 27 Memorial Dr West, Alumni Memorial Bld Bethlehem PA 18015 E-mail: gcf2@lehigh.edu.

FARRIS, MARKETTA BLACKBURN, elementary educator; b. Pikeville, Ky., Mar. 5, 1954; d. Henry Herbert and Olga (Lowe) Blackburn; m. Edgar Boyd Farris, Nov. 26, 1983; children: Christopher Boyd, Edgar Alexander. BS, Pikeville Coll., 1977; MA in Edn., Morehead (Ky.) State U., 1984. Cert. elem. and resource tchr., Ky.; cert. elem. tchr., Va. Elem. tchr. Buchanan County Schs., Grundy, Va., 1977-84, Pike County Schs., Pikeville, 1984-88, Montgomery County Schs., Mt. Sterling, Ky., 1988—. Program leader 4-H Club, Pike County, 1984-85; sec. PTA, Pike County, 1985-87. Named Tchr. of Yr., Brushy Elem. Sch., Pikeville, 1984. Mem. NEA, Ky. Edn. Assn. Democrat. Methodist. Avocations: reading, gardening, cooking, interior decorating, cross-stitching. Office: Camargo Elem Sch 4307 Camargo Rd Mount Sterling KY 40353-8866

FARRIS, VERA KING, former college president; b. Atlantic City, July 18, 1940; BA in Biology magna cum laude, Tuskegee Inst., 1959; MS in Zoology, U. Mass., 1962, PhD in Zoology/Parasitology, 1965; LHD (hon.), Marymount Manhattan Coll., 1985; LLD (hon.), Monmouth Coll., West Long Branch, N.J., 1987; DSc honoris causa, Johnson and Wales Coll., 1988. Dean spl. programs, assoc. prof. pathology and biology SUNY, Stony Brook, 1968-72, vice provost acad. affairs, prof. biological sci. Brockport, 1973-80; v.p. acad affairs, prof. biological sci. Kean Coll. N.J., Union, 1980-83; pres. Stockton State Coll., Pomona, NJ, 1983—2003. Contbr. articles to profl. jours. Founding mem. Gov.'s Pride award acad., 1986—, Gov.'s adv. coun. Holocaust Edn. in N.J., 1982—. Recipient Golden Trefoil award, Delaware Valley Coun. Girl Scouts Am., 1987,Chancellors Medal for Exemplary and Extraordinary Svc., U. Mass., 1986, Honor Roll Ednl award Wash. Ctr. for Internships and Acad. Seminars, Commendation for Outstanding Achievement in Edn., N.J. Assembly, 1993, others; named Lifetime Honorary citizen of Atlanta, 1984, N.J. Woman or Yr. N.J. Woman's Mag. Mem. Am. Coun. Edn. (bd. dirs. 1988-91), Coun. Post-Secondary Accreditation (bd. dirs. 1988—), Middle States Assn. Colls. and Secondary Schs. (pres. bd. trustees), Am. Assn. State Colls. and Univs. (nominating com.), N.J. State Bd. Examiners, N.J. State Coll. Pres. (chair 1987-89), B'naiB'rith (life hon.), Cosmos Club (Washington).*

FARSHIDI, ARDESHIR B. cardiologist, educator; b. Kerman, Iran, June 13, 1945; arrived in U.S., 1972, naturalized, 1977; s. Jamshid and Farangis Farshidi; m. Katayoon Kavoussi, Jan. 2, 1982. MD, Tehran U., 1969. Diplomate Am. Bd. Internal Medicine, Am. Bd. Cardiovasc. Disease, Am. Bd. Cardiac Electrophysiology. Intern, Washington, 1972—73; resident U. Pa., Phila., 1973—75, resident in cardiology, 1975—77, electrophysiologist, 1977—78; asst. prof., assoc. prof. medicine U. Conn., Farmington, 1978—84; dir. electrophysiology LA Heart Inst., 1984—90; dir. arrhythmia ctr. Los Robles Regional Med. Ctr., 1990—. Dir. electrophysiologist U. Conn., Farmington, 1982—84, attending cardiologist, 1982—84; co-dir. electrophysiology, asst. prof. medicine Yale U., 1979—82; attending cardiologist Yale U. Hosp., 1979—82; chief cardiology sect. VA Hosp., Newington, Conn., 1982—84. Rschr. Am. Heart Assn., 1981. Lt. Iranian Army, 1969—72. Fellow: ACP, Am. Heart Assn., Am. Coll. Cardiology; mem.: Am. Electrophysiologic Soc., Am. Fedn. Clin. Rsch. Achievements include research in clin. cardiac electrophysiology and arrhythmia. Home: 3011 Grandoaks Dr Westlake Village CA 91361-5563 Office: 2100 Lynn Rd Ste 220 Thousand Oaks CA 91360-8036

FARWELL, HAROLD FREDERICK, JR., English language educator; b. Oak Park, Ill., Apr. 9, 1934; s. Harold Frederick and Dorothy Delma (Cobb) F.; m. Joyce G. Farwell, Feb. 10, 1961; children: Douglas G., Beth Elene, Amy Kathleen, Ellen Claudia. BA, U. Chgo., 1960, MA, 1961; PhD, U. Wis., Madison, 1970. Instr. English Drake U., Des Moines, 1960-61; asst. prof. U. Cin., 1966-70; assoc. prof., prof. Western Carolina U., Cullowhee, N.C., 1970—, dir. English grad. program, 1980-90, 97-00. Ranger U.S. Park Svcs., Great Smokies Nat. Park, 1983. Editor: Smoky Mountain Voices, 1993; reporter Opera News, 1982—; editor, reporter The Arts Jour. With USN, 1956-58. Fulbright sr. lectr., The Phillipines, 1986-87, Indonesia, 1991; rsch. grantee Western Carolina U., 1974, 93, 94, 97; SDIP grantee U. Tex., 1981; China Field Study grantee, 1995, 96; Ctr. for Tchg. Excellence fellow Western Carolina U., 1992-94; fellow East-West Ctr., Honolulu, 1997, 99. Mem.: Dictionary Soc. N.Am., Melville Soc. Avocations: nature study, gardening. Home: PO Box 838 Cullowhee NC 28723-0838 E-mail: hal_farwell@aol.com., farwell@wcu.edu.

FARWELL, HERMON WALDO, JR., parliamentarian, educator, former speech communication educator; b. Englewood, NJ, Oct. 24, 1918; s. Hermon Waldo and Elizabeth (Whitcomb) Farwell; m. Martha Carey Matthews, Jan. 3, 1942. AB, Columbia U., 1940; MA, Pa. State U., 1964. Commd. USAF, 1940, advanced through grades to maj., various positions, 1940—66, ret., 1966; instr. aerial photography Escola Tecnica de Aviaçao, Brazil, 1946—48; mem. faculty U. So. Colo., Pueblo, 1966—84, prof. emeritus speech comm., 1984—; cons., tchr. parliamentary procedure. Author: Point of Opinion: The Majority Rules - A Manual of Procedure for Most Groups: Parliamentary Motions: Majority Motions, Point of Opinion - An Anthology of Parliamentary Simplicity; editor: The Parliamentary Jour., 1981—87; contbr. articles to profl. jours. Mem.: VFW, Nat. Assn. Parliamentarians, Ret. Officers Assn., Commn. on Am. Parliamentary Practice (chmn. 1976), Am. Inst. Parliamentarians (nat. dir. 1977—87), Air Force Assn., Am. Legion. Home and Office: 65 MacAlester Rd Pueblo CO 81001-2052

FARWELL, MARGARET WHEELER, elementary education educator; b. Ware, Mass., Nov. 20, 1934; d. Joseph Otis and Margaret (Carter) Sawtell; m. Norman Dale Farwell, July 23, 1955; children: Mary, Nancy, Bradford. BA, U. Mass., 1956; MEd, Antioch, 1976. Cert. early childhood, elem. tchr. and experienced tchr., N.H. Tchr. primary Ervingside Sch., Erving, Mass., 1959-60; founder, dir. New Hampton (N.H.) Community Kindergarten, 1962-65; adminstrv. asst. Macduffie Sch., Springfield, Mass., 1973-75; tchr. Warwick (Mass.) Ctr. Sch., 1977, Bement Sch., Deerfield, Mass., 1977-81, head lower sch., 1977-81; tchr. The Am. Sch. in Switzerland Eng. Am. Sch., Thorpe Surrey, U.K., 1981-82, head lower sch., 1982-91; chpt. I teaching asst. Hebron (Maine) Elem. Sch., 1991-92; dir. lower sch. Hebron Acad., 1992-96; retired. Mem. accreditation team European Coun. Internat. Schs./New Eng. Assn. Schs. and Colls., Dublin, Dusseldorf, Brussels, Luxembourg, 1985-87; mem. accreditation team New Eng. Assn. Schs. and Colls., Milton Acad., 1991; mem. The Am. Sch. in Switzerland Eng. Sch. Governing Bd., Surrey, 1981-91, mem. acad. com., 1981-91; presenter in field. Organizer, leader Girl Scouts of Am.; dir. Jr. Ch. Choir, 1975-81. Mem. ASCD, Nat. Coun. Tchrs. Math. Republican. Avocations: music, skiing, doll collecting. Home: PO Box 191 Melvin Village NH 03850-0191

FASEL, IDA, English language educator, writer; b. Portland, Maine, May 9, 1909; d. I.E. Drapkin and Lilian Rose Harwich; m. Oscar A. Fasel, Dec. 24, 1946 (dec. Apr. 1973). BA summa cum laude, Boston U., 1931, MA, 1945; PhD, U. Denver, 1963. Mem. faculty English U. Conn., New London, Midwestern U., Wichita Falls, Tex., Colo. Woman's Coll., Denver; prof. English U. Colo., Denver, 1962-77, prof. emerita of English, 1977. Presenter in field; contest judge. Translator from French and Italian, editl. cons.: Baroque and Renaissance Lyrics, 1962; author (poetry): On the

Meanings of Cleave, 1979 (Nortex Publ. award); author: The Study of Writing Poetry, 1983; author: (poetry) Where Is the Center of the World?: Selections From Seven Chapbooks, 1981-1991, 1999 (U. Fla. and Before the Rapture Press prize chapbooks), All Real Living Is Meeting, 1999, The Difficult Inch, 2000, Journey of a Hundred Years, 2002, Air, Angels and Us, 2002, Waking to Light, 2002 (Best Chapbook Angels Without Wings Found. 2003), Aureoles, 2002; translator: Renaissance and Baroque Lyrics, 1962; contbg. author: The Study and Writing of Poetry, 1983; contbr. articles to profl. jours., chpts. to books, poetry to anthologies and jours. Faculty Rsch. fellow U. Colo., 1979; recipient Disting. Alumni honor Boston U., 1979, Alumni Poetry prize, 1983, 85, Before the Rapture Chapbook prize, 1985, Colo. Poet Honor, Friends of Denver Pub. Libr., 1991, Panhandler Chapbook prize, U. West Fla., 1991, Prize Poems award Colo. Authors League, 1993-94. Mem. Milton Soc. Am. (life), Friends of Milton's Cottage (charter), Assn. Literary Scholars and Critics, Conf. on Christianity and Lit., Poetry Soc. Tex., Colo. Ctr. for the Book, Denver Woman's Press Club, Phi Beta Kappa. Avocations: ballet, Star Trek, collecting angels, piano, translating French poetry. Home: 165 Ivy St Denver CO 80220-5846

FASH, WILLIAM LEONARD, retired architecture educator, college dean; b. Pueblo, Colo., Feb. 9, 1931; s. James Leonard and Jewel Dean (Rickman) F.; m. Maria Elena Shaw, June 5, 1982; children: Cameron Shaw, Lauren Victoria; children by previous marriage: Victoria Ruth, William Leonard B.Arch., Okla. State U., 1958, M.Arch., 1960; postgrad., Royal Acad. Fine Arts, Copenhagen, 1960-61. Asst. prof. U. Ill., Urbana, 1961-64, assoc. prof., 1967-70, prof., 1970-76; assoc. prof. Okla. State U., Stillwater, 1964-66, U. Oreg., Eugene, 1966-67; prof., first dean coll. architecture Ga. Inst. Tech., Atlanta, 1976-92, prof., 1992-93, prof., dean emeritus, 1997—. Vis. prof. Chulalongkorn U., Bangkok, Thailand, 1973-74; bd. dirs. Nat. Archtl. Accreditation Bd., 1981-85 (commendation award 1985); mem. edn. com. adv. bd. Nat. Coun. Archtl. Registration Bds., 1982-85; profl. cons. U.S. Navy Trident Submarine Base, Kings Bay, Ga., 1980-89; mem. adv. bd. Atlanta Urban Design Commn.; cons. Atlanta High Mus. Art Bldg. Com., 1982-84. Author, editor monographs Chmn. tech. adv. com. Gov.'s Commn. State Growth Policy, 1982-83; mem. Mayor's transition team for housing, Atlanta, 1989, Atlanta Symphony New Hall Com., 1991. Recipient awards for design, recognition citations for teaching excellence, 1975, 76; Spl. Recognition cert. Atlanta Coll. Architecture, 1986, Recognition award Indsl. Designers Soc. Am., 1990, Spl. award Atlanta chpt. AIA, 1994; Fulbright-Hays fellow, Copenhagen, 1960-61. Mem. AIA (award juries 1968, 75, 76, 79, spl. recognition award Atlanta chpt. 1994), Assn. Collegiate Schs. Architecture (recognition award 1985), Phi Kappa Phi, Sigma Tau, Pi Mu Epsilon, Alpha Rho Chi, Omicron Delta Kappa. Clubs: Bent Tree Country (Jasper, Ga.). Home: 2854 Ridgemore Rd NW Atlanta GA 30318-1448 E-mail: fashdomain@worldnet.att.net.

FASTENAU, FREDERICK HENRY, III, principal; b. Carlisle, Pa., Oct. 2, 1952; s. Frederick H. Jr. and Dorothy (Dee) F.; m. Rhonda L. Alltop, May 29, 1982; children: Victoria A., Catherine E. BS in Edn., Ohio U., 1973; MEd, Kent State U., 1976, EdS, 1984. Elem. tchr. Elyria (Ohio) City Schs., 1973-76, 77-78, cadet prin., 1976-77; asst. prin. Midview Local Schs., Grafton, Ohio, 1978-82, dir. community svcs., 1982-85; elem. prin., adminstr. govt. programs and pers. Sheffield (Ohio)-Sheffield Lake City Schs., 1985-91; elem. prin. Oberlin (Ohio) City Schs., 1991—. Co-dir. Intervention Assist. Team tng. project Ohio Dept. Edn., Columbus, 1990-92, trainer IAT project, 1990-91, reading recovery site coord. Ohio Dept. Edn., Sheffield Lake. Contbr. articles to profl. jours. Mem. Kiwanis, Grafton, 1980-85; co-chair Community Action Team, Sheffield Lake, 1986-91. Mem. Nat. Assn. Elem. Sch. Prins., Ohio Assn. Elem. Sch. Adminstrs. (committeeman 1985-92), Buckeye Assn. Sch. Adminstrs., Lorain County Assn. Elem. Sch. Adminstrs. (past pres. 1986-87), Kappa Delta Pi. Avocations: travel, cooking, writing, water sports. Office: Prospect Elem Sch 36 S Prospect St Oberlin OH 44074-1410

FATEMI, SAEID, language educator, writer, researcher; b. Yazd, Iran; s. Mohammad Ali and Saltanat Fatemi; m. Minoo Varzegar; children: Delaram, Arezou. BA in French Lang. Lit., BA in Law, U. Tehran, 1947, PhD in Persian Lit., 1950; PhD in Comparative Lit., U. Paris, 1953. Assoc. prof. U. Tehran, 1953-65, prof., 1965—. Translator of French into Persian UNESCO; vis. prof. Princeton U., Kent State U.; over 70 presentations at nat. and intern. confs. Author: Greek and Roman Mythology, A Collection of Poems; author, translator: Formation of the Rural Education; translator: Human Rights, Human Against Ignorance; chief editor Bakhtare-Emruz Daily Newspaper, Tehran; translator Courier, Payam; editor PAYAM; contbr. over 500 articles to profl. jours. Leader Iran-e-Emruz Polit. Party, 1978-80; elected mem. supreme coun. Nat. Front Iran, 1960—; del. Internat. Ct. of Justice; polit. prisoner in Iran, 1953-62. Mem. Internat. Coun. Philosophy and Human Scis., Assn. Writers and Poets. Avocations: reading, writing. Home: 290 Anderson Ave # 6K Hackensack NJ 07601 E-mail: varzegar@aol.com.

FATUM, DELORES RUTH, school counselor; b. Kingston, NY, Aug. 1, 1945; d. Robert and Dorothy Beatrice (Van Demark) F. BS, Winthrop U., 1968; MEd, Ga. Coll., Milledgeville, 1973; EdS, Ga. So. U. Cert. couselor, Ga.; practice tchr. supr. Sch. couselor Laurens County Bd. of Edn., Dublin, Ga.; EdS counseling educator Ga. So. U. Regional coordinator Outdoor Edn., Ga. Dept. of Natural Resources, Atlanta. Author: (manuals) Georgia Outdoor Education, Student Services for Lauren County. Mem. Am. Counseling Assn., Am. Sch. Counselors Assn., Nat. Mid. Sch. Assn., Profl. Assn. Ga. Educators. (v.p. Laurens county chpt.), Ga. Sch. Counselors Assn. (chair U.S. Congl. Dist. 8). Home: 573 Coleman Ln Dublin GA 31021-4439 Office: W Laurens Mid Sch 332 W Laurens School Rd Dublin GA 31021-1570

FAUBER, ANITA P. special education educator; b. Chgo., Feb. 1, 1957; d. Roy L. and Louise E. (Perry) Pilson; m. Wilson L. Fauber, June 3, 1977; children: Heather Dawn, Christy Renee. BA, Bridgewater Coll., 1979; MEd, James Madison U., 1991. Cert. tchr., Va. Pvt. practice tchr. pre-sch., Staunton, Va., 1988-89; deve. technician DeJarnett Ctr., Staunton, 1989-90; grad. asst. James Madison U., Harrisonburg, Va., 1990; educator Edn. and Tng. Corp., Staunton, 1990-91; tchr. Highland Elem. Sch., 1991-93, Augusta County, 1993—. Mem. com. Highland County Spl. Edn. Adv. Bd., 1991—. Mem. NEA, Va. Edn. Assn., Va. Coun. Learning Disabilities, Coun. for Exceptional Children, Highland County Edn. Assn. Republican. Baptist. Avocations: reading, piano, traveling. Home: 503 Victoria Dr Staunton VA 24401-2148

FAUCETTE, MERILON COOPER, retired elementary educator; b. Washington, Ark., Oct. 17, 1931; d. Andrew and Narciss (Tyus) Cooper; m. Clarence William Faucette, Jr., May 17, 1958 (dec. 1982); children: Billie Reneé, Gwenevere Yvetta. BS, Ark. Bapt. Coll., Little Rock, 1953; MEd, Henderson State U., Arkadelphi, Ark., 1975. Tchr. Searcy (Ark.) Sch. Dist., 1953-61, Pulaski County Spl. Sch. Dist., Searcy, 1961-86; ret., 1986. Mem.: Telephone Pioneers Am. (assoc.).

FAUCHIER, DAN R(AY), mediator, arbitrator, educator, construction management consultant; b. Blackwell, Okla., Sept. 27, 1946; s. Wallace Monroe and Betty Lou F.; m. Sylvia Stephanie Chan Fauchier, Mar. 15, 1969; 1 child, Angele Calista Fauchier; m. Jonah Keri, 1997. BA cum laude, Southwestern Coll., 1964-68; student, Sch. Theology, Claremont, Calif., 1968-69, Claremont Grad. Sch., 1969-70. Lic. bldg. contractor, Calif.; cert. arbitrator and mediator. Min. of youth First United Meth. Ch., Winfield, Kans., 1964-68, First Congl. Ch., Riverside, Calif., 1968-69; adminstr. Calif. Youth Authority, Chino and Paso Robles, Calif., 1969-76; tchr. Chaffey Coll., Rancho Cucamonga, Calif., 1971-74; dir. Pacific Fin. Svcs., Beverly Hills, Calif., 1977-81; pres. Littlefields Corp., Santa Maria and Corona del Mar, Calif., 1978-81; cons. Hughes Helicopters, Oasis Oil, Jakarta, Indonesia, 1981; systems designer Teltrans Corp., L.A., 1982-85; project mgr. Pacific Sunset Builders, L.A., 1985-87, DW Devel., Fontana, Calif., 1987-90; owner Fauchier Group Builders, San Diego, 1988—; pres. Empire Bay Devel. Corp., San Bernardino, Calif., 1991-92; project mgr. White Sys. L.A. Ctrl. Libr., 1993; dir. project mgmt. White Sys. divsn. Pinnacle Automation, Inc., San Diego, 1993-95; dir. project mgmt.; dir. design logistics White Systems divsn. Pinnacle Automation, Inc., San Diego, 1995-97; v.p. SDC & Assocs., San Diego and Washington, 1997-2000; tchr. Power Summit, 2000—, dir., bd. advisors, 2001—. Founding dir. Neighborhood Restoration Project, San Bernardino, Calif., 1991-92; cons. project mgr. White Sys., Inc., Cin. Pub. Libr., 1997, FCC Document Mechanization Project, 1998; instr. U. Calif. San Diego, 1998-2001; Inst. Constrn. Mgmt., arbitrator and mediator Arbitration Works, 1999—, Saddle Island Inst., 1999—; instr. San Diego State U., 2001—, mediator panelist La Jolla Ctr. Dipsute Resolution, 2003-. Contbr. cons.: President's Commission on Criminal Justice, 1972; co-author: Consumer Credit, 1984. Deputy Registrar Voters San Bernardino, Calif., 1975; mem. Skid Row Mental Health Adv. Bd., L.A., 1986, Chaffey Coll. Adv. Bd. Rancho Cucamonga, Calif., 1991-95, chmn. Bus. Security Alliance, San Bernardino, Calif., 1992. Named Nat. fellow Woodrow Wilson Fellowship, Princeton, N.J., 1968-69; Grad. scholar State of Calif., Claremont, 1969. Mem. Associated Gen. Contractors (chmn. edn. com. 1999-2001), Am. Subcontractor Assn. (chmn. mktg. com. 1999-2000), Associated Builders and Contractors, Nat. Elec. Contractors Assn., Forensics Cons. Assn., Nat. Found. for Dispute Rev. Bds., Engrng. Gen. Contractors Assn. (pub. works advocate), ABA Constrn. Industry Forum, Self-Realization Fellowship, Christmas in April (bd. dirs., v.p. 1999-2000), Habitat for Humanity, Internat. Platform Assn., Inst. for Cmty. Econ., Homeless Coalition, People for Ethical Treatment of Animals, Rainforest Alliance. Avocations: painting, photography, writing. Home: PMB249 9921 Carmel Mountain Rd San Diego CA 92129-2813 E-mail: dan@danzpage.com.

FAUL, JUNE PATRICIA, education specialist; b. Detroit; d. John William and Shirley Olive (Block) Lynch; m. George Johnson Faul, EdD, Dec. 22, 1949; children: Robert M., Alison. BA, U. Calif., Berkeley, 1952. Cert. elem. tchr., Calif. Tchr. Tulare County (Calif.) Schs., 1945-46, Tulare City Schs., 1946-48, Visalia (Calif.) City Schs., 1948-49, Richmond (Calif.) City Schs., 1951-52, Pacific Grove (Calif.) Sch. Dist., 1965-85; designated English tchg. specialist State of Calif., 1969—; edn. cons. Leo A. Meyer Assocs., Inc., Hayward, Calif., 1993—. Prin. Group Four Assocs.; lectr. Calif. State U., Fresno, 1969, U. Calif., Santa Cruz, 1970. Co-author: The New Older Woman, 1996. Apprd. mem. first human rels. commn. City of Richmond, 1962-64; mem. adv. bd. Family Resource Ctr.; founding mem., 1st pres. Monterey (Calif.) Peninsula Child Abuse Prevention Coun., 1974; hon. life mem. Calif. PTA; bd. dirs. Carmel Cultural Commn., 1964-67, Harrison Meml. Libr. Bd., Carmel, Calif., 1978-84; bd. dirs. Monterey Peninsula Airport Dist., 1980—; co-founder 100 Women Supporting Women, Monterey Peninsula Coll., 1997. Mem. Am. Assn. Airport Execs., Friends of Hopkins Marine Sta. (founer, bd. dirs.), Carmel Heritage (founder, bd. dirs.), Monterey NAACP (life), Monterey Mus. Art (life), Monterey Symphony Guild (life). Democrat. Avocation: writing. Home: PO Box 4365 Carmel CA 93921-4365 E-mail: patfaul@aol.com.

FAULES, BARBARA RUTH, retired elementary education educator; b. Austin, Tex., Mar. 10, 1940; d. Milton Friedrich Hausmann and Ruth Elizabeth Hornbuckle; m. John Wilson Faules, May 30, 1967. BA cum laude, Harding U., 1962; MA in Curriculum and Instrn., U. Mo., Kansas City, 1995. Cert. elem. tchr., Mo. Tchr. 4th grade Searcy Grammar Sch., Ark., 1962-64, Pulaski County Spl. Sch., Little Rock AFB Elem., Jacksonville, Ark., 1964-67; tchr. grades 3, 4, and 6 Butcher Greene Elem. Consol. Sch. Dist. #4, Grandview, Mo., 1967-98, ret., 1998. Contbr. (poetry) Sunrise and Soft Mist, 1999 (Editor's Choice 1999). Mem. Nat. Congress Parents and Tchr. (hon. life mem.). Mem. Ch. of Christ. Avocations: freelance photography, writing, gardening, reading, traveling. Home: 305 Valley Ct Smyrna TN 37167-5509 E-mail: Tchow1101@aol.com.

FAULKNER, JUANITA WILLIAMS, educational administrator; b. Trenton, N.J., Jan. 1, 1933; d. John Earl Williams and Lillie Lee (Powell) Williams-Randolph; 1 child, Robin Lee Ann. BS, Kean Coll., Union, N.J., 1957; MA, Columbia U., 1974, postgrad., 1990; MA, Rider Coll., 1975. Cert. elem. tchr., N.J. Tchr. Trenton Pub. Sch. System, 1958-68; dir. day care svc. United Progress, Inc., Trenton, 1968-75; instr. Kean Coll., 1975-76; program adminstr. Dept. Health, Recreation & Welfare, Trenton, 1977-78; ednl. planner N.J. Dept. Edn., Trenton, 1978—. Test. cons. N.J. Dept. Pers., Trenton; ednl. cons. Trenton Bd. Edn., Div. Youth and Family Svcs., 1970-75. Bd. dirs. YWCA, Trenton, 1968-83, v.p., 1975-77; bd. dirs. Mercer Comprehensive Planning Coun., Trenton, 1970-80; chmn. bd. dirs. Mercer County Head Start, 1987; chmn. bd. dirs. Community Coordinated Child Care, Mercer County; mem. Mercer County Commn. Child Abuse, 1984-89; chmn. Coalition for Healthy Mothers/Healthy Babies, 1986-90. Named Woman of Yr., Trenton Jr. Women United, 1976; U.S. Office Edn. fellow, 1966. Mem. Assn. for Supervision and Curriculum Devel., NAFE, Kappa Delta Pi, Alpha Kappa Alpha. Mem. Ch. of God in Christ. Avocations: collecting dolls, reading, singing, swimming, pub. speaking. Home: 619 Lincoln Ave Morrisville PA 19067-2137 Office: 2238 Hamilton Ave Trenton NJ 08619-3006

FAULKNER, LARRY RAY, university official, chemistry educator; b. Shreveport, La., Nov. 26, 1944; s. James Clifford and Doris Louise (Koch) Faulkner; m. Mary Ann Jordan, Aug. 14, 1965; children: Brian Jordan, Susan Louise. BS, So. Meth. U., 1966; PhD, U. Tex., Austin, 1969; DSc (hon.), So. Meth. U., 2000. Asst. prof. chemistry Harvard U., Cambridge, Mass., 1969—73; prof. chemistry U. Tex., Austin, 1983—84, pres., 1998—; asst. prof. U. Ill., Urbana-Champaign, 1973—75, assoc. prof., 1975—79, prof., 1979—83, prof. chemistry, dept. head, 1984—89, dean Coll. Liberal Arts and Sci., 1989—94, provost and vice chancellor acad. affairs, 1994—98. Mem. Materials Rsch. Lab, 1978—90. Author (with A.J. Bard): Electrochemical Methods, 1980, 2d edit., 2001; editor: Jour. Electroanalytical Chemistry, 1980—85; mem. edit. bd.: Jour. Electrochem. Soc., 1975—80. Recipient U.S. Dept. Energy award, 1986. Fellow: Electrochem. Soc. (v.p. 1988—91, pres. 1991—92, Edward Weston fellow 1969, Young Author's prize 1976, Edward Goodrich Acheson medal 2000), Am. Acad. Arts and Scis.; mem.: Soc. Electroanalytical Chemistry (Charles N. Reilly award 1998), Am. Chem. Soc. (award in analytical chemistry 1992), Phi Kappa Phi, Phi Beta Kappa (Grad. Rsch. award Tex. Gamma chpt. 1969—70). Home: 5310 Western Hills Dr Austin TX 78731-4822 Office: Office of Pres U Tex at Austin PO Box T Austin TX 78713-8920 E-mail: president@po.utexas.edu.

FAUST, JOHN JOSEPH, JR., theatre educator, director; b. St. Louis, Feb. 16, 1939; s. John J. and Elinor (Cafferata) F.; m. Deborah Doyle, Aug. 18, 1969; children: John Charles, Mark Doyle. AB in Speech, St. Louis U., 1961; MA in Speech and Dramatic Arts, State U. Iowa, 1964. Tchr. speech/theatre Columbus High Sch., Waterloo, Iowa, 1963-64; chair English dept., dir. theatre Augustinian Acad., St. Louis, 1964-70; chair fine arts dept., dir. activities De Smet Jesuit High Sch., St. Louis, 1970-79; dir. theatre John Burroughs Sch., St. Louis, 1979-88, Barrington (Ill.) High Sch., 1988-94. Dir. nat. high sch. inst. theatre Northwestern U., Evanston, Ill., 1963-72, 89, Webster U. High Sch. Inst., St. Louis, 1978-80, creative drama workshop Barrington Area Arts Coun., 1990-93; adjudicator, panel mem. arts recognition and talent search Nat. Found. Advancement Arts, Miami, Fla., 1978-88; tchr. Mark Twain Summer Inst., St. Louis, 1985-88; founder, exec. dir. Theatre Whatever A Prodn. Co. For, By and With Young Adults, 1996. Assoc. editor: Theatre Technology & Design, 1984; contbg. editor: Model/Theatre Curriculum. Americorps vol. in HIV/AIDS awareness in teenagers ARC, 1994-95. Mem. Am. Alliance Theatre and Edn. (John Barner award 1992, Secondary Theatre Tchr. of Yr.), Ednl. Theatre Assn.

FAUST, NAOMI FLOWE, education educator, poet; b. Salisbury, N.C. d. Christopher Leroy and Ada Luella (Graham) Flowe; m. Roy Malcolm Faust, Aug. 16, 1948. AB, Bennett Coll; MA, U. Mich., 1945; PhD, NYU, 1963. Elem. tchr. Pub. Schs. Gaffney (S.C.); tchr. English, French, phys. edn. Atkins H.S., Winston-Salem; instr. English Bennett Coll. and So. U., Scotlandville, La., 1944-46; prof. English Morgan State Coll., Balt., 1946-48; tchr. English Greensboro (N.C.) Pub. Schs., 1948-51, N.Y.C. Pub. Schs., 1954-63; prof. edn. Queens Coll. of CUNY, Flushing, 1964-82; writer, lectr., poetry readings, 1982—. Lectr. in field. Author: Discipline and the Classroom Teacher, 1977; (poetry) Speaking in Verse, 1974, All Beautiful Things, 1983, And I Travel by Rhythms and Words, 1990; contbr. poetry to jours. Named Tchr.-Author of 1979, Tchr.-Writer; recipient Cert. of Merit for Poem Cooper Hill Writers Conf., 1970, Achievement award L.I. br. AAUW, 1985, Poet of the Millennium award Internat. Poets Acad., Excellence in World Poetry award Internat. Poets Acad., 2002; named Internat. Eminent Poet, Internat. Poets Acad. Mem. AAUP, AAUW, Acad. Am. Poets, Nat. Coun. Tchrs. English, Nat. Women's Book Assn., Nat. Assn. Univ. Women (L.I. br.), World Poetry Soc. Intercontinental, N.Y. Poetry Forum, Poetry Soc. Am., NAACP, United Negro Coll. Fund, Alpha Kappa Alpha, Alpha Kappa Mu., Alpha Epsilon. Home: 11201 175th St Jamaica NY 11433-4135

FAVELA-LOZOYA, FERNANDO, engineering educator; b. Durango, Mex., Dec. 13, 1927; s. Jesus Favela and Gabina (Lozoya) F.; m. Sonia Vara Melero, June 22, 1956; children: Fernando, Sonia, Jesus, Elia and Alejandra. M in Constrn. Engrng. Civil engr. Nat. Autonoma U. Mex., Mexico City, 1952; jefe de frente y de obra ICA Group, Mexico City, 1950-56, supt. y jefe de superintendentes, 1956-64, gerente, 1964, dir., 1965-66, v.p., 1967-77, exec. v.p., 1977-92, chmn Mex. com. of Internat. engrng. practice, 1992-99; adviser of gen. dir. Federal Commn. Electricity, Mexico City, 1993-94; pres. Mex. Union of Engrng. Assn., Mexico City, 1995-99; proprietor Chateau Camou, S.A. de C.V., 1994—; prof. Nat. U. Mex., Mexico City, 1966—. Mem. Nat. Reconstruction Commn., 1985; pres. Fedn. Colls. Civil Engrng. Mex., 1991-92; pres. Soc. Ex-Alum engrng. faculty UNAM, 1997-99. Named Excellent and Eminent Prof., U. Cauca, Colombia, 1981; recipient Honor medal Engrng. Coll. Spain, 1982. Mem. ASTM, Am. Concrete Inst., Engrs. and Architects Mex. Assn., Civil Engrng. Mex. Coll. (pres. 1984-86), Mex. Soc. Engrs. (v.p. 1989-92), Internat. Road Fedn. (dir. 1991-99). Roman Catholic. Home: Creston 336 Pedregal de San Angel 01900 Mexico City Mexico Office: Roberto Gayol # 55 Col del Valle 03100D F Mexico City Mexico E-mail: ffavela@correo.unam.mx.

FAVERTY, PATRICK WILLIAM, educational administrator; b. Gary, Ind., Jan. 20, 1949; s. Marion W. and Margaret (Bailey) F.; children: Scott, Andra, Shannon. BA in Secondary Edn., Utah State U., 1971; MEd in Counseling, U. Calif., Santa Barbara, 1990; EdD in Orgnl. Mgmt., U. LaVerne, 1995. From tchr. to headmaster Ojai (Calif.) Valley Sch., 1972-80; owner, dir. Potrero Canyon Sch., Camp Carmel, Calif., 1980-88; dir. Alumni Vacation Ctr. U. Calif. Santa Barbara, 1989-90; dist. counselor Saugus Union Sch. Dist., Santa Clarita, Calif., 1990-92; prin. Bennett Valley Union Sch. Dist., Santa Rosa, Calif., 1992-93; prin. McDowell Sch. Petaluma (Calif.) City Schs., 1992-97; prin. American Canyon Mid. Sch., Napa Valley, Calif., 1997-99; supt. Cold Spring Sch. Dist., Santa Barbara, Calif., 1999—. Cons. Shandra Corp., Santa Barbara, 1986—; cons./workshop presenter. Author (poetry) Contemporary American Poets, 1987, Hon. Mention, 1987. Mem. ASCD, Assn. Calif. Sch. Adminstrs., Phi Delta Kappa. Avocations: tennis, horseback riding, writing.

FAWCETT, LEE C. retired dean; b. Omaha, Nebr., May 15, 1941; s. Paul Wayne and Helen Rivola F.; m. Rita Margaret West, June 20, 1964; children: David, Daniel, Michael. BA in Polit. Sci., U. Chgo., 1963; MA in Ancient History, Wayne State U., 1970. Intern Detroit Country Day Sch., Birmingham, Mich., 1963—65; dir. fin. aid Kendall Coll., Evanston, Ill., 1965—68; assoc. dir., dir. fin. aid Wayne State U., Detroit, 1968—70; assoc. dean admissions and fin. aid Ea. Mich. U., Ypsilanti, Mich., 1970—75, dir. fin. aid, 1975—80, asst. to v.p. student svcs., 1980—81; assoc. dean student svcs. Clackamas C.C., Oregon City, Oreg., 1981—91, assoc. dean rsch. and planning, 1991—97; ret., 1997. Pres. Mich. Student Fin. Aid Assn., Detroit, 1969—71; chair C.C. Rsch. and Planning Coun., Salem, Oreg., 1991—93. Treas. ACLU, Ann Arbor, Mich., 1972—76; cubmaster Boy Scouts Am., Ann Arbor, 1973—75; city councilor City of Lake Oswego (Oreg.), 1985—90; treas. Unitarian Ch., 1999—2001. Recipient Disting. Svc. award, Mich. Student Fin. Aid Assn., 1981. Democrat. Mem. Unitarian Ch. Avocations: reading, distributing library books to local shelters. Home: Apt 105 416 NW 13th Ave Portland OR 97209-2932 E-mail: lee_ritafawcett@attbi.com.

FAXON, ALICIA CRAIG, art educator, department chairman; b. N.Y.C., July 27, 1931; d. William Donald and Clara Alicia (Harnecker) Craig; m. Richard Bremer Faxon, Feb. 21, 1953; children: Richard Paul, Thomas Hardwick. AB, Vassar Coll., 1952; MA, Radcliffe Coll., 1953, Boston U., 1971, PhD, 1979; DHL (hon.), Simmons Coll., 1998. Lectr. New Eng. Sch. Art and Design, Boston, 1974-77; acting dir. Danforth Mus., Framingham, Mass., 1977; teaching assoc. Boston U. Sch. for Art, 1978-79; vis. lectr. Simmons Coll., Boston, 1979-80, asst. prof. art, 1980-86, assoc. prof., 1986-91, chmn. dept. art and music, 1987-93, prof. art, 1991-93, alumnae endowed chair, 1992-93. Lectr. Sch. for Lifelong Learning, Harvard U., Cambridge, Mass., 1978-80; program chmnn. Women's Studies Adv. Bd., 1982-84; R.I. editor Art New Eng., 1994-99. Author: Catalog Raisonnè of Prints of J.-L. Forain, 1982, Pilgrims and Pioneers, 1987, Dante Gabriel Rossetti, 1989; co-author: (with Liana Cheney and Kathleen Russo) Self-Portraits of Woman Painters, 2000; co-editor (with Susan Casteras) Pre-Raphaelite Art in its European Context, 1995; mem. editl. bd. Woman's Art Jour., 1989—. Mem. acquisitions com. Danforth Mus., 1974-89, trustee, 1975-77. Recipient Nan award for art criticism Art New Eng., 1987; grantee Nat. Endowment for Arts, 1982, Simmons Coll., 1984, NEH, 1989, 92. Mem. Coll. Art Assn. (chmn. preRaphaelite session 1990), Women's Caucus for Art (program co-chmn. 1986-88), Victorian Soc., 19th Century Art Historians Group, Vassar Coll. Alumnae Assn. Democrat. Episcopalian. Avocations: travel, writing.

FAY, CAROLYN M. education marketing business owner; b. Cambridge, Ohio, June 15, 1958; d. Frederick Russell and Lillian Marianna Mbiad; m. Michael Elliott Fay, Oct. 22, 1988. BA in Mass Comm., U. South Fla., 1984. Mktg. dir. Specialty Restaurants Corp., Clearwater, Fla., 1984-85; account exec. Landers & Ptnrs. Advt., St. Petersburg, Fla., 1986-87; mktg. mgr. Patchington Fashions, Inc., Clearwater, 1987-90; sr. project mgr. Modern Talking Picture Svc., St. Petersburg, 1990-92; pres., owner MarketingWorks Edn. Sys., Inc., Safety Harbor, Fla., 1992—. Creative dir., editor tchg. materials for various Fortune cos. programs; co-author, creative dir., editor tchg. materials Am. Egg Bd., 1991—. Recipient Excellence for Creation of Client Direct Mktg. award Fla. Dir. Mktg. Assn., 1994, 95, 98, Merit award Chgo. Nat. Agri-Mktg. Assn., 1994, Internat. Assn. Bus. Communicators, 1994, 96, What's New in Home Econs. Healthy Living award, 1996, 98, Prodn. Excellence award Consol. Papers, 1995-96, Judges award Printing Industry Fla., 1996, Nat. Mature Market Media award (2), 1998, S.E. Regional Silver Quill award of Excellence Internat. Assn. Bus. Commicators, 1998. Mem. Fla. Dir. Mktg. Assn., Pinellas County (Fla.) Home Econ. Tchrs. Assn. Democrat. Avocation: travel. Office: PO Box 273 Safety Harbor FL 34695-0273

FAY, GLENN MILLS, JR., science educator; b. Middlebury, Vt., July 3, 1954; s. Glenn Mills Sr. and Virginia Field (Powers) F.; m. Donna Sutton, Jul. 11, 1987; children: Addison, Lillian. BS, U. Vt., 1976, EdD, 1995; MEd, Colo. State U., 1981. Sci. tchr. Lake Region Union H.S., Orleans, Vt., 1976—79, Shelburne (Vt.) Mid. Sch., 1982—83, Champlain Valley H.S., Hinesbury, Vt., 1983—. Adj. prof. U. Vt. Burlington, Trinity Coll. Vt. Author: Science in the Service of Reform, 1992; contbr. articles to profl. jours. Recipient Gustav Ohaus award NSTA Ohaus, 1990, Scimat fellowship NSF, 1993, Presdl. award in Excellence in Teaching NSF, 1993. Mem. Vt. Sci. Tchrs. Assn. (bd. dirs. 1991—), Vt. Profl. Standards Bd (bd. dirs. 1995-2001), Nat. Sci. Tchrs. Assn. Avocations: running, hiking. Home: PO Box 177 South Hero VT 05486-0177 Office: Champlain Valley Union HS 369 CVU Rd Hinesburg VT 05461-9403

FAZZI, CHARLES, accounting educator; b. Phila., Sept. 10, 1948; s. Benjamin Carl and Connie (DiFranco) F.; m. Millicent Yvonne Andrews, May 15, 1976; children: Matthew, Stephen. BS, Pa. State U., 1970, MBA, 1974, PhD, 1983. Asst. prof. acctg. Ariz. State U., Tempe, 1977-79; bus. adminstrn. lectr. U. North Tex., Denton, 1979-82; asst. prof. acctg. Tex. Christian U., Ft. Worth, 1982-83; assoc. prof. acctg. Bucknell U., Lewisburg, Pa., 1983-88; Edgar T. Bitting prof. acctg. Elizabethtown (Pa.) Coll., 1988-92; prof., acad. dept. head Robert Morris Coll., Pitts., 1992—2002; prof., dir. grad. programs in acctg. St. Vincent Coll., Latrobe, Pa., 2002—. Vis. prof. acctg. Old Dominion U., Norfolk, Va., 1988; cons. Nat. Steel Corp., Inc., Pitts., 1988-90, Hercules, Inc., Wilmington, Del., 1984-90, Nat. Tax Seminars, Portland, Oreg., 1984-88; mem. acctg. adv. bd. McGraw-Hill, Inc., N.Y.C., 1992-93. Author: Study Guide for Financial Reporting and Analysis, 2002, Instructor's Manual for Advanced Accounting, 2003; co-author: Study Guide for Advanced Financial Accounting, 1986; contbr. articles to profl. jours. Recipient Dedication to Edn. award Beta Alpha Psi, 1981, Outstanding Grad. Asst. Tchr. award Pa. State U. Alumni Assn., 1975; fellow Deloitte & Touche, 1974, Book Industry Study Group, 1987. Mem. Am. Acctg. Assn. (various coms.), Inst. Mgmt. Accountants (nat. v.p. 1994-95). Avocations: golf, reading. Home: 1600 Whitney Court Dr 40 Latrobe PA 15650 Office: St Vincent Coll 300 Fraser Purchase Rd Latrobe PA 15650 E-mail: charles.fazzi@email.stvincent.edu.

FEAL, GISELE CATHERINE, foreign language educator; b. Froges, France, July 5, 1939; PhD in Spanish, U. Paris, 1964; PhD in French, U. Mich., 1973. Instr. Ea. Mich. U., Ypsilanti; lectr. U. Mich., Ann Arbor; asst. prof. SUNY Coll., Buffalo, 1974-80; chair dept. SUNY, Buffalo, 1977-80, assoc. prof., 1980-83, assoc. v.p., 1983-88, prof., 1992—2002. Author: Le Théatre de Crommelynck, 1976, La Mythologie Matriarcale, 1993, Ionesco. Un Theatre Onirique, 2001. Mem. Cercle Culturel de Langue Française (bd. dirs. 1980-93).

FEARN, HEIDI, physicist, educator; b. Sutton-in-Ashfield, Eng., Aug. 21, 1965; came to U.S., 1989; d. Lawrence Leonard and Erika Hanna Elfrede (Kröger) F. BS in Theol. Physics with honors, Essex U., Colchester, Eng., 1986, PhD in Theol. Quantum Optics, 1989. Grad. lab. demonstrator Essex U., 1986-89; postdoctoral rsch. asst. Max Planck Inst. Quantum Optics, Garching, Germany, 1989; rsch. assoc. U. N.Mex., Albuquerque, 1989-91; lectr. physics Calif. State U., Fullerton, 1991-92, asst. prof. physics, 1992-95, assoc. prof. physics, 1995-97, prof. physics, 1997—. Vis. scholar U. Ariz., Tucson, 1989-91; cons. Los Alamos (N.Mex.) Nat. Lab., 1994—. Kavli Inst. Theoretical Physics scholar, 2003—. Mem. AAAS, Am. Phys. Soc. Office: Calif State U Physics Dept 800 N State College Blvd Fullerton CA 92831-3547

FEARS, JESSE RUFUS, historian, educator, academic dean; b. Atlanta, Ga., Mar. 7, 1945; s. Emory Binford Fears; m. Charlene Louise Bauer, July 9, 1966; children: Laura Elizabeth, Jesse Rufus IV. BA summa cum laude, Emory U., 1966; MA, Harvard U., 1967, PhD, 1971. Asst. prof. classical langs. Tulane U., New Orleans, 1971-72; asst. prof. history Indiana U., Bloomington, 1972-75, assoc. prof. history, 1975-80, prof. history, 1980-86; prof., chair classical studies Boston U., 1986-90, assoc. dean Coll. Liberal Arts, 1987-89, dir. humanities found., 1988-90; dean Coll. Arts and Scis. U. Okla., Norman, 1990-92, prof. Classics, 1990—, G.T. and Libby Blankenship prof. history of liberty, 1992—, dir. Ctr. for History of Liberty, 1992—; adj. scholar Okla. Coun. Pub. Affairs, 1996—. Adj. scholar Okla. Coun. Pub. Affairs, 1996—. Author: Princeps A Diis Electus, 1977, (monographs) The Cult of Jupiter, 1981, The Theology of Victory, 1981, The Cult of Virtues, 1981; books on audio and video tape: A History of Freedom, 2001, Famous Greeks, 2001, Famous Romans, 2001, The Life and Times of Winston Churchill, 2001; editor: (3 vols.) Selected Writings/Lord Acton, 1985-88; contbr. chpts. to books, numerous articles to profl. jours. Bd. dirs. Okla. Sch. Sci./Math., Oklahoma City, 1990—; pres. Vergilian Soc., 2002—. Recipient Judah P. Benjamin award, Military Order of Stars and Bars, 1996; Danforth fellow Danforth Found., 1966-71; fellow Am. Acad. in Rome, 1969-71, Guggenheim Found., 1976-77, Howard Found., 1977-78, Alexander Von Humboldt, 1977-78, 80-81, Ctr. for History of Freedom, Wash. U., 1989-90; grantee Am. Philos. Soc., 1972, 79, NEH, 1974, Am. Coun. Learned Soc., 1979, Woodrow Wilson, 1983, Kerr Found., 1994, 99, 2003, Zarrow Found., 2000, 2001, 2002; Sigma Chi Scholar in Residence, Miami U., 2003. Mem. AAUP, Am. Philol. Assn., Classical Assn. Middle West and South, Archaeol. Inst. of Am., Phi Beta Kappa, Golden Key Nat. Honor Soc. Office: U Okla Dept Classics Ctr History of Liberty Kaufman Hall Norman OK 73019 E-mail: jrfears@ou.edu.

FEASTER, CHARLOTTE JOSEPHINE S. school administrator; b. Asheboro, N.C., Aug. 5, 1951; d. Earlie Lenan Staley and McCoy (Cheek) Staley Gathings; m. Jasper Nathaniel Feaster, July 23, 1983. BS in Intermediate Edn., Winston-Salem State U., 1973; MS in Intermediate Edn., N.C. Agrl. and Tech. State U., 1981, MS in Ednl. Leadership, 1993; postgrad., U. N.C., Chapel Hill and Asheville, 1995-96, East Carolina U., 1996. Cert. tchr., N.C., La. Dormitory asst. Winston-Salem (N.C.) State U., 1969-73; emergency rm. receptionist Reynolds Meml. Hosp., Winston-Salem, 1969-73; office asst. Employment Security Commn., Asheboro, 1969-71; cottage home parent asst. Guilford County Dept. Social Svcs., High Point, N.C., 1971-73; intermediate grade tchr. Randolph County Bd. Edn., Asheboro, 1973-94, summer sch. instr., 1987-91, 4th and 5th grade tchr., 1983-94, Ramseur (N.C.) Sch., 1973-94; asst. prin. Randleman (N.C.) Elem. Sch., 1994-95, Liberty (N.C.) Sch., 1995—. Enrichment camp instr. N.C. Agrl. & Tech. State U., Greensboro, 1982-87; Can. studies group leader Duke U., Durham, N.C., 1991-93; 4-H summer camp leader N.C. Randolph County, Asheboro, 1973-82; co-leader N.C. Tchr. Acad., Meredith Coll., Raleigh, N.C., 1993-94; site mgr. N.C. Tchr. Acad., Fayetteville (N.C.) State U., 1995, E. Carolina U., Greenville, 1996; mem. Asst. Prins. Exec. Program U. N.C., Chapel Hill, 1996—. 4-H leader Randolph County Agrl. Ext., Ramseur, 1983-85; Christian edn. dir. Deep River Assn. Bapt. Chs., Lee, Chatham and Randolph Counties, 1980-93; youth edn. resource person Oakland Bapt. Ch., Ramseur, 1983-93. Recipient Lay Leadership award Deep River Assn. Chs., 1990, Gold Clover award Randolph County Home Ext., 1989, Excellence First Project award Greensboro Area Math & Science Edn. Ctr., U. N.C. at Greensboro, 1991-93; grantee First Am. Bank, 1990; named one of Outstanding Young Educators Jaycees, 1990. Mem. N.C. Conf. Tchrs. Math. (workshop presenter 1988-93, Outstanding Math. Tchr. award 1992), N.C. Assn. Educators (county pres. 1992-95), Order Eastern Star (fin. sec. 1987-93), Gamma Omicron (award Eta Phi Beta chpt. 1991). Avocations: water sports, crocheting, ceramics, arts and crafts. Home: 361 Thornbrook Rd Ramseur NC 27316-8853 Office: Liberty Sch Asst Prin Exec Program 206 N Fayetteville St Liberty NC 27298-3205

FEATHERSTONE, JOHN DOUGLAS BERNARD, biochemistry educator; b. Stratford, New Zealand, Apr. 26, 1944; arrived in U.S., 1980. s. Alfred Douglas and Yvonne May (Richmond) F.; children: Michelle, Mark. BS chemistry and math., Victoria U., Wellington, New Zealand, 1962-64; MS phys. chemistry, U. Manchester, 1975; PhD chemistry, Victoria U., Wellington, New Zealand, 1977. Quality control chemist Unilever, New Zealand, 1965-66; tech. mgr. chem. Industries, Wellington, New Zealand, 1966-72; prodn. mgr. Quinoderm Pharms., Oldham, England, 1972-74; lect.r pharm. chemistry Ctrl. Inst. Tech., New Zealand, 1977-78; sr. rsch. fellow Med. Rsch. Coun., New Zealand, 1979-80; cons., dental chemistry and dental products, 1980—; asst. prof., part-time U. Rochester, NY, 1980-83; sr. rsch. assoc. Eastman Dental Ctr., Rochester, NY, 1980-88, chmn. dept. oral scis., 1983-95; assoc. prof. U. Rochester, NY, 1983-95; prof. Eastman Dental Ctr., Rochester, NY, 1988-95; prof. dept. of restorative dentistry U. Rochester, NY, 1995; prof. U. Calif., San Francisco, 1995—99, prof, San Francisco, 1995—99, prof., chmn. dept. of preventive and restorative dental sci., 1999—. Contbg. articles to profl. jour. Leader scouts, New Zealand, 1962-71; mem. New Zealand Nat. Tchg. Team, 1968-71; asst. nat. commr. Venturer Scouts New Zeland, 1968-70; mem. New Zeland Outdoor Tchg. Adv. Bd., 1978-79; New Zealand Mountain Rescue, 1976-80. Recipient Colgate Rsch. prize New Zeland Internat. Assn. Dental Rsch., 1976; Colgate Travel Award, Internat. Assn. Dental Rsch., Australia, 1976; Edward Hatton Award, World Internat. Assn. Dental Rsch. Meeting, Copenhagen, 1977; Hamilton Award Royal Soc. New Zeland, 1979. Distinguished Scientist Award, Internat. Assn. Dental Rsch, 2000; Zsolnai Rsch. Award; European Orgn. for Caries Rsch., 2002; Rsch. Lctr. of the Yr., Sch. of Dentistry, U. Calif., San Francisco, 2003. Fellow New Zeland Inst. Chemistry; mem. AAAS; Am. Chem. Soc.; European Orgn. Caries Rsch. (sr.); Internat. Assn. Dental Rsch. Home: 311 Miramontes Ave Half Moon Bay CA 94019-1821 Office: U Calif San Francisco Dental Sch Dept Preventive Restorative Dental Sci 707 Parnassus Ave San Francisco CA 94143-0001 E-mail: jdbf@itsa.ucsf.edu.

FEBRES-SANTIAGO, SAMUEL F. retired academic administrator; BA in Secondary Edn.-Hispanic Studies, Inter Am. U. P.R.; MA in Spanish-Am. Literature, MEd in Curriculum and Instrn., Temple U.; MA in Sch. Mgmt., U. P.R.; postgrad., Harvard U.; EdD in Adminstrn. of Ednl. Instns., Seton Hall U. Chancellor Guayama Campus, Interam. U. P.R., 1989-99. Recipient Disting. Alumni award Inter Am. U. Mem. Am. Assn. Higher Edn., Hispanic Assn. Colls. & Univs., Mid. State Assn. Colls. & Univs., Lions (pres. edn. com., bd. dirs.), Phi Delta Kappa. Office: InterAm U PR Guayama Campus PO Box 10004 Guayama PR 00785-4004 E-mail: sffebre@ns.inter.edu.

FECTEAU, ROSEMARY LOUISE, educational administrator, educator, consultant; b. Niagara, Wis., Aug. 7, 1930; d. Andrew Raymond and Julianna Agnes (Wodenka) Waitrovich; m. Jack Richard Fecteau Sr. (dec. Dec. 1994), June 12, 1954; children: Michele, Julienne, Gervaise, Jack Jr., Andrew, Anne-Marie. BA with high distinction, U. R.I., 1974; MS in Edn., U. Maine, 1976; MS in Ednl. Adminstrn., U. So. Maine, 1979; PhD, Columbia Pacific U., 1999. Cert. supt. schs. K-12. Sec. A.O. Smith Corp., Milw., 1949-54; sec. to Judge Irving W. Smith, Niagara, 1954-55; asst. tchr. Regional Resource Rm., Yarmouth, Maine, 1974-75; prin. Breakwater Sch., Cape Elizabeth, Maine, 1975-78; tchr. grades 6-8 Wells (Maine) Jr. H.S., 1978-79; dir. spl. svcs. Maine Sch. Adminstrv. Dist. 75, Bowdoin, Bowdoinham, Harpswell, Topsham, Maine, 1979-84; ednl. cons. various states, 1984—; mem. policy adv. group for Maine Gov. John Baldacci, 2002. Owner Serendipity Acres Sheep Farm; secondary handicapped task force State Dept. Edn., Augusta, 1980-81; chairperson nat. insvc. network U. Ind., Topsham, Maine, 1981-84; mem. policy adv. group Gov. John Baldacci, Maine, 2002. Mem. Maine Spl. Edn. Rev. Team; founder Project Co-Step and Project S.E.A.R.C.H.; mem. focus group Casco Bay Estuary Project Maine; brownie leader, girl scout cons. Girl Scouts Am., Erie, Pa., 1965-66; dir. women's Cursillo Movement, Erie, 1967; co-chair publicity St. Vincent Hosp., Erie, 1966-67; chair conservation commn. Town of North Yarmouth, 1987; del. Maine Dem. Conv., 1986; mem. policy adv. group Maine Gov. John Baldacci, 2002 Mem.: AAUW, Columbia Pacific U. Alumni Assn., Maine Children's Alliance, Physicians for Social Responsibility, Union of Concerned Scientists, Consumers for Affordable Health Care, Maine Organic Farmer and Gardener Assn., North Yarmouth Hist. Soc., U. So. Maine Alumni Assn. Avocations: music, arts, nutrition, physical fitness. Home: Serendipity Acres 140 W Pownal Rd North Yarmouth ME 04097-6819 E-mail: romyphd99@aol.com.

FEDAK, BARBARA KINGRY, retired technical center administrator; b. Hazleton, Pa., Feb. 7, 1939; d. Marvin Frederick and Ruth Anna (Wheeler) Siebel; m. Raymond F. Fedak, Mar. 27, 1993; children: Sean M., James Goldey. BA, Trenton State Coll., 1961; MEd, Lesley Coll., Cambridge, Mass., 1986. Registered respiratory therapist. Dept. dir. North Platte (Nebr.) Community Hosp., 1974-75; newborn coord. Children's Hosp., Denver, 1975-79; edn. coord. Rose Med. Ctr., Denver, 1979-81; program dir. respiratory tech. program Pickens Tech., Aurora, Colo., 1981-86; mktg. rep. Foster Med. Corp., Denver, 1986-87; staff therapist Porter Meml. Hosp., Denver, 1987-88; dir., br. mgr. Pediatric Svcs. Am., Denver, 1988-90; dir. clin. edn. Pickens Tech., Aurora, Colo., 1991—2000, divsn. chair health occupations, 1991—2000; ret., 2000. Site evaluator Joint Rev. Com. for Respiratory Therapy Edn., Euless, Tex. Co-editor: Am. Assn. Respiratory Care Record, 1998-2000. Met. coun. mem. Am. Lung Assn., 1987-91. Mem.: Colo. Assn. Respiratory Educators (chair 1991—96), Colo. Soc. Respiratory Care (sec. 1980—81, program com. 1982—92, dir. at large 1983—86, 1990—92), Am. Assn. for Respiratory Care (edn. sect. program com. 1992—2000, abstract rev. com. 1993—96, alt. del. ho. dels. 1997—98, del. 1999—2000, treas. ho. dels. 2001, 2002), Lambda Beta (sec./treas. exec. bd. 2003). Methodist. Avocations: reading, mountain biking, golf, singing, piano playing. Home: 11478 S Marlborough Dr Parker CO 80138-7318 E-mail: bobbinkf@aol.com.

FEDAK, JOHN G. biology education educator; b. Wilkes Barre, Pa., Nov. 10, 1962; s. John J. and Lillian A. (Eget) F. AS in Wildlife Tech., Pa. State U., 1982; B in B in Biology, B in Secondary Edn., Lock Haven U., 1986; MS in Edn., Clarion U., 1989. Sci. tchr. Redbank Valley Sch. Dist., New Bethlehem, Pa., 1986—. Coach for wrestling, softball, and volleyball; bd. dirs. Beaver Creek Nature Ctr., Clarion/Knox, Pa. Columnist: Leader-Vindicator Newspaper, 1994; contbr. articles to profl. jours. Named Conservation Educator of the Yr. Clarion County Conservation Dist., 1992-93. Mem. Am. Birding Assn., Audubon Soc. (chpt. v.p. 1990, pres. 1993-95, newsletter editor 1991-92). Democrat. Avocations: birdwatching. rock-climbing, hiking, nature study. Home: 26 Race St Bradford PA 16701-2348

FEDDER, DONALD OWEN, pharmacist, educator; b. Balt., Nov. 20, 1926; s. William Samuel and Rose Fedder; m. Michaeline R. Fedder; children: Debra M. Fedder Goren, Ira Louis. Student, Western Md. Coll., 1944-47; BS in Pharm., U. Md., 1950; MPH, Johns Hopkins U., 1978, DrPH, 1982. Staff pharmacist Pikesville (Md.) Pharmacy, 1950-51; chief pharmacist, owner Fedder's Pharmacy & Fedder Med. Svcs., Balt., 1951-74; prof., dir. cmty. pharm., pharm. high blood pressure prgms. U. Md., 1974—, prof. epidemiology and preventive medicine, 1992—. Chmn. Md. Commn. on High Blood PRessure and Related Cardiovasc. Risk Factors, 1984-91; chmn. hyptension com. Md. affiliate Am. Heart Assn., 1984-86, sec., bd. dirs., 1984-86, chmn. health care site com., 1987-92, New Initiatives Com., 1992-95; pres., CEO Bd. Orthotist/Prosthetist Cert., 1984—; cons. in field. Contbr. articles to profl. jours. Bd. dirs. Dundalk Concert Assn., 1963-75; candidate Md. Legis., 1970. With U.S. Army, 1944-45. Recipient Order Double Star, Alpha Zeta Omega, 1972, 75; Beta chpt. award Phi Alpha, 1950; Bowl of Hygiea award, 1980, Disting. Achievement award Md. Pharmacists Assn., 1988, Alumnus of Yr. Alumni Assn. Sch. Pharmacy, U. Md., 1990, Martin Luther King Jr. Diversity award, 2003. Fellow Am. Pharm. Assn. (dir., chmn. 1976-77), Soc. Pub. Health Edn.; mem. Md. Pharm. Assn. (Pres.'s award 1971), Am. Assn. Colls. Pharmacy, Nat. Orgn. for Competency Assurance (sec.-treas. 1994-95), Md. Pub. Health Assn. (life, pres. 1995-96, Vol. of Yr. 1988, Innovation in Pub. Health award 1997, award named in his honor 2002), Acad. Pharmacy Practice (pres. 1973-74), Balt. Met. Pharm. Assn. (pres. 1968, hon. pres. 1994), U. Med. Sch. Pharm. Alumni Assn. (Hon. Alumnus award 1990), Optimist Club (pres. local club 1963-64). Sigma Xi, Rho Chi. Democrat. Jewish. Home: 136 Welcome Aly Baltimore MD 21201-2432 Office: 515 W Lombard St Ste 170 Baltimore MD 21201

FEDELI, SHIRLEY ANN (MARTIGNONI), secondary school educator; b. Rockford, Ill., Aug. 19, 1935; d. Peter William and Catherine Gertrude (Domino) Martignoni; m. Eugene Anthony Fedeli, Oct. 24, 1959; 1 child, Lisa Marie. BA in Child Devel., Rockford Coll., 1957. Elem. tchr. Bloom Sch., Rockford, 1957-68; social studies chair St. Peter Cathedral Sch., Rockford, 1980—. Founder Pappagallo--Italian Culture News, 1995—. Tour dir. Columbus Day com., Rockford, 1992, 1994, 1995, 1999, 2002; founder, dir. Amici Italiani-Folk Dancers Adult and Youth, Rockford, 1986—; bd. dirs., v.p. Ethnic Heritage Mus., Rockford, 1987—, pres., 1999—, Graham-Ginestra Hist. Home, Rockford, 1976—; initiation bd. Outdoor Edn. Pub. Atwood, city of Rockford Schs. Program, 1958—68; gov. apptd. Multi-Cultural Svc. Com. Bd. of Mental Health, Springfield, Ill., 1997—; founder Club La Vita Italiana, 1995—; culture, edn. chmn. Italians in N.W. Ill., 1980—; source vol. Rockford City Schs., 1999, 2000—03; apptd. Rockford Diocese Social Studies Curriculum Devel., 1998—2000; chair Ethnic Village Fundraiser, Rockford; tchr. leader Ctr. in Learning in Retirement; SOURCE vol. Rockford Pub. Schs.; mem. Rfd. Hist. Soc., Burpee Nat. Hist. Mus., program: Leornardo Da Vinci for Pub. Sch.; celebration supporter Rockford's Millennium; coord. Gourmet Alley, Rockford, emcee; coord. On the Waterfront Event (Admiral's Club) city-wide fest, 1998—2003; hist. tour guide River Dist.; mem. Rockford Sesquicentennial Interfaity City program; mem. Columbus spl. event com. Klehm Arboretum; spkr. at various civic and religious orgns.; mem. Winnebago County Vision Project; mem. Golden Apple selection com. Rockford Pub. Schs.; intergenerational com. Rock Valley Coll. Recipient Studs Terkel Humanities Svc. award, 2002, Futurists award Rockford Sesquicentennial, 2002, Lifescape Comty. Svc. award, 2002, Bishop O'Neill award; inducted in Italian Am. Hall of Fame, 1996; named Outstanding Social Studies Tchr. State of Ill., 1989; recognition in Rockford Register Star newspaper, Rockford Pub. Libr. Newsletter. Mem.: AAUW, Italian Folk Art Fedn. Am. (bd. dirs.), Nat. Cath. Soc. Foresters (v.p., youth leader), Delta Kappa Gamma Internat. Hon. Tchg. Soc. (1st v.p., 2d v.p., sec., coms.). Roman Catholic. Avocations: touring italy/europe, volunteering, reading. E-mail: esfedeli@aol.com.

FEDERMAN, DANIEL DAVID, medical educator, educational administrator, endocrinologist; b. N.Y.C., Apr. 16, 1928; m. Elizabeth Buckley; children: Lise, Carolyn. BA, Harvard U., 1949, MD, 1953. Diplomate Am. Bd. Internal Medicine. Instr. to prof. Harvard Med. Sch., Boston, 1961—72, prof. medicine and dean for students and alumni, 1977—92, Carl W. Walter prof. medicine and med. edn., dean med. edn., 1992—; chmn. medicine Stanford Med. Sch., Palo Alto, Calif., 1972—77. Author: (med. textbook) Abnormal Sexual Development, 1967; editor: Scientific American Medicine. Master: ACP (pres. Phila. 1982—83). Office: Harvard Med Sch Office of Dean Bldg A-101 25 Shattuck St Boston MA 02115-6027

FEERICK, JOHN DAVID, law educator; b. N.Y.C., July 12, 1936; s. John D. and Mary J. F.; m. Emalie Platt, Aug. 25, 1962; children: Maureen, Margaret, Jean, Rosemary, John, William. BS, Fordham U., 1958, LL.B., 1961; hon. degree, Coll. New Rochelle, 1991. Bar: N.Y. 1961. Assoc. Skadden, Arps, Slate, Meagher & Flom, N.Y.C., 1961-68, partner, 1968-82; prof. law Fordham U. Sch. Law, 1982—, dean, 1982—2002. Author: From Failing Hands: The Story of Presidential Succession, 1965, The 25th Amendment, 1976; co-author: The Vice Presidents of the United States, 1967, NLRB Representation Elections-Law, Practice and Procedure, 1980; also articles; editor-in-chief Fordham Law Rev., 1960-61. Chmn. N.Y. State Commn. Govt. Integrity, 1987-90. Recipient Eugene J. Keefe award Fordham U. Law Sch., 1975, 85, spl. award Fordham U. Law Rev. Assn., 1977. Fellow Am. Bar Found.; mem. ABA (chmn. spl. com. election law and voter participation 1976-79, spl. award 1966), N.Y. State Bar Assn. (chmn. com. fed. constrn. 1979-83, exec. com. 1985-87), Assn. Bar City N.Y. (v.p. 1986-87, pres. 1992-94), Am. Arbitration Assn. (chair exec. com. and bd. dirs. 1995, chair Fund for Modern Cts. 1995—), Fordham U. Law Sch. Alumni Assn. (dir. 1972—, medal of achievement 1980), mem. Homeless Panel of N.Y. and Comn. on Jud. Elections, 2003, Phi Beta Kappa. Office: Fordham U Sch Law 33 W 60th St 2nd Fl New York NY 10023

FEESER, LARRY JAMES, civil engineering educator, researcher; b. Hanover, Pa, Feb. 23, 1937; s. Cyrus Myers and Arelia Cecilia (Stonesifer) F.; m. Patricia Marianne Reinhold, Aug. 19, 1961; children— Anne Elizabeth, David John BS in Civil Engring., Lehigh U., 1958; MS, U. Colo., 1961; PhD, Carnegie-Mellon U., 1965. Registered profl. engr., Colo., 1963, N.Y., 1974. From instr. to prof. civil engring. U. Colo., Boulder, 1958-74; prof., chmn. dept. civil engring. Rensselaer Poly. Inst., Troy, NY, 1974-82, assoc. dean engring., 1982-85, vice provost for computing and info. tech., 1985-90, prof. civil engring., 1990—, dir. ctr. for infrastructure and transp. studies, 1993-95. Cons. Jorgensen & Hendrickson Engrs., Denver Contbr. articles to profl. jour. Named to Those Who Made Marks in 1981, Engring. News Record, 1982; Ford Found. fellow, 1961-63; NSF Sci. Faculty fellow, 1971-72 Fellow Am. Concrete Inst., ASCE (hon., nat. dir. 1979-82), fellow, Nat. Soc. Profl. Engrs. (nat. v.p. 1998-99); mem. Am. Soc. Engring. Edn. Office: Rensselaer Poly Inst Dept Civil and Environ Engring Troy NY 12181

FEHLER, POLLY DIANE, neonatal nurse, educator; b. Harvard, Ill., Jan. 6, 1946; d. Arthur William and Charlotte (Stewart) Eggert; m. Gene L. Fehler, Dec. 26, 1964; children: Timothy, Andrew. AS, summa cum laude, Kishwaukee Coll., 1974; BSN, magna cum laude, No. Ill. U., DeKalb, 1977, MSN, summa cum laude, 1980. Cert. BLS, neonatal resuscitation instr., 1989-00. Ob-gyn. staff nurse Kishwaukee Hosp., 1977; community health nurse DeKalb County Health Dept., 1977-79; grad. teaching asst. No. Ill. Univ., 1978-80; adj. maternity instr. Auburn Univ., Montgomery, Ala., 1980-81; maternal/newborn nurse USAF Regional Hosp. Maxwell, Montgomery, Ala., 1980-81, nurse internship coord., 1981-83; edn. coord. USAF Hosp., Bergstrom, Austin, Tex., 1983-87; neonatal ICU & transport RN St. Mary's Hosp., Athens, Ga., 1988-90; nursing instr. Tri-County Tech. Coll., Pendleton, S.C., 1990-97, dept. head nursing program, 1998—. EMT, course lectr. U. Tex., Austin, 1984-86; counselor, vol. Hospice, 1984-87; sec., v.p. Shared Resources for Nurses, Austin, 1984-87; high blood pressure instr.-trainer Am. Heart Assn., 1986-87, home health staff nurse Interim Health Care, Anderson, S.C., 1991-94; expert witness St. Mary's Hosp., Athens, 1991-92; coord. NCLEX rev. course Health Edn. Systems, Inc., 1993-96; lectr. on interculturalism in nursing, 1993-99; mem. adv. bd. Tri-County Student Competencies, 1990-99, mem. advising team, 1995-2002, mini grant sel. com., 1992-93, 95-97, com. chmn., 1996-97, Tri-County Instrnl. Affairs com., 1998-2000, Y2K Coll. Planning Group, 1999-2000. Nursing textbook reviewer Addison Wesley Pubs., 1993-99, Mosby Yearbook, 1995-99, Saunders Publisher, 1999-2000. Nurse, med. evaluator Mass Casualty Exercises, Austin, 1984-87; tchr., sec. United Meth. Chs., Ill., Ala., Ga., S.C., 1970—; mem. alumni bd. No. Ill. U., DeKalb, 1979-80; mem. Malta Dist. Bd. Edn., 1979-80; judge Austin Sch. Dist. Sci. and Math. Fair, Austin, 1983-84; S.C. Gov.'s Guardian ad Litem Vol., 1995-99; vol. Oconee County Healthy Visions Task Force, 1996-98, S.C. Good Health Appeal Coll. Campaign Mgr., 1996, Oconee County Humane Soc., 1996-2002; mem. adv. coun. Oconee Kid's Health, 1997-99, Planning Work Force, 1998-99; mem. SC Nurses Assn. Continuing Edn. Approval Com., 1998-2000, SC Maternal Child Health Counc., 1999-2001. Capt. USAF, 1980-88. Decorated USAF Commendation medal with oak leaf cluster; recipient Sr. Nursing Class of Tri-County Tech. Coll. Instr. of the Yr. award, 1992, Nat. Inst. for Staff and Orgnl. Devel. Excellence award, 1995; Duke Power grantee Alliance 2020, 1997-02; Amy Cockcroft Leadership fellow, U. S.C., 2002-03. Mem. ANA, Nat. League for Nursing, S.C. Nurses Assn., S.C. Assn. Perinatal Nurses, S.C. Tech. Edn. Assn. (Educator of Yr. 2000), Nursing Faculty Orgn. (v.p. 1991-94, pres. 1998-2003), United Meth. Women (pres. 1998-99), S.C. Nursing Deans and Dirs. Coun. (nom. com. 2000-01), S.C. League for Nursing (bd. dirs.), RN-BSN-MSN Co-0p. Initiative (pres. 2002—), Sigma Theta Tau, Lambda Chi Nu. Meth. Avocations: reading, swimming, writing, walking. Home: 106 Laurel Ln Seneca SC 29678-2705 Office: Tri-County Tech Coll PO Box 587 Pendleton SC 29670-0587 E-mail: pfehler@tctc.edu.

FEHR, RALPH EDWARD, III, electrical engineer, educator; b. Reading, Pa., Aug. 15, 1961; s. Ralph Edward II and Estelle Carolyn (Hill) F. BSEE, Pa. State U., 1983; M.Elec. Engring., U. Colo., 1987. Registered profl. engr., N.Mex., Fla. Elec. engring. coop. Gilbert/Commonwealth, Reading, Pa., 1980-83; ops. engr. Pub. Svc. Co. of N.Mex., Albuquerque, 1984-86, distbn. engr., 1986-88; dep. assoc. dir. energy matters USAF, Kirtland AFB, N.Mex., 1988-92; project engr. transmission design Fla. Power Corp., St. Petersburg, 1992-95, sr. engr. transmission and substa. design tech., 1995-96, sr. engr. sys. control, 1996-98, sr. engr. sys. planning, 1998—2000; sr. cons. engr. Tampa Electric Co., 2000—02, ind. engr. cons., 2003—; instr., elec. engring. Pa. State U., Monroeville, 2001—. Computer instr. U. N. Mex., Albuquerque, 1986—92; adj. instr. math. St. Petersburg Jr. Coll., Clearwater, Fla., 1994—97; adj. instr. elec. engring. U. So. Fla., Tampa, 1997—. Author: Industrial Power Distribution; contbr. articles various profl. mags. Pets Uplifting People, St. Petersburg, 1995-2002 Sr. mem. IEEE (profl. activities chmn. 1996-98), Tau Beta Pi, Eta Kappa Nu. Achievements include development of three-dimensional modeling techniques and software for power transmission line design and analysis. Home and Office: 2738 Roosevelt Blvd Apt 106 Clearwater FL 33760-2503 E-mail: r.fehr@ieee.org.

FEHRING, MARY ANN, secondary education educator; Secondary tchr. Bishop Noll Inst., Hammond, Ind. Named Outstanding High Sch. tchr. Inland Steel Ryerson Found., 1992. Office: Bishop Noll Inst 1518 Hoffman St Hammond IN 46327-1769

FEI, LIN, engineering educator, engineering executive; b. Ningbo, Zhejiang, China, Oct. 15, 1957; s. Shen Shen F. and Ai Mei Zhou; m. Jiu Ru Chen, Jan. 27, 1986; 1 child, Xi. BS in Physics, Fu Dan U., Shanghai, China, 1982; Promotion, Munich U., 1987-89; Mittlestufe III, Goethe-Inst. Freiburg, Germany, 1987. Sr. engr. in laser and optoelectronics. Asst. rschr. N. China No. 3, Tianjin, China, 1982-86; vis. scholar Max-Planck Inst. Quantumoptik, Munich, 1987-89; rschr. Inst. Chem. and Phys. Engring., Tianjin, China, 1989-91, assoc. prof., 1992—; vice mng. dir., sales mktg. mgr. Lexel Laser Beijing Co. Ltd., 1995-99; product mgr. Cantronic Sys. Inc., 2000—. Cons. as liaison Venture Capital Cons., Encino, Calif., 1996; rschr. in field. Mem. editl. bd. China Laser Focus, The Buyer Guide, 1996-99; inventor in field. Recipient Second prize Communicate of Saving Electricity and Energy, 1992, First place Photography Com. Shen-Jian, 1993. Fellow Fed. Com. Tianjin Youth. Avocations: swimming, music, dancing, table-tennis, photography. Office: Cantronic Sys Inc 63A Clipper St Coquitlam BC Canada V3K 6X2 Office Fax: 604-516-6618. E-mail: linfei@cantronic.com.

FEIG, BARBARA KRANE, elementary school educator, author; b. Mitchell, S.D., Nov. 8, 1937; d. Peter Abraham and Sally (Gorchow) Krane; m. Jerome Feig, June 8, 1963; children: Patricia Lynn, Lizabeth Ann. Student, Washington U., St. Louis, 1955-58; BE, Nat. Coll. Edn., 1960; postgrad., Northeastern Ill. U. Tchr. various schs., 1960-68, Anshe Emet Day Sch., Chgo., 1966-68, Sacred Heart, Chgo., 1982—, New City Day Sch., Chgo., 1983-90, Chgo. Pub. Schs., 1990—. Pres. J.B. Pal & Co., Inc., Chgo., 1975—; bd. dirs. Barclee Cosmetics, Inc., Chgo., Media Merchandising, Chgo.; meeting planner Ismes, Bergamo, Italy, 1987—, Technica, Chgo., 1987—, Meeting Network, Chgo., 1987—. Author: Now You're Cooking: A Guide to Cooking For Boys and Girls, 1975, The Parents' Guide to Weight Control For Children, 1980; mem. editorial staff Other Voices, 1985—; developer ednl. toy, 1985. Mem. womens bd. Francis Parker Sch., Chgo., 1972—; trustee Chgo. Inst. for Psychoanalysis, 1975—; bd. dirs. Juvenile Diabetes Found., Chgo., 1976—. Mem. Women of the Professions and Trades, Jewish Fedn. Avocations: skydiving, scuba diving, mountain climbing, skiing, marathons. Home: 1340 N Astor St Apt 2906 Chicago IL 60610-8438

FEIGERT, FRANK BROOK, retired political science educator, writer; b. N.Y.C., Nov. 10, 1937; s. Morris Samuel Feigert and Anna (Frank) Spelke; m. Frances Goodside, June 17, 1961; children: Benjamin, Daniel. BA, Allegheny Coll., 1959; MA, U. Md., 1965, PhD, 1968. Instr. to asst. prof. Knox Coll., Galesburg, Ill., 1966—70; asst. to prof. SUNY, Brockport, 1970—77; prof. then regents prof. polit. sci. U. North Tex., Denton, 1997—2002; ret., 2002. Author: Canada Votes, 1988, Parties and Politics in America, 1976, Politics and Process of American Government, 1982, American Political Parties, 1984, American Party System and The American People, 1985; author: (with others) Political Analysis, 1972, 1976. Precinct leader Monroe County Dem. Com., NY, 1972—77, registration chmn., 1972; campaign chmn. State Assembly Campaign, Monroe County, 1974; bd. dirs. Participation, 2000—03. Served to capt. USAF, 1959—64. Fulbright-Hays sr. fellow, 1977—78. Mem.: Midwestern Polit. Sci. Assn., So. Polit. Sci. Assn., Am. Polit. Sci. Assn., U.S. Sailing Club, Dallas Corinthian Yacht Club (Oak Point, Tex.) (treas. 1983—89). Jewish. Avocations: reading, photography, travel. Home: 500 Court Sq Apt 404 Charlottesville VA 22902

FEILER GOLDSTEIN, PAULETTE, secondary education educator, researcher; b. Paris, Mar. 27, 1933; came to U.S., 1949; d. Bernard Berel and Rachel Leja (Gimelsein) Feiler; widowed; children: Robert Bart Goldstein Feiler, Hillary Renee Goldstein. BA, Queens Coll., 1973; MA in Philosophy, CUNY, 1977, PhD in French, 1987. Cert. tchr. N.Y. Acct. Seligman & Latz, N.Y.C., 1950-58; dance tchr. Henry St. Playhouse, N.Y.C., 1959-65; tchr. Bd. Edn., N.Y.C., 1973—. Yearbook advisor Flushing H.S., 1992—. Mem. Nat. Assn. For the Children Of The Holocaust, N.Y.C., 1992. Mem. PhD Alumni Assn., Warthwatch, Smithsonian, Harvard Health Letter, Women's Health Watch, Temple Beth El of Great Neck, Earthwatch. Jewish. Avocation: swimming. Home: 5 Brokaw Ln Great Neck NY 11023-1159

FEIN, ADRIENNE MYRA, nursing administrator; b. N.Y.C., Oct. 30, 1936; d. Sidney and Mae (Chaikin) Englander; children: Ellen, Harold, Aaron. Diploma, Newark Beth Israel Hosp. Sch. Nursing, 1957. Cert. psychoprophylactic childbirth educator. Staff nurse obstetrics unit Newark Beth Israel Med. Ctr., asst. head nurse, head nurse, nursing educator; dir. inservice edn. Hamilton Park Health Care Ctr.; dir. nursing svcs. Delaire Nursing and Convalescent Ctr., Linden, NJ. Mem. ANA, NJ. Nurse's Assn., Congress on Policy, Newark Beth Israel Hosp. Sch. Nursing Alumnae Assn. (sec.), Nat. Assn. Dirs. Nursing, Cmty. Assn. Inst.

FEINBERG, ARTHUR WARREN, medical educator; b. Bklyn., June 17, 1923; BA, Columbia Coll., 1943; MD, Columbia U., 1945. Intern Lenox Hill Hosp., Bklyn., 1945-46; resident Maimonides Hosp., Bklyn., 1948-51; physician pvt. practice, Great Neck, N.Y., 1951-74; attending physician North Shore U. Hosp., Great Neck, N.Y., 1951-74, assoc. dir. dept. medicine, 1975-88, chief geriatric medicine Manhasset, N.Y., 1988—; med. dir. Ctr. Extended Care Rehab., Manhasset, N.Y., 1988—; prof. clin. medicine NYU Sch. Medicine, N.Y.C., 1996—. Bd. dirs. L.I. Alzheimer's Found., N.Y., 1996—. Capt. U.S. Army Med. Corps, 1946-48. Fellow N.Y. Acad. Medicine; master ACP; mem. Am. Fedn. Clin. Rsch., Am. Geriatrics Soc., Gerontological Soc. Am., N.Y. Med. Dirs. Assn., Met. Area Geriatrics Soc. (bd. dirs., v.p., pres.). Office: NSUH/CECR 330 Cmty Dr Manhasset NY 11030

FEINBERG, ELEN AMY, artist, educator; b. N.Y.C., Jan. 22, 1955; d. S.J. Feinberg. BFA, Cornell U., 1976; student, Tyler Sch. of Art, Rome, 1974-75; MFA, Ind. U., 1978. Regent's prof. of art U. N.Mex., Albuquerque, 1978—, assoc. dean. Coll. Art. One-woman shows include Eason Gallery, Santa Fe, 1981, Touchstone Gallery, N.Y.C., 1984, Roger Ramsay Gallery, Chgo., 1987, Mekler Gallery, L.A., 1988, Graham Gallery, Albuquerque, 1992, Locus Gallery, St. Louis, 1996, 98, Inpost Gallery, Albuquerque, 1997, Sarah Morthland Gallery, N.Y.C., 1999, Ruth Bachofner Gallery, L.A., 1999, Galerie Rauminhalt, Vienna, 1999, Dist. Fine Arts, Washington, 2000, Plains Art Mus., Fargo, N.D., 2000, Insap III, Palermo, Italy, 2000, St. James Ctr. for Creativity, Vallella, Malta, Dist. Fine Arts, Washington, 2003, others; exhibited in group shows at Okun Gallery, Santa Fe, 1994, Ruth Siegel Gallery, N.Y.C., 1987, Bill Bace Gallery, N.Y.C., 1990, Locus Gallery, 1997, 98, Works Gallery, Long Beach, Calif., 1991, Mus. Fine Arts, Santa Fe, 1992, Albuquerque Mus., 1992, Thomas Barry Fine Arts, Mpls., 1993, Gallery A., Chgo., 1995, Ruth Bachofner Gallery, Santa Monica, Calif., 1998, Dist. Fine Arts, Washington, 1998, South Bend (Ind.) Regional Mus. Art, 1998, Byron Cohen Gallery for Contemporary Art, Kansas City, Mo., 1998, U.S. Dept. State Art in Embassies Program, Lilonque, Malawi, 1998, Cedar Rapids Mus. Art, 1998, Dist. Fine Arts, Washington, 1998-99, Ruth Bachofner Gallery, L.A., 1999, Locus Gallery, St. Louis, 1999, Dowd Fine Arts Mus., SUNY, Cortland, N.Y., 2000, Common Ground, Albuquerque, N.Mex., 2000, Tenn. Repertory Theatre. Nashville, 2001, Lost City Arts, N.Y.C., 2001, Graphic Arts Coun., N.Y C., 2001, Harrison Gallery, Williamstown, Mass., 2001, Metaphor Contemporary Art, Bklyn., N.Y., 2002, Oxford U., Magdalen Coll., Eng., 2003, Albuquerque Mus., 2003, Johnson Gallery Fire Arts Mus., U. N.Mex., Albuquerque, Saks Fifth Ave., N.Y.C., 2003, others; represented in pub. collections Israel Mus., Jerusalem, Fed. Chancellery Bundeskanzleramt, Vienna, Morgan Guarantee Trust, N.Y.C., IBM, Atlanta, others; pub. in The Inspiration of Astronomical Phenomena: Edition Malta, 2002. N.Mex. state rep. Friends of Art & Preservation in the Embassies. Recipient Ingram Merrill Found. award in painting, 1989, Ruth Chenven Found. award in painting, 1991, Basil H. Alkazzi award in painting, 1997; Painting fellow NEA, 1987, MacDowell Colony fellow, Peterbough, N.H., 1987, Burlington rsch. fellow U. N.Mex., 1991, Va. Ctr. for the Creative Arts fellow, Sweet Briar, 1998, Painting fellow St. James Ctr. for Creativity, Vallella. Malta, 2001, Presdl. Tchg. fellow U. N.Mex., 2002; grantee Montalvo Ctr. for Arts, Saratoga, Calif., 1981, 84, Rsch. grantee U. N.Mex. Coll. Fine Arts, 1992-99, Fulbright scholar Germany, 2000; named Regents Prof., U. N.Mex., 1994-97; Presdl. Tchg. fellow U. N.Mex., 2002—. Office: U NMex Dept Arts and Art Hist 1 Univ Campus Albuquerque NM 87131-0001

FEINBERG, RICHARD ALAN, consumer science educator, consultant; b. N.Y.C., June 12, 1950; s. Irving and Belle (Kolkwitz) F.; m. Fran Susan Jaffe, Jan 21, 1973; 1 child, Seth Jason. BA, SUNY, Buffalo, 1972; MS, SUNY, Cortland, 1974; PhD, U. Okla., 1976. Asst. prof. psychology Ohio State U., 1976-78, Juniata Coll., Huntington, Pa., 1978-80; asst. prof. consumer scis., retailing and environ. analysis Purdue U., West Lafayette, Ind., 1980-85, assoc. prof. consumer and retailing, 1985-89, prof., dept. head., 1989-97, dir. ctr. customer driven quality, 1997—. Dir. Purdue Retail Inst., 1990-97, coord. retail mgmt. program, 1988-89; bd. dirs. Paul Harris Stores, Purdue Univ. Press. Contbr. articles in field to profl. jours. David Ross fellow, 1980; NIHM fellow, 1975; Purdue Agrl. Expt. Sta. grantee, 1981. Mem. AAAS, Am Psychol. Assn., Assn. for Consumer Rsch. Office: Purdue U Retail Inst 320 Matthews Hall West Lafayette IN 47907

FEINFELD, DONALD ALLEN, nephrologist, educator; b. N.Y.C., Nov. 12, 1944; s. Theodore and Anne (Reiken) F.; m. Daryl Drury, June 26, 1970; 1 child, Michael Jay. BA in Math., U. Rochester, 1965; MD, Columbia U., 1969. Diplomate Am. Bd. Internal Medicine. Dir. nephrology Harlem Hosp. Ctr., N.Y.C., 1978-86; assoc. prof. Columbia U., N.Y.C., 1984-86, Albert Einstein Coll. Medicine, Bronx, N.Y., 1986-89; co-dir. nephrology Nassau County Med. Ctr., East Meadow, NY, 1989—2000, dir. biomed. rsch. facility, 1991—2001; dir. nephrology Nassau U. Med. Ctr., East Meadow, NY, 2001—02, chmn. dept. medicine, 2002—; assoc. prof. SUNY Health Sci. Ctr., Stony Brook, 1990-95, prof., 1995—. Cons. N.Y. Poison Control Ctr., N.Y.C., 1985—, L.I. Regional Poison Control Ctr., 1995—; chmn. institutional rev. bd. Harlem Hosp. Ctr., 1986. Author: (chpts.) Nephrotoxicity, 1989, Goldfrank's Toxicologic Emergencies, 1990, 94, 98, 2002, Pediatric Kidney Disease, 1992, Cardiovascular Pharmacotherapeutics, 1996, Clinical Management of Poisoning and Drug Overdose, 1997. Recipient rsch. fellowship Nat. Kidney Found., 1974-76. Fellow ACP; mem. Am. Soc. Nephrology, Am. Acad. Clin. Toxicology, European Renal Assn. (assoc.), N.Y. Soc. Nephrology (pres. 2002-2003). Achievements include discovery that kidney failure causes increase in urinary myoglobin more frequently than the reverse; research showing a difference in isoenzymes of glutathione transferase between human male and female kidneys. Office: Nassau County Med Ctr 2201 Hempstead Tpke East Meadow NY 11554-1859

FEINGOLD, RONALD SHERWIN, physical education educator; b. Chgo., Feb. 28, 1942; s. Albert and Nettie (Zafran) F.; m. Donna Jean Bennett, Aug. 13, 1970. BS, U. Ill., 1965; MEd, U. Ariz., 1966; PhD, U. New Mex., 1972. Mem. faculty U. Ariz., Tucson, 1966-67, U. Ill., Chgo., 1967-69; mem. faculty dept. phys. edn. Adelphi U., Garden City, N.Y., 1972—, chmn. dept., 1974—, prof., 1983—; dir. Inst. Sports Medicine and Fitness, 1975—; pres. faculty senate, 1981, 84, 88. Mem. N.Y. State Gov.'s Adv. Com. on Sport and Fitness, 1992-94, health and phys. edn. curriculum and assessment com. N.Y. State Dept. Edn., 1992-96; Sargent lectr. Nat. Assn. Phys. Edn. in Higher Edn., 1994; Assn. Internat. des Ecoles Supieureurs d'Education Physique Cagagal lectr., 1995. Author: Outlines for Fitness, 1969, Sport Pedagogy: myths, Models and Methods, 1987; contbr. articles to profl. jours.; patentee physiol. testing equipment. Mem. exec. bd. Nassau Heart Assn., Mineola, N.Y., 1984; bd. dirs. n.Y. chpt. Am. Heart Assn., 1988-92, chmn. bd. dirs. Nassau region, 1989-91. Recipient Alumni award U. New Mex., 1980, 94; Svc. award Nassau Heart Assn., 1981, Leadership award Nassau Heart Assn., 1984, 91, Svc. award Nat. Assn. Phys. Edn. in Higher Edn., 1995, James Dowling Lifetime Achievement award, 1996. Mem. Eastern Dist. Assn., AAHPERD (v.p. 1987—, Merit award 1987, R. Tait McKenzin Nat. award 1993, pres. 1992-93, pres. elect 1998—, bd. dirs. 1993-95, 98—, Honor award 1990, 95), Am. Coll. Sports Medicine, Nat. Assn. Coll. Phys. Edn. Assn. (editor 1980, v.p. 1984, pres. 1992), N.Y. State Profl. Preparation Coun. (pres. 1976), N.Y. State Assn. for Health, Phys. Edn., Recreation and Dance (pres. 1984, Svc. award 1985, Disting. Svc. award 1988), N.Y. Acad. Sci., Nat. Assn. Phys. Edn. in Higher Edn. (editor 1980, v.p. 1984, 88, pres. 1992-93, named Profl. of Yr., 2002), Assn. Internat. des Ecoles Supieureurs d'Education Physique (bd. dirs. 1985—, pres. 1998—, Gold Cross award 2002), Nassau Sports Commn. (bd. dirs. 1992—2001). Home: 3604 Summer Dr Wantagh NY 11793-2780 Office: Adelphi U Woodruff Hall Garden City NY 11530

FEINSILVER, DONALD LEE, psychiatry educator; b. Bklyn., July 24, 1947; s. Albert and Mildred (Weissman) Feinsilver. BA, Alfred U., 1968; MD, Autonomous U., Guadalajara, Mexico, 1974. Diplomate Am. Bd. Psychiatry and Neurology, Am. Bd. Forensic Psychiatry. Intern in medicine L.I. Coll. Hosp., Bklyn., 1975—76; resident in psychiatry SUNY-Bklyn., 1977—78, chief resident, 1979; asst. prof. psychiatry and surgery Med. Coll. Wis., Milw., 1980—85, assoc. prof., 1985—; dir. psychiat. emergency svc. Milw. County Mental Health and Med. Complexes, 1980—88; dir. med.-psychiat. unit Milw. Psychiat. Hosp./West Allis Meml. Hosp., 1988—. Contbr. articles to profl. jours.; editor: Crisis Psychiatry: Pros and Cons, 1982; mem. editl. bd.: Psychiat. Medicine Jour., 1983—. Mem.: AAAS, AMA, Acad. Psychosomatic Medicine, Am. Acad. Psychiatry and the Law, Am. Psychiat. Assn. Office: West Allis Psychiat Assocs 2424 S 90th St Milwaukee WI 53227-2455 E-mail: DFeinsilver@prodigy.net.

FEINSTEIN, ALVAN RICHARD, physician, educator, epidemiologist, educator; b. Phila., Dec. 4, 1925; s. Joel B. and Bella (Ukasz) Feinstein. BS, U. Chgo., 1947, MS in Math., 1948, MD, 1952; MA (hon.), Yale U., 1969; ScD (hon.), McGill U., Montreal, Que., Can., 1997, U. Toronto, 2002. Intern, then resident Yale-New Haven Hosp., 1952—54; research fellow Rockefeller Inst., 1954—55; resident Columbia-Presbyn. Med. Center, N.Y.C., 1955—56; clin. dir. Irvington House, N.Y.C., 1956—62; instr., then asst. prof. N.Y. U. Sch. Medicine, 1956—62; chief clin. pharmacology VA Hosp., West Haven, Conn., 1962—64, chief clin. biostatistics, 1964—74; mem. faculty Sch. Medicine, Yale U., from 1962, prof. medicine and epidemiology, from 1969, dir. clin. scholar program, from 1974, Sterling prof., from 1991. Chief Ea. Rsch. Support Ctr. VA, 1967—74; pres. New Haven area chpt. Assn. Computing Machinery, 1968—69. Author: Clinical Judgment, 1967, Clinical Biostatistics, 1977, Clinical Epidemiology, 1985, Clinimetrics, 1987, Multivariable Analysis, 1996; editor: Jour. Clin. Epidemiology; contbr. articles to profl. jours. With U.S. Army, 1944—46. Recipient Francis G. Blake award for outstanding tchg., Yale Med. Sch., J. Allyn Taylor Internat. prize, awards, Soc. for Gen. Internal Medicine, U. Chgo., Ludwig Heilmyer Soc., Europe, Gairdner Found. Internat., Can., 1993. Master: ACP (disting. tchr. award); mem.: AMA, Am. Assn. History Medicine, Biometric Soc., Assn. Computing Machinery, Am. Statis. Assn., Am. Soc. Clin. Pharmacology and Therapeutics (Oscar B. Hunter Meml. award 1999), Am. Fedn. Med. Rsch., Am. Bd. Internal Medicine, Inst. Medicine, Am. Epidemiol. Soc., Am. Soc. Clin. Investigation, Assn. Am. Physicians, Alpha Omega Alpha. Home: Branford, Conn. Died Oct. 25, 2001.

FEINSTEIN, SASCHA, English language educator; b. N.Y.C., Mar. 13, 1963; s. Samuel L. and Anita (Askild) F.; m. Marleni Rajakrishnan, June 3, 1989; children: Kiran Anders, Divia Anita. BA, U. Rochester, 1985; MFA, Ind. U., 1990, PhD, 1993. Assoc. prof. English Lycoming Coll., Williamsport, Pa., 1995—. Author: Jazz Poetry, 1997, A Biographic Guide to Jazz poetry, 1998, Misterioso, 2000 (Hayden Carruth award for poetry Copper Canyon Press, 2000); co-editor: The Jazz Poetry Anthology, 1991, The Second Set, 1996; editor-in-chief Brilliant Corners: A Jour. of Jazz and Lit., 1996—. Mem. Phi Kappa Phi, Phi Beta Kappa. Office: Lycoming Coll 700 College Pl Williamsport PA 17701-5157

FEIR, DOROTHY JEAN, entomologist, physiologist, educator; b. St. Louis, Jan. 29, 1929; d. Alex R. and Lillian (Smith) F. BS, U. Mich., 1950; MS, U. Wyo., 1956; PhD, U. Wis., 1960. Instr. biology U. Buffalo, 1960-61; mem. faculty St. Louis U., 1961—, prof. biology, 1967-99, prof. biology emeritus, 1999—. Mem. tropical medicine and parasitology study sect. NIH, 1980-84 Editor Environ. Entomology, 1977-84; mem. editl. bd. Jour. Med. Entomology, 1995-99, chair editl. bd., 1999. Fellow Entomol. Soc. Am. (hon.; pres. 1989, Riley Achievement award north ctrl. br. 1993), Mo. Acad. Sci. (v.p. 1987-88, pres.-elect 1988-89, pres. 1989-90, Most Disting. Scientist award 1995); mem. AAAS, Am. Physiol. Soc., N.Y. Acad. Sci., Phi Beta Kappa, Sigma Xi. E-mail: feirdj@slu.edu.

FEIR-STILLITANO, ELISABETH, gifted/talented education educator; b. N.Y.C., Feb. 27, 1971; d. Sherman Stuart and Olivia Terry (Gordon) F. BA, U. Buffalo, 1993; MEd, Lehigh U., 1994. Cert. elem. edn., secondary English edn., Pa., N.Y. Asst. kindergarten tchr. Allentown (Pa.) Jewish Cmty. Ctr., 1993-94; gifted and talented educator Island Park (N.Y.) Union Free Sch. Dist., 1994—. Mem. Nat. Coun. for Tchrs. English, Nat. Coun. for Tchrs. Math., Internat. Reading Assn., Assn. for Edn. Young Children, Nat. Assn. for Gifted Children. Democrat. Jewish. Avocations: reading, singing, dancing, skiing, acting. Home: 2103 Seneca Dr N Merrick NY 11566-3628 Office: Island Park Union Sch Dist Trafalgar Blvd Island Park NY 11558

FEISEL, LYLE DEAN, retired dean, electrical engineer, educator; b. Tama, Iowa, Oct. 16, 1935; s. Clyde Edward and Clara Maria (Ehlers) F.; m. Dorothy Evelyn Stadsvold, June 15, 1957; children: Patricia, Margaret, Kenneth. BSEE, Iowa State U., 1961, MSEE, 1963, PhDEE, 1964. Registered profl. engr., S.D. Engr. Honeywell, Mpls., 1961-62; staff engr. IBM Corp., Poughkeepsie, N.Y., 1963, Burlington, Vt., 1967; mem. faculty of elec. engring. S.D. Sch. of Mines, Rapid City, 1964-83, head elec. engring. dept., 1975-83; dean Watson Sch. SUNY, Binghamton, 1983—2001. Vis. prof. Cheng Kung U., Tainan, Taiwan, 1969-70; rsch. engr. Northrop Corp., L.A., 1974; Wachmeister prof. engring. Va. Mil. Inst., 1982; mem. engring. accreditation commn. Accreditation Bd. Engring. and Tech., 1987-92, bd. dirs., 1992-97. Nat. Def. fellow, 1961-64; recipient profl. achievement citation Iowa State U., 1984, Ednl. Achievement award N.Y. State Soc. Profl. Engrs., 1989, Nat. Soc. Profl. Engrs. award, 2002. Fellow IEEE (pres. edn. soc. 1978-79, v.p. ednl. activities 2000-2002, Meritorious Svc. award, Ben Dasher award 1983, Centennial medal 1984, Ronald J. Schmitz award 1989, achievement award Edn. Soc. 1999, Third Millennium medal 2000), Am. Soc. Engring. Edn. (bd. dirs. 1982-83, 94-99, pres. 1997-98); mem. S.D. Renewable Energy Assn. (pres. 1979-81, N.Y. State Engr. of Yr. 2000), Tau Beta Pi (Disting. Alumnus award 2002). Democrat. Lutheran. Address: PO Box 839 Saint Michaels MD 21663 E-mail: l.feisel@ieee.org.

FEIT, ALAN, cardiologist, internist, medical educator; b. N.Y.C., Sept. 24, 1946; BS, CCNY, 1968; MS, Syracuse U., 1971; MD, Columbia U., 1975. Diplomate Am. Bd. Internal Medicine, Am. Bd. Cardiovasc. Disease. Intern, resident, cardiology fellow Roosevelt Hosp., N.Y.C., 1975-80; pvt. practice N.Y.C., 1980-81; asst. prof. medicine Bklyn. VA Hosp., 1981-84, SUNY Health Sci. Ctr., Bklyn., 1984-91, assoc. prof. medicine, dir. cardiac catheterization lab., 1991-96, asst. dean for edn., 1994—, prof. medicine, 1996—. Contbr. articles to profl. jours. Trustee Tenafly (N.J.) Nature Ctr., 1984-88. Fellow ACP, Am. Coll. Cardiologists. Office: SUNY Health Sci Ctr 450 Clarkson Ave Brooklyn NY 11203-2056

FELBECK, DAVID KNISELEY, mechanical engineering educator; b. Mt. Vernon, N.Y., Apr. 2, 1926; s. George Theodore and Helen Mildred (Kniseley) F. BSME, Cornell U., 1948; MS, MIT, 1949, mech. engr., 1951, ScD, 1952. Registered profl. engr., Mich. Asst. prof. mech. engring. MIT, Cambridge, Mass., 1953-55; exec. dir. ship structures com. NAS, Washington, 1955-61; assoc. prof. mech. engring. U. Mich., Ann Arbor, 1961-65, prof. mech. engring., 1965—. Chmn. bd. dirs. Materials Tech. Corp., An Arbor. Author: Introduction to Strenthening Mechanisms, 1968, Strength and Fracture of Engineering's Solids, 1984; editor: Fracture, 1959; contbr. numerous articles to profl. jours. Rhodes Found. scholar candidate, 1948; U.S. Fulbright lectr. Tech. U. of Delft, Holland, 1952-53; Adams Meml. mem. Am. Welding Soc. Fellow ASME; mem. AIME, Am. Soc. Metals (Wilson award), Rotary, Barton Hills Country Club. Home: 2060 Scottwood Ave Ann Arbor MI 48104-4511

FELD, MARJORIE NAN, history educator; b. Harrisburg, Pa., Mar. 10, 1971; d. Arthur Michael and Rosalind Ilene (Sperling) F.; m. Michael Fein, Oct. 10, 1999. BA in History and Judaic Studies, SUNY, Binghamton, 1993; PhD, Brandeis U., 2003. Rsch. asst. SUNY, Binghamton, 1991-94; environ. project coord. Henry St. Settlement, N.Y.C., 1993; rsch. asst. Brandeis U., Waltham, 1994-96; instr. Urban Scholars Program, Boston, 1996-99; instr. Am. studies U. Mass., Boston, 2001—02; vis. prof. of history Babson Coll., 2002—03, asst. prof. of history, 2003—. Bd. dirs. Radical Tchr., manuscript editor, 1999—. Contbr. articles to profl. jours. Pres. Coll. Democrats,

SUNY, Binghamton, 1991-93. Recipient Crown fellowship Brandeis U., Waltham, 1994-98 Jewish. Avocations: swimming, reading. Home: 100 Walnut St Watertown MA 02472-4028

FELD, MICHAEL STEPHEN, physics educator; b. N.Y.C., Nov. 11, 1940; s. Albert and Lillian R. Norwalk; children: David A., Jonathan R., Alexandra A. SB in Humanities and Sci., SM in Physics, MIT, 1963; PhD in Physics, M.I.T., 1967. Postdoctoral fellow MIT, Cambridge, 1967-68, asst. prof., 1968-73, assoc. prof., 1973-79, prof. physics, 1979—, dir. George R. Harrison Spectroscopy Lab., 1976—, dir. Laser Research Ctr., 1979—; dir. Laser Biomed. Research Ctr., 1985—. Co-editor: Fundamental and Applied Laser Physics, 1973, Coherent Nonlinear Optics, 1980. Alfred P. Sloan rsch. fellow, 1973; recipient Disting. Svc. award MIT Minority Cmty., 1980, Gordon Y. Billard award, 1982, Thomas award Spectrochimica Acta, 1991, Vinci d'Excellence, France, 1995, Disting. Baltzer Colloquim spkr. Princeton U., 1996, Lamb medal Physics of Quantum Electronics Soc., 2003. Fellow AAAS, Am. Optical Soc., Am. Phys. Soc., Am. Soc. Laser Medicine and Surgery (bd. dirs.), Sigma Xi. Home: 66 Dunster Rd Jamaica Plain MA 02130 Office: MIT George R Harrison Spectroscopy Lab 77 Massachusetts Ave Cambridge MA 02139-4307

FELD, STEVE, data coordinator; b. Jan. 5, 1948; s. Herbert and Ida Feld. BA, Hunter Coll., 1969. Cert. fine arts secondary tchr., N.Y. Instr. photography Audio Visual Tng. Ctr., N.Y.C., 1979-80; assoc. prodr. MAGI, Elmsford, N.Y., 1981; dialogue leader Internat. Ctr. of Photography, N.Y.C., 1983-85; Kennedy Cares coord. J.F. Kennedy H.S., Bronx, 1988-90, computer graphics instr., 1982—; pres. Tropical Opticals, 1980—. Momentum for the 90's computer coord. N.Y. State Art Tchrs. Assn., 1990; condr. workshops in field; lectr. in field. Contbr. articles to profl. jours.; software developer N.Y.C. Bd. Edn.; contbr. spl. effects for Hot Dogs for Gaugrin, 1971; assoc. prodr. MAGI, 1976. Funding coord. Media House, 1995. Internat. Grand Prize winner Computer Learning Month Learning Found., 1991; recipient 7th Ann. Bklyn. Mus. Film Festival award for The Monster that Ate the Bronx, 1969, Nat. Kodak Film award for The Giant Girl, 1969, Impact II Develop award Impact II Network, 1988. Mem. Nat. Art Edn. Assn., Media Art Tchrs. Assn. (pres. 1987-88, v.p. 1986-87). Office: Tropical Opticals PO Box 91 New York NY 10034-0091

FELDBAUER, JAMES FREDERICK, retired school system administrator; b. Angelica, N.Y., Jan. 11, 1930; s. Harry and Viola (Graham) Feldbauser; m. Carolyn M. Feldbauer, July 25, 1970; children: Kathryn Ann, James M., Michael J., Mark J., Martin J., Mary J. BS, SUNY-Buffalo, 1952; MEd, St. Bonaventure U., 1961. Cert. dist. adminstr. High sch. tchr., Bolivar, NY, 1952—57; supt. schs. Woodhull, NY, 1959—62, Bradford, NY, 1962—63, Belmont Central Sch., NY, 1963—85; pvt. practice gen. contracting Belmont, 1985—87; dir. Physical Plant, Alfred U., 1988—93; ret., 1993—. Bd. dirs. ARC of Allegany County, NY, 1986—92; councilman Town of Amity, NY; parish coun. St. Mary's Cath. Ch., Belmont, 1987—2003. Mem.: N.Y. State Coun. Sch. Supts., Pittsburgh Shawmut & No. R.R. Hist. Assn., Town and Village Rep. Club (Devoted Svc. award 2003). Roman Catholic. Home: 7 Martin St Belmont NY 14813-1003

FELDBERG, MEYER, university dean; b. Johannesburg, Mar. 17, 1942; s. Leon and Sarah (Kretzmer) F.; m. Barbara Erlick, Aug. 9, 1965; children: Lewis Robert, Ilana. BA, Witwatersrand U., Johannesburg, 1962; MBA, Columbia U., 1965; PhD, Cape Town (South Africa) U., 1969. Product mgr. B.F. Goodrich Co., Akron, Ohio, 1965-67; dean Grad. Sch. Bus., U. Cape Town, 1968-79; assoc. dean J.L. Kellogg Sch. Mgmt., Northwestern U., Evanston, Ill., 1979-81; prof., dean Sch. Bus., Tulane U., New Orleans, 1981-86; pres. Ill. Inst. Tech., Chgo., 1986-89, chmn. bd. govs. Rsch. Inst.; dean Grad. Sch. Bus. Columbia U., N.Y.C., 1989—, Sanford C. Bernstein prof. leadership and ethics, 2003—. Bd. dirs. Federated Dept. Stores, UBS Funds, Revlon, Inc., Primedia Inc., Select Med. Corp., Sappi Ltd.; vis. prof. MIT, 1974, Cranfield Inst. Tech., 1970, 76. Author: Organizational Behaviour: Text and Cases, 1975; contbr. articles to profl. jours. Named Jaycee Young Man of Yr., 1972 Mem. Univ. Club (N.Y.C. and Chgo.), Econ. Club (N.Y.C. and Chgo.). Office: 101 Uris Hall Columbia U Grad Sch Bus 3022 Broadway New York NY 10027-6945

FELDER-WRIGHT, PAMELA THERESA, education educator; b. Natchez, Miss., Aug. 1, 1956; d. Albert and Yvonne (McMorris) Evans; m. Marion Wright; children: D'Antwanette, Demetricstepchildren: Keon, Crystal. BS, Alcorn State U., 1977, MS, 1980; PhD, Kans. State U., 1982. Resource rm. specialist Jefferson Elem. Sch., Fayette, Miss., 1977-79; GED instr. Alcorn State U., Lorman, Miss., 1980-81; dir. child devel. assn. Rust Coll., Holly Springs, Miss., 1982-84; dir. early childhood ctr. Winston Salem (N.C.) State U., 1984-90; owner Pam's Unique Technique, Winston Salem, 1990-93; coord. Uplift, Inc., Greensboro, N.C., 1993-94; dir. med. ctr. child care N.C. Bapt. Hosp., Winston-Salem, 1994—; assoc. prof. edn., coord. spl. edn. Alcorn State (Miss.) U., 2002—. Author: Dream....but Dream Big, 1992, I'm Black and I'm Beautiful, 1993, (poetry) Best Poems, 1996 (Merit 1996). Bd. visitors Tech. Assistance Ctr., Winston-Salem, 1996. Recipient Golden Poet award World of Poetry, 1995, Best Poem Nat. Libr. of Poetry, 1995, Internat. Poet of Merit award, 2002; named Best Poet, 2000, Poet of Merit 2002-03, Poet of Yr., 2002. Mem. ASCD, N.C. Day Care Assn., N.C. Assn. of Educators, So. Assn. for Edn. for Children, Coun. Exceptional Children. Avocations: reading, exercising. Office: Dept Edn and Psychology 100 ASU Dr Alcorn State MS 39096-7500

FELDHUSEN, HAZEL JEANETTE, elementary education educator; b. Camp Douglas, Wis., Feb. 20, 1928; d. Vincent O. and Helen (Johnson) Artz; m. John F. Feldhusen, Dec. 18, 1954; children: Jeanne V., Anne M. B, U. Wis., 1965; M, Purdue U., 1968; postgrad., U. Wis. Tchr. Suldal Sch., Mauston, Wis., 1947-50, Lake Geneva (Wis.) Schs., 1950-55, West Lafayette (Ind.) Schs., 1965-91. Presenter World Conf., Hamburg, 1985, Juneau (Alaska) Schs., 1986, Vancouver (B.C., Can.) Schs., 1990, Norfolk (Va.) Schs., 1991, Taiwan Nat. U., 1992, U. New South Wales, Sydney, Australia, 1993, New Zealand Schs., Auckland, 1993; 2d Nat. Conf. Gifted, Taiwan, 1992, Sarasota, Fla., 1998. Author: Individualized Teaching of the Gifted, 1993, 2d edit., 1997; contbr. articles to profl. jours., chpts. to books, 1981-2002. Mem. Tchr. of Yr. Com., West Lafayette, 1988. Recipient Outstanding Tchr. award Elem. Tchrs. Am., 1974, Appreciation award U. Stellenbosch, 1984, Appreciation award Australian Assn. for the Gifted, 1987; winner Golden Apple Tchg. award Greater Lafayette C. of C., 1989, Disting. Alumnus award Purdue U., 1996. Mem. NEA, Ind. State Tchrs. Assn., West Lafayette Edn. Assn. (Outstanding Achievement award 1984), Phi Delta Kappa, Delta Kappa Gamma (v.p 1983-85). Avocations: reading, interior decorating. Home: Sarasota Bay Club 1301 N Tamiami Apt 205 Sarasota FL 34236 E-mail: feldhusenjf@aol.com.

FELDKAMP, JAMES NORBERT, athletics, physical education director; b. Lorain, Ohio, 1947; BS, Ea. Mich. U., 1970, MS, 1972; EdS in Adminstrn., Wayne State U., 1984. Cert. edn. specialist. Tchr., coach Romeo (Mich.) Community Schs., 1970-71; tchr., coach, athletic dir., asst. prin. Anchor Bay Schs., New Baltimore, Mich., 1971-85; dir. health, phys. edn., athletics West Bloomfield (Mich.) Schs., 1985-88; dir. phys. edn., athletics Troy (Mich.) Pub. Schs., 1988—. Cons. Fitness For Youth, Ann Arbor, Mich., 1986-88; bd. dirs. Oakland County Athletic Adminstrs. Assn.; cert. instr. Pace Edn. Program, 1991; athletic dept. goal setting Nat. Athletic Adminstrs. Assn., 1991. Author (chpts.) Pace Coaching Manual, 1990. Tournament dir. Troy Daze Community Fair, 1988—; coach Youth Baseball, Softball, Basketball, 1980—, AAU Basketball, Detroit, 1988—; dir. Oakland County Slam Dunk and 3 Point Shooting Contest, 1991—. Recipient 1st place Phys. Edn. Video, Inst. Creative Rsch. and Sport Art Acad., 1989. Mem. AAPERD, Oakland County Athletic Dirs. Assn., Mich. Assn. Phys. Edn., Recreation, and Dance, Mich. Interscholastic Athletic Adminstrs. Assn., Nat. Interscholastic Athletic Adminstrs. Assn. Avocations: travel, coaching, basketball, softball, golf. Office: 4420 Livernois Rd Troy MI 48098-4777

FELDMAN, ELAINE BOSSAK, medical nutritionist, educator; b. N.Y.C., Dec. 9, 1926; d. Solomon and Frances Helen (Fania) Nevler Bossak; m. Herman Black, Dec. 23, 1951 (div. 1957); 1 child, Mitchell Evan; m. Daniel S. Feldman, July 19, 1957; children: Susan, Daniel S. Jr. AB magna cum laude, NYU, 1945, MS, 1948, MD, 1951. Diplomate Am. Bd. Internal Medicine, Nat. Bd. Med. Examiners; cert. in Clin. Nutrition. Rotating intern Mt. Sinai Hosp., N.Y.C., 1951-52, resident in pathology, 1952, asst. resident, 1953, fellow in medicine, resident in metabolism, 1954-55, rsch. asst. in medicine, 1955-58, clin. asst. physician Diabetes Clinic, 1957; asst. vis. physician Kings County Hosp., Bklyn., 1958-66, assoc. vis. physician, 1966-72; asst. attending physician Maimonides Hosp., Bklyn., 1960-68; spl. fellow USPHS Dept. of Physiol. Chemistry U. of Lund, Sweden, 1964-65; attending physician Eugene Talmadge Meml. Hosp., Augusta, Ga., 1972-92, Univ. Hosp., Augusta, 1972-92, cons., 1973; prof. medicine Med. Coll. Ga., Augusta, 1972-92, prof. emeritus, 1992—, chief sect. of nutrition, 1977-92, chief emeritus, 1992—, acting chief sect. of metabolic/endocrine disease, 1980-81, prof. physiology and endocrinology, 1988-92, prof. emeritus physiology and endocrinology, 1992—; instr. medicine SUNY Downstate Med. Ctr., 1957-59, asst. prof. medicine, 1959-68, assoc. prof. medicine, 1968-72. Tchg. fellow dept. zoology U. Wis. Grad. Sch., 1945-46, dept. biology NYU Grad. Sch., 1946-47; cons. N.Y.-N.J. Regional Ctr. for Clin. Nutrition Edn., 1983-92; vis. prof. and Harvey lectr. Northeastern Ohio Sch. Medicine, Youngstown, 1985; cons., vis. prof. U. Nev. Sch. Medicine (NCI grant), 1989-94; mem. nat. adv. com. nutrition fellowship program Nat. Med. Fellowship Inc., 1988-95; dir. Ga. Inst. Human Nutrition, 1978-92, dir. emeritus, 1992—; dir. Clin. Nutrition Rsch. Unit, 1980-86; mem. med. nutrition curriculum initiative adv. bd. U. N.C., Chapel Hill, 1992-2001; advisor ednl. materials Am. Inst. Cancer Rsch., 1997—. Author: Essentials of Clinical Nutrition, 1988; (with others) Conference on Biological Activities of Steroids in Relation to Cancer, 1969, Nicotinic Acid, 1964, The Menopausal Syndrome, 1974, Hyperlipidemia, Medcom Special Studies, 1974, Medcom Famous Teaching in Modern Medicine, 1979, Harrison's Principles of Internal Medicine, 1980, Health Promotion: Principles and Clinical Applications, 1982, The Encyclopedic Handbook of Alcoholism, 1982, The Climacteric in Perspective, 1986, Selenium in Biology and Medicine, Part A., 1987, Medicine for the Practicing Physician, 1988, Clinical Chemistry of Laboratory Animals, 1989, Ency. Human Biology, 1991, Laboratory Medicine: The Selection and Interpretation of Clinical Laboratory Studies, 1993, Modern Nutrition in Health and Diseases, 1994, Nutrition Assessment-A Comprehensive Guide for Planning Intervention, 1995, The Women's Complete Healthbook, 1995, The American Medical Women's Association's Guide to Nutrition and Wellness, 1996, Normal Nutrition and Therapeutics, 1996, Handbook of Nutrition and Food, 2001; editor: Nutrition and Cardiovascular Disease, 1976, Nutrition in the Middle and Later Years, 1983 (paperback edit. 1986), Nutrition and Heart Disease, 1983, Handbook of Nutrition and Food, 2001, Human Nutrient Needs in the Life Cycle, 2001; mem. editl. adv. bd. Contemporary Issues in Clin. Nutrition, 1980-92; mem. edit. bd. Am. Jour. Clin. Nutrition, 1983-91, 92-98, Jour. Clin. Endocrinology and Metabolism, 1984-88, MidPoint: Counseling Women through Menopause, 1984-85, Jour. Nutrition, 1985-89; cons. editor Jour. Am. Coll. Nutrition, 1982-94; mem. edit. bd. Complementary Med. for the Physician, 1996-2000; contbg. editor Nutrition Rev., 1997-2002; mem. editl. bd. Nutrition Today, 1999—; reviewer Jour. Lipid Rsch., Biochm. Pharmacology, Sci., The Physiologist, Jour. Am. Acad. Dermatology, Israel Jour. Med. Scis., N.Y. State Jour. Medicine, Jour. of Nutrition Edn., Jour. Am. Dietetic Assn., Am. Jour. Medicine, Am. Jour. Med. Sci., So. Med. Jour., Jour. AMA, Jour. NCI; author 176 published articles in field, numerous abstracts and presentations. Mem. tech. adv. com. for sci. and edn. Rsch. Grants Program, Human Nutrition Grants Peer Panel, USDA, 1982, mem. bd. sci. counselors human nutrition; Community Svc. Block Grant Discretionary Program Panel; vice chmn. Urban and Rural Econ. Devel. Panel, Dept. HHS, 1982, grant reviewer, 1983; mem ad hoc and spl. rev. coms. and groups NIH, 1979-93, mem. nutrition study sect., 1976-80; mem. Rev. Panel Nat. Nutrition Objectives, Life Scis. Rev. Office, Fed. Am. Socs. Exptl. Biology, 1985-86; mem. subcom. Women's Health Trial Nat. Cancer Inst., 1987, mem. bd. sci. counselors cancer prevention and control program, 1990-94; mem. adv. com. Clin. Nutrition Rsch. Unit, U. Ala., 1986-94, Ga. Nutrition Steering Com., 1974-75, Ctrl. Savannah River Area Nutrition Project Coun. 1974-75, ednl. adv. com. Health Central, 1980; mem. geriatrics and gerontology rev. com. Nat. Inst. on Aging, 1986-90; breast cancer initiative peer rev. Dept. of Def., 1997, 98. N.Y. Heart Assn. rsch. fellow, 1955-57. Fellow Am. Heart Assn. Coun. on Atherosclerosis (nominating com. 1978, chmn. nominating com., mem. exec. com. 1979-80, Spl. Recognition award 1995), Am. Inst. Nutrition (grad. nutrition edn. com. 1980-83, 89-93); mem. Am. Coll. Nutrition (chmn. com. pub. affairs), Am. Soc. for Clin. Nutrition (com. on nutrition edn. 1982, chmn. subcom. on nutrition edn. in med. schs. 1983-84, chmn. com. on med./dental residency edn., 1985-87, com. on subsplty. tng. 1988-92, nominating com. 1982, 90, chair nominating com. 1994, com. on clin. practice issues in health and disease 1989-92, Nat. Dairy Coun. award 1991, rep. coun. acad. socs. 1990-96, membership com. 1996—, chair 1999, 2000), Fedn. Am. Socs. Exptl. Biology. Am. Oil Chemists Soc., Am. Physiol. Soc., Endocrine Soc., Soc. Exptl. Biology and Medicine, So. Soc. Clin. Investigation, Am. Diabetes Assn., Am. Fedn. Clin. Rsch., Am. Gastroent. Assn., AMA (Joseph B. Goldberger award 1990), Am. Med. Women's Assn. (profl. resources com. 1975-76, med. edn. and rsch. fund com. 1976-79, chmn. 1978-90, chmn. student liaison subcom. of membership com. 1981-84, pres. Br. 51, Augusta 1977-80, treas. 1980-97, Calcium Nutrition Edn. award 1991, CSRA Girl Scout Women of Excellence award 1994), Am. Soc. Parenteral and Enteral Nutrition, Am. Heart Assn. (Ga. affiliate, nutrition com., chmn. sci. session for nutritionists, 1978, chmn. nutrition com. 1979-90, mem. long range planning com. 1980-81, rsch. com. 1980-83, bd. dirs. 1987-90, profl. edn. task force, 1988-89), Richmond Country Med. Assn., Augusta Opera Assn. (bd. dirs. 1973—, recording sec. 1973-74, pres. 1974-75, coord. audience devel. 1975-77, at-large exec. com. 1994-96, chair nominating com. 1994-96, corr. sec. 1998-99, 1st v.p. 1999-2000, chair search com., gen. dir. 2002), Augusta Sailing Club (women's com. 1973), Greater Augusta Arts Coun. (Arts Festival Collage 1982 chmn. promotion and publicity com., Festival coms. 1983-86, 89-93, 95, 96, 98, 99, bd. dirs. 1984-94, Vol. of the Yr., 2001), Gertrude Herbert Inst. Art (bd. dirs. 1987-92), Authors Club Augusta, Philomathic Club (sec. 1999—), Phi Beta Kappa, Sigma Xi (chpt. sec. 1982-83, pres. elect 1983-84, pres. 1984-85), Alpha Omega Alpha. Avocations: opera, wine tasting, travel. Home: 2123 Cumming Rd Augusta GA 30904-4333 E-mail: efeldman7@comcast.net.

FELDMAN, GARY JAY, physicist, educator; b. Cheyenne, Wyo., Mar. 22, 1942; married; 2 children. BS, U. Chgo., 1964; AM, Harvard U., 1965, PhD in Physics, 1971. Research assoc. in physics Stanford Linear Accelerator Ctr., Stanford U., Calif., 1971-74, staff physicist, 1974-79, assoc. prof., 1979-83, prof., 1983-90; prof. physics Harvard U., Cambridge, Mass., 1990-92, Frank B. Baird, Jr. prof. sci., 1992—, chmn. dept. physics, 1994-97. Sci assoc. CERN, Switzerland, 1982-83. Fellow Am. Phys. Soc. (chmn. divsn. particles and fields 1992), Am. Acad. Arts and Scis. Office: Harvard U Lyman Lab Cambridge MA 02138

FELDMAN, LILLIAN MALTZ, early childhood education consultant; b. N.Y.C. d. Jacob and Ida (Burko) Maltz; m. Harry A. Feldman (dec. Jan. 1985); children: Ronald, Donna Feldman Weisman, Jeffrey, Robert. AB, George Washington U., 1937, MA, 1939; EdD in Early Childhood Edn., Syracuse U., 1987; HLD (hon.), SUNY, 1993. Cert. tchr., guidance counselor, sch. adminstr., N.Y. Elem. sch. guidance counselor Syracuse (N.Y.) Sch. Dist., 1963-65, Kindergarten tchr., 1957-63, dir. early children edn., 1965-83; dir. Syracuse Head Start, summers 1968-70; cons. early childhood edn. Syracuse, 1985—. Adj. instr. child, family and community studies Syracuse U., 1988-89, adj. prof. child and family studies, 1990-91. Author invited papers in early child devel. and care, 1988, 89, 95, 96. Adv. com. network adv. bd. Dr. Martin Luther King Jr. Cmty. Sch., Syracuse, 1988—. Named Woman of Achievement in Edn., Post-Standard, Syracuse, 1969; recipient Hannah G. Solomon Award Nat. Coun. Jewish Women, Syracuse, 1979, Honoree Na'amat USA 1988, Friend of Children award Women's Commn. Task Force on Children, 1992. Mem. Syracuse Assn. for Edn. Young Children (Outstanding Early Childhood Educator award 1984), Consortium for Children's Svcs. (Silver Dove award 1985, Friend of Family award 1992), Onondaga County Child Care Coun. (Community Svc. award 1983, Friend of Children award 1992), Delta Kappa Gamma, Phi Delta Kappa. Democrat.

FELDMAN, MARTHA SUE, political scientist, educator; b. Oak Ridge, Tenn., Mar. 31, 1953; d. Melvin J. and Nancy Ann (McCarty) F.; m. Hobart Taylor III, Oct. 30, 1993; 1 child, Bruce Alexander Feldman Taylor. BA in Polit. Sci., U. Wash., 1976; MA in Polit. Sci., Stanford U., 1980, PhD in Polit. Sci., 1983. Asst. prof. dept. polit. sci., asst. rsch. sci. Inst. Pub. Policy Studies U. Mich., Ann Arbor, 1983-89, assoc. prof. dept. polit. sci., 1989—2001, assoc. prof. Sch. Pub. Policy, 1995—2001, prof. polit. sci. and pub. policy, 2001—03, assoc. dean Ford Sch. Pub. Policy, 2001—03; prof., Johnson chair for civic governance and pub. mgmt., dept. policy, planning and design Sch. Social Ecology, U. Calif. Irvine, 2003—. Health svcs. rschr. U. Wash., Seattle, 1975—76; cons. to Com. on Ability Testing NAS, Washington, 1980; regulatory impact analyst for fossil fuels Dept. Energy, Washington, 1980—81; vis. scholar Stanford (Calif.) U. Ctr. Orgns. Rsch., 1990—91; vis. prof. Luigi Bocconi U., Milan, 1991, Swedish Sch. Econs., Helsinki, Finland, 1992, U. Bergen, Norway, 2002. Author: Order Without Design: Information Production and Policy Making, 1989, Strategies for Interpreting Qualitative Data, 1994; co-author: Reconstructing Reality in the Courtroom, 1981, Gaining Access, 2003; contbr. articles. Ameritech fellow, 1986, Rackham Faculty Rsch. grantee, 1984-85, Brookings Instn. Rsch. fellow, 1979-80, NIMH fellow, 1978-79, others. Office: U Calif Irvine Dept Policy Planning and Design 226G Social Ecology I Irvine CA 92697-4252 E-mail: feldmanm@uci.edu.

FELDMAN, ROGER LAWRENCE, artist, educator; b. Spokane, Wash., Nov. 19, 1949; s. Marvin Lawrence and Mary Elizabeth (Shafer) Feldman; m. Astrid Lunde, Dec. 16, 1972; children: Kirsten B., Kyle Lawrence. BA in Art Edn., U. Wash., 1972; postgrad., Fuller Theol. Sem., Pasadena, Calif., 1972-73, Regent Coll., Vancouver, B.C., 1974; MFA in Sculpture, Claremont Grad. U., 1977. Teaching asst. Claremont (Calif.) Grad. U.; prof. art Biola U., La Mirada, Calif., 1989-2000, Seattle Pacific U., 2000—. Adj. instr. Seattle Pacific U., 1979, 80, 82, 83, Linfield Coll., 1978, Edmonds C.C., 1978-80, Shoreline C.C., 1978; guest artist and lectr. One-man shows include Art Ctr. Gallery, Seattle Pacific U., 1977, 83, 84, Linfield Coll., McMinnville, Oreg., 1979, Blackfish Gallery, Portland, 1982, Lynn McAllister Gallery, Seattle, 1986, Biola U., 1989, 93, Coll. Gallery, La. Coll., Pineville, 1990, Gallery W, Sacramento, 1991, 96, Aughinbaugh Gallery, Grantham, Pa., 1992, Riverside Art Mus., 1994, Azusa Pacific U., 1995, Cornerstone '96, Bushnell, Ill., 1996, Davison Gallery, Roberts Wesleyan Coll., Rochester, N.Y., 1997, Concordia U., Irvine, Calif., 1999, Northwestern Coll., St. Paul, 2000, Union U., Jackson, Tenn., 2001, F. Schaeffer Inst., St. Louis, 2001, Seattle Pacific U., Seattle, 2002, G. Fox U., Newberg, Oreg., 2001; group shows include Pasadena Artists Concern Gallery, 1976, Libra Gallery, Claremont, 1977, Renshaw Gallery, McMinnville, 1978, Cheney Cowles Mus., Spokane, 1979, 80, 83, Lynn McAllister Gallery, Seattle, 1985, Bumbershoot, Seattle, 1985, 86, 87, Pacific Arts Ctr., Seattle, 1987, Grand Canyon U., Phoenix, 1990, Connemara, Dallas, 1991, West Bend (Wis.) Gallery, 1992, L.A. Mcpl. Satellite Gallery, 1990, 93, Greenbelt 93, Northamptonshire, Eng., 1993, Claremont Sch. Theology, 1994, Queens Coll. Cambridge U., Eng., 1994, Jr. Arts Ctr. Gallery, Barnsdall Park, L.A., 1994, Bade Mus. Pacific Sch. of Religion, Berkeley, Calif., 1995, Ctrl. Arts Collective, Tucson, 1995, L.A. Mcpl. Gallery Barnsdall Art Park, 1996, Reconstructive Gallery Santa Ana, Calif., 1997, Guggenheim Gallery, Chapman U., Orange, Calif., 1997, Weaver Art Gallery, Bethel Coll., Mishawaka, Ind., 1998-, Concordia U. Art Gallery, Mequon, Wis., 1999, Palos Verdes Art Ctr., Calif., 1999, Grand Canyon U.,Phoenix, 2000, Tryon Ctr. Visual Arts, Charlotte, N.C., 2001, U. Dallas, 2001, Weaver Gallery, 2001, John Brown U., Siloam Springs, Ark., 2001, Sweetwater Ctr. for the Arts, Sewickley, Pa., 2002, Ind. Wesleyan U., Marion, 2002, others; comms. Wheaton, Pasadena, Calif., 1999, Renton Vocat. Tech Inst., 1987-89. Recipient King County Arts Commn. Individual Artist Project award, Seattle, 1988, Natl. Endowment for the Arts Individual Artist fellowship in Sculpture, 1986, David Gaiser award for sculpture Cheney Cowles Mus., 1980, Disting. Award for Harborview Med. Ctr. "Viewpoint", Soc. for Tech. Comm., 1987, Design award for "Seafirst News", Internat. Assn. Bus. Comm., 1987, Pace Setter award, 1987, others; Connemara Sculpture grant, 1990, Biola U., 1991; Faculty Rsch. grantee Seattle Pacific U., 2001-2002. Office: Seattle Pacific U 3307 Third Ave West Seattle WA 98119 E-mail: rfeldman@spu.edu.

FELDMAN, SANDRA, labor union executive; b. N.Y.C. m. Arthur Barnes. M in English Lit., NYU. Tchr. Pub. Sch. 34, N.Y.C.; field rep. United Fedn. Tchrs., 1966-83, exec. dir., 1983-86, sec., 1983-86, pres., 1986-97, Am. Fedn. Tchrs., 1997—. Exec. com. Edn. Internat.; exec. coun. AFL-CIO, 1997—. Active Coun. on Competitiveness, Internat. Rescue Com., Freedom House, A. Philip Randolph Inst., Jewish Labor Com., Coalition Labor Union Women, Nat. Coun. Ams. to Prevent Handgun Violence, N.Y. Urban League, Women's Forum, Women's Commn. on Refugee Children; co-chair Child Labor Coalition; nat. bd. mem. Profl. Tchg. Stds.; chair AFL-CIO Com. on Social Policy; mem. U.S. com. UNICEF Named one of N.Y.C. 75 Most Influential Women, Crain's New York Bus. Avocations: collecting african art, jazz, reading. Office: Am Fedn Tchrs 555 New Jersey Ave NW Washington DC 20001-2029 E-mail: online@AFT.org.*

FELDMAN, STEPHEN, academic administrator; b. N.Y.C., Sept. 11, 1944; s. Harry and Mae (Morris) F.; m. Constance M. Lerudis, June 1, 1969; children— Jennifer Dawn, Timothy Richard. BBA, CCNY, 1966, MBA, 1968, PhD (fellow), 1971. Chmn. dept. banking, fin. and investments Hofstra U., Hempstead, N.Y., 1969-77, assoc. prof., 1974-77; dean Ancell Sch. of bus. Western Conn. State U., Danbury, 1977-81, pres., 1981-92, Nova Southeastern U., Ft. Lauderdale, Fla., 1992-94; v.p. real estate Ethan Allen Inc., Danbury, 1995-96; v.p. univ. rels., devel. Calif. State U., Long Beach, 1996-99; pres. Astronaut Meml. Found., Kennedy Space Ctr., Fla., 1999—. Bd. dirs. Ethan Allen Inc., Sci. Horizons Inc.; cons. IBM, N.Y. Telephone Co. Editor: Credit Unions, 1974, Handbook of Wealth Management, 1977, Smarter Money, 1985; contbr. articles to profl. jours. Trustee Danbury Hosp., United Way. Mem. Am. Assn. State Colls. and Univs. (chmn. corp. coll. rels.), Greater Ft. Lauderdale C. of C. Office: Astronaut Meml Found Ctr Space Mail Code Amf Kennedy Space Center FL 32899-0001 E-mail: sfeldman@amfcse.org.

FELDMAN, STEPHEN MICHAEL, retired periodontist, dental educator; b. Phila., Nov. 1, 1942; s. Meyer and Annette (Gaurd) F.; m. Anna Ruth Workman; 1 child, Samantha Aileen. DDS, Temple U., 1967; periodontics cert., Loyola U., Maywood, Ill., 1971; MSEd, U. So. Calif., 1974. Asst. prof. N.J. Dental Sch., Newark, 1971-73, 74-76; trainee, fellow, vis. asst. clin. prof. U. So. Calif. Sch. Medicine, Los Angeles, 1973-74; asst. prof. U. Louisville Sch. Dentistry, 1976-79, assoc. prof., 1979—2002, dir. cmty. svcs., 1997—2002; ret., 2002. Cons. Ft. Knox Dental Activity, Ky., 1979—89; dental exhibit fundraising com. Louisville Sci. Ctr., 1985—86, cons., 1986. Contbr. articles to profl. jours. Fund raising com. for dental exhibit Louisville-Jefferson County Bd. Health, 1988-90; consumer adv. coun. Louisville water Co., 2000-02; bd. dirs. Temple Shalom, Louisville, 1986-89. Capt. USAF, 1967-69, col. USAR, ret. 1996. Recipient Disting. Achievment award, Ky. Dept. Edn., 1979. Mem. ADA, Ky. Dental Assn. (nutrition cons. 1984-86), Louisville Dental Soc. (dental health com. 1987-2002, chair dental health com. 1990-2002, Lifetime Superior Achievement award 2002), Ky. Soc. Periodontists (bd. dirs. 1987-89). Democrat. Avocations: photography, physical fitness, skiing. Home: 149 Harvest Dr Vacaville CA 95687-7220

FELDMAN, WALTER SIDNEY, artist, educator; b. Lynn, Mass., Mar. 23, 1925; s. Hyman and Fradel (Gordon) F.; m. Barbara Rose, June 4, 1950; children— Steven, Mark. B.F.A., Yale U., 1950, M.F.A., 1951; studied with, Willem de Kooning, 1950-51; MA (hon.), Brown U., 1953. Instr. painting Yale U., 1951-53; mem. faculty dept. art Brown U., 1953—, prof., 1961—, John Hay prof. bibliography, 1993—, chmn. studio div., 1973—; founder Ziggurat Press, 1985—; dir. Brown/Ziggurat Press, 1990—. Vis. prof. Harvard U., 1968, U. Calif., Riverside; artist-in-residence Dartmouth Coll., 1978; cons. Providence Lithography Co.; artist-in-residence Rutgers Ctr. for Innovative Printmaking, 1993. One-man shows include Kruaushaar Galleries, N.Y.C., 1958, 61, 63, Obelisk Gallery, Boston, 1965-66, 67, Inst. Contemporary Arts, London, 1967-68, Bristol Mus., 1975, Hopkins Ctr., Dartmouth Coll., 1978; group shows include Mus. Modern Art, 1954, 55, Bklyn. Mus., 1957-58, 60, Corcoran Gallery, Washington, 1959, Butler Inst. Am. Art, Youngstown, Ohio, 1960, Harvard U. Carpenter Ctr. for Visual Arts, 1963, Lowe Art Ctr., Syracuse, 1964, Inst. Contemporary Art, Boston, 1961, 66; represented in permanent collections at Brown U., Fogg Mus., L.A. County Mus., Met. Mus. Art, Mus. Modern Art, Phoenix Art Mus., Princeton U., Yale U. Art Gallery, Lehigh U. Art Collection, U. Mass., Mex.-Am. Inst., U. Florence, Italy, Folger Shakespeare Libr., Washington, Fuller Mus., Brockton, Mass., Victoria and Albert Mus., London and others. Served with U.S. Army, 1943-46. Decorated Purple Heart, Combat Inf. Badge; Alice Kimball English fellow Yale U., 1950, Fulbright fellow, Italy, 1956-57; Eliza Howard fellow Mex., 1961; recipient Gov.'s award for arts, 1980. Home: 107 Benevolent St Providence RI 02906-3154 Office: Brown U 64 College St Providence RI 02912-9021

FELDMANN, JUDITH GAIL, language professional, educator; b. Grenova, N.D., Feb. 10, 1938; d. Jule and Evelyn (Hagen) F.; children: Robert, Carole Elizabeth. BA magna cum laude, Minot State Tchrs. Coll., 1962; MA, Mich. State U., 1971; postgrad, U. Oslo, 1980, U. London, 1982, 85; postgrad., Western Mich. U., 1987, Eastern Mich. U., 1992-93, Harvard U., 1994. Cert. tchr., secondary adminstrn., Mich. English tchr. Minot Pub. Schs., N.D., 1961, Charlotte Pub. Schs., Mich., 1962; grad. asst. instr. Mich. State Univ., East Lansing, Mich., 1963; reading specialist, English educator Jackson (Mich.) Pub. Schs., 1964—2003, English educator, 1964—2003. Mem. Internat. Reading Assn., Mich. Reading Assn. (presenter Grand Rapids 1995), Assn. for Supervision and Curriculum Devl., Jackson Edn. Assn. (v.p.). Home: 2791 Brookside Blvd Jackson MI 49203-5532 E-mail: jfeldman2456@aol.com.

FELDSCHER, SHARLA, writer, public relations executive; b. Phila., Nov. 8, 1945; d. Irwin and Evelyn (Heisen) Stupine; m. Barry Feldscher, June 18, 1967; children: Amy, Hope. BS in Edn., Temple U., 1967. Cert. tchr., Pa. Kindergarten tchr. Lawton Sch., Phila., 1967-71; dir. pub. affairs Please Touch Mus., Phila., 1979-83; pres. Sharla Feldscher Pub. Rels., Phila., 1984—. Clients include Sesame Place, Peter Nero; lectr. numerous schs. and ms. Author: The KIDFUN Activity Book, 1990 (bestseller 1990), The KIDFUN Activity Book Expanded Edition, 1995, Engl. and Russian transl., Help! The Kid Is Bored, 1979 (Book of Month 1980), 148 Do-Its for Early Leaners, 1977, Readiness Week by Week, 1972. Chmn. Read Together Coalition Phila., 1989; pres. Phila. Pub. Rels. Assn., 1988; bd. dirs. Variety Club, Phila. Named to PPRA Hall of Fame; recipient Sarah award WIC. Mem. Ctr. for Literacy (bd. mem. 1985-90), Phila. Music Alliance, (bd. dirs. 1987—). Avocation: choir. Office: Sharla Feldscher Pub Rels 325 Cherry St Philadelphia PA 19106-1815

FELDSTEIN, JOSHUA, educational administrator; b. Russia, Apr. 12, 1921; arrived in U.S., 1939, naturalized, 1944; s. Cemach and Fania B. Feldstein; m. Miriam Myzel, Dec. 24, 1944; children: Theodore Lee, Daniel Ethan. BS, Delaware Valley Coll., 1952; MS, Rutgers U., 1956, PhD, 1962. Instr. horticulture Delaware Valley Coll., Doylestown, Pa., 1952—56, asst. prof. horticulture, 1956—60, assoc. prof. horticulture, 1960—65, prof. horticulture, 1965—, chmn. dept., 1959—69, chmn. plant sci. divsn., 1966—73, assoc. dean, 1969—73, dean, 1973—75; pres. Delaware Valley Coll. Sci. and Agr., Doylestown, Pa., 1975—87, pres. emeritus, 1987—, interim pres., 1995—97. Coord. nat. tchg. fellowships, student fin. aid, chmn. admissions, curriculum, athletics, student affairs, acad. std. coms. Delaware Valley Coll. Sci. and Agr. Author (with N.F. Childers): Effect of Irrigation on Fruit Size and Yield of Peaches in Pennsylvania, 1957; author: Peach Irrigation in a Humid Region, 1964, Effects of Irrigation on Peaches in Pennsylvania, 1965. Recipient Legion of Honor, Chapel of Four Chaplains, Phila., 1974, award, Pa. Future Farmers Am., 1980. Mem.: Commn. of Ind. Colls. and Univs., Pa. Assn. Colls. and Univs., Soil Conservation Soc. Am., Ea. Assn. Coll. Deans and Advs. to Students, Am. Inst. Biol. Scis., Am. Soc. Hort. Sci. Jewish.

FELDSTEIN, MARTIN STUART, economist, educator; b. N.Y.C., Nov. 25, 1939; s. Meyer and Esther (Gevarter) Feldstein; m. Kathleen Foley, June 19, 1965; children: Margaret, Janet. AB summa cum laude, Harvard U., 1961; MA, Oxford U., 1964, DPhil, 1967; LLD (hon.), Rochester U., 1984; LLD (hon.), Marquette U., 1985. Research fellow Nuffield Coll., Oxford U., 1964—65, ofcl. fellow, 1965—67, lectr. pub. fin., 1965—67; asst. prof. econs. Harvard U., 1967—68, assoc. prof., 1968—69, prof., 1969—, George F. Baker prof., 1984—; pres. Nat. Bur. Econ. Research, 1977—82, 1984—; chmn. Council Econ. Advisers, 1982—84. Bd. dirs. AIG, HCA, Eli Lilly; mem. internat. adv. coun. J.P. Morgan, Daimler-Chrysler, Robecco. Bd. contbrs.: Wall St. Jour. Fellow: Am. Philos. Soc., Nat. Assn. Bus. Economists, Econometric Soc. (coun. 1977—82), Nuffield Coll. (hon.), Brit. Acad. (corr.), Am. Acad. Arts and Scis.; mem.: Trilateral Commn. (exec. com. 1987—), Coun. on Fgn. Rels. (bd. dirs. 1998—), Inst. Medicine-NAS, Austrian Acad. Scis. (fgn.), Corp. Mass. Gen. Hosp., Am. Econ. Assn. (exec. com. 1980—82, v.p. 1988, pres.-elect 2003, John Bates Clark medal 1977), Phi Beta Kappa. Home: 147 Clifton St Belmont MA 02478-2603 Office: Nat Bur Econ Rsch Inc 1050 Massachusetts Ave Cambridge MA 02138-5317 E-mail: mfeldstein@harvard.edu.

FELDT, GLENDA DIANE, educational administrator; b. Mobile, Ala., Sept. 15, 1950; d. William and Thelma G. (Sullivan) Sanderson; m. Fitzhugh M. Nuckols, 1969 (div. 1979); children: Thomas F., William L.; m. Everett R. Feldt, Jr., July 26, 1980; 1 child, Everett R., III. Student, Radford Coll., 1967-69; BA, Averett Coll., 1974; M of Pub. Adminstrn., Old Dominion U., 1981; EdD in Ednl. Leadership, Nova U., Ft. Lauderdale, Fla., 1993. Cert. tchr. voct. edn., adminstr., sociology, evaluator, work adjustment specialist, sch. supt., Va. Welfare eligibility technician Danville (Va.) Social Svc. Bur., 1971-73, social worker I, 1973-74; counselor, evaluator Fred T. Hatcher Ctr., Danville, 1974-75; vocat. evaluator Va. Dept. Vocat. Rehab., Danville, 1975-78, Va. Beach City Pub. Schs., 1978-80, work adjustment specialist, 1980-87; program leader vocat. spl. needs Norfolk (Va.) Pub. Schs., 1987-93; asst. prin. Bayside High Sch., Virginia Beach, Va., 1993-94; prin. New Horizons Regional Edn. Ctr., Newport News, Va., 1994-97, Franklin (Va.) H.S., 1997—99; with U.S. Army, 2000—01, U.S. Coast Guard, 2001—. Project dir. Tidewater (Va.) Regional Nursing Articulation Project, 1988-90; cons. Johnson & Wales U., Norfolk, 1992-93; project dir. High Schs. that Work So. Regional Edn. Bd., 1993-94; presenter numerous confs. Presenter Coun for Exceptional Children, Boston, 1985, Nashville, 1987, Albuquerque, 1993; keynote speaker W. Va. Tech. prep. health occupations, Charleston, 1991. Bd. dirs Goodwill Industries, Danville, 1977-78; pres. PTA, 1977-78. Mem. NEA, ASCD, Nat. Assn. Secondary Sch. Prins., Va. Edn. Assn., Am. Vocat. Edn. Assn. (bd. dirs. Va. 1987-93, 96), Nat. Assn. Vocat. Edn. Spl. Needs Pers., Va. Assn. Vocat. Spl. Needs Pers. (pres. 1983-85, Va. Tchr. of Yr. 1986, Va. Adminstr. Yr. 1993), Jr. League Hampton Rds., Va. Women's Network, Exch. Club of York, Franklin Rotary Club. Baptist. Avocations: reading, crafts, walking, bicycling. Home: 405 Marlbank Dr Yorktown VA 23692-4306 Office: US Coast Guard Tng Ctr Yorktown End of Route 238 Yorktown VA 23690-5000

FELDT, LEONARD SAMUEL, university educator and administrator; b. Long Branch, New Jersey, Nov. 2, 1925; s. Harry and Bessie (Doris) F.; m. Natalie Ruth (Fischer), Aug. 29, 1954; children: Sarah Feldt Roach, Daniel C. BS in Edn., Rutgers Univ., 1950, EdM, 1951; PhD, U. Iowa, 1954. Asst. prof. to prof. U. Iowa, Iowa City, 1954-94, dir. testing programs, 1981-94, Lindquist prof. ednl. measurement, 1981-94, prof. emeritus, 1994. Pres. Iowa Measurment Rsch. Found., Iowa City, 1978—; editor standardized tests, Iowa Tests Ednl. Devel., 1960—. With U.S. Army, 1943—46. Recipient Disting. Svc. Award Rutgers U., 1999; Disting. Achievement Award, Nat. Ctr. for Rsch. on Evaluation Stds. and Student Testing, 1999. Mem.: Am. Stats. Assn., Psychometric Soc., Nat. Coun. on Measurement in Edn. (Career Contbns. award 1994), Am. Ednl. Rsch. Assn. (E.F. Lindquist award 1995), Sigma Xi, Phi Beta Kappa. Avocation: golf. Home: 810 Willow St Iowa City IA 52245-5438 Office: Univ Iowa Lindquist Ctr Iowa City IA 52242 E-mail: leonard-feldt@uiowa.edu.

FELGAR, RAYMOND E(UGENE), pathologist, medical educator; b. Mt. Pleasant, Pa., Mar. 2, 1963; s. Samuel Hurst and Anna June (Stull) F. BS in Microbiology with honors, Pa. State U., 1985; PhD in Pathology, U. Pitts., 1990, MD, 1992. Diplomate Am. Bd. Pathology in Anatomic and Clin. Pathology, Am. Bd. Pathology, cert. subspecialty in Hemotology Am. Bd. Pathology. Resident in anatomic and clin. pathology U. Pa. Med. Ctr., Phila., 1992-96; fellow in hematopathology dept. pathology Vanderbilt U., Nashville, 1996-98; dir. hematopathology and clin. flow cytometry Hahnemann Hosp., Phila., 1998; asst. prof. dept. pathology and lab medicine MCP-Hahnemann Sch. Medicine, Phila., 1998; dir. clin. flow cytometry lab., hematopathologist and dir. hematopathology Strong Meml. Hosp., Rochester, N.Y., 1998—; asst. prof. Dept. Pathology & Lab. Medicine U. Rochester Sch. Medicine & Dentistry, 1998—. Co-dir. Course on T-cell lymphomas, ASCP Nat. Meeting. Contbr. articles to profl. jours., chpt. to book. NIH med. scientist tng. fellow, 1987-92. Mem. AMA, Coll. Am. Pathologists, Am. Soc. Clin. Pathologists (co-dir. course t-cell lymphomas nat. mtg.), Am. Soc. Hematology, U.S. and Can. Acad. Pathology, Soc. for Hematopathology, European Assn. for Hematopathology, Eastern Coop. Oncology Group (pathology com.), Southwestern Oncology Group, Children's Oncology Group, Pa. State U. Alumni Assn., Phi Beta Kappa.

FELGER, RALPH WILLIAM, education educator, retired military officer; b. Hamilton, Ohio, Oct. 14, 1919; s. Edward Lewis and Blanche Esther (House) F.; m. Bernice Regina Moeller, Dec. 28, 1944 (dec.); 1 child, Mary Karen. BA, Whitworth Coll., 1950; MBA, U. Denver, 1952; MS, Trinity U., 1954. Cert. instr. bus. and psychology, Calif. Commd. 2d lt. U.S. Army, advanced through grades to 1st lt., pers. tng. officer, 1942-46, relieved from active duty, 1946; commd. 1st lt. USAF, 1951, advanced through grades to col., edn. and pers. officer, 1951-67, ret., 1967; asst. prof. Bakersfield (Calif.) Coll., 1967-68; dean continuing edn. Lincoln Land C.C., Springfield, Ill., 1968-72; dir. corp. tng. Sangamo Electric Co., West Union, S.C., 1972-74; asst. campus dir. Ohio State U., Marion, 1974-79, asst. to v.p. Columbus, 1979-83; exec. v.p. Internat. Mgmt. Inst., Westerville, Ohio, 1983-84; dir. continuing edn. N.Mex. Inst. Mining and Tech., Socorro, 1984-85; part-time cons. edn. and mktg. Midwest Human Resource Sys., Columbus, Ohio, 1985-89; acad. counselor Franklin U., Columbus, 1990-91; edn. program mgr. Jr. Achievement of Ctrl. Ohio, Columbus, 1991-92; v.p. Career Mgmt. Ctrs., Inc., Columbus, 1991-92; ret., 1992. Ill. divsn. chmn. United Way, Springfield, 1972; mem. Police Human Rels. Com., Springfield, 1970-72; bd. dirs. ARC, Oconee, S.C., 1973; edn. chmn. Marion (Ohio) Econ. Coun., 1975-79, Marion County chpt. Am. Heart Assn., 1975-79. Decorated Legion of Merit, U.S. Joint Chiefs of Staff Badge, 3 USAF Commendation medals; recipient 2 commendations United Way Community Service. Mem.: U.S. Ret. Mil. Officers Assn., Am. Biog. Inst. (rsch. bd. advisors), Pers. Mgrs. Club (v.p. 1972—74), Delta Sigma Pi (life). Avocations: fishing, camping, travel, cooking, reading. Home: 1300 O Ave #106 Anacortes WA 98221

FELICETTI, DANIEL A. academic administrator, educator; b. N.Y.C., Apr. 25, 1942; s. Ernest and Rose (DiAdamo) F.; m. Barbara D'Antonio, July 13, 1969. BA in Polit. Sci., Hunter Coll., 1963; MA in Polit. Sci., NYU, 1966, PhD in Polit. Sci., 1971. From asst. to assoc. prof. Fairfield (Conn.) U., 1967-77, chmn. dept. politics, 1973-76, spl. asst. to pres., 1977; acad. v.p., acad. dean Wheeling (W.Va.) Coll., 1977-80; sr. v.p. for acad. affairs Coll. New Rochelle, N.Y., 1980-81, Southeastern U., Washington, 1982-84; v.p. acad. affairs U. Detroit, 1984-89; pres. Marian Coll., Indpls., 1989-99, Capital U., Columbus, Ohio, 1999-2001; founder Higher Edn. Leadership Projects Consulting Svc., 2001—. Participant Am. Coun. on Edn., Washington, 1976-77, vis. assoc., 1984-85; intern Inst. for Ednl. Mgmt. program Harvard U., 1981; cons. Coun. for Ind. Colls., Washington, 1986. Trustee Am. Heart Assn., Mich.; bd. dirs. Am. Heart Assn., Ind., Mental Health Assn. Marion County, Econ. Club Indpls., Coun. Ind. Colls.; mem. health and substance abuse com. New Detroit, Inc., 1986-89; mem. Greater Indpls. Progress Com.; mem. Pub. Safety Task Force Ind.; mem. Colls. Ind. Found.; mem. Indpls. delegation to Pres.'s Summit for Am.'s Future, 1997. Trustee Am. Heart Assn., Mich.; bd. dirs. Am. Heart Assn., Ind., Mental Health Assn. Marion County, Econ. Club Indpls., Coun. Ind. Colls.; mem. health and substance abuse com. New Detroit, Inc., 1986-89; mem. Greater Indpls. Progress Coml; mem. Pub. Safety Task Force Ind.; mem. Colls. Ind. Found.; mem. safety vision coun. United Way Columbus. Named to Hunter Coll. Hall of Fame, Hunter Coll. Alumni Assn., 1986; recipient Cert. of Recognition Sen. Lugar, 1994; Lilly Found. vis. faculty fellow Yale U., 1975; named Sagamore of the Wabash Gov. of Ind., 1990. Mem. Indpls. Athletic Club, received hon. doctoral degree from Marian Coll., 1999, Columbus C. of C. (pub. rels. com.), Rotary, Alpha Sigma Nu (hon.), Beta Gamma Sigma (hon.). Democrat. Roman Catholic. Avocations: baseball, reading, antiques.

FELL, MICHAEL JOHN, mathematics educator; b. Balt., Oct. 20, 1961; s. John Francis and Elizabeth Ann (Kozak) F.; m. Judith Marie Kwiatkowski, Aug. 4, 1990; children: Stephen Michael, Trevor Austin. BA in Math., Towson State U., 1985; MA in Edn., Loyola Coll., 1995. Cert. math. tchr. Math. and German tchr. Curley High Sch., Balt., 1985-95, chmn. math. dept., 1992-95; tchr. math. Kent County H.S., Worton, Md., 1995—2001, Elkton (Md.) H.S., 2001—. Math. tchr. summer sch. Curley HS, Balt., 1989-94, varsity tennis coach, 1989—, intramural athletic dir., 1988-95, acad. coun., 1992-95, faculty rep. to sch. bd., 1989-91, goals 2000 instr., 1996—, coll. bd. pacesetter instr., 1998—, SIT chair, 1998-2000; item writer, content coordinating com., Md. HSA, 2000—. Recipient Tchr. of Yr. award Curley HS Student Govt., 1992, Coach of Yr., 2000. Mem. ASCD, Nat. Coun. Tchrs. Math., Md. Coun. Tchrs. Math. (Outstanding Math. Tchr. 1992, 99, Outstanding Math. Tchr. finalist 1993, 94), U.S. Tennis Assn. Republican. Avocations: tennis, basketball, bowling. Office: Elkton HS Elkton MD 21921

FELL, RICHARD D. entomology educator; BA in Biology, U. Pa.; MS and PhD in Entomology and Apiculture, Cornell U. Prof. entomology Va. Poly. Inst., State U. Blacksburg. Ext. specialist on bees and stinging insects. Recipient Disting. Achievement award in Teaching. Achievements include research in honey bee and ant biology. Office: VPI & State U Dept of Entomology Blacksburg VA 24061

FELLER, WILLIAM FRANK, surgery educator; b. St. Paul, Nov. 2, 1925; s. William and Eva Caroline (Nordstrom) F.; m. Margareta Elizabeth Helm, Sept. 5, 1964; children: William Frank III, Elizabeth Suzanne. BA magna cum laude, U. Minn., 1948, BS, 1952, MD, 1954, PhD, 1962. Diplomate Am. Bd. Surgery. Intern U. Minn., Mpls., 1954-55; asst. prof. Georgetown U., Washington, 1964-69, assoc. prof., 1969-92; ret., 1992. Contbr. articles to profl. jours. Warden St. John's Episc. Ch., Chevy Chase, Md., 1975-76. Recipient St. George's medal Am. Cancer Soc., 1987. Mem. AAAS, ACS, Am. Assn. Cancer Rsch., Am. Scandinavian Found. (chpt. pres. 1969-71), Med. Soc. D.C., Am. Cancer Soc. (D.C. divsn. pres. 1984-85, St. George's medal 1987), Washington Acad. Medicine, Washington Acad. Surgery (pres. 1982-83), Cosmos Club (Washington). Achievements include 2 patents for Cancer Detection Methods. Home: 7028 Barkwater Ct Bethesda MD 20817-4402

FELLOWS, DIANA POTENZANO, educational administrator; b. N.Y.C., Aug. 29, 1939; d. Paul John and Frances (Castrovinci) P.; m. William Thomas Fellows, June 16, 1962; children: Paul Warren, Joan Fellows Madden. BA, St. Joseph's Coll., 1960; MA, Fordham U., 1963, Coll. St. Joseph, Rutland, Vt., 1979. Cert. guidance, early childhood, spl. edn. tchr., Vt., N.Y. Tchr. N.Y.C. Pub. Schs., 1960-68; guidance counselor Rutland Pub. Schs., 1968-86, Colchester (Vt.) H.S., 1986-88; dir. guidance Otter Valley Union H.S., Brandon, Vt., 1988-91, Burr & Burton Sem., Manchester, Vt., 1991-94, Colchester Sch. Dist., 1994—. Grant writer Rutland N.E. Supervisory Union; bd. dirs. Rutland County Parent/Child Ctr.; presenter in field; crisis intervention specialist, state activities coord. Vt. Student Assistance Corp., Winooski. Author: School-to-Work Resource Guide, 1997, Crisis Manual, 1997, Workbase Learning Manual, 1998. Vol. Dismiss House of Vt., Rutland, 1988—, Rutland Regional Med. Ctr., 1972-90; mem. Cmty. Choir of Rutland, 1976—; organizer teen vol. program Rutland Hosp., 1972; organizer Rutland County Parent/Child Ctr., 1983; organizer literacy vol. program Otter Valley Union H.S., 1989; bd. dirs. Vt. State Hugh O'Brian Youth Leadership Found., 1993, Lake Champlain Sch.-to-Work Collaborative, DARE Am., 2000—; crisis intervention specialist Rutland Cen. Supervisory Union; drug/alcohol coord. Colchester Sch. Dist.; edn. specialist Vt. Student Assistance Corp. Grantee in field, 1985-2000; named Vt. Counselor of Yr., State Orgn., 1983; recipient Cert. of Merit, Rutland N.E. Supervisory Union, 1989, Lake Champlain Regional Sch. to Work award, 1997. Mem. ACA, New Eng. Conf. for Counseling and Devel. (bd. dirs. 1986-92, co-chair Vt. chpt. 1990, bd. dirs. 1990-92), Vt. Assn. Counselors (treas. 1984-86), Vt. Counseling Assn. (membership chair, treas. 1996-99, pres. elect 1999-2000, pres. 2000—), Manchester C. of C. (bd. dirs.), Rotary. Roman Catholic. Avocations: china painting, chinese caligraphy. Home: 25 Howard Ave Rutland VT 05701 Office: Vt Student Assistance Corp PO Box 2000 Champlain Mill Winooski VT 05404 also: Vt Student Assistance Corp PO Box 2000 Winooski VT 05404-2601 E-mail: fellows@vsac.org.

FELLOWS, ESTHER ELIZABETH, musician, music educator; b. Miami, Ariz., Nov. 5, 1952; d. John Wilmont and Flora Elizabeth (Eyestone) Walker; m. James Michael Fellows, Aug. 20, 1976; children: Joy Christine, Rachel Lindsay, Daniel Matthew, Jessica Grace. B in Music Edn., U. Colo., 1975. Co-dir. Children's Piano Lab. U. Colo., Boulder, 1975-76; instr. So. Calif. Conservatory Music, Sun City, 1976-78; pvt. instr. Ft. Lauderdale, 1978-84; instr. Ft. Lauderdale Christian Sch., 1981-83; sect. violinist Signature Symphony Tulsa Ballet, 1984—, Bartlesville (Okla.) Symphony, 1990—; pvt. instr. Broken Arrow, Okla., 1984—. Pvt. instr. Ft. Lauderdale, 1978-84. Mem. Music Tchrs. Nat. Assn. (cert. piano, violin and viola), Am. String Tchrs. Assn., Am. Viola Soc., Okla. Music Tchr. Assn., Suzuki Assn. Am., Hyechka Music Club Tulsa, Tulsa Accredited Music Tchrs. Assn. (chair scholarship com.). Avocation: biking. Home: 19821 S Harvard Ave Mounds OK 74047-5049

FELLOWS, MARILYN KINDER, elementary education educator; b. Louisville, July 21, 1952; d. Clyde White and Violet (Nicklies) Kinder; m. Steven Anthony Fellows, Jan 5, 1973; children: Suzann Renee, Amber Marie. BA in Edn., U. Ky., 1974; MS in Edn., U. Louisville, 1978; MS in Counseling, Ind. U. S.E., 1991; trained reading recovery tchr., Purdue U., 2000. Tchr. profoundly handicapped Jefferson County Pub. Schs., Louisville, 1975-77; tchr. learning disabled Greater Clark County Schs., Jeffersonville, Ind., 1977, tchr. 1st grade, tchr. learning disabled, 1978-92; coord. spl. needs students Jonathan Jennings/Greater Clark County Schs., 1992-94; 1st grad. tchr., 1994—. Chmn. performance based accreditation team Charlestown, Ind., 1988-89, team leader, 1998-99. Leader 4-H, New Wash., Ind. 1989—. Recipient recognition Ind. Dept. Edn., Indpls., 1990, Teacher Excellence award Louisville Courrier Jour. and WHAS-TV, 1992; grantee Greater Clark County Schs., 1989, 90, 99. Mem. ASCD, Internat. Reading Assn., Ind. State Tch. Assn. (presentor 1978), Assn. Supervision Curriculum Devel., Phi Dela Kappa. Avocations: reading, swimming, waterskiing. Home: 7013 Taflinger Rd RR 1 Nabb IN 47147-9801 Office: Utica Elem Sch 210 Maplehurst Dr Jeffersonville IN 47130

FELLOWS, ROBERT ELLIS, medical educator, medical scientist; b. Syracuse, N.Y., Aug. 4, 1933; s. Robert Ellis and Clara (Talmadge) F.; m. Karlen Kiger, July 2, 1983; children: Kara, Ari. AB, Hamilton Coll., 1955; MD, CM, McGill U., 1959; PhD, Duke U., 1969. Intern N.Y. Hosp., N.Y.C., 1959—60, asst. resident, 1960—61, Royal Victoria Hosp., Montreal, Canada, 1961—62; asst. prof. dept. medicine Duke U., Durham, NC, 1966—76, asst. prof. dept. physiology and pharmacology, 1966—70, assoc. prof. dept. physiology and pharmacology, assoc. dir. med. scientist tng. program, 1970—76; prof., chmn. dept. physiology and biophysics U. Iowa Coll. Medicine, 1976—2002, dir. med. sci. tng. program, 1976—97, dir. physician sci. program, 1984—88, dir. neurosci. program, 1984—88. Mem. Nat. Pituitary Agy. Adv. Bd.; mem. NIH Population Rsch. Com., 1981-86, VA Career Devel. Rev. Com., 1985-88; cons. NIH, NSF March of Dimes. Mem. editorial bd.: Endocrinology, Am. Jour. Physiology. Mem. AAAS, Am. Chem. Soc., Am. Fedn. Clin. Rsch., Am. Physiol. Soc., Am. Soc. Biol. Chemists, Am. Soc. Cell Biology, Assn. Chairmen Depts. Physiology, Biochem. Soc., Biophys. Soc., Endocrine Soc., Internat. Soc. Neuroendocrinology, N.Y. Acad. Scis., Soc. for Neurosci., Assn. Neurosci. Depts. and Programs (pres. 1995-96), Sigma Xi, Alpha Omega Alpha. Home: 135 Pentire Cir Iowa City IA 52245-1575 Office: 5-660 Bowen Sci Bldg Iowa City IA 52242 E-mail: robert-fellows@uiowa.edu.

FELNER, ROBERT DAVID, psychology educator, researcher, consultant; b. Norwich, Conn., June 3, 1950; s. Joseph and Roslyn (Aptaker) Felner. BA, U. Conn., 1972; MA, U. Rochester, 1975, PhD, 1977. Lic. psychologist. Clin. psychology intern Convalescent Hosp. for Children, Rochester, NY, 1973—74, Center for Cmty. Studies, Rochester, 1974—75, U. Rochester Med. Ctr., 1975—76; asst. prof. psychology Yale U., New Haven, 1976—81; assoc. prof., dir. doctorlal program in clin./cmty. psychology Auburn U. (Ala.), 1981—86; prof. psychology U. Ill., Champaign, 1986—90, prof. pub. policy edn., social welfare, 1990—96, dir. doctoral program in clin./cmty. psychology, dir. clin. tng., 1986—90; prof., dir. sch. edn. and Nat. Ctr. on Pub. Edn. and Social Policy U. R.I., Kingston, 1996—. Mem. NIMH Small Grants Panel, 1978—82, NIMH Child/Family/Prevention Panel, 1983—87; NSF grants reviewer, 1983; cons. Conn. Bar Assn., 1978—82, Charles Henderson Child Health Ctr., 1981—86, Office for Prevention, NIMH, 1973—90, Alcohol, Drug and Mental Health Adminstrn., 1981—82, Office of Substance Abuse Prevention, Office of Health and Human Services, 1986—88. Author: Preventive Psychology: Theory Research and Practice, 1983, A Multidisciplinary Approach to Prevention, 1987; contbr. chapters to books, articles to profl. jours. in field; mem. editl. bd. Jour. Clin. Child Psychology, Jour. Divorce, Am. Jour. Cmty. Psychology, Jour. Social and Clin. Psychology, Profl. Psychology: Theory and Research, Suicide and Life Threatening Behavior, Jour. of Consulting and Clin. Psychology, Jour. Primary Prevention. Grantee, NIH, 1976—77, Edward W. Hazen Found., 1978—81, NSF rsch. grantee, 1980—82, 1983—85, Carnegie Corp. of N.Y., 1989—, Lilly Endowment, 1993—98, Kellogg Found., 1994—98, E.M. Kaufmann Found., 1995—99, R.I. Dept. Edn., 1997—. Fellow: APA, Am. Orthopsychiat. Assn.; mem.: Am. Assn. Sociology (bd. dirs. 1988—92, chair Council of Community Psychology Program Dirs. 1983), Soc. for Research in Child Devel. Republican. Jewish. Office: Univ RI Sch Edn 705 Chafee Hall Kingston RI 02818 E-mail: rfelner@uri.edu.

FELS, RENDIGS, economist, educator; b. Cin., June 11, 1917; s. Clifford George and Estella Luella (Rendigs) F.; m. Beatrice Carmichael Baker, Dec. 27, 1941, (dec.); children: Charles Wentworth Baker, Carmichael (dec.); m. Marilyn W. Whiteman, July 15, 2001. AB, Harvard U., 1939, PhD, 1948; AM, Columbia U., 1940. Mem. faculty Vanderbilt U., 1948—, prof. econs., 1956-82, prof. emeritus, 1982—, dir. grad. program econ. devel., 1956- 57, chmn. dept. econs. and bus. adminstrn., 1962-65, 77-79. Chmn. Univs.-Nat. Bur. Com., 1962-67 Author: American Business Cycles, 1865-1897, 1959, Challenge to the American Economy, an Introduction to Economics, 1961, 2d edit, 1966, (with C. Elton Hinshaw) Forecasting and Recognizing Business Cycle Turning Points, 1968; Editor: (with Stephen Buckles) Casebook of Economic Problems and Policies, 5th edit, 1981. Served with USAAF, 1942-46. Mem. Am. Econ. Assn. (sec.-treas. 1970-75, treas. 1976-87), Midwest Econ. Assn. (pres. 1984-85), So. Econ. Assn. (pres. 1967-68) Home: Apt 109 4400 Belmont Park Ter Nashville TN 37215-3643

FELSENSTEIN, FRANK ARJEH, educator; b. London, July 28, 1944; came to U.S., 1998; s. Ernest Maurice and Vera Lotte F.; m. Carole Alison Jaffe, Dec. 22, 1985; children: Kenny, Joanna. BA with honors, U. Leeds, England, 1966, PhD, 1971. Asst. lectr. English U. Geneva, Switzerland, 1968-70; lectr. English U. Leeds, England, 1971-86, sr. lectr. English, 1986-96, reader 18th century studies, 1996-98; vis. prof. book history Drew U., Madison, NJ, 1998—; dir. honors program Yeshiva Coll., N.Y.C., 1998—2001; Reed D. Voran honors disting. prof. Ball State U., Muncie, Ind., 2002—. Vis. prof. English Vanderbilt U., Nashville, 1989-90. Author: Anti-Semitic Stereotypes, 1995; editor: Travels Through France and Italy, 1979, A Practical Treatise of Flowers, 1985, English Trader, Indian Maid, 1999, Ann Yearsley and the Politics of Patronage, 2002-03 Mem. Am. Soc. 18th Century Studies. Avocation: antiquarian books and prints. Home: 8 Manor Dr Morristown NJ 07960-2611 Office: Ball State U Dept English Muncie IN 47306 E-mail: felsenstein@bsu.edu.

FELSENTHAL, STEVEN ALTUS, lawyer, educator; b. Chgo., May 21, 1949; s. Jerome and Eve (Altus) F.; m. Carol Judith Greenberg, June 14, 1970; children: Rebecca Elizabeth, Julia Alison, Daniel Louis Altus. AB, U. Ill., 1971; JD, Harvard U., 1974. Bar: Ill. 1974, U.S. Dist. Ct. (no. dist.) Ill. 1974, U.S. Ct. Claims 1975, U.S. Tax Ct. 1975, U.S. Ct. Appeals (7th cir.) 1981. Assoc. Levenfeld, Kanter, Baskes & Lippitz, Chgo., 1974-78; ptnr. Levenfeld & Kanter, Chgo., 1978-80, Levenfeld, Eisenberg, Janger, Glassberg & Lippitz, Chgo., 1980-84; sr. ptnr. Sugar, Friedberg & Felsenthal, Chgo., 1984—. Lectr. Kent Coll. Law, Ill. Inst. Tech., Chgo., 1978-80. Mem. ABA, Ill. Bar Assn., Chgo. Bar Assn., Chgo. Coun. Lawyers, Harvard Law Soc. Ill., Standard Club, Harvard Club, Phi Beta Kappa. Office: Sugar Friedberg & Felsenthal 30 N La Salle St Ste 3000 Chicago IL 60602-3327 E-mail: saf@sff-law.com.

FELSKE, JAMES DAVID, mechanical engineering educator; b. Detroit, Feb. 22, 1949; s. Edward William and Marion Katherine (Schassburger) F.; m. Joyce Ellen Espenmiller, July 31, 1971; children: Jonathan David, Jenny Elizabeth. BSME, U. Mich., 1971; MSME, U. Calif., Berkeley, 1972, PhD in Mech. Engring., 1974. Asst. prof. mech. engring. MIT, Cambridge, Mass., 1974-77; from asst. prof. to assoc. prof. mech. engring. SUNY, Buffalo, 1977-86, prof. mech. engring., 1986—. Mem. tech. adv. com. N.Y. State Solid Waste Combustion Inst., Ithaca, N.Y., 1988-94; cons. numerous cos. in chem., thermal and mfg. industries. Contbr. rsch. articles to profl. jours.; reviewer archival jours. in heat transfer, combustion, energy sys., instrumentation and optics. Elder Cleveland Dr. Presbyn. Ch., Cheektowaga, N.Y., 1979—. Named Scholar of Yr., Evans Scholars Found., 1971; NSF grad. fellow, 1971-74; recipient Best Paper award Ctrl. States meeting Combustion Inst., 1992. Mem. ASME (K-11 com. 1980—, Outstanding Review Jour. Heat Transfer 1993) AIAA, Tau Beta Pi (Outstanding Sr. Engr. award 1971), Pi Tau Sigma, Phi Eta Sigma. Avocations: cosmology, sports. Home: 119 Capen Blvd Amherst NY 14226-3052 Office: SUNY Dept Mech & Aero Engr 330 Jarvis Hall Buffalo NY 14260-4400 E-mail: felske@buffalo.edu.

FELSTINER, MARY LOWENTHAL, history educator; b. Pittsburgh, Feb. 19, 1941; d. Alexander and Anne Lowenthal; m. John Felstiner, Feb. 19, 1966; children: Sarah Alexandra, Aleksandr. BA, Harvard U., 1963; MA, Columbia U., 1966; PhD, Stanford U., 1971. Prof. history San Francisco State Univ., 1972—. Author: To Paint Her Life, 1994. Mem.: Phi Beta Kappa. Office: San Francisco State Univ History Dept 1600 Holloway Ave San Francisco CA 94132-1722

FELT, JENNIFER RUTH, elementary physical education educator; b. Toledo, Ohio, Sept. 10, 1950; d. Albert Edward and Joyce Muriel (Haynes) Chiles; m. William Nickolas Felt, Dec. 30, 1983. BS, U. Iowa, 1972; MS in edn., Northern Ill. U., 1988. Cert. physical edn. tchr., Ill. Physical edn. tchr. C.U.S.D. # 303, St. Charles, Ill., 1972—. Volleyball coach 8th grade C.U.S.D. # 303, track coach 8th grade, girls athletic dir., h.s. asst. volleyball coach; intramural dir. Munhall Elem. Sch., presenter creative drama Arts At Night, St. Charles, 1994; part edn. leadership conf., 1994-95; mem. state acad. stds. project Ill. State Bd. Edn., 1995-96, external team mem. for quality rev., 1997, 98. Active Curriculum revision C.U.S.D. #303, 1991-96, Fine Arts curriculum work, 1993-94; mentor Golden Apple Scholars of Ill., 1994—. Recipient Tech. grant Ill. State Bd. Edn., 1994. Mem. IAHPERD (presenter state conv. 1995), AAHPERD, NEA, IEA, SCEA, IAAE. Avocations: aerobics, boating, biking, traveling. Office: Munhall Elem Sch 1400 S 13th Ave Saint Charles IL 60174-4405

FELTON, CYNTHIA, educational administrator; b. Chgo., Apr. 1, 1950; d. Robert Lee Felton Sr. and Julia Mae (Cheton) Felton-Phillips. BA, Northeastern, 1970; MEd, National Coll., 1984; MA, DePaul U., 1988; PhD, Loyola U., Chgo., 1992. Cert. tchr, adminstrv., Ill. Tchr. Chgo. Pub. Schs., 1971-86, adminstr., 1986-89, asst. prin., 1989-92, prin., 1992-97; dir. Chgo. Acad. for Sch. Leadership, 1997—. Mem. ASCD, Nat. Staff Devel. Coun., Nat. Coun. Tchrs. Math, Nat. Coun. Suprs. Math, Ill. Coun. Tchrs. Math (bd. dirs. 1992-95). Office: Chgo Acad Sch Leadership 221 N Lasalle St Chicago IL 60601-1206

FELTON, ZORA BELLE, emerita museum educator; b. Allentown, Pa., June 22, 1930; d. James Edward and Elizabeth (Cobbs) M.; m. Edward Pernizer Felton, July 12, 1975. BA, Moravian Coll., 1952; MEd, Howard U., 1980. Asst. dir. teenage programs Dayton (Ohio) YWCA, 1952-57, dir. teenage programs, 1957-58; dir. edn. and group work Southeast Neighborhood House, Washington, 1958-67; chief, edn. dept. Anacostia Mus.-Smithsonian Inst., Washington, 1967-89, acting dir., 1989, asst. dir., edn. and outreach dept., 1989-94. Bd. dirs., recording sec. E.J. Williams Scholarship, Inc., Washington. Co-author: A Different Drummer: John R. Kinard and the Anacostia Museum, 1967-1989, Washington D.C.: Anacostia Museum, 1992; author: A Walk Through "Old Anacostia", rev., 1991. Bd. dirs. Anacostia Coordinating Coun. Named to D.C. Women's Hall of Fame, Washington, 1994; recipient Mus. Educator's award for Excellence, Am. Assn. Museums, 1991, African Am. Museums M. Burroughs award for Exceptional Contbns. to Edn., 1989, John Amos Comenius award, Moravian Coll., Bethlehem, Pa., 1992, Katherine Coffee Museum award, 2000. Mem. Delta Sigma Theta. Democrat. Avocations: travel, cooking, writing. Home: 1438 Whittier St NW Washington DC 20012-2840

FELTS, GEORGE WILLIAM, SR., special education educator; b. Greenwood, S.C., Dec. 8, 1933; s. Green Franklin and Katie Mae (Evans) F.; m. Rosemary Lawton, Jan. 2, 1958; children: George II, Michael, Aprol. BS in Phys. Edn., S.C. State Coll., 1963; MEd in Counseling Edn., Antioch U., 1985. Cert. spl. edn. tchr., Pa. From counselor to probation officer City of Phila., 1960-69, 71-73; counselor Youth Devel. Ctr., Cornwell Heights, Pa., 1970, 75-77, Phila. Housing Authority, 1973-75, Phila. Drug Treatment Ctr., 1977-79, Giuffre Med. Ctr., Phila., 1979-81; asst. Sch. Dist. Phila., 1979-86, spl. edn. tchr., 1986—. Inventor Extension on an umbrella, 1975. Swim instr. YMCA; bd. mgrs. Columbia/North YMCA; commr. Boy Scouts Am.; governing bd. E. Luther Community Ctr.; block capt. Yorktown Civic Orgn., Phila., 1992. With U.S. Army, 1958-60. Mem. Am. Pers. and Guidance Assn., Prince Hall Free and Accepted Masons, Shriner. Democrat. Baptist. Avocations: bowling, swimming, roller skating, drawing, reading. Home: PO Box 16561 Philadelphia PA 19122-0261

FENG, ALBERT, science educator, researcher; b. Bandung, Java, Indonesia, Feb. 10, 1944; s. Shu-San and Yi (Chow) F.; m. Phoebe Lifei Wang, Oct. 14, 1974; children: Jeffrey Thomas, Jacqueline A. BSEE, U. Miami, 1968, MSc, 1970; PhD, Cornell U., 1975. Reliability engr. Singer Corp. Kearfott Div., Little Falls, N.J., 1970; asst. rsch. neuroscientist U. Calif. at San Diego, La Jolla, 1974-76; postdoctoral fellow Washington U., St. Louis, 1976-77; asst. prof. U. Ill., Urbana, 1977-83, assoc. prof., 1983-89, prof., 1989—, head dept. molecular and integrative physiology, 1992-97. Mem. adv. bd. Parmly Hearing Inst., Chgo., 1982-88; mem. review panel NSF, Washington, 1986-88; chmn. neurosci. program U. Ill., Urbana, 1987-90; mem. hearing rsch. study sect. NIH, Washington, 1991-95, chmn., 1993-95. Contbr. articles to profl. jours. including Jour. Neurophysiology, Jour. Comparative Physiology, Science, Jour. Comparative Neurology, Jour. Acoustical Soc. Am., Jour. Neurosci. Fellow AAAS, Acoustical Soc. of Am.; mem. Assn. for Rsch. Otolaryngology, Internat. Soc. Neuroethology (treas. 1992-98, pres.-elect 1998-2001, pres. 2001—), Soc. of Neurosci. Achievements include research in neural mechanisms of sound localization and sound pattern recognition. Home: 1209 Wilshire Ct Champaign IL 61821-6916 Office: U Ill 405 N Mathews Ave Urbana IL 61801-2325

FENISON, EDDIE, health science educator; b. Montgomery, Ala., Feb. 17, 1935; s. Oliver and Rachel (Boyd) F.; m. Selena Viola, July 10, 1958; children: Michel, Anthony, Michelle, Cynthia, Chantelle. BA, Calif. State U., Los Angeles, 1975, MEd, 1976. Cert. Nat. Bd. Respiratory Care, Calif.; cert. class A tchr., Calif. Mem. staff UCLA Med. Ctr. Respiratory Dept., Los Angeles, 1965-67; dir. respiratory dept. Daniel Freeman Hosp., Inglewood, Calif., 1967-68, Centinela Valley Hosp., Inglewood, 1968-69; instr. health scis. Mt. San Antonio Coll., Walnut, Calif., 1969—. Instr. CPR, ARC, 1976—. Mem. Am. Assn. Respiratory Therapy (chmn. continuing edn. subcom. 1970-71), Calif. Assn. Respiratory Therapy (pres. 1972-75). Democrat. Seventh-day Adventist. Avocations: baseball, basketball, football, travel, nature. Home: 6288 Hellman Ave Alta Loma CA 91701-3416

FENNO, RICHARD FRANCIS, JR., political scientist, educator; b. Winchester, Mass., Dec. 12, 1926; s. Richard Francis and Mary Brooks (Trendennick) Fenno; m. Nancy Davidson, Sept. 10, 1948; children: Mark Richard, Craig Pierce. Student, Williams Coll., 1944-46; AB, Amherst Coll., 1948, LLD (hon.), 1986; PhD, Harvard U., 1956; LHD (hon.), Union Coll., 1989. Instr. govt. Wheaton (Mass.) Coll., 1951-53; instr. polit. sci. Amherst Coll., 1953-56, asst. prof., 1956-57; mem. faculty U. Rochester, NY, 1957—, prof., 1964—, Don Alonzo Watson prof. polit. sci., 1971-78, William R. Kenan prof. polit. sci., 1978—, Disting. Univ. prof., 1985—. Author: (book) The President's Cabinet, 1959, The Power of the Purse, 1966, Congressmen in Committees, 1973, Home Style: U.S. House Members in Their Districts, 1978 (Woodrow Wilson Found. award, 1979, D. B. Hardeman prize, 1980); author: (with F. Munger) National Politics and Federal Aid to Education, 1962; author: The Making of a Senator: Dan Quayle, 1989, The Presidential Odyssey of John Glenn, 1990, Watching Politicians, 1990, The Emergence of a Senate Leader: Pete Domenici and the Reagan Budget, 1991, Learning to Legislate: The Senate Education of Arlen Specter, 1991, When Incumbency Fails: The Senate Career of Mark Andrews, 1992; editor: The Yalta Conf., 1956, 1973, (book) Senators on the Campaign Trail: The Politics of Representation, 1996, Learning to Govern: An Institutional View of the 104th Congress, 1997, Congress at the Grassroots: Represntational Change in the South, 1970-1998, 2000, Going Home: Black Representatives and Their Constituents, 2003. With USNR, 1944—46. Rockefeller Found. fellow, 1963—64, Ford fellow, 1971—72, Guggenheim fellow, 1976—77, Russell Sage Found. grantee, 1978, 1980—85. Mem.: Am. Philos. Soc., Am. Acad. Arts and Scis., Social Sci. Rsch. Coun. (dir. 1973—75, fellow 1960—61), Nat. Acad. Scis., Am. Polit. Sci. Assn. (coun. 1971—73, v.p. 1975—76, pres. 1984—85), Phi Beta Kappa. Home: 108 Farm Brook Dr Rochester NY 14625-1519

FENSKE, EDWARD CHARLES, special education educator, consultant; b. West Palm Beach, Fla., Oct. 28, 1949; s. Edward and Frances (Frankenberger) F.; m. Susan Louise Schaeffer, Dec. 29, 1971; children: Joanna S., Melissa S. BS, U.S. Mil. Acad., 1971; MA, Trenton State Coll., 1976, EdS, 1981. Cert. tchr. handicapped, tchr. cons. learning disabilities, prin.-supr., N.J. Tchr. aide Carolyn Stokes Day Nursery, Trenton, N.J., 1974-75; child therapist Princeton (N.J.) Child Devel. Inst., 1975-76, head tchr., 1976-77, edn. program coord., 1977-95, dir. edn. programs, 1995—. Contbr. articles to profl jours.; mem. edit. rev. bd. Edn. and Treatment Children Jour., 1983. Pres. Sherbrooke II Civic League, Trenton, 1990, Ewing Girls Softall Assn., 1998-00. 1st Lt. U.S. Army, 1971-74. Mem. Coun. Exceptional Children, Autism Soc. Am. (Mercer County chpt.), Assn. for Behavior Analysis, Kappa Delta Pi. Office: Princeton Child Devel Inst 300 Cold Soil Rd Princeton NJ 08540-2002 Fax: (609) 924-4119. E-mail: info@pcdi.org.

FENSTER, SAUL K. university president emeritus; b. N.Y.C., Mar. 22, 1933; s. Samuel and Rose (Glass) F.; m. Roberta Schamis, Jan. 11, 1959; children: Deborah, Lisa, Jonathan. Student, Bklyn. Coll., 1949-51; B of Mech. Engring., CUNY, 1953; MS, Columbia U., 1955; postgrad., NYU, 1955-56; PhD, U. Mich., 1959; LLD, Rutgers U., 2002, William Paterson U., 2002; DHL (hon.), N.J. Inst. Tech., 2002. Lectr. mech. engring. CUNY, 1953-56; teaching fellow engring. mechanics U. Mich., 1956-57, with univ. Rsch. Inst., 1957-58; rsch. engr. Sperry-Rand Corp., 1959-62; prof. engring. Fairleigh Dickinson U., Teaneck, N.J., 1962-78, chmn. dept. physics, 1962-63, chmn. dept. mech. engring., 1963-70, grad. adminstrv. asst. to dean, 1965-70, assoc. dean, 1970-71, exec. asst. to pres., 1971-72, provost Rutherford campus, 1972-78; pres. N.J. Inst. Tech., Newark, 1978—2002, N.J. Inst. Tech. (Found.), 1978—2002. Bd. dirs. various Prudential Mut. Funds, IDT Corp.; vice-chmn. Bus.-Higher Edn. Forum, 1992; cons., 1962—. Author: (with Wallace Arthur) Mechanics, 1969, (with A. Cahit Ugural) Advanced Strength and Applied Elasticity, 1975, 87, 94; contbr. chpts. to books, tech. papers. Mem. Hudson River Waterfront Study and Planning Commn., 1979-80; bd. dirs. N.J. Assn. Colls. and Univs., 1980-2002, N.J. Alliance for Action, 1982-2002, R&D Coun. N.J., 1994-2002, Regional Bus. Partnership, 1994-95, Prosperity N.J., Inc., Soc. Mfg. Engrs. Edn. Found., 1998—; trustee Newark Boys Chorus Sch., 1980-84, Newark Acad., 1984-86; mem., vice chmn. N.J. Water Supply Authority, 1981-88; mem. N.J. Commn. on Sci. and Tech., 1985—; bd. govs. Union County Coll.; mem. Commn. Def. Conversion and Cmty. Assistance, 1993; mem. Commn. on Jobs, Growth and Econ. Devel., 2003—; mem. N.J. Coun. on Job Opportunities; bd. visitors Air U., 1993-98. Shell fellow U. Mich., 1957-58. Fellow ASME, Am. Soc. Engring. Edn.; mem. AAAS, Assn. Ind, Colls. and Univs. N.J. (chmn. bd. 1978-80, bd. dirs. 1980-96), Greater Newark C. of C. (bd. dirs. 1980-91), N.J. State C. of C. (bd. dirs. 1987-2002), Coun. on Competitiveness, Sigma Xi, Tau Beta Pi, Omicron Delta Kappa, Pi Tau Sigma. Home: 524 Bernita Dr Westwood NJ 07675-5902 Office: NJ Inst Tech Office of Pres University Heights Newark NJ 07102

FENTIMAN, AUDEEN WALTERS, nuclear engineer, educator; b. Athens, Ohio, Aug. 29, 1950; d. Rob Roy and Mary Frances (Bean) Walters; m. Allison F. Fentiman, June 2, 1984. BS in Math., Glenville (W.Va.) State Coll., 1972; MA in Math., W.Va. U., 1974; MS in Nuclear Engring., Ohio State U., 1977, PhD in Nuclear Engring., 1982. Tchr. math. St. Marys (W.Va.) High Sch., 1974-76; rsch. asst. Ohio State U., Columbus, 1976-79; rsch. scientist Battelle-Nuclear Systems Sect., Columbus, 1979-85; sr. engr. Battelle-Office Nuclear Waste Isolation, Columbus, 1985-87; assoc dept. mgr. Battelle-Ordnance Systems and Tech., Columbus, 1987-89; sr. specialist EG&G Mound Applied Techs., Miamisburg, Ohio, 1989-90; asst. prof. engring. graphics Ohio State U., Columbus, 1990-96, assoc. prof. civil and environ. engring., 1996—, dir. environ. sci. grad. program, 1998—2001, assoc. dean Coll. Engring., 1999—2001, chair, nuclear engring. program, 2001—, interim dir., nuclear reactor lab., 2002—. Mem. Dayton-Montgomery County Math. Collaborative, Ohio, 1989-90; mem. indsl. and profl. adv. coun. Pa. State Coll. Engring., 1989-95. Contbr. articles and abstracts to nuclear tech. Ohio Jour. Sci., Jour. Engring. Edn., Engring. Design Graphics Jour., Health Physics; author bulletins or fact sheets on low-level radioactive waste. Battelle Meml. Inst. fellow, 1982. Fellow AAAS; mem. Am. Nuclear Soc. (local sect. pres. 1991-92, bd. dirs. 2003—), Ohio Acad. Sci., Am. Soc. for Engring. Edn., Sigma Xi. Office: Ohio State U Dept Civil and Environ Engring and Geodetic Sci 2070 Neil Ave Columbus OH 43210-1226

FENTON, MARJORIE, university official, consultant; b. Warren, Ohio, Feb. 7, 1935; d. Leland Reed and Elma Arlene Titus; m. Harold W. Fenton, June 11, 1955 (div. Sept. 1984); children: Brian, Amy. BS in Edn., Kent State U., 1985, M in Edn. Adminstrn., 1988. Treas. Champion Local Sch. Dist., Warren, 1967-80, Trumbull County Joint Vocat. Sch. Dist., Warren, 1980-89; pres., cons. Sch. Mgmt. Svcs., Inc., Worthington, Ohio, 1989—; coord. Ashland U., Ohio, 1989—. Cons. Ohio Dept. Edn., Columbus, 1980—84, 1989—, Kemper Securities, Inc., 1993—94; trustee Champion Cmty. Sr. Housing, Inc., Warren, 1982—90, Trimble & Julian, Inc., 1996—98, Franklin County Ednl. Svc. Ctr., 2001—. Mem. Trumbull County Bd. Edn., Warren, 1968-93. Recipient Exemplary Service to Edn. award Champion Local Schs., Warren, 1980. Mem. Ohio Assn. Sch. Bus. Ofcls. (state pres. 1979-80, state legis. chmn. 1980-89, Pres.'s Disting. Svc. award 1984, Recognition Outstanding Svc. 1985), Assn. Sch. Bus. Ofcls. Internat. (chair profl. devel. rsch. com.), Ohio Sch. Bds. Assn., Phi Delta Kappa. Avocations: travel, reading.

FENTON, ROBERT EARL, electrical engineering educator; b. Bklyn., Sept. 30, 1933; s. Theodore Andrew and Evelyn Virginia (Brent) F.; m. Alice Earlyn Gray, Dec. 13, 1934; children: Douglas Earl, Andrea Leigh. BEE, Ohio State U., 1957, MEE, 1960, PhD in Electrical Engring., 1965. Registered profl. engr., Ohio. Engr. rsch. N. Am. Aviation, Columbus, Ohio, 1957; instr. electric engring. Ohio State U., Columbus, 1960-65, prof., 1965-95, prof. emeritus, 1995—. Cons. transp. sys. divsn. GM, Warren, Mich., 1974-80, Battelle Meml. Inst., Columbus, Ohio, 1991-93. Inventor kinesthetic-tactile display; contbr. articles to profl. jours. Capt. USAF, 1957-60. Recipient Outstanding Tchr. award Eta Kappa Nu, 1963, Neil Armstrong award Ohio Soc. Profl. Engrs., 1971, Pioneering Rsch. award Nat. Automated Hwy. Systems Consortium, 1997, Significant Achievement award Intelligent Vehicle Hwy. Sys. Ohio, 1993. Fellow IEEE (IEEE Millennium medal 2000), Radio Club Am., IEEE Vehicular Tech. Soc. (pres. 1985-87, v.p. 1983-85, treas. 1981-83, prize paper 1980, Stuart F. Meyer Meml. award 1998), NAE, Sigma Xi. Avocations: bicycling, swimming, classical music. Home: 2177 Oakmount Rd Columbus OH 43221-1229 Office: Ohio State Univ Dept Elec Engring 2015 Neil Ave Dept Elec Columbus OH 43210-1210 E-mail: fenton.2@osu.edu.

FER, AHMET F. electrical engineer, educator; b. Ankara, Turkey, July 31, 1945; came to U.S., 1959; s. Muslih F. and Hayrunnisa (Gurkan) F.; m. Esther Elizabeth Horvath, Nov. 14, 1987; children: Danyal, Adam. BSEE, Mid. East Tech. U., 1967, MSEE, 1970; PhD, U. Birmingham, Birmingham, U.K., 1975. Asst. dept. chmn. elec. engring. dept. Mid. East Tech. U., Ankara, 1979-81, asst. prof., 1975-83, assoc. prof., 1983-84; exec. sec. Engring. Rsch. div. Sci. and Tech. Rsch. Coun., Ankara, 1984-85; assoc. prof. engring. and tech. Purdue U., Indpls., 1985-91, 95-96; dir. tech. programs Inst. for Forensic Imaging Ind. U.-Purdue U., Indpls., 1998—. Permanent cons. Technalysis, Inc., Indpls., 1989-98. Contbr. Microwave Techniques, 1978; contbr. articles to profl. jours. Fund raiser Multiple Sclerosis Soc., Indpls., 1989-90; mem. electromagnetic wave propagation panel AGARD/NATO. Mem. IEEE, Scientech Club, Phi Delta Kappa. Home: 5219 Wiltonwood Ct Indianapolis IN 46254-9665 Office: IFI-IUPUI 723 W Michigan St Ste SI174 Indianapolis IN 46202-5191

FERBEL, THOMAS, physics educator, physicist; b. Radom, Poland, Dec. 12, 1937; arrived in U.S., 1949, naturalized, 1955; s. Joseph and Natalie (Gotfryd) F.; m. Barbara G. Goolnick, Apr. 20, 1963; children: Natalie, Peter Jordan. BS, Queens Coll., 1959; MS, Yale U., 1960, PhD, 1963. Research staff physicist Yale U., New Haven, 1963-65; asst. prof. physics U. Rochester, N.Y., 1965-69, assoc. prof., 1969-73, prof., 1973—, assoc. dean grad. studies, 1989-91; sci. assoc. CERN, Geneva, 1980-81. Vis. scientist cen. design group Superconducting Supercollider, Lawrence-Berkeley Lab., U. Calif., 1988-89; vis. prof. LAL, Orsay, France, 1995.U. Mainz, Germany, 2001. U. Freiburg, Germany, 2002; mem. program adv. com. Stanford Linear Accelerator Ctr., Calif., 1974-76, Brookhaven Lab., Upton, N.Y., 1981-84; exec. com. Users' Orgn. of Brookhaven Lab., 1972-74; exec. com. Fermi Nat. Accelerator Lab., 1973-75, chmn., 1986-87; sci. dir. Biennial Advanced Study Inst. on High Energy Physics, St. Croix. Author: (with A. Das) Introduction to Nuclear and Particle Physics, 1993; editor: Techniques and Concepts of High Energy Physics, Vol. 1-X, Silicon Detectors in High Energy Physics, 1982, Experimental Techniques in High Energy and Nuclear Physics, 1991; mem. editl. bd. Phys. Rev., 1978-80, Zeitschrift fur Physik, 1981-85, Internat. Jour. Modern Physics, 1995—. Recipient Alexander von Humboldt prize, 1995; Alfred P. Sloan fellow, 1970, John S. Guggenheim fellow, 1971; Particle Physics and Astronomy Rsch. Coun. sr. fellow Imperial Coll., London, 2002-03. Fellow Am. Phys. Soc. (sec.-treas. divsn. particles and fields 1983-85, chmn. com. on internat. freedom of scientists 1990-92, mem. com. on internat. sci. affairs 1999-2001). Office: U Rochester Dept Physics Rochester NY 14627

FERENCZ, CHARLOTTE, pediatrician, epidemiology and preventive medicine educator; b. Budapest, Hungary, Oct. 28, 1921; came to U.S., 1954; d. Paul Ferencz and Livia deFekete. BSc, McGill U., 1944, MD, CM, 1945; MPH, Johns Hopkins U., 1970. Cert. pediatrics Royal Coll. Physicians and Surgeons, Can., pediatric cardiology Am. Bd. Pediatrics. Demonstrator McGill U., Montreal, 1952-54; asst. prof. pediatrics Johns Hopkins U., Balt., 1954-58, U. Cin., 1959-60; asst. prof. SUNY, Buffalo, 1960-66, assoc. prof., 1966-73; assoc. prof. epidemiology and preventive medicine U. Md. Sch. Medicine, Balt., 1973-74, prof., 1974-98, prof. pediatrics, 1985—, prof. emeritus, 1998—. Prin. investigator population based study Etiology of Congenital Heart Disease, 1981-89; mem. epidemiology and disease control study sect. NIH, 1984-88; pres. Delta Omage Alpha chpt. Pub. Health Soc., 1990-92. Recipient M.E.S. Abbott scholarship McGill U., 1943-45, M.E.R.I.T. award Nat. Heart, Lung & Blood Inst.,

1987, Fogarty Internat. Ctr. Health Sci. Exchange award NIH, 1988, Helen B. Taussig award Am. Heart Assn. Md. Affiliate, 1991, Achievement award Univ. Ctr. Life Scis., Balt., 1993, Johns Hopkins U. Disting. Alumnus award, 2001. Fellow Am. Acad. Pediatrics (Spl. Achievement award Md. chpt. 1994), Am. Coll. Cardiology; mem. Teratology Soc. Democrat. Office: U Md Sch Medicine 660 W Redwood St Baltimore MD 21201-1541

FERENS, MARCELLA, educator, business executive; b. Pitts.; d. Ignatius and Marcella (Buzas) Slevinskas; student Greensburg Bus. Coll., 1934-35, Maison Frederic Cosmetology, 1936, Kree Inst. Electrolysis, N.Y., 1952; B.S., U. Pitts., 1957; postgrad. Mid-Western U., 1962; M.Ed., Duquesne U., 1964; m. Joseph J. Ferens, Nov. 27, 1937; children: Joseph Ferens, James. Cosmetologist and electrologist, Manor and Darragh, Pa., 1937—; research in hair regrowth, Darragh, 1954—; tchr. cosmotology Uniontown (Pa.) Vocat. High, 1954-55; tchr. algebra, reading and drama dir. Harold Jr. High Sch., Greensburg, Pa., 1958—; pres. Marcella Ferens Inc.; treas. Schumacher Labs. Inc., Darragh. Insp., Chem. Corps, Dept. Army, N.Y., 1951. Mem. Nat. Coun. Tchrs. Math., Nat. Edn. Assns., Pa. Edn. Assns. Patentee in field. Home: PO Box 84 Darragh PA 15625-0084

FERGUS, PATRICIA MARGUERITA, English language educator emeritus, writer, editor; b. Mpls., Oct. 26, 1918; d. Golden Maughan and Mary Adella (Smith) Fergus. BS, U. Minn., 1939, MA, 1941, PhD, 1960. Various pers. and editing positions U.S. Govt., 1943-59; mem. faculty U. Minn., Mpls., 1964-79, asst. prof. English, 1972-79, coord. writing program conf. on writing, 1975, dir. writing centre, 1975-77; prof. English and writing, dir. writing ctr., assoc. dean Coll. Mt. St. Mary's Coll., Emmitsburg, Md., 1979-81; dir. writing seminars Mack Truck, Inc., Hagerstown, Md., 1979-81; writer, 1964—. Editor, 1997—; vocal soloist, 1997—; editl. asst. to pres. Met. State U., St. Paul, 1984-85; coord. creative writing, writer program notes for Coffee Concerts, The Kenwood, 1992-94; dir. Kenwood Scribes Presentation, 1994; spkr. and cons. in field; dir. 510 Groveland Assocs.; bus. mgr. Eitel Hosp. Gift Shop; freelance manuscript editor, 1997-99; writer, reviewer Whittier Publs., Long Beach, N.Y., 1997; instr. Elderlearning Inst., 1999-2000, Univ. Coll., U. Minn., 1999-2000; poetry and prose reading, retirement cmtys., 2002-03. Author: Spelling Improvement, 5th edit., 1991; contbr. to Downtown Cath. Voice, Mpls., Mountaineer Briefing, ABI Digest, Women in the Arts The Penletter; contbr. poems to Minn. English Jour., Women in the Arts, Decatur Area Arts Coun. Newsletter, Mpls. Muse, The Moccasin, Heartsong and Northstar Gold, The Pen Woman, Midwest Chaparral, Rhyme Time, The Best of Rhyme Time, 1998, Fantasy, 1998; contbr. short stories to anthologies, including Seeking the Muses, Inspired Works of Creativity, 2000; musical works performed at St. Olaf Ch., 1997, Nat. League Am. Pen Women, 1998. Mem. spl. vocal octet St. Olaf Ch. Choir, 1977-79, 81-92, St. Olaf Parish Adv. Bd., 1982-84, Windmore Found. for the Arts., 1996. Recipient Outstanding Contbn. award U. Minn. Twin Cities Student Assembly, 1975, Horace T. Morse-Amoco Found. award, 1976; Golden Poet award World of Poetry, 1992; Ednl. Devel. grant U. Minn., 1975-76, Mt. St. Mary's Coll. grant, 1980; 3d prize vocal-choral category Nat. Music Composition Contest, Nat. League Am. Pen Women, poetry prize No. Dist. Women's Club, Va., 1996. Mem.: Midwest Fedn. Chaparral Poets (poetry judge, numerous poetry prizes including 1st prize 1998, 1999, 2001, 2003), Mpls. Poetry Soc. (pres. 2000—02, numerous poetry prizes including 1st prize 1999, 2d prize 2003), World Lit. Acad., Nat. League Am. Pen Women (Minn. br. past pres., 1st pl. Haiku nat. poetry contest 1992), Minn. Coun. Tchrs. English (chmn. career and job opportunities comm., spl. com. tchr. licensure, sec. legis. com.), Nat. Coun. Tchrs. English (regional judge 1974, 1976—77, state coord. 1977—79), Mpls. Woman's Club (critic writers group). Roman Catholic. Home and Office: # 612 3535 Bryant Ave S Minneapolis MN 55408-4134

FERGUSON, BETTIE JEAN, secondary education educator; b. Boise, Idaho, July 29, 1935; d. Benjamin Jackson and Louise M. (Radke) Hoyt; m. Jerry C. Ferguson, July 30, 1957; children: Jeri Lou Timmons, Bonnie Nichols, Scott Ferguson. BA, Albertson Coll. Idaho, 1957; MA in History, Ctrl. Wash. U., 1990. Social studies, English tchr. Homedale (Idaho) High Sch., 1957-59, Boise (Idaho) S. Jr. High Sch., 1959-60; English tchr. Sunnyside (Wash.) High Sch., 1960-63, Grandview (Wash.) H.S., 1966-78, history and English tchr., 1978—. Mem. Grandview Cmty. Libr. Bd., 1980-90; chmn. Grandview Curriculum Coun., 1990-92. Campfire leader Campfire Girls, Grandview, Wash., 1969-74; bldg. rep. H!Grandview (Wash.) Edn. Assn., 1990—; mem of deacons Bethany Presbyn. Ch., Grandview, Wash., 1980-83, bd. elders, 1985-87, 93—. Named Grandview (Wash.) Secondary Tchr. of Yr Grandview Sch. Dist., 1986-87. Mem. PEO, Delta Kappa Gamma. Republican. Presbyterian. Avocations: reading, travel, bridge, golf, skiing. Home: 6291 N Charleston Pl Boise ID 83703-2606

FERGUSON, CLEVE ROBERT, lawyer, educator; b. Long Beach, Calif., Dec. 31, 1938; s. Frank H and Ruth S Ferguson; m. Kathryn Jane Weaver, Apr. 10, 1965 (div. June 25, 1995); children: Sharon Anne, Robert Timothy; m. Peggy Burke Daniell, Nov. 19, 1995. AB in Econs., U. So. Calif., 1961, JD, 1965. Bar: Calif 1966, US Dist Ct (cent dist) Calif 1966, US Ct Appeals (9th cir) 1987, US Supreme Ct 1975. Assoc. Musick, Peeler & Garrett, L.A., 1965-69, Hayes & Hume, Beverly Hills, Calif., 1969-74; pvt. practice Pasadena/Claremont, Calif., 1974—; adj. prof. physics and astronomy U. La Verne (Calif.), 1993—; pres., CEO Mars Manned Mission Corp.; adj. prof. Coll. Law U. La Verne (Calif.), 1994—2001. Mem. alcohol and drug abuse com. Calif. State Bar, 1990—91; instr. astronomy and bus. law Chapman U., 1992—93; arbitrator Am. Arbitration Assn., Nat. Arbitration Forum; lectr. in field; instr. telescope use and telescope optics UCLA, U. Calif., Irvine. Editor: (book) Tall Tales and Memories, 1987. Mem. Stony Ridge Obs., 1985—, pres., 1994—97; co-founder, bd govs. Mt. Wilson Inst., Calif., 1987, co-founder, trustee, 2003—; lectr., cons. Mcpl. Officers for Redevel. Reform, Calif., 1996—; mem. L.A. Opera League; bd. dirs. Clan Fergusson Soc. N.Am., 1987—2000. With U.S. Army, 1961—62. Decorated Knights Templar of Jerusalem, Grand Priory of the Scots. Fellow: Soc. Antiquaries Scotland; mem.: Sons of the Revolution, Univ. Club Pasadena, Beta Theta Pi (past pres). Avocations: astronomy, mountaineering, dry fly fishing, skiing. Office: C Robert Ferguson Atty at Law 237 W 4th St Claremont CA 91711-4710 Office Fax: 909-624-7291. E-mail: crflawyer@earthlink.net., crf@marsmannedmission.org.

FERGUSON, JENNIFER LEE BERRY, education educator, educator; b. Houston, Feb. 4, 1946; d. Carnie Delton and Martha June (McAlexander) Berry; m. David Eugene Wilson Jr., May 31, 1968 (div. Apr. 1978); m. Jerry Duane Ferguson, Dec. 12, 1982; 1 child, Shawn Berry Benton. BA, Houston Bapt. U., 1969; MEd, Stephen F. Austin U., 1979; EdD, U. Houston. Cert. tchr., Tex. Tchr., coach Aldine Ind. Sch. Dist., Houston, 1968-75, Spring Br. Ind. Sch. Dist., Houston, 1975-86; grad. asst. Stephen F. Austin U., Nacogdoches, Tex., 1978-79; prof. Houston Bapt. U., 1986—. Presenter in field. Active Houston Jr. League, 1987—; exec. coun. dist. IV Nat. Assn. Intercollegiate Athletics, 1990-93; vol. Houston Heritage Soc., 1989—. Mem. AAHPERD, Tex. Assn. Health, Phys. Edn., Recreation and Dance, Phi Mu (advisor, 1989—, v.p. alumni 1990-92, pres. 1992-95, area alumni bd. dirs. 1995—), Kappa Delta Pi, Delta Psi Kappa. Baptist. Avocations: interior decorating, sewing, choreography, cooking. Home: 2910 Kismet Ln Houston TX 77043-1322

FERGUSON, JOHN BARCLAY, biology educator; b. Balt., July 5, 1947; s. John Miller and Helen (Sucro) F.; m. Jane Hough, June 28, 1970 (div. 1987); children: Hallam H., Gillian D.; m. Valeri J. Thomson, July 1, 1988; children: Samantha T., Fiona T. BS, Brown U., 1969; PhD, Yale U., 1973. Asst. prof. Bard Coll., Annandale, NY, 1977-83, assoc. prof., 1983-92, prof., 1992—, health professions advisor, 1985—. Contbr. to Microsoft Encarta 97 CD-ROM, 1 book and articles to profl. jours. Bd. trustees Ch. St. John Evangelist, Barrytown, N.Y., 1988—. NIH Postdoctoral fellow, 1974-76. Mem. AAAS, Am. Soc. Microbiology, N.Y. Acad. Scis., Sigma Xi. Home: 1 W Bard Ave Red Hook NY 12571-1109 Office: Bard Coll Dept Biology Annandale On Hudson NY 12504 E-mail: ferguson@bard.edu.

FERGUSON, JOHN DUNCAN, medical research educator; b. Saskatoon, Sask., Can., Aug. 20, 1929; s. George Alexander and Urdine (LeValley) F.; m. Tamara van den Bergh, Sept. 12, 1958. MA, U. Toronto, Ont., Can., 1956; PhD, Columbia U., 1966. Project dir. Bur. Applied Social Rsch., Columbia U., N.Y.C., 1958-64; asst. prof. Northeastern U., Boston, 1966-68; from assoc. prof. to prof. U. Windsor, Ont., 1968—; mem. assoc. med. staff Harper Hosp., Detroit, 1982-2000, rsch. cons., 2000—. Author reports in field. Grantee Ont. Cmty. and Social Svcs. Ministry, 1991-93. Presbyterian. Home: 1516 Iroquois Ave Detroit MI 48214-2747 Office: U Windsor Windsor ON Canada N9B 3P4 E-mail: tamjackferg@worldnet.att.net.

FERGUSON, JOHN FRANKLIN, music educator; b. Council Bluffs, Iowa, Jan. 18, 1942; s. Ora Franklin and Francis Elizabeth (Sprague) F.; m. Cynthia Claire Hauge, June 21, 1969; children: Klaus, Erik, Scott. Student, Western Oreg. State Coll., 1960-62, Tchr. Tng. Inst., 1963-64; MusB, U. Oreg., 1966; MusM, U. Idaho, 1969. Dir. high sch. and elem. band Riddle (Oreg.) Sch. Dist., 1966-67; dir. concert band U. Idaho, Moscow, 1967-68, supr. undergrad. directed studies in music edn., 1967-68; music specialist elem. sch. Sutherlin (Oreg.) Sch. Dist., 1968-78; salesman Ricketts Music Store, Roseburg, Oreg., 1978-87; music specialist elem. sch. Roseburg Sch. Dist., 1987—. Dir. Roseburg Barbershop Chorus, 1973-77, Roseburg German Band, 1981—; mem. Ch. Choir, Roseburg, 1970—, Vintage Singers, Roseburg, 1991-93. Mem. Music Educators Nat. Conf., Masons. Republican. Presbyterian. Avocations: fishing, water skiing, travel, hunting, tennis. Home: 128 W Bodie St Roseburg OR 97470-2308

FERGUSON, JULIE ANN, physical education educator; b. Maquoketa, Iowa, June 19, 1958; d. Donald Hayes and Bonnie Lea (Bullock) Maxey; m. John Stephan Ferguson, Aug. 10, 1985; children: Dawn Ann, John Ryan, John Scott. BS in Edn., U. Mo., 1980; MS in Athletic Adminstrn., U. Ill., 1982. Cert. tchr. Mo. Sub. tchr. Ritenour Dist., St. Louis, 1978-80; asst. women's basketball coach U. Ill., Champaign, 1980-82, instr. phys. edn., 1981-82, adminstrv. asst. Athletic Assn., 1982-83; dir. championships, supr. officials Big Eight Conf., Kansas City, Mo., 1983-90; instr. phys. edn., head volleyball and girls basketball coach Lee's Summit (Mo.) Sch. Dist., 1990—. Speaker, clin. coord. Fellowship Christian Athletes, Kansas City, 1986; selection com. U. Mo., Kansas City, 1987, 88; scholar athlete Kansas City Star, 1989; coach, tour adminstr. Athletes in Action Basketball Team to China and Far East, 1984; tour adminstr. Big Eight Conf. Basketball Tour to Czechoslovakia, 1990. Deacon Lee's Summit Christian Ch., 1990-. Named to, Ritenour H.S. Hall of Fame, 1998. Mem. (life) U. Mo. Columbia Alumni Assn., (life) U. Ill. Alumni Assn., Women's Basketball Coaches Assn., Am. Volleyball Coaches Assn., Coun. Collegiate Women Athletic Adminstrs., Am. Alliance Health, Physical Edn., Recreation and Dance Fellowship Christian Athletes (Tchr. of Yr. finalist Lee's Summit Sch. Dist. 1997—, Excellence in Tchg. award). Avocations: horseback riding, cross stitch, sports, family. Home: 4151 SE Paddock Cir Lees Summit MO 64082-4926

FERGUSON, MARTHA ANN, elementary school educator; b. Pitts., Apr. 3, 1947; d. Edward Lawrence and Mary I. (Livingston) Hora; m. June 14, 1969 (div.); 1 child, Matthew Lawrence. BA in English, Calif. State U., Long Beach, 1969; postgrad., UCLA, Pepperdine U., 1970—, Marymount Loyola U., 1987—; Cert. Lang. Devel., 1994; M in Classroom Guidance, U. LaVerne, 1997. Lang. devel. spl. cert. Tchr. kindergarten Lawndale (Calif.) Sch. Dist., 1970-73, tchr. first grade, 1973-74, early childhood educator, 1974-81, tchr. intermediate, 1981-92, tchr. bilingual, 1992—. Math. chair Lawndale Sch. Dist., 1987—, math. mentor, 1987-90; trainer Tchr. Expectations and Student Achievement, 1980—; family math. trainer L.A.C.O.E., 1988—, Nat. Coun. Tchrs. Math. Assn., 1987—; master tchr. Loyola Marymount U., Calif. State U., Dominguez, 1985—; equals math. trainer, 1989—; cons. Program Quality Rev., 1998—; participant Tech. Cohort, 2000—, Lucent/UCLA Algebra Project, 1999—. Mem. NEA, 1978—, NEA Polit. Action Com., Washington, 1980—, NEA Equity Watch, Washington, 1984—. Recipient scholarship Valley Forge Freedom Found., 1987. Mem. AAUW, Nat. Coun. Tchrs. Math., Calif. Assn. Bilingual Educators, Lawndale Tchrs. Assn. (pres. 1979-84, grievance chair 1987-91, negotiations chair 1980-86, v.p. 1989-91), Calif. Tchrs. Assn. (state coun. rep. 1981-94, credentials and profl. devel. com. 1983-94, competancy panel 1986, apptd. to elections and credentials com. 1994-98), Internat. Reading Assn. Democrat. Avocations: travel, reading, politics, lang. Home: 810 E Grand Ave Apt A El Segundo CA 90245-4130 Office: William Green Elem Sch 4520 W 168th St Lawndale CA 90260-3246

FERGUSON, PAMELA ANDERSON, mathematics educator, educational administrator; b. Berwyn, Ill., May 5, 1943; d. Clarence Oscar and Ruth Anne (Stroner) Anderson; m. Donald Roger Ferguson, Dec. 18, 1965; children: Keith, Amanda. BA, Wellesley Coll., 1965; MS, U. Chgo., 1966, PhD, 1969. Asst. prof. Northwestern U., Evanston, Ill., 1969—70, U. Miami, Coral Gables, Fla., 1972—77, assoc. prof., 1978—81, prof. math., 1981—91, dir. honors program, 1985—87, assoc. provost, dean Grad. Sch., 1987—91; pres. Grinnell Coll., Iowa, 1991—97, prof. math., 1991—2003, Breid McFarland prof. of sci., 2003—. Mem. Nat. Sci. Bd., 1998—2004; vis. com. phys. scis. divsn. U. Chgo., 1996—. Contbr. articles to profl. jours. Mem. Iowa Rsch. Coun., 1993—97. Grantee NSF grantee. Mem.: Am. Women in Math., Am. Math. Soc., Wellesley Club, Phi Beta Kappa, Omicron Delta Chi, Sigma Xi. Lutheran. Avocations: hiking, reading, skiing. Office: Grinnell Coll Dept Math PO Box 805 Grinnell IA 50112-0805

FERGUSON, RICHARD L. educational administrator; Pres. Am. Coll. Testing Program, Iowa City. Office: Am Coll Testing Program Instl Srvcs 2201 N Dodge St Iowa City IA 52243-0001

FERGUSON, WANDA RENEE, art educator; b. South Boston, Va., Dec. 6, 1954; d. Owen Coleman and Ruby Ann (Hall) F. BS in Art Edn., Radford U., 1976. Sales rep. W Atlee Burpee Co., Warminster, Pa., 1978-80; territory mgr. Am. Express Corp., Richmond, Va., 1980-84; regional sales mgr., asst. v.p. Signet Bank, Richmond, Va., 1984-86; account exec. Control Data Corp., Richmond, 1987-90; art educator Elkhardt Mid. Sch., Richmond, 1990—. Art instr. Richmond City Schs. Artists of sculptures and paintings at various shows. Vol., Big Bros./Big Sisters, 1978-81, 84-86; steering com. Va. Environ. Assembly, Richmond, 1989, vol. chair, 1989. Mem. Richmond Craftsman's Guild (sec., bd. dirs. 1989—, pres. 1990-92), Metro. Artists Assn., Sierra Club (Chair polit. com. 1989—, exec. com. 1991-92), Control Data K Club. Methodist. Home: 3705 Floyd Ave Richmond VA 23221-2615 Office: Elkhardt Mid Sch 6300 Hull Street Rd Richmond VA 23224-2632

FERGUSON, WENDELL, private school educator; b. Sandersville, Ga., May 6, 1954; d. Isadore and Willie Mae (Roberts) Jordan; m. Larry Brown Sr., May 28, 1971 (div. Dec. 1985); children: Larry Brown Jr., Dwyne Lamont Brown, Anthony Patrick Brown; m. Jerry Lang Ferguson, Sept. 28, 1992 (div.). Diploma, Alphena C.C., 1972; student, Ga. State U., 1983-87. Sales clk. U.S. NAS, Albany, Ga., 1972-74, 76-77; substitute tchr. Ga. Dept. Edn., Houston County, 1976-77; nutritionist (nursery) Howard AFB, Panama Canal, 1980; joined Sweet Adelines, Inc., Tulsa, 1981; data entry operator dept. budget mgmt. Atlanta City Hall, 1982; mgr., operator Atlanta Connections, 1982-83; asst. supr. micro-film Ga. Dept. Revenue, Atlanta, 1986-88; promotional sales rep. RG Clothier/L.B. Holyfield, Atlanta, 1992-95; substitute tchr. Old Nat. Christian Acad., College Park, Ga., 1995—; loan broker Cherokee Funding Inc., Thomaston, Ga., 1989—; owner, wholesale dist. Dells' Clevor Enterprises, 2000. Libr. YWCA, Rochester, N.Y., 1999; co-prodr., writer, owner Jeri-Del Prodns., Atlanta. Actress, singer, dancer various prodns. (Irving Berlin award 1982); author: Times In Life, 1996. Vol. persona bus. broker Asst. Sec. of State, Atlanta, 1994, J.D. Sims Recreation Ctr., 2000, Atlanta; Gospel Fest judge, 1995, coord. nominees judgeship position Fayette, Pike, Upson & Spaulding Counties, Ga., 1992; surveyor for st. lights, Atlanta, 1982; vol. Fulton County Dept. Parks and Recreation, Burdett Gym, 1996—; active We Are Today and Tomorrow; founder Steadfast Children Learning Systems Atlanta Coalition of Chs., 1997. Recipient Gold Citizens Acheivement award Mayor William Campbell, 1997, Outstanding People of 20th Century, Internat. Biog. Assn. Democrat. Avocations: horseback riding, chess, painting, cooking, tennis. Home: Fergusons' Entertainment PO Box 492383 College Park GA 30349 E-mail: dellthangs@aol.com.

FERGUSSON, FRANCES DALY, college president, educator; b. Boston, Oct. 3, 1944; d. Francis Joseph and Alice (Storrow) Daly. BA, Wellesley Coll., 1965; MA, Harvard U., 1966, PhD, 1973; DLitt, U. Hartford, 2000, U. London, 2001. Asst. prof. Newton Coll., Mass., 1969—75; assoc. prof. U. Mass., Boston, 1974—82, asst. chancellor, 1980—82; provost, prof. Bucknell U., Lewisburg, Pa., 1982—86; pres. Vassar Coll., Poughkeepsie, NY, 1986—. Bd. dirs. HSBC Bank N. Am., 1990—. bd. dirs., Foreign Policy Assn. Bd. overseers Harvard U., 2002—; trustee Mayo Found., 1988—2002, chair, 1998—2002; trustee Ford Found., 1989—2001, Historic Hudson, 1990—99. Recipient Founder's award Soc. Archtl. Historians, 1973, Eleanor Roosevelt at Val-Kill medal, 1998, Centennial medal Harvard Grad. Sch. of Arts and Scis., 1999. Fellow: Am. Acad. Arts and Scis.; mem.: Fgn. Policy Assn. (bd. dirs. 2003—). Avocation: piano. Office: Vassar Coll PO Box 1 Poughkeepsie NY 12604-0001

FERNANDER, KAREN GENEINE, secondary school educator; b. Ft. Lauderdale, Fla., Feb. 18, 1957; d. Wilbur Franklin and Gloria Elaine (Chunn) Fernander. BA, Wesleyan Coll., Macon, Ga., 1978; MS, Nova U., Ft. Lauderdale, Fla., 1987. Cert. tchr. Fla. Author: (book) Hired Help, 1996. Charter mem. Dem. Women's Club of Ctrl. Broward, Ft. Lauderdale, 1990—91; mem. Dem. Exec. Com., Broward County, 1995—96; bd. dirs. Gwen Cherry Polit. Caucus, Ft. Lauderdale, 1988—90. Recipient Plaque for Svc./MAC chair, Broward Tchrs. Union, Tamarac, Fla., 1990. Mem.: Fla. Edn. Assn. (minority leadership cert. trainer 2001—), Broward Tchrs. Union (area v.p. 1985—, mem. exec. bd. 1985—). Democrat. Baptist. Avocations: travel, snorkeling, theater. Home: 27 SW 7th Ave Dania FL 33004

FERNANDEZ, HENRY A. lawyer, consultant; b. Bklyn., Dec. 5, 1949; s. Henry and Pura (Perez) F. BA Sociology, St. John's U., 1971; student, Empire State Military Acad. Army Reserve Nat. Guard, Peekskill, N.Y., 1972-73; JD, Bklyn. Law Sch., 1977. Bar: N.Y. 1978, U.S. Dist. Ct. (so. and ea. dists.) N.Y. 1978, U.S. Dist. Ct. (no. dist.) N.Y. 1981. Supr. Hornblower & Weeks Hemphill-Noyes, 1967-72; ednl. counselor, devel. exec. Aspira of N.Y. and Am., Inc., 1972-74; field placement counselor Bur. Coop. Edn. N.Y.C. Bd. Edn., 1974-75; dir. Coll. Adapter Program Higher Edn. Devel. Fund, 1975-77; vis. atty., grad. honors fellow Puerto Rican Legal Defense and Edn. Fund Inc., 1977-79; staff atty. Williamsburg Legal Svcs., 1979-81; asst. counsel N.Y. State Office Mental Health, 1981-86; dir. adminstrn. Capital Dist. Psych. Ctr., 1986-88; dir. Bur. Investigation and Audit N.Y. State Office Mental Health, 1988; state rev. officer N.Y. State Edn. Dept., 1990-93; dep. commr. U. State N.Y., 1988-93; pres., CEO Assn. of Univ. Programs in Health Adminstrn., Arlington, Va., 1993-98; mng. dir. KPMG/Peat Marwick LLP, Atlanta, Ga., 1998—. Bd. dirs., pres. Coun. Licensure Enforcement & Regulation, program com., fin. com. 1989, vice chair fin. com. 1989-90, pres.-elect 1991-92, treas. 1991-92, pres. 1992-93; nat. bd. cert. Occpl. Therapy, 1994—. Mem. N.Y. State Coun. Grad. Med. Edn., 1990-93; bd. dirs. N.Y. State Divsn. Youth Independent rev. bd., 1977-88, Legal Aid Soc. Northeastern N.Y., chair labor rels. com., exec., policy, nomination com., 1984-89. Recipient Disting. Svc. Citation N.Y. State Chiropractic Assn., 1991, Presdl. Citation Assn. Architects, AIA, 1991; Hispanic Health Leadership fellow Nat. Coalition Hispanic Health and Human Svc. Orgns., Kellogg Found., 1990-91; DeGray Meml. scholar St. John's U., 1967-71; Bklyn. Law Sch. scholar, 1973-77. Fellow N.Y. Acad. Medicine, N.Y. State Bar Found.; mem. N.Y. State Bar Assn. (chair com. Minorities in Profession 1990-94, Labor and Employment law sect. 1982-92, com. Mental and Phys. Disabilities 1986-88, com. atty. professionalis 1989-92, Action Unit 4 1993-94), Puerto Rican Bar Assn. (Capital dist. chpt. pres. 1986-88), N.Y. Health Careers (adv. coun.), Coun. State Govs. (exec. com. 1992-93, VA bd. nursing home adminstrn. 1993-97), Coalition Hispanic Health Human Svc. Orgn. (sec., bd. dirs. 1994—), AIHA, Inst. for Diversity. Home: 211 Colonial Homes Dr NW Atlanta GA 30309-1262 Office: KPMG/Peat Marwick LLP 303 Peachtree St NE Ste 2000 Atlanta GA 30308-3261

FERNANDEZ, MARTIN ANDREW, secondary school educator; b. Gary, Ind., Dec. 5, 1969; s. Luther Fritz and Martha June (Yingling) F. BA in Edn., Olivet Nazarene U., Kankakee, Ill., 1992; MS, Purdue Univ., 2002. Cert. tchr. English/Spanish, Ind. From server to mgr. Wingfield's Restaurant, Chesterton, Ind., 1988-95; custodian Duneland Cmty. Ch., Chesterton, 1991-97; tchr. North Newton H.S., Morocco, Ind., 1993—2000, Lafayette Jefferson H.S., Lafayette, Ind., 2000—. Vacation bible sch. leader Duneland Ch. of Nazarene, Chesterton, 1993-95; drama dir., sr. class sponsor, N. Newton H.S., Morocco, 1994—, retention com. mem. 1995-96. Hon. mem. FFA, N. Newton H.S., 1996. Mem. Nat. Coun. Tchrs. of English, Ind. State Tchrs. Assn. (rep. 1993—). Republican. Avocations: golf, tennis, reading, acting, jigsaw puzzles. Office: Lafayette Jefferson HS 1801 S 18th St Lafayette IN 47905-8267 Home: 826 Harrington Dr Lafayette IN 47909-6263

FERNANDEZ, RICARDO R. university administrator; b. Santurce, P.R., Dec. 11, 1940; s. Ricardo F. and Margarita (Marchese) F.; m. Patricia M. Kleczka, Aug. 7, 1965; children: Ricardo F., Amanda M., Daniel E., David R., Jose M. BA, Marquette U., 1962, MA, 1965, Princeton U., 1967, PhD, 1970. Asst. prof. Marquette U., Milw., 1968-70, U. Wis., Milw., 1973, assoc. prof., 1978-90, prof. ednl. policy, 1990, asst. vice chancellor; pres. CUNY Herbert H. Lehman Coll., Bronx, 1990—. Pres. Nat. Assn. Bilingual Edn., 1980-81; fellow ACE, 1981-82; chmn. bd. dirs. Hispanic Ednl. Telecommunicaton Sys.; chmn. Bronx Ednl. Alliance. Co-author: Reducing the Risk, 1989, Effective Desegregation Strategies, 1983, IEM, 1992. Bd. dirs. P.R. Legal Def. and Edn. Fund; chmn. bd. dirs. Jerome Park Conservancy. Recipient Promesa Cmty. Svc. award 1992, Ednl. Excellence award Com. Noiembre, award Nat. Soc. Hispanic MBAs, 2002; fellow Nat. Ctr. Effective Secondary Schs., 1986-87. Mem. Hispanic Assn. of Colls. and Univs. (bd. dirs., P. Gus Cárdenas award 2000), Intercultural Devel. Rsch. Assn., Am. Assn. for Higher Edn. Office: CUNY Herbert H Lehman Coll 250 Bedford Park Blvd W Bronx NY 10468-1527 E-mail: rrf@ehman.cuny.edu.*

FERNANDEZ-ARRONDO, MARIA DEL CARMEN, secondary education educator; b. Guines, Cuba, Mar. 26, 1931; came to U.S., 1960; d. Guillermo and Amada (Mendiandua) Fernandez-Arrondo; m. Santiago J. Fernandez-Pichs, Jan. 16, 1954; children: Santiago Sam Fernandez, Julio G. Fernandez. BA, U. Havana, 1953, Pacific U., Oregon, 1965; MA, Pacific U., 1969; postgrad., U. Calif. Riverside. Cert. Spanish/polit. sci. tchr., Calif. Educator of gifted and talented, 1970-89; faculty Desert Sands U. Sch. Dist., 1965-90; tchr. Indio (Calif.) High Sch., 1965-88, Palm Desert (Calif.) High Sch., 1988-90. Chmn. Fgn. Lang. dept. IndioHigh Sch., 1977-82; advisor Spanish Honor Soc., 1970-89. Co-author: The Tutor System, Books 1 and 2, 1976 (patentee), The New Spanish System, 1969. Named Outstanding Tchr. Indio High Sch., 1980, Tchr. of Month Indio High Sch. Student Body, 1986; recipient Golden Apple Desert Sands Tchr. Assn.,

1988, Achievement award Bd. Edn., Desert Sands U. Sch. Dist., 1990. Mem. Calif. Tchrs. Assn. (life), NEA, Am. Assn. Tchrs. of Spanish and Portugese, Desert Sands Tchrs. Assn., Delta Kappa Gamma. Republican. Roman Catholic. Avocations: reading, writing poetry, travel.

FEROZ, EHSAN HABIB, accounting educator, researcher, writer; b. Chittagong, Bangladesh, Jan. 9, 1952; came to U.S., 1979, permanent resident, 1983, naturalized, 1990; s. Mohammad Obaidul and Sabera (Begum) Hakim; m. Kishwar Sultana Beg, Oct. 16, 1982; children: Rubens, Jonas, Amran. BA with honours, U. Dacca, 1972, MA first class first, 1974; MA, Carleton U., 1978; PhD, U. Chgo., 1982. Cert. fraud examiner; cert. govt. fin. mgr. Asst. prof. acctg. SUNY, Buffalo, 1983-86; asst. prof. acctg. CUNY, Baruch, 1986-89; vis. asst. prof. acctg. Carlson Sch. of Mgmt. U. Minn., 1989-91, assoc. prof. acctg., assoc. mem. grad. faculty, 1991-93, prof. acctg., assoc. mem. grad. faculty, 1993—. Invited guest Ctr. For Internat. Studies, MIT, 1979; disting. faculty mentor U. Minn., 1990, 91; faculty mentor sch. bus. and econs., mem. honors and awards com., dean search com., outcome measures com., student behavior judiciary com., libr. policy com. U. Minn., Duluth, spl. project assoc. of vice-chancellor for acad. adminstrn., spring, 1995; invited presenter Jour. Acctg. Rsch. Conf., 1991; invited nominator Seidman Disting. Award in Polit. Economy, 1991, 92. Contbr. numerous articles to profl. jours., including Advances in Acctg., Acctg. Horizons, Australian Jour. Mgmt., Acctg. Orgns. and Soc., Acctg. Rev., Jour. Acctg. Rsch., Jour. Bus. Fin. and Acctg., Pub. Adminstrn. Quarterly, Fin. Accountability and Mgmt., Jour. Acctg. Abstracts, IEEE Transactions on Neural Networks, Encyclopedic Dictionary of Acctg.; mem. editl. bd. Internat. Jour. Acctg., Internat. Jour. Acctg. and Bus. Soc., Rsch. in Govtl. and Non Profit Acctg. Bd. dirs. Duluth Children's Mus., 1996—; mem. affirmative action rev. com. Minn. Edn. Assn., 1996-98. Mem. Assn. Govt. Accts., Assn. Cert. Fraud Examiners, Acad. Internat. Bus., Am. Acctg. Assn. (rsch. com. GNP sect. 1982-93, fin. com. 1992), Minn. Coun. Acctg. Educators. Avocations: walking, swimming, classical music. Office: U Minn-Dept Acctg 125 Sch Bus and Econs 10 University Dr Duluth MN 55812-2403

FERRANTE, OLIVIA ANN, retired educator, consultant; b. Revere, Mass., Nov. 9, 1948; d. Guy and Mary Carmella (Prizio) F. BA, Regis Coll., 1970; MEd, Boston Coll., 1971, postgrad., 1977-81, Middlebury Coll., 1974, Lesley Coll., 1982. Cert. history tchr., tchr. of blind. Chmn. Braille dept. Nat. Braille Press, Boston, 1971-74; tchr. of visually impaired, spl. needs dept. Revere H.S., 1974-92. Steven J. Rich scholarship com., 1993—; cons. Revere PTA, 1984—. Contbr. articles to profl. jours. Vol. Morgan Meml., Boston, 1983—, tchr. braille, 1993—, tchr. literacy program, 1993—; mem. Revere Com. for Handicapped Affairs, 1985—, Everett (Mass.) Chorus, 1974-76, Adult Music Ministry, 1989, Revere First Com., 1993, publicist; soloist Revere Music Makers, 1977-79; mem. partnership com. Internat. Year Disabled, 1980-81; mem. adult choir Immaculate Conception Ch., 1966—, lectr., 1995—, cantor, 1997; publicist Revere Commn. on Disabilities, 1985—, Revere Hist. Commn., 1996—, Cath. Daus., SHARE, 1995—, A Woman's Concern, 1996; mem. adv. bd. Mass. Commn. of Blind, 1988—, governing bd. on ind. living, 1989; access monitor Mass. Orgn. on Disability, 1988—; mem. adv. bd. Radio Reading Svc. for Blind, 1989; mentor Nat. Braille Literacy Project, 1992, Braille Lib., 1995—; mem. Friends of the Sick Children's Trust, 1992; vol. Birthright, 1992, ProLife Office, 1992; active Arts Coun. Coop, 1992—; mentor Vision Found., 1993—; friend Wang Ctr., 1993—, Boston Pub. Garden and Common, 1993—, Boston Pops, 1992—; mem. mobility adv. bd. Mass. Com. for Blind, 1994—; mem. Historic Mass., 1994—, Cath. League, 1994—; friend Paul Revere House, 1994—; mem. Peregrine Fund, 1994—, Ctr. for Marine Preservation, 1994—; sponsor Rite of Cath. Initiation for Adults, 1995—; publicist Next Door Theater Group, 1996, Animal Umbrella Cat Shelter, 2003—; mem. access task force Revere Pub. Libr., 1996; mem. Revere 2000 Com., 1998-99. Mem. NEA, Internat. Soc. for Endangered Cats, Mass. Tchrs. Assn. Revere Tchrs. Assn., Nat. Space Soc., Nat. Cath. Assn. for Persons with Visual Impairment, Cath. Daus. of Am. (publicist), Soc. Bl. Kateri Tekakwitha, 1997, Friends of Revere Pub. Libr., Friends of Librs. for Blind, Friends of Boston Symphony Orch., Nat. Writers Union, Amnesty Internat., Soc. Creative Anachronism, Women Affirming Life, Michael Crawford Internat. Fan Assn., Revere Soc. for Cultural and Hist. Preservation (publicist, life mem., v.p. 1998—, chmn. grants com. 1998, 2000 com., 1998), Chelsea Hist. Soc., Mass. Aviation Hist. Soc., Brian Boitano Fan Club, Barry Manilow Fan Club, Michael Feinstein Fan Club, Feregrine Fund, Paul Revere House, Greater Lynn Arts and Crafts Soc.. Roman Catholic. Avocations: travel, music, swimming, ice skating, crafts. Home: 115 Reservoir Ave Revere MA 02151-5825 Office: Revere High Sch Spl Needs Dept 101 School St Revere MA 02151-3099

FERRARA, FRANK GREGORY, middle school educator; b. Bklyn., Aug. 11, 1952; s. Frank William and Gloria (Rossicone) F. BA in English, SUNY, Stony Brook, 1974, MA in Liberal Arts, 1987, postgrad., 1974-90; cert., SUNY, New Paltz, 1976. Cert. secondary English tchr., N.Y. Group leader Brookhaven Country Day Sch., Yaphank, N.Y., 1972-87; substitute tchr. Longwood Schs., Middle Island, N.Y., 1976-78, secondary English tchr., 1978—. Foster parent, N.Y. State, 1990-92, Childreach, 1994-95; vol. SUNY-Stony Brook Med. Ctr., 1989; active Longwood Schs. PTA, 1978—, mentor for gifted program, 1996—. Mem. Soc. Children's Book Writers. Roman Catholic. Avocations: writing, children, educational policy decision making, music, nephews. Office: Longwood Mid Sch Yaphank-Middle Island Rd Middle Island NY 11953

FERRARA, JAMES LAWRENCE MICHAEL, medical educator, physician, scientist; b. N.Y.C., Dec. 17, 1952; s. Lawrence Andrew and Mary Theresa (Fichter) F.; m. Flora Eleanor Viola Watson, June 27, 1981; children: Andrew, David, Michael. Diploma d'etudes, La Sorbonne, Paris, 1973; AB summa cum laude with honors, Xavier U., 1974; MA, Oxford U., 1976; MD cum laude, Georgetown U., 1980. Diplomate Am. Bd. Pediat. Intern in pediatrics Children's Hosp., Boston, 1980, resident in pediatrics, 1981; fellow pediatric hematology/oncology Children's Hosp. and Dana-Farber Cancer Inst., Boston, 1982, rsch. fellow pediatric hematology/oncology, 1983; rsch. fellow pediatrics Harvard Med. Sch., 1982, clin. instr. pediatrics, 1980, 85, asst. prof. pediatrics, 1987, assoc. prof. pediatrics, 1993; pediat. oncologist Dana Farber Cancer Inst., 1985-98; prof. medicine and pediatrics U. Mich. Med. Sch., 1998; dir. bone marrow transplant program U. Mich. Cancer Ctr., 1998. Lectr. Sydney, 1992, Munich, 1993, Chustchuch, New Zealand, 1993, Okayama, Japan, 1996, Innsbruck, Austria, 1997, Geneva, 1997, Bologna, 2000, Stockholm, 2001, Beijing, 2001, Seoul, 2002, Rio de Janiero, 2002. Author (with others): Graft Versus Host Disease, 1990, 2nd edit., 1996; editor Hematology Revs. and Comm., 1985, Transplantation, 1988, Jour. Immunology, 1993, Transplantation Immunology, 1993, Bone Marrow Transplantation, 1994; contbr. numerous articles to profl jours., chpts. to books. Recipient Physician Sci. award NIH, 1985, Stohlman scholar Leukemia Soc. Am., 1997, Alexander von Humoldt award, 1998, Doris Duke Disting. Clin. Scientist award, 2002; Am. Cancer Soc. Rsch. grantee, 1991, NIH grantee, 1992, 93. Mem. NIH (study sect. 1996), Am. Assn. Immunologists, Am. Soc. Hematology, Am. Soc. Clin. Investigation, Soc. Pediat. Rsch., Transplantation Soc., Am. Acad. Pediat., Am. Assn. Physicians. Avocations: opera, antique books and maps. Office: U Mich Cancer Ctr 1500 E Medical Center Dr Ann Arbor MI 48109-0005 E-mail: ferrara@umich.edu.

FERRARA-SHERRY, DONNA LAYNE, education educator; b. Trenton, N.J., Aug. 19, 1946; d. Joseph and Rita Marie (Cerra) F.; m. Peter P. Barsczeski Jr., July 20, 1968 (div. Sept. 1974); 1 child, Lisa Ayn; m. James John Sherry, Jan. 20, 1980; 1 child, Jaymes John Joseph; stepchildren: Jennifer, Kimberly. BA, Manhattanville Coll., 1968, MA in Teaching, 1973; profl. diploma, L.I. U., 1985; PhD, NYU, 1992. Cert. English and social studies tchr., N.Y. Tchr. Holy Rosary Sch., Port Chester, N.Y., 1968; adminstrv. asst. for curriculum coord. Blind Brook High Sch., Port Chester, 1973—; English tchr. Rye (N.Y.) Country Day Sch., 1973-75, Hampton Bays (N.Y.) Jr. and Sr. High Schs., 1975-87, English coord., 1985-87, dist. curriculum coord., 1987-89; asst. dir. Southampton (N.Y.)-Hampton Boys Tchr. Ctr., 1986-89; coord. curriculum planning rsch. and evaluation Suffolk Dist. 2 BOCES, Patchogue, N.Y., 1989; prof. edn. L.I. U., Southampton, 1993—, outcomes assessment coord., TEAC coord., 1995—99. Exec. dir. Smith-Layne Ednl. Cons. Svc., Hampton Bays, N.Y., 1988—; assoc. Shared Edn. Decisions Assocs., 1992—; exec. dir. Sch. Transformation, 1992—. Mem. Community Awareness Program, Hampton Bays; mem. facilities planning com. Hampton Bays Schs., 1987-88, co-chair AIDS adv. com., 1988-89; mem. steering com. Shared Decision Making Dist., 1993. Mem. ASCD, Am. Ednl. Rsch. Assn., Spl. Edn. Parent Tchrs. Assn., NYU Adminstr.'s Roundtable (com.), Kappa Delta Pi, Phi Delta Kappa, Delta Kappa Gamma. Roman Catholic. Achievements include research in school reform, decentralization, autonomy, international studies, school indicators, evaluation, staff development, shared decision making, leadership. Office: LIU Southampton 239 Montauk Hwy Southampton NY 11968-4100 E-mail: ferrara@optonline.net., dottoressadlf@yahoo.com., schooltransformation@yahoo.com.

FERRARI, DENNIS M. secondary education educator; Tchr. Burlington (Vt.) High Sch. Recipient Tchr. Excellence award Internat. Tech. Edn. Assn., 1992. Office: Burlington High Sch 52 Institute Rd Burlington VT 05401-2721

FERRARI, L. KATHERINE, speaker, consultant, entrepreneur; b. Chgo. d. August and Aurora (Lenzi) Puccinelli; m. Charles Wasserman; children: Michael John, Alexandra Marie; m. Gordon Wharton Holt Jr. MA in Architecture, MS in Engring., Stanford (Calif.) U., 1972; BA in Polit. Sci., Northwestern U.; M in Hypnotism, Hypnotism Tng. Sch. L.A., 1989. Educator Moreland Sch. Dist., San Jose, Calif., 1961-65; pres. Ferrari Design, Los Gatos, Calif., 1970—; project dir. AIA Energy Conservation Retrofit, San Jose, Calif., 1978—81, AIA/N.A.S.A. tech. house of future, Moffet Field, 1982—85; pres. Internat. Laughter Soc. Inc., Los Gatos, 1983—, Ferrari Communications, Los Gatos, 1989—. Bd. dirs. Pacific We. Bank, San Jose; bldg. cons. & design in field; product designer Internat. Laughter Soc. Inc., Los Gatos, 1983—; trainer non-profit groups. Contbr. articles to profl. jours. Mem. Advanced Tech. Advancement Com., Moffett Field, Calif., 1977-89; pres., v.p. League of Eastfield Children's Ctr., Campbell, Calif., 1964-66; pres., treas. Triton Mus. of Art, Santa Clara, Calif., 1979-81; bd. dirs. Coun. Environ. & Econ. Improvement, San Jose, Calif., 1976-79. Art Inst. scholar. Mem. AIA (hon. assoc., bd. dirs. San Jose chpt.), A.S.I.D., Nat. Speakers Assn., Am. Coun. Hypnotists, Nat. Guild Hypnotists. Avocations: travel, reading. Office: Ferrari Communications 16000 Glen Una Dr Los Gatos CA 95030-2911

FERRARI, MERCEDES V, secondary education educator; English tchr. Milford (Del.) High Sch.; spl. assignment Dept. Edn., 2000—. Named Del. State English Tchr. of Yr., 1992. Office: Dept Edn PO Box 1402 Dover DE 19903-1402

FERRARI, MICHAEL RICHARD, JR., university administrator; b. Monongahela, Pa., May 12, 1940; s. Michael Richard and Lillian Ann (Cristina) F.; m. Janice Bjurstrom, Sept. 5, 1964; children: Elizabeth Anne, Michael, III. BA, Mich. State U., 1962, MA, 1963, DBA (Ford Found. fellow), 1968; D of Pub. Svc. (hon.), Bowling Green State U., 1991. Asst. to dean men U. Cin., 1965-66; asst. to dir. residence life, resident hall head advisor Mich. State U., 1966-68; acting chmn. dept. adminstrv. scis. Kent (Ohio) State U., 1970-71; mem. adminstrv. staff Bowling Green (Ohio) State U., 1971-73, v.p. resource planning, 1973-78, provost, exec. v.p., 1978-81, interim pres., 1981-82; vis. scholar U. Mich., 1982-83; prof. mgmt., provost Wright State U., Dayton, 1983-85; pres. Drake U., Des Moines, 1985-98; chancellor Tex. Christian U., Ft. Worth, 1998—2003, chancellor emeritus, 2003—; pres. Ferrari and Assocs., 2003—. Bd. dirs. Pier One Imports; mgmt. cons., 1968—. Author: Profiles of American College Presidents, 1970, Measuring the Quality of Universities, 1970, National Study of Student Personnel Manpower Planning, 1972. Research fellow Am. Coll. Testing Program, 1970 Mem. Acad. Mgmt., Omicron Delta Kappa, Phi Kappa Phi, Beta Gamma Sigma, Pi Gamma Mu, Alpha Tau Omega. Episcopalian. Office: 570 Greenway Dr Lake Forest IL 60045

FERREE, MYRA MARX, sociologist, educator; b. Morristown, N.J., Oct. 10, 1949; d. Irwin F. and Marguerite (Sosnoski) Marx; m. G. Donald Ferree. Student, U. Hamburg, Fed. Republic Germany, 1969-70; BA, Bryn Mawr (Pa.) Coll., 1971; PhD, Harvard U., 1976. Sr. research assoc. Boston Coll., 1975-76; asst. prof. sociology U. Conn., Storrs, 1976-81, assoc. prof., 1981-87, prof., 1987—, dir. Women's Studies Program, 1985-87; prof. U. Wis., Madison, 2000—. Guest prof. J.W. Goethe U., Frankfurt, Fed. Republic Germany, 1985. Co-author (with Beth Hess) Controversy and Coalition: The New Feminist Movement, 1985 (Choice Best Book, 1985), revised and expanded, 2000, Shaping Abortion Discourse, 2002; co-editor: Analyzing Gender, 1987, Feminist Organizations, 1995, Revisioning Gender, 1998; assoc. editor Gender and Society, 1986-90, The Sociol. Quar., 1985-89, Contemporary Sociology, 1980-83; mem. editl. bd. Am. Sociol. Rev., 1990-93, Am. Jour. Sociology, 1999-2002. German Acad. Exchange Svc. Rsch. fellow, 1982-85; recipient German Marshall Fund fellowship, 1990-91; named Outstanding Conn. Woman in Edn. UN/USA Assn., 1988. Mem. Am. Sociol. Assn. (chair sex and gender sect. 1985-86, com. on nominations, 1986-88, com. on coms. 1984-86, chair collective behavior and social movements sect. 1991-92, coun. 1990-93, v.p. 1995-96), Ea. Sociol. Soc. (chair com. on women 1977-79, Disting. lectr. 2000), Soc. for Study of Social Problems (program com. 1984), Sociologists for Women in Soc. Episcopalian. Office: Dept Sociology U Wis Social Sci Bldg 1180 Observatory Dr Madison WI 53706-1320 E-mail: mferree@ssc.wisc.edu.

FERREIRA, DANIEL ALVES, secondary education Spanish language educator; b. Lisbon, Portugal, Feb. 24, 1944; came to U.S., 1959, naturalized, 1963; s. Manuel and Lourdes (Alves) F.; m. Cheryl R. Jann, July 1, 1978; children: Jeffrey, Douglas, Peter. BA, U. Ill., 1966, MEd, 1970; Diploma Superior, U. Salamanca, Spain, 1994. Cert. tchr., Ill. Tchr. Homewood-Flossmoor (Ill.) High Sch., 1966-2000, Marian Cath. H.S., 2002—. Boys and girls Soccer Coach at Homewood-Flossmoor (Ill.). Bd. dirs. Grace Migrant Day Care Ctr., Park Forest, Ill., 1971-80. Named Chgo. Area Tchr. of Yr., U. Chgo., 1985. Mem. Am. Assn. Tchrs. of Spanish and Portuguese, Ill. High Sch. Soccer Coaches Assn., Nat. Soccer Coaches Assn. Am., Ill. Edn. Assn., NEA, Homewood-Flossmoor Edn. Orgn. (pres. 1981-82), Phi Delta Kappa. Avocations: soccer, golf. Home: 21343 Ginger Ln Frankfort IL 60423-9428 E-mail: daferreira12@hotmail.com.

FERREIRA, JOSEPH JOHN, JR., history educator, theatre/drama educator; b. Newport, R.I., May 13, 1964; s. Joseph John and Frances Marian (Watson) F. BA in History and Social Sci., R.I. Coll., 1987, MA in Tchg. History, 1996; Cert. Grad. Study, U. Western Ont., London, Can., 1988. Cert. tchr. Mass., R.I. Tchr. history and social studies Middletown (R.I.) Pub. Schs., 1989-96, King Philip Regional H.S., Wrentham, Mass., 1996—. Drama dir. King Philip Regional H.S., 1998—; editor, mem. tchg. com. H-Net: Humanities and Social Scis. On-Line. Co-editor: H-Net Humanities and Social Sciences On-Line, 1997—. Trustee Middletown Pub. Libr., 1985-87; history rep. Soc. Grad. Students, U. Western Ont., 1987-88; project dir./fundraiser Irene Kennedy Meml. Fund, Wrentham, Mass., 1998. Recipient Tchg. fellowship Taft Inst. Govt., 1994, Civil War Inst., 1996, Stratford Hall Inst. Slavery, 1998, Nat. History Day/U. Md., 1999. Mem. Am. Hist. Assn., Nat. Coun. History Edn., Mass. Coun. for the Social Studies, Hon. Order Ky. Cols. Unitarian Universalist. Avocations: reading, wine tasting, travel to historic sites, gourmet cooking, classic films. Office: King Philip Regional HS 201 Franklin St Wrentham MA 02093-2404 Fax: 508-384-1006. E-mail: ferreiraj@kingphilip.org.

FERRELL, EVA BOIKO, principal; b. Hopkinsville, Ky., Sept. 2, 1954; d. Peter Steffen and Vivian Jean (Hutchins) Boiko; m. Layne Ferrell, June 18, 1976; 1 child, Holly Suzanne. BS, Mid. Tenn. State U., 1976. Lic. tchr. history/edn., Tenn. Tchr. Cannon County Bd. Edn., Woodbury, Tenn., 1978-83; tchr. jr. high sch. F.C. Boyd Sr. Christian Sch., McMinnville, Tenn., 1990-92, prin., 1992—. Editor: Cannon County 1836-1986, 1986; editor slide presentation/documentary Historic Homes of Cannon County, 1986. Bd. dirs. Tenn. 4-H alumni, Nashville, 1988; mem. Upper Cumberland Tourism Bd., Cookeville. Avocation: antique dealing. Home: 307 Hayes St Woodbury TN 37190-1311 Office: F C Boyd Sr Christian Sch 806 Morrison St Mc Minnville TN 37110-2900

FERRIER, MARIA HERNANDEZ, federal official, educator; BA in Speech, MEd in Gidance and Counseling, Our Lady of the Lake U.; EdD in Ednl. Adminstrn., Tex. A&N U. Dir. ESL San Antonio Norteast Ind. Sch. Dist. Cmty. Edn. Program, Tex.; dir. Office Bilingual Edn. and Minority Langs. Affairs, Washington, 1992; exec. dir. City Year; host and exec. prodr. City Spirit; dir. office English Lang. Acquisition U.S. Dept. Edn., Washington, 2002—. Founding mem., creator Comty. Edn. Leadership Program; mem. San Antonio Literacy Commn.; nat. bd. dirs. City Yr.; San Antonio Air Force Comty. Named United Way Vol. of Yr.; recipient Minority Leadership award, Nat. Comty. Edn. Assn., Imagineer award, Mind Sci. Found., Edn. award, Hispanic Heritage Month. Mem.: Rotary Club San Antonio (bd. dirs.). Office: 400 Maryland Ave SW Washington DC 20202 E-mail: maria.ferrier@ed.gov.

FERRITOR, DANIEL E. chancellor emeritus; b. Kansas City, Mo., Nov. 8, 1939; m. Patricia Jean Ferritor; children: Kimberly Ann, Kristin Marie, Sean Patrick. BA, Rockhurst Coll., 1962; MA, Washington U., St. Louis, 1967, PhD, 1969. Tchr. grade sch., Raytown, Mo., 1962-64; program assoc., asst. dir. Nat. Program on Early Childhood Edn., 1970-71; asst. program dir. CEMREL Inc., St. Ann, Mo., 1969-70, assoc. dir. instrnl. systems program, 1970-71; asst. prof. sociology U. Ark., Fayetteville, 1967-68, assoc. prof., 1973-79, prof., 1979-85, chmn. dept., 1973-85, vice chancellor for acad. affairs, provost, 1985-86, chancellor, 1986-97, prof., 1997—, chancellor emeritus, 1998—. Author: (with Robert L. Hamblin, D. Buckholdt, M. Kozloff and L. Blackwell) The Humanization Processes, 1971; contbr. articles to profl. jours. Office: Dept Sociology Social Work Criminal Justice U Ark Fayetteville AR 72701 E-mail: def@uark.edu.*

FERRO-NYALKA, RUTH RUDYS, librarian, educator; b. Chgo., June 2, 1930; d. Joseph F. and Anna (Serbenta) Rudys; children: Keith A. Krisciunas, Kevin L. Krisciunas, Kenneth M. Krisciunas; stepchildren: Anita L. Abbate, Vincent A. Abbate. BA, U. Chgo., 1950; MALS, Rosary Coll., 1972. Tchr. elem. sch, Westmont, Ill., 1961-63; libr. Dist. 105 Pub. Schs., La Grange, Ill., 1972-95; mem. youth svcs. dept. Hinsdale (Ill.) Pub. Libr., 1995—. Tchr. program for gifted children, 1979-81, 82-85, coord. gifted program, 1981-82. Mem. ALA, NEA, AAUW, Ill. Edn. Assn., Dist. 105 Tchrs. Assn. (pres. 1983-85, 91-93). Roman Catholic. Home: 5800 Doe Cir Westmont IL 60559-2138 Office: Hinsdale Pub Libr 20 E Maple St Hinsdale IL 60521-3490

FERRY, JOAN EVANS, school counselor; b. Summit, N.J., Aug. 20, 1941; d. John Stiger and Margaret Darling (Evans) F. BS, U. Pa., 1964; cert., Coll. of Preceptors, London, 1966; EdM, Temple U., 1967; postgrad., Villanova U., 1981. Cert. elem. sch. tchr., elem. sch. counselor; cert. vol. Dale Carnegie. Indsl. photographer Bucksco Mfg. Co., Inc., Quakertown, Pa., 1958-59; math. and German tutor St. Lawrence U., Canton, N.Y., 1959-61; research asst. U. Pa., Phila., 1963; tchr. elem. sch. Pennridge Schs., Perkasie, Pa., 1964-74, 75-77, elem. sch. counselor, 1981—2001; pvt. practice counselor, real estate partnership Perkasie, 1981—; chair child study team Perkasie Elem. Sch., 1988-94; editor Princeton (NJ) Pub. Group, 2000—. Tutor math., German, St. Lawrence U., Canton, N.Y., 1959-61; supervisory tchr. East Stroudsburg U., Pennridge Schs., 1971-74; research asst. U. Pa., Phila., 1963; mem. acad. coms. for Pennridge Schs.; adj. faculty Bucks County Community Coll., 1983—; instr. Am. Inst. Banking, 1982—; notary pub., 1986—; mcpl. auditor, sec. bd. auditors, 1984-90, mcpl. auditor 1990—, chmn. bd. auditors 1990—; cons. in field. Author (with others) Life-Time Sports for the College Student: A Behavioral Objective Approach, 1971, 3d rev. edit. 1978, Elementary Social Studies as a Learning System, 1976. Vol. elem. sch. counselor Perkasie, 1979-80; mem. Hilltown Civic Assn., 1965-70, 92—; exec. com. chairperson Hilltown PTO, 1965-73; soloist Good Shepherd Episcopal Ch. Choir, Hilltown, 1964-77; steering com. Perkasie Sch., 1989-95; poll watcher, 1993; med. vol. Olympics, Atlanta, 1996; vol. Dublin Ambulance Squad, 1996—, House Rabbit Soc., Chadds Ford, Pa., 1998—, Special Olympics World Games, Summer, North Carolina, 1999, Silverdale Quick Response Med. Svc., 1999; mem. Dublin Vol. Fire and Ambulance Co., Silverdale Fire Co., Silverdale, Pa.; mem. prin.'s round table Perkasie (Pa.) Sch., 1997; vol. House Rabbit Soc. Southeastern Pa./Del. Foster Home and Sanctuary, Chadds Ford, Pa., 1998—; vol. marshal First Union USPro Championship Cycling Race, Phila., 1999, 2000; vol. spl. driver Bush Family and Friends at Rep. Nat. Conv., Phila., 2000, Bucks County Crisis Response Team, 2001-; mem. Nat. Arbor Day Found., Best Friends Animal Sanctuary. NSF grantee, Washington, 1972-73, Philanthropic Edn. Orgn. grantee, Doylestown, Pa., 1982; recipient Judith Netzky Meml. Fellowship award B'nai B'rith, Phila., 1979; Durning scholar Delta Delta Delta, Arlington, Tex., 1981, Am. Mgmt. Assns. scholar, N.Y.C., 1983, Statesman's award World Inst. Achievement, 1989, Achievement award Women's Inner Circle, 1990, Golden Acad. award for lifetime achievement, 1991; named to Internat. Tennis Hall of Fame, 2000 Notable Am. Women Hall of Fame, 1989, Cmty. Leaders of Am. Hall of Fame, 1990, Internat. Book of Honor Hall Of Fame, 1990, Internat. Bus. & Profl. Women's Hall of Fame, 1994, Lifetime Achievement Acad. Humane Soc. of U.S., Internat. Honor Soc. In Edn., Certificate of appreciation in recognition and acknowledgement for outstanding service and dedication as a member of the 1996 Atlanta Olympics Med. Team, 1997, Certs. of Appreciation Spring Mountain Ski Patrol, 1997, Honorary Educator certificate, St. Joseph's Indian Sch., 1996, ARC, 1986, Cert. Achievement in Recognition of Contbn. as Med. Svcs. Vol. at 1996 Centennial Olympic Games, 1996, Honor Award for Svc. to Edn. and Tchg. Profession, 1996, 99, award for Outstanding Svc. to Edn. Pennridge Schs., 1999, Certificate of appreciation for dedication to the success of the 1999 Special Olympics World Summer Games, 1999. Fellow Internat. Biog. Assn.; mem. AAUW, NEA, NAFE, Humane Soc. U.S., World Inst. Achievement, Pa. State Edn. Assn. (polit. action com. for edn., chair Pennridge Schs. 1986—, del. leadership conf. 1987, 89, Honor award for svc. to edn. and tchg. profession, 1996, 99), Pennridge Edn. Assn. (faculty rep. 1986-88, exec. coun. 1986—, negotiations resource com. 1987-89, 1990-93, steering com. Perkasie Sch. 1989-95, chairperson Child Study Team, 1988-94, Instructional Support Team, 1992—, selection com. for asst. supt. Pennridge Schs. 1993, selection com. for prin. Perkasie Sch. 1994, prin. round table 1997—), Am. Inst. Banking (chairperson 1987), U.S. Tennis Assn. (hon. life), Pa. and Mid. States Tennis Assn. (hon. life), U.S. Profl. Tennis Registry, Mid. States Profl. Tennis Registry, Women's Internat. Tennis Assn., Nat. Ski Patrol (Svc. Recognition award 1994), Spring Mountain Ski Patrol (Outstanding Aux. 1993, MOM Dedication award 1995, Outstanding Svc. and Dedication award 1996, 98, certificate of appreciation, 1997, svc. award, Nat. Ski Patrol, 1999), Pa. Elected Women's Assn., Bucks County Assn. Twp. Ofcls., Bucks County Sch. Counselors Assn., Pa. Sch. Counselors Assn., Pa. Assn. Notaries, Am. Soc. Notaries, Internat. Fedn. Univ. Women, Internat. Platform Assn., World Inst. Achievement, Am. Biog. Inst. Rsch. Assn. (rsch. bd. advisors, bd. govs. 1989—), World Inst. of Achievement, Lifetime Achievement Acad., Rails-to-Trails

Conservancy, World Wildlife Fund, Bucks County Sch. Counselors Assn., Highpoint Athletic Club, Pennridge Cmty. Rep. Club. (recording sec. 1986-91, publicity chmn. 1991-92, Pen care chmn. 1992—), Assn. Tennis Profls. Tour Tennis Ptnrs., Sierra Club, The Nature Conservancy, Nat. Wildlife Fedn., John Wayne Found., Mediterranean Club, Philadelphia Sports Club, Delaware Valley Jaguar Club, Jaguar Clubs of North Am., Nockamixon Boat Club, Peace Valley Yacht Club, Kappa Delta Pi. Episcopalian. Avocations: land and water sports, flying, music, parasailing, photography. Home and Office: 834 Rickert Rd Perkasie PA 18944

FERSHLEISER, STEVEN BUCKLER, secondary education educator; b. N.Y.C., Feb. 14, 1943; s. Bernard Aaron and Caryl (Buckler) F.; m. Lorraine Carol McGinnis, July 13, 1974; 1 child, Alexandra Margaret. Student, Cape Cod C.C., 1973-74; BA, Boston U., 1974-76; MA, Northeastern U., 1976-77; postgrad., Carnegie-Mellon U., 1977—. Cert. social studies tchr., Fla., N.Y., Conn. Instr. Northeastern U., Boston, 1976-77, Carnegie Mellon U., Pitts., 1977-81, Clark County C.C., Las Vegas, Nev., 1982-86; spl. edn. tchr. N.Y.C. Bd. Edn., 1982-86; history tchr. Van Wyck Jr. High Sch., Wappingers, N.Y., 1986-87, Circleville (N.Y.) Sch. Dist., 1987-88; instr. social sci. Am. Heritage, Plantation, Fla., 1988—. Cons. Pitts. Tchr. Ctr., 1980-81, Sylvan Learning Ctrs., 1994—; co-dir. Carnegie-Mellon Edn. Ctr., Pitts., 1978-81. Editor book series: The American Slave, 1979. With USN, 1961-64. Northeastern U. fellow, 1976. Mem. ASCD, Am. Hist. Assn., Phi Alpha Theta. Avocations: coaching basketball, track and tennis. Home: 1500 NW 110th Ave Apt 368 Plantation FL 33322-6444 Office: Am Heritage 12200 W Broward Blvd Fort Lauderdale FL 33325-2404

FERSTENFELD, JULIAN ERWIN, internist, educator; b. Des Moines, Sept. 5, 1941; m. Sharon Rukas, Mar. 8, 1975; children: Megan Ann, Adam Justin. B.A., U. Iowa, 1963, M.D., 1966. Intern Milwaukee County Gen. Hosp., Milw., 1966-67, resident in internal medicine, 1969-71, fellow in infectious diseases, 1972-73; instr. internal medicine Med. Coll. Wis., Milw., 1974-75, asst. prof. medicine, 1975-78, asst. clin. prof. medicine and family practice, 1978-83, assoc. clin. prof. family practice and medicine, 1983—, internal medicine dir. Waukesha family practice residency, 1978— ; practice medicine specializing in infectious diseases, Milw., 1974— ; mem. staff Waukesha Meml. Hosp. (Wis.), West Allis Meml. Hosp. (Wis.), Elmbrook Meml. Hosp., Brookfield, Wis., Froedtert Meml. Hosp., Milw. Served as capt. M.C., U.S. Army, 1967-69; Korea. Fellow ACP; mem. Wis. Thoracic Soc., Am. Fedn. Clin. Research, Phi Beta Kappa. Contbr. articles, abstracts to profl. jours.

FERZACCA, PAMELA ANN, elementary education educator; b. Detroit, Sept. 28, 1963; d. John Joseph and Lois Susan (Henson) F. BS, Grand Valley State Coll., Allendale, Mich., 1987. Cert. spl. edn. tchr. Substitute tchr. Almont (Mich.) Community Schs., 1987-88, bilingual tchr., 1988-90; 1st grade tchr. Almont Summer Migrant Edn. Program, •1988, tchr. kindergarten, 1989, 90, recruiter, 1990; tchr. 3d grade Almont Elem. Sch., 1990-94; tchr. educably mentally impaired Almont Jr./Sr. H.S., 1994-95; tchr. 3d grade Almont Elem. Sch., 1995—. Mem. Nat. Assn. Migrant Educators, Coun. Exceptional Children, Mich. Edn. Assn., Almont Edn. Assn. Democrat. Roman Catholic. Avocations: attending the theater, travel, fgn. travel, basketball, reading. Home: PO Box 120 132 N Main St Almont MI 48003 Office: Almont Elem Sch 401 Church St Almont MI 48003-1030

FESSLER, PATRICIA LOU, retired library and media coordinator; b. Chgo., Dec. 01; d. Eugene Rickert and Dorothy May McKeen; m. Kermit John Fessler, June 23, 1951; children: Barbara, Peter, James. BA, Cornell Coll., 1950; MS, Chgo. State U., 1970. Cert. tchr., supr., Ill. Tchr. phys. edn. Harlan (Iowa) Pub. Schs., 1950-51, Blue Island Community High Sch. Dist. # 218, Oak Lawn, Ill., 1960-63, 67-70; coord. library, media A.B. Shepard High Sch., Oak Lawn, Ill., 1971-93; ret. Mem. adv. coun. Grad. Sch. Libr. Scis. U. Ill., Champaign, 1977-80; mem. libr./media adv. coun. State Bd. Edn., Springfield, Ill., 1980-83. Deacon Palos Park (Ill.) Presbyn. Ch., 1991-93. Named as one of Those Who Excel Ill., State Bd. Edn., 1987. Mem. AAUW (ednl. found. honoree 1992), Assn. for Ednl. Comms. and Tech. (bd. dirs. 1981-84, Spl. Svc. plaque 1989, bd. trustees 1984—, found. sec. 1988—), Ill. Ednl. Comms. and Tech. (pres. 1977-78, 80-82, Disting. Svc. award 1982-84, Meritorious Svc. award A.V. Am. 1983). Avocations: reading, knitting, needlework, golf, watching sports.

FETLER, PAUL, retired composer; b. Phila., Feb. 17, 1920; s. William Basil and Barbara (Kovalevski) Fetler-Malof; m. Ruth Regina Pahl, Aug. 13, 1947; children: Sylvia, Daniel, Beatrix. MusB, Northwestern U., 1943; MusM, Yale U., 1948; PhD, U. Minn., 1956. From instr. to prof. music theory and composition U. Minn., Mpls., 1948—91, ret., 1992. Vis. composer, condr. and lectr. various colls. and univs. Composer: Symphonic Fantasia, 1941, Passacaglia for orch., 1942, Dramatic Overture, 1943, Prelude for orch., 1946, Orchestral Sketch, 1949, A Comedy Overture for Orchestra, 1952, Gothic Variations for Orchestra, 1953, Contrasts for orch., 1958, Sing Unto God for mixed voices, 1958, Nothing but Nature for mixed voices and orchestra, 1961, Soundings for orch., 1962, Jubilate Deo for voices and brass, 1963, Te Deum for mixed voices, 1963, Four Symphonies, 1948-67, Cantus Tristis for orch., 1964, Five Pieces for guitar, 1964; opera Sturge Maclean, 1965, A Contemporary Psalm for chorus, organ and percussion, 1968, Prayer for Peace for mixed voices, 1969, Hosanna for mixed voices, 1970, Cycles for percussion and piano, 1970, The Words From the Cross for mixed voices, 1971, First Violin Concerto, 1971, Four Movements for guitar, 1972, Dialogue for flute and guitar, 1973, Six Pastoral Sketches for guitar, 1974, Lamentations for chorus, narrator, percussion and flute, 1974, Three Venetian Scenes for guitar, 1974, Dream of Shalom for mixed voices, 1975, Songs of the Night for voices, narrator and flute, 1976, Three Poems by Walt Whitman for narrator and orch., 1975, Pastoral Suite for piano trio, 1976, Celebration for orch., 1976, Three Impressions for guitar and orch., 1977, Five Piano Games, 1977, Sing Alleluia, 1978, Song of the Forest Bird for voices and chamber orch., 1978, Six Songs of Autumn for guitar, 1979, Second Violin Concerto, 1980, Missa de Angelis for three choirs, orch., organ and handbells, 1980, Serenade for chamber orch., 1981, Rhapsody for violin and piano, 1982; song cycle The Garden of Love for voice and orch., 1983, Piano Concerto, 1984; Capriccio for chamber orch., 1985; Frolic for Flute, Winds and Strings, 1986, Three Excursions, A Concerto for Percussion, Piano and Orchestra, 1987, String Quartet, 1989, Toccata for Organ, 1990, numerous sacred and secular choral works, 1949-93, Twelve Sacred Hymn Settings, 1993, Divertimento for Flute and Strings, 1994, December Stillness for Flute, Harp and Voices, 1994, Suite for Woodwind Trio, 1995, Up the Dome of Heaven, Three Pieces for Mixed Voices and Flute, 1996; The Raven for basso, clarinet, percussion and string, 1998, Saraband variations for guitar, Folia Lirica,, 1999 . Served with AUS, 1943-45. Recipient Guggenheim awards, 1953, 60, Soc. for Publ. Am. Music award, 1953, Yale U. Alumni Assn. cert. of merit, 1975, NEA award, 1975, 77, 87; Ford Found. grantee, 1958. Mem. ASCAP (ann. award 1962—), Sigma Alpha Iota (nat. arts assoc.) Home: 174 Golden Gate Pt Apt 32 Sarasota FL 34236-6602 Office: U Minn 100 Ferguson Hall Minneapolis MN 55455 E-mail: pf-tonus8@webtv.net.

FETT, DIANE P. child development specialist; b. Chgo., Sept. 14, 1958; d. William Leo and Patricia June (Cunradi) Kuhn; m. Michael A. Fett; children: Jonathan, David; stepchildren: Ryan, Rob. BA, Concordia Tchr.'s Coll., River Forest, Ill., 1980; MEd, U. Ill., Chgo., 1987. Cert. elem. tchr., Ill., Wis. 1st grade tchr. Rhodes Sch., River Grove, Ill., 1980-82, kindergarten tchr., 1982-92, New Holstein (Wis.) Elem. Sch., 1992-93; coord. of svcs. birth to three Fond du Lac County Dept. of Community Programs, Fond du Lac, Wis., 1993—. Early interventionist U. Ill., Chgo., 1985-87; dir. dept. cmty. programs, Fond du Lac, Wis., 1994—; adj. prof. Marian Coll., Fond du Lac, Wis., 1998. Mem. Wis. Divsn. for Early Childhood Exec. Bd.; advocate Head Start Policy Coun., 1995-98. U.S. Dept. Edn. grantee, 1986. Mem. ASCD, Nat. Assn. Edn. of Young Children, Coun. for Exceptional Children. Lutheran. Avocations: reading, music, tennis. Office: Dept Community Programs 459 E 1st St Fond Du Lac WI 54935-4505 Home: W651 Danes Rd New Holstein WI 53061-9713

FETTER, ALEXANDER LEES, theoretical physicist, educator; b. Phila., May 16, 1937; s. Ferdinand and Elizabeth Lean Fields (Head) F.; m. Jean Holmes, Aug. 4, 1962 (div. Dec. 1994); children: Anne Lindsay, Andrew James. AB, Williams Coll., 1958; BA, Balliol Coll., Oxford U., 1960; PhD, Harvard U., 1963. Miller rsch. fellow U. Calif., Berkeley, 1963-65; mem. faculty dept. physics Stanford U., 1965—, prof., 1974—, chmn. dept. physics, 1985-90, assoc. chmn. dept. physics, 1998-99, asso. dean undergrad. studies, 1976-79, assoc. dean humanities and sci., 1990-93, dir. Hansen Exptl. Physics Lab., 1996-97, dir. lab. for adv. materials, 1999—2002; vis. prof. Cambridge U., 1970-71; Nordita vis. prof. Tech. U., Helsinki, Finland, 1976. Author: (with J.D. Walecka) Quantum Theory of Many Particle Systems, 1971, Theoretical Mechanics of Particles and Continua, 1980. Alumni trustee Williams Coll., 1974-79. Rhodes scholar, 1958-60; NSF fellow, 1960-63; Sloan Found. fellow, 1968-72; Recipient W.J. Gores award for excellence in teaching Stanford U., 1974 Fellow Am. Physics Soc. (chmn. divn. condensed matter physics 1991), AAAS; mem. Sigma Xi. Home: 904 Mears Ct Palo Alto CA 94305-1029 Office: Stanford U Physics Dept Stanford CA 94305-4045

FETTERLY, MARY E. counseling administrator; b. Wenatchee, Wash., Aug. 9, 1960; d. Jesus Gonzalez Pliego, Anita Maria Castillo; m. Roger Dale Fetterly, Aug. 14, 1982 (div. Nov. 20, 2000). Grad. H.S., Burien, Wash. Cert. completion fgn. credentials analysis. Internat. admissions evaluator U. Wash. Office Grad. Admissions, Seattle, 1980—91, internat. admissions counseling svcs. coord., 1991—. Recipient Cert. Appreciation to Region 1 Conf., Nat. Assn. for Fgn. Student Affairs, 1997. Mem.: Nat. Assn. for Fgn. Student Affairs (nat. com. on edn. and tng. 2001—), Nat. Assn. Grad. Admissions Profls., Assn. Wash. State Internat. Student Affairs, Seattle Athletic Club. Roman Catholic. Avocations: Karate, travel, collecting thimbles, bicycling, skiing. Office: U Wash Grad Admissions #301 Loew Hall Box 352191 Seattle WA 98195-2191

FETTERMAN, DAVID MARK, anthropologist, education evaluator; b. Danielson, Conn., Jan. 24, 1954; s. Irving and Elsie (Blumenthal) F.; 1 child, Sarah Rachel. BA, BS, U. Conn., 1976; MA in Anthropology, Stanford U., 1977, MA in Edn., 1979, PhD in Anthropology, 1981. Cert. tchr. Calif., Conn. Tchr. Richard C. Lee High Sch., New Haven, 1975-76; dir. Office of Econ. Opportunity Anti-Poverty, Danielson, 1976; tchr. Beth Am and Beth David, Cupertino and Palo Alto, Calif., 1976-78; sr. assoc., project dir. RMC Rsch. Corp., Mountain View, Calif., 1978-82; prin. rsch. scientist Am. Insts. Rsch., Stanford, Calif., 1982-91; dir. MA policy analysis and evaluation Stanford U., 1991-93, dir. evaluation tng. program, 1993—, dir. evaluation, career devel. and alumni rels., 2003; dir. rsch. and evaluation Calif. Inst. Integral Studies, San Francisco, 1993—. Mem. adv. bd. Ednl. Leadership, U.S. Dept. Edn., Washington, 1987—, mem. adv. bd. Nat. Rsch. Ctr. Gifted & Talented; trustee Nueva Learning Ctr., Hillsborough, Calif., 1990—; chair accreditation team Calif. Inst. Integral Studies, San Francisco, 1994—. Author: Excellence and Equality, 1988 (Mensa award 1990), Ethnography: Step by Step, 1989, (G. & L. Spindler award Am. Anthropol. Assn., 1990), 2d edit., 1998, Foundations of Empowerment Evaluation, 2002 (Paul Lazarsfield award for contbns. to evaluation theory, Am. Evaluation Assn. 2002); editor: Speaking the Language of Power, 1993, Empowerment Evaluation, 1995. Pres. Mini-Infant Day Care Ctr., Palo Alto, 1992-93. Fellow Am. Anthrop. Assn. (bd. dirs. 1993), Soc. Applied Anthropology (liaison 1989); mem. Am. Evaluation Assn. (pres. 1992-94, Myrdal award 1999), Coun. Anthropology and Edn. (life, pres. 1988-92, Ethnographic Evaluation award 1988), Collaborative, Participatory, and Empowerment Group (chair 1995—, Pres.'s prize 1984). Avocations: computers, internet. Home: 520 Barron St Menlo Park CA 94025-3593 Office: Stanford U Sch Edn Stanford CA 94305

FEUER-STERN, BARBIE SHNIDER, elementary and secondary school educator; b. Cin., Mar. 27, 1949; d. Edward and Nilda Ruth (Ostrovsky) Shnider; children: Courtney, Jennifer, Brian; m. Geoffrey Stern, 1985. Student, U. Cin., 1967-68, U. Tel Aviv, 1968-70; BS in Edn., Ohio State U., 1972; postgrad., U. Dayton, 1989—. Cert. tchr., Ohio. Adminstr., prin. Ashland U. Bd. mem. advisor Interdisciplinary Coun., Columbus, Ohio, 1991-92; tribes leader Columbus Pub. Schs., 1989-90. Author: (edn. texts) You and Your Sexuality, 1973, Famous Black American Personalities, 1988; contbr. articles to various ednl. publs. Mem. discipline coun. Ohio State Tchrs., Columbus, 1988-90; v.p. B'nai B'rith Women, Columbus, 1973. Mem. NEA, Columbus Edn. Assn., Hadassah, Nat. Assn. of Profl. Adminstrs. Jewish. Avocations: downhill skiing, traveling.

FEVURLY, KEITH ROBERT, educational administrator; b. Leavenworth, Kans., Oct. 30, 1951; s. James R. Fevurly and Anne (McDade) Barrett; m. Peggy L. Vosburg, Aug. 4, 1978; children: Rebecca Dawn, Grant Robert. BA in Polit. Sci., U. Kans., 1973; JD, Washburn U. of Topeka Sch. Law, 1976; postgrad., U. Mo. Sch. Law, 1984; MBA, Regis U., 1988; LLM, U. Denver, 1992. Bar: Kans. 1977, Colo. 1986; cert. fin. planner. Pvt. practice, Leavenworth, 1977; atty. estate and gift tax IRS, Wichita and Salina, Kans., Austin, Tex., 1977-83; atty., acad. assoc. Coll. for Fin. Planning, Denver, 1984-91, program dir., 1991-95, v.p. edn., 1995-98; COO, U. St. Augustine (Fla.) for Health Scis., 1998-2000; exec. dir. fin. planning edn. program Kaplan Coll., Denver, 2000—. Adj. prof. taxation Met. State Coll., Denver; adj. faculty in retirement planning and estate planning Coll. Fin. Planning. Contbg. author tng. modules, articles on tax mgmt., estate planning. Mem. Colo. Bar Assn., Toastmasters Internat., Rotary Internat., Delta Theta Phi, Pi Sigma Alpha. Republican. Presbyterian. Avocations: softball, racquetball. Home: 3007 E Otero Pl Littleton CO 80122-3666 Office: Kaplan Coll 1401 19th St Denver CO 80202 E-mail: KFevurly@KaplanCollege.edu.

FICHT, ANGELA KAY, middle school counselor; b. Chgo. d. Robert J. and Ruth K. (Binder) F. BA in Edn., Calif. State U., Long Beach, 1961; MA in Cirriculum and Instruction, Univ. St. Thomas, 1980. Life gen. pupil personnel credential, life elem. teaching credential. Elem. tchr. Long Beach Unified Sch. DIst., 1961-77, math specialist, 1977-81, counselor, 1981—98. Mem. Los Angeles County Personnel and Guidance Assn. (pres. 1986), Long Beach Pupil Personnel Assn. (pres. 1984—), Assn. Long Beach Ednl. Mgrs., Calif. Assn. Counseling and Devel., Delta Delta Delta Alumnae. Avocations: music, reading, travelled to 90 countries, volunteering.

FICHTHORN, FONDA GAY, gifted and talented educator, retired principal; b. Jamestown, Ohio, Sept. 4, 1949; d. Robert William and Evelyn Elizabeth (Schmitt) Fichthorn. BS, Otterbein Coll., 1970; MEd, Wright State U., 1983. Cert. tchr., prin., supr., elem. music, gifted edn. Ohio. Elem. tchr. Groveport (Ohio) Madison Schs., 1970-71, Miami Trace Schs., Washington Court House, Ohio, 1971-92, prin., 1992-2000, ret., 2000. Part-time gifted coord. Clark County Schs., Ohio; part-time intervention coord. Miami Trace Schs., Ohio. Bd. dirs. Scioto Paint Valley Mental Health Ctr., crisis vol. Recipient Class Act award Sta. WDTN-TV, 1990. Mem. AAUW, Phi Delta Kappa, Delta Kappa Gamma. Republican. Avocations: piano, flute, travel, gardening. Home: 7313 State Route 729 NW Washington Court House OH 43160-9526

FICK, WALTER HENRY, range research scientist, educator; b. O'Neill, Nebr., June 13, 1951; m. Marilyn Sue Boelter, May 27, 1973; children: Alissa, Adam, Angela. MS, U. Nebr., 1975; PhD, Tex. Tech. U., 1978. Grad. rsch. asst. U. Nebr., Lincoln, 1973-75, Tex. Tech. U., Lubbock, 1975-78; asst. prof. dept. agronomy Kans. State U., Manhattan, 1978-84, assoc. prof., 1984—. Contbr. articles to Jour. Range Mgmt., Down to Earth, Kans. Agr. Exptl. Sta. Bull., Jour. Dairy Sci., many others; author abstracts, procs. profl. confs.; assoc. editor crops Agronomy Jour., 1987-89. Mem. Am. Soc. Agronomy, Weed Sci. Soc. Am., Soc. Range Mgmt. (pres. Kans.-Okla. sect. 1987), Sigma Xi, Phi Eta Sigma, Alpha Zeta, Gamma Sigma Delta (pres. Kans. State U. chpt. 1996-97, Outstanding Advising award 2002), Phi Kappa Phi. Achievements include research in the effect of stage of growth and environmental conditions on effectiveness of herbicides for musk thistle control, the determination of effectiveness of foliar and soil-applied herbicides for brush control, production and quality of eastern gamagrass; integrated control of invasive weeds; the utilization of 14CO2 to study carbohydrate translocation in warm season grasses and mesquite. Office: Kans State Univ Dept Agronomy Manhattan KS 66506 E-mail: whfick@ksu.edu.

FIDDLE, LORRAINE ANNE, artist, art educator; b. N.Y.C. d. Seymour and Adele (Gottdiener) F. BFA, Sch. Art Inst. Chgo., 1979, MFA, 1982. Cert. art tchr., N.Y. Artist-in-residence Studio in a Sch. Assn., N.Y.C., 1983-91, Bronx (N.Y.) Coun. for Arts, 1984, N.Y.C. Dept. Cultural Affairs, 1985, N.Y. Found. for Arts, N.Y.C., 1985; interdisciplinary art coord. Dodge Vocational H.S., Bronx, N.Y., 1993-94; art instr. Lehman Coll., South Bronx H.S., 1994—. Tchr., advisor The Whitney Mus. Am. Art, 1993. Exhbns. include Bronx (N.Y.) Mus. of Arts, 1987, Sch. Art Inst. Chgo., 1991, Artists Space, 1995, Cork Gallery, Lincoln Ctr., N.Y.C., 1995, Sotheby's, N.Y.C., 1996, Queens (N.Y.) Theater in the Park, 1996, Longwood Art Gallery, Bronx, 1997, Lehman Coll. Art Gallery, 1998, Ann. N.Y. Art Tchr. Assn. Exhbn., Ark Gallery/Lincoln Ctr., 1999. Grantee Ill. Arts Coun., 1983, Arts in Edn. grantee NEA, 1987. Avocations: swimming, hiking, reading. Home: 7240 Huntington Ln Apt 604 Delray Beach FL 33446-2912 Office: South Bronx HS Art Dept 701 Saint Anns Ave Bronx NY 10455-1446

FIEDLER, FRED EDWARD, organizational psychology educator, consultant; b. Vienna, July 13, 1922; came to U.S., 1938; s. Victor and Hilda (Schallinger) F.; m. Judith Joseph, Apr. 14, 1946; children: Decky, Ellen Victoria, Carol Ann. AM, U. Chgo., 1947, PhD, 1949. Clin. psychol. trainee US VA, Chgo., 1947-50; rsch. assoc., instr. U. Chgo., 1949-51; asst. prof. psychology to prof. U. Ill., Urbana, 1951-69; prof. U. Wash., Seattle, 1969-93, prof. emeritus psychology, 1993—. Vis. prof. U. Amsterdam, 1958-59; guest prof. U. Louvain, Belgium, 1963-64; vis. rsch. fellow Templeton Coll., Oxford, 1986; cons. State of Wash., 1981-84, King County, Wash., 1970-80; cons. various govt., mil., pvt. orgns., U.S., Europe, 1953—; apptd. to SLA Marshall chair U.S. Army Rsch. Inst., 1988-89. Author: Boards, Management and Company Success, 1959; A Theory of Leadership Effectiveness, 1967; Improving Leadership Effectiveness, 1976; Leadership and Effective Management, 1974; New Approaches to Effective Leadership—Cognitive Resources and Organizational Performance, 1987; contbr. numerous articles to profl. jours. Mem. Wash. Gov.'s Transition Team, 1980, Task Force on Pers. Selection of Apptd. Ofcls; co-chmn. Tech. Transfer, State of Wash., 1980-81; pub. mem. State Med. Disciplinary Bd., 1981-85. With Med. Dept. and Mil. Govt. br. U.S. Army, 1942-45. Recipient Outstanding Rsch. award Am. Pers. and Guidance Assn., 1953, Stogdill award for disting. contbns. to leadership, 1978, award Outstanding Sci. Contbns. to Mil. Psychology, 1979; named Disting. Bicentennial lectr. U. Ga., 1985; Claremont Grad. Sch. and Claremont-McKenna Coll. 1991 Leadership Conf. dedicated to him. Fellow APA (Rsch. award in cons. psychology 1971), Soc. for Indsl./Orgnl. Psychology (Disting. Sci. Contbns. award 1996), Am. Psychol. Soc. (James McKeen Caltell award 1999), Am. Acad. Mgmt. (Disting. Educator award), Internat. Assn. Applied Psychology (Disting. Contrbns. award 2002), Internat. Assn. Applied Psychology (past pres. orgnl. psychology divsn.), Soc. Orgnl. Behavior. Office: Univ Wash Dept Psychology # 351525 Seattle WA 98195-0001

FIEGEL, JOHN, federal agency administrator; BS in Edn., U. Tex., El Paso. Elem. sch. math. tchr.; dir. arts programs El Paso Boys' Clubs; joined U.S. Dept. Edn., Washington, 1976—, dir. Parental Options and Info., Office Innovation and Improvement. Office: US Dept Edn OESE FOB-6 Rm 3E122 400 Maryland Ave SW Washington DC 20202*

FIEL, MAXINE LUCILLE, journalist, behavioral analyst, lecturer; b. N.Y.C. d. William Jack and Rowena (Burton) Stempel; m. David H. Fiel; children: Meredith Susan, Lisa Beth. Student in psychology and humanities, NYU. Nat. columnist, contbg. editor Mademoiselle Mag., N.Y.C., 1972—2001; nat. columnist Womens World, Englewood, N.J., 1979-89; contbg. editor Overseas Promotions, N.Y.C., 1979—; articles and features editor Japanese Overseas Press, 1976—; feature editor N.Y. Now, N.Y.C., 1980-91; contbg. editor Woman's World mag., 1979-89, Bella mag., Eng., 1987-89; nat. columnist First mag. for women, 1989-91; founder Starcast Astrological Svcs., Floral Park, N.Y., 1993—; columnist Borderland Mag., Japan, 1995—2000, IM Mag., Japan, 1997—2000. Cons. legal profession jury selection, 1984—; mktg. cons. Imperial Enterprises, Tokyo and Princeton, N.J., 1983—; cons. spokesperson Rowland Co., N.Y.C., 1972-81, Allied Chem. Co., N.Y.C., 1972-75; lectr., cons. Atlanta and Fla. Bar Assns., 1986—; creator Touch Game Parker Bros., Salem, Mass., 1971-76; behavior analystand communications advisor multi-nat. bus. corps.; cons. Chesebrough-Ponds, Footwear Coun., Grand Marnier Liquor; founder Starcast Astrological Svcs., 1993; pres. Interglobal Mktg. Co., 1999. Pioneer field of polit. body lang., 1969; author: Lovescopes, 1998, The Little Book of Body Language, 1998; contbr. articles to News Am., L.A. Times, Newhouse News Svc., Newspaper Enterprise Assocs., King Features, Borderland Mag.; adv. bd. mem. Writers Digest Mag., 2002; TV appearances on morning and afternoon shows including A Current Affair, The Regis Philbin Show, Eyewitness News, Cable News Networks, Tonight Show, Today Show, Good Morning Am., Joan Rivers Show, Jenny Jones, Entertainment Tonight, Hard Copy, Inside Edition, BBC Breakfast Show, Good Morning Japan, Fox News Channel, MSNBC, many others; appears in daily segment Good Morning Japan, own daily TV show on Nippon Network, Japan, 1989—. Active Sister Cities, Tokyo and N.Y.C.; charter mem. Elem. Sch. Cultural Exchange, Toyko and N.Y.C., Ctr. Environ. Edn.; bd. dirs. Periwinkle Prodns. Anti-Drug Abuse, N.Y.C., Adirondacks Save-A-Stray. Recipient Achievement award field behavioral sci. and photojournalism, Tokyo, 1974, Outstanding Rsch. award field psychology of gesture, Tokyo, 1976, Outstanding Achievement award Internat. Conf. Soc. Para-Psychology, 1974-75; honored guest at award dinner for involvement and support in the merging of Eye Rsch. Inst. Boston and Harvard Med. Sch., 1991. Mem. AFTRA, Internat. Found. Behavioral Rsch. (past v.p.), Nat. Writers Assn. (profl.), Profl. Writers Assn., Authors Guild, Authors League, World Wildlife Fund, Whale Protection Fund, Environ. Def. Soc., Nature Conservancy, Greenpeace, People for Ethical Treatment Animals, Humane Assn. U.S., Sea Shepherd Conservation Soc., Defenders of Wildlife, Guiding Eyes for Blind, Braille Camps for Blind Children, Save the Children, Lotos Club (N.Y.C.), East End Yacht Club (Freeport, N.Y.). Office: 338 Northern Blvd Ste 3 Great Neck NY 11021-4808

FIELD, ALEXANDER JAMES, economics educator; b. Boston, Apr. 17, 1949; s. Mark George and Anne (Murray) F.; m. Valerie Nan Wolk, Aug. 8, 1982; children: James Alexander, Emily Elena. AB, Harvard U., 1970; MS, London Sch. Econs., 1971; PhD, U. Calif., Berkeley, 1974. Asst. prof. econs. Stanford (Calif.) U., 1974-82; assoc. prof. Santa Clara (Calif.) U., 1982-88, acad. v.p., 1986-87, prof., chmn. dept. econs., 1988-93, assoc. dean Leavey Sch. Bus. and Adminstrn., 1993-96, dean, 1996-97, Michel and Mary Orradre prof. econs., 1992—. Mem. bd. trustees Santa Clara U., 1988-91. Author: Educational Reform and Manufacturing Development in Mid-Nineteenth Century Massachusetts, 1989, Altruistically Inclined: The Behavioral Sciences, Evolutionary Theory and the Origins of Reciprocity, 2001; author, editor: The Future of Economics, 1995, assoc. editor: Jour. Econ. Lit., 1981—98, 1999—; editor: Rsch. in Econ. History, 1993—; mem. editl. bd.: Explorations in Econ. History, 1993—, Jour. Econ. History,

2001—. Recipient Nevins prize Columbia U., 1975; NSF rsch. grantee, 1989. Mem. Phi Beta Kappa, Beta Gamma Sigma. Home: 3762 Redwood Cir Palo Alto CA 94306-4255 Office: Santa Clara Univ Dept Econs Santa Clara CA 95053-0001

FIELDEN, C. FRANKLIN, III, early childhood education consultant; b. Gulfport, Miss., Aug. 4, 1946; s. C. Franklin and Georgia (Freeman) F.; children: Christopher Michaux (dec.), Robert Michaux, Jonathan Dutton. Student, Claremont Men's Coll., 1964-65; AB, Colo. Coll., 1970; MS, George Peabody Coll. Tchrs., 1976, EdS, 1979. Tutor Proyecto El Guacio, San Sebastian, P.R., 1967-68; asst. tchr. GET-SET Project, Colorado Springs, Colo., 1969-70, co-tchr., 1970-75, asst. dir., 1972-75; tutor Early Childhood Edn. Project, Nashville, 1975-76; pub. policy intern Donner-Belmont Child Care Ctr., Nashville, 1976—77; asst. to urban min. Nashville Presbytery, 1977; intern to prin. Steele Elem. Sch., Colorado Springs, 1977-78, tchr., 1978-86; resource person Office Gifted and Talented Edn. Colorado Springs Pub. Schs., 1986-87; tchr. Columbia Elem. Sch., Colorado Springs, 1987-92; tchr., pre-sch. team coord. Helen Hunt Elem. Sch., Colorado Springs, 1992-93; validator Nat. Acad. Early Childhood Programs, 1992—, mentor, 1994—, commr., 1996-2000, 2001—; cons. Colo. Dept. Edn., Denver, 1993—96, sr. cons., 1996—2001, state coord. Even Start Family Literacy Program, 1997—, prin. cons., 2001—. Lectr. Arapahoe C.C., Littleton, Colo., 1981-82; instr. Met. State Coll., Denver, 1981; cons. Jubail Human Resources Devel. Inst., Saudi Arabia, 1982; mem. governing bd. GET-SET Project, 1969-79, 91-93. Ad hoc bd. trustees Tenn. United Meth. Agy. on Children and Youth, 1976-77; mem. So. Regional Edn. Bd. Task Force on Parent-Caregiver Relationships, 1976-77; day care com. Colo. Commn. Children and Their Families, 1981-82; active Nashville Children's Issues Task Force, 1976-77, Tenn. United Meth. Task Force on Children and Youth, 1976-77, Citizens' Goals Leadership Tng., 1986-87, Child Abuse Task Force, 4th Jud. Dist., 1986-87, First Impressions (Colo. Govs. Early Childhood Initiative) Task Force, 1987-88, El Paso County Placement Alternatives Commn., 1990-96, White Ho. Summit on Early Childhood Cognitive Devel., 2001; proposal rev. team Colo. Dept. Edn., 1992—; co-chair City/County Child Care Task Force, 1991-92; charter mem. City/County Early Childhood Care and Edn. Commn., 1993-96; bd. dirs. Colo. Office of Resource and Referral Agys., 1996-99; appeals panel Divsn. Child Care, Colo. Dept. Human Svcs., 2002—. Recipient Arts/Bus./Edn. award, 1983, Innovative Tchg. award, 1984; fellow NIMH, 1976. Mem.: ASCD, Pikes Peak Assn. Edn. Young Children, Nat. Assn. Early Childhood Specialists in State Depts. of Edn. (v.p. 1997—99, pres. 1999—2001, past. pres. 2001—03), Colo. Assn. Edn. Young Children (legis. com. 1979—84, governing bd., sec., exec. com. 1980—84, rsch. conf. chmn. 1982, tuition awards com. 1983—86, governing bd. 1985—86, chmn. tuition awards com. 1985—86, governing bd. 1989—95, pub. policy com. 1989—96, exec. com., treas. 1993, primary grades conf. chmn. 1994), Nat. Assn. Edn. Young Children (founding mem. primary-grades caucus 1992—2001, co-chair Western States Leadership Network 1993, Membership Action Group grantee 1993, panel profl. ethics in early childhood edn. 1993—97, nominating panel 2000—02, co-facilitator primary-grades interest forum 2001—), Nat. Trust Hist. Preservation, Huguenot Soc. Gt. Britain and Ireland., Phi Delta Kappa. Presbyterian. Home: PO Box 7766 Colorado Springs CO 80933-7766 Office: 201 E Colfax Ave Denver CO 80203-1704

FIELDS, GEORGE D., JR., former college president; Former pres. Spartanburg (S.C.) Meth. Coll. Home: 113 Starline Drive Spartanburg SC 29307-3713*

FIELDS, HALL RATCLIFF, finance educator; b. Gilbert, La., Nov. 24, 1937; s. Frederick Deacue and Mary Elodie (Moore) F.; 1 child, Demetria Charise Gable Fields Hunt; m. Ruby Jean James, Feb. 23, 1980 (dec. May 1998); 1 child, Brandon Hall. BS, So. U., Baton Rouge, 1965; MEd, McNeese State U., 1975; Coop. Edn. cert., La. Tech. U., 1968; postgrad., Grambling State U., 1990, Nova Southeastern U., 1991-98, U. Sarasota, Union Inst., 2001. Lic. ins. agt. Bus. tchr., head dept. bus. edn. Armstrong High Sch., Rayne, La., 1965-70; bus. edn. tchr., advisor Future Bus. Leaders Am. Rayne High Sch., 1970-80, gen. coop. edn. coord., 1978-80; acct., bookkeeper Housing & Urban Devel. Community Block, Grambling, La., 1980-81; bus. edn. tchr. Ft. Necessity (La.) High Sch., 1981-82, Ruston (La.) High Sch., 1982-83; acct. Grambling State U., 1983-87, acad. counselor, asst. prof., 1987—. Bus. edn. and career counselor vact. edn. Acadia Parish Sch. Bd., Crowley, La., 1965-78; adv. sec. Minority Affairs, La. Commr./Ins., Baton Rouge, 1989—, com. 1994; mem. Gov.'s Adv. Com. Equal Opportunity, Baton Rouge, 1991, sec., 1994; lectr. continuing edn. spkrs. bur. Grambling State U.; bus. counselor career, pres., CEO Fields Career and Fin. Svcs., 1990. Chmn. Accreditation Sub-Com. III, Grambling State U., 1989, Accreditation, Adminstrn., Rayne H.S., So. Assn. Colls. and Schs., 1979. Photographer, lectr., organizer Ivy Camera Club, Ft. Lewis, Wash., 1961-62; treas. Acadia Parish Edn. Assn., Crowley, 1967-71; pres. Acadia Assn. Edn., Crowley, 1980; deacon Starlight Bapt. Ch., Rayne, La., 1966; deacon, Mt. Olive Bapt. Ch., Grambling, 1980, chmn. deacon bd., 1993—; chmn. sustaining membership enrollment Boy Scouts Am., Grambling, 1993, scoutmaster, mem. bd. Ouachita Valley Coun., 1994. With U.S. Army Signal Corps, 1960-63, Vietnam. Recipient Thunderbird Dist. award Boy Scouts Am., 1994; named Outstanding Tchr. Yr., 1991. Mem. AACD, Am. Assn. Christian Counselors (charter), Nat. Career Devel. Assn., Am. Coll. Personnel Assn., Am. Assn. Multi-Cultural Counseling & Devel., Am. Counseling Assn., Internat. Platform Assn., La. Assn. Multi-Cultural Counseling & Devel., Am. Assn. Religious & Values Issues in Counseling, La. Assn. Religious & Values Issues in Counseling, Nat. Acad. Advising Assn., La. Acad. Advising Assn., Southern U. Alumni Fedn. (life), Omega Psi Phi (Pi Tau chpt. editor, historian). Democrat. Avocations: travel, camping, fishing, photography, bicycling. Home: 703 College Ave Grambling LA 71245-2413 Office: Grambling State U Coll Bas Study PO Box 567C Grambling LA 71245-0567

FIELDS, HARRIET GARDIN, counselor, educator, consultant; b. Pasco, Wash., Feb. 25, 1944; d. Harry C. and Ethel Jenell (Rochelle) Gardin; m. Avery C. Fields; 1 child, Avery C. BS in Edn., S.C. State U., Orangeburg, 1966; MEd, U. S.C., 1974. Lic. profl. counselor and supr.; nat. bd. cert. counselor and career counselor. Tchr. Richaldn Sch. Dist., Columbia, S.C., 1966-67 73-76; counselor supr. S.C. Dept. Corrections, Columbia, 1971-73; counselor Techinal Edn. System, West Columbia, S.C., 1967-70; exec. dir. Bethlehem Community Ctr., Columbia, 1976-79; human rels. cons. Calhoun County Schs., St. Matthews, S.C., 1979-82; admission counselor Allen U., Columbia, 1982-83; pres., cons. H.G. Fields Assn., Columbia, 1973—. Exec. dir. Big Bros./Big Sisters, Columbia, 1984-87 Mem. Richland County Coun., Columbia, 1989-97, chair, 1993, 94, 95, 96, 97; 2d vice chair Richland County Dem. Party, Columbia, 1984-88; sec. Statewide Reapportionment Com., 1990-97; mem. Richland Lexington Immunization Com., Hope for Kids, The Lifeline: Mission to Families; commr. Midlands Tech. Coll., 2001—. Recipient inaugural Woodrow Wilson award Greater Columbia C. of C., 1994, Pres.'s Disting. Svc. award Nat. Orgn. Black County Ofcls., 1996, numerous human rels. and outstanding svc. awards. Mem. ACA (resolutions chair So. br. 1993-94, parlimentarian 1998, 99-2000), SC Counseling Assn. (chair govt. rels. 1985-97, 98-99, pres. 1982-83), Assn. Multicultural Counseling Devel. (v.p. for African Am. concerns 1999-2000, rep. to Am. governing coun. 2000-2003), SC Coalition Pub. Health, Nat. Assn. Counties (d. dir. 1996, bylaws and election cm. 1996, 97, employment steering com. 1997), Nat. Assn. Counties (employment steering com. 1993-97, chair youth subcom. employment steering 1995-97, vice chair 1993-94), Am. Bus. Women's Assn. (pres. Midlands chpt. 1998-99), Columbia C. of C. Democrat. Methodist. Avocations: travel, reading. Home and Office: HG Fields and Assocs 412 Juniper St Columbia SC 29203-5055

FIELDS, HENRY WILLIAM, college dean; b. Cedar Rapids, Iowa, Sept. 25, 1946; m. Anne M. Fields; children: Benjamin Widdicomb, Justin Riley. AB in Psychology, Dartmouth, Hanover, N.H., 1969; DDS in Dentistry, Univ. Iowa, Iowa City, 1973, MS in Pedodontics, 1975; MSD in Orthodontics, Univ. Wash., Seattle, 1977. Cert. dentistry Iowa 1973, N.C. 1978, Ohio 1991. Staff, Dept. Hosp. Dentistry Univ. Iowa Hosps., Iowa City, 1973; grad. supr. Muscatine (Iowa) Migrant Program, 1974; grad. instr., Undergrad. Pedodontic Clinic and Lab. Univ. Iowa, 1974-75; AFDH tchr. tng. fellow, Dept. Orthodontics Univ. Wash., 1975-77, clin. asst., Undergrad. Pediatric Dentistry Clinic and Seminars, 1977; active participant Dental Faculty Practice, Sch. Dentistry Univ. N.C., Chapel Hill, 1977-91, asst. prof., Depts. of Pediatric Dentistry and Orthodontics, 1977-82; with N.C. Meml. Hosp., Chapel Hill, 1978-91; assoc. prof., Depts. of Pediatric Dentistry and Orthodontics Univ. N.C., Chapel Hill, 1982-87, grad. program dir., Dept. Pediatric Dentistry, 1984-89, prof., Dept. Pediatric Dentistry and Orthodontics, 1987-91, acting dir. grad. studies, Sch. Dentistry, 1989, asst. dean acad. affairs, Sch. Dentistry, 1990-91; chair, Dept. Dentistry OSU Hosps., Columbus, Ohio, 1991—, adj. prof. of Orthodontics, Sch. Dentistry, 1992—; participant, Faculty Practice OSU Coll. of Dentistry, Columbus, Ohio, 1991—, prof. Dept. Orthodontics, 1991—, dean, 1991—; staff Columbus Children's Hosp., 1992—. Mem. human subjects com. Sch. Dentistry, Univ. N.C., 1989-91, chmn. curriculum com., 1990-91, chmn. dirs. com. adv. edn. program, 1989-91, health promotion disease prevention task force, 1990-91; deans coun. computerization com. The Ohio State Univ., 1991—; bd. dirs. IADR-AADR Craniofacial Biology Group, 1988-90; cons. to com. to review grad. Pediatric Dentistry Univ. Pitts., 1991; co-chair cont. edn. com. Am. Acad. Pediatric Dentistry/ Am. Assoc. of Orthodontic, 1991—; cons. Callahan award commn., 1992; external examiner BDS and MDS programs Dept. Pediatric Dentistry and Orthodontics Univ. Hong Kong, 1991-93; course dir. and coord. for numerous grad. and undergrad. programs. Contbr. chpts. to books, articles to profl. jours. Recipient NIDR grantee, 1980-83, NIDR Inst. grantee, 1985-86, 1988-93. Home: 4066 Fenwick Rd Columbus OH 43220-4870 Office: Ohio State U Coll Dentistry 1159 Postle Hall Columbus OH 43210-1241

FIELDS, KEITH ALLEN, secondary education educator; b. Salisbury, Md., Nov. 5, 1958; s. John Mark and Ruby Lee (Staton) F. BA, Salisbury State U., 1980, Cert. Secondary Edn., 1982; MA, U. Del., 1984. Cert. tchr., Md. Tchr. Wicomico County, Salisbury, Md., 1984—. Mem. Md. State Tchrs. Assn. (assn. rep. 1986-94), Wicomico County Tchrs. Assn. (assn. rep. 1986-94), Nat. Coun. for Social Studies, Phi Alpha Theta, Kappa Delta Pi. Avocations: reading, sports/baseball, football and basketball, travel.

FIELDS, RUTH KINNIEBREW, secondary and elementary educator, consultant; b. Notasulga, Ala. d. Lee Wesley and Olivia S. (Scruggs) Kinniebrew; m. Benjamin Belton Fields, Dec. 24, 1950; children: Ivan W., Benjamin B. Jr. BS, Tuskegee Inst., 1949, MEd, 1954, postgrad., 1971—75. Cert. vocat. home econs. tchr., Ala.; cert. supt. edn., Ala. Prin., tchr. Choctaw County Bd. Edn., Butler, Ala., 1950-56; dietician, tchr. home econs. Hale County Bd. Edn., Greensboro, Ala., 1957-62; prin., tchr. Tuscaloosa (Ala.) County Bd. Edn., 1962-64, tchr. home econs., 1964-67, home sch. worker, 1967-76, tchr. kindergarten, 1976-85. Supervising tchr. of students Ala. A&M U., Normal, U. Ala., Tuscaloosa, 1976-85; sec./treas. Dist. II Attendance Suprs., Ala., 1974-75. Bd. dirs. ARC, Tuscaloosa, 1967-73, Girl Scouts, Tuscaloosa, 1967-73, Am. Red Cross, Tuscaloosa, 1968-74, LWV, Tuscaloosa; treas. Planned Parenthood, Tuscaloosa, 1967-76, Cmty. Svc. Programs, Tuscaloosa, 1968-74; advisor Chpt. 2/Title II Adv. Coun., Tuscaloosa, 1985-89. Recipient Presdl. Assoc. award Tuskegee U., 1990; named to Nat. Women's Hall of Fame, 1995. Mem. NEA, AAUW, LWV (dir. Greater Tuscaloosa chpt. 2003), Ala. Edn. Assn. (Excellence in Edn. 1982), Tuscaloosa County Edn. Assn., Nat. Women's History Mus., The Links, Inc., Delta Kappa Gamma, Alpha Kappa Alpha, Gamma Sigma Sigma. Democrat. Baptist. Avocations: reading, working puzzles, walking, cooking, traveling. Home: PO Box 1755 Tuscaloosa AL 35403-1755

FIELDS, W(ADE) THOMAS, dental educator; b. McKenzie, Tenn., Oct. 15, 1942; s. Thomas N. and Rachel (Reynolds) Fields; m. Sherry J. Jolly, Aug. 12, 1966; children: Jeffrey Thomas, Susan Michele. DDS, U. Tenn., 1965; MPH, U. N.C., 1970. Clin. dentist N.C. State Bd. Health, Raleigh, 1966-69; asst. prof. U. Louisville, 1972-75, assoc. prof., dept. chmn., 1975-79, U. Tenn., Memphis, 1979-83, assoc. prof., divsn. dir., 1983-90, prof., 1990—, divsn. dir., 1990—, dept. chair, 1998-99. Faculty cons. Memphis (Tenn.) VA Hosp., 1981—; project cons. Am. Bd. Dental Pub. Health, Gainesville, Fla., 1984; cons. to asst. surgeon gen. and chief dental officer USPHS, Washington, 1985; presenter in field. Reviewer Jour. Acad. Gen. Dentistry, 1984—; author: 6 tchg. manuals; contbr. articles to profl. jours. Head coach Little League, Elizabeth City, NC, 1968—69, Peewee Baseball, Louisville, 1976—78; asst. den leader Boy Scouts Am., Louisville, 1978—79; pres. Germantown (Tenn.) HS Band Boosters, 1985—86, 1989—90. Recipient Traineeship, USPHS, 1969—71. Mem.: ADA (content cons. monographs 1983, 1986), Deans' Odontological Soc. (elected mem.), Am. Assn. Pub. Health Dentistry (sec.-treas. 1979—82, pres. 1982—84, abstract reviewer 1985, pres.-elect), Am. Dental Edn. Assn., Memphis Dental Soc. (editor newsletter 2002—), Tenn. Dental Assn. (cons. Coun. Dental Edn. 1984—87), Omicron Kappa Upsilon. Avocations: chess, golf. Home: 1536 Carr Ave Memphis TN 38104-4901 Office: Univ Tenn Coll Dentistry 875 Union Ave Memphis TN 38163-0001 E-mail: tfields@utmem.edu.

FIERRO, MARCELLA, language educator; b. Las Cruces, N.Mex., Apr. 9, 1950; d. J. Arturo and Estella M. Fierro. BA French, NMex. State U., 1973, MA Spanish, 1975. Residential faculty Scottsdale C.C., Scottsdale, Ariz., 1990—92, Mesa C.C., Mesa, Ariz., 1992—, evening supr., 1998—2000, 2002—03, dept. chairperson, 2003—. Acad. adv. Ariz. State U. Cross Coll. Advising Svcs., Tempe, Ariz., 1990—2000. Office: Mesa CC 1833 W Southern Ave Mesa AZ 85202-4868 Office Fax: 480-461-7458. Business E-Mail: fierro@mail.mc.maricopa.edu.

FIES, JAMES DAVID, elementary education educator; b. Chgo., May 19, 1950; s. Arthur Herbert Sr. and Ruth Paulina (Rehm) F.; m. Ruth Elaine Carlson, June 24, 1972; children: Samuel Jacob, Sarah Rae. BA, Purdue U., 1972, MS, 1975. Cert. elem. edn. tchr., Ind. Tchr. math. Morton Elem./Mid. Sch., Hammond, Ind., 1972-82, Eggers Elem./Mid. Sch., Hammond, 1982-88, Gavit Jr./Sr. High Sch., Hammond, 1988—, interim asst. prin., 1992. Dept. chair Eggers Mid. Sch., 1983-86. Bldg. union rep. Hammond Tchrs. Fedn. Local 394, 1981-87; trustee Trinity Luth. Ch., Hammond, 1976-82, 86-87, bd. fin., 1993—. Mem. Nat. Coun. Tchrs. of Maths., Hammond Tchrs. Fedn., Am. Fedn. of Tchrs. Avocations: traveling, fishing, family activities. Home: 544 Hickory Ln Munster IN 46321-2409

FIFE, BETTY H. retired librarian; b. Indpls., Mar. 31, 1925; d. Otho Cova and Mae Craddock (Paxton) Hay; m. James A. Fife, Aug. 30, 1945; children: Andrew, Marlie, John, Laurie. BS, Boston U., 1967, MS, 1969; student, Northeastern U. Classroom tchr., libr. Town of Hanover (Mass.); elem. libr. City of Newburgh (N.Y.); ret., 1999. Fellow Northeastern U. Mem. NCTE. Home: 174 Cedar Acres Rd Marshfield MA 02050-6036

FIFE-LAFRENZ, JANET KAY, elementary school educator; b. Creston, Iowa, Dec. 26, 1944; d. Cleve Hoiser and Eiffle Laurene (White) Seley; m. Bruce D. Fife, Aug. 15, 1965 (div. Nov. 1977); 1 child, Menda S.; m. Stanley C. LaFrenz, May 26, 1997. AA, Creston Community Coll., 1965; BS in Edn., Western Ill. U., 1967; MA in Edn., N.E. Mo. State U., 1978. Sch. tchr. Keokuk (Iowa) Community Schs., 1967—. Sec., treas. Tri State Coalition Against Family Violence, 1983-93, dir., 1983—96; city councilperson Keokuk City, 1986—2000; dir. Sister Cities, 1990-92, S.E. Iowa League of Municipalities, 1990—95; trustee Southeastern C.C., Keokuk/Burlington, Iowa, 1992—, pres. 1994—96; pres. YMCA, 1992-93, bd. dirs., 1992—96; pres. Iowa Women's Polit. Caucus, 1994—96. Mem. AAUW (pres. 2002—), Internat. Reading Assn., Assn. Univ. Women, Bus. and Profl. Women (pres. 1992-94), Delta Kappa Gamma (corr. sec. 2002—). Avocations: sewing, traveling, gardening. Home: 1122 Grand Ave Keokuk IA 52632-4127 Office: Keokuk Community Schs 727 Washington St Keokuk IA 52632-2438

FIGGS, LINDA SUE, educational administrator; b. Westhope, N.D., Dec. 19, 1946; d. Clifford James and Ethel Grace (Geise) Drake; m. Tom R. Figgs, Dec. 27, 1969. Student, Minot State U., 1964-66; B.Music Edn., U. Kans., 1968, M.Music Edn., 1972, EdD, 1978; postgrad., U. del Valle de Mex., 1996, Habla Hispana Lang. Inst. San Miguel de Allende, Guanajuato, Mex., 1997. Cert. secondary music tchr., ednl. adminstr., Kans., Iowa, Nebr., N.D. Music tchr. Jefferson County N. High Sch., Winchester, Kans., 1968-76, 89-91, supr. student tchrs., 1970-75; rsch. asst. to assoc. dean of edn. U. Kans., Lawrence; prin. McKinley Elem., Liberal, Kans., 1992-95, Maynard Elem., Emporia, Kans., 1995-96, Stanton Street Early Childhood Ctr., 1995-96; gen. dir. Academia Cultural de Espanol, San Miguel de Allende, Mex., 1997—. Rsch. asst. Sch. Edn., U. Kans., Lawrence, 1977; piano tchr. Toon Shop, Atchison, Kans., Leavenworth, Kans.; music tchr. Little Flower Sch., Minot, N.D., Effingham, Kans.; mgr. music store, Effingham; sec. humanities Minot State U.; counselor Internat. Music Camp, Dunseith, N.D., Midwestern Music and Art Camp, Lawrence; summer counselor, unit leader Nat. Music Camp, Interlochen, Mich.; sponsor 5th grade Positive Peer Group; mem. edn. adv. panel TeleKansas Alliance; mem. U.S. D.480 Action Team Mem., McKinley Action Team Mem.; reader adv. bd. S.W. Daily Times; chmn. rural residency coordinating team Chamber Music Am. and NEA; mem. tech. com. for Unified Sch. Dist. 480 and McKinley Quality Performance Accreditation Team; elem. adminstrn. rep. Stakeholders Com., Sch. Site Coun., strategic planning teams Unified Sch. Dist. 480, McKinley preassessment team, 504 team, intensive assistance team, skunk works, supervision, stakeholders, McKinley Drug Team; bd. dirs., patron, docent Baker Arts Ctr.; coord. ESL and migrant summer sch.; coord. for Unified Sch. Dist. 253 Migrant/ESL program, 1995—; 1st grade prin. rep. for Supt.'s Curriculum Coun. for Sci., elem. prin. rep. sci. com. Singer, pianist, dir. San Miguel Chorale; contbr. articles to profl. pubs. Bd. dirs. Am. Youth Symphony Band and Orch., Nebr., 1970-76; music dir. United Meth. Ch., Atchison, 1988-92; mem. choir United Meth. Ch., Liberal, 1992-95; choir dir. 1st Christian Ch., Liberal, 1995, McKinley Elem. PTA, S.W. Kans. Humane soc.; bd. dirs. Cmty. Concert, 1994-95; vol. Mid Am. Air Mus.; mem. 500 Club, Leadership Liberal, 1995, Leadership Emporia, 1996, Maynard Elem. PTO, Maynard Elem. Sch. Site Coun., Flint Hills Humane Soc., SOS, Emporia Arts Coun., Emporia Area Friends of the Zoo. Mem. ASCD, NEA, AAUW (edn. and scholarship com.), Nat. Assn. Elem. Sch. Prins., United Sch. Adminstrs., Kans. Assn. Sch. Adminstrs., Kans. ASCD, Kans. Assn. Elem. Sch. Prins., Kans. Edn. Assn., Nat. Mid. Sch. Assn., Kans. Assn. Mid Level Edn., Kans. Reading Assn., Knas. Reading Coun., Profl. Devel. Coun. (co-pres., insvc. com.), U. Kans. Alumni Assn. (life), S.W. Symphony Soc. (pres. 1993-95), Assn. Cmty. Art Agys. Kans., Emporia Area C. of C. (bus. edn. com.), Sigma Alpha Iota, Pi Kappa Lambda, Phi Delta Kappa. Presbyterian. Avocations: reading, walking, piano performance, computers, stained glass. Address: 1007 Dickinson Rd Effingham KS 66023-5130

FIGUEIRA, ROBERT CHARLES, history educator; b. N.Y.C., Jan. 30, 1951; s. Charles Manoel and Marion (Gentile) F.; m. Jan Friedewald, Oct. 14, 1995. BA in History and German, Wesleyan U., Middletown, Conn., 1973; MA in Medieval Studies, Cornell U., 1976, PhD in History, 1980. Asst. prof. history Trinity Coll., Washington, 1979-83; asst. dean Emory Coll. Emory U., Atlanta, 1983-85; vis. asst. prof. history So. Meth. U., Dallas, 1986-87, Wright State U., Dayton, 1987-88; assoc. prof. history St. Mary's Coll. Minn., Winona, 1988-91; assoc. prof. and prof. history Lander U., Greenwood, S.C., 1991—. Book reviewer; presenter papers at confs., 1983—; faculty peer reviewer Bush Found. Grants St. Mary's Coll., Minn., 1988; manuscript referee Ch. History, 1988, 2001, 2002, U. Pa. Press, 1987, 94, Yale U. Press, 1996, Allyn & Bacon, 2003; grant applications referee NEH, 1993, 97; state examiner Bavarian Ministry for Edn. and Culture, 1986; vis. scholar U. Calif., Berkeley, Inst. Medieval Canon Law/Robbins Collection, 1982, 84, 88, 90, 91. Contbr. articles to profl. jours. Bd. dirs. S.C. Humanities Coun., 1996—2002. Recipient scholarships Wesleyan U., 1969-73, N.Y. State Regents, 1969; grantee NEH, 1988, 91, 92, 93, Lander Found., 1991, 93, 94, 95, 99, 2002, 03, Bush Found., 1988-89, 89-90; rsch. fellow Deutscher Akademischer Austauschdienst, 1993; Cornell U. fellow, 1977-78, Fulbright, 1973-74. Mem. Am. Cath. Hist. Assn., Am. Hist. Assn., Medieval Acad. Am., Am. Soc. Ch. History, Soc. for Medieval Canon Law, S.C. Hist. Assn.(co-editor, 2002, 04), Selden Soc., Phi Beta Kappa, Phi Alpha Theta. Roman Catholic. Office: Lander U Willson St Greenwood SC 29649

FIKES, JAY COURTNEY, anthropology educator, art dealer; b. San Luis Obispo, Calif., June 14, 1951; s. J.C. and Virginia Lee (Roberts) F.; m. Lebriz N. Tosuner, Apr. 17, 1979; 1 child, Leyla Tupina. BA in Comparative Culture, U. Calif., Irvine, 1973; MEd in Bilingual Edn., U. San Diego, 1974; MA in Anthropology, U. Mich., 1977, P in Anthropology, 1985. Tutor Palomar Coll., Pala Indian Reservation, Calif., 1974; instr. anthropology Allan Hancock Coll., Santa Maria, Calif., 1975-76; land use planner Navajo Nation, Windowrock, Ariz., 1983; instr. anthropology U.S. Internat. U., Oceanside, Calif., 1985—. Instr. research methods in soc. sci. Marmara U., Istanbul, Turkey, 1985-87; lobbyist Friends Com. on Nat. Legislation, 1990; instr. anthropology Yeditepe U., Istanbul, 1998—; owner Cuatro Esquinas Traders, Carlsbad, Calif., 1979—. Author: Huichol Indian Identity and Adaptation, 1985, Carlos Castaneda,Academic Opportunism and the Psychedelic Sixties, 1993, Reuben Snake, Your Humble Serpent, 1996, Huichol Indian Ceremonial Cycle, 1997; contbr. articles on edn. and anthropology to profl. jours. Coord. Fiestas Patrias, Carlsbad Bicentennial Com., 1975. Anthropology teaching fellow U. Mich., Ann Arbor, 1976-79, Postdoctoral fellow Smothsonian Instn., Washington, 1991-92; acad. scholar dept. anthropology, U. Mich., 1981-82; doctoral dissertation grantee Rackham Grad. Sch. U. Mich., 1981. Mem. Internat. Platform Assn., Am. Anthropol. Assn., N.Y. Acad. Scis., Rotary (dir. internat. svc. 1982-83). Mem. Religious Soc. Friends. Home: 2421 Buena Vista Cir Carlsbad CA 92008-1601

FILCHOCK, ETHEL, education educator; BS in Edn., Kent State U. Tchr. Cleve. Pub. Schs.; with EFC Creations, Solon, Ohio. Author: Voices in Poetics: Vol. 1, 1985 (Merit award), Hall of Fame, Ethel Filchock, Vol. 1, 1991, (book of poetry) Softer Memories Across a Lifetime, 1989, (poetry chapbook) A Glimpse of Love, 1991; composer: Praise God, The Lord is Coming; lyricist (songs) He Is Born, 1991, An Old-Fashioned Christmas, Let's Wave the Stars and Stripes Forever, 1991, Be There for Me Music of America, 1993, Christmas Joy, Happy Holidays, 1993, Beautiful Lady of Medugorje, 1993 (Harmonious Honor award), Christmas Joy, There is a Story, 1994, Hilltop Country, Love is Not a Game, 1994, High Country, Loving is Caring, 1995, Mistletoe and Holly, 1996, The Joy of Christmas, This Land is Called America, 1996, Together We Stand, 1996, Everyday, 1997, America Sounds of the Street, Music of America, 1997, Hilltop Country Songbook Songs, Just Love, Love is Not a Game, 1997, Hilltop Records, album, Christmas in My Heart Song, This Holy Morning, 1998, Christmas Songbook, Songs, Mistletoe and Holly, 1998, There Is a Story, 1998, This Holy Morning, 1998 (Award for Excellence, 2000), Adore Him Today, 2000, Christmas Time, 2000, Love Came Down, 2001, Santa Came to our House, 2001, This Land is Called America, 2001, We Will Remember September, 2001, I Will Be With You, 2002, America Is Our Land, 2002. Chmn. sch. United Way, 1985-86. Recipient Cert. of Achievement N.Y. Profl./Amateur Song Jubilee, 1986, Editor's Choice award Disting. Poets of Am., Outstanding Achievement in Poetry, Nat. Libr. of Poetry, 1993, Outstanding Poets of 1994, Interregnum Nat. Libr. of Poetry, Best Poets of

1995, Transformation, Nat. Libr. of Poetry, Editor's Choice award Outstanding Achievement in Poetry, 1996, 2000, 01, 02, Nat. Libr. of Poetry, 1995, 96, 2001, Outstanding Poets of 1998 for Magnanimous Beauty, Nat. Libr. of Poetry, 1998, Editor's Choice award for outstanding achievement in poetry, 1998. Mem. NAFE, Am. Fedn. Tchrs. Clubs: Akron Manuscript. Roman Catholic. Avocations: painting, traveling, dancing, fishing.

FILIPPELLI, ALICE MARIE, special education educator; b. Paterson, N.J., Feb. 24, 1962; d. William Carl Jr. and Donna Marie (Altavilla) F. BA in Psychology, William Paterson Coll., Wayne, N.J., 1985, postgrad., 1985-88, 91—. Cert. tchr. of handicapped, N.J. Substitute tchr. United Cerebral Palsy League, Union, N.J., 1985; grad. asst. infant psychology program William Paterson Coll., 1985-87; classroom tchr. St. Patricks Spl. Classes Sch., Newark, 1985-88; spl. edn. tchr. Paterson Pub. Sch. # 27, 1988—. Mem. ann. conv. Assn. Schs. and Agys. for Handicapped, Atlantic City, 1985-88. Vol. helper, fund raiser Eva's Kitchen/Homeless Shelter, Paterson, 1986—; polit. worker, poll worker Young. Dems. (Riverside) Assn., Paterson, 1978—. Recipient Sponsor Appreciation award Paterson PASSPLAN Orgn., 1991. Mem. NEA, N.J. Edn. Assn., Passaic County Edn. Assn., Paterson Edn. Assn. (bldg. del. 1989—). Democrat. Roman Catholic. Avocations: arts and crafts, reading, physical training, personal growth courses, peer counseling group talk. Home: 1036 E 24th St # 2nd-flr Paterson NJ 07513-1628

FILISKO, FRANK EDWARD, physicist, educator; b. Lorain, Ohio, Jan. 29, 1942; s. Joseph John and Mary Magdalene (Cherven) F.; m. Doris Faye Call, Aug. 8, 1970; children: Theresa Marie, Andrew William, Edward Anthony. BA, Colgate U., 1964; MS, Purdue U., 1966; PhD, Case Western Res. U., 1969. Post doctoral fellow Case Western Res. U., Cleve., 1968-70; prof. materials sci. engring. and macromolecular sci. U. Mich., Ann Arbor, 1970—, acting dir. macromolecular sci. and engring., 1987-96. Dir. Polymer Lab., U. Mich. Editor: Progress in Electrorheology, 1995; contbr. more than 125 articles to profl. jours. Mem. Am. Phys. Soc., Am. Chem. Soc., KC, Soc. of Rheology. Roman Catholic. Achievements include patents for Electric field dependent fluids and Electric dependent fluids-CIP. Office: U Mich Materials Sci & Engring Ann Arbor MI 48109 E-mail: fef@engin.umich.edu.

FILLER, ROBERT, chemist educator; b. Bklyn., Feb. 2, 1923; s. Alfred Louis and Ethel (Schwab) F.; m. Lael Carol Rosenbloom, Oct. 7, 1945 (dec. 1954); children: Susan, Rebecca Filler Helgesen, Debby; m. Miriam G. Holland, Sept. 20, 1959; children: Michael Knize, Daniel. BS, CCNY, 1943; MS, U. Iowa, 1947, PhD, 1949. Asst. prof. Union U., 1949-50; postdoctoral research fellow Purdue U., 1950-51; research chemist Wright Air Devel. Center, Dayton, Ohio, 1951-53; instr., asst. prof. Ohio Wesleyan U., 1953-55; asst. prof. chemistry Ill. Inst. Tech., Chgo., 1955-61, assoc. prof., 1961-66, prof., 1966—, acting chmn. dept., 1966-68, 90-93; chmn. chemistry, 1968-76; prof. emeritus, sr. rsch. fellow, 1994—; dean Lewis Coll. Scis. and Letters Ill. Inst. Tech., Chgo., 1976-86. Rsch. assoc. Ben May Lab. for Cancer Rsch., U. Chgo., 1956-57; cons. U. Ill. Coll. Medicine, 1958-59, IIT Rsch. Inst., 1964-66; vis. scientist Weizmann Inst. Sci., Israel, 1974; guest prof. Ruhr U., Germany, 1987; v.p. TechDrive, Inc., Chgo., 1997—. Contbr. articles to profl. jours.; editor 3 books on chemistry; mem. editorial bd. Fluorine Chem. Revs., Jour. Fluorine Chemistry. Served with AUS, 1944-46. Recipient Excellence in Teaching award Ill. Inst. Tech., 1990; NIH spl. postdoctoral fellow U. Cambridge, Eng., 1962-63 Fellow AAAS; mem. AAUP, Am. Chem. Soc. (sec.-treas. div. fluorine chemistry 1972-74, chmn. 1976), Royal Soc. Chemistry (London), N.Y. Acad. Scis., Sigma Xi, Phi Lambda Upsilon. Home: 8453 Linder Ct Skokie IL 60077-2014 E-mail: filler@ut.edu.

FILLGROVE, KEVIN, principal; BS Edn. in Secondary Math., Clarion U., 1988; postgrad., Allentown Coll., 1990—91, Wilkes Coll., 1990—91, Millersville U., 1992—93; MEd in Secondary Adminstrn., Shippensburg U., 1994. Math. tchr. Columbia (Pa.) Jr.-Sr. H.S., 1988—94, dean students, 1989—94, middle sch. coord., asst. prin., 1994—97; asst. middle sch. prin. Hershey (Pa.) Middle Sch., 1997—99, prin., 1999—. Spkr. in field. Baseball and basketball coach Little League; umpire Amateur Softball Assn.; weekend camp vol.; elder, single adult Sunday sch. tchr. Calvary Ch., Lancaster. Mem.: ASCD, Pa. Coun. Tchrs. Math., Pa. Assn. for Supervision and Curriculum Devel., Pa. Middle Sch. Assn., Pa. Assn. Secondary Sch. Prins. (chmn. awards com., mem. pub. rels. com.), Nat. Coun. Tchrs. Math., Nat. Staff Devel. Coun., Nat. Middle Sch. Assn., Nat. Assn. Secondary Sch. Prins. Office: Hershey Middle Sch Homestead Rd PO Box 898 Hershey PA 17033*

FILOMENO, LINDA JEAN HARVEY, elementary education educator; Bilingual tchr. Phila. Pub. Sch. Sys., 1976-79, Woodrow Wilson Elem. Sch., Trenton, N.J., 1979-83; head presch. tchr. YWCA Greater R.I., Central Falls, 1984-88; tchr. in language, culture William D'Abate Elem. Sch., Providence, 1988-95; tchr. lang. and culture dept. Providence Pub. Schs., 1995—; coord. literacy and profl. devel. Woonsocket Edn. Dept. Named R.I. State Tchr. of Yr., 1993, 94; recipient Milken Family Educator award, 1995.*

FILSTON, HOWARD CHURCH, pediatric surgeon, educator; b. NYC, Dec. 29, 1935; s. Howard Samuel and Marion (Church) F.; m. Nancy Lee Jameson, June 3, 1961 (dec. Nov. 2002); children: Scott Jameson (dec.), Timothy Howard, Megan Lee Johnson. AB, Harvard U., 1958; MD, Case Western Res. U., 1962. Diplomate Am. Bd. Med. Examiners. Intern in gen. surgery Univ. Hosps., Cleve., 1962-63, asst. resident in gen. surgery, 1963-64, 66-68, chief resident, 1968-69; asst. chief resident pediatric surgery Children's Hosp. Phila., 1969-70; instr. pediatric surgery U. Pa. Sch. of Medicine, Phila., 1969-71, chief resident pediatric surgery, 1970-71; asst. prof. pediatric surgery Case Western Res. U. Hosp., Cleve., 1971-76; assoc. prof. pediatric surgery and pediatrics Duke U. Med. Ctr., Durham, NC, 1976-82, chief pediatric surgery, 1976-90, prof. pediatric surgery and pediats., 1982—90, prof. pediatric surgery and pediatrics, U. Tenn. Med. Ctr., Knoxville, 1990-2000, chief pediatric surgery, 1990-2000, vice chmn. dept. surgery, 1992-2000; emeritus prof.of pediat. surgery, 2000—. Specialist site visitor, pediatric surgery, Accreditation Coun. Grad. Med. Edn., 1982-90, 1995—. Author: Surgical Problems in Children, 1982; author: (with others) The Surgical Neonate, 1978, rev. 1985; assoc. editor, Jour. Pediatric Surgery, 1985-2000; mem. editorial bd. Pediatrics, 1990-97; contbr. articles to profl. jours. Bd. dirs. Pediatric Family Ctr. of N.C. (Ronald McDonald House), Durham, 1980-90, Surgeon Gen.'s Workshop on Drunk Driving, chmn. Citizens Adv. Panel, 1988; mem. exec. bd. Met. Drug Commn., Knoxville, 1993-2000, v.p., 1997-2000, chair DUI task force, 1994-99. Served to capt. U.S. Army, 1964-66. Nat. scholar Harvard U., 1954-58. Fellow ACS (gov. 1992-98), Am. Acad. Pediatrics (surg., exec. com. 1984-91, chmn. 1989-90), Am. Pediatric Surg. Assn. (edn. com. 1984-90, sec., bd. govs. 1994-97), Am. Surg. Assn., So. Surg. Assn.; mem. Alpha Omega Alpha. Republican. Presbyterian. Avocations: family activities, water sports, sailing. Office: Univ of Tenn Med Ctr Dept Surgery Box U-11 1924 Alcoa Hwy Knoxville TN 37920-6900 Fax: (865) 544-6898. E-mail: hnfilston@earthlink.net.

FINAISH, FATHI ALI, aeronautical engineering educator; b. Tripoli, Libya, July 22, 1954; came to U.S., 1981; s. Ali Finaish and Zuhra (Lamin) Mahfud; m. Deborah Lynn Demijohn, Dec. 28, 1984. BS in Aero. Engring., U. Al-Fateh, Tripoli, 1978; MS in Aerospace Engring., U. Colo., 1984, PhD in Aerospace Engring., 1987. Lic. pvt. pilot; FAA airframe and power plant cert. mechanic. Rsch. asst. U. Colo., Boulder, 1984-87, adj. asst. prof., 1987-88; asst. prof. aero. engring. U. Mo., Rolla, 1988-94, assoc. prof., 1994-2000, prof., 2000—, assoc. chair aerospace engring., 1999—. Dir. Mo. NASA Space Grant, 1999—; airworthiness engr. Dept. Civil Aviation, Tripoli, 1979-81; ground sch. instr. Tripoli Flight Ctr., 1980-81; rsch. fellow Naval Under Water Systems Ctr., Newport, R.I., 1991, NASA Langley Rsch. Ctr., Hampton, Va., 1992; lectr. various univs.; advisor Licking High Sch., St. James High Sch.; summer rsch. fellow U.S. Navy-Am. Soc. Engring. Edn., 1991, NASA-Am. Soc. Engring. Edn., 1992. Contbr. articles to profl. jours. Head coach Rolla Soccer Club, asst. to soccer head coach, 1997-99. Grantee U. Mo., Rolla, 1988-92, U. Mo. Systems, 1991-92, U. Mo. Rsch. Bd., 1994-95, Office Naval Rsch., 1991, NASA, 1993-95, Precision Environ. Sys., 1995-96, Ctr. Indoor Rsch., 1998—, ASHRAE, 1999—. Fellow AIAA (assoc., Outstanding Tchr. award U. Mo. chpt. 1993); mem. ASEE, ASHRAE (grantee 1992-93, 99). Achievements include development of several ednl. computer codes and courses in aerospace engring.; design and bldg. an exptl. system that generates and visualizes impulsive and accelerating motions and other unsteady airflow histories; designed and developed several wind tunnels for steady and unsteady aerodynamic testing at the University of Missouri-Rolla. Office: U Mo Dept Mech Engring Rolla MO 65401

FINALE, FRANK LOUIS, elementary school educator, writer; b. Brookyln, Mar. 10, 1942; s. Ralph and Mary (Guidone) F.; m. Barbara Ann (Long), Oct. 20, 1973; children: Michael, Alan, Steven. BS in edn., Ohio State U., 1964; MA in human devel., Fairleigh Dickinson U., 1976. Tchr. Toms River Regional Sch., NJ, 1964—2002. Presenter, Young Authors Conf., 1985—, voted tchr. of the yr., 2002-2003, East Dover Elementary and named to the State of New Jersey's 2002 Governor's Tchr. Program. Author: To the Shore Once More, 1999, To the Shore Once More Vol. II, 2001, Jersey Shor Publ. A Gull's Story,2002,Jersey Shore Publ.; editor-in-chief Without Halos, 1985-95; poetry editor the new renaissance, 1996—; co-editor: Under A Gull's Wing, 1996; author poems and essays. Recipient: Exemplary Svc. Award, Internat. Reading Assn. and Ocean County Reading Coun., 1993; Nominated for Excellence in Edn. Award, 2002 Mem. NEA, Poetry Soc. Am., N.J. Edn. Assn., Ocean County Poets Collective (founding mem.). Avocations: reading, films, music, comedians. Office: East Dover Elem Sch 725 Vaughn Ave Toms River NJ 08753-4567

FINCH, CAROL ANNE, former secondary education educator; b. N.Y.C., Oct. 22, 1942; d. William George and Anna Frances (O'Connell) Simpson; m. Aug. 1, 1970 (div.); children: Robert A., James J. BA, William Paterson Coll., 1964, MA, 1968. Cert. English, reading and learning disabilities tchr., N.J. Tchr. Bridgewater-Raritan (N.J.) Sch. Dist., 1964-67, Ramsey (N.J.) Bd. of Edn., 1967-71; office mgr. Maywood (N.J.) Pub. Libr., 1985-86; tchr. Teaneck (N.J.) Bd. of Edn., 1987-88, Passaic County Tech. & Vocat. High Sch., Wayne, N.J., 1988-91, Elizabeth (N.J.) Bd. Edn., 1991-93; collections asst. Party Rental, Teterboro, N.J., 1994-98; adminstrv. asst. Randy Hangers, LLC, East Rutherford, N.J., 1998, Bryant Staffing, Emerson, NJ, 1999; shareholder rels. Mellon Investor Svcs., Ridgefield Park, NJ, 1999—. Mem. NEA, Internat. Reading Assn., N.J. Edn. Assn., N.J. Reading Assn. Avocations: reading, crocheting, ceramics, crewel work. Home: 279 Clark St Apt A15 Hackensack NJ 07601-1062 Office: Mellon Investor Svcs 85 Challenger Rd Ridgefield Park NJ 07660-2104

FINCH, ROBERT DAVID, mechanical engineer, educator, consultant; b. Westcliff, Essex, England, Aug. 18, 1938; came to U.S., 1963; s. David Nichols and Winifred Laura (Davey) F.; m. Sheila Ann Field, Jan 19, 1963; children: Matthew John, Christine Victoria. BSc, Imperial Coll., London U., 1959; MSc, Chelsea Coll., London U., 1960; PhD, Imperial Coll., London U., 1963. Asst. prof. U. Houston, 1965-67, assoc. prof., 1967-72, prof. mech. engring., 1972—98, prof. emeritus, 1998—. Pres. Am. Acoustics Corp., Sugarland, Tex., 1971—. Contbr. papers on acoustics to tech. publs. Fellow Acoustical Soc. Am. (Biennial award 1972); mem. ASME, Am. Phys. Soc. Home: 211 Lombardy Dr Sugar Land TX 77478-3420

FINCHER, MARGARET ANN, librarian, educator; b. Harrodsburg, Ky., June 2, 1934; d. Henry Alexander and Minnie Bee (White) Cathey; m. Willie John Fincher, Jr., Apr. 1, 1955; children: John Richard, Joseph Michael, Judy Darlene, James Andrew. BS in Bus. Edn., Auburn U., 1955; MEd, U. New Orleans, 1978. Bookkeeper, Markle's Drug Store, Auburn, Ala., 1952-54; asst. to dir. Auburn U. Library, 1955; elem. tchr., Birmingham, Ala., 1958-64; bus. edn. tchr. Abramson High Sch., New Orleans, 1964-2001; ret., 2001; owner, mgr. craft shop Fanci Krafts, New Orleans, 1977-78; asst. supr. Shaklee Corp., 1979-85; libr., media ctr. dept. chmn. Abramson Sr. High Sch. Orleans Parish Sch. Bd., 1984-89. Supr. adult Bible tng. dept. Word of Faith Temple, 1982, cons. library devel., 1982, tchr., 1975-80, deaconess, 1983—; bd. dirs. Lamb Day Care Center, 1979-81; sustaining mem. Meth. Hosp. Aux., 1967—; adv./sponsor Christian Life on Campus Club. Recipient Am. Legion citation of appreciation, 1981; Future Bus. Leaders Am., award of Appreciation, 1976. Mem. ALA, Donna Villa Improvement Assn., Metro. Ednl. Media Orgn., Ch. and Synagogue Library Assn., So. Bus. Edn. Assn., Nat. Bus. Edn. Assn., La. Assn. Bus. Edn., La. Library Assn., La. Vocat. Assn., United Tchrs. New Orleans, Policemen's Assn. New Orleans (hon.), Tamaron Homeowners Assn. (treas. 1992—), Abramson Libr. Media Club (sponsor 1986—), Phi Delta Kappa. Republican. Mem. Christian Ch.

FINDLEY, CARTER VAUGHN, historian, educator; b. Atlanta, May 12, 1941; s. John Clarke and Elizabeth (Steed) F.; m. Lucia LaVerne Blackwelder, Aug. 31, 1968; children: Madeleine Vaughn, Benjamin Carter. BA, Yale U., 1963; PhD, Harvard U., 1969. Asst. prof. Ohio State U., Columbus, 1971-79, assoc. prof., 1979-87, prof. Middle East and world history, 1987—. Vis. mem. Inst. for Advanced Study, Princeton U., 1981-82; enseignant invité Ecole des Hautes Etudes en Scis. Sociales, Paris, 1994. Author: Bureaucratic Reform in the Ottoman Empire: The Sublime Porte, 1789-1922, 1980, Ottoman Civil Officialdom, 1989 (Book award Ohio Acad. of History 1990, Turkish Studies Assn. 1990), An Ottoman Occidentalist in Europe: Ahmed Midhat Meets Madame Gulnar, 1889, 1998; co-author: Twentieth-Century World, 1986, 3d edit., 1994; contbr. articles to profl. publs. Capt. USAR, 1969-71. Joint Com. on Near and Middle East/Am. Coun. Learned Socs./SSRC fellow, 1976-77, 79, 85-86; Fulbright grantee, 1983, 94, Inst. Turkish Studies grantee, 1986. Fellow Middle East Inst., Middle East Studies Assn.; mem. ACLU, Am. Hist. Assn., Am. Oriental Soc., Ohio Acad. History, Turkish Studies Assn. (pres. 1990-92), World History Assn. (exec. coun. 1991-94). Home: 2515 Sherwin Rd Columbus OH 43221-3623 Office: Ohio State U Dept History 106 Dulles Hall 230 W 17th Ave Columbus OH 43210-1361 E-mail: findley.1@osu.edu.*

FINDLEY, MARTHA JEAN, elementary education educator; b. King City, Mo., Apr. 2, 1945; d. Lloyd Lester and Vola Dell (O'Neal) Beattie; m. Drexel David Findley, Oct. 21, 1962; children: Pamela Findley Bernard, James, Jerald. BS, Mo. Western State Coll., 1982; MA, U. Mo., Kansas City, 1989. Tchr. 1st grade East Buchanan C-I Sch. Dist., Gower, Mo., 1982-88, tchr. Chpt. I reading, 1988—2001; owner, operator Martha's This and That Store (now Martha's Floral, Gift, Collectibles and Miscellaneous), Gower, Mo., 1995—. Coord. sci. club, 1988-2000, recycling program, 1988-2000, facilitator at-risk com. East Buchanan C-I Sch. Dist., 1993-94, at risk com., 1993-2001; parent facilitator Practice Parenting Partnership, 1994-97. Editor MSC/IRA Newsletter, 1993-98. Mem. Title I Sch. Support Team State Mo.; assoc. mem. Clinton County Libr. Bd., 2003. Mem. ASCD, Mo. Reading Assn. (chair scholarship com. 1991-93, chair state poster contest com. 1993-95), Cert. Tchrs. Assn. (treas. Gower chpt. 1989-90), Internat. Reading Assn. (pres. Kansas City area coun. 1988-91, chair hospitality com. 1994 Mo. State Conv., Celebrate Literacy award 1991), Mo. Tchrs. Assn., U. Mo.-Kansas City Alumni Assn., Mo. Western State Coll. Alumni Assn., Phi Kappa Phi, Phi Delta Kappa (treas. St. Joseph chpt. 1996-98), Kappa Delta Phi. Home: 504 W Riley St Plattsburg MO 64477-1358 Office: Martha's 314 Railroad Ave Gower MO 64454-9187

FINE, DAVID JEFFREY, hospital executive, educator, consultant, lecturer; b. Flushing, N.Y., Oct. 10, 1950; s. Arnold and Phyllis F.; m. Susan Gory, Dec. 29, 1985; children: Jeffrey Jacob, Christopher Lee. BA, Tufts U., 1972; MHA, U. Minn., 1974. Asst. to dir. U. Calif. Hosp. and Clinics, San Francisco, 1974-76, asst. dir., 1976-78; sr. assoc. dir. U. Nebr. Hosp. and Clinic, Omaha, 1978-83; adminstr. W.Va. Univ. Hosp., Morgantown, 1983-84; pres. W.Va. Univ. Hosps., Inc., Morgantown, 1984-87; pres., chief oper. officer Health Net, Inc., Charleston, 1985-87; vice provost for health affairs, chief exec. officer U. Cin. Health System, 1987-90; pres. U. Cin. Med. Assocs., 1988-90; vice chancellor Tulane U. Med. Ctr., New Orleans, 1990-95, emeritus vice chancellor, 1995—; prof., chmn. dept. health sys. mgmt. Sch. Pub. Health and Tropical Medicine Tulane U., New Orleans, 1990—; prof., chmn. dept. health systems mgmt. sch. pub. health Tulane U. Med. Ctr., New Orleans, 1990—; pres., CEO New Orleans Region Columbia/HCA Healthcare Corp., 1995—. Chmn. bd. dirs. Allied Health Svcs., Morgantown, W.Va.; prof. med. econ. and pharmacy U. Cin., 1987-90; cons. Merck, Sharp & Dohme, West Point, Pa., 1983—, Eli Lilly & Co., Indpls., 1984, DuPont Critical Care, Chgo., Johnson and Johnson, 1988-91, Ethicon, Somerville, N.J., 1988-90, Standard Textile, Cin., 1989, Baxter, 1990—; bd. dirs., exec. com. Univ. Hosp. Consortium, Atlanta, 1983-90; vis. fellow King Fund Coll.; adj. prof. dept. pharmacy adminstrn. Xavier U., New Orleans, 1990—; chmn. bd. dirs. S.E. Med. Alliance; bd. dirs. Premier Bank New Orleans. Mem. editl. bd. Hospital Formulary, 1982-87, Health Adminstrn. Press, 1991-94, Jour. Health Adminstrn. Edn., 1991—; contbr. jour. articles, book chpts. and films. Trustee Monongalia Arts Coun., 1984-86, Cin. Chamber Orch., 1987-91; sec.-treas. Internat. Found. for Pharmacy Edn. Recipient James A. Hamilton prize, U. Minn., 1974; W. K. Kellog fellow. Fellow Am. Coll. Hosp. Adminstrs. (Robert S. Hudgens Young Adminstr. of Yr. award 1985, mem. com. on awards and testimonials), Royal Coll. Medicine; mem. Am. Hosp. Assn. (mem. regional policy bd., mem. ho. of dels., mem. governing coun. sect. on met. hosps.), New Orleans City Club, English Turn Country Club, Rotary, Omicron Delta Epsilon. Jewish.

FINE, MIRIAM BROWN, artist, educator, poet, writer; b. Vineland, N.J., Mar. 8, 1913; d. Abraham and Katie (Walidarsky) Brown; m. Irvin Fine, Nov. 3, 1935; children: Ruth Eileen Fine, Adele Aviva Fine Gross. BFA, The U. the Arts (formerly Indsl. Sch. Arts) and U. Pa., 1935; postgrad., Cheltenham (Pa.) Art Sch., 1968-77, Temple U., 1976-91. Tchr. art and watercolor painting Phila. Pub. Schs., 1953-60; lectr., watercolor tchr. Assn. Ret. Profls. Temple U., 1976-92. Pvt. tchr. art, Phila., 1952-77; geriatric poster contest judge and program cover design Pa. Podiatric Med. Assn., 1984-95; tchr., vis. artist Abington Friends Com., 1989-90; tchr. watercolor N.E. Cultural Art Coun. Phila., 1987-90; tchr. watercolor, speaker poetry forum David G. Neuman Sr. Ctr., Jewish Community Ctr. Phila., 1991—. Executed 7 murals at Spruance Elem. Sch., Phila., 1951, Holocaust oils and watercolors displayed in Temple Sholom Synagogue, Oxford Cir. Synagogue, UN Women's Conf., Nairobi, Kenya, 1985—, Libr. Nat. Mus. Women in Arts, Washington, 1992—; 16 one-person exhbns. John Wanamaker's Fine Art Gallery, The Hahn Gallery, Cida Art Gallery, First Pa. Bank, Revsin Art Gallery, Frankford Trust Co., Temple U. Ctr. City, Northeast Regional Libr., Phila., 1996, Spring Art Exhbn. N.E. Regional Libr., 1997, Printmaking Gallery U. of Arts, Phila., 1998; group shows include: U.N. Women's Conference, Nairobi, Phila. Art Show, Provident Nat. Bank, Cheltenham Art Ctr., Art Alliance, Pa. Acad. Fine Arts, Phila. Mus. Art, Camden County Hist. Soc., Rutgers Coll., Frankford Women's Art League, Pennock Art & Flower Show, Nat. Coun. Jewish Women, Immaculata Coll., Ocean City Art League, Artist Equity, Cape May Art Ctr.; author: (poetry and illustrations) Word and Drawings, 1984, (in braille) 1996, Mom I Didn't Know It Was Like That, Family History, 1984, The Full Moon Energises My Creativity, 1988, You Are in My Galaxy, 1990, That's Life, 1992, Flowers I, 1993 (Nat. Mus. Women in Arts, Washington), Treasures of Miriam Brown Fine for You, 1993; author, illustrator: My Bible, 1994; contbr. watercolor paintings on boxes and book covers Continental Box Co., 1995, Flower Book VII, 1996, Flower Book VIII, 1996, Flower Book IX, 1997, Flower Book X, 1998, Flower Book XI, 1999, Flower Book XII, 2000-02, cover (Passover prayer book) The Haggadah, 1998 (honored by Am. Jewish Congress, Pa. region, 1998); author: Poetry from My Soul, 1998. Did benefit for St. Christopher's Children's Hosp., Phila., 1984-87; mem. Torch of Life chpt. City of Hope, Phila., 1935—, mem. Herman chpt., 1992—; vol. Overbrook Sch. for the Blind, Phila., 1991—. Recipient Phila. Art Tchrs. award, 1956, Chapel of Four Chaplains Humanitarian award Torch of Life chpt. City of Hope, 1964, Nat. Synagogue Women's League award, Frankford Women's League award, 50 Yr. Svc. award 1981, 60 Yr. Svc. award 1991, Solomon Schector Illustrated Book award, City Coun. Citizen award City of Phila., 1996, award City of Hope, 1996; Bd. Edn. Art scholar, 1931; Citation in honor of Miriam Brown Fine for her artistic and literary contbn. to the life of the City of Phila. and N.E. Regional Libr., 1996. Mem. NOW, Artists Equity Inc., Phila. Watercolor Club (hon.), Women's Caucus for Art, Univ. Arts Alumni Assn., Acad. Am. Poets, Nat. Fedn. State Poetry Socs., Writers Cadence Crafters, Poets Study Group, Nat. Mus. of Women in Arts (charter mem.), Temple U. Assn. Ret. Profls. (pres. emeritus, award), Pa. State Poetry Socs., Fight for Sight. Republican. Jewish. Avocations: music, teaching, sharing knowledge, learning. Home: Brith Sholom House 3939 Conshohocken Ave Apt 820 Philadelphia PA 19131-5470

FINE, SALLY SOLFISBURG, artist, educator; b. Aurora, Ill., July 20, 1948; d. Roy John Jr. and Edith Warrick (Squires) Solfisburg; m. Philip Clark Fine, May 5, 1973 (div. 1997); children: Alexander, Arielle. BFA, Ohio U., 1970; postgrad., Boston U., 1978-82, MFA, 1985. Graphic designer Mus. of Sci., Boston, 1970-72; teaching fellow Boston U., 1980-81; instr., lectr. U. Mass., North Dartmouth, 1993-95; sr. lectr. Bradford Coll., 1995-96, asst. prof., 1996-2000; assoc. prof. art. Regis Coll., Weston, Mass., 2000—. Prin. S.S. Fine Design, Boston, 1970—. Solo shows include Viridian Gallery, N.Y.C., Bradford Coll., Chapel Gallery; exhibited in group shows at DeCordova Mus., Lincoln, Mass., Danforth Mus. of Art., Framingham, Mass., Brockton (Mass.) Art Mus., Newport (R.I.) Art Mus., A.I.R. Gallery, N.Y.C., Cité Internationale Gallerie, Paris. Bd. dirs. Kendall Ctr. for the Arts, 1983-86. Visual Artists grantee Mass. Coun. for the Arts, 1995, Sculpture fellow New Eng., Found. for the Arts, 1995, others. Mem. AAUP, Coll. Art Assn. Avocations: swimming, gardening, biking. Office: Regis Coll 235 Wellesley St Weston MA 02493-1571 E-mail: sally.fine@regiscollege.edu.

FINEMAN, MORTON A. chemistry and physics educator; b. Kearny, N.J., Aug. 9, 1919; s. Abram and Esther (Deiksal) F.; m. Mary Theresa Zoza, Feb. 4, 1949; children: Marcia Anne, Paul Mark. BA, Ind. U., 1941; PhD, U. Pitts., 1948. Teaching asst. U. Pitts., Pitts., 1941-44; rsch. staff Sprague Elect. Co., N. Adams, Mass., 1948-50; rsch. fellow U. Minn., Mpls., 1950-52; asst. prof. to prof. chemistry Providence (R.I.) Coll., 1952-61; postdoctoral Nat. Bur. of Stnds., Washington, 1959-60; sr. rsch. staff Gen. Atomic, San Diego, Calif., 1961-66; prof. physics Lycoming Coll., Williamsport, Pa., 1966-84; adj. prof. San Diego State U., 1984-89; cons. Separations Systems Tech., San Diego, 1990-92. Vis. scholar, U. Calif., San Diego, 1994-2003. Contbr. articles to profl. jours. Mem. Am. Physical Soc., Am. Chem. Soc., Phi Beta Kappa, Phi Lambda Upsilon, Sigma Xi, Sigma Pi Sigma. Avocation: tennis. Home: 4085 Rosenda Ct Unit 262 San Diego CA 92122-1962

FINGER, IRIS DALE ABRAMS, elementary school educator; b. Ironton, Ohio, Jan. 22, 1939; d. Frank Abrams and Pearl (Moore) Schwab; m. Robert James Roderick Sr., July 20, 1957 (div. Nov. 1971); children: Robert James Roderick Jr., Elizabeth Ann Roderick Travis; m. Henry Waterman Bromley Jr., May 14, 1972 (div. June 1987); child: Henry Waterman Bromley III; m. Grover Cleveland Finger III, Apr. 1, 1989. Degree in early childhood and elem. edn., U. South Fla.; degree in design, Jackson Coll., Honolulu. Cert.

middle sch. math. tchr.; cert. TESOL; cert. gifted edn. Children's libr. Ft. Myers (Fla.) Pub. Libr., 1955-57; workmen's compensation payroll adminstr. San Diego, 1964-66; permanent substitute tchr. Sigsbee Elem. Sch., Key West, Fla., 1968-70; part-time libr. Danielson (Conn.) Libr., 1970-71; residential design Bateman Homes, Leigh Acres, Fla., 1971-72; structural steel designer So. Machine and Steel, Ft. Myers, 1972-73; dir. Ft. Myers Bus. Coll., 1973-77; structural prestress concrete designer Southland Prestress, Dean Steel and Kirby MaCumber Steel, 1977-83; tchr. Lee County Sch. Bd., Ft. Myers, 1983—, team leader, math. coach, 1983, 94-95; with Bonita Spring Mid. Sch., 1994-96, equity coord., 1995-96. Pres. PTA, Key West, 1966-68, Fla. Art League, Ft. Myers, 1984-86; dir. Ft. Myers Bus. Coll., 1973-77; hosp. nurse ARC, 1964-66; med. evacuation for Vietnam wounded Philippine Islands Subic Hosp.; mem. Treasury of Island Coast Uni-Serve; rep. to Lee County Safety Com. Recipient Pres. Regan Achievement award, 1976, Pres. Johnson People to People award and plank award for sch. constrn. at San Meguel, the Philippines, 1960. Mem.: Am. Legion, VFW Aux., Navy Wives and Navy Relief Soc., Pioneer Club Ft. Myers, Lee County Math. Coun., Fla. Math. Coun., Rep. Assembly, Tchrs. Assn. Lee County, Fla. Tchrs. Profession, NEA, Phi Beta Kappa, Alpha Delta Kappa. Republican. Methodist. Avocations: arts and crafts, reading, vacationing at the beach, family socials, swimming. Home: PO Box 7068 Naples FL 34101-7068

FINIFTER, ADA WEINTRAUB, political scientist, educator; b. NYC; d. Isaac and Stella (Colchamiro) Weintraub. BA, CUNY, Bklyn., 1959; MA, U. Mich., 1961; PhD, U. Wis., 1967. Prof. polit. sci. Mich. State U., East Lansing, 1967—. Author: Using Your IBM Personal Computer: Easywriter, 1984; editor: Political Science: The State of the Discipline, 1983, Alienation and the Social System, 1970, Political Science: The State of the Discipline II, 1993; editor Am. Polit. Sci. Rev., 1996-2001; contbr. articles to polit. sci. jours. Vol. U.S. Peace Corps, Venezuela, 1962-64. Rsch. grantee Russell Sage Found., 1979-82, NSF, 1977-78; fellow NSF, 1966, 73. Mem. Am. Polit. Sci. Assn. (v.p. 1983-84, program chmn. 1982), Midwest Polit. Sci. Assn. (pres. 1986-87). Office: Mich State U Dept Polit Sci 303 S Kedzie Hall East Lansing MI 48824-1032 E-mail: finifter@msu.edu.

FINK, DOLORES HESSE, special education educator; b. Long Branch, N.J., Feb. 19, 1938; d. Charles Joseph and Laura Rita (Ellis) Hesse; m. John Charles Fink, Jr., Apr. 23, 1960; children: John Charles Fink III, Thomas Anthony, Anthony Gerard. BA, Marymount Coll., Tarrytown, N.Y.; MA, Gerogian Ct., Lakewood, N.J. Cert. learning disability tchr. cons., N.J. Elem. tchr. Shrewsbury (N.J.) Boro Bd. Edn., 1959-61, Middletown Twp. (N.J.) Bd. Edn., 1962-63, tchr. handicapped, 1980-90; cons. Stevenson Lang. Skills, Attleboro, Mass., 1988—; learning disability tchr. cons., dir. Alternative Learning Ctr., Atlantic Highlands, N.J., 1990—; learning disability tchr., cons. Lakewood (N.J.) Pub. Schs., 1991-95. Mem. Coun. Exceptional Children, N.J. Assn. Learning Cons., N.Y. Orton Soc. Avocations: tennis, traveling, reading, golf. Home: 15 Beacon Hill Rd Atlantic Highlands NJ 07716-2006

FINK, EDWARD LAURENCE, communications educator; b. NYC, Aug. 24, 1945; s. Leo and Beatrice (Berger) F.; m. Varda Naomi Schwartzman, June 18, 1967 (div. Sept. 1994); children: Elana Esther, Rebecca Eve; m. Sharon Manette Doner, Feb. 4, 1996 (div. Feb. 2003). BA, Columbia U., 1966; MS, U. Wis., 1969, PhD, 1975. Lectr. U. Wis., Madison, 1970; asst. prof. U. Notre Dame, South Bend, Ind., 1971-73; instr. Mich. State U., East Lansing, 1973-75, asst. prof., 1975-81; assoc. prof. U. Md., College Park, 1981-87, prof., 1987—, acting assoc. dean grad. studies and rsch., 1993—95, chmn., 1997—. Cons. in field; adv. com. Nat. Endowment for Arts, Washington, 1986; Lady Davis vis. prof. Hebrew U., Jerusalem, 1998. Author: (with J. Woelfel) Measurement of Communication Processes, 1980; editor Human Comm. Rsch., 1998-2000; contbr. articles to profl. jours. Bd. dirs. Lansing br. ACLU, 1978-81, Health Cen., Inc., Lansing, 1977-79, Ind. Civil Liberties Union, Indpls., 1972. Disting. scholar-tchr. U. Md., 1988-89 Mem. APA, Internat. Comm. Assn. (v.p. 1981-83, bd. dirs. 1988-91, B. Aubrey Fisher Mentorship award 2003), Am. Sociol. Assn., Nat. Comm. Assn., Soc. for Personality and Social Psychology, Soc. for Chaos Theory in Psychology and the Life Scis., Sigma Xi (pres. U. Md. chpt. 1999-2000), Omicron Delta Kappa. Jewish. Office: U Md Dept Comm 2130 Skinner Bldg College Park MD 20742-7635 E-mail: elf@umd.edu.

FINK, EDWARD MURRAY, lawyer, educator; b. N.Y.C., Mar. 11, 1934; s. Nathaniel and Elsa Charlotte (Lenrow) F.; divorced; children: Jeffrey Neil, Andrea Sue; m. Rita Toby Cohen, Aug. 11, 1985. BS in Chemistry, CCNY, 1955; JD, Georgetown U., 1959. Bar: D.C. 1960, U.S. Dist. Ct. D.C. 1960, U.S. Ct. Appeals (D.C. cir.) 1960, N.Y. 1962, N.J. 1970, U.S. Dist. Ct. N.J. 1970, U.S. Patent and Trademark Office 1960. Patent examiner U.S. Patent Office, Washington, 1955-60; atty. Bell Labs., Murray Hill, N.J., 1960-83, Bell Comm. Rsch. Inc., Livingston, N.J., 1984-91, Edward M. Fink, P.A., Edison, N.J., 1991—; v.p., gen. counsel Eastern R.R. Investment Corp., Bridgewater, N.J., 2000—, chmn. bd. dirs., 2001—, Somerset Terminal R.R. Corp., 2001—02. Adj. prof. torts, bus. law and civil litigation Middlesex County Coll., Edison, N.J., 1980-2000; adj. prof. partnerships and corps, contract law Montclair State U., Upper Montclair, N.J., 1984-2000. Mem. ABA, Am. Intellectual Property Assn., N.J. Patent Law Assn., N.J. State Bar Assn., Middlesex County Bar Assn., D.C. Bar Assn., N.Y. State Bar Assn. Democrat. Jewish. Home and Office: 51 Jamaica St Edison NJ 08820-3726 E-mail: patemf@aol.com.

FINK, HILARY LYNN, Slavic languages educator; b. Northampton, Mass., May 11, 1966; d. Lawrence Alfred and Barbara Louise (Gross) F. AB, Smith Coll., 1987; MA, Columbia U., 1990, MPhil, 1993, PhD, 1996. Preceptor Columbia U., N.Y.C., 1990-94; lectr. Princeton U., 1992-93; instr. Middlebury (Vt.) Coll., 1991-94; asst. prof. Slavic langs. and lit. Yale U., New Haven, 1996—2002, Sara Ribicoff assoc. prof. Slavic langs. and lit., 2002—. Author: (book) Bergson and Russian Modernism, 1999; (poetry) American Poetry Anthology, 1990, Wind in the Night Sky, 1993, The Best Poems of the '90s, 1992 (2nd prize 1992). Pepsi Co. jr. fellow, 1991-92, Harriman Inst. jr. fellow Columbia U., N.Y.C., 1992-93, 93-94, Whiting Found. fellow, 1994-95, Individual advanced rsch. fellow Internat. Rsch. & Exchs. Bd., 1995, Morse fellow, 2000-01; recipient Sarai Ribicoff award for Encouragement of Tchg. Yale U., 2000. Mem. MLA, Am. Assn. Advancement Slavic Studies, Internat. Assn. for Philosophy and Lit., Am. Assn. Tchrs. Slavic and East European Langs. Office: Yale U Dept Slavic Langs PO Box 208236 New Haven CT 06520

FINK, JOSEPH RICHARD, academic administrator; b. Newark, Mar. 20, 1943; s. Joseph Richard and Jean (Chorazy) F.; m. Donna Gibson, 1965 (div. 1986); children: Michael, Taryn; m. Christine Gaudenzi, oct. 4, 1992; children: Madison, Joseph. AB, Rider U., 1963; PhD in Am. History, Rutgers U., 1971; DLitt (hon.), Rider U., 1982, Coll. of Misericordia, 1992, Golden Gate U., 1994. Asst. then assoc. prof history Immaculata (Pa.) Coll., 1964-72, adminstrv. asst. to pres., 1969-72; dean of Arts & Scis. City Colls. Chgo., 1972-74; pres. Raritan Valley Coll., Somerville, N.J., 1974-79, Coll. Misericordia, Dallas, 1979-88, Dominican U of Calif, San Rafael, 1988—. Pres. Regional Planning Coun. Higher Edn., Region 3/Northeastern Pa., 1986-88. Mem. exec. com. Philharm. Soc. Northeastern Pa., 1986-89; bd. dirs. Marin Symphony, 1989-, San Francisco Ballet, 1994-97, Ind. Coll. No. Calif., 1992—, Marin Forum, 1991—, Guide Dogs for the Blind, 1994-97; bd. dirs. Am. Land Conservancy, 1995—, exec. com.; mem. campaign cabinet United Way San Francisco, 1990; bd. dirs. North Bay Coun., 1993—, chmn., 1996, exec. com. Mem. Nat. Assn. Ind. Colls. and Univs. (secretariat 1986), Nat. Assn. Intercollegiate Athletics (pres.'s adv. coun. 1986), Am. Coun. on Higher Edn. (commn. leadership devel. higher edn. 1978-82, commn. on internat. edn. 1993-96, acad. adminstrn. fellow 1974-75), Assn. Mercy Colls. (pres. 1985-87, exec. com. 1981-87), Coun. for Ind. Colls. (bd. dirs. 1989-92), Am. Hist. Assn., World Affairs Coun. No. Calif. (bd. dirs. 1990-96), Commonwealth Club Calif. (quar. chmn. 1989, chmn. Marin County chpt. 1989—, bd. dirs. 1992—, exec. com. 1997—, pres., 2003). Office: Dominican U Calif 50 Acacia Ave San Rafael CA 94901-2230

FINK, KRISTIN DANIELSON, secondary education educator; b. Camden, N.J., Sept. 23, 1951; d. Ralph J. and Marguerite J. (Bickerstaff) Danielson; m. Garl L. Fink, Nov. 23, 1976; children: Karl Tony, Tracy Denise, Brittany Mar. BA in English, U. Utah, 1973, MA in Edn., 1979. Cert. secondary edn. tchr., Utah; endorsements in English, theatre, speech, reading, journalism and gifted/talented edn. Tchr. Kearns (Utah) Jr. H.S., 1973-85, Hunter Jr. High, West Valley City, Utah, 1986-93; tchr. English Olympus H.S., Salt Lake City, 1993-95; character edn. specialist Utah State Office Edn., Salt Lake City, 1995—; bd. dirs. Character Edn. Partnership, Washington, 1998—; exec. dir. Cmty. of Caring, 2001—. Adj. instr. U. Utah, 1993-94, U. So. U., 1998—; chair dept. performing arts Kearns Jr. H.S., 1978-80, 83-85; chair dept. performing arts Hunter Jr. H.S., 1987-93; grad. com. adv. Westminster Coll., 1979; dir. Hunter Acting Co., 1985-93; attended White House Conf. on Character, 1996-98; bd. dirs. Character Edn. Partnership; presenter in field. Lead tchr. Cmty. of Caring; cons. Joseph P. Kennedy Found.; peer leadership team advisor Olympus H.S., 1993-95; mem. Gov.'s Commn. on Centennial Values, 1996. Named Tchr. of Yr., Hunter PTA, WVC, 1988; recipient Granite Dist. Employees Ptnrs. in Edn. Outstanding Svc. award, 1989-90, 1st Pl. award Best Jr. H.S. Newspaper in the State of Utah, Utah Press Assn., 1990, Holladay Rotary Club Svc. award, 1994, Excel Outstanding Educator award, 1995, Gov.'s Friends to Families award, Utah, 1998, Educator of Yr., Joseph P. Kennedy Found. Cmty. of Caring, 1999. Avocations: reading, travel, music. Office: 1325 G St NW Ste 500 Washington DC 20005 Home: Apt 307 2410 27th Ct S Arlington VA 22206-2863

FINK, LESTER HAROLD, engineering company executive, educator; b. Phila., May 3, 1925; s. Harold D. and Edna B. (Hopkins) F.; m. R. Naomi Veit, Dec. 10, 1955; children: Lois Hope, Carol Anne. BSEE, U. Pa., 1950, MSEE, 1961. Supr. engr. rsch. divsn. Phila. Electric Co., 1950-74; asst. dir. Electric Energy Systems divsn. Dept. Interior, Washington, 1974-75, ERDA, Washington, 1975-77, Dept. Energy, 1977-79; pres. Systems Engring. for Power, Inc., Vienna, Va., 1979-83; chmn. Carlsen & Fink Assocs., Inc., 1983-89; exec. v.p. ECC, Inc., 1989-96, ret.; pvt. cons. Adj. prof. Drexel U., 1961-74, U. Pa., 1973, U. Md., 1979-80; Attwood assoc. Conf. Internationale de Grande Reseaux Electrique. Patentee underground power transmission and automatic generation control; contbg. author: Large Scale Systems, 1982, Power System Analysis and Planning, 1983; contbr. chpt. to electronics engring. handbook, 1982; editor, contbg. author: Power Systems Restructuring, 1988. With U.S. Army, 1943-46. Recipient Meritorious Svc. award Dept. Energy, 1979. Fellow IEEE (life), Instrument Soc. Am., Sigma Tau, Eta Kappa Nu, Tau Beta Pi. Presbyterian. Home: 250 Pantops Mountain Rd # WCBR-4 Charlottesville VA 22911-8694

FINK, NORMAN STILES, lawyer, educational administrator, fundraising consultant; b. Easton, Pa., Aug. 13, 1926; s. Herman and Yetta (Hyman) F.; m. Helen Mullen, Sept. 1, 1956; children: Hayden Michael, Patricia Carol. AB, Dartmouth Coll., 1947; JD, Harvard U., 1950. Bar: N.Y. 1951, U.S. Dist. Ct. (ea. and so. dists.) N.Y. 1954, U.S. Supreme Ct. 1964. Mem. legal staff Remington Rand, Inc., N.Y.C., Washington, 1949-54; ptnr. Lans & Fink, N.Y.C., 1954-68; counsel devel. program U. Pa., Phila., 1969-80; v.p. devel. and univ. rels. Brandeis U., Waltham, Mass., 1980-81; dep. v.p. devel., alumni rels., assoc. gen. counsel devel. Columbia U., N.Y.C., 1981-89; sr. counsel John Grenzebach & Assocs., Inc., Chgo., 1989-91. Cons. v.p. Engle Consulting Group, Inc., Chgo. Editor: Deferred Giving Handbook, 1977; author: (with Howard C. Metzler) The Costs and Benefits of Deferred Giving, 1982. V.p. Am. Australian Studies Found.; mem. bd. visitors Brevard (N.C.) Coll., 1995-99, life trustee, 1999; Warren Wilson Coll., 1997—, Killough Trustee, N.Y.C. With U.S. Army, 1945-46. Recipient Alice Beeman award for excellence in devel. writing Coun. Advancement and Support of Edn., 1984, Silver medal for fundraising comms., Coun. Advancement and Support of Edn., 1988; Lilly Endowment grantee, 1979-80. Master Mason; mem. ABA (mem. com. on exempt orgns. sect. taxation and com. estate planning and drafting, charitable givint), Coun. Advancement and support of Edn. (various coms.), Am. Arbitration Assn. (panelist), Assn. of Bar of City of N.Y.C. (com. on tax-exempt orgns. 1987-90), Dartmouth Lawyers Assn., Harvard Law Sch. Assn., Nat. Assn. Fundraising Profls. (Contbn. to Knowledge award 1985), Harvard Club Western N.C., Elks. Democrat. Jewish.

FINKELSTEIN, NORMAN HENRY, librarian; b. Chelsea, Mass., Nov. 10, 1941; s. Sydney and Mollie (Fox) F.; m. Rosalind Brandt, July 4, 1967; children: Jeffrey, Robert, Risa. BS, Boston U., 1963, MEd, 1964; MA, Hebrew Coll., 1986. Dir. edn. Hebrew Coll. Sch. & Camp, Northwood, N.H., 1982-87; instr. Hebrew Coll., Brookline, Mass., 1982—; libr./media specialist Brookline Pub. Schs., 1970—. Author: Remember Not to Forget: A Memory of the Holocaust, 1985, The Other 1492: Jewish Settlement in the New World, 1989, The Emperor General: A Biography of Douglas MacArthur, 1989, Theodor Herzl: Architect of a Nation, 1991, Captain of Innocence: France and the Dreyfus Affair, 1991, Sounds in the Air: The Golden Age of Radio, 1993, Thirteen Days/Ninety Miles: The Cuban Missile Crisis, 1994, With Heroic Truth: The Life of Edward R. Murrow, 1997, Heeding The Call, 1997, Friends Indeed, 1998, The Way Things Never Were, 1999, Forged in Freedom, 2002.. CBE/NEH fellow, Washington, 1992; Study grantee Brookline Found., 1987; recipient study award Kennedy Presdl. Libr., 1987, Ford Presdl. Libr., 1996, Golden Kite Honor award, 1997, Nat. Jewish Book award, 1998, 2002. Mem. Mass. Sch. Libr./Media Assn. (com. chair 1977-82), Wayfarer's Club, Phi Delta Kappa. Office: Edward Devotion Libr 345 Harvard St Brookline MA 02446-2907 E-mail: nfinkelstein@hebrewcollege.edu.

FINKELSTEIN, STANLEY MICHAEL, engineering educator, research biomedical engineer; b. Bklyn., June 16, 1941; BSEE, Poly. Inst. Bklyn., 1962, MSEE, 1964, PhD in Elec. Engring. and Sys. Sci., 1969. Asst. prof. Poly. Inst. Bklyn., 1968-74, assoc. prof., 1974-77, U. Minn., Mpls., 1977-89, prof., 1990—. Contbr. articles to profl. jours. Grad. fellow NDEA, 1962-64, faculty fellow sci. NSF, 1975-77. Fellow Am. Inst. for Med. and Biol. Engring.; mem. AAAS, Engring. Medicine and Biology Soc. (sr.; adminstrv. com. 1987-92), Biomed. Engring. Soc. (sr.), N.Y. Acad. Scis., Assn. for Advancement Med. Instrumentation, Cardiovasc. Sys. Dynamics Soc., Sigma Xi. Achievements include cardiovascular dynamics, patient home monitoring, medical informatics, telemedicine. Office: U Minn Div Health Informatics Scis MMC 609 Minneapolis MN 55455

FINKL, CHARLES WILLIAM, II, geologist, educator; b. Chgo., Sept. 19, 1941; s. Charles William and Marian L. (Hamilton) F.; m. Charlene Bristol, May 16, 1965 (div.); children: Jonathan William Frederick, Amanda Marie. BSc, Oreg. State U., 1964, MSc, 1966; PhD, U. Western Australia, 1971. Instr. natural resources Oreg. State U., 1967; demonstrator U. Western Australia, Perth, 1968, staff geochemist for S.E. Asia, Internat. Nickel Australia Pty. Ltd., 1970-74; chief editor Ency. Earth Sci., N.Y.C., 1974-87; dir. Inst. Coastal Studies Nova. U., Port Everglades, Fla., 1979-83; pres. Resource Mgmt. & Mineral Exploration Cons., Inc., Ft. Lauderdale, Fla., 1974-85, Info. Mgmt. Corp. (IMCO), Ft. Lauderdale, 1985-87; exec. dir., v.p. Coastal Edn. and Rsch. Found., Charlottesville, Va., 1983-89, pres., 1990—; prof. dept. geology Fla. Atlantic U., Boca Raton, 1983—; pres. Earth Systems Analysis, Inc., 1995-97. Mem. IGU survey and mapping and sub-commn. on morphotectonics, 1983-95; exec. bd. dirs. Internat. Geol. Correlation Program project 274 on Quaternary Coastal Evolution, 1989-93; mem. exec. bd. Skagen Odde Project Mus. for Coastal Geomorphology, Denmark, 1989—; mem. marine adv. bd. com. Broward County Bd. Commrs., 1990-96; radio and TV appearances. Author: Soil Classification, 1982; vol. editor, contbg. author: The Encyclopedia of Soil Science, Part I: Physics, Chemistr, Biology, Fertility and Technology, 1979; editor, contbg. author: The Encyclopedia of Applied Geology, 1983, The Encyclopedia of Field and General Geology, 1988; vol. editor The Encyclopedia of Soil Science and Technology, 1991—; editor in chief Jour. Coastal Rsch.: An Internat. Forum for the Littoral Scis., 1984—; series editor Benchmark Papers in Soil Sci., 1982-86; editor: Current Titles in Ocean, Coastal, Lake and Wateway Sciences, 1985-88 Fellow Assn. Exploration Geochemists, Geol. Assn. Can.; mem. ASCE, Am. Geophys. Union, Am. Geog. Soc., Am. Soc. Photogrammetry and Remote Sensing, Am. Shore and Beach Preservation Assn., Coun. Editors of Learned Jours., Coastal Soc., European Assn. Earth Sci. Editors, Estuarine and Coastal Scis. Assn., Fla. Acad. Sci., Geol. Soc. Am., Geol. Soc. Australia, Internat. Soc. Reef Studies, Internat. Soil Sci. Soc., Internat. Geographical Union (mem. neotectohics, commn. on rapid geomorphological hazards working group, corr. mem. working group on paleosols, commn. on coastal systems), Internat. Union Geol. Scis. (mem. project 317, paleoweathering records and paleosurfaces), Soil Sci. Soc. Am., Soc. Econ. Paleontologists and Mineralogists, Soc. Scholarly Publ., Soc. Mining Engrs. AIME, Fla. Acad. Scis., Soc. Wetland Scientists (cert. profl. wetland scientist), Am. Inst. Profl. Geologists (cert. profl. geol. scientist), Am. Registry Cert. Profls. in Agronomy Crops and Soils (cert. profl. soil scientist), Soil and Water Conservation Soc., Internat. Soc. For Prevention and Mitigation of Natural Disasters, Gamma Theta Upsilon. Republican. Roman Catholic. Home: 1656 Cypress Row Dr West Palm Beach FL 33411-5108 Office: Fla Atlantic U Dept Geography and Geology Boca Raton FL 33431 E-mail: cfinkl@gate.net.

FINKS, ROBERT MELVIN, paleontologist, educator; b. Portland, Maine, May 12, 1927; s. Abraham Joseph and Sarah (Bendette) F. BS magna cum laude, Queens Coll., 1947; MA, Columbia U., 1954, PhD, 1959. Lectr. Bklyn. Coll., 1955-58, instr., 1959-61; lectr. Queens Coll., CUNY, 1961-62, asst. prof., 1962-65, acting chmn., 1963-64, assoc. prof. geology, 1966-70, prof., 1971—2002, prof. emeritus, 2002—; geologist U.S. Geol. Survey, 1952-54, 63—; rsch. assoc. Am. Mus. Natural History, 1961—77, Smithsonian Instn., 1968—; rsch. assoc. in paleontology N.Y. State Mus.; rsch. prof. dept. geology Union Coll., Schenectady, NY. Doctoral faculty CUNY, 1983—; cons. in field. Author: Late Paleozoic Sponge Faunas of the Texas Region, 1960; Editor: Guidebook to Field Excursions, 1968; Contbr. articles profl. jours. Queens Coll. Scholar, 1947. Fellow AAAS, Geol. Soc. Am., Explorers Club; mem. AAUP, Paleontol. Soc. (vice chmn. Northeastern sect. 1977-78, chmn. 1978-79), Paleontol. Assn. Britain, Soc. Econ. Paleontologists and Mineralogists, Internat. Palaeontol. Assn., Geol. Soc. Vt. (charter mem.), Planetary Soc. (charter), Phi Beta Kappa (v.p. Sigma chpt. N.Y. 1993-95, pres. 1995-99), Golden Key (hon.), Sigma Xi (exec. sec. Queens Coll. chpt. 1982-85). Office: Queens Coll CUNY Sch Earth and Environ Scis Flushing NY 11367 Address: Geology Dept Union Coll Schenectady NY 12308

FINLAY, AUDREY JOY, environmental educator, consultant, naturalist; b. Davidson, Sask., Can., Sept. 18, 1932; d. Leonard Noel and Vilhemine Marie (Rossander) Barton; m. James Campbell Finlay, June 18, 1955; children: Barton Brett, Warren Hugh, Rhonda Marie. BA, U. Man., Can., 1954; profl. diploma in edn., U. Alta., 1974, MEd, 1978. Social worker Children's Aid, Brandon, Man., 1954-55; foster home worker Social Services Province of Sask., Regina, 1955-56, City of Edmonton, Alta., 1956-59, naturalist, 1965-74; tchr., cons., adminstr. Edmonton Pub. Sch. Bd., 1974-88. Cons. edn., interpretation numerous projects, 1965—. Author: Winter Here and Now, 1982; co-author: Parks in Alberta, 1987, Ocean to Alpine, A British Columbia Nature Guide, 1992; contbr. nature articles to profl. jours. Chmn., chief exec. officer Wildlife '87: Canadian Centennial Wildlife Conservation, 1985-87. Named Ms. Chatelaine, Chatelaine mag., 1975; recipient Order of Bighorn award Alta Gov., Ralph D. Bird award, 1987, Can. Park Svc. Heritage award Environ. Can., 1990, Order of Can. award, 1990, Reeve's award of Distinction County of Strath, 1991, Douglas Pimlot award Can. Nat. Fedn., 1991, Greenways Achievement award Victoria Provincial Capital Commn., 2001, Queen's Jubilee medal 2002. Fellow Alta. Tchrs. Assn., Environ. Outdoor Coun. (founder, 1st pres., disting. mem.); mem. Canadian Nature Fedn. (v.p. 1984-90), Edmonton Natural History Soc. (Loran Goulden award 1980), Am. Nature Study Soc. (bd. dirs. 1984-91, pres. 1991-94), N.Am. Environ. Edn. Assn. (bd. dirs. 1983-89), Fedn. Alta Naturalists (bd. dirs. 1970s). Home and Office: 270 Trevlac Pl Victoria BC Canada V9E 2C4

FINLEY, CARMEN JOYCE, psychologist, former research administrator; b. Santa Rosa, Calif., Mar. 9, 1926; d. Perry E. and Ardith (Bobst) F.; m. J. Hayes Hunter, Dec. 20, 1956 (div. 1968). AB in Speech and Math, U. Calif.-Berkeley, 1947; MA, Tchrs. Coll., Columbia U., 1952, PhD, 1962; postdoctoral in computer sci., Sonoma State U., 1983-84. Cert. genealogist. Tchr. math. Porterville (Calif.) Union High Sch., 1948-51; sch. psychologist, cons. in adminstrv. research, dir. research and data processing Sonoma County Schs., Santa Rosa, 1952-67; assoc. dir. Nat. Assessment Ednl. Progress, Ann Arbor, Mich., 1968-70, Denver, 1971; prin. research scientist Am. Insts. for Research, Palo Alto, Calif., 1972-83. Cons. in planning and evaluation San Mateo County Schs., 1974-75; vis. asst. prof. stats. Sonoma State Coll., Rohnert Park, Calif., summer 1963, lectr. counseling dept., 1976; vis. assoc. prof. U. Rochester, N.Y., summer 1964; project asso. in ednl. psychology U. Wis., Madison, summer 1965; mem. com. on research and devel. Coll. Entrance Examination Bd., 1966-67; mem. European seminar on learning and ednl. process Skepparholmen, Hasseludden, Sweden, summer 1968; mem. Calif. Adv. Council on Ednl. Research, 1964-68, 72-73; cons. to Calif. State Dept. Edn., 1965, 75-82, Maine State Dept. Edn., 1972-73, Mo. State Dept. Edn., 1973-74, Minn., Ill., Mich. depts. edn., 1973-80, La., Ohio depts. edn., 1975, Santa Rosa, Sonoma County city schs., 1973; sub-regional rep. Far West Lab. Ednl. Research, 1966; mem. Johns Hopkins U. Nat. Symposium on Ednl. Research, 1979-83 Adv. editor Jour. Ednl. Measurement, 1968-70; editorial bd. Calif. Jour. Ednl. Rsch., 1964-69, 72-73; cons. Am. Ednl. Rsch. Jour., 1974; rev. editor Measurement and Evaluation in Guidance, 1977-82; author monograph, tests in field; contbr. numerous articles on ednl. and psychol. measurement to profl. jours.; contbr. to 11th Mental Measurement Yearbook. Mem. adv. com. Redwood Caregiver Resource Ctr., pres., 1987-90; trustee, chmn. long range planning com., chair computer applications com., mem. grants com. Sonoma County Mus., 1987-91, 2d v.p., 1989, 1st v.p., 1990, chmn. internal ops., pers., 1990; mem. adv. bd. devel. office, bd. dirs. Acad. Found. Sonoma State U., 1990—; bd. dirs. Sonoma County Hist. Soc., 1992-98, mem. sec. 1994—. Broderbund scholar Inst. Geneal. and Hist. Rsch.-Samford U., 1998; recipient award for Outstanding Contbns. to Tech. and Geneal. Quality, GenTech, 1998; established Dr. Carmen Finley Hist. Web Site award Sonoma County Hist. Soc., 2000. Mem. APA (rsch. com. 1966), Am. Ednl. Rsch. Assn. (chmn. com. state and regional rsch. assns. 1967-69, chmn. nominating com. div. D 1969, chmn. award com. 1975, reviewer ednl. evaluation and policy analysis), Calif. Ednl. Rsch. Assn. (sec. treas. 1963-64, v.p. 1965-66, pres. 1966-67), Calif. Ednl. Data Processing Assn., Am. Pers. and Guidance Assn., Calif. Tchrs. Assn., Assn. Measurement and Evaluation in Guidance (publ. com. 1965), Nat. Coun. on Measurement in Edn. (newsletter reporter 1969-82, program chmn. western region 1968, dir. 1970-71, chmn. publs. policy com. 1971, editor Measurement in Edn. 1972-75), Sonoma County Supts. Staff Assn. (pres. 1955-56), Nat. Geneal. Soc. (chair family history writing contest 1991—, mem. edit. bd. Nat. Geneal. Soc. Quar., 2003—, Disting. Svc. award 1996), Sonoma County Geneal. Soc. (v.p. 1986-87, program chmn. 1986-87, pres. 1987-88, v.p. 1992-94, project bd., 1990—, editorial bd. 1994—, project dir. 1996—), IBM PC User's Group of Redwoods, Nichols Founders Soc. (charter Sonoma State U. 1989), Sigma Xi, Kappa Delta Pi, Pi Lambda Theta. Home: 4820 Rockridge Ln Santa Rosa CA 95404-1912 E-mail: finleyc@somona.edu.

FINLEY, GERRY, special education educator, primary school educator; b. Evergreen Park, Ill., Nov. 18, 1948; d. James Thomas and Lorraine Frances (Ploszek) Houlihan; m. David Anthony Finley, Aug. 29, 1970; children: Joanne, Robert Joseph, Sara Kristine. BA, Loyola U., 1970; MS in Edn., No. Ill. U., 1987. Cert. tchr., Ill. Pre-sch. tchr. Wesley Pre-Sch. Program, Aurora, Ill., 1981-85; Kindergarten tchr. St. Rita Sch., Aurora, Ill., 1985-86; spl. edn. tchr. Little Friends, Inc./Krejci Acad., Naperville, Ill., 1987—94; kindergarten tchr., reading coord. K-5th grade Sts. Peter & Paul Sch., Naperville, 1994—. Site trainer on autism Ill. State Autism Assn., Naperville, 1990—; program coord. for Entice, Krejci Acad. Team, Naperville, 1990-92. Sch. bd. mem. St. Rita Sch., Aurora, 1984, 85. Mem. ASCD, Ill. Assn. for Supervision & Curriculum Devel., Assn. Childhood Edn. Internat., Kappa Delta Pi (historian 1987-90). Roman Catholic.

FINLEY, MARGARET MAVIS, retired elementary school educator; b. Jackson, Mich., Dec. 2, 1927; d. Allen Aaron and Minnie Mavis (Graham) Lincoln; m. Duane Douglas Finley, Aug. 23, 1952; 1 child, Linda Louise. BS, Ea. Mich. U., 1960; postgrad., Pepperdine U., 1968-72. Cert. tchr., Mich., Calif. Tchr. Jackson Sch. Dist., 1960-67, Pomona (Calif.) Sch. Dist., 1967-88. Editor Calif. Ret. Tchrs. Assn. Divsn. 82 Newsletter; contbr. poetry and articles to profl. jours. Mem. AAUW, Calif. Ret. Tchrs. Assn., Calif. Tchrs. Assn. (life). Avocations: writing, reading, hiking, travel, theater. Home: 1072 Cypress Point Dr Banning CA 92220-5404

FINLEY, ROBERT COE, III, interventional cardiologist, consultant, educator; b. Aurora, Ill., July 14, 1947; s. Robert Coe Jr. and Elizabeth Lorraine (Winkenweder) F.; m. Celia Ann Oberg; children: Robert IV, Timothy, Rebecca; children: Erik, Jacquelyn. BS magna cum laude, U. Ill., 1970, postgrad., 1970-72; MD, Loyola U, Chicago, 1976. Diplomate Am. Bd. Med. Examiners, Am. Bd. Internal Medicine, Am. Bd. Cardiovasc. Disease. Resident internal medicine Loyola U. Med. Ctr., Maywood, Ill., 1976-79, cardiology fellow, 1979-81, attending physician, asst. prof. medicine, 1981-83, clin. asst. prof., 1983—; physician, ptnr. Suburban Cardiologist, Hinsdale, Ill., 1983—. Dir. founder Cardiac Rehab. Ctr., Maywood, 1982-83; dir., founder cardiac catherization lab. Hinsdale Hosp., 1984-91, dir. coronary angioplasty program, founder, 1989-91, dir., founder outpatient inotropic support program, 1989-91, chmn. cardiac catheterization com., 1984—, chmn. dept. medicine, 1996-97. Co-founder, co-dir. Men's Bible Group, Riverside Presbyn. Ch., 1983-85; physician vol. advanced cardiac life support tag com. Chgo. Heart Assn., 1988-91; physician vol. Cmty. Nurse Assn., La Grange, Ill., 1995-2000. Commendation for Caring and Bravery City Woodstock, Ill., 1983; Edmund James James scholar U. Ill., 1966-70. Fellow Am. Coll. Cardiology, Soc. Cardiac Angiography and Interventions, Am. Coll. Chest Physicians; mem. Alpha Sigma Nu. Avocations: martial arts, snow and water skiing, hiking, bicycling. Home: 136 Circle Ridge Dr Burr Ridge IL 60527-8379 Office: Suburban Cardiologist 333 Chestnut St Hinsdale IL 60521-3247

FINLEY-MORIN, KIMBERLEY K. educator; b. San Angelo, Tex., Nov. 23, 1954; d. James Griffith Jr. and Imogene (Powers) Finley; m. Michael Morin, Feb. 15, 1986. BA cum laude, Pan Am. U., 1982. Cert. Acupressuriest. Tchr. Dallas Theatre Ctr., Greenfield (Mass.) Child Care Ctr.; site coord., tchr. Greenfield Girls Club; tchr. theatre/acting Shea Theatre, Turners Falls, Mass.; prof. theatre/speech Greenfield Com. Coll., 1996—. Resident dir. Fellowship Players of South Deerfield, 1996—. Pres. Arena Civic Theatre, 1992—. With USN, 1976-80. Mem. Tex. Ednl. Theatre Assn., Alpha Omega. Home: 62 High St Turners Falls MA 01376-1709

FINNEMORE, DOUGLAS KIRBY, retired physics educator; b. Cuba, N.Y., Sept. 9, 1934; s. David Jerome and Mildred (Bosworth) F.; m. Faith Romaine Watson, June 16, 1956; children: Martha, Susan, Sara. BS, Pa. State U., 1956; MS, U. Ill., 1958, PhD, 1962. Mem. faculty Iowa State U., Ames, 1962—, assoc. prof. physics, 1965-68, prof., 1968—, Disting. prof. sci. and humanities, 1987—, program dir. solid state physics, 1978-83, assoc. dir. Ames Lab, 1983-88, chair dept. physics and astronomy, 1994—99, ret., 2002—. Program dir. quantum solids and liquids program NSF, 1976-77; detailee U.S. Dept. Energy, 1993-94; vis. fellow U. Coll. Oxford, 1989. Fellow Univ. Coll. Oxford, 1989. Fellow Am. Phys. Soc.; mem. Sigma Xi. Home: 3312 Oakland St Ames IA 50014-3520

FINNERTY, EDWARD PATRICK, neuroscience educator, clinical chemist; b. Terre Haute, Ind., Aug. 19, 1951; s. Thomas Joseph and Helen Beatrice (Clifton) F.; m. Marilyn L. Burns, June 7, 1975; children: Jennifer, Kathleen, Jessica. BS, Ind. State U., 1973, MA, 1975, PhD, 1982; postgrad., Wake Forest U., 1976-77. Cert. specialist in chemistry Am. Soc. Clin. Pathology. Lab. technician St. Anthony Hosp., Terre Haute, 1970-73, Valley Med. Lab., Terre Haute, 1973-75; clin. chemist Community Hosp. Indpls., 1975-76; grad. fellow Ind. State U., Terre Haute, 1977-80; clin. chemist Terre Haute Regional Hosp., 1977-80; asst. prof. U. Minn., Mpls., 1980-83; asst. prof. neurosci. U. Osteo. Med. and Health Scis. (now Des Moines U.), Des Moines, 1983-86, assoc. prof., 1986-94, prof., 1994—. Contbr. numerous articles to sci. jours. Mem. Urbandale (Iowa) Cmty. Sch. Bd., 1987-99, pres., 1989-90, 95-96, 97-98, v.p., 1994-95, 96-97. Recipient faculty award phys. therapy class U. Osteo. Medicine and Health Scis., 1992, rsch. grantee, 1984-87, 94-96. Mem. Soc. for Neurosci., Am. Assn. for Clin. Chemistry, Am. Coll. Neuropsychiatrists (affiliate), Iowa Acad. Sci., Internat. Assn. Med. Sci. Educators (bd. dirs. 2000-02, v.p. 2002—), Sigma Xi. Roman Catholic. Avocations: reading, swimming, golf, genealogy. Office: Des Moines U 3200 Grand Ave Des Moines IA 50312-4104 E-mail: edward.finnerty@dmu.edu.

FINNERTY, JOHN DUDLEY, financial consultant; b. Glen Ridge, NJ, Apr. 23, 1949; s. John Patrick and Patricia (Conover) F.; m. Christine Watt, Dec. 29, 1973 (div. Jan. 1987); m. Louise Hoppe, May 21, 1988; 1 child, William Patrick Taylor. AB, Williams Coll., 1967-71; BA, U. Cambridge (Eng.), 1971-73, MA, 1977; PhD, Naval Postgrad. Sch., 1977. Adj. prof. Naval Postgrad. Sch., Monterey, Calif., 1973-77; sr. assoc. Morgan Stanley and Co. Inc., NYC, 1977-82; v.p. Lazard Frères and Co., NYC, 1982-86; exec. v.p., CFO Coll. Savs. Bank, Princeton, NJ, 1986-89, also bd. dirs.; gen. ptnr. McFarland Dewey & Co., NYC, 1989-95; dir. Houlihan Lokey Howard & Zukin, NYC, 1995-97; ptnr. PricewaterhouseCoopers LLP, NYC, 1997—2001; mng. prin. Analysis Group, Inc., NYC, 2001—03, Finnerty Econ. Cons., LLC, NYC, 2003—. Adj. prof. Fordham U., NYC, 1987-89, prof., 1989—. Author: Bond Refunding Analysts, 1984, Corporate Fin. Analysis, 1986, Fin. Mgr. Guide, 1988, Principles of Fin. with Corp. Applications, 1991, Yearbook of Fixed Income Investing, 1995, Project Fin., 1996, Corporate Fin. Mgmt., 1997, Principles of Fin. Mgmt., 1998, Debt Mgmt., 2001, Corp. Fin. Mgmt., 2d edit., 2004; assoc. editor Jour. of Corp. Fin., 1987-89, Fin. Mgmt., 1982-93; Jour. of Applied Fin., 1999-; mem. editl. bd. Jour. Portfolio Mgmt., 1990—, Jour. Fin. Engring., 1992-99; patentee Restructuring Debt Obligations, 1987, 88, Funding a Future Liability of Uncertain Cost., 1988, Insuring the Funding of a Future Liability of Uncertain Cost, 1989; editor: Fin. Mgmt., 1993-99, FMA Online, 2001-. Co-chmn. fund-raising in NJ for Williams Coll., 3d Century Campaign, 1990-93. Lt. USNR, 1973-77. Marshall Commn. scholar, London, 1971. Mem. Fin. Mgmt. Assn. (bd. dir. 1984-86, 91-99), Am. Fin. Assn., Western Fin. Assn., Fixed Income Analysts Soc. (program chmn. 1989-90, v.p. 1990-91, pres. 1991-92, bd. dir. 1990-92, 2001-), Williams Club (NYC), Spring Lake Bath and Tennis Club (NJ). Republican. Roman Catholic. Avocation: coin collecting. Home: 400 Park Ave Rye NY 10580-1213

FINNEY, LINNEA RUTH, tailor, accountant, writer; b. Seattle, May 4, 1952; d. Donald Bruce and Ethel Ruth (Hagli) Deans; m. Raymond Howard Finney, Oct. 5, 1977; children: Sean Howard, Chelan Kimber. A of A of Arts and Scis., A of Applied Arts and Scis. in Acctg., Shoreline C.C., Seattle, 1995. Dental asst., technician Dr. Donald Bruce Deans, Seattle, 1966-74; dental technician Zundel Dental Lab., Seattle, 1976-79; tailor Carol McClellan Suedes & Leathers, Seattle, 1982, 84; wardrobe asst. Diana Ross on Tour, Seattle, 1982, Harry Belafonte on Tour, Seattle, 1987, Rod Stewart on Tour, Seattle, 1988, Dream Girls Nat. Tour, Seattle, 1988; home tchr. Mukilteo (Wash.) Sch. Dist., 1991-94, Stanwood (Wash.) Sch. Dist., 1995-96. Tailor Haute Couture, Bothell, Wash., 1964-74, 81-84, Seattle, 1977-80, Everett, Wash., 1984-95, Stanwood, Wash., 1995—. Vol. Habitat for Humanity, 1992. Avocations: reading, medicine. Home: 7719 274th St NW Stanwood WA 98292-5927

FINNEY, PATRICIA ANN, elementary education educator; b. Ft. Worth, Aug. 7, 1936; d. Thomas Lee and Mary Myrtle (Austin) Carleton; m. Roy Jack Finney, Nov. 9, 1957; children: Roy Jack Finney III, Thomas Lee Finney. BS in Edn., North Tex. State U., 1957. Cert. tchr., Tex. Tchr. art Ft. Worth Ind. Sch. Dist., Ft. Worth, 1957-67; tchr. Ft. Bend Ind. Sch. Dist., Sugar Land, Tex., 1979-85, tchr. elem. art, 1985—. One-woman gallery shows, 1972—; wildlife artist, naturalist; illustrator children's books, 1991—. Vol. artist Audubon Soc. newsletter, Houston, 1991—; vol. Houston Mus. Natural Sci., 1994—. Mem. Tex. Art Edn. Assn., Nat. Art Edn. Assn., Soc. Children's Book Writers, PTA. Methodist. Avocations: painting, gardening. Home: 10019 Towne Brook Ln Sugar Land TX 77478-1642

FINOCCHIARO, PENNY MORRIS, secondary school educator; b. Glendale, Calif., Sept. 30, 1949; d. C. Harold and Margaret (Nelson) Morris; m. Paul D. Finocchiaro, Apr. 9, 1996; children from previous marriage: E. Pierce III, Hailey M. BA in Speech and English, Muskingum Coll., New Concord, Ohio, 1971; MA in Edn., Nat. U., Sacramento, 1991. Cert. multiple and single subject tchr. Assoc. prodr. Alhecama Players, Santa Barbara (Calif.) C.C. Dist., 1972-86; docent Santa Barbara Mus. Art, 1975-86; importer Cambridge Place Corp., Santa Barbara, 1974-86; promotions and fund raising Stewart-Bergman Assocs., Nevada City, Calif., 1986-89; travel columnist The Union, Grass Valley, Calif., 1987-90; tchr. drama and English Bear River H.S., Grass Valley, 1991-98, dept. chair visual and performing arts, 1993-98; tchr. English lit. Lyçee Françise La Perouse, San Francisco, 1999—, chair dept. English, 2001—. Art docent coord. Deer Creek Sch., Nevada City, 1986-90, pres. Parent Tchr. Club, 1987-88. Recipient award for valuable contbn. to schs. Nevada City Sch. Dist., 1990, Dir.'s award Santa Barbara C.C., 1982, Tchrs. Who Make a Difference award Assn. of Calif. Sch. Adminstrs., 1998. Mem.: No. Calif. Ednl. Theatre Assn., Calif. Ednl. Theatre Assn., Ednl. Theatre Assn., Calif. Assn. Tchrs. English, Nat. Coun. Tchrs. of English. Avocations: art and antique collecting, rollerblading, travel, biking, swimming, theatre. Home: 2123 Jones St San Francisco CA 94133-2582 Office: Lycee Francais Internat 755 Ashbury St San Francisco CA 94117-4013

FINSTER, DIANE L. STELTEN, secondary school educator, media specialist, home economics educator; b. St. Cloud, Minn., Sept. 11, 1953; d. George Henry and Theresa Lucy (Becker) Stelten; m. Jon Gregory Dane, Aug., 1976 (dec. Oct. 1981); m. James Robert Finster, June 1, 1985 (div. Feb. 1993); children: James Andrew, Nicholas William. BS in Home Econs., U. Wis. at Stout, Menomonie, 1975; MS in Ednl. Media, U. Wis., LaCrosse, 1987. Cert. in vocat. and gen. home econs. edn., ednl. media specialist, Wis., Minn. With Hagerty Catering, Chgo., Tri-R Vending, Chgo.; instr. home econs. Blair (Wis.) Pub. Schs.; edn. media specialist Brillion (Wis.) Pub. Schs.; home econs. dept. head Blair-Taylor Pub. Schs., Blair, Wis., 1980-87; libr. media specialist Brillon Pub. Schs., 1987-88; dist. libr., audio/visual coord. Pardeeville (Wis.) Pub. Schs., 1989-90; dist. media dir. St. Croix Falls (Wis.) Pub. Schs., 1990—. Contbr. articles to profl. jours. Coach Spl. Olympics, Blair, 1980-87; homemaking divsn. chairperson. Cheese Festival, Blair, 1980-87; mem. adv. bd. Com. Tech., Vocat. Adult Edn., Blair, 1980-87, Sch. Evaluation Consortium, Blair, 1980-87, St. Croix Falls Pub. Libr., 1990—; with Boy Scouts of Am.; vol. CRA-Battered Women, Children's Shelter, hosp. aux.; soccer coach River Valley Soccer Club. Mem. AAUW, ALA, Am. Home Econs. Assn., Wis. Ednl. Media Assn., Wis. Libr. Assn., Wis. Assn. Sch. Librs., Phi Upsilon Omicron. Avocations: travel, outdoor sports, gourmet cooking, sketching, reading. Home: PO Box 182 Dresser WI 54009-0182 Office: St Croix Falls High Sch PO Box 130 Saint Croix Falls WI 54024-0130

FINSTER, JAMES ROBERT, library media specialist; b. Milw., Sept. 29, 1947; s. Milton Robert Finster and Eleonore B. (Worgull) Helvey; children: James Andrew, Nicholas William. BS in Edn., Dr. Martin Luther Coll., 1971; BS in Resource Mgmt., U. Wis., Stevens Point, 1976; MS in Edn. Media, U. Wis., LaCrosse, 1987. Cert. libr. media specialist, Wis., Minn. Ski instr. various ski clubs, resorts, Wis. and Colo., 1971—; elem. tchr. pvt. and pub. schs. Wis., 1971-73, 78-81; teaching asst. U. Wis., Stevens Point, 1975; park ranger Nat. Park Svc., various locations, 1976-77; ski. sch. dir. Whitecap Mountain, Montreal, Wis., 1982-83, Coffee Mill Ski Area, Wabasha, Minn., 1983-84; grad. asst. U. Wis., LaCrosse, 1986-87; libr. media specialist Chilton (Wis.) High Sch., 1987-93; libr. media specialist K-12 Rib Lake (Wis.) Pub. Schs., 1993-94, Elcho (Wis.) Pub. Sch., 1994-96; ski instr. Trollhaugen, 1997—. Mem. Wis. Ednl. Media Assn. Republican. Lutheran. Avocations: downhill skiing, travel, sports, games, music. Home: 200 Seminole Ave Lot 78 Osceola WI 54020-8076

FINTA, FRANCES MICKNA, secondary school educator; b. Stafford Springs, Conn., June 17, 1927; d. John Joseph Mickna and Mary Frances Breslin; m. Quinn Finta, Aug. 21, 1951; children: John Wright, Susan Frances Finta Phillips. BA in Math., Boston U., 1949; postgrad., U. Va., 1963—69, Prince George's C.C., Largo, Md., 1982, No. Va. C.C., Alexandria, 1982—84, postgrad., 1994, U. Va., Fairfax, 1988—89; MEd in Guidance and Counseling, George Mason U., 1975. Cert. tchr. Va. Food prodn. mgr., dining rm. mgr., waitress, field ops. rep., liaison to airlines Marriott Corp., Marriott In-Flight Svcs., Inc., Washington, 1950—62; tchr., guidance counselor Arlington (Va.) Pub. Schs., 1963—. Substitute tchr. Fairfax (Va.) Pub. Schs., 1972—73; 'substitute tchr. Arlington (Va.) County Pub. Schs., 1972—. Mem. Arlington County Scholarship Fund for Tchrs., Inc., 1995—, sec., 1996—2001, treas., 2002—; mem. Friends of Arlington Parks, 1995—, Maywood Cmty. Assn., 1966—; treas. Washington-Lee H.S. Band Booster Club, 1979—81, Evelyn Staples for County Bd., 1991; vol. coord. David Foster for Sch. Bd., 1994; Maywood del. Arlington County Civic Fedn., 1982—; mem. Arlingtonians for a Better County, 1999—2002; membership chmn. Arlington County Civic Fedn., 1984—, treas., 2000—; mem. Arlington County Rep. Com., 1994—, chmn. hdqrs., 2000—, mem. fin. com., 1994—95, canvass chmn., 2000—03, chmn. nominations com., 2000—01; mem. steering com. John Hager for Gov., 2000; del. to state conv. Rep. Party Va., 1996, 1998, 2000, Va. Fedn. Rep. Women, 1996—; mem. credential com. Va. 8th Dist. Rep. Conv., 1998; sec. adv. com. Commonwealth of Va., 1998—2002; mem. Organized Women Voters of Arlington, 1997—, mem. nominating com., 2000, treas., 2000—. Recipient Hon. Guardian of Srs.' Rights award, 60 Plus Assn., 1999, Vol. Svc. award, Arlington County Rep. Com., 1995—99, Hilda Griffith Lifetime Achievement award, 1999, Leon Delyannis Cmty. Involvement award, 1997, Cert. of Appreciation, Arlington County Civic Fedn., 1988, 1997, Jour. Newspapers trophy, 2001, Parent Vol. award, Washington-Lee H.S. Band Boosters Club, 1979, Appreciation award, 1981, Parent Vol. award, Woodmont Elem. Sch., 1975, Patrick Henry award, Commonwealth of Va., 2001, Disting. Meritorious Svc. award, Arlington Co. Civic Found., 2003. Mem.: AAUW (del. to Arlington County Civic Fedn. 1994—, co-1st v.p. programs 2001—03, exec. com. 2001—03, co-1st programs exec. com. 2001—03, 1st v.p. programs 2002—03), NEA, Arlington Ret. Tchrs. Assn., Arlington Edn. Assn., Va. Edn. Assn., Va. Ret. Tchrs. Assn. (life), Arlington County Taxpayers' Assn., Arlington Rep. Women's Club (auditor 1996, asst. treas. 1997, pres. 1998—99, newsletter editor 1998—99, chmn. achievement awards 2000, chmn. bylaws com. 2000, chmn. Barbara Bush literacy com. 2000, dir. 2000—01, chair fin. com. 2002—). Republican. Roman Catholic. Avocations: civic and political activities, reading. Home: 3317 23d St N Arlington VA 22201-4310

FIORE, JAMES LOUIS, JR., public accountant, educator, professional speaker, trainer consultant; b. Jersey City, Oct. 7, 1935; s. James Louis and Rose (Perrotta) F.; m. Alberta W. Pope, July 21, 1957; children: Carolyn Leigh, James Louis III, Toni Lynn. BS in Acctg., Seton Hall U., 1957; MBA, We. Colo. U., 1972; PhD, Calif. We. U., 1979. Lic. acct. Pa., N.J. Field auditor State of N.J., Trenton, 1958-60; supr. internal auditing Ronson Corp., Woodbridge, N.J., 1960-64; surp. gen. acctg. Electronic Assocs., West Long Branch, N.J., 1964-65; pvt. practice acctg., 1965—. Pres. Bucks County Rsch. Inst., Inc., 1972-79; mem. adj. faculty Allentown Coll. St. Francis de Sales, Ctr. Valley, Pa., 1979-81, Pa. Coll. Chriopractic, 1986-94, Holy Family Coll., Phila., 1995; sec.-treas. Cordian Group Internat., Inc. Bus. Cons., 2001— Author: (with others) Shareholder Loans, The National Public Accountant, 1988, Financial Problems and Your Profession, 1989, Non-Absorption of Nitrofurazone from the Urethra in Men, 1976, Comparative Bioavailability of Doxycycline, 1974; contbr. articles to profl. jours. Founder Brick Twp. (N.J.) Scholarship Fund, 1963-67; mem. adv. coun. Inst. for Accts., Pa. State U.; trustee Pa. Coll. Chiropractic, 1986-94; founder, treas. Cath. Acad. Sci. in U.S.A., Washington. Lt. U.S. Army, 1957. Named Jayce of Yr., 1962; recipient Legion of Honor, Chapel of Four Chaplains, 1979. Mem. Calif. We. U. Alumni Assn., We. Colo. U. Alumni Assn., Seton Hall U. Alumni Assn. (Crest and Centrury Clubs), Masons, Shriners, Scottish Rite, K.T. Home: 265 Thompson Mill Rd Newtown PA 18940-3105 E-mail: James.Fiore@speakerjim.com.

FIREBAUGH, GLENN ALLEN, sociology educator; b. Charleston, W.Va., Oct. 23, 1948; s. George Lawrence and Rosanelle (Grose) Firebaugh; m. Judy Rae Thompson, Nov. 21, 1970; children: Heather, Joel, Rose Marie. BA, Grace Coll., 1970; MA, Ind. U., 1974, PhD, 1976. Prof. sociology Pa. State U., University Park, 1988—, head dept. sociology, 2001—. Author: The New Geography of Global Income Inequality, 2003; editor: (jour.) Am. Sociol. Rev., 1997—99; editor: (editl. bd.) Sociol. Quar., Sociol. Methods and Rsch., Social Forces, Am. Jour. Sociology; contbr. articles to profl. jours. Recipient Disting. Scholar award, Pa. State U., 2001; fellow, NIMH, 1972—76; grantee, NSF, 1983—84, 1988—2001. Office: Pa State Univ Dept Sociology 206 Oswald Tower University Park PA 16802

FIRESTONE, JUANITA MARLIES, sociology educator; b. Wurzburg, Germany, Jan. 30, 1947; d. Harrison and Marlies (Breit) Gillette; m. Kenneth Todd Firestone, Aug. 31, 1968 (div. Oct. 1993); children: Jason Dean, Krystillin Elisabeth; m. Richard J. Harris, Apr. 19, 1995. BS in Sociology cum laude, Black Hills State U., 1979; MA in Sociology, U. Tex., 1982, PhD in Sociology, 1984. Office mgr. Silver Wings Aviation, Rapid City, S.D., 1975-76; pub. rels. mgr. Pacer Mining Co., Custer, S.D., 1976-79; lectr. sociology U. Tex., Austin, 1980-87, asst. prof. sociology San Antonio, 1987-94, assoc. prof., 1994—99, prof., 1999—. Cons. in field; attendee Nat. Security Forum, 1994; mem. Chancellor's Faculty Adv. Coun., U. Tex. Sys., 1994-96; testimony U.S. Congress Black Polit. Caucus, 1996; mem. peer rev. panel Am. Inst. Biol. Scis., 1998-99; mem. Internat. Demography Workshop, 1999; Fulbright Disting. chair in gender studies U. Klagenfurt, Austria, 2001-02; Fulbright Sr. Specialist, 2003—, Disting. Chair Gender Studies, Klagenfurt, Austria, 2001-03. Contbr. articles to profl. jours. Mem. spkrs. bur. Rape Crisis Ctr., Austin and San Antonio, 1984-94; bd. dirs. AIDS Found., San Antonio, 1992; coord. workshop Expanding Your Horizons, San Antonio, 1992-2001; mem. Task Force on Crime and Violence, San Antonio, 1990. Recipient Rsch. award U. Tex. Sys., Austin, 1991, 95, 98, 2000, U. Tex., San Antonio, 1999; Congrl. fellow, Washington, 1983. Mem. Internat. Sociol. Assn., Am. Sociol. Assn., S.W. Soc. Social Sci. (pres. women's caucus 1994-95), Golden Key (faculty advisor 1990-96), Inter Univ. Consortium Armed Forces and Soc. (bd. dirs. 1998—), Alpha Kappa Delta. Avocations: swimming, skiing, water skiing, reading. Office: U Tex at San Antonio Divsn Social and Policy Sci San Antonio TX 78249

FIRESTONE, SHEILA MEYEROWITZ, retired gifted and talented education educator; b. Bronx, N.Y., Dec. 20, 1941; d. Boris and Bella Meyerowitz; m. Bruce Firestone, Oct. 1, 1961; children: Wayne, Evan. AA, Miami-Dade Community Coll., North Miami, Fla., 1969; BA in Edn., Fla. Atlantic U., 1972; MS in Spl. Edn., Fla. Internat. U., 1973. Cert. learning disabilities, elem., gifted, early childhood, emotionally disturbed, Fla. Tchr. to gifted Highland Oaks Elem. Sch., North Miami Beach, Fla., 1973-98; ret., 1998. Chairperson Dade County Very Spl. Arts Festival, 1989-93. Composer: Premiere - Psalm 117, Because I Love, South Florida Youth Symphony, 1994; rec. artist Songs for a New Day, 2002, Neoclassical and Postmodern Compositions, Piano Favorites #1, 2002, Sing and Think interactive songs and curriculum for early childhood, Peaceful Journeys, Music for Meditation and Healing. Mem. choir Temple Sinai, North Miami Beach, 1979-92; state evaluator Future Problem Solving, 1989-96; creative writing supt. Dade County Youth Fair, 1982-87; founder "Songs for a New Day; pub. teaching curriculum and leadership/citizenship tng. thematic music and interdisciplinary whole lang. learning units, 1990; mem. choir Aventura Turnberry Jewish Ctr., 1993. Named Master Tchr., State of Fla., 1985; recipient Very Spl. Arts Honor award Dade County Bd. Pub. Instns., 1990, 1st pl. Jim Harbin Fame award Fla. Media Educators, 1994, Tchr. of Note, Young Patronesses of the Opera, 1996; Freedom Found. grantee, summers, 1983, 84, 87, 90, Nancy Givens Instrnl. grantee, Fla. Coun. Exceptional Children, 1995, Javitts grant Nat. Evaluator F.P.S., 1992-93, grantee Dade Pub. Edn. Fund Impact II Adapter, 1994; recipient Tchr. of Note award Young Patronesses of the Opera, 2002. Mem. ASCAP Coun. for Exceptional Children (various offices 1963-97, chpt. pres. 1988, Fla. Exceptional Tchr. of Yr. finalist 1989, Chpt. 121 Dade County Exceptional Student Tchr. of Yr. award 1989, Highland Oaks Elem. Sch. Tchr. of Yr. 1990), Nat. League Am. Pen Women, Sigma Alpha Iota (patroness 1996—, pres. patroness chpt. U. Miami 1998—, composer spring Vespers program 1997). Democrat. Avocation: studying and composing music. E-mail: shesong@songsforanewday.com.

FIRE THUNDER, SONDRA NADINE, elementary educator; b. Monmouth, Ill., Dec. 13, 1943; d. Robert Clair and Marjorie Nadine (Pierce) Stevens; m. Edgar William Fire Thunder, Dec. 7, 1973 (div. 1979); children: Kathleen, April, William. BS in Edn., Western Ill. U., 1970. Cert. tchr., Ariz. Tchr. elem. sch. Monmouth Pub. Schs., 1970-73, Bur. Indian Affairs, Allen, S.D., 1973-74, Cherry Creek, S.D., 1976-77, Sells, Ariz., 1977—, equal employment opportunity counselor, 1987—. PTO fundraising rep. Santa Rosa Boarding/Day Sch., 1988—; sec. PTO, 1992—. Mem. Ariz. Archaeol. Soc. (dir. Casa Grande chpt. 1985-87). Avocations: beading, reading, archaeology. Home: HCR Box 483K Sells AZ 85634 Office: Santa Rosa Boarding/Day Sch Sells AZ 85634

FIRIMITA, FLORIN ION, artist, educator, writer; b. Bucharest, Romania, July 30, 1965; came to the U.S., 1990; s. Ion and Anica (Manu) F. AA magna cum laude, Naugatuck Valley Coll., 1995; BS summa cum laude, Ctrl. Conn. State U., 1997, postgrad. Cert. art edn. grades K-12. Asst. stage designer Nat. Theatre of Opera and Ballet, Bucharest, 1986-90, prodn. mgr., 1988-90; curator, mem. adv. bd. Gallery on the Green, Canton, Conn., 1996—; artist-tchr. Middlebury (Conn.) Elem. Sch., 1997—. Mgr., owner Fif Studio, Winchester, Conn., 1995—. Works exhibited at various group and solo shows York Sq. Gallery, New Haven, 1994, Miss Porter's Sch., Farmington, Conn., 1995, Pat Steier Gallery, Litchfield, Conn., 1995, Emporium Gallery, Mystic, Conn., 1996; represented in various pvt. and pub. collections; co-author: The Art of Leaving; author of essays, short stories and art criticism. Vis. artist and educator Vol. Outreach Program, New Britain, Conn., 1997. Recipient Honorable mention Nat. Arts Program,

Hartford, Conn., 1992, Nat. prize for lit. NYU, Suffern, 1994. Mem. NEA, Conn. Edn. Assn., Washington Art Assn., Canton Art Guild. Avocations: classical music, jazz, travel, reading. Home: 155 Smith Hill Rd Winsted CT 06098-2217

FIRST, HARRY, law educator; b. 1945; BA, U. Pa., 1966, JD, 1969. Bar: Pa. 1969, N.Y. 1979. Law clk. to justice Supreme Ct. Pa., 1969-70; atty. U.S. Dept. Justice, Washington, 1970-72; asst. prof. U. Toledo Coll. Law, 1972-76; vis. assoc. prof. NYU Law Sch., N.Y.C., 1976-77, assoc. prof., 1977-79, prof., 1979—; counsel Loeb & Loeb, N.Y.C. and Los Angeles, 1985-99; chief antitrust bur. N.Y. State Office of Atty. Gen., 1999-2001. Mem. editl. bd. Pa. Law Rev. Mem. Pa. Law Rev., Order of Coif, Phi Beta Kappa. Office: NYU Law Sch Vanderbilt Hall 40 Washington Sq S New York NY 10012-1099 E-mail: hf3@nyu.edu.*

FISCH, ARLINE MARIE, artist, educator; b. Bklyn., Aug. 21, 1931; d. Nicholas H. and Elizabeth (Fischer) F. BS in Art, Skidmore Coll., 1952; MA in Art, U. Ill., 1954; postgrad., Kunsthaandvaerkerskolen, Copenhagen, 1956-57; DHL (hon.), Skidmore Coll., 2002. Instr. Wheaton Coll., Norton, Mass., 1954-56, Skidmore Coll., Saratoga Springs, N.Y., 1958-61; prof. art San Diego (Calif.) State U., 1961—2000. Summer sch. instr. Haystack Mt. Sch. of Crafts, Deer Isle, Maine, 1965, 66, 78, 83, 85, 87, 90, 95, Penland (N.C.) Sch., 1968, 71, 74, 79, 86, 94, 2003; lectr. World Crafts Coun. and others, 1970—, workshop, seminar leader Textile Techniques in Metal, 1970—; vis. prof. Boston U., 1975-76; design cons. Reed and Barton, Taunton, MAss., 1977-78; juror, curator Craft Eshbns., 1977—. Jewelry artist solo exhbns. Pasadena Mus. Art, 1962, Am. Craft Mus., 1968, Mus. Fur Angewandie Kunst, Vienna, Austria, 1982, Mus. Fine Arts, Montevideo, Uruguay, 1989, The Textile Mus., Washington, 2001, Am. Craft Mus., N.Y., 2002; represented in pub. collections Schmuck Mus., Pforzheim, 1979, 85, 90, Detroit (Mich.) Inst. Art, 1988, Victoria and Albert Mus., London, 1989, Kunstindustrimuseet, Copenhagen, 1989, Renwick Gallery/Smithsonian, Washington, 1990. Trustee Haystack Mt. Sch. of Crafts, 1973-82, 91-2000; v.p. World Craft Coun., 1976-80; commr. U.S. Nat. Com. for Unesco, 1977-82. Recipient Fulbright award for student rsch. USEF, Denmark, 1956-57, 66-67, Fulbright Tchg. awards U.S. State Dept., Austria, 1982, Uruguay, 1989; Faculty Rsch. grantee San Diego State U., 1970, 88, 90, 93; Craftsmen's fellow Nat. Endowment in the Arts, 1973-74. Fellow Am. Craft Coun. (trustee 1972-75, 94-2000, lectr.); mem. Soc. N.Am. Goldsmiths (founding mem., pres. 1982-85, lectr.).

FISCH, NATHANIEL JOSEPH, physicist; b. Montreal, Quebec, Can., Dec. 29, 1950; s. Mandel and Helene (Greenfield) F.; m. Tobe Michelle Mann, Aug. 12, 1984; children: Jacob, Benjamin, Adam. BS, MIT, 1972, MS, 1975, PhD, 1978. Researcher Princeton (N.J.) Plasma Physics Lab., 1978-91, assoc. dir. for acad. affairs, 1993—; dir. program in plasma physics Princeton U., 1991—, prof. astrophys. scis., 1991—. Cons. Exxon Rsch. and Engring., Clinton, N.J., 1981-86; vis. scientist IBM, Yorktown Heights, N.Y., 1986. Recipient fellowship Guggenheim Found., 1985, 1992 APS award for Excellence in Plasma Physics, Am. Phys. Soc., 1992. Fellow Am. Phys. Soc. (vice chair divsn. of plasma physics 1996, chair-elect 1997, chair 1998). Achievements include patents in new ways to produce current in plasmas. Office: Princeton U Forrestal Campus PO Box 451 MS30 Princeton NJ 08543-0451 E-mail: nfisch@pppl.gov.

FISCHBACH, RUTH LINDA, ethics educator, social scientist, researcher; b. NYC, June 7, 1940; d. Edward Joseph and Bess (Wolsk) Zeitlin; m. Gerald David Fischbach, July 8, 1962; children: Elissa, Peter, Mark and Neal (twins). Attended, Mt. Holyoke Coll., 1958-60; BS, RN, Cornell U., 1963; MS, Boston U., 1975, PhD, 1983; MPE, Washington U., 1990. Dir. patient edn. Beth Israel Hosp., Boston, 1978-80; postdoctoral fellow Washington U. Sch. Medicine, St. Louis, 1983-86, asst. rsch. prof., 1986-90, asst. dean, 1989-90; asst. prof. Harvard Med. Sch., Boston, 1990-98; sr. advisor for biomed. ethics Office of Dir. for Extramural Rsch./NIH, Bethesda, Md., 1998—2001; prof. bioethics Coll. Physicians and Surgeons, Mailman Sch. Pub. Health Columbia U., NYC, 2001—, dir. Ctr. Bioethics, 2001—. Dir. Program for Humanities in Medicine Washington U. Sch. Medicine, 1988—90, Program in Practice of Sci. Investigation Harvard Med. Sch., 1990—98; bd. dir. Pub. Responsibility in Med. and Rsch., Boston, 1992—; reviewer Univ.-wide AIDS Rsch. Program State Calif., 1995; adv. bd. Beth Israel Clin. Investigator Tng. Program, Boston, 1995—; vice chmn. bd. dirs. Pub. Responsibility in Med. and Rsch., Boston, 2002—. Producer: (dramatization) Miss Evers' Boys, 1993; editl. bd. Sci. & Engring. Ethics, 1994—; contbr. articles to profl. jours., chpts. to books. Pres. Lincoln Sch. PTA, Brookline, Mass., 1978—80; vol. Mass. Coalition of Battered Women Svc. Groups, Boston, 1993—98; trustee Penzance Point, 1998—, Parc Somerset Condo., Chevy Chase, Md., Morris Jumel Mansion, 2002—; med. and profl. adv. coun. Gold Found., 2002—; bd. dirs. Joint Com. on Status of Women, Boston, 1990—97. Fellow Exec. Inst. of Advanced Study, St. Louis, 1988; recipient Disting. Alumna award Cornell U., 2003. Mem. Applied Rsch. Ethics Nat. Assn. (bd. dirs. 1994—), Mass. Bioethics Forum (bd. dirs. 1994—), Md. Mothers of Twins (pres. 1969-70), Sigma Theta Tau. Avocations: horticulture, travel, music. Home: 100 Riverside Dr # 3A New York NY 10024

FISCHER, ALICE EDNA WALTZ, computer science educator; b. Detroit, May 20, 1942; d. Robert Beatty and Frances Marie (Schell) Waltz; m. Michael John Fischer, June 1, 1963; children: Edward Michael, Robert Patrick, David Frederick. BA in Math., U. Mich., 1964; MA in Applied Math., Harvard U., 1967, PhD in Computer Sci., 1985. Cert. tchr. secondary edn., Mich. Programmer Loyal Protective Life Ins. Co., Boston, 1964-66; analyst Computer Assocs., Wakefield, Mass., 1967-68; vis. instr. Ga. Inst. Tech., Atlanta, 1980; adj. instr. U. Wash., Seattle, summer 1980, U. New Haven, West Haven, Conn., spring 1982, from instr. to prof. computer sci., 1982—, chair dept. computer sci., 1997—, chair faculty senate, 1994-95. Reviewer textbook manuscripts Addison-Wesley Pub. Co., West Pub. Co. Author: The Anatomy of Programming Languages, 1993. Mem. Rep. Town Com., Hamden, Conn., 1992—, Bd. of Edn., Hamden, 1992-97 Mem. Assn. Computing Machinery, Yale Figure Skating Club (membership chair 1989-96, vol. instr. 1990-96). Republican. Avocations: figure skating, music performance and listening. Office: Univ of New Haven Dept of Computer Science 300 Orange Ave West Haven CT 06516-1999

FISCHER, FRED WALTER, physicist, engineer, educator; b. Zwickau, Germany, June 26, 1922; s. Fritz and Louiska (Richter) F.; m. Yongja Kim, Oct. 1, 1970. BS in Mech. Engring., Columbia U., 1949, MS, 1950; MS in Physics, U. Wash., 1957; D in Elec. Engring., Tech. U. Munich, 1966. Analyst Boeing Co., Seattle, Germany, 1950—84, cons., 1984—88; owner Fischer Cons., 1984—88. Instr. physics, math., and engring. North Seattle Community Coll., 1973-93; guest tchr. Perkins Sch. Author: Analysis for Physics and Engineering, 1982, Renaissance Mathematics, 1992. First v.p., trustee Wedgwood Cmty. Coun., 1994-2000; mem. Wedgwood Elem. Sch. Site Coun., Eckstein Middle Sch. Site Coun. With AUS, 1943-46. Boeing scholar Max Planck Inst. Plasma Physics, 1964-65. Mem. AAAS, N.Y. Acad. Sci., Mercedes Benz Club (Seattle sect. bd. dirs.), Sigma Xi (life). Office: North Seattle CC 9600 College Way N Seattle WA 98103-3514

FISCHER, GAYLE, elementary education educator; b. Fort Worth, Mar. 27, 1950; d. Noble Eugene and Myrtle Mildred (Aycock) Chandler; m. Roger William Harlin, May 23, 1979 (div. 1987); children: Jesse Chandler Harlin, Laura Claire Harlin; m. Terry Wayne Fischer, Mar. 18, 1990. BS in Edn., U. Ga., 1973; MS in Edn., U. Okla., 1990, PhD in Ednl. Psychology, 1998. Cert. tchr., Nat. Bd. Tchrs., 2002, Tex., Okla.; cert. elem. prin., spl. edn., Okla. Tchr. Cobb County Dist., Marietta, Ga., 1973-75; tchr. of emotionally disturbed Spring Br. Acad., Houston, 1976-78; 4th grade tchr. Aldine Sch. Dist., Houston, 1979-81; tchr. of emotionally disturbed Mid-Del Schs., Midwest City, Okla., 1979-81; 3d grade tchr. Mid Del Schs., Midwest City, Okla., 1989-99; 6th and 8th grade tchr. Norman (Okla.) Sch. Dist., 1988-89; tchr. children with emotional disturbance Norman Pub. Schs., 1999—. Trainer behavioral mgmt. Mid-Del Schs., 1990-95; chmn. adminstrv. com. Okla. Commn. on Tchr. Preparation, Oklahoma City, 1991-95; adj. instr. U. Okla., Norman, 1999—; appointed to program accreditation com. Okla. Commn. for Tchr. Preparation, 2001; mem. profl. accreditation com. Okla., 2000-03. Mem. NEA, ASCD, Coun. for Exceptional Children, Coun. for Children with Behavioral Disorders, Coun. Adminstrs. in Spl. Edn., Nat. Coun. for Accreditation of Tchr. Edn., Okla. Assn. Colls. Tchr. Edn. (presenter winter conf. 1993), Assn. Classroom Tchrs., Okla. Edn. Assn. (mem. task force to develop competencies for licensure and cert. 1996-97, credentials com. del. assembly 1996-97). Avocations: writing, research, sailing, boating. Home: 6028 SE 104th St Oklahoma City OK 73165-9606

FISCHER, JOEL, social work educator; b. Chgo., Apr. 22, 1939; s. Sam and Ruth (Feiges) F.; m. Renee H. Furuyama; children: Lisa, Nicole. BS, U. Ill., 1961, MSW, 1964; D in Social Welfare, U. Calif., Berkeley, 1970. Prof. sch. social work U. Hawaii, Honolulu, 1970—. Vis. prof. George Warren Brown Sch. Social Work, Washington U., St. Louis, 1977, U. Wis. Sch. Social Welfare, Milw., 1978-79, U. Natal, South Africa, 1982, U. Hong Kong, 1986; cons. various orgns. and univs. Author: (with Harvey L. Gochros) Planned Behavior Change: Behavior Modification in Social Work, 1973, Handbook of Behavior Therapy with Sexual Problems, vol. I, 1977, vol. II, 1977, Analyzing Research, 1975, Interpersonal Helping: Emerging Approaches for Social Work Practice, 1973, The Effectiveness of Social Casework, 1976, (with D. Sanders and O. Kurrem) Fundamentals of Social Work Practice, 1982, Effective Casework Practice: An Eclectic Approach, 1978, (with H. Gochros) Treat Yourself to a Better Sex Life, 1980, (with H. Gochros and J. Gochros) Helping the Sexually Oppressed, 1985, (with Martin Bloom) Evaluating Practice: Guidlines for the Helping Professional, 1982, (with Kevin Corcoran) Measures for Clinical Practice, 1987, (with Daniel Sanders) Visions for the Future: Social Work and Pacific-Asian Perspectives, 1988, (with Martin Bloom and John Orme) Evaluating Practice, 2nd edit., 1995, (with Kevin Corcoran) Measures for Clinical Practice, 2nd edit., vol. 1, 1994, Couples, Children, Families, vol. 2, 1994, Adults, 1994, East-West Connections: Social Work Practice Traditions and Change, 1992, (with Martin Bloom and John Orme) Evaluating Practice, 3d edit., 1999, (with Martin Bloom and John Orme) Instructor's Manual for Evaluating Practice, 1999; (with Kevin Corcoran) Measures for Clinical practice, 3d edit, vol. 1, 2000, Couples, Children and Families, Adults, vol. 2, 2000, (with Martin Bloom and John Orme) Evaluating Practice, 4th edit., 2003, Instructor's Manual for Evaluating Practice, 2d edit., 2003; mem. editl. bd. 12 profl. jours.; contbr. over 150 articles to profl. jours. Bd. dirs. U. Hawaii Profl. Assembly; precinct pres. Dem. Party. With U.S. Army, 1958. Mem. NASW, ACLU, Hawaii Com. for Africa, Coun. Social Work Edn., Acad. Cert. Social Workers, Nat. Conf. Social Welfare, AAUP, Unity Organizing Com., Hawaii People's Legis. Coalition, Bertha Reynold Soc., Amnesty Internat. Democrat. Home: 1371-4 Hunakai St Honolulu HI 96816-5501 Office: U Hawaii Sch Social Work Henke Hall Honolulu HI 96822-2217 E-mail: jfischer@hawaii.edu.

FISCHER, JOHN MARTIN, education educator, researcher; b. Cleve., Dec. 26, 1952; s. Joseph and Armeda F.; m. Tina Louise Astrolio, Feb. 2, 1991; children: Aja Marie Newton, Ariel Marton, Zoe Sigrid. BA, MA, Stanford U., 1975; MA, Cornell U., 1980, PhD, 1982; MA (hon.), Yale U., 1981. From asst. to assoc. prof. Yale U., New Haven, Conn., 1981-88; assoc. prof. U. Calif., Riverside, 1988-90, prof., 1990—. Dir. honors program U. Calif., Riverside, 1996—. Author: The Metaphysics of Free Will, 1994, Responsiblity and Control, 1998; editor: Moral Responsibility, 1986, The Metaphysics of Death, 1993. Faculty adv. Golden Key Nat. Honor Soc., 1999—; sec.-treas. Phi Beta Kappa, Riverside, 1999—; faculty rep. Rhodes, Marshall and Udall Scholarships, Riverside, 1998—. NEH fellow, 1983-84, 94-95, Residential fellow Nat. Humanities Ctr., Research Triangle Park, 1990-91, 93-94, Australian Nat. U. Rsch. Ctr., Canberra, Australia, 1994. Mem. Am. Philos. Assn. Home: 821 S University Dr Riverside CA 92507 Office: Univ Calif Dept Philosophy Riverside CA 92521 E-mail: john.fischer@ucrac1.ucr.edu.

FISCHER, JOSEPH EDWARD, secondary school mathematics educator; b. Vincennes, Ind., June 12, 1942; s. Russell C. and Grace (Dunham) F.; m. Laura Lea Vachet, Dec. 27, 1965; children: Eric, Kevin, Matthew. AA, Vincennes U., 1962; BA, Ind. State U., Terre Haute, 1964, MS, 1965; postgrad., U. Ill., 1967-68. Cert. tchr., Ind. Instr. in math. Vincennes U., 1965-66, asst. prof. math., 1966-67; math. tchr. North Ctrl. H.S., Indpls., 1968—, chair math. dept., 1992—. Edn. advisor U.S. Senate candidate, Ind., 1988; mem. Friends of Indpls. Marion County Libr., 1988—. Grantee Eli Lilly Found., 1989, MSDWT Found., 1989; recipient Golden Apple award Indpls. Power and Light, 1993. Mem. NEA, Nat. Coun. Tchrs. Math., Ind. Coun. Tchrs. Math., Sch. Sci. and Math. Assn., Math. Assn. Am., Ctrl. Ind. Coun. Tchrs. Math. (bd. dirs. 1972-76), Fractional Currency Collectors' (bd.), Assn. for Recorded Sound Collections, Leopold Stokowski Soc., Serge Koussevitzky Soc., Kappa Delta Pi. Home: 5759 Guilford Ave Indianapolis IN 46220-2642 Office: North Ctrl HS 1801 E 86th St Indianapolis IN 46240-2396

FISCHER, KURT WALTER, education educator; b. Balt., June 9, 1943; s. Kurt Wilhelm and Irmgaard Louise (Funke) Fischer; m. Sandra Pipp (div.); 1 child, Seth; m. Jane Haltiwanger, Dec. 7, 1986; children: Johanna, Lukas, Kara. BA in Psychology summa cum laude, Yale U., 1965; MA in Soc. Rels., Harvard U., 1968, PhD in Soc. Rels., 1971. Asst. prof. Univ. Denver, 1972-78, assoc. prof., 1978-85, prof., 1985-87; prof. edn. Harvard U., Cambridge, Mass., 1986—, Charles Bigelow prof., chair human devel., 1989—92, 1994—95, 1999—2000, dir. mind, brain and edn., 1999—. Vis. scholar Univ. Geneva, 1978—79; vis. prof. U. Pa., Phila., 1985—86; master lectr. U. Groningen, The Netherlands, 1996; vis. prof. Nanjing Normal U., China, 2000. Author: Cognitive Development, 1981, Levels and Transitions in Cognitive Development, 1983; co-author: (with P. Shaver and A. Lazerson) Psychology Today: An Introduction, 2d and 3d edits., 1972, 75; co-author: Human Development from Conception to Adolescence, 1984, Development in Context, 1993, Human Behavior and the Developing Brain, 1994, Self Conscious Emotions, 1995, Development and Vulnerability in Close Relationships, 1996, Socioemotional Development across Cultures, 1998; contbr. articles to profl. jours. Fellow James McKeen Cattell Fund, 1985-86, Ctr. for Advanced Study, Palo Alto, Calif., 1992-93; grantee Carnegie Found., Nat. Inst. Child Health and Devel., 1994—, Sloan Found., Spencer Found., Rose Found., 1995—. Mem. Jean Piaget Soc. (pres. 1988-91), Phi Beta Kappa, Sigma Xi. Home: 29 Vincent Ave Belmont MA 02478-4418 Office: Harvard U Human Devel Grad Sch Edn Cambridge MA 02138 E-mail: kurt_fischer@harvard.edu.

FISCHER, LEROY HENRY, historian, educator; b. Hoffman, Ill., May 19, 1917; s. Andrew LeRoy and Effie (Risby) F.; m. Martha Gwendolyn Anderson, June 20, 1948; children: Barbara Ann, James LeRoy, John Andrew. BA, U. Ill., 1939, MA, 1940, PhD, 1943; postgrad., Columbia U., 1941. Grad. asst. history U. Ill., 1940-43; asst. prof. history Ithaca (N.Y.) Coll., 1946. Okla. State U. at Stillwater, 1946-49, assoc. prof. history, 1949-60, prof. history, 1960-73, Oppenheim Regents prof. history, 1973-78, Oppenheim prof. history, 1978-84, Oppenheim prof. emeritus, 1984—. Exec. sec. honors program, 1959-61; exec. coun. Emeriti Assn., 2000-02. Author: Lincoln's Gadfly, Adam Gurowski, 1964; (with Muriel H. Wright) Civil War Sites in Oklahoma, 1967, The Civil War Era in Indian Territory, 1974, The Western States in the Civil War, 1975, Territorial Governors of Oklahoma, 1975, The Western Territories in the Civil War, 1977, Civil War Battles in the West, 1981, Oklahoma's Governors 1907-1979, 3 vols., 1981-85, Oklahoma State University Historic Old Central, 1988; co-author: A History of Governance at Oklahoma State University, 1992; editor: The History of the Oklahoma State University Centennial Histories Project, 1993; contbr articles to profl. jours. Vice chmn. Honey Springs Battlefield Park Commn., 1968-92, Okla. Civil War Centennial Commn., 1958-65; chmn. Old Ctrl. com. Okla. State U., 1971-98; mem. Okla. State Hist. Preservation Rev. Commn., 1978—, vice chmn., 1978-81, chmn., 1981-83, 97—; bd. dirs. Nat. Indian Hall of Fame, 1969-2002, YMCA, 1951-54, 83-85, 91—; bd. dirs. Assocs. Western History Collections, U. Okla., 1981-2002, pres., 1989-90; bd. dirs. Stillwater Mus. Assn., 1987-93, pres., 1990-91; mem. Okla. Chisholm Trail Centennial Commn., 1967-68; bd. dirs. Friends of Honey Springs Battlefield Park, 1991—, pres., 1994-97, sec. 1997-2000. With Signal Corps, AUS, 1943-45. Recipient Lit. award Loyal Legion U.S., 1963; named tchr. of Yr., Okla. State U.-Okla. Edn. Assn., 1969; inducted in Okla. Historians Hall of Fame, 1995, Centralia (Ill.) Hall of Fame, 1997, Okla. Higher Edn. Hall of Fame, 2002. Mem. Am. Hist. Assn., Southern Hist. Assn., Western History Assn., Am. Assn. State and Local History, AAUP, Okla. Heritage Assn. (Disting. Svc. award 1989), Okla. Hist. Soc. (bd. dirs. 1966—, treas. 1984-87), Ill. Hist. Soc., Orgn. Am. Historians, Omicron Delta Kappa, Pi Gamma Mu, Phi Alpha Theta, Alpha Kappa Lambda. Methodist (chmn. various coms. 1946—, adminstrv. bd. 1950-77, chmn. 1976-77, lay leader 1970-71). Home: 1010 W Cantwell Ave Stillwater OK 74075-4603

FISCHER, LINDA MARIE, nursing educator; b. Paterson, N.J., Sept. 26, 1959; d. William Jr. and Marie (Bilz) F. BSN cum laude, Coll. Misericordia, 1981; MSN magna cum laude, Bloomsburg U., 1996, clin. nurse specialist, 1996. RN, Pa.; CCRN-R. Staff nurse cardiac ICU Geisinger Med. Ctr., Danville, Pa., 1981-90, clin. nurse II cardiac ICU, 1987-90, clin. instr. cardiac ICU and cardiovasc. spl. care unit, 1990—, med. leave, 1990. Chair adv. group profl. pers. case record rev. subcom. Columbia-Montour Home Health/Vis. Nurses Assn., Inc. Contbr. articles to profl. jours. Active Montour-Riverside chpt. Am. Heart Assn., 1989-92. Mem. AACN, Sigma Theta Tau (nominating com. Theta Zeta chpt. 1995-97, 97-99, 99-01).

FISCHER, MARY CHRISTINE, artist, art and elementary education educator; b. May 23, 1951; d. James Richard and Gilda Marie (Tomasso) Joyce; m. Arthur T. Fischer, Jr. BS, U. South Ala., Mobile, 1986; MFA, U. New Orleans, 1998. Tchr. elem. sch. Mobile Pub. County Schs., 1985-89; tchr. Maryvale Elem. Sch., Mobile, 1986-88, Meadowlake Elem. Sch., Mobile, 1988-89; fin. aid counselor U. New Orleans, Mobile, 1990-91, grad. tchg. asst., 1998, adj. instr. fine arts dept., 1999; dental asst. Dr. P. Shannon Allison, Mandeville, La., 1999—2000; lead bookseller Barnes and Noble Bookstore, Mandeville, La., 1999—2000; instr. GED, lead tchr. adult basic skills dept. Adult H.S., Haywood C.C., Clyde, NC, 2001—03, instr. dept. liberal arts, distance lng. dept., 2003; elem. tchr. Marywood Country Day Sch., Palm Desert, Calif., 2003—. One-woman show U. New Orleans, 1998; group shows U. So. Ala., 1985, include St. Tammany, New Orelans, 1993, 94, 95, World Trade Ctr., New Orleans, 1994, U. New Orleans, 1996, 97, Lino, 1998. Paul Harris fellow Rotary Internat., 1988-89; recipient 6th pl. award USTF Southeastern Championships Marathon Event, 1979. Mem. Omicron Delta Kappa, Alpha Theta Epsilon, Kappa Delta Pi.

FISCHER, MARY E. special education educator; b. Kansas City, Mo., July 7, 1948; d. Tom Earl and Sue Turner (Fitts) Walker; m. Timothy Montgomery Fischer, Sept. 4, 1971; children: Ethan David, Elizabeth Louise. AB, U. Mo., 1971; MSE, Cen. Mo. State U., Warrensburg, 1981; PhD, U. Wash., 1997. Occupl. therapy asst. Children's Therapy Ctr., 1971-73, tchr., 1976-78, psychometrist, 1978-79; program coord. United Cerebral Palsy, Camp Wonderland, Lake of the Ozarks, Mo., 1983; developmental presch. tchr. Children's Therapy Ctr., 1979-84, 75-76; project assoc. Early Childhood Follow Along Study, U. Wash., 1985-87; rsch. assoc. U. Wash., 1987-88; project assoc. Rsch. and Evaluation Network, U. Wash., 1989; project mgr. ChildFind project, Child Devel./Mental Retardation Ctr., Seattle, 1989-90; project coord. N.W. Insvc. Coop. for Transdisciplinary Teams U. Wash., Seattle, 1990-93; project coord. Choices, 1992-95; coord. Wash. Statewide Sys. Change Project, 1993-94; regional dir. Ctr. for Supportive Edn., Seattle, 1994-97; elem/early childhood spl. edn. and readiness to learn coord. Olympic Ednl. Svc. Dist. 114, Bremerton, Wash., 1997—. Adj. prof. Western Wash. U., 1999-2001; instr. Seattle Pacific U. Contbr. articles to profl. jours. Mem. Kitsap Infant Mental Health Coalition; pers. and tng. com. Infant/Toddler Early Intervention Program; family resource coord. tng. project; mem. Kitsap County Commn. on Children and Youth, 2002—; dir. children's choir Lake City Presbyn. Ch., 1999—2002. Mem.: ASCD, Assn. for Persons with Severe Handicaps, Coun. for Exceptional Children (sec. divsn. for early childhood 2001—), Nat. Assn. Edn. Young Children, Soc. Creative Anachronism, Bremerton Kiwanis Club, Pi Lambda Theta (Outstanding Mem. 1990), Phi Kappa Phi. Avocations: singing, camping. Home: 1514 N Montgomery Bremerton WA 98312

FISCHER, PATRICIA ANN, middle school educator; b. Cleve., Apr. 11, 1951; d. Norman Stanley and Teresa (Domagalski) Michaels; m. David Leland Stroh, June 1, 1973 (div. June 1977); m. Lawrence Joseph Fischer, June 14, 1986. BA in Edn., Ohio No. U., 1973; MBA in Edn., Mt. St. Joseph Coll., Cin., 1986; postgrad., Miami U., Oxford, Ohio, 1985—, Ohio State U., 1988. Cert. K-8 tchr., 7-12 history tchr., Ohio. Mid. sch. tchr. St. Gerard Sch., Lima, Ohio, 1973-79, Our Lady of Rosary Sch., Cin., 1980-89, Little Flower Sch., Cin., 1989—, coord. sci., 1989—. Recipient award Project Bus., Cin., 1986, 87, 88, 89, 98, 99 Civic Achievement award Burger King Corp., Cin., 1990, 91, 92, Sci. Tchr. award NSTA, 1993, 20-Yr. award for Cath. educator Diocese of Cin., 1994, Time Warner Cable Nat. Tchr. award, 2003. Mem. Nat. Cath. Edn. Assn., Ohio Edn. Assn., European Am. Study Ctr. Alumni Assn., Order Ea. Star, Alpha Omicron Pi. Roman Catholic. Avocations: painting, travel, needlework, reading. Home: 5450 Cecilia Ct Cincinnati OH 45247-7508 Office: Little Flower School 5555 Little Flower Ave Cincinnati OH 45239-6898

FISCHER, STANLEY, bank executive, economist, educator; b. Lusaka, Zambia, Oct. 15, 1943; came to U.S., 1966, naturalized, 1976; s. Philip and Ann (Kopelowitz) F.; m. Rhoda Keet, Dec. 12, 1965; children: Michael Adam, David Benjamin, Jonathan Phillip. BSc, London Sch. Econs., 1965, MSc, 1966; PhD, MIT, 1969. Fellow U. Chgo., 1969-70, asst. prof. econs., 1970-73; assoc. prof. MIT, 1973-77, prof., 1977—, Killian prof., 1992-94; chief economist, v.p. devel. econs. World Bank, 1988-90; 1st dep. mgr. dir. IMF, 1994—2001; vice chmn. Citigroup, N.Y.C., 2002—; pres. Citigroup Internat., 2002—. Vis. sr. lectr. Hebrew U. Jerusalem, 1972; fellow Ctr. for Advanced Studies Hebrew U., 1976-77; vis. fellow Hoover Instn., Stanford U., 1981-82; cons. on Israeli economy Dept. State, 1984-87, 91-94; cons. IMF, 1991-92. Author: Indexing Inflation and Economic Policy, 1986, (with R. Dornbusch and R. Schmalensee) Economics, 1988, (with O. Blanchard) Lectures in Macroeconomics, 1989, (with R. Dornbusch and R. Startz) Macroeconomics, 8th edit., 2001; editor Nat. Bur. Econ. Rsch. Macroecons. Ann., 1986-94; contbr. articles to profl. jours. Guggenheim fellow. Fellow Econometric Soc.; mem. Am. Acad. Arts and Scis., Coun. on Fgn. Rels. Office: Citigroup 399 Park Ave New York NY 10043

FISCHER, THOMAS COVELL, law educator, consultant, writer, lawyer; b. May 2, 1938; s. Vilas Uber and Elizabeth Mary (Holland) F.; m. Katherine Brenda Andrew, Sept. 29, 1972. AB, U. Cin., 1960; postgrad., U. Wash., 1960-62, Loyola U., Chgo., 1964-66; JD, Georgetown U., 1966. Asst. dir. U. Ill.-Chgo., 1964-66; asst. dean Georgetown U. Law Ctr., 1966-72; cons. Antioch Sch. Law, 1972-73; asst. exec. dir. Am. Bar Found., Chgo., 1974-76; assoc. dean, prof. law U. Dayton, 1976-78; dean, prof. law New Eng. Sch. Law, Boston, 1978—81, prof., 1981—2003, prof. emeritus, 2003—; disting. acad. in residence Seattle U. Law Sch., 2003—. Vis. scholar, Cambridge, 1991, Exeter, 91, Edinburgh, 91, Konstanz U., 1993, Muenster U., 1993; fellow Inst. Advanced Legal Studies, U. London, Inns Court, 1997; vis. fellow Wolfson Coll., Cambridge, England, 1997; sr. vis.

fellow U. Southampton Law Faculty, 2001; cons. in field. Author: Due Process in the Student/Institutional Relationship, 1970; author: (with Duscha) The Campus Press: Freedom and Responsibility, 1973; author: (with Zenhle) Introduction to Law and Legal Reasoning, 1977, Legal Education, Law Practice and the Economy: A New England Study, 1990, The Europeanization of America: What Americans Need to Know About the European Union, 1996, The United States, the European Union, and the Globilization of World Trade: Allies or Adversaries?, 2000; author: (with Cox) Quick Review of Conflict of Laws, 4th edit., 2001. Project dir. Commn. on Legal Edn. and Practice and the Economy of New Eng. Recipient Elaine R. Maham award U. Cin., 1960; Pi Kappa Alpha Meml. scholar 1960-62. Fellow Inns of Ct.; mem. Delta Theta Phi, Pi Delta Epsilon, Phi Alpha Theta. Roman Catholic. Office: New Eng Sch Law 154 Stuart St Boston MA 02116-5616

FISCHETTI, MICHAEL JOSEPH, accounting educator; b. Bklyn., Sept. 20, 1939; s. Anthony Joseph and Nicolina Rose (Marchitello) F.; m. Carlotta Theresa Cannarili, Sept. 25, 1960; children: Christine, Doreen, Clorissa, Diana. BBA, Pace U., 1968, MBA, 1970. CPA, N.Y. Audit mgr. Arthur Young & Co., N.Y.C., 1973-77, prin. Reston, Va., 1978-81; sr. mgr. Friedman & Fuller, Rockville, Md., 1982-86, Hoffman & Dykes, Vienna, Va., 1987-91; asst. dir. U.S. Gen. Acctg. Office, Washington, 1991—. Lectr. U. Md., Marymount U., Potomac Coll. Pace U. teaching fellow, 1967. Mem. AICPAs (chair computer edn. subcom. 1973-74), Christian Businessmen's Com. (chair 1988-91). Avocations: swimming, walking, bible study. Office: US Gen Acctg Office 441 G St NW Washington DC 20548-0001 E-mail: fischettim@msn.com.

FISCHLER, BARBARA BRAND, librarian; b. Pitts., May 24, 1930; d. Carl Frederick and Emma Georgia (Piltz) Brand; m. Drake Anthony Fischler, June 3, 1961 (div., Oct. 1995); 1 child, Owen Wesley. AB cum laude, Wilson Coll., Chambersburg, Pa., 1952; MM with distinction, Ind. U., 1954, AMLS, 1964. Asst. reference librarian Ind. U., Bloomington, 1958-61, asst. librarian undergrad. library, 1961-63, acting librarian, 1963; circulation librarian Ind. U.-Purdue U., Indpls., 1970-76, pub. services librarian Univ. Library, sci., engring. and tech. unit, 1976-81, acting dir. univ. libraries, 1981-82, dir. univ. libraries, 1982-95; retired, 1995; dir. Sch. Libr. and Info. Sci. Ind. U.-Purdue U., Indpls., 1995—. Vis. and assoc. prof. (part-time) Sch. Libr. and Info. Sci. Ind. U., Bloomington, 1972-95, counselor-coord., Indpls., 1974-82, dir. sch. libr. and info. sci. campus Ind. U.-Purdue U., Indpls., 1995—; resource aide adv. com. Ind. Voc. Tech. Coll., Indpls., 1974-86; adv. com. Area Libr. Svcs. Authority, Indpls., 1976-79; mem. core com., chmn. program com. Ind. Gov.'s Conf. on Librs. and Info. Svcs., Indpls., 1976-78, mem. governance com., del. to conf., 1990; mem. Ind. State Libr. Adv. Coun., 1985-91; cons. in field. Contbr. articles to profl. jours. Fund-raiser Indpls. Mus. Art, 1971, Am. Cancer Soc., Indpls., 1975; vol. tchr. St. Thomas Aquinas Sch., Indpls., 1974-75; fund-raiser Am. Heart Assn., Indpls., 1985; bd. dirs., treas. Historic Amusement Found., Inc., Indpls., 1984-91; bd. advisors N.Am. Wildlife Park Found., Inc., Battle Ground, Ind., 1985-91, bd. dirs., 1991—; mem. adv. bd. Ind. U. Ctr. on Philanthropy, 1987-90. Recipient Outstanding Svc. award Ctrl. Ind. Area Libr. Svc. Authority, 1979, Outstanding Libr. award Ind. Libr.-Ind. Libr. Trustee Assn., 1988, Louise Maxwell award for Outstanding Achievement, 1989, William Jenkins award for Outstanding Svc. to Ind. U. Libr. and the Libr. Profession, 1996. Mem. ALA, Libr. Adminstrn. and Mgmt. Assn. (vice chair and chair elect fund raising and fin. devel. sect. 1991-92), Ind. State Libr. Adv. Coun., Midwest Fedn. Libr. Assns. (chmn. local arrangements for conf. 1986-87, sec. 1987—, bd. dirs. 1987-91), Ind. Libr. Assn. (chmn. coll. and univ. div. 1977-78, chmn. libr. edn. div. 1981-82, treas. 1984-86), German Shepherd Dog Club of Cen. Ind. (pres. 1978-79, treas. 1988-89, v.p. 1989-90, pres. 1990-93, bd. dirs. 1993—), Wabash Valley German Shepherd Dog Club (pres. 1982-83), Cen. Ind. Kennel Club (bd. dirs. 1984-86), Pi Kappa Lambda, Beta Phi Mu. Republican. Presbyterian. Avocations: ethology, exhibiting american saddlebred horses. Home: 735 Lexington Ave Apt 3 Indianapolis IN 46203-1000 Office: Ind-Purdue U 755 W Michigan St Indianapolis IN 46202-5195

FISCHMAN, GARY JOSEPH, podiatrist, educator; b. N.Y.C.; s. Isidore and Sally (Gold) F.; m. Elaine Sue Dworkin, July 12, 1981; 1 child, Isadora Sydnie. BA, Hunter Coll., 1963; Dr, Pa. Coll. Podiatric Medicine, 1972; PhD in Pathology, Thomas Jefferson U., 1980. Technician dept. microbiology Dalhousei U., Halifax, N.S., Can., 1964-67; rsch. scientist Pa. Coll. Podiatric Medicine, Phila., 1968-72, instr. histology and anatomy, 1972-75; pvt. practice podiatry, Phila., 1972-75, Long Island City, 1976-85, Bklyn., 1985—; prof. Rockland C. C., 1994—; fellow community health and adminstrn. N.Y. Coll. Podiatric Medicine, N.Y.C., 1977-78, asst. prof. pathology, 1978-84, rsch. cons., 1984—; podiatry cons. Rockland Psychiat. Ctr., 1985—. Recipient Am. Podiatry Assn. fellow, 1972-75. Fellow Am. Soc. Podiatric Medicine, V.P. Daxor Corp., 1998-; mem. Am. Acad. of Pain Mgmt. (diplomate), Am. Auto. Soc., Am. Assn. of Tissue Banks, Microscopy Soc. of Am.

FISCHMAN, STUART LEE, oral medicine educator, dentist; b. Buffalo, Nov. 29, 1935; s. Ben and Lillian (Friedland) F.; m. Jane Ann Vogel, June 25, 1960; 1 child, Lisa. Student, Cornell U., 1953-56; DMD, Harvard U., 1960. Diplomate Am. Bd. Oral Pathology, Am. Bd. Oral Medicine. Resident Boston VA Hosp., 1960-61; prof. SUNY, Buffalo, 1961-97, prof. emeritus, 1997—. Vis. prof. U. P.R., San Juan, 1974, Hebrew U., Jerusalem, 1981, 89. 96; cons. Cheseborough Ponds, Trumbull, Conn., 1965-2001, ADA, Chgo., 1975—, Unilever Rsch., Eng., 1985—, Pfizer, Morris Plains, N.J., 1998—, Colgate-Palmolive, Piscataway, N.J., 1998—, Procter-Gamble, Cin., 1998—; Cedbury-Schweppes, Morris Plains, N.J., 2003, hon. prof. Nat. U., Paraguay, 1976; dir. dentistry Erie County Med. Ctr., Buffalo, 1973-97. Contbr. numerous articles to profl. jours.; contbr. 6 textbooks. Named Disting. Alumnus, Harvard U., 1988. Fellow Am. Acad. Oral Pathology, Am. Coll. Dentists, Internat. Coll. Dentists. Jewish. Avocations: cross country skiing, photography. Home: 255 Louvaine Dr Buffalo NY 14223-2757 Office: SUNY Buffalo 355 Squire Hall Buffalo NY 14214-8006

FISH, ANDREW JOSEPH, JR., electrical engineering educator, researcher; b. New Haven, Conn., Aug. 15, 1944; s. Andrew Joseph and Katherine Pauline (Frey) F.; m. Paula Jean Bosiclaré, June 21, 1985; 1 child, Ashley Marie. BSEE, Worcester Poly Inst., 1966; MSEE, U. Iowa, 1973; MS in Math., St. Mary U., San Antonio, 1974; PhD, U. Conn., 1980. Assoc. prof. elec. engring. U. Hartford, West Hartford, Conn., 1979-84, Western New Eng. Col., Springfield, Mass., 1984-87, U. New Haven, 1987—90, chmn. dept. elec. engring., 1992-94, chmn. dept. elec. and computer engring., 1993—, prof. elec. engring., 1990—. Co-chmn. nonlinear systems group Am. Control Conf., 1980. Contbr. articles to profl. jours., publs. Gate keeper Suffield Grange, 1982. Fellow Yale U., 1982-83. Mem. IEEE (co-chmn. large scale and nonlinear sys. gorup 22nd Conf. on Decision and Control), ASME. Achievements include research on modeling, analysis, control of nonlinear systems, particularly hybrid analog-digital systems. E-mail: andy.fish@home.com.

FISH, ELIZABETH ANN, physical education educator; b. Bryn Mawr, Pa., June 24, 1964; d. George David and Elizabeth Fish. BS in Health and Phys. Edn., U. Del., 1987; MS in Health Edn., Saint Joseph's U., Phila., 1990. Dept. head phys. edn. Springside Sch., Phila., 1987—. Coach Eastern Field Hockey Camp, Pottstown, Pa., 1983-93, Pvt. I's All-Star Field Hockey Team, Pa., 1990. Mem. Am. Alliance for Health, Phys. Edn., Recreation and Dance, U.S. Field Hockey Assn., Pa. Assn. for Health, Phys. Edn., Recreation and Dance, Phi Kappa Phi, Kappa Delta Pi. Avocations: woodworking, gardening, fitness, golf. Home: 279 Deerfield Ct New Hope PA 18938-1805 Office: Springside Sch 8000 Cherokee St Philadelphia PA 19118-4135

FISH, JACOB, civil engineer, educator; b. Vilnius, Lithuania, Oct. 4, 1956; came to U.S., 1986; s. David and Gutia (Shmukler) F.; m. Ora Kogan, July 12, 1985; children: Efrat, Adam. BS, Technion, Haifa, Israel, 1982, MS, 1984; PhD, Northwestern U., Evanston, Ill., 1989. Registered profl. engr., N.Y., Israel. Structural engr. Bikshpan-Consulting, Tel Aviv, 1982-84; rsch. engr. Israel Aircraft Industries, Lod, Israel, 1984-86; rsch. asst. Northwestern U., 1986-89; asst. prof. Rensselaer Poly. Inst., Troy, N.Y., 1989-94, assoc. prof., 1994-98, prof., 1998—, prof. civil, mech. and aerospace engring. and info. tech., 1998—. Cons. Lockheed Missiles, Palo Alto, Calif., 1990-91, ANSYS Software House, Pitts., 1991-92, EHRC Software House, Troy, Mich., 1995—, N.Y. Dept. Law, Albany, 1995. Editor-in-chief U.S. Assn. Computational Mechs. Bull., 1993—, Internat. Jour. for Computational Civil and Structural Engring, Internat. Jour. of Civil and Structural Engring., 1998—; contbr. over 60 articles to profl. jours. Recipient Presdl. award NSF, 1991, Best Paper award AIAA/Structural Dynamics and Materials, 1993, Young Investigator award USACM, 1994, Best Paper award ASME, 1995. Home: 7 Burton Ln Loudonville NY 12211-1472 Office: Rensselaer Poly Inst Troy NY 12180

FISH, THOMAS EDWARD, English language and literature educator; b. Redbud, Ill., Aug. 1, 1952; s. Edward Charles and H. Grace (Thomas) F.; m. Kathryn Jane Griffith, Nov. 17, 1979; children: Dana Rose, Sally Kathryn. BA, Iowa State U., Ames, 1974; MA, U. Kans., 1976, MPhil, 1979, PhD, 1981. Asst. instr. in English U. Kans., Lawrence, 1974-81, staff mem. communications resource ctr., 1978, 80; adj. asst. prof. English Iowa State U., 1981-84; asst. prof. English Cumberland Coll., Williamsburg, Ky., 1984-86, assoc. prof. English, 1986-96, prof. English, 1996—. Dir., SACS self-study Cumberland Coll., 2003—09. Self-study editor SACS, 1992-95, 2002—, dir. re-accreditation, 2003—. Elder Corbin (Ky.) Presbyn. Ch., 1986, 90-92, 2002—. Lilly grantee Cumberland Coll., 1990, named Prof. for Excellence in Teaching, 1990; tchg. grantee Cumberland Coll., 1998; faculty-student rsch. grantee Appalachian Coll. Assn., 1999; recipient Cutting Edge award for Tchg. with Technology, Appalachian Coll. Assn., 1999. Mem. MLA, Nat. Coun. Tchrs. English, Popular Culture Assn., Browning Inst., South Atlantic MLA, Appalachian Coll. Assn. (Tchg. with Tech. coord. for English 2000-03), Phi Beta Kappa, Phi Kappa Phi. Democrat. Home: 260 Brush Arbor Rd Williamsburg KY 40769-1717 Office: 7193 College Station Dr Williamsburg KY 40769-1382 E-mail: tfish@cumberlandcollege.edu.

FISH, TOM, vocational school educator; b. Wyandotte, Mich., Mar. 18, 1936; s. Kenneth Lyle and Ann Julia Fish; m. Beverley Anderson, June 18, 1956 (div. Aug. 1976); children: Robert, Toni, Kenneth; m. Lynne Coates, Dec. 12, 1992. BA, Adrian (Mich.) Coll., 1962; MA, U. Pacific, Stockton, Calif., 1985. Food svc. dir. Saga Adminstrv. Corp., Adrian, 1961-75, Cleve. Browns Pro Football Team, Hiram, Ohio, 1965-68, Del Monte Corp., San Francisco, 1975-80, Placer County Corrections, Auburn, Calif., 1980-83; intern Devel. Disabilities Svcs. Orgn., Sacramento, 1984-85; vocat./edn. tchr. Stockton (Calif.) Unified Sch. Dist., 1985—. Founder Campus Cafe, A.A. Stagg High Sch., Stockton, 1987—, Deli Delivery, 1989, Greystone Cons. Group., 1992. Recipient Ednl. Enrichment award Stockton Enrichment Found., 1989, 90, Program Devel. award Jr. Aid Stockton, 1989, 90, Outstanding Person award San Joaquin County Juvenile Justice and Deliquency Prevention Commn., 1991. Mem. NEA, Coun. Exceptional Children (membership chair 1988-89, community svc. award 1989), Calif. Tchrs. Assn., Phi Delta Kappa (U. pacific chpt.). Democrat. Lutheran. Avocations: marathon runner, carousel horse collector, vegetarian, lecturing on spiritual devel. Home: 944 Lake Front Dr Sacramento CA 95831-5609 Office: AA Stagg High Sch 1621 Brookside Rd # H-8 Stockton CA 95207-7804

FISHBACK, PATRICIA DAVIS, academic administrator, educator; b. Lexington, Va., Apr. 8, 1940; d. Allen Edward and Mildred (Beeton) Davis; m. James Kemper Fishback, Mar. 3, 1962; children: Edward, Jill. BS, Madison Coll., Harrisonburg, Va., 1961; MEd, U. Va., 1975; PhD, Va. Commonwealth U., Richmond, 1992. Cert. Tchr. Physics, Math., Va. Pilot sci. tchr. Hicksville (N.Y.) Pub. Schs., 1961-62; tchr. Henrico County Schs., Richmond, Va., 1962-64; cons. tchr. Math. and Sci. Ctr., Richmond, Va., 1975-77; tchr. The Collegiate Schs., Richmond, Va., 1977-83; program specialist The Math. and Sci. Ctr., Richmond, Va., 1983—. Founding mem. Greater Richmond (Va.) Coun. Sci. Educator, 1986—; governing bd. Jr. Acad. Sci., Richmond, Va., 1984-90; dir. Spl. Projects for Elderly, Richmond, Va., 1983—. Del. Dem. pary of Va., Norfolk, 1984; mem. Va. Equal Rights Amendment Ratification Coun., Richmond, 1978—; bd. mem. Lewis Ginter Community Assn., richmond, Va., 1977-79. Grantee Inst. for Profl. Edn. Inc., Washington, 1991. Mem. Phi Kappa Phi, Phi Delta Kappa. Democrat. Avocations: painting, travel. Home: 1617 Princeton Rd Richmond VA 23227-3727 Office: Mathematics and Science Ctr 2401 Hartman St Richmond VA 23223-2458

FISHBACK, WILLIAM THOMPSON, educator; b. Milw., Jan. 28, 1922; s. Richard and Loraine (Thompson) F.; m. Joan Landers, Dec. 26, 1960; 1 child, Paul. AB, Oberlin Coll., 1943; MA, Harvard U., 1947, PhD, 1952. Staff mem. MIT Radiation Lab., Cambridge, Mass., 1943-46; instr. to asst. prof. U. Vt., Burlington, 1950-53; asst. prof. to prof. Ohio U., Athens, 1953-66; prof. Earlham Coll., Richmond, Ind., 1966-87, prof. emeritus, 1987—. Author: Projective and Euclidean Geometry. 1962, 2d edition 1968. Mem. Nat. Coun. Tchrs. Math., Math. Assn. Am., Am. Math. Soc., Phi Beta Kappa, Sigma Xi.

FISHBAUGH, CAROLE SUE, middle school educator; b. Newark, Ohio, Mar. 11, 1938; d. Lawrence William and Thelma Irene Baird; m. Emerson LaVern Fishbaugh, Sept. 11, 1961. BS in Edn., Ohio U., 1962; postgrad., Ohio State U., 1963-65, U. North Fla., 1985—, Jacksonville U., 1994. Cert. elem., 1-6 reading tchr., K-12 tchr. mentally retarded, Fla. Elem. tchr. Greenfield (Ohio) Exempted Village Schs., 1958-60, Newark Pub. Schs., 1960-61, tchr. mentally retarded, 1961-62. 63-65, Alexandria (Va.) Pub. Schs., 1962-63; vice prin. Lincoln Jr. High Sch., Newark, 1963—65; tchr. reading Nassau County Pub. Schs., Fernandina Beach, Fla., 1986-93. Contact person reading dept. Fernandina Beach Mid. Sch., 1990-93, sch. adv. coun., 1991—, contact person for alternative edn., chair dept. alternative edn., 1993-94, chair sch. improvement adv. coun., 1994-96, tchr. varied exceptionalities, 1994-99, ESE dept. chair, 1996-98, dist. team, 1994-96, remedial reading tchr. 6th-8th grades, 1999-2002, tchr. GED adult edn., 2000-02, reading tchr. 6th grade, 2001—; grant com. Fernandina Beach Mid. Sch., 1992-98, tech. com.; tchr. Cities in Schs., 2000-02. Mem. ch. and soc. com., organizer drug abuse fight Meml. United Meth. Ch., Fernandina Beach, 1987; mem. adminstrv. coun. Meth. Children's Home Soc. for United Meth. Ch., 1987-98; mem. Fernandina Beach Task Force to Fight Crime, 1992-96; dist. rep. Sch. Adv. Coun., 1994-96; vol., mem. adv. coun. Quality Health Nursing Home, Fernandina Beach, 1996-99. Mem. ASCD, Nat. Mid. Sch. Assn., Nassau Tchrs. Assn. (sch. rep. 1987-90, treas. 1988-90, rep. on sch. improvement 1992, sec. 1994, treas. 1995-98), Nat. Alzheimers Assn. Democrat. Avocations: travel, pet therapy, birdwatching, photography, music, swimming. Office: Fernandina Beach Mid Sch 315 Citrona Dr Fernandina Beach FL 32034-2716

FISHER, ANITA JEANNE (KIT FISHER), language educator; b. Atlanta, Oct. 22, 1937; d. Paul Benjamin and Cora Ozella (Wadsworth) Chappelear; m. Kirby Lynn Fisher, Aug. 6, 1983; 1 child from previous marriage, Tracy Ann. BA, Bob Jones U., 1959; postgrad., Stetson U., 1961, 87, U. Fla., 1963, 87, 90; MAT, Rollins Coll., 1969; PhD in Am. Lit., Fla. State U., 1975; postgrad., U. Ctrl. Fla., 1978, NEH Inst., 1979, U. Ctrl. Fla., 1987, Disney U./U. Ctrl. Fla., 1996, Jacksonville U., 1996; student, Agnes Scot Coll. AP Inst., 1998, Duke Univ. AP TIP Summer Inst., 1999. Cert. English, gifted and adminstrn. supr., in ESOL. Chairperson basic learning improvement program secondary sch. Orange County, Orlando, Fla., 1964-65; chmn. composition Winter Park (Fla.) HS, 1978-80; chmn. English depts. Orange County Pub. Schs., Fla., 1962, 71; reading tchr. Woodland Hall Acad., Reading Rsch. Inst., Tallahassee, 1976; instr. edn., journalism, reading, Spanish, thesis writing Bapt. Bible Coll., Springfield, Mo., 1976-77; prof. English S.W. Mo. State U., Springfield, 1980-84, instr. continuing edn. music and creative writing, 1981-82, editor LAD Leaf; tchr. Volusia County Schs., Fla., 1984-88, 95-97, gifted students, 1986-88; tchr. Lee County Schs., 1988-95; gifted students Lake Mary HS, 1997; tchr. Seminole Pub. Schs., 1997—. Instr. Seminole CC; adj. prof. Edison CC, 1989—95, U. So. Fla., 1990—95, Barry U., 1993; mem. steering com. So. Assn. Colls. and Schs.; active Fla. Coun. Tchrs. English; assessor tchr. performance Nat. Bd. Profl. Tchg. Stds.; panel mem. PSAT/NMSQT Descriptive Score Report Ednl. Testing Svc.; spkr. in field.; chair advanced placement vertical team Lake Mary HS, 2000—01, chair dept. English, chair vertical team curriculum implementation, 2001—. Contbr. writings to publs. in field, papers to nat. profl. confs.; co-editor: Fla. English Jour., 1998—2000. Vol. Green County Action Com., 1977, Heart Fund, 1982; book reviewer Voice Youth Advs. Writing Program fellow U. Ctrl. Fla., 1978; mem. Rep. Nat. Com., 1994—; active Rep. Presdl. Task Force, 1998—2000. Named Lee County Tchr. of Distinction, 1994—95. Mem.: Seminole County Tchrs. English (chartered, pres. 1998—2000), Volusia Coun. Tchrs. English (pres. 1997), Fla. Coun. Tchrs. English (chair commn. ESL 1997—99, sch. adv. coun.), Nat. Count. Tchrs. English, Phi Delta Kappa (historian). Presbyterian.

FISHER, BRUCE DAVID, elementary school educator, education educator; b. Long Beach, Calif., Dec. 24, 1949; s. Oran Wilfred and Irene (May) F.; m. Mindi Beth Evans, Aug. 15, 1976; 1 child, Jenny Allison Viola. BA, Humboldt State U., 1975, standard elem. credential, 1976, learning handicapped credential, 1977. Instrnl. svcs. specialist Blue Lake (Calif.) Elem. Sch.; resource specialist Fortuna (Calif.) Union Sch. Dist., tchr. 3d grade, tchr. 5th grade, 1988—; prof. Humboldt State U., 1996—, disting. tchr.-in-residence, 1999—. Sci. cons. Pitsco, 1995; cons. Newton's Apple, 1995-97, NASA, 1995; site leader tchr., cons., 1998-99, curriculum writer Calif. Sci. Internet, 1995-97; cons. U.S. Forest Svc., 1999; mem. J.P.L./NASA/Johns Hopkins U. Core Curriculum Devel. Team Project KidSat and CASOE; mem. ednl. adv. bd. Calif. Dairy Coun., 1998-99, advisor, 1998; rep. Calif. Tech. Assistance Project, 1998; mem. Calif. Ski Industry and U.S. Forest Svc. Vice chmn. Tchrs. Edn. and Cmty. Helpers, Arcata, Calif., 1990—; v.p. Sequoia Pk. Zool. Soc., Eureka, 1989-90, chmn. Whale Fair, 1989—; mem. selection com. Christa McAuliffe Fellowship; bd. dirs. Redwood Environ. Edn. Fair, Eureka, 1990—, Family Wellness Project, 1991; apptd. to Calif. Curriculum and Supplemental Materials Commn.; commr. Calif. Curriculum Commn., 1992-95; chairperson math. assessment Calif. Dept. Edn., 1995; cons. PITSCO Sci., 1995, NASA/JPL, 1995-97; mem. NASA/JPL and Johns Hopkins U. CORE Curriculum Devel. Team, 1995-96; lead tchr. KidSat and CASDE projects Calif. Sci. Internat. Site. Named Calif. Tchr. of Yr. Dept. Edn., 1991, Favorite Tchrs. ABC-TV, 1991, Humboldt County Tchr. of Yr., 1991, Disting. Alumni, Humboldt State U., 2000; recipient Leadership Excellence award Calif. Assn. Sci. Specialists, 1990, Masonic Meritorious Svc. award for Pub. Edn., 1991, Profl. Best Leadership award Learning Mag., Oldsmobile Corp., and Mich. State U., 1991, Nat. Educator award Miliken Found. Calif. State Dept. Edn., 1991, NASA/NSTA Newest award, 1993, Newton's Apple Multimedia Inst., 1995, Lifetime Achievement award Humboldt County Bd. Edn., 1996. Mem. Calif. Tchrs. Assn., Calif. Sci. Tchrs. Assn., Calif. Assn. Health, Phys. Edn., Recreation, and Dance. Democrat. Avocations: whale watching, curriculum development, photography, sports, aviation, travel. Home: 4810 14th St Arcata CA 95519-9778 Office: Fortuna Elem Sch 843 L St Fortuna CA 95540-1997

FISHER, CHARLES HAROLD, chemistry educator, researcher; b. Hiawatha, W.Va., Nov. 20, 1906; s. Lawrence D. and Mary (Akers) F.; m. Elizabeth Dye, Nov. 4, 1933 (dec. 1967); m. Lois Carlin, July 1968 (dec. June 1990); m. Elizabeth Snyder Kiser, Nov. 29, 1991. BS in Chemistry, Roanoke Coll., 1928, ScD (hon.), 1963; MS in Chemistry, U. Ill., 1929, PhD, 1932; DSc (hon.), Tulane U., 1953. Tchg. asst. in chemistry U. Ill., Urbana, 1928-32; instr. Harvard U., 1932-35; rsch. group leader US Bur. Mines, Pitts., 1935-40; head carbohydrate divsn. Ea. Regional Rsch. Ctr. USDA, 1940-50; dir. So. mktg. and nutrition rsch. div. So. Regional Rsch. Ctr., USDA, New Orleans, 1950-72. Adj. rsch. prof. Roanoke Coll., Salem, Va., 1972—; established Elizabeth Snyder Fisher Scholarship, Roanoke Coll., 1992. Co-author: Profiles of Eminent American Chemists, 1988; contbr. over 200 articles to profl. jour. Co-inventor 72 patents. Pres. New Orleans Sci. Fair, 1967-69; bd. dir. Salem Hist. Soc., 1982-85, Salem Ednl. Found., 1991-99; established Lawrence D. and Mary A. Fisher Scholarship Roanoke Coll., 1978, Lois Carlin Fisher Scholarship, 1991. Recipient So. Chemists award, 1956, Herty medal, 1959; named Polymer Science Pioneer, 1981, Roanoke Coll. medal, 1996; named to Hall of Fame, Salem Ednl. Found., 1996; Charles H. Fisher Lectures established in his honor Roanoke Coll., 1990; Laboratory of Organic Chem. named in his honor Roanoke Coll., 2002. Mem. AAAS, Am. Inst. Chemists (hon., pres. 1962-63, chmn. bd. dir., Chem. Pioneer award 1966, Presdl. citation of merit 1986), Oil Chem. Soc., Am. Chem. Soc. (dir. region IV 1969-71), Chemurgic Coun. (dir.), Am. Assn. Textile Chemists and Colorists, Hidden Valley Country Club (Salem, Va.), Cosmos Club (Washington), Internat. House, Round Table Club (New Orleans); Chemists Club (NYC). Achievements include co-inventor of acrylic rubber. Office: Roanoke Coll Dept Chemistry 221 College Ln Salem VA 24153-3742

FISHER, DEENA KAYE, social studies education administrator; b. Elk City, Okla., Dec. 20, 1950; d. Earl Dean and Rosa Lee (Stone) Music; m. Mike Fleck, May 29, 1970 (div. June 1988); children: DeeAnna Michelle, Carrie Denise, William Michael; m. Tom Fisher, Nov. 13, 1993; 1 stepchild, Eleni. BA in Edn.-Social Sci., Southwestern Okla. State U., 1979, MEd in Social Sci., 1983, MEd in Sch. Counseling, 1987; postgrad., U. Okla., 1999. Instr. in social sci. Cordell (Okla.) H.S., 1979-85, El Reno (Okla.) C.C., 1985-88, Upward Bound guidance and career counselor, instr., 1987-89; instr. Am. History Yukon (Okla.) H.S., 1986-87; instr. polit. sci. and Am. history Southwestern Okla. State U., 1987-89; chair dept. Am. history, instr. Am. govt. Woodward (Okla.) H.S., 1989-96; instr. social studies Northwestern Okla. State U., Alva, 1989—, dir. Woodward campus, 1996—. Author ednl. materials in field. Del. Dem. Nat. Conv., Okla. Dem. Party, Chgo., 1996; law day coord. Okla. Bar Assn., Woodward, 1990-96; regional coord. Citizen Bee, Tulsa World, 1994-97; panelist U.S. History Nat. Assessment of Ednl. Progress, St. Louis, 1994. Recipient Outstanding Am. History Tchr. award Okla. Soc. DAR, 1993, Tchr. of Yr. award Okla. Supreme Ct., 1992; Bill of Rights Edn. Collaborative grantee, 1991. Mem. Nat. Coun. for Social Studies (ho. dels., co-chmn. resolution com. 1996), Okla. Social Studies Suprs.' Assn. (membership bd. 1997), Okla. Coun. for Social Studies (del.-at-large 1996, pres. 1994-96), Woodward Edn. Assn. (pres. 1996), Woodward C. of C. (mem. edn. com. 1997), Delta Kappa Gamma (pres. Psi chpt. 1996-98), Phi Delta Kappa. Mem. Christian Ch. (Disciples Of Christ). Avocations: reading, chess. Home: 3308 Bent Creek Dr Woodward OK 73801-6931 Office: Northwestern Okla State U Woodward Campus PO Box 1046 Woodward OK 73802-1046

FISHER, ELIZABETH ANN, classics educator; b. Mpls., Oct. 25, 1944; d. George Lee and Karleen Elizabeth (Fawcett) F.; m. Robert Arthur Hadley, June 19, 1976. BA, Northwestern U., 1966; MA, Harvard U., 1971, PhD, 1972. Asst. prof. classics U. Minn., Mpls., 1971-76; from asst. to prof. George Washington U., Washington, 1978—, chair dept. classics/semitics, 1998—. Adj. assoc. prof. Georgetown U., Washington, 1976-78, sec. U.S. Nat. Byzantime com., 2002—. Editor: M. Psellus Orationes hagiographicae, 1994; contbr. articles to profl. jours. Woodrow Wilson fellow Woodrow Wilson Found., Harvard U., 1966-67, Dumbarton Oaks fellow, Washington, 1990-91, Jr. fellow Ctr. for Hellenic Studies, Washington, 1974-75. Mem. Am. Philol. Assn., Archaeol. Inst. of Am. (D.C. Soc. bd. mem. 1994-97, sec.

1987-90), Medieval Acad. of Am., Classical Assn. of Atlantic States, Dumbarton Oaks Alumni Assn. (pres. 1991-93). Episcopalian. Office: George Washington U Dept Classics Acad Ctr T 345 Washington DC 20052-0001 E-mail: eaf@gwu.edu.

FISHER, ELLEN ROOP, retired librarian, educator; b. Washington, Dec. 16, 1944; d. Robert Wendell and Katherine (Booth) Roop; m. Allan Campbell Fisher, June 14, 1969; children: Bradford Booth, Katherine Thayer. BA, Smith Coll., Northampton, Mass., 1966; MA, U. Chgo., 1974. Cert. library sci. edn., Pa. Rsch. asst. Indsl. Rels. Ctr. Library, U. Chgo., 1967-68; asst. sys. libr. U. Chgo. Libraries, 1968-71; reference asst. Toledo (Ohio) Pub. Libr., 1972; libr. Cleve. Orch. Chorus Library, 1973-74; reference libr. Harford County Library Sys., Bel Air, Md., 1975; computer tchr. Lawrence Twp. Sch. Dist., Indpls., 1982-84; music tchr. Hegvik Sch. of Music, Wayne, Pa., 1984-86; libr. Edn. Resource Ctr., Cabrini Coll., Wayne, Pa., 1986—87; libr. Radnor Twp. Sch. Dist., Wayne, Pa., 1987—94, head libr., 1994—2001. Author: Sources and Nature of Errors in Transcribing Bibliographic Data into Machine Readable Form, 1974; co-author: The University of Chicago Bibliographic Data Processing System, 1970. Singer St. Cecilia Chamber Choir, Newcastle, Maine, Tapestry Singers. La Verne Noyes scholar U Chgo., 1966. Mem.: ALA, Am. Recorder Soc. Unitarian Universalist. Avocations: travel, genealogy. Home: 13 Pilot Circle PO Box 134 Nobleboro ME 04555-0134

FISHER, FRANKLIN MARVIN, economist; b. NYC, Dec. 13, 1934; s. Mitchell Salem and Esther (Oshiver) F.; m. Ellen Jo Paradise, June 22, 1958; children— Abraham Samuel, Abigail Sarah, Naomi Leah. AB summa cum laude, Harvard U., 1956, MA, 1957, PhD, 1960; PhD (hon.), Hebrew U., Jerusalem, 2001. Asst. prof. econs. U. Chgo., 1959-60; asst. prof. econs. MIT, 1960-62, assoc. prof., 1962-65, prof., 1965-2000, Jane Berkowitz Carlton and Dennis William Carlton prof., 2000—; chair Mid. East Water Project, 1992—. Cons. various law firms; dir. cons. Charles River Assocs., Inc., vice chmn., 1997—2002, chmn., 2002—; bd. dirs. Nat. Bur. Econ. Rsch. Editor: Econometrica, 1968-77. Trustee Combined Jewish Philanthropies, Boston, 1975—, bd. mgrs., 1979-92; trustee Beth Israel Hosp., Boston, 1979-97; chmn. faculty adv. cabinet United Jewish Appeal, 1975-77; bd. govs. Tel Aviv U., 1976-92, Acad. Coll. Tel Aviv-Yafo, 2000—; bd. dirs. New Israel Fund, 1983—, treas., 1984-96, pres. 1996-99; pres. Boston Friends of Peace Now, 1984-85, N.E. region Am. Jewish Congress, 1993-95; chmn. steering com. N.Am. Friends of Peace Now, 1986-88, bd. dirs., treas., 1988-91. NSF fellow, 1962-63; Ford Found. Faculty Research fellow, 1966-67; Guggenheim fellow, 1981-82; Erksine fellow U. Canterbury, N.Z., 1983. Fellow Econometric Soc. (council 1972-76, v.p. 1977-78, pres. 1979), Am. Acad. Arts and Scis.; mem. Am. Econ. Assn. (John Bates Clark medal 1973) Home: 130 Mt Auburn St Cambridge MA 02138-5757 Office: MIT 50 Memorial Dr # E52 359 Cambridge MA 02142-1347

FISHER, JACK CARRINGTON, environmental engineering educator; b. Cortland, N.Y., Aug. 30, 1932; s. William J. and Jeannette (Carrington) F.; m. Sally Key Retzer, Nov. 15, 1981; children by previous marriage— John C., Margaret Lynn. BA, Syracuse U., 1956, MA, 1958, PhD (Ford Found. fellow), 1961. Asst. prof. city and regional planning Cornell U., Ithaca, N.Y., 1962-68; assoc. prof., assoc. dir. urban studies Wayne State U., Detroit, 1969-72; prof. geography and environ. engring. Johns Hopkins U., Balt., 1972—; dir. Center for Met. Planning and Research, 1972-86; spl. asst. to pres. for oversees univ. liaison, dir. spl. projects Johns Hopkins U., 1985-89, coord. internat. internship program Sch. Engring., 1992-98. Author: Yugoslavia: A Multinational State; editor: City and Regional Planning in Poland; contbr. articles to profl. jours. Served with U.S. Army, 1952-55. Recipient Golden Placket award U. Ljubljan, Slovenia, 1997. Mem. Am. Assn. Planning Ofcls., Am. Inst. Planning, Am. Assn. Geographers, Regional Sci. Assn. Office: Johns Hopkins U 210 Ames Hall Baltimore MD 21218

FISHER, JANET WARNER, secondary school educator; b. San Angelo, Tex., July 7, 1929; d. Robert Montell and Louise (Buckley) Warner; m. Jarek Prochazka Fisher, Oct. 17, 1956 (div. May 1974); children: Barbara Zlata Harper, Lev Prochazka, Monte Prochazka. BA, So. Meth. U., 1950, M of Liberal Arts, 1982; student various including, Columbia U., U. Dallas, U. Colo., U. London and others. Cert. English, German and ESL tchr., K-12, Tex., N.Y. Bd. dirs., sec. Masaryk Inst., N.Y.C., 1968-71; with orphan sect. Displaced Persons Commn., Washington, 1950; fgn. editor Current Digest of the Soviet Press, N.Y.C., 1953-55; cable desk clk. Time, Inc., N.Y.C., 1955-56; tchr. of English and reading, langs. Houston Ind. Sch. Dist., 1975-80; tchr. Carmine Ind. Sch. Dist., Round Top, Tex., 1980-82; tchr. German Region IV Interactive TV, 1983-85; adj. prof. English U. Houston, 1983-87; tchr. Royal Ind. Sch. Dist., Brookshire, Tex., 1989-92, Hempstead Ind. Sch. Dist., Waller County, Tex., 1992-94. Adj. prof. English, U. Houston, Houston C.C., 1983-87, 1997—; tchr. Amnesty Program, Houston, 1988-90; adj. prof. English Blinn Coll., Brenham, Tex., 1995-97. Candidate sch. bd., South Orangetown, N.Y., 1962, state rep., Houston, 1980; del. Houston Tchrs. Assn., 1975-80; officer LWV, Nyack, N.Y., 1960-62; trustee, chair adminstrn. bd. Shepherd Drive United Meth. Ch., Houston, 1994-2003; del. Tex. ann. conf. United Meth. Ch., 1994-2001; del. Tex. State Dem. Conv., 1996, 2000, 02. Recipient award for Svc. to Missions, United Meth. Ch., Houston, 1985. Mem. AAUW, NOW, WILPF, Harris County Women's Polit. Caucus. Avocations: Russian and German literature, real estate development. Home: PO Box 66067 Houston TX 77266-6067 E-mail: jsufish@aol.com.

FISHER, JANINE GALMICHE, educator, counselor; b. New Brunswick, NJ, Dec. 30, 1948; d. Francis Edward and Anna Margaret (Bailey) Galmiche; m. Herbert O. Fisher Jr., Aug. 4, 1973; 1 child, Jennifer Ann. BBA, Wilmington Coll., 1972; cert., Tex. Women's U., 1986. Cert. econ. and bus. tchr. Tex. Registrar Wilmington Coll., New Castle, Del., 1972-73; adminstrv. sec. Tex. Women's U., Denton, 1973-79, accreditation coord. Sch. of Pt., 1981-82; corp. sec., treas. Tex. Airport Mgmt. Svcs., Lewisville, 1980-84, tchr. Child Care Ctr., 1986; substitute tchr. Lewisville Ind. Sch., 1986-87; tchr. PASS Delay Mid. Sch., Lewisville, 1987-89, tchr. transition, 1989-90; alternative tchr. Lewisville Learning Ctr., 1990—91, at-risk tchr., 1991—. Leader Girl Scouts USA, Lewisville, 1986-98, trainer, 1987-90, bd. dir. day camp, 1987-94; tchr. St. Phillips Roman Cath. Ch., Lewisville, 1984-86; treas. Hot Shots Soccer Team, Lewisville, 1988-89. Mem. Nat. Bus. Edn. Assn., Tex. Edn. Assn., Tex. Tchr. Assn., Sigma Phi Beta. Avocations: reading, sewing, crafts, soccer. Home: 532 Auburn Dr Lewisville TX 75067-5202 Office: Lewisville Learning Ctr 1601 S Edmonds Ln Lewisville TX 75067-5637

FISHER, MARGARET ELEANOR, psychologist, lawyer, arbitrator, mediator, educator; d. John T. and Mary (Worden) F. BS cum laude in Psychology, Seton Hall U., 1958; postgrad., U. Paris, 1958, Carl Jung Inst., Switzerland, 1958-59, NYU, 1959-60, U. Md., 1960-63; MA magna cum laude in Ednl. Psychology, San Diego State U., 1966; postgrad. (NDEA grantee), U. Alaska, 1965, MBA, MPA, 1991; Phd cum laude in Psychology, U. Wash., 1970; JD magna cum laude, La Salle U., 1993. Lic. pilot comml. helicopter, fixed wing, psychologist, Mass., Ind., Alaska. Resident counselor Children's Ctr., NYC, 1959-60; tchr. Am. Dependent's, Turkey, 1960—64, 1960—64, 1960—64, Am. Dependent's Sch., Japan, 1960-64; tchr. English as fgn. lang. Jean Giraudoux Lycée, Chateauroux, France, 1963-64; tchr. English and French Sweetwater Sch. Dist., Chula Vista, Calif., 1964-66; asst. to editor Rev. of Ednl. Rsch. Jour., Seattle, 1967-68; psychologist vocat. rehab. program Edmonds Sch. Dist., Lynnwood, Wash., 1968-70; cons. psychologist Charles Denny Youth Ctr., Everett, Wash., 1969-71; instr. psychology Seattle Cmty. Coll., 1971; asst. prof. dept.social sci., humanities and edn. Purdue U., Lafayette, Ind., 1971-72; lang. evaluation specialist Def. Lang. Inst., Monterey, Calif., 1972; rsch. psychologist U. Calif., San Francisco, 1972, asst. prof. psychology Santa Cruz, 1973, Mass. State Coll., 1973-76; pvt. practice psychology Mass., 1976-78; psychologist NY State Dept. Mental Hygiene, 1978, AK divsn. mental health Harborview Devel. Ctr., Valdez, 1978-79, AK Psychiat. Inst., Anchorage, 1979-95; psychologist, atty. AK Psychol., Arbitration & Mediation Svc., Inc., 1995—; with AK Civil Air Patrol, 1987. Adj. prof. law and psychology La Salle U. Contrb. articles to psychol. and law jour. Arbitrator, mediator forensic psychologist Am. Arbitration Assn.; pres. Internat. Coun. Psychologists, 1992, world area chairs coord.; mem. AK State Bd. Psychologists and Psychol. Assoc. Examiners, 1984—88; amb. to Mauritius Anchorage organizing com. 1994 Winter Olympics, 1988—. With Alaska Civil Air Patrol, 1987—. Recipient Internat. travel award Purdue U., 1972, scholarly support award Mass. State Coll., 1974, 75, 76. Fellow: Am. Coll. Forensic Examiners (cert. forensic examiner); mem.: DAR, Internat. Coun. Psychologists (past pres. 1992, diplomate), AK Psychol. Assn., Mensa. Home and Office: 7935 Hillside Way Anchorage AK 99516 Fax: (907) 345-6234.

FISHER, MICHAEL ELLIS, mathematical physicist, chemist; b. Trinidad, W.I., Sept. 3, 1931; m. Sorrel Castillejo; children: Caricia J., Daniel S., Martin J., Matthew P.A. BS with 1st class honors in Physics, King's Coll., London, 1951, PhD, 1957; DSc (hon.), Yale U., 1987, Tel Aviv U., 1992. Lectr. math. RAF, 1952-53; lectr. theoretical physics King's Coll., 1958-62, reader physics, 1962-64; prof. physics U. London, 1965-66; prof. chemistry and math. Cornell U., 1966-73, Horace White prof. chemistry, physics and math., 1973-89, chmn. dept. chemistry, 1975-78; Disting. prof. Inst. for Phys. Sci. and Tech. U. Md., 1987—, Regents prof. Inst. for Phys. Sci. & Tech., 1993—. Guest investigator Rockefeller Inst., 1963-64; vis. prof. applied physics Stanford U., 1970-71; Buhl lectr. theoretical physics Carnegie-Mellon U., 1971; Richtmyer Meml. lectr. Am. Assn. Physics Tchrs., 1973; S. H. Klosk lectr. NYU, 1975; 17th F. London Meml. lectr. Duke U., 1975; Walker-Ames prof. U. Wash., Seattle, 1977; Loeb lectr. physics Harvard U., 1979; vis.prof. physics MIT, 1979; Welsh Found. lectr. in physics U. Toronto, Ont., Can., 1979; 21st Alpheus Smith lectr. Ohio State U., 1982; Fairchild scholar Calif. Inst. Tech., 1984; Cherwell-Simon lectr., vis. prof. Oxford U., 1985; Schlapp scholar Edinburgh U., 1987; Marker lectr. Pa. State U., 1988, Nat. Sci. Coun. lectr., Taiwan, 1989; Hamilton Meml. lectr. Princeton U., 1990, 65th J. W. Gibbs lectr. Am. Math. Soc., 1992; E. U. Condon lectr. U. Colo., 1992; M. S. Green Meml. lectr. Temple U., 1992; R&B Sackler Disting. lectr. in solid state physics Tel Aviv U., 1992; 1st Lars Onsager lectr., Norway, 1993; Phi Beta Kappa vis. scholar, 1994; Lennard-Jones lectr. Royal Soc. Chemistry, 1995; Joseph O. Hirschfelder Prize lectr. U. Wis., 1995; Gilbert Newton Lewis Meml. lectr. U. Calif., Berkeley, 1995; George Fisher Baker lectr. chemistry Cornell U., 1997. Author (with d.M. MacKay): Analogue Computing at Ultra-High Speed, 1962; author: The Nature of Critical Points, 1964, The Theory of Equilibrium Critical Phenomena, 1967; assoc. editor Jour. Math. Physics, 1965—68, 1972—75, 1986—89, mem. adv. bd. Jour. Theoretical Biology, 1969—82, Chem. Physics, 1972—84, Discrete Math., 1971—78, Jour. Statis. Physics, 1978—81, mem. editl. bd. Comms. Math. Phys., 1984—2000. Recipient award in phys. and math. scis. N.Y. Acad. Scis., 1978, Guthrie medal and prize Inst. Physics, London, 1980, Wolf prize in physics, 1980, Michelson-Morely award Case Western Res. U., 1982, Boltzmann medal IUPAP, 1983, Hirschfelder prize U. Wis., 1995; Guggenheim fellow, 1970-71, 78-79. Fellow: AAAS, Kings Coll. London, Am. Phys. Soc., Phys. Soc. London, N.Y. Acad. Scis. (hon.), Royal Soc. Edinburgh (hon.), Am. Acad. Arts and Scis., Royal Soc. London (regional editor 1989—93, v.p. 1993—95); mem.: NAS (fgn. assoc.), Indian Acad. Scis., Brazilian Acad. Scis. (fgn. assoc.), Math. Assn. Am., Soc. Indsl. and Applied Math., Am. Philos. Soc., Am. Chem. Soc. Office: U Md Inst Phys Sci & Tech College Park MD 20742-0001

FISHER, MILES MARK, IV, education and religion educator, minister; b. Huntington, W.Va., Sept. 25, 1932; s. Miles Mark and Ada Virginia (Foster) F. BA, Va. Union U., 1954, M.Div., 1959; MA, N.C. Central U., 1968; D.Min., Howard U., 1978. Ordained to ministry Baptist Ch., 1961; tchr. pub. schs. Durham, N.C., 1959-67; assoc. min. White Rock Bapt. Ch., Durham, N.C., 1959-65; asst. prof. edn., counselor Norfolk (Va.) State U., 1967-69; cons. Model Cities Area of Recreation, Norfolk, 1968-69; exec.-sec., CEO Nat. Assn. Equal Opportunity in Higher Edn., Washington, 1969-78; spl. cons. Inst. for Services to Edn., Washington, 1969-70; vis. asst. prof. Sch. Divinity Howard U., 1978-80; staff dir., com. clk. Com. of Whole, Council of D.C., Washington, 1979-83; spl. asst. to v.p. acad. affairs U. D.C., Washington, 1983-84, dir. policy rev. and analysis Office of the Bd. of Trustees, 1985-88, exec. dir. Office of the Bd. of Trustees, 1989-90, interim pres., 1990-91, disting. U. prof., 1991—. Chaplain counselor Lincoln Hosp. Sch. Nursing, Durham, N.C., 1962-67; chaplain Fisher Funeral Parlor, Durham, 1963-67; mem. task force employment of minority populations Nat. Recreation and Park Assn., 1970-71; mem. task force on edn. and Vietnam Era vet. VA, 1971-72; mem. steering com. U.S. Office of Edn. Common Core Data for the 70's, 1971-78, Congl. Black Caucus Nat. Policy Conf. on Black Edn., 1972; mem. Nat. task force on Student Financial Aid Problems, 1974-75; bd. trustees Consortium of U. of the Washington Met. Area, 1990-91; bd. dirs. Washington Rsch. Libr. Consortium, 1990-91. Bd. dirs. Cooperative Coll. Registry, 1973-75; mem. adv. bd. Four-Year Servicemen's Opportunity Coll., 1974-77; mem. adv. com. to bd. dirs. Nat. Student Ednl. Fund, 1974-78; v.p. bd. dirs. Reading is Fundamental Program, 1977-79, Vis. Nurse Assn., 1974-80; bd. dirs. D.C. Citizens for Better Public Edn., 1977, pres., 1981-83; bd. dirs. Voice Informed Community Expression, pres., 1982-84; trustee Va. Union U., 1983-85, Shaw U. Div. Sch., 1982-88. Mem. ACA, Am. Assn. Higher Edn., Am. Acad. Polit. and Social Scis., Am. Acad. Religion, Assn. Multicultural Counseling and Devel., Assn. Spiritual Ethical and Religious Values in Counseling, Am. Soc. Ch. History, Internat. Alumni Assn. Va. Union U. (pres. 1983-85), Am. Tennis Assn. (life), Assn. for Study of Afro-Am. Life and History (life), Assn. for Study of Higher Edn., U.S. Tennis Assn. (life). Home: 4444 Connecticut Ave NW Apt 402 Washington DC 20008-2319 Office: PO Box 2340 Washington DC 20013-2340

FISHER, PEARL BEATRICE, retired reading specialist educator; b. Northrop, Minn., June 10, 1913; d. Robert H. and Flora Ella (Sloneker) Unke; m. Harlan Lloyd Fisher, June 10, 1936. BS in Elem. Edn., Mankato (Minn.) State U., 1935. Tchr. 3rd grade Lakefield (Minn.) Elem. Sch., 1935-37; tchr. 2d grade Shaw Elem. Sch., Austin, Minn., 1942-43; tchr. kindergarten, jr. h.s. phys. edn. Bayport (Minn.) Elem. Sch., 1943-54; tchr. elem. Minn. Sch. Dist. 834, Stillwater, 1954-63, tchr. reading specialist, 1963-73. Mem. Literary Club, Mower County, Minn., 1938-41; vol. ARC, Afton-Lakeland, Minn., 1942, 68-76, Food Shelf and Meals on Wheels, Stillwater, Minn., 1973-76; assoc. mem. Bayport (Minn.) Libr., 1993—; chair, Ch. Women's Guild Memls. Bd., Bayport, 1979-84, 93-95, 94-96. Mem. Nat. Edn. Assn., Minn. Edn. Assn., Tuesday Reading Club, Ret. Tchrs. Assn. Congregationalist. Avocations: world travel, camping, sports, reading, gardening. Home: 1411 Old Toll Bridge Rd Lakeland MN 55043-9713

FISHER, PHILIP J. English language and literature educator; b. Pitts., Oct. 11, 1941; s. Leo and Anna (Walker) F.; 1 child, Mark. BA, U. Pitts., 1963; AM, Harvard U., 1966, PhD, 1970. Asst. prof. U. Va., Charlottesville, 1970-72, Brandeis U., Waltham, Mass., 1973-80, assoc. prof. English and Am. lit., 1980-87, prof., 1987—; Reid prof. English Harvard U., Cambridge, Mass., 1988-91, chair dept. English, 1990-93. Asst. prof. Andrew Mellon Harvard U., 1976-77; vis. prof. Free U. Berlin, 1981, Yale U., 1985-86, U. Konstanz, W.Ger., 1986, Harvard U., 1986-87. Author: Making Up Society, 1981, Hard Facts: Setting and Form in the American Novel, 1984, Making and Effacing Art: Modern American Art in a Culture of Museums, 1991, The New American Studies, 1991, Wonder, the Rainbow and the Aesthetics of Rare Experiences, 1998, Still The New World, American Literature in a Culture of Creative Destruction, 1999, The Vehement Passions, 2002. Recipient Howard Mumford Jones prize Harvard U., 1971, Nat. Endowment Humanities fellow, 1972-73, Mellon fellow, 1976-77, Exxon fellow program in sci., tech. and soc., MIT, 1984-85, Inst. Advanced Study fellow, Berlin, 1987-88, adv. bd., 1994—, Guggenheim fellow, 1996-97; sr. fellow Getty Mus., 1998-99; fellow Stanford Ctr. for Advanced Study in the Behavioral Scis., 2003—. Office: Harvard U Dept English Barker Ctr Cambridge MA 02138 E-mail: PJFisher@fas.harvard.edu.

FISHER, RAMONA FAYE, hospital child care center administrator; b. Birdsnest, Va., May 8, 1960; d. Willie Upsher and Willia Mae (Kates) Harmon; 1 child, Rashad Eugene. Cert., Thomas Nelson, Hampton, Va., 1981; student, Tidewater C.C., Portsmouth, Va., 1990, Ea. Shore C.C., Meifa, Va., 1991, Old Dominion U., Norfolk, Va., 1990, 91, 93—. TMR asst. Northampton County Pub. Schs., Eastville, Va., 1983-84; instr. TMR adults Ea. Shore Community Svc. Bd., Belle Haven, Va., 1985-86; ednl. dir. East Coast Migrant Headstart, Parksley, Va., 1982-91; dir. Short Stop Child Care and Presch. Northampton-Accomack Meml. Hosp., Nassawadox, Va., 1989—. Facilitator Parent Anonymous Group, Eastville, 1989—; mem. adv. bd., v.p. Children and Parents of The Shore, Eastville, 1989—; head pub. rels. Child Care Task Force, Eastville, 1992—; mem. career studies com. Ea. Shore C.C., Melfa, 1992; mem. Interagy. Task Force for Children, 1990; parent rep. Eastern Shore Comprehensive Svc. Mgmt. Team, 1992. Ch. clk. Antioch Bapt. Ch., Trehernville, Va., 1991—; sec. W.R. Ponds Gospel Choir, Trehernville, 1989—; mem. Voters League Northampton County, Eastville. Recipient Vol. awards Children and Parents of the Shore, Eastville, 1990, 91, Project Migrant Headstart, Parksley, Va., 1981-88, 89-90. Mem. NAACP (Freedom Fund Queen contest participant award 1990), ASCD, Tidewater Child Care Assn. Democrat. Avocations: reading, advocating for rights fo children. Home: 11233 Sealey Rd Birdsnest VA 23307-1615 Office: Short Stop Child Care & Presch 9507 Hospital Ave Nassawadox VA 23413-1821

FISHER, RANDALL EUGENE, lawyer, educator; b. Wichita, Kans., June 3, 1949; s. George Allen Fisher and LaVonna (Brooks) Jackson; m. Arlena L. Eveleigh, May 20, 1970 (div. 1976); 1 child, Scott N.; m. Kathy R. Vetter, July 21, 1978 (div. 1985); m. Deena M. Bolton, Aug. 2, 1986; children: Anthony Michael, Nicholas Wade. BA, Wesleyan U., Salina, Kans., 1971; JD, Washburn U., 1976. Bar: Kans. 1976, U.S. Dist. Ct. Kans. 1976, U.S. Ct. Appeals (10th cir.) 1981, U.S. Supreme Ct. 1981. Law clk. to assoc. justice Kans. Supreme Ct., Topeka, 1976-78; assoc. Barta & Barta, Salina, 1978-80; staff atty. Legal Aid of Wichita, 1980-81; ptnr. McDonald, Tinker, Skaer, Quinn & Herrington PA, Wichita, 1981-87, also bd. dirs.; judge U.S. Dist. Ct. Kans., 1987-89; assoc. Michaud, Hutton & Bradshaw, Wichita, 1989—. Adj. prof. Wichita State U., 1982—; trustee, vice chmn. Wichita Legal Aid, 1983—, now chmn.; faculty mem. Nat. Inst. Trial Advocacy, 1985—. Author: (with others) Settling Personal Injury Cases in Kansas, 1986, KBA KS Worker's Compensation Practice Manual, 1985-88, Kansas Uninsured and Underinsured Motorist Issues, 1987, (with others) Current Issues in Kansas Auto Insurance, 1988; ann. supplements. Advisor Law Explorer Post, Wichita, 1985-86. Recipient Dist. Advocacy Internat. Trial Lawyers Assn., 1975. Mem. ABA, Kans. Bar Assn., Wichita Bar Assn., Assn. Trial Lawyers Am., Kans. Trial Lawyers Assn. (bd. editors 1978-80), Internat. Trial Lawyers Assn., Am. Judge's Assn., Kans. Dist. Judge's Assn., Order of Barristers, Am. Judicature Soc. Methodist. Avocations: photography, writing, computers, conservation. Address: Michaud Hutton Fisher Hutton PO Box 638 Wichita KS 67201-0638

FISHER, ROGER DUMMER, lawyer, educator, negotiation expert; b. Winnetka, Ill, May 28, 1922; s. Walter Taylor and Katharine (Dummer) F.; m. Caroline Speer, Sept. 18, 1948; children: Elliott Speer, Peter Ryerson. AB, Harvard U., 1943, LLB magna cum laude, 1948; LHD, Conn. Coll., 1994; DHL, Bay Path Coll., 1999. Bar: Mass. 1948, D.C. 1950. Asst. to gen. counsel, then asst. to dep. U.S. spl. rep. ECA, Paris, 1948-49; with firm Covington & Burling, Washington, 1950-56; asst. to solicitor gen. U.S., 1956-58; lectr. law Harvard Law Sch., Cambridge, Mass., 1958-60, prof. law, 1960-76, Samuel Williston prof. law, 1976-92, prof. emeritus, 1992—, dir. Harvard negotiation project, 1980—. Vis. prof. internat. rels. dept. London Sch. Econ., 1965-66; cons. pub. affairs editor WGBH-TV, Cambridge, 1969; tech. advisor Found. for Internat. Conciliation, Geneva, 1984-87. Originator, 1st exec. editor: (pub. TV series) The Advocates, 1969-70, moderator, 1970-71; co-originator, exec. editor: (pub. TV series) Arabs and Israelis, 1975; author: International Conflict for Beginners, 1969, Dear Israelis, Dear Arabs, 1972, International Mediation: A Working Guide, 1978, International Crises and the Role of Law: Points of Choice, 1978, Improving Compliance with International Law, 1981; co-author: Getting to Yes: Negotiating Agreement Without Giving In, 1981, 2d edit., 1991, Getting Together: Building Relationships as We Negotiate, 1988, Beyond Machiavelli: Tools for Coping with Conflict, 1994, Getting Ready to Negotiate: The Getting to Yes Workbook, 1995, Coping with International Conflict: A Systematic Approach to Influence in International Negotiation, 1997, Getting It Done: How to Lead When You're Not in Charge, 1998; co-author, editor: International Conflict and Behavioral Science--The Craigville Papers, 1964; lectr., contbr. articles on internat. rels., negotiation, internat. law and TV. Bd. dir. Coun. for Livable World; trustee Hudson Inst., 1962-95. 1st lt. USAF, 1942-46. Recipient Sziland Peace award 1981, Peace Advocate award Lawyers Alliance for Nuclear Arms Control, 1988, Spl. Contbn. award Ctr. Pub. Resources, 1993, Steve Brutsché award Assn. Atty. Mediators, 1994, D'Alemberte-Raven Outstanding Achievements and Contributions to Dispute Resolution award, 1995, Honorato Vasquez Nat. Order Insignia Great Cross Republic Ecuador, 1999, helping settle in 1998 the fifty-yr. boundary war between Ecuador and Peru, Lifetime Achievement award Am. Coll. Civil Trial Mediators, 1999, Pioneer award New Eng. Soc. Profls. Dispute Reolution, 1999, St. Thomas More award St. Mary's U. Law Sch., 1999; named Guggenheim fellow 1965-66. Fellow Am. Acad. Arts and Sci.; mem. ABA (sect. dispute resolution), Am. Soc. Internat. Law (exec. coun. 1961-64, 66-69, v.p. 1982-84), Mass. Bar Assn., Commn. to Study Orgn. of Peace, Coun. Fgn. Rels., Phi Beta Kappa. Clubs: Metropolitan (Washington); Harvard (NYC). Office: Harvard U Law Sch Harvard Negotiation Project Pound Hall # 525 Cambridge MA 02138 also: Conflict Mgmt Group 9 Waterhouse St Cambridge MA 02138-3607

FISHER, SANDRA IRENE, English educator; b. Massillon, Ohio, Aug. 7, 1947; d. Samuel Arnold and Pearl Irene (Wood) Sells; m. John Jay Fisher, July 23, 1978; children: Melissa Pearl, Benjamen Jay. BA in Edn., Harding U., Searcy, Ark., 1969; postgrad., Ohio U., 1980—; M in Tchg. and Tech., Nova Southeastern U., 2001. Cert. tchr. English grades 7-12, health/phys. edn. K-12, Ohio. Tchr. phys. edn. and health Shenandoah H.S., Sarahsville, Ohio, 1969-72; tchr. English grades 9-12 Belmont Career Ctr., St. Clairsville, Ohio, 1973—. Advisor Lit. Club, St. Clairsville, 1978-97, Skills-USA Vocat. Indsl. Clubs Am.; sec.-treas. Barnesville (Ohio) Track/Cross Country Orgn., 1993-2001; sec., charter mem. Mt. Olivet Water Trustees, Barnesville, 1994-96. Martha Jennings scholar, 1979-80. Mem. Belmont County Lang. Arts Coun. (v.p. 1998-2003), Ohio Coun. Tchrs. English Lang., Iota Lambda Sigma. Mem. Ch. of Christ. Avocations: singing, writing, reading, floral designing, traveling. Home: 36815 Morse Ln Barnesville OH 43713-9456 Office: Belmont Career Ctr 110 Fox Shannon Pl Saint Clairsville OH 43950-8751

FISHER, SHIRLEY IDA A. photography and humanities educator; b. Cleve., Aug. 7, 1935; d. E. and I. (Morley) F. BFA, Ohio U., 1957, MFA, 1959; postgrad., U. Calif., Berkeley, from 1964, U. Calif., Santa Cruz, from 1964. Instr. Detroit Community Ctr., 1960-63; med. photographer Ford Hosp., Detroit, 1961-63; comml. photographer Detroit, 1960-63; photo producer San Jose State U., 1963-70, prof. photography, 1966-67; prof. digital photography and humanities, coord. dept. De Anza Coll., Cupertino,

Calif., 1967-99, founder digital photography dept., 1985-99. Photojournalist to Mexican, Puerto Rican and Costa Rican dept. tourism; photographer in over 67 countries; owner Hispanic and Anglo Publs., San Jose, 1986—, World Images Photography, Cupertino, 1963—; 1st invited Am. photographer to Ecuador. Work in internat. mus., embassies, bi-nat. ctrs. and pvt. collections; author, editor: Argentine and Chilean Photo, 1984, Cinco de Mayo en San Jose, 1987; author/editor/photographer: El Dia de Las Muertos, 1999; author/editor/photographer, The Sea, 2000; editor: Self Reflections, 1987. Am. participant USIS serving in Ecuador, Uruguay, Chile, Bolivia, Venezuela, Brazil, Argentina, 1981-86. Mem. Soc. Photog. Edn., Sister Cities San Jose (Calif.), Friends of Photography, Peninsula Advt. Photographers Assn., Bookies Art Caucas, Adobe Users Group, Phi Theta Kappa, Kappa Alpha Mu. Avocations: travel, writing, photographic exhibiting, theme projects, private photo classes, metaphysics. Died Oct. 2.

FISH-LACEY, HELEN THERESE, educator, author; b. Mpls., Mar. 17, 1944; d. John Howard and Helen Therese (Ochs) Berg; m. Ronald Bruce Fish, Oct. 13, 1967 (div. May 1994); children: Eric James, Angela Diane, Christine Ann; m. Richard Ellis Lacey, Feb. 1, 2003. BS, U. Minn., Mpls., 1966; postgrad., U. Minn., Mankato, 1969-70, U. Wis., Whitewater, 1970-72; MEd, Brenau Coll., 1986; EdS, U. Ga., 1992, EdD in Ednl. Leadership and Lifelong Learning, 2002. Cert. elem. tchr., Minn., Wis., Ill., Kans., Ga. Tchr. kindergarten Lincoln Hills Sch., Mpls., 1966-68, Mapleton (Minn.) Pub. Schs., 1968-69; tchr. 1st grade Hoover Sch., Mankato, 1969-70; kindergarten tchr. Todd Sch., Beloit, Wis., 1970-73; tchr. presch., K-1 Wilson Sch., Janesville, Wis., 1973-75; tchr. gifted and reading specialist (remedial) Lakewood Sch., Park Forest, Ill., 1975-77; tchr. kindergarten, 1st and 3d grades Sibley Sch., Albert Lea, Minn., 1977-82; tchr. kindergarten Most Pure Heart Sch., Topeka, 1983-85, Enota Sch., Gainesville, Ga., 1985-88, chronicler Danforth grant, 1988-91; tchr. kindergarten Centennial Sch., Gainesville, Ga., 1992—; adj. asst. prof. Brenau U., Gainesville, Ga., 1988—, U. Ga., 1990, 94—, Barton Coll., 2002. Cons. and field test tchr. Rsch. and Devel. Ctr. U. Wis., Madison, 1970-79, Ency. Britannica Edn. Corp.; workshop leader for adminstrs. and tchrs. in Pre-Reading Skills; demonstration tchr. Internat. Reading Assn. Conv., New Orleans, 1975; field rschr. U. Ga.2002, Ga. Dept. Edn., 2002. Author: Starting Out Well: A Parent's Approach to Exercise and Nutrition, 1989; editor Y's Menettes newsletter, 1971-75. Sec., treas. PTA, Mpls, Mankato, Albert Lea, Beloit, Janesville, Park Forest, Topeka, Gainesville; leader Girl Scouts U.S., Blue Birds, Topeka; asst. softball coach, Gainesville H.S. Recipient award for contbns. to edn. and participation in Tchr. in Space Program NASA, 1986; Cert. of World Leadership, Cambridge, Eng., 1990. Mem. Ga. Edn. Assn., Assn. for Supervision and Curriculum Devel., Ga. Presch. Assn., Internat. Platform Assn., Pi Lamda Theta (Hon. Teaching Soc. award). Roman Catholic. Avocations: writing, inventing, learning, teaching, sports. Home: 3650 Brown Well Ct Gainesville GA 30504-5774 Office: Enota Sch Gainesville GA 30501

FISHMAN, CLAIRE, media specialist; b. Croydon, Surrey, Eng. came to U.S., 1968; d. Jack and Anne (Greenberg) Ritoff; m. Leon Fishman, Sept. 2, 1962 (dec. July 1976); children: Jonathan David, Simon Andrew. Cert. in edn., Bognor Regis Tchrs.' Tng. Coll. Southampton, Eng.; BA in History summa cum laude, U. Bridgeport; M. in Libr. Sci. and Tech., So. Conn. State U.; postgrad., Fairfield U. Cert. sch. libr., media specialist, elem. and secondary tchr. Tchr. Ecclesbourne Road Boy's Elem. Sch., Croydon, Bridge Road Elem. Sch., Willesden, Eng.; gen. subjects and libr. Caulfield High Sch., Melbourne, Australia, Ashburton Secondary Modern for Girls; pub. libr. Ferguson Libr., Stamford (Conn.) Pub. Schs., 1968-73; libr. Convent of the Sacred Heart, Noroton, Conn., 1973-74; media specialist, learning facilitator Dundee Elem. Sch., Cos Cob Elem. Sch., Greenwich (Conn.) Pub. Schs., 1974—. Mem. Bd. Reps., Stamford, chmn. pers., charter revision, 1984-87; asst. sec., sec., chmn. policy, ad hoc breakfast Stamford Bd. Edn., 1988-91; dist. rep. Stamford Dem. City Com., 1983-91, treas., 1992—; bd. dirs. First Night Stamford, 1988-90, pres., 1990; mem. Pub. Arts Adv. Panel, Stamford; bd. dirs. Stamford Emergency Med. Svcs., 1996—, sec., 1997—, Congregation Agudath Sholom, Stamford; Justice of the Peace. Mem. Greenwich Edn. Assn. (computer adv. com., bd. dirs., profl. rights and responsibilities com., negotiation team, chair pub rels. com., nat. del., state del.), Conn. Ednl. Media Assn., Alpha Sigma Lamba, Phi Alpha Theta, Delta Kappa Gamma (legis. chmn.). Jewish. Home: 1 Clover Hill Dr Stamford CT 06902-1601 Office: Cos Cob Elem Sch Boston Post Rd Cos Cob CT 06807

FISHMAN, GAIL BARBARA, special education educator; b. Boston, Sept. 3, 1942; d. Morris and Sylvia (Steinberg) Katzman; m. Robert A. Fishman, Sept. 15, 1963; chldren: Jeffrey P., Ina S. Fishman Rosenthal. BS in Elem. Edn., Spl. Edn., Am. Internat. Coll., 1974, cert. advanced grad. studies in Counseling/Spl. Edn., 1980; MEd in Spl. Edn., Deaf Edn., Smith Coll.-Am. Internat. Coll, 1977; postgrad., U. Mass., 1984-87. Cert. tchr., spl. edn. tchr., elem. sch. prin., counseling tchr. of handicapped, tchr. of hearing impaired, Mass.; nat. cert. in deaf edn. Asst. tchr. of deaf Willie Ross Sch. for Deaf, Longmeadow, Mass., 1974-76; substitute tchr. spl. edn. Mass. Pub. Schs., Chicopee, 1976-77, specialist hearing-impaired students, 1977-88, tchr. spl. edn. resource rm., 1988—. Mem. bilingual curriculum com., curriculum com. Chicopee Pub. Schs.; cons. computers in spl. edn. Mass. Office Edn., 1988; mem. nat. tchrs. adv. bd. Star Serve, Santa Monica, Calif., 1992-93; advisor Selser Sch. Coun. Newspaper, 1988—; presenter multicultural conf U. Mass., 1993; advisor Jr. USO, 1993—. Contbr. articles to profl. publs. Mem. NEA, Mass. Tchrs. Assn., Chicopee Edn. Assn. (bldg. rep. 1988—), Hampden County Tchrs. Assn., Selser Sch. PTO, Citywide PTO (Spl. Merit award 1986). Jewish. Avocations: mah jongg, reading, travel, card games. Home: 9892 Summerbrook Ter Apt D Boynton Beach FL 33437-6107 Office: Selser Sch 12 D A R E Way Chicopee MA 01022

FISKE, SANDRA RAPPAPORT, psychologist, educator; b. Syracuse, N.Y., Sept. 25, 1946; d. Sidney Saul and Helen (Lapides) Rappaport; m. Jordan J. Fiske, June 22, 1974. BS, Cornell U., 1968; M.Ed., Tufts U., 1969; MA, Columbia U., 1971, PhD., 1974. Supervising sch. psychologist St. Elizabeth's Sch., N.Y.C., 1971-76; instr. clin. psychology Tchrs. Coll. Columbia, N.Y.C., 1973, clin. asst. dept. psychology, 1975-76; adj. prof. Syracuse U., 1976; sch. psychologist Syracuse Bd. Edn., 1976-77; prof. psychology Onondaga Community Coll., Syracuse, 1976-87, prof., 1988—, chair social sci. dept., 1993-99; pvt. practice psychology Syracuse, 1976—. NIMH fellow, 1969-72. Mem. APA, Ctrl. N.Y. Psychol. Assn., Sigma Xi, Psi Chi. Home: 2 Signal Hill Rd Fayetteville NY 13066-9674 Office: Onondaga Community Coll Dept Psychology Syracuse NY 13215 E-mail: fiskes@mail.sunyocc.edu.

FISS, OWEN M. law educator, educator; b. 1938; BA, Dartmouth Coll., 1959; BPhil, Oxford U., 1961; LLB, Harvard U., 1964. Bar: N.Y. 1965. Law clk. to Judge Thurgood Marshall U.S. Ct. Appeals 2d Cir., 1964—65; law clk. to Justice Brennan U.S. Supreme Ct., 1965; spl. asst. atty. gen. civil rights divsn. U.S. Dept. Justice, Washington, 1966—67; acting dir. Office of Planning Coordination, 1968; prof. U. Chgo. Law Sch., 1968—74, Yale Law Sch., New Haven, 1974—84, Alexander M. Bickel prof. pub. law, 1984—92, Sterling prof., 1992—. Vis. prof. Stanford U., 1972; mem. Harvard Law Rev. Author: Injunctions, 1972, The Civil Rights Injunction, 1978; author: (with R.M. Cover) The Structure of Procedure, 1979; author: (with D. Rendleman) Injunctions 2d edit., 1984; author: (with Cover and J. Resnick) Procedure, 1988; author: (with Cover and Resnick) The Fed. Procedural Sys., 1988, The Fed. Procedural Sys. 3d edit., 1991, Holmes Devise Hist. of the Supreme Ct.: Troubled Beginnings of the Modern State, 1888-1910, 1993, Liberalism Divided, 1996, The Irony of Free Speech, 1996, A Cmty. of Equals, 1999, A Way Out, 2003; mem. edtl. bd.: Philosophy and Pub. Affairs and Found. Press, Yale Jour. Criticism, Yale Jour. Law and Humanities, Law, Econs. and Orgns.

FISTELL, IRA J. newspaper editor, adult education educator, newswriter, radio and television personality; b. Chgo., Mar. 31, 1941; s. Harry and Marian L. (Wolfe) F.; m. Tonda R. Sloane, Aug. 20, 1978; children: Kelly, Christopher, Katherine, Mary Ellen, Sara, Andrea. AB with honors, U. Chgo., 1962, JD, 1964; MA in U.S. History, U. Wis., 1967. Bar: Ill. 1964. Radio personality Sta. WKOW-AM, Madison, Wis., 1968-71, Sta. WEMP-AM, Milw., 1971-77, Sta. KABC-AM, L.A., 1977-95; nat. radio personality ABC Talkradio Network, L.A., 1982-88, TalkAmerica Radio Network, 1998—2001; TV personality USA & ESPN Cable Networks, 1980-84; editor L.A. Jewish Times, 1995-96; radio personality Sta. KABC-AM, L.A., 2001—. Mem. faculty U. Phoenix, 1998—; instr English Concord Sch., Santa Monica, Calif, 1998—. Author: America By Train, 1982, Oddball America, 1986, Encounters with Mark Twain, 1995. Recipient Golden Spike award for svc. to rail passengers, NARRP, Anaheim, Calif., 1987. Mem. AFTRA, SAG, Milw. Press Club. Avocations: music, reading, travel.

FITCH, FRANK WESLEY, pathologist educator, immunologist, educator, administrator; b. Bushnell, Ill., May 30, 1929; s. Harold Wayne and Mary Gladys (Frank) F.; m. Shirley Dobbins, Dec. 23, 1951; children—Mary Margaret, Mark Howard. MD, U. Chgo., 1953, S.M., 1957, PhD, 1960; MD (hon.), U. Lausanne, Switzerland, 1990. Postdoctoral research fellow USPHS, 1954-55, 57-58; faculty U. Chgo., 1957—, prof. pathology, 1967—, Albert D. Lasker prof. med. sci., 1976—, emeritus prof., 1996, assoc. dean med. and grad. edn. div. biol. scis., 1976-85, dean acad. affairs, 1985-86, dir. Ben May Inst., 1986-95. Vis. prof. Swiss Inst. Exptl. Cancer Research, Lausanne, Switzerland, 1974-75. Editor-in-chief The Jour. of Immunology, 1997-2002; contbr. chpts. to books, articles to profl. jours. Recipient Borden Undergrad. Research award, 1953, Lederle Med. Faculty award, 1958-61; Markle Found. scholar, 1961-66; Commonwealth Fund fellow U. Lausanne (Switzerland) Institut de Biochimie, 1965-66; Guggenheim fellow, 1974-75 Mem. Fedn. Am. Socs. for Exptl. Biology (pres. 1993-94), Am. Assn. Immunologists (pres. 1992-93), Am. Soc. for Investigative Pathology, Am. Assn. for Cancer Rsch., Chgo. Path. Soc., Transplantation Soc., Sigma Xi, Alpha Omega Alpha. Home: 5449 S Kenwood Ave Chicago IL 60615-5312 E-mail: ffitch@uchicago.edu.

FITCH, LINDA BAUMAN, elementary school educator; b. Elmira, N.Y., Jan. 6, 1947; d. Floyd Theodore Bauman and Wilma Mildred Rennie; m. H. Taylor Fitch, Feb. 15, 1969; children: Trevor Andrew, Matthew Taylor. BS, Keuka Coll., Keuka Park, 1969. Elem. tchr. Penn Yan (N.Y.) Ctrl. Sch. Dist., 1972-73, tchg. asst. K-5, 1999—; computer coord. Fitch Auto Supply, Penn Yan, 1973-99. Com. chmn. troop 48 Boy Scouts Am., Branchport, N.Y., 1986-92; v.p. Penn Yan Cen. Sch. Bd., 1984-92, 95-97, pres., 1992-95; chmn. pub. rels. Yates Day Care Ctr., Penn Yan, 1980-82; mem. Bd. Coop. Ednl. Svcs., 1992-99. Mem. AAUW, Nat. Sch. Bds. Assn. (fed. rels. network 1988-99), N.Y. State Sch. Bds. Assn. (state legis. network 1991-99), Four County Sch. Bds. Assn. (legis. chmn., 2d v.p., 1st v.p., pres., mem. commr.'s adv. coun. sch. bd. mems. 1995). Republican. Presbyterian. Avocations: needlework, reading, swimming. Home: 3120 Kinneys Corners Rd Bluff Point NY 14478-9752 E-mail: tnlfitch@adelphia.net.

FITE, KATHLEEN ELIZABETH, education educator; b. Houston, June 26, 1948; d. Daniel Patrick and Edith Elizabeth (Burnett) F. BS in Edn., S.W. Tex. State U., 1969, MEd, 1970; EdD, N. Tex. State U., 1972. Cert. tchr., Tex. Prof. doctoral faculty S.W. Tex. State U., San Marcos, 1973—, dir. Ctr. for Study of Basic Skills, 1980, dir. Race Integration Tng. Inst., 1982-83, dir. elem. edn. dept., 1983-84, assoc. dir. sponsored projects, 1984-86, dir. sponsored projects, 1986-87. Cons. U.S. Dept. Edn., numerous pub. cos.; mem. adv. bd. Dushing Pub. Group, Inc. Author: Strutters: A few Favorites of the Total Teacher, The Super Ideas Book, Creative Art Ideas; asst editor SW Tex. U. Faculty Bull., 1977-78, editor, 1978-81; contbr. articles to profl. jours. Mem. sr. citizens adv. com. San Marcos City Coun., Commn. for Women; facilitator, dir. cmty. workshops; pres. Jr. Svc. League; activity chmn. Tex. Spl. Olympics. Named Ky. Col., 1975, named to Hall of Fame, San Marcos Commn. for Women, 1991; grantee U.S. Dept. Edn., L.B. Johnson Inst., 1988-89. Mem. ASCD, Nat. Assn. Edn. Young Children, Tex. Assn. Tchr. Educators, Kindergarten Tchrs. Tex., Tex. Computer Edn. Assn. (bd. dirs. 1984-87, publs. editor, state conf. asst. 1984-88), San Marcos Assn. for Edn. Young Children (treas.), S.W. Tex. State U. Alumni Assn. (Tchg. award of honor, Key of Excellence award, Strutter Hall of Fame), Golden Key, Phi Delta Kappa (pres. 1981, v.p., faculty advisor, ritual team 1986-89), Kappa Delta Pi (hon.). Methodist. Avocations: sewing, needle crafts, painting. Home: 602 Larue Dr San Marcos TX 78666-2410 Office: SW Tex State U Dept Curriculum & Instrn San Marcos TX 78666

FITTING, MELVIN CHRIS, computer scientist, educator; b. Troy, N.Y., Jan. 24, 1942; s. Chris Philip and Helen Gertrude (Van Denburgh) Fitting; m. Greer Aladar Russell, Jan. 17, 1971 (div. July 1983); children: Miriam Amy, Rebecca Jo; m. Roma Simon, Jan. 11, 1992. BS, Rensselaer Polytechnic Inst., 1963; MA, PhD, Yeshiva U., 1968. Prof. computer sci., philosophy, math. CUNY, Bronx, 1969—. Author: (book) Intuitionistic Logic Model Theory and Forcing, 1969, Fundamentals of Generalized Recursion Theory, 1981, Proof Methods for Modal and Intuitionistic Logics, 1983, Computability Theory, Semantics and Logic Programming, 1989, First-Order Logic and Automated Theorem Proving, 1990, Types, Tableaus and Goedel's God, 2002; author: (with Greer Fitting) In Praise of Simple Things, 1975; author: (with Raymond Smullyan) Set Theory and the Contiuum Problem, 1996; author: (with Richard Mendelsohn) First-Order Modal Logic, 1998. Grantee, NSF, 1987, 1989, 1991. Democrat. Home: 11 Kings Ln Montrose NY 10548-1307 Office: Lehman Coll Math Dept Bedford Park Blvd W Bronx NY 10468-1589

FITTS, LEONARD DONALD, educational administrator; b. Montgomery, Ala., Aug. 19, 1940; s. William Leonard and Mary Alice (Brown) F.; m. Sherrell Adrienne Thomas, June 4, 1966. BS, Tuskegee (Ala.) U., 1961, EdM, 1964; EdD, U. Pa., 1972; MBA, Drexel U., 1981. Lic. psychologist, Pa.; diplomate Vocat. Knowledge, Sch. Adminstrn., N.J. Math. coord., assoc. ednl. dir. Tuskegee U., 1964-65; guidance counselor U. Wis., Sparta, 1966-67; adminstr. Radio Corp. of Am., N.Y.C., 1967-69; sch. psychologist Phila. Bd. of Edn., 1971-75; dir. spl. svcs. Camden (N.J.) Bd. Edn., 1975-81; asst. supt. of schs. Lower Camden County Regional Sch. Dist., Atco, N.J., 1981-87; supt. of schs. Pa.-Grove Carneys Point, Penns Grove, N.J., 1987-92; Union county supt. of schs. N.J. Dept. of Edn., Westfield, 1992—. Vocat. sch. counselor Camden Co. Vocat. Sch., Pennsauken, N.J., 1968-73; psychol. cons. Rutgers U., Camden, 1969, Narcotic Addict Rehab. Ctr., Atlantic City, 1971-74; parent edn. cons. Dept. of Health, Edn. and Welfare, Phila., 1974—; chairperson commr.'s adv. coun. for handicapped State of N.J., 1982, Comprehensive System for Pers. Devel., 1982, White House conf. of Handicapped Individuals, 1976; adv. chmn. Al-Assist Recovery and Counseling Program. Contbr. articles to profl. publs. Bd. dirs. Union County Coll., Cranford, N.J., 1992, March of Dimes, N.J., 1994; elder 1st Presbyn. Ch., 1995. Lt. USAF, 1961-63. Watson Kinter scholarship U. Pa., 1969-72; recipient U.S. Dept. of Health, Edn. and Welfare, 1976; named Outstanding Alumni N.J. United Negro Coll. Fund, 1990. Mem. N.J. Assn. of Sch. Adminstrs. Avocation: rebuilding old cars. Home: 50 Cove Rd Moorestown NJ 08057-3950 Office: State Dept Edn 300 North Ave Westfield NJ 07090

FITZ-CARTER, ALEANE, elementary school educator, composer; b. Council Bluffs, Iowa, July 24, 1929; d. Andrew Wilburt and Beatrice Mildred (Maddox) Fitz; m. James Benny Carter, Dec. 10, 1958 (wid. Aug. 1964); children: Angel Beatrix, Angel Sherrie. BSEd, U. Nebr., 1956. Elem. sch. tchr. Omaha Pub. Schs., 1956-69; instr. Black history and music U. Nebr., Omaha, 1970-74; nat. faculty mem. Gospel Music Workshop Am. Inc., 1986; music tchr. Ascension Luth. Sch., L.A., 1990-94; min. music Messiah Luth. Ch., L.A., 1996—2003; church musician Tamarind Seventh Day Adventist Ch., Compton, Calif., 1997—; performing artist Nebr. Arts Coun., Omaha, 1980—, Iowa Arts Coun., Des Moines, 1998—; tchr. adult edn. L.A. Unified Schs., 1998—; ednl. cons. Torrance (Calif.) Unified Schs., 1997—99; min. of music Olivet Luth. Ch., Hawthorne, Calif., 2003—. Program prodr. KETV TV, Omaha, 1970-73; radio talk show host, KOWH Radio, Omaha, 1973-74; comms. cons. Mayor's Human Rels. Bd., Omaha, 1970-73; midwest bd. rep. Nat. Black Media Coalition, Washington, 1973-76, others; tchr. Black Awareness Opportunities Industrialization Ctr., 1969-74; instr. history of jazz, Oasis, L.A., 1997-2001; arranger, librettist, lyricist, elocutionist, storyteller, lectr. in field. Founder, dir. Omaha Gospel Choir, 1965—68, recs. include I Love Jesus, 1965, A Mighty Fortress, 1986; performer: (one-woman show) Rosa Parks, 1979—, Omaha Junior Theater, 1980—85; actress appearing in I Elvis, Hard Copy, 1992, Ice Cube video Dead Homie MTV, 1990, A Man Apart, 2003, music dir. (stage show) One Last Look, Marla Gibbs Theater, 1990; contbr. articles to profl. jours.; composer: One Child, 1993, (sacred hymns) Psalm 91, 1993—97, Children's TV workshop, Strawberry Square II: Take Time, NETV, 1983; invitee South African churches of KwaZulu Natal and African Enterprises to do a piano performance for country's celebration of 1st yr. anniversary freedom, Durban, S. Africa, 1995. Presentation vis. with Huell Howser, KCET; rschr. soul food history and cooking; min. music Olivet Luth. Ch., Hawthorne, Calif., 2003—. Nominee Best Supporting actress, Great White Hope Ctr. Stage, Omaha, Nebr., 1982; recipient Comty. Christian Leadership award, Salem Baptist Ch., Omaha, Nebr., 1987, Woman in Fine Arts award, Alyce Wilson Womens Ctr., Omaha, 1987, 5 yr. ACT-SO award, NAACP, Omaha, 1986, Outstanding Songwriter award, 1987—88, Psalm 91 Song of Yr. award, Thurston Frazier Chorale, 1987, Nebr. Chpt. GMWA award, 1987—88, Fine Arts award, Bethesda Seventh Day Adventist Ch., 1988, Comty. Guest Day, Bethesda Seventh Day Ch., Omaha, Nebr., 1988, Outstanding Svc. award, L.A. Union Seventh Day Acad., 1992, Creativity in music award, Thurston Frazier Chorale, GMWA, 1993, Svc. comty. award, Salem Baptist Mission, Norfolk, Nebr., 1995; grantee, L.A. Dept. of Cultural Affairs. Mem.: ASCAP, SAG, Rec. Acad., Profl. Musicians Union - Local 47, Nebr. Congress of Parents and Tchrs. (hon. life), Gold Star Wives Am., L.A. Pianist Club, VFW Ladies Aux., Sigma Gamma Rho (Gamma Beta Sigma chpt.). Seventh Day Adventist. Avocations: walking, swimming, cooking. Mailing: PO Box 90087 Los Angeles CA 90009 Home: 200 E Hyde Pk Blvd #1 Inglewood CA 90302 Personal E-mail: Psalm91@mymailstation.com.

FITZGERALD, EDWIN ROGER, physicist, educator; b. Oshkosh, Wis., July 14, 1923; s. James C. and Edwina (Brown) F.; m. Carolyn H. Johnson, Aug. 30, 1946; children: Lucia Edwina, Margaret Mary, William Maurice, Alice Ann, Roger Edwin, Douglas Brendan, Thomas Michael, Jane Carolyn. BS in Elec. Engring, U. Wis., 1944, MS in Physics, 1950, PhD in Physics, 1951. Registered profl. engr., Md. Physicist Phys. Research Lab., B.F. Goodrich Co., 1944-46; Project asso. chemistry U. Wis., 1951-52; faculty Pa. State U., 1953-61, prof. physics, 1959-61; prof. dept. mechanics Johns Hopkins U., 1961—99; ret., 1999. Vis. prof. chemistry U. Wis., Madison, 1981. Author: Particle Waves and Deformation in Crystalline Solids, 1966; contbr. articles to profl. jours., sects. in books; patentee in field. Fellow: Am. Phys. Soc. (exec. com., chmn. high polymer physics 1958—59); mem.: Am. Chem. Soc. (poly. materials divsn.), Materials Rsch. Soc., Acoustical Soc. Am., Tau Beta Pi, Eta Kappa Nu, Sigma Xi, Phi Beta Kappa. Achievements include research in mechanical and dielectric properties solids including dynamic mechanical properties of violin wood in relation to tone qualities of violins and viscoelastic properties of marine mammal tissues, dynamic mechanical measurements during freezing and thawing of ice. Home: 2445 Traceys Store Rd Parkton MD 21120-9642

FITZGERALD, JOHN THOMAS, JR., religious studies educator; b. Birmingham, Ala., Oct. 2, 1948; s. John Thomas and Annie Myrtle (Walters) Fitzgerald; m. Karol Bonneaux, May 23, 1970; children: Kirstin Leigh, Kimberly Anne. BA, Abilene Christian U., 1970, MA, 1972; MDiv, Yale U., 1975, PhD, 1984. Instr. Yale Coll., New Haven, 1979, Yale Divinity Sch., New Haven, 1980-81; from instr. to asst. prof. U. Miami, Coral Gables, Fla., 1981—88, assoc. prof., 1988—, dir. honors program, master Hecht Residential Coll., 1987—91. Vis. assoc. prof. Brown U., Providence, 1992, Yale Div. Sch., New Haven, 1998—99. Author: Tabula of Cebes, 1983, Cracks in an Earthen Vessel, 1988; editor: Friendship, Flattery and Frankness of Speech, 1996, Christian Origins sect. Religious Studies Rev., 1994—2002, Greco-Roman Perspecitve on Friendship, 1997, Early Christianity and Classical Culture, 2003; contbr. articles to profl. jours. Judge for Silver Knight awards Miami (Fla.) Herald, 1988, 1990. Named Two Bros. fellow, Yale Div. Sch., 1974—75; recipient Max Orvitz Summer Rsch. award, U. Miami, 1985, 1987, 1994, 1995, 1998, 2002; fellow, Rotary, Tuebingen, Germany, 1974—76. Mem.: Soc. Bibl. Lit. (chmn. com. 1989—96, editor Texts and Translations Series: Greco-Roman Religion 1993—2000, editor Writings from the Greco-Roman World Series 2001—, chmn. com. 2003—, mem. coun. 2003—, rsch. grantee 1997—99), Golden Key Nat. Honor Soc., Iron Arrow Hon. Soc., Omicron Delta Kappa, Phi Kappa Phi (chpt. pres. 1988—89). Home: 15215 SW 78 Ct Palmetto Bay FL 33157-2349 Office: U Miami PO Box 248264 Coral Gables FL 33124-4672 E-mail: john.fitzgerald@miami.edu.

FITZGERALD, SUSAN HELENA, elementary educator; b. Ft. Washington, Pa., Sept. 28, 1953; d. John Robert and Helen Etta (Groscost) Payne; m. Richard Michael Fitzgerald, June 8, 1974 (dec. June 1998); children: Kevin Michael, Gregory Thomas, Wendy Elaine. BS in Edn., West Chester (Pa.) U., 1975, M, Reading Specialist, 1992. Cert. reading specialist, elem., spl. edn. tchr. Head start tchr. Chester County IU, Coatesville, Pa., 1987-89; intermediate spl. edn. tchr. Coatesville Sch. Dist., 1989-91, 5th grade tchr., 1991-92, 1st grade tchr., 1992-97, instrl. support tchr., 1997-99, title I reading splst., 1999—. Coach Spl. Olympics Coatesville Sch. Dist., 1989—91, mem. instn. support team, 1994—99; summer sch. tchr. Youth Writing Project, 1995—; part-time prof. West Chester U., 2001, site coord. young readers/young writers program, 2003—. Tchr. Pennington Presbyn. Ch., Atglen, Pa., 1992—93, Sunday sch. tchr., 2000—03, choir mem., 2000—, deacon, 2003—. Grantee Coatesville Sch. Dist., 1990, 92. Republican. Presbyterian. Avocations: reading, writing, gardening. Home: 175 Upper Valley Rd Christiana PA 17509-9771

FITZGIBBON, WILLIAM EDWARD, III, mathematician, educator, academic administrator; b. Cambridge, Mass., July 21, 1945; s. William Edward Jr. and Florence Ethel (Steuville) F.; m. Jan Brooks; 1 child, William Edward IV. BA, Vanderbilt U., 1968, PhD, 1972. NASA trainee Vanderbilt U., Nashville, 1968-72; asst. prof. U. Houston, 1972-76, assoc. prof., 1976-82, prof. math., 1982—, chair dept. math., 1999—2003, dean Coll. Tech., 2003—. Summer visitor Argonne (Ill.) Nat. Lab., 1981; vis. prof. U. Calif., San Diego, 1980-82, U. Bordeaux II, France, 1996. Contbr. over 130 articles to profl. jours. Mem. Am. Math. Soc., Soc. Indsl. Applied Math., Irish Math. Soc., Sigma Xi, Omicron Delta Kappa, Phi Kappa Phi. Avocations: hunting, reading, skiing, athletics. Home: 5000 Montrose Blvd Unit 14F Houston TX 77006-6562 Office: U Houston Dept Math Houston TX 77204-0001

FITZPATRICK, M. LOUISE, dean, nursing educator; b. South River, N.J., May 24, 1942; d. John Francis and Bettina (Galassi) F. Diploma in nursing, Johns Hopkins U., 1963; BSN, Cath. U. Am., 1966; MA, Columbia U., 1968, MEd, 1969, EdD, 1972; cert., Harvard U., 1985. Former assoc. prof., dept. nursing edn. Tchrs. Coll., Columbia U., N.Y.C.; dean, prof. Villanova (Pa.) U. Coll. Nursing, 1978—. Cons. Mid. States Assn., Phila.; cons. to numerous univs., also univs. in Morocco, Egypt, Jordan, West Bank, Sultanate of Oman; cons., reviewer USPHS; bd. dirs. Nurses Ednl. Funds, Inc., N.Y.C. Author: The National Organization for Public Nursing, Development of a Practice Field, 1975; editor: Present Realities/Future Imperatives, 1977, Historical Studies in Nursing, 1978, Nursing in Society:

A Historical Perspective, 1983; also 21 articles in profl. jours. Recipient Disting. Alumni award Columbia U. Tchrs. Coll., 1966, Cath. Univ. McManus medal, 1992; WHO fellow, Scandinavia and U.K., 1974; Am. Acad. Nursing fellow, 1978. Mem. Am. Nurses Assn. (past chmn. cabinet on nursing edn.), Am. Assn. Colls. Nursing, Nat. League for Nursing (bd. of govs.). Democrat. Roman Catholic. Avocations: music, theater, cooking, international travel. Home: 80 Woodstone Ln Villanova PA 19085-1425 Office: Villanova U Coll Nursing Villanova PA 19085

FITZPATRICK, RUTH ANN, education educator; b. Brockton, Mass., July 12, 1941; d. Lenard Burton and Alva D.M. (Goranson) Parent; m. Richard Noll Fitzpatrick, July 9, 1966; 1 child, Elizabeth Ann. BS in Edn., Bridgewater State Coll., 1963, MEd, 1966, cert. advanced grad. study, 1985. Cert. elem. tchr. and prin., reading tchr. and supr., Mass. Tchr. Sharon Pub. Sch., Mass., 1963-72, 79-81; assoc. prof. edn., tchr. Bridgewater State Coll., Mass., 1982-98. Presenter in field. Contbr. articles to The Reading Tchr., NALS Jour., The Edn. Digest. Chair gifts and memls. com. 1st United Meth. Ch. Stoughton, 1968—, supt. ch. sch., 1968-74, liturgist, 1976-86, 95-2002, chair pastor/staff/parish com., 1994-97; tutor, bd. dirs. Literacy Vols. Am., Stoughton, 1998—. Mem. Nat. Assn. Lab. Schs. (life, chmn. N.E. conf. 1990, 95, exec. bd. dirs. 1991—, audit com. 1992-01, nominating com. 1993-94, 97, 2003, pres.-elect 1996, pres. 1997, historian 1998—, Disting. Svc. award 1999), Mass. Reading Assn. (mem. editl. bd. 1990-94), Delta Kappa Gamma (Alpha Beta chpt. corr. sec. 1985-92, treas. 1992—, presenter N.E. conf. Stockholm 1997), Phi Delta Kappa (charter mem. Bridgewater chpt., found. chair 1998-2000).

FITZSIMMONS, ROBERT WILLIAM, social science educator; b. Beloit, Wis., May 6, 1954; s. Leo Fitzsimmons and Ethel Fitzsimmons Dhom; m. Mary Reinhardt, June 27, 1981; children: Kathryn, Theodore. BS in Edn., U. Wis., 1977; MS in Bus., U. Wis., Whitewater, 1988. Cert. tchr., sch. bus. mgr., Wis. Tchr. Sioux City (Iowa) Sch. Dist., 1978, Delavan (Wis.) Sch. Dist., 1979-82; dist. rep. Sen. Tim Cullen, Madison, 1982-83; sales mgr. Agri Supply Co., Beloit, 1983-85; tchr. Beloit Sch. Dist., 1985—; instr. Beloit Coll., 1990—. Campaign treas. Rock County (Wis.) Treas. Peg Ross, 1988—; mem. mil. svc. acad. bd. Congressmen Aspin and Barca, 1990—; coach Youth Softball League, Beloit, 1991—. Named Tchr. of Month Rotary Club of Beloit, 1994. Mem. NEA, Wis. Edn. Assn. (bd. dirs. 1998—), Rock Valley United Tchrs. (pres. 1989), Wis. Coun. Social Studies. Home: 1209 Ridgeway St Beloit WI 53511 Office: Beloit Sch Dist 1225 4th St Beloit WI 53511-4437

FITZSIMMONS, TERRI KATHLEEN, educator, counselor; b. Vancouver, B.C., Can., June 1, 1949; came to the U.S., 1975; d. Boyce William and Rose (Stangle) Banner; m. Charles Russell Fitzsimmons, Sept. 3, 1989; stepchildren: Charles, Richard. AS, Mt. San Jacinto Coll., 1989; BA, Calif. State U., San Bernardino, 1991, MS in Pupil Pers. Svcs.-Counseling, 1994; tchg. credential, Chapman Coll., 1995; postgrad., Asuza Pacific U. Clk. admissions and records, registration clk. Mount San Jacinto (Calif.) Coll., 1988-91; career counselor Calif. State U., San Bernardino, 1992—; substitute tchr. Hemet (Calif.) Sch. Dist., 1993—; spl. edn. tchr. Nueview Sch. Dist., Nuevo, Calif., 1994-95; substitute tchr. San Jacinto (Calif.) Sch. Dist., 1995—. Instr. grad. studies Calif. State U., San Bernardino; sociology tchr., tutor, trainer instr., coord. for welfare reform Mt. San Jacinto (Calif.) Coll.; pvt. practice career cons., Hemet, 1992—. Vol. Valley Resource, San Jacinto, 1994-95. Scholar Mount San Jacinto Coll., 1988, CACD, 1993. Mount San Jacinto Coll. scholar, 1988; mem. Univ. Assn. Women, Calif. Assn. Counselors (scholar 1993). Home: 27189 Roger St Hemet CA 92544-8311

FIXLER, MICHAEL H. elementary education educator; b. N.Y.C., June 26, 1951; s. Robert and Thelma Gladys (Altman) F.; m. Barbara Lynn Hesselson, Oct. 11, 1987; children: Nathan, Judy, David. BA in Polit. Sci., U. Rochester, 1973; MS in Reading Edn., Syracuse U., 1982. Cert. elem. tchr., reading tchr., Ark., N.Y. VISTA worker ACTION Agy., Little Rock, 1975-76; rsch. asst. U. Ark., Little Rock, 1976-78; 2d grade tchr. Little Rock Pub. Schs., 1978-81; grad. asst. Syracuse (N.Y.) U., 1981-82; 1st grade tchr. Jordan (N.Y.) Elbridge Ctrl. Schs., 1982-90, 3d grade tchr., 1990—. Religious educator Temple Concord, Syracuse, 1984—; conflict resolution cons., 1985—, mem. nat. governing bd., 1988-91; jazz announcer Sta. KLRE Radio, 1976-81. Jewish. Avocations: jazz, jewish folk music, long distance running. Home: 103 Meadow Dr Elbridge NY 13060-9712 Office: Ramsdell Elem Sch Chappell St Jordan NY 13080

FIZER, MARILYN DAHLE, elementary education educator; b. San Antonio, Tex., Dec. 12, 1947; d. Richard Ivy and Marjory Blanche (Rookstool) Gold; m. Lawrence Franklin Fizer, Aug. 31, 1968; 1 child, Lawrence Scott. BS, Southwest Tex. State U., San Marcos, 1969. Tchr. Tex., 1969. Tchr. Northeast Ind. Sch. Dist., San Antonio, 1969-74, Katy (Tex.) Ind. Sch. Dist., 1979—. Mem. NEA, Nat. Coun. Tchrs. Math., Tex. State Reading Assn., Tex. State Tchrs. Assn., Greater Houston Area Reading Coun., Katy Edn. Assn., Bear Creek Elem. PTA, Internat. Reading Assn. Home: 15810 Echo Canyon Dr Houston TX 77084-3119 Office: Bear Creek Elem Sch 4815 Hickory Downs Dr Houston TX 77084-3654

FJORTOFT, NANCY FAY, univeristy administrator, educator; b. Osseo, Wis., Sept. 20, 1953; d. Willard c. and Rachel M. (Hubbard) Schmidt; m. Jon M. Fjortoft, May 10, 1986. BA, Blackburn Coll., 1975; MA, DePaul U., 1980; PhD, U. Ill., Chgo., 1994. Circulation mgr. DePaul U., Chgo., 1977-84; registrar, bus. mgr. Chgo. Sch. of Profl. Psychology, 1984-88; asst. to dean U. Ill., Chgo., 1988-93, asst. dean, 1993-97; asst. dean, assoc. prof. Coll. Pharmacy Midwestern U., Downers Grove, Ill., 1997-2000, assoc. dean, assoc. prof., 2000—. Lay leader First United Meth. Ch., Oak Park, Ill., 1993-98. Recipient Lyman award Am. Assn. of Colls. of Pharmacy, 1994. Office: Midwestern Uo 555 31st St Downers Grove IL 60515-1235 E-mail: nfjort@midwestern.edu.

FLACK, MIGNON SCOTT-PALMER, elementary educator; b. Silver Spring, Md., July 09; d. Lawrence Henry and Dorothy Elizabeth (Still) Scott; m. Harley Eugene Flack; children: Oliver S. Palmer II, Michael Scott Palmer; stepchildren: Harley E. II, Christopher F.; m. Frank W. Hale Jr., July, 2003. BS, D.C. Tchrs. Coll., 1966; MS, Johns Hopkins U., 1977. Cert. tchr., Md. Elem. tchr. D.C. Pub. Schs., Washington, 1968-71; dir. Home Day Care Ctr., Columbia, Md., 1973-77; from elem. tchr. to resource tchr. gifted and talented Howard County Pub. Schs., Columbia, Md., 1977-90; elem. tchr. Cherry Hill (N.J.) Pub. Schs., 1990-94. Lang. arts rep. Howard County Pub. Schs., Columbia, 1977-86, student tchr. coord., 1984-90, tchr. recruiter, 1986-90; cons., tutor Village Reading Ctr., Columbia, 1986-90. Bd. trustees Children's Mus. Dayton, Ohio, 1995—, Opera Guild Dayton, 1995—, Muse Machine, Dayton, 1995—, Dayton Mus. Natural History, 1996; planning com. Centennial Flight-Yr. 2003, 1995—; first lady of Wright State U., Dayton. Recipient Cmty. Svc. award United Way Ctrl. Md., 1982; named Outstanding Supt., Breath of Life Ch., 1981, First Lady of Wright State U., 1994-98. Mem. AAUW, Nat. Assn. State U. and Land Grant Colls., Am. Assn. State Colls. and U., Wright State Orgn. for Women, Phi Delta Kappa, Alpha Lambda Delta. Avocations: reading, travel, music, cooking, entertaining. Home: 9222 Snow Shoe Ln Columbia MD 21045-1826

FLAGAN, RICHARD CHARLES, chemical engineering educator; b. Spokane, Wash., June 12, 1947; s. Robert and Frances F.; m. Aulikki Pekkala, Aug. 4, 1979; children: Mikko, Suvi, Taru. BME, U. Mich., 1969; MME, MIT, 1971, PhDME, 1973. Research assoc. MIT, Cambridge, 1973-75; from asst. prof. environ. engring. sci. to Irma and Ross McCollum prof. Chem. Engring. Calif. Inst. Tech., Pasadena, 1975—2000, Irma and Ross McCollum prof. Chem. Engring., 2000—. Exec. officer chem. engring. Calif. Inst. Tech., Pasadena, 1996, 97; vis. prof. Helsinki U. Tech., 1987. Assoc. editor Aerosol Sci. and Tech.; editor-in-chief Aerosol Sci. and Tech., 2003—. Mem. AIChE (Thomas Baron award in fluid particle sys. 1997), Am. Assn. Aerosol Rsch. (pres. 1996-97, Sinclair award 1993), Gesellschaft fur Aerosolforschung (Smoluchowski award 1990). Office: Calif Inst of Tech Dept Chem Engring Pasadena CA 91125-0001

FLAGG, E(LOISE) ALMA WILLIAMS, educational administrator; b. City Point, Va., Sept. 16, 1918; d. Hannibal Greene and Caroline Ethel (Moody) Williams; m. J. Thomas Flagg, Jr., June 24, 1942 (dec. Apr. 1994); children: Thomas L., Lois Luisa. BS, Newark State Coll., 1940, LittD (hon.), 1968; MA, Montclair (N.J.) State Coll., 1943; EdD, Columbia U., 1955. Tchr., Washington, 1941-43; with Newark Pub. Schs., 1943-83, vice-prin., 1963-64, prin., 1964-67, asst. supt., 1967-78, dir., 1978-83; bd. dirs. Krueger-Scott Mansion Cultural Ctr., Share-N.J., v.p., 1996—; cons. edn., 1972—; adj. instr., spkr. in field, poet-in-residence various pub. schs. Author: (poetry) Lines and Colors, 1979, Feelings, Lines, Colors, 1980, Twenty More with Thought and Feeling, 1981, Lines, Colors, and More, 1998; editor: Cardiac Valve Bioprosthesis. Mem. Newark Bicentennial Commn. Recipient various profl. awards; E. Alma Flagg Sch. erected, 1984; E. Alma Flagg Scholarship Fund established, 1984. Mem. NAACP (life), LWV (pres. Newark 1982-84), AAUW, N.J. Hist. Soc., Nat. Assn. Negro Bus. and Profl. Women's Clubs (Truth award, 1985) Nat. Alliance Black Sch. Educators, Nat. Coun. Negro Women (life), Newark Sr. Citizen's Commn. (editl. cons. 1989—), Alpha Kappa Alpha (life), Kappa Delta Pi. Presbyterian. Home: 67 Vaughan Dr Newark NJ 07103-3470

FLAKE, LEONE ELIZABETH, special education educator; b. New Orleans, Jan. 12, 1938; d. Alfred Charles and Ione (Mills) Ittmann; m. Allen Oliver Flake, July 25, 1959; children: Diana Lee, Alan Mark, Wendy Lynn. BA, St. Mary's Dominican, New Orleans, 1973; MEd, U. New Orleans, 1979, postgrad., 1980. Cert. elem. tchr., learning disabled, social maladjusted, emotionally disturbed, kindergarten, mild moderate, severe profound, computer literacy, La. Tchr. grade 2 Jefferson Parish Sch. Board, Metairie, La., 1973-74, tchr. grade 3, 1974-75, tchr. grade 1, 1975-79, spl. edn. tchr. emotionally disturbed, 1979-87, generic tchr., spl. edn., 1987—, spl. edn. tchr., exptl. tchr., 1991—. Substitute prin. Marie Riviere Elem., Metairie, 1992—. Spl. edn. chair, Marie Riviere Elem., 1987—, sch. rep., 1987—, sch. dir. very spl. arts., 1987—, spl. needs tchr., 1991—, elem. discipline com., 1987—, sch. bld. level com. for project read, 1992—, elem. safety com., 1987—, sch. effectiveness action plan com., 1987—, sch. bldg. level com., 1987—, spl. program to upgrade reading task force, 1984-85; counselor, At Risk Students for Project Charlie, 1991—. Recipient cert. of Merit Jefferson Parish Coun. Of Charitable Involvement, 1985, Jefferson Parish key to the City, 1985, Appreciation cert. Coun. for Exceptional Children, 1991, Outstanding Tchr. award Am. Petroleum Inst., 1992-93. Mem. The Orton Dyslecic Soc., Internat. Reading Assn., La. Reading Assn., Coun. for Exceptional Children, Children Adults with Attention Deficit Disorders, J.C. Ellis Coop. Club (v.p. 1984-84), Phi Delta Kappa, Kappa Delta Pi, Beta Sigma Phi (internat. mem, preceptor 1973—), Avocations: travel, painting, reading. Home: 3701 Wanda Lynn Dr Metairie LA 70002-4523

FLAKS, J. MARGOT, retired elementary school educator; b. Phila. d. Benjamin Charles and Frances (Lupu) Hoffman; m. Joel G. Flaks, Dec. 24, 1961; children: Sarah Elise, Judith Alison. BS, Temple U., 1953, MS in Edn., 1958; postgrad. in Am. Studies, U. Pa. Cert. tchr., Pa. Tchr. Sch. Dist. Phila., 1953—2002, ret., 2002. Curriculum cons. Sch. Dist. Phila., 1990-91, Jewish Childrens Sch., Phila., 1980-88; tchr., mentor Sch. Dist. Phila., 1989—; cons. Pa. Geography Alliance, 1992-98; building rep. Phila. Fedn. Tchrs., Phila., 1987-89, 92-93, instructional support tchr., test coord., 1997-98. V.p., bd. dirs. Merion (Pa.) Civic Assn., 1987—; active Lower Merion Conservancy; rschr. Marian Civic Assn. PATHS fellow, 1988, Pa. Geography fellow Pa. Geography Alliance, 1992. Mem.: Cure Assn. (v.p. 2001—), Merion Hist. Soc. Democrat. Avocations: gardening, reading, concerts, theatre, cooking.

FLAM, BERNARD VINCENT, retired secondary education educator; b. Bronx, N.Y., June 6, 1945; s. Abraham and Anna (Aptowitzer) F.; m. Lydia Esther Nieves, June 7, 1969 (div. Sept. 1989); children: Rachel, Elliot. BS in Psychology, CCNY, 1969. Registered jr. high sch. math. tchr., N.Y.C. Actuarial clk. Nat. Health & Welfare, N.Y.C., 1968-69; tchr. math. Intermediate Sch. 52X, Bronx, 1969-75, Intermediate Sch. 192X, Bronx, 1975—2002. Pres. Stratford Ave. Block Assn., Bronx, 1969-71; sec. Throgs Neck-Soundview Mental Health Ctr., Bronx, 1970; mem. 801 Bronx River Rd. Coop Bd., 2001-03. Recognized as Inspirational Tchr. Fordham Prep. Sch., 1995. Mem. United Fedn. Tchrs. (chpt. chmn. Intermediate Sch. 192X 1992-94), Am. Fedn. Tchrs. Jewish. Avocations: running (finished N.Y.C. marathon 1987), flood relief (St. Louis 1993), opera, rock and roll, supporting homeless shelter in N.Y.C. Home: 811 Bronx River Rd Bronxville NY 10708-8020

FLAMING, IRETHA MAE, elementary education educator; b. Goodwell, Okla., Oct. 30, 1935; d. Loren Sherman and Irene (Fry) Flanagan; m. Kenneth G. Flaming, June 9, 1957; 1 child, Kyelene. BS, Panhandle State U., 1957; MS, Okla. State U., 1961. Cert. tchr., Kans. Classroom tchr. Guymon Pub. Schs., 1957-58, Boise City (Okla.) Pub. Schs., 1958-60; media specialist Holly (Colo.) Pub. Schs., 1961-66, Unified Sch. Dist. 490, El Dorado, Kans., 1966-70, 74—. Mem. NEA, ASCD, Kans. Edn. Assn., El Dorado Edn. Assn., Kans. Assn. Sch. Librs., AAUW, Aux. Gideons Internat., Lambda Sigma Tau (life). Home: 2430 Country Club Rd El Dorado KS 67042-4124 Office: El Dorado Pub Schs #490 1518 W 6th Ave El Dorado KS 67042-1425

FLANAGAN, ANNE PATRICIA, art educator, artist; b. Methuen, Mass., Jan. 26, 1927; d. John Joseph and Kathryn Josephine (Conley) Kane; m. Robert William Flanagan, Dec. 27, 1951; children: Robert W. Jr., Kathryn A., Joan Marie. B in Music Edn., Boston U., 1948; BFA, U. N.H., 1982. Cert. tchr. Mass. Supr. music Town of Middetown, R.I., 1948-50; asst. supr. music Towns of Littleton, Harvard and Stow, Mass., 1951-52; adj. therapist music Bayberry Psychiat. Hosp., Hampton, Va., 1973-74; relief mgr. Fidelity House, Lawrence, Mass., 1979-82, asst. mgr., 1982; instr. oil painting Adult Edn. Program, Derry, N.H., 1984-86; art tchr., dept. chair St. Joseph's Regional Sch., Salem, N.H., 1989—. Charter mem. Alley Art Gallery, Portsmouth, N.H., 1982-84; mem. Art Group Gallery, Manchester, N.H., 1988-91. Exhibited works in numerous one-woman and group shows including Art Group Gallery, 1989, 88, Newburyport (Mass.) Art Assn., 1987 (1st prize), St. Matthew's Art Show, Windham, N.H., 1985 (1st prize), Alley Gallery, 1983-84, U. N.H., 1982. Vol. art tchr. St. Joseph's Regional Sch., Salem, 1989-91; vol. Korean Orphange, Seoul, 1966-67; vol. tchr. artistically gifted children after sch. program St. Joseph Regional Sch., 1991-94; tchr. art sr. citizens group Royal Crest, Andover, Mass., 1983-84; tchr. developmentally retarded adults Fidelity House, 1979-82. Recipient cert. of achievement Republic of Korea, Seoul, 1967, cert. of appreciation U.S. Army, 1976. Roman Catholic. Avocations: painting, sculpting, traveling, cooking. Home: 138 Shadow Lake Rd Salem NH 03079-1438 Office: St Josephs Regional Sch 40 Main St Salem NH 03079-1923

FLANAGAN, CLYDE HARVEY, JR., psychiatrist, psychoanalyst, educator; b. Louellen, Ky., Aug. 21, 1939; s. Clyde H. Sr. and Ruby M. Flanagan; m. Gloria Kay Glymph, June 1, 1961 (div. Feb. 1974); children: Clyde H. III, Christopher Shane; m. Carol Anne Ross, Apr. 13, 1974; children: Patrick Ross, Colleen Helen. BS, Maryville Coll., 1962; MD, U. Tenn. Med. Unit, Memphis, 1966. Cert. Am. Bd. Psychiatry and Neurology in Adult, Child, Adolescent Psychiatry; diplomate Nat. Bd. Med. Commd. 2d lt. U.S. Army, 1965, advanced through grades to col. MC, 1980; rotating med. intern U.S. Army Tripler Gen. Hosp., Honolulu, 1966-67; gen. psychiatry resident U.S. Army Walter Reed Gen. Hosp, Washington, 1967-69, child psychiatry resident, 1969-71; asst. chief child guidance svc. Walter Reed Army Med. Ctr., Washington, 1971-80; chief cmty. mental health activity Ft. Belvoir, Va., 1980-86; asst. head tri-svc. alcohol rehab. dept. Nat. Navy Hosp., Bethesda, Md., 1986-88, ret., 1988; dir. gen. psychiat. residency program W.S. Hall Psychiat. Inst., Columbia, S.C., 1988-92; prof. psychiatry dept. of psychiatry/behavioral sci. Sch. Medicine U. S.C., Columbia, 1988—, dir. divsn. psychoanalysis dept. psychiat./behavioral sci., 1992—. Candidate in psychoanalysis Washington Psychoanalytic Inst., 1978-88; tng. and supervising analyst U. N.C./Duke PSA Ednl. Program, Chapel Hill, 1991—. Contbr. chpt. to books in field. Recipient Tchr. Yr. award Resident's Gen. Psychiat. Rsch. Program William S. Hall Psychiat. Inst., 1995, Spl. Alumni citation Maryville Coll., 2000. Fellow Am. Psychiat. Assn. (disting. life fellow), Am. Coll. Psychiatrists (com. pub. edn. 1998-99, Laughlin fellow selection com. 2000-03, membership devel. com. 2003—), Am. Acad. Child and Adolescent Psychiatry (Franklin Robinson award 1975); mem. Am. Psychoanalytic Assn. (councilor 1989—, cert. in adult, adolescent, and child psychoanalysis Bd. Profl. Stds. 1991), N.C. Psychoanalytic Soc. (councilor 1989-98), S.C. Psychiat. Soc. (membership chmn. 1991—), Am. Group Psychotherapy Assn. (founder, cert. group psychotherapist), Internat. Psychoanalytic Assn., Am. Assn. Child Psychoanalysis. Avocations: fishing, boating. Office: U SC Sch Medicine Dept Neuropsychiatry 3555 Harden Street Ext Ste 104A Columbia SC 29203-6894

FLANAGAN, JAMES HENRY, JR., lawyer, writer, business educator; b. San Francisco, Sept. 11, 1934; s. James Henry Sr. and Mary Patricia (Gleason) F.; m. Charlotte Anne Nevins, June 11, 1960; children: Nancy, Christopher, Christina, Alexis, Victoria, Grace. AB in Polit. Sci., Stanford U., 1956, JD, 1961. Bar: Calif. 1962, U.S. Dist. Ct. (no. dist.) Calif. 1962, U.S. Ct. Appeals (9th cir.) 1962, U.S. Dist. Co. (so. dist.) Calif. 1964, U.S. Dist. Ct. (ea. dist.) Calif. 1967, Oreg. 1984. Assoc. Creede, Dawson & McElrath, Fresno, Calif., 1962-64; ptnr. Pettitt, Blumberg & Sherr and successor firms, Fresno, 1964-75; pvt. practice, Clovis, Calif., 1975—92, North Fork, Calif., 1992-98; counsel for Standing Chpt. 13 Trustee, 2003—. Instr. Humprey's Coll. Law, Fresno, 1964-69; instr. bus. Calif. State U., Fresno, 1986—; instr. MBA program Coll. of Notre Dame, Belmont, 1990-91; instr. Nat. U., 1991—, Emerson Inst., 1998—; judge pro tem Fresno County Superior Ct., 1974-77; gen. counsel Kings River Water Assn., 1976-79; founder, CEO Bus. and Non-profit Devel. Ctr. Author: California Water District Laws, 1962; columnist. Choir mem. Our Lady of Sierra, 1998—; exec. com. parish coun. St. Helen's Ch., 1982-85, chmn. exec. com., 1985; pres. parish coun. St. John's Cathedral, 1974-82; pres. bd. dirs. 3d Floor Ctrl. Calif.; bd. dirs. Fresno Facts Found., 1969-70, Fresno Dance Repertory Assn., St. Anthony's Retreat Ctr., Three Rivers, Calif.; sec. Coarsegold Resource Conservation Dist.; co-founder Clovis Big Dry Creek Hist. Soc.; chmn. Sierra Vista Nat. Scenic Byway Assn.; judge advocate Mountain Detachment, Marine Corps League. Recipient President award Fresno Jaycees, 1964. Mem. Calif. Bar Assn., Fresno County Bar Assn., Calif. Trial Lawyers Assn. (chpt. pres. 1975, 83, state bd. govs. 1990-94), Fresno Trial Lawyers Assn., Am. Arbitration Assn., Stanford Alumni Assn. (life, svc. award), Fresno Region Stanford Club (pres. 1979-80), Celtic Cultural Soc. Ctrl. Calif. (pres. 1977-78), Fresno County and City C. of C. (chmn. natural resources com. 1977-78), Clovis C. of C., North Fork C. of C. (pres. 1993-96, sec. 1998-2000, exec. dir. 2000—), Serra Club (pres. Fresno chpt. 1980-81, v.p. 1986-87), Rotary, Elks, KC (4th degree grand knight), Superchex, Western Assn. Chamber Exec. Republican. Roman Catholic. Avocations: writing, music, gardening, sailing, fishing. Office: PO Box 1555 North Fork CA 93643-1555 E-mail: jayflanagan@netptc.net.

FLANAGAN, JAMES LOTON, electrical engineer, researcher, engineering educator; BSEE, Miss. State U., 1948; SMEE, MIT, 1950, ScDEE, 1955; PhD (hon.), U. Madrid, 1992, U. Paris, 1996. Elec. engring. faculty Miss. State U., 1950-52; tech. staff Bell Labs., Murray Hill, N.J., 1957-61, head dept. speech and auditory rsch., 1961-67, head dept. acoustics rsch., 1967-85, dir. info. prins. rsch. lab., 1985-90; dir. ctr. for advanced info. processing Rutgers U., Piscataway, NJ, 1990—, v.p. for rsch. Piscataway, NJ, 1993—. Evaluation panel Nat. Bur. Standards/NRC, 1972—77; adv. panel on White House tapes U.S. Dist. Ct. for D.C., 1973—74; sci. adv. bd. Callier Center, U. Tex., Dallas, 1974—76; sci. adv. panel on voice comm. Nat. Security Agy., 1975—77. Author: Speech Analysis, Synthesis and Perception, 1972; contbr. articles to profl. jours. Recipient Disting. Svc. award in sci., Am. Speech and Hearing Assn., 1977, L.M. Ericsson Internat. prize in telecomms., 1985, Nat. Medal Sci., Nat. Medal Sci. Com., Pres. Clinton, 1996, N.J. R&D Coun. Sci. and Tech. medal, 2000; fellow, Marconi Internat., 1992. Fellow: IEEE (selection com. 1979—81, Edison medal 1986), Am. Acad. Arts and Scis., Acoustical Soc. Am. (assoc. editor Speech Comm. 1959—62, exec. coun. 1970—73, v.p. 1976—77, pres. 1978—79, Gold medal 1986); mem.: NAS (chmn. engring. sect. 1996—99), NAE, Acoustics, Speech and Signal Processing Soc. (v.p. 1967—68, pres. 1969—70, Achievement award 1970, Soc. award 1976), Eta Kappa Nu. Achievements include patents in field. Office: Rutgers U Advanced Info Processing Piscataway NJ 08854-8088 E-mail: jlf@caip.rutgers.edu.

FLANAGAN, JOAN MARIE, nursing educator, dean; b. Decatur, Ind., June 8, 1952; d. Donald Nicholas and Joan Claudette Rochstron (Schnippel) Minnich; m. Charles Michael Flanagan, Feb. 19, 1977 (div. Nov. 1991); children: Lyle, Erin, Kelsey. BS, Ball State U., 1976; MS, No. Ill. U., 1987. RN, Ill., Ind. Staff nurse surg. ICU Univ. Hosp., Indpls., 1976-77; asst. head nurse, staff nurse neonatal ICU Meml. Med. Ctr., Savannah, Ga., 1977-78; neonatal nurse educator Improved Pregnancy Outcome Grant, Savannah, 1978-79; maternal child educator St. Joseph's Hosp., Savannah, 1979-80; staff nurse obstetrics Sherman Hosp., Elgin, Ill., 1980-83; exec. dir. Well Child Conf., Elgin, 1983-87; ADN program supr., instr. Waubonsee C.C., Sugar Grove, Ill., 1987-94, assoc. dean for health and life scis., 1994-2000; preceptor coord. Rural Adult Nurse Practitioner Project, No. Ill. U., DeKalb, 2000—. Nursing instr. Elgin (Ill.) C.C., 1981-83. Author (booklet) Baby Care, 1979. Bd. dirs. Am. Cancer Soc., South Kane County, Ill., 1994—. Mem. Sigma Theta Tau. Roman Catholic. Avocations: reading, dancing. Office: Rural Adult Nurse Prac Project No Ill U Dekalb IL 60115 E-mail: j.flanagan@mchsi.com.

FLANAGAN, JOAN WHEAT (MAGGIE FLANAGAN), educational therapist; b. Covina, Calif., Feb. 3, 1941; d. George Stanley Wheat and Elizabeth Virginia (Wilde) von Brecht; m. Connell O'Brien Cowan, Sept. 1959 (div. 1971); children: Sean O'Brien Cowan, Coby Burke Cowan. BA in English, Fontbonne Coll., 1985, teaching cert., 1987. Cert. secondary tchr., Mo. Counselor, instr. DeNovo Ctr., St. Louis, 1982-83; tchr., counselor Logos High Sch., Olivette, Mo., 1987-88; ednl. coord. Care Unit Hosp., St. Louis, 1988-89; treatment coord. Luth. Hosp. New Beginnings, St. Louis, 1989-90; dir. Creative Learning and Counseling Ctr., University City, Mo., 1990—; ednl. cons. University City High Sch., 1992-96; English instr. Logos Sch., 1996-97; instr. Torah Prep, 1997—. Cons. University City Bd. Edn., 1992. Pres. Fair in the Square Com., University City, 1991—; bd. dirs. Drug Free Schs. and Communities Adv. Coun., University City, 1992—, Community Partnership for Prevention of Substance Abuse, 1992, CALOP, 1998—; receptionist/sec. U.S. Senate, L.A., 1972-73; vol. various Dem. campaigns, L.A. and St. Louis, 1972-92. Mem. AAUW, Women's Consortium St. Louis, Optimist Internat. (pres. University City club 1992, 96-97, Community Svc. award 1992). Avocations: politics, civic involvement, writing. Home: 9322 Manchester Rd Saint Louis MO 63119-1450 Office: 9322 Manchester Rd Saint Louis MO 63119-1450

FLANAGAN, JUDY, special events professional, entertainment and marketing specialist, professional public speaker; b. Lubbock, Tex., Apr. 28, 1950; d. James Joseph II and Jean (Breckenridge) F. BS in Edn., Memphis State U., 1972; postgrad., Disney U., 1975-81, Valencia C.C., 1977-79, Rollins Coll., 1979; MS in Comm., U. Tenn., 2003. Cert. festival exec. Area/parade supr. Entertainment div. Walt Disney World, Orlando, Fla., 1972-81; parade dir. Gatlinburg (Tenn.) C. of C., 1981-85; entertainment prodn. mgr. The 1982 World's Fair, Knoxville, 1982; cons. Judy Flanagan Prodns./Spl. Events, Gatlinburg, 1982—, Miss U.S.A. Pageant, Knoxville, 1983; prodn. coord. Nashville Network, 1983; dir. sales River Terr. Resort, Gatlinburg, 1985-86; account exec. Park Vista Hotel, Gatlinburg, 1986-88; project coord. Universal Studios, Fla., 1988-90; dir. spl. events U. Tenn., Knoxville, 1990—. Dir. Neyland Stadium Expansion Dedication, 1996—; Vt. Bicentennial Events, 1994, 21st Century Campaign Major Events; prodn. mgr. 1984 World's Fair Parades and Spl. Events, New Orleans, Neil Sedaka rock video, Days of Our Lives daytime soap opera. Recipient Gatlinburg Homecoming award, 1986, World Lifetime Achievement award, 1993. Mem.: ASPCA, Tenn. Festivals and Events Assn. (bd. dirs.), Internat. Festivals and Events Assn. (cert. festival exec., found. bd.), Internat. Spl. Events Soc., Doris Day Animal League, Defenders of Wildlife, Humane Soc. U.S., U. Tenn. Soc. Pres. Club. Roman Catholic. Home: 350 Bruce Rd Gatlinburg TN 37738-5612 E-mail: judy-flanagan@utk.edu.

FLANAGAN, ROBERT JOSEPH, economics educator; b. New Haven, Dec. 16, 1941; s. Russell Joseph and Anne (Macauley) F.; m. Susan Rae Mendelsohn, Aug. 23, 1986. BA, Yale U., 1963; MA, U. Calif., 1966, PhD, 1970. Economist U.S. Dept. Labor, Washington, 1963-64; asst. prof. labor econs. Grad. Sch. Bus. U. Chgo., 1969-75; assoc. prof. labor econs. Grad. Sch. Bus. Stanford (Calif.) U., 1975-86; sr. staff economist Coun. of Econ. Advisors, Washington, 1978-79; sr. fellow The Brookings Instn., Washington, 1983-84; prof. labor econs. Grad. Sch. Bus., Stanford (Calif.) U., 1987-92, Matsushita prof. internat. labor econs. and econ. policy, 1993—, assoc. dean, 1996-99. Cons. OECD, Paris, 1988, U.S. Civil Rights Commn., Washington, 1982-83, NOAA, Washington, 1981; vis. scholar IMF, 1994, Australian Nat. U., 1990, 2000. Author: Labor Relations and Litigation Explosion, 1987; (with others) Unionism, Economic Stabilization and Income Policy, 1982, Economics of the Employment Relationship, 1989, numerous others; contbr. articles to profl. jours. Mem. Am. Econs. Assn., Indls. Rels. Rsch. Assn., Soc. Labor Economists. Office: Stanford U Grad Sch Bus Palo Alto CA 94305

FLANAGAN, ROSEMARY, psychologist, educator; b. Bklyn., Jan. 13, 1956; d. Patrick W. and Angela (Lauro) F. BS, St. Francis Coll., Bklyn., 1976; MA, New Sch. for Social Rsch., 1980, Hofstra U., 1982, PhD, 1986; cert. advanced study, Queens Coll., 1989. Diplomate Am. Bd. Profl. Psychology; lic. psychologist, N.Y. Supr. labs. St. Francis Coll., Bklyn., 1977-81; psychologist West Hempstead (N.Y.) Union Free Sch. Dist., 1984-85, East Williston (N.Y.) Union Free Sch. Dist., 1985-86, Copiague (N.Y.) Union Free Sch. Dist., 1986-87, Baldwin (N.Y.) Union Free Sch. Dist., 1987—2002. Asst. prof. Hofstra U., Hempstead, N.Y., 1989-91, adj. assoc. prof., 2000-2002; asst. prof. St. John's U., Jamaica, N.Y., 1991-96, assoc. prof. 1996-2001; pvt. practice, Hempstead, 1988—; dir. MA program in sch. psychology Adelphi U., Garden City, N.Y., 2002—. Fellow Am. Acad. Sch. Psychology (pres. 2000-02), Am. Bd. Sch. Psychology (pres. 2003), Inst. Rational Emotive Therapy (assoc.), Soc. Personality Assessment; mem. APA, Assn. Advancement Behavior Therapy, N.Y. State Psychol. Assn. (pres. sch. psychology divsn. 1992-93, 2000, sch. psychology rep. to governing coun. 1996—), Nat. Assn. Sch. Psychologists, Nassau County Psychol. Assn., Nassau County Psychol. Svcs. Inst. (trustee), N.Y. Assn. Sch. Psychologists, Sch. Psychology Educators Coun. of N.Y. State Office: 7 Shepherd St Rockville Centre NY 11570-2247

FLANDERS, HENRY JACKSON, JR., religious studies educator; b. Malvern, Ark., Oct. 2, 1921; s. Henry Jackson and Mae (Hargis) F.; m. Tommie Lou Pardew, Apr. 19, 1944; children: Janet Flanders Mitchell, Jack III. BA, Baylor U., 1943; BD, So. Bapt. Theol. Sem., 1948, PhD, 1950. Ordained to ministry Bapt. Ch., 1941. Asst. prof., assoc. prof. Furman U., Greenville, S.C., 1950-55, prof., chaplain, chmn. dept. religion, 1955-62; pastor First Bapt. Ch., Waco, Tex., 1962-69; prof. religion Baylor U., Waco, Tex., 1969-92, chmn. dept., 1980-83. Chmn., trustee Golden Gate Bapt. Theol. Sem., Mill Valley, Calif., 1966-76; chaplain Tex. Ranger Commn., 1965—; mem. exec. com. Bapt. Gen. Conv. Tex., Dallas, 1966-68. Author: (with R.W. Crapps and D.A. Smith) People of the Convenant, 1963, 73, 88, 96; (with Bruce Cresson) Introduction to the Bible, 1973; TV spkr. Lessons for Living, WFBC-TV, 1957-62. Trustee Baylor U., Waco, Tex., 1964-68; trustee Hillcrest Bapt. Hosp., 1963-64; chmn. Heart of Tex. Red Cross, 1967-68; narrator Waco Cotton Palace Pageant, 1970-80; chaplain Tex. Aero Commn., 1986—; pastor emeritus First Bapt. Ch., Waco, 1987; mem. grievance oversight com. Tex. Bar, 1979-87. Served to 1st. lt. USAAC, 1943-45, ETO. Named disting. alumnus Baylor U., 1986; grantee Furman U., 1960; grantee Baylor U., 1977, 82 Mem. Assn. Bapt. Profs. Religion (pres. 1958-59), AAUP (chpt. pres. 1973), Soc. Bibl. Lit., Am. Acad. Religion, Inst. Antiquity and Christianity, Waco Bapt. Ministerial Assn. (pres. 1967-68) Lodges: Rotary; Shriners. Home: 3820 Chateau Ave Waco TX 76710-7102 Office: Baylor U Religion Dept Waco TX 76798

FLANIGAN, ANNETTE LIPSCOMB, secondary education educator; b. Gainesville, Ga., Apr. 22, 1945; d. Demory S. Sr. and Willie Mae (Jackson) Lipscomb; m. Everett Flanigan, Aug. 31, 1968; children: Kyle Yusef, Ryan Llyn, Asa Karl, Erika. BS, Howard U., 1968; MA in Edn., Olivet Nazarene U., 1987. Cert. chemistry, physics and gen. sci. tchr. grades 6-12, middle sch. phys. sci. and social sci. tchr., Ill. Rsch. scientist Washington U., St. Louis, 1968-69, Jewish Hosp./Children, St. Louis, 1969-70, Brookhaven Nat. Labs., L.I., 1971-72; educator, counselor sci. Title 7 Alternative Sch., Kankakee, Ill., 1974-76; dir. alternative sch. Cmty. Action Program, Kankakee, 1975-77; mgr. sales Mid-Hudson Tupperware, Peekskill, N.Y., 1981-83; educator biology and gen. sci. Kankakee (Ill.) Sch. Dist., 1987-88; educator Riverside Med. Ctr./Partial Hospitalization Program, Kankakee, 1988-90; life sci. educator/tchr. Kankakee (Ill.) Sch. Dist. 111 Jr. H.S., 1990—. Mem. Urban Rural Sch. Devel., Kankakee, 1976-77; leadership trainer Boy Scouts Am., Westchester-Putnam, N.Y., 1980-83; bd. dirs. Kankakee Pub. Libr., 1994—; Kankakee area cmty. adv. panel Henkel/Rohm & Haas, 1995—. Grantee traineeship program Ill. State Bd. Edn., Springfield, Ill., 1985. Mem. ASCD, Am. Assn. for the Advancement Sci., Nat. Sci. Tchrs. Assn., Nat. Middle Sch. Assn., Ill. Sci. Tchrs. Assn., Assn. Ill. Middle-Level Schs., Sigma Pi Sigma. Lutheran. Avocations: traveling, reading, stamp collecting, classical music, gardening. Home: 1290 S Lincoln Ave Kankakee IL 60901-5504 Office: Kankakee Jr HS 2250 E Crestwood St Kankakee IL 60901-2803

FLANNIGAN, SANDRA F. secondary education educator; b. Mt. Pleasant, Pa., Dec. 22, 1946; d. James and Esther Pauline (Jordan) F. BS in Edn., Taylor U., Upland, Ind., 1968. Tchr. English, Mentor (Ohio) High Sch., 1968-70; tchr. speech Glenbrook High Sch., Glenview, Ill., 1970-71; tchr. English, Batavia (Ill.) High Sch., 1971—, chair English dept., 1996—. Cons. Chgo. Area Writing Project, Evanston, 1979-81; dir. The Writing Exch., Lombard, Ill., 1987—. Editor, author: The Writing Exchange, 1987, Network, 1987-89. Chgo. Area Writing Project fellow, 1979, Christa McAuliffe Found. fellow/grantee, Washington, 1987, Nat. Humanities Ctr. fellow, Research Triangle Park, N.C., 1989, NEH Tchr.-Scholar fellow, 1992-93. Mem. Nat. Coun. Tchrs. English, Ill. Assn. Tchrs. English. Republican. Avocations: needlework crafts, travel, creative writing, attending plays and concerts. Home: 1342 S Finley Rd Apt 1P Lombard IL 60148-4321 Office: Batavia High Sch 1200 W Wilson St Batavia IL 60510-1628

FLATTÉ, STANLEY MARTIN, physicist, educator; b. Los Angeles, Dec. 2, 1940; s. Samuel and Henrietta (Edelstein) F.; m. Renelde Marie Demeure, June 26, 1966; children: Michael, Anne. BS, Calif. Inst. Tech., 1962; student, NYU, 1960-61; PhD, U. Calif.-Berkeley, 1966. Research particle physicist Lawrence Berkeley Lab., Calif., 1966-71; asst. prof. physics U. Calif.-Santa Cruz, 1971-73, assoc. prof., 1973-78, prof., 1978—; dir. Ctr. for Studies of Nonlinear Dynamics La Jolla Inst., 1982-86, dept. chmn., 1986-89. Cons. phys. oceanography and underwater sound U.S. Govt.; vis. researcher, Cern, Geneva, 1975, Scripps Inst. Oceanography, 1980, Cambridge U., Eng., 1981 Author: (with others) Sound Transmission Through a Fluctuating Ocean, 1979; contbr. (with others) articles profl. jours. Woodrow Wilson fellow, 1962; NSF fellow, 1962-66; Guggenheim Found. fellow, 1975 Fellow AAAS, Am. Phys. Soc., Acoustical Soc. Am., Optical Soc. Am.; mem. Am. Geophys. Union, Sigma Xi (pres. Santa Cruz chpt. 1999-2000). Achievements include discovery of cusp phenomenon in particle physics; developed methods for using sound and light waves to probe statis. atmosphere, ocean and earth processes. Office: Univ Calif Physics Dept Santa Cruz CA 95064 E-mail: sflatte@ucsc.edu.

FLATTMANN, ALAN RAYMOND, artist, educator; b. New Orleans, Aug. 6, 1946; s. Louis Eusabe and Julia Margaret (Kastner) Flattmann; m. Rebecca Regina Price, Oct. 6, 1972. Cert., John McCrady Art Sch., New Orleans, 1968. Tchr. John McCrady Art Sch., New Orleans, 1967—82; instr. painting workshops coll. and art socs., 1970—. Lectr., travel art tour leader Hellenic Arts Soc., New Orleans, 1987, Webster's World, Falls Church, Va., 1993—2003. Author: The Art of Pastel Painting, 1987; subject of book: The Poetic Realism of Alan Flattmann, 1981, Alan Flattmann's French Quarter Impressions, 2002; one-man shows include Lauren Rogers Mus. Art, Laurel, Miss., 1970, 1975, 1981, Okla. Arts Ctr., Oklahoma City, 1975, Bryant Galleries, New Orleans, Jackson, Birmingham, Atlanta, Palm Beach, 1975—, exhibited in group shows at Columbus Club, N.Y.C., 1981, Represented in permanent collections New Orleans Mus. Art, Miss. Mus. Art, Okla. Art Ctr., Lauren Rogers Mus. Art, Meriden Art Ctr., Longview Mus. Art, Ogden Mus. So. Art. Recipient Tchr. award, Am. Artist Art Masters, 1996; grantee Study, Elizabeth T. Greenshields Found., 1973; scholar, New Orleans Art Assn., 1964. Mem.: Southeastern Pastel Soc. (award 1993—96), Pastel Soc. Am. (award 1979, 1986, 1991, 1998, 2002), Degas Pastel Soc. (founder, pres. 1999—, award 1987—88, 1990, 1993—95, 1997—2000, 2002). Avocations: photography, travel. Office: 1202 Main St Apt A Madisonville LA 70447-9742 E-mail: art@alanflattmann.com.

FLEAGLE, ROBERT GUTHRIE, meteorologist, educator; b. Woodlawn, Md., Aug. 16, 1918; s. Benjamin Edward and Frances Taylor (Guthrie) F.; m. Marianne Diggs, Dec. 19, 1942; children: Robert Guthrie, John B. AB, Johns Hopkins U., 1940; MS, N.Y. U., 1944, PhD, 1949. Asst. prof. U. Wash., 1948-51, assoc. prof., 1951-56, prof., 1956-87, prof. emeritus, sr. fellow Joint Inst. Study of Atmosphere and Ocean, 1978—, chmn. dept. atmospheric scis., 1967-77. Cons. various businesses, instns., govt. agys.; staff specialist Office Sci. and Tech., Exec. Office of Pres., 1963-64; mem. com. on atmospheric scis. NAS, 1962-76, chmn., 1969-73; mem. panel on oceanography Pres.'s Sci. Adv. Com., 1965-66; mem. U.S. com. Global Atmospheric Rsch. Program, 1968-73;mem. adv. panel on meteorology NATO, 1970-73; chmn. adv. panel BOMAP, 1969-73; mem. assembly of math. and phys. scis. NAS, 1976-79. Author: (with J.A. Businger) An Introduction to Atmospheric Physics, 1963, 2d edit., 1980, Global Environmental Change: Interactions of Science, Policy, and Politics in the United States, 1994, Eyewitness: Evolution of the Atmospheric Sciences, 2001; editor: Weather Modification: Science and Public Policy, 1968, Weather Modification in the Public Interest, 1974; contbr. articles to sci. jours. Trustee Univ. Corp. for Atmospheric Research, 1970-78, chmn. bd., 1975-77, chmn. council mems., 1966-67, chmn. membership com., 1987-89. Served from pvt. to capt. AUS, 1942-46. NSF fellow Imperial Coll., London, 1958-59. Fellow AAAS (chmn. sect. atmospheric and hydrological scis. 1977-78), Am. Geophys. Union (pres. meteorol. sect. 1967-70), Am. Meteorol. Soc. (Meisinger award 1959, Cleveland Abbé award 1971, Brooks award 1985, commn. sci. and technol. activities 1965-69, council 1957-60, 73-76, 80-84, pres. 1981); mem. Sigma Xi. Home: 7858 56th Pl NE Seattle WA 98115-6331 Office: Dept of Atmospheric Scis U Washington Seattle WA 98195-0001

FLECHTNER, HARRY MARSHAL, law educator; b. Fostoria, Ohio, Apr. 8, 1951; s. August Marshal and Dorothy Mary (Reardon) F.; m. Joan Patricia Kammer, Aug. 5, 1978; children: Emily Lora, Andrew Robert. AB, Harvard U., 1973, AM, 1975, JD, 1981. Bar: D.C. 1981. Assoc. Wilmer Cutler and Pickering, Washington, 1981-84; asst. prof. law U. Pitts., 1984-88, assoc. prof. law, 1988-94, prof. law, 1994—. Faculty adviser Journal Law and Commerce Sch. Law U. Pitts., 1986—. Contbr. articles to profl. jours. Mem. ABA, Assn. Am. Law Schs., Am. Bankruptcy Inst. Office: U Pitts Sch of Law Pittsburgh PA 15260

FLEETWOOD, M. FREILE, psychiatrist, educator; b. Valparaiso, Chile, Nov. 20, 1915; d. Alfonso Larrea and Berta (Cordovez) Freile; children: Harvey Blake, Francis Freile. MD, U. Chile, 1941; PhD, Pedagogic Inst., Santiago, Chile, 1947; MD, U. of State of N.Y., 1950. Instr. biochemistry to asst. in pub. emergencies U. Chile, Santiago, 1937-41, resident in neurology at neurol. clinic, 1941-42, head of rsch. lab. in psychiatry, 1944-48; resident in psychiatry Henry Phipps Clinic, John Hopkins U., Balt., 1942-44; provisional asst. in psychiatry to out-patient psychiatrist N.Y. Hosp., N.Y.C., 1948-61; attending psychiatrist Gracie Square Hosp., N.Y.C., 1961—; clin. asst. prof. psychiatry Cornell Univ., N.Y. Hosp., N.Y.C., 1970-88, emeritus status, 1988—. Instr. psychiatry, Payne Whitney Clinic, Cornell U., N.Y. Hosp., N.Y.C., 1950-63; cons. Family Svc. of Patterson, N.J., 1955-56, East Harlem Project Community Svc. Soc., N.Y.C., 1960-61, Manhattan Family Svc. Ctr. Community Svc. Soc., N.Y.C., 1960-61; asst. psychiatrist NYU, U. Hosp., Bellevue Med. Ctr., N.Y.C., 1954, psychiatrist 1954-55, and others. Contbr. articles to profl. publs. Recipient Rockefeller Found. grantee, 1942-43, 43-44, 44-45, Sagin Fund grantee, 1952-53, Squibb Fund grant, 1952-53. Mem. AAAS, Med. Soc. State and County of N.Y., Am. Med. Soc. on Alcoholism and Other Drug Dependencies, Am. Psychiat. Assn. (N.Y. county dist. br.), N.Y. Acad. Sci., Spanish Am. Med. Soc., Pan Am. Med. Soc., N.Y. Soc. for Adolescent Psychiatry, The N.Y. County Review Orgn., Women's Med. Assn. N.Y., Am. Med. Women's Assn. Office: PO Box 1955 28 Central Ave Amagansett NY 11930 also: 69 W 83rd St New York NY 10024-5248

FLEETWOOD, MARY ANNIS, education association executive; b. Winfield, Ala., July 31, 1931; d. George A. and Martha Ann (Perry) Sullivan; m. Lewis N. Fleetwood, Aug. 19, 1950; children: Juanita, Dexter Lewis, Melanie Louise. Student, HCC Community Coll., 1973-80. Gen. office staff Able Rose Mercentile Co., Birmingham, Ala., 1949-51; with auditing dept. Bank for Savs. & Trusts, Birmingham, Ala., 1951; account receivables clk. I.W. Phillips, Tampa, Fla., 1972-77; account clk. Sch. Bd. Hill County, Tampa, Fla., 1980, office mgr., 1981-90. V.p. PTA, 1961-62; pres. Woman's Missionary Union, Birmingham, 1963-64. Mem. DAR, Nat. Inst. Govt. Purchasing (cert. profl. buyer). Baptist. Avocations: photography, genealogy, travel.

FLEISCHACKER, DONNA M. middle school educator; b. Atwood, Kans., Mar. 31, 1948; d. Math J. and Lorraine W. (Dankert) F.; m. Andreas Maheras, Apr. 21, 1991. BA, Kans. State U., 1970; MA, Ft. Hays State U., 1977. Tchr. 5th and 6th grades, Edson, Kans., 1970-71; tchr. phys. edn. and health Victoria, Kans., 1971-72, Unified Sch. Dist. 489, Hays, 1972—; master tchr. Kennedy Mid. Sch., Felten Mid. Sch., 2001—02. Coord. Jump Rope for Heart, Hays, 1979-91, Hoops for Heart, 1996—; deliverer Meals on Wheels, Hays, 1990; active Rep. campaign Gov. Hayden, Hays, Topeka, 1990. Named Kans. Phys. Edn. Tchr. of Yr., AAHPERD, 1985-86. Mem. NEA, Kans. Nat. Edn. Assn., Kans. Assn. Health and Phys. Edn. (mem. nominating com. 1989), Kans. Dept. Health, Govs. Coun. on Fitness (chairperson 1989), Phi Delta Kappa (pres. 1985, 89, $1000 stipend 1986). Lutheran. Avocations: travel, piloting, photography. Home: 305 E 20th St Hays KS 67601-3232 Office: Unified Sch Dist #489 1309 Fort St Hays KS 67601-3742

FLEISCHAUER, JOHN FREDERICK, retired English language educator, administrator; b. Dayton, Ohio, Apr. 29, 1939; s. Paul J. and Ruth (Hedgecock) F.; m. Janet Elaine Patterson, June 17, 1961; children: John Eric, Marc Lawrence, Scott Christopher. BA, Cornell U., 1961; MA, Ohio State U., 1966; PhD, 1970. Tchg. fellow Denison U., 1968-69; asst. prof. English Ohio U., Athens, 1970-74; dir. 100-level English, 1973-74; div. chmn., prof. English Columbus (Ga.) State U., 1974-81; dean coll. Coll. Mt. Union Coll., 1981-87; dean liberal arts Edinboro U., Pa., 1987-88; provost, v.p. acad. affairs, 1989-95; acting pres., 1990-91; provost, v.p. acad. and student affairs, 1995; provost Wright State U., 1995-98; spl. asst. to pres., 1998-99; ret., 1999. Cons., lectr. bus. communications, humanities, acad. adminstrn., strategic planning, academic standards, 1975—; moderator Northwest Pa. Health Care Cost Summit, 1993—; co-writer academic grants, 1981—; chair Nat. Aerospace Conf., 1997-98. Author: Writing Skills, 1978; contbr. articles to profl. jours. Served with USN, 1961-65. Rsch. grantee Ohio U., 1973, grantee NEH, 1978. Mem. SOCHE (chair trustees), Am. Assn. State Colls. and Univs., Middle States Assn. (evaluator), Dayton Art Inst. (trustee), Alliance for Edn. (trustee), Ohio Humanities Coun. (scholar), Kiwanis Internat. (dir.). Methodist. Avocations: choral music, canoeing, art.

FLEISCHER, CYNTHIA SILVERMAN, special education educator; b. Chgo., May 6, 1951; d. Herbert Sanford and Francine Patricia (Leeb) Silverman; m. Cary Steven Fleischer, June 3, 1973; 1 child, Holly Anne. BA, Washington U., St. Louis, 1973; MA, Northwestern U., 1974; cert. advanced study, Nat.-Louis U., Evanston, Ill., 1992. Cert. in elem. edn., early childhood edn., learning disabilities, behavioral disorders, gen. adminstv. and supervisory, Ill. Spl. edn. tchr. Julia Molloy Edn. Ctr., Morton Grove, Ill., 1974-79; dir., tchr. St. Elisabeth's Nursery Sch., Glencoe, Ill., 1984-85, 86-87; coord. Hillel Torah North Suburban Day Sch., Skokie, Ill., 1987-90; spl. edn. tchr. Sch. Dist. 29, Northfield, Ill., 1991—. At risk cons. Hillel Torah North Suburban Day Sch., 1990-91. Bd. dirs., mem.-at-large assoc. bd. Chgo. Lighthouse for the Blind, 1988-94; bd. dirs. PTO, Deerfield, 1987-92; adult literacy vol. Mem. ASCD, Orton Dyslexia Soc., Phi Beta Kappa. Avocations: gardening, reading. Office: Sch Dist 29 525 Sunset Ridge Rd Northfield IL 60093-1025

FLEISCHER, JOHN RICHARD, retired secondary education educator; b. Milw., Mar. 7, 1934; s. Ernest William and Ruth Ida (Braun) F.; m. Barbara Ann Seidel, June 11, 1955; children: Lisa (dec.), Kurt Richard. BS in Art Edn., U. Wis., Milw., 1960. Cert. art tchr., Wis. Art tchr. Kenosha (Wis.) Pub. Schs., 1960-62, Westosha High Sch., Salem, Wis., 1963-94; ret., 1994. Art instr. adult classes Gateway Tech. Inst., Kenosha County, 1970-74, Kenosha Pub. Mus., 1961-62; speaker various community groups, S.E. Wis., 1960—; judge art shows, 1960—. Exhibited in group shows at Nat. Air and Space Mus., 1984, The Exptl. Aircraft Assn., 1980-86. With U.S. Army, 1957-59. Mem. NEA, Wis. Edn. Assn., Salem Cen. Edn. Assn. (pres. 1974-75), Lions Club of Greater Kenosha, Internat. Assn. Lions (dist. gov. 1978-79, Gov. award 1979), Westosha Lions Club (pres. 1973-74, Pres. award 1974). Avocations: painting, gardening, military collectables, travel. Home: 210 Walnut Rd Twin Lakes WI 53181-9367

FLEISCHER, REBECCA, federal agency administrator; Degree in Secondary Edn. cum laude, Ball State U. Chief of staff Greater Ednl. Opportunities Found., Indpls.; exec. assoc. dir. White House Office Mgmt. and Budget; dir. outreach and planning Office Innovation and Improvement U.S. Dept. Edn., Washington. Office: US Dept Edn 400 Maryland Ave SW Washington DC 20202*

FLEISCHMAN, KATHRYN AGNES, secondary education educator; b. Buffalo, Jan. 3, 1937; d. Charles Joseph and Catherine (Rydzynski) Baker; m. Jerome Joseph Fleischman, July 16, 1960. Student, Buffalo Sem., 1954; BA in Math., U. Buffalo, 1958; MS in Math., SUNY, Buffalo, 1964. Cert. secondary math. tchr., N.Y. Chmn. math. dept., tchr., enrichment coord. Amherst Cen. Schs., Snyder, N.Y., 1958-92; instr. Niagara C.C., Niagara Falls, N.Y., 1964-65. Cons. N.Y. State Edn. Dept., Bur. Math. Edn., 1962-64, 74, 84-86, Addison-Wesley Pubs., 1963-64; instr. U. SC Creative Retirement Ctr. Women's com. Buffalo Philharm. Orch. Soc., 1977-95, edn. com., 1986-90, bd. dirs., 1993-94; bd. dirs. World Hospitality Assn., 1987-88; active Encore Soc. Metropolitan Opera, N.Y.C., 1992—, Heritage Soc. Buffalo Seminary, 1992—, Women's Assn. Hilton Head Island, Women's Assn. Hilton Head Plantation, Low Key Piano, Scribblers. Jesse Ketchum scholar, 1950; recipient Citizenship award Am. Legion, 1950, George Washington medal Freedom Found. at Valley Forge, 1988. Mem. Assn. Math. Tchrs. of N.Y. State (pres. 1974-75, exec. com., speaker, coun., county chmn., corr. sec., rec. sec., 2d v.p., 1st v.p), Nat. Coun. Tchrs. of Math. (program com., speaker, nat. del. assembly, jour. referee, rep. to bd. govs. Mu Alpha Theta), Delta Kappa Gamma. Roman Catholic. Avocations: travel, piano, organ. Home: 15 Oyster Bay Pl Hilton Head Plantation Hilton Head Island SC 29926-2687

FLEISCHMANN, WILLIAM ROBERT, JR., microbiologist, educator; b. Balt., Oct. 16, 1944; s. William Robert Sr. and Margaret Mary (Finecey) F.; m. Christina Margaret Goetz, Aug. 20, 1966 (dec. Sept. 1996); 1 child, Kenneth Robert; m. Linda Carol Perkowski, Nov. 17, 2001. BS, Capital U., 1966; PhD, Purdue U., 1972. Asst. prof. Idaho State U., Pocatello, 1973-76; James W. McLaughlin postdoctoral fellow U. Tex. Med. Br., Galveston, 1976-77, asst. prof., 1977-80, assoc. prof., 1980-86, prof., 1986—, dir. grad. program, 1993-97, course dir. Pathobiology and Host Defenses, 1998—. Mem. editl. bd. Jour. Biol. Regulators and Homeostatic Agt., Milan, 1991—, Antiviral Rsch., Jour. Interferon and Cytokine Rsch., 1998—; contbr. articles to Jour. Gen. Virology, Jour. Interferon and Cytokine Rsch., Cancer Rsch., Antiviral Rsch., Jour. Biol. Resp. Modif., Jour. Interferon Rsch., Investigative Radiology, Jour. Immunology, Acta Medica Saliniana, Jour. Infectious Diseases, Jour. Immunology Methods, Molecular and Cellular Biology of Cytokines, Ednl. and Psychol. Rsch., among others. Recipient Grad. Student Orgn. Disting. Tchg. award, 1982, 90, Excellence in Edn. award Class of 1947, 2001, Continued Execllence in Tchg. award, 2002. Mem. Am. Soc. for Microbiology, Am. Soc. for Virology, Soc. for Exptl. Biology and Medicine, Internat. Soc. for Interferon Rsch., N.Y. Acad. Scis. Achievements include 6 patents for Methods and Compositions Employing Interferons. Office: Dept Microbiology and Immunology Univ Tex Med Br Galveston TX 77555-0001 E-mail: rfleisch@utmb.edu.

FLEISHER, PAUL, elementary education educator; BA, Brandeis U., 1970; MEd, Va. Commonwealth U., 1975. Tchr., coord. Providence Free Sch., 1970-72; tchr. corps intern Va. Commonwealth U., Richmond, 1973-75; 6th grade tchr. Petersburg (Va.) Pub. Schs., 1975-76, Williamsburg (Va.) Pub. Schs., 1976-78; tchr. programs for gifted Richmond Pub. Schs., 1978—, trainer computer programming and applications, 1983-85. Instr. div. continuing studies Va. Commonwealth U., 1981-86; instr. adult continuing studies U. Richmond, 1998—; adj. faculty Ctr. for Talented Youth, Johns Hopkins U., Balt., 1989-90; leader workshops in field. Author: Secrets of the Universe, 1987, Understanding the Vocabulary of the Nuclear Arms Race, 1988, Write Now!, 1989, (with Patricia Keeler) Looking Inside, 1991, Changing the World: A Handbook for Young Activists, 1992, The Master Violinmaker, 1993, Ecology A-Z, 1994, Our Oceans, 1995, Life Cycles of a Dozen Diverse Creatures, 1996, Webs of Life: Tide Pool, Coral Reef, Saguaro Cactus, Oak Tree, 1997, Brain Food: Games That Teach Kids to Think, 1997, Webs of Life: Salt Marsh, Pond, Alpine Meadow, Mountain

Stream, 1998, Tanglers Too, 1998, Gorilla, 2000, Secrets of the Universe, (5 vols.), 2001, ce Cream Treats: The Inside Scoop, 2001, Ants, 2002, 21st Century Writing, 2003; also computer software in field; contbr. articles to profl. jours.; editor: Va. Educators for Peace newsletter, 1982-86 Mem. adv. bd, Chespeake Bay Found. CLEAN, 1996—97; faculty advisor S.T.O.P. Nuclear War, 1982—86; bd. dirs. ACLU of Va., 2002—. Recipient Award for Peace and Internat. Rels., Va. Edn. Assn., 1988, Thomas Jefferson medal for outstanding contbns. to nat. sci. edn., Va. Mus. Nat. History, 1999; finalist R.E.B. awards for Teaching Excellence, 1995, Pub. Schs. Tchr. of Yr., Richmond, 1997. Mem. NEA (editor Peace Caucus News 1987-88), Va. Edn. Assn.(award for peace and internat. rels., 1988), Richmond Edn. Assn. (faculty rep., del. to convs., editor REAlworld and Actionline, 1980-85). Home: 2781 Beowulf Ct Richmond VA 23231-7366

FLEISHHACKER, DAVID, school administrator; b. San Francisco, May 30, 1937; s. Mortimer and Janet (Choynski) F.; m. Victoria Escamilla, Aug. 1965; children: William, Eleanor, Jeffrey. AB, Princeton U., 1959; MA, U. Calif., 1965. Tchr. Lick-Wilmerding High Sch., San Francisco, 1959-61, Peace Corps, Afghanistan, 1962-64, Marin Country Day Sch., Corte Madera, Calif., 1965, Town Sch., San Francisco, 1965-70; headmaster Katherine Delmar Burke Sch., San Francisco, 1970-95; ret.; interim head Hillbrook Sch., Los Gatos, 1997-98, South Peninsula Hebrew Day Sch., 1998-99. Pvt. ednl. cons. Author: (book) Lessons from Afghanistan, 2002; contbr. articles to profl. jours. Trustee Internat. Ho., Berkeley, Calif., 1987—95; pres. Fleishhacker Found., San Francisco, 1990—; bd. dirs. St. Joseph's Hosp./Queen of Angels, L.A., 1976—, San Francisco Youth Orch., 1981—, San Francisco Boys Chorus, 1997—, Educating Girls Globally, 2002—, Booker T. Washington Cmty. Ctr., 1995—. Mem. Nat. Assn. Prins. Schs. Girls. (bd. dirs. 1979-82), Elem. Sch. Heads Assn., Calif. Assn. Ind. Schs. (treas. 1978-81). Home: 3424 Jackson St San Francisco CA 94118-2021 E-mail: trampc@aol.com.

FLEMENBAUM, ABRAHAM, psychiatrist, educator; b. Cali, Colombia, Sept. 17, 1942; came to U.S., 1966; s. Moises R. and Ana (Safirstein) F.; m. Lily Gorenstein, Apr. 3, 1965 (div. Oct. 1988); children: Arieh M., Joel N., Judith S.; m. Elsa Slifstein, Aug. 1993. Pre-med. degree magna cum laude, U. Andes, 1960; MD, U. del Valle, Cali, 1964; MS, U. Minn., 1973; PhD in Psychopharmacology, 1974. Diplomate Am. Bd. Psychiatry and Neurology. Intern Univ. Hosp. Cali, 1964-65, Mt. Sinai-Chgo. Med. Sch., 1966-67; resident in psychiatry U. Minn., 1969-70, research fellow in psychiatry, 1970-73; asst. to assoc. prof. Tex. Tech U. Sch. Medicine, Lubbock, 1973-78; prof. La. State U., Shreveport, 1978-79; clin prof. psychiatry U. Miami, 1979-91; practice medicine specializing in psychiatry and psychopharmacology, Hallandale, Fla., 1980-88, Broward County, 1989—; mem. staff and chief unit 4B, VA Med. Ctr., Miami, 1979-88; bd. dirs. Hineni, Jewish Family Svcs. Recipient Alfredo Correa Henao Basic Sci. award U. Del Valle, 1962; William C. Menninger award Central Neuropsychiat. Assn., 1970. Fellow Am. Psychiat. Assn. (past pres. West Tex. chpt.); mem. Soc. Biol. Psychiatry, South Fla. Psychiat. Soc. Lodge: B'nai B'rith. Contbr. numerous articles to profl. jours. Office: 4900 W Oakland Park Blvd Fort Lauderdale FL 33313-7500 also: 1000 N Hiatus Rd Ste 160 Pembroke Pines FL 33026-3096

FLEMING, BLANCHE MILES, educational administrator; b. Salem, N.J., Nov. 4, 1918; d. William Alford and Mary Blanche (Cottman) Miles; m. Daniel Edward Fleming II, Apr. 12, 1952 (dec. Mar. 1970); 1 child, Daniel Edward III. BS, Del. U., 1939; MA, Columbia U., 1947; PhD, Union Grad. Sch., Yellow Springs, Ohio, 1976. Cert. profl. edn., Del.; lic. bus. cert., Del. Tchr. English Wilmington (Del.) Bd. Edn., prin. Bayard Jr. H.S., supr. social studies, intern to supt. of schs., 1974-75; coord. undergrads. Del. State U., Dover, 1971; exec. dir. Nat. Tchr. Corps U. Del., Newark, 1970-72; dir. secondary edn. Del. Bd. Edn., Wilmington, 1980-83; pres. B.M. Fleming & Assocs. Charter mem. Helping Hands Cmty. Svc., Inc., Wilmington, 1996—; bd. dirs. Common Cause of Del., Wilmington, 1984—, Housing Opportunity of No. Del., Wilmington, 1987—, Del. state adv. com. U.S. Commn. on Civil Rights, Washington, 1991—; chair housing com. LWV, Wilmington, 1997—. Recipient Legacy from Del. Women award Chesapeake Bay Girl Scouts, Wilmington, 1987. Mem. Nat. Assn. Univ. Women (pres. 1990-94, cert. of appreciation 1994), Wilmington Women in Bus. (bd. dirs. 1983-85), Delta Kappa Gamma Internat. (corr. sec. 1991-93), Phi Delta Kappa, Kappa Delta Pi, Pi Beta Lambda. Avocations: photography, painting, poetry. Office: Fleming & Assocs 2806 W 5th St Wilmington DE 19805-1824

FLEMING, CHRISTINA SAMUSSON, special education educator; b. Ft. Belvoir, Va., Dec. 20, 1950; d. Lewis Frew and Gayle Virginia (Pribnow) Samusson; m. Hal Alex Fleming, July 16, 1977; children: Hilary Anne, Alex Andrew. BS, Tex. Woman's U., 1972, MEd, 1974. Cert. tchr., Tex. Spl. edn. tchr. Richardson (Tex.) Ind. Sch. Dist., 1972-81; ednl. diagnostician Mental Health Mental Retardation, Plano, Tex., 1985-90; pre-kindegarten tchr. U. Gymnastics, Plano, 1987-90; spl. edn. tchr. Plano Ind. Sch. Dist., 1990—. Mem. spl. edn. task force Plano Ind. Sch. Dist., 1994-97; ednl. diagnostician Collin County Mental Health Mental Retardation, Plano, 1985-90; mem. Blue Ribbon Sch. Writing Team, 1996, 2000; master tchr. Tech. in Edn., 1998, mem. site based improvement coun., 1999—; math specialist TEXTEAMS, 2001—; Herman Method trainer, 2003—. Author: (manuals) Self Concept in the Primary Years, 1974, The Dick and Jane Guide to Paraeducators, 2002; (booklet) Heart to Heart: A Parent's Guide to Congenital Heart Disease, 1981. Exec. bd. Child Guidance Clinic, Plano, 1984-91, Shepard Elem. Sch. PTA, Plano, 1985-89, pres., 1987, life; exec. bd., founding mem. Heart to Heart, Dallas, 1980-86; leader Girl Scouts U.S.A., Tex., 1985-94; regional problem chair Destination Imagination, 2001--. Tech. in Edn. Fed. grantee, 1998, Plano Futures Found. grantee, 1998-99, 2002-03. Mem. Tex. Assn. Gifted and Talented, Richardson Learning Disabilities Assn. (exec. bd. 1974-87), Assn. Tex. Profl. Educators, Parent Tchr. Student Assn. (life), Destination Imagination (regional problem capt. 2001-). Republican. Methodist. Avocations: reading, creative problem solving. Home: 1217 Monterey Cir Plano TX 75075-7315 Office: Plano ISD Weatherford Elem 2941 Mollimar Dr Plano TX 75075-6306 E-mail: txfleming@comcast.net.

FLEMING, DONALD HARNISH, historian, educator; b. Hagerstown, Md., Aug. 7, 1923; s. Donald Harnish and Luciphene (Beery) F. AB, Johns Hopkins U., 1943; A.M., Harvard U., 1944, PhD, 1947. With Brown U., 1947-58, successively lectr., asst. prof., asso. prof., 1953-55, prof. history, 1955-58; prof. history of sci. Yale U., 1958-59; vis. prof. Harvard U., 1958-59, prof. history, 1959-70, Jonathan Trumbull prof. Am. history, 1970—. Dir. Charles Warren Center for Studies in Am. History, 1973-80 Author: John William Draper, 1950 (Beveridge prize Am. Hist. Assn.), William Henry Welch and the Rise of Modern Medicine, 1954; co-author: Glimpses of the Harvard Past, 1986; co-editor: Perspectives in American History, 1967-80, 85—, The Intellectual Migration: Europe and America, 1930-1960, 1969. Fellow Am. Acad. Arts and Scis.; mem. History of Sci. Soc., Antiquarian Soc.

FLEMING, JANE WILLIAMS, retired educator, writer; b. Bethlehem, Pa., May 26, 1926; d. James Robert and Marion Pauline (Melloy) Groman; m. George Elliott Williams, July 2, 1955 (div. July 1965); children: Rhett Dorman, Santee Stuart, Timothy Cooper; m. Jerome Thomas Fleming, Sept. 25, 1980 (dec. 2002). BS, UCLA, 1951; MA, Calif. State U., Long Beach, 1969. Tchr. San Diego Unified Sch Dist., 1951-55, Costa Mesa (Calif.) Sch. Dist., 1955-56, Long Beach (Calif.) Sch. Dist., 1956-58, 62-87, 90-92; ret. Author: Why Janey Can't Teach, 2001. Mem. Phi Kappa Phi, Ret. Tchrs. Assn., UCLA Alumni Assn., Planetary Soc. (charter), Mus. of Tolerance. Avocations: theater, travel. Address: PO Box 13053 Long Beach CA 90803-8053 E-mail: jwilli5687@aol.com.

FLEMING, JANELLE SMITH, gifted and talented education educator; b. Atlanta, Sept. 21, 1944; d. Rufus Herbert and Pauline Kirven (Bartlett) Smith; m. Arthur Taft Fleming, June 19, 1973. BA, Ga. State U., 1966; MEd, West Ga. Coll., 1972. Cert. secondary edn., gifted edn. and social studies tchr., Ga. Tchr. Babb Jr. High Sch., Forest Park, Ga., 1966-74, Mundy's Mill Jr. High Sch., Jonesboro, Ga., 1974-89; tchr., literary coord. Mt. Zion High Sch., Jonesboro, 1989—. Active Hist. Jonesboro-Clayton County, 1987—. Mem. Nat. Coun. Social Studies, Ga. Coun. Social Studies, Coun. for Exceptional Children, Phi Delta Kappa. Democrat. Baptist. Avocations: travel, reading, historical re-enactment. Home: 155 Planters Walk Locust Grove GA 30248-2809 Office: Mt Zion High Sch 2535 Mt Zion Pky Jonesboro GA 30236-2501

FLEMING, JANICE J. elementary education educator; b. Louisburg, N.C., June 30, 1940; d. William Bennett and Estelle Joyner; m. William Harrison Fleming, Mar. 7, 1959; children: Lynn Fleming Will, Angela Fleming Provost. BS, Radford Coll., 1972, MS, 1981. Kindergarten and elem. edn. tchr. Roanoke City (Va.) Sch. Bd., 1972-89; asst. prof. dept. edn. N.C. Wesleyan Coll., Rocky Mount, 1990—. Insvc. leader-coord. of "Farm" math. program, Roanoke City Schs. Mem. ASCD, Internat. Reading Assn., Assn. Tchr. Educators N.C., Nat. Assn. Edn. Young Children, Delta Kappa Gamma. Home: RR 3 Box 336 Whitakers NC 27891-9213

FLEMING, JEAN ANDERSON, adult and community education educator; b. Cleve., May 17, 1952; d. Evert Ludwig Walter and Martha Fay (Oehling) A. BA, Colo. State U., 1973, MEd, 1977; EdD, U. No. Colo., 1996. Coord. adult basic edn. Poudre Valley Schs. and Vols. Clearinghouse, Ft. Collins, Colo., 1975-80; tchr. trainer Colo. Dept. Edn., Denver, 1981-83, cons. spl. projects, 1993-95; instnl. mgr., exec. dir. Cmty. Tech. Skills Ctr., Denver, 1987-91; dir. workplace edn. program Arapahoe C.C., Denver, 1991-92; cons. adult edn., 1992-97; asst. prof. adult and cmty. edn. Ball State U., Muncie, Ind., 1997-00; vis. asst. prof. U. Tenn., 2000, asst. prof. mgmt., 2003—; asst. prof. grad. edn. Coll. of the S.W., Hobbs, N.Mex., 2000—03, dir. Ctr. for Ednl. Excellence, 2000—03. Dir. Commn. of Affiliate Orgns. of Am. Assns. for Adult and Continuing Edn., 1998—2001; mem. exec. bd. Commn. of Profls. of Adult Edn., 1999-2001, co-chmn. future directions com., 2001-02. Editor: New Perspectives on Designing and Implementing Effective Workshops, 1997; mem. editl. bd. Jour. Adult Edn. Mem. Colo. Assn. for Continuing Adult Edn. (treas., bd. dirs., pres. 1989-90, Disting. Leadership award 1983, 90, 94), Mountain Plains Adult Edn. Assn. (bd. dirs. 1988—, pres. 1996, cert. of appreciation 1990), Colo. Alliance for Lifelong Learning (chair 1994-96), Am. Assn. for Adult and Continuing Edn. (mem. found. task force 2003—). Avocations: reading, camping, travel, baking. E-mail: JeanColo@aol.com., jfleming@csw.edu.

FLEMING, SUSAN ELAINE, elementary school educator; b. West Chester, Pa., Apr. 11, 1954; d. Earl Alexander and Leah Edna (Crowle) Masteller; m. Kevin John Fleming, Aug. 13, 1988. BMus magna cum laude, U. Miami, 1976; MMus, West Chester U., 1984; MA in Edn. Adminstrn., Villanova U., 1990. Cert. elem tchr. and prin., Pa. Tchr. music Ridley Sch. Dist., Ridley Park, Pa., 1977-78, Sch. Dist. Lancaster, Pa., 1979—. Community rep. spl. edn. Solanco Sch. Dist., Quarryville, Pa., 1990-91; adminstrv. intern Donegal Sch. Dist., Mount Joy, Pa., 1991; action team mem. Sch. Dist. Lancaster, 1990-91. Citizen rep. for Providence Twp. Lancaster County Redevel. Authority, Quarryville, Pa., 1990. Mem. ASCD, Pa. Staff Devel. Coun., Lancaster Edn. Assn. (spl. svcs. chairperson), Music Educators Nat. Conf., Phi Kappa Phi. Avocations: walking, skiing, playing musical instruments, gardening, travel. Home: 10 Garvin Rd Denver PA 17517-9407 Office: Sch Dist Lancaster 225 W Orange St Lancaster PA 17603-3782

FLEMING, THOMAS A. former special education educator; Spl. asst. to the provost Ea. Mich. U., Ypsilanti, Mich. Named Tchr. of Yr. Mich., 1991, Nat. Tchr. of Yr., 1992. Office: Ea Mich U 106 Welch Hall Ypsilanti MI 48197-2214

FLEMMING, NAOMI VERNETA, elementary school educator; b. Las Vegas, Nev., Oct. 13, 1953; d. James Major and Mable Audrey (Mack) F. BS in Edn., U. Nev., 1976. Inventory clk. Woolco Dept. Stor, Las Vegas, 1969; student aide U.S. AEC, Las Vegas, 1971-75; telephone sales person Sears, Roebuck & Co., Las Vegas, 1973-74; clk., typist U.S. Energy, Rsch. and Devel. Adminstrn., Las Vegas, 1975-77; div. sec. U.S. Dept. Energy, Las Vegas, 1977-79; investigator U.S. Office Personnel Mgmt., Las Vegas, 1979-85; employment security specialist State of Nev., Las Vegas, 1988; counselor NutriSystem Weight Loss Ctr., Las Vegas, 1988-89; tchr. Mabel Hoggard Sixth Grade Ctr. (name now to Mabel Hoggard Math & Sci. Magnet Sch.), Las Vegas, 1988—; Title I reading tchr. Mabel Hoggard Math. and Sci. Magnet Sch., 1994—. Mem. black history program com. Mabel Hoggard Sch., Las Vegas, 1989-90, student coun. advisor, 1990-91, tchr. liaison Parent Tchr. Student Assn., 1991-92, mem. Martin Luther King Jr. parade com. 1991-92, Just Say No To Drugs Computer Club advisor, 1992-93; Hoggard Magnet sch. lang. arts rep., drill team sponsor, Clark County Sch. Dist. mentor, 1993-94, Hoggard Magnet Sch. Title I reading tchr., 1994—. Mem. Martin Luther King Jr. Parade Com., 1991-92; advisor Just Say No To Drugs Club, 1992-93; chairperson hospitality com. Am. Bus. Women's Assn., 1976-77; mem. women's adv. com. U.S. Energy, R&D Adminstrn., Las Vegas, 1976-78; facilitator, vol. Fully Alive Self-Help Ctr., 1992, 93-94. Mem. Las Vegas Alumnae chpt. Delta Sigma Theta (publicist 1976-78). Democrat. Avocations: aerobics, walking, self-help groups, owl collecting. Home: 1220 W Washington Ave Las Vegas NV 89106-3543 Office: Mabel Hoggard Math & Sci Magnet Sch 950 N Tonopah Dr Las Vegas NV 89106-1902

FLETCHER, BRADY JONES, vocational education career specialist; b. Natchitoches, La., Apr. 17, 1928; d. Louis Benjamin and Isadore Hannah (Stephens) Jones; m. Donald Greene Fletcher, Aug. 13, 1950; children: Donald Bruce, Nathan Louis, Debra Patrice. BA, Clark Coll., 1950; MA (fellow), Howard U., 1953; postgrad. (NDEA fellow), Ind. U., 1965; EdS in Guidance, George Washington U., 1967, EdD, 1977. Tchr. math. and sci. Fairmont Heights (Md.) High Sch., 1951-54; tchr. math. and sci. Douglas High Sch., Upper Marlboro, Md., 1955-57, Prince George's County (Md.) Pub. Schs., 1951-59, Banneker Jr. High Sch., Washington, 1959-63; chmn. guidance dept. Garnet/Patterson Jr. High Sch., 1963-67; counselor Lincoln Jr. High Sch., D.C. pub. schs., 1967-69, Kensington (Md.) Jr. High Sch., 1969-73, Banneker Jr. High Sch., 1975-77; career edn. specialist Montgomery County (Md.) Schs., 1973-75; counselor Frederic Douglass Middle Sch., Indpls., 1999—. Cons. Md. State Dept. Edn., 1973, Balt. City Pub. Schs., 1973, Balt. County Pub. Schs., 1973, D.C. Pub. Schs.; mem. adv. com. for spl. needs population Montgomery Coll., Rockville, Md., Am. Coll. Testing Bd., Washington, 1987—; project dir. InterAmerica Rsch. Assoc., Inc., Rosslyn, Va., 1977. Editor: Career Edn., 1973-75; Increasing Collaboration in Career Education (2 vols.). Rep. to Cmty. Action Bd. for Montgomery County Edn. Assn.; dir. D.C. Summer Youth Job Program, 1981; tech. cons., del. to Russia, Czech Republic and Poland with citizen amb. program People to People Internat., 1993. Inst. Ednl. Leadership fellow, summer 1984, Montgomery County Vocat. Assessment Ctr. (recipient dedicated service award 1987); recipient Educators award Clinton A.M.E. Ch., 1988, Multicultural Counseling award Founders of Orgn., 1987, award Montgomery County Coun., 1990; resolution in her honor Md. State Senate, 1990; Adminstr. of Yr. for I-Star Program, Ind. Say No to Drugs, 1994; named Alumnus of Yr. George Washington U., 1999, keynote spkr. opening conf. edn. and tech.; inducted into Hall of Fame, Englewood H.S., Chgo., 1999. Mem. AACD (Nat. award for govt. rels.), Am. Pers. and Guidance Assn. (Human Rels. Com. award 1974, editor conv. newsletter 1983), Am. Assn. Specialists in Group Work (nat. chairperson human rels. 1993, Recognition award 1993), Md. Pers. and Guidance Assn. (award 1975), Nat. Capital Pers. and Guidance Assn. (award 1975-76), Ind. Counseling Assn. (v.p. ctrl. chpt. 1992), Ind. Sch. Counselors Assn., Ind. Career Devel. Assn. (Ind. sch. counselor), Ind. Multicultural Assn., D.C. Assn. Counseling and Devel. (pres. 1986-87, del. to North Atlantic region assembly, recipient award disting. profl. leadership 1987, award for profl. devel. of assn. 1986, trustee 1988-89, co-chairperson govt. rels. com., Nat. awards Govt. Rels. Com. Boston 1989 and Cin. 1990), Nat. Vocat. Guidance Assn., Assn. Non-White Concerns, Nat. Assn. Career Edn., Nat. Sch. Counselor Assn., Internat. Platform Assn., Indpls. Urban League, Alpha Kappa Alpha, Phi Delta Kappa. Home: 7340 Steinmeier Dr Indianapolis IN 46250-2567 E-mail: dgflet1098@prodigy.net.

FLETCHER, CHARLES, secondary school educator; Instr. music dept. Fernley (Nev.) H.S. Mem. Nev. Commn. on Profl. Stds. in Edn., 1996—99. Recipient Marna Zachry award for disting. svc., Lyon County Edn. Assn., 1999. Mem.: No. Zone Nev. Music Educators Assn. (sec.-treas. 1989—99), Nat. Bd. for Profl. Tchg. Stds. (bd. mem.). Office: Fernley High Sch Music Dept 1300 Hwy 95A Fernley NV 89408*

FLETCHER, J. S. health educator; b. Hollister, Calif., Aug. 9, 1946; BSN, Calif. State U., Fresno, 1968, MS in Nursing, 1971; EdD, U. San Francisco, 1980. RN, Calif. Instr., chmn. div. Modesto Jr. Coll., Calif., 1973—83; staff nurse Scenic Gen. Hosp., 1983—90; prof. Calif. State U., Stanislaus, Turlock, 1983—, chair dept. physical edn. and health, 2002—. Co-Author: Essentials in Mental Health Nursing, 4d edit.; mng. editor peer rev. sect. CAHPERD Jour. Times, 1999-; bd. assoc. editors Am. Jour. Health Edn., 2002-. Pres. Mercer City Sch. Dist. Bd. Edn., 1995-96; pres. Merced County Sch. Bds. Assn., 1995-97. Mem. AAHPERD (v.p. Southwest Regional health divsn. 2002-2003), Calif. Nurses Assn. (pres. region 8 1992-94), Calif. Assn. for Health, Phys. Edn., Recreation and Dance (v.p. health divsn. 2000-).

FLETCHER, JOHN LYNN, psychology educator; b. Springdale, Ark., Apr. 18, 1925; s. Lynn Harrington and Elsie Irene (Jones) F.; m. Mary Lou Campbell, Aug. 21, 1949 (div. July 1974); children: Lynn Gray, Jana Lee. BA, U. Ark., 1950, MA, 1951; PhD, U. Ky., 1955. Commd. 2nd lt. U.S. Army, 1953, advanced through ranks to lt. col., 1968; chief audition br. Med. Rsch. Lab. Ft. Knox, Ky., 1953-70; ret. U.S. Army, 1970; prof. psychology Memphis State U., 1970-75; prof., dir. rsch. dept. otolaryngology U. Tenn. Ctr. for Health Sci., Memphis, 1975-81; prof., chair psychology dept. U. Mo., Rolla, 1981-87; lectr. psychology S.W. Tex. State U., San Marcos, 1987—. Cons. NASA Space Shuttle, Kennedy Space Ctr., 1972-76; mem. Commn. on Hearing and Bio Acoustics, 1956—. Editor: Effects of Noise on Animals, 1978; contbr. articles to profl. jours. Decorated Bronze Star. Fellow Acoustical Soc. Am., Am Speech, Lang. Hearing Soc.; mem. NAS, NRC, N.Y. Acad. Scis. (life), Human Factors Soc. Republican. Presbyterian. Achievements include patents for Acoustic Reflex Ear Defender. Home: PO Box 309 Martindale TX 78655-0309 Office: SW Tex State Univ Dept Psychology San Marcos TX 78666

FLETCHER, LAWRENCE FRANCIS, guidance counselor; b. Phila., June 9, 1946; s. Frank Louis and Lorraine Marie (Lawrence) F.; m. K. Star Yoham; children: Christopher Powell, Heather L., Michael L. BA, Villanova U., 1971, MA, 1973. Cmty. cons., counselor Sch. Dist. Phila., Pa., 1973-76; guidance counselor Delaware County Intermediate Unit, Media, Pa., 1976-83, Salesianum Sch., Wilmington, Del., 1983—, dir. guidance, 2003—. Poll watcher, Wilmington, 1992, poll greeter, 1994. Recipient 2d pl. Superstars in Edn., Del. State C. of C., 1994. Mem. ASCD, ACA, Del. State Counseling Assn., Coll. Bd. Avocations: reading, computers. Office: Salesianum Sch 1801 N Broom St Wilmington DE 19802-3891

FLETCHER, MARY BETH, reading specialist, educator; b. Miami, Fla., Oct. 12, 1949; d. James Richard and Elmira (Neal) Brooks; m. Howard Martin Fletcher, Jr., Sept. 5, 1971; 1 child, Sarah Lindsey. BA, U. Fla., 1971; MA, U. So. Fla., 1976; EdM, Harvard U., 1985, EdD, 1990. Cert. reading specialist, elem. tchr., early childhood educator. Tchr. Pinellas County Schs., 1971-72, Lake Trafford Elem., Immokalee, Fla., 1976-78, reading tchr., 1978-80; teaching fellow Harvard U., Grad. Sch. of Edn., Cambridge, Mass., 1984-85, instr. edn., 1988-90; lectr., reading supr. and cons. Lesley U. Grad. Sch., Cambridge, 1986; instr. in reading Lesley Coll. Grad. Sch., Cambridge, 1987—2003; reading specialist, chair dept. language arts Buckingham, Browne & Nichols Sch., Cambridge, 1989—2002; Lower Sch. Lang. dept. head The Carroll Sch., Lincoln, Mass., 2002—. Vol. Peace Corps, Afghanistan, 1972-74; sponsor for Afghan refugee family, 1982. Mem. Internat. Reading Assn., Internat. Dyslexia Assn., Mass. Reading Assn. (chmn. parents and reading com. 1988-90, chmn. scholarship com. 1991-92), Phi Kappa Phi, Phi Delta Kappa. Avocation: bird watching. Office: 25 Baker Bridge Rd Lincoln MA 01773

FLETCHER, MARY H. English language educator; b. Tehran, Iran, May 25, 1927; d. Ralph Cooper and Harriet T. (Thompson) Hutchison; m. Robert Fletcher (dec.); children: Edward John Clark, Elizabeth Clark Kendall, Lynn Clark Barbieri, Lori Clark Corrochano, Ralph Hutchison Clark; m. Wesley Moses Smith, 1969 (dec. 1993). BA, Wilson Coll., 1948; postgrad., U. Pa., 1948-49, Rollins Coll., 1963-65, Stetson U., 1973-74. Cert. tchr., Fla. Tchr. Leesburg (Fla.) Sr. H.S., 1963-68, 85-86, 90-91, Carver Heights Mid. Sch., 1968-84; English tutor Learning Lab. Lake Sumter C.C., 1991—. Co-author: (with Ann Meador) Saving Our Schools From the Religious Right The Lake County Florida Story, 1995. Dir. Fla. Fedn. Womens Clubs Dist. 5, 1955-57, 2d v.p., 1958; women's dir. Dale Carson Campaign Sheriff Duval County, 1956; elder New Life Presbyn. Ch., 1980-95; mem. Conservation Coun. Lake County, 1991-93, People for Mainstream Values, 1994-95; grad. Leadership Lake County, 1996; elected mem. Lake County Sch. Bd. Dist. 2, 1996. Mem. LWV (pres. 1991-93), Phi Delta Kappa. Republican. Avocations: writing, theatre. Home: 32423 Mabel Ln Leesburg FL 34788-3941 Office: Lake Sumter CC Learning Ctr Leesburg FL 34788

FLETCHER, PATRICE TOMASKY, special education educator; b. Euclid, Ohio, Aug. 19, 1958; d. George William and Margaret Louise (Zapotosky) Tomasky; m. Richard Jan Fletcher, Dec. 30, 1988. BA, W.Va. U., 1982; BS, California U. Pa., 1987; MS, Nova U., 1990. Cert. tchr., spl. edn. tchr., Pa., Mass., Fla., edn. leadership, Fla. Residential program worker Greene County Assn. Retarded Citizens, Waynesburg, Pa., 1985-87, Twin Trees, Inc., Connellsville, Pa., 1985-87; spl. edn. tchr. May Inst. Autistic Children, Chatham, Mass., 1987-88, Eckerd Youth Devel. Ctr., Okeechobee, Fla., 1988-90, Cypress Hammock Sch., Canal Point, Fla., 1990-92, Crestwood Mid., Royal Palm Beach, Fla., 1992-95, H.L. Johnson Elem. Sch., Royal Palm Beach, Fla., 1993—. Presenter workshops in field. Mem. Fla. Edn. Assn., Coun. Exceptional Children. Avocations: aerobics, camping, photography, travel.

FLETCHER, REGINA ROBERSON, school system administrator; b. Cartersville, Ga., Jan. 4, 1949; d. Walter and Emma Lois (Shaw) Roberson; 1 child, Bryan Walter. BA, Spelman Coll., 1971; MEd, Va. Commonwealth U., 1973; EdS, Ga. State U., 1990; EdD Candidate, Clark Atlanta U., 2003. Cert. elem. adminstr., supr.; cert. elem. tchr., Ga. Tchr. Richmond (Va.) Pub. Schs., 1971-76; tchr., instructional lead tchr., Chpt. I tchr. and coord. DeKalb County Schs., Decatur, Ga., 1976—. Fed. programs adminstr.; dir. Chpt. 1 Programs; dir. Title I Programs, state funded prekindergarten theme schs., 1999-2002, sr. advisor to Supt.'s Office, adminstrv. exec. asst. Author: (handbook) Text Wiseness. Mem. ASCD, Nat. Coun. Tchrs. Math., Ga. Compensatory Edn. Leaders (treas., pres.). Office: 3770 N Decatur Rd Decatur GA 30032-1005

FLETCHER, SARAH LEE, retired elementary school educator; b. Webb, Ala., May 7, 1925; d. James Harvey and Emma Freddie (Scarborough) Lee; m. Gaston Maurice Fletcher, June 24, 1948; children: S. Daphne, Lee Maurice, Timothy J. Student, Bob Jones Coll., 1943-44, assoc. bus. cert., 1947; student, Calhoun Coll., 1968-70, Troy State U., 1970-72; BRE, Bethany Theol. Seminary, 1995, MRE, 1996. With Atlanta and St. Andrews Bay Rwy. Co., 1944-46; sec. to pub. Dothan (Ala.) Eagle, 1947-48; tchr. Morgan County Schs., Decatur, Ala., 1967-69, Newton (Ala.) Pub. Schs., 1969-72, Trinity Christian Schs., Oxford, Ala., 1972-73, Berachah Christian Acadamy, Huntsville, Ala., 1973-75; sec. Dominion Textile, Yarmouth, Nova Scotia, 1975-76; tchr. Mueller Christian Sch., Miami, 1976-79, Berean Christian Sch., Dothan, 1979-86, Grace Bible Acad., Dothan, 1987-90, Clinton Christian Acad., Upper Marlboro, Md., 1990-91. Cons. Mary Kay Cosmetics, 1982-99. Author: To Love Again, 1996, Love in Bloom, 2001; compiler, contbg. author: (book of short stories) The Set of the Sails, 1997; contbr. articles to Christian papers and mags. Active in ch. Mem. Troy State U. Creative Writing Club, Dothan Creative Writing Group. Baptist. Avocations: helping the elderly, writing, walking, speaking. Home: 1119 Garden Ln Dothan AL 36301-3407

FLETCHER, SHERRYL ANN, higher education administrator; b. Wyandotte, Mich., July 1, 1956; d. Richard Charles and Pauline L. (Fisher) Seavitt; m. Alan Morris Fletcher, July 26, 1980; children: Christopher Richard, Cameron Morris. BA summa cum laude, Albion Coll., 1978; MA with honors, U. Mich., 1986. Elem. art tchr. East Grand Rapids (Mich.) Schs., 1978-80; asst. dean students, dir. student activities Northwood U., Midland, Mich., 1981-83; admissions counselor Office of Undergrad. Admissions, U. Mich., Ann Arbor, 1983-84, sr. admissions counselor, 1984-88, asst. dir. admissions, 1988-93, assoc. dir. admissions, 1993-95; exec. dir., founder Coll. Access for Rural Am., 1995—; sr. assoc. dir. Office of Undergrad. Admissions Johns Hopkins U., 1996—. Adminstrv. univ. liaison Cook Family Found., Mich., 1986—; speaker in field. Chair future planning Jr. League Ann Arbor, 1993-94, chair pub. rels., 1990-93; sustainer Jr. League Annapolis, 1995—; mem. David Hallissey scholarship com., Hightower Scholars, Inc., bd. trustees. Mem.: Potomac Chesapeake Assn. Coll. Admissions Counselors (chair conf. devel. 1997—98, membership chair 1998—, dir. selection mil. dependents scholarship selection com.), Mich. Assn. Coll. Admissions Counselors (state sec. 1992—), Nat. Assn. Coll. Admissions Counselors (nat. presdl. com. 1993, 1997), Alumnae Club Annapolis, Albion Coll. Shield Club, U. Mich. Alumni Club of Washington, Alpha Chi Omega. Methodist. Avocations: tennis, golf, watercolor painting, power walking, travel. Office: Johns Hopkins U Of Undgrad Adm 3400 N Charles St Baltimore MD 21218-2608

FLETCHER, SHIRLEY FAYE, counselor; b. Stilwell, Okla., Feb. 27, 1945; d. Roy Jefferson and Lillie Bernice (Doyle) Clinton; m. Jerry Dale Fletcher, Jan. 21, 1966; children: Carmen Dee, Matthew Dale, Jason Doyle, Benjamin Wade. BS, N.E. Okla. U., 1966, MEd, 1991. Tchr. Sapulpa (Okla.) Pub. Schs., 1967-75, 87-91, counselor, 1991—. Active Parents Educators Orgn., Sapulpa, 1983—. Mem. NEA, Okla. Edn. Assn., Sapulpa Edn. Assn., Order Eastern Star. Democrat. Methodist. Avocations: snow skiing, gardening, sports spectator, swimming. Home: 822 Henshaw Ave Sapulpa OK 74066-6012

FLETCHER, WINONA LEE, theater educator emeritus; b. Nov. 25, 1926; m. Joseph Grant; 1 child, Betty. BA, Johnson C. Smith U., 1947; MA, U. Iowa, 1951; PhD, Ind. U., 1968. Prof. speech and theatre Ky. State U., Frankfort, 1951-78; prof. theatre and afro-Am. studies Ind. U., Bloomington, 1978-94, prof. emeritus, 1994; assoc. dean COAS, 1981-84. Costumer, dir. summer theatre, U. Mo., Lincoln, 1952-60, 69. Recipient Lifetime Achievement award, 1993; Am. Theatre fellow, 1979. Mem. Am. Theatre for Higher Edn., Black Theatre Network, Nat. Assn. Dramatic and Speech Arts, Nat. Theatre Conf., Alpha Kappa Alpha. Home: 317 Cold Harbor Dr Frankfort KY 40601-3011

FLEXNER, JOSEPHINE MONCURE, musician, educator; b. Marion, Va., Oct. 11, 1919; d. Walter Raleigh Daniel and Harriet Ashby (Ogburn) M.; m. Kurt Fisher Flexner, Dec. 20, 1942; children: Thomas Moncure, Peter Wallace. BA, Univ. Richmond, 1941; tchr. cert. in piano, Peabody Conservatory, 1945; MS in piano, Juilliard Sch. Music, 1950. Class piano tchr. Balt. Pub. Sch., 1945-46; mem. piano faculty Peabody Conservatory Prep., Balt., 1945-46, Pius X Sch. Manhatanville Coll. Sacred Heart, N.Y.C., 1946-50, Henry Street Settlement Sch., N.Y.C., 1949-50; piano tchr. Bronxville, N.Y., 1950-54; mem. piano faculty Rhodes Coll., Memphis, Tenn., 1970-82; piano tchr. St. Mary's Episcopal Sch., Memphis, 1982-87. Judge for Tenn. piano auditions, 1980-85, judge in Tenn. Nat. Guild Auditions, 1983-84. Contbr. articles to profl. jours. Den mother Boy Scouts Am., 1963-65, vice chmn., 1964-65; precinct worker, capt. Nat. Elections, Memphis, 1972, 74; mem. Memphis Arts Coun., 1977-79; area chmn. Westchester Soc. Performing Arts, 1964-66, chmn. cultural activities Sch. No. 8, Yonkers, N.Y., 1963-66; vice chmn. music dept. Bronxville Women's Club, 1964-66; pres. chancel choir Dutch Reformed Ch., Bronxville, 1963-66; program chmn. Seoul Internat. Women's Assn., Seoul, Korea, 1967-68, chmn. cultural activities Seoul Am. Schs., 1966-68, chmn. cultural seminars Am. Women's Club, Seoul, 1967-68; treas., pres. Greater Memphis Music Tchrs. Assn., 1975-79; bd. dirs. Young Peoples Piano Concerto Competition, 1979-85, Tenn. Music Tchrs. Assn., 1977-79. Named Tchr. of Yr., Greater Memphis Music, 1983, Tchr. of Yr., Tenn. Music Tchrs. Assn., 1985. Democrat. Presbyterian. Avocations: writing, reading, playing piano. Home: The Fountains at Millbrook 17 Crestview Rd Millbrook NY 12545

FLIER, MICHAEL STEPHEN, Slavic languages educator; b. L.A., Apr. 20, 1941; s. Albert and Bonnie F. BA, U. Calif., Berkeley, 1962, MA, 1964, PhD, 1968. Acting vis. asst. prof. Slavic langs. and lits. U. Calif., Berkeley, 1968; asst. prof. Slavic langs. and lits. UCLA, 1968-73, assoc. prof., 1973-79, prof., 1979-91, chmn. dept., 1978-84, 87-89. Vis. prof. Slavic langs. Columbia U., fall 1988, Harvard U., fall 1989; Oleksandr Potebnja prof. Ukrainian Philology Harvard U., 1991—, chmn. dept. Linguistics, 1994-99, chmn. dept. Slavic langs. and lits., 1999—, acting chmn. dept. linguistics, 2002; acting dir. Harvard Ukrainian Rsch. Inst., 2001. Author: Aspects of Nominal Determination in Old Church Slavic, 1974, Say It In Russian, 1982; editor: Slavic Forum: Essays in Slavic Linguistics and Literature, 1974, Am. Cont. to the Intl. Congress of Slavists, 1983, Ukrainian Philology and Linguistics, 1994; co-editor: Medieval Russian Culture, 1984, Issues in Russian Morphosyntax, 1985, The Scope of Slavic Aspect, 1985, Language, Literature, Linguistics, 1987, Medieval Russian Culture, vol. 2, 1994, For SK: In Celebration of the Life and Career of Simon Karlinsky, 1994, The Language and Verse of Russia: In Honor of Dean S. Worth on His Sixty-fifth Birthday, 1995; mem. editl. bd. Slavic and East European Jour., 1989—, Movoznavstvo, 1991—, Harvard Ukrainian Studies, 1991—, Russkii iazyk v nauchniom osveshchenii, 2000—. Vice chmn. Am. Com. Slavists, 1989-94, chmn., 1994—. Internat. Rsch. and Exchs. Bd. travel grantee Russia, Czechoslovakia, 1966-67, 71, 78, 93, 96; U. Calif. Pres.'s fellow, 1990, John Simon Guggenheim Meml. Found. fellow, 1990-91. Mem. Linguistics Soc. Am., Am. Assn. Tchrs. Slavic and East European Langs., Am. Assn. Advancement Slavic Studies, Western Slavic Assn., Coll. Art Assn., Am. Assn. for Ukrainian Studies (sec.-treas. 1989-93, bd. dirs.). Home: 76 Fresh Pond Ln Cambridge MA 02138-4641 Office: Harvard U Dept Slavic Langs and Lits Barker Ctr, 12 Quincy St Cambridge MA 02138

FLINK, CHARLES LAWRENCE, education director; b. Boston, Dec. 10, 1945; s. Ira and Lillian Frances (Novak) F.;' m. Adrian Marie Mangan, Apr. 16, 1983. BA, U. Mass., 1969, MA, 1971. Cert. tchr., prin. and supr., Mass. Tchr. Mid. Coll. High Sch., Springfield, Mass., 1971-91, program dir., 1991-97; dir. truency project, liaison Budd Youth Svcs. Ctr., Springfield, 1997—. Scorer Mass. Edn. Assesment Program, Quincy, 1987-92; mem. hist. curriculum com. Mass. Dept. Edn., Quincy, 1992—. Mem. com. Ward 6 Dem. Com., Springfield, 1986-91, chmn., 1992; mem. exec. com. Dem. City Com., Springfield, 1992. Sgt. USAF, 1963-67. Mem. NEA, Mass. Tchrs. Assn. (del. annual meeting 1980-92, bd. dirs. 1991-93, ethics com. 1992), Springfield Edn. Assn. (exec. bd. 1983-92, grievance chair 1987-91), Forest Park Civic Assn. (bd. dirs. 1987-92). Democrat. Avocations: historian, card collecting. Home: PO Box 248 Feeding Hills MA 01030-0248 Office: Budd Youth Svc Ctr 450 Cottage St # 5 Springfield MA 01104-3219

FLINN, MARY AGNES, artist, educator; b. Balt., July 31, 1962; d. Eugene Aloyisious and Rose Flora F. BFA, Swain Sch. Design, New Bedford, Mass., 1985; MFA, CUNY, 1991. Art handler, conservation technician NAD Mus., NYC, 1992—. Tchr. Kundalini Yoga, dir./tchr. training program in Yoga at the Energy Ctr., NYC, 2003-2003, Yoga tchr. Hunter Coll., NYC, 2000-2003, Yoga tchr. Pratt Inst., NYC, 2002-2003; tchr. art Melrose Cmty. Ctr., Bronx, N.Y., 1993, Saraswati Prodns., Bklyn., 1996; vis. artist Fairleigh Dickinson Coll., N.J., 1994. One-woman shows include Prince St. Gallery, N.Y.C., 1995, 1997, 1999, two person show, Dartmouth Coll., N.H., 2001, exhibited in group shows at Balt. City Hall, 1995, Prince St. Gallery, 1996, also pvt. collections, restored mural, Grand Ctrl. Sta., N.Y.C.; featured: article (Mary's Loft) Ascent mag., 2001. Vol. Meth. Hosp., Bklyn., 1995-96. Fellow Vt. Studio Ctr., 1987. Mem. Women's Mus., Amnesty Internat. Avocations: yoga, healing arts.

FLINNER, BEATRICE JEFFREYS ALLAYAUD, retired library and media sciences educator; b. Uledi, Pa., Feb. 8, 1924; d. Charles Robert and Esther Marjorie (Sickles) Jeffreys; m. Donald Allayaud, May 18, 1944 (dec.); 1 child, Donald Allayaud; m. Lyle P. Flinner, June 27, 1947; 1 child, Carol Jean Flinner Dorough. AB summa cum laude, So. Nazarene U., 1974; MLS, U. Okla., 1977; MA in Social Studies, So. Nazarene U., 1978, MA in Early Childhood, 1981. Cataloging dept. Asbury Theol. Sem., Wilmore, Ky., 1949-52; aquisitions Geneva Coll., Beaver Falls, Pa., 1959-62, audio visual coord., 1965-68; assoc. prof., head pub. svcs. So. Nazarene U., Bethany, Okla., 1968-96, adj. prof. grad. edn., 1980-2000; ret., 1996. Adv. bd. Bethany Libr., rep. to bd. trustees, 1986-87. Book reviewer The Christian Librarian, 1980-94; indexer Christian Periodical Index, 1988-96; contbr. articles to profl. jours. Mem. AAUW (directory), Assn. Christian Librs. (v.p. 1991-93, program chair internat. conf. 1992), Univ. Women's Club, U. Okla. Sch. Libr. Info. Sci. Alumni Assn., Assn. Christian Librs. (conf. coord. 1992-95), Rsch. Interest Group, Acad. Sr. Profls. (libr. resources columnist, named one of 2000 Notable Am. Women), Phi Delta Lambda. Republican. Nazarene.

FLINT, BETTY RUTH, elementary school educator; b. Cin., Jan. 14, 1943; d. Clarence Lovelle Weaver and Dorothy Regina (Haynes) Copeland; m. Virgil Eugene Flint, Apr. 2, 1994; children: Cassandra Haynes, Aaron Ellis. BS in Elem. Edn., U. Cin., 1972, MA in Reading, 1978. Tchr. Cin. Bd. of Edn., 1973-76, Oceanside (Calif.) Unified Sch. Dist., 1976-96, Chpt. I reading tchr., 1996—2000; reading recovery tchr. San Diego Unified Sch. Dist., 2001—. Clin. instr. U. San Diego, Inter Am. Coll.; presenter in field. Mem. Internat. Reading Assn., Calif. Reading Assn., Whole Lang. Coun. of San Diego. Democrat. Avocations: reading, traveling, music. Office: Marshall Elem Sch 3550 Altadena Ave San Diego CA 92105 Home: 3020 Plaza Lorenzo Bonita CA 91902-1606 E-mail: bflint@sdcoe.k12.ca.us.

FLINT-FERGUSON, JANIS DEANE, English language and literature educator; b. Chgo., June 6, 1953; d. Warren Francis Jr. and Dorajean (Buch) F.; m. Robert Rex Ferguson, Sept. 2, 1978. BA, North Ctrl. Coll., 1975; MS, Ill. State U., 1985, DA, 1993. Tchr. lang. arts Paris (Ill.) Union Schs., 1977-79, Gibson City (Ill.) Cmty. Schs., 1979-90; assoc. prof. Gordon Coll., Wenham, Mass., 1990—. Dept. chair Gordon Coll., Wenham, Mass., 1997—, cons., inservice provider mid. schs.; regional and nat. presenter. Co-editor: Readings are Writing, 1995; contbr. articles to profl. jours. Named Coll. Educator of Yr., Mass. Assn. Tchr. Educators, 1997. Mem. Nat. Coun. Tchrs. English, Northeast Alliance Mid. Schs. (chair 1995-2002, treas. 2002—), New England League Mid. Schs. (com. chair 1994-2002). Congregationalist. Avocation: adolescent literature. Office: Gordon Coll 255 Grapevine Rd Wenham MA 01984-1813

FLOCK, CAROL ANN, secondary education educator; b. Emporia, Kans., May 9, 1947; d. Carol Franklin and Hartsel Laverne (Norton) Storrer; m. Phillip W. Flock, Feb. 15, 1970; children: Erin Rebecca, Joanna Renee. BS in Home Econs. Edn., Kans. State U., 1970. Cert. tchr., Kans. Tchr. home econs., advisor Family, Career and Cmty. Leaders Am. Unified Sch. Dist. 389, Eureka, Kans., 1970-74, 80—. Active Etude Jr. Federated, 1971-79, Jaycee-Jaynes, 1971-75; Sunday sch. tchr., v.p. congregation, pres. congregation Cen. Christian Ch. Named Young Educator of Yr., Eureka Jaycees, 1973. Mem. AAUW (v.p., pres.), Kans. Assn. Vocat. Home Econs. Tchrs. (state bd. dirs. 1982-84), Kans. Home Econs. Assn. (chmn. state elem., secondary and adult edn. 1992—, Dist. Tchr. of Yr. 1992, sec. 1999-2001), Eureka Tchrs. Assn. (v.p. 1990-92, pres. 1992, Tchr. of Yr. 1991. 02), Greenwood County Cattlewomen (pres. 2002-03), Greenwood Hist. Soc., Greenwood County Alumni Assn. (sec. 1999, v.p. 2001, pres. 2003), Delta Kappa Gamma (v.p. 2002-03). Republican. Avocations: cooking, reading, golf, shopping. Home: RR 2 Box 605 Madison KS 66860-9538 E-mail: caflock@madtel.net., caflock@389us.org.

FLORENCE, ERNEST ESTELL, JR., special education educator; b. Grayson, Ky., Feb. 19, 1954; s. Ernest Estell Florence and Margaret Jean (Tittsworth) Ikemire; m. Ginger Lynn Miller, Apr. 19, 1980; children: Ashley Michelle, Charles Todd. BS in Edn., Ea. Ill. U., 1975; MS in Edn., No. Ill. U., 1980. Behavior disorder tchr. Project Advocate Northwestern Ill. Assn., Geneva, 1976-80; behavior disorder tchr. O'Donnell Elem. Sch. Dist. 131, Aurora, Ill., 1980-85, behavior disorder/learning disability tchr. Bardwell Elem., 1985-93; behavior disorder tchr. Prairie Elem. sch. Dist. 203, Naperville, Ill., 1993—, mem. Spl. Edn. Inst. Day com., 1998-2000. Vol. Spl. Olympics, Aurora, 1990-93; com. mem. Just Say No Com., City of Aurora, 1991-95; com. mem. Aurora 2000 Com., 1993; chmn. scholarship com. Boulder Hill Sch. PTA, Montgomery, Ill., 1992—, reflections chmn., 1995-98; vol. bell ringer Salvation Army, 1995—; vol. Prairie Sch. Market Day, 1995—; mem. Prairie Sch. Bldg. Leadership Team, 1995-98. Named Tchr. of Yr., Bardwell Sch. PTA, 1989, Educator of Yr., Ill. Learning Disabilities Assn., 1989; recipient Chpt. Recognition award Ill. Learning Disabilities Assn., 1992. Mem. NEA (local sch. rep. 1998-2000), Coun. for Exceptional Children, Learning Disabilities Assn. Am. (chmn. Proud Projects 1997-98, state pres. rep. to Nat. Bd. 1998-99, affiliate support com. 1998-2000), Learning Disabilities Assn. Ill. (regional dir. 1991-94, pres.-elect 1994-96, pres. 1996-98, chmn. scholarship 1992-96, chmn. prin. scholarship programs 1992—, chair nominations com. 1999-2000), Ill. Coun. for Children with Behavior Disorders, Kane Kendall Learning Disabilities Assn. (v.p. 1987—, Kane Kendall Recognition award 1994), Ill. br. Orton Dyslexia Soc., Aurora Moose. Democrat. Avocations: travel, reading, music. Home: 113 Circle Dr W Montgomery IL 60538-2725 Office: Naperville Comty Unit Sch Dist 203 203 W Hillside Rd Naperville IL 60540-6500

FLORES, CHRISTINA ROSALIE, elementary education art educator; b. Tamuning, Guam, Nov. 17, 1947; d. George Pangelinan Franquez; m. Larry Blas Flores, June 20, 1970 (div. Nov. 1974); children: Tanisha, Briana. AA, Sacred Heart Coll., 1967; BA, San Diego State U., 1970; MA, Long Beach State U., 1979. Cert. art tchr., Guam. 5th grade tchr. Price Elem. Sch., Mangilao, Guam, 1970-80; 6th grade tchr. Harmon (Guam) Loop Elem. Sch., 1980-82; 6th and 7th grade art tchr. Agueda Johnston Mid. Sch., Ordot, Guam, 1982—; art tchr. George Washington H.S., 1999—. Gifted and talented edn. art tchr. various elem. schs., Guam, summers, 1984-95; art instr. Fun in the Sun camp for handicapped children, summers 1975-82, Parks and Recreation Summer Camp, 1983-85; instr., tchr. workshops in art Simon Sanchez H.S., Yigo, Guam, 1988-92; mem. adv. bd. Coun. Arts and Humanities, Maite, Guam, 1991-94, 2002, bd. dirs., 1995-99; chief advisor Crime Stoppers Agueda Mid. Sch., 1992—; advisor Nat. Jr. Honor Soc. Agueda Johnston Mid. Sch., 1987-99; part time art methods instr. Coll. Edn., U. Guam, 1994-2000; art dir. mural painting KGTF TV Sta., cmty walls Internat. Reading Assn., Guam, 2000—. Chief advisor Students Against Drunk Driving, Agueda Johnston Mid. Sch., 1987—; mem. Driver's Edn. Consortium, Guam, 1993-94; vol. Spl. Olympics, Guam, 1974—, ARC, Guam, 1992—, Festival of the Arts, Tahiti, 1985, Australia, 1988, Cook Islands, 1992, Western Samoa, 1996, New Caledonia, 2000, Am. Cancer Soc., Guam, 2001—, Relay for Life, 1999-2003, BLood Dr. Gift of Life, 2003, ARC Disaster Relief, 1997-2003; instr. Pacific Region Ednl. Lab., 1993—. Tchr. Inst. scholar Nat. Art Gallery, Washington, 1991. Mem. ASCD, Nat. Art Edn. Assn., Nat. Assn. Student Activity Advisers. Avocations: weaving, swimming, dancing, paddling. Home: PO Box 1654 Hagatna GU 96932-1654

FLORES, FRANK CORTEZ, public health researcher, educator, administrator; b. L.A., Mar. 13, 1930; s. Frank Chaves and Jane (Cortez) F.; m. Juliette Carmen Sotelo, Nov. 24, 1951; children: Patricia Marie, Marie Juliette, Frank Anthony, Gregory Steven, Mark Adam, Jon Eric, Aaron Michael. AA, East L.A. Coll., 1951; BS, U. So. Calif., L.A., 1955, DDS, 1957, MSEd, cert. in med. edn., U. So. Calif., L.A., 1988; cert. in risk mgmt., Golden Gate U., San Francisco, 1981; PhD Fellow in Higher Edn., Claremont U., 1991, MA and PhD, 1992; MPH, Loma Linda U., 1996. Lic. dentist, real-estate broker, ins. broker. Dental care implementor Specialist Ctr. For Dental Therapy, Riyadh, Saudi Arabia, 1984-86; asst. clin. prof. Univ. So. Calif. Sch. Dentistry, L.A., 1987—; rsch. assoc. in internat. pub. health Loma Linda U., 1997, asst. prof., 1997—; rschr. in border pub. health U. Tex. Houston Health Sci. Ctr., 1997-98. Dentist Am. Dental Vols. for Israel, Jerusalem, 1987—; vis. fellow rsch. in higher edn. Claremont Grad. Sch., 1993. Fundraiser various colls. and univs., 1988—; 2nd v.p. Project Hosp. Ship Oceanic, Upland, Calif., 1986—. With USNR, 1947-52. Mem. AAUP, APHA, Am. Assn. Dental Schs., Nat. Coun. for Internat. Health, Am. Assn. Pub. Health Dentistry, U.S.-Mex. Border Health Assn. Democrat. Avocations: sailing, backpacking, photography, golf, archaeology. Office: PO Box 3729 San Dimas CA 91773-7729

FLORES, SYLVIA A. principal; BS in elem. edn., U. Houston, 1979; MS in sch. adminstrn., N. Mex. State U., 1995. Tchr. 1st grade Floresville (Tex.) Elem., 1980-82, tchr. 3d grade, 1982-85; tchr. 1st grade Ctrl. Elem., Artesia, N. Mex., 1985-87, Yucca Elem., Artesia, N. Mex., 1987-92; tchr. 4th grade, asst. prin. Hermosa Elem., Artesia, N.Mex., 1992—95; prin. Yucca Elem., Artesia, 1996—. Recipient N. Mex. Tchr. of the Year, 1995. Mem. Assn. Supr. and Curriculum Devel., Legis. and Salary Chairperson for Artesia Pub. Sch. Network. Home: 103 Marsha Dr Artesia NM 88210-9251 Office: 900 North 13th St Artesia NM 88210*

FLORES, YOLANDA, literature educator; b. Bakersfield, Calif., Mar. 2, 1962; d. Simon and Micaela Flores. BA, U. Calif., Berkeley, 1987; MA, U. Chgo., 1989; PhD, Cornell U., 1995. Lectr. Cornell U., Ithaca, N.Y., 1994-95; prof. Chapman U., Orange, Calif., 1995-99, U. Vt., Burlington, 1999—. Author: The Drama of Gender: Feminist Theater by Women of the Americas, 2000, 2d edit., 2002; contbr. articles to profl. publs. Mem. MLA, L.Am. Studies Assn., Am. Soc. for Theater Rsch., Feministas Unidas, Assn. Theater in Higher Edn. Democrat. Roman Catholic. Avocations: film, music, aerobics, travel. Office: Romance Langs and Lit Dept U Vt 517 Waterman Bldg Burlington VT 05405-0001 E-mail: yflores@uvm.edu.

FLORY, BETSY J. educator; b. Grand Rapids, Oct. 16, 1936; Divorced; 2 children. AA, Grand Rapids C.C., 1955; AB, Calvin Coll., 1956; MA, U. Mich., 1977, EdS, 1987; SPADA, Western Mich. U., 1992. Dem. nom. for Mich. House of Reps., 1978, Kent County Commn., 1982; Dem. candidate 3d dist. Mich. U.S. House of Reps., 1996. Congregationalist. Office: 309 Palmer St NE Grand Rapids MI 49505-4723

FLOSS, FREDERICK GEORGE, economics and finance educator, consultant; b. Buffalo, Feb. 12, 1957; s. Frederick H. and Mary (White) F.; m. Lauren Bodziak, July 26, 1986. BA in Econs. and English, SUNY, Oswego, 1979; MA in Econs., SUNY, Buffalo, 1982, PhD in Econs., 1986. Instr. econs. SUNY, Buffalo, 1980-85, asst. prof., 1986-90, mem. faculty senate, 1986-2000, assoc. prof., 1990-99, prof., 1999—, co-dir. Ctr. for Econ. Edn., 1997—. Rsch. assoc. Ctr. for Applied Rsch. in Urban and Regional Devel., 1983—; exec. bd. United Univ. Professions, 2000—; presenter in field. Contbr. articles to profl. jours. Committeeman Erie County Dem. Com., 1979—; mem. cmty. needs assessment com. United Way Western N.Y., 1987-92; mem. adv. coun. Erie-Niagara Planning Bd., 1987-92; chmn. bd. regional dirs. Young Dems. Am., 1988-90; bd. dirs. Literacy Vols. of Buffalo and Erie County, 1992-98, Summitt Edn.; sec. Literacy Vol. of Buffalo and Erie County, 1995-97. Regents scholar, 1975-79; fellow Ctr. for Devel. Human Svcs., 1987-88, 89-98. Roman Catholic. Home: 27 Landers Rd Buffalo NY 14217-2405 Office: SUNY Dept Econs and Fin 1300 Elmwood Ave Dept Econsand Buffalo NY 14222-1004 E-mail: flossfg@buffalostate.edu.

FLOURNOY, JACOB WESLEY, internal audit director; b. Odessa, Tex., June 18, 1956; s. Dan Dunn and Vonnie Rea (Morrow) F.; m. Tina Charlene Hargis, Jan. 5, 1980; children: Daniel Edward, Samuel Wesley. BBA, U. North Tex., 1978; MBA, U. Okla., 1984. CPA, cert. internal auditor; cert. info. sys. auditor; cert. fraud examiner. Asst. bank examiner Fed. Deposit Ins. Corp., Oklahoma City, Okla., 1978-80; internal auditor City of Oklahoma City, 1980-82; sr. internal auditor U. Okla., Norman, 1982-86; internal audit dir. U. Tex. Health Sci. Ctr., San Antonio, 1986-91, U. Ark. Sys., Little Rock, 1991—; instr. AICPA, 2000—. Fellow: AICPA (instr.); mem. Inst. Internal Auditors, Info. Sys. Audit and Control Assn., Assn. Coll. and Univ. Auditors, Assn. Cert. Fraud Examiners, Ark. Soc. CPAs. Office: U Ark 2404 N University Little Rock AR 72207-3608 E-mail: jwflournoy@uasys.edu.

FLOWER, JEAN FRANCES, art educator; b. Schenectady, N.Y., Apr. 12, 1936; d. Francis Tunis and Marjorie (Colcord) Fort; m. Wesley Allen Flower, Aug. 23, 1958; children: Kimberly Lynn, Kristina Kathleen. BA, Syracuse U., 1958; BFA cum laude, Western Mich. U., 1984, MFA magne cum laude, 1989. Free-lance artist, 1981-86; tech. grad. asst. Western Mich. U., Kalamazoo, 1988, grad. asst. early mgmt., 1989, instr. art, 1989-93, Kalamazoo Inst. Art, 1993—. One-woman shows include Peoples Ch., Kalamazoo, 1991; exhibited in group shows Kalamazoo Area Art Show, 1992, 94 95, 97, Nat. Art Show, Dallas, 1993, Libr., Parchment, Mich., 1993, EAA Aviation Internat. Art Show, 1992, 95; murals executed Kalamazoo Valley Pub. Mus., 1995, Kalamazoo Aviation History Mus., 1996. Pres., mem. Anna Cir. 1st United Meth. Ch., Kalamazoo, 1980—, mem. communications commn., 1994—; sec.-treas. Airward, Plainwell, Mich., 1986—. Mem. Am. Assn. Aviation Artists, Plainwell Pilots Assn., Kalamazoo Aviatrix Assn. (past v.p.). Avocations: flying, painting, golf, tennis, cross-country skiing. Home: 8745 Marsh Rd Plainwell MI 49080-8818

FLOWERS, SANDRA JOAN, elementary education educator; b. Newport, R.I., July 17, 1943; d. Joseph A. and Dolores A. (Martino) F. BA, Salve Regina Coll., 1965; MA in Teaching, R.I. Coll., 1968; postgrad., Salve Regina U., 1990—, cert. advanced grad. study, 1994. Cert. elem. tchr., R.I. Tchr. Newport Sch. Dept., 1965-95; ret., 1995; instr., edn. Salve Regina U., Newport, 1979—. Mem. adv. bd. Underwood Sch., Newport, 1986, mem. site-based mgmt. team, 1993—; mem. basic ednl. planning ream R.I. Dept. Edn., Barrington Pub. Schs., 1986; mem. planning team, reader Children's Reading Hour, Literacy Outreach, Newport. Mem. Funding and

Expenditures Alternatives Strategic Planning, Newport, 1989—; mem. grad. student coun. Salve Regina U.; religious edn. tchr. St. Joseph's Parish, Newport, 1995—, chair liturgy com., 2000—, sec. parish coun., 2001—; bd. dirs. Aquidneck Collaborative for Edn., 1993—. Moore scholar Salve Regina Coll., 1961-65, R.I. State scholar, 1961-65; recipient Feinstein Enriching Am. award, 1999. Mem.: LWV, AAUW, ASCD, Newport County Ret. Tchrs. Assn., R.I. Ret. Tchrs. Assn., R.I. Assn. Tchr. Educators. Roman Catholic. Avocations: writing for children, reading, church work, drawing, painting. Home: PO Box # 114 16 Keeher Ave Newport RI 02840-2320 E-mail: flowerss@salve.edu.

FLOYD, ANN R. elementary education educator; b. Mullins, S.C., June 29, 1951; d. Harry Theodore and Mary Elizabeth (Winburn) Richardson; m. Larry Dwight Floyd, Sr., Feb. 20, 1971; 1 child, Larry Dwight Jr. Student, Coastal Carolina, 1969-71; BA in Early Childhood Edn., Clemson U., 1981; MEd in Reading, Francis Marion U., 1990. Cert. early childhood edn., elem. edn. Fourth grade tchr. McKissick Elem., Easley, S.C., 1981-82; first grade tchr. Concrete Elem., Easley, 1983-84, third grade tchr., 1984-85; fourth grade self contained tchr. Royall Elem., Florence, S.C., 1985-91, sixth grade sci./health tchr., 1991-93, sci. specialist, 1993—99; 3rd grade tchr. Red Bank Elem., Lexington, SC, 1999—. Mem. Supts. Faculty Adv. Bd., 1993-99. Loyalty fund mem. Clemson U., 1981—, mem. Iptay, 1981—; active Friends of the Mus., S.C. State Mus., Columbia, 1988—, S.C. Wildlife Orgn., 1990—, Supt.'s Adv. Bd., Florence, 1993. Recipient Presdl. award for excellence in sci. tchg. NSF, 1995; grantee Pee Dee Edn. Found., 1995. Mem. NSTA, Internat. Reading Assn., S.C. Ednl. TV Endowment, S.C. Sci. Coun., S.C. Middle and Elem. Sch. Sci. Coun. (bd. dirs., charter mem.), S.C. Children's Sci. Coun. (exec. bd. 1995—), Nat. Wildlife Assn., Nat. Geographic Soc. Office: Red Bank Elem Sch 246 Community Dr Lexington SC 29073

FLOYD, CINTHIA ANN, secondary school educator, coach; b. Mobile, Ala., July 26, 1961; d. Joe Merle and V. Marolyn (Whiddon) Crump; children: Cory James, Courtney Marie; m. Martin A. Floyd, Aug. 12, 1994. BS in Phys. Edn., U. South Ala., 1983, MEd, 1984. Cert. phys. edn. tchr., Ala. Grad. tchg. asst. U. South Ala., Mobile, 1984-85; tchr. phys. edn., volleyball coach Palmer Pillans Mid. Sch., Mobile, 1985-98; volleyball and track coach Cranford Burns Mid. Sch., Mobile, 1998—. Softball coach B.C. Rain H.S., Mobile, 1989-93; mem. health curriculum adv. bd. Mobile County Pub. Sch. Sys., 1990-91; program dir. Racquetball Club Mobile, 1980-8; track coach Palmer Pillans Mid. Sch., 1994-98. Named Outstanding Tchr. of Yr., Mobile C. of C., 1991, one of Top Three in Nation, Disney's Am. Tchr. awards, 1993. Mem. AAHPERD, NEA, Nat. Assn. Girls and Women in Sports, Ala. Assn. Health Phys. Edn. Recreation and Dance (State Coach of Yr. 1991), Ala. Edn. Assn., Ala. H.S. Athletic Assn., Coaches and Phys. Educators Mobile (v.p. 1989-91), Kappa Kappa Iota (pres. 1991). Baptist. Avocations: volleyball, softball, beach activities, swimming. Home: 607 Montclaire Way Mobile AL 36609-6539 Office: Cranford Burns Mid Sch 6175 Girby Rd Mobile AL 36693-3323

FLUEGGE, GLENN WILLIAM, secondary education educator; b. Jackson, Mo., Apr. 28, 1943; s. Edwin W. and Laura A. (Aufdenberg) F.; m. Nancy L. Wills, Aug. 17, 1963; children: Julie C. Fluegge Holland, Christopher G., Steven A. BS in Edn., S.E. Mo. State U., 1965, MA in Teaching, 1973. Life cert. secondary edn. tchr., Mo. Tchr. indsl. tech. Marquand (Mo.)-Zion R-II Schs., 1965-68, Ste. Genevieve (Mo.) R-II Dist., 1968—. Draftsman Miss. Lime, Ste. Genevieve, 1979-94; com. mem. North Ctrl. Sch. Accreditation Bd., Bayless, Mo., 1972, Perryville, Mo., 1979, Herculaneum, Mo., 1988; mem. adv. com. indsl. tech. dept. S.E. Mo. State U., Cape Girardeau, 1992-93. Trustee, elder Luth. ch., Ste. Genevieve, 1968—; mem. nat. alumni coun. S.E. Mo. State U., 1994-95. With U.S. Army, 1960-64. Grantee Mo. Dept. Edn., 1984-89. Mem. Am. Fedn. Tchrs., S.E. Mo. State U. Alumni Assn. (sec. Ste. Genevieve-Perry Counties chpt. 1992, v.p. 1993, pres. 1994), Iota Lambda Sigma (v.p. 1984). Avocations: hunting, fishing, woodworking, metalworking. Home: 13 Saint Ann St Sainte Genevieve MO 63670-1905 Office: 715 Washington St Sainte Genevieve MO 63670-1237

FLUHARTY, CHARLES WILLIAM, policy institute director, consultant, policy researcher; b. Wheeling, W.Va., Apr. 21, 1947; s. Irwin Adrian and Mary Elizabeth (Foster) F.; m. Marsha Jean Prospal, June 27, 1970; children: Matthew, Joshua, Megan. BA cum laude, U. Steubenville, Ohio, 1969; MDiv with distinctions, Yale U., 1973. Co-dir. Rural Policy Rsch. Inst. U. Mo., Columbia, 1990-92, dir. Rural Policy Rsch. Inst., 1992—, rsch. prof. Truman Sch. Pub. Affairs, 1998—, interim dir. Mo. inst. pub. policy, 1998—. Human resources cons., 1987—; presenter numerous Congl. hearing/briefing testimonies. Author numerous rural policy rsch. studies, publs., reports, briefings. Recipient Recognition award Nat. Rural Devel. Partnership, 1999, Disting. Svc. award Nat. Assn. Counties, 1998, Recognition award Nat. Orgn. of State Offices of Rural Health, 1998, Columbia Devlin Outstanding Educator award, 1977, Disting. Svc. to Rural Life award Rural Sociol. Soc., 2002, Sec.'s Honor award for superior svc. USDA, 2002, Pres.'s award Nat. Assn. of Devel. Orgns., 2002. Mem. Baconian Soc., Alpha Chi. Office: U Mo Rural Policy Rsch Inst Mumford Hall Columbia MO 65211

FLUKER, JAY EDWARD, middle school visual arts educator; b. Hackensack, N.J., Sept. 26, 1943; s. J. Edward and Betty B. (Berkey) Flucker; m. Eileen Elizabeth Owens, June 22, 1968; children: Colleen Sharon, Maureen Jaye. BA in Art Edn., William Paterson Coll. N.J., 1966, MEd in Art Edn., 1972, MA in Comm. Arts, 1974. Cert. art tchr., elem. tchr. Art tchr. South Plainfield (N.J.) Bd. Edn., 1966-67, Chester (N.J.) Bd. Edn., 1967—. Co-developer workshop instr. Visual Arts Gifted and Talented Consortium, NJ, 1990—2003; spkr. Nat. Conf. Sch. Restructuring, Atlanta, 1991, Phila., 93, Shore Consortium, Rumson, NJ, 1986; mem. Crayola Art Edn. Coun., 1998. Solo landscape painting exhibit Roxbury, N.J., 1989, 92, Chester, N.J., 1972; solo photograph exhibits Roxbury, N.J., 2000, Chester, N.J., 2001; creator of weaving, 1966 (pub. in Weaving Without A Loom). With U.S. Army Mil. Police, 1968-71, Vietnam. PTA grantee, 1991-97. Mem. NEA, N.J. Edn. Assn., N.J. Assn. for Mid. Level Edn. (conf. guest spkr. 1991-94, workshop presenter), Art Educators N.J. (presenter 1992, 94-99, 2001), Art Assn. in Roxbury (historian 1991-93, exhibitor 1989, 92, 2000), HUB Camera Club (Denville, N.J., 3 First pl. photo competition awards, 1 Second pl. award, 1 Hon. mention 2001-02). Roman Catholic. Avocations: painting, travel, avid sci. fiction Star Trek and Star Wars fan. Office: Black River Mid Sch Rte 513 Chester NJ 07930

FLUSCHE, JOANNE MARTINI, secondary education educator; b. Wichita Falls, Tex., Aug. 29, 1938; d. Joseph Albert and Elizabeth Pearl (Meurer) Martini; m. Arnold Joseph Flusche, Aug. 5, 1957; children: Angela Diane, Michael David, Darryl Glen. BS, Tex. Tech. U., 1985, MEd, 1988. Cert. reading specialist; cert. libr; cert. master reading tchr.; cert. elem. tchr., Tex. Libr. Idalou Elem. Sch., 1985-96, Slaton HS, 1996—. Mem. Internat. Reading Assoc., Tex. Classroom Tchr., Tex. State Reading Assn. (Region XVII Svc. Ctr., staff devel. specialist), Caprock Reading Assn. (v.p., sec. 199-94), Tex. Assn. Sch. Libr. E-mail: jflusche@slaton.esc17.net.

FLYNN, GEORGE WILLIAM, chemistry educator, researcher; b. Hartford, Conn., July 11, 1938; s. George William and Rose Margaret (Tummillo) F.; m. Jean Pieri, Oct. 3, 1970; children: David Kenneth, Suzanne MacKay BS, Yale U., 1960; A.M., Harvard U., 1962, PhD, 1965. Postdoctoral fellow MIT, Cambridge, 1965-67; asst. prof. chemistry Columbia U., N.Y.C., 1967-72, assoc. prof., 1972-76, prof., 1976—, Thomas Alva Edison prof. chemistry, 1986-92, Higgins prof. chemistry, 1994—, dir. lab., 1979-2000, chmn. dept. chemistry, 1994-96, co-chair dept. chem. engring. and applied chemistry, 1997-2000. Research collaborator Brookhaven Nat. Lab., Upton, N.Y., 1969-78, cons., 1978— Contbr. articles to profl. jours. Fellow Sloan Found., 1968-70, Guggenheim Found., 1974-75; A. Cressy Morrison award N.Y. Acad. Scis., 1983; recipient Advancement Basic and Applied Sci. award Yale U. Sci. and Engring. Assn., 1994, NAS, 2001. Fellow Am. Phys. Soc. (Herbert P. Broida prize 2003); mem. Am. Acad. Arts and Scis., Am. Chem. Soc. (chmn. divsn. phys. chemistry, 1996-97), N.Y. Acad. Scis., Sigma Xi Roman Catholic.

FLYNN, JOHN DAVID, writer, educator; b. Jackson, Tenn., Apr. 4, 1948; s. John Aloysius Flynn and Mary Evelyn Groom; m. Deborah Ann Coleman, Jan. 28, 1978 (div. Dec. 1989); 1 child, Caitlin Rose; m. Jennifer Leigh O'Saile, Jan. 2002. BA, B of Journalism, U.Mo., 1971; MA, U. Denver, 1972, Boston U., 1980; PhD, U. Nebr., 1984. Reporter Memphis Press-Scimitar, 1973-74; editor Chapin Pub. Co., Mpls., 1976-77; instr. Tenn. State U., Nashville, 1978-79, asst. prof., 1988-89, U. Hawaii, Honolulu, 1989-91; dir. English Hawaii Tokai Internat. Coll., Honolulu, 1992-93; assoc. prof. Vol. State C.C., Gallatin, Tenn., 1993—. Fulbright sr. specialist, Ukraine, 2002; cons. in field; with Japan Exch. and Tchg. Program, Osaka, 1987—88; adj. instr. Am. Intercontinental U. Online, 2002—. Author numerous poems, short stories and novels; writer-in-residence Millay Colony for the Arts, 1987, Tyrone Guthrie Ctr., Ireland, 1991, Israeli Ctr. for the Arts, 1992, Helene Wurlitzer Found., Taos, N.Mex., 1993, 97-98, 2002. Bd. dirs. Hawaii Literary Arts Coun., Honolulu, 1991-92; congrl. intern U.S Congress, Washington, 1972. Fulbright scholar award Macedonia, 2001. Mem.: PEN, Poets and Writers, Acad. Am. Poets, Marion James Musicians Aid Soc. (pres. 2002, bd. dirs. 2001—), Music City Blues Soc. (bd. dirs. 1996—, v.p. 1999—2002, pres. 2002—), Am. Radio Relay League. Avocations: amateur radio, stained glass, astronomy, hiking. Office: Vol State C C 1480 Nashville Pike Gallatin TN 37066-3148 Home: 127 Brixworth Ln #11 Nashville TN 37205

FLYNN, PAMELA, artist, educator; b. Bellmore, N.Y., Dec. 24, 1948; d. Robert S. and Amalie M. (Debler) Williams; m. Dennis M. Flynn, Aug. 7, 1971; children: Matthew, Amalie. BA, Monmouth U., West Long Branch, N.J., 1971; MA, Kean U., Union, N.J., 1995; MFA, N.J. City U., 1996. Tchr. Freehold (N.J.) Regional Continuing Edn., 1978-95, St. Leo the Great Sch., Lincroft, N.J., 1985—; asst. prof. Holy Family Coll., Phila., 1999—. Adj. instr. New Jersey City State U., 1996-99, Bergen C.C., 1997-99, Brookdale (N.J.) C.C., 1997-99, Ocean County (N.J.) C.C., 1997—, asst. prof. art Holy Family Coll., Phila., 1996—. One-woman shows include Monmouth U., 1995, Abney Gallery, N.Y.C., 1994, Art Space, New Jersey City State U., 1996; exhibited in group shows at Nude/Naked Union St. Gallery, Chgo. Women in the Visual Arts, 1998, Erector Gallery, New Haven, Aljira Nat. 4, Newark, 1998. Mem. FATE, Coll. Art Assn., Phi Kappa Phi. Home: 13 Dogwood Ln Freehold NJ 07728-1868

FLYNN, PATRICIA M. director, special education educator, gifted and talented educator; b. East Cleveland, Ohio, Sept. 11, 1952; d. Harry L. and Eleanore (Mahon) Flynn. BS in Edn. magna cum laude, St. John Coll., Cleve., 1974, MS in Edn., 1975; cert., Notre Dame Coll., 1992, Ursuline Coll., 2001. Cert. elem. edn., prin., edn. handicapped Ohio Detp. Edn. Reading specialist East Cleveland City Schs., 1974—98, reading coord., 1998—2000, curriculum specialist, 2000—01; dir. pupil svcs. Fairview Park (Ohio) Schs., 2001—. Local coord. Reading Is Fundamental Project, East Cleveland, 1996—2000; coord. East Cleveland Elem. Acad., East Cleveland, 1999. Scholar, St. John Coll., 1974. Mem.: Nat. Assn. Fed. Edn. Program Adminstrs., Internat. Reading Assn., Ohio Assn. Adminstrs. State and Fed. Edn. Programs, Ohio Assn. Pupil Svcs. Adminstrs., Irish Am. Club, City Club Cleve., Kappa Gamma Pi. Roman Catholic. Office: Fairview Park City Schs 20770 Lorain Rd Fairview Park OH 44126

FLYNN, PATRICIA MARIE, economics educator; b. Lynn, Mass. BA in Econs., Emmanuel Coll., 1972; MA in Econs., Boston U., 1973, PhD in Econs., 1980. Rsch. assoc. Inst. for Employment Policy, Boston U., 1975-83; prof. econs. Bentley Coll., Waltham, Mass., 1976—; sr. rsch. fellow New Eng. Bd. Higher Edn., Boston, 1980-82; vis. sch. Fed. Res. Bd., Boston, 1983-84; exec. dir. Inst. for Rsch. & Faculty Devel., Bentley Coll., Waltham, 1986-90; assoc. dean faculty Bentley Coll., Waltham, Mass., 1991-92, dean grad. sch., 1992—2002, Trustee prof. econs. and mgmt., 2002—. Mem. faculty Inst. in Employment and Tng. Adminstrn. Harvard U., Cambridge, Mass., summers, 1979-81; cons. U. Mo., Columbia, 1983-84, First Security Svcs. Corp., Boston, 1985, Devel. Alternatives, Inc., Jakarta, Indonesia, summer, 1987, ABT Assocs., Cambridge, 1987-89; bd. dirs. Fed. Savs. Bank, Waltham, Mass. Author: Technology Life Cycles and Human Resources, 1993; co-author: Turbulence in the American Workplace, 1991; contbr. articles to profl. jours. Adv. panel mem. Office Tech. Assessment, U.S. Congress, Washington, 1989-91; accreditation team mem. New Eng. Assn. Schs. and Colls., 1985—; mem. Newton (Mass.) Econ. Devel. Commn., 1984-87; bd. dirs. Big Sisters Assn., US Trust, 1998-2000, Boston Fed. Savs. Bank, 2000—, BostonFed Bancorp, Inc., 2000—; trustee Mass. Taxpayers Found., Sloan Found., 1995-98. Grantee Dept. Labor, 1982-84, 88-89, Nat. Inst. Edn., 1982-83, NSF, 1990-93, Sloan Found., 1995-98; recipient Gregory H. Adamian award for tchg. excellence Bentley Coll., 1986, Scholar of Yr., 1991, New Eng. Woman's Leadership award, 1998. Mem. Fin. Womens Assn., Am. Econ. Assn., Com. on the Status of Women in Econs. Professions, The Boston Club, The Boston Econ. Club. Office: Bentley Coll 175 Forest St Waltham MA 02452-4713

FLYNN, PAULINE T. speech pathologist, educator; d. William J. and Pauline F. Flynn. BA, Paterson State Coll., 1963; MA, Seton Hall U., 1966; PhD, U. Kans., 1970; cert. specialist in aging, U. Mich., 1982. Lic. speech pathologist, Ind.; cert. of clin. competence in speech pathology, Am. Speech Lang. Hearing Assn. Tchr., speech pathologist Bd. Edn., Parsippany-Troy Hills, N.J., 1963-67; prof., chmn. dept. audiology and speech scis. Ind. U. Purdue U., Ft. Wayne, 1970—. Ednl. cons. Retirement Ctr., Ft. Wayne, 1982-85. Contbr. articles to nat. and internat. jours. Recipient Outstanding Alumna award William Paterson Coll., 1973, Woman of Achievement award Ft. Wayne YWCA, 1992. Fellow Am. Speech, Lang. and Hearing Assn.; mem. Am. Speech, Lang., Hearing Assn., Ind. Speech, Lang. and Hearing Assn., Phi Kappa Phi. Office: Ind U Purdue U Ft Wayne Dept Audiology & Speech Scis 2101 E Coliseum Blvd Fort Wayne IN 46805-1445

FLYNN, WILLIAM BERCHMAN, JR., psychology educator, clinical psychologist; b. Worcester, Mass. s. William Berchman and Elizabeth (Caplis) F.; m. Priscilla Flynn, Oct. 8, 1983; children: Meghan, Alexander. BA in Psychology, Lyndon State Coll., 1972; MA in Counseling Psychology, Assumption Coll., Worcester, 1972, cert. advanced grad. study in counseling, 1973; EdD in Counseling Psychology, Boston U., 1985. Cert. psychologist, N.H.; lic. psychologist, Mass. Asst. prof. psychology Rivier Coll., Nashua, N.H., 1975-79; dir., psychologist Merrimack Valley Counseling, Nashua, 1980—; assoc. prof. Franklin Pierce Coll., Rindge, N.H., 1992—. Adj. prof. U. N.H., Manchester, 1978—, Northeastern U., Boston, 1979—. Fellow Am. Bd. Med. Psychotherapists, 1989—. Mem. APA, Mass. Psychol. Assn., N.H. Psychol. Orgn., Am. Assn. Marriage and Family Therapy. Office: Merrimack Valley Counseling 39 Simon St Ste 2A Nashua NH 03060-3043

FLYNN-FRANKLIN, GERTRUDE ELIZABETH, elementary education educator, social worker; b. Wardell, Mo., Feb. 16, 1938; d. Oren Henry and Mary Elizabeth (Haywood) Flynn; m. Cleophus P. Franklin, Aug. 10, 1954; children: Webster, Gary, LaCreasia, Canessa, Cleophus, Jr., Emory, Mark, Stephen, Alesia. AA, Loop Coll., Chgo., 1972; BA in Sociology, Roosevelt U., 1975, MEd, 1992; MA in Human Svcs., Goddard Coll., 1978; M in Edn., Adminstrn. & Supervision, Roosevelt U., 1993. Ordained minister Christian Meth. Episc. Ch.; cert. social worker, Ill.; cert. pediatric aide III; cert. surg. technician. Career instr., various other positions Model Cities, Chgo., from 1965, housing specialist, to 1978; social worker Chgo. Com. Urban Opportunity- Model Cities, to 1978; asst. dir. CAM-Austin Industries, Chgo., 1978-80; social worker Carlinshor Inst., Chog., 1980-90; elem. sch. tchr. Chgo. Pub. Schs., 1990—. Mem. The Royal Eagle chpt. 88 Prince Hall affiliation, Chgo.; chair Black Community Developer Com., Chgo. Home: 4131 W 21st Pl Chicago IL 60623-2832

FLYNN-TRACE, PATRICIA M. secondary education educator; b. Flushing, N.Y., June 7, 1964; d. Daniel J. and Margaret Flynn; m. Stephan D. Trace, Dec. 21, 1990. BA in Communications, SUNY, Oswego, 1986; MS in Secondary Edn., Hofstra U., 1988; postgrad., L.I. U., 1988-93. Cert. tchr., sch. dist. adminstr., N.Y. Tchr. social studies, English Center Moriches (N.Y.) Jr./Sr. High Sch., 1988—. Office: Center Moriches High Sch 311 Frowein Rd Center Moriches NY 11934-2229

FOBES, JACQUELINE THERESA MITCHELL, psychologist, educator; b. June 5, 1946; came to U.S., 1966; d. Jack and Marie Jane (Powell) Mitchell; m. James Lewis Fobes, Feb. 28, 1970. AA, Pasadena City Coll., 1969; BA, U. Ariz., 1973, MEd, 1974; postgrad., U. Wis., 1975; PhD in Ednl. Psychology, Claremont Grad. Sch., 1988. Lic. ednl. psychologist, Calif.; lic. marriage, family and child therapist, Calif. Edn. psychologist L.A. Unified Schs., 1976-82, Fobes Assocs., Pacific Grove, Calif., 1978-89, Monterey Unified Schs., Calif., 1982-89, Pajaro Valley Schs., Watsonville, Calif., 1984-85; devel. cons. Monterey County Office Edn., Salinas, Calif., 1983-89; assessment psychologist Psychiat. Inst., Washington, 1990-93; ednl. psychologist Pleasantivlle (N.J.) Pub. Schs., 1993—99; Pajara Valley Sch, Watsonsville, Calif., 1999—. Author: A Papapo Boy and His Friends, 1979; editor Ostomy Quar., 1985. Sr. sci. Mainstreaming Spl. Edn. Students Study, 1981; program initiator, cons. Writing adn Thinking Workshops Children, Monterey, 1983-86; cons. Agnese N. Lindley Found., Tucson, 1984-92; project dir. Salinas Reduction Minority Isolation Study, Calif., 1985; initiator, leader Sexual Assault Victims Group, Rape Crisis Ctr., Monterey. Mem. AAUW (bd. dirs. 1984-86, program initiator, chmn. workshop series 1985), Ostomy Soc., Atlantic County Sch. Psychologists Assn., Monterey Bay Women's Sch. Psychol. Assn. Roman Catholic. Avocations: writing, gourmet cooking, walking, gardening, restoration of antique furnitures. Office: Pajaro Valley Unified Sch Dist SELPA/Special Svc 294 Green Valley Rd Watsonville CA 95076-2137 Office Fax: 831-728-8107. E-mail: jackie_Fobes@pvusd.net., jtfobes@yahoo.com.

FODREA, CAROLYN WROBEL, educational researcher, publisher, consultant; b. Hammond, Ind., Feb. 1, 1943; d. Stanley Jacob and Margaret Caroline (Stupeck) Wrobel; m. Howard Frederick Fodrea, June 17, 1967 (div. Jan. 1987); children: Gregory Kirk, Lynn Renee. BA in Elem. Edn., Purdue U., 1966; MA in Reading and Lang. Devel., U. Chgo., 1973; postgrad., U. Colo., Denver, 1986—87. Cert. elem. tchr., Ind., Ill. Tchr. various schs., Ind., Colo., 1966-87; founder, supr., clinician Reading Clinic, Children's Hosp., Denver, 1969-73; pvt. practice in reading and lang. rsch. clinic Denver, 1973-87; pvt. practice in reading rsch. ctr. Deerfield, Ill., 1973—; creator of pilot presch.-kindergarten lang. devel. program Gary, Ind. Diocese Schs., 1987—, therapist lang. and reading disabilities, 1987—; pres. Reading Rsch. Ctr., Arlington Heights, Ill., 2000—. Conducted Lang. Devel. Workshop, Gary, Ind. 1988; tchr. adult basic edn. Dawson Tech. Sch., 1990, Coll. Lake County, 1991, Prairie State Coll., 1991—, Chgo. City Colls., 1991, R.J. Daley Coll., 1991, Coll. DuPage, 1991—; condr. adult basic edn. workshops for Coll. of DuPage, R.J. Daley Coll., 1992, Ill. Lang. Devel. Literacy Program; tchr. Korean English Lang. Inst., Chgo., 1996, Lang. Devel. Program for Minorities, 2000; dir. pilot study Cabrini Green Tutoring Ctr., Chgo., 2000; presenter in field. Author: Language Development Program, 1985, Presch. Kindergarten Lang. Devel. Program, 1988, A Multi-Sensory Stimulation Program for the Premature Baby in Its Incubator to Reduce Medical Costs and Academic Failure, 1986, Predicting At-Risk Babies for First Grade Reading Failure Before Birth A 15 Year Study, A Language Development Program, Grades 1 to Adult, 1988, 92; editor, pub.: ESL For Native Spanish Speakers, 1996, ESL for Native Korean Speakers, 1996. Active Graland Country Day Sch., Denver, 1981-83, N.W. Ind. Children's Chorale, 1988—; Ill. state chair Babies and You com. March of Dimes, 1999—. Mem. NEA, Am. Ednl. Rsch. Assn., Internat. Reading Assn., Am. Coun. for Children with Learning Disabilities, Am. Acad. Environ. Medicine (presenter pilot study at conf. 2002), Assn. for Childhood Edn. Internat., Colo. Assn. for Edn. of Young Children, Infant Stimulation Edn. Assn., Art Inst. Chgo., U. Chgo. Alumni Club (Denver area ann. fund, Pres. fund com. 1988—, numerous positions Denver area chpt. 1974-87). Roman Catholic. Avocations: sports, health and nutrition, literary and cultural activities, sewing. E-mail: cfodrea@readingresearch.com.

FOGARTY, JAMES VINCENT, JR., special education administrator, educator; b. N.Y.C., Dec. 12, 1945; s. James Vincent and Dorothy (Hummender) F.; divorced; children: Ann Denise, Brian James. BS in Biology, SUNY, Stony Brook, 1967; MS in Spl. Edn., Adelphi U., 1971; CAS in Adminstrn., Hofstra U., 1974. Tchr. curriculum and mentally handicapped Bd. of Coop. Edn. Svcs.- Rosemary Kennedy Ctr., Nassau County, N.Y., 1967-74; tchr., lead tchr. Town of Oyster Bay, Syosset/Woodbury, N.Y., 1970-74; asst. ctr. adminstr. Bd. of Coop. Edn. Svcs., 2d Supervisory Dist., Patchogue, N.Y., 1974-77, dep. asst. dir., 1977-83, dir. spl. edn., 1983-96, dir. instrnl. programs divsn. spl. edn. & occ./tech. edn., 1996—, exec. dir., 1997—. Adj. faculty C. W. Post U., Greenvale, N.Y., 1980—; cons. N.Y.C. Bd. Edn., 1981—; adj. prof. Hofstra U., Hempstead, N.Y., 1986—, Dowling Coll., Oakdale, N.Y., 1988—. Pres. chpts. 72 and 653 Coun. Exceptional Children, 1968—; active Nat. Christina Found., 1985—, Suffolk County Handicapped Adv. Bd., Hauppauge, N.Y., 1985—. Rsch. scholar, grantee NSF, 1967; recipient Svc. award Assn. Children with Down's Syndrome, 1981, Stephen Apter Leadership award N.Y. State Educators Emotionally Disturbed, 1989, Comty. Svc. award St. Charles Hosp., 1997. Mem. Phi Delta Kappa (internat. bd. dirs., internat. v.p. 1991-95, internat. pres.-elect 1995-97, pres. 1997-99, Outstanding Kappan award 1971-80, Educator of Yr., Columbia U. 1989). Home: PO Box 1392 Patchogue NY 11772-0796 Office: Eastern Suffolk BOCES James Hines Adminstrn Bldg 201 Sunrise Hwy Patchogue NY 11772

FOGARTY, ROBERT STEPHEN, historian, educator, editor; b. Bklyn., Aug. 30, 1938; s. Michael Joseph and Marguerita (Carmody) F. BS, Fordham U., 1960; PhD, U. Denver, 1968. Instr. Mich. State U., 1963-67; asst. prof. Antioch Coll., Yellow Springs, Ohio, 1968-73, chmn. humanities area, 1973-74, 78-79, assoc. prof., 1974-80, prof. history, 1980—; prof. Advanced Internat. Studies, Ctr. for Chinese-Am. Johns Hopkins U., 1986-87; editor Antioch Rev., 1977—; dir. Associated Colls. Midwest/Gt. Lakes Coll. Assn., Program in Humanities, Newberry Library, 1978-79; cons. Nat. Endowment for Arts, 1975-81, U. Waterloo, Ont., Can., 1981. Vis. fellow NYU Inst. for Humanities, 1992—93; Darwin lectr. human biology Galton Inst., London, 1994. Author: Dictionary of American Communal and Utopian History, 1980, The Righteous Remnant-The House of David, 1981, All Things New: Communes and Utopian Movements, 1860-1914, 1990, Special Love/Special Sex, 1994, Desire and Duty at Oneida: Tirzah Miller's Intimate Memoir, 2000; editor Antioch Rev., 1977—; contbr.: American Encyclopedia of American Culture, 2001; contbr. essays to The Nation, TLS, Mo. Rev. Recipient Martha K. Cooper award for editl. achievement, 1981, Nora Magid Award for Editing PEN Am. Ctr., 2003; grantee Am. Philos. Soc., 1976, Am. Coun. Learned Socs.; fellow NEH, 1980, All Souls Coll., Oxford U., 1988, Lloyd Lewis fellow Newberry Libr., 1995, Galton Inst. fellow, 1995; Fulbright Disting. Lectr. to Korea, 2000, Gilder Lehrman fellow 2001. Mem.: PEN/Am. Ctr., Orgn. Am. Historians, Nat. Hist. Communal Sites Assn. (exec. com. 1975—2002), Am. Studies Assn. (bibliography com. 1981—). Office: Antioch Rev Inc PO Box 148 Yellow Springs OH 45387-0148

FOGED, LESLIE OWEN, mathematician, educator; b. Cheyenne, Wyo., Sept. 26, 1953; s. Leif Clifford and Darlene Ann (Lutz) F.; m. Robyn Rachel Gilliom, May 30, 1981 (div. 1984); 1 child, Leif Erik. BA in Math., Midland Luth. Coll., 1974; PhD in Math., Washington U., St. Louis, 1979. Asst., assoc. prof. U. Tex., El Paso, Tex., 1979—, chmn. dept. math., 1987-88. Dir. U. Tex. H.S. Math. Contest, 1990—. Contbr. articles to profl. jours. Recipient Master Tchr. award Midland Luth. Coll., 1991. Achievements include discovery of an internal characterization of topological spaces which are closed images of metric spaces, constrn. of a consistent example of a quotient space of a separable metric space which is not stratifiable; construction of open-compact image of metric space with no point-countable closed quasibase. Office: U Tex at El Paso Dept Math El Paso TX 79968-0001

FOGEL, RICHARD, lawyer, educator; m. Sheila Feldman; children: Bruce, Lori Ellen. BA, York Coll., CUNY, 1971; JD, N.Y. Law Sch., 1974. Bar: N.J. 1976, U.S. Dist. Ct. N.J. 1976, N.Y. 1981, U.S. Dist. Ct. (so. dist.) N.Y. 2000, U.S. Tax. Ct. 1977. Tax law specialist IRS, Newark, 1975-77; sr. pension cons., atty. N.Y. Life, N.Y.C., 1977-81; pvt. practice Franklin, N.J., 1981-85, Wayne, N.J., 1985-88, McAfee, N.J., 1988—. Lectr. Inst. for Continuing Legal Edn., Newark, 1977—; mem. adj. faculty Upsala Coll., East Orange, N.J., 1978-88; presenter 34th ann. meeting. Internat. Soc. for Systems Scis., Portland State U., 1990. Recipient Certs. of Appreciation, IRS, Newark, 1977, Inst. Continuing Legal Edn., Newark, 1981-82, 84, Cert. in Recognition of Accomplishments, Coop. Extension Cook Coll., Rutgers U., 1982, Disting. Grad. award York Coll., 1984, Founder's Day Dist. Alumni award, 1992. Home: 28 Elizabeth Dr Sussex NJ 07461-3402 Office: Vernon Colonial Pla PO Box 737 Rt 94 Mc Afee NJ 07428

FOGEL, ROBERT WILLIAM, economist, educator, historian; b. N.Y.C., July 1, 1926; s. Harry Gregory and Elizabeth (Mitnik) Fogel; m. Enid Cassandra Morgan, Apr. 2, 1949; children: Michael Paul, Steven Dennis. AB, Cornell U., 1948; AM, Columbia U., 1960; PhD, Johns Hopkins U., 1963; MA (hon.), U. Cambridge, Eng., 1975, Harvard U., 1976; DSc (hon.), U. Rochester, 1987, U. de Palermo, Argentina, 1994, Brigham Young U., 1995. Instr. Johns Hopkins U., 1958—59; asst. prof. U. Rochester, 1960—64; Ford Found. vis. research prof. U. Chgo., 1963—64, asso. prof., 1964—65, prof. econs., 1965—69, prof. econs. and history, 1970—75; prof. econs. U. Rochester, 1968—71, prof. econs. and history, 1972—75; Taussig research prof. Harvard U., Cambridge, Mass., 1973—74, Harold Hitchings Burbank prof. polit. economy, prof. history, 1975—81; Charles R. Walgreen Disting. Svc. prof. Am. instns. U. Chgo., 1981—. Pitt prof. Am. history and insts. U. Cambridge, 1975—76; chmn. com. math. and statis. methods in history Math. Social Sci. Bd., 1965—72; rsch. assoc. Nat. Bur. Econ. Rsch., 1978—; dir. DAE program, 1978—91; dir. Ctr. for Population Econ., Chgo. Author: The Union Pacific Railroad: A Case in Premature Enterprise, 1960, Railroads and American Economic Growth: Essays in Econometric History, 1964, Ten Lectures on the New Economic History, 1977, Without Consent of Contract: The Rise and Fall of American Slavery, Vol. 1, 1989, The Fourth Great Awakening and the Future of Egalitarianism, 2000, The Slavery Debates, 1952-1990: A Retrospective, 2003; author: (with others) The Reinterpretation of American Economic History, 1971, Dimensions of Quantitative Research in History, 1972, Without Consent of Contract: The Rise and Fall of American Slavery, Vols. 2-4, 1992; author: (with S.L. Engerman) Time on the Cross: The Economics of American Negro Slavery, 1974; author: (with G.R. Elton) Which Road to the Past? Two Views of History, 1983. Co-recipient The Bancroft prize, 1975, Gustavus Myers prize, 1990, Nobel prize, Nobel Found., 1993; recipient Arthur H. Cole prize, 1968, Schumpter prize, 1971, Disting. Alumnus award, Johns Hopkins U., 2000; fellow, Gilman, 1957—60, Social Sci. Rsch. Coun., 1960, Ford Found. Faculty Rsch., 1970; grantee Faculty Rsch., 1966, NSF, 1967, 1970, 1972, 1975—76, 1978, 1992—96, Fulbright, 1968, NIH, 1991—. Fellow: AAAS, Royal Hist. Soc., Econometric Soc., Brit. Acad. (corr.); mem.: NAS, Am. Philos. Soc., Internat. Union for Sci. Study of Population, Population Assn. Am., Am. Acad. Arts and Scis., Agrl. History Soc., Social Sci. History Assn. (pres. 1980—81), Assn. Am. Historians, Am. Hist. Assn., Econ. History Soc., Econ. History Assn. (trustee 1972—81, pres. 1977—78), Royal Econ. Soc., Am. Econ. Soc. (pres. 1998), European Acad. Arts, Scis. and Humanities, Phi Beta Kappa. Office: U Chgo Grad Sch Bus Ctr for Population Econ 1101 E 58th St Chicago IL 60637-1511

FOGELBERG, PAUL ALAN, continuing education company executive; b. St. Paul, May 18, 1951; s. Harry William and Dorothy Marie (Dokmo) F.; m. Melissa Rosanne Ormsbee, Oct. 1980; children: Emily Lauren, Julia Christine, Sara Ellen. BS, U. Minn., 1975; JD, Hamline U., 1978. Pub. affairs asst. The Pillsbury Co., Mpls., 1974-75; dir. Nat. Practice Inst., Mpls., 1978-81; CEO The Profl. Edn. Group, Inc., Minnetonka, Minn., 1981—. Pres. Ctrl. States Dressage & Combined Tng. Assn., 2000-2002. Mem. Hamline U. Pres. Club, Hamline U. Sch. Law Alumni Assn. (Disting. Svc. 1988, pres. 1985-86), Cen. States Dressage and Combined Training Assn. (bd. dirs. 1999—, pres. 2000-02), Opportunity Internat. Minn. (bd. dirs.). Presbyterian. Office: The Profl Edn Group Inc 12401 Minnetonka Blvd Minnetonka MN 55305-3994 E-mail: paul@proedgroup.com.

FOGELSON, BRIAN DAVID, educational administrator; b. Newton, N.J., Sept. 25, 1953; s. Edwin Malcolm and Marylyn Jean (Post) F. MusB, Westminster Choir Coll., 1975; EdM, Stetson U., 1989; EdD, Fla. State U., 1992. Cert. music tchr. grades K-12, N.J., tchr. class VIII, N.S., Can.; cert. music tchr., tchrs. K-12, adminstr., ednl. leader, Fla.; cert. elem. and secondary prin., Pa.; cert. prin., sch. adminstr., N.J. Tchr. Lunenburg County Dist. Sch. Bd., Bridgewater, N.S., 1975-90; grad. asst., coord. alt. tchr. preparation program Stetson U., Deland, Fla., 1988-89; grad. asst., coord. tutors for at risk students Fla. State U., Tallahassee, 1989-92, rsch. assoc., asst. prof., 1992-93; program adminstr. Fla. Acad. for Excellence in Teaching and the Fla. League Tchrs., Fla. State Univ., Tallahassee, 1992-93; asst. prin. Key West (Fla.) H.S., 1993-95, Catasauqua (Pa.) H.S., 1995-97, prin., 1997-2000, Delaware Valley Regional H.S., Frenchtown, N.J., 2000—. Cons. Fla. Sch. Dists., 1989-95, Fla. Dept. Edn., Tallahassee, 1991-95. Vol. asst. conductor Steton U. Children's Chorus, Deland, 1988-89; mem. sect. leader, soloist Tallahassee (Fla.) Community Chorus, 1989-93; dir. Tallahassee Civic Chorale, 1993. Mem. ASCD, NASSP, Nat. Assn. Multicultural Edn., Nat. Coun. of the States, Internat. Soc. for Tchr. Edn., N.J. Prins. and Suprs. Assn., N.J. Assn. Sch. Adminstrs., Kappa Delta Pi, Phi Delta Kappa (newsletter editor 1992-93), Free and Accepted Masons (past master), Order of the Ea. Star (past worthy patron). Avocations: reading, singing, golfing. Office: Delaware Valley Regional HS 19 Senator Stout Rd Frenchtown NJ 08825-3721 E-mail: brian.fogelson@DVRHS.K12.NJ.US.

FOGLEMAN, GUY CARROLL, physicist, mathematician, educator; b. Lake Charles, La., Dec. 29, 1955; s. Louis Carroll and Peggy Joyce (Trahan) F.; m. Jenny S. Kishiyama, Mar. 14, 1993; children: Elyssa Mayumi, Myles Masaru. BS in Physics, La. State U., 1977; MS in Physics, Ind. U., 1979, MA in Math., 1981, PhD in Physics, 1982. Rsch. assoc. Tri Univ. Meson Facility U. B.C., Vancouver, Canada, 1982—84; assoc. prof. San Francisco State U., 1984—87, adj. prof., 1987—; project scientist RCA Govt. Svcs., Moffett Field, Calif., 1987—88; prin. investigator Search for Extraterrestrial Intelligence Inst., Mountain View, Calif., 1988—89; mgr. advanced programs life scis. divsn. NASA Hdqrs., Washington, 1990—93; acting chief environ. sys. and tech. br. Life and Biomed Scis. and Applications divsn. NASA Hdqrs., Washington, 1993—95; program exec. human exploration and devel. of space advanced human support techs. program Life Scis. divsn. NASA, Washington, 1996—2000; acting dir. bioastronautics rsch. divsn. NASA Hdqrs., Washington, 2000—03, dir. bioastronautics rsch. divsn., 2003—. Vis. physicist Stanford (Calif.) Linear Accelerator Ctr., 1984-86. Contbr. articles to sci. jours. Travel grantee NSF and NATO, 1980; rsch. grantee NASA, 1988, 89. Mem. AIAA (sr.), AAAS, Am. Phys. Soc., Prometheus Soc. (ombudsman 1998-99), Mega Soc., Sigma Xi (assoc.), Sigma Pi Sigma. Achievements include research in physics of particles in microgravity, theoretical elementary particle physics, technologies for the collection of cosmic dust particles, the origins of life and the philosophy of mind. Office: NASA Hdqrs Code UB Washington DC 20546-0001 E-mail: gfoglema@hq.nasa.gov.

FOGLESONG, PAUL DAVID, molecular biology and microbiology educator; b. Marion, Va., June 24, 1949; s. Everett Paul and Thelma Broucelle (Conner) F.; m. Clare Maria Wright, July 1, 1978 (div. Jan. 1985). BS, Va. Tech., 1971; PhD, SUNY, Stony Brook, 1980. Cost analyst Irving Trust Co., N.Y.C., 1973; rsch. asst. SUNY, Stony Brook, 1973-80; fellow Albert Einstein Coll. of Medicine, Bronx, N.Y., 1980-82, rsch. fellow, 1982; rsch. asst. St. Jude Children's Rsch. Hosp., Memphis, 1982-86; dir. biochemistry Biotherapeutics Inc., Memphis, 1986-88; asst. prof. Memphis State U., 1988-89, Rutgers U., Camden, N.J., 1989-96, U. Incarnate Word, San Antonio, 1996-97, assoc. prof., 1997—; pres. Progressive Capital Svcs., 2002—. Cons. So. Rsch. Inst., Birmingham, Ala., 1989—. Contbr. articles to Jour. Virology, Cancer Immunol. Immunother., Anal. Biochem., Virology, Jour. Heredity, Virus Genes. Treas. Am. Guild Organists, Memphis, 1988-89; trustee St. Mark's Ch., Phila., 1993-96, treas., 1991-95, acctg. warden, 1995-96; asst. organist St. Mary's Cathedral, Memphis, 1984-89. Gov. Westmoreland Davis scholar, 1967-71. Mem. AAAS, Am. Soc. Microbiology, Am. Soc. Virology, Am. Assn. Cancer Rsch., Soc. Exptl. Biology and Medicine, Phi Kappa Phi. Achievements include characterization of the inhibition of type I DNA topoisomerase by ATP analogs, antibiotics, and antitumor drugs; characterization of DNA topoisomerase levels in tumor tissues by immunohistochemistry; development of an in vitro system for faithful transcription of vaccinia virus genes, map of Frog Virus 3 genome. E-mail: davidf@universe.uiwtx.edu.

FOLAND, KAY LYNN, nurse therapist, nursing educator; b. Kadoka, S.D., Dec. 23, 1955; d. Vern K. and Carrol G. (Thorson) P. BSN, S.D. State U., Brookings, 1980; MSN, U. Nebr. Med. Ctr., 1982; PhD, U. Tex., 1989. RN, S.D. Instr. Rapid City Area Schs., 1982-84; clin. nurse specialist West River Mental Health Ctr., Rapid City, 1982-83; instr. U. Tex., Austin, 1985-86, 87-88; asst. prof. to assoc. prof. S.D. State U., Rapid City, 1982—; therapist Behavior Mgmt. Systems, 1989—99. Mem. ANA, Coun. Nurse Researchers, Midwest Nursing Rsch. Soc., Gerontol. Soc. Am., Phi Kappa Phi, Sigma Theta Tau. Home: 4908 Stoney Creek Dr Rapid City SD 57702-9238 Office: 1011 11th St Rapid City SD 57701-3530

FOLBERG, HAROLD JAY, lawyer, mediator, educator, university dean; b. East St. Louis, Ill., July 7, 1941; s. Louis and Matilda (Ross) F.; m. Diana L. Taylor, May 1, 1983; children: Lisa, Rachel, Ross. BA, San Francisco State U., 1963; JD, U. Calif., Berkeley, 1968. Bar: Oreg. 1968. Assoc. Rives & Schwab, Portland, Oreg., 1968-69; dir. Legal Aid Service, Portland, 1970-72; exec. dir. Assn. Family and Conciliation Cts., Portland, 1974-80; prof. law Lewis and Clark Law Sch., Portland, 1972-89; clin. asst. prof. child psychiatry U. Oreg. Med. Sch., 1976-89; judge pro-tem Oreg. Trial Cts., 1974-89; dean, prof. U. San Francisco Sch. Law, 1989-99, prof. law, 1999—. Chair jud. coun. Calif. Task Force on Alternative Dispute Resolution and the Jud. Sys., 1998-99, Calif. Blue Ribbon Panel Experts on Arbitration Ethics, 2001-2002, chair jud. coun.; Rockefeller Found. scholar in residence Bellagio, Italy, 1996; vis. prof. U. Wash. Sch. Law, 1985-86; mem. vis. faculty Nat. Jud. Coll., 1975-88; mem. Nat. Commn. on Accreditation for Marriage and Family Therapists, 1984-90; cons. Calif. Jud. Coun., U.S. Dist. Ct. (no. dist.) Calif. Author: Joint Custody and Shared Parenting, 1984, 2d edit., 1991; (with Taylor) Mediation-A Comprehensive Guide to Resolving Conflicts without Litigation, 1984; (with Milne) Divorce Mediation-Theory and Practice, 1988; mem. editorial bd.Family Counts Rev., Jour. of Divorce, Conflict Resolution Quar.; contbr. articles to profl. jours. Bd. dirs. Internat. Bioethics Inst., 1989-95, Oreg. Dispute Resolution Adv. Coun., 1988-89. Recipient Bernard E. Witkin award, Jud. Coun. Calif., 2002. Mem. ABA (chmn. mediation and arbitration com. family law sect. 1980-82, chmn. ethics com. dispute resolution sect. 2002-), Oreg. State Bar Assn. (chmn. family and juvenile law sect. 1979-80), Am. Bd. Trial Advs., Multnomah Bar Assn. (chmn. bd. dirs. legal aid svc. 1973-76), Am. Arbitration Assn. (mem. panel of arbitrators), Assn. Family and Conciliation Cts. (pres. 1983-84), Assn. Marriage and Family Therapists (disting. mem.), Am. Assn. Law Schs. (chmn. alternative dispute resolution sect. 1988), Acad. Family Mediators (bd. dirs., pres. 1988), Assn. Conflict Resolution, World Assn. Law Profs. (sec.-gen. 1995-2000). Office: U San Francisco Sch Law 2130 Fulton St San Francisco CA 94117-1080 E-mail: folbergj@usfca.edu.

FOLDESI, ROBERT STEPHEN, education administrator, management educator; b. Mt. Pleasant, Mich., Aug. 3, 1946; s. Julius and Imogene Mary (Walker) F.; m. Nancy Bernadette Guiser, Dec. 1, 1967; children: Robert, Todd, Amy. BA in Sociology, Cen. Mich. U., Mt. Pleasant, 1968, MA in Mgmt., 1977. Indsl. relations specialist Ford Motor Co., Dearborn, Mich., 1971-76; mgr. devel. Cen. Mich. U., Mt. Pleasant, 1976-80; personnel dir. St. Mary's Coll., South Bend, Ind., 1980-84, dir. of admn. srvcs., 1984-86; asst. v.p., human resources Ill. State U., Normal, Ill., 1986—97; v.p. and dir. human resources U. Iowa, 1997—2001; v.p. human rels. U. Notre Dame, Ind., 2001—. Instr. external degree program, Cen. Mich. U., 1978—. Vice chmn. projects with industry Goodwill, South Bend, 1980-81; chmn. campaign St. Mary's County United Way, South Bend, 1984-86; mem. planning div. St. Joseph County United Way, South Bend, 1985-86. Served to capt. U.S. Army, 1968-71, Vietnam. Mem. Am. Soc. Personnel Profls. (sec. 1985-86), Am. Soc. Personnel Adminstrs. (mem. local bd. 1985), Coll. and Univ. Personnel Assn. (dir. membership 1984-85). Roman Catholic. Avocation: running.*

FOLEY, CHARLES BRADFORD, university dean, music educator; b. Indpls., Jan. 30, 1953; s. Charles Lyman and Barbara Ann (Shaw) F.; m. Diane Ellen Berger, June 6, 1976; children: Carolyn Berger, David Bradford. BA with honors, Ball State U., 1975; MusM, U. Mich., 1977, D of Musical Arts, 1983. Grad. tchg. asst. U. Mich., Ann Arbor, 1975-77; instr. Stephen F. Austin State U., Nacogdoches, Tex., 1977-79, East Carolina U., Greenville, N.C., 1979-81, asst. prof., 1981-86, assoc. prof., 1986-92, prof., 1992—2002, asst. dean Sch. Music, 1984-95, dean Sch. Music, 1995—2002, mem. adv. bd. Friends of Music, 1984—2002, mem. adv. bd. Music Alumni Soc., 1985—2002; prof., dean sch. music U. Oreg., 2002—. Contbr. articles to profl. jours.; performer Brad Foley in Concert, 1984, soloist, chamber music, 1979—. Pres., bd. dirs. Greenville Choral Soc. and New Carolina Sinfonia, 1990—91; bd. dirs. Oreg. Bach Festival, 2002—. Grantee So. Arts Fedn., 1997-02, A.J. Fletcher Found., 1995-02, Presser Found., 1995-02, N.C. Arts Coun., 1997. Mem. N.Am. Saxophone Alliance (regional dir. 1982-88, treas. 1988-93, jour. editor 1989), N.C. Music Tchrs. Assn., Music Tchrs. Nat. Assn. Methodist. Avocations: reading fiction, swimming, travel. Home: 743 Brookside Dr Eugene OR 97405-4935 Office: Music Sch 1225 U Oreg Eugene OR 97403-1205 Fax: 541-346-0723.

FOLEY, DAVID RAY, middle school educator; b. Greenville, Mich., Feb. 15, 1947; s. Norman Peter and Bernice Florence (Utter) F.; m. Cynthia Stewart Cheney, Sept. 19, 1970; children: Benjamin, Betsy. AA, Grand Rapids Jr. Coll., 1967; BA, Albion Coll., 1969; MA, Mich. State U., 1976. Cert. tchr., Mich. Tchr. middle sch. Cadillac (Mich.) Area Schs., 1974—. Author: Guide to the AuSable Marathon, 1991; editor Mich. Runner, 1984-99; contbr. articles to Mich. Out-of-Doors, Runner's World. Served with U.S. Army, 1969-71. Recipient Outstanding Person in Edn. award, Cadillac Area Pub. Schs., 2002. Mem. Cadillac Tchrs. Assn. Presbyterian. Avocations: wilderness canoe trips, running, canoe paddling, cross country skiing, fishing. Home: 203 Peninsula Dr Cadillac MI 49601-9621 Office: Cadillac Area Schs 500 Chestnut St Cadillac MI 49601-1824

FOLEY, JAMES DAVID, computer science educator, consultant; b. Palmerton, Pa., July 20, 1942; s. Marvin Winfield and Stella Elizabeth (Ziegler) F.; m. Mary Louise Herrmann, Aug. 22, 1964; children: Heather, Jennifer. BSEE, Lehigh U., 1964; MSEE, U. Mich., 1965, PhD, 1969. Group mgr. Info. Control Systems, Ann Arbor, Mich., 1969-70; asst. prof. U. N.C., Chapel Hill, 1970-76; sr. systems analyst Bur. of Census, Washington, 1976-77; assoc. prof. George Washington U., Washington, 1977-81, prof., 1981-90, chmn. dept. elec. engring. and computer sci., 1988-90; prof. Ga. Inst. Tech., Atlanta, 1991—, assoc. dean coll. computing, 2001—03; dir. Graphics Visualization and Usability Ctr., Atlanta, 1991-96, Mitsubishi Electric Rsch. Lab. (MERL), Cambridge, Mass., 1996-97; exec. v.p. Mitsubishi Electric Info. Tech. Ctr. Am., Cambridge, 1996-97, chmn., CEO, 1998-99; exec. dir. Ga.'s Yamacraw Mission, 1999—2000. Pres. Computer Graphics Cons., Washington, 1979-96; mem. industry program adv. com. NAS, 1997-99. Author: (with others) Fundamentals of Computer Graphics, 1982, (with others) Computer Graphics: Principles and Practice, 1990, (with others) Introduction to Computer Graphics, 1993; co-author (graphics standard) Core System, 1977. Bd. dirs. Patriot Trails coun. Girl Scouts. U.S., 1998-99. Fellow: IEEE, Computing Rsch. Assn. (bd. dirs. 1996—, treas. 1998—2000, chmn. 2001—), Assn. for Computing Machinery; mem.: Assn. for Computing Machinery/Computer-Human Interaction Acad. (Spl. Interest Group for Graphs Coons award 1997), Nat. Computer Graphics Assn. (bd. dirs. 1982—84), Spl. Interest Group for Graphics (vice chmn. 1973—75), Human Factors Soc. Avocations: skiing, sailing, model railroading. Office: Georgia Inst Tech College of Computing Atlanta GA 30332-0280 Home: 1588 Friar Tuck Rd Atlanta GA 30309 Business E-Mail: foley@cc.gatech.edu.

FOLEY, JANE DEBORAH, foundation executive; b. Chgo., May 30, 1952; d. Colin Gray Stevenson and Bette Jane (Cullenbine) Coleman; m. George Edward Foley, Jan. 29, 1972; children: Sy Curtis, Shelly. BA, Purdue U., 1973, MS, 1977, PhD, 1992. Cert. elem. adminstr., Ind., cert. elem. adminstrn. and supervision. Tchr. phys. edn. and health Lafayette (Ind.) Jefferson H.S., 1973-74; tchr. music and phys. edn. Valparaiso (Ind.) Cmty. Schs., 1974-79, tchr. elem. phys. edn., 1979-90; prin. South Ctrl. Elem. sch., Union Mills, Ind., 1990-93, Flint Lake Elem. Sch., Valparaiso, 1993-98; v.p. Milken Family Found., Santa Monica, Calif., 1998—2003, sr. v.p., 2003—. Mem. panel of experts The Master Tchr., 1996-98; key note spkr., presenter state and nat. confs. Contbr. articles to profl. jours. Mem. Valparaiso Sch. Sys. PTA, mem. exec. bd., 1993-98; bd. dirs. Hold Onto Your Music, Wings Inc. Recipient Hoosier Sch. award, 1992, Ind. 2000 Designation award 1994, Outstanding Dissertation award Internat. Soc. Ednl. Planning, 1993, Nat. Educator award, Milken Family Found., 1994, Ind. Bell Ringer award Ind. Dept. Edn., 1994, Ind. 4 Star Sch. award, 1995, 96, 97, 98, Internat. Tech. Edn. Assn. award, 1995, Cmty. Improvement award Valparaiso C. of C., 1994, NCREL Pathways to Improvement Pilot Site, 1995, Ind. Sch. Improvement award, Ind. Dept. Edn., 1998, others; Ind. 2000 Planning grantee, 1993, Milken Educator Tech. Project leader, 1997, other grants. Mem. ASCD (assoc.), NAESP, Ind. Assn. Sch. Prins., Valparaiso Tchrs. Assn. (treas. 1989-90), Phi Kappa Phi. Avocations: running, reading, writing, computers. Office: Milken Family Found 1250 4th St Santa Monica CA 90401-1350 E-mail: jfoley@mff.org.

FOLEY, MICHAEL PATRICK, marketing professional educator; b. Bethesda, Md., May 15, 1952; s. Patrick Walter and Marguerite Augusta (Boyer) F.; m. Marykate Maag, Aug. 25, 1973; children: Joshua, Erin, Natalie. Student, U. Dayton, 1970-71; BS in Edn., Va. Tech., 1975, MS in Edn., 1979. Cert. mktg. educator. Mktg. educator Fauquier H.S., Warrenton, Va., 1975-78, Osbourn Park H.S., Manassas, Va., 1979—. Mem. Distributive Edn. Clubs Am. (officer, advisor), Va. Assn. Mktg. Educators (Tchr. of Yr. nominee 1990), Va. Vocat. Assn., U.S. Golf Assn., Va. State Golf Assn., PGA Tour Ptnrs. Roman Catholic. Avocations: golf, reading, crossword puzzles, outdoor sports. Home: 8028 Gracie Dr Manassas VA 20112-3738 Office: Osbourn Park H S 8909 Euclid Ave Manassas VA 20111-2404 E-mail: foleymp@pwcs.edu.

FOLEY, TRACY YEVONNE LICHTENFELS, special education educator; b. Cheecktowaga, N.Y., May 3, 1966; d. Vaughn Glen and Georgia Zoanne (Carroll) Lichtenfels; m. Duane Paul Foley, Aug. 4, 1990. Student, Hiram Coll., 1984-85, U. S.C., Conway, 1985-88; BS in Edn., Kent State U., 1989; postgrad., U. S.C., Columbia, 1992-95, Kent State U., 1995-97; MA in Edn., Mt. Vernon Nazarene Coll., 2000. Cert. elem. tchr., spl. edn. tchr., tchr. of emotionally disabled, S.C. Pvt. tutor, Cuyahoga Falls, Ohio, 1988-90; spl. edn. tchr. Pinecrest Elem. Sch., Aiken, S.C., 1991-93, North Aiken Elem. Sch., Aiken, 1993-95, Newcomerstown (Ohio) Mid. Sch., 1995-98; instr. Nat. Inst. Crisis Prevention, 1995—, East Knox Jr./Sr. H.S., Howard, Ohio, 1998-99, Kearsley Early Childhood Ctr., Bucyrus, Ohio, 1999—. Cons. North Aiken County Textbook Adoption Coun., 1992-93; mentor Aiken County Pub. Schs., 1992-93, Bucyrus City Pub. Schs., 2000—; spkr. in field. V.p. North Aiken Sch. Improvement Coun., 1993-95; pres. Pinecrest Sch. Improvement Coun., Aiken, 1991-93; mem. comms. strategic action plan com. Bucyrus City Schs., 2000—; mem. profl. devel. com. Bucyrus City Schs., 2000—. Recipient EIA Tchr. grant State of S.C., Coun. for Exceptional Children chpt. 165 grant, 1994-95, Cert. of Honor Kidz Express Pub. Program, 1993-94; Martha Jennings Scholarship Series lectr., 1996-97. Mem. S.C. Edn. Assn., Ohio Edn. Assn. (mem. profl. rights and responsibility com. 1988-90, Cert. of Honor 1988-89), Coun. for Exceptional Children, S.C. Curriculum Congress, Healthy People 2000 Coalition (mem. tobacco awareness com.), Newcomerstown Edn. Assn. (mem. exec. com. 1995-98), Bucyrus Edn. Assn. (exec. com. 2000—). Democrat. Roman Catholic. Home: 1391 Spring Village Dr Mansfield OH 44906-5010 Office: Bucyrus City Schs Kearsley Early Childhood Ct 630 Jump St Bucyrus OH 44820-1525

FOLGATE, CYNTHIA A. social services administrator; b. Chgo., Jan. 27, 1950; d. William C. and Cassie Edna (Sisemore) F. BA, No. Ill. U., 1974, MA, 1983. Sec. No. Ill. U., DeKalb, 1974—80, 1983—84, instr., 1984—92; outreach coord. Safe Passage, DeKalb, 1992—96, crisis intervention/outreach coord., 1996—97, systems advocacy coord., 1997—2002, cmty. edn. and tng. coord., 2002—. Instr. Waubonsee C.C., Sugar Grove, Ill., 1990—; mem. DeKalb County Domestic Violence Forum, 1990-91; family violence coord. coun. Ill. 16th Jud. Cir.; mem. adv. bd. Coop. Edn. Internship Office No. Ill. U. Speech cons. for various election campaigns DeKalb County, 1988—90; coord. DeKalb County Domestic Violence Initiative, 1998—2000; mem. bd. deacons 1st Congregational United Ch. of Christ, DeKalb, 1989—92. Mem. Friends of Barb City Manor. Office: Safe Passage PO Box 621 Dekalb IL 60115-0621

FOLK, FRANK ANTON, surgeon, educator; b. Chgo., Dec. 15, 1925; s. Frank A. and Anna (Pilisauer) F.; m. Lorna C. Hill, June 18, 1949; children: Laura, Lawrence, Patricia, Elizabeth, Thomas, James, Mary, Tracy Ann, William. BS, Northwestern U., 1945; postgrad., U. Wis., 1945-46; MD, U. Ill., 1949. Diplomate Am. Bd. Surgery, Nat. Bd. Med. Examiners; lic. Ill., Wis. Rotating intern Cook County Hosp., Chgo., 1949-51; resident in gen. surgery Cook County/Columbus Hosp., Chgo., 1951, Cook County Hosp., Chgo., 1954-57, surgeon, 1958-69, dir. of surgery, 1969-72; mem. faculty Stritch Sch. Medicine Loyola U., Maywood, Ill., 1958—, prof. surgery Stritch Sch. Medicine, 1972-96; prof. emeritus, 1997—; rsch. fellow Hektoen Inst., Chgo., 1959-64; asst. chief surgery VA Hosp., Hines, Ill., 1972-95, chief surg. svc., 1995-96. Mem. editl. bd.: The Am. Surgeon, 1984-92; contbr. articles to med. jours. including Am. Jour. Physiology, Jour. Occupl. Medicine, Annals of Surgery, Archives of Surgery, Jour. Trauma, Surg. Clinics of N.Am. Unit pres., exec. bd. Am. Cancer Soc., Chgo., 1972-89; mem. pres.'s adv. com. Benedictine U., Lisle, Ill., 1965-90. Lt. USN, 1951-53, Korea. Decorated Bronze Star, 1953. Fellow ACS (gov., chmn. gen. surgery Chgo. com. on trauma 1975-83, pres. met. chpt. 1977-78, mem. SESAP com. II and III, instr. ACS advanced trauma life support course 1980-87); mem. Am. Surg. Assn., Am. Assn. for Surgery of Trauma, Assn. Mil. Surgeons of U.S., Assn. for Acad. Surgery, Soc. for Surgery of Alimentary Tract, Assn. VA Surgeons, Collegium Internat. Chirurgiae Digestivae, Cen. Surg. Assn., Midwest Surg. Assn. (pres. 1974-75), Western Surg. Assn., Ill. Surg. Soc. (pres. 1971-72), Chgo. Surg. Soc. (pres. 1989-90), Inst. Medicine of Chgo. Roman Catholic. Avocations: medical history, civil war history, central american civilizations. Office: VA Hosp Surg Svc PO Box 5000 Hines IL 60141-1489 Fax: (708) 202-2180.

FOLK, JUDITH ALYNN, school librarian, educator; b. Wash., June 1, 1946; d. Alwyn Vaughan and Laura Nelda Folk. BA in Elem. Edn., U. Oreg., 1968, MA in Curriculum and Instrn., 1969; M in Libr., Info. Svcs., U. Hawaii, 1989. Cert. pvt. schs., Hawaii. Tchr. 6th grade Coos River Elem. Sch., Coos Bay, Oreg., 1968-69; tchr. grades 2-3 Hawaii Prep. Acad., Kamuela, 1969-71, tchr. grades 3,4 & 5, 1973-92, sch. libr. K-8, 1992—, tchr. 7th grade, 2002—. Editor: Around the World Through Stories, vol. 2, 1989. Youth chmn. Waimea Outdoor Cir., Kamuela, 1994; vol. North Hawaii Hospice, Kamuela, 1992—, Children's Lit. Hawaii, 1998—; bd. dir. Waimea Arts Coun., Kamuela, Hawaii, 2002—; co-coord. HPA Horse Trials and Dressage Show, 1996—. Mem. Internat. Reading Assn., Hawaii Isle Dressage and Combined Tng. Assn. (v.p. 1989-94, pres. 1995, 96), Hawaii Quarter Horse Assn., Hawaii Libr. Assn., Hawaii Assn. Sch. Librs., Phi Beta Mu. Avocations: equestrian instructor, traveling, reading, photography. E-mail: jfolk@hpa.edu.

FOLK, ROBERT LOUIS, geologist, educator; b. Cleve., Sept. 30, 1925; s. George Billmyer and Marjorie Marshall (Kinkead) F.; m. Marjorie Thomas, Sept. 7, 1946; children: Robert T., Jennifer Louise, Charles Marshall. BS, Pa. State Coll., 1946, MS, 1950, PhD, 1952. Research geologist Gulf Oil Co., Houston, 1951-52; mem. faculty U. Tex., Austin, 1952—, prof. geol. scis., 1960—, Dave Carlton prof. geol. scis., 1977-88. Vis. lectr. Australian Nat. U., Canberra, 1965, Tong-Ji U., Shanghai, China, 1980; vis. researcher Universita degli Studi, Milan, Italy, 1973 Author: Petrology of Sedimentary Rocks, 1980; contbr. articles to sci. publs. Neil Miner award Nat. Assn. Geology Tchrs., 1989, H.C. Sorby medal Internat. Assn. Sedimentologists, 1990. Fellow Geol. Soc. Am. (Penrose medal 2000); mem. Soc. Econ. Paleontologists and Mineralogists (hon., Twenhofel medal 1979). Methodist. Achievements include first discovery of mineralized nannobacteria on earth; the same-appearing organisms were discovered by NASA in Martian meteorite. Home: 1107 Bluebonnet Ln Austin TX 78704-2005 Office: U of Tex Dept Geol Scis Austin TX 78801

FOLLAND, SHARON KAY, secondary education educator; b. Salt Lake City, May 6, 1950; d. Noel Lee and Geraldine (Potts) Payne; m. Don T. Folland, Aug. 4, 1976 (div. Mar. 1984). BS, Utah State U., 1972. Bus. tchr. Cardston (Alberta) High Sch., Can., 1972-74, Kennedy Jr. High Sch. Granite Sch. Dist., Salt Lake City, 1974-75, Kearns (Utah) Jr. High Sch., 1975-79, Eisenhower Jr. High Sch., Salt Lake City, 1979—. Community sch. tchr. Granite Sch. Dist., Salt Lake City, 1975-86; chair person bus. dept. Eisenhower Jr. High Sch., 1979-88, promotion com., 1984-85, accreditation com., bldg. com., 1985-86. Vol. Community Svc. Reach for Recover, Am. Cancer Soc. Mem. NEA, Utah Edn. Assn., Granite Edn. Assn., Nat. Bus. Edn. Assn. Democrat. Mem. Lds Ch. Avocations: tole painting, crafts, volley ball. Home: 2762 Stafford Cir Salt Lake City UT 84119-5839 Office: Eisenhower Jr High Sch 4351 S Redwood Rd Salt Lake City UT 84123-2298

FOLLET, ROBERT EDWARD, music librarian; b. Syracuse, N.Y., Aug. 12, 1942; s. Robert Edward and Grace (Weymer) F.; m. Diane Weber, June 15, 1968 (div. Apr. 1997). MusB, Oberlin Coll., 1964; MusM, U. Ill., 1966; MLS, U. Tex., 1979. Asst. music libr. U. North Tex., Denton, 1980-89; music libr. Rice U., Houston, 1989-92; head music libr. U. Ariz., Tucson, 1992-95, Ariz. State U., Tempe, 1995—2002, Arthur Freidheim Libr., Peabody Conservatory, Balt., 2002—. Author: Albert Roussel: A Biobibliography, 1986; contbr. over 75 revs. to Am. Record Guide, L.Am. Music Rev. and Notes. Violist Tempe and Mesa Symphony Orch. Mem. Music Libr. Assn. (co-chmn. local arrangements for nat. meeting 1999-2002, chmn. Mountain Plains chpt. 1998-2000), Internat. Assn. Music Librs. (treas. U.S. br. 1991-98). Episcopalian. Avocations: reading, tennis. Address: 1733 E Pratt St Baltimore MD 21231

FOLLICK, EDWIN DUANE, law educator, dean, chiropractor; b. Glendale, Calif., Feb. 4, 1935; s. Edwin Fulfford and Esther Agnes (Catherwood) Follick; m. Marilyn K. Sherk, Mar. 24, 1986. BA, Calif. State U., LA, 1956, MA in Edn., 1961; MA in Social Sci., Pepperdine U., 1957, MPA, 1977; PhD, DTh, St. Andrews Theol. Coll., Sem. Free Prot. Episc. Ch., London, 1958; MS in LS, U. So. Calif., 1963, MEd in Instructional Materials, 1964, AdvMEd in Edn. Adminstrn., 1969; postgrad., Calif. Coll. Law, 1965; LLB, Blackstone Law Sch., 1966, JD, 1967; DC, Cleve. Chiropractic Coll., L.A., 1972; PhD, Academia Theatina, Pescara, 1978; MA in Orgnl. Mgmt., Antioch U., L.A., 1990. Tchr., libr. adminstr. L.A. City Schs., 1957-68; law librarian Glendale U. Coll. Law, 1968-69; coll. librarian Cleve. Chiropractic Coll., L.A., 1969-74, dir. edn. and admissions, 1974-84, prof. jurisprudence, 1975—, dean student affairs, 1976-92, coll. chaplain, 1985—, dean of edn., 1989—, rector, 2003—; assoc. prof. Newport U., 1982; extern prof. St. Andrews Theol. Coll., London, 1961; dir. West Valley Chiropractic Health Ctr., 1972-2000, West Valley Chiropractic Consulting, 2001—. Contbr. articles to profl. jours. Chaplain's asst. U.S. Army, 1958—60. Decorated cavaliere Internat. Order Legion of Honor of Immaculata (Italy); Knight of Malta, Sovereign Order of St. John of Jerusalem; Knight Grand Prelate, comdr. with star, Order of Signum Fidei; comdr. chevalier Byzantine Imperial Order of Constantine the Gt.; comdr. ritter Order St. Gereon; chevalier Mil. and Hospitaller Order of St. Lazarus of Jerusalem (Malta), Chaplain to the Order of St. Stanislas; numerous others. Mem. ALA, NEA, Am. Assn. Sch. Librarians, L.A. Sch. Libr. Assn., Calif. Sch. Libr. Assn., Assn. Coll. and Rsch. Librarians, Am. Assn. Law Librarians, Am. Chiropractic Assn., Internat. Chiropractors Assn., Nat. Geog. Soc., Internat. Platform Assn., Phi Delta Kappa, Sigma Chi Psi, Delta Tau Alpha. Democrat. Episcopalian. Home: 6435 Jumilla Ave Woodland Hills CA 91367-2833 Office: 590 N Vermont Ave Los Angeles CA 90004-2115 also: 7022 Owensmouth Ave Canoga Park CA 91303-2005 E-mail: follicke@cleveland.edu.

FOLSOM, HYTA PRINE, educational grant writer, consultant; b. Day, Fla., Jan. 6, 1948; d. John Wesley and Estelle Melissa (Weaver) Prine; m. Terrence Franklin Folsom, Aug. 25, 1968 (div. 1995); children: Heather V., Laura E., Teresa A., Tyson F. AA, North Fla. Jr. Coll., Madison, 1967; BS in Elem. Edn., Fla. State U., 1969, cert. in early childhood edn., 1981; MS in Ednl. Leadership, Nova U., 1991. Cert. Fund Raising Executive (CFRE) Nat. Soc. of Fund Raising Execs. (NSFRE), 1996. Tchr. Gladys Morse Elem. Sch., Perry, Fla., 1969-72, 73-74; owner, operator Hyta's Presch. and Nursery, Mayo, Fla., 1979; tchr. Lafayette Elem. Sch., Mayo, 1975-77, 81-93; grants writer Lafayette County Sch. Dist., Mayo, 1989-93; cons. Grant Writers Directory, Jostens Learning Corp., 1991—; dir. alt. resources Coun. of Govts., Odessa, Tex., 1993-97; owner, CEO Devel. Strategies, Inc., 1996—; title III coord. Odessa Coll., 1998—2000, dir. grants and fed. projects, 1998—2000. Mem. tchr. edn. coun. Layafette County Sch. Dist., 1983-85, coord. pre-kindergarten program, 1989-93; rep. Nat. Child Devel. Assocs., 1992; mem. Lafayette Dist. Adv. Coun., 1990-93, Schoolyear 2000 Pub. Schs. Coun., 1991-93; chair Lafayette County Early Childhood Coun., 1989-92; bd. dirs. Permian Basin chpt. Assn. Fundraising Profls., 2003—. Co-author: Rainbows of Readiness, 1990. Leader Brownie troop Girl Scouts U.S., 1984-85; mem.-at-large Suwannee River Resource Conservation Devel., 1991, sec., 1992-93; nursery coord., tchr. Sunday sch., leader children's ch. Brewer Lake Bapt. Ch., 1984-85; bd. dirs. Bynum Sch., 2003—. Named Master Tchr., State of Fla., 1986. Mem. Assn. Fundraising Profl. (chmn. edn. forum, 2003), Lafayette Edn. Assn. (v.p. 1976-77, 87-89, pres. 1990), Am. Diabetes Assn. (Odessa chpt. v.p. 1997, pres. 1998), Kiwanis (sec. Mayo chpt. 1992), Alpha Delta Kappa. Democrat. Avocation: reading. Home and Office: 1513 Custer Ave Odessa TX 79761-3230 E-mail: hytafols@apex2000.net.

FOLSOM, LOWELL EDWIN, language educator; b. Pitts., Sept. 30, 1947; s. Lowell Edwin and Helen Magdalene (Roeper) Folsom; m. Patricia Ann Jackson, Aug. 30, 1969; 1 child, Benjamin Bradford. BA, Ohio Wesleyan U., 1969; MA, U. Rochester, 1972, PhD, 1976. Chmn. English dept. Lancaster (Ohio) H.S., 1969-70, 71-72; instr. Eastman Sch. Music, Rochester, NY, 1974-75; vis. asst. prof. SUNY, Geneseo, 1975-76; asst. prof. U. Iowa, Iowa City, 1976-82, assoc. prof., 1982-87, prof., 1987—, chair English dept., 1991-95, F. Wendell Miller disting. prof., 1997—2002, Carver prof., 2002—. Cons. Am. Coll. Testing Co., Iowa City, 1980—, Nat. Assessment Ednl. Progress, Denver, 1980—84; dir. Walt Whitman Centennial Conf., Iowa City, 1992, Walt Whitman Conf., Beijing, 2000; Fulbright sr. prof. U. Dortmund, Germany, 1996. Author: Walt Whitman's Native Representations, 1994 (Choice Best Acad. Book, 1995); editor: Walt Whitman: The Centennial Essays, 1994, Walt Whitman: The Measure of His Song, 1981 (Choice Best Acad. Book, 1982), rev. edit., 1998 (Ind. Publisher Book award, 1999), Walt Whitman and the World, 1995, (CD-ROM) Walt Whitman, 1997 (Choice Best Acad. Book, 1998), Walt Whitman Quar. Rev., 1983—, Whitman East and West, 2002; co-dir.: Walt Whitman Hypertext Archive, 1997—; editl. bd. Walt Whitman Encyclopedia, 1994—98, PMLA, 1999—2002, Profession, 2002—. Named Disting. Scholar, U. Rochester, 1995; recipient Rsch. award, NEH, 1991—94, Collaborative Rsch. award, 2000—, Faculty Excellence award, Iowa Bd. Regents, 1996. Mem.: MLA, Whitman Scholars Assn. (dir. 1992—), Am. Studies Assn., Am. Lit. Assn. Home: 739 Clark St Iowa City IA 52240-5640 Office: Univ Iowa Dept English 308 EPB Iowa City IA 52242 E-mail: ed-folsom@uiowa.edu.

FOLTINY, STEPHEN VINCENT, special education educator; b. Syracuse, N.Y., Feb. 1, 1952; s. Stephen and Ilona T. (Kovacs) F. BA, Rutgers U., 1974; MA, Rider Coll., 1982; EdS, Rider U., 2002. Tchr. Princeton (N.J.) Child Devel. Inst., 1986-87; assoc. teaching parent devel. disabilities div. State of N.J. Human Svcs., Trenton, 1988-91; trainer Mercer County (N.J.) Assn. Retarded Citizens, 1991; tchr., job coach EDEN W.E.R.C., Montgomery Twp., N.J., 1991—; behavioral cons. N.J. Ctr. Outreach and Svcs. for Autism Cmty., Trenton, N.J., 1992. Assoc. teaching parent divsn. Youth and Family Svcs., Autism unit, State of N.J., 1988-91; respite cons. New Horizons in Autism, Cranbury, N.J., 1997-; intern presch. program Mercer County Sp; Sch. Dist., 1999; intern Ctr. for Innovative Family Achievement, 2001. Recipient N.J. State scholarship, 1970-74. Mem. ACA, Nat. Tchg. Family Assn. (cert.), Coun. Exceptional Children, Coun. Children with Behavioral Disorders, N.J. Assn. for Persons in Supported Employment, United Chess Fedn. (cert. chess coach 1998). Avocations: coaching, sports, reading, stamp and coin collecting.

FOLZ, KATHLEEN LOUISE, elementary education educator; b. Chgo. d. Roman Louis and Dorothy Irene (Krueger) Salik; m. Thomas F. Folz. BS in Edn., Loyola U., Chgo., 1971; MS, St. Xavier U., 1997. Elem. tchr. St. Veronica Sch., Chgo., 1971-73, St. Robert Bellarmine Sch., Chgo., 1973-79; substitute tchr. St. Mary's Sch., Des Plaines, Ill., 1979-80, kindergarten and presch. tchr., 1980-86; kindergarten tchr. South Elem. Sch., Franklin Park, Ill., 1986-92, head tchr., 1989-90, tchr., 1992-93, 1992-93, tchr. kindergarten, 1993-97; tchr North Elem. Sch., Franklin Park, 1997—. Master tchr. Archdiocese of Chgo., 1982-86. Creator/tchr. kindergarten program, 1975, perceptual-motor program, 1976-86; sold 2 ideas (Spl. Spiders and Little Sprouts to The Mailbox mag., 1995), Plant a Little Flower, 1997, others.

FOMON, SAMUEL JOSEPH, physician, educator; b. Chgo., Mar. 9, 1923; s. Samuel and Isabel (Sherman) F.; m. Betty Lorraine Freeman, Aug. 20, 1948 (div. Apr. 1978); children: Elizabeth Ann Fomon Seiberling, Kathleen Lenore Fomon Anderson, David Bruce, Christopher, Mary Susan Fomon; m. Louise G. Thomson, June 27, 1986. AB cum laude, Harvard U., 1945; MD, U. Pa., 1947; D (hons.), U. Catolica de Cordoba, Argentina, 1974. Diplomate Am. Bd. Pediatrics, Am. Bd. Nutrition. Intern Queen's Gen. Hosp., Jamaica, N.Y., 1947-48; resident Children's Hosp., Phila., 1948-50; research fellow Cin. Children's Hosp. Research Found., 1950-52; asst. prof. pediatrics U. Iowa, Iowa City, 1954-58, assoc. prof., 1958-61, prof., 1961-93, prof. emeritus, 1993—. Adj. prof. pediat. Baylor Med. Coll., Houston, 2002—; rev. com. child health and human devel. program project NIH, 1966-69, nutrition study sect., 1978-81; select com. GRAS-Generally Recognized as Safe substances Life Sci. Rsch. Office, 1974-80; expert to US Food and Agrl. Orgn. of UN and WHO, 2003—, mem. working group on infant formulas export to U.S., 2003. Author: Infant Nutrition, 1st edit., 1967, 2d edit., 1974, Nutrition of Normal Infants, 1993. Recipient Career Devel. award NIH, 1962-67, Rosen von Rosenstein award Swedish Pediatric Soc., 1975, McCollum award Am. Soc. Clin. Nutrition, 1979, F. Cuenca Villoro Found. award, Zaragosa, Spain, 1981, Commr.'s spl. citation FDA, 1984, Nutricia Found. award, Rotterdam, The Netherlands, 1991, Bristol-Myers Squibb/Mead Johnson award, 1992, Harry Schwachman award N.Am. Soc. Pediatric Gastroenterology and Nutrition, 1992, A.O. Atwater 2000 Lectureship, Spl. award L.Am. Nutrition Soc., 2000. Fellow AAAS; mem. Am. Inst. Nutrition (pres. 1989-90, fellow 1989, Conrad A. Elvehjem award 1990), Am. Acad. Pediatrics (chmn. com. nutrition 1960-63, Borden award 1956), Am. Soc. Clin. Nutrition (pres. 1981-82), Fedn. Am. Socs. Exptl. Biology, Midwest Soc. Pediat. Rsch. (pres. 1963-64, Founder's award 1986), Am. Dietetic Assn. (hon.), El Colegio de Pediat. de Jalisco (hon.). E-mail: samfomon@aol.com.

FONDAW, ELIZABETH LOUISE, vocational school educator; b. Nashville, Nov. 11, 1942; d. Robert Herchell and Della Mae (Swoner) Bridges; m. Edward D. Fondaw, June 14, 1958; children: Herchell Steven, Tonya Ann Fondaw Hamlin. BS in Edn., U. Tenn., 1989; trade cert. for edn., Memphis State U., 1993; student, various cosmetology courses. Lic. cosmetology instr., lic. cosmetologist/instr., Tenn.; cert. skin care tng. Cosmetologist Harvey's Beauty Salon; cosmetology sr. tchr. Tenn. Tech. Ctr. at Nashville. Tchr. esthetics Memphis State Continuing Edn. Adv. com. Metro Schs. Artist for runner-up Hair Fashion Model of Yr., Nat. Hairdresser and Cosmetology Assn., 1982; recipient Cert. of Recognition, Dudley Products, Inc., 1988. Mem. ASCD, Nat. Assn. Cosmetology Schs., Inc. (Tchrs. Coun. Cert. of Achievement 1980), Golden Key. Home: 7753 Dice Lampley Rd PO Box 941 Fairview TN 37062-0941 Office: Nashville Area Vo-Tech Sch 100 White Bridge Rd Nashville TN 37209-4515

FONER, ERIC, historian, educator; b. N.Y.C., Feb. 7, 1943; s. Jack D. and Liza F.; m. Lynn Garafola, May 1, 1980. BA, Columbia U., 1963, PhD, 1969; BA, Oxford (Eng.) U., 1965. Prof. history City Coll., CUNY, N.Y.C., 1973-82, Columbia U., N.Y.C., 1982—; Pitt prof. Am. history and instns. Cambridge (Eng.) U., 1980-81. Harmsworth prof. Am. history Oxford (Eng.) U., 1993-94. Author: Free Soil, Free Labor, Free Men, 1970, Tom Paine and Revolutionary America, 1976, Politics and Ideology in the Age of the Civil War, 1980, Nothing But Freedom, 1983, Reconstruction: America's Unfinished Revolution, 1988, Readers' Encyclopedia of American History, 1991, Freedom's Lawmakers, 1993, The Story of American Freedom, 1998, Who Owns History?, 2002, Give Me Liberty!: An American History, 2004; editor: The New American History, 1990, The Reader's Companion to American History, 1991. Recipient Bancroft prize Columbia U., 1989, L.A. Times Book award, 1989, Parkman prize Soc. Am. Historians, 1989, Owsley prize So. Hist. Assn., 1989, Lit. Lion prize N.Y. Pub. Libr., 1994; named Scholar of Yr., N.Y. Coun. for the Humanities, 1995; fellow ACLS, 1972-73, NEH, 1983-84, Guggenheim fellow, 1974-76. Mem. Am. Hist. Assn. (pres. 2000), Orgn. Am. Historians (Avery O. Craven prize 1989, pres. 1993-94), Am. Antiquarian Soc., Am. Acad. Arts and Scis., British Acad. Home: 606 W 116th St New York NY 10027-7011 E-mail: ef17@columbia.edu.

FONES, MONTY GARTH, secondary school educator; b. Dalhart, Tex., Dec. 5, 1932; s. Wilbur Leslie and Bernice Hazel (Wiley) F.; m. Nancy Jeanne Mills, Dec. 23, 1972. BS in Math., Panhandle State U., Goodwell, Okla., 1955; MA in Edn., San Diego State U., 1964. Tchr. math. Redwood High Sch., Visalia, Calif., 1960-61, Costa Mesa (Calif.) High Sch., 1961-63, Corona Del Mar High Sch., Newport Beach, Calif., 1963-66; tchr. math. and sci. Estancia High Sch., Costa Mesa, 1966-68; resource tchr. Space Sci. Learning Project, Costa Mesa, Newport Beach, 1968-72, Sanborn Instructional Media Ctr., Newport Beach, 1972-74; alternative educator secondary math. and sci. Alternative Edn. Ctr., Costa Mesa, 1974-89; ret., 1989. Editor: Colonizing A Planet, 1968, Metric Guide Book, 1972-75; author: Model Rocket Guidebook, 1972; author, editor: Technology in Curriculum, 1989. Lt. (j.g.) USNR, 1956-59. Grantee Calif. Assn. for Educators in Media and Tech., 1974; recipient Beacon award NMEA, 1975, Newport Schs. Found., 1987-88, 88-89. Methodist. Avocations: computers, photography, music. Home: 910 Powell Ct Costa Mesa CA 92626-2942 Personal E-mail: montyfones@comcast.com.

FONG, BERNADINE CHUCK, academic administrator; BA, MA, PhD, Stanford U. Psychology and child devel. prof.; pres. Foothill Coll., Los Altos Hills, Calif., 1994—. Vis. prof., scholar Stanford U. Sch. Edn.; vice-chair Univ. Bd. Trustees Minority Alumni Rels. Task Force; bd. mem. Nat. Ctr. for Postsecondary Improvement Bd. Sr. Scholars, SCT Corp. Exec. Adv. Coun., Am. Inst. for Fgn. Study Bd. Acad. Advisors; trustee Stanford U., Menlo Coll., Am. Assn. C.C., CEO's of Calif. C.C., Assn. for Calif. C.C. Adminstrs., ACE Leadership Devel. Commn., Coun. for Internat. Edn. and Exch. Recipient Phenomenal Woman award, Harold Washington Coll. Chpt., Am. Assn. Women in C.C., 2002. Mem.: Carnegie Found. for Advancement Tchg. (bd. mem.). Office: Foothill Coll 12345 El Monte Rd Los Altos CA 94022*

FONG, NELSON S. secondary education educator; b. San Francisco, Aug. 23, 1950; m. Lorraine Hom, Aug. 15, 1973; children: Keith, Kevin. AA, City Coll. San Francisco, 1970; BA, U. Calif., Berkeley, 1972. Tchr. Livermore Valley Joint Unified Sch. Dist., Livermore, Calif., 1973—. Recipient Cert. of Honor, Westinghouse Found., 1991. Mem. Nat. Coun. Tchrs. Math., Calif. Tchrs. Assn., Livermore Edn. Assn., Am. Assn. Physics Tchrs. Avocations: stamp collecting, computer simulations, baseball. Home: 1312 Kathy Ct Livermore CA 94550-3713 Office: Livermore HS 600 Maple St Livermore CA 94550-3298

FONKALSRUD, ERIC WALTER, pediatric surgeon, educator; b. Balt., Aug. 31, 1932; s. George and Ella (Fricke) F.; m. Margaret Ann Zimmermann, June 6, 1959; children: Eric Walter Jr., Margaret Lynn, David Loren, Robert Warren. BA, U. Wash., 1953; MD, Johns Hopkins U., 1957. Diplomate Am. Bd. Surgery, Am. Bd. Thoracic Surgery, Am. Bd. Pediatric Surgery. Intern Johns Hopkins Hosp., Balt., 1957-58, asst. resident, 1958-59, U. Calif. Med. Ctr., Los Angeles, 1959-62, chief resident surgery, 1962-63, asst. prof. surgery, chief pediatric surgery, 1965-68, assoc. prof., 1968-71, prof. LA, 1971—2001, emeritus prof., 2001—, vice chmn. dept. surgery, 1981-89; resident pediatric surgery Columbus (Ohio) Childrens Hosp. and Ohio State U., 1963-65; practice medicine specializing in pediatric surgery LA, 1965—. Mem. surg. study sect. NIH; James IV surg. traveller to, Gt. Britain, 1971 Mem. editl. bd. Jour. Surg. Rsch., Archives Surgery, Am. Jour. Surgery, Annals Surgery, Surgery, Current Problems in Surgery, Jour. Pediat. Surgery, World Jour. Surgery, Japanese Jour. Surgery, Turkish Jour. Pediat. Surgery, Med. Video Jour. Surgery; contbr. over 650 articles to profl. jours., chpts. to books. Recipient Golden Apple award UCLA Sch. Medicine, 1968; John and Mary R. Markle scholar, 1963-68; named Tree Farmer of Yr. Western Wash., 1998. Fellow ACS (surg. forum com., bd. govs. 1978-84, pres. So. Calif. chpt. 1995-96, Mead Johnson award 1963), Am. Acad. Pediat. (exec. bd., chmn. surg. sect. 1986-87, Salzberg award 2000), German Assn. for Surgery (hon.), Polish Assn. Pediat. Surgery (hon.), Japanese Pediat. Surgery Assn. (hon.), John Hopkins Soc. Scholars (hon.); mem. AMA, Am. Thoracic Surg. Assn., Am. Acad. Sci., Soc. Univ. Surgeons (pres. 1976, sec. 1972-76), Calif. Med. Assn., Crohns and Celitis Found. of So. Calif. (Man of Yr. 1999), Internat. Surg. Group (treas. 1993—), Lilliputian Surg. Soc. (chmn. 1989), L.A. County Med. Assn., Am. Surg. Assn., Pan Pacific Surg. Assn., Pacific Coast Surg. Assn. (recorder 1979-85, pres. 1989), Am. Pediat. Surg. Assn. (bd. govs. 1975-78, pres. 1989), Pacific Assn. Pediat. Surgeons (pres. 1983-84, Coe medal 1998), S.W. Pediatric Soc., L.A. Pediat. Soc., Soc. for Clin. Surgery, Transplantation Soc., Pediat. Surgery Biology Club, Bay Surg. Soc., L.A. Surg. Soc. (sec. 1988-90, pres. 1991), Town Hall (L.A.), Pithotomy Club (pres. 1956-57), Sigma Xi, Alpha Omega Alpha. Methodist. Home: 428 24th St Santa Monica CA 90402-3102 Office: U Calif Med Ctr Dept Surgery Los Angeles CA 90095 E-mail: efonkalsrud@mednet.ucla.edu.

FONNER, KELLY S. educational technologist, consultant; b. Harrisburg, Pa., Nov. 22, 1961; d. Richard L. and Frances (Szivos) Fonner. BS in Spl. Edn. cum laude, Millersville (Pa.) U., 1983; MS in Ednl. Tech. summa cum laude, Johns Hopkin's U., 1988; postgrad., U. Wis., Milw., 1995—. Asst. tchr. Bucks County Easter Seal Soc., Levittown, Pa., 1983-84; instructional media technologist Easter Seal Soc., Phila., 1984-87, ednl. technologist, 1987-90; assistive technology specialist Penn Tech, Harrisburg, 1990-95. Pvt. practice tech. cons., 1985—; instr. Johns Hopkins U., 1990, U. Wis., Milw., 1996—; presenter in field; edn. cons. Instrnl. Support Sys. Pa., 1997-99. Co-author: Getting off to a Great Start, Closing the Gap, 1994, Using Family Dreams to Develop Meaningful Goals, Closing the Gap, 1995. Cen. Dauphin Edn. Assn. scholar, 1979, 96. Mem. Coun. for Exceptional Children, Internat. Soc. for Augmentative and Alternative Comm., Internat. Soc. for Tech. in Edn. Democrat. Presbyterian. Avocations: sports, gardening, drum and bugle corps. Office: U Wisc Milwaukee Dept Occpl Therapy PO Box 413 Milwaukee WI 53201-0413

FONTANA, SANDRA ELLEN FRANKEL, special education educator; b. N.Y.C., July 12, 1951; d. Robert Lowell and Mildred (Tropan) Sharoff; m. Jay Tommy Frankel, May 25, 1973 (div. 1993); children: Austin, Lauren; m. David Fontana, July 27, 2002; stepchildren: Troy, Tara. BS in Med. Tech., Rochester (N.Y.) Inst. Tech., 1973; MA in Linguistics, Gallaudet U., 1984. Cert. comprehensive permanent S.I.G.N. Nat. Assn. Deaf SIGN Instr. Guidance Network, 1985, profl. Am. Sign Language Tchr. Assn. (ASLTA), 1986. Coord. bus. affairs/sign lang. program dept. bus. affairs Gallaudet U., 1980-83; head tchr. dept. sign communication faculty retreat N000, winter 1981; instr. dept. interpreter/translator instruction Gallaudet U., 1981-84, instr. in sign lang. dept. sign communication, spring 1982, ASL instr. dept. sign communication, 1982-84, coord. NDC sign lang. program dept. sign communication, 1984-88, instr. dept. sign communication, 1984-88, head instr./trainer, ASL instr. dept. sign communication, 1988-89, ASL instr. Coll. Continuing Edn. extension/summer programs, 1988; assoc. prof. interpreting preparation program C.C. Balt. County, 1990—2002, Riverside (Calif.) C.C., 2002—. Evaluator Sign Instr. Guidance Network, Indpls., 1989-90; mem. Sign Instr. Guidance Network; bd. dir. State Md. Office Govr. Assistive Tech. Guaranteed Loan Program, 1999-2002. Mem. Am. Sign Lang. Tchr. Assn. (evaluator 1990-), Nat. Assn. of the Deaf, Metro. Wash. Assn. of the Deaf, Md. Assn. of the Deaf. Home: 1540 Highridge Rd Riverside CA 92506 Office: Riverside CC 4800 Magnolia Ave Riverside CA 92506

FONTANA, SHARON MARIE, early childhood education educator; b. Pitts., Feb. 3, 1951; d. Tony and Thelma (Pereira) Simarro; m. Ernest J. Fontana, Aug. 26, 1973; children: Alison, Santino. BS, Calif. State U.,

Chico, 1973. Cert. secondary tchr., Calif., vocat. tchr., Wash. Home econs. tchr. Antioch (Calif.) Unified Schs., 1973-78, Lodi (Calif.) Unified Schs., 1989-92; early childhood edn. tchr. Kennewick (Wash.) Sch. Dist., 1992—. Mem. GATE adv. bd. Lodi Unified Schs., 1986-92; cons. Home and Family Life Adv. Com., Kennewick, Wash., 1992-94. Master food preserver Coop. Extension, Davis, Calif., 1988-92; mem. Triaeyc, PTA. Mem. ASCD, Wash. Vocat. Assn., Nat. Assn. Edn. of Young Children. Democrat. Roman Catholic. Home: 205 Pacific Ct Richland WA 99352-8700 Office: Tri Tech Skills Ctr 5929 W Metaline Ave Kennewick WA 99336-1495

FONTANEZ-PHELAN, SANDRA MARIA, special education director, consultant; b. Las Piedras, P.R., June 1, 1952; came to U.S., 1955; d. Santos and Felicita (Velazquez) Fontánez; m. Patrick Mallon Phelan, July 23, 1983; children: Patrick Brandon, Cory Michael. Student, U. P.R., 1969-70; BA, U. Ill. at Chgo., 1973, MA in Edn., 1980; postgrad., So. Ill. U., Carbondale, 1986, Ill. State U., Normal, 1988—. Cert. tchr., adminstr., learning disabilities, behavior disorders, emotionally disturbed, educable mentally disabled, trainable mentally disabled, Spanish K-12, bilingual edn. and ESL tchr. Tchr. Spanish Chgo. Pub. Schs., 1974-77, tchr., counselor behavior disorders, 1977-80, tchr. home and hosp., 1980-81, resource tchr. bilingual learning disabilities, 1981, master tchr. bilingual spl. edn., 1981-83, ednl. diagnostician, 1983-85, dir. spl. edn., 1991—; tchr. communications Fermi Lab. Sci. and Engring. Program, Batavia, Ill., 1980; facilitator Chgo. Pub. Sch. Compliance and Due Process, 1985-89; grad. asst. Ill. State U., Normal, summer 1989; prin. John Hancock Elem. Sch., Chgo., 1989-91; dir. spl. edn. Chgo. Pub. Schs., 1991—. Counselor Chgo. City Colls., 1982-85; hearing officer level I Ill. State Bd. Edn., Springfield, 1988—; cons. Bilingual and Spl. Edn. Issues, Chgo., 1988—; mem. adv. coun. Truman Coll., Chgo., 1988—; tchr. rep. U. Chgo. Mock Congress, Chgo., 1979, translator law offices, Chgo., 1979. Mem. adv. coun. Truman Coll., Chgo., 1988—, Dover St. Block Club, Chgo., 1983—, Sheridan Pk. Neighbors Assn., Chgo., 1983—, Our Lady of Lourdes Ch.-Womens Guild, Chgo., 1983—. Ill. Consortium for Ednl. Opportunity Ill. State U. fellow, 1989—; So. Ill. U. fellow, 1986. Mem. Nat. Conf. of P.R. Women (pres. 1990—), Ill. Coun. of Adminstrs. for Spl. Edn., Coun. for Exceptional Children, Chgo.'s Prin. Assn. (dist. 7 staff devel. 1989-90), Southwest Community Congress (edn. com. 1989-90), Nat. Assn. Bilingual Edn., Learning Disabilities Assn. Democrat. Roman Catholic. Avocations: drawing, needlework, antiquing, calligraphy, public speaking. Office: Chgo Pub Schs 1819 W Pershing Rd Chicago IL 60609-2300

FONTANIVE, LYNN MARIE, special education administrator; b. Detroit, June 29; d. Edward and Violet Fontanive; m. Paul Adasek Jr., Nov. 8, 1985; 1 child, Paul Fontanive. BA, Marygrove Coll., Detroit; MA, Mich. State U.; EdS, Wayne State U., Detroit; EdD, Wayne State U. Audiologist Plymouth (Mich.) Ctr. for Human Devel.; assoc. dir. Deaf Hearing & Speech Ctr.; from ednl. audiologist to dept. dir. ctr. programs Oakland Schs., Waterford, Mich., 1976—99; dir. presch. and assessment ctr. Macomb Intermed. Sch. Dist., Clinton Twp., Mich., 1999—. Lectr. in field. Adv. bd. Mich. Sch. for Deaf, Flint, 1986—91; pres. Suprs. for Programs for Hearing Impaired; bd. dirs. Career Leadership and Devel. Bd., 1987—90; bd. dirs., human svcs. coord. bd. HSCB, 1999—; pres. local coord. coun. LICC, 1999—; bd. dirs. State Spl. Edn. Adv. Com., 1994—98; adminstr. Macomb County Adminstrn. Spl. Edn., 1999—. Mem. Am. Speech and Hearing Assn., Mich. Speech, Lang., Hearing Assn. (v.p. 1986-90), Coun. for Exceptional Children Macomb County (membership chmn. 1988-90), Adminstrs. of Spl. Edn., Mich. Suprs. of Pub. Sch. Programs for Hearing Impaired (treas. 1996-97, pres. 1997-2000). Roman Catholic. Avocations: dance, aerobics, travel, biking, tennis. Office: Macomb ISD 44001 Garfield Rd Clinton Township MI 48038-1100

FOOS, K. MICHAEL, biology educator; b. Bellfontaine, Ohio, Jan. 16, 1943; s. Kenneth Boyd and Alberta (Storms) F.; m. Karen A. Adams, June 25, 1966 (div. 1990); 1 child, David Michael; m. Catherine Ludlum, Oct. 4, 1997. BS in Edn., Ohio State U., 1965, MS, 1970, PhD, 1972. Sci. tchr. Ridgemont High Sch., Ridgeway, Ohio, 1965-66, Bowling Green (Ohio) High Sch., 1966-67, Jefferson Local Schs., Gahanna, Ohio, 1967-70; teaching assoc. Ohio State U., Columbus, 1970-72, vis. asst. prof., 1972-73; asst. prof. Lake Erie Coll., Painesville, Ohio, 1973-83; prof. Ind. U. East, Richmond, 1983—, div. chmn., 1985-95. Program dir. Cleveland Clinic Lake Erie Coll., 1976-78. Editor Jour. of Coll. Sci. Teaching, 1988-91; contbr. articles to profl. jours. Mem. AAUP, Mycological Soc. Am., British Mycological Soc., Nat. Sci. Tchrs. Assn., Soc. Coll. Sci. Tchrs., Nat. Assn. Biology Tchrs., Nat. Assn. Scholars, Ind. Acad. Sci., Sigma Xi. Avocations: photography, mountain climbing. Office: Ind U East 2325 Chester Blvd Richmond IN 47374-1220 E-mail: foos@indiana.edu.

FOOTE, AVON EDWARD, web developer/producer, communications educator; b. Sept. 24, 1937; s. Avon Ruble and Lila Frances (Broughton) F.; m. Dorothy Veronica Gargis, Mar. 15, 1960; children: Anthony E., Kevin A., Michele. Cert., NYU, 1961; BS, Florence State U., 1963; MS, U. So. Miss., 1968; PhD, Ohio State U., 1970. Announcer Sta. WJOI, Florence, Ala., 1958-60; prodn. mgr. Sta. WOWL-TV, Florence, 1960-64; advt. coord. Plough Inc., Memphis, 1964-66; faculty adviser Sta. WMSU, U. So. Miss., Hattiesburg, 1966-67; prodr.-dir. telecomm. Ohio State U., Columbus, 1967-69; assoc. prof. broadcasting U. Miss., Oxford, 1971-72; project dir. Ohio Valley TV Sys., Columbus, 1972-74; faculty, coord. grad. studies Sch. Journalism/Mass Comm. U. Ga., Athens, 1974-80; prof. broadcasting U. North Ala., Florence, 1980—. Prof., London, 1990, 91; awards judge Ohio State Awards, 1968-73; chmn. faculty screening com. Peabody Radio-TV Awards, 1976-79; jury chair N.Y. Festivals TV awards, 2002—; founder Worldwide Web pages including Worldserver, 1995; Web cons. chotank.com, others, 1996—; collection developer: Gulf War Video Collection, 1992-2001, Libr. of Am. Broadcasting, U. Md., College Park, 2002—. Editor: The Challenges of Educational Communications, 1970, CBS and Congress: The Selling of the Pentagon Papers, 1972, Nat. Assn. Ednl. Broadcasters Broadcasting Rev., 1969-73 ; author: (with Koenig and others) Broadcasting and Bargaining, 1970, Chotankers, 1982; prodr. ednl. TV programs; editor ref. shelf materials Nat. Pub. Broadcasting Archives, U. Md., College Park, 2002. Bd. dirs. Florence YMCA, 1982-86. Recipient Cmty. Svc. award Florence Civitan Club, 1990, 1st pl. award Corp. Video Profl. Competition Nat. Broadcasting Soc., 1991, regional 1st pl. award, Nat. 3d pl. award Coll. Emmy award Hollywood Acad. TV Arts and Scsi., 1984, Honorable Mention Comedy awards Nat. Broadcasting Soc., 1987; Industry Faculty Seminar fellow Internat. Radio-TV Soc., 1987, NDEA fellow, 1967, NATAS Meml. fellow, 1970. Mem.: BBC Networking Club, Radio TV News Dirs. Assn. Republican. Anglican. Home: 222 Shirley Dr Florence AL 35633-1434 Office: Comm Bldg PO Box 5158 Florence AL 35632-0001 E-mail: chotank@aol.com.

FOOTE, CHANDRA JEANET, education educator, writer, elementary school educator; b. Rochester, N.Y., Jan. 20, 1970; d. Theron A. and Patricia M. Foote; m. Christopher A. Robins, July 3, 1999. BS, Syracuse U., 1992, MA, 1994, PhD, 1996. Cert. in elem. edn., N.Y. Tchg. assoc. Syracuse (N.Y.) U., 1994-96; assoc. prof. edn. Niagara U., N.Y., 1996—. Project dir. Niagara Falls (N.Y.) Bd. Edn., 1998-99. Co-author: (book) Constructionist Teaching Practices; contbr. chpt. to books, articles to profl.jours. Leadership rep. The Higher Edn. Task Force for Quality Inclusion, N.Y. State, 1998—; cmty. rep. LaSalle Mid. Sch. Quality Coun., 2001—. Recipient Golden Apple award Niagara Falls City Sch. Dist., 1998-99, Dean's award Coll. Edn. at Niagara U., 1998; Goals 2000 grantee N.Y. State Dept. Edn., 1998-99; Office of Vocat. and Ednl. Svcs. for Individuals with Disabilities grantee, 2000, 02,03. Mem. Am. Ednl. Rsch. Assn., Assn. Tchr. Educators. Avocations: reading, travel. Office: Niagara U Dept Edn B 11 O'Shea Hall Niagara University NY 14109-2042 Fax: (716) 286-8561. E-mail: cjf@niagara.edu.

FOOTE, DOROTHY GARGIS, nursing educator; b. Sheffield, Ala., Jan. 27, 1942; d. Tracy E. and Mary Helen (Cox) Gargis; m. A. Edward Foote, Mar. 15, 1960; children: Anthony E., Kevin A., Michele. Student, U. So. Miss., 1966-67; AS in Nursing, NW Coll., 1985; BS in Nursing, U. N. Ala., Florence, 1987; MS in Nursing, U. Ala., Huntsville, 1989; postgrad., U. North Ala., England and Scotland, 1990, 91; PhD in Higher Edn. Adminstrn., Miss. State U., 2003. RN, Ala.; cert. family nurse practitioner, cert. gerontol. nurse practitioner. Real estate assoc. McWaters Realty & Appraisal Co., Athens, Ga., 1977-79; acctg. clk. U. Ga., Athens, 1979-81; nurse practitioner Mitchell Hollingworth annex Eliza Coffee Meml. Hosp., Florence, 1985-92; v.p. Thornwood Books, Florence, 1982-93; prof. N.W. C.C., Phil Campbell, Ala., 1992-93, U. Ala., Huntsville, 1993—. Rsch. dir. Leadership in Long Term Care, 1995—; co-donor Gulf War video collection U. Md., College Park, 2002. Editor newsletter Dames Digest, 1970. Pres. Band Boosters, Athens, 1976. Mem.: ANA, Ala. State Nurses Assn. (pres. dist. 1 1989—92, bd. dirs. 1989—92, chair gerontol. coun. 1992—93), Phi Theta Kappa, Beta Sigma Phi, Sigma Theta Tau (Beta Phi chpt. pres 2002—). Home: 222 Shirley Dr Florence AL 35633-1434 Business E-Mail: footed@uah.edu.

FOOTE, EDWARD THADDEUS, II, university president, lawyer; b. Milw., Dec. 15, 1937; s. William Hamilton and Julia Stevenson (Hardin) F.; m. Roberta Waugh Fulbright, Apr. 18, 1964; children: Julia, William, Thaddeus. BA, Yale U., 1959; LLB, Georgetown U., 1966; LLD (hon.), Washington U., St. Louis, 1981, Barry U., 1991; hon. degree, Tokai U., Tokyo, 1984; LLD (hon.), Barry U., 1991. Bar: Mo. 1966. Reporter Washington Star, 1963-64, Washington Daily News, 1964-65; exec. asst. to chmn. Pa. Ave. Commn., Washington, 1965-66; assoc. Bryan, Cave, McPheeters & McRoberts, St. Louis, 1966-70; vice chancellor, gen. counsel, sec. to bd. trustees Washington U., St. Louis, 1970-73, dean Sch. Law, 1973-80, spl. adv. to chancellor and bd. trustees, 1980-81; pres. U. Miami, Coral Gables, Fla., 1981—. Mem. exec. com., bd. dirs. Am. Coun. Edn., 1986-88; chmn. citizens com. for sch. desegregation, St. Louis, 1980; chmn. desegregation monitoring and adv. com., St. Louis, 1980-81. Author: An Educational Plan for Voluntary Cooperation Desegregation of School in the St. Louis Met. area, 1981 Mem. Coun. on Fgn. Rels.; founding pres. bd. New City Sch., St. Louis, 1967-73; mem. gov.'s task force on reorganization State of Mo., 1973-74, steering com., chmn. governance com. Mo. Gov.'s Conf. on Edn., UN Assn. Greater St. Louis chpt., 1977-79, adv. com. Naval War Coll., 1979-82, Fla. Coun. of 100, Southern Fla. Metro-Miami Action Plan, exec. com. Miami Citizens Against Crime; founding chmn. Miami Coalition for a Drug Free Community, 1988—. Recipient Order of Sun (Peru). Democrat. Office: U Miami PO Box 248006 Miami FL 33124-8006

FOOTE, STEPHANIE, English educator; b. Bangor, Maine, Feb. 24, 1966; d. Rachel Thibodeau; m. Cris Susan Mayo. BA, Oberlin Coll., 1988; PhD, U. Buffalo, 1995. Assoc. prof. English U. Ill., Champaign, 2000—. Vis. prof. Colby Coll., Waterville, Maine, 1993-94, Duke U., Durham, N.C., 2001. Author: Regional Fictions, 2001; contbr. articles to profl. jours. Activist, founder Buffalo United for Choice, 1992; rape crisis counselor, Champaign, 1995—.

FORBES, CYNTHIA ANN, small business owner, marketing educator; b. Richmond, Calif., Dec. 27, 1951; d. James Martin and Mary Jane (Clafferty) Forbes; m. Larry Charles Osofsky, Mar. 20, 1970 (div. 1980); 1 child, Anna; m. William Charles Ham, Aug. 30, 1986. BA, U. Calif., 1977; MS, Golden Gate U., 1981; AS, Butte Coll., 2002. Rsch. asst. U. Calif., Berkeley, 1975-77, Chevron Rsch., Richmond, 1977-79; specialist dealer affairs Chevron USA, San Francisco, 1979-80, sales rep. San Rafael, Calif., 1981-84, adminstrv. supr. San Ramon, Calif., 1984-85; advt. mgr. Chevron Chem. Co., San Francisco, 1986-88; assoc. prof. Golden Gate U., San Francisco, 1981-92. Vol., lectr. child abuse prevention; vol. children's theatre dir.; firefighter, paramedic, tng. dir. Downieville Fire Dept. Democrat. Avocations: mountaineering, bicycling. Home: PO Box 427 Downieville CA 95936-0427 E-mail: cynthiaforbes@excite.com.

FORBES, FELICIA RENÉ, art educator; b. Jackson, Miss., Apr. 10, 1978; d. Clyde Thomas and Gladys Merl (Gray) Forbes. BA in Art Edn., Delta State U., Cleveland, Miss., 2001. Art tchr. Northeast Madison Middle Sch., Canton, Miss., 2001—. Home: 501 Pine Ridge Rd Florence MS 39073

FORBES, FRANKLIN SIM, lawyer, educator; b. Kingsport, Tenn., Sept. 21, 1936; s. Harvey Sim and Virginia Smith (Pooler) F.; m. Suzanne Marie Willard, June 30, 1962; children— Franklin Sim, Anne Marie. BA, U. Hawaii, 1959; JD, U. Iowa, 1963. Bar: Hawaii 1963, Nebr. 1964. Law clk. Hawaii Supreme Ct., 1963; mem. faculty U. Nebr. Coll. Bus. Adminstrn., Omaha, 1965—, prof. law, 1965—, chmn. dept. law and society, 1970-97, acting chmn. dept. profl. acctg., 1986-87, Peter Keweit disting. prof. law, 1987-93; pvt. practice, Omaha, 1964—. Author: Going Into Business in Nebraska: The Legal Aspects, 1983, Instructor's Resource Guide-Business Law, 1983-88, Starting and Operating a Business in Nebraska, 1995, Debtors and Creditors Rights, 1988, Legal Environment of Telemarketing, 1991; contbr. articles to legal publs. Mem. integration com. Omaha Sch. Bd., 1974; mem. St. James Bd. Edn., Omaha, 1974; pres. parish coun. St. James Roman Cath. Ch., 1975, St. Elizabeth Ann Ch., 1983-84, 90-91. Recipient Real Dean award U. Hawaii, 1959, Gt. Tchr. award U. Nebr., 1978, 81, Chancellor's medal U. Nebr., 1977, Outstanding Achievement award U. Nebr. Coll. Bus. Adminstrn., 1983, 84, 85, 87, 88; Rotary Found. grantee Australia, 1972 Mem. ABA, Am. Arbitration Assn., Am. Judicature Soc., Midwest Bus. Adminstrs. Assn., Midwest Bus. Law Assn. (pres. 1975), Nebr. Bar Assn., Omaha Bar Assn. (del. conf. Future Law 1979), Hawaii Bar Assn., Nat. Golden Key Soc., Alpha Phi Omega, Phi Alpha Delta, Beta Gamma Sigma, Phi Theta Chi. Clubs: Rotary. Democrat. Office: Univ Nebr Coll Bus Adminstrn Omaha NE 68182-0001

FORBES JOHNSON, MARY GLADYS, retired primary education educator; b. Bend, Oreg., June 19, 1929; d. Percy Lloyd and Bertha May (Gettman) F.; married, 1996 BA in Edn. magna cum laude, Cascade Coll., 1951; BS in Edn., Western Oreg. State Coll., Monmouth, 1951, MS in Edn., 1968. Cert. tchr., Oreg. Tchr. Christian & Missionary Alliance, Mamou, Guinea, West Africa, 1952-54, Bend (Oreg.)-Redmond Christian Day Sch., 1954-56, Dalat Sch., Asia, 1956-76, Bend-LaPine Sch. Dist. 1, Bend, 1976-99, adminstr., tchr., 1981-87, tchr. kindergarten Thompson Sch., 1989-99. Cons. Chpt. I Program in Spl. Edn., 1976-88; supt. Sunday sch. Christian and Missionary Alliance, 1976-80, Faith Fellowship Four Sq., Madras, Oreg., 1981-88. Mem. Citizens for the Republic, Washington, 1989; mem. Rep. Nat. Com., 1990—. Recipient cert. of appreciation Hale Found., 1986, 87, Skyhook II Project, 1987, Concerned Women Am., 1987, Nat. Law Enforcement Officer Meml., 1991, Am. Indian Relief Coun., 1992. Mem. Am. Def. Inst., Nat. Right to Life Com., Coun. for Inter-Am. Security, Nat. Assn. for Uniformed Svcs., Concerned Women for Am., Capitol Hill Women's Club, Christian Coalition, Am. Ctr. for Law and Justice, Am. Life League, Oreg. Citizens Alliance, Heritage Found., Delta Kappa Gamma. Avocations: gardening, cycling, hiking, farming. Home: PO Box 107 Bend OR 97709-0107 Office: Bend LaPine Sch Dist 1 520 NW Wall St Bend OR 97701-2608

FORCE, CRYSTAL ANN, school counselor; b. Atlanta, Jan. 4, 1947; d. Raymond Ralph and Mary Ellen (Sticher) Bennett; m. Edward James Force, June 26, 1971; children: Lane Bennett, Patrick Brendan. BA, Carson-Newman Coll., 1969; MEd, Fla. Atlantic U., 1971. Cert. sch. counselor, Ga. Tchr. English Clewiston (Fla.) High Sch., 1969-71, sch. counselor, 1971-72, Greenport (N.Y.) Sch., 1972-75; dir. after sch. program LaBelle Elem. Sch., Marietta, Ga., 1985-89; sch. counselor LaBelle and Fair Oaks Elem. Schs., Marietta, 1989-90, LaBelle and King Springs Elem. Schs., Marietta, Smyrna, Ga., 1990-91, King Springs Elem. Sch., Smyrna, 1991—, creator Peacewalk and Peacegardens. Co-dir. Smart Kids Orgn., Smyrna, 1992—; trainer Real Colors of Nat. Curriculum and Tng. Inst., Inc. Chair parent edn. com. Griffin Mid. Sch. Parent Teacher Student Assn., Smyrna, 1993-94, exec. bd. sec. 1988; chmn. celebrating differences multicultural com. King Springs Elem., chmn. parent edn. com. PTA; mem. Citizens Adv. Coun., Smyrna, 1984-85, 93-94; mentor Campbell High Sch., Smyrna, 1992-93; mem. nat. adv. coun. Inst. Human Resource Devel., Building Esteem in Students Today Program; vol. Hands on Atlanta Project, Egleston Children's Hosp. Rainbow Buddies; coord., facilitator Rainbows Support Group. Recipient Am. Hero in Edn. award Reader's Digest Assn., 1993, Today's Kids award Brawner Hosp., 1993, Elem. Sch. Counselor of Yr. for Cobb County, Ga., 1994. Mem. AAUW, Am. Counseling Assn., Am. Sch. Counselor Assn., Ga. Sch. Counselor Assn., Nat. Sch. Age Child Care Alliance, Ga. Sch. Age Child Care Assn., Cobb County Sch. Counselor Assn. (program chmn. 1995-96, profl. recognition com. 1994-95, cmty. outreach co-chmn. 1996-97, elem. v.p. 1997-98, treas. 1999—, Most Unique Student Involvement in a Counseling Program award 1997), Campbell High Sch. Booster Club. Republican. Baptist. Avocations: collecting sheila houses, reading books on islands and maine, writing, walking, bible study. Home: 4227 Deerwood Pky Smyrna GA 30082-3929 Office: King Springs Elem Sch 1041 Reed Rd Smyrna GA 30082-4230

FORD, ANDREW THOMAS, academic administrator; b. Cambridge, Mass., May 22, 1944; s. Francis Lawler and Eleanor (Vahey) F.; m. Anne M. Monahan, July 2, 1966; 1 dau., Lauren Elizabeth. BA, Seton Hall U., 1966; MA, U. Wis., 1968; PhD, U. Wis., 1971. Asst. prof. history Stockton State Coll., Pomona, N.J., 1971-72, asst. to v.p. for acad. affairs, 1972-74; acting dir. Nat. Materials Devel. Ctr. for French and Portuquese, Bedford, N.H., 1976-77; acad. programs coordinator N.H. Coll. and Univ. Council, Manchester, 1975-78; v.p. acad. affairs R.I. Sch. Design, Providence, 1978-81; dean Allegheny Coll., Meadville, Pa., 1981-93, provost, 1983-93; pres. Wabash Coll., Crawfordsville, Ind., 1993—. Mem. adv. bd. Marine Bank, 1987-93; founding mem. Commonwealth Partnership. Author: (with R. Chait) Beyond Traditional Tenure, 1982; mem. editl. bd. Liberal Edn., 2000—. Bd. dirs. Vis. Nurse Assn., Providence, 1979-81, Allegheny Summer Music Festival, Meadville, 1981-89, Meadville Med. Ctr., 1985-87; bd. incorporators Spencer Hosp., 1981-85; mem. Nat. Com. on U.S.-China Rels., 1986—; trustee Higher Learning Commn. North Ctrl. Assn. Schs. and Colls., 2002—; dir. Crawfordsville Main St. Program, 2001—. Democrat. Home: 400 E Pike St Crawfordsville IN 47933-2520 Office: Wabash Coll Office of Pres Crawfordsville IN 47933

FORD, ANNA MARIA, language educator; b. Starachowice, Poland, Aug. 17, 1940; arrived in U.S., 1954; d. Antoni Niedzwiedzki and Wanda Gluszkiewicz; married; 1 child, Alexandra Johanna Paszowski. BA, Wayne State U., 1963, MA, 1970. Cert. secondary edn. tchr. French, Spanish, English Mich., S.C., Advanced Placement French tchr. cert. S.C., 1999, cert. tchr. adolescence young adulthood English lang. arts Nat. Bd., 2001. Tchr. French and Spanish Ford Mid. Sch., Highland Park, Mich., 1965-66; tchr. fgn. lang. dept. Highland Park Cmty. HS, 1966-97, head fgn. lang. dept., 1968-70, 73-78, lang. arts facilitator, 1991-94; owner, founder Horizons-Internat., Grosse Pointe Park, Mich., 1993-97; dist.-wide lang. cons./coord. Highland Park Pub. Schs., 1994-97; Spanish, French and English lang. tchr. Georgetown (S.C.) County Sch. Dist., 1997—. Ind. contractor, cons. Langs. and Svcs. Agy., 1993—; assessor, field study, tchr. performance lang. arts Nat. Bd. Profl. Tchg. Stds., Mich., 1994; scorer writing proficience assessments Mich. Dept. Edn., 1994—97, trainer of tchrs., 1995, trainer of trainers, 1995—97, mem. elem. and secondary content literacy com., 1995—; instrnl./profl. devel. task force Mid. Cities Assn., Lansing, Mich., 1995—97; mem. North Ctrl. Accreditation Evaluation Teams, 1970—97; cons. Coastal Area Writing Project, SC, 1998—; TEAM evaluator, asst. tng. evaluator, SC, 1999—; advisor H.S. yearbook Polar Bear, 1985—86. Editor: (newsletter) Happenings, 1977—79, Mich. Writing Assessment News, 1994—97. Bd. dirs. Friends of Polish Art, Mich., 1995—97, French Inst. Mich., Southfield, 1985—97. Recipient Big E award, Josten's Printing Divsn., 1986, cert. appreciation for participation in Classrooms of Tomorrow program, Mich. Gov., 1990. Mem.: AAUW, Alliance Francaise (Detroit/Grosse Pointe/Charleston), Alpha Mu Gamma. Roman Catholic. Avocations: travel, sailing, skiing, literature, music. Home: 38 Wexford Ln River Club Pawleys Island SC 29585-7614 Office: Horizons Internat 38 Wexford Ln Pawleys Island SC 29585-7614

FORD, BARBARA FOREMAN, middle school educator; b. Denver, Jan. 31, 1947; d. Haymond and Rosetta (Weaver) Foreman; m. Roscoe Orme Ford, Dec. 28, 1968; 1 child, Derrick Foreman. BA in History, Colo. State U., 1969; MEd, U. Hawaii, 1972, postgrad., 1990—. Cert. tchr. secondary social studies, Hawaii. Teacher Booth Meml. Sch., Honolulu, 1972-76; chpt. I tchr. Leilehua High Sch., Wahiawa, Hawaii, 1979-81; tchr. Aiea (Hawaii) High Sch., 1981-82, Radford High Sch., Honolulu, 1982-83, Mililani (Hawaii) High Sch., 1983, Aliamau Intermediate Sch., Honolulu, 1984, Waialua (Hawaii) High Sch., 1985; tchr., team leader, 7th grade St. Andrews Priory Sch., Honolulu, 1985—. Mem. profl. improvement com. St. Andrew's Priory Sch., Honolulu, 1985-87, acad. com. 1990—. Named Middle Sch. Tchr. of Yr., 1992; Sachs Found. scholar Colo. State U., 1965-69; U. Denver grantee, 1987. Mem. Nat. Coun. Social Studies, Hawaii State Coun. Social Studies, Hawaii Assn. Middle Schs. Methodist. Avocations: reading, 60's music, collecting elephants.

FORD, BARBARA JEAN, library studies educator; b. Dixon, Ill., Dec. 5, 1946; BA magna cum laude with honors, Ill. Wesleyan U., 1968; MA in Internat. Rels., Tufts U., 1969; MS in Libr. Sci., U. Ill., 1973. Dir. Soybean Insect Rsch. Info. Ctr. Ill. Natural History Survey, Urbana, 1973-75; from asst. to assoc. prof. U. Ill., Chgo., 1975-84, asst. documents libr., 1975-79, documents libr., dept. head, 1979-84, acting audiovisual libr., 1983-84; asst. dir. pub. svcs. Trinity U., San Antonio, 1984-86, assoc. prof., assoc. dir., 1986-91, acting dir. librs., 1989, 91; prof., dir. univ. libr. svcs. Va. Commonwealth U., Richmond, 1991-98; asst. commr. Chgo. Pub. Libr., 1998—2002; dir., disting. prof. Mortenson Ctr. Internat. Libr. Programs, U. Ill., Urbana, 2003—. Mem. women's re-entry adv. bd. U. Ill., Chgo., 1980-82, student affairs com., 1978-80, student admissions, records, coll. rels. com., 1981-84, univ. senate, 1976-78, 82-84, chancellor's libr. coun. svcs. com. 1984, campus lectrs. com. 1982-83; admissions interviewer for prospective students Trinity U., 1987-91, reader for internat. affairs theses, 1985-91, libr. self-study com., 1985-86, internat. affairs com., 1986-91, inter-Am. studies com., 1986-91, faculty senate, 1987-90; with libr. working group U.S./Mex. Commn. Cultural Coop., 1990. Contbr. articles to profl. publs., papers to presentations. Bd. dirs. Friends of San Antonio Pub. Libr., 1989-91; adv. com. chair Office for Libr. Pers. Resources, 1994-95; mem. steering com. Virtual Libr. Va., 1994-98, chair user svcs. com., 1995-96. Celia M. Howard fellow Tufts U., 1969; sr. fellow UCLA Grad. Sch. Libr. and Info. Sci., 1993. Mem. ALA (conf. program com. 1985-91, libr. edn. assembly 1983-84, membership com. 1978-79, status of women in librarianship com. 1983-85, exec bd., 1996-99, Lippincott Award Jury 1979-80, Shirley Olofson Meml. award 1977), ALA Coun. (at-large councilor 1985-89, chpt. councilor Ill. Libr. Assn. 1980-84, com. on coms. 1987-88, spl. coun. orientation com. 1982-83, ALA exec. bd., 1996-99, pres.- elect 1996-97, pres. 1997-98), Assn. Coll. and Rsch. Librs. (bd. dirs. 1989-92, pres.-elect 1989-90, pres. 1990-91, publs. com. 1990-91, conf. program planning 1990-91), Nat. Assn. State Univs. and Land Grant Colls. (commn. info. tech. 1992-94), Internat. Fedn. Libr. Assns. and Instns. (sec. ofcl. pubs. sect., gen. info. com. 1985 conf., moderator Latin Am. seminar on ofcl. pubs. 1991, univ. and other rsch. librs. sect. standing com. 1999—), Spl. Librs. Assn. (program com. 1976-77, 80-82, publicity com. 1977-79, chair 1978-79, chair spl. projects com. 1981-82, sec./treas. divsn. social sci. internat. affairs sect. 1984-86), Assn. Libr. Info. Sci. Edn. (chair local arrangements conf. planning com. 1988, 92), Ill. Libr. Assn. (chair election com. 1976-77, exec. bd. 1978-79, 80-84, bd. govt. documents round table

1976-79, chair 1978-79, long range planning com. 1980-84), Tex. Libr. Assn. (pubs. com. 1985-87, legis. com. 1986-87, judge best of exhibits award 1987, task force Amigos Fellowship 1990, del. conf. on librs. and info. svcs., 1991), Va. Libr. Assn. (ad hoc. com. distance learning 1992), Va. State Libr. and Archives (Va. libr. and info. svcs. task force 1991-93, steering com. Arbuthnot lecture 1992-93, coop. continuing edn. adv. com. 1992-94), VIVA (steering com. 1994-98), Chgo. Libr. Club (2d v.p. 1983-84), Richmond Acad. Libr. Consortium (v.p. 1991-92, pres. 1992-93), Beta Phi Mu, Phi Kappa Phi, Phi Alpha Theta, Kappa Delta Pi. Office: Chicago Pub Libr Box 2033 400 S State St Chicago IL 60605-1216

FORD, FREDERIC HUGH, secondary school educator; b. Woonsocket, R.I., Feb. 5, 1939; s. Robert Saunders and Catherine Esther (Hudson) Ford; m. Kathleen Marie Hoffman, Oct. 12, 1968; children: Amy Meredith Ford Fitzgerald, Geoffrey Duncan. AB, Harvard Coll., 1960; MA in Music Edn., Harvard U., 1962, MA in Tchg.; MA in Music History, SUNY, Buffalo, 1969, PhD in Music History, 1990. Instr. U. Va., 1966—67; asst. prof. Wabash Coll., Crawfordsville, Ind., 1972—79, Rutgers U., New Brunswick, NJ, 1979—86; dir. N.J. State Teen Arts Program, New Brunswick, 1988—89; tchr. Bridgewater (N.J.)-Raritan Regional H.S., 1990—. Pres. Ea. divsn. Am. Choral Dirs. Assn., 1998—2000, chair 2000 divsn. conv., pres. N.J. chpt.; scorer Praxis exams for tchr. cert. Ednl. Testing Svc., Princeton, NJ. Lt. USNR, 1962—65. Mem.: NEA, Am. Musicol. Soc., Music Educators Nat. Conf. (condr. 1995, 2003). Unitarian Universalist. Home: 12 Melvin Ave East Brunswick NJ 08816 Office: Bridgewater-Raritan Regional HS PO Box 6569 Bridgewater NJ 08807

FORD, GORDON BUELL, JR., literature educator, writer; b. Louisville, Sept. 22, 1937; s. Gordon Buell Sr. and Rubye (Allen) F. AB summa cum laude in Classics, Medieval Latin, and Sanskrit, Princeton U., 1959; AM in Classical Philology and Linguistics, Harvard U., 1962, PhD in Linguistics, Slavic and Baltic Langs. and Lits., 1965; postgrad., U. Oslo, 1962-64, U. Sofia, Bulgaria, 1963, U. Uppsala, Sweden, 1963-64, U. Stockholm, 1963-64, U. Madrid, 1963. CPA. Yeager, Ford, and Warren Found. Disting. prof. Indo-European, Classical, Slavic, and Baltic linguistics, Sanskrit, and Medieval Latin Northwestern U., Evanston, Ill., 1965—; Lybrand, Ross Bros., and Montgomery Found. Disting. prof. English and linguistics U. No. Iowa, Cedar Falls, 1972—; sr. exec. v.p. for real estate acctg. fin. mgmt., bd. dirs. The Southeastern Real Estate Co., Inc., Louisville, 1976-93; sr. exec. v.p. reimbursement and rates acctg. fin. mgmt., hosp. acctg. divsn. Humana Inc., The Hosp. Co., Louisville, 1976-93; ret., 1993; bd. dirs. Southeastern Investment Trust, Inc., Louisville, 1976-93; ret., 1993; rsch. prof. The Southeastern Investment Trust, Inc. Rsch. Found., Louisville, 1976—. Vis. prof. Medieval Latin, U. Chgo., 1966—; vis. prof. linguistics U. Chgo., Downtown Ctr., 1966—; prof. English evening divs. Northwestern U., Chgo., 1968-69, prof. anthropology, 1971-72. Author: The Ruodlieb: The First Medieval Epic of Chivalry from Eleventh-Century Germany, 1965, The Ruodlieb: Linguistic Introduction, Latin Text with a Critical Apparatus, and Glossary, 1966, The Ruodlieb: Facsimile Edition, 1965, 3d edit. 1968, Old Lithuanian Texts of the Sixteenth and Seventeenth Centuries with a Glossary, 1969, The Old Lithuanian Catechism of Baltramiejus Vilentas (1579): A Phonological, Morphological, and Syntactical Investigation, 1969, Isidore of Seville's History of the Goths, Vandals, and Suevi, 1966, 2d edit. 1970, The Letters of Saint Isidore of Seville, 1966, 2d edit. 1970, The Old Lithuanian Catechism of Martynas Mazvydas (1547), 1971, others; translator: A Concise Elementary Grammar of the Sanskrit Language with Exercises, Reading Selections, and a Glossary (Jan Gonda), 1966, The Comparative Method in Historical Linguistics (Antoine Meillet), 1967, A Sanskrit Grammar (Manfred Mayrhofer), 1972; contbr. numerous articles to many scholarly jours. Appointed to Hon. Order Ky. Cols. (life). Mem. Linguistic Soc. Am. (life, Sapir life patron), Internat. Linguistic Assn. (life), Societas Linguistica Europaea (charter, life), Am. Philol. Assn. (life), Classical Assn. of the Atlantic States (life), Classical Assn. of the Middle West and South (life), Classical Assn. of N.Eng. (life), Medieval Acad. of Am. (life), Renaissance Soc. of Am. (life), MLA (life), Am. Assn. Tchrs. Slavic and East European Langs. (life), Am. Assn. Advancement Slavic Studies (life), Am. Coun. Tchrs. Russian (life), Assn. for Advancement Baltic Studies (life), Inst. Lithuanian Studies (life), Tchrs. of English to Speakers of Other Langs. (charter, life), SAR (life), Princeton Club (N.Y.C., Chgo.), Princeton Alumni Assn. (Louisville), Harvard Club (N.Y.C., Chgo., Louisville, Lexington, Ky.), Pres.'s Soc. Bellarmine Coll. (life), Louisville Country Club, KC (life), Phi Beta Kappa (life). Baptist. Home: 3619 Brownsboro Road Louisville KY 40207-1863 also: PO Box 2693 Clarksville Br Jeffersonville IN 47131-2693

FORD, JEAN ELIZABETH, former English language educator; b. Branson, Mo., Oct. 5, 1923; d. Mitchell Melton and Annie Estella (Wyer) F.; m. J.C. Wingo, 1942 (div. 1946; m. E. Syd Vineyard, 1952 (div. 1956); m. Vincent Michel Wessling, Feb. 14, 1983 (div. Dec. 1989). AA in English, L.A. City Coll., 1957; BA in English, Calif. State U., 1959; MA in Higher Edn., U. Mo., 1965; postgrad., UCLA, 1959-60, U. Wis., 1966, U. Mo. Law Sch., 1968-69. Cert. English tchr., real estate broker, Mo. Dance instr. Arthur Murray Studios, L.A., 1948-51; office mgr. Western Globe Products, L.A., 1951-55; pvt. dance tchr., various office jobs L.A., 1955-59; social dir. S.S. Matsonia, 1959; social worker L.A. County, 1959-61; 7th grade instr. Carmenita Sch. Dist., Norwalk, Calif., 1961-62; English instr. Leadwood (Mo.) High Sch., 1962-63; dance instr. U. Mo., 1963-66, SW Mo. State U., 1966-68, NW Mo. State U., 1970-76, Johnson County Community Coll., 1976-77; tax examiner IRS, Kansas City, Mo., 1978-80; tax acct. Baird, Kurtz & Dobson, Kansas City, Mo., 1981; dance tchr. Singles Program Village, Presbyn. Ch., Kans., 1981-96. Substitute tchr. various sch. dists., 1976-85; dance chmn. Mo. Assn. Health, Phys. Edn. and Recreation, 1965-66, 68-69, dance chmn. ctrl. dist. AAHPER, 1972-73; vis. author Young Author's Conf., Ctrl. Mo. State U., 1987, 88, 89; speaker Am. Reading Assn., Grandview, Mo., 1990; real estate sales agt., Kansas City, 1980-84; real estate sales broker, Mo., 1990—, Kans., 1990-2000; pvt. practice tax acct., dance tchr., 1984-2002. Author, pub.: Fish Tails and Scales, 1982, 2d edit., 2000; spkr. at librs. Mem. Am. Contract Bridge League, Kansas City Ski Club. Democrat. Presbyterian. Avocations: tennis, swimming, skiing, sailing, bridge. Home and Office: 142 Grandview Dr Bldg 4 #7 Branson MO 65616

FORD, JOHN T., JR., art, film and video educator; b. Rotan, Tex., Feb. 17, 1953; s. John T. and Lala Fern (Shipley) F.; m. Betty Jean Crawford; children: Casey, Craig, Kirk. BA, U. Redlands, 1975. Cert. tchr. Calif. Tchr. art, film, video Yucaipa (Calif.) Joint Unified Sch. Dist., 1976-88; tchr. art and crafts Vacaville (Calif.) Unified Sch. Dist., 1990-92, tchr. video prodn., 1992—, sr. prodn. video, 1994—. Cons. Dist. Fine Arts Insvc., Yucaipa, 1987; co-sponsor Art Club, Will C. Wood High Sch., Vacaville, sponsor Video Club. Creator, coord. (conceptual art) Whole School Environments, Caves, Tubes and Streamers, Forest Edge, 1980-84; creator (comml. art prints) Toy Horse Series, 1982-83; prodr. ann. sr. video, 1994—. Mem. Yeoman Svc. Orgn., U. Redlands, 1972, Vacaville Sch. Dist. Tech. Com., Dist. Fine Arts Task Force, Yucaipa, 1984-87, Dist. Task Force for Vocat. Edn., 1992; interim dir. Hosanna House, Redlands, Calif., 1975; liaison Sch. Cmty. Svc./San Bernardino County (Calif.) Fire Dept., 1980-81. Recipient Golden Bell award Calif. Sch. Bd. Rsch. Found., 1987, Ednl. Svc. award Mason's, 1987-88; named one of Outstanding Young Men of Am., 1987, Tchr. of Yr. Calif. Continuation Edn. Assn., 1987-88; grantee Calif. Tchrs. Instructional Improvement Program, 1985; scholar U. Redlands, 1975. Mem. Am. Film Inst. Avocations: art, media fabrication, writing, collecting books, backpacking. Office: Buckingham Charter Sch 188 Bella Vista Dr Vacaville CA 95687-5735

FORD, LORETTA C. lecturer, consultant, retired university dean, nurse; b. N.Y.C., Dec. 28, 1920; d. Joseph F. and Nellie A. (Williams) Pfingstel; m. William J. Ford, May 2, 1947; 1 child, Valerie. BSN, U. Colo., Boulder, 1949, MS, 1951, EdD, 1961; DSc (hon.), Ohio State Med. Coll., 1997; DSc (hon.), Simmons Coll., 1997, U. Colo., 1997; LLD (hon.), U. Md., 1990; DSc (hon.), U. Rochester, 2000; LHD (hon.), Binghamton U., 2001. RN N.J. Staff nurse New Brunswick Vis. Nurse Svc., 1941—42; supr., dir. Boulder County (Colo.) Health Dept., 1947—58; from asst. prof. to prof. U. Colo. Sch. Nursing, 1960—72; dean Sch. Nursing, DON, prof. U. Rochester, NY, 1972—86, acting dean Grad. Sch. Edn. and Human Devel., 1988—89; vis. prof. U. Fla., 1968, U. Wash., Seattle, 1974, St. Lukes Coll. Nursing, Tokyo, 1987. Mem. educators adv. panel GAO; dir. Security Trust Co., Rochester, Rochester Telephone Co.; internat. cons. in field. Contbr. chapters to books, articles to profl. jours. Mem. adv. com. Commonwealth Fund Exec. Nurse Fellowship PRogram; bd. dirs. Threshold Alt. Youth Svcs., Easter Seal Soc., ARC, Monroe Cmty. Hosp. With Nurse Corps USAF, 1942—46. Named Colo. Nurse of Yr., Colo. Nurses Assn., Alumni of Century, U. Colo. Sch. Nursing Alumni Assn., 1998; recipient N.Y. State Gov.'s award for women in sci., medicine and nursing, Modern Healthcare Hall of Fame award, Modern Health Care Jour., 1994, Lillian D. Wald Spirit of Nursing award, N.Y. Vis. Nurse Svc., 1994, Lifetime Achievement award, Nat. Conf. Nurse Practitioners, 1999, Trailblazer award, Am. Coll. Nurse Practitioners, 2003, Elizabeth Blackwell award, Hobart and William Smith Colls., 2003. Fellow: Nat. League Nursing (Linda Richards award), Am. Acad. Nursing (Living Legend award 1999); mem.: NAS Inst. Medicine (Gustav O. Leinhard award 1990), ANA, APHA (Ruth B. Freeman award), Am. Coll. Nurse Practitioners (Crystal Trailblazers award 2003), Am. Coll. Health Assn. (Boynton award), Sigma Theta Tau, Alpha Omega Alpha (hon.). E-mail: lorettaford@cfl.rr.com.

FORD, PATRICK KILDEA, Celtic studies educator; b. Lansing, Mich., July 31, 1935; s. Oliver Patrick and Ina Mildred (Spence) F.; m. Carol Mae Larsen, June 20, 1959 (div. 1978); children: Anne Kristina, Paul Kildea, James Oliver; m. Chadine Pearl Bailie, Nov. 17, 1979. BA, Mich. State U., 1959; MA, Harvard U., 1966, PhD, 1969. Asst. prof. English Stanford U., 1968-70; asst. prof. Indo-European studies UCLA, 1970-71, asst. prof. English, 1971-74, assoc. prof., 1974-79, prof. English and Celtic studies, 1979-91, dir. Folklore and Mythology Ctr., 1979-84, chmn. Indo-European studies program, 1972-73, 74-75, 79-82, dir. writing programs, 1989-91; Margaret Brooks Robinson prof. Celtic Harvard U., Cambridge, Mass., 1991—; Wallace E. and Grace Connolly prof. Celtic Stanford U., 1986. Founder, pres. Ford & Bailie Pubs./Book Distbrs. Author: The Poetry of Llywarch Hen, 1974, The Mabinogi and Other Medieval Welsh Tales, 1977, Ystoria Taliesin, 1992, The Celtic Poets: Songs and Tales from Early Ireland and Wales, 1999, Math uab Mathonwy, 1999, Manawydan uab Llyr, 2000; editor, contbr.: Celtic Folklore and Christianity: Essays in Memory of William W. Heist, 1983; co-author: Sources and Analogues of Old English Poetry: Celtic and Germanic, 1984, The Irish Literary Tradition, 1992. With AUS, 1956-57. NEH fellow, 1972, UCLA fellow, 1973, Fulbright fellow, 1973-74; grantee Skaggs Found., 1981-83, Am. Council Learned Socs., 1985, NEH, 1986, 94, 96, 99, 2002; hon. fellow Ctr. for Advanced Welsh and Celtic Studies/U. Wales. Mem. MLA, Internat. Arthurian Soc. (pres. N.Am. br. 1981-83), Medieval Acad. Am., Celtic Studies Assn. N.Am. (v.p. 1984-86, pres. 1987-89). Office: Harvard U Dept Celtic Lang and Lit Barker Ctr 12 Quincy St Cambridge MA 02138-2030

FORD, RUTH ALICE, elementary education educator; b. LaFollette, Tenn., May 30, 1955; d. Gilford H. and Mabel (Burris) Lovely; m. Lyle K. Blair, Dec. 18, 1976 (div. Aug. 1984); children: Frances Ann, Sarah Beth; m. Marvin A. Ford, June 10, 1986. BS in Home Econ. Edn., U. Tenn., 1976, MEd in Curriculum and Instrn., 1993. Elem. tchr. Franklin County Bd. Edn., Winchester, Tenn., 1977-78, mid. sch. tchr. math., 1978-79; tchr. vocat. home econs. Campbell County Bd. Edn., Jacksboro, Tenn., 1984-92; tchr East La Follette Elem. Sch., La Follette, Tenn., 1992—2003, LaFollette Mid. Sch., 1998—2003; Appalachia math./sci. coord. tchr. Appalachiaian Rural Sys., 2003—; tchr. ptnr. Appalachia Rural Sys. Initiative, 1999—2003. Advisor Future Homemakers Am., Stony Fork High Sch., Caryville, Tenn., 1984-92; tchr., ptnr. Appalachian Rural Systemic Initiative. Troop leader Girl Scouts U.S., Jacksboro, 1984-87, Centerville, Tenn., 1982, 83; leader 4-H Club, Campbell County, 1984-93; mem./pianist Mt. Zion United Meth. Ch., LaFollette; mem. Tenn. Gov.'s Drug Alliance, 1989-90; adv. bd. Campbell County Talent Search. Recipient cert. 4-H Vol. Leader, 1988, 89, 90, 92. Mem. NEA, Am. Vocat. Assn., Nat. Sci. Tchrs. Assn., Tenn. Sci. Tchrs. Assn. (bd. dirs. 2002—), Tenn. Vocat. Assn., Am. Home Econs. Assn., Tenn. Edn. Assn., Campbell County Edn. Assn., Knox County Home Econs. Assn., Order Ea. Star (officer Caryville chpt. 1987, 88, 90), Delta Kappa Gamma. Democrat. Avocations: quilting, sewing, cooking, crafts, reading. Home: 315 Lakeshore Ln La Follette TN 37766-4164 Office: Materials Ctr Jacksboro TN 37757

FORD, VANDELETTE, mental health educator; b. July 31, 1942; d. Edna L. Cooke; 1 child, Stephanie Ford-Aaron. AA, N.Y.C. Community Coll., 1968; BA in Sociology/Psychology, CUNY, 1973; MA in Psychology/Sociology, New Sch. for Social Rsch., 1979; MSW, Yeshiva U., 1984, post masters cert. in Advanced Gerontological Counseling, 1986. Cert. social worker, N.Y. Social worker, dept. psychiatry Downstate Med. Ctr., Bklyn.; asst. prof. N.Y. City Tech. Coll., Bklyn. Cons. ednl. vocat. rehab. program Kings County Hosp., Bklyn.; adjunct prof. human svcs. Audrey Cohen Coll., N.Y.C.; adjunct instr. Coll. of New Rochelle, N.Y.C. Child sponsor Save the Child. Mem. Nat. Assn. Social Workers, NOHSE, Child Welfare League of Am. Home: 6755 Ann Arbor Dr College Park GA 30349-1101

FORDEMWALT, JAMES NEWTON, microelectronics engineering educator, consultant; b. Parsons, Kans., Oct. 18, 1932; s. Fred and Zenia (Chambers) F.; m. Suzan Lynn Hopkins, Aug. 26, 1958 (div. June 1961); m. Elizabeth Anna Hoare, Dec. 29, 1963; children: John William, James Frederick. BS, U. Ariz., 1955, MS, 1956; PhD, U. Iowa, 1960. Sr. engr. GE Co., Evandale, Ohio, 1959-60, U.S. Semcor, Inc., Phoenix, 1960-61; sect. mgr. Motorola Semiconductor Products Div., Phoenix, 1961-66; dept. mgr. Philco-Ford Microelectronics Div., Santa Clara, Calif., 1966-68; assoc. dir. R & D Am. Microsystems Inc., Santa Clara, 1968-71; assoc. rsch. prof. U. Utah, Salt Lake City, 1972-76; dir. microelectronics lab. U. Ariz., Tucson, 1976-87; assoc. prof., lab. mgr. Ariz. State U., Tempe, 1987—2001, prof. emeritus, 2001—, assoc. chair microelectronics, 1992—2001, asst. chair dept. electronic and computer tech., 1993—2001. Cons. Integrated Cirs. Engring., Scottsdale, Ariz., 1976—, Western Design Ctr., Mesa, Ariz., 1980—; mem. semiconductor com. United Techs. Corp., Hartford, Conn., 1978-87. Author: Silicon Wafer Processing Technology, 1979; editor: Integrated Circuits, 1965; contbr.: MOS Integrated Circuits, 1972. Mem. IEEE, Internat. Soc. for Hybrid Microlectronics (chpt. pres. 1982-83), Electrochem. Soc. Avocations: pilot, photographer. Home: 613 W Summit Pl Chandler AZ 85225-7798 E-mail: jfordemwalt@cox.net.

FOREMAN, MARY LU, educator; b. Trenton, Mo., Feb. 23, 1938; d. Carl and Hariette Lee (Moore) Kelley; m. Charles Foreman, Nov. 23, 1974; children: Lucinda, Melinda. BSEd, U. Kans., 1960; MA, U. Mo., Kansas City, 1965. Cert. tchr. English, Spanish, journalism, speech, Mo. Tchr. English Colegio Bolivar, Cali, Colombia; tchr. English as a 2nd lang. U. del Valle, Cali; tchr. English Shawnee Mission East High Sch., Prairie Village, Kans.; tchr. journalism Center Sr. High, Kansas City, Mo. Computer cons. Center Sch. Dist.; adj. prof. Johnson County C.C., Overland Park, Kans. Named Journalism Tchr. of Yr., 1984; NCTE grantee, 1985-87, 87-89; Nat. Found. for Improvement of Edn. grantee, 1990—; state grantee, 1988-93. Mem. NCTE, JEA, Mo. Journalism Edn. Assn. (past. pres., past v.p.), Phi Delta Kappa (sec.), Alpha Delta Kappa. Home: 6925 Park St Shawnee Mission KS 66216-2349

FOREMAN, ROBERT CHARLES, physical education educator; b. Cin., Dec. 18, 1969; s. Mary Janice (Woeste) F. BS in Phys. Edn., Meth. Coll., 1992. Cert. tchr., N.J. Sports dir. Town and Country Day Camp, Old Tappan, N.J., 1989-90; substitute tchr. Passaic County Bd. Edn., Wanaque, N.J., 1990-92; sports dir. Cupsaw Lake, Ringwood, N.J., 1991—; asst. basketball coach Meth. Coll., Fayetteville, N.C., 1992—. Substitute tchr. Riverdale (N.J.) Pub. Schs.; dir. teen programs Skylands YMCA, Ringwood, N.J., 1993—, bd. dirs.; founder, dir. Lancer Summer Basketball Camp, Wanaque, N.J. Vol. Spl. Olympics, Fayetteville, 1990—; del. Statewode Alcohol Awareness Convention, Raleigh, N.C., 1990, 91; mem. Pres.'s Coun. for Physical Fitness, 1991; del. nat. conv. Nat. Assn. for Campus Activities, Nashville, 1991, Dallas, 1992; mem. steering com. Alliance of Wanaque and Ringwood for Edn. and Awareness for Substance Abuse Prevention. Recipient award Pres.'s Coun. for Phys. Fitness, established leader award NACA. Mem. AAPHERD. Roman Catholic. Avocations: collecting baseball cards, sports, television, basketball. Home: 80 Cedar Rd Ringwood NJ 07456-1813

FORER, ARTHUR H. biology educator, researcher, editor; b. Trenton, N.J., Dec. 17, 1935; arrived in Can., 1972; s. Bernard and Rose Ethel Forer; m. Alexandra Engberg Westengaard, Dec. 18, 1964; children— Michael, David. B.Sc., MIT, Cambridge, 1957; postgrad., U. Rochester, 1957-59, U. Wash.-Friday Harbor, summer 1959; PhD in Molecular Biology, Dartmouth Med. Sch., 1964. Postdoctoral fellow Am. Cancer Soc. Carlsberg Labs., Copenhagen, 1964-66; research asst. Cambridge U., Eng., 1966-67, Helen Hay Whitney Found. fellow, 1967-69, Duke U., Durham, N.C., 1969-70; lektor Odense U., Denmark, 1970-72; assoc. prof. biology York U., Toronto, Canada, 1972—75, prof. biology, 1975—2001, prof. emeritus, sr. scholar, 2001—. Mem. grant selection panel Natural Scis. and Engring. Rsch. Coun., 1976-78. Editor: Mitosis/Cytokinesis, 1981; mem. editorial bd. Jour. Cell Sci., 1972-84, Can. Jour. Biochemistry and Cell Biology, 1982-93, Cell Biology Internat. Reports, 1984—; contbr. articles to profl. jours. Active Amnesty Internat., Ottawa, Ont., 1980—, Cmty. Theatre Orchs., Toronto, A Pack-O-Lips Now Saxophone Quartet, Toronto. Fellow Royal Soc. Can., Acad. Scis.; mem. AAAS, Am. Soc. Cell Biology, Stankel Ben Soc. (charter mem. 1960—), Tarragon Theatre, Shaw Festival (supporting). Avocations: music, gardening, cycling, hiking. Home: 17 Michigan Dr Willowdale ON Canada M2M 3H9 Office: York U Biology Dept 4700 Keele St Downsview ON Canada M3J 1P3 E-mail: aforer@yorku.ca.

FORESTER, JEAN MARTHA BROUILLETTE, innkeeper, retired librarian, educator; b. Port Barre, La., Sept. 7, 1934; d. Joseph Walter and Thelma (Brown) Brouillette; m. James Lawrence Forester, June 2, 1957; children: Jean Martha, James Lawrence. BS La. State U., 1955; MA, George Peabody Coll. Tchrs., 1956. Libr. Howell Elem. Sch., Springhill, La., 1956—58; asst. post libr. Fort Chaffee, Ark., 1958; command libr. Orleans Area Command, U.S. Army, Orleans, France, 1958—59; acquisitions libr. Northwestern State U., Natchitoches, La., 1960; serials libr. La. State U., New Orleans, 1960—66, mem. faculty Eunice, 1966—85, asst. libr., 1972—85, assoc. libr., 1985—87, acting libr., 1987—88, dir. libr., 1988—89, libr. emeritus, 1989—, asst. prof., 1972—85, faculty senator, 1978—80, 1985—86, 1987—89; innkeeper Crown'n'Anchor Inn, Saco, Maine, 1989—. Co-author: Robertsons's Bill of Fare; contbr. articles to profl. jours. Active Eunice Assn. Retarded Children. Fellow Carnegie, 1955—56. Mem.: UDC, La. Libr. Assn. (sect. sec. 1971—72, coord. serials interest group 1984—85), Delta Kappa Gamma (chpt. parliamentarian 1972—74, rec. sec. 1984—86), Order Ea. Star, Phi Mu, Phi Gamma Mu, Alpha Beta Alpha. Democrat. Baptist.

FORGIONE, PASCAL D., JR., state superintendent; 3 children. BA, St. Mary's Seminary and Univ., 1967; MEd, Loyola Coll., 1969; MA, Stanford U., PhD, 1977. Tchr. Balt. Pub. Schs., pub. sch. adminstr.; dir. divsn. rsch., evaluation and assessment State Dept. Edn., Conn., 1979-91; exec. dir. Nat. Edn. Goals Panel, Washington, 1991; state supt. State of Del., Dover, 1991—96; commr. Nat. Ctr. Edn. Stats., 1996—99; supt. Austin Ind. Sch. Dist., Tex., 1999—. Expert advisor Nat. Ctr. Edn., Economy of Nat. Examination System; active Nat. Ctr. Applied Linguistics, Nat. Program Effectiveness Panel; mem. adv. bd. Nat. Ctr. Rsch. Tchr. Edn.; mem. chancellor's commn. minimum standards N.Y.C. Pub. Schs. Mem. Am. Fedn. Tchrs., Nat. Alliance Bus., Nat. Gov. Assn., Nat. Rsch. Coun. Office: 1111 W 6th St Austin TX 78703*

FORINA, MARIA ELENA, gifted education educator; b. Santiago, Cuba, Apr. 10, 1942; came to U.S., 1972; d. Jorge Fernando and Maria Elena (De Gongora) Chaves; m. Antonio Forina, May 28, 1961; children: Maria Elena, Amalia, Jose, Jorge Antonio. AA, Somerset County Coll., 1975; BS magna cum laude, U. Tex. Pan Am., Edinburg, 1982, M in Gifted Edn., 1995. Cert. elem. tchr., bilingual tchr., gifted edn. tchr., Tex.; SOI cert. trainer. 1st grade tchr. Pharr-San Juan-Alamo (Tex.) Ind. Sch. Dist., 1981-83, gifted edn. resource tchr., 1983-88, 6th grade gifted edn. tchr., 1988—, AMS writing trainer, 1991—. Eucharistic minister Resurrection Cath. Ch., Alamo, 1982—, CCD tchr., 1986—, mem. blue ribbon com., 1988—, mem. pastoral coun., 1993-97; mem. adv. bd. Lalo Arcaute Pub. Libr., 2000—. Mem. ASCD, Nat. Coun. Tchrs. Math., Nat. Coun. Tchrs. English, Tex. Assn. for Gifted and Talented, Phi Kappa Phi, Delta Kappa Gamma. Republican. Avocations: classical music, opera, reading, gourmet cooking. Home: 842 Fannin Box 3901 Alamo TX 78516 Office: Alamo Mid Sch 1819 W Us Highway 83 Alamo TX 78516-2102

FORMAN, JUDITH AVIS, retired secondary school educator; b. Chgo., Oct. 12, 1937; d. Bernard L. and Bettie (Bluhm) Becker; m. Larry S. Forman, Aug. 23, 1959; children: Mark, Kenneth, James. BA, U. Mich., 1959; MEd, Calif. Luth. U., Thousand Oaks, 1979. Life tchg. credential. Tchr. Redford Twp. (Mich.) Jr. H.S., 1959-60, Santa Maria (Calif.) H.S., 1960-61, Monte Vista Intermediate Sch., Camarillo, Calif., 1971-90, Oak Park H.S., Agoura, Calif., 1990—2001, chmn. English dept., 1999—2001, ret., 2001. Fellow Nat. Writing Project, U. Calif. Santa Barbara, 1987, returning fellow, 1995; Tech. in Classroom fellow U. Calif. Santa Barbara, 1985; mentor tchr. Pleasant Valley Sch. Dist., Camarillo, 1983-86, Oak Park Sch. Dist., Agoura, 1995. Author, editor: The American Experience, 1995; contbr. articles to profl. jours. Grantee Calif. Ednl. Initiative Fund, 1992, creative ideas grantee Oak Park, 1994-95. Mem. Nat. Coun. Tchrs. English, Assn. Secondary Curriculum Devel., Calif. Assn. Tchrs. English, Smithsonian, Oak Park Tchrs. Assn. Avocations: hiking, gardening, cooking, painting watercolor, reading. Office: Oak Park HS 899 Kanan Rd Oak Park CA 91377-3904

FORMAN, MICHELE, secondary school educator; b. Biloxi, Miss., Apr. 7, 1946; m. Dick Forman; children: Elissa, Laura, Tim. BA in hist., Brandeis U., 1967; MA in tchg., U. Vt. Cert. Profl. Tchg. Standards Nat. Bd. Tchr. Middleburg (Vt.) Union HS, 1986—. Alcohol drug edn curriculum spec. Vt. Dept. Edn. Mem. Vt. State Dept. Edn., Task Force HS Reform; vol. Peace Corp., Nepal, 1960. Named Nat. Tchr. of Yr., 2001, Vt. State Tchr. of Yr., 2001; recipient mary K. Bonsteel Tachau Pre-Collegiate Tchg. award, 1999. Mem.: Academic Coun. The Coll. Bd., Hist. Soc. Studies Academic Adv. Com., Nat. Bd Profl. Tchg. Standards. Office: Middlebury Union HS Hist Social Studies Dept 73 Charles Ave Middlebury VT 05753

FORMICA, JOSEPH VICTOR, retired microbiology educator; b. N.Y.C., July 3, 1929; s. Joseph and Carmela (LaRosa) F.; m. Philomena Theresa Moretti, June 26, 1956; children: Diane, Jody Ann. BS, Syracuse U., 1953, MS, 1954; PhD, Georgetown U., 1967. Bacteriologist Biol. Warfare, Ft. Detrick, Frederick, Md., 1954-58; biochemist NIH, Bethesda, Md., 1958-63; asst. prof. dept. pediatrics Georgetown Med. Ctr., Washington, 1967-69; assoc. prof. dept. microbiology Med. Coll. Va., Richmond, 1969—2001, assoc. dean Sch. Basic Scis., 1977-81; ret., 2001. Author: (chpt.) Pathobiology of Neoplasma, 1989; patentee in field; contbr. articles to profl. jours.

With U.S. Army, 1946-48, Korea. Grantee Ctr. for Innovative Tech., Herndon, Va., 1986-89, NIH, 1970, 72, 78. Fellow Am. Acad. Microbiology; mem. Soc. Wine Educators (pres. 1985-87). Avocation: wine educator. Office: Va Commonwealth U PO Box 980678 Richmond VA 23298-0678

FORNEY, RONALD DEAN, elementary school educator, consultant, educational therapist; b. Kearney, Nebr., June 28, 1954; s. Carl Roger and Florence Alyce (Gordon) F. Student, Community Coll. Denver, 1972-73; BA in Liberal Arts, Loretto Heights Coll., Denver, 1975; AS in Devel. Psychology, Arapahoe Community Coll., Denver, 1977; MBA, Calif. State Coll., San Bernardino, 1992; MS in Ednl. Adminstrn., Nat. U., 1993. Cert. tchr., English tchr., Calif.; cert. ednl. therapist. Tchr. Lake Elsinore (Calif.) Sch. Dist., 1985-87, Banning (Calif.) Unified Sch. Dist., 1987—, master tchr., classroom mgmt.-assertive discipline cons., 1990—, asst. prin. Ctrl. Elem. Sch., 1996-98. Cons. visual and performing arts, motivation and self-esteem bldg; ednl. therapist in pvt. practice, 1998—. Recipient cert. in affective domain Lake Elsinore Sch. Dist., 1986, Outstanding Tchr. award Hemmerling Sch., Banning, 1989. Avocations: theatre, reading, writing and reading haiku poetry.

FORNIA, DOROTHY LOUISE, physical education educator; b. Youngstown, Ohio, Feb. 14, 1918; d. Joseph and Margaret Alice (Berner) F. BS in Edn., Ohio State U., 1941, MA, 1944; EdD, U. So. Calif., 1957. Cert. tchr., Ohio. Tchr. Ohio Solders and Sailors Orphans Home, Xenia, Ohio, 1941-43; grad. asst. Ohio State U., Columbus, 1943-44; asst. prof. Wilmington (Ohio) Coll., 1944-45, Ohio Wesleyan U., Delaware, 1945-47, Bowling Green (Ohio) State U., 1947-53; teaching asst. U. So. Calif., L.A., 1953-56; prof. Calif. State U., Long Beach, 1956-92, prof. emeritus phys. edn., gerontology, 1992. Mem. task force Calif. State U., Long Beach, 1982-84; cons. grad. edn. Calif. State U., Long Beach, 1992—, also founder, chmn. Sr. Univ. Mem. adv. bd. Interfaith Action for Aging, Long Beach, 1978—; mem. L.A. County Commn. on Aging, 1989-93, v.p. 1992—; founder Sr. Care Action Network, 1979, gov., 1988; vice chair Area Programs on Aging, 1992-93; chair, sr. univ. bd. Calif. State U. Recipient Founders award Sr. Care Action for Aging, 1988. Fellow Am. Sch. Health Assn.; mem. Sr. Care Action Network, Calif. Women in Higher Edn. (v.p. 1980-84, 89—), Soroptimist Internat. (chair Long Beach chpt. 1990-92). Avocations: gardening, photography, theater, travel, walking. Home: 6941 E Driscoll St Long Beach CA 90815-4810

FORREST, KATHLEEN, secondary education educator; b. Attleboro, Mass., Nov. 28, 1955; d. Joseph Paul and Josephine Joan (Dziedzic) Poholek; m. Wayne J. Forrest, Aug. 9, 1980. BA, Wheaton Coll., Norton, Mass., 1977; MEd, R.I. Coll., 1978. Cert. tchr. Spanish, French, bilingual edn., Mass., R.I. Foreign lang. tchr. Pawtucket (R.I.) School Dept., 1977—. Adj. prof. R.I. Coll., Providence, 1990—; advisor Shea H.S. Key Club, Pawtucket, 1987-93. Home: 11 Doro Pl Rumford RI 02916-1913

FORRESTER, ALFRED WHITFIELD, psychiatrist, educator; b. Springfield, Mass., May 15, 1953; s. Wallace Lomax and Alma Mae (Brooks) F. BA magna cum laude, Yale U., 1975; MD, Johns Hopkins U., 1979. Diplomate Nat. Bd. Med. Examiners, Am. Bd. Psychiatry and Neurology. Med. resident dept. medicine Mt. Auburn Hosp., Cambridge, Mass., 1979-82; psychiatry resident dept. psychiatry and behavioral scis. Johns Hopkins Med. Insts., Balt., 1982-85, research fellow, 1985-86, instr., 1986-93; clin. asst. prof. dept. psychiatry U. Md., Balt., 1987—; pvt. psychiat. practice, 1988—. Staff psychiatrist Cann Health Resources, Fallston, Md., 1987-88, The Sheppard and Enoch Pratt Hosp., 1988-97; dir. psychiat. svcs. Chase-Brexton Health Svcs., Balt., 1988-90, staff psychiatrist, 1985-2000; med. dir. Behavioral Sci. Assocs., Lutherville, Md., 1993-97, Nicotine Addiction Treatment Ctrs., Lutherville, 1997-2002; med. cons. Bon Secours Hosp., Balt., 1983-90; psychiat. cons. Shock-Trauma Ctr. U. Md. Hosp., 1987-90. Contbr. articles to profl. jours. Active Groton (Mass.) Sch. Bd. Govs., 1983-85, AIDS com., Med. and Chirurgical Faculty State of Md., 1988-91. Nat. Achievement scholar, 1971-75. Fellow APA; mem. Am. Coll. Physicians, Med. and Chirurgical Faculty State Md., AMA, Md. Psychiatric Soc., Md. Psychiat. Liaison Assn., Yale Alumni Assn. (fundraiser 1975—), Greater Balt. Bus. Profl. Assn. Clubs: Mory's Assn. (New Haven), Yale (Md.). Democrat. Episcopalian. Avocations: classical music, theater. Home: 115 Saint Dunstans Rd Baltimore MD 21212-3311 Office: 9515 Deereco Rd Ste 1001 Timonium MD 21093 E-mail: a.w.forrester@att.net.

FORRESTER, DONALD DEAN, educational administrator; b. Laporte, Ind., Feb. 8, 1945; s. Grady Wesley and Margaret Elizabeth (Meadows) F.; m. Anne Gaskill, June 17, 1967; 1 child, Shannon Anne. BS in Edn., Frostburg State U., 1967; MEd in Edn., Bowie State U., 1972; EdD in Edn., Nova Southeastern U., 1978; MA in Theology, St. Mary's Sem. and U., 1990. Tchr. Montpelier Elem. Sch., Laurel, Md., 1967-73, ESAA Floating Faculty, Suitland, Md., 1973-74; vice prin. Rogers Heights Elem. Sch., Bladensburg, Md., 1974-76; prin. Somerset Elem. Sch., Bowie, Md., 1976-77, Montpelier Elem. Sch., Laurel, 1977-92, Yorktown Elem. Sch., Bowie, 1992-95; ednl. cons., Mountain Lake Park, Md., 1995-97; lectr., univ. supr. Frostburg State U., 1995-97; prin. Rowlesburg (W.Va.) Sch., 1997—. V.p. Montpelier Elem. Sch. PTA, Laurel, 1972-73, pres., 1973-74. Lay reader Trinity Episcopal Ch., Waterloo, Elkridge, Md., 1980-86, lay min., 1986-95; sr. warden Trinity Episcopal Ch. Vestry, Waterloo, Elkridge, 1986-90; lay reader chalicist, vestry St. Matthew's Episcopal Ch., Oakland, Md., 1995—; dir. Woodbridge Crossing Homeowners Assn., Laurel, 1990-92. Mem. ASCD, Nat. Assn. Elem. Sch. Prins., Md. Assn. Elem. Sch. Adminstrs., Md. Congress PTAs (hon. life), Am. Assn. Christian Counselors, Lions, Masons, Phi Delta Kappa, Phi Mu Alpha Sinfonia. Republican. Avocations: reading, photography, travel. Home: RR 1 Box 255 Rowlesburg WV 26425-9600 Office: Rowlesburg Sch Rowlesburg WV 26425

FORST, EDMUND CHARLES, JR., communications educator, administrator, consultant; b. Chgo., June 25, 1961; s. Edmund Sr. and Patricia Ann (Dopek) Forst; m. Kelly Lee Globke; children: Morgan Mae, Shannon Rose, Maximillian. BA, Ea. Ill. U., 1983, MA, 1984; EdD, W. Va. U., 1994. Leader, mem. staff Neighborhood Boys Club, Chgo., summer 1975-84; instr. in communication DePaul U., Chgo., 1988-93; instr. Waubonsee C.C., Sugar Grove, Ill., 1993-94, assoc. dean comms. and humanities, 1994-98; dean arts & scis. Triton Coll., River Grove, Ill., 1998—. Cons. comm. for Leon Spinks, 1990; pres.-elect Ill. Coun. CC Adminstrs., 2003—. Contbr. articles to profl. jours. Euracharist minister Our Lady of Mercy, Chgo., 1989-90; bd. dirs. Neighborhood Boys Club, Chgo., 1988-92,; bd. dirs. St. Leonard Sch., Berwyn, Ill., 2000-2001, mem. parish coun., 2002, mem. fin. com. 2003. Mem. Aurora-Naperville Rotary, Forest Park C. of C. Republican. Roman Catholic. Avocations: sports, reading, movie collecting, model railroads. Home: 6509 Sinclair Ave Berwyn IL 60402-3737 E-mail: eforst@triton.cc.il.us.

FORSTER, BRUCE ALEXANDER, dean; b. Toronto, Ont., Can., Sept. 23, 1948; m. Margaret Jane Mackay, Dec. 28, 1968 (div. Dec. 1979); 1 child, Kelli Elissa; m. Valerie Dale Pendock, Dec. 8, 1979 (div. Oct. 2003); children: Jeremy Bruce, Jessica Dale. BA in Math., Econs., U. Guelph, Ont., 1970; PhD in Econs., Australian Nat. U., Canberra, 1974. From asst. prof. to prof. U. Guelph, 1973-87; vis. assoc. prof. econs. U. B.C., Vancouver, 1979; vis. assoc. fellow U. Wyo., 1979-80, vis. prof., 1983-84, 87, prof. econs., 1987-2000, dean Coll. Bus., 1991-2000; prof. econs., dean Sch. Mgmt. Ariz. State U. West, Phoenix, 2000—. Vis. prof. Profl. Tng. Ctr., Ministry of Econ. Affairs, Taiwan, 1990-2002; cons. in field; Jayes-Qantas vis. scholar U. Newcastle, Australia, 1983. Author: The Acid Rain Debate: Science and Special Interest in Policy Formation, 1993; co-author: Economics in Canadian Society, 1986; assoc. editor: Jour. Applied Bus. Rsch., 1987, mem. edit. adv. bd., 1987—; editl. coun.: Jour. Environ. Econs. and Mgmt., 1989, assoc. editor, 1989-91; contbr. articles to profl. jours. Trustee Wyo. Retirement Sys., 1995-2000, Laramie Sr. Housing, Inc., 1995-96; mem. City of Surprise Econ. Devel. Adv. Bd., 2002—, Ariz. C. of C. Econ. Devel. com., 2002—. Mem. Assn. to Advance Collegiate Schs. of Bus., Am. Econ. Assn., Assn. Environ. and Resource Economists, Mid-West Assn. Bus. Deans and Divsn. Heads (pres. 1995-96), Faculty Club U. Guelph (treas. 1981-82, v.p. 1982-83, 85-86, pres. 1986-87). Avocations: weight lifting, swimming, skiing, scuba diving. Office: Ariz State UWest Office of Dean Sch Mgmt Phoenix AZ 85069 E-mail: Bruce.Forster@asu.edu.

FORSTER, SUSAN BOGART, computer educator; b. Hackensack, N.J., June 6, 1944; d. Charles William and Lillian (Vito) Bogart; m. John D. Forster, June 17, 1967; children: Gregory, Brian. BA, Mt. Holyoke Coll., 1966; MEd, George Mason U., 1985. Tchr. adult edn. Fairfax (Va.) County Pub. Schs., 1983-84; programmer Fairfax County Pub. Schs., Annandale, Va., 1984-85; computer dir. Potomac Sch., McLean, Va., 1985-93; computer trainer, tchr. The Langley Sch., McLean, Va., 1994—; dir. computer Summer Inst., Washington, 1993—. Program developer Adult Computer Literacy Program, McLean, 1991-92; adj. prof. edn. Marymount U., 1993—, George Mason U., Fairfax, Va., 1993—. Mem. Computer Assn. Ind. Schs. (program chair 1990-91). Avocations: needlework, water aerobics. Home: 1283 Wedgewood Manor Way Reston VA 20194-1329

FORSYTH, BEVERLY K. language educator, writer; b. Memphis, June 05; d. Marian Davidson Roy and Oakley Eugene Stover, Johnny Roy. AA in Mass Comm., Odessa (Tex.) Coll.; BA in Mass Comm., U. Tex., Odessa, MA in English, 1995; PhD in English, Union Inst., Cin., 2001. Author: (travel guide book) The Texas Monthly Guidebook to Texas. 3rd edition, 1993; co-author: (anthology) American Women Writers, 1900-1945, A Bio-Bibliographical Critical, 2000; author: (short stories) La Gringa Is My Name, 1999, Pontotoc Witch, 2000, The Knock, 2002, Shadow's Edge, 2003; contbr. articles to profl. jours. Grantee Grace Mitchell/Learner Coun. Rsch. Travel, Union Inst., 2000; scholar, 2000, Agnes Rettig, 2000. Mem.: W. Tex. Writers, Tex. Assn. Creative Writing Tchrs., Tex. Coun. Tchrs. English (Pres.'s Classroom Rsch/Travel Study grantee 2001), Tex. C.C. Tchrs. Assn., Conf. Coll. Tchrs. English (exec. bd. councilors 2002—), S. Ctrl. MLA, Tex. Popular Culture Assn., S.W. Popular Culture Assn., Am. Culture Assn., Sigma Kappa Delta, Sigma Tau Delta (life). Office: Odessa Coll 201 W University Odessa TX 79764 Office Fax: 432-335-6846. Personal E-mail: bforsyth@cableone.net. Business E-Mail: bforsyth@odessa.edu.

FORSYTH, ROSALYN MOYE, middle school educator; b. Pavo, Ga., Sept. 14, 1942; d. David Cody and Mary (Chapman) Moye; m. Jamos Floyd Forsyth, Aug. 7, 1965. AB, Wesleyan Coll., Macon, Ga., 1964. Cert. paraprofl. Tchr. edn. Dougherty County Bd. of Edn., Albany, Ga., 1965-70, substitute tchr., 1972-88, paraprofl., 1988—. Editor: Membership Roll and Register of Ancestors, 1986. Mem. at large exec. com. South Ga. conf. United Meth. Women, 1972-74, dist. pres. Thomasville dist., 1977-78, rec. sec., 1979-83, sec. publicity and pub. rels., 1983-87, mem. com. on nominations Southeastern jurisdiction 1988-92). Mem. Profl. Assn. Ga. Educators, Bus. and Profl. Woman's Club (pres. 1973-75, dist. dir. Ga. Fedn., state chmn. Young Careerist 1977-79, state chmn. nat. found. 1979-81), DAR (regent Thronateeska chpt. 1986-88, state chmn. Am. Heritage 1986-88, dist. dir. Ga. soc. 1988-90, state officer, historian 1990-92, state chmn. textbook study nat. soc. 1992-94, state officer, registrar 1994-96, state officer, libr. 1996-98). Methodist. Avocations: reading, jogging, georgia bulldog activities, basketball, football. Home: 1706 Pineknoll Ln Albany GA 31707-3770 Office: Alice Coachman Elem 1425 Oakridge Dr Albany GA 31707

FORSYTHE, ROBERT ELLIOTT, economics educator; b. Pitts., Oct. 25, 1949; s. Robert Elliott and Dolores Jean (Davis) F.; m. Lynn Maureen Zollweg, June 17, 1970 (div. July 1978); m. Patricia Ann Hays, June 20, 1981; 1 child, Nathaniel Ryan. BS, Pa. State U., 1970; MS, Carnegie-Mellon U., Pitts., 1972, MS, 1974, PhD, 1975. Ops. rsch. analyst PPG Industries Inc., Pitts., 1970-72; instr. Carnegie-Mellon U., Pitts., 1974-75; asst. prof. Calif. Inst. Tech., Pasadena, 1975-81; assoc. prof. U. Iowa, Iowa City, 1981-86, prof. econ., 1986-90, chmn. dept. econ., 1990-94, sr. assoc. dean Coll. Bus., 1994—, Cedar Rapids Area Bus. Chair, 1992-2000, Leonard A. Hadley Chair in Leadership, 2000—. Founder Iowa Polit. Stock Market; pres. Iowa Market Systems, Inc., 1993-2000. Author: Forecasting Presidential Elections: Polls, Markets, Models; assoc. editor Jour. Econ. Behavior and Orgn., Jour. Exptl. Econs., 1997—. Recipient State of Iowa Regents award for faculty excellence, 2002; Univ. faculty scholar U. Iowa, 1985-88. Mem. Econometric Soc., Am. Econ. Assn., Econ. Sci. Assn. (sect. head 1989-92, pres.-elect 1992-93, pres. 1993-95). Congregationalist. Home: 1806 E Court St Iowa City IA 52245-4643 Office: U Iowa Tippie Coll Bus 108 Pappajohn Bus Bldg Iowa City IA 52242-1000 E-mail: robert-forsythe@uiowa.edu.

FORT, ARTHUR TOMLINSON, III, physician, educator; b. Lumpkin, Ga., Sept. 24, 1931; s. Thomas Morton and Gladys (Davis) F.; m. Jane Wilmer McClelland, June 15, 1957; children: Abby Lucinda, Arthur Tomlinson IV, Juliana Melody, Ernest Arlington, II. BBA, U. Ga., 1952; MD, U. Tenn., 1962. Diplomate: Am. Bd. Ob-Gyn, Am. Bd. Family Practice. Intern, then resident in ob-gyn U. Tenn.-City of Memphis Hosp., 1962-66; asst. prof. U. Tenn. Med. Sch., 1966-70; prof. ob-gyn, head dept. Sch. Medicine La. State U., Shreveport, 1970-73; prof. maternal-child health and family planning, head program family health Sch. Pub. Health Tulane U., 1973-74; practice medicine specializing in rural family medicine Vacharie, La., 1974-79; prof. ob-gyn and family medicine, head dept. family medicine and comprehensive care Sch. Medicine La. State U., Shreveport, 1980—. Author articles in field. Adv. bd. mem. State of La. Dept. Health and Human Resources, 1986-88. With USAF, 1952-57. Recipient Golden Apple Teaching award Student AMA, 1969, Golden Apple Teaching award Western Interstate Commn. on Higher Edn., 1973 Fellow Am. Coll. Ob-Gyn, Am. Acad. Family Practice; mem. AMA. Office: PO Box 33932 Shreveport LA 71130-3932

FORT, EDWARD BERNARD, university chancellor; b. Detroit, Apr. 14; s. Edward Clark and Inez Corrine (Baker) F.; m. Lessie Covington; children: Clarke, Lezlie. BS, MS, Wayne State U., LLD (hon.), 1986; Doctorate, U. Calif., Berkeley, 1964. Supt. Inkster (Mich.) Schs., 1967-71; adj. prof. adminstrn./urban edn. U. Mich., Ann Arbor, 1968-71; supt., dep. supt. schs. Sacramento, 1971-74; chancellor U. Wis. Center System, Madison, 1974-81, N.C. Agricultural and Technological State U., Greensboro, 1981-99, chancellor emeritus, endowed prof. edn., 1999—. Vis. prof. Mich. State U., East Lansing, 1974; mem. White House Sci. Adv. Com.; mem. fin. adv. bd. HBCU Capital, 1993—; mem. NASA adv. coun., 1992—. Bd. editorial cons., Phi Delta Kappa, 1980-83. Bd. dirs. Sacramento Urban League, 1973-74, Madison Urban League, 1979-81; bd. advisors Fund for Improvement Post Secondary Edn., 1980-82; mem. pres.'s commn. N.C. Athletic Assn., 1984-90; mem. century alliance exec. com. Guilford County Sch. Sys., 1986-87, White House Sci. Adv. Com.; bd. advisors Ctr. for Creative Leadership; mem. N.C. Farm Task Force, NIH Adv. Coun. for Environ. Health Svcs. With AUS, 1954-56. Mem. N.C. Assn. Coll. and Univs. (pres.-elect 1993-94, exec. com. 1985—), Nat. Collegiate Athletic Assn. (pres.'s commn. 1984-90), Am. Assn. State Colls. and Univs. (exec. bd.), Nat. Assn. State Univs. and Land Grant Colls., N.C. Bd. Sci. and Tech., N.C. Biotechnology Bd., Greensboro C. of C. Office: NC Agrl & Tech State U Chancellor's Ofc Bluford Libr Ste 357 Greensboro NC 27411-0001

FORTALEZA, JUDITH ANN, school system administrator; b. Dayton, Ohio, Sept. 10, 1936; d. Jesse Beldon and Vivian (Bussert) Moore; m. Alfred Little, Aug. 28, 1954 (div. Oct. 1974); m. Leslie Comdey, July 8, 1988; children: Allen Dale, Jeffrey, Stuart. BS, Wright State U., 1971, MA, 1976; EdD, U. Sarasota, Fla., 1981. Tchr. Bellbrook (Ohio) City Schs., 1969-73, Greene Vocat. Sch., Xenia, Ohio, 1973-74, London (Ohio) City Schs., 1974-75; cons. C.O.S.E.R.R.C., Columbus, Ohio, 1975-78; coord. Hopewell Special Edn. Regional Resource Ctr., Hillsboro, Ohio, 1978-81, Ctrl. Ohio Special Edn. Regional Resource Ctr., Columbus; supr. Westerville (Ohio) City Schs., 1986-90; dir. Newark (Ohio) City Schs., 1990—. Lectr. U. Dayton, 1976, Capital U., Columbus, 1983, Ohio U., Athens, 1986-89. Co-author: Identification of SBH Students, 1975, Intervention Assistant Teams, 1983. Mem. Coun. of Exceptional Children (exec. com. 1989-90), Coun. of Adminstrs. of Spl. Edn. (nat. bd. dirs. 1989-90, pres. 1990). Home: 22 Pinckney Dr Bluffton SC 29910-4471 Office: Newark City Schs 85 E Main St Newark OH 43055-5605

FORTE, VIRGINIA FRANCES, secondary educator; b. Bklyn. d. James and Francesca (Clemente) Anselmi; m. Stephen Palmer Forte; children: Stephen Joseph, Diane Marie, Robert James, Lisa Francesca. BA in English magna cum laude, Queens Coll., 1978, MS in English, Edn., 1987. Cert. tchr., N.Y. Tchr. St. Rita's Sch., Bklyn., 1978; tchr. English St. Sylvester Sch., Bklyn., 1979-85, Christ the King Regional High Sch., Middle Village, N.Y., 1985—. Mobile unit vol. Bklyn. Tuberculosis Assn., 1963; social dir. Parish St. Rita, Bklyn., 1964-66; chair bd. elections Regular Dem. Orgn., Bklyn., 1965-75. Mem.Alpha Sigma Lambda. Roman Catholic.

FORTENBERRY, JACK CLIFTON (CLIFF FORTENBERRY), mass communications educator; b. Laurel, Miss., Jan. 6, 1955; s. Claude Henry and Margaret Ann (Jordan) F.; m. Melanie Caroline Leigh, Oct. 29, 1983; children: Elizabeth, Ryan. Student, Jones County Jr. Coll., Ellisville, Miss., 1973-74; BS, Miss. Coll., Clinton, 1975, MS, 1976; PhD, U. So. Miss., Hattiesburg, 1991. Salesman Surplus City, Jackson, Miss., 1977; instr. U. So. Miss., Hattiesburg, 1977-78; minister music Pattison (Miss.) Bapt. Ch., 1978-79; dir. media svcs. St. Dominic/Jackson Meml. Hosp., 1979-82; instr. gen. studies Southeastern La. U., Hammond, 1982-83; minister music Westside Bapt. Ch., Ponchatoula, La., 1983-85, Bowie St. Bapt. Ch., Hattiesburg, 1979-83; instr. communications Southeastern La. U., Hammond, 1983-85, media cons., 1983-85; asst. prof. mass communications Miss. Coll., Clinton, 1985—. Pres. faculty coun. Miss. Coll., 1994—. Contbr. articles to profl. jours. Minister music Twin Lakes Bapt. Ch., 1991. Mem. Speech Communication Assn., Miss. Speech Communication Assn. (v.p. elect 1991-92, pres. 1992-93). Baptist. Avocations: hunting, fishing, beekeeping, woodwork, gardening. Office: Miss Coll PO Box 4207 Clinton MS 39058-0001

FORTIER, MARDELLE LADONNA, English educator; b. Brookings, S.D., Sept. 15, 1947; d. Leon Doneval and Edna Pearl (Rosenstock) Eide; m. Robert Frederic Fortier, July 27, 1974. BA, U. Minn., 1970; MA, U. Ill., 1971, PhD, 1978. Instr. Berlitz, Hinsdale, Ill., 1983-84, North Ctrl. Coll., Naperville, Ill., 1985; sr. lectr. Loyola U., Chgo., 1984-95; instr. Coll. DuPage, Glen Ellyn, Ill., 1985—; English instr. Benedictine U., Lisle, Ill., 1985, 95—. Cons. in field. Author: The Utopian Thought of St. Thomas More, 1994; author numerous poems. Mem. Ill. State Poetry Soc., Poets and Patrons, Inc. (1st prize 1992, 2d prize 1995), Poets Club Chgo. Roman Catholic. Avocations: music, travel. Home: 5515 E Lake Dr Apt A Lisle IL 60532-2664

FORTIER, SHARON MURPHY, special education educator; b. Alice, Tex., July 22, 1939; d. Henry Barcus and Burnice Ruth (Clifft) Murphy; m. James Robert Fortier, Sept. 30, 1967; children: Mikaron, Robynlea. BS in Elem. Edn., Tex. Woman's U., Denton, 1961; MEd in Early Childhood Spl. Edn., U. Wash., 1988. Cert. tchr., Tex., K-12 spl. edn. tchr., Wash. Ctrl. Agy. dir. Tex. Intercollegiate Student Assn., Austin, 1960-61; tchr. Denver Pub. Schs., 1961-62, Deer Park (Tex.) Sch. Dist., 1962-66, Anchorage Sch. Dist., 1966-70, spl. reading tchr., 1970-72; dir. St. Mary's Creative Playsch., Anchorage, 1976-79; resource specialist/coord. Alaska Resource Access Project, Anchorage, 1981-83, co-dir., 1983-86; spl. edn. tchr. Northshore Sch. Dist., Bothell, Wash., 1988—. Mem. task force on regulation Nat. Head Start Nat. Resource Access Project, Washington, 1982; presenter workshops. Compiler, editor: (libr. catalog) Alaska Special Services Resource Library Catalog and Addenda, 1979-81; co-editor, producer: (video) Like Any Child, 1993-94; editor newsletter Rapline, 1981-86. Troop leader Girl Scouts U.S., Anchorage, 1978-84; block chmn. Am. Cancer Soc., Seattle, 1992-93; asst. in organizing telethon Easter Seals, Anchorage, 1985-86. Kindergarten Inclusion grantee Assn. Wash. Sch. Prins., 1993-94. Mem. AAUW, Coun. for Exceptional Children (divsn. early childhood). Democrat. Episcopalian. Avocations: camping, travel, reading, sewing. Home: 15316 Old Redmond Rd Redmond WA 98052-6837 Office: Woodmoor Elem Sch 12225 NE 160th St Bothell WA 98011-4167

FORTMAN, MARVIN, law educator, consultant; b. Bklyn., Oct. 20, 1930; s. Herman and Bess (Smith) F.; m. Sorale Esther Elpern, Aug. 3, 1958; children: Brian E., Anita J., Deborah J. BS in Acctg., U. Ariz., 1957, JD magna cum laude, 1960; LLM, NYU, 1961. Bar: Ariz. 1960, N.Y. 1961, U.S. Tax Ct. 1962, U.S. Ct. Appeals 1962, U.S. Supreme Ct. 1962. Assoc. Aranow, Brodsky, Bolinger, Einhorn & Dann, N.Y.C., 1961-63, O'Connor, Cavanaugh, Anderson, Westover & Beshears, Phoenix, Ariz., 1963-65; prof. bus. law, bus. and pub. adminstrn. U. Ariz., Tucson, 1965—. Legal cons. various corps., 1963—. Author: Legal Aspects of Doing Business in Arizona, 1970; contbr. articles to profl. jours. Mem. legal com. Ariz. Coun. on Econ. Edn., Tucson, 1975—, Sabbar Shrine Temple, Tucson, 1978—, legal advisor, chmn. wills and gifts, 1981-84, 1990-00, 1990—. With U.S. Army, 1951-53; ETO. Kenneson fellow NYU, 1960-61. Mem. N.Y. State Bar Assn., Ariz. Bar Assn. (wills, trusts, estates sect.), Phi Kappa Phi, Beta Gamma Sigma (v.p., treas. 1972—), Beta Alpha Psi, Alpha Kappa Psi (vp. treas. 1972-01). Home: 5844 E 15th St Tucson AZ 85711-4508 Office: U Ariz Coll Of Bus And Pub Adminstr Tucson AZ 85721-0001

FORTSON, EDWARD NORVAL, physics educator; b. Atlanta, June 16, 1936; s. Charles Wellborn and Virginia (Norval) F.; m. Alix Madge Hawkins, Apr. 3, 1960; children— Edward Norval, Lucy Frear, Amy Lewis BS, Duke U., 1957; PhD, Harvard U., 1963. Research fellow U. Bonn., Federal Rep. Germany, 1965-66; research asst. prof. physics U. Wash., Seattle, 1963-65, asst. prof., 1966-69, assoc. prof., 1969-74, prof., 1974—. Fulbright travel grantee, 1965-66; Nat. Research Council fellow Oxford, Eng., 1977; Guggenheim fellow, 1980-81 Fellow AAAS, Am. Phys. Soc.; mem. NAS. Office: U Wash Dept Physics PO Box 351560 Seattle WA 98195-1560

FORTSON-RIVERS, TINA E. (THOMASENA ELIZABETH FORTSON-RIVERS), information technology specialist; b. Anderson, S.C. d. Thomas Henry and Mary (Oliver) Fortson; m. Michael M. Rivers, Sept. 12, 1962 (div. 1973); children: Michael II (dec.), George Thomas, Kashiya Elaine. BA, Spelman Coll., 1962; MEd, Bowie State U., 1979; MS, Johns Hopkin U., 1982. Cert. adminstrn., supervision, Md. Tchr. Tulip Grove Elem. Sch., Bowie, Md., 1973-79, Kenmoor Elem. Sch., Landover, Md., 1979-82; computer coord. Benjamin Stoddert Mid. Sch., Temple Hills, Md., 1982-86; info. tech. specialist Prince Georges County Pub. Schs., Upper Marlboro, Md., 1986—. Ednl. cons. Wicat, Provo, Utah, 1985-91; design cons. Computer Lady, Capitol Heights, Md., 1990-92; del. U.S.-Russia Conf. on Edn., 1994; del. Initiative for Edn., Sci. and Tech. to Republic of South Africa, 1995. Author: Education Software Correlation to PGCPS Socal Studies Curriculum, 1992. Mem. Com. of 100, Prince Georges County Schs., Upper Marlboro, 1985; bd. trustees Gethsemane United Meth. Ch. Mem.: Nat. Coun. for Social Studies (membership com. chmn. 1994, task force on governance 1999), Prince Georges County Coun. for Social Studies (pres. 1981—82), Md. Coun. for Social Studies (treas. 1982—83), Mid. States Coun. for Social Studies (bd. dirs. 1979—, conf. program chair 1989, 1997, regional conf. coord. 1992—93, pres. 1994—96, awards chair 1996—99, sec. 1999—), Alpha Delta Kappa (sec. Md. ETa

1992—94, membership chair 1994—96, pres.-elect 1996—98, 2000—, pres. 1998—2000, Md. dist. chair 1994—96, Md. state rec. sec. 1998—, corr. sec. 1996—98, state pres.-elect 2000—02, pres. 2002—). Avocations: watercolor painting, sewing. Office: Prince Georges County Pub Schs 8437 Landover Rd Hyattsville MD 20785-3502

FORTUNATO, JOANNE ALBA, athletic director; b. Phila. d. Frank and MaryAnn (Vasquez) Torcaso. BS, Temple U., 1957, MS, 1959; PhD, U. So. Calif., L.A., 1973, Northwestern U., Chgo., 1986. Tchr. Phila. Pub. Sch. System, 1957-64; asst. prof. Trenton (N.J.) Coll., 1964-68, Cen. Conn. State Coll., New Britain, 1968-69; teaching asst. U. So. Calif., L.A., 1970-71; asst. prof. CUNY, Bklyn., 1971-75; assoc. athletic dir. and prof. Northwestern U., Chgo., 1975-80; athletic dir. Keene (N.H.) State Coll., 1981-93; commr. athletics New Eng. Collegiate Conf., 1990-93, Calif. C.C.'s, 1995—. Commr. CCLC Commn. on Athletics, 1990-93; chair infraction com. Ea. Collegiate Athletic Conf., Centerville, Mass., 1984-89; regional chair W soccer Nat. Collegiate Athletic Assn., 1987-90; commr. Div. I champ, AIAW, Washington, 1983-86. Recipient Instl. Svc. award Italian Olympic Com., Rome, 1965, Ann. Leadership award Internat. Orgn. Women Execs., 1978, Citation of Recognition USVBA, 1972. Mem. AAHPERD, Nat. Assn. Coll. Women Athletic Adminstrs., Nat. Assn. Coll. Dirs. of Athletics. Home: 3090 Sierra Blvd Sacramento CA 95864-4931 Office: CCLC/COA 2017 O St Sacramento CA 95814-5211

FORTUNE, LAURA CATHERINE DAWSON, elementary school educator; b. Louisville, Feb. 2, 1931; d. Lewis Harper and Zelma Ruth (Hocutt) Dawson; m. James Ralph Fortune, Jan. 10, 1950; children: Elaine, Jean, Tom, Joe. BS, R.I. Coll., 1969, MEd, 1972; postgrad., Longwood Coll., Farmville, Va., 1980-88, U. Va., 1977-90. Elem. sch. tchr. North Kingston (R.I.) Schs., 1969-74; 6th grade tchr. Campbell County Schs., Altavista, Va., 1974-92, sch. divsn. grantwriter, 1992-96, instructional coord., 1987-91. Active Gov.'s Commn. Champion Schs., 1994—96; leader Girl Scouts U.S., parent com., 1961—69; treas. Narrow River Preservation Assn., 1970—74; mem. Edn. Commn. States Investment Com., 1997—98; edn. com. Va. Bd. for People with Disabilities, 1997—2001, sec., 1999—2001; mem. Edn. Commn. States, 1994—2002; past chmn., tchr. adv. coun. Reps., Va. Mem.: ASCD, NEA (past chair Rep. educators caucus), Va. Edn. Assn. (past chair Rep. educators caucus), Phi Delta Kappa. Baptist. Address: 2645 Johnson Creek Rd Evington VA 24550-4133 E-mail: lauracatherine@att.net.

FORVOUR, JACK EDWIN, adapted physical education educator, consultant; b. Cherry Hill, N.J., Sept. 2, 1946; s. Joseph William and Ethel Estelle (Duffield) F.; children: Jason Daniel Forvour, Jared Scott Forvour. BA, Lynchburg Coll., 1969; MA, Glassboro (N.J.) State Coll., 1975; EdD, Temple U., 1985. Phys. edn. tchr. Pennsauken (N.J.) Bd. of Edn., 1969-78; supr. student tchrs. Temple U., Phila., 1978-79; tchr., cons. phys. edn. Pennsauken Pub. Schs., 1979—. Cons. Forvour Consulting, Cherry Hill, 1985—. Recipient N.J. Gov.'s Tchr. of Yr. award, 1994. Mem. AAHPERD, NEA, N.J. Edn. Assn. Lutheran. Avocations: boating, fishing, camping, hiking, bowling. Home: 54 Grant Ave Cherry Hill NJ 08002-3535

FOSS, DONALD JOHN, university dean, research psychologist; b. Mpls., Mar. 28, 1940; s. Bernard J. and Elizabeth (Cody) F.; m. Patricia R. Diamond, Sept. 18, 1965; children— Melissa, Lara BA, U. Minn., 1962, PhD, 1966. Postdoctoral fellow Harvard U., Cambridge, Mass., 1966-67; asst. prof. psychology U. Tex., Austin, 1967-71, assoc. prof., 1971-75, prof., 1975-95, chmn. dept., 1983-95; dean Coll. Arts and Scis., Fla. State U., Tallahassee, 1995—. Author: (with others) Psycholinguistics, 1978, Mental Health Research in Texas, 1990; editor Contemporary Psychology, 1980-85; assoc. editor Am. Psychologist, 1987-92, Ann. Rev. of Psychology, 1994-98; contbr. articles to profl. jours. Mem. adv. coun. Hogg Found., 1988-91, USAF Cognition Group, 1989-93, Mellon Found. Literacy Coun., 1989-93, U. Corp. Atmospheric Rsch. 1995—, Fla. State U. Rsch. Found, 1995—, bd. dirs., 1993—; co-chair Nat. Rsch. Agenda Steering Com., NIE, 1973-75, Am. Psychology Soc., 1995—. Grantee NSF, 1969-72, NIMH, 1976-81, Army Rsch. Inst., 1982-85, Tex. Advanced Rsch., 1988-92; recipient Outstanding Grad. Tchg. award U. Tex., 1986, Outstanding Achievement award U. Minn., 1993. Fellow AAAS, APA (mem. publs. and comm. bd. 1985-94, chmn. 1991-93), Am. Psychol. Soc.; mem. Psychonomics Soc., Soc. Engring. Psychologists, Chancellors Coun. U. Tex., Pres.'s Club U. Minn. Home: 3933 Bobbin Brook Cir Tallahassee FL 32312-1239 Office: Fla State U Coll Arts and Scis Tallahassee FL 32312

FOSTER, CHARLES CRAWFORD, lawyer, educator; b. Galveston, Tex., Aug. 1, 1941; s. Louie Brown and Helen (Hall) F.; m. Marta Brito, Sept. 7, 1967 (div. Apr. 1986); children: John, Ruth; m. Lily Chen, Jan. 7, 1989; children: Zachary, Anthony. AA, Del Mar Jr. Coll., 1961; BA, U. Tex., 1963, JD, 1967. Bar: Tex. 1967, N.Y. 1969. Assoc. Reid & Priest, N.Y.C., 1967-69, Butler & Binion, Houston, 1969-73; ptnr. Tindall & Foster, Houston, 1973—. Hon. consul gen. Kingdom of Thailand, 1996—; adj. prof. immigration law U. Houston, 1985-89; bd. dirs. Greater Houston Partnership, 1997-2003, chmn. econ. devel. adv. bd., 2000 World Trade Adv. Bd., 1997; chmn. Asia Soc.-Tex., bd. trustees, 1990—; bd. dirs. Houston World Affairs Coun., 1990; chmn. Inst. Internat. Edn., The Houston Club, 1999—, Houston Ballet Found., Assn. of Cmty. TV, Houston Holocaust Mus.; mem. Mayoral Adv. Bd. for Internat. Affairs and Devel./Asia, 1999—; pres. Houston Forum, 2002. Contbr. articles to profl. jours. Chmn. immigration reform Gov.'s Task Force of Tex., 1984—87; mem. Bush-Cheney Transition Adv. Com., 2000—01. Admiral Texan Navy, 2003. Decorated comdr. 3d class Order of the Crown (Thailand), comdr. Exalted Order of White Elephant (Thailand); Rotary Internat. fellow U. Concepción, Chile, 1964; recipient Houston Internat. Svc. award Houston Jaycees, 1996, Disting. Friend of China award U.S. China Friendship Found., 2000; honoree Am. Immigration Law Found., 1998' commd. adm. Tex. Navy, Gov. Rick Perry, 2003. Mem. ABA (chmn. immigration com. internat. law and practice sect. 1982-90, chmn. coordinating com. on immigration and law 1987-89, fgn. rels. com. 2000—), Am. Immigration Lawyers Assn. (pres. 1981-82, Outstanding Svc. award 1985), Tex. Bar Assn. (chmn. com. law on immigration and nationality 1984-86), Tex. Bd. Legal Specialization (chmn. immigration adv. commn. 1979—), Houston Bar Assn., Asia Soc. (trustee 1992—, chmn. Houston Ctr. 1992—), Rotary, Houston Club (pres. 2001). Methodist. Avocations: mountain climbing, photography, travel. Home: 17 Courtlandt Pl Houston TX 77006-4013 Office: Tindall & Foster 2800 Chase Tower 600 Travis St Ste 2800 Houston TX 77002-3094

FOSTER, CHARLES THOMAS, JR., geology educator; b. Fremont, Ohio, Aug. 30, 1949; s. Charles Thomas Sr. and Evelyn May (Reed) F.; m. Darcy Lipsius, May 3, 1990; children: Hillary Suzanne, Charles Robert, Elena Ruth. BA, U. Calif., Santa Barbara, 1971; MA, Johns Hopkins U., 1974, PhD, 1975. Acting asst. prof. geology UCLA, 1975-77; asst. prof. geology U. Iowa, Iowa City, 1978-83, assoc. prof., 1983—2001, prof., 2001—. Cons. Unocal/Molycorp, Brea, Calif., 1982-87. Contbr. articles to profl. jours. Fellow: Geol. Soc. Am., Mineral. Soc. Am. Office: U Iowa Dept Geology Dept Geology 123 S Capitol St Iowa City IA 52240-3806

FOSTER, DALE WARREN, political scientist, educator, management consultant, real estate broker, accountant; b. Bryan, Tex., Mar. 7, 1950; s. William Henry and Maysie Blanche (Hembree) F. BBA, Tex. A&M U., 1972, MA, 1979, Cert. in Profl. Teaching, 1987; BS, U. Houston, 1981, MEd, 1983; AAS, Houston C.C. Sys., 1982. Cert. in property mgmt. Dept. mgr. J.C. Penney Co., Bryan, 1973-74; shopper advt. mgr. Harte-Hanks Newspapers/Daily Eagle, Bryan, 1975-76; bus. mgr., contr. S.M. Hardee Enterprises, College Station, Tex., 1976-78; ops. mgr. Western Food Svcs., Inc., Pasadena, Tex., 1978-80; internal auditor Hermann Hosp., Houston, 1980-82; high sch. tchr. Cypress-Fairbanks Independent Sch. Dist., Houston, 1983-84; alternative sch. tchr. Alief Independent Sch. Dist., Houston, 1984-88; gov. prof. Houston C.C. System, 1980—, chmn. govt. dept. co-op program, 1992—; lead instr. Houston C.C. Sys., 1993—; supr. student tchr. U. Houston, 1989-90. Adj. instr. North Harris County Coll., Houston, 1983-96; fin. cons. Pro-Trac Econ. Planning Adv. Bd., Denver, 1985-86; Presdl. Scholars lectr. Minority Students Honors Program, Houston, 1986-89; coord. legis. practicum Harris County Congl. Internship Program, 1988—; exch. tchr., The Netherlands, 1992. Co-editor textbook supplement, curriculum guide, departmental political reader; author classroom instructional project. Mem. adv. com. Hermann Affiliated Fed. Credit Union, Houston, 1980-82; mem. fin. coun. Harris County Dem. Com., 1991-93; mem. dean's coun. U. Houston, 1992-96; trustee, treas. Wilmington-Barnard Found., 1992—. Named Tchr. of Yr., Cy.-Fair H.S., 1984, Alief Individualized Study Ctr., 1987, Master Tchr. Nat. Leadership Inst. U. Tex., Austin, 1991, host tchr. Washington Week Intern Program, 1995; recipient Adj. Teaching and Comty. Svc. award North Harris County Coll. Dist., 1990, Teaching Excellence medal Nat. Inst. Staff and Orgn. Devel., 1991, 98; Fulbright scholar, 1992, 98; Robert A. Taft fellow L.B.J. Sch. Pub. Affairs, 1995, Fulbright-Hays fellowship U.S. Dept. Edn., 1998. Fellow Am. Bd. Master Educators; mem. Tex. Jr. Coll. Tchrs. Assn., Tex. Coun. Social Studies, Inst. Mgmt. Accts.,, Am. Fin. Assn., Fulbright Assn., Houston C.C. Sys. Faculty Assn. (treas. 1997-2000, v.p. 2000-01, pres.-elect 2001-02, pres. 2002-03, Outstanding Tchr. award 1991, Tchr. of Yr. 1997), Phi Theta Kappa, Alpha Phi Omega, Kappa Delta Pi. Democrat. Baptist. Avocations: travel, reading, bowling, water sports, outdoor activities. Office: Houston C C NW 1010 W Sam Houston Pkwy N Houston TX 77043 E-mail: corps1972@yahoo.com.

FOSTER, DEBORAH SIMMONS, educator; b. Memphis, Nov. 1957; d. William Thomas Simmons and Maxie Lee (Broadway) Carter; m. Larry Allan Foster, June 5, 1983 (dec.); children: Ashley Nicole, Kelly Elizabeth, David William. BS in Elem. Edn., Spl. Edn., Memphis State U., 1980. Nat. Bd. cert. tchr., 2001. Tchr. Ednl. Svcs., Memphis, 1979-83; tchr. spl. edn. Southaven (Miss.) Jr. High/High Sch., 1981-83; tchr. spl. edn. learning disabled and regular edn. Whitesburg Mid. Sch., Huntsville (Ala.) City Schs., 1985—87, elem. tchr., 1987—. Mem., exec. bd., faculty rep. PTA, 1989—. Mem. NEA, Coun. for Exceptional Children, Nat. Assn. Acad. Suprs. and Prins., Ala. Edn. Assn., Huntsville Edn. Assn. Avocations: drawing, reading. Home: 1014 Riviera Ave SE Huntsville AL 35802-2647

FOSTER, DELORES JACKSON, retired elementary school principal; b. Halltown, W. Va., Jan. 24, 1938; d. Daniel David and Mary (Taylor) Jackson; m. Robert L. Bailey, Aug. 24, 1957 (div. 1968); 1 child, Mark D.; m. James Hadlei Foster, Sept. 25, 1982; stepchildren: James H. Jr., Arthur. BA, Shepherd Coll., 1960; MA, Jersey City State, 1973. Tchr. Dickinson H.S., Jersey City, 1961-73, guidance counselor, 1973-82, vice prin., 1982-84, prin., 1985-86; vice prin. Snyder H.S., Jersey City, 1987-91, prin., 1991, Pub. Sch. # 34, 1991-2000; exec. coach Prin. Ctr. for Garden State, 2001—. Cons. cmtys. in schs.; cons. Jersey City State Career Ctr., 1975; mem. prin.-tchr. team Johns Hopkins U. Ctr. for Talented Youth Optimal Match Inst., 1994. Co-author: Integrating School with the World of Work, 1975; featured in documentary Quicksand and Banana Peels, Geraldine R. Dodge Found., 1998. Vol. Jersey City Med. Ctr., 1991—. Geraldine R. Dodge Found. grantee, 1993; recipient Grant to attend Harvard Summer Inst. for Prins. to Jersey City Sch. Dist., 1993, Grant to attend Inst. for Optimal Match Instrn. and Instl. Design at Franklin & Marshall Coll., 1994. Mem. ASCD, NAACP, N.J. Prins. and Suprs. Assn. (mem. sensitivity com.), Jersey City Prins. and Suprs. Assn., Coll. Women Inc. (pres., v.p., parliamentarian), No. Jersey Alumnae, Delta Sigma Theta, Prin.'s Ctr. for Garden State (mem. adv. bd.). Democrat. Mem. A.M.E. Ch. Avocations: sewing, music, dancing, collecting antiques, travel. Home: 97 Pagoda Ln Freehold NJ 07728-4163 E-mail: deloresdeefoster@aol.com.

FOSTER, DIANE MARIE, elementary school counselor; b. St. Louis, June 17, 1946; d. Perry and Florence (Eubanks) F. AA, Meramec Jr. Coll., Kirkwood, Mo., 1966; BA, Webster Coll., 1968; MEd, U. Mo., 1975. Cert. classroom tchr., math specialist, counselor, psychol. examiner, sch. psychologist. Classroom tchr. Valley Park (Mo.) Sch. Dist., 1968-80, elem. sch. counselor, 1980—96. Chpt. I grant writer Valley Park (Mo.) Sch. Dist., 1980—, spl. edn. entitlement writer, 1982-85; tax preparer. Sunday sch. tchr. Manchester (Mo.) Heights Ch., 1977-78, Kirkwood (Mo.) Bapt. Ch., 1981-86. Mem. ACA, Am. Sch. Counseling Assn. Avocations: painting, dog obedience, breeding golden retrievers, writing. Home: 411 S Ballas Rd Kirkwood MO 63122-5303

FOSTER, DOROTHY JEAN PECK, language educator; b. Guatemala, Dec. 5, 1934; came to U.S., 1948; d. H. Dudley and Dorothy Gertrude (Miller) Peck; m. Stanley O. Foster, June 23, 1956; children: Williams, Andrew, Paul, Rebecca. BA, Coll. Wooster, 1956; MA in Edn., U. Rochester, 1959; MAT, Sch. Internat. Tng., 1990. Tchr. Spanish Brighton Schs., Rochester, N.Y., 1956-60; tchr. ESOL Sunbeams Sch., Dhaka, Bangladesh, 1975-76; tchr. fgn. lang. Dekalb County Schs., Atlanta, 1977-79, tchr. ESOL, 1979-99. Adj. prof. ESOL Endorsement Courses; vol. English and Spanish tchr., tutor; cons Cornerstones Counseling Ctr.; for spkrs. of other langs. Session mem. Cristo Para Todas las Naciones, 1996-99; outreach chair, session mem. Cacoochee Presbyn. Ch., 2001-03. Mem. Internat. TESOL (mem. awards com. 1992-95, co-chair refugee concerns intrest sect. 2001-02), Ga. TESOL (bd. dirs. 1983, pres. 1996-97). Democrat. Avocations: swimming, sewing. E-mail: dfoster@hemc.net.

FOSTER, DUDLEY EDWARDS, JR., musician, educator; b. Orange, N.J., Oct. 5, 1935; s. Dudley Edwards and Margaret (DePoy) F. Student Occidental Coll., 1953-56; AB, UCLA, 1957, MA, 1958; postgrad. U. So. Calif., 1961-73. Lectr. music Immaculate Heart Coll., L.A., 1960-63; dir. music Holy Faith Episcopal Ch., Inglewood, Calif., 1964-67; lectr. music Calif. State U., L.A., 1968-71; assoc. prof. music L.A. Mission Coll., 1975-83, prof., 1983—, also chmn. dept. music, 1977—; mem. dist. acad. senate L.A. Community Colls., 1991-92; mem. acad. senate L.A. Mission Coll., 1993-97; dir. music 1st Luth. Ch., L.A., 1968-72. Organist, pianist, harpsichordist; numerous recitals; composer O Sacrum Convivium for Trumpet and Organ, 1973, Passacaglia for Brass Instruments, 1969, Introduction, Arioso & Fugue for Cello and Piano, 1974. Fellow Trinity Coll. Music, London, 1960. Recipient Associated Students Faculty award, 1988. Mem. Am. Guild Organists, Am. Musicol. Soc., Nat. Assn. of Scholars, Acad. Senate, Town Hall Calif., L.A. Coll. Tchrs. Assn. (pres. Mission Coll. chpt. 1976-77, v.p., exec. com. 1982-84), Mediaeval Acad. Am. Republican. Anglican. Office: LA Mission Coll Dept Music 13356 Eldridge Ave Sylmar CA 91342-3200 E-mail: fostermusic@eartlink.net., defoster@lamc.org.

FOSTER, EDWARD JOHN, engineer physicist; b. N.Y.C., Aug. 10, 1938; s. John Paul and Mildred Julia (Hassiak) F.; m. Sandra Thornton Christie (div. 1989); children: Sandra Foster Swindler, Mary Elizabeth Foster. BS in Physics cum laude, Fordham U., 1959; MS in Physics, Syracuse (N.Y.) U., 1965; MBA, Iona U., 1973. Mgr. magnetics dept. Shephard Industries, Inc., Nutley, N.J., 1960-61; founder, CEO S.E.D. Memories, Inc., Rutherford, N.J., 1961-63; br. mgr. rsch. CBS Labs., Stamford, Conn., 1963-73; v.p. tech. ByWord Corp., Armonk, N.Y., 1973-76; pres. Diversified Sci. Labs., Marco Island, Fla., 1976—. Cons. Electronics Industries Assn., Washington; dep. tech. advisor to U.S Nat. Com. Internat. Electrotech. Com. TC100, Geneva, Switzerland, 1982—. Author: Effects and Degrees of Error of Modulation-Demodulation, 1965; contbg. editor: Acquisition Reduction and Analysis of Acoustical Data, 1974; contbr. articles to profl. jours. Woodrow Wilson fellow, 1959, fellowship NSF, 1959-60. Fellow Audio Engring. Soc. (v.p. ea. U.S./Can.); mem. IEEE, Sigma Xi, Delta Mu Delta. Achievements include patents for Automatic Recording Level Control, Directional Microphone Arrays. Home and Office: 1952 San Marco Rd Marco Island FL 34145-6723 E-mail: DivSciLab@worldnet.att.net.

FOSTER, LUCILLE CASTER, school system administrator, retired; b. Vallejo, Calif., Sept. 28, 1921; d. Lewis Caster and Mabel Estelle (Witt) Beidleman; m. Donald Foster, Nov. 21, 1942 (deceased). AB in History, U. Calif., Berkeley, 1943; MA in Elem. Edn., San Francisco State U., 1953; EdD, Stanford U., 1959. Cert. sch. adminstr., Calif. Elem. tchr. Alameda (Calif.) Unified Sch. Dist., 1948-55; curriculum cons. Laguna Salada Elem. Sch. Dist., Pacifica, Calif., 1955-60, asst. supt., 1960-81; ret., 1981. Fir br. Children's Med. Ctr. No. Calif. Co-author (handbooks) Selling Ventures, 2000, Grant Writing 4th edit., 2002, Fundraising, 2d edit., 2002, Resource Development, 2002; contbr. articles to Calif. Jour. Elem. Edn., 1957, 61. Mem. AAUW (Santa Rosa br.), Can. Fedn. Univ. Women (hon. life), Internat. Fedn. U. Women, Calif. Sch. Adminstrs. Assn. (life), Calif. Tchrs. Assn. (life), Calif. Sch. Personnel Commrs. Assn. (life), Nat. Assistance League, Assistance League Sonoma County (hon. life), Pi Lambda Theta, Delta Zeta. Avocations: community volunteer, bridge, travel. Home: 245 Mockingbird Cir Santa Rosa CA 95409-6245 Fax: 707-538-2584.

FOSTER, MARCIA VERONICA, gifted and talented education educator; b. Kingston, Jamaica; d. Vivian Hollingsworth and Olivene Idona (Smith) Foster. BS, Columbia U., 1961, MA, 1963, profl. diploma, 1967. Cert. tchr. Tchr. reading summer schs. Bd. Edn., N.Y.C.; tchr. Ministry of Edn., Kingston, 1948-58; tchr. English Jr. High Sch. 45 Manhattan, N.Y.C., 1964-91, retired, 1991. Vol. tchr. english. and reading North East Bronx Orgn., New York, 1991—. Tchr. of the Year award Dist. #4, N.Y.C., 1979. Mem. AAUW, ASCD, Knickerbocker Internat. Bus. and Profl. Women's Soc. Inc., Nat. Coun. Tchrs. of English. Home: 1870 Andrews Ave Bronx NY 10453-5202

FOSTER, MARGARET ANN, elementary school educator; b. Washington, Dec. 3, 1957; d. Edward Hugh and Mary Joanne (Garrity) Jones; children: Elise Marie, Eric Louis. B in Music Edn., U. Lowell, 1979. Elem. sch. music educator, choir dir., band dir. Town of Easthampton (Mass.), 1985-90; elem. sch. music educator City of Springfield, 1993—. Mem. curriculum frameworks com. Mass. Dept. Edn., Malden, 1994—; darts tchr. Tanglewood-Boston Symphony, Lenox, Mass., 1993—; mem. Springfield Symphony Orchestra Edn. Com., 1995—. Vol. Easthampton (Mass.) Pub. Schs., 1993—. Mem. ASCD, Music Educators Nat. Conf. Avocations: dance skating, skiing. Office: Glickman Elem Sch 120 Ashland Ave Springfield MA 01119-2704

FOSTER, MARTHA TYAHLA, educational administrator; b. Coaldale, Pa., Apr. 22, 1955; d. Stephen and Frances (Solomon) Tyahla; m. David Marion Foster, Jan. 3, 1981. BA with distinction, U. Va., 1977, MEd, EdS, U. Va., 1981. Legis. asst. U.S. Ho. of Reps., Washington, 1977-79; asst. dean summer session U. Va., Charlottesville, 1981; program cons. campus activities U. Houston, 1981; coord. student affairs Capitol Inst. Tech., Kensington, Md., 1982-83, asst. dean students Laurel, Md., 1983-84, assoc. dean students, 1984-86, dean students, 1986-87. Bd. dirs. Curry Sch. Edn. Found. U. Va., 1987-90. Mem. Arlington County Commn. on Status of Women, 1985-88; chmn. Christian edn. Christ Meth. Ch., 1994-97; dir. Resurrection Luth. Presch., 1997—; coun. mem.-at-large Arlington United Way, 1995-98; pres. PTA Arlington Traditional Sch., 1997-98, treas., 1994-96. Named Woman of Yr., Bus. and Profl. Women's Club, Vienna, Va., 1986. Mem. Order Eastern Star (worthy matron 1988-89, trustee 1993-96). Methodist.

FOSTER, MARY JEAN SMITH, elementary educator, reading specialist; b. Alexandria, La., Dec. 2, 1944; d. Harry Wallace and Mary K. (Goodie) Smith; m. Stephen Carroll Foster, May 25, 1968; children: Amanda, Benjamin. BS in Edn., U. So. Maine, 1967; MEd, U. N.H., 1970. Cert. elem. tchr., reading specialist, Mass. Elem. tchr. West Sch., Portland, Maine, 1967-68, Veazie (Maine) Elem. Sch., 1968-69, Henniker (N.H.) Elem. Sch., 1970-73; cons. N.H. Dept. Edn., Concord, 1973-78; elem. tchr. Emerson Sch., Bolton, Mass., 1980—; master tchr. grades K-4 Sawyer Sch., Bolton, 2002—. Author: A Model for the Use of Computers in the First Grade, 1987, A Concrete Approach to the Teaching of Mathematics in Grade One, 1988. Pres. Bedford (N.H.) Jr. Women's Club, 1977-78; lector St. Teresa's Cath. Ch., Harvard, Mass., 1990-94. Experienced tchr. fellow U. N.H., 1969; Horace Mann grantee, 1982, 87. Mem. NEA, Mass. Tchrs. Assn., Bolton Tchrs. Assn. (pres. 1988-89). Avocations: tennis, swimming, reading. Home: PO Box 298 Harvard MA 01451-0298 Office: Florence Sawyer Sch Mechanic St Bolton MA 01740

FOSTER, MERRILL WHITE, geology and marine biology educator; b. South Gate, Calif., Mar. 18, 1939; s. Samuel Merrill and Ruth Duval (Johnson) F.; m. Patricia Leigh Blodgett, Sept. 1963 (div. Aug. 1971); children: Warren Duval, Alden Lowell; m. Wilma Marie Rinsch, Aug. 1, 1976 (div. Sept. 1984); 1 child, Jonathan David; m. Glenda Sugiura Hoppe, Oct. 1989. AA, Pasadena City Coll., 1959; BA, U. Calif., Berkeley, 1961, MA, 1964; PhD, Harvard U., 1970. Grad. research asst. U. Calif., Berkeley, 1962, teaching asst., 1962-64; teaching fellow Harvard U., Cambridge, Mass., 1964-66; asst. investigator Harvard U., NSF, Cambridge, 1966-69; instr., asst. prof., assoc. prof. dept. geol. scis. Bradley U., Peoria, Ill., 1969-78, prof. chmn. dept. geol. scis., 1978—. Lead tchr. NSF Field Sci., Peoria, 1979, 80, 81; scientist in residence East Peoria Sch. Dist., 1990; cons. in research. Author: Antarctic and Subantarctic Brachiopods, 1974; cons. editor Rocks and Minerals, 1988—; contbr. articles to sci. jours. and books. Chmn. Peoria City/County Landfill Com., 1990-92, Peoria County Solid Waste Adv. Com.; mem. Ill. River Bluffs Ecosys. Partnership and Local Partnership Coun., 1996—. Recipient Putnam award for Tchg. Excellence Bradley U., 1984, Rothberg award for Profl. Excellence, 1985, Disting. Svc. medallion Sun Found., 1993. Mem. AAAS, Peoria Acad. Sci. Internat. Paleontol. Assn., Paleontol. Soc., Soc. Econs. Paleontol. and Minerals, Mid-Am. Paleontol. Soc., Paleontol. Rsch. Inst., Sigma Xi (past pres. local group), Phi Beta Kappa. Avocations: history, nature study, photography, numismatics, hiking. Home: 1119 N Maplewood Ave Peoria IL 61606-1037 Office: Dept Geol Sci Bradley U Peoria IL 61625-0001 E-mail: fossil@bradley.edu.

FOSTER, MICHELE, educator; b. May 5, 1947; BA, U. Mass., Boston, 1968; PhD, Harvard U., 1987. Asst. prof. U. Pa., Phila., 1987-91; assoc. prof. U. Calif., Davis, 1991-94; prof. Claremont (Calif.) Graduate U., 1994—. E-mail: mlynnf94525@yahoo.com.

FOSTER, PAMELA LYNN, elementary education educator; b. Front Royal, Va., Mar. 3, 1963; d. Frederick Philip and Betty Maxine (Blakely) F. BA in Early Childhood Edn., Sacred Heart Coll., 1985; MS in Edn., Shenandoah U., 1994. 2d grade tchr. Saint Gabriel's Parochial Sch., Charlotte, N.C., 1986-87; kindergarten tchr. Warren County Pub. Schs., Front Royal, 1987—. Faculty rep. tchr. liaison com. Ressie Jeffries Elem. Sch., Front Royal, 1993-95, coach Odyssey of the Mind, Front Royal, 1991-95, faculty rep. ednl. fair com., 1990-94. Mem. NEA, Va. Edn. Assn., Warren County Edn. Assn. (rep. 1991-93, sec. 1994, v.p. 1995), Beta Sigma Phi. Presbyterian. Avocations: softball, reading, theater. Home: 227 Polk Ave Front Royal VA 22630-4329 Office: Ressie Jeffries Elem Sch 320 E Criser Rd Front Royal VA 22630-2244

FOSTER, REBECCA ANNE HODGES, secondary school educator; b. Waurika, Okla., Mar. 29, 1941; d. Robert Lee and Ouida (Gregory) Hodges; m. Jim Foster, Sept. 27, 1963; children: Krista Michelle, Lisa Rene. BS, Abilene Christian U., 1963; MEd, Middle Tenn. State U., 1989; student, SW Mo. State U., North Tex. State U. Cert. vocat. home econs., English, libr.

Tchr. English and home econs. Dallas Christian Sch., 1963-70; tchr. vocat. home econs. Garland (Tex.) High Sch., 1971-73; tchr. English, home econs. Alternative Edn. Ctr., Corpus Christi, Tex., 1974-77; tchr. English, Mid. Tenn. Christian Sch., Murfreesboro, 1984-90; tchr. English, Coyle Mid. Sch., Garland Ind. Sch. Dist., 1990-92, libr. Meml. Prep. Sch., 1992—. Mem. ASCD, NEA, Tex. State Tchrs. Assn., Garland Edn. Assn., Tex. Libr. Assn., Phi Kappa Phi. Home: PO Box 460009 Garland TX 75046-0009 Office: 2825 S 1st St Garland TX 75041-3429

FOSTER, WILLIAM ANTHONY, management consultant, educator; b. Washington, Nov. 26, 1929; s. Willard Hill and Evelyn Marie (Serrin) F.; m. Donna Roy Hayden, Feb. 5, 1955 (div. July 1985); children: Serrin M., Donna L., Shickel, Laura A. Valentine; m. Frances Christian Meacham, Dec. 6, 1995. BS in Bus. and Pub. Adminstrn., U. Md., 1956; MSPA, Nova Southeastern U., 1975, DPA, 1977. Registered profl. engr., Calif. Dir. indsl. engring. Washington region U.S. Postal Svc., 1969-71, mgr. indsl. engring. and plant maintenance Ea. Region, 1971-72, mgr. indsl. engring., 1972-80, nat. coord., 1980-83, program mgr. tng., 1983-86; pres., educator, trainer, cons. William A. Foster Assoc., Washington, 1986—. Educator, trainer, cons. U.S. Postal Svc., Washington, 1983-86, Embry-Riddle U., Daytona Beach, Fla., 1993, U. D.C., Washington, 1977-83, Southeastern U., 1980; dir., mgr. ops. U.S. Postal Svc., Washington, 1962-83. Author exec. tng. books; moderator TV show (Inaugural award 1991). Charter mem. Charleston Assn., Springfield, Va., 1968-84. Mem. ASTD (com. mem. 1986—), Am. Inst. Indsl. Engrs. (govt. liaison 1976-80, Nat. award for excellence 1969), Am. Soc Pub. Adminstrn. (cons. 1980-84), D.C. Coun. Engring. and Archtl. Socs. (chmn., PBS chair 1979-81, Outstanding Svc. award 1981, Bicentennial Engring. and Archtl. award 1976). Republican. Roman Catholic. Avocations: public speaking, american history, family, travel. Home: 1441 Northgate Sq Apt 12B Reston VA 20190-3754

FOSTER, WINFRED ASHLEY, JR., aerospace engineering educator; b. Greensboro, N.C., Jan. 30, 1945; s. Winfred Ashley and Pauline Crouse Foster; m. Doris Thelma Murphree, Aug. 28, 1966; children: Kimberly Ann, Elizabeth Carol. B of Aerospace Engring., Auburn U., 1967, MS of Aerospace Engring., 1969, PhD of Aerospace Engring., 1974. Registered profl. engr., Fla., Ala. Student trainee NASA George C. Marshall Space Flight Ctr., Huntsville, Ala., 1963, NASA/ASEE faculty rsch. fellow, summer 1977; grad. rsch. and teaching asst. dept. aerospace engring. Auburn (Ala.) U., 1967-69, instr. dept. aerospace engring., 1969-70, grad. teaching and rsch. asst. dept. aerospace engring., 1970-74, asst. prof. dept. aerospace engring., 1974-78, 79-83, assoc. prof. dept. aerospace engring., 1983-96; prof. dept. aerospace engring., 1996—; sr. design engr. Pratt & Whitney Aircraft Co., West Palm Beach, Fla., 1978-79. Presenter in field. Patentee aerial seeder and method; contbr. articles to profl. jours. Recipient Award for aircraft row-seeder Indsl. Rsch. Mag., 1973. Mem. AIAA, Sigma Xi, Sigma Gamma Tau, Phi Kappa Phi. Republican. United Methodist. Avocations: tennis, golf. Home: 903 Cherokee Rd Auburn AL 36830-2724 Office: Auburn U Dept Aerospace Engring 211 Aerospace Engring Bldg Auburn AL 36849

FOTI, MARGARET MAI, education consultant; b. Hoboken, N.J., Mar. 6, 1938; d. Angelo Julius and Margaret (Egan) Mai; m. Henry Carl Koenig, June 25, 1960 (div. May 1981); children: Mai Anne, Jo Ellen; m. Anthony Philip Foti, Aug. 1987. EdB, Jersey City State U., 1959; Ms in Edn., Psychology, Rutger su., 1973; cert. learning cons., Kean Coll., 1986. Tchr. Ridgefield (N.J.) Bd. Edn., 1960-61; tchr. sci., math. and reading St Bartholomews Sch., Scotch Plains, N.J., 1971-77; tchr. program math. underachievers South Plainfield (N.J.) Bd. Edn., 1977-78; tchr. handicapped Plainfield (N.J.) Bd. Edn., 1981-86; learning cons. Union County Vocat. Tech. Sch., Scotch Plains, N.J., 1986-89, Flemington (N.J.) Raritan Sch. Dist., 1989—. Developer, implementer vocat. edn. program for pregnant teens and unmarried mothers; ednl. therapist Summit Learning Ctr.; developer, trainer of spl. edn. pers. as part of staff devel. Vol. Spl. Olympics, Plainfield, 1987. Mem. Orgn. Learning Cons. Roman Catholic. Avocations: swimming, walking, classical music, reading. Home: 270 Pompano Dr Beach Haven NJ 08008-6152 Office: Flemington Raritan Spl Svcs 50 Court St Flemington NJ 08822-1325

FOUBERG, GLENNA M. career planning administrator; b. Ashley, N.D., Sept. 1, 1942; m. Rod Fouberg; children: Robert, Dan. Student, N.D. State U., 1960—61; BS in Secondary Edn., No. State U., 1963, psychol. examiner's endorsement, 1980, Doctorate (hon.), 2002; MEd in Guidance and Counseling, S.D. State U., 1968; postgrad., 1971—. English tchr., drama dir., Sisseton, SD, 1963—64; English tchr., 1965—67, Eielson AFB, Fairbanks, Alaska, 1964—65; English tchr., guidance counselor Bristol, SD, 1967—69, Webster, SD, 1968—71; tchr. Holgate Jr. H.S., Aberdeen, SD, 1973—90; coord., tchr. Alt. Learning Ctr. Cntl. H.S., SD, 1990—2002; chief examiner GED testing Aberdeen Career Planning Ctr., 2002—. Mem. S.D. State Bd. Edn., 1998—, pres., 2002—; mem. editl. com. Ctr. Applied Rsch.; mem. nominating com. Nat. State Tchrs. Yr.; adj. prof. English No. State U.; presenter in field. Co-chair Aberdeen Arts Festival; bd. mem., membership drive chmn., pres. Cmty. Concert Assn.; mem. health adv. com. Northeastern Mental Health Ctr. and Brown County; block worker Am. Cancer Soc., Heart Fund, March of Dimes, Easter Seals; active Alexander Mitchell Libr. Found. Bd.; co-chair Rails Club United Way; bd. dirs., office coord. Abderdeen Swim Club; fund raising com. Act II Cmty. Theater, S.D. Humanities Fund; co-chair Jr. Achievement, 2001—03. Recipient Sertoma Svc. to Mankind award, F.O.E. Eagles Edn. award, Golden Deed award, Exch. Club, George award, Aberdeen Area C. of C., award, Optimist Club, Spl. Contbns. award, S.D. Assn. Guidance Counselors, 2001, Outstanding Grad. award, S.D. State U. Guidance and Human Resources Dept., 2002. Mem.: NEA, State Profl. Practices Commn. (charter), Local Reading Coun., N.E. S.D. Reading Coun., Aberdeen Edn. Assn. (mem. comm. com.), S.D. Edn. Assn., Nat. Coun. Tchrs. English, Kappa Delta Pi, Phi Delta Kappa (v.p. membership, pres.), Delta Kappa Gamma (mem. rsch. com.). Office: Aberdeen Career Planning Ctr 420 S Roosevelt Aberdeen SD 57402-4730 also: 203 Third Ave SE Aberdeen SD 57401*

FOUCART VINCENTI, VALERIE, retired art educator; m. Stephen C. Vincenti; 1 child, Kayla. BS in Art Edn., Mansfield (Pa.) State U., 1975; MFA in Weaving, Marywood U., Scranton, Pa., 1993. Art tchr. Lycoming Valley Mid. and Roosevelt Mid. Schs., Williamsport, Pa., 1975—2003. Tchr. gifted arts program Pa. State U., Wilkes-Barre, Lehman Campus, 1990; presenter Pa. Art Edn. Assn. Art Conf., 2002. Editor The Lion newsletter St. Mark's Luth. Ch., Williamsport, 1985-88; editor, layout and design Roosevelt Roundup, 1997-2003. Playground arts instr. Williamsport Recreation Commn., summers 1980's; vol. ARC, Williamsport, 1980's; mem. ELCA Luth. Ch. Women; mem. planning com. PAEA State Conf. for 2002; sch. art exhbn. coord. Lycoming County Fair, 2000-03. Recipient 3rd pl. award painting and photography Bald Eagle Art League and Williamsport Recreation Commn., 1975-76, Nat. Program Stds. award Nat. Art Edn. Assn., 1994. Mem.: Williamsport Edn. Assn. (faculty rep.), Pa. State Edn. Assn., Pa. Art Edn. Assn. (com. state conf. 2000—02), Nat. Art Edn. Assn., Lycoming County Hist. Soc., Williamsport-Lycoming Arts Coun., Coalition Ind. Artists and Artisans, Handweavers Guild Am., Bald Eagle Art League, Susquehanna Valley Spinners and Weavers Guild, Ea. Star, Kappa Pi (Zeta Omicron chpt.). Democrat. Lutheran. Avocations: weaving, racquetball, travel, collecting art. Home: 801 Clearview Ave Pittsburgh PA 15205-3203

FOUCHT, JOAN LUCILLE, retired elementary school educator, retired counseling administrator; b. Glenford, Ohio, Feb. 26, 1931; d. Byron Ralph and Elsie Pauline (Tavenner) Foucht. BS in Elem. Edn., Ohio State U., 1953, MA in Guidance, 1967. Elem. sch. tchr. Southwood Elem. Sch., Columbus, Ohio, 1953—55, Suffern (N.Y.) Pub. Sch., 1955—56, N.E. Elem. Sch., Upper Montclair, NJ, 1956—60, Hubbard Elem. Sch., Columbus, 1960—67, Medary Elem. Sch., Columbus, 1986—93; counselor Medina Jr. H.S., Columbus, 1967—70; elem. sch. counselor various schs., Columbus, 1970—86; ret., 1993; sub. tchr., 1996—. Elected delegate Ohio Edn. Assn. and Nat. Edn. Assn. Conv., 1966—77; treas. Columbus Assn. of Classroom tchr., 1964—66, pres. elect, 1966—67, pres., 1967—69; human rels. chairperson, coorndinated tchr. edn. study with Ohio State Univ., Sch. desegregation. Columbus Edn. Assn., 1973—77. Contbr. articles Career Education Interest Groups Ohio Sch. Coun., 1968. Counselor, advisor 4H Club, Columbus, 1971—73; pres. Women's Assn. Columbus Symphony Orch., 1991—92, Women's Assn. Symphony Columbus Orch., 2000—01; program chairperson bus. and prof. unit Women's Assn. Columbus Symphony Orch., 1990—2000, 2002—03; choir mem. Overbrook Presbyn. Ch., Columbus, 1945—. Recipient Rsena B. Willis Award, Nat. Edn. Assn. Convention, 1975, Coun. Award of the Yr. for Creative Multicultral Programs, Ohio Sch., 1982. Mem.: AAUW (choral group 1988—2002, membership treas. 1996—2001, co chairperson 2002—04), Clintonville Women's Club (chairperson bridge groups 1988—2001), Alpha Delta Kappa (chpt. pres. 1986—88). Democrat. Presbyterian. Avocations: gardening, music, travel, theater, reading. Home: 225 Webster Pk Columbus OH 43214

FOUGHT, SHARON GAVIN, nursing educator; b. Fort Dodge, Iowa, May 25, 1949; d. George J. and Velma E. (Smith) Gavin; m. Jeffrey R. Fought, Sept. 7, 1974. BS in Nursing, U. Md., Washington, 1971; MSN, U. Tex., Austin, 1974, PhD, 1983. Staff RN Walter Reed Army Hosp., Washington, 1971-73; head nurse ICU 121 Evac. Hosp., Seoul, Korea, 1973-74; clin. nurse specialist Brackenridge Hosp., Austin, 1976-78; clin. instr. U. Tex., Austin, 1978-79; asst. prof. U. Tex. Health Sci. Ctr., San Antonio, 1981-86; asst. prof. dept. physiol. nursing U. Wash., Seattle, 1986-92, assoc. prof., dir. nursing program Tacoma, 1992-98, assoc. dean, 1996—2001, assoc. vice chancellor acad. affairs, 2001—. Contbr. articles to profl. jours. Lt. US Army Nurse Corps, 1971-74. WRAIN scholar, 1967-71; recipient Nursing Rsch. award Micromedex/ENA Best Original, 1989, 90, ENA Rsch. award, 1990; Nat. Inst. Drug Abuse/Nat. Inst. Alcohol Abuse & Alcoholism faculty fellowship, 1989-92. Mem. ANA, AACN, Emergency Nurses Assn. (chair 1984-86, Nat. Com. Rsch. 1986-90, mem. spl. com. on trauma nat. faculty), Nat. League Nursing, Soc. Critical Care Medicine, Sigma Theta Tau. Home: 4613 144th Pl SE Bellevue WA 98006-3159 Office: U Wash Tacoma Office of Chancellor Campus Box 358430 1900 Commerce St Tacoma WA 98402-3112

FOUNTAIN, ANDRE FERCHAUD, academic program director; b. Oklahoma City, Nov. 12, 1951; s. J. E. and Neaumatta Abilene (Edwards) F.; m. Linda K. Young. BS in Nursing, U. Okla., 1978. RN, Okla; cert. master hyrdotherapist, Kniepp Inst., Germany, massage therapist. Exec. dir. New Life Programs, Oklahoma City, 1981-87; dir. Praxis Coll. Health, Arts and Scis., Oklahoma City, 1988—. Speaker in field. Author: A Psychoprophylactic Workbook, 1981; co-author: Psychological Reports, 1977. Found. Caucus for Men in Nursing, Norman, 1976. Recipient 1st Pl. award Internat. Sci. Fair Balt., 1970; honored for Oklahoma City bombing vol. work, U.S. Dept. Justice. Mem. Internat. Childbirth Edn. Assn. (state coord. 1982-84), Am. Soc. Psychoprophylaxis in Obstetrics, Body Workers and Wellness Therapies Assn., Okla. Sports Massage Assn., Masons.

FOUNTAIN, CORNELIA WILKES, special education educator; b. Towns, Ga., Apr. 30, 1942; d. Kermit Lee and Marion Wilhemenia (Clark) Strickland; m. John H. Fountain, Dec. 15, 1974; children: Reginald K. Wilkes, Myrian R. Wilkes. AA, Fla. Jr. Coll., 1973; BA in Edn., U. Fla., 1975. Tchr. asst. career opportunity program Duval County Sch. Bd., Jacksonville, Fla., 1968-75, tchr. exceptional edn., chair dept. exceptional student edn., 1975—. Dir. classroom scouting Northwestern Mid. Sch., Jacksonville, 1988—; tchr. rep. Child Study Team, Jacksonville, 1991—; beginning tchr. observer, Jacksonville, 1990—. Recipient Varsity award Boy Scouts Am., 1993. Mem. Coun. Exceptional Children, U. Fla. Nat. Alumni Assn., Life Study Fellowship Assn., Women's Missionary Soc. (Keynote Speaker award 1990), Emancipation Proclamation Assn. Methodist. Avocations: reading, speech writing and public speaking, Scrabble, church work.

FOUNTAIN, LINDA, secondary education educator; b. LaPorte, Ind., Dec. 2, 1950; d. Richard Raymond and Myrtle Irene (Sigle) Hartwick; m. Donald Henry Nebelung, Dec. 23, 1972 (div. June 1991); children: Michele Lynette, Trent Howard; m. Franklin C. Fountain, Jan. 20, 1996. BS, Purdue U., 1972; MA, U. Ariz., 1996. Cert. secondary tchr., Ariz. Tchr. math. Williamsport (Ind.) Jr. High Sch., 1973-74, Jefferson County Schs., Louisville, Ky., 1974-75; substitute tchr. Crawford County Schs., Bucyrus, Ohio, 1975-77; tchr. math. Emily Gray Jr. High Sch., Tucson, Ariz., 1989—, basketball coach, 1991-94. Pvt. math. tutor, Tucson, 1985—92. Mem. choir Tanque Verde Luth. Ch., Tucson, 1980—96, chmn. presch. com., 1982-89, leader Sunday sch., 1984—95. GIFT fellow, 1993. Mem. Nat. Coun. Tchrs. Maths., Ariz. Assn. Tchrs. Maths. Lutheran. Avocations: tennis, golfing, hiking, tandem bicycling. Home: 6280 E Placita de Fuego Tucson AZ 85750-1285 Office: Emily Gray Jr H S 11150 E Tanque Verde Rd Tucson AZ 85749-8524

FOUQUET, ANNE (JUDY FUQUA), musician, music educator; b. Wurtland, Ky., Oct. 2, 1938; d. John Paul and Garnet May (Gibson) Hillman; m. Warren Russell Fuqua, Dec. 21, 1961 (div. Dec., 1992); children: Bryan David, Faith Fuqua-Purvis, Paul Carroll. BMus., Am. Conservatory, Chgo., 1962; MMus., No. Ill. U., 1967; MFA, U. Iowa, 1971, D in Musical Arts, 1997. Organist various churches and denominations, Ill., 1960—; profl. accompanist Wis., Ill., 1970—; piano instr. Beloit (Wis.) Coll., 1972—; instr. Rockford (Ill.) Coll. Acad., 1991—; ind. instr. Keyboard Studio, Rockford, Ill., 1971—; clarinet player Rockford (Ill.) Park Band, 1995—. Composer: (song cycle soprano) Spinner of the Seasons, 1987, (suite for flute and hapsichord) Issar Suite, 1992; author: (play) Miracle of Love, 1982; (novel) If It Hadn't Been for Joel, 1980; (memoirs) Daddy Was a Farmer, Mother Was a City Girl, 1999; concert artist duo-piano with Robin Wooten, 1999, 2001; solo harpsichord recitals, 2001, 02. Mentor Helping One Student To Succeed, Structured Reading, Kishwaukee Sch., Rockford, Ill., 1997-98, adult lit. tutor READ Chatanooga, 1999—; interim organist, choirmaster Trinity Luth. Ch., 2000, Northminster Presbyn. Ch., Chattanooga, summer 2001; organist St Thaddeus Episcopal Ch., 2003—; Suzuki piano instr. Tenn. Valley area, 1998--; active concert artist, harpsichord, and piano. Nominee Best Classical Pianist Rockford Area Music Industry, 1996. Mem. Am. Guild of Organists, Music Tchrs. Nat. Assn., Ill. Music Tchrs. Assn. (adjudicator 1994-97), Kishwaukee Valley Concert Band, Szuki Assn. of the Americas, Midwest Hist. Keyboard Soc., Mendelsson Club (founder composer showcase concerts Rockford 1991-97, bd. dirs. 1993-97), Am. Fedn. of Musicians, Tenn. Music Tchrs. Assn. (adjudicator 1999-2000), Sierra Club. Avocations: hiking, langs. (German, French, Hebrew), cooking, gardening, astronomy. Office: Cadek Conservatory Music U Tenn Chattanooga 724 Oak St Chattanooga TN 37403-2406

FOURNIER, MAUREEN MARY, physical education educator; b. Chgo., Feb. 27, 1952; d. George Joseph and Lauretta Marie (Tangney) Lewis; m. Thomas Joseph Fournier, Sept. 21, 1979; children: Jennifer Lynn, Michele Marie. BS in Edn., No. Ill. U., 1973; MS in Edn., Chgo. State U., 1983. Recreation leader Alsip (Ill.) Pk. Dist., Alsip, 1973-75; tchr. phys. edn. Sch. Dist. 126, Alsip, 1974—. Pres. Alsip Coun. Local 943 IFT, 1976—80, 1985—87, 1992—97, chair tchrs. negotiation team, 1993, 96, chmn. phys. edn. curriculum com., 1992—94, mem. curriculum steering com., 1992—97, chmn. fine arts curriculum com., mem. sch. improvement plan com. Mgr. Oak Lawn (Ill.) Girls Softball, 1990—91, 1994—98, sec., 1998, Richard Area Swim Club, 1997—98; mem. internal rev. com. Sch. Dist. 126, Alsip, 1999—2003; NCA com. mem., sec. Richards HS Parent Boosters Club, 2000—. Mem.: AAHPERD, Ill. Assn. Health, Phys. Edn., Recreation and Dance (evaluator Blue Ribbon com.). Avocations: bowling, swimming, reading. Office: Sch Dist 126 Lane Sch 4600 W 123rd St Alsip IL 60803-2522

FOUSE, ANNA BETH, education educator; b. Austin, Tex., Jan. 11, 1947; d. Wilfred Davis and Doris Faye (Thomas) Chrisner; m. William Douglas Fouse; children: Douglas Lee, Alan Dale, Michael Wade, Robert Lynn. BS, U. Tex., Austin, 1967; MEd, Tex. Woman's U., 1973, PhD, 1976; various postgrad., Tex., 1980-81, 85-89. Cert. elem. tchr., spl. edn. tchr., Tex. 1st grade tchr. Austin Ind. Sch. Dist., 1967-68, Pasadena Ind. Sch. Dist., 1968-69; 3rd grade tchr. Harlingen (Tex.) Ind. Sch. Dist., 1969-70; homebound tchr. Irving (Tex.) Ind. Sch. Dist., 1970-71, tchr. emotionally disturbed, 1971-73; spl. edn. dir. Paris (Tex.) Ind. Sch. Dist., 1975-85, Region VII ESC, Kilgore, Tex., 1985-91; instr. U. Tex., Tyler, 1990-91, asst. prof., 1991-96, assoc. prof., 1996-98; ednl. cons., autism specialist, 1995—; pres. Ark-La-Tex Shredding Co., Inc., 2000—. Consulting editor bd. Acad. Therapy Jour., Austin, 1988-89. Author: Creating a Win-Win/EP for Students with Autism, 1996, 2nd edit., 1999; co-author: (tech. asst. manual) Assessment Manual for Appraisal Personnel, 1987, Guidelines for Speech Pathologists, 1987, Accreditation for Special Educators, 1988, A Primer About Attention Deficit Disorder, 1993, A Treasure Chest of Behavioral Strategies for Individuals with Autism, 1997. Chair Paris Regional Habilitation Ctr. Adv. Bd., 1980-85, High Priority Infant Transitional Svcs. Adv. Bd., Longview, Tex., 1989-90; chair mental retardation/DD adv. bd. Sabine Valley Ctr., 1997-99, mem. human rights and behavior mgmt. com., 2002-03; profl. adv. bd. so. region Attention Deficit Disorders Assn., 1990—; mem. adv. bd. Lamar County Alcohol and Drug Ctr., Paris, 1984-86; mem. citizens planning and adv. com. Tex. Dept. Mental Health and Mental Retardation, 1999-2003, vice chmn., 2003-03; bd. dirs., treas. Real Jobs for Youth, Inc., 2003. Mem. Autism Soc. of Ams., Tex. Coun. for Exceptional Children (v.p., pres., pres.-elect, bd. dirs.), Tex. Coun. of Adminstrs. in Spl. Edn., Assn. for Children with Learning Disabilities, Tex. Ednl. Diagnosticians Assn., Internat. Coun. for Exceptional Children, Phi Delta Kappa (pres. chpt. 1324 1991-93). Avocations: ceramics, crocheting, reading. Home and Office: 517 E Fairmont St Longview TX 75601-3804 E-mail: bfouse@worldnet.att.net.

FOUST, KAREN, art educator; b. Kokomo, Ind., June 10, 1956; d. Max Henry and ELizabeth Irene (Black) Comer; m. Jeffrey Scott Foust, Aug. 5, 1978; children: Adam Michael, Justin Thomas. BS in art edn., Ind. State U., 1978, MS in secondary edn., 1981; gifted edn., Purdue U., 1990. Art tchr. Kokomo Cen. Schs., 1978—. Curriculum writing Kokomo Cen. Schs., 1987, 21st century planning com., 1994. Sec. Friendship Home, Kokomo, 1993-94. Recipient fine arts grant State of Ind., 1993. Mem. Delta Kappa Gamma, Sigma Eta (pres. 1986, v.p. 1985, sec. 1984, treas. 1983). Methodist. Avocations: reading, swimming, painting, ceramics. Home: 926 S Co Rd 600 W Kokomo IN 46901 Office: Kokomo HS 2501 S Berkley Kokomo IN 46901 E-mail: kfoust@kokomo.k12.us.

FOUTCH, GARY LYNN, chemical engineering educator, entrepreneur; b. Poplar Bluff, Mo., Aug. 26, 1954; s. Cecil Foutch and Edith Frances Gardner Wood; m. Pamela Lynn Smith, May 28, 1977; children: Aaron Lloyd, Brendan Lee, Keely Anne. BS, U. Mo., Rolla, 1975, MS, 1977, PhD, 1980. Asst. prof. chem. engring. Okla. State U., Stillwater, 1980-85, assoc. prof., 1985-89, prof. chem. engring., 1989—, Kerr-Mcgee chmn., regents prof., 1999—. NASA-ASEE fellow Jet Propulsion Lab., Pasadena, Calif., summers 1981, 82; engr. Dow Chem. Co., Freeport, Tex., summer 1983; vis. scientist Smith Kline and French, Phila., summer 1985, Phillips Petroleum, Bartlesville, Okla., summer 1987, 92; chair faculty coun. Okla. State U., 1992-94; founder, pres. Focus Software, 1996—; lectr. in field. Contbr. articles to profl. jours. Witness Okla. State Senate Subcom., Oklahoma City, 1985. Halliburton Young faculty, Coll. Engring., Arch. & Tech., 1985, 90; named Outstanding Young Engr. Okla. Soc. Profl. Engrs., 1987; Fulbright scholar Loughborough U. of Tech., Eng., 1990-91; DOD summer faculty fellow, U.S. Navy, Anapolis, 1995. Mem. NSPE, AIChE, Am. Chem. Soc., Soc. Chem. Industry Eng. Achievements include 1 patent. Office: Okla State Univ Chemical Engring Dept Chemical Engring # 423en Stillwater OK 74078-0001

FOWLER, ARDEN STEPHANIE, music educator; b. N.Y.C., May 24, 1930; d. Arthur Simon and Lenore Irene (Strouse) Bender; m. Milton Fowler, Aug. 6, 1951; children: Stacey Alison, Crispin Laird. Student, Traphagen Sch., 1947-49; BA, Marymount Coll., Tarrytown, N.Y., 1976; MusM, U. So. Fla., 1978. Designer Rubeson's Sportswear, N.Y.C., 1949-51; free-lance designer Dobb's Ferry, N.Y., 1952-72; organist/choir dir. Children's Village, Dobb's Ferry, N.Y., 1972-74; music specialist Highland Nursery Sch., Chappaqua, N.Y., 1972-76; pvt. voice tchr., vocal coach, 1972—; music therapist Cedar Manor Nursing Home, Ossining, N.Y., 1974-76; founder, pres. Gloria Musicae Chamber Chorus, Sarasota, Fla., 1979-85, mng. dir., 1979—89. Soloist various chs. and choruses, N.Y., Fla., 1953-97; mem. faculty vocal music dept. St. Boniface Conservatory, Sarasota, 1979-81; music critic Sarasota Herald Tribune, 1986-91; lectr. music history Edn. Ctr., Longboat Key, Fla., 1991-2001; vol. music for early childhood Head Start, 1991-2001. Freelance travel writer, 1985—. Mem. Dem. Exec. Com of Manatee County, Fla. Mem. Chorus Am., Assn. Profl. Vocal Ensembles, Friends of the Arts (hon.), Sigma Alpha Iota, Phi Kappa Phi. Episcopal. Avocations: sailing, sewing, artwork, fgn. travel. Home: 4244 Marina Ct Cortez FL 34215-2518

FOWLER, CHARLES WILLIAM, school administrator; b. White Plains, N.Y., Oct. 21, 1938; s. Arthur Sherwood and Mary Hall (Buckhout) F.; m. Yolanda Elinor Iversen, July 19, 1963; children: Geoffrey, Pamela, Craig. BS, SUNY, 1960, MS, 1961; EdD, Columbia U., 1969. Rsch. asst. Capital Area Sch. Devel. Assn., Albany, N.Y., 1960-61; tchrs. Fox Lane H.S., Mt. Kisco, N.Y., 1961; asst. supt. schs. Bedford (N.Y.) Sch. Dist., 1962-70; supt. DeKalb (Ill.) Sch. Dist., 1970-76, Fairfield (Conn.) Sch. Dist., 1976-85, Sarasota County (Fla.), 1985-95; dist. supt. Nassau County, N.Y., 1995-98; supt. Hewlett-Woodmere Sch. Dist., 1998—. Contbr. articles to profl. jours. Mem. Am. Assn. Sch. Adminstrs. (officer), Conn. Assn. Sch. Adminstrs., So. Fairfield County Supts. Assn. (chmn.), Suburban Sch. Supts. U.S.A. (pres.). Presbyterian. Home: 223 Main St East Hampton NY 11937-2723 Office: Hewlett-Woodmere Pub Schs One Johnson Place Woodmere NY 11598

FOWLER, DAVID WAYNE, architectural engineering educator; b. Sabinal, Tex., Apr. 25, 1937; s. Otis Lindley and Sadie Gertrude (Cox) F.; m. Maxine Yvonne Thomson, Mar. 31, 1961; children: Teresa, Leah. BS in Archtl. Engring., U. Tex., 1960; MS, U. Tex., Austin, 1962; PhD in Civil Engring., U. Colo., 1965. Design engr. W.C. Cotten (Cons. Engr.), Austin, Tex., 1961-62; asst. prof. archtl. engring. U. Tex., Austin, 1964-69, assoc. prof., 1969-75, prof., 1975—, Taylor prof., 1981—, dir. Ctr. Aggregates Rsch., 1992—, Joe J. King chair, 1998—. Vis. prof. Nihon U., Japan, 1981, Chulalongkorn U., Thailand, 2001; bd. dirs. Univ. Fed. Credit Union, 1976-84; pres. Internat. Congress on Polymers in Concrete, 1981-87, bd. dirs. Univ. Coop, 2000—. Editor procs. 2d Internat. Congress on Polymers in Concrete, 1978, 2001; contbr. articles to profl. jours. Recipient Teaching award Gen. Dynamics, 1975, Teaching award Amoco Found., 1978, Disting. Engring. Alumnus award U. Colo., 1993, Owen Nutt award ICPIC, 1995, Joe J. King Profl. Achievement award, 2000, Claude Hocott Rsch. award, 2002; named to Acad/ Disting. Tchrs., 2000; cited by Engring.-News Record, 1975, Concrete Repair, 1995; Ford Found. faculty devel. grantee, 1962-64. Fellow ASCE (pres. Austin br. 1976-77), Am. Concrete Inst. (Delmar L. Bloem award 1985, bd. dirs. 1993-96, Robert Philleo award 2003); mem. NAE, Concrete Rsch. Coun. (chmn. 1996-2002), Concrete Rsch. Found. (chmn. 2000-2001), Am. Soc. Engring. Edn. (chmn. archtl. engring. divsn. 1971-72), Tex. Soc. Profl. Engrs. (bd. dirs. Travis chpt.

1968), Russian Acad. Engring. (hon.), Tau Beta Pi, Chi Epsilon. Mem. Ch. of Christ. Home: 612 Brookhaven Trl Austin TX 78746-5455 Office: Univ Tex ECJ 5208 Archtl Engring Group Austin TX 78712 Personal E-mail: dwfowlerpe@austin.rr.com. Business E-Mail: dwf@mail.utexas.edu.

FOWLER, KATRINA JOAN, special education educator; b. Concord, N.H., Feb. 6, 1958; d. Richard Tripp and Joan (Crosbie) F. BS in Edn., R.I. Coll., 1980; MA in Edn., U. N.H., 1992. Cert. elem., spl. edn. tchr., N.H. Spl. edn. tchr. Spaulding Youth Ctr., Tilton, N.H., 1980-82, Berlin (N.H.) Mid. Sch., 1982—. Coord. Theater Works, Berlin, 1989—; mem. area mgmt. com. Spl. Olympics, Berlin; trustee Gorham United Ch. of Christ. Named Young Career Woman Bus. and Profl. Women, Berlin, 1990. Mem. Internat. Reading Assn., New Eng. Reading Assn., Coun. for Exceptional Children, North Country Assn. for Spl. Needs Children, Theatre North (v.p. 1988-89), Berlin Jazz Band. Avocations: theater, reading, travel, music, arts and crafts. Home: 386 High St Berlin NH 03570-1810 Office: Berlin Mid Sch 200 State St Berlin NH 03570-1897

FOWLER, LINDA MCKEEVER, hospital administrator, management educator; b. Greensburg, Pa., Aug. 7, 1948; d. Clay and Florence Elizabeth (Smith) McKeever; m. Timothy L. Fowler, Sept. 13, 1969 (div. July 1985). Nursing diploma, Presbyn. U. Hosp., Pitts., 1969; BSN, U. Pitts., 1976, M in Nursing Adminstrn., 1980; D in Pub. Adminstrn., Nova U., 1985. Supr., head nurse Presbyn. Univ. Hosp., Pitts., 1969-76; mem. faculty Western Pa. Hosp. Sch. Nursing, Pitts., 1976-79; acute care coord. Mercy Hosp., Miami, 1980-81; asst. adminstr. nursing North Shore Med. Ctr., Miami, 1981-84, v.p. patient care, 1984-88, Golden Glades Regional Med. Ctr., Miami, 1988-89, Humana Hosp.-South Broward, Hollywood, Fla., 1989-91, assoc. exec. dir. nursing; v.p., chief nursing officer Columbia Regional Med. Ctr., Bayonet Point, 1991-96; COO, chief nursing officer Greenbrier Valley Med. Ctr., 1996-97; quality mgmt. coord. Greenbrier Valley Hospice, 1997-98; pvt. practice healthcare cons., 1998-99; chief nursing officer Marlboro Park Hosp., 1999—2002; pvt. practice healthcare cons., 2002—; chief clin. officer Intermedical Hosp. of S.C., 2003—. Mem. adj. faculty Barry U., Miami, 1984-97, Broward C.C., Ft. Lauderdale, 1984-85, Nova U., 1986-87; cons. Strategic Health Devel. Inc., Miami Shores, Fla., 1986-90, So. Coll., Cleveland, Tenn., 1995-96. Dept. HEW trainee, 1976, 79-80; bd. dirs. Pasco County Am. Cancer Soc., 1992-95. Mem. Am. Orgn. Nurse Execs. (legis. com. 1988-90), Fla. Orgn. Nurse Execs. (bd. dirs. 1986-88), S.C. Orgn. Nurse Execs., South Fla. Nurse Adminstrs. Assn. (sec. 1983-84, bd. dirs. 1984-86), U. Pitts. Alumni Assn., Presbyn. U. Alumni Assn., Portuguese Water Dog Club Am. (bd. dirs. 1988-89), Ft. Lauderdale Dog Club (bd. dirs. 1981-82, 83-85, v.p. 1982-83), Am. Kennel Club (dog judge), Moore County Kennel Club, Sigma Theta Tau. Lutheran. Office: Taylor at Marion Sts Columbia SC 29220

FOWLER, MARTI, fine arts consultant; b. St. Louis, Mar. 25, 1952; d. Chester Felix and Emily (Kohout) Czarcinski; m. Robert Lee Fowler, Mar. 26, 1988. BA, So. Ill. U., 1973, MA, 1981. Cert. tchr. English, speech and theatre, Mo. Tchr. asst. Hazelwood Sch. Dist., St. Louis, 1974-76; instr. Jefferson Coll., 1991-92, St. Louis C.C. at Meramec, St. Louis, 1990-98; tchr. Hazelwood East H.S., St. Louis, 1976-97; dept. chair fine arts Hazelwood East H.S. and Kirby Jr. H.S., 1997-99; cons. fine arts Hazelwood Sch. Dist., 1999—2003; owner, prodr. Interactive Ednl. Video LLC, 2003—. Co-playwright/lyricist: (musical theatre) Difficult Choices, 1988; dir. and choreographer numerous prodns., 1973—; co-producer: Practical Technical Theatre-Interactive Educational DVD Series, 2003-. Recipient Adminstr. of Yr. award, Mo. Thespians Ednl. Theatre Assn., 2001—02. Mem. Am. Alliance for Theatre in Edn. (Mo. state chmn. 1993-97, Dina Reese Evans award 1998), Theatre Edn. Assn. (Mo. State chmn. 1993-97, coord. Mo. State Thespian Conf. 1996, 99, Dina Rees Evans award for theatre in our schs. advocacy), Mo. State Thespian Bd. Dirs., Speech Theatre Assn. of Mo., Internat. Thespian Soc., Zeta Phi Eta (pres. 1972-73). Avocations: attending theatre, reading. Home: 15685 Silver Lake Ct Chesterfield MO 63017-5128 E-mail: marti@interactiveeducationalvideo.com.

FOWLER, WALLACE T. engineering educator; BA in Math., U. Tex., 1960, MS in Engring. Mechanics, 1961, PhD, 1965. Prof. Dept. Aerospace Engring. U. Tex., Austin, Tex., 1965—. Disting. vis. prof. astronautics & computer sci. U.S. Air Force Acad., 1981-82; chair advanced design program faculty group U. Tex., Austin, 1991-92; ad hoc aerospace engring. program Accreditation Bur. Engring. & Tech.; presenter in field. Recipient Fred Merryfield Design award, 1994. Mem.: Am. Soc. Engring. Edn. (pres. 2000—01). Office: U Tex Dept Aerospace Engring Austin TX 78712-1085*

FOWLER, WALTON BERRY, franchise developer, educator; b. Tulsa, Dec. 4, 1946; s. Walton Rector Fowler and Martha Jean (Berry) Oliver; m. Deborah Martz, Oct. 1, 1972 (div. Feb. 1985); 1 child, Cullen Brian; m. Anne Sadler, Sept. 23, 1985; children: Nicole Anne, William Dean, Catherine Elizabeth. BA, Chapman Coll., 1972; teaching cert., Calif. State U., Fullerton, 1973. Mgr. Al Mayton Prodns., Universal City, Calif., 1968-72; dept. chmn., tchr. Anaheim (Calif.) High Sch. Dist., 1973-78; founder, chmn. Sylvan Learning Corp., Montgomery, Ala., 1979-88; v.p., treas. Vincent, Hanna, Fowler Investments, Bellevue, Wash., 1987-92; chmn. The Little Gym Internat. Inc., Kirkland, Wash., 1992-94; founder, pres. Krypton Inst., Spokane, Wash., 1995-97; pres. W. Berry Fowler & Assocs., 1997—. Dept. chmn., tchr. Anaheim (Calif.) High Sch. Dist., 1968-72; bd. dirs. The Wilcox Group, Mercer Island; lectr. Nat. Honor Soc. Mem. Com. for Tchr. Tng. Chapman Coll., Orange, Calif., 1973, planning com. Boy Scouts Am., Mercer Island; founder, chmn. A Thousand Points of Knowledge Learning Ctrs. Mem. NEA, Internat. Franchise Assn., Venture Founders Assn. Republican. Avocations: boating, traveling, reading, art. Office: A Thousand Points of Knowledge Inc 3016 S Grand Blvd Fl 3 Spokane WA 99203

FOX, EDWARD A. business executive; b. N.Y.C., July 17, 1936; s. Herman and Ruth F.; divorced; children: Brian, Laura, Jacqueline. AB, Cornell U., 1958; MBA, NYU, 1975. Pres., CEO, Student Loan Mktg. Assn., Washington, 1973-90; dean Amos Tuck Sch. Dartmouth Coll., Hanover, N.H., 1990-94; chmn. SLM Corp., Reston, Va., 1997—. Bd. dirs. Delphi Fin. Group, Inc., Greenwich Capital Holdings, Inc. Trustee U. Maine sys.; vice chmn. bd. dirs. Am. Ballet Theater. Office: SLM Corp 11600 Sallie Mae Dr Reston VA 20190-4796

FOX, ELEANOR MAE COHEN, lawyer, educator, writer; b. Trenton, N.J., Jan. 18, 1936; d. Herman and Elizabeth (Stein) Cohen; children: Douglas Anthony, Margot Alison, Randall Matthew. BA, Vassar Coll., 1956; LLB, NYU, 1961. Bar: N.Y. 1961, U.S. Dist. Ct. N.Y. 1964, U.S. Supreme Ct. 1965. Ptnr. Simpson Thacher & Bartlett, 1970—76, of counsel, 1976—; prof. Law Sch. NYU, N.Y.C., 1976—, Walter J. Derenberg prof. trade regulation, 1999—. Lectr. on antitrust and interntat. competition policy, globalization markets; mem. Pres. Carter's Nat. Commn. Rev. Antitrust Laws and Procedures, 1978-79; mem. adv. bd. Bur. Nat. Affairs Antitrust and Trade Regulation Reporter, 1977—; trustee NYU Law Ctr. Found., 1974-92; trustee Lawyers' Com. Civil Rights Under Law, 1988—; mem. Coun. Fgn. Rels., 1993—; mem. Pres. Clinton's internat. competition policy adv. com. to advise the U.S. Atty. Gen., 1997-2000. Author: (with Byron E. Fox) Corporate Acquisitions and Mergers, Vol. 1, 1968, Vol. 2, 1970, Vol. 3, 1973, Vol. 4, 1981, rev. edit., 2003; (novel) W.L., Esquire, 1977, (with Lawrence A. Sullivan) Antitrust—Cases and Materials, 1989, supplement, 1995, (with G. Bermann, R. Goebel, W. Davey) European Union Law, Cases and Materials, 2002, The Competition Law of the European Union--Cases and Materials, 2002; (with J. Fingleton, D. Neven, P. Seabright) Competition Policy and the Transformation of Central Europe, 1996; mem. bd. editors N.Y. Law Jour., 1976-99, Antitrust Bull., 1986—; mem. adv. bd. Rev. Indsl. Orgn., 1990-2001, EEC Merger Control Reporter, 1992—, Gaceta Juridica de la CE y de la Competencia, 1992-2001, World Competition: Law and Economics Review, 1999—, Inst. for Consumer Antitrust Studies, 2002--. Fellow Am. Bar Found., N.Y. Bar Found.; mem. ABA (chmn. merger com. antitrust sect. 1974-77, chmn. publs. com. 1977-78, chmn. Sherman Act com. 1978-79, mem. council antitrust sect. 1979-83, 90-94, vice chmn. antitrust sect. 1992-94, chair NAFTA Task Force, 1993-99), N.Y. State Bar Assn. (chmn. antitrust sect. 1978-79, mem. exec. com. antitrust sect. 1979-83), Fed. Bar Council (trustee 1974-76, v.p. 1976-78), Assn. of Bar of City of N.Y. (v.p. 1989-90, exec. com. 1977-81, chmn. trade regulation com. 1973-76, lawyer advt. com. 1976-77, chmn. com. on U.S. in a global economy, 1991-94), Am. Law Inst., Assn. Am. Law Schs. (chmn. sect. antitrust and econ. regulation 1981-83), NYU Law Alumni Assn. (bd. dirs. 1974-79, 87-91), Am. Fgn. Law Assn. (v.p. 1979-82, 98-2001).

FOX, FRANK G. school librarian, writer; b. Lake Charles, La., Oct. 16, 1956; s. Hubert Jackson Fox and Mary Margaret Hebert. BS in Fin., McNeese State U., 1980; MS in Econs., La. State U., 1982, MS in Libr. Sci., 1985. Cert. journeyman wireman. Br. libr. Westwego, Jefferson Parish Libr., Metairie, La., 1986—87; asst. dir. St. Charles Parish Libr., Luling, La., 1987—89; info. broker Frankenstein's Fax, Harvey, La., 1990—94; sch. libr. Plaquemines Parish Sch. Bd., Belle Chasse, La., 1994—98; regional libr. FDIC, Memphis, 1998—2000; evening reference libr. S.W. Tex. State U., San Marcos, 2000—. Author: (book) Funky Butt Blues, 1996, Bizarre New Orleans, 1997 (River Rd. award, 1998), 19 1/2 Revelations, 2002, Jean Lafitte and the Big Ol' Whale, 2003. Mem.: ALA, Internat. Brotherhood Elec. Workers, Assn. Ind. Info. Profls., Tex. Libr. Assn., Phi Kappa Phi. Democrat. Roman Catholic. Avocations: reading, writing, travel. Home: 109 Craddock Ave San Marcos TX 78666 Office: Tex State U Alkek Libr 601 University Dr San Marcos TX 78666 Office Fax: 512-245-3002. Personal E-mail: fgf01@yahoo.com. E-mail: ff10@txstate.edu.

FOX, JOAN MARIE, educator; b. Flint, Mich., July 8, 1948; d. Elmer William and Elizabeth (Fisher) Skolnik; m. Richard Charles Fox, Dec. 19, 1970; children: Elizabeth Grace, Julie Anne. BA in Edn., Mich. State U., 1970; postgrad., Ind. U., 1982-83; MEd, U. Md., 1988; postgrad., Loyola Coll., 1989—. Tchr. math. Dayton (Ohio) Pub. Schs., 1970-71; tchr. 5th grade Mt. Orab (Ohio) Elem., 1971-75; docent Indpls. Mus. of Art, 1979-81; substitute instrional aide Washington Twp. Schs., Indpls., 1981-83; ednl. cons. Mastery Edn. Corp., Watertown, Mass., 1983-85; tchr. Howard County Pub. Schs., Ellicott City, Md., 1985—. Bd. dirs. Mt. Hebron Nursery Sch., Ellicott City, 1984—; employee recognition com. Howard County Pub. Schs., 1988—. Mem. Md Com. for Children, Balt., 1983—, Smithsonian, Washington, 1983—, ARC, Balt. Mem. NEA, Nat. Coun. Tchrs. of Math., Phi Delta Kappa (sec. 1985-86, v.p. 1986-87, pres. 1987-88). Democrat. Episcopalian. Avocations: reading, travel, visiting museums. Home: 9990 Old Annapolis Rd Ellicott City MD 21042-5602 Office: Howard County Pub Schs 4200 Centennial Ln Ellicott City MD 21042-6270

FOX, JOHN BAYLEY, JR., university dean; b. Cambridge, Mass., Nov. 6, 1936; s. John Bayley and Eunice (Jameson) F.; m. Julia Garrett, July 22, 1967; children— Sarah Cleveland, Thomas Bayley AB, Harvard U., 1959; BA, Oxford U., Eng., 1961, MA, 1962. Assoc. div. internat. fellowships Commonwealth Fund of N.Y., N.Y.C., 1963-67; dir. Office Career Services Harvard U., Cambridge, 1967-71, spl. asst., asst. dean of faculty, 1971-76, dean Harvard Coll., 1976-85, adminstrv. dean Grad. Sch. Arts and Scis., 1985-94; sec. faculty arts and scis., sec. faculty coun., 1992—. Unitarian. Home: 125 Prince St West Newton MA 02465-2603 Office: Harvard U Faculty Arts and Scis University Hall 1 Cambridge MA 02138-5722 E-mail: John_Fox@harvard.edu.

FOX, MARGARET LOUISE, retired secondary education educator; b. Newport News, Va., Nov. 27, 1919; d. Preson Curtis and Lydia Enos (Diggs) Watson; m. Jesse Emerson Todd, Sr., Apr. 5, 1947 (dec. 1992); children: Frances Diggs, Jesse Emerson Jr.; m. Russell E. Fox, Aug. 3, 1996. AB, Coll. William and Mary, 1943; MA, Hampton U., 1978. Elem. tchr. Newport News (Va.) Sch. System, 1943-45; newspaper reporter Times-Herald, 1945-46; tchr. English George Wythe Jr. High, 1946-47, Bethel High Sch., Hampton, 1970-82, ret., 1982. Speaker in field and tchr. workshops. Author: (with others) Hampton From the Sea to the Stars, 1985; author: (biograph) C. Alton Lindsay: Educator and Community Leader, 1994; contbr. articles to profl. jours. Cert. lay spkr. United Meth. Ch., Peninsula, 1970s-95; judge Va Forensics Debate, 1970s-82; debate coach Bethe H.S., Hampton, 1971-82; pres. Hampton PTA Coun., 1966-68. Mem. AAUW (life), Va. Ret. Tchrs. Assn. (trustee Va. conf. UM Hist. Soc.), Nat. Assn. Parliamentarians, Great Books Group, Planned Parenthood (pres. 1967-68), Hampton Hist. Found., Nat. Blackstone Coll. Alumnae Assn. (pres. 1995—). Avocations: reading, visiting historical sites, teaching, travel. Home: 3 Carrington Ct Hampton VA 23666-6030

FOX, MARK RICHARD, lawyer, educator, political consultant; b. Fulton, N.Y., Nov. 26, 1953; s. Herman and Marilyn (Miller) F.; m. Anita Gail Raby, June 15, 1992; children: Tyler Jacob, Meredith Eve, Gregory Aaron. BA, U. Vt., 1975; JD cum laude, Thomas M. Cooley Law Sch., Lansing, Mich., 1986. Bar: Mich. 1987, Fla. 1987, D.C. 1990, U.S. Dist. Ct. (ea. and we. dists.) Mich.1987, U.S. Dist. Ct. (mid. and so. dists.) Fla. 1990, U.S. Dist. Ct. Colo. 1997, U.S. Ct. Appeals (6th cir.) 1987, U.S. Ct. Appeals (8th cir.) 1992, U.S. Ct. Appeals (11th cir.) 1997, U.S. Supreme Ct. 1992. Polit. columnist Valley Voice, 1974-75; radio reporter WJOY-AM Radio, Burlington, Vt., 1974-75; rsch. aide U.S. Senator Patrick J. Leahy, Washington, 1975; newspaper reporter Rutland Daily Herald and Barre-Montpelier (Vt.) Times Argus, Burlington, 1975; polit. media cons. East Lansing, Mich., 1976-85; adj. prof. law Thomas M. Cooley Law Sch., Lansing, 1987—92; shareholder Fraser Trebilcock Davis & Foster, P.C., Lansing, 1987—. Mediator Gov. Jennifer Granholm, 2002, Sen. Debbie Soobenon, 2002; legal counsel Granholm-Cherry Inaugeral Com. Polit. cons. Congressman Howard Wolpe, Mich., 1994, U.S. Senator Carl Levin, 1990. Recipient Am. Jurisprudence awards Thomas M. Cooley Law Sch., 1984-85. Mem. State Bar of Mich. (antitrust coun. 1993-94). Democrat. Office: Fraser Trebilcock Davis & Dunlap 1000 Michigan Nat Tower Lansing MI 48933

FOX, MARY ANN WILLIAMS, librarian; b. Savannah, Ga., Jan. 16, 1939; d. Alton F. and Arthur (Colquitt) Williams; m. William Francis Fox, Dec. 26, 1960 (div. 1984); children: Katherine Frances, William Francis Jr. BA, U. Ga., 1960; MLS, Rutgers U., 1984. Libr. Metuchen (N.J.) Pub. Libr., 1983-85, Mable Smith Douglas Libr. Rutgers U., New Brunswick, N.J., 1984, Firestone Libr. Princeton (N.J.) U., 1985, The Hun Sch. of Princeton, 1985—. Bd. dirs. Ctrl. Jersey Regional Libr. Coop., 1997—, Region 5 Libr. Coop., N.J., 1985-92. Trustee East Brunswick (N.J.) Pub. Libr., 1979-92; bd. dirs. Ctrl. Jersey YWCA, New Brunswick, 1985-88, Ctrl. Atlantic Conf. United Ch. of Christ, 1985-88. Mem. ALA, N.J. Libr. Assn., N.J. Ind. Sch. Assn. (chair libr. sect. 1988—), Edn. Media Assn. N.J. (bd. dirs. 1987-92), Librs. of Middlesex (pres.). Democrat. Mem. United Ch. of Christ. Home: 10 Redcoat Dr East Brunswick NJ 08816-2759 Office: Hun Sch Princeton 176 Edgerstone Rd Princeton NJ 08540 E-mail: mafox@hun.k12.nj.us.

FOX, MAURICE SANFORD, molecular biologist, educator; b. N.Y.C., Oct. 11, 1924; s. Albert and Ray F.; m. Sally Cherniavsky, Apr. 1, 1955; children: Jonathan, Gregory, Michael. BS in Meteorology, U. Chgo., 1944, MS in Chemistry, PhD, U. Chgo., 1951; Docteur Honoris causa, Université Paul Sabatier, Toulouse, France, 1994. Instr. U. Chgo., 1951-53; asst. Rockefeller Inst., 1953-55, asst. prof., 1955-58, assoc. prof., 1958-62, MIT, Cambridge, 1962-66, prof., 1966-79, Lester Wolfe prof. molecular biology, 1979-96, head dept. biology, 1985-89. Mem. Radiation Effects Rsch. Found., Hiroshima, 1997—2000. Mem. Internat. Bioethics Com. UN Ednl., Sci. and Cultural Orgn., 1997-2003. Served with USAAF, 1943-46. USPHS fellow, 1952-53; Nuffield Research fellow, 1957; Fogarty scholar, 1991. Fellow AAAS; mem. NAS, Am. Acad. Arts and Scis., Inst. Medicine. Office: MIT Dept Biology 77 Massachusetts Ave Cambridge MA 02139-4307

FOX, MICHAEL DAVID, retired art educator; b. Dec. 29, 1937; s. Donald F. and Ethel (Allen) Sullivan; m. Carol Ann Hamptston, Nov. 5, 1967; 1 child, Kathryn Gabrielle. BS, SUNY, Buffalo, 1962, MS, 1969; cert. in sculpture, Bklyn. Mus. Sch., 1964. Tchr. art City Schs., Rochester, NY, 1962-63, 64-65; prof. art Morehead State U., Ky., 1965-67, SUNY, Oswego, 1967—2000; ret., 2000. Vis. artist univs. and art ctrs., United States, Canada; dir. Popular Image Gallery, Oswego, 1967—2003; spkr. in field; lectr. in field. Work featured on CBS-TV, 1976, 1978, 1980, also featured in N.Y. Times, Look, Evergreen Rev., Nat. Lampoon, Scanlon's Monthly, Cavalier, Sch. Arts, others, featured in texbooks Sculpture: Techniques, Form and Content, 1988, Represented in permanent collections, U.S., Can., Japan, Africa, Asia, Europe, S.Am.; reviewer textbooks. Recipient Outstanding Tchg. award, Morehead State U., 1967—2000, Chancellors award for excellence in tchg., State Univ. Coll., Oswego, NY, 1981, numerous awards for drawing, painting and sculpture, 1962—. Mem.: United Univ. Profs. (v.p., del). Home: 38 W End Ave Oswego NY 13126-1758

FOX, MICHAEL VASS, Hebrew educator; b. Detroit, Dec. 9, 1940; s. Leonard W. and Mildred (Vass) F.; m. Jane Schulzinger, Sept. 4, 1961; children: Joshua, Ariel BA, U. Mich., 1962, MA, 1963; PhD, Hebrew U., Jerusalem, 1972. Ordained rabbi, 1968. Lectr. Haifa U., Israel, 1971-74, Hebrew U., Jerusalem, 1975-77; prof. Hebrew U. Wis., Madison, 1977—, chmn. dept., 1982-88, 92-99, Weinstein-Bascom prof. in Jewish studies, 1990—, Halls-Bascom prof., 1999—. Author: The Song of Songs and the Ancient Egyptian Love Songs, 1985, Shirey Dodim Mimitzrayim Ha'atiqa, 1985, Qohelet and his Contradictions, 1988, The Redaction of the Books of Esther, 1991, Character and Ideology in the Book of Esther, 1991, 2001, A Time to Tear Down and a Time to Build Up: A Rereading of Ecclesiastes, 1999; editor: Anchor Bible: Proverbs, vol. I, 2000; contbr. articles to profl. jours. Named Vilas assoc., U. Wis., 1988—90; recipient Wahrburg prize, Hebrew U., 1971—72, Kellett Mid-Career award, U. Wis., 1999; fellow, Brit. Friends of Hebrew U., Liverpool, 1974—75, NEH, 1992; Leverhulme fellow, U. Liverpool, Eng., 1974—75, Am. Coun. Learned Socs. fellow, 2001, Am. Acad. for Jewish Rsch. fellow. Mem. Soc. for Bibl. Lit. (editor SBL Dissertation Series 1994-99, editl. bd. Jour. Bibl. Lit. 1991-95; pres. midwest region 1998-2000), Nat. Assn. Profs. Hebrew (editor Hebrew Studies 1985-93, v.p. 2000—). Home: 2815 Chamberlain Ave Madison WI 53705-3607 Office: U Wis Dept Hebrew 1220 Linden Dr Rm 1338 Madison WI 53706-1525

FOX, RAYMOND GRAHAM, educational technologist; b. Portland, Oreg., May 31, 1923; s. George Raymond and Georgia Dorothy (Beckman) F.; B.S., Rensselaer Poly. Inst., 1943; m. Harriet Carolyn Minchin, Apr. 17, 1948; children: Susan, Christine, Ellen, Laura, John. Salesman IBM Corp., N.Y.C., 1946-48, br. mgr., 1949-56, systems mgr., 1957-65, edn. systems devel. mgr., 1965-76; chmn. bd. Learning Tech. Inst., Warrenton, 1975— . Mem. Va. Council for Deaf, 1978-84; chmn., 1980-83; mem. Sec. of Navy Adv. Bd. on Edn. and Tng., 1972-77; cons. for tech. Va. Legis. Adv. Com. on Handicapped, 1970; mem. Nat. Def. Exec. Reserve, 1970-83; mem. emeritus, 1983— . Served with USNR, 1943-46. Mem. Soc. Applied Learning Tech. (pres. 1972—), Nat. Security Indsl. Assn. (chmn. tng. group 1974-76). Anglican. Clubs: Army & Navy (Washington); Fauquier (Warrenton, pres. 1993-94); Columbia Country (Chevy Chase, Md.); Moorings (Vero Beach, Fla.). Patentee interactive multimedia instruction delivery sys. Home: PO Box 376 Warrenton VA 20188-0376 Office: 50 Culpeper St Warrenton VA 20186-3207

FOX, RENÉE CLAIRE, sociology educator; b. N.Y.C., Feb. 15, 1928; d. Paul Fred and Henrietta (Gold) F. AB summa cum laude, Smith Coll., 1949, LHD, 1975; PhD, Harvard U., 1954; MA (hon.), U. Pa., 1971, U. Oxford, 1996; ScD (hon.), Med. Coll. Pa., 1974, St. Joseph's Coll., Phila., 1978; D (hon.), Katholieke U., Leuven, 1978; LHD (hon.), La Salle U., Phila., 1988; DSc (hon.), Hahnemann U., 1991, U. Nottingham, UK, 2002. Rsch. asst. Bur. Applied Social Rsch., Columbia U., 1953-55, rsch. assoc., 1955-58; lectr. dept. sociology Barnard Coll., 1955-58, asst. prof., 1958-64, assoc. prof., 1964-66; lectr. sociology Harvard U., 1967-69; rsch. fellow Center Internat. Affairs, 1967-68, research assoc. program tech. and soc., 1968-71; prof. sociology, psychiatry and medicine U. Pa., Phila., 1969-98, Annenberg prof. social scis., 1978-98, chmn. dept. sociology, 1972-78, Annenberg prof. social scis. emerita, 1998—. Rsch. assoc. Refugee Studies Centre, Queen Elizabeth House, U. Oxford, 1998—; sci. advisor Centre de Recherches Sociologiques, Kinshasa, Zaïre, 1963-67; vis. prof. sociology U. Officielle du Congo, Lubumbashi, 1965; vis. prof. Sir George Williams U., Montreal, Que., Can., summer 1968; Phi Beta Kappa vis. scholar, 1973-75; dir. humanities seminar med. practitioners NEH, 1975-76; maitre de cours U. Liège, Belgium, 1976-77; vis. prof. Katholieke U., Leuven, Belgium, 1976-77; Wm. Allen Neilson prof. Smith Coll., Mass., 1980; dir. d'Etudes Associè, Ecole des Hautes Etudes en Sciences Sociales, Paris, summer 1989; George Eastman vis. prof. Oxford U., 1996-97; vis. scholar Tokyo Med. and Dental U., 2001; mem. bd. clin. scholars program Robert Wood Johnson Found., 1974-80; mem. Pres.'s Commn. on Study of Ethical Problems in Medicine, Biomed. and Behavioral Rsch., 1979-81; dir. human qualities of medicine program James Picker Found., 1980-83; Fae Golden Kass lectr. Harvard U. Sch. Medicine and Radcliffe Coll., 1983, Kate Hurd Mead lectr. Med. Coll. Pa./Coll. Physicians Phila., 1990, Lori Ann Roscetti Meml. lectr. Rush-Presbyn.-St. Luke's Med. Ctr., Chgo., 1990; vis. scholar Women's Ctr., U. Mo., Kansas City, 1990, vis. scholar Case Western Reserve Sch. of Med., 1992; opening address 13th Internat. Conf. on Social Scis. and Medicine, Hungary, 1994, vis. prof. U. Calif., San Francisco Sch. of Med., 1994; lectr. founds. of medicine Faculty of Medicine McGill U., Montreal, Can., 1995; Supernumerary fellow Balliol Coll. Oxford U., 1996-97; WHR Rivers disting. lectr. Dept. of Social Medicine, Harvard Med. Sch., 1998; assembly series lectr. Washington U., St. Louis, 1998; William J. Rashkind Meml. lectr, Am. Heart Assn., 1998, Salinger-Forlang lectr. U. Tex. Health Scis. Ctr. at San Antonio, 1999, Frances H. Schlitz lectr. U. Kans., Wichita, 2002; affiliated faculty Solemon Asch. Ctr. for Study of Ethnopolitical Conflict, U. Pa., 2001—. sr. fellow, Ctr. Bioethics, U. of Pa., 1999-. Author: Experiment Perilous, 1959, (with Willy DeCraemer) The Emerging Physician, 1968, (with Judith P. Swazey) The Courage to Fall, 1974, rev. edit. 1978, 2002, Essays in Medical Sociology, 1979, 2d edit., 1988, L'Incertitude Medicale, 1988, The Sociology of Medicine: A Participant Observer's View, 1989, (with Judith P. Swazey) Spare Parts: Organ Replacement in American Society, 1992, In the Belgian Château: The Spirit and Culture of European Society in an Age of Change, 1994, French language edit., 1997, Organ Transplantation: Meanings and Realities (edited with Stuart Youngner and Laurence O'Connell), 1996, (in Japanese) Looking Intimately at Bioethics: Fifty Years as a Medical Sociologist, 2003; assoc. editor: Am. Sociol. Rev., 1963-66, Social Sci. and Medicine; mem. editl. com.: Ann. Rev. Sociology, 1975-79; assoc. editor Jour. Health and Social Behavior, 1985-87, Perspectives in Biology and Medicine, 1996—; mem. editl. adv. bd. Tech. in Soc., Sci., 1982-83; mem. editl. bd. Bibliography of Bioethics, 1979—, Culture, Medicine and Psychiatry, 1980-86, Jour. of AMA, 1981-94, Am. Scholar, 1994-99, Current Revs. in Publs., 1994—, Am. Jour. Bioethics, 1999—; vice chair adv. bd. Am. Jour. Ethics and Medicine; contbr. articles to profl. jours.; A Festschrift published in his honor: Society and Medicine: Essays in Honor of Renée Fox, 2003. Bd. dirs. Medicine in Pub. Interest, 1979-94; mem. tech. bd. Milbank Meml. Fund, 1979-85; mem. overseers com. to visit univ. health svcs. Harvard Coll., 1979-86; trustee Russell Sage Found., 1981-87; vice chmn. bd. dirs. Acadia Inst., 1990-97; mem. adv. com. Sch. Nursing LaSalle U., 1998—; mem. external bd. Ctr. for Bioethics, Columbia U., mem. advancement com. King Baudouin Found. U.S. Inc., 1998—, mem., sec. bd. dirs. Acadia Inst.,

2002—; mem. info. sci. adv. coun. Innovia Found., The Netherlands, 2002—; mem. external bd. Ctr. for Bioethics, Columbia U., 2002—; mem. Internat. and Sci. Adv. Coun., 2002—. Recipient E. Harris Harbison Gifted Teaching award Danforth Found., 1970, Radcliffe Grad. Soc. medal, 1977, Lindback Found. award for teaching U. Pa., 1989, Centennial medal Grad. Sch. Arts and Scis. Harvard U., 1993, Chevalier de l'Ordre de Leopold II (Belgium), 1995; Wilson Ctr., Smithsonian Instn. fellow, 1987-88, Guggenheim fellow, 1962, Sr. fellow Ctr. Bioethics U. Pa., 1999—; Fulbright Short-Term Sr. scholar to Australia, 1994; 1st W.H.R. Rivers Disting. lectr. Harvard Med. Sch., 1998. Fellow African Studies Assn., AAAS (dir. 1977-80, chmn. sect. K 1986-87), Am. Sociol. Assn. (council 1970-73, 79-81, v.p. 1980-81), Am. Acad. Arts and Scis. (co-chair Class III section I membership com., 1994-96), Inst. Medicine (Nat. Acad. Scis., council 1979-82), Inst. Soc., Ethics and Life Scis. (founder, gov.); mem. AAUP, AAUW, Assn. Am. Med. Colls., Social Sci. Research Council (v.p., dir.), Eastern Sociol. Soc. (pres. 1976-77, Merit award 1993), N.Y. Acad. Scis., Soc. Sci. Study Religion, Inst. Intercultural Studies, 1969-93, (asst. sec. 1969-78, sec. 1978-81, 89-92, v.p. 1987-89), Am. Bd. Med. Specialists, Coll. of Physicians of Phila. (coun. 1993-98), Phi Beta Kappa (senate 1982-87, Ralph Waldo Emerson book award com. 1998-2001). Home: The Wellington 135 S 19th St #1104 Philadelphia PA 19103-4912 E-mail: rcfox@ssc.upenn.edu.

FOX, ROBERT WILLIAM, mechanical engineering educator; b. Montreal, Que., Can., July 1, 1934; s. Kenneth and Jessie (Glass) F.; m. Beryl Williams, Dec. 15, 1962; children— David, Lisa. BS in Mech. Engring, Rensselaer Poly. Inst., 1955; MS, U. Colo., 1957; PhD, Stanford U., 1961. Instr. mech. engring. U. Colo., Boulder, 1955-57; research asst. Stanford (Calif.) U., 1957-60; mem. faculty Purdue U., Lafayette, Ind., 1960-99, assoc. prof., 1963-66, prof., 1966-99, asst. head mech. engring., 1971-72, asst. dean engring. for instrn., 1972-76; acting head Purdue U. (Sch. Mech. Engring.), 1975-76, asso. head, 1976-98, chmn. univ. senate, 1971-72, prof. emeritus, 1999. Cons. Owens-Corning Fiberglass Co., Edn. Services Inc., Nelson Mfg. Co., Peoria, Ill., B. Offen Co., Chgo., Agard Co., Johns-Marsville Co., Richmond, Ind., Babcox & Wilcox, Alliance, Ohio. Named Standard Oil Outstanding Tchr. Purdue U., 1967; recipient Harry L. Solberg Outstanding Tchr. award, 1978, 83, Donald E. Marlowe awd., Am. Soc. for Engineering Education, 1992. Fellow ASME, Am. Soc. for Engring. Edn.; mem. Sigma Xi, Pi Tau Sigma, Tau beta Pi, Delta Tau Delta. Home: 3627 Chancellor Way Lafayette IN 47906-8809 Office: Purdue U Sch Mech Engring Lafayette IN 47907

FOX, SUSAN FRANCES, mathematics educator, education educator; b. Gilmer, Tex., Aug. 12, 1948; d. Byron J. and Olga Patricia (Green) Smith; m. Al Fox, Nov. 20, 1970 (dec.); children: Michelle A., Amanda L. BS in Secondary Edn., Coll. of Artesia, 1971; MEd in Edn., Ea. N.Mex. U., 1985. Cert. instrnl. leader, secondary math. tchr., N.Mex. Math. tchr. Artesia (N.Mex.) Pub. Schs., 1971-75; asst. prof. math./edn. Coll. of S.W., Hobbs, N.Mex., 1989—. Adult mem. Girl Scouts, Hobbs, 1993-94. Mem. Delta Kappa Gamma (treas. 1994-96). Avocations: crafts, golf, bowling. Home: 905 W Lead Ave Hobbs NM 88240-2197 Office: Coll of Southwest 6610 N Lovington Hwy Hobbs NM 88240-9120

FOY, HERBERT MILES, III, lawyer, educator; b. Statesville, N.C., Mar. 22, 1945; s. Herbert Miles Jr. and Perci Aileen (Lazenby) F.; m. Eleanor Jane Meschan, June 27, 1970; children: Anna Meschan, Sarah Aileen. AB, U. N.C., 1967; MA, Harvard U., 1968; JD, U. Va., 1972. Bar: N.C. 1973, U.S. Dist. Ct. (mid. and we. dists.) N.C., 1973, U.S. Ct. Appeals (4th cir.), 1975, U.S. Supreme Ct., 2002. Jud. clk. U.S. Ct. Appeals (5th cir.), Atlanta, 1972-73; assoc. Smith, Moore, Smith, Schell & Hunter, Greensboro, N.C., 1973-77, 81-83, ptnr., 1983-84; sr. atty. advisor office legal counsel U.S. Dept. Justice, Washington, 1977-81; assoc. prof. Sch. Law Wake Forest U., Winston-Salem, N.C., 1984-87, prof., 1987—, assoc. dean acad. affairs, 1990-95, Law Sch., Wake Forest U., Winston-Salem, 2000—. Contbr. articles to legal jours. Morehead scholar, 1963; Woodrow Wilson fellow, 1968. Mem. ABA, N.C. Bar Assn., N.C. State Bar Assn., Fosythe County Bar Assn., Order of Coif, Phi Beta Kappa. Democrat. Methodist. Avocations: banjo playing, gardening, athletics, poetry. Home: 2328 Oak Ridge Rd Oak Ridge NC 27310-9701 Office: Wake Forest U Sch Law PO Box 7206U Winston Salem NC 27109-7206

FRAGALE, RICHARD P. academic administrator; BA, Muhlenberg Coll., 1958; MEd, Western Md. Coll., 1968; postgrad., U. South Calif. Supt. Cen. Union H.S. Dist., El Centro, Calif., 2000—, Trona (Calif.) Joint Unified Sch. Dist. Mem.: Small Sch. Dists. Assn. Calif. (treas. declining enrollment sch. dists. of Calif.), Am. Assn. Sch. Adminstrs. (pres. Imperial Valley chpt., region XVIII legis. com., Region XVIII Adminstr. of Yr. award 1992). Office: Cen Union H S Dist 351 Ross Ave El Centro CA 92243*

FRAKER, BARBARA J. elementary education educator, school system administrator, middle school education educator; b. Kansas City, Mo., Apr. 22, 1950; d. Theodore and Donna Ruth (Beitman) Van Alden; children: Tamara Amanda, Everett Nathaniel. BS, Taylor U., Upland, Ind., 1972; MA, U. Mo., Kansas City, 1978, EdS, 1983. Cert. elem. tchr., K-12 reading tchr., elem. adminstr., mid. sch. social studies, 9-12 social studies and early childhood tchr., spl. edn. tchr., Mo. Tchr. Scarritt Elem. Sch., Kansas City, Mo., 1972-73, Richardson Elem. Sch., Kansas City, 1973-76, Willard Elem. Sch., Kansas City, 1976-80, Linwood Elem. Sch., Kansas City, 1980-81; title I tchr. Kalihi Waena Elem. Sch., Honolulu, 1981-82; instrnl. asst. to prin., tchr. C.A. Franklin Elem. Sch. Kansas City Sch. Dist., 1983-86; tchr., reading resource Lincoln Middle Sch., 1986-92; tchr. social studies resource Kansas City Sch. Dist., 1992-93; curriculum coord. Lincoln Middle Math/Sci. Magnet Sch., Kansas City, 1993-95; social studies intervention provider Chester Anderson Alternative Sch., 1995—2002; spl. edn. tchr. Missouri City (Mo.) Sch., 2002—. Mem. ASCD (assoc.), Nat. Coun. Social Studies, Internat. Platform Assn., Internat. Reading Assn., Phi Delta Kappa (v.p. Zeta Delta chpt. membership 1991-92, pres. 1992-96, advisor 1996-98). Office: Chester Anderson Alt Sch 1600 Forest Kansas City MO 64106

FRAMPTON, LISA, elementary education educator; b. Greenville, S.C., July 8, 1957; d. Lewis John and Lenora (Donnelly) F. BS in Edn., U. Ga., 1979, MEd, 1980. Cert. tchr., S.C. Tchr. elem. phys. edn. Sara Collins Elem. Sch., Greenville, 1980—. Elder Prsbyn. Ch. U.S.A., Greenville, 1987-90; mem. S.C. Tchr. Forum, 1991-92, Greenville County Tchr. Forum, 1993-96. Recipient Milken Nat. Educator award, 1994; named Greenville Young Educator Greenville Jaycees, 1992, Tchr. of Yr. S.C. PTA. Mem. AAHPERD, S.C. Assn. Health, Phys. Edn., Recreation and Dance (adapted phys. edn. chairperson 1989-91, Phys. Educator of Yr. awrd 1991-92), Phi Delta Kappa (membership com. 1992). Presbyterian. Avocations: racquetball, swimming, hiking, camping, scuba diving. Home: 206 Bloomfield Ln Greer SC 29650-3807 Office: Sara Collins Elem Sch 1200 Parkins Mill Rd Greenville SC 29607-3699

FRANCE-DEAL, JUDITH JEAN, language educator; b. Falls City, Nebr., June 27, 1941; d. Paris and Georgia Elizabeth (Reiger) France; m. Gary Arthur Deal, Dec. 30, 1960; children: Kevin, Timothy. Student, Bapt. Inst. Christian Workers, Bryn Mawr, Pa., 1959; grad., Liberty Bible Inst., 1994, Barbizon Sch. Modelling, 1998. Cert. and lic. chaplain. Vol. worker with many orgns., 1957—; receptionist Central Ins. Co., Omaha, Nebr., 1960-62; vol. PTA, Cub Scouts, etc., Wis., 1966-76; tchr. spl. edn. First Bapt. Ch., Dallas, 1985-88, vol. tutor ESL, 1985—. Inspirational spkr.; tchr. English and Bible studies 1st Bapt. Ch., Richardson, Tex., 1989—; pres., founder God's Internat. ABCs, Inc.; model for numerous advts. and commls. Author: Center of Our Lives, 1994. Chaplain-min. to cancer patients Tulsa Cancer Treatment Ctr.; vol. chaplain Plano Specialty Hosp. Recipient numerous writing awards. Mem. Internat. Platform Assn. Republican. Avocations: sewing, reading, writing poetry, helping others, songs. Office: Gods Internat ABC 1000 14th St Ste 122 Plano TX 75074-6220

FRANCE-LITCHFIELD, RUTH A. reading and early literacy specialist; b. Cleve., Mar. 17, 1945; d. Elizabeth Ann (Way) France; children: Katherine Ann, C. Robert. AA, Christian Coll., Columbus, Mo., 1965; BS in Elem. Edn. and French, U. Mo., 1969; MEd in Reading, U. Hawaii, 1974; cert. advanced grad. study, Boston U., 1995. Cert. advanced grad. study, consulting tchr. of reading, French K-9, Mass., K-12 reading tchr.; trained and cert. Orton Gillingham. Tchr. Severence Millikin Sch., Cleveland Heights, Ohio, 19699; elem. tchr. Claude O. Markoe Sch., Fredericsted, St. Croix, V.I., 1969-70; tchr. Ecole Active Bilingue, Paris, 1970-71; elem. tchr. Punahou Sch., Honolulu, 1971-74; nat. cons., asst. editor, editor, asst. to mng. editor The Economy Co.-McGraw Hill Divsn., Oklahoma City, 1974-81; pvt. cons., tutor U.S. Army, West Germany, 1981-84; tchr., substitute Community Nursery Sch., Lexington, Mass., 1985-89; substitute tchr. Lexington (Mass.) Pub. Schs., 1989-91; instrnl. aide Bridge Elem. Sch., Lexington, 1991-92, reading recovery trainee, 1992-93; reading recovery tchr. Davis Elem. Sch., Bedford, Mass., 1994, Bridge Elem. Sch., Lexington, 1992—; rsch. asst. Harvard U. Sch. Edn., 1993—; pvt. tutor, 1995—; reading/early literacy specialist, 1997—. Workshop presenter in field. Contbr. articles to profl. publs. Mem. ASCD, Internat. Reading Assn. (local bd. dirs., pres. 1998-99),. Nat. Reading Assn., Mass. Reading Assn., Ohio Reading Assn., New Eng. Reading Assn., Mass. Assn. Bilingual Edn., Reading Recovery Coun. of N.Am., Phi Delta Kappa, Pi Lambda Theta, Delta Kappa Gamma. Avocations: reading, swimming, knitting, cooking/baking, sewing, crafts. Home: 6 Conestoga Rd Lexington MA 02421-6427 Office: 55 Middleby Rd Lexington MA 02421-6920 E-mail: ruthkb3@hotmail.com., rfrance@sch.ci.lexington.ma.us.

FRANCIS, ALBERT W. elementary education educator; b. St. Louis, Jan. 9, 1952; s. Joseph T. and Alberta M. (Hoeltge) F. BS in Elem. Edn., SE Mo. State U., 1974. Cert. elem. edn. Elem. tchr. Warren County R-III, Warrenton, Mo., 1974-79, Montgomery County R-II, New Florence, Mo., 1980—. Pres. PTO. Mem. ASCD, Mo. Tchrs. Assn., Montgomery County CTA (pres., v.p.). Home: 10210 Shamrock Ln Saint Ann MO 63074-2934 Office: New Florence Elem Sch PO Box 47 Bellflower MO 63333-0047

FRANCIS, CAROLYN RAE, music educator, musician, author, publisher; b. Seattle, July 25, 1940; d. James Douglas and Bessie Caroline (Smith) F; m. Barclay Underwood Stuart, July 5, 1971. BA in Edn., U. Wash., 1962. Cert. tchr., Wash. Tchr. Highline Pub. Schs., Seattle, 1962-64; musician Olympic Hotel, Seattle, 1962-72; 1st violin Cascade Symphony Orch., 1965-78; tchr. Bellevue (Wash.) Pub. Schs., 1965-92; founder Innovative Learning Designs Strategies for Music Edn., Mercer Island, Wash., 1984-96. Profl. violinist for hotels, restaurants, TV, recs., mus. shows, 1962-85; violist Eastside Chamber Orch., 1984-86; pvt. tchr. string instruments, 1959-96; spkr., presenter in-svc. workshops, convs., music educators numerous cities, U.S., Can., London, 1984-96; adjudicator music festivals; instr. Music Instrument Digital Interface applications for educators, 1992-96, also related activities. Author-pub. Music Reading and Theory Skills (curriculum series), Levels 1, 2, 3, 4, 1984-2000; contbr. articles to profl. jours. Mem. Snohomish Indian Tribe. Bellevue Schs. Found. grantee, 1985-86, 86-87, 89-90; scholar U. Wash., 1959-62, We. Wash. State Coll., 1958-59; named Wash. All-State Orch., 1958. Mem. NEA, Am. String Tchrs. Assn. (regional mem. chmn. 1992-94), Music Educators Nat. Conf., Music Industry Coun., Nat. Sch. Orch. Assn. Avocations: hiking, traveling, reading, sewing, sketching. Office: Innovative Learning Designs PO Box 578 Mercer Island WA 98040-0578 E-mail: cfrancis@musicreading.com.

FRANCIS, ELIZABETH ROMINE, secondary school educator, theater director; b. Clarksburg, WVa., Sept. 10, 1920; d. John Ransel and Virginia Snider Romine; m. Jack Stanley Francis, Feb. 13, 1943; children: Michael Stanley, John Maurice. BM, WVa. U., 1942, MM, 1963, JD; grad. drama, Ohio U., 1980. Tchr. Elem. Sch., Clarksburg, W.Va., 1942—43, Jr. H.S., Clarksburg, W.Va., 1943—44, Sr. H.S., Clarksburg, W.Va., 1943—45, New Martinville, W.Va., 1960—93; tchr. adult edn. WVa. U. Ext., New Martinville, 1960—70; Fred Waring workshop staff mem. Waring Enterprises, Delaware Water Gap, 1988—90; dir. theater activities Park & Recreation, New Martinsville, W.Va., 1993—2001. Chmn. theater divsn. Parks and Recreation, New Martinsville, W.Va., 1993—2001. Prodr., dir. : (musical theater) Cmty. Theater, 1993—2001. Recipient Acad. Excellence award, State of WVa., 1985. Republican. Methodist. Avocations: golf, bridge. Office: New Martinsville Parks and Recreation 191 Main St New Martinsville WV 26155 Personal E-mail: eliza@ovis.net.

FRANCIS, FREDERICK JOHN, food science educator; b. Ottawa, Ont., Can., Oct. 9, 1921; came to U.S., 1954; s. Roland and Mary (Dyble) F.; m. Jean Dalton Burrows, Mar. 15, 1952; children: Margaret A. Clayton, John B., Laurie J. BA, U. Toronto, 1946, MA, 1948; PhD, U. Mass., 1954. Instr. dept. food chemistry U. Toronto, 1946-50; asst. prof. dept. horticulture U. Guelph, Ont., Can., 1950-54; prof. dept. food sci. U. Mass., Amherst, 1954-90. Author 13 books; contbr. over 400 articles to profl. jours. With RCAF, 1944-45. Recipient 10 nat. and internat. sci. awards. Fellow AAAS; mem. Am. Coun. of Sci. Health (chmn. bd. dirs. 1992-94), Coun. Agr. Sci. Tech. (bd. dirs. 1990-97). Republican. Congregationalist. Home: 123 Pine St Amherst MA 01002-1125 Office: U Mass Dept Food Sci Amherst MA 01003

FRANCIS, MAXINE BETH, special education educator; b. Brown's Town, St. Ann, Jamaica, Dec. 28, 1964; came to U.S., 1985; d. Earl B. and Mable (Corrodus) F. Diploma in deaf edn., Mico Tchrs. Coll., Kingston, Jamaica, 1984; BSc in Early Childhood Edn., Bowie State U., 1992; MSc in Ednl. Tech., Gallaudet U., 1994. Cert. std. profl., Md., advanced prof., Md. Pre-sch./kindergarten tchr. Gallaudet U. Child Devel. Ctr., Washington, 1985-91; elem. spl. edn. resource tchr. Prince George's County Pub. Sch., Bowie, Md., 1992—. Mem. home and sch. com. Emmanuel Seventh-Day Adventist Ch., Brinklow, Md., 1993—. Mem. Kappa Delta Pi. Avocations: reading, board games, old movies, interior decorating. Office: Yorktown Elem Sch 7301 Race Track Rd Bowie MD 20715-1437

FRANCIS, SHARI, federal agency administrator; BA in edn., Southeast Mo. State U., 1970; MA in edn., U. Mo., St. Louis, 1976. V.p., state relations Nat. Coun. Accreditation Tchr. Edn., Wash., 1992—; sr. policy analyst Nat. Edn. Assn., Wash., DC, 1981—92; staff US Dept. Edn., Elem. Secondary Edn., Wash., 1980; reading spec., tchr., 1970—79. Mem.: Nat. Bd. Profl. Tchg. Standards. Office: Nat Coun Accreditation Tchr Edn 2010 Mass Ave NW Ste 500 Washington DC 20036 E-mail: shari@ncate.org.*

FRANCISCO, DEBORAH ANTOSH, educational administrative professional; b. Wilkes-Barre, Pa, Mar. 8, 1952; d. Albert and Marie Iris (Stuka) Antosh; m. John Thomas McCauley, Sept. 11, 1970 (div. Sept. 1983); 1 child, John-Austen; m. John Patrick Francisco, July 28, 1988; 1 child, Theresa. BA, Cedar Crest Coll., Allentown, Pa., 1984; EdM in Ednl. Adminstrn., Rutgers U., 2003. Cert. elem. tchr., Pa.; cert. elem. and nursery sch. tchr., N.J. Elem. tchr. Allentown Sch. Dist., 1984-88; tchr. basic skills Perth Amboy Sch. Dist., NJ, 1988-89, elem. tchr., 1989—90; tchr. St. Matthias, Somerset, NJ, 1993—96; order processor divsn. housing and confs. Rutgers U., 1997—99, asst. mgr. adminstrn. Coll. Ave. campus, 1999—. Democrat. Roman Catholic. Home: 14 Canadian Woods Rd Marlboro NJ 07746-1672

FRANCO, KENNETH LAWRENCE, surgery educator; b. Hartford, Conn., Sept. 27, 1951; s. Nicholas Lawrence and Mary Elizabeth (LaRosa) F.; m. Jody Mazer, Oct. 10, 1981; 1 child, Jonathan Lawrence. BS, Fairfield U., 1973; MS, Georgetown U., 1975, MD, 1979. Surgical intern, resident Johns Hopkins Hosp., Balt., 1979-81; rsch. fellow Harvard Med. Sch., Boston, 1981-82; resident in surgery Georgetown U. Hosp., Washington, 1982-85, fellow in cardiothoracic surgery, 1985-86; fell in chest and cardiothoracic surgery Columbia-Presbyn. Med. Ctr., N.Y.C., 1986-88; asst. prof. cardiothoracic surgery Yale U. Sch. Medicine, New Haven, 1988-94, assoc. prof., 1994—2000, co-dir. heart and lung transplant program, 1988, dir. surg. rsch. labs., 1988—, dir. mech. assist device program, 1988—, dir. lung volume reduction surgery program, 1994—; dir. heart and lung failure programs Coll. Medicine U. Nebr., 2000—03. Invited reviewer Jour. of Cardiac Surgery, Annals of Thoracic Surgery, Chest, New Eng. Jour. Medicine, Jour. Heart/Lung Transplantation, 1989—. Assoc. editor Jour. Cardiac Surgery, 1997—. Biorsch. grantee Harvard U. Med. Sch., 1981. Fellow ACS, ACCP, STS, ASAIO, ISAO, ASTS; mem. Internat. Soc. Heart Transplantation, Johns Hopkins Med. and Surg. Soc., Alpha Omega Alpha. Roman Catholic. Avocations: golf, swimming, skiing. Fax: 203-307-5525. E-mail: jkjfranco@aol.com.

FRANCOIS, JOSEPH RUFUS, parochial school educator; b. Choiseul, St. Lucia, Feb. 2, 1947; came to U.S., 1984; s. Jean Baptiste and Petronilla (Xavier) F.; m. Olivia Grant, Sept. 27, 1987; children: Norris, Kelsie; 1 child by previous marriage, Ricardo. Cert. edn., U. W.I., St. Lucia, 1970; diploma bus. edn., C.A.S.T., Jamaica, 1984; BA, CUNY, 1992. Lic. tchr. bus. and distributive edn. Tchr. trainer Dept. Edn., St. Lucia, 1976-78; tchr. math. Choiseul Secondary Sch., St. Lucia, 1972-81, Holy Cross Sch., Bronx, N.Y., 1985—. Chmn. faculty com. Holy Cross Sch., Bronx, 1986-87, coord. mid. sch., 1990-92. Union rep. St. Lucia Tchrs. Union, 1975-79. Mem. ASCD. Roman Catholic. Avocations: reading, politics, country music, ping pong. Office: Holy Cross Sch 1846 Randall Ave Bronx NY 10473-2997

FRANK, ELIZABETH AHLS (BETSY FRANK), art educator, artist; b. Cin., Sept. 27, 1942; d. Edward Henry and Constance Patricia (Barnett) Ahls; m. James Russell Frank, Aug. 10, 1963; children: Richard Scott, Robert Edward. Student, Hiram (Ohio) Coll., 1960-63; BA, U. Denver, 1964; MA, U. South Fla., 1988. Cert. profl. educator, Fla. Remedial reading tchr. Willoughby-Eastlake (Ohio) Schs., 1971-72; elem. tchr., grade level chmn. Lee County Pub. Schs., Ft. Myers, Fla., 1972-79, tchr. art, 1979—, mem. arts coun., long range and model schs. planning coms., 1997-98. Contbg. author Davis Art Edn. Publs., Worcester, Mass. Vol. Mann Performing Arts Hall, Fort Myers, 1986-98, Harborside Convention Ctr., 1991-95; sec. Colonial Acres Homeowners Assn., North Fort Myers, Fla., 1994-99. Named Golden Apple Tchr. of Distinction, Lee County Schs. Found., 1991—2002; recipient, Seminar Fla. Humanites Coun., 2000. Mem.: NEA, Edison African Violet Soc. (1st v.p. 1997—2000), Tchrs. Assn. Lee County (rep. bd. 1972—99, mem. exec. bd. 1990—91, M.M. Bethune Humanities award 1992), Fla. Edn. Assn., Lee Art Edn. Assn. (pres. 1991—92, founder, Art Educator of Yr. 1991—92), Calusa Nature Ctr., Southwest Fla. Rose Soc., Fla. Art Edn. Assn. (workshop presenter), Nat. Art Edn. Assn., Audubon of S.W. Fla.. (recording sec. 2002—03, Educator of Yr. 1998), Delta Kappa Gamma (v.p. 1986—88, pres. 1988—90, sec. 1996—98, state chmn. arts and crafts com. 1997—99, sec. 2001—03, state mem. world fellowship com., Fla. scholar 1988), Phi Delta Kappa, Phi Kappa Phi. Democrat. Avocations: gardening, camping, boating, arts and crafts, birdwatching. Home: 4583 S Sawgrass Cir Homosassa FL 34446-3602 Office: North Ft Myers Acad Arts 1858 Suncoast Ln Fort Myers FL 33917-1898 E-mail: jrfrank@mindspring.com.

FRANK, KARL HEINZ, civil engineer, educator; b. San Francisco, Apr. 16, 1944; s. Heinz Benno and Jessie (Johnson) F.; m. Jeanne Doelp, June 28, 1969; children: Erik, Ilse. BCE, U. Calif., Davis, 1966; MCE, Lehigh U., 1969, PhD in Civil Engring., 1971. Registered profl. engr., Tex. Rsch. asst. Fritz Engring. Lab. Lehigh U., Bethlehem, Pa., 1967-71; asst. prof. civil engring. U. Tex., Austin, 1974-80, assoc. prof., 1980-88, prof., 1988—, dir. Ferguson Structural Engring. Lab., 1991-94, Warren S. Belloios prof. civil engring. Structural rsch. engr. Fed. Hwy. Adminstrn., 1971-74; cons. in field. Named one of Outstanding Young Men Am., 1974. Mem. ASCE (assoc., mem. com. structural fatigue, 1971-77, flexural mems. com. 1974-77, chmn. subcom. on longitudinally stiffened plate girders, mem. com. structural connections 1980-83, sec., vice chmn., chmn. structures group Tex. sect. 1984-87, Raymond C. Reese award, Croes award 1999), Am. Welding Soc. Avocations: auto racing, golf. Home: 6005 Ivy Hills Dr Austin TX 78759-5522 Office: U Tex Dept Civil Engring Balcones Rsch Ctr Ferguson Structural Engring Lab 10100 Burnet Rd Austin TX 78758-4445

FRANK, MARY LOU, retired elementary school educator; b. Cleve., May 18, 1915; d. William Henry and Martha Ann (Brown) Parsons; m. Russell Edward Frank, May 18, 1935; children: Richard Edward, James Russell. BS in Edn., Cleve. State U., 1960; MS in Edn., U. Akron, Ohio, 1967, Miami U., Oxford, Ohio, 1934-35; student, Baldwin-Wallace Coll., 1933-34. Cert. tchr., Ohio. Substitute tchr. Cleve. Pub. Schs., 1963; tchr. elem. Brecksville (Ohio) City Sch. Dist., 1953-71, Lee County Bd. of Edn., Ft. Myers, Fla., 1971-74, ret., 1974. Mem. ambassadors to China from Fla., Children's Palaces Homes Hosps., 1980. Martha Holden Jennings Found. scholar, 1963-64, grantee, 1965. Mem. U.S. Power Squadron Aux. (pilot), Collier Reading Coun., Delta Kappa Gamma. Avocations: boating, travel, oil painting. Home: 61 Impala Ct # 23 Fort Myers FL 33912-6338

FRANK, MARY LOU BRYANT, psychologist, educator; b. Denver, Nov. 27, 1952; d. W. D. and Blanche (Dean) Bryant; m. Kenneth Kerry Frank, Sept. 9, 1973; children: Kari Lou, Kendra Leah. BA, Colo. State U., 1974, MEd, 1983, MS, 1986, PhD, 1989. Tchr. Cherry Creek Schs., Littleton, Colo., 1974—80; grad. dir. career devel. Colo. State U., Ft. Collins, 1980—86; intern U. Del., Newark, 1987—88; psychologist Ariz. State U., Tempe, 1988—93; assoc., lead prof. psychology Clinch Valley Coll. U. Va., Wise, 1992—96, asst. acad. dean, 1993—95; head psychology dept., prof. North Ga. Coll. and State U., Dahlonega, 1996—2001; dean undergrad. and univ. studies, prof. psychology Kennesaw State U., 2001—. Chmn. bd. regents adv. com. Psychology, 2000—01; instr. Colo. State U., Ft. Collins, 1981—82, counselor, 1984—85, Ft. Collins, 1986—87; psychologist Ariz. State U., Tempe, 1989—92; assoc. prof. psychology Clinch Valley Coll. U. Va., 1992—96; spkr. in field. Author: (program manual) Career Development, 1986; contbr. book chpts. on eating disorders and existential psychotherapy, 1996, 1998, 1999, 2002; reviewer: Buros Mental Measurements Yearbook. Bd. dirs. Ct. Apptd. Spl. Advocates, 2000—, Enotah Legis. Dist., Helping Teens Succeed, 2003; Youth Adv. Coun. Lumpkin County, 2000—. Mem.: AACSU, AAUP, AAHE, ACES, APA, AACD, Am. Counseling Assn., Ga. ACE Network (mem. exec. com. 2001—), Ga. Assn. Women Higher Edn. (pres. 2001—), Southeastern Psychol. Assn. (chair undergrad. rsch. 1996—2000), Odeka, Phi Beta Kappa, Psi Chi (Ga. Woman of the Yr. com. 1999—2003, vice chair 2003—, documentary project), Pi Kappa Delta, Phi Kappa Phi (Internat. Womans Day program com. 2003, planning com. so. women in pub. svc. conf. 2003—, pres. 2003—, Promotion of Excellence grantee 2002—03). Avocations: music, hiking, reading. Office: Kennesaw State U Off Dean Undergrad & Univ Studies 1000 Chastain Rd - Kennesaw Hall 4443 Kennesaw GA 30144-5591 E-mail: mlfrank@kennesaw.edu.

FRANK, RONALD EDWARD, marketing educator; b. Chgo., Sept. 15, 1933; s. Raymond and Ethel (Lundquist) F.; m. Iris Donner, June 18, 1958; children: Linda, Lauren, Kimberly. BSBA, Northwestern U., 1955, MBA, 1957; PhD, U. Chgo., 1960. Instr. bus. statistics Northwestern U., Evanston, Ill., 1956-57; asst. prof. bus. adminstrn. Harvard U., Boston, 1960-63, Stanford U., 1963-65; assoc. prof. mktg. Wharton Sch., U. Pa., 1965-68, prof., 1968-84, chmn. dept. mktg., 1971-74, vice dean, dir. rsch. and PhD programs, 1974-76, assoc. dean, 1981-83; dean, prof. mktg. Krannert Grad. Sch. Mgmt., Purdue U., 1984-89; dean, Asa Griggs Candler prof. mktg. Goizueta Bus. Sch. Emory U., Atlanta, 1989-98, dean, Asa Griggs Candler prof. mktg. emeritus, 1998-99; mktg. cons., 1999—; pres. Singapore Mgmt. U., 2001—. Bd. dirs. Lafayette (Ind.) Life Ins. Co., The MAC Group, Home Hosp., Lafayette; cornerstone rsch. cons. to industry; mem. strategic issues com. Am. Assembly Collegiate Schs. of Bus., 1988-92, bd. dirs., 1992-96, chmn. audit com., 1993-94, mem. strategic planning and ops. com,. 1994-95; chmn. Orgn. for the Future Task Force, 1996-97; trustee Singapore Mgmt. U., 2000-01. Author: (with Massy and Kuehn) Quantitative Techniques in Marketing Analysis, 1962, (with Matthews, Buzzell and Levitt) Marketing: an Introductory Analysis, 1964, (with William Massy) Computer Programs for the Analysis of Consumer Panel Data, 1964, An Econometric Approach to a Marketing Decision Model, 1971, (with Paul Green) Manager's Guide to Marketing Research, 1967, Quantative Methods in Marketing, 1967, (with Massy and Lodahl) Purchasing Behavior and Personal Attributes, 1968, (with Massy and Wind) Market Segmentation, 1972, (with Marshall Greenberg) Audience Segmentation Analysis for Public Television Program Development, Evaluation and Promotion, 1976, The Public's Use of Television, 1980, Audiences for Public Television, 1982. Bd. dirs., fin. com. Home Hosp. of Lafayette, 1985-89; bd. dirs. The Washington Campus, 1984-89, 95-98. Recipient pub. TV rsch. grants John and Mary R. Markle Found., 1975-82. Mem. Am. Mktg. Assn. (dir. 1968-70, v.p. mktg. edn. 1972-73), Inst. Mgmt. Sci., Assn. Consumer Rsch. Office: Singapore Mgmt Univ 469 Bukit Timah Rd Oei Tion Singapore 259756 Singapore Home: 1609 Wind Song Ln Aurora IL 60504-5561 E-mail: ref@bus.emory.edu.

FRANK, STEPHEN IRA, political science educator; b. Seattle, Oct. 14, 1942; s. Nancy Ann (Schwartz) Frank; m. Barbara Ann Covey; 1 child, Thomas Aaron. BS in Edn., History and Polit. Sci., Ctrl. Mich. U., 1966, MA in Polit. Sci., 1969; PhD in Polit. Sci., Wash. State U., Pullman, 1976. Tchr. social sci. Clarkston HS, Mich., 1967-69; instr. in polit. sci. Gogebec Cmty. Coll., Ironwood, Mich., 1967-69, Lamar U., Beaumont, Tex., 1975-76; prof. polit. sci. N.E. La. U., Monroe, La., 1976-78, St. Cloud State U., Minn., 1978—, chair dept. polit. sci., 2001—03. Co-dir., founder St. Cloud State U. Survey. Author: We Shocked the World: A Case Study of Jesse Ventura's Election As Governor of Minnesota, 1999, 2d edit., 2001; contbr. articles to profl. jour., and chapters to books. Mem. Am. Polit. Sci. Assn., Minn. Polit. Sci. Assn. (bd. dir., treas.), Am. Assn. Pub. Opinion, Nat. Assn. Prelaw Advisors, Midwest Prelaw Advisors Assn. (bd. dir. 1999-2002), St. Cloud State U. Faculty Assn. (pres. 1993-94), Phi Kappa Delta. Avocations: gardening, walking, reading. Office: St Cloud State U Dept Polit Sci 319 Brown Hall Saint Cloud MN 56301-4444

FRANK, WALTER MONROE, JR., media specialist; b. Portsmouth, N.H., May 1, 1945; s. Walter Monroe and Ida (Gammon) F.; divorced; children: Kathleen Seeley, Kelley, Walter Monroe III, Pradel. BS in Edn., U. Maine, 1970; MS in Edn., Nova U., 1985, media specialist, 1989; postgrad., U. Miami, 1989—. Cert. K-8 tchr., Maine, K-12 media tchr., Fla. Tchr. St. Peter's Sch., Lewiston, Maine, 1967-69, Sacred Heart Sch., Auburn, Maine, 1969-71, Town of Jay, Maine, 1971-75; site supr. Androscoggin County Head Start, Lewiston, 1975-81; tchr. St. Mary's Cath. Sch., Miami, Fla., 1981-82, Dade County Pub. Schs., Miami, 1982-89, media specialist, 1989—; dir. media ctr. Miami Jackson Sr. High, 1992—. Instr. tchr. cert. program Dade County, 1985—. Leader 4-H Club; treas. PTA; mem. Ptnrs. in Edn. Scholarship Fund; site coord. Inner City Marine Project; mem. Fairchild Gardens. Recipient mayor's cert. of appreciation City of Miami, 1982, cert. of recognition Fla. Coop. Extension Svc., U. Fla., 1985, 86, 87, Outstanding Svc. award Dade County Pub. Schs., 1986, award of merit Dade Coun. Math. Tchrs., 1987, vol. cert. Informed Families Dade County, 1990. Mem. Fla. Assn. Media Educators, Dade Sci. Tchrs. Assn., Dade County Assn. Vocat. Tchrs., Dade County Reading Assn., United Tchrs. Dade County (rep.), Dade County Media Specialists Assn. Republican. Roman Catholic. Home: 679 NE 87th St Miami FL 33138-3512 Office: Miami Jackson Sr High 1751 NW 36th St Miami FL 33142-5439

FRANKEL, GENE, theater director, writer, producer, educator; b. N.Y.C., Dec. 23, 1923; s. Barnet and Anna (Talerman) F.; m. Pat Ruth Carter, May 1, 1963; children: Laura Ann, Ethan-Eugene. BA, NYU, 1943. Artistic dir. Gene Frankel Theatre, N.Y.C., 1963—; exec. dir. Gen. Frankel Theatre, N.Y.C., 1973—; founding dir. Berkshire Theatre Festival, Stockbridge, Mass., 1965-66. Vis. Arena Stage, Washington, 1969-71; cultural exchange dir. U.S. Dept. State, Belgrade, Yugoslavia, 1968-69; dir. Hartman Theatres, Stamford, Conn., 1976-79; vis. prof. Boston U., 1967-69, Queens Coll., N.Y.C., 1969-71, Columbia U., N.Y.C., 1972-73; cons. dir. Nat. Shakespeare Co., N.Y.C., 1966— ; dir. various regional theaters, 1969-80 Dir.: Broadway, 1969 (Burns Mantle 1969, Best Play award), Emperor Jones, European tour, 1970, Oh Dad, Poor Dad, Belgrade, Yugoslavia, 1969, Lost in the Stars, Broadway, 1971, The Night That Made American Famous, 1975, Cry of Players, 1967, The Blacks, Off-Broadway, 1961 (Obie award 1963), also European tour, Brecht on Brecht, Off-Broadway, 1965, To Be Young Gifted and Black, Off-Broadway, 1970, Enemy of the People, Off-Broadway, 1969, Indians, On Broadway, 1979, Pueblo, 1981, 27 Wagons Full of Cotton, 1985, Talk To Me Like the Rain, 1985, War Play, 1986, The Marriage, 1986, Private Wars, 1987, Sister Aimee, 1987, The Dutchman, 1988, Carreno, 1989—; author, dir. The Actor Then Ma, 1979; co-author, dir.: (play/concert) Carreno, 1990, See Moscow and Die, 1991, (play) Hallowed Ground The Private Thoughts of Abraham Lincoln, 1997; author: So This is the Wicked Stage, 1993, Notes on Othello, 1998, What's Absurd About the Theatre of the Absurd?, 1998, People do Not Want to Suffer, Only Actors Do, 1999; taught and directed numerous actors and actresses including Anne Bancroft, Maya Angelou, Morgan Freeman, Vincent Gardenia, Frank Langella, Fred Gwynne, Louis Gosset, Jr., Walter Matthau, Rod Steiger, Beau Bridges, James Earl Jones, Loretta Swit, Judd Hirsh, Stacy Keach, Lee Marvin, Raul Julia, others. With U.S. Army Air Force, World War II. Recipient Lola D'Annunzio award, 1958; recipient Obie award for Volpone, Village Voice, 1958, Obie award for Machinal Village Voice, 1963, Vernon Rice award for Machinal, Drama Desk-N.Y. Post, 1963; Ford Found. fellow, 1969-71. Mem. SAG, Soc. Choreographers and Dirs., Actors Equity Assn. Office: 4 Washington Square Vlg New York NY 10012-1936 also: Gene Frankel Theatre 24 Bond St New York NY 10012-2424 E-mail: genefrankel@genefrankel.com.

FRANKINO, STEVEN P. lawyer, law educator; b. 1936; AB, Cath. U. Am., 1959, JD, 1962. Bar: D.C. 1963, Nebr. 1977. Tchg. fellow Northwestern U. Sch. Law, Chgo.; asst. prof. Cath. U. Am., Washington, 1963-65, dean sch. law, gen. counsel, 1979-86; prof. law Villanova U., 1965-71; dean Creighton U. Sch. Law, Omaha, 1971-77; ptnr. Kutak, Rock & Huie, Omaha, 1977-79; dean Villanova (Pa.) U. Law Sch., 1987-97, prof. law, 1997—. Rsch. editor Cath. U. Law Jour. Mem. Am. Law Inst., Am. Bar Found., Pa. Bar Found., Knight of Malta, Order of Coif. Office: Villanova U Law Sch Garey Hall Villanova PA 19085 E-mail: frankino@law.villanova.edu.

FRANKL, RAZELLE, management educator; BA in English, Temple U., 1955; MA in Polit. Sci., Bryn Mawr Coll., 1966; MBA in Organizational Devel., Drexel U., 1973; PhD, Bryn Mawr Coll., 1984. Chair codes and ordinance com. Exec Com. Neighborhood Improvement Program, Lower Merion Twp., 1967-68; pres. LWV Lower Merion Twp., 1967-68; v.p. for organizational affairs LWV, Springfield, Mass., 1968-70; chair environ. quality com. LWV Radnor Twp., 1970-71; instr. applied behavioral sci. Drexel U. Sch. Bus., 1972-73; planner office of mental health/mental retardation Dept. Pub. Health, City of Phila., 1971-73, planner office of health planning, 1971-73; coord. for health programs Phila. '76 Inc. (Official Bicentennial Corp.), 1972-74; adj. faculty dept. mgmt. adminstrv. studies divsn. Coll. Bus. Rowan U. (formerly Glassboro State Coll., Rowan Coll.), 1974-77, 81-82; asst. prof. Glassboro (N.J.) State Coll., 1982-88, assoc. prof. dept. mgmt., 1988-95, prof., 1995—2002, prof. emerita, 2002—. Author: Televangelism: The Marketing of Popular Religion, 1987, Popular Religion and the Imperatives of Television: A Study of the Electric Church, 1984; author: (with others) Religious Television: Controversies and Conclusions, 1990, Teleministries as Family Businesses, 1990, New Christian Politics, 1984, Culture Media and Religious Right, 1997, The Encyclopedia of Religion and Society, 1997; contbr. (book chpt.) Transformation of Televangelism: Repackaging of Christian Family Values, 1997, articles to profl. jours. Dir. nat. bd. Allegheny U. Health Scis., chair spring program; chair, bd. dirs. Anti-Violence Partnership of Phila.; founder, chair Friends of Rowan U. Libr., 1995—. Rsch. grantee Rowan Coll. N.J. (formerly Glassboro State Coll.), 1986-87, 90, 91, 93-94, 94-95, All-Coll. Rsch. grantee, 1987-88. Mem. Am. Acad. Mgmt. (chair membership com. div. mgmt. edn. and devel., chair media rels. com., div. women in mgmt.), Soc. for Human Resource Mgmt., Am. Sociol. Assn., Ea. Sociol. Soc., Assn. for Sociology Religion, Religious Rsch. Assn., Soc. for Sci. Study Religion (chair womens caucus), Internat. Sociol. Assn. Home: 536 Moreno Rd Wynnewood PA 19096-1121 E-mail: frankl@rowan.edu.

FRANKL, WILLIAM STEWART, cardiologist, educator; b. Phila., July 15, 1928; s. Louis and Vera (Simkin) F.; m. Razelle Sherr, June 17, 1951; children: Victor S. (dec.), Brian A. BA in Biology, Temple U., 1951, MD, 1955, MS in Medicine, 1961. Diplomate Am. Bd. Internal Medicine, Am. Bd. Cardiovasc. Disease. Intern Buffalo Gen. Hosp., 1955-56; resident in medicine Temple U., Phila., 1956-57, 59-61; faculty Temple U. Sch. Medicine, 1962-68, dir. EKG sect. dept. cardiology, 1966-68, dir. cardiac care unit, 1967-68; prof. medicine, dir. divsn. cardiology Med. Coll. Pa., Phila., 1970-79; prof. medicine, assoc. dir. cardiology divsn. Thomas Jefferson U., Phila., 1979-84; physician-in-chief Springfield (Mass.) Hosp., 1968-70; prof. medicine, co-dir. William Likoff Cardiovascular Inst. Hahnemann U., Phila., 1984-86, dir. William Likoff Cardiovascular Inst., dir. div. cardiology, 1986-92, Thomas J. Vischer Prof. medicine, chmn. dept. medicine, 1987-92; prof. medicine, dir. cardiovascular regional programs Allegheny U. of the Health Scis., 1992-98; dir. cardiovascular regional programs Allegheny U. Hosps., 1992-98; v.p. cardiovascular program devel. Allegheny U. Hosps. System, 1995-98; prof. medicine cardiology divsn. dept. medicine Temple U. Sch. Medicine, 1998-2000. Cons. cardiology Phila. Va Hosp., 1970-79; Fogarty Sr. Internat. fellow Cardiothoracic Inst., U. London, 1978-79; pres. Pa. affiliate Am. Heart Assn., 1985-86; clin. prof. of medicine, Temple U. Sch. of Medicine, 2000—. Contbr. articles to profl. jours. Capt. (M.C.), U.S. Army, 1957-59. Cardiovascular Rsch. fellow U. Pa., Phila., 1961-62; recipient Golden Apple award Temple U. Sch. Medicine, 1967; award Med. Coll. Pa., 1972; Lindback award for disting. teaching, 1975. Fellow ACP, Am. Coll. Cardiology (gov. Ea. Pa. 1986-89), Phila. Coll. Physicians, Am. Coll. Clin. Pharmacology (regent 1980-85, 93-98), Coun. Clin. Cardiology of Am. Heart Assn. (coun. on arteriosclerosis); mem. AAUP, AAAS, N.Y. Acad. Scis., Am. Fedn. Clin. Rsch., Assn. Am. Med. Colls., Am. Heart Assn. (bd. govs. S.E. Pa. chpt. 1972-84, pres. 1976, Pa. affiliate pres. 1984-85), Am. Soc. Clin. Pharmacology and Exptl. Therapeutics, Phila. County Med. Soc. (pres. 1993-94, 1st dist. trustee to Pa. Med. Soc. bd. trustees 1998-2001). Home and Office: 536 Moreno Rd Wynnewood PA 19096-1121 E-mail: wfrankl@earthlink.net.

FRANKLIN, BILLY JOE, international higher education specialist; b. Honey Grove, Texas, Jan. 30, 1940; s. John Asia and Annie Mae (Castle) F.; m. Sonya Kay Erwin, June 1, 1958; children: Terry Daylon, Shari Dea. BA, U. Tex., 1965, MA, 1967, PhD, 1969. Asst. prof. sociology U. Iowa, Iowa City, 1969-71; chmn. Western Carolina U., Cullowhee, NC, 1971-72, Wright State U., Dayton, Ohio, 1973-75; dean SW Tex. State U., San Marcos, Tex., 1975-77; v.p. acad. affairs Stephen F. Austin State U., Nacogdoches, Tex., 1977-81; pres. Tex. A&I U., Kingsville, Tex., 1981-85, Lamar U., Beaumont, Tex., 1985-91; exec. v.p. Tex. Internat. Edn. Consortium, Austin, 1991-96, pres., 1996-2000. Adj. prof. U. Tex., Austin, 2000—; mem. nat. agrl. rsch. com. USDA, 1982-85; policies and purposes com. Am. Assn. State Colls. and Univs., 1985-91, nominating com., 1986-88, mem. exec. com. bd. dir., 1990-91; pres. Assn. Tex. Colls. and Univs., 1985-86, Tex. Acad. Sci., 1986-87; commr. commn. on coll. So. Assoc. Coll. and Sch., 1985-90, chmn., 1987-90, pres.-elect, 1990-91; chmn. Coun. Pub. Univ. Pres. and Chancellors, 1988-91; bd. dir. Tex. Ptnr. of Am., Scheriner U. Co-editor: Research Methods: Issues and Insights, 1971, Social Psychology and Everyday Life, 1973; contbr. articles to profl. jour. Mem. sr. adv. bd. Tex. Lyceum, Inc., 1982-88; bd. dir. United Way of Coastal Bend, 1981-84, United Way of Beaumont, Tex., Tex. Ptnr. of . Energy Mus., 1987, pres., 1987-90; mem. exec. com. Muscular Dystrophy Assoc., 1985-91. Presbyterian. Fellow Tex. Acad. Sci.; mem. Am. Sociol. Assn., Kingsville C. of C. (bd. dir. 1981-83, pres. 1984), Beaumont C. of C. (bd. dir. 1986-91, chmn. 1988-89), East Tex. C. of C. (bd. dir. 1985-87), East Tex. Venture Capital Group (bd. dir. 1985-87), Schreiner Univ. (bd. trustees, 2003-). E-mail: billf@gvtc.com.

FRANKLIN, BOBBY JO, state education agency administrator; b. Canton, Miss., Nov. 14, 1951; s. Robert Lee and Gladys Julia (Thompson) F.; m. Nelda Ann Allbritton, Apr. 5, 1986; children: Elizabeth Leann, Caleb Lee, John Winston. AS, East Cen. Jr. Coll., Decatur, Miss., 1971; BS, U. So. Miss., 1973; MEd, Auburn U., 1987; PhD, La. State U., 1992. Cert. tchr., Miss., La. Tchr. Warren County Schs., Vicksburg, Miss., 1973-84; environ. technician U.S. Corps Engrs., Vicksburg, 1981-84; grad. asst. dept. chemistry La. State U., Baton Rouge, 1984-85, grad. asst. dept. curriculum and instrn., 1986-89; lab. technician Baddley Chem. Co., Baton Rouge, 1985-87; adminstr. edn. sect. office of R&D La. Dept. Edn., Baton Rouge, 1989-97, dir. divsn. planning, analysis and info. resources, 1997—. Cons. La. Acad. Rally, U. So. La., 1987; mem. Parkview Bapt. Sch. Bd., Baton Rouge, 1992-94; chair AERA Sig: Sch. Indicators and Report Cards, 1994-96; mem. edn. info. adv. com. Coun. Chief States Sch. Officers; adj. prof. La. State U., 2002; mem. bd. examiners NCATE. Contbr. articles to profl. jours. Mem. Warren County Rep. party, 1983-84. Named Star Tchr. Miss. Econ. Coun., 1983; recipient tchr. commendation Internat. Sci. and Engring. Fair, 1983. Mem. NSTA, Nat. Assn. Rsch. in Sci. Teaching, Am. Edn. Rsch. Assn., Nat. Forum on Edn. Statistics, Mid-South Edn. Rsch. Assn., La. Edn. Rsch. Assn., Phi Delta Kappa. Baptist. Avocations: hunting, fishing, refinishing furniture. Home: 2131 Firewood Dr Baton Rouge LA 70816-2814 Office: La Dept Edn 626 N 4th St Baton Rouge LA 70802-5363

FRANKLIN, DOLORES ROBERTS, elementary education educator; b. Commerce, Tex. d. David Roberts and Earnestine (Massey) Ivory; children: Ronald Tyrone Franklin, Angela Franklin, Jocelyn Franklin. BS in Elem. Edn., Tex. Coll., 1956; MS in Elem. Edn., Portland (Oreg.) State U., 1978. Elem. tchr. Commerce Ind. Sch. Dist., 1960-61, Portland Pub. Sch. Dist., 1972—. Author sch. dist. curriculum. Impact II disseminator grantee Portland Pub. Schs., 1992. Mem. NEA, Oreg. Edn. Assn., Oreg. Sci. Tchrs. Assn., Portland Assn. Tchrs. (rep. 1989—, Impact II disseminator grantee 1992). Home: 3961 NE 19th Ave Portland OR 97212-1410

FRANKLIN, DOROTHY ANN, guidance counselor; b. West Point, Ky., June 30, 1938; d. Raymond and Laura B. (Robards) Williams; m. Herbert Franklin, Mar. 31, 1962; children: Marcus, Lori. BS, Ky. State U., 1960; MEd, U. Louisville, 1969; postgrad., Ind. U., 1973-74, U. Dayton. Cert. in guidance supervision. Tchr. Cardinal Cmty. High Sch., Eldon, Iowa, 1960-61; tchr., counselor Louisville/Jefferson County Schs., Louisville, 1961-72; counselor Monroe County Schs., Bloomington, Ind., 1972-74, Alachua County Schs., Gainesville, Fla., 1974-80, Franklin County Schs., Frankfort, Ky., 1980-84, Sidney (Ohio) City Schs., 1984—. Bd. trustees United Way, Sidney, 1993-96, Riverview Behavior Health Care Ctr., Sidney, 1993-96; mem. steering com., mem.-at-large City of Sidney Comprehensive Plan, 1996-97; mem. adv. bd. Bank One, Sidney, 1994-97; mem. adv. coun. Planned Parenthood, Sidney, 1993-98. Mem. AAUW, NEA, Am. Assn. Counseling Devel., Ohio Edn. Assn., Ohio Sch. Counselors Assn., Sidney Edn. Assn., Tri-County Br. NAACP, Kappa Delta Pi, Alpha Kappa Alpha. Democrat. Baptist. Avocations: real estate, reading, travel. Home: 954 Lakepointe Ct Union KY 41091-9558

FRANKLIN, GENE FARTHING, engineering educator, consultant; b. Banner Elk, N.C., July 25, 1927; s. Burnie D. and Delia (Farthing) F.; m. Gertrude Stritch, Jan. 1952; children: David M., Carole Lea. BSEE, Ga. Inst. Tech., 1950; MSEE, MIT, 1952; DEngSc, Columbia U., 1955. Asst. prof. Columbia U., N.Y.C., 1955-57; prof. elec. engring. Stanford (Calif.) U., 1957-95, prof. emeritus, 1995—. Cons. IBM, Rochester, Minn., 1982-94. Author: Sampled-Data Control, 1958, Digital Control, 1980, 3d edit., 1997, Feedback Control, 1986, 4th edit., 2001. With USN, 1945-47. Recipient Edn. award Am. Automatic Control Coun., 1985. Fellow IEEE (life), Control Soc. of IEEE (Bode lectr. 1994). Democrat. Office: Stanford U Dept Elec Engring Stanford CA 94305

FRANKLIN, INGA SIVILLS KNUPP, special education educator; b. Norfolk, Va., Sept. 24, 1955; d. Stanley Allen and Margaret (DeVane) K.; m. John Walter Franklin, Aug. 21, 1976; 1 child, John Allen. BS in Spl. Edn., Pembroke State U., 1976; MEd, U. N.C. Chapel Hill, 1982; AG cert., St. Andrews, 1982. Cert. tchr., including H.S. sci., math. grades 6-9, lang. arts grades 6-9, learning disabilities, mentally handicapped, behavior/emotionally handicapped, N.C. Spl. edn. tchr. Lee County Schs.; owner 3J Home Repair Svcs.; co-owner Barn Again. Sch.-based com. chair, adminstrv. placement com., tchr. learning disabilities workshops. Contbr. article to profl. jour., 1985. Art. dir. VBS, First Bapt. Ch., Dublin, N.C., 1992-93, mem. children's com., 1990-93, crusader dir., 1992—; asst. leader Wieblo Scouts, 1992-93. Mem. Bladen County Coun. Exceptional Children (pres. 1985, 92, sec. 1993, Presdl. award 1992). Democrat. Avocations: music, reading, travel, crafts.

FRANKLIN, JOEL NICHOLAS, mathematician, educator; b. Chgo., Apr. 4, 1930; m. Patricia Anne; 1 dau., Sarah Jane. BS, Stanford, 1950, PhD, 1953. Research asso. N.Y. U., 1953-55; asst. prof. math. U. Wash, 1955; mem. faculty Calif. Inst. Tech., 1957—, prof. applied sci., 1966-69, prof. applied math., 1969—. Author: Matrix Theory, 1968, Methods of Mathematical Economics, 1980, also articles. Mem. Am. Math. Soc., Soc. Indsl. and Applied Math., Phi Beta Kappa. Home: 1763 Alta Crest Dr Altadena CA 91001-2130 Office: Calif Inst Tech 217 50 Pasadena CA 91125-0001

FRANKLIN, JULIAN HAROLD, political science educator; b. N.Y.C., Mar. 26, 1925; s. Jerome A. and Molly (Seidenstein) F.; m. Paula Angle, Feb. 23, 1928. BA summa cum laude, Queens Coll., 1946; MA, Columbia U., 1950, PhD, 1960. Instr. Columbia U., N.Y.C., 1951-59, assoc. prof., 1962-68, prof., 1968-96, prof. emeritus, 1997—; vis. asst. prof. New Sch. for Social Research, N.Y.C., 1959-60; asst. prof. Princeton (N.J.) U., 1960-62. Acting chmn. summer session Columbia U., 1962—, dir. grad. studies polit. theory, 1968—, dept. rep., 1971-72, 86—, dept. del. com. on instruction faculty polit. sci., 1971-73, 81-82, chmn., 1973-74, co-founder, adj. chmn. sem. on polit. and social thought; mem. adv. council dept. politcs. Princeton U., 1973-76. Author: Jean Bodin and the Sixteenth Century Revolution in the Methodology of Law and History, 1963, Constitutionalism and Resistance in the Sixteenth Century, 1969, Jean Bodin and the Rise of Absolutist Theory, 1973, rev. edit. (in French), 1993, John Locke and the Theory of Sovereignty, 1978; editor and translator: Jean Bodin on Sovereignty, 1992; editl. cons. in polit. theory Polity, 1977-79; mem. editl. bd. Polit. Theory; contbr. articles to profl. jours. Served with USAF, 1943-46. Queens Coll. scholar, 1946, Social Sci. Research Council fellow, 1950-51, William Bayard Cutting travelling fellow, 1950-51, NEH fellow, 1975-76, 89-90, Phi Beta Kappa fellow, 1990. Mem. Conf. for Study Polit. and Social Thought. Jewish. Office: Columbia U Dept Polit Sci 116th St And Broadway New York NY 10027

FRANKLIN, MARC ADAM, law educator; b. Bklyn., Mar. 9, 1932; s. Louis A. and Rose (Rosenthal) Franklin; m. Ruth E. Korzenik, June 29, 1958 (dec. Dec. 2000); children: Jonathan, Alison. AB, Cornell U., 1953, LLB, 1956. Bar: N.Y. 1956. Assoc. Proskauer Rose Goetz & Mendelsohn, N.Y.C., 1956-57; law clk to Hon. Carroll C. Hincks, New Haven, 1957-58; prof. law Stanford U., Calif., 1962-76, Frederick I. Richman prof. law, 1976—2001, emeritus, 2001—; prof. law Columbia U., 1959-62; law clk to to Earl Warren, U.S. Supreme Ct., Washington, 1958-59. Author: Biography of a Legal Dispute, 1968, Dynamics of American Law, 1968, Cases and Materials on Tort Law and Alternatives, 1971; co-author (with R.L. Rabin): Cases and Materials on Tort Law and Alternatives, 7th edit., 2001; author: Mass Media Law, 1977; co-author (with D.A. Anderson and F.H. Cate): Mass Media Law, 6th edit., 2000; author: The First Amendment and the Fourth Estate, 1977; co-author (with T.B. Carter and J.B. Wright): The First Amendment and the Fourth Estate, 8th edit., 2001; author: The First Amendment and the Fifth Estate, 1986; co-author (with T.B. Carter and J.B. Wright): The First Amendment and the Fifth Estate, 6th edit., 2003. Fellow Ctr. for Advanced Study in Behavioral Scis., 1968—69; scholar Fulbright, Victoria U., 1973. Home: 999 Green St # 2005 San Francisco CA 94133 Office: Stanford U Law Sch Nathan Abbott Way Stanford CA 94305

FRANKLIN, MARY ANN WHEELER, educator, higher education and management consultant; b. Boston; d. Arthur E. Wheeler Sr. and Madeline Ophelia (Hall) Wheeler-Brooks; m. Carl Matthew Franklin; 1 child, Evangeline Rachel Hall Franklin. BS, U. N.H., 1942; MEd, U. Buffalo, 1948; EdD, U. Md., 1982. Cert. tchr., N.Y., Ga. Instr. sci. edn. W.Va. State Coll., 1947; tchr. gen. sci. John Marshall Jr. High Sch., Bklyn., 1952-58, 59-60; assoc. prof. sci. Elizabeth City State Coll., 1960-67; asst. dean of the coll. Morgan State Coll., Balt., 1967-77; asst. dean Coll. Arts and Scis. Morgan State U., Balt., 1977-78, asst. v.p. acad. affairs, 1978-82; asst. prof. bus. Catonsville (Md.) Community Coll., 1982; asst. to dean evening and weekend coll. So. U. New Orleans, 1983-92. Cons. numerous locations including Herford County Tchrs., Murfreesboro, N.C., 1961, St. Catherine's Sch., Elizabeth City, N.C., 1962-64, St. Elizabeth Cath. Sch., Elizabeth City; cons., bd. dirs. Archbishop Keough H.S., Balt., 1970-80, Hampton (Va.) Inst., 1971, St. Paul Coll., 1972; presenter confs., seminars and workshops; spkr. in field. Editor Morgan State U. Acad. Affairs Newsletter, 1980-82; editor, pub. Morgan State U. Catalog, 1969-82, So. U. New Orleans Catalog, 1986-84, 89-92; author: The How and Why of Testing at Elizabeth City State College, 1962, Report on Princeton University Program for Physics Teachers in HBCU's, 1964, A Descriptive Report of Pre-College Study Booster Program, 1965, 66, Learning Summer Camp Code, National Library of Poetry, 1992, Interrogations of a Metropolis of the Day, Who Are We/Who We Are, 1994. Mem. com. higher edn. Citizens League, Balt., 1979-81; assoc. dir. youth camp NCCJ, 1974-75, bd. dirs., 1969-80; dir., originator Vestibule Program and Parents Workshop for New Citizens and Residents, SUNO Summer Learning Camp, 1984-95, Ctr. Women Against Crime Conf.; pres. Lake Willow Homeowners Assn., 1994-96. Fellow NSF, Harvard U., 1958-59, Carnegie-Ford-NSF, Princeton U., 1964; recipient Education award Am. Assn. of Coll. Tchrs. Edn., 1966. Mem. AAUW, Am. Mgmt. Assn., Nat. Coun. Negro Women, Am. Assn. Higher Edn., Am. Assn. Continuing Higher Edn., Nat. Assn. Trainers and Educators for Alcohol and Substance Abuse Counselors (bd. dirs.), La. Assn. Continuing Higher Edn., Md. Assn. Higher Edn., Urban League, Delta Sigma Theta, Phi Sigma, Pi Lambda Theta. Avocations: fine arts, portraits, pastels, listening to classical music and popular show tunes, swimming.

FRANKLIN, PATRICIA LYNN POWELL, special education educator; b. East St. Louis, Ill., Nov. 28, 1953; d. William and Alice Alfreda (Sowers) Powell; 1 child, Ashley Lynn. BS in Edn., So. Ill. U., 1976, MS in Elem. Edn., 1992. Cert. elem. edn., early childhood spl.edn., learning disabilities, behavior disorder, and educable mentally handicapped tchr., Ill. Primary spl. edn. tchr. Highland (Ill.) Community Sch. Unit #5, 1976—; devel.

therapist/early interventionist Child and Family Connections, Ill. Dept. of Human Svc., 2002—. Mentor tchr., insvc. presenter Madison County Region II Svc. Ctr., Edwardsville, Ill., 1976, 89, 91, 92, coach, supr. Spl. Olympics, 1977-90; supervising tchr. So. Ill. U., Edwardsville, 1976, 91, 93, 96—, Greenville (Ill.) Coll., 1976-84; chmn. exec. orgnl. com. Very Spl. Arts Festival, Madison County Supr. Schs., Edwardsville, 1983; chmn. com. Very Spl. Arts Festival, Ill. Arts for Handicapped, 1983-855; participating tchr. Title IV-C learning disabilities program St. Clair County Supr. Schs., 1979-81; spl. edn. summer program tchr. Madison County Region II Svc. Ctr., 1998—. Vol. Angel choir St. Paul United Meth. Ch., Rosewood Heights, Ill., 1990-92; Sunday sch. tchr. St. John's United Meth. Ch., Edwardsville, brownie leader Girl Scouts U.S., 1991—; v.p., program chair Heritage Herb Assn., 1998-2000, pres. 2000—. Mem. Ill. Reading Assn., Tchrs. Applying Whole Lang., Zoo Tchrs., Coun. for Exceptional Children, Highland Profl. Educators, Lewis & Clark Reading Coun., Ill. Whole Lang., Early Childhood Spl. Interest Coun.; clubs: Edwardsville Garden Club. Avocations: needlework, crafts, gardening, fishing, travel. Office: 1800 Lindenthal St Highland IL 62249-2206

FRANKLIN, PHYLLIS, retired professional society administrator; b. N.Y.C., Apr. 21, 1932; d. Matthew Pine and Helen Lutsky; m. Irwin Franklin, Apr. 21, 1958 (div. 1971); children: James, Jody. AB, Vassar Coll., 1954; MA, U. Miami, 1965, PhD, 1969; LHD (hon.), George Washington U., 1986. From asst. to assoc. prof. U. Miami, Coral Gables, 1969-80; spl. asst. to dean Coll. Arts & Scis. Duke U., Durham, N.C., 1980-81; dir. English programs MLA, N.Y.C., 1981-85, exec. dir., 1985—2001, ret., 2001. Adj. prof. English programs NYU, 1987-88. Editor ADE Bull., 1981-85. Fellowship, Danforth Found., 1966-68, Am. Council on Edn., 1980-81; stipend NEH, 1971. Mem. USSR Acad. Scis., Am. Coun. Learned Socs. (bd. dirs. 1987-89, commn. on humanities and social scis. 1987-88, chair conf. secs. 1987-90), Nat. Humanities Alliance (bd. dirs. 1986-88, v.p. 1990-91, pres. 1991-96), Nat. Fedn. Abstracting and Info. Svcs. (bd. dirs. 1994-96). Democrat. Jewish.*

FRANKLIN, VIRGIL L. school administrator, education educator; b. Waterbury, Conn., July 26, 1940; s. Virgil Sr. and Frances (Edmonds) F.; m. Dionet Ruth Jordan, Nov. 2, 1962; children: Tracey, Jacqueline, Bara, Dakar, Jordan, Mildred. BS, Fayetteville State U., 1962; MA, U. Conn., Storrs, 1968; EdD, U. Bridgeport, 1989. Tchr. Martin County (N.C.) Bd. Edn., 1962-63, Waterbury Bd. Edn., 1963-68; adj. faculty U. Hartford, Conn., 1968-69; adj. faculty, lab. sch. tchr. So. Conn. State U., New Haven, 1969; prin. Barbour Elem. Sch., Hartford, 1970-73, Walsh Elem. Sch., Waterbury, 1973-86, West Side Mid. Sch., Waterbury, 1986—; prof. edn. Western Conn. State U., Danbury, 1990-92; assoc. prof. Va. State U., Petersburg, 1992—. Coord. edn. leadership; dir. youth enrichment program N.O.W., Inc., Waterbury, 1965, 66; adj. faculty Mattatuck C.C., Waterbury, 1971; adj. prof. Western Conn. State U., 1989; reading instr. U. Hartford, 1973; instr., team leader U. Conn., Storrs, 1984; lectr. in field; mem. rev. panel secondary sch. recognition program U.S. Dept. Edn., 1990; mem. com. to set criteria for elem. edn. proficiency exam Conn. State Dept. Edn., 1990; mem. Waterbury Curriculum Revision Com., 1979; assessor Va. Prins. Assessment Ctr., 1993. Mem. Waterbury Substance Abuse Policy Com., 1988-89; sch. coord. Ptnrs. in Edn. program, Waterbury, Peer Helpers program, Waterbury, 1988-89. Mem. NEA, Am. Fedn. Sch. Adminstrs. Am. Assoc. Univ. Prof., Sch. Adminstrs. Waterbury, Fayetteville State U. Alumni Assn. Conn. (pres. 1990-92), Masons, Kappa Delta Pi, Phi Delta Kappa, Omega Psi Phi. Home: 5603 Melbeck Cir Richmond VA 23234-5280 Office: Va State U PO Box 9055 Petersburg VA 23803

FRANKS, ALLEN P. research institute executive, educator; b. Cleve., Nov. 12, 1936; s. Stanley Arthur and Helen Dorothy (Kulwicki) F.; m. Cary Bajko, Feb. 2, 1963; children: Mathew, Sara. BS, U. Miami, 1959; LLB, Case Western Res. U., 1963, JD, 1968. Cert. chem. engr. Patent atty. B.F. Goodrich Co., Akron, Ohio, 1963-65; chemist, mgr. paint testing lab. PPG Industries, Barberton, Ohio, 1965-66; tech. dir., lab. mgr. Reichhold Chems., Inc., Cuyahoga Falls, Ohio, 1966-76; instr. Inst. Astral Studies, Inc., Akron, 1974-80, pres., 1977-80; mgr. tech. sales Sovereigh Chem. Co., Cuyahoga Falls, 1980-86; pres. I.A.S. Inc., 1986-94; sec.-treas. rsch. divsn. IAA, 1990-95, pres., 1995—; CEO Cary Franks Inc., 1995—. Lectr. astrology, biorhythms, tennis Akron U., 1974-79, Kent (Ohio) State U., 1973-77. Contbr. articles to profl. jours. Bd. dirs. Persephone Found., Bath, Ohio, 1974-80, chmn., 1981-86; instr. tennis YWCA, Goodyear Racquet Club. With USCGR, 1954-62. Fellow Am. Inst. Chemists; mem. AAAS, N.Y. Acad. Scis., Ohio Inst. Chemists (treas. 1976-84, pres. 1984-90), Am. Chem. Soc., Akron Rubber Group, N.E. Ohio Rubber Group, Theosophical Soc. South Fla. (treas. 1996-99), Mensa, Intertel, Crystal Lake Country Club, Am. Legion, Fraternal Order Police, Univ. Club, Goodyear Racquet Club, Phi Delta Phi. Home: 1887 NW 70th Ln Margate FL 33063-2487 E-mail: A8531A@cs.com.

FRANKS, LOU ELLA, school system administrator, educator; b. Shreveport, La., July 2, 1950; d. Melvin (Watt) and Robbie Lee (Jelks) F.; m. Clyde Beavers, July 1, 1972 (div.); children: Lateecia Beavers, Nelobie Beavers, Martin Beavers. Student, Grambling State U., La., 1968; BS, U. Oreg., 1972, MS, 1977; EdD, Seattle U., 1991. Cert. prin., vice prin., biology and math. tchr., supt., Wash. Civil engr. intern U.S. Army Corp. Engrs., Portland, Oreg., 1978-79; math. instr. Portland (Oreg.) State U., 1985, 91; math. and biology instr. Portland Pub. Schs., 1977-90, adminstrv. asst., 1986-87; supt. intern Ridgefield (Wash.) Sch. Dist., 1990—. Coord. project reassurance, Sigma Gamma Rho Sorority, 1986-90; tamiochus Sigma Beta Eta Chpt., 1986-90; real estate agt. Farrell and Assocs. Realty, 1992-93. Author: Mathematics African American Style; cons. Electrical Power Plant; counselor Social Character Renewal, 1977. Mem. Blacks in Govt., 1985; state statistician Ch. of God in Christ Jurisdiction, 1987, pastor Abundant Life Ministries; mem. 21st Century Planning Com./Schs., 1988. Mem. ASCD, Oreg. Edn. Assn. Avocations: singing, bowling, skating, skiing, basketball. Office: Ridgefield School Dist #122 Ridgefield WA 98642

FRANKS, PETER JOHN, educational administrator; b. Lexington, Mass., Feb. 25, 1948; s. Charles Henry and Evelyn Rebecca (Anderson) F.; m. Jane Karen Campbell, Sept. 9, 1972; children: Andrew C., Meredith C. BA, Northeastern U., 1971, MEd, 1974. Adminstrv. asst. to dir. suburban campus Northeastern U., Boston, 1971-72, asst. to dean of students, 1972-77, asst. dean of students, 1977-84; v.p. Nat. Commn. for Coop. Edn., Boston, 1984-95; CEO World Assn. for Coop. Edn., Boston, 1995—. Mem. site-based mgmt. coun. Lexington (Mass.) Sch. Sys., 1990-94; chmn. edn. com. Hancock Ch., 1989-94, endowment com., 1995-2000, co-chair 1998-2000; bd. trustees Charles I. Travelli Fund. Named one of Outstanding Young Men of Am., U.S. Jaycees, 1979. Mem. New Eng. Assn. Field Experience, World Assn. for Coop. Edn., Coop. Edn. and Internship Assn., Employment Mgmt. Assn. Found. (bd. dirs. 1995—, sec.-treas. 1997-98, pres., 1998-2000), Soc. for Human Resource Mgmt., Internat. Scholars Soc., Kappa Delta Pi, Phi Beta Delta. Home: 7 Dexter Rd Lexington MA 02420-3303 Office: World Assn for Coop Edn Ste 384 CP 360 Huntington Ave Boston MA 02115-5005

FRANSE, JEAN LUCILLE, secondary school educator; b. Comanche, Okla., Jan. 24, 1932; d. Robert Sydney and Mary Lee (Hooper) McDonald; children: Steven E. Franse, John K. Franse, James M. Franse. BS, Eastern N.Mex. U., 1969, MA, 1976; PhD, Tex. Tech. U., 1998. Cert. ESL, mid-mgmt. Telephone operator Mountain States Telephone, Clovis, N.Mex., 1950-51; mktg. rschr. Opinions Unltd., Amarillo, Tex., 1985-88; sch. tchr. Farwell (Tex.) Ind. Schs., 1969—; bookkeeper, pres. Franse Irrigation, Inc., Farwell, 1985—. Author: (poetry) World of Poetry Anthology, 1991 (Golden Poet award 1991), Our World's Favorite Poems (Outstanding award 1993), Outstanding Poets of 1994, 1994 (Merit award 1994). Mem. Christian Coalition, Dallas, 1994, Ctr. for Am. Values, Washington, 1993-94, Liberty Alliance, Forest, Va., 1994. Mem. ASCD. Home: PO Box 580 Farwell TX 79325-0580 Office: Farwell Ind Sch Dist Box F Farwell TX 79325

FRANSEN, CHRISTINE IRENE, mathematics educator; b. Chgo., Sept. 3, 1947; d. Henry and Irene Antoinette (Ross) F. BS in Maths. Edn., U. Ill., 1969; MS in Maths., Northeastern Ill. U., 1971. Cert. math. tchr., Ill., adolescent and young adulthood math.; nat. bd. cert. tchr. Tchr. Senn Met. Acad., Chgo., 1969—. Mentor for NTL assisting CPS tchrs. in nat. bd. certification. Recipient Dedicated Tchr. award Kate Maremont Found., 1982, Ednl. Svc. award Blum-Kovler Found., 1989, Presdl. award for excellence in math. tchg., 1996. Mem. Nat. Coun. Tchrs. Math., Ill. Coun. Tchrs. Math. (spkr. at confs.). Avocations: photography, gardening. E-mail: c_fransen@hotmail.com.

FRANSON, C(ARL) IRVIN, aerospace material and process engineer, educator; b. Hibbing, Minn., Oct. 17, 1934; s. Gunnar Theodore and Ina Selena (Kamb) F.; m. Adele Esther Haselton, June 29, 1968 (div. 1969). BSChemE, Purdue U., 1956; MBA, Santa Clara U., 1963. Cert. secondary tchr., Calif. Process engr. Wyandotte (Mich.) Chem. Corp., 1956-59; materials and process engr. Lockheed Missiles and Space Co., Sunnyvale, Calif., 1959-62, staff engr., 1963-68; devel. engr. Raychem Corp., Menlo Park, Calif., 1962-63; project engr. McCormick Selph, A Teledyne Co., Hollister, Calif., 1968-69; sr. devel. engr. Johnson Controls-Globe Union, Milw., 1969-70; sr. chem. engr. Gen. Telephone-Lenkurt, San Carlos, Calif., 1970-71; sr. materials engr. Ford Aerospace (Loral), Palo Alto, Calif., 1971-91. Prin., entrepreneur Sigmaform Corp., Menlo Park, 1963-66; educator Golden Gate U., San Francisco, 1973, Chabot Coll., Hayward, Calif., 1970. Contbg. author: International Encyclopedia of Composites, 1990. Treas. Valley League-San Francisco Symphony, 1987-98; docent San Francisco Symphony, 1993-03. Mem. Soc. for Advancement of Material and Process Engrng. (exhibits chmn. 1986 nat. symposium, historian 1974, co-founder No. Calif. chpt. 1960), Internat. Exec. Svc. Corps. (registered), No. Calif. Golf Assn. Avocations: photography, travel, golf, classical music. Home: 8162 Park Villa Cir Cupertino CA 95014-4009

FRANTZEN, ALLEN JOHN, English language educator; b. New Hampton, Iowa, Oct. 20, 1947; s. John Victor and Dorothy Mae (Birmingham) F. BA, Loras Coll., Dubuque, Iowa, 1969; MA, U. Va., 1973, PhD, 1976. Asst. prof. English Oberlin (Ohio) Coll., 1976-78, Loyola U., Chgo., 1976-82, assoc. prof., 1983-88, prof., 1988—. Author: Literature of Penance, 1983, King Alfred, 1986, Desire for Origins, 1990, Before the Closet: Same-Sex Love from "Beowulf" to "Angels in America", 1998, Bloody Good: Chivalry, Sacrifice, and The Great War, 2003; editor: Speaking Two Languages, 1991, Troilus and Criseyde: The Poem and the Frame, 1993, (with D. Moffatt) The Work of Work, 1994, (with J. Niles) Anglo-Saxonism and the Construction of Social Identity, 1997. Pres. Edgewater Cmty. Coun., Chgo., 1984-85. With U.S. Army, 1969-72, Korea. Named Alexander von Humboldt Found. grantee, 1979, NEH fellow, 1990-91, Guggenheim Found. fellow, 1994; recipient Tempo All-Professor Team, Humanities, Chicago Tribune, 1993. Office: Loyola U Lake Shore Campus Dept English 6525 N Sheridan Rd Dept English Chicago IL 60626-5344 E-mail: afrantz@luc.edu.

FRANTZVE, JERRI LYN, psychologist, educator, consultant; b. Huntington Beach, Calif., Sept. 9, 1942; d. Rolland and Marjorie Weiland. Student, Purdue U., 1964-68; BA in Psychology and History, Marian Coll., 1969; MS in Organizational Psychology, George Williams Coll., 1976; PhD in Indsl. and Organizational Psychology, U. Ga., 1979. Sr. mktg. rsch. analyst Quaker Oats Co., Barrington, Ill., 1971-75; asst. prof. sch. of mgmt. SUNY, Binghamton, 1979-83; dir. employee rels. Conoco/DuPont, Ponca City, 1983-88; cons. psychologist Mass., 1988-89; assoc. prof. psychology Radford (Va.) U., 1989-94; mgmt. cons. J.L. Frantzve & Assocs., Bklyn., 1994—; divsn. head human svcs. Coll. New Rochelle, 1994-99; affiliate prof. Milano Grad. Sch. of Mgmt. New Sch. U., N.Y.C., 1999—. Instrn. cons. USAF, Rome, N.Y., 1979-83; dir. Israel Overseas Rsch. Program, Ginozar, Israel, 1982, Japanese Overseas Rsch. Program, Tokyo, 1983; coord. rsch. Ctr. for Gender Studies, Radford U., 1989-99; adj. prof. dept. psychology Bklyn. Coll., 2000—. Author: Behaving in Organizations: Tales from the Trenches, 1983, Guide to Behavior in Organizations, 1983; contbr. articles to profl. jours. Bd. dirs. Broome County Alcoholism Clinic, Binghamton, N.Y., 1980-83, bd. dirs. Broome County Mental Health Clinic, Binghamton, 1981-83; del. Dem. Caucus, Okla., 1985. Mem. APA (com. on women in psychology 1986-88), AAUW, Acad. Mgmt., Internat. Pers. Mgmt. Assn., Assn. for Women in Psychology. Avocations: ceramics, jazz, murder mysteries. Home and Office: 1804 Glenwood Rd Brooklyn NY 11230-1816 E-mail: drj4647@aol.com.

FRANZ, CAROL ANNE, special education educator; b. Andrews AFB, Md., July 15, 1968; d. David Joseph and Joanne Elizabeth (Bara) Lynch; m. George Frederick Franz, July 7, 1990. BS, George Mason U., 1990; MA, U. West Fla., 1993. Cert. early childhood educator, spl. edn. tchr., Va. Tchr. asst. Creative Learning Ctr., Pensacola, Fla., 1991-92; student advisor, grad. asst. U. West Fla., Pensacola, 1991-92; spl. edn. tchr. Virginia Beach (Va.) Schs., 1992—. Mem. NEA, Va. Edn. Assn., Virginia Beach Edn. Assn., Coun. for Exceptional Children, Coun. for Children with Behavior Disorders, Coun. on Learning Disabilities. Roman Catholic. Avocations: rollerblading, crafts, reading. Home: 47294 Silver Slate Dr Lexington Park MD 20653-2410 Office: Princess Anne Mid Sch 2509 Seaboard Rd Virginia Beach VA 23456-3501

FRANZ, FRANK ANDREW, university president, physics educator; b. Phila., Sept. 16, 1937; s. Russell Ernest and Edna (Keller) F.; m. Judy Rosenbaum, July 11, 1959; 1 child, Eric Douglas. BS in Physics, Lafayette Coll., 1959; MS in Physics, U. Ill., 1961, PhD in Physics, 1964. Research assoc. U. Ill., Urbana, 1964-65; asst. prof. physics Ind. U., Bloomington, 1967-70, assoc. prof., 1970-74, prof., 1974-85, assoc. dean Coll. Arts and Scis., 1974-77, dean faculties, 1977-82; prof. physics, provost, v.p. academic affairs and research W.Va. U., Morgantown, 1985-91; prof. physics, pres. U. Ala., Huntsville, 1991—. Guest scientist Swiss Fed. Inst. Tech., Zurich, 1965-67, U. Munich, 1978. Contbr. articles to profl. jours. NSF fellow, 1965-67, Alfred P. Sloan fellow, 1968-70. Fellow Am. Phys. Soc.; mem. AAAS, AAUP (pres. Bloomington, Ind. chpt. 1972-73), Am. Assn. Physics Tchrs., Sigma Xi. Avocation: tennis. Office: U Ala in Huntsville Office of the President Huntsville AL 35899-0001

FRANZ, JUDY R. physics educator; BA in Physics, Cornell U., 1959; MS in Physics, U. Ill., 1961, PhD in Physics, 1965. Rsch. physicist IBM Rsch. Lab., Zurich, Switzerland, 1965-67; asst. prof. dept. physics Ind. U., 1968-74, assoc. prof., 1974-79, prof., 1979-87; prof. dept. physics W.Va. U., 1987-91, U. Ala. Huntsville, 1991—; exec. officer Am. Phys. Soc., 1994—. Vis. prof. Tech. U. Munich, 1978-79, Cornell U., 1985-86, 88, 90; assoc. dean coll. arts and scis. Ind. U., 1980-82; mem. coun. on materials sci. Dept. of Energy, 1997-2002; mem. rev. com. for materials sci and tech. divsn. Los Alamos Nat. Lab., 1999-2002; sec. gen. Internat. Union Pure & Applied Physics, 2002—, assoc. sec. gen., 1999-2002. Mem. editorial bd. Am. Jour. Physics, 1985-88; contbr. numerous articles to profl. jours. Mem. divsn. materials rsch. adv. com. NSF, 1986-89, mem. divsn. undergrad. edn. adv. com., 1991-93. Humboldt rsch. fellow Munich, 1978-79; recipient Distinguished Service Citation awd., Am. Assn. of Physics Teachers, 1993, Disting. Alumni award Coll. Eng., U. Ill., Urbana-Champaign, 1997. Fellow AAAS (coun. 1995-98), Am. Phys. Soc. (various coms. and offices, chair exec. com. divsn. condensed matter physics 1993-94); mem. Am. Assn. Physics Tchrs. (pres. 1990-91), Assn. Women in Sci., Am. Inst. Physics (various coms., gov. bd. 1994—, exec. com. 1996-00), Coun. Sci. Soc. Pres. (exec. bd. 1990), Phi Beta Kappa, Sigma Xi (pres. local chpt. 1981-82). Avocations: tennis, reading. E-mail: franz@aps.org.

FRASE, RICHARD STOCKWELL, law educator; b. Washington, June 19, 1945; BA, Haverford Coll., 1967; JD, U. Chgo., 1970. Bar: Ill. 1970, Minn. 1977. Law clk. to L. Swygert, Chief Judge U.S. Ct. Appeals 7th Cir., Chgo., 1970-71; assoc. atty. Sidley & Austin, Chgo., 1972-74; rsch. assoc. U. Chgo. Law Sch., 1974-77; assoc. prof. law U. Minn. Law Sch., Mpls., 1977-81, prof. law, 1981-91, Davis prof. law, 1988-89, Berger prof. law, 1991—. Reporter Speedy Trial Act Planning Group, U.S. Dist. Ct. (no. dist.) Ill., Chgo., 1975-80; adv. bd. Fed. Sentencing Reporter, 1994—. Co-author: (textook) Criminal Justice System, 1980, (practice treatise) Minnesota Misdemeanors, 1982, 3d edit., 1999; author: (practice treatise) Criminal Evidence, 1985; co-author: (fgn. code translation) French Code of Criminal Procedure, 1988; co-editor: Encyclopedia of Crime and Justice, 2d edit., 2001, Sentencing and Sanctions in Western Countries, 2001; mem. U. Chgo. Law Rev. Mem. Phi Beta Kappa. Office: U Minn Law Sch 229 19th Ave S Minneapolis MN 55455-0400

FRASER, ARVONNE SKELTON, former United Nations ambassador; b. Lamberton, Minn., Sept. 1, 1925; d. Orland D. and Phyllis (Du Frene) Skelton; m. Donald M. Fraser, June 30, 1950; children: Thomas Skelton, Mary MacKay, John Du Frene, Lois MacKay (dec.), Anne Tallman (dec.), Jean Skelton Fraser. BA, U. Minn., 1948; LLD (hon.), Macalester Coll., 1979. Staff asst. Office Congressman Donald M. Fraser, 1963-70, adminstrv. asst., campaign mgr., 1970-76; regional coord. Carter-Mondale Com., 1976; counsellor office presdl. pers. The White House, 1977; coord. office women in devel. U.S. Agy. Internat. Devel., Washington, 1977-81; dir. Minn. and Chgo. coms. peace petition dr. Albert Einstein Peace Prize Found., Chgo., 1981-82; co-dir. ctr. on women and pub. policy Hubert H. Humphrey Inst. Pub. Affairs, U. Minn., Mpls., 1982-94; head U.S. del. Commn. On The Status of Women, UN, 1993-94, U.S. rep., amb., 1994; co-founder, dir. Internat. Women's Rights Action Watch, 1985-93. Bd. dirs. Minn. DFL Edn. Found., Internat. Women's Yr. Conf., Mexico City, 1975, UN Commn. on Status of Women, 1974, 78, Internat. Bur. Edn. Conf., Geneva, 1977; cons. Kenya Women's Leadership Conf., 1984; organizer, chairperson Orgn. Econ. Coop. and Develp./Devel. Assistance com./Women in Devel. experts group for aid-donor nations, 1978-80; dir. Ford. Found. Women's Equity Action League Fund Intern Project and World Plan Project, treas. 1974-77, bd. dirs. 1970-77, 81-83, nat. pres. 1972-74, past legis. chairperson Washington office. Author: U.N. Decade for Women: Documents and Dialogue, 1987; (with others) Women in Washington: Advocates for Public Policy, 1983, Women, Politics and the United Nations, 1995. Trustee Macalester Coll., St. Paul, 1982-84; candidate Lt. Gov. Minn., 1986; pres. Friends of Minneapolis Pub. Libr. Recipient Disting. Svc. award Women's Equity Action League, 1977, Superior Honor award U.S. Agy. Internat. Devel., 1981, Elizabeth Boyer award Women's Equity League, 1984, Leader of Leaders Outstanding Achievement award Mpls. YWCA, 1979, Resourceful Woman award Tides Found., 1992; sr. fellow Humphrey Inst. Pub. Affairs U. Minn., 1981-94, emeritus 1995; Prominent Women in Internat. Law award Am. Soc. of Internat. Law, 1995, Mpls. Internat. Citizen award, 1995. Mem. Minn. Bd. Law Examiners. Home and Office: 821 7th St SE Minneapolis MN 55414-1331

FRASER, BEVERLY ANN, assistive technology and special education consultant, physical therapist; b. Washington, Sept. 28, 1938; d. John Cabot and Esther (Smith) White; m. Alan R. Fraser, Oct. 21, 1961; children: Gregory A., Joyce E. BS in Edn., Tufts U., 1960; MA in Spl. Edn., Ea. Mich. U., 1983; PhD in Spl. Edn., Temple U., 1994. Phys. therapist Portsmouth Rehab. Ctr., NH, 1960-61, Henry Ford Hosp., Detroit, 1961-63, Wayne County Intermediate Sch. Dist., Mich., 1974-89; prin. invest., 8 rsch. studies Beverly A. Fraser, PhD, New Smyrna Beach, Fla., 1978—96; part-time faculty Temple U., Phila., 1990-93; ind. cons. Beverly A. Fraser, PhD, New Smyrna Beach, Fla., 1994—. Author: (textbooks) Gross Motor Management of Severely Impaired Students, Vol. I, 1980, Vol. II, 1980, Managing Physical Handicaps, 1983, Physical Management of Multiple Handicaps, 1987, 2d edit., 1990, Physical Characteristics Assessment, 1993, 2d edit., 1996; contbr. articles to profl. jours. Mem. AAUW (pres. New Smyrna Beach br. 1996-98), physical characteristics assessment: computer access for persons with Cerebral Palsey-Doctoral Dissertation (1993), Dir. of Ed. Found., Fla. (1999-2001), Am. Phys. Therapy Assn., Internat. Soc. Augmentative and Alt. Comm., Rehab. Engrng. and Assistive Tech. Soc. N.Am. Home and Office: 4722 Van Kleeck Dr New Smyrna Beach FL 32169-4208

FRASER, FREDERICK EWART, art educator; b. Dec. 10, 1939; m. Mary Louise Washburn Fraser, Aug. 8, 1965; children: Carol Louise, Paul Frederick. AA, Boise Jr. Coll., 1960; BS in Edn., U. Idaho, 1967; MS, U. Oreg., 1970. Elem. tchr. Emmett (Idaho) Pub. Schs., 1961-62, Nampa (Idaho) Pub. Schs., 1962-66, Boise (Idaho) Pub. Schs., 1967-69; elem. art tchr. Eugene (Oreg.) Pub. Schs., 1969-70; elem. art specialist Richland (Wash.) Pub. Schs., 1970-98, chmn. art dept., 1983-84; prof. painter and photographer, 1999—. Adj. prof. Ea. Wash. State U., Cheney, 1980-83; adj. instr. art Columbia Basin Coll., Pasco, Wash., 1999-2002; workshop presenter Wash. Art Edn. Assn., 2000; pvt. art instr., 2000-; guest lectr. Wash. State U., Tri-Cities. Prin. works include 2-D sculpture American Me, 1994; prints and paintings in numerous pvt. collections. Campaign worker Richland Dem. Com., 1972. Grantee Ednl. Dist. Svc. No. 123, Pasco, 1978, computer graphics in elem. art grantee Richland Pub. Schs., 1991. Mem. NEA, Nat. Art Edn. Assn. (workshop presenter 1997), Wash. Art Edn. Assn. (chmn. Pasco 1972, state elem. art educator of yr. award 1995), Columbia Basin Model A Ford Club, Three Rivers Model T Ford Club. Methodist. Avocations: art, photography, antique auto restorer.

FRASIER, RALPH KENNEDY, lawyer, banker; b. Winston-Salem, N.C., Sept. 16, 1938; s. LeRoy Benjamin and Kathryn O. (Kennedy) F.; m. Jeannine Quick, Aug. 1981; children: Karen D. Frasier Alston, Gail S. Frasier Cox, Ralph Kennedy Jr., Keith Lowery, Marie Kennedy, Rochelle Doar. BS, N.C. Cen. U., Durham, 1963, JD, 1965. Bar: N.C. 1965, Ohio 1976. With Wachovia Bank and Trust Co., N.A., Winston-Salem, N.C., 1965-70, v.p., counsel, 1969-70; asst. counsel, v.p. parent co. Wachovia Corp., 1970-75; v.p., gen. counsel Huntington Nat. Bank, Columbus, Ohio, 1975-76, sr. v.p., 1976-83, sec., 1981-98, exec. v.p., 1983-98, cashier, 1983-98. V.p. Huntington Bancshares Inc., 1976-86, gen. counsel, 1976-98, sec., 1981-98; sec., dir. Huntington Mortgage Co., Huntington State Bank, Huntington Leasing Co., Huntington Bancshares Fin. Corp., Huntington Investment Mgmt. Co., Huntington Nat. Life Ins. Co., Huntington Co., 1976-88; v.p., asst. sec. Huntington Bank N.E. Ohio, 1982-84; asst. sec. Huntington Bancshares Ky., 1985-97; sec. Huntington Trust Co., N.A., 1987-97, Huntington Bancshares Ind., Inc., 1986-97, Huntington Fin. Services Co., 1987-98; dir. The Huntington Nat. Bank, Columbus, Ohio, 1998—; of counsel Porter Wright Morris & Arthur LLP, Columbus, 1998—; trustee OCLC Online Computer Libr. Ctr., Inc., Dublin, Ohio, 1999—, mem. fin. com., 2000—, mem. audit com., 2000—, chair 2002—, exec. com., 2002—, pers. and compensation com., 2002-03; dir. ADATOM.COM, Inc., Milpitas, Calif., 1999-2001, mem. compensation com., 1999-2001, chair audit com., 1999-2001. Bd. dirs. Family Svcs. Winston-Salem, 1966-74, sec., 1966-71, 74, v.p., 1974; chmn. Winston-Salem Transit Authority, 1974-75; bd. dirs. Rsch. for Advancement of Personalities, 1968-71, Winston-Salem Citizens for Fair Housing, 1970-74, N.C. United Community Svcs., 1970-74; treas. Forsyth County (N.C.) Citizens Com. Adequate Justice Bldg., 1968; trustee Appalachian State U., Boone, N.C., 1973-83, endowment fund, 1973-83, Columbus Drug Edn. and Prevention Fund, Inc., 1989-92; trustee, vice chmn. employment and Edn. Commn. Franklin County, 1982-85; mem. Winston-Salem Forsyth County Sch. Bd. Adv. Coun., 1973-74, Atty. Gen's Ohio Task Force Minorities in Bus.,

1977-78; bd. dirs. Inroads Columbus, Inc., 1986-95, Greater Columbus Arts Coun., 1986-94, Columbus Urban League Inc., 1987-94, vice chmn., 1990-94; trustee Riverside Meth. Hosp. Found., 1989-90, Grant Med. Ctr., 1990-95, Grant/Riverside Meth. Hosps., 1995-97; trustee Ohio Health Corp., 1997—, treas., chair Fin./Audit Com., 2001—, exec. com., 2002—; dir. Cmty. Mutual Ins. Co., 1989-92, mem. audit com., 1989-92; trustee N.C. Ctrl. U., Durham, N.C., 1993-2001, vice-chmn., 1993-94, chmn. 1995, chair ednl. planning and acad. affairs com., 1995-98, audit, devel. and personnel coms., 1998-2001, chair audit com., 1999-2001; mem. Ohio Bd. Regents, 1987-96, vice-chmn., 1993-95, chmn., 1995-96; trustee Nat. Jud. Coll., Reno, Nevada, 1996-2002, fin. and audit com., 1997-2002 treas., chair, 1999-2002, Columbus Bar Found., 1998— (fellows com. 1998—, grants com., 1998—); AEFC Pension Adminstrn. Com. defined benefit plan of the ABA, Am. Bar Endowment, Am. Bar Found., and Nat. Jud. Coll., Chgo, Ill., 1998-2002. With AUS, 1958-64. Fellow Ohio Bar Found. (life); mem. ABA, Nat. Bar Assn., Ohio Bar Assn., Columbus Bar Assn. Office: Porter Wright Morris & Arthur LLP 41 S High St Ste 3100 Columbus OH 43215-6194 E-mail: rfrasier@porterwright.com., rfrasier@columbus.rr.com.

FRASURE, CARL MAYNARD, political science educator; b. Morgantown, W.Va., Aug. 21, 1938; s. Carl Maynard and Louise (Durham) F.; m. Beverly Brown, Sept. 1, 1962 (div. Aug. 1980); 1 child, Stephanie Frasure Goff. BS, W.Va. U., 1962, MA, 1965, MS, 1966, PhD, 1980; postgrad., Ohio U., 1985. Cert. secondary tchr., W.Va. Extension prof. W.Va. U., Morgantown, 1966-82; dir. student svcs. Bluefield (W.Va.) State U., 1982-83; prof. Salem (W.Va.)-Teikyo U., 1983—2001, chmn. polit. sci. dept., 1983—2001, asst. to acad. dean, 1984-86; prof. Fairmont (W.Va.) State Coll., 2001—. Cons. W.Va. Dept. Edn., Charleston, 1990; chair social scis. divsn., 1994-2001. Author, editor: W.Va. U. Non-credit Programs Catalog, 1980. Treas. Polit. Action Com. for Better Edn., Clarksburg, 1990; mem. Bridgeport (W.Va.) Police Civil Svc. Commn., 1993—; mem. Clarksburg Police Civil Svc. Commn, 1994—. Sgt. U.S. Army, 1957-65. U.S. Dept. Edn. grantee, 1966-70, 82-87, Options grantee Brown U., 1991. Mem. Am. Polit. Sci. Assn., W.Va. Polit. Sci. Assn., Phi Delta Kappa (treas. W.Va. U. chpt. 1984), Lions (treas. Bridgeport chpt. 1987-93, pres. 1993—), Elks (essay judge Clarksburg chpt. 1983—). Democrat. Episcopalian. Avocations: reading, politics, travel. Home: 1088 Taylor St Clarksburg WV 26301-4227 Office: Fairmont State Coll Locust Ave Salem WV

FRATESCHI, LAWRENCE JAN, economist, statistician, educator; b. Chgo., Oct. 7, 1952; s. Lawrence and Olga (Los) F. BS in Math. and Psychology, U. Ill., Chgo., 1975, MA in Econs., 1979, MS Pub. Health in Biostats. and Epidemiology, 1990, PhD in Econs., 1992. Teaching asst. dept. math, lectr. dept. info. and decision scis. U. Ill., Chgo., 1978-80, rsch. assoc. epidemiology and biostatistics Sch. Pub. Health, 1989-90; statistician Argonne (Ill.) Nat. Labs., 1980-81; asst. prof. econs. and stats. Coll. of DuPage, Glen Ellyn, Ill., 1981-86, assoc. prof., 1986-90, prof. econs., stats., 1990—; rsch. prof. epidemiology and biostats. Sch. Pub. Health U. Ill., Chgo., Ill., 1993—. Contbr. articles to profl. publs. Mem. Am. Econ. Assn., Am. Statis. Assn., Am. Pub. Health Assn., Soc. Epidemiologic Rsch., Midwest Econs. Assn., Ill. Econs. Assn., Ill. Pub. Health Assn., Phi Eta Sigma, Phi Kappa Phi, Delta Omega. Office: Coll of DuPage 425 22nd St Glen Ellyn IL 60137-6784 E-mail: fratesch@cdnet.cod.edu.

FRAUTSCHI, STEVEN CLARK, physicist, educator; b. Madison, Wis., Dec. 6, 1933; s. Lowell Emil and Grace (Clark) F.; m. Mie Okamura, Feb. 16, 1967; children: Laura, Jennifer. BA, Harvard U., 1954; PhD, Stanford U., 1958. Research fellow Kyoto U., Japan, 1958-59, U. Calif.-Berkeley, 1959-61; mem. faculty Cornell U., 1961-62, Calif. Inst. Tech., Pasadena, 1962—, prof. theoretical physics, 1966—, exec. officer physics, 1988-97, master student houses, 1997—2002. Vis. prof. U. Paris, Orsay, 1977-78 Author: Regge Poles and S-Matrix Theory, 1963, The Mechanical Universe, 1986. Guggenheim fellow, 1971-72 Mem. Am. Phys. Soc. Achievements include research and publications on Regge poles, bootstrap theory, cosmology. Home: 1561 Crest Dr Altadena CA 91001-1838 Office: 1201 E California Blvd Pasadena CA 91125-0001

FRAWLEY-O'DEA, MARY GAIL, clinical psychologist, psychoanalyst, educator; b. Lowell, Mass. d. John Edward and Mary Gail (Quinn) Frawley; m. Dennis Michael O'Dea, Jan. 1, 1996; 1 stepson, Daniel Patrick; children: Igor Ibradzic, Mollie Gilmore Chun O'Dea, Sally Kivlan Ying O'Dea. BA, St. Mary's Coll., Notre Dame, Ind., 1972; MBA, So. Meth. U., 1975; PhD, Adelphi U., 1988, postdoctoral diploma in psychoanalysis, 1996. Psychologist II Pomona (N.Y.) Mental Health Clinic, 1987-91; asst. clin. prof. Adelphi U., Derner Inst., Garden City, NY, 1989—91; pvt. practice clin. psychologist/psychoanalyst Nyack, NY, 1990—2000, New City, NY, 2000—. Faculty supr. Minn. Inst. Contemporary Psychoanalysis, Mpls.-St. Paul, 1996—; continuing edn. faculty N.Y. Psychol. Assn. for Psychoanalysis, 1998—; supr. and faculty Nat. Tng. Program for psychoanalysis, N.Y., 2000—; co-dir. Manhattan Inst. Psychoanalysis, 2001—; exec. dir. Manhattan Inst. Psychoanalysis Trauma Treatment Ctr., 2001—; mem. faculty supervisory tng. program Nat. Inst. for Psychotherapies, NY, 2002—; mem. adv. bd. Nat. Orgn. for Male Sexual Victims, 2002—, Psychoanalytic Perspectives; chair victims rights com. Archdiocese of Boston. Co-author: treating the Adult Survivor of Childhood Sexual Abuse, 1994, The Supervisory Relationship, 2000; mem. editl. bd. Studies in Gender and Sexuality; mem. adv. bd. Psychoanalytic Perspectives, 2003—; contbr. chpts. to books, articles to profl. jours. Mem.: APA (mem. pub. com. div. psychoanalysis 2001—), Manhattan Inst. Psychoanalytic Soc., N.Y. State Psychol. Assoc., Westchester Soc. Psychoanalysis and Psychotherapy. Avocations: hiking, cooking, theater, symphony, reading. Home and Office: 5 Opal Ct New City NY 10956 E-mail: mgfod@aol.com.

FRAZER, RICARDO AMANDO, psychology educator; b. Kingston, Jamaica, May 11, 1953; came to U.S., 1959; s. Neman Wesley and Vera Olive (Reid) F.; m. Katana L. Hall, May 15, 1987 (div. Mar. 10, 1995). BS, BA, U. Conn., 1977; EdM, Harvard U., 1979; PhD, Bowling Green State U., 1993. Dir. Dittmar Gallery, Evanston, Ill., 1992—99; art svcs. mgr. Northwestern U., 1992—99; asst. prof. psychology Atlanta Met. Coll. Editor: (univ. publ.) Cultural Crossroads, 1994, (jour.) Crucial Roots, 1987, Assn. Coll. Unions Internat., 1996, Human Rels. Jour., 2001. Trustee Bowling Green State U., 1989-90. Recipient Jacob Lawrence award Bowling Green State U., 1990. Mem. Am. Psychol. Soc., Assn. Black Psychologists, Ritual Artists Group (founder 1996). Avocations: poetry, photography, conga drumming, oil painting. Office: Atlanta Met Coll 1630 Metropolitan Pkwy SW Atlanta GA 30310-4448 Home: 203 Solomon Dr Ellenwood GA 30294-4508

FRAZIER, JAMES R. management educator; b. Hays, Kans., Mar. 8, 1946; s. James G. and Esta P. (Chalfant) F.; div.; 1 child, James A. AA, Hutchinson Jr. Coll., 1966; BA, Kans. Wesleyan U., 1968; AAS, USAF C.C., 1988; MA, Webster U., 1988. Cert. tchr., N.Mex., flight instr., law enforcement trainer. Commd. 2d lt. USAF, 1973, advanced through grades to capt., survival instr., 1972, B-52 aircraft comdr., 1981, command post contr., 1983, edn. specialist Albuquerque, 1986, learning resources mgr., 1988, ret., 1989; tchr. Albuquerque Pub. Schs., 1990, Embry Riddle Aero. U., Prescott, Ariz., 1990; cons. Cen. Tng. Acad., Albuquerque, 1990, sr. instr., 1990—. Co-author tng. manuals. Mem. ASTD, ASCD, Am. Mgmt. Assn. Avocations: hot-air ballooning, outdoor activities, music. Home: 2812 Alcazar St NE Albuquerque NM 87110-3516 Office: Cen Tng Acad PO Box 18041 Albuquerque NM 87185-0041

FREASIER, AILEEN W. special education educator; b. Edcouch, Tex., Nov. 12, 1924; d. James Ross and Ethel Inez (Riley) Wade; m. Ben F. Freasier, Mar. 9, 1944 (dec.); children: Ben. C., Doretha J. Christoph, Barbara F. McNally Protzman, Raymond E. (dec.), John F. BS HE, Tex. A and I Coll., 1944; MEd, La. Tech. U., 1966; postgrad. 90 hours, La. Tech. U. Tchr. Margaret Roane Day Care Ctr., Ruston, La., 1965-71; tchr. spl. edn. Lincoln Parish Schs., Ruston, 1971-81; individualized edn. program facilitator La. Tng. Inst. Monroe Spl. Sch. Dist. # 1, 1981-89; ednl. diagnostician LTI Monroe (La.) SSD # 1, 1985-95. R.S.V.P. vol. tutor, Lincoln Parish Detention Ctr., 1995—; citizen amb. People Conf. on Edn., Beijing, 1992, South Africa, 1995; presenter in field. Mem. editl. bd.: Jour. Correctional Edn., 1983—95, editor learning tech. sect.:, 1991—95; contbr. articles to ednl. publs. and profl. jours. Treas. Ruston Mayor's Commn. on Women, 1996—. Named Spl. Sch. Dist. #1 Tchr. of Yr., 1988; recipient J.E. Wallace Wallin Educator of Handicapped award La. Fedn. CEC, 1994, Meritorious Svc. award La. Dept. Pub. Safety and Corrections, 1995, Pres.'s award La. CEC-Tech. and Media, 1997. Mem. AAUW (pres. Ruston br. 1995—, state co-chair diversity task force 1993-94, state chmn. diversity com. 1994-2002, state treas. 2001-03, La. Named Gift honoree AAUW Edn. Found. 1994), CEC-Tech. and Media (treas. La. divsn. 1993-96, 2001—, Pres.'s award 1997), Internat. Correctional Edn. Assn. (spl. edn. spl. interest group, newsletter editor 1991-94, chmn. 1994-96, editl. bd. CEA Yearbook of Correctional Edn. 1998—), Nat. Soc. DAR (Long Leaf Pine chpt., regent 1997-99, constitution week chmn. 2000—), Lincoln Parish Ret. Tchrs. Assn. (yearbook editor 1996—, pres. 1998-2000), Phi Delta Kappa (past pres. chpt. 1994-96, newsletter editor 1989-93, 97-98, treas. 2002—), Kappa Kappa Iota (state pres. 1991-92, nat. scholarship com. 1995-97, nat. tech. com. 1997-99, chmn. nat. tech. com. 1999-2000, nat. profl. devel. com. 2001-03, chmn. Eta State Scholarship Com., 2002-03, chmn. bylaws com. 2003—, v.p. 2003—, chmn. Eta State Loretta Doerr award 1995, Epsilon conclave pres. 1985-87, 99-2000). Home: PO Box 1595 Ruston LA 71273-1595 E-mail: aileenwf@bayou.com.

FRECKLETON, JON EDWARD, engineering educator, consultant, retired military officer; b. Rochester, N.Y., Feb. 23, 1939; s. William Howard and Kathryne Ann (Staud) F.; m. Terence Quirke Washburn, Mar. 15, 1966 (div. Mar. 1975); children: Melinda Leigh (DVM), Jon Karl. BSME, U. Rochester, 1961; MS in Edn., Nazareth Coll., Rochester, 1986. Profl. engr., N.Y. Engr. Eastman Kodak, Rochester, 1961-67; tree farmer Rochester, 1963—; ins. agt. W. Howard Freckleton Agy., Rochester, 1967-69; engr. N.Y. Dept. Transp., Rochester, 1969; mgr. Xerox Corp., Rochester, 1969-84; tchr. McQuaid Jesuit High Sch., Rochester, 1984-85; engring. cons. Rochester, 1984—; assoc. prof. emeritus Coll. Engring. Rochester Inst. Tech., 1985-98. Vis. assoc. prof. CAST RIT, 1998—; cons. RIT Rsch. Corp., Rochester, 1987—; workshop leader Boothroyd Dewhurst Inc., Wakefield, R.I., 1985—; workshop presenter RIT Profl. Tng. & Devel., Rochester, 1989—; com. mem. Ctr. for Integrated Mfg., Rochester, 1990-96. Editor graphics text; co-author software program; contbr. articles to profl. jours. Mem. region fish and wildlife mgmt. bd. N.Y. State Dept. Environ. Conservation, Avon, 1991-99; mem. Penfield (N.Y.) Planning Bd., 1987-89; treas. N.E. Penfield Fire Dist., 1990-97, commr., 1998—, chmn., 1999—; mem., treas. Webster Vol. Fire Dept., N.Y., 1979-83, bd. dirs., 1998-2002; committeeman Rep. Town & Country Com., Penfield & Monroe Cty, 1972—. With USAF, 1961-89, lt. col. USAFR ret. Named Fireman of Yr. Webster Fairport Elks, 1986; recipient N.Y. State Conspicuous Svc. Cross, 1994; Mosey fellow U. Western Australia, Perth, 1989. Mem. NSPE, N.Y. State Soc. Profl. Engrs. (life), Monroe County Soc. Profl. Engrs. (bd. dirs. 1995-97), Am. Soc. Engring. Edn., N.Y. State Forest Owners, N.Y. State Christmas Tree Growers, Adirondack Mountain Club (treas. Genesee chpt. 1991-93), Tau Beta Pi. Republican. Roman Catholic. Avocations: mountain climbing, photography, woodworking, travel, gardening. Home: 1651 Harris Rd Penfield NY 14526-1815 Office: Rochester Inst Tech 1 Lomb Memorial Dr Rochester NY 14623-5603

FREDERICK, ALBERT BRUCE, historian, educator; b. Norristown, Pa., June 8, 1930; s. Miles L. and Mary E. (Kready) F.; m. Norma S. Nai, Apr. 4, 1953; children: Carl, Paula, Neil, Adam. BS, West Chester (Pa.) State Tchrs. Coll., 1952; MEd, Temple U., 1961; PhD, U. Minn., 1974. Tchr. Del. Pub. Schs., 1952-66; assoc. prof. phys. edn. U. Wis. Superior, 1966-76; prof. SUNY, Brockport, 1976-84, U.S. Sports Acad., Riyadh, Saudi Arabia, 1984-87; curator Internat. Gymnastics Hall of Fame, Oceanside, Calif., 1987-97; ednl. cons. Midatlantic Am. Automobile Assn., Phila., 1988—. Founder Am. Assn. Advancement Tension Control, Mpls., 1971; hon. mem. Del. Soccer Ofcls., Wilmington, Del., 1989. Author: 212 Ideas for Physical Education, 1963, Gymnastics for Women (Author's Day honoree 1981), Gymnastics for Men, 1969, Roots of American Gymnastics, 1995, 2d edit., 1997; editor: Total Health and Fitness, 1988. With USN, 1947-60. Recipient McCloy Rsch. award Gymnastic Coaches Assn., 1973, Rsch. award Nat. Assn. Collegiate Gymnastic Coaches, 1983; named to Gymnastics Hall of Fame, 1990. Mem. AAHPERD (emeritus), Sport Psychology Acad., Del. Assn. Health, Phys. Edn., and Recreation (pres., Honor award 1965), Lions, Phi Delta Kappa. Roman Catholic. Avocations: sport history, rotoscopic drawing, gymnastic genealogy. Home: 1043 11th Ave Wilmington DE 19808-4970

FREDERICK, SUSAN LOUISE, preschool educator; b. Somers Point, N.J., May 2, 1964; d. Ingeborg Louise (Böhmer) Kimbark; m. R. Scott Frederick, Oct. 6, 1984; 1 child, Taylor Scott. BS in Edn. with honors, Millersville (Pa.) U., 1993; postgrad., Millersville U., 2002—. Cert. elem. and early childhood tchr. Graphic artist Datcon Instrument Co., East Petersburg, Pa., 1984-86; day care provider Small Steps Early Learning Ctr., Lancaster, Pa., 1986-89; substitute elem. tchr. Lancaster County Sch. Dists., 1993-94; elem. co-op tchr. Manheim Twp. Parent's Co-op, Lancaster, 1993; day care provider Small Frey's Children's Ctr., Manheim, Pa., 1991-96; pre-kindergarten, presch. tchr. St. Peter's Presch., Lancaster, 1993—; elem. co-op. tchr. Manheim Twp. Parent's Co-op., Lancaster, 1995, 1997—2000, supr. student tchr., 2003. Mem. bd. Christian edn. St. Paul's United Ch. of Christ, Manheim, Pa., 1985-87, co-dir. vacation bible sch., 1987; mem. Manheim Area Jaycees, 1988-89; v.p. Stiegel Elem. Sch. P.T.O., 2001-2002, pres., 2003-; sponsor Youth Encouragement program St. Paul's U.C.C., Manheim, Pa., 2001—. Mem. ASCD, Phi Kappa Phi. Avocations: crafts, reading, gardening, decorating, indoor soccer. Home: 125 E Ferdinand St Manheim PA 17545-1605

FREDERICKS, MARGARET MATTERSON, elementary education educator; b. Syracuse, N.Y., Nov. 9, 1930; d. Curtiss Dutton and Elizabeth Logan (Morrison) Matterson; m. Roland S. Fredericks, Sept. 1951; children: Margaret Jean, Elizabeth Clara. Degree, Syracuse U., 1952, Moray House, Edinburgh U., Scotland, 1966; M of Liberal Learning, Marietta Coll., 1984. Sch. savs. Amsterdam (N.Y.) Savs. Bank, 1967-70; 5th grade tchr. Amsterdam Pub. Schs., 1970; elem. edn. tchr. Marietta City Schs., 1971-98, ret., 1998; organizer, founder Marietta Boys and Girls Club of Washington County, 1998—. Course of study lang. arts. Marietta City Schs. Mem. Dems. for Ohio; elder Presbyn. Ch. Recipient Citizen of Yr., Civitan Club, 2002. Mem. AAUW, LVW, Ohio Coun. Tchrs. English, Ret. Tchrs. Ohio, Ret. Tchrs. Washington County, Marietta Natural History Soc., Rotary Anne, Betsey Mills Club (women's bd. dirs.), Delta Kappa Gamma. Avocations: hiking, canoeing, reading. Home: 303 Ohio St Marietta OH 45750-3139

FREDERICKS, WILLIAM JOHN, chemistry educator; b. San Diego, Sept. 18, 1924; s. William and Jenney (Cunnion) F.; m. Lola M. Schneider, Sept. 20, 1942. BS, San Diego State Coll., 1951; PhD, Oreg. State U., 1955. Technician, planner USN, San Diego, 1942-46; electronics technician Waldorf Appliance Co., San Diego, 1946-47; jr. civil engr. Calif. Div. Architecture, San Diego, 1947-51; phys. chemist, solid state mgr. Stanford Research Inst., Menlo Park, Calif., 1956-62; prof. chemistry Oreg. State U., Corvallis, 1962-87, prof. chemistry emeritus, 1988—. Rsch. prof. chemistry and materials sci. U. Ala., Huntsville, 1988-94, ret.; vis. acad. Atomic Research Establishment, Harwell, Eng., 1973-74; sr. vis. fellow U. Western Ont. Ctr. Chem. Physics, 1982; cons. in field; faculty advisor Oreg. State U. Flying Club. Contbr. articles to profl. jours. Chmn. Corvallis Airport Commn., 1979-83. Fulbright fellow 1955-56. Mem. AAAS. Am. Assn. Crystal Growth (mem. exec. bd. West Sect. 1976-86), Am. Chem. Soc. (sect. chmn.), Am. Phys. Soc., Materials Research Soc. Democrat. Avocations: flying, fishing, bonzai, golfing. Office: 11443 SW 82nd Court Rd Ocala FL 34481-3566

FREDERKING, KATHY HAHN, elementary school librarian; b. Dodge City, Kans., Mar. 24, 1954; d. Donald and V. June (West) Hahn; m. Hal Frederking, Aug. 20, 1978; children: Jerrod, Joel, Emileigh. BS, Ft. Hays State U., 1975; MLS, Emporia State U., 1994. Cert. elem. edn. tchr., Kans. Tchr. Unified Sch. Dist. 328, Wilson, Kans., 1976-79, Unified Sch. Dist. 443, Dodge City, 1979—. Mem. tech. com. Unified Sch. Dist. 443, Dodge City, 1992-95. Co-dir. youth fellowship Holy Cross Luth. Ch., Dodge City, 1991-2000. Mem. NEA (bldg. rep. 1987-94, 99—, chief negotiator 2001-02, treas. 2002-03, Ark Valley Reading Cir. commr. 1996-2003), Kans. Reading Assn. (exec. bd. 1994-2000, pres. 1998-99, zone 5 coord. 1991-93, William Allen White book selection com. 1998-2002, Bill Martin Jr. picture book award com. 1995—), Delta Kappa Gamma (sec. 2002—), Phi Delta Kappa (chpt. treas. 1999—). Republican. Lutheran. Avocations: following children's sports, reading, counted cross-stitching.

FREDRICKSON, GEORGE MARSH, history educator; b. Bristol, Conn., July 16, 1934; s. George Fredrickson and Gertrude (Marsh) F.; m. Helene Osouf, Oct. 16, 1956; children: Anne, Laurel, Thomas, Caroline. AB, Harvard U., 1956, PhD, 1964. Instr. history Harvard U., Cambridge, Mass., 1963-66; assoc. prof. history Northwestern U., Evanston, Ill., 1966-71, prof., 1971-84, William Smith Mason prof. Am. history, 1979-84; Edgar E. Robinson prof. U.S. history Stanford U., Calif., 1984—2002, prof. emeritus, 2002—. Fulbright prof. Moscow U., 1983, Harmsworth prof. Am. history Oxford U., 1988-89. Author: The Inner Civil War, 1965, 2d edit., 1993, The Black Image in the White Mind, 1971, 2d edit., 1987 (Anisfield-Wolf award 1972), White Supremacy, 1981 (Ralph Waldo Emerson award 1981, Merle Curti award, 1982, Pulitzer prize finalist 1982), The Arrogance of Race, 1988, Black Liberation, 1995, The Comparative Imagination, 1997, Racism: A Short History, 2002; co-author: America: Past and Present, 6th edit., 2002; editor: A Nation Divided, 1975. Served to lt. USN, 1957-60. Guggenheim fellow, 1967-68; NEH fellow, 1973-74; Ctr. for Advanced Studies in Behavioral Scis. fellow, 1977-78; NEH fellow, 1985-86; Ford sr. fellow DuBois Inst., Harvard U., 1993. Fellow Soc. Am. Historians, Am. Antiquarian Soc., Am. Acad. Arts and Scis.; mem. Am. Hist. Assn., Orgn. Am. Historians (pres. 1997-98), So. Hist. Assn. Home: 741 Esplanada Way Palo Alto CA 94305-1013 Office: Stanford Univ Dept History Stanford CA 94305 E-mail: fredrick@stanford.edu.

FREEBURG, RICHARD L. primary education educator; Elem. tchr. Nicollet Jr. High Sch., tchr. tech. edn. Recipient Tchr. Excellence award Internat. Tech. Edn. Assn., 1992. Office: Nicollet Jr High Sch 400 E 134th St Burnsville MN 55337-4010

FREED, DEBOW, academic administrator; b. Hendersonville, Tenn., Aug. 26, 1925; s. John Walter and Ella Lee (DeBow) F.; m. Catherine Carol Moore, Sept. 10, 1949; 1 child, Debow II. BS, U.S. Mil. Acad., 1946; grad., U.S. Inf. Sch., 1953, U.S. Army Command and Gen. Staff Coll., 1959; MS, U. Kans., 1961; PhD, U. N.Mex., 1966; grad., U.S. Air War Coll., 1966; LLD, Monmouth (Ill.) Coll., 1987; DLitt (hon.), Ohio No. U., 1999. Comdg. officer U.S. Army, 1946; comdr. 35th Inf. Japan, 1947-48; asst. to cmdr. 17th Airborne Div., 1948-49; comdr. 26th Inf., Federal Republic of Germany, 1949-51; asst. to chief U.S. Mission, Iran, and chief Middle Ea. Affairs, 1951-53; instr. The Inf. Sch., 1953-56; comdr. 32d Inf., Korea, 1956-57; instr. Command and Gen. Staff Coll., 1957-58; chief nuclear br. U.S. Atomic Energy Agy., 1961-65; chief plans divsn. US Army, Vietnam, 1966-67; prof. physics dept. U.S. Mil. Acad., 1967-69, ret., 1969; dean Mt. Union Coll., 1969-74; pres. Monmouth Coll., 1974-79, Ohio No. U., Ada, 1979—99, pres. emeritus, 1999—; pres. U. Findlay, 2003—. Chmn. Assoc. Colls. of Midwest, 1977-79, others. Author: Using Nuclear Capabilities, 1959, Pulsed Neutron Techniques, 1965; contbr. articles, revs. to profl. publs.; editor: Atomic Development Report, 1962-64. Bd. dirs. Presbyn. Coll. Union, 1974-79; trustee Ctr. Sci. and Industry, 1982—, Toledo Symphony, 1994—, Blanchard Valley Health Assn., 1999—, Blanchard Valley Health Found., 2000—; chmn., bd. trustees, COSI Endowment Found., 2001; v.p., dir. Buckeye coun. Boy Scouts Am., 1972-74, dir. Prairie coun., 1974-78. Decorated Bronze Star, (2) Legion of Merit, Legion of Honor Iran, Army Commendation medal, Air medal, Joint Svcs. Commendation medal, others; recipient various civic awards; Associated Western Univs. fellow, 1963-65; AEC fellow, 1963-65; Fgn. Policy Rsch. Inst. fellow, 1966; named Ohio Commodore, 1990. Mem. Assn. Meth. Colls. and Univs. (bd. dirs. 1979-99), Ohio Coll. Assn. (bd. dirs. 1980-84, 85-88, pres. 89-90), Ohio Found. Independent Colls. (bd. dirs. 1979-99), Am. Assn. Pres. of Colls. and Univs. (bd. dirs. 1988-99, treas. 1997-98, v.p. 1998-99), Ohio Commodores, Sixma Xi, Phi Kappa Phi, Phi Eta Sigma, Delta Theta Phi, Omicron Delta Kappa. Home: 205 W Lima Ave Ada OH 45810-1635 Office: Ohio No U Office of Pres Emeritus Ada OH 45810 E-mail: d-freed@onu.edu.

FREED, MELVYN NORRIS, retired higher education administrator and educator, writer; b. Kansas City, Mo., Apr. 30, 1937; s. Carl and Betty (Wachtel) F.; m. Janet Lea Triplitt, Dec. 26, 1971; children: David A., Edward L. BA in Econs. with distinction, U. Mo., Kansas City, 1959; MS in Edn., So. Ill. U., Carbondale, 1962, PhD in Higher Edn., 1965. Dir. instl. rsch. Ark. State U., Jonesboro, 1965-72, v.p. for adminstrn., 1972-76, Govs. State U., University Pk., Ill., 1977-82, univ. prof., rsch. assoc., 1982-87; writer, 1987—. Co-founder, past dir. measurement and rsch. So. Ctrl. Region Edn. Lab., Little Rock; past evaluator rsch. grants U.S. Office of Edn., Washington; mem. Evans Scholars Found., 2002—; co-founder U.S. River Acad. (chartered by Congress) in the late 1960s. Co-author: The Educator's Desk Reference, 1989 (1 of 30 Best Reference Books 1989, Best Single Vol. Reference Book in Edn. 1989), 2d edit., 2002, Business Information Desk Reference, 1991, Patient's Desk Reference, 1994, others; contbr. articles to profl. jours.; editor: Handbook of Statistical Procedures and Their Computer Applications, 1991; tool inventor. Village trustee, Hazel Crest, Ill., 1997—; plan commr., 1988—97; adminstrv. asst. Congressman William Alexander, Washington, 1969; v.p., bd. dirs. Calumet Coun. Boy Scouts Am., Munster, Ind., 1978—95, 2001—; bd. dirs. Bremen H.S. Dist. 228 Ednl. Found., 1998—, pres., 2002—. Recipient U.S. Congl. citation, Washington, 1971, Silver Beaver award Boy Scouts Am., 1976, Disting. Svcs. award Ark. State U., 1975, Nat. Endowment award; James E. West fellow Calumet Coun. Boy Scouts Am., 2002, Daniel Carter Beard Masonic Scouter award Boy Scouts Am., 2003. Mem. Masons (past master), Scottish Rite (knight comdr. Ct. of Honor 1979), Par Club (life), Alpha Epsilon Pi, Phi Kappa Phi, Omicron Delta Kappa. Home: 17023 Magnolia Dr Hazel Crest IL 60429-1020

FREEDBERG, DAVID ADRIAN, art educator, historian; b. Capetown, South Africa, June 1, 1948; s. William and Eleonore (Kupfer) F.; children: Hannah, William. BA, Yale U., 1969; DPhil, Oxford U., 1973. Lectr. art Westfield Coll., U. London, 1973-76, Courtauld Inst. Art, U. London, 1976-84; prof. Barnard Coll., Columbia U., N.Y.C., 1984-86, Columbia U., 1986—, dir. Italian Acad. Advanced Studies in Am., 2000—. Slade prof. fine art U. Oxford, 1983-84; dir. Print Quar., London, 1983—; Andrew W. Mellon prof. Nat. Gallery Art, 1996-98. Author: Dutch Landscape Prints of the Seventeenth Century, 1980, Rubens: The Life of Christ After the Passion, 1984, Iconoclasts and Their Motives, 1985, Iconoclasm and Painting in the Revolt of the Netherlands, 1566-1609, 1988, The Prints of Pieter Bruegel the Elder, 1989, The Power of Images: Studies in the History and Theory of Response, 1989, Joseph Kosuth the Play of the Unmentionable, 1992, Peter Paul Rubens: Paintings and Oil Sketches, 1995, The Eye of the Lynx: Galileo, His Friends, and the Beginnings of Modern Natural History, 2002; author: (with E. Baldini) The Paper Museum of Cassiano dal Pozzo: Citrus Fruit, 1997; author: (with A. Scott) The Paper Museum of Cassiano dal Pozzo: Fossil Woods, 2000. Mem. Am. Acad. Arts and Scis., Am. Philos. Soc. Office: Columbia University Schermerhorn Hall New York NY 10027

FREEDMAN, DAVID AMIEL, statistics educator, consultant; b. Montreal, Que., Can., Mar. 5, 1938; came to U.S., 1958; s. Abraham and Goldie (Yelin) F.; children: Deborah, Joshua. B.Sc., McGill U., Montreal, 1958; MA, Princeton U., 1959, PhD, 1960. Prof. stats. U. Calif.-Berkeley, 1961—, Miller prof., 1991, chmn. dept. stats., 1981-86. Cons. Bank of Can., Ottawa, 1971-72, WHO, 1973, Carnegie Commn., 1976, Dept. Energy, 1978-87, Bur. Census, 1983, 98, Dept. Justice, 1984, 89-92, 96, 2002, Brobeck, Phleger & Harrison, 1985-89, Skadden Arps, 1986, 2002, County of Los Angeles, 1989, Fed. Jud. Ctr., 1993. Author: Markov Chains, 1971, Brownian Motion and Diffusion, 1971, Approximating Countable Markov Chains, 1972, Mathematical Methods in Statistics, 1977, Statistics, 1978, 3d edit., 1997; contbr. numerous articles to profl. publs. Recipient John J. Carty award for Advancement of Sci., NAS, 2003; fellow, Can. Coun., 1960, Sloan Found., 1964. Mem.: Am. Acad. Scis., Nat. Acad. Scis. Home: 901 Alvarado Rd Berkeley CA 94705-1551 Office: U Calif-Berkeley Dept Stats Berkeley CA 94720-3860

FREEDMAN, DAVID NOEL, religious studies educator; b. NYC, May 12, 1922; s. David and Beatrice (Goodman) F.; m. Cornelia Anne Pryor, May 16, 1944; children: Meredith Anne, Nadezhda, David Micaiah, Jonathan Pryor. Student, CCNY, 1935-38; AB, UCLA, 1939; BTh, Princeton Theol. Sem., 1944; PhD, Johns Hopkins U., 1948; LittD, U. Pacific, 1973; ScD, Davis and Elkins Coll., 1974. Ordained to ministry Presbyn. Ch., 1944; supply pastor in Acme and Deming, Wash., 1944-45; tchg. fellow, then asst. instr. Johns Hopkins U., 1946-48; asst. prof., then prof. Hebrew and Old Testament lit. Western Theol. Sem., Pitts., 1948-60; prof. Pitts. Theol. Sem., 1960-61, James A. Kelso prof., 1961-64; prof. Old Testament San Francisco Theol. Sem., 1964-70, Gray prof. Hebrew exegesis, 1970-71, dean of faculty, 1966-70, acting dean of sem., 1970-71; prof. Old Testament Grad. Theol. Union, Berkeley, Calif., 1964-71; prof. dept. Nr. Ea. studies U. Mich., Ann Arbor, 1971-92, Thurnau prof. Bibl. studies, 1984-92, dir. program on studies in religion, 1971-91; prof., endowed chair in Hebrew Bibl. studies U. Calif., San Diego, 1987—, dir. religious studies program, 1989-97. Danforth vis. prof. Internat. Christian U., Tokyo, 1967; vis. prof. Hebrew U., Jerusalem, 1977, Macquarie U., N.S.W., Australia, 1980, U. Queensland (Australia), 1982, 84, U. Calif., San Diego, 1985-87; Green vis. prof. Tex. Christian U., Ft. Worth, 1981; dir. Albright Inst. Archeol. Rsch., 1969-70, dir., 1976-77; lectr. in field. Author: The Published Works of W.F. Albright, 1975, Pottery, Poetry and Prophecy, 1980, The Unity of the Hebrew Bible, 1991 (paperback edit., 1993), Divine Commitment and Human Obligation, 1997, Psalm 119, 1999, The Nine Commandments, 2000; co-author: (with J.D. Smart) God Has Spoken, 1949, (with F.M. Cross, Jr.) Early Hebrew Orthography, 1952, (with John M. Allegro) The People of the Dead Sea Scrolls, 1958, (with R.M. Grant) The Secret Sayings of Jesus, 1960, (with F.M. Cross, Jr.) Ancient Yahwistic Poetry, 1964, rev. edit., 1975, 97, (with M. Dothan) Ashdod I, 1967, (with L.G. Running) William F. Albright: Twentieth Century Genius, 1975, 2d edit., 1991, (with B. Mazar, G. Cornfeld) The Mountain of the Lord, 1975, (with W. Phillips) An Explorer's Life of Jesus, 1975, (with G. Cornfeld) Archaeology of the Bible: Book by Book, 1976, (with K.A. Mathews) The Paleo-Hebrew Leviticus Scroll, 1985, The Unity of the Hebrew Bible, 1991, (with D. Forbes and F. Andersen) Studies in Hebrew and Aramaic Orthography, 1992, (with Sara Mandell) The Relationship between Herodotus' History and Primary History, 1993; co-author, editor: (with F. Andersen) Anchor Bible Series Hosea, 1980, Anchor Bible Series Amos, 1989, Micah, 2000; editor: (with G.E. Wright) The Biblical Archaeologist, Reader I, 1961, (with E.F. Campbell, Jr.) The Biblical Archaeologist, Reader 2, 1964, Reader 3, 1970, Reader 4, 1983, (with W.F. Albright) The Anchor Bible, 1964—, including, Genesis, 1964, James, Peter and Jude, 1964, Jeremiah, 1965, Job, 1965, 2d edit., 1973, Proverbs and Ecclesiastes, 1965, I Chronicles, II Chronicles, Ezra-Nehemiah, 1965, Psalms I, 1966, John I, 1966, Acts of the Apostles, 1967, II Isaiah, 1968, Psalms II, 1968, John II, 1970, Psalms III, 1970, Esther, 1971, Matthew, 1971, Lamentations, 1972, 2d edit., 1992, To the Hebrews, 1972, Ephesians 1-3, 4-6, 1974, I and II Esdras, 1974, Judges, 1975, Revelation, 1975, Ruth, 1975, I Maccabees, 1976, I Corinthians, 1976, Additions, 1977, Song of Songs, 1977, Daniel, 1978, Wisdom of Solomon, 1979, I Samuel, 1980, Hosea, 1980, Luke I, 1981, Joshua, 1982, Epistles of John, 1983, II Maccabees, 1983, II Samuel, 1984, II Corinthians, 1984, Luke II, 1985, Judith, 1985, Mark, 1986, Haggai-Zechariah 1-8, 1987, Ecclesiasticus, 1987, 2 Kings, 1988, Amos, 1989, Titus, 1990, Jonah, 1990, Leviticus I, 1991, Deuteronomy I, 1991, Numbers 1-20, 1993, Romans, 1993, Jude and 2 Peter, 1993, Zechariah 9-14, 1993, Zephaniah, 1994, Colossians, 1995, Joel, 1995, James, 1995, Obadiah, 1996, Tobit, 1996, Ecclesiastes, 1997, Ezekiel 21-37, 1997, Galatians, 1997, Malachi, 1998, Acts of the Apostles, 1998, Exodus 1-18, 1999, Jeremiah 1-20, 1999, Mark 1-8, 2000, Numbers 21-36, 2000, 1 Peter, 2001, Isaiah 1-39, 2000, Thessalonians 1&2, 2000, Leviticus 17-22, 2000, Proverbs 1-9, 2000, Micah, 2000, Philemon, 2000, Timothy 1&2, 2001, Hebrews, 2001, Leviticus 23-27, 2001, Habakkuk, 2001, 1 Kings, 2001, Isaiah 40-55, 2002, Isaiah 56-66, 2003; editor Anchor Bible Ref. Libr., Jesus Within Judaism, 1988, Archaeology of the Land of the Bible, 1990, The Tree of Life, 1990, A Marginal Jew Vol. 1, 1991, The Pentateuch, 1991, The Rise of Jewish Nationalism, 1992, History and Prophecy, 1993, Jesus and the Dead Sea Scrolls, 1993, The Birth of the Messiah, 1993, The Death of the Messiah, 2 vols., 1994, Introduction to Rabbinical Literature, 1994, A Marginal Jew, vol. 2, 1994, vol. 3, 2001, The Scepter and the Star, 1995, The Gnostic Scriptures, 1995, Reclaiming The Dead Sea Scrolls, 1995, An Introduction to the New Testament, 1997, Education in Ancient Israel, 1998, Warrior, Dancer, Seductress, Queen, 1998, A History of the Synoptic Problem, 1999, Archaeology of the Land of the Bible, vol. 2, 2001, A Marginal Jew, vol. 3, 2001, Peoples of an Almighty God, 2002, Introduction to the Gospel of John, 2003; editor: Eerdmans Critical Commentary, 1 and 2 Timothy, 1999, Biblical Resource Series, The Parables of Jesus, 2000, The Rivers of Paradise, 2000, Biblein its World Series: David's Secret Demons, 2001, Music in Ancient Israel/Palestine, 2002, Injustice Made Legal: Deuteronomic Law and the Plight of Widows, Strangers, and Orphans in Ancient Israel, 2002, The Psalms, 2003, Piety and Politics, 2003; (with J. Greenfield) New Directions in Biblical Archaeology, 1969; (with J.A. Baird) The Computer Bible, 1971, A Critical Concordance to the Synoptic Gospels, 1971, An Analytic Linguistic Concordance to the Book of Isaiah, 1971, I, II, III John: Forward and Reverse Concordance and Index, 1971, A Critical Concordance to Hosea, Amos, Micah, 1972, A Critical Concordance of Haggai, Zechariah, Malachi, 1973, A Critical Concordance to the Gospel of John, 1974, A Synoptic Concordance of Aramaic Inscriptions, 1975, A Linguistic Concordance of Ruth and Jonah, 1976, A Linguistic Concordance of Jeremiah, 1978, Syntactical and Critical Concordance of Jeremiah, 1978, Synoptic Abstract, 1978, I and II Corinthians, 1979, Zechariah, 1979, Galatians, 1980, Ephesians, 1981, Philippians, 1982, Colossians, 1983, Pastoral Epistles, 1984, 1 & 2 Thessalaians, 1985, Density Plots in Ezekiel, 1986, Exodus, 1987, Hebrews, 1988, Ruth, 1989, James, 1991, 1 & 2 Peter, 1991, 1, 2 & 3 John and Jude, 1991, Psalms, Job and Proverbs, 1992, Apocalypse, 1993, The Pentateuch, 1995, Aramaic Inscriptions, 1975, (with T. Kachel) Religion and the Academic Scene, 1975, Am. Schs. Oriental Research publs; co-editor: Scrolls from Qumran Cave I, 1972, Jesus: The Four Gospels, 1973, Palestine in Transition, 1983, The Bible and its Traditions, 1983, Pomegranates and Golden Bells, 1995; Reader's Digest editor: Atlas of the Bible, 1981, Family Guide to the Bible, 1984, Mysteries of the Bible, 1988, Who's Who in the Bible, 1994, The Bible Through the Ages, 1996, Complete Guide to the Bible, 1998; The Leningrad Codex, 1998, Untold Stories: The Bible and Ugaritic Studies in the Twentieth Century, 2001; assoc. editor Jour. Bible Lit., 1952-54, editor, 1955-59; cons. editor Interpreter's Dictionary of the Bible, 1957-60, Theologisches Wörterbuch des Alten Testaments, 1970—, English Translation Theological Dictionary of the Old Testament, 1975—; editor in chief The Anchor Bible Dictionary, 6 vols., 1992, Eerdmans Dictionary of the Bible, 2000; co-editor (with W.H. Propp and Baruch Halpern) The Hebrew Bible and Its Interpreters, 1990; contbr. articles to profl. jours. Recipient prize in New Testament exegesis Princeton Theol. Sem., 1943, Carey-Thomas award for Anchor Bible, 1965, Layman's Nat. Bible Com. award, 1978, 3 awards for Anchor Bible Bibl. Archaeol. Soc., 1993; William H. Green fellow in Old Testament, 1944, William S. Rayner fellow Johns Hopkins U., 1946, 47, Guggenheim fellow, 1959, Am. Assn. Theol. Schs. fellow, 1963; Am. Coun. Learned Socs. grantee-in-aid, 1967, 76; named Disting. Faculty lectr. U. Calif., San Diego, 2002. Fellow U. Mich. Soc. Fellows (sr., chmn. 1980-82); mem. Soc. Bibl. Lit. (pres. 1975-76), Am. Oriental Soc., Am. Schs. Oriental Rsch. (v.p. 1970-82, editor bull. 1974-78, editor Bibl. Archeologist 1976-82, dir. publs. 1974-82), Archaeol. Inst. Am., Am. Acad. Religion, Bibl. Colloquium (sec.-treas. 1960-90), Bibl. Colloquium West (sec., treas. 2000—). Presbyterian. Office: U Calif San Diego Dept History 0104 9500 Gilman Dr La Jolla CA 92093-0104 E-mail: dnfreedman@ucsd.edu.

FREEDMAN, JAMES OLIVER, former university president, lawyer; b. Manchester, N.H., Sept. 21, 1935; s. Louis A. and Sophie (Gottesman) Freedman, Louis A. and Sophie (Gottesman) Freedman. AB, Harvard U., 1957; LLB, Yale U., 1962; LLD (hon.), Cornell Coll., 1982; LLD (hon.), So. Meth U., 1988; LLD (hon.), Mt. Holyoke Coll., 1988, Vt. Law Sch., 1992, U. N.H., 1992; LHD (hon.), St. Ambrose U., 1984, Colby-Sawyer Coll., 1995, Dartmouth Coll., 1998, Hebrew Union Coll., 1998, Brown U., 1999, Whitman Coll., 1999; LHD (hon.), U. Rochester, 2002. Bar: N.H. 1962, Pa. 1971, Iowa 1982. Prof. law U. Pa., 1964—82, assoc. provost, 1978, dean, 1979—82, also univ. ombudsman, 1973—76; pres., disting. prof. law and polit. sci. U. Iowa, 1982—87; pres. Dartmouth Coll., Hanover, 1987—98, Am. Acad. Arts and Scis., 2000—01; Henry N. Rapaport lectr. Jewish Theol. Sem., 2001. 8th ann. Roy R. Ray lectr. So. Meth. U. Sch. Law, 1985; Tyrell Williams lectr. Washington U. Sch. Law, 1984; Francis Greenwood Peabody lectr. MIT, 1999; W.E.B. du Bois lectr. U. Md.-Balt. County, 1999; bd. dirs. Houghton Mifflin Co., 1991—2001; Howard R. Bowen lectr. Claremont Grad. U., 1997; Simon H. Rifkind lectr. CCNY, 2000. Author: Crisis and Legitimacy: The Administrative Process and American Government, 1978, Idealism and Liberal Education, 1996; contbr. Bd. govs. Am. Jewish Com., 1999—; mem. Phila. Bd. Ethics, 1981—82; chmn. Pa. Legis. Reapportionment Commn., 1981, Iowa Gov.'s Task Force on Fgn. Lang. Studies and Internat. Edn., 1982—83; trustee Jewish Pub. Soc., 1979—88, Brandeis U., 2000—, Hebrew Union Coll., 2001—; bd. dirs. Am. Coun. on Edn.; bd. dirs. Jacob K. Javits fellows program U.S. Dept. Edn., 1993—97; bd. dirs. Salzburg Seminar Am. Studies, 1988—92, 1994—97. Recipient Am. Book award, 1990, William O. Douglas First Amendment award, Anti-Defamation League, 1991, Gilda Radner award, Wellness Cmty. Greater Boston, Frederic W. Ness award, Assn. Am. Coll. and Univ., 1997; fellow, NEH, 1976—77; scholar Pa. chpt., Order of Coif, 1981, vis., Phi Beta Kappa, 1999—2000. Mem.: Am. Phil. Soc., Am. Acad. Arts & Scis., Am. Law Inst., Clare Hall Cambridge U. (life). Office: Dartmouth Coll 236 Baker Libr Hanover NH 03755-3529*

FREEDMAN, MONROE HENRY, lawyer, educator, columnist; b. Mt. Vernon, N.Y., Apr. 10, 1928; s. Chauncey and Dorothea (Kornblum) F.; m. Audrey Willock, Sept. 24, 1950 (dec. 1998); children: Alice Freedman Korngold, Sarah Freedman Izquierdo, Caleb (dec. 1998), Judah. AB cum laude, Harvard U., 1951, LLB, 1954, LLM, 1956. Bar: Mass. 1954, Pa. 1957, D.C. 1960, U.S. Dist. Ct. (ea. dist. N.Y.), U.S. Ct. Appeals (D.C. cir.) 1960, U.S. Supreme Ct. 1960, U.S. Ct. Appeals (2d cir.) 1968, N.Y. 1978, U.S. Ct. Appeals (9th cir.) 1982, U.S. Ct. Appeals (11th cir.) 1986, U.S. Ct. Appeals (Fed. cir.) 1987. Assoc. Wolf, Block, Schorr & Solis-Cohen, Phila., 1956-58; ptnr. Freedman & Temple, Washington, 1969-73; dir. Stern Community Law Firm, Washington, 1970-71; prof. law George Washington U., 1958-73; dean Hofstra Law Sch., Hempstead, N.Y., 1973-77, prof. law, 1973—, Howard Lichtenstein Disting. prof. legal ethics, 1989—2003; Drinko-Baker & Hostetler chair in law Cleve. State U., 1992; CFO Olive Tree Mktg. Internat., 1998—. Faculty asst. Harvard U. Law Sch., 1954-56, instr. trial advocacy and legal ethics, 1978—; lectr. on lawyers' ethics; exec. dir. U.S. Holocaust Meml. Coun., 1980-82, gen. counsel, 1982-83, sr. adviser to chmn., 1982-87; cons. U.S. Commn. on Civil Rights, 1960-64, Neighborhood Legal Services Program, 1970; legis. cons. to Senator John L. McClellan, 1959; spl. com. on courtroom conduct N.Y.C. Bar Assn., 1972; exec. dir. Criminal Trial Inst., 1965-66; expert witness on legal ethics state and fed. ct. proceedings, U.S. Senate and House Coms., U.S. Dept. Justice, FDIC; spl. investigator Rochester Inst. Tech., 1991; reporter Am. Lawyer's Code of Conduct, 1979-81; mem. Arbitration panel U.S. Dist. Ct. (ea. dist.) N.Y., 1986—; Inaugural Wickwire lectr. Dalhousie Law Sch., N.S., 1992; lectr. S.C. Bar Found., 1993, numerous profl. confs; adv. subgroup on ethics U.S. Dist. Ct. (ea. dist.) N.Y., 1994-96. Author: Contracts, 1973, Lawyers' Ethics in an Adversary System, 1975 (ABA gavel award, cert. of merit 1976), Teacher's Manual Contracts, 1978, American Lawyer's Code of Conduct, 1981, Understanding Lawyers' Ethics, 1990, (with Abbe Smith) 2d edit., 2002, Group Defamation and Freedom of Speech—The Relationship Between Language and Violence, 1995; co-editor; columnist Cases and Controversies, Am. Lawyer Media, 1990-96, (with Supreme Ct. Justice Ruth Bader Ginsburg) Freedom, Life, & Death: Materials on Comparative Constitutional Law, 1997; mem. panel acad. contbrs. Black's Law Dictionary, 2002-2003; television appearances include Donohue, CNN Money Line, CBS 60 Minutes, CNN Late Edition, Court TV, and others; contbr. articles to profl. jours. Recipient Martin Luther King Jr. Humanitarian award, 1987, The Lehman-LaGuardia Award for Civic Achievement, 1996. Fellow Am. Bar Found. (life); mem. ABA (ethics adv. to chair criminal justice sect. 1993-95, Michael Franck award 1998), ACLU (nat. bd. dirs. 1970-80, nat. adv. coun. 1980—, spl. litigation counsel 1971-73), Am. Law Inst. (consultative group on the law governing lawyers, 1990-99, consultative group on Uniform Comml. Code art. 2 1990-2002), Soc. Am. Law Tchrs. (mem. governing bd. 1974-79, exec. com. 1976-79, chmn. com. on profl. responsibility 1974-79, 87-90), ABA (vice chmn. ethical considerations com. criminal justice sect. 1989-90, ethics advisor to chmn. criminal justice sect., 1993-96), N.Y. State Bar Assn. (com. on legal edn. and admission to bar 1988-92, criminal justice sect. com. on profl. responsibility, 1990-92, award for Dedication to Scholarship and pub. svc. 1997), Assn. Bar City N.Y. (com. on profl. responsibility 1987-90, com. on profl. and jud. ethics 1991-92), Fed. Bar Assn. (chmn. com. on profl. disciplinary standards and procedures 1970-71), Am. Soc. Writers on Legal Subjects (mem. com. on constitution and bylaws 1999—), Am. Bd. Criminal Lawyers (hon. 2003-), Am. Jewish Congress (nat. governing coun. 1984-86), Am. Arbitration Assn. (arbitrator, nat. panel arbitrators 1964—, cert. svc. award 1986), Nat. Network on Right to Counsel (exec. bd., exec. com. 1986-90), Nat. Prison Project (steering com. 1970-90), Nat. Assn. Criminal Def. Lawyers (vice chmn. ethics adv. com. 1991-93, co-chmn., 1994). Democrat. Jewish.

FREEDMAN, SARAH WARSHAUER, education educator; b. Wilimington, N.C., Feb. 23, 1946; d. Samuel Edward and Miriam (Miller) Warshauer; m. S. Robert Freedman, Aug. 20, 1967; 1 child, Rachel Karen. BA in English, U. Pa., 1967; MA in English, U. Chgo., 1970; MA in Linguistics, Stanford U., 1976, PhD in Edn., 1977. Tchr. English Phila. Sch. Dist., 1967-68, Lower Merion H.S., 1968-69; instr. English U. N.C., Wilmington, 1970-71; instr. English and linguistics Stanford U., 1972-76; asst. and assoc. prof. English San Francisco State U., 1977-81; asst. prof. edn. U. Calif., Berkeley, 1981-83, assoc. prof. edn., 1983-89; dir. Nat. Ctr. for the Study of Writing and Literacy, 1985-96; prof. edn. U. Calif., 1989—. Resident Bellagio Conf. and Study Ctr., Rockefeller Found., 1997; mem. nat. task force Nat. Writing Project, 1998—. Author: Response to Student Writing, 1987, Exchanging Writing, Exchanging Cultures, Lessons in School Reform from the United States and Great Britain, 1994, (with E.R. Simons, J.S. Kalnin, A Casareno and M-Class teams) Inside City Schools, Investigating Literacy in Multi-cultural Classrooms, 1999; editor: The Acquisition of Written Language: Response and Revision, 1985; contbr. chpts. to books and articles to profl. jours. Recipient Richard Meade award for Pub. Rsch. in Tchr. Edn. Nat. Coun. Tchrs. English, 1989, 94, Ed Fry book award, 1996, 2000, Multicultural Book award, Nat. Assn. Multicultural Edn., 2000; fellow Nat. Conf. on Rsch. in English, 1986, Ctr. Advanced Study Behavioral Scis., 1999-00; Spencer Found. grantee, 1996-2003, Rockefeller Found. grantee Bryn Mawr Coll., 1992, Nat. Ctr. for Study of Writing and Literacy grantee Office Ednl. Rsch. and Improvement, 1985-95, Minority Undergrad. Rsch. Program grantee U. Calif., 1988, 89, 92, 93, numerous other grants. Mem. Nat. Coun. Tchrs. English (standing com. on rsch. 1981-87, ex-officio 1987—, chair bd. trustees rsch. found. 1990-93, co-chair rsch. assembly 1999—), Am. Ednl. Rsch. Assn. (chair spl. interest group on rsch. in writing 1983-85, numerous other coms.), Linguistic Soc. Am., Am. Assn. Applied Linguistics, Internat. Reading Assn. Office: U Calif Dept Edn Berkeley CA 94720-0001

FREEHLING, DANIEL JOSEPH, law educator, law library director; b. Montgomery, Ala., Nov. 13, 1950; s. Saul Irving and Grace (Lieberman) L. BS, Huntingdon Coll., 1972; JD, U. Ala., 1975, MLS, 1977. Ref. libr., asst. to assoc. dean U. Ala. Sch. Law, Tuscaloosa, 1975-77; assoc. law libr. U. Md., Balt., 1977-79, Cornell U., Ithaca, N.Y., 1979-82; law libr. dir., assoc. prof. U. Maine, Portland, 1982-86; law libr. dir., assoc. prof. law Boston U., 1986-92, prof., 1992—, assoc. dean for adminstrn., 1993-97, assoc. dean for info. svcs., 1999—. Mem. steering com., law program com. Rsch. Librs. Group, 1989-91; treas. New Eng. Law Libr. Consortium, 1989-91; vice chair, chair-elect sect. on law librs. Assn. Am. Law Schs., 1990-91, chair, 1992. Mem.: ABA (accreditation com. 1995—2001, coun. sect. legal edn. and bar admission 2002—), Am. Assn. Law Librs. (chair acad. law librs. spl. interest sect. 1981—82, edn. com. 1982—83, membership com. 1983—84, program chair 1987—88, local arrangements co-chair 1992—93, chair mentoring and retention com. 1995—96). Home: 106 Washington St Topsfield MA 01983 Office: Boston U Law Sch Pappas Law Libr 765 Commonwealth Ave Boston MA 02215-1401

FREELAND, ALAN EDWARD, orthopedic surgery educator, physician; b. Youngstown, Ohio, July 30, 1939; s. Harold Edward and Esther Amelia (Hanley) F.; m. Janis Ann Foerschl, Oct. 11, 1969; children: Matthew, Jennifer, Rebecca, Michael. BA, Johns Hopkins U., 1961; MD, George Washington U., 1965. Cert. hand surgery Am. Bd. Orthopaedic Surgery. Intern Church Home and Hosp., Balt., 1965-66; resident Johns Hopkins Hosp., Balt., 1967-70, Letterman Army Med. Ctr., San Francisco, 1973-75; prof. dept. orthopaedic surgery U. Miss. Med. Ctr., Jackson, 1978—, dir. hand surgery fellowship program, 1991—, chief of staff, 1986-87, also bd. dirs. Rowland Med. Libr., 1996-98. Chief surgery Miss. Meth. Rehab. Ctr., Jackson, 1991-93, pres. elect med. staff, 1994, pres. med. staff, bd. dirs., 1995-97. Author: Stable Internal Fixation of the Hand and Wrist, 1986, The First Twenty-Five Years: History of the American Association for Hand Surgery, 1996, Hand Fractures: Repair, Reconstruction and Rehabilitation, 2000; mem. editl. bd. Orthopedics, Slack, Inc., 1986—, Jour. Orthop. Trauma, 1993—2002, Year Book of Hand Surgery, 1997, Trauma Update, Orthop., 1989—; sect. editor, sr. editor hand surgery: Jour. Orthop. Trauma, 1997—2002; bd. editors Microsurgery, 2001—, sect. editor Trauma Update, Orthop., 1989—, Hand Surgery, 1997—2002. Mem. Fire Protection Dist., Brandon, Miss., 1990-93; bd. dirs. Miss. Sports Hall of Fame, 2002—. Lt. col. U.S. Army, 1971-78. Fellow: Am Acad. Orthopaedic Surgeons; mem.: S.E. Hand Club (sec.-treas. 1998—2000, v.p. 2001, pres.-elect 2002, pres. 2003), Miss. State Orthopaedic Assn. (pres. Jackson chpt. 1985, pres. 1986), Internat. Fedn. Socs. for Surgery of Hand (chmn. bone and joint com. 1992—), Am. Assn. Hand Surgeons (parliamentarian 1994, exec. com., bd. dirs. 1994—, historian 1995, treas. 1996—98, historian 1999, v.p. 2000, pres.-elect 2001, pres. 2002), Am. Soc. Surgery of Hand (governing coun. 1989—92), Am. Orthopaedic Assn. Home: 303 Swallow Dr Brandon MS 39047-6454 Office: 2500 N State St Jackson MS 39216-4500

FREELAND, DEBORAH JANE, English educator; b. Rushville, Ill., May 28, 1949; d. Donald Rosell and Alma Darlene (Farrar) Rohn; m. Jerry Douglas Freeland, Nov. 17, 1973; 1 child, William T.D. BA in English, Western Ill. U., 1972. Cert. tchr., Ill., Iowa. Subs. tchr. Dallas City (Ill.) Community Schs., 1972, tchr., 1973; tchr. high sch./middle sch. English Burlington (Iowa) Community Schs., 1973—. Mem. Supt.'s Adv. Coun., Burlington, 1989-90; co-chair Iowa Alternative Edn. State Conf., 1990-91; participant Level III-Iowa Writing Project, 1993-94; co-chair historian com. Iowa Assn. Alternative Educators, 1993-94. Author: He's A Keeper (prose), 1989; contbr. poetry to profl. jours. Mem. PTO, Burlington, Fireman's Aux., Burlington; co-sponsor Dem. Party Fund Raisers, 1991-94. Mem. NEA, Iowa Edn. Assn. (rep. del. assembly 1990-91), Burlington Edn. Assn. (election chair 1988-90, bldg. rep. 1990—, exec. bd. 1993, elections chair 1994, pres. 1994—), Iowa Assn. of Alternative Schs. (bd. dirs. com. mem. 1991, election chair alternative edn. assn. 1991—), Nat. Coun. Tchrs. English, Iowa Coun. Tchrs. English, Iowa Policeman's Assn. Methodist. Avocations: travel, boating, camping, swimming, cooking. Home: 5517 Ferres Ln Burlington IA 52601-9028 Office: University High Sch 1200 Market St Burlington IA 52601-4232

FREELAND, RICHARD MIDDLETON, academic affairs administrator, historian; b. Orange, N.J., May 13, 1941; s. Harry Middleton and Margaret Lyons (Child) F. BA in Am. Studies, Amherst Coll., 1963; PhD in Am. Civilization, U. Pa., 1968; DHL (hon.), Amherst Coll., 1998, Am. Coll. Greece, 2000. Asst. to pres. U. Mass., 1970, asst. to chancellor, 1971-72, dir. Office of Ednl. Planning, asst. prof., 1972-74, dean Coll. Profl. Studies, 1974-79, assoc. prof., 1974-92, dean Coll. of Arts and Scis., 1982-92, prof. history, 1992; prof. history Grad. Sch. & Univ. Ctr. CUNY, 1992-96; vice chancellor for acad. affairs, pres. CUNY Rsch. Found., 1992-96; pres., prof. history Northeastern U., Boston, 1996—. Proposal reviewer NEH, Divsn. Rsch., 1989, Divsn. Edn. Programs, 1985, R.I. Bd. Higher Edn., 1987, Fund for the Improvement of Post Secondary Edn., 1988, Rockefeller Found., 1985, Am. Univ., 1988, 89, 90; cons. Am. Coun. Edn., 1994, U.S. Dept. Edn., 1989-90, 92; dir. Mass. Bus. Roundtable, Citizens Bank Mass., The Boston Globe, Boston Plan for Excellence, Assn. Ind. Colls. and Univs. Mass. Author: The Truman Doctrine and the Origins of McCarthyism, 1972, Academia's Golden Age, 1992; reader, reviewer numerous profl. jours. Recipient Rsch. grants Ford Found., 1979-80, NEH, 1980-81, Rockefeller Found., 1988. Office: Northeastern U 110 Churchill Hall 380 Huntington Ave Boston MA 02115-5000 E-mail: r.freeland@neu.edu.

FREEMAN, CAROLE COOK, education educator; b. Hanover, N.H., Oct. 14, 1949; d. Sidney Leighton and Ruth Mary (Tyler) Cook; m. Michael Stuart Freeman, July 5, 1974; children: Alice Pearl, Josie Eleanor. BS in Edn., U. Vt., 1971; MEd, U. Ill., 1974; PhD, U. Pa., 1991. Elem. sch. tchr. Middlebury, Winooski, and Norwich schs., Vt., 1971-78; intern advisor Upper Valley Tchr. Tng., Hanover, N.H., 1978-80; asst./acting coord. svcs. for learning disabled students Coll. of Wooster, Ohio, 1982-85; 4th grade tchr. Friends Select Sch., Phila., 1986-87; supr. student tchrs. U. Pa., Phila., 1987-88, 90-91; coord. field experiences U. pa., Phila., 1988-89; asst. prof. edn. LaSalle U., Phila., 1991-97, assoc. prof., chmn. dept. edn., 1997-2000; prin. Waits River Valley Sch., East Corinth, Vt., 2000—. Cons. Ctr. for Schs. Stucy Coun., Grad. Sch. Edn. U. Pa., Phila., 1988-2000. Co-author: Pets and Me: A Thematic Learning Experience Built on the Relationship Between People and Animals, 1991; author: A Literate Community: Common Threads and Unique Patterns in Teaching and Learning, 1995. Cmty. Svc. Rsch. grantee Pa. Campus Compact, 1994, Am. Counts grantee NSF, 1999. Mem. ASCD, Nat. Assn. for Edn. of Young Children, Nat. Acad.

Early Childhood Programs (validator), Nat. Coun. Tchrs. English, Am. Ednl. Rsch. Assn., Assn. Childhood Edn. Internat., Phi Delta Kappa. Home: PO Box 192 East Corinth VT 05040-0192 Office: Waits River Valley Sch 6 Waits River Valley Rd East Corinth VT 05040 E-mail: cfreeman@wrvs.us.

FREEMAN, GORDON RUSSEL, chemistry educator; b. Hoffer, Sask., Can., Aug. 27, 1930; s. Winston Spencer Churchill and Aquila Maud (Chapman) Freeman; m. Phyllis Joan Elson, Sept. 8, 1951; children: Mark Russel, Michèle Leslie. BA, U. Sask., 1952, MA, 1953; PhD, McGill U., 1955; D.Phil., Oxford (Eng.) U., 1957. Postdoctoral fellow Centre D'Etudes Nucléaires, Saclay, France, 1957-58; asst. prof., then assoc. prof. chemistry U. Alta. (Can.), Edmonton, 1958-65, prof., 1965-95, chmn. divsn. phys. and theoretical chemistry, 1965-75, dir. radiation rsch. ctr., 1968-95, prof. emeritus, 1995—; exec. Chem. Inst. Can., 1974-80, chmn. phys. chemistry div., 1976-78, councillor, 1978-80. Author: Kinetics of Nonhomogenous Processes: A Practical Introduction for Chemists, Physicists, Biologists and Materials Scientists, 1987; contbr. over 450 articles to profl. jours., chapters to books. Grantee Rsch., Nat. Rsch. Coun. Can., 1959—78, Natural Scis. and Engring. Rsch. Coun. Can., 1978—98, Def. Rsch. Bd. Can., 1965—72. Mem.: Can. Assn. Archaeologists, Am. Phys. Soc., Chem. Inst. Can. Achievements include research in archaeoastronomy and sociology. Office: U Alta Chemistry Dept Edmonton AB Canada T6G 2G2 E-mail: k.np@ualberta.ca.

FREEMAN, JOHN HENRY, mathematics educator; b. Orleans, Mass., Mar. 16, 1938; s. Charles Otis and Dorothy Walker (Moulton) F.; m. Mary Elizabeth Peters, July 3, 1965; children: James, John, Colleen, Patricia. BA, Harvard U., 1960; MEd, Tufts U., 1961. Coach mid. sch. baseball, h.s. varsity soccer Roslyn Mid. Sch., NY, 1961-96; retired, 1997; with Town of Orleans Pk. Dept., Mass., 1999—, Friends Acad., Glen Cove, NY, 1998—2001. Recreation dir. Orleans (Mass.) Recreation, 1967-91. Dir. Glen Head (N.Y.) Little League, 1970-80; dir., coach North Shore Soccer Club, Glen Head, 1970-95; mem. parish coun. St. Marys Ch., pres., 1986-92. Mem. Nassau County Soccer Coaches Assn. (pres., Coach of Yr. 1994, Nassau County champions 1994, N.Y. State Boys Soccer champions 1978, 80, Cape Cod referee 1999—). Roman Catholic. Avocations: soccer, music, tennis, reading. Home: Box 788 49 Meetinghouse Rd Orleans MA 02653-0788

FREEMAN, MARJORIE SCHAEFER, mathematician, educator; b. Chevy Chase, Md., Sept. 23, 1924; d. Herbert Stanley and Helen (Hummer) Schaefer; m. John C. Freeman, June 14, 1947; children: John C. III, Walter H., Jill F. Hasling, Cathryn F. Disch, Helen, Paul D. AB, Randolph-Macon Womans Coll., 1946; MS, Brown U, 1949; postgrad., U. Houston, 1973-75. Computer asst. Inst. for Advanced Study, Princeton, NJ, 1949-50; rsch. asst. Tex. A&M Rsch. Found., College Station, 1954-55; instr. Tex. A&M U., College Station, 1955; cons. Gulf Cons., Houston, 1955-56; instr. South Tex. Jr. Coll., Houston, 1961-74; asst. prof. U. Houston-Downtown, 1974-90, asst. prof. emeritus, 1990—. Sys. analyst, programmer TERA, Inc., Houston, 1985; cons. Inst. Storm Rsch., Houston, 1979—86; adv. bd. Weather Rsch. Ctr., Houston, 1987—. Mem.: Math. Assn. Am., S.W. Tracking Assn., Alamo Area Chesapeake Bay Retriever Club, Am. Chesapeake Club, S. Tex. Obedience Club. Avocations: dog training, camping, crafts. Home: 4404 Mount Vernon St Houston TX 77006-5814 E-mail: jfreeman9@houston.rr.com.

FREEMAN, MARY COLEMAN, special education educator; b. Pontotoc, Miss., Dec. 1, 1956; d. John Roland and Juanita (Pipkin) Coleman; m. William C. Freeman, Feb. 10, 1978; children: Holly Michelle, Blake and Corey. Assoc. Edn., N.W. Jr. Coll., 1976; M Reading, M Spl. Edn., U. Miss., 1980. Spl. edn. tchr. Senatobia (Miss.) City Schs., 1978—. Mem.: TEAAM (Together Enhancing Autism Awareness in Miss.), Coun. Exceptional Children. Avocations: Karate, knit and needle crafts, writing poems, reading, horseback riding. Home: PO Box 235 Senatobia MS 38668-0235

FREEMAN, MELVIN IRWIN, ophthalmic surgeon, educator, municipal official; b. Seattle, Mar. 17, 1935; s. Joseph and Rally (Arensberg) F.; m. Nanette Jean Dreyfuss, Feb. 17, 1979; children: Robert Eliot, Jacqueline Dreyfuss, Joseph Dreyfuss. BS, U. Wash., Seattle, 1957; MD, U. Wash., 1960. Intern VA Hosp., L.A., 1960-61; resident Washington U., St. Louis, 1961-66; head sect. ophthalmology The Mason Clinic, Seattle, 1969-95; dir. continuing med. edn. Virginia Mason Med. Ctr., Seattle, 1984-95; head contact lens clinic, clin. prof. ophthalmology U. Wash., Seattle, 1969—. Chmn. Tel-Med Trust King County, Seattle, 1977-85; nat. commissionaire nat. secretariat edn., exec. v.p., pres., 1996-2002, The Joint Commn. Allied Health Personnel Ophthalmology, St. Paul, 1986—; pres., sec., treas. exec. com. Alliance Continuing Med. Edn., Northbrook, Ill., 1984-2002; cons. in field. Author, co-author numerous sci. papers, book chpts. and presentations. Mayor pro tempore, councilman Town of Yarrow Point, Wash., 1974-94; trustee, treas., v.p., pres. Temple De Hursch Sinai, Seattle and Bellevue, 1976-94; trustee Virginia Mason Rsch. Found., Seattle, 1978-84. Capt. U.S. Army, 1961-63. Recipient Williams prize med. rsch. U. Wash., 1960, Contact Lens Assn. Ophthalmologist Disting. Svc. award, 1996, Joint Commn. Allied Health Personnel Ophthalmology Scientists award, 1999, Alliance Cert. Med. Edn. award, 1998, 2003; fellow Retina Found., Boston, 1966-69, Mass. Eye and Ear Infirmary, Boston, 1967-69, USPHS, 1957, 58, 59, NSF, 1959, Nat. Inst. Neurol. Disease and Blindness, 1961, 64-69, Fight for Sight, 1966. Fellow ACS, Am. Acad. Ophthalmology (honors award 1984, sr. honors award 1995), Wash. State Acad. Ophthalmology (officer, trustee 1976—), Pacific Coast Oto-Ophthal. Soc., Seattle Surg. Soc.; mem. AMA (del.), Washington Athletic Club (Seattle). Home: 4625 92nd Ave NE Bellevue WA 98004-1336 Office: The Mason Clinic 1100 9th Ave Seattle WA 98101-2799

FREEMAN, NEIL, accounting and computer consulting firm executive; b. Reading, Pa., Dec. 27, 1948; s. Leroy Harold and Audrey Todd (Dornhecker) F.; m. Pamela Hong, May 30, 2000. BS, Albright Coll., 1979; MS, Kennedy-Western U., 1987, PhD, 1988. Cert. systems profl., data processing specialist, info. system security profl. Acct. Jack W. Long & Co., Mt. Penn, Pa., 1977-78; comptroller G.P.C., Inc., Bowmansville, Pa., 1978-79; owner Neil Freeman Cons., Bowmansville, 1980-81; program mgr., systems cons. Application Systems, Honolulu, 1981-82; instr. Chaminade U., Honolulu, 1983-96; owner Neil Freeman Cons., Kaneohe, Hawaii, 1982-96, Grand Junction, Colo., 1996—. Instr. Mesa State Coll., Grand Junction, 1997—. Author: (computer software) NFC Property Management, 1984, NFC Mailing List, 1984; (book) Learning Dibol, 1984. Served with USN, 1966-68, Vietnam. Mem. Nat. Assn. Accts., Am. Inst. Cert. Computer Profls., Assn. Systems Mgmt. Office: 1620 Canon Ave Grand Junction CO 81503

FREEMAN, PETER KENT, chemist, educator; b. Modesto, Calif., Nov. 25, 1931; s. Russell Arthur and Helen Aleth (Surryhne) F.; m. Marilyn Taber, June 15, 1955 (div.); children: Diane, Irene, Theodore, Michael; m. Judith W. Farrahi, May 14, 1995. BS, U. Calif., Berkeley, 1953; PhD, U. Colo., 1957. Research assoc. Pa. State U., University Park, 1958; asst. prof. chemistry U. Idaho, Moscow, 1959-62, assoc. prof., 1962-65, prof., 1965-68, Oreg. State U., Corvallis, 1968-97; prof. emeritus, 1998—. Contbr. articles to profl. jours. Mem. Am. Chem. Soc., Sigma Xi, Phi Kappa Phi, Phi Lambda Upsilon., Home: 3342 NW Roosevelt Dr Corvallis OR 97330-1170

FREESE, KATHERINE, physicist, educator; b. Freiburg, Germany, Feb. 8, 1957; came to U.S., 1957; d. Ernst and Elisabeth Gertrude Maria (Bautz) F.; 1 child, Douglas Quincy Adams. BA, Princeton U., 1977; MA, Columbia U., 1981; PhD, U. Chgo., 1984. Postdoctoral fellow Harvard/Smithsonian Ctr. for Astrophysics, Cambridge, Mass., 1984-85, Inst. for Theoretical Physics, Santa Barbara, Calif., 1985-87, U. Calif., Berkeley, 1987-88; asst. prof. physics MIT, Cambridge, 1988-91; prof. physics U. Mich., Ann Arbor, 1991—. Gen. mem. Aspen Ctr. for Physics, 1991—; bd. dirs. Inst. for Theoretical Physics. Contbr. articles to profl. jours. William Rainey Harper fellow U. Chgo, 1982; Sloan Found. fellow, 1989; Presdl. Young Investigator NSF, 1990, rsch. grantee, 1991, 94; Presdl. fellow U. Calif., 1987. Mem. Am. Phys. Soc., Assn. for Women in Sci. Democrat. Avocations: water polo, swimming, skiing, tennis. Office: U Mich Dept Physics Ann Arbor MI 48109

FREESE, MELANIE LOUISE, librarian, professor, assistant dean; b. Mineola, N.Y., May 12, 1945; d. Walter Christian and Agnes Elizabeth (Jensen) F. BS in Elem. Edn., Hofstra U., 1967, MA in Elem. Edn., 1969; MLS, L.I. U., 1977. Cert. tchr., N.Y. Bibliographic searcher acquisitions dept. Adelphi U. Swirbul Libr., Garden City, N.Y., 1973-79, res. desk libr., 1979-83; catalog libr., assoc. prof. Hofstra U. Axinn Libr., Hempstead, N.Y., 1984—, asst. dean, chair libr. tech. svcs., 1998—2000, sr. cataloger, 2000—. Ch. librarian St. Peters Evang. Luth. Ch., Baldwin, N.Y., 1977—. Founder libr. Salvation Army Wayside Home and Sch. for Girls, Valley Stream, N.Y., 1993. Mem. ALA, Nassau County Libr. Assn. (cor. sec. acad. and spl. librs. divsn. 1986-88, v.p., pres.-elect 1989-90, pres. 1991), Bus. and Profl. Women's Club (pres. Nassau County chpt. 1990-92, 95-97, Woman of Yr. 1994). Republican. Avocations: needlework, knitting, crocheting. Office: Hofstra U Axinn Library 1000 Fulton Ave Hempstead NY 11550-1030

FREESE, RAYMOND WILLIAM, mathematics educator; b. Foristell, Mo., Dec. 17, 1934; s. Herman E. and Lydia D. (Giessmann) F.; m. Celia Ann Staubach, Aug. 10, 1957; children: Carl, William, Timothy. BS in Agrl., U. Mo., 1956, BS in Edn., MA in Math., U. Mo., 1958, PhD in Math., 1961. Asst. prof. math. St. Louis U., 1961-64, assoc. prof. math., 1964-67, prof. math., 1967-83, prof. math., chmn. dept., 1971-83, prof. math. and computer sci., chmn. dept., 1983-86, prof. math. and computer sci., 1983—, prof. edn., 1989—, acting dept. chair, 1999-2000. Contbr. articles to profl. jours. Mem. Francis Howell Sch. Dist. Bd. Edn., St. Charles, Mo., 1967-69. Mem. Mo. Sch. Bd. Assn. (exec. com. 1968-70), Math. Assn. Am. (Mo. sect. chmn. 1964-65, Mo. sect. gov. 1973-76), Am. Math. Soc., Math. Educators of Greater St. Louis, Nat. Coun. Tchrs. of Math., Sigma Xi. Mem. United Ch. of Christ. Avocations: ham radio, sci. fiction. Office: St Louis U Dept Math/Computer Sci 221 N Grand Blvd Saint Louis MO 63103-2006 E-mail: freeserw@slu.edu.

FREGETTO, EUGENE FLETCHER, marketing educator; b. Milw., Oct. 18, 1947; s. Fletcher Eugene and Eva Mary F.; m. Judith Ann Shafel, Dec. 26, 1969; children: Katherine Ann, Julie Lynn. Student, Mich. State U., 1965-67; BA in Journalism, Marquette U., 1970; AS in Architecture and Structural Engring., Milw. Sch. Engring., 1972; MBA in Mktg., De Paul U., 1983; PhD in Pub. Policy Analysis, U. Ill., Chgo., 1997. Tech. writer Chemetron Corp., Chgo., 1972-73; specification engr. Chgo. Transit Authority, 1973-83, procurement engr., 1983-84, sr. procurement engr., 1984-88, supt. procurement engrs., 1988-89, sr. contract adminstr., 1990-97, ret., 1997; mem. mktg. faculty U. Ill., Chgo., 1983—. Lectr. in mgmt. De Paul U., Chgo., 1983-91, co-developer grad. entrepreneurship program, purchasing mgmt. program, De Paul U.; lectr. in mktg. U. Ill., Chgo., 1983—; founder, pres. MidwestTechnology Access Group, Inc., 1992—. Contbr. articles profl. jours. Civil Svc. Commnr. City of Des Plaines, Ill., 1989—. Athletic scholar Mich. State U., 1965; scholar Milw. Sch. Engring., 1970-72. Fellow U.S. Assn. for Small Bus. and Entrepreneurship (founding, v.p. fin. 1983-90); mem. Nat. Assn. Purchasing Mgmt. (cert.), Purchasing Mgrs. Assn. Chgo. (chmn. 1986-91), Ill. Assn. Pub. Procurement Officials. Avocations: photography, fishing, hunting, camping. Home: 800 Laurel Ave Des Plaines IL 60016-7121 Office: U Ill at Chgo Managerial Studies Dept (M/C 243) 601 S Morgan St Chicago IL 60607 E-mail: fregetto@uic.edu., fregetto@mtag.org.

FREIBERGER, CHRISTINE HOLMBERG, biologist; b. Southhampton, N.Y., June 4, 1935; d. Frank and Mildred (Anderson) Holmberg.; m. Walter F. Freiberger; Oct. 6. 1956; children: Christopher, Andrew, Nils. BA, Brown U., 1956, MAT, 1959. Cert. biology instr. Tchr. Hope H.S., Providence, 1960-69; instr. biology Roger Williams Coll., Providence, 1970-85. Republican. Episcopalian. Home: 24 Alumni Ave Providence RI 02906-2310

FREIBERGER, KATHERINE GUION, composer, retired piano educator; b. Mineral Wells, Tex., May 2, 1927; d. Waldo Burton and Kate Francis (Guion) Lasater; m. John Jacob Freiberger, July 22, 1950. AA, HocKaday Jr. Coll., Dallas, 1946; BA, U. Tex., 1949; MusB, So. Meth. U., 1966. Tchr. Dallas Ind. Schs., 1949-50; pvt. practice piano tchr. Dallas, 1961-85. Composer piano solos and duets, chamber, choral and incidental music. Mem. Dallas Civic Chorus, 1962-69, 72-76, chorus Dallas Civic Opera, 1959; alto soloist Preston Hollow Presbyn. Ch., Dallas, 1956-63; alto soloist, dir. youth choir Churchill Way Presbyn. Ch., Dallas, 1963-70; sole trustee David W. Guion Edn. and Religious Trusts I and II, Dallas, 1978-91; bd. dirs. Dallas Music Tchrs. Assn., 1979-91, Voices of Change, Dallas, 1980s, Dallas Civic Music, 1970s-80s, Durango/Purgatory Music in the Mts., Colo., 1990—, The Dallas Opera, 1989-97;artist in residence com. Ft. Lewis Coll., Durango, Co., 1998—.) Recipient; Elizabeth Mathias Award, Prof. Achievement, 2001. Mem. Musical Arts Club, Mu Phi Epsilon Alumni (First prize for composition 1989, Elizabeth Mathias award 2001). Home: 3825 Hawthorne Ave Dallas TX 75219-2212

FREIBERGER, WALTER FREDERICK, mathematics educator, actuarial science consultant, educator; b. Vienna, Feb. 20, 1924; came to U.S., 1955, naturalized, 1962. s. Felix and Irene (Tagany) F.; m. Christine Mildred Holmberg, Oct. 6, 1956; children: Christopher Allan, Andrew James, Nils H. BA, U. Melbourne, 1947, MA, 1949; PhD, U. Cambridge, Eng., 1953. Rsch. officer Aero. Rsch. Lab. Australian Dept. Supply, 1947-49, sr. sci. rsch. officer, 1953-55; tutor U. Melbourne, 1947-49, 53-55; asst. prof. divsn. applied math. Brown U., 1956-58, assoc. prof., 1958-64, prof., 1964—2002; prof. applied math., prof. cmty. health Brown U. Med. Sch., 1994—2002; prof. emeritus applied math. Brown U., 2002—, dir. Computing Center, 1963-69, dir. Ctr. for Computer and Info. Scis., 1969-76, chmn. divsn. applied math., 1976-82, chmn. grad. com., 1985-88, assoc. chmn. divsn. applied math., 1988-91, chmn. univ. ctr. for statis. sci., 1991—2002; joint appointment Brown U. Med. Sch., 1994—2002. Fmr. lectr., cons. program in applied actuarial sci. Bryant Coll.; joint appointment as prof. cmty. health Sch. Medicine Brown U., 1994-2002; mem. fellowship selection panel NSF, Fulbright fellowship selection panel; mem. Rep. Nat. Com. Author: (with U. Grenander) A Short Course in Computational Probability and Statistics, 1971; editor: The International Dictionary of Applied Mathematics, 1960, (with others) Applications of Digital Computers, 1963, Advances in Computers, Volume 10, 1970, Statistical Computer Performance Evaluation, 1972; mng. editor: Quarterly of Applied Mathematics, 1965—; Contbr. numerous articles to profl. jours. Served with Australian Army, 1943-45. Fulbright fellow, 1955-56; Guggenheim fellow, 1962-63; grantee NSF Office Naval Rsch. NIH. Mem. Am. Math. Soc. (assoc. editor Math. Reviews 1957-62), Soc. for Indsl. and Applied Math., Am. Statis. Assn., Inst. Math. Stats., Assn. Computing Machinery, Bristol Yacht Club, Univ. Club. Republican. Episcopalian. Home: 24 Alumni Ave Providence RI 02906-2310 Office: Box F Brown U 182 George St Providence RI 02912-9056 E-mail: Walter_Freiberger@Brown.edu.

FREIER, SUSAN MARCIE, violinist, music educator; b. Bklyn., Dec. 13, 1953; d. George David and Ruth (Hollenberg) F.; children: Sarah, Rachel, Zachary. BS in Biology, BA in Music, Stanford U., 1975, MA, 1976; MusM, Eastman Sch. Music, 1980. Asst. prof. violin Ind. U., South Bend, 1980-88, assoc. prof., 1988; mem. faculty Stanford (Calif.) U., 1989—; mem. Stanford Quartet; mem. violin faculty Rocky Ridge, Estes Park, Colo., 1993—; mem. Ives Quartet, 1997—. Artist-in-residence Grand Teton Music Festival, Wyo., 1980-84, Garth Newel Music Camp, 1985-87, Downeast Music Camp, Maine, 1984, 85, Somerset Music Festival, 1987, San Miguel de Allende Chamber Music Festival, Mex., 2002-; vis. resident string quartet Tex. Christian U., Ft. Worth, 1985-87; pedagogue Ft. Worth Suzuki Inst., 1986, 87, Chgo. Suzuki Inst., 1987; mem. Chester String Quartet, 1978-89; coach, South Bend Youth Symphony, 1980-89, master classes Oberlin Conservatory, Cleve. Inst. Music, 1988; mem. Newport (R.I.) Music Festival, 1989, 90, Chamber Music West, San Francisco, 1990, Strings in the Mountains, Steamboat Springs, Colo., 1990-93, Sedona (Ariz.) Music Festival, 1990-94, Telluride (Colo.) Music Festival, 1992—, Port Townsend (Wash.) Chamber Music Festival, 1999-2001; mem. San Francisco Contemporary Mus. Players, 1994—. Winner top awards in quartet competitions, Munich, Portsmouth, Eng., Chgo. Mem. Chamber Music Assn., Am. String Tchrs. Assn. Avocations: hiking, jogging.

FREIFELD, MURIEL ISRAEL, early childhood consultant; b. N.Y.C., Aug. 2, 1923; d. Eli Israel and Anna Becker; m. Milton Freifeld, Nov. 18, 1943; children: Martin, Nina Freifeld Giles, Alison Freifeld Cowan. BA in Psychology, Hunter Coll., 1945; MA in Teaching, Trinity Coll., 1985. Lic. tchr. trainer and lectr. Md. Child Care Adminstrn. Tchr. Atlantic Highlands (N.J.) Pub. Schs., 1946-47, Dayton (Ohio) Pub. Schs., 1947-48; dir. presch. Jewish Cmty. Ctr., Springfield, Mass., 1954-57, Cin., 1958-60, dir. nursery sch. Easton, Pa., 1962-67; tchr. kindergarten Rockaway Twp. (N.J.) Pub. Schs., 1967-75; dir., tchr. Head Start Easton (Pa.) Pub. Schs., 1965; tchr., specialist Head Start Montgomery County Schs., Rockville, Md., 1975-85; pres., founder New Visions for Child Care, Potomac, Md., 1991—; founder, CEO New Visions for Caregivers, 1996—; ret. Chair adv. bd. New Visions for Child Care, 1993-94; cons. Head Start Peer Rev., Phila., 1993—; mem. Cons. Pool for Region IV Head Start Quality Improvement Ctrs., 2000—; rschr. in field. Artist paintings, pen and ink drawings. Vol. Children's Inn, Bethesda, Md., 1991—, Hebrew Home, Rockville, 1993—, NIH-Pediatric Oncology, Bethesda, 1993-94; hospice worker Jewish Social Svcs., Rockville, 1994—. Project Head Start grantee, 1965. Mem. Nat. Assn. for Edn. of Young Children (validator 1990—), Assn. Childhood Edn. Internat., Hunter Coll. Alumni Assn. (program chair 1991-93, bd. dirs.). Avocations: reading, painting, piano. Home and Office: 6 Deerfield Ct Palm Coast FL 32137-5903

FREIMAN, ALVIN HENRY, cardiologist, educator; b. N.Y.C., Jan. 26, 1927; s. Maurice and Beatrice (Freeman) Freiman; m. Nadine Roehr, June 12, 1959; children: Audrey L., Gail L., Marshall A. BA, N.Y. U., 1947, MD, 1953; MS, U. Ill., 1949. Diplomate Am. Bd. Internal Medicine. Intern Montefiore Hosp., N.Y.C., 1953—54; resident in medicine and cardiology Beth Israel Hosp., Boston, 1954—56; fellow in cardiology Meml. Hosp., N.Y.C., 1956—58; individual practive medicine specializing in internal medicine and cardiology N.Y.C., 1954—. Attending staff cardiology Meml. Sloan-Kettering Cancer Ctr., N.Y.C., 1971—, dir. clin. info. ctr., 1974—; attending physician Sloan-Kettering Inst., N.Y.C., 1995; prof. medicine Cornell U. Med. Coll., N.Y.C., 1995—. Contbr. articles to profl. jours. With USNR, 1945—46. Mem.: AAAS, Internat. Coll. Angiology, N.Y. Acad. Scis., Am. Heart Assn., Am. Coll. Angiology, Am. Coll. Chest Physicians, Am. Coll. Cardiology, A.C.P., Nat. Cancer Inst., Sigma Xi, Alpha Omega Alpha. Home: 74 Homestead Rd Tenafly NJ 07670-1109 Office: 178 E End Ave New York NY 10128-7762

FREIMAN, LELA KAY, retired secondary school educator; b. Canton, Miss., Oct. 2, 1939; d. Lyle K. and Mae Susan (Billman) Linch; m. James F. Freiman, Sept. 5, 1965 (div. Feb. 1975); 1 child, Jennifer Leigh. Student, Northwestern State Coll., Natchitoches, La., 1957-59; BA, U. Iowa, 1962; MEd, U. Ariz., 1977. Tchr. speech, English and drama Sturgeon Bay (Wis.) H.S., 1962-65; spl. edn. tchr. Naylor Jr. H.S., Tucson, 1975-83; tchr. drama Sahuaro H.S., Tucson, 1983-97. Summer camp dir. Sahuaro coun. Girl Scouts U.S.A., Tucson, 1977-87; mem. adv. coun. drama dept. U. Ariz., Tucson; participant Nat. faculty for Humanities, Santa Fe, Tucson, 1988-89; bd. dirs. Live Theatre Workshop, 2001-; sec. Ariz. Alliance Arts Ed., 2001-03. Former leader, trainer, camp dir. Girl Scouts U.S.A., Sturgeon Bay, Wis. Rapids, Waukesha, Wis., Ariz., rep. Nat. Leadership Conf., Washington, 1983, bd. dirs. Sahuaro coun., 1992-95; first aid com., instr. AFA, CPR ARC, Tucson; instr. CPR Am. Heart Assn.; Sunday sch. tchr., supt., mem. coun. Luth. Chs., Wis. Rapids, Waukesha, now Tucson; v.p. bd. dirs. S.W. Actors Studio, Tucson, 1987-92; adult mem. Ariz. State Thespian Bd., 1992-97; h.s. page editor Tucson Theatre Scene; sec. Live Theatre workshop Bd., 2002—. Recipient Thanks Badge, Sahuaro coun. Girl Scouts U.S.A., 1976, 88, Cross and Crown award Luth. Scouters So. Ariz., 1983, Mainstream Tchr. of Yr. award Assn. for Retarded Citizens So. Ariz., 1989. Mem. NEA (ret.), Am. Alliance for Theatre and Edn., Ariz. Theatre Alliance (state sec. 1989-90, state treas. 1990-91, state bd. 1998, 2000-03, exec. dir. 1998-2000, com. to draft curriculum guidelines for Ariz. Ho. of Reps., Theatre Educator of Yr. 1994-95), Ariz. Edn. Assn. (ret.), Ariz. Prodn. Assn. (sec. so. Ariz. chpt. 1997-99), Cougar Found. (bd. dirs. 1997-2002), Pima County Ret. Tchrs. Assn., Sahuaro Speculators. Avocations: camping, travel, reading. Home: 7517 E Beach Dr Tucson AZ 85715-3649

FREITAG, PATRICIA KOENIG, education educator; b. Mar. 17, 1962; BA, Boston U., 1984, EdD, 1991; MS, U. Md., 1988. Asst. rschr. U. Wis., Milw., 1991-93, assoc. rschr. Madison, 1992-95; asst. prof. ednl. rsch. George Washington U., Washington, 1995—. Office: NSG 4201 Wilson Blvd 885 Arlington VA 22230

FREITAS, FRANCES ANNE, nursing educator, consultant; b. Buffalo, Aug. 11, 1956; d. Daniel Dominic and Frances Anne Freitas. BSN, SUNY, Buffalo, 1978; MSN, Edinboro U. Pa., 1986. Cert. neonatal intesive care and school nurse. Asst. prof. Kent State U., Ashtabula, Ohio, 1995—. Program evaluator Nat. League Nursing Accrediting Commn., N.Y.C., 1999—. Mem. Nat. League Nursing, Sigma Theta Tau. Office: Kent State U 3325 W 13th St Ashtabula OH 44004 E-mail: ffreitas@kent.edu.

FRENCH, ELIZABETH CHAMBERLAIN, musician; b. Altoona, Pa., Aug. 16, 1929; d. Alton Francis and Margaret (Griffith) Chamberlain; children: Eugene Thurman Vest, Jonathan Mark Vest, Harry Allan Vest, Michael Robert Vest. BMus in Edn. with honors, Wheaton Coll., 1951; MMus, U. Cin., 1963; postgrad., Peabody Conservatory Music, 1967—70; D of Music Arts, Boston U., 1975; postgrad., U. Ariz., 1978. Dir. music Westminster Presbyn. Ch., Bluefield, W.Va., 1951—53; dir. music Bland St. Meth. Ch., Bluefield, 1959—70, Episcopal Ch. St. Matthew, Tucson, 1973—76; organist Trinity Presbyn. Ch., Tucson, 1976—78; sr. staff assoc. for acad. affairs Ala. Commn. on Higher Edn., Montgomery, 1978—82, asst. dir., 1982—87, dir., 1987—. Instr. music Concord Coll., Athens, W.Va., 1964—66, asst. prof., 1966—70; mus. dir. Barter Theater, Abingdon, Va., 1968, Temple Beth Or, Montgomery, Ala., 1980—. Musician (harpsichord): Birmingham Musica Antiqua, 1980—83; musician: appearances as harpsichord and recitalist; contbr. articles to profl. jours. Govs. study commn. on libr. coop. State of Ala., 1979—81; exec. bd. Pres. Coun. Montgomery, 1981—83; adv. coun. Ala. Pub. Libr. Svc., 1981—84, chmn., 1982; task force Ala. Hist. Records Adv. Bd., 1984—85; chmn. State Higher Edn. Officers Nat. Planning Com., 1984; active Montgomery Bus. Com. for the Arts, 1983—; Active Episcopal Diocesan Music Commn. State Ariz., Ariz., 1973—78; bd. dirs. Friends of Temple of Music and Art, Tuscson, 1975—78; bd. dirs. Montgomery chpt. Ala. Symphony, 1980—81; bd. dirs. Arrowhead Townhouse Owners Assn., 1979—80, 1984—85, pres., 1984—85. Mem.: AAUW, Southeastern Hist. Keyboard Soc., Am. Guild Organists (Ala. state chmn. 1981—87, regional chmn. ednl. concerns

1985—89), Coll. Music Soc., Capital City Club, Phi Kappa Phi. Home: 37 Tecumseh Dr Montgomery AL 36117-4123 Office: PO Box 302000 100 N Union St Montgomery AL 36130-2000 Business E-Mail: efrench@ache.state.al.us.

FRENCH, ELIZABETH IRENE, biology educator, violinist; b. Knoxville, Tenn., Sept. 20, 1938; d. Junius Butler and Irene Rankin (Johnston) F. MusB, U. Tenn., 1959, MS, 1962; PhD, U. Miss., 1973. Tchr. music Kingsport (Tenn.) Symphony Assn., 1962-64, Birmingham (Ala.) Schs., 1964-66; NASA trainee in biology U. Miss., Oxford, 1969-73; asst. prof. Mobile (Ala.) Coll. (name now U. Mobile), 1973-83, assoc. prof., 1983-94, prof., 1994—. Orch. contractor Am. Fedn. Musicians, 1983—; 1st violin Kingsport Symphony Orch., 1962-64, Birmingham Symphony Orch., 1964-66, Knoxville Symphony Orch., 1955-62, 66-68, Memphis Symphony Orch., 1970-73, Fairhope (Ala.) Concert Series, 1998, Mobile Symphony Orch., 1974—, Pensacola Symphony Orch., Gulf Coast Symphony Orch. Violin recitalist Ala. Artists Series, 1978-81, Fairhope (Ala.) Concert Series, 1998. Mem. project Choctaw Nat. Wildlife Refuge, 1997-98. Named Career Woman of Yr., Gayfer's, Inc., 1985. Mem. Assn. Southeastern Biologists, Human Anatomy and Physiology Soc. (nat. com. to construct standardized test on anatomy and physiology), Wilderness Soc., Ala. Acad. Scis. (presenter 1996), Ala. Ornithol. Soc., Mobile Bay Audubon Soc. (bd. dirs. 1997—), Am. Fedn. Musicians, Ala. Fedn. Music Clubs (chmn. composition contest 1986-90, historian 1991-94), Schumann Music Club (pres. 1977-79, 85-87, 94-97, 2000-03). Republican. Roman Catholic. Avocations: camping, photography, birdwatching. Home: 36 Ridgeview Dr Chickasaw AL 36611-1317 Office: U Mobile PO Box 13220 Mobile AL 36663-0220

FRENCH, HENRY PIERSON, JR., historian, educator; b. Rochester, N.Y., Nov. 21, 1934; s. Henry Pierson and Genevieve Lynn (Johnson) F.; m. Beverly Anne Bauernschmidt, Aug. 22, 1959; children: Henry Pierson III, Donna Lynn (dec.), William Dean, Susan Gayle, John Douglas. AB, U. Del., 1960; MA, U. Rochester, 1961, MA in Edn., 1962, EdD, 1968. Tchr. Pittsford (N.Y.) Ctrl. H.S., 1962-66; field svc. assoc. U. Rochester, N.Y., 1962-66, assoc. lectr., 1967-68, vis. asst. prof. Coll. Edn. and East Asian Ctr., 1968-69, asst. prof. edn., 1969-70, assoc. prof. Ctr. Spl. Degree Programs, 1970-72, lectr. East Asian studies, 1972-74, sr. lectr., 1974-95. Adj. asst. prof. history SUNY-Monroe C.C., 1964-67, asst. prof. history, 1967-70, assoc. prof., 1970-74, prof., 1974—, chmn. dept. history and polit. sci., 1979-85, chmn. tenure, promotion com., 1985—, sabbatical leave, 1986, chair history and polit. sci. cluster in dept. anthropology, history, polit. sci. and sociology, 2001--, coord. history and polit. sci. in dept. anthropology/history/polit. sci., sociology, 2001--; moderator, host Disciplines Within the Social Scis. series, 1968; moderator, permanent panelist Fgn. Policy Assn. and Rochester Assn. for UN Great Decisions, 1973, 77, 78 series Channel 21 Ednl. TV, Rochester; cons., panelist Great Decisions TV series, 1982, 84; vis. prof. history, 1988-89; prof. Canisius Coll., 1968, 69, 71, 73, 89, Dunlop Tire Corp. Japan Inst. faculty, 1989, Rochester Inst. Tech., 1969-70, spring 1977, 98, SUNY, Brockport, 1971; adj. mentor SUNY-Empire State Coll., 1976, 88, 89, spring/fall 1997; bd. dirs. polit. insts. Robert A. Taft Inst. Govt., 1962-65; co-dir., adminstr. NDEA insts., 1965-69; bd. dirs. Rochester Assn. UN, 1972-83, 85-91, chmn. policy com., 1972-74, v.p., 1975-77, pres., 1977-78, chmn. bd., 1978-79, chmn. nominating com., 1983-84; panelist 10th conf. Internat. Assn. Historians of Asia, 1986, 12th conf., 1991, 13th conf., chair, 1994, 14th conf., Bangkok, Thailand, 1996; presenter Gannett News Svc., Rochester, N.Y., 1994; contbr. CNN.com/china article on People's Rep. of China and Dynasticism, 1999. Contbr. articles to profl. jours. Vestryman St. Thomas Episcopal Ch., Rochester, 1965-68, Christ Episc. Ch., Pittsford, 1976-79, jr. warden, 1979-80, sr. warden, 1980-81, chmn. rector selection com., 1982; del. to diocesan Conv., 1989-91, 94-97; 1st provisional lay dep. 1991; lay dep., 1994, 97; mem. commn. on Ordained Ministry, Episc. Diocese of Rochester, 1987-94, chmn., 1992-94; advisor Shanghai-Rochester Bishops' Visitation in U.S. and China, 1989-90, co-leader lay delegation to Shanghai and China Christian Couns., China, 1992, 94, 97; coord. visit of Bishop Shen Yifan and Hong Luming to Rochester, Nov. 1-8, 1993; presenter Symposium on Protestant Christianity in Modern China and East Asia, Chongging and Nanjing, 1994; trustee Reynolds Libr. Bd., 1991—, Mendon Pub. Libr., 1996-97, Rochester Pub. Libr., 1992-2003, v.p., 1996-98, pres., 1998-2000; trustee Friends of Rochester Pub. Libr., 1983-2003, v.p., 1986-88, pres., 1988-91; trustee Rochester Regional Libr. Coun., 1998—; chmn., presenter Rochester Lit. award to James Baldwin, 1986; mem. Edn. Adv. Bd., 1988—, Preferred Care HMO, 1988—; mem. N.Y. State Citizens' Com. for the Bicentennial of the French Revolution, 1988-90. Programs and Comparative Studies grantee, 1970; recipient SUNY Chancellor's medal for philanthropy for estab. endowed chair Henry Pierson French Sr. chair in bus. adminstrn./econs. at Monroe C.C. Rochester, 1999, establish scholarship fund in polit. sci. in the name of Henry Pierson French, III at Monroe C.C. Rochester, 2002. Mem. Assn. Asian Studies, Mid. Atlantic and New Eng. Conf. for Can. Studies, Torch (bd. dirs. Rochester chpt. 1973-76, 97—, pres. 1974-75, Silver Torch award Internat. Assn. 2001), Brighton Schs. Alumni Assn. (co-chair 1998—), Univ. Club (v.p. 1975-76, sec. 1988-90, pres.-elect 1991-92, pres. 1992-93), Genesee Valley Club, Twenty Club, Delta Tau Delta. Episcopalian. Home: 78 Smith Rd Pittsford NY 14534-9727 also: SUNY-Monroe C C Rochester NY 14623 E-mail: hfrench@monroecc.edu.

FRENCH, KATHLEEN PATRICIA, educational administrator; b. Elizabeth, N.J., July 31, 1951; d. Raymond Patrick and Dorothy Ann (Gerber) F. BA, Kean U. N.J., 1974; MS in Edn., Fordham U., 1978; MS in Edn. Admin., Kean U., 1998. Cert. learning disabilities tchr.-cons., prin., supr., spl. edn. tchr., elem. sch. tchr., N.J. Tchr. spl. edn. Elizabeth Sch. Dist., 1974-87; with pub. affairs dept. Merck and Co., Inc., Rahway, N.J., 1987-89; tchr. spl. edn. Woodbridge (N.J.) Twp. Sch. Dist., 1989-92; intervention strategist Phillipsburg (N.J.) Sch. Dist., 1992-93; adj. prof. Kean U. N.J., Union, 1992-94; learning cons. on child study team Union Twp. Sch. Dist., N.J., 1993-99; supr. spl. edn. Piscataway Twp. Schs., Piscataway, N.J., 1999—. Alumni vol. to undergrad. admissions office Fordham U., N.Y.C., 1990-97; adviser Union County Narcotics Bd., Elizabeth, 1992-97. Mem. Assn. Learning Cons., Coun. for Exceptional Children, Kappa Delta Pi. Avocation: travel. Home: 183 Gibson Blvd Apt 8 Clark NJ 07066-1455 Office: Piscataway Twp Schs Adminstrn Bldg PO Box 1332 Piscataway NJ 08855-1332

FRENCH, KENNETH ALFRED, chemistry educator; b. Louisville, Ky., May 24, 1945; s. Bernard George Sr. and Anna Mary (Ray); m. Patricia Ann Brogan, June 22, 1985. BA, Bellarmine Univ., Louisville, Ky., 1967; PhD, Ga. Inst. Tech., 1975. Asst. prof. chemistry Tarkio Coll., Mo., 1975-78, No. Va. C.C., Annandale, 1978; head sci. dept. Idia Coll., Benin City, Nigeria, 1979-81; instr. chemistry, divsn. chmn. Blinn Coll., Brenham, Tex., 1983—. Contbr. articles to profl. jours. Capt. U.S. Army, 1973—75, ret. active duty USAR. Pres.'s scholar, 1963-67; NDEA fellow, 1967-70, Welch fellow, 1982; Rsch. Corp. grantee, 1977. Mem.: Two Yr. Coll. Chem. Conf., Tex. CC Tchrs. Assn., Am. Chem. Soc., Lions Club Internat. (local bd. mem.), Gideons Internat. Avocations: wood-working, volunteer working, traveling. Home: 1406 Kevin Ln Brenham TX 77833-3920 Office: Blinn Coll 902 College Ave Brenham TX 77833-4049 E-mail: kfrench@blinn.edu.

FRENCH, LAURENCE ARMAND, social science educator, psychology educator; b. Manchester, NH, Mar. 24, 1941; s. Gerald Everett and Juliette Teresa (Boucher) F.; m. Nancy Picthall, Feb. 13, 1971. BA cum laude, U. N.H., 1968, MA, 1970, PhD, 1975; postdoctorate, SUNY, Albany, 1978; PhD, U. Nebr., 1981; MA, Western N.M. U., 1994. Diplomate Am. Bd. Forensic Medicine, Am. Bd. Forensic Examiners, Am. Bd. Psychol. Specialties in Forensic Psychology & Neuropsychology, Am. Coll. Advanced Practice Psychologists; lic. psychologist, Ariz. Instr. U. So. Maine, Portland and Gorham, 1971-72; asst. prof. Western Carolina U., Cullowhee, N.C., 1972-77, U. Nebr., Lincoln, 1977-80; psychologist I N.H. Hosp., Concord, 1980-81; psychologist II Laconia (N.H.) State Sch., 1981-88; sr. psychologist N.H. Divsn. for Children & Youth Svcs., Concord, 1988-89; prof., chair dept. social scis. Western N.Mex. U., Silver City, 1989—2003, prof. emeritus of psychology, 2003—; rsch. assoc. justiceworks U. NH Inst. for Policy and Social Sci. Rsch., 2002—; prof., head dept. psychology Coll. Juvenile Justice and Psychology, Prairie View A&M U., 2003—. Profl. adv. bd. Internat. Coll. Prescribing Psychologists; cons. N.C. Dept. Mental Health, 1972—77, Cherokee (N.C.) Indian Mental Health Program, 1974—77, Nebr. Indian Commn., Lincoln, 1977—80; cons. alcohol program Lincoln Indian Ctr., 1977—80; adj. assoc. prof. U. So. Maine, 1980—84; faculty adviser Psi Chi Nat. Honor Soc. in psychology Western N.Mex. U., 1995—2003; mem. Psi Chi Rocky Mountain Regional Steering Com., 2001—02; faculty adviser Psi Chi Nat. Honor Soc. in psychology A&M U., 2003—. Author: The Selective Process of Criminal Justice, 1976; author: (with Richard Crowe) Wee Wish Tree: Special Qualla Cherokee Issue, 1976; author: (with Hornbuckle) Cherokee Perspective, 1981; author: (with Letman et al.) Contemporary Issues in Corrections, 1981; author: Indians and Criminal Justice, 1982, Psychocultural Change and the American Indian, 1987, The Winds of Injustice, 1994, Counseling American Indians, 1997, The Qualla Cherokee Surviving in Two Worlds, 1998, Addictions and Native Americans, 2000, Native American Justice, 2003; spl. issue editor Quar. Jour. Ideology, Vol. II, 1987, mem. editl. bd. Jour. Police and Criminal Psychology; contbr. articles to profl. jours. Commr. Pilsbury Lake Village Dist., Webster, N.H., 1985-90. With USMC, 1959-63, Badge of Honor, Republic of China, 1998. Recipient Hon. medal Rep. China, 1998, Nat. Int. Drug Abuse 1st Leadership in Rsch. award, 1999; Dissertation Yr. fellow U. N.H. 1971-72, Nebr. U. System grad. faculty fellow, 1978. Fellow: APA, Am. Coll. Forensic Examiners (diplomate), Soc. Psychol. Study Social Issues, Prescribing Psychologists Register (diplomate); mem.: VFW (life), N.Mex. Alcohol and Drug Abuse Counselors Assn. (Educator of Yr. 1997), Am. Soc. Criminology (life), Nat. Assn. Alcohol and Drug Abuse Counselors (clin. issue com. 1996—98, nat. chmn.), Internat. Coll. Prescribing Psychologists Inc. (profl. adv. bd.), Nat. Assn. Sch. Psychologists, 3rd Marine Divsn. Assn. (life), Psi Chi (steering com. Rocky Mountain region 2001—, Regional Faculty Advisor award 2002—03), Phi Delta Kappa (treas. Rocky Mountain region 1990—91, pres. 1991—92). Office: Dept Psychology Prairie View A&M Univ Prairie View TX 77446 E-mail: Laurence_French@pvamu.edu., frogwnmue@yahoo.com.

FRENCH, LEURA PARKER, secondary educator; b. Owensville, Ind., June 4, 1926; d. Arthur William and Mildred Ruth Parker; m. Alvin L. French, July 14, 1947 (dec. Sept. 1996); children: Bruce A., Dwight L. BA cum laude, God's Bible Sch. and Coll., 1950; BS in Edn., Wesleyan U., Marion, Ind., 1952; MS in Edn., Butler U., 1962; postgrad., U. Calif., Davis, 1970-73. Tchr. Moorhead Jr. H.S., Indpls., 1957-58, Washington H.S., Indpls., 1962-63, Bella Vista H.S., Fair Oaks, Calif., 1963-65, Casa Roble H.S., Orangevale, Calif., 1967-84, Valley Oak H.S., Oakdale, Calif., 1987—. Study tours for WWII in Europe, China, Hong Kong, Bangkok, Singapore. Co-author booklet: Goals and Objectives for the San Juan Unified School District's Reading Program, 1972. Active Free Meth. Ch., Indpls., 1953-62, Orangevale, 1963-85, 89-96, Oakdale, 1985-89. Fellow Calif. Tchrs. Assn. Republican. Avocations: reading, research, writing, travel. Home: 1100 Roseville Pkwy #317 Roseville CA 95678-5351

FRENCH, MICHAEL FRANCIS, non-profit education agency administrator; b. La Crosse, Wis., July 25, 1948; s. Albert Frank Jr. and Kathryn Patricia (MacKoske) F.; m. Janet Alan Streeter Head, Nov. 26, 1991. BS in Edn., U. Wis., 1972. Cert. emergency med. technician. Tng. coord. emergency med. svcs. Wis. Dept. Health and Social Svcs., Madison, 1975-80, tng. dir. emergency med. svcs., 1980-84, chief emergency med. svcs., 1984-90; co-dir. Area Health Edn. Ctrs. office Kirksville (Mo.) Coll. Osteo. Medicine, 1990—, adj. instr. family medicine and cmty. health, 1990—. Emergency med. svcs. cons., Kirksville, 1984—; founding mem. Continuing Edn. Coordinating Bd. for Emergency Med. Svcs., Inc., Kirksville, 1992. Author: (tng. curriculum) EMS Instructor Training Course-U.S. Dept. Transportation, 1985; editor newsletter, editor-in-chief publs. Nat. Assn. Emergency Med. Technicians, 1983-91; author book chpts. V.p., pres. bd. dirs. Adair County Ret. Sr. Vol. Program, Kirksville, 1992-95; com. chair, bd. dirs. Mo. Rural Opportunities Coun., 2000—. Recipient Lunda Trauma award Am. Trauma Soc., 1982, Svc. awards Nat. Coun. State EMS Tng. Coords., 1982, 83, A. Roger Fox Founders award Nat. Assn. Emergency Med. Technicians, 1989, others. Mem. ASTM, ASCD, ASTD, APHA, Nat. Rural Health Assn. (rural health policy bd. 1998—, gov. affairs com. 2000—), Mo. Rural Health Assn. (bd. dirs. 1995-96, 99—, pres.-elect 1996-97, pres. 1997-99, exec. com. 1999—), Mo. PEW Health Professions Partnership (chair exec. com. 1994-95), Mo. Pub. Health Assn. (awards chair 1996), Wis. Emergency Med. Tech. Assn., Am. Coll. Healthcare Execs. (assoc.), Nat. Orgn. Area Health Edn. Ctr. Program Dirs. (nominations com. 1996), Mensa. Avocations: bicycling, reading, computer games. Office: KCOM AHEC Program 800 W Jefferson St Kirksville MO 63501-1443

FRENCH, PHYLLIS OLIVIA, artistic director, dance instructor; b. N.Y.C., Jan. 8, 1933; d. John Rossiter and Olivia Alvina (Lutz) F.; m. Herbert Edwin Boepple, Mar. 3, 1956; children: Lynn, Lauren, Leanne. Studies with Constantin Kobeleff, N.Y.C., 1940-45; student, Sch. Am. Ballet, N.Y.C., 1944-49; studies with Vitale Fokine, N.Y.C., 1944-50, studies with Jean Yazvinsky, 1950-57. Dancer corps de ballet Radio City Music Hall, N.Y.C., 1949-50, 53-54, Ballet Russe de Monte Carlo, N.Y.C., 1951-51; dancer Broadway prodns. Seventeen, N.Y.C., 1950, Two on the Aisle, N.Y.C., 1952; dancer Perry Como TV Show, N.Y.C., 1953; dancer U.S. tour Oklahoma!, 1954; actress Studio One TV, CBS, N.Y.C., 1958-59; actress, dancer film Edge of the City, N.Y.C., 1959; dance dir. Westwood (N.J.) Recreation Dept., 1970—. Columnist Westwood News, 1970-77; contbr. to local publs; choreographer: Magic in Dance, Westwood, N.J., 1997; subject of film Untapped, 2003.. Pres. PTA Westwood Regional Schs., 1968-71, officer coordinating coun., 1970-73, dir. Phyllis French Sch. Dance Arts, 1977-89, Pascack Art Assn., sec., 1990—; instr. dance programs YWHA, Washington Twp., N.J., 1992-93. Avocations: writing, sculpting, oil-painting. Home: 70 Roosevelt Ave Westwood NJ 07675-2334

FRENCH, RONALD WAYNE, physical education educator; b. L.A., Sept. 17, 1942; s. Herbert Gale and Della Marie (Jackino) F.; m. Janet Lee William, Sept. 3, 1960 (div. June 1989); children: Kelly Lyn, Michael Paul, Niki Marie; m. Lisa Marie Silliman, Mar. 11, 1995. BA, Humboldt State Coll., 1966, MA, 1967; EdD, UCLA, 1971. Cert. nat. adapted phys. educator. Instr. UCLA, 1972-73; asst. prof. SUNY, Brockport, 1972-77; assoc. prof. U. Utah, Salt Lake City, 1977-84, Tex. Woman's U., Denton, 1984-88, prof., 1988—. Presenter numerous state, nat. and internat. confs. and meetings in field. Co-author: When Warm Fuzzies Don't Work, What Next,1990, Creative Approaches to Managing Student Behavior in Physical Education, 1992, Psychomotor Domain Training and Serious Disabilties, 1993, Motor Development of Down's Syndrome Children, 1993, Special Physical Education, 1994, Positive Behavior Management Strategies for Physical Educators, 1997; author chpts. to books; contbr. articles to profl. jours. Soccer coach North Tex. State Soccer Assn., Denton, 1991-94. Grantee N.Y. State Divsn. of Handicapped Children, 1974, 75, Rsch. Found. SUNY, 1975, Bur. Edn. for Handicapped, 1976, HEW, 1977, 78, 79, 80, 81, Utah State Resource Ctr., 1980, Dept. Edn., 1985—, U. Utah Biomed. Rsch., 1979, Tex. Woman's U., 1985, 86. Mem. AAHPERD, Tex. Assn. Health, Phys. Edn., Recreation and Dance, Nat. Consortium of Phys. Edn. and Recreation for Individuals with Disabilities. Roman Catholic. Avocation: racquetball. Office: Tex Womans U PO Box 23717 Denton TX 76204-1717 Home: 3320 Cooper Br E Denton TX 76209-7906 E-mail: f_french@twu.edu.

FRENDER, GLORIA G. secondary school educator; b. Spokane, Mar. 20, 1948; d. Clark and Nylene Collier; m. W. Dean Frender; children: Kevin, Kimberly. BA in Elem. Edn., Wash. State U., 1970. Cert. tchr., Colo. Elem. tchr. Northshore Sch. Dist., Bothell, Wash., 1970-72; middle sch. tchr. Adams County # 12 Sch. Dist., Northglenn, Colo., 1972-73; elem. tchr. Boulder (Colo.) Valley Sch. Dist., 1973-77, secondary English tchr., 1987—. Ednl. cons. Brain Power, Inc., Boulder, 1987—. Author: Learning to Learn, 1990; editor: Right to Read Materials, 1976. Boulder Valley Found. for Schs. grantee, 1990, 91, 92. Mem. ASCD, CEC, Colo. Lang. Arts Soc. Home and Office: 4350 Sage Ct Boulder CO 80301-3965

FRENETTE, LUC, anesthesiologist, educator; b. LaTuque, Que., Can., June 14, 1958; came to U.S., 1990; s. Liguori and Colette (Charland) Frenette. BS, Coll. Three Rivers, Trois-Riviere, Que., Can., 1978; MD, U. Montreal, Que., Can., 1984; BA, U. Pitts., 1991. Chief dept. anesthesiology Hotel Dieu Hosp., Amos, Que., Can., 1988-90; assoc. prof. anesthesiology U. Ala., Birmingham, 1991—. Cons. R.I.S., Boantree, 1991—, Tonorstric, Hoskinton, 1992—. Mem. internat. editl. bd. Practical Cases on Gynaecology; author numerous abstracts; contbr. articles to profl. jours. Mem. AMA, Internat. Soc. Perioperative Care in Liver Transplantation, Internat. Anesthesia Rsch. Soc., Am. Soc. Anesthesiology, Am. Soc. Regional Anesthesiologists, Can. Med. Assn., Can. Soc. Anesthesiologists, Quebec Med. Assn., Quebec Soc. Anesthesiologists. Achievements include discovery that the use of Tonometric shows early allograft viability (up to 60 minutes) in Orthotopic Liver Transplantation, Estrogen decreases blood product needs during Orthotopic Liver Transplantation; designed a 14 Fr catheter for specific use during Orthotopic Liver Transplantation providing on demand veno-venods bypass. Target thera pies coagulation to determinated earlier which specific blood product or pharmaceutical treatment the patient needs during liver transplantation. Office: Univ Ala Dept Anesthesiology 619 19th St S # 845 Birmingham AL 35233-0001 E-mail: luc.frenette@ccc.uab.edu.

FRENKEL, EDWARD VLADIMIR, mathematician, educator; b. Kolomna, Russia, May 2, 1968; came to U.S., 1989; s. Vladimir Iosifovich and Lidia Vladimirovna Frenkel. BA, Gubkin Inst., Moscow, 1989; PhD, Harvard U., 1991. Jr. fellow Soc. Fellows, Harvard U., Cambridge, Mass., 1991-94, assoc. prof. math., 1994-97; prof. U. of Calif., Berkeley, 1997—. Vis. prof. Kyoto (Japan) U., 1992, 93, 95, U. Paris VII, 1992, 2003, U. Paris VI, 1996, Ecole Normale Superieure, Paris, 1998, 2002, Weizmann Inst., Israel, 1992; invited spkr. Internat. Congress Mathematicians, Zurich, Switzerland, 1994, Internat. Congress Math. Physics, Paris, 1994; mem. Inst. for Advanced Study, Princeton, 1997. Editl. bd. Inventiones Mathematicae, Internat. Math. Rsch. Notices, Transformation Groups. Lett. Math. Physics; contbr. articles to profl. jours. Recipient Hermann Weyl prize, 2002; Harvard prize fellow, 1989, Packard Found. fellow, 1995-2000; grantee NSF, 1992, 95, 2003, Sloan Found., 1995-97. Mem. Am. Math. Soc. Office: U Calif at Berkeley Dept Math 970 Evans Hall Berkeley CA 94720-3840

FRERKER, JEFFREY CARL, secondary education educator; b. Breese, Ill., Jan. 11, 1962; s. Leo Henry and Bernice Cathrine (Richter) F.; m. Denise Marie Spihlman, June 27, 1987; 1 child, Joshua Robert. BS in Secondary Edn., So. Ill. U., 1985, MS in Secondary Edn. and History, 1992. Cert. secondary educator grades 6 thru 12, Ill. Tchr. Belleville (Ill.) West High Sch., 1986—. Advisor Belleville West Model U.N. club, Amnesty Internat. club. Mem. KC, Breese, Ill., 1982—. Named to Nat. Dean's List, 1985-86. Mem. Nat. Coun. for Social Studies, Ill. Fedn. Tchrs., Phi Kappa Phi. Home: 617 E 4th St Trenton IL 62293-1757 Office: Belleville West High Sch 2600 E Main St Belleville IL 62221-5032

FRESCHI, BRUNO BASILIO, architect, educator; b. Trail, B.C., Can., Apr. 18, 1937; s. Giovanni and Irma (Pagotto) F.; m. Vaune Ainsworth, Dec. 13, 1986; children from previous marriage: Dea Rachelle, Anna Nadine, Aaron Basilio, Reuben Alessandro. BArch with honors, U. B.C., 1961; postgrad., Archtl. Assn., London; cert., Royal Can. Acad. Art, 1973. Assoc. Erickson Massey Architects, Vancouver, B.C., 1964-70; prin. Keith, King, Freschi, Vancouver, 1970-74; prin., owner Bruno Freschi, Architects, Vancouver, 1986; prof. architecture U. B.C., Vancouver, 1969-79; prof., dean Profl. Sch. Architecture and Planning SUNY, Buffalo, 1988-2000, prof., dean emeritus, 2000—; design prin. Cannon Design, Buffalo, 1997—. Lectr. in field; chief architect Expo '86. Prin. works include Peace Bridge design proposal, Buffalo, Waterfront Regeneration plans for Tacoma, Wash., Buffalo, Vancouver, Jamatkhana Mosque, Expo '86 Master Plan, Expo Centre, Burnaby Mcpl. Hall, Cathedral Sq. and Ga. Place; cons. Teleport, Vancouver. Chmn., Italian Heritage Plz., Vancouver, 1985; past mem. numerous civic and cultural orgns. Decorated officer Order of Can.; recipient Man of Yr. award, Confratellanza Italo-Canadese, 1983, Gov. Gen. medal, 1984, 1st prize, Wheel-Expo Symbol Competition, 1984, Nat. Columbus Day Citation of Honor, 1992, Commemorative Medal of Honor, 125th Anniversary of Can. Confedn., 1992. Fellow: Royal Archtl. Inst. Can. (medal 1961); mem.: AIA (assoc.), Alta. Assn. Architects, Royal Can. Acad. Arts (academician), Archtl. Inst. B.C., World Acad. Art and Sci., Christopher of Columbus Lodge. Avocations: painting, hiking, bike riding. Home: 1003 New Hampshire Ave NW Washington DC 20037-1814 Office: Cannon Design 3299 K St NW Washington DC 20007 also: 200-1450 Creekside Dr Vancouver BC Canada V6J 5B3 E-mail: bfreschi@cannondesign.com.

FRESHWATER, MICHAEL FELIX, plastic surgeon, educator; b. N.Y.C., Feb. 4, 1948; s. Jack and Rhonda Freshwater. BS magna cum laude, Bklyn. Coll., 1968; MD, Yale U., 1972. Diplomate Nat. Bd. Med. Examiners, Am. Bd. Plastic Surgery. Asst. resident in surgery Yale New Haven Hosp., 1972-74; fellow in plastic surgery Med. Sch. Johns Hopkins U., Balt., 1974-77; resident, then chief resident in plastic surgery Jackson Meml. Hosp., 1977-78; Kleinert fellow hand and microsurgery Jewish Hosp., Louisville, 1979; pvt. practice medicine specializing in plastic/hand surgery Miami, Fla., 1979—; pres., dir. Miami Inst. Hand and Microsurgery, 1980—; dir. hand and microsurgery Cedars Med. Ctr., 1985—, chief surgery, 1988-90, bd. dirs., 1990-92. Vol. assoc. prof. plastic surgery U. Miami Sch. medicine, 1979—; vol. faculty mem. Barry U. Sch. Podiatric Medicine and Surgery, 1989—; vis. prof. Javeriana U., Bogota, 1983—85, Centro Medico de los Andes, 1983—86; cons. Fla. Children's Med. Svc., Tallahassee, 1979—, Fla. Elks Crippled Children Soc., Orlando, 1983—, Fla. Dept. Profl. Regulation, Tallahassee, 1984—95, League Against Cancer, 1983—, Scientists Inst. Pub. Info., 1985—, USCG, Miami Beach, 1992—. Contbr. chapters to books, articles to profl. jours.; mem. bd. reviewers: Plastic and Reconstructive Surgery, 1976—. Trustee Yale U. Med. Libr., New Haven, 1972—77, 2000—, D. R. Millard Found., 1987—; bd. dirs. V. and A. Gildred Found., 1980—86, Yale Sch. Medicine Fund, 1991—97, Campaign for Stuyvesant, 2003—; mem. nat. campaign com. Yale Sch. Medicine, 1993—97; mem. Fla. Bar Grievance Com., 1998—2001. Recipient Letter Commendation, Gov. Bob Graham, 1984; fellow Weinberger, NIH, 1974—76; scholar Jonas Salk, CUNY, 1968—72. Fellow: Internat. Coll. Surgeons; mem.: AMA (Physicians Recognition award 1976, 1979, 1982, 1985, 1988, 1990, 1993, 1996, 1999, 2001), Miami Assn. for Surgery of Hand (dir. 1991—), Am. Soc. Peripheral Nerve, Miami Soc. Plastic Surgeons (sec.-treas. 1987—88, v.p. 1988—89, pres. 1989—90), Royal Soc. Medicine, Internat. Soc. Reconstructive Microsurgery, Am. Soc. Reconstructive Microsurgery, Am. Burn Assn., Am. Assn. Hand Surgery, Assn. Yale Alumni in Medicine (bd. dirs. 1998—2000), Grove Isle Club (Miami), Yale Club (Miami, N.Y.), Phi Beta Kappa. Avocation: skiing. Office: 1 Datran Ctr Ste 502 Miami FL 33156-7814 E-mail: miamihandsurgery@bellsouth.net.

FRETER, LISA, non-profit association administrator; b. Washington, Aug. 25, 1951; d. Theodore Henry and Elizabeth Crawford (Stout) Freter; m. David O'Shea Dawkins, Dec. 10, 1975 (div. May 1995); 1 child, Meghan Elizabeth. Student, Towson State Coll., 1969-70, U. de las Americas,

Cholula, Puebla, Mex., 1972-73; BSBA, U. Phoenix, 1992. Owner B&B Liquors, Denver, 1979-81; dir. pubs. Gt. Western Assn. Mgmt., Denver, 1985-88; adminstrv. asst., conf. coord. Employment and Tng. divsn. Arapahoe County, Aurora, Colo., 1988-93; dir. confs. 3AI Affiliated Advt. Agys. Internat. Inc., Aurora, Colo., 1994-95; office mgr. Cin. Works, 1996—. Author: (poems) The San Miguel Writer, 1970, Xalli, 1971; exec. producer Law Enforcement Torch Run for Spl. Olympics Video, 1986, videotaped pub. svc. announcements, 1987; producer, dir. (video) Private Industry Council, 1989; contbr. articles to mags.; editor various newsletters. Exec. dir. Colleagues Police for Edn., Support, Denver, 1983-85; liaison Colo. Assn. Chiefs of Police, 1983-85; coord. Law Enforcement Torch Run for Spl. Olympics, 1986-88. Mem. Freedoms Found. Valley Forge (v.p. pub. rels. 1988-92, 93-94, pres. 1992-93), Colo. Gang Investigators Assn. (exec. dir. 1989-90, v.p. membership 1993-94, newsletter editor 1994-95), Colo. Soc. Assn. Execs., Profl. Conv. Mgmt. Assn., Cin. Soc. Assn. Execs. Avocations: reading, writing, swimming. Office: Cincinnati Works 37 W 7th St Ste 200 Cincinnati OH 45202-2414 Home: 7175 W Alabama Dr Lakewood CO 80232-5509

FREUDIG, DAVID WAYNE, elementary educator; b. Bethlehem, Pa., Mar. 9, 1943; s. Rudolph Arthur and Sarah Ann (Pflueger) F.; m. Patty Lynn Schumacher, Dec. 12, 1986 (div. Dec. 1991). BA, Gettysburg Coll., 1965; MEd, Lehigh U., 1968. Cert. social studies and history tchr., Pa. Tchr. 5th and 6th grades Salford Hills Elem. Sch., Woxall, Pa., 1965-70, 71-86; elem. tchr. social studies Indian Valley Mid. Sch., Harleysville, Pa., 1987—. Mem. NEA (life), Pa. State Edn. Assn. (life), Masons. Republican. Lutheran. Avocations: skiing, golf. Home: 84 Aspen Way Schwenksville PA 19473-2330 Office: Indian Valley Mid Sch 130 Maple Ave Harleysville PA 19438-1796

FREY, BOB HENRY, psychotherapist, sociologist, educator, poet, canon lawyer; b. Porterdale, Ga., Mar. 7, 1953; s. George Loyd Sr. and Betty Montine (Canup) F.; m. Deborah Ann Dunn Mar. 8, 1980. BA, Immanuel Coll., Peachtree City, Ga., 1976; MA, Immanuel Sem., Peachtree, 1977, DRE, 1980; EdD in Counseling and Adminstrn., Immanuel Sem., Atlanta, 1988; PhD in Sociology, Columbia Pacific U., 1985; MA in Counseling, Luther Rice Sem., 1992; PhD in Christian Counseling, Am. Bible Coll. and Seminary, 1998; postgrad., South Fla. Bible Coll. & Sem., 1996—; D Canon Jurisprudence, Romano-Byzantine Coll., Duluth, Minn., 1997; LLD (hon.), Christian Bible Coll., 1996; PhD in Psychology, All Am. U., 2003. Cert. med. psychotherapist, Am. Bd. Med. Psychotherapists and Psychodiagnosticians, bd. cert. disability analyst Am. Bd. Disability Analysts; cert. sociologist, cert. profl. sociol. practitioner, Am. Acad. Profl. Sociol. Practitioners and Nat. Assn. Forensic Counselors; lic. Mercian practitioner, Romano-Byzantine Synod Commn. on Religious Counseling and Healing. Dean Calvary Bapt. Bible Coll., Jonesboro, Ga., 1977-78; chief of police City of Hagan, Ga., 1986-87; caseworker prin. Toombs County Dept. Family and Children Svcs., Lyons, Ga., 1987; adj. faculty mentor Columbia Pacific U., San Rafael, Calif., 1987-89; adj. prof. Newport U., Newport Beach, Calif., 1989—; coord., mgr. Tidelands Community Mental Health, Mental Retardation and Substance Abuse Ctr., Savannah, Ga., 1990-91; psychotherapist, clin. dir. social and clin. svcs. Mel Blount Youth Home Ga., Vidalia, Ga., 1992—95; psychotherapist, clin. supr. Clayton Ctr. for Mental Health, Substance Abuse and Devel. Svcs., Riverdale, Ga., 1994—97, psychotherapist, auditor, monitor, 1997—2001; pres., CEO Christian-Frey Assn. Connection Elite Svcs., 2000—. Mentor adj. faculty Christian U. Kuaui, Hawaii, 1993-97; adj. faculty St. Martin's Coll. and Sem., Milw., 1995-2000; poet, Nat. Libr. Poetry, Owings Mills, Md.; canon lawyer, 1997-99. Author: A Biblical Perspective-The Writing of Divorcement, 1993, A Biblical Study Guide, 1993, The Frey Initiative on Accreditation-Discriminatory Practices Regional vs National, 1994, (pamphlets) The Bible, The Christian, Non-Christian and Nudism, 1982, The Frey Manifesto On Accreditation Issues, 1995, Christians Out-Of-Step With God, 1985; contbg. poet: Life, Not Fair, The Flight, The Old House Analogy, The Old Car Analogy. Lobbyist MADD, Atlanta, 1983; rsch. bd. advisors nat. divsn. Am. Biographical Inst., Raleigh, N.C., 1994—; vol. police/city chaplain, capt. City of Riverdale, Ga. Sgt. U.S. Army, 1970-77; hosp. adminstr. Ga. Dept. Def., Ga. State Def. Force, Air Med. Detachment, Savannah, Ga., 2003—. Scholar, Columbia Pacific U., 1982. Fellow Am. Bd. Disability Analysts; mem. Internat. Soc. Poets (disting.), Am. Coll. of Profl. Mental Health Practitioners (diplomate), Nat. Assn. of Forensic Counselors, Am. Acad. of Profl. Sociological Practitiioners. Democrat. Avocations: hunting, fishing, swimming, boating, camping. Home: 324 Green Oak Rd Lyons GA 30436 E-mail: annbob@stealthport.com., dafann@stealthport.com., dafbob@stealthport.com.

FREY, FREDERICK AUGUST, geochemistry researcher, educator; b. Milw., Apr. 1, 1938; s. Frederick August and Evelyn Dorothy (Lange) F.; m. Julie Ann Golden; 1 child, Oren. BSCE, U. Wis., 1960, PhD in Chemistry, 1967. Prof. dept. earth, atmospheric and planetary scis. MIT, Cambridge, 1966—, Francqui Found. prof., 1996-97. Assoc. editor: Geochimica et Cosmochimica Acta; contbr. over 185 articles to profl. jours. Fellow Geochem. Soc., European Assn. Geochemist, Am. Geophys. Union (pres. VGP sect. 2000-2002, VGP Bowen award 1986); mem. Geol. Soc. Am., European Union Geoscis. Office: MIT Dept Earth Atmos & Plan Sci 54 # 1226 Cambridge MA 02139

FREY, JOANNE ALICE TUPPER, art educator; b. Wakefield, Mass., Jan. 16, 1931; d. Arthur Andrew Tupper, Elva June Goddard, Joanne Alice Tupper; m. John Oscar Frey, June 14, 1953 (dec. Oct. 2000); children: David J., Donald A., Dale R., Alexandria Brennan. Grad. honors, Vesper George Sch. Art, Boston, 1951; student art history, NTL Art Gallery, London, 1979. Tchr. art Wishing Well Cards, Everett, Mass., 1951—54, Sarrin Studio, Wakefield, Mass., 1960—96; tchr. art oil, acrylic, and watercolor Wakefield H.S., Wakefield, 1997—. Antique and current doll authority; lectr. in field. Asst. resident dir. Boit Home for Women, Wakefield, Mass., 1996—; bd. dirs. The Hartshorne House. Mem.: Collie Rescue League of N.E., The Kosmos Club (decorator 1997—). Republican. Congregationalist. Avocations: painting, reading, walking, gardening, art history. Home: 701 Haverhill St Reading MA 01867

FREY, JUDITH LYNN, elementary education educator; b. Ashland, Ohio, Sept. 10, 1956; d. Lloyd Baeder and Norma Claire (Hostettler) Wygant; children: Jennifer Lynn, Lynnette Danielle. BS in Edn., Otterbein Coll., 1978. Elem. remedial reading tchr. Norwalk (Ohio) City Schs., 1978-79, Bucyrus (Ohio) City Schs., 1979-81, 87-98, kindergarten tchr., 1981-87, 7th grade English tchr., 1998-99; title I tchr., 1999—. Co-dir. Holy Trinity Cath. Ch. Pre-Sch. Religion, Bucyrus, 1987-92. Mem. DAR, Internat. Reading Assn. (Crawford County chpt., bldg. rep. 1991-94), Eden Homemakers Club (sec./treas. 1995—), Bucyrus Acad. Boosters. Avocations: reading, bike riding, walking, crafts. Home: 9940 County Highway 134 Nevada OH 44849-9763 Office: Kilbourne Elementary Sch 1130 S Walnut St Bucyrus OH 44820-3265

FREY, KATIE MANCIET, education educator; b. Tucson, Ariz., Dec. 31, 1952; d. Hector Encinas and Lilian Eloisa (Hanna) Manciet; m. Richard Patrick Frey, Jul. 20, 1974; 1 child, Stacy Ann. BS, U. Ariz., 1974, MEd, 1982, PhD, 1987. Tchr. physical edn. Amphitheater Pub. Schs., Tucson, 1974-81, rsch. specialist, 1982-85, dir. rsch. & devel., 1985-88, asst. supt., 1988-89, assoc. supt., 1989—2001; tng. coord. LINKS U. Ariz., 2002—03. Gymnastics coach Amphitheater Pub. Schs., Tucson, 1974-81, rsch chair Ad Hoc Adv. Coun. on Sch. Dropouts, Ariz., 1987, mem. Gov. Edn. Conf., Ariz., 1989, mem. State Supr. Task Force on Sch. Violence, Ariz., 1993-94, Mayor's Sch. Dist. Action Task Force, Tucson. 1993—; mem. NCAA recertification equity subcom. U. Ariz., 1997-98. Mem. APEX, Tucson, 1987-99, Traveler's Aid Soc. of Tucson, 1993-98, Citizen's Adv. Coun. U. Ariz., 1994-96; mem. tech. adv. bd. Town of Oro Valley, 1995-96; mem. exec. steering com. K-16 Edn. Coun. So. Ariz., 1995-96; bd. dirs. YWCA, 1999—; chair Tucson Resiliency Initiative, 1999—. Recipient APEX Apple award U. Ariz., 1994, Women on the Move award, 2000. Mem.: AAUW, NOW, U. Ariz. Hispanic Alumni Assn., U. Ariz. Letterwinners Assn. Avocations: reading, travel, family, Tai Chi, landscaping. E-mail: tucsonkatie@aol.com.

FREY, LUCILLE PAULINE, social studies educator, consultant; b. Huggins, Mo., Aug. 1, 1932; d. Albert Raymond and Gladys Pearl (Maxville) F. BS in Edn., Southwest Mo. State U., 1955; MA in English, Mo. U., 1963; MAT, Ala. Pacific U., 1975; PhD in Women's Studies, Union Grad. Inst., 1985. Tchr. Tex. County Rural Schs., Plato, Mo., 1949-53, Sullivan (Mo.) Pub. Schs., 1953-57, Anchorage Pub. Schs., 1957-70, social studies coord., 1970-75; ednl. cons. The Learning Tree, Alaska, 1975-85. Adj. prof. U. Alaska, 1970-77; owner Women's Bookstore, Anchorage, 1981-84; comml. fisherwoman Net Prophets, Bristol Bay, Alaska, 1980-85; real estate salesperson Dynamic Properties, Anchorage, 1989-94, Century 21 Peterson, Hermitage, Mo., 1995—. Author: (textbook) Eyes Toward Icebergia, 1963; editor: Women of Alaska Workbook, 1974, Alaska Studies Curriculum, 1975, Athabaskan Curriculum, 1980. Founding mem. Alaska Women's Edn. Caucus, Anchorage, 1970; mem. Alaska Women's Polit. Caucus, Anchorage, 1972; organizer various state edn. confs., 1976-83, women's conf., Alaska, 1982. Recipient Gov's. Vol. award, Alaska, 1984; named to Women's Hall of Fame, Alaska, 1991. Mem. NEA (Women's Right award 1979, Renowned Alaskan award, 1986), Profl. Women's Assn. (sec.), Mo. Realtor's Assn., Union Grad. Inst. (mem. doctoral com.), Ozark Bd. Realtors, Lake Area Friendship Club. Democrat. Avocations: gardener, birdwatcher, historian, political activist. Home: RR 1 Box 1965 Urbana MO 65767-9639

FREY, MARGO WALTHER, career counselor, columnist; b. Watertown, Wis., July 1, 1941; d. Lester John and Anabel Marie (Bergin) Walther; m. James Severin Frey, June 29, 1963; children: Michelle Marie Frey Loberg, David James. BA in French, Cardinal Stritch Coll., 1963; MS in Ednl. Psychology, U. Wis., Milw., 1971; EdD in Adult Edn., Nova U., 1985. Nat. bd. cert. career counselor; approved profl. counselor, Wis. Acad. counselor biology dept. Ind. U., Bloomington, 1975-76; dir. career planning and placement Cardinal Stritch Coll., Milw., 1977-89; pres. Career Devel. Svcs., Inc., Milw., 1989—. Weekly columnist Milw. Journ. Sentinel, 1994-95, 98—. Mem. Bloomington (Ind.) women's commn. com. on employment assessment Displaced Homemakers Task Force, 1975. Named to Practitioner's Hall of Fame, Nova U., 1985. Mem. ASTD (bd. dirs. 1992), Wis. Career Planning and Placement Assn. (bd. dirs. 1987), Wis. Assn. Adult and Continuing Edn. (bd. dirs. 1983-85), Milw. Coun. Adult Learning, Human Resource Mgmt. Assn., Tempo (bd. dirs. 1995-97). Avocations: reading, swimming. E-mail: margocds@execpc.com.

FREYD, PETER JOHN, mathematician, computer scientist, educator; b. Evanston, Ill., Feb. 5, 1936; s. Paul Robert and Pauline Margaret (Pattinson) F.; m. Pamela Parker, Jan. 1, 1957; children: Jennifer Joy, Gwendolyn Ann. AB magna cum laude, Brown U., 1958; MA (Woodrow Wilson fellow), Princeton U., 1959, PhD, 1960. Tchr. art Conti Art Sch., Providence, 1952—54; tchr. carpentry Camp Cragged Mountain Farm, Freedom, NH, 1954; instr. stats. Batton Barton Durstine and Osborn, N.Y.C., 1956; asst. instr. math. Brown U., Providence, 1957, instr. math. NSF program, 1958—59, instr. Acad. Potential project, 1960; asst. instr. math. Princeton U., 1959—60; tchr. dramatics Am. Sch., Shiraz, Iran, 1968; J.F. Ritt instr. math. Columbia U., N.Y.C., 1960-62; faculty U. Pa., Phila., 1962—, prof. math., 1968—, chmn. grad. group math., 1982-87, prof. computer info. sci., 1987—; dir. Lab. for Logic and Computation, 1993—. Adviser Pahlavi U., Shiraz, Iran, 1968; lectr. Canadian Nat. Rsch. Seminar, 1974; vis. rschr. Swiss Fed. Inst. Tech., Zurich, 1969; vis. researcher U. Mex., 1975, U. Sydney, 1985, U. Milan, 1986, U. Parma, 1990; vis. prof. U. Chgo., 1980, U. Louvain, Belgium, 1981; vis. prof. in computer sci. Carnegie Mellon U., 1988-89. Author: Abelian Categories, 1964; (with Andre Scedrov) Categories, Allegories, 1990; founder Jour. Pure and Applied Algebra, 1970; editor Theoretical Computer Sci., 1988—, Math. Structures in Computer Sci., 1989—, Internat. Jour. Algebra and Computation, 1990—, Jour. Knot Theory and its Ramifications, 1991—. Fulbright scholar Australia, 1971; fellow St. John's Coll., Cambridge U., Eng., 1980-81 Mem. Isaac Newton Inst. 1995, Phi Beta Kappa, Sigma Xi. Home: 2020 1/2 Addison St Philadelphia PA 19146-1307 Office: U Pa Dept Maths 33 E Walnut Ln Philadelphia PA 19144-2002

FREYERMUTH, VIRGINIA KAREN, art educator; BFA cum laude, Boston U., 1973, MFA, 1975; edn. cert., Suffolk U., 1975; PhD in Interdisciplinary Studies, Art Edn., Union Inst. and U., 2003. Cert. art tchr., Mass. Grad. asst. Boston U., Mass., 1973-75; art tchr. Quincy Pub. Sch., Mass., 1975-76, Plymouth Pub. Sch., Mass., 1976-78, 83-85; painting tchr. Brockton Fuller Mus. Art, Mass., 1978-79; art coord. grades K-12 Duxbury Pub. Sch., Mass., 1985-99; vis. lectr. art edn. U. Mass., Dartmouth, Mass., 1999—. Art reviewer Patriot Ledger, Quincy, 1975-85; dir. Freyermuth Fine Arts Ctr., Plymouth, 1990-94; mem. adv. coun. Mass. Field Ctr. Tchg. & Learning, 1993-96; tchr. in electronic residence MCET, Cambridge, 1993-95; instr. art Massasoit C.C., Brockton, 1991-92; dir. Helen Bumpus Gallery, Inc., Duxbury, 1992-94; forum tchr. Goals 2000 U.S. Dept. of Edn., 1994—, internat. space camp, 1994. Columnist Learning for Life, 1994. Mem. commn. on common core of learning Mass. Dept. Edn., 1993-94; bd. dirs. Mass. Alliance for Arts Edn., 1994-95. Named Mass. Tchr. of Yr., Mass. Dept. Edn., 1994, Nat. Outstanding Visual Art Tchr., Walt Disney and McDonald's, 1995, 1995-96 Profiled in Disney Channel. Mem. Mass. Art Edn. Assn., Nat. Art Edn. Assn., Tchr. Leadership Acad. Mass. (bd. dirs.), Lucretia Crocker Acad. of Tchg. Fellows (bd. dirs.). Office: PO Box 6132 Plymouth MA 02362-6132

FRIAS, JAIME LUIS, pediatrician, educator; b. Concepcion, Chile, Mar. 20, 1933; came to U.S., 1970; s. Luis Humberto and Olga Ana (Fernandez) F.; m. Jacqueline May Steel, Apr. 8, 1961; children: Jaime Arturo, Juan Pablo, Patricio Andres, Maria Josefina. MD, U. Chile, 1959. Diplomate Am. Bd. Pediatrics, Am. Bd. Human Genetics. Intern Hospital Regional, Concepcion, 1958-59; resident in pediatrics Calvo Mackenna Hosp., Santiago, Chile, 1960-62; clin. genetics and dysmorphology fellow U. Wis., Madison, 1965-66, U. Wash., Seattle, 1966-67; asst. prof. pediatrics U. Concepcion, 1967-69, U. Fla. Coll. Medicine, Gainesville, 1970-74, assoc. prof., 1974-77, prof., 1977-86, chief divsn. genetics, 1977-86, chmn. med. sch. admissions com., 1983-86; prof., chmn. dept. pediatrics U. Nebr. Med. Ctr., 1986—91; prof. pediatrics U. South Fla. Coll. Medicine, Tampa, 1991—, chmn. dept. pediatrics, 1991-99, dir. Birth Defects Ctr., 1999—. Chmn. Com. for Protection of Human Subjects, 1975-78; chmn. Fla. Com. on Prevention Devel. Disabilities, 1979-82, chmn. infant hearing screening adv. coun., 1982-86; cons. Spanish Collaborative Project on Congenital Malformation, Madrid, 1983—. Contbr. chpts. to books, articles to profl. jours. Trustee All Children's Hosp., 1991-99, Ronald McDonald Charities Tampa Bay, 1999-2001; exec. com. Assn. Med. Sch. Pediat. Dept. Chmn., 1993-96; steering com. Nat. Folic Acid Coun., 1999-2003. Named Tchr. of Yr., U. Fla. Coll. Medicine, 1978-79, Lewis A. Barness Endowed Chair Pediatrics, 1994-99. Mem. ACP (affiliate; W.K. Kellogg fellow 1965-67), Am. Acad. Pediatrics (com. genetics 1995-2002), Am. Pediatric Soc., Am. Soc. Human Genetics, Assn. Clin. Scientists, Tampa Yacht and Country Club. Democrat. Roman Catholic. Office: U South Fla Dept Pediat 17 Davis Blvd Ste 200 Tampa FL 33606-3438 E-mail: jfrias@hsc.usf.edu.

FRIBOURGH, JAMES HENRY, university administrator; b. Sioux City, Iowa, June 10, 1926; s. Johan Gunder and Edith Katherine (James) F.; m. Cairdenia Minge, Jan. 29, 1955; children: Cynthia Kaye, Rebecca Jo, Abbie Lynn. Student, Morningside Coll., 1944-47; BA, MA, U. Iowa, 1949, PhD, 1957; LHD (hon.), DHL (hon.), Morningside Coll., 1989. Instr. Little Rock Jr. Coll., 1949-56; assoc. prof. biology Little Rock U., 1957-60, prof., chmn. div. life scis., 1960-69; vice chancellor U. Ark., Little Rock, 1969-72, interim chancellor, 1972-73, exec. vice chancellor for acad. affairs, 1973-82, interim chancellor, exec. vice chancellor for acad. affairs, 1982, provost, exec. vice chancellor, 1983—, disting. prof., 1984-94, disting. prof. emeritus, 1994—. Cons. in field; assoc. Marine Biol. Lab., Woods Hole, Mass. Contbr. articles to profl. jours. Mem. Ark. Gov.'s Com. on Sci. and Tech., 1969-71; bd. dirs., mem. nat. adv. bd. Nat. Back Found., 1979; vice chmn. NCCJ, 1981-82; div. rep. United Way of Pulaski County, 1980-82; bd. dirs. Ark. Dance Theatre, Little Rock, 1980-82; vestryman Good Shepherd Episcopal Ch.; del. Episcopal Diocese of Ark.; fellow Ark. Mus. Sci. and History, 1987. Fribourgh Hall named in his honor, U. Ark., Little Rock, 1994; NSF fellow History of Sci. Inst., 1959-60. Fellow AAAS, Coll. Preceptors (London), Am. Inst. Fishery Rsch. Biologists, Ark. Mus. Sci. and History; mem. Am. Fisheries Soc. (chmn. com. on internationalism cert. fisheries scientist), AAUP (pres. Ark. conf.), Electron Microscopy Soc. Am., Am. Soc. Swedish Engrs. (corr. mem.), Ark. Acad. Sci. (pres. 1966), Ark. Dean's Assn. (pres. 1982), Am. Assn. State Colls. and Univs., Am. Swedish Inst., Swedish Club (Chgo.), Rotary (Paul Harris fellow), Vasa Order Am. Lodge, Sigma Xi, Phi Kappa Phi. Clubs: Swedish, Vasa Order Am. Lodges: Rotary (Paul Harris fellow). Democrat. Office: U Ark 33rd and University Ave Little Rock AR 72204 E-mail: jhfribourgh@ualr.edu.

FRICK, GENE ARMIN, university administrator; b. Huntingburg, Ind., Oct. 13, 1929; s. Armin John and Naomi S. (Kemp) F.; m. Barbara Sue Partenheimer, Feb. 12, 1955; children: David Alan, Barbara Jean. BS in Acctg., Butler U., 1951. Acct. Huntingburg Machine Works, 1947-51; auditor Army Audit Agy., Louisville, 1952-53; property acct. E.I. DuPont, Louisville, 1954; acting internal auditor Purdue U., West Lafayette, 1955-57, contract adminstr., 1957-76, dir. contracts, 1976-93, dir. emeritus, 1993—. Treas. Purdue Calumet Devel. Found., East Chicago, Ind., 1955-57; sec., treas. East Chicago Housing Corp., 1955-57; mem. com. on contracts Coun. Govt. Rels., Washington, 1975-82, com. on costing, 1982-84, bd. dirs., 1978-84; lectr. Nat. Grad. U., 1976-80. Cpl. U.S. Army, 1951-53. Named Outstanding Regional Dir., Toastmaster Internat., 1978, Ky. Col., 1989, Sagamore of the Wabash, State of Ind., 1993. Mem. Elks, Lafayette Country Club, John Purdue Club, Sigma Nu (pres. housing corp. 1977-87). Republican. Avocations: golf, spectator sports, reading. Home: 2166 Tecumseh Park Ln West Lafayette IN 47906-2182 Office: Purdue U Hovde Hall West Lafayette IN 47905

FRIED, BELLE WARSHAVSKY, education educator; b. N.Y.C., Apr. 14, 1917; d. Maurice and Sarah (Brown) Bennett; m. Henry Warshavsky, Feb. 22, 1941 (dec.); children Barry Alyn, Beth, Benes; m. Joseph Fried, Jan. 13, 1986. BBA, St. Johns U., 1940; MSEd, Hofstra U., 1957; postgrad., NYU, 1962, profl. diploma in reading, 1965; PhD, Walden U., 1975; postgrad., C.W. Post U., 1994. Cert. gerontologist. Pvt. sec. real estate div. Home Owners Loan Corp., N.Y.C., 1935-39; pers. interviewer N.Y. State Arsenal, Bklyn., 1940-41; brokerage agt. Mut. Trust Life Ins. Co., N.Y.C., 1950-55; instr. Cen. Sch. Dist. No. 4, Plainview, N.Y., 1955-60, cons. in reading, 1961-85, dir. summer reading program, 1962-85. Instr. Kindergarten Workshops, 1961-63, Hofstra U. Reading Clinic, 1965-66; adj. instr. Queensboro C.C., 1970-79, asst. prof. 1994—, adj. prof., 1994—. Contbg. author: The Non-graded Primary—A Case History, 1986. Vice chmn. Nassau County Rep. Com., 1981; vice chmn. Rep. Com. Town of North Hempstead, 1983—; exec. leader Great Neck North Rep. Com.; mem. presdl. Task Force; leader Girl Scouts U.S., 1940-42; instr. 1st aid course for adults CD, 1941; aid welfare commr. Saddle Rock Civic Assn., 1962-80; rep. Long Term Care Ins. Mem. NEA, Nat. Soc. Study Edn., N.Y. State Tchrs. Assn., Nassau County Tchrs. Assn., Classroom Tchrs. Assn. (v.p., sec. 1958-60), Great Neck Edn. Assn. Nassau County, Internat. Reading Assn., Internat. Platform Assn., Sigma Tau Delta, Phi Delta Kappa. Home: 35 Cooper Dr Great Neck NY 11023-1908 Address: 4302 Martinique Cir Coconut Creek FL 33066-1482

FRIED, CHARLES, law educator; b. Prague, Czechoslovakia, Apr. 15, 1935; came to U.S., 1941, naturalized, 1948; s. Anthony and Marta (Winterstein) F.; m. Anne Sumerscale, June 13, 1959; children: Gregory, Antonia. AB, Princeton U., 1956; BA, Oxford (Eng.) U., 1958, MA, 1961; LLB, Columbia U., 1960; LLD (hon.), New Eng. Sch. of Law, 1987, Pepperdine U., 1994, Suffolk U., 1996. Bar: D.C. 1961, Mass. 1966. Law clk. to Hon. John M. Harlan U.S. Supreme Ct., 1960; from asst. prof. to prof. law Harvard U., Cambridge, 1961-85, Carter prof. gen. jurisprudence, 1981-85, 89-95, Carter prof. emeritus, disting. lectr. Law Sch., 1995-99, Beneficial prof. law, 1999—; assoc. justice Supreme Jud. Ct. Mass., Boston, 1995-99. Spl. cons. Treasury Dept., 1961—62; cons. White House Office Policy Devel., Washington, 1982, Dept. Transp., Washington, 1981—82, Dept. Justice, 1983; solicitor gen. U.S., 1985—89. Author: An Anatomy of Values, 1970, Medical Experimentation: Personal Integrity and Social Policy, 1974, Right and Wrong, 1978, Contract as Promise: A Theory of Contractual Obligation, 1981, Order and Law: ArgSayiuing the Reagan Revolution, 1991, (with David Rosenberg) Making Tort Law: What Should Be Done and Who Should Do It, 2003, Saying What The Law Is: The Constitution in The Supreme Cour, 2004; contbr. legal and philos. jours. Guggenheim fellow, 1971-72 Fellow Am. Acad. Arts and Scis.; mem. Inst. Medicine, Am. Law Inst., Century Assn., Mass. Hist. Soc., Phi Beta Kappa. E-mail: fried@law.harvard.edu.

FRIED, ELEANOR REINGOLD, psychologist, educator; b. Quantico, Va., Jan. 4, 1943; d. Morris and Eleanor (Wilson) R.; divorced, 1984; children: Joshua Mark, Noah Seth, Adam Lawrence. BS cum laude, Boston U., 1964; MS in Clin. Sch. Psychology, CUNY, 1971; postgrad. Fordham U., 1971-73; MA in Clin. Psychology, The Fielding Inst., 1980, PhD in Clin. Psychology, 1981. Lic. psychologist, N.J. Psychology intern Roosevelt Hosp., N.Y.C., 1971-73; cons. Inwood House, N.Y.C., 1971-83; staff therapist Univ. Consultation Center Mental Hygiene, Bronx, N.Y., 1974-79, clin. instr., 1976-80; sr. clin. psychologist moderate security unit North Princeton Developmental Ctr., 1983-98; cons. Early Childhood Learning Center, Paramus, N.J., 1978-80, Found. for Religion and Mental Health, Briarcliff Manor, N.Y., 1979-82, Inwood House, N.Y.C., 1981-83, prin. clin. psychologist Ewing Residential Ctr., Trenton, N.J., 1987-88, Ind. Child Study Teams, East Orange, N.J; pvt. practice, Princeton, N.J.; ct. expert in forensic psychology; exec. dir. Ea. Profl. Group. Fellow Am. Bd. Forensic Examiners; mem. APA (assoc.), N.J. Psychol. Assn., Nat. Assn. Treatment Sex Offenders, Kappa Tau Alpha. Office: Ea Profl Group 601 Ewing St Ste C20 Princeton NJ 08540-2758 E-mail: fried@nerc.com.

FRIED, JOEL ROBERT, chemical engineering educator; b. Memphis, Dec. 9, 1946; s. Samuel J. and Mathilda (Kleinman) F.; m. Ava S. Krinick, June 8, 1969; children: Marc S., Aaron M. BS, Rensselaer Poly. Inst., 1968, 71, ME, 1972; MS, U. Mass., 1975, PhD, 1976. Mem. assoc. rsch. staff GE, Schenectady, N.Y., 1972-73; sr. rsch. engr. Monsanto Co., St. Louis, 1976-78; asst. prof. chem. engring. U. Cin., 1978-83, assoc. prof. chem. engring., 1983-90, dir. grad. studies, 1986-90, dir. polymer rsch. ctr., 1989-92, prof. chem. engring., 1990—, acting dir. membrane ctr., 1994, dir. Ohio Molecular Computation and Simulation Network, 1995—, interim head dept. chem. engring., 1998-99, head dept. chem. engring., 2000—02. Pres. Polymer Rsch. Assocs., Inc., Cin., 1984—. Author: Polymer Science and Technology, 1995, 2d edit., 2003; contbr. articles to sci. jours. Recipient Faculty Achievement award, 1994, Outstanding Prof., 96; Jr. Morr ow rsch. chair U. Cin., 1980; USAF summer faculty rsch. fellow, 1981, 93, 94, 2003. Mem. Am. Chem. Soc., Am. Inst. Chem. Engrs., Soc. Plastics Engrs. Achievements include patents in permeation modified separation membranes. Office: U Cin Dept Chem and Materials Engring Cincinnati OH 45221-0012

FRIED, MORRIS LOUIS, retired humanities educator; b. N.Y.C., Jan. 26, 1925; s. Abraham and Tillie (Marrus) F.; m. Helen Gorson, Feb. 26, 1949; children: Stephanie Fried, Pamela Crawford. BA, U. Buffalo, 1951; MA, New Sch. for Social Rsch., N.Y.C., 1958; PhD, New Sch. for Social Rsch., 1964. Verbatim reporter UN Security Coun./U.S. Dist. Cts., N.Y.C., 1958-62; lectr. in Sociology Fairleigh Dickinson U., Teaneck, N.J., 1962-64; lectr. in Labor Rels. Cornell U./Western N.Y. Dist. Internat. Labor Rels. Sch., Buffalo, 1972-78; vis. prof. Leicester (Eng.) U., 1970-71; asst., assoc. prof. Sociology SUNY, Buffalo, 1964-78; prof. Labor Studies & Sociology Ga. State U., Atlanta, 1978-81; ext. prof. continuing edn., adj. prof. sociology U. Conn., Storrs, 1981-92, ext. prof. emeritus, 1992—. Dir. Office of Pub. Svc. & Applied Rsch., U. Conn., 1988-92 Contbr. articles to profl. jours. Bd. dirs. Conn. Joint Coun. on Economic Edn., Storrs, 1987-91, Indsl. Rels. Rsch. Assn., Hartford, Conn. (pres. 1983-85); nat. chair Am. Hist. and Cultural Inst., N.Y.C., 1982-84; cons. Conn. State Dept. Labor, Hartford, 1987-89. Active in educating seniors and retired persons Shepherd's Ctr., Columbia, S.C., 1998—, Emory U., Atlanta, 1997, U. Conn., 1988-91. Named prin. investigator constrn. industry OSHA, 1978-81, mining industry Mine Safety & Health Adminstrn., 1982-88. Mem. Ctr. for Learning in Retirement (life). Avocations: computers, teaching, writing, developing new ideas for seniors. Home: 147 Old Hampton Ln Columbia SC 29209-1981 E-mail: MLFLCTR@earthlink.net.

FRIEDBERG, ERROL CLIVE, pathology educator, researcher; b. Johannesburg, Oct. 2, 1937; s. Edward and Rena (Berman) F.; children: Malcolm, Andrew, Jonathan, Lawrence. BSc, Witwatersrand U., Johannesburg, 1957, MB BCh, 1961. Intern King Edward VIII Hosp./U. Natal, Durban, South Africa, 1962; resident pathologist Witwatersrand U., 1963-64, Cleve. Met. Gen. Hosp., 1965; postdoctoral fellow dept. biochemistry Case Western Res. U., Cleve., 1966-68; rsch. investigator divsn. nuclear medicine Walter Reed Army Inst. Rsch., Washington, 1969-70; asst. prof. pathology Stanford (Calif.) U., 1971-77, assoc. prof. pathology, 1977-84, prof. pathology, 1984-90; prof., chair dept. pathology U. Tex. Southwestern Med. Ctr., Dallas, 1990—, Senator Betty and Dr. Andy Andujar chair pathology, 1990-93, Senator Betty and Dr. Andy Andujar disting. chair pathology, 1993—. Co-organizer symposia and confs. in field. Editor or co-editor: DNA Repair Mechanisms, 1978, DNA Repair: A Laboratory Manual of Research Procedures, Vol. 1, 1981, Cellular Responses to DNA Damage, 1983, DNA Repair: A Laboratory Manual of Research Procedures, Vol. 2, 1983; author: DNA Repair, 1984; editor-in-chief:, editor or co-editor: Scientific American Reader: Cancer Biology, 1985, Mechanisms and Consequences of DNA Damage Processing, 1988, DNA Repair: A Laboratory Manual of Research Procedures, Vol. 3, 1988; author: Cancer Answers: Encouraging Answers to 25 Questions You Were Always Afraid to Ask, 1992, 1993; author: (with others) DNA Repair and Mutagenesis, 1995; author: Correcting the Blueprint of Life, 1997; author: (with others) Sydney Brenner: My Life in Science, 2001; author: The Waiting Life of James D. Watson, Professor, Promotor, Provacateur, 2003; contbr. numerous articles to profl. pubs. Recipient Rsch. Career Devel. award USPHS, 1974-79, Merit award USPHS, 1988—, Rous-Whipple awrd Am. Soc. Investigative Pathology, 2000; Andrew W. Mellon Found. rsch. fellow, 1973-76; Joshua Macy Jr. Found. faculty scholar, 1978-79. Fellow: Royal Coll. Pathology; mem.: Am. Acad. Microbiol. Office: U Tex Southwestern Med Ctr Dept Path 5323 Harry Hines Blvd Dallas TX 75390-7208

FRIEDEN, BERNARD JOEL, urban studies educator; b. N.Y.C., Aug. 11, 1930; s. George and Jean (Harris) F.; m. Elaine Leibowitz, Nov. 23, 1958; 1 child, Deborah Susan. BA, Cornell U., 1951; MA, Pa. State U., 1953; MCP, MIT, 1957, PhD, 1962. Asst. prof. urban studies and planning MIT, Cambridge, 1961-65, assoc. prof., 1965-69, prof., 1969—, Ford prof. urban devel., 1989—, assoc. dean architecture and planning, 1993—; dir. rsch. Ctr. for Real Estate Devel., mem. faculty com. Ctr. for Real Estate, Cambridge, 1985-87; chmn. faculty MIT, 1987-89; dir. MIT-Harvard U. Joint Center for Urban Studies, 1971-75, mem. exec. com., 1975-82. Cons. HUD, 1966-68, DOD, 1994—; staff Pres. Johnson's Task Force Urban Problems, 1965; mem. Pres. Nixon's Task Force Urban Problems, 1968, The White House Task Force Model Cities, 1969, Pres. Carter's Urban Policy Adv. Com., 1977-80; vis. scholar U. Calif., Berkeley, 1990-91, 96. Author: The Future of Old Neighborhoods, 1964, Metropolitan America, 1966, (with Robert Morris) Urban Planning and Social Policy, 1968, (with William W. Nash) Shaping an Urban Future, 1969, (with Marshall Kaplan) The Politics of Neglect, 1975, 77, (with Wayne E. Anderson and Michael J. Murphy) Managing Human Services, 1977, The Environmental Protection Hustle, 1979, (with Lynne B. Sagalyn) Downtown, Inc., 1989; editor: Jour. Am. Inst. Planners, 1962-65; contbr. to various books and encys. Bd. dirs. Citizens Housing and Planning Assn., 1966-75. Served with AUS, 1952-54. Guggenheim fellow U. Calif., Berkeley, 1975-76, rsch. fellow Urban Land Inst., 1978-89, sr. fellow, 1989-98. Mem. Am. Inst. Cert. Planners, Am. Planning Assn. Jewish. Home: 7 Diamond Rd Lexington MA 02420-1610 E-mail: bfrieden@mit.edu.

FRIEDEN, JANE HELLER, art educator; b. Norfolk, Va., Aug. 25, 1926; d. Samuel Ries and Saida (Seligman) Heller; m. Joseph Lee Frieden, Dec. 23, 1950 (dec. 1990); children: Nancy Frieden Crowe, Robert M., Andrew M. AA, Coll. of William and Mary, Norfolk, Va., 1945; BA, Coll. of William and Mary, Williamsburg, Va., 1947; MA, Columbia U., 1950. Lic. pvt. pilot. Tchr. art City of Norfolk Pub. Schs., 1947-48, Hudson Day Sch., New Rochelle, N.Y., 1948-49, Mt. Vernon (N.Y.) Pub. Schs., 1949-50, City of Norfolk Pub. Schs., 1950-51; prof. art Coll. William and Mary Extension, Williamsburg, 1957-72, U. Va. Extension, Norfolk, 1972-78, Cmty. Colls. State of Va., Chesapeake and Hampton, 1978-82, St. Leo Coll., Norfolk, 1982-95; advocate Chrysler Mus. Art, 2003—. Travel agt., 1977-89. Author: (dictionary) A is For Art, 1978-82; artist water color paintings and ink drawings at several shows. Asst. Gen. Douglas MacArthur Meml. Archives, Norfolk, 1945—95; vol. Chrysler Mus. Art, Norfolk, 1991—, advocate, 2003—; vol. Va. Symphony Aux., 1992—98, Norfolk Little Theatre Box Office, 1991—, Meals on Wheels, 1962—66, Make a Wish Found., 1996, ARC, 1953—95, Grey Lady Project, 1956—62, Bloodmobile Project, 1966—80, Va. Zool. Soc., 1996; tchr. drawing Ghent Venture, 1993; reader for the visually handicapped Intouch Network WHRO-Radio, 1991—; archives com. Ohef Sholom Temple; bd. dirs. Norfolk Little Theatre, 1996; vol. career svcs. Coll. William and Mary, 1992—; drawing tchr. Norfolk Sr. Ctr., 1998—99; vol. docent USS Wisconsin BB 64, Hampton Roads Naval Mus., 2001—. Mem. Ninety-Nines (treas. 1978-85), Tidewater Artists Assn. (bd. dirs. 1975-80, 91—, treas. membership com.), Tidewater Orchid Soc., Am. Orchid Soc., Norfolk Soc. Arts, United Daus. Confederacy, Hermitage Soc., Norfolk Ex Libris Soc. Coll. William & Mary (steering com. 1993—), Va. Belles (reunion com. 1993—), Chesapeake Watercolor Soc. Republican. Jewish. Avocations: drawing and water color painting, raising orchids, travel. Home: 221 Oxford St Norfolk VA 23505-4354 E-mail: flymum@earthlink.net.

FRIEDENTHAL, JACK H. former dean; b. Denver, Sept. 22, 1931; m. Jo Anne Marder; 3 children. BA, Stanford U., 1953; JD, Harvard U., 1958. Bar: Calif. 1959, D.C. 1990. Sole practice, 1959—; from asst. prof. to assoc. prof. Stanford (Calif.) U., 1958-64, prof., 1964-88, George E. Osborne prof. law, 1980-88, assoc. dean, 1984—87; dean, prof. George Washington U. Nat. Law Ctr., Washington, 1988-98, Freda H. Alverson prof. law, 1998—. Vis. prof. U. Mich. Law Sch., Ann Arbor, 1965, 71, Harvard Law Sch., 1976-77; cons. Law Revision Commn., 1964. Coauthor: Introduction to Evidence, 1985, Civil Procedure (text), 2d edit., 1993, 6th edit. 1993, Civil Procedure (casebook) 7th edit., 1997, 1993 Civil Procedure Supplement, Pleading Joinder Discovery, 1968, Gilbert Law Summaries: Civil Procedure & Practice, 1992-93; contbr. articles to profl. jours. Office: George Washington U Law Sch 2000 H St NW Washington DC 20006-4234*

FRIEDHEIM, JAN V. education administrator; b. Corpus Christi, Tex., Oct. 20, 1935; d. Roy Lee Conyers and Bertha Victoria (Ostrom) Hamm; m. John R. Eisenhour, Nov. 22, 1962 (div. 1983); m. Stephen B. Friedheim, Sept. 1, 1984; children: Neenah, Stephen II, Robert. BS, U. Tex., 1957; PhD (hon.), Constantinian U., Malta, 1994. Chmn. bd. Exec. Secretarial Sch., Dallas, 1960—2001; ptnr. Edn. Sys. and Solutions, 2001—. Vice-chmn. Tex. Vocat.Adv. Bd., Austin, 1979-86; mem. adv. com. Dept. Edn., Washington, 1980-84; commr. So. Assn. Colls. and Schs. Commn. on Occupl. Edn. Instns., 1994-97; adv. com. State Postsecondary Rev. Entity, 1994; bd. dirs. Tex. Assn. Pvt. Schs., Career Coll. and Schs. of Tex.; commr. Coun. on Occupl. Edn., 1995-2001. Bd. dirs. Career Colls. and Schs. of Tex., 1995—. Named Disting. Evaluator, Accrediting Coun. Ind. Coll. Schs., 1999. Mem. Career Coll. Assn. (bd. dirs. 1999—), Assn. Ind. Colls. and Schs. (chmn. bd. dirs. 1980-81, commn. 1978-79, commr. 1974-79, Disting. Mem. 1974, 81, Mem. of Yr. 1979), Southwestern Assn. Pvt. Schs. (pres. 1982), Metroplex Assn. Pvt. Schs. (pres. 1989-90, 92-93), So. Assn. Colls. and Schs. (trustee 1981-85, commn. on occupational edn. instns. 1994-97), Tex. Assn. Pvt. Schs. (bd. dirs. 1992—), Career Colls. and Schs. Tex. (bd. dirs. 1995—, chmn.-elect 1998, chmn. 1999). Home: 6450 Patrick Dr Dallas TX 75214-2444

FRIEDL, RICK, lawyer, former academic administrator; b. Berwyn, Ill., Aug. 31, 1947; s. Raymond J. and Ione L. (Anderson) F.; m. Dawn Friedl; children: Richard, Angela, Ryan, Ariana. BA, Calif. State U., Northridge, 1969; MA, UCLA, 1976, postgrad., 1984; JD, Western State U., 1987. Bar: Calif. 1988, U.S. Dist. Ct. (ctrl. dist.) Calif. 1992. Dept. mgr. Calif. Dept. Indsl. Rels., 1973-78; mem. faculty dept. polit. sci. U. So. Calif., 1978-80; pres. Pacific Coll. Law, 1981-86; staff counsel state fund Calif., 1988-89; prin. Law Offices of Rick Friedl, 1989—. Author: The Political Economy of Cuban Dependency, 1982; tech. editor Glendale Law Rev., 1984; contbr. articles to profl. jours. Calif. State Grad. fellow, 1970-72. Mem. ABA, Calif. State Bar Assn., Los Angeles County Bar Assn., Am. Polit. Sci. Assn., Latin Am. Studies Assn., Acad. Polit. Sci., Pacific Coast Coun. Latin Am. Studies, Calif. Trial Lawyers Assn. Home: PO Box 2095 California City CA 93504-0095

FRIEDLANDER, JOHN BENJAMIN, mathematician, educator; b. Toronto, Can., Oct. 4, 1941; s. Daniel Theodore and Beatrice Adele (Axler) Friedlander; m. Cheryl Lynn Thompson, Sept. 1, 1974; children: Jonathan, Diana, Amanda, Keith. BSc, U. Toronto, 1965; MA, U. Waterloo, Ont., Can., 1966; PhD, Pa. State U., 1972. Asst. to A. Selberg, Inst. Advanced Study, Princeton, NJ, 1972-73, mem. Sch. Math, 1973-74, 83-84, 95-96, 99-2000; lectr., dept. math MIT, Cambridge, 1974-76; vis. prof. Scuola Normale Superiore, Pisa, Italy, 1976-77; from asst. prof. to assoc. prof. U. Toronto, 1977—82, prof. math, 1982—, chair dept. math., 1987-91; lectr. U. Ill., Urbana, 1979-80; rsch. prof. Math Sci. Rsch. Inst., Berkeley, Calif., 1991-92. Mem. grant selection com. Nat. Scis. and Engring. Rsch. Coun. Can., 1991—94; lectr. ICM, 1994; mem. sci. adv. bd. Banff Internat. Rsch. Sta., 2003—, Field Inst. Rsch. Math. Sci., 1996—2000; math. convenor Royal Soc. Can., 1990—93; mem. gen. assembly Internat. Math. Union, 1994; lectr. in field. Mem. editl. bd. 3 jours. in field; contbr. articles and revs. to profl. jours. Recipient CRM Fields prize, 2002; Acad. Sci. fellow, Royal Soc. Can., 1988—, Killam Rsch. fellow, 2003—. Mem.: Can. Math. Soc. (Jeffery-Williams prize lectr. 1999), Am. Math. Soc. Avocations: bridge, chess, sailing, barbecue. Home: 22 Stonemanse Ct Scarborough ON Canada M1G 3V3 Office: U Toronto Dept Math Toronto ON Canada M5S 3G3 also: Scarborough Coll Dept of Math Scarborough ON Canada M1C 1A4 Fax: (416) 978-4107. E-mail: frdlndr@math.toronto.edu.

FRIEDLANDER, MYRNA LOIS, psychologist, educator; b. Washington, Dec. 10, 1947; d. Leon Herbert and Ada (Slater) F.; 1 child, Lee Kara. BA cum laude, Case Western Res. U., 1969; MA, George Washington U., 1978; PhD, Ohio State U., 1980. Lic. psychologist, N.Y. Prof. U. at Albany (SUNY), 1981—, dir. doctoral tng., 1999—. Clin. adj. asst. prof. Albany Med. Coll., 1984—. Contbr. articles to profl. jours. Fellow Am. Psychol. Assn., Am. Psychol. Soc., Am. Assn. Applied and Preventive Psychology. Democrat. Jewish. Avocation: travel. Office: U at Albany 1400 Washington Ave Albany NY 12222-1000

FRIEDLANDER, SHELDON KAY, chemical engineering educator; b. N.Y.C., Nov. 17, 1927; s. Irving and Rose (Katzewitz) F.; m. Marjorie Ellen Robbins, Apr. 16, 1934; children: Eva Kay, Amelie Elise, Antonia Zoe, Josiah. BS, Columbia U., 1949; SM, MIT, 1951; PhD, U. Ill., 1954. Asst. prof. chem. engring. Columbia U., N.Y.C., 1954-57, Johns Hopkins, Balt., 1957-59, assoc. prof. chem. engring., 1959-62, prof. chem. engring., 1962-64; prof. chem. engring., environ. health engring. Calif. Inst. Tech., Pasadena, 1964-78; prof. chem. engring. UCLA, 1978—, Parsons prof., 1982—, chmn. dept. chem. engring., 1984-88, chmn. steering com. Ctr. for Clean Tech., 1989-92. Chmn. EPA Clean Air Sci. Adv. Com., 1978-82. Author: Smoke, Dust, and Haze: Fundamentals of Aerosol Dynamics, 2nd edit., 2000. Served with U.S. Army, 1946-47. Recipient Sr. Humboldt prize Fed. Republic of Germany, 1985, Internat. prize Am. Assn. for Aerosol Rsch./Gesellschaft für Aerosolforschung/Japan Assn. for Aerosol Sci. and Tech., Fuchs Meml. award, 1990, Christian Junge award European Aerosol Assn., 2000; Fulbright scholar, 1960-61; Guggenheim fellow, 1969-70. Mem.: AIChE (Colburn award 1959, Alpha Chi Sigma award 1974, Walker award 1979, Lawrence K. Cecil award in environ. chem. engring. 1995, Particle Tech. Forum Lifetime Achievement award 2001), NAE, Am. Assn. for Aerosol Rsch. (pres. 1984—86). Office: UCLA Dept Chem Engring 5531 Boelter Hl Los Angeles CA 90095-0001

FRIEDMAN, AVNER, mathematician, educator; b. Petah-Tikva, Israel, Nov. 19, 1932; arrived in U.S., 1956; s. Moshe and Hanna (Rosenthal) Friedman; m. Lillia Lynn, June 7, 1959; children: Alissa, Joel, Naomi, Tamara. MSc, Hebrew U., Jerusalem, 1954, PhD, 1956. Prof. math. Northwestern U., Evanston, Ill., 1962—85; prof. Purdue U., West Lafayette, Ind., 1985—87, dir. Ctr. Applied Math., 1985—87; prof. math., dir. Inst. Math. and Its Applications U. Minn., Mpls., 1987-97, dir. Minn. Ctr. for Indsl. Math., 1994—2002; prof. Ohio State U., Columbus, 2002—; dir. Math. Bioscis. Inst., 2002—. Author: (book) Generalized Functions and Partial Differential Equations, 1963, Partial Differential Equations of Parabolic Type, 1964, Partial Differential Equations, 1969, Foundations of Modern Analysis, 1970, Advanced Calculus, 1971, Differential Games, 1971, Stochastic Differential Equations and Applications, Vol. 1, 1975, Vol. 2, 1976, Variational Principle's and Free Boundary Problems, 1983, Mathematics in Industrial Problems, 10 vols., 1988—98; author: (with D.S. Ross) Mathematical Models in Photographic Science, 2001; contbr. articles to profl. jours. Recipient Creativity award, NSF, 1983—85, 1990—92; fellow, Sloan Found., 1962—65, Guggenheim, 1966—67. Mem.: NAS, AAAS, Soc. Indsl. Applied Math. (pres. 1993, 1994, chair bd. math. scis. 1994—97), Am. Math. Soc. Office: Ohio State U Math Dept 231 18th Ave Columbus OH 43210 Business E-Mail: afriedman@mbi.osu.edu.

FRIEDMAN, BARRY DAVID, political scientist, educator; b. Meriden, Conn., Sept. 29, 1953; s. Edward Louis and Esia (Baran) F.; m. Cynthia Joy Landis, July 8, 1990 (div. Feb. 17, 2003). BA in Polit. Sci., BS in Engring., U. Hartford, 1976; MPA, MBA, U. Conn., 1983, PhD in Polit. Sci., 1991. Forecasting analyst Northeast Utilities, Berlin, Conn., 1976-82; pers. specialist ARC, Fairfax, Va., 1986-87; asst. prof. polit. sci. Valdosta (Ga.) State U., 1987-92; prof. polit. sci. North Ga. Coll. & State U., Dahlonega, 1992—; dir. MPA program North Ga. Coll., Dahlonega. Conf. presentations, 1988—. Author: Regulation in the Reagan-Bush Era: The Eruption of Presidential Influence, 1995; book rev. editor Internat. Social Sci. Rev., 2002—; contbr. articles to profl. jours. Nat. instr.-trainer ARC 1990-96. Recipient Outstanding Lt. Gov. award New Eng. dist. Key Club Internat., 1971, Phi Kappa Phi Promotion of Excellence in Higher Edn. award, 1999, Disting. Prof. award North Ga. Coll. and State U. Alumni Assn., 1997, 2002; named Bd. Mem. of Yr., ARC, Valdosta, 1991. Mem. ASPA (life, sec.-treas., pres., editor Ga. chpt. 1994—), Ga. Polit. Sci. Assn. (exec. bd. 1997-99), Am. Red Magen David for Israel (internat. life, nat. adv. coun., 2002—), Phi Beta Kappa, Phi Kappa Phi (chpt. pres. 1989-90), Pi Alpha Alpha, Pi Sigma Alpha, Pi Gamma Mu (gov. Ga. 1995-2002, vice chancellor Atlantic region 1999-2002, chancellor, 2002—), Beta Gamma Sigma, Alpha Chi, Kappa Mu, Omicron Delta Kappa, Alpha Kappa Delta. Jewish. Office: North Ga Coll & State U Dept Polit Sci Dahlonega GA 30597-0001 E-mail: bfriedman@ngcsu.edu.

FRIEDMAN, BENJAMIN MORTON, economics educator; b. Louisville, Ky., Aug. 5, 1944; s. Norbert and Eva (Lipsky) F.; m. Barbara Allan Cook, Dec. 17, 1972; children: John Norton, Jeffrey Allan. AB summa cum laude, Harvard U., 1966, AM, 1969, PhD, 1971; MSc King's Coll., Cambridge U., 1970. Economist Morgan Stanley & Co., N.Y.C., 1971-72; asst. prof. econs. Harvard U., Cambridge, Mass., 1972-76, assoc. prof., 1976-80, prof., 1980-89, William Joseph Maier prof. polit. economy, 1989—, chmn. dept. of econs., 1991-94. Dir. fin. markets and monetary econs. Nat. Bur. Econ. Rsch., Cambridge, 1977—93; dir. Pvt. Export Funding Corp., NYC, 1981—, Britannica.com, 2000—. Author: Economic Stabilization Policy, 1975, Monetary Policy in the United States, 1981, Day of Reckoning, 1988; co-author: Does Debt Management Matter?, 1992; editor: New Challenges to the Role of Profits, 1978, The Changing Roles of Debt and Equity in Financing U.S. Capital Formation, 1982, Corporate Capital Structures in the United States, 1985, Financing Corporate Capital Formation, 1986, Handbook on Monetary Economics, 1990; assoc. editor Jour. Monetary Econs., 1977-95. Trustee Coll. Retirement Equities Fund, N.Y.C., 1978-82, Standish Mellon Investment, 1989—; dir. Am. Friends of Cambridge U., 1994-2000. Marshall scholar Cambridge U., 1966-68; Soc. Fellows jr. fellow Harvard U., 1968-71. Mem. Coun. Fgn. Rels., Brookings Panel Econ. Activity, Am. Econ. Assn., Harvard Club N.Y.C. Home: 74 Sparks St Cambridge MA 02138-2238 Office: Harvard U 127 Littauer Center Cambridge MA 02138

FRIEDMAN, DEBORAH LESLIE WHITE, educational administrator; b. Grand Rapids, Mich., July 5, 1950; d. Edward Charles and Luella Jane (Carr) White; children: Karen Elizabeth, David Edward. BS, Cen. Mich. U., 1972; MBA, U. Toledo, 1980; D in Higher Ednl. Adminstrn., N.C. State U., 1995. Traffic mgr. WTOL-TV, Toledo, 1972-74; catering cons. Gladieux Food Svcs., Toledo, 1974-75; mktg. rsch. analyst Owens-Ill., Toledo, 1978; instr. Sampson C.C., Clinton, N.C., 1980-81, chmn. acctg., bus. adminstrn., real estate, 1981-98, divsn. chair bus. and pub. svc. programs, 1998-2001; dean bus. programs Fayetteville Tech. C.C., 2001—03, v.p. for human resources, 2003—. Faculty advisor Phi Beta Lambda, 1981-88; adj. trainer N.C. Dept. Community Colls., Raleigh, 1989-2001; bd. dirs. Sampson County United Way, Inc., 1995-1998, State Employees Credit Union, Clinton br., 1998-2001. Bd. dirs. Found. for Edn., 1984-89, appropriations chmn., 1984-88, sec., 1988-89; com. mem. Clinton City Schs. Com. on Stds. of Excellence, 1986-87; vol. Girl Scouts Am., Clinton, 1983, 85; mem. N.C. C.C. Leadership Program, 1990; pres. Sunday Sch. Class, 1997-98; bd. ch., Acad. of Fin., 2001—, bd. chair, 2002—; mem. Leadership Fayetteville, 2001-02; mem. faculty for leadership Fayetteville and Leadership Fayetteville Youth Acad., 2002-03. Named Outstanding Young Educator, Clinton Jaycees, 1985; recipient Outstanding Svc. award Clinton Student Govt. Assn., 1982, Excellence in Tchg. award N.C. State Bd. C.C., 1989, 98, Cert. of Appreciation, State of N.C. for Vol. Svcs., 1987, Leadership Challenge awrd Fayetteville C. of C., 2002. Mem. Am. Assn. Women in Cmty. Colls. (membership dir. 1988-89), N.C. Assn. Bus. Chair and Dept. Heads (pres. 1997-99), Am. Bus. Women Assn. (pres. 1983-84, Sampson County Woman of Yr. 1984), Kiwanis, NetWorth, Beta Gamma Sigma, Phi Kappa Phi, Phi Theta Kappa. Avocations: tennis, running, golf. Home: 585 Broyhill Rd Fayetteville NC 28314-2522 Office: Fayetteville Tech CC PO Box 35236 Fayetteville NC 28303 E-mail: friedmad@faytechcc.edu.

FRIEDMAN, DEBRA RENEÉ, elementary education educator; b. Kenmore, N.Y., Oct. 29, 1964; d. Nelson Marvin and Barbara Ann (Alberella) Colley; m. Adam Friedman, July 18, 1987. BS in Elem. Edn., SUNY, Geneseo, N.Y., 1985; postgrad., U. South Fla., 1990—. Cert. tchr. early childhood, elem. edn. 1-6, ESL, Fla. Elem. educator Wider Horizons Pvt. Sch., Brooksville, Fla., 1986; kindergarten tchr. N.W. Elem. Sch./Pasco County Schs., Hudson, Fla., 1986-89, Mary Giella Elem. Sch./Pasco County Schs., Hudson, Fla., 1989-91; Kindergarten tchr. Pembroke Lakes (Fla.) Elem. Sch./Broward County Schs., 1991-92; elem. generalist Sawgrass Elem. Sch./Broward County Schs., Sunrise, Fla., 1992—; pres. founder Learning Lines Inc., 1993—. Cons., presenter in field; vis. com. So. Assn. Colls. and Schs., 1988—. Club sponsor Fla. Future Educators of Am., 1988-90; sch. improvement team mem. Pembroke Lakes Elem. and Sawgrass Elem., 1990—, tchr. mem. PTA, 1989—. Grantee Rigby Books Inc., 1992, Humana Hosp., 1992, 93. Mem. Nat. Assn. for Edn. of Young Children, Fla. Reading Assn., Broward County Reading Coun., Dade County Reading Coun., Internat. Reading Assn., Broward County Generalists Assn., So. Assn. for Edn. Children Under 6, Fla. Assn. for Edn. Children Under 6. Republican. Roman Catholic. Avocations: scuba diving, boating, fishing, stained glass art, reading. Office: Sawgrass Elem Sch 12655 NW 8th St Fort Lauderdale FL 33325-1354

FRIEDMAN, DIAN DEBRA, elementary education educator; b. Balt., June 12, 1943; d. Bernard Maurice and Sondra Seletta (Dolgoff) Jacobs; m. Irving Joel Friedman, June 24, 1965; children: Benjamin Aaron, Joshua Jason. AA, Miami (Fla.)-Dade Jr. Coll., 1963; BS in Elem. Edn., Fla. State U., 1965. With contracts and grants Fla. State U., Tallahassee, 1965-66; substitute tchr. Chicopee (Mass.) Sch. Systems, 1965-66; elem. tchr. City of Springfield, Mass., 1966-76; real estate salesperson Gene Kelly Real Estate, Suffield, Conn., 1985-87; ednl. tutor Suffield (Conn.) Sch. Sys., 1987—, mem. curriculum coun., 1986-91. Tchr. Computer Tots; substitute tchr., tchr. asst. Agawam (Mass.) Jr./Sr. H.S. Bd. dirs. The Village for Families and Children, Inc., Hartford, Conn., 1986-97, pub. issues com., 1994-96; bd. dirs. Child and Family Charities, Inc., Hartford; chairperson Suffield Aux. The Village for Families and Children, Inc., 1978-80, mem. 1973—; mem. Citizens for Suffield, 1990—, Friends of Suffield Libr., 1973—, Springfield Mass. Cyclonauts, Franklin Hampshire Freewheelers Bicycle Clubs. Mem. Mass. Tchr.'s Assn., Fla. State Alumni Club, Suffield Woman's Club, Franklin/Hampshire Free Wheelers, Fla. State Univ. Alumni Assn. Democrat. Jewish. Avocations: skiing, reading, bicycling, jogging, painting. Home: 119 Marbern Dr Suffield CT 06078-1542

FRIEDMAN, ERICK, concert violinist, educator; b. Newark, N.J., Aug. 16, 1939; s. Abraham David and Lillian Edith (Herman) F. Artist tchr. N.C. Sch. for the Arts, Winston-Salem, 1973-78; artist faculty Manhattan Sch. Music, N.Y.C., 1978-83; artist-in-residence So. Meth. U., Dallas, 1983-89; prof. music Yale U., New Haven, 1989—. Music dir., condr. Garrett Lakes Arts Festival, 1986—; guest panelist Nat. Endowment for the Arts, Washington, 1983-88; guest juror panels various internat. competitions including Dealey Competition, Taipei Internat. Competition, Amb. in Washington, Can. Music Competitions. Performer numerous recordings RCA Red Seal, Monitor, also Kultur videocassettes; recorded Bach Double Violin Concerto with Sir Malcolm Sargent, Jascha Heifetz and New Symphony Orch. of London, 1961, Paganini Concerto, Cadenza, 1962. Nominee Grammy awards, 1963, 64. Avocations: chess, drawing. Address: 70 Autumn St New Haven CT 06511-2221

FRIEDMAN, GERALD MANFRED, geologist, educator; b. Berlin, July 23, 1921; came to US, 1946, naturalized, 1950; s. Martin and Frieda (Cohn) F.; m. Sue Tyler Theilheimer, June 27, 1948; children: Judith Fay Friedman Rosen, Sharon Mira Friedman Azaria, Devorah Paula Friedman Zweibach, Eva Jane Friedman Scholle, Wendy Tamar Friedman Spanier. Student, U.

Cambridge, Eng., 1938-39; BSc, U. London, Eng., 1945, DSc, 1977; student, U. Wyo., 1949; MA, Columbia U., 1950, PhD, 1952; DSc (hon.), U. Heidelberg, Fed. Republic Germany, 1986. Agrl. laborer, England, 1938-39; baker, 1940-42; internee Brit. Army, 1940; lectr. Chelsea Coll., London, 1944-45; analytical chemist J. Lyons & Co., 1945—46, E.R. Squibb & Sons (now Bristol Myers-Squibb), New Brunswick, 1946—49; asst. geology Columbia U., 1950; temp. geologist NY State Geol. Survey, 1950; from instr. to asst. prof. geology U. Cin., 1950-54; cons. geologist Sault Ste. Marie, Ont., Can., 1954-56; from sr. rsch. scientist to supr. sedimentary geology rsch. Pan Am. Petroleum Corp. (now BP), 1956-64; Fulbright vis. prof. geology Hebrew U., Jerusalem, 1964; prof. geology Rensselaer Poly. Inst., 1964-84, prof. emeritus, 1984—; prof. geology Bklyn. Coll., 1984—88, Disting. prof. geology, 1988—; prof. earth and environ. sci. Grad. Sch. CUNY, 1984—88, disting. prof. earth and environ. sci., 1988—, dep. exec. officer, 1992-94; pres. Gerry Exploration Inc., 1982-88. Rsch. sci. Hudson Labs., Columbia, 1965-69, rsch. assoc. dept. geology Lamont Geol. Obs., 1968-73; vis. prof. U. Heidelberg, 1967; cons. sci. Inst. Petroleum Rsch. and Geophysics, Israel, 1967-71; lectr. Oil & Gas Cons. Internat., 1968-98; pres. Northeastern Sci. Found. Inc., 1979—; vis. scientist Geol. Survey of Israel, 1970-73, 78; mem. Com. Sci. Soc. Pres., 1974-76; Gerald M. Friedman fellow Inst. Earth Sci., Hebrew U., Israel, 1990—; vis. prof. Martin-Luther-Univ., Halle-Wittenberg, Germany, 1998. Co-author: Principles of Sedimentology (Outstanding Acad. Books, Choice, 1978/79), 1978, Exploration for Carbonate Petroleum Reservoirs, 1982, Exercises in Sedimentology, 1982, Principles of Sedimentary Deposits: Stratigraphy and Sedimentology, 1992; pub. Northeastern Environ. Sci., 1982-90; editor: Jour. Sedimentary Petrology, 1964-70 (Best Paper award 1961, hon. mention 1964, 66), Northeastern Geology (now Northeastern Geology and Environ. Sci.), 1979—, Earth Sci. History, 1982-93, Carbonates and Evaporites, 1986—, 10th Internat. Congress on Sedimentology, 1978, Oil Industry History, 1999-2003; sect. co-editor: Chem. Abstracts (Mineral. and Geol. Chemistry), 1962-69, abstractor, 1952-69; editl. bd. Jour. Geol. Edn., 1951-55, Sedimentary Geology, 1967-95, Israel Jour. Earth Sci., 1971-76, Coral Reef Newsletter, 1973-75, Jour. Geology, 1977—, GeoJour., 1977-83, Facies, 1987—; mng. editor Sedimentology for Earth Sci. Revs., 1992—; contbg. co-editor: Carbonate Sedimentology in Central Europe, 1968, Hypersaline Ecosystems: The Gavish Sabkha, 1985, editor, contbr.: Depositional Environments in Carbonate Rocks, 1969; co-editor: Modern Carbonate Environments, 1983, Lecture Notes in Earth Sci., 1985—; founding editor: Earth Sci. History, 1982, hon. life mem.; contbr. articles to profl. jour.; patentee in field. Phys. edn. com., judo instr. Tulsa YMCA, 1958-64, chmn. awards com., 1962-64; adviser, instr. Judo Club, Rensselaer Poly. Inst., 1964-84; bd. dir. Troy Jewish Cmty. Coun., 1966-72, 74-77; v.p. Temple Beth El, 1986-89, pres., 1989-91, bd. dir., 1965-76; bd. dir. Leo Baeck Inst., NYC, 1986—; v.p., chmn. pub. com. Drake Well Found., 1998-2003, v.p., 2002—. Recipient award for devoted svc. Tulsa YMCA, 1963, Hon. W.Va. award, 1998; named hon. alumnus dept. geology Bklyn. Coll., 1989; grantee Office Naval Rsch., AEC, Dept. Energy, Petroleum Rsch. Fund, NY Gas Assn., NY State Energy Rsch. and Devel. Authority. Fellow: AAAS (councillor 1979—80, soc. rep. geology/geography sect. 1989—97), Soc. Econ. Geologists, N.Y. Acad. Sci. (vice chair geol. sci. sect. 1993—94, chmn. 1994—96, vice chair geol. sci. sect. 1996—97, chmn. 1997—2001), Geol. Assn. Can., Geol. Soc. London (life, chartered geologist, hon. fellow 1996), Mineral Soc. Am. (mem. nominating com. fellows 1967—69, mem. awards com. 1977—78), Mineral Soc. Gt. Brit. (abstractor mineralogical abstracts 1963—64), Geol. Soc. Am. (sr. chmn. sect. program com. 1969, candidate sect. chmn. 1969, publ. com. 1980—82, chmn. overseas pub. rels. com. internat. divsn. 1996—97, vice chair history geology divsn. 1997—99, chair 1999—2000, mem. awards nom. com. sedimentary geol. divsn. 1999—2000, chair history geology awards com. 2000—01); mem.: So. Venezolana Historia Geociencias (internat. corr. mem.), Sigma Xi, Sigma Gamma Epsilon (nat. pres. 1982—86), Kodokan, Empire State Judo Assn., Amateur Athletic Union (judo com. 1963, Okla.), Okla. Judo Fedn. (pres 1959—60, v.p. 1961—64), U.S. Judo Fedn. (San Dan, cert. judo tchr.), Cin. Mineral Soc. (v.p. program chmn. 1953—54), N.Y. State Mus.-N.Y. State Geol. Survey (James Hall medal 1997), N.Y. State Geol. Assn. (pres. 1978—79, bd. dir. 1979—84), Geosci. Info. Soc. (mem. membership com. 1983—85, ad hoc com. to devel. criteria for reviewing geosci. jour. 1985—86), Assn. Earth Sci. Editors (v.p. 1970—71, pres. 1971—72, host 1991, Outstanding Editorial Pub. Contributions Award 1993), Nat. Assn. Geosci. Tchr. (nat. treas. 1951—55, subscription and circulation mgr. 1951—55, chmn. organizing and nominating com. establish east-ctrl.sect. 1952—53, assoc. editor Jour. of Geosci. Edn. 1953—55, pres. Okla 1962—63, pres. Ea. sect. 1983—84, Disting. Svc. Award 2001), Geol. Vereinigung, Deutsche Geol. Gesellschaft, Soc. Venezolana Historia Geociencias (intenat. corr. mem.), Indian Assn. Sedimentologists (mem. governing coun. 1978—82), Serbian Yugoslavian Geol. Soc. (hon. 1998), History of the Earth Sci. Soc. (hon.; co-founder 1981), Geol. Soc. Israel (hon. 1992), Internat. Assn. Sedimentologists (nat. corr. USA 1971—73, v.p. 1971—75, pres. 1975—78, program com. Internat. Sedimentological Congress 1978, excursion com. Internat. Sedimentological Congress 1982, hon. mem. 1986), Geologists' Assn. (life), Am. Geol. Inst. (governing bd. 1971—72, 1974—75), New Eng. Intercollegiate Geol. Conf. (convenor, editor 1979), Capital Dist. Geologists Assn. (chmn. program 1966—73), Hudson-Mohawk Profl. Geologists Assn. (bd. dir. 1995—2001, program com. 1996—97, chmn. program com. 1997—2001), Paleontological Soc. (hon. mention to Outstanding Paper award Jour. Paleontology 1971, Twenhofel medal 1997), Soc. for Sedimentary Geology (sect. pres. pro tem 1966—67, chmn. Shepard award selection com. 1966—67, sect. pres. 1967—68, pres. 1974—75, Best Paper award Gulf Coast sect. 1974, Twenhefel medalist 1997), Am. Assn. Petroleum Geologists (chmn. carbonate rock com. 1965—69, mem. rsch. com. 1965—71, lectr. continuing edn. program 1967—88, chmn. Persian Gulf liaison com. 1968—70, mem. marine geology com. 1970—74, Disting. lectr. 1972—73, adv. coun. 1974—75, mem. disting. lectr. com. 1975—78, mem. rsch. com. 1976—82, ho. of dels. 1977—80, Eastern Section sect. sec. 1979—80, sect. treas. 1980—81, alt. del. 1980—83, sect. v.p. 1981—82, sect. pres 1982—83, mem. vis. geologists program com. 1982—85, membership com. 1982—87, div. profl. affairs rep. from Eastern sect. 1983—84, hon. mem. Eastern sect. 1984, com. on convs. 1984—85, nat. v.p. 1984—85, ho. of dels. 1984—87, mem. select com. on future petroleum geologist 1985—86, chmn. sect. awards com. 1989—92, nat. hon. mem. 1990, ho. of dels. 1991—93, alt. del. 1993—98, sect. chmn. tech. program com. 1994—95, vice chair standing com. hist. petroleum geology 1997—2000, chair 2000—01, ho. of dels. 2002—, John T. Galey Meml. Award medal 1993, sect. cert. of merit 1995, Disting. Educator award 1996, Nat. Disting. Svc. award 1998, Sidney Powers Meml. award 2000, Divsn. Environ. Scis. Tchg. award 2001, award for excellence and dedication in tchg. environ. geology 2001), Am. Chem. Soc. (group leader 1962—63), Am. Inst. Profl. Geologists (cert.), Russian Acad. Nat. Sci. US sect. (Kapitsa Gold medal of honor 1996), Ky. Cols., Explorers Club NY. Home: 32 24th St Troy NY 12180-1915 Office: Bklyn Coll/Grad Sch CUNY Dept Geology Brooklyn NY 11210 E-mail: gmfriedman@juno.com.

FRIEDMAN, H. HAROLD, cardiologist, internist; b. N.Y.C., July 31, 1917; s. Morris and Sarah (Rudnitsky) F.; m. Charlotte Lostfogel, Mar. 7, 1943; children: Alan Edward, Marsha Lynn, Betsy Ellen. BS, NYU, 1936, MD, 1939. Intern Jewish Hosp., Bklyn., 1939-41, resident, 1941-42, 46, Bellevue Hosp., N.Y.C., 1947; practice medicine specializing in cardiology and internal medicine Denver, 1948—; attending physician, dir. electrocardiographic lab. Rose Med. Ctr., pres. med. staff, 1959; attending physician St. Joseph Hosp., Denver; fellow in medicine NYU Coll. Medicine, 1947; pres. med. staff Nat. Jewish Hosp., 1959; assoc. clin. prof. medicine U. Colo. Sch. Medicine, Denver, 1963-75, prof., 1975—. Mem. Colo. State Bd. Med. Examiners, 1962-67 Author: Outline of Electrocardiography, 1963, Diagnostic Electrocardiography and Vectorcardiography, 1971, 3d edit., 1985; editor: Problem-Oriented Medical Diagnosis, 1975, 7th rev. edit.2001. Served to capt. M.C. AUS, 1942-46. Recipient Outstanding Clin. Faculty Teaching award U. Colo. Sch. Medicine, 1981-82, Outstanding Clin. Faculty Svc. award U. Colo. Sch. Medicine, 1991, Outstanding Clin. Faculty Acad. Pubs. award U. Colo. Sch. Medicine, 1992; Rose Med. Ctr. Physicians Recognition award for Excellence in Teaching Rsch., 1993. Fellow ACP, Am. Coll. Cardiology, Am. Coll. Chest Physicians, Council on Clin. Cardiology, Am. Heart Assn.; mem. Denver Med. Soc., Colo. Med. Soc., Phi Beta Kappa. Home: 405 Hodenkamp Rd Apt 304 Thousand Oaks CA 91360

FRIEDMAN, HERBERT A. rabbi, educator, fund raising executive; b. New Haven, Sept. 25, 1918; s. Israel and Rae (Aaronson) F.; children from previous marriage: Judith Rae, Daniel Stephen, Joan Michal; m. Francine Bensley, June 28, 1963; children: David Herbert, Charles Edward. BA, Yale U., 1938; MHL, Jewish Inst. Religion, 1943; DD (hon.), Hebrew Union Coll., 1969; PhD (hon.), Tel Aviv Univ., 2002. Ordained rabbi, 1944. Rabbi Temple Emanuel, Denver, 1943-52, Milw., 1952-55; exec. chmn. Nat. United Jewish Appeal, N.Y.C., 1955-75; pres. Am. Friends of Tel Aviv U., N.Y.C., 1982-85, Wexner Heritage Found., 1985-95, founding pres. emeritus, 1995—. Author: Collected Speeches, 1971, Roots of the Future, 1999. Chaplain (capt.) U.S. Army, 1944—47, ETO. Mem. Central Conf. Am. Rabbis, Yale Club (N.Y.C.). Home: 500 E 77th St Apt 2519 New York NY 10162-0008 Office: Wexner Heritage Found 551 Madison Ave New York NY 10022-3212

FRIEDMAN, JEFFREY ROBERT, psychiatrist, educator; b. Mpls., May 26, 1956; s. Harry Samuel and Gertrude (Rotenberg) F.; m. Laura Jean Weisblatt, July 14, 1985; children: Gabrielle Eve, Daniel Adam. BA, Yale U., 1978; MD, U. Chgo., 1982. Diplomate Am. Bd. Psychiatry and Neurology. Intern in medicine Mt. Auburn Hosp., Cambridge, Mass., 1982-83; intern in neurology Mass. Gen. Hosp., Boston, 1982-83; resident in psychiatry McLean Hosp., Belmont, Mass., 1983-86, asst. psychiatrist, 1986-88, asst. clin. psychiatrist, 1988—; instr. psychiatry Harvard U. Med. Sch., Boston, 1986-88, clin. instr., 1988—99, asst. clin. prof. psychiatry, 2000—, psychiatrist Harvard Community Health Plan, 1988-96; assoc. residency dir. Harvard Longwood Psychiatry Residency, Boston, 1995-99; psychiatrist Harvard Pilgrim Health Care, Boston, 1996-97. Candidate Boston Psychoanalytic Soc. and Inst., 1986-97; grad. analyst Boston Psychoanalytic Soc. and Inst. Recipient Paul Howard award McLean Hosp., 1986; Group for Advancement Psychiatry Ginsburg fellow, 1984-86. Mem. Am. Psychiat. Assn., Boston Psychoanalytic Soc. and Inst., Am. Bd. Geriatric Psychiatry, Am. Bd. Forensic Psychiatry, Am. Psychoanlytic Assn., Am. Acad. Psychiatry and Law. Avocations: tennis, squash, cross-country skiing. Office: 875 Massachusetts Ave Ste 51 Cambridge MA 02139-3015

FRIEDMAN, JEROME ISAAC, physics educator, researcher; b. Chgo., Mar. 28, 1930; married, 1956; 4 children. AB, U. Chgo., 1950, MS, 1953, PhD in Physics, 1956. Research assoc. in physics U. Chgo., 1956—57; research assoc. in physics Stanford U., Calif., 1957—60; from asst. prof. to assoc. prof. MIT, Cambridge, 1960—67, prof. physics, 1967—, dir. lab. nuclear sci., 1980—83, head dept. physics, 1983—88, William A. Collidge prof., 1988—90, inst. prof., 1990—. Recipient Nobel prize in Physics, 1990. Fellow: AAAS, Am. Phys. Soc. (co-recipient W.H.K. Panofsky prize 1989); mem.: NAS, Am. Acad. Arts and Scis. Office: MIT Room 24-512/Dept Physics 77 Massachusetts Ave Cambridge MA 02139-4307*

FRIEDMAN, LAWRENCE M. law educator; b. Chgo., Apr. 2, 1930; s. I. M. and Ethel (Shapiro) F.; m. Leah Feigenbaum, Mar. 27, 1955; children: Jane, Amy. AB, U. Chgo., 1948, JD, 1951, LLM, 1953; LLD (hon.), U. Puget Sound, 1977, CUNY, 1989, U. Lund, Sweden, 1993, John Marshall Law Sch., 1995, U. Macerata, Italy, 1998. Mem. faculty St. Louis U., 1957-61, U. Wis., 1961-68; prof. law Stanford U., 1968—, Marion Rice Kirkwood prof., 1976—; David Stouffer Meml. lectr. Rutgers U. Law Sch., 1969; Sibley lectr. U. Ga. Law Sch., 1976; Wayne Morse lectr. U. Oreg., 1985; Childress meml. lectr. St. Louis U., 1987. Jefferson Meml. lectr. U. Calif., 1994; Higgins vis. prof. Lewis and Clark U., 1998; Tucker lectr. Washington and Lee U., 2000. Author: Contract Law in America, 1965, Government and Slum Housing, 1968, A History of American Law, 1973, 2d edit., 1985, The Legal System: A Social Science Perspective, 1975, Law and Society: An Introduction, 1977, American Law, 1984, Total Justice, 1985, Your Time Will Come, 1985, The Republic of Choice, 1990, Crime and Punishment in American History, 1993, The Horizontal Society, 1999, Law in America: A Short History, 2002; author: (with Robert V. Percival) The Roots of Justice, 1981; co-editor (with Stewart Macaulay): Law and the Behavioral Sciences, 1969, 2d edit., 1977; co-editor: (with Stewart Macaulay and John Stookey) Law and Society: Readings on the Social Study of Law, 1995; co-editor: (with Harry N. Scheiber) American Law and the Constitutional Order, 1978; co-editor: Legal Culture and the Legal Profession, 1996; co-editor: (with George Fisher) The Crime Conundrum, 1997; contbr. articles to profl. jours. Served with U.S. Army, 1953-54. Recipient Triennial award Order of Coif, 1976, Willard Hurst prize, 1982, Harry Kalven prize, 1992, Silver Gavel award ABA, 1994, Rsch. award Am. Bar. Found., 2000-01; Ctr. for Advanced Study in Behavioral Sci. fellow, 1974-75, Inst. Advanced Study fellow, Berlin, 1985. Mem. Law and Soc. Assn. (pres. 1979-81), Am. Acad. Arts and Scis., Am. Soc. for Legal History (v.p. 1987-89, pres. 1990-91), Soc. Am. Historians, Rsch. Com. Sociology of Law (hon. life, pres. 2003—). Home: 724 Frenchmans Rd Palo Alto CA 94305-1005 Office: Stanford U Law Sch Nathan Abbott Way Stanford CA 94305-9991 Business E-Mail: lmf@stanford.edu.

FRIEDMAN, LAWRENCE SAMUEL, gastroenterologist, educator; b. Newark, May 11, 1953; s. Maurice and Esther (Slansky) F.; m. Mary Jo Cappuccilli, Apr. 12, 1981; 1 child, Matthew Jacob. Student, Princeton U., 1971-73; BA, Johns Hopkins U., 1975, MD, 1978. Diplomate in internal medicine and gastroenterology Am. Bd. Internal Medicine. Intern dept. medicine Johns Hopkins Hosp., Balt., 1978-79, resident dept. medicine, 1979-81; fellow Mass. Gen. Hosp./ Harvard Med. Sch., Boston, 1981-84; asst. prof. Jefferson Med. Coll., Phila., 1984-87, assoc. prof., 1987-93, vice chmn., 1987-92; assoc. prof. Harvard Med. Sch., Boston, 1993-2001, prof. medicine, 2001—; physician Mass. Gen. Hosp., Boston, 1993—; chief Bauer Firm, 1997—2003; chmn. dept. medicine Newton-Wellesley Hosp., Newton, Mass., 2003—. Chmn. Gastroenterology Leadership Coun. Tng. Com., 1994. Editor: Gastrointestinal Disorders in the Elderly, 1990, 2001, Gastrointestinal Bleeding I, 1993, Gastrointestinal Bleeding II, 1994, Viral Hepatitis, 1994, Training in Endoscopy, 1995, Management of Chronic Liver Disease, 1996, Handbook of Liver Disease, 1998, Sleisenger & Fordtran's Gastrointestinal and Liver Disease, 2002; contbr. articles contbr. articles to profl. jours. Fellow ACP, Am. Coll. Gastroenterology, Coll. Physicians of Phila.; mem. Am. Assn. for Study of Liver Diseases, Am. Fedn. for Med. Rsch., Am. Soc. Gastrointestinal Endoscopy (treas. 1998-2000, Disting. Svc. award 2001), Am. Gastroenterol. Assn., Am. Liver Found., Assn. Subsplty. Profs., Crohn's and Colitis Found. Am., Am. Bd. Internal Medicine Gastroenterology (chair 2003—). Jewish. Avocations: american history, woodwind instruments, travel, basketball. Office: Mass Gen Hosp GI Unit 456D Baker St Boston MA 02132-4235

FRIEDMAN, MARK JOEL, cardiologist, educator; b. N.Y.C., 1944; s. Hyman and Sylvia (Baumgarten) F.; m. Barbara Lynn Rauch, Oct. 11, 1969; 1 child, Gregory N. BA cum laude, Syracuse U., 1967; MD, N.Y. Med. Coll., 1971. Cert. in internal medicine, specialty in cardiovasc. disease. Intern Mt. Sinai Hosp., N.Y.C., 1971-72, resident in medicine, 1972-74; fellow in cardiology U. Ariz., 1976-78; active staff St. Francis Hosp., Tulsa, 1981—. Prof. medicine U. Okla. Tulsa Med. Coll., 1982—. Contbr. articles to profl. jours. Fellow Am. Coll. Cardiology, Am. Heart Assn.; mem. AMA, Alpha Omega Alpha. Office: Springer Clinic Cardi 6151 S Yale Ave Tulsa OK 74136-1907 E-mail: marktul@email.msn.com.

FRIEDMAN, MILES, trade association executive, financial services company executive, university lecturer; b. N.Y.C., Apr. 18, 1950; s. Sol and Rose (Schenkerman) F.; m. Susan Liles, Apr. 26, 1975; children: David Andrew, Diana Leigh. BA in Pub. Affairs, George Washington U., 1971, MA in Polit. Sci., 1972, PhD candidate in Polit. Sci., 1976. Dep. commr. pub. works Town of Ramapo, Suffern, N.Y., 1971; grad. teaching fellow George Washington U., Washington, 1972-75; sr. assoc. Lazar Mgmt. Group, Washington, 1976-77; dir. legis. and policy Nat. Council Urban Econ. Devel., Washington, 1977-80; pres., CEO Nat. Assn. State Devel. Agys., Washington, 1980—. Founder, instr. trade specialist tng. program, Phoenix, 1980—, founder, instr. fgn. investment tng. program, 1988-96; instr. Fgn. Svc. Inst., U.S. and Fgn. Comml. Svc. Inst., Georgetown U., Washington, 1991, U. N.C. Basic Econ. Devel. Inst., Chapel Hill, 1984-85; cons. Pres.' Drug Abuse Prevention Office, Washington, 1972; lectr. George Washington U., Washington, 1975-77. Mem. editl. bd., contbg. editor Econ. Devel. Rev., 1991—; contbg. author to several books, directory; contbr. articles to profl. jours. including Wall St. Jour, Area Devel. mag., Export Today mag., others. Mem bd. dirs., sec./treas. Pub. Sector Devel. Found., Washington, 1983—; pres. Am. Devel. Fin., Inc., 1986-95, also bd. dirs.; liaison subcom. Pres.'s Export Council, Washington, 1981-82; Pinewood Forest Council Owners, 1977-78; chmn. Washington Symposium Higher Edn., 1970-71; pres. Coles Little League, 1997-98; chmn. Prince William County Econ. Devel. Coun., 1998—; bd. dirs. Friends of Brentsville Courthouse Hist. Ctr., 1998—. Recipient Pres.'s E award for Excellence in Export Svc., NASDA, 1993. S. C. of C., Am. Soc. Assn. Execs., Nat. Assn. Execs., Tau Kappa Epsilon, Delta Phi Epsilon, Lambda Alpha. Office: Nat Assn State Devel Agys 750 1st St NE Ste 710 Washington DC 20002-8004

FRIEDMAN, MONROE, psychologist, educator; b. NYC, Oct. 16, 1934; s. Isadore and Pearl Friedman; m. Rita Joyce Shaffer, Sept. 2, 1956; children: Ethan, Mark, Jordan. BS, Bklyn. Coll., 1956; PhD, U. Tenn., 1959. Human factors scientist Sys. Devel. Corp., Santa Monica, Calif., 1959-64; prof. Ea. Mich. U., Ypsilanti, 1964—, dir. Contemporary Issues Ctr., 1970—79. Vis. prof. Tilburg (The Netherlands) U., 1982—83, U. Leuven, Belgium, 1990—91; cons. Pres.'s Com. (Lyndon Johnson) on Consumer Interests, Washington, 1966, Consumer Interests Found., Washington, 1972—73; cons. NSF, Washington, 1973—74, U.S. Gen. Acctg. Office, Washington, 1973—74, FTC, Washington, 1976—77, ACLU Found., NY, 2001—02; bd. dirs. Consumer Interest Rsch. Inst., Washington; presenter in field. Author: A Brand New Language, 1991, Consumer Boycotts, 1999 (Outstanding Acad. Title of Yr., Assn. for Coll. and Rsch. Librs. 2000); contbr. Jour. Consumer Affairs, 1998; issue editor Jour. Social Issues, 1991; co-editor: Frontier of Research in the Consumer Interest, 1988; contbr. over 100 articles to profl. publs.; editl. bd. Jour. Consumer Affairs, Jour. Consumer Rsch., Jour. Consumer Policy; editor: Jour. Consumer Affairs, 1980-84. Pres. Am. Coun. Consumer Interests, 1989—90. Rsch. grantee AARP Andrus Found., 1990, 92, Mich. Coun. for Humanities, 1975; Congl. fellow Am. Polit. Sci. Assn., 1966-67; recipient Disting. Faculty award Mich. Bd. Regents, 1983. Fellow APA (divsn. Population and Environ. Psychology, divsn. Tchg. of Psychology, divsn. Internat. Psychology, divsn. Media Psychology and divsn. Adult Devel. and Aging), Am. Psychol. Soc. (charter), Am. Assn. Applied and Preventive Psychology (charter), Am. Coun. on Consumer Interests (disting., Applied Consumer Econs. award, 1991, 97), Soc. for Consumer Psychology, Soc. for the Psychol. Study of Social Issues, Soc. for Psychology of Aesthetics, Creativity, and the Arts, Soc. for the Study of Peace, Conflict and Violence; mem. Internat. Assn. for Rsch. in Econ. Psychology (U.S. rep. bd. trustees 1982—), Internat. Assn. Applied Psychology (U.S. rep. bd. trustees econ. psychology divsn. 1988—). Home: 1613 E Stadium Blvd Ann Arbor MI 48104-4452 Office: Ea Mich U Psychology Dept Ypsilanti MI 48197

FRIEDMAN, ROBERT SIDNEY, political science educator; b. Balt., Mar. 1, 1927; s. Harry N. and Eva (Cohen) F.; m. Renee Cohen, Aug. 11, 1953 (dec. Oct. 4, 2002); children: Helene, David. BA, Johns Hopkins U., 1948; MA, U. Ill., 1950, PhD, 1953. Rsch. asst. Bur. Govt. Rsch., Md., 1953-55; instr. govt. and politics U. Md., 1955-56; from instr. to assoc. prof. govt. La. State U., 1956-61; rsch. assoc. Inst. Pub. Adminstrn., U. Mich., 1961-67, acting dir., 1967-68; assoc. prof. polit. sci. U. Mich., 1961-66, prof., 1966-68; prof., head dept. polit. sci. Pa. State U., 1968-78; dir. Center for Study Sci. Policy, Inst. for Policy Research and Evaluation, 1978-88, dir. policy analysis program, 1991-94; prof. emeritus, 1994—. Cons. in field. Co-author: Local Government in Maryland, 1955, Government in Metropolitan New Orleans, 1959, Political Leadership and the School Desegregation Crisis in New Orleans, 1963; author: The Michigan Constitutional Convention and Administrative Organization: A Case Study in the Politics of Constitution-Making, 1971; contbg. author: Politics in the American States, 1965, 5th edit., 1990; contbr. articles to profl. jours. Bd. dirs. Pa. Civil Liberties Union, 1969-72; mem. State College (Pa.) Zoning Hearing Bd., 1976-79; chmn. study com. State College Mcpl. Govt., 1991-93; active State College Planning Commn., 1996-99; safety adv. bd. Three Mile Island-2 Cleanup, 1981-89; Pa. bd. Common Cause, 1998—; pres. Friends of Schlow Meml. Libr., 1999-2002, trustee, 2002—. With AUS, 1945-46. Recipient McKay Donkin award for disting. svc., 1980. Mem. Am. Polit. Sci. Assn. Home: 205 Horizon Dr State College PA 16801-8615 Office: Pa State U Burrowes Bldg University Park PA 16802 E-mail: rsf3@psu.edu.

FRIEDMAN, SALLY, artist, educator; b. NYC, Jan. 21, 1932; d. Isaac Mercado and Delicia (Elias) Hazan; children: Michael, Deborah. BA, Queens Coll., 1953, MA, 1959; postgrad., Ruskin Sch. Art, 1962-64, Art Students League, 1964-70. One-woman shows include Waverly Gallery, 1974, NYU, 1977, L.I. U., 1977, 92, Queens Coll., 1980, 90, Fairleigh Dickinson U., 1982, 93, Phoenix Gallery, 1978, 81-82, 84, Pratt Inst., 1985, Donnell Libr. Ctr., 1987, 97, Queens Coll., 1990, Coach Gallery, 2001, Clayton-Libertore Gallery, 2002, Kingsfoot Gallery, 2003; exhibited in group shows at Bklyn., Mus., 1975, Butler Inst. 1975, Phila. Mus., 1978, Sara Lawrence Coll., 1978, Marymount Coll., 1983, Adelphi U., 1987, Berkshire Mus., 1989, Art Expo, NYC, 2000, Guild Hall, East Hampton, NY, 2001, Ashawagh Hall, East Hampton, 2003; represented in permanent collections Oklahoma City Art Mus., Mus. Arts & Scis., Daytona Beach, Fla., New England Ctr. Contemporary Art, Brooklyn, Conn. Mem. Nat. Assn. Women Artists (Paley prize 1975, Cotton prize 1978, Grumbacher award 1980, Winston Meml. prize 1982, Erlanger Meml. prize 1986), Art Students League (life). Avocations: skiing, golf, folk guitar. Home: 255 W 88th St Apt 4D New York NY 10024-1717

FRIEDMAN, SHARON MAE, science journalism educator; b. Phila., Apr. 28, 1943; d. Thomas and Evelyn Eva (Gordon) Berschler; m. Kenneth A. Friedman, July 12, 1963; children: Melissa, Michael. BA in Biology, Temple U., 1964; MA in Journalism, Pa. State U., 1974. Sci. writer/editor Pa. State U., University Park, 1966-67; assoc. info. officer Nat. Acad. Sci., Washington, 1967-70; editor Ctr. for Study of Higher Edn., University Park, 1970-71; adminstrv. and info. officer U.S. Com. for Internat. Biol. Program, State College, Pa., 1971-74; asst. prof., then assoc. prof. journalism Lehigh U., Bethlehem, Pa., 1974-86, dir. sci. writing program, 1977—, prof., 1986—, chmn. dept. journalism, 1986-95, Iacocca prof., 1992—. Cons. Pres.'s Commn. on the Accident at Three Mile Island, Washington, 1979, Clement Internat. Corp., Washington, 1988-90, Environ. Unit, UN Econs. and Social Commn. for Asia/Pacific, Bangkok, 1987-89; mem. adv. bd. Environ. Reporting Forum, Radio-TV News Dirs. Found., 1991-93; participant environ. journalism program Found. Am. Comm., 1992-94; mem. bd. trustees Internat. Food Info. Coun. Found., 1992—, vice chairperson, 1995—; Fulbright Disting. lectr., Brazil, 1982, Bosch Found. lectr., Germany, 1984, 92; cons. in field. Co-author: Reporting on the Environment - Handbook for Journalists, 1988; sr.-editor: Scientists and Journalists: Reporting Science as News, 1986, Communicating Uncertainty: Media Coverage of New and Controversial Science, 1999; assoc. editor: Risk: Health Safety & Environment; mem. editl. bd. Science Communication;

contbr. articles to profl. jours., chpts. to books. EPA grantee, 1990, 92, GM grantee, 1986-93, Ctr. for Fgn. Journalists grantee, 1994. Fellow AAAS (sect. Y officer 1991-95, coun. del., 1999—); mem. Sci. Writing Educators Group (chmn. 1985-91), Assn. for Edn. in Journalism and Mass Comm. (mag. divsn. officer 1988-91), Nat. Assn. Sci. Writers Soc. Environ., Soc. Environ. Jounalists. Achievements include research on mass media coverage of science, environment and technology issues, environmental risk communication, coverage of Alar, radon, dioxin, Chernobyl and Three Mile Island radiation issues, and international environmental journalism and training. Office: Lehigh Univ Dept Journalism & Comm 29 Trembley Dr Bethlehem PA 18015-3066

FRIEDMAN, WILLIAM JOHN, psychology educator; b. May 22, 1950; BA in Psychology with honors, Oberlin Coll., 1972; PhD in Psychology, U Rochester, 1977. Asst. instr. grad. stats. U. Rochester, 1973-74, instr. devel. psychology, 1975-76; trainee in devel. psychology U.S. Dept. Pub. Health, 1972-76; asst. prof. psychology Oberlin (Ohio) Coll., 1976-84, assoc. prof. psychology, 1984-91, prof., 1991—, chair dept. psychology, 1992-2000. Vis. scientist Applied Psychology Unit, Med. Rsch. Coun., Cambridge, Eng., 1983; vis. scientist lab. exptl. psychology U. Grenoble II, 1988-89; vis. scientist U. Canterbury, 1994; U. Otago, 2000-2001. Author (book) About Time: Inventing the Fourth Dimension, 1990; editor (book) The Developmental Psychology of Time, 1982; co-editor (book) Time, Action & Cognition, 1992; contbr. articles to profl. jours. Mem. Soc. for Rsch. in Child Devel., Cognitive Devel. Soc. Office: Oberlin Coll Dept Psychology Oberlin OH 44074

FRIEDMANN, PAUL, surgeon, educator; b. Vienna, Dec. 2, 1933; came to U.S., 1938; s. Erich and Rochelle (Behar) F.; m. Janee Armstrong, Apr. 24, 1962; children: Pamela, Cynthia. BA, U. Pa., 1955; MD, Harvard U., 1959. Diplomate Am. Bd. Surgery, Am. Bd. Vascular Surgery. Chmn. dept. surgery Baystate Med. Ctr., Springfield, Mass., 1971-98, sr. v.p. acad. affairs, 1996—; prof. surgery Sch. Medicine Tufts U., Boston, 1985—. Prof. of surgery, Tufts U. Sch. Medicine, Boston, 1985—, chmn. ad interim dept. surgery, 1996-2001; mem. residency rev. com., 1985-91, chmn., 1989-91; chmn. RRC Coun., Accreditation Coun. for Grad. Med. Edn., 1989-91, mem., 1994-2000. Contbr. articles to profl. jours. Served to capt. USAF, 1961-63. Fellow ACS (bd. govs. 1978-84, 94—, vice chmn., 1998-99, pres. Mass. chpt. 1987, exec. com. bd. govs. 1996-99, adv. coun. for gen. surgery 1996—, chmn. 2001—); mem. Am. Surg. Assn., Assn. Program Dirs. in Surgery (sec. 1985-87, pres. 1987-89), Coun. Med. Specialty Socs. (bd. dirs., sec. 1995-96, pres. elect 1996-97, pres. 1997-98), New Eng. Soc. Vascular Surgery (recorder 1989-90, pres.-elect 1990-91, pres. 1991-92), New Eng. Surg. Soc. (treas. 1991-95, pres.-elect 1995-96, pres. 1996-97), Accreditation Coun. for Grad. Med. Edn. (exec. com. 1995—, chmn. designate 1997-98, chmn. 1998-2000, John Gienapp award 2003). Office: Baystate Med Ctr 759 Chestnut St Springfield MA 01199-1001 E-mail: paul.friedmann@bhs.org.

FRIEDMANN, ROSELI OCAMPO, microbiologist, educator; b. Manila, Nov. 23, 1937; came to U.S., 1968; d. Eliseo Amio and Generosa (Campana) Ocampo; m. Emerich Imre Friedmann ; children: Maria Roseli, Rodolfo. BSc in Botany, U. Philippines, 1958; MSc in Biology, Hebrew U. of Jerusalem, 1966; PhD in Biology, Fla. State U., 1973. Rsch. assoc. Inst. Sci. and Tech., Manila, 1958-67; rsch. asst. Queen's U., Kingston, Ont., Can., 1967-68; tchg. asst. Fla. State U., Tallahassee, 1968-73, rsch. assoc., 1973—75; from asst. prof. dept. biology to assoc. prof. Fla. A&M U., 1975-87, prof., 1987—2000, prof. emeritus, 2000—; prin. investigator NASA Ames Rsch. Ctr., Moffett Field, Calif., 2000—. Contbr. articles to profl. jours. Recipient Resolution of Commendation, State of Fla., Tallahassee, 1978, Antarctic Svc. medal U.S. Congress, NSF, 1981. Mem. Soc. Phycologique France, Phycological Soc. Am., Planetary Soc., AAAS, U.S. Fedn. Culture Collections, Am. Soc. Microbiology, Assn. Women in Sci., Sigma Xi. Avocations: cooking, classical music, photography, travel, cats. Office: NASA Ames Rsch Ctr Mail Code 245 3 Moffett Field CA 94035-1000 E-mail: ifriedmann@mail.arc.nasa.gov.

FRIEDRICH, KATHERINE ROSE, educational researcher; b. Ft. Benning, Ga., Mar. 16, 1964; d. Robert Louis and Judith Ann (Dupont) F. BS in Math. and Psychology, S.W. Tex. State U., 1987; MS in Ednl. Psychology, Tex. A&M U., 1990, PhD in Ednl. Psychology, 1997. Grad. rsch. asst. dept. sociology Tex. A&M U., College Station, 1989, grad. rsch. asst. dept. ednl. psychology, 1989-91, grad. teaching asst., 1991-92; program evaluator Ctr. for Alternative Programs Bryan (Tex.) Ind. Sch. Dist., 1991; rsch. specialist dept. rsch. and evaluation Houston Ind. Sch. Dist., 1993—. Rsch. cons. U. Oreg., Eugene, 1987-88, Tex. A&M U., 1991-92. Vol. Doing Something, Washington, 1992-93. Am. Ednl. Rsch. Assn. rsch. fellow with NSF, 1992-93; scholar for acad. excellence Tex. A&M U., 1990-91. Mem. Advanced Studies of Nat. Databases (sec. 1994-95), Am. Ednl. Rsch. Assn., So. Ednl. Rsch. Assn. Roman Catholic. Avocations: reading, exercise, volunteer work. Office: Houston Ind Sch Dist Dept Rsch Evaluation 3830 Richmond Ave Houston TX 77027-5802

FRIEDRICH-FOX, MARILYN DALE, secondary school educator; b. Chgo., June 12, 1932; d. Arnold Alfred and Ruth Maria Johnson; m. Jerome William Friedrich, Feb. 14, 1952 (div.); children— Rochelle, Denise, Steven; m. Lloyd Francis Fox, Feb. 9, 1990. Student Purdue U., 1951-52; B.A.E., U. Nev., 1955; postgrad. Ind. U., 1958-60, 82-84; M.A.E., Ball State U., 1962. Life cert. tchr., Ind. Recreation dir. Reno City Parks (Nev.), summer 1954; secondary tchr. Kokomo High Sch. (Ind.), 1956-65, cheerleader, block sponsor, 1956-65, 84—, Girls' Athletic Assn. sponsor, 1956-61, curriculum chmn., writer, 1966; recreation dir. Kokomo City Parks (Ind.), summers 1960-62; secondary tchr. Haworth High Sch., Kokomo, Ind., 1968-84, cheerleader, block sponsor, 1968-73, girls' tennis coach, 1975-84, Ind. High Sch. Athletic Assn. swim official, 1973-82; recreation dir. Crystal Beach Cottagers' Assn., Frankfort, Mich., summers 1963-82; dir., writer synchronized swim shows Internat. Aquatic Art Festival, 1959-68; mem. computer core com. Kokomo-Center Schs., 1983—; mem. Handi-Hands Art Guild, . Mem. NEA, Ind. State Teachers' Assn., Kokomo Tchrs. Assn., Internat. Order Foresters, Internat. Platform Assn., Lions Internat., Phi Delta Kappa, Delta Kappa Gamma, Psi Iota Xi (chpt. pres., dist. officer). Roman Catholic. Club: Interracial. Office: Kokomo High Sch Downtown Campus 303 E Superior St Kokomo IN 46901-4841

FRIEMAN, EDWARD ALLAN, academic administrator, educator; b. N.Y.C., Jan. 19, 1926; s. Joseph and Belle (Davidson) F.; m. Ruth Paula Rodman, June 19, 1949 (dec. May 1966); children: Jonathan, Michael, Joshua; m. Joy Fields, Sept. 17, 1967; children: Linda Gatchell, Wendy. BS, Columbia U., 1946, MS in Physics, 1948; PhD in Physics, Poly. Inst. Bklyn., 1952. Prof. astrophys. scis., dep. dir. Plasma Physics Lab. Princeton U., N.J., 1953-79; dir. energy rsch. Dept. Energy, Washington, 1979-81; exec. v.p. Sci. Applications Internat. Corp., La Jolla, Calif., 1981—; dir. Scripps Instn. Oceanography, La Jolla, 1986-96; vice-chancellor marine scis. U. Calif., San Diego, 1986-96, rsch. prof., dir. emeritus, 1996—. Vice-chmn. White House Sci. Coun., 1981-89, Def. Sci. Bd., Washington, 1984-90; mem. Joint Oceanog. Insts., Inc., 1986—, chmn., 1991—; chmn. supercollider site evaluation com. NRC, 1987-89; sci. adv. com. GM, 1987-93, corp. Charles Stark Draper Lab., Inc., 1989—, Sec. Energy Adv. Bd., 1990—, v.p. Space Policy adv. bd., 1992—; bd. dirs. Sci. Applications Internat. Corp.; chmn. NASA Earth Observing Sys. Engring. Rev., 1991-92, v.p.'s space policy adv. bd., 1992—; chmn. Pres.'s Com. on Nat. Medal Sci., 1992-93; chmn. bd. global change NAS/NRC, 1993-94, chmn. bd. on sustainable devel., 1995—; active Joint Oceanog. Insts., Inc., 1986—, chmn., 1991-94; spl. study group NRAC, 1995—; mem. law and policy adv. bd. Ctr. for Oceans, 1994—; mem. Def. Sci. Bd. Task Force on Future Submarines, 1997—. Contbr. articles to profl. jours. With USN, 1943-46, PTO. Recipient Disting. Service medal Dept. Energy, Compass Disting. Achievement Award, Marine Technology Soc., 1995; Disting. Alumni award Poly. Inst. Bklyn.; NSF sr. postdoctoral fellow; Guggenheim fellow Fellow Am. Phys. Soc. (Richtmyer award); mem. AAAS, NAS, Am. Philos. Soc., Cosmos Club (Washington). Avocations: piano, tennis, literature. Home: 1001 Genter St Ph 6 La Jolla CA 92037-5539 Office: Univ Calif San Diego Inst Geophys & Plan Physics 1241 Cave St La Jolla CA 92037-3602

FRIERSON, JIMMIE LOU, retired vocational education educator; b. Mize, Miss., Apr. 12, 1936; d. Eathel Mathew and Lottie Mae (Martin) Maddox; m. Robert Lynn Frierson Jr., Nov. 28, 1957; children: Robert Lynn III, Benjamin Luckie, Arthur Maddox. BS in Home Econs., Miss. U. Women; MA in Home Econs., U. Miss. Cert. tchr., Miss. Tchr. East Prairie (Mo.) Schs., 1957-58; computer operator U. Miss., University, 1959-60, dir. nursery sch., 1973-74; home economist Northeast Miss. Electric Power Assn., Oxford, 1960-62; social worker Lafayette County Welfare Dept., Oxford, 1963-65; tchr. Pontotoc (Miss.) County Sch. System, 1965-70, College Hill Acad., Oxford, 1971-73; tchr. vocat. home econs. Water Valley (Miss.) H.S., 1973-96; ret., 1996. Co-editor The Informed Citizen Non Profit Newsletter; cons. and lectr. in field. Vice chmn. Lafayette County Libr. Bd., Oxford, 1969-97; vol. Am. Cancer Soc., College Hill, Miss., 1992; mem. College Hill Cmty. Assn. Recipient Disting. Svc. award Miss. Future Homemakers Am., 1994. Mem. NEA, Miss. Edn. Assn., Miss. Libr. Assn., Kappa Omicron Nu. Presbyterian. Avocations: gardening, writing.

FRIERSON, MARIE HOLMES, middle school educator; b. Lee County, S.C., Apr. 30, 1946; d. Alex and Marie (Herriott) Holmes; m. Charles Henry Frierson, June 24, 1972; children: Kenneth Marlo, Tobe Renita. BS in Math., Morris Coll., 1968; MEd, S.C. State U., 1975. Tchr. Manning (S.C.) Tng. High Sch., 1968-70, Manning Mid. Sch., 1970—. Adv. coun. Manning Mid. Sch., 1990-92, Clarendon Sch. Dist. #2, Manning, 1991-92. Mem. NEA, S.C. Edn. Assn., Clarendon County Edn. Assn., Nat. Coun. Tchrs. Math., S.C. Coun. Tchrs. Math. Baptist. Avocations: reading, bowling, computer games. Home: 476 Alpine Dr Sumter SC 29154-5402 Office: Manning Mid Sch 311 W Boyce St Manning SC 29102-2628

FRIES, MARY KIM, AIDS education educator, educational consultant; b. Pitts., Nov. 12, 1956; d. Franklin Herr and Lorraine (Sondecker) F. Bachelor degree, U. South Fla., 1979, Master degree, 1994. Educator Pasco County Schs., Land O'Lakes, Fla., 1979-85; educator, nat. trainer, curriculum, developer, mktg. C.E. Mendez Found., Tampa, Fla., 1985-92; ednl. cons. Wediko Children's Svcs., Boston, 1985—; AIDS resource team leader Hillsborough County Schs., Tampa, 1992—. Contbr. articles to profl. jours. Mem. child care bd. YMCA, Tampa, 1991—; vol. Tampa AIDS Network, 1992—; mem. com. Am. Cancer Soc., Tampa, 1982-85, Am. Lung Assn., St. Petersburg, Fla., 1982-85, Am. Heart Assn., New Port Rickey, Fla., 1980-82. Mem. AAHPERD, ASCD, U. South Fla. Alumni Assn., Kappa Delta Pi, Phi Kappa Phi. Avocations: athletics, aquatics. Office: Hillsborough County Schs 1202 E Palm Ave Tampa FL 33605-3512

FRIESEN, BRUCE K. education educator; b. Saskatoon, Can., July 20, 1958; s. John W. Friesen and Ruth S. Nickel; m. Deborah K. Zuercher, Aug. 14, 1982; children: Brittany, Justin. BA, U. Waterloo, Can., 1983; MA, U. Calgary, Can., 1986, PhD, 1993. Assoc. prof. Kent State U., Canton, Ohio, 1995—. Author: Perceptions of the Amish Way, 1996. Office: Kent State U 6000 Frank Ave NW Canton OH 44720-7599 E-mail: bfriesen@kent.edu.

FRIESEN, RONALD LEE, economics educator; b. Inman, Kans., Mar. 2, 1939; s. J.D. and Hilda Marie (Neufeld) F.; m. Phyllis Ruth Sawatzky, June 2, 1961; children: Janine Renee, Jon Alan, Julie Dyan. BA, Bethel Coll., 1961; MA in Econs., U. Kans., 1962; PhD in Econs., Columbia U., 1973. Tchr. Alliance Secondary Sch., Dodoma, Tanzania, 1962-65; prof. econs. Bluffton (Ohio) Coll., 1969—. Past faculty chmn., past chmn. econ., bus. adminstrn. and acctg. dept. Bluffton Coll.; cons. in field. Contbr. book reviews and articles to profl. jours. and collected vols. Recipient Rsch. and Lectr., C. Henry Smith Trust, 1981-82; scholar faculty U. Kans., Lawrence, 1961-62, faculty fellow Columbia U., N.Y.C., 1965-69; Albert Schweitzer Chair fellow, N.Y.C., 1969. Mem. Am. Econs. Assn., African Studies Assn., Ohio Assn. Economists and Polit. Scientists, Economists Allied for Arms Reduction. Avocations: tennis, stamp collecting, coin collecting, antique collecting. Office: Bluffton Coll Dept Econs Bluffton OH 45817

FRIESS, DONNA LEWIS, children's rights advocate; b. LA, Jan. 16, 1943; d. Raymond W. Lewis, Jr. and Dorothy Gertrude (Borwick) McIntyre; m. Kenneth E. Friess, June 20, 1964; children: Erik, Julina, Daniel. BA in Comm., U. So. Calif., 1964; MA in Comm., Calif. State U., Long Beach, 1966; PhD in Psychology, U.S. Internat. U., San Diego, 1993. Cert. tchr., Calif. Prof. human comm. Cypress (Calif.) Coll., 1966—. Lectr. survivors of abuse, 1990—, mental health profls., 1990—; guest expert (TV) Sally Jessy Raphael, 1993, Leeza Gibbons Talk Show, 1994, Sonja: Live, 1994, Oprah Winfrey Show, 1991, others; presenter, spkr. in field. Author: Relationships, 1995, Just Between Us: A Guidebook for Survivors of Childhood Trauma, 1995, Cry the Darkness, 1993, European edit. 1995, Danish edit., 1999, Korean edit., 1995, Norwegian edit., 1998, Circle of Love: Secrets to Successful Relationships, 1996, 2d edit., 2002, Whispering Waters: The Story of Historic Weesha, 1998, Chronicle of Historic Weesha and the Upper Santa Ana River Valley, 2000; contbr. articles to mags. Del. to round table discussion on victims' issues U.S. Justice Dept., 2002, apptd. consortium for victims affairs, 2003; nat. consortium of victim assistance experts U.S. Dept. Justice, 2003—, adv. bd. Recipient Author's award U. Calif. Friends of Libr., 1996, recognition from U.S. Justice Dept. for outstanding efforts to stop child abuse, 1995, Lee Steelmon award, Recognition cert. for work to prevent child abuse Calif. State Senate, 2000, Orange County (Calif.) Bd. Suprs.' Resolution for Outstanding Efforts for Children, 2000, Outstanding Speech Faculty award Calif. State U., 2001. Mem. Am. Coalition Against Child Abuse (founder), Task Force for ACCA to Educate American Judges on Issues of Sexual Abuse, One Voice, Calif. Psychol. Assn., Western Social Sci. Assn., Child Abuse Listening and Mediating (bd. dirs.), Am. Profl. Soc. on Abuse of Children, Mother Against Sexual Abuse (bd. dirs.), Laura's House for Battered Women (bd. dirs.), Calif. Tchrs. Assn., Faculty Assn. Calif. C.Cs., Speech Communication Assn. of Am., U.S. Internat. U. Alumni Assn. (bd. dirs.). Avocation: painting on porcelain. Office: Cypress College Dept Human Communications Cypress CA 90630 E-mail: donafriess@aol.com.

FRIIS, ROBERT HAROLD, epidemiologist, health science educator; b. San Jose, Calif., July 15, 1941; s. Harold Hector and Florence Marie (Brant) F.; m. Carol Ann Speer, Oct. 28, 1966; children: Michelle Alanna, Erik Adler. BA, U. Calif., Berkeley, 1964; MA, Columbia U., N.Y.C., 1966, PhD, 1969. Postdoctoral fellow U. Mich., Ann Arbor, 1969-71; asst. prof. Sch. Pub. Health Columbia U., 1971-74, Albert Einstein Coll. Medicine, Bronx, N.Y., 1974-76; assoc. prof. CUNY, Bklyn. Coll., 1976-78; dir. field epidemiology Orange County Pub. Health, Santa Ana, Calif., 1978-79; assoc. clin. prof. U. Calif., Irvine, 1979-93; prof., chairperson dept. health sci. Calif. State U., Long Beach, 1988—, now mem. acad. senate. Vis. rschr. Karolinska Inst., Stockholm, 1993; dir. Joint Studies Inst. Calif. State U. and VA Med. Ctr., Long Beach, 1995—; adv. bd. Ctr. for Health Care Innovation Calif. State U., Long Beach; guest scientist Max Planck Inst. Psychiatry, Munich, 2001; vis. prof. clin. psychology and psychotherapy unit Dresden (Germany) Tech. U., 2001; bd. dirs. Long Beach (Calif.) Global Health Initiative, Ctr. for Health Care Innovation, Long Beach, Long Beach Tobacco Edn. Program; clin. prof. cmty. and environ. medicine U. Calif., Irvine, 2003; cons. in field. Sr. author: Epidemiology Public Health Practice, 1996, 3d edit. 2004; co-author: Introductory Biostatistics for the Health Sciences, 2003; contbr. articles to profl. jours. Faculty mentor Ptnrs. for Success, Long Beach, 1992. Grantee U. Calif., Irvine, 1995, Mexus com. U. Calif., 1988, U. Calif. systemwide, 1988, U. Calif. Tobacco Related Disease Rsch. Program, 1998, 2003. Mem. APHA, Am. Statis. Assn. (So. Calif. sect.), Soc. Epidemiol. Rsch., Am. Assn. Health Edn., U. Calif. Berkley Alumni Assn., So. Calif. Pub. Health Assn. (bd. dirs.), Eta Sigma Gamma. Democrat. Avocations: reading, travel, coin collecting, computers, gardening. Office: Calif State U Long Beach Dept Health Sci 1250 N Bellflower Blvd Long Beach CA 90840-0006 E-mail: rfriis@csulb.edu.

FRISCH, IVAN THOMAS, computer and communications company executive; b. Budapest, Hungary, Sept. 21, 1937; came to U.S., 1939, naturalized, 1941; s. Laszlo and Rose (Balog) F.; m. Vivian Scelzo, June 6, 1962; children: Brian, Bruce. BS, MS, Columbia U., 1958, PhD, 1962. Asst. prof. elec. engring. and computer sci. U. Calif., Berkeley, 1962-65, assoc. prof., 1965-69; Ford Found. resident engring. practice Bell Labs., Holmdel, N.J., 1965-66; founding mem. Network Analysis Corp., Great Neck, N.Y., 1969—, sr. v.p., 1971—, gen. mgr., 1978-85; v.p. Contel Bus. Networks, 1985-87; dir. Ctr. on Advanced Tech. in Telecommunications, prof. Poly. U., Bklyn., 1987—; provost Polytech. U., 1992—. Adj. prof. computer sci. SUNY, Stony Brook, 1975—, Columbia U., N.Y.C., 1977—; cons. in field. Author: (with Howard Frank) Communication, Transmission and Transportation Networks, 1971; Founding editor-in-chief: Networks, 1971—; contbr. articles to profl. publs. Guggenheim fellow, 1969 Fellow IEEE (Eric E. Sumner award 1999, 3d Millenium award 2000); mem. N.Y. Acad. Scis., Cable TV Assn. Am., Nat. Acad. Engring., Phi Beta Kappa, Tau Beta Pi, Eta Kappa Nu. Office: Poly U Six Metrotech Ctr Rm JB-555 Brooklyn NY 11201-2907

FRISCH, PAUL ANDREW, librarian; b. Madison, Wis., Oct. 23, 1950; s. Arthur Joseph and Ruth Beverly (Myers) F.; m. Claudia Anna Maria Hirsch, Aug. 1, 1990. BA History, UCLA, 1975, MA History, 1977, MLS, 1986, PhD History, 1992. Social scis. libr. Trinity Univ., San Antonio, 1986-88; head ref. dept., libr. Southwest Mo. State U., Springfield, 1988-92; head of ref. dept., libr. U. Ill., Chgo., 1992-95; head libr. Washington & Jefferson Coll., Washington, Pa., 1995-2000; dir. Old Westbury Libr. SUNY, Old Westbury, NY, 2000—01; dean libr. Our Lady of the Lake, San Antonio, 2001—. Contbr. articles to profl. jours. Treas., trustee Citizens Libr., Washington, Pa., 1995-2000. Summer rsch. grantee S.W. Mo. State U., 1990. Mem. ALA, Assn. Coll. and Rsch. Libs. Office: Sueltenfuss Libr Our Lady of the Lake U San Antonio TX 78207-4689

FRISINA, ROBERT DANA, sensory neuroscientist, educator; b. Evanston, Ill., Sept. 11, 1955; s. D. Robert and Louise (Boaz) F.; m. Susan Taylor Frisina, July 31, 1982; children: Laurin Taylor, Taylor Robert. AB in Exptl. Psychology summa cum laude, Hamilton Coll., 1977; PhD in Neurosci., Syracuse U., 1983. Rsch. asst. Hamilton Coll., Clinton, NY, 1977; Root fellow in sci. Inst. Sensory Rsch., Syracuse (N.Y.) U., 1977-78, NSF grad. fellow, 1978-81, grad. rsch. assoc., 1981-83; NIH rsch. fellow Ctr. Brain Rsch. U. Rochester, NY, 1983-85; asst. prof. physiology and otolaryngology U. Rochester, 1985-91, assoc. prof. surgery, neurobiology and anatomy, 1991-99, prof. surgery, neurobiology, anatomy, and biomed. engring., 1999—, dir. rsch. otolaryngology, 1988-92, assoc. chmn. otolaryngology, 1992—; v.p. and founder Auditory Sys. Technologies, Inc., Pittsford, NY, 1989-98; adj. assoc. prof. comm. scis. Nat. Tech. Inst. Deaf, 1993—; adj. clin. instr. comm. scis. U. Buffalo, 1998—; disting. rsch. prof. Rochester Inst. Tech., 2003—. Staff mem. Nat. Tech. Inst. for Deaf, Rochester, 1975; charter mem. adv. bd. Internat. Ctr. for Hearing and Speech Rsch., 1988—; assoc. editor Jour. Acoustical Soc. Am., 1996-99; chmn. study sect. NIH, 2000-02. Author: Hearing, 1989; mem. editl. bd. Hearing Rsch. Jour., 1997—; contbr. articles to profl. jours. Dir. Vols. Hamilton Coll. Aspect of Marcy (N.Y.) Psychiat. Ctr., 1974-77. Recipient 1st Award in Communicative Disorders, NIH, 1988-94. Fellow Am. Acad. Otolaryngology-Head and Neck Surgery, Acoustical Soc. Am.; mem. Assn. Rsch. in Otolaryngology, Soc. Neurosci., Am. Speech-Hearing-Lang. Assn., Acoustical Soc. Found. (charter, bd. dirs. 1996—, gen. sec. and chief fin. officer 1998—), Phi Beta Kappa, Sigma Xi, Psi Chi. Roman Catholic. Achievements include patents for a noise suppression electronic circuit for enhancing speech in the presence of background noise; a hearing aid circuit which can be custom fit to a patient's hearing loss using laser trimming. Office: U Rochester Med Ctr Otolaryngology Divsn Rochester NY 14642-8629 E-mail: rdf@q.ent.rochester.edu.

FRITCH, RONALD J. vocational education educator; b. Deckerville, Mich., Sept. 16, 1935; s. Lawrence Thomas and Catherine Aseneth (Sweet) F.; m. Lois Marie Hooper, Aug. 8, 1958; children: Lucinda, Lynnette, Robert, Russel, Lenore. BS, Mich. State U., 1957, MA, 1962, spl. edn. cert., 1972. Tchr. vocat. agrl. Yale (Mich.) Pub. Schs., 1957-58; tchr. biology and gen. sci. Deckerville Community Schs., 1958-59; tchr. vocat. agrl. Britton (Mich.) Macon Area Schs., 1959-63; tchr. vocat. agrl., spec. edn. Elkon Pigeon (Mich.) Bay Port Schs., 1963-70; spl. edn. coord. Port Huron (Mich.) Area Schs., 1970-75; vocat. bldg. and grounds St. Clair County Schs., Port Huron, 1975-87; vocat. agrl. tchr. Volusia County Schs., De Land, Fla., 1988—. Owner R.J. Fritch Builders, Port Huron, 1975-87; mgr. Outrigger Time Share, Ormond Beach, Fla., 1987-88. Chmn. Fort Gratiot (Mich.) Zoning Bd. of Appeals, 1983-87; unit commr. Boy Scouts Am., Orlando, Fla., 1992. Mem. F.W. Hubbard Lodge Free and Accepted Mason (master 1969), Port Huron Chpt. Royal Arch Mason (high priest), Marine City Coun., Port Huron Commandery, York Rite Bodies. United Methodist. Avocation: boy scout leader training and membership. Home: 1420 E Euclid Ave Deland FL 32724-6118

FRITSCH, CARLA E. secondary education educator; b. Milw., Dec. 10, 1958; d. Thomas A. and Blanche E. (Palsgrove) F. BA, John Carroll U., 1980, MA, 1986; MEd, Ursuline Coll., 2001. Cert. tchr., Ohio. Asst. dir. St. Augustine Acad., Lakewood, Ohio, 1980—; cons. Ctr. for Learning, Westlake, 1987—. Tchr. High Sch. Religion Series, Lakewood, 1993. Author: Church History, 1990, Understanding Scripture, 1992, Faith: Developing an Adult Spirituality, 1994, Church: Tracing Our Pilgrimage, 1995, (curriculum unit) The Lord of the Rings, 1991. Named for Excellence in Edn. Cath. Diocese of Cleve., 1992. Democrat. Roman Cath. Avocations: reading, writing, cooking, theatre. Office: Saint Augustine Acad 14808 Lake Ave Lakewood OH 44107-1391

FRITSCHLER, A. LEE, retired college president, public policy educator; b. Schenectady, N.Y., May 5, 1937; s. George A. and Jane E. (Green) F.; m. Aliceann Wohlbruck, Sept. 2, 1961 (div. 1976); children: Craig A., Eric G.; m. Susan Torrence, Dec. 31, 1977. BA, Union Coll., Schenectady, 1959; MPA, Syracuse U., 1960, PhD, 1965; LLD, The Dickinson Sch. of Law, 1993. Asst. prof. Am. U., Washington, 1964-67, prof., 1967-79, acad. dir. Washington semester program, 1964-67, dir. pub. adminstrn. program, 1971-72, dean Coll. Pub. and Internat. Affairs, 1977-79; chmn. U.S. Postal Rate Commn., 1979-81; dir. ctr. pub. policy edn. Brookings Instn., Washington, 1981-87; pres. Dickinson Coll., Carlisle, Pa., 1987-99. Guest prof. U. Cologne, Fed. Republic Germany, 1971; vis. prof. Union Coll., 1984; lectr Nat. War Coll., 1969; lectr. on bus.-govt. rels. to exec. devel. programs at IBM Corp., AT&T, GE, Gulf Corp.; co-founder, former chair, treas. The Annapolis Group, 1991—. Author (with B.H. Ross) (textbook) Business Regulation and Government Decision-Making, 1980, (trade book) Executive's Guide to Government: How Washington Works, 1980, Smoking and Politics: Policymaking and the Federal Bureaucracy, 1983, 5th edit., 1996, How Washington Works: The Executive's Guide to Government, 1987; mem. editl. bd. Pub. Adminstrn. Rev., 1976-80, Internat. Jour. Pub. Adminstrn., 1979-88; contbr. numerous articles to profl. jours. Mem. Harrisburg Acad. Cmty. Adv. Bd., 1991-96, Commonwealth Partnership Adv. Bd., 1997—; hon. bd. dirs. Friends of the Joseph Priestly House; mem. exec. com. Am. Collegiate Consortium for East-West Cultural and Acad. Exch., 1993-96. Mem. Am. Soc. Pub. Adminstrn. (nat. pres. 1982-83, bd. dirs. govt.-bus. relations sect.), Nat. Acad. Pub. Adminstrn. (bd. dirs.), Assn.

of Governing Bds. Univs. and Colls. (adv. coun. of pres.), Bd. Orgn. Resources Counsellors, Indsl. Rels. Counselors, Inc., Internat. Inst. Adminstrv. Scis. (mem. N.Am. bd. govs. schs. and insts. sect.), Nat. Capital Area Polit. Sci. Assn. (pres. 1975), Nat. Assn. Schs. Pub. Affairs and Adminstrn. (bd. dirs. 1975), Libr. of Congress (coun. scholars), Internat. Assn. Univ. Presidents, Am. Coun. on Edn. (comn. on internat. edn.), Nat. Acad. Found. Acad. Pub. Sbvc. (bd. dirs.), Northeast-Midwest Inst. (bd. dirs.), Ctr. for Regional Policy, Pa. Commn. for Ind. Colls. and Univs. (exec. com.), Assn. Ind. Colls. and Univs. Pa. (bd. dirs. 1997—). Avocations: tennis, furniture repair, golf.

FRITZ, JAN MARIE, planning educator, mediator, clinical sociologist; b. Cleve., Nov. 4, 1941; d. Andrew and Julia (Zrencsik) F.; m. Richard Lerner; children: Hyunjin, Karin. BA, Bowling Green State U.; MA, Ohio State U.; PhD, Am. U. Cert. clin. sociologist, 1984. Asst. prof. Georgetown U., Washington, 1975-85; sci. assoc. Nat. Cancer Inst., Washington, 1986-89; assoc. prof. Calif. State U., San Bernardino, 1989-93, U. Cin., 1993—. Mem. Nat. Environ. Justice Adv. Coun., U.S. EPA, 2002—. Mediator U.S. Equal Opportunity Commn. U.S. Postal Svc. Grantee U.S. EPA, 1996-97; Kellogg Found. Nat. fellow, 1982-85, NEH fellow, 1991-92, Ohio Campus Compact Faculty fellow, 1999-2000; recipient Peres-Rabin Peace award, 1999. Mem.: AAUP, Internat. Assn. Facilitators, Nat. Network Forest Practioners, Am. Health Planning Assn. (bd. dirs. 1995—2000), Assn. Conflict Resolution, Am. Sociol. Assn., Sociol. Practice Assn. (pres. 1980—82, Disting. Career award 1992), Internat. Sociol. Assn. (pres. clin. sociology divsn. 1992—94, exec. bd. 1994—2002, rep. to UN 1999—2002, v.p. sociotechnics-sociol. practice divsn. 2002—). E-mail: jan.fritz@uc.edu.

FRITZ, KRISTINE RAE, secondary education educator; b. Monroe, Wis. BS in Phys. Edn., U. Wis., LaCrosse, 1970; MS in Phys. Edn., U. N.C., Greensboro, 1978. Softball and fencing program coord. Mequon (Wis.) Recreation Dept., 1970; phys. edn., health and English tchr. Horace Jr. H.S., 1970—81; phys. edn. and health tchr. Sheboygan (Wis.) South H.S., 1982—; basketball and volleyball coach, 1972—89; girls track coach, 1972—. Mem. dist. wide curriculum and evaluation coms., 1978—; mem. sch. effectiveness team, 1991—94; sch. evaluation consortium evaluator, 1988—; inbound/outbound coach Sport for Understanding, 1991—96. Contbr. articles to profl. jours. Active Sheboygan (Wis.) Spkrs. Bur., 1987—95, Women Reaching Women. Recipient Nat. H.S. Coaches award for girls track, 1987. Mem.: AAHPERD (Midwest dist. Tchr. of Yr. 1995, Pathfinder award 1997), NEA, Sheboygan Edn. Assn., Wis. Assn. Health, Phys. Edn., Recreation and Dance (pres.-elect 1998—99, pres. 1999—2000, Phys. Edn. Tchr. Yr. 1993), Phi Delta Kappa. Home: 1841 N 26th St Sheboygan WI 53081-2008

FRITZ, MADELINE MILIDONIS, art educator, professional artist; b. Akron, Ohio, Mar. 8, 1949; d. Michael and Mary Hope (Anuta) Milidonis; children: Jared Micah, Justin Ray. BS in Art Edn., Western Mich. U., 1970, MA in Watercolor/Textiles, 1974; postgrad., Eastern Mich. U., 1981, 87, 89, Ctrl. Mich. U., 1990, U. Cin., 1992, Cranbrook Acad. of Art, 1993. Cert. tchr., Mich. Art tchr. Crestwood Cmty. Schs., Dearborn, Mich., 1971-75, Allen Park (Mich.) Pub. Schs., 1975-80; mid. sch. tchr. Mio (Mich.)-AuSable Schs., 1983-86; art tchr. Gaylord (Mich.) Cmty. Schs., 1986—, quality sch. trainer, 1997-99. Inservice trainer P.A.C.E. Telecomm., Indian River, Mich., 1993-94. One woman show Jesse Besser Mus., Alpena, Mich., 1989; exhibited in group shows at Bay Window Gallery, Garden City, Mich., 1988, McCune Art Ctr., Petoskey, Mich., 1989, Jesse Besser Mus., Alpena, 1990, 91, The Arts Castle, Delaware, Ohio, 1990, Artisans Gallery, Petoskey, 1992. Recipient Hon. Mention award Mich. Art Edn. Electronic Gallery, 1993, grand prize winner N.E. Juried Art Exhibit, 1999, award N.E. Mich. Artists Guild, 1998, 1st place award Jesse Besser Mus., Alpena, 1999. Mem. Nat. Art Edn. Assn., Mich. Art Edn. Assn. (liaison Region 14 1989-91, presenter and trainer, Mich. Art Educator of the Yr. award 1993, cons. visual arts curriculum assessment), Gaylord Area Coun. for the Arts (sec. 1990-92, v.p. 1993, pres. 1994). Avocations: gardening, weaving, painting, reading.

FRITZ, MARY NOONAN, elementary school educator, consultant; b. N.Y.C., Jan. 6, 1932; d. James Patrick and Kathleen (O'Connor) Noonan; m. Howard Philip Fritz, Nov. 12, 1955; children: Howard Jr., Maura, James, Sharon. BA in English, St. John's U., 1954; MS in Elem. Edn., Fordham U., 1956; Profl. Diploma in Adminstrn., St. John's U., 1984, EdD in Adminstrn., 1993. Cert. elem. tchr., sch. dist. adminstr., N.Y. Tchr. West Hempstead (N.Y.) U.F.S.D., 1955-56; tchr. Farmingdale (N.Y.) U.F.S.D., 1962-77; cons. Open Ct. Pub. Co., Peru, Ill., 1977-90; pre-kindergarten dir., prin. Westbury (N.Y.) U.F.S.D. Freelance cons., 1990—; mem. N.Y. State Edn. Dept. Pre-K Adv. Bd., 1993—, Permanent Inter-Agy. Com. on Early Childhood, 1993—; sr. cons. Nassau County Alliance for Family Literacy. Contbr. to textbook, tchr.'s guide. Recipient Educator of Yr.-Gary Mintz award St. John's U., 2000. Mem. ASCD, Phi Delta Kappa (v.p. 1994-95, pres. 1995-96). Avocations: reading, writing, gardening, antiques. Home: 43 Ridge Dr Plainview NY 11803-2505 Office: St Joseph's Coll Child Study Dept Patchogue NY

FRITZ, NANCY H. educational researcher, administrator; b. Greenfield, Mass., Nov. 21, 1944; d. Gerard Martin and Helen (Cassidy) F. BA in English, Western New Eng. Coll., 1970; EdM in Psychology and Edn., Smith Coll., Northampton, Mass., 1982. Cert. tchr., Mass., N.Y., Vt. Title I reading recovery tchr., dir., Amherst, Mass.; ret. Lectr. in field. Contbr. articles to profl. jours. Recipient Eckel Human Rels. Cup, WRA Highest Achievement award. Mem. NEA, AAUW, Internat. Reading Assn., Nat. Coun. Tchrs. English, Nat. Coun. Tchrs. Math., Mass. Reading Assn. Home: The Deerfield Commons South Deerfield MA 01373-9620

FRIZELL, SAMUEL, law educator; b. Buena Vista, Colo., Aug. 30, 1933; s. Franklin Guy and Ruth Wilma (Noel) F.; m. Donna Mae Knowlton, Dec. 26, 1955 (div. June 1973); children: Franklin Guy III, LaVerne Anne; m. Linda Moncure, Jul. 3, 1973 (div. June 1996); m. Jeannette Graham, Jan. 1997. AA cum laude, Ft. Lewis Coll., 1957; BA cum laude, Adams State Coll., 1959, EdM, 1960; JD, Hastings U. Calif., 1964. Bar: Calif. 1965. Assoc. atty. McCutcheon, Black, Verleger & Shea, Calif., L.A., 1964-67; atty. Law Offices Samuel Frizell, Santa Ana, Calif., 1967-82; adj. prof. Cerritos Coll., Norwalk, Calif., 1977-81, Western State U., Fullerton, Calif., 1982-84, assoc. prof., 1984-90, prof., 1990-98, prof. emeritus, 1998—; cons. Law Offices Samuel Frizell, Mira Loma, Calif., 1982-98. Author: Frizell's Torts Tips, 1992; contbr. articles to profl. jours.; editor law jour. Mem. Main St. Adv. Panel, Garden Grove, Calif., 1975-76; judge pro-tem Orange County Superior Ct., Santa Ana, 1979-80; chair, com. atty. advertising Orange County Bar Assn., 1975; bd. dirs. Orange County Trial Lawyers Assn., 1972-75; adv. panel to legal assts. Cerritos Coll., Norwalk, 1982-86. Fellow Soc. Antiquaries; mem. Order of the Coif. Avocations: history, reloading and target shooting, saddle making. Office: Western State U 1111 N State College Blvd Fullerton CA 92831-3000 E-mail: SJFrizell@Earthlink.net.

FRODSHAM, OLAF MILTON, music educator; b. Bournemouth, Eng., Oct. 25, 1915; came to U.S., 1921; s. Sydney Herbert and Oline Magarethe (Espersen) F.; m. Grace Elaine Bessey, Aug. 17, 1946; 1 child, Lance Philip. AB, U. Redlands, 1937, MA, 1938; postgrad., Royal Sch. London, 1962, Exeter U., 1967. Cert. life gen. secondary credential, life gen. jr. coll., life gen. elem. Tchr. Porterville HS, Calif., 1938-41, Kamehameha Sch., Honolulu, 1941-42; instr., dir. choral music Long Beach City Coll., Calif., 1946-50; assoc. prof. Occidental Coll., LA, 1950-78; dir. choral music. Calif. Inst. Tech., Pasadena, Calif., 1953-82; dir. music St. Bede the Venerable Sch., LaCanada, Calif., 1982-92, Santa Clara Elem. Sch., Oxnard, Calif., 1992-95, Luth. Ch. of Our Redeemer, Oxnard, Calif., 1994-99. Adj. asst. prof. Long Beach State U., 1948-52. Dir. choral recs. God of Abraham Praise, 1978; Liszt: Messe fur Vierstimmigen Männerchor, 1979-80. Staff sgt. U.S. Army, 1942-46, PTO. Recipient Leadership in Edn. Athenaeum award U. Redlands, 1972; named Hon. Alumnus, Calif. Inst. Tech., Pasadena, 1970. Mem. Am. Choral Dirs. Assn., Music Educators Assn., Choral Conductors Guild, Pacific Southwest Choral Assn. (sec.-treas. 1970-78, pres. 1978-79), Calif. Tchrs. Assn. Roman Catholic. Avocations: weight tng., cooking, singing. Home: Apt 410 842 E Villa St Pasadena CA 91101-1284

FROGGE, JAMES LEWIS, secondary school educator; b. Kankakee, Ill., Nov. 1, 1950; s. Calvin Lewis and Marietta Katherine (McCue) F.; m. Margaret Hansen, Oct. 11, 1980; children: Jessica, Sarah, Nathan. BS, Yale U., 1972; postgrad., Northwestern U., Evanston, Ill., 1976-77; MA, Governors State U., University Park, Ill., 1982. Instr. sci. Bishop McNamara H.S., Kankakee, 1972-76, 77—. Engring. cons. Argonne (Ill.) Nat. Labs, 1975-76, Armour Pharm. Co., Kankakee, 1976-77; assoc. prof. Governors State U., 1984-85. Site steward Nature Conservancy, Bourbonnais, Ill., 1990—; interviewer Yale Alumni Schs. Com., Kankakee, 1980—; site coord. Ill. Rivers Project, Kankakee, 1990—. Named Gov.'s Master Tchr., State of Ill., 1983, Dreyfus Master Tchr., Woodrow Wilson Found., 1982; First of Am. Bank grantee, 1991, 95, Kankakee County Conservation Tchr. of Yr., 1995. Mem. AAAS, Am. Chem. Soc., Am. Assn. Physics Tchrs., Nature Conservancy, Sierra Club. Democrat. Roman Catholic. Avocations: canoeing, prairie restoration, mathematics, computing. Home: 1298 S Sandbar Rd Kankakee IL 60901-7606 Office: Bishop McNamara High School Brookmont at Entrance Kankakee IL 60901 E-mail: mcnamarajlf@hotmail.com.

FROHMAN, LAWRENCE ASHER, endocrinology educator, scientist; b. Detroit, Jan. 26, 1935; s. Dan and Rebecca (Katzman) F.; m. Barbara Hecht, June 9, 1957; children: Michael, Marc, Erica, Rena. MD, U. Mich., 1958. Diplomate: Am. Bd. Internal Medicine. Intern Yale-New Haven Med. Ctr., 1958—59, resident in internal medicine, 1959—61; asst. prof. medicine SUNY, Buffalo, 1965—69, assoc. prof., 1969—73; prof. medicine U. Chgo., 1973—81; dir. endocrinology Michael Reese Hosp., Chgo., 1973—81; prof., dir. div. endocrinology and metabolism U. Cin., 1981—92; prof. medicine U. Ill., Chgo., 1992—, chmn. Dept. Medicine, 1992—2001; dir. Med. Svcs. U. Ill. Hosp., Chgo., 1992—2001. Dir. Gen. Clin. Rsch. Ctr., 1986-90; mem. sci. rev. com. NIH, Bethesda, Md., 1972-76; mem. sci. rev. bd. VA, Washington, 1979-82; mem. endocrine adv. bd. FDA, Washington, 1982-86; mem. adv. com. Nat. Inst. Diabetes, Digestive and Kidney Diseases, NIH, 1983-94, chmn., 1991-93; mem. sci. adv. bd. Edison Biotech. Inst., Ohio U. Editor: (with others) Endocrinology and Metabolism, 2001; editl. bd. 7 med. and sci. jours., 1970—; contbr. articles to profl. jours. NIH research grantee, 1967-98, Endocrine Soc. Rorer Clin. Investigator award, 1991. Mem.: ACP, Am. Clin. Climatological Assn., Pituitary Soc., Internat. Soc. Neuroendocrinology, Am. Diabetes Assn., Am. Soc. Clin. Investigation, Assn. Am. Physicians, Endocrine Soc. Office: U Ill at Chgo Section Endocrinology M/C 640 1819 W Polk St Chicago IL 60612-7333 E-mail: frohman@uic.edu.

FROLICK, PATRICIA MARY, retired elementary school educator; b. Portland, Oreg., May 17, 1923; d. Fred Anthony and Clara Cecelia (Riverman) F. BS in Edn., Marylhurst Coll., 1960; MS in Edn., Portland State U., 1970; student, U. Oreg., 1975; MA in Theology, St. Mary's Coll., Moraga, Calif., 1977. Joined Roman Cath. Order Sisters of Holy Names of Jesus and Mary, 1943. Left order in 1974. Elem. sch. tchr. Catholic Sch. System, Oreg., 1943-69; tchr., libr. Hood River Pub. Schs., 1970-74, Bend-La Pine (Oreg.) Pub. Schs., 1981-93; ret., 1993. Part-time tchr.'s asst., Portland, 1993—2000. Mem. NEA, Oreg. Edn. Assn., Met. Mus. Art (assoc.), Nat. Mus. Women in Arts (charter). Democrat. Roman Catholic. Avocation: watercolor and oil painting. Home: 3465 SE 153rd Ave Portland OR 97236-2265

FROMAN, ANN DOLORES, computer education educator; b. Phila., June 3, 1938; d. Matthew and Anna (Daniels) Kennedy; m. Joseph S. Froman, Nov. 11, 1965; children: Michael, Joseph, Thomas. AB in Social Science, Immaculata Coll., 1973; MA in History, Villanova U., 1976; postgrad., U. Vt. Cert. elem. tchr., Pa. Tchr. St. Rose of Lima Sch., Phila., 1958-60, Good Shepherd Sch., Phila., 1960-61, St. Cecilia Sch., Phila., 1961-63, St. Anselm Sch., Phila., 1963-66, St. Elearnor Sch., Collegeville, Pa., 1966-68, St. Rose of Lima Sch., North Wales, Pa., 1973-74, St. Stanislaus Sch., Lansdale, Pa., 1974-84; computer specialist St. Matthew Sch., Conshohocken, Pa., 1984—, St. Agnes/Sacred Heart Sch., Hilltown, Pa., 1987—. Mem. computer com. Archdiocese of Phila., 1980-91, chairperson, 1991—; tchr. Pa. Higher Edn. Assistance Agy. program Temple U., Phila., West Chester State Coll., Phila. Textile & Scis.; presenter Ea. Pa. Edn. and Computer Conf., 1990, 92; guest speaker Rosemont (Pa.) Coll., Chestnut Hill Coll., Phila., Cabrini Coll. Author: The Computer Teacher, 1992. Mem. Nat. Cath. Edn. Assn., Mid. Atlantic Social Studies. Avocations: reading, travel, swimming, computers. Office: St Matthew Sch 205 Fayette St Conshohocken PA 19428-1893

FROMBERG, JEAN STERN, school system administrator; b. Roanoke, Va., Jan. 4, 1943; d. Ernest George and Marianne (Stamm) Stern; m. Aug. 26, 1968 (div. 1989); children: Nathan, Eric, Craig, Brian, Laura; m. Zachary Fromberg, Nov. 14, 1999. BA, Coll. William and Mary, 1965; MA, Wichita State U., 1986, specialist degree, 1989. Cert. permanent tchr. German, N.Y.; cert. supt., bldg. adminstr., Kans., Colo., N.Y., Va., N.H., Ohio, Ariz., Pa., Ky. Rural community devel. vol. Peace Corps, Turkey, 1965-67; tchr. German, Spanish and English Kenmore (N.Y.)-Tonawanda Sch. Dist., 1967-70; tchr. German Grand Island (N.Y.) Sch. Dist., 1978-82, coord. adult edn., prin., 1982; grad. rsch. asst. Wichita (Kans.) State U., 1984-86, instr. German, 1985; asst. prin. Unified Sch. Dist. 259, Wichita, 1986-88; supt., high sch. prin. Unified Sch. Dist. 3l4, Brewster, Kans., 1988-91; supt. Unified Sch. Dist. 271, Stockton, Kans., 1991-93; dir. edn. Computer Learning Ctr., Alexandria, Va., 1993; sr. dir. distbr. Nat. Safety Assocs., Lorton, Va., 1993-96; dir. KinderCare Learning Ctr., Alexandria, 1994; dir. edn. Gesher Jewish Day Sch. of No. Va., Fairfax, 1994; dir. Kinder Care Learning Ctr., Vienna, Va., 1994-95, Children's World Learning Ctr., Lake Ridge, Va., 1995-98; dir. adminstrn. Sanz Sch., Inc., Washington, 1998—. Mem. sch. community adv. coms., N.Y., Kans., 1975-86; chmn. Com. To Revise Fgn. Lang. Curriculum, Grand Island, 1981-83; judge Kans. Fgn. Lang. Competition, 1987. Contbr. numerous articles on ednl. leadership to profl. jours. Pres. Grand Island Food Coop., 1978-83, Waterford Food Coop., Wichita, 1983-88. Mem. ASCD, Am. Assn. Sch. Adminstrs., Nat. Assn Secondary and Elem. Sch. Prins., Am. Assn. Tchrs. German, Kans. Assn. Sch. Adminstrs., Kans. Unified Sch. Adminstrs., AAUW (active local, regional and state levels 1973—), Phi Kappa Phi, Phi Delta Kappa, Nat. Supts. Acad., Ankadaslar-Returned Peace Corps Vols. of Turkey (bd. dirs. 1993-99, pres. 1996-98, area coord. 1993-2002). Avocations: gourmet cooking and baking, reading, gardening, swimming, sewing. Home: 8513 Farrell Dr Chevy Chase MD 20815-3849 Office: Sanz Sch Inc 2nd Fl 8455 Colesville Rd Silver Spring MD 20910 Fax: 301-608-3685. E-mail: jean@sanzschool.erols.com.

FROMHAGEN, CARL, JR., obstetrician, gynecologist; b. Tampa, Fla., 1926; s. Carl Frederick and Minnette Gertrude (Douglass) Von Fromhagen; children: Dana Lynn, Carol Leslie, Carl Scott. BS, U. Miami, 1950; student U. Utah, 1949; grad. mil. pilot tng. USAF, 1951; MS, U. Colo., 1952; MD, Emory U., 1955. Diplomate Am. Bd. Ob-Gyn. Intern, Baylor U., 1955-56, resident in ob-gyn, 1956-59; instr. Sch. Medicine U. Miami, Coral Gables, Fla., 1959-62, asso. prof., 1975—; obstetrician, gynecologist, specialist in aviation medicine, FAA sr. med. examiner, Clearwater, Fla., 1960—; pres. Fromhagen Aviation Inc., 1969—; chmn. bd. Navigate Inc., 1970-73; med. cons. Planned Parenthood, 1963-67; chief of staff Clearwater Community Hosp., 1991-92. Mem. Fla. State Aviation Coun., 1966-67; mem. Com. of 100 Pinellas County, pres. Honduras Relief Soc., 1970; bd. dirs. Am. Cancer Soc., 1962-68; bd. dirs. Interprofl. Family Coun., 1967-68. Served to col. USAFR. Named outstanding resident Baylor U. Med. Sch., 1959; recipient award merit Res. Officers Assn., 1964; Silver Wings Frat. award of honor, 1981. Fellow ACOG, ACS, Am. Coll. Abdominal Surgeons, Internat. Coll. Surgeons; mem. Pan Am. Med. Assn., Fla. Soc. for Preventive Medicine (pres. 1968), Aerospace Med. Assn., Civil Aviation Med. Assn., Flying Physicians (v.p. 1967-68, dir., 1968-74, state pres. 1966-74), Res. Officers Assn. Fla. (Clearwater chpt. pres. 1963-67, state surgeon 1964), N.Y. Acad. Sci., Confederate Air Force, Clan Douglas Soc., Aviation Maintenance Found., U.S. Power Squadron (fleet surgeon), Iron Arrow, Omicron Delta Kappa, Pi Kappa Alpha, Beta Beta Beta. Clubs: Carlouel Yacht. Home: 1666 Robinhood Ln Clearwater FL 33764-6431 Office: 1838 Southwood Ln Clearwater FL 33764-2468

FROMMER, HERBERT HENRY, educator; b. N.Y.C., May 28, 1933; s. Benjamin and Ethel (Trencher) F.; m. Eleanor Goldman, Aug. 21, 1960; children: Ross, Daniel. AB, Columbia Coll., 1954, DDS, 1957. Diplomate Am. Bd. Oral & Maxillofacial Radiology. Instr. Seton Hall Coll. Dentistry, Jersey City, N.J., 1958-60, asst. prof., 1960-65; assoc. prof. N.J. Coll. Dentistry, Jersey City, 1965-68; assoc. clin. prof. NYU Coll. Dentistry, N.Y.C., 1968-78, clin. prof., 1978-88, assoc. prof., 1987-94, prof., 1994—. Mem. FDA Sel. Criteria Panel, Washington, 1983-88; chmn. NYU Faculty Senate, 1993-94. Author: Radiology for Dentistry, 1996. Comdr. USNR. Fellow Am. Acad. Mexillfacial Radiology (pres. 1990-91), N.Y. Acad. Medicine, N.Y. Acad. Dentistry, Omicron Kappa Upsilon, Sigma Xi. Jewish. Avocations: rowing, tennis. Home: 60 E 96th St New York NY 10128-0757 Office: NYU Coll Dentistry 345 E 24th St New York NY 10010-4020

FROOM, DAVID, composer, music educator; b. Calif., 1951; Student, U. Calif., Berkeley, U. So. Calif., Columbia U.; studies with, Chen Wen-chung, Mario Davidovsky, Alexander Goehr, William Kraft. Tchr. Baruch Coll., U. Utah, Peabody Conservatory; prof. music St. Mary's Coll., Md., 1989—. Bd. dirs. N.Y. New Music Ensemble. Composer: music performed by numerous ensembles. Recipient commn., Fromm and Koussevitsky Found., Friedheim Awards 1st Prize, Kennedy Ctr., 3 Individual Artist award, State of Md.; Charles Ives scholar, fellow, John Simon Guggenheim Meml. Found., 2003, Tanglewood Music Festival, Wellesley Composers Conf., MacDowell Colony, grant, NEA, Fulbright grant, Cambridge U. Mem.: League of Composers/ISCM (mem. nat. adv. bd.). Office: St Mary's Coll Md 18952 E Fisher Rd Saint Marys City MD 20686-3001*

FROST, EVERETT LLOYD, anthropologist, academic administrator; b. Salt Lake City, Oct. 17, 1942; s. Henry Hoag Jr. and Ruth Salome (Smith) F.; m. Janet Owens, Mar. 26, 1967; children: Noreen Karyn, Joyce Lida. BA in Anthropology, U. Utah, 1965; PhD in Anthropology, U. Oreg., 1970. Field researcher in cultural anthropology, Taveuni, Fiji, 1968-69; asst. prof. in anthropology Ea. N.Mex. U., Portales, 1970-74, assoc. prof., 1974-76, asst. dean Coll. Liberal Arts and Scis., 1976-78, dean acad. affairs and grad. studies, 1978-80, v.p. for planning and analysis, dean rsch., 1980-91, dean grad. studies, 1983-88, pres., 1991-2001, pres. emeritus, prof. anthropology emeritus, 2001—. Cons., evaluator N. Ctrl. Assn. Accreditation Agy. for Higher Edn., 1989-93—, mem. rev. bd., 1993-95—; bd. mem. emeritus N.Mex. First; commr., past pres. Western Interstate Commn. for Higher Edn., 1993—; pres. Lone Star Athletic Conf. Pres.'s Commn., 1992-93; chmn. rsch. com. N.Mex. First, 1989-91. Chmn. N.Mex. Humanities Coun., 1980-88; mem. N.Mex. Gov.'s Commn. on Higher Edn., 1983-86; mem. exec. bd. N.Mex. First, 1987-92; bd. dirs. Roosevelt Gen. Hosp., Portales, 1989-92; pres. bd. dirs. San Juan County Mus. Assn., Farmington, 1979-82; vice chair Portales Pub. Schs. Facilities Com., 1990-91. NDEA fellow, 1969-70; grantee NEW, 1979-80, NSF, 1968-69, Fiji Forbes, Ltd., 1975-76, others. Fellow Am. Anthropol. Assn., Am. Assn. Higher Edn., Soc. Coll. and Univ. Planning, Assn. Social Anthropologists Oceania, Anthropol. Soc. Washington, Sch. Am. Rsch., Western Assn. Grad. Deans, Current Anthropology (assoc.) Polynesian Soc., Phi Kappa Phi.

FROST, JAMES ARTHUR, former university president; b. Manchester, Eng., May 15, 1918; came to U.S., 1926, naturalized, 1942; s. Harry Arthur and Janet (Wilson) F.; m. Elsie Mae Lorenz, Sept. 14, 1942 (dec.); children: Roger Arthur (dec.), Janet Linda Frost Naleski, Elise Anita Frost Alair. BA, Columbia U., 1940, MA, 1941, PhD, 1949; LLD, So. Conn. State U., 1993. Tchr. Am. history high sch., Nutley, N.J., 1946-47; instr. SUNY Coll.-Oneonta, 1947-49, asst. to pres., 1949-52, dean, 1952-64; assoc. provost acad. planning Cen. Adminstrn., SUNY, 1964-65, exec. dean for four year colls., 1965-68, vice chancellor for univ. colls., 1968-72; exec. dir. Conn. State Colls., 1972-83; pres. Conn. State U., 1983-85, pres. emeritus, 1985—; instr. Am. history Columbia U., summers, 1947-48; Smith-Mundt prof. Am. history U. Ceylon, 1959-60. Mem. com. on research and devel. Coll. Entrance Exam Bd., 1973-76; mem. adv. bd. Conn. Rev., 1972-76; mem. commn. on higher edn. Middle States Assn. Colls. and Secondary Schs., 1966-72; mem. Nat. Coun. Heads of Systems of Pub. Higher Edn., 1976-85, pres., 1979-80, now hon. mem. Author: Life on the Upper Susquehanna, 1783-1860, 1951; (with David M. Ellis, Harold Syrett, Harry J. Carman) A Short History of New York State, 1957, 2d edit., 1967; (with David M. Ellis and William B. Fink) New York: The Empire State, 1961, 5th edit., 1980; (with R.A. Brown, D.M. Ellis, William B. Fink) A History of the United States: The Evolution of a Free People, 1967, 2d edit., 1969, The Establishment of the Connecticut State University, 1965-85; Notes and Reminiscences, 1991, The Country Club of Farmington, Connecticut, 1892-1995, 1996; mem. editl. bd. SUNY Press, 1964-72; contbr. articles on history and edn. to mags. Treas. Conn. State U. Found., Inc., 1999—2003, bd. dirs., 1983—, treas., 1986—95, 1995—2003, pres., 1995—98, chmn. investment com., 1995—2003; trustee Robinson Sch., Hartford, 1973—77; sponsor Soc. Columbia Scholars, 1997—. Maj. AUS U.S. Army, 1941—46, lt. col. USAFR. Rockefeller grantee, 1959 Fellow N.Y. State Hist. Assn.; mem. Country Club of Farmington, Conn. Congregationalist. Home: 17 Neal Dr Simsbury CT 06070-2801 Office: Conn State U 39 Woodland St Hartford CT 06105-2337

FROST, JERRY WILLIAM, religion and history educator, library administrator; b. Muncie, Ind., Mar. 17, 1940; s. J. Thomas and Margaret Esther (Meredith) F.; m. Susan Vanderlyn Kohler; 1 son, James. BA, DePauw U., Greencastle, Ind., 1962; postgrad., Yale Div. Sch., 1962-63; MA, U. Wis.-Madison, 1965, PhD, 1968. Instr. Vassar Coll., 1967-68, asst. prof. history, 1968-73; assoc. prof. religion Swarthmore Coll., 1973—, prof. religion, 1980—, Howard M. and Charles F. Jenkins prof. of Quaker history and rsch., 1981—2002, sr. rsch. scholar, 2003—. Author: The Quaker Family in Colonial America, 1973, Connecticut Education in Revolutionary Era, 1974, A Perfect Freedom: Religions Liberty in Pennsylvania, 1990; co-author: The Quakers, 1988, Christianity: A Social and Cultural History, 1998; editor: The Keithian Controversy in Early Pennsylvania, 1980, Quaker Origins of Antislavery, 1981, Records and Recollections of James Jenkins, 1984, Seeking the Light: Essays in Quaker History, 1987; editor Pa. Mag. of History and Biography, 1981-86; contbr. articles to profl. publs. Bd. dirs. Friends Hist. Assn., 1973—. John Carter Brown Libr. fellow, 1970, Eugene M. Lang fellow, 1980-81, 97, Phila. Ctr. fellow, 1986; U.S. Inst. of Peace grantee, 1992. Mem. Soc. Of Friends. Home: 890 Millington Rd Sudlersville MD 21668 Office: Swarthmore Coll Friends Hist Libr Swarthmore PA 19081

FROSTICK, ROBERT MAURICE, secondary education educator; b. Charleston, W.Va., Aug. 31, 1954; s. Frederick Charles and Florence (Barber) F. BS, W.Va. U., 1977; MA, W.Va. U. Grad. Studies, 1989. Cert. permanent profl. 5-12 tchr., W.Va. Tchr. Gauley Bridge (W.Va.) Mid. Sch., 1977-84, Geary Sch., Left Hand, W.Va., 1986, Marmet (W.Va.) Jr. H.S., 1988-90; sci. dir. Sunrise Mus., Charleston, 1984-86; tchr. Horace Mann Jr.

H.S., Charleston, 1990-97, John Adams Jr. H.S., Charleston, 1997—2002, George Washington H.S., 2002—. Instr. sci. W.Va. State Coll., Institute, 1984—, W.Va. Grad. Coll., Institute, 1990—, W.Va. Inst. Tech., Montgomery, 1992—; trainer AIMS Found., Fresno, Calif., 1990—, project wild, 1990—, Bell Atlantic World Sch., 1994—, steering com. project WET, 1995—; curriculum developer W.Va. Dept. Edn., Charleston, 1982, mem. videotape materials selection com., 1990; curriculum developer Roane County Bd. Edn., Spencer, W.Va., 1987; mem. W.Va. Commn. for Porfl. Tchg. Stds., 1997—, W.Va. Licensure Appeals panel, 1997-2002, W.Va. State Sci. Textbook Selection com., 1999, PBS tchr. adv. bd. 1999-2000. Bd. dirs. Cave Conservancy of Vas., 1984-86. Recipient Gov.'s Cmty. Svc. award State of W.Va., 1982, Presdl. Conservation Edn. award, 1982, 83, award of honor Presdl. awards for excellence in math. and sci. tchg., 1993, Outstanding Young Educator Jaycces, 1994, First award BEAMS Acad., 1994, Golden Apple Achiever award Ashland Oil, 1995, Rising Star award STARS Tech. Competition, 1997, N.E. Region winner Tech. and Learning Tchr. of Yr., 1997, Svc. Recognition award PBS, 2000; named Tech. and Learning Tchr. of Yr., 1996, 97; Christa McAuliffe fellow, 1993. Mem. NSTA, Geol. Soc. Am. (award of excellence 1993), Nat. Speleological Soc., Nat. Assn. Earth Sci. Tchrs., W.Va. Sci. Tchrs. Assn., Kanawha Valley Astron. Soc. Avocations: exploring caves, photography, computers, astronomy. Home: PO Box 6885 Charleston WV 25362-0885 E-mail: bfrostic@access.k12.wv.us.

FROUM, STUART JAY, periodontist, educator; b. Bklyn., Oct. 2, 1946; s. Solomon and Florence F.; B.A. (N.Y. Regents scholar), Bklyn. Coll., 1966; D.D.S., NYU, 1970. Resident in periodontia VA Hosp., Bklyn., 1969-70, NYU, 1971-73; dir. periodontal residency tng. program VA Med. Center, N.Y.C., 1978-82; mem. staff NYU Coll. Dentistry, assoc. clin. prof., 1978-94, clin. prof. surg. scis. and implant dentistry, 1994—; mem. staff N.Y. Inst. Hypnotherapy; research assoc. Morton Prince Clinic for Hypnotherapy; pres. Northeast Soc. of Pero, 1995. Mem. ADA, Am. Acad. Periodontology, Am. Acad. Oral Medicine, Am. Assn. Mil. Surgeons, Am. Acad. Implant Prosthodontics, Am. Acad. Osseointegration, Sigma Xi. Office: 17 W 54th St New York NY 10019-5404

FRUCHTER, ROSALIE KLAUSNER, elementary school educator; b. Bklyn., May 1, 1940; d. Marcus and Sarah (Twersky) Klausner; m. Marvin Fruchter, Aug. 15, 1970; children: Marcus, Alexander. BA, Bklyn. Coll., 1960; MA, Nat. Louis U., Evanston, Ill., 1988; postgrad., U. Chgo., 1962-65, Northeastern Ill. U., 1997—. Cert. Irlen Syndrome scotopic sensitivity syndrome screener 2001. Tchr. William H. Ray Sch./Chgo. Bd. Edn., 1961—; lead tchr. primary lang. arts structured curriculum project Chgo. Bd. Edn., 1997—; tchr. reading resource Dixon Elem. Sch., 1999—2003. Cons. math project U. Chgo., 1985-87; presenter in field. Contbr. to math book: One Minute Math, 1990, (Chgo. pub. schs. writing program) Read Write Well, Lesson Resource Book, 1998, Handbook of Kids Primary Assessment Tools, 1998. Bd. dirs. Jewish Community Ctr. of Hyde Park, Chgo., 1978-84, Congregation KAM Isaiah Israel, Chgo., 1984-91, 93—; co-founder Nurit chpt. Hadassah, Hyde Park, 1980; mem. Hyde Park Neighborhood Club, Chgo., 1975—; mem. adv. bd. Humana Michael Reese Hyde Park HMO. Recipient Kate Maremont award Chgo. PTA, 1980, award Chgo. Found. for Edn., 1994; Chgo. Found. for Edn. grantee, 1990, 92, 93, 94, Oppenheimer grantee, 1991. Mem. ASCD, Nat. Coun. Tchrs. Math., Nat. Coun. Tchrs. English, Acad. Econ. Edn., Ill. Sci. Tchrs. Found., Chgo. Area Reading Assn. (bd. dirs. 1997—, treas. 1998—, pres.-elect 1999-2000, pres. 2000-01, past pres. 2001-02, mem. co-chair 2002-03), Chgo. Tchrs. Union, Internat. Reading Assn., Ill. Resource Coun., Pi Lambda Theta. Democrat. Avocations: embroidery, art, cross country skiing, walking, reading, history, drama, judaica. Home: 5434 S Hyde Park Blvd Chicago IL 60615-5802

FRUEN, LOIS, secondary education educator; Chemistry tchr. Breck Sch., Mpls. Recipient James Bryant Conant award High Sch. Chemistry Teaching, 1992. Office: The Breck Sch 123 Ottawa Ave North Minneapolis MN 55422*

FRUG, GERALD E. law educator; b. 1939; AB, U. Calif.-Berkeley, 1960; JD, Harvard U., 1963. Bar: Calif. 1964, N.Y. 1969. Frank Knox fellow London Sch. Econs., 1963-64; law clk. to chief justice Supreme Ct. Calif., 1964-65; assoc. Heller, Ehrman, White & McAuliffe, San Francisco, 1965-66; spl. asst. to chmn. EEOC, 1966-69; assoc. Cravath, Swaine & Moore, N.Y.C., 1969-70; gen. counsel Health Services Adminstrn., N.Y.C., 1970-72, 1st dep. adminstr., 1972-73, adminstr., 1973-74; assoc. prof. U. Pa. Law Sch., Phila., 1974-78, prof., 1978-81, Harvard U. Law Sch., 1981-94, Samuel R. Rosenthal prof. law, 1994-2000, Louis D. Brandeis prof., 2000—. Mem. Phi Beta Kappa. Office: Law Sch Harvard U Cambridge MA 02138

FRUIHT, DOLORES GIUSTINA, artist, educator, poet; b. Portland, Oreg., Mar. 9, 1923; d. Erminio and Irene (Onorato) Giustina; m. Thos. Herman Fruiht, Dec. 20, 1947 (div. 1976); children: Justina, Bryce, Bradford, Erica, Renee. BS, RN, U. Portland, 1944; attended, U. San Francisco, 1971. Nurse, Nurse Corps U.S. Army, 1944-46; intravenous nurse St. Vincent's Hosp., Portland, 1946; staff nurse Dr. Shepard, Eugene, Oreg., 1947-49; surg. nurse Sacred Heart Hosp., Eugene, Oreg., 1949-52; tchr. Ursulina High Sch., Santa Rosa, Calif., 1976-78; artist Angela Ctr. for Adult Edn., Santa Rosa, Calif., 1978-88. Juror Bodega Bay Fisherman's Festival, Calif., 1992, Sebastopol Ctr. for the Arts, 1995. One woman shows include: "Expressions in Art", Abstract Photography, Paintings, and Images in Clay, Sonoma County Mus., Santa Rosa, 1992, Pottery Exhibit, Angela Ctr., 1980, Sonoma, 1976; exhibited in group shows at: Oreg. State U., 1999, Cultural Arts Coun. Sonoma County, 1998, Sebastopol Libr., 1992, Bodega Bay Allied Arts, 1991, 93-96, Nor Cal. State Art Exhibit, Nat. League of Am. Pen Women, Souverain Winery, 1985, "Tibetan Faces", Photography, Calif. Mus. of Art, Santa Rosa, 1985, Photography Exhibit, Angela Ctr., 1982, "The Healing Celebration of Art", Photography, San Francisco Civic Auditorium, 1981, Photography Show, Angela Ctr., 1980, Pottery Exhibit, 1975; contbr. articles to numerous profl. jours.; disting. lectr. Diplomat City of Sonoma, Russia, 1988. 1st Lt. U.S. Army Nurse Corps, 1944-46. Decorated Bronze Star for Luzon Campaign U.S. Army. Mem. Nat. League of Am. Pen Women (Biennial Selection award, 1986, Excellence award, 1985). Roman Catholic. Avocations: hiking, golfing, reading. Office: PO Box 823 Bodega Bay CA 94923-0823

FRUITS, CHERYL ANN, elementary education educator; b. Evansville, Ind., July 4, 1949; d. Donald C. and Mary Margaret (Summers) Appler; m. Dennis G. Fruits, June 21, 1974; children: Karen, Brian, Michelle. BA, U. Evansville, 1972; MS, Ind. U., 1978; postgrad., U. Nebr., 1984-85, Belmont Abbey Coll., 1993-95, N.C. Ctr. Advancement in Tchg., 1993. Cert. tchr., N.C. 4th grade tchr. Gibson Elem. Sch., Norwich, N.Y., 1971-72; 3d and 4th grade tchr. Cannelton (Ind.) Elem. Sch., 1975-76; 1st through 6th grade tchr. Desert Sch., Dhahran, Saudi Arabia, 1978-80; presch. tchr., co-dir. Rainbows and Sunshine Presch., RasTanura, Saudi Arabia, 1981-83; presch. dir., tchr. Ralston (Nebr.) Found. Presch., 1984-86; 1st grade tchr. Meadows Elem. Sch., Ralston, 1986-87; 3d and 4th, 1st grade tchr. Woodhill Elem. Sch., Gastonia, N.C., 1988-93; reading tchr. Cherryville (N.C.) East Primary Sch., 1993-94, Brookside Elem. Sch., Gastonia, 1994—. Asst. leader Girl Scouts U.S.A., Gastonia, 1992—, leader, Dhahran, 1982-83, Boy Scouts Am., Gastonia, 1990-92. Grantee Glenn Found., 1991, Nat. Diffusion Network, 1991, Carolina Electric Cooperatives Bright Ideas grantee, 1994. Mem. NEA, Assn. for Childhood Edn. Internat., Alpha Delta Kappa. Avocation: sewing. Home: 351 Wagontree Ct Dallas NC 28034-7758

FRUNDT, HENRY JOHN, sociologist, educator; b. Blue Earth, Minn., May 22, 1940; s. John Henry and Mary Ellen (Kane) F.; m. Bette Jule Swatzki, June 13, 1970; children: Michael, Laura, James, Daniel, Janine, Paul. BA, St. Louis U., 1964, MA, PhL, 1967; PhD, Rutgers U., 1975. Tchr. Creighton Prep. Sch., Omaha, 1965-68; program developer U.S. Dept. Labor, Omaha, 1969; instr. sociology U. Wis., Superior, 1969-71; cons. UN, N.Y.C., 1978-85; prof. sociology Ramapo Coll., Mahwah, N.J., 1973—, dir. sch. social sci., assoc. dean, 1989-93, convenor Latin Am. studies, 1995-2000, convenor sociology, 2000—01. Rsch. assoc. conservation of human resources Columbia U., N.Y.C., 1980-82; rsch. assoc. inter-Am. devel. program Am. U., Washington, 1982-84; Fulbright lectr. U. Rafael Landivar, Guatemala City, 1987-88, 2002; Fulbright sr. specialist peer rev. com., 2003. Author: Agribusiness Manual, 1978, Refreshing Pauses, 1987, Trade Conditions and Labor Rights, 1998 (Whitaker prize: Outstanding Book award labor sect. Latin Am. Studies Assn.); contbr. articles to profl. jours. Co-chair N.J. Labor Com. on Ctrl. Am., 1987-93; bd. dirs. U.S./Labor Edn. in Americas Project, 1990—; choral singer N.J. Oratorio Soc., Essex County, N.J., 1994—, pres., 2003—; commr. commn. on disarmament edn. UN, 1995-2002. Orgn. Am. States fellow, 1982, Faculty fellow NYU, 1996-97; grantee Soc. for the Psychol. Study of Social Issues, 2002. Mem. Soc. for Psychol. Study of Social Issues, Latin Am. Studies Assn., Guatemala Scholars Network, Am. Fedn. Tchrs. (local pres. 1984-87, coun. del. 1997—). Roman Catholic. Office: Ramapo Coll Mahwah NJ 07430

FRY, CHARLES GEORGE, theologian, educator; b. Piqua, Ohio, Aug. 15, 1936; s. Sylvan Jack and Lena Freda (Ehle) F. BA, Capital U., 1958; MA, Ohio State U., 1961, PhD, 1965; BD, Evang. Lutheran Theol. Sem., 1962, MDiv, 1977; DMin, Winebrenner Theol. Sem., 1978; DD, Cranmer Sem., 2001; M of Sacred Theology, Holy Trinity Coll. and Sem., 2002, M Religious Edn., 2003. Ordained to ministry Lutheran Ch. U.S.A, 1963; diplomate Am. Psychotherapy Assn. Pastor St. Mark's Luth. Ch. and Martin Luther Luth. Ch., Columbus, Ohio, 1961-62, 63-66; instr. Wittenberg U., 1962-63, 71-72, Capital U., 1963-75, asst. prof. history and religion, 1966-69, assoc. prof., 1969-75; theologian-in-residence North Community Luth. Ch., Columbus, 1971-73; assoc. prof. hist. theology, dir. missions edn. Concordia Theol. Sem., Ft. Wayne, Ind., 1975-84; sr. minister First Congl. Ch., Detroit, 1984-85; Protestant chaplain St. Francis Coll., Fort Wayne, 1982-92; prof. philosophy and theology Luth. Coll. of Health Professions, Ft. Wayne, 1992-98, U. St. Francis, Ft. Wayne, 1998-99, Winebrenner Theol. Sem., U. Findlay, Ohio, 1999—. Interim min. Arbor Grove Congl. Ch., Jackson, Mich., 1980, hon. minister emeritus 1996, First Presbyn. Ch., Huntington, Ind., 1988-89, St. Luke's Luth. Ch., Ft. Wayne, 1989-90, Mt. Pleasant Luth. Ch., 1990-91, St. Mark's Luth. Ch., 1990-91, Mt. Zion Luth. Ch., Ft. Wayne, 1991-93; interim min. Cmty. Christian Ch., New Carlisle, Ind., 1993-94, First Luth. Ch., Stryker, Ohio, 1994-95, Zion Luth. Ch., West Jefferson, Ohio, 1994-97, 98-2000, Agape Congl. Ch., Bowling Green, Ohio, 1997-98; interim min. Fairfield Parish, Lancaster, Ohio, 2000—; vis. prof. Damavand Coll., Tehran, 1973-74, bd. dirs., 1976-94; vis. prof. Ref. Bible Coll., 1975-80, Concordia Luth. Sem. at Brock U., summers 1977, 79, Grad. Sch. Christian Min., Huntington (Ind.) Coll., 1986-89, Wheaton Coll., 1987-88; vis. scholar Al Ain U., United Arab Emirates, 1987; theologian-in-residence, tchg. theologian Queentown Luth. Ch., Singapore, 1991, 99, 2000, 02; adj. faculty history Ind. U./Purdue U., Ft. Wayne, 1982-98, Winebrenner Theol. Sem., Findlay, Ohio, 1992, 99, 2000, Holy Trinity Coll. and Sem., 1999—, Tung Ling Bible Coll., Singapore, 2000, 02, North Tenn. Bible Inst., 1998—; pastor-in-residence Wittenberg U., Springfield, Ohio, 1992, Deaconess Cmty. Evang. Luth. Ch. Am., Phila., 1993. Author books including Age of Lutheran Orthodoxy, 1979, Lutheranism in America, 1979, Islam, 1980, 2d edit. 1982, The Way, The Truth, The Life, 1982, Great Asian Religions, 1984, Francis: A Call to Conversion, 1988, Brit. edit., 1990, The Middle East: A History, 1988, Congregationalists and Evolution: Asa Gray and Louis Agassiz, 1989, Pioneering a Theology of Evolution: Washington Gladden and Pierre Teilhard de Chardin, 1989, Avicenna's Philosophy of Education: An Introduction, 1990, Explorations in Protestant Theology, 1992, Life's Little Lessons, 1997, Kant's Three Questions, 1997, Four Little Words, 1997, Goethe: Life and Truth, 2001, Washington Gladden as a Preacher of the Social Gospel, 1882-1918, 2003, others; co-producer Global Perspectives, IPFW-TV, Ft. Wayne, 1987-97. Bd. dirs. Luth. Liturgical Renewal, 1983-90, 94-2000, pres., 1999-2000; v.p. Internat. Luth. Fellowship, 1995-98, pres., 1998-2001; consecrated bishop, so. region Internat. Luth. Fellowship, 1996; assoc. St. Augustine's Fellowship, 1996—; bd. dirs. Zwemer Inst., Ft. Wayne, Ind., 1997—. Recipient Praestantia award Capital U., 1970, Concordia Hist. Inst. citation, 1977, Archbishop Robert Leighton award Nat. Anglican Ch., 1997; Regional Coun. for Internat. Edn. rsch. grantee, 1969; Joseph J. Malone postdoctoral fellow Egypt, 1986, Malone postdoctoral fellow, United Arab Emirates, 1987; named Ky. Col., 1999. Fellow Brit. Interplanetary Soc., Coll. Pastoral Counseling (diplomate), Am. Assn. Integrated Medicine (diplomate, bd. coll. pastoral counseling 2001-), Oxford Soc. Scholars; mem. Am. Hist. Assn., Am. Acad. Religion, Mid. East Inst. Gen. Soc. War of 1812 (compatriot 1994—, chaplain Ohio chpt. 1996—, chaplain gen. 2001-), German Soc. Md., Mil. and Hospitaller Order of St. Lazarus of Jerusalem (chaplain 2000—), Phi Alpha Theta. Democrat. Home: 158 W Union St Circleville OH 43113-1965 Office: 950 N Main Street Findlay OH 45840-4416

FRY, DAVID FRANCIS, computing educator; b. Richland Center, Wis., Nov. 17, 1957; s. Francis Perry and Mary Lou (Noble) F.; m. Barbara Diane Gleisner, Aug. 11, 1979; children: Matthew David, Dana Marie. BS in Elem. Edn., U. Wis., 1980, MEd, 1987. Cert. in elem. edn. Tchr. St. Mary's Sch., Richland Center, 1980-83; history, math., computing tchr. Dodgeville (Wis.) Sch. Dist., 1983—. Newsletter editor Dodgeville Revitalization Program, 1994-95; asst. soccer coach Iowa County League, Dodgeville, 1991-94. Named computer educator of yr. 1990 Wis. Ednl. Computer Consortium. Mem. Dodgeville Edn. Assn. (v.p. 1985-86, pres. 1986-87, negotiator 1987-94), Wis. Soc. Tech. in Edn. (computer educator of yr. 1994). Roman Catholic. Avocations: coins, pencils, news, cameras, bowling. Office: Dodgeville Mid Sch 951 W Chapel St Dodgeville WI 53533-1021 Home: 407 Lora Ct Dodgeville WI 53533-1059

FRY, DONNA MARIE, military officer, educator; b. Altadena, Calif., Oct. 16, 1947; d. Hampton Scott and M. Genevieve (Wolff) F.; 1 child, Alicia Fay. BA, Rutgers U., 1981; MS, Air Force Inst. Tech., 1986. Enlisted USAF, 1968, advanced through grades to master sgt., 1981, commd. 2d lt., advanced through grades to capt., staff cost analyst Cost Rsch. Office, 1986-88, instr. Air Force Inst. Tech. Wright-Patterson AFB, Ohio, 1989-91, chief divsn. exec. communications Maxwell AFB, Ala., 1991-92, chief divsn. analysis for resource mgrs., 1992-95, instr. Ctr. Profl. Devel., Profl. Mil. Comp. Sch., 1991-95, ret., 1995; sr. analyst, curriculum developer Budget Info. Sys. FIRST, MCR Fed., Inc., Maxwell AFB, Montgomery, Ala., 1999-2000; v.p. curriculum devel. Knowledge Mgmt. Solutions, Prattville, Ala., 2000—02; substitute tchr. Lighthouse Christian Acad., 2001—, Evangelical Christian Acad., 2001—, Montgomery Cath. Prep. Sch., 2001—. Tchr. speech/pub. speaking, computers Covenant Acad., 1995-97; adj. faculty J. Patterson State Tech. Coll. (now H. Coun. Trenholm State Coll.), 1996—; cons. in field. Mem. NAFE, Am. Soc. Mil. Comptrollers (v.p., project officer 1988-91, v.p. for Profl. Mil. Comptrollers' Sch. 1992), Air Force Assn. (life), Soc. Cost Estimating and Analysis, SALSAW (pres. Dayton chpt. 1990-91), Res. Officers Assn. (life), Non-Commd. Officers Assn. (life), Rutgers U. Alumni Assn. Republican. Roman Catholic. Avocations: travel, costume design, reading, swimming, knitting. Home: 7537 Halcyon Forest Trl Montgomery AL 36117-3493 E-mail: wafretiree@aol.com.

FRY, EDWARD BERNARD, education educator, retired; b. L.A., Apr. 4, 1925; s. Eugene Bernard and Frances (Dreier) F.; m. Carol Addison Adams, 1950 (div. 1970); m. Cathy Ruwe, Jan. 8, 1974; children: Shanti, Christopher. BA, Occidental Coll., 1949; MS in Edn., U. So. Calif., 1954, PhD, 1960. Asst. prof. Loyola U., L.A., 1953-63; prof. edn. Rutgers U., New Brunswick, N.J., 1963-86, prof. emeritus, 1986—; pub., author Tchr. Created Materials Jamestown Glenoe McGraw-Hill. Fulbright lectr., Uganda, 1961, Zimbabwe, 1985; pub., owner Laguna Beach Ednl. Books, 1991-98; founder Africa Univ. Press, 1999. Author: How to Teach Reading, 1992; co-author: Reading Teachers Book of Lists, 4th edit., 2000; author of over 25 textbooks for schs. and colls. With U.S. Mcht. Marine, 1943-46. Recipient Disting. Svc. award N.J. Reading Assn., 1979. Mem. Nat. Reading Conf. (pres. 1974-76, Oscar Causey award 1980), Internat. Reading Assn. (Reading Hall of Fame 1992). Democrat. Methodist. Avocations: skiing, docent in laguna coast wilderness park. Home: 245 Grandview St Laguna Beach CA 92651-1518

FRY, JOHN ANDERSON, university president; m. Cara Fry; children: Mia, Nathaniel, Phoebe. BA in Am. Civilization, Lafayette Coll., 1982; MBA, NYU, 1986; postgrad., U. Pa. Staff acct. Peat, Marwick, Mitchell & co., N.Y.C., 1982—84; adj. instr. NYU Stern Sch. Bus., 1985, Hunter Coll. CUNY, 1990; cons. KPMG Peat Marwick, N.Y.C., 1984—86, sr. cons., 1986—88, mgr., 1988—89, sr. mgr., 1989—91; mng. assoc. Coopers & Lybrand, N.Y.C., 1991—93, ptnr., 1993, ptnr.-in-charge, 1994—95; exec. v.p. U. Pa., Phila., 1995—2002; pres. Franklin & Marshall Coll., Lancaster, Pa., 2002—. Sr. fellow Inst. for Rsch. on Higher Edn. U. Pa.; pres., CEO Penn to Bus.; bd. dirs. Sovereign Bancorp, Ban Franklin Tech. Ptnrs.; trustee Del. Investments. Bd. dirs., mem. exec. com. Phila. Indsl. Devel. Corp.; trustee Morris Arboretum; bd. dirs., vice chmn. Univ. City Sci. Ctr.; founding mem., chmn. bd. dirs. Univ. City Dist.; trustee Pa. Acad. Fine Arts, Lafayette Coll.; bd. dirs., exec. com. Greater Phila. C. of C.; bd. dirs. Greater Phila. Tourism and Mktg. Corp. Office: Office of the Pres Franklin & Marshall Coll Lancaster PA 17604

FRY, ROY H(ENRY), librarian, educator; b. Seattle, June 16, 1931; s. Ray Edward and Fern Mildred (Harmon) F.; m. Joanne Mae Van de Guchte, Sept. 12, 1970; 1 child, Andrea Joy. BA in Asian Studies, BA in Anthropology, U. Wash., 1959; MA in Libr. Sci., Western Mich. U., 1965; MA in Polit. Sci., Northeastern Ill. U., 1977; archives cert., U. Dever, 1970; advanced studies program cert., Moody Bible Inst., 1990. Cert. tchr., Wash.; cert. pub. libr., N.Y.; cert. Med. Libr. Assn. Libr. and audio-visual coord. Zillah (Wash.) Pub. Schs., 1960-61; libr. Mark Morris H.S., Longview, Wash., 1961-64; evening reference libr. Loyola U. of Chgo., 1965-67, head reference libr., 1967-73, bibliog. svcs. libr., 1973-74, head circulation libr., 1974-76, coord. pub. svcs., 1976-85, gov. documents libr., 1985-91; ind. libr. cons., 1991-94; ref. libr. Trinity Evang. Divinity Sch., Deerfield, Ill., 1994—2001, reference and archives libr., 2001—. Tchg. asst. in anthropology Loyola U. of Chgo., 1966-67, instr. libr. sci. program for disadvantaged students, 1967, 68, univ. archivist, 1976-78, bibliographer for polit. sci., 1973-91, instr. corr. study div., 1975-85. Mem. Niles Twp. Regular Rep. Orgn., Skokie, Ill., 1982-98, sec. 1986-98; mem. Skokie Caucus Party, 1981-98; vol. Dep. Registration Officer, 1986—; mem. Skokie Traffic Safety Commn., 1984—, Skokie 4th July Parade com., 1986—; election judge Niles Twp., 1983-98, Avon Twp., 1999—. With USNR, 1951-52. Mem. Nat. Librs. Assn. (founding mem., bd. dirs. 1975-76), Asian/Pacific Am. Librs. Assn. (founding mem.), Chgo. Area Theol. Librs. Assn., Pacific N.W. Libr. Assn., Chgo. Area Archivists (founding mem.), Midwest Archives Conf. (founding mem.), ALA, Assn. Coll. and Rsch. Librs., Ill. Prairie Path Assn., Royal Can. Geog. Soc., Skokie Hist. Soc. (recording sec. 1986—), Ballard Hist. Soc. (Seattle), Macon County Hist. Soc. (Decatur, Ill.), Nat. Right to Life Com., Ill. Fedn. for Right to Life, Am. Legion, VFW, Korean War Vets. Assn., Pi Sigma Alpha. Republican. Evangelical Free. Office: Trinity Evang Divinity Sch Rolfing Meml Libr 2065 Half Day Rd Deerfield IL 60015-1241 Address: 335 S Arrowhead Ct Round Lake IL 60073-4209 E-mail: rfry@tiu.edu., lexifry@netzero.net.

FRYE, LINDA BETH (LINDA BETH HISLE), elementary, secondary education educator; b. Apr. 15, 1947; d. Roland Earl Jr. Hisle and Paralee M. Jones; m. Dennis Franklin Frye; children: Byron Franklin, Cody Earl, Matthew Cole. BA in Art and Elem. Edn., E. Ctrl. State U., Ada, 1970; M.Ed. in Elem. Edn., E. Tex. State U., Commerce, 1975. Tchr. Sherman (Tex.) Ind. Sch. Dist., 1969—2002. Specialist in lang., learning disabilities in spl. edn. Recipient Tex. Instrument Invention Conv. award, Tchr. award, Tex. Instrument Invention Convention; grantee Ada City Sch. Foundation, Ada City Sch. Foun. Mem.: Church of Christ. Home: 8380 CR 3510 Ada OK 74820-9619 Office: P O Box 2015 Ada OK 74821-1701

FRYXELL, GRETA ALBRECHT, marine botany educator, oceanographer; b. Princeton, Ill., Nov. 21, 1926; d. Arthur Joseph and Esther (Andreen) Albrecht; m. Paul A. Fryxell, Aug. 23, 1947; children: Karl Joseph, Joan Esther, Glen Edward. BA, Augustana Coll., 1948; MEd, Tex. A&M U., 1969, PhD, 1975. Tchr. math and sci. jr. high schs., Iowa, 1948-52; research asst. Tex. A&M U., College Station, 1968-71, research scientist, 1971-80, asst. prof. oceanography, 1980-83, assoc. prof., 1983-86, prof., 1986-94, prof. emeritus, 1994—; adj. prof. botany U. Tex., Austin, 1993—. Vis. scientist U. Oslo, 1971; chmn. adv. commn. Provasoli-Guillard Ctr. for Culture Marine Phytoplankton, Bigelow Lab, Maine, 1985-87; hon. curator N.Y. Bot. Garden, 1992—; courtesy prof. U. Oreg., 1994—; sr. rsch. scientist U. Tex. Marine Sci. Inst., 1996—. Editor: Survival Strategies of the Algae, 1983; contbr. articles to profl. jours. Recipient Outstanding Woman award Brazos County, College Station, 1979, Outstanding Achievement award Augustana Coll., Rock Island, Ill., 1980; Faculty Disting. Achievement award in rsch. Tex. A&M U., 1991, Geoscis. and Earth Resources Adv. Coun. medal, 1993; grantee NSF. Fellow: AAAS; mem.: ACLU, Oceanographic Soc., Tex. Assn. Coll. Tchrs., Internat. Diatom Soc. (coun. 1986—92), Am. Soc. Plant Taxonomists, Internat. Phycol. Soc., Brit. Phycol. Soc., Phycol. Soc. Am. (editl. bd. 1976—79, 1982—85, chair Prescott award com. 1991, award of Excellence in Phycology 1996). Democrat. Unitarian-Universalist. Office: U Tex Sch Biol Scis Sect Integrative Biology Austin TX 78712

FRYZ, BETTY FARINA, educator; b. Pitts., Mar. 29, 1930; d. Frank Joseph and Theresa (Pagliaro) Farina; m. Joseph Michael Fryz Sr., Aug. 6, 1955; children: Joseph Michael Jr., Deborah Lynn. BS in Music Edn., Ind. U., 1951; postgrad., Carnegie-Mellon U., 1953. Tchr. music elem. sch., jr. and sr. high schs. Moon Area Sch. Dist., Coraopolis, Pa., 1951-93, choral dir., tchr. piano, 1987—, head humanities dept., 1987—; pvt. piano tchr., 1994—. Pvt. practice piano tchr., Pa., 1960-80; cons. music Prentice-Hall, Pa., 1971-73; chmn. jr. high music curriculum com. Dist. 1, Pa., 1984-86. Mem. Mid. States Evaluating Com.; bd. dirs. Am. Youth Symphony and Chorus; Pa. State Rep. for Retired Music Tchrs., 1997—; choir dir. St. Margaret Mary Ch., 1999—. Named one of Outstanding Secondary Educators of Am., 1974. Mem. NEA, AAUW, Music Educators Nat. Conf. (chairperson 1987—), Pa. Music Educators Assn. (Citation of Excellence award 1989; rep. ret. music tchrs. 1997), Pi Kappa Sigma (pres. 1949-51). Roman Catholic. Avocations: tennis, golf. Office: Moon Area Sch Dist 1407 Beers School Rd Coraopolis PA 15108-2597

FU, SHOUCHENG JOSEPH, biomedicine educator; b. Beijing, Mar. 19, 1924; s. W.C. Joseph and W.C. (Tsai) F.; m. Susan B. Guthrie, June 21, 1951; children: Robert W.G., Joseph H.G., James B.G. BS, MS, Cath. U., Beijing, 1944; PhD, Johns Hopkins U., 1949. Postdoctoral fellow Nat. Insts. Health, Bethesda, Md., 1949—51, scientist, 1951—55; Gustav Bissing fellow Johns Hopkins U. at Univ. Coll. London, 1955—56; chief enzyme and bioorganic chemistry lab. Children's Cancer Rsch Found (now Dana Farber Cancer Inst.), 1956—65; rsch. assoc. Harvard U. Med. Sch., Boston, 1956—65; prof., chmn. bd. chemistry Chinese U., Hong Kong, 1966—70, dean sci. faculty, 1967—69; vis. prof. Coll. Physicians and Surgeons Columbia U., N.Y.C., 1970—71; prof. biochemistry and molecular biology U. Medicine and Dentistry of N.J., Newark, 1971—2003, prof. emeritus, 2003—, asst. dean, 1974—77; acting dean Grad. Sch. Biomed. Scis., 1977—78, prof. ophthalmology, 1989—2003, prof. emeritus, 2003—.

Founder, pres. CMDNJ Credit Union (now North Jersey Fed. Credit Union), 1974-75. Contbr. articles to profl. jours. Capt. USPHS Res., 1959—. Named Hon. Disting. Prof. and Acad. Advisor Inner Mongolia Med. U., Huthot, Peoples Republic of China, 1988—. Fellow AAAS, Royal Soc. Chemistry (U.K.); mem. Royal Hong Kong Jockey Club, Am. Club Hong Kong, Sigma Xi (Newark chpt. pres. 1976-80, sec. 1974-76, 81-82). Home: 693 Prospect St Maplewood NJ 07040-3105 Office: U of Medicine and Dentistry NJ Med Sch Med Sci Bldg 185 S Orange Ave Newark NJ 07103-2757 E-mail: fujo@umdnj.edu.

FUCHS, VICTOR ROBERT, economist, educator; b. New York, Jan. 31, 1924; s. Alfred and Frances Sarah ((Scheiber)) Fuchs; m. Beverly (Beck), Aug. 29, 1948; children: Nancy, Frederic, Paula, Kenneth. BS, N.Y. Univ., 1947; MA, Columbia Univ., 1951, PhD, 1955. Internat. fur broker, 1946—50; lectr. Columbia Univ., N.Y.C., 1953—54, instr., 1954—55, asst. prof. econ., 1955—59; assoc. prof. econ. N.Y. Univ., N.Y.C., 1959—60; program assoc. Ford Found. Program in econ., devel., and adminstrn., 1960—62; mem. sr. rsch staff Nat. Bur. Econ. Rsch., 1962—; prof. econ. Grad. Ctr. City Univ. of N.Y., N.Y.C., 1968—74; prof. cmty. medicine Mt. Sinai Sch. Medicine, 1968-74; v.p. rsch. Nat. Bur. Econ. Rsch., 1968—78; prof. econ. Stanford U., Stanford Med. Sch., 1974—95; Henry J. Kaiser Jr. prof. Stanford U., Stanford Med. Sch., 1988—95, prof. emeritus, 1995—. Author: The Economics of the Fur Industry, 1957; co-author (with Aaron Warner): Concepts and Cases in Econ. Analysis, 1958; author: Changes in the Location of Mfg. in the U.S. Since 1929, 1962, The Svc. Economy, 1968, Prodn. and Productivity in the Svc. Industries, 1969, Policy Issues and Rsch. Opportunities in Indsl. Orgn., 1972, Essays on the Economics of Health and Med. Care, 1972, Who Shall Live? Health, Economics, and Social Choice, 1975; co-author (with Joseph Newhouse): The Economics of Physician and Patient Behavior, 1978; author: Economic Aspects of Health, 1982, How We Live, 1983, The Health Economy, 1986, Women's Quest for Econ. Equality, 1988, The Future of Health Policy, 1993, Individual and Social Responsibility: Child Care Edn., Med. Care, and Long-term Care in Am., 1996, Who Shall Live? Health, Economics and Social Choice, expanded edit., 1998; contbr. articles to profl. jour. Served in USAF, 1943—46. Fellow: Am. Econ. Assn. (disting., pres. 1995), Am. Acad. Arts and Sci.; mem.: Am. Philos. Soc. (John R. Commons award), Am. Inst. Medicine of NAS, Beta Gamma Sigma, Sigma Xi. Home: 796 Cedro Way Stanford CA 94305-1032 Office: NBER 30 Alta Rd Stanford CA 94305-8006

FUCHS, W. KENT, engineering educator; b. Elk City, Okla., Nov. 3, 1954; BS, Duke U., 1977; MDiv, Trinity Evang. Div. Sch., 1984; PhD, U. Ill., 1985. Asst. prof. U. Ill., Urbana, 1985-89, assoc. prof., 1989-93, prof., 1993-96; Disting. prof., head Sch. Elec. and Computer Engring., Purdue U., West Lafayette, Ind., 1996—2003; prof. Cornell U. Coll. Engring., Ithaca, NY, 2003—. Contbr. numerous articles to profl. jours. Recipient Best Paper award design automation conf. Assn. Computing Machinery, 1986; scholar U. Ill., 1991. Fellow IEEE (assoc. editor 1992—), Assn. for Computing Machinery. Office: Cornell U Coll Engring 242 Carpenter Hall Ithaca NY 14853-2201

FUCHSBERG FISHMAN, ADELE RAQUEL, school district administrator; b. Havana, Cuba, Nov. 13, 1949; came to U.S., 1959; d. Meyer and Rosalie (Pincus) Fuchsberg; m. Calvin M. Tannenbaum, July 19, 1971 (div. 1982); children: Lenny M. Tannenbaum, David Gary Tannenbaum; m. Harold M. Fishman, Apr. 9, 1982; 1 child, Michael Alan. BS in Edn. cum laude, Syracuse U., 1972; MS in Edn., L.I. U., 1980, Sch. Dist. Adminstr., Sch. Adminstr./ Supr., 1991-92. Educator ESL Shellbank Jr. High Sch., Bklyn., 1980-82; tchr. Spanish Forest Hills. (N.Y.) Jr. High Sch., 1989-90; educator bilingual lang. support program NASSAU Bur. Coop. Edn. Svcs., Westbury, N.Y., 1991-92, sch. dist. adminstr., 1992—. Presenter in field. Dir. film Adaptations on the Instruction for the LEP Student, 1992. Del. liason Gifted Children's Orgn., Great Neck, N.Y., 1977-92; mem. parent exec. bd. U. Pa., Phila., 1989-92; lead educator Hispanic Youth Leadership Program, Albany, N.Y., 1992, Somos Unos, Somos el Futuro, Albany, 1992. Faculty scholar L.I. U., 1979, Dr. Arnold Reisner scholar, 1990. Fellow Omicron Nu; mem. Benjamin Franklin Soc., Phi Kappa Phi, Phi Delta Kappa. Democrat. Avocations: classical music, art, travel, swimming, gardening. Home: 22 Sycamore Dr Sands Point NY 11050-1133

FUDGE, MARY ANN, vocational school educator; b. Traverse City, Mich., July 21, 1947; d. Thomas C. and Mildred M. (Garey) Moran; m. Lew Fudge, June 28, 1969; children: Brian M., Cheryl M. BS, Cen. Mich. U., 1969; MA, Ea. Mich. U., 1975. Jr. HS tchr. math. St. Charles Sch., Mich., 1969-71; mid. sch. tchr. Gallatin County Sch., Bozeman, Mont., 1972-73; substitute tchr. Lincoln Consol. Sch., Ypsilanti, Mich., 1973-77; tchr. adult edn. Benton Harbor Area Sch., Mich., 1980-82; instr. math. Southwestern Mich. Coll., Dowagiac, Mich., 1983-84; high. sch. tchr. math. Coloma Pub. Sch., Mich., 1984-86; tchr. adult edn. math. Van Buren Technology Ctr., Lawrence, Mich., 1982-83, math. cons., coord., 1986-99, tech. coord., 1999—. Dep. clk. Hagar Twp., Riverside, Mich., 1987-88. Mem. Nat. Coun. Tchr. Math., Mich. Coun. Tchr. Math. Roman Catholic. Home: 25403 63rd Ave Mattawan MI 49071-9594 Office: Van Buren Intermediate Sch Dist 490 S Paw Paw St Lawrence MI 49064-9599 E-mail: mfudge@vbisd.org.

FUERTES, RAUL A. psychologist, educator; b. Havana, Cuba, Nov. 4, 1940;, U.S., 1961; s. Raul and Luisa Elvira (Pichardo) Fuertes. BA, U. Miami, Fla., 1967; EdB, U. Miami, 1968; MS, Barry U., 1972, EdS, 1992; AA, Miami Dade U., 1977; PsyD, LaSalle U., 1995. Acad. dean, dir. admissions Miami Mil. Acad., 1967—74; sch. psychologist, guidance counselor Dade County (Fla.) Pub. Schs., Miami, 1974—. Instr. Miami Dade C.C., 1980—; instr. psychology St. Thomas U., 1974; mem. adv. bd. Ednl. Testing Svc., NJ. Mem.: Guidance Counselors Assn. Fla., Nat. Assn. Sch. Psychologists, Am. Assn. Counseling and Devel., Am. Mental Health Counselors Assn., Nat. Assn. Soccer Coaches. Republican. Roman Catholic. Home: 1705 SW 125th Ct Miami FL 33175-1413 Office: Miami Palmetto Sr High Sch 7460 SW 118th St Miami FL 33156-4599

FUGAZZI, HAVEN HARDIN, elementary education educator; b. Cin., Apr. 14, 1953; d. Oliver Wendell and Carol (Lockwood) Hardin; m. Steven Charles Fugazzi, Dec. 28, 1974; children: Kolbe, Michael, Andrew, Dominick. BE, U. Miami, 1975. Tchr. Broward County Schs., Ft. Lauderdale, Fla., 1975-82; sales rep. Fitz and Floyd, Dallas, 1982-87; adminstrv. asst. Guardian Ad Litem, State of Fla., Ft. Lauderdale, 1987-88; tchr. Saint Coleman Sch., Pompano Beach, Fla., 1988—. Vol. Jr. League, Ft. Lauderdale, 1977, Guardian Ad Litem, Ft. Lauderdale, 1982. Mem. Rho Lambda, Delta Gamma (alumni). Republican. Roman Catholic.

FUGELBERG, NANCY JEAN, music educator; b. Tarentum, Pa., Mar. 6, 1947; d. Stanley and Mary (Struhar) Homer; m. Darrell Marvin Fugelberg, Aug. 27, 1977. B in Music Edn., Mt. Union Coll., 1969; postgrad., Kent State U., 1973-76; EdM in Curriculum and Instrn., Ashland U., 1989. Cert. master piano classes and music lit. Mozarteum, Salzburg, Austria. Music tchr. Alliance (Ohio) Sch. Dist., 1969-70, Minerva (Ohio) Sch. Dist., 1970-99. Pianist musicals Carnation Players, Alliance, 1969—72. Asst. organist, accompanist various chs.; organist 1st Imannuel United Ch. of Christ, Alliance, 1969—85. Named to Outstanding Young Women Am., 1981. Mem.: NEA, Ohio Edn. Assn., Minerva Tchrs. Assn., Alliance Area Ret. Tchrs. Assn., S.C. Ret. Tchrs. Assn., Ohio Ret. Tchrs. Assn., Mu Phi Epsilon (chpt. v.p. 1980—82, pres. 1982—84, historian and music therapy chmn. 1984—, Alumni Svc. award 1983, 1984). Republican. Avocations: plants, travel, keyboards, gives various musical programs. Address: 345 S Rockhill Ave Alliance OH 44601-2257

FUGGI, GRETCHEN MILLER, education educator; b. Westerly, R.I., Aug. 26, 1938; d. John Louis and Harriet (Scheid) M.; m. William Joseph Fuggi, Aug. 15, 1960; children: Gretchen, Juliann, John, Kristen. BS, So. Conn. State U., 1960, MS, 1969, 6th yr. diploma, 1991, 6th yr. Ednl. Leadership diploma, 1994. Reading cons. Washington Magnet Sch., West Haven, Conn., 1974—; adj. prof. So. Conn. State U., New Haven, 1988—. Pres. Cath. Charity League of Greater New Haven, 1989-90; bd. dirs. New Haven Symphony Aux., 1992—. Named Tchr. of Yr., West Haven Fedn. Tchrs., 1998-99. Mem. AAUP, Internat. Reading Assn., Conn. Reading Assn., Stonington Hist. Soc. of Conn., Delta Kappa Gamma Soc. Internat., Grad. Club New Haven. Roman Catholic. Home: 19 Westview Rd North Haven CT 06473-2013 E-mail: Fuggi@Juno.com.

FUHRMAN, SUSAN H, education educator; BA in history with highest honors, Northwestern U., 1965, MA in history, 1966; PhD in polit. sci. and edn., Columbia U., 1977. Prof. of edn. policy Eagleton Inst. of Polit. at Rutgers U., 1989—95; prof., dept. of pub. policy Rutgers Edward J. Bloustein Sch. of Planning and Pub. Policy, 1994—95; dean grad sch. edn. U. Penn, 1995—. Bd. mem. Carnegie Found. for the Advancement of Tchg.; founder and chmn. Consortium for Policy Rsch. in Edn. (CPRE), 1985—; mem. of coun. Corp. and Sch. Partnerships of the Coca-Cola Found.; former co-chair Nat. Adv. Panel for the Third Internat. Math and Sci. Study. Editor: From the Capitol to the Classroom: Standards-Based Reform in the States, One Hundredth Yearbook of the National Society for the Study of Education, 2001, Designing Coherent Education Policy: Improving the System, 1993; co-editor (with Jennifer O'Day): Rewards and Reform: Creating Educational Incentives that Work, 1996; co-editor: (with Melissa Carr) Making Money Matter: Equity and Adequacy in Education Finance, 1999. Achievements include research in state education reform, state local relationships, state differential treatment of districts, federalism in education, incentives and systemic reform, legislatures and education policy. Office: The Graduate Sch Penn State U 114 Kern Bldg University Park PA 16802

FUJIOKA, JO ANN OTA, educational administrator, consultant; b. Bellflower, Calif., Apr. 30, 1939; d. Richard Masayoshi and Lillian Chiyono (Ihara) Ota; m. Arthur Fujioka, Feb. 19, 1961; 1 child, Dana Kay. BSN, U. Colo., 1961, MSN, 1970; PhD, Colo. State U., 1987. RN; cert. adminstr., supt., spl. edn. dir., sch. nurse, vocat. edn. adminstr., instr. Nurse pub. health, psychiat. Denver Gen. Hosp., Denver Vis. Nurse Svc., 1961-71; sch. nurse Jefferson County Sch. Dist., Golden, Colo., 1971-76, mgr. program, supr. sch. health program, 1976-79, mgr. spl. edn. and related svcs., adminstr. elem. bldg., 1979-95; cons. Fujioka Cons., Denver, 1995—. Cons. Ctrl. Kans. Bd. Coop. Ednl. Svcs., Salina, 1992, Denver Children's Home, 1996, Colo. Assn. of Family and Children's Agencies, 1997, Colo. Mediation Project, 1998. Contbr. articles to profl. jours. Vice chmn. bd. dirs. Creative Exch., 1997—99, chmn. bd. dirs., 1999—2001, mem. adv. bd., 2002—; mem. edn. adv. com. PBS, 2001—; mem. Cross Cultural Dialogue, 2001—; hon. bd. dirs. Colo. Women's Hall of Fame, 2002—. Mem.: AAUW, NOW, Jefferson County Adminstrs. Assn., Colo. Sch. Health Coun. (pres. 1978—80), U. Colo. Health Scis. Ctr. Srs. Assn. (chpt. pres. 1992—94, Internat. Dist. IV project grant dir. 1993, fall conf. chair 1993—, bd. dirs., sec. 1997—, Internat. Dist. IV project grant dir. 1999, internat. coord. for ethical leadership project 2000—, bd. dirs. 2000—, sec. 2000—03, v.p. internat. bd. dirs. 2001—), Am. Assn. Sch. Execs., Alliance Profl. Cons. (exec. bd.), Colo. Women's Hall of Fame (hon. bd. dirs. 2002—), Public Broadcasting System (edn. adv. bd. 2001—), Japanese Am. Nat. Mus., Cross Cultural Dialogue, Phi Delta Kappa (internat. del. 1993, area coord. 1996—2001, internat. v.p. bd. dirs. 2001—, internat. pres. elect 2003—, Douglas County Chpt. award 1999, Denver U. Chpt. Svc. award 1999, Jefferson County Chpt. Svc. award 2001). Democrat. Buddhist. Avocations: crossword puzzles, jigsaw puzzles, crocheting, tai chi, reading. Home and Office: 540 S Forest St #K Denver CO 80246-8164

FULCO, JOHN DOMINICK, diagnostic radiologist; b. Flushing, N.Y., Dec. 5, 1941; s. Vincent Carl and Lucy (Serpi) F.; m. S. Claire Bailey, Oct. 2, 1965; children: Vincent, Christie, Dana. BA in Biology, BA in Chemistry, L.I. U., 1965; D Medicine and Surgery cum laude, U. Bologna, Italy, 1974. Diplomate Am. Bd. Radiology. Rotating intern L.I. Jewish-Hillside Med. Ctr., New Hyde Park, N.Y., 1974-75; intern Queens Hosp. Ctr., Jamaica, N.Y., 1974-75, resident in radiology, 1975-78, chief resident, 1977-78, cons. interventional radiologist, 1979-81; fellow in cardiovasc. and interventional radiology Tufts-New Eng. Med. Ctr., Boston, 1978-79; attending radiology Ellis Hosp., Schenectady, N.Y., 1979—; pvt. practice, Schenectady, 1979—. Cons. in diagnostic radiology Sunnyview Hosp., Schenectady, 1980-, chief radiology, 1981-92; attending diagnostic radiology St. Clares Hosp., Schenectady, 1995-; clin. instr. radiology Sch. Medicine, SUNY, Stony Brook, 1975-80; asst. prof. diagnostic radiology Albany Med. Coll., 1985-97, 2001-; clin. instr. med. scis. N.Y. Sch. Med. and Dental Assts., Forest Hills, 1974-78, cons., 1974-79; cons. radiologic tech. adv. com. Hudson Valley C.C., Troy, N.Y., 1980-, physician chmn., 1981-; house physician Doctors Hosp., Freeport, N.Y., 1976-78; rsch. assoc. dept. surgery, divsn. exptl. surgery St. Vincent's Hosp. and Med. Ctr., N.Y.C., 1972-73; athletic physician Bellmore (N.Y.)-Merrick Sch. Dist., 1976-78; emergency room physician Lydia E. Hall Hosp., Freeport, 1975-77; mem. abstract rev. staff Jour. Surgery, Jour. Ob-Gyn., 1977; presenter paters to profl. confs., U.S., Can., Japan. Contbr. articles to med. jours. Bd. dirs. Sunnyview Hosp. and Rehab. Ctr., Schenectady; bd. dirs. Am. Cancer Soc., Schenectady, 1986—, mem. profl. edn. com., 1982-89, mem. pub. edn. com., 1982—. Named Intern of Yr., L.I. Jewish-Hillside Med. Ctr., 1975; recipient award for sci. exhibit Can. Assn. Radiologists, 1978, spl. award for clin. rsch. conducted outside Can., 1978. Fellow Cardiovasc. Internventional Radiol. Soc., Am. Heart Assn., Am. Coll. Radiology; mem. AMA (chmn. vascular caucus, chmn. sect. coun. on radiology), Radiol. Soc. N.Am. (cert. of merit 1977), Royal Soc. Health (London), Newng. Roentgen Ray Soc., Med. Soc. State N.Y. (v.p. 4th dist., councilor 1994-2000, awards in clin. rsch. 1976, 77), Med. Soc. County Schenectady (v.p. 4th dist. 1985-86, pres.-elect 1986-87), Northeastern N.Y. Radiol. Soc. (pres. 1983-84), Mohawk Valley Health Plan, N.Y. Acad. Scis. (co-chmn. Schenectady County com. on health care issues). Office: Schenectady Radiologists PC 2546 Balltown Rd Ste 100 Schenectady NY 12309-1080 E-mail: jfulco@nycap.rr.com.

FULDA, MICHAEL, space policy researcher; b. Liverpool, Eng., Apr. 21, 1939; came to U.S., 1962, naturalized, 1966; s. Boris and Catherine (Von Dehn) F.; m. Rosa Bongiorno, July 19, 1970; children: Robert, George. Student, Polytechnique, Grenoble, France, 1956-57, Tech. U., West Berlin, Germany, 1957-58, Karl Eberhardt U., Tubingen, Germany, 1963-66; MA, Am. U., 1968, PhD in Internat. Studies, 1970. Prof. polit. sci. Fairmont State Coll., W.Va., 1971—. Vis. prof. Bauman Moscow State Tech. U., 2002; internat. rels. specialist NASA, Washington, 1979. Author: Oil and International Relations, 1979; (with others) United States Space Policy, 1985; contbr. articles to profl. jours. Bd. dirs. Fairmont Chamber Music Soc., 1983—; W.Va. state com. chmn., dir. space policy Nat. Unity Campaign for John Anderson, 1980; mem. nat. adv. com. John Glenn Presdl. Com., 1984, space policy group Dukakis/Bentsen Com., 1988; dist. advancement com. Boy Scouts Am.; active psychol. ops. Vets. Assn. With U.S. Army, 1962-66. Fellow NASA Marshall Ctr., Huntsville, Ala., 1977, Langley Ctr., Hampton, Va., 1976, Woodrow Wilson Found., 1969-70; grantee Humanities Found. W.Va., 1978-80, NASA W.Va. Space Grant Consortium, 1991—; named del. to Aerospace States Assn. by Gov. of W.Va., 2001. Fellow AIAA (assoc.), Brit. Interplanetary Soc.; mem. Am. Astronautical Soc., Nat. Space Soc. (dir. 1991-93), German Assn. for Luft and Raumfamrt, Soc. Espacial Mexicana, Nat. Space Club, Assn. Argentina Tech. Space, Inst. for Social Sci. Study of Space (pres. 1988—), Fairmont Elks Lodge (edn. com.). Avocations: physical fitness, weightlifting, tango, triathlons. Home: 2 Briarwood Terr Fairmont WV 26554-1331 E-mail: mfulda@mail.fscwv.edu.

FULGHUM, ROBERT SCHMIDT, microbiologist, educator; b. Washington, Mar. 3, 1929; s. James Hooks and Frances (Schmidt) F.; m. Esther Marie Slagle, June 17, 1953; children: Deborah (dec.), Robert Slagle, David James, Joseph Christopher. BS in Biology, Roanoke Coll., 1954; MS in Bacteriology, Va. Poly. Inst. and State U., 1959, PhD in Bacteriology, 1965. Approved cons. bacteriologist, Pa. Grad. asst. Va. Poly. Inst. and State U., Blacksburg, 1956-60; instr. Susquehanna U., Selinsgrove, Pa., 1960-63, asst. prof., 1963-64, N.D. State U., Fargo, 1964-68; asst. prof. Coll. Dentistry U. Ky., Lexington, 1968-71; dir. anaerobic products Robbin Lab. div. Scott Labs., Carrboro, N.C., 1971-72; assoc. prof. East Carolina U. Sch. Medicine, Greenville, 1972-90, prof., 1990-96, asst. chair dept., 1989-96, prof. emeritus, 1996—. Cons. Scott Labs., Fiskeville, R.I., 1972-73; cons., spkr. Norwich Eaton Pharm, Inc., 1987, Abbott Labs., Chgo., 1988, Otitis Media Rsch. Ctr. Children's Hosp., Pitts., 1988; program co-chmn. 3d ednl. strategies workshop tchg. microbiology and immunology Med. Students Assn., Med. Sch. Microbiology and Immunology Chairs, 1990, 4th ednl. stratgies workshop, 1992, 5th ednl. strategies workshop, 1994, 6th ednl. strategies workshop, 1996; mem. organizing com. Ednl. Strategies for Basic Scis. Workshop, Charleston, S.C., 1993. Regional editor newsletter The Anaerobist, 1973-75; contbr. articles to profl. jours. Troop committeeman, treas. Boy Scouts Am., Lexington, Ky., 1968-71, Greenville, 1981-83; bd. dirs. Wesley Found., Greenville, 1979-82; bd. dirs., fin. com. Greenville Community Shelter, 1989-91. With USAF, 1952-56. Rsch. grantee Nat. Inst. Dental Rsch., Washington, 1969, N.C. United Way, 1974, Deafness Rsch. Found., N.Y.C., 1979-88, Block Drug Co., N.J., 1991. Mem. Am. Soc. Microbiology (alternate councilor N.C. br. 1972, 83, ednl. rep. 1973-77, sec.-treas. 1978-81, 89-94, treas. 1994-96, v.p. 1983-84, pres. 1984-85, editor 1988-91), Sigma Xi (Helms award 1982). Methodist. Avocations: genealogy, home maintenance, history. Home: PO Box 20664 Greenville NC 27858-0664 E-mail: RFULGHUM@prodigy.net.

FULKERSON, WILLIAM MEASEY, JR., college president; b. Moberly, Mo., Oct. 18, 1940; s. William Measey and Edna Frances (Pendleton) F.; m. Grace Carolyn Wisdom, May 26, 1962; children: Carl Franklin, Carolyn Sue. BA, William Jewell Coll., 1962; MA, Temple U., 1964; PhD, Mich. State U., 1969. Asst. to assoc. prof. Calif. State U., Fresno, 1981—; asst. to pres. Calif. State U.-Fresno, 1971-73; assoc. exec. dir. Am. Assn. State Colls., Washington, 1973-77; acad. v.p. Phillips U., Enid, Okla., 1977-81; pres. Adams State Coll., Alamosa, Colo., 1981-94, State Colls. in Colo., 1994—. Interim pres. Met. State Coll., Denver, 1987-88, Western State Coll., 1996. Author: Planning for Financial Exigency, 1973; contbr. articles to profl. jours. Commr. North Ctrl. Assn., Chgo., 1980—; bd. dirs. Acad. Collective Bargaining Info. Svc., Washington, 1976, Office for Advancement Pub. Negro Colls., Atlanta, 1973-77, Colo. Endowment for Humanities, 1988-2000, pres., 1998-99. Named Disting. Alumni William Jewell Coll., 1982, Outstanding Alumnus Mich. State U. Coll. Comm., Arts & Scis., 1987. Mem. Am. Assn. State Colls. and Univs. (parliamentarian, bd. dirs. 1992-94), Am. Coun. on Edn. (bd. dirs.), Assn. Pub. Coll.s and Univs. Pres.s (pres. 1994-95), Nat. Assn. Sys. Heads, Alamosa C. of C. (dir., pres. 1984 Citizen Yr. award), Rotary. Office: State Colls Colo 1580 Lincoln St Ste 750 Denver CO 80203-1505

FULLER, ELTHOPIA VIVENS, gifted and talented education educator; b. Stockton, Calif., Sept. 16, 1948; d. Simon and Hattie (Giles) Vivens; m. Frederick T. Fuller; children: Shamie Tzelota Fuller, Tia Lashawn Fuller, Ashton. BA, U. No. Colo., 1970; MA in Ednl. Adminstrn., U. Denver, 1980-82. English instr. Manual High Sch., 1970-72; lay reader Denver Pub. Schs., 1972-75; reading tutor Colo. State Dept. Edn., 1973; instr. drama, English, speech Cole Jr. High Sch., Cole Middle Sch., 1975-91; gifted and talented coord. and resource tchr. Morey Middle Sch., 1991—. Mem. Personnel Com., Cole Middle Sch., Denver, 1991, Justina Ford Community History Project Com., Denver, 1990-91, Sch. Improvement and Accountability Com., Denver, 1985-86; coord. Foot Locker Stay in Sch. video; state rep. Legacy Inst., July 1993. Performer, vocalist At First Annual Fund Raiser Dinner, NAACP, Denver, 1988, At Colo. Easter Seals Dance for those Who Can't, 1984, United Negro Coll. Fund Brunch and Banquet, 1985, 88. Recipient Outstanding Tchr. award Cole Jr. High Sch. Student Body, Denver, 1982, Tchr. award Morey Mid. Sch. Faculty, Denver, 1992, Outstanding Drama Tchr., Cole Sch. Student Coun., Denver, 1980; nominee Nat. Coun. of Negro Women Excellence in Tchng. award 1994. Mem. ASCD, Jack and Jill, Denver Assn. for Gifted and Talented (Excellence in Teaching award, mem. state bd./adv. coun. 1994), Denver Gifted and Talented Adv. Coun., Denver Classroom Tchrs. Assn., Denver Assn. for Performing Arts Tchr. Focus Group, Colo. Educators Assn. Democrat. Home: 13321 E Idaho Pl Aurora CO 80012-4337

FULLER, JOHN WILLIAMS, economics educator; b. Phoenix, Nov. 8, 1940; s. John W. and Myrtle Arabella (Parr) F.; m. Annette Cunkle, June 16, 1962 (dec. 1977); m. Kathy J. Fait, Feb. 17, 1980; children: Helen, Douglas, Andrew, Elizabeth. AB, San Diego State U., 1962; PhD, Wash. State U., 1968. Chief econ. analysis Wis. Dept. Transp., Madison, 1968-74, dir. environ. and policy analysis, 1974-76; hwy. commr. State Of Wis., 1976-77; deputy exec dir. Nat. Transp. Policy Study Commn., Washington, 1977-79; prof. econs., urban and regional planning and geography U. Iowa, Iowa City, 1979—, chair grad. program in urban and regional planning, 1996-99; cons. Bur. Transp. Stats., Washington, 1993—. Cons. Fed. Hwy. Adminstrn., Washington, 1980-82, legis. coun. Iowa Gen. Assembly, Des Moines, 1980-91; dir. Legis. Extended Assistance Group, Iowa City, 1979—. Contbr. articles to profl. jours. Mem., vice chair Johnson County Broadband Telecom. Comm., 1982-88; chmn. Zoning Bd. Adjustment, Johnson County, 1987-92; mem. West Branch Zoning Bd. of Adjustment, 1993—; trustee West Branch Libr., 1995—, pres. 1997-98. Recipient Fulbright award, Venezuela, 1985. Mem. Transp. Rsch. Bd., Am. Assn. RR Supts., Am. Soc. Transp. and Logistics, Assn. Am. Geographers, Nat. Assn. Environ. Profls., Am. Econ. Assn., Am. Planning Assn., Transp. Rsch. Forum, Am. Inst. Cert. Planners. Congregationalist. Office: U Iowa 340 Jessup Hall Iowa City IA 52242-1316

FULLER, JUDITH KAY ALTENHEIN, special education educator; b. Battle Creek, Mich. d. Emmett Bernard and Wilmuth Alice (Lichty) Altenhein; m. David LeRoy Fuller, July 29, 1967; children: Christine Cae, Sheila Beth, Eric David, Erin Judith, Karen Sue Petersen, Daniel Lynn Fuller. BA, Mich. State U., 1970, MA in Tchr. Edn., 1980; MA, cert. learning disabilites/tchr cons, Cen. Mich. U., 1984. Cert. elem. edn., tchr. cons. mentally impaired, tchr. cons. learning disabilities. Devel. regular kindergarten tchr., 5th grade tchr. Olivet (Mich.) Community Schs., 1st and 2nd grade tchr., mentally impaired type A tchr., learning disabilities tchr., tchr. cons. resource rm. Mem. adv. bd. agrl. edn. Olivet High Sch., 1992-93. Author: Diagnosis and Treatment of ADD, Spelling and Memory Strategies Easier if Visual., Vocational Education or Elimination, 1991. Ch. photographer 1st Assembly of God, 1990-97; missions coord. Olivet First Assembly, 1995-97. Named Tchr. of Yr. PTA, 1983; recipient Cert. Appreciation for Mich. Discovery Sci. Fair, Gov. Mich., Statewide Communication and Dissemination System award, 1990; named LDA Mich. Tchr. of Yr., 1989. Mem. NEA, Mich. Assn. Learning Disabilities Educators (newsletter chair 1990, exec. bd., Cert. Appreciation 1988, 89), Mich. Edn. Assn., Olivet Edn. Assn., MOSNA, Learning Disabilities Assn. Am. (chair fall conf. 1991), Mich. Learning Disabilities Assn. (state newsletter editor 1989-93, exec. bd. news letter editor 1990-94). Home: 5194 W Baseline Hwy Olivet MI 49076-9709

FULLER, MAXINE COMPTON, retired secondary school educator; b. Tiny, Va., Aug. 23, 1921; d. Perry and Lillie (Sutherland) Compton; m. David Thompson Fuller Jr., 1946 (dec. Mar. 1975); children: Davine Miller, Patricia Machen, Shirley Brodeur, Dorothy Brunson, David Thompson III. BS, Longwood Coll., 1943; MA, U. Ala., 1966; AA in Edn., U. Ala., Birmingham, 1980. Receptionist Goodyear Tire and Rubber Co., Richmond, Va., 1943, office mgr. trainee Selma, Ala., 1943-44; office mgr. Goodyear Service, Bessemer, Ala., 1944-46; sec., ops. mgr. Birmingham So. Coll., 1966; tchr. Manpower-Bessemer State Tech. Coll., 1966-68, McAdory H.S., 1968-71; bus. edn. coord. Hueytown (Ala.) H.S., 1971-88; ret. Hueytown H.S., 1988. Vis. com. mem. So. Assn. Secondary Schs. and Colls., 1980, 84. Sunday sch. tchr. Pleasant Ridge Bapt. Ch., Hueytown, 1962-88, pers. com., 1980-83; mem. Hueytown High PTA, 1986-87; liaison officer Adopt-A-Sch. program Hueytown High/Lloyd Noland Hosp., 1987-88; chmn. bus. edn. dept. Hueytown H.S., 1971-88. Mem. NEA, Nat. Ret. Tchrs. Assn., Ala. Ret. Tchrs. Assn., former mem. Echo Study Club (pres. 1987-88, sec. 1991-92), former mem. Culture Club of Hueytown (pres. 1994-96), Longwood Coll. Alumni Assn., former mem., Alpha Delta Kappa (corr. sec. XI chpt. 1982-84), Delta Kappa Gamma (treas. Gamma Lambda chpt. 1976-80). Baptist.

FULLER, NANCY MACMURRAY, mathematics educator, tutor; b. Great Barrington, Mass., Sept. 19, 1945; d. Robert Waight and Nancy MacMurray (Robinson) F. BA, MacMurray Coll., 1968; postgrad., George Mason U., 1981, U. Va., 1983—95, Mt. Vernon U., 1983, postgrad., 2000—. Cert. tchr. Ohio. Tchr. Brandon Hall Sch., Dunwoody, Ga., 1969-78, The Scheaffer Sch., Fall Church, Va., 1978-79, Flint Hill Preparatory Sch., Oakton, Va., 1979-87; pvt. tutor Vienna, Va., 1987—. Tutor Atlanta area, also Fairfax and Loudon counties, Va., Vienna, Va.; math tutor, Columbus, Ohio, Morrow, Knox and Delaware Counties, Ohio. Asst. dir. cassette ministries and sound depts. Christian Fellowship Ch., Vienna, Va., 1987-91, cassette ministries Gilead Friends Ch., 2002—; co-dir. sound, dir. cassette ministry Christian Fellowship Ch. of Leesburg (Va.)/Cornerstone Chapel, 1992-95; mem. Glorybound Singers, 1989-95, Trinity Singers, 1997—.

FULLER, THEODORE, JR., elementary education educator; b. Hempstead, Tex., Nov. 4, 1937; s. Theodore and Bernice V. (Rutledge) F.; B.S., Prairie View (Tex.) A&M U., 1959, M.Ed., 1980. Tchr. vocat. agr., Richards, Tex., 1960; elem. tchr. Houston Ind. Sch. Dist., 1963—. Served with USAR, 1961-63. Mem. NEA, Nat. Council Tchrs. English, Assn. Childhood Edn., Assn. Supervision and Curriculum Devel., Internat. Reading Assn., Soc. Children's Book Writers, Tex. Tchrs. Assn., Houston Tchrs. Assn., Audubon Soc., Sierra Club, Nature Conservancy. Author feature stories, articles in field. Home: 7709 Claiborne St Houston TX 77016-3909 Office: 10130 Aldine Westfield Rd Houston TX 77093-5449

FULLER, WRENDA SUE, music and secondary school educator; b. Aberdeen, S.D., Oct. 21, 1947; d. LeRoy William and Annette Karlene (Robinette) Herther; m. Larry Fray Fuller, Aug. 22, 1970; 1 child, Heather Sue. BA in Music, History, Dakota Wesleyan U., 1969; MA in Govt., U. Va., 1970. Sr. state human resources planner Commonwealth of Va., Richmond, 1970-73; cons. Social Security Adminstrn., S.W. Va., 1973-74; educator Russell County Sch. Bd., Lebanon, Va., 1974—. Mem. faculty Va. Gov.'s Sch., 2000; founder/artistic dir. S.W. Va. Children's Choir, 2003—. Author: (directory) Listing and Evaluation of Available Human Services in Russell County, 1975; also articles. Mem. Health Svcs. Adv. Bd., S.W. Va., 1982-84; pres. Lebanon Women's Club, 1982-84; minister of music, Lebanon Meml. United Meth. Ch., 1982—; sponsor Boy Scouts Bloomington, Ind. (nat. winner mock trial), 1994, 96-98, 2000, Nat. Hist. Day, College Park, Md., 1994—. Named Outstanding Young Educator Jaycees, 1980, Econs. fellow U. Va., Charlottesville, 1988, Robert Cross History award, 1998, Gov.'s Coun. for the Arts award, 2000, UFW Citizenship award, 1998, Alumni Edn. award Dakota Wesleyan U., 2001. Mem. NEA, Music Educators Nat. Conf. (chmn. dist. VII, Va., 1989-91, 95—), Am. Choral Dirs. Assn. Avocations: reading, directing musicals, piano. Home: RR 4 Box 81 Lebanon VA 24266-9734 E-mail: wsfull@naxs.com.

FULLERTON, NANCY LEE, elementary school and music educator; b. Wheeling, W. Va., June 28, 1951; d. Harley Richard and Dannie Lou (Burkett) Lilley; m. Thomas Michael Fullerton, May 15, 1977; children: April Dawn, Shawn Michael, Jennifer Lynn. BA in Music Edn., Fairmont State Coll., 1973; postgrad. studies in Edn. Adminstrn., W. Va. U., 1993—. Travelling music tchr. Upshur County Schs., Buchannon, W. Va., 1973-76; substitute tchr. Marshall County Schs., Moundsville, W. Va., 1976-90, elem. music specialist Cameron, W. Va., 1990—; min. of music Cameron Bapt. Ch., 1998—. Dir. chancel choir First Christian Ch., Cameron, 1977-97, program chmn., 1986-88, Sunday sch. supt., 1992-97; advisor Camerette Theta Rho Girls' Club, 1979—. Election worker Marshall County, Cameron, 1990-91; troop leader Girl Scouts U.S., 1984—; dir. Cameron Cmty. Choir, 1996—. Mem. NEA, W.Va. Edn. Assn., Music Educators Nat. Conf., W.Va. Music Educators Assn., Sunmbeam Rebekah Lodge, Sigma Alpha Iota (pres.). Republican. Mem. Christian Ch. (Disciples Of Christ). Avocations: reading, needle craft, sewing, ceramics, performing with alumni music groups. Office: Cameron Elem Sch 12 Church St Cameron WV 26033-1217

FULTON, JO ANN, lawyer; b. 1951; BA in History, U. Wyo., JD, 1989. Atty. Fulton Law Office, Laramie, Wyo., 1992—. Mem. Wyo. State Bd. Edn., 2000—, chmn., 2003—. Office: Fulton Law Office PC PO Box 1267 1002 S 3rd St Laramie WY 82073-1267 Address: Wyo Dept Edn Hathaway Bldg 2nd Fl 2300 Capitol Ave Cheyenne WY 82002-0050*

FULTON, ROBERT LESTER, sociology educator; b. Toronto, Ont., Can., Nov. 30, 1926; s. Edgar John and Mary Grace (Ouderkirk) F.; m. Patricia Alma Brown, July 29, 1948 (div.); children: David, Richard; m. Julie Ann Rockman, June 13, 1964; 1 son, Regan. AB cum laude, U. Ill., 1951; MA, U. Toronto, 1953; PhD, Wayne State U., 1959. Instr. U. Wis., 1957-58; asst. prof. sociology Calif. State U., L.A., 1958-65, prof. sociology, 1965-66, U. Minn., Mpls., 1966-97; dir. Ctr. for Death Edn. and Rsch., 1969-97. Vis. prof. U. Minn., 1963-65, U. Osmania, India, 1967, St. Christopher's Hospice, London, 1975, Radium Hemmet, Stockholm, 1975, U. Calif.-Irvine, 1975, U. Calif.-San Diego, 1978, 79, U. Calif.-San Francisco, 1986, U. Vt., 1983, 84, 86, 88, 89, 92, St. Luke's Coll., Tokyo, 1985, U. Cape Town, 1993, Rikkyo U., Tokyo, 1993, Nankai U., Tianjin, China, 1995. Author: Death and Identity, 1965, 3rd rev. edit., 1993; Education and Social Crisis, 1967, Death, Grief and Bereavement: Bibliography 1845-1975, 1977, Death and Dying: Challenge and Change, 1978; assoc. editor Omega, 1970-73. With Royal Can. Navy, 1944. Fellow Am. Sociol. Assn.; mem. Internat. Workgroup on Death, Dying and Bereavement, Société de Thanatologie de la Langue Française. Home: 139 Nina St Saint Paul MN 55102-2129 E-mail: fult001@tc.umn.edu.

FULTON, THOMAS, theoretical physicist, educator; b. Budapest, Hungary, Nov. 19, 1927; came to U.S., 1941; s. Michael and Irene (Weisz) F.; m. Babette Pilzer, June 14, 1952; children: Ruth Carol, Judith Pamela. BA, Harvard U., 1950, MA, 1951, PhD, 1954. Prof. emeritus Johns Hopkins U., Balt., 2000—; Frank B. Jewett Found. postdoctoral fellow Inst. Advanced Studies, Princeton, N.J., 1954-55; NSF postdoctoral fellow Princeton, N.J., 1955-56; from asst. prof. to assoc. prof. physics Johns Hopkins U., Balt., 1956-64, prof., 1964-2000. Rsch. cons. and vis. scientist numerous orgns., 1954—. Author: (with others) Resonances in Strong Interaction Physics, 1963; assoc. editor Jour. Math. Physics, 1968-71; contbr. over 100 articles to profl. jours. Bd. dirs. Shriver Hall Concert Series, Balt., 1981-91. With U.S. Army, 1946-47. John Simon Guggenheim Found. fellow, U. Vienna, 1964-65, Fulbright sr. rsch. fellow, 1964-65; prin. investigator rsch. grantee NSF, Johns Hopkins U., 1960-92. Fellow Am. Phys. Soc.; mem. Archeol. Inst. Am., Sigma Xi. Home: 5600 Roxbury Pl Baltimore MD 21209-4502 Office: Johns Hopkins U Dept Physics And Astro Baltimore MD 21218

FULTON, WILLIAM, mathematics educator; b. Aug. 29, 1939; BA, Brown U., 1961; PhD, Princeton U., 1966. Instr. Princeton (N.J.) U., 1965-66; from instr. to asst. prof. Brandeis U., 1966-69; assoc. prof. Brown U., 1970-75, prof., 1975-87, U. Chgo., 1987-98, Charles L. Hutchinson Disting. Svc. prof., 1995-98; Keeler prof. math. U. Mich., Ann Arbor, 1998—. Vis. asst. prof. Princeton U., 1969-70; vis. prof. U. Genoa, 1969, Aarhus U., 1976-77, Orsay, 1987; vis. mem. Inst. des Hautes Etudes Scis., 1981, Inst. Advanced Study, 1981-82, 94, Math. Scis. Rsch. Inst., 1992-93, Ctr. Advanced Study, Oslo, 1994; Erlander prof. Mittag-Leffler Inst., 1996-97; lectr. in field. Author: Intersection Theory, 1984, Introduction to Intersection Theory in Algebraic Geometry, 1984, Introduction to Toric Varieties, 1993, Algebraic Topology, 1995, Young Tableaux, 1997; (with R. MacPherson) A Categorical Framework for the Study of Singular Spaces, 1981; (wih S. Lang) Riemann-Roch Algebra, 1985, (with J. Harris) Representation Theory; a first course, 1991; (with S. Bloch and I. Dolgachev, editors) Proceedings of the US-USSR Symposium in Algebraic Geometry, Univ. of Chicago, June-July, 1989, 1991; assoc. editor Duke Math. Jour., 1984-93, Jour. Algebraic Geometry, 1992-93; editor Jour. Am. Math. Soc., 1993-99, mng. editor, 1995-98; mem. editl. bd. Cambridge Studies in Advanced Math., 1994—, Chgo. Lectures in Math., 1994-98. Grantee NSF, 1976—, Sloan Found., 1981-82; Guggenheim fellow, 1980-81; named Erlander prof. Swedish Sci. Found., 1996-97. Mem.: NAS, AAAS, Royal Swedish Acad. Sci. Office: U Mich 525 E University Ave Ann Arbor MI 48109-1109

FULTZ, JOHN HOWARD, retired middle school educator; b. East Liverpool, Ohio, Mar. 4, 1949; s. John C. and Irene (Christy) F.; m. Sandra Liebhart, 1975. BS in Edn., Kent State U., 1971, MEd, 1976. Cert. tchr., Ohio. Laborer Union Labor Local 809, Steubenville, Ohio, 1967-71; clk. Montgomery Ward, East Liverpool, 1967-71; tchr., tutor Wellsville (Ohio) Schs., 1968-70; tchr. Kent (Ohio) City Schs., 1971—. Chmn. curriculum adv. com. Kent City Schs., 1982. Editor monthly publ. for pub. speakers Phantastic Phunnies, 1978-91. Active Make-A-Wish Found., Cleve., 1989—, Rails to Trails Conservation, Washington, 1992—, Spl. Olympics Ohio, Columbus, 1991—, No. Ohio chpt. Leukemia Soc. Am., 1995—; vol. Meml. Sloan Kettering Cancer Found., N.Y.C., 1991—; rep. to South Africa in Citizen Amb. Program, 1997. Martha Holden Jennings Found. scholar, Cleve., 1972; recipient Coast to Coast marathon award Mercedes-Benz Co., 1991, Vol. award Meml. Sloan Kettering Cancer Found., 1991-93, Leukemia Soc. Am., 1995. Mem. ASCD, Fraternal Order of Police, Masons (brother), Kent State Alumni and Blue and Gold Club, U.S. Athletics Congress, Ohio Athletics Congress, N.Y.C. Road Runners Club, Erie (Pa.) Road Runners Club, Summit Athletic Club, Scotish Rite, Phi Delta Kappa, Kappa Sigma. Avocations: marathon running, intramural sports, cooking, writing, reading, traveling. Home: 1450 Loop Rd Kent OH 44240-4619 Office: Stanton Middle Sch 6662 Cleveland Canton Rd Kent OH 44240

FUMENTO, ROCCO, retired English and film educator; b. North Adams, Mass., Feb. 12, 1923; s. Mauro-Vincenzo and Antonia Cifrese Fumento; m. Tobey Baer Fumento, Mar. 10, 1956; children: David, Michael, Andrew, Matthew. BS, Columbia U., 1950; MFA, U. Iowa, 1952. Prof. English and film U. Ill., Urbana, 1952—92; ret. Author: (novels) Devil By the Tail, 1953, Tree of Dark Reflection, 1964, A Decent Girl Always Goes to Mass on Sunday, 2002, short stories; contbr. articles to profl. jours. Staff sgt. U.S. Army, 1944—46. Mem.: Italian-Am. Orgns. (film festival organizer Oct. celebrations 2001—02). Avocations: traveling, reading, film studios. Home: 1100 Main St Dalton MA 01226-2202

FUNG, SUN-YIU SAMUEL, physics educator; b. Hong Kong, Dec. 27, 1932; came to U.S., 1953; s. Lok-Chi and Lai-Lan Fung; m. Helen Wu, Feb. 9, 1964; children: Eric, Linette. BS, U. San Francisco, 1957; PhD, U. Calif., 1964. Rsch. physicist Rutgers U., New Brunswick, N.J., 1964-66; asst. prof. physics U. Calif., Riverside, 1966-70, assoc. prof., 1970-76, prof., 1976—, chmn. physics dept., 1980-85, 90-91. Chmn. Chinese Meml. Pavilian Com., Riverside, 1985-88; commr. City Riverside Human Rels., 1994-2000. Mem. AAAS, Am. Phys. Soc., Overseas Chinese Physicist Assn., Chinese Am. Faculty Assn. (pres. 1988-89, 90-92, pres. scholarship found., 2001—). Office: U Calif Riverside CA 92521-0001

FUNK, DAVID ALBERT, retired law educator; b. Wooster, Ohio, Apr. 22, 1927; s. Daniel Coyle and Elizabeth Mary (Reese) F.; children— Beverly Joan, Susan Elizabeth, John Ross, Carolyn Louise; m. Sandra Nadine Henselmeier, Oct. 2, 1976 Student, U. Mo., 1945-46, Harvard Coll., 1946; BA in Econs., Coll. of Wooster, 1949; MA, Ohio State U., 1968; JD, Case Western Res. U., 1951, LLM, 1972, Columbia U., 1973. Bar: Ohio 1951, U.S. Dist. Ct. (no. dist.) Ohio 1962, U.S. Tax Ct. 1963, U.S. Ct. Appeals (6th cir.) 1970, U.S. Supreme Ct. 1971. Ptnr. Funk, Funk & Eberhart, Wooster, Ohio, 1951-72; assoc. prof. law Ind. U. Sch. Law, Indpls., 1973-76, prof., 1976-97, prof. emeritus, 1997—. Vis. lectr. Coll. of Wooster, 1962-63; dir. Juridical Sci. Inst., Indpls., 1982—. Author: Oriental Jurisprudence, 1974, Group Dynamic Law, 1982; (with others) Rechtsgeschichte und Rechtssoziologie, 1985, Group Dynamic Law: Exposition and Practice, 1988; contbr. articles to profl. jours. Chmn. bd. trustees Wayne County Law Library Assn., 1956-71; mem. Permanent Jud. Commn., Synod of Ohio, United Presbyn. Ch. in the U.S., 1968. Served to seaman 1st class USNR, 1945-46 Harlan Fiske Stone fellow Columbia U., 1973; recipient Am. Jurisprudence award in Comparative Law, Case Western Res. U., 1970 Mem. Assn. Am. Law Schs. (sec. comparative law sect. 1977-79, chmn. law and religion sect. 1977-81, sec.-treas. law and social sci. sect. 1983-86), Am. Soc. for Legal History, Pi Sigma Alpha. Republican. Home: 6208 N Delaware St Indianapolis IN 46220-1824

FUNK, WILLIAM HENRY, retired environmental engineering educator; b. Ephraim, Utah, June 10, 1933; s. William George and Henrietta (Hackwell) F.; m. Ruth Sherry Mellor, Sept. 19, 1964 (dec.); 1 dau., Cynthia Lynn; m. Lynn Bridget Robson, Mar. 30, 1996. BS in Biol. Sci, U. Utah, 1955, MS in Zoology, 1963, PhD in Limnology, 1966. Tchr. sci., math. Salt Lake City Schs., 1957-60; research asst. U. Utah, Salt Lake City, 1961-63; head sci. dept. N.W. Jr. High Sch., Salt Lake City, 1961-63; mem. faculty Wash. State U., Pullman, 1966-99, assoc. prof. environ. engring., 1971-75, prof., 1975-99, chmn. environ. sci./regional planning program, 1979-81; dir. Environ. Research Center, 1980-83, State of Wash. Water Research Ctr., 1981-99; ret., 1999. Cons. U.S. Army C.E., Walla Walla, Wash., 1970—74, Harstad Engrs., Seattle, 1971—72, Boise Cascade Corp., Seattle, 1971—72, Wash. Dept. Ecology, Olympia, 1971—72, ORB Corp., Renton, Wash., 1972—73, U.S. Civil Svc., Seattle, Chgo., 1972—74; mem. High Level Nuclear Waste Bd., Wash., 1986—89, Wash. 2010 Com., 1989, Pure Water 2000 Steering Com., 1990; co-dir. Inst. Resource Mgmt.; co-founder Terrene Inst., Washington, 1991, pres., 1993—2002. Author publs. on water pollution control and lake restoration. Served to capt. USNR, 1955-88. Grantee NSF Summer Inst., 1961, U.S. Army C.E., 1970-74, 94-96, 97-98, Office Water Resources Rsch., 1971-72, 73-76, EPA, 1980-83, 93-94, 95-96, U.S. Geol. Survey, 1983-94, 95-96, 97-98, 99-00, Nat. Parks Svc., 1985-87, Colville Confederated Tribes, 1990-92, Nez Pierce Tribe, 1992-95, Wash. Conservation Commn., 1992-95, Clearwater Co., 1992-93, Idaho Dept. Environ. Quality, 1995-96, U.S. Bur. Reclamation, 1995-98; USPHS fellow, 1963; recipient Pres.'s Disting. Faculty award Wash. State U., 1984. Mem. Naval Res. Officers Assn. (chpt. pres. 1969), Res Officers Assn. (U.S. Naval Acad. info. officer 1973-76), N.Am. Lake Mgmt. Soc. (pres. 1984-85, Secchi Disk award 1988), Pacific N.W. Pollution Control Assn. (editor 1969-77, pres.-elect 1982-83, pres. 1983-84), Water Pollution Control Fedn. (Arthur S. Bedell award Pacific N.W. assn. 1976, nat. bd. dirs. 1978-81, bd. dirs. Rsch. Found. 1990-92), Nat. Assn. Water Inst. Dirs. (chair 1985-87, bd. dirs. univ. council on water resources 1986-89), Wash. Lakes Protection Assn. (co-founder 1986, Friend of Lakes award 1999), Am. Water Resources Assn. (v.p. Wash. sect. 1988), Am. Soc. Limnology and Oceanography, Am. Micros. Soc., N.W. Sci. Assn., North Am. Lake Mgmt. Soc. (co-founder 1972), Sigma Xi, Phi Sigma. Home: 330 SW Kimball Ct Pullman WA 99163-2176

FUQUA, CHARLES JOHN, retired classics educator; b. Paris, Oct. 5, 1935; s. John Howe and Gillian Elynor (Quennell) F.; m. Mary Louise Morse, Aug. 26, 1961; children— Andrew Morse, David Reed, Gillian Quennell. BA magna cum laude, Princeton, 1957; MA, Cornell U., 1962, PhD, 1964. Instr. classics Dartmouth Coll., Hanover, NH, 1964, asst. prof., 1965-66; assoc. prof. classics, chmn. dept. classics Williams Coll., Williamstown, Mass., 1966-72, Garfield prof. ancient langs., chmn. dept. classics, 1972-86; ret., 2003. Mem. adv. council Am. Acad. in Rome, 1966, chmn. exec. com., 1974 Served to lt. (j.g.) USNR, 1957-60. Mem.: Vergilian Soc., Classical Assn. Mass., Classical Assn. New Eng., Am. Philol. Assn., Phi Beta Kappa, Phi Kappa Phi. Home: 96 Grandview Dr Williamstown MA 01267-2528 E-mail: cfuqua@williams.edu.

FUQUA, JUDY See FOUQUET, ANNE

FURCI, JOAN GELORMINO, early childhood education educator; b. Torrington, Conn., Jan. 3, 1939; BS, Western Conn. State Coll., Danbury, 1960; MS, U. Hartford, 1966; EdD, Nova U., Ft. Lauderdale, Fla., 1975. Tchr., Conn., 1960-68; dir. Early Childhood Program, Univ. Sch., Nova U., 1971-90; asst. prof. Nova Coll., 1990-94; early childhood tchr. N.C. Tng. and Tech. Assistance Ctr., Morganton, 1995—; cons. Early Childhood Program, N.Y., N.C., 1968—. Bd. dirs. United Way Child Care Centers, Broward County. Pres. Kids in Distress, 1987-88. Mem. Nat. Assn. for Edn. Young Children, Assn. for Children Edn. Internat. Home: 704 Baytree Dr Titusville FL 32780-2310

FURGASON, ROBERT ROY, university president, engineering educator; b. Spokane, Wash., Aug. 2, 1935; s. Roy Elliott and Margaret (O'Halloran) F.; m. Gloria L. Althouse, June 14, 1964; children: Steven Scott, Brian Alan. BSChemE, U. Idaho, 1956, MSCE, 1958; PhD in Chem. Engring., Northwestern U., 1961; postdoctoral, U. Wis., 1961. Registered profl. engr., Idaho. Design engr. Phillips Petroleum Co., Bartlesville, Okla., 1956; rsch. engr. Martin Marietta Co., Denver, 1958; instr. chem. engring. U. Idaho, Moscow, 1957-59, asst. prof., 1961-63, assoc. prof., 1963-67, acting head dept. chem. engring., 1964-65, chmn. dept. chem. engring., 1965-74, prof., 1967-84, dean Coll. Engring., 1974-78, v.p. acad. affairs and rsch., 1978-84; prof., vice chancellor acad. affairs U. Nebr., Lincoln, 1984-90; prof., pres. Tex A&M U.-Corpus Christi, 1990—. NSF advisor scientists and engrs. in econ. devel. program Escuela Politecnica Nacional, Quito, Ecuador, 1973-74, 76; proposal reviewer NSF, 1965-84; program reviewer Clearwater Econ. Devel. Assn., 1978-84; mem. long-range planning commn. Idaho State Bd. Edn., 1978-80, Gov.'s Com. Faculty Salary Equity, 1980, State of Idaho Energy Policy Bd., 1980-84, adv. com. Northwest Power Policy Coun., 1982-84, engring. accreditation commn. Accreditation Bd. Engring. and Tech., 1981-96, exec. bd., 1984-89, vice chmn., 1985-87, chmn., 1988-89, bd. dirs., 1989-95, fellow, 1990, pres., 1993-94; bd. dirs. Hanover Cos.; adv. bd. dirs. Am. Bank. Bd. of trustees, Driscoll Hospital Founnd., 2002— . Contbr. articles to profl. jours. Chmn. Idaho-Ecuador Ptnrs. of Ams., 1975-77; commr. Moscow Parks and Recreation Commn., 1977-81; mem. charter revision commn. City of Lincoln, 1989-90; chair Nebr. Energy Mgmt. Plan Adv. Com., 1989-90; mem. chem. engring. vis. com. Colo. Sch. Mines, 1989-99; exec. adv. bd. Coastal Bend United Way, 1991-93; bd. dirs. S.W. Moscow Cmty. Assn., 1977-84, Am. Festival Ballet, 1978-80, Lincoln Cancer Ctr., 1988-90, Tex. Econ. Edn. Commn., 1991-2001, Ada Wilson Children's Rehab. Ctr., 1993-96, Tex. State Aquarium, 1994—; adv. bd. Sta. KEDT-TV, Sta. KEDT-FM. Recipient Pub. Svc. award Idaho State Libr. Assn., 1978, Phillip Carrol Nat. award Soc. Advanced Mgmt., 1996, Grinter award Accreditation Bd. Engring. and Tech., 1996, Baldwin award Corpus Christi C. of C., 2000; named Citizen of Yr. Kappa Sigma, 1980, Newsmaker of the Yr., Corpus Christi Caller-Times, 1997, Newsmaker of the Decade, 2000; CASE Chief Exec. Leadership award, 2001; Walter P. Murphy fellow. Fellow AIChE (chmn. nat. tech. sessions 1967, sec. dept. heads forum 1971-72, chmn. 1981, nat. vis. lectr. 1977-79, edn. and accreditation com. 1981-92, chair 1989-91, accreditation visitation group 1977—); mem. Am. Soc. Engring. Edn. (Pacific Northwest coord. effective tchg. 1962-64, bd. dirs. chem. engring. divsn. 1974-77, Centennial medal 1993), Idaho Soc. Profl. Engrs. (No. Idaho chpt. pres. 1970, state pres. 1980, Idaho's Young Engr. of Yr. 1967), Northwest Coll. and Univ. Assn. Scis. (exec. com. bd. dirs. 1976-80, 81-84, chmn. bd. dirs. 1979-80), Corpus Christi C. of C. (bd. dirs. 1990-94), Crucible Club, Wranglers Club, Lions (program chmn., corr. sec., bd. dirs.), Rotary, Sigma Xi, Phi Kappa Phi, Phi Eta Sigma, Sigma Tau. Avocations: piloting, skiing, camping, woodworking. Home: 1334 Sandpiper Dr Corpus Christi TX 78412-3818 Office: Tex A&M U Office of Pres 6300 Ocean Dr Corpus Christi TX 78412-5503 E-mail: furgason@tamucc.edu.

FURHT, BORIVOJE, computer engineer, educator, researcher; b. Belgrade, Yugoslavia, June 11, 1946; came to U.S., 1981; s. Pavle and Nina (Jakoljevic) F.; married; 1 child, Tanya. BSEE, U. Belgrade, 1970, MSEE, 1973, PhD, 1978. Research engr. Inst. Boris Kidric-Vinca, Belgrade, 1970-73, sr. research engr., 1973-78, project leader, mgr., 1978-82; project engr. Siemens Corp., Erlangen, Fed. Republic Germany, 1974-75; asst. prof. electrical and computer engring. U. Miami, Coral Gables, Fla., 1982-84, assoc. prof., 1984-88; prin. engr. Cordis Corp., Miami, Fla., 1983-87; sr. dir. Modcomp/AEG, Ft. Lauderdale, Fla., 1988-92; prof., dir. multimedia lab. Fla. Atlantic U., Boca Raton, 1992—, chmn., 2002—. Cons. Hewlett Packard, Ft. Collins, Colo., 1992, NASA-Kennedy Space Ctr., Cape Canaveral, Fla., 1985, Honeywell, Inc., Clearwater, Fla., 1985, IBM Almaden Rsch. Ctr., San Jose, Calif., 1990-94, Rank Xerox, London, 1993-94, GE, Milw., 1997, Cylex, 2000. Author: Microprocessor Interfacing, 1986, Real-Time UNIX Systems, 1990, Video and Image Processing in Multimedia Systems, 1995, A Guided Tour of Multimedia Systems and Applications, 1995, Multimedia Systems and Techniques, 1996, Multimedia Tools and Applications, 1996, Real-Time Video Compression: Techniques and Algothims, 1997, Motion Estimation Techniques for Video Compression, 1997; Multimedia Technologies and Applications for the 21st Century, 1997, Handbook of Multimedia Computing, 1999, Handbook of Internet and Multimedia Systems and Applications, 1999, Handbook of Internet Computing, 2000, Content-Boxed Image and Video Retrieval, 2002, Handbook of Video Databases, 2003, Handbook of Wireless Internet, 2003; editor-in-chief Multimedia Tools and Applications Jour., Internat. Jour. Computers and Applications; editor: Computer Architecture, 1987, A Guided Tour of Multimedia Systems and Applications, 1995; contbr. articles to sci. and tech. jours. Recipient Sci. award Modcomp, 1991, Cordis, 1987, Inst. Boris Kidric-Vinca, 1983. Mem. IEEE (sr.), Computer Soc. of IEEE, Assn. Computing Machinery. Avocations: tennis, chess, hockey, skiing. Home: 2641 NW 45th St Boca Raton FL 33434-2578 Office: Dept Computer Sci & Engring Fla Atlantic Univ Boca Raton FL 33431 E-mail: borko@cse.fau.edu.

FURLONG, DENNIS J. education minister, physician; b. St. John's, Newfoundland, 1945; B in Physical Edn., U. New Brunswick; MS in Edn., U. Oregon; MD, Meml. U., Newfoundland, 1977. Tchr. Newfoundland Pub. Schs.; family physician Dalhousie Med. Clinic, Canada, 1977—99; elected min. New Brunswick Legis. Assembly, Fredricton, 1999—, min. for health and comty., 1999—2000, health and wellness min., 2000—01, min, edn. and min. responsible for culture and sport secretariat, 2001—. Rep. Restigouche Premier's Coun, Status of Disabled Persons, 1986—92, chmn, 1991—94. Mem. Com. to hold Winter Olympics 2003 in Chleur region; bd. dirs. New Brunswick Lung Assn, 1992—, pres., 1998. Mem.: New

Brunswick Med. Soc. (pres. 1988—89), Coll. Physicians and Surgeons (pres. 1977—80, 1985—87). Office: Legis Assembly New Brunswick PO Box 6000 Fredricton E3B SH1 Canada

FURNISH, DALE BECK, lawyer, educator; b. Iowa City, Iowa, Feb. 11, 1940; s. William Madison and Eula Bernice (Beck) F.; m. Roberta Rae Mahnke, Aug. 23, 1963 (div. Oct. 1975); 1 child, Katherine Elizabeth; m. Hannah Rose Arterian, May 27, 1978 (div. May 1994); children— William, Susannah, Diana, Cordelia; m. Diane Larkey, June 11, 1994. B.A., Grinnell Coll., 1962; J.D., U. Iowa, 1965; LL.M., U. Mich., 1970. Bar: Iowa, 1965; U.S. Ct. Appeals (8th cir.) 1966, Ariz. 1973, U.S. Ct. Appeals (9th cir.), Ariz. 1992; U.S. Dist. Ct. Ariz. 1976. Law clk. U.S. Ct. Appeals (8th cir.), Sioux City, Iowa, 1965-66; asst. prof. law U. Iowa, Iowa City, 1966-68; vis. prof. law Ford Found. Internat. Legal Ctr., Santiago, Chile, 1969-70; prof. law Ariz. State U., Tempe, 1970— ; ptnr. Molloy, Jones & Donahue, P.C., 1988-92; vis. prof. law U. Nacional Autonoma de Mexico, Mexico City, 1974-75; Fulbright prof. Pontificia U. Católica del Peru, 1984, 88, prof. law U. of Sonora, Mexico, 1994—; lectr. USIA, Latin Am., 1972—; chmn. Ariz. Supreme Ct. Project on Judicial Cooperation with Sonora, Mex., 1993—, Nat. Law Ctr. Inter-Am. Free Trade, 1991—. Author: Usury and the Monetary Control Act of 1980, 1981, Legal Aspects of the North American Free Trade Agreement, 1992. Bd. editors Am. Jour. Comparative Law, 1972-89, 96—, Revista Peruana del Derecho Internat., 1979— . Mem. Fgn. Relations Com., Phoenix, 1979—, mem. exec. bd. 1986-91; mem. Gov.'s Ariz.-Mex. Commn., 1981—, chmn. legal adv. com., 1988-93. Mem. Am. Assn. Law Schs. (chmn. creditor debtor sect. 1978, chmn. comparative law sect. 1979), ABA, Ariz. Bar Assn., Iowa Bar Assn., Interam. Bar Assn., Am. Bankruptcy Inst. (bd. dirs. 1984-91), Order of Coif. Republican. Office: Ariz State U Coll Law Tempe AZ 85287-7906

FURR, CYNDI J. secondary school educator; b. Indio, Calif., Jan. 28, 1974; d. Johnny George and Sandra Sue (Anderson) Furr. AA in English Composition, Coll. of the Desert, Palm Desert, Calif., 1994; BA in English Literature, Calif. State U., San Bernadino, 1996, MA in Instrl. Tech., 2003. Cert. tchr., Calif. Chiropractic asst. Rapp Chiropractic Health Ctr., Palm Desert, Calif., 1995-97; English tchr. Palm Desert H.S., 1997—. Recipient Rogers Scholar award Rogers Family Trust, 1996; Inland Area Writers Project fellow, 1999. Mem. Calif. Assn. Tchrs. English, Calif. Tchrs. Assn., Inland Area Writers Project (facilitator 2001), Phi Kappa Phi. Avocations: reading, scrapbooks, crafts, karaoke singing. Office: Palm Desert HS Phyllis Jackson Ln Palm Desert CA 92260

FURSTE, WESLEY LEONARD, II, surgeon, educator; b. Cin., Apr. 19, 1915; s. Wesley Leonard and Alma (Deckebach) F.; m. Leone James, Mar. 28, 1942; children: Nancy Dianne, Susan Deanne, Wesley Leonard III. AB cum laude (Julius Dexter scholar 1933-34); Harvard Club scholar 1934-35), Harvard U., 1937, MD in Anatomy, 1941. Diplomate: Am. Bd. Surgery. Intern Ohio State U. Hosp., Columbus, 1941-42; fellow surgery U. Cin., 1945-46; asst. surg. resident Cin. Gen. Hosp., 1946-49; sr. asst. surg. resident Ohio State U. Hosps., 1949-50, chief surg. resident, 1950-51; limited practice medicine specializing in surgery Columbus, 1951—; instr. Ohio State U., 1951-54, clin. asst. prof. surgery, 1954-66, clin. assoc. prof., 1966-74, clin. prof. surgery, 1974-85, clin. prof. emeritus, 1985—. Mem. surg. staff Mt. Carmel Med. Center, chmn. dept. surgery, 1981-85, dir. surgery program, 1981-82; mem. surg. staff Children's, Grant Med. Ctr., Univ., Riverside, Meth. Hosps., St. Anthony Med. Ctr., Park Med. Ctr. (all Columbus); surg. cons. Dayton (Ohio) VA Hosp., Columbus State Sch., Ohio State Penitentiary, Mercy Hosp., Benjamin Franklin Hosp., Columbus, Columbus Cmty. Hosp.; regional adv. com. nat. blood program ARC, 1951-68, chmn., 1958-68; invited participant 2d Internat. Conf. on Tetanus, WHO, Bern, Switzerland, 1966, 3d, São Paulo, Brazil, 1970, 4th, Dakar, Sénégal, 1975, 5th, Ronneby Brunn, Sweden, 1978, 6th, Lyon, France, 1981, 7th, Copanello, Italy, 1984, 8th, Leningrad, USSR, 1987, 9th, Granada, Spain, 1991; invited rapporteur 4th Internat. Conf. on Tetanus, Dakar, Sénégal, 1975; mem. med. adv. com. Medic Alert Found. Internat., 1971-73, 76-80, bd. dirs., 1973-76; Douglas lectr. Med. Coll. of Ohio, Toledo; founder Digestive Disease Found; lectr. U.S. Army M.C. on WWII Chinese activities during 1943-46; invited orator for new citizens at naturalization ceremonies U.S. Dist. Ct. (so. dist.) Ohio. Prime author: Tétanos; Tetanus: A Team Disease; contbg. author: Advances in Military Medicine, 1948, Management of the Injured Patient, Immediate Care of the Acutely Ill and Injured, 1978, Anaerobic Infections, 1989, Procs. of Internat. Tetans Confs. in Switzerland, Brazil, Sweden, Sénégal, France, Italy, USSR, Current Therapy in Emergency Medicine, Surgical Infectious Diseases (3 edits.), Currenty Emergency Therapy, Surgical Infections, Current Diagnosis (multiple edits.), Current Therapy (multiple edits.), Surgical Infections, 5 Minute Clinical Consult, 8 edits. (4 and 5 CD-Rom, Internet), Medical Microbiology and Infectious Diseases, editor Surgical Monthly Review; contbr. articles to profl. jours. Mem. Ohio Motor Vehicle Med. Rev. Bd., 1965-67, Pres. Club, Ohio State Univ.; bd. dirs. Am. Cancer Soc. Franklin County, pres., 1964-66; adv. coun. Upper Arlington Sr. Ctr., 2000. Served to maj., M.C. AUS, 1942-46, CBI, 1951-53. Recipient China Liberation medal, 2 commendations for surg. service in China U.S. Army; cert. of merit Am. Cancer Soc.; award for outstanding achievement in field clostridial infection dept. surgery Ohio State U. Coll. Medicine, 1984, Outstanding Service award, 1985; award for outstanding and dedicated service Mt. Carmel Med. Ctr., 1985; award for over 25 yrs. service St. Anthony Med. Ctr., U.S.A. Nat. Softball Squash Champion for age group, (1975—), Houston, 1995, (1980—), Denver, 96. Mem. AMA, AAAS, APHA, Cen. Surg. Assn., Surgical Infection Soc., Internat. Biliary Assn., Shock Soc., Soc. Am. Gastrointestinal Endoscopic Surgeons (com. on stds. of practice, resident and fellow edn., com. legis. review), Soc. Surgery of Alimentary Tract, A.C.S. (gov.-at-large, chmn. Ohio com. trauma; nat. subcom. prophylaxis against tetanus in wound mgmt., Ohio chapter Disting. Service award 1987; regional credentials com.), Am. Assn. Surgery of Trauma, Internat. Fedn. of Surg. Colls., Ohio Surg. Assn., Columbus Surg. Assn. (hon. mem.; pres. 1983), Am. Trauma Soc. (founding mem., dir.), Ohio Med. Assn., Acad. Medicine Columbus and Franklin County (Award of Merit for 17 yrs. service, chmn. blood transfusion com., 50 Year Svc. award), Acad. Medicine Cin., Am. Med. Writers Assn., Grad. Surg. Soc. U. Cin., Robert M. Zollinger Surg. Ohio State U. Surg. Soc., Mont Reid Grad. Surg. Soc., Am. Geriatrics Soc., N.Y. Acad. Scis., Assn. Program Dirs. in Surgery, Assn. Physicians State of Ohio, Collegium Internationale Chirurgiae Digestivae, Assn. Am. Med. Colls., Internat. Soc. Colon and Rectal Surgeons, Soc. Internat. de Chirurgie, Am. Assn. Sr. Physicians, Société Internationale sur le Tētanos, Am. Physicians Art Assn., Am. Assn. Retired Persons (bd. dirs. Franklin County Unit), China-Burma-India Vets., Assn. Columbus Basha (vice comdr. 1992-93, comdr. 1993-94, V-J Day coord., surgeon gen. 1994—), Am. Legion NW Post # 443, Am. Med. Golfing Assn., Internat. Brotherhood Magicians, Soc. Am. Magicians, N.Y. Cen. System Hist. Soc., U.S. Squash Racquets Assn. (mem. ranking com., med. adv. com., Nat. Softball Champion, 1992, 1996), Am. Platform Tennis Assn., Columbus Squash Racquets Assn. (bd. dirs.), VFW of U.S. (lectr.), Pres.'s Club (Ohio State U.). Presbyterian. Home and Office: Ohio State Univ 3125 Bembridge Rd Columbus OH 43221-2203 Fax: 614-457-5119. E-mail: wfursteii@aol.com.

FUSCO, RICHARD, English literature educator; b. Phila., Apr. 27, 1952; BA, U. Pa., 1973, MA, 1974, U. Miss., 1982; PhD, Duke U., 1990. Instr. English St. Joseph's U., Phila., 1988-91, asst. prof. English, 1997—2003, assoc. prof. English, 2003—. Author: Maupassant and the American Short Story: The Influence of Form at the Turn of the Century, 1994, (pamphlet) Fin de millénaire: Poe's Legacy for the Detective Story, 1993; contbr. articles to profl. jours. Served as intelligence officer U.S. Navy, 1975-79. Mem. MLA. Home: 2237 S 23rd St Philadelphia PA 19145-3321 Office: Dept English St Joseph's U 5600 City Ave Philadelphia PA 19131-1308 E-mail: fusco@sju.edu.

FUSSELL, PAUL, author, English literature educator; b. Pasadena, Calif., Mar. 22, 1924; s. Paul and Wilhma Wilson (Sill) F.; m. Betty Ellen Harper, June 17, 1949 (div. 1987); children: Rosalind, Samuel; m. Harriette Behringer, Apr. 11, 1987. BA, Pomona (Calif.) Coll., 1947, LittD (hon.), 1981; MA, Harvard U., 1949, PhD, 1952; MA (hon.), U. Pa., 1983; LittD (hon.), Monmouth U., N.J., 1985. Instr. English, Conn. Coll., 1951-55; mem. faculty Rutgers U., 1955—, John DeWitt prof. English lit., 1976-83; Donald T. Regan prof. English lit. U. Pa., Phila., 1983-94, prof. emeritus, 1994—. Cons. editor Random House, 1963-64; lectr. Am. univs., 1965—; vis. prof. Kings Coll., London, 1990-92. Author: The Rhetorical World of Augustan Humanism, 1965, Poetic Meter and Poetic Form, 1965, rev., 1979, Samuel Johnson and The Life of Writing, 1971, The Great War and Modern Memory (Nat. Book Critics Circle award 1975, Nat. Book award 1976), Abroad: British Literary Traveling Between the Wars, 1980, The Boy Scout Handbook & Other Observations, 1982, Class: A Guide through the American Status System, 1983, Thank God for the Atom Bomb & Other Essays, 1988, Wartime: Understanding and Behavior in the Second World War, 1989; BAD: or The Dumbing of America, 1991, The Anti-Egoist: Kingsley Amis, Man of Letters, 1994, Doing Battle: The Making of a Skeptic, 1996, Uniforms: Why We Are What We Wear, 2002; contbg. editor Harper's, 1979-83, The New Republic, 1979-85. Served with AUS, 1943-46. Decorated Purple Heart, Bronze Star; recipient James D. Phelan award Phelan Found., 1964; Lindback Found. award, 1971; Ralph Waldo Emerson award Phi Beta Kappa, 1976; sr. fellow Nat. Endowment Humanities, 1973-74; Guggenheim fellow, 1977-78; Rockefeller Found. fellow, 1983-84 Fellow Royal Soc. Lit., Soc. Am. Historians; mem. MLA, Acad. Lit. Studies. Home: 2020 Walnut St Philadelphia PA 19103-5635

FUTRELL, ALVIN, director; BSE in Phys. Edn., MSE in Phys. Edn., Henderson State U.; EdS in Ednl. Adminstrn., Ark. State U.; EdD in Secondary Edn., Ball State U., 1987. Prof. dept. secondary edn. Henderson State U., Arkadelphia, Ark., 1975—88, dir. tchr. admissions and field experiences, 1988—99, asst. to pres. for diversity, 1999—. Mem.: S.W. Ednl. Lab. (bd. mem. 2003—). Office: Henderson State Univ WO 311 1100 Henderson St Arkadelphia AR 71999-0001

FUTTER, JOAN BABETTE, former school librarian; b. N.Y.C., Nov. 15, 1921; d. Samuel S. and Helen (Mosher) Feinberg; m. Victor Futter, Jan. 26, 1943; children: Jeffrey Leesam, Ellen Victoria, Deborah Gail Futter Cohan. AB, NYU, 1941; MS, L.I. U., 1966. Sch. libr. Carrie Palmer Weber Jr. High Sch., Port Washington, N.Y., 1966-91. Mem. LWV, AAUW, L.I. Sch. Media Assn., C.W. Post Libr. Assn., Cold Spring Harbor Beach Club, Manhasset Bay Yacht Club. Home: 17 Sunnyvale Rd Port Washington NY 11050-4519

FYFE, ALISTAIR IAN, cardiologist, scientist, educator; b. Hobart, Tasmania, Australia, Sept. 5, 1960; came to U.S., 1991; s. Ian John and Merrill Millicent (Faragher) F.; 1 child, Alexander Jonathan. B of Med. Sci., U. Tasmania, 1980, B of Med. Sci. with honors, 1981, MBBS, 1984; PhD in Molecular Biology, UCLA, 1995. Diplomate Am. Bd. Internal Medicine and Cardiovasc. Disease. Intern Royal Hobart Hosp., 1985-86; resident in internal medicine U. B.C., Vancouver, Can., 1986-89; cardiology fellow U. Toronto, Ont., Can., 1989-91; cardiac rsch. fellow UCLA, 1991-95, asst. prof. medicine and cardiology, 1995-99, dir. Ctr. for Cholesterol and Lipid Mgmt., 1995-98, assoc. mem. Molecular Biology Inst., 1996-98; dir. clin. rsch. Heart Place, Dallas, 1999—. Author: (with others) Progress in Pediatric Cardiology, 1993; contbr. articles to profl. jours. Recipient Fellowship Clinician Scientist award Med. Rsch. Coun., Can., 1992. Fellow Royal Coll. Physicians Can., Am. Coll. Cardiology, Coun. Arterial Sclerosis; mem. Internat. Heart Transplant Soc., Am. Heart Assn. (fellow arteriosclerosis coun., reviewer 1993—, Young Investigator award, 1993, 95), Am. Soc. Clin. Investigation, Am. Diabetes Assn. Achievements include first demonstration of genetic modification of solid organ transplants. Office: Heart Place 7777 Forest Ln Ste A341 Dallas TX 75230-2500

FYFE, DORIS MAE, elementary school educator; b. Shelby, Nebr., Sept. 5, 1930; d. Harold William Fyfe and Mae Emma Schmid. Assoc. in Elem. Edn., Scottsbluff Jr. Coll., Nebr., 1957; BS in Elem. Edn., Peru State Tchrs. Coll., Nebr., 1963; M in Urban Edn., U. Nebr., Omaha, 1980. Cert. K-12 tchr. Nebr. Tchr. K-8, Polk County Schs., Shelby, 1947—50, Banner County Schs., Harrisburg, Nebr., 1950—53; tchr. 2d grade Albin Consol. Schs., Albin, Wyo., 1953—57; prin., tchr. K-2, Union Pub. Schs., Nebr., 1957—61; tchr. 2d grade Nebraska City Pub. Schs., Nebr., 1961—63; intermediate tchr. Omaha Pub. Schs., 1963—90, substitute tchr., 1990—; adj. faculty Grace U., Omaha, 1984—. 4-H leader Agr. Coll. Ext. Svc. Polk County, 1947—50; vol. tutor Uta Halee Girls' Village, Omaha, 1995—; active Harvey Oaks Bapt. Ch., 1962—; dir. Midway Bible Camp, Thompson, Canada, 1970—90. Mem.: Omaha Area Ret. Tchrs. Assn., Olympian Club. Republican. Avocations: philately, doll collecting, pencil collecting. Home: 6222 Ponderosa Dr Omaha NE 68137-4231

FYFE, WILLIAM SEFTON, geochemist, educator; b. New Zealand, June 4, 1927; s. Colin Alexander and Isabella Fyfe; m. Patricia Walker, Feb. 27, 1981; children: Christopher, Catherine, Stefan. BSc, U. Otago, New Zealand, 1948, MS, 1949, PhD, 1952; DSc (hon.), Meml. U., Lisbon, Portugal, 1989, 90, Lakehead U., 1992, Guelph U., 1994, St. Mary's U., Otago, New Zealand, 1994, Otago U., New Zealand, 1995, U. Western Ont., 1995. Prof. chemistry in, N.Z., 1955-58; prof. geology U. Calif., Berkeley, 1958-66; research prof. Manchester U. and Imperial Coll., London, 1966-72; chmn. dept. geology Western Ont. U., 1972-84, prof. dept. geology, 1984-92, prof. emeritus dept. earth sci., 1992—, dean faculty sci., 1986-90. Decorated companion Order of Can.; Commemorative medal (New Zealand), Commemorative medal (Canada); recipient Logan medal Geol. Assn. Can., Arthur Holmes medal European Union of Geoscis., Can. Gold medal for Sci. and Engring., 1991; Guggenheim fellow, 1964, 83; named hon. prof. U. Beijing. Fellow Geol. Soc. London (hon.; Wollaston medal 2000), Royal Soc. London, Geol. Soc. Am. (hon. life, Day medal), Mineral Soc. Am. (Roebling medal); mem. AAAS (chmn. geology geography sect. 2000—), Internat. Union Geoscis. (pres. 1992-96, Grand Cross Ordem Nacional do Merito Cientifico, Brazil, 1996), Nat. Sci. and Engring. Rsch. Coun. Can., Royal Soc. Can., Acad. Sci. Brazil, Brit. Chem. Soc., Russian Acad. Sci., Indian Acad. Sci., Chinese Acad. Sci. Home: 1197 Richmond London ON Canada N6A 3L3 Office: U Western Ont Dept Earth Scis London ON Canada N6A 5B7 Fax: 519-661-2179. E-mail: pjfyfe@uwo.ca.

FYLER, JOHN MORGAN, English language educator; b. Chgo., Sept. 17, 1943; s. Earl Harris and Harriet (Morgan) F.; m. Julia Ann Genster, Aug. 5, 1978; children: Amanda, Lucy. AB, Dartmouth Coll., 1965; MA, U. Calif., Berkeley, 1967, PhD, 1972. Asst. prof. Tufts U., Medford, Mass., 1972-78, assoc. prof., 1978-88, prof., 1988—. Author: Chaucer and Ovid, 1979; contbg. editor: Riverside Chaucer, 1986. ACLS fellow, 1975-76, Guggenheim fellow, 1982-83, Camargo Found. fellow, 2002; fellow Clare Hall, U. Cambridge, 2003. Home: 126 Central St Concord MA 01742-2911 Office: Dept English Tufts U Medford MA 02155 E-mail: john.fyler@tufts.edu.

GAAR, MARILYN AUDREY WIEGRAFFE, political scientist, educator, property manager; b. St. Louis, Sept. 22, 1946; d. Arthur and Marjorie Estelle (Miller) W.; m. Norman E. Gaar, Apr. 12, 1986. AB, Ind. U., 1968, MA, 1970, MS, 1973. Mem. faculty Stephens Coll., Columbia, Mo., 1971-73, Johnson County CC, Overland Park, Kans., 1973—. Interviewer Fulbright Hayes Tchr. Exch. fellowship candidates, Kansas City, Mo., 1982-92; mem. state selection com. Congress Bundestag Youth Exch. Program, Kans., 1985; pres. faculty del. Kans. Assn. C.C.s, 1984-85; gov.'s appointee, admissions interviewer, mem. selection panel Sch. Medicine U. Kans., 1991-95, mem. admissions criteria and admissions process rev. com., 1992. Author: Profile of Kansas Government, 1990; contbg. editor to instr.'s manual Am. Democracy (by Thomas Patterson). Pres. LWV Johnson County, 1987—89, prodr. candidates forum, mem. governing bd., 1993—95; mem. Johnson County Elder Net Coalition, 1988; mem. governing bd. Johnson County Mental Health Ctr., 1981—86, chmn., 1985—86; vol., translator Russian Refugee Resettlement Program of Jewish Family and Children Svcs., Kansas City, 1979—81; treas. Heart of Am., Japan Am. Soc., 1979; hon. dir. Rockhurst Coll., Kansas City; sec. Ctrl. Slavic Conf., 2000—; alt. mem. Rep. State Com., Kans., 1984—86; chmn. Rep. City Com., Shawnee, Kans., 1982—86; program chmn. Kans. Fedn. Rep. Women, 1984—87; bd. dirs. Internat. Rels. Coun. Kansas City, 2001—, Substance Abuse Ctr., Johnson County, 1983—85, Huntington Farms Homes Assn., Leawood, Kans., 1984—87. Grantee Europaische Akademie, West Berlin, 1984, 92, 97, Fulbright Hayes, The Netherlands, 1982, Japan, 1975; Univ. fellow NEH, 1990; Scholars in Residence grant, Johnson County C.C., 1998, 1999, 2001, 2003. Mem. Russian and Am. Internat. Studies Assn. (sec. 1999—), C.C. Humanities Assn., Kans. Polit. Sci. Assn., Internat. Rels. Coun., Assn. Russian and Am. Historians (sec. 1998-99), Ctrl. ASsn. Russian Tchrs. Am. (bd. dirs. 2003—), People to People, Soc. Fellows, Nelson-Atkins Mus. Arts, Dobro Slovo Nat. Slavic Honor Soc., Phi Beta Kappa, Phi Sigma Alpha. Episcopalian. Avocations: piano, gardening. Office: Johnson County C C 12345 College Blvd Shawnee Mission KS 66210-1283

GABALDON, PAUL JAMES, high school principal; b. Jerome, Ariz., July 25, 1946; s. Paul G. and Mercedes M. (Gonzales) G.; m. Diana N. Jenkins, Aug. 31, 1968; children: Paul Jr., Adam, Jill. BS in Edn., Ariz. State U., 1969; MA in Counseling, No. Ariz. U., 1973; EdS in Adminstrn., U. Ariz., 1980. Tchr., coach Lyle (Wash.) H.S., 1969-71, Amphitheater H.S., Tucson, 1971-75, counselor, coach, 1975-81; asst. prin., athletic dir. Nogales (Ariz.) H.S., 1981-83; asst. prin. Prescott (Ariz.) H.S., 1983-89; prin. Westview H.S., Avondale, Ariz., 1989-92, Monte Vista (Colo.) H.S., 1992—. Coach Little League Baseball, Prescott, 1988, Babe Ruth Baseball, Monte Vista, 1993; treas. White Tonks Rotary, Avondale, Ariz., 1992; vol. Big Bros., Big Sisters, Prescott, 1985-87. Named Ariz. Baseball Coach of Yr., Ariz. Republic, 1980, Ariz. Daily Star, 1980, Tchr. of Yr., Oreg. Mus. Sci. and Industry, 1970. Mem. ASCD, Nat. Assn. Secondary Sch. Prins., Colo. H.S. Activities Assn. (mem. com. 1984—), Inter Mountain League (pres. 1994-95), Monte Vista C. of C. (conquistadores br.), Phi Delta Kappa. Democrat. Roman Catholic. Avocations: fishing, hunting, reading, camping. Office: Monte Vista HS 349 Prospect Monte Vista CO 81144 Home: 800 N Spring Creek Trl Cornville AZ 86325-5811

GABBOUR, ISKANDAR, city and regional planning educator; b. Mansura, Egypt, Feb. 6, 1929; s. Iskandar Gabbour and Mathilde Louli; m. Amy Surur, Feb. 4, 1956; children: May, Tamer, Rami. B.Arch. with honors, Cairo U., 1953; M.Arch., M.C.P., U. Pa., 1963, PhD, 1967. Arch., chief designer Devel. & Popular Housing Co., Cairo, 1954-61; rschr. assoc. U. Pa., Phila., 1966-67; prof. city and regional planning U. Montreal, Que., Can., 1967-97, vice dean acad. affairs, faculty environ. design, 1993—97, hon. prof., 1997—, interim chmn. dept. landscape architecture, 2000—02. Cons. UN Ctr. for Human Settlements, Nairobi, Kenya, 1985; vol. advisor Tech. Studies and Devel. Office, Abidjan, Ivory Coast, 1998. Contbr. numerous articles to profl. jours. Mem. Am. Planning Assn. (charter), Am. Inst. Cert. Planners (charter), Can. Inst. Planners, Royal Archtl. Inst. Can., Assn. Collegiate Schs. Planning, Order Urbanists of Que. Home: 5510 Ashdale Ave Montreal QC Canada H4W 3G4 Fax: (514) 484-8245. E-mail: iskandar.gabbour@umontreal.ca.

GABEL, CONNIE, chemist, educator; b. Green Bank, W.Va. d. William Ashby and Marie Lowry; m. Richard Gabel; children: Greg, Keith, Debbie. BS in Chemistry magna cum laude, James Madison U.; MA in Ednl. Adminstrn. summa cum laude, U. Colo., 1984, PhD in Ednl. Leadership and Innovation, 2001. Tchg. asst. U. Wis., Madison, 1969-70, specialist endocrinology, 1970-71; tchr. Dept. Def. Schs., Tokyo, 1972-74, Poudre R-1 Schs., Ft. Collins, Colo., 1975-78, Boulder (Colo.) Valley Schs., 1985-87, 96-98, intern asst. prin., 1984-85; intern supt. Jefferson County Schs., Golden, Colo., 1992; tchr. Mapleton Pub. Schs., Thornton, Colo., 1992-95; internat. studies Egyptian program Regis U., Denver, 1994; instr. chemistry Colo. Sch. Mines, 1995-98; dean students Horizon HS, Thornton, Colo., 1995-96; project 2061 coord. dept. chemistry/edn. U. Colo., Denver, 1998-2000; instr. St. Mary's Acad., Englewood, Colo., 2000—. Cons. sch. fin. Colo. Dept. Edn., Denver, 1984; rschr. AMC Cancer Rsch. Ctr., Denver, 1993, Colo. U. Med. Ctr., Denver, 1994; display tech. Boulder-Chemistry Rsch., 1995. Charter mem., pres. Friends Louisville (Colo.) Libr., 1985—; charter mem. Nat. Women's History Mus.; charter mem., pres., v.p. Coal Creek Rep. Women, Louisville, 1987—; sec., mem. Boulder County Reps., 1988—98, precinct chair; mem. Nat. Rep. Women, Washington, 1987—; sec. Dist. 17 Colo. Senate, Dist. 13 Colo. Ho., 1993—2002; mem. Colo. Fedn. Rep. Women, 1987—, Colo. Rep. Ctrl. Com. Mem.: AAUW, AAAS, ASCD, N.Y. Acad. Scis., Math., Engring. and Sci. Achievement (dir., advisor 1992—97, mem. state level adv. bd. 1992—96), Colo. Chemistry Tchrs. Assn., Colo.-Wyo. Acad. Sci., Colo. Assn. Sci. Tchrs., Nat. Soc. Study Edn., Nat. Assn. Rsch. Sci. Tchg., Am. Chem. Soc., Nat. Assn. Sci. Tchrs., Am. Ednl. Rsch. Assn., Phi Delta Kappa. Avocations: reading, hiking, gardening. Office: St Marys Academy 4545 S University Blvd Englewood CO 80110-6099 E-mail: connie_gabel@ceo.cudenver.edu.

GABEL, KATHERINE, retired academic administrator; b. Rochester, N.Y., Apr. 9, 1938; d. M. Wren and Esther (Conger) G.; m. Seth Devore Strickland, June 24, 1961 (div. 1965). AB, Smith Coll., Northampton, Mass., 1959; MSW, Simmons Coll., 1961; PhD, Syracuse U., 1967; JD, Union U., 1970; bus. program, Stanford U., 1984. Psychol. social worker Cen. Island Mental Health Ctr., Uniondale, N.Y., 1961-62; psychol. social worker, supt. Ga. State Tng. Sch. for Girls, Atlanta, 1962-64; cons. N.Y. State Crime Control Coun., Albany, 1968-70; faculty Ariz. State U., Tempe, 1972-76; supt. Ariz. Dept. of Corrections, Phoenix, 1970-76; dean, prof. Smith Coll., 1976-85; pres. Pacific Oaks Coll. and Children's Sch., Pasadena, Calif., 1985-98; western region v.p. Casey Family Program, Pasadena, 1998—2001; cons. svcs., 2001—. Advisor, del. UN, Geneva, 1977; mem. So. Calif. Youth Authority, 1986-91. Editor: Master Teacher and Supervisor in Clinical Social Work, 1982; author report Legal Issues of Female Inmates, 1981, model for rsch. Diversion program Female Inmates, 1984, Children of Incarcerated Parents, 1995. Vice chair United Way, Northampton, 1982-83; chair Mayor's Task Force, Northampton, 1981. Mem. Nat. Assn. Social Work, Acad. Cert. Social Workers, Nat. Assn. Edn. Young Children, Western Assn. Schs. and Colls., Pasadena C. of C., Athenaeum, Pasadena Rotary Club. Democrat. Presbyterian. Avocations: collecting, S.W. Indian art, aviary. Fax: 626-449-8501. E-mail: gabelk@prodigy.net.

GABLE, JOHN ALLEN, historian, association executive, educator; b. Rockford, Ill., Nov. 14, 1943; s. Allen Herman and Mary Jane (Kirkpatrick) G. AB, Kenyon Coll., 1965; PhD in History, Brown U., 1972. Asst. prof. history Briarcliff Coll., Briarcliff Manor, N.Y., 1974-77; exec. dir. Theodore Roosevelt Assn., Oyster Bay, N.Y., 1974—; adj. assoc. prof. C.W. Post L.I. U., Greenvale, N.Y., 1977-89; adj. prof. New Coll. Hofstra U., Hempstead, N.Y., 1989—. Editor, founder Theodore Roosevelt Assn. Jour., 1975—; author, editor 6 books in field; contbr. articles to profl. jours. Vestry Christ Ch., Oyster Bay, 1979-2002. Mem. Orgn. Am. Historians. Episcopalian. Home: 64T Glen Keith Rd Glen Cove NY 11542-3515 Office: Theodore Roosevelt Assn PO Box 719 Oyster Bay NY 11771-0719 E-mail: tra_gable@sprynet.com.

GABLE, KAREN ELAINE, health science educator; b. Des Moines, Nov. 12, 1939; d. John E. and Mabel I. (Davis) Clay; m. Robert W. Gable, Jr., Feb. 4, 1961; children: Susan Kay, Barbara Lynne, R. J. Kent. AS, 1969; BS in Edn., Ind. U., Indpls., 1976, MS in Edn.; 1979, EdD, 1985. Registered dental hygienist Ind. U., cert. dental asst. Ind. U. Clin. instr. dental hygiene program Sch. Dentistry Ind. U., Indpls., 1976, asst. prof., coord. program dir. health scis. edn. Sch. Medicine, 1977-81, asst. prof. Sch. Edn., 1981-94, assoc. prof. health scis. edn. Sch. Allied Health & Medicine, 1994—, program dir., 1994—. Contbr. articles to profl. jours. Recipient Disting. Dental Hygiene Alumna award, Ind. U. Sch. Dentistry. Mem.: ACTE/Health Occupations Edn. (mem. policy bd. 2002—), Ind. Career and Tech. Edn. Assn. (Outstanding Svc. awards), Ind. Dental Hygienists Assn. (sec.), Ind. Health Careers Assn. (pres.-elect, pres.), Health Occupations, Supvs. and Tchr. Educators Coun. (treas., pres.), Sigma Phi Alpha.

GABLIK, SUZI, art educator, writer; b. N.Y.C., Sept. 26, 1934; d. Anthony Julius and Geraldine (Schwartz) G. BA, Hunter Coll., 1955. Vis. prof. art Sydney Coll. Arts, 1980, U. of the South, Sewanee, Tenn., 1982, 84, U. Calif., Santa Barbara, 1985, 86, 88, Va. Commonwealth U., Richmond, 1987, Va. Tech., Blacksburg, 1990, U. Colo., Boulder, 1990. Endowed lectr. U. Victoria, B.C., 1983, Colo. Coll., 1983, U. Santa Barbara, 1985, Va. Tech., 1989. Author: Magritte, 1979, Has Modernism Failed?, 1984, The Reenchantment of Art, 1991, Conversations Before the End of Time, 1995, Living the Magical Life, 2002. Recipient Lifetime Achievement award, Women's Caucus for Art, 2003. Home: 3271 Deer Run Rd Blacksburg VA 24060-9075 E-mail: suzi@swva.net.

GABRICK, ROBERT WILLIAM, secondary education educator; b. Mpls., Nov. 11, 1940; s. Michael Jr. and Helen Marie (Lendt) G.; children: Brad William, Ross Michael. BS, U. Minn., 1962, postgrad., 1962, 63; MEd, Macalester Coll., 1969; postgrad., U. Wis., River Falls, 1968-69, 71, 84, U. Va., 1988, UCLA, summer 1990, U. Minn., 1991, U. Mass., 1995. Cert. social studies tchr. Tchr., River Falls, Wis., 1962-70, White Bear Lake (Minn.) Schs., 1970-84, 87—, social studies curriculum leader, 1994—; tchr. Blaine (Minn.) Sr. H.S., 1984-87. Cons. teaching Ednl. Growth, 1974—; reviewer, panelist tchr. scholar program NEH, 1989, mem. summer seminar, 1993; cons. Ednl. Testing Svc., Tex. Assessment of Acad. Skills, Austin, 1990; adj. faculty history U. Minn., 1989—; reviewer, panelist innovative projects tech. U.S. Office Edn., 1993; reviewer Minn. State rev. com. Nat. Stds. Civics and Govt., 1993-94; reviewer, panelist NEH, Humanities Focus grant, 1995, 98, Tchg. Am. History Grant Program, U.S. Office Edn., 2001; judge Nat. History Day, 1996—; congl. dist. coord. We the People program Ctr. Civic Edn., 1998-2003, judge state finals, 1998; summer inst. participant Nat. Gallery of Art, 1999; adv. bd. Coll. in the Schs., U. Minn., 2002—; rsch., evaluation and assessment com. LA County Office Edn., 2002—; presenter in field. Author: Humanities Focus grant: Victorian America: The Birth of Modern American Culture, 1860-1915, 1995-96, Autocar Trucks, 1950-1987, Photo Archive, 2002, Freightliner Trucks, 1937-1981, Photo Archive, 2003; co-author (curriculum for website): Thank You, Mr. Edison: Electricity, Innovation and Social Change; co-author: The Great Depression and the Arts, 1998; contbr. articles to profl. jours. Scholar Am. Studies Inst., COE Found., 1965, NDEA Fgn. Policy Inst., U. Wis., 1968, Inst. for Staff Devel., White Bear Lake Schs., 1972-73, Minn. History Tchg. Alliance, 1987-88, Monticello-Stratford Hall Seminar for Tchrs., 1988, Fgn. Policy Rsch. Inst., 1998, 2000, Nat. Archives, 1998; Allen J. Ellander fellow Close-Up Program, 1973, Nat. fellow Coun. for Basic Edn., 1988, Montpelier Program Nat. Trust for Hist. Preservation fellow, 1989, Ctr. for Civic Edn./UCLA fellow, 1990; grantee NEH, 1989-90, 2000, 02-03, Minn. Humanities Commn., 1990-91, Bill of Rights Summer Inst., U. Minn., 1991, Bill of Rights Edn. Collaborative, 1991-92, NEH Summer Inst., 1992, 94-96, U.S. Dept. Edn., 2003-05; Am. Memory fellow Libr. of Congress, 1999, Gilder Lehrman Summer Seminar for Tchrs., 2002, Assumption Coll., 2003.. Mem. NEA, Assn. Tchr. Educators, Orgn. Am. Historians (presenter ann. mtg. 1995, 98, 2001), Nat. Coun. Social Studies, Nat. Coun. History Educators, Wis. Assn. Tchr. Educators (exec. bd. 1984-90, pres. 1989-90), St. Croix Valley Assn. Tchr. Educators (pres. 1984-86, 95-97), Minn. Assn. History Educators (v.p. 1994—), Minn. Edn. Assn., Phi Delta Kappa (chpt. pres. 1986-88, v.p. pres. membership 1998-2001, found. rep. 2001-2003). Home: 424 165th Ave Somerset WI 54025-7011 Office: White Bear Lake Pub Sc Saint Paul MN 55110 E-mail: rwgabrick@aol.com.

GABRIEL, BARBARA JAMIESON, educator; b. Pasadena, Calif., Jan. 21, 1929; d. Hamer Hershal and Hazel (Kendall) Jamieson; m. Albert Lawrence Gabriel, June 28, 1947; children: Sam Winston, Bryn Patricia Petersen. B.A. magna cum laude, Calif. State U.-Long Beach, 1971, M.A. in Ednl. Adminstrn., 1982. Cert. tchr., sch. adminstr., Calif. Bilingual tchr. Parkview Sch., 1973-78, minimum essential tchr., 1978-80; instructional materials specialist Mountain View Sch. Dist., El Monte, Calif., 1980—, bilingual program cons., 1985—; dir. Title VII project, 1988-89. Mem. State Book Rev. Com., 1979, Four Dist. Task Force, 1979; sec. El Monte/So. El Monte Coordinating Council; mem. 1989, 91, 93 CABE Conf. Planning Com.; supporting mem. Aero-Space Mus., Globe Theatre. Mem. ASCD, Internat. Reading Assn., WSGV Assn. Calif. Sch. Adminstrs. (bd. dirs. 1991-93), Nat. Council Tchrs. English, San Diego Zool. Soc., Long Beach Art Mus., Audubon Soc., Phi Kappa Phi, Kappa Delta Pi, Phi Delta Kappa. Clubs: Alamitos Bay Yacht, (Long Beach, Calif.). Office: 3320 Gilman Rd El Monte CA 91732-3226

GABRIEL, DONALD EUGENE, science educator; b. Brush, Colo., May 24, 1944; s. Max and Vera Ellen (Coleman) G.; m. Evonne Kay Asheim, Sept. 27, 1964; children: Shawn Lee, Dawn Kay. AA, Northeastern Jr. Coll., Sterling, Colo., 1964; BA, Colo. State Coll., 1967; MA, U. No. Colo., 1972. Cert. secondary chemistry tchr. Tchr. sci. and math. Brush (Colo.) H.S., 1967—. Adv. bd. mem. Colo. Sci. and Engring. Fair, Fort Collins, 1980—; ea. zone chairperson Colo.-Wyo. Jr. Acad. Sci., Fort Morgan, Colo., 1980—; co-dir. Morgan-Washington BiCounty Sci. Fair, Fort Morgan, 1975—. Contbr. articles to profl. jours. Pres. South Platte Valley BOCES, Fort Morgan, 1993-99, v.p., 1991-93; Eagle Scout reviewer Boy Scouts Am., Fort Morgan, 1990—; sec., treas. Brush Pub. Schs., 1995-99. Grantee Tandy Corp., 1989, Joslin Needhams Found., 1990; recipient Presdl. award NSF, 1994; named Milken Nat. Educator, Milken Found., 1991, Tandy Tech. Scholars Outstanding Tchr., 1994-95, Pub. Svc. Co. of Colo. Classroom Connection awards, 1993-99, S. Platte Valley Bd. of Coop. Ednl. Svcs. grants, 1995-98. Mem. Nat. Sci. Tchrs. Assn. (Presdl. award 1994), Colo. Assn. Sci. Tchrs. (regional dir. 1993-96, Outstanding Tchr. 1990). Republican. Lutheran. Avocations: arrowhead hunting, rock hounding. Home: 26137 MCR S 2 Brush CO 80723 Office: Brush HS PO Box 585 Brush CO 80723-0585

GABRIEL, JUDITH A. bodywork therapist, educator, writer; b. Reading, Pa., July 14, 1949; d. Daniel Jacob and Alma Geraldine (Wengel) Tobias; m. Cleon Jay Hertzog, Oct. 5, 1974 (div. 1987). BS, Kutztown U., 1971, MEd, 1977; cert. massage therapist, Pa. Sch. Muscle Therapy, Phila., 1989; further tng., U.S. and Sweden. Cert. tchr. Pa., bodywork therapist. Tchr. Hamburg (Pa.) Area Sch. Dist., 1971-96; bodywork therapist, owner, operator Judith Gabriel Integrational Bodywork, Reading, Pa., 1989—; Rebirther (breathwork counseling) Reading, Pa., 1988—. Presenter WIOV Radio, 1997; asst. Patrick Collard's Internat. Apprenticeship, 1997, 98, 99; prodr. concert A Tribute to John Denver: The Man and His Music, Kempton, Pa., 2000; prodr. A Tribute to John Denver: The Man and His Music concert, Kempton, Pa., 2001; organizer Hibernia County Park, Pa., 2002; pres., CEO, The John Denver Meml. Found., Inc.; presenter Tuly's Conf. for Women, Reading, Pa., 2003; prodr., pres./CEO John Denver Meml. Found., Inc.; prodr. concert A Tribute to John Denver: The Man and His Music, Hibernia County Park, Pa., 2002; presenter Tulip Conf. for Women, Reading, Pa., 2003. Choir singer various chs., Reading; stress mgmt. demonstrator Berks Advocates Against Violence, Reading, 1997. Recipient Corp. Achiever award, Multiple Sclerosis Found., 2002. Mem.: Berks C. of C., Assoc. Bodyworkers and Massage Profs. (cert. massage therapist, cert. bodywork therapist). Avocations: reading, walking, singing, meditation, travel.

GABRIEL, MICHAEL, psychology educator; b. Phila., May 5, 1940; s. Michael and Josephine (Alesio) G.; m. Linda Prinz, June, 1967 (div.); 1 child, Joseph Michael; m. Sonda S. Walsh, 1984. AB in Psychology, St. Joseph's Coll., 1962; MA, U. Wis., 1965, PhD, 1967. Asst. prof. Pomona Coll., Claremont, Calif., 1967—70; staff psychologist Pacific State Hosp., Pomona, Calif., 1968-70; NIMH sr. postdoctoral fellow U. Calif.-Irvine, 1970-72; asst. prof. U. Tex.-Austin, 1973-77, assoc. prof., 1977-82; prof. psychology U. Ill., Urbana, 1982—, appointee Ctr. for Advanced Study, 1990-91. Area chmn. Biol. Psychology Program, U. Tex., Austin, 1979-82; mem. rev. panel in behavioral and neural scis. NSF, 1988-91, prin. investigator database system for neuronal pattern analysis project, 1992—, ad hoc mem. biopsychology rev. panel, 1997-98; faculty Beckman Inst., U. Ill., Urbana, 1989—; chmn. Neuronal Pattern Analysis Group, Beckman Inst., mem. neuroinformatics rev. panel, NIH, 2000-. Co-editor: (with J. Moore) Learning and Computational Neuroscience: Foundations of Adaptive Networks, 1989, (with B. Vogt) Neurobiology of Cingulate Cortex and Limbic Thalamus, 1993; mem. editl. bd. Neural Plasticity, Neurobiology of Learning and Memory. Grantee NIMH, 1978-88, 98—, NIH, 1988—, Air Force Office Sci. Rsch., 1988-91, NSF, 1992—, NIDA, 1996-2001. Fellow Am. Psychol. Soc., Internat. Behavioral Neurosci. Soc.; mem. Sigma Chi. Office: U Ill Beckman Inst 405 N Mathews Ave Urbana IL 61801-2325 E-mail: mgabriel@uiuc.edu.

GACNIK, BONITA L. computer science, mathematics educator; b. Pueblo, Colo., Feb. 3, 1948; d. Stanley J. Sr. and Viola M. (Wolf) G. BS in Math, U. So. Colo., 1970; MA in Math, U. S.D., 1988, MA in Computer Sci., 1989; Edn. Specialist, Nova S. Ea. U., 2003. Software engr. Nat. Ctr. for Atmospheric Rsch., Boulder, Colo., 1970-84; assoc. prof. Mount Marty Coll., Yankton, 1989—, dir. acad. computing, 1991—2000. Cantor, choir Sacred Heart Monastery, Yankton, 1985—; vol. Kiwanis, Yankton, 1989—. Mem. Pi Mu Epsilon, Upsilon Pi Epsilon. Democrat. Roman Catholic. Avocations: golf, music, photography, sports, travel.

GADDIS, RICHARD WILLIAM, management educator; b. Tulsa, May 29, 1941; s. Preston Gilbert and Gladys Leona (Booton) G.; m. Janet Gail Roché, Nov. 23, 1974; 1 child, Jennifer Lee. BA, Northeastern State U., Tahlequah, Okla., 1966, MEd, 1971; EdD, U. Ark., 1988; MS in Mgmt., So. Nazarene U., Bethany, Okla., 1994; grad., Tulsa Citizens Police Acad., Broken Arrow, Okla., 1998. Bus. edn. tchr. Vinita (Okla.) High Sch., 1966-74, Oologah (Okla.) High Sch., 1974-77; bus. edn. instr. N.W. Tech. Inst., Springdale, Ark., 1977-86; asst. prof. bus./mktg. edn. SUNY, Oswego, 1988-90; asst. prof. office adminstrn. Lamar U., Beaumont, Tex., 1990-92; MBA/MSM program dir. grad. studies mgmt. So. Nazarene U., Bethany, Okla., 1992—, asst. prof. mgmt., 1992-94, assoc. prof. mgmt., 1994—2001, prof. mgmt., 2002—. Cons., lectr. in field. Contbr. articles to profl. jours. and mags. Mem. Class of XXII, Leadership Tulsa, 1995-96, Spring class Broken Arrow Citizens Police Acad., 2001. Recipient leadership tng. award Mountain-Plains Bus. Edn. Assn., 1974, Dale Carnegie pers. progress award, 1982, Golden Apple award Lamar U. Student Edn. Assn., 1991. Mem. NEA, Am. Vocat. Assn. (new profl. award 1989), Nat. Bus. Edn. Assn., Okla. Edn. Assn. (outstanding educator award 1975, outstanding univ. tchr. of yr. 1997), Okla. Bus. Edn. Assn. (adminstr. of yr. 1994), Northeastern State U. Alumni Assn. (citation of merit 1992), Mountain-Plains Bus. Edn. Assn. (Okla. rep. 1999-2002), Okla. Bus. Edn. Assn. (exec. bd. mem. 1999-2002), Alpha Phi Omega, Delta Mu Delta, Delta Sigma Pi, Kappa Delta Pi, Phi Delta Kappa, Pi Omega Pi, Rho Theta Sigma, Sigma Tau Delta, Delta Pi Epsilon. Nazarene. Home: 704 N Kalanchoe Ave Broken Arrow OK 74012-2273 Office: So Nazarene U 10159 E 11th Ste 200 Tulsa OK 74128

GADSDEN, MARIE DAVIS, educational agency administrator; b. Douglas, Ga., Apr. 27; d. Thomas Jethro Sr. and Louella Helen (Mayberry) Davis; m. Benjamin Franklin Cochrane (div. 1948); m. Robert Washington Gadsden Jr., 1954 (dec. Mar. 24, 1993). BS in Biology, Ga. State Coll., 1939; MA in English/Communications, Altanta U., 1945; postgrad., Oxford (Eng.) U., 1951-53; PhD in English/Lang., U. Wis., 1954, LHD (hon.), 1982; LHD (hon.), U. New Eng., 1991. Cert. English, ESL tchr. Tchr. pub. schs., Cairo, Thomasville and Albany, Ga., 1939-43; tchr. Reed's Bus. Coll., Atlanta, 1943-45; asst. prof. drama, English So. U., Baton Rouge, 1945-47; assoc. prof. Dillard U., New Orleans, 1953-54, Howard U., Washington, 1954-57; researcher, prof. teaching English as a fgn. lang. Am. U., Washington, 1956-59; coordinator, specialist TEFL English Lang. Services, Inc., Conakry, Guinea, 1959-61; chmn. dept. humanities Alcorn U., Lorman, Miss., 1961-63; tng. officer, coordinator TEFL U.S. Peace Corps, Washington, 1963-65, vis. prof., supr. with Tchrs. Coll., Columbia U. Nairobi (Kenya) and Kampala (Uganda), 1965-67, tng. coordinator Africa region Washington, 1967-70, country dir. Lome, Togo, 1970-72; prof. Tchrs. English to Speakers of Other Langs. dept. Am. Lang. Inst., Georgetown U., Washington, 1972; v.p., exec. dir. Phelps-Stokes Fund, Washington, 1972-83; conf. coordinator Africare, Washington, 1983-84; dep. dir. Nat. Assn. Equal Opportunity Higher Edn./AID Coop. Agreement, Washington, 1984-89; ret., 1989. Mem. overseas liaison com. Am. Coun. on Edn., Washington, 1978-80; team cons. internat. edn. transition team U.S. Dept. Edn., Washington, 1980; bd. dirs. fgn. svc. selection bds. U.S. Info. Agy. Author: Minor Playwrights of the Abbey Theatre 1899-1914, 1953, Aesthetic of John Addington Symonds, 1964; editor: Update-NAFEO/AID Quar., 1984-89. Chair panel mem. Africa panel Coun. for Internat. Exch. of Scholars, Washington, 1975-78; pres., treas. Emergency Svc. for African Students, Washington, 1978-92; bd. dirs. Acad. for Ednl. Devel., N.Y.C. and Washington, 1978—; chair Oxfam Am., 1981-89. Recipient citation Philomathians, 1979, White House Presdl. Award for Outstanding Achievement in Internat. Devel. Assistance, 1990. Disting. Alumni award U. Wis., 1988; honoree Nat. Assn. Coll. Deans, Registrars, Admissions Officer, 1978, Club 20, 1983; named one of Top 50 Women in U.S. Govt. Pres. of U.S., 1963; named to Ga. Hall of Fame Chatham County (Ga.) Lions, 1979; named one of Women of Achievement Sta. WETA Radio-TV, 1981; Atlanta U. scholar, 1943-45; fellow La. State Dept. Edn., 1947-51, U.S. Council for Internat. Exchange of Scholars, 1951-53, UNESCO, 1952. Mem. AAUW, MLA, Nat. Coun. Tchrs. English, Nat. Coun. Negro Women (internat. honoree 1982), Teaching English to Speakers of Other Langs., African Am. Women's Assn. (chair edn. and scholarship com. 1973—). Democrat. Mem. A.M.E. Ch.

GAEBE, MORRIS J. academic administrator; From mem. faculty to pres., chancellor Johnson and Wales U., Providence, 1997—, pres., chancellor. Named Disting. Citizen of Yr., R.I., 1989. Office: Johnson & Wales U Office of Chancellor 8 Abbott Park Pl Providence RI 02903-3775*

GAELENS, ALBERT ROBERT, educational administrator, priest; b. Rochester, N.Y., Oct. 3, 1932; s. Gaston and Adrienne (Dhont) G. BA, U. Toronto, Ont., Can., 1955; MEd, U. Rochester, 1958; STB, U. St. Michael's, Toronto, 1961; MA, Cath. U. Am., 1967. Joined Congregation St. Basil., Roman Cath. Ch., 1950, ordained priest, 1960. Tchr. Aquinas Inst., Rochester, 1955-57, 61-62, dean students, 1962-64, vice prin., 1964-66, prin., 1970-77; tchr. Assumption High Sch., Windsor, Ont., 1967-69; asst. prin. St. Thomas High Sch., Houston, 1978-82, dir. guidance, 1982-87, prin., 1987—, mem. found. bd., 1982—. Sch. rep. Coll. Bd., 1980—; religious rep. Diocesan Priest Coun., 1975-77; mem. Basilian Fathers High Sch. Com., 1970-77, 87—; mem. adv. bd. Dewey-Ridge br. Community Savs. Bank, 1972-75. Bd. dirs. U. St. Thomas, Houston, 1988—; sch. leader United Way, Houston, 1987-89; mem. Project Hope, 1971-72, Rochester Civic Music Assn., 1971-77, Urban League Rochester, 1972-77, Maplewood Neighborhood Assn., 1975-77; chaplain Camp Massawepie, Boy Scouts Am., N.Y., 1962, 63, dist. chmn. Otetiana coun., 1974-75; chmn. Longhorn dist. nominating com., 1977 Recipient Disting. Svc. award Tex. Assn. Student Couns., 1986, award Inroads of Houston, Inc., 1986, Nat. Leadership award Soc. Disting. Am. High Sch. Students, 1988. Mem. ASCD, Nat. Cath. Edn. Assn., Nat. Assn. Secondary Sch. Prins., Tex. Assn. Secondary Sch. Prins., Basilian High Sch. Prins. Assn. (chmn. 1989-91), Tex. Assn. Coll. Admission Counselors, Tex. ASCD, Tex. Pers. and Guidance Assn., Houston Pers. and Guidance Assn., Phi Delta Kappa (program com. 1971-72, dist. del. 1972-73). Avocations: gardening, walking, travel. Home and Office: St Thomas High Sch 4500 Memorial Dr Houston TX 77007-7332

GAFFIN, JOAN VALERIE, secondary school educator; b. N.Y.C., Nov. 25, 1947; d. William John and Louise Eleanor (Liebig) Philibert; m. Ira Martin Gaffin, May 7, 1981. BS in Bus. Edn., Rider U., 1971; MA in Student Personnel Svcs., Montclair State U., 1978. Cert. coop. bus. edn. coord., bus. edn. adminstr. and coord. Bus. edn. instr., coord. Econ. Manpower Corp., N.Y.C., 1971-72; bus. edn. coord., educator Northern Valley Regional H.S., Old Tappan, N.J., 1972—; gymnastics instr. Twp. of Teaneck, NJ, 1985—2000. Adj. grad. prof. Montclair State U., Upper Montclair, N.J., 1994—. Recipient N.J. Gov.'s Outstanding Tchr. of Yr. award, 1986. Mem. NEA, Nat. Bus. Edn. Assn., N.J. Bus. Edn. Assn. (legis. com. 1990-92, bd. dirs. 1991-95, chmn. critical issues task force 1991-95, N.J. Bus. Tchr. of Yr. 1993), N.J. Edn. Assn., Eastern Bus. Edn. Assn. (Educator of Yr. 1993), N.J. Cooperative Bus. Edn. Coord.'s Assn. (Bergen sector sec. and pres., Coord. of Yr. 1993), Northeast Bergen Ind. Assn. (treas., bd. dirs. 1978—), Northern Valley Edn. Assn. (sec. 1978-80, 85-86, 91-92, Tchr. Recognition award 1990-91). Avocations: traveling, reading, cooking, exercising, antiquing. Home: 852 W Crescent Ave Allendale NJ 07401-2129 Office: Northern Valley Regional HS Central Ave Old Tappan NJ 07675

GAFFNEY, PAUL GOLDEN, II, academic administrator, military officer; b. Attleboro, Mass., May 30, 1946; s. Paul G. and Elfrieda L. (Piepenstock) G.; m. Linda L. Myers; 1 child, Crista L. BS, U.S. Naval Acad., 1968; MS in Engring., Cath. U. Am., 1969; grad. with highest distinction, Naval War Coll., Newport, R.I., 1979; MBA, Jacksonville U., 1986, LHD (hon.), 2002, U. S.C.; degree (hon.), Jacksonville U., 2002, U.S.C., 2002, Catholic U. of Am., 2003. Commd. ensign USN, 1968, advanced through grades to vice adm., 1994, ops. officer USS Whipporwill, 1969-71, advisor Vietnamese Combat Hydrog. Survey Team, 1971-72, ocean svcs. officer Fleet Weather Cen., 1972-75, exec. asst. Office of Oceanographer Alexandria, Va., 1975-78, rsch. fellow Naval War Coll Ctr. Advanced Rsch. Newport, R.I., 1978-78, comdg. officer Oceanographic Unit 4, 1979-80, dir. Arctic and Earth Scis. Rsch. Office Naval Rsch., 1980-81; mil. asst. internat. security affairs to Asst. Sec. Def. Washington, 1981-83; comdg. office Oceanography Command Facility USN, Jacksonville, Fla., 1983-86, dir. resources Office of Oceanographer Washington, 1986-89, asst. chief, Office Chief of Naval Rsch. Arlington, Va., 1989-91, comdg. officer Naval Rsch. Lab. Washington, 1991-94, commdr. Naval Meteorology and Oceanography Command Stennis Space Ctr., Miss., 1994-97, chief naval rsch. and naval test/evaluation/tech. requirements for the Navy Staff, dep. comdt. USMC for sci. and tech. Arlington, Va., 1996-2000; pres. Nat. Def. U., Washington, 2000—03; commr. U.S. Commn. Ocean Policy, 2000—; pres. Monmouth U., West Long Branch, NJ, 2003—. Grad. rsch. asst. Cath. U. Am., Washington, 1968—. Mem. policy com. Jour. Def. Rsch., 1989-91. Acad. adv. bd. NATO Def. Coll., Rome, 2000—03, U.S. Inst. of Peace; bd. dirs. Marymount U., 2000—03, Fla. State U. Rsch. Found., Jacksonville U., 2002—03, Jacksonville (Fla.) U., 2002—03. Decorated DSM, Legion of Merit with three gold stars, Bronze Star with V; recipient Middendorf prize Naval War Coll., 1979. Fellow Am. Meteorol. Soc., Explorer's Club; mem. Naval Acad. Alumni Assn., Sigma Xi. Roman Catholic. Avocations: running, track and field and cross country announcing and officiating. Office: Office of the Pres Monmouth U 400 Cedar Ave West Long Branch NJ 07764-1898

GAFFORD, MARY MAY, humanities educator; b. Paris, Tex., Jan. 4, 1936; d. Benjamin Earl and Mary Elizabeth (Perfect) Grimes; m. Frank Hall Gafford, Dec. 31, 1958; children: Michelle Marguerite, Georgette Marie. BA in English and Social Studies, North Tex. State U., Denton, 1957, MA in English, Spanish and History, 1958; postgrad., U. Nev., summer 1970. Tchr. English Alpine (Tex.) Pub. Schs., 1959-61; tchr. English and history Houston Sch. Dist., 1957-58; tchr. English and Spanish Grapevine (Tex.) Sch. Dist., 1958-59, Amarillo (Tex.) Sch. Dist., 1962-65; tchr. English, Spanish and Journalism Fabens (Tex.) Schs., 1965-67; tchr. English and Spanish Flagstaff (Ariz.) Schs., 1967-68, Mesa County Schs., Grand Junction, Colo., 1968-71; tchr. English Clark County Schs., Las Vegas, Nev., 1976—. Editor: Ethnic Etchings, 1990-93 (award of Excellence 1991, 92). Vol. Am. Cancer Soc., Las Vegas, 1974—, So. Nev. Dems., Las Vegas, 1980, Very Spl. Arts Festival, 1990-92, youth health fair Nev. Bus. Svcs., Las Vegas, 1989; mem. Nev. Symphony Guild; chair Christopher Columbus Quincentinnial 1990—; bd. dirs., hospitality and publicity chair Summer Theatre; cultural arts bd. State Pks., 1990-2001; publicist Nev. Women's History Project, 1998-2002, 1st v.p., 2002-03; cultural chair Roy Martin Middle Sch., 2000-03. Recipient Nat. Defense Edn. Act. award U. Alaska, Fairbanks, 1966, Spanish Inst. Calif. Luth. Coll., Thousand Oaks, 1968; named Outstanding Woman of Las Vegas, Las Vegas (Nev.) Mus., 2003 Mem. DAR (chair com. Am. Indians), Clark County Classroom Tchrs., Soc. Nev. Tchrs. of English, State Pks. Cultural Arts Bd., DAR (vice-regent 1983-90, regent 1990-92, chair Christopher Columbus Quincentennial 1990—, chair WWII 50th Anniversary Commemoration 1992—, chair U.S. Constn. week 1992—), AAUW (life chair teen-age pregnancy study group chpt. 1983-92, pres. 1976-77, chair coupon clippers 1984-93), Pilot Club (pres. 1989-90, hospitality chair 1993), Nev. Soc. Descs. Mayflower (lt. gov. 1997—, sec. 2002—). Methodist. Avocations: numismatics, antiques, native Am. artifacts, creative writing. Home: 5713 Balzar Ave Las Vegas NV 89108-3184 Office: Roy Martin Jr High 2800 Stewart Ave Las Vegas NV 89101-4799

GAGLIARDI, UGO OSCAR, systems software architect, educator; b. Naples, Italy, July 23, 1931; came to U.S., 1956; s. Edgardo and Lina (Valenzuela) G.; m. Anna Josephine Italiano, July 7, 1954 (div. May 1972); children: Oscar Marco, Alex Piero. Diploma in Math. and Physics, U. Naples, Italy, 1951; DEng in Elec. Engring., U. Naples, 1954. Chief scientist U.S. Air Force, Hanscom AFB, Mass., 1965-66; rsch. fellow Harvard U., Cambridge, Mass., 1965-66; v.p. tech. ops. Interactive Scis., Inc., Braintree, Mass., 1968-70; dir. engring. Honeywell Info. Systems, Waltham, Mass., 1970-75; lectr. Harvard U., Cambridge, Mass., 1966-74, prof. practice computer engring., 1974-83, Gordon McKay prof. practice computer engring., 1983—2000; pres. Gen. Systems Group, Salem, N.H., 1975—; chmn. Ctr. for Software Tech., Inc., 1982-99; vis. prof. Harvard Grad. Sch. Design, 2000—. Mem. NAS rsch. coun. panel Nat. Computer Systems Lab. (formerly Inst. Computer Scis. and Tech.), Nat. Inst. Standards and Tech. (formerly Nat. Bur. Standards), 1985-91, chmn., 1988-91. Fulbright scholar Columbia U., 1955-56. Office: Harvard U 335 Gund Hall 48 Qincy St Cambridge MA 02138 also: General Systems Group 16 Glen Rd Salem NH 03079 E-mail: uog@deas.harvard.edu., uog@gsg.com.

GAGLIOTI, LINDA CRISTA, nurse midwife, educator; b. Bklyn., Apr. 14, 1961; d. Nicholas Cosmo and Emily Marie (Romani) G.; m. Eugene Joseph Venezia, June 22, 1985 (div. Feb. 1991); children: Crista Nicole, Jenna Rosemarie. BSN, Adelphi U., 1983, MS in Perinatal CNS, 1993. Cert. nurse midwife, midwifery preceptor. Staff nurse Luth. Med. Ctr., Bklyn., 1983-89, asst. coord. nursing care, 1989-94; nurse midwife Maimonides Med. Ctr., Bklyn., 1994—. Clin. adj. faculty Coll. Staten Island, 1991-93, Borough Manhattan C.C., N.Y.C., 1993; pvt. practice childbirth educator, Bklyn., 1988—. Mem.: Am. Coll. Nurse Midwives. Republican. Roman Catholic. Office: Maimonides Midwifery Svc 967 48th St Brooklyn NY 11219-2919

GAGNA, CLAUDE EUGENE, molecular biologist, biochemist, anatomist; b. N.Y.C., Sept. 16, 1956; s. Alexander and Leontina (Coda) G. BS, St. Peter's Coll., 1979; MS, Fairleigh Dickinson U., 1983; PhD in Basic Med. Scis., NYU, 1990. Tchg. fellow NYU, N.Y.C., 1982-84, rsch. asst. in biochemistry basic med. scis., 1984-90, instr. human anatomy basic med. scis., 1988-91, instr. anatomy basic med. scis., 1991—, instr. biochemistry basic med. scis., 1991-93, postdoctoral fellow basic med. scis., 1991-93; rsch.-tchg. specialist dept. physiology/dept. ophthalmology U. Medicine and Dentistry Med. Sch., Newark, 1992—. Biomed. cons. Herbert Law Firm, Palisades Park, N.J., 1990—; asst. prof. dept. pathology UMDNJ-Med. Sch., 1998—; asst. prof. dept. life scis. N.Y. Inst. Tech., 1999—; vis. rsch. prof. dept. biology Fairleigh Dickinson U., 1998—; postdoctoral fellow UMDNJ, 1996-98, asst. prof. dept. medicine, 2001—. Author: Cellular and Molecular Aspects of Eye Research, 1990; contbr. articles to profl. jours. Recipient Leonardo Da Vinci award Leonardo Da Vinci Soc., 1976, First Author award Am. Assn. Anatomists, 1986, 89, 90. Mem. Internat. Soc. for Eye Rsch., Histochem. Soc., Am. Soc. Microbiology, Tissue Culture Assn. Achievements include the identification and quantification of Z-DNA and Z-RNA in both normal and diseased, adult and embryonic, mammalian tissues; development of novel molecular biological techniques, and DNA immuno-probes (anti-Z-DNA antibodies, Z-DNA metal probes, Z-DNA chem. probes and Z-DNA binding proteins) for the investigation of the structure and function of human left-handed Z-helical nucleic acids; development of novel DNA probes to turn off mutated genes. Home: 157 Morningside Ln Palisades Park NJ 07650-1917 Office: U Medicine and Dentistry-Med Sch 185 S Orange Ave Newark NJ 07103-2757 also: NY Inst Tech Dept Life Sci Old Westbury NY 11568

GAGNA, ANN MARIE, special education educator; b. Elmont, N.Y., Feb. 21, 1956; d. Wilfred Alfred and Anita Agnes (Henne) G. BA in Edn., U. Miss., 1978, MEd, 1979; postgrad., Nicholl State U., 1982-85, U. Memphis, 1989-92. Tchr. learning disabled So. Elem. Sch., Southaven, Miss., 1979-82; tchr. spl. edn. Labodieville (La.) Elem. Sch., 1982-84, Bayou Bay (La.) Elem. Sch., 1984-86; tchr. physically disabled and medically fragile Shrine Sch., Memphis, 1986-97; tchr. comprehensive devel. class primary class Knight Rd. Sch., Memphis, 1997—. Career ladder III tchr. 21st century classroom tchr.; athletic sports coach Spl. Olympics, wheelchair events dir.; parent contract advisor Tenn. Infant Parent Svcs., 1997—, parent advisor, intake splst. Active human rights com. Open Arms Corp.; mem. tech. adv. panel United Cerebral Palsy; mem. assistive tech. adv. panel U. Memphis. Mem. Coun. Exceptional Children, Friends of Orpheum, Open Arms Corp. Human Rights Com., Delta Kappa Gamma. Roman Catholic. Avocations: cross-stitch, reading, walking. Home: Apt 105 840 Schilling Farm Rd Collierville TN 38017-7060

GAGNÉ, DOREEN FRANCES, nursing educator; b. Altoona, Pa., Jan. 9, 1960; d. Arch Leon and Kim (Youngja) Gunnett; m. Philip Bast Gagné, Sept. 4, 1984; children: Philip Alexander, Laura Elizabeth. BSN, Pa. State U., 1989. Staff nurse pediatric oncology/transplant unit The Children's Hosp., Phila., 1981-85, Johns Hopkins Hosp. Children's Ctr., Balt., 1985-89; educator nursing Anne Arundel C.C., Arnold, Md., 1993—. Co-chair cmty. and project rsch. Jr. League Annapolis (Md.), 1992. Mem. Social Register Assn., Sigma Theta Tau. Republican. Avocations: skiing, running, aerobics. Home: 21 Windward Dr Severna Park MD 21146-2442 Office: Anne Arundel C C Allied Health Bldg Arnold MD 21012

GAGNE, MARGARET LEE, accounting educator; b. Miller, S.D., June 23, 1953; d. E.A. and Helen A. (Simonds) Andersen; m. Ronald W. Gagne, Jan. 2, 1988. B summa cum laude, Huron Coll., 1975; MBA, U. S.D., 1979; PhD, Ind. U., 1989. Tchr. Hitchcock (S.D.) Ind. Schs., 1975-77; staff auditor Banco, Inc., Sioux Falls, S.D., 1979-81; instr. acctg. U. S.D., Vermillion, 1981-83; from instr. to asst. prof. U. Colo., Colorado Springs, 1987-96, assoc. prof., 1996-2000, Marist Coll., Poughkeepsie, N.Y., 2000—. Cons. Walter Drake, Colorado Springs, 1994, Johns Manville, Denver, 1998. Contbr. articles to profl. jours. Treas. St. Luke's Luth. Ch., Colorado Springs, 1987-88; vol. Ecumenical Social Ministries, Colorado Springs, 1995-96. Ind. U. fellow, 1983-86. Mem.: Inst. Mgmt. Accts., Inst. Internal Auditors (bd. govs. 1980—81), Am. Acctg. Assn. Republican. Avocations: reading, walking, crocheting. Office: Marist Coll 3399 North Rd Poughkeepsie NY 12601-1350 E-mail: margaret.gagne@marist.edu.

GAGNON, MARGARET ANN CALLAHAN, secondary education educator; b. St. Paul, Apr. 8, 1952; d. Leo N. and Ursula A. (Iverson) Callahan; m. Stephen A. Gagnon, July 16, 1977; children: Stephanie, Irlonde, Joseph. BA, U. Minn., 1974; postgrad., Idaho State U., 1979-81. Cert. secondary English, French and German edn. Translator, paralegal computer support Control Data, Bloomington, Minn., 1974-75; home svcs. aide Vis. Home Svcs., Salt Lake City, 1975-76; tchr. Glenwood (Minn.) High Sch., 1976-77; bartender Sunwood Inn., Morris, Minn., 1976-78; waitress Papa John's Pizza, Morris, 1978-79; teaching asst. Idaho State U., Pocatello, 1979-81; tchr. Carden Sch., Pocatello, 1980-81; substitute tchr. Pocatello (Idaho) Sch. Dist., 1981-82; tchr.,speech coach Jackson (Wyo.) Hole High Sch., 1982—. Named Tchr. of Yr., Wyo. Fgn. Lang. Assn., 1995. Mem. Wyo. Fgn. Lang. Tchrs. (bd. mem. 1992, sec. treas. 1993-96, pres. elect 1996-98, pres. 98-2000), Wyo. High Sch. Speech Coaches (sec./treas. 1988-93, v.p. 1993-95, pres. 1995-99, Coach of Yr. 1992-93). Avocations: camping, skiing, traveling. Office: Teton County Schs # 1 PO Box 568 Jackson WY 83001-0568

GAGNON, MARIE FRANCES, elementary school educator; b. Fall River, Mass., Jan. 3, 1951; d. Joseph A. and F. Lorraine (Rogers) Goulart; m. Russell L. Gagnon, July 10, 1976; children: Ann Marie, Kristine, Nicole. BA in English & Elem. Edn., Salve Regina Coll., 1973. Cert. tchr., life R.I., 1973, tchr. Mass., 2000. From tchr. 3rd grade to sch. wide enrichment k-8 Wilbur McMahon Sch., Little Compton, RI, 1973—94, sch. wide enrichment k-8, 1994—96; tchr. lang. arts 6-8 Holy Name Sch., Providence, 1997—98; tchr. math & sci. 7-8 St. James St. John Sch., New Bedford, Mass., 1998—2003. State evaluator Future Problem Solving, Little Compton, 1996—2003. Coach Future Problem Solving, 1997—2003; coord. Feinstein Hunger Brigade, Little Compton, 1997, 1998; coord St. Catherine's Ch., Little Compton, 1984—94. Nominee Disney's Tchr. award, Disney Learning, 1999; recipient Marion award, Cath. Girl Scouts, 1991. Roman Catholic. Avocations: gardening, cross stitch, sewing, walking. Home: 49 Amesbury Lane Little Compton RI 02837 Office: St James St John School 180 Orchard St New Bedford MA 02740

GAGOSIAN, ROBERT B. chemist, educator; b. Medford, Mass., Sept. 17, 1944; m. Susan Gagosian; children: Travis, Alex. SB in Chemistry, MIT, 1966; PhD in Organic Chemistry, Columbia U., 1970; hon. degree, L.I. Univ., 2000, Northeastern U., 2000. Asst. scientist Woods Hole Oceanog. Instn., Mass., 1972-76, assoc. scientist, 1976-82, sr. scientist, 1982—, chmn. dept. chemistry, 1982-87, assoc. dir. rsch., 1987-92, sr. assoc. dir., dir. rsch., 1992-93, acting dir., 1993, pres., 2001, pres., dir., 2002—. Vis. lectr. dept. geology and geophysics Yale U., 1975, cons., lectr. in field; mem. numerous vis. coms. and rsch. panels NSF, Office Naval Rsch., univs. and rsch. orgns. in U.S. and fgn. countries; mem. corp. Bermuda Biol. Sta. for Rsch., Sea Edn. Assn. Contbr. chpts. to books, articles to profl. jours. Grantee and fellow numerous profl. and ednl. instns. including vis. scholar U. Wash., 1983, Australian Inst. Marine Scis., 1983; vis. fellow Australian Nat. U., 1983; William Evans fellow, U. Otago, Dunedin, New Zealand, 1987. Mem. Am. Chem. Soc., AAAS, Geochem. Soc. Am., Am. Geophys. Union, European Assn. Organic Geochemists, Sigma Xi. Office: Woods Hole Oceanographic Inst Fenno House MS 40A Woods Hole MA 02543

GAIA, H. VERONIKA, middle school educator; b. Bklyn., Nov. 11, 1947; d. Anthony Paul and Helen Madeline (Callahan) Romeo. BS in Health and Phys. Edn., So. Conn. State Coll., 1971, MS in Health Edn., 1977; postgrad., Southwest Coll., 1986-87. Tchr. health and phys. edn. Chalk Hill Sch., Monroe, 1971—; tchr. Stepney Elem. Sch., Monroe, Conn., 1984-85. Recipient Profl. Devel. award Conn. Assn. for Health, Phys. Edn., Recreation and Dance, 1982, Susan B. Anthony award Conn. Edn. Assn. Human Rels., 1984, Tchr.'s medal Freedom Found., Valley Forge, 1991. Mem. Conn. Edn. Assn., NEA. Home: 27 White Deer Rock Rd Woodbury CT 06798-2935

GAINES, JERRY LEE, retired secondary education educator; b. Seminole, Okla., Feb. 18, 1940; s. Frank Gaines and Jane M. (Crowe) Gring; m. Lorraine Louise Paulson, Oct. 7, 1961; children: Paul Martin, Mark Edwin. AA, Pasadena City Coll., 1960; BA, Calif. State U., L.A., 1964; MA, Calif. State U., Long Beach, 1969. Tchr. bus. Rolling Hills High Sch., Rolling Hills Estates, Calif., 1965-91, Palos Verdes Peninsula High Sch., Rolling Hills Estates, 1991—2002. Coord. driver edn. Palos Verdes Peninsula Unified Sch. Dist., Palos Verdes Estates, Calif., 1970-91, mentor tchr., 1984-93. Co-author driver edn. workbook; contbr. articles to traffic safety publs. Chmn. San Pedro (Calif.) Citizens Adv. Com., 1985-88; pres. South Shores Homeowners Assn., San Pedro, 1986-90, 95-96, San Pedro and Peninsula Homeowners Coalition, 1990-93; commr. City of L.A. Charter Reform Commn., 1997-99, City of L.A. Planning Commn., 2000-02; County of L.A. Workforce Investment Bd., 2002—; bd. dirs. South Bay Credit Union, 1997—. With USN, 1960-62. Mem. NEA, Calif. Tchrs. Assn., Palos Verdes Faculty Assn., Nat. Bus. Edn. Assn., Calif. Bus. Edn. Assn., Am. Driver and Traffic Safety Edn. Assn. (bd. dirs. 1982-88), Calif. Assn. Safety Edn. (pres. 1982-83, 1998-2000), Elks, Lions, Phi Delta Kappa. Avocations: travel, model railroading. Home: 2101 W 37th St San Pedro CA 90732-4707 E-mail: jgaines852@aol.com.

GAINES, KENDRA HOLLY, English language educator, editorial and writing consultant; b. Chgo., Dec. 6, 1946; d. Reuben B. and Frances P. Gaines; m. Kenneth C. Wolfgang, Feb. 18, 1989. BA with distinction, Mt. Holyoke Coll., 1968; MA with honor, Claremont Grad. Sch., 1971; MA, Northwestern U., 1974, PhD, 1982. Cert. life secondary and community coll. tchr., Calif., Ariz. Tchr. English, Claremont (Calif.) Collegiate Sch., 1969-72; teaching asst. Northwestern U., Evanston, Ill., 1975-78; instr. English, U. Mich., Ann Arbor, 1978-79; assoc. editor Scott, Foresman Co., Glenview, 1983-85; instr. English, sr. career tutor U. Ariz., Tucson, 1985—2002, mgr. Grad. Writing Resource website, 2002—; instr., faculty advisor Chapman U., Davis-Monthan AFB, Ariz., 1987—2002. Head Grad. Writing Inst., U. Ariz., 1996—2002; editl. cons., freelance writer, 1969—; lectr. Suzhou U., Nanjing Normal U., China, 1999; mem. adv. bd. translation studies Pima C.C.; writing cons. U. Ariz. Coll. Law; trainer S.W. Gas Corp.; writing cons., mgr. writing resource website U. Ariz., Tucson, 2002—. Contbr. articles to various publs.; writer radio scripts Holiday World of Travel, 1969—. Elected to The Imperial Russian Order of St. John of Jerusalem Ecumenical Found. (Knights of Malta), N.Y.; grantee State of Calif., 1970; Mills fellow, 1971; fellow Northwestern U., 1973-76. Mem. MLA, Nat. Coun. Tchrs. English, AAUW. Avocations: travel, photography, music, creative writing, aerobics. Home: 925 N Jerrie Ave Tucson AZ 85711-1153 Office: U Ariz Grad Coll Tucson AZ 85719 E-mail: kgaines@email.arizona.edu.

GAINES, SARAH FORE, retired foreign language educator; b. Roxobel, N.C., Aug. 21, 1920; d. Stonewall Jackson Fore and Ethel Gattis; m. Clyde Ritchie Bell (div. 1974); m. John Coffman Gaines. AB, U. N.C., 1941, MA, 1944, PhD, 1968, MLS, 1982. Instr. U. N.C., Greensboro, 1967-69, asst. prof., 1970-75, assoc. prof., 1976-85, assoc. prof. emeritus, 1985—. Author: Charles Nodier, 1971; also articles, book revs. Avocations: reading, travel, cats. Home: 3017 Robin Hood Dr Greensboro NC 27408-2618

GAINEY, KATHYRN O'REILLY, art education educator; b. Red Wing, Minn., Nov. 14, 1950; d. Wilfred and Edna (Buchholtz) O'Reilly; children: Jeb, Josh, Seth. BS in Art and Elem. Edn. cum laude, Winona State U., 1972; MS in Curriculum and Instrn., St. Cloud State U., 1978; EdD in Ednl. Leadership, U. Minn., 1996. Tchr. 3rd grade, 6th grade, then secondary art Sauk Rapids (Minn.) Sch. Dist., 1972-81, 82—; asst. prof. art edn. St. Cloud (Minn.) State U. Exch. tchr. to New Zealand, 1995; weekend host to internat. students U. Minn.; designer, implementer K-12 art curriculum Sauk Rapids Sch. Dist. 47, implementer, coord. art and acad. awards program. Artwork exhibited in juried art show; poetry included in lit. publs. Mem. Ctrl. Minn. Arts Bd., 1997—99, v.p. Recipient Excellence in Art Edn. award, 1999. Mem.: AAUW (exec. bd. 1990—96), NEA, Minn. Edn. Assn., Minn. Alliance for Arts in Edn., Art Educators of Minn. (exec. bd. 2001—), Nat. Art Edn. Assn., Kappa Pi, Phi Kappa Phi. Home: 1193 59th Ave SE Saint Cloud MN 56304-9741

GAITER, JATRICE MARTEL, educational administrator; b. Bad Constatt, Germany, Aug. 27, 1953; (parents Am. citizens); d. Leonce and Lulene (Jones) G. BA, Univ. Md., 1974; JD, Syracuse Univ., 1977. Dir. pub. affairs United Way, Indpls., 1977-84; dir. fed. govt. rels. United Way of Am., Washington, 1985-88; sr. v.p. community devel. United Way of Dade County, Miami, Fla., 1988-91; v.p. Mich. Partnership for New Edn., (Mich. State Univ.), East Lansing, Mich., 1991-95; exec. dir. SOS Children's Villages-USA Inc., Alexandria, Va., 1995—. Comm. chmn. Women in Govt. Rels., Washington, D.C., 1986; vice chmn. Human Svcs. Council, Indpls., 1983; speaker in the field. Author: (manual) United Way of America Goverment Relations Manual, 1987; (handbook) City-County Council Handbook, 1980; (directory) Legal Services to the Poor in Indianapolis, 1979; Editor: Immigration Directory, 1989. Pres. Coalition of 100 Black Women, Indpls, 1982-84, Wash., 1986, fin. sec. Wash., 1981-88; govt. rels. com. Jr. League, Indpls., Wash., Miami, E. Lansing, 1983—; chair, Pre Natal Care Task Force Met. Dade County Childrens Svcs Coun., 1991; active mem. Miami Foster Care Action Project, 1989-90, Mich. State U. Distressed Communities Working Group, 1992—, Civic Coalition of Hispanic Am. Women, 1990-91; bd. dirs. Nat. Child Labor Com. Jatrice Gaiter Day proclaimed by City of Indpls., 1984. Mem. Nat. Soc. Fundraising Execs., Nat. Alliance of Black Sch. Educators, Nat. Community Edn. Assn., Washington Jr. League, Alpha Kappa Alpha Sorority. Roman Catholic. Avocations: caribbean/latin art collecting, black collectibles, antiques, travel, power walking. Home: 400 Madison St Apt 1004 Alexandria VA 22314-1750 Office: SOS Children's Villages-USA Inc 1317 F St NW Fl 5 Washington DC 20004-1105

GAJEWSKI, RONALD S. consulting and training company executive; b. Chgo., Feb. 3, 1954; s. Stanley B. and Irene M. (Onak) G.; m. D. June Easley, Nov. 22, 1980; 1 child, Mary Anne. BSEE summa cum laude, DeVry Inst., Irving, Tex., 1977; MBA summa cum laude, U. Dallas, Irving, 1981. Product mgr. Docutel Corp., Irving, 1975-82; v.p. Automated Banking, Dallas, 1983-85; asst. v.p. MTech subs. MBank, Dallas, 1986-87; dir. bus. devel. Uccel Corp., Dallas, 1987-89; dist. sales mgr. Goal Systems Internat., Dallas, 1989-90; v.p., gen. mgr. Acclivus Corp., Dallas, 1991—. Editor: (sales skills handbook) Building on the Base, 1995; mem. editl. adv. com. Sales and Mktg. Mgmt., 1996-97. Bd. dirs. Hickory Creek (Tex.) Property and Zoning Bd., 1995—. Mem. ASTD, Assn. for Svcs. Mgmt. Internat. (bd. dirs. 2003—), Instructional Systems Assn. (bd. dirs. 2003—, v.p. 2003—). Roman Catholic. Avocation: building period antique furniture reproductions. Office: Acclivus Corp 14500 Midway Rd Dallas TX 75244-3109

GAJIC, RANKA PEJOVIC, educator; b. Mostar, Bosnia-Herzegovina, Apr. 30, 1928; came to U.S., 1953; d. Radovan Ilija and Darinka Ducic Pejovic; m. Sreten Gajic, Sept. 26, 1954 (dec. Apr. 1991). Student, Belgrade (Yugoslavia) U., 1947-52; B Art Edn., Northeastern Ill. U., 1973; M Slavic Langs. and Lit., U. Ill., Chgo., 1979, ABD, 1990; MLS, Chgo. State U., 1987; PhD in Edn., Century U., 1995. Acct. Field Enterprises Ednl. Corp., Chgo., 1955-59; ins. policy writer Alexander & Co. Ins., Chgo., 1959-64; fgn. ind. travel agt. Am. Express, Chgo., 1964-69; tchr. Chgo. Pub. Schs., 1974-84, 85—; tchg. asst. U. Ill., Chgo., 1984-85. Exhibited paintings in group shows at Northeastern Ill. U., Chgo., 1976 (3d prize) Mus. Sci. and Industry, Chgo., 1976 (Hon. Mention), North River Gallery, Chgo., 1977, 79 (2d prize 1977, Hon. Mention 1979). Chgo. State U. scholar, 1986; recipient Nat. Collegiate award U.S. Achievement Acad., 1987, Am. Medal of Honor ABI, 2000, Lifetime Achievement award IBC, Cambridge, Eng., 2002, Women of Yr. award ABI, 2002. Mem. Am. Assn. for Advancement of Slavic Studies, U. Ill. Alumni Assn. (life), Mus. Contemporary Art (comm. chair North Side Affiliates chpt. 1999—), Golden Key Nat. Honor Soc. Avocations: art, literature, languages, travel. Home: 5901 N Sheridan Rd Apt 12J Chicago IL 60660-3638

GALANTER, EUGENE, psychologist, educator; b. Phila., Oct. 27, 1924; s. Max and Sarah (Honigman) G.; m. Patricia Anderson, Dec. 22, 1962; children: Alicia, Gabrielle, Michelle. AB, Swarthmore Coll., 1950; A.M., U. Pa., 1951, PhD, 1953. From instr. to prof. psychology U. Pa., 1952-62; research fellow Harvard U., 1955-56, Center Advanced Study Behavioral Scis., 1958-59; chmn. dept. psychology U. Wash., 1962-64, prof., 1964-66; Joseph Klingenstein vis. prof. social psychology Columbia U., N.Y.C., 1966-67, prof. psychology, 1967—. Cons. NIH, NSF, also to industry; mem. Coun. for Biology in Human Affairs; chmn. commn. on biology, learning and behavior Salk Inst.; founder Children's Computer Sch., 1980, sold to CompuServe, 1984; founder, chmn. bd. dirs. Children's Progress Inc., 1999—. Author: Plans and Structure of Behavior, 1960, 2d edit., 1986, New Directions in Psychology, 1962, Textbook of Elementary Psychology, 1966, Kids & Computers: The Parents' Microcomputer Handbook, 1983, Kids & Computers: Elementary Programming for Kids in BASIC, 1983, Kids & Computers: Advanced Programming Handbook, 1984; editor: Handbook of Mathematical Psychology, 3 vols., 1963-64, Readings in Mathematical Psychology, 2 vols., 1963-65, Psych Tech Notes, 1988, version 2.1, 1994. Served with AUS, 1942-46. Decorated Bronze Star. Fellow AAAS, APA, Acoustical Soc. Am., N.Y. Acad. Scis.; mem. Eastern Psychol. Assn., Assn. Aviation Psychologists (pres. 1970-71), Human Factors Soc., Internat. Soc. for Psychophysics, Sigma Xi (past chpt. pres.). Achievements include patent in field. Office: Columbia U 324 Schermerhorn Hall 1190 Amsterdam Ave # 5501 New York NY 10027-7054

GALATIANOS, GUS A. computer executive, information systems consultant, real estate developer, educator; b. Hermoupolis, Siros, Greece, Jan. 18, 1947; came to U.S., 1973; s. Athanassios Constantine and Despina Athanassios (Stefanou) G.; m. Katerina E. Saridis, Sept. 29, 1974; children: Athanassios, Deborah. BSEE, N.Y. Inst. Tech., 1974; MSEE, Columbia U., 1977; MS in Computer Sci., Stevens Inst. Tech., 1977; PhD in Computer Sci., Poly. U., N.Y.C., 1986. Mgr. ops. Solomos Bus. Machines, Athens, Greece, 1970-73; computer cons. Univ. Computer Ctrs., N.Y.C., 1973-77; tech. dir. Computer Dynamics Corp., N.Y.C., 1977-79; assoc. prof., chmn. dept. computer sci. SUNY, Old Westbury, 1979-93, prof., 1993-2000, chmn. dept. computer sic., 1995-98; computer cons. Keane Inc., N.Y.C., 1986—98, Ins. Svcs. Office, N.Y.C., 1981-82, Computer Corp. Am., N.Y.C., 1983-84; mgr. fin. systems Singer/Electronic Systems Div., Little Falls, N.J., 1984-87. Pres. Advanced Computer Cons. Internat., N.Y.C., 1988—; pres. ACCI Properties, Inc., N.Y.C., 1988—. Author: Principles of Software Engineering, 1986, Principles of Database Systems, 1986; contbr. articles to profl. jours. Mem. Statue of Liberty Found. Inc., N.Y.C., 1984, Nat. Fedn. Blind, Balt., 1988, Rep. Presdl. Task Force, Washington, 1984—, Greater Whitestone Taxpayers Civic Assn., N.Y.C., 1984—. Served with Greek Air Force, 1965-67. Mem. IEEE, AAAS, Assn. Computing Machinery, N.Y. Acad. Scis., Am. Mgmt. Assn., Am. Assn. Artificial Intelligence, Am. Cons. League, Hellenic Univ. Club (N.Y.C.). Republican. Greek Orthodox. Avocations: music, hunting, travel, reading. Home: 17-24 Parsons Blvd Whitestone NY 11357-3041 Office: SUNY 160 Havemeyer St Brooklyn NY 11211 E-mail: accidrg@aol.com.

GALBRAITH, BRUCE W. educational administrator; b. Detroit, Apr. 4, 1940; s. Hugh T. and Sybil Louise (Cook) G.; m. Karen Anne Van Dam, Sept. 1, 1962; children: Michael, Elizabeth, Sarah. MusB, U. Mich., 1962, MA in Edn., 1963. Dir. bands Chelsea (Mich.) H.S., 1964-68, asst. prin., 1968-69; exec. sec. Mich. Sch. Band and Orch. Assn., Ann Arbor, 1968-77; dir. arts acad. Interlochen (Mich.) Ctr. for Arts, 1977-87, v.p., 1979-87; mem. exec. com. Mich. Cun. for Arts, 1980-87; headmaster Park Tudor Sch., Indpls., 1987—. Chmn. bd. Met. Indpls. Pub. Broadcasting, 1994-97, exec. com.; music adjudicator Performing Arts Abroad, U.S. and Europe; condr. U.S. Collegiate Choir European tour, 1988—; registrar gen. Cum Laude Soc., 1994—. Editor music jour. Mich. Sch. Band and Orch. Assn., 1969-77; music syllabus, 1971. Bd. dirs., mem. governance Exec. com. Ind. State Symphony Soc., 1994—, chmn., 1994-97. Recipient Gov.'s award State of Mich., 1977; named Outstanding Mich. Prin., Mich. Alliance for Arts in Edn., 1985. Mem. Ind. Schs. Assn. Ctrl. States (1st vice chmn. 1985-87, chmn. 1987-89), Network Performing and Visual Arts Schs. (pres. 1985-86), Assn. Ind. Mich. Schs. (prs. 1982-84), Coun. Am. Pvt. Edn. (Exemplary Pvt. Sch. award 1984), Nat. Assn. Ind. Schs. (bd. dirs. 1991-95), Internlochen c. of C. (v.p. 1984), Meridian Hills Country Club, Skyline Club. Presbyterian. Office: Park Tudor Sch 7200 N College Ave Indianapolis IN 46240-3016

GALBRAITH, FRANCES LYNN, educational administrator; b. Phila., Jan. 16, 1950; d. Noble Galbraith and Frances J. Griffin; divorced; 1 child, Frances Lynn Witucki; m. Spencer McPherson Kuhn, June 23, 1989, (div.); children: Arthur McPherson, Edward James. BA, Rutgers U., Camden, N.J., 1974; EdD, Rutgers U., New Brunswick, N.J., 1986; MA, Glassboro State Coll., 1977. Tchr. of English Lenape Regional H.S., Medford, N.J., 1974-90, cmty. rels. coord., 1977-90, supr. curriculum, 1990-94; tchr. English Shawnee H.S., 1994-96; dir. adult and continuing edn. Lenape Regional H.S. Dist., 1996—. Adj. prof. Rutgers U., New Brunswick, 1981—; chmn. writing com., test devel. N.J. Dept. Edn., Trenton, 1982-94, cons. N.J. Div. Gen. Acad. Edn.; reader, table leader, Ednl. Testing Svc., Princeton, N.J., 1981—; mem. reading and writing adv. coun. N.J. Dept. Higher Edn., 1980-81; manuscript reviewer Harcourt, Brace, Jovanovich; test devel. cons., item developer, Nat. Evaluation Systems, Westinghouse/Am. Coun. on Edn.; cons., workshop presenter Ednl. Info. Resource Ctr. South, 1987—; presenter in field. Mem. Nat. Coun. Tchrs. English (mem. commn. on composition 1986-90, writing achievement awards adv. com. 1984-87; chmn. numerous confs., asst. editor Quarterly Rev. of Doublespeak, 1980-84, other), N.J. Coll. English Assn. (presenter 1983 spring conf.), NEA (presenter conf. 1983), N.J. Edn. Assn., N.J. Assn. Learning Cons., N.J. Assn. Supervision and Curriculum Deve. (exec. bd. 1980-81, editor FOCUS newsletter 1980-81, other offices), Assn. South Jersey English Depts. Home: 118 Sheridan Dr Cape May NJ 08204-3833 Office: Lenape Regional High Sch 235 Hartford Rd Medford NJ 08055-4001

GALBRAITH, MARIAN, elementary school educator; Tchr. West Side Mid. Sch., Reading and Lang. Arts Dept., Groton, Conn., 1991—, various U., 1986—96; with Conn. State Dept. Edn., Fist Assessment Devel. Lab. Served various com. State Dept. Edn., 1986—93. Bd. dirs. Nat. Edn. Assn., 1993—99. Office: West Side Mid Sch Reading and Lang Arts Dept 250 Brandegee Ave Groton CT 06340

GALDI-WEISSMAN, NATALIE ANN, secondary education educator; b. N.Y.C., Nov. 28, 1948; d. Alphonse Vincent and Jean (Banek) Galdi; m. David Allen Weissman, Feb. 7, 1987; 1 child, Adam Justin Weissman. BA, Adelphi U., 1970, MA, 1971; PhD, NYU, 1978. Tchr. Jr. High Sch. 101, N.Y.C., 1971-81, Evander Child High Sch., N.Y.C., 1981-82, South Bronx High Sch., N.Y.C., 1982—. Adj. prof. Mercy Coll., Dobbs Ferry, N.Y., 1976-88; prep. coord. South Bronx High Sch., acad. olympics coach,

1985-87, curriculum developer, 1987-90, 2000-03; tutor, 2002-03. Mem. Union Fedn. Tchr. Avocations: gardening, environmental wildlife affairs, needlepoint, knitting, dog training. E-mail: natalie797@aol.com.

GALE, ROBERT LEE, retired American literature educator and critic; b. Des Moines, Dec. 27, 1919; s. Erie Lee and Miriam (Fisher) G.; m. Maureen Dowd, Nov. 18, 1944; children: John Lee, James Dowd, Christine Ann. BA, Dartmouth Coll., 1942; MA, Columbia U., 1947, PhD, 1952. Lectr. Columbia U., N.Y.C., 1947-48; instr. U. Del., Newark, 1949-52; asst. prof. U. Miss., Oxford, 1952-56, assoc. prof., 1956-59; asst. prof. U. Pitts., 1959-60, assoc. prof., 1960-65, prof. Am. lit., 1965-87; ret., 1987. Fulbright prof. Inst. Univ. Orientale, Naples, Italy, 1956-58, U. Helsinki, Finland, 1975. Author: Thomas Crawford, 1964, The Caught Image: Figurative Language in Henry James, 1964, Richard Henry Dana, Jr., 1969, Francis Parkman, 1973, Plots and Characters in Mark Twain, 1973, John Hay, 1978, Luke Short, 1981, Will Henry, 1984, Louis L'Amour, 1985, rev. edit., 1992, A Henry James Encyclopedia, 1989, Matt Braun, 1990, A Nathaniel Hawthorne Encyclopedia, 1991, The Gay Nineties: A Cultural Dictionary of the 1890s in the U.S., 1992, A Cultural Encyclopedia of the American 1850s, 1993, A Herman Melville Encyclopedia, 1995, An F. Scott Fitzgerald Encyclopedia, 1998, A Sarah Orne Jewett Companion, 1999, A Dashiell Hammett Companion, 2000, An Ambrose Bierce Companion, 2001, A Lafcadio Hearn Companion, 2002, A Ross Macdonald Companion, 2002, A Mickey Spillane Companion, 2003; contbr. articles to profl. jours., chpts. to books, revs. Served with U.S. Army, 1942-46, ETO. Mem. MLA, Phi Beta Kappa. Home: 131 Techview Ter Pittsburgh PA 15213-3820

GALIN, JERRY DEAN, college dean; b. Cullman, Ala., May 22, 1945; s. Herman William and Evelyn B. (McManus) G. BA, St. Bernard (Ala.) Coll., 1967; MA, U. Ala., Tuscaloosa, 1970; EdD, Nova U., 1981. Tchr. math. Morgan County Sch. Sys., Eva, Ala., 1967-74; chmn. mgmt. dept. Wallace State Coll., Hanceville, Ala., 1974-90, dean faculty devel., 1990-93, acad. dean, 1993-98. Pres. Cullman Tchrs. Credit Union, 1982-85; mem. survey team So. Assn. Colls. and Schs., 1984—; ptnr. G & G Properties, Cullman, 1989—; participant radio and TV shows. Bd. dirs., mem. fin. com. Hospice of Cullman County, Cullman, 1989-91; bd. dirs. Helen Keller Eye and Temporal Bone Bank, Florence, Ala., 1990-91, Ala. Sight Conservation Assn., Birmingham, 1990-91, Cullman County Family Recreational Complex, 1990—; pres. Cullman County Electric Coop. Operation Round-Up Commn., 1995—; chmn. Cullman County Quality Cmty. Coun., 1991-93; mem. Cullman Rural Devel. Com., 1989—; lectr. to social, civic and cmty. groups; master of ceremonies for local events. Recipient Knights of Blind award Eye and Temporal Bone Bank, 1990, 100 percent Dist. Govs. award Internat. Lions Club, 1991, Henry and Lucille Sweet award Ala. Lions Club, 1992. Mem. Ala. Econ. Devel. Orgn., Cullman Area C. of C. (pres. bd. dirs. 1993-94), Wallace State Athletic Assn. (treas. 1989—), Cullman Investment Club (pres. 1989—), Lions (numerous offices 1972—, Lion of Yr. award 1988, Melvin Jones fellow 1991). Democrat. Methodist. Avocations: coin collecting, travel. Home: 294 County Road 591 Hanceville AL 35077-8054

GALINSKY, DENNIS LEE, radiation oncologist, educator; b. Des Moines, Sept. 16, 1948; s. Sam and Joyce Geraldine (Givant) G.; m. Daryl Lee Goldstein, Nov. 9, 1975; children: Dana Lauren, David Lawrence. BS, Drake U., 1970; MD, U. Iowa, 1974. Diplomate Am. Bd. Radiology. Intern U. Ariz., Tucson, 1974-75, resident in radiation oncology, 1975-77, U. Minn., Mpls., 1977-78; assoc. attending physician Evanston (Ill.) Hosp., 1978-80; dir. radiation oncology Copley Meml. Hosp., Aurora, Ill., 1980-89, U. Ill. Hosp., Chgo., 1991-93, DuPage Oncology Ctr., Winfield, Ill., 1993; assoc. prof. Rush U., Chgo., 1994—, 1994—; pvt. practice, Chgo., 1978. Clin. assoc. Northwestern U., Evanston, 1978-80; co-dir. rev. course Osler Inst., Lisle, Ill., 1991; presenter Internat. Congress Radiology, 1989, European Soc. Radiation Oncology, 1990. Contbr. articles to med. jours. Bd. dirs. Congregation Beth Shalom, Naperville, Ill., 1984-85; mem. Dist. 27 Sch. Bd., Northbrook, Ill., 1990—. Grantee NSF, 1968; recipient gold medal Am. Coll. Radiation Oncology, 2003. Fellow: Am. Coll. Radiation Oncology (vice chmn. 1991—92); mem.: AMA (del. 1996—), Chgo. Met. Area Radiation Oncology Soc. (pres. 1987—88), Beta Beta Beta. Avocations: golf, coin collecting. Office: Nuclear Oncology SC 6929 Ogden Ave Berwyn IL 60402-3649

GALIZZI, MONICA, economics educator; b. Piacenza, Italy, Nov. 12, 1961; arrived in U.S., 1987; d. Giovanni and Giuliana (Vecchiotti) G.; m. Enrico Cagliero, June 25, 1994; children: Diana Anna, Erica B. BS, U. Cattolica, Milan, Italy, 1986; M in Polit. Economy, Boston U., 1990, PhD in Econs., 1994; D in Polit. Economy, U. Milan, Italy, 1990. Rsch. asst. dept. econs. Cath. U., Milan, Italy, 1986-87; instr. micro- and macro-economics, dept. econs. Boston U., 1989-92; postdoctorate rsch. fellow in econs. of labor markets U. Limburg, Maastricht, The Netherlands, 1993-94; economist Workers Compensation Rsch. Inst., Cambridge, Mass., 1994-98; adminstrv. dir. program on children Nat. Bur. Econ. Rsch., Cambridge, 1998-99; asst. prof. dept. econs. U. Mass., Lowell, 1999—. Co-author (with L. Boden): What Are the Most Important Factors Shaping Return to Work? Evidence from Wisconsin, 1996; co-author: (with Boden and T. Liu) The Workers' Story: Results from a Survey of Workers injured in Wisconsin, 1998; co-author: (with G. Gotz and T. Lin) Predictors of Multiple Workers' Compensation Claims in Wisconsin, 2000; contbr. articles to profl. jours. Mem.: Workers' Compensation Rsch. Group, European Econ. Assn., Am. Econ. Assn. Home: 76 Paul Revere Rd Lexington MA 02421-6638 Office: U Mass Lowell Dept Econs 1 University Ave Lowell MA 01854-2881 E-mail: monica_galizzi@uml.edu.

GALL, ERIC PAPINEAU, physician, educator; b. Boston, May 24, 1940; s. Edward Alfred and Phyllis Hortense (Rivard) G.; m. Katherine Theiss, Apr. 20, 1968; children: Gretchen Theiss Gall, Michael Edward. AB, U. Pa., 1962, MD, 1966. Asst. instr. U. Pa., Phila., 1970-71, post doctoral trainee, fellow, 1971-73; asst. prof. U. Ariz., Tucscon, 1973-78, assoc. prof., 1978-83, prof. internal medicine, 1983-94, prof. surgery, 1983-94, prof. family/community medicine, 1983-94, chief rheumatology allergy and immunology, 1983-93, dir. arthritis ctr., 1986-94; Herman Finch Univ. of Health Scis. prof. of medicine The Chgo. Med. Sch., North Chicago, Ill., 1994—, prof. microbiology and immunology, 1994—, chmn. dept. medicine, 1994—, chief rheumatology sect., 1994-98, assoc. dean clin. affairs, 1996-97, dir. metabolic bone unit, 1998—. Author, editor: Rheumatoid Arthritis: Illustrated Guide to Path DX and Management of Rheumatoid Arthritis, 1988, Rheumatic Disease: Rehabilitation and Management, 1984, Primary Care, 1984; editor Clin. Care in The Rhematic Diseases, 1996; contbr. numerous articles to profl. jours. Chmn. med. and scientific com. Arthritis Found., Tucson, 1979-81. Maj. M.C., U.S. Army; Vietnam. Decorated Bronze Star; recipient Addie Thomas Nat. Svc. award Arthritis Found., 1988. Fellow ACP (coun. Ill. chpt. 1995—, Laureate award 2002), Am. Coll. Rheumatology (founding chair ednl. materials com. 1986-89, bd. dirs. 1992-95, chmn. rehab. sect. 1992-95), Chgo. Inst. Medicine; mem. AMA (rep. sect. on med. schs. 1995—), Arthritis Health Professions Assn. (nat. pres. 1982-83), Am. Assn. Med. Colls., Am. Fedn. Clin. Rsch., Inst. Medicine of Chgo., Ctrl. Soc. Clin. Investigation, Arthritis Found. (nat. vice chmn. 1982-83, chmn. profl. edn. com. 1996—, chmn. ednl. materials com. 1991-96, blue ribbon com. on quality of life, trustee Greater Chgo. chpt. 1997—, exec. com. 1998—, bd. dirs. 1997—, treas. 2003—), Assn. Profs. Medicine, Ill. Med. Soc., Lake County Med. Soc. (treas. 1998-99, sec. 2000—, pres. 2002-03), Sigma Xi, Alpha Omega Alpha (counselor Chgo. Med. Sch. chpt., 1995—, regional counselor 1998—), Alpha Epsilon Delta. Avocations: photography, fishing. Office: The Chgo Med Sch Dept Medicine 3333 Green Bay Rd North Chicago IL 60064-3037 E-mail: egall@aol.com., ericgall@finchcms.edu.

GALL, KEITH M. director; Dir. Enterprise Village, Largo, Fla. Office: Enterprise Village 12100 Starkey Rd Largo FL 33773-2729

GALL, LENORE ROSALIE, educational administrator; b. Bklyn., Aug. 9, 1943; d. George W. Gall and Olive Rosalie (Weekes) Gall Bryant. AAS, NYU, 1970, cert. tng. and devel., 1975, BS in Mgmt., 1973, MA in Counselor Edn., 1977; EdM, EdD, Columbia U., 1988. Various positions Ford Found., N.Y.C., 1967-75; dep. dir. career devel. Grad. Sch. Bus., NYU, N.Y.C., 1976-79; dir. career devel. Pace Lubin Sch. Bus., N.Y.C., 1979-82, Sch. Mgmt., Yale U., New Haven, 1982-85; asst. to assoc. provost Bklyn. Coll., 1985-88, asst. to provost, 1988-91; asst. to v.p. acad. affairs Fashion Inst. Tech., 1991-94; asst. provost curriculum and instrn. N.Y.C. Tech. Coll., 1994-2000, dean students and acad. svcs., 2000—. Adj. asst. prof. LaGuardia C.C., L.I. City, N.Y., 1981-90, Sch. Continuing Edn. NYU, 1983-84; dir., sec. devel. workshop Coll. Placement Svcs., Bethlehem, Pa., 1978-81. Bd. dirs. Langston Hughes Cmty. Libr., Corona, N.Y., 1975-83, 86-92, chair, 1975-79, 82-83, 89-92, 2d v.p., 1986, 1st v.p., 1987-88, chair awards com. Dollars for Scholars, Corona, 1976-99, pres., 1999-2003; active audience devel. task force Dance Theatre of Harlem, 1992-98, hon. co-chmn., 1994-95; active alumni coun. Tchrs. Coll., Columbia U., 2000—; bd. trustees Renaissance Charter Sch., 2002, Queens (N.Y.) Borough Pub. Libr., 2003. Recipient Concerned Women of Bklyn., Inc., 1994, Edn. award Stuyvesant Heights Lions Club, Bklyn., N.Y., 1997, Edn. award Girls HS Alumni Assn., Bklyn., N.Y., 2003, Edn. award Key Women Am., Concourse Village Beach, 2003; grantee Jewish Fedn. for the Edn. of Women, 1986-87. Mem. AAUW, Assn. Black Women in Higher Edn. (exec. bd., membership chair, pres.-elect 1988, pres. 1989-93), Am. Assn. Univ. Adminstrs., Nat. Assn. Univ. Women (chaplain 1987-88, 2d v.p. 1988, 1st v.p. 1988-92, dir. N.E. sect. 1993-96, nat. 2d v.p. 1996-98, nat. first v.p. 2000-2002, nat. pres. 2002), Tchr.'s Coll./Columbia U. Alumni Coun. (chmn. nominating com. 2001-), Nat. Assn. Women in Edn., Black Faculty and Staff Assn. Bklyn. Coll. (1st vice-chair 1986-87, chair 1987-88), New Haven C. of C. (chmn. women bus. and industry conf. 1984), Nat. Coun. Negro Women Inc. (life, 1st v.p. North Queens sect. 1986-89, pres. 1989-93), Nat. Assn. Negro Bus. & Profl. Women's Club (Sojourner Truth award 1991), Phi Delta Kappa, Kappa Delta Pi, Pi Lambda Theta, Delta Sigma Theta (chmn. nominating com. Queens Alumni chpt. 2001-03, chmn. tri-com.-arts and letters, project ch., May Week 1999-2002). Mem. A.M.E. Ch. Office: NYC Coll Tech 300 Jay St Jackson Heights NY 11201-1909

GALL, PATIENCE BETH, elementary education educator; b. Battle Creek, Mich., July 9, 1936; d. Richard Bernhart and Martha Helen (Luedders) Hervig; m. Bruce John Gall, Mar. 18, 1967; children: Bethann, John. BA in Edn., U. Mich., 1958. Cert. tchr., Minn. Tchr. Mpls. Pub. Schs., 1958—70, 1979—2000; ret. Dir. Christian edn. Osseo (Minn.) United Meth. Ch., 1979-84; dir. Osseo Sch. Bd., Maple Grove, Minn., 1979-97, chair, 1983-84, 89-90, 95-97; crew dir. U.S. Dept. Census, Mpls., 1979, with census crew, 1980; chairperson com. to elect state sen., Minn., 1972; leader Girl Scouts U.S.A., Maple Grove, 1979-88; sch. bd. liaison PTA, Maple Grove, 1975-78. Recipient Leadership award Greater Mpls. coun. Girl Scouts U.S.A., 1987, Sch. Bd. Mem. of Yr. award Minn. Sch. Bds. Assn., 1993. Mem. Phi Kappa Phi, Delta Kappa Gamma. Home: 8123 Maple Ln N Maple Grove MN 55311-2203

GALLAGER, ROBERT GRAY, electrical engineering educator; b. Phila., May 29, 1931; s. Jacob Boon and May (Gray) G.; m. Ruth Atwood, Oct. 19, 1957 (div. July 1981); children: Douglas, Ann, Rebecca; m. Marie Tarnowski, July 18, 1981. BEE, U. Pa., 1953; MEE, MIT, 1957, ScD, 1960. Mem. tech. staff Bell Telephone Labs., Murray Hill, N.J., 1953-54; rsch. asst. MIT, Cambridge, Mass., 1956-60, asst. prof., 1960-64, assoc. prof., 1964-67, prof., 1967—. Co-dir. Lab. Info. and Decision Systems, 1986-96; chmn. adv. com. NSF Div. on Networking and Comm. Rsch. and Infrastructure, Washington, 1989-92; mem. adv. coun. Elec. Engring. Dept., U. Pa., 1991-93; chair adv. com. Elec. Engring. Dept., The Technion, Haifa, Israel, 1999. Author: Information Theory and Reliable Communication, 1968, Discrete Stochastic Processes, 1995; co-author Data Networks, 1987, 2d edit. 1992; patentee in field. Recipient Gold medal Moore Sch., U. Pa., 1973, Harvey prize The Technion, 1999, Eduard Rhein Basic Rsch. award, 2002; Guggenheim fellow, 1978. Fellow IEEE (Baker prize 1966, Medal of Honor 1990); mem. AAAS, NAS, NAE, Infor. theory Soc. of IEEE (bd. govs. 1965-72, 79-88, pres. 1971, Shannon Award 1983). Avocations: piano, skiing. Home: 13 Strawberry Cove Gloucester MA 01930-4128 Office: MIT Dept Elec Eng/Comp Sci Rm 35-206 Cambridge MA 02139 E-mail: gallager@mit.edu.

GALLAGHER, GARY W(AYNE), educational services executive; b. Ponca City, Okla., May 13, 1954; s. Linden B. and Lenna J. (Greenshields) Wilson; m. Carole B. Stewart, May 1, 1979 (div. Mar. 1994); children: Heather, Danielle; m. Jani B. Viljoen, Aug. 5, 1998; children: Trevor, Derek, Stephen. BA in Polit. Sci., L.Am. Area Studies cert., Okla. State U., 1975, MS in Curriculum Studies, Supt. and Prin. Adminstrv. cert., Okla. State U., 1995, postgrad., 1995—. Tchr. Ponca City (Okla.) Pub. Schs., 1987-88; transitional sch. and work program instr. seriously emotionally disturbed children Am. Legion Children's Home, Ponca City, 1988-89; social scis. instr. Olive Pub. Schs., 1989-90; social scis. and tech. applications instr. Ponca City (Okla.) Pub. Schs., 1990-98; foundr., curriculum theorist Advanced Academics, Ponca City, Okla., 1999—2001; dir. comml. mktg. Okla. ops. Applied Techs. divsn. Sci. Rsch. Corp., 2002—. Yearbook and sch. newspaper organizer, sponsor organizer West Jr. High Parent Tchr. Student Assn., 1991; student coun. sponsor, 1991—; mem. Okla. Close-Up Exec. Com., 1992; chmn. Middle Sch. Bldg. Budget Com., 1994. Bd. dirs. Jour. Curriculum Discourse, Okla. State U., 1994—, coord. editor, 1995—. Commr. Marland Estate Commn., Fin. and Mktg. Subcoms.; coord. for ednl. activities Cherokee Strip Celebration Com., 1991-93; participant Okla. Bar Assn. Grant Writing Workshop, 1991, Okla. Bar Assn. Programs Advancing Citizenship Edn., 1991, ABA Law Related Edn. Working Conf. on Tech., Boston, 1992, Okla. Bar Assn. Advanced Grant Writing Workshop, 1993; tchr. mentor Okla. Bar Assn., PACE III Inst., 1992; tchr. coord. AT&T Learning Network, 1993; mem. State Dept. Edn. Adv./Planning Com. on Svc. Learning, 1993; chmn. fin. com. Pioneer Free-Net Steering Com., 1994—; active Ponca City Literacy Coun., Ponca City 101 Ranch Old-Timers Assn.; tchr. cons. Nat. Geographic Soc. Recipient Carl Albert Ctr. Bill of Rights Symposium scholarship, Nat. Bicentennial Competition of the Constn. and the Bill of Rights scholarship, 1991, 92, Gov.'s Commendation for Volunteerism, 1993, 94; named Okla. Tech. Tchr. of the Yr., Tech. and Learning Mag., 1990. Mem. ASCD, Am. Assn. Sch. Adminstrs., Nat. Assn. Secondary Sch. Prins., Nat. Assn. Elem. Sch. Prins., Internat. Internet Learning Assn., Internat. Soc. Tech. in Edn., Nat. Coun. for the Social Studies (instrnl. media/tech. com.), Am. Ednl. Rsch. Assn., Nat. Youth Leadership Coun., Okla. Alliance for Geographic Edn., Internat. Assn. Sch. Bus. Officials, Okla. Coun. for the Social Studies, Okla. Hist. Soc., Assn. Ednl. Comm. and Tech., Assn. Childhood Edn. Home: 1813 E Hartford Ave Ponca City OK 74604-2521 E-mail: gwg@cableone.net., ggallagh@scires.com.

GALLAGHER, JANICE MORI, school administrator; b. Brownwood, Tex., Apr. 15, 1944; d. Wade and Mildred Jeanne (Balthaser) M., m. Anthony Patrick Gallagher, Nov. 1, 1964; children: Barbara Petsch, Todd, Timothy, Brenda. BS in edn., Kent State U., 1966; MS in edn., U. Akron, 1985; PhD, Kent State U., 1994; cert. gifted edn., Ashland U., 1984. Eng. tchr. Barberton (Ohio) City Schs., 1966-67, Cloverleaf Local Schs., Lodi, Ohio, 1973-91; gifted coord. Euclid (Ohio) City Schs., 1991-98, asst. supt. schs., dir. spl. programs, 1998—. Instr. Cleve. State U. Inst. Reading Instrn., 1999-2003; art coord., spring conf. OCETLA, Columbus, 1993-94, planning com., 1994-95. Contbr. articles to profl. jours.; illustrator Springboard to Creative Writing, 1988. Active AAUW, Wooster, Ohio, 1994—; Euclid Women's caucus, 1993—; instr., curator Wayne Ctr. for the Arts, Wooster, 1985—; facilitator Word Works/Cmty. Writing Group, Wooster, 1994—. Recipient Career Explorations award Martha Holden Jennings, Cleve., 1993-94, All Things are Connected Ohio Arts Coun., 1994, Teaching Art Criticism, 1991-94, Creative Hook video Sta. WVIZ, Cleve., 1990. Mem. AAUW, Euclid Assn. Sch. Adminstrn. (sec. 1993-95), Ohio Eng. Language Arts, Internat. Reading Assn., Nat. Assn. Gifted Children, Ohio Assn. Gifted Children, Nat. Coun. Eng. Tchrs., Cleve. Coord. of Gifted, Word Works Writers Group, Wooster Artists Group Efforts. Home: 241 E Beverly Rd Wooster OH 44691-2266 Office: Euclid City Schs 651 E 222nd St Euclid OH 44123-2031 E-mail: jgallagher@euclid.k12.oh.us.

GALLAGHER, JOHN FRANCIS, education educator; s. John Charles Edward and Marion (McKeon) G.; m. Georgiana Frances Cole; children: Kristen Marie, John David. BA in Philosophy, Mary Immaculate Coll.; STD in Theology, U. Fribourg, Switzerland; MS in Indsl. Rels., EdD, Rutgers U. Instr. Mary Immaculate Coll., Northampton, Pa., 1962-65; asst. prof. Coll. St. Vincent De Paul, Boynton Beach, Fla., 1965-69, pres., 1966-70, assoc. prof., 1969-70; advisor instructional resources SUNY, Plattsburgh, 1970-71; dean humanities Brookdale Community Coll., Lincroft, N.J., 1971-73, v.p. acad., 1973-81; dir. Rockland Campus Iona Coll., New Rochelle, N.Y., 1981-83, dean Sch. Gen. Studies, 1983-89, provost, v.p. acad. affairs, 1989-95, prof. edn., 1995—. Mem. coll. evaluation team N.J. Dept. Higher Edn., Trenton, 1975-77, N.Y. State Edn. Dept., Albany, 1980—; coord. coll. activities to achieve accreditation by Nat. Coun. for Accreditation of Tchr. Edn., 1999—, chief instnl. rep., 1999—. Chair County Arts Festival, Monmouth County, N.J., 1972; trustee Monmouth County Arts Coun., Red Bank, N.J., 1973-76. Mem. Am. Ednl. Studies Assn., Philosophy of Edn. Soc., Soc. for History Edn., Mid. States Assn. Colls. and Scis. (coll. evaluation team 1976—), Phi Delta Kappa. Avocations: photography, classical music, tennis. Office: Iona Coll Dept Edn New Rochelle NY 10801 E-mail: jgallagher@iona.edu.

GALLAGHER, KATHRYN KASICH, elementary school educator; b. Litchfield, Ill., Dec. 30, 1951; d. William and Joan Teresa (Jatcko) Kasich; m. Larry Eugene Gallagher, Oct. 25, 1980; children: Vanita Eleanor, Michael Edward. BA in French, So. Ill. U., Edwardsville, 1974, MS in Elem. Edn., 1978, BA in Music, 1988. Ind. piano/voice tchr., Edwardsville, 1971—; instructional aide Edwardsville Jr. H.S., 1978-79, Montessori Sch., Edwardsville, 1979-80; organist St. Boniface Ch., Edwardsville, 1988-91; singer/soprano St. Louis Chamber Chorus, 1989-94; music dir. Sts. John & James, Ferguson, Mo., 1991-95; tchr. Our Lady of Fatima, Florissant, Mo., 1994-97, St. Ambrose Sch., Godfrey, Ill., 1997—. Music dir. Cath. Campus Ministries, Edwardsville, 1998—. Mem. pastoral coun. St. Boniface Ch., Edwardsville, 1988-93; mem. friends of Music, So. Ill. U.-Edwardsville, 1997—, friends of Watershed Nature Ctr., Edwardsville, 1996—; cantor St. Boniface/St. Mary's, 1986-94. Mem. Nat. Guild of Piano Tchrs., Nat. Music tchrs. Assn., Ill. State Music Tchrs. Assn., Choristers Guild. Democrat. Roman Catholic. Avocations: swimming, knitting, cooking. Office: St Ambrose Catholic Sch 820 Homer Adams Pkwy Godfrey IL 62035

GALLAGHER, M. CATHERINE, English literature educator; b. Denver, Feb. 16, 1945; d. John Martin and Mary Catherine Sullivan; m. Martin Evan Jay, July 6, 1974; children: Margaret Shana, Rebecca Erin. BA, U. Calif., Berkeley, 1972, MA, 1974, PhD, 1979. Asst. prof. U. Denver, 1979-80, U. Calif., Berkeley, 1980-84, assoc. prof., 1984-90, prof., 1990—. Author: The Industrial Reformation of English Fiction, 1985, Nobody's Story, 1994; co-author: The Making of the Modern Body, 1987, Practicing New Historicism, 2000; editor Representation, 1983—. Guggenheim fellow Guggenheim Found., 1989; fellow NEH, 1990, ACLS, 1990, Mem. MLA (del. assembly mem. 1985-86, exec. com. lit. criticism divsn. 1991-94), Am. Acad. Arts and Scis., Acad. Lit. Studies, Brit. Studies Assn., The Dickens Soc. Office: U Calif Dept English Berkeley CA 94720-0001

GALLAGHER, PATRICIA HIRSCH, nurse, educator; b. Erie, Pa., Nov. 24, 1945; d. Albert and Gertrude (Fiolek) Hirsch; m. William B. Gallagher Jr., Feb. 2, 1974; children: Michelle, Nichole. BS, Villa Maria Coll., 1967; postgrad., U. Pitts., 1969-71; MS, Duquesne U., 1973. Instr. Presbyn. Sch. Nursing, Pitts., Duquesne U., Pitts., Allegheny Community Coll., Pitts.; asst. chair BSN program Waynesburg (Pa.) Coll. Profl. test writer C. Mosby Co.; expert witness nursing stds. Contbr. to nursing publs. Grantee Pa. State Dept. Nursing, Helene Fuld Health Trust. Mem. Nat. League Nursing, Villa Maria Coll. Alumnae, Sigma Theta Tau. Home: 2594 Rossmoor Dr Pittsburgh PA 15241-2584

GALLAGHER, ROSANNA BOSTICK, elementary educator, administrator; b. Kingman, Ariz., May 16, 1949; d. Charles Topp and Mary (Lisalda) Bostick; m. Richard Kent Gallagher, June 18, 1971; children: Richard Jonathon, Ryan Charles. BA in Elem. and Spl. Edn., U. Ariz., 1971, MA in Bilingual Adminstrn., 1986, postgrad., 1995—. Cert. tchr., spl. edn. tchr., adminstr., Ariz. Tchr. learning disabled students Tucson (Ariz.) Unified Sch. Dist., 1973-75, curriculum specialist Davis Sch., 1975-77, multi-cultural resource tchr., 1979-81, curriculum generalist, 1981-87, prin. Drachman Primary Magnet Sch., 1987-93, prin. Robins Elem., 1994—. Mentor Prescott Coll., Tucson, 1988—; instr. U. Phoenix, Tucson, 1988—; nat. cons., presenter Curriculum Assocs. Pub., 1990—; GAPS adv. bd. Pima County Health Dept., Tucson, 1991—; pres. Teaching Rainbow Publs., Tucson,1 980-83. Author: Rainbow of Activities, 1982, Chalkboard Activities, 1985, Counting Creatures, 1990, Abracadabra ABCs, 1990, Tantos Niñoto/So Many Children, 1993, Rub-a-Dubb-Dub/Uno Dos Tres, 1993, Sometimes..., 1995. Adv. bd. Tucson area Girl Scouts U.S., 1988; choir mem. St. Mark's Meth. Ch., Tucson, 1988-92, coord. Time-With-Children program, 1991-93; com. mem. Pima County Interfaith Coun. Edn., Tucson, 1992; pres. Tucson Unified Ednl. Leaders Inc., 1997—; bd. dirs. GAP program PIma County Health Dept., 1990—. Recipient Outstanding Adminstr. award Tucson Assn. Bilingual Edn., 1990, Copper Letter award City of Tucson, 1994; named Tucson Woman on the Move YWCA, 1989. Mem. Tucson Adminstrs. Assn. (bd. dirs. 1988-89), Tucson Assn. Bilingual Adminstrs., U. Ariz. Coll. Edn. Alumni Bd. Home: 867 W Placita Mesa Fria Tucson AZ 85704-4746 Office: Robins Elem Sch 3939 N Magnetite Ln Tucson AZ 85745-9167

GALLAHER, CAROLYN COMBS, secondary education educator; b. Lakewood, Ohio, June 27, 1939; d. Andrew Grafton and Wilhelmina D. (Jackson) Combs; m. Thomas F. Gallaher, Apr. 2, 1966; children: Andrew Brooks, Sloan T.F., Sarah Jane Bloodworth. BA, Duke U., 1961; MA, Columbia U., 1965; MA in ESL, Manhattanville Coll. Cert. history and Spanish tchr., N.Y. Tchr. Am. High Sch., San Salvador, El Salvador, 1961-62; Peace Corps vol. Ednl. TV, Colombia, South America, 1965-67; tchr. Tarrytown (N.Y.) High Sch., 1969-70, The Masters Sch., Dobbs Ferry, N.Y., 1979-93, dept. head, Lightner endowed history chair, 1988-93; grad. asst. ESL inst. Manhattanville Coll., Purchase, N.Y., 1994-95; adj. prof. ESL Equal Opportunity Ctr. Westchester C.C., 1994—98; tchr. Ursuline Sch., New Rochelle, NY, 1997—. Originator ann. Conf. Advanced Placement Students; curriculum cons.; presenter Western Europe Inst. Workshop Columbia U.; Newly Ind. States-US Tchr. Exchange Program; grader Advanced Placement European History, Coll. Bd. Mem. various bds. Life Ctr.-Environ. Organ, Larchmont, N.Y., 1976—; vestry St. John's Episcopal Ch., Larchmont, 1986-89. Recipient Fulbright grant U.S. Govt., Yugoslavia, 1989, NEH grant U.S. Govt., Dept. Edn. grant U.S. Govt. Mem. Nat. Coun. Social Studies, Westchester Coun. Social Studies, Phi Delta Kappa. Home: 2 Lyons Pl Larchmont NY 10538-3810

GALLAS, MARTIN HANS, librarian; b. Berlin, Nov. 23, 1947; came to U.S., 1953; s. Ernst Gallas and Kate Lesser; m. Myoung Ok Lee, Dec. 23, 1977; children: Monica, Matthew. AA, Springfield (Ill.) Coll., 1971; AB, U. Ill., 1973, MLS, 1974. Reference libr. Starved Rock Libr. Sys., Ottawa, Ill., 1979—81; libr. dir. Springfield Coll., 1974—79, Oakland City U., Ind.,

1981—86, Ill. Coll., Jacksonville, 1986—. Translator: German POW documents for www.kriegsgefangen.de. With U.S. Army, 1965-68. Avocation: shortwave radio. Office: Ill Coll Schewe Libr 1101 W College Ave Jacksonville IL 62650-2212

GALLATIN, NANCY MAE, retired elementary education educator; b. Downing, Mo., Oct. 5, 1934; d. Russell W. and Louise I. (Farland) Morgan; m. Harlie Kay Gallatin, Aug. 5, 1954; children: Kaylene Cox, Rhonda Proffitt, Morgan. A in Edn., Hannibal-LaGrange Coll., 1954; BA, SW Baptist Coll., 1970. 2d grade tchr. Englewood Elem. Sch., Kansas City North, Mo., 1954-57; libr. sec. U. Ill., Urbana, 1965-69; 1st, 2d grade tchr. Fair Play (Mo.) Elem. Sch., 1970-77; kindergarten tchr. Bolivar (Mo.) R-I Sch., 1977-85, reading tchr. grades 1-3, 1985-95; reading tchr. grades 4-5 Bolivar Intermediate Sch., 1995-99, ret., 1999. Active PTA, Bolivar, 1969-99; Sunday sch. tchr. 1st Bapt. Ch., Bolivar, 1962—. Mem. Mo. State Tchrs. Assn., Mo. Ret. Tchrs. Assn. (pres. 2003—), Polk County Ret. Tchrs. Assn., Kappa Kappa Iota (pres. local chpt. 1992-95, pres. S.W. area coun. 1995-97, 2003). Avocations: collecting cardinals and bells, gardening, roses, reading.

GALLAWAY, GLADYS MCGHEE, elementary education educator; b. Detroit, Oct. 5, 1931; d. William A. and Elsie P. (Cooper) McGhee; m. Lowell E. Gallaway, Dec. 18, 1953; children: Kathleen, Michael, Ellen. BSc, Ohio State U., 1953; student, U. Minn., Ohio U. Cert. elem. edn. Instr. Ohio U., Athens; tchr. grade 5 Athens City Schs. Pres. conf. Coun. Tchrs. English, 1988, conf. Ohio Reading Coun., 1988. Author: Take Me To Your Leaders, 1993. Martha Holden Jennings grantee, 1984; Martha Holden Jennings scholar, 1989; recipient Literacy award Appalacian Reading Coun., 1992. Mem. Appalachian Reading Coun. (past pres.), Internat. Reading Assn., OCIRA (field rep. area 9), Ohio Coun. for Social Studies (Tchr. of Yr. 1989), Phi Delta Kappa (hon.). Home: 33 Longview Heights Rd Athens OH 45701-3335

GALLEN, MARYANNE B. special education educator; b. St. Louis, Sept. 13, 1960; d. Leonard and Patricia (Brennan) Dino. BA, Maryville U., St. Louis, 1983. Cert. tchr., Mo. Primary tchr. St. Joseph Sch., Manchester, Mo., 1983-87, 88-90; kindergarten tchr. St. Andrew Sch., Lemay, Mo., 1987-88; jr. high tchr. Dept. Spl. Edn., St. Christopher's Learning Ctr., Florrisant, Mo., 1991—. Mem. Nat. Cath. Educators Assn. Roman Catholic. Office: St Christophers Sch 11755 Mehl Ave Florissant MO 63033-7208

GALLETTI, MARIE ANN, English language and linguistics educator; b. N.Y.C., Nov. 25, 1944; d. Fidel G. and Marie Theresa (Chaumard) G.; m. Wayne Lee Mitchell. BA cum laude, Queens Coll. CUNY, 1965; MA, Hunter Coll. CUNY, 1971; M in Counseling, Ariz. State U., 1981. Prof. English Glendale (Ariz.) Cmty. Coll. Maricopa Cmty. Coll. Dist., 1975—. Co-editor: (anthologies) Native American Substance Abuse, 1982, American Indian Families: Developmental Strategies, 1982. Mem. Nature Conservancy, 1984—, World Wildlife Fund, 1984—, Humane Soc. of U.S., 1984—, Ellis Island Found., 1986—; founding mem. 390th Meml. Mus. Found., Tuscon, 1994. Recipient Regents' scholarship N.Y. State Bd. Regents, 1961. Mem. AAUP, Phi Beta Kappa (founding v.p. Phoenix met. area chpt. 1981-83), Phi Delta Kappa. Office: Glendale Cmty Coll 6000 W Olive Ave Glendale AZ 85302-3006

GALLI, JOHN RONALD, physicist, educator; b. Salt Lake City, Oct. 10, 1936; s. John Lester and Ella Mae (Lewis) G.; m. Marica Lee Jackson, Mar. 21, 1960 (div. July 1, 1977); children: Shawnee Sue Galli Petersen, Sherri Kay Galli Bond; m. Cheryl Maur Corley, June 2, 1978; children: Debora Maur Galli Baird, Diana Lynn, John David. PhD in Physics, U. Utah, 1963. Physicist Naval Weapons Ctr., China Lake, Calif., summer 1958, 59, Aerojet Gen., Downy, Calif., 1963; prof. Physics Weber State U., Ogden, Utah, 1963—, dept. chair physics, 1964-70, 83-95, dean Coll. of Sci., 1995—2003. Inventor: Mechanical Twisting Cat, 1993; contbr. various publs. and presentations, 1963-95. Mem. Golden Key, Am. Assn. Physics Tchrs., Phi Kappa Phi. Mem. Lds Ch. Avocations: skiing, golf.

GALLIAN, JOSEPH ANTHONY, mathematics educator; b. New Kennington, Pa., Jan. 5, 1942; s. Joseph Anthony Gallian and Alvira Helen (Gardner) Strauss; m. Charlene Toy, May 29, 1965; children: William, Ronald, Kristin. BA, Slippery Rock State U., 1966; MA, U. Kans., 1968; PhD, Notre Dame U., 1971. Vis. asst. prof. Notre Dame (Ind.) U., 1971-72; asst. prof. U. Minn., Duluth, 1972-76, assoc. prof., 1976-80, prof., 1980—. Nat. coord. Math. Awareness Month, 2003; adv. bd. Math. Horizens, 1993—; chmn. Math. and Computer Sci. Divsn. Coun. Undergraduate Rsch. Author: Contemporary Abstract Algebra, 1990, 5th edit., 2002, For All Practical Purposes, 6th edit., 2003, Principals and Practices of Mathematics, 1997; editor: American Mathematical Society, 2000; assoc. editor Math. Mag., 1981-85, Am. Math. Monthly, 1992—, MAA OnLine, 1997—. Fellow Coun. Undergraduate Rsch., 2002. Mem.: Math. Assn. Am. (2d v.p. 2002—, Trevor Evans award 1996, Deborah and Franklin Tepper Haimo award 1993, Allendoerfer award 1977). Home: 1522 Triggs Ave Duluth MN 55811-2742 Office: Univ Minn Dept Math and Stats Solon Campus Ctr 140 1117 University Dr Duluth MN 55812-3000*

GALLIHER, CLARICE A. ANDREWS, secondary education educator; b. Laporte, Minn., June 28, 1922; d. Clarence Ray and Luella Anna (Leitch) Andrews; m. Ralph Galliher, June 5, 1943 (dec. Oct. 1985); children: William, Rosemary, Rosanne, Andrew. BS in Secondary Edn., St. Cloud State Coll., 1942; MS, Bemidji State U., 1967. Tchr. math. Ind. Sch. Dist. 111, Baudette, Minn., 1942-43; tchr. math. and sci. Ind. Sch. Dist. 306, Laporte, Minn., 1943-47; tchr. math. Ind. Sch. Dist. 564, Thief River Falls, Minn., 1965-79. Clk. Ind. Sch. Dist. 303 Bd. Edn., Guthrie, Minn., 1948-65; mem. sch. survey com. Hubbard county, Minn., 1961-65. Author of poems; contbr. travel articles to pubs. Mem. United Way, Thief River Falls, 1975-77, pres., 1977; mem. Bus. and Profl. Women's Club, Thief River Falls, 1973-89, pres., 1977-78, chair Pennington County Ind. Reps., 1974; life mem. N.W. Med. Ctr. Aux., 1980—, sec., 1989-92, v.p., 1992-93, pres., 1993-94; v.p. United Meth. Women, 1987-90, pres., 1993-97; adminstrv. coun. sec. Thief River Falls United Meth. Ch., 1984-91. Named Pennington County Outstanding Sr. Citizen, 2001. Mem. AARP, AAUW (Woman of Honor 2000), NEA (life), Nat. Coun. Tchrs. Math. (life), Minn. Edn. Assn. (life), N.W. Minn. Ret. Educators (v.p. 1983-94, co-pres. 1999-2000), Ret. Educators Assn. Minn. (life), Am. Legion Aux. (life), Thief River Falls Nutrition Coun., N.W. Minn. Sr. Fedn. (sec. 1998-2003), Mensa (life), Delta Kappa Gamma Soc. Internat. (editor MN newsletter 1981-95). Avocations: travel, crafts, photography, gardening, writing.

GALLINOT, RUTH MAXINE, educational consultant; b. Carlinville, Ill., Feb. 16, 1925; d. Martin Mike and Augusta (Kumpus) G. BS, Roosevelt U., Chgo., 1971, MA with honors, 1974; PhD, The Union Inst., Cin., 1978. Adminstrv. asst., exec. sec. Karoll's Inc., Chgo., 1952-66; asst. dean Cen. YMCA Community Coll., Chgo., 1966-81, dir. life planning inst., 1979-80; pres. Gallinot & Assocs., Chgo., St. Louis and Bethalto, Ill., 1980—. Mem. task force Office Sr. Citizens and Handicapped, City of Chgo., 1971-79; mem. criteria and guidelines com. Internat. Assn. for Continuing Edn. and Tng., 1983-86, survey and rsch. com., 1984-88; team chair accreditation evaluation team Accrediting Commn. Ind. Colls. and Schs., Washington, 1983-88; instr. Grad. Sch., USDA, 1984—, Coun. Rehab. Affiliates, Chgo., 1985—. Developer leisure time adult edn. series for elderly Uptown model cities area dept. human resources City of Chgo., 1970; editor: Certified Professional Secs. Rev., 1983; reporter Greater Alton Pub. Co., 1987-89; contbr. articles to profl. jours. Chmn. Commn. Status of Women in State of Ill., 1963-68; del. White House Conf. on Equal Pay, 1963, White House Conf. on Civil Rights, 1965, City of Chgo. White House Conf. on Info. and Libr., 1976, State of Ill. White House Conf. Info. Svcs. and Libr. Svcs., 1977; life mem. Mus. Lithuanian Culture, Chgo., 1973—; pub. mem. Fgn. Svc. Selection Bd. U.S. Dept. State, 1984; bd. dirs. Luths. for Chgo., 1978-83, also founding member; member adv. edn. com. Chgo. Commn. Human Rels., 1968-75 fundraising chmn. Bethalto (Ill.) Sr Citizens new bldg. furnishings, 1990-91, pres. 1995-97; mem. dist. adv. com. Bethalto (Ill.) Cmty. Unit Sch. Dist. # 8, 1997—. Recipient Leadership in Civic, Cultural and Econ. Life of the City award YWCA, Chgo., 1972, Achievement in Field Edn. award Operation P.U.S.H., Chgo., 1975. Mem.: Literacy Coun. Chgo. (bd. dirs. 1979—86), Nat. Assn. Parliamentarians (Ill. and Chgo. chpts.), Assn. Cert. Profl. Secs., Edn. Network Older Adults (v.p., sec. 1979—86), Internat. Assn. Adminstrv. Profls. (pres. 1961—63, ednl. cons. 1980—84), Zonta Internat. (treas. Chgo. club 1965—66). Lutheran. Home and Office: Gallinot & Assocs 210 James St Bethalto IL 62010-1318

GALLO, DONALD ROBERT, retired English educator; b. Paterson, N.J., June 1, 1938; s. Sergio and Thelma Mae (Lowe) G.; m. C.J. Bott, Feb. 14, 1997; 1 child, Brian Keith; 1 stepchild, Christian Perrett. BA in English, Hope Coll., 1960; MAT in English Edn., Oberlin Coll., 1961; PhD in English Edn., Syracuse U., 1968. English tchr. Bedford Jr. High Sch., Westport, Conn., 1961-65; rsch. assoc. Syracuse (N.Y.) U., 1965-67; from asst. prof. to assoc. prof. edn. U. Colo., Denver, 1968-72; reading specialist Golden Jr. High Sch., Jefferson County Pub. Schs., Colo., 1972-73; prof. English Cen. Conn. State U., New Britain, 1973-97. Instr. composition Onondaga C. C., Syracuse, 1967; vis. faculty grad. liberal studies program Wesleyan U., 1983; staff writer reading assessment Nat. Assessment Ednl. Progress, Denver, 1972-73; speaker in field; cons. to schs. and librs. Mem. editl. bd. Nat. Coun. Tchrs. English, 1985-88; compiler, editor: Speaking for Ourselves, 1990, Speaking for Ourselves, Too, 1993; editor: Connections: Short Stories by Outstanding Writers for Young Adults, 1989, Visions: Nineteen Short Stories by Outstanding Writers for Young Adults, 1987, Center Stage: One-Act Plays for Teenage Readers and Actors, 1990, Sixteen: Short Stories by Outstanding Writers for Young Adults, 1984, Books for You, 1985, Authors' Insights: Turning Teenagers into Readers and Writers, 1992, Short Circuits: Thirteen Shocking Stories by Outstanding Writers for Young Adults, 1992, Within Reach: Ten Stories, 1993, Join In: Multiethnic Short Stories by Outstanding Writers for Young Adults, 1993, Ultimate Sports: Short Stories by Outstanding Writers for Young Adults, 1995, No Easy Answers: Short Stories About Teenagers Making Tough Choices, 1997, Time Capsule: Short Stories About Teenagers Throughout the Twentieth Century, 1999, On The Fringe, 2001, Destination Unexpected, 2003; author: Presenting Richard Peck, 1989, Bookmark Reading Program, Seventh and Eighth Grade Texts and Workbooks, 1979, Heath Middle Level Literature, 1995; co-author: (with Sarah K. Herz) From Hinton to Hamlet: Building Bridges Between Young Adult Literature and the Classics, 1996; interviewer of authors for Authors4Teens.com website. Recipient Disting. Svc. award Conn. Coun. Tchrs. English, 1989, ALAN award Assembly on Lit. for Adolescents of the Nat. Coun. Tchrs. English, 1992, Cert. of Merit award Cath. Libr. Assn., 1995, Ted Hipple Svc. award NCTE, 2001. Mem. Nat. Coun. Tchrs. English, Assembly on Lit. for Adolescents, Ohio Coun. Tchrs. English Lang. Arts (named an Outstanding English Lang. Arts Educator 2003), Soc. Children's Book Writers and Illustrators, Authors Guild. Avocations: gardening, cooking, traveling, photography. Address: 34540 Sherbrook Park Dr Solon OH 44139-2046 E-mail: gallodon@aol.com.

GALLOWAY, KENNETH FRANKLIN, engineering educator; b. Columbia, Tenn., Apr. 11, 1941; s. Benjamin F. and Carrie (Dowell) G.; m. Dorothy Elise Lamar; children: Kenneth Jr., Carole A. BA, Vanderbilt U., 1962; PhD, U. S.C., 1966. Rsch. assoc. Ind. U., Bloomington, 1966-67, asst. prof., 1967-72, assoc. prof., 1972; rsch. physicist Naval Weapons Support Ctr., Crane, Ind., 1972-74; tech. staff Nat. Bur. Standards, Gaithersurg, Md., 1974-77, chief sect., 1977-79, chief divsn., 1980-86; prof. elect. enging. U. Md., 1980-86; prof., dept. head elect. and computer engring. U. Ariz., Tucson, 1986-96; dean engring., prof. elec. engring. Vanderbilt U., Nashville, 1996—. Contbr. articles to profl. jours. Sci. and Tech. fellow U.S. Dept. Commerce, 1979-80. Fellow IEEE (gen. chmn. Nuc. and Space Radiation Effects Conf. 1985, v.p. Nuc. and Plasma Sci. Soc. 1990, chmn. radiation effects com. 1991-94, chmn. engring. rsch. and devel. policy com. 1994, gen. chmn. Internat. Electron Devices Meeting 1997), AAAS, Am. Phys. Soc.; mem. Electrochem. Soc., Am. Soc. Engring. Edn., Sigma Xi, Eta Kappa Nu, Tau Beta Pi. Office: Vanderbilt U Sch Engring VU Sta B 351826 Nashville TN 37235-1826 E-mail: kenneth.f.galloway@vanderbilt.edu.

GALLOWAY, SISTER MARY BLAISE, mathematics educator; b. Mendota, Ill., June 30, 1933; d. Otto William and Rita Irene (Cannon) G. BS in Math., St. Joseph's Coll., 1965; MS in Math. Edn., U. Ill., 1970; MS in Adminstrn., U. Notre Dame, 1985. Tchr. elem. edn. St. Augustine Sch., Richmond, Mich., 1952-58, Holy Rosary Sch., Duluth, Minn., 1958-65; asst. prin. Sacred Heart Acad., Springfield, Ill., 1983-85, co-prin., 1985-87; instr. math. Marian Cath. H.S., Chicago Heights, Ill., 1965-75, 90—, instr. math., chair math. dept., 1975-83, asst. prin., 1987-90. Mem. curriculum com., adv. bd., registrar Marian Cath. H.S., Chicago Heights, 1987-90, faculty coun., 1994—. Recipient Disting. Life Svc. award, Marian Cath. H.S. Alumni Assn., 2002; grantee, U. Ill., 1990, Ohio State U., 1992, Ill. State U., 1992, 1995. Mem. Nat. Coun. Tchrs. Math., Ill. Coun. Tchrs. Math., Math. Tchrs. Assn. Chgo. (Master Tchr. 1994, pres. 1996-98). Roman Catholic. Avocations: gardening, music, reading. Home and Office: 700 Ashland Ave Chicago Heights IL 60411-2073

GALLOWAY, PAMELA EILENE, university official emeritus; b. Tucson, Dec. 2, 1952; d. David Barnes and Nancy (Harrison) Galloway. BA in Journalism, U. Nev., 1974. Feature writer Reno Gazette Jour., 1973-74; feature writer Reno Newspapers, Inc., 1974-78, lifestyle editor, 1978-80, mem. copy desk/gen. assignment, 1980-81, edn. beat reporter, 1981-84; stairds dir. pub. info. U. Nev. System, 1984-94; dir. student advisement, Coll. Edn. U. Nev., Reno, 1994-97, dir. student advisement emeritus, 1997—. Mem. First United Meth. Ch., 1982—; publicity chair Homeowners Assn.; bd. dirs. prison program Kairos, 1984-86; bd. dirs., fund raising chmn. Cursillo Interdenom. Group, 1981-84; no. Nev. publicity chair Gov's. Conf. Women, 1987. Active Citizen's Alert, Friends of the Libr. Recipient Planned Parenthood Pub. Svc. award for no. Nev., 1983. Mem. ACLU, Nev. State Press Assn. (numerous writing awards 1977-78), Nat. Fedn. Press Women (two nat. interview awards), Inc., Internat. Assn. Press Women, Inc., Toastmasters (10 Most Watchable Women No. Nev. 1984).

GALLOWAY, SHARON LYNNE, special education educator; b. Pensacola, Fla., Jan. 2, 1951; d. Richard Earl and Beatrice Kathlyn (Stone) G. AA, Pensacola Jr. Coll., 1995; BA, U. West Fla., 1998, MEd, 2000. Professionaly Recognized Spl. Educator. Travel counselor, trainer Gulf Breeze (Fla.) Travel, 1985-95; sign lang. interpreter Pensacola Jr. Coll., 1995-97; tchg. intern Sherwood Elem., Pensacola, 1997-98; tchr. Sherwood Elementary, Pensacola, FL, 1998—. Coord. deaf ministries Gulf Breeze United Meth. Ch., 1995-2000, interpreter, 1995—, youth counselor anchor program, 1996-98; vol. Habitat for Humanity, Gulf Breeze, Pensacola, 1994-96, Gulf Coast Sports Ability Games, 1996, Special Olympics, 1999-02; interpreter Ala.-West Fla. Annual Conf. United Meth. Ch., Montgomery, Ala., 1996—; server, cleanup com. Loaves and Fishes, Pensacola, 1996-97; reading camp tchr. U. West Fla., Pensacola, 1997, 99. Mem. NEA, Internat. Reading Assn., Student Coun. Exceptional Children (mem. chair 1996-98) Golden Key Internat. Honor Soc. (chpt. webmaster 1998-2002, chpt. treas. 1998), Coun. for Exceptional Children, Coun. for Children with Behavioral Disorders, Coun. for Children with Learning Disabilities, Alpha Sigma Lambda, Phi Delta Kappa (bd. dirs., chpt. webmaster, 2001—). Avocations: gardening, carpentry, interior design, webpage design. Home: 3367 Crestview Ln Gulf Breeze FL 32563 Office: Sherwood Elem Sch 501 Cherokee Trl Pensacola FL 32506-3519

GALLUZZO, CHARLES ANTHONY, special education educator; b. Buffalo, Aug. 13, 1962; s. Salvatore Peter and Maria Angeline (Picone) G.; m. Josie Andolina; children: Gianna May, Nicholas Giovanni. BS in Edn., SUNY, Buffalo, 1986, MS in Edn., 1991, CAS in Ednl. Adminstrn., 1995. Cert. elem., nursery and spl. edn. tchr., N.Y. Spl. edn. tchr. Oswego County BOCES, Mexico, N.Y., 1986-88; spl. edn. tchr., baseball, football, track & swimming coach Orchard Park (N.Y.) Sch. Dist., 1988-92; educator severely emotionally disturbed students Stanley G. Falk Sch., Buffalo; prin. Windham Elem. Sch., Orchard Park, NY, 1998—. Mem. ASCD, NAESP, Phi Delta Kappa. Democrat. Roman Catholic. Avocations: camping, baseball, reading, golf. Home: 3 Timberlake Dr Orchard Park NY 14127-3547

GALOFRE, ALBERTO, medical educator; b. Santiago, Chile, Dec. 10, 1937; children— Ana Margarita, Christine Elizabeth, Mary Kay. B.Sc., Catholic U. Chile, 1959; M.D. summa cum laude, U. Chile, 1962; M.Ed., U. Ill.-Urbana, 1974. Instr. pediatrics Catholic U., Santiago, 1963-70, asst. prof. pediatrics, 1970-73; asst. prof. pediatrics and human devel. Mich. State U., East Lansing, 1974-78; asst. prof. internal medicine St. Louis U., 1978-85, assoc. prof., 1985—2002, prof., 2002—, asst. dean curriculum Med. Sch., 1979-85, assoc. dean, 1985— ; mem. adv. panel WHO, Geneva, 1980— ; cons. med. edn. Panam. Health Orgn., Washington, 1975— ; dir. pediatric research U. Chile, Santiago, 1964-72; mem. sci. adv. com. Latin Am. Ctr. Ednl. Tech. for Health Scis., Mexico City, 1979-81, Rio de Janeiro, Brazil, 1980-83. Contbr. chpts. to books, articles to med. jours. Recipient Merrel Flair award in med. edn., 2002; Nat. Fund Med. Edn. grantee, 1982-84; W.K. Kellogg fellow, 1967-68; USPHS fellow, 1974-75; Harvard-Macy fellow, 1997-98. Mem. ACP, Am. Ednl. Research Assn., Nat. Council Measurement in Edn., AAAS, Am. Pub. Health Assn., Am. Assn. Higher Edn. Avocations: nature photography, birding, golf. Office: Saint Louis U Sch Med 1402 S Grand Blvd Saint Louis MO 63104-1004

GALVAN, MARY THERESA, economics and business educator; b. Rockford, Ill., Dec. 19, 1957; d. Dino F. and Ida M. Dal Fratello; m. John D. Galvan, June 27, 1987; children: Marie K., John M., Kathleen T. BA, Rockford Coll., 1979; MA, No. Ill. U., 1981, PhD, 1988. Instr. No. Ill. U., DeKalb, 1979-81; asst. prof. Rockford Coll., 1981-87; assoc. prof. bus. and econs. St. Xavier Coll., Chgo., 1987-92; assoc. prof. mktg. North Ctrl. Coll., Naperville, Ill., 1992—, dir. Ctr. for Rsch., 1994—, chmn. bus. dept., 1998—, chair dept. bus., 1998. Chmn. grad. studies com. North Ctrl. Coll., 1996—; cons. Fed. Res. Bank Chgo., 1988—. Lector, St. Elizabeth Seton Parish, Naperville, 1987—, mem. edn. commn., Pastoral counc., 1998—, pres. Women's Network. Earhart Found. fellow, 1988; Hegelar Carus scholar, 1987.. Mem. AAUW, Am. Econs. Assn., Am. Mktg. Assn., Am. Statis. Assn. (v.p. 1994—), Western Econs. Assn. Internat., Midwest Bus. Adminstrn. Assn., Midwest Econs. Assn., Phi Beta Kappa, Omicron Delta Epsilon. Avocations: tennis, golf, sewing, hiking, reading. Office: North Ctrl Coll 30 N Brainard St Naperville IL 60540-4607

GALVIN, NOREEN ANN, nurse, educator; b. New Haven, Dec. 9, 1943; d. John Joseph and Helen Jane (Doherty) G.; divorced; children: Eileen M., Paula T., Beth A. Diploma in Nursing, Hosp. St. Raphael Sch. Nursing, 1964; BSN, Cath. U. Am., 1967, MSN, 1979. Staff nurse Greater S.E. Community Hosp., Washington, 1970-72, asst. head nurse, 1972-75; nurse assoc. Guy W. Gargour, M.D., Bethesda, Md., 1975-76; lectr. Prince George's Community Coll., Largo, Md., 1975-78; asst. dir. nursing So. Md. Hosp. Ctr., Clinton, 1977-82, dir. planning, 1982-85; nursing adminstr. Parkwood Hosp., Clinton, 1985-86; staff nurse Phsycians Meml. Hosp., La Plata, Md., 1986-88; prof. Charles County C.C., La Plata, 1988—. Nurse cons. Nancy C. Taber, Ft. Washington, Md., 1983-85. Pres. Brandywine (Md.) Dem. Club, 1979, 88, Brandywine Heights Citizens Assn., 1980—; vice chmn. So. Md. Health Systems Agy., Clinton, 1985-90. St. Raphaels Hosp. scholar, 1964. Mem. ANA, Acad. of Med.-Surg. Nursing, Orgn. for the Advancement Assoc. Degree Nursing, Md. Nurses Assn. (bd. dirs. 1989—, dist. 9 sec. 1995—), Lioness (3d v.p. Brandywine chpt. 1985-86, pres. 1994—), Sigma Theta Tau. Roman Catholic. Avocations: crocheting, dancing. Home: 15515 Baden Naylor Rd Brandywine MD 20613-8679

GAMARRA, EDUARDO A. political scientist, educator; BA in Polit. Sci., U. Ark., 1979, MA in Econs., 1980; PhD in Polit. Sci., U. Pitts., 1987. Assoc. prof. dept. polit. sci. Fla. Internat. U., Miami, 1986—2003, prof., dir. L.Am. and Carribean Ctr., 2003—. Co-author: Revolution and Reaction: Bolivia 1964-1985, 1988, Dictators, Democrats, and Drugs, 1994; co-editor: Latin American Political Economy in the Age of Neoliberal Reform, 1994, Democracy, Markets, and Structural Reform in Latin America, 1994, La lay para mis enemigos, 1994; editor Hemisphere mag., 1994—. Rsch. grantee Heinz Endowment, 1991-92, North-South Ctr., 1992. Mem. Am. Polit. Sci. Assn., L.Am. Studies Assn. Office: Fla Internat U LAm & Caribbean Ctr Univ Park Dm 353 Ctr Miami FL 33199-0001*

GAMBET, DANIEL G(EORGE), college president, clergyman; b. June 9, 1929; Student, DeSales Hall Sch. Theology, 1953-57; AB in Latin and Greek, Niagara U., 1954; MA in Latin and Greek, Cath. U. Am., 1957; PhD in Classical Studies, U. Pa., 1963, postgrad. in higher edn. adminstrn, 1964; LHD (hon.), Lehigh U., 1986; HHD (hon.), Moravian Coll., 1988; DD (hon.), Lafayette Coll., 1994, Muhlenberg Coll., 1999. Ordained priest Roman Catholic Ch. (Order of Oblates of St. Francis de Sales), 1957; tchr. Latin Father Judge High Sch., Phila., 1957-58; dean of men. instr. Latin, French and German Salesianum Sch., Wilmington, Del., 1958-61; instr. history Oblate Coll., Childs, Md., 1962-64, St. Mary's Coll., Wilmington, 1962-64; acad. dean, instr. Latin and history Allentown Coll. of St. Francis de Sales, 1965-70, v.p., acad. dean, instr. Latin, 1970-72, v.p., 1972-78, pres., 1978—99, pres. emeritus, 1999—. Provincial Eastern Province Oblates of St. Francis de Sales, 1972-78; mem. Allentown Diocesan Bd. Edn., 1978-81, chmn., 1968-70, 79-81; pres. bd. trustees DeSales Hall Sch. Theology, 1972-77; pres. bd. dirs. Salesianum Sch., 1972-77; chmn. vis. com. dept. classica Lehigh U., 1977-85; mem. instl. survey com. Commn. for Ind. Colls. and Univs. in Pa., 1977-81, chmn. instl. survey com., 1980-81, exec. com., 1980-89; exec. com. Found. Ind. Colls., 1984—; chmn. vis. com. for religious studies Lehigh U., 1985-94; bd. dirs. Pa. Power and Light Co. Trustee Allentown Coll. of St. Francis de Sales, 1972-99; bd. dirs. Better Bus. Bur. of Ea. Pa., 1978, United Way of Lehigh County, 1979-88, Health East Inc., 1987-91, Moravian Acad., 1991-98, Ben Franklin Mfrs. Resource Ctr., 1994-97, Lehigh Valley Cmty. Fedn., 1996—; exec. com. Minsi Trails coun. Boy Scouts Am., 1980; trustee Valley Youth House, 1991-97; vice-chmn. bd. dirs. Lehigh Valley Hosp. Ctr., 1983-88. Mem. Pa. Assn. Colls. and Univs. (bd. dirs. 1994-99), Lehigh Valley Assn. Ind. Colls. (bd. dirs. 1978-99, chmn. 1980-81), Ctr. for Agile Pa. Edn. (chair bd. dirs. 1996-99), Assn. Governing Bds. Univs. and Colls., Allentown-Lehigh County C. of C. Office: DeSales U Office of the Pres Emeritus 2755 Station Ave Center Valley PA 18034-9568

GAMBLE, STEVEN G. academic administrator; Pres. Southern Ark. U., Magnolia. Office: Southern Arkansas U Office of The President PO Box 9392 Magnolia AR 71754-9392

GAMBLE, THOMAS ELLSWORTH, academic administrator; b. Chgo., Nov. 14, 1941; s. Slade LeBlount and Anna Marie VanDuzer G.; m. Donna Kay Dersch, Nov. 3, 1973; children: Brendan, Shari, Oscar, Rebecca, Slade, Aubrey, David, Donna. BA in Biology, Northwestern U., 1964; MEd in Ednl. Psychology, U. Ill., 1970, PhD in Higher Ednl. Adminstrn., 1973. Asst. to dean student pers. U. Ill., Urbana-Champaign, 1968-71, asst. prof. edn., 1972, asst. dean Coll. Medicine, 1972—76, assoc. prof. Coll. Medicine Chgo., 1976—83; exec. asst. to chancellor U. Ill. Med. Ctr., Chgo., 1976-78, asst. chancellor, 1976—83; dean intercampus affairs Ill. Ea. C.C., Olney, 1983-84; dean of instrn. Wabash Valley Coll., Mt. Carmel, Ill., 1984—89, dean of coll., 1989-90; pres. Dodge City (Kans.) C.C., 1990-95, Joliet (Ill.) Jr. Coll., 1995-98; dist. pres. Brevard C.C., Cocoa, Fla.,

1999—. Asst. prof. U. Ill. Coll. Edn., 1972-77; assoc. prof. U. Ill. Coll. Medicine, 1982-83; pres. Kans. Jayhawk C.C. Athletic Conf., 1993-94, Ill. N4C C.C. Athletic Conf., 1996-97. Contbr. articles to profl. jours. Bd. dirs. Kans. Newman Coll., Wichita, 1994-96, U.S. Naval Inst., 1968—, Jr. Achievement East Ctrl. Fla., Econ. Devel. Com. Fla. Space Coast, Brevard County Workforce Devel. Bd., Brevard C.C. Found.; chmn. Fla. Coun. Pres.; mem. Am. Coun. on Edn., Commn. on Adult Learning and Ednl. Credentials, 2002—; mem. policy adv. bd. Fla. Solar Energy Ctr.; mem. First Bapt. Ch. Merritt Is., Fla. Capt. USNR, 1964-87, ret. Mem. VFW (life), Am. Assn. Cmty. Colls., Am. Coun. Edn., Fla. Assn. Colls. and Univs., Fla. Assn. C.C.'s, Fla. Space Rsch. Inst., Fla. Sterling Coun., Inc. (bd. dirs.), U. Ill. Coll. Edn. Alumni Assn. (life, sr. advisor, pres. 1988-90), Rotary, Beta Beta Beta, Chi Gamma Iota, Kappa Delta Pi, Phi Delta Kappa, Phi Kappa Phi. Avocations: non-fiction reading, children, classical music, naval science. Office: Brevard CC Office of Pres 1519 Clearlake Rd Cocoa FL 32922-6598 E-mail: gamblet@brevardcc.edu.

GAMBLIN, CYNTHIA MACDONALD, mathematics educator, lobbyist; b. Chgo., Sept. 12, 1946; d. Robert Eugene and Janice (Billings) MacD.; m. James Bradford Gamblin, Sept. 6, 1969 (div. June 1980). BS, Washington U., St. Louis, 1969, MA in Teaching, 1971. Cert. tchr., Fla., Mo.; lic. basic ground instr. FAA. Tchr. maths. Mary Inst., St. Louis, 1969-70; exec. sec. Coalition for the Environment, St. Louis, 1971-72; office mgr. Around the World Food Corp., St. Louis, 1972-73; tchr. maths. Dunedin (Fla.) High Sch., 1973—. Mem. pub. policy com. Juvenile Welfare Bd., St. Petersburg, Fla., 1979-98, co-chmn. legis. subcom., 1989-90; advisor DHS Sailing Club, 2002—. Mem. Pinellas Classroom Tchrs. Assn. (lobbyist St. Petersburg chpt. 1979-92), Ctr. for Fla.'s Children, Jr. League of Clearwater, Phi Delta Kappa. Republican. Avocations: pilot, sailing, reading. Home: 1441 Fairway Dr Dunedin FL 34698-2270

GAMBOA, GEORGE CHARLES, retired oral surgeon, educator; b. King City, Calif., Dec. 17, 1923; s. George Angel and Martha Ann (Baker) G.; m. Winona Mae Collins, July 16, 1946; children: Cheryl Jan Gamboa Granger, Jon Charles, Judith Merlene Gamboa Hiscox. Pre-dental cert., Pacific Union Coll., 1943; DDS, U. Pacific, 1946; MS, U. Minn., 1953; AB, U. So. Calif., 1958, EdD, 1976. Diplomate Am. Bd. Oral and Maxillofacial Surgery. Fellow oral surgery Mayo Found., 1950-53; clin. prof. grad. program oral and maxillofacial surgery U. So. Calif., L.A., 1954-99; assoc. prof. Loma Linda (Calif) U., 1958-99, chmn. dept. oral surgery, 1960-63; pvt. practice oral and maxillofacial surgery San Gabriel, Calif., 1955-93. Dir. So. Calif. Acad. Oral Pathology, 1995-2002. Mem., past chmn. first aid com. West San Gabriel chpt. ARC. Fellow Am. Coll. Dentists, Am. Coll. Oral and Maxillofacial Surgeons (founding fellow), Pierre Fauchard Acad., Am. Inst. Oral Biology, Internat. Coll. Dentists, So. Calif. Acad. Oral Pathology (pres. 2001); mem. Calif. Assn. Oral and Maxillofacial Surgeons, Am. Assn. Oral and Maxillofacial Surgeons, Internat. Assn. Oral Surgeons, So. Calif. Soc. Oral and Maxillofacial Surgeons, Western Soc. Oral and Maxillofacial Surgeons, Am. Acad. Oral and Maxillofacial Radiology, Marsh Robinson Acad. Oral Surgeons, Profl. Staff Assn. L.A. County-U. So. Calif. Med. Ctr. (exec. com. 1976-99), Am. Cancer Soc. (Calif. div., profl. edn. subcom. 1977-90, pres. San Gabriel-Pomona Valley unit 1989-90), Am. Dental Assn. (sci. session chmn. sect. on anesthesiology, 1970), Calif. Dental Soc. Anesthesiology (pres. 1989-94), Calif. Dental Found. (pres. 1991-93), Calif. Dental Assn. (jud. coun. 1990-96), So. Calif. Acad. Oral Pathology (dir. 1995-2002, pres. 2000-01), San Gabriel Valley Dental Soc. (past pres.), Xi Psi Phi, Omicron Kappa Upsilon, Delta Epsilon. Seventh-Day Adventist. Home: 1102 Loganrita Ave Arcadia CA 91006-4535

GAMBRELL, RICHARD DONALD, JR., endocrinologist, educator; b. St. George, S.C., Oct. 28, 1931; s. Richard Donald and Nettie Anzo (Ellenburg) G.; m. Mary Caroline Stone, Dec. 22, 1956; children: Deborah Christina, Juliet Denise. BS, Furman U., 1953; MD, Med. U. S.C., 1957. Diplomate Am. Bd. Obstetrics and Gynecology, Diplomate Div. Reproductive Endocrinology. Intern Greenville Gen. Hosp., S.C., 1957-58, resident, 1961-64; commd. USAF, 1958, advanced through grades to col., chmn. dept. ob-gyn, cons. to surgeon gen. USAF Hosp., 1966-69, chief gynecologic endocrinology Wilford Hall USAF Med. Ctr. Lackland AFB, Tex., 1971-78, ret., 1978; clin. prof. ob-gyn and endocrinology Med. Coll. Ga., Augusta, 1978—2001; practice medicine specializing in reproductive endocrinology Augusta, 1978—. Fellow in endocrinology Med. Coll. Ga., 1969-71; mem. staff Westlawn Bapt. Mission Med. Clinic, San Antonio, 1972-78; assoc. clin. prof. U. Tex. Health Sci. Ctr., San Antonio, 1971-78; internat. lectr.; mem. ob-gyn. adv. panel U.S. Pharmacopeial Conv., 1986-90; mem. sci. adv. bd. Nat. Osteoporosis Found., 1988-91. Co-author: The Menopause: Indications for Estrogen Therapy, 1979, Sex Steroid Hormones and Cancer, 1984, Unwanted Hair: Its Cause and Treatment, 1985, Estrogen Replacement Therapy, 1987, Hormone Replacement Therapy, 3rd edit., 1992, 4th edit., 1995, 5th edit., 1997, Estrogen Replacement Therapy Users Guide, 1989, 2d edit., 1997; mem. editl. bd. Jour. Reproductive Medicine, 1982-85, Maturitas, 1982-99, The Female Patient, 1992—, Menopause: Jour. of the N.Am. Menopause Soc., 1995—; mem. editl. bd. Internat. Jour. Fertility, 1986-91, assoc. editor, 1988-91; contbr. articles to med. jours., chpts. to books. Deacon, Sunday sch. tchr. Baptist Ch., 1971—; mem. sci. adv. bd. Nat. Osteoporosis Found., 1988-91. Recipient Chmn.'s Best Paper in Clin. Rsch. from Tchg. Hosp. award Armed Forces Dist. Am. Coll. Ob-Gyn., 1972, 88, Host award, 1977, Chmn.'s award, 1978, Purdue-Frederick award, 1979, Outstanding Exhibit award Am. Fertility Soc., 1983, Am. Coll. Obstetricians and Gynecologists award, 1983, Thesis award South Atlantic Assn. Ob-Gyn., Winthrop award Internat. Soc. Reproductive Medicine, 1985, Chmn.'s Best Paper award Pan Am. Soc. for Fertility, 1986, Outstanding Sci. exhibit award Am. Acad. Family Physicians, 1986, 87, 92, Boston, 1994, New Orleans, 1996, Merit award ACS, 1994, Cert. of Appreciation for Sci. Exhibit, 1995, Best Doctors for Women award Good Housekeeping, 1997; named to Hall of Fame, Lloyd Meml. H.S., Erlanger, Ky., 1996. Fellow ACOG (mem. subcom. on endocrinology and infertility 1983-86, Kermit Krantz award 2000); mem. Pacific N.W. Ob-Gyn Soc. (hon.), So. Med. Assn. (2nd place Sci. Exhibit award 1992), Am. Fertility Soc., Ga. Obstetric and Gynecologic Soc., Tex. Assn. Ob-Gyn., Augusta Obstetric and Gynecologic Soc., San Antonio Ob-Gyn. Soc. (v.p. 1975-76), Chilean Soc. Ob-Gyn. (hon.), South Atlantic Assn. Obstetricians and Gynecologists (v.p. 1997-98, pres.-elect 1998-99, pres. 1999-00), Soc. Obstetricians and Gynecologists of Can. (hon.), Internat. Family Planning Rsch. Assn., Internat. Menopause Soc. (mem. exec. com. 1981-84), Internat. Soc. for Reproductive Medicine (program chmn. 1980, pres. 1986-88), Am. Assn. of Pro-Life Obs. and Gyn. (exec. bd. 1995—), Christian Med. and Dental Assn., Am. Geriat. Soc. (mem. editl. bd. 1981-83), N.Am. Menopause Soc. (Ortho-McNeil Pharm. Rsch. award 2001), Nat. Geog. Soc., Phi Chi, Alpha Epsilon Delta. Home: 3542 National Ct Augusta GA 30907-9517 Office: 903 15th St Augusta GA 30901-2607

GAMER, FRANCES, elementary school educator; b. Boston, Feb. 12, 1946; d. Morris and Rose Garner. BS in Edn., Boston State Coll., 1967, MEd, 1969; EdD, U. Mass., 1991. Cert. elem. tchr., reading tchr., supr., prin. Mass. Lead tchr. Boston Pub. Schs., Dorchester, Mass., 1967-80, tchr.-in-charge Roxbury, Mass., 1980—, stds. facilitator, 1995—, mem. instrnl. leadership team, mem. curriculum devel. team, 1997—. Cons. Renaissance Charter Sch., Boston, 1994—, Apple Seed Inst. Edn. Reform, Washington, 1997; mem. adv. bd. Apple Seed Inst. Ednl. Innovation, Washington, 1996—97; mem. Harvard U./Boston Pub. Schs. Leadership Initiative, 1997—. Contbr. articles to profl. jours. Friend John F. Kennedy Libr., Boston; active Wang Ctr. Performing Arts, Boston; mem. adv. bd. Horace Mann Ednl. Found., Boston, 1992—. Mem.: AS/CD, Boston Reading Coun., Whole Lang. Assn. Mass., Coun. Tchrs. English, Learning Disabilities Network, Coun. Exceptional Children, Phi Delta Kappa. Office: Mendell Elem Sch 164 School St Roxbury MA 02119-3113

GAMIERE, CONSTANCE ANNE, education educator, counselor; b. Cleve., Nov. 26, 1942; d. Charles Lincoln and Mary Carmella (Zappola) G.; m. Conlon Stephan Keator, Sept. 11, 1974. BS in Edn., Miami U., 1965, MEd, 1969, Pupil Pers. Degree, 1971. Cert. c.c. instr., Calif. Coll. instr., counselor Monterey (Calif.) Peninsula Coll., 1974—, co-chair creative arts divsn., 1997—; tchr. Rushville Consold. Sch., Ind., 1973-74; grad. asst./instr. Miami U., Oxford, Ohio, 1968-71; tchr. Lakewood (Ohio) Schs., 1966-68, Cleveland Heights (Ohio) Schs., 1965-66. Costume designer Mac N Ava Film Prodn., Monterey, 1984-90, make-up designer, 1984-90, Chapparrel Prodns., Monterey, 1988, costume asst., John Pytka Prodns., Hollywood, Calif., 1988. Designer theatre costumes All Main Stage Prodns., 1974-97 (ann. Bay Area Region Best awards). Costume designer for Larkin House, Calif. Parks Dept., Monterey, 1987, Squid Festival, Monterey Chamber, 1985. Mem. Calif. Tchrs. Assn., Faculty Assn. of Calif. C.C., NEA, Costume Soc. Am., Bay Area Costumer's Guild. Avocations: gardening, travel, art collecting, play flute, piano. Home: 949 14th St Pacific Grove CA 93950-4901 Office: Monterey Peninsula Coll 980 Fremont St Monterey CA 93940-4799

GAMMILL, STEPHEN MARK, school administrator; b. Tampa, Fla., Apr. 15, 1955; s. L.C. and Helen Gennetta (Branscum) G.; m. Vickie Ann Jennings, June 5, 1982; children: James Ryan, Jeffrey Mark. AA, So. Bapt. Coll., 1976; BS in Edn., Ouachita Bapt. U., 1978; MS in Edn., U. Cen. Ark., 1982. Cert. tchr., Ark. Tchr. Delight (Ark.) Elem. Sch., 1978-79; tchr. reading Hughes (Ark.) High Sch., 1979-81; tchr. Hughes Elem. Sch., 1981-83, prin., 1983-88, Shirley (Ark.) Elem. Sch., 1988-91, Cowsert Elem. Sch., Clinton, Ark., 1991—. Pres. Hughes Rotary Club, 1987, mem. Fairfield Bay (Ark.) Club, 1990-91. Mem. ASCD, Nat. Assn. Elem. Sch. Prins., Ark. Assn. Elem. Sch. Prins., Van Buren County Prins.' Assn., Phi Delta Kappa. Baptist. Avocations: camping, golf, softball, computers, woodworking. Office: Cowsert Elem Sch RR 6 Box 103-1 Clinton AR 72031-9021

GAMPP, TERESA LEE LAVENDER, special education educator; b. Columbus, Ohio, Mar. 17, 1953; d. Danny Lee and Roberta Faye (Holsinger) Lavender; m. Rick Joe Gampp, Jul. 5, 1974; children: Kara, Erick. BS in hearing and speech scis., Ohio U., 1975; MA, Ohio State U., 1983. Cert. hearing handicapped and speech pathology tchr., lic. Ohio State Bd. of Speech Pathology. Speech pathologist Scioto County Schs., Portsmouth, Ohio, 1975-76; presch. tchr. Samkel Presch., Obetz, Ohio, 1976-77; speech pathologist Fairfield County Bd. Edn., Lancaster, Ohio, 1977-78, Berne Union Local Schs., Sugar Grove, Ohio, 1978-80, Pickerington (Ohio) Local Schs., 1980-89; tchr. hearing handicapped Columbus (Ohio) Pub. Schs., 1992—. Speech pathology cons. Fairfield County Schs., Lancaster, 1990-92; coord. Sertoma speech clinics, Sertoma Clubs, Lancaster, 1976-84. Author: Introduction to Reading Aloud for Parents of Hearing Impaired Children, 1994. Girl scout leader Girl Scout Coun. Ohio, 1989-91; program adv. bd. Columbus Hearing Impaired Program, Columbus, 1993—. Mem. NEA, Ohio Edn. Assn., Columbus Edn. Assn. (bldg. rep. 1992-93), Ohio Conf. Tchrs. Eng. Lang., Children with Attention Deficit Disorder Assn., Ohio Speech and Hearing Assn. Avocations: camping, reading, crafts, calligraphy, piano. Home: 6860 Ridgeway Ct Pickerington OH 43147-8972 Office: Columbus Hearing Impaired Program AB Bell Sch 1455 Huy Rd Columbus OH 43224-3563

GAMSON, JOSHUA PAUL, sociology educator; b. Ann Arbor, Mich., Nov. 16, 1962; s. William Anthony and Zelda (Finkelstein) G. BA, Swarthmore Coll., 1985; MA, U. Calif., Berkeley, 1988, PhD, 1992. Asst. editor Moment Mag., Boston, 1985-86; tchr. h.s. The Cambridge Sch., Weston, Mass., 1986-87; instr. U. Calif., Berkeley, 1992, lectr., 1993; asst. prof. Yale U., New Haven, 1993—98, assoc. prof., 1998—2002, U. San Francisco, 2002—. Author: Claims to Fame: Celebrity in Contemporary America, 1994, Freaks Talk Back: Tabloid Talk Shows and Sexual Nonconformity, 1998; contbr. articles to profl. jours. Activist, media coord. Act Up/San Francisco, 1988-90. Spencer fellow Woodrow Wilson Nat. Fellowship Found., 1991-92, Regents-Intern fellow U. Calif., 1987-92, program on non-profit orgns. fellow Yale U., 1994. Mem. Am. Sociol. Assn. (coun. mem. coun. on stats. of lesbians, gays and bisexuals in sociology 1995—, Fund for the Advancement of the Discipline award 1995), Ea. Sociol. Assn. Office: Univ San Francisco 2130 Fulton Street San Francisco CA 94117

GAMST, FREDERICK CHARLES, social anthropologist; b. N.Y.C., May 24, 1936; s. Rangvald Julius and Aida (Durante) G.; m. Marilou Swanson, Jan. 28, 1961; 1 child, Nicole Christina. AA, Pasadena City Coll., 1959; AB, UCLA, 1961; PhD, U. Calif., Berkeley, 1967. Instr. anthropology Rice U., Houston, 1966-67, asst. prof., 1967-71, assoc. prof., 1971-75; prof. dept. anthropology U. Mass., Boston, 1975—2001, chmn. dept. anthropology, 1975-78, assoc. provost for grad. studies, 1978-83, prof. emeritus, 2001—. Cons. in social rels., human factors and ops. to R.R. industry, 1970—; acting dir. Houston Inter-Univ. African Studies Program, 1969-71, Behavioral Sci. Grad. Program, Rice U., 1974-75; mem. Joint Internat. Observer Group (for observation of Ethiopian elections), 1992; mem. com. on human factors for railroads and other fixed guideway transp. sys. Transp. Rsch. Bd., 1999—; adj. prof. anthrology U. Wyo., 2001—. Author: Travel and Research in Northwestern Ethiopia, 1965, The Qemant: A Pagan-Hebraic Peasantry of Ethiopia, 1969, Peasants in Complex Society, 1974, The Hoghead: An Industrial Ethnology of the Locomotive Engineer, 1980, Highballing with Flimsies: Working under Train Orders, 1990; editor: Studies in Cultural Anthropology, 1975, Letters from the United States of North America on Internal Improvements, Steam Navigation, Banking, Etc., 1990, Anthropology Quar., Golden Anniversary Spl. Issue on Indsl. Ethnology, 1977, (with Edward Norbeck) Ideas of Culture: Sources and Uses, 1976, Meanings of Work: Consideration for the Twenty-First Century, 1995, Early American Railroads: Franz Anton Ritter von Gerstner's Die Innern Communicationen (1842-1843), 2 vols., 1997, (video documentary) T-Time: The History of Mass Transit in Boston, 1984; contbr. articles and revs. to profl. publs., chpts. to books. Mem. adv. com Quincy Quarries Hist. Site, Met. Dist. Commn. Mass., 1987—2001; bd. dirs. Cheyenne Depot Found., 2002—. N.Y. State Regents scholar 1954-58, UCLA scholar 1959-60, Haynes Found. scholar 1960-61; Woodrow Wilson Nat. fellow 1961-62, Ford Found. Fgn. Area fellow 1962-63, Social Sci. Rsch. Coun. and ACLS Fgn. Area fellow 1963-66; Rice U. rsch. grantee 1967, NSF grantee 1970-72, NIMH grantee 1972-74, others. Fellow AAAS, Am. Anthrop. Assn. (Conrad Arensberg award 1995, Festschrift Session honoring life's work 2002), Soc. Applied Anthropology, Royal Anthrop. Inst. Gt. Britain and Ireland; mem. Sci. Rsch. Soc., Ry. and Locomotive Hist. Soc. (dir., editor 4 vol. Franz Anton Ritter von Gerstner project 1988—), Indsl. Rels. Rsch. Assn., Soc. for History Tech., Lexington Group in Transp. History, Ry. Fuel and Operating Officers Assn., Am. Assn. R.R. Supts., Soc. Anthrop. Work (pres. 1984-87, bd. dirs. 1987-90), Internat. Union Anthrop. and Ethnol. Scis. (chmn. curriculum com. Commn. Study of Peace 1983-86), Assn. for Study Lang. in Prehistory (bd. dirs. 1988—), Mass. Tchrs. Assn. (mem. exec. com. Faculty Staff Union 1996-2001), Cheyenne Depot Found. (bd. dirs. 2002—). Office: U Mass Dept Anthropology Harbor Campus Boston MA 02125-3393 E-mail: fcgamst@aol.com.

GANDY, GERALD LARMON, rehabilitation counseling educator, psychologist, writer; b. Thomasville, Ga., Feb. 9, 1941; s. Larmon Brinkley and Ruby Wylene (Vickers) G.; m. Patricia Kay Haltiwanger, Jan. 22, 1966. BA, Fla. State U., 1963; MA, U. S.C., 1968, PhD, 1971. Lic. profl. counselor, Va.; lic. clin. psychologist, Va.; nat. cert. rehab. counselor; nat. cert. counselor; nat. registered psychologist; cert. profl. qualification in psychology Assn. of State and Provincial Psychology Bds. Profl. counselor U. S.C. Counseling Ctr., Columbia, 1968-70; counseling psychologist VA Regional Office, Columbia, 1970-75, chief counseling psychologist, 1974-75; ind. cons., prof. emeritus Med. Coll. Va., Va. Commonwealth U., Richmond, 1996—, prof., program dir., 1975-95. Chair nat. com. on undergrad. rehab. edn. Nat. Coun. on Rehab. Edn., 1984-89; mem. numerous state and govt. adv. coms., 1970—; cons. in field.. Author: Mental Health Rehabilitation, 1995; co-author: Rehabilitation and Disability, 1990; co-author/editor: Rehabilitation Counseling and Services, 1987, Counseling in the Rehabilitation Process, 1999; co-editor: International Rehabilitation, 1980, 89; contbr. numerous articles to profl. jours. Faculty pres. Sch. of Community and Pub. Affairs, VA Commonwealth U., 1989-93. Capt. U.S. Army, 1963-66. Recipient Disting. Svc. award Sch. of Community and Pub. Affairs, 1988, School and U. Leadership award, 1993. Fellow Internat. Acad. of Behavioral Medicine, Counseling and Psychotherapy (diplomate); mem. APA, ACA, World Fedn. for Mental Health, Phi Kappa Phi. Home and Office: Highland Springs 300 Southern Ct Richmond VA 23075-1519 E-mail: ggandy@vcu.org.

GANGSTEAD, SANDRA KAY, physical education educator, administrator; b. Ft. Dodge, Iowa, Dec. 12, 1950; d. James Elliott and Beverly Jean (Patton) G. BS with highest honors, U. Wis., LaCrosse, 1973; MS, U. Wyo., 1979; PhD, U. Utah, 1982. Cert. tchr., Wyo. Grad. asst. phys. edn. U. Wyo., Laramie, 1973-74; instr. Albany County Sch. Dist., Laramie, 1974-79; teaching fellow U. Utah, Salt Lake City, 1979-81, instr., 1981-82; asst. prof. Okla. State U., Stillwater, 1982-85, assoc. prof., 1986-87, coord. phys. edn., 1987-90; coord. Sch. Human Performance & Recreation, U. So. Miss., Hattiesburg, 1990-91, asst. dir., 1991-92, dir., 1992—. Assoc. editor editorial rev. bd. Phys. Educator, 1989-92, Phys. Edn. Index, 1988-91; editor Okla. Assn. Health, Phys. Edn., Recreation and Dance Jour., 1984-90; author video tape prodn. Utah Skills Analysis Tests I and II, 1981, 82. Active Miss. Coalition for Disabled Individuals, Jackson, 1992-93, Coalition for Youth Miss., Jackson, 1992-94, Miss. Gov.'s Commn. on Phys. Fitness and Sport, 1993—, chair higher edn. sub.-coun., amend IV task force. Nat. Youth Sports grantee Nat. Collegiate Athletic Assn., 1991-96; recipient Outstanding Faculty award Okla. State U., 1986. Mem. AAHPERD, Nat. Assn. for Phys. Edn. in Higher Edn., So. Dist. Assn. of Health, Phys. Edn. and Recreation, Miss. Assn. for Health, Phys. Edn., Recreation and Dance (coll. sect. chair 1992—, v.p. gen. 1994-94, coll. sect. chair 1992-94, exec. dir.), Okla. Assn. for Health, Phys. Edn., Recreation and Dance (v.p. 1989-90, coll. sect. chair 1988-89, rsch. sect. chair 1986-87, Presdl. citation 1987), Sigma Xi. Democrat. Avocations: pottery, fencing, golf, gardening, woodworking. Office: U So Miss Sch Human Performance & Rec Southern Sta 5142 Hattiesburg MS 39406-5142

GANLEY, BEATRICE, English educator, writer; b. Oct. 21, 1932; BS in Edn., Nazareth Coll., 1958, BA in English, 1964; MA in English, SUNY, Brockport, 1995. Tchr. elem. schs. Diocese of Rochester (N.Y.), 1955-66; tchr. English dept. Nazareth Acad. High Sch., Rochester, 1967-82; dir. comms. Sisters of St. Joseph, Rochester, 1984-89; lectr. English Nazareth Coll., Rochester, 1989—. Office: 150 French Rd Rochester NY 14618 E-mail: bganley@ssjrochester.org.

GANN, PAMELA BROOKS, academic administrator; b. 1948; BA, U. N.C., 1970; JD, Duke U., 1973. Bar: Ga. 1973, N.C. 1974. Assoc. King & Spalding, Atlanta, 1973; 1975assoc. Robinson, Bradshaw & Hinson, P.A., Charlotte, 1974; asst. prof. Duke U. Sch. Law, Durham, 1975—78, assoc. prof., 1978—80, prof., 1980—99, dean, 1988—99; pres. Claremont McKenna Coll., Claremont, Calif., 1999—. Vis. asst. prof. U. Mich. Law Sch., 1977; vis. assoc. prof. U. Va., 1980 Author: (with D. Kahn) Corporate Taxation and Taxation of Partnerships and Partners, 1979, 83, 89; article editor Duke Law Jour. Mem. Am. Law Inst., Coun. Fgn. Rels., Order of Coif, Phi Beta Kappa Office: Claremont McKenna Coll Office Pres 500 E 9th St Claremont CA 91711-5903

GANNON, PATRICIA J. academic administrator; b. Methuen, Mass., June 25, 1965; d. Richard Edward and Barbara Lee Gannon. BA, Coll. Holy Cross, 1987; MPA, Suffolk U., 1997. Mng. dir. adminstrn., dir. non-profit fin. Mass. Indsl. Fin. Agy., Boston, 1989-95, exec. dir., 1995; sr. mng. dir. fin. programs Mass. Devel. Fin. Agy., Boston, 1996-99; v.p. fiscal affairs, CFO Merrimack Coll., North Andover, Mass., 1999—. Mem. Nat. Mus. Women in the Arts, Pi Alpha Alpha. Avocations: decorative furniture painting, gardening, travel. Office: Merrimack Coll Office of Fiscal Affairs 315 Turnpike St North Andover MA 01845-5806

GANS, HERBERT J. sociologist, educator; b. Cologne, Germany, May 7, 1927; came to U.S., 1940, naturalized, 1945; s. Carl M. and Elise (Plaut) G.; m. Louise Gruner, Mar. 19, 1967; 1 son, David. PhB, U. Chgo., 1947, MA, 1950; PhD, U. Pa., 1957, DSc (hon.), 2003. Planner pvt. and pub. planning agys., Chgo. and Washington, 1950-53; from lectr. to assoc. prof. urban studies and planning U. Pa., 1953-64; from asso. prof. to adj. prof. sociology Tchrs. Coll., Columbia, also sr. staff scientist Center Urban Edn., 1964-69; prof. sociology and planning Mass. Inst. Tech., also Mass. Inst. Tech.-Harvard Joint Center for Urban Studies, 1969-71; prof. sociology Columbia (Ford Found. Urban chair), 1971—; Robert S. Lynd prof. sociology Columbia U., 1985—. Sr. fellow Gannett Ctr. for Media Studies, fall 1985-86, Media Studies Ctr., 1996-97; vis. scholar Russell Sage Found., 1989-90; film critic Social Policy mag., 1971-78; cons. Ford Found., HEW, Nat. Adv. Commn. Civil Disorders. Author: The Urban Villagers, 1962, 2d edit., 1982, The Levittowners, 1967, 1982, People and Plans, 1968, More Equality, 1973, Popular Culture and High Culture, 1974, rev. edit., 1999, Deciding What's News, 1979, Middle American Individualism, 1988, 1991, People, Plans and Policies, 1991, 2d edit., 1994, The War Against the Poor, 1995, 1996, Making Sense of America, 1999, Democracy and the News, 2003; co-editor: On the Making of Americans, 1979; editor: Sociology in America, 1990; adv. editor Jour. Am. Inst. Planners, 1965—75, Jour. Contemporary Ethnography, 1971—, Am. Jour. Sociology, 1972—74, Society, 1971—76, Social Policy, 1971—, Pub. Opinion Quar., 1972—86, Jour. Comm., 1974—91, Jour. Ethnic and Racial Studies, 1977—89, 1995—2003, Internat. Ency. Comm., 1984—88, The Am. Sociologist, 1991—95, Georgetown Jour. Fighting Poverty, 1992—, Critical Studies in Mass Comm., 1992—96, Rose Monograph Series, 1998—, Qualitative Sociology, 1998—2001. Bd. dirs. Ams. for Dem. Action, 1969-75, Met. (formerly Suburban) Action Inst., 1974-85, Human Serve Inst., 1987—, Workers Def. League, 1992—, Working Today, 1995—, Rsch. Coun. Jt. Project on Equality, 1996—, Nat. Jobs for All Coalition, 1996. With AUS, 1945-46. Recipient Excelsior award SUNY, Albany, 1987, award for disting. contbn. to media and media studies Freedom Forum Media Studies Ctr., 1995; Guggenheim fellow, 1977-78, Rsch. fellow German Marshall Fund, 1984. Fellow Am. Acad. Arts and Scis.; mem. Am. Sociol. Assn. (exec. coun. 1968-71, pres. 1988, Lynd award for lifetime contbn. to rsch. cmty. and urban sociology sect. 1992, Pub. Understanding Sociology award 1999), Ea. Sociol. Soc. (pres. 1972, Merit award, 1995), Sociol. Rsch. Assn., German Sociol. Assn. (hon.). Office: Columbia U 404 Fayerweather Hall New York NY 10027 E-mail: hjg1@columbia.edu.

GANTZ, SUZI GRAHN, special education educator; b. Chgo., May 17, 1954; d. Robert Donald and Barbara Edna (Ascher) Grahn; m. Louis Estes Gantz, July 11, 1976; children: Christopher, Joshua. BS in Edn. of Deaf and Hard of Hearing, U. Ill., 1976. Tchr. A.G. Bell Sch., Chgo., 1976-80, 88—, facilitator Edn. Connection grant, 1999-2001; sales asst. Bob Grahn & Assocs., Chgo., 1982-84; with sales dept. Isis/My Sisters Circus, Chgo., 1984-86; interpreter Glenbrook North High Sch., Northbrook, Ill., 1986-87; interpreter, aide Lake Forest (Ill.) Dist. 67, 1987-88. Mem. Northbrook Citizens for Drug and Alcohol Alliance, 1988—; cubmaster Boy Scouts Am., Northbrook, 1990-93. Mem. Ill. Tchrs. of the Hearing Impaired, A.G. Bell Soc., Coun. on Exceptional Children. Avocations: dancing, swimming. Home: 485 Laburnum Dr Northbrook IL 60062-2259 Office: AG Bell Sch 3730 N Oakley Ave Chicago IL 60618-4813

GANZ, WILLIAM ISRAEL, radiology educator, medical director, researcher; b. Munich, Jan. 2, 1951; s. Lazar and Jean Ganz; m. Susan Rebecca Sirota, June 22, 1980; children: Tova, Debora, Harry. BA, Adelphi U., 1972; MS, MD, Albert Einstein Coll. Medicine, Medicine, 1979. Diplomate Am. Bd. Nuclear Medicine. NIH med. scientist trainee Albert Einstein Coll. Medicine, Bronx, N.Y., 1972-78, pharmacology rsch. fellow, 1978-79, NIH cardiovasc. fellow, 1979-80, resident in radiology, 1980-83; radiology/nuc. medicine fellow Barnes Hosp./Inst. Radiology, St. Louis, 1983-85; from asst. prof. to assoc. prof. U. Miami Sch. Medicine, Fla., 1985-97, coord. nuc. medicine tchg. program, 1990-97; radiation safety officer, coord. clin. nuc. medicine South Shore Hosp., 1994-97; dir. nuc. medicine Animal Rsch. Lab., 1995-97; med. dir. PET/Nuc. Medicine Ctr. and Bone Mineral Density Cts. Metabolic Imaging of Boca Raton, Fla., 1996-98; instr. radiology, nuc. medicine Mt. Sinai Med. Ctr., Miami Beach, Fla., 1998-99; staff cons. nuclear cadiology Cedars Med. Ctr., 1985—; medical dir. Imaging Ctr. and Diagnostic Testing Group, Miami, 1996—. Staff South Shore Hosp., 1994—; prof. panel Pfizer Pharms., Miami, 1986-95; guest editor Nuc. Medicine Ednl. Review, 1996—; med. dir. Diagnostic Testing Ctr. and Imaging Ctr., Atlantis, Fla., 1998—; staff physician nuclear medicine Holy Cross Hosp., Ft. Lauderdale, Fla., 1999, Clin. Neurosci. Inst. Brain Rsch. Group, 1999—; rsch. reviewer NIH, 2000—. Reviewer Jour. Nuc. Medicine, 2001—; exhibitor in field; contbr. articles to profl. jours. Recipient, RSNA cum laude award, 1990-91, NIH Svc. awards 1975-78, NSF award 1976. Mem. AMA (lectr. 2000—), Am. Coll. Nuc. Physicians, Am. Coll. Cardiology, Radiol. Soc. N.Am., Soc. Nuc. Medicine, Soc. Magnetic Resonance Imaging, Am. Soc. Orthodox Jewish Scientists. Democrat. Jewish. Home: 4333 Adams Ave Miami FL 33140-2927

GANZEL, DEWEY ALVIN, English language educator; b. Albion, Nebr., July 5, 1927; s. Dewey Alvin Ganzel Sr. and Frances Gross; m. Carol Henderson, July 27, 1955; children: Rebecca, Catherine, Emily. BS, U. Nebr., 1949; MA, U. Chgo., 1954, PhD, 1958. Prof. English Oberlin (Ohio) Coll., 1958-97. Chair Oberlin City Coun., 1976-84. Served in U.S. Navy, 1945-47, PTO. Fulbright scholar, 1952-53, 55-56. Office: Oberlin Coll Rice Hall Oberlin OH 44074 E-mail: dewey.ganzel@oberlin.edu.

GAO, LUJI, foreign language educator, columnist; b. Tian Jin, China, May 18, 1941; s. Shaohua and Guoqin (Yang) G.; m. Leiping (Ding), Feb. 3, 1969; children: Grace Jie, Yang. BS civil engring., Qing Hua U., Beijing, China, 1965, MS arch., 1980; M Christian ministry, Christian Witness Theol. Seminary, Calif., 2001—. Chief civil engr. First Constrn. Corp., Beijing, 1965-80; gen. mgr. Golden East Products Com., Morton Grove, Ill., 1981-82; corr. Wen Wei Po, Hong Kong, 1983-97; Mandarin Chinese instr. Coll. San Mateo, Calif., 1989—. Author: The Bronze Sword, 1981 (award Nat. Sci. Short Story Contest, Ministry of Culture, China 1981), editor-in-chief Hua Sheng TV, San Mateo, 1991-98; pres., editor-in-chief China Jour., San Francisco, 1994-95; columnist Hong Kong Econ. Jour., 1997—; contbg. articles to profl. jour. Deacon, San Francisco Mandarin Bapt. Ch., 1997-2000. Avocations: art appreciation and collection, travel, watching movies, singing. Home: 185 Santa Cruz Ave Daly City CA 94014-1051

GARABEDIAN, BETTY MARIE, retired elementary school educator; b. Worcester, Mass., June 24, 1928; d. Henry L. and Marie A. (Holquist) Olson; m. Peter Garabedian, Aug. 20, 1960. BA in humanities, Bob Jones U., 1950; MEd, Boston U., 1961. Elem. tchr. Town of Shrewsbury, Mass., 1950-54, remedial reading tchr., 1950-57; elem. supr. Auburn, Mass., 1957-67; elem. tchr. grades 5th & 6th and music tchr. Douglas, Mass., 1967-87. Pres. Shrewsbury Tchrs. Club Assn., 1954-56, Auburn Tchrs. Assn., 1960-61. Recipient Horace Mann Outstanding Tchr. award, State of Mass., 1985-86. Mem. Boston U. Alumni, AAUW, Christian Appalachian Project; Delta Kappa Gamma (pres. 1961-62). Baptist. Avocations: sacred, Gospel, and classical music, reading the Bible, non-fiction/biographies, making wreaths, cooking, knitting.

GARABEDIAN, CHARLES, JR., mathematician, educator; b. Whitinsville, Mass., July 16, 1943; s. Charles and Sadie (Mandanjian) Garabedian; m. Manoushag Manougian. BS, Worcester State Coll., 1965; MEd, Framingham State Coll., 1970; PhD, U. Conn., 1981. Cert. secondary tchr. Mass. Math. tchr. Holliston (Mass.) High Sch., 1965—2001; assoc. prof. math. Framingham (Mass.) State Coll., 1971-75, 84—; math. instr. Ea. Conn. State Coll., Willimantic, 1976. Cons., math. instr. Huntington Learning Ctr., Shrewsbury, Mass., 1993—; vis. lectr. Quinsigamond C.C., Worcester, Mass., 2002—. Recipient Presdl. Disting. Tchr. award, 1991, Practitioner award, Harvard U., 1988, Disting. Tchr. award, White Ho. Commn. Presdl. Scholars, 1991, Christa Corrigan McAuliffe award, Christa McAuliffe Ctr. Edn. and Tchg. Excellence, 1996, Disting. Tchr. award, Border's Books, 2000. Mem.: Mass. Assn. Supervision and Curriculum Devel., Nat. Coun. Tchrs. Math., Nat. Assn. RR Passengers, Mass. Assn. RR Passengers, Knights of Vartan, Phi Delta Kappa. Armenian Evang. Ch. Avocations: music, photography, model railroads, cooking, reading. Home: PO Box 452 Shrewsbury MA 01545-0452

GARATE, REBECCA, elementary school bilingual educator; b. Denver City, Tex., Aug. 27, 1956; d. Joe and Amparo (Manzano) Nevarez; m. Jesse Garate, June 30, 1975; 1 child, Rebecca Diane. AA, N.Mex. Jr. Coll., 1983; BS, Coll. of S.W., 1986; bilingual endorsement, Tex. Tech U., 1988. Spl. edn. aide Denver City Jr. H.S., 1977-87; 3d grade tchr. Kelley Elem. Sch., Denver City, 1987-89, 2d grade bilingual tchr., 1989—. Mem. textbook proclamation adv. com. Tex. Edn. Agy., Austin, 1990. Mem. Assn. Tex. Profl. Educators. Avocations: reading, sports. Home: PO Box 1464 Denver City TX 79323-1464

GARBARINO, ROBERT PAUL, retired administrative dean, lawyer; b. Wanaque, N.J., Oct. 6, 1929; s. Attillio and Theresa (Napello) G.; m. Joyce A. Sullivan, June 29, 1957; children: Lynn, Lisa, Mark, Steven. BBA cum laude, St. Bonaventure U., 1951; JD with highest class honors, Villanova U., 1956. Bar: Pa. 1956, U.S. Dist. Ct. (ea. dist.) Pa. 1956, U.S. Ct. Appeals (3d cir.) 1962, U.S. Supreme Ct. 1962, U.S. Tax Ct. 1966, U.S. Ct. Internat. Trade 1966. Law clk. U.S. Dist. Ct. (ea. dist.) Pa., Phila., 1956-57; asst. counsel Phila. Electric Co., Phila., 1957-60, asst. gen. counsel, 1960-62; ptnr. Kania & Garbarino & predecessor firm, Phila. and Bala Cynwyd, Pa., 1962-81; assoc. dean adminstrn. Sch. Law Villanova (Pa.) U., 1981-96. Right-of-way cons. Edison Electric Inst., N.Y.C., 1960—62; trustee reorgn. Tele-Tronics Co., Phila., 1962—64; mem. bd. consultors Law Sch. Villanova U., 1967—81, mem. bd. consultors (life mem.), 1996—2003, chmn., vice chmn. bd. consultors, 1971—76; chmn. Profl. Sports Career Counseling Panel Villanova U.; mem. pres.'s adv. coun. St. Bonaventure U., NY, 1975—86, chmn., 1976—78. Contbr. articles to profl. jours.; 1st editor-in-chief Villanova U. Law Rev., 1954. Mem. community leadership seminar Fels Inst. Local and State Govt., 1961. Staff sgt. USMC, 1951-53. Mem. ABA, Phila. Bar Assn., Order of Coif. Home: 120 Ladderback Ln Devon PA 19333-1815

GARCIA, ANGÉLICA MARIA, elementary education educator; b. Tijuana, Mex., Mar. 22, 1963; came to U.S., 1967; d. Juan José Quijada and Paula (Magallanes) Garcia. AA, L.A. Harbor Coll., Wilmington, Calif., 1985; BA, Calif. State U., Carson, 1990, MA, 1993. Tchr. asst., tutor L.A. Harbor Coll., 1982-85; elem. tchr. asst., tutor Ambler Avenue Sch., Carson, 1985-90; bilingual elem. tchr. Hooper Avenue Sch., L.A., 1991—; mentor tchr. Hooper Avenue Elem. Sch., L.A., 1997—, mem. coordinated compliance rev. team, 1998. Jefferson cluster tchr. trainer dist. stds. L.A. Unified Sch. Dist., 1996—, tchr. trainer early literacy, 1997—; stakeholder Instrnl. Transformation Team, 1995-96; mem. pupil quality rev. team, 1995-96; co-chair local sch. leadership coun., 1998; mentor Latino Tchr. Project, U. So. Calif., 1993—; primary math. coach Hooper Ave. Sch., 2003--. Counselor Pathfinders, Carson Seventh Day Adventist Ch., 1980; treas. Carson Spanish Seventh-Day Adventist Ch., 1994; pianist Harbor City Seventh Day Adventist Ch., 1995-96; mem. ednl. com. Lynwood Seventh Day Adventist Ch., 1999, ch. pianist, 2001, ch. clk., 2002. Mem. TESOL, United Tchrs. L.A. (co-chmn. 1994, chpt. chmn. 1995-98). Democrat. Avocations: playing piano, photography, reading, playing softball, drawing. Home: 320 E 181st St Carson CA 90746-1815 E-mail: angieq@earthlink.net.

GARCIA, CELSO-RAMON, obstetrician, gynecologist, educator; b. N.Y.C., Oct. 31, 1921; s. Celso García y Ondina and Oliva (Menèndez del Valle) G.; m. Shirley Jean Stoddard, Oct. 14, 1950; children: Celso-Ramón Jr., Sarita Garcia Cole. BS, Queens Coll., 1942; MD, SUNY Downstate Med. Ctr., 1945; MA (hon.), U. Pa. Intern Norwegian Hosp., Bklyn., 1945-46; resident, rsch. fellow in gynecology Cumberland Hosp., Bklyn., 1949-50; assoc. in ob-gyn. U. P.R., San Juan, 1953-54; asst. prof. ob-gyn. Sch. Medicine and Tropical Medicine, San Juan, 1954-55; co-dir. Rock Reproductive Study Ctr.; asst. obstetrician and gynecologist Boston Lying-In Hosp.; assoc. surgeon Free Hosp. for Women, Brookline, Mass., 1955-65; sr. scientist, dir. tng. program in physiology reprodn. Worcester Found. for Exptl. Biology, Shrewsbury, Mass., 1960-62; asst. surgeon, chief Infertility Clinic, Mass. Gen. Hosp.; from asst., instr. to clin. assoc. ob-gyn. Harvard Med. Sch., 1962-65; prof. obstetrics and gynecology U. Pa., Phila., 1965-92, William Shippen, Jr. prof. human reprodn., 1970-92, William Shippen, Jr. prof emeritus, 1992—, dir. infertility and reproductive endocrinology and surgery, 1987-95. Extraordinary prof. U. San Luis Potosi, Mex., 1974; rapporteur com. of experts on clin. aspects oral gestogens WHO, Geneva, 1965; mem. ad hoc adv. com. contraceptive devel., contract program Nat. Inst. Child Health and Human Devel., 1971-75; original team mem. which developed clin. application of 1st FDA approved progestagen-estrogen combinations for oral contraception (the Pill); developer, dir. 1st tng. program in physiology of reprodn. in U.S.; innovator surg. approach to infertility of women; cons. Pa. Hosp., 1973-94; asst. staff Faulkner Hosp., Jamaica Plain, Boston; courtesy staff Glover Meml. Hosp., Needham, Mass., 1962-65; adv. bd. Global Alliance for Women's Health, 1995—. Chmn. nat. med. adv. com. Planned Parenthood World Population, 1971-74; mem. nat. adv. child and human devel. coun. Nat. Inst. Child Health and Human Devel., 1981-84. With AUS, 1943-48. Recipient Carl G. Hartman award Am. Soc. Study of Sterility, 1961, Sesquicentennial award U. Mich., 1967, MD Master Tchg. award Alumni Assn. SUNY, 1989, Recognition award APGO Wyeth-Ayerst, 1993, Frank L. Babbott award SUNY, 1995, Sci. Leadership award Global Alliance Women's Health, 2000; Sidney Graves fellow in gynecology Harvard Med. Sch., 1955. Fellow: ACOG, ACS, Coll. Physicians Phila.; mem.: AMA, Boston Obstet. Soc. (emeritus), Phila. Obstet. Soc., Am. Soc. Reproduction Medicine (bd. dirs., past pres.), Soc. Reproductive Surgeons (founding pres.), Assn. Planned Parenthood Physicians (past pres.), Fedn. Columbian Socs. Ob-Gyn. (hon.), Cuban Soc. Ob-Gyn. (hon.; in exile), Am. Physiol. Soc., Am. Gynecol. and Obstet. Soc., Am. Soc. Gynecol. Surgeons, Global Alliance Women's Health (adv. bd. 1994—, rep. to U.N. Econ. and Social Coun. 1998), Alpha Omega Alpha, Sigma Xi, Masons. Democrat. Presbyterian. Home: 109 Merion Rd Merion Station PA 19066-1734 Office: 3701 Market St Philadelphia PA 19104 Business E-Mail: cgarcia@mail.obgyn.upenn.edu. E-mail: crgsr@snip.net.

GARCIA, F. CHRIS, academic administrator, political science educator, public opinion researcher; b. Albuquerque, Apr. 15, 1940; s. Flaviano P. and Crucita A. Garcia; m. Sandra D. Garcia; children: Elaine L., Tanya C. BA, U. N.Mex., 1961, MA in Govt., 1964; PhD in Polit. Sci., U. Calif., Davis, 1972. Froma asst. prof. polit. sci. to pres. U. N.Mex., Albuquerque, 1970—2002, pres., 2002—03, prof., 1978—; founder Zia Rsch. Assocs., Inc., Albuquerque, 1973-94, also chmn. bd. dirs. Cons.-evaluator North Ctrl. Assn. Higher Learning Commn., 1994—. Author: Political Socialization of Chicano Children, 1973, La Causa Politica, 1974, The Chicano Political Experience, 1977, State and Local Government in New Mexico, 1979, New Mexico Government, 1976, 81, 94, Latinos and the Political System, 1988, Latino Voices, 1992, Pursuing Power, 1997. Mem. charter rev. com. City of Albuquerque, 1999, Alburquerque Goals Commn.; bd. dirs. Nat. Hispanic Cultural Ctr., 2002—. With N.Mex. Air Nat. Guard, 1957-63. Recipient Disting. Svc. award, Am. Polit. Sci. Assn., 2001. Mem. Western Polit. Sci. Assn. (pres. 1977-78), Am. Polit. Sci. Assn. (v.p. 1994-95, exec. coun. 1984-86, sec. 1992-93, Disting. Svc. award 2001), Am. Assn. Pub. Opinion Rsch., Coun. Colls. of Arts and Sci. (bd. dirs. 1982-85), Nat. Assn. State Univs. and Land Grant Colls. (coun. acad. affairs 1987-90, exec. com. 1989), We. Social Sci. Assn. (exec. coun. 1973-76), Phi Beta Kappa, Phi Kappa Phi, Gold Key. Home: 1409 Snowdrop Pl NE Albuquerque NM 87112-6331 Office: U N Mex Polt Sci Dept Social Scis Bldg 2053 Albuquerque NM 87131-1121 E-mail: cgarcia@unm.edu.

GARCIA, FRANCISCO, federal agency administrator; MA in edn., Boise State U.; BA Coll. of Idaho. Dir. Migrant Edn. US Dept. Edn., Wash., 1998—; exec. dir. Interface Cons.; dir. Ctr. for Bilingual Edn., NW Regional Edn. Lab.; tchr. Boise State U., Idaho; equity spec. Dept. Edn., (Reg.); fellow Coun. for Excellence in Govt. Program. Office: US Dept Edn Off Migrant Edn Rm 3E317 400 Maryland Ave SW Washington DC 20202*

GARCIA, JULIET VILLARREAL, university administrator; m. Oscar E. Garcia; two children. Grad. in Comm. and Linguistics, U. Tex. Pres. U. Tex. at Brownsville, Tex. Southmost Coll. Bd. dirs. Fed. Res. of Dallas/San Antonio br. of Tex. Commerce Bancshares Inc.; past bd. dirs. Am. Coun. Edn., chmn. bd. dirs. 1995. Bd. dirs. Carnegie Found. for Advancement of Teaching, Pub. Welfare Foun.; vice-chair adv. com. on Fin. Aid; appointed mem. White House Initiative on Ednl. Excellence for Hispanic-Ams. Named Woman of Distinction Nat. Conf. of Coll. Women Student Leaders, 1995, one of most influential Hispanics Hispanic Bus. Mag. Office: U Tex & Tex Southmost Coll Office of Pres 80 Fort Brown St Brownsville TX 78520-4956

GARCIA, YOLANDA VASQUEZ, educational services manager, educator; b. San Antonio, Nov. 27, 1948; d. Eleodoro and Antonia (Hernandez) Vasquez; (div. 1985); children: Yvette Flores, Marisa Flores, Julie Garcia. BA, Our Lady of the Lake, 1971; MA, U. Tex., San Antonio, 1977. Cert. counseling and guidance. Elem. sch. tchr. San Antonio (Tex.) Ind. Sch. Dist., 1972-76, Northside Ind. Sch. Dist., San Antonio, 1977-81, itenerant ESL tchr., 1981-87, sch. counselor, 1988-93, adminstr.; student tchr. supr. U. Tex., Austin, 1993—. Scholar Our Lady of the Lake, San Antonio, 1968, U. Tex., San Antonio, 1976, Inst. de Cooperacion, Madrid, Spain, 1985; fellow U. Tex., Austin, 1993. Mem. TESPA, Am. Edn. Rsch., Coun. for Exceptional Children, Tex. Assn. Bilingual Edn., Kappa Delta Pi. Democrat. Roman Catholic. Office: Northside Elem Alt Edn Program 7111 Huebner Rd San Antonio TX 78240-3121 Home: 6515 Pavona Rdg San Antonio TX 78240-3069

GARCIA-GODOY, CRISTIAN, historian, educator; b. Mendoza City, Argentina, June 3, 1924; came to the U.S., 1963; s. Cristián García Pontis and Renee Godoy Ponce; children: María Celina Heeter, María Inés García Robles, María Susana García Robles. Degree in law, U. Buenos Aires, 1950; diploma, U. Nacional de Cuyo, 1952; postgrad., Washington U., 1969, Cath. U., 1971. Official various banks, Argentina, 1941-62; sec. gen. Secretaria de Comercio de la Nación, Argentina, 1958-59; cabinet mem. Ministro de Economía, Río Negro, Argentina, 1959-60; pres.-organizer Banco de la Provincia de Río Negro, Argentina, 1960; internat. civil servant GS/OAS, 1962-89; prof. history Argentine Sch., Washington, 1977—99. Author: Asociados Eminentes de San Martin, 1998, San Martin en el Reino Unido, 1996, Jefes Espanoles en la Formacion Militar de San Martin, 1995, Correspondencia Inedita de Tomas Godoy Cruz con su Padre Clemente Godoy y Videla, 1993, The Essential San Martin, 1993-94, Tomas Godoy Cruz: Su tiempo, su vida, su drama, 1991, Tomas Godoy Cruz, Dictamen Federalista, Introduccion y estudio, 1991, Los XII Presidentes 1850-1910, 1989, 2d edit., 1999, The San Martin Papers, 1988, Selected U.S. Supreme Court Decisions Related to Constitutional Law, 1986, San Martin y Unanue en la Liberacion del Peru, 1983, Evolucion Historica y Constitucional de la Argentina, 1982, San Martin, Selected Bibliography, 1978, Ampliación y Actualizacion 1978/96, Tribute to the Liberator General San Martin, 1978, Diario Secreto de San Martín, 2003; contbr. articles to profl. jours. Lt. Argentine Army, 1946. Decorated comdr. Order of St. Lazarus of Jerusalem; recipient Premio al Merito Historico, U.S. Belgrano Soc., 2000, Premio Educacion Premio Republica Argentina condecoracion, Palmas Sanmartinianas I.N.S. Argentina. Mem. Acad. Nat.de la Historia, Soc. Argentina de Historiadores Buenos Aires, Nat. Geneal. Soc. USA, Inst. Argentino de Ciencias Genealogicas, Inst. Bonaerense de Numismatica y Antiguedades, Acad. Nacional Sanmartiniana Buenos Aires, Junta de Estudios Historicos Mendoza, Inst. de Estudios Ibericos Buenos Aires, Inst. Urquiza de Estudios Historicos, Internat. Inst. Pub. Adminstrn. (U.K.), Acad. Polit. Sci. USA, Am. Soc. Internat. Law, Washington Fgn. Law Soc. USA, San Martin Soc. (pres.), Hermandad Ysabel la Catolica (chancellor), Instituto Urquiza de Estudios Históricos. Avocations: collecting art, rare books, maps, antiques and military decorations and historical medals. Home: 1128 Balls Hill Rd Mc Lean VA 22101-2653 Office: San Martin Soc PO Box 33 Mc Lean VA 22101-0033 E-mail: cggodoy@email.msn.com.

GARCIA-VARELA, JESUS, language educator, literature educator; b. Madrid, Nov. 26, 1944; came to U.S., 1982; s. Onofre Garcia and Josefa Varela; m. Margarita Lliteras; children: Susana, Nuria. Atty. in Law, U. Madrid, 1968; MA in Spanish Lit., Ind. U., 1984, PhD in Spanish Lit., 1989. Asst. prof. Spanish lit. U. Louisville, 1989-95, assoc. prof., 1995—. Contbr. articles to profl. jours. Mem. MLA, Assn. Hispanic Classical Theater, Assn. Internat. de Hispanistas, Am. Renaissance Soc., Assn. Internat. del Siglo de Oro, Assn. de Licenciados y Doctores de España Avocations: swimming, outdoor activities. Office: U Louisville Classical Modern Langs Louisville KY 40292-0001

GARD, GARY LEE, chemistry educator, researcher; b. Goodland, Kans., Nov. 17, 1937; s. Edward and Grace O. (Campbell) G.; m. Elizabeth Ann Kester; children: Timothy Lee, Dolores Ann, Julie Ann; m. Christina Huprich, Mar. 18, 1972; 1 child, Jason Lee. AA, Clark Coll., 1957; BA in Edn., U. Wash., 1959, BS in Chemistry, 1960, PhD in Chemistry, 1964. Sr. rsch. chemist Allied Chem. Co., Morristown, N.J., 1964-66; asst. prof. Portland State U., 1966-70, assoc. prof., 1970-75, prof., 1975—99, emeritus prof., 1999—. Coord. Environ. Sci. PhD Program, 1979-81, acting dean Coll. Sci., 1979-81, Chemistry Dept. Head, 1971-77, 1992-94, Portland, Oregon; cons. C3S, 1983-96. Contbr. more than 200 articles to profl. jours. Recipient Fulbright Sr. Prof. award, 1989-90, Branford Price Millar award, Portland State U., 1990-91, Camille and Henry Dreyfus Sr. Scientist Mentor, 2003—. Mem. Am. Men. and Women of Sci., Sigma Xi., Phi Delta Kappa, Phi Theta Kappa, Phi Kappa Phi. Avocations: fishing, reading, sports exercise. Office: Portland State U Dept Chemistry PO Box 751 Portland OR 97207-0751 E-mail: gardg@pdx.edu.

GARDNER, CAROL ELAINE, elementary school educator; b. Savannah, Ga., Dec. 12, 1958; d. Marshall Lee and Carol Elaine (Brown) Williams; m. Jacky Lee Gardner, Sept. 29, 1979; children: Brian Alexander, Brandon Lee, Brent Matthew. BE, Cameron U., Lawton, Okla., 1979. Cert. elem. tchr., Okla. Tchr. grade 4 Swinney Elem. Sch., Lawton, 1980, tchr. grade 1, 1980—. Lawton Sch. Dist curriculum adv. bd., 1990-91; rep. Profl. Planning Devel. Coun., 1992—, chmn. fin. com., 1996-97; mem. Bldg. Leadership Team, 1991—; mentoring tchr. Cameron U., 1995-2002; mem. Dist. Ednl. Instrn. Coun., 2002—. Chair youth program Lawton Pub. Sch. Recipient Environ. award, Pub. Svc. Co. Okla., 1996. Mem. NEA, Lawton Area Reading Coun., Profl. Sci. Curriculumn Alignment Coun. Jehovah'S Witness. Avocations: reading, biking, hiking, coin collecting. Home: 2306 NW 72nd St Lawton OK 73505-1007

GARDNER, DAVID CHAMBERS, adult education educator, psychologist, business executive, author; b. Charlotte, N.C., Mar. 22, 1934; s. James Raymond and Jessica Mary (Chambers) Bumgardner m. Grace Joely Beatty, 1984; children: Joshua Avery, Jessica Sarah. BA, Northeastern U., 1960; MEd, Boston U., 1970, EdD, 1974; PhD, Columbia Pacific U., 1984. Diplomate Am. Bd. Med. Psychotherapists. Mgr. market devel. N.J. Zinc Co., N.Y.C., 1961-66, COMINCO, Ltd., Montreal, Que., Can., 1966-68; dir. Alumni Ann. Giving Program, Northeastern U., Boston, 1968-69; dir. career and spl. edn. Stoneham (Mass.) Pub. Schs., Boston, 1970-72; assoc. prof. divsn. instructional devel. and adminstrn. Boston U., 1974—, prof. emeritus, 1999—; sr. ptnr. Gardner Beatty Group, 1990—; chmn. bd. CyberHelp, Inc., 1995—; v.p. for edn. and mktg. Kaleidoscope Software, Inc., 1997-98; exec. v.p. ISMChina, Ltd., Rancho La Costa, Calif., 1998—; prin. The Human Factors Rsch. Group, Foster City, Calif., 2001—; dir. human factors rsch. Titoma, Inc., Taipei, Taiwan, 2003—. Coord. program career vocat. tng. for handicapped, Boston U., 1974-82, chmn. dept. career and bus. edn., 1974-79, also dir. fed. grants, 1975-77, 77-79; co-founder Am. Tng. and Rsch. Assocs., Inc., chmn. bd., 1979-83, pres., chief exec. officer, 1984—; dir. La Costa Inst. Lifestyle Mgmt., 1986-87. Author: Careers and Disabilities: A Career Approach, 1978; co-author: (with Grace Joely Beatty) Dissertation Proposal Guidebook: How to Prepare a Research Proposal and Get It Accepted, 1980, Career and Vocational Education for the Mildly Learning Handicapped and Disadvantaged, 1984, Stop Stress and Aging Now, 1985, Never Be Tired Again, 1990; co-author: The Visual Learning Guide Series, 1992, 93, 94, 95, 96, 97, Internet for Windows: America Online Edition, 1995, Cruising America Online for Windows, 1995, Windows 95: The Visual Learning Guide, 1995, Quicken 5 for Windows, 1995, The Visual Learning Guide, 1995, Excel for Windows 95: The Visual Learning Guide, 1995, Word for Windows 95, The Visual Learning Guide, 1995, Windows NT 4.0 Visual Desk Reference, 1997, Discover Netscape Communicator, 1997, Discover Internet Explorer, 1997, A Visual Guide to Installing Linux-Mandrake 7.1 onto a Windows Machine, Visual Desk Reference, 2000, A Visual Guide to Installing Linux Red Hat 6.2 on a Windows Machine, 2000, How to Import from China, 2000; editor Career Edn. Quar., 1975-81; contbr. articles to profl. jours. With AUS, 1954-56. U.S. Office Edn. fellow Boston U., 1970, U.S. Office Edn.-Univ. Boston rsch. fellow, 1974. Fellow Am. Assn. Mental Deficiency (Ann. Profl. Tchr. and Rsch. award Region X 1979); mem. Nat. Assn. Career Edn. (bd. dirs., past pres.), Coun. for Exceptional Children, Ea. Ednl. Rsch. Assn. (founding dir.), Am. Vocat. Assn., Phi Delta Kappa, Delta Pi Epsilon.

GARDNER, ELMER CLAUDE, academic administrator; b. Marmaduke, Ark., Jan. 16, 1925; s. O.A. Gardner and Edna (Sutton) Rowe; m. Delorese Tatum, June 17, 1945 (dec.); children: Phyllis, Rebecca, Claudia, David; m. Glenda Jacobs, Sept. 10, 2002. AA, Freed-Hardeman Coll., 1944; BS, Abilene Christian U., 1946; MA, SW Tex. State U., 1947; postgrad., George Peabody Coll., 1951; LLD (hon.), Magic Valley Christian Coll., 1962, Pepperdine U., 1969; LittD (hon.), Okla. Christian U., 1969; HHD (hon.), Morehead State U., 1973; LLD (hon.), Freed-Hardeman U., 1990. Chmn. dept. edn. and psychology Freed-Hardeman U., Henderson, Tenn., 1949-56, registrar, 1950-68, dean, 1956-69, v.p., 1969, pres., 1969-90, chancellor, 1990-92, pres. emeritus, 1992—; chancellor Ga. Christian Sch., 1993—, Crowley's Ridge Coll., 2002—. Bd. dirs. Chester County Bank, Henderson; col. on former Gov. McWherter's staff, 1988—. Editor: Brigance's Sermons, 1951, Van Dyke's Sermons, 1971; contbr. numerous articles to Gospel Advocate and other publs. Former commr. Edn. Commn. of States, 1991; mem. pub. svcs. coun. Tenn. State Cert. Commn., 1988-91; past pres. Heritage Towers Bd., Henderson; past chmn. Crime Stoppers of Henderson and Chester County. Named Civitan of Yr., Civitan Internat., Henderson. Mem. Tenn. Coll. Assn. (pres. 1986-87), Chester County C. of C. (founder), Alpha Chi. Democrat. Mem. Ch. of Christ. Home and Office: 372 E Mill St Henderson TN 38340-2428

GARDNER, GEOFFREY, writer, English educator; b. Chgo., Mar. 23, 1943; s. Alan and Marion Gardner; m. Frieda Gardner, Sept. 16, 1966 (div. Oct. 1985); 1 child, Kate; m. Christin Payack, Dec. 1, 1986. BA in English, NYU, 1964; postgrad., Columbia U., 1965-67, U. Minn., 1970-72; MA in Philosophy, New Sch., N.Y.C., 1971. Lectr. Bklyn. Coll., N.Y.C., 1966-67, CUNY, 1967-69; instr. N.Y. Inst. Tech., N.Y.C., 1968-70; dir. interlibrary loan Hamline U., St. Paul, 1974-81; lectr. Tufts U., Medford, Mass., 1984—. Lit. executor Estate of George Dennison, 1987—. Editor: The Ark, 1976-84, For Rexroth: A Festschrift, 1980, Swords that Shall not Strike: Poems of Protest and Rebellion by Kenneth Rexroth, 1999; translator: The Horses of Time: Poems of Jules Supervielle, 1985; co-editor: Temple, 1994, An Existing Better World: Notes on the Bread and Puppet Theater, 1999. Bd. dirs. Minn. Tenants Union, Mpls., 1979-81, Southside Family Sch., 1979-81; co-chair steering com. Cambridge (Mass.) Tenants Union, 1987-91. Small Press Editor's grantee Coordinating Coun. Lit. Mags., 1976-80, Editor's grantee NEA, 1979, Translation grantee NEA, 1987. Mem. Poetry Soc. Am., Acad. Am. Poets. Home: 461 Gilsum Rd Sullivan NH 03445 Office: Tufts U English Dept 212 East Hall Medford MA 02155

GARDNER, HOWARD GARRY, pediatrician, educator; b. Gary, Ind., Oct. 5, 1943; s. Oscar and Anita (Arenson) G.; m. Judith (Geen), June 21, 1986; children: Molly, Joseph. BA, Ind. U., 1965, MD, 1968. Intern, resident St. Louis U., 1969-73; pvt. practice Hinsdale (Ill.) Pediatrics, 1973-79, DuPage Pediatrics, Darien, Ill., 1979—; attending staff Hinsdale Hosp., 1973—, chmn. dept. pediatrics, 2000—02; courtesy staff Childrens Meml. Hosp., Chgo., 1988—. Clin. prof. dept. pediatrics Loyola U. Sch. of Medicine, Maywood, 1983-2002; chmn. dept. pediatrics Hinsdale Hosp., 1983-85, 2000-02; prof. clin. pediatrics Northwestern U. Med. Sch.; med. adv. bd. YMCA of the USA, Chgo., 1989—. Mem. editl. bd. Pediatric News, 1990—; contbr. articles to profl. jours. Co-chmn. med. adv. bd. DuPage Easter Seal Ctr., Villa Park, Ill.; past, founding mem. bd. dirs. Loyola Ronald McDonald House; co-founder, past pres. Ill. Child Passenger Safety Assn.; mem. med. adv. bd. Pathways Awareness Found.; officer, steering com. DuPage Interagy. Coun. on Early Intervention. Lt. USN, 1969-71. Recipient Outstanding Clin. Tchr. award Loyola Med. Sch., 1978, Tchr. of Yr. Hinsdale Hosp. Family Practice Residency, 1981, Chgo. Caring Physician's award Met. Chgo. Health Care Coun., 1987, Buckle Up Am.! award Ill. Coalition for Safety Belt Use, 1991, Parent and Child Edn. Soc. 20th Anniversary Achievement award, 1992, Outstanding Vol. award West Suburban United Way, 1999, Carol Sanicki Crystal Heart award Easter Seals, DuPage, 2002. Fellow Am. Acad. Pediat. (past pres. Ill. chpt., past mem. nat. nominating com., instnl. rev. bd., com. on injury and poison prevention, Pisani Pediatrician of Yr. award 1986); mem. Chgo. Pediat. Soc. (past pres., Archibald Hoyne Pediatrician of Yr. 1994), Ill. Maternal and Child Health Coalition (bd. dirs., pres., 2000-2002, Advocacy award 1996), DuPage County Med. Soc. (bd. dirs.). Democrat. Jewish. Avocations: reading, skiing, photography. Office: DuPage Pediatrics 1306 Plainfield Rd Darien IL 60561-5038

GARDNER, JOHN WILLIAM, writer, educator; b. Los Angeles, Oct. 8, 1912; s. William and Marie (Flora) G.; m. Aida Marroquin, Aug. 18, 1934; children: Stephanie Gardner Trimble, Francesca Gardner. AB, Stanford U., 1935; PhD, U. Calif., 1938, LL.D. (hon.), 1959; hon. degrees from various colls., univs.; hon. fellow, Stanford U., 1959. Teaching asst. in psychology U. Calif., 1936-38; instr. psychology Conn. Coll., 1938-40; asst. prof. psychology Mt. Holyoke Coll., 1940-42; head Latin-Am. sect. FCC, 1942-43; from lt. to captain USMC, 1943—46; mem. staff Carnegie Corp. of N.Y., 1946-47, exec. assoc., 1947-49, v.p., 1949-55, pres., 1955-65, cons., 1968-77; pres. Carnegie Found. Advancement of Teaching, 1955-65; sec. U.S. Dept. HEW, 1965-68; chmn. Urban Coalition, 1968-70; founder and chmn. Common Cause, 1970-77; chmn. Pres.'s Commn. on White House Fellowships, 1977-80; co-founder, chmn. Independent Sector, 1980-83, dir. leadership studies program, 1984-89; Miriam and Peter Haas prof. pub. svc. Stanford (Calif.) U., 1989-96. Cons. prof. Stanford Sch. Edn., 1996—; mem. Pres. Kennedy's Task Force on Edn., 1960; chmn. U.S. Adv. Commn. Internat. Ednl. and Cultural Affairs, 1962-64, Pres. Johnson's Task Force on Edn., 1964, White House Conf. Edn., 1965; dir. N.Y. Telephone Co., 1961-65, Shell Oil Co., 1962-65, Am. Airlines, 1968-71, Time, Inc., 1968-72 Author: Excellence, 1961, rev. edit., 1984, Self-Renewal, 1964, rev. edit, 1981, No Easy Victories, 1968, The Recovery of Confidence, 1970, In Common Cause, 1972, Morale, 1978, On Leadership, 1990; editor: To Turn the Tide (John F. Kennedy); co-editor: Know or Listen to Those Who Know, 1975, reissued as Quotations of Wit and Wisdom, 1980. Chmn. Nat. Civic League, 1994-96; trustee N.Y. Sch. Social Work, 1949-55, Met. Mus. Art, 1957-65, Stanford U., 1968-82, Rockefeller Bros. Fund, 1968-77, Jet Propulsion Lab., 1978-82, Enterprise Found., 1982-91. Served to capt. USMC, 1943-46. Recipient USAF Exceptional Svcs. award, 1956; Presdl. Medal of Freedom, 1964; Nat. Acad. Scis. Pub. Welfare medal, 1966; U.A.W. Social Justice award, 1968; Eem. Legacy award Anti-Defamation League, 1968; AFL-CIO Murray Green medal, 1970. Home: Stanford, Calif. Died Feb. 16, 2002.

GARDNER, JUDITH WARREN, retired elementary educator; b. Hartford, Conn., Oct. 4, 1940; d. Henry Stanley and Madeline Warren; m. Fred Marvin Gardner, Dec. 28, 1963; children: Warren, Charles, Kevin, Eric. BA, Mt. Holyoke Coll., 1962; MEd, U. Hartford, 1976. Cert. profl. educator, Conn. Pre-kintergarten tchr. Hebron (Conn.) Elem. Sch., 1977-78; elem. tchr. Hopewell Sch., Glastonbury, Conn., 1978-94, Hebron Ave. Sch., Glastonbury, Conn., 1994—2003, ret., 2003—. Cons. dept. psychology U. Hartford, 1989; rep. Internat. Ctr. Adv. Com., Glastonbury, 1990-92; framework com. mem. East Hartford (Conn.) Glastonbury Magnet Sch., 1992; Glastonbury team leader Yale U. East Asian Group Project in China and Taiwan, New Haven, 1992-93. Author: (with others) A Look At Contemporary Chinese Culture in Taiwan Through the Family: Case Studies for the Classroom, 1994; co-author: (tchr. manual) Grade 3 Sci. Notebook, 1987-88. Recipient Celebration of Excellence award State of Conn. and So. New Eng. Tel. Co., 1988, Commendation awards Glastonbury Bd. Edn., 1989, 91, 93; grantee Glastonbury Bd. Edn., and PTO, 1986-89, 93, fellow Programs Internat. Edn. Resources, 1996. Mem. NEA, Conn. Edn. Assn., Glastonbury Edn. Assn. (elem. v.p. 1996-99), Conn. Sci. Suprs. Assn., Tchr. Fund Com., Book Club (founding mem.), Parent Tchr. Student Orgn. (mini-grant com. 1991-93). Avocations: reading, gardening. Home: 111 Stockade Rd South Glastonbury CT 06073-2118

GARDNER, SANDI B. biology educator; b. Chicago Heights, Ill., June 24, 1959; d. Robert S. and Lenore M. (D'Arcy) Bushor; m. Daniel E. Gardner, Apr. 16, 1988 (div. 1997); 1 child, C(atherine) J. BS in Phys. Edn./Recreation, U. Ill., Chgo., 1981; MS in Environ. Biology, Govs. State U., University Park, Ill., 1988; postgrad., Ill. Inst. Tech., Chgo., 1993-95; PhD, Walden U., Mpls., 1997. Profl. scout Wau Bon Girl Scout Coun., Fond Du Lac, Wis., 1981-82; pre-sch. tchr. Anita M. Stone Ctr., Flossmoor, Ill., 1982-84, Alsip (Ill.) Pre-Sch., 1984-85; tchg. asst. Govs. State U., 1986-89; park ranger Ind. Dunes Nat. Lakeshore, Porter, 1986-92; prof. biology South Suburban Coll., South Holland, Ill., 1990-96. Adj. prof. Ind. U.-N.W., Gary, 1990—92, Govs. State U., 1989—93; mem. spl. populations adv. bd. South Suburban Mental Health, South Holland, 1992—94; staff develop./curriculum specialist Purdue U., 1995—96, adj. faculty, 1996; prof. biology Triton Coll., River Grove, Ill., 1996—, chair sci. dept., 2001—, adv. pre-profl. orgn., 2002; cons. Taylor U., Ft. Wayne, Ind., 1999—2001; workshop presenter, cons. in field. Author: Relationship Between Computer Anxiety and Computer Use, 1996, WebWeaver Environmental Science Online, 2001, Lab Manual Genetics, 2002; co-author: Case Studies for Anatomy and Physiology, 1992, Lab Manual for General Biology, 1994, 1999, 2001, Teachers/Student Guide to Virtual Biology Laboratory CD-ROM, 1997, WebWeaver Study Guide, 1998. Leader, vol., trainer Calumet coun. Girl Scouts U.S., Highland, Ind., 1981-84, 93—; vol. Lincoln Park Zoo, 1986-88, Brookfield Zoo, 1996-2000; coach AYSO Soccer, River Forest, Ill., bd. dirs. 1999; adv. Phi Theta Kappa Triton Coll, River Grove, Ill., 1996-2000; vol. mentor West Lake Hosp., 2002; vol. Amb. Walden U., 2002; co-chair accreditation com. NCA, 2003. Recipient Spl. Achievement award Nat. Park Svc., 1988; Hand-On Sci. for Tchrs. award EPA, 1992; grantee R&D Triton, 1998—, On-line Biology, 1999, Plastination, 1999, HECA, 1999-2000, On-Line Tutoring Ctr., 2000-01. Mem. Nat. Sci. Tchrs. Assn., Nat. Assn. Biology Tchrs., Ill. Assn. C.C. Biology Tchrs. (pres. 1999-2001), Phi Delta Kappa (v.p. membership 1999-2003). Home: PO Box 5922 River Forest IL 60305 Office: Triton Coll 2000 N 5th Ave River Grove IL 60171-1907 E-mail: sbgardner@aol.com.

GARDNER, TERESA GABRELS, elementary education educator; b. Spartanburg, S.C., Sept. 1, 1947; d. Frank Marion and Mary Veril (Williams) Gabrels; children: Taylor, Andrew. BA, Limestone Coll., 1982; MEd, U. S.C., 1984, postgrad., 1992. Teller, head teller, new accounts rep. various banks, Spartanburg, 1972-80; tchr. Startex (S.C.) Elem. Sch., 1983-96, River Ridge Elem., Moore, S.C., 1996—. Mem. Internat. Reading Assn., Spartanburg Writing Project. Baptist. Avocations: reading, walking, antiques. Home: 123 Bain Dr Spartanburg SC 29307-3014 E-mail: gardnetg@spart5.k12.sc.us.

GARDNER, WILLIAM ALLEN, electrical engineering educator; b. Palo Alto, Calif., Nov. 4, 1942; s. Allen Frances McLean and Francis Anne Demma; m. Nancy Susan Lenhart Hall, June 19, 1966. MS, Stanford U., 1967; PhD, U. Mass., Amherst, 1972. Engr. Bell Telephone Labs., North Andover, Mass., 1967-69; asst. prof. U. Calif., Davis, 1972-77, assoc. prof., 1977-82, prof. elect. engring., 1982—. Pres. Statis. Signal Processing Inc., 1982—; chmn., organizer workshop on Cyclostationary Signals, NSF, Air Force Office of Sci. Rsch., Army Rsch. Office, Office Naval Rsch. Author: Introduction to Random Processes with Applications to Signals and Systems, 1985, 2d edit., 1989, Statistical Spectral Analysis: A Nonprobabilistic Theory, 1987, Cyclostationarity in Communications and Signal Processing, 1994; contbr. over 100 articles to profl. jours.; patentee in field. Recipient Disting. Engring. Alumnus award U. Mass., 1987; grantee Air Force Office Sci. Rsch., 1979-82, 92-93, NSF, 1983-84, 89-96, Electromagnetic Sys. Labs., 1984-92, Army Rsch. Office, 1989-96, Office of Naval Rsch., 1991-94. Fellow IEEE (S.O. Rice Prize Paper award in Comm. Theory, 1988); mem. European Assn. Signal Processing (Best Paper award 1986), Sigma Xi, Eta Kappa Nu, Tau Beta Pi. Office: U Calif Dept Elec and Computer Engring Davis CA 95616

GARFIELD, JOAN BARBARA, statistics educator; b. Milw., May 4, 1950; d. Sol L. and Amy L. (Nusbaum) Garfield; m. Michael G. Luxenberg, Aug. 17, 1980; children: Harlan Ross and Rebecca Ellen (twins). Student, U. Chgo., 1968; BS, U. Wis., 1972; MA, U. Minn., 1978, PhD, 1981. Prof. ednl. psychology Coll. Edn., U. Minn., Mpls., 1995—. Disting. tchg. prof. stats., 1995—. Mem. Nat. Rsch. Coun.'s Applied and Theoretical Stats., 1996-99. Co-editor books on assessment and tech. in stats. edn. Fellow Am. Statis. Assn. (newsletter co-editor 1994-2000, chair sect. on statis. edn. 2003-04); mem. Am. Ednl. Rsch. Assn., Nat. Coun. Tchrs. Math., Internat. Assn. for Statis. Edn. (v.p. 1997—), Internat. Statis. Inst. Jewish. Office: U Minn Dept Edn Psychology 315 Burton Hall Minneapolis MN 55455

GARFIELD, PHYLLIS H. international program administrator, educational consultant; b. Columbus, Nebr., Aug. 21, 1950; d. Carl and Wilma (Phillips) Rafferty; m. Alan J. Garfield, Sept. 2, 1979; children: Eliot, Margaret, Carolan. AA, Platt C.C., Columbus, Nebr., 1972; BA, Midland Luth. Coll., Fremont, Nebr., 1974; student, Phillips U., Marburg, Germany, 1973-74; postgrad., Creighton U., 1975-79. Asst. to dean of students Marycrest Coll., Davenport, Iowa, 1980-83; cons. and v.p. Digigraphic Systems, Inc., Davenport, 1985—, internat. travel advisor Meenaleck, Ireland, 1992—; internat. study advisor Teikyo Marycrest U., Davenport, 1981-99; info. dir. internat. studies program U. Dubuque, 2000—. Pres. Temple Emanuel Sisterhood, Davenport, 1993-94. Fulbright fellow, Marburg, 1973-74. Avocations: travel, making baskets, community volunteering. Home: 2378 Beacon Hill Dr Dubuque IA 52003-0202 Address: Meenaleck Letterkenny County Donegal Ireland E-mail: phyllisgarfield@hotmail.com.

GARFINKEL, ALAN, language educator; b. Chgo., Sept. 6, 1941; s. Bernard D. and Tillie (Schaffner) G.; m. Sonya Pickus, July 10, 1965; children: Eli Louis, Noah Baruch. BA, U. Ill., 1961, MA, 1963; PhD, Ohio State U., 1969. Tchr. Spanish Waukegan (Ill.) Twp. H.S., 1964-65; asst. prof. Okla. State U., Stillwater, 1969-72, Purdue U., West Lafayette, Ind., 1972-74, assoc. prof., 1974-93, prof., 1993—. Cons. Cath. U. of Chile, Santiago, 1976; vis. scholar U. Queensland, Brisbane, Australia, 1993; fgn. expert Beijing Fgn. Studies U., People's Republic China, 2000; cons. in field. Co-author: Modismos al Momento, 1978, Trabajo y Vida, 1983, Explorando en la Casa de los Monstruos, 1997, Navidad en España, 2002, Let's Get Together, 2003; contbr. articles to profl. jours. Bd. dirs. Congregation Sons Abraham, Lafayette, 1986-93; committeeman Dem. Party, West Lafayette, 1993-99. Recipient Sr. Lectr. award Fulbright Commn., 1978, Acad. Specialist award U.S. State Dept., 1985, Tchr. Ctr. award U.S. Dept. Edn., 1978-81. Mem. Am. Coun. Teaching Fgn. Langs. (nat. textbook com. 1992), Ind. Fgn. Langs. Tchr.'s Assn. (pres. 1993-95), Lafayette Adult Resource Acad. (mem. adv. bd.), Lafayette Daybreak Rotary Club (Rotarian of the Yr.) 1997-98, Phi Delta Kappa (del., chpt. pres. 2000—). Jewish. Avocation: philatelist. Home: 2229 Carberry Dr West Lafayette IN 47906-1943 Office: Purdue U FLL-SC West Lafayette IN 47907-1359 E-mail: alangarf@purdue.edu.

GARFINKEL, BARBARA ANN, pianist, educator, musicologist; b. Elizabeth, N.J., Dec. 19, 1931; d. Irving and Lillian (Treister) Slavin; m. Burton Garfinkel, June 28, 1952; children: Steven, Joan Struss. BS in Edn., Boston U., 1953. Cert. vocal music instr., piano instr. Pvt. piano tchr., Millburn, N.J., 1949-52, Livingston, N.J., 1968-90; elem. sch. tchr. Nahant (Mass.) Pub. Schs., 1953-54, Maplewood (N.J.) Pub. Schs., 1954-56; profl. pianist, vocalist, 1984—. Music tchr. Downs Syndrome Children, Livingston, 1982-85; choir dir. Daughters of Miriam, Clifton, N.J., 1986, Cranford (N.J.) Home Continuing Care, 1990. Composer liturgical and show music; performer one woman shows vocal and piano. Vol. pianist Grotta Nursing Home, West Orange, N.J., 1988-93; judge teen piano finalists Garden State Art Ctr., Holmdel, N.J., 1985-95; local leader Dem. Party, Livingston, 1990—; v.p. Christ Hosp. Auxiliary, Jersey City, 1980-85; instrs. Russian, Israeli, Chinese immigrants, 1980-93; diplomat World Jewish Congress, 1995—. Mem. N.J. Music Tchrs. Assn., Schumann Music Study Club (program chair 1994-95), Pro Musica Hon. Music Club, Pi Lambda Theta. Avocations: swimming, boating, gardening, writing, movies. Home: 2 Tiffany Ct Montville NJ 07045-9165

GARFINKEL, LAWRENCE SAUL, academic administrator, educator, television producer; b. N.Y.C., Mar. 9, 1932; s. Benjamin and Rose (Rochkind) G.; m. Adrienne Rederer, June 26, 1960; children: Andrew, Rodger, Craig. BS in Art Edn., NYU, 1953, MA in Higher Edn., 1955, postgrad. in Edn. Comm., 1975. Tchr., supr. art, prin. high schs. West Hempstead Pub. Schs., N.Y., 1954-56, dir. related arts, 1957-69, dir. cmty. rels., 1961-71; prof. edn. adminstrn. and comm., dir. instrnl. comm. program Hofstra U., Hempstead, N.Y., 1969-76; dir. summer television & media insts.; dir. gifted programs Sachem Pub. Schs., Lake Ronkonkoma, N.Y., 1978-79; dir. ednl. comm. Coll. Dentistry, Kriser Dental Ctr., NYU, 1979-91, ret.; adj. prof. dept. speech Baruch Coll., CUNY, 1980-91, Adelphi U., Stern Coll.-Yeshiva U., St. Johns U., Temple U., N.Y. Inst. Tech.; adj. prof. dept. media arts C.W. Post-L.I. U., 1991—. Adj. assoc. prof. art dept. Nassau C.C.; cons. bd. regents N.Y. State Edn. Dept., Ctr. Urban Edn., N.Y.C. Pub.: Restorative Dentistry, 1985; illustrator: Classroom Television, 1970; illustrator N.Y. Times, John Huston Prodns., Century Theatres, Nat. Audio Visual Assn., and numerous publs.; editl. cartoonist Merrick Life; asst. prodr. WPIX-TV, programming Dumont Network; pub. Garson Assocs.; contbr. articles to profl. jours. Coord. youth edn. Mothers Against Drunk Driving, Long Island Area, 1997-99; bd. dirs. Hist. Soc. Merricks, 1983— pres., 2001-; bd. dirs. Higher Edn. Assn. TV, 1972; v.p. Health Equities, N.Y.C.; oral historian Bi Centennial Commn., 1975. Nominee, Woodrow Wilson Found.; named alt., Fulbright award; recipient Grad. Arch award medal, NYU, scholarship masters NYU, numerous awards, Nat. Com. Sch. Pub. Rels.; grad. tchg. fellow, NYU. Mem. N.Y. Acad. Sci., L.I. Art Tchrs. Assn. (pres. 1967-68), Nat. Com. Art Edn. (co-pres. 1967). Avocations: illustrating, lecturing on communications theory, arts, visual literacy, nostalgia therapy. Home and Office: Garson Assocs 172 Babylon Tpke Merrick NY 11566-4407

GARLAND, CARL WESLEY, chemist, educator; b. Bangor, Maine, Oct. 1, 1929; s. Cecil G. and Blandena Couillard (Wadell) G.; m. Joan A. Donaghy, July 30, 1955; children: Leslie J., Andrew E. BS, U. Rochester, 1950; PhD, U. Calif.-Berkeley, 1953. Instr. chemistry U. Calif.-Berkeley, 1953; faculty MIT, 1953—, assoc. prof. chemistry, 1959-68, prof. chemistry, 1968-98; prof. emeritus, 1998—. Vis. prof. U. Calif., San Diego, 1972, U. Rome, 1974, Cath. U. Leuven, Belgium, 1977, Ben Gurion U., Israel, 1980, U. Paris, 1981, 82, U. Bordeaux, France, 1990; chmn. Gordon Rsch. Conf. Orientational Disorder in Crystals, 1984. Author: (with J.W. Nibler, D.P. Shoemaker) Experiments in Physical Chemistry, 7th edit., 2003; editor: Optics and Spectroscopy, 1960-81, Liquid Crystals, 1991-95; contbr. over 200 articles to profl. jours. A.P. Sloan fellow, 1954-60; Guggenheim fellow, 1963 Fellow Am. Acad. Arts and Sci.; mem. Am. Phys. Soc. Home: 4 Edward St Belmont MA 02478-2343 Office: MIT Rm 2-121 Cambridge MA 02139-4307 E-mail: cgarland@mit.edu., carlwgarland@aol.com.

GARLAND, CONNIE JO, secondary health and physical education educator; b. Ft. Wayne, Ind., Jan. 5, 1954; d. George Joseph and Dorothy R. (Wallace) Dobbelaere; m. Robert Lloyd Garland, Mar. 18, 1978; children: Brian Robert, Casie Jo, Brenton Taylor. BEd cum laude, Bowling Green State U., 1976, MEd, 1977. Cert. tchr., Nebr., Ohio. Grad. asst. Bowling Green (Ohio) State U., 1976-77; tchr. health and phys. edn. Mayfield (Ohio) City Schs., 1977-79, Westside Community Schs., Omaha, 1979-92; tchr. phys. edn. S.H.A.P.E., Cin., 1992—93; health and phys. edn. tchr. Lakota Local Sch. Dist., West Chester, Ohio, 1993—. Volleyball, track and gymnastics coach. Mem. AAHPERD, Ohio Assn. for Health, Phys. Edn. and Recreation (chair health, pub. and community sect. 1978-79), Alpha Xi Delta, Delta Psi Kappa, Kappa Delta Pi. Roman Catholic. Avocations: reading, water skiing, swimming, arts and crafts. Home: 7612 Legendary Ln West Chester OH 45069-4603

GARLAND, LARETTA MATTHEWS, nursing educator; b. Jacksonville, Fla. d. Wilburn L. and Clyde-Marian (Chamberlin) Matthews; m. John B. Garland, Mar. 2, 1946; children: John Barnard, Brien Freeling, Amy-Gwin. Diploma, Fla. State Sch. Nursing, 1942; BSN, Emory U., 1950, MA, 1953; BA in Edn., U. Fla., 1951; cert. cardiovascular nurse specialty, Tex. Med. Ctr., 1965; EdD, U. Ga., 1975; postgrad. in counseling and guidance, Ga. State U., 1969; grad. cert. in gerontology, 1981. Cert. nat. counselor. Office and staff nurse, Lakeland, Fla., 1942, 45; nurse ARC, Buffalo, 1956; asst. prof. nursing Med. Coll. Ga., 1965-67; instr. Emory U., 1952-54, assoc. prof., 1967-71, prof., 1972-86, prof. emeritus, 1987—. Ednl. psychologist, dir. gerontol. nurse practitioner program, 1978-80, asst. to dean, 1983-86. Author: (with Carol Bush) Coping Behavior and Nursing, 1982; contbr. articles to profl. jours. With Nurse Corps, U.S. Army, 1942-45. Decorated 2 Bronze Stars; recipient Outstanding Tchg. award Emory U. Sch. Nursing Grad. Srs., 1977, Appreciation award So. Region Constituent Leagues, Nat. League for Nursing award, 1987, Mabel Korsell award of appreciation Ga. League Nursing, 1987, Spl. Recognition award Ga. Nurses Assn., 1988, 90, Nurse of Yr. award, 1992, Appreciation award Ga. Assn. Nursing Students, 1990, Van de Vrede award Ga. League Nursing, 1993; HEW fellow, 1967-68. Mem. APA, AACD, ANA, Ga. Assn. Nursing Students (hon.), Nat. League Nursing, Bs. and Profl. Women, China Burma India VA Assn. (mem. nat. bd. 1993—), 14th Air Force Asssn. (Flying Tigers), Hump Pilots Assn., Ormond Beach Womens Club, Ormond Beach Hist. Trust, Nat. Assn. Women Vet. (steering com.), Women in Mil. Svc. Meml. Found. (charter), ARC Nurses, Panhellenic Assn., Hist. Trust, Alpha Chi Omega, Sigma Theta Tau, Kappa Delta Pi, Alpha Kappa Delta, Omicron Delta Kappa. Office: Emory U Nell Hodgson Woodruff Sch Atlanta GA 30322-0001

GARN, SUSAN LYNN, middle school art educator; b. Astoria, Oreg., July 12, 1948; d. Everett Leslie and Jeanne Esther (Linquist) G. BA in Art, U. Nev., Reno, 1970; MEd in Ednl. Adminstrn. and Higher Edn., U. Nev., Las Vegas, 1990. Registered mem. federally recognized Chinook Indian tribe. Tchr. art Desert Sands Unified Sch. Dist., Indio, Calif., 1973-74; art. resource tchr. Trinity County Schs., Weaverville, Calif., 1974-75; multi-subject tchr., primarily in visual arts, digital art edn. Clark County Sch. Dist., Las Vegas, 1975-80, 87—; tchr. English, reading Jordan Sch. Dist., Sandy, Utah, 1982-84; lead community sch coord. Lincoln County Sch. Dist., Newport, Oreg., 1984-87. Sole propr. Sue Garn and Kids Art, Las Vegas, 1988-98; presenter at profl. confs.; long term substitute tchr. Chemawa Indian Sch., Salem, Oreg., 1984. Work displayed at Educators as Artists exhibit, 1990, 92, 93, 2001, 02, 03. Bd. dirs. Las Vegas Indian Ctr., 1996-99. Named Tchr. of Yr. Nev. State PTA, 1990; Excellence in Edn., CCSD, 1991. Mem. Art Educators So. Nev., Am. Indian C. of C. Avocations: german short haired pointer, wirehaired terrier and weimaraner dogs, travel, movies, art. Home: 3709 El Jardin Ave Las Vegas NV 89102-3821 Office: James Cashman Mid Sch 4622 W Desert Inn Rd Las Vegas NV 89102 E-mail: sgarninlv@hotmail.com.

GARNER, BRYAN ANDREW, law educator, consultant, writer; b. Lubbock, Tex., Nov. 17, 1958; s. Gary Thomas and Mariellen (Griffin) G.; m. Pan Anurugsa, May 26, 1984; children: Caroline Beatrix, Alexandra Bess. BA, U. Tex., 1980, JD, 1984; LLD (hon.), Thomas M. Cooley Law Sch., 2000. Bar: Tex. 1984, U.S. Ct. Appeals (5th cir.) 1985, U.S. Dist. Ct. (no. dist.) Tex. 1986. Law clk. to judge U.S. Ct. Appeals (5th cir.), Austin, Tex., 1984-85; assoc. Carrington, Coleman, Sloman & Blumenthal, Dallas, 1985-88; dir. Tex./Oxford Ctr. for Legal Lexicography U. Tex. Sch. Law, Austin, 1988-90; adj. prof. law So. Meth. U., Dallas, 1990—. Vis. assoc. prof. law U. Tex., 1988—90; pres. LawProse, Inc., 1990—; vis. scholar U. Salzburg, 1995, 98, U. Glasgow, 1996, U. Cambridge, England, 1997; chmn. plain-lang. com. State Bar Tex., 1989—95; lectr. in field; cons. in field. Author: A Dictionary of Modern Legal Usage, 1987, A Dictionary of Modern Legal Usage, 2d edit., 1995, The Elements of Legal Style, 1991, Guidelines for Drafting and Editing Court Rules, 1996, A Dictionary of Modern American Usage, 1998, Securities Disclosure in Plain English, 1999, The Winning Bried, 1999, Legal Writing in Plain English, 2001, The Redbook: A Manual on Legal Style, 2002; editor: Scribes Jour. Legal Writing, 1989—2000, Tex, Our Texas, 1984, Black's Law Dictionary, 1996, Black's Law Dictionary, 7th edit., 1999, A Handbook of Basic Law Terms, 1999; A Handbook of Business Law Terms, 1999; editor: A Handbook of Family Law Terms, 2001; mem. editl. bd.: Tex. Law Rev., 1984; contbr. articles to profl. jours. Recipient Henry C. Lind award, Assn. Reporters Judicial Decisions, 1994, Clarity award, State Bar Mich, 1997, Outstanding Young Tex. Ex. award, 1998. Fellow: Tex. Bar Found.; mem.: ABA, Tex. Bar Assn. (chmn. plain lang. com. 1990—), Am. Law Inst. (commn. on bylaws & coun. rules 1993—94), Scribes (exec. bd. 1990—2001, pres. 1997—98), Dictionary Soc. N.Am., Am. Dialect Soc., Philos. Soc. Tex., Friars (abbot 1981—84), Bent Tree Country Club, Phi Beta Kappa. Republican. Avocation: golf. Home: 6478 Lakehurst Ave Dallas TX 75230-5131

GARNER, CHARLES WILLIAM, educational administration educator, consultant; b. Pine Grove Mills, Pa., Apr. 18, 1939; s. Adam Krumrine and Blanche Ella (Gearhart) G.; m. Karyl J. Packer, Sept. 8, 1962; children:

Ronald Adam, Juliet Paige. Student, U.S. Navy Electronics Airborne Sonar Sch., 1959; BS in Bus. Edn., Pa. State U., 1965, MEd in Higher Edn. Adminstrn., 1968, EdD in Vocat. Indsl. Edn., 1974. Cert. govt. fin. mgr. Adminstrv. asst. dept. psychology Pa. State U., 1965-75; asst. prof., site adminstr. March AFB, Calif. for So. Ill. U., 1975-77; asst. prof., coordinator Ft. Knox Ctr.- U. Louisville, 1977-78; assoc. prof., acting vice dean Rutgers U., Camden, N.J., 1978-79, assoc. prof. urban edn., chmn. dept. edn. Univ. Coll. New Brunswick, N.J., 1978-81, assoc. prof. vocat. tech. edn. Grad. Sch. Edn., 1981—, chmn. dept. vocat. tech. edn., 1982-85, assoc. prof. edn. adminstrn., 1985—, exec. dir. Vocat. Edn. Resource Ctr., 1983-88, dir. continuing edn., 1987-89, program chair edn. adminstrn., 1990-96; cons. CWG Assocs., McElhattan, Pa., 1989—; pres. Penn State Auto Repair, Inc., Williamsport, Pa., 1997-2000. Author: Accounting and Budgeting in Public and Nonprift Organizations: A Manager's Guide, 1991, Financial Management of School Districts in New Jersey: For School Leaders, 1996, Education Finance for School Leaders: Strategic Planning and Administration, 2004; contbr. articles to profl. jours.; co-editor: Occupational Edn. Forum, 1979-85; editl. reader Jour. Indsl. Tchr. Edn., 1981; producer, host talk show pilot for pub. TV, 1979; producer, host: TV tape series Rutgers U.: Current Issues in Vocat. Edn., 1979; editor edn. sect. Pub. Budgeting and Financial Management, 1995. Bd. dirs., treas. Cerebral Palsy League of Union County, N.J., 1996-99. With USN, 1959-62. Grantee N.J. Dept. Edn. Divsn. Vocat. Edn., 1978-88; grantee HEW, 1979-80. Mem.: AAUP, DAV (life), Nat. Soc. for Study of Edn., Spl. Needs Pers. (exec. coun. 1980—81, pres. 1981—82), Assn. Govt. Accts., Am. Edn. Rsch. Assn., Non-Commd. Officers Assn. (life), Elks (exalted ruler 1972—73), Epsilon Pi Tau (trustee 1983—88), Omicron Tau Theta, Phi Delta Kappa. Home: PO Box 456 Mc Elhattan PA 17748 Office: Rutgers U Dept Ednl Theory Admin New Brunswick NJ 08903 E-mail: wgarner@rci.rutgers.edu.

GARNER, DORIS TRAGANZA, education educator, director; b. Phila., Oct. 13, 1934; d. Charles Thomas and Elizabeth Marie (Blatteau) Traganza; m. Joseph Anthony DeMatteo, Apr. 12, 1958 (dec. Aug. 1968); children: Maria Louise, Carol Ann, Nicholas Joseph, Elizabeth Joan, Charles Traganza, Ann Seton; m. Doyle Daniel Garner, July 11, 1970 (div. Feb. 1989); 1 child: Jean Estelle. Student in piano with, Leo Ornstein, Phila., 1948—54; BA in Psychology cum laude, U. Pa., 1955; postgrad., Temple U., 1955-59; MS in Ednl. Adminstrn., SUNY, Albany, 1978, PhD in Ednl. Adminstrn. and Higher Edn., 1983. Cert. tchr., N.Y. Elem. tchr. Phila. Sch. Dist., 1955-59; asst. to asst. dean grad. studies SUNY, Albany, 1977-78, asst. to asst. v.p. acad. affairs, 1979; curriculum rsch. assoc. John Jay Coll., CUNY, N.Y.C., 1979; asst. in higher edn. doctoral office N.Y. State Edn. Dept., Albany, 1979-84, coord. program rev. master's programs, 1985-87, assoc. in higher edn. coll./univ. evaluation, 1987-89, asst. to dep. commr. higher edn. and professions, 1989-95, divsn. dir. coll./univ. evaluation, 1995-96, staff dir. N.Y. State Regents Task Force on Tchg., 1996-98, supr. acad. program rev., 1998—2002; supr. higher edn. N.Y. State Edn. Dept., 2002—; conf. panelist on preparing tchrs. to use technology, 2002. Featured spkr. CUNY conf. on tchr. edn. reform, 2000, NYACTE/NYSATE conf. on tchr. edn., 2001, plenary spkr., 2003; expert witness for plaintiffs, Campaign for Fiscal Equity v. N.Y. State, 1999; invited participant Inaugural Portfolio Conf., Annenberg Inst. for Sch. Reform, Boston, 1998; chair session on state policy Am. Assn. Colls. for Tchr. Edn., New Orleans, 1988; plenary session panelist on tchg. reform Edn. Conf. of Empire State Reports, 1998; presenter in field. Editor (manuscript) Regents College: The Early Years by D.J. Nolan, 1998. Mem. Shaker H.S. Theater Support, Latham, N.Y., 1988-89; pianist at non-profit functions, Albany, N.Y., 1992-94; cmty. theater actor Stagecrafters, Phila., 1951. Avocations: grandchildren and children, reading on social and political issues, piano, plays, concerts, nature.

GARNER, DOUGLAS MICHAEL, gymnastics fitness center executive, team coach; b. Camden, Ark., Sept. 10, 1959; s. Thomas Clark and Naomi (Colvert) G.; m. Becky Lynn Cathcart, Dec. 26, 1982; children: Tyler, Michael. BA in Psychology and Sociology, Centenary Coll., Shreveport, La., 1980; MS in Behavioral Sci., Kennedy Western U. Instr. Am. Coaching Effectiveness Program; meet dir. USGF; dir. U.S. Gymnastics Fedn. Men's Program; co-owner, head team coach Hot Springs Gymnastics Fitness Ctr., 1980—. Adj. prof. Garland County C.C.; instr. elem. phys. edn. pvt. sch.; dir. Ark. Springers Gymnastics Camp; guest presenter Youth Clinics, Head Start Conf. for Movement Edn. Mem. adv. bd. Collegiate Press. Youth coach Wheelchair Sports, H.S. Boys Club; dir., head coach Ark. Jr. Rollin' Razorbacks Wheelchair Sports Team; vol. youth coach, Hot Springs, Shreveport; rated ofcl. Ark. Activities Assn. Mem. AAPHERD, ASCD, APA, Nat. Assn. Girls and Women Sports (citizen amb. program del. to Russia 1993), U.S. Assn. Ind. Gym Clubs, U.S. Gymnastics Fedn. (safety cert.), Ark. Ofcls. Assn., Wheelchair Sports USA, Nat. Handicapped Sports, Nat. Wheelchair Basketball Coaches Assn. Avocations: reading, sports. Home: 122 Mesa Trl Hot Springs National Park AR 71913-9088 Office: Hot Springs Gymnastics and Fitness 1510 Lakeshore Dr Hot Springs National Park AR 71913-6652

GARNER, GIROLAMA THOMASINA, retired educational administrator, educator; b. Muskegon, Mich., Sept. 15, 1923; d. John and Martha Ann (Thomas) Funaro; student Muskegon Jr. Coll., 1941; B.A., Western Mich. U., 1944, M.A. in Counseling and Guidance, 1958; Ed.D., U. Ariz., 1973; m. Charles Donald Garner, Sept. 16, 1944 (dec.); 1 dau., Linda Jeannette Garner Blake. Elem. tchr., Muskegon and Tucson, 1947-77; counselor Erickson Elem. Sch., Tucson, 1978-79; prin. Hudlow Elem. Sch., Tucson, 1979-87, adj. prof. U. Ariz., 1973-98, Tuscon Pima Community Coll., 1981-93, Prescott Coll., 1986-93; mem. Ariz. Com. Tchr. Evaluation and Cert., 1976-78; del. NEA convs. Active ARC, Crippled Children's Soc., UNESCO, U.S.-China People's Friendship Assn., DAV Aux., Rincon Renegades; bd. dirs. Hudlow Community Sch., 1973-76. Recipient Apple award for teaching excellence Pima Community Coll., 1982. Mem. Nat. Assn. Sci. Tchrs., Tucson Edn. Assn., Ariz. Edn. Assn., NEA, Assn. Supervision and Curriculum Devel., AAUW, Tucson Adminstrs., Pima County Retired Tchrs., Delta Kappa Gamma, Kappa Rho Sigma, Kappa Delta Pi. Democrat. Christian Scientist. Home: 6922 E Baker St Tucson AZ 85710-2230

GARNER, JO ANN STARKEY, retired elementary and special education educator; b. Ft. Hamilton, N.Y., Dec. 25, 1934; d. Joseph Wheeler and Irene Dorothy (Vogt) Starkey; m. James Gayle Garner, Mar. 2, 1957; children: Mary Vivian Pine, Margaret Susan Gillis, Kathryn Lynn. BA in History, Govt., Law, U. Tex., Austin, 1956; postgrad., Trinity U., 1973. Cert. deaf edn. and elem. tchr., Tex. Kindergarten tchr. Platenstrasse Internat. Sch., Frankfurt, Fed. Republic Germany, 1964-66; tchr. of deaf Sunshine Cottage Sch. for Deaf, San Antonio, 1966-2000; ret., 2000. Speech cons. Trinity U., 1978, cooperating tchr., 1978-87; fiesta coord. Sunshine Cottage. Active San Antonio Fiesta Commn., Powesheik County Iowa Geneal. Soc.; chmn. book com. San Antonio Geneal. and Hist. Soc. Mem. Tex. (charter) and Nat. Alexander Graham Bell Assn., Tex. State Geneal. and Hist. Soc., Rep. Nat. Com., German-Texan Heritage Soc., Pioneers of Ind., Olde Mecklenburg Geneal. Soc. N.C., Pioneers of Ill., Ill. Geneal. Soc., Madison County (Ill.) Geneal. Soc., Tex. Pioneers, Alpha Delta Pi. Republican. Mem. Catholic Episcopal Ch. Avocations: writing, painting, history, genealogical research, science. Home: 2027 Edgehill Dr San Antonio TX 78209-2023

GARNER, JULIE LOWREY, occupational therapist; b. Paris, Tex., Aug. 6, 1953; d. John Robert and Rachel (Garner) Lowrey; m. Kenneth Wayne Garner, Jan. 29, 1983. BS, U. Tex., Galveston, 1975; MS, Tex. Woman's U., 1982; MEd, Tex. A&M U., Commerce, 2001. Cert. occupational therapist, Tex.; cert. to administer and interpret So. Calif. Sensory Integration Tests Sensory Integration Internat., neurodevel. treatment approach to cerebral palsy. Occupational therapist Presbyn. Hosp. Dallas, 1976-77; occupational therapist region X Ednl. Svc. Ctr., Richardson, Tex., 1977; occupational therapist Duncanville (Tex.) Ind. Sch. Dist., 1977-81, 89-90, Grand Prairie (Tex.) Ind. Sch. Dist., 1978-81, U. Tex., Dallas, 1981-83, Lewisville (Tex.) Ind. Sch. Dist., 1983-85, Collin County Coop. Spl. Svcs., Wylie, Tex., 1983-89, Commerce (Tex.) Ind. Sch. Dist., 1990-97, M.J. Care, Gunter, Tex., 1997-99. Bd. dirs. United Cerebral Palsy Assn. Dallas, 1980-84. Recipient Hurdle Cert. of Honor Soroptimist Internat., Dallas, 1976. Mem. Am. Occuptl. Therapy Assn. Methodist. Avocations: sewing, arts and crafts, computers. Home: 1313 Flameleaf Dr Allen TX 75002-4424

GARNER, SHIRLEY NELSON, English language educator; b. Waxahachie, Tex., Aug. 8, 1935; d. Cleo and Ruby D. Nelson; m. Frank L. Garner, Nov. 24, 1972; children: Hart Phillip, Celia Ann. AB magna cum laude, U. Tex., 1957; MA, Stanford U., 1966, PhD, 1972. Instr. Stanford (Calif.) U., 1964-65, instr., asst. to dir. fresh composition, 1967-70; asst. prof. U. Minn., Mpls., 1972-76, assoc. prof., 1976-86, assoc. mem. faculty Women's Studies, 1980—, prof., 1986—, chair Women's Studies, 1989-90, dir. Ctr. Advanced Feminist Studies, 1990-94, chair English dept., 1994—2000, assoc. dean grad. sch., 2001—. Editor: (with Personal Narratives Collective) Interpreting Women's Lives: Feminist Theory and Personal Narratives, 1989, (with Madelon Sprengnether) Shakespearean Tragedy and Gender, 1995, Antifeminism in the Academy, 1996, (with VeVe Clark, Ketu Katrak, and Marianne Higonnet) Is Feminism Dead?, 2000; editor, contbg. author: (with Clare Kahane and Madelon Sprengnether) The (M)other Tongue: Essays in Feminist Psychoanalytic Interpretation, 1985; contbg. author: Bad Shakespeare: Revaluations of the the Shakespeare Canon, 1988, Seduction and Theory: Readings of Gender, Representation and Rhetoric, 1989, Shakespeare's Personality, 1989, Novel Mothering, 1991, Feminism and Psychoanalysis, Feminism and Philosophy: Essential Readings in Theory, Reinterpretation and Application, 1992, The Intimate Critique: Autobiographical Literary Criticism, 1993; founder, mem. editl. bd. Hurricane Alice, 1983—; mem. editl. bd. Signs, 1992—; contbr. articles, revs. to profl. jours. Scholar Phillips Petroleum Found., 1953-57; Woodrow Wilson fellow, 1959-60, Sorptimists' fellow, 1965-66, 66-67; grantee U. Minn. 1974-76, 81, 87-88, Bush Sabbatical, 1984-85, Office Internat. Edn., 1988, CIA, 1981, 84-90, UROP, 1991-92. Mem. MLA (co-chairperson Marriage and the Family in Shakespeare divsn., Shakespeare sect. 1979, chairperson 1980-82, chair, co-chair various seminars, symposia), Nat. Women's Studies Assn., Midwest Modern Lang. Assn. (sec. Shakespeare sect. 1972, chairperson 1973, nominations com. 1974-77, sec. Women and Lit. sect. 1978-79, chairperson 1980-81, nomination com. Women and Lit. sect. 1981-84), Shakespeare Assn. Office: U Minn English Dept 207 Church St SE Minneapolis MN 55455-0134

GARNETTE, CHERYL PETTY, government agency administrator; BS in Math., MA in Measurement and Stats., U. Md. With Model Secondary Sch. for the Deaf; dir. tech. in edn. programs Office Innovation and Improvement U.S. Dept. Edn., Washington. Comm. dir. Assn. for Ednl. Comm. and Tech. Editor: (Rsch. Notes column) Jour. Ednl. Computing Rsch. Office: US Dept Edn Rm 522G Capitol Pl 555 New Jersey Ave NW Washington DC 20208*

GARNISS, JOAN BREWSTER, musician, educator; b. Bangor, Maine, Aug. 10, 1940; d. William Ayer Brewster and Constance Miriam (Witham) Page; adopted d. Woodrow Evans Page; m. Howard Freeman Garniss, Aug. 26, 1962; children: Gretchen, Jonathan. MusB, Boston U., 1962, MusM, 1991. cert. music tchr., Music Tchr. Nat. Assn. Pvt. practice, Dover-Foxcroft, Maine, 1954-58, Hingham, Mass., 1963-65, Waltham, Mass., 1974—. Musician: (albums) En blanc et noir, 2001, Duo Con Anima, 1987, (accompanist) Wintersauce Chorale, 1984—86, U. Mass., 1988—. Co-founder, pres. Waltham Band Parents, 1979-82, Waltham Music Festival, 1994-97; pres. Friends Waltham Pub. Libr., 1980-83 (bd. dir. 1980-89, 1995—); trustee Waltham Pub. Libr., 1986—, co-chmn. fundraising com., 1995-96; dir. children's choir, All Saints Ch., 1963-66; vol. Boston Pub. Sch., 1969-73; active City Coun. Citizens Com. Transp., Waltham, 1977. Mass. Cultural Affairs Coun. grantee, 1988-89. Mem. UUA/MA N.E. Dist. (human rels. chmn. 1967-70), LWV (v.p. 1979-83, pres. 1983-85, sec. 1997-2003, bd. dir., 2003—, Outstanding Mem. award, 1995), Music Tchrs. Nat. Assn.(rep. East Divsn. Cmty. Outreach, 1995-97,) Ind. Music Tchr. Forum oversight com., 1997-99, Mass. Music Tchrs. Assn. (v.p. 1987-91, pres.-elect 1991-93, pres. 1993-97, immediate past pres. 1997-99), New England Piano Tchr. Assn. (co-chmn. junior recitals com. 1982-88, student master class 1988-90, dir. 1988-90, chair Ensemble Festival, 2000—), Mass. Libr. Trustees Assn., Lexington Music Club, Mu Phi Epsilon, Pi Kappa Lambda. Avocations: needlework, travel, reading, grandchildren.

GAROFALO, VINCENT JAMES, secondary education educator; b. Oneida, N.Y., July 6, 1939; s. Leonard John and Ethel Ida (Reick) G.; m. Patricia Sue Schieble, Jan. 15, 1966; children: Gitana, Leonardo, Prudence Keyes, Dove Rose. BA in History, Albright Coll., 1961; MAT in Social Studies, Colgate U., 1962; PhD in Reading Edn., Syracuse U., 1969. Admission, placement, fin. aid office Morgan State Coll., Balt., 1964-65; dir. reading ctr. Md. State Coll., Princess Anne, 1968-71; dir. spl. edn. Clarksdale Pub. Sch., Miss., 1971-72; secondary sch. team leader Title I Standing Rock Sioux Tribe, Ft. Yates, N.D., 1972-74; dir. skills learning program U. Wis., Green Bay, 1974-77; dir. spl. svcs. project SUNY, Plattsburg, 1977-79; chair edn. Aquinas Coll., Grand Rapids, Mich., 1979-98, dean sch. edn., 1998—. Part-time mid. sch. tchr. Wyoming Mich. Pub. Schs., 1987-94, reading cons., 1995—; dir. Migrant Rsch. Project, Syracuse U., N.Y., 1968; coord and cons. to various confs. and tng. projects, 1968—; instr. edn. COPE Montcalm C.C., 1980—; guest instr. Ctrl. mich. U., 1989-99, Nazareth Coll., 1990-92; presenter numerous workshops. Contbr. articles to profl. jours. Vol. U.S. Peace Corps, 1962-64. Mem. AAUP, ACLU, NEA, Mich. Edn. Assn., Miss. Mental Health Assn., N.D. Edn. Assn., Congress Racial Equality, Coll. Reading Assn., Internat. Reading Assn., Alpha Psi Omega. Avocations: organic gardening, piano, classical and jaz music, hiking, reading. Office: Aquinas Coll Sch Edn 1607 Robinson Rd SE Grand Rapids MI 49506-1741

GAROFOLO, RONALD JOSEPH, secondary education drafting and architecture educator; b. Omaha, July 10, 1949; s. Salvator A. and Louise (Marino) G.; m. Pamela J. Garofolo, Oct. 22, 1971; children: Amy, Timothy. BS in Secondary Edn., U. Nebr., 1971, MS, 1975, cert. in ednl. adminstrn., 1993. Indsl. edn. tchr. Bryan Jr. High Sch., Omaha, 1971-78; archtl. drafting tchr. Tech. High Sch., Omaha, 1978-84, Bryan Sr. High Sch., Omaha, 1984—. Recipient Alice Buffett Outstanding Tchr. award, 1988, Norwest Bank Outstanding Tchr. award, 1990, Tchr. Excellence award (Nebr.), Internat. Tech. Edn. Assn., 1992. Mem. NEA (rep. nat. assembly del.), Internat. Tech. Edn. Assn. (Tchr. Excellence award 1993), Nebr. State Edn. Assn. (state del. assembly del.), Nebr. Indsl. Tech. Edn. Assn. (Tchr. of Yr. 1992, Nebr. Coaches Assn. (mem. adv. com., tennis rep., Tennis Coach of Yr. 1992), Omaha Edn. Assn. (bd. dirs.), Nat. High Sch. Athletic Coaches Assn. (mem. nat. tennis com.), Phi Delta Kappa. Office: Bryan Sr High Sch 4700 Giles Rd Omaha NE 68157-2641

GARONE, FRANK, English language educator; b. Bklyn., Feb. 16, 1944; s. Charles and Elizabeth (Basta) G.; children: Elizabeth, Christopher. BA, St. Francis Coll., Bklyn., 1966; MA, Duquesne U., 1968. 7th grade tchr. St. Brigid's Sch., Bklyn., 1965-66; philosophy tchr. Duquesne U., Pitts., 1967-69, Point Park Coll., Pitts., 1968-70; English tchr. L.I. Luth. High Sch., Brookville, N.Y., 1970-73, head of rsource ctr., 1973-74; English tchr. Oyster Bay (N.Y.) High Sch., 1974-93, Vernon Middle Sch., East Norwich, N.Y., 1988-90. Author: (play) You the Crusader, 1992, Kiss Her First, Judas, 1992. Recipient Duns Scotus Honor Soc. St. Francis Coll., Bklyn., 1966; named hon. mem. Nat. Honor Soc. Oyster Bay High Sch., 1988; recipient Rotary Club award for svc. Oyster Bay Rotary, 1987. Office: Oyster Bay High Sch E Main St Oyster Bay NY 11771

GARR, WANDA FAYE, secondary education educator; b. Jamestown, Ky., May 7, 1950; d. Clarence and Willie Mae (Clayton) G. BS, Ea. Ky. U., 1972; MA, U. Ky., 1976; MPA, Ky. State U., 1981; postgrad., U. Ky. Cert. secondary tchr., supr. instruction, Ky. Tchr. bus. Jefferson County Pub. Schs., Louisville, Ky., 1972-73, Fayette County Pub. Schs., Lexington, Ky., 1973—. Tchr. observer Tchr. Internship Program, 1992—. Civil svc. commr. Lexington Fayette Urban County Govt., 1977-78; cons. Ky. Coun. Econ. Edn., Louisville, 1986-89. Mem. NEA, ASCD, Ky. Edn. Assn., Nat. Assn. for Advancement Black Ams. in Vocat. Edn., Fayette County Edn. Assn., Parent, Tchr., Student Assn., Nat. Bus. Edn. Assn., Am. Black Book Writers Assn., Inc., Ky. Assn. Gifted Edn. Democrat. Baptist. Avocations: writing fiction, piano.

GARRETSON, RICHARD A. principal; b. Stephenson, W.Va., Nov. 10, 1936; s. Kermit and Nellie Madeline (Miller) G.; m. Edna May Butterworth, Mar. 26, 1960; children: Richard A. Jr., John Carroll, Kristin Cheryl, Nancy Michelle, Melissa Dawn. BS, W.Va. Inst. Tech., 1964; MA, W.Va. U., 1968; cert. of adminstrn., W.Va. Coll. Grad Studies, 1978. Cert. tchr., W.Va., Mass. Tchr. Baileysville (W.Va.) Grade Sch., 1964-68, Herndon (W.Va.) Grade Sch., 1968-75, 77-86; prin. Matheny (W.Va.) Grade Sch., 1975-77, Glen Rogers (W.Va.) Grade Sch., 1986-88, Mullens (W.Va.) Mid. Sch., 1988-89, Herndon Consol. Sch., 1989—. Pres., owner Mullens Taxi Co., 1980—. With U.S. Army, 1956-59, Korea. Republican. Home: PO Box 400 Bud WV 24716-0400

GARRETT, DONNA IRVIN, librarian; b. Nashville, Nov. 4, 1946; d. Donald and Violet Loucile (Nelson) Irvin; m. Billy Gene Garrett, July 14, 1979. BA, Tenn. Tech. U., 1969; MS, Memphis State U., 1976, student, 1977-79. Cert. libr. and tchr., Tenn. Tchr. Met. Nashville Schs., 1970-73, Shelby County Schs., Germantown, Tenn., 1973-75, libr. Memphis, 1975—. Recipient Career Ladder III Libr. award Tenn. State Dept. of Edn., 1986—; named S.W. Tenn. Region Tchr. of Yr., 1993. Mem. ALA, NEA, Tenn. Assn. Sch. Librs. (v.p. 1992-93, pres. 1993-95), Tenn. Edn. Assn., Shelby County Edn. Assn. (Outstanding Tchr. award 1985), Soc. Sch. Librs. Internat., Memphis State U. Alumni (Disting. Edn. Alumni award 1986), Delta Kappa Gamma (treas. 1990-92). Mem. Ch. of Christ. Avocations: reading, gardening, walking.

GARRETT, GEORGE PALMER, JR., creative writing and English language educator, writer; b. Orlando, Fla., June 11, 1929; s. George Palmer and Rosalie (Toomer) G.; m. Susan Parrish Jackson, June 14, 1952; children: William, George, Rosalie. Grad., Hill Sch., 1947; AB, Princeton U., 1952, MA, 1956, PhD, 1985; DLitt (hon.), U. South, 1995. Asst. prof. English Wesleyan U.; writer-in-residence, resident fellow in creative writing Princeton U., 1964-65; former assoc. prof. U. Va.; prof. English Hollins Coll. Va., 1967-71; prof. U. S.C., Columbia, 1971-73, Princeton U., 1974-78, U. Mich., 1979-80, 83-84; Hoyns prof. creative writing U. Va., Charlottesville, 1984—2001; prof. Bennington Coll., 1980; Coal Royalty chair U. Ala., 1994. Author The Reverend Ghost: Poems (Poets of Today IV), 1957, King of the Mountain, 1958, The Sleeping Gypsy and Other Poems, 1958, The Finished Man, 1959, Which Ones Are the Enemy, 1961; (poems) Abraham's Knife, 1961, In the Briar Patch, 1961; (plays) Sir Slob and the Princess, 1962, Cold Ground Was My Bed Last Night, 1964; (screenplays) The Young Lovers, 1964, The Playground, 1965, Do, Lord, Remember Me, 1965, For a Bitter Season, 1967, A Wreath for Garibaldi, 1969, Death of the Fox, 1971, The Magic Striptease. 1973, Welcome to the Medicine Show, Postcards/Flashcards/Snapshots, 1978, To Recollect a Cloud of Ghosts: Christmas in England 1602-03, 1979, Luck's Shining Child: Poems, 1981, The Succession: A Novel of Elizabeth and James, 1983, The Collected Poems of George Garrett, 1984, James Jones, 1984, An Evening Performance: New and Selected Short Stories, 1985, Poison Pen, 1986, Understanding Mary Lee Settle, 1988, Entered from the Sun, 1990, The Sorrows of Fat City, 1992, Whistling in the Dark, 1992, My Silk Purse and Yours, 1992, The Old Army Game, 1994, The King of Babylon Shall Not Come Against You, 1996, Days of Our Lives Lie in Fragments, 1998, Bad Man Blues, 1998, Going to See the Elephant, 2001; editor The Girl in the Black Raincoat, 1966, The Sounder Few, 1971, Film Scripts I-IV, 1971, Craft So Hard to Learn, 1973, The Writer's Voice, 1973, Intro V, 1974, Intro 6: Life As We Know It, 1974, Intro 7: All of Us and None of You, 1975, Botteghe Obscure Reader, 1975, Intro 8: The Liar's Craft, 1977, Intro 9: Close to Home, 1978, Eric Clapton's Lover, 1990, The Wedding Cake in the Middle of the Road, 1992, Elvis in Oz, 1992, That's What I Like (About the South), 1993, The Yellow Shoe Poets, 1999. Served in occupation of Trieste, Austria and Germany. Recipient Rome prize Am. Acad. Arts and Letters, 1958-59, Sewanee Rev. fellow poetry, 1958-59, Am. Acad. and Inst. of Letters award, 1985, T.S. Eliot award Ingersoll Found., 1990, Pen/Malamud award, 1990, Hollins Coll. medal, 1992, U. Va. Pres.'s Report award, 1992, Aiken-Taylor award, 1999, Gov.'s award Commonwealth of Va., 2000; named Cultural Laureate of Va., 1986; Ford Found. grantee in drama, 1960, Nat. Found Arts grantee, 1966; Guggenheim fellow, 1974, resident fellow Bellagio Ctr., 2000. Fellow: Am. Acad. in Rome; mem.: PEN, MLA, Fellowship So. Writers (vice chancellor 1988, chancellor 1993—97), Poetry Soc. Am., Writers Guild Am. East, Authors League. Democrat. Episcopalian. Home: 1845 Wayside Pl Charlottesville VA 22903-1630 Office: Univ Va Dept English Charlottesville VA 22903 E-mail: gpg@virginia.edu.

GARRETT, JAMES LEO, JR., theology educator; b. Waco, Tex., Nov. 25, 1925; s. James Leo and Grace Hasseltine (Jenkins) G.; m. Myrta Ann Latimer, Aug. 31, 1948; children: James Leo III, Robert Thomas, Paul Latimer. BA, Baylor U., 1945; BD, Southwestern Bapt. Theol. Sem., 1948, ThD, 1954; ThM, Princeton Theol. Sem., 1949; PhD, Harvard U., 1966; postgrad., Oxford U., 1968—69, St. John's U., 1977, Trinity Evang. Div. Sch., 1989. Ordained to ministry Baptist Ch., 1945. Pastor Bapt. chs. in Tex., 1946-48, 50-51; successively instr., asst. prof., assoc. prof., prof. theology, disting. prof., disting. prof. emeritus Southwestern Bapt. Theol. Sem., Ft. Worth, 1949-59, 79—, assoc. dean for PhD degree, 1981-84; prof. Christian theology So. Bapt. Theol. Sem., Louisville, 1959-73; dir. J.M. Dawson Studies in Ch.-State, prof. religion Baylor U., Waco, Tex., 1973-79, Simon M. and Ethel Bunn prof. Ch.-State Studies, 1975-79. Interim pastor Bapt. chs. in Tex., D.C., Ind. and Ky.; guest prof. Hong Kong Bapt. Theol. Sem., 1988; coord. 1st Conf. on Concept of Believers' Ch., 1967; chmn. Study Commn. on Coop. Christianity, Bapt. World Alliance, 1968-75; sec. Study Commn. on Human Rights, 1980-85; co-chmn. Study and Rsch. Divsn., 1995-99; theol. lectr. Wake Forest, N.C., Torreon, Mex., Cali, Colombia, Recife, Brazil, Montevideo, Uruguay, Oradea, Romania, Dallas, Yalta and Odessa, Ukraine. Author: The Nature of the Church According to the Radical Continental Reformation, 1957, Baptist Church Discipline, 1962, Evangelism for Discipleship, 1964, Baptists and Roman Catholicism, 1965, Reinhold Niebuhr on Roman Catholicism, 1972, Living Stones: The Centennial History of Broadway Baptist Church, Fort Worth, Texas, 1882-1982, 2 vols., 1984—85, Systematic Theology Vol. 1, 1990, Vol. 2, 1995, 2d edit. Vol. 1, 2000, Vol. 2, 2001; co-author: Are Southern Baptists "Evangelicals"?, 1983; co-editor: The Teacher's Yoke: Studies in Memory of Henry Trantham, 1964; editor: The Concept of the Believers' Church, 1970, Baptist Relations with Other Christians, 1974, Calvin and the Reformed Tradition, 1980, We Baptists, 1999, The Legacy of Southwestern, 2002, Southwestern Jour. Theology, 1958—59, Jour. of Ch. and State, 1973—79. Mem. Am. Soc. Ch. History, Bapt. Hist. and Heritage Soc., Conf. on Faith and History, Nat. Assn. Bapt. Profs. Religion. Home: 5525 Full Moon Dr Fort Worth TX 76132-2309 Office: PO Box 22117 Fort Worth TX 76122-0117

GARRETT, LELAND EARL, nephrologist, educator; b. Spartanburg, S.C., Jan. 8, 1949; s. Leland Earl and Mary Lillian (Butler) G.; m. Sarah Anne Pryor, Aug. 13, 1970 (div. 1978); 1 child, Katherine; m. Nancy Jean Swenson, May 3, 1980; children: Christopher, Jennifer. BS, N.C. State U.,

1971; MD, Med. U. S.C., 1976. Commd. 2d lt. USAF, 1971, advanced through grades to lt. col., 1985, ret., 1991; intern Wilford Hall, USAF Med. Ctr., 1976-77; resident USAF Med. Ctr., 1977-79; fellowship Duke U. Med. Ctr., 1979-81; pvt. practice Wake Nephrology Assocs., Raleigh, N.C., 1991—. Clin. prof. medicine U. N.C., Chapel Hill, 1998—. Contbr. articles to profl. jours. Chair-elect Urban Ministries, 2000—01, chmn., 2001—02; mem. adv. chmn. N.C. affiliate Nat. Kidney Found., Charlotte, 1994—2001; med. dir. Open Door Clinic, 1996—98; chmn. Carolina Renal Care, 2000—02; pres. med. staff Raleigh Cmty. Hosp., 2000—02; data chair, bd. dirs. Southeastern Kidney Coun., Raleigh, 1993—97, 1998—, treas., 2000—01, chmn., 2002—; bd. dirs. South Tex. Organ Bank, San Antonio, 1984—86, Urban Ministries, 1997—, treas., 1998—2000; bd. dirs. Carolina Renal Care, 1999—2002. Named Physician of Yr. N.C. affiliate Nat. Kidney Found., 1995. Fellow ACP, Am. Soc. Nephrology, Internat. Soc. Nephrology. Lutheran. Avocation: medical informatics. Office: Wake Nephrology Assocs 3604 Bush St Raleigh NC 27609-7511

GARRETT, NORMAN ANTHONY, business education educator; b. San Diego, Aug. 30, 1947; m. Margaret Ann Florence, Dec. 11, 1970; children: Rachel, Ethan, Joshua, Aaron, Emily. BA, Brigham Young U., 1971; MA, Ariz. State U., 1975, EdD, 1986. High sch. tchr. Tolleson (Ariz.) Union High Sch., 1973-80; systems engr. Electronic Data Systems, Phoenix, 1980-83; acad. computing specialist Ariz. State U., Tempe, 1983-84; assoc. dir. Ariz. State U. Computer Inst., Tempe, 1984-86; instr. South Mountain Community Coll., Phoenix, 1986-89, assoc dean instrn., 1989-90; assoc. prof. bus. edn./ adminstrv. info. systems Eastern Ill. U., Charleston, 1990-95, prof., 1995—. Author: Great Bread Machine Recipes, 1992, Quick and Delicious Bread Machine Recipes, 1993, Advanced Microcomputer Applications, 1994, Favorite Bread Machine Recipes, 1994; contbr. numerous articlesto profl. jours. 1st lt. USAF, 1972-73. Mem. Nat. Bus. Edn. Assn., Office Systems Rsch. Assn., Ill. Bus. Edn. Assn., Internat. Soc. Tech. in Edn., Internat. Assn. for Computer Info. Systems. Office: Ea Ill U Sch Bus Bus Edn and Adminstrv Info Systems Charleston IL 61920

GARRETT, SANDY LANGLEY, school system administrator; b. Muskogee, Okla., Feb. 8, 1943; 1 child, Charles Langley (Chuck). BS in Elem. Edn., Northeastern U., Tahlequah, Okla., 1968, MS in Counseling, 1980; grad. John F. Kennedy Sch. Govt., Harvard U., 1989. Lic. tchr., adminstr., supt. std., Okla. Tchr. Hilldale Schs., Muskogee, Okla., 1968-80; coord. gifted program Hillsdale Schs., Muskogee, Okla., 1980-82; coord. gifted and talented State Dept. Edn., Oklahoma City, 1982-85, dir. rural edn., 1985-87, exec. dir. ednl. svcs., 1987-88, state supt. pub. instrn., 1991-95; sec. edn. Gov.'s Office, Oklahoma City, 1988—; state supt. pub. instrn. State Dept. Edn., Oklahoma City, 1991—. Chair State Bd. Edn., Oklahoma City, 1991—, State Vo-Tech. Edn., Oklahoma City, 1991—; bd. dirs. So. Regional Edn. Bd.; regent Okla. Colls., 1991—; mem. Nat. Coll. Bd. Equality Project; chair. Okla. Lit. Initiatives Commn.; mem. So. Regional Ednl. Bd. Co-author: (curriculum guide) Gifted Galaxy; mem. editorial bd. Rural and Small Schs.; contbr. articles to profl. jours. Co-chair Dem. Party, Muskogee, 1978; del. Dem. Nat. Conv., N.Y.C., 1980, 82; mem. Leadership Okla., 1990. Recipient Cecil Yarbrough award, 1989, Claude Dyer Legis. award, 1989. Mem. Muskogee County Ednl. Assn., Delta Kappa Gamma, Phi Delta Kappa, Delta Kappa Gamma. Methodist. Avocations: tennis, swimming, computer programming, travel, politics. Office: State Dept Edn 2500 N Lincoln Blvd Oklahoma City OK 73105-4503*

GARRISON, ANNE-MARIE DICKINSON, middle school educator; b. Fredericksburg, Va., May 21, 1947; d. Robert DuVal and Anne (Dawideit) Dickinson; m. Gary Leroy Garrison, Dec. 23, 1972; children: Stephen, Christine. BA in Math., Duke U., 1969. Cert. tchr., Va. Tchr. Stafford (Va.) County Schs., 1972—. Mem. Fredericksburg Full Gospel. Full Gospel fellow, Pentecostal Ch. Mem. Nat. Coun. Math. Tchrs. Republican. Mem. Pentecostal Ch. Avocation: reading. Home: 1525 Clover Dr Fredericksburg VA 22407-4820 Office: Stafford Mid Sch 101 Spartan Ln Stafford VA 22554-5453

GARRISON, GUY GRADY, librarian, educator; b. Akron, Ohio, Dec. 17, 1927; s. Grady and Emma (Dodson) G.; m. Joanne Ruth Sergeant, Mar. 22, 1964; 1 dau., Anne Olivia. BA, Baldwin-Wallace Coll., 1950; MS, Columbia U., 1954; PhD, U. Ill., 1960. Mem. staff Oak Park (Ill.) Pub. Library, 1954-58; head reader services Kansas City (Mo.) Pub. Library, 1960-62; prof., dir. library research center Grad. Sch. Library Sci., U. Ill., 1962-68; prof., dean Coll. Info. Studies, Drexel U., 1968-87, Alice B. Kroeger prof., 1987-91, dean emeritus, prof. emeritus, 1992—. Contbr. articles to profl. jours. Served with AUS, 1950-52. Mem. ALA, Assn. for Library and Info. Sci. Edn., Beta Phi Mu. Home: 731 Limehouse Rd Wayne PA 19087-2856 E-mail: guy.garrison@drexel.edu.

GARRISON-FINDERUP, IVADELLE DALTON, writer, educator; b. San Pedro, Calif., Oct. 4, 1915; d. William Douglas and Olive May (Covington) Dalton; m. Fred Marion Garrison, Aug. 8, 1932 (dec. Nov. 1984); children: Douglas Lee, Vernon Russell, Nancy Jane; m. Elmer Pedersen Finderup, Apr. 8, 1994 (dec. Oct. 1997). BA, Calif. State U., Fresno, 1964; postgrad., U. Oreg., 1965, U. San Francisco, 1968. Cert. secondary tchr., Calif. Tchr. Tranquillity (Calif.) H.S., 1964-78, West Hills Coll., Coalinga, Calif., 1970-74. Lectr. in field. Author: Roots and Branches of Our Garrison Family Tree, 1988, Roots and Branches of Our Dalton Family Tree, 1989, The History of James' Fresno Ranch, 1990, 3d edit., 1993, There is a Peacock on the Roof, 1993; (with Vernon R. Garrison) William Douglas Dalton, a Biography, 1995, Sam (The Cat That Thought He Was a Boy), 1997, Amanda and Her Feathered Friends, 1997, Freddy Goes on a Trailer Outing, 1998, David Learns to Count, 1998, Laura and the Lizard: a fairy tale, 2001. Mem. DAR (sec. 1987-89, regent 1989-91, regent Fresno chpt. 1999-2001, scholarship chmn. 2002, nat. recognition for excellence in cmty. svc. Cert. of Award 1995), Nat. Trust for Hist. Preservation, Frazier Clan N.Am., Fresno City and County Hist. Soc. (life), Fresno Archaeology Soc. (sec. 1994), Children of the Am. Revolution (life patriot, sr. pres. 1991-97), Westerners Internat., Fresno Gem and Mineral Soc., Thora # 11 Dannebrog, Friends of the Libr. (Fresno), Chaffee Zoolog. Gardens of Fresno, Archaeological Inst. Am. (San Joaquin Valley chpt., charter mem.), Fresno County Archaeological Soc, Fresno Met. Mus., Baker Hist. Mus. (life), Fresno Gem and Mineral Soc. Republican. Lutheran. Avocations: quilting, knitting. Office: Garrison Libr 3427 Circle Ct E Fresno CA 93703-2403

GARRISS, PHYLLIS WEYER, music educator, performer; b. Hastings, Nebr., Dec. 25, 1923; d. Frank Elmer and Mabelle Claire (Carey) Weyer; m. William Philip Garriss, Aug. 28, 1954; children: Daniel, Meredith, Margaret. AB, MusB, Hastings Coll., 1945; MusM, U. Rochester, 1948. Instr. DePauw U., Greencastle, Ind., 1948-51; assoc. prof. music Meredith Coll., Raleigh, N.C., 1951-94, assoc. prof. emerita, part-time prof., 1994—. Instr. Cannon Music Camp, Appalachian State U., Boone, N.C., 1973-98; vis. instr. Ball State U., Muncie, summers 1951, 53; dir. Lamar Stringfield Chamber Music Camp, Meredith Coll., 1980—; bd. dirs. Raleigh Symphony Orch., Raleigh Chamber Music Guild; mem. various symphonic groups as violinist, including Roanoke Symphony, Raleigh Civic Symphony, Duke U. Symphony, Tri-City Chamber Orch., Raleigh Symphony Orch., Capital Chamber Music Ensemble. Mem. Raleigh Civic Coun., 1958-60; bd. dirs. Raleigh Comty. Mus. Sch., 1993-97, N.C. Fedn. Music Clubs, 1988-96; mem. PEO. Recipient Medal of Arts, City of Raleigh Arts Commn., 1987. Mem. Am. String Tchrs. Assn. (corr. sec. 1950-54, Disting. Svc. award 1979), Music Tchrs. Nat. Assn., Music Educators Nat. Conf., Local 500 Musicians Assn. (bd. dirs. 1980—), Raleigh Music Club (pres. 1958-60, 93-95), Pi Kappa Lambda, Mu Phi Epsilon. Democrat. Presbyterian. Avocations: cooking, traveling. Home: 3400 Merriman Ave Raleigh NC 27607-7004 Office: Meredith Coll 3800 Hillsborough St Raleigh NC 27607-5237

GARRITY, ROBERT JOHN, philosophy and English language educator; b. Pitts., Mar. 6, 1931; s. John Joseph and Ann Theresa (Kelly) G.; m. Gloria Mary Giegerich, May 4, 1957; children: Robert Jr., Judith, Kathleen, Patricia, Michael. BA in German and Edn., LaSalle U., 1953, MA in Religion, 1954; MA in Philosophy, Duquesne U., 1962, PhD in Philosophy, 1964; MA in English, Purdue U., 1983. Tchr. Ctrl. Cath. H.S., Canton, Ohio, 1954-56; instr. U.S. Army Signal Sch., Ft. Gordon, Ga., 1956-58; tchg. asst. Duquesne U., Pitts., 1958-60, instr. in philosophy, 1960-64; asst. prof. in philosophy Franciscan U., Steubenville, Ohio, 1964-66, assoc. prof., 1966-70, assoc. dean, 1968-72, prof. philosophy, 1970-72; v.p. for acad. affairs St. Joseph's Coll., Rensselaer, Ind., 1972-84, prof. philosophy and English, 1972—. Cons. in field. Author of poetry. Cpl. U.S. Army, 1956-58. Republican. Roman Catholic. Avocation: community theater. Home: 900 E Stewart Dr Rensselaer IN 47978-3221 Office: St Josephs Coll PO Box 904 Rensselaer IN 47978-0904 E-mail: cyrano@netnitco.net., rjg@saintjoe.edu.

GARRITY, RODMAN FOX, psychologist, educator; b. Los Angeles, June 10, 1922; s. Lawrence Hitchcock and Margery Fox (Pugh) G.; m. Juanita Daphne Mullan, Mar. 5, 1948; children: Diana Daphne, Ronald Fox. Student, Los Angeles City Coll., 1946-47; BA, Calif. State U., Los Angeles, 1950; MA, So. Meth. U., Dallas, 1955; Ed.D., U. So. Calif., 1963. Tchr. elem. sch. Palmdale (Calif.) Sch. Dist., 1952-54; psychologist, prin. Redondo Beach (Calif.) City Schs., 1954-60; asst. dir. ednl. placement lectr., ednl. adviser U. So. Calif., 1960-62; asso. prof., coordinator credentials programs Calif. State Poly. U., Pomona, 1962-66, chmn. social sci. dept., 1966-68, dir. tchr. preparation center, 1968-71, coordinator grad. program, 1971-73, prof. tchr. preparation center, 1968—, coordinator spl. edn. programs, 1979—. Cons. psychologist, lectr. in field. Pres. Redondo Beach Coordinating Council, 1958-60; mem. univ. rep. Calif. Faculty Assns., 1974-76. Served with Engr. Combat Bn. AUS, 1942-45. Mem. Prins. Assn. Redondo Beach (chmn. 1958-60), Nat. Congress Parents and Tchrs. (hon. life), Am. Psychol. Assn., Calif. Tchrs. Assn. Democrat. Office: Calif State U Dept Special Edn Pomona CA 91768

GARROTT, CARL LEE, foreign language educator; b. Indpls., Dec. 4, 1948; s. George Richard and Rosie (Diggs) G. BA, Ky. State U., 1970; MA, Tenn. State U., 1974; EdS, Western Ky. U., 1977; EdD, U. Ky., 1985; postgrad., U. Guadalajara (Mex.), 1999—2000, Inst. de Filologia Hispanica, 1990, 91, 93, Monteverde Inst., Costa Rica, 2002—03. Instr. Cath. High Sch., Frankfort, Ky., 1969-70, Christian County Schs., Hopkinsville, Ky., 1974-81; prof. Chowan Coll., Murfreesboro, N.C., 1984-95; assoc. prof. Hampton U., 1995-98; prof. Va. State U., 1998—. Author: (monograph) The Thinking Man in France, 1977, (book) José Martí Poesía, Cuentos, Teatro, 2001, A systematic Approach to Teaching Intonation Patterns in French, 2003; contbr. articles to profl. jours. Donor Sci. Enrichment Scholarship, Hertford County, 1984-91, 93; founder African-Am. Forum, Franklin, Southampton, 1987—. Sgt. U.S. Army, 1971-73. Woodrow Wilson Found. fellow, 1970, U. Ky. fellow, 1970-71, 81-84; grantee Ford Found., Starr Found., Va. Found. Humanities; faculty rsch. grantee Hampton U. Mem. MLA, Am. Assn. Tchrs. Spanish and Portuguese, Am. Assn. Tchrs. French, N.E. Conf. on the Tchg. Fgn. Langs., Am. Assn. for Applied Linguistics, Coll. Lang. Assn., Afro-Latin Am. Rsch. Assn., County Alliance for Sci., Cmty. Concert Assn., Alpha Phi Alpha, Alpha Mu Gamma. Democrat. Baptist. Avocation: shortwave radios. Office: Va State Univ Dept Langs and Lit Petersburg VA 23806 E-mail: cgarrott@vsu.edu.

GARRUTO, RALPH MICHAEL, research anthropologist, educator, biologist, neuroscientist; b. Binghamton, N.Y., Nov. 20, 1943; s. Ralph Anthony and Josephine Janet (DiMartino) G.; children: Jessica Anne, Jason Michael, John Ralph. BS, Pa. State U., 1966, MA, 1969, PhD, 1973. Postdoctoral fellow NIH, Bethesda, Md., 1972-73, staff, then sr. staff fellow, 1973-78, from rsch. biologist to supervisory rsch. biologist, 1978—2003; adj. prof. med. genetics Coll. Medicine U. South Ala., Mobile, 1982—; adj. sr. scientist biol. anthropology Pa. State U., University Park, 1985; rsch. prof. biomedical anthropology neuroscis. SUNY, Binghamton, 1997, assoc. dir. Inst. Biomed. Tech., 2000—, dir. biomed. anthropology program, 2002—; adj. clin. prof. pathology Upstate Med. U., Syracuse, 1998—. Participant anthropol. and biomed. fieldwork, Asia, Pacific Islands, L.Am., 1969—; mem., NIH rep. U.S. Nat. Com. U.S. Man and the Biosphere Program, 1993-95; founding mem. bd. trustees Nat. Mus. Health and Medicine Found., Washington, 1989-91; exec. sec. Commn. on Aging and the Aged, Zagreb, Yugoslavia, 1985-89; cons. WHO, 1987; chair selection com. Paul T. Baker Disting. lectr. in human biology and anthropology Pa. State U., 1986-98; adj. clin. prof. pathology SUNY Upstate Med. U., Syracuse; Wellcome Found. lectr., vis. prof. U. Mich., Dearborn, 2001. Co-editor: Biological Anthropology and Aging: Perspectives on Human Variation over the Lifespan, 1994, Dermatoglyphics: Science in Transition, 1991; contbr. articles on neurodegenerative disorders, neurosci. and aging to profl. jours.; patentee bil. agts. Recipient Commendation for Rsch., Guam Legislature, 1987, Spl. Achievement award, 1990, Merit award NIH, 1991, Dir.'s award, 1993; Wenner-Gren Found. leadership grantee, 1986, grantee, 1993-95; Alumni fellow Pa. State U., 1987. Fellow AAAS, Am. Coll. Epidemiology, Am. Dermatoglyphics Assn. (sec.-treas. 1981-82, pres. 1987-89, disting. achievement award 1995), Human Biology Assn. (pres./pres.-elect 1993-96, exec. com. 1991-93), Internat. Assn. of Human Biologists (pres. 1999-2002, Gorjanović-Krambergeri medal 1999-2000), Internat. Genetic Epidemiology Soc. (founding fellow), NAS, Third World Acad. Scis. (assoc.); mem. Soc. for Neurosci., World Fedn. Neurology (rsch. com. on neurepidemiology). Avocations: field trialing, environmental projects. E-mail: rgarruto@binghamton.edu.

GARSTKA, JOHN EDWARD, interior design educator; b. Holyoke, Mass., Dec. 28, 1940; s. Edward Joseph and Viola (Delage) G.; m. Caron Paula McKane, June 30, 1972; children: John Paul, Caron. BFA in Interior Architecture, R.I. Sch. Design, 1962; MS, U. Mass., 1975; PhD, U. Tex., 1994. Designer R.J. Hubert, AIA, South Hadley, Mass., 1962-68, Bernard Vinick Assocs., Hartford, Conn., 1968-69; tchr. Palmer (Mass.) High Sch., 1969-75; instr. interior design Tex. Tech. U., Lubbock, 1975-78, U. Ky., Lexington, 1978-81, Southwest Tex. State U., San Marcos, 1982—. Design cons. P.K. Design Assocs., Lexington, 1980-81; cons., San Marcos, 1982—. Mem. Am. Soc. Interior Designers (profl.), Interior Design Educators Council (treas. 1983-84, co-editor I.D.E.C. Bibliography 1983), Am. Soc. Archtl. Historians. Home: 302 Blueridge Trl Austin TX 78746-5409

GARTHWAITE, GENE RALPH, historian, educator; b. Mt. Hope, Wis., July 15, 1933; s. Ralph Albert and Merle I. (Quarne) G.; div.; children: R. Andrew, Alexander, Martin. BA, St. Olaf Coll., 1955; postgrad., U Chgo., 1958-59; PhD, U. Calif., 1969; MA, Dartmouth Coll., 1987. From instr. to prof. history Dartmouth Coll., Hanover, N.H., 1968-98, chair Asian studies, 1980-92, chair history dept., 1992-96, Jane & Raphael Bernstein prof. in Asian studies, 1998—. Author: Khans and Shahs, 1983; contbr. articles to profl. jours. Capt. USAF, 1955-58. Grantee Social Sci. Rsch. Coun., NEH, 1979-80, 91-93. Mem. Middle East Studies Assn. (dir. 1968—), Soc. Iranian Studies (exec. sec. 1969—), Phi Beta Kappa. Democrat. Episcopalian. Avocation: gardening. Office: Dartmouth Coll Dept History Hanover NH 03755

GARTNER, ALAN P. municipal official; b. N.Y.C., Apr. 4, 1935; s. Harold J. and Mary T.; children: Jonathan, Rachel, Daniel. BA, Antioch Coll., 1956; MA, Harvard U., 1960; PhD, Union Grad. Sch., 1973. Tchr. Newton (Mass.) H.S., 1961—65; cmty. rels. dir. Congress of Racial Equality, 1965-66; exec. dir. Econ. Opportunity Coun. of Suffolk County, 1966-68; dir. New Careers Tng. Lab., N.Y.C., 1968-81; prof. Queens Coll., 1972-76, Grad. Sch., CUNY, 1976—81, dir. Ctr. for Advanced Study in Edn. Grad. Sch., 1978-81, dir. Office of Sponsored Rsch., 1983-92, dean Rsch. and Univ. Progs., 1992-98, prof., 1983—2002; dir. policy rsch. Office of Mayor, City of NY, 2002—; exec. dir. N.Y.C. Charter Revision Commn., 2003—. Exec. dir. divsn. spl. edn. N.Y.C. Pub. Schs., 1981-83; exec. dir. N.Y.C. Districting Commn., 1990-92; pub. Social Policy mag., N.Y.C., 1971-93; exec. dir. task force on N.Y.C. Cmty. Sch. Bd. Governance, 1998; exec. dir. Charter Revision Commn., 2003—. Author: Paraprofessionals and Their Performance, 1971, The Preparation of Human Services Professionals, 1976; co-author: Children Teach Children, 1971, The Service Society and Consumer Vanguard, 1974, Self Help in the Human Services, 1977, Help: A Working Guide to Self-Help Groups, 1979, Supporting Families With a Child With Disabilities, 1991, Inclusion and School Reform, 1997, Inclussion: A Service, Not a Place, 2002; co-editor: After Deschooling, What?, 1973, Public Service Employment, 1973, What Nixon is Doing to Us, 1973, The New Assault on Equality, 1974, What Reagan is Doing to Us, 1982, The Self-Help Revolution, 1985, Beyond Reagan, 1985, Images of the Disabled/Disabling Images, 1987, Caring for America's Children, 1989, Beyond Separate Education, 1989, Inclusion and School Reform, 1997. Bd. dirs. N.Y. Civil Liberties Union, 1973—2002; bd. dirs. Antioch Coll., 1974-75; treas. Congress Racial Equality, N.Y.C., 1962-64, chairperson, Boston, 1960-64. Ford Found. fellow, 1956-58; Florina Lasker fellow, 1961-62; Poynter fellow, 1976 Office: Office of Mayor City Hall New York NY 10007 E-mail: agartner@cityhall.nyc.gov.

GARVEY, DANIEL EDWARD, foundation administrator, educator, academic administrator; b. Westfield, Mass., Apr. 25, 1950; s. John Henry and Ruth Marie (Long) G.; m. Barbara Nelson, Apr. 28, 1973; children: Kathryn, Connor. BA in Sociology, Worcester State Coll., 1973; MA in Social Change, Cambridge Goddard Coll., 1974; PhD in Edn., U. Colo., 1990. Dir. Upward Bound U. N.H., Durham, 1974-79, assoc. dean students, 1979-88, adj. assoc. prof., 1988—; exec. dir. Assn. for Exptl. Edn., Boulder, Colo., 1988-91; v.p. Am. Youth Found., Ossipee, N.H., 1991—; pres. Prescott Coll., 2001—. Adj. assoc. prof. Moscow State U.; cons. in field. Guest editor Multi-Cultural Issues in Edn., 1992; author Management Development Directory, 1989; contbr. articles to profl. jours.; editorial reviewer Assn. for Exptl. Edn. Coach Youth Soccer, South Berwick, Maine. Avocations: music, woodworking. Office: Prescott Coll Office of Pres 220 Grove Ave Prescott AZ 86301

GARVEY, MICHAEL STEVEN, veterinarian, educator; b. Chgo., Dec. 5, 1950; s. Charles Anthony and Jane O. G. BS in Vet. Medicine, U. Ill., 1972, DVM, 1974; cert. internship, The Animal Med. Ctr., N.Y.C., 1976, cert. med. residency, 1978; cert. advanced mgmt. program, Wharton Sch., U. Pa., 1992. Diplomate Am. Coll. Vet. Internal Medicine, Am. Coll Vet. Emergency and Critical Care. Staff veterinarian Bevlab Vet. Hosp., Blue Island, Ill., 1974-75; intern in medicine and surgery The Animal Med. Ctr., N.Y.C., 1975-76, resident in medicine, 1976-78; staff internist Bevlab Vet. Hosp., Blue Island, 1978-81; dir. medicine The Animal Med. Ctr., N.Y.C., 1981-83, chmn. dept. medicine, 1983-97, vice-chief of staff, 1993—; dir. The Elmer and Mamdouha Bobst Hosp., 1995—, chmn. dept. emergency medicine and critical care, 1997—. Cons. Office of Animal Care, U. Chgo. Sch. Medicine, 1979-94, Nat. Bd. Vet. Examiners, Schaumburg, Ill., 1981—, Mercy Coll. Animal Health Tech., Dobbs Ferry, N.Y., 1984-95, Reader's Digest and Good Housekeeping mags., N.Y.C., 1984—, Pfizer Animal Health, Westchester, Pa., 1994—; tech. cons. Sesame St., N.Y.C., adv. bd. Profl. Examination Svc., N.Y.C., 1981—, vice chmn., 1991—; vet. adv. panel Alpo Pet Foods, Inc., Allentown, Pa., 1981-95; vet. adv. panel Friskies Pet Care, 1995-96; adj. prof. vet. medicine Tex. A&M U., 1986—; faculty assoc. U. Maine Animal Health Tech., Orono, 1976-78; chmn. vet. adv. panel Schering Plough Inc., Madison, N.J., 1993—; mem. cmty. adv. bd. N.Y. Hosp./Cornell U. Med. Sch., 1995—; chmn. emergency room oversight com. N.Y. Presbyn. Hosp. Cornell Campus, 1998—. Author: Animal Medical Center Hospital Formulary, 1990, 96, (with others) Keeping Your Dog Healthy, 1985, Canine Emergencies, 1985, Symptoms of Illness in Dogs, 1985, Infectious and Contagious Diseases in Dogs, 1985, Feline Emergencies, 1985, Sysmtoms of Illness in Cats, 1985, Infectious and Contagious Diseases in Cats, 1985, Feeding the Sick Cat, 1989, The Veterinarian's Guide to Your Dog's Symptoms, 1999, The Veterinarian's Guide to Your Cat's Symptoms, 1999; editor: Canine Allergic Inhalant Dermatitis, 1982; cons. editor Small Animal Medicine, 1990; editorial review bd. Jour. of Am. Animal Hosp. Assn., 1985-93, Jour. Vet. Emergency Critical Care, 1992—; contbr. articles to profl. jours. Bd. dirs. Blue Island Cmty. Theatre, 1974-75, 78-80, treas., 1984-94, pres., 1985—; treas. 440 E 62d St Owners' Corp., N.Y.C.; mem. cmty. adv. bd. N.Y. Hosp./Cornell U. Med. Sch., 1995—; mem. N.Y.C. Office Emergency Mgmt. Task Force Biol. Terrorism, 1997—. Recipient Disting. Leadership award Am. Biog. Inst., 1993, 96. Mem. AVMA (del. 1990-91), Am. Animal Hosp. Assn. (Friskie's award for excellence in feline medicine 1993), Am. Assn. Vet. Clinicians (exec. bd. 1986—, pres. 1988-89, President's Gavel award 1989, Faculty Achievement award 1993), Am. Coll. Vet. Emergency Critical Care (v.p. 1993-95), Am. Coll. Vet. Internal Medicine (pres. internal medicine splty. 1994-97), Acad. Vet. Cardiology, N.Y. State Vet. Med. Soc. (Outstanding vet. award 1995), Soc. Gastroenterology Soc., Vet. Med. Assn. N.Y.C. (Outstanding Svc. award 1984, Outstanding Vet. award 1995), Vet. Endoscopy Soc., Soc. Internat. Vet. Symposia (bd. dirs. 1990—, pres. 1992-94), Vet. Intern and Resident Matching Program (co-chmn. 1986—). Republican. Roman Catholic. Avocations: golf, swimming, snorkeling, personal computers. Home: 440 E 62nd St Apt 2B New York NY 10021-8341 Office: The Animal Med Ctr 510 E 62nd St New York NY 10021-8314

GARVEY, SHEILA HICKEY, theater educator; b. Erie, Pa., Dec. 23, 1949; d. Robert Francis and Mary Virginia (Sullivan) H.; children: Sean Timothy, Darragh Burgess. BS, Emerson Coll., 1971; MA, Northwestern U., 1973; PhD, NYU, 1984; grad., The Circle in the Square, N.Y.C., 1975. Preceptor NYU, N.Y.C., 1978-80; sabbatical replacement Rutgers U., Camden, N.J., 1980-81; asst. prof. Dickinson Coll., Carlisle, Pa., 1981-88; full prof. So. Conn. State U., New Haven, 1988—. Editor: Jason Robards Remembered, 2002; contbr. articles to profl. jours. Scholar JFK Ctr. Performing Arts, Am. Coll. Theatre Festival, 1993; Rsch. grantee Dickinson Coll., 1987-88, So. Conn. State U., 1988-90, 92, 94, 98, 2003, Faculty Devel. grant, 1988-90, 92, 94, 97; Dana fellow Dickinson Coll., 1987. Mem. New Eng. Theatre Conf. (bd. dirs., coll. divsn. 1992-95, chair coll. and univ. com. 1991-95, life mem. Coll. Fellows), Eugene O'Neill Soc. (pres. 2000-02, v.p. 2001—), Conn. Critics' Cir., Conn. Critics Cir. (bd. dirs.). Roman Catholic. Home: 273 Knob Hill Dr Hamden CT 06518-2737 Office: So Conn State U 501 Crescent St New Haven CT 06515-1330

GARY, JANET LYNNE CARLOCK, middle school educator; b. Bowling Green, Ky., July 31, 1956; d. Dorris Dixon and Sarah Jane (Coates) C.; children: Gary, Carlock, Janet, Lynne. BS in Elem. Edn., Western Ky. U., 1978, MA in Elem. Edn., 1980, cert. rank I in ednl. adminstrn., 1995. Cert. tchr., Ky. Tchr. Owen County Elem. Sch., Owenton, Ky., 1979-86, Richardsville (Ky.) Elem. Sch., 1986-88, Henry Moss Mid. Sch., Bowling Green, Ky., 1988—. Resource tchr. Ky. Internship Program, Frankfort, 1986—. Recipient Oustanding Young Educator, Jaycees, 1995. Mem. ASCD, Ky. ASCD, Ky. Mid. Sch. Assn., Nat. Mid. Sch. Assn., Ky. PTA, Nat. Coun. Social Studies, Internat. Reading Assn., Three Springs Reading Coun. (sec. 1992—), Parent/Tchr. Orgn. (bd. dirs. 1992—), Phi Eta Sigma. Office: Henry Moss Mid Sch 2565 Russellville Rd Bowling Green KY 42104

GARY, TONI BERRYHILL, psychology educator, psychotherapist; b. Belzoni, Miss., Mar. 2, 1951; d. Thomas Richard and Alyene Cornealia (Ellis) Berryhill; m. Clarence Addison Hall III, Feb. 3, 1972 (div. Mar. 1976); 1 child, Clarence Addison IV; m. Mark Loftin Gary, Dec. 23, 1977 (div. Apr. 1990); children: Kristina Lynn, James Thomas. BS, Miss. State U. for Women, Columbus, 1972; MEd, Delta State U., Cleve., 1991, MS, 1998. Lic. profl. counselor; nat. cert. counselor, nat. cert. sch. counselor. Social worker Humphreys County Welfare Dept., Belzomi, Miss., 1974-76; bookkeeper Gary Flying Svc., Inverness, Miss., 1978-90; counselor The Indianola (Miss.) Acad., 1991-98; psychology instr. Miss. Dela C.C., Moorhead, 1998—. Part-time pvt. practice psychotherapy Editor: The Share-Cropper, 1977. Cons., counselor Teen Pregnancy Prevention Project, Sunflower County Make a Difference Day, 1995; pres. PTO, Ctrl. Delta Acad., 1975-78. Recipient Pres. award Miss. Women's Agrl. Aviation Assn., 1985; named Woman of Yr. Miss. Agrl.Aviation Assn., 1986. Mem. ACA, Am. Sch. Counselor Assn., Miss. Women's Agrl. Aviation Assn. (pres. 1987), Miss. Counseling Assn., Delta Counseling Assn., Chi Sigma Iota, Phi Kappa Phi. Baptist. Avocations: reading, walking, computer internet, travel. Home: 702 3rd St Inverness MS 38753-8710 Office: The Indianola Acad Dorsett Dr Indianola MS 38751

GARZA, CUTBERTO, nutrition educator; b. San Diego, Tex., Aug. 26, 1947; s. Cutberto and Diamantina (Salinas) G.; m. Yolanda, Mar. 21, 1970; children: Luis-Andres, Carlos-Daniel, Ariel-Abram. BS summa cum laude, Baylor U., 1969; MD, Baylor Coll. Medicine, 1973; PhD, MIT, 1976. Asst. prof. Baylor Coll. Medicine, Houston, 1977-85, assoc. prof., 1984-86, prof., 1986-88, Cornell U. Divsn. Nutritional Sci., Ithaca, NY, 1988—, dir., 1988—98, 2003—; vice-provost Cornell U., 1998-2000; dir. food nutrition program UN Univ., Cornell U., 1998—. Chmn. Inst. Medicine Food and Nutrition Bd., Washington, 1995-2002; mem. WHO expert adv. panel on nutrition; adv. com., chmn. Nat. Dietary Guidelines, 2000. Contbr. articles to profl. jours. on normal growth of young children, Nutritional Mgmt. of Prematures, Comparison of Energy Expenditure, Energy Expenditure and Deposition. Bd. dirs. Tex. Rehab. Commn., Houston, 1985-88; mem. N.Y. State Pub. Health Coun., 1990-98. Recipient Disting. Achievement award Baylor U., 1986, Alan S. Feinstein World Hunger prize for Edn. and Rsch., Brown U., 1996, Lydia J. Roberts prize U. P.R., 1993. Mem. AAAS, NAS (nat. assoc.), Inst. of Medicine, Am. Soc. Clin. Nutrution, Am. Inst. Nutrition, Am. Pediatric Soc., Soc. Pediatric Rsch. Roman Catholic. Achievements include definition of energy requirements of infants, identification of functional outcomes of infants fed human milk or formula.

GARZA, DEBORAH JANE, bilingual education educator; b. L.A., July 25, 1952; d. Nicholas and Mary Jane (Hover) Maloof. AA in Gen. Edn., Rio Hondo Coll., 1973; BA in Sociology, Calif. State U., Fullerton, 1978; MS in Sch. Mgmt., U. La Verne, 1988. Calif. life teaching credential; bilingual cert. competence; cert. sch. adminstr.; profl. adminstr. svcs. credential. Bilingual classroom tchr. Norwalk (Calif.)-La Mirada Unified Sch. Dist., 1981—87, 1989—2002, categorical aid program specialist, 1987—88; instrnl. specialist Whittier (Calif.) City Sch. Dist., 1987—88; prin. South Whittier Sch. Dist., 2002—. Master tchr. Norwalk (Calif.)-La Mirada Unified Sch. Dist., 1985-90, dist. mentor tchr., 1989-90, presenter/instr., 1991—; panel mem. ednl. tv. broadcast Schooling and Language Minority Students, 1990. Treas. Edmondson Sch. PTA, Norwalk, 1989-94, sec., 1994—. Recipient Merit Scholarship award U. of La Verne (Calif.) Faculty, 1991, Hon. Svc. award Edmondson Sch. PTA, Norwalk, 1992; named Tchr. of Yr., Edmondson Sch., 1990. Mem. Calif. Assn. for Bilingual Edn., Assn. Calif. Sch. Adminstrs., Norwalk-La Mirada Adminstrs. Assn. Avocations: tennis, reading, writing children's stories, attending concerts, movies and plays.

GARZA, MARGUERITE SCOTT, physical education educator; b. Ft. Worth, Mar. 31, 1961; d. James Hernandez and Nina Jean (Seevers) Scott; m. Severo Garza, Nov. 24, 1990; 1 child, Victoria Leigh. AA, Ferrum Coll., 1981; BS, Tex. Christian U., 1984. Paraprofl. phys. edn. Chula Vista Acad. Fine Arts, Corpus Christi, Tex., 1984-86; tchr. phys. edn. Flour Bluff Ind. Sch. Dist., Corpus Christi, 1986—, coach jr. high volleyball, basketball, track, 1986-90, coach high. sch. swim team, 1990-92. Mem. Assn. Tex. Profl. Educators, Tex. AAPHERD. Republican. Episcopalian. Avocations: swimming, cross-stitch. Home: 2213 Bird Island Dr Corpus Christi TX 78418-3619 Office: Flour Bluff Ind Sch Dist 2505 Waldron Rd Corpus Christi TX 78418-4706

GARZA, ROBERTO JESUS, retired education educator; b. Hargill, Tex., Apr. 10, 1934; s. Andres and Nazaria (De La Fuente) G.; m. Idolina Alaniz, Aug. 24, 1957; children: Roberto Jesus Jr., Sylvia Lynn. BA in Psychology, Tex. A&I Coll., 1959, MA in Spanish, 1964; EdD in Curriculum and Instrn., Higher Edn., Okla. State U., 1975. High sch. tchr. and counselor, Tex., Ill., Wyo., 1959-64; instr., chmn. dept. St. Joseph (Mo.) Jr. Coll., 1964-65; teaching asst. U. Wash., Seattle, 1965-66; instr., chmn. dept. S.W. Tex. Jr. Coll., Uvalde, 1966-68; prof. Spanish Sul Ross State U., Alpine, Tex., 1968-70; adminstr. Office of Equal Opportunity, Edinburg, Tex., 1970-71; NEH rsch. fellow U. Notre Dame, Ind., 1972-73; prof., chmn. dept. higher edn. U. Tex., Brownsville, 1973-96; ret., 1996. Cons. migrant edn. S.W. Lab., Austin, 1966-67; psychometrist Peace Corps, San Marcos, Tex., 1965; counselor Job Corps, San Marcos, 1966; higher edn. tchr. edn. evaluator Tex. Edn. Agy., Austin, 1980-85; mem. Tex. Edn. Agy. Accreditation Team, 1979—; journalism scholarship com. KGBT-TV and KRGV-TV, 1979—; mem. So. Assn. Schs. and Colls. Accreditation Team, 1990—; cons. U.S. Dept. Edn., 1993—. Author, editor Contemporary Chicano Theatre: An Anthology, 1975. Trustee, v.p., pres. Brownsville Ind. Sch. Dist., 1985-87; mem. Cameron County Appraisal Dist., Brownsville, 1985-87, Tex. Ho. Reps. Resolution #521, 1987; assoc. dir. Reynaldo Garza Law Sch., Edinburg, 1985-87. With U.S. Army, 1954-56. Recipient recognition/appreciation award Brownsville Ind. Sch. Dist., 1987; grantee NDEA, 1963, John Hay Whitney Found., 1970-71; NEH fellow Notre Dame U., 1972-73. Mem. AAUP, So. Assn. of Colls. and Schs., Tex. Assn. Coll. Tchrs., Am. Assn. for Higher Edn., Smithsonian Assocs., Phi Delta Kappa. Democrat. Roman Catholic. Home: 2 Alvarado Ave Rancho Viejo TX 78575-9501

GASAWAY, LAURA NELL, law librarian, educator; b. Searcy, Ark., Feb. 24, 1945; d. Merel Roger and Carnell (Miller) Gasaway. BA, Tex. Woman's U., 1967, MLS, 1968; JD, U. Houston, 1973. Bar: Tex. 1973. Catalog libr. U. Houston, 1968—70, catalog-circulation libr., 1970—72, asst. law libr., 1972—73, asst. prof. law, 1973—75; dir. law libr. U. Okla., Norman, 1975—85, prof. law, 1975—85; dir. law libr. U. N.C., 1985—, prof. law, 1985—. Copyright cons. Author: Growing Pains: Adapting Copyright for Libis., Edn. and Soc., 1997; co-author (with Maureen Murphy): Legal Protection for Computer Programs, 1980; co-author: (with James Hoover and Dorothy Warden) Am. Indian Legal Materials, A Union List, 1981, 1981; co-author: (with Bruce S. Johnson and James M. Murray) Law Libr. Mgmt. during Fiscal Austerity, 1992; co-author: (with Sarah K. Wiant) Libraries and Copyright: A Guide to Copyright in the 1990s, 1994; co-author: (with Michael D. Chiorazzi) Law Librarianship: Hist. Perspectives, 1996. Recipient Calvert prize, U. Okla., 1973, 1981, Compton award, Ark. Librs. Assn., 1986. Fellow: Spl. Librs. Assn. (H.W. Wilson award 1983, John Cotton Dana award 1987, Fannie Simon award 1992); mem.: ABA, Am. Assn. Law Librs. (pres. 1986—87), N.C. Bar Assn., State Bar Tex. Democrat. Office: U NC Law Libr Clb # 3385 Chapel Hill NC 27599-0001

GASBARRO, NORMAN JOHN, JR., educational administrator; b. Atlantic City, N.J., Jan. 27, 1944; s. Norman J. and Kathryn E. (Dietrich) G.; m. Jeanette Scoglio, Nov. 20, 1971; 1 child, Annette Helen. AB, Muhlenberg Coll., 1966; MA, Glassboro State Coll., 1970; EdM, EdD, Columbia U., 1992. Cert. sch. adminstr., prin., supr., N.J., sch. dist. adminstr., N.Y. Tchr. social studies Atlantic City High Sch., 1966-71, chmn. social studies dept., 1971-76, supr. social studies, 1976-89, supr. curriculum and instruction, 1989-94; dir. tchr. edn. Richard Stockton Coll. N.J., Pomona, 1994—. Mem. N.J. Task Force on Multicultural Edn., Trenton, 1989-93, N.J. Social Studies Standards Panel, 1992-93; mem. edn. adv. com. Stockton State Coll., Pomona, N.J., 1976-91; mem. adv. com. N.J. Commn. of Edn., 1979-81; head of delegation to USSR, People to People and Gov. Thomas Kean, Spokane, Wash. and Trenton, 1987. Editor, pub.: (newsletter) Pres.'s Letter: N.J. Coun. for the Social Studies, 1977-88; editor: (newsletters) Bulletin of Atlantic City Schools, 1979-82, Phi Delta Kappa So. N.J., 1991-92. Mem. UN Assn. of U.S., N.Y.C., 1986—; bd. dirs. Citizens' Scholarship Found., Atlantic City, 1973-90, past v.p.; bd. dirs. St. Leonard's Assn. of Property Owners, Ventnor, N.J., 1971—; mem. South Jersey Festival Chorus, Margate, 1969, pres., 1993—; bd. dirs. Atlantic City Boys Choir, 1993—. Recipient Outstanding Svc. award N.J. Model Congress, Sewell, 1984, award for Outstanding Contbn. to Internat. Edn., Internat. Model UN Assn., N.Y.C., 1990. Mem. Atlantic City Adminstrs. Edn. Assn. (pres. 1988-90, Svc. award 1990), N.J. Coun. for Social Studies (pres. 1979-81, pres. emeritus 1988, Outstanding Educator of Yr. 1984), Nat. Coun. for Social Studies (mem. chmn. 1984-86), ASCD, NEA, N.J. Assn. Supervision and Curriculum Devel., N.J. Edn. Assn., Phi Delta Kappa (faculty advisor 1993—). Republican. Lutheran. Avocations: philately, home repair, choral singing. Home: PO Box 2477 Ventnor City NJ 08406-0477 Office: Richard Stockton Coll NJ Jim Leeds Rd Pomona NJ 08240

GASCHEL-CLARK, REBECCA MONA, special education educator; b. Hudson, N.Y., Sept. 10, 1972; d. Michael Anthony and Ellen Michele (Wright) Gaschel; m. Eric Clark, Nov. 8, 1997. BS in Spl. Edn., Early Childhood Edn., U. Hartford, 1994, MEd, 1997. Cert. spl. edn. tchr., Conn., pre-kindergarten-12. Spl. edn. educator Regional Sch. Dist. #1, Falls Village, Conn., 1994—. Mem. consultation team Salisbury Ctrl. Sch., Lakeville, Conn., 1996—, Lector Ch. of the Resurrection, Germantown, N.Y., 1989—. Named tchr. of elem. sch. Exemplary Program, Conn. Assn. of Schs., 1996. Mem. Phi Delta Kappa, Alpha Chi, Kappa Delta Pi. Democrat. Roman Catholic. Avocations: water skiing, opera, cooking, camping. Office: Regional Sch Dist # 1 246 Warren Tpke Falls Village CT 06031-1600

GASINK, WARREN ALFRED, speech communication educator; b. Sioux City, Iowa, Sept. 1, 1927; s. George A. and Maud (Hatter) G.; children: Roxanne L. Cope Reyna, John A. Gasink. BA, Morningside Coll., 1953; MA, U. So. Calif., 1955; postgrad., UCLA, 1958-59. Educator Long Beach (Calif.) Community Coll., 1954-55, San Gabriel (Calif.) High Sch., 1956-58, Portland (Oreg.) State Coll., 1959-61, DuPont High Sch., Jacksonville, Fla., 1961-62, U. Maine, Orono, 1963-65; prof. speech communication East Stroudsburg (Pa.) U., 1965-91; ret. Composer: (music lyrics) The Christmas Star, The Desert Fiend, Victory Over the Desert Fiend, My Saviour Lives, Your Love, The Virgin, Fear Not, others; author: (booklets) Avoiding Statspeak, Lovingly Building Relationships, Two Patterns for Speech Organization, Tips for Taking Tests, Beating the SAT, Nine Poems (A series of five articles on Beating the SAT), others; (poetry) Desert Victory, 1990, The Desert Fiend, 1991, Children of War, 1993, Haitian Dreams, 1994, My Enemy's Walls, 1996, My Woman, My Love, 1996, Our Mother's Faith, 1996, Saguaro, 1996, others (awards); contbr. articles to mags. With USN, 1945-48, USNR, 1950-51. Recipient Outstanding Leadership award Nat. Multiple Sclerosis Soc., 1990, also numerous forensics and poetry awards; elected to Internat. Poetry Hall of Fame, 1977. Mem. Pi Kappa Delta (vice gov. N.E. province 1971-73), many others. Democrat. Methodist. Avocations: composing, writing poetry, playing viola. Home: RR 3 Box 3915 East Stroudsburg PA 18301-9579

GASIOR, DAWN MARIE, elementary education educator; b. Chgo., Nov. 30, 1957; d. Joseph Anthony and LaVerne Theresa (Ptacin) Slowinski; m. Thomas Joseph Gasior, Aug. 22, 1986; children: Daniel Thomas, Aimee Elizabeth, Sara Marie, Nathan Joseph. BA in Elem. Edn., Northeastern Ill. U., 1979. 1st grade tchr. Our Lady of Guadalupe Sch., Chgo., 1979-80; kindergarten and 2nd grade tchr. St. Symphorosa Sch., Chgo., 1980—. Mem. Assn. Childhood Edn. Internat. Roman Catholic. Avocations: country music, vegetable gardening, photography, family travel. Office: St Symphorosa Sch 6125 S Austin Ave Chicago IL 60638-4349

GASIOROWICZ, STEPHEN GEORGE, physics educator; b. Gdansk, Poland, May 10, 1928; came to U.S., 1946, naturalized, 1952; s. Alexander A. and Maria K. (Landau) G.; m. Hilde E. Fromm, Apr. 4, 1953; children: Nina E., Catherine A., Mara E. BA, UCLA, 1948, MA, 1949, PhD, 1952; postgrad., U. Delhi, 1945-46. Physicist Lawrence Radiation Lab., U. Calif. at Berkeley, 1952-60; assoc. prof. physics U. Minn., 1960-63, prof., 1963-97, prof. emeritus, 1997—. NSF fellow Bohr Inst., Copenhagen, Denmark, 1957-58; cons. Argonne Nat. Lab., 1961-70; vis. scientist Max Planck Inst. Physics and Astrophysics, Munich, Germany, 1959-60, Nordita, 1964, Deutsches Elektronen Synchrotron, Hamburg, Germany, 1968-69, 80, Tokyo U., 1982; acting dir. Theoretical Physics Inst. U. Minn., 1987-89. Author: (Book) Elementary Particle Physics, 1966, Quantum Physics, 1974, 3rd rev. edit., 2003, Structure of Matter, 1979; co-author: Physics for Scientists and Engineers, 1993, 3d rev. edit., 2004, Modern Physics, 2000. Trustee Aspen Center for Physics, 1980-86. Fellow Am. Phys. Soc. (chair divsn. particles and fields 1977). Home: 2630 Glenhurst Ave Minneapolis MN 55416-3957

GASKELL, IVAN GEORGE ALEXANDER DE WEND, art museum curator; b. Weston-super-Mare, Somerset, U.K., Feb. 26, 1955; came to U.S., 1991. s. William George Keith de Wend and Johanna Catharina (van Leeuwen) G.; m. Jane Susan Whitehead, May 9, 1981; 1 child, Alexander Leo Ralph de Wend. Attended, Worcester Coll., Oxford, 1973-76, Courtauld Inst. Art, London, 1976-80; MA in Modern History, Oxford U.; MA in History of Western Art, London U.; PhD in History of Art, Cambridge U. Rsch. fellow, acad. curatorial asst. Warburg Inst. London U., 1980-83; fellow Wolfson Coll. Cambridge U., 1983-91, mem. faculty architecture, history of art, 1983-91; sr. lectr. fine arts Harvard U., Cambridge, Mass., 1991—, head dept. paintings and sculpture Fogg Art Mus., 1991—, Margaret S. Winthrop curator of paintings, 1991—, sr. lectr. history, 2002—; 8. Presenter papers at numerous internat. confs., 1978—; chair seminars in field; lectr. Royal Acad., Nat. Gallery, London, Courtauld Inst. Art, 1982—. Author: The Thyssen-Bornemisza Collection: Dutch and Flemish Painting, 1990, Vermeer's Wager: Speculations on Art History, Theory and Art Museums, 2000; co-editor: The Language of Art History, 1991, Landscape, Natural Beauty and the Arts, 1993, Explanation and Value in the Arts, 1993, Nietzsche, Philosophy and The Arts, 1998, Vermeer Studies, 1998, Sketches in Clay for Projects by Gianlorenzo Bernini, 1999, Performance and Authenticity in the Arts, 1999, Politics, Aesthetics and The Arts, 2000; joint gen. editor: Cambridge Studies in Philosophy and the Arts, 1988-2000; contbr. articles, revs. to profl. jours. Mem. Coll. Art Assn., Am. Soc. for Aesthetics. Avocation: sight-seeing. Office: Harvard U Fogg Art Mus 32 Quincy St Cambridge MA 02138-3845 E-mail: gaskell@fas.harvard.edu.

GASKILL, JOHN WILLIAM, secondary school educator; b. Wendell, Idaho, Oct. 18, 1945; s. Charles William and Mae Merton (Hundley) G.; m. Lanae Anelda Reece, Feb. 2, 1968; children: William, Malinda, Jason, Cynthia, Jonathan. BA, Coll. of Idaho, 1967; MA in Teaching History, U. Idaho, 1972. Cert. secondary tchr., Oreg. Social studies tchr. Ontario (Oreg.) Jr. H.S., 1967-89, Ontario H.S., 1989-99; subst. tchr., 1999—. Mem. leadership team Ontario Sch. Dist., 1989-94, mem. curriculum coord. team, 1992-94; mem. social studies curriculum com. Oreg. State Dept. of Edn., Salem, 1987-89; counselor Ontario City, 2000—. Mem. scout com. 2d ward LDS Ch., Ontario, 1985-87; charter treas. Malheur Hist. Soc., Ontario, 1971, pres., 1972-73. Mem. Oreg. Coun. for Social Studies, Oreg. Geog. Alliance. Republican. Home: 1006 SW 6th Ave Ontario OR 97914-3308 Office: Ontario HS 1115 W Idaho Ave Ontario OR 97914-2146

GASPAR, ANNA LOUISE, retired elementary school educator, consultant; b. Chgo., May 12, 1935; d. Miklos and Klotild (Weiss) G. BS in Edn., Northwestern U., 1957. Cert. elem. tchr., Calif. Tchr. 6th grade Pacific Palisades Elem. Sch., L.A., 1957-58; tchr. 1st grade Eastman St. Elem. Sch., L.A., 1959, Glassell Park, L.A., 1959-62, Stoner Ave. Elem. Sch., L.A., 1962-67; 2nd-4th grade tchr. Brentwood Elem. Sch., L.A., 1967-78; tchr. 4th and 5th grades Brockton Ave. Elem. Sch., L.A., 1978-90; vol., established Swakopmund Tchrs. Resource Ctr., Peace Corps, Namibia, 1991-93; tchr. English, Atlantic Sr. Primary Sch., Swakopmund, Namibia, 1992; career info. cons. Peace Corps., 1991—; substitute tchr. Hebrew Acad./Pre-Primary, Las Vegas, 1994-2000. Mem. Elderhostel Programs: Alaska, 2000, Victoria BC, 2000, Hungary, 2001, Banff Ctr. Can. 2002, Mpls., 2002, San Francisco, 2002, Phoenix Valley, 2003, Santa Fe, 2003, Taos, N.Mex., 2003, Albuquerque, 2003; mem. Bet Knesset Bamidbar Temple. Mem.: Calif. State Ret. Tchrs. Assn., So. Nev. Peace Corps Assn., Peace Corps, Northwestern U. Alumni Assn. Democrat. Jewish. Avocations: world travel, playing piano, art, collecting costume dolls, folk music. Home: 2700 Hope Forest Dr Las Vegas NV 89134-7322

GASPAROVICH, SANDRA, educator; b. Peoria, Ill., Apr. 8, 1947; d. Richard Lee and Lucille Ann (Gorman) Augusburger; m. M. Stephen Gasparovich, June 7, 1969; children: Stephen, Scott. BS, Western Ill. U., 1969, student. Cert. quest instr. Tchr. East Peoria (Ill.) Elem. Sch., 1969-75, Cen. Jr. High. Sch., East Peoria, 1977—. Coord. East Peoria Drug Prevention. Recipient Cert. of Appreciation USDA; named Sci.-Math. Tchr. of Yr., 1988. Mem. NEA, Ill. Edn. Assn., Ill. Tchrs. Assn., East Peoria Elem. Edn. Assn., NSTA, ISTA (Sci. Tchr. of the Yr., 2001), Sigma Xi. Home: 4920 W Woodwind Ct Peoria IL 61607-1322

GASPER, GEORGE, JR., mathematics educator; b. Hamtramck, Mich., Oct. 10, 1939; s. George Gregory and Anastasia Gasper; m. Brigitta Gasper, July 1, 1967; children: Karen, Kenneth. BS, Mich. Technol. U., 1962; MA, Wayne State U., 1964, PhD, 1967. Predoctoral traineeship NASA, 1966-67; vis. lectr. U. Wis., Madison, 1967-68; postdoctoral fellow U. Toronto, Ont., Can., 1968-69, vis. asst. prof., 1969-70; asst. prof. math. Northwestern U., Evanston, Ill., 1970-73, assoc. prof., 1973-77, prof., 1977—. Co-author: Basic Hypergeometric Series, 1990; assoc. editor Jour. Math. Analysis and Applications, 1985-95, The Ramanujan Jour., 1995—. Fellow Alfred P. Sloan Found., 1973-75. Mem. Am. Math. Soc., Soc. Indsl. and Applied Math. (assoc. editor Jour. Math. Analysis 1984-85, vice chair activity group on orthogonal polynomials and spl. functions 1993-95). Office: Northwestern U Dept Math Lunt Bldg Evanston IL 60208-0001

GASS, SAUL IRVING, retired education educator; b. Chelsea, Mass., Feb. 28, 1926; s. Louis and Bertha Gass; m. Gertrude Gass, June 30, 1946; children: Ronald S., Joyce A. BS in Edn., MA in Math., Boston U., 1949; PhD in Engring. Sci., U. Calif., Berkeley, 1965. Mathematician USAF, 1949-55; applied sci. rep. IBM, Washington, 1955-58; dir. ops. rsch. CEIR, Inc., Arlington, Va., 1959; mgr. project mercury IBM Fed. Systems, Gaithersburg, Md., 1960-63, mgr. civil programs, 1965-69; sr. v.p. World Systems Lab., Bethesda, Md., 1969-70; v.p. Mathematica, Inc., Bethesda, 1970-75; prof. U. Md., College Park, 1975—2001, prof. emeritus, 2001—. Cons. Nat. Inst. Std. and Tech., Gaithersburg, 1976—. Author: Linear Programming, 1958, Illustrated Guide to Linear Programming, 1970, Decision Making, Models and Algorithms, 1985; editor: Encyclopedia of Operations Research and Management Science, 1996. Pres. Ops. Rsch. Soc. Am., 1976. With U.S. Army, 1944-46. Fulbright scholar Fulbright Commn., 1995-96, Fulbright Sr. specialist, 2002; recipient Steinhardt Meml. award Ctr. of Naval Analysis, 1996, Kimball award Ops. Rsch. Soc. of Am., 1991. Fellow Inst. for Ops. Rsch. and the Mgmt. Scis. (Expository Writing award 1997); mem. Assn. for Computing Machinery (coun. mem. 1960-62), Math. Assn. of Am., Soc. for Indsl. and Applied Math., Math. Programming Soc.

GASTEYER, CARLIN EVANS, museum administrator, museum studies educator; b. Jackson, Mich., Mar. 30, 1917; d. Frank Howard and Marian (Spencer) Evans; m. Harry A. Gasteyer, Jan. 8, 1944; 1 dau., Nancy Catherine. Student, Barnard Coll., 1934-35; BA, CUNY, 1983. Clk. First Nat. City Bank, 1939-42; statistician Bell Tel. Labs., 1942—45; dir. asst. S.I. Mus., 1956-61; bus. mgr. Mus. City N.Y., 1961-63; asst. dir., 1967-70; mus. adminstr., 1963-66; asst. dir. Monmouth (N.J.) Mus., 1966-67; vice dir. admisntr. Bklyn. Mus., 1970-74; dir. planning Snug Harbor Cultural Ctr., S.I., NY, 1975—79; cable tv cons., 1980—2003. Adj. lectr. mus. studies Coll. S.I. CUNY, 1985-94, asst. higher edn. officer, 1995. Active Girl Scouts; co-founder, pres. Jr. Mus. Guild, S.I. Mus., 1956-58; mem. N.Y.C. Local Sch. Bd. 54, 1960-61. Mem. Am. Assn. Mus., Mus. Coun. N.Y.C. Home: Eatontown, NJ. Died Feb. 26, 2003.

GASTON, BONNIE FAYE JAMES, elementary education educator; b. Littlefield, Tex., Apr. 17, 1931; d. John William and Kittie (Drake) James; m. Milburn Fenton Gaston, May 26, 1954; children: Terry Lynn, Dale Weldon, Randy Lee. BS in Edn., Tex. Tech U., 1952, postgrad. Tchr., Plainview, Tex., 1952-54, 55-58, San Angelo, Tex., 1954-55, Hale Ctr., Tex., 1968-72, 74-76, Olton, Tex., 1977-93. Condr. elem. tchrs. workshops, mem. sch. evaluating vis. team, elem. math. and reading cons. Author, pub.: Gaston Enrichment Skills, 1979. Dist. sec. PTA. Recipient Outstanding Young Homemaker award State Senator Andy Rogers, Notable Women of Tex. award, 1984-85. Mem. Tex. Assn. for Improvement Reading (cons. West Tex. U.), Assn. Tex. Profl. Educators (local pres., sec. dist. 17), AAUW, Smithsonian Assocs., Nat. Mus. Women in Arts, Delta Kappa Gamma. Baptist. Avocations: art, reading, developing children's materials. Home: 1119 Holiday St Plainview TX 79072-6045

GASTON, MARGARET ANNE, retired business educator; b. Regina, Sask., Can., Aug. 28, 1930; Came to U.S., 1948. d. William Julius and Mary Josephine (Collins) Grogan; m. Robert F. Gaston, 1955 (dec. Mar. 1970); 1 child, Robert. BA in Bus. Edn., Cen. Wash. U., 1959; MEd, Western Wash. U., 1972; postgrad., Boston U., 1984. Cert. tchr. K-12, cert. vocat. tchr., Wash. Bus. educator Manson (Wash.) Sch. Dist., 1956-59; instr. K-12 Eastmont Sch. Dist., East Wenatchee, Wash., 1959-63; instr., chmn. dept. bus. Skagit Valley Coll. Whidbey Campus, Oak Harbor, Wash., 1970-90. Part-time instr. bus. edn. Wenatchee Valley Coll., 1959-65. Contbr. articles to profl. jours. Fellow Western Wash. U., Bellingham, 1968-69. Mem. AAUW, NEA, Wash. Edn. Assn., Bus. and Profl. Women, Delta Pi Epsilon, Beta Sigma Phi. Home: 20 Little Mountain Estates 2610 E Section St Mount Vernon WA 98274-6100

GASTON, PAT BENEFIELD, educational administrator; b. LaGrange, Ga., Aug. 11, 1950; m. Larry Gaston, Dec. 20, 1968; children: Tara Jenning, Tiffany, Tabatha. Student, West Ga. Tech. Sch., LaGrange, 1969, So. Union Coll., 1972, Ga. State U., 1986. Data processing clk. Rubber Maid, LaGrange, 1971-76; owner, dir. Ms. Pat's Christian Learning, LaGrange, 1986—. Mem. svc. bd. Ga. Childcare, 1990-91, conf. chair, 1991. Active Mission Union, LaGrange, 1982—, Troup County Chamber, 1987-92; svc. bd. March of Dimes, LaGrange, 1990-92; mem., past pres. Ga. Gideons, LaGrange, 1976—; dir. Rock Ridge Camp, Franklin, Ga., 1991—. Mem. ASCD, Nat. Assn. Educators, Nat. Assn. Edn. Young Children, Ga. School-Age Childcare Coun., Ga. Childcare Coun., Ga. Preschool Assn. Avocations: running, outdoors recreation. Office: Ms Pat's Christian Ctr 3009 Westpoint Rd Lagrange GA 30240-8627

GASTON, PAUL LEE, academic administrator, language educator; b. Hattiesburg, Miss., Aug. 23, 1943; s. Paul Lee and Ruth (Gooch) Gaston; m. Eileen Margaret Higgins, June 29, 1968; children: Elizabeth, Tyler Lee. BA, S.E. La. U., 1965; MA, U. Va., 1966, PhD, 1970. Ordained min. Episc. Ch., 1990. Prof. English So. Ill. U., Edwardsville, 1969-88, assoc. v.p., 1984-88; dean Coll. Arts and Scis. U. Tenn., Chattanooga, 1988-93; provost, exec. v.p. No. Ky. U., Highland Heights, 1993-99; provost Kent (Ohio) State U., 1999—. Author: W. D. Snodgrass, 1978, Concordance Conrad, Arrow of Gold, 1980; contbr. articles to profl. jours. Bd. dirs. Ohio Learning

Network, Ohio Lik. Mem.: Nat. Assn. State U. and Land Grant Colls., Assn. Specialized and Profl. Accreditors, Phi Beta Kappa. Democrat. Avocations: softball, hiking, calligraphy. Office: Kent State U Office of Provost PO Box 5190 Kent OH 44242-0001 E-mail: pgaston@kent.edu.

GATCH, CHARLES EDWARD, JR., academic administrator; b. St. George, S.C., Feb. 26, 1939; m. Dolores Bull, Aug. 13, 1961; children: Michael and Jerald (twins), Victoria. BSEd, U. S.C., 1962; MMEd, La. State U., 1964; EdD in Adminstrn., U. S.C., 1991. Cert. supt., elem. prin., secondary prin., instrumental music tchr. Band dir. Westdale Elem. Sch., Baton Rouge, 1962-64; asst. prof. music edn. Campbell U., Buies Creek, N.C., 1964-70; grad. asst. La. State U., 1970-72; band dir. Episcopal High Sch., Baton Rouge, 1970-72; asst. prof. music edn. U. S.C., Columbia, 1972-74; prin. Pelion (S.C.) High Sch., 1974-77; tchr., band dir. part-time Oak Grove Elem. Sch., Lexington, S.C., 1977-78; tchr., choral dir. part-time Gilbert (S.C.) High Sch., 1977-78; prin. Lexington Mid. Sch., 1978-93; intern S.C. State Dept. of Edn., 1993-94; coord. student svcs. Lexington Sch. Dist. I, 1995—. Part-time adminstrv. asst. dist. office Lexington County Sch. Dist. I, 1977-78, coord. tech. prep and at risk programs, 1994-96, coord. student svcs., 1996—; presenter Nat. NAESP Conv., 1987, SCASSP Conf., 1990; mem. prin. evaluation adv. com. S.C. State Dept. Edn. Com., 1984-87, trainer for new prins., 1985—; mem. adv. com. NTE Successor Project, 1989; mem. panel conf. on Preventing Teen Pregnancies and Enhancing Human Sexuality, 1985; mem. supt. internship program S.C. Dept. Edn. Leadership Acad., 1986; presenter U. Pa. Ethnography in Edn. rsch. Forum, 1987, Summer Leadershp Inst., Myrtle Beach, S.C., 1987, Leadership Acad., 1986, trained as an assessor, 1986. Site visitor Nat. Blue Ribbon Schs. Award, 1993; mem., adult choir dir. Lexington United Meth. Ch., 19 yrs., former mem. adminstrn. bd., former Sunday sch. tchr. grades 9-12 and adult Sunday sch., former youth choir dir.; dir. Columbia Youth Orch., 1978-83; prin. trombonist S.C. Philharm. Orch., 1983-84; participant Lexington musical revues Lexington County Arts Assn.; musical conductor Annie, 1989; musical dir. Lexington Musical Revue, 1973; dir. Lexington Bicentennial Chorus, 1976; judge state music competition Richland Sch. Dist. 2, 1985. Recipient Outstanding Contributions award S.C. ASCD, 1991, Nat. Disting. Prin. award S.C., 1987; named one of Outstanding Young Men of Yr., Jaycees, 1968. Mem. S.C. Mid. Sch. Assn. (pres. 1985-86, pres.-elect 1984-85, program com. 1981-82, 85, 86, presenter S.C. Leadership Acad. Workshop, prin. evaluation adv. com., SCASA rep. exec. com. for S.C. Alliance for Arts Edn.), S.C. Assn. Elem. and Mid. Sch. Prins. (presenter conf. for new prins. and asst. prins., program com. 1983 for Spring 1984 conf., Palmetto's finest com. 1983-84, judge 1985, 86, 90, program com. for workshop asst. prins. 1983, chmn. fin. com. 1986-87, entertainment com. for S.E. prins. conf. 1990, program participant discussion of EIA 1984), S.C. Assn. Mid. Level Prins. (chmn. winter conf. 1993, pres.-elect 1992-93, pres. 1993—, rep. SCASA legis. com.), PTA (life), Lexington Lions Club (2d v.p. 1985-86, 1st v.p. 1986-87, pres. 1987-88, zone chmn. 1988-89, 89-90, program chmn. Ladies Night 1985, chmn. Candy Day Sale 1984), Rotary Club Lexington. Avocations: jogging, golf, fishing, dance band leader, swing set jazz dance band. Home: 129 Foxglen Cir Lexington SC 29072-9199 Office: Lexington Sch Dist I PO Box 1869 Lexington SC 29071-1869

GATCHEL, DENNIS LEROY, assistant principal; b. Decatur, Ill., Jan. 6, 1949; s. Omer LeRoy and Betty (Zientara) G.; m. Mary Kathryn Cohorst, Aug. 2, 1975; 1 child, Cara Lynn. BS in Edn., Ea. Ill. U., 1971; MS in Edn., So. Ill. U., 1981. Ind. art tchr., coach N. Greene High Sch., White Hall, Ill., 1971-72, Bement H.S., Ill., 1972-76; shop foreman Schrock Cabinets, Arthur, Ill., 1976; ind. art tchr., coach Ctrl. HS, Breese, Ill., 1976-85; ind. art tchr., head football and track coach Macon HS, Ill., 1985-94; asst. football coach Millikin U., Decatur, Ill., 1990-93; asst. prin./AD/Head football coach Meridian HS, Macon, Ill., 1994—. Head coach state playoffs, Normal, 1986; head coach state playoffs, Champaign, 1999, coach Ill. Shrine Football Game, Normal, 1987, coach Ill. Shrine football Game, Peoria, 2000. Named Area Football Coach of Yr. Decatur Herald Rev., 1986 & 1999. Mem. Ill. Football Coaches Assn. (presenter 1987 & 2000), Knights of Columbus, Sigma Tau Gamma. Avocations: woodworking, golf, fishing, gardening, cars. Office: Meridian High Sch 720 S Wall St Macon IL 62544-9540

GATES, DONNA MARIE, special education educator; b. Milton, Fla., Dec. 14, 1961; d. Lawrence C. and Theresa M. (Bechard) Bonneau; m. David J. Gates, June 25, 1994; children: Matthew, Michael. BS in Edn., Fitchburg State Coll., 1983; MEd, Wheelock Coll., 1997. Head counselor, counselor WAARC-Camp Joy, Worcester, Mass., 1977-81; house staff Cape Cod Summer Vacation Program, Hyannis, Mass., 1982; case mgr. NCM Friends of Retarded Coop. Apt. Program, Fitchburg, Mass., 1983; head tchr. May Inst., Chatham, Mass., 1983-85; tchr. Assabet Valley Collaborative Elem. Spl. Needs Program, Marlborough, Mass., 1985-88; primary resource tchr. Town of Auburn (Mass.), 1988—. Tchr. Project Challenge Assabet Valley Collaborative, 1993. Mem. Mass. Tchrs. Assn., Nat. Assn. Edn. Young Children. Avocations: camping, hiking.

GATES, JAMES DAVID, retired association executive, consultant; b. East Cleveland, Ohio, July 9, 1927; s. James Adelbert and Margaretta (Voigt) G.; m. Carol Marie Schreiber, June 9, 1956; children: David, Keith, Robert. AB, Hiram (Ohio) Coll., 1951; MA, Columbia, 1956; EdD, George Washington U., 1975. Tchr. Maple Heights (Ohio) City Schs., 1951-61; profl. asst. Nat. Council Tchrs. Math., Reston, Va., 1961-63, exec. sec., 1963-76, exec. dir., 1976-95. Mem. faculty U. Va., 1963-66, George Washington U., 1966-75; assoc. dir. Math. Scis. Edn. Bd., Ctr. for Sci., Math., and Engring. Edn., Nat. Rsch. Coun., 1997-99. Mem. Va. Coalition Math. and Sci.; bd. dirs. MathCounts Found.; sec.-treas. Jr. Engring. Tech. Soc. Served with AUS, 1945-46. Fellow AAAS; mem. NEA, ASCD, Nat. Coun. Suprs. Math., Nat. Coun. Tchrs. Math., Math. Assn. Am., Assn. State Suprs. Math., Benjamin Banneker Assn., Assn. Math. Tchr. Educators, Am. Math. Assn. Two-Yr. Colls., Rotary. Home: 11303 Fieldstone Ln Reston VA 20191-3905 E-mail: jamgate@aol.com.

GATES, ROBERTA PECORARO, nursing educator; b. Elmira, N.Y., May 22, 1948; d. Patrick George and Verle Elizabeth (Warriner) Pecoraro; m. William Franklin Gates III, May 20, 1972; 1 child, William Franklin IV. BSN, U. Ariz., 1970; MSN in Family Nursing, U. Ala., Huntsville, 1981. Cert. clin. specialist in med.-surg. nursing; bd. cert. Advanced practice nurse; cert. lactation counselor. Charge nurse St. Mary's Hosp. and Mental Health Ctr., Tucson, 1970-72; asst. head nurse Torrance (Calif.) Meml. Hosp., 1973-74; dist. nurse Sierra Sands Sch. Dist., Ridgecrest, Calif., 1974-76; instr. Albany (Ga.) Jr. Coll., 1978-80, John C. Calhoun Coll., Decatur, Ala., 1981-83; learning resources coord. Albany State Coll., 1984-85; asst. prof. Sinclair C.C., Dayton, Ohio, 1990-91, Darton Coll., Albany, 1986-89, 92—. Bd. dirs. Network Trust, Albany; cons. Cmty. Health Inst., Albany, 1993, Early County Bd. Edn., Blakely, Ga., 1994, Ga. State U., 1996—, Ga. Interagy. Coordinating Coun., 1997—; mem. Dist. Health Perinatal Bd., 2002; mem. Breastfeeding Task Force, 2002; cons. Project SCEIs, Ga. State U., 1996—. Author: A Model for Adolescent Health Promotion in the Dougherty County Community, 1993. Mem. Ga. Coun. Prevention of Child Abuse, Albany, 1988, 93; mem. Albany Mus. Art, 1993—; mem. Cmty. Ptnrs. Health Care Initiative, Dayton, 1990-91; bd. dirs. March of Dimes, Albany, 1986-89; mem. Albany-Dougherty 2000, DOCO Alternative Adv. Bd., State Consortium Early Intervention, Babies Can't Wait, 1995. Recipient NISOD award tchg. excellence, 2002; Named to Outstanding Young Women of Am., 1983. Mem. Ga. Higher Edn. Consortium, Sigma Theta Tau, Phi Kappa Phi. Avocations: gardening, walking, boating, reading. Office: Darton Coll 2400 Gillionville Rd Albany GA 31707-3023

GATEWOOD, LINDA LAYNE, special education educator; b. Tampa, Fla., Sept. 25, 1947; d. Donald Paul and Kathryn (Taylor) Gatewood. BA in Secondary Edn., U. Fla., 1969; MA in Ednl. Psychology, U. Hawaii, 1972; MA in Adult Edn., U. South Fla., 1986, MA in Counseling and Guidance, 1989. Cert. tchr., Fla. Vocat. and rehab. counselor HRS, Sarasota, Fla., 1972-73; tchr. emotionally handicapped Monroe County Schs., Key West, Fla., 1973-74; tchr. adult English Hillsborough County Schs., Tampa, 1977-87, tchr. specific learning disabilities, 1974—. Dir. City of Tampa Recreation Dept., 1965-69, Ctr. for Learning Strategies and Career Counseling, Tampa, 1990—; assoc. del. Nicaragua in Spl. Edn., Washington, 1990, del. Pres.'s Coun. on Mental Retardation, Honolulu, 1972. Pres. U. Fla. Alpha Nu Found., 1993-94. Recipient Internat. award for Tchrs. of Handicapped, Rotary, 1976, Prin. award Dunbar Elem. Sch., 1992, Community Svc. award Sta. WQYK-Radio, 1993; Fla. State fellow, 1965-69, Phi Mu scholar, 1972, Pi Lambda scholar, 1976. Mem. NEA, Phi Mu (v.p. 1992-93), Phi Delta Kappa, Bay Sailors, St. Petersburg Sailing Club. Home: 3308 W Palmira Ave Tampa FL 33629-7138

GATHERCOLE, PATRICIA MAY, modern foreign languages educator; b. Erie, Pa., Oct. 5, 1920; d. John William and Iris (Beech) G. BA with 1st class hons., U. B.C., Vancouver, 1941; MA, U. B.C., 1942; PhD, U. Calif., Berkeley, 1950. Teaching asst. U. Calif., Berkeley, 1945-50; instr. U. B.C., Vancouver, 1950-53, U. Wash., Seattle, 1952, U. Oreg., Eugene, 1953-56; asst. to assoc. prof. Roanoke Coll., Salem, 1956—, prof. modern fgn. lang., to 1992, prof. emeritus modern fgn. lang., 1992—. Author: Laurent de Premierfait's "Des Cas", Tension in Boccaccio, 1975, Selected Poems of U. Liberatore, 1967, Animals in Medieval French Manuscript Illumination, 1995, The Landscape of Nature in Medieval French Manuscript Illumination, 1997, The Depiction of Women in Medieval French Manuscript Illumination, 2000; contbr. articles to profl. jours. Fulbright fellow, 1954, Mellon fellow, 1978, others. Mem. Fgn. Lang. Assn. Va. (v.p.), Am. Assn. Tchrs. French, Southeastern Medieval Assn., S. Atlantic Modern Lang. Assn., Big Lick Stamp Club (sec. 1988-90, bd. dirs. 2000—), Star City Cat Fanciers (sec. 1980-2002, pres. 2003—). Republican. Episcopalian. Avocations: stamp collecting, gardening, dancing. Home: 423 Highfield Rd Salem VA 24153-3263 E-mail: gathercole2@yahoo.com.

GATHERS, EMERY GEORGE, computer science educator; b. Meadville, Pa., Oct. 10, 1942; s. George Edward and Martha Elizabeth (McCaughty) G.; m. Judith Ann Harbison, Aug. 5, 1967; children: Ann D., Adam E. BS in Math., Edinboro U. Pa., 1964; MA in Math., Bowling Green State U., 1967; Ed.S. in Higher Edn., Okla. State U., 1975, ED.D. in Higher Edn., 1982. Math. tchr. Toms River HS, NJ, 1964-65; grad. asst. Bowling Green State U., Ohio, 1965-66; tchr. Fostoria Jr. HS, Ohio, 1967; prof. math., computer sci. U. Tenn, Martin, 1967—; grad. asst. Okla. State U., Stillwater, 1977-78. Acad. student advisor U. Tenn., 1985—, promotion and tenure com., 1990—, faculty senate, 1990—93, 1995—, grad. coun., 1995—, personnel policy, 2000. Contbr. articles to UTM Math. Placement Exam, Spl. Interest Group on Computer Sci. Edn. Bull. Tchr. Sunday sch. First Bapt. Ch., Martin, Tn., 1990—, treas., 1993—. Recipient Meritorious award Phi Kappa Phi, 1988, Outstanding Tchg. award U. Tenn Alumni, 1989; Kappa Alpha Order Tchr. of the Yr. Award, 2000; named Outstanding Adv. Coll. Bus. and Pub. Affairs, 2002; Faculty Devel. grant U. Tenn, 1984, 95-97. Mem. IEEE, Assn. Computing Machinery, Sigma Xi (treas. 1984—), Masons. Democratic. Achievements include development of student retention model for higher education. Home: 112 Clark St Martin TN 38237-2904 Office: U Tenn Dept Computer Sci and Info Sys Martin TN 38238-0001

GATI, WILLIAM EUGENE, architect, designer and planner; b. Apr. 10, 1959; s. John and Edith Gati. Student, The Juilliard Sch. of Music, 1965-77; BS in Architecture, CCNY, 1980, BArch cum laude, 1982; MS in Urban Planning, CUNY, 1985. Registered architect, N.Y., N.J. Freelance designer, N.Y.C., 1978-83; designer Urban Living, Inc., N.Y.C., 1983-84, Robert L. Henry, Architect, N.Y.C., 1984-86, Glass & Assocs., N.Y.C., 1986-87; prin. architect William E. Gati, RA, AIA, N.Y.C., 1987—; prin. Architecture Studio, N.Y.C., 1991—; writer Home Editor Resident Publs., 1995-97. Prof. architecture N.Y. Inst. Tech., Old Westbury, 1985-89; instr. religious architecture Cooper Union, N.Y.C., 1989; instr. architecture St. John's U., N.Y.C., 1995—; curator Fundamentals of Architecture, N.Y. Inst. Tech., 1987; bd. dir. Queen's (N.Y.) Design Ctr.; lectr. in field. Archtl. designs include offices for Here's Life, N.Y.C., alterations to Calvary Bapt. Ch., N.Y.C., El Eden Ch., Bklyn., Living Word Christian Ctr., N.Y.C., All Saints Ch., Queens, N.Y.C., Dr. Aviles Med. Ctr., Queens, Tampellini Residence, Queens, Beninen Residence, Queens, Khafi Residence, Queens, expansion for Flushing Christian Sch., Queens, N.Y., Faith Assembly Ch., Queens, P.S. 68 annex, Queens, Perkovich Residence, Queens, Kaufman Residence, L.I., Cardinal Residence, Mas, Lindas Natural Kitchen, Queens, Resurrection Ch., Bklyn., Dr. Peter Chin's Med. Offices, Queens, Dr. Peter Murowski's Med. Offices, Queens, Dr. Larry Weinstein med. offices, Quantum Feet Store, Queens, Greenberg Residence, Queens, Parson Residence, Queens, Malik Residence, Queens, Benenati Residence, Queens; author: Solar Energy Techniques, 1979 (AIA Recognition 1979), Frank L. Wright, 1981, Theory of Modern Architecture, 1981, Boston's Pub. Space, 1985, Vacant Lots, Architectural League N.Y.C., 1987; contbg. illustrator Jonathan Friedman Creations in Space, Fundamentals of Architecture. Chmn. religious architecture com., organized series: Places for Worship, N.Y.C. 1990; planning bd. Kew Gardens; dir. Queens Design Ctr. Recipient Design award, Queens County Builder's Assn., 2002, Builders award, 2002. Mem. AIA (mem. religious arch. com. N.Y.C., v.p. Queens chpt., head coms., bd. dirs. N.Y. State chpt.), Mcpl. Art Soc. (assoc.), Archtl. League (assoc.), CCNY Alumni Assn. (v.p. 1983-92), N.Y. Arts Group, Christian Architects Fellowship (pres.). Avocations: photography, chess, piano, art. Office: 11231 84th Ave Jamaica NY 11418-1321 E-mail: wgati@williamgati.com.

GATIPON, BETTY BECKER, medical educator, consultant; b. New Orleans, Sept. 8, 1931; d. Elmore Paul and Theresa Caroline (Sendker) Becker; m. William B. Gatipon, Nov. 22, 1952 (dec. 1986); children: Suzanne, Ann Gatipon Sved, Lynn Gatipon Pashley. BS magna cum laude, Ursuline Coll., New Orleans, 1952; MEd, La. State U., 1975, PhD, 1983. Tchr. Diocese of Baton Rouge, 1960-74, edn. cons. to sch. bd., 1974-78; dir. Right to Read program Capital Area Consortium/Washington Parish Sch. Bd., Franklington, La., 1978-80; dir. basic skills edn. Capital Area Consortium/Ascension Parish Sch. Bd., Donaldsonville, La., 1980-82; instr. Coll. Edn. La. State U., Baton Rouge, 1982-84; evaluation cons. La. Dept. Edn., Baton Rouge, 1984-85; dir. basic skills edn. Capital Area Basic Skills/East Feliciana Parish Sch. Bd., Clinton, La., 1985-86; program coord. La. Bd. Elem. and Secondary Edn., New Orleans, 1987-89; dir. divsn. of med. edn., dept. family medicine Sch. Medicine La. State U. Med. Ctr., New Orleans, 1989—. Evaluator East Feliciana Parish Schs., 1982-86; presenter math. methods workshops Ascension Parish Schs., 1980-84. Author curriculum materials, conf. papers; contbr. articles to edn. jours. Curatorial asst. La. State Mus., New Orleans, 1987—; soprano St. Louis Cathedral Concert Choir, New Orleans, 1988—; chmn. Symphony Store, New Orleans Symphony, 1990—; lector St. Francis Xavier Ch. Mem. Am. Ednl. Rsch. Assn., Assn. Am. Med. Colls., Midsouth Ednl. Rsch. Assn., La. Ednl. Rsch. Assn., Soc. Tchrs. Family Medicine, New Orleans Film and Video Buffs, Phi Kappa Phi, Phi Delta Kappa. Roman Catholic. Avocations: music, aerobic walking, classic movies. Home: 105 10th St New Orleans LA 70124-1258 Office: LA State U Med Ctr Sch Medicine 1542 Tulane Ave New Orleans LA 70112-2825

GATJE, GEORGE CARLISLE, retired secondary education educator; b. Patchogue, N.Y., Apr. 29, 1931; s. George Henry and Marion (Shand) G.; m. Peggy Grady, Aug. 2, 1968; children: Jean C., Amy E. B Aerospace Engring., Rensselaer Polytech Inst., 1952, MS in Aerosapce Engring., 1958; MS in Bus. Adminstrn., George Washington U., 1969; MS in Secondary Edn., Math., Old Dominion U., 1983. Teaching asst. Rensselaer Polytech Inst., Troy, N.Y., 1955-57; tchr. math. Western Br. High Sch., Chesapeake, Va., 1983-2000; ret., 2000. Capt. USN, 1952-82. Mem. AIAA, Nat. Coun. Tchrs. Math., U.S. NAval Inst. Presbyterian. Home: 1221 Botetourt Gdns Norfolk VA 23517-2201

GATTAZ, WAGNER FARID, psychiatry educator; b. Rio Preto, Sao Paulo, Brazil, Feb. 10, 1951; s. Farid and Laila G.; m. Gabriele Cornelia Gattaz; children: Moritz, Leonardo. Medical degree, Faculty Medicine Found. ABC, Sao Paulo, 1975; MD, U. Heidelberg, Fed. Republic Germany, 1979, habilitation in psychiatry, 1983. Resident in psychiatry U. Sao Paulo, 1976-77; vis. scientist Cen. Inst. Mental Health, Mannheim, Germany, 1978-80, vis. prof., 1981-83, prof. psychiatry, 1984—, dir. neurobiology unit, 1991—. Co-editor: Search for the Causes of Schizophrenia: (jour.) European Archives Psychiatry and Neurol. Scis.; mem. editorial bd. European Jour. Psychiatry, Schizophrenia Rsch., Psiquiatria Biologica, Psychopharmacology and Biological Psychiatry (sec.). Mem. Soc. Biol. Psychiatry, World Psychiatric Assn., Internat. Soc. Human Biologists, German Soc. Biological Psychiatry (sec.). Avocation: painting. Home: M6 16 68161 Mannheim 68161 Mannheim Germany

GAUDEAMUS, See JORDAN, JOHN LESTER

GAUDET, JEAN ANN, retired librarian, educator; b. Oakland, Calif., Dec. 28, 1949; d. Edwin Joseph and Teresa Maureen (McDonnell) G. BS, Madison Coll., Harrisonburg, Va., 1971; MLS, George Peabody Coll. for Tchrs, Nashville, 1973. Libr., gifted edn. tchr. Prince William County Schs., Manassas, Va., 1971—2003, ret., 2003. Chmn. PSHS Site-Based Mgmt. Com., Dumfries, Va., 1989-92, 98-2001; chmn. Cmty. Choir, Woodbridge, Va., 1983-85; citizen ambassador People to People, Russia and Poland, 1992, China, 1993, 2000, Australia, 1994. Named Prince William Assn. for Edn. of Gifted Tchr. of Yr., 1998. Mem. ALA, Va. Edn. Media Assn., Va. Assn. for Edn. of Gifted, Delta Kappa Gamma (sec. 1994—), Beta Phi Mu, Alpha Beta Alpha. Home: 16820 Francis West Ln Dumfries VA 22026-2110 E-mail: gaudetja@cs.com.

GAUDIANI, CLAIRE LYNN, retired academic administrator; b. Venice, Fla., Nov. 10, 1944; d. Vincent Augustus and Vera (Rossano) Gaudiani; m. David Graham Burnett; children: David Graham, Maria. BA, Conn. Coll., 1966; MA in French and Italian, Ind. U., 1969, PhD in French and Italian, 1975; PhD (hon.), Purdue U., 1989, Whitman Coll., 1989. Asst. prof. Purdue U., W. Lafayette, Ind., 1977—80, Emory U., Atlanta, 1980—81; sr. fellow in romance langs., acting assoc. dir. Joseph H. Lauder Inst. Mgmt. and Internat. Studies U. Pa., Phila., 1981—88; pres. Conn. Coll., New London, 1988—2001; sr. rsch. scholar Yale Law Sch., 2001—. Mem. commn. internat. edn. Am. Coun. Edn.; bd. dirs. So. NEw ENg. Telephone Co.; cons. Dana Found., Exxon Found., Rockefeller Found. Author: The Cabaret Peotry oof Theophile de Viau: Texts and Traditions, 1980, Teaching Writing in the Foreign Language Curriculum, 1981; co-author (with Carol Herron and others): Strategies for Development of Foreign Language and Literature Programs, 1984; contbr. articles to profl. jours.; author: The Greater Good: How Philanthropy Saves American Capitalism, 2003. Chair assessment task force United Way, New London, 1988; hon. chair Summer Music Fund, 1988; trustee Hazen Found.; bd. dirs. Eugene O'Neill Theatre Ctr. Recipient Coll. medal, Conn. Coll., 1987; fellow rsch. fellow, Nat. Humanities Ctr., 1980—81, Am. Coun. Learned Socs., 1976—77. Mem.: MLA (adv. com. fgn. lang. programs 1988—), Conn. World Trade Assn. (bd. dirs.), Am. Assn. Higher Edn. (bd. dirs. 1988—), Phi Beta Kappa. Roman Catholic. Office: Yale Law School P O Box 208215 New Haven CT 06520*

GAUDIN, TIMOTHY J. paleontologist, biology educator; b. Atlanta, June 2, 1966; s. James M. and Elaine M. (Kaminski) G.; m. Suzanne M. Rusmisel, Aug. 18, 1990; children: Thomas M., Eleanor M. BS summa cum laude, U. Ga., 1987; PhD, U. Chgo., 1993. Vis. asst. prof. dept. biology Coll. Holy Cross, Worcester, Mass., 1993-94; asst. prof. dept. biology and environ. sci. U. Tenn., Chattanooga, 1994—98, assoc. prof. dept. biology and environ. sci., 1999—. Rsch. assoc. Field Mus. Natural History, Chgo., 1994—. Contbr. articles to profl. jours. Rsch. assoc. Carnegie Mus. Natural History, Pitts., 1999—. Grad. fellow NSF, 1987-90, Harper Dissertation fellow U. Chgo., 1992-93; UC Found. asst. professorship U. Tenn., 1996—. Mem. Am. Soc. Mammalogists, Soc. Integrative and Comparative Biology, Tenn. Acad. Sci., Soc. Vertebrate Paleontology. Achievements include studies of phylogeny and evolution of edentate mammals, including sloths, armadillos, anteaters and pangolins. Office: U Tenn Dept Biology & Environ Sci 615 Mccallie Ave Chattanooga TN 37403-2504

GAUDREAU, GAYLE GLANERT, computer resource educator; b. Hartford, Conn., June 10, 1944; d. Edward Eugene and Evelyn Ruth (Manning) Glanert; m. George C. Gaudreau, Nov. 15, 1974; children: Christopher, Matthew, Nathan. BS in Bus. Edn., Ctrl. Conn. State U., New Britain, 1969, MS in Edn., 1974; postgrad., U. Conn. Cert. tchr. bus. edn., coord. coop. work experience, Conn. Group leader Pratt & Whitney Aircraft, East Hartford, Conn., 1964-67; coord. bus. edn. Wethersfield H.S., 1969-92; computer resource tchr. Wethersfield (Conn.) Bd. Edn., 1992—. Part-time instr. Manchester (Conn.) C.C., 1973-74; mem. adv. bd. State of Conn. Bus. Edn., 1992; mem. adv. bd. bus. edn. Ctrl. Conn. State U., 1993—; cooperating tchr. State of Conn.; mem. Wethersfield Technology Com., 1993—. Named Disting. Educator, Wethersfield Bd. Edn.; recipient edn. alumni award Ctrl. Conn. State U. Sch. Bus., 1996. Mem. USTA (capt. sr. team), Conn. Educators Computer Assn., Conn. Bus. Educators' Assn., Am. Fedn. Tchrs., Wethersfield Fedn. Tchrs., Phi Delta Kappa, Pi Lambda Theta, Delta Pi Epsilon. Avocations: tennis, cooking, hiking, boating. Home: 1 Falcon Ln Glastonbury CT 06033-2731 Office: Wethersfield HS 411 Wolcott Hill Rd Wethersfield CT 06109-2981 E-mail: GayleG8198@aol.com.

GAULT, JANICE ANN, ophthalmologist, educator; b. Hammond, Ind., Sept. 3, 1965; d. William Wallace and Waltraud Anna (Konhäuser) G. BS, Duke U., 1987, MD, 1991. Diplomate Am. Bd. Ophthalmology. Intern in internal medicine Santa Barbara (Calif.) Cottage Hosp., 1991-92; resident in ophthalmology Wills Eye Hosp., Phila., 1992-95, asst. surgeon, 1995—. Contbr. articles to med. jours. Fellow ACS; mem. Am. Acad. Ophthalmology, World Affairs Coun., Jr. League Phila., Duke Club Phila. (pres., treas. 1992—), Phi Beta Kappa, Alpha Omega Alpha. Avocations: tennis, scuba diving, photography, wine, travel. Office: Wills Eye Hosp 840 Walnut St Ste 1240 Philadelphia PA 19107-5599

GAULT, TERESSA ELAINE, special education educator; b. South Williamson, Ky., Feb. 25, 1959; d. Donald Lee and Glenna Faye (Kirk) Varney; m. Marc Allen Widener, Sept. 1, 1979 (div. Aug. 1994); 1 child, Dawn Elise Widener; m. Robert William Gault III, July 29, 1995. EdB, Ohio U., 1980, MEd, 1992. Cert. tchr. grades 1-8, Ohio; cert. tchr. multiple, severely, profoundly retarded grades K-12, Ohio. Substitute tchr. Lancaster City (Ohio) Schs., 1980-81, tchr. multihandicapped, 1990—; tchr. St. Mary Elem. Sch., Lancaster, Ohio, 1981-88; habilitation specialist II Licking County Bd. Mental Retardation/Developmental Disabilities, Heath, Ohio, 1988-89; presch. instr. MH Perry County Cmty. Schs., New Lexington, Ohio, 1989-90. Instr. computer Fairfield Career Ctr., Carroll, Ohio, 1988, Southeastern Bus. Coll., Lancaster, Ohio, 1988-89. Recipient Letter of Commendation The Ohio House of Reps., 1993. Mem. Nat. Edn. Assn., Ohio Edn. Assn., Lancaster Edn. Assn. Democrat. Methodist. Avocations: swimming, beading, making jewelry, cross stitch. Home: 2656 Heidelberg Dr Lancaster OH 43130-8842 Office: West Elem Sch Lancaster City Schs 625 Garfield Ave Lancaster OH 43130-2497

GAUMOND, LYNN E. elementary school educator; b. Meriden, Conn., July 15, 1953; d. Richard Drake and Jean (Hall) Anderson; m. Gary Williams Gaumond, June 28, 1975; children: Jeffrey Ross, Kara Marie. BS in Edn. magna cum laude, Plymouth (N.H.) State Coll., 1975; MEd summa cum laude, U. Hartford, 1978. Tchr. grade 6 Squadron Line Sch., Simsbury, Conn., 1975-84, tchr. grade 3, 1984-86, tchr. kindergarten, 1986-89; tchr. grade 1 Tootin Hills Sch., West Simsbury, Conn., 1989—2000. Adj. prof. U. Hartford, 2002-; tchr. in residence bur. program and tchr. evaluation Conn. State Dept. Edn., 2000-2001, U. Hartford Magnet Sch., West Hartford, Grades 1, 2001-2003; logical math. essentialist, 2003-; cons. math program Primary Math. Series, Scholastic Book Pub., 1992-93; cons. math. manipulative project LEGO/DACTA, Enfield, Conn., 1990-91; tchr. PIMMS math recovery, 2002-. Contbg. writer/editor math program: Math Place, 1993-94; contbg. writer: CSDE Tchg. Handbook Portfolio. Mem. faculty, portfolio benchmarking, trainer, scorer, leader CSDE elem. edn., 1997-; trainer Ind. State Tchr.'s Portfolio, 2001, 2002; instr. CSDE Numeracy Acad., 1998-2000; com. mem. troop 177 Boy Scouts Am., Canton, Conn., 1992; coun. mem. Girl Scouts U.S., Canton, 1991—, leader troop 828, Canton, 1991—; mem. PTO, Canton Pub. Schs., 1985—; mem. Concerned Citizens for Canton, 1992—; bd. dirs. Canton Youth for Environ. Awareness, 1994—. Recipient Presdl. Award for Excellence in Sci. and Math. Teaching, NSF, 1993, state awardee, 1992, 93; Assoc. Tchrs. of Math. in Conn. grantee, 1993; semifinalist Conn. Tchr. of Yr., 2003, CREC Tchr. of Yr., 2003. Fellow Acad. for Edn. in Math., Sci. and Tech.; mem. NEA, ASCD, Conn. Edn. Assn., Simsbury Edn. Assn., Nat. Coun. Tchrs. Math., Assoc. Tchrs. of Math. in New Eng., Assoc. Tchrs. Math. in Conn., Coun. of Presdl. Awardees in Math., Soc. of Elem. Presdl. Awardees, Coun. for Elem. Sci. Internat., Nat. Sci. Tchrs. Assn. Democrat. Avocation: gardening. Home: 18 High Hill Rd Canton CT 06019-2225 Office: U Hartford Magnet Sch 196 Bloomfield Ave West Hartford CT 06117

GAUS, LYNN SHEBESTA, school administrator; b. Manitowoc, Wis., Dec. 16, 1955; d. Joseph J. Shebesta and Shirley Ann (Pietras) Kent; m. John Michael Gaus, Jr. BS, U. Wis., La Crosse, 1978; MS, Mankato State U., 1986; postgrad., Harvard U., 1992. Admissions counselor Silver Lake Coll., 1980-83; asst. dir. admissions Mankato (Minn.) State U., 1983-88; dir. admissions Lakeland Coll., Sheboygan, Wis., 1988-90; dean of admissions and fin. aid Wayland Acad., Beaver Dam, Wis., 1990-95; econ. devel. profl. N.E. Wis. Tech. Coll., Green Bay, 1995-2000; adminstr., prin. St. Mary's Sch., Luxemburg, Wis., 2000—01, St. Philip the Apostle Sch., Green Bay, 2001—02; dir. Am. Red Cross, Manitowoc, 2002—. Cons. to admissions Northwestern Military/Naval Acad., Lake Geneva, Wis., 1992; adj. instr. N.E. Wis. Tech. Coll., Lakeland Coll.; presenter, workshop presenter in fiel. Editor, designer, publisher (ednl. insts. brochures, viewbooks), 1986-93. Bd. dirs. Big Bros.-Big Sisters, Manitowoc, 1989, Girl Scouts U.S.A., Green Bay, 1996-98. Mem. Green Bay Area C. of C. (advance econ. devel. com., advance retention com.), Civitan (bd. dirs., v.p. Mankaato 1986-88), Rotary (bd. dirs., pres. DePere, Wis.). Avocations: skiing, camping, golf, cooking, gardening. Home: 448 N Good Hope Rd De Pere WI 54115-2405 Office: Am Red Cross 205 N 8th St Manitowoc WI 54220 E-mail: arclynng@lsol.net.

GAUSTAD, EDWIN SCOTT, historian, educator; b. Rowley, Iowa, Nov. 14, 1923; s. Sverre and Norma (McEachron) G.; m. Helen Virginia Morgan, Dec. 19, 1946; children— Susan, Glen Scott, Peggy Lynn. BA, Baylor U., 1947; MA, Brown U., 1948, PhD, 1951. Instr. Brown U., 1951-52, Am. Council Learned Socs. scholar in residence, 1952-53; dean Shorter Coll., 1953-57; prof. humanities U. Redlands, 1957-65; assoc. prof. history U. Calif., Riverside, 1965-67, prof., 1968-89, prof. emeritus, 1989; prof. Princeton (N.J.) Theol. Sem., 1991-92, Auburn U., 1993. Vis. prof. Baylor U., 1976, U. Calif., Santa Barbara, 1986, U. Richmond, 1987. Author: The Great Awakening in New England, 1957, New Historical Atlas of Religion in America, new edit., (with P.L. Barlow), 2001, Religious History of America, revised edit., (with Leigh E. Schmidt), 2002, Dissent in American Religion, 1973, Baptist Piety: The Last Will and Testimony of Obadiah Holmes, 1978, George Berkeley in America, 1979, Faith of Our Fathers, 1987, Liberty of Conscience: Roger Williams in America, 1991, Revival, Revolution, and Religion in Early Virginia, 1994, Sworn on the Altar of God: A Religious Biography of Thomas Jefferson, 1996, Church and State in America, 1998, 2d edit., 2003, Memoirs of the Spirit, 1999, Roger Williams: Prophet of Liberty, 2001. Served to 1st lt. USAAC, 1943-45. Decorated Air medal; Am. Council Learned Socs. grantee, 1952-53, 72-73; Am. Philos. Soc. grantee, 1972-73 Mem. Am. Soc. Ch. History (pres.), Orgn. Am. Historians, Phi Beta Kappa. Democrat. Baptist. Home: 599 Vista De La Ciudad Santa Fe NM 87501-6300 E-mail: egaustad@aol.com.

GAUTSCHI, WALTER, mathematics educator; b. Basel, Switzerland, Dec. 11, 1927; came to U.S., 1955, naturalized, 1961; s. Hans and Margrit Eugster G.; m. Erika Wuest, Apr. 8, 1960; children: Thomas, Theresa, Doris, Caroline PhD, U. Basel, 1953. Research mathematician Nat. Bur. Standards, Washington, 1956-59; mathematician Oak Ridge Nat. Lab., 1959-63; prof. math. and computer scis. Purdue U., Lafayette, Ind., 1963—2000, prof. emeritus, 2000—. Vis. prof. Tech. U. Munich, Germany, 1970-71, Math. Research Ctr., U. Wis., Madison, 1976-77; cons. Argonne Nat. Lab., Ill., 1967-77, vis. prof ETH Zurich, 1996-98, U. Padua, Italy, 1997, U. Basel, 2000. Assoc. editor Math. of Computation, 1966-84, 96-98, mng. editor, 1984-95; assoc. editor Soc. Indsl. and Applied Math., Math. Analysis, 1970-73, Numerische Mathematik, 1971—, hon. editor, 1991—; assoc. editor Calcolo, 1975-87. Fulbright research scholar, Munich, 1970-71 Mem. Am. Math. Soc., Math. Assn. Am., Soc. Indsl. and Applied Math., Schweizerische Mathematische Gesellschaft, Bavarian Acad. Scis. (fgn.), Turin Acad. Scis. (fgn. 2001). Office: Purdue Univ Dept Computer Scis Lafayette IN 47907

GAVALAS, GEORGE R. chemical engineering educator; b. Athens, Greece, Oct. 7, 1936; s. Lazaros R. and Belouso A. (Matha) G. BS, Nat. Tech. U., 1958; MS, U. Minn., 1962, PhD, 1964. Asst. prof. chem. engring. Calif. Inst. Tech., 1964-67, assoc. prof., 1967-75, prof., 1975—. Cons. in field. Author: Nonlinear Differential Equations of Chemically Reacting Systems, 1968, Coal Pyrolysis, 1983; contbr. articles to profl. jours. Mem. AIChE (Tech. award 1968, Wilhelm award 1983), Am. Chem. Soc., N.Am. Membrane Soc. Home: 707 S Orange Blvd # F Pasadena CA 91105-1779 Office: Caltech 210-41 Pasadena CA 91125-0001 E-mail: garalas@cheme.caltech.edu.

GAVIN, JOAN ELAINE, special education educator; b. Onalaska, Wis., July 26, 1950; d. Vernon and Helen Ruth Weinberg; m. A.M. Gavin, June 13, 1986; stepchildren: John Edward, Daniel James, Mark Ambrose, Scott Michael. BS in Elem. Edn., U. Wis., La Crosse, 1973, MS in Spl. Edn., ED/LD, 1975. Cert. 1-8 elem. tchr., tchr. emotionally disturbed and learning disabled, Wis.; cert. crisis prevention intervention; cert. CPR. Tchr. emotionally disturbed and learning disabilities De Soto (Wis.) Area Schs., 1975-79; tchr. elem. emotionally disturbed coop. program Elroy-Kendall-Wilton Schs., Elroy, Wis., 1979-84, Wilton, Wis., 1984-86, Kendall, Wis., 1986-93, elem. tchr. Elroy, 1993-2000, Ithaca Schs., 2000—01; spl. edn. ED/LD tchr. Wonewoc (Wis.) Ctr. Schs., 2001—. Mem. dist.-wide insvc. com. Elroy-Kendall-Wilton Schs., 1986-2000, facilitator AODA program, mem. CORE com. AODA, 1994-2000, chairperson dist. wide insvc. com. 1997-2000. Developer, bd. dirs., treas. Kinship of Elroy, Inc., 1980-89; pres., coord. County-Wide Kinship, Kinship, Inc., 1984-94; active Kids for Kids. Honor scholar, 1968; grantee NSF Sci. Enhancement Project, U. Wis., 1985, 86, 88, 89, 90. Mem. Am. Legion Aux., U. Wis.-LaCrosse Alumni Assn. Avocations: collecting coins, stamps, antiques, depression and carnival dishes. E-mail: gavijoa@wc.k12.wi.us.

GAY, CHARLES W., JR., academic administrator; b. Tulsa, June 30, 1937; s. Charles W. Sr. and Juanita T. (Reeder) G.; m. Sarah E. Frost Smith, Sept. 8, 1953 (div. June 1967); children: Timothy L., Patrick N.; m. Louise M. Kiser, Dec. 22; stepchildren: Beth L., Richard E. Macatee. BS in Forest Mgmt., Okla. State U., 1962, MS in Range and Livestock Mgmt., 1964. Range rsch. asst. Santa Rita Explt. Range/U.S. Forest Svc., Tucson, 1962; range mgmt. extension specialist to assoc. prof. N.Mex. State U., 1964-68, chief of party livestock devel. project in Paraguay, 1969-72; gen. mgr. agr. divsn. Collier Cobb and Assocs./Hudson Farms and Farm Svcs., Pike Road, Ala., 1973-79; v.p. Gay Sales and Svcs., Inc., Tulsa, 1979-83; assoc. chief of party, adj. prof. on range mgmt. project Utah State U., Rabat, Morocco, 1983-86, rsch. asst. prof. of range sci. Logan, 1986-87, acting dept. head range scie., 1987-88, asst. to dean for adminstrv. affairs, ext. program leader, 1989—2001, asst. dean extension & adminstrn., 2001, assoc. v.p. for university extension. Invited lectr. Bank of Am. Symposium, 1978, Global Natural Resources Monitoring and Assessments Conf., Venice, Italy, 1989, Icelandic Soil Conservation Svc., Iceland, 1989; invited vis. scientist N.W. Plateau Inst. of Biology, Haibei Alpine Rsch. Sta., China, 1992; co-chmn. U.S. Range Mgmt. Task Force/USDA and Mex.'s Dept. Agr. and Water Resources. Editorial bd., assoc. editor: Arid Soil Rsch. and Rehab. jour.; contbr. articles to profl. jours. Pres. bd. dirs. Nora Eccles Harrison Mus. Art, 1994-97; bd. dirs. USU Comty. Credit Union, 1991-97, Utah Festival Opera Co., 1995-99; trustee, past dir. Devel. for the Logan Chamber Music Soc., 1988-89; chmn. joint com. for Mendon Ward, Boy Scouts Am., 1989-90; Dem. Party chmn., Mendon, 1990—; mem. Kiwanis Youth Devel. Com., Logan; bd. advisors Stokes Nature Ctr., Logan, Utah, 2000. Recipient Phillips Petroleum Grad. Rsch. scholarship, Ala. Coop. Extension Leadership award 1978, Goodyear award for land stewardship and resource conservation, 1998, Disting. Svc. award Epsilon Sigma Phi, 2000, Internat. Svc. award, 2002. Mem. N.Y. Acad. Scis., Soc. Range Mgmt. (sec., chmn. internat. affairs com., others), Soc. Am. Foresters (chair range ecology work group), Am. Mgmt. Assn., Soc. Internat. Devel. (mentor), Utah Soc. Environ. Edn., Intermountain Assn. Environ. Edn., Assn. of Natural Resources Ext. Profls. (pres. 2001), Joint Coun. Ext. Profls. Avocations: sailing, classical music and theatre, lit., tennis, gardening. Office: Utah State Univ Ext 4900 Old Main Hill Logan UT 84322-4900 E-mail: chuckg@ext.usu.edu.

GAY, PETER, history educator, author; b. Berlin, June 20, 1923; came to U.S., 1941, naturalized, 1946; s. Morris Peter and Helga (Kohnke) G.; m. Ruth Slotkin, May 30, 1959; stepchildren: Sarah Khedouri, Sophie Glazer Cohen, Elizabeth Glazer. BA, U. Denver, 1946; MA, Columbia U., 1947, PhD, 1951; LHD (hon.), U. Denver, 1970, U. Md., 1979, Hebrew Union Coll., Cin., 1983, Clark U., 1985, Suffolk U., Boston, 1987, Tufts U., 1988, U. Ill., 2003. Faculty Columbia U., N.Y.C., 1947-69, prof. history, 1962-69, William R. Shepherd prof. history, 1967-69; prof. comparative European intellectual history Yale U., New Haven, 1969—, Durfee prof. history, 1970-84, Sterling prof., 1984-93, Sterling prof. emeritus, 1993—; dir. Ctr. for Scholars and Writers N.Y. Pub. Libr., 1997—. Dir. Ctr. Scholars and Writers N.Y. Pub. Libr. Author: The Dilemma of Democratic Socialism: Eduard Bernstein's Challenge to Marx, 1952, Voltaire's Politics: The Poet as Realist, 1959, The Party of Humanity: Essays in the French Enlightenment, 1964, A Loss of Mastery: Puritan Historians in Colonial America, 1966, The Enlightenment: An Interpretation, vol. I, The Rise of Modern Paganism, 1966, Weimar Culture: The Outsider as Insider, 1968, The Enlightenment, vol. II, The Science of Freedom, 1969, The Bridge of Criticism: Dialogues on the Enlightenment, 1970; author: (with R.K. Webb) Modern Europe, 1973; author: Style in History, 1974, Art and Act, 1976, Freud, Jews, and Other Germans, 1978, Education of the Senses, 1984, Freud for Historians, 1985, The Tender Passion, 1986, A Godless Jew: Freud, Atheism, and the Making of Psychoanalysis, 1987, Freud: A Life for Our Time, 1988, A Freud Reader, 1989, Reading Freud: Explorations and Entertainments, 1990, The Cultivation of Hatred, 1993, The Naked Heart, 1995, Pleasure Wars, 1998, My German Question: Growing Up in Nazi Berlin, 1998, Mozart, 1999, Schnitzler's Century: The Making of Middle-Class Culture, 1815-1914, 2001, Savage Reprisals, Bleak House, Madame Bovary, 2002. Fellow Am. Coun. Learned Socs., 1959-60, Ctr. Advanced Study Behavioral Scis., 1963-64; Guggenheim fellow, 1967-68, 77-78; Overseas fellow Churchill Coll., Cambridge, 1970-71; Rockefeller Found. fellow, 1979-80; Wissenschaftskolleg zu Berlin, 1984; recipient First Amsterdam prize in Hist. Sci., 1991. Mem. Am. Philos. Soc., Am. Inst. Arts and Letters (gold medal in history 1996), Ctr. for Scholars and Writers (dir. emeritus), N.Y. Pub. Libr., Phi Beta Kappa. Home: Apt 15A 760 W End Ave New York NY 10025-5524

GAYLOR, JAMES LEROY, biomedical research educator; b. Waterloo, Iowa, Oct. 1, 1934; s. David P. and Lena (Livingston) G.; m. Marilyn Louise Gibson, Mar. 25, 1956; children: Douglas, Ann, Robert, Kenneth. BS, Iowa State U., 1956; MS, U. Wis., 1958, PhD, 1960. From asst. prof. to prof. biochemistry Cornell U., Ithaca, N.Y., 1960-77, chmn. biochemistry, molecular and cell biology sect., 1970-76; prof., head dept. biochemistry U. Mo., Columbia, 1977-80; assoc. dir. life scis. rsch. E.I. duPont Cen. Rsch., Wilmington, Del., 1981-83, dir. health sci. rsch., 1984-85; dir. biol. rsch. E.I. duPont Pharms., Wilmington, Del., 1986-87; v.p. sci. and technology Johnson & Johnson, New Brunswick, NJ, 1987-97; adj. prof. biochemistry Emory U. Sch. Medicine, 1997-01. Vis. prof. U. Ill., summer, 1964-65; sabbatical leave U. Oreg. Sch. Medicine, 1966-67, U. Osaka, Japan, 1973-74; vis. lectr. La Molina, Peru, summer 1962; nutrition cons. Pew Found., Phila., 1986-92; mem. bd. sci. counselors div. cancer prevention Nat. Cancer Inst., NIH, Bethesda, Md., 1987-91. Contbr. over 150 rsch. articles to profl. jours.; mem. edit. bd.: Jour. Biol. Chemistry, 1970-76, Biochimica Biophysica Acta, 1971-81, Jour. of Lipid Rsch., 1972-87, assoc. editor, 1983-87. NIH fellow, 1958-60, Spl. fellow, 1966-67, Guggenheim fellow, 1973-74. Fellow: Am. Heart Assn. (emeritus); mem.: Am. Chem. Soc. Achievements include patents for specific synthetic inhibitors of cholesterol synthesis; research on biosynthesis of cholesterol and other membrane-bound enzymes including inborn errors of cholesterol synthesis. Home: 14125 Bounty Ave Corpus Christi TX 78418

GAYMON, WILLIAM EDWARD, psychology educator; b. Bryn Mawr, Pa., Nov. 11, 1929; s. Frederick and Victoria (Brown) G.; m. Estelle Smith (dec. 1985); children: William Victor, Nicole Gabrielle; m. Violeta Nedkova, Aug. 6, 1988. BS in Psychology, Howard U., 1951, MS in Psychology, 1956; PhD in Psychology, Temple U., 1964. Dir. Peace Corps, Liberia, 1967-69, 1969-71; assoc. dir. Office of Naval Rsch., Arlington, Va., 1971-74; sr. rsch. fellow Am. Insts. for Rsch., Washington, 1974-77; sr. rsch. assoc. Richard A. Gibboney Assocs. Inc., Washington, 1977; dir. Africa Region U.S. Peace Corps, Washington, 1977-79; dep. chief UN Sudano Sahelian Regional Office, Ouagadougou, 1979-84; dep. resident rep. UN Devel. Programme, Cotonou, Benin, 1984-88; resident rep., resident coord. operational activities UN System, Sao Tome & Principe, 1988-89; rsch. prof. of Internat. Affairs, dir. Ctr. Pub. Policy & Diplomacy Lincoln University (Pa.), 1990—. Mem. adv. bd. Fgn. Policy Assn., N.Y.C., 1991—. Contbr. articles to profl. jours. 1st lt. USAF, 1953-55. Mem. APA. Home: 2044 Hermitage Hills Dr Gambrills MD 21054-2006 Office: Ctr Pub Policy & Diplomacy Lincoln University PA 19352

GAZAWAY, BARBARA ANN, music educator, art educator; b. Lebanon, Pa., Jan. 7, 1942; d. Ammon Mark Brubaker and Margaret (Lesher) Dierwechter; m. Hal Prentiss Gazaway; children: Farideh Dunford, Ramin Dunford, Ammon Dunford, Lavada Kahumoku, Rene Dunford. BS in Music Edn., West Chester State U., 1963; cert. in elem. edn., Brigham Young U., 1979. Cert. Multiple Subject Tchg. Credential 1984, type A tchg. cert. 1990. Elem. music tchr. Oxford (Pa.) Sch. Dist., 1963—65; elem. classroom tchr. Lebanon (Pa.) Sch. Dist., 1965—67; elem. music tchr. U.S. Dept. Edn., European Area, Bad Kreuznach, Germany, 1968—70, elem. classroom tchr. Darmstadt, Germany, 1972—74, elem. music tchr. Alconbury, England, 1974—75; instrumental music instr. Lebanon (Pa.) Cath. H.S., 1976—78, h.s. music tchr., 1976—77; music instr. Brigham Young U., Provo, Utah, 1978—79; elem. vocal music tchr. Bennett Valley Union, Santa Rosa, Calif., 1987—89; elem. vocal music instr. Anchorage Sch. Dist., 1990—2000; pvt. practice, 2001—. Owner, dir. Millcreek Nursery Sch., Newmanstown, 1975—76; instr. Homestay Am. Japanese Exch. Program, Santa Rosa, Calif., 1987; show pianist Marquee Theater, Santa Rosa, Calif., 1985—85; governess, Stuttgart, Germany, 1967—68; opermädchen Internat. Student Info. Svc., Mautern, Austria, 1967; singer, waitress The Harbor View, Martha's Vineyard Is., Mass., 1964; singer, baker, pianist The Inn, Mt Gretna, Pa., 1963; active Experiment in Internat. Living Home Stay Program, Switzerland, 1962; gasthaus worker Am. Student Info. Svc., Feldkirch, Austria, 1965; pres. Internat. Reading Assn. Campus Chpt. Singer: Sister Quartet, 1956—64. Family Coun. sec. Anchorage Pioneer Home, 2001—02; sec. Alpine Condominium Assn., Anchorage, 2001—02; chair Beautification Com., Anchorage, 2001—02; co-chair County Rep. Com., Santa Rosa, 1984—84; co-chair mission com. Trinity Christian Reformed Ch., Anchorage, 2001—02, co-facilitator divorce recovery program, 1999—; praise and worship team Anchorage First Free Methodist Ch. Mem.: NEA, Internat. Reading Assn. (pres.), Music Educators Nat. Conv. First Free Meth. Avocations: travel, hiking, reading, gardening, cooking. Personal E-mail: gazaway_barbara@hotmail.com.

GEALT, ADELHEID MARIA, museum director; b. Munich, May 29, 1946; came to U.S., 1950; d. Gustav Konrad and Ella Sophie (Daeschlein) Medicus; m. Barry Allen Gealt, Mar. 15, 1969. BA, Ohio State U., 1968; MA, Ind. U., 1973, PhD, 1979. Registrar Ind. U. Art Mus., Bloomington, 1972-76, curator Western art, 1976—, acting/interim dir., 1987-89, dir., 1989—. Adj. assoc. prof. H.R. Hope Sch. Fine Arts, Ind. U., Bloomington, 1985—89, assoc. scholar, 1986, assoc. prof., 1989—; mem. nat. adv. coun. Valparaiso U. Art Mus.; commr. Indiana Arts Commn., 1997—2001. Author: Looking at Art, 1983, Domenico Tiepolo The Punchinello Drawings, 1986; co-author: Art of the Western World, 1989, Painting of the Golden Age: A Biographical Dictionary of Seventeenth-Century European Painters, 1993, Domenico Tiepolo: Master Draftsman, 1996, Giandomenico Teipolo, Disegni dal mondo, 1996; contbg. author Critic's Choice, 1999. Grantee Nat. Endowment for Arts, 1982, 83, Am. Philos. Soc., 1985, NEH, 1985, Samuel H. Kress Found., 1999-2000. Mem. Assn. Art Mus. Dirs. Office: Ind U Art Mus 7th St Bloomington IN 47405-3024

GEARHART, MARILYN KAYE, mathematics and biology educator; b. Tucson, Apr. 11, 1950; d. Raymond Fred and Joan Gazell (White) Hagerty; m. Lon David Gearhart, Mar. 22, 1975; children: Amanda Kaye, Shannon Leigh. BA in Elem. Edn. with distinction, Manchester Coll., 1972; MS in Elem Edn. summa cum, Ind. U., 1976; BS in Math. with high honors, Tri-State U., 1985; postgrad., Ind. U., 1983-89, postgrad., 2001—, Purdue U., 1998-99, Loyola U., Chgo., 1999, St. Mary's U., 2002. Sub. tchr. South Bend (Ind.) Community Sch. Corp., 1971-72; tchr. DeKalb County Ea. Community Sch. Dist., Butler, Ind., 1972-77; founder, tchr. Pleasant View Christian Early Learning Ctr., Angola, Ind., 1981-85, also bd. dirs.; micro computer tchr. Purdue U., Ft. Wayne, Ind., 1984; substitute tchr. Met. Sch. Dist. Steuben County, Angola, 1985; tchr. math. and biology DeKalb County Ctrl. United Sch. Dist., Auburn, Ind., 1985—, math. dept. chair, 1999—2001. Assoc. prof. math. Purdue U., 1998-2001. Author: (textbook) The Impossibility of Achieving and Maintaining an Utopia, 1971. Sponsor freshman class DeKalb H.S., 1987-89, sophomore class, 1989-96, Students Against Drunk Driving, Auburn, 1985-90, Butler Elem. Little Hoosiers, 1973-77; mem. attendance and gifted and talented coms. DeKalb H.S., 1989-90; coach Acad. Decathlon and Hoosier Acad. Super Bowl, 1989-97, Hoosier Spell Bowl, 1993-97; leader Girl Scouts U.S., 1986-91, mem., coord. product sales svc. Unit, 1989-90; del. Rep. State Conv., 1996; mem. DeKalb Band and Show Choir Parents. Recipient Dir's. award Ind. Jr. Hist. Soc., 1981-85; math. and sci. scholar Tri-State, 1985; grantee Tchrs. Retng. Fund. Ind.-State, 1983-85. Mem. NEA, AAUW (treas. 1987-89), Ind. Tchrs. Assn. (dist. del. to rep. assembly 1997, 99, 2000), DeKalb Edn. Assn. (bldg. rep. 1997-98, dist. membership chair 1998-2001), Beta Beta Beta. Mem. Christian Ch. Avocations: reading, swimming, canoeing, computers, working with young people. Home: 910 Duesenberg Dr Auburn IN 46706-3223

GEARY, ALLYSON, secondary education educator; Tchr. secondary geography Ctrl. High Sch., Independence, Oreg. Recipient Disting. Tchr. K-12 award Nat. Coun. for Geog. Edn., 1992.*

GEARY, BARBARA ANN, recital and concert pianist, music educator; b. Chgo., July 2, 1935; d. Edmond Francis and Helen Mary (Brophy) G. BA in French, St. Mary's Coll., Notre Dame, Ind., 1957; postgrad., Middlebury Coll., 1958; MusM in Piano, Ind. U., 1961; postgrad., U. Paris, 1966-67, 69-70. Grad. asst. Ind. U., 1962-63; prof. piano Ohio U., 1963-69; mem. piano faculty U. N.C., 1970; prof. piano Okla. State U., 1973-78. Debut piano recital Wigmore Hall, London, 1972; touring pianist in U.S., 1971—, in western Europe, 1972, 76-83, 91-92; producer-performer narrated concerts Gottschalk Gala, Lisztomania, From Paris With Love, Fiesta Hispanica, Gottschalk to Gershwin: The Ragtime Connection, Piano Concerts for Kids; lecture-recitals in French on French piano music.; performed in festivals in U.S., France, on QE2. Activist for Eviron. Sustainability. Recipient scholarship French govt., 1970. Mem. Am. Liszt Soc., Coll. Music Soc., Gottschalk Soc. Internat. (founding mem.). Roman Catholic. Avocations: French and German langs., playing chamber music. Home and Office: 2545 S Birmingham Pl Tulsa OK 74114-3225 E-mail: bgearypiano@alumni.indiana.edu.

GEBAIDE, STEPHEN ELLIOT, retired mathematics and computer science educator; b. Bklyn., Oct. 28, 1946; s. David and Ruth (Kaplan) G. BS, Bklyn. Coll., 1968; MS, Pratt Inst., 1975. Tchr. math., computer sci., coach math/computer teams Robert H. Goddard Jr. High Sch., Ozone Park, NY, 1968—2002, mentor tchr.; ret., 2002; adj. asst. prof. computer info. systems Fiorello H. LaGuardia C.C., Long Island City, NY, 1984—. Math. team coach and advisor, computer team coach and advisor, mentor tchr., math. curriculum devel., computer sci. curriculum devel. Robert H. Goddard Jr. High Sch., Ozone Park; microcomputer instr. for sch. dist. pers. Cmty. Sch. Dist. 27, Ozone Park. Recipient 1st place team award N.Y.C. Interscholastic Math. League, 1981, NSPE, 1988. Mem. United Fedn. Tchrs., Assn. Computer Educators, Assn. Tchrs. Math. N.Y.C., Nat. Coun. Tchrs. Math., Assn. Math. Tchrs. N.Y. State, Mensa. Jewish. Avocations: logical puzzles, physical fitness, volleyball. Home: 67-15 Dartmouth St Forest Hills NY 11375-4024

GEBHARDT, RICHARD GEORGE, therapist, educator; b. Old Forge, N.Y., Aug. 19, 1928; s. William Frederick Gebhardt and Wilhelmina May (Vrooman) Forsch. BS in Elem. Edn., Akron (Ohio) U., 1963; MSW, Ohio State U., 1969, PhD in Adult Edn., 1978. Police officer City of Akron Police Dept., 1950-57; scheduler Goodyear Tire & Rubber Co., Akron, 1957-60; detention supr. intake referee Summit County Juvenile Ct. Ctr., Akron, 1960-65; tchr. elem. sch. Akron Pub. Schs., 1963—64; dep. supt., asst. chief, youth counselor Ohio Youth Commn., Akron and Columbus, 1965-70; asst. dir., treatment dir. Buckeye Boys Ranch, Inc., Grove City, Ohio, 1970-78; exec. dir. St. Vincent Children's Ctr., Inc., Columbus, 1978—88; outpatient therapist Sandusky Valley Ctr., Inc., Tiffin, Ohio, 1988-91; clin. therapist North Community Counseling Ctrs., Inc., Worthington, Ohio, 1991-92; rsch. project dir. Measurement Inc., Durham, N.C., 1994—. Part-time classroom instr. Ohio State U. Coll. of Social Work, Columbus, 1976-82; part-time asst. prof. Heidelberg Coll., Tiffin, 1990-91; rsch. evalation specialist Columbus Met. Human Svc. Commn., 1987-88. With USMC, 1946-48. Mem. Coun. on Accreditation for Svcs. of Families and Children (site surveyor 1983-88). Avocations: set design and construction, home remodeling. Office: Measurement Inc 423 Morris St Durham NC 27701-2128 E-mail: dgebhardt@measinc.com.

GEBLER, MARY ANNE, elementary school educator; b. Roanoke, Va., June 2, 1947; d. Robert E. and Mary Reeves (Hale) Jones; m. Arnold F. Gebler III, June 22, 1968; children: Glenn F., Lisa Reeves. BA, Am. U., 1969; MEd, Ctrl. Mich. U., 1980. Cert. tchr., Md. Tchr. Nye Elem. Sch., Laredo, Tex., 1969-70, Christ the King Luth., Universal City, Tex., 1971-72, Port Tobacco (Md.) Elem. Sch., 1972-76, Eva Turner Elem. Sch., Waldorf, Md., 1978-79, Mt. Calvary Sch., Forestville, Md., 1982-90, J.C. Parks Elem. Sch., Bryans Road, Md., 1990—. Team evaluator Middle States Assn., La Plata, Md., 1988; staff developer Charles County, La Plata, 1993—; adj. prof. We. Md. Coll., 1995—. Facilitator for women's spirituality group St. Paul's Episcopal Ch., Waldorf, 1989-94; spiritual mentor Episcopal Diocese of Washington, Washington, 1994—. Mem. NEA, ASCD, Charles County Edn. Assn., Md. State Tchrs. Assn., Nat. Coun. Tchrs. Math. Democrat. Episcopalian. Avocations: writing fiction and poetry, collecting antiques. Home: 5761 Linden Farm Pl La Plata MD 20646-2854 Office: JC Parks Sch 3505 Livingston Rd Indian Head MD 20640-3200

GEDIMINSKAS, REBECCA ANN, critical care nurse, nurse educator; b. Pitts., Aug. 7, 1956; d. Jokubas Edward Gediminskas and Anna Elizabeth (Jurgaitis) Zupick; m. John Rawlings Kalberer, Oct. 18, 1980; children: Jacob, Alexander, Rachel Ann. BSN, U. Pitt., 1978, MSN, 1985. Critical care staff nurse Monsour Med. Ctr., Jeannette, Pa., 1978, West Penn Hosp., Pitts., 1978-79; head nurse Monsour Med. Ctr., Jeannette, 1979-80, educator, critical care nurse, 1980-81, asst. dir. nursing, 1981-83, dir. edn., 1983-87; part-time clin. instr. Westmoreland County C.C., Youngwood, Pa., 1987-90, clin. instr., 1990-93, asst. prof. nursing, 1993—2003, prof. nursing, 2003—. Mem. sch. bd. Norwin Sch. Dist., 2000. Recipient Outstanding Educator award WCCC, 1999. Democrat. Roman Catholic. Avocations: needlepoint, reading. Office: Westmoreland County Community Coll Armbrust Rd Youngwood PA 15697

GEE, CHUCK YIM, dean; b. San Francisco, Aug. 28, 1933; s. Don Yow Elsie (Lee) G. AA, City Coll. of San Francisco, 1953; BSBA, U. Denver, 1957; MA, Mich. State U., 1958; PhD (hon.), China Acad. Chin. Cultural U., 1972; D of Pub. Svc. (hon.), U. Denver, 1991. Assoc. dir. Sch. of Hotel and Restaurant Adminstn. U. Denver, 1958-68; cons. East West Ctr., Honolulu, 1968-74; assoc. dean and prof. Sch. of Travel Industry Mgmt. U. Hawaii, 1968-75, dean and prof. Sch. Travel Industry Mgmt., 1976-99, interim dean Coll. Bus. Adminstrn., 1998-99, dean emeritus, 2000—. Vis. prof. Sch Bus. and Commerce, Oreg. State U., 1975; hon. prof. Nankai U., Tianjin, China, 1987—, Shanghai Inst. Tourism, 1994—, Dept. Tourism Huaqiao U., Xiamen, China, 1995—; cons. Internat. Sci. and Tech. Inst., Washington, 1986-90; trustee Pacific Asia Travel Assn. Found., San Francisco; chmn. Govs. Tourism Tng. Coun., Honolulu, 1989-92, chmn., 1992-96, chmn. industry coun. PATA, 1994-96, PATA Human Resource Devel. Coun., 1996-99, chmn. PATA Coun. on Ednl. Devel. and Certification, 2000-02; mem. State Workforce Devel. Coun., 1997-98, Pacific Asia Travel Assn. Human Resource Devel. Coun, 1996-98; acad. Inst. Cert. Travel Agts., Wellesley, Mass., 1989—; mem. Coun. on Hotel, Restaurant and Edn., 1967-2000, Honolulu Commn. on Fgn. Rels., 1979-98; mem. Pacific Asian Affairs Coun.; sr. acad. adv. China Tourism Assn. Cons., Inc., 1993—; adv. World Tourism Orgn. Internat. Tourism Edn. and Tng. Ctr., 1991-2000; external examiner sch. accountancy and bus. Nanyang Tech. U., Singapore, 1996-98; bd. dirs. ProjectonNet.com. Author: Resort Devel. and Mgmt., 1988, 2d edit., The Story of PATA, 2d edit., co-editor, 2001; co-author: The Travel Industry, 1988, 3d edit., 1997, Profl. Travel Agency Mgmt., 1990, Internat. Hotels: Devel. and Mgmt., 1994; editor: Internat. Tourism: A Global Perspective, 1997; founding dir., Hong Kong, China, Hawaii Chamber of Commerce, 1998-; mem. adv. bd. Asian Hotelier mag., 1997-99, Get2Hawaii.com, 2001—. Bd. dir. Hawaii Visitors Bur., 1993-95, Kaukini Med. Ctr., Honolulu, 1986-95, KMC, 1996-, Travel and Tourism Adv. Bd., US Dept. Commerce, Washington, 1982-90, Pacific Rim Found., Honolulu, 1987-93, Cmty. Entrepreneurs, Hawaii Dept. Edn., 1997—; vice-chmn. Tourism Policy Adv. Coun., Dept. Bus. and Econ. Devel., Honolulu, 1978-92; chmn. Kaukini Geriat. Care, Inc., bd. dir., 1992-95; trustee Pata Found., 1984-95, Kuakini Health System, 1988-2003; consulting com. Beijing Inst. Tourism, 1992—; v.p. Hawaii Vision 2020, 1992-93; mem. Mayor's Task Force on Waikiki Master Plan, 1992-93; devel. bd. Miss Hawaii Scholarship Pageant, 1993-; workforce devel. coun. Hawaii Dept. of Labor and Indsl. Rels., 1996-98; bd. dir., Cmty. Enterprises, Hawaii Dept. Edn., 1997—, Hong Kong Hawaii C. of C., 1999—. Served US Army, 1953-55. Recipient NOAH award Acad. Tourism Orgns., 1987, Gov.'s Proclamation honors State of Hawaii, 1998,1999,2003; named Mayor's Proclamation, 2003; named State Mgr. of Yr., State of Hawaii, 1995; named one of 100 Who Made a Difference in Hawaii during 20th Century, Star Bull., 1999. Mem. Acad. for Study of Tourism (emeritus), Pacific Asia Travel Assn. (hon. life Hawaii chpt., bd. dirs. 1993-96, chmn. industry coun. 1994-96, 50th Anniversary Hall of Honors, 2001, Grand award 1991, Life award 1990, Presdl. award 1986), Travel Industry Am. (Travel Industry Hall of Leaders award 1988), China Tourism Assn. (award of excellence 1992), China-Hawaii C. of C. (founding dir. 1998), Hong Kong-China-Hawaii C. of C. (bd. dirs. 1999—), Golden Key. Office: U Hawaii Sch Travel Industry Mgmt 2560 Campus Rd Honolulu HI 96822-2217 E-mail: cgee@hawaii.edu.

GEE, DAVID E. academic administrator; BS, Muskingum Coll., 1966; MA, U. Bridgeport, 1974, Columbia U., 1969, EdD, 1988. Supt. Western Suffolk Bd. Coop. Ednl. Svcs., Dix Hills, NY, 1998—, Queensbury (N.Y.) Union Free Sch. Dist. Exec. com. liaison Leadership Adv. Com., Suburban Schs. Adv. Com.; mem. Am. Assn. Sch. Adminstrs./N.Y. State Resolutions Com. Mem.: N.Y. State Coun. Sch. Supts. (past pres.), Am. Assn. Sch. Adminstrs. (presenter, presider nat. confs., chair fin. com., mem. governance com., mem. new bldg. com., past chair suburban schs. adv. com., mem. exec. dir.'s nat. adv coun., mem. blue ribbon evaluation task force). Office: Western Suffolk Bd Coop Ednl Svcs 507 Deer Park Rd Dix Hills NY 11746-5297

GEE, ELWOOD GORDON, academic administrator; b. Vernal, Utah, Feb. 2, 1944; s. Elwood A. and Vera (Showalter) Gee; m. Elizabeth Dutson, Aug. 26, 1968 (dec. Dec. 1991); 1 child, Rebekah; m. Constance Bumgarner, Nov. 26, 1994. BA, U. Utah, 1968; JD, Columbia U., 1971, EdD, 1972. Asst. dean U. Utah, Salt Lake City, 1973—74; jud. fellow U.S. Supreme Ct., Washington, 1974—75; assoc. dean Brigham Young U., Provo, Utah, 1975—79; dean W.Va. U., Morgantown, 1979—81, pres., 1981—85, U. Colo., 1985—90, Ohio State U., Columbus, 1990—97, Brown U., Providence, 1998—2000; chancellor Vanderbilt U., Nashville, 2000—. Author: Education Law and Public Schools, 1975, Law and Public Education, 1980, Violence, Values and Justice in American Education, 1982, Fair Employment Practice, 1982. Fellow, W.K. Kellogg, 1971—72, Mellon fellow, 1977—78. Mem.: ABA, Adminstrv. Conf. U.S., Phi Kappa Phi, Phi Delta Kappa. Mem. Lds Ch. Office: Vanderbilt U Chancellors Office 211 Kirkland Hall Nashville TN 37240 E-mail: gordon.gee@vanderbilt.edu.

GEE, ROGER ALLAN, accounting educator, writer; b. Ithaca, N.Y., May 9, 1941; s. Charles F. and Helen Elenore (Knuutila) G.; m. Linda Dorman Campbell, June 11, 1966; children: Jennifer Anne, John Allan. BS in Acctg., Ithaca Coll., 1964; MS in Taxation, Nat. U., 1990. CPA, Calif. Staff acct. Touche, Ross & Co., CPAs, San Diego, 1969-71; owner Roger A. Gee, CPA, San Diego, 1971-89; prof. acctg. San Diego Mesa Coll., 1986—. Mem. dist. acctg. adv. com. San Diego C.C., 1986—. Author: Computer Accounting Applications Using Microsoft Excel with a Mouse, 1993, Computer Accounting Applications Using Lotus 1-2-3, 1993, Financial Accounting Computer Applications Using Microsoft Excel '97, 1998; Computer Accounting Applications Using BusinessWorks 10.0, 1995. Lt. (j.g.) USN, 1964-67. Named Two-Yr. Coll. Educator of Yr., 1996-97. Mem. AICPA, Am. Acctg. Assn., Calif. Soc. CPAs, Kiwanis (disting. club pres. Scripps-Mira Mesa chpt. 1984). Avocations: photography, travel, jazz, reading. Office: San Diego Mesa Coll 7250 Mesa College Dr San Diego CA 92111-4902

GEE, SHARON LYNN, funeral director, educator; b. Berea, Ohio, Jan. 11, 1963; d. Donald Edward Gee and Janet Lee Floyd. Cert. in mortuary sci., Wayne State U., 1986, BS Psychology, 1987. Mortuary sci. lic. Mich., Nat. Bd. Cert. Funeral Dir. Mgr., funeral dir. Pixley Funeral Home, Keego Harbor, Mich., 1996—; lectr. instr. dept. mortuary sci. Wayne State U., Detroit, 1996—2003, asst. prof. embalming, 2003—. Recipient Residential Beautification award, City of Royal Oak, Mich., 1993. Mem.: West Bloomfield C. of C., Tri City Bus. Assn., Mich. Embalmers Soc. (pres. 2000—), Mich. Funeral Dirs. Assn., Nat. Funeral Dirs. Assn. (pursuit of excellence achievement award 1997—), Optimist Internat., Keego Harbor Chpt. (Keego Harbor chpt.), A-Dock Sailing Club. Avocations: sailing, circa 1910 home renovation and restoration. Office: Pixley Funeral Home Godhardt-Tomlinson Chapel 2904 Orchard Lake Rd Keego Harbor MI 48320 Office Fax: 248-681-2147. Business E-Mail: ad7158@wayne.edu.

GEELHOED, GLENN WILLIAM, surgeon, educator, writer; b. Grand Rapids, Mich., Jan. 19, 1942; s. William and Alice (Stuk) G.; m. Sally Ryden (div. 1972); children: Donald W., Michael A. AB, BS cum laude, Calvin Coll., Grand Rapids, 1964; MD cum laude, U. Mich., 1968; DTMH, U. London, 1990; MA in Internat. Affairs, Elliott Sch. Internat. Affairs, Washington, 1991; MPH, George Washington U., 1992, MA in Anthropology, 1994, MPhil in Human Scis., postgrad., George Washington U., 2003—. Intern Peter Bent Brigham Hosp./Harvard Med. Sch., Boston, 1968-69; resident in surgery Boston Children's Hosp. Med. Ctr., Boston, 1968-70; clin. investigator NIH, Bethesda, Md., 1971-73; prof. surgery George Washington U., Washington, 1973—, prof. internat. med. edn., 1985—, prof. microbiology and tropical medicine, 2000—. Chmn. clin. rsch. Nat. Cancer Inst., 1972—73. Mem. editl. bd. Factline, 1984—, Surg. Rsch. Comm., 1985—, Sound Surg. Collections, 1986, CINE-Med. Inc., 1986, Peptide Therapy: Index & Revs., 1989; contbr. over 500 articles to profl. jours. Chmn. med. adv. com. ARC, Washington, 1980—. Comdr. USN, 1970-73. Robert Wood Johnson Found. clin. scholar, 1975-78, James IV Surg. Assn. Traveling scholar, 1986, Sr. Fulbright scholar, 1996. Fellow ACS; mem. Acad. de Chirurgie, Wash. Acad. Surgery (pres. 1984), D.C. Med. Soc. (chmn. com. on blood sect., tissue transplant 1973-83), Washington Area Transplant Soc. (chmn. promotions and organ procurement com. 1975-85), So. Med. Assn. (spl. edn. sub-com. sect. surgery D.C. 1989-91), Southeastern Surg. Congress (councillor 1984-89). Republican. Mem. Christian Reformed Ch. Office: George Washington U Med Ctr Ross Hall 741 2300 I St NW Washington DC 20037-2336

GEERTZ, CLIFFORD JAMES, anthropology educator; b. San Francisco, Aug. 23, 1926; s. Clifford James and Lois (Brieger) G.; m. Hildred Storey, Oct. 30, 1948 (div. 1981); children: Erika, Benjamin; m. Karen Blu, 1987. AB, Antioch Coll., 1950; PhD, Harvard U., 1956, LL.D. (hon.), 1974; L.H.D. (hon.), No. Mich. U., 1975, U. Chgo., 1979, Bates Coll., 1980, Knox Coll., 1982, Brandeis U., 1984, Swarthmore Coll., 1984, New Sch. for Social Research, Yale U., 1987, Williams Coll., 1991, Princeton U., 1995, Cambridge (Eng.) U., 1997; L.H.D. (hon.), Colby Coll., 2003. From asst. prof. to prof. dept. anthropology U. Chgo., 1960-70; prof. dept. social sci. Inst. for Advanced Study, Princeton, N.J., 1970—, Harold F. Linder prof. social sci., 1982-2000, prof. emeritus, 2000—; Eastman prof. Oxford U., 1978-79. Author: The Religion of Java, 1960, Peddlers and Princes, 1963, The Social History of an Indonesian Town, 1965, Islam Observed, 1968, The Interpretation of Cultures, 1973, (with H. Geertz) Kinship in Bali, 1975, (with L. Rosen and H. Geertz) Meaning and Order in Moroccan Society, 1979, Negara: The Theatre State in Nineteenth-Century Bali, 1980, Local Knowledge, 1983, Works and Lives, 1988, After the Fact, 1995, Available Light, 2000. Served with USNR, 1943-45. Nat. Acad. Scis. fellow, 1973—; recipient Asian Cultural prize, 1992, Bintang Jasa Utama, Govt. of Indonesia, 2002; recipient award Republic of Indonesia. Fellow AAAS, Am. Philos. Soc., Am. Acad. Arts and Scis., Brit. Acad. (corr.); mem. Am. Anthrop. Assn., Assn. for Asian Studies, Middle East Studies Assn. Office: Inst for Advanced Study Princeton NJ 08540 E-mail: geertz@ias.edu.

GEFTER, WILLIAM IRVIN, physician, educator; b. Phila., Jan. 29, 1915; s. Samuel and Pauline (Bulmash) G.; m. Winnie Neiman, June 17, 1939; children: Sharon Gefter Greene, Warren, Gail Gefter Simon, Ellen. AB, U. Pa., 1935, MD, 1939. Diplomate Am. Bd. Internal Medicine. Intern, then resident medicine Phila. Gen. Hosp., 1939-43; mem. faculty Med. Coll. Pa., 1943-66, Mullen prof. medicine, 1959-66; prof. medicine Temple U. Sch. Medicine, 1966-74; chief medicine Phila. Gen. Hosp., 1959-66; dir. dept. medicine Episcopal Hosp., Phila., 1966-74, pres. med. bd., 1970-72; dir. profl. services St. Joseph Hosp., Stamford, Conn., 1974-77, dir. med. edn., 1977-92, dir. emeritus, 1992—; clin. prof. medicine N.Y. Med. Coll., 1975-92, prof. emeritus, 1992—. Author: Synopsis of Cardiology, 1965, Quality Living in the Semiircle of Life, 2001; also numerous articles. Served to capt. M.C., USAAF, 1943-46. Recipient Disting. Service citation Med. Coll. Pa., 1966, Disting. Service citation Phila. Gen. Hosp., 1964; named to Cultural Hall of Fame, So. High Sch., Phila., 1983 Fellow ACP, Coll. Physicians Phila., Am. Coll. Cardiology; mem. Am., Conn., Fairfield County med. assns. Home: West Ln and Toilsome Brook Rd Stamford CT 06905

GEHRING, DONALD D. education educator; b. Trenton, N.J., Oct. 9, 1937; s. Philip F. and Elsie E. (Jackson) G.; m. Bettie Groover, Aug. 6, 1960; children: Lisa Anderson, David. BS, Ga. Inst. Tech., 1960; MEd, Emory U., 1966; EdD, U. Ga., 1971. Asst. to dean men Emory U., Atlanta, 1962-66; dir. housing West Ga. Coll., Carrollton, 1966-69; dean student devel. Mars Hill (N.C.) Coll., 1971-78; prof. higher edn. U. Louisville, 1978-91; prof. Bowling Green State U., 1991-2000. Tchr. People's Republic China, El Salvador Editor Coll. Student Affairs Jour.; contbr. numerous articles to profl. jours. Founder Assn. Student Jud. Affairs. Lt. USN, 1960-62. Recipient S. Earl Thompson award Assn. Coll. and Univ. Housing Officers, Outstanding Tchr. Sch. Edn. award. Mem. Nat. Assn. Student Pers. Adminstrn. (Outstanding Contbr. to Lit. or Rsch. award, Excellence as Grad. Faculty Mem. award), Am. Coll. Pers. Assn. (sr. scholar), Assn. Student Jud. Affairs (Disting. Svc. award), Am. Assn. for Higher Edn., So. Assn. for Coll. Student Affairs (past pres., Melvene Hardee and H. Howard Davis awards). E-mail: dgehrin1@earthlink.net.

GEIB, GEORGE WINTHROP, history educator; b. Buffalo, Oct. 31, 1939; s. Irving G. and Jessie A. (Hammond) G.; m. Mirian K. Orelup, Aug. 17, 1973; children: Helen K., Geoffrey W. BA, Purdue U., 1961; MA, U. Wis., 1963, PhD, 1969. Prof. history Butler U., Indpls., 1965—. Author: Indianapolis: Hoosier Circle City, 1981, Lives Touched by Faith, 1987 (IRHA Best Book 1991), Indianapolis First, 1990. Pres., mem. Indpls. Civilian Fire Merit Bd., 1980-87, Indpls. Hist. Preservation Com., 1989—; Presdl. elector from Ind. U.S. Electoral Coll., 1984; mem. Marion County Sheriff's Pension Bd., Indpls., 1987—2002, Ind. Constitution Bicentennial Com., Indpls., 1987-91; bd. dirs. Ind. Humanities Coun., Indpls., 1980-85, Ind. Ass. Historians, Indpls., 1989-91. Fellow Woodrow Wilson Found., 1961, Henry Vilas, 1964, English Speaking Union, 1979; Jenn Rsch. grantee Jenn Found., 1987, C-SPAN ednl. grantee, 1995. Mem. Ind. Acad. of the Social Scis. (bd. dirs. 1991). Republican. Presbyterian. Avocations: military miniatures, austrian philately. Office: Butler U Dept History 4600 Sunset Ave Dept History Indianapolis IN 46208-3487

GEIB, VIOLET M. elementary education educator; Tchr. Sporting Hill Elem. Sch., Manheim, Pa. Named Pa. State Tchr. of Yr., 1993. Office: Sporting Hill Elem Sch 65 S Colebrook Rd Manheim PA 17545-1901

GEIER, SHARON LEE, special education educator; b. Dayton, Ohio, Nov. 21, 1943; d. Robert Stanley Murphy and Mary Frances (Ross) Briggs; m. Arthur M. Geier, Jan 23, 1965; children: Arthur William, Bradford Robert. BA, Wilmington (Ohio) Coll., 1965; cert. spl. edn., Wright State U., 1976; MS in Edn., U. Dayton, 1995. Cert. elem. tchr., Ohio, edn. handicapped. Tchr. 1st grade Fairborn (Ohio) City Schs., 1965-66, Kettering (Ohio) City Schs., 1967-71, Xenia (Ohio) City Schs., 1975-81, tchr. 3rd grade, 1981-82, tchr. learning disabled, 1982—. Tchr. specifically learning disabled Camp Progress Centerville (Ohio) Schs., summers, 1977, 78; coord. MicroSoc. Program, 1995-2000, 2002-04. Founder, pres. Twig 6 Children's Med. Ctr. Aux., Dayton, 1971-73, chmn. Jr. Aux., 1972-74. Recipient Doer award Miami Valley Regional Ctr. and Dayton Area Citizens for Spl. Edn., 1988; Martha Holden Jennings scholar, 1980-81; named Spl. Educator of Yr., Spl. Edn. dept. Ctrl. State U., 1993. Mem. AAUW, ASCD, Coun. Exceptional Children (Outstanding Chpt. Pres. Ohio Fedn. 1989, pres. Greene County chpt. 1987-89, treas. Ohio divsn. learning disabilities 1989-91, pres. 1991-93, treas. Greene County chpt. 1999—), Ohio Fedn. Coun. for Exceptional Children (liaison S.W. region 1989-94, liaison chmn. 1992-93, 93-94, sec. 1994-97, v.p. 1997-98, pres. elect 1998-99, pres. 1999-2000, past pres. 2000-01), Green Key Honor Soc. Republican. Avocations: reading, music, painting, plants, aerobics. Home: 1134 Napa Rdg Centerville OH 45458-6017 E-mail: sgeier89@aol.com.

GEIGER, ANNE ELLIS, secondary education educator; b. Washington, Jan. 20, 1932; d. George Joseph and Katherine Martha (Johnson) Ellis; m. John James Gallagher, June 12, 1954 (div. 1972); children: Sean James Jr., Michael William, Anne Cecilia Gallagher Jones; m. Gerald Lewis Geiger, May 28, 1983. BA, Trinity Coll., Washington, 1953; MEd, U. Md., 1972. Cert. tchr., Md. Social studies tchr. Notre Dame Acad., Washington, 1953-54; assoc. dir. Office of Edn., Laon (France) AFB, 1954-56; elem. tchr. Our Lady of Lourdes Sch., Bethesda, Md., 1956-57; social studies tchr. Albert Einstein Sr. High Sch., Kensington, Md., 1966-76; social studies tchr., head dept. Randolph Jr. High Sch., Rockville, Md., 1976-79, Argyle Jr. High Sch., Silver Spring, Md., 1979-81, Eastern Mid. Sch., Silver Spring, 1981—. Mem. title IX adv. com. Montgomery County Pub. Schs., Rockville, 1977-78; cons. Nat. Geog. Soc., Washington, 1991-92. Chmn. econs., v.p., dir. focus women project Montgomery County Commn. for Women, Rockville, 1976-80. Recipient Meritorious Civilian Community Svc. award Republic of France, 1956. Mem. Montgomery County Ednl. Assn. (del. 1977-81), Rockville Bus. and Profl. Women's Club (pres. 1982-83), Phi Alpha Theta. Avocations: antiques, cooking, scripture reading, swimming, contemporary issues. Home: 5011 Westport Rd Chevy Chase MD 20815-3714 Office: Eastern Mid Sch 300 University Blvd E Silver Spring MD 20901-2896

GEIGER, MARK WATSON, management educator; b. Grand Forks, N.D., Aug. 22, 1949; s. Louis George and Helen Marjorie (Watson) G.; children: Harley, Uintah, Klaus. BA, Carleton Coll., 1971; MBA, U. Pa., 1975; MA, U. Mo., 2000. CPA, N.Y. Bldg. contractor Spiral Remodeling, Phila., 1976-78; EDP project mgr. Ariz. State Govt., Phoenix, 1978-81; mgr. internal audit Gulf & Western Industries, N.Y.C., 1981-85; v.p. spl. projects Kidder, Peabody & Co., Inc., N.Y.C., 1986-90; v.p., chief adminstrv. officer Analytical Bio-Chemistry Labs., Inc., Columbia, Mo., 1990-92; ind. mgmt. cons. Columbia, 1992-94; asst. prof. fin. William Woods U., Fulton, Mo., 1994—. Rsch. grantee William Woods U., 1994, Mo. State Hist. Soc., 1997, 2001. Mem. AICPA, Mensa, SAR, Am. Hist. Assn., So. Hist. Assn., Mo. Hist. Soc., Phi Alpha Theta. Avocations: creative writing, long-distance swimming, target shooting, horseback riding. Home: 1508 Hickam Dr Columbia MO 65202

GEIMAN, STEPHEN ROYER, secondary school educator, coach; b. Waynesboro, Va., Aug. 10, 1947; s. David Samuel and Frances Elizabeth (Davis) G.; m. Donna Lisa Hanger, Aug. 9, 1974; children: Stephen Colburn, Charles Dolan, Brecken Elisabeth. BS in Phys. Edn., Appalachian State U., 1969. Cert. tchr., Va. Phys. edn. instr. Orange (Va.) County H.S., 1969-70; driver edn. instr. Wilson Meml. H.S., Fishersville, Va., 1970-72, phys. edn. instr., coach, 1974—; phys. edn. instr., English tchr. Fishburne Mil. Sch., Waynesboro, Va., 1972-74. Mem. Waynesboro/Augusta County Drug Advocacy Com., 1972-74; mem. adv. com. State Dept. Edn. Spl. Edn. Phys. Edn. Va., 1982; mem. quality com. State Dept. Edn. Phys. Edn. Stds., 1983; mem. sch. evaluation team State Dept. Edn., 1983. Mem. ASCD, AAHPERD, Nat. H.S. Coaches Assn., Va. H.S. Coaches Assn. (legis. coun. 1982-85, 92—), Va. Assn. Health, Phys. Edn., Recreation and Dance, Am. Running and Fitness Assn., Assn. for the Advancement of Health Edn., Nat. Assn. Sport and Phys. Edn., Nat. H.S. Track Coaches Assn. Avocations: martial arts, motorcycling. Home: RR 2 Box 310 Waynesboro VA 22980-9550 Office: Wilson Meml HS RR 1 Box 260 Fishersville VA 22939-9801

GEIS, TARJA PELTO, educational coordinator, consultant, counselor, teacher, professor; m. John J. Geis; children: Jeffrey, Steven. BS in Edn. and Art, Towson U., 1967, MEd in Elem. Edn., 1970; EdD in Edn., Nova Southeastern U., 1986. Nat. bd. cert. tchr., 2002. Tchr. Balt. County, Balt., 1967-70, Prince George's County, Bowie, Md., 1970-73, Dade County, Miami, Fla., 1979-84, ednl. specialist fed. programs, 1984-85, tchr., chairperson, 1985-89; co-originator, saturn coord. Dr. Gilbert L. Porter Elem., Miami, 1990-96; counselor Kendale Lakes, Miami, 1995—, advanced acads. eductator, 1997—. Adj. prof. Barry U., 1996—; presenter South Fla. Thinking Skills Conf., 2001, M-DCPS Advanced Acad. Conf., 2001—02. Editor: Chapter I Connection newsletter, 1984, Leo-T Times newsletter, 1987, Phi Delta Kappa newsletter, 1987. Validator NAEYC, Dade Reading Coun., 1999—; chair Restructuring Pub. Edn. Internat. Conf., Miami, 1990; mem. Lindgren Lakeowner Assn., Miami; svc. Feeding the Needy, Miami, 1990—. Named Tchr. of the Yr., South Area Dade County Pub. Schs., 1987, 2002, Fla. Master Tchr., Dept. Edn. Fla., 1988; grantee, Found. Excellence, 1986, 1988, 1989, 1991, 2001—02; DRC Literacy grantee, 2001—02. Mem.: NAEYC, Nat. Bd. Professionalization of Tchg. Stds., Internat. Reading Assn. (assoc. supervision and curriculum devel.), Fla. Reading Assn. (presenter 39th Conf. 2001), Phi Delta Kappa (pres. U. Miami chpt. 1991—92, Svc. Key award 1994, Travel scholarship 1997—98). Avocations: art and design, writing, travel, Reiki master, master hypnotherapist. Home: 12764 SW 112th Ter Miami FL 33186-4721

GEISELHART, LORENE ANNETTA, English language educator; b. Rake, Iowa, June 28, 1929; d. Charles Tobias and Altha May (Mills) Knutson; m. James Willis Geiselhart, June 1, 1947 (div. 1971); children: Nancy Joyce, Larry Paul, Richard Ray, Kathleen Ann. Cert., Luther Coll., 1949; BA, U. No. Iowa, 1965, MA, 1989; postgrad., U. Iowa, 1990—. Pub. sch. tchr., Postville, Iowa, 1947-48; adminstrv. asst. to county supt. schs. Decorah, Iowa, 1948-49; pub. sch. tchr. Galesville and Trempealeau, Wis., 1949-51, Iowa Braille and Sight-Saving Sch., Vinton, 1959-70, South Winneshiek Community Sch., Ossian, Iowa, 1970-94; instr. English to univ. students Nanchong Inst. Edn., Sichuan, China, 1995-96. Student tchr. supr. Luth. Coll., Decorah, 1971-94. Sec. Calmar (Iowa) Improvement Assn., 1987-92; active Calmar Luth. Ch. Coun., 1975-80, 89-91, mem. choir, 1975-80, pres. Ch. Circle, 1975-77, 88-92. Mem. AAUW (pres. 1969-70, 96-2000, sec. 1990-92), NEA, Iowa Reading Coun., Iowa State Edn. Assn., NE Iowa Rosemaling Assn. (sec. 1991-94), Delta Kappa Gamma (pres. Beta Eta chpt. 1978-81, state fellowship com. 1982-84, grantee 1988). Democrat. Avocations: rosemaling, golf, bridge, painting, reading.

GEISINGER, KURT FRANCIS, university administrator, psychometrician; b. Danville, Pa., Jan. 11, 1951; s. Karl William and Florence Eva (Graber) G.; m. Janet Frances Carlson, Sept. 22, 1984. AB with honors, Davidson Coll., 1972; MS, U. Ga., 1974; PhD, Pa. State U., 1977. Instr. Pa. State U., University Park, 1975-76; dir., rsch. svcs. Bartell Assocs., State College, Pa., 1976-77; asst. prof. to prof. and chmn. dept. psychology Fordham U., Bronx, N.Y., 1977-92; prof. psychology, dean of arts and scis.

SUNY, Oswego, 1992-97; acad. v.p., prof. psychology LeMoyne Coll., 1997—2001; v.p. acad. affairs U. St. Thomas, Houston, 2001—, prof. psychology, 2001—. Mem. tech. adv. com. on Grad. Record Exam., Ednl. Testing Svc., Princeton, N.J., 1995-2003, chair, 2000-03, vis. rsch. assoc., 1976, bd. dirs., 2001—; mem. SAT com. Coll Bd., 2001-03; cons. expert witness N.Y.C. Depts. Law and Pers., 1981-92, Fox and Fox Counsellors at Law, N.Y.C., 1986-98; cons. Assessment Alternatives, Florham Park, N.J., 1987-92; co-chair Joint Com. on Testing Practices, 1993-97. Cons. editor Ednl. Rsch. Quar., Coll. Bd. Rev., Internat. Jour. Testing, Practical Assessment Rsch. and Evaluation. Fellow APA (Com. on Psychol. Testing and Assessment 1998-2000), Am. Psychol. Soc.; mem. Am. Ednl. Rsch. Assn., Nat. Coun. on Measurement in Edn., Northeastern Ednl. Rsch. Assn. (newsletter editor 1988-91, pres. 1986-89, bd. dirs. 1984-86), Phi Kappa Phi (Fordham U. chpt. pres. 1984-86), Psi Chi, Sigma Xi, Alpha Sigma Mu. Democrat. Lutheran. Avocations: swimming, softball, golf, computer activities. Home: 3935 Indian Point Missouri City TX 77459 Office: Office VP Acad Affairs Univ St Thomas 3800 Montrose Blvd Houston TX 77006 E-mail: kurtgeis1@aol.com.

GEISSER, PETER JAMES, artist, educator for hearing impaired; b. Providence, Oct. 19, 1945; s. John H. and Helen L. (Callaghan) G.; m. Maura Jane McNamara, May 14, 1972; 1 child, Mary Alicia. BS in Edn., Tufts U., 1969, MFA, 1971; diploma, Sch. Mus. Fine Arts, Boston, 1970, grad. cert., 1971; DFA (hon.), RISD, 1997. Cert. tchr., R.I. Art instr. Mus. Fine Arts, Boston, 1967-73; painting instr. Belvoir Terr. Fine Arts Camp, Lenox, Mass., 1969; art instr. H.S. Scholarship Program, Boston, 1969-70; art coord. Boston Sch. for Deaf, Randolph, Mass., 1970-73; art dir. R.I. Sch. for Deaf, Providence, 1973—. Summer lectr. in Rome, Am. Leadership Study Groups, Clarke U., Worcester, Mass., 1971-72; art instr. RISD Continuing Edn., Providence, 1987—; dir. Cir. of Clay project Very Spl. Arts R.I., Pawtucket, 1992-96; spl. needs adv. bd. Mus. Fine Arts, Boston, 1979—; tchr. adv. bd. R.I. Com. on Humanities, 1984—, RISD, Providence, 1989—, Nat. Gallery of Art, Washington, 1991-92; mem. bd. dirs. Perishable Theatre, Providence, 1994-96. Group exhbns. include Cohen Art Ctr., Tufts U., Medford, Mass., 1971, Warwick (R.I.) Mus., 1988, R.I. Sch. Design, 1989, R.I. Tchrs. Assn., 1992, 93, 94, R.I. Art Edn. Assn. 2nd prize, 1996; Circle of Clay ceramic murals Hasbro Children;s Hosp.; commd. stained glass installations include AS 220, Providence, St. Joseph's Rectory/Regina Caeli, Providence, Hasbro Children's Hosp., Providence, St. Mark's Ch., Cranston, R.I., Notre Dame Coll., Manchester, N.H., Roger Williams Park Mus., Providence, Trinity Ch., Concord, Mass., St. Michael's Ch., Providence, Cathedral Sts. Peter and Paul, Providence, other churches, pvt. collections. Named 50th Anniversary scholar Nat. Gallery of Art, Washington, 1991; recipient R.I. State of Arts award R.I. Coun. on Arts, 1992, Humanitarian award Bus. Vols. for Arts/R.I., 1994, 1st prize NAEA Electronic Gallery '97, New Orleans; grantee R.I. State Coun. on the Arts, 2000, L.E.F. Found., 2000. Mem. Nat. Art Educators Assn., R.I. Art Edn. Assn (exec. bd. 1995—, pres.-elect 1997, pres. 1999-2001), R.I. Forum for Humanities. Home: 19 Philmont Ave Cranston RI 02910-5814 Office: RI Sch for Deaf Corliss Park Providence RI 02903

GEISSER, SEYMOUR, statistics educator; b. Bronx, N.Y., Oct. 5, 1929; s. Leon and Rose (Kielmanowicz) G.; m. Mary Lee George, Jan. 30, 1955 (div. Apr. 21, 1977); children— Mindy Sharon, Dan Levi, Georgia Lynn, Adam Dov.; m. Anne S. Flaxman, Mar. 21, 1982. BA, CCNY, 1950; MA, U. N.C., 1952, PhD, 1955. Mathematician NIMH, Bethesda, Md., 1955-61; chief biometry sect. Nat. Inst. Arthritis and Metabolic Diseases, Bethesda, 1961-65; prof. stats. SUNY-Buffalo, 1965-70, chmn., 1965-70; prof. Sch. Stats. U. Minn., 1971—, dir., 1971—2001. Professorial lectr. George Washington U., 1960-65; vis. asso. prof. Iowa State U., Ames, 1960; vis. prof. U. Wis., Madison, 1964, U. Tel-Aviv (Israel), 1971, U. Waterloo (Can.), 1972, Stanford U., 1976, 88, Carnegie-Mellon U., Pitts., 1976, U. Orange Free State, Bloemfontein, South Africa, 1978, 93, Harvard U. Sch. Public Health, 1981, U. Chgo., 1985, U. Warwick, Coventry, Eng., 1986, Univ. Modena, Italy, 1996, Nat. Chiao Tung Univ., Tawain, 1998; mem. biometric and epidemiological methodology adv. com. FDA, 1976-78, mem. arthritis adv. com., 1978-84; mem. NIH Biometry and Epidemiology Study sect. 1974-76; com. on Nat. Stats., 1984-87; chmn. Nat. Acad. Panel on Occupational and Health Stats., 1985-86; expert witness on forensic statistics; Lady Davis vis. prof. Hebrew U. Jerusalem, 1991, 94, 99. Author: Predictive Inference, 1993; assoc. editor Jour. Am. Statis. Assn., 1968-70, 86-88; editor: Bayesian and Likelihood Methods in Statistics and Econometrics, 1989, Statistics in Genetics, 1999, Diagnosis and Prediction, 1999; contbr. articles to sci. jours. Bd. dirs. Savage Trust, 1978—2000; bd. of trustees Nat. Inst. of Statistical Sci., 1999—2001. Scholar Merck Rsch. Lab., 2002—03. Fellow Inst. Math. Stats. (mem. coun. 1978-80), Royal Statis. Soc., Am. Statis. Assn. (bd. dirs. 1964-65); mem. Biometric Soc., Math. Assn. Am., Internat. Statis. Inst., Psychometric Soc., Can. Statis. Soc., Sigma Xi. Home: 1770 Summit Ave Saint Paul MN 55105-1834

GELDER, DONNA RAE, elementary school educator, retired; b. Canton, N.Y., Jan. 14, 1943; d. William Raymond and Elizabeth Helen (Winship) G. BA, SUNY, Potsdam, 1965, MS in Reading, 1972, reading specialist cert., 1974. Cert. elem. tchr., reading tchr., N.Y. 1st grade tchr. Queensbury (N.Y.) Sch., 1965-67, 73-81, developmental 1st grade tchr., 1967-72, summer Headstart tchr., 1986-88, supervising tchr., 1968-81, reading tchr., 1981-98, summer sch. reading tchr., 1984, 87, 88,94; ret., 1998. Leader, chair classroom clinic N.Y. State Reading Conf., Kiameska Lake, N.Y., 1976. Author: Reading Is Magic, 1974, Spotlight on Fifty Years - A History of the Glens Falls Operetta Club, 1986; complier: Fifty Years of Directors, Casts, and Crews, Glens Falls Operetta Club Programs, 1985. Mem. com. Mohican coun. Boy Scouts Am., Glens Falls, 1983-98, mem. exec. bd., 1987-98, mem. Twin Rivers coun., exec. bd., Albany, 1998—; mem. com. Adirondack coun. Girl Scouts U.S.A., Queensbury, 1965—, 1st v.p. Adirondack coun. Queensbury, 2000-2002, pres., 2003—.; mem. com., bd. dirs., historian Glens Falls Operetta Club/Glens Falls Cmty. Theater, 1965—. Recipient Appreciation award Adirondack coun. Girl Scouts U.S., 1984, Silver Beaver award Mohican coun. Boy Scouts Am., 1991, 3d Pl. Hon. Mention award N.Y. State Assn. Compensatory Educators, 1994, Execs. award Wakpominee Dist. Boy Scouts Am., 1999, Thanks Badge, Girl Scouts U.S.A., 2001. Mem. AAUW, DAR, Internat. Reading Assn., Soc. Children's Book Writers and Illustrators, Friends in Coun., Kappa Delta Pi. Republican. Methodist. Avocations: reading, writing children's stories, lighting design, performing arts, biking.

GELDERMAN, CAROL, English educator, writer; b. Detroit, Dec. 2, 1938; d. Albert John and Irene Ellen (Kelly) Wettlaufer; m. Gregory Anthony Gelderman, Sept. 26, 1959 (dec.); children: Gregory Anthony III, Margot, Irene (dec.). BA, Manhattanville Coll., Purchase, N.Y., 1960; MA, Northwestern U., 1968, PhD, 1972. Asst. prof. English U. New Orleans, 1972-76, assoc. prof. English, 1976-81, prof. English, 1981-88, rsch. prof. English, 1988-92, disting. prof. English, 1992—. Cons. in field. Author: Henry Ford, The Wayward Capitalist, 1981, Mary McCarthy, A Life, 1988 (named One of Best Books of Yr., N.Y. Times Book Rev. 1988), Better Writing for Professionals, 1982, Better Business Writing, 1990, Conversations with Mary McCarthy, 1990, Louis Auchincloss, A Writer's Life, 1993, All the Presidents' Words, The Bully Pulpit and the Creation of the Virtual Presidency; also articles. Mem. PEN. Democrat. Roman Catholic. Avocations: new orleans food, restaurants, politics. Home: 1527 4th St New Orleans LA 70130-5917 Office: U New Orleans English Dept New Orleans LA 70148-0001

GELDIEN, JUDITH RUTH MOTTER, elementary educator; b. Ravenna, Ohio, June 3, 1944; d. Theodore James and Lois Ethel (McHenry) Motter; m. Robert James Geldien, Aug. 29, 1964; children: Christopher Scott, Wendy Lynne. BS, Ind. U., Ft. Wayne, 1980, MS, 1983; postgrad., Ball State U., 1991-95. Elem. tchr. East Allen County Schs., New Haven, Ind., 1981—. Tchr. Sci. Day Camp, 1992—; mem. Enriching Activities for Creative Sciencing, 1994—. Mem. subcom. Dist. Planning Commn., East Allen County Schs., New Haven, 1991-92; vol. Sci. Ctrl., 1990—. Mem. NEA, Internat. Reading Assn., Hoosier Assn. Sci. Tchrs. (presenter convs. 1992-95), East Allen County Schs. Assn., Ind. Educators Assn., East Allen Educators Assn. (bldg. rep. 1987-89, 92—), Delta Kappa Gamma (chmn. attendance 1987-89, treas. 1989—). Republican. Avocations: hiking, reading, camping, travel, crafts. Home: 3914 Scarborough Dr New Haven IN 46774-2710 Office: Monroeville Elem Sch 401 Monroe St Monroeville IN 46773-9362

GELEHRTER, THOMAS DAVID, medical and genetics educator, physician; b. Liberec, Czechoslovakia, Mar. 11, 1936; married 1959; 2 children. BA, Oberlin Coll., 1957; MA, U. Oxford, Eng., 1959; MD, Harvard U., 1963. Intern, then asst. resident in internal medicine Mass. Gen. Hosp., Boston, 1963-65; rsch. assoc. in molecular biology NIAMD NIH, Bethesda, Md., 1965-69; fellow in med. genetics U. Wash., 1969-70; asst. prof. human genetics, internal medicine and pediatrics Sch. Medicine Yale U., 1970-73, assoc. prof., 1973-74, U. Mich., Ann Arbor, 1974-76, prof. internal medicine and human genetics, 1976-87, dir. divsn. med. genetics, 1977-87, chmn. dept. human genetics, prof. human genetics and internal medicine, 1987—. Josiah Macy, Jr. Found. faculty scholar and vis. scientist Imperial Cancer Rsch. Fund Labs., London, 1979-80; vis. fellow Inst. Molecular Medicine; Keeley vis. fellow Wadham Coll., U. Oxford, Wellcome Rsch. Travel grantee, 1995. Mem. editl. bd. Jour. Biol. Chemistry, 1995-2000. Trustee Oberlin Coll., 1970-75; mem. adv. com. NIH Recombinant DNA, 2002—. Rhodes scholar, 1957-59. Fellow AAAS, Am. Coll. Med. Genetics; mem. Am. Soc. Human Genetics (bd. dirs. 1994-96), Am. Soc. Clin. Investigation, Am. Soc. Biochemistry and Molecular Biology, Assn. Am. Physicians. Office: 1241 Catherine St PO Box 0618 Ann Arbor MI 48109-0618 E-mail: tdgum@umich.edu.

GELFAND, LAWRENCE EMERSON, historian, educator; b. Cleve., June 20, 1926; s. Maurice Hirsch and Rachel S. (Shapiro) G.; m. Miriam J. Ifland, June 14, 1953; children: Julia M., Daniel B., Ronald S. BA, Western Res. U., 1949, MA, 1950; PhD, U. Wash., 1958. Asst. prof. history U. Hawaii, 1956-58; acting asst. prof. history U. Wash., 1958-59; asst. prof. history U. Wyo., 1959-62, U. Iowa, Iowa City, 1962-64, assoc. prof., 1964-66, prof., 1966-94, chmn. history dept., 1989-92; prof. emeritus, 1994—; vis. prof. U. Oreg., summer 1966, U. Mont., summer 1970, U. Wash., 1974. Mary Ball Washington prof. Am. History, Univ. Coll., Dublin, Ireland, 1987-88. Author: The Inquiry: American Preparations for Peace 1917-1919, 1963; contbg. editor: The Treaty of Versailles: A Reassessment after 75 Years, 1999; editor: A Diplomat Looks Back (Memoirs of Lewis Einstein), 1968; Essays on the History of American Foreign Relations, 1972; Herbert Hoover: The Great War and Its Aftermath 1914-1923, 1979; contbr. chapters to books. Bd. curators State Hist. Soc. Iowa, 1970-72; mem. adv. bd. Nat. Archives for Region VI, 1968-74; chmn. Ctr. for Study Recent History of U.S., Iowa City, 1981-91; mem. rsch. and book prize com. Hoover Presdl. Libr., 1996-99. Served with AUS, 1944-46. Decorated Purple Heart; Am. Council Learned Socs. grantee in Korean studies, summer 1951; Rockefeller Found. grantee, 1964-65. Mem. Am. Hist. Assn., Orgn. Am. Historians, Soc. for Historians of Am. Fgn. Relations (v.p. 1981, pres. 1982) Home: 1437 Oakcrest St Iowa City IA 52246-1622

GELFER, JEFFREY IAN, early childhood education educator; b. Bklyn., June 18, 1952; s. George Ralph and Ruth (Seltzer) G.; m. Peggy Gardner Perkins, Dec. 7, 1980; children: Sacha, Daniel. BA, Wilmington Coll., 1974; MS, U. Oreg., 1975; PhD, Fla. State U., 1981. Reading and learning disability specialist Columbia County Schs., Westport, Oreg., 1975-77; kindergarten tchr. Creative Presch., Tallahassee, 1978-79; asst. prof. SUNY, Fredonia, 1985-87; dir. Easter Seal Soc. of S.W. Fla., Sarasota, 1987-89; assoc. prof. Univ. Nev., Las Vegas, 1989—. Vis. asst. prof. U. S. Fla., Tampa, 1981-85; cons. Clark County Sch. Dist., Las Vegas, 1991, Sarasota County Sch. Dist., 1984-85, Fla. State U., Tallahassee, 1979; presenter/participant workshops in field. Contbr. articles to profl. jours. Grantee Health Rehab. Svcs. of State of Fla., 1987, 88, Sarasota County Sch. Dist., 1988, Frank Stanley Beveridge Foun., 1989, Univ. Nev. Las Vegas, 1991. Mem. Assn. Childhood Edn. Internat. (mem. rev. com. 1991—), Nat. Assn. Edn. Young Children, ASCD, Coun. Exceptional Children, Nat. Coalition Campus Child Care, Am. Evaluation Assn., Phi Delta Kappa. Avocations: mountain climbing, piano, film making, jogging, golf. Home: 401 Donner Pass Dr Henderson NV 89014-3401 Office: Univ Nev Las Vegas 4505 S Maryland Pky Las Vegas NV 89154-9900

GELLER, HAROLD ARTHUR, earth and space sciences executive, educator; b. Bklyn., June 14, 1954; s. Morris and Minnie (Kaplan) G. BS, SUNY, Albany, 1983; MA, George Mason U., 1992, postgrad. cert. in C.C. Edn., 2002. Rsch. asst. SUNY at Downstate Med., Bklyn., 1972-74; rsch. asst. CUNY at Bklyn. Coll., 1974-75; engring. aide FBI, Washington, 1977-78; lab. supr. ENSCO Inc., Springfield, Va., 1978-80; assoc. engr. Def. Systems Inc., McLean, Va., 1980-83; staff scientist/systems engr. Sci. Applications Internat. Corp., McLean, 1983-87; systems engr. Grumman Aerospace, Reston, Va., 1987-88, Sci. Applications Internat. Corp., McLean, 1988-90; rsch. asst. Naval Rsch. Lab., George Mason U., 1990-91; project mgr. Rsch. and Data Systems Corp., Greenbelt, Md., 1991-92; dep. dir. Washington ops. Consortium Internat. Earth Sci. Info. Network, Washington, 1992-96; instr. physics and astronomy George Mason U., 1993—; sr. sys. engr. Sci. Applications Internat. Corp., McLean, Va., 1996-99. Computer cons., Burke, Va., 1986—87. Commonwealth fellow, 1992-93. Mem.: Astronomical League (media relations officer 2000-01), Asn. Community Col. Educ. (v.p. 2000-01), Potomac Geophys. Soc. (1st v.p. 1994-95, 2000-01, pres. 1995-96, 2001-02), Am. Geophys. Union, Am. Astron. Soc., AAAS, AIAA (chmn. corp. liason com. 1989-90, chmn. pub. affairs com. 1990-91). Democrat. Jewish. Office: George Mason U Dept Physics 4400 University Dr Fairfax VA 22030-4444 E-mail: hgeller@gmu.edu.

GELLER, MARGARET JOAN, astrophysicist, educator; b. Ithaca, N.Y., Dec. 8, 1947; d. Seymour and Sarah Geller. AB, U. Calif., Bekeley, 1970; MA, Princeton U., 1972, PhD, 1975; DSc (hon.), Conn. Coll., 1995, Gustavus Adolphus Coll., 1997, U. Mass., Dartmouth, 2000. Rsch. assoc. Harvard Coll. Obs., Cambridge, Mass., 1978-80; asst. prof. Harvard U., Cambridge, 1980-83; astrophysicist Smithsonian Astrophys. Obs., Cambridge, 1983—. Goodspeed-Richardo lectr. U. Pa., 1992; Brickwedde disting. lectr. JHU, 1993; Hogg lectr. Royal Astro. Soc. Can., 1993; Bethe lectr. Cornell U., 1996; Hilldale lectr. U. Wis., 1999. Contbr. articles to profl. jours.; mem. editl. bd. Sci., 1991—94. Named Libr. Lion, N.Y. Pub. Libr., 1997; recipient Newcomb-Cleve. prize, 1989—90, Klopsteg award, Am. Assn. Physics Tchrs., 1996, ADION medal, 2002; fellow, MacArthur Found., 1990—95. Fellow: AAAS, APS; mem.: NAS (coun. mem. 2000—), Assoc. Univs. Rsch. in Astronomy (dir.-at-large), Am. Astron Soc. (councillor), Am. Acad. Art and Scis. (coun. mem.), Internat. Astron Union, Phi Beta Kappa (senator 1998—99). Office: Smithsonian Astrophys Obs 60 Garden St Cambridge MA 02138-1516

GELMONT, BORIS L. engineering research educator; b. Leningrad, USSR, Sept. 7, 1937; came to U.S., 1990; s. Lev Gendlerfeld and Zinaida Gelmont; m. Evelyn Galbraikh; 1 child, Maria; m. Tatiana Globus, Feb. 11, 1976. MSEE, Elec. Engring. U., 1960; PhD in Physics, Ioffe Inst., 1965; DS, Ioffe Inst., Leningrad, 1975. Mem. rsch. staff Ioffe Inst. Physics and Tech., Leningrad, 1964-80, leading scientist, 1980-90; prof. engring. Poly. U., Leningrad, 1984-90; sr. scientist U. Va., Charlottesville, 1990-95, rsch. assoc. prof., 1999—. Recipient State prize in sci. and tech. Presidium of Supreme Soviet, USSR, 1982. Mem. IEEE (sr.), Internat. Union Radio Sci. (mem. commn.). Office: U Va Thornton Hall Charlottesville VA 22903

GELTMAN, EDWARD MARK, cardiologist, educator; b. Oceanport, N.J., Feb. 22, 1946; s. Irving Robert and Goldie (Bazoll) G.; m. Nancy Milner, Aug. 25, 1968; 1 child, Joshua Aaron. BS, MIT, 1967; MD, NYU, 1971. Diplomate Am. Bd. Internal Medicine, Am. Bd. Cardiovasc. Disease. Intern Bellevue Hosp., N.Y.C., 1971-72, resident in internal medicine, 1972-74; fellow in clin. cardiology Washington U., Barnes Hosp., St. Louis, 1976-78, instr. medicine, 1978-79, asst. prof., 1979-84, assoc. prof., 1984-92, prof., 1992—, dir. heart failure and transplant program, 1994—. Steering com., chmn. ancillary studies, publs. com. SAVE Study (Bristol-Myers Squibb), Princeton, N.J., 1987-92; steering com. MACH-1 Study, Roche, 1995-98; lectr. in field. Reviewer of 16 med. jours.; contbr. over 100 articles to profl. jours. and chpts. to books. Pres. St. Louis chpt. Am. Heart Assn., 1987-88, also bd. dirs., pres. Mo. affiliate, 1992-94, bd. dirs, exec com. coun. on clin cardiology 1990-92. Maj. M.C., USAF, 1974-76. Fellow ACP, Am. Coll. Cardiology (regional councilor Mo. chpt. 1993-2001). Avocations: photography, golf, rowing. Home: 15 Crosswinds Dr Olivette MO 63132-4303 Office: Washington Univ Sch of Medicine Campus Box 8086 660 S Euclid Ave Saint Louis MO 63110-1010 E-mail: egeltman@lm.wustl.edu.

GEMMING, MARY FRANCES, college educator, writer, astrologer; b. Elmira, N.Y., June 3, 1941; d. Walter and Antoinette Grybos; m. Curtiss Gemming, Dec. 30, 1981. AAS in Bus. Adminstrn., Corning (N.Y.) C.C., 1966; PhD, U. Metaphysics, Studio City, Calif., 1998; BSBA, Rochester Inst. Tech., 1984. Adminstrv. asst. Gannett Newspapers, Rochester, N.Y., 1968-79; cost analyst Eastman Kodak Co., Rochester, 1979-92; tchr. Sch. Bd. Manatee County, Bradenton, Fla., 1993—. Part-time tchr. Bd. Continuing Edn., Fairport, N.Y., 1977-91. Author: Mystical Secrets of the Stars, 1999, Discovering Treasures of Peace, 2000. Recipient Wall St. Jour. award, Corning C.C., 1966. Mem. Assn. for Rsch. and Enlightenment, Am. Fedn. Astrologers, Rochester Astrological Assn. (pres. 1980-82). Avocations: yoga, swimming.

GENDRON, SUSAN ANN, commissioner, educator; b. Tewksbury, Mass. m. Mark Gendron; children: Stacey, Matthew. BS in Elem. and Secondary Edn., MS in Ednl. Adminstrn., U. So. Maine, Gorham. From tchr. to supt. Scarborough Pub. Schs., Maine; supt. Windham Sch. Dist., 1997—2003; commr. of edn. State of Maine, Augusta, 2003—. Mem.: Maine Sch. Supts Assn. (Disting. Educator award 2001, Supt. of Yr. award 2002). Office: Commr of Edn State House Sta #23 Augusta ME 04333 Office Fax: 207-624-6601. E-mail: susan.gendron@maine.gov.

GENEL, MYRON, pediatrician, educator; b. York, Pa., Jan. 6, 1936; s. Victor and Florence (Mowitz) G.; m. Phyllis Norma Berkman, Aug. 25, 1968; children: Elizabeth, Jennifer, Abby. Grad., Moravian Coll., 1957; MD, U. Pa., 1961; MA (hon.), Yale U., 1983; DSc (hon.), Moravian Coll., 1995. Diplomate Am. Bd. Pediat. Intern Mt. Sinai Hosp., N.Y.C., 1961-62; resident in pediat. Children's Hosp. Phila., 1962-64; trainee pediat. endocrinology Johns Hopkins Hosp., Balt., 1966-67; instr. pediat. U. Pa. Sch. Medicine, 1967-69, assoc. in pediat., 1969-71; trainee in genetics, inherited metabolic diseases Children's Hosp. Phila., 1967-69, assoc. physician, 1969-71; attending physician Yale-New Haven Hosp., 1971—; faculty Yale U. Sch. Medicine, New Haven, 1971—, dir. pediat. endocrinology, 1971-85, program dir. Children's Clin. Rsch. Ctr., 1971-86, prof., 1981—, assoc. dean, 1985—, dir. Office Govt. and Cmty. Affairs, 1985—. Genetic adv. bd. State of Conn., 1979—82, 1994—; cons. subcom. investigations, oversight com. sci. and tech. U.S. Ho. of Reps., 1982—84; mem. adv. bd. New Eng. Congenital Hypothyroidism Collaborative; cons. Hosp. St. Raphael, Milford Hosp., Norwalk Hosp., Stamford Hosp., Danbury Hosp., Greenwich Hosp.; chmn. transplant adv. com. Office of Commr. Conn. Dept. Income Maintenance, 1984—92; health policy fellowship bd. Inst. Medicine, 1989—95; clin. rsch. roundtable Inst. Medicine Nat. Rsch. Coun., 2000—. Contbr. articles to profl. jours. Bd. dirs. Rsch. America!, 1997—2000. Capt. USAR, 1964—66. Robert Wood Johnson Health Policy fellow Inst. Medicine NAS, Washington, 1982-83; recipient ann. award Conn. Campaign Against Cooley's Anemia, 1979, Ann. Comenius Alumni award Moravian Coll., 1990, Abraham Jacobi Meml. award Am. Acad. Pediat. and AMA, 1999. Fellow: AAAS; mem.: AMA (med. schs. sec. 1985—, coun. on sci. affairs 1994—2001, task force on fin. grad. med. edn. 1995, alt. del. governing coun., med. schs. sec. 1995—98, task force on privacy and confidentiality 1998—99, del. 1998—2002, chair 2003—), APHA, Assn. Patient Oriented Rsch., N.Y. Acad. Medicine, Conn. Acad. Sci. and Engring. (coun. 2000—), Soc. Pediat. Rsch. (Disting. Svc. award 2003), Endocrine Soc. (rsch. initiative com. 1995—99, legis. affairs com. 2002—), Conn. United for Rsch. Excellence (chmn. steering com. 1989—90, pres. 1990—93, chmn. bd. dirs. 1993—94), Conn. Endocrine Soc., Nat. Assn. Biomed. Rsch. (bd. dirs. 1990—93, exec. com. 1991—93), Assn. Program Dirs. (pres.-elect 1980—81, pres. 1981—82), New Haven County Med. Assn. (bd. govs. 1990—2002), Assn. Am. Med. Colls. (adminstrv. bd. coun. acad. socs. 1987—92, chmn.-elect coun. acad. socs. 1989—91, exec. coun. 1989—92, adv. panel on rsch. 1999—2003), Am. Soc. Bone and Mineral Rsch., Am. Pediat. Soc., Am. Fedn. Med. Rsch., Am. Diabetes Assn. (co-recipient Jonathan May award 1979), Am. Coll. Preventive Medicine, Am. Coll. Nutrition, Am. Assn. Clin. Endocrinologists, Am. Acad. Pediat. (task force organ transplants, com. on fed. govt. affairs), Sigma Xi. Jewish. Office: Yale Sch of Med PO Box 208000 New Haven CT 06520-8000 Home: 30 Richard Sweet Dr Woodbridge CT 06525-1126 E-mail: myron.genel@yale.edu.

GENERAS, GEORGE PAUL, JR., finance educator, lawyer; b. Erie, Pa., Dec. 24, 1943; s. George Paul and Helen Sophie (Chesney) G.; m. Darlene Ann Hosey, Nov. 8, 1980; 1 child, George Paul III. BS, U. Scranton, 1966, MBA, 1968; JD, U. Conn., 1991. Bar: Conn., CPA, Conn., N.Y., U.S. Dist. Ct. Conn., U.S. Supreme Ct. Sr. acct. Arthur Andersen & Co., N.Y.C., 1968-74; controller JOC Oil Ltd., Bermuda and Holland, 1974-78; asst. prof., chair U. Hartford, Conn., 1979-85, dir. MBA, 1985-86, asst. prof., chair, 1986-94; assoc. dean, 1994-95; lawyer, 1995—; of counsel Rome McGuigan. Chair Ednl. Adv. Commn. State Bd. Acct., Hartford, Conn., 1983-89, 92-94; bd. mem. Community Acctg. Aid and Svcs., Hartford, Conn., 1991-94. Co-author: Collaboration Between Higher Education and Big Six Accounting Firms, 1991. Bd. dirs. No. Conn. chpt. Leukemia Soc., 1992-97, treas., 1994-97. Mem. AICPA, Conn. Soc. CPAs, Am. Acctg. Assn., ABA, Conn. Bar Assn. Roman Catholic. Home: 9 Old Barge Rd Simsbury CT 06070-1741 Office: Univ Hartford 200 Bloomfield Ave Hartford CT 06117-1599 E-mail: generas@mail.hartford.edu.

GENERLETTE, BERTRAM B. elementary school educator; b. St Johns, Antigua and Barbuda, Apr. 25, 1956; Came to U.S., 1981. s. Theodore Bedford and Octavia Edith (Samuel) G.; m. Patricia Aileen Lee, Aug. 22, 1985; children: Amber Leeana, Cory Bedford, Danielle Aileen. Diploma in edn., Antigua State Coll., St. Johns, 1979; BS with honors, Columbia Union Coll., Takoma Park, Md., 1986; postgrad., U. Md., College Park, 1993; MS in Edn., Johns Hopkins U., 1995. Cert. tchr., Md. Elem. tchr. Montgomery County Pub. Schs., Rockville, Md., 1986—. Private math. tutor, Montgomery County, Md., 1984—. Recipient Sharon Christa McAuliffe Scholarship award Md. State Scholarship Adminstrn., 1994-95; fellow OAS, 1984-86; scholar Orgn. Am. States, Washington, 1986. Mem. ASCD, Nat. Coun. Tchrs. Math, Montgomery County Math Tchrs. Assn. (first v.p. 1997—). Avocations: piano, photography, swimming. Office: Montgomery County Pub Schs 850 Hungerford Dr Rm 257 Rockville MD 20850-1718

GENEROUS, WILLIAM THOMAS, JR., (TOM GENEROUS), educator, coach; b. Pawtucket, R.I., Feb. 20, 1939; s. William T. and Marjorie Myette (Smith) Generous; m. Diane B. Kowalchuck, Oct. 24, 1964; children: Michelle Elizabeth, Suzanne Felice. AB, Brown U., 1963; MA, Stanford U., 1968, PhD, 1971. Tchg. asst. Stanford (Calif.) U., 1968-71; Charles T. Wilson jr. tchr. of history Choate Rosemary Hall, Wallingford,

Conn., 1971-97, girls squash coach, 1975-96, boys squash coach, 1996—99; coach Wallingford Jr. Squash, 1992—99; squash coach U. N.C., 1999—. History tchr. summers St. Paul's Sch., Concord, NH, 1985, Concord, 87; adj. assoc. prof. phys. edn., squash coach U. N.C., adj. assoc. prof. Peace, War and Def. Author: (books) Swords and Scales: The Development of the Uniform Code of Military Justice, 1950-69, 1973, History of Choate Rosemary Hall 1890-1990, 1997. Lt. USN, 1956—67. Mem.: U.S. Squash Racquets Assn. Avocation: advanced flute. Home: 206 Wild Oak Ln Carrboro NC 27510-4140 E-mail: tomgenerous@hotmail.com.

GENGOR, VIRGINIA ANDERSON, financial planning executive, educator; b. Lyons, N.Y., May 2, 1927; d. Axel Jennings and Marie Margaret (Mack) Anderson; m. Peter Gengor, Mar. 2, 1952 (dec.); children: Peter Randall, Daniel Neal, Susan Leigh. AB, Wheaton Coll., 1949; MA, U. No. Colo., 1975, MA, 1977. Cert. fin. planner Coll. Fin. Planning. Chief hosp. intake svc. County of San Diego, 1966-77; chief Kearny Mesa Dist. Office, 1977-79, Dept. Children of Ct., 1979-81, chief child protection svcs., 1981-82; registered rep. Am. Pacific Securities, San Diego, 1982-85; registered tax preparer State of Calif., 1982—; registered rep. (prin.) Sentra Securities, 1985—; assoc. Pollock & Assocs., San Diego, 1985—86; pres. Gengor Fin. Advisors, 1986—. Cons. instr. Nat. Ctr. for Fin. Edn., San Diego, 1986-88; instr. San Diego Community Coll., 1985-88. Mem. allocations panel United Way, San Diego, 1976-79; children's cir. Child Abuse Prevention Found., 1989—; chmn. com. Child Abuse Coord. Coun., San Diego, 1979-83; pres. Friends of Casa de la Esperanza, San Diego, 1980-85, bd. dirs., 1980—; 1st v.p. The Big Sis. League, San Diego, 1985-86, pres., 1987-89. Mem. NAFE, AAUW (bd. dirs.), Fin. Planning Assn., Inland Soc. Tax Cons., Nat. Assn. Securities Dealers (registered prin.), Nat. Ctr. Fin. Edn., Am. Bus. Women's Assn., Navy League, Freedoms Found. of Valley Forge, Internat. Platform Assn. Presbyterian. Avocations: community service, travel, reading. Home: 6462 Spear St San Diego CA 92120-2929 Office: Gengor Fin Advisors 4950 Waring Rd Ste 7 San Diego CA 92120-2700 E-mail: vgengor@cox.net.

GENIN, JOSEPH, engineering educator, researcher; b. Norwalk, Conn., Sept. 9, 1936; s. Kalman and Ida (Kaplan) G.; m. Grace Ann Gale; children: Kent, Guy, Hugh. BS, CCNY, 1956; MS, U. Ariz., 1958; PhD, U. Minn., 1963. Aeronautics and engring. mechanics instr. U. Minn., Mpls., 1959-63; sr. engr. Gen. Dynamics Corp., Ft. Worth, 1963-64; prof. aeronautics and astronautics Purdue U., West Lafayette, Ind., 1964-73, dir. Advanced Transp. Ctr., 1971-76, head engring. mechanics, 1975-81; dean Coll. Engring. N.Mex. State U., Las Cruces, 1981-85, dir. Optics & Material Scis. Lab., 1985-92, dir. Ctr. Dynamics Mechs. and Control, 1997—. Cons. engr., Tucson, 1956-60; instr. civil engring. U. Ariz., Tucson, 1956-58. Author: Statics-Dynamics, 1974, Introduction to Applied Math, 1970. Mem. econ. devel. bd. State of N.Mex., 1981-85. Fellow ASME; mem. Am. Soc. for Engring. Edn., AIAA (pres. Ctrl. Ind. sect. 1967-68). Avocations: reading, writing, jogging. Office: NMex State U Dept Mech Engring Las Cruces NM 88003 E-mail: jgenin@nmsu.edu.

GENNARO, GLENN JOSEPH, principal; b. New Orleans, Feb. 11, 1949; s. Tony Paul and Rosemary Lucy (Cartazzo) G. BA, U. New Orleans, 1970, MEd, 1975. Cert. tchr., supr. and prin., La. Debate coach Archbishop Rummel High Sch., Metairie, La., 1969-71; rschr. Resource Mgmt. Corp., Bethesda, Md., 1971; tchr., devel. dir. Redemptorist High Sch., New Orleans, 1971-74; asst. prin. Acad. of the Holy Angels, New Orleans, 1974-77; prin. St. Christopher Sch., Metairie, 1977-80, mem. sch. bd., 1967-70; prin. Pope John Paul II High Sch., Slidell, La., 1980-84; dir. guidance and admissions Jesuit High Sch., New Orleans, 1984-92; prin., coordinating coun. St. Clement of Rome Sch., Metairie, 1992—. Mem. sch. bd. Archdiocese of New Orleans, 1984-91; bd. dirs. Clarion Herald Newspaper. Author newspaper column Ask Mr. G., 1984-87, book rev. Sch. Safety, 1985. Campaign staff Fitzmorris for Lt. gov., New Orleans, 1971-75, Fitzmorris for Gov., Metairie, 1979; pres. Jefferson Livestock Protective Coun., Metairie, 1971-80; publicity chmn. Friends of WYES-tV, New Orleans, 1973-74; v.p. Conservative Polit. Action Com., Slidell, La., 1983-84. Named Hon. State Senator, La. Senate, 1975, Ambassador of Goodwill, State of La., 1978, Hon. Citizen, City of New Orleans, 1981, Aide-de-Comp, Gov. La., 1983; Cert. of Appreciation, City of Slidell, 1984. Mem. ASCD, NASSP, La. Assn. Prins., Nat. Catholic Edn. Assn., Nat. Assn. Student Activity Advisors, Nat. Forensic League. Democrat. Roman Catholic. Avocations: stained glass, gardening, furniture refinishing, travel, reading. Office: St Clement of Rome Sch 3978 W Esplanade Ave Metairie LA 70002

GENOVESE, LAWRENCE MATTHEW, secondary education educator; b. N.Y.C., Jan. 1, 1949; s. Robert Pascuale Sisto and Jean Laura (Lundari) G.; m. Laura Gail Vukich, Aug. 9, 1975; 1 child, Lawrence Matthew II. BS, Queens Coll., 1971, MS, 1973; profl. diploma, St. John's U., Jamaica, N.Y., 1976. Cert. elem. speech and English tchr., sch. adminstr., supr., sch. dist. adminstr., N.Y. Cluster tchr. Mark Twain Middle Sch., Yonkers, N.Y., 1971-72; elem. tchr. N.Y.C. Pub. Schs., 1972-75; English, lang. arts tchr. Burr's Ln. Jr. High Sch., Dix Hills, N.Y., 1975—; lang. arts tchr. Half Hollow Hills High Sch., Dix Hills, N.Y., Candlewood Middle Sch, Dix Hills, N.Y., 1975—. Supr. Summer Youth Employment Program, N.Y.C., 1971—. Author: No One Would Play With Peppe, 1970, We Are Children of the Zuni, 1972, How to Teach the Recorder, 1974. Recipient Humanitarian award Half Hollow Hills Parent Tchrs. Students Assn., 1979, Dr. Jenkins award, 1990. Mem. L.I. Bd. Realtors, Masons, Phi Delta Kappa. Avocations: piano, gardening, theater, opera, real estate.

GENOVICH-RICHARDS, JOANN, health care services consultant, educator; b. Detroit, July 23, 1954; d. Steven Edward and Catherine Ann (Malaspina) Genovich; m. David Edward Richards, Aug. 15, 1975. BSN, U. Mich., 1976; MSN, Wayne State U., 1978; MBA, Oakland U., 1985; PhD, U. Mich., 1993. Mental health coord. Midland (Mich.) Hosp. Ctr., 1978-79; outpatient nursing supr. Henry Ford Hosp., Detroit, 1979-82; adminstrv. dir. nursing St. John Hosp. Macomb Ctr., Mt. Clemens, Mich., 1986; dir. quality svcs., cons., dir. nursing Mercy Health Svcs., Farmington Hills, Mich., 1983-89; instr. nursing Oakland U., Rochester, Mich., 1985-92, interim dean Nursing Sch., 1992; asst. prof. Sch. Nursing and Pub. Health, U. N.C., Chapel Hill, 1993; asst. v.p. planning and devel. Nat. Com. Quality Assurance, 1993-95; expert appointment Ctr. Quality Measurement & Improvement Agy. for Health Care Policy & Rsch. Bd. dirs. Sisters of St. Joseph Health System, Ann Arbor; clin. faculty Joint Commn. on Accreditation of Healthcare Orgns., Chgo., 1986-90. Contbr. chpt. to book and articles to profl. jours. Recipient Project grant, Inst. of Medicine, 1989. Mem. ANA, Mich. Nurses Assn., Nat. Assn. Quality Assurance Profls., Am. Soc. for Quality Control, Aircraft Owners and Pilots Assn. Roman Catholic. Avocations: gardening, golfing, flying. Home: 12322 Prairie Dr Sterling Heights MI 48312-5230

GENOWAYS, HUGH HOWARD, systematic biologist, educator; b. Scottsbluff, Nebr., Dec. 24, 1940; s. Theodore Thompson and Sarah Louise (Beales) G.; m. Joyce Elaine Cox, July 28, 1963; children: Margaret Louise, Theodore Howard. AB, Hastings Coll., 1963; postgrad., U. Western Australia, 1964; PhD, U. Kans., 1971. Curator Mus. of Tex. Tech U., Lubbock, 1972-76, lectr. Mus. Sci. Program, 1974-76; curator Carnegie Mus. Natural History, Pitts., 1976-86; dir. U. Nebr. State Mus., Lincoln, 1986-94; chair mus. studies program U. Nebr., 1989—95, 1997—, prof. state mus., 1986—2003, prof. mus. studies, 1989—, prof. natural resource scis., 1997—2003, prof. phase d retirement program, 2003—. Author, editor:(with Michael A. Mares) Mammalian Biology in South America, 1982, (with Marion A. Burgwin) Natural History of the Dog, 1984; (with Mary R. Dawson) contbns. in Vertebrate Paleontology, 1984, Species of Special Concern in Pennsylvania, 1985, Current Mammalogy, 1987, 90, Biology of the Heteromyidae, 1993, Storage of Natural History Collections: A Preventive Conservation Approach, 1996, (with Robert J. Baker) Mammalogy: A Memorial Volume Honoring Dr. J. Knox Jones, Jr., 1996, (with Ted Genoways) A Perfect Picture of Hell: Eyewitness Accounts by Civil War Prisoners from the 12th Iowa, 2001, (with Lynne M. Ireland) Museum Administration: An Introduction; editor: Collections: A Journal for Museum and Archive Professionals, 2003--. Packmaster Allegheny Trails coun. Boy Scouts Am., 1981-83, asst. scoutmaster, 1983-86. Grantee Fulbright Found., 1964, NSF, 1977-86, R.K. Mellon Found., 1981-86, Smithsonian Fgn. Currency Program, 1983-84, Inst. Mus. Svcs., 1989-96. Mem. Am. Soc. Mammalogists (pres. 1984-86, C. Hart Merriam award 1987, editor Spl. Pubs. 1995-96, historian 1997—, elected hon. mem. 2002), Internat. Theriological Congress (steering com. 1985—), Southwestern Assn. Naturalists (pres. 1984-85, trustee 2003--), Am. Assn. Mus., Nebr. Mus. Assn. (pres. 1990-92, 1st Hugh H. Genoways Achievement award 1994, sec. 1997-2000), Assn. Systematics Collections (bd. dirs. 1993-94), Nat. Inst. for Conservation Cultural Property (bd. dirs. 1993-94), Sociedad Argentina para Estudio Mamiferos, Lincoln Attractions and Mus. Assn. (chair 1987-94), Soc. Systematic Biologists, Rotary (bd. dirs. Lincoln N.E. club 1990-92). Office: U Nebr-Lincoln State Mus W436 Nebraska Hall Lincoln NE 68588-0514

GENT, ALAN NEVILLE, physicist, educator; b. Leicester, Eng., Nov. 11, 1927; came to U.S., 1961, naturalized, 1972; s. Harry Neville and Gladys (Hoyle) G.; m. Jean Margaret Wolstenholme, Sept. 1, 1949; children: Martin Paul Neville, Patrick Michael, Andrew John; m. Ginger Lee, Sept. 4, 1997. BS, U. London, 1946, BS in Physics, 1949, PhD in Sci., 1955; DHC, U. Haute-Alsace, France, 1997; DSc (hon.), De Montfort U., Eng., 1998. Lab. asst. John Bull Rubber Co., Leicester, Eng., 1944-45; research physicist Brit. (now Malaysian) Rubber Producers' Research Assn., 1949-61; prof. polymer physics U. Akron, Ohio, 1961-88, Dr. Harold A. Morton prof. polymer physics and polymer engring., 1988-94; prof. emeritus, 1994—; dean grad. studies and research U. Akron, 1978-86. Vis. prof. dept. materials Queen Mary Coll., U. London, 1969-70; vis. prof. dept. chem. engring. McGill U., 1983; Hill vis. prof. U. Minn., 1985; cons. Goodyear Tire & Rubber Co., 1963-2002, Gen. Motors, 1973-87. Contbr. articles to profl. publs. Served with Brit. Army, 1947-49. Recipient Mobay award, Cellular Plastics divsn. Soc. of Plastics Industry, 1963, Colwyn medal Plastics and Rubber Inst. Gt. Brit., 1978, Adhesives award Com. F-11, ASTM, 1979, Internat. Rsch. award Soc. Plastics Engrs., 1980, Whitby award Rubber Chem. divsn. Am. Chem. Soc., 1987, Pub. Svc. medal NASA, 1988, Charles Goodyear medal Rubber Chem. divsn. Am. Chem. Soc., 1990; installed Ohio Sci. Tech. and Industry Hall of Fame, 1993. Mem. NAE, Soc. of Rheology (pres. 1981-83, Bingham medal 1975), Adhesion Soc. (pres. 1978-80, 3M award 1987, Pres.'s award 1997), Am. Phys. Soc. (chmn. divsn. high polymer physics 1977-78, High Polymer Physics prize 1996). Democrat. Office: U Akron Inst Polymer Science Akron OH 44325-3909 E-mail: gent@uakron.edu.

GENTILCORE, EILEEN MARIE BELSITO, elementary school principal; b. Glen Cove, N.Y. d. Samuel Francis and Nellie Theresa (McKenna) Belsito; m. James Matthew Gentilcore, Aug. 4, 1951; children: Kevin, John, Scott. BS in Edn., SUNY, Potsdam; MS in Edn., Hofstra U., 1968, profl. diploma, 1976, EdD, 1979. Tchr., first grade Sea Cliff, N.Y., 1951-52; founder, pre-K Germany Officers Sch., Munich, 1952-53; tchr., first grade Peekskill (N.Y.) Schs., 1953-54; tchr., second grade Syosset, N.Y., 1954-55, reading cons., 1970-84, head tchr., 1974-84, prin., 1985-96; ret., 1996. Bicentennial adv. bd. Syosset Community, 1976; adv. bd. mem. Telicare, Uniondale, N.Y., 1978-80; cons. in field. Author: Developmental Learning, 1979. Organizer med. team to Honduras, 1998; mem. Nassau County Graffiti Task Force, 1994—. N.Y. State PTA fellow, 1971, 72, 73, Hofstra fellow, 1971; recipient Jenkins award N.Y. State PTA, 1968, Hon. Life, 1976, Pius X award Rockville Ctr. Diocese, 1985, Disting. Svc. award, N.Y. State PTA Dist., 1996, Teddy Roosevelt Achievement award, 1999, Award for outstanding svc. Rotary Internat., 1999, Abe Gordon Rotary Internat. V.P. Outstanding Svc. award, 2000, R.I. Internat. Achievment award, 2000. Citation for meritorious svc., R.I. Internat. Found., 2002, Rotary Internat. Svc. Above Self award, 2003, Zone 32 Disting. Past Dist. Gov. award, Barcelona, Spain, 2002; named Woman of Distinction, N.Y. State Senate, 1998, Woman of Distinction, Syosset-Woodbury Rep. Club and Senator Carl Marcellino, 1999; grantee Karla Project, 1998; honoree Gift of Life Inc., 1999, Internat. Task Force for Children at Risk, Rotary Internat. Literary Task Force Coord. Zone 32, 2003-04. Mem.: Syosset Prins. (pres. 1992), Rotary (pres. Syosset-Woodbury 1993—95, gov. aide 1995, Gift of Life pres. 1996—97, vocat. dir. dist. 7250 1996—97, med. mission to Honduras 1997, 1st woman dist. gov. dist. 7250 1998—99, Children at Risk Task Force 2000—, conf. chair Zone 32 2000—, coord. RI literacy task force zone 32 2003—, chair RI centennial com. dist 7250 2003—, med. mission to Russia 1995 dist. 7250, coord. Internat. Children at Risk task force, v.p., coord. Internat. Avoidable Blindness task force 2002—, launched Operation Mitch, Honduras, N.Y. State Senate Woman of Distinction 1998, Internat. Achievement award 1999, Meritorious Svc. citation 2002, Disting. Past Dist. Coord. citation 2002, Internat. Global award 2002, Paul Harris fellow, Svc. Above Self award 2003), Kappa Delta Pi, Alpha Sigma Omicron. Roman Catholic. Avocations: swimming, writing, reading, gardening. Fax: 516-921-0206.

GENTILCORE, JOHN C. principal; Prin. Mt. Sinai (N.Y.) Union Free Sch Dist.

GENTILE, GLORIA IRENE, computer designer, educator, watercolor artist; b. NYC, Jan. 4, 1929; d. Pasquale Francesco and Giusepinna (Dittore) G. Grad., Cooper Union Art Sch., 1950; B.F.A., Yale U., 1952, M.F.A., 1954. Instr. Sch. Visual Arts, N.Y.C., 1967—, Gentille Mini Sch., N.Y.C., 1968—, Parsons Sch. Design, N.Y.C., 1972—, Cooper Union, N.Y.C., 1974—; Queens Coll., 1977, Fashion Inst. Tech., 1980, Pratt Inst., 1981-88; founder, dir. Gentille Sch. Graphics, N.Y.C., 1975—; lectr. in field. Designer promotion-collateral, 1955—; conceptual art dir. French Curve Studio, N.Y.C., 1966—, book designer, Harcourt Brace Jovanovich, N.Y.C., 1965-67, mag. designer United Bus. Publs., 1975-78, design supr. Holt, Rinehart & Winston, 1981-89, Gentille Studio of Computer Graphics, L.A., N.Y.C., 1989—, Knightbridge Pub. Co., 1990-91; exhibited in one woman shows; devel. articulated bronze sculpture; conceptualist happening: Impromptu, Mus. Modern Art, 1972; appeared on radio and TV shows including The Mike Douglas Show, Captain Kangaroo, Joe Franklin, others; author: Kinaesthetics: Analysis of Cat Drawings by Famous People, 1971, Kinaesthetics: Cats Tell Tales, 1972; contbr. sculpture and story to New Worlds of Reading, 1969; contbr. over 30 articles to profl. jours. Recipient Desi award, 1978, award Bookbinders' Guild N.Y., 1986, Graphic Arts competition award, 1986, Gold award Lehigh Press, 1986, Silver award York Graphic, 1986, Pia award, 1987. Designer, developer only live hybrid Rumpie Persian-Manx cat. Home and Office: 333 E 46th St New York NY 10017-7401

GENTILE, JOSEPH F. principal; b. Sept. 3, 1949; married; 3 children. BA, SUNY, Buffalo, 1972, MA, 1975; secondary math. cert., Niagara U., 1978; adminstrn. cert., Canisius Coll., 1987. Cert. elem. edn., secondary math. and secondary social studies, secondary and elem. adminstrn. Tchr. computer tech., math., social studies Buffalo Pub. Sch. Sys., 1972—85; asst. prin. Sch. 71, 1985—86; prin. Hutch-Tech, 1986—90; acting asst. supt. secondary, 1990—91; prin. Hutchinson Cen. Tech. H.S., 1991—94, Clarence H.S., NY, 1994—. Adj. prof. Canisius Coll., 1986—. Avocations: family, computers, sports.

GENTILE, PATRICIA M. elementary education educator; b. Bklyn., June 7, 1945; d. Cosmo D. and Anne D. (Citrola) G. BS, SUNY, New Paltz, 1967; MA with distinction, Hofstra U., 1972; postgrad., L.I. U. Cert. permanent elem. tchr., N.Y. Mem. mentor adv. bd. Lindenhurst (N.Y.) Sch. Dist., grade chmn., linker in ednl. rsch. and dissemination program, pilot tchr. for health and lang. programs; tchr. 2d grade Daniel St Sch., Lindenhurst, N.Y., 1967-68—. Author ednl. materials. Active community orgns. Mem. ASCD, NEA, Bldg. Liaison Team Cultural Arts Com. Home: 4 Spruce St Centereach NY 11720-1736 Office: Daniel St School 289 Daniel St Lindenhurst NY 11757-3598

GENTRY, ALBERTA ELIZABETH, elementary education educator; b. Richter, Kans., Feb. 18, 1925; d. John Charles and Dessie Lorena (Duvall) Briles; m. Kenneth Neil Gentry, June 1, 1947; children: Michal Neil, Alan Dale, Elisa Ann. BE, Emporia (Kans.) Tchrs. Coll., 1975. Cert. tchr., Kans. Tchr. Chippewa Rural Sch., Ottawa, Kans., 1943-44; prin., tchr. Pomona (Kans.) Grade Sch., 1944-47, tchr., 1960-61, Silverlake Rural Sch., Pomona, 1947-48, Hawkins Rural Sch., Ottawa, 1948-49, Davy Rural Sch., Ottawa, 1950-53, Eugene Field Sch., Ottawa, 1953-54, Centropolis Grade Sch., Ottawa, 1964, Appanoose Elem. Sch., Pomona, 1964-90, ret., 1990. Trainer student tchr., 1985-86. Author: Proven Ideas for Classroom Teachers, 1988. Project leader, supporter 4-H, Franklin County, Kans., 1963-67; den mother Boy Scouts Am., Ottawa, 1955-66; dir. Bible sch., tchr. Trinity Meth. Ch., Ottawa, 1955-70, supt., 1955-66, mem. choir, 1947—. Named to Kans. Tchrs. Hall of Fame, 1991. Mem. NEA, Kans. Tchrs. Assn., Kans. Edn. Assn., Alpha Delta Kappa (sec. 1988-90). Republican. Methodist. Avocations: bird watching, arts and crafts, family genealogy, flower gardening, music. Home: PO Box 2 Pomona KS 66076-0002

GENTRY, BARBARA BEATRICE, educational consultant; b. Utica, N.Y., Oct. 21, 1948; d. James Russell and Beatrice Hazel (Vanderhoop) G. BS in Social Work, Utah State U., 1974; MA in Guidance and Counselor Edn., U. Wyo., 1975. Head counselor U. Wyo. Divsn. Student Ednl. Opportunity, Laramie, 1976-78, assoc. dir. Laromie, 1985-86; edn. unit dir. N.Am. Indian Ctr. of Boston, 1978-83; ptnr. Indian and Mexican Crafts, Oak Bluffs, Mass., 1986-93; multicultural coord. Ea. Mich. U., Ypsilanti, 1990-92; Wampanoag tribal edn. dir. Wampanoag Tribe of Gay Head, Gay Head, Mass., 1992-93; sr. assoc. ORBIS Assocs., Washington, 1993—. Cons. Indian Vocat. Edn. U.S. Dept. Edn., Washington, 1990, Springfield (Mass.) Mus., 1992, Nat. Indian Adult Edn. Conf., 1994, 95, Mich. Indian Critical Issues Conf., 1994, 95, N.Y. State Indian Edn. Conf., 1996, U.S. Dept. of Edn., Office of Indian Edn., 1981. Mem. election com. Boston Indian Coun., 1980-81. Mem. Nat. Indian Edn. Assn. (Wampanoag Tribe), Nat. Indian Adult Edn. Assn., Mich. Assn. Programs, Ea. Mich. U. Woman's Assn., Wampanoag Tribe of Gay Head. Office: Orbis Assocs 1411 K St NW Ste 700 Washington DC 20005-3404

GENTRY, DONNA JEAN, librarian; b. Anderson, Ind., Oct. 31, 1947; d. Lyman Siler and Marjorie Lois (Clark) Balser; m. John M. Gentry, July 19, 1969; children: Malinda, Catherine. BS, Ball State U., 1969, MA, 1972; endorsement in libr. sci., Butler U., 1978. Cert. English, govt., libr. media svcs. English tchr. Noblesville (Ind.) Jr. High, 1969-77; libr. Tipton (Ind.) H.S., 1978—. Mem. task force 21st Century, Tipton (Ind.) Cmty. Schs., 1993-94, mem. tech. com., 1994—. Sec. Hamilton Heights Ednl. Found., Arcadia, Ind., 1987-91, Hamilton Heights Bldg. Corp., Arcadia, 1991—; mem. Hamilton County Future Search, Noblesville, 1994—. Mem. Assn. for Ind. Media Educators, Delta Gamma Sorority, Lambda Iota Tau, Pi Gamma Mu, P.E.O. Republican. Methodist. Home: 16440 E 266th St Atlanta IN 46031-9725 Office: Tipton High Sch 619 S Main St Tipton IN 46072-9796

GENTRY, ROBERT BRYAN, humanities educator, writer; b. Knoxville, Tenn., July 21, 1936; s. Robert Bryan Sr. and Inez (Barnes) G.; m. Sharon Ann Norvell, Mar. 18, 1967 (div. Apr. 1977); children: Mark Bryan, Brannon John; m. Mary Sue Koeppel, May 31, 1980. BS, U. Tenn., 1958, MA, 1966. Cert. tchr. Fla. Sales rep. Humble Oil (now Exxon), Tenn., 1961-63; instr. Ga. State U., Atlanta, 1966-68; from tchg. asst. to instr. U. Ga., Athens, 1971-72; adminstr. Fla. C.C., Jacksonville, 1972-80, prof., 1980—2002; ret., 2002. Mem. faculty Nat. Inst. Tchrs. Writing, Greenfield, Mass, 1985-88. Author: A College Tells Its Story-An Oral History of Florida Community College at Jacksonville, 1991 (Gold Star award Fla. C.C. Bd. Trustees 1992), (textbooks) Insights into Love and Freedom, 1997, 5th rev. edit., 2001, Twentieth-Century Western Culture: An Introduction, 2000. With U.S. Army, 1958-61; 1st lt. USAR, 1964-68. Study grantee NEH, 1993; recipient 1st place award in short fiction 1st Coast Writers' Festival Contest, 1997. Mem. C.C. Humanities Assn., U.S. English. Avocations: swimming, reading, gardening. Home: 3879 Oldfield Trl Jacksonville FL 32223-2022

GEORGALAS, ROBERT NICHOLAS, English language educator; b. N.Y.C., Nov. 11, 1951; s. Nicholas and Dora (Patisso) G.; m. Joanne Louise Pepe, Sept. 5, 1981. BA, Lehman Coll., 1972; MA, CCNY, 1974; MFA, Columbia Coll., Chgo., 1997. Mktg. coord. Am. Express Co., N.Y.C., 1978-79; media supr. Wunderman Ricotta & Kline, N.Y.C., 1979-82, Needham Harper & Steers, N.Y.C., 1982-84; v.p., media dir. J. Walter Thompson Direct, N.Y.C., 1984-88, Leo Burnett USA, Chgo., 1988-91; prof. English Coll. of DuPage, Glen Ellyn, Ill., 1991—. Adj. assoc. prof. English Marymount Manhattan Coll., N.Y.C., 1979-88; voting judge Echo Awards, N.Y.C., 1987. Contbr. fiction to mags. Recipient Gold Effie award Am. Mktg. Assn., 1983, 91. Mem. NEA, MLA, Nat. Coun. Tchrs. English. Avocations: writing, swimming, traveling, theater, cinema. Home: 360 E Randolph St Chicago IL 60601-5069 Office: Coll of DuPage 425 Fawell Blvd Glen Ellyn IL 60137-6784 E-mail: georgala@cdnet.cod.edu.

GEORGE, ALBERT RICHARD, mechanical and aerospace engineering educator; b. N.Y.C., Mar. 12, 1938; s. Albert Richard and Tekla (Kovtoun) G.; m. Carol Mae Frerichs, June 21, 1959; children— Albert Frederick, David Kovtoun, Amy Margaret. BSE., Princeton U., 1959, MA, 1961, PhD, 1964. Vis. asst. prof. U. Wash., Seattle, 1964-65; asst. prof. Cornell U., 1965-69, assoc. prof., 1969-77, prof., 1977—, John F. Carr prof. mech. engring., 1992—, asst. dir. mech. and aerospace engring. dept., 1972-77; dir. mech. and aero. engring., 1977-87; dir. mfg. engring. and productivity program Cornell U., 1991—, dir. Ctr. Mfg. Enterprise, 1993—; head sect. BMW AG Automobile Mfrs., Fed. Republic of Germany, 1987-88; NRC sr. research assoc. NASA Ames Research Ctr., 1988; scholar-in-residence Harley-Davidson Motor Co., 1996—97; dir. systems engring. Cornell U., 1999—2002. Mem. Univ. Grants Com., Hong Kong, 1991-02; vis. sr. fellow U. Southampton, Eng., 1971-72; cons. in field. Contbr. articles to profl. jours. Mem. AIAA (fellow), ASME, Soc. Automotive Engrs., Am. Helicopter Soc. Congregationalist. Office: Cornell U 100 Rhodes Hall Ithaca NY 14853-3801 Home: 315 Savage Farm Dr Ithaca NY 14850-6503

GEORGE, CHARLENE COLETTE, mathematics educator; b. Pitts., Sept. 17, 1960; d. George James and Mildred Marie (Gorra) G. AS in Bus. Adminstrn., Community Coll., West Mifflin, Pa., 1980; BS in Bus. Adminstrn., Duquesne U., 1982, MS in Edn., 1990. Cert. math. and social studies tchr., Pa. Tchr. St. Wendelin Sch., Pitts., 1987-90; retail salesperson Leslie Dresbold Typewriter Store, Upper St. Clair, Pa., 1990-91, The Teacher's Store, Brentwood, Pa., 1991-92; substitute tchr. various sch. dists., Pa., 1990-92; tchr. Canon McMillan Sch. Dist., 1992—. Tchr. sponsor Pa. Jr. Acad. of Sci., Pitts., 1986-90, judge, 1986-91, mem. state juding com., 1991—; tchr. sponsor Superbowl of Problem Solving, Pitts., 1987-90, judge 1987, 91—; coach MathCounts, Pitts., 1988-90. Vol. Pitts. Regional Ctr. for Sci. Tchrs., 1989-90. Mem. Nat. Coun. Tchrs. Math. (Pa., Western Pa. chpts.), Nat. Coun. for the Social Studies (Pa. chpt.). Democrat. Roman Catholic. Avocations: swimming, cross country skiing, ice skating, roller skating, boating. Home: 5054 Parkvue Dr Pittsburgh PA 15236-2055

GEORGE, DIANE ELIZABETH, school media specialist, educational technology and computer education educator; b. L.I., N.Y., July 12, 1952; d. Arnold J. and Jeanette A. (Hester) G. BS, So. Conn. State U., 1974, MS in Libr. Sci., 1976, MS in Ednl. Tech., 1977. Cert. intermediate adminstr., libr. media specialist K-12, elem. edn. 1-8, driver's edn. Libr. media specialist New Canaan (Conn.) Pub. Schs., 1976-77, North Haven (Conn.) Pub. Schs., 1977-80, Branford (Conn.) Pub. Schs., 1980—. Ednl. cons. to SEED Project, New Haven; Conn. del. N.E. Regional Ednl. Leadership Conf., 1983; participant forum Linking Children with Nature, Roger Tory Peterson Inst., 1988. Mem. libr. power adv. com. New Haven Pub. Edn., 1995-97. Recipient Faculty Excellence award Branford Intermediate Sch., 1985-86. Mem. Conn. Educators Computer Assn. (bd. dirs. 1989—), Conn. Ednl. Media Assn. (bd. dirs. 1984-85, cert. of appreciation 1984). Office: Francis Walsh Intermediate Sch 185 Damascus Rd Branford CT 06405-6107

GEORGE, DONALD RICHARD, retired principal; b. Coffeyville, Kans., Oct. 1, 1926; s. Murl C. and Georgia M. (Leib) G.; m. Zepha Lowry, June 5, 1949; children: Donna L. Kellison, David L., Mary M. Tribby. BS in Edn., Pitts. State U., 1960; MS in Edn., Emporia State U., 1965. Tchr., asst. prin. Hugoton (Kans.) Elem. Sch., 1954-75; prin. Nelson Elem. Sch., Haysville, Kans., 1975-80, W.D. Munson Primary Sch., Mulvane, Kans., 1980-93, ret., 1993. IDEA Kettering Found. fellow, 1978-83. Mem. Nat. Assn. Elem. Sch. Prins., Kans. Assn. Elem. Sch. Prins., United Sch. Adminstrs. Kans., Lions, Phi Delta Kappa. Mem. Ch. of God. Avocations: farming, golf, woodworking. Home: 713 Tristan Dr Mulvane KS 67110-1212

GEORGE, RONALD BAYLIS, physician, educator; b. Nov. 17, 1932; MD, Tulane U., 1958. Diplomate in internal medicine and pulmonary diseases Am. Bd. Internal Medicine. Intern Charity Hosp. La., New Orleans, 1958-59, resident, 1962-64, Tulane Med. Svc., New Orleans, 1959-60; assoc. prof. medicine Tulane U. Sch. Medicine, New Orleans, 1969-72, La. State U. Sch. Medicine, Shreveport, 1972-74, prof. medicine, 1974—, chief pulmonary sect., 1972-92, acting chmn. dept. medicine, 1991-92, chmn. dept. medicine, 1992—2000; chief med. svc. VA Med. Ctr., Shreveport, 1978-82. Capt. USAF, 1960-62. Recipient H.M. Cotton Faculty Excellence award La. State U., Shreveport, 1987, Owls Club award Tulane U., 1968. Fellow ACP, Am. Coll. Chest Physicians (pres. 1993-94); mem. Am. Thoracic Soc., Am. Soc. for Clin. Investigation, Am. Assn. for Respiratory Care, Shreveport Med. Soc., Alpha Omega Alpha. Office: La State U Med Sch Dept Medicine PO Box 33932 Shreveport LA 71130-3932

GEORGE, STEPHEN CARL, reinsurance executive, educator, medical and life consultant, expert witness, expert witness; b. Miami, Fla., July 11, 1959; s. Joseph P. and Beatrice P. George; 3 children. BS in MIS, Fla. State U., 1983; MBA in Health Adminstrn., U. Miami, 1986. Provider rels. spec. Travelers Health Network, Phila., 1987-89; prin. Tyler & Co., Atlanta, 1989-93; risk mgmt. cons. John Alden - Provider Group, Miami, 1994; pres. Provider Risk, Inc., Miami, 1995—. Spkr. U. Miami, 1995-97; adj. prof. Nova U. Southeastern, 1996—; speaker in field. Contbr. articles to profl. jours. Vol. Habitat for Humanity, Miami, Fla., 1995—, innkeeper Covenet House.; del. U. So. Calif.-L.A.—People to People Amb. Programs, Moscow and St. Petersburg and Tallinn, Estonia A.A. Green scholar. Mem. Am. Coll. of Health Care Execs. (regents adv. coun. 1995-97), Toastmasters Internat. (CTM), South Fla. Exec. Forum, Alpha Kappa Psi. Avocations: family, water sports, scouting. Office: Provider Risk Inc 9761 SW 123rd St Miami FL 33176-4929 E-mail: reinsurance@providerrisk.com.

GEORGI, HOWARD, physics educator; b. San Bernardino, Calif., Jan. 6, 1947; married, two children. BA magna cum laude with high honors, Harvard Coll., 1967; PhD, Yale U., 1971. Rsch. fellow Harvard U., Cambridge, Mass., 1971-73, jr. fellow Soc. of Fellow, 1973-76, assoc. prof. physics, 1976-80, prof. physics, 1980—, sr. fellow, 1982-98, chmn. dept. physics, 1991-94. Co-chair com. on women in sci. and engring. NRC, 1996-99; master Leverett House, 1998—. Author: Lie Algebras in Particle Physics, 1981, Weak Interactions and Modern Particle Theory, 1984, The Physics of Waves, 1993; editor: Physics Letters B, 1982—. NSF postdoctoral fellow 1971-73, Alfred P. Sloan Found. fellow, 1976-80, Am. Phys. Soc. Divsn. Particles and Fields fellow, 1994; recipient Dirac medal Abdus Salam Internat. Ctr. Theoretical Physics, 2000, Levenson Meml. Tchg. award, 1999, Phi Beta Kappa Tchg. award, 2002. Fellow Am. Acad. Arts and Scis., Am. Phys. Soc. (com. on status of women in physics 1994-97, exec. com. Forum on Edn. 1995-98, Sakurai prize 1995); mem. NAS. Office: Harvard Univ Lyman Lab Of Physics Cambridge MA 02138 E-mail: georgi@physics.harvard.edu.

GEORGOPOULOS, NENOS ARISTIDES, philosophy educator; b. Thessaloniki, Greece, Feb. 19, 1938; m. Anna Terri Challenger; children: Alexis, Phillip, Stephan. BA, U. Vt., 1963; MA, Northwestern U., 1967; PhD, Pa. State U., 1973. Lectr. in philosophy Purdue U., West Lafayette, ind., 1964-65; teaching fellow Pa. State U., University Park, 1969-71; instr. in philosophy Kent (Ohio) State U., 1971-73, asst. prof., 1973-85, assoc. prof., 1985—. Vis. prof. U. Thessaloniki, 1988-89. Editor: Art and Emotion, 1989, Tragedy and Philosophy, 1993; co-editor: Continuity and Change in Marxism, 1982, Being Human in the Ultimate, 1993; contbr. articles to profl. publs. With U.S. Army, 1959-61. Recipient numerous teaching awards. Democrat. Avocations: travel, cooking, fencing. Office: Kent State U Dept Philosophy Kent OH 44242-0001

GEPHARDT, DONALD LOUIS, university official; b. St. Louis, Mar. 27, 1937; s. Louis Andrew and Loreen Estelle (Cassell) G.; m. Zenaida Otero Gephardt, June 10, 2000; children from previous marriage: Lisa Diane, Francis Joseph. B Music Edn., Drake U., 1959; BS, Juilliard Sch., 1961, MS, 1962; EdD, Washington U., St. Louis, 1978. Clarinet instr. Henry Street Settlement Music Sch., N.Y.C., 1961-64; music tchr. Wantagh (N.Y.) Elem. Schs., 1962-67; music tchr., band and orch. dir. W.C. Mepham High Sch., Bellmore, N.Y., 1967-70; assoc. prof. music, band and jazz ensemble conductor Nassau C.C., Garden City, N.Y., 1970-83, chmn. music dept., 1977-83, dean instrn., 1984-90; dean Coll. Fine and Performing Arts, Rowan U., Glassboro, N.J., 1990—, acting exec. v.p., provost, 1994-95. Clarinetist Des Moines Symphony Orch., 1956-59, Aspen (Colo.) Festival Orchestra, 1959-60, Henry Schuman's Wind Ensemble Workshop, 1965-69, L.I. Symphony Orch., 1970-82; clarinetist Seuffert Band, 1962-90, Great Neck (N.Y.) Symphony, 1967-80; contbr. articles to profl. jours. Bd. dirs. L.I. Symphony, 1980-82; surrogate speaker Richard Gephardt for Pres., 1987-88. Mem. Music Educators Nat. Conf. (chpt. advisor 1970-83, 2-yr. coll. chmn. Ea. divsn. 1982-83), N.Y. State Sch. Music Assn. (chmn. rsch. 1982-84), N.J. Music Educators Assn., Alliance for Arts Edn. N.J. (past pres.), Nassau Music Educators Assn. (rec. sec. 1968-69, 1st v.p. 1969-70, pres. 1970-71), Coll. Music Soc., Internat. Coun. of Fine Arts Deans (pres.-elect 2001-02, pres. 2003—), Young Audiences of N.J. (bd. dirs.), Arts Edn. Partnership (steering com.), Phi Mu Alpha Sinfonia. Democrat. Avocations: cooking, reading. Office: Rowan U NJ Coll Fine-Performing Arts Glassboro NJ 08028

GEPHART, MICHELE MARIE, elementary education educator; b. Buffalo, Sept. 16, 1969; d. Michael Raymond and Nancy Marie (Young) M.; m. Joseph Donald Gephart, July 15, 1989. AA, Villa Maria Coll., 1989; BEd, Daemen Coll., 1992; M in Reading Edn., Canisius Coll., 1995. Tchr. Queen of Martyrs Sch., Cheektowaga, N.Y., 1992, Our Lady of Czestchowa Sch., Cheektowaga, 1992-98, St. Bernard's, Buffalo, 1999—2001, St. Benedict's, Amherst, NY, 2001—02; reading tchr. Buffalo Pub. Schs., 2002—. Avocations: ceramics, sports. Home: 9453 E Eden Rd Eden NY 14057

GERACE, ROBERT F. secondary school principal; Prin. Alcott Mid. Sch., Wolcott, Conn. Recipient Blue Ribbon Sch. award U.S. Dept. Edn., 1990-91. Office: Alcott Mid Sch 1490 Woodtick Rd Wolcott CT 06716-1538

GERARD, SUSAN JANE, secondary education educator; b. Spokane, Wash., Feb. 8, 1962; d. Michael Arthur and Jane Carol (Sheppard) Hussey; m. Thomas Roy Gerard, Dec. 20, 1986; children: Andrew Thomas, Stephen Michael, Kymberley Sue. BA in History and Edn. with honors, Gonzaga U., 1984, MA in Tchg. and History, 1987, postgrad., 1990, Ea. Wash. U., 1990. Cert. tchr., adminstrn., Wash. Tchr. social studies Lewis and Clark H.S., Spokane, 1984—, freshman track coach, 1984-88, debate coach, 1986-88, mem. sch. care team, 1985—. Adj. prof. edn. Whitworth Coll., 1995—; advanced placement European history essay exam grader, 1996—, table leader, 2002—; mem. sch. attendance discipline com., 1995—, sch. faculty adv. group leader, site coun., 2000-03; coll. bd. faculty cons., workshop presenter, 1998—; racial and cultural equality adv. Lewis and Clark HS, Spokane, Wash., 1996—. Author: A.P. Teacher's Guide to European History, 1998; contbr. articles to profl. publs. Voter registrar Spokane County Election Bd., 1983—; leader, Cub Scouts, 1996-2001, Girl Scouts Am., 2002—; chmn. com. Boy Scouts Am., 2002—. Named Wash. State Profl. Woman of Yr., 1997, Tchr. of Yr., VFW, 1998; Cataldo acad. scholar Gonzaga U., 1984-87; recipient 20th Century achievement award, Cambridge, 1998, Outstanding Scholar award, Cambridge Press, 1999. Mem. ASCD, NEA, Wash. Edn. Assn., Spokane Edn. Assn. (bldg. rep. 1985-87), Phi Alpha Theta, Kappa Delta Pi, Alpha Sigma Nu. Roman Catholic. Avocations: camping, family activities, cooking, reading. Home: 14025 E 23rd Ave Veradale WA 99037-9330 Office: Lewis and Clark HS 521 W 4th Ave Spokane WA 99204-2692

GERBA, CHARLES PETER, microbiologist, educator; b. Blue Island, Ill., Sept. 10, 1945; s. Peter and Virginia (Roulo) G.; m. Peggy Louise Scheitlin, June 6, 1970; children: Peter, Phillip. BS in Microbiology, Ariz. State U., 1969; PhD in Microbiology, U. Miami, 1973. Postdoctoral fellow Baylor Coll. Medicine, Houston, 1973-74, asst. prof. microbiology, 1974-81; assoc. prof. U. Ariz., Tucson, 1981-85, prof., 1985—. Cons. EPA, Tucson, 1980—, World Health Orgn., Pan Am. Health Orgn., 1989—; advisor CRC Press, Boca Raton, Fla., 1981—. Editor: Methods in Environmental Virology, 1982, Groundwater Pollution Microbiology, 1984, Phage Ecology, 1987, Pollution Sci., 1996; contbr. numerous articles to profl. and sci. jours. Mem. Pima County Bd. Health, 1986-92; mem. sci. adv. bd. EPA, 1987-95. Recipient McKee medal Water Environ. Fedn., 1996; named Outstanding Research Scientist U. Ariz., 1984, 92, Outstanding Rsch. Team, 1994. Fellow AAAS (environ. sci. and engring.), Am. Acad. Microbiology, Am. Soc. Microbiology (divsn. chmn. 1982-83, 87-88, pres. Ariz. chpt. 1984-85, councilor 1985-88); mem. Internat. Assn. Water Pollution Rsch. (sr. del. 1985-91), Am. Water Works Assn. (A.P. Black award 1997), Water Quality Assn. (Hom. Mem. award 1998). Achievements include research in environmental microbiology, colloid transport in ground water, wastewater reuse and risk assessment. Home: 1980 W Paseo Monserrat Tucson AZ 85704-1329 Office: U Ariz Dept Microbiol & Immunol Wat Tucson AZ 85721-0001 E-mail: gerba@ag.arizona.edu.

GERBER, GWENDOLYN LORETTA, psychologist, educator; b. Calgary, Alta., Can. came to U.S., 1958; d. Ernest and Alma (Tesky) G. AB, UCLA, 1961, MA, 1964, PhD, 1967; cert. in psychoanalysis, NYU, 1970. Lic. psychologist, N.Y. Clin. psychologist Hillside Hosp., Glen Oaks, N.Y., 1970-73; asst. prof. psychology John Jay Coll. of Criminal Justice CUNY, N.Y.C., 1973-77, assoc. prof. psychology, 1977-90, prof., 1991—; pvt. practice in psychotherapy N.Y.C., 1970—. Contbr. chpts. to books and numerous articles to profl. jours. USPHS fellow, 1962-63, 66-67, NIMH fellow, 1967-69; CUNY grantee, 1989-92, 99-2000, 45 Found. grantee, 1991-96. Fellow: APA (bd. dirs. sect. III 1988—92, liaison divsn. 35 1989—, bd. dirs. sect. III 1994—95, bd. dirs. divsn. 39 1997—2004), N.Y. Acad. Scis. (chair psychology com. 1992—94); mem.: N.Y. State Psychol. Assn. (pres. acad. divsn. 1989—90, coun. rep. 1991—96, 2003—05, William Wundt award 1993, Disting. svc. award 1996, Kurt Lewin award 1999), Phi Beta Kappa, Psi Chi, Chi Delta Pi. Office: John Jay Coll CUNY 445 W 59th St New York NY 10019-1104

GERBER, LINDA MAXINE, epidemiology educator; b. N.Y.C., Apr. 12, 1953; d. Kenneth K. and Hilda (Butschowitz) S.; m. Michael Leit, Feb. 27, 1982; children: Benjamin Kenneth Leit, Rachel Joanna Leit. BA, SUNY, Binghamton, 1973; MA, U. Colo., 1976, PhD, 1978. Rsch. assoc. Inst. Behavioral Sci., U. Colo., Boulder, 1978; rsch. assoc. Cornell U. Med. Coll., N.Y.C., 1979-81, asst. prof. pub. health, 1982-84, 87-95, preceptor dept. pub. health, 1980-84, 87—, assoc. prof. pub. health, 1995—; rsch. scientist, epidemiologist Nassau County Dept. Health, Mineola, N.Y., 1984; clin. asst. prof. pub. health Cornell U. Med. Coll., N.Y.C., 1984-86; dir. office epidemiology Nassau County Dept. Health, Mineola, 1985-86; asst. prof. clin. community and preventive medicine SUNY Sch. Medicine, Stony Brook, 1985-87; asst. prof. epidemiology in medicine and pub. health Cornell U. Med. Coll., N.Y.C., 1987-95; dir. Clin. Rsch. Methodology Core Facility; assoc. prof. epidemiology in medicine Cornell U. Med. Coll., 2002—. Rsch. intern East-West Population Inst., East-West Ctr., Honolulu, 1976-77; cons. Inst. Behavioral Sci. U. Colo., Boulder, 1974; mem. institutional rev. bd. Fordham U., N.Y.C., 1980-98; presenter numerous confs.; organizer symposia. Author: Evolutionary Perspectives on Chronic Degenerative Diseases, 1999; guest editor Am. Jour. Human Biology, Vol. 7, 1995, Human Biology, Vol. 71, 1999; contbr. articles to profl. jours. Mem. N.Y. Heart Assn., N.Y.C., 1980-88. Post-doctoral fellow Pub. Health Svc., Cornell U. Med. Coll., 1979-81, Fleischmann fellow U. Colo., 1978, NIMH predoctoral fellow U. Colo., 1975-78. Fellow Am. Phys. Anthropologists (career devel. com.), Human Biology Assn. (exec. com.), Am. Heart Assn. (coun. on epidemiology), Am. Soc. Hypertension, N.Y. Acad. Medicine (fellow 1998—). Avocations: swimming, tai-chi. Office: Weill Med Coll Cornell U Dept Pub Health 411 E 69th St Dept Pub New York NY 10021-5608 E-mail: lig2002@med.cornell.edu.

GERBER, LUCILLE D. elementary education educator; b. Adrian, Mich., Nov. 22, 1952; d. William C. and V. Lucille (Wilson) Brooks; m. Gerald F. Gerber, Aug. 3, 1985. BS, Ea. Mich. U., 1976, cert. in continuing edn., 1981, 87—. Tchr. 3d grade Ypsilanti (Mich.) Pub. Schs., 1977-78; tchr. 1st grade Adams Elem. Sch. Ypsilanti (Mich.) Pub. Schs., 1978—. Contbr. poetry to various publs. Mem. NEA, Mich. Edn. Assn. Address: 615 N Mansfield St Ypsilanti MI 48197-2028 Office: Ypsilanti Pub Schs 1885 Packard Rd Ypsilanti MI 48197-1846

GERBER, SANDRA LEE, secondary education educator; b. St. Louis, June 25, 1953; d. Louis Wilford and Lillian Elizabeth (Hohnbaum) G. BA in Edn., Harris Tchrs. Coll., St. Louis, 1975; MAT in Math., Webster Coll., St. Louis. Cert. tchr. elem. edn. and math. Lectr. Harris Tchrs. Coll., St. Louis, 1976-79; math. resource tchr. Stix Investigative Learning Ct., St. Louis, 1979-82; computer math. tchr. Sumner High Sch., St. Louis, 1982-99; math. tchr. Cleve. Jr. Naval Acad., 1999—. Participant tchr. in bus. program St. Louis Pub. Schs. Partnership Program and Southwestern Bell Telephone, 1988; mem. math. contest com. St. Louis Pub. Schs., 1987—, math. curriculum com., 2003. Mem. Bd. Evangelism, St. Johns Luth. Ch., 1988—. Recipient Gus Clark Tchr. of Yr. award Urban Math. Collaborative St. Louis, 1991. Mem. Nat. Coun. Tchrs. Math., Mo. Coun. Tchrs. Math., Mo. State Tchrs. Assn., Math. Educators Greater St. Louis, Alpha Delta Kappa (treas. 1984-88, 2000--, v.p. 1992-94, pres. 1994-96), Kappa Delta Pi. Lutheran.

GERBERDING, WILLIAM PASSAVANT, retired university president; b. Fargo, N.D., Sept. 9, 1929; s. William Passavant and Esther Elizabeth Ann (Habighorst) G.; m. Ruth Alice Albrecht, Mar. 25, 1952; children: David Michael, Steven Henry, Elizabeth Ann, John Martin. BA, Macalester Coll., 1951; MA, U. Chgo., 1956, PhD, 1959. Congl. fellow Am. Polit. Sci. Assn., Washington, 1958-59; instr. Colgate U., Hamilton, N.Y., 1959-60; research asst. Senator E.J. McCarthy, Washington, 1960-61; staff Rep. Frank Thompson, Jr., Washington, 1961; faculty UCLA, 1961-72, prof., chmn. dept. polit. sci., 1970-72; dean faculty, v.p. for acad. affairs Occidental Coll., Los Angeles, 1972-75; exec. vice chancellor UCLA, 1975-77; chancellor U. Ill., Urbana-Champaign, 1978-79; pres. U. Wash., Seattle, 1979-95. Cons. Dept. Def., 1962, Calif. Assembly, 1965. Author: United States Foreign Policy: Perspectives and Analysis, 1966; co-editor, contbg. author: The Radical Left: The Abuse of Discontent, 1970. Trustee Macalester Coll., 1980—83, 1996—2001, Gates Cambridge Trust, U. Cambridge, England, 2000—. With USN, 1951—55. Recipient Distinguished Teaching award U. Calif., Los Angeles, 1966; Ford Found. grantee, 1967-68 Office: Univ Wash PO Box 352800 Seattle WA 98195-2800

GERBI, SUSAN ALEXANDRA, biology educator; b. N.Y.C., 1944; d. Claudio and Jeannette Lena (Klein) Gerbi; m. James Terrell McIlwain, Apr. 10, 1976. BA, Barnard Coll., 1965; MPhil, Yale U., 1968, PhD, 1970. NATO and Jane Coffin Childs Fund fellow Max-Planck Institut fur Biologie, Tubingen, Fed. Republic Germany, 1970-72; asst. prof. biology Brown U., Providence, 1972-77, assoc. prof., 1977-82, prof., 1982—. Dir. grad. tng. program in molecular and cell biology, 1982-87, asst. dir. grad. program in molecular biology, cell biology and biochemistry, 1987-89, vice-chair sect. molecular, cellular and devel. biology, 1990-94, chair dept. molecular biology, cell biology and biochemistry, 1994—; vis. assoc. prof. Duke U., Durham, N.C., 1981-82; mem. genetics research grants rev. panel NSF, 1979-80; mem. genetic basis of disease com. NIH, 1980-84. Contbr. articles to profl. jours. Dist. commr. Palmer River Pony Club, 1973-75. N.Y. State Regents scholar, 1965; NIH fellow, 1966-70; NIH research grantee, 1974—, research career devel. award, 1975-80; recipient Gov.'s award for sci. achievement State of R.I., 1993. Mem. Fedn. Am. Socs. Exptl. Biology (pub. policy com. 1994-97, chair consensus conf. on grad. edn. 1996), Assn. Am. Med. Colls. (pub. policy com. 1994-98, chair grad. rsch. edn. and tng. group 1999), Am. Soc. for Cell Biology (program chair 1986, council mem. 1988-90, pub. policy com. 1991-97, pres. 1993), Soc. for Devel. Biology, Genetics Soc., RNA Soc., Sigma Xi (nat. lectr.). Office: Brown Univ Biomedical Divsn Providence RI 02912-0001

GERBRACHT, ROBERT THOMAS (BOB GERBRACHT), painter, educator; b. Erie, Pa., June 23, 1924; s. Earl John and Lula Mary (Chapman) G.; m. Delia Marie Paz, Nov. 27, 1952; children: Mark, Elizabeth, Catherine. BFA, Yale U., 1951; MFA, U. So. Calif., 1952. Cert. tchr., Calif. Art tchr. William S. Hart Jr. and Sr. High Sch., Newhall, Calif., 1954—56; stained glass artist Cummings Studios, San Francisco, 1956—58; art tchr. McKinley Jr. High Sch., Redwood City, Calif., 1958—60, Castro Jr. High Sch., San Jose, Calif., 1960—79; portrait artist, tchr. San Jose, San Francisco, 1979—. Instr. art Coll. of Notre Dame, Belmont, Calif., 1955-60, San Jose City Coll., 1967-71, Notre Dame Novitiate, Saratoga, 1976-79, U. Calif., Santa Cruz, 1980-81; art cons. Moreland Sch. Dist., Campbell, Calif., 1979-80; instr. nationwide workshops, Calif., Colo., Fla., Kans., Mass., Nebr., Nev., N.Mex., N.Y., Oreg., S.C., Vt., Wash., Wis., Mex., 1980—; presenter guest portrait demonstrations to numerous art assns. and clubs, San Francisco area including The Commonwealth Club of Calif., 1992, The Acad. of Art Coll., 1998, The G-40 chpt. Prime Timers, 2002; juror several art exhbn. awards. Exhibited in Charles and Emma Frye Mus. Fine Art, Seattle, Rosicrucian Mus., San Jose, Calif., San Jose Mus. of Art, Denver Art Mus., Erie Mus. Art, Triton Mus. of Art, Santa Clara, Calif., Commonwealth Club Calif., 1992, San Francisco Acad. of Art Coll., 1998, 2000, Israel, Austria, China; represented in permanent collection Triton Mus. Art, Santa Clara, Calif.; portraits include Marie Gallo, Mrs. Bruce Jenner, Austin Warburton, Rev. Jack La Rocca, Rev. Cecil Williams, Jordan Lee; subject of articles in Today's Art and Graphics, Art and Antique Collector, Am. Artist, U.S. ART, Pastel Jour., Internat. Artist, Pastel Artist Internat.; work reproduced and included in Best of Pastel, Best of Oil Painting, 1996, Pastel Highlights, 1996, Portrait Inspirations, The Best of Portrait Painting, 1997, Best of Pastel 2, 1998, Creative Computer Tolls for Artists, 2001, The Little Book of Pastel, 2002. Cpl. U.S. Army, 1943-46. Recipient Am. Artist Achievement award Tchr. of Pastels, 1993, Gold medal Amsterdam Art Competition, 1998, Life Achievement award Sonoma Plein Air, 2002. Mem. Pastel Soc. Am. (master pastellist), Pastel Soc. West Coast (advisor, Best of Show 1988), Soc. Western Artists (trustee 1989-97, Best of Show 1982, 85, 90, Best Portrait award 1984, Best of Show Nat. Open Exhbn. 1999). Home and Office: 1301 Blue Oak Ct Pinole CA 94564-2145

GERDES, LILLIAN ANNA, elementary education educator; b. Ft. Atkinson, Iowa, July 8, 1933; d. Hugo Henry and Mathilda Rose (Schrandt) Lensing; m. James Chester Gerdes, June 30, 1956 (div. 1970); children: Heather, Julia, John. Student, UCLA, 1954-55; BA, Calif. Coll., 1955-58; MA, U. South Fla., 1969-72, EdS, 1984-88. Cert. tchr., Fla. 4th grade tchr. Heights Elem. Sch., Ft. Myers, Fla., 1967-68; 4th and 2d grade tchr. Orange River Elem. Sch., Ft. Myers, 1968-91; tchr. 2d and 3d grade gifted program Orangewood Elem. Sch., Ft. Myers, 1991—. Adult tchr. Tice Community Sch., Ft. Myers, 1978-79, Riverdale Community Sch., Ft. Myers, 1979-80; presenter Young Authors Conf., Ft. Myers, 1989-94. Author: (curriculum) Law Education, 1986; costume designer (madrigal costumes) The Rout, 1975 (award 1976), The Lusistrata, 1990; game designer for country schs.' centennial Cowboy Tournament, 1986 (award, 1986); booth designer for country schs.' "Hometown Heroes": Orangewood-A Kaleidddoscope, 1993-94; designer for Edison Players Community Theater, Ft. Myers, 1971-75, Lee County Dance Coun., Ft. Myers, 1972-77. Vol. Abuse Counseling and Treatment Ctr., Ft. Myers, 1989—, Arts for Act, 1989—; organizer Orangewood Bicentennial Mural Restoration Project, 1992; bd. mem. Orangewood Sch. PTA, tchr. parent liaison, 1992-94, Sch. Restructuring Tng. Team and Restructing Governance Team, 1990-92. Named Tchr. of Distinction Golden Apple Tchr. Recognition Program, Ft. Myers, 1991-93. Mem. Fla. Coun. Tchrs. English, S.W. Fla. Collegium for Advancement Teaching (cert.), Lee Coun. tchrs. of English (sec. 1985-87, 1st v.p. 1987-88, pres. 1988-89, state liaison 1989-90, elem. liaison 1990-94, Recognition Cmty. Support award 1977, Betterment Sch. award 1986, English Tchr. of Yr. award 1989), Tchrs. Assn. of Lee County (newsletter editor 1990-92), Grad. Sch. Assn. U. South Fla. Ft. Myers (officer 1985-88), Phi Delta Kappa (hon.). Avocations: reading, painting, hiking, home restoration, gardening. Home: 207 Kingston Dr Fort Myers FL 33905-2517 Office: Orangewood Elem Sch 4001 Deleon St Fort Myers FL 33901-8906

GERDES, NEIL WAYNE, library director, educator; b. Moline, Ill., Oct. 19, 1943; s. John Edward and Della Marie (Ferguson) G. AB, U. Ill., 1965; BD, Harvard U., 1968; MA, Columbia U., 1971; MA in Libr. Sci., U. Chgo., 1975; DMin, U. St. Mary of the Lake, 1994. Ordained to ministry Unitarian Universalist Assn., 1975. Copy chief Little, Brown, 1968-69; instr. Tuskegee Inst., 1969-71; libr. asst. Augustana Coll., 1972-73; editl. asst. Library Quar., 1973-74; libr., prof. Meadville Theol. Sch., Chgo., 1973—; libr. program dir. Chgo. Cluster Theol. Schs., 1977-80; dir. Hammond Libr., 1980—; prof. Chgo. Theol Sem., 1980—. Affiliated minister 1st Unitarian Church, Chgo., 2002—. Mem. exec. bd. Sem. Coop. Bookstore, Chgo., 1982-2002, Ctr. for Religion and Psychotherapy, Chgo., 1984-97, Ind. Voters of Ill., 1986-89, Hyde Park-Kenwood Cmty. Orgn., Chgo., 1988-89; pres. Hyde Park-Kenwood Interfaith Coun., 1986-90, Inst. for Spiritual Leadership, 2000—; chair libr. coun. Assn. Chgo. Theol. Sch., 1984-88, 96-98; trustee Civitas Dei Found., 1994—; mem. alumni coun. Harvard Divinity Sch., 1999—, sec., 2001—. Mem. ALA, Am. Theol. Library Assn., Chgo. Area Theol. Library Assn., Unitarian Universalist Mins. Assn. (sec., treas. nat. body 1990-94), Assn. Liberal Religious Scholars (sec., treas. 1975—), Phi Beta Kappa Office: Chgo Theol Sem Hammond Libr 5757 S University Ave Chicago IL 60637-1507

GERDNER, LINDA ANN, nursing researcher, educator; b. Burlington, Iowa, Sept. 17, 1955; d. Richard Paul and Edna Marie Gerdner. AA, Southeastern C.C., 1975, ADN, 1977; BSN, Iowa Wesleyan Coll., 1980; MA, U. Iowa, 1992, PhD, 1998. RN, Iowa, Ark., Minn. Staff devel. coord. Elm View Care Ctr., Burlington, Iowa, 1985—88, DON, 1988—89; tchg./rsch. asst. U. Iowa Coll. Nursing, Iowa City, 1989-92; nursing faculty Grand View Coll., Des Moines, 1992-93; project dir. Nat. Caregiver Tng. Project, U. Iowa Coll. Nursing, 1992-97, predoctoral fellow, 1996-98; postdoctoral fellow/faculty dept. psychiatry U. Ark. Med. Scis., VA Med. Ctr., Little Rock, 1998—2000; asst. prof. U. Minnesota Sch. Nursing, 2001—. Presenter in field; cons. Alverno Health Facility, Clinton, Iowa, 1997—. Mem. referee panel Clin. Nursing Rsch., 1997—, Western Jour. Nursing Rsch., 1998—, Jour. Gerontol. Nursing, 1999—, Internat. Jour. Geriatric Psychiatry, 2000—, Internat. Psychogeriatrics, 2002—, Alzheimer's Disease and Related Disorders, 2002—, Nursing Research, 2003—; contbr. chapters to books, articles to profl. jours. Recipient AARP Andrus Found. grad. fellowship in gerontology Assn. Gerontology in Higher Edn., 1996-97, Rsch. award Am. Soc. Aging, 1999. Mem.: ANA, Coun. Nursing and Anthropology, Am. Assn. Geriatric Psychiatry, Midwest Nursing Rsch. Soc. (Outstanding Poster award 1993), Mid-Am. Contress on Aging (Best Grad. Paper award 1994), Am. Geriatric Soc., Internat. Psychogeriatric Assn. (task force on behavioral and psychol. symptoms of dementia 1999—, scientific advisory com. 2001, IPA/Bayer Rsch. award 1999), Sigma Theta Tau (Best of Image award 1997). Avocations: reading, traveling, walking, music, photography. Home: 1160 Cushing Cir Apt 318 Saint Paul MN 55108 Office: Weaver-Densford Hall 308 Harvard St SE Minneapolis MN 55455-0353 E-mail: gerdn001@umn.edu.

GERETY, TOM, academic administrator, lawyer, educator, philosopher; b. NYC, July 22, 1946; m. Adelia Moore, Oct. 7, 1972; children: Finn, Carrick, Amias, Rowan. BA, Yale U., 1969, MPhil, 1974, JD, PhD, Yale U., 1976; MA, Amherst Coll., 1995; LLD (hon.), Williams Coll., 1995; LHD, Doshisha U., 1996; LLD (hon.), Wesleyan U., 2001. Tchr. Peru project Joint Ctr. Urban Studies Harvard-MIT, Lima, 1966—67; bilingual tchr. Boston Pub. Schs., 1970—71; assoc. lectr. philosophy, master's asst. Morse Coll. Yale U., New Haven, 1972—74; asst. prof., fellow Ctr. Profl. Ethics Chgo. Kent Coll. Law, Ill. Inst. Tech., 1976—78; prof. law U. Pitts., 1978—86; dean, Nippert prof. Coll. Law U. Cin., 1986—89; pres., prof. philosophy Trinity Coll., Hartford, Conn., 1989—94, Amherst (Mass.) Coll., 1994—2003; exec. dir., Brennan prof. Brennan Ctr. for Justice, NYC, 2003—. Vis. asst. prof. Ind. U. Sch. Law, Bloomington, 1977—78; vis. prof. constl. law and jurisprudence Stanford U. Sch. Law, 1983—84; occasional appellate litigation in constl. law ACLU, 1981—; chair New Engl. Small Coll. Athletic Conf., 1991—92, 2000—01; chair bd. dirs. Consortium on Financing Higher Edn., 1993—95; testimony before the Senate Judiciary Com., Subcom. on Constitution on various proposed amendments. Writer, cons., on-air corr., fundraiser Visions of the Constitution, Nat. Endowment for Humanities TV series in constl. law, 1985—88, commentaries in various media Washington Post, Boston Globe, Chgo. Tribune, Christian Sci. Monitor, L.A. Times, MacNeil Lehrer Report, Nat. Pub. Radio; contbr. articles to profl. jours. Bd. mem. Internat. Rescue Com., 1989—, Save the Children U.S., Conn. State Bd. Edn., 1992—94. Fellow Kent fellow, Danforth Found., 1972—76, Woodrow Wilson fellow, 1983. Office: Brennan Ctr for Justice 12th Fl 161 Avenue of the Americas New York NY 10013

GERHARD, LEE CLARENCE, geologist, educator; b. Albion, N.Y., May 30, 1937; s. Carl Clarence and Helen Mary (Lahmer) G.; m. Darcy LaFollette, July 22, 1964; 1 dau., Tracy Leigh. BS, Syracuse U., 1958; MS, U. Kans., 1961, PhD, 1964. Exploration geologist, region stratigrapher Sinclair Oil & Gas Co., Midland, Tex. and Roswell, N.Mex., 1964-66; asst. prof. geology U. So. Colo., Pueblo, 1966-69, assoc. prof., 1969-72; assoc. prof., asst. dir. West Indies Lab. Fairleigh Dickinson U., Rutherford, N.J., 1972-75; asst. geologist State of N.D., Grand Forks, 1975-77, geologist, 1977-81; prof., chmn. dept. geology U. N.D., Grand Forks, 1977-81; mgr. Rocky Mountain div. Supron Energy Corp., Denver, 1981-82; owner, pres. Gerhard & Assocs., Englewood, Colo., 1982-87; prof. petroleum geology Colo. Sch. Mines, Denver, 1982—, Getty prof., 1984-87; state geologist, dir. geol. survey State of Kans., Lawrence, 1987-99, prin. geologist, 1999—; founder, co-dir. Energy Rsch. Ctr., U. Kans., 1990-94. Presdl. appointee Nat. Adv. Com. on Oceans and Atmosphere, 1984-87. Contbr. articles to profl. jours. Served to 1st lt. U.S. Army, 1958-60. Danforth fellow, 1970-72; named to Kans. Oil and Gas Hall of Fame, 2002. Fellow Geol. Soc. Am.; mem. Am. Assn. Petroleum Geologists (hon. mem., Disting. Svc. award 1989, Journalism award 1996, pres. divsn. environ. geosci. 1994-95, hon. mem. divsn. environ. geoscis. 1998, v.p., Pub. Outreach award 1999, 2003), Am. Inst. Profl. Geologists, Rocky Mountain Assn. Geologists, Colo. Sci. Soc., Kans. Geol. Soc. (hon.), Sigma Xi, Sigma Gamma Epsilon. Home: 1628 Alvamar Dr Lawrence KS 66047-1714 Office: Kans Geol Survey 1930 Constant Ave Lawrence KS 66047-3724 E-mail: leeg@sunflower.com.

GERHARD, NANCY LUCILE DEGE, school counselor, educator; b. St. Paul, July 23, 1939; d. Carl H. and Mildred L. (Toenjes) Dege; m. Rick A. Gerhard, June 25, 1960; children: Geoffrey Austin, Mark Alan. BS in Elem. Edn. magna cum laude, Gustavus Adolphus Coll., 1960; MA in Sch. and Guidance Counseling, Chapman U., 1978. Cert. English tchr., guidance counselor, elem. tchr., adminstr., Calif. Tchr. English Orange (Calif.) Unified Sch. Dist., 1987—99, mentor tchr., 1990-93, coach Middle Sch. Demonstration Program, 1990-93, h.s. counselor, 1993—99; ret., 1999. Mem. Calif. Lang. Arts Instructional Materials Evaluation Panel, 1988; consulting tchr. Calif. Dept. Edn., 1999—. Mem. Ret. Calif. Tchrs. Assn. Office: Orange High Sch 525 N Shaffer St Orange CA 92867-6898

GERHARDT, LESTER A. engineering educator, dean; b. Bronx, N.Y., Jan. 28, 1940; s. David and Mary G.; m. Karen Rita Zimmerman, Sept. 2, 1961; children: Brian, Douglas. BEE, CUNY, 1961; MSEE, SUNY, Buffalo, 1964, PhD, 1969; Doctorate (hon.), Danish Tech. U., 2000. Engr., asst. dir rsch. Bell Aerospace, Buffalo, 1961-70; assoc. prof. Rensselaer Polytechnic Inst., Troy, N.Y., 1970-74, prof., 1974—, chmn. elect., computer and systems engrng. dept., 1975-86, dir. CIM Program, 1986-91, assoc. dean engrng., 1991—. Acting dir. Ctr. for the Mfg. Productivity, 1991-92, founding dir., 1979-80, dir. Ctr. for indsl. Innovation, 1993—; nat. del. NATO, 1980—, chair Rsch. Collaborative Grants Programme; mem. AFSB com. on Robotics and Artificial Intelligence, 1986-89, mem. com. Tactical Communications Nat. Acad. Scis.; mem. adv. bd. N.Y. Gov. Carey's Panel on Telecommunications, NSF, chair. adv. bd.; active internat. cons. to industry, the gov't, and other Universities. Recipient Inventor of Yr. award N.Y. State Intellectual Property Law Assn., 1997, Rsch. adminstrn. award Engrng. Rsch. Coun., 2002. Fellow: ASEE (chmn. engrng. rsch. coun. 1996—98, bd. dirs. 1996—98, inaugural award for rsch. adminstrn. engrng. rsch. coun. 2002), IEEE. Avocations: sailing, photography, tennis. Office: Rensselaer Poly Inst Deans Office Sch Engrng JEC 3002 Troy NY 12180

GERHART, JAMES BASIL, physics educator; b. Pasadena, Calif., Dec. 15, 1928; s. Ray and Marion (van Deusen) G.; m. Genevra Joy Thomesen, June 21, 1958; children: James Edward, Sara Elizabeth. BS, Calif. Inst. Tech., 1950; MA, Princeton, 1952, PhD, 1954. Instr. physics Princeton, 1954-56; asst. prof. physics U. Wash., Seattle, 1956-61, assoc. prof., 1961-65, prof., 1965-98, prof. emeritus, 1998—. Exec. officer Pacific Northwest Assn. for Coll. Physics, 1972-94, bd. dirs., 1965-99, chmn., 1970-72; governing bd. Am. Inst. Physics, 1973-76, 78-81. Recipient Disting. Teaching award U. Wash. Regents and Alumni Assn., 1982, Ann. Gerhart lectr., 1997. Fellow Am. Phys. Soc, AAAS; mem. Am. Assn. Physics Tchrs. (sec. 1971-77, v.p. 1977, pres.-elect 1978, pres. 1979, Millikan medal 1985). Home: 2134 E Interlaken Blvd Seattle WA 98112-3433 E-mail: gerhart@dirac.phys.u.wahington.edu.

GERHART, LORRAINE PFEIFFER, reading specialist, educator; b. Porterfield, Wis., Mar. 13, 1939; d. Frank William and Michalena Mary (Kroll) Pfeiffer; m. Adolph Dietrich Gerhart, June 20, 1964; 1 child, Monika. BS, U. Wis., Oshkosh, 1961; cert. reading specialist, Carroll Coll., 1966; MA in Reading, Cardinal Stritch Coll., 1975. Classroom tchr. Elmbrook Schs., Brookfield, Wis., 1961-67, reading specialist, 1967—, team leader and specialist, 1988—95; lectr., workshop coord. Cardinal Stritch Coll., 1975—95. Acad. staff U. Wis., Oshkosh, Madison. Co-author: Study Skills, 1977; cons. author for manuals with filmstrip set, 1979; cons. for reading strategies Scott Foresman Soc. St. text, 1988, 90; contbr. Middle School Content Reading, Middle School Thematic Series. Mem. fin. com. Village of Lac La Belle, 1983-84. Recipient Celebrate Literacy award Waukesha Reading Coun., 1986, 96. Mem. ASCD, Internat. Reading Assn. (mem. adv. bd. Jour. of Reading 1989-90, book reviewer Signal, 1975—90), N.E. Reading Coun., Wis. State Reading Assn. (pres. 1990-91, Friend of Literacy award 2000), Milw. Area Reading Coun., Nat. Coun. Tchrs. English., Delta Kappa Gamma. Republican. Roman Catholic. Avocations: reading, gardening, hiking, taking rubbings, making books. Home: 901 Fj St Crivitz WI 54114-1544 Office: 901 FJ St Crivitz WI 54114-1549

GERITY, PATRICK EMMETT, university executive director; b. Cleve., Aug. 31, 1949; s. James Emmett and Helen Louise (Rouse) Gerity; m. Cynthia Lee Fetterolf, July 21, 1979; children: Rya Jenae, Jaissa Liane, Shayla Denae. BS in Health/Phys. Edn., Pa. State U., 1971-79, MS in Exercise and Sport Sci., 1986, PhD in Exercise and Sport Sci., 1999. Phys. edn. instr. Pa. State U., University Park, 1972-79, asst. intramural dir., 1973-78; dir. continuing edn., bus., and industry Community Coll. of Allegheny County, West Mifflin, Pa., 1986—98; nat. tournament dir. Am. Amateur Racquetball Assn., Colorado Springs, Colo., 1978—; exec. dir. U. Ctr. Southwest Pa., Pa. State Sys. Higher Edn., 1998—2002, Office Corp. Partnerships, Slippery Rock U., Pa., 2002—. Cons. racquetball and phys. fitness promotion, Bethel Park, 1978—; phys. edn. instr. C.C. of Allegheny County, 1981—; state liaison for Pa. for cmty. coll. workforce devel. Am. Assn. of Cmty. Colls., Pa., 1992—, mem. commn. for workforce and econ. devel., 1996—. Co-editor: (book) Linking Workforce Development Training to Performance: A Guide for Workforce Development Professionals in Community Colleges and Other Higher Educational Institutions, 2003; contbr. articles to profl. pubs. Program dir. YMCA, 1988-93. Named Coach of Yr. for Racquetball Skyline Athletic Conf., 1984. Mem. Am. Amateur Racquetball Assn. (regional dir. 1987-91), Am. Soc. Tng. and Devel., Nat. Coun. for Continuing and Community Edn., C. of C., Am. Assn. Cmty. Colls. Commn. for Cmty. and Workforce Devel. Lutheran. Avocations: racqueball, basketball, fitness. Home: 124 Thunderwood Dr Bethel Park PA 15102-1352 Office: Community Coll Allegheny 1750 Clairton Rd West Mifflin PA 15122-3029

GERLACH, JEANNE ELAINE, English language educator; b. Charleston, W.Va., Oct. 20, 1946; d. Lafayette and Edith Lorraine (Robinson) Marcum; m. Roger Thomas Gerlach Sr., Dec. 30, 1966; children: Roger Thomas Jr., Kristen Elaine. BS, W.Va. State Coll., Institute, 1974; MA, W.Va. State Coll., 1979; EdD, W.Va. U., 1985, U. North Tex., 1992. Lang. arts tchr. Ohio County Schs., Wheeling, W.Va., 1974-79; English instr. West Liberty (W.Va.) State Coll., 1979-82; continuing edn. instr. Seattle Pacific U., 1982-85; asst. prof. English W.Va. U., Morgantown, 1985-86, Tarrant County Jr. Coll., Ft. Worth, 1986-88; dir. Communications Unlimited, Dallas, Pitts., 1986—; assoc. prof. English edn. W.Va. U., Morgantown, 1989-97, spl. asst. to the provost, 1994-97, dir. ctr. women's studies, 1993-94; dean sch. of edn. U. Tex., Arlington, 1997—, assoc. v.p. K-16 initiatives, 2003—. Cons. to bus. and corps., 1986—; co-dir. advanced writing project W.Va. U., Morgantown, 1989, lang. arts camps, 1988, 89, 90, young writers inst. Editor: English Internat.; contbr. articles to profl. jours. Mem. LWV, W.Va., DAR, Young Republicans, W.Va. Faculty Devel. grantee W.Va. U., 1989; recipient 1st. place Creative Writing award W.Va. Women's Clubs, 1976. Mem. AAUW, AAUP, Nat. Coun. Tchrs. English (chair women's com. 1986—, chair nominating com. 1988-89, Outstanding Tchr. in Coll. of Human Resources and Edn. award W.Va. U. 1992, Rewey Belle Inglis award 1992), Am. Ednl. Rsch. Assn., W.Va. U. Alumni Assn. (sec. 1990, pres.), Nat. Women's Studies Assn., Nat. Soc. Daus. Am. Revolution. Republican. Methodist. Avocations: tennis, golf, writing poetry, photography, doll collecting.

GERLE, RICHARD DARLINGTON, radiologist, educator; b. Great Neck, L.I., N.Y., Feb. 11, 1930; s. Eric P. and Helen M. (Darlington) G.; student Denison U., 1949-53; B.S., U. Rochester, 1957, M.D., 1957; children from a previous marriage: Gretchen, Kirsten, Wendy; m. Janice Bettinger, Oct. 23, 1987. Intern, Mary Imogene Bassett Hosp., Cooperstown, N.Y., 1957-58; resident U. Rochester (N.Y.) Med. Center, 1958-61; asso. radiologist Mary Imogene Bassett Hosp., 1962-63; asst. prof. radiology Emory U. Sch. Medicine, Atlanta, 1963-65; attending radiologist Crouse-Irving Meml. Hosp., Syracuse, N.Y., 1965-79; practice medicine specializing in radiology, Syracuse, 1979— ; mem. staff VA Med. Center, Upstate Med. Center; clin. assoc. prof. SUNY Upstate Med. Center, Syracuse, 1979—. Mem. AMA, Am. Coll. Radiology, Radiol. Soc. N. Am., Am. Roentgen Ray Soc., N.Y. State Med. Soc., Am. Acad. Sci., N.Y. Acad. Scis., Onondaga County Med. Soc., Sigma Xi. Republican. Contbr. articles to med. jours. Office: 310 S Crouse Ave Syracuse NY 13210-1775

GERMAN, LYNNE CUMMINGS, music educator; b. Columbus, Ohio, Feb. 25, 1958; d. W. Dean and Naomi Faye (Cook) Cummings; m. Kenneth W. German, July 31, 1982; children: Madelaine Anne, Eliza Lynne, Brooke Nicole, Iris Noel. BS in Music Edn., Bob Jones U., 1980, MA in Piano, 1982. Dir. Southside Christian Sch. Flute Choir, Greenville, S.C., 1981-82; founder, owner, tchr. German Piano Studio, Mt. Crawford, Va., 1983—; tchr. James Madison U., Harrisonburg, Va., 1989-94; dir. Harrisonburg Flute Choir, 1994-95, Grace Covenant Ch. Vocal Choir and Brass Choir, Harrisonburg, 1995—. Spkr. in field. Contbr. articles to profl. jours. Mem. Nat. Guild Piano Tchrs., Musi. Tchrs. Nat. Assn., Va. Music Tchrs. Assn. (western Va. chpt. music theory chmn. 1995—), Harrisonburg Piano Tchrs. Forum. Avocations: composing, arranging music, writing, hiking, bicycling. Home and Office: 5006 Cross Keys Rd Mount Crawford VA 22841-2535

GERNER, EDWARD WILLIAM, medical educator; b. N.Y.C., Nov. 8, 1940; s. David and Anne (Robbins) G.; m. Judith E. Delbaum, June 5, 1983; 1 child, Danielle. BA magna cum laude, Clark U., 1961; MD, NYU, 1965. Diplomate Am. Bd. Ophthalmology, Am. Bd. Neurology. Intern Presbyn. U. Pitts. Hosp., 1965-66; resident Hosp. U. Pa., Phila., 1967-69; instr. dept. neurology U. Pa. Sch. Medicine, Phila., 1967-69, instr. dept. ophthalmology, 1972-74; attending neurologist Tulane U. Sch. Medicine, New Orleans, 1969-71; asst. surgeon Wills Eye Hosp., Phila., 1981-88, assoc. surgeon, 1988—; asst. prof. dept. neurology T. Jefferson U. Sch. Medicine, Phila., 1978-88, asst. prof. dept. ophthalmology, 1982-88, assoc. prof., 1988—. Bd. dirs. Pa. Physicians Healthcare Plan, Harrisburg. Contbr. chpts. to books and articles to profl. jours. Lt. comdr. USPHS, 1969-72. N.Y. State Regent scholar N.Y. State Bd. Regents, 1957-61; Jones fellow Mayo Clinic, Rochester, Minn., 1965. Fellow Am. Acad. Ophthalmology, Am. Acad. Neurology; mem. Royal Soc. Medicine (affiliate), Phi Beta Kappa. Avocations: photography, gardening. Office: 1015 Chestnut St # 1125 Philadelphia PA 19107-5127

GERNSBACHER, MORTON ANN, psychology educator; b. Ft. Worth, Nov. 22, 1955; d. Larry Morton and Phyliss (Berwald) G.; m. H. Hill Goldsmith, Aug. 12, 1983. BS, U. North Tex., 1976; MS, U. Tex., Dallas, 1980; PhD, U. Tex., 1983. High sch. tchr. Richardson (Tex.) Ind. Sch. Dist., 1976-80; rsch. and tech. asst. U. Tex., Austin, 1980-83; asst. prof. U. Oreg., Eugene, 1983-88, assoc. prof., 1989-91, prof., 1991-92, U. Wis., Madison, 1992—, Sir Frederic C. Bartlett prof. psychol., 1994—. Ad hoc reviewer for Jour. Memory and Lang., Cognitive Psychology, Jour. of Exptl. Psychology, Psychol. Rev., Cognitive Sci. Soc., NSF, Air Force Office of Sci. Rsch., NIH, NIMH, Natural Scis. and Engring. Rsch. Coun. of Can.; speaker First NSF Korea-US Coop. Conf. on Cognitive Sci., Seoul, 1991, First Evan L. Brown Meml. lectr., U. Nebr., Omana, 1991, Third Annual CUNY Conf. on Human Sentence Processing, 1990, 68th Annual Meeting Western Psychol. Assn., 1988, among others. Author: Language Comprehension as Structure Building, 1990, Handbook of Psycholinguistics, 1994, Fundamentals of Psycholinguistics, 1995; mem. editl. bd. Jour. Explt. Psychology; contbr. articles to profl. jours. Recipient Rsch. Career Devel. award NIH, 1989, Ersted award for Disting. Univ. Teaching U. Oreg., 1986; Fulbright Rsch. scholar 1989; grantee NSF 1985-85, Air Force Office of Sci. Rsch., 1989-90, 90-91, 91-92, Nat. Inst. Neurol. and Communication Disorders and Stroke, 1989-94, 91-96. Mem. APA (Edwin B. Newman Excellence in Rsch. award 1982), AAAS, Am. Psychol. Soc., Western Psychol. Assn., Psychonomic Soc., Cognitive Sci. Soc., Soc. for Computers in Psychology, Linguistic Soc. Am., Found. for Behavioral Rsch., Phi Kappa Phi, Psi Chi. Avocations: running, music. Office: U Wis Madison Dept Psychology 1202 W Johnson St Madison WI 53706-1611

GERRARD, RUTH ANN, retired English educator; BA, Coll. of Wooster, 1962, MA in Tchg., 1967; postgrad., Youngstown (Ohio) State U., 1975-79, Kent (Ohio) State U. Cert. tchr., supr. English instr. Orrville (Ohio) City Schs., 1962-64, Boardman Local Schs., Youngstown, Ohio, 1964-66, Wooster (Ohio) City Schs., 1967-69, Youngstown State U., 1969-71; gifted coord. Austintown Local Schs., Youngstown, 1977-96, English instr., 1971-96. Curriculum coms. Austintown Schs., workshop leader state and nat. orgns. Contbr. to publs. Spkr. various orgns.; elder Presbyn. Ch., 1985-90, 93—. Martha Holden Jennings scholar Jennings Found., 1987-88; recipient Tchr. of Yr. PTA. Mem. AAUW, Phi Delta Kappa, Delta Kappa Gamma 1968— (chapt. pres. 1996-98), docent Butler Inst. Am. Art. Avocations: painting, sketching, reading, gardening.

GERRINGER, ELIZABETH (THE MARCHIONESS DE ROE DEVON), writer, lawyer; b. Edmund, Wis., Jan. 7, 1934; d. Clyde Elroy and Matilda Evangeline Knapp; m. Roe (Don Davis) Devon Gerringer-Busenbark, Sept. 30, 1968 (dec. Dec. 1972). Student, Madison Bus. Coll., 1952, San Francisco State Coll., 1953-54, Vivian Rich Sch. Fashion Design, 1955, Dale Carnegie Sch., 1956, Arthur Murray Dance Studio, 1956, Biscayne Acad. Music, 1957, L.A. City Coll., 1960-62, Santa Monica (Calif.) Jr. Coll., 1963; JD, U. Calif., San Francisco, 1973; postgrad., Wharton Sch., U. Pa., 1977, London Art Coll., 1979; PhD, U. Cambridge, 1979; student, Goethe Inst., 1985. Bar: Calif., 1965. Ordained to ministry, 1978. Atty. Dometrik's JIT-MAP, San Francisco, 1973—. Cons. in field; pres., tchr. Environ Improvement, Originals by Elizabeth. Actress Actors Workshop San Francisco, 1959, 65, Theatre of Arts Beverly Hills, Calif., 1963, also radio; artist, poet, singer, songwriter, playwright, dress designer; author: The Cardinal, 1947, Explorations in Worship, 1965, The Magic of Scents, 1967, New Highways, 1967, The Grace of Romance, 1968, Happening-Impact-Mald, 1971, Seven Day Rainbow, 1972, The Day of the Lone Survivor, 1972, Zachary's Adversaries, 1974, Fifteen from Iowa, 1977, Bart's White Elephant, 1976, Skid Row Minister, 1978, Points in Time, 1979, Special Appointment-A Clown in Town, 1979, Happenings, 1980, Candles, 1980, The Stranger in the Train, 1983, Votes from the Closet, 1984, Wait for Me, 1984, The Stairway, 1984, The River is a Rock, 1985, Happenings Revisited, 1986, Comparative Religion in the United States, 1986, Lumber in the Skies, 1986, The Fifth Season, 1987, Summer Thoughts, 1987, Crimes of the Heart, 1987, Toast Thoughts, 1988, The Contrast of Russian Literature Through the Eyes of an American Artist, 1988, A Thousand Points of Light, 1989, The Face in The Mirror, 1989, Sea Gulls, 1990, Voices on the Hill, 1991, It's Tough to Get a Matched Set, 1991, Equality, 1991, Miss Geranium, 1991, Forest Voices, 1991, Golden Threads, 1991, Castles in the Air, 1991, The Cave, 1991, Angels, 1991, Real, 1991, An Appeal to Reason, 1992, We Knew, 1992, Like It Is, 1992, Politicians Anonymous, 1993, Wheels Within Wheels, 1994, A Tree for All Seasons, 1995, The Visitor, 1995, Time Frames, 1996, Save the Dance, 1998, Flowers For My Grandfather, 1999, Last Day at Mission Rock, 1999, Waiting for the Train, 1999, The Influence of Rural Life Upon Culture, 1999, The Crowd, 2001, Without Saying Goodbye, 2002, The Moon's Agreement, 2003. Steering com. Explorations in Worship. Address: 1008 10th St #275 Sacramento CA 95814-3502 Fax: 916-442-3735.

GERRITY, THOMAS P. management educator; b. Savannah, Ga., July 13, 1941; s. Thomas Patrick and Margaret Ellen Gerrity; m. Anna Rita Zablocki, Sept. 22, 1984. BSEE, MIT, 1963, MSEE, 1964, PhD, 1970; Masters (hon.), U. Pa., 1991. Mem. faculty Sloan Sch. Mgmt. MIT, Cambridge, Mass., 1968-72; chmn., CEO Index Group, Inc. (formerly Index Systems, Inc.), Cambridge, 1969-89; pres. CSC Consulting, Cambridge, 1989-90; dean Wharton Sch. U. Pa., Phila., 1990-99, prof. mgmt., dir. Wharton Electronic Bus. Initiative. Bd. dirs. Fannie Mae, Washington, Sunoco., Inc., Phila., Reliance Group Holdings, N.Y.C., CVS Corp., Woonsocket, R.I., Internet Capital Group, ICG Commerce; exec. com. Tech. Leaders, Phila., 1991—, Knight-Ridder Inc., San Jose, 1998—. Rhodes scholar Oxford U., 1964-65. Episcopalian. Office: U Pa Wharton Sch 3620 Locust Walk Philadelphia PA 19104-6302

GERSON, MARTIN LYONS, secondary school educator; b. Morristown, Tenn., Sept. 12, 1961; s. Allan Jerome and Bernice (Misner) G. BS, Purdue U., 1984; MA for Tchrs., Ga. State U., 1986, cert. ednl. specialist, 1994. Cert. secondary math. tchr., Ga. Tchr. math. Cross Keys H.S., Atlanta, 1984—97; tchr. S. Gwinnett H.S., Snellville, Ga., 1997—2003, Peachtree Ridge H.S., 2003—. Instr. math. Ga. State U., Atlanta, 1988-90, Dekalb Coll., Atlanta, 1990-96. Named Tchr. of Month math. students Cross Keys High Sch., 1989, South Gwinnett H.S., 2001, HERO Club, Cross Keys H.S., 1990, Tchr. of Yr. faculty Cross Keys H.S., 1990, West Dekalb Rotary Club, Atlanta, 1991. Mem. Nat. Coun. Tchrs. Math., Ga. Coun. Tchrs. Math., B'nai B'rith. Jewish. Avocations: bowling, collecting bobbleheads, hats and crystal figures. Home: 1196 Mandalay Ct SW Lilburn GA 30047-4227 Office: Peachtree Ridge HS 1555 Old Peachtree Rd Suwanee GA 30024 E-mail: marty_gerson@gwinnett.k12.ga.us.

GERSOVITZ, SARAH VALERIE, painter, printmaker, playwright; b. Montreal, Que., Can., Sept. 5, 1920; d. Solomon and Eva Gamer; m. Benjamin Gersovitz, June 22, 1944; children: Mark, Julia, Jeremy. Student, MacDonald Coll., Montreal Mus. Fine Arts; diploma communication arts, MA, Concordia U. Tchr. painting and drawing Bronfman Centre, Montreal, 1972—. One-woman shows include Montreal Mus. Fine Arts, 1962, 65, Art Gallery Greater Victoria, 1966, U. Alta, 1968, Burnaby Art Gallery, 1969, Art Gallery Hamilton, 1969, Mt. St. Vincent U., 1971, Coll. St. Louis, 1972, Inst. Cultural Peruano, Lima, 1973, Confedn. Art Gallery, 1976, St. Mary's U., 1976, U. Sherbrooke, 1979, 83, 95, Peter Whyte Gallery, 1982, London Regional Art Gallery, 1982, Holland Coll., 1982, Stewart Hall Art Gallery, 1984, U. Kaiserslautern (W. Ger.), 1984, Bibliothèque Nat. Québec, 1997, Galérie de la ville, D.D.O., Québec, 1999, Retrospective, Stewart Hall, Print Claire, Québec, 2000, Galérie Auguste-Chénier, Ville Marie, Québec, 2003, others; represented in permanent collections Libr. of Congress, N.Y. Pub. Libr., Nat. Gallery South Australia, Inst. Cultural Peruano, Lima, Am. Embassy, Ottawa, House of Humour and Satire, Gabrovo, Bulgaria, Israel Mus., Jerusalem, numerous Can. mus., univs. and embassies including Nat. Gallery Can., Montreal Mus. Fine Arts, Le Musée du Québec, Le Musée d'Art Contemporain; group exhbns. include most recently 3d Internat. Art Biennial Ville Marie, Que., 1996, 2000, 02, III Trienale, Harirov, Czech Republic, 2002, Sichuan Exlibris Assn., China, 2002, 2d Internat. Biennale d'art miniature, Ostow, Poland, 2002, numerous others U.S. and Abroad;

author: A Prtrait of Portia, 1989. Recipient numerous art awards including 1st prize 9th Internat. Biennale Gabrovo, Bulgaria, 1989, 1st prize Seagram Fine Arts Expn., 1968, Travel award, 1991; Graphic Art prize Winnipeg Art Gallery Bienial, 1962; Anaconda award Can. Soc. Painters-Etchers, 1963, 67; 1st prize Concours Graphique, U. Sherbrooke, 1977; purchase award Mus. de Que., 1966, Nat. Gallery South Australia, 1967, Dawson Coll., 1974, Thomas More Inst., 1977, Law Faculty U. Sherbrooke, 1979, 1st prize and 2 gold medals Nat. Playwriting Competition, Ottawa, 1982, 1st prize prize Country Playhouse, 1985, Jacksonville U., 1988. Mem. Royal Can. Acad. Arts (coun. 1981-82, 92-94), Dramatists Guild. Address: 4360 Montrose Ave Westmount QC Canada H3Y 2B1

GERSTENBERGER, VALERIE, media coordinator; b. Amherst, Ohio, Sept. 7, 1913; d. Frank Abraham Eppley and Ethel Elizabeth Dute; m. William Jacob Jenkins, Aug. 13, 1944 (div. May 1964); m. Henry Louis Gerstenberger, Nov. 8, 1984 (dec. Aug. 2001). BA, Baldwin-Wallace Coll., 1936; MA, Kent State U., 1963; postgrad., U. Iowa, 1938—39. Asst. drama dir. Baldwin-Wallace Coll., Berea, Ohio, 1936—38; English/speech tchr. St. Elmo (Ill.) H.S., 1940—42, Clearview H.S., Lorain, Ohio, 1942—57; speech tchr. Kent State U., Elyria, Ohio, 1963—66, Cleve. State U., Lakewood, Ohio, 1966—70; media coord. Amherst (Ohio) Pub. Schs., 1957—80; drama dir. Amherst (Ohio) Pub. H.S., 1957—60, 1975—78. Mem./pres. Amherst Pub. Libr. Bd., 1963—92; cons. for libr. expansion Am. Pub. Libr., 1972—73; costume designer various orgns. Various civic positions and contbns. including founding of Community Theater, local edn. programs and cataloging documents for Amherst Hist. Soc. Named to Gallery of Success, Amherst (Ohio) HS, 1987, Ohio Cmty. Theatre Assn. Hall of Fame, 2003; recipient Merit award, Baldwin Wallace Coll., 1986; Paul Harris fellow, Rotary Internat., 1983. Mem.: Amherst Hist. Soc., Phi Mu. Republican. Congregationalist. Home: 439 Shupe Ave Amherst OH 44001

GERSTING, JUDITH LEE, computer scientist, educator, computer scientist, researcher; b. Springfield, Vt., Aug. 20, 1940; d. Harold H. and Dorothy V. (Kinney) MacKenzie; m. John M. Gersting, Jr., Aug. 17, 1962; children: Adam, Jason. BS, Stetson U., 1962; MA, Ariz. State U., 1964, PhD, 1969. Assoc. prof. computer sci. U. Ctrl. Fla., Orlando, 1980-81; asst. prof. Ind. U.-Purdue U., Indpls., 1970-73, assoc. prof., 1974-79, prof., 1981-93, U. Hawaii, Hilo, 1994—. Staff scientist Indpls. Ctr. Advanced Rsch., 1982—84. Author: Mathematical Structures for Computer Science, 1996, 2003; contbr. articles to sci. jours. Mem.: Assn. Computing Machinery. Avocations: youth soccer, reading. Office: U Hawaii 200 W Kawili St Hilo HI 96720-4075 E-mail: gersting@hawaii.edu.

GERT, BERNARD, philosopher, educator; b. Cin., Oct. 16, 1934; s. Max and Celia (Yarnovsky) G.; m. Esther Libbye Rosenstein, Aug. 3, 1958; children: Heather Joy, Joshua Noah. BA, U. Cin., 1956; PhD, Cornell U., 1962. Instr. philosophy Dartmouth Coll., Hanover, NH, 1959-62, asst. prof. philosophy, 1962-66, assoc. prof., 1966-70, prof., 1970—, chmn. dept. philosophy, 1971—74, 1979—81, 1998—2001, Stone prof. intellectual and moral philosophy, 1981—92, 1998—, Eunice and Julian Cohen prof. ethics and human values, 1992-98. Vis. assoc. prof. philosophy Johns Hopkins U., Balt., 1967-68; vis. prof. philosophy Edinburgh U., fall 1974, Hebrew U. Jerusalem, 1985-86, Nacional U. de la Plata and U. Buenos Aires, Argentina, fall 1995; adj. prof. psychiatry Dartmouth Med. Sch., 1976—. Author: The Moral Rules: A New Rational Foundation for Morality, 1970, 1973, 1975, German edit. 1983, Morality: A New Justification of the Moral Rules, 1988, Morality: Its Nature and Justification, 1998; co-author: Philosophy in Medicine: Conceptual and Ethical Issues in Medicine and Psychiatry, 1982, Japanese edit. 1984; first author: Morality and the New Genetics: A Guide for Students and Health Care Providers, 1996, Bioethics: A Return to Fundamentals, 1997; editor: Hobbes' Man and Citizen, 1972, reprinted with revisions, 1991, Rationality, Rules, and Ideals: Critical Essays on Bernard Gert's Moral Theory, 2002; contbr. chpts. to books, articles to profl. jours. NEH fellow, 1969-70, Hastings Ctr. fellow, 1986—; recipient NSF-NEH Sustained Devel. award, 1980-84, Fulbright lectureship, Israel, 1985-86, Argentina, fall 1995; prin. investigator NIH, 1990-93. Fellow Nat. Humanities Ctr. 2001-2002; mem. Am. Philos. Assn., Am. Soc. Polit. and Legal Philosophy, Soc. Ethics Across the Curriculim, Assn. Practical and Profl. Ethics. Avocations: squash, poker. Home: 8 Bridgman Rd Hanover NH 03755-1302 Office: Dartmouth Coll Dept Philosophy Hanover NH 03755 E-mail: bernard.gert@dartmouth.edu.

GERTH, DONALD ROGERS, university president; b. Chgo., Dec. 4, 1928; s. George C. and Madeleine (Canavan) G.; m. Beverly J. Hollman, Oct. 15, 1955; children: Annette, Deborah. BA, U. Chgo., 1947, AM, 1951, PhD, 1963. Field rep. S.E. Asia World Univ. Svc., 1950; asst. to pres. Shimer Coll., 1951; Admissions counselor U. Chgo., 1956-58; assoc. dean students, admissions and records, mem. dept. polit. sci. San Francisco St. U., San Francisco, 1958-63; assoc. dean instnl. relations and student affairs Calif. State Univ., 1963-64; chmn. commn. on extended edn. Calif. State Univs. and Colls., 1977-82; dean of students Calif. State U., Chico, 1964-68, prof. polit. sci., 1964-76, assoc. v.p. for acad. affairs, dir. internat. programs, 1969-70, v.p. acad. affairs, 1970-76, pres., prof. polit. sci. Dominguez Hills, 1976-84, pres., prof. pub. policy and adminstrn. Sacramento, 1984—2003, pres., prof. emeritus, 2003—; co-dir. Danforth Found. Research Project, 1968-69; coordinator Inst. Local Govt. and Public Service, 1968-70. Past chair Accrediting Commn. for Sr. Colls. and Univs. of Western Coll. Assn.; chmn. admissions coun. Calif. State U., 1974-2003; bd. dirs. Ombudsman Found., L.A., 1968-71; lectr. U. Philippines, 1953-54, Claremont Grad. Sch. and Univ. Ctr., 1965-69; chair Sacramento World Trade Ctr.; chmn. Calif. State U. Inst., No. Calif. World Trade Ctr.; pres. Internatl. Assn. U. Pres. 1996-99. Co-author: The Learning Society, 1969; author, editor: An Invisible Giant, 1971; contbg. editor Education for the Public Service, 1970, Papers on the Ombudsman in Higher Education, 1979. Mem. pers. commn. Chico Unified Sch. Dist., 1969-76, chmn., 1971-74; adv. com. on justice pgorams Butte Coll., 1970-76; mem. Varsity Scouting Coun., 1980-84; chmn. United Way campaign Calif. State Univs., L.A. County, 1981-82; bd. dirs. Sacramento Area United Way, campaign chmn., 1991-92, exec. com., 1991-96, vice chmn., 1992-94, chmn.-elect, 1994-95, chmn., 1995-96; mem. bd. dirs. South Bay Hosp. Found., 1979-82; mem. The Cultural Commn., L.A., 1981-84; mem. com. govtl. rels. Am. Coun. Edn. Capt. USAF, 1952-56. Mem. Internat. Assn. Univ. Pres. (pres. 1996-99), Am. Polit. Sci. Assn., Am. Soc. Pub. Adminstrn., Soc. Coll. and Univ. Planning, Western Govtl. Rsch. Assn., World Affairs Coun. No. Calif., Assn. Pub. Adminstrn. Edn. (chmn. 1973-74), Western Polit. Sci. Assn., Am. Assn. State Colls. and Univs. (bd. dirs.), Calif. State C. of C. (edn. com.), Assn. Governing Bds. of Univs. and Colls., Calif. State U. Inst. (chmn. bd. dirs.), UN Ednl., Sci. and Cultural Orgn. (mem. adv. com.), UN Univ. Coun., World Trade Ctr. Sacramento, Sacramento Club (bd. dirs.), Comstock Club. Democrat. Episcopalian. Avocations: tennis, skiing, reading. Home: 7132 Secret Garden Loop Roseville CA 95747-8339 Office: Calif State U 2000 State Univ Drive East Rm 3022 Sacramento CA 95819

GERYE, ROBERT ALLEN, secondary school administrator; b. Topeka, Oct. 6, 1953; s. Allen Francis and Marye Ruth (Webster) G.; m. Cathy Jean Dunaway, June 19, 1981; 1 child, Rebecca Ann; stepchildren: Zachary Shelton, Gabriel Shelton. BA, Washburn U., 1974; MA, U. Kans., 1977, postgrad., 1991. Cert. principal, Kans., tchr., Colo. Tchr., chmn. dept. lang. arts Blue Valley High Sch., Overland Park, Kans., 1974-81; pres. Kids' Express, Inc., Topeka, 1981-87; asst. prin., dir. lang. arts Ft. Scott (Kans.) High Sch., 1987-88; prin. Jefferson West High Sch., Meriden, Kans., 1988-91; adminstr. Bonanza High Sch., Las Vegas, Nev., 1991; asst. prin. Western High Sch., Las Vegas, 1992—; founding prin. Las Vegas Acad. Internat. Studies, Performing and Visual Arts, Las Vegas, 1992—; prof. edn. U. Phoenix, Las Vegas, 1996—. Adj. instr. English Johnson County C.C., Overland Park, 1977-91; adj. asst. prof. Washburn U., Topeka, 1981-87; lectr. English U. Kans., Lawrence, 1985-87; speaker at profl. confs; adj. prof. English, C.C. So. Nev., 1991—, adj. prof. English and Edn., 1992—; prof. edn. Sierra Nevada Coll.; facilitor Adminstrs. Retreat, 1991; presenter in field. Author: Grasping the Sunset, 1978, Auroral Spring, 1979; developer Ft. Scott Writing Program, 1987-88. 2d v.p. Internat. Network Performing and Visual Arts Schs., 1998—2002; bd. dirs. Las Vegas Sister Cities Assn., 1997—2000. Recipient Community Svc. Edn. award Las Vegas C.C., 1998; inducted into Edn. Hall of Fame Clark County Sch. Dist., 2000. Mem. Nat. Assn. Secondary Sch. Prins., ASCD, Nat. Coun. Tchrs. of English, Nat. Sch. Conf. Inst. Exec. Leadership Acad. Office: Las Vegas Acad Internat Studies and Performing Arts 315 S 7th St Las Vegas NV 89101-5894

GESKIN, ERNEST S(AMUEL), science administrator, consultant; b. Dnepropetrovsk, Ukraine, USSR, June 4, 1935; came to U.S., 1977; s. Samuel A. and Rosa M. (Raskin) G.; m. Doris M. Osherenko, June 12, 1964; 1 child, Ellen. M in MetE, Inst. Mettalurgy, Dnepropetrovsk, 1957; PhD in ME, Inst. Steel and Alloys, Moscow, 1967. Engr. Inst. Automation, Dnepropetrovsk, 1957-67, mgr. lab., 1967-74; assoc. rsch. prof. George Washington U., Washington, 1977-78; assoc. prof. Clarkson Coll. Tech., Potsdam, N.Y., 1979-80; rsch. scientist, lab. mgr. Revere Rsch. Inc., Edison, N.J., 1981-83, dir. waterjet cutting lab., 1986—. Spl. lectr. N.J. Inst. Tech., Newark, 1984-85, assoc. prof., 1986-90, prof. 1991—. Author/co-author over 90 papers and presentations; editor various symposia (Cert. Recognition 1984, 89), 22 U.S. and USSR patents, 1969—. Mem. Internat. Soc. Waterjet Tech., Waterjet Tech. Assn., Sigma Xi. Avocations: swimming, gardening. Office: NJ Inst Tech 323 King Blvd Newark NJ 07102-1824 E-mail: geskin@njit.edu.

GESSAMAN, MARGARET PALMER, mathematician, educator, retired dean; b. Florence, Ariz., Oct. 7, 1934; d. William Lee Sr. and Lillian Maude (Henkle) Palmer; m. Paul Hayden Gessaman, June 11, 1965. BS, Mont. State Coll., 1956, MS, 1965, PhD, 1966. Statistician Fatstock Mktg. Corp., London, 1957-59; ops. researcher Richard, Thomas and Baldwin, Ebbw Vale, South Wales, 1959-60; market researcher Nestle Co., Inc., London, 1960-61; instr. Mont. State U., 1966-67; asst. prof. math. Ithaca Coll., 1967-70; asst. prof., assoc. prof., prof. math. U. Nebr., Omaha, 1970—, chmn. dept. math., computer sci., 1973-80, 98—, dean grad. studies rsch., 1980-93. Cons. grad. and rsch. activities, Coll. Bd., Chgo., 1981-88, Ednl. Testing Svc., Princeton, N.J., 1976-80, various govt. units, univs.; panelist NSF, Washington. Contbr. articles to profl. jours. Program chair Nebr. Commn. United Ministries in Higher Edn., Lincoln, 1976-81, 88-90. Mem. Coun. Grad. Schs. (bd. dirs.), Inst. Math. Stats., Am. Statis. Assn., Grad. Women in Sci.(nat. treas. 1994-95), Fulbright Assn., Mid-Am. State Univs. Assn. (chair 1988-89), Midwestern Assn. Grad. Schs. (chair-elect, chair, past chair 1986-89). Methodist. Avocations: travel, mayan history, cat lore.

GETS, LISPBETH ELLA, ret. educational administrator; b. Jhelum, Pakistan, Mar. 18, 1931; came to U.S., 1952, naturalized, 1955; d. Henry Ellis and Constance Selina (Bodell) Glenn; m. Terence Mathew Gets, Jan. 19, 1952; children: Erik Charles, Alison Beth, Hugh Malcolm, Adrienne Lea. AA, Santa Fe Community Coll., 1973-74; BA with high honors U. Fla., 1976, postgrad., 1977-89, MS, edn1. specialist cert., 1989. Cert. adminstr., supr., Fla. Editorial asst. John Trundell Pub., London, 1950-52; exec. secretarial positions, various cos., Chgo., Ft. Smith, Ark. and Jamestown, N.Y., 1952-58; tchr. spl. edn. Buchholz High Sch., Gainesville, Fla., 1976-81; asst. prin. Sidney Lanier Sch., Gainesville, 1981-83, 1987-2003, ret. 2003; prin. Monarch Ctr. for Exceptional Students, Gainesville, 1983-87 . Named Tchr. of Yr. Gatorland chpt. Coun. for Exceptional Children, 1981. Mem. Council Exceptional Children (chpt. pres. 1983—), Fla. Assn. Exceptional Sch. Adminstrs. (state chmn. 1988-90), Phi Delta Kappa. Democrat. Episcopalian. Home: 4601 NW 13th Ave Gainesville FL 32605-4534

GETZ, MICHAEL DAVID, elementary school educator; b. Altoona, Pa., May 22, 1968; s. Ronald J. and Sandra L. (Adelson) G.; m. Lisa Renee Ferdinandi, Aug. 23, 1992. BS in Elem. Edn., Pa. State U., 1990. Cert. elem. tchr., Pa. Tchr. 6th grade Downington (Pa.) Sch. Dist., 1990—. Coach Intramural Sports, Downington Sch. Dist., 1991—, mem. Lang. Arts Implementation Team, co-capt. Corp. Cup Team. Mem. NEA, Pa. Edn. Assn., Downington Area Edn. Assn. Jewish. Avocations: sports, reading, writing. Office: Bradford Heights Elem Sch 1330 Romig Rd Downingtown PA 19335-3689

GETZ, WAYNE MARCUS, biomathematician, researcher, educator; b. Johannesburg, Republic of South Africa, Apr. 26, 1950; came to U.S., 1979; m. Jennifer Bryna Gonski, Feb. 15, 1972; children: Stacey Lynn, Trevor Russell. BSc with honors, U. Witwatersrand, South Africa, 1972, PhD, 1976; DSc, U. Cape Town, South Africa, 1995. Rsch. scientist Coun. for Sci. and Indsl. Rsch., Pretoria, South Africa, 1974-79; biomathematician U. Calif., Berkeley, 1979—, prof. entomology, 1987-93, prof. environ. scis., 1993—, chair divsn. insect biology, 1995—2000, Berkeley chancellor's prof., 1998—2001. Extraordinary prof. U. Pretoria, South Africa, 2003—, fellow Mammal Rsch. Inst.; cons. Nat. Marine Fisheries Svc., 1980—89. Author: (with R. Haight) Population Harvesting: Demographic Models of Fish, Forest, and Animal Resources, 1989; editor Oxford U. Press book series Biol. Resource Mgmt., 1983-97; mem. editl. bd. Ecol. Applications, 1994-96, Annales Zoologica Fennici; contbr. articles to profl. jours. Rsch. grantee NSF, NIH, James S. McDonnell Found., Whitehall Found., Alfred P. Sloan Found., Def. Advanced Rsch. Programs Adminstrn.; Alexander von Humboldt U.S. Sr. Scientist awardee, 1993. Fellow AAAS, Calif. Acad. Scis., Stellanbosch Inst. for Advanced Studies; mem. Soc. Am. Naturalist, Internat. Soc. for Ecol. Modelling, Ecology Soc. Am., Resource Modelling Assn. (pres. 1995-96, bd. dirs. 1992-98), Soc. for Math. Biology. Office: Univ Calif Dep Env Sci Policy Mgmt Berkeley CA 94720-0001

GEWERTZ, BRUCE LABE, surgeon, educator; b. Phila., Aug. 27, 1949; s. Milton and Shirley (Charen) G.; children: Samantha, Barton, Alexis; m. Diane Weiss, Aug. 31, 1997. BS, Pa. State U., State Coll., 1968; MD, Jefferson Med. Coll., Phila., 1972. Diplomate Am. Bd. Surgery. Surg. resident U. Mich., Ann Arbor, 1972-77; asst. prof. U. Tex., Dallas, 1977-81; assoc. prof. U. Chgo., 1981-87, prof. surgery, 1988—, faculty dean med. edn., 1989-92, Dallas Phemister prof., chmn. dept. surgery, 1992—. Teaching scholar Am. Heart Assn., Dallas, 1980-83; pres. Assn. Surg. Edn., 1983-84. Author: Atlas of Vascular Surgery, 1989, Surgery of the Aorta and its Branches, 2000; editor Jour. Surg. Rsch., 1987—; patentee removable vascular filter. Recipient Jobst award Coller Surg. Soc., 1975, Coller award Mich. chpt. Am. Coll. Surgeons, 1975, Outstanding Sci. Alumnus award Pa. State U., 2003. Mem. Soc. Vascular Surgery, Midwestern Vascular Soc. (pres. 1993, 94-95), Soc. Clin. Surgery, Soc. Univ. Surgeons, Chgo. Surg. Soc. (treas. 1989-92, pres.-elect 2003), Am. Surg. Assn., Point O'Woods Club (Benton Harbor, Mich.). Office: U Chgo MC 5029 5841 S Maryland Ave Chicago IL 60637-1463

GEWIRTZ, PAUL D. lawyer, legal educator; b. May 12, 1947; s. Herman and Matilda (Miller) Gewirtz; m. Zoë Baird, June 8, 1986; children: Julian, Alec. AB summa cum laude, Columbia U., 1967; JD, Yale U., 1970. Bar: D.C. 1973, U.S. Supreme Ct. 1976. Law clk. to Hon. Marvin E. Frankel U.S. Dist. Ct (so. dist.) N.Y., 1970—71; law clk. to Justice Thurgood Marshal U.S. Supreme Ct., Washington, 1971—72; assoc. Wilmer, Cutler & Pickering, Washington, 1972—73; atty. Ctr. Law and Social Policy, Washington, 1973—76; assoc. prof. then prof. Yale Law Sch., New Haven, 1976—, Potter Stewart prof. Law, 1992—, dir. The China Ctr., 1999—. Dir. Clobal Constitutionalism Project, 1996—; spl. rep. the Presdl. Rule of Law Initiative US Dept. of State, 1997—98; US rep. European Commn. on Democracy through Law, 1996—2000. Author: Law's Stories, 1996, The Case Law Sys. in Am., 1989; contbr. numerous articles to profl. jours. Mem.: Am. Law Inst., Coun. on Fgn. Rels. Office: Yale U Law Sch PO Box 208215 New Haven CT 06520-8215 E-mail: paul.gewirtz@yale.edu.

GHALI, ANWAR YOUSSEF, psychiatrist, educator; b. Cairo, May 30, 1944; arrived in U.S.A., 1974, naturalized, 1980; s. Youssef and Insaf Wahba (Soliman) G.; m. Violette Fouad Saleh, May 23, 1968; 1 child, Susie MD, Cairo U., 1966, DPM, 1970, DM, 1971; MPA, NYU, 1999. Diplomate Am. Bd. Psychiatry and Neurology; cert. adminstrv. psychiatry. Registrar in psychiatry Woodilee Hosp., Glasgow, Scotland, 1973-74; resident in psychiatry N.J. Med. Sch., Newark, 1974-77, instr., 1977-78, clin. asst. prof., 1978-79, asst. prof., 1979-83, clin. assoc. prof., 1983—; chief Outpatient Dept.-Community Mental Health Ctr., N.J. Med. Sch., Newark, 1978-86; dir. Emergency Psychiat. Svcs. Univ. Hosp., U. Medicine and Dentistry of N.J., Newark, 1986-87; med. dir. Profl. Counsel Ctr., Westfield, NJ, 1984-87; med. chief ambulatory psychiat. svcs. Elizabeth (N.J.) Gen. Hosp., 1987-89; dir. psychiat. tng. VA Med. Ctr., East Orange, NJ, 1989—2001, asst. chief psychiatry, 1990—91, assoc. chief psychiatry, 1991—2001; chmn. psychiatry Trinitas Hosp., Elizabeth, NJ, 2001—. Contbr. articles to profl. jours. Recipient Exceptional Merit award Coll. Medicine & Dentistry, Newark, 1981 Mem. AMA, Christian Med. Soc., Am. Psychiat. Assn., N.J. Psychiat. Assn., N.Y. Acad. Scis. Republican. Presbyterian. Home: 22 Benvenue Ave West Orange NJ 07052-3202

GHALY, EVONE SHEHATA, pharmaceutics and industrial pharmacy educator; b. Cairo; d. Shehata Ghaly Shenouda and Amalia Elias Tadros; m. Nagdy Roshdy Mehany; children: Maichel Nagdy Roshdy, Mary Nagdy Roshdy. B in Pharm. Scis., Assiut U., Egypt, 1970; M in Pharm. Sci., Cairo U., 1979, PhD of Pharmaceutics, 1984; postdoctoral fellow, Phila. Coll. Pharm., 1986-88. Specialist and pharmacist in R&D Arab Drug Co., Cairo, 1970-75, sr. pharmacist in R&D, mgr. rsch. devel., 1975-86; assoc. rschr. Phila. Coll. Pharm., 1988-89; vis. prof., asst. prof. Sch. Pharmacy U. P.R., San Juan, 1989-92, assoc. prof., 1992-97, prof., 1997—. Cons. Smith Kline & Beecham, Inc., P.R., 1990—, Eli Lilly found., P.R., 1993—, Merck Sharp and Dohme Inc., P.R., 1994; instr., lectr. FDA, 1991, Warmer Lambert Inc., P.R., 1993-94, Ciba Geigy Inc., P.R., 1995. Contbr. articles to profl. jours. Grantee Colorcon Pharm. Inc., 1993-94, Baker Norton Pharm. Inc., 1993, INDUNIV Rsch. Ctr., 1990-92, 92-93, IBM, NIH-BRSG, 1991-92, Knoll AG Co., 1983, others. Mem. AAAS, Fed. Internat. Pharmaceutics, Am. Assn. Pharm. Scientists, Am. Pharm. Assn., Am. Assn. Coll. Pharmacy, Controlled Release and Bioactive Material, Sigma Xi, Rho Chi. Avocations: chess, piano, photography, sports, travel. Home: Condominio Puerta Sol 2000 San Juan PR 00926 Office: Univ PR Sch Pharmacy PO Box 5067 San Juan PR 00936-5067

GHORMLEY, WILLIAM FREDERICK, elementary school educator, music educator; b. Yakima, Wash., Oct. 5, 1954; s. John Thomas and Eileen Marie (Clyde) G. B in Music Edn., U. Portland, 1977; MS in Tchg. and Music, Portland State U., 1992. Cert. tchr., Wash. Elem. music specialist Evergreen Sch. Dist., Vancouver, Wash., 1977—, mem. bldg. project team, 1990-92; grad. tchg. asst. Portland (Oreg.) State U., 1990-92. Composer, arranger (choral music) Spirit of God, 1986, Peace Like a River, 1990, Blow Ye Winds, 1991. Mem. sect. chair Portland Symphonic Choir, 1990-92; conductor Vancouver's (Wash.) Men's Chorus, 1993—, Centennial Civic Chorale, Vancouver, 1984-89; mem. S.W. Wash. Fairness Coalition, 1993—. Recipient Conductor's award Vancouver's Men's Chorus, 1994. Mem. Wash. Music Educators Assn. (conf. planning team 1993-94), Music Educators Nat. Conf., Soc. for Gen. Music (adv. bd. 1983-85). Office: Evergreen Sch Dist PO Box 8910 Vancouver WA 98668-8910

GHOSH, ARUN KUMAR, economics, social sciences and accounting educator; b. Burdwan, West Bengal, India, Feb. 1, 1930; came to U.S., 1986, naturalized, 1997; s. Ashu Tosh and Indu Prova (Roy Mitter) G.; m. Krishna Datta, De. 10, 1986. BA with Honors in Econs. and Polit. Sci., U. Calcutta, India, 1948, MA in Econs., 1950. Asst. tchr. Burdwan Town Sch., 1950-51; rsch. fellow Dept. Econs. U. Calcutta, 1952-55, examiner, re-examiner, scrutineer BA and B of Commerce exams., 1952-66, asst. prof., 1955-56, rsch. asst. in indsl. fin., 1956-66; tutor Inst. Cost and Works Accts. India, Calcutta, 1966-69, asst. dir. rsch., 1970-85, faculty mem. exec. and profl. devel. programs, 1970-86, head rsch. directorate, 1981-84, asst. dir. exams., 1985-88. Socio-polit. commentator, analyst The Radical Humanist, 1950-62; vis. prof. Indian Inst. Mgmt., Calcutta, 1973-74; chmn. exams com. Internat. Inst. Mgmt. Scis., Calcutta, 1984-86, papersetter MBA exams, 1985; cons. U.S. AID, Indonesia, 1992-93; researcher and cons. in field. Author: The Collective Economy and the Cooperative Economy, 1954, Individual Freedom, Economic Planning and Cooperation, 1956, Government and Private Enterprise: Their Place in the Economy, 1957, Economic Growth and Integral Humanism, 1957, Fiscal Problem of Growth with Stability, 1959, Fiscal Policy and Economic Growth I and II, 1962 and 1963, Inflation and Price Control, 1975, (with C.R. Sengupta) Bank Finance Criteria and the Tandon Committee Report, 1975, Cost Accounting in Commercial Banking Industry, 1979, Introduction to Cost Accounting in Commercial Banking Industry, 1983, Cost Accounting and Farm Product Costing, 1990, Fiscal Policy, Stability and Growth: Experience and Problems of the Underdeveloped Economies, 1929-39, 1945-65, 1990, Fiscal Debt Management, Monetary-Credit Policy, and Growth-with-Stability, 1963, Management Accountants' Role in Monitoring Bank Finance, 1982; founder, editor rsch. bull. Inst. Cost and Works Accts. India, 1982-84; contbr. over 30 articles to profl. jours. Active Radical Humanist Movement in India, Indian Renaissance Inst., 1950-62. Mem. Am. Econ. Assn., Cine Club Calcutta, Am. Univ. Ctr. Jazz Club. Avocations: painting, sculpture, architecture, performing arts, international and indian history and culture. Address: 11500 Bucknell Dr Apt 3 Wheaton MD 20902-2888 Home: Punascha 72/1 BC Rd Burdwan 713 101 India

GHOUL, WAFICA ALI, finance educator; b. Beirut, Aug. 27, 1956; came to U.S., 1983; d. Ali H. and Anissa A. G. BS in Chemistry, Lebanese U., Beirut, 1978; PhD in Chem. Physics, U. East Anglia, Norwich, England, 1983; MBA in Fin., Wayne State U., 1992. Rschr. Wayne State U., 1984-87, Biosym Tech., San Diego, 1987-89, Sterling Drug, Albany, N.Y., 1989-90; prof. fin. Davenport U., Dearborn, Mich., 1993-98, chair fin., 1998—2003, assoc. prof. fin., 2003—. Presenter in field of chem. physics. Contbr. articles to profl. jours. Scholar Wayne State U., 1991-92; Lebanese U. fellow, 1979-83; recipient Disting. Students award U. Beirut, 1974-78. Mem. MBA Assn., Am. Lebanese U. Grads., Beta Gamma Sigma. Office: Davenport Univ Ea Region 4801 Oakman Blvd Dearborn MI 48126-3755

GIACCHI, JUDITH ADAIR, elementary education educator; b. Rochester, N.Y., Dec. 8, 1947; d. William Robert Peters and L. Virginia (Coulter) Peters Sweet; m. Alphonse Robert Giacchi, Aug. 8, 1970; children: Christina Marie, Anthony Robert. BS, SUNY, Buffalo, 1969. Permanent cert. tchr., N.Y. Data processing control clk. Neisner Bros., Inc., Rochester, 1969-70; tchr. Syracuse (N.Y.) City Sch. Dist., 1970—. Tchr. insvcs. and workshops Syracuse sch. dists., 1972—; master tchr. Syracuse U., 1983—; chmn. bldg. level team, 1988—98; collaborative Field Team Rep., mem., 1988—; trainer, ednl. rsch. and dissemination thinking math I, II and III, 2001—; rep. N.Y. State Tchrs. Retirement Sys. convs. and N.Y. State United Tchrs. convs., 1987—89. Contbr. articles to profl. publs. Corr. sec., rec. sec., legis. chmn. Nate Perry Sch. PTA, Liverpool, N.Y., 1983-95; troop aide Girl Scouts U.S.A., Liverpool, 1982-86; rep., mem. strategy com. Syracuse Labor Coun., 1995-97; mem. Union Cities Planning Com., 1997. Recipient award N.Y. State Legislature, 1994, various minigrants. Mem. N.Y. State United Tchrs. Fedn. (rep. convs. 1990-92), Ctrl. N.Y. Romance Writers Group, Onondaga County Tchrs. Assn. (award 1989), Syracuse Tchrs. Assn. (various coms., chief bldg. rep. 1984-2000). Avocations: reading, writing, needlecrafts, music, computers. Office: Porter Magnet Sch Tech and Career Exploration 512 Emerson Ave Syracuse NY 13204

GIACCIO, MARIA, special education educator, administrator; b. Bronx, Apr. 26, 1961; d. Salvatore Elio and Luigia Ginetta (Romagnoli) G. BA, Iona Coll., 1983. Developmental specialist Assn. for the Help of Retarded Children, Bronx, N.Y., 1983-87, supr., 1987—. Mem. ASCD, Nat. Bus. Women's Assn. Roman Catholic. Office: Assn Help of Retarded Children 1954 Mayflower Ave Bronx NY 10461-4007 Home: 206 Warren Ave Mamaroneck NY 10543-1328

GIACCONI, RICCARDO, astrophysicist, educator; b. Genoa, Italy, Oct. 6, 1931; arrived in U.S., 1956, naturalized, 1967; s. Antonio and Elsa (Canni) Giacconi; m. Mirella Manaira, Feb. 15, 1957; children: Guia Giacconi Trutter, Anna Lee, Marc A. PhD, U. Milan, Italy, 1954; ScD (hon.), U. Chgo., 1983; laurea honoris causa in astronomy, U. Padua, 1984; ScD (hon.), Warsaw U., 1996; laurea honoris causa in physics, U. Rome, 1998; Dr Tech. and Sci. (hon.), U. Uppsala, 2000. Asst. prof. physics U. Milan, 1954—56; rsch. assoc. Ind. U., 1956—58, Princeton U., 1958—59; exec. v.p., dir. Am. Sci. & Engring. Co., Cambridge, Mass., 1959—73; prof. astronomy Harvard U.; also assoc. dir. high energy astrophysics divsn. Center Astrophysics, Smithsonian Astrophys. Obs./Harvard Coll. Obs., Cambridge, 1973—81; dir. Space Telescope Sci. Inst., Balt., 1981—92; prof. astrophysics Johns Hopkins U., 1981—99, U. Milan, Italy, 1991—99; dir.-gen. European So. Obs., Garching, Germany, 1993—99; pres. Assoc. Univs., Inc., Washington, 1999—; rsch. prof. Johns Hopkins U., 1999—. Richtmeyer meml. lectr. Am. Assn. Physics Tchrs., 1975; mem. space sci. adv. com. NASA, 1978—79, mem. adv. com. innovation study, 1979—; mem. NASA Astrophysics Coun., mem. adv. com. innovation study astronomy adv. com., 1979—; mem. high energy astronomy survey panel Nat. Acad. Scis., 1979—80, mem. Space Sci. Studies Bd., 1980—84, 1989—; mem. adv. com. Max-Planck Inst. für Physik und Astrophysik; chmn. bd. dirs. Instituto Guido Donegani, Gruppo Montedison, 1987—89; mem. vis. com. to divsn. of phys. scis. U. Chgo., U. Padua; chmn. ISC E-1 (galactic and extragalactic astrophysics) Com. on Space Rsch. (COSPAR), 1982—93; Russell lectr. Co-editor: X-ray Astronomy, 1974, The X-Ray Universe, 1985, author numerous articles and papers in field.; inventor x-ray telescope, discoverer of x-ray stars. Decorated Targhe d'Oro della Regione Puglia, Cavaliere di Gran Croce dell'Ordine al Merito della Repubblica Italiana; recipient Röntgen prize in astrophysics, Physikalish-Medizinische Gesellschaft, Wurzburg, Germany, 1971, Exceptional Sci. Achievement medal, NASA, 1971, 1980, Disting. Pub. Svc. award, 1972, 2003, Space Sci. award, AIAA, 1976, Elliot Cresson medal, Franklin Inst., 1980, Gold medal, Royal Astron. Soc., 1982, A. Cressy Morrison award, N.Y. Acad. Sci., 1982, Bruce medal, 1987, Heinneman award, 1987, Wolf Prize in Physics, 1987, Nobel prize in physics, 2002; fellow, Fulbright, 1956—58. Mem.: Am. Philos. Soc., Royal Astron. Soc., Max-Planck Soc. (ext. mem.), Academia Nazionale dei Lincei (fgn.), Md. Acad. Sci. (sci. coun. 1982—), Internat. Astron. Union, Am. Acad. Arts and Scis., Italian Phys. Soc. (Como prize 1967), Am. Astron. Soc. (Henry Norris Russel lectr. 1981, Darwin lectr. Royal Soc. 1993, chmn. high energy astrophysics divsn., Helen B. Warner award 1966), NAS (rep. 1979—82), AAAS, Cosmos Club (Washington). Office: Associated Univs Inc 1400 16th St NW Ste 730 Washington DC 20036-2252

GIACOBBE, ANNA GRETCHEN STEINHAUER, elementary education educator; b. Oswego, N.Y., May 13, 1938; BS in Edn., SUNY, Oswego, 1959; MS in Edn., Elmira (N.Y.) Coll., 1987; postgrad., Syracuse U., 1991—. Cert. tchr., N.Y.; lic. real estate salesperson, N.Y. Elem. tchr. Holland Patent (N.Y.) Ctrl. Sch., 1966—, Poland (N.Y.) Ctrl. Sch., Whitesboro (N.Y.) Ctrl. Sch. Adj. prof. L.I. U., 1987—, Elmira Coll., 1992; tour guide Mohawk Valley Tour, 1982—; vis. practioner parent involvement rsch. Am. Fedn. Tchrs., Washington, 1993; presenter in field. Trustee Barneveld Libr., v.p., 1988—; grant writer, policy bd. chair Holland Patent Tchr. Ctr., 1988—; sec. Town of Trenton (N.Y.) Planning Bd., 1982—, Town of Trenton (N.Y.) Zoning Bd. Appeals, 1991—; bd. dirs. Big Bros./Big Sisters, nominating com., 1975-80; mem. adv. com. peer counseling group Planned Parenthood, 1979; active United Way, 1978-80; v.p., pres. Jr. League of Greater Utica; active scouts, libr., Meals on Wheels, others. Mem. ASCD, Am. Fedn. Tchrs., N.Y. State United Tchrs., Nat. Coun. for Social Studies, N.Y. State Coun. for Social Studies, AAUW (v.p.), Snow Ridge Ski Club (pres.), Phi Delta Kappa, Delta Kappa Gamma (state scholar, 1993). Office: Gen Wm Floyd Elem Sch Holland Patent CS Holland Patent NY 13354

GIAMARTINO, GARY ATTILIO, university administrator, management educator; b. Syracuse, N.Y., Feb. 19, 1952; s. Albert J. and Margaret M. (Palange) G.; m. Maryellen McDonald, July 23, 1988; children: Anna, Mary. AB, SUNY, Fredonia, 1974; MA, Western Ky. U., 1976; PhD, Vanderbilt U., 1979. Asst. prof. Coll. Charleston, S.C., 1979-84, The Citadel, Charleston, 1984-86; assoc. prof. mgmt. St. Joseph's U., Phila., 1986-93, dir. Inst. Internat. Trade, 1990-93; dean Sch. Bus., Social andPub. Policy, Wilkes U., 1993—97; dean Coll. Bus. Adminstrn. U. of Detroit Mercy, 1997—2002; dean Sch. Bus., So. Ill. U., Edwardsville, 2002—. Cons. various bus. and govt. orgns. Contbr. articles to profl. jours. Bd. dirs. Greater Wilkes-Barre C. of C., Internat. Visitors Coun. Phila., 1991-93, Jr. Achievement of S.E. Mich., 1999-2002; mem. adv. bd. Brazil U.S. Cen. Culture and Edn., Phila., 1986-90; mem. exec. com. East Pa. Ptnrs. Ams., Pittston, 1986-93. Internat. Devel. fellow Kellogg Found., Ptnrs. Ams., 1988-90. Mem. Internat. Coun. Sml. Bus., U.S. Assn. Sml. Bus. and Entrepreneurs, Acad. Mgmt., Psi Chi. Home: 6200 Timberwolfe Dr Glen Carbon IL 62034 Office: So Ill Univ Edwardsville Sch of Business Edwardsville IL 62026

GIAMBALVO, VINCENT SALVATORE, secondary education educator; b. Bklyn., Jan. 29, 1958; s. Leonardo and Emanuela (Annino) G. BA in Philosophy and Sociology, Queens Coll., 1982. Social work counselor Cath. Charities, Jackson Heights, N.Y., 1982-84; jr. high sch. tchr. St. Joseph, Jamaica, N.Y., 1984-86, Blessed Sacrament, Bklyn., 1986-92, St. Rita, Bklyn., 1993-94; salesperson Crifasi Real Estate, Ridgewood, N.Y., 1986—; pres. RP Prospects, Inc., L.I., N.Y., 1996—. CCD instr. Our Lady of the Miraculous Medal, Queens, 1992—, St. Pancras, Queens, 1984—, St. Matthias, Queens, 1982—, Immaculate Conception Ch., Queens, 1996—. Mem. L.I. Bd. of Realtors. Democrat. Roman Catholic. Avocations: classical music, films, videography, model trains. Home: 85-46 Chevy Chase St Jamaica NY 11432 Office: Crifasi Real Estate Inc PO Box 863930 Ridgewood NY 11386-3930 also: RP Prospects PO Box 381 Roslyn NY 11576-0381

GIANELLI, VICTOR F. mathematics and physics educator; b. Valparaiso, Chile, June 27, 1939; came to the U.S., 1966; s. Santiago and Elena Teresa (Gil) G.; m. Margaret Kay Carter, Feb. 3, 1967; children: Paul, James. BS, U. So. Colo., 1970; MA, U. No. Colo., 1973. Cert. secondary edn. in math. and physics. Physics and chemistry tchr. Re-3 Platte Valley Sch. Dist., Sedgwick, Colo., 1970-75; head physics divsn. Chilean Ministry of Edn., Santiago, 1975-78; math. and physics tchr. Ysleta Ind. Sch. Dist., El Paso, Tex., 1978—. Math, physics and electronics instr. El Paso (Tex.) C.C., 1979—; state textbook selection com. mem. Tex. Edn. Agy., Austin, 1982; prin.'s adv. com. pres. Riverside H.S., El Paso, 1986-87; math curriculum alignment mem. Ysleta Ind. Sch. Dist., El Paso, 1992-95. Co-author: Projecto de Mejoramiento de la Ensenanza de la Fisica, 1977, Curriculum Para la Ensenanza de la Fisica, 1977. Recipient Student Body award Revere Student Coun., Sedgwick, 1975; named Tchr. of Most Influence by Ex-Students, MIT, Cambridge, 1980. Mem. NEA, Nat. Coun. Math. Tchr., Tex. State Tchrs. Assn., Greater El Paso Coun. Tchrs. Math. Home: 1948 Preview Pl El Paso TX 79936-3932

GIANGRECO, CARMINE CHARLES, superintendent; b. N.Y.C., Dec. 26, 1945; s. Louis and Dorothy (Fernandez) G.; children: LouAnne Lane, Carmine Joseph, Joseph Anthony. BA, Franklin Pierce Coll., 1966; MS in Edn., Iona Coll., 1975; postgrad., Fordham U., 1978. Tchr. English and history St. Cecilia High Sch., Englewood, N.J., 1966-69; tchr. English Wallingford (Vt.) High Sch., 1969-70, Woodcliff Sch., Woodcliff Lake, N.J., 1970-79; prin. Lin-Wood Coop. Sch., Lincoln, N.H., 1979-84; dir. ednl. devel. Cambridge (N.Y.) Ctrl. Sch., 1984-87; asst. supt. Sch. Adminstrn. Unit # 19, Goffstown, N.H., 1987-90; supt. Indian Lake (N.Y.) Ctrl. Sch., 1990-1997; supt., mid. sch. prin. Greenwood Lake Union Free sch. dist., Greenwood Lake, NY, 1996—2003; supt. Schoharie (N.Y.) Sch. Dist., 2003—. Bd. trustees Franklin Pierce Coll., 1991—, pres. alumni bd. dirs. Umpire softball & baseball Mountain & Valley League, Section VII, N.Y., 1992-1997; dir. Hamilton County Cmty. Svc. Bd. dirs., Indian Lake, 1992-1997. Avocation: acting. Home: 159 Hilgert Pkwy Schoharie NY 12157 Office: Schoharie CSD Schoharie NY 12157 E-mail: ceegee123@yahoo.com.

GIANLORENZI, NONA ELENA, painter, art dealer, educator; b. Virginia, Minn., July 20, 1939; d. Teto Nicholas and Lena Dora (Zini) Gianlorenzi; m. George Michael Devlin, July 20, 1966 (dec. Feb. 1990); children: Gian Loren Kjellesvig Waering, Helena Nicole Devlin Seidel. BA, Bklyn. Coll./CUNY. Painter self employed, N.Y.C., 1960—; asst. dir. Am. Art Gallery, N.Y.C., 1961-67; owner, dir. Asage Art Gallery, N.Y.C., 1977-88; pvt. art dealer Art Space Inc., Bklyn., 1989—. Tchr. art and aesthetics St. Francis Sch. Deaf, Bklyn., 1968-71, Mt. Carmel, Queens, N.Y., 1968-71, Charles Borromeo Sch., Bklyn., 1968-71. Ford fellow, 1992-94, Loy fellow, 1992-94; Art Studio scholar, 1961. Address: 415 Rugby Rd Brooklyn NY 11226-5611

GIANNINI, A. JAMES, psychiatrist, educator, researcher, author; b. Youngstown, Ohio, June 11, 1947; s. Matthew and Grace Carla (Nistri) G.; children: Juliette Nicole, Jocelyn Danielle. BS, Youngstown State U., Ohio, 1970; MD, U. Pitts., 1974; postgrad., Yale U., 1974-78, U. London, 1996-97. Diplomate Nat. Bd. Med. Examiners. Intern St. Elizabeth Med. Ctr., Youngstown, 1974, assoc. dir. family medicine, psychiatry, 1978-80; resident in psychiatry Yale U., New Haven, 1975-78, chief resident, 1977-78; assoc. psychiatrist Elmcrest Psychiat. Inst., Portland, Conn., 1976-78; acting ward chief Conn. Mental Health Ctr., New Haven, 1977; assoc. dir. family medicine, psychiatry St. Elizabeth Med. Ctr., Youngstown, 1978-80; from asst. prof. to assoc. prof. dept. psychiatry N.E. Ohio Med. Coll., 1978-84, program dir., 1980-88, prof., 1984-90, vice-chmn., 1985-89; assoc. clin. prof. dept psychiatry Ohio State U., 1983-89, clin. prof., 1989-96; chmn. depts. psychiatry and toxicology Western Res. Care System Hosp., 1985-87, med. dir. toxicology, 1987. Dir. Alumni Schs. Com., Yale U., New Haven, Conn., 1997—; vis., prof. Inst. for Scis. Comm. and Sci. Edn., Columbia Coll., Chgo.; vis. prof. U. Naples, Italy, 1990; examiner in psychology LaTrobe U., Bundoora, Australia, 1988-89; sr. mentor U. Pitts., 2001—; sr. cons. Fair Oaks Hosp., Summit, N.J., 1979, Regent Hosp., N.Y.C., 1981-96, chmn. Nat. Adv. Council Prevention and Control of Rape, NIMH, Rockville, Md., 1983-86, spl. reviewer mood disorders com., 1995-97; mem. drug abuse clin., behavioral and rsch. rev. com. Nat. Inst. Drug Abuse, Rockville, Md., 1987-88; chief forensic psychiatrist Mahoning County Prosecutor, 1989-97; Am. Participant USIA Drug Abuse program to Cyprus, Italy, Can., Barbados, St. Lucia and Yugoslavia, 1990-94; panelist Renaissance Weekend, Hilton Head, S.C., 1997—; cons. Smith-Kline Labs., McNeil Labs., Excerpta Medica Pubs., Amino Labs., Fund for Am. Renaissance; dir. clin. rsch. Princeton Diagnostic Labs., South Plainfield, N.J., 1987-89; med. dir. med. adv. bd. Neurodata Inc., 1987-89, pres., 1989—, med. dir. Chem. Abuse Ctrs. Inc., 1987; spl. reviewer initial review group, 1995-97, health, behavior and prevention review com. NIH, Rockville, Md.; corp. med. dir. Chemical Abuse Ctrs., Inc., 1987-97; ethics com. Mahoning County Mental Retardation Bd., Youngstown, Ohio, 1995-98, treas. 1996-97, vice-chmn., bd. treas., 1997-98; psychiatrist emeritus Stony Lodge Hosp., Briar Cliff Manor, NY; book reviewer Psychiat. Times, 2000—. Author: (with Henry Black) Psychiatric, Psychogenic, Somatopsychic Disorders, 1978; (with Robert Gilliland) Neurologi and Neuropsychiatric Disorders, 1983; (with Andrew Slaby) Overdose and Detoxification Emergencies, 1983; Biological Foundation of Clinical Psychiatry, 1988, (with Andrew Slaby and Mark Gold) Drugs of Abuse, 1989, 2d edit., 1996, Comprehensive Laboratory Services in Psychiatry, 1986; (with Philip Jose Farmer) Red Orc's Rage, 1991; (with Andrew Slaby) The Eating Disorders, 1993, 2d edit., 1997, Drugs of Abuse, 2d edit., 1998, Drug Abuse: A Family Guide to Recognition and Treatment, 1999; contbr. numerous articles to profl. jours. Vice chmn. Mahoning County (Ohio) Mental Health Bd., 1982-84, chmn., 1984-86; councilor Nat. Italian Am. Found. Recipient Physician's Recognition award, 1978—, rsch. award Fair Oaks Hosp., 1979, bronze award Brit. Med. Assn., 1983, Outstanding Leadership award Mahoning County Mental Health Bd., 1986, Silver Rose award Assn. Italiano Donati d'Organo, Milan, 1990, Excellence award Yale U. Admissions Com., 2002. Fellow Royal Acad. Medicine (Eng.), APA (disting. 2003—), N.J. Acad. Medicine, Acad. Medicine, Am. Coll. Cin. Pharmacology (sec.-treas. Ohio chpt. 1990-97, pres. 1997—, steering coun., exec. com. Ohio chpt. 1990—, mem. nat. govt. affairs com. 1990-2003, nat. edn. com. 2003—), Am. Psychiat. Assn. (Disting. fellow 2003—); mem. Soc. Neurosci., Brit. Brain Soc., European Neurosci., Royal Coll. Medicine, N.Y. Acad. Scis., Am. Psychiat. Assn., Acad. Clin. Psychiatry, Youngstown C. of C. (vice-chmn. health com. 1986-89, chmn. 1989-96), Yale Club (Cleve, Pitts.), Youngstown Club, Atrium Club (Warren, Ohio), Domus (London), Morey's (New Haven), Cercola di Corso (Italy), Swim and Racquet Club (Poland, Ohio), Sigma Xi. Republican. Roman Catholic. Office: 721 Boardman Poland Rd Ste 200 Boardman OH 44512-5105

GIANNOTTA, STEVEN LOUIS, neurosurgery educator; b. Detroit, Apr. 4, 1947; s. Louis D. and Betty Jane (Root) G.; m. Sharon Danielak, June 13, 1970; children: Brent, Nicole, Robyn. Student, U. Detroit, 1965-68; MD, U. Mich., 1972. Diplomate Am. Bd. Neurol. Surgeons. Surg. intern U. Mich., Ann Arbor, 1972-73, neurosurg. resident, 1973-78; asst. prof. neurosurgery UCLA, 1978-80, U. So. Calif., Sch. Medicine, L.A., 1980-83, assoc. prof. neurosurgery, 1983-89, prof. neurosurgery, 1989—. Bd. dirs. Am. Bd. Neurol. Surgery, 1995—2001, sec., 1999—2000, chmn., 2000—01. Fellow ACS, Am. Heart Assn. (stroke coun., rsch. grantee 1980, 84), So. Calif. Neurol. Soc. (pres. 1993-94), Congress Neurol. Surgeons (sec. 1986-89, v.p. 1993) Soc. Clin. Neuroscis. (L.A. pres. 1992-93), Am. Assn. Neurol. Surgeons (bd. dirs. 2001-). Democrat. Roman Catholic. Avocations: golf, skiing, sports cars. Office: Dept Neurosurgery Ste 5046 1200 N State St Los Angeles CA 90033-1029

GIARRUSSO, ALENA LOUISA, elementary education educator; b. Pitts., Oct. 22, 1951; d. Nicholas Anthony and Antonina P. (Mazzotta) G. BE, Duquesne U., 1973; MEd, U. Pitts., 1974. Cert. elem. and secondary counselor, spl. edn. tchr., Pa. Diagnostician Assn. for Children with Learning Disabilities, Pitts., 1975-77; tchr. of emotionally disturbed children Highland Sch., Bethel Park, Pa., 1974-77; resource tchr. Peters Twp. Mid. Sch., McMurray, Pa., 1977-91; trainer U. Pitts., 1980-82; elem. and spl. edn. tchr. Elm Grove Sch., McMurray, 1991-92; tchr. grade 4 Pleasant Valley Sch., Mc Murray, Pa., 1992—. Adv. bd. Penn Star Computer System in Spl. Edn., Harrisburg, Pa., 1990-91; facilitator videotape Orientation to Peters Twp. Mid. Sch., 1990-91. Contbr. articles to profl. jours. Active Pitts. Ctr. Arts; dance study group South Side Presbyn. Ch., Pitts., 1991; usher Pitts. Pub. Theatre, 1981. Recipient Am. Legion Leadership award Immaculate Conception Sch., Pitts., 1965; fellow Dept. Def., 1973-74; Mainstreaming fellow U. Pitts., 1975. Mem. Am. Liturgical Planning Holistic Approach, Am. Fedn. Tchrs., Am. Film Inst., Pa. State Edn. Assn., Explorers CLub. Democrat. Roman Catholic. Avocations: dancing, walking, aerobics, music and art. Office: Pleasant Valley Sch 250 E Mcmurray Rd Mc Murray PA 15317-2948

GIBALA, RONALD, metallurgical engineering educator; b. New Castle, Pa., Oct. 3, 1938; s. Steve Anthony and June Rose (Frank) G.; m. Janice Claire Grichor; children: Maryellen, Janice, David, Kristine. BS, Carnegie Inst. Tech., 1960; MS, U. Ill., 1962, PhD, 1964. Engring. technician Crane Co., New Castle, Pa., 1956-59; engr. U.S. Steel Rsch. Labs., Monroeville, Pa., 1960; rsch. asst. U. Ill., Urbana, 1960-64; asst. prof. metallurgy Case Western Res. U., Cleve., 1964-69, assoc. prof., 1969-76, prof. metallurgy and materials sci. and macromolecular sci., 1976-84, co-dir. materials rsch. lab., 1981-84; dir. metallurgy program NSF, 1982-83; prof., chmn. dept. materials sci. and engring. U. Mich., Ann Arbor, 1984-94, L.H. and F.E. Van Vlack prof. materials sci. and engring., 1998—. Dir. electron microbeam analysis lab. U. Mich., Ann Arbor, 2002—. Contbr. articles to profl. jours.; editor: Hydrogen Embrittlement and Stress Corrosion Cracking, 1984. Pres. Woodhaven Hills Homeowners Assn., 1989-91. Recipient Alfred Noble prize ASCE, 1969, NASA Materials Sci. Divsn. Paper award, 1992; named Outstanding Young Mem. Cleve. chpt. Am. Soc. Metals, 1971; Tech. Achievement award Cleve. Tech. Socs. Council, 1972; vis. research fellow C.E.N.G. Labs., Grenoble, 1973-74; Matthias fellow Los Alamos Nat. Lab., 1991-92, Disting. Merit award U. Ill., 1998; vis. scientist Sandia Nat. Labs., 1998-99. Fellow TMS/AIME (dir. 1981-87), Am. Soc. Metals (chpt. chmn. 1975-76); mem. AAAS, Materials Research Soc. (councillor 1995-97, v.p. 1998, pres. 1999), Am. Ceramic Soc., Sigma Xi, Tau Beta Pi, Alpha Sigma Mu. Clubs: Suburban Ski (pres. 1981-82). Democrat. Home: 1543 Stonehaven St Ann Arbor MI 48104-4149 Office: U Mich Dept Materials Sci Engring Ann Arbor MI 48109-2136

GIBBONS, DONA LEE, principal; b. San Diego, Mar. 22, 1949; d. Donald Leland and Joan Elaine (Gray) Riley; children: Lee, Nicole. BA, U. Mo., Kansas City, 1972, MA, 1988, EdS, 1989. Vol. U.S. Peace Corps, Micronesia, 1972-74; tchr. Koror Palan Dept. Edn., Micronesia, 1974-80; tchr. bilingual edn. Kansas City (Mo.) Sch. Dist., 1983-84, tchr. gifted program, 1984-87, instnl. asst., 1987-88, prin., 1988—; prin. Maplewood Elem. Sch. North Kansas City Sch. Dist., Kansas City, Mo., 1995—. Mem. dist. adv. com. Kansas City Schs., 1992—. Mem. ASCD, Nat. Assn. Elem. Sch. Prins., Advocates of Lang. Learning, Nat. Assn. Yr. Round Edn., Fgn. Lang. Assn. Mo., Mo. Assn. Elem. Sch. Prins., North Kansas City Prins. Assn., Clay-Platte Prins. Assn. Roman Catholic. Avocations: art, gardening. Home: 3735 Kimstin Cir Blue Springs MO 64015-4577 Office: Maplewood Elem Sch 6400 NE 52nd St Kansas City MO 64119-3298

GIBBONS, JAMES FRANKLIN, electrical engineering educator; b. Leavenworth, Kans., Sept. 19, 1931; s. Clifford Hugh and Mary Jewel (Petty) G.; m. Mary Lynn Krywick; children: Robert, Sally, Laura BS, Northwestern U., 1953; PhD, Stanford U., 1956. Prof. elec. engring. Stanford U., Calif., 1956—84, 1996—2002, Reid Weaver Dennis prof. elec. engring., 1983-84, 96—, dean Sch. Engring., 1984-96, Frederick Emmons Terman prof. engring., 1984-96. Bd. dirs. Centigram, Cisco Systems, El Paso (Tex.) Energy; founder, chmn. Sera Learning Techs.; cons. Shockley Transistor Corp., 1957-63, Fairchild Semiconductor, 1964-71, Avantek, Inc., 1964-91; chmn. grad. fellowship panel NSF, 1967-70; mem. Newman com. HEW Task Force on Higher Edn., 1969-74; mem. ednl. tech. panel Pres. Sci. Adv. Com., 1971-73; Fulbright guest lectr. European univs.; vis. prof. nuclear physics dept. Oxford U., 1970-71; vis. prof. U. Tokyo, 1971; cons. electronics br. Atomic Energy Research Establishment, 1971; mem. sci. team for exchanges on ion implanation and beam processing U.S. Nat. Acad. Scis., 1971, 76, 77, 79, 81. Author: (with J. G. Linvill) Transistors and Active Circuits, 1961, (with P. E. Gray, D. DeWitt and A. R. Boothroyd) SEEC Vol. 2: Physical Electronics and Models of Transistors, 1964, Semiconductor Electronics, 1966; editor: Fundamentals of Electronic Science, 1970-78; contbr. articles to profl. jours.; inventor tutored video instruction technique Recipient Western Electric Fund award Am. Soc. Engring. Edn., 1971, award for Outstanding Achievement, No. Calif. Solar Energy Assn., 1975, Founder's prize Tex. Instruments, 1983, Outstanding Alumni award Northwestern U., 1985, Rappaport award IEEE Electron Devices Soc., 1990, Univ. Rsch. award Semicondr. Industry Assn., 1996, Medal of Achievement award Am. Electronics Assn., 1966; NSF and NAS fellow, 1953-56; Fulbright fellow Cambridge (Eng.) U., 1956-57; NSF postdoctoral fellow, 1963-64; inducted Santa Clara County Bus. Hall of Fame, 1997, Silicon Valley Engring. Hall of Fame, 1997; Prof. James Gibbons award established by Internat. Conf. on Advanced Thermal Processing of Semicondrs., 1999. Fellow IEEE (Jack A. Morton award 1980, Edn. medal 1985, Solid State Sci. and Tech. award Electrochem. Soc. 1989, 3d Millenium medal 2001); mem. Nat. Acad. Engring., Nat. Acad. Sci., Swedish Acad. Engring. Scis., Norwegian Acad. Tech. Scis., Am. Acad. Arts and Scis., Sigma Xi, Tau Beta Pi (award for outstanding undergrad. engring. teaching 1976), Eta Kappa Nu. Home: 320 Tennyson Ave Palo Alto CA 94301-3835 Office: Elec Engring Dept CISX-201X Paul G Allen Bldg Stanford CA 94305-4075

GIBBS, ELIZABETH DOROTHEA, developmental psychologist; b. Ithaca, N.Y., July 4, 1955; d. Robert Henry and Sarah Preble (Bowker) G. AB, Cornell U., 1976; MA, U. Vt., 1981, PhD, 1984. Lic. psychologist, Vt.; cert. N.H. Postdoctoral fellow Brown U. Child Devel. Ctr., R.I. Hosp., Providence, 1984-85; asst. prof. Rutgers U., New Brunswick, 1986-87; assoc. dir. rsch., asst. prof. Clin. Genetics and Child Devel. Ctr., Dartmouth Med. Sch., Hanover, N.H., 1987-92; owner Positive Devel. Cons., Newport, N.H., 1992—. Coord. presch. programs Sch. Adminstrv. Unit # 43, Newport, 1992—; presenter in field. Editor: Interdisciplinary Assessment of Infants: A Guide for Early Intervention Professionals, 1990; contbr. articles to profl. jours.; videotape producer: Early Use of Total Communication: Parents' Perspectives on Using Sign Language with Young Children with Down Syndrome. Pres. Early Intervention Network of N.H., Concord, 1993—. Grantee Dartmouth Med. Sch., 1988-89, N.H. Dept. Edn., 1989-92, Dept. Edn. Office of Spl. Edn. Programs, Handicapped Children's Early Edn. Programs, 1988-91, 88-91, Dartmouth Med. Sch., 1988-89. Mem. Soc. for Rsch. in Child Devel., Nat. Ctr. for Clin. Infant Programs, Coun. for Exceptional Children (div. early childhood), Am. Psychol. Assn. (developmental psychology div.), N.H. Early Intervention Network. Avocations: knitting, sailing, gardening, cross country skiing, birdwatching. Office: 4 Fletcher Rd Newport NH 03773-2313

GIBERT, CHARLENE WEST, gifted education educator; b. Ft. Worth; m. Wayne Gibert, 1975; 1 child, Christine. MusB, Tex. Tech U., 1964; MEd, U. Houston, 1978, EdD, 1991. Cert. tchr., profl. counselor, Tex. Elem. tchr. music Lubbock (Tex.) Ind. Sch. Dist., 1965-68; jr. high sch. tchr. lang. arts Clear Creek Ind. Sch. Dist., Houston, 1968-79, tchr. gifted and talented edn. Spring Br. Ind. Sch. Dist., 1981—. Cons. gifted and talented field. Editor, contbr: Biographical Dictionary of Gifted Education, 1988; also articles. Mem. First Presbyn. Ch., Houston. Mem. Nat. Assn. for Gifted Children, Tex. Assn. for Gifted and Talented, T Avocations: music, travel. Home: 1926 Abby Aldrich Ln Katy TX 77449-2817

GIBSON, DAVID M. dean; b. Phila., Apr. 13, 1940; s. Robert Allen and Rose Frances (Morris) G.; m. Margaret M. Reilly, Apr. 15, 1945; children: Geoffrey, John. BA, St. Charles Borromeo Seminary, Phila., 1964; attended, St. Charles Borromeo Seminary, 1968; MA, Seton Hall U., 1983, EdD, 1992. Ordained to ministry, 1968. Exec. v.p. Gar Raymond Co., Inc., Lafayette Hill, Pa., 1970-75; exec. asst. dean U. Medicine and Dentistry N.J., Newark, 1975-79, asst. dean, 1979-85, assoc. dean, 1986-89, acting dean, 1989-92, dean, 1992—. Cons. Suez Canal U., Ismalia, Egypt, 1992-95, 1st Med. Faculty Charles U., Prague, Czech Republic, 1994. Contbr. articles to profl. jours., chpts. to books; artist medical illustration Jour. Neurosurgery, 1985. Pres., bd. edn. Our Lady of Sorrows Sch., South Orange, N.J., 1980-84; pres. doctoral assn. Seton Hall, South Orange, 1986-89; mem. bd. health, South Orange, 1989-92; mem. task force N.J. Dept. Labor, Trenton, 1992-96. Grantee Multi-Lab Stillman Trust Fund, 1993; recipient Excellence award Nat. Assn. State Mental Health Program

Dirs., 1995, Gov. award N.J., 1982-83. Mem. Northea. Deans (chair), Assn. Schs. Allied Health Profs. (chair gov. rels. com.), Task Force on Basic Skills, Am. Health Info. Mgmt. Assn. (mem. gov. rels. com. 1993, chair 1995), N.J. Soc. Allied Health Profs. (pres.-elect 1995-96). Avocations: woodworking, water colors, caligraphy, cooking, walking. Office: U Medicine & Dentistry NJ 65 Bergen St Newark NJ 07107-3001

GIBSON, ELISABETH JANE, retired principal; b. Salina, Kans., Apr. 28, 1937; d. Cloyce Wesley and Margaret Mae (Yost) Kasson; m. William Douglas Miles, Jr., Aug. 20, 1959 (div.); m. Harry Benton Gibson Jr., July 1, 1970. AB, Colo. State Coll., 1954-57; MA, San Francisco State Coll., 1967-68; EdD, U. No. Colo., 1978; postgrad., U. Denver, 1982. Cert. tchr., prin., Colo. Tchr. elem. schs., Santa Paula, Calif., 1957—58, Salina, Kans., 1958—63, Goose Bay, 1963—64, Jefferson County, Colo., 1965—66, Topeka, 1966—67; diagnostic tchr. Ctrl. Kans. Diagnostic Remedial Edn. Ctr., Salina, 1968—70; instr. Loretta Heights Coll., Denver, 1970—72; co-owner Ednl. Cons. Enterprises, Inc., Greeley, Colo., 1974—77; resource coord. region VIII Resource Access Project Head Star Mile High Consortium, Denver, 1976—77; exec. dir. Colo. Fedn. Coun. Exceptional Children, Denver, 1976—77; asst. prof. Met. State Coll., Denver, 1979; dir. spl. edn. N.E. Colo. Bd. Coop. Edn. Svcs., Haxtun, Colo., 1979—82; prin. elem. jr. h.s. Elizabeth, Colo., 1982—84; prin., spl. projects coord. Summit County Schs., Frisco, Colo., 1985—92; prin. Frisco Elem. Sch., 1985—91; ret., 2002. Cons. Mont. Dept. Edn., 1978-79, Love Pub. Co., 1976-78, Colo. Dept. Inst., 1974-75, Colo. Dept. Edn., 1984-85, mem. proposal reading com., 1987—; pres. Found. Exceptional Children, 1980-81; pres. bd. dirs. N.E. Colo. Svcs. Handicapped, 1981-82; bd. dirs. Dept. Ednl. Specialists, Colo. Assn. Sch. Execs., 1982-84; mem. Colo. Title IV Adv. Coun., 1980-82; mem. Mellon Found. grant steering com. Dolo. Dept. Edn., 1984-85; mem. Colo. Dept. Edn. Data Acquisition Reporting and Utilization Com., 1983, Denver City County Commn. for Disabled, 1978-81; chmn. regional edn. com. 1970 White House Conf. Children and Youth; bd. dirs. Advs. for Victims of Assault, 1986-91; mem. adv. bd. Alpine Counseling Ctr., 1986-92; mem. placement alternatives commn. Dept. Social Svcs., 1986—; mem. adv. com. Colo. North Ctrl. Assn., 1988-91; sec. Child Care Resource and Referral Agy., 1992—; mem. Child Care Task Force Summit County, 1989-92; mem. tchr. cert. task force Colo. State Bd. Edn., 1990-91; chmn. Summit County Interagy. Coord. Coun., 1989-93. Co-author: (with H. Padzensky) Goal Guide: A minicourse in writing goals and behavioral objectives for special education, 1975, Assaying Student Behavior: A minicourse in student assessment techniques, 1974; contbr. articles to profl. jours. Recipient Vol. award Colo. Child Care Assn., 1992, Ann. Svc. award Colo. Fedn. Coun. Exceptional Children, 1981; San Francisco State Coll. fellow, 1967-68; named Vol. of Season, Hospice of Metro Denver, 2003. Mem. ASCD, Nat. Assn. Elem. Sch. Prins., Colo. Assn. Retarded Citizens, North Ctrl. Assn. (state adv. com. 1988-91), Order Ea. Star, Kappa Delta Pi, Pi Lambda Theta, Phi Delta Kappa. Republican. Methodist. Home: 4505 S Yosemite St Unit 114 Denver CO 80237-2520 E-mail: ejgibson@netzero.net.

GIBSON, KATHLEEN RITA, anatomy and anthropology educator; b. Phila., Oct. 9, 1942; d. Keath Pope and Rita Irene (Shewell) G. BA, U. Mich., 1963; MA, U. Calif., Berkeley, 1969, PhD, 1970. Teaching assoc. U. Calif., Berkeley, 1965-69; lectr., adj. assoc. prof., then adj. prof. Rice U., Houston, 1973-2000; asst. prof. U. Tex. Health Sci. Ctr., Houston, 1970-73, assoc. prof., 1973-80, prof., 1980—, chair dept. basic sci., 1998—2002. Mem. com. on parenting behavior Social Sci. Rsch. Coun., N.Y.C., 1980-89; mem. fellowship rev. panel NSF, 1992-95; vis. fellow Cambridge U., 1993; vis. scholar Oxford U., 1996. Editor: (with M. Thames and K. Molokon) Genealogy and Demography of the West Main Cree, 1989, (with S. Parker) Language and Intelligence in Monkeys and Apes, 1990, 94, (with A. Petersen) Brain Maturation and Cognitive Development, 1991, (with Tim Ingold) Tools, Language and Intelligence in Human Evolution, 1993, 94, 98, (with Paul Mellars) Modelling the Early Human Mind, 1996, (with Hilary Box) Social Learning in Mammals: Comparative and Ecological Perspectives, 1999 (with Dean Falk) Evolutionary Anatomy of the Primate Neocartin, 2001; contbg. editor Anthropology Newsletter, 1990-93; contbr. articles, commentaries and abstracts in profl. jours. Conf. grantee Wenner Gren Found., 1990, Sloan Found., 1985, travel grantee NSF, 1984, 86, Brit. Soc. Devel. Biology, 1982. Fellow Am. Assn. Phys. Anthropologists, Am. Assn. Anthropologists; mem. AAAS, Am. Assn. Anatomists, Internat. Primatol. Assn., Am. Assn. Dental Schs. (chmn. sect. anatomical scis. 1990), Am. Anthropol. Assn. (chmn.-elect biolog. anthropology sect. 1994-96, chair 1997-98, co-chmn. com. on ethics, 1994-95, chair 1996, chair com. scientific comm. 1997, mem. exec. bd. 1997, 99—2002, chmn. assn. oper. com. 2000—02, mem. nominations com., 2002—), Lang. Origins Soc., Am. Assn. Primatologists (publs. com. 1987-89). Office: Dept Basic Scis U Tex Houston Houston TX 77225

GIBSON, ORPHA RAY, retired education educator; b. Blue Eye, Mo., Feb. 20, 1934; s. Claude Bertrum and Sylvia Jane Hudson G.; m. Nancy Lou Lawson, Dec. 23, 1962; children: Gregory Ray, Nancy Ann, Bethany Jane. BS, Southwest Mo. State U., 1961; MEd, U. Ark., 1964, EdD, 1968. Tchr., coach Blue Eye Pub. Schs., 1960-61, Bradleyville (Mo.) Pub. Schs., 1961-62, Waynesville (Mo.) Pub. Schs., 1962-66; assoc. prof. Southwest Bapt. U., Bolivar, Mo., 1967-71; supt. schs. Pleasant Hope (Mo.) Pub. Schs., 1971-72, Cabool (Mo.) Pub. Schs., 1972-73; prof., dir. tchr. edn. Coll. of the Ozarks, Point Lookout, Mo., 1973-97, prof. edn. emeritus, 1997—. Coun. of faculty athletics rep. Nat. Assn. of Intercollegiate Athletics, Tulsa, 1989-95, faculty athletics rep., Tulsa, 1973-97; coach State Championship Basketball Team, Bradleyville, Mo., 1962. Sec. Sch. Bd. of Edn., Blue Eye, 1974-95; deacon First Bapt. Ch., Blue Eye, 1986—. With U.S. Army, 1956-58, Japan. Named to Hall of Fame Nat. Assn. Intercollegiate Athletics, Tulsa, 1997, Coll. of the Ozarks, Point Lookout, 1997. Mem.: Kappa Delta Pi, Phi Delta Kappa. Baptist. Achievements include coaching Missouri State Class S basketball championship team from Bradleyville in 1962. Avocations: spectator sports, reading, horseback riding, family activities, travel.

GIBSON, SHERE CAPPARELLA, foreign language educator; b. Norristown, Pa. d. Anthony and Patsy (Robbins) Capparella. BA in Spanish and French, Rosemont (Pa.) Coll., 1978; BA in Mktg., Ursinus Coll., 1991; student, Institut Internat. D'Enseignement de la Langue Française, France, 1992, Escuela de Idiomas, Spain, 1992; MEd in Multicultural Edn., Eastern Coll., 1993; ballet student, Novak and Kovalska; Spanish flamenco/castanet student, José Greco; dance student, Harrisburg Dance Conservatory; postgrad., Clayton Coll. of Natural Health, 2001—. Cert. in French/Spanish. Salesperson Spectrum Communications Corp., Norristown, 1977-79, sales and mktg. mgr., 1986-87; asst. sales and adminstrv. asst. Tettex Instruments, Inc., Fairview Village, Pa., 1979-83; owner, instr. Shere's World of Dance and Fine Arts, Jeffersonville, Pa., 1982-88; multilingual adminstrv. asst. Syntex Dental Products, Inc., Valley Forge, 1984-86; v.p. Captrium Devel. Corp., Exton, Pa., 1987-89; cons. Mary Kay Cosmetics, 1988-96; sales mgr. Spectrum Communications, 1989-92; tchr. Spanish and French Middletown (Pa.) Area Sch. Dist., 1992-94; adj. prof. Spanish Messiah Coll., Grantham, Pa., 1996—; market rsch. analyst Capital Health Sys., Harrisburg, Pa., 1995; Spanish and French tchr. Elizabethtown (Pa.) Area Sch. Dist., 1996-97; Spanish, French, and German tchr. The Milton Hershey Sch., 1997-98; tng. cons., 1999—; tech. recruiting specialist SHS Staffing Solutions, Harrisburg, Pa., 2000—01; trainer/curr. developer Capital Region Health Sys., 2002—; world lang. tchr. Milton Hershey Sch., 2002, world lang. chair, mem. multicultural com., mem., 2002—. V.p. La Bella Modeling Agy., Collegeville, Pa., 1979-82; choreographer and dance instr. La Bella Sch. Performance, Collegeville, 1979-82. Judge state and nat. pageants Miss Am. Scholarship, Jr. Miss. Nat. Teen and Pre-Teen, All-Am. Talent, Ofcl. Little Miss Am., Little Miss Diamond, Talent Olympics, Talent Unltd., 1979—; producer, choreographer Miss Montgomery County Pageant, Plymouth Meeting, Pa., 1985; co-producer, choreographer Miss Del. Valley Pageant, Horsham, Pa., 1983-84; confraternity Christian Doctrine kindergarten tchr. Visitation Parish, 1987-88; adult leadership acad., Milton Hershey Sch., 2003. Recipient award Internat. Leaders in Achievement, 1989, Community Leaders of Am., 1989, Internat. Woman of Yr., 1999-2000. Mem. Am. Soc. Tng. and Devel., Am. Holistic Health Assn., Am. Naturopathic and Holistic Assn., Nat. Integrative Medicine Coun., Am. Coun. Tchrs. Fgn. Langs., Am. Assn. Tchrs. French, Pa. State MLA, Pa. State Edn. Assn., Christian Children's Fund, Am. Assn. Tchrs. Spanish, Kappa Delta Pi. Roman Catholic. Avocations: health and fitness, travel, dance, house restorations. Home: 4700 Cumberland St Harrisburg PA 17111-2725

GIBSON, WALKER, retired English language educator, poet, writer; b. Jacksonville, Fla., Jan. 19, 1919; s. William Walker Sr. and Helen (Jones) G.; m. Nancy Close, 1942; children: David R., Susan M., William Walker. III, John S. BA, Yale U., 1940; MA, U. Iowa, 1946. Rsch. asst. writers workshop U. Iowa, 1945-46; instr. English Amherst (Mass.) Coll., 1946-48, asst. prof., 1948-54, assoc. prof., 1954-57; assoc. prof., dir. freshman English Washington Square Coll. NYU, N.Y.C., 1957-61, prof., 1961-67; prof. English U. Mass., Amherst, 1967-87, dir. freshman English, 1967-70, dir. rhetoric program, 1970-72, dir. undergrad. studies in English, 1974-76, prof. emeritus, 1984. Lectr. Yale Summer Music Sch., 1948-56; dir. NYU Summer Inst. for Secondary Tchrs. English, 1962, NDEA Summer Inst. for Secondary Tchrs. English, NYU, 1965, Summer Seminars for Coll Tchrs, NEH, 1973-75; prof. summer intern teaching program Smith Coll., 1963, 64, 66, 67; vis. prof. Swarthmore Coll., 1965-66; prof. NDEA Summer Inst. at Mass., 1968, Bread Loaf Sch. English, Middlebury Coll., 1976, 77. Author: (verse) The Reckless Spenders, 1954 Come As You Are, 1957, (texts) Seeing and Writing: Fifteen Exercises in Composing Experience, 1959, Tough Sweet & Stuffy, 1966, Persona: A Style Study for Readers and Writers, 1969, (antholgy text) Poems in Progress, 1963; co-author: The Macmillan Handbook of English, 1960, 2nd edit, 1965; contbg. author: Traditions of Inquiry, 1985, The Legacy of Language, 1987, others; editor: Limits of Language, 1962, New Students in Two-Year Colleges, 1979; co-editor: The Play of Language, 1971; prose and verse published in The New Yorker, Story, Atlantic, Harpers, Saturday Review, The Nation, Furioso, Carleton Miscellany, Mass. Review, N.Y. Times Mag., others, reprinted in anthologies and texts; book reviews in N.Y. Times Book Review, Coll. English, Poetry, Nation, others; acad. articles in Victorian Studies, Modern Language Notes, N.Y.U. Law Review, Coll. Composition and Comm., ADE Bulletin, Coll. English, English Jour., The Quarterly Review of Doublespeak, Rhetoric Review, Chronicle of Higher Edn., others; contbns. to TV and film include Sunrise Semester, CBS-TV, full-year course Modern Literature: British and American, 1962-63, semester course Studies in Style, 1966-67, film The Speaking Voice and the Teaching of Composition, 1963, videotapes on dramatic role-playing in student writing, 1971, 84. 1st lt. U.S. Army Air Corps, 1941-45. Ford Found. fellow 1955-56; John Simon Guggenheim Found. fellow, 1963-64; grantee NEH, 1973-77. Mem. MLA (selection com. for scholar's libr. 1968-71, del. assembly 1976-77, exec. com. divsn. on tchg. of writing 1976-80, chmn. divsn. 1979), Nat. coun. Tchrs. English (commn. on curriculum 1962-65, chmn. coll. sect. 1969-71, pres. elect and pres. coun. 1971-73, com. pub. doublespeak 1972-90, chmn. emeritus assembly 1986-87, Disting. Lectr. award 1969, Disting. Svc. award 1988), CCCC (exec. com. 1966-69), 5 Coll. Learning in Retirement (pres. 1990-91). Avocations: reading, writing. Home: 38 Lessey St Amherst MA 01002-2118

GIBSON, WILLIAM WILLARD, JR., law educator; b. Amarillo, Tex., Mar. 5, 1932; s. William Willard and Genelle (Works) G.; m. Beth Smyth, July 31, 1953; children— William Willard, Michael Murray, Timothy Thomas, Elizabeth Mills. BA, U. Tex., Austin, 1954, LLB, 1956. Assoc. Gibson, Ochsner, Harlin, Kinney & Morris, Amarillo, Tex., 1956-60, ptnr., 1960-65; assoc. prof. U. Tex.-Austin Sch. Law, 1965-69, prof., 1969-76, Albert Sydney Burleson prof. law, 1976-83, Sylvan Lang prof. law, 1983-98, Sylvan Lang prof. emeritus, 1998—, dir. continuing legal edn., 1981-85, assoc. dean, 1979-86; Austin. Provost jud. edn. Supreme Ct. Tex., 1992-93. Author: Teaching Materials on Wills and Estates, 1967; Selected Provisions from Texas Statutes Pertaining to Wills and Estates, 1973; also articles Vice chancellor Diocese of Tex., Protestant Episcopal Ch. Recipient Leon Green award Tex. Law Rev. Assn. of Ex-Editors, Austin, 1983. Mem. Am. Coll. Real Estate Lawyers. Democrat. Avocations: walking, fishing, hunting. Office: U Tex Sch Law 727 E Dean Keeton St Austin TX 78705-3224 E-mail: bgibson@mail.law.utexas.edu.

GICOLA, PAUL, middle school science educator, administrator; b. Bklyn., Nov. 21, 1950; s. Frank and Ann G.; m. Rosanne Signa, Aug. 3, 1974; children: Sabrina, Elise. BS, Southampton Coll., 1972; MS, L.I. U., 1976, profl. diploma in sch. bus. adminstrn., 1982, profl. diploma in sch. dist. adminstrn., 1983. Tchr. sci. Amityville (N.Y.) Pub. Schs., 1972—, asst. prin. summer sch., 1987, 88, chair sci. dept., 1986-89, dist. dir. sci., 1989-92. Advisor Sci. Soc., Amityville Jr. High Sch., 1974-85, mem. mid. states steering com., 1979-81, audio-visual coord., 1986-89; mem. bldg. planning team Amityville H.S., 1990-92, chmn., 1991-92; middle level sci. mentor N.Y. State, 1991-95. Co-author dist. textbooks. Mem. ASCD, Nat. Sci. Tchrs. Assn., Sci. Tchrs. Assn. N.Y. State (dir. 1996-99), N.Y. State United Tchrs., Nat. Sci. Suprs. Assn., L.I. Inst. Sci. and Tech., Suffolk County Sci. Tchrs. Assn. (exec. bd., v.p. 1991-94, chmn. elect 1995, chmn. 1996-98), Phi Delta Kappa. Avocations: computers, travel. Office: EW Miles Mid Sch Rt 110 Amityville NY 11701-3858

GIDEON, SHARON LEE, secondary education educator; b. Roswell, N.Mex., Mar. 24, 1955; d. Talmage Dever and Maggie Lee (Payton) Dever Franklin. BA, Baylor U., 1977; MLA, So. Meth. U., 1985. Cert. tchr., Tex. Tchr. Sulphur Springs (Tex.) Ind. Sch. Dist., 1977-80, Klein Ind. Sch. Dist., Spring, Tex., 1980-82, Plano (Tex.) Ind. Sch. Dist., 1982—, So. Meth. U., 2001—02. Author: History and Relationship to it Environment. Named Notable Woman of Tex., 1984-85. Mem. NEA, Tex. State Tchrs. Assn. (bd. regions 1991-94), Plano Edn. Assn. (area rep. coord. 1990, 2002-03, chmn. external comm. 1989, pres. 1991-94, 98-99, chair 2002-03), Classical Assn. Mid. and S.Am., Tex. Jr. Classical League, Tex. Fgn. Lang. Assn., Order Ea. Star. Republican. Unity. Home: 1501 Rockshire Dr Plano TX 75074-4007 Office: Clark High Sch 523 W Spring Creek Pkwy Plano TX 75023-4699

GIEBISCH, GERHARD HANS, physiology educator; b. Vienna, Jan. 17, 1927; s. Hans Otto and Valery (Friedlaender) G.; m. Ilse Riebeth, Dec. 10, 1952; children— Christina Marie, Robert Gerhard. MD, U. Vienna, 1951, PhD (hon.), 1996, U. Uppsala, Sweden, 1977, U. Bern, Switzerland, 1979, U. Lausanne, 1991. Asst. prof. physiology Cornell U., N.Y.C., 1957-60, assoc. prof., 1960-65, prof. physiology, 1965-68; chmn. dept. physiology Yale U., New Haven, 1968-73, Sterling prof. cellular and molecular physiology, 1970—. Mem. coun. Nat. Inst. Diabetes and Digestive and Kidney Disease, NIH, 1989-92. Editor: Biology of Membrane Transport, 1980, Physiol. Reviews, 1985-91; sect. editor Am. Jour. Physiology, 1967-69, Annual REv. Physiology, 2002—; contbr. articles to profl. jours. Recipient Homer Smith award N.Y. Heart Assn., 1971, Faculty Scholar award Josia Macy, Jr. Found., 1974, Disting. Svc. award Cornell U. Med. Coll., 1983, Johannes Muller medal German Physiol. Soc., 1980, Alexander von Humboldt award, 1987, Volhard medal German Nephrol. Soc., 1988, Jung-Stiftung for Wissenschaft and Forschung prize, 1990, A.N. Richards award Internat. Soc. Nephrology, 1992, Disting. Svc. award Chairmen of Depts. of Physiology, 1992, Berliner award, 1994. Mem. NAS, Am. Acad. Arts and Scis., Am. Physiol. Soc. (coun. 1988-90, Cannon lectr. 1993), Biophys. Soc., Soc. Gen. Physiologists (coun. 1980-82, pres. 1986-87), Am. Soc. Nephrology (pres. 1971-72, Berliner award 1994), Soc. Clin. Rsch. Home: 5 Carriage Dr Woodbridge CT 06525-1212 Office: Yale Sch Medicine Dept Cellular & Molecular Physiol 333 Cedar St New Haven CT 06520-8026

GIES, FREDERICK JOHN, education educator; b. Chgo., Sept. 4, 1938; s. Leo M. and Gertrude E. (Demmer) G.; m. Margaret Meads, May 30, 1964; children: Frederick Meads, Edward Michael, Nicholas John, Maria Louise BA, DePaul U., 1960; MEd, U. Mo., 1964, EdD, 1970. Cert. secondary English and Latin tchr., h.s. prin. Assoc. prof., assoc. dir. U. Mo., Columbia; prof., dean Seattle U. Sch. Edn.; prof., dean Coll. Edn. and Behavioral Scis., Northwestern State U.; prof. ednl. leadership, former dean, prof. Wright State U. Coll. Edn. and Human Svcs., Dayton, Ohio. Editor pub. Record in Ednl. Leadership; mem. editl. bd. Teaching Edn.; mem. editl. rev. Jour. Ednl. Pub. Rels.; contbr. over 200 publs., grants, tech. reports. Editor: Record in Ednl. Leadership; mem. editl. bd. Teaching Edn., AASA Profl., Jour. Ednl. Pub. Rels.; contbr. over 200 publs., grants, tech. reports. Former site dir. Nat. Network for Ednl. Renewal; chmn. bd. trustees Dayton Area Higher Edn. Consortium; chmn. bd. Leadership Svcs. Internat., Dayton. Recipient numerous rsch. grants. Home: 3672 Northern Dr Dayton OH 45431-3129 Office: Wright State U Kettering Ctr Dayton OH 45435

GIESE, SALLY JEAN, parochial school educator; b. Waukesha, Wis., Feb. 6, 1957; d. Ernest and Orva June (Koch) G. BS in Elem. Edn., Dr. Martin Luther Coll., New Ulm, Minn., 1979; MA in Elem. Edn., Mich. State U., 1983. Cert. tchr., Mich., Fla. Multi-grade tchr. Christ Luth. Sch., Saginaw, Mich., 1979-87; elem. tchr. Hope Luth. Sch., Pompano Beach, Fla., 1987-88; primary tchr., curriculum coord. Our Savior Luth. Sch., Plantation, Fla., 1988—, supt. Vacation Bible Sch., 1990, prin., 1993—. Workshop leader Mo. Luth. Synod Tchrs. Conf., Orlando, Fla., 1989; trainer, evaluator Fla. Performance Measurement System, Fla. Dept. Edn., Tallahassee, 1990—. Youth group leader Christ Luth. Ch., Saginaw, 1979-87; br. v.p. Aid Assn. for Lutherans, Pompano Beach, 1990-91. Recipient award for 10 yrs. teaching in Luth. edn. Fla.-Ga. dist. Luth. Ch.-Mo. Synod, 1989. Mem. ASCD, Internat. Reading Assn. Republican. Avocations: volleyball, reading. Office: Our Savior Luth Sch 8001 NW 5th St Plantation FL 33324-1914

GIESSELMANN, MICHAEL GUENTER, electrical engineer, educator, researcher; b. Basel, Switzerland, Oct. 15, 1956; came to U.S., 1986; s. Guenter Fritz and Hedwig Giesselmann. MSEE, Tech. U. Darmstadt, Fed. Republic Germany, 1981, PhDEE, 1986. Registered profl. engr., Tex. Rsch. assoc. Tech. U. Darmstadt, 1981-86; asst. prof. Tex. Tech U., Lubbock, 1986-92, assoc. prof., 1992—, grad. advisor, chair grad. com., 1994—. Cons. West Pub., San Francisco, 1988, OCR Diasonics, Salt Lake City, 1990-92, ESP Inc., 1995—; researcher Lawrence Livermore (Calif.) Nat. Lab., 1988-90, Tex. Advanced Tech. program, 1992-94, Ballistic Missile Def. Orgn., 1995—; conf. chmn., Dallas, Tex., 2003. Contbr. tech. papers and reports to confs., symposia and profl. jours. Charter mem., exec. com. mem. Tex. Tech. U. Tchg. Acad. Recipient Halliburton award Halliburton Edn. Found., 1988, New Faculty award Tex. Tech. U. Ex-Students Assn., 1990, Outstanding Faculty award, 1991, Charles L. Burford Faculty award, 1994, Pres.'s Excellence in Teaching award, 1995. Mem. IEEE (sr., sec. 1990-91, treas. 1992-95), Aircraft Owners and Pilots Assn. Avocations: aviation, pvt. pilot. Office: Tex Tech U Elec Engring Ms # 3102 Lubbock TX 79409 E-mail: m.giesselmann@coe.ttu.edu.

GIESSER, BARBARA SUSAN, neurologist, educator; b. Bronx, N.Y., Jan. 21, 1953; d. David and Evelyn (Cohen) G.; m. Philip D. Kanof, June 17, 1979; children: David, Marisa. BS, U. Miami, 1972; MS, U. Tex., Houston, 1974; MD, U. Tex., San Antonio, 1978. Diplomate Am. Bd. Psychiatry and Neurology. Intern Montefiore Hosp., Bronx, 1978-79; resident Bronx Mcpl. Hosp. Ctr. (Albert Einstein Coll. Medicine), 1979-82; asst. prof. neurology Albert Einstein Coll. Medicine, Bronx, 1983-91; med. dir. Gimbel MS Comprehensive Care Ctr., Teaneck, N.J., 1985-90, Rehab. Inst. of Tucson, 1991-95; assoc. prof. clin. neurology Ariz. Health Scis. Ctr., Tucson, 1993—2002; assoc. clin. prof. neurology UCLA, 2002—. Author: Neurology Specialty Board Review, 3d edit., 1986, 4th edit., 1996; contbr. articles to profl. publs. Dean's Tchr. scholar Ariz. Health Scis. Ctr., 1995. Fellow Am. Acad. Neurology (undergrad. edn. subcom. 1999—, Tchr. Recognition award 2002); mem. Nat. Multiple Sclerosis Soc. (rsch. grant 1989, 97, 2003, mem. profl. adv. com. Desert S.W. chpt. 1994-2000, bd. dirs. 1994-2000, counselor Am. Acad. Neurology sect. on Multiple Sclerosis 1997-99, nat. chair client edn. com. 1999-2003, mem. med. adv. bd. 1999-2002). Office: UCLA Sch Medicine Neurology Reed Neurologic Rsch Ctr 710 Westwood Plz Los Angeles CA 90095

GIFFIN, BARBARA HAINES, education coordinator; b. Mt. Holly, N.J., July 2, 1944; d. Harvey and Loris (Mantell) H.; m. Donald William Giffin, Mar. 25, 1967; children: Sherri Christine, Darrell Wesley. BS, Ind. U. of Pa., 1966; MEd, U. South Fla., 1982. Cert. tchr. Fla., N.J., Pa. Instr. No. Burlington (N.J.) County H.S., 1966-68, Sterling H.S., Sommerville, N.J., 1968-71, U. Tampa, Fla., 1975-77; industry svcs. coord. Pinellas Tech. Edn. Ctr., St. Petersburg, Fla., 1997—, Fire Chief's Assn., 1994-97. Adv. bd. Operation Par, Inc., St. Petersburg, 1992-93; mem. exec. bd. Pinellas Adult Vocat. Edn., St. Petersburg, 1991-92; treas., membership chair PAVE, 1994-95; v.p. Bus. Edn. Assn. Pinellas, 1988. Active All Children's Guild, 1995—98; corr. sec. Dillard's Career Club, 1994—97, coun. of ten, 1997—2000. Recipient Nat. Recognition award for Exemplary Vocat. Edn. Programs, 1991. Mem. Am. Vocat. Assn., Shriners Aux. Republican. Episcopalian. Home: 12338 Capri Cir N Treasure Island FL 33706-4974 Office: Pinellas Tech Edn Ctr 901 34th St S Saint Petersburg FL 33711-2209

GIFFORD, DONALD GEORGE, legal educator; b. Medina, Ohio, July 26, 1952; s. George W. and Ruth Ann (Reed) G.; m. Nancy Ray Aten, Mar. 24, 1973; children: Rebecca, Caroline. BA, Wooster Coll., 1973; JD, Harvard U., 1976. Bar: Ohio 1976, Fla. 1984. Assoc. Gallagher, Sharp, Fulton, Norman & Mollison, Cleve., 1976-77; ptnr. Noble & Gifford, Millersburg, Ohio, 1977-79; asst. prof. law U. Toledo, 1979-82, assoc. prof. law, 1982-84; prof. U. Fla., Gainsville, 1984-89; assoc. dir. academic task force for rev. ins. and tort systems Fla. Gov.'s Office, Gainsville, 1986-88; dean, prof. law W.Va. U., Morgantown, 1989-92; prof. law U. Md., Balt., 1992—, dean, 1992-99. Contbr. articles to profl. jours.; author 3 books. Chmn. Gov.'s Lead Paint Poisoning Commn., Md., 1992-94; vice chair Md. Alt. Dispute Resolution Task Force, 1997-2000. Mem. Ohio Bar Assn., The Fla. Bar. Am. Law Inst. Office: U Maryland Sch Law 500 W Baltimore St Baltimore MD 21201-1602 E-mail: dgifford@law.umaryland.edu.

GIFFORD, MARY ANN, retired special education educator; b. Three Rivers, Mich. d. Lorenzo Lyman and Anna Marie (Rumsey) Swartwout; m. David Carlton Gifford, June 20, 1964; children: Tammy, Corey. BA, Western Mich. U., 1966. Cert. tchr. mentally impaired, Mich. Tchr. kindergarten Mendon (Mich.) Elem. Sch., 1967-69; tchr. 6th grade Sturgis (Mich.) Pub. Sch., 1969; tchr. mentally impaired Pathfinder Ctr., Centreville, Mich., 1970—2001; ret., 2001. Former bereavement coord. Hospice Care, Inc.; del. People to People Internat. Amb. Programs, Russia, 1994, China, 1999, Cuba, 2000; short term missionary to Russia/Ukraine, 1995-2003. Editor: Hospice Care Inc. Bereavement Newsletter, 1990-91, bereavement coord., 1989—. Named Vol. of Yr. Hospice Care Inc., 1991. E-mail: Magifford@juno.com.

GIL, LIBIA SOCORRO, school system administrator; Tchr. L.A. Unified Sch. Dist., 1970; elem. sch. prin. ABC Sch. Dist.; area adminstr., asst. supt. for curriculum and instrn. Seattle Pub. Schs.; supt. Chula Vista (Calif.) Elem. Sch. Dist., 1993—2002; chief acad. officer New Am. Schs., 2002—.

Author: Principal Peer Evaluation, Promoting Change From Within; co-author: Eight at the Top. Recipient McGraw prize in edn., 2002. Office: New Am Schs Ste 220 675 N Washington St Alexandria VA 22314*

GILBERT, CREIGHTON EDDY, art historian; b. Durham, N.C., June 6, 1924; s. Allan H. and Katharine (Everett) G. BA, NYU, 1942, PhD, 1955; DHL (hon.), Adelphi U., 1990, U. Louisville, 1997. Assoc. prof. Brandeis U., 1961-65, Sidney and Ellen Wien prof. history of art, 1965-69; prof. Queens Coll. City U. N.Y., 1969-77; Jacob Gould Schurman prof. art history Cornell U., 1977-81; prof. Yale U., 1981-2000, prof. emeritus, 2000—. Fulbright sr. lectr. U. Rome, 1951-52; fellow Netherlands Inst. for Advanced Study, 1972-73; vis. prof. U. Leiden, 1974-75; Zacks Found. vis. prof. Hebrew U. Jerusalem, 1985. Author: Change in Piero della Francesca, 1968, History of Renaissance Art, 1972, The Works of Girolamo Savoldo, 1986, Poets Seeing Artists' Work: Instances from the Italian Renaissance, 1991, Michelangelo On and Off the Sistine Ceiling, 1994, Piero della Francesca et Giorgione: Problèmes d'Interpretation, 1994, Caravaggio and His Two Cardinals, 1995, The Saints' Three Reasons for Paintings in Churches, 2001, How Fra Angelico and Signorelli Saw the End of the World, 2002; editor: Italian Art 1400-1500, Sources and Documents, 1979, enlarged Italian edit., 1988; editor-in-chief: The Art Bull, 1980-85; translator: Complete Poems and Selected Letters of Michelangelo, 1963, 3d edit., 1979. Recipient Mather award Coll. Art Assn., 1964 Fellow Am. Acad. Arts and Scis., Ateneo Veneto (fgn.). Office: Yale U Dept Art History Box 208272 New Haven CT 06520-8272

GILBERT, DAVID ERWIN, retired academic administrator, physicist; b. Fresno, Calif., June 23, 1939; s. Erwin Azel and Hester (Almond) G.; m. Carolyn Faye Parker, June 24, 1960; children: Ronald David, Joan Elaine. AB, U. Calif.-Berkeley, 1962; MA, U. Oreg., 1964, PhD, 1968. Prof. physics Eastern Oreg. U., La Grande, 1968-98, dean. acad. affairs, 1977-83, pres., 1983-98; pres. emeritus. Vis. rschr. Obs. Paris, 1975-82; commr. N.W. Assn. Schs. and Colls., 1982-88. Contbr. articles on physics to profl. jours. V.p. Ea. Oreg. Regional Arts Coun., 1979-80; vice chair, bd. dirs. Oreg. Ed-Net, 1989-97, Oreg. Pub. Broadcasting Found., 1991-93; mem. Oreg. Task Force Superconducting Super Collider, 1987, Oreg. Pub. Broadcasting Commn., 1991-01, Oreg. Bd. Forestry, 1991-2002, chair, 1996-2002; mem. Gov.'s Transition Team, 1990, Oreg. visibility adv. com. Dept. Environ. Quality, 1990-91; bd. dirs. Blue Mountains Natural Resources Inst., 1990-98, N.E. Oreg. Area Health Edn. Ctr., Gov.'s Telecomms. Forum Coun., 1996-97; bd. dirs. Keep Oreg. Green Assn., 1999-2001, Tillamook Forest Heritage Trust, 1999-2002, North Ctrl. U., Ariz., 2002—. Grantee NATO; grantee Research Corp. U.S.A., U.S. Govt., pvt. founds. Mem. Am. Assn. Colls. and Univs. (bd. dirs. 1995-97, chmn. com. econ. and cmty. devel. 1990-92), Am. Assn. Physics Tchrs. (pres. Oreg. chpt. 1973-74), Pacific N.W. Assn. Coll. Physics (bd. dirs. 1970-74), Sigma Xi, Sigma Pi Sigma, Phi Kappa Phi. Democrat. Home: PO Box 36 Joseph OR 97846-0036 E-mail: deg@starband.net.

GILBERT, FREDERICK FRANKLIN, academic administrator, natural resource sciences educator; b. Toronto, Ont., Can., Aug. 5, 1941; came to U.S., 1981 PhD, U. Guelph (Ont.), 1968. Cert. wildlife biologist. Big game project leader Maine Inland Fish and Game, Orono, 1968-72; asst. prof. U. Maine, Orono, 1968-72, U. Guelph, 1972-75, assoc. prof., 1975-81; dir. Ecol. Svcs. for Planning, Guelph, 1975-77; prof. zoology, wildlife biology, natural resources scis. Wash. State U., Pullman, 1981-92, dept. chmn., 1988-91; dean faculty natural resources and environ. studies U. No. B.C., Prince George, 1992-97; vice provost Colo. State U., 1997-98; pres. Lakehead U., Thunder Bay, Ont., Can., 1998—. Chair U.S. TAG, ISO/TC191 Am. Nat. Standards Inst., N.Y.C., 1986-92; cons., Ont., Wash., 1971-; mem Living Legacy Trust Bd., 1999-, Adv. Council for Nuclear Waste Mgmt. Org., 2002-, Northwestern Ont. Tech. Ctr. Bd., 1999—. Author: Philosophy and Practice of Wildlife Management, 1987, 2d edit., 1991, 3d edit., 2001; editor: Proceedings Symposium Wildlife in Urban Canada, 1976; contbr. 57 articles to profl. jours., chpts. to books. Grantee Ont. Ministry Environ., Guelph, 1976-81, U.S. Forest Svc., Pullman, 1984-88, Internat. Fur Trade Fedn., Pullman, Guelph, 1978-81, 83-85, Fur Inst. Can., Pullman, 1988-90; recipient award Humane Trap Devel. Com., Guelph, 1980, Merit award Govt. Can., 1998, Queen's Golden Jubilee Medal award, 2003. Mem. AAAS, Am. Assn. Higher Edn., The Wildlife Soc. Office: Lakehead U 955 Oliver Rd Thunder Bay ON Canada P7B 5E1 Home: 340 Intola Rd RR 12 Thunder Bay ON Canada P7B 5E3

GILBERT, HOWARD ALDEN, economics educator; b. Spokane, Wash., Feb. 1, 1935; s. Alden Phineas and Hester Anne (Warner) G.; m. Lucille Dorothy Weaver, June 28, 1957; children: Douglas Alden, Daniel William, Dawnna Faye Gilbert Berndt, Debra Anne Gilbert La Croix. BA, Cen. Bible Inst., Springfield, Mo., 1957; BS, Wash. State U., 1961, MA, 1962; PhD, Oreg. State U., 1967; postgrad., Vanderbilt U., 1971. Asst. prof. S.D. State U., Brookings, 1966-70, assoc. prof., 1970-76, prof., 1976—2001; ret., 2001. Expert witness retained by various attys. Mem. Mensa (pres. S.D. chpt. 1989-91, v.p. 1992-94, 96-97), Mortar Bd., Phi Kappa Phi (pres., v.p., sec., marshall), Pi Gamma Mu (sec., v.p., pres.), Gamma Sigma Delta (treas., pres.), Alpha Zeta, Omicron Delta Epsilon, Lambda Chi Alpha (head advisor 1967-97, ednl. advisor 1997—, order of merit, Alumni Hall of Fame). Democrat. Avocations: motorcycling, building restoration, running, piano, photography. Home: 708 8th St Apt 7 Brookings SD 57006-1559

GILBERT, JAMES EASTHAM, academic administrator; b. Bridgeport, Conn., July 1, 1929; s. Carl Ludwig and Anna Maude (Eastham) G.; m. Betty Lee Blankenship, Aug. 26, 1953; 1 child, Gregory Eastham. BS in Psychology, U. N.Mex., 1952, MA in Psychology, 1959; PhD in Psychology, Am. U., 1969. Interviewer Va. State Employment Service, Alexandria, 1952-53; tng. officer Nat. Security Agy., Washington, 1953-55, rsch. psychologist Ft. Meade, Md., 1957-64, Hdqrs., Sec. to Air Staff, USAF, Washington, 1955-57; assoc. dean adminstrn. Northeastern U., Boston, 1964-71; assoc. vice-chancellor Ind. U.-Purdue U., Ft. Wayne, 1971-78; v.p. acad. affairs Pittsburg (Kans.) State U., 1978-86, interim pres., 1983; pres. East Stroudsburg (Pa.) U., 1986-96, pres. emeritus, 1996—; spl. asst. to provost Med. U. S.C., 1996—. NCES fellow, 1998. Mem. Sigma Xi, Psi Chi, Phi Kappa Phi, Omicron Delta Kappa. Democrat. Home: 1296 Waterfront Dr Mount Pleasant SC 29464-9493 E-mail: gilbertj@musc.edu.

GILBERT, MELBA CALDWELL, special education and early childhood educator; b. Daytona Beach, Fla., Apr. 15, 1941; d. William Bradford and Melba (Selman) Caldwell; m. Douglas Allison, Dec. 28, 1963 (div. Apr. 1983); children: Steve Allison, Sally Allison Abele; m. John Lockee Gilbert, Mar. 6, 1987. BS, Auburn U., 1963; MS, Samford U., 1978; M, U. Ala., 1993. Cert. early childhood edn., early childhood educationally handicapped tchr., Ala., Montessori I. Tchr. spl. edn. Birmingham (Ala.) City Schs., 1963-65; dir. kindergarten Birmingham Cath. Schs., 1969-78; tchr. kindergarten Vestavia Hills Pub. Schs., Vestavia, Ala., 1978-83; tchr. Creative Montessori Schs., Birmingham, 1986-91; tchr. early childhood educationally handicapped Concord Elem. Sch., Jefferson County Pub. Schs., Birmingham, 1991-95; tchr. Early Childhood Educationally Handicapped Hueytown Elem. Sch., 1995—. Instr. Samford U., Birmingham, 1976-78; participant Tchr. Expectations of Student Achievement; team mem. Effective Quality Schs., 1994-95, 4-Mat team mem., 1996-97. Named among Outstanding Women of Am., 1973. Mem. NEA, Nat. Assn. Edn. Young Children, Ala. Edn. Assn., Internat. Montessori Soc., So. Early Childhood Assn., Coun. Exceptional Children (divsn. early childhood), Ala. Fedn. Coun. for Exceptional Children, Jefferson County Edn. Assn. (faculty rep. 1992-96, 97—), Auburn Alumni Assn., Kappa Delta Pi, Phi Kappa Phi, Alpha Delta Kappa (historian 1998—). Republican. Methodist. Avocations: counted cross stitch, gardening, bridge, reading. Home: 2322 Old Rocky Ridge Rd Birmingham AL 35216-6106 Office: Hueytown Elem Sch 112 Forest Rd Hueytown AL 35023-2499

GILBERT, MONTINE FOX (TINA GILBERT), elementary and middle school educator; b. Albany, Ga., Nov. 26, 1949; d. Gaston Meredith and Ruth Montine (Harris) Fox; m. Samuel Claude Gilbert, Sept. 11, 1971; children: Samuel Claude III, Charles Meredith. AA, Stephens Coll., Columbia, Mo., 1969; BA, Queens Coll., Charlotte, N.C., 1980. Tchr. Charlotte Country Day Sch., 1981, tchr., grade coord., 1988-92, tchr., dept. head, 1993—. Coach junior varsity volleyball and softball teams; presenter workshop History through Lit., 1992. Co-author curriculum manuals on novel studies and math. enrichment. Pres., treas., sec. Charlotte Panhellenic Congress, 1974-78. Mem. ASCD, Nat. Coun. Tchrs. of English, Nat. Coun. Tchrs. of Math., Nat. Coun. Social Studies, N.C. Conf. for Social Studies, Queens Coll. Alumnae, Pi Beta Phi Alumnae (pres.), Delta Kappa Gamma (com. chairperson 1993—). Avocations: music, travel, theater, sports, horses. Office: Charlotte Country Day Sch 1440 Carmel Rd Charlotte NC 28226-5096 Home: 4633 River Bluff Ct Charlotte NC 28214-8835

GILBERT, NAN VARLEY, retired principal; b. Arcata, Calif., Jan. 30, 1945; d. Willard David and Mabel Lantz (McMaster) Varley; m. James Marion Gilbert Jr., Mar. 5, 1983. BS in English, East Carolina U., 1968, MA in Edn., 1976, Edn. Specialist, 1984. Cert. academic adminstr., N.C. Tchr. Brinson Meml. Sch., New Bern, N.C., 1968-70, James City sch., New Bern, N.C., 1970-71, Ft. Barnwell Elem. Sch., Dover, N.C., 1971-77, asst. prin., 1977, prin., 1978-86; coord. initial cert. program Craven County Schs., New Bern, 1986-90; asst. prin., coord. summer sch. Edwards Elem. Sch., New Bern, 1990—97; asst. prin. Havelock Mid. Sch., 1997—2002. Author poem. Mem. adv. bd. State Employees Credit Union, Kinston and New Bern, 1975-85; vol. various cmty. svcs., New Bern, 1975—. Mem. ASCD, Profl. Educators N.C., Internat. Reading Assn. (parliamentarian 1993-94), Delta Kappa Gamma (corr. sec. 1984-86, pres. 1998-2000). Avocations: water color painting, jewelry designing, writing. Home: 2109 Perrytown Loop Rd New Bern NC 28562-8583

GILBERT, RICHARD JOSEPH, economics educator; b. N.Y.C., Jan. 14, 1945; s. Michael N. and Esther (Dillon) G.; m. Sandra S. Waknitz, Sept. 7, 1974; children: Alison, David. BEE with honors, Cornell U., 1966, MEE, 1967; MA in Econs., PhD, Stanford U., 1976. Rsch. assoc. Stanford U., Calif., 1975-76; from assist. prof. to assoc. prof. econs. U. Calif., Berkeley, 1976-83; assoc. prof engring-econ. systems Stanford U., 1982-83; prof. econs. U. Calif., Berkeley, 1983—, dir. energy rsch. inst., 1983-93, prof. bus. adminstrn., 1990—; dep. asst. atty. gen. antitrust divsn. U.S. Dept. Justice, 1993-95. Prin. Law & Econ. Cons. Group, Berkeley, 1989—. Contbr. numerous articles to profl. jours.; editor scholarly jours. Adv. U.S. Dept. Energy, Washington, 1983—, World Bank, Washington, 1980—, NSF, Washington, 1985—, Calif. Inst. Energy Efficiency, Berkeley, 1990—. Fulbright scholar Washington, 1989; vis. scholar Cambridge U., 1979, Oxford U., 1979. Mem. Tau Beta Pi, Eta Kappa Nu, Sigma Xi. Office: U Calif Dept Economics Berkeley CA 94720-0001

GILBERT, RICHARD KEITH, education educator, researcher; b. St. Louis, Apr. 23, 1958; s. William Ray and Janice Sylvia (Rephlo) Gilbert. BA, U. Calif., Santa Barbara, 1981, MA, 1990, postgrad., 1993; PhD, U. So. Calif., 1997. Cert. secondary tchr. Calif. Rschr. Marine Sci. Inst., Santa Barbara, 1979-82; rschr., coord. Catalina Isl. Marine Inst., Calif., 1983-85; tchr. sci. LA Unified Sch. Dist., 1985-87; sci. and calculus educator Am. Internat. Sch., Johannesburg, 1987-89; rschr. psychotherapy U. Calif., Santa Barbara, 1990-92; cons. advanced tech. divsn. spl. projects Gen. Rsch. Corp., Santa Barbara, 1992-94; instr., rschr. U. So. Calif., LA, 1993—; head dept. sci. Valley HS, 2002—. Rschr., cons. Human Scis. Rsch. Coun., Pretoria, South Africa, 1995; cons. spl. project divsn. binary sys. and geog. area specialist Akela Corp., 1994; team leader, cons. Tertiary Edn. Linkages Project USAID, Pretoria, 1996; profl. expert rsch. and evaluation dept. alternative edn. L.A. County Office Edn.; adj. prof., rschr. U. So. Calif., 1993—; cons. tech. Capabilities, Assessment Geog. Info. Sys.; evaluator NSF, 1999—; adj. prof. rsch. U. Phoenix; evaluator MSP Projects NSF, 2002—; cons. UN Bangladesh Sci. Project, 2002; chair sci. dept. Hacienda La Punta Sch. Dist., 2002—; evaluator TPC programs NSF, 2003—. Active re-election campaign Hon. Robert Lagomarsino, Santa Barbara, 1992. Named Outstanding Tchr. Advanced Biol. Sci., NSF, Calif. State U. Northridge, 1986—87, Internat. Man of Yr. Sci. and Edn., 1996—97, Internat. Scientist of Yr., 2003; recipient Outstanding Mentor award, NSF Rsch. Dir. Fellow Program, 2002—, Am. Medal of Honor, 2003; fellow Calif. State U., U. So. Calif., 1993, Eisenhower fellow in marine rsch., NSF, 2002—, 2002; Calif. Sci. Project fellow, 2002—, Robotics edn. grantee, NASA. Mem.: AAAS, Am. Ednl. Rsch. Assn., Comparative Internat. Edn. Soc., NY Acad. Sci., Order Internat. Ambs., Phoenix Soc. (Outstanding Achievement award 1987), US Naval Inst., Phi Beta Delta. Presbyterian. Avocations: scuba diving, photography, music, climbing, trekking. Home: 6285 Avenida Ganso Goleta CA 93117-2063 Office: 123 S Figueroa St Apt 702 Los Angeles CA 90012-5485 E-mail: richard.gilbert@mindspring.com.

GILBERT, SCOTT FREDERICK, biologist, educator, author; b. N.Y.C., Apr. 13, 1949; s. Marvin Marshall and Elaine (Caplan) G.; m. Anne Marie Raunio, Dec. 30, 1971; children: Daniel, Sarah, David. BA, Wesleyan U., 1971; MA, PhD, Johns Hopkins U., 1976; PhD (hon.), U. Helsinki. Postdoctoral assoc. U. Wis., Madison, 1976-78, 1978-80; asst. prof. Swarthmore (Pa.) Coll., 1980-86, assoc. prof., 1986-92; prof., 1992—. Author: Developmental Biology, 1985, 88, 91, 94, 97, 2000, Embryology, 1997; zoology editor Jour. Irreproducible Results, 1979-93, Com. de Patronage, Annales Hist. Philosophie Sci.; mem. editl. bd. Am. Jour. Med. Genetics, Jour. Exptl. Zoology, Internat. Jour. Devel. Biol., Ency. of Life Scis.; contbr. articles to sci. jours. Grantee Dwight J. Ingle award Perspectives in Biology and Medicine, 1984, medal of François I, Coll. de France, 1996; Guggenheim fellow, 1999., Hon. Fel., St. Petersburg Soc. Nat., 2001. Fellow AAAS; mem. Soc. Devel. Biology (Viktor Hamburger prize 2002), Soc. Integrative Comparative Biology, Internat. Soc. for Differentiation (exec. bd.), Soc. Human Genetics, Hist. Sci. Soc., St. Petersburg Soc. Naturalists, Internat. Soc. Hist. Phil. Soc. Stud. Biology, Phi Beta Kappa, Sigma Xi. Democrat. Jewish. Home: 224 Cornell Ave Swarthmore PA 19081-1932 Office: Swarthmore Coll Dept Biology 500 College Ave Swarthmore PA 19081-1306 E-mail: sgilber1@swarthmore.edu.

GILBERT, SHANDEL SUE, reading educator, educational director; b. Wheeling, W.Va., Apr. 20, 1941; d. Meyer and Gertrude (Viess) Spiro; m. Sheldon Ian Gilbert, Dec. 23, 1967; children: John Harrison, Rebecca Jo. BA, Brandeis U., 1962; MEd, U. Pitts., 1964, reading specialist, 1992. Editorial asst. Jewish Chronicle, Pitts., 1962-63; tchr. Pitts. Pub. Schs., 1965-67, Long Lots Jr. High Sch., Westport, Conn., 1964-65; instr. English C.C. Beaver County, Monaca, Pa., 1968-70; dir. Readers and Writers Workshop Beaver Falls, Pa., 1983-92, Pitts., 1993—; acad. counselor Academic Support Svcs. for Student Athletes, U. Pitts., 1992—, reading coord., 1993—; columnist News-Tribune, Beaver Falls, 1978-79. Assoc. editor: BEV and BEV N.Y., summer 1965; writer, pub.: (lang. arts newsletter) Letterbug, 1985-93. Pres. Beaver Valley Hadassah, 1975-77; co-chmn. State of Israel Bonds, Beaver Falls, 1976; bd. dirs. Merrick Free Art Gallery, 1986-91. Recipient Disting. Achievement award Ednl. Press Assn. Am., 1989. Mem. Nat. Assn. Athletic Academic Advisors, Internat. Reading Assn. Home: 5600 Munhall Rd Apt 205 Pittsburgh PA 15217-2039 Office: U Pitts Acad Support Svc Athletic Bldg 520 Pittsburgh PA 15213

GILBERT, WALTER, molecular biologist, educator; b. Boston, Mar. 21, 1932; s. Richard V. and Emma (Cohen) G.; m. Celia Stone, Dec. 29, 1953; children: John Richard, Kate. AB, Harvard U., 1953, AM, 1954; PhD, Cambridge U., 1957; DSc (hon.), U. Chgo., 1978, Columbia U., 1978, U. Rochester, 1979, Yeshiva U., 1981. NSF postdoctoral fellow Harvard U., Cambridge, Mass., 1957-58, lectr. physics, 1958-59, asst. prof. physics, 1959-64, assoc. prof. biophysics, 1964-68, prof. biochemistry, 1968-72, Am. Cancer Soc. prof. molecular biology, 1972-81, prof. biology, 1985-86, H.H. Timken prof. sci., 1986-87, Carl M. Loeb Univ. prof., 1987—, chair dept. cellular and devel. biology, 1987-93; chmn. sci. bd. Biogen, 1978-83, co-chmn., supervisory bd., 1979—81, chmn. supervisory bd., chief exec. officer, 1981—84; vice chmn., bd. dirs. Myriad Genetics, Inc., 1992—; chmn. bd. dirs. Paratek Pharms., Inc., 1996—, Myriad Proteomics, Inc., 2001—. Mem. bd. sci. govs. The Scripps Rsch. Inst., 1994-; bd. dirs. Memory Pharms., Inc., mem. sci. adv. bd., 1998-; chmn. bd. dirs., sci. adv. bd. Pintex Pharms., Inc., 1999—; bd. dirs., mem. sci. adv. bd. Trankaryotic Therapies Inc., 2000-; bd. dirs. HospitalCareOnline.com., Inc., 2001—; V.D. Mattia lectr. Roche Inst. Molecular Biology, 1976. Recipient U.S. Steel Found. NAS, 1968, Ledlie prize Harvard U., 1969, Warren triennial prize Mass. Gen. Hosp., 1977, Louis and Bert Freedman Found. N.Y. Acad. Scis., 1977, Prix Charles-Leopold Mayer Academie des Scis., Inst. de France, 1977, Nobel prize in chemistry, 1980, New Eng. Entrepreneur of Yr. award, 1991; co-winner Louisa Gross Horwitz prize Columbia U., 1979, Gairdner prize, 1979, Albert Lasker Basic Sci. award, 1979; Guggenheim fellow, 1968-69; hon. fellow Trinity Coll., Cambridge, U.K., 1991. Mem. Am. Phys. Soc., Nat. Acad. Scis., Am. Soc. Biol. Chemists, Am. Acad. Arts and Scis., Royal Soc. (fgn.). Office: The Biol Labs 16 Divinity Ave Cambridge MA 02138-2020

GILBERTI, JUDITH ANNE, secondary school educator; b. Jersey City, Jan. 6, 1957; d. Charles Joseph and Rose Elizabeth (Mastropasqua) G. BS in Home Econs., Saint Mary-of-the-Woods Coll., 1979; MS in Edn., Monmouth Coll., 1994. Tchr., cheerleading coach Essex Catholic Girls H.S., Irvington, N.J., 1979-86; tchr., coach Middletown (N.J.) Twp. Bd. Edn., 1986—. Cheer coach, judge Met. Cheerleading Judges Assn., 1995; class sec., alumnae assn. Saint Mary-of-the-Woods Coll., 1990—; adv. bd. mem. alumnae assn. Mother Seton Regional H.S., Clark, N.J., 1994—. Vol., supporter Muscular Dystrophy Assn., ALS divsn. N.J./N.Y., 1990—. Recipient Cheer Coach of Yr. award Nat. Cheerleaders Assn., 1982-83, Gov. Tchrs. Recognition award N.J. State Dept. Edn., 1989. Mem. NJ-EFACS (officer), Am. Counseling Assn., Am. Assn. Family and Consumer Scis., Nat. Fedn. Interscholastic Spirit Assn., N.J. Assn. Mid. Level Educators, N.J. Assn. Family and Cons. Scis., Alpha Delta Kappa (historian, treas., pres., Membership Svc. award 1997), Kappa Delta Pi, Phi Delta Kappa. Roman Catholic. Avocations: cheerleading, culinary cuisine, sewing, skiing, travel. Home: 401 Aldene Rd Roselle NJ 07203-1802 Office: Middletown Twp Bd Edn 59 Tindall Rd Middletown NJ 07748-2799

GILBERTSON, ERIC RAYMOND, academic administrator, lawyer; b. Cleve., Mar. 5, 1945; s. Ewald R. and Esther V. (Johnson) G.; m. Cynthia F. Forrest, Jan. 25, 1974; children: Sara, Seth. BS, Bluffton Coll., 1966; MA in Econs., Ohio U., 1967; JD cum laude, Cleve. State U., 1970; DLitt (hon.), U. Mysore, Karnataka, India, 1993. Bar: Ohio 1970, Vt. 1984, U.S. Dist. Ct. (no. and so. dists.) Ohio 1971, U.S. Supreme Ct. 1981. Instr. econs. Kent State U., Ohio, 1969-70; law clk. Supreme Ct. of Ohio, Columbus, 1970-71; asst. atty. gen. State of Ohio, Columbus, 1971-73; exec. asst. to pres. Ohio State U., Columbus, 1973-79; assoc. Vorys, Sater, Seymore & Pease, Columbus, 1979-81; pres. Johnson State Coll., Vt., 1981-89, Saginaw Valley State U., University Center, Mich., 1989—. Bd. dirs. Citizens Bank. Contbr. articles to profl. jours. Exec. com. Mich. Campus Compact; pres. coun. State Univs. Mich.; cmty. affairs com. Diocese Saginaw; active Bay County Bus. and Edn. Adv. Coun., Mich. Cmty. Svc. Commn., Saginaw County Crime Prevention Coun., Vision Tri-County Steering Com.; trustee Citizens Rsch. Coun. Mich., 2003—. Mem. Am. Assn. State Colls. and Univs., Saginaw County C. of C., Torch Club, Saginaw Club, Bay City Country Club. Home: 7371 Glen Eagle Dr Bay City MI 48706-9316 Office: Saginaw Valley State U Office Of Pres University Center MI 48710-0001 E-mail: erg@svsu.edu.

GILCHRIST, GERALD SEYMOUR, pediatric hematologist, oncologist, educator; b. Springs, Transvaal, South Africa, May 25, 1935; arrived in U.S.A., 1962; s. David and Anne (Lipschitz) G.; m. Antoinette E. Besset, May 7, 1967; children: Daniel J., Michael A., Lauren D. MB BCh, U. Witwatersrand Med. Sch., Johannesburg, South Africa, 1957; Diploma in Child Health, Royal Coll. Physicians and Surgeons, London, 1961. Diplomate Am. Bd. Pediatrics (chmn. Sub-Bd. Pediatric Hematology-Oncology 1990-92). Intern Johannesburg Gen. Hosp., 1958-59; resident Transvaal Meml. Hosp. for Children and Baragwanath Hosp., Johannesburg, 1959-60; resident in pediatrics Hosp. for Sick Children, London, 1961, Children's Hosp., Cin., 1962-63; fellow pediatrics, hematology/oncology Children's Hosp. of L.A., 1963-65, cons. hematology and blood banking, 1965-71; attending physician Childrens Hosp. L.A., 1968-71; asst. prof. pediatrics U. So. Calif., Los Angeles, 1966-71; assoc. prof. pediatrics Mayo Med. Sch., Rochester, Minn., 1972-78, chmn. dept. pediatrics, 1984-96; cons. pediatric hematology/oncology Mayo Clinic and Found., Rochester, 1971-2000; prof. pediatrics Mayo Med. Sch., Mayo Clinic and Found., Rochester, Minn., 1978-2000; Helen C. Levitt prof. Mayo Clinic and Found., Rochester, Minn., 1987-2000; prof. emeritus Mayo Found. and Med. Sch., 2000—. Mem. Commn. on Cancer ACS, 1982—85; bd. dirs. Hemophilia Ctr., Dept. Maternal and Child Health, Rockville, Md., 1978—2000; prin. investigator Children's Cancer Study Group Nat. Cancer Inst., Bethesda, 1981—99; mem. Accreditation Coun. Grad. Med. Edn. Residency Rev. Com. Pediat., 1997—2002. Co-author: You and Leukemia, 1976; contbr. chpts. to books, numerous articles to profl. jours. Med. advisor Northland Childrens Oncology Svcs., Rochester, Minn., 1978-80; bd. dirs. Minn. chpt. Nat. Hemophilia Found. Found., Mpls., 1981-84; chpt sec. Physicians for Social Respinsibility, Rochester, 1982-85; bd. dirs. Nat. Childhood Cancer Found., 1990-97; chair med. and scientific adv. bd. Nat. Children's Cancer Found., 1995-97. Fellow: Am. Acad. Pediat. (chmn. sect. on pediat. hematology-oncology 1988—90, chair coun. on sects. 1999—2002, com. on pediat. edn. 1999—, com. on pediat. workforce 2003—); mem.: Am. Soc. Pediat. Hematology/Oncology (trustee 1996—98), Soc. Pediat. Rsch. (mem. accrediation coun. grad. med. edn. residency rev. com. pediatrics 1997—2002), Am. Bd. Pediat. (chmn. sub-bd. pediat. hematology-oncology 1989—91, bd. dirs. 1990—91), Am. Pediat. Soc., Am. Soc. Hematology, Am. Soc. Clin. Oncology. Democrat. Jewish. Avocations: sailing, bicycling, kayaking, scuba diving.

GILDEN, ROBIN ELISSA, elementary education educator; b. Albany, N.Y., Aug. 1, 1950; d. Avrom Irwin and Virginia (D'Arcangelo) G. BS, Pa. State U., 1972, cert. in teaching, 1977. Cert. elem. tchr., Pa. Tchr. West Allegheny Sch. Dist., Imperial, Pa., 1972—. Fundraiser Mary Rensel Meml. Fund, Pitts., 1992—, Fanconi Anemia, 1996—; participant Race for the Cure, 1998—. Recipient NASA Tchr. in Space Program, 1986. Mem. Pa. Edn. Assn. (bldg. rep. 1984-86, 91-93, 99—), Pa. Framework, PTA, Pa. State U. Alumni Assn., ASCD. Avocations: reading, travel, body building, theater. Home: 1256 Pennsbury Blvd Pittsburgh PA 15205-1638 Office: McKee Sch 1501 Oakdale Rd Oakdale PA 15071-3638 E-mail: rgilden@westallegheny.k12.pa.us.

GILE, MARY STUART, state legislator, educational executive; b. Montreal, Que., Can., Mar. 24, 1936; d. William Gillies and Hazel Irene (Stuart) Sinclair; m. Robert Hall Gile, Mar. 29, 1974; children: D. Christopher, Julia Mary, Robertson Sinclair. BS, McGill U., 1957; EdM, U. NH, 1971; EdD, Vanderbilt U., 1982. Specialist phys. edn. Protestant Sch. Bd. Greater Montreal, 1957-64; kindergarten tchr. White Mountains Sch. Bd., Littleton, NH, 1965-67; dir. Open Door Kindergarten, Salem, NH, 1967-69; coord. State Follow Through, NH, 1969-80, Right to Read, NH, 1973-74; coord. US Sec.'s Initiative in Excellence; Chpt. 1 Edn. Consol. and Improvement Act, 1983-84; sr. cons. edn. State Dept. Edn., Concord, NH, 1969-85; v.p. edn. and devel. Acad. Applied Sci., Concord, NH, 1985-90; prof., dept. head early childhood edn. NH Tech. Inst., Concord, NH, 1990-98. State dept. staff assoc. to U. NH, Durham, 1970—74; mem. Gov.'s Task Force on Sexual Harassment, Concord, NH, 1981—83; chair Trust Fund for Prevention of Child Abuse and Neglect, NH, 1988—92; mem. state child abuse neglect prevention leadership team; mem. State Child Care Adv. Coun., NH, 1994—99; pres. faculty Tech. Inst. and C.C., NH, 1995—97; chmn. State Child Care Adv. Coun., NH, 1997—2001. Pres. Concord Parents and Children, 1977—82; chmn. Citizens Adv. Bd. to Cmty. Devel., 1978—82; bd. gov. Merrimack County United Way, 1983—88; pres. Assn. for Mental Health, NH, 1984—86; Founder Legis. Caucus for Young Children, NH, 1997—; elected to NH legis. Merrimack Dist. 38, 1996—; apptd. to exec. dept. and adminstrn., 1997—98; apptd. to children and family law, 1999—; U. NH Alumni Assn., 1999. Recipient cert. outstanding achievement NH State Bd. Edn., 1985, NH Dept. Children, Youth and Families award for exemplary leadership and svc., 1999, Providian Child Care leader award, 1999, Honoree DCYF Mary Stuart Gile Award presented to group committed to devel. leadership in early childhood. Mem. NH Assn. for Edn. Young Children (Svc. for Young Children award 1998), Phi Delta Kappa. Congregationalist. Avocations: skiing, music, theater, hiking.

GILES, MELVA THERESA, nursing educator; b. Balt. 1 child, Meya Elizabeth. AA in Nursing, Catonsville (Md.) Community, 1970; BSN, Calif. State U., L.A., 1981; MSN, Calif. State U., Dominguez Hills, 1988; EdD, Pepperdine U., 1993. RN, Calif. Guest lectr. Rsch. Edn. Inst. UCLA, 1987-89; DON and in-svc. edn. CompCare Corp., 1986-87; clin. nurse specialist, educator County of L.A., 1987-89; prof. nursing L.A. Pierce Coll., 1989—; prof. grad. sch. nursing sci. U. Phoenix, 2002—. Lectr. Calif. State U., Dominguez Hills Statewide Grad. Sch. Nursing, 1990-98. Fellow Nightingale Soc.; mem. Calif. Nurses Assn., Coun. Black Nurses, Future Soc., Assn. Pan-African Doctoral Scholars Inc., Phi Delta Kappa, Sigma Theta Tau, Chi Eta Phi (Delta chpt.).

GILES, PATRICIA CECELIA PARKER, retired art educator, graphic designer; b. Chgo., Mar. 8, 1925; d. Frederick Louis and Bernice Clara (Kennedy) Parker; m. Lewis Wentworth Giles, June 20, 1946 (div. 1960); children: Alan Julian, Kay Celeste. BS in Fine Arts, U. Ill., Urbana, 1946; postgrad., Howard U., Washington D.C., 1947, U. Mass., Amherst, 1974-75, Washington Sch. Psychology, 1962. Reg. sec. tchr. art Ill., 1972. Sec. tchr. art Randall Jr. High, Washington, D.C., 1947-48; art cons. Elem. Sch., Washington, 1952-53; tchr., chmn. art dept. Theodore Roosevelt H.S., Washington, 1959-60, Boys Sr. H.S., Washington, 1961-63, Carter G. Woodson Jr. H.S., Washington, 1963-72, Howard D. Woodson Sr. H.S., Washington, 1973-85; mgr. Foreverl Living Products, Washington, 1985—. V.p. D.C. Art Assn., 1964-65; cons. art-math. with humanities Upward Bounders U. Md., College Park, 1966-67; potential supr. of student tchg. in art therapy Planning Program Staff George Washington U., Washington, 1972; visual arts coord. D.C. Congress PTA Cultural Arts, Washington, 1972; artist-in-residence Washington Srs. Wellness Ctr., 1987-88, 97—, art therapist, 2002—; tennis instr. Tenn. Edn. Found.; calligraphy instr. D.C. Parks and Recreation, 34th Smithsonian Folklife Festival, 2000. Painter: (oil painting) Mud and Roots, 1971 (award), Mural: Infinite Joy, 1991 (Golden Dolphins Commendation award 1991), Kenkin, oils, 1992 (award); author: (poetry) Mud and Roots, 1976; illustrator: (children's book) Short Fuzzy Hair, 1999; exhibited at two Washington pub. librs., 2002. Taught art workshop in cmty. Fort DuPont Civic Assn., Washington, 1960, defining creative art WOOK-TV, Washington, 1963, comparing and interacting with cultures and govts. Am. Forum for Internat. Study, Senegal, Ghana, Ethiopia, Kenya, Tanzania, 1970; peer leader in tennis and yoga Washington Seniors Wellness Ctr., Washington, 1995—; charter mem. Nat. Mus. Art Women. Recipient Commendation award, Ft. DuPont Civic Assn., Washington, 1960, 1st prize for watercolor, Arch.'s Wives Assn., 1962, Gold medal, D.C. Sr. Olympics in Tennis, 1993, 1995—97, Silver medal, 1998—99, Gold medal in Swimming, 1993, 2d Pl. trophy, NATA, 2001, 2 Gold medals, Sr. Olympics in Tennis, 2000, Am. Tennis Assn. Nat. Competition, 65 Doubles, Silver Plate (2d. Pl.), 2002, U.S. Tennis Assn./Mid-Atlantic Sectional Orgn. of the Yr. award, 2002, Dir. of Yr. award, Wash. Seniors Wellness Ctr., Tennis Set., U.S. Tennis Assn., Wash. Tennis Assn. Orgn., 2002. Mem.: Am. Art League (D.C.), Nat. Conf. of Artists, U.S. Tennis Assn., U.S. Wash. Tennis Assn., U.S. Nat. Tennis Assn., Deltakas Social Club, Swim Club Golden Dolphins (Outstanding Swimming Trophy 1993), Alpha Kappa Alpha. Democrat. Seventh Day Adventist. Avocations: tennis, swimming, yoga, gardening, painting. Home: 3942 Blaine St NE Washington DC 20019-3333

GILES, SCOTT ANDREW, finance company executive; b. Ithaca, NY, Aug. 6, 1960; s. Peter Giles and Marilyn Kay Redman; m. Catherine Elizabeth Lalley, Oct. 10, 1987; children: Abagael Brennan, Eliza Roe, William Samuel. BA, St. Lawrence U., 1982; MA, U. Va., 1995, postgrad., 1995—. Spl. asst. to Hon. Frank Horton, Washington, 1982-84, legis. dir., 1984-86; assoc. Cassidy & Assocs., Washington, 1986-90, interim dir. rsch., 1991-92; pub. affairs cons. Charlottesville, Va., 1990-97; editl. asst. Biolaw, 1993—97; mem. profl. staff Senate Labor and Human Rels. Com., 1997-99, Senate Com. on Health, Edn., Labor and Pensions, 1999—2001; dep. staff dir. House Com. on Sci., 2001—03; v.p. policy, rsch. and planning Vt. Student Assistance Corp., 2003—. Presenter Am. Assn. Cmty. Colls., Nat. Leadership Acad.; keynote spkr. Calif. C.C., 1996. Adv. to bd. dirs. Tougaloo Coll., 1987-90; adv. to bd. Alexander Graham Bell Assn. for Deaf, 1986-92; mem. St. Marks Episcopal Ch. Mem. AAAS, Soc. for Health and Human Values, Soc. for Christian Ethics, Kennedy Inst., Hastings Ctr., Raven Soc. Home: 73 Yacht Haven Dr Shelburne VT 05482

GILGEN, JOY RENÉ, elementary education educator; b. Neosho, Mo., July 1, 1966; d. Darrell and Mary Margaret (McNew) S. BS, Evangel Coll., 1988. Cert. English and elem. tchr., Mo. 5th grade tchr. Berryville (Ark.) Elem. Sch., 1988-93; jr. high English tchr. Noel (Mo.) Jr. H.S., 1993-97; English tchr. Southwest City (Mo.) Jr. H.S., 1997—2002; counselor Southwest City Elem. Sch., 2002—. Mem.: Mo. Sch. Counselors Assn. Home: 15009 W Hwy 90 Noel MO 64854-9737

GILHAUS, BARBARA JEAN, secondary education home economics educator; b. Hindsboro, Ill., Aug. 30, 1940; d. Garold Wayne and Lois Marie (Gaede) Farthing; m. Robert Lee Gilhaus, Sept. 28, 1963; 1 child, Gregory Lee. BS in Edn., Ea. Ill. U., Charleston, 1962; postgrad., Ill. State U., 1975-85, No. Ill. U., 1978. Tchr. home econs. and consumer edn. Heritage High Sch., Broadlands, Ill., 1962-93. Consumer edn. cons. Ill. State Bd. Edn., Springfield, 1976-80; mem. Ill. White House Conf. on Children, 1980; chair, mem., sec. Edn. Svc. Ctr. 13, Rantoul, Ill., 1985-91. Author booklet and consumer edn. articles; participant radio program In the Consumer Interest, 1975. Chair Homer (Ill.) Zoning Bd. Appeals, 1980—; active in voter registration Champaign County, Urbana, Ill., 1980—. Recipient Ednl. Excellence award Ill. State Bd. Edn., 1985, award Ill. Ho. of Reps., 1985, Educator's award Champaign/Ford County, 1989. Mem. NEA, Ill. Edn. Assn. (bd. dirs. 1982-88), Ill. Consumer Edn. Assn. (bd. dirs., sec., treas., Gladys Bahr award 1985), Ill. Vocat. Home Edn. Tchrs. Assn., Heritage Edn. Assn. (all offices). Methodist. Avocations: sewing, attending sports events, cooking. Home: 607 W 4th St Homer IL 61849-1017

GILL, DIANE LOUISE, psychology educator, university official; b. Watertown, N.Y., Nov. 7, 1948; d. George R. and Betty J. (Reynolds) G. BS in Edn., SUNY, Cortland, N.Y., 1970; MS, U. Ill., 1974, PhD, 1976. Tchr. Greece Athena High Sch., Rochester, N.Y., 1970-72; asst. prof. U. Waterloo, Ont., Can., 1976-78, U. Iowa, Iowa City, 1979-81, assoc. prof., 1981-86; assoc. prof. sport & exercise psychology U. N.C., Greensboro, 1987-89, prof. Greenboro, 1989—, assoc. dean Greensboro, 1992-97, head dept. exercise and sport sci., 1997-2000, dir. Ctr. for Women's Health and Wellness, 2002—. Author: Psychological Dynamics of Sport and Exercise, 1986, 2000; editor Jour. of Sport and Exercise Psychology, 1985-90; contbr. articles to profl. jours. Fellow AAHPERD (rsch. consortium pres. 1987-89), APA (pres. divsn. 47 exercise and sport 1999-2001), Am. Psychol. Soc., Assn. for Advancement of Applied Sport Psychology, Am. Acad. Kinesiology and Phys. Edn.; mem. N.Am. Soc. for Psychology of Sport and Phys. Activity (pres. 1988-91). Democrat. Office: U NC Dept Exercise and Sport Sci Greensboro NC 27402-6170 E-mail: diane_gill@uncg.edu.

GILL, GERALD LAWSON, librarian; b. Montgomery, Ala., Nov. 13, 1947; s. George Ernest and Marjorie (Hackett) G.; m. Nancy Argroves, Mar. 5, 1977 (div. 1982). AB, U. Ga., 1971; MA, U. Wis., 1973. Cert. profl. libr., Va. Cataloger James Madison U., Harrisonburg, Va., 1974-76, reference libr., 1976-87, bus. reference libr., 1987-99, govt. documents libr., 1998—2003, head of reference and govt. documents, 2003—, instr., 1974-80, asst. prof., 1980-90, assoc. prof., 1990—2002, prof., 2002—. Lectr., spkr. nat. and regional groups; cons. in field; mem. faculty senate James Madison U., 1975-79, 96-98, sec. curriculum and instrn. com., 1976-78, chair, 1978-79, univ. coun., 1996-98. Mem. editl. bd. James Madison Jour., 1977-80; reviewer Am. Reference Books Ann.; contbr. articles to profl. jours. Mem. libr. adv. com. State Coun. for Higher Edn. in Va., 1986-87; virtual Va. Coord. Mgmt. Bus. com. Mem. ALA (chmn. bus. reference svcs. com. 1984-86, sec. law and polit. sci. sect. 1982-85, chmn. bus. reference svcs. discussion group 1986-87, chmn. bus. reference in acad. librs. com. 1988-91, Gale Rsch. award 1991), AAAS, Am. Soc. for Info. Sci., Va. Libr. Assn. (coun. 1986-87, parliamentarian 1979, 81), Spl. Librs. Assn. (treas. Va. chpt. 1983-85, pres. 1986-87), World Future Soc., Harrisonburg C. of C., Sierra Club. Democrat. Roman Catholic. Avocations: art collecting, travel. Home: 326 Westfield Rd Charlottesville VA 22901-1660 Office: James Madison U Library Harrisonburg VA 22807-0001 E-mail: gillgl@jmu.edu.

GILL, JO ANNE MARTHA, middle school educator; b. L.A., July 8, 1940; d. James Hurse Wilson and Martha Grace (Hanson) Wilson Horn; m. Richard Martin Gill, Apr. 18, 1959; 1 child, Richard James. BA in Interdisciplinary Studies, Nat. U., San Diego, 1989; MA in Edn. Adminstrn., Calif. State U., San Bernardino, 1992. Cert. tchr. pre-sch. through adult edn., social sci., adminstrn. Tchr. grades 6 and 7 Palm Springs (Calif.) Unified Sch. Dist., 1989-94, tchr. 8th grade U.S. history, gifted/regular, 1994-2001; prof. edn. Calif. State U., San Bernardino, 2001—; ednl. cons.; cons. tchr. PAR/BTSA, 2001—. Cons. Desert Schs. Consortium, Palm Springs, 1993-95, Inland Empire History/Social Studies, Riverside, Calif., 1991-95, Palm Springs Unified Sch. Dist.; adv. bd. Inland Empire Lit. Project, 1994-98; mem. leadership team Inland Area History/Social Sci. Summer Inst., U. Calif., Riverside, 1994-98; presenter in field. Contbr. articles to profl. jours. Mem. Calif. State History Standards and Course Models Commn.; coach mid. sch. demonstration program. Inland Area History/Social Sci. Adv. Acad. fellow, 1991, NEH fellow, 1993, Calif. History/Social Sci. Project/UCLA fellow, 1994; recipient 1st pl. award/tchr. multimedia group presentation Nat. History Day, 1996, 98. Mem. AAUW (home tour guide 1993), Calif. Coun. for the Social Studies (presenter conf. workshop 1993, 95, 96), Calif. Assn. for Gifted (presenter ann. conf. workshop 1994, 96, 98, Calif. Outstanding Middle Sch. Educator Area 9 1997), Inland Empire Coun. for the Social Studies (pres. 1994-96, Outstanding Middle Sch. Educator area 9 local award 1997), Delta Kappa Gamma (scholarship fundraising com. 1993-94, Theta Zeta Chi (pres. 1998-2000). Democrat. Roman Catholic. Avocations: hiking, fishing, reading, travel, writing. Office: Palm Springs Unified Schs 980 E Tahquitz Canyon Way Palm Springs CA 92262-6786

GILL, MARY LOUISE GLANVILLE, educator of classics and philosophy; b. Alton, Ill., July 31, 1950; d. John Glanville and Evalyn Ruth (Pierpoint) G. BA, Barnard Coll., 1972; MA, Columbia U., 1974; BA, Cambridge (Eng.) U., 1976, MA, PhD, 1981. Instr. U. Pitts., 1979-81, asst. prof., 1981-88, assoc. prof., 1988-94, prof., 1994—2001, Brown U., Providence, 2001—. Vis. asst. prof. Dartmouth Coll., Hanover, N.H., 1984, Stanford (Calif.) U., 1985; dir. program in classics, philosophy, and ancient sci. U. Pitts., 1988-93; vis. prof. philosophy and classics Harvard U., Cambridge, Mass., 1998-99; vis. assoc. prof. UCLA, 1994; vis. prof. U. Calif., Davis, 1995; chair of classics U. Pitts., 1994-97; vis. scholar Princeton (N.J.) U., 1989; vis. fellow Clare Hall, Cambridge (Eng.) U., 1994; mem. Inst. for Advanced Study, Princeton, 1999-2000. Author: Aristotle on Substance, 1989; book review editor Ancient Philosophy Jour., 1983-88, co-editor, 1988—; co-translator, author introduction: Plato: Parmenides, 1996; co-editor: Self-Motion: From Aristotle to Newton, 1994, Unity, Identity and Explanation in Aristotle's Metaphysics, 1994; series editor: Ashgate Publs., 1999—; mem. editl. bd. History of Philosophy Quar., 1990-93, Philosophy and Phenomenological Research, 2002—. Faculty rsch. grant U. Pitts., 1981, Am. Coun. of Learned Socs. Travel grant, 1989; Ethel Wattis Kimball fellow Stanford Humanities Ctr., 1985-86; recipient Pres. Disting. Rsch. award U. Pitts., 1990. Mem. Am. Philol. Assn., Am. Philos. Assn., N.Y. Ancient Philosophy Colloquium. Home: 36 Bowen St Providence RI 02903 Office: Dept Philosophy Brown U Box 1918 Providence RI 02912

GILLAM, PAULA SAMPLE, artist, educator; b. Cleve., Mar. 1, 1939; d. Howard Donaldson and Elizabeth Minerva (Slater) Sample; d. Virginia W. (stepmother) Sample; m. Jerry Michael Gillam, Sept. 14, 1962 (div. May 1974); children: Thea Elizabeth, Chad Michael; m. James W. Butler, Aug. 1, 1981 (div. May 1986). BFA, Cleve. Inst. Art, 1975; postgrad., Kent State U., 1979-81, U. Akron, 1979-81; MFA in Visual Art, Norwick U., 1999. Instr. Cleve. Mus. Art, 1965-68, 72-78, Cooper Sch. Art, Cleve., 1974-78, Cuyahoga C.C., Cleve., 1977, U. Akron, Ohio, 1978-81, Art Inst. Fort Lauderdale, Fla., 1981—. Artist-in-residence traveling summer program Akron Mus. Art, 1978. One person shows include Coral Springs (Fla.) Libr., 1983, Gilles Patrick Studio/Gallery, Fort Lauderdale, 1984, Art Inst. Fort Lauderdale, 1985, 87, Margate Libr., 1985; exhibited in group shows at Cleve. Mus. Art, 1961, 62, 63, 64, 65, 68, Chautauqua (N.Y.) Inst., 1963-67, 69, 74, Canton (Ohio) Inst. Art, 1974, Cooper Sch. Art, Cleve., 1975-79, Women's Caucus Art, Akron, 1978, Summit County Libr., Akron, 1978, Massillon (Ohio) Mus., 1979, U. Akron, 1979, 80, Kent (Ohio) State U., 1980, Boca Raton (Fla.) Mus. Art, 1982-85, 91, 93, Art Inst. Fort Lauderdale, 1982—, Moosart Gallery, Miami, Fla., 1984, Mus. Art, Fort Lauderdale, 1984, 87, 91, 95, Gilles Patrick Studio/Gallery, 1985, 86, Barbara Gillman Gallery, Miami, 1986, Main Libr., Miami, 1986, Palm Beach C.C., Lake Worth, Fla., 1993, Soc. Four Arts, Palm Beach, Fla., 1993, Broward C.C., Davie, Fla., 1996. Substitute tchr. sch. and workshops Cuyahoga County Bd. Mental Retardation, Cleve.; active swim program for spl. edn. students, West Shore YMCA, 1971-74; coord. vols. for George McGovern, Fairview Park, 1972; v.p. 23rd Dist. Caucus, Cleve., 1973; campaign chairperson Robert Weller for Ohio Senate, Cleve., 1973-74; bd. mem. Women's Polit. Caucus, Cleve., 1973-75; den mother Cub Scouts, 1979, asst. to den mother, 1980. Mem. Met. Mus. Art, Mus. Art Fort Lauderdale, Mus. Art Boca Raton. Democrat. Unitarian Universalist. Avocations: gardening, racewalking, traveling. Home: 325 NW 5th Ave Boca Raton FL 33432-3611 Office: Art Inst Ft Lauderdale 1799 SE 17th St Fort Lauderdale FL 33316-3000

GILLAN, CHESTER, education commissioner; b. Prince Edward Island, Canada; m. Fran Gillan; children: Jennifer, Alana. BA, St. Dunstan's Coll.; BEd, MEd, U. New Brunswick. Tchr. Charlottetown H.S., Canada; elected minister for Dist. II Prince Edward Island, Charlottetown, Canada, 1996—. Past pres. Canadian Coun. Ministers of the Environ., Ottawa, Ontario, Canada; chair Coun. Ministers of Edn. Canada, 1996—97. Nat. vice chair small craft safety divsn. Red Cross Soc., 1985—88; mem. bd. mgmt., v.p. Human Resources Divsn. Canada Winter Games, 1991; chmn.vol. com. East Coast Music Awards; bd. dirs. Island Nature Trust. Mem.: (charter) Can. Environ. Edn. Assn., Prince Edward Island Alpine Ski Assn., Prince Edward Island Canoeing Assn., Can. Recreational Canoeing Assn. Office: Prov Prince Edward Island PO Box 2000 Charlottetown PE Canada CIA 7NB

GILLANI, NOOR VELSHI, atmospheric scientist, researcher, educator; b. Arusha, Tanzania, Mar. 8, 1944; came to the U.S., 1963, naturalized, 1976; s. Noormohamed Velshi and Sherbanu (Kassam) G.; children: Michael, Michelle, Nicole. Gen. Cert. of Edn., U. Cambridge, 1960; advanced level, U. London, 1963; AB cum laude, Harvard U., 1967; MSME, Washington U., St. Louis, 1969, DSc, 1974. Rsch. assoc. Washington U., 1975-76, rsch. scientist, 1976-77, asst. prof., 1977-80, assoc. prof., 1981-84, prof. mech. engring., 1984-91, faculty assoc. Ctr. Air Pollution Impact and Trend Analysis, 1979-91, dir. air quality spl. studies data ctr., 1981-88, dir., mech. engring. rsch. computing facility, 1988-90; pres. N.V. Gillani & Assocs., Inc., 1991—; prin. rsch. scientist NASA-UAH Nat. Space Sci. & Tech. Ctr., Ala., 1995—; adj. prof. atmospheric sci. U. Ala., Huntsville, 1995—. Vis. scientist Stockholm U., 1977, Brookhaven Nat. Lab., 1990—91, EPA/RTP, 1992—93, TVA Environ. Rsch. Ctr., 1994—95; organizer NATO CCMS 15th internat. tech. meeting on air pollution modeling and its applications, St. Louis, 1985; mem. Sci. Bd. NATO/Commn. for the Challenges of Modern Soc. Air Pollution Pilot Study, 1984—92; mem. tech. adv. bds. U.S. EPA, DOE and others, 1980—; hon. mem. Aga Khan Edn. Bd. for U.S.A. (AKEB/USA), 1987—90; vis. prof. NC State U., NC, 1993—94. Author: (with others) Critical Assessment Document on Acidic Depositions, 1984, EPA Criteria Document for Particulate Matter, 1994-95; editor: Air Pollution Modeling and Its Applications V, vol. 10, 1986; contbr. chpts. to book and articles to profl. jours. Dir., founder AKEB/USA Program (PIAR)for Parental Involvement in Children's Edn., 1987-97; pres. Pyar Found. for Humanitarian Assistance, 2000—. Scholar, Harvard Coll., 1963—67; Aga Khan travel grantee, 1961—63, grad. fellow, Washington U., 1967—74, rsch. grantee, EPA, DOE, Elec. Power Rsch. Inst., NASA, NOAA, NSF, TVA, Tex. Commn. Environ. Quality, 1978—. Mem. Am. Meteorol. Soc., Am. Chem. Soc., Am. Geophys. Union, Nat. Assn. for Edn. Young Children, N.Y. Acad. Scis. Achievements include research on superconductivity, bioengring., atmospheric scis., air pollution and Islamic humanism. Office: NASA-UAH Nat Space Sci and Tech Ctr 320 Sparkman Dr Huntsville AL 35805 E-mail: gillani@nsstc.uah.edu.

GILLASPIE, LYNN CLARA, education educator, educator; b. Winchester, Ky., Oct. 23, 1953; d. Bramblette Francis and Annette (Faulconer) G. BS in Elem. Edn., U. Tenn., 1976, MS in Elem. Edn./Reading, 1979; EdD in Curriculum and Supervision, Vanderbilt U., 1993. Cert. elem. educator, reading, gifted educator, Ky., Tenn. Tchr. lang. arts Morristown (Tenn.) City Schs., 1976-78; tutor, grad. asst. U. Tenn., Knoxville, 1978-79; reading tchr., migrant math. tchr., adult basic educator Clark County Schs., Winchester, Ky., 1979-90; vis. instr., supr. student interns Eastern Ky. U., Richmond, 1990-91; teaching asst. Vanderbilt U., Nashville, 1991-93; assoc. prof., dir. clin. experiences U. North Ala., Florence, 1993-98, mem. grad. faculty, former dir. clin. experiences, 1996-97; assoc. prof. edn. Miss. State U., 1997—. Cost ctr. head, tchr. edn. coun. mem., first yr. tchr. survey task force, U. North Ala., Florence, 1993-97, internat. prog. steering com., graphics standards com., 1996-97. Co-author: University of North Alabama Teacher Education Handbook, 1994, Facilitating Reform: One Laboratory School's Collaborative Enterprise, 1994; author: University of North Alabama Student Internship Handbook, 1994; contbr. articles to profl. jours. Recipient Eliza Claybrooke Meml. scholarship Vanderbilt U., 1993. Mem. ASCD, AAUW (North Ala. chpt. scholarship com. 1996), Internat. Reading Assn., Am. Ednl. Rsch. Assn., Assn. Tchr. Educators, Ala. Assn. Tchr. Educators (sec.-treas. 1995-97), Kiwanis, Phi Delta Kappa (v.p. U. North Ala. chpt. 1994-95), Alpha Upsilon Alpha, Kappa Delta Pi, Alpha Delta Kappa. Mem. Christian Ch. (Disciples Of Christ). Avocations: study of sea mammals, travel, reading, needlework. Office: PO Box 9705 Mississippi State MS 39762-9705

GILLEO, SANDRA V. elementary education educator; b. Somerville, N.J., May 8, 1944; d. Sam B. and Frances (Green) Hammer; m. Robert James Gilleo (div. Dec. 1981); children: Robert T.I., Felise V. BA, Trenton (N.J.) State Coll., 1967; MA, Newark State Coll., 1971. Cert. tchr., N.J., Pa. Tchr. elem. Franklin Twp. Sch. Dist., Quakertown, N.J., 1966-67, Bricktown (N.J.) Twp. Sch. Dist., 1967-69; reading specialist Lawrence Twp. Sch. Dist., Lawrenceville, N.J., 1969-72; elem. tchr. New Hope-Solebury (Pa.) Sch. Dist., 1972—. Libr. Village Libr. of Wrightstown, Pa., 1972—; vol. John B. Anderson presdl. campaing, Bucks County, Pa., 1980; mem. Second Monday adv. com. for women, Doylestown, Pa., 1982-894; tchr. Temple Judea of Bucks County, 1991; active James Michener Art Mus., Churchville Nature Ctr. With USNR, 1965-71. Mem. Franklin Twp. Edn. Assn., Brick Edn. Assn., Lawrenceville Edn. Assn., New Hope-Solebury Edn. Assn., Churchville Nature Ctr., Michener Art Mus. Jewish. Avocations: volunteering, tennis, hiking, tap and country western dance. Home: 2650 Windy Bush Rd Newtown PA 18940-3601 Office: New Hope-Solebury Elem Sch N Sugan Rd Solebury PA 18963-9998

GILLESPIE, CORNELIA MESSLER (CONNIE GILLESPIE), retired reading specialist; b. Springfield, Ill., Oct. 17, 1935; d Harold Vandenburg and Helen Covert (Donaldson) Welch; m. Bruce Edward Gillespie, June 29, 1957; children: Anne Elizabeth Gillespie Phelps, Marsha Ellen Gillespie Bell. Student, Bradley U., Peoria, 1953-55, U. Wis., 1955-57, U. Hawaii, 1956; BA, U. Mich., 1970; MA, Oakland U., 1975. Cert. Elem. Edn. reading specialist. Tchr. elem. grades Linden (Mich.) Community Schs, 1970-93; reading and math. specialist Linden (Mich.) Community Schs., 1985-93. Co-owner Internat. Mktg. Mem. DAR, Lioness Club, Lion's Aux., Huguenot Soc., Humane Soc. Genesee Co. Republican. Presbyterian. Avocations: reading, gardening, ceramics; Lions Youth Exch. host family, 1974—. Home and Office: 6276 Greenview Dr Burton MI 48509-1361 E-mail: coniegille@aol.com.

GILLESPIE, EILEEN ROSE, elementary education educator; b. Chgo., Sept. 18, 1933; d. William Joseph and Eileen Rose (McFarland) G. BA, Clarke Coll., 1965; MS, Queens Coll., 1967; PhD, Fordham U., 1982. Tchr. Sisters of Charity of the Blessed Virgin Mary, various cities, 1954-70, Ctrl. Islip (N.Y.) Pub. Schs., 1970—, dir. tchr. ctr., 1980-89. Acting prin. St. Patrick Sch., Dubuque, Iowa, 1960-61; asst. prin. Holy Name Sch., Wilmot, Wis., 1966-67. Bd. dirs., v.p. Timber Ridge Homeowners Assn., Holbrook, L.I., 1989-92. Grantee N.Y. State Edn. Dept., 1989-90. Mem. N.Y. State United Tchrs. (regional coord. effective teaching program Suffolk County 1981-89, instr. 1980—), Nat. Thespian Soc. (charter), Phi Delta Kappa, Kappa Delta Phi, Delta Kappa Gamma. Roman Catholic. Avocations: comedy, ballet, italian opera, training dogs, drama. Office: Mulligan Sch Off Broadway Central Islip NY 11722 Home: 420 Sunset Dr Wilmette IL 60091-3031

GILLET, PAMELA KIPPING, special education educator; EdB in Elem. Edn., Chgo. Tchrs. Coll., 1963; MA in Mental Retardation, Northeastern Ill. U., 1966; PhD in Gen. Spl. Edn./Adminstrn., Walden U., 1976. Cert. elem. edn., early childhood edn., learning disabled, mental retardation, behavior disorders, supt., supr. and dir. spl. edn. 4th grade tchr. Dist. # 83 Mannheim, Frankling Park, Ill., 1963—64; h.s. spl. edn. tchr. Dist. # 207 Maine Twp., Park Ridge, Ill., 1964—67, prevocational coord., 1967—69, dept. chmn. spl. edn. dept., 1969—70; dir. EPDA tchr. tng. program Chgo. Consortium Colls. and Univs., Northwest Ednl. Coop., Palatine, Ill., 1970—71; prin. West Suburban Spl. Edn. Ctr., Cicero, Ill., 1971—73; supr. West Suburban Assn. Spl. Edn., Cicero, 1973—75; asst. dir. Northwest Suburban Spl. Edn. Orgn., Palatine, 1975—78, supt. Mt. Prospect, Ill., 1978—96; spl. edn. cons., 1996—. Adj. instr. Northeastern Ill. U., Chgo. State U., Corcordia Coll., Barat Coll., Nat. Coll. Edn., Roosevelt U.; mem. task forces ISBE, 1975—2007, cons. career edn. project, 1977—78, spl. edn. demandate study group, 1983—85; cons. Ednl. Testing Svc.; tchr. edn. coun. Northeastern Ill. U., 1981—97, dean's grant program, 1982—97; workshop leader, 1974—; lectr., cons. in field. Author: Auditory Processes, 1974, rev., 1992, Career Education for Children, 1978, Of Work and Worth: Career

Education Programming for Exceptional Children and Youths, 1981; contbr. articles to profl. jours., chapters to books. Bd. dirs. Found. Exceptional Children, 1996—, pres., 1999—. Recipient Cmty. Svc. award, Am. Legion, 1976, 1980, Alumnus of Yr. award, Northeastern Ill. U., 1984, Learning Disabilities of Am. Contributors award, Coun. Understanding Learning Disabilities, 1992, Those Who Excel award of excellence, Ill. State Bd. of Edn., 1994, Outstanding Svc. award, Divsn. Mental Retardation and Devel. Disabilities, 1994, Sleznick award, Coun. of Admin. of Spl. Edn., 1996, Outstanding Contbr. award, Coun. Exceptional Children, 1996, Burton Blatt award, Divsn. on Metal Retardation and Devel. Disabilities, 1997, Spl. Edn. Leadership award, Ill. Adminstrs. of Spl. Edn., 1995, Outstanding Spl. Edn. Adminstr. of Yr. award, 1997. Mem.: ASCD, Found. for Exceptional Children (pres. 2000—), Ill. Adminstrs. Spl. Edn. (pres. 1994—95), Coun. Exceptional Children (pres. Ill. chpt. 1975—77, bd. govs. 1977—80, 1996—2000, pres. mental retardation divsn. 1983—85, bd. govs. 1986, exec. com. 1989—92, v.p. internat. 1992—93, pres.-elect 1993—94, pres. 1994—95, bd. dirs. 2000—, Meritorious Svc. award Ill. 1983), Assn. Children with Learning Disabilities, Am. Assn. Sch. Adminstrs. Home and Office: 413 Courtley Oaks Blvd Winter Garden FL 34787

GILLETT, JAMES WARREN, ecotoxicology educator; b. Sept. 18, 1933; s. Ira Elijah and Atha Arthela (Morlan) Gillett; m. Mary Francis Hebert, Aug. 7, 1970; children: Grant Jameson, Iain; m. Mary Alexia Stuart, June 26, 1958 (div. Apr. 1970); children: John Stuart, Peter Warren. BS, U. Kans., 1955; PhD, U. Calif., Berkeley, 1962. Postdoctoral rsch. chemist U. Calif., Berkeley, 1962-64; asst. prof. agrl. chemistry Oreg. State U., Corvallis, 1964-69, assoc. prof., 1969-74; rsch. ecologist EPA/Environ. Rsch. Lab., Corvallis, 1974-81, rsch. environ. scientist, 1981-83; prof. ecotoxicology dept. natural resources Cornell U., Ithaca, N.Y., 1983—, dir. superfund basic rsch. program, 1992—2001. Dir. Inst. for Comparative and Environ. Toxicology, 1986-92, Risk Analysis Studies minor field of grad study. Editor, pub.: Biological Impact of Pesticides in the Environment, 1971; editor: Terrestrial Microcosms, 1979; editor: (jour.) Hazard Assessment, Environ. Toxicology & Chemistry, 1988-93; contbr. articles to profl. jours. Chmn. bd. Oreg. Mus. Sci. and Industry, 1969-71, Cmty. Action Program, 1970-72; sec. Willamette Soccer League, 1970-74; coach Corvallis Womens Soccer Team, 1979-81; pres., founder Esophagal Cancer Awareness Assn., 2002-. Summerfield scholar, 1951-54. Mem. Soc. Environ. Toxicology and Chemistry (bd. dirs. 1984-88), Alpha Kappa Lambda, Toastmasters (pres. 1974). Office: Cornell U Ctr for Environment 216 Rice Hall Ithaca NY 14853 E-mail: jwg3@cornell.edu.

GILLETT, PATRICIA, family and acute care nurse practitioner, clinical nurse; b. Mass., Jan. 2, 1948; d. Clyde and Estelle (Carter) Gleason; m. Warren Gillett, July 1968; children: Michael, James. ADN, Berkshire Community Coll.; BSN, U. N.Mex.; MSN, U. Tex., El Paso; FNP, Tex. Tech. Univ. Nursing instr. U. Albuquerque, Albuquerque T-VI; critical care edn. coord. St. Joseph Med. Ctr., Albuquerque VA Med. Ctr.; faculty U. N. Mex., Coll. of Nursing. Mem. ANA, AACN (Outstanding Cricital Care Educator 1989), Am. Acad. Nurse Practitioners, N.Mex. Nurses Assn. (award for clin. excellence 1994), Sigma Theta Tau.

GILLETTE, HALBERT GEORGE, mathematics educator; b. Kansas City, Mo., Sept. 18, 1926; s. Halbert Reginald and Vinada Pearl (Varnado) G.; m. Dorothy Helene Youmans, Apr. 20, 1947; children: Richard Wayne, Susan Helene, Kenneth George, Eric Glen. BA, U. Nebr., 1964; MEd, Tulane U., 1974; EdS, Stetson U., 1983; postgrad., Calif. Coast. U., 1999—. Math., sci. and sci. research tchr. L.B. Johnson Jr. High Sch., Melbourne, Fla., 1974-76; math tchr. J. Madison Middle Sch., Titusville, Fla., 1976-77; math./sci. tchr. Titusville High Sch., 1977-78; tchr. math. Cocoa H.S., Fla., 1978-94. Chmn. dept. math. Cocoa H.S., 1987-94; adj. math. instr. Brevard C.C., Cocoa, 1983-2001; assoc. math. instr. Keiser Coll., Melbourne, Fla., 1996; math./sci. facilitator grad. tchr. edn. program Nova Southeastern U., Ft. Lauderdale, 1997-2001; question writer Fla. H.S. Acad. Tournament, 1985-1992, judge 1985—; question writer Nat. Tournament for Acad. Excellence, 1987-92, judge, 1987—. Del. leader People-to-People Friendship Caravan to USSR, 1990, to Australia, 1991; mem. del. 1st Joint U.S./Russia Conf. on Math. Edn., 1993. Lt. comdr. USN, 1944-74, ret. Named Tchr. of the Yr., Cocoa High Sch., 1983-84. Mem. Nat. Coun. Tchrs. Math., Fla. Coun. Tchrs. Math., Brevard Coun. Tchrs. Math. (treas. 1983—), Assn. Former Intelligence Officers (Nat. and Satellite chpts., v.p. Satellite chpt. 1994-96, pres. 1997-2000), Ret. Officers Assn. (Nat. and Cape Canaveral chpts. 1974—), Navy League U.S., Naval Investigative Svc. Retirees Fla. (sec. 1994—, treas. 1998—), Assn. Ret. Naval Investigative Svc. Spl. Agts., Astronaut Trail Shell Club, Fla. Ret. Educators Assn., Ctrl. Brevard Ret. Educators Assn. Home: 3740 Ocean Beach Blvd # 404 Cocoa Beach FL 32931-5405 E-mail: g4169@bellsouth.net.

GILLEY, EDWARD RAY, school system administrator; b. Jenkins, Ky., Sept. 17, 1939; s. Farley and M. Darlene (Mullins) G.; m. Shirley Gilley; children: David, Steven, Diana, Gary, Ed Jr. BS, US Naval Postgrad. Sch., 1973; MA, Cen. Mich. U., 1980; EdD, U. So. Miss., 1985; postgrad., Vanderbuilt U., 1988. Cert. tchr., Miss., Tenn., Alaska. Commd. ensign USN, 1954, advanced through grades to lt. comdr., 1979; tchr. Bradley County Cen. High Sch., Cleveland, Tenn.; prin.-facilitator-asst. supt. Monroe County Tenn. Sch. System, Tellico Plains; supt. Vicksburg (Miss.) Warren Sch. Dist., Adak (Alaska) Region Sch. Dist. Decorated Bronze Star medal, Air medal, Meritorious Svc. medal. Mem. Alaska Assn. Sch. Adminstrs., Alaska Coun. Sch. Adminstrs., NASSP, Horace Mann League Educators, Phi Kappa Delta, Phi Delta Kappa. Home and Office: Adak Region Sch Dist 801 W 10th St Ste 200 Juneau AK 99801-1878

GILLIAM, M(ELVIN) RANDOLPH, retired urologist, educator; b. Jan. 5, 1921; s. Adolphus and Grace (Thornsberry) Gilliam; m. Sara Dee Rainey, May 15, 1948; children: Elizabeth Neal, Virginia Dee, Bryan Randolph, Frank Stuart, Grace Carroll. Student, Centre Coll. of Ky., 1938-41; MD, U. Louisville, 1944. Diplomate Am. Bd. Urology. Intern Norfolk (Va.) Marine Hosp., 1944-45; resident in urology Nichols VA Hosp., Louisville, 1947-50; pvt. practice medicine specializing in urology Lexington, Ky., 1950-98; retired, 1998. Ptnr. Commonwealth Urology, P.S.C., Lexington, Ky., 1971—98; clin. prof. urology U. Ky. Med. Sch., 1964—98, prof. emeritus, 1998—; chief urology Good Samaritan Hosp.; staff mem. Ctrl. Bapt. Hosp., St. Joseph's Hosp. Capt. U.S. Army, 1945—47. Mem.: AMA, Fayette County Med. Soc. (past pres.), Ky. Med. Assn., Am. Urology Assn. Republican. Methodist. Home: 1244 Summitt Dr Lexington KY 40502-2273

GILLIAM, VINCENT CARVER, religion educator, minister, writer; b. Boston, Mar. 24, 1944; s. Wayland Westfield and Belle (Vincent) G.; m. Linda Hassan, June 22, 1970 (div. 1979); children: Halima K., Sumaiya B., Fatimah Z.; m. Nandini Vasudev Katre, Sept. 1, 1991; children: Raphael K. AB in English Lit., Stanford U., 1968; M of Religion, Claremont Sch. Theology, 1970; MA, PhD in Religious Studies and Humanities, Stanford U., 1990. Ordained to ministry United Ch. of Christ, 1982. Asst. and youth min. Lincoln Meml. Congl. Ch., L.A., 1968-69, adj. assoc. min., 1982-86; exec. dir. Coalition for Haitian Asylum, Oakland, Calif., 1983-84; rsch. asst. Martin Luther King Jr. Papers Project, Stanford, Calif., 1985-87; President's fellow U. Calif., Berkeley, 1990-92, rsch. fellow, 1992-95. Bd. dirs. United East Oakland Clergy, 1982-84, Am. Friends Svc. Com., San Francisco, 1983—, exec. com., 1990—. Pres.'s fellow U. Calif., Berkeley, 1990-92. Fellow Soc. for Values in Higher Edn.; mem. Am. Acad. Religion, Soc. Bibl. Lit., Am. Hist. Assn., Am. Soc. Ch. History, Medieval Acad. Am., MLA, Renaissance Soc. Am. Democrat. Office: PO Box 1002 Solana Beach CA 92075-1002

GILLIES, DONALD RICHARD, marketing and advertising consultant, educator; b. Sioux Falls, SD, Jan. 14, 1939; s. Donald Franklin and Gladys O. (Gullickson) G.; m. Twyla Elaine Bloomquist, Apr. 7, 1962; children: Dawn, Trent, Tara. BA in Journalism/Advt., U. Minn., 1961. Writer, producer Sta. WCCO-TV, Mpls., 1954-60; mgmt. supr., sr. v.p., bd. dirs. Campbell-Mithun Advt., Mpls., 1960-86; pres., chief oper. officer Colle & McVoy Inc., Mpls., 1987-89; prin. Gillies group inc. (Gg), Minnetonka, Minn., 1989—. Adj. prof. U. St. Thomas, 1990-97, asst. prof., 2001—. Bd. dirs. Guthrie Theater, Mpls., 1979-84; ch. coun. Mt. Olivet Ch., Mpls., 1988-94; Midwest adv. rev. bd. BBB, 1996—. Mem. Am. Assn. Advt. Agencies (regional gov.), Minn. Advt. Fedn. (bd. dirs. 1973-76). Lutheran. Home and Office: Gillies group inc (Gg) 5942 Fairwood Ln Minnetonka MN 55345-6533 E-mail: dongillies@prodigy.net.

GILLIGAN, SANDRA KAYE, private school director; b. Ft. Lewis, Wash., Mar. 22, 1946; d. Jack G. and O. Ruth (Mitchell) Wagoner; m. James J. Gilligan, June 3, 1972 (div. June 1998); 1 child, J. Shawn Gilligan. BS in Edn., Emporia State U., 1968, MS in Psychology, 1971; postgrad., Drake U., 1976, U. Mo., St. Louis, 1977-79. Tchr. Parklane Elem. Sch., Aurora, Colo., 1968-69, Bonner Springs (Kans.) Elem., 1970; stewardess Frontier Airlines, Denver, 1969; grad. teaching asst. Emporia (Kans.) State U., 1970-71; lead tchr. Western Valley Youth Ranch, Buckeye, Ariz., 1971-74; staff mem. program devel., lead tchr. The New Found., Phoenix, 1974; ednl. therapist Orchard Pl., Des Moines, 1974-76; ednl. cons. Spl. Sch. Dist. of St. Louis County, 1976-79; founding dir. The Churchill Sch., St. Louis, 1978—. Instr. Webster Coll., Webster Groves, Mo., 1978-80; adj. prof. Maryville Coll., St. Louis, summer 1985; keynote spkr. Miss. Learning Disabilities Assn. Conv., 1991; site visitor blue ribbon schs. program U.S. Dept. Edn., 1992; mem. Evaluation Review Com. Indep. Sch. of Ctrl. States; cert. trainer Human Potential Seminars; presenter in field. Mem. Learning Disabilities Assn., Internat. Dyslexia Assn., St. Louis Jr. League. Avocations: gardening, painting. Office: The Churchill Sch 1035 Price School Ln Saint Louis MO 63124-1596

GILLILAND, DIANE, elementary school educator; b. Clinton, Iowa, July 14, 1951; d. Carl J. and Maxine L.M. Jessen; m. Rick E. Gilliland, June 2, 1972; children: Michael, Gina. AA, Mt. St. Clare Coll., 1971; BA in Elem. Edn., Augustana Coll., 1973; MS in Ednl. Adminstrn., Western Ill. U., 1990. Cert. elem. edn. Tchr. 5th and 3rd grade Rockridge Sch. Dist. 300, Taylor Ridge, Ill.; tchr. 5th and 6th grades Rock Island Sch. Dist. Mem. ASCD, NEA, Rock Island Ed. Assn.(RIEA), Ill. Edn. Assn., Frances Willard PTA, Andalusia Libr. Bd., Andalusia Baseball Assn. (v.p.), Andalusia Lions, Phi Delta Kappa, Delta Kappa Gamma. Home: 853 2nd Ave W Andalusia IL 61232-9999

GILLILAND, RICK E. elementary education educator; b. Ottumwa, Iowa, July 9, 1948; s. Donald Franklin and Lorreta Vondean (Manos) White; m. Diane M. Gilliland, June 3, 1972; children: Michael, Gina. AA, Centerville Community Coll., 1968; BSEd, SE Mo. State U., 1970; MS, Western Ill. U., 1975. Cert. elem. edn. K-8th grades, secondary edn. 6th-12th grades, phys. edn. specialist K-14th grades. Phys. edn. tchr. K-6 Rock Island (Ill.) Sch. Dist., 1981—2002; dir. phys. edn. Clinton (Iowa) YMCA, 1970-71; elem. tchr. Rock Island Sch. Dist. 41, 1985—. Co-author: Rock Island School District Physical Education Curriculum Guide. Trustee Andalusia Village. Mem. Phi Delta Kappa, Phi Kappa Phi. Home: 853 2nd Ave W PO Box 272 Andalusia IL 61232-0272

GILLIN, CAROL ANN, middle school educator; b. Phila., July 19, 1942; d. Harry Joseph and Louise Dolores (Hewitt) G. AB in English Lit., Chestnut Hill Coll., 1972; MEd in Reading, Temple U., 1978, postgrad., 1990—. Cert. elem. educator, reading specialist, N.J., Pa. Tchr. Phila. and N.J. Parochial Schs., 1962-76; reading specialist Camden (N.J.) Bd. Edn., 1976-80, Corpus Christi Sch., Lansdale, Pa., 1980-82; asst. prof. edn., supr. student tchrs. Rosemont (Pa.) Coll., 1982-86, acting dir. edn., asst. acad. dean, 1985-88; mid. sch. tchr. Phila. Sch. System, 1988—. Tchr. cons. Phila. Writing Project; presenter, lectr. in field; mem. rsch. project Taking Stock, Making Change, U. Pa.; instr. Chestnut Hill Coll., 1998—; sr. career tchr. Phila. Sch. Sys., enhanced compensation project, 2003—; adv. bd. Schuykill Ctr. Environ. Edn., Phila, 1999—; participant enhanced compensation sys. pilot, 2003 Bd. dirs. Archbishop Prendergast H.S. Alumnae, Drexel Hill, Pa., 1989-95. Mem. Internat. Reading Assn., Am. Assn. Univ. Adminstrs., Nat. Coun. Tchrs. English. Avocations: reading, needlepoint, walking club, cooking. E-mail: Carolanngillin@aol.com.

GILLIS, MALCOLM (STEPHEN GILLIS), academic administrator, economics educator; b. Dothan, Ala., Dec. 28, 1940; s. Stephen Malcolm and Eva May (Mac Kinnon) Gillis; m. Elizabeth Cifers, Aug. 18, 1962; children: Eva Leanora, Heather Elizabeth, Stephen Malcolm. BA, U. Fla., 1962, MA, 1963; PhD, U. Ill., 1968; LLD (hon.), Rocky Mountain Coll., 1992. Asst. prof. econs. Duke U., Durham, NC, 1967—69; lectr. in econs. Harvard U., Cambridge, Mass., 1969—73, inst. fellow, 1974—84; prof. econs., pub. policy Duke U., 1984—93, dean grad. sch., vice provost acad. affairs, 1986—91, Z. Smith Reynolds Disting. prof. pub. policy, 1990—93, dean faculty arts and scis., 1991—93; pres. Rice U., Houston, 1993—, Irvin Kenneth Zingler prof. econs., 1998—. Com. on energy taxation NRC/NAS, 1979—80; coun. econ. policy Office of Gov. State of Alaska, Juneau, 1982—83; mem. seminar on Southeast Asia in world affairs Columbia U., 1982—84; adv. com. energy divsn. Oak Ridge Nat. Lab., 1984—87, chmn. adv. com., 1985—86; internat. adv. bd. KPMG Peat Marwick Policy Econs. Group, 1988—; cons. World Bank, Washington; Disting. Fulbright prof. Cath. U., Chile, 1989; adv. bd. Internat. Ctr. for Econ. Growth, 1986—, Inst. for Policy Reform, 1990—; so. regional adv. bd. Inst. Internat. Edn., 1993—; bd. dirs. Houston Advanced Rsch. Ctr.; presenter in field; bd. dirs. Fed. Res. Bank, Dallas. Author (with others): Fiscal Reform For Colombia, 1971, Taxation and Mining, 1978, Tax and Investment Policies for Hard Minerals, 1980, Economics of Development, 1983; editor: Export Diversification and the New Protectionism, 1981, Public Policy and Misuse of Forest Resources, 1988, The Value-Added Tax in Developing Countries, 1991; mem. editl. bd.: Pakistan Devel. Rev, 1977—80, Quar. Jour. Econs., 1978—79, co-editor; mem. editl. bd.: Tex. Bus. Rev., 1979—83, Pakistan Jour. Applied Econs., 1980—83, Comparative Econ. Studies, 1986—88, referee: various jours.; contbr. articles to profl. jours. Adv. Navajo Indian Nation, Ship Rock, N.Mex., 1983—84; trustee Found. for Hosp. Art, 1989, Francisco Marroquin Found., 1989—, Friends of Edn. in Chile, 1989—, United Way of Tex. Gulf Coast; vice-chmn. higher edn. sector Houston area U.S. Savs. Bond Campaign, 1994; bd. adv. Houston Symphony, 1995; chmn. March of Dimes Gulf Coast Walk Am., 1995; chmn. bd. trustees Ctr. for World Environ. and Sustainable Devel., 1969, 1975, 1983—87, Harvard Inst. Internat. Devel., 1984—; bd. dirs. Am. Forestry Assn., 1989—92; chair U.S. Savs. Bonds, Gulf Coast Region, 2002—04; bd. dirs. South Main Ctr. Assn., 1993—, Greater Houston Partnership, 1993—, St. Luke's Episc. Hosp., 1994—2003, Amigos de las Ams., Consortium on Financing Higher Edn., 1994—, Ind. Colls. and Univs. Tex., 1995—; exec. com. Houston Advanced Res. Ctr. Bd., 1994—, Assn. Am. Univs., 1993—; mem. Houston Lifestock Show and Rodeo; bd. dirs. Indo-Am. C. of C., 2000—, Houston Tech. Ctr., 1999—, BioHouston, 2000—, Tex. Aviation Hall of Fame, 1998—. Grantee, U.S. AID, Washington, 1986—87. Mem.: Houston Philos. Soc., Assn. Pub. Policy Analysis and Mgmt., Nat. Tax Assn., Am. Econ. Assn. Republican. Episcopalian. Office: Rice U Office of Pres PO Box 1892 Houston TX 77251-1892

GILLISON, JEANETTE SCOTT, elementary school educator; b. Phila., Aug. 17, 1931; d. Swinton O'Neal and Lillie (Roberts) Scott; m. Everett A. Gillison, Dec. 10, 1955 (div. Apr. 1965); children: Everett A. Jr., Sharida L., Katanya L. BA in Elem. Edn., Cheney State Tchrs. Coll., 1953. Elem. sch. tchr. Sch. Dist. Phila., 1953—, Meade Sch., Phila., 1953-58, Martha Washington Sch., Phila., 1960—. Liaison tchr. for Sch. Dist. Phila., World Affairs Coun., 1969-73. Mem. adv. bd. Belmont YMCA educators to Africa, Phila., 1973—. Mem. NAACP (life), Nat. Coun. Negro Women (life), Black Women's Ednl. Alliance, Alpha Kappa Alpha (life). Home: 18 S 50th St Philadelphia PA 19139-3538

GILLMOR, CHARLES STEWART, history and science educator, researcher; b. Kansas City, Mo., Nov. 6, 1938; s. Charles Stewart and Evelyn (Noland) G.; m. Rogene Marie Godding, Nov. 28, 1964; children: Charles Stewart III, Alison Bogue. BSEE, Stanford U., 1962; MA, Princeton U., 1966, PhD, 1968; postgrad., U. Colo., 1963. Ionospheric physicist Bur. Standards, Antarctica and Boulder, Colo., 1960-62; instr. history Wesleyan U., Middletown, Conn., 1967-68, asst. prof., 1968-72, assoc. prof., 1973-79, prof. history and sci., 1979—, chmn. dept. history, 1986-88, 91-94; cons. Office Sci. Edn., AAAS, 1973-75. Adv. com. Coun. Internat. Exch. Scholars, 1978—82; cons. NSF, 1983; Hennebach vis. prof. Colo. Sch. Mines, 1996—97; vis. prof. elec. engring. Stanford u., 1998—2001. Author: Coulomb and the Evolution of Physics and Engineering in 18th Century France, 1971; editor: The History of Geophysics, Vol. 1, 1984, Vol. 2, 1986, Vol. 4, 1990, Vol. 7, 1997; jour. editor: Transactions Am. Geophys. Union, 1983-86; mus. dir. Nutmeg Foxtrot-Jazz Orch., 1990-96; contbr. articles to profl. jours.; recording artist with Leo Records, 1998. Deacon Higganum Congl. Ch., Conn., 1978-96. Mt. Gillmor in Antarctica named in his honor, 1963; Social Sci. Research Council grantee, 1971; NSF research grantee, 1972-74, 75-77, 76-79; sr. Fulbright research scholar Cambridge U., Eng., 1976; NASA History scholar, 1980-81; U.S.-France NSF research fellow, Paris, 1984-85; Joseph J. Malone fellow to Tunisia Nat. Coun. U.S.-Arab Rels., 1989 Fellow Am. Phys. Soc. (sec.-treas. history of physics divsn. 1988-94, exec. com. 1996-98, chair 1997-98); mem. AAAS, IEEE, Am. Geophys. Union, History of Sci. Soc., Soc. History of Tech. (adv. coun. 1978-82), Sigma Xi. Home: 29 Spencer Rd Higganum CT 06441-4034 Office: Wesleyan Univ Dept History Middletown CT 06459-0002 E-mail: sgillmor@wesleyan.edu.

GILLON, STEPHEN JOHN, business educator, consultant; b. Ft. Sheridan, Ill., June 13, 1948; s. Eli and Joan Rodgers Gillon; children: Barron August, Sterling Joseph. AA, Reedley Coll., 1981; BS, U.S. Mil. Acad., 1972; MBA, Calif. State U., Fresno, 1984; MS in Accountancy, Calif. State U., Chico, 1989; D Edn., Boston U., 1997. Cert. airframe and powerplant mech., pvt. pilot, FAA. Sports info. officer Reedley (Calif.) Coll., 1978-81; instr. Calif. State U., Fresno, 1981, Chico, 1987-90, U. Alaska, Anchorage, 1991-94, Ivy Tech. C.C., Marion, Ind., 1996-97; instr., sys. mgr. MILA, Inc., Anchorage, 1991-94; asst. prof. Cleve. State C.C., 1997-2000, U. Alaska-Anchorage, Homer, 2000—. Mem. com. Vocat. Ednl. Task Force, Homer, Alaska, 2000—03; dir., treas. Homer Co. on Arts, 2001—03. Capt. USAF, 1973—77. Sam M. Walton fellow, 1997-2000. Mem. Exptl. Aircraft Assn. Home: 137 E Danview Homer AK 99603-0724 Office: U Alaska 533 E Pioneer Dr Homer AK 99603 Fax: (907) 235-2199. E-mail: gillon@uaa.alaska.edu.

GILLOZ, ANDRÉ-PIERRE, urologist, educator; b. Sallanches, France, Dec. 16, 1926; s. Louis Edmond and Clémence Marie Gilloz; m. Micheline Marie Fouletier, Mar. 3l, l955. BA, BA, Coll. Bonneville, 1944; MD, U. Lyon (France), 1955. Intern Hosp. Lyon, 1950-54, chief clin. faculty, 1955-60; surgeon Hosp. Nord, St. Etienne, France, 1961—; prof. urology Faculty Medicine, St. Etienne, 1974—. Chief dept. Ctr. Hosp. Univ., St. Etienne, 1966—. Contbr. articles to med. jours., chpts. to books. Decorated chevalier Ordre Palmes Academiques (France). Mem. French Urol. Assn., French Soc. Urology, Internat. Soc. Urology, European Assn. Urology, Swiss Soc. Urology, Loire Urol. Club (pres. 1977—). Roman Catholic. Avocation: skiing. Home: 8 Pl de l'Hotel de Ville F-42000 Saint Etienne France Office: Hosp Nord Ave Albert Raimond F-42277 Saint Priest en Jarez France

GILMAN, TODD SEACRIST, librarian, scholar, educator, musician; b. Cambridge, Mass., Feb. 15, 1965; s. Sidney and Linda Louise (Lamlein) G. BA, U. Mich., 1987; MA, U. Toronto, 1988, PhD, 1994; MS, Simmons Coll., 2001. Artistic dir. Arbor Oak Trio, Toronto, 1988-96; lectr., tutor, writing cons. U. Toronto, 1994-96; lectr. Boston U., 1996-97; vis. fellow Houghton Libr., Harvard U., Cambridge, Mass., 1996-97; lectr. dept. English, Suffolk U., Boston, 1997-99; lectr. lit. sect. MIT, Cambridge, 1998-99; libr. assoc. collection maintenance and pub. svcs. Mus. Libr., Mus. of Fine Arts, Boston, 2000-01; libr. for lit. in English, Sterling Meml. Libr., Yale U., New Haven, 2001—. Adj. asst. prof. dept. info. and libr. sci. and dept. English So. Conn. State U., 2002—. Book reviews editor: Yale Jour. Law and the Humanities, 2002—; contbr. articles to profl. jours. Bd. dirs. Toronto Early Music Ctr., 1993-95. Fletcher Jones fellow The Huntington Libr., San Marino, Calif., 1995, fellow Ezra Stiles Coll., Yale U., 2002-. Mem. ALA, MLA (field bibliographer English lang and lit. sect.), AAUP, Assn. Coll. and Rsch. LIbrs., Viola Gamba Soc. Am.-N.E., Am. Soc. 18th Century Studies (McMaster fellow 1994), Am. Handel Soc. (rsch. fellow 1998), Soc. Theatre Rsch. (travel grantee 1998), Early Music Am., Beta Phi Mu. Democrat. Office: Yale U PO Box 208240 New Haven CT 06520-8240 E-mail: toddgilman@aol.com.

GILMORE, CONNIE SUE, director; b. Nashville, Sept. 3, 1951; d. Earl C. and L. Louise (Coleman) G. AA, Stephens Coll., 1971; BA, Vanderbilt U., 1973; MA, Cumberland U., 1992, postgrad., 1992—. Cert. tchr., Tenn. Tchr. Bellevue Presbyn. Ch., Nashville, 1980-83, dir., 1983-86; presch. tchr. St. Henry's Ch., Nashville, 1985-89, dir., 1986-90; comparative fin. analyst Vanderbilt U., 1998—. Tutor BellSouth Grant Reading Program, Lebanon, Tenn., 1990. Editor, author: Leadership, 1992. Mem. Nat. Assn. for Edn. Young Children, So. Assn. for Children Under Six, Tenn. Assn. for Young Children, Nashville Area Assn. for Young Children, So. Literacy Soc. (charter)., Kappa Delta Pi

GILMORE, JENNIE RAE, elementary education educator; b. Bellflower, Calif., Mar. 22, 1941; d. Jake and Agnes (Mooren) Elzenga; (widowed); children: Mike, Steve. AA, Modesto (Calif.) Jr. Coll., 1961; BA, Calif. State U., Chico, 1963. Tchr. Modesto City Schs., 1963-67, Stockton (Calif.) Unified Schs., 1975-78, substitute tchr., 1980—. Mem. AAPHERD, Modesto Tchrs. Assn. Avocations: sports, gardening, reading. Home: 1320 Kearney Ave Modesto CA 95350-4843

GILMORE, JENNIFER A.W. computer specialist, educator; b. San Fernando, Trinidad, Jan. 12, 1954; came to U.S., 1972; d. Fitzroy Grant and Zelma (Williams) Oudkerk; m. Frederick R. Gilmore, June 17, 1983. BA, MA, Bklyn. Coll., 1984; BBA, MS, Baruch Coll., 1993; MBA, L.I. U., 1994; PhD, Walden U./Kennedy-Western U., 2001. COBOL programmer MetLife, N.Y.C., 1972-86; project mgr., human resources adminstrn. mgmt. info. sys. City of N.Y., 1990—. Adj. prof. N.Y.C. Coll. Tech., 1997, Kingsborough C.C., 1998, St. Francis Coll., Bklyn., 1998, Medgar Evers Coll., 1998, Borough of Manhattan C.C., 1998, Touro Coll., 1999—, Baruch Coll., 1999—2000, Monroe Coll., 1999—, U. Md., 2003—. Home: 47 Mckeever Pl Apt 16J Brooklyn NY 11225-2537 Office: NYC-HRA-MIS 111 8th Ave New York NY 10011-5201 E-mail: jgilmore102716560@yahoo.com.

GILMORE, LINDA LOUISE TRAYWICK, nursing educator, educator; b. Alexander City, Ala., Dec. 4, 1962; d. James Winston and Vena Louise (Curlee) Traywick; m. Gerald Bates Gilmore, Aug. 24, 1985; 1 child, Ethan Bates Gilmore. AS, Alexander City State Jr. Coll., 1984; RN, Sylacauga Hosp. Sch. Nursing, 1985; BSN, U. Ala., Birmingham, 1988; MSN, Troy State U., 1992. Cert. surg. nurse, chemotherapy nurse, oncology nurse, BLS instr., diabetes educator; RN Ala.; cert. vol. firefighter Ala., 1995. Staff nurse U. Ala. Hosps., Birmingham, 1985-89, S.E. Ala. Med. Ctr., Dothan, 1989-94; ADN instr. Wallace Coll., Dothan, 1991-95; asst. prof. BSN program Troy (Ala.) State U., 1996-97; staff nurse Flowers Hosp., Dothan, Ala., 1997—99, diabetes edn. coord., 1999—. Quality assurance rep. perinatal divsn. Univ. Hosp., Birmingham, 1986-88; discharge planning rep. S.E. Ala. Med. Ctr., Dothan, 1989-91; faculty advisor Wallace Assn. Nursing Students, Dothan, 1993-95; mem. courtesy com. Wallace Coll., 1994-95; mem. drug computation com. Wallace ADN, 1994-95; mem. admission and progression com. BSN, Troy State U., 1996-97; instr. chemotherapy Flowers Hosp., 2001-; chair, developer Flowers Hosp. Diabetes Edn. Program, 1999-. Guest speaker Hospice Care Sr. Citizen Group, 1992; guest speaker nursing Bible Sch. Class, 1993; guest speaker Bay Springs Bapt. First Place Group, 1998—2000; discipleship tng. tchr., 1993—96; dir. children's choir grades 1-3, 1995—96; ch. nursery worker, 1996—; children's ch. worker, 1998—2003; vol. firefighter Bay Springs Vol. Fire Dept., Dothan, 1993—, sec., 2003—; choir mem., soloist Bay Springs Bapt. Ch., Dothan, 1990—. Named Bay Springs Vol. Firefighter Yr., 1997, Houston County Vol. Firefighter Yr., 1997. Mem.: ANA, Am. Diabetes Assn., Am. Assn. Diabetes Educators, Ala. State Nurses Assn. (v.p. dist. 7 1993—95), Oncology Nursing Soc. Baptist. Avocations: singing, fishing, crafts, walking.

GILMORE, NORMA J. special education educator; b. Mancelona, Mich., Mar. 16, 1924; d. Glen Brereton and Olive (Tinker) Blair; m. Douglas M. Gilmore, Dec. 28, 1945 (div. Oct. 1969); children: George, Glenn, James, Anne. BA, U. No. Ariz., 1955; MA, Mich. State U., 1969; EdD, U. No. Colo., 1976. Cert. tchr., Colo., Mich. Elem. tchr. Lansing (Mich.) Pub. Schs., 1959-60, adminstr. learning impaired and adjustment programs, 1976-78; elem. tchr. Holt (Mich.)-Dimondale Sch. Dist., 1960-61, 68-72; cons. Boulder (Colo.) Valley Schs., 1972-73; dir. spl. edn. Mountain Bd. Coop. Ednl. Svcs., Leadville, Colo., 1973-75, South Platte Valley Bd. Coop. Ednl. Svcs., Ft. Morgan, Colo., 1978-80, 82-84; prof. Peru (Nebr.) State Coll., 1980-82, 88-92, Western State Coll. Colo., Gunnison, 1984-88; with rsch. project Vocat. Edn./Spl. Edn. Program Cen. Mich. U., Mt. Pleasant, 1975-76, adj. prof. spl. edn., 1992-95, U. No. Ariz., Prescott, 1995-97; dir. spl. edn. South Platte Valley BOCES, 1997—. Various position Presbyn. Ch., 1952—; vol. Western State Coll. Colo. Friends of Western. Mem. Internat. Platform Assn., Found. for Exceptional Children (bd. dirs. 1984-90, sec. 1985-90), Coun. for Exceptional Children (various offices 1969—, pres. 1979-80, faculty advisor 1984-85, 90-92), P.E.O., Order Ea. Star (Martha 1988-92, Esther, 1997—), Delta Kappa Gamma (pres. 1986-88, sec. 1990-92), Phi Delta Kappa. Avocation: travel.

GILMORE, PHILIP NATHANAEL, finance educator, accountant; b. Northville, Mich., Mar. 13, 1944; s. Herbert Earl and Ruth Elaine (Shull) G.; m. JoAnn Wilson, Aug. 7, 1965; children: Martha K., David P., Rebecca J., Laurel A. BBA, U. Mich., Dearborn, 1967; MBA, U. Mich., 1968; DBA, Nova Southeastern U., 2001. CPA, Va.; cert. internal auditor Inst. Internal Auditors; cert. mgmt. acct. Inst. Mgmt. Accts.; fin. mgr. Inst. Fin. Mgmt. Dir. acctg. Moody Bible Inst., Chgo., 1973-76, asst. mgr. investments, 1976-79; contr. Old Time Gospel Hour, Lynchburg, Va., 1979-81, dir. estates & trusts, 1981-83; prin. Philip N. Gilmore, CPA, Lynchburg, Va., 1984; from asst. to assoc. prof. Liberty U., Lynchburg, Va., 1985—. Acctg. cons., Lynchburg, Va., 1979—. Mem. AICPA, Inst. Cert. Mgmt. Accts. Baptist. Avocations: music, investing, sports. Home: 328 Colington Dr Lynchburg VA 24502-2506 Office: Liberty U 1971 University Blvd Lynchburg VA 24506-8001 E-mail: pngilmor@liberty.edu.

GILMORE, ROGER, college consultant; b. Phila., Oct. 11, 1932; s. Wheeler and Edith Seal (Thompson) G.; m. Beatrice Reynolds, Sept. 17, 1952 (dec. Sept. 1994); children: Christopher, Jennifer E., Lesley Margaret; m. Elizabeth McOuat Lameyer, Oct. 1, 1995. AB, Dartmouth Coll., 1954; postgrad., U. Chgo. Div. Sch., 1958-63; DFA (hon.), Sch. Art Inst. Chgo., 1993; DHL (hon.), Maine Coll. Art, 2002. Social worker N.H. Dept. Pub. Welfare, Woodsville, 1954-55; adminstrv. asst. Furn Corp. Lisbon, N.H., 1955-56; office mgr., asst. to pres. Cole's Mill Inc., Littleton, N.H., 1956-58; acct., office supr. U. Chgo., 1958-61, asst. dir. fin. aid, 1961-63; asst. to dean Sch. Art Inst. Chgo., 1963-65, acting dean, 1965-68, dean, 1968-87, provost, v.p. for acad. affairs, 1987-89; pres. Maine Coll. Art (formerly Portland Sch. Art), 1989-2001, pres. emeritus, 2001—. Dir. Commn. Accreditation and Membership Nat. Assn. Schs. of Art and Design, 1975-78, v.p. 1984-87, pres., 1987-90; mem. Joint Commn. on Dance and Theatre Accreditation, 1978-82; bd. dirs. Internat. Coun. Fine Arts Deans, 1986-88; pres., bd. dirs. Ox-Bow Summer Sch. and Artists Colony, 1987-89; treas. Assn. Ind. Colls. Art and Design, 1991-95; mem. exec. com. Maine Higher Edn. Coun., 1991-95. Bd. dirs. Maine Alliance for Arts Edn., 1992-94, Greater Portland Landmarks, 1993-99, Stanley Mus., 1993-95, World Affairs Coun., 1993-95. Fellow Nat. Assn. Schs. Art and Design (life); mem. Maine Citizens for Hist. Preservation, Nat. Trust for Hist. Preservation, Maine Alliance for Arts Edn. Democrat. Episcopalian. Home: 24 Fairmount St Portland ME 04103-3051

GILSTRAP, LEAH ANN, media specialist; b. Seneca, S.C., Sept. 12, 1950; d. Raymond Chester and Eunice Hazel (Long) G. AA, Anderson Coll., 1973; BA in History, Furman U., 1976, MEd, 1982; MLS, U. S.C., 1991. Cert. tchr., media specialist, S.C. Tchr. Greenville (S.C.) County Sch. Dist., 1978-92, media specialist, 1992—. Mem. NEA (del. 1991-95), ALA, S.C. Assn. Sch. Librs., S.C. Edn. Assn. (bd. dirs. 1994-96), Greenville County Edn. Assn. (bd. dirs. 1988-98, governance chair 1988-98, v.p. 1996-97, pres. 1997-98), Greenville County Coun. Media Specialists (bd. dirs. 1993-94). Democrat. Baptist. Avocations: travel, reading, ednl. studies. Home: 19 Anson Ct Simpsonville SC 29681-5560 Office: Bryson Mid Sch 3657 S Industrial Dr Simpsonville SC 29681-3295 E-mail: lgistra@greenville.k12.sc.us.

GIMBO, ANGELO, veterinary pathology educator, researcher; b. Biancavilla, Catania, Italy, June 18, 1928; s. Carmelo and Sara (papotto) G.; m. Francesca Olga DeSalvo (div. 1980); m. Francesca Domina, July 24, 1988; 3 children. DVM, U. Messina (Italy), 1953. Instr. vet. pathology U. Messina, 1960-75, prof., 1975—, inst. dir., 1975—. Contbr. articles to profl. jours. Mem. Italian Soc. Vet. Sci., Italian Soc. Buiatria, Italian Soc. Pathology, AAAS, N.Y. Acad. Scis. Office: U Messina Vet Med Faculty Via S Cecilia 30 98123 Messina Italy

GIMENEZ, LUIS FERNANDO, physician, educator; b. Antofagasta, Chile, Mar. 3, 1952; came to U.S., 1979; s. Luis Sr. and Nelly (Basulto) G.; m. Diane Marie Salazar, Sept. 20, 1957; children: Luis Andres, Pilar Elizabeth, Nicholas Miguel, Catherine Anne. MD, U. Chile, Valparaiso, 1976. Diplomate Am. Bd. Internal Medicine, Am. Bd. Nephrology. Intern U. Chile Sch. Medicine, Valparaiso, 1975-76; resident U. Concepcion Sch. Medicine, Chile, 1976-77, U. Chile Sch. Medicine, Valparaiso, 1977-79; research fellow in nephrology Johns Hopkins U. Sch. Medicine, Balt., 1979-81; intern Johns Hopkins Hosp., Balt., 1981-82, resident, 1982-84, clin. fellow nephrology div., 1984-85; instr. Johns Hopkins U. Sch. Medicine, Balt., 1985-86, asst. prof. medicine, 1986—. Dir. dialysis unit The Good Samaritan Hosp., Balt., 1985—, chief renal div., 1990; mem. med. adv. bd. Am. Kidney Found., Balt., 1987—. Contbr. articles to profl. jours. Recipient Outstanding Civic Svc. award Chilean Med. Assn., Valparaiso, 1974. Mem. Am. Fedn. for Clin. Research., Am. Soc. Nephrology, Am. Coll. Physicians, Internat. Soc. Nephrology, Internat. Soc. Peritoneal Dialysis, Am. Coll. Clin. Pharmacology. Avocation: philatelist. Office: Johns Hopkins Hosp Renal Divsn 1830 Bldg Baltimore MD 21205-2109

GINGERICH, OWEN JAY, astronomer, educator; b. Washington, Iowa, Mar. 24, 1930; 3 children. BA, Goshen Coll., 1951; MA, Harvard U., 1953, PhD in Astronomy, 1962. Dir. obs. Am. U., Beirut, 1955-58, from instr. to asst. prof., 1955-58; lectr. astronomy Wellesley Coll., 1958-59; astrophysicist Smithsonian Astrophys. Obs., 1961-87, sr. astronomer, 1987-2000; from lectr. to assoc. prof. astronomy and history of sci. Harvard U., 1960-69, prof., 1969-2000, chmn. history of sci. dept., 1992-93, rsch. prof., 2000—; Sigma Xi nat. lectr., 1971; George Darwin lectr. Royal Astron. Soc., 1971. Astronomy cons. Harvard Project Physics, 1964-69; dir. ctrl. telegram bur. Internat. Astronomical Union, 1965-67, pres. commn. history astronomy, 1970-76, chmn. U.S. nat. com., 1982-84; adv. com. Ctr. Theol. Inquiry, Princeton, 1988-97; adv. bd. John Templeton Found., 1994-99, 2001-2003, trustee, 2003—. Assoc. editor: Jour. History Astronomy, 1975— ; mem. editorial bd. Am. Scholar, 1975-80; dir. Harvard mag., 1978-85, incorporator, 1986—. Overseer Boston Mus. Sci., 1979-96, 98—. Decorated Order of Merit comdr. class People's Republic of Poland, 1981 Fellow AAAS (chmn. sect. L 1974, sect D 1981); mem. Academie Internationale d'Histoire des Sciences, Am. Acad. Arts and Scis., Am. Philos. Soc. (v.p. 1982-85, John F. Lewis prize 1976, councilor 1994-2000), Am. Astron. Soc. (chmn. hist. astronomy div. 1983-85, Doggett prize 2000), Royal Astron. Soc. Can. (hon.), Phi Beta Kappa. Clubs: Examiner. Achievements include research and publications on model stellar atmospheres (to 1971) and in history of astronomy. Office: Harvard-Smithsonian Ctr for Astrophysics Cambridge MA 02138 Business E-Mail: ginger@cfa.harvard.edu.

GINGERICH, PHILIP DERSTINE, paleontologist, evolutionary biologist, educator; b. Goshen, Ind., Mar. 23, 1946; s. Orie Jacob and Miriam (Derstine) G.; m. B. Holly Smith, 1982 AB, Princeton U., 1968; PhD, Yale U., 1974. Prof. U. Mich., Ann Arbor, 1974—, dir. Mus. Paleontology, 1981-87, 1989—. Contbr. articles to sci. jours. Recipient Henry Russel award U. Mich., 1980; Shadle fellow Am. Soc. Mammalogists, 1973-74, NATO fellow, 1975, Guggenheim fellow, 1983-84 Fellow Am. Assn. Adv. Scis., Am. Acad. Arts Sci., Geol. Soc. Am.; mem. Paleontol. Soc. (Schuchert award 1981), Soc. Study Evolution, Am. Soc. Mammalogists, Soc. Vert. Paleontology. Office: U Mich Mus Paleontology 1109 Geddes Ave Ann Arbor MI 48109-1079

GINN, VERA WALKER, director; b. Jacksonville, Fla., Dec. 22, 1949; d. Grady and Pearl Walker; m. Perry L. Ginn, Mar. 16, 1969; children: Perry Jr., Spencer. BA in Edn., Fla. Atlantic U., 1972; MS, Nova U., 1985; specialist in edn., Barry U., 1991. Cert. ednl. leadership, reading, elem. edn. ESOL. Tchr. grades 3 and 4 Plantation (Fla.) Park Elem., 1973-82, Griffin Elem., Cooper City, Fla., 1982-85; tchr. grades 6-8 Seminole Mid., Plantation, 1985-90; lead tchr. Chpt. 1 Adminstrv. Office, Ft. Lauderdale, Fla., 1990-92, tchr. on spl. assignment, 1992-93, dir. title 1 migrant & spl. programs, 1997—. Advisor Fla. Future Educators Am., Plantation, 1990—91; adj. prof. Fla. Atlantic U., Ft. Lauderdale, 1995—97. Mem.: ASCD, Fla. Assn. Sch. Adminstrs., Fla. Reading Assn., Internat. Reading Assn., Fla. Assn. State and Fed. Ednl. Program Adminstrs., Phi Delta Kappa. Democrat. Baptist. Avocations: reading, travel, entertaining, bowling. Home: 6700 SW 20th St Plantation FL 33317-5107 Office: Title 1 Adminstrv Office 701 NW 31st Ave Fort Lauderdale FL 33311-6627

GINOP, ANITA LEUOLLA, elementary education educator; b. Cheboygan, Mich., Mar. 8, 1966; d. Gerald Allen Brown and Patricia D. Hershey Thornton; m. Kenneth Edward Ginop, Aug. 6, 1988; children: Zachary Emil, Kelsey Catherine. BS, Ctrl. Mich. U., Mt. Pleasant, 1988. Tchr. sixth grade math. and sci. Littlefield Schs., Alanson, Mich., 1990—. Office: Littlefield Schs 7400 North St Alanson MI 49706-9247

GINORIO, ANGELA BEATRIZ, university research administrator, educator; b. Hato Rey, P.R., Jan. 30, 1947; d. Melquiades Alejandro and Juana del Carmen (Morales) G.; m. Charles H. Muller; 1 child, Emilia Beatriz Muller-Ginorio. BA, U. P.R., 1968, MA, 1971; PhD, Fordham U., 1979. Instr. U. P.R., Rio Piedras, 1970-71; asst. prof. Bowling Green (Ohio) State U., 1978-80; counselor Office of Minority Affairs, Seattle, 1981-82; dir. Women's Info. Ctr., Seattle, 1983-87; dir. N.W. Ctr. for Rsch. on Women and Women's Info. Ctr. U. Wash., Seattle, 1987-92, affiliate asst. prof. psychology, 1986-93, dir. N.W. Ctr. Rsch. on Women, 1993—99, asst. prof. women studies, adj. asst. prof. psychology, 1993—99, assoc. prof., adj. prof., 1999—. Cons. U. Hawaii, Honolulu, 1989, AAUW Rsch. Found., 1994—. Mem. editl. bd. Internat. Jour. of Intercultural Rels., Sex Roles, Signs; co-editor: (spl. issue) Women's Studies Quar., 1990; author: (monograph) Warming the Climate for Woman in Academic Science, Si, se puede! Yes We Can! Bd. dirs. Mexican Am. Women Nat. Assn.-N.W., Seattle, 1988-89, Planned Parenthood, King County, Wash., 1991-93; mem. Wash. state com. Nat. Mus. Women in the Arts, 1989-92. Recipient Travel awards NIMH, 1979, APA/NSF, 1981; named Woman of Yr., Bus. and Profl. Women Campus chpt., 1986; grantee for evaluation Ford Found., 1989-91, grantee for summer sci. camp Discuren Found., 1992-93, NSF grantee, 1994-97. Fellow APA (bd. ethnic and minority affairs 1987-90); mem. Assn. for Women in Psychology. Office: Univ Wash Padel Ford Hall 35-4345 NW Ctr Rsch Women 35 130 Hl Seattle WA 98195-4345

GINOSAR, D. ELAINE, elementary education educator; b. Red Lodge, Mont., June 14, 1937; d. Alvin Henry and Dorothy Mary (Roberson) Wedemeyer; children: Nathan B., Daniel M., David M. BA, Calif. State U., Northridge, 1964, MA, 1977. Cert. edn. tchr., reading and learning disabilities. Tchr. Sacramento City Unified Sch. Dist., 1977—; math. leader, 1992-95. Owner, operator rental properties. Pres. Davis (Calif.) Flower Arrangers, 1993-96. Host family for U. Calif. Davis to 15 fgn. students from Japan, Thailand, Mexico, South Korea, 1990-95. Named Woman of Yr. Am. Biog. Soc., 1996. Mem. AAUW (edn. equity chair 1993-95, edn. chair 1965-93, readers theater, women's history week 1990, 91, treas. 1993-98, pres. 1990-91, 98-2000), Calif. Tchrs. Assn., Delta Kappa Gamma (pres. 2000-02). Republican. Presbyterian. Home: 3726 Chiles Rd Davis CA 95616-4346

GINSBERG, NORMAN ARTHUR, physician, educator; b. Chgo., May 28, 1946; m. Denise Ginsberg; children: Melinda, Sara. BA, So. Ill. U., 1968; postgrad., Ill. Coll. Pharmacy, 1968-69, U. Guadalerjara, 1969-72; MD, Chgo. Med. Sch., 1974. Diplomate Am. Bd. Ob-gyn. Intern Michael Reese Hosp. and Med. Ctr., Chgo., 1974-75, resident in ob-gyn., 1975-79, mem. staff, 1979—; pvt. practice in ob-gyn. Chgo. Mem. staff Northwestern Hosp. and Med. Ctr., 1984—; investigator 1st trimester diagnosis of inheritable diseases WHO. Bd. dirs. Nat. Abortion Rights League Ill. Fellow Am. Coll. Ob-gyn., Am. Soc. Human Genetics, Ctrl. Assn. Ob-gyn.; mem. AMA, Am. Fertility Soc., Chgo. Med. Soc. Achievements include pioneering of chorionic villi sampling in U.S.; first trimester screening for Down's Syndrome; pre-implantation genetis in U.S. Home: 1520 Eastwood Ave Highland Park IL 60035-2729 Office: Assn for Women's Health Care Ltd 30 N Michigan Ave Ste 607 Chicago IL 60602-3405

GINSBURG, ALAN L. federal agency administrator; PhD in Econ., U. Mich. Dir. Planning and Evaluation Svcs., Washington; dir. policy and program studies svc. U.S. Dept. Edn., rep. to edn. forum of Asia-Pacific Econ. Coop. Contbr. articles to profl. jours. Recipient Gunnar Myrdal award, Am. Evaluation Assn., 1993. Office: Planning & Evaluation Services 400 Maryland Ave SW Rm 6W324 Washington DC 20202-0001*

GINSBURG, KENNETH ALAN, obstetrician-gynecologist, educator; b. San Diego, Jan. 7, 1954; s. Arthur and Ruth Muriel (Hyken) G.; m. Bonnie Jean Sowa, June 14, 1981; children: Katherine Amara, Kevin Benjamin. BA, U. Calif., San Diego, 1976; MD, Chgo. Med. Sch., 1981. Diplomate Am. Bd. Ob.-Gyn. divsn. reproductive endocrinology and infertility, Nat. Bd. Med. Examiners. Intern Cook County Hosp., Chgo., 1981-82; resident Baylor U. Coll. Medicine, Houston, 1982-85; fellow Wayne State U., Detroit, 1985-87; assoc. prof. divsn. reproductive endocrinology, infertility Sch. Medicine, Wayne State U., Detroit, 1987—, dir. andrology sect., 1987—, asst. dean for clin. edn. Contbr. articles, revs. to profl. jours., chpts. to books. Fellow ACOG (Cognate award 1989, 91); mem. AMA (Physicians Recognition award 1989, 91), Am. Fertility Soc., Endocrine Soc., Soc. for Study of Reprodn., Am. Soc. Andrology, Wayne County Med. Soc. (mem. com. 1988—), Sigma Xi. Jewish. Avocations: computers, music, reading. Office: Acad Student Programs Wayne State U Sch Medicine 540 E Canfield Rm 1206 Detroit MI 48201 E-mail: kginsbur@med.wayne.edu.

GINSBURG, MARK BARRY, comparative sociology of education educator; b. LA, Dec. 9, 1949; s. Norman Leslie and Blanche Dorothy (Burg) G.; m. Barbara Iris Chasin, Sept. 5, 1971; children: Jolie Richelle, Kevin Eran, Stefanie Alyse. AB in Sociology magna cum laude, Dartmouth Coll., 1972; MA in Sociology, UCLA, 1974, PhD in Edn., 1976. Lectr. U. Aston, England, 1976-78; asst. prof. U. Houston, Tex., 1979-82, assoc. prof. sociology of edn., 1982-87; dir. Inst. Internat. Studies in Edn. U Pitts., Pa., 1987-93, 96—, prof. edn. and sociology, 1989—, co-chair faculty social responsibility, 1990—95. Contbr. articles to profl. jours. Mem. steering com. Tex. Mobilization for Peace, Jobs and Justice, Houston, 1985—87; bd. dirs. Alliance for Progressive Action, 1990—; active Free South Africa Movement, Houston, 1985—87, Pitts. Peace Inst., 1989—98, co-chmn., 1990—92; bd. dirs. Pitts.-Matanzas (Cuba) Sister City Project, 1998—; treas. Metro Pitts. Labor Party chpt., 1997—99, steering com., 1997—. Rufus Choate scholar Dartmouth Coll., 1972. Mem.: United Faculty of the U. Pitts. (v.p. 1990-92, pres. 1992-), Coun. on Anthropology and Edn. (co-chmn. transnat. issues com. 1984-86), Brit. Sociol. Assn., Am. Ednl. Studies Assn. (exec. bd. 1988-91), Am. Ednl. Rsch. Assn. (exec. com. internat. studies spl. interest group, 1991-94, chmn. peace edn. spl. interest group 1992-96), Comparative and Internat. Edn. Soc. (v.p., pres.-elect, pres. 1989—93, co-editor 2003—), Phi Delta Kappa (rsch. rep. 1983-85). Avocations: bicycle touring, coin collecting. Home: 365 N Craig St 2 Pittsburgh PA 15213 Office: U Pitts Inst Internat Studies in Edn 5K01 Posvar Hall Pittsburgh PA 15260-7455 E-mail: mbg@pitt.edu.

GINSBURG, MARTIN DAVID, lawyer, educator; b. N.Y.C., June 10, 1932; s. Morris and Evelyn (Bayer) Ginsburg; m. Ruth Bader, June 23, 1954; children: Jane, James. AB, Cornell U., 1953; JD, Harvard U., 1958; LLD (hon.), Lewis and Clark Coll., 1992, Wheaton Coll., 1997. Bar: N.Y. 1959, D.C. 1980. Practiced in N.Y.C., 1959-79; mem. firm Weil, Gotshal & Manges, N.Y.C., 1963-79; of counsel firm Fried, Frank, Harris, Shriver and Jacobson, Washington, 1980—; Charles Keller Beekman prof. law Columbia U. Law Sch., N.Y.C., 1979-80; prof. law Georgetown U. Law Center, Washington, 1980—; lectr. U. Leiden, The Netherlands, 1982; lectr. Salzburg Seminar Austria, 1984; mem. tax divsn adv. group Dept. Justice, 1980-81; mem. adv. group to Commr. Internal Revenue, 1978-80; mem. adv. bd. U. Calif. Securities Regulation Inst., 1973-91. Adj. prof. law NYU, 1967—79; vis. prof. law Stanford U., Calif., 1978, Harvard U., Cambridge, Mass., 1986, U. Chgo., 1990, NYU, 1993; cons. joint com. on taxation U.S. Congress, 1979—80, acad. advisor, 2000—01; chmn. tax adv. bd. Commerce Clearing House, 1982—94; mem. bd. advisors NYU/IRS Continuing Profl. Edn. Program, 1983—88, co-chmn., 1986—88; sub coun. on capital allocation, co-chmn. taxation expert group Competitiveness Policy Coun., 1993—95; chmn. tax adv. bd. Little, Brown, 1994—96; bd. dirs. Millennium Chems., Inc., 1996—2003, Chgo. Classical Rec. Found.; lectr. various tax insts. Co-author: Mergers, Acquisitions, and Buyouts, 4 vols., 2003; contbr. articles to legal jours. Mem. vis. com. Harvard Law Sch., 1994—98. 1st lt. arty. U.S. Army, 1954—56. Recipient Chair named in his honor, Georgetown U. Law Ctr., 1986, Marshall-Wythe Medallion, Coll. of William and Mary Sch. Law, 1996, Outstanding Achievement award, Tax Soc. NYU, 1993, Viccenial medal, Georgetown U., 2000. Fellow: Am. Bar Found. (bd. dirs. 2000—03), Am. Coll. Tax Counsel; mem.: ABA (mem. com. corp. taxation, tax sect. 1973—, chmn. com. simplification 1979—81, mem. tax sect. coun. 1984—87, tax systems task force 1995—97), Assn. Bar City N.Y. (chmn. com. taxation 1977—79, mem. audit com. 1980—81), N.Y. State Bar Assn. (mem. tax sect. exec. com. 1969—, chmn. tax sect. 1975, ho. of dels. 1976—77), Am. Law Inst. (cons. Fed. Income Tax Project 1974—93). Office: 600 New Jersey Ave NW Washington DC 20001-2022 E-mail: ginsbma@ffhsj.com.

GINTER, VALERIAN ALEXIUS, urban historian, educator; b. Chgo., Nov. 4, 1939; s. Valerian Adalbert and Bernice (Podraza) G.; m. Linda Garner Tadlock, Feb. 24, 1968 (div. 1973). BS in Speech, Northwestern U., 1962; postgrad., L.I.U., 1979-81. Investigator Acme Secret Service Ltd., Chgo., 1960-62; producer, dir. Sta. WAAY-TV, Huntsville, Ala., 1965-68; comml. coordinator CBS TV, N.Y.C., 1968-70; buyer SSC&B Lintas Worldwide, Furman-Roth Inc., SFM Media Corp., N.Y.C., 1970-79; prin. Ginter-Gotham Urban History, N.Y.C., 1981—. Adj. lectr. Kingsborough C.C., N.Y., 1990—, LaGuardia C.C., N.Y., 1998—. Author: Manhattan Trivia: The Ultimate Challenge, 1985; contbr. articles to profl. jours., The Ency. N.Y.C., 1995. Cons., lectr. Mcpl. Art Soc., N.Y., 1975—, dir. video tng., St. Bartholomew's Cmty. House, N.Y.C., 1974-77. With U.S. Army, 1962-65. Mem. Theatre Hist. Soc., Victorian Soc. Am., Nat. Trust Historic Preservation, Soc. Archtl. Historians. Roman Catholic. Avocation: jazz accordionist. Home and Office: 50 W 72nd St Ste 312 New York NY 10023-4132 E-mail: gintgotham@aol.com.

GIORDANO, ANTONIO, medical educator; b. Naples, Italy, Oct. 11, 1962; came to U.S., 1987; s. Giovan Giacomo and Maria Teresa (Sgambati) G.; m. Mina Massaro, July 4, 1992; children: Maria Teresa, Giovan Giacomo, Luca. MD summa cum laude, U. Naples, 1986; PhD in Pathology summa cum laude, U. Trieste, 1990. Intern U. Naples, 1983-86; postdoctoral fellow N.Y. Med. Coll., 1987-88, Cold Spring Harbor Lab., N.Y.C., 1988-92; fellow Irvington Inst. for Med. Rsch., 1990-92; asst. prof. pathology/biochemistry Temple U., Phila., 1992-94; pres., chmn. bd., founder Sbarro Inst. for Cancer Rsch. and Molecular Medicine, 1993—; asst. prof. pathology Thomas Jefferson U., Phila., 1994-96, assoc. prof., 1996—2001, prof., 2001—02, Temple U., Phila., 2002—. Adj. prof. Thomas Jefferson U., Phila., 2002—; prof. human pathology and oncology U. Siena, Italy, 2003. Editl. bd. Jour. Cellular Biochemistry, Jour. Cellular Physiology, Anticancer Rsch., La Clinica Terapeutica, Jour. Clin. Pathology and Molecular Pathology, Frontiers in Bioscience, Cancer Biology and Therapy, Women's Oncology Rev., Jour. Exptl. Clin. Cancer Rsch., Jour. Neurovirology; contbr. numerous articles to profl. jours. and books. Knighted by Pres. of Republic of Italy, 2001; recipient Nat. Achievement award in med. rsch., Nat. Italian-Am. Polit. Action Com., 2003. Mem. Societá Italiana Tumori, Am. Assn. for Cancer Rsch., N.Y. Acad. of Scis. Achievements include identification of a novel tumor suppressor gene and a development of a new test for lung cancer; patent for tumor suppressor protein pRB2, related gene products, and DNA encoding, patents include novel human cyclin-dependent kinase-like proteins and methods of using the same, human retinoblastoma-related, genomic DNA and methods of detecting mutations therein, lung, prostate, breast cancer screening on pRb2 gene expression; pRb2/p130 peptide inhibitors of cdk2 kinase activity; determination of cyclin dependent kinase inhibitor p27 as prognostic factor in cancer patient. Home: 1230 Gulph Creek Dr Radnor PA 19087-4686 Fax: 610-964-9834. E-mail: g_tonio@hotmail.com.

GIORDANO, DIANE E. middle school educator; b. Worcester, Mass., Mar. 30, 1946; d. George Joseph and Elouise Marie (McClure) Vincent; m. Richard Allen Giordano, Aug. 8, 1970; children: Elizabeth, Lisa, Julie. BA in Biology, Bridgewater State Coll., 1967; MEd, Cambridge Coll., 1993. Cert. tchr., Mass. Tchr. Blackstone (Mass.) Pub. Sch., 1967-69, Norwood (Mass.) Jr. High Sch., 1969-71, Norton (Mass.) Mid. Sch., 1980-81, 84—, team leader, 1987—. Awards chair, judging chair Mass. Region III Sci. Fair Com., 1986—. Chair Recycling Com., Norton, 1979-81. Recipient Levine Meml. award Mass. Region III Sci. Fair Com., 1991. Mem. ASCD, NEA, Mass. Tchrs. Assn., Norton Tchrs. Assn. (v.p. 1985-87, pres. 1987-88),

Bristol County Tchrs. Assn. (Disting. Svc. award 1988), Mass. Tchrs. Assn., Kappa Delta Pi. Avocations: reading, needlework. Office: Norton Mid Sch 64 W Main St Norton MA 02766-2713

GIORDANO, JAMES JOSEPH, neuroscientist, pathologist, pain specialist; b. Staten Island, N.Y., Sept. 22, 1959; s. James and Gloria (Timpone) G. BS, St. Peter's Coll., Jersey City, 1981; MA, Norwich U., 1982; MPhil, CUNY, 1985, MS, PhD cum laude, 1986. Diplomate Am. Acad. Pain Mgmt., Am. Soc. Behavioral Medicine, Am. Bd. Clin. Sexuality; bd. cert. in pain mgmt. and behavior medicine. Rsch. asst. Einstein Med. Coll., Bronx, N.Y., 1983-86; rsch. fellow Johns Hopkins U., Balt., 1986-88; asst. prof. neurosci. Drake U., Des Moines, Iowa, 1988-92; dir. pain rsch. Iowa Meth. Hosp., Des Moines, 1990-92; commd. lt. USN, 1992, divsn. officer, 1992-93, dept. head aerospace physiology Cherry Point, N.C., 1993-95; neurology prof. Lamar U., Tex., 1996—; dir. pain program, behavioral medicine HealthSouth Rehab. Hosp., 1996—. Vis. prof. dept. pathology/psychiatry U. Tex. Med. Br., Galveston, 1996—. Textbook author; contbr. articles to profl. jours. Recipient Presdl. Point of Light award Pres. George Bush, 1991. Fellow Am. Bd. Disability Analysts, Internat. Aerospace Med. Assn., Soc. USN Flight Surgeons, Aeromed. Engring. Soc., Nat. Acad. Neuropsychiatrists. Avocations: commercial pilot, weight lifting, equestrian activities, Judo, piano.

GIORDANO, LOIS LYDIA, elementary school educator, consultant, writer; b. Port Washington, Wis., May 19, 1948; d. Theodore R. and Lydia E. (Riemer) Bartell; m. Thomas A. Giordano, June 27, 1970; 1 child, Jon. BA, Concordia Tchrs. Coll., River Forest, Ill., 1970; MA, Cardinal Stritch Coll., 1991. Cert. tchr. Ill., Wis., reading tchr., Wis. Tchr. preschool and kindergarten Hope Luth. Sch., Pk. Forest, Ill., 1970-72; tchr. grade 2 Brookwood Sch. Dist. 167, Glenwood, Ill., 1975-79, tchr. gifted and talented, 1979-80; gifted-enrichment coord. Emmanuel Luth. Sch., Fresno, Calif., 1980-86, interim prin., 1983-84; tchr. grade 4 1st Immanuel Luth. Sch., Cedarburg, Wis., 1986-92; tchr. grade eight Slinger Mid. Sch., Wis., 1992—, mid. sch. gifted coord., 1995-97. Cons., spkr. at confs. Luth. Schs. Wis. and Calif., 1981—; freelance writer. Mem. Ch. Coun. Emmanuel Luth. Ch., Fresno, 1982-84; v.p. Zone Luth. Women's Missionary League, Fresno, 1984-86; supt. Sunday sch. First Immanuel Luth. Ch., Cedarburg, 1987-92. Mem. NEA, Wis. Edn. Assn., Luth. Edn. Assn. Avocations: travel, reading, writing, church choir. Office: Sch Dist of Slinger 207 Polk St Slinger WI 53086-9585

GIOVALE, VIRGINIA GORE, health products executive, volunteer; b. Salt Lake City, Oct. 12, 1943; d. Wilbert Lee and Genevieve (Walton) Gore; m. John Peter Giovale, June 20, 1965; children: Peter, Daniel, Michael, Mark. BS in Math., Westminster Coll., Salt Lake City, 1965. With W.L. Gore & Assocs., Inc., Flagstaff, Ariz., 1976-84, bd. dirs., 1976—. Trustee Westminster Coll., Salt Lake City, 1977—, chair, 1988—, Ariz. Cmty. Found., 1995—. Recipient Heritage award, Westminster Coll., 1994. Avocations: travel, backpacking, skiing. Office: WL Gore & Assocs Inc 1505 N 4th St Flagstaff AZ 86004-6102

GIPSON, JEFFERY, chemistry educator; b. Waco, Tex., Aug. 7, 1922; s. Jeffery and Johnnie (Donahue) G. BS, Tillotson Coll., 1944; MS, Howard U., 1949; PhD, U. Tex., 1955. Assoc. prof. chemistry So. U., Baton Rouge, 1954-59; prof. chemistry, chmn. dept. St. Augustine's Coll., Raleigh, N.C., 1959-76; prof. chemistry Va. Union U., Richmond, 1981—. Vis. prof. chemistry Met. State coll., Denver, 1974; vis. prof. sci. U. Va., Charlottesville, summer 1985; cons. USAID, Bangalore, India, 1965, 67; rsch. scientist DNA Lawrence Radiation Lab., Livermore, Calif., summer 1970; rsch. trichina Los Alamos (N.Mex.) Sci. Lab., summer 1971; mem. colloid chem. conf. U. So. Calif., L.A., summer 1983; environ. scientist U.S. EPA, Arlington, 1987, Chgo., 1988, Phila., 1989, 91, 92, Research Triangle Park, N.C., 1990, Phila., 1991-92. Editor: Experiments in Physical Science, 1989; contbr. articles to profl. jours. Sgt. U.S. Army, 1944-46, PTO, 50-51. Mem. AAAS, AAUP, Am. Assn. Retired Profs., Nat. Space Acad. Am. Legion. Avocations: walking, create science crosswords. Home: Apt 134 7608 Forest Hill Ave Richmond VA 23225-1556

GIRARD, LOUIS JOSEPH, ophthalmologist, educator; b. Spokane, Wash., Mar. 29, 1919; s. Harry and Agnes (Cain) G.; m. Bonita Crossnay, Mar. 31, 1945; children: Hilaire Michelle (Mrs. Cliff Richey), Bryan, Suzanne (Mrs. R. Thackston), Christina Ann, Michael Sanford (dec.), Hugh Ashley, Gabrielle Inez; m. Loraine McMurrey, June 30, 1967; 1 son, Louis McMurrey; m. Louise Bell, June 14, 1975. BA, Rice U., 1941; MD, U. Tex., 1944; postgrad., NYU, Med. Sch., 1947-48. Diplomate: Am. Bd. Ophthalmology. Intern Jersey City Med. Ctr., 1944-45; assoc. Dr. Conrad Berens, NYC, 1947—49; asst. attending St. Clare's Hosp., 1948—53; resident ophthalmology NY Eye and Ear Infirmary, 1949-51; asst. attending Willard Parker Hosp., 1949-53; dir. chronic infection project, 1949-52; asst. attending N. Country Community Hosp., 1951-53; assoc. Dr. Conrad Berens, 1951—53; asst. surgeon, 1951-53; assoc. dir. dept. rsch., 1953—57; asst. attending Nassau Hosp., 1951-53; cons. ophthalmologist Southside Hosp., 1951-53; attending ophthalmologist Jefferson Davis Hosp., 1953-59, VA Hosp., Houston, 1954—98, Tex. Children's Hosp., 1954—98, St. Luke's Episcopal Hosp., 1954—98, Meth. Hosp., 1955—98; cons. Montgomery County Hosp., 1955—, Tex. Children's Hosp., 1957—98; assoc. prof., assoc. chmn. dept. ophthalmology Baylor Coll. Medicine, Houston, 1957—70, prof., chmn. dept., 1957-70; cons. VA Hosp., Houston, 1958—98; sr. attending Ben Taub Gen. Hosp., 1959—98, Meth. Hosp., 1959—98; cons. St. Luke's Episcopal Hosp., 1961—98, St. Joseph's Hosp., 1965—98; chief ophthalmology, co-chief surgery Ctr. Pavilion Hosp., 1970-76; clin. prof. Baylor Coll. Medicine, Houston, 1971—. Coord. grad. course ophthalmology NYU Postgrad. Med. Sch., 1948-49, instr., 1951-53; clin. asst. prof. U. Tex. Postgrad. Sch. Medicine, 1953-57, lectr., 1946 ; assoc. mng. dir. Ophthal. Found., N.Y., 1951-55, cons., 1957; founder Tex. Med. Ctr.-Lions Eye Bank, 1953; exec. dir. Girard Ophthal. Found., 1971—; cons. Meth. Hosp., St. Luke's Hosp.; founder, exec. dir. Inst. Ophthalmology, Tex. Med. Ctr., 1958—70; founder opthal. tissue culture lab. Baylor U., 1954; mem. Am. Orthoptic Coun., 1962-72; pres. Internat. Eye Film Library, 1967-71; med. adv. bd. Internat. Eye Bank, 1965-70; Pres. IX Pan Am. Congress Ophthalmology, 1972; presenter in field. Author: Advanced Techniques in Ophthalmic Microsurgery, Vol. I: Ultrasonic Fragmentation for Intraocular Surgery, 1979, Vol. II: Corneal Surgery, 1981; author, editor. over 7 books; prodr. 70 films.; editor: Corneal Contact Lenses, 1964, 2d edit., 1971, Corneal Scleral Contact Lenses, 1967, Proceedings of XI Pan Am Congress of Ophthalmology, 1974; mem. editl. bd. Ophthalmologia, 1965-72, Annals of Ophthalmology, 1968-74; contbr. articles to profl. jours.; cons. Highlights Ophthalmology, 1972; founded the Lions Ey Bank; founded the just Tissue laboratory devoted to ophthalmology in the world, 1959; established the first institute of ophthalmology in southwestern USA at Taylor College of Medicine, 1961. Recipient Alfred H. Bond award for rsch. in ophthalmology, 1950, Prof. Ignacio Barraquer Meml. award Inst. Barraquer, 1965, 2d prize Internat. Eye Film Festival, 1966, 1st prize, 1970, 1st prize, 1972, Golden Eagle award Internat. Film Festival Nantes, France, 1970, 71, Alumnus award Baylor U., 1984, First Disting. Alumnus award NY Eye and Ear Infirmary, 1984, Disting. Alumnus award Rice U., 1985, Disting. Alumnus award U. Tex. Med. Br. at Galveston, 1991; named to Hall of Fame, Alcon Labs., 1990. Fellow ACS (bd. gov. 1966-72); mem. Am. Acad. Ophthalmology (2d pl. award sci. exhibits 1960, Honor award, Sr. Honor award), Pan Am. Assn. Ophthalmology (1st pl. award sci. exhibits 1960, 62, vis. prof. 1967, v.p. 1972), Assn. Research Ophthalmology, N.Y. Acad. Medicine, NY Acad. Sci., Nassau, Houston ophthal. socs., French Soc. Ophthalmology, Houston Neurol. Soc., Jules Gonin Club, Tex. Ophtal. Assn., Alumni Assn. NY Eye and Ear Infirmary, AMA (certificate of merit sci. exhibit 1961), So. Med. Assn., Nat. Med. Found. Eye Care, Assn. Am. Physicians and Surgeons, Am. Assn. Ophthalmologists, Nat. Med. Found. Eye Care, Tex. Rehab. Assn., Harris County Med. Soc., Am. U. Prof. Ophthalmologists (founder, chmn. com. on ophthalmic asst.), Med. Rsch. Found. Tex., Contact Lens Soc. Ophthalmologists (Exceptional Merit award 1968), Inst. Horacio Ferrer (corr., lectr. 1959), Am. Eye Study Club (pres.) Achievements include inventing several instruments; originator numerous surg. techniques. Home: 20126 Indigo Lake Dr Magnolia TX 77355-3163

GIRGUS, JOAN STERN, psychologist, university administrator; b. Albany, N.Y., Mar. 21, 1942; d. William Barnet and Louise (Mayer) Stern; m. Alan Chimacoff, Jan. 2, 1981; 1 child, Katherine Louise Stern. BA, Sarah Lawrence Coll., 1963; MA, The Grad. Faculty New Sch. for Social Research, 1965, PhD, 1969. Asst. prof. dept. psychology CCNY, N.Y.C., 1969-72, assoc. prof., 1972-77, assoc. dean div. social sci., 1972-75, dean, 1975-77; prof. psychology Princeton U., 1977—, dir. Pew Sci. Program Undergrad. Edn., 1987—2002, chair dept. psychology, 1996—2002. Contbr. articles and chpts. to profl. jours. and books. NSF fellow, NIH fellow; Research grantee CUNY, 1971-74; Nat. Inst. Child Health and Human Devel. research grantee, 1972-74; NSF grantee, 1975-79; NIMH grantee, 1985-91. Fellow APA, Am. Psychol. Soc.; mem. Eastern Psychol. Assn., Soc. Rsch. in Child Devel. Home: 1 Boudinot St Princeton NJ 08540-3007 Office: Princeton U Green Hall Princeton NJ 08544

GIROLAMI, GREGORY SCOTT, chemistry educator; b. Honolulu, Oct. 16, 1956; s. Guido and Kristine Merle (White) G.; m. Vera Virginia Mainz, July 14, 1979. BS in Chemistry, BS in Physics, U. Tex., 1977; MS in Chemistry, U. Calif.-Berkeley, 1979, PhD in Chemistry, 1981. NATO postdoctoral fellow Imperial Coll. Sci. and Tech., London, 1982-83; asst. prof. chemistry U. Ill. at Urbana-Champaign, 1983-89, assoc. prof. chemistry, 1989-93, prof. chemistry, 1993—, head dept., 2000—. Vis. scientist AT&T Bell Labs., Murray Hill, N.J., 1991; cons. Exxon, 1991-95. Bd. editors Inorganic Chemistry, 1989-91, Organometallics, 1998-00; N.Am. editor Jour. Chem. Soc. Dalton Trans., 1995-98; contbr. over 120 articles to sci. jours. Recipient Young Investigator award in Chemistry, Office of Naval Rsch., 1986, Sloan Rsch. award A.P. Sloan Found., 1988, Dreyfus Tchr.-Scholar award Dreyfus Found., 1988; Univ. scholar U. Ill., 1990. Mem. Am. Chem. Soc. (treas. inorganic divsn. 1997-99), Royal Soc. Chemistry, Materials Rsch. Soc. Home: 2709 Holcomb Dr Urbana IL 61802-7724 Office: U Ill at Urbana-Champaign 600 S Mathews Ave Urbana IL 61801-3617 E-mail: girolami@scs.uiuc.edu.

GIROUARD, TANDY DENISE, special education educator, psychology educator; b. Ft. Worth, Tex., Aug. 25, 1960; d. Nolan Ray and Barbara Gale (Miller) Rutledge; m. Jan. 22, 1980 (div. Dec. 1995); children: Michael, Christopher, Kaneissa. BS in Generic Spl. Edn., U. of Mary Hardin-Baylor. Tchr. asst. spl. edn. Hurst-Euless-Bedford Ind. Sch. Dist., Bedford, Tex., 1988; tchr. asst. in spl. edn. McLennan County Dept. Edn., Waco, Tex., 1988-90; tchr. spl. edn. Moody Ind. Sch. Dist., 1991—94; tchr. resource reading LaVega Ind. Sch. Dist., 1994—95; tchr. life skills Waco Ind. Sch. Dist., 1996—98; tchr. 2d grade/tchr. spl. edn. Emma L. Harrison Charter Sch., 1998—99; tchr. resource Belton Ind. Sch. Dist., 1999—2000; tchr. spl. edn. Connally Ind. Sch. Dist., 2000—02. Mem. Internat. Assn. of Pers. in Employment Security, Assn. Tex. Profl. Educators, PTA, Bedford-Euless Soccer Assn., Tex. State Edn. Assn., Pi Gamma Mu. Home: 500 Greenfield Dr Waco TX 76705-1705

GIRVIN, SHIRLEY EPPINETTE, retired elementary education educator, journalist; b. New Orleans, Apr. 16, 1947; d. Woodie Trevillion and Thelma Elizabeth (Axline) E.; m. Russell Robertson Girvin, Nov. 30, 1996. AA, East L.A. Coll., 1967; BA, Calif. State U., L.A., 1969, postgrad., 1969-70, U. So. Calif., 1982, Chapman Coll., 1983, Loyola Marymount U., L.A., 1986-87. Elem. tchr. Covina-Valley Unified Sch. Dist., 1970-74, San Gabriel (Calif.) Sch. Dist., 1974-75, Alhambra (Calif.) City Sch. Dist., 1976-78; elem. and program mentor tchr., faculty rep. L.A. City Unified Sch. Dist., 1978—2003; ret., 2003. Rewrite editor, staff writer San Gabriel Valley Newspaper Publs., 1975-76. Contbr. articles to profl. publs. Recipient TAP award Alhambra-San Gabriel dist. Soroptimist Club, 1975; Calif. State PTA scholar, 1981, Journalism Alumni Assn. scholar East L.A. Coll., 1967, Arthur J. Baum Journalism scholar Calif. State U., 1969. Mem. AAUW (mem. com. internat. rels. 1977-78, chmn. ednl. com. 1978-79), NEA, Calif. Tchrs. Assn., L.A. City Tchrs. Math. Assn., United Tchrs. L.A. (chpt. chairperson 1994-95), Women in Comm., Nat. Press Women, Humane Soc. U.S., Soc. for the Prevention of Cruelty to Animals, Handgun Control Inc., Sigma Delta Chi. Avocations: breeding, selling, and racing Thoroughbred race horses, gardening. Home: 8730 S East Ave Fresno CA 93725

GISCHLAR, KAREN LYNN, psychologist; b. Trenton, NJ, Sept. 18, 1964; d. William Peter and Carol Patricia G. BS, Trenton State Coll., 1986, MA, 1993; Ed.S., Rider U., 2003. Cert. early childhood/elem. tchr., guidance counselor, sch. psychologist, NJ. Pre-kindergarten tchr. William Penn Ctr., Morrisville, Pa., 1986-87; kindergarten tchr. Sunnybrae Sch., Yardville, NJ, 1987—2002; psychologist East Windsor Regional Sch. Dist., Hightstown, NJ, 2002—. Named Sunnybrae Tchr. of Yr., Gov.'s Tchr. Recognition Program, 2000. Mem. NEA, Nat. Assn. Sch. Psychologists, NJ Edn. Assn., EWRSD Edn. Assn., NJ Assn. Sch. Psychologists, Kappa Delta Pi, Chi Sigma Iota.

GISH, ROBERT FRANKLIN, English language educator, writer; b. Albuquerque, Apr. 1, 1940; s. Jesse Franklin and Lillian J. Gish; m. Judith Kay Stephenson, June 20, 1961; children: Robin Elaine Butzier, Timothy Stephen, Annabeth. BA, U. N.Mex., Albuquerque, 1962, MA, 1967, PhD, 1972. Tchr. Albuquerque Pub. Schs., 1962-67; prof. U. No. Iowa, Cedar Falls, 1968-91; dir. ethnic studies, prof. English Calif. Poly. State U., San Luis Obispo, 1991-2000, prof., 1992-2000, prof. emeritus, 2000—. Vis. prof. U. N.Mex., 2001—. Author: Hamlin Garland: Far West, 1976, Paul Horgan, 1983, Frontier's End: Life of Harvey Fergusson, 1988, William Carlos Williams: The Short Fiction, 1989, Songs of My Hunter Heart: A Western Kinship, 1992, Frist Horses: Stories of the New West, 1993, North American Native American Myths, 1993, When Coyote Howls: A Lavaland Fable, 1994, Nueva Granada: Paul Horgan and the Southwest, 1995, Bad Boys and Black Sheep: Fateful Stories from the West, 1996, Beyond Bounds: Cross-Cultural Essays, 1996, Beautiful Swift Fox: Erna Fergusson and the Modern Southwest, 1996, Dreams of Quivira: Stories in Search of The Golden West, 1997. Avocation: guitarist. E-mail: rfg@robertfgish.com.

GISOLFI, DIANA (DIANA GISOLFI PECHUKAS), art history educator; b. N.Y.C., Sept. 12, 1940; d. Anthony M. and Eleanor (Hayes) Gisolfi; m. Philip Pechukas, June 15, 1963 (div. Sept. 1991); children: Rolf, Maria, Sarah, Fiona (dec.), Amy. Student, Manhattanville Coll., 1958-60; BA magna cum laude, Radcliffe Coll., 1962; postgrad., Yale U., 1962-63; MA, U. Chgo., 1964, PhD, 1976. Instr. CUNY, 1967-68, Marymount Manhattan Coll., N.Y.C., 1977-79; asst. prof. art history Pratt Inst., Bklyn., 1979-84, assoc. prof., 1984-90, prof., 1990—, chmn. dept., 1980-99. Vis. asst. prof. Pratt Inst., 1976-79; dir. Pratt in Venice, Italy, 1984—; spkr. Conv. on Veronese, Venice, 1988, Conv. on Tintoretto, Venice, 1994, Symposium on Italian Art in Am., Fordham U., 1993, Mass. Coll. Art, 1998, AM Berger lecture, Manhattanville Coll., 2001; invited participant Veronese Reconsidered, CASVA, Washington, 1988; spkr. in field. Illustrator (book) On Classic Ground, 1982; designer (book) Caudine Country, 1987; author: (with S. Sinding-Larsen) The Rule, the Bible, and the Council: The Library of the Benedictine Abbey at Praglia, 1998; contbr. articles on Veronese, Tintoretto and other sixteenth-century artists in North Italy and Venice to Art Bull., 1982, Artibus et Historiae 1987, 96, Arte Veneta 1989-90, Nuovi Studi su Paolo Veronese, 1990, Burlington Mag., 1995, Dictionary of Art, 1996, Tintoretto Convegno Acts, 1996, Renaissance Quar., 1997, 2000, 01, Encyclopedia of Italian Renaissance and Mannerist Art, 2000, and others. Coord. Park Slope Freeze, Bklyn., 1984-86, Peace and Justice Com., St. Francis Xavier, 1984-86. Am. Philos. Soc. grantee, 1989, Delmas Found. grantee, 1995-96. Mem. Italian Art Soc., Renaissance Soc., Coll. Art Assn., Caucus for Design History, Phi Beta Kappa. Democrat. Roman Catholic. Home: 843 President St Brooklyn NY 11215-1405 Office: Pratt Inst Dept Art History East 250 Brooklyn NY 11205 E-mail: dgisolfi@pratt.edu., Dianagisolfi@aol.com.

GIST, JOSEPH ANDREW, JR., retired elementary school educator; b. Garland, Wyo., Jan. 15, 1925; s. Joseph Andrew and Vida Edith Gist; m. Barbara Mills Gist, June 20, 1949; children: Barbara Gist Hanneloré, Herschel Mills Gist. AA, Napa (Calif.) Jr. Coll., 1947; BA, Chico (Calif.) State U., 1949; MA, San Jose (Calif.) State U., 1974. Elem. tchr. Redding (Calif.) Sch. Dist., 1949-57, elem. sch. prin., 1958—68, Franklin-McKinley Sch. Dist., San Jose, 1968—75, elem. sch. tchr., 1975-91. Shasta County conf. coord. Calif. Assn. Elem. Sch. Prins., 1965—67. Author: Rancher T.J. Trager and Little Tracey, Gold Rush Boy, Dutch Harbor, Dead Reckoning. Mem. County Dem. Com., Shasta County, Calif., 1964. With USN, 1943-46. Mem. NEA (life), Calif. Tchr. Assn., Calif. Assn. Elem. Sch. Prins., Phi Delta Kappa. Methodist. Avocations: writing music, writing novels, woodwork. Home: 4343 Miranda Ave Palo Alto CA 94306

GIST, MARILYN ELAINE, organizational behavior and human resource management educator; b. Tuskegee, Ala., May 9, 1950; d. Lewis A. and Grace (Perry) G. BA in Edn., Howard U., 1972; MBA, U. Md., 1982, PhD in Bus. Adminstrn. Organizational Behavior, 1985. Tchr. Montgomery County Pub. Schs., Rockville, Md., 1972-76; mgmt. intern NASA Goddard Space Flight Ctr., Greenbelt, Md., 1976-79, procurement mgr., 1980-81, staff asst. to dir. mgmt. ops., 1983-85; dir. contracts OAO Corp., Greenbelt, 1981-83; prof. organizational behavior U. N.C., Chapel Hill, 1985-87; Boeing Endowed prof. bus. mgmt. U. Wash., Seattle, 1987—2002. Staff cons. U. Md., Coll. Park, 1979-84; adj. prof. human resources Cornell U., 1995-96; pres., exec. dir. Millennium Resources, Inc., 1999—. Contbr. articles to profl. jours. Recipient Outstanding Student award Alumni Assn. Internat. U. Md., 1985, Alan Nash Outstanding Doctoral Student award U. Md., 1985, Chancellor's Disting. lectr. award U. Calif., Irvine, 1993; U. Md. Acad. Rsch. grantee, 1982-85. Mem. APA, Acad Mgmt. (Outstanding Paper award 1987). Democrat. Roman Catholic. Avocations: stained glass, photography, guitar. Office: 1001 4th Ave Ste 3200 Seattle WA 98154

GITLOW, ABRAHAM LEO, retired dean; b. N.Y.C., Oct. 10, 1918; s. Samuel and Esther (Boolhack) G.; m. Beatrice Alpert, Dec. 12, 1940; children: Allan Michael, Howard Seth. BA, U. Pa., 1939; MA, Columbia U., 1940, PhD, 1947. Substitute instr. Bklyn. Coll., 1946-47; instr. NYU, N.Y.C., 1947-50, asst. prof., 1950-54, assoc. prof., 1954-59, prof. econs., 1959-89, prof. emeritus, 1989—; acting dean NYU Coll. Bus. and Pub. Adminstrn., 1965-66, dean, 1966-85, dean emeritus, 1989—. Hon. dir. Bank Leumi Trust Co. N.Y.; pres. bd. edn. Ramapo (N.Y.) Cen. Sch. Dist. 2, 1963-66; pres., sec. Samuel and Esther Gitlow Found., N.Y.C. Author: Economics of the Mt. Hagen Tribes, New Guinea, 1947, Economics, 1962, Labor and Manpower Economics, 1971, Being the Boss: The Importance of Leadership and Power, 1992, NYU's Stern School: A Centennial Retrospective, 1995, Reflections on Higher Education: A Dean's View, 1995; co-editor: General Economics: A Book of Readings, 1963; contbr. articles to profl. jours. Served to 1st lt. USAAF, 1943-46, PTO. Recipient Univ. medal Luigi Bocconi U., 1983 Mem. Am. Econ. Assn. Home and Office: 9 Island Ave Apt T3 Miami Beach FL 33139-1349 E-mail: abgit@earthlink.net.

GITNER, DEANNE, retired school system administrator; b. Lyons, NY, Jan. 8, 1944; d. Myron and Mary (Kurland) Gebell; m. Gerald L. Gitner, June 24, 1968; children: Daniel Mark, Seth Michael. AB, Cornell U., 1966. Cert. English tchr. Tchr. English Gates (N.Y.) Chili Cen. Sch., 1966-68, Wantagh (N.Y.) Jr. and Sr. High Sch., 1968-70, F. Weiner Sch., Houston, 1980-81; writer Bellaire Texan, Houston, 1980; rep. sales McDougal Littel & Co., Chgo., 1981-83; writer Millburn Short Hills Ind., New Providence, N.J., 1987-93; comm. coord. Millburn Twp. (N.J.) Pub. Schs., 1993—2002; ret., 2001. Contbr. articles to profl. publs. Bd. dirs. United Way of Millburn-Short Hills, NJ, 1998—2001, sec., 1999—2002. Mem.: NJ Sch. Pub. Rels. Assn., NJ Press Women (newsletter editor 1992, hon. mention 1990, 2nd prize comm. contest 1992, 1st prize 1993, 1994, 3rd prize nat. contest 1994, Hon. Mention Nat. Contest 1995), Nat. Fedn. Press Women, Soc. Profl. Journalists, Cornell Alumni Assn. Admissions Network (chmn. 1990—2001), Nat. Coun. Jewish Women (v.p. Houston sect. 1976—79, pres. 1980—81, pub. rels. com. 1981—90, v.p. Essex County NJ sect. 1983—88, chmn. nat. bull. subcom. 1990—93, Vol. award), Cornell Alumni Fedn. (bd. dirs. 1995—, v.p. 1999—), Cornell Club N.Y.C., Cornell Club No. NJ (v.p. 1992, 1993, pres. 1994, 1995, co-pres. 1997—98, bd. dirs. 1999—).

GITTLEMAN, SOL, university official, humanities educator; b. Hoboken, N.J., June 5, 1934; s. Frank and Edna (Schlanger) G.; m. Robyn Singer, Sept. 9, 1956; children: Julia, Peter Thomas. BA, Drew U., 1955; MA, Columbia U., 1956; PhD, U. Mich., 1961; LHD (hon.), Hebrew Coll., 1993, Stonehill Coll., 1996. Asst. prof., German Mt. Holyoke Coll., South Hadley, Mass., 1962-64; asst. prof. Tufts U., Medford, Mass., 1964-70, prof. German, 1971—, chmn. dept. German and Russian, 1966-81, McCollester prof. religious studies, 1978—, provost, 1981—2002, acad. v.p., from 1981, now sr. v.p., Alice and Nathan Gantcher prof. Judaic studies, 1992, disting. univ. prof., 2002—. Dir. summer seminars NEH Author: Frank Wedekind, 1969, Sholem Aleichem, 1974, From Shtetl to Suburbia, 1978. Recipient Harbison award Danforth Found., 1970; named Alice and Nathan Gantcher Prof. of Judaic Studies, 1992, Disting. Prof., 1992, Gantcher Univ. prof., 2002—. Mem. MLA, Am. Assn. Tchrs. Yiddish, Am. Assn. Tchrs. German Office: Tufts U Ballou Hall Medford MA 02155

GITTLER, JOSEPHINE, law educator; b. Richmond, Va., May 13, 1943; d. Joseph and Lamie G. BA, Barnard Coll.; JD, Northwestern Coll., 1968. Bar: Conn. 1969. Law clk. U.S. Dist. Ct., New Haven, 1969-70, Conn. Supreme Ct., Hartford, 1970-71, U.S. Dist. Ct. Conn., 1971-72; from assoc. prof. Coll. Law to prof. Coll. Pub. Health U. Iowa, Iowa City, 1973—2002, prof. Coll. Pub. Health, 2002—. Chief counsel subcom. investigate juvenile deliquency jud. com. U.S. Senate, Washington, 1977-78; coord. U.S. Surgeon Gen.'s Conf., Washington, 1988; mem. exec. com. Consortium Ctrs. on Children Families & Law, 1989—2000; legis. cons. Nat. Assn. State and Territorial Maternal and Child Health and Crippled Children's Programs, 1982-86, recipient Pub. Svc. award 1982, 84; counsel interim study com. juvenile justice Iowa Gen. Assembly, Des Moines, 1975-77; vis. scholar Justice Ctr. of Atlanta, 1999; cons. in field. Contbr. articles to profl. jours. Chair Iowa Maternal and Child Health Adv. Coun., Des Moines, 1983-88; mem. Iowa Juvenile Justice Adv. Com., Des Moines, 1975—83, Iowa Crime Commn., Des Moines, 1974-75, interim com. Penal Reform and Correction, Des Moines, 1973-74. Office: U Iowa Coll Law Iowa City IA 52242

GITTMAN, ELIZABETH, education educator; b. NYC, Mar. 15, 1945; d. Kallman and Rebecca (Santcroos) Gittman; children: Stephen Loeb, Leslie Gulkis, Sherry Loeb. BS, NYU, 1966; MS, CUNY Queens Coll., 1969; PhD, Hofstra U., 1979, Cert. Advanced Study, 1987. Cert. ednl. adminstr., N.Y. Tchr. NYC Bd. Edn., Kew Gardens, NY, 1966-68; instr. New Sch. for Social Rsch., NYC, 1980-81; ind. cons., 1981-84; coord. instl. rsch. and evaluation Bd. Coop. Ednl. Svc. of Nassau County, Westbury, NY, 1984-94; assoc. prof. NY Inst. Tech., Old Westbury, NY, 1994-97; cons., 1997-98; dir. instrnl. support svc. Commack Pub. Sch., NY, 1998-2000; ind. cons., 2002—03. Adj. prof. L.I. U., Brookville, N.Y., 1987-93. Mem. high risk youth rev. com. Ctr. Substance Abuse Prevention, U.S. Dept. HHS, 1990-95; developer numerous ednl. programs. Recipient NYU Founders Day award, 1966; Hofstra U. Doctoral fellow, 1976. Mem.: ASCD, APA,

Northeastern Ednl. Rsch. Assn. (membership com. 1989—90, program com. 1989—2003, nominating com. 1991—2003, program co-chair 1993, editor 1993—95, bd. dirs. 1993—98, treas. 1996—98), Nat. Coun. Measurement in Edn., Am. Evaluation Assn., Am. Ednl. Rsch. Assn., Phi Delta Kappa (rsch. rep. 1990—91, exec. bd. 1990—2003, sec. 1991—93, conf. co-chair 1992, v.p. 1993—94, pres. 1995—96, nominating com. 1996—2000, Svc. award 1998), Kappa Delta Pi. Republican. Jewish. Avocations: computer applications, reading, writing. E-mail: elarn@optonline.net.

GIVEN, MAC F. biologist, educator; b. Abington, Pa., June 14, 1955; s. Peter Simmonds and Eleanor Jane (McFadden) G.; m. Barbara E. Scott, June 6, 1987; 1 child, Gabriel Scott. AB magna cum laude, Brown U., 1977; PhD, U. Conn., 1987. Sci. tchr. Friends' Ctrl. Sch., Phila., 1977-81; dir. Camp Dark Waters Conf. Ctr., Medford, N.J., 1981-82; adj. asst. prof. Providence (R.I.) Coll., 1987-89; prof. Neumann Coll., Aston, Pa., 1990—. Bd. dirs. Pendle Hill Conf. Ctr., Wallingford, Pa., 1995—. NSF grantee, 1992. Mem. AAAS, Assn. Study of Animal Behavior, Herpetologists' League, Sigma Xi. Mem. Soc. Friends Ch. Office: Neumann Coll One Neumann Dr Aston PA 19014

GIVEN, MELISSA ANN, elementary school educator, educational consultant; b. Charleston, West Virginia, June 5, 1961; d. Robert Carl and Janet (Barnette) Rehe; m. Bruce Owen Given. BS, West Va. State Coll., 1983; MA, West Va. U., 1989. Cert. elem. edn., mental retardation K-12, preschool handicapped, severe,profound handicapped. Tchr. Kanawha County Sch., Charleston, 1984—91, Monongalia County Sch., Morgantown, W.Va., 1991—94, Gwinnett County Sch., Buford, Ga., 1995—98, Kanawha County Sch., Dunbar, W.Va., 1998—. Course grader W.Va. U., Morgantown, 1991—94; cons., cadre tchr. Office Spl. Edn. W.Va. Dept. Edn., Charleston, 1999—; qualified mental retardation profl. Braley & Thompson, St. Albans, W.Va., 2000—01; qualified mental retardation prof. cons., 1999—. Named Tchr. of the Yr., West Va. Fedn. Coun. Exceptional Children, 2001. Mem.: Coun. Exceptional Children, La Belle Garden Club (co-v.p. 2001—). Episcopalian. Avocations: boating, swimming, photography. Home: 848 Alta Rd Charleston WV 25314 Office: Kanawha County Sch Dunbar Middle Sch 325 27th St Dunbar WV 25064 Business E-Mail: Wvcatlover39@aol.com.

GIVENS, PAUL EDWARD, industrial engineer, educator; b. Pwhuska, Okla., Aug. 12, 1934; s. George Edward Givens and Myrtle Elizabeth (Whipkey) Stewart; m. Ann Elizabeth Piper, Oct. 26, 1957; children: Scott Andrew, Mark Edward. BS in Indsl. Engring., Univ. Ark., 1957; MBA, Creighton Univ., 1968; PhD in Engring., Univ. Tex., Arlington, 1974. Sr. field engr. Svc. Pipeline Co., Tulsa, 1957-63; mgr. indls. relations Northern Natural Gas Co., Omaha, 1963-69; personnel mgr. The Western Co. of N.A., Ft. Worth, 1969-72; grad. teaching assoc. Univ. Tex., Arlington, 1972-74, instr., 1974; mgmt. cons. Cooperative Extension Svc. Miss. State Univ., Starkville, 1977-80, assoc. prof., 1974-80; v.p. ops. Stapccotn Cooperative, Greenwood, Miss., 1980-83; assoc. prof. Univ. Mo., Rolla, 1983-87; prof., chmn. indsl. and mgmt. systems engring. dept. U. South Fla., Tampa, 1987—2001; assoc. dean U. South Fla. Coll. Engring., Tampa, 2001—. Cons. in field. Author: (with others) Team Effort Advances Missouri, 1985; co-prodr.: (video) Industrial Engineering—Past, Present, and Future; contbr. papers to profl. jours. TV host PBS series, Miss., 1979; bd. dirs. Mo. Incutech Found., Rolla, 1984-85; tribal mem. Osage Indian nation, Pawhuska, Okla., 1934—; pres. ch. coun. St. Joseph's Cath. Ch., Starkville, 1978; mem. subcom. Fla. High Tech. Coun., Tampa, 1988—; mem. Boy Scouts Am., Ft. Worth, dist. chmn. 1970-72. Recipient 1st Edward A. Smith Rsch. award, Tulsa, 1985. Fellow Inst. Indsl. Engrs. (dir. mgmt. divsn. 1978-79), Am. Soc. Engring. Mgmt. (charter, bd. dirs. 1981-82, fellow 2001), Ark. Acad. Indsl. Engrs.; mem. KC, Soc. Engring. and Mgmt. Sys. (pres. 1991-92, sr. v.p. profl. devel. 1994-96), Am. Soc. Engring. Edn. (Bernie Sarchet award 1996), Acad. Mgmt. Republican. Avocations: golf, fishing. Home: 11501 Moffatt Pl Tampa FL 33617-2415

GIVENS, RANDAL JACK, communications educator; b. Borger, Tex., Mar. 17, 1951; s. Fred Frank and Doris Mae (Bley) G.; m. Carol Marie Griffin, May 21, 1973; children: Mary Leanna, Anna Elizabeth. BA in Speech, Lubbock (Tex.) Christian Coll., 1973; MA in Speech Comm., Tex. Tech. U., 1974; MAR in Counseling Psychology, Harding U., Memphis, 1977, MAR in Missiology, MTh in Philosophy, 1978; diploma in French, IFCAD, Brussels, 1982. Diploma in French, I.F.C.A.D., Brussels, 1982. Missionary (in French) Eglise du Christ, Brussels, 1979-82; dir. Internat. Sch. Conversational English, Brussels, 1982-89; acad. dean Internat. Christian U., Vienna, Austria, 1989-94; chmn. dept. comm., dir. forensics York (Nebr.) Coll., 1994-97, dir. grants and program devel., 1997—. Counselor Memphis Mental Health Ctr., 1976-78; group therapy coord. Memphis Rehab. Svc., 1976-78; chief coord. of translating 2 internat. confs., Strasbourg, France, 1983, Metz, France, 1987; bd. dirs. Grant Profls. Cert. Inst., 2003—; lectr. in field; ind. grants cons., 1998—; bd. dirs. Grant Profls. Cert. Inst. Author: Induced Feedback, 1974; translator (book): Johnson's Notes, 1989; editor Vienna Views newsletter, 1989-94. Bd. dirs. Blue Valley Cmty. Action Agy., 2001—, Grant Profls. Cert. Inst., Blue Valley Cmty. Action Agy.; mem. tech. panel Grant and Program Devel. Inst., 1999—. Recipient Svc. award Lubbock Christian Schs., 1992; Tex. Tech. U. grantee, 1974, 91. Mem. Nat. Soc. Fundraising Execs., Speech Comm. Assn. Am., Nebr. Speech Comm. Assn. (liaison for univ. affairs 1994), Speech Comm. Assn., Martial Arts Black Belt Assn., L'Association de l'Ordinateur (mem. tech. panel grant and program devel. inst.), Am. Assn. Grant Profls. (founding pres. 1998, pres. 1999, 2000—). Republican. Ch. of Christ. Avocations: martial arts, drummer, woodworking, computers. Home: 1315 Blackburn Ave York NE 68467-2011 Office: York College 1125 E 8th St York NE 68467-2699

GIZA, MARIE THERESA, elementary school educator, secondary school educator; b. Balt., May 1, 1931; d. Joseph Frank and Frances Theresa (Staniec) G.; B.A., Coll. of Notre Dame of Md., 1953; M.A., Cath. U. Am., 1960; Cert. Advanced Studies in Edn., Johns Hopkins U., 1972, M.S., 1982; postgrad. (scholar) U. Oslo, 1973. Elem. tchr. St. Jerome's Sch., Balt., 1953-56; social studies tchr. Cath. High Sch. of Balt., 1956-62, guidance counselor, 1962; Polish language instr. evening coll. Essex Community Coll., 1975-77; primary and intermediate tchr. Balt. Highlands Elem. Sch., 1962-92, ret., 1992; instr. in-service creative writing course for tchrs., Balt. County, 1978-80; cons. on social studies and econs. Carroll County Schs., 1983. Sec. Polish Nat. Alliance, Group 692, 1975-78; treas. PTA, 1974-76; mem. ethnic adv. com. for Balt. City Sch. Tchrs., 1979-83; pres. St. Stanislaus Parish Council, 1978-80, former pres. Southeast Area Council, Balt. Archdiocese; instr. Polish Nat. Alliance Language Sch. Father Koble Soc. Language Sch. St. Casimir's Parish, 1978-82; seminar lectr. to Lithuanian tchrs., Vilnius, Lithuania 1995; tchr. of English Lujiang U., Xiamen, China, 1992; 1st sec. Archdiocesan Pastoral Council, Balt. Recipient Elinor Pancoast award for excellence in teaching econs., 1978; cert. of merit Joint Council on Econ. Edn. and Internat. Paper Co. Found., 1982; Balt. Polish Community award, 1980; NDEA fellow in lang. arts to Kutztown State Tchrs. Coll., 1956; Russian scholar, Georgetown U., 1963-64, Fulbright scholar, India, 1990; recipient scholarships Jagiellonian U., Cracow, Poland, 1974. Cath. U. Lublin, Poland, 1976, Mikotaj Kopernik U., Torun, Poland, 1978, tchr. of yr. award in social studies Md. Coun. for Social Studies, 1992. Mem. NEA, Nat. Coun. Tchrs. English, Nat. Coun. for the Social Studies, Nat. Coun. Geographic Edn., Nat. Assn. for Ethnic Studies, Md. Geographic Alliance, Md. Tchrs. Assn., Tchrs. Assn. Baltimore County (One of Outstanding Tchrs. award 1983), Md. Coun. Tchrs. English Language Arts (disting. svc. award 1993, tchr. of yr. elementary 1985), Md. Council Tchrs. of English (tchr. of yr. award 1988), Women Educators of Balt. County (pres. 1992-93), Smithsonian Assn., Eta Sigma Phi, Delta Epsilon Sigma, Phi Delta Gamma, Pi Lambda Theta (cert. award for outstanding presentation on China 1994). Democrat. Roman Catholic. Contbr. articles to Creative Teacher; contbr. articles to profl. jours.; speaker in field. Home: 4000 N Charles St Apt 701 Baltimore MD 21218-1790

GLAD, JOAN BOURNE, retired clinical psychologist, educator; b. Salt Lake City, Apr. 24, 1918; d. E. LeRoy and Ethel G. (Rogers) Bourne; m. Donald D. Glad, Sept. 10, 1938 (dec. 1978); children: Dawn JoAnne Lundquist, Toni Ann Saunders, Sue Ellen Winmill, Roger Bruce. BA, UCLA, 1955; MA, U. Utah, 1960, PhD, 1965. Psychologist Utah State Dept. Health, Salt Lake City, 1960-65; founder, dir. adminstr. Child and Family Guidance Clinic, Primary Children's Hosp., Salt Lake City, 1965-68; dir. parent edn. Children's Hosp., Orange County, 1968-75; founder, adminstr. Family Learning Ctr., Santa-Ana Tustin Cmty. Hosp., Santa Ana, Calif., 1975-77; dir. Glad & Assocs., Tustin, Calif., 1977—2003, ret., 2003. Instr. Grad. Sch., Chapman Coll., Orange, Calif., 1970-73; cons. Calif. Assn. Neurologically Handicapped Children, Orange, 1970-77; lectr. self esteem Fullerton (Calif.) Coll., 1980-82; pres. Profl. Corp., Orange, Calif., 1999. Author: Reading Unlimited, 1965; editor newsletter Between You and Me, 1998—. Past Pres. Friends of Tustin (Calif.) Libr.; docent Tustin Hist. Soc. Mem. Assn. Holistic Health (a founder San Diego), Assn. Mormon Counselors and Psychotherapists, Redwood Psychol. Assn. Mem. Lds Ch. Home and Office: Glad & Assocs 309 Orangewood Dr Healdsburg CA 95448-4322 E-mail: joanglad@sonic.net.

GLADDEN, KATHLEEN ANN, anthropologist, educator; b. Grove City, Pa., Mar. 5, 1960; d. William Henry and Elizabeth Ann (Breaden) Gladden. BA, Allegheny Coll., 1982; MA, Tulane U., 1984; PhD in Anthropology, U. Fla., 1991. Vis. asst. prof. U. Pitts., 1993, asst. prof., 1994; vis. asst. prof. Carnegie Mellon U., Pitts., 1993, Indiana U. Pa., Kittaning, 1993, 1993; rsch. assoc. Womens Studies Ctr., 1993-94; instr. humanities and social scis. Pa. State U., Erie, 1998-99. Adj. faculty mem. U. Pitts., 1992—95, Pa. State U., Shenango, 1999—2000. Contbr. articles to sci. and profl. jours. Active Sacred Heart Ch., 2001—03, St. Leos Ch., 2003—. Fulbright scholar, Nat. U., Bogota, Columbia, 1992, U. Los Andes, 1992, Fulbright Tchg. fellow, 1992, Fulbright grantee, 1988—89. Mem.: Am. Anthrop. Assn. Republican. Avocation: flute. Home: 101 N Mill St # 415 Ridgway PA 15853 Personal E-mail: kathleengladden@hotmail.com.

GLADFELTER, WILBERT EUGENE, physiology educator; b. York, Pa., Apr. 29, 1928; s. Paul John and Marea Bernadette (Miller) G.; m. Ruth Isabelle Ballantyne, Jan. 26, 1952; children: James W., Charles D., Mary A. AB magna cum laude, Gettysburg (Pa.) Coll., 1952; PhD, U. Pa., 1960. NSF fellow U. Pa., Phila., 1956-58, NIH fellow, 1958-59, asst. instr., 1954-56; instr. physiology W.Va. U., Morgantown, 1959-61, asst. prof., 1961-69, assoc. prof., 1969-96, prof. emeritus, 1996—. Contbr. articles to profl. jours. Treas., Monongalia County chpt. W. Va. Heart Assn., 1976-95. With USN, 1946-48. NSF fellow, 1956-58. Mem. Am. Physiol. Soc., Soc. Neurosci., Soc. for Integrative and Comparative Biology, Sigma Xi, Phi Beta Kappa, Beta Beta Beta. Lutheran. Home: 70 Pine Tree Ln Morgantown WV 26508-2929 Office: WVa U Health Sci Ctr Dept Physiology Morgantown WV 26506

GLADSTONE, CAROL LYNN, education educator; b. N.Y.C., Aug. 14, 1944; d. Albert Ludwig and Jeanne Adler; m. Edward Gladstone, Nov. 20, 1973. BA, Hunter Coll., 1965; MA, CCNY, N.Y.C., 1967; PhD, Columbia Pacific U., 1988, postgrad., 1993-94. Cert. tchr. English, French, sch. dist. adminstr., Ariz., Conn., N.J., N.Y. English/reading tchr. Jr. High Sch. #120, N.Y.C., 1965-66; reading coord. Dewitt Clinton High Sch., Bronx, 1966-74; asst. chair John F. Kennedy High Sch., Bronx, 1974-85; asst. prin. James Monroe High Sch., Bronx, 1985-97, Morris High Sch., 1997-98, Flags H.S., 1998-99. Prin. PM/Saturday Sch. James Monroe H.S., 1993-94; trainer of adminstrv. staff Bronx. Supt.'s Office, 1992-2002, Manhattan Supt.'s Office, 1989-90; adj. prof. Coll. of New Rochelle, N.Y., 1988-89, Lehman Coll., Bronx, 1987-88, Manhattanville Coll., 1999-2002; grad. edn. advisor Mercy Coll., 2003—. Contbr. articles to profl. jours.; author: Competence in Cloze, 1989; author series of books: Gladstone Comprehensive Writing Program, 1986-88; study guides Broadway shows, 1999-2001, EverStar Classics and Related Readings, 2001—, Brooklyn Academy of Music's Screening Guides, 2001. Sec. Westchester (N.Y.) Alzheimer's Disease Assn., 1980-87; reporter Pub. Access Cable TV, Westchester, 1982-83. Named Supr. of Yr. Bronx Supt.'s Office, 1990-91, 94-95, Educator of Yr. Assn. Tchrs. N.Y., 1987-88, 90-91, Educator as Writer Mayor of City of N.Y., 1986; N.Y. Inst. for Humanities fellow, 1994. Mem. ASCD (assoc.), N.Y. State English Coun. (Educator of Excellence 1992-93, 95-96, regional dir. 1994-98, v.p. supervision 1998), N.Y. State Reading Assn., Bronx Assn. Prins. of English (chmn. 1990-98), N.Y.C. Assn. Asst. Prins. (exec. bd. 1995-98), Nat. Bd. for Profl. Teaching Standards, Nat. Coun. Tchrs. English (chancellor's com. new stds. 1997, ESL/ELA new stds., 1997, dist. literacy com., 1997). Avocations: travel, reading, gourmet cooking, computer technology.

GLANERT, KAREN LOUISE, secondary education educator; b. Sheboygan, Wis., July 21, 1954; d. Alvin H. and Laverne E. (Haun) G. GS Summa cum laude in Edn., U. Wis., Whitewater, 1976; postgrad. Tchr. Lakeland (Wis.) Mfg. Co., 1972-76; instr. Sheboygan Pub. Schs., 1978—. Counselor emotionally disturbed children; coach. Mem. Coun. Exceptional Children, Nat. Ret. Tchrs. Assn., Wis. Edn. Assn., Sheboygan Edn. Assn., PTA, Assn. Supervision and Curriculum Devel., Coun. Basic Edn., Luth. Women's League, Beta Sigma Phi. Lutheran. Office: Farmsworth Middle Sch 1017 Union Ave Sheboygan WI 53081-5936 Home: 2733 N 26th St Sheboygan WI 53083-3712

GLANZER, MURRAY, psychology educator; b. N.Y.C., Nov. 18, 1922; s. Max and Norma (Reichenthal) G.; m. Mona Naomi Sorcher, Sept. 20, 1953; children: Michael, Marla, James. BA, City Coll., N.Y.C., 1943; MA, U. Mich., 1948, PhD, 1952. Instr. Bklyn. Coll., 1949-53; project dir. to program dir. Am. Inst. Rsch., 1954-58; lectr. U. Pitts., 1955-58; rsch. assoc. Walter Reed Army Inst. Rsch. U. Md. Sch. Medicine, 1958-63; prof. N.Y.U., 1963—. Numerous publications; contbr. articles to profl. jours. Fellow Ford Found. U. Chgo., 1953-54, Guggenheim, Hebrew U., Jerusalem, 1969-70. Mem. Am. Psychol. Assn., Psychonomic Soc., Soc. Exptl. Psychologists. Home: 17 Weston Pl Lawrence NY 11559-1524 Office: NYU 6 Washington Pl New York NY 10003-6634

GLASCO, JOANN, adult education educator, consultant; b. Oxford, N.C., Apr. 8, 1965; d. McLeonard and Doris Elizabeth (Harris) G. BA in Early Childhood Edn., Shaw U., 1988; postgrad., N.C. Ctrl. U., 1989—. Dir. Kid's World Child Care, Creedmoor, N.C., 1990-91; edn. cons. Shaw U., Raleigh, N.C., 1991—. Edn. advisor Wake/Orange Head Start, Raleigh, 1993—; rep. Coun. for Early Childhood Profl. Recognition, Washington, 1993—; field assoc. Child Care Assessment Project, Raleigh, summer 1994. Mem. Nat. Head Start Assn., Nat. Assn. for Edn. of Young Children, Nat. Black Child Devel., N.C. Day Care Assn., N.C. Head Start Assn., Alpha Kappa Alpha. Democrat. Baptist. Avocations: music, reading, theatre arts, church and community activities, family gatherings. Office: Operation Breakthrough Head Start 200 E Umstead St Durham NC 27707-1850

GLASEL, JAY ARTHUR, biochemistry educator; b. N.Y.C., Apr. 30, 1934; s. Rudolph Louis and Mildred Rose (Weber) G.; m. Jean Muriel Stewardson, Oct. 2, 1962. BS, Calif. Inst. Tech., 1955; PhD; U. Chgo., 1959. Postdoctoral fellow U. Calif., San Diego, 1959-60, Imperial Coll., London, Eng., 1960-61; asst. prof. Columbia U., N.Y.C., 1964-69; assoc. prof. Health Ctr. U. Conn., Farmington, 1970-74, prof. Health Ctr., 1975—2000. Vis. rsch. fellow sch. chemistry Australian Nat. U., Canberra, 1988; vis. scientist NAS; exch. vis. Biol. Rsch. Inst., Szeged, Hungary, 1990; prof. emeritus Health Ctr., 2000-; mng. mem. Global Sci. Consulting LLC, 2000-. Capt. USAF, 1962-64. NSF fellow, 1959-61, NIH Fogarty Sr. Internat. fellow, 1979-80. Mem. Am. Soc. Biol. Chemists, Am. Chem. Soc., Am. Physical Soc. Office: U Conn Health Ctr Dept Biochemistry Farmington CT 06030-0001

GLASER, LUIS, biochemistry educator; b. Vienna, Mar. 30, 1932; came to U.S., 1953, naturalized, 1961; s. Hermann and Gisela (Kohn) G.; m. Ruth Walliser, May 18, 1961; children: Miriam, Nicole. BA, U. Toronto, Ont., Can., 1953; PhD, Washington U., St. Louis, 1956. Asst. prof. biol. chemistry Washington U., 1959-62, asso. prof., 1962-67, prof., 1967-75, chmn. dept. biol. chemistry, 1975-86; dir. Div. Biology and Biomed. Scis., 1980-86; exec. v.p., provost U. Miami, 1986—. Contbr. numerous articles on bacterial and mammalian metabolism to profl. jours.; editor Jour. Biol. Chemistry, 1969-74, 81-86, Jour. Supramolecular Structures, 1979-86, Jour. Cell Biology, 1981-92. Helen Hay Whitney fellow, 1956-59; NIH grantee; NSF grantee. Mem. Am. Soc. Biol. Chemists, Am. Chem. Soc., Am. Soc. Microbiology, Am. Soc. Neurochemists, AAAS. Democrat. Jewish. Office: PO Box 248033 Coral Gables FL 33124-8033 E-mail: lglaser@umiami.edu.

GLASGOW, KAREN, principal; b. N.Y.C., May 20, 1954; d. Douglas G. Glasgow. BS in Edn., U. Wis., 1976; MS in Spl. Edn., U. So. Calif., 1979; MA, Calif. State Univ., Los Angeles; PhD, Claremont Univ., 2001. Prin. Toluca Lake Elem. Sch., 2000—; adj. prof. Calif. State U. Northridge, Northridge, 2001—. Mem. Assoc. Adminstrs. L.A., Women in Ednl. Leadership, Assoc. of Calif. Sch. Adminstrn. of L.A.

GLASHEEN, GLORIA D. secondary school educator; b. June 30, 1945; m. Michael J. Glasheen, Aug. 1, 1970; children: Catharine, Jeffrey, Gregory, Theresa. BA, Cedar Crest Coll., 1967. Tchr. English Bethlehem (Pa.) Area Schs., 1967-70, Prince George's County Schs., Upper Marlboro, Md., 1970-73; tchr., English, gifted program Pennsbury HS, Fairless Hills, Pa., 1997—. Leader Boy Scouts Am., Holland, Pa., 1986-93. Recipient award, USA Today. Mem. NEA, NCTE, Pa. State Edn. Assn., Pa. Coun. Tchrs. English. Office: Pennsbury HS 705 Hood Blvd Fairless Hills PA 19030-3199

GLASS, DOROTHEA DANIELS, physiatrist, educator; b. N.Y.C. d. Maurice B. and Anna S. (Kleegman) Daniels; m. Robert E. Glass, June 23, 1940; children: Anne Glass Roth, Deborah, Catherine Glass Barrett, Eugene. BA, Cornell U., 1940; MD, Woman's Med. Coll. Pa., 1954; postgrad., U. Pa., 1960-61; DMS (hon.), Med. Coll. Pa., 1987. Diplomate Am. Bd. Phys. Medicine and Rehab. (guest bd. examiner 1978, 89). Intern Albert Einstein Med. Center, Phila., 1954-55, clin. asst. dept. medicine, 1956-59, attending phys. medicine and rehab., 1968-70, chmn. dept. phys. medicine and rehab., sr. attending, 1971-85; chief rehab. medicine VA Med. Ctr., Miami, Fla., 1985-95; clin. prof. dept. orthopaedics and rehab. U. Miami Sch. Medicine, 1985—. Lois Mattox Miller fellow preventive medicine Woman's Med. Coll. Pa., 1955-56, instr. preventive medicine, 1956-59, instr. medicine, 1960-62; resident phys. medicine and rehab. VA Hosp., Phila., 1959-62, chief phys. medicine and rehab., 1966-68, cons., 1968-82; asst. clin. dir. Jefferson Med. Coll. Hosp., Phila., 1963-66; Camden County Stroke Program, Cooper Hosp., Camden, N.J., 1963-66; gen. practice medicine, Phila., 1956-59; asst. med. dir., chief rehab. medicine and rehab. Moss Rehab. Hosp., Phila., 1968-70, med. dir., 1971-82, sr. cons., 1982— ; mem. active staff Temple U., Phila., 1968—, asso. prof. rehab. medicine, 1968-73, prof., 1973—, dir. residency tng. rehab. medicine, 1968-82; program dir. Rehab. Research and Tng. Center, 1977-80, chmn. dept. rehab. medicine, 1977-82; staff physician Hosp. Med. Coll. Pa., Phila., 1955-59, vis. asso. prof. neurology, 1973-79, clin. prof., 1977-82, vis. prof., 1982-96; mem. cons. staff Frankford Hosp., Phila., 1968-82, Phila. Geriatric Center, 1975-82; mem. active staff Willowcrest-Bamberger Hosp., Phila., 1980-82; asso. phys. medicine and rehab. U. Pa. Sch. Medicine, Phila., 1962-66; asst. prof. clin. phys. medicine and rehab., 1966-68; asst. clin. dir. dept. phys. medicine and rehab. Jefferson Med. Coll., Phila., 1963-66; cons. Vols. in Medicine Clinic, Stuart, Fla., 1996—. Contbr. articles to profl. jours. Mem. profl. adv. com. Easter Seal Soc. Crippled Children and Adults Pa., 1975-82; active Goodwill Industries Phila., 1973-82, Cmty. Home Health Svcs. Phila., 1974-82, Ea. Pa. chpt. Arthritis Found., 1968-82. Recipient humanitarian svc. cert. Gov.'s Com. on Employment Handicapped, 1974, Outstanding Alumnae award Commonwealth of Pa. Bd., Hosp. Med. Coll. Pa., 1975, humanitarian award Pa. Easter Seal Soc., 1981, John Eiselie Davis award Am. Kinesiotherapy Assn., 1988, Carl Haven Young svc. award, 1994, Disting. Career award Moss Rehab. Hosp., 1997, Outstanding Svc. and Accomplishments award Fla. Soc. Phys. Medicine and Rehab., 2001, Susan B. Anthony award LWV of Martin County, 2002. Mem. AMA, Am. Acad. Med. Dirs., Am. Acad. Phys. Medicine and Rehab. (disting. clinician award 1995, Krusen award 2000), Am. Assn. Electromyography and Electrodiagnosis (assoc.), Am. Assn. Sex Educators, Counselors and Therapists, Am. Burn Assn., Am. Coll. Angiology, Am. Coll. Utilization Rev., Am. Congress Rehab. Medicine (bd. govs. 1979-85, pres. 1986-87, gold Key award 1989), Am. Heart Assn. (coun. on cerebrovascular disease), Am. Lung Assn. Phila. and Montgomery County (bd. dirs. 1977-79), Am. Med. Women's Assn., Assn. Acad. Physiatrists, Assn. Med. Rehab. Dirs. and Coordinators, Coll. Physicians Phila., Emergency Care Rsch. Inst., Gerontol. Soc., Internat. Assn. Rehab. Facilities, Internat. Rehab. Medicine Assn., Pan Am. Med. Assn., Fla. Med. Assn., Fla. Soc. Phys. Medicine and Rehab. (pres. 1975-77, Award for Outstanding Svc. in Rehab. Medicine 2001), Pa. Med. Soc. (phys. medicine and rehab. adv. com. 1975-82), Pa. Thoracic Soc., Delaware Valley Hosp. Coun. Forum, Phila. Med. Soc., Phila. PSRO (bd. dirs. 1975-82), Phila. Soc. Phys. Medicine and Rehab. (pres. 1968-69), Laennec Soc. Phila., Royal Soc. Health, Alpha Omega Alpha. E-mail: glassrd@earthlink.net.

GLASSCOCK, ELIZABETH ANNE (LIBBY GLASSCOCK), kindergarten educator, adjunct college instructor; b. Florence, Ala., Nov. 11, 1952; d. Harold Owen and Marjorie (Hudson) G. BS, U. N. Ala., 1974, EdS, 1985; MA, U. Ala., Tuscaloosa, 1977. Cert. early childhood and elem. tchr., Ala. Title I reading tchr. Athens (Ala.) City Schs., 1974-75, kindergarten tchr., 1975—. Adj. instr. Athens State Coll., 1981, 86—. Active kindergarten task force Plan for Excellence for Ala.'s Schs., 1984. Named Outstanding Young Educator, Athens Jaycees, 1980-81. Mem. NEA, Ala. Edn. Assn., Athens City Educators (sec. 1986-87, bldg. rep. 1975-76, 80-81, 84-85), Alpha Delta Kappa (sec. Tau chpt. 1980-82, treas. 82-84, v.p. 88-90, pres. 90-92).

GLASSER, CHARLES EDWARD, university president emeritus; b. Chgo., Apr. 3, 1940; s. Julius J. and Hilda (Goldman) G.; m. Hannah Alex, Mar. 8, 1987; children: Gemma Maria, Julian David. BA in History, Denison U., 1961; MA in Polit. Sci., U. Ill., 1967; JD, John F. Kennedy U., 1970. Bar: Calif. 1970, U.S. Ct. Appeals (9th cir.) 1970. Pvt. practice Hineser, Spellberg & Glasser, Pleasant Hill, Calif., 1971-77; dean Sch. Law John F. Kennedy U., Orinda, Calif., 1977-83, pres., 1990—2003, pres. emeritus, 2003—; v.p., gen. counsel Western Hosp. Corp., Emeryville, Calif., 1983-90. Author: The Quest for Peace, 1986. Mem. Calif. Bar Assn. Office: John F Kennedy U 12 Altarinda Rd Orinda CA 94563-2603

GLASSICK, CHARLES ETZWEILER, academic foundation administrator; b. Wrightsville, Pa., Apr. 6, 1931; s. Gordon J. and Melva G. (Etzweiler) G.; m. Mary Williams, Feb. 27, 1952; children: Bruce, Judith, Jeffrey, Robert, Jonathan. BS with honors, Franklin and Marshall Coll., 1953; MA, PhD, Princeton U., 1957; D.Sc. (hon.), U. Richmond, 1977; L.L.D. (hon.), Dickinson Sch. Law, 1986; LLD, Pepperdine U., 1996, Adrian Coll., 1997; LHD (hon.), Franklin & Marshall Coll., 1997. Research chemist Rohm & Haas Co., Phila., 1957-62; instr. gen. chemistry Temple U., Phila., 1957-62; prof. chemistry Adrian (Mich.) Coll., 1962-68; v.p. Great Lakes Colls. Assn., Ann Arbor, Mich., 1968-69; asso. dean for acad. affairs Albion (Mich.) Coll., 1969-71, v.p. for acad. affairs, 1971-72; pres.

Va. Inst. Scientific Research, Richmond, 1972-77; provost, v.p. for acad. affairs U. Richmond, Va., 1972-77; pres. Gettysburg (Pa.) Coll., 1977-89, Woodruff Arts Ctr., Atlanta, 1990-96; sr. scholar Carnegie Found. for Advancement of Tchg., Menlo Park, Calif., 1989-90, acting pres., 1995, interim pres., 1996-97, sr. assoc., 1997-2001, sr. assoc. emeritus, 2001—; interim pres. N.C. Wesleyan Coll., 2000-01, Reinhardt Coll., 2001—02. Cons. NEH, 1971-72, NSF, 1963-67, Va. Coun. High Edn., 1972-76; mem. exec. com. Luth. Ednl. Conf. of N.Am., 1983-86; mem. Pres.'s Commn. Nat. Collegiate Athletic Assn., 1988-89; interim pres. Converse Coll., 1998-99; interim dir. Scholars Press, 1999-2000; vis. fellow Cambridge U., 2002. Mem. editorial bd. Liberal Education, 1978-82, Educational Record, 1985-97. Mem. Mental Health and Mental Retardation Task Force Manpower Devel., Richmond, 1975—77, ACE Commn. on Minorities; bd. dirs. Meth. Conf. Homes Aging, 1985—89, Hist. Gettysburg/Adams County, 1979—89, Midtown Alliance, 1991—97; mem. exec. com. Atlanta Cultural Olympiad, 1991—96; trustee, vice-chmn. Carnegie Found. Advancement in Tchg., 1991—97, Eisenhower Soc., 1985—95, Ga. Found. Ind. Colls., 1992—, Literacy Action, Inc., 1994—97, Found. Hosp. Art, 1994—; bd. curators Ga. Hist. Soc., 1997—99; bd. regents Am. Arch. Fedn., 1998—; Fulbright sr. scholar specialist, 2002—. Mem. AAAS, AAUP, Am. Chem. Soc., N.Y. Acad. Scis., Danforth Assocs., Am. Chem. Soc., Phi Beta Kappa (hon.), Beta Gamma Sigma, Omicron Delta Kappa, Alpha Chi Omega. Methodist. Home: 216 Mills Ave Spartanburg SC 29302 E-mail: CEGlassick@aol.com.

GLASSMAN, ARMAND BARRY, physician, pathologist, scientist, educator, administrator; b. Paterson, N.J., Sept. 9, 1938; s. Paul and Rosa (Ackerman) G.; m. Alberta C. Macri, Aug. 30, 1958; children: Armand P., Steven B., Brian A. BA, Rutgers U., N.J., 1960; MD magna cum laude, Georgetown U., Washington, 1964. Diplomate Am. Bd. Pathology, Am. Bd. Nuclear Medicine. Intern Georgetown U. Hosp., Washington, 1964-65; resident Yale-New Haven Hosp., West Haven VA Hosp., 1965-69; asst. prof. pathology, Coll. Medicine U. Fla.; chief radioimmunoassay lab. Gainesville VA Hosp.; practice lab. and nuc. medicine, 1969-71; dir. clin. labs., assoc. prof., prof. pathology, cellular, molecular biology Med. Coll. Ga., Augusta, 1971-76; cons. physician in nuclear medicine Univ. Hosp., Augusta, 1973-76; med. dir. clin. labs. Med. U. S.C. Hosp., Charleston, 1976-87; attending physician in lab. and nuclear medicine Med. U. S.C., Charleston, 1976-87, assoc. med. dir. Med. U. Hosp. and Clinics, 1982-86; med. dir. clin. labs. Charleston Meml. Hosp., S.C., 1976-87; cons. VA Hosp., Charleston, 1976-87; prof., chmn. dept. lab. medicine Med. U. S.C., 1976-87, med. dir. MT and MLT programs, 1976-87, clin. prof. pathology, lab. medicine, and radiology, 1987—, acting chmn. dept. immunology and microbiology, 1985-87, assoc. dean Coll. Medicine, 1979-85, asst. and assoc. dean Coll. Allied Health Sci., 1984-87, chmn. hosp. exec. com., 1985-86, acting med. dir. Univ. Hosp. and Clinics, 1985-86; sr. v.p. med. affairs, prof. lab. medicine and nuclear medicine Montefiore Med. Ctr. and Albert Einstein Coll. Medicine, Bronx, N.Y., 1987-89; v.p., lab. dir. Nat. Reference Lab., Nashville, 1989-92; from clin. prof. to prof. dept. pathology Vanderbilt U., Nashville, 1990-94; dir. Vanderbilt Pathology Lab. Svcs., 1992-94; dir. clin. labs. Vanderbilt U. Med. Ctr., 1993-94, O. Stribling chair, prof., 1994—; head and chair divsn./dept. lab. medicine U. Tex., M.D. Anderson Cancer Ctr., Houston, 1994-96, also med. dir. Med. Tech. & Cytogenetic Tech. programs, 1994-96, 2001—, also dir. sect. cytogenetics, 1994—, also dir. sect. cytogenetic, 2002—, chair ops. and improvement mgmt. com. dept. hematopathology, 1998—2002, prof. Grad. Sch. Biol. Scis., 1994—. Adj. prof. Grad. Sch. Biol. Scis. and U. Tex. Health Scis. Med. Sch., 1994—; adv. coun. Trident Tech. Coll., 1976-87; bd. dirs. Fetter Family Health Ctr.; mem. steering com. pathology and lab medicine U. Tex. M.D. Anderson Cancer Ctr., 1998-2000, mem. radiation safety com., 1998-, pharmacy and therapeutics com., 2000-, credentials com., 2002—, radiation drug rsch. com., 2003—, chmn. task force on antiemetic drugs, 2003—; founding dir. Sealite, Inc., 1987-99, chmn. bd. dirs., 1995-99; med. adv. com. Nashville Red Cross Blood Ctr., 1991-94, acting med. dir., 1991-92; bd. sci. advisors Nat. Health Labs./Nat. Reference Lab., 1992-94; trustee, bd. dirs. Gulf Coast Cmty. Blood Ctr., 1994—; cons. in field. Editor, co-editor 4 books; bd. editors Annals of Clin. and Lab. Scis., 1981—; contbr. over 170 articles to profl. jours., 30 chpts. to books. Trustee Coll. Prep. Sch., 1979-84, chmn. bd., 1983-84; trustee, bd. dirs., v.p. Mason Prep. Sch., 1984-87; bd. dirs. United Way, 1983-87, Am. Cancer Soc., 1984-87; co-founder, bd. dirs. Glassman Family Fund, 1998—. With USMCR, 1956-64. Johnson and Avalon Found. scholar Georgetown U., 1961-64, State scholar Rutgers U., 1956-60. Fellow ACP, Coll. Am. Pathologists (numerous coms.), Assn. Clin. Scientists (Diploma of Honor 1987, pres. 1990-91, exec. com. 1990-95, Clin. Scientist of Yr. 1993, C.P. Brown lectr. 1995), Am. Soc. Clin. Pathology (coun. immunohematology and blood banking 1983-89, coun. grad. med. edn. and rsch. 1998—, Commr.'s award for Continuing Edn. 1989, nat. contbg. editor to Resident In-Svc. Exam. 2000-) Am. Bd. Pathology (transfusion medicine/blood bank test com. 1984-88), Am. Coll. Nuc. Medicine, N.Y. Acad. Medicine; mem. Internat. Acad. Pathology, Am. Assn. Pathologists, Soc. Nuc. Medicine (chmn. edn. com. 1973-77, acad. coun. 1979-92), AMA (Physician's Recognition award, instnl. rep. to sect. on med. schs., 1987-94, 2003—), So. Med. Assn., Am. Geriat. Soc. (founding fellow So. divsn.), Am. Soc. Microbiology, Am. Assn. Blood Banks (chmn. cryobiology com. 1974-83, edn. com. 1978-85, sci. program com. 1981-84, autologous transfusion com. 1979-83, bd. dirs. 1984-87, transfusion practices com. 1992-96), Assn. Schs. Allied Health Professions (bd. editors jour. 1979-83), Soc. Cryobiology (treas., bd. dirs. 1978-80), AAAS, N.Y. Acad. Scis., Acad. Clin. Lab. Physicians and Scientists (exec. coun. 1978-85, pres. 1982-83), S.E. Area Blood Bankers (pres. 1979-81, exec. coun. 1980-85), Tenn. Assn. Blood Banks (treas. 1993-94), Am. Coll. Physician Execs., Sigma Xi, Alpha Eta, Alpha Omega Alpha. Avocations: jogging, tennis, community service. Office: U Tex MD Anderson Cancer Ctr Hematopathology Unit 350 1515 Holcombe Blvd Houston TX 77030-4009 E-mail: aglassma@mail.mdanderson.org.

GLASSMAN, IRVIN, mechanical and aeronautical engineering educator, consultant; b. Balt., Sept. 19, 1923; s. Abraham and Bessie (Snyder) G.; m. Beverly Wolfe, June 17, 1951; children: Shari Powell, Diane Geinger, Barbara Ann. B.E., Johns Hopkins U., 1943, D.Eng., 1950. Research asst. Manhattan Project, Columbia U., N.Y.C., 1943-46; mem. faculty Princeton U., N.J., 1950—, prof. mech. and aero. engring., 1964—, Robert H. Goddard prof. mech. and aero. engring., 1988—99, prof. emeritus, 1999—, dir. Ctr. for Energy and Environ. Studies, 1972-79. Cons. to industry; vis. prof. U. Naples, Italy, 1966-67, 78-79, Stanford U., 1975. Author: (with R.F. Sawyer) Performance of Chemical Propellants, 1971, Combustion, 1987, 3d edit., 1996; editor Combustion Sci. & Tech. Jour., also 3 books; contbr. articles to tech. jours. Served with U.S. Army, 1944-46. NSF fellow, 1966-67 Fellow AIAA (Propellants and Combustion award 1998); mem. AAUP, Nat. Acad. Engring., Combustion Inst. (Sir Alfred Egerton Gold medal 1982), Am. Soc. Engring. Edn. (Roe award 1984), Am. Chem. Soc., Tau Beta Pi. Achievements include 3 rocket propellant and burner patents. Home: 160 Longview Dr Princeton NJ 08540-5641 Office: Princeton U Dept Mech & Aero Engring Princeton NJ 08544-5261 E-mail: glassman@princeton.edu.

GLAYSHER, FREDERICK, English language educator; b. Detroit, Mich., Feb. 9, 1954; B in Gen. Studies, U. Mich., 1980, MA, 1981. Instr. English Gunma U., Maebashi, Japan, 1982-83, Ill. State U., Normal, 1983-86, Ariz. Western Coll./Colorado River Indian Tribes Reservation, Parker, 1990-92; instr. creative writing Mohave C.C., Lake Havasu, Ariz., 1991-92; instr. non-western lit. and English Lewis and Clark C.C., Godfrey, Ill., 1992-94; instr. multicultural lit. Oakland U., Rochester, Mich., 1994—. Participant Fulbright-Hays Group Project, China, 1994, NEH Summer Seminar on India, 1995, UN Millennium Forum, 2000. Author poems; author: Into the Ruins: Poems, 1999, The Bower of Nil: A Narrative Poem, 2002; editor: Robert Hayden's Collected Prose, 1984, Robert Hayden's Collected Poems, 1985; contbr. articles, poems and revs. to profl. jours. Mem. Baha'i Faith. E-mail: fglaysher@hotmail.com.

GLAZE, LYNN FERGUSON, development consultant; b. Oakland, Calif., May 24, 1933; d. Kenneth Loveland and Constance May (Pedder) Ferguson; m. Harry Smith Glaze, Jr., July 3, 1957; children: Catherine, Charles Richard. BA, Stanford U., 1955, MA, 1966. Devel. dir. Greenwich Acad., Conn., 1982-84; devel. cons. Del. Learning Ctr., Brandywine Mus., Opera Del., others, 1984—. Author: Seasons of the Trail, 2000. Pres. Darien-Norwalk YWCA, Conn., 1973-76; sec. Darien Republican Town com., 1974-79; dist. chmn. Darien Rep. Meeting, 1974-76, mem. Rep. Nat. Conv. Platform Com., 1988; vestry St. Luke's Ch., Darien, 1979-82; justice of the peace, Darien, 1981-84; bd. dirs. Ingleside Homes, Inc., 1986-92, Henrietta Johnson Med. Ctr., 1994-97; pres. Del. ProChoice Med. Fund, 1997-99; mem. Gov.'s Small Bus. Coun., 1987, EEOC, New Castle County, 1991-94, Del. Common Cause, 1999-2003, Coro Found. fellow.

GLEASON, ABBOTT, history educator; b. Cambridge, Mass., July 21, 1938; s. Sarell Everett and Mary Eleanor (Abbott) G.; m. Sarah Caperton Fischer, June 11, 1966; children— Nicholas Abbott, Margaret Holliday BA, Harvard U., 1961, PhD, 1969. Asst. prof. history Brown U., Providence, 1969-73, assoc. prof. history, 1973-78, prof. history, 1978—, Keeney prof. history, 1993—; sec. Kennan Inst. for Advanced Russian Studies, Woodrow Wilson Ctr., Washington, 1980-82, chmn. history, 1989-92; dir. Watson Inst., 1999-2000, dir. univ. rels., 2000—. Mem. overseers com. to visit Davis Ctr. for Russian Studies, Harvard U., Cambridge, 1981-85, 91-97; bd. dirs. Fabergé Arts Found. Author: European and Muscovite, 1972, Young Russia, 1980, Totalitarianism, 1995 (with William Taubman and Sergei Khrushchev), Nikita Khrushchev, 2000; co-editor: Bolshevik Culture, 1985, Shared Destiny, 1985, Nineteen Eighty-Four: George Orwell and our Future, 2003. Howard Found. fellow, 1973-74; Rockefeller fellow Aspen Inst., 1977; Mellon fellow Harvard U., 1985 Mem. Am. Hist. Assn., Am. Assn. Advancement Slavic Studies (del. to Am. Coun. Learned Socs. 1984-87, bd. dirs. 1991-97, exec. com. 1994-97, pres. 1995). Democrat. Home: 30 John St Providence RI 02906-1043 Office: Brown U Dept History 142 Angell St Providence RI 02912-9040 E-mail: abbott_gleason@brown.edu.

GLEASON, WALLACE ANSELM, JR., medical educator and researcher; b. Fargo, N.D., July 26, 1944; s. Wallace Anselm and Elizabeth Madeline (Powers) G.; m. Mary Jo-Ann Hofer, Nov. 25, 1972; children: Michael Andrew, Dennis Patrick. Student, Creighton U., 1962-65; BS, U. Minn., 1967, MD, 1969. Diplomate Am. Bd. Pediatrics. Intern St. Louis Children's Hosp., 1969-70, resident, 1970-72; asst. in pediatrics Washington U., St. Louis, 1969-73, instr., 1973-74; instr. pediatrics St. Louis U., 1974-75, asst. prof., 1975-77, U. Tex. Health Sci. Ctr., San Antonio, 1977-82, assoc. prof., 1982-84; assoc. prof., chief divsn. pediat. gastroenterology U. Tex. Med. Sch., Houston, 1984-96, prof. pediat., chief divsn. gastroenterology, hepatology & nutrition, 1996—, asst. dean admissions and student affairs, 1998—. Contbr. articles to profl. jours. Fellow Am. Acad. Pediat.; mem. Am. Gastroenterol. Assn., N.Am. Soc. Pediatric Gastroenterology, So. Soc. Pediat. Rsch., Soc. Pediat. Rsch., Houston Pediat. Soc., Houston Gastroenterol. Soc. Roman Catholic. Home: 6720 Rutgers Houston TX 77005-3855 Office: Univ Tex Med Sch 6431 Fannin #3142 Houston TX 77030

GLEDHILL, ROGER CLAYTON, statistician, engineer, mathematician, educator; b. Parkersburg, W.Va., July 14, 1943; s. Arthur Clayton and Frances Marie (Freeman) G.; m. Barbara Louise Baker, June 12, 1965; children: Diane Michelle, David Arthur. BBA, Miami U., Oxford, Ohio, 1965; MA, U. Mass., 1972; MS, PhD, Va. Poly. Inst. and State U., 1976. Assoc. prof. statistics Ea. Mich. U., Ypsilanti, 1976—. Author: Numerical Methods, 1993; contbr. articles to profl. publs. Ford Found. fellow, 1975. Mem. Mensa, Alpha Iota Delta, Phi Kappa Phi, Alpha Pi Mu, Pi Mu Epsilon, Omicron Delta Epsilon, Alpha Kappa Psi, Tau Beta Phi, Beta Gamma Sigma, Tau Kappa Epsilon. Avocations: computers, sailing, photography, travel, astrophysics. Office: Ea Mich Univ Owen Hall Ypsilanti MI 48197

GLEICHMANN, FRANCES EVANGELINE, retired elementary educator; b. Marion, N.C., Sept. 24, 1920; d. Alexander Rudolph and Margaret Katherine (McNeely) McCulloch; m. August O. Gleichmann, Dec. 1, 1945. Diploma, Pfeiffer Jr. Coll., 1940; BS in Edn., Asheville Coll., 1942; postgrad., Mount St. Agnes Coll., Johns Hopkins U., U. Md., U. R.I. Elem. tchr. Balt. City Pub. Schs., 1942-85. Cooperating tchr. for student tchrs. from Towson State U. Balt. City Pub. Schs., 1957-59. Co-author: Tales of the Smokies and Blue Ridge Mountains1, 1997; contbr. poetry to poetry-.com, poetry to Internat. Libr. Poetry. Recipient Econ. Edn. Tchr, award Econ. Edn. Program Com., 1985, Disting. Alumni award Pfeiffer Coll., 1973, Tate award Balt. C. of C. and Tate Industries, 1975, Salute 13 award Sta. WJZ TV, 1980, Golden Poet award World of Poetry, 1985-88. Mem. NEA, Md. State Ret. Tchrs. Assn., Balt. City Ret. Tchrs. Assn., Alpha Delta Kappa (Md. state publicity chmn. 1988-90, Alpha Delta Kappa week chmn. 1986-88). Home: 10 Dungarrie Rd Baltimore MD 21228-3401

GLENN, CORNELIA JARMON, education educator; m. James H. Glenn; children: Kimberly L., James H. Glenn III. BS, Wis. State U., 1971; MS of Spl. Edn., U. Wis., 1974; EdD, U. Ky. Elem. tchr. Greendale (Wis.) Pub. Schs., 1971-72; primary tchr., spl. edn. Wauwatosa (Wis.) Pub. Schs., 1975-76, 1976-77; elem. tchr. Dist. 88, Bellwood, Ill., 1987-88; prof. Ky. Cmty. and Tech. Colls., Owensboro, 1988—2003. Mem. primary assessment task force Ky. Dept. Edn.; mem. adv. com. Commonwealth Ky. Goals 2000, Ky. Edn. Reform Act Regional Svc. Ctr. V.p., state and local edn. chair LWV, Owensboro, 1988-2003; bd. dirs. Owensboro Dance Theatre, 1989-95, Girls Inc. Am., Owensboro, 1989-95; scholarship chmn. Owensboro Career Devel., 1990-94; v.p. adv. bd. Daviess County Extension Svc., 2001—; chr. wealth coach Owensboro Saves, 2002—. Grantee Dept. Edn., Frankfort, 1992. Mem. ASCD, AAUW, NAACP, Assn. Childhood Edn. Internat., Am. Assn. Women in C.C., O.H.R.C. (bd. dirs.), Ky. Blacks in Higher Edn. (conf. chair), Human Devel. Coun. (bd. dirs.), Ky. Assn. Devel. Edn., Laubach Internat. Avocations: painting, gardening, down hill skiing, reading. Home: 1001 Michaels Ct Owensboro KY 42303-6443 Office: Owensboro Community Coll 4800 New Hartford Rd Owensboro KY 42303-1800 E-mail: cornelia.glenn@kctcs.edu.

GLENN, EVELYN NAKANO, social sciences educator; b. Sacramento, Aug. 20, 1940; d. Makoto and Haru (Ito) Nakano; m. Gary Anthony Glenn, Nov. 20, 1962; children: Sara Haruye, Antonia Grace, Patrick Alexander. BA, U. Calif., Berkeley, 1962; PhD, Harvard Coll., 1971. Asst. prof. sociology Boston U., 1972-84; assoc. prof. sociology Fla. State U., Tallahassee, 1984-86; prof. sociology SUNY, Binghamton, 1986-90; prof. sociology women's and ethnic studies U. Calif., Berkeley, 1990—. Mem. bd. scholars Am. Nat. Mus., L.A., 1989—; vis. rsch. scholar Murray Rsch. Ctr., Radcliffe Coll., 1989-90. Author: Issei, Nisei, Warbride, 1986, Unequal Freedom: How Race and Gender Shaped American Citizenship and Labor, 2002; editor: Mothering: Ideology, Experience and Agency, 1994; adv. editor Gender and Soc., 1986-90, Frontiers, 1991-93, Editl. Collective Feminist Studies, 1999-; dep. editor Am. Sociol. Rev., 1999-2003; contbr. articles to profl. publs. Named Japanese Am. of Biennum, Japanese Am. Citizens League, 1994; recipient Article prize Assn. Black Women Historians, 1993. Mem. Am. Sociol. Assn. (mem. coun. 1990-94), Soc. for Study of Social Problems (pres. 1998-99, v.p. 1988-90, bd. dirs. 1984-87). Office: Univ Calif 2241 College Ave Berkeley CA 94720-1002

GLENN, JAMES FRANCIS, urologist, educator; b. Lexington, Ky., May 10, 1928; s. Cambridge Francis and Martha (Morrow) G.; children: Cambridge Francis II, Sara Brooke, Nancy Carrick, James Morrison Woodworth; m. Gay Elste Darsie, Jan. 11, 2002. Student (Yale Regional scholar), Univ. Sch., Lexington, 1946; BA in Gen. Sci. (Bausch and Lomb Nat. Sci. scholar), U. Rochester, 1949; MD, Duke U., 1952; DSc, U. Ky., 1998. Diplomate Am. Bd. Urology (mem.), Nat. Bd. Med. Examiners. Intern Peter Bent Brigham Hosp., Boston, 1952-54; asst. resident urology Duke U. Med. Ctr., 1956-58, resident, 1958-59; instr. urology Duke U., 1958-59, prof., chief div. urology, 1963-80; asst. prof. Yale U., 1959-61; assoc. prof. Bowman Gray Sch. Medicine, Wake Forest Coll., 1961-63; practice medicine specializing in urology New Haven, 1959-61, Winston-Salem, N.C., 1961-63, Durham, N.C., 1963-80; prof. surgery, dean Med. Sch., Emory U., 1980-83; pres. Mt. Sinai Med. Ctr., 1983-87; prof. surgery U. Ky. Coll. Medicine, Lexington, 1987—; CEO Markey Cancer Ctr., 1989-93; chief staff Univ. Hosp., Lexington, 1993-95, chmn. dept. surgery, 1996-97. Sci. dir. Coun. for Tobacco Rsch. U.S.A., 1987-91, chmn. bd., 1991—. Contbg. author: Renal Neoplasia, 1967, Urodynamics, 1971, Textbook of Surgery, 1972, Plastic and Reconstructive Surgery of The Genital Area, 1973, Current Operative Urology, 1975, Campbell's Urology, 1977; author, editor: Diagnostic Urology, 1964, Ureteral Reflux in Children, 1966, Urologic Surgery, 1969, rev. edit., 1975, 84, 90; contbr. numerous articles to profl. jours. Capt. M.C., USAF, 1954-56. Mem. Am. Assn. Genitourinary Surgeons (pres. 1992-93, hon. 1998), Am. Surg. Assn., ACS, AMA (sec. sect. urology 1972-73, chmn. 1975-77), Assn. Am. Med. Colls., Internat. Urol Soc. (v.p. 1985-91, pres. 1991-94), Clin. Soc. Genito-Urinary Surgeons (pres. 1990-91), N.Y. Acad. Medicine, Soc. Pediatric Urology (pres. 1972-73), Soc. Pelvic Surgeons (pres. 1980-81), Soc. Univ. Surgeons, Soc. Univ. Urologists (pres. 1971-72), Royal Coll. Surgeons (hon. fellow 1987), German Urol. Assn. (hon.), Australasian Urologic Soc. (hon.), Brit. Assn. Urologic Surgeons (hon.) Home: 101 Idle Hour Dr Lexington KY 40502-1166 Office: Univ Ky Med Ctr Hosp Adminstrn 800 Rose St Lexington KY 40536-0001 E-mail: drjglenn@aol.com.

GLENN, JAMES H., JR., business educator; b. Birmingham, Ala., Feb. 17, 1948; s. James H. and Betty J. G.; m. Cornelia J., July 1, 1972; children: Kimberly, James III. BS, Wis. State U., 1971; MBA, U. Wis., 1974; EdD, U. Ky., 1991. Adj. faculty Concordia Coll., River Forest, Ill., 1985-88; assoc. prof. bus. technology Owensboro (Ky.) C. C., 1988—. Adj. faculty Brescia Coll., Owensboro, Ky., 1990-95, Ivy Tech. State Coll., Evansville, Ind., 1991. Contbr. articles to profl. jours. Bd. dirs. Citizen Com. on Edn., Owensboro, Ky., 1989-99, River Park Ctr., Owensboro, 1992-99, Owensboro Mus., 1993-96; vol. 4-H, Owensboro, 1990—. Grad. fellow U. Wis., 1973, Lyman T. Johnson fellow U. Ky., 1998, U. Ky. Extended Campus Coll. Edn. fellow, 1998, 2000. Mem. Ky. Blacks in Higher Edn. (conf. chair 1996), Midwest Bus. Adminstrn. Assn., So. Assn. Colls. and Schs. (mem. vis. team 1995-00). Avocations: fishing, cooking, reading about business. Office: Owensboro C C 4800 New Hartford Rd Owensboro KY 42303-1800

GLENN, JEROME T. secondary school principal; Prin. San Lorenzo (Calif.) High Sch., to 1999; dir. secondary edn. San Lorenzo (Calif.) Sch. Dist., 1999—. Recipient Blue Ribbon Sch. award U.S. Dept. Edn., 1990-91. Office: San Lorenzo Dist Ednl Svcs 15510 Usher St San Lorenzo CA 94580-1641

GLENN, NORVAL DWIGHT, sociologist, educator; b. Roswell, N.Mex., Aug. 13, 1933; s. William N. and Mary E. (Cochrain) G. BA, N.Mex. State U., 1954; PhD, U. Tex., 1962. Instr. Miami U., Oxford, Ohio, 1960-61; instr. U. Ill., 1961-63, asst. prof., 1963-64, U. Tex., Austin, 1964-65, assoc. prof. sociology, 1965-70, prof. sociology, 1970-84, Ashbel Smith prof. sociology, 1984—, Raymond Dickson, Alton C. Allen and Dillon Anderson centennial prof., 1990-91, Stiles prof. Am. studies, 1991—. Author: (with Leonard Broom) Transformation of the Negro American, 1965, Cohort Analysis, 1977, (with Elizabeth Marguardt) Hooking Up, Hanging Out, and Looking for Mr. Right; editor: (with Charles Bonjean) Blacks in the United States, 1969, (with Marion Coleman) Family Relations, 1989; editor Contemporary Sociology, 1977-80, Jour. Family Issues, 1984-89; compiler: (with Jon Alston and David Weiner) Social Stratification: A Research Bibliography, 1969; contbr. articles to profl. jours. Mem. coun. Inter-Univ. Consortium for Polit. and Social Rsch., 1980-84, assoc. dir., 1984—2000. Served to 1st lt AUS, 1954-56. Mem. Am. Sociol. Assn., Am. Assn. Public Opinion Rsch., Nat. Coun. on Family Rels., Population Assn. Am. Home: 13309 Villa Park Dr Austin TX 78729-3733

GLENNEN, ROBERT EUGENE, JR., retired university president; b. Omaha, Mar. 31, 1933; s. Robert E. and La Verda (Elledge) G.; m. Mary C. O'Brien, Apr. 17, 1958; children: Maureen, Bobby, Colleen, Billy, Barry, Katie, Molly, Kerry AB, U. Portland, 1955, M.Ed., 1957; PhD, U. Notre Dame, 1962. Asst. prof. U. Portland, 1956-60; asst. prof., assoc. prof. Eastern Mont. Coll., Billings, 1962-65; assoc. dean U. Notre Dame, South Bend, Ind., 1965-72; dean, v.p. U. Nev.-Las Vegas, 1972-80; pres. Western N.Mex. U., Silver City, 1980-84, Emporia (Kans.) State U., 1984-97; acting vice-chancellor U. Ark., Montecello, 1999; interim provost U. So. Colo., 1999-2000, interim pres., 2001—02. Bd. dirs. Emporia Enterprises; cons. HEW, Washington, 1964-84 Author: Guidance: An Orientation, 1966. Contbr. articles to profl. jours. Pres. PTA, South Bend, Ind., 1970-71; bd. trustees Am. Coll. Testing Corp., Iowa City, 1977-80; chmn. Kans. Regents Coun. of Pres., 1986-87, 92-93, 95-96. Recipient award of excellence Nat. Acad. Advising Assn., Disting. Alumnus award U. Portland, 1993, Kans. Master Tchr. award, 1994; named Coach of Yr., Coach and Athletic mag., 1958, Pub. Adminstr. of Yr., 1994, Athletic Hall of Fame, Portland, 1995; Rotary Paul Harris fellow, 1995, Ford Found. fellow, 1961-62. Mem. Kans. C. of C. (bd. dirs.), Emporia C. of C. Regional Devel. Assn. (bd. dirs., Bank IV), Am. Personnel and Guidance Assn., Am. Assn. State Colls. and Univs. (chair pres's. commn. on tchr. edn.), Am. Assn. Higher Edn., Nev. Personnel and Guidance Assn., Assn. Counselor Educators and Suprs., Am. Assn. Counseling and Devel., Nat. Assn. Student Personnel Adminstrs. Republican. Roman Catholic. Avocations: racketball, walking, reading; hiking.

GLESK, IVAN, physicist, educator, researcher; b. Martin, Czechoslovakia, Sept. 1, 1957; arrived in U.S., 1990; s. Pavol and Elena (Orszaghova) G.; m. Helena Gleskova, Aug. 18, 1984; 1 child, Ivan. BS, MS in Physics, Comenius U., Bratislava, Slovak Republic, 1981, PhD in Quantum Electronics and Optics, 1989; DSc, Slovak Acad. Scis., 1998. Asst. prof. Comenius U., Bratislava, 1986-95, assoc. prof., 1996—2002, prof., 2003—; vis. fellow Princeton (N.J.) U., 1990-91, vis. rsch. staff mem., 1991-94, rsch. staff mem., 1994-96, rsch. scientist in physics, 1996-2000, sr. rsch. scholar, 2000—. Chmn. Slovak Com. for Optics, 1998—; presenter at numerous confs. Contbr. over 160 articles to profl. jours., 2 US patents; contbr. chapters to books. IREX Bd. fellow, 1990. Mem.: SPIE, IEEE (sr.), Optical Soc. Am. Achievements include first to 1st demonstration of ultrafast all-optically controlled routing switch capable of Tb/s operation; first demonstration of all-optical demultiplexing of TDM data at 250 Gb/s; first demonstration of 100 Gb/s optical shuffle network; work in ultra fast all-optical switching; first demonstration of 100 Gb/s optical comptuer interconnect; patents in field.

GLICK, JOHN H. oncologist, medical educator; b. N.Y.C., May 9, 1943; s. Arthur W. and Sybil (Goldman) Glick; m. Jane Mills, May 25, 1968; children: Katherine, Sarah. AB magna cum laude, Princeton U., 1965; MD, Columbia U., 1969. Diplomate Am. Bd. Med. Oncology, (sec. subsplty. com. med. oncology 1976-83, mem. subsplty. bd. med. oncology 1983-87, chmn. 1987-89, cert. exam. com. 1986-88, mem. bd. govs. 1987-89) Am. Bd. Internal Medicine. Intern in medicine Presbyn. Hosp., N.Y.C., 1969-70, asst. resident in medicine, 1970-71; commd. surgeon, clin. assoc. medicine br. Nat. Cancer Inst., USPHS, Bethesda, Md., 1971-73; postdoctoral fellow in med. oncology Stanford (Calif.) U., 1973-74; asst. prof. medicine U. Pa.,

Phila., 1974-79, Ann B. Young asst. prof. cancer rsch., 1974, assoc. prof., 1979-83, prof., 1983—, Madlyn and Leonard Abramson prof. clin. oncology, 1988—; dir. clin. trials U. Pa. Cancer Ctr., Phila., 1977-79, assoc. dir. for clin. rsch., 1980-85, dir. Cancer Ctr., 1985—; mem. numerous acad. coms., dept. medicine coms., hosp. coms., 1974—; pres. Abramson Family Cancer Rsch. Inst., Phila., 1998—, also bd. dirs. Attending physician Hosp. U. Pa., 1974—, dir. Hematology-Oncology Clinic, 1974—76; cons. Phila. VA Hosp., 1974—; mem. clin. trials rev. com. NIH, 1980—83, mem. radiosensitizer /radioprotector working group, radiotherapy devel. br., 1980—85, chmn. consensus devel. panel conf. adjuvant therapy for breast cancer, 1985; mem. com. accreditation med. oncology tng. programs Accreditation Coun. Grad. Med. Edn., 1983—, mem. appeals panel, 1984—94; prin. investigator Ea. Coop. Oncology Group, U. Pa.; pres., dir. Abramson Family Cancer Rsch. Inst., 1987—; dir. Pa. Cancer Ctr., 1985—. Mem. editl. bd.: Am. Jour. Clin. Oncology, 1983—89, Blood, 1983—86, Jour. Clin. Oncology, 1987—93, mem. bd. editors: Internat. Jour. Radiation Oncology, Biology and Physics; editor (assoc. editor): Cancer Rsch., 1984—88; contbr. articles to profl. jours. Recipient Faculty Rsch. award, Am. Cancer Soc., 1982—86; grantee Rsch., Nat. Cancer Inst., Ea. Coop. Oncology Group, Am. Cancer Soc., others. Fellow: ACP (mem. various splty. coms. 1983—84, master), Coll. Physicians and Surgeons; mem.: John Morgan Soc. U. Pa., Am. Fedn. Clin. Rsch., Am. Soc. Hematology, Am. Radium Soc. (mem. exec. com. 1986—87), Am. Assn. Cancer Rsch., Am. Assn. Cancer Edn., Am. Soc. Clin. Oncology (chmn. program com. 1983—84, nominating com. 1983—84, mem. pub. issue com. 1984—85, bd. dirs., pres. 1995—96), Alpha Omega Alpha, Phi Beta Kappa. Office: U Pa Cancer Ctr 3400 Spruce St Philadelphia PA 19104-4283

GLICK, KAREN LYNNE, college administrator; b. Bucyrus, Ohio, Sept. 2, 1945; d. Phillip Dole and Bernice Grace Glick; children: M. Todd, K. Christine. BSJ, Bowling Green State U., 1967, MA, 1979. Editor Bowling Green (Ohio) State U., 1972-74; account exec. Howard E. Mitchell, Jr., Advt., Findlay, Ohio, 1974-77; asst. to dir. Student Devel. Program Bowling Green State U., 1977-79; dir. pub. info. Bluffton (Ohio) Coll., 1980-83; asst. to v.p. for instl. advancement Findlay (Ohio) Coll., 1983-85; assoc. dir. devel. Bluffton Coll., 1985-90; assoc. dir. divsnl. support Miami U. Ohio, Oxford, 1990-93; sr. regional dir. devel. U. Ill. Found., Urbana, 1993—. Bd. dirs. Provena Behavioral Health. Mem. Fla. Sea Kayaking Assn., Bowling Green U. Press Club (charter 1983). Anglican. Office: U Ill Found Harker Hall MC-386 1305 W Green St Urbana IL 61801-2945 E-mail: glick@uif.uillinois.edu.

GLICK, THOMAS F. history educator; b. Cleve., Jan. 28, 1939; s. Lester G. and Ruth (Rothstein) G.; m. Elizabeth Ladd, Nov. 10, 1963; children: Rachel, Amos. BA, Harvard U., 1960, PhD, 1968; MA, Columbia U., 1963. Asst. prof. history U. Tex., Austin, 1968-72; prof. Boston U., 1972—, chmn. dept., 1984-89, 94-95; dir. Shtetl Econ. History Project, 2003—. Fulbright sr. lectr. U. of Republic, Montevideo, Uruguay, 1988, 90; pres. New England Medieval Conf., 1999-2000. Author: From Muslim Fortress to Christian Castle, 1995, Einstein in Spain, 1988; editor: The Reception of Darwinism in the Iberian World, 1999. Guggenheim fellow, 1987-88, Dibner Inst. Sr. fellow, 2000-01; grantee NSF, 1989-90, NEH, 1993-94. Mem. Soc. for Preservation of Old Mills (pres. N.E. chpt.), Reial Acad. Bones Lletres (corr.) Home: 132 Brook St Holliston MA 01746-1304 Office: Boston U Dept History Boston MA 02215 E-mail: tglick@bu.edu.

GLICKMAN, MICHAEL RICHARD, social studies educator; b. N.Y.C., Nov. 15, 1946; s. George Osiris Glickman and Hilda Ann Milmed; m. Irma S. Glickman, June 10, 1990; stepchildren: Scott D., Shari E. BA, Franklin (Ind.) Coll., 1969; MS, Coll. of S.I., 1997. Cert. tchr. social studies, N.Y. Paraprofl. N.Y.C. Bd. of Edn., Bklyn., 1974-92, tchr. social studies, 1992—. Adj. prof. sociology Kings Borough Coll., Bklyn., 1998—; tutor Williamsburg Settlement House, Bklyn., 1966-67; computer svcs. for children John Jay H.S., 1990-91. Head Young Dems., Dem. Party, Franklin Coll., Ind., 1968; vol. VISTA, 1969-70; tchr. Literacy Program John Jay H.S. Mem. United Fedn. of Tchrs., Am. Fedn. of Tchrs. Republican. Jewish. Avocations: reading, astronomy, computers, painting, music. Home: 1111 Schmidt Ln North Brunswick NJ 08902 Office: Murray Bergtraum High School 411 Pearl St New York NY 10002 E-mail: glickmoid13@cs.com.

GLICKMAN, NORMAN JAY, economist, urban policy analyst; b. Bklyn., July 27, 1942; s. Harry and Beatrice (Frankel) G.; m. Elyse M. Pivnick, May 8, 1983; children: Katy Rose, Madeline Claire. BA, U. Pa., 1963, MA, 1967, PhD, 1969. Prof. urban and regional planning U. Pa., Phila., 1980-82; Hogg prof. urban policy U. Tex., Austin, 1983-89; State of N.J. prof. urban planning Rutgers U., New Brunswick, 1989, dir. Ctr. for Urban Policy Rsch. State of N.J., 1989—, Disting. Univ. prof., 2000—. Vis. scholar U.S. HUD, Washington, 1978-79; fellow Netherland Inst. Advanced Studies, Wassenaar, 1981-82; sr. rsch. scholar Internat. Inst. Applied Systems Analysis, Laxenburg, Austria, 1977; appointee N.J. Coun. on Job Opportunities, N.J., 1992—. Co-author: The New Competitors, 1989 (Top 10 Bus. Week 1989). Chmn. Econ. Devel. Commn., Austin, 1985-89. Recipient Lindback award U. Pa., 1976, named Disting. Fulbright Prof., Monterrey (Mex.) Inst. of Tech., 1985; fellow Japan Found., 1976. Mem. EEFMS (charter), Regional Sci. Assn. (v.p. 1988-89), Am. Econ. Assn. Office: Rutgers U Ctr Urban Pol Rsch 33 Livingston Ave Ste 400 New Brunswick NJ 08901-1982

GLICKSMAN, LEON ROBERT, mechanical engineering educator; b. Chgo., May 12, 1938; s. Aaron and Daisy Merium (Rosenbaum) G.; m. Judith Kidder, Oct. 25, 1969; children: Shayna G. Swartz, Eric K., David W. BSME, MIT, 1959, PhD in Mech. Engring., 1964; MS in Mech. Engring., Stanford U., 1960. Instr. dept. mech. engring. MIT, Cambridge, 1962-64, asst. prof., 1966-70, assoc. prof., 1970-73, lectr., program mgr., rsch. coord. Energy Lab., 1973-78, sr. rsch. scientist, 1979-87, sr. Joint Program for Energy Efficient Bldgs. and Systems, 1982—, sr. lectr. mech. engring. dept., 1988—, prof. thermal sci. and bldg. tech. arch. dept., 1987—, prof. mech. engring. dept., 1993—. Cons. Alumiseal Corp., 1973—, Birdair Corp., 1984, Babcock and Wilcox, 1986—, BPAm., 1988—, Camp Dresser and McKee, 1985, Crown Zellerback, 1986—, Dept. Commerce, 1980—, Los Alamos Nat. Lab., 1983—, Nat. Bur. Stds., 1975—, Owens-Corning Fiberglas Corp., 1970—, Raytheon, 1986—, Riley Stoker, 1987—, TVA, 1980—, Underground Systems Inc., 1979—, United Techs., 1976—, U.S. Army, 1966-70, Dept. Energy, 1985-86, others; mem. energy rsch. ctr. vis. com. Lehigh U., Bethelehem, Pa.,1993—. Capt. U.S. Army, 1964-66. Recipient Melville medal ASME, Robert T. Knapp award ASME. Home: 8 Maiden Ln Lynnfield MA 01940-2419 Office: MIT Dept Arch & Mech Engring 5-418 77 Massachusetts Ave Cambridge MA 02139-4307

GLICKSMAN, MARTIN EDEN, materials engineering educator; b. N.Y.C., Apr. 4, 1937; s. Nathan Henry and Ruth Elaine (Rosensaft) G.; m. Lucinda Jeanette Mulder, May 7, 1967 B in Metall. Engring., Rensselaer Poly. Inst., 1957, PhD, 1961. Metall. engr. Procter & Gamble Co., Cin., 1957-58; research metallurgist Naval Research Lab., Washington, 1961-75, assoc. supt. materials sci. divsn., 1974-75; chmn. materials engr. dept. Rensselaer Poly. Inst., Troy, N.Y., 1975-86, prof., 1986—; prof. materials engring., chmn. dept. materials engring. Rensselaer Poly. Inst., Troy, N.Y., 1975-86, John Tod Horton prof. materials engring., 1986—. Van Horn lectr. Case Western Res. U., 1984; cons. in field. Author: Diffusion in Solids, 2000; contbr. in articles to profl. jours. Recipient Pure Sci. Rsch. award Rsch. Soc. of Am., 1968, Arthur Flemming award Washington Jr. C. of C., Space Processing medal AIAA, 1998; Minerals Metals and Materials Soc. fellow AIME, 1994. Fellow AAAS, ASM (M.E. Grossman award 1971); mem. AIME (Bruce Chalmers award 1992), Am. Soc. Metals Internat. (Gold medal 2003), Univ. Space Rsch. Assn. (chmn. bd. trustees 1986, dir. microgravity divsn. 1986—), Nat. Acad. Engring. (Alexander von Humboldt Rsch. prize, 2001). Home: 22 Schuyler Hills Rd Albany NY 12211-1445 Office: Rensselaer Poly Inst CII-9111 Troy NY 12180-3590

GLICKSTEIN, HOWARD ALAN, law educator; b. N.Y.C., Sept. 14, 1929; s. Samuel and Fannie (Greenblat) G. BA magna cum laude, Dartmouth Coll., 1951; LLB, Yale U., 1954; LLM, Georgetown U., 1962. Bar: N.Y. 1954, U.S. Supreme Ct. 1962, D.C. 1980. Assoc. Proskauer, Rose, Goetz & Mendelsohn, N.Y.C., 1956-60; staff atty. Civil Rights divsn. Dept. of Justice, 1960-65; gen. counsel U.S. Commn. on Civil Rights, Washington, 1965-68, staff dir., 1968-71. Cons. in law, 1971-73; adj. prof., dir. Ctr. for Civil Rights U. Notre Dame, 1973-75; prof., dir. equal employment litigation clinic Howard U. Sch. Law, Washington, 1976-80; dir. Task Force on Civil Rights Reorgn., Exec. Office of Pres., Washington, 1977-78; dean, prof. U. Bridgeport Sch. Law, Conn., 1980-85, Touro Coll. Law, 1986—. Contbr. articles to profl. jours. Bd. dirs. Fund for Modern Cts.; commr. Suffolk County Human Rights Commn.; chair Town Huntington Bd. Ethics and Fin. Disclosure, 1999—. With U.S. Army, 1954-56. Mem. ABA (former chmn. affirmative action com., sect. legal edn. and admissions to bar), Soc. Am. Law Tchrs. (bd. dirs., former pres.), N.Y. State Commn. on Fiduciary Appointments, N.Y. State Bar Assn. (mem. spl. com. pub. trust and confidence in the legal sys.). Office: Touro Coll Sch Law Jacob D Fuchsberg Law Ctr 300 Nassau Rd Huntington NY 11743-4346

GLIER, INGEBORG JOHANNA, German language and literature educator; b. Dresden, Germany, June 22, 1934; came to U.S., 1972; d. Erich Oskar and Gertrud Johanne (Niese) G. Student, Mt. Holyoke Coll., 1955-56; Dr. phil. (Studienstiftung des deutschen Volkes), U. Munich, Germany, 1958; Dr. phil., Habilitation, 1969; MA (hon.), Yale U., 1973. Asst., lectr. U. Munich, 1958-69, universitätsdozentin, 1969-72; vis. prof. Yale U., 1972-73, prof. German, 1973—, chmn. dept., 1979-82, chmn. Medieval Studies, 1986-93, chmn. Women's Studies, 1995-96, sr. faculty fellow, 1974-75; vis. prof. U. Cologne, Germany, 1970-71, U. Colo., Boulder, spring 1983, U. Tubingen, summer 1984. Author: Struktur und Gestaltungsprinzipien in den Dramen John Websters, 1958, Deutsche Metrik, 1961, Artes amandi, Untersuchung zu Geschichte, Überlieferung und Typologie der deutschen Minnereden, 1971; contbr. articles, book reviews to profl. jours. Mem.: Wolfram von Eschenbach Gesellschaft, Internat. Courtly Lit. Soc., Am. Assn. Tchrs. German, Medieval Acad. Am., MLA, Internat. Germanisten-Verband. Home: 111 Park St Apt 12T New Haven CT 06511-5421 Office: Yale Univ Dept Germanic Langs PO Box 208210 New Haven CT 06520-8210 E-mail: ingeborg.glier@yale.edu.

GLIKLICH, JERRY, physician, educator; b. Jelenia Góra, Poland, May 6, 1948; came to U.S., 1958; s. Henry and Henia (Gotajner) G.; m. Jane Salmon, Sept. 12, 1976; children: David, Benjamin. AB, Columbia U., 1969, MD, 1975. Intern N.Y. Hosp., N.Y.C., 1975-76, resident, 1977-78; fellow in cardiology Presbyn. Hosp., N.Y.C., 1978-81, attending physician, 1981—, assoc. clin. prof., 1991-97, clin. prof., 1997—2001, David A. Gardner prof. medicine, 2001—; asst. prof. medicine Columbia U., N.Y.C., 1981-91. Cons. in field. Contbr. articles to profl. jours. Mem. ACP, Am. Coll. Cardiology, Phi Beta Kappa. Office: Presbyn Hosp 161 Fort Washington Ave New York NY 10032-3713

GLIME, ANN ELIZABETH, special education educator; b. Waterloo, Iowa, May 28, 1952; d. Robert Narber and Mabel Alice (Sloan) Glime. BS in Elem. Edn., Iowa State U., 1974; MA in Spl. Edn., U. No. Iowa, 1979. Tchr. 4th grade St. Boniface Sch., New Vienna, Iowa, 1975-77; elementary resource tchr. Edgewood Colesburgh Sch., Colesburg, Iowa, 1977-87; tchr. spl. class with integration Edgewood Colesburg Sch., Colesburg, Iowa, 1987—. Mem.: Autism Soc. Iowa, Profl. Educators Iowa, Assn. Am. Educators, Delta Kappa Gamma.

GLINES, JON MALCOLM, secondary education educator; b. Nashua, N.H., Jan. 2, 1942; s. Richard N. and Patricia (Tinker) Russell; m. Doris Blouin Glines, July 4, 1992. BS in Edn., Lyndon State Coll., 1967; MS in Social Sci., Rivier Coll., 1977. Cert. tchr., N.H. Tchr. social studies Spring St. Jr. High Sch., Nashua, 1969-75, Elm St. Jr. High Sch., Nashua, 1975—. Mem. ASCD, Nat. Coun. Social Studies, Nashua Tchrs. Union, Elks, History Book Club, U.S. Golf Assn., Book of the Month Club. Avocations: golf, reading, history, travel. Home: 11 Timberwood Dr Unit 306 Goffstown NH 03045-2576

GLOBIG, SABINE A. biology educator; b. Stuttgart, Germany, Nov. 13, 1949; came to U.S., 1953; d. Herbert and Ursula Ruth (Vesely) G. BA in Internat. Studies, Am. U., 1972; MS in Horticulture, Rutgers U., 1988. Cert. tchr. h.s., N.J. Adj. instr. biology Union County Coll., Cranford, N.J., 1980-91; teaching asst./adj. Rutgers U., New Brunswick, N.J., 1984-87; tchr. biology Millburn (N.J.) H.S., 1987-89; rsch. asst. Ctr. for Agrl. Molecular Biology Rutgers U., 1990; teaching lab. mgr. William Paterson Coll., Wayne, N.J., 1991-92; assoc. prof. Hazard (Ky.) C.C., 1992—. Author poster presentation Internat. Horticultural Congress, 1986. Mem. Perry County Humane Soc., Hazard, 1993—. Mem. Ky. Acad. Scis., Mensa (area coord.), AAWCC. Avocations: reading science, science fiction, mystery books, horticulture, animal welfare work. Office: Hazard C C Divsn Natural Sci Hwy 15 N Hazard KY 41701

GLOSSON, JULIE ANN MCDADE, language educator; b. Dallas, Apr. 11, 1969; d. Richard Warren and Barbara Ann (Bennett) McDade; m. Jimmy A. Glosson, Dec. 18, 1993; 1 child, Sierra Noel. BA, Union U., Jackson, Tenn., 1991; MA, U. Memphis, 1995, EdD, 2002. Spanish tchr. Bolivar (Tenn.) Ctrl. H.S., 1992—93; Spanish tchg. asst. U. Memphis, 1993—95; conversation instr. Rhodes Coll., Memphis, 1995; Spanish instr. Union U., Jackson, Tenn., 1995—99, Spanish asst. prof., 1999—. Lang. cons. Jackson-Madison County Gen. Hosp., Jackson, Tenn., 2000—01. Mem.: Tenn. Fgn. Lang. Tchg. Assn. Avocations: singing, acting. Office: Union U Lang Dept 1050 Union University Dr Jackson TN 38305-3697

GLOTZBACH, PHILIP A. academic administrator; m. Marie B Glotzbach; children: Jason, Elizabeth. BA summa cum laude, U. Notre Dame, 1972; PhD, Yale U., 1979. Assoc. prof. to chair of Philosophy dept. to chair of the faculty sen. Denison U., Granville, Ohio, 1977—92; dean of coll. of arts then v.p. for academic affairs U. of Redlands, 1992—2003; pres. Skidmore Coll., 2003—. Mem.: Phi Beta Kappa. Office: Skidmore Coll 815 N Broadway Saratoga Springs NY 12866

GLOVER, CINDY, secondary school educator; b. Seminole, Tex., June 13, 1948; d. Maitland Gilbert and Billie Faye (Thompson) Allen; m. Ron Glover, July 10, 1971; children: Will, Jennie. BA, Sul Ross State U., Alpine, Tex., 1970; MEd, Sul Ross State U., 1996. Cert. elem. and secondary English and Spanish tchr., gifted and talented, Tex. Elem. tchr., tchr. gifted and talented edn. Socorro (Tex.) Ind. Sch. Dist.; elem. tchr. to gifted and talented Clint (Tex.) Ind. Sch. Dist.; tchr. humanities 7th El Paso Ind. Sch. Dist. Dist. coord gifted Clint I.S.D.; instr. specialist secondary lang. El Paso I.S.D. Recipient award Socorro Ind. Sch. Dist., Kiwanis Club, El Paso, Tex. Mem. Tex. Assn. Gifted and Talented (Region XIX Tchr. of Yr. 2002). Home: 15337 Mineral Ct El Paso TX 79928-7029

GLOVER, DELORIS DICKSON, history educator; b. Charleston, S.C., Mar. 9, 1947; d. William II and Victoria (McDaniel) Dickson; m. Arthur Richard Glover, Nov. 14, 1966; children: Penelope, Shana, Kimberly. BA, Claflin Coll., 1971; MA, State U., Orangeburg, S.C., 1982. Tchr. history Branchville (S.C.) High Sch., 1971-72, Dantzler Elem., Holly Hill, S.C., 1973-78, Bowman (S.C.) High Sch., 1979—; tchr. history Upward Bound Claflin Coll., Orangeburg, summer 1990, 92. Chairperson Sch. Improvement Coun., Bowman, 1991-92; parent coord. Kenan Program, Bowman, 1991. Grantee Strom Thurmond Inst., Clemson, S.C., 1992, Woodrow Wilson Inst. Coll. Charleston, S.C., 1992. Mem. NEA, Nat. Coun. Social Studies, Orangeburg County Edn. Assn. (pres. 1991-92, Svc. award 1992), Law Related Summer Inst. U. S.C. Democrat. Baptist. Avocations: traveling, reading, sewing, gardening. Office: PO Box 186 Bowman SC 29018-0186

GLOVER, MARIE ELIZABETH, special education educator, speech language pathologist; b. Sacramento, Aug. 19, 1943; d. Melvin Edward and Edith Maria (Brown) Thomas; m. Robert John Glover, May 26, 1967. BA in Speech Pathology, Edn., San Jose State U., 1965; MA in Speech Pathology, Ea. Mich. U., 1980; MS in Spl. Edn./Learning Disabilities, Emporia State U., 1984. Tchr. Calif., N.Y., Wis., Ark., Oreg., Mich., Wash., 1965—. Speech pathology cons. Coffey County Hosp., Burlington, Kans., 1983-85. Precinct leader Rep. Party, Ann Arbor, Mich., 1975-80; leader Girl Scouts, London, Ark., 1970-74. Mem. Am. Speech-Lang. Hearing Assn. (cert. speech lang. pathology), Wash. Speech, Hearing and Lang. Assn., Coun. Exceptional Children (state mem.-at-large 1991-94, local pres. 1994-95), Learning Disabilities Assn. (pres. 1989), Internat. Reading Assn., Phi Delta Kappa (v.p. 1990-93). Avocations: woodcarving, private pilot, music (flute and irish tin whistle). Home: 331 Basalt Springs Way Naches WA 98937-9235

GLOVER, NANCY ELLIOTT, elementary school administrator; b. Nashville, Dec. 10, 1950; d. Walter Leroy and Mary Ruth (Draughon) Elliott; m. Donald R. Hamlett, Aug. 1971 (dec. Nov. 1981); children: Joshua Hamlett, Kyle Hamlett; m. Charles H. Glover, Feb. 14, 1986; stepchildren: Chris, Troy. BS, David Lipscomb Coll., 1971; MA, Austin Peay State U., 1975; Edn. Degree Specialist, Tenn. Tech. U., 1982; EdD, Tenn. State U., 1994. Asst. ext. agt. U. Tenn. Ext. Svc., Dover, 1971-73; kindergarten/resource tchr. Lakeside Elem. Sch., New Johnsonville, Tenn., 1974-76; 3d grade tchr. Union Elem. Sch., Gallatin, Tenn., 1976-78; 1st grade tchr. Vena Stuart Elem. Sch., Gallatin, Tenn., 1978-81; 7th grade sci. tchr. Gallatin Mid. Sch., 1984-85; 5th and 6th grade math./sci. tchr. Friendship Christian Sch., Lebanon, Tenn., 1985-87; Home Bound/resource tchr. Gallatin H.S., 1988-89; 4th and 5th grade tchr. Clyde Riggs Elem. Sch., Portland, Tenn., 1989-93; asst. prin. Howard Elem. Sch., Gallatin, 1993—2002, Jack Anderson Elem. Sch., Hendersonville, Tenn., 2002—. Vis. evaluation com. So. Assn. Colls. and Schs., 1994. Vol. coll. coord. United Way Howard Elem. Sch., Gallatin, 1993—2002, Tenn. Child Abuse Prevention, 1998—; campaign vol. various polit. candidates, Sumner County, 1968—; Bible sch. tchr. Ch. of Christ, Castalian Springs, Tenn., 1976—. Recipient Gras. assistantship Tenn. State U., 1982-83, scholarship David Lipscomb U., 1968-71. Mem. ASCD, NEA, Tenn. Edn. Assn., Sumner County Edn. Assn., Gallatin Edn. Assn., Phi Delta Kappa. Democrat. Avocations: sports, reading, photography, crafts. Home: 160 Graystone Dr Gallatin TN 37066-4619 Office: Jack Anderson Elem Sch Hendersonville TN

GLOVER, PEGGY ANN, elementary education educator; b. Pontiac, Ill., Jan. 6, 1946; m. Gordie Glover, Jan. 27, 1968; children: David, Rebecca, Kathy. BS in Elem. Edn., Ill. State U., 1971, MS in Edn., 1991. Cert. elem. tchr., cert. reading tchr. 2nd grade tchr. Unit 5 Eugene Field Elem. Sch., Normal, 1985—. Rep. Reading Selection Com., Normal, 1994, Lang. Arts Selection Com., Normal; supr. Patrol Eugene Field Sch., Normal, 1994-95; resource tchr. Gifted Program, Normal, 1986— Mem. NEA, Unit Five Edn. Assn., Ill. Edn. Assn. Avocations: reading, traveling. Office: Unit Five Eugene Field Sch 412 E Cypress St Normal IL 61761-1777

GLUCK, CAROL, history educator; b. Newark, Nov. 12, 1941; d. David E. and Doris S. Newman; m. Peter L. Gluck, May 1, 1966; children: Thomas Edward, William Francis. Student, U. Munich, 1960-61, U. Tokyo, 1972-74; BA, Wellesley Coll., 1962; MA, Columbia U., 1970, PhD, 1977. Asst. prof. Columbia U., N.Y.C., 1975-83, assoc. prof., 1983-86, prof., 1986-88, George Sansom prof. history, 1988—. Vis. rsch. assoc. faculty law Tokyo U., 1978-79, 85-86, 92; vis. prof. Harvard U., Cambridge, Mass., 1991, Inst. Social Sci. Tokyo U., 1993, Ecole des Hautes Etudes en Scis. Sociales, Paris, 1995, 98; fellow Inst. for Advanced Studies in the Behavioral Scis., 1999-2000; publs. bd. Columbia U. Press, N.Y.C., 1991-96; co-dir. project on Asia in the core Curricuclm NEH, N.Y.C., 1987—; Am. adv. com. Japan Found., 1986-96, chair, 1991-96; disting. lectr. N.E. Area Coun., 1988, Japan Soc. for Promotion of Sci., 1989. Author: Japan's Modern Myths, 1985 (Fairbank prize 1986, Trilling award 1987); co-editor: Showa: The Japan of Hirohito, 1992, Asia in Western and World History, 1997; contbr. numerous articles to profl. publs. Mem. Coun. on Fgn. Rels., U.S.-Japan Friendship Commn., 1994—2001; mem. com. on rsch. librs. N.Y. Pub. Libr., 1987—, mem. humanities adv. coun., 1996—. Recipient Fulbright 50th Anniversary Disting. Fellow award, 2002; fellow, Woodrow Wilson Found., Fgn. Area fellow; grantee Fulbright grantee, 1985—86, Japan Found. grantee. Fellow: Am. Acad. Arts and Scis.; mem.: Am. Philos. Soc., Asia Soc. (trustee 1992—98, 2002—), Japan Soc. (bd. dirs. 1990—), Assn. Asian Studies (coun. 1981—84, nominating com. 1985—86, pres. 1996—97, bd. dirs. 1995—99), Am. Hist. Assn. (coun. 1987—90), Phi Beta Kappa. Home: 440 Riverside Dr New York NY 10027-6828 Office: Columbia U East Asian Inst 420 W 118th St New York NY 10027-7213

GLUCK, LUCILLE GINDOFF, educator; b. Lakewood, N.J., May 16, 1940; d. Louis and Georgiana (Klass) Gindoff; m. James E. Brodes, May 1, 1962 (div. 1979); children: Victor James, Jill Sharon; m. Joseph Gluck, May 10, 1981. BA, Georgian Ct. Coll., 1977, MA, 1985. Tchr. 6th grade Princeton Ave Sch. Lakewood (N.J.) Schs., 1980-83, tchr. 3d grade Oak St. Sch., 1983-87, tchr. 5th grade Oak St. Sch., 1987-88, 89-92, tchr. 3d grade Oak St. Sch., 1988-89, 92-93. Coor. sci. Oak St. Sch. Mem. The Coun. for Elem. Sci. (bd. dirs.), Nat. Sci. Tchrs. Assn., N.J. Sci. Tchrs. Assn., Alpha Delta Kappa. Avocation: travel. Home: 2304 Hunters Ct Toms River NJ 08755-1381

GLYNN, JAMES A. sociology educator, author; b. Bklyn., Sept. 10, 1941; s. James A. and Muriel M. (Lewis) G.; m. Marie J. Gates, Dec. 17, 1966 (div. Apr. 1995); 1 child, David S. AA, Foothill Coll., 1961; BA in Sociology, San Jose (Calif.) State U., 1964, MA in Sociology, 1966; PhD, U. Calif. at Riverside, 1972. Instr. in sociology Bakersfield (Calif.) Coll., 1966-98, prof. sociology, 1972—; prof. sociology State Ctr. Cmty. Coll. Dist. Clovis Ctr. and Madera Ctr., 1998—2002, prof. emeritus State Ctr. Cmty. Coll. Dist., 2003. Adj. prof. Fresno (Calif.) State U., 1971-72, Chapman Coll., Orange, Calif., 1972, Calif. State U., Bakersfield, 1989-98, Chapman U., Visalia, Calif., 1997-98; del. acad. senate Calif. C.C., Sacramento, 1980-89; mem. coun. Faculty Assn. Calif. C.Cs., 1981—; columnist Madera Tribune, 1999-2001, www.maderainfo.com. Author: Studying Sociology, 1979, Writing Across the Curriculum Using Sociological Concepts, 1983, Hands On: User's Manual for Data Processing, 1986; (with Elbert W. Stewart) Introduction to Sociology, 1972, 4th edit., 1985; (with Crystal Dea Moore) Guide to Social Psychology, 1992, Understanding Racial and Ethnic Groups, 1992, 98, 2001, Guide to Human Services, 1994, Focus on Sociology, 1994, 98; (with Charles F. Hohm and Elbert W. Stewart) Global Social Problems, 1996; contbg. editor Introduction to Sociology, 1996; contbg. author: California's Social Problems, 1997; editor, contbg. author (with Charles F. Hohm) California's Social Problems, 2d edit., 2001 Mem. Madera County Arts Coun., 2000—, co-chair fin. com., 2001—02, pub. rels. chmn., exec. bd., 2001—, v.p., 2002—03, pres., 2003—04. Recipient Innovator Yr. award League Innovations C.C., 1989, Innovator Yr. award Kern C.C. Dist., 1992. Mem. Am. Sociol. Assn., Calif. Sociol. Assn. (founder, treas. 1990-92, editor newsletter 1991-92, pres. 1992-93, exec. dir. 1993-2001), Commn. on Tchg., Pacific Sociol. Assn. (mem. editl. bd. Sociol. Perspectives 1996-99, awards com. 2000-03, Disting. Prof. award for Contbn. to Edn. 1997,), Population Reference Bur., World Watch Inst., World Future Soc., Kiwanis (editor newsletter 2001—, pres. 2001-02). Democrat. Home: 135 N Park Dr Madera CA 93637-3041 Home Fax: 559-674-4490.

GMEINER, WILLIAM HENRY, science educator; b. East Cleveland, Ohio, May 12, 1961; s. Francis James and Thelma Ruth G.; m. Susan Cathryn Stucki, Sept. 10, 1988; children: Robert James, Michael William, Karl Henry. BA, U. Chgo., 1982; PhD, U. Utah, 1989. Rsch. assoc. U. Alta., Edmonton, Canada, 1989-91; asst. prof. U. Nebr. Med. Ctr., Omaha, 1991-97, assoc. prof., 1997-2000; prof. Wake Forest U., Winston-Salem, NC, 2000—, chair, 2000—03. Vis. prof. U. Calif., San Francisco, 1998; mem. edn. com. Am. Med. Grad. Dept. Biochemistry, 2001-03; vis. scholar Duke U., 2002-03; pres. Wake Forest U., Sigma Xi, 2002; cons. in field. Inventor/patentee in field. Pres. Habitat for Humanity, Omaha, 1999—2000, Neighbor's South Coalition; chair property com. St. Matthew's Evang. Luth. Ch., Omaha, 1996—2000; active Luth. Ch. of the Epiphany, Winston-Salem, 2000—. Recipient Chmn.'s Challenge award, 2002; Alta. Heritage Med. Rsch. fellow, Edmonton, 1990-91. Mem. Am. Chem. Soc., Am. Assn. Cancer Rsch., Fedn. Am. Socs. Exptl. Biology, Internat. Soc. Antiviral Rsch. Democrat. Lutheran. Avocations: camping, reading, sports, music. Office: Wake Forest U Dept Biochemistry Med Ctr Blvd Winston Salem NC 27157-1016 E-mail: bgmeiner@wfubmc.edu.

GOBAR, ALFRED JULIAN, retired economic consultant, educator; b. Lucerne Valley, Calif., July 12, 1932; s. Julian Smith and Hilda (Millbank) G.; m. Sally Ann Randall, June 17, 1957; children: Wendy Lee, Curtis Julian, Joseph Julian. BA in Econs., Whittier Coll., 1953, MA in History, 1955; postgrad., Claremont Grad. Sch., 1953-54; PhD in Econs., U. So. Calif., 1963. Asst. pres. Microdot Inc., Pasadena, Calif., 1953-57; regional sales mgr. Sutorbilt Corp., L.A., 1957-59; mkt. rsch. assoc. Beckman Instrument Inc., Fullerton, Calif., 1959-64; sr. marketing cons. Western Mgmt. Consultants Inc., San Diego, 1964-66; ptnr., prin., chmn. bd. Darley/Gobar Assocs., Inc., San Diego, 1966-73; pres., chmn. bd. Alfred Gobar Assocs., Inc., Placentia, Calif., 1973—. Asst. prof. finance U. So. Calif., L.A., 1963-64; assoc. prof. bus. Calif. State U., L.A., 1963-68, 70-79, assoc. prof. Calif. State U.-Fullerton, 1968-69; mktg., fin. adviser 1957—; bd. dirs. Quaker City Bancorp, Inc.; pub. spkr. seminars and convs. Contbr. articles to profl. publs. Trustee Whittier Coll., 1992—. Home: 1100 W Valencia Mesa Dr Fullerton CA 92833-2219 Office: 721 W Kimberly Ave Placentia CA 92870-6343 E-mail: agobar@gobar.com.

GOBUS, BARBARA CHATTERTON, secondary education educator; b. Leeds, Yorkshire, Eng., Dec. 30, 1941; d. Ernest and Gertrude Emma (Balmforth) Chatterton; 1 child, Roger Eggers. AA with hons., Santa Monica Coll., 1987; BA summa cum laude, Calif. State U., Northridge, 1991; MA, 1994. Exec. sec., office mgr. Med. and Legal Field, L.A., 1966-82; docent Greater L.A. Zoo Assn., 1983-92; tutor, lang. lab. Calif. State U., Northridge, 1990-91, tchg. assoc., 1991-92; English tchr. Marlborough Sch., L.A., 1993—. Bd. dirs. The Doheny Sch., L.A., 1984—. Founder, contbg. editor: Inform. and Ednl. mag., 1983-85. Reader recordings for blind, Braille Inst., L.A., 1992-93; sec. PTSA Palms Jr. High Sch., L.A., 1987-89. Mem. Nat. Coun. Tchrs. of English, Golden Key, Phi Kappa Phi, Sigma Tau Delta. Avocations: music, jungian psychology, walking, nature, reading. Office: Marlborough Sch 250 S Rossmore Ave Los Angeles CA 90004-3739

GOCHÉ, JOYCE PRISCILLA HUGHEY, special education and gifted education educator; d. Joseph A. Sr. and Dora R. Hughey. BA, Howard U., 1970, MEd, 1973; MS, U. D.C., 1985. Cert. tchr. K-12, cert. libr. media specialist, D.C. Tchr. D.C. Pub. Schs., Washington, 1970—, coord. gifted/talented program, 1978—, coord. summer sch., 1987. Coach Odyssey of the Mind, Washington, 1980-95, bd. dirs.; coach Future roblem Solving, Washington, 1991. Bd. dirs. Housing Coop., Washington, 1984—; judge Odyssey of the Mind, 1992-94; bd. rep. Washington Tchrs. Union, 1994—, PTA pres. 1996—, chair Local Sch. Restructuring Team. Fellowship U. D.C., 1983-85, Honors Workshop, NSTA. Mem. ASCD, ALA, AASL, D.C. Assn. Sch. Librs., D.C. Reading Coun., Am. Fedn. Tchrs., Washington Tchrs. Union, Nat. Coun. Tchrs. Math., Nat. Sci. Tchrs. Assn. (local com. mem. 1991). Avocations: travel, theater, storytelling, sewing, painting, reading.

GODDARD, SANDRA KAY, elementary education educator; b. Steubenville, Ohio, Oct. 31, 1947; d. Albert Leonard and Mildred Irene (Hill) G. BS in Edn., Miami U., Oxford, Ohio, 1969; MEd, Miami U., 1973. Tchr. Gregg Elem. Sch., Bergholz, Ohio, 1969; tchr. elem. grades Springfield Mid. Sch., Bergholz, 1999—, media club advisor, 2002—; Praxis III assessor Ohio Dept. Edn., 2002—. Curriculum and textbook com. Jefferson County Schs., Steubenville, 1994-95, textbook com., 2002; cooperating tchr. Franciscan U., 1972-77, 2002; presenter Ohio Regional Tchrs. Workshop, 1998, County Tchrs. Workshops for ARC/Jefferson County Tchrs., 1992-97, Jefferson County coord. Presch./Kindergarten Workshop for ARC first aid course, 2000, 2002. Publicity chmn., rec. sec., box office chmn., lead actress, asst. dir. Steubenville Players, 1981-83; mem. Edison Local Adv. Coun. on Drug Edn., 1987-99; mem. Edison Local Curriculum Instrn. Com., 1993-99; state judge Ashland Oil Tchr. Achievement awards, 1988-90; regional and state judge Odyssey of the Mind, 1992-97, bd. dirs. Region XI, 1993-97, regional dir., chair governing bd., bd. dirs. Ohio chpt., 1994-97; exec. com. Gregg Elem. PTO, 1990-92; instr. 1st aid and CPR, ARC, 1990—, county disaster team, profl. rescuer status, 1997—, instr. trainer educator, 2002; instr. CPR for Profl. Rescuer, 2002—. Martha Holden Jennings scholar, 1972-73; mini-grantee Jefferson County Schs., 1991, 94. Mem. NEA (del. to rep. assembly 1979, 85-88), Ohio Edn. Assn. (exec. com. 1983-89, pres.'s cabinet 1985-87, appeals bd. 1994-2002), Ea. Ohio Edn. Assn. (pres. 1978-79, exec. com. 1983-89), Edison Local Edn. Assn. (pres. 1974-75, v.p. 1986-91, exec. com. 1991-94, negotiation's team 1987, 90, 93), Ohio Valley UNISERV Coun. (treas. 1986-92), Delta Kappa Gamma (legis. chair 1990-92). Democrat. Methodist. Avocations: singing, reading, theater, collecting hummels and bells, photography. Home: 200 Fernwood Rd Apt 11 Wintersville OH 43953-9200 Office: Springfield Mid Sch 4569 County Hwy 75 Bergholz OH 43908-9801

GODFREY, ALBERT BLANTON, former research and management consulting company executive, writer, educator; b. Greenbelt, Md., Feb. 21, 1941; s. Albert Barney and Alice Lallage (Green) G.; m. Judith Lynn Cashion, Aug. 11, 1962; 1 child, Parke Tremayne. BS, Va. Poly Inst. & State U., 1964; MS, Fla. State U., 1970, PhD, 1974. Mem. tech. staff AT&T Bell Labs., Holmdel, N.J., 1973-76, supr., 1976-80, dept. head, 1980-87; chmn./chief exec. officer Juran Inst., Inc., Wilton, Conn., 1987—2000; dean, Joseph D. Moore disting. prof. N.C. State U., 2000—. Assoc. editor Jour. of Quality Tech., Milw., 1978-84; adj. prof. Columbia U., N.Y.C., 1982—, N.C. State U., 1994—; vis. com. mem. Fordham U. Grad. Bus. Sch., N.Y.C., 1989—. Co-author: (books) Modern Methods For Quality Control & Improvement, 1986, 2d edit., 2002 (book of the yr. 1987), Curing Health Care, 1990, 2d edit., 2003; contbr. numerous articles to profl. jours.; editorial adv. bd. Quality Mgmt. Jour., 1992-2000; co-editor in chief Juran's Quality Handbook, 1999; founding editor Six Sigma Forum Mag., 2001—. Co-principle investigator Nat. Demonstration Project in Quality Improvement for Health Care, Boston, 1986-90; judge Malcolm Baldrige Nat. Quality Award, Washington, 1987-90. Capt. U.S. Army, 1963-68, Germany, Vietnam. Fellow Am. Statistical Assn. (bd. dirs. 1986-89), Am. Soc. Quality Control; mem. N.Y. Acad. Scis., Internat. Acad. for Quality, World Acad. Productivity Scis., Quality Mgmt. Network (exec. bd. dirs. 1990-92), Inst. Healthcare Improvement (exec. bd. dirs. 1991-95), Quality Mgmt. Healthcare (editorial adv. bd. jour. 1992-2000), Sigma Xi. Democrat. Baptist. Avocations: photography, travel, tennis, bicycling. Office: NC State U Coll Textiles 2401 Rsch Dr Raleigh NC 27606 Home: 5002 Kingpost Dr Fuquay Varina NC 27526-8674

GODFREY, ALINE LUCILLE, music specialist, church organist; b. Providence, R.I., Dec. 4, 1943; d. Bernard Almasse and Rita Linda (Laramee) Brindamour; m. George Ruben Godfrey, Aug. 22, 1981; 1 child, Murray Aaron. BA, Rivier Coll., 1970; cert. of attendance, Am. Conservatory of Music, Fontainebleau, France, 1972; M of Music, U. Notre Dame, 1975. Cert. tchr. profl. all level music, provisional elem.-gen., Tex. Choir dir. Scituate (R.I.) High Sch., 1970-74; tchr. grade 4 McDowell Intermediate Sch., Hondo, Tex., 1974-75; tchr. grade 5 Wilson Elem. Sch., Harlingen, Tex., 1975-76; organist St. Albans Episcopal Ch., Harlingen, 1977-80; music specialist St. Mary's Sch. and Immaculate Conception Sch., Brownsville, Tex., 1977-79; choral accompanist Harlingen H.S., 1979-80; tchr. grade 6 Sam Houston Sch., Harlingen, 1980-81; music dir. St. Alban's Episcopal Sch., Harlingen, 1987-90; choral accompanist Marine Military Acad., Harlingen, 1988-90; tchr. Stuart Place Elem. Sch., Harlingen, 1990-91; msic specialist Harlingen Ind. Sch. Dist., 1991—. Organist St. James Ch., Manville, R.I., 1972-74, First United Meth. Ch., Mercedes, Tex., 1987-93; pianist, accompanist Cardinal Chorale, Harlingen, 1979-80. Composer: Songs for Tots, 1983; playwright: (musical) Why the Bells Rang, 1988, American Tribute, 1995; arranger, dir. (musicals) Across the U.S.A., 1988, Around the World at Wilson School, 1992; dir. Under the Big Top, 1989, United We Stand, 1991; music dir.: Together, 1995, Christmas in the West, 1995, Every Day is Earth Day, 1996. Vol. Hosts Program, Harlingen, 1981, Riofest, 1983, Dishman Spring Festival, Combes, Tex., 1993, 94, Wilson Spring Fest, 1996; dir. Crockett Sch. dedication, 1993. Mem.: Am. Assn. Ret. Persons, Smithsonian Instn., Tex. Music Educators Assn., PEO Sisterhood (pres. 1999—2001, v.p. 2001—). Avocations: travel, reading, sewing, aerobics, swimming. Home: PO Box 875 Combes TX 78535-0875 Office: Primera Rd PO Box 240 Harlingen TX 78551-0240 E-mail: aligod@harlingen.isd.tenet.edu.

GODFREY, EUTHA MAREK, elementary school educator, consultant; b. Balt., Mar. 25, 1937; d. Louis Joseph and Estella Virginia (Stickels) Marek; m. Stanley I. Lewis (div. June 1970); children: Mark W. Lewis, Ronald A. Lewis, Kari S. Howard; m. Carl Godfrey Sr., Nov. 20, 1983 (dec. July 1993). BM in Music Edn., Johns Hopkins U., 1959; postgrad., N.C. A & T State U., 1972-75, U. N.C., 1974-76. Cert. early childhood edn. Tchr. Murray County Schs., Chatsworth, Ga., 1959-60, Fulton County Schs., Roswell, Ga., 1960-62; music tchr. Balt. County Schs., Baltimore, Md., 1962-63; band, chorus tchr. Guilford County Schs., Greensboro, N.C., 1963-67, kindergarten tchr., 1967-73; cons., early childhood State Dept. Pub. Instruction, Raleigh, N.C., 1972-76; early childhood tchr. Peeler and Erwin Magnet Schs., Greensboro City Schs., N.C., 1973-91; cons. Divsn. of Reading, State Dept. Pub. Instruction, Raleigh, N.C., 1976-82; dir. music Palm Coast United Methodist Ch., Palm Coast, Fla., 1993-98; min. coord. St. John's United Meth. Ch., 1999—. Cons., presenter, Individually Guided Edn., St. Louis, 1977; workshop presenter, Greensboro City Assn. for Edn. of Young Children, 1980-90; accreditation team, Southern Assn. of Schs. and Colls. State of N.C., 1977-91. Bd. dirs. Family Life Ctr., Palm Coast, 1992-95; mem. exec. com. Dem. Party, Greensboro, N.C., 1975. Greensboro Pub. Sch. Fund grantee, 1987-88; Full Competative scholar Peabody Conservatory, 1955. Mem. N.C. Ret. State Employees, Fellowship of United Meth. in Music and Worship Arts, Royal Sch. Ch. Music, Am. Choral Dir.'s Assn., Mu Phi Epsilon. Avocations: music, writing, cooking. Home: 5100 Eagle Perch Way Greensboro NC 27407

GODMAN, GABRIEL CHARLES, pathology educator; b. Albany, N.Y., Jan. 24, 1921; s. Hyman S. and Bertha R. Godman. AB, NYU, 1941, MD, 1944. House officer medicine Bellevue Hosp., N.Y.C., 1944-45; resident in pathology New Haven Hosp.; asst. in pathology Yale U. Med. Sch., New Haven, 1948-50; fellow in pathology Mt. Sinai Hosp., N.Y.C., 1950-51; mem. faculty Columbia U. Coll. Physicians and Surgeons, N.Y.C., 1952—; prof. pathology Columbia U. Coll. Physicians and Surgeons., N.Y.C., 1969—. Assoc. Rockefeller U., 1957-60. Contbr. articles and chpts. to jours. and texts in field. Served to capt. M.C., U.S. Army, 1945-47. Mem. Am. Assn. Pathologists, Am. Soc. Cell Biology, Harvey Soc., Internat. Acad. Pathology, Assn. U. Pathologists. Home: 900 W 190th St New York NY 10040-3633 Office: 630 W 168th St New York NY 10032-3702 E-mail: gcg2@columbia.edu.

GODSEY, CHERYL PARTRIDGE, administrator; b. Haleyville, Ala., Feb. 16, 1955; d. Herman Eugene and Gladys (Lackey) Partridge; m. Willard Lanier Godsey, Jr., Sept. 23, 1972; children: Laurel Eugenia, Erin Ruth. BS magna cum laude, U. N. Ala., 1983; MA, U. Ala., 1987, postgrad. Cert. spl. edn. tchr., Ala., ednl. leadership, Ala. Tchr. spl. edn. Winston County Sch. System, Double Springs, Ala., 1983-84; tchr. learning disabilities Morgan County Sch. System, Danville, Ala., 1984-85; grad. asst. emotional conflict U. Ala., Birmingham, 1985-86; tchr. learning disabilities Shelby County Sch. System, Birmingham, 1986—, chair spl. edn. dept., 1990—. Mem. NEA, Ala. Edn. Assn., Divsn. Learning Disabilities (sec. 1991-93), Coun. Exceptional Children (pres. 1988-89), Coun. Children with Behavioral Disorders, Optimist Club, Delta Kappa Gamma. Avocations: reading, travel, sports. Home: PO Box 623 Mc Calla AL 35111-0623

GODSEY, MARTHA SUE, speech-language pathologist; b. Abilene, Tex., Jan. 24, 1956; d. John Holbrook and Stella Mae (Blankenship) Chalmers; children: Bo Kilpatrick, Ryan Smith; married, Dec. 18, 1993; 1 child, J. Jordan Godsey. BSN, Tex. Chritian U., 1979; MA, Abilene Christian U., 1988. RN, Tex. RN Hendrick Med. Ctr., Abilene, 1979-80; speech pathologist Abilene Ind. Sch. Dist., 1989-92, Tri-County Edn. Co-op, 1992-94; pvt. practice, 1994-96; speech therapist Therapy Assocs., Inc., 1996-97, Sundance Rehab. Corp., 1997, West Tex. Rehab. Ctr., 1997-99, Abilene Ind. Sch. Dist., Tex., 1999—. Mem. Am. Speech/Lang. and Hearing Assn., Tex. Speech/Lang. and Hearing Assn. Avocation: reading. Home: 421 Pollard Abilene TX 79602

GODSHALL, BARBARA MARIE, educational administrator; b. Newark, N.Y., Jan. 5, 1958; d. Edward Franklin and Joan Marie (Moon) Moll; m. Clark J. Godshall, Oct. 26, 1985. AS, Cazenovia Coll., 1978; BS summa cum laude, Keuka Coll., 1989; MS, Nazareth Coll., 1991; CAS in Adminstrn., SUNY, Brockport, 1992; postgrad., U. Buffalo, 1995—. Cert. spl. edn. and elem. tchr., adminstr. Spl. edn. tchr. Lockport (N.Y.) Ctrl. Sch. Dist., 1991-92, Barker (N.Y.) Ctrl. Sch. Dist., 1992-93, dir. pupil pers. svcs. and spl. programs, 1993-97, Roy-Hart Ctrl. Sch. Dist., Lockport, 1997—. Pres., ednl. cons. elem., secondary and spl. edn.; spl. edn. tchr. Niag-Wheat Cen. Sch. Dist., 1995-97. Bd. dirs. ARC, Lockport, 1990—, Lockport Pub. Libr., 1990—. N.Y. State scholar, 1991. Mem. ASCD, Coun. for Exceptional Children, Phi Delta Kappa. Avocations: traveling, bicycling, reading, crafts, gardening. Home and Office: 9211 Somerset Dr Barker NY 14012-9542

GODT, EARL WAYNE, II, technology education educator; b. Coco Solo, Canal Zone, Panama, Aug. 10, 1953; came to U.S., 1955; s. Earl Wayne and Theresa May (Hymel) G.; m. Pamela Rollefson Terry, Aug. 1, 1987; 1 child, Anne Louise Terry. AS, Kilgore Coll., 1983; BS, U. Tex., Tyler, 1984; MS, Purdue U., 1985; postgrad., Ind. U., 1987-91; PhD, Kensington U., 1993. Tech. writer USMC/Civil Svc., Cherry Point, N.C., 1974-77; mgr. Pizza Hut, N.C., Tex., 1977-81; refinery worker Shore Oil Corp., Kilgore, Tex., 1981; lab. asst. Stewart Blood Ctr., Tyler, Tex., 1982; quality assurance engr. East Tex. Lighthouse for the Blind, Tyler, Tex., 1983-84; grad. teaching asst. Purdue U., West Lafayette, Ind., 1984-85; instr. GMC/Chevrolet-Pontiac-Can., Doralville, Ga., 1986; asst. prof. Ind. State U., Terre Haute, Ind., 1986-93, Western Ill. U., Macomb, 1993-96, Spoon River Coll., Canton, Ill., 1996-98, 2000—, Heartland C.C., Bloomington, Ill., 1998-2000. Cons. Covered Bridge Spl. Edn. Dist., Terre Haute, 1990; judge Student Contest Robotics Internat., 1989, 94, 95; developer/instr. robotics grades 3-6 Ind. State U. Sch., Terre Haute, 1988—; curriculum evaluator Assn. Ind. Colls. and Schs., Washington, 1989—. Presented robotics tutorial 4th Annual Nat. Robotics and Automation Systems Conf., 1987; contbr. articles profl. jours. Chairperson Unitarian-Universalist congregation, Terre Haute, 1990. Faculty devel. grantee TRW Found., 1989, Higher Edn. Cooperation Act grantee Ill. Bd. Higher Edn., 1996, Macomb fellow, 2001. Mem. Soc. Mfg. Engrs., Robotics Internat. (cert. sr. indsl. technologist, cert. mfg. technologist), Nat. Assn. Indsl. Tech. (dir. region 2 1994-96, 98-2001, pres. elect 2001-2002, pres. 2002-, chair ann. program com.), Ill. Assn. Electricity/Electronics Educators (treas. 1998—). Democrat. Avocations: golf, bowling, chess. Home: 1719 W Adams St Macomb IL 61455-1203 Office: Spoon River Coll Canton IL 61520 E-mail: egodt@spoonrivercollege.edu.

GODWIN, ANNABELLE PALKES, retired early childhood education educator; b. St. Louis, Dec. 23, 1920; d. Louis Aaron and Sadie (Galperin) Palkes; m. Robert Franklin Godwin, Jr., June 7, 1942 (dec. Aug. 1991); children: Sara, Jo Beth, Robert Franklin III. BS in Edn. and Drama, Washington U., St. Louis, 1945; MA in Early Childhood Edn., UCLA, 1967. Cert. secondary English and drama tchr., Mo.; cert. C.C. child devel. tchr., Calif. Tchr. L.A. Child Devel. Ctrs., 1946-47, Burbank (Calif.) Child Devel. Ctrs., 1947-49, Adventure Sch., Studio City, Calif., 1952-53; dir. nursery sch. Temple Emanuel, Burbank, 1959-67, Temple Beth Hillel, North Hollywood, Calif., 1967-75; prof. child devel. L.A. C.C. Dist., 1968-92, prof. emeritus, 1992—. Instr. UCLA Ext., 1968-78. Co-chair prodn. com. Setting Up for Infant Care, 1988; prodr. ednl. film Creative Experiences with Body Movement, 1975, Infant/Toddler Environments: Adult/Child Interaction, 1991. Bd. dirs. Calif. Children's Lobby, 1980-92; bd. dirs., legis. chmn., v.p. L.A. Mayor's Adv. Com. on Childcare, 1976—, chair, 1994-95; pres. exec. bd. Childcare Resource Ctr. San Fernando Valley, Calif., 1990—. Scholarship named in her honor L.A. Mission Coll., 1996, play day named in her honor San Fernando Valley, Calif., 1997. Mem. Assn. for Early Jewish Edn. (charter, past pres., bd. dirs., plaque 1975), So. Calif. Assn. for Edn. Young Children (bd. dirs., v.p. 1965—). Democrat. Avocation: working on behalf of children. Home: 1825 Rosita Ave Burbank CA 91504-2818

GODWIN, HAROLD NORMAN, pharmacist, educator; b. Ransom, Kans., Oct. 9, 1941; s. Harold Joseph and Nora Elva (Welsh) G.; m. Judy Rae Ricketts, June 9, 1963; children: Paula Lynn, Jennifer Joy. BS in Pharmacy, U. Kans., 1964; MS in Hosp. Pharmacy, Ohio State U., 1966. Lic. pharmacist, Kans., Ohio. Instr. Ohio State U. Coll. Pharmacy, Columbus, 1966-69; asst. dir. pharmacy Ohio State U., Columbus, 1966-69; dir. pharmacy U. Kans. Med. Ctr., Kansas City, 1969—; asst. prof. U. Kans. Sch. Pharmacy, Kansas City, 1969-74, assoc. prof., 1974-80, prof. pharmacy, 1980—, asst. dean pharmacy, 1975-89, assoc. dean pharmacy, 1989—, chmn. pharmacy practice, 1984—. John W. Webb lectr., vis. prof. Northeastern U., 1999; chmn. pharmacy exec. com. U. HealthSys. Consortium, 2001—. Author: Implementation Guide to IV Admixtures, 1977; (with others) Remington's Pharmaceutical Sciences, 1980, 85, 90, 95, 2000; contbr. over 100 articles to profl. jours. Recipient Clifton J. Latiolais award Ohio State U. Residents Alumni, 1986, Disting. Alumni award Ohio State U. Coll. Pharmacy, 1995; named Tchr. of the Yr., U. Kans. Sch. of Pharmacy, 2001. Fellow: Am. Soc. Health System Pharmacists (bd. dirs. 1978—81, pres. 1982—83, bd. dirs. rsch. and edn. found. 2002—, Harvey A.K. Whitney award 1991); mem.: Am. Coun. Pharm. Edn. (bd. dirs. 1988—2000, pres. 1992—96), Greater Kansas City Soc. Hosp. Pharmacists (pres. 1972), Kans. Soc. Hosp. Pharmacists (Kans. Hosp. Pharmacist of Yr. 1982, Harold N. Godwin award 1984), Kans. Pharmacists Assn. (pres 1977, Kans. Pharmacist of Yr. 1982), Am. Pharm. Assn. (Disting. Achievement award 2000). Republican. Methodist. Avocations: tennis, biking, cooking, wine tasting. Home: 10112 W 98th St Shawnee Mission KS 66212-5238 Office: U Kans Med Ctr Rainbow Blvd At 39th St Kansas City KS 66106-7231

GODWIN, SANDRA DONNA, secondary school educator; b. Blackshear, Ga., May 8, 1963; d. William Clinton Sr. and Margaret Louisa (Williams) G. AA, Waycross Coll., 1982; BA in History and English, Tift Coll., 1984; MEd in Secondary Social Studies, Valdosta State Coll., 1986, MEd in Secondary English, 1987, Ednl. Specialist in Secondary Social Studies, 1990. Cert. secondary history, English, social studies tchr., Ga. English tchr. Ware County Sr. H.S., Waycross, Ga., 1986-87, social studies tchr., 1987—, chair dept. social studies. Mem. Ga. Profl. Practices Commn., 1995-98, exec. com., 1998. Mem. state exec. bd. Future Ga. Educators, Clarkston, 1987-89, 92-97, state advisor, 1988-89, 93-94; Sunday sch. tchr. Emmanuel Bapt. Ch., Blackshear, Ga., 1986-87, First Bapt. Ch., Blackshear, 1994—; faculty advisor Ware County Students Against Driving Drunk, Waycross, 1986-87. Named Advisor of Yr., Future Ga. Educators, 1994. Mem. ASCD, Profl. Assn. of Ga. Educators, Nat. Coun. for Social Studies. Democrat. Avocations: genealogy, local history, music, swimming, travel. E-mail: dgodwin@ware.k12.ga.us.

GOEHRING, MAUDE COPE, retired business educator; b. Persia, Tenn., Jan. 5, 1915; d. James Lawrence and Bobbie C. (Ross) Cope; m. Harvey John Goehring Jr., Aug. 12, 1950 (dec. Mar. 1992). Student, Lebanon Valley Coll., 1944-45; grad., Am. Inst. Banking, 1945; BS in Edn., Indiana U. of Pa., 1948; MEd, U. Pitts., 1950. Tchr. Penn Hills Sr. High Sch., Pitts., 1948-68, U. Pitts., 1959-60, ret., 1968; vol. chmn. ICU, operating rm. info. desk Margaret R. Pardee Meml. Hosp., Hendersonville, N.C., 1989-95; vol. Carolina Village Health Ctr., 1994-99. Coord. Henderson County Ct. House Vols., Hendersonville, 1983-89; cons., counselor tax aid program Am. Assn. Ret. Persons, Hendersonville, 1981-96. Neighborhood chmn. Girl Scouts U.S., Butler County Pa., 1976-79; bd. dirs. ARC, Hendersonville, 1986-91; sec.-treas., bd. dirs. Crime Stoppers of Henderson County, 1991-96; nat. bd. dirs. Second Wind Hall of Fame, 1991-95. Mem. AAUW (officer 1975-76), Gideon Internat. Aux. (pres., sec. 1969-70), Delta Pi Epsilon (life, Gamma chpt., pres., sec. 1956-59, nat. del. 1957). Republican. Lutheran. Avocations: gardening, crafts, sewing, reading.

GOERKE, GLENN ALLEN, university administrator; b. Lincoln Park, Mich., May 15, 1931; s. Albert W. and Cecile P. (Crowl) Goerke; m. Joyce Leslie Walker, Mar. 3, 1973; children: Lynn, Jill, Kurt. AB, Eastern Mich. U., 1952, MA, 1955; PhD, Mich. State U., 1964; LhD (hon.), U. Tech. Santiago, Domincan Republic, 1995, U. Houston, 1997. Dean univ. svcs. Fla. Internat. U., Miami, 1970—71, assoc. dean faculty, 1971—72, assoc. v.p. acad. affairs, provost North campus, 1972—73; v.p. community affairs Fla. Internat U., Miami, 1973—78; dean coll. continuing edn. U. R.I., 1978—81; chancellor Ind. U. East, Richmond, 1981—86; pres. U. Houston, Victoria, 1986—89; interim chancellor U. Houston Sys., 1989; pres. U. Houston, Clear Lake, 1991—95, 1995—97, pres. emeritus, 1997; dir. Inst. for Future of Higher Edn., U. Houston, 1997—98. Recipient Disting. Alumni award, Eastern Mich. U., 1982. Mem.: Internat. Assn. Univ. Pres. (bd. dirs., v.p. 1991—98), Am. Assn. Univ. Adminstrs. (bd. dirs. 1991—96), Nat. Univ. Continuing Edn. Assn. (pres. 1973—74), Golden Key, Phi Delta Kappa, Phi Kappa Phi, Omicron Delta Kappa.

GOERLICH, SHIRLEY ALICE BOYCE, publishing executive, educator, media consultant; b. Oneonta, N.Y., May 17, 1937; d. John Orlo and Nella Virginia (Bartow) Boyce; m. Robert Frank Goerlich, Aug. 19, 1967; children: Robert John, Daniel Lee. AAS, SUNY, Cobleskill, 1957; BA, Parsons Coll., 1962. Cert. tchr. N.Y., bus. owner N.Y. Tchr. Milw. Pub. Schs., 1962-64, Huntington (N.Y.) Pub. Schs., 1964-67, Fairfax (Va.) County Adult Edn., 1970-76; pvt. practice Greene, NY, 1979-83; prin., owner RSG Pub., Sidney, NY, 1984—. Cons. Cemetery Bds. Trustees, Chenago, Delaware and Otsego counties. Author: (book) Genealogy: A Practical Research Guide, 1984 (CSG award, 1987), 2d edit., 1995, At Rest in Unadilla, Otsego Co., N.Y, 1987 (CSG award, 1988, Otsego County Local History award, 1993), Etched in Stone in Sidney, Delaware County N.Y., 1997, East Guilford Cemetery, 1997, History of Unadilla, 4 vols., 1998, History of West Unadilla, 1999, Town of Guliford, Chenango County, N.Y., Book 2 (Guilford, Chenango County, N.Y.) Cemeteries and Burial Grounds, 2000; pub.: Author Unknown, 2001, transcribed and pub.: N.Y.

State Censuses for Guilford, Chenango County, N.Y., 1855, 1865, 1875, 1905, Sidney (Delaware County, N.Y.) 1850, Masonville (Delaware County, N.Y.) 1845 along with the Civil War Roster for this town, transcriber, pub.: N.Y. State censuses for Unadilla, N.Y., 1855, 1865, 1875, 1892, Civil War roster town of Franklin, Delaware County, N.Y. Historian Town of Unadilla, NY, 1989—98; trustee Evergreen Hill Cemetary Assoc., Unadilla, 1996—2000, advisor, 2001—; v.p. Prospect Hill Cemetary Assn., Sidney, NY, 2000, bd. dirs., 2001—, v.p. bd. dirs., 2001, pres., 2002—03, sexton, 2003—. Recipient Nat. award, Nat. Soc. New Eng. Women, 1989, award for Excellence, Otsego County Local History Adv. Com., 1995, Civil War Re-enactors award, Bainbridge Hist. Soc., 2002. Mem.: Nat. Soc. New Eng. Women, N.Y. State Hist. Assn., Conn. Soc. Genealogists (Spl. Outstanding award 1989), Nat. Soc. Daus. Union Vets., Nat. Soc. DAR (chmn. 1989—91, organizing regent Gen. John Paterson chpt. 1978, Nat. Lineage Rsch. award 1987, 1988, 1989), Sidney Hist. Assn. (life). Republican. Presbyterian. Avocations: cooking, painting. Home: 217 County Highway 1 Bainbridge NY 13733-9307 Office: RSG Publishing 217 County Highway 1 Bainbridge NY 13733-3399 Home (Winter): PO Box 441 Sidney NY 13838-0441

GOERTZ, ROGER LAMAR, retired education counselor; b. Freer, Tex., Apr. 24, 1938; s. Albert F. and Dorothy N. Goertz; m. Jean L. Humphrey, Mar. 29, 1980. BA, S.W. Tex. State U., 1964; MEd, Sul Ross State U., 1974. Cert. vocat. and spl. edn. counselor. Tchr., coach Knippa (Tex.) Schs., 1964-65, Sanderson (Tex.) Schs., 1965-69, Big Spring (Tex.) Schs., 1969-76, vocat. counselor, 1981-94, career svcs. coord., 1994-98; plan a counselor Plainview (Tex.) Schs., 1976-78; vocat. counselor Svc. Ctr. XV, San Angelo, Tex., 1978-81; ret., 1998. Mem. goals com. Future Goals City of Big Spring, 1995. Mem.: Big Spring Optimist Club (pres. 2000—02). Lutheran. Avocations: plays, jazz concerts, athletic events.

GOES, KATHLEEN ANN, secondary education educator, choral director; b. New Bedford, Mass., Jan. 13, 1951; d. Filento Andrade and Lillian (Cabral) G. BA in Psychology, U. Mass., North Dartmouth, 1976; postgrad., Ctrl. Conn. State U., 1987—98. Cert. K-8 elem. tchr., K-12 music tchr., Mass. Social worker Dept. Social Svcs., Cambridge, Mass., 1980-85; pvt. tchr. voice and piano, New Bedford, 1985-88; tchr. vocal music New Bedford Pub. Sch., 1985-90; tchr. music, choral dir. Fairhaven (Mass.) H.S., 1991—. Singer, actress, southeastern New Eng., 1974—; dir. music ministry St. Mary's Ch., South Dartmouth, Mass., 1988—; bd. dirs., sec. New Bedford Festival Theatre, 1990-97, v.p., 1997-99, mem. adv. bd., 1999—. Dir. musicals The Sound of Music, Cinderella, My Fair Lady, Bye, Bye Birdie, You're a Good Man Charlie Brown, How to Succeed in Business Without Really Trying, Little Shop of Horrors, The Boyfriend, Godspell, Jesus Christ Superstar; performed the mother in Amahl and the Night Visitors; actress, singer in musicals Fiddler on the Roof, Godspell, Phantom, The Sound of Music. Bd. dirs. New Bedford Symphony Orch., 1994-96. Named Promising Young Artist, Crescendo Club, Boston, 1981; recipient outstanding leadership award Fairhaven Assn. for Music Edn., 1995. Mem. NEA, Am. Choral Dirs. Assn., Nat. Pastoral Musicians Assn., New Eng. Theatre Conf., Drama League, Music Educators Nat. Conf., Mass. Tchrs. Assn., Mass. Music Educators Assn., Whale Hist. League. Roman Catholic. Avocations: cooking, crafts, computers, boating, scenic design. Home: 363 Maple St New Bedford MA 02740-1075 Office: Fairhaven HS 12 Huttleston Ave Fairhaven MA 02719-3122

GOETHE, ELIZABETH HOGUE, music educator; b. Balt., May 4, 1943; d. Paul Robert and Charlotte H. (Rigney) H.; m. Frederick Martin Goethe, June 30, 1973; children: Elizabeth Anne, Jonathan David. BS, Towson U., 1965; MEd in Music, U. Md., 1972. Cert. tchr. piano. Accompanist Vera Hax Dance Studio, Balt., 1962-66; music tchr. Balt. County Pub. Schs., 1965-74; ch. choir dir. Glyndon, Ellicott City, Md., 1976-79; class piano tchr. Balt. County Pub. Schs., 1980—83; piano tchr. Reisterstown, Md., 1978—; pvt. piano tchr., 1978—; music tchr. St. John's Episcopal Pre-Sch., Glyndon, 1978—2000. Mem. Choristers Guild, 1976-79. Mem. Music Tchrs. Nat. Assn. (ea. divsn. sec. 1996-98), Md. State Music Tchrs. Assn. (convention chair 1991-93, v.p. student activities 1993-97, cert. com. 1991-97), Greater Columbia Music Tchrs. Assn. (sec. 1996-98), Greater Balt. Music Tchrs. Assn. (treas. 1997—), Nat. Guild of Piano Tchrs. (adjudicator), Am. Coll. Musicians. Republican. Episcopalian. Avocations: family, teaching, profl. activities. Home and Office: 120 Nicodemus Rd Reisterstown MD 21136-3245

GOETZ, MARY ANNA, artist, educator; b. Oklahoma City, Oct. 7, 1946; d. Richard V. and Edith Jean (Day) G.; m. James David Cox, Sept. 20, 1971; children: Nathan, Julianna. BA, Oklahoma City U., 1968; post grad., Malden Bridge Sch. Art, 1967-71, Cape Sch. Art, 1970, N.Y. Acad. Art, 1981-82. instr. landscape and still life painting Woodstock, N.Y. Sch. Art, 1992-03. Juror Salmagundi Art Club, N.Y.C., 1985; Pastel Soc. Am., N.Y.C., 1992; Catherine Lorrilard Art Club, N.Y.C., 1993. Editor: (newsletter) Nat. Assn. Women Artists, 1988—; author: (periodicals) The Illuminator, 1979; The American Artist, 1992; (book) Painting Landscapes in Oil, 1992. Mem. Nat. Arts Club; Nat. Assn. Women Artists (bd. mem.); Artists Fellowship; Woodstock Artists Assn. Avocations: travel, reading. Home: PO Box 4666 Willow NY 12495

GOETZ, WILLIAM WALTER, education and history educator; b. Union City, N.J., Dec. 2, 1928; s. William Martin and Carmela Anastasia (Grosson) G.; children: Margaret Ann, William Joseph. BSin Fgn. Svc., Georgetown U., 1950; MA in History, Fordham U., 1960; profl. diploma, Columbia U., N.Y.C., 1967, EdD, 1981. Tchr. Latin and history Holy Trinity High Sch., Westfield, N.J., 1959-61; supr. social studies New Providence (N.J.) Pub. Schs., 1965-85; mem. adj. faculty dept. history William Paterson Coll., Wayne, N.J., 1989—; mem. adj. faculty Sch. Edn., Kean Coll. N.J., Union, 1989—. NSF seminar participant Stevens Inst. Tech., 1981; participant N.J. Com. for Humanities, Rutgers U., 1986; NEH inst. participant Princeton U., 1984, Columbia U., 1987. Contbr. articles and book revs. to profl. publs. With U.S. Army, 1950-52. Coun. for Basic Edn. nat fellow, 1988. Mem. ASCD, Nat. Coun. Social Studies (mem. coll. and univ. faculty assembly 1989—), N.J. Coun. Social Studies. Avocations: sports, current events, physical fitness. Home: 14 Artillery Park Rd Bedminster NJ 07921-2045 Office: William Paterson Coll Dept History 300 Pompton Rd Dept History Wayne NJ 07470-2103

GOFF, JANE E. secondary school educator; b. Denver, Nov. 12, 1949; d. Donald F. and Susanna L. (Commerford) Gallion; m. Harry M. Goff, June 12, 1982. BA, Colo. State U., 1971; student, U. Colo. Cert. modern lang. tchr., Colo. Tchr. French Jefferson County Pub. Sch., Golden, Colo. Adminstr. Alternative Compensation/Student Outcomes Task Forces; project dir. Tchr. Performance Pay Pilot, 1995-98, Columbine anniversary com., Coordinator of World Lang. and Internat. Student Exchange Program, 2003-; mem. Nat. Bd. for Profl. Tchg. Std. Workgroup. Hon. chmn. West Chamber Good News Breakfast; design group West Chamber Links for Learning; mem. Jefferson County Sch. Anchor Group, 1998-2000, Jefferson County Sch. Fin. Task Force, Leadership Jefferson County Steering Com., Jefferson County Schs. 50th Anniversary Com.; bd. dir., v.p. for edn. programs Jefferson Symphony. Mem. NEA, Am. Assn. Tchr. French, Colorado Congress of Fgn. Lang. Tchrs. Jefferson County Edn. Assn. (bd. dir., by-laws chair, bldg. rep., sec. 1990-94, v.p. 1994-98, pres. 1998-2000, budget com./negotiations team, JCEA Award 2003), Colo. Edn. Assn. (v.p. 2000—, quality tchg. task force, pub. edn. advocacy team)Western States Quality Schs. Cadre, Jefferson County Coun. PTA (bd. dirs. 1990-2000), Phi Delta Kappa Internat. E-mail: jgoff@nea.org.

GOFF, NADINE FARABEE, elementary education educator; b. Bartow, Fla., June 6, 1944; d. Edward Theodore and Sarah Eileen (Jenkins) Farabee; m. Dale Warren Goff, Sept. 2, 1967; children: Ginger Danine, Shelly Eileen. B in Music Edn., Lee Coll., 1976; postgrad., Mid. Tenn. State U., 1979. Cert. tchr., Tenn. Tchr. music Dunbar Secondary Sch., Ft. Myers, Fla., 1967; tchr. 1st grade McDonald Elem. Sch., Cleveland, Tenn., 1970; tchr. 2d grade Waterville Elem. Sch., Cleveland, 1970-71; music tchr. Gallatin, Tenn., 1980-82; tchr. 6th grade Wessington Place Elem., Hendersonville, Tenn., 1982-83, Lakeside Park Elem., Hendersonville, 1984-85, Mayfield Elem. Sch., Cleveland, 1987-89, tchr. 4th grade, 1989-92, tchr. 2d grade, 1992—. Recipient 21st Century classroom computer equipment, 1994. Mem. Ch. of God. Avocations: piano, needlecrafts, reading, walking. Home: 3675 Crown Colony Dr NW Cleveland TN 37312-2714

GOFF, RENEE ROSENSTOCK, middle school educator; b. Chgo., May 15, 1956; d. Alfred and Alice (Bronstein) Rosenstock; m. Gerald M. Goff; children: Gregory Scott, Carly Michelle. BA, Northeastern Ill. U., Chgo., 1978; MEd, Nat. Louis U., 2001. Tchr. 5th and 6th grades Talala Elem. Sch., Park Forest, Ill., 1978-88; tchr. lang. arts and social studies West Oak Middle Sch., Diamond Lake, Ill., 1989—2003; tchr. gifted grades 2-5 Diamond Lake Sch. Dist., 2003—. Leader 4-H Clubs, Park Forest and Diamond Lake, 1978—; Washington trip sponsor/assembly chairperson. Recipient Disney Am. Tchr. award nominee, 2001, Golden Apple nominee, 2003. Mem. Nat. Middle Sch. Assn., NAGC (Nat. Assn. Gifted Children).

GOFF, THOMAS M. secondary education educator; b. Seattle, Feb. 28, 1942; s. Ralph E. and Hazel R. (Hamilton) G.; m. Marianne Fattorini, June 8, 1968; children: Maria, Diana, Tom, Krista. BA in History, Seattle U., 1967, MA in Am. Hist., 1971. Tchr. history Enumclaw (Wash.) High Sch., 1971—. With USMC. Mem. NEA, Orgn. of Am. Historians, Nat. Coun. for Social Studies, Wash. Edn. Assn. Home: 18701 126th Pl SE Renton WA 98058-7949 Office: Enumclaw High Sch 226 Semanski St Enumclaw WA 98022-2099

GOFFE, ESTHER, elementary school educator; b. Devils Lake, N.D., Jan. 3, 1944; d. Harold Melvin and Myrtle Gilene (Johnson) Hanson; m. Stanley M. Goffe, July 14, 1965; 1 child, Bryan. BA, Jamestown (N.D.) Coll., 1966; postgrad., Pacific Luth. U., Tacoma, 1972. Elem. tchr. Plains (Mont.) Sch. Dist., 1966-68, Sch. Dist. 216, Enumclaw, Wash., 1968—, bldg. coord. after sch. enrichment, 1989-90, trainer coop pluralism, 1990-93. Dist. coord. Young Authors' Celebration, 1991-93; mem. Joint Assn./Dist. Forum, 1987-92; mem. Joint Assn./Dist. Formative Evaluation Com., 1991-93, legis. bargaining team, 1991, sec., 1991-93; mem. elem. instrnl. coun., 1994—, grade level chair, 1994—. Mem. AAUW, NEA, ASCD, Wash. ASCD, Wash. Edn. Assn. (del. rep. assembly 1990—, del. endorsement conv. 1992), Enumclaw Edn. Assn. (v.p. 1987-91, pub. rels. 1987-93, negotiator 1986-90, 94—, pres. 1990-92), Puget Sound Uniserv Coun. (pres. 1993-95), Enumclaw C. of C. (edn. com. 1990—, chair 1992-94, Peer Coach 1992-94).

GOFORTH, MARY ELAINE DAVEY, secondary education educator; b. Barnesville, Ohio, Sept. 9, 1922; d. Frederick Richard and Lola (Knox) Davey; m. Richard Eugene Goforth, Sept. 9, 1944; 1 child, Diane Lynell Goforth-Ohning. B.M.Ed., Oberlin Coll., 1944; MA in Edn., Coll. of Mt. St. Joseph, 1987. Cert. edn. Music tchr., Leipsig, Ohio, 1944-45, Perry Local, 1945-47; English tchr. Ohio No. Univ., 1946; English and music tchr. Perry Sch., Lima, Ohio, 1945-47; English tchr. Stone Creek (Ohio) Sch., 1947—51, Conotton Valley Sch., Bowerston, Ohio, 1961—68, New Philadelphia (Ohio) Sch., 1973—88, Indian Valley Sch., Midvale, Ohio, 1988—93. Author poems. Pres. New Philadelphia (Ohio) Tchrs.' Assn., 1967. Named Indian Valley Tchr. of Yr., 1985, Candidate for Ohio Tchr. of the Yr., 1985; Martha Holden Jennings scholar, 1985. Home: 2123 E High Ave New Philadelphia OH 44663-3323

GOGGIN, JOAN MARIE, school system administrator; b. Boston, Nov. 15, 1956; d. Richard and Florence Muriel (Stone) G. BS in Edn., Westfield State Coll., 1978; MS in Edn., Lesley Coll., 1981; Cert. Adv. Grad. Studies in Adminstrv. Leadership, U. Mass., 1999. Spl. needs tchr. Supervisory Union # 53, Pembroke, N.H., 1978-79; grad. intern, head tchr. Ednl. Collaborative Greater Boston, Brookline, Mass., 1979-80; vocat. counselor Charles River Assn. for Retarded Citizens, Needham, Mass., 1981-83; dir. vocat. svcs. Community Assistance Corp., New Orleans, 1983-84; tchr. of pre-sch. children with severe spl. needs St. Charles Parish Pub. Schs., Luling, La., 1985-88; career placement and tng. specialist Plymouth (Mass.) Carver Regional Sch. Dist., 1988-92; inclusion facilitator Plymouth Pub. Schs., 1992-98, asst. dir. spl. edn., 1999—. Cons. on self advocacy Mass. Assn. for Retarded Citizens, 1980-83; ednl. cons. Human Devel. Ctr., La. State U., New Orleans, 1984-85, D.K. Hollingsworth & Assocs., Metairie, La., 1984-88; vocat. cons. United Cerebral Palsy, Harahann, La., 1984-85; program coord. JTPA Project, Plymouth Sch. Dist., 1989-91, program. adminstr., 1991-93, exec. prodr. Bridging the Gap, We All Belong Together, 1991-93. Exec. prodr.: Bridging the Gap: Transition to Independence, We All Belong Together; author tng. program for paraprofls; curriculum devel. with adaptive modifications for learners with spl. needs, 1997. Active tadk force on criteria for spl. edn. svcs. Mass. Dept. Edn., 1992-93, mem. com. individual edn. plan, 1990-93, mem. com. on profl. devel., 2000—. Recipient Hon. Mention Tchr. of Yr. award Mass. Coun. Exceptional Children; grantee Mass. Dept. Edn., 1988—. Mem.: ASCD, NEA, Mass. Assn. Spl. Edn. Adminstrs., Assn. for Severely Handicapped. Democrat. Avocations: t'ai chi, yoga, travel, reading, gourmet cooking. Office: Pupil Personnel Svcs 253 S Meadow Rd Plymouth MA 02360-4739 E-mail: jgoggin@plymouth.k12.ma.us.

GOGOLIN, MARILYN TOMPKINS, language pathologist, retired educational administrator; b. Pomona, Calif., Feb. 25, 1946; d. Roy Merle and Dorothy (Davidson) Tompkins; m. Robert Elton Gogolin, Mar. 29, 1969. BA, U. LaVerne, Calif., 1967; MA, U. Redlands, Calif., 1968; postgrad., U. Wash., 1968-69; MS, Calif. State U., Fullerton, 1976. Cert. clin. speech pathologist; cert. teaching and sch. adminstrn. Speech and lang. pathologist Rehab. Hosp., Pomona, 1969-71; diagnostic tchr. L.A. County Office of Edn., Downey, Calif., 1971-72, program specialist, 1972-74, cons. lang., 1975-76, cons. orgns. and mgmt., 1976-79, dir. adminstrv. affairs, asst. to supt., 1979-95; dep. supt., 1995—2001; acting supt. L.A. County Office of Edn., Downey, Calif., 2001—02; COO Pulliam Group, 2003—. Cons. lang. sch. dists., Calif., 1975—79; cons. orgn. and mgmt. and profl. assns., Calif., 1976—; exec. dir. L.A. County Sch. Trustees Assn., 1979—2003; treas. L.A. County Edn. Found., 1996—2003; mem. NAEP task force, 1998; mem. adv. bd. Lightspan Partnerships, 2001. Founding patron Desert chpt. Kidney Found., Palm Desert, Calif., 1985. Doctoral fellow U. Washington, 1968; named One of Outstanding Young Women Am., 1977. Mem. Am. Mgmt. Assn., Am. Speech/Hearing Assn., Calif. Speech/Hearing Assn., Am. Edn. Research Assn. Baptist. Avocation: travel. Office: The Pulliam Group 1980 Orange Tree Ln Redlands CA 92374-

GOHEEN, JANET MOORE, counselor, sales professional; b. Everett, Mass., Sept. 29, 1945; d. Franklin Pierce and Virginia Louise (Murphy) Moore; m. Peter Arthur Goheen, Apr. 2, 1967; children: Kevin Murphy Moore Goheen, Andrew Hudson Moore Goheen. BA, Ohio Wesleyan U., 1967; MS, U. Bridgeport, 1979. Cert. profl. guidance counselor, Ohio. Tchr. English Nordinia Hills High Sch., Macedonia, Ohio, 1967-69, White Plains (N.Y.) High Sch., 1969-71, Hudson (Ohio) High Sch., 1982-83; tchr. emotionally disturbed Palisades Learning Ctr., Paramus, N.J., 1986-87; sales cons. The Longaberger Co., Dresden, Ohio, 1983-84, br. advisor, 1984-90, regional advisor, 1990—; middle sch. counselor Hudson Middle Sch., 1988—. Tchr. ESL Hitchcock Presbyn. Ch., Scarsdale, N.Y., 1976-79, Aurora (Ohio) City Schs., 1979-81, Hudson Local Schs., 1980-82. Mem. Jr. League of Scarsdale, 1976-79, Jr. League of Akron, 1979-82, Jr. League No. N.J., Ridgewood, 1983-85; mem. alumni bd. dirs. Ohio Wesleyan U., Delaware, Ohio, 1990-93; trustee Am. Found. for Suicide Prevention N.E. Ohio, 1997—; founder Hudson Presbyn. Ch., 1980; founder Anna Lee chpt. Questers, Hudson, 1981. Mem. Am. Sch. Counselors Assn., Ohio Sch. Counselors Assn., Kappa Kappa Gamma, Kappa Delta Pi. Home: 97 Manor Dr Hudson OH 44236-3406 Office: Hudson Middle Sch 77 N Oviatt St Hudson OH 44236-3043

GOLBY, JAMES L. school system administrator; b. Kewanee, Ill., Mar. 2, 1927; s. John Thomas and Margaret Elizabeth (Larkin) G.; m. Alice Ann Simons, July 25, 1964; children: Katherine Golby Stewart, Margaret Golby Gustafson, Angela, James. BA, U. Ill., 1950, MA, 1952; postgrad., Bradley U., U. Chgo. Cert. tchr., Ill. Agrl. instr. Geneseo (Ill.) H.S., 1950-51; agrl. and sociology instr. Kewanee (Ill.) H.S., 1951-62, prin., 1962-67; supt. Kewanee Cmty. Unit Schs., 1967-98, supt. emeritus, 1998—. Bd. dirs. Kewanee Devel. Corp., 1970s. Sgt. U.S. Army, 1945-46. Named one of Outstanding Young Men in Am., Kewanee Jaycees, 1965, Citizen of Yr., City of Kewanee, 1984, Outstanding Adminstr., State of Ill. Supts. Office, 1977, Hon. State Farmer, Future Farmers Am., 1958; named to Hall of Fame, Blackhawk Coll., 1992. Mem. Am. Assn. Sch. Adminstrs., Ill. Assn. Sch. Adminstrs., Kewanee C. of C. (bd. dirs. 1970s), Kiwanis (pres. 1966, George Hixson award 1997). Democrat. Roman Catholic. Home: 611 McKinley Ave Kewanee IL 61443-3015 Office: Kewanee Cmty Unit Sch Dist 1101 E Third St Kewanee IL 61443-2951

GOLD, MARLYN H. art educator; b. N.Y.C., Mar. 10, 1952; d. John Joseph and Irene (Turney) Hommel; m. Daniel Wayne Gold, Mar. 6, 1976; children: Jacob, Olivia. BA in Teaching Art., Sam Houston State U., 1976. Art tchr. Conroe (Tex.) Ind. Sch. Dist., 1977-85, Kerrville (Tex.) Ind. Sch. Dist., 1988—. Ednl. adv. bd. Cowboy Artist of Am., Kerrville, 1992-94; assoc. in fabric and craft Walmart; presenter in field. Mem. Nat. Art Educators Assn., Tex. Art Educators Assn. (presenter convs. 1994). Roman Catholic. Avocations: learning folk art techniques (weaving, spinning wheel), family and home, sewing, gardening, hand made ceramic tiles. Office: Peterson Mid Sch K ISD 605 Tivy St Kerrville TX 78028-4600 E-mail: lyn.gold@kerrville.isd.net.

GOLD, PAUL ERNEST, psychology educator, behavioral neuroscience educator; b. Detroit, Jan. 7, 1945; s. Hyman and Sylvia Gold; children: Scott David Gold, Zachary Alexander Korol-Gold. BA, U. Mich., 1966; MS, U. N.C., 1968; PhD, 1971. NIH postdoctoral fellow, lectr. psychobiology U. Calif., Irvine, 1972-76; asst. prof. U. Va., Charlottesville, 1976-78, assoc. prof., 1978-81, prof., 1981-97, Commonwealth prof., 1997—99, dir. neurosci. grad. program, 1991-95; prof. Binghamton (N.Y.) U., 1999-2000, U. Ill., Urbana-Champaign, 2000—. Dir. Med. Scholars Program U. Ill. Coll. Medicine, Urbana-Champaign, 2000—02, mem. exec. com. Inst. Aging, 2001—. Editor Psychobiology, 1990-97, Neurobiology of Learning and Memory, 1998—; contbr. numerous articles to sci. publs. Mem. Commonwealth of Va. Alzheimer's and Related Disorders Commn., 1998-99. Recipient James McKeen Cattell award, 1983, Sesquicentennial Assn. award, U. Va., 1983, 90-93, Disting. Alumni award U. N.C., Chapel Hill, 2000; named APA Master Lectr., 2000; NIH fellow, 1967. Fellow APA (com. animal rsch. & ethics), AAAS, Am. Psychol. Soc. (mem. com. 1990-91, program com. 1991); mem. Soc. for Neurosci. (com. on animals in rsch. 1993-98), NSF Adv. Panel for Behavioral and Computational Neurosci., 1993-96. Office: U Ill at Urbana-Champaign Dept Psychology Champaign IL 61820 E-mail: pgold@uiuc.edu.

GOLD, PHRADIE KLING See KLING, PHRADIE

GOLD, ROSLYN, social worker, educator; b. Bklyn., July 17, 1924; d. Abraham and Esther (Steinberg) Smith; m. Simon Gold; children: Jay Alexander, Alice Louise. BS, Queens Coll., 1972; MSW, Yeshiva U., N.Y.C., 1977; M in Gerontalogy, Yeshiva U., 1980; DSW, Yeshiva U., N.Y.C., 1990. Cert. psychoanalytical psychotherapy, group psychotherapy. Tchr. home econs., food and nutrition, family and child enrichment N.Y. Bd. Edn., Queens, 1972-75; dir. sr. ctr. Jewish Assn. for Svcs. to the Aged, Queens, 1977-81; case mgr. JASA, Queens, 1981-85; pvt. practice Queens, 1985—; dir. svcs. to the aged L.I. Consultation Ctr., 1988-90; pvt. practice Forest Hills, N.Y., 1987—; founder/dir. Hillcrest Leisure Group, 1992—. Mem. (pres. Queens chap. 1990-92) N.Y. Soc. Clin. Social Workers. Home: Bldg 1-26D 27126 Grand Central Pkwy Floral Park NY 11005-1209 Office: 10923 71st Rd Apt 2J Forest Hills NY 11375-4856 E-mail: gzahav@aol.com.

GOLD, RUTH FORMAN, education educator; b. Bklyn., Oct. 10, 1932; d. Louis and Bertha (Wolkowitz) Forman; m. Bernard Gold, Nov. 23, 1952 (dec. May 1994); children: Alan Mark, Anyta Joan Costales. BA, Bklyn. coll., 1953, MA, 1955; EdD, Columbia U., 1973. Tchr. N.Y.C. Pub. Schs., Bklyn., 1953-58, East Meadow (N.Y.) Schs., 1958-60; lectr. Hofstra U., Hempstead, N.Y., 1961-72; from asst. prof. to prof. Adelphi U., Garden City, N.Y., 1972-86; prof. spl. edn. Hofstra U., 1986—2000, chair dept. counseling, rsch., spl. edn. and rehab., 1993-96, coord. gerontology, 1996—2003, dir. Ctr. for Gerontology, 1997—. Mem. adv. bd. C.W. Post Tchr. Tng. Grant, Greenvale, N.Y., 1992-95, C.W. Post Tapp Project, 2001-2002; cons. Ctr. for Devel. Disabilities, Woodbury, N.Y., 1991-94. Co-author: Education the Learning Disabled, 1982; contbr. chpts. to books. Named Person of the Yr. Long Is. Assn. Spl. Edn. Adminstrs. Mem. Assn. for Children with Learning Disabilities (mem. adv. bd. 1972-84, bd. dirs. 1984-90, bd. trustees 1990—), Coun. for Exceptional Children (v.p. N.Y. State chpt. 1987-88, pres. N.Y. state divsn. for early childhood 1984-85). Office: Hofstra U Hempstead Tpke Hempstead NY 11549-0001

GOLDBERG, ALAN MARVIN, toxicologist, educator; b. Bklyn., Nov. 20, 1939; s. William and Celia Ida (Rudman) G.; m. Helene Schoenbach, Aug. 14, 1960; children: Michael David, Naomi Jill BS, Bklyn. Coll. Pharmacy, 1961; PhD in Pharmacology, U. Minn., 1966; DSc (hon.), L.I. U, 1995. Rsch. asst. U. Wis., 1961-62, U. Minn., 1962-66; rsch. assoc. Inst. Psychiat. Rsch. Ind. U., 1966-67, asst. prof. dept. pharmacology, 1967-69; asst. prof. environ. medicine Johns Hopkins U., Balt., 1969-71, assoc. prof., 1971-78, prof. dept. environ. health scis., 1978—, assoc. chmn. dept., 1978-80, acting dir. div. toxicology, 1979-80, dir. div. toxicology, 1980-82, dir. Ctr. Alternatives to Animal Testing, 1981—, assoc. dean rsch., 1984-94; assoc. dean corp. affairs Sch. Pub. Health, Balt., 1994-99; adminstrv. head health edn. program Johns Hopkins U./Nat. Basketball Player Assn., 1990-95; cons. OECD, Paris, 1998—. Prin. rsch. scientist Chesapeake Bay Inst., 1979-84; mem. health hazard evaluation team of chem. waste dumps State of Tenn., 1980; mem. rev. panel EPA, 1980-82; mem. working group on harmonization of in vitro methods Orgn. Econ. and Cmty. Devel., 1995—; organizer 1st World Congress on Alternative and Animal Use in Life Scis., 1993; sci. adv. bd. subcom. on toxicology U.S. FDA, 1996-2001; mem. interagy. coord. com. for validation of alternative method HHS, 1998-2002; bd. sci. advisors Xenogen, Inc.; mem. sci. adv. com. Alternative Tchg. Methods, NIEHS, 2002— vis. prof. U. Utrecht Ctr. Animals and Society, 2002. Mem. editorial bd. Jour. Am. Coll. Toxicology, assoc. editor In Vitro Toxicology; contbr. articles to profl. jours. Trustee Hildergard Doerenkamp-Gerhard Zbinden Found., 1985-2001, hon. mem., 2002-. Recipient award Ind. Neurol. Soc., 1967, Russell and Burch award Human Soc. of U.S., 1991; named Disting. Alumnus, L.I. Univ., 1992. Mem. AAAS, Am. Soc. Pharmacology and Exptl. Therapeutics, Soc. Neurosci. (pres. Balt. chpt. 1971-73), Am. Soc. Neurochemistry, Am. Epilepsy Soc., Assn. Univ. Tech. Mgrs., Internat. Soc. Neurochemistry, Soc. Toxicology (Ambassador Mid-Atlantic sect. 1998), Soc. Toxicology (Enhancement of Animal Welfare award 2001, Hildergard Doerenkamp-Kerhard Zbinden award 2001), Internat. Study Group on Memory Disorders, Internat. Union Pharmacology, Office of Tech. Assessment Panel on Alternatives to Animal Use in Rsch. Testing and Edn. and Frontiers in Neuroscience, Nat. Acad. Sci., Inst. for Lab. Animal Resources. Office: 111 Market Pl Ste 840 Baltimore MD 21202-7113 E-mail: goldberg@jhsph.edu.

GOLDBERG, ERWIN, biochemistry educator; b. Waterbury, Conn., Jan. 14, 1930; m. Geraldine Bloom, Aug. 26, 1951 (div. Sept. 1983); m. Pauline Bentley, May 12, 1985; children: Samuel, Larry, Jeffrey, Thomas, Katherine. BA, Harpur Coll., 1951; PhD, U. Iowa, 1956. Asst. prof. W.Va. U., Morgantown, 1958-61; from asst. prof. to assoc. prof. N.D. State U., Fargo, 1961-63; from asst. prof. to prof. dept. biochem., molecular biol., cell biol. Northwestern U., Evanston, Ill., 1963—. Contbr. over 170 articles to profl. jours. NSF, NIH Rsch. grantee, 1958—. Fellow AAAS; mem. Am. Soc. Biochem. Molecular Biology, Am. Soc. Andrologists, Soc. Study Reproduction, Protein Soc. Office: Northwestern U Dept BMBCB 2205 Tech Dr Evanston IL 60208-0001

GOLDBERG, STEVEN EDWARD, history and philosophy educator; b. Chgo., Sept. 10, 1951; s. Richard and Arlene (Simon) G.; m. Katherine Anne Neill, Sept. 18, 1981; children: Sarah Anne, Emily Allison. BA with high honors, So. Ill. U., 1974; MA, De Paul U., 1976; PhD with distinction, DePaul U., 1983. cert. tchr. secondary edn. Lectr. in philosophy DePaul U., Chgo., 1977-85, asst. dean, 1979-81, dir. advt. and assessment ctr., 1981-84, asst. to v.p. acad. affairs, 1985-86; tchr. history and philosophy Oak Park & River Forest H.S., Ill., 1987—; tchr. philosophy and religion Saffron Walden County (England) H.S., 1992-93. Scholar in residence Ill. Bell, Chgo., 1984; rsch. assoc. Inst. for Bus. Ethics DePaul U., 1984-86; instr. philosophy gifted program Northwestern U., Evanston, 1992, 94; Fulbright exchg. tchr. Saffron Walden County H.S., 1992-93; sem. leader U. Chgo. Ctr. South Asian Studies, 2001; mem. faculty World History Summer Inst. St. Edward's U., 2000. Co-editor, author: (book) Modern Technology and the Transformation of America, 1987; author: (book) Two Patterns of Rationality in Freud's Writings, 1988 (selected for seminar NEH); contbr. article to philosophical jour. Workshop leader, applicant interviewer Fulbright Agy., Washington D.C., 1993—. Recipient Arthur T. Schmitt fellow DePaul U., 1977-79; DePaul Competitive Rsch grantee DePaul U., 1986; recipient Fullbright-Hays Sem. Abroad to India, 2001, recipient Fulbright Mem. Fund. Scholarship to Japan, 2003. Mem. Am. Philosophical Assn., Am. Hist. Assn., Nat. Coun. Social Studies, Assn. for Curriculum and Instrn., World History Assn. Avocations: running, cycling, hiking, travel. Home: 134 Ashland Ave River Forest IL 60305-2106 Office: Oak Park River Forest HS 201 N Scoville Ave Oak Park IL 60302-2264 E-mail: sgoldberg@oprfhs.org.

GOLDBERGER, MARVIN LEONARD, physicist, educator; b. Chgo., Oct. 22, 1922; s. Joseph and Mildred (Sedwitz) G.; m. Mildred Ginsburg, Nov. 25, 1945; children: Samuel M., Joel S. BS, Carnegie Inst. Tech., 1943; PhD, U. Chgo., 1948. Research assoc. Radiation Lab., U. Calif., 1948-49; research assoc. Mass. Inst. Tech., 1949-50; asst.-assoc. prof. U. Chgo., 1950-55, prof., 1955-57; Higgins prof. physics Princeton U., 1957-77, chmn. dept., 1970-76, Joseph Henry prof. physics, 1977-78; pres. Calif. Inst. Tech., Pasadena, 1978-87; dir. Inst. Advanced Study, Princeton, N.J., 1987-91; prof. physics UCLA, 1991-93, U. Calif., San Diego, 1993-2000, dean divsn. natural scis., 1994-99, prof. emeritus, 2000—. Mem. President's Sci. Adv. Com., 1965-69; chmn. Fedn. Am. Scientists, 1971-73. Fellow Am. Phys. Soc., Am. Acad. Arts and Scis.; mem. Nat. Acad. Scis., Am. Philos. Soc., Council on Fgn. Relations. E-mail: mgoldberger@ucsd.edu.

GOLDBLATT, EILEEN WITZMAN, art director, director, management consultant; b. N.Y.C. d. Ben and Sylvia Witzman; m. Myron Everett Goldblatt Jr.; children: Tracy Ellen, David Laurence. BS, Russell Sage Coll., 1967; MS, Bank Street Coll., 1980. Tchr., tchr. trainer N.Y.C. Bd. Edn., 1967-73, dir. mus. and cultural programs, 1984-89; ednl. cons. Cooper-Hewitt Mus., N.Y.C., 1979-80; dir. mus., collaborative sch./cultural voucher programs Mus. Collaborative, Inc., N.Y.C., 1981-84; exec. dir. Young Audiences/N.Y., 1990-97; pres., CEO Nat. "I Have a Dream" Found., N.Y.C., 1997-2000, LBD Systems, Inc., 2001—; supr. regional arts N.Y.C. Dept. Edn., 2003—; internet cons. Creator N.Y.C. Arts and Cultural Edn. Network and Arts and Cultural Edn. Network Menu, 1986-90, Cultural Instn. Network Menu, 1984-85; creator N.Y.C. Cultural Instn. Network. Author: (workbook) Electroworks, 1980, (exhbn. guide) Smithsonian: A Treasure Hunt, 1979, (curriculum) The Ancient Egyptians, 1980. Trustee N.Y.C. Sch. Art League; mem. cultural del. People to People Internat., People's Republic China, 1988, 96, India Initiative, 1997; mem. Class of 1990 Leadership Am. Mem. Am. Assn. Mus., Nat. Arts Club, Women's City Club N.Y.

GOLDBLATT, STEVEN HARRIS, law educator; b. Bklyn., Apr. 30, 1947; s. J. Irving and Ethel (Epstein) G.; m. Irene P. Burns, June 12, 1981; children: Sarah P., Elizabeth G.B. BA, Franklin & Marshall Coll., 1967; JD, Georgetown U., 1970. Bar: Pa. 1970, D.C. 1981. With Phila. Dist. Atty.'s Office, 1970-81; dir. Appellate Litigation Program Georgetown U. Law Ctr., Washington, 1981-83, prof. law, dir. Appellate Litigation Progam, 1983—. Chair rules adv. com. U.S. Ct. Appeals for Armed Forces, 1998—. Co-author: Analysis and Commentary to the Pennsylvania Crime Code, 1973, Three Prosecutors Look at the Crimes Code, 1974, Ineffective Assistance of Counsel: Attempts to Establish Minimum Standards for Criminal Cases, 1983; reporter Criminal Justice in Crisis, 1988, Achieving Justice in a Diverse America, 1992, An Agenda for Justice: ABA Perspectives on Criminal and Civil Justice Issues, 1996. Mem. ABA (criminal justice sect. chmn. amicus curiae briefs com. 1981-99, crisis in criminal justice com. 1990-91, criminal justice standards com.). Office: Georgetown U Law Ctr 600 New Jersey Ave NW Washington DC 20001-2075 E-mail: goldblat@law.georgetown.edu.

GOLDE, DAVID WILLIAM, physician, educator; b. N.Y.C., Oct. 23, 1940; BS in Chemistry, Fairleigh Dickinson U., 1962; MD, McGill U., 1966. Diplomate: Am Bd. Internal Medicine, Am. Bd. Med. Oncology, Nat. Bd. Med. Examiners. Asst. research chemist Gen. Foods Corp., 1962; intern. U. Calif. Hosps., San Francisco, 1966-67, resident in medicine, 1970-72, fellow Cancer Research Inst., 1971-72; staff cons. continuing edn. and tng. br. div. regional med. program (NIH), 1967-68, resident in clin. pathology, 1968-70; hematology fellow NIH, 1969-70; instr. medicine U. Calif., San Francisco, 1972-73, asst. prof., 1973-74; asst. prof. medicine UCLA, 1974-75, assoc. prof., 1975-79, prof., 1979-91, chief divsn. hematology-oncology, 1981-91, prof. emeritus, 1991—, co-dir. Clin. Rsch. Ctr., 1974-87, dir., 1987-91, dir. AIDS Ctr., 1986-90; Enid A. Haupt prof. hematologic oncology Meml. Sloan-Kettering Cancer Ctr., N.Y.C., 1991—, attending physician Meml. Hosp. for Cancer and Allied Diseas, 1991—, head divsn. hematologic oncology, 1991-96; mem. Sloan-Kettering Inst. for Cancer Rsch., 1991—; prof. medicine Cornell U. Med. Coll., N.Y.C., 1991—; prof. molecular pharmacology and therapeutics Cornell U. Grad. Sch. Med. Scis., N.Y.C., 1992—; physician-in-chief Meml. Hosp. Cancer and Allied Diseases, 1996—2002. Mem. editl. bd. Blood, 1978-81, Peptides, 1979-83, Leukemia, 1986—;, Scandinavian Jour. Haematology (now European Jour. Haematology), 1986-99; editor: Blood Revs., 1986-93, Cytokines, Cellular & Molecular Therapy, 1997—; assoc. editor: Cancer Rsch., 1989—; contbr. numerous articles to profl. jours. With USPHS, 1967-70. Fellow ACP; mem. AAAS, Am. Assn. Cancer Rsch., Am. Fedn. Clin. Rsch., Am. Soc. Clin. Investigation, Am. Soc. Clin. Oncology, Am. Soc. Hematology, Assn. Am. Physicians, Endocrine Soc., Internat. Soc. Exptl. Hematology (councillor 1995-97), Soc. Biol. Therapy, Internat. Assn. for Comparative Rsch. on Leukemia, Soc. Exptl. Biology and Medicine, Western Soc. Clin. Investigation (pres. 1989-90), Western Soc. Clin. Rsch., Alpha Omega Alpha. Office: Meml Sloan-Kettering Cancer Ctr 1275 York Ave New York NY 10021-6094 E-mail: d-golde@ski.mskcc.org.

GOLDEN, BETH, Special Olympics administrator; 1 child, Molly E. Student, Eureka Coll., 1970; BA, U. N.C., Asheville, 1985; postgrad., Western Carolina U., 1993. Instr. adult basic edn. Blue Ridge C.C., Flat Rock, N.C., 1988, 90-91, tng. rep., 1989-90, compensatory edn. and spl. populations specialist, 1990-91, coord. spl. populations office, 1991-96; area dir. Spl. Olympics N.C., 1996-99, field svcs. dir., 1999—. Cognitive retraining therapist Thoms Rehab. Hosp., Asheville, 1988-89, cons. in field; pvt. practice, 1997—. Chair Henderson County Mayor's Com. for Persons with Disabilities, 1992-97; chair respite care com. Parents' Assistance League, 1994-95. Recipient Lockhart Follin-Mace Advocacy award N.C. Employment Network/Divsn. Vocat. Rehab., 1999; Grantee State of N.C., 1985, Ednl. Found., 1991, 92, 93, Melvin Lane Charitable Trust, 1992, 93. Mem. N.C. Head Injury Found. (profl. coun.), Henderson County Coun. on Women (pres. 1991-93), Job Devel. Coun. Henderson County, Inter-Agy. Coun.

GOLDEN, JUDITH GREENE, artist, educator; b. Chgo., Nov. 29, 1934; d. Walter Cornell and Dorothie (Cissell) Greene; m. David T. Golden, Oct. 10, 1955 (div.); children: David T. Golden III, Lucinda Golden Rizzo. BFA, Art Inst. Chgo., 1973; MFA, U. Calif., Davis, 1975; PhD Art (hon.), Moore Coll. Art, 1990. Assoc. prof. art U. Ariz., Tucson, 1981-88, prof. art, 1989-96, prof. emerita, 1996—. NEA forum pub. grants panelist, 1987; project dir. U. Calif. L.A. NEA Lecture series, 1979, 84. One woman shows include Women's Bldg., L.A., 1977, G. Ray Hawkins Gallery, L.A., 1977, Quay Gallery, San Francisco, 1979, 81, A. Nagel Galerie, Berlin, 1981, Ctr. Creative Photography, U. Ariz., 1983, Colburg Gallery, Vancouver, Can., 1985, Etherton Gallery, Tucson, 1985, 89, 91, 95, Mus. Photog. Arts, San Diego, 1986, Friends of Photography, Carmel, Calif., 1987, Tucson Mus. Art, 1987, Mus. Contemporary Photography, Chgo., 1988, Visual Arts Ctr., Anchorage, Alaska, 1990, Temple Music and Art, Tucson, 1992, 97, Scottsdale (Ariz.) Ctr. Arts, 1993, Arte de Oaxaca, Mex., 1995, Etherton Gallery, Tucson, 1995, Columbia Art Ctr., Dallas, 1997, U. Arts, Phila., 2002; exhibited in group shows at Centre Georges Pompidou, Paris, 1981, Security Pacific Bank, L.A., 1985, Phoenix Mus. Art, 1985, L.A. County Mus. Art, 1987, Tokyo Met. Mus. Photography, 1991, Laguna Art Mus., 1992, U. N.M. Mus. Art, Albuquerque, 1993, L.A. County Mus., 1994, Hara contemporary Mus., Tokyo, 1995, Mus. Women in Arts, Washington, 1997, Santa Barbara Mus. Art, Calif., 1997, Mus. Cont. Photography, 1998, Tucson Mus. Art, 1999, Calif. Mus. Photography, 1999, Ctr. for Creative Photography, 1999, Santa Barbara Mus. Art, 1999, Mus. Fine Arts, Santa Fe, N.Mex., 2002, U. Ariz. Mus. Art, 2003, Akron (Ohio) Mus. Art, numerous others; represented in permanent collections at Art Inst. Chgo., Calif. Mus. Photography, Ctr. Creative Photography U. Ariz., Denver Art Mus., Fed. Reserve Bank San Francisco, Fogg Mus. Art, Grunwald Ctr. Graphic Arts, Internat. Mus. Photography George Eastman House, L.A. County Mus. Art, Mpls. Inst. Arts, Mus. Photographic Arts, San Diego, Calif., Mus. Fine Arts, Santa Fe, N.Mex., Newport Harbor Mus. Art, Oakland Mus. Art, Photography Mus. Osaka, Polaroid Corp., San Francisco Mus. Modern Art, Security Pacific Bank, Tokyo Met. Mus. Photography, Tucson Mus. Art, Weisman Found., L.A., Mus. Cont. Photography, Chgo., Seattle Art Mus., Wash., Akron (Ohio) Art Mus., Avon Collection, N.Y.C. Individual artist grantee Tucson Pima Arts Coun., 1987; faculty rsch. grantee U. Ariz., 1986-87, 93-94; Ariz. Found. grantee U. Ariz., 1984; fellow Ariz. Commn. Arts, 1984; individual photography fellow NEA, 1979; Regent's faculty fellow Creative Rsch. U.Calif. L.A., 1977. Achievements include appearance of works in archive of artists' works and other material established at Center for Creative Photography.

GOLDEN, LILY OLIVER, humanities educator; b. Tashkent, Uzbekistan, USSR, July 18, 1934; d. Oliver John and Bertha Alexander (Bialik) Golden; m. Abdulla Kassim Hanga, Mar. 13, 1960 (dec. 1966); 1 child, Yelena; m. Boris Vladimirovitch Yakovlev, Aug. 14, 1979 (dec. Mar. 1997). PhD, Soviet Acad. of Sci., 1966; LHD (hon.), Chgo. State U., 1992. Jr. rschr. Inst. of Oriental Studies Acad. of Sci., Moscow, 1957-59; sr. scientific rschr. Inst. of African Studies Acad. of Sci. of Russia, 1959-60; disting. scholar-in-residence Chgo. State U., 1992—. Vis. prof., lectr. Lumumba U., Moscow, Inst. of Asia and Africa, Moscow State U., Leningrad State U., Tbilici State U., History Inst. Tbilici State U., Columbia U., N.Y.C., NYU, Rutgers U., N.J., Peoria U., Ill., Loyola U., Chgo., Calif. State U., Cape Town U., South Africa, Libreville U., Gabon, Dakar U., Senegal, Zurich U., Switzerland, Benjinsu, China, Seoul, Republic of Korea, numerous others; presenter and lectr. in field. Author: Africans in Russia, 1966, The Tendencies of Development of African Music, 1967, Pan-Africanism, 1972, (with others) Trade Unions in Africa, 1964, Dr. Dubois-A Scholar Humanitarian and a Fighter for Freedom, 1971, USSR and Africa (also editor), 1977, Ideology of Revolutionary Democrats, 1981, Political Parties in Africa, 1964, Nationalism in Modern Africa, 1983, Marxism in Africa, 1987, African Musicology, 1984, others; editor: African Encyclopedia, Dr. Dubois-Scholar, Humanist, Fighter for Freedom, 1971, Presence Africain; contbr. articles to profl. jours. Bd. dirs. Internat. Intercultural Black Woman's Study Inst., Ctr. Am. Citizens, San Francisco, 1996—; chmn. Black-White Jews, Chgo., 1996—. Named hon. spkr. Black Caucuses U.S. Congress, Calif. State Congress; proclamation Lily Golden Day City of Mobile, Ala., City of Juno; recipient Award for Contbn. to Elimination of Racism Nat. Orgn. for Men Against Sexism, Internat. Achievement award Tau Gamma Delta; named to Educators Hall of Fame,Sacramento. Avocations: tennis, music. Home: 5530 S South Shore Dr Chicago IL 60637-1945 E-mail: lilygold@aol.com.

GOLDENBERG, LINDA (LINDA ATKINSON), librarian, author; b. Bklyn., Mar. 3, 1941; d. Harry Louis and Sara (Nathanson) G.; children: William C. Murphy, Sara H. Atkinson. MA in Philosophy, NYU, 1964; MLS, CUNY, 1989. Libr. Chambers Sch., Kingston, N.Y. Author: Mother Jones: The Most Dangerous Woman in America (Notable Children's Trade Book in Social Science 1979), Alternatives to College, 1980, Psychic Stories: Strange But True, 1981, Hit and Run, 1981, Incredible Crimes, 1982, Your Legal Rights as a Minor, 1982, Have We Lived Before?, 1983, Women in the Martial Arts: A New Spirit Rising, 1983 (Best Books for Teenage N.Y. Libr. Assn. 1984), In Kindling Flame: The Story of Hannah Senesh, 1984 (Nat. Jewish Book award 1985, Kenneth B. Smilen award 1985). Mem. ALA, NOW, N.Y. Libr. Assn., Sch. Libr. Media Specialists of Southeastern N.Y., Nat. Women's Studies Assn. Jewish.

GOLDENBERG, MYRNA GALLANT, English language/literature and Holocaust educator; b. Bklyn., Mar. 8, 1937; d. Harry and Fay (Solomon) Gallant; m. Neal Goldenberg, Jan. 27, 1957; children: Elizabeth, David Brian, Eve Lisa. BS cum laude, CCNY, 1957; MA, U. Ark., 1961; PhD, U. Md., 1987. Faculty dept. English Montgomery Coll., Rockville, Md., 1971—2003, chair dept., 1979-81, coord. gen. edn., 1981-90, coord. women's studies program, 1990-94, dir. Paul Peck Humanities Inst., 1997—2003. Lectr. Sch. Arts and Scis., Johns Hopkins U.; lectr. Holocaust and genocide studies, women's studies, Jewish women's studies, honors coll. English U. Md.; dir. project to integrate scholarship on women and minorities into the curriculum Ford Found., 1993-94; co-dir. project integrating scholarship of women in curricula of selected Md. C.C.s, FIPSE, 1988-90; chmn. Montgomery County Commn. on Humanities, 1984-91; chmn. Title IX adv. com. Montgomery County Pub. Schs., 1985-89; lectr. in field. Contbg. author/author: Common and Uncommon Concerns: The Complex Role of Community College Department Chairpersons/Enhancing Department Leadership, 1990, Different Horrors/Same Hell: Women Remembering the Holocaust, Thinking the Unthinkable: Human Meanings of the Holocaust, 1990, Writing Everybody In: Two-Year College English: Essays for a New Century, 1994, Testimony, Narrative and Nightmare: Experience of Jewish Women in the Holocaust: Active Voices/Women and Jewish Culture, 1995, Lessons Learned from Gentle Heroism: Women's Holocaust Narratives, 1995; The Beautiful Days of My Youth, 1997, Memoirs of Auschwitz Survivors: The Burden of Gender, 1998, Experience and Expression: Women, the Nazis, and the Holocaust, 2003; editor: Community College Guide to Curriculum Change, 1990, Experience and Expression: Women, the Nazis and the Holocaust; contbg. editor: Belles Lettres, 1989-98; editor C.C. Humanities Rev., 1990—; contbr. articles to profl. jours. Bd. dirs. Jewish Cmty. Coun., 1997-2002, Md. Humanities Coun., 1997-2003, Jewish Hist. Soc. Greater Washington, 1997—, Arts and Humanities Coun., 2000-02. Recipient Disting. Humanities Educator award C.C. Humanities Assn., 1989, Outstanding Faculty Mem. award Montgomery Coll., 1990, Teaching award Md. Assn. for Higher Edn., 1991; Acad. Adminstrn. fellow Am. Coun. on Edn., 1981-82; Lowenstein Wiener fellow Am. Jewish Archives, 1983; recipient William H. Meardy Faculty award Assn. of Comm. Coll. Trustees, 1996, Comcast Excellence in the Humanities award, 2002. Mem. MLA (sec.), Nat. Women's Studies Assn. (sec.), Assn. Jewish Studies, Nat. Coun. Tchrs. English, Jewish Hist. Soc. Greater Wash. (bd. dirs. 1997—2002, Phi Kappa Phi. Avocations: walking, travel, writing, reading, cooking. Office: Montgomery Coll 51 Mannakee St Rockville MD 20850-1101 E-mail: myrnagoldenberg@hotmail.com.

GOLDFARB, HELENE DIANE, school counselor, retired; b. N.Y.C., Sept. 24, 1929; d. Joseph and Fay E. (Hirschhorn) G. BA, Hunter Coll., 1951; MA, NYU, 1953. Sci. and social studies tchr. Hunter Coll. H.S., N.Y.C., 1951-53; sci. tchr. Isaac E. Young Jr. H.S., New Rochelle, N.Y., 1953-56; asst. prodr. Tic Tac Dough-NBC, N.Y.C., 1956-59; sci. tchr. Albert Leonard Jr. H.S., New Rochelle, 1960-68; guidance counselor, key counselor Albert Leonard Jr. H.S. and Mid. Sch., New Rochelle, 1968-95; ret., 1995. Adminstr. O'Neill Critics Inst., Eugene O'Neill Theater Ctr., Waterford, Conn., summers 1981-86, 94-; sec. bd. dirs. Westchester Arts and Sci. Program, Scarsdale, N.Y., 1970-97; bd. dirs. New Rochelle H.S. Scholarship Fund, 1975-95. Pres. Alumni Assn. Hunter Coll., N.Y.C., 1979—81, 1996—99, treas., pres. Queens chpt., 1953—, 1st v.p. Scholarship and Welfare Fund, 1999—; bd. dirs. Hunter Coll. Found., 1996—99, chair subcom. on planned giving; mem. fin. com., bd. dirs. Lenox Hill Neighborhood Ho., N.Y.C., 1979—; treas. The Caring Neighbor, 2003—; chair bd. The Feminist Press at CUNY, 1987—2002, nat. chair, 1999—, Thomas Hunter Soc.; bd. dirs. Hunter Coll. Hillel Found., 2001—; chmn. subcom. planned giving HC Found. Recipient Alumni Recognition award Alumni Assn. Hunter Coll., 1984, Pres. medal Hunter Coll., 1999, Femmy award Feminist Press at CUNY, 1995; named to Hall of Fame, Hunter Coll. Alumni Assn., 1978. E-mail: hdgoldfarb@aol.com.

GOLDFARB, RONALD C. lawyer, educator; b. Bklyn., Apr. 20, 1947; s. Abe and Minnie G.; Marianne Kelleher, Apr. 10, 1983; 1 child, Rachel. BA, Richmond Coll., 1971; JD, New York Law Sch., 1975. Bar: N.Y. 1976, U.S. Dist. Cts. (so. and ea. dists) N.Y. 1976, U.S. Ct. Appeals (2d cir.) 1976, N.J. 1977, U.S. Supreme Ct. 1979. Pvt. practice, N.Y.C., N.J., 1976-94; assoc. prof, chmn. acctg. and legal studies Middlesex County Coll., Edison, NJ, 1995—2001, dean divsn. bus., computer sci and engring. techs., 2001—. Adj. instr. Middlesex County Coll., 1988-94; adj. asst. prof. Fordham U. Grad. Sch. Bus., 1991-93. Contbr. articles to profl. jours. Arbitrator N.Y. Civil Ct., 1978—88; mem. standing com. on legal asst. approval comm. Am. Bar Assn., 2002—. Mem. ABA (standing com. on paralegals approval commn. 2002—), Am. Assn. Paralegal Edn. (bd. dirs.), North East Acad. Legal Studies in Bus. (past pres.), Phi Delta Phi. Jewish. Office: Middlesex County Coll 2600 Woodbridge Ave Edison NJ 08837-3604 E-mail: ronald_goldfarb@middlesexcc.edu.

GOLDFARB, RUTH, poet, educator; b. Bklyn., Aug. 13, 1936; d. Nathan Alter and Florence Goldfarb. BA in Psychology, L.I. Univ., 1980; MA in Edn., NYU, 1984. Tchr. kindergarten N.Y.C. Bd. Edn., 1963-64, early childhood tchr., 1993-94, N.Y.C., Bklyn., 1970-84; tchr. common br. Bklyn. Bd. Edn., 1986-93; clk. Primary Health Care Ctr. North Broward Med. Ctr., Pompano Beach, Fla., 1998—. Author (poetry) Whispers and Chants, 1997; CD recs. include Christmas Memories, 1999, The Miracle of Christmas, 2000, Songs of Praise, 2000. Mem.: AARP, Gold Coast Poetry Group, Acad. Am. Poets, Internat. Soc. Poets. Avocations: poetry, music, sculpture, writing stories.

GOLDFARB, WARREN (DAVID GOLDFARB), philosophy educator; b. N.Y.C., Aug. 25, 1949; s. Norman J. and Ella (Kaback) G. AB, Harvard U., 1969, A.M., 1971, PhD, 1975. Asst. prof. philosophy Harvard U., Cambridge, Mass., 1975-80, assoc. prof., 1980-82, prof., 1982—, Pearson prof. math. logic, 1995—, chmn. dept. philosphy, 1984—91, 1993—94, 1999—2000. Vis. prof. U. Calif.-Berkeley, 1984 Author: Deductive Logic, 2003, (with Burton Dreben) The Decision Problem, 1979; editor: Jacques Herbrand, Logical Writings, 1971; co-editor: K. Godel, Collected Works, vol. III, 1995, vols. IV-V, 2003. Mem. Am. Philos. Assn., Assn. Symbolic Logic (exec. com. 1982-84) Office: Harvard U Dept Philosophy Cambridge MA 02138 E-mail: goldfarb@fas.harvard.edu.

GOLDFINE, HOWARD, microbiology and biochemistry educator, researcher; b. Bklyn., May 29, 1932; s. Samuel and Ida (Cohen) G.; m. Norah C. Johnston, Jan. 25, 1963; children: Cynthia A. Kaiser, Sarah C. Ward. BS, CCNY, 1953; PhD, U. Chgo., 1957; MS (hon.), U. Pa., 1970. Instr. Med Sch. Harvard U., Boston, 1962-63, assoc., 1963-66, asst. prof., 1966-68; assoc. prof. U. Pa., Phila., 1968-76, prof. microbiology, 1976—, chmn. grad. program in microbiology, 1986-88. Vis. scientist Microbial Genetics Rsch. Unit, London, 1967-68; mem. physiol. chemistry study sect. NIH, 1968-73. Exec. editor Analytical Biochemistry, 1989—; mem. editorial bd. Jour. Bacteriology, 1970-75, Jour. Biol. Chemistry, 1974-80, 82-87, Jour. Lipid Rsch., 1972-82, 87-90, assoc. editor., 1983-86. Trustee, v.p. Bala Cynwyd (Pa.) Libr., 1995—2000. Am. Cancer Soc. scholar, 1960-63; NIH grantee, 1962— ; Macy Found. scholar, 1976-77; Fogarty Sr. Internat. fellow, 1985. Fellow AAAS, Am. Acad. Microbiology; mem. Am. Soc. Biochemistry and Molecular Biology, Am. Soc. Microbiology (chmn. div. K 1981-82), Soc. Gen. Microbiology. Business E-Mail: goldfinh@mail.med.upenn.edu.

GOLDICH, SANDRA MCGINTY, secondary school educator, consultant; b. Alexandria, La., Aug. 3, 1945; d. Herschel McGinty and Patricia (Hammonds) Corley; m. Ward Christopher Hooter II, Nov. 29, 1960 (div. Sept. 1977); children: Ward Christopher III, Patricia Lynlee Hooter Linke; m. Mark S. Goldich, July 1, 1978. BA in Edn., La. State U., New Orleans, 1966. Cert. tchr., La. Tchr. Andrew Jackson H.S., Arabi, La., 1966-69, Alexandria (La.) Country Day Sch., 1978-84, Peabody Sixth Grade Ctr., Alexandria, 1984—2001; tchr., chair dept. social studies Alexandria Mid. Magnet Sch., 2001—. Geography tchr., cons. La. Geography Edn. Alliance, Baton Rouge, 1992—, Nat. Geog. Soc. Summer Geography Inst., 1992; reviewer Nat. Geography Standards Goals 2000, 1992-93, Nat. Geog. Standards Workshop, 1995; mem. exercise devel. team Nat. Comprehensive Social Studies Assessment Project; presenter, cons. in field. Contbr. articles to profl. jours. Life mem., pres. St. Frances Cabrini Hosp. Aux., Alexandria, 1976-78; ptnr. in literacy Alexandria Daily Town Talk, 1991—; mem. discipline policy com. Rapides Parish Sch. Bd., 1996—; adv. coun. Town Talk Editl. Bd.; active La. Social Studies Textbook Adoption Com., 1999; mem. Cmty. Adv. Bd., 1998—. Recipient award Nat. Geog. Soc., Expect the Best award, 1989-92, Competetive Grant award La. Quality Edn. Support Fund, 1995-97; named Rapides Parish Tchr. of Yr., 1996; grantee Rand McNally, 1990, Jr. League of Alexandria, 1993-94, La. State L.E.A.R.N., 1998. Mem. NEA, AAUW (pres. 1976-78), Nat. Coun. Geog. Edn., So. Assn. Cur. and Schs. (mem. commn. on elem. and mid. schs. 1997), La. Mid. Sch. Assn. (Excellence in Tchg. award 1995-96), La. Coun. for Social Studies (bd. dir.), La. Geography Edn. Alliance (sec.-treas. 1995—, Faculty Inst. award 1992—), La. Social Studies Content Stds. Reviewer, Assessment Team and Lesson Plan Samplers (assessment mem.), Rapides Assn. Educators (sec. 1992-94), Delta Kappa Gamma (pres. Beta Xi 1994-96, quad. pres. Ctrl. La. 1994-95, Dist. Tchr. of Yr. award 1996-97), Alpha Delta Kappa (pres. 1997), Accelerated Schs. Assn. Republican. Roman Catholic. Avocations: reading, grandparenting, antique hunting, collecting music boxes, playing bridge. Home: 1703 Shirley Park Pl Alexandria LA 71301-4040 Office: Alexandria Middle Magnet School 122 Maryland Alexandria LA 71309

GOLDIN, LEON, artist, educator; b. Chgo., Jan. 16, 1923; s. Joseph P. and Bertha (Metz) G.; m. Meta Solotaroff, July 30, 1949; children: Joshua, Daniel. BFA, Art Inst. Chgo., 1948; MFA, U. Iowa, 1950. From instr. to assoc. prof. Columbia U., N.Y.C., 1964-82, prof., 1982-92, prof. emeritus, 1992—, 1992—. Former tchr. Calif. Coll. Arts and Crafts, Phila. Coll. Art, Queen's Coll., Cooper Union; vis. prof. painting Stanford, summer 1973 One-man shows Oakland Art Mus., 1955, Felix Landau Gallery, L.A., 1956, 57, 59, Galleria L'Attico, Rome, 1958, Kraushaar Galleries, N.Y.C., 1960, 64, 68, 72, 84, 88, 90, 93, 96, 98, 2001, U. Houston, 1981, Binghamton U. Art Mus., 2000, Ctr. for Maine Contemporary Art, 2000; represented in permanent collections Bklyn. Mus., City Mus. St. Louis, Worcester Mus., Addison Gallery Am. Art, Pa. Acad. Fine Arts, L.A. County Mus., Santa Barbara Mus., Oakland Art Mus., Munson Proctor Inst., Va. Mus. Fine Arts, Portland (Maine) Mus., Everson Mus., U. Ark., Okla. Art Ctr., Cleve. Mus. Fine Art. Served with AUS, 1943-46, ETO. Recipient Prix de Rome, Am. Acad. Rome, 1955-58, Jennie Sesnan Gold medal Pa. Acad. Fine Arts, 1966, Benjamin Altman Landscape prize Nat. Acad. Design, 1993, Adolph and Clara Obrig prize NAD; Tiffany grantee, 1951; Fulbright scholar to France, 1952; Guggenheim fellow, 1959, Nat. Endowment for Arts grantee, 1967, 80; Nat. Inst. Arts and Letters grantee, 1968; N.Y. Caps grantee, 1981, Benjamin Altman prize, NAD, 2003. Mem. NAD. Home: 438 W 116th St New York NY 10027-7203

GOLDING, LAWRENCE ARTHUR, physiology educator; b. Capetown, South Africa, May 8, 1926; s. Reginald Gerald and Maizie (Mitchell) Golding; m. Carmen Golding, Aug. 9, 1952; children: Scott Mitchell, Neal Lawrence, Kirk Louis. BS, U. Ill., 1950, MS, 1953, PhD, 1958. Asst. prof. U. Idaho, Moscow, 1953—58, U. Ill., Champaign, 1956—58; prof. physiology exercise Kent State U., Ohio, 1958—76; prof. U. Nev., Las Vegas, 1976—. Cons. Nat. YMCA, Chgo., 1958—, Cleve. Indians, 1960—66, Akron Civil Svc. Commn., 1970—76. Author: Scientific Foundations of Physical Fitness, Y's Way to Physical Fitness, 1967; contbr. articles to profl. jours. Grantee, NIH, 1960—65, NSF, 1960—62, Portage County Heart Assn.; Barrick fellow, 1983. Fellow: Am. Coll. Sports Medicine (Healthy Am. award 1992); mem.: AAHPERD, Acad. Sci., Am. Coll. Sports Medicine (editor-in-chief Health and Fitness Jour.), Phi Epsilon Kappa, Sigma Xi. Republican. Congregationalist. Home: 3258 Redwood St Las Vegas NV 89146-6508 Office: U Nev Las Vegas Exercise Physiology Lab Las Vegas NV 89154-3034

GOLDINGER, SHIRLEY ANNE, elementary education educator; Spl. edn. tchr. La Esperanza Sch., San Juan, P.R. Name P.R. State Spl. Edn. Tchr. of Yr., 1993.

GOLDMAN, BERT ARTHUR, psychologist, educator; b. N.Y.C., Apr. 4, 1929; children: Lisa, Linda. BA, U. Md., 1951; M.Ed., U. N.C., 1956; Ed.D., U. Va., 1960. Mem. faculty U. N.C., Greensboro, 1965—, prof. ednl. psychology, 1971-85, dean acad. advising, 1970-85, prof. higher ednl. adminstrn., 1985—86, acting chair dept. ednl. adminstrn., higher edn. and ednl. rsch., 1987-88, dept. coord. of higher edn., 1991—. Served with U.S. Army, 1951-53. Mem. APA, Am. Coun. Measurement Edn., N.C. Assn. for Rsch. in Edn., Am. Ednl. Rsch. Assn. Office: U NC at Greensboro Dept Curriculum and Instrn PO Box 26170 Greensboro NC 27402-6170

GOLDMAN, GLENN, architecture educator, architect; b. N.Y.C., Apr. 7, 1952; s. Herbert and Tamara G.; m. Elizabeth Anne Strub, May 31, 1982; children: Aaron, Nathan, Jacob. BA, Columbia U., 1974; M in Architecture, Harvard U., 1978. Registered arch. and planner. Instr. career discovery program Harvard U., Cambridge, Mass., 1978; asst. prof. architecture Iowa State U., Ames, 1978-80; design critic Boston Architectural Ctr., 1981; prof., dir. imaging lab. N.J. Inst. of Tech., Newark, 1982—. Graphic designer Skidmore, Owings and Merrill, Boston, 1975; designer Moshe Safdie Archs., Ltd., Jerusalem, 1976; arch. Jung/Brannen Assocs., Boston, 1980-82, J.F. Caulfield Assocs., Hoboken, N.J., 1983-86, Glenn Goldman, Arch., Tenafly, N.J., 1984—. Author: Architectural Graphics: Traditional and Digital Communication, 1997; co-author, photographer: (video) Iowa: Downtowns in Transition, 1980; co-editor: Reality and Virtual Reality, 1991; contbr. articles to profl. jours. Recipient Applied Rsch. citation, Progressive Architecture Awards Program, 1991; grantee Tech. Engrng. Pre-Visualization Archl. Design grantee, N.J. Dept. Higher Edn., 1985, 1989, Imaging Lab grantee, numerous corp. sponsors, 1990—2003. Mem.: AIA (honorable mention edn.honors program 1989), Assn. Computer Aided Design in Architecture (pres. 1996—97), N.J. Soc. Archs. (edit. bd. Architecture N.J. 1983—93), Assn. Computing Machinery Spl. Interest Group in Graphics, Tenafly United Soccer Club (youth soccer coach 1999—, v.p.), Tenafly Swim Club (trustee 1999—, pres. 2001—). Home: 11 Ravine Rd Tenafly NJ 07670-2124 Office: NJ Inst Tech Sch of Architecture Newark NJ 07102 E-mail: glenn_goldman@hotmail.com.

GOLDMAN, NATHAN CARLINER, lawyer, educator; b. Charleston, S.C., Mar. 19, 1950; s. Reuben and Hilda Alta (Carliner) G.; m. Judith Tova Feigon, Oct. 28, 1984; children: Michael Reuben, Miriam Esther. BA, U. S.C., 1972; JD, Duke U., 1975; MA, Johns Hopkins U., 1978, PhD, 1980. Bar: N.C. 1975, Tex. 1985, U.S. Dist. Ct. (mid. dist.) N.C. 1975. Paralegal City Atty.'s Office, Durham, N.C., 1975-76; asst. prof. govt. dept. U. Tex., Austin, Tex., 1980-85; pvt. practice Houston, 1985-86; assoc. Liddell, Sapp, Zivley, Hill & LaBoon, Houston, 1986-88; pvt. practice Houston, 1988-2000; atty. Amour Law Office, 2000—. Adj. prof. space law U. Houston, 1985-88; rsch. assoc. Rice U. Inst. Policy Analysis, 1986—; lectr. bus. law, 1988-95; mem. coordinating bd. Space Architecture, U. Houston, 1985—; v.p. Internat. Design in Extreme Environments Assn., U. Houston, 1991—; vis. asst. prof. U. Houston-Clear Lake, 1989-91, 99—; adj. prof. South Tex. Coll. Law, 1994-95; gen. counsel Internat. Space Enterprises, 1993—, Globus Ltd. Co., 1994—; info. officer Israel Consulate, 1996-97, atty. Judith G. Cooper, P.C. Author: Space Commerce, 1985, American Space Law, 1988, 2d edit., 1996, Space Policy: A Primer, 1992; editor: Space and Society, 1984; assoc. editor Jour. Space Commerce, 1990-91; exec. editor Space Governance, 1996-99; also articles. Mem. com. on governance of space U.S. Bicentennial Commn., 1986-88, Clear Lake (Tex.) Area Econ. Devel. Found., 1987, Space Collegium, Houston Area Rsch. Ctr., 1987; pres. Windermere Civic Assn., 1990-92; bd. dirs. Hebrew Acad., 1994-96, Men's Club United Orthodox Synagogues, 1994—, pres., 1999-2002. U.S. Dept. Justice grantee, 1979-80, U. Tex. Inst. for Constructive Capitalism U. grantee, 1983; E.D. Walker Centennial fellow, 1984; NASA Summer fellow U. Calif., 1984. Fellow Internat. Inst. Space Law; mem. ABA, Tex. Bar Assn., Nat. Space Soc. (v.p. 1989-91), Inst. for Social Sci. Study Space (mem. adv. bd. 1990, editor Space Humanization Jour. 1993-2000), Am. Astronautical Soc., Inst. for Design in Extreme Environment Assn. (v.p. 1991-96), Space Bus. Roundtable. Avocations: reading, hiking, baseball, softball. Home: 9406 Cliffwood Dr Houston TX 77096

GOLDMAN, STANFORD MILTON, medical educator; b. Salt Lake City, Nov. 28, 1940; s. Osher and Miriam (Solomon) G.; m. Harriet Kaplow, Apr. 2, 1965; children: Etan, Nava. BA, BRE, Yeshiva U., 1961; MD, Einstein Coll. Medicine, 1965. Intern Jefferson U. Sch. Medicine, Phila., 1965-66; resident Einstein Coll. Medicine, Bronx, 1966-69; chmn. dept. radiology USPHS Phoenix Indian Med. Ctr., 1969-71; asst. prof. radiology Einstein Coll. Medicine, Bronx, 1971-72; from instr. to asst. prof. radiology Johns Hopkins U. Sch. Medicine, Balt., 1972-79; from asst. prof. to assoc. prof. U. Md., Balt., 1975-81; assoc. prof. Johns Hopkins U., 1979-86; clin. prof. Uniformed Svcs. U., Bethesda, Md., 1981-94; prof. radiology Johns Hopkins U., 1986-94, prof. urology, 1988-93; prof., chmn. radiology U. Tex. Med. Sch., Houston, 1993—2000, prof. urology, 1995—, prof. radiology, 1993—. Adj. prof. radiology and urology Baylor Coll. Medicine, Houston, 1994—; med. dir. radiol. sch. tech. Houston C.C., 1994, ultrasound sch. tech., 1999—; prof. radiology M.D. Anderson Cancer Ctr., Houston, 1995—. Editor: Computed Tomography of Kidneys & Adrenals, 1983, CT & MRI of the Genitourinary Tract, 1990, Tc E Rm Del Trattos Genito-Urinario, 1994; assoc. editor: Urologic Radiology, 1982-85, Radiology, 1986-94; cons. editor Urology, 1998—. Mem. Radiation Control Adv. Bd., Md., 1989—93. Lt. comdr. USPHS, 1969—71. Recipient Albert Einstein Disting. Alumni award, 1996. Mem.: AMA (CPT adv. bd. 1995—2000), Johns Hopkins Med. and Surg. Assn., Assn. Univ. Radiologists (rep. AMA CPT adv. bd. 1995—2000, ethics com. 1997, nominating com. 1997—98), European Soc. Urogenital Radiology, Houston Radiol. Soc. (treas. 2000—, pres.-elect 2001, pres. 2002, past pres. 2003, chmn. nominating com. 2003—), Houston Med. Soc., Tex. Radiol. Soc. (program com. 1994—96, chmn. long range planning com. 1996—97, bd. dirs. 1996—, fellowship nominating com. 1998—2000, 2d v.p. 2001, 1st v.p. 2002, chmn. program com. 2002—03, exec. com., pres.-elect 2003, chmn. legis. com.), Tex. Med. Soc., Soc. Uroradiology (bd. dirs. 1992—98, med. equipment com. 2000—01, ethics com.), Radiol. Soc. N.Am. (chmn. sci. exhibits awards com. 1988—90, chmn. program coms. subcom. on gu radiology 1996—99), Am. Urol. Assn. (hematuria guidelines panel 1998—99), Am. Soc. Emergency Medicine (bd. dirs. 1994—, indsl. com. 1994—, abstract com. 1995—97, chmn. audit com. 1995—99, chmn. sci. program com. 1996—97, fin. com. 1996—98, site com. 1996—98, vice chair program com. 1996—, ad hoc audit com. 1996—, sec.-treas. 1998—2000, 2001, pres.-elect 2001—02, nominating com. 2002—, chair site selection com. 2002—, pres. 2002—, site selection com.), Am. Roentgen Ray Soc., Am. Coll. Radiology (alt.-counselor from Tex. 1995—96, counselor from Tex. 1996—2002, mem. com. on coding and nomenclature of commn. on econs. 1996—, nominating com. 1999, co-chmn. nominating comm. 2000—01, alt. counselor 2002—03), U.S.-Israel Bi-Nat. Sci. Found., Albert Einstein Alumni Assn. (bd. dirs. 1991—, Disting. Alumni award 1996), U. Md. Alumni Assn. (assoc.). Jewish. Avocations: swimming, music. Office: U Tex Med Sch Dept Radiology 6431 Fannin St Ste 2100 Houston TX 77030-1501

GOLDOFF, ANNA CARLSON, public administration educator; m. Barry Goldoff, June 2, 1968; children: David, William, Jacqueline. BA, Hunter Coll., 1969; PhD, CUNY, 1974. Asst. prof. pub. adminstrn. John Jay Coll. Criminal Justice, N.Y.C., 1974-80, assoc. prof. pub. adminstrn., 1980—. Mem. editl. bd. Public Adminstrn. & Mgmt.; an Interactive Jour., Internat. Jour. of Orgn. Theory & Behavior. Author, editor: The Essence of Decision Redux Crisis Decision Making, 1999; contbg. editor: Ency. Pub. Adminstrn., 1999—2002. Bd. dirs. St. Christopher's, Inc., N.Y.C., 1997—; elder Rye (N.Y.) Presbyn. Ch., 1994-97; trustee Rye (N.Y.) Presbyn. Ch., 2001-03. Mem.: Women's Coalition, Am. Soc. Pub. Adminstrn., Am. Polit. Sci. Assn. Democrat. Avocations: reading, swimming, walking.

GOLDSBOROUGH, EDMUND LEE, III, retired secondary school educator; BA in English, Allegheny Coll., 1961; MS, U. Pa., 1969. Secondary sch. tchr. English Lower Merion Sch. Dist., 1966-94; founder, dir. Lower Merion/Harriton High Schs. Alumni Assn., 1988—2000; ret. Vol. fireman Union Fire Assn., Bala Cynwyd's Fire Dept.; dir., sec., treas. Neighborhood Club; scoutmaster troop 187, Boy Scouts Am., Bala, Pa.; founder, chmn. Concerned Cyclists Com. Lower Merion; mem. Lower Merion Cmty. Watch, 1984-89; sponsor Lower Merion Bike Hike to Benefit the Retarded, Lower Merion H.S., 1984-89; founder, dir. Friends of Jim Brown Fund, 1987-89; spokesperson for Citizens to Save Ardmore Jr. H.S., 1988-92; pres. Lower Merion Hist. Soc., 1988-99; pres. bd. trustees Lower Merion Acad., 1988—; mem. Narberth Pub. Sch. Reunion Com., 1994-95. Capt. USAF, 1962-64. Recipient award Freedom's Found., Valley Forge, Pa., 1964, Montgomery County Assn. Retarded Citizens, 1986, Fritz Brennan award for cmty. svc. Lower Merion H.S. Student Coun., 1989; named Outstanding Young Man of Yr., Main Line Jaycees, 1974, Disting. Alumnus, Lower Merion H.S., Ardmore, Pa., 1996. Mem. NEA, Pa. Edn. Assn. (life mem., del.).

GOLDSCHEIDER, FRANCES K. sociologist, educator; b. Balt., June 12, 1942; d. George Hyde and Ida Thomas (Sledge) Engeman; m. David R. Kobrin, Sept. 23, 1961 (div. 1978); children: Sarah, Janet; m. Calvin Goldscheider, Aug. 18, 1983. BA, U. Pa., 1965, MA, 1967, PhD, 1971. Asst. prof. sociology Skidmore Coll., 1969-74, Brown U., Providence, 1974-86, prof., 1986—, chair dept. sociology, 1984-87, dir. Social Sci. and Data Ctr., 1984-85, dir. Population Studies and Tng. Ctr., 1989-92, 94-95; rsch. assoc. RAND Corp., 1980—, Inst. Social Rsch., U. Mich., Ann Arbor, 1989—. Vis. assoc. prof. demography The Hebrew U., 1983-84, vis. prof. sociology Stockholm U. Author: (with C. Goldscheider) The Ethnic Factor in Family Structure and Mobility, 1978, Ethnicity and the New Family Economy, 1989, (with Linda Waite) New Families, No Families: The Transformation of the American Home, 1991, (with C. Goldscheider) Leaving Home Before Marriage, 1993, (with C. Goldscheider) The Changing Transition to Adulthood: Leaving and Returning Home, 1999; editor: Demography, 1994-95; assoc. editor: Jours. of Gerontology, 1992-94, Am. Sociol. Rev., 1990-92, Jour. Marriage and Family, 1987—;contbr. articles to profl. jours. NEH grantee, 1973-74; Fulbright fellow, 1983-84, 2001-02. Mem. Am. Sociol. Assn. (chair population sect. 1988-89), Internat. Union for Sci. Study of Population, Population Assn. Am. (bd. dirs. 1987-90, 2nd v.p. 1991-92, chair Dorothy Swaine Thomas Award com. 1985-86). Home: 185 Taber Ave Providence RI 02906-3338 Office: Brown U Dept Sociology Providence RI 02912-0001

GOLDSCHMIDT, WALTER ROCHS, anthropologist, educator; b. San Antonio, Feb. 24, 1913; s. Hermann and Gretchen (Rochs) G.; m. Beatrice Lucia Gale, May 27, 1937 (dec.); children: Karl Gale, Mark Stefan. BA, U. Tex., 1933, MA, 1935; PhD, U. Calif. at Berkeley, 1942. Social scientist Bur. Agrl. Econs., 1940-46; mem. faculty UCLA, 1946—, prof. anthropology, 1956—, chmn. dept., 1964-69, prof. anthropology and psychiatry, 1970-83, prof. emeritus, 1983—. Vis. lectr. Stanford, summer 1945, U. Calif. at Berkeley, 1949, Harvard, 1950 Dir. radio program: Ways of Mankind, 1951- 53, Culture and Ecology in E. Africa, 1960-68. Spl. editor: World of Man Series, Aldine Pub. Co., 1966-75. Author: Small Business and the Community, 1946, As You Sow, 1947, 2nd edit., 1978, Nomlaki Ethnography, 1951, Ways to Justice, 1953, Man's Way, 1959, Exploring the Ways of Mankind, 1960, 3rd edit., 1977, Comparative Functionalism, 1966, Sebei Law, 1967, Kambuya's Cattle, The Legacy of an African Herdsman, 1968, On Being an Anthropologist, 1970, Culture and Behavior of the Sebei, 1976, The Sebei: A Study in Cultural Adaptation, 1986; The Human Career: The Self in The Symbolic World, 1990; co-author: Haa Aaní, Our Land: Tlingit and Haida Land Rights and Use, 1998; editor: The U.S. and Africa, rev, 1963, French edit., 1965, The Anthropology of Franz Boas, 1959, (with H. Hoijer) The Social Anthropology of Latin America, 1970, The Uses of Anthropology, 1979, Anthropology and Public Policy: A Dialogue, 1986, Am. Anthropologist, 1956-59; founding editor: Ethos, 1972-79. Fulbright scholar U.K., 1953; grantee Social Sci. Rsch. Coun., 1953; grantee Wenner-Gren. Found., 1953; NSF postdoctoral fellow, 1964-65; fellow Center Advanced Study Behavioral Scis., 1964-65; sr. sci. fellow NIMH, 1970-75; disting. lectr. U. Indonesia, 1993. Fellow Am. Anthrop. Assn. (pres. 1975-76, Dist. Svc. award 1994), African Studies Assn. (founding, bd. dirs. 1957-60); mem. Southwestern Anthrop. Assn. (pres. 1950-51), Am. Ethnol. Soc. (pres. 1969-70), Phi Beta Kappa, Sigma Xi. Home: 978 N Norman Pl Los Angeles CA 90049-1535 E-mail: walterg@ucla.edu.

GOLDSMITH, CATHY ELLEN, retired special education educator; b. NYC, Feb. 18, 1947; d. Eli D. and Gertrude A. G. BS, NYU, 1968, MA in Elem. Edn., 1971, MA in Ednl. Psychology, 1974. Cert. phys. handicapped, K-6 elem. edn. tchr., N.Y. 2d grade tchr. N.Y.C. Bd. Edn., 1968-69, tchr. learning disabled students (spl. edn.), 1969-86, tchr. emotionally disturbed learning disabled students, 1986-87, tchr. learning disabled students, 1987-88, tchr. trainable retarded students, 1988-2000, tchr. mixed disabilities class, 2000-01; ret., 2001. Represented in permanent collections Bobst Libr. NYU. Recipient Charles Oscar Maas Essay award in Am. History, 1968, Disting. Alumni Svc. award NYU, 1987. Mem. AAUW, Nat. Mus. Women in Arts, NYU Alumni Assn. (past rec. sec., v.p.), NYU Alumni Assn., NYU Alumnae Club (past v.p.), Pi Lambda Theta (past pres., past historian). Home: 418 Beach 133d St Rockaway Park NY 11694-1416

GOLDSMITH, MICHAEL ALLEN, oncologist, educator; b. Bronx, Jan. 28, 1946; s. Walter and Bertha (Tannenberg) G.; m. Judith Harriet Plaut, June 6, 1971; children: Sharon, Esther, Eva, Steven. BA, Yeshiva U., 1967; MD, Albert Einstein Coll. Medicine, 1971. Diplomate Am. Bd. Internal Medicine. Intern Bronx Mcpl. Hosp. Ctr., 1971-72; staff assoc. Nat. Cancer Inst., Bethesda, Md., 1972-74; resident in medicine Mt. Sinai Hosp., N.Y.C., 1974-75, fellow in neoplastic diseases, 1975-77, asst. clin. prof. medicine and neoplastic diseases, 1977—; attending physician Oncology Consultants, P.C., N.Y.C., 1977—. Assoc. editor Cancer Investigation. 2001—; reviewer Jour. AMA, 1988-90, New Eng. Jour. Medicine, 1995—. Contbr. articles to med. jours. Vice-pres. Congregation Orach Chaim, N.Y.C., 1978-83. Lt. comdr. USPHS, 1972-74. Fellow ACP; mem. Am. Soc. Clin. Oncology, Am. Assn. Cancer Rsch. Achievements include research in new anticancer drugs. Office: Oncology Cons PC 1045 5th Ave New York NY 10028-0138

GOLDSMITH, NANCY CARROL, business and health services management educator; b. Conemaugh, Pa., May 11, 1940; d. John and Mary (Appley) Stinich; m. Sidney Goldsmith, Apr. 2, 1966. RN, Temple U., 1961; Assoc. summa cum laude, C.C. Phila., 1984; BS in Health Care Mgmt. summa cum laude, Phila. Coll. Textiles and Sci., 1986; MA in Health Care Adminstrn. summa cum laude, Antioch U., Yellow Springs, Ohio, 1988; PhD in Health Svcs. and Hosp. Adminstrn. summa cum laude, Southwest U., New Orleans, 1990. Nurse, head nurse to med. surg. supr. Temple U. Hosp., Phila., 1961-67; nursing rsch. assoc. Smith Klein & French, Inc. and Ames Med. Co., Phila. and Elkhart, Ind., 1967-69; sr. nursing rsch. assoc. NIH, Washington, 1969-75; adminstrv. supr. nursing svcs. Rolling Hill Hosp. and Diagnostic Ctr., Elkins Park, Pa., 1975-87, lectr. legal aspects nursing, 1980-90, dir. cost containment strategies, 1987-89, lectr. in health svcs. mgmt., 1989—, asst. dir. nursing svcs., 1988-89, nursing svcs. dir., 1989-90; prof. health svcs. adminstrn. and svcs. Phila U., 1991—, prof. bus. mgmt., 1992—, mem. adv. bd. health and wellness programs, 1993—, advisor, counselor, 1997—. Prof. managed care in health svcs. adminstrn. Ea. Coll., St. Davids, Pa., 1996—; lectr. Sr. Edn. League, 1992—; lectr. healthcare fin. and health svcs. adminstrn. Pa. State U., 1994; lectr. health svcs. reform C.C. Phila., 1993—, Free Libr. Phila., 1994—; instr. med./surg. nursing Sch. Nursing, Temple U., 1964-67, chmn. ann. fundraising, 1978-86. Author 2 books. Inventor use of dextrostix in hypoglycemic range, 1972 (Rsch. award 1974); co-patentee multipurpose biopsy needle, 1972; mem. editl. bd. Phila. U. Newletter, 1993—. Recipient Mayor's Liberty Bell award City of Phila., 1978, Legion of Honor award Chapel of Four Chaplains, 1981, Capitol award Nat. Leadership Coun., 1991; named to Hall of Fame, Internat. Profl. and Bus. Women's Assn., 1994. Mem. Am. Hosp. Assn., Am. Mgmt. Assn., Temple U. Nurse's Alumni Assn. (bd. dirs., v.p. 1991-92, pres. 1993-94, dir. continuing edn. com. 1986—), Temple U. Gen. Alumni Assn. (bd. dirs. 1980-88, 93—, Disting. Svc. award 1984), Downtown Club Temple U., Phi Beta Kappa, Phi Theta Kappa (pres. Delta of Pa. chpt. 1991-94, Honors Hall of Fame 1991). Jewish. Avocations: tennis, golf, home computing. Office: Phila U School House Ln Henry Ave Philadelphia PA 19144

GOLDSMITH, STANLEY JOSEPH, nuclear medicine physician, educator; b. Bklyn., Aug. 17, 1937; s. Jack and Mae (Greenzweig) G.; m. Miriam Schulman, June 6, 1959; children: Ira, Arthur, Beth, Mark. BA, Columbia U., 1958; MD, SUNY, Bklyn., 1962. Diplomate Am. Bd. Internal Medicine, Am. Bd. Nuclear Medicine (bd. dirs. 1990-96, treas. 1995-96). Intern SUNY-Kings County Med. Ctr., Bklyn., 1962-63, resident, 1965-66, chief resident, 1966-67; fellow in endocrinology Mt. Sinai Hosp., N.Y.C., 1967-68, dir. physics nuclear medicine, 1973-92; clin. dir. nuclear medicine Meml. Sloan-Kettering Cancer Ctr., N.Y.C., 1992-95; dir. nuclear medicine N.Y. Hosp.-Cornell Med. Ctr., N.Y.C., 1995—. Rsch. assoc. radioisotope svc. Bronx (N.Y.) VA Hosp., 1968-69; dir. nuclear medicine, asst. dir. endocrine dept. Nassau County Med. Ctr., East Meadow, N.Y., 1969-73; asst. prof. medicine radiology SUNY-Stony Brook Health Sci. Ctr., 1971-73; asst. prof. medicine Mt. Sinai Sch. Medicine, 1973-76, assoc. prof., 1976-84, prof. clin. medicine, 1985-91, prof. radiology and medicine, 1991-92, Cornell U. Med. Coll., 1993—, prof. radiology, medicine; bd. dirs. Capintec, Inc., Ramsey, N.J.; rsch. collaborator Brookhaven Nat. Labs., Upton, N.Y., 1971-75; cons. nuclear medicine; cons. dept. health State of N.Y., 1973-77, Health Svcs. Adminstrn., N.Y.C., 1976; mem. radiopharm. adv. com. FDA, 1987-90, low level radioactive waste disposal site commn., N.Y., 1987-95. Assoc. editor Newline, 1984-93, Jour. Nuclear Medicine, editor-in-chief, 1993-98; mem. editl. bd. Am. Jour. Cardiology, 1978-82, European Jour. Nuclear Medicine, 1993-98, Cancer Biotherapy and Radiopharm., 1998—; reviewer Israeli Jour. Med. Scis., 1979, JAMA, 1983-92, Jour. Am. Coll. Cardiology, 1984-94, Jour. Nuclear Medicine, 1989-93, 99—. Capt. U.S. Army, 1963-65. Recipient Radiology Educator award, SUNY Downstate Alumni, 2001. Fellow Am. Coll. Cardiology, ACP, Am. Coll. Nuclear Physicians (chmn. nuclear med. tech. affairs, chmn. Washington oversight com.), N.Y. Acad. Sci.; mem. AAAS, Am. Fedn. Clin. Rsch., Am. Coll. Radiology, Endocrine Soc., N.Y. Acad. Medicine (pres-elect sect. on nuclear medicine 2002-), Radiol. Soc. N.Am., Soc. Nuclear Medicine (trustee 1982-84, pres.-elect 1984-85, prse. 1985-86, chmn. govt. rels. com. 1991-93, sec. Greater N.Y. chpt. 1975-78, pres. 1979-80, pres. therapy coun. 2001-2003, named Outstanding Educator, 2000). Home: 72 Ivy Way Port Washington NY 11050-3817 Office: NY Presbyn Hosp Weill Cornell Med Ctr 525 E 68th St New York NY 10021-4885 E-mail: sjg2002@med.cornell.edu.

GOLDSON, TERRI DREW, special education educator, consultant; b. Ansonia, Conn., Jan. 27, 1958; s. Bruce Robert and Dorothy May (Edwards) G.; m. Ronja Darleen Redd, June 14, 1980; children: Tiffany D., Tegan D., Terri D. Jr. BS in Elem. and Spl. Edn., Am. Internat. Coll., 1980, MEd in Spl. Edn., 1988; Cert. Advanced Studies Adminstrn., Fairfield (Conn.) U., 1994. Cert. spl. edn. and elem. edn. educator., Conn., Mass. Apl. edn. tchr. Dept. Correction, Somers, Conn., 1980-83, State of Conn. Unified Dist. #1, New Haven, 1983-87, State of Conn. Dept. Mental Retardation, New Haven, 1986-87, Prendergast Sch., ansonia, Conn., 1987—. Adj. instr. So. Conn. State U., New Haven, 1994-95; assessor Conn. State Dept. Edn., Hartford, 1990-94. Coach Ansonia Pop Warner, 1980—, Girls City Wide Basketball, Ansonia, 1989—, Ansonia Cmty. Action Basketball, 1986, Girls Mid. Sch. Basketball, Ansonia, 1989-97; co-dir. Ansonia Drug-Free Leadership Club, 1990-94; nom. dir. Conn. Trails coun. Girl Scouts U.S., North Haven, Conn., 1991-93; bd. dirs. Valley YMCA, Ansonia Cmty. Action. Recipient Community Svc. Citation award Mass. House Reps., Springfield, 1980, Outstnading Young Leader award Macedonia Bapt. Ch., Ansonia, 1987, NAACP Freedom Fund award, 1997, Citation, Conn. State Gen. Assembly, 1997; inductee Ansonia Football Hall of Fame, 1997. Mem. ASCD, Coun. Exceptional Children, Correctional Edn. Assn., Assn. Children and Audlts with Learning Disabilities, Alpha Phi Alpha (pres. 1989-90). Baptist. Avocations: golf, photography, basketball, running, fishing. Home: Hunters Lane Ansonia CT 06401 Office: Pendergast Elem Sch 59 Finney St Ansonia CT 06401-2738

GOLDSTEIN, ABRAHAM SAMUEL, lawyer, educator; b. N.Y.C., July 27, 1925; s. Isidore and Yetta (Crystal) G.; m. Ruth Tessler, Aug. 31, 1947 (dec. Feb. 1989); children: William Ira, Marianne Susan; m. Sarah Feidelson, May 7, 1995. BBA, CCNY, 1946; LL.B., Yale U., 1949, MA (hon.), 1961, Cambridge (Eng.) U., 1964; LL.D. (hon.), N.Y. Law Sch., 1979, DePaul U., 1987. Bar: D.C. bar 1949. Law clk. to judge U.S. Ct. Appeals, 1949-51; partner firm Donohue & Kaufmann, Washington, 1951-56; mem.

faculty Yale Law Sch., 1956—, prof. law, 1961—, dean, 1970-75, Sterling prof. law, 1975—. Vis. prof. law Stanford Law Sch., summer 1963; vis. fellow Inst. Criminology, fellow Christ's Coll. Cambridge U., 1964-65; faculty Salzburg Seminar in Am. Studies, 1969, Inst. on Social Sci. Methods on Legal Edn., U. Denver, 1970-72; vis. prof. Hebrew U., Jerusalem, 1976, UN Asia and Far East Inst. for Prevention Crime, Tokyo, 1983, Tel Aviv U., 1986; cons. Pres.'s Com. Law Enforcement, 1967; mem. Conn. Bd. of Parole, 1967-69, Conn. Commn. Revise Criminal Code, 1966-70; mem. of the Conn. Planning Com. on Criminal Adminstrn., 1967-71; sr. v.p. Am. Jewish Congress, 1977-84, mem. exec. com., 1977-89, gov. coun., 1989-94. Author: The Insanity Defense, 1967, The Passive Judiciary, 1981, (with L. Orland) Criminal Procedure, 1974, (with J. Goldstein) Crime, Law and Society, 1971; contbr. numerous articles and revs to profl. jours. Served with AUS, 1943- 46. Guggenheim fellow, 1964-65, 75-76, Am. Acad. Arts & Scis., 1975—. Office: Yale Law Sch PO Box 208215 New Haven CT 06520-8215

GOLDSTEIN, CHARLES MEYER, dental educator; b. Providence, Apr. 21, 1921; s. Sigmund Alexander and Beatrice Goldstein; m. Shirley Eleanor Spector, Apr. 28, 1943; children: Jeffrey, Jonathan, Judith, Joel. BS, DDS, U. Calif., San Francisco, 1944; MPH, UCLA, 1967. Pvt. practice, Santa Monica, Calif., 1946-71, West Los Angeles, Calif., 1971-83; dir. mobile clinic sch. dentistry U. So. Calif., LA, 1970-81, prof., chmn. dept. practice dynamics, 1981-87, clin. prof. pub. health and cmty. dentistry, sect. chmn., 1989—; prof. and dir. Clin. Dentistry and Cmty. Outreach Programs, LA, 2001. Mem. adv. com. dental sect. Calif. Dept. Health, 1979-82; founder Tel Aviv U. Dental Sch., 1981, Hebrew U. Dental Sch., Jerusalem, 1976; mem. adv. bd. Clinica Oscar Romero, LA, 1988—; sponsor mobile clinic to El Salvador, Monsenor Oscar Romero C.Am. Refugee Com., Santa Cruz, Calif., 1990—; hon. prof. U. Autonoma Guadalajara, Mex., 1975; mem. adv. bd. East LA Occupl. Ctr. Dental Assts. Program, 1996—; bd. dir. LA Coalition of Mobile Med. Units, 1996—. Author: Ethics in Dentistry, 1989; co-author: Ethics in Dentistry; contbr. articles to dental jour., chpt. to Geriatric Dentistry, 1991. Dental cons. United Farm Workers, Calif., 1965-67; cons. dental program Synanon, Calif., 1961-87; cons. fluoride rinse bill Calif. Dept. Edn., 1981-83. Lt. USN, 1944-46, PTO. Recipient humanitarian award Latin Am. Dental Soc., 1974, svc. award, 1997; recognition award ADA, 1989, presdl. commendation award for meritorious svc. U. S.C. Dental Sch. Alumni, 1994, Dean's Spl. Recognition award for svc. to children in Calif. and Mexico U. So. Calif. Sch. Dentistry, 1997; named Citizen of Week, Sta. KNX, 1993, Citizen of Yr. Lions Club L.A., 1996-97, inductee, U. So. Calif. Sch. of Dentistry, Hall of Fame, 2001. U. So. Calif. Sch. of Inducted Dentistry Hall of Fame, 2001; Fellow Am. Soc. Geriatric Dentistry, Acad. Dentistry Internat., Am. Coll. Dentists, Internat. Coll. Dentists; mem. Am. Soc. Dentistry for Children (pres. So. Calif. sect. 1983-84, Disting. Svc. award 1974), Pierre Fauchard Acad. Democrat. Jewish. Avocations: reading, classical music. Home: 3485 Mandeville Canyon Rd Los Angeles CA 90049-1019 Office: U So Calif Sch Dentistry 925 W 34th St Los Angeles CA 90089-0641

GOLDSTEIN, DONALD MAURICE, historian, educator; b. Dec. 15, 1932; s. Max A. and Jean M. Goldstein; m. Mariann Norma Zinck, Aug. 5, 1961; children: Tammie, Timmie, Tommie, Teri. BA, U. Md., 1954, MA, 1962; MS, Georgetown U., 1963; MPA, George Washington U., 1965; PhD, U. Denver, 1970; grad., War Coll., 1973, Air Command and Staff Coll., 1965. Commd. 2d. lt. USAF, 1955, advanced through grades to lt. col., 1972, comdr. missile site, 1958-59; staff officer US Strike Command, 1961-64; rsch. assoc. Airstaff Pentagon; assoc. prof. history USAF Acad., 1965-71, asst. track coach, 1965-71; ret., 1977; assoc. prof. history Troy State U., Ala., 1971-74; prof. aerospace studies U. Pitts., 1975-77, assoc. prof. pub. and internat. affairs, 1975-92, prof., 1993, dir. placement and alumni, 1977-85, assoc. dean, 1985-88. Author: Ennis C. Whithead Aerospace Commander, 1970, Adolph Hitler in the Perspective of the Am. Press, 1961, Adolph Hitler Administr. of a Society, 1965, (with others) Miracle at Midway, 1982, 2001, 3d edit., 2002, Target Tokyo: The Story of the Surge Spy Ring in Japan, 1984, 3d edit., 2001; collaborator: At Dawn We Slept: The Untold Story of Pearl Harbor, 1981, 3d edit., 2001, Pearl Harbor: The Verdict of History, 1985, 3d edit., 2001, December 7, 1941: The Day the Japanese Attacked Pearl Harbor, 1990, Fading Victory: The Diary of Matome Ugaki, 1991, The Way It Was: A Pictorial Hist.of Pearl Harbor, 1991, The Williwar War: The Arkansas Nat. Guard in World War II, 1992, The Pearl Harbor Paper, 1993, Classics in Internat. Affairs with Others, 1993, 2d edit., 1998, D Day: A Pictorial Hist., 1994, Nuts: The Battle of the Bulge, 1994, Security in Korea: War, Stalemate and Negotiation, 1994, Rain of Ruin: A Photographic Hist. of Hiroshima and Nagasaki, 1995, Amelia Earhart: A Biography, 1997, Vietnam: A Pictorial History, 1997, The Spanish American War: A Centennial Hist., 1998, The Korean War: The Story and Photographs, 2000, World War I: The Story and Photographs, 2002, God's Samurai: Lead Pilot at Pearl Harbor, 2003; asst. editor papers on fgn. policy for House Com. on Internat. Affairs, 1947-54; contbr. articles on def. policy and nat. security affairs to profl. jour. Decorated Soldiers medal, Meritorious Svc. medal with 2 oak leaf clusters, Joint Svc. Commendation medal, Air Force Commendation medal with oak leaf cluster. Mem. Am. Hist. Assn., Internat. Studies Assn., Am. Soc. Pub. Adminstr., Am. Polit. Sci. Assn., Air Force Assn., Toastmasters, Omicron Delta Kappa, Phi Kappa Phi, Phi Alpha Theta, Sigma Nu. Roman Catholic. Home: 2146 Meadowmont Dr Upper St Clair Pittsburgh PA 15241 Office: U Pitts Grad Sch Pub Int Affairs Dean's Office Forbes Complex 3J-11 Pittsburgh PA 15260

GOLDSTEIN, GEORGE A. school system administrator; b. Bklyn., Sept. 28, 1942; s. Alex and Mary (Zeluck) G. AAS, N.Y.C. Community Coll., 1962; BS, L.I. U., 1965, MS, 1969; EdD, Nova U., 1975. Cert. sch. dist. adminstr., fin. planner. Tchr. Sewanhaka Cen. High Sch. Dist., Elmont, N.Y., 1965-71, chair dept., 1971-77, asst. supt., 1978-84, dep. supt., 1984-86; asst. prof. CUNY, Bklyn., 1971-78, Staten Island, 1980-86; supt. schs. Sewanhaka Cen. High Sch. Dist., Elmont, N.Y., 1986—. Area leader State Edn. Dept., Albany, N.Y., 1974-77, chair bd. trustees, 1975-78; pvt. mgmt. cons., 1980—; disting. fellow Harvard U. Supts. Symposium, 1989; examiner N.Y. State Excelsior Awards Program. Contbr. articles to profl. jours. Bd. dirs. Patchogue Homes Corp., Howard Beach, N.Y., 1984, S.E. Sr. Citizens, Howard Beach, 1985, Elmont Youth Outreach, 1987. NSF computer/data processing fellow, Stanford, Calif., 1969, IDEA fellow Kettering Found., San Diego, 1984, IBM Corp. exec. leadership fellow, San Jose, Calif., 1987; recipient AASA award, 1994. Mem. Am. Assn. Sch. Adminstrs. (apptd. mem. Nat. Supts. Acad. 1985), Nat. Assn. Secondary Prins., Soc. Profl. Mgmt. Cons. (v.p. 1984-87), Am. Mgmt. Assn., Am. Bd. Masters Edn., Internat. Assn. Planning Cons., Assn. Cert. Fin. Planners (bd. dirs. 1986—), Phi Delta Kappa (Educator of Yr. 1990). Lodges: Lions (v.p. Elmont chpt. 1985). Jewish. Avocations: travel, theater. Home: PO Box 81 Elmont NY 11003-0081 Office: Sewanhaka Cen High Sch Dist 555 Ridge Rd Floral Park NY 11003-3524*

GOLDSTEIN, HOWARD, art educator; b. NYC, Feb. 10, 1933; s. Charles and Mary (Dubin) G.; m. Marilyn Sunshine, June 27, 1954; children: Marcia Renee, Brian Daniel. BS, Buffalo State Coll., 1954; MA, N.Y.U., 1957; EdD, Columbia U., 1973. Art tchr. East Meadow (N.Y.) Pub. Schs., 1956-60; prof., chmn. art dept. Trenton (N.J.) State Coll., 1960-94; ret., 1994; prof. emeritus, 1995—. Exec. dir. Commn. to Study the Arts in N.J., Trenton, 1964-66; commr., chmn. Mercer County Cultural and Heritage Commn., Trenton, 1971-2003; chmn. Ewing (NJ) Twp. Arts Coun. Ewing Twp. Mcpl. Govt., 1982-92. Exhibited paintings in group shows at 23d New Eng. Exhibition (Videorecord award 1972), 21st New Eng. Exhibition (Union Trust award 1970), N.J. Artists Exhibition (1st prize 1964, 66); retrospective exhibition Trenton City Mus., 1989. With U.S. Army Corp Engrs., 1954-56. Recipient 1st prize for painting, Emily Lowe Found. Competition, N.Y.C., 1960, N.J. Tercentary award, State of N.J., Trenton, 1964, purchase award, The N.J. State Mus., Trenton, 1971, Gov. of N.J. purchase award, N.J. State Mus., 1973. Mem. Nat. Art Edn. Assn., Assoc. Artists N.J. Office: Art Dept Coll NJ Hillwood Lakes CN 4700 Trenton NJ 08650-4700

GOLDSTEIN, IRVIN L. elementary school educator; b. Louisville, Aug. 12, 1929; s. Henry S. and Dorothy (Zillman) G.; m. Daisy Baker, Aug. 21, 1955; children: Steven, Alan, Sara, Lynne. BA in Edn., U. Ky., 1951; MEd in Supervision and Adminstrn., U. Louisville, 1961. Camp dir. Jewish Community Ctr., Louisville; elem. tchr. Louisville Pub. Schs.; elem. tchr., coord. camping New Albany (Ind.) Floyd County Schs. Speaker profl. confs.; prin. religious sch. The Temple, Louisville, 1957-98, life mem. bd. trustees, 1998; exch. tchr., Vancouver, B.C., Can., 1955-56; mem. leadership edn. adv. bd. Bellarmine Coll., 1987-96. Contbr. articles to profl. mags. Mem. Floyd County Comprehensive Health Planning Coun., South Ind. Comprehensive Health Plan; active numerous community orgns. Named Valley Forge Classroom Tchr. of Yr., 1963, Floyd County Conservation Classroom Tchr. of Yr., 1973, 88, Reform Jewish Educator, 1986; recipient Tchr. of Yr. award Floyd County Schs., 1990; finalist Ind. Tchr. Yr., 1990; Ind. Coun. on Econ. Edn. grantee, 1989, 90, 91, 92, 93, Olin Davis award, Tchr. Creativity award Lilly Found., 1992. Mem. NEA, Nat. Assn. Temple Educators, Ind. Tchrs. Assn., Environ. Edn. Assn. Ind., NAFCEA, Leadership Edn. Alumni Assn. (pres. 1990-91), Phi Delta Kappa. Home: 3430 Bryan Way Louisville KY 40220-1930

GOLDSTEIN, IRVING ROBERT, mechanical and industrial engineer, educator, consultant; b. Jersey City, Apr. 28, 1916; s. David and Anna (Krug) G.; m. Natalie E. Glattstein, Jan. 30, 1949; children: Barbara Joy, David Lee. BSME, Newark Coll. Engring., 1939; MSME, Stevens Inst. Tech., 1947. Registered profl. engr., N.J., Calif. Field worker N.J. Dept. Edn., 1938-39; indsl. engr. Maidenform Co., 1939-40; cost analyst William Bal Corp., 1940-41; resident insp. N.Y. Ordnance Dist., War Dept. U.S. Army, 1941-43; sales rep. Eagle Hosiery Co., 1946-47; instr. dept. indsl. and mgmt. engring. N.J. Inst. Tech., 1947-50, asst. prof., 1950-55, assoc. prof., 1955-70, prof., 1970-81, prof. emeritus, 1981—. Prof. dept. info. sci. and sys. Fairleigh Dickinson U., 1992; cons. engr. Irving R. Goldstein, P.E., Springfield, N.J., 1967—; lectr. in field; examiner profl. engring. exam State of N.J., 1967-82; rep. Am. Nat. Stds. Inst., 1970-83, Engr. Joint Coun. Com. for Am. Bicentennial, 1975-78; vice-chmn. N.J. Engrs. Com. for Student Guidance, 1981-83, state meetings coord., 1974-81, treas., 1983-86. Contbr. articles to profl. jours. Scoutmaster Hausen coun. Boy Scouts Am., Jersey City, 1937—43, 1946—50. With U.S. Army, 1943—46, ETO. Decorated 7 mil. svc. medals. Fellow Inst. Indsl. Engrs. (life, dir. work measurement and method engring. div. 1970-73, conf. chmn. 1973-81, publs. chmn. 1966-70, Phil Carroll Achievement award 1975, pres. Met. N.J. chpt. 1977-78, v.p. rsch. and edn. 1968-73, 75-76, 79-81, chmn. bd. gov.'s Metro N.J. chpt. 1966-68, 81-82, faculty advisor N.J. Inst. Tech. U. chpt. 1962-77, Disting. Svc. award Met. N.J. chpt. 1970, 76, 85, Walter Salabun award 1989, author, historian Metro N.J. chpt. 1982—, dir. student affairs Dist. 2, 1989-90); mem. NSPE, ASME (life), Informs, Am. Soc. Metals, Order of Engr., Alpha Pi Mu, Pi Tau Sigma. Home and Office: 21 Janet Ln Springfield NJ 07081-2714

GOLDSTEIN, IRWIN STUART, philosophy educator; b. Windsor, Ont., Can., July 12, 1947; arrived in U.S., 1951; s. Allen and Idelle (Wasserman) G.; children: Rebecca, Rachel Louise, Sheena Miriam. BA, Carleton U., 1970; MLitt, U. Bristol, Eng., 1974; PhD, U. Edinburgh, Eng., 1979. Vis. positions U. Tex., Dallas, 1982-83; asst. prof. philosophy Loyola U., Chgo., 1980-81; asst. prof. Davidson (N.C.) Coll., 1983-87, assoc. prof., 1987-98, prof., 1998—. Lectr. Soc. for Classical Realism, Berkeley, Calif., 1989—, Rochester (N.Y.) Inst. Tech., 1989—, Am. Philos. Assn., British Soc. for Ethical Theory, others. Contbr. articles to numerous profl. jours. Carleton U. grantee, 1969-70; U. Edinburgh scholar, 1977-79, 84; Davidson Coll. rsch. grantee, 1984-85. Mem. Am. Philos. Assn. (lectr.), Internat. Soc. for Value Inquiry, So. Soc. Philosophy and Psychology, N.C. Philos. Soc. Avocations: art, swimming, travel, reading. Office: Davidson Coll Box 6950 Davidson NC 28036-6950

GOLDSTEIN, JEFFREY JAY, astrophysicist, educator; b. N.Y.C., Dec. 3, 1957; s. Gustave and Gloria Pauline (Simon) G. BA in Physics, Queens Coll., CUNY, 1980; MS in Astron. & Astrophysics, U. Pa., 1987, PhD in Astrophysics, 1989. Instr., astrophysics Univ. Pa., Phila., 1981-85; astrophysicist lab. for astrophysics Nat. Air & Space Mus., Smithsonian Instn., 1988—95, chmn., 1996; dir. space sci. rsch. dept. Challenger Ctr. for Space Sci. Edn., Alexandria, Va., 1996—99, v.p. space sci. rsch., 1999—; rsch. assoc. Nat. Air and Space Mus. Smithsonian Instn., 1996—. Ednl. cons., 1988—. Contbr. articles to profl. jours. Lectr. on space sci. to schs., ednl. workshops and popular talks, 1983—. Grad. student researcher NASA Goddard Space Flight Ctr., Greenbelt, Md., 1985-88; recipient Outstanding PhD Thesis award Sigma Xi Sci. Rsch. Soc., Univ. Pa. chpt., 1990. Mem. AAAS, Am. Geophysical Union, Am. Astron. Soc. (div. planetary scis.). Achievements include research on measurement of winds in planetary atmospheres. Home: 10020 Howell Dr Upper Marlboro MD 20774-9473 Office: Challenger Ctr for Space Sci Edn Nat Air & Space Mus 1250 N Pitt St Alexandria VA 22314-1542 E-mail: jgoldstein@challenger.org.

GOLDSTEIN, JILL M. psychiatric epidemiologist, clinical neuroscientist, psychiatry educator; b. New Haven, Sept. 18, 1954; d. Paul and Betty (M.) G.; m. Phillip S. Freeman, Sept. 23, 1984; children: Sonya, Eliana. AB with honors, Brown U., 1976; MPH, Columbia U., 1979, MPhil, 1984, PhD, 1985. Rsch. scientist N.Y. State Psychiat. Inst., N.Y.C., 1976-81, 81-84; rsch. fellow Columbia U., N.Y.C., 1984-85; sr. rsch. assoc. Brandeis U., Mass., 1985-89; instr. psychiatry Harvard Med. Sch., Boston, 1986-89, cons. psychiat. rsch. project, 1987—, asst. prof. psychiatry, 1989-95, assoc. prof. psychiatry, 1996—; dir. rsch. on women's mental health Inst. Psychiat. Epidemiology and Geneticx. Mem. exec. com. Harvard Med. Sch./Mysell, Boston, 1992—; mem. NIMH sci. rev. com. Behavioral Sci. Track Awards for Rapid Transition, 1994—; exec. mem. rsch. com. Mass. Mental Health Ctr., Boston, 1995—. Reviewer, ad hoc jour. referee Am. Jour. Med. Genetics, Neuropsychiat. Genetics, Am. Jour. Psychiatry, Archives of Gen. Psychiatry, Biol. Psychiatry, Hosp. and Cmty. Psychiatry, Jour. Nervous and Mental Disease, Jour. Psychiat. Rsch., Psychiatry, Psychiatry Rsch., Schizophrenia Bull., Schizophrenia Rsch.; guest editor Schizophrenia Bull., 1990; contbr. articles to profl. jours. Grant reviewer Needham (Mass.) Edn. Found., 1992-94; fundraiser Countryside Sch., Newton, Mass., 1996—. NIMH fellow in psychiat. epidemiology, 1980-84; recipient Investigator award Nat. Alliance Rsch. on Schizophrenia and Depression, 1989, Investigator award Internat. Congress on Schizophrenia Rsch., 1989-91, NIMH Scientist Devel. award, 1992-94. Mem. AAAS, Phi Beta Kappa. Avocations: tennis, skiing, violin. Office: Harvard Med Sch/Mass Mental Health Ctr 74 Fenwood Rd Boston MA 02115-6113

GOLDSTEIN, JOEL, finance and statistics educator, researcher; b. N.Y.C., Mar. 29, 1938; s. Jack and Regina (Gross) G.; m. Marcia Rosen, Sept. 5, 1966; children: Jennifer Ann, Carol Lynn. BME, CCNY, 1967; MS, NYU, 1971; PhD, Polytech U., 1980. Analyst Allied Corp., N.Y.C., 1963-67; automation engr. Ebasco Svcs., N.Y.C., 1967-68; mgr. Bunker Ramo Corp., Trumbull, Conn., 1969-74; sr. analyst Getty Oil Co., N.Y.C., 1974-77; dir. Am. Express Co., N.Y.C., 1978-83; v.p. Citicorp, NA, N.Y.C., 1983-86; assoc. prof. Western Conn. State U., Danbury, 1987-96, prof. fin. and stats., 1997—. Coord. MBA program Ancell Sch. Bus., 1994-97. Author: (with R. Montague) Lotus 1-2-3 The Easy Way, 1989; contbr. articles to profl. jours. Mem. Internat. Assn. Fin. Engrs., INFORMS. Office: Western Conn State Univ 181 White St Danbury CT 06810-6826

GOLDSTEIN, JUDITH SHELLEY, reading and learning specialist; b. Bklyn., Mar. 5, 1935; d. Maurice and Mary (Goldstein) G. BA, Adelphi U., 1956; MA, Columbia U., 1957; EdD, Hofstra U., 1984. Cert. permanent tchr. in reading, spl. and elem. edn., N.Y. Early childhood tchr. N.Y.C. Sch. System, Bklyn., 1957-80; reading specialist Southampton (N.Y.) Unified Sch. Dist., 1981-87; spl. edn. tchr. Amagansett (N.Y.) Sch., 1987-88; mem. adj. faculty C.W. Post Campus, L.I. U., Brookville, N.Y., 1984-88, supr. clin. practice Southampton Campus, 1988-95. Exec. dir. nursery sch. Jewish Ctr. of Hamptons, East Hampton, N.Y., 1988-89; adj. assoc. prof. Southampton Campus L.I. U., 1989-94, Dowling Coll., 1990-92; chmn. edn. Hadassau, 2003-; adj. asst. prof. Suffolk County C.C., 1989-95, adj. assoc. prof. 1995—. Mem. Guild Hall, East Hampton, 1980—; v.p. edn. Hadassah, East Hampton, 1989-92, chmn. edn., 2003; chair Am. Affairs, 1993-96, Hadassah edn. chair 2002-03; tchr. religious ch. Jewish Ctr. of the Hamptons, 1990-98; vol. Bay St. Theatre, Sag Harbor, N.Y., Long House Res., East Hampton; mem., vol. Friends of Guild Hall, East Hampton. Mem. ASCD, AAUW (v.p. programming 1987-89, sec. 1993-99, 2003), Internat. Reading Assn. Democrat. Avocations: gardening, museums, theater. Home: 138 Windward Rd East Hampton NY 11937-3189

GOLDSTEIN, KATHERINE H. technology educator, computer consultant; b. N.Y.C., Oct. 17, 1968; d. Leon and Patricia (Chambers) G. BA, CUNY, 1991; MA, Columbia U., 1995. Lic. pub. h.s. tchr., N.Y.C.; lic. pub. h.s. tchr., N.Y. State. Acctg. asst. Biller & Schnyer, N.Y.C., 1984-89; salesperson retail electronics Crazy Eddie, N.Y.C., 1986-87; tchr. Hebrew sch. Larchmont (N.Y.) Temple, 1987-93; youth dir. United Synagogue Youth Forest Hills JCC, Kane St. and Town & Village Synagogue, N.Y., 1988—; computer tech. coord. Middle Coll. H.S. at LaGuardia Coll., Long Island City, N.Y., 1994—; computer tchr. Murry Bergtraun Adult Edn., N.Y.C., 1996—; computer instr. Monroe Coll., Bronx, 1996—. Adminstr. Camp Ramah, Nyack, N.Y., summer 1985-92, 96, 97; counselor, staff USY Pilgramage, Israel, and Poland sem. summer 1993-95; educator AIDS Ctr. Queens County, Queens, 1990-93; vol. Nat. Jewish Dem. Coun., N.Y.C., 1995—; vol., educator, mentor United Synagogue of Am., N.Y.C., 1987—. Mem. NOW, ACM, Coalition for Advancement of Jewish Edn., Delta Kappa Phi, Kappa Delta Phi. Democrat. Jewish. Avocations: rollerblading, swimming, traveling, woodworking. Office: Middle Coll HS at LaGuardia Coll Rm L101 31-10 Thomson Ave Long Island City NY 11101

GOLDSTEIN, MARC, microsurgeon, urology and reproductive medicine educator, administrator; b. N.Y.C., Mar. 22, 1948; BS cum laude, CUNY, Bklyn., 1968; MD summa cum laude, SUNY, Bklyn., 1972. Diplomate Nat. Bd. Med. Examiners, Am. Bd. Urology. Surgical intern Columbia-Presbyn. Med. Ctr., N.Y.C., 1972-73, surgical resident, 1973-74; asst. instr., resident, chief resident dept. urology Downstate Med. Ctr. SUNY, Bklyn., 1977-80, asst. prof. urology dept. urology Downstate Med. Ctr., 1980-82; asst. attending surgeon Univ. Hosp., SUNY Downstate Med. Ctr., and Kings County Hosp. Ctr., Bklyn., 1980-82; fellow-in-residence Population Coun. Rockefeller U., N.Y.C., 1980-82, rsch. assoc., 1980-83; assoc. physician Rockefeller U. Hosp., N.Y.C., 1980-86, vis. assoc. physician, 1986-87; asst. attending surgeon urology N.Y. Hosp., N.Y.C., 1982-88; asst. prof. surgery Cornell U. Med. Ctr., N.Y.C., 1982-88; staff scientist Population Coun. Ctr. Biomed. Rsch., N.Y.C., 1982—; dir. divsn. male reproductive medicine and microsurgery, dept. urology N.Y. Hops.-Cornell Med. Ctr., N.Y.C., 1982—; assoc. attending surgeon N.Y. Hosp., N.Y.C., 1988-94; assoc. prof. surgery Cornell U. Med. Coll., N.Y.C., 1988-94; attending surgeon N.Y. Hosp., 1994—; prof. urology Cornell U. Med. Coll., N.Y.C., 1994—, prof. urology and reproductive medicine, 1999—, dir. ctr. for male reproductive medicine and microsurgery, 1982—, co-exec. dir. Cornell Inst. Reproductive Medicine, 1999—; surgeon-in-chief Inst. Reproductive Medicine Cornell Ctr., 2001—. Mem. adv. com. Assn. Voluntary Surgical Contraception, 1984—; participant concept clearance meeting NIH, 1989; mem. editorial bd. Microsugery, 1983—, Jour. of Andrology, 1991-93, Andrology Report, 1992—. Author: (with M. Feldberg) The Vasectomy Book: A Complete Guide to Decision Making, 1982, 2nd edit., 1985, (with G. Berger, M. Fuerst) The Couples Guide to Fertility, 1989, 2nd edit., 1995, 3rd edit., 2001, (with Doubleday Co.) Surgery of Male Infertility, 1995, Atlas of the Urology Clinics: Surgery for Male Infertility, 1999; contbr. chpts. to books, articles to profl. jours.; patentee in field. Maj. USAF, 1974-77, USAFR, 1977-90. Honor scholar Downstate Med. Ctr., 1969; Summer Rsch. fellow Downstate Med. Ctr., 1969-70, Ferdinand C. Valentine fellow N.Y. Acad. Medicine, 1980-82; recipient Ferdinand C. Valentine Urology prize N.Y. Acad. Medicine and N.Y. sect. Am. Urological Assn., 1981, Best Movie award Am. Fertility Soc. and Can. Fertility and Andrology Soc., 1986, 96, Excellence in Video Prodn. award Video Urology, 1987, 90; commd. Ky. Col., Commonwealth of Ky., 1988. Fellow ACS; mem. AMA, Am. Soc. Andrology (mem. various coms.), Am. Fertility Soc., Am. Urological Assn. (scholar 1980-82, mem. various coms.), N.Y. County Med. Soc., Internat. Microsurgical Soc., Soc. Study Reproduction, Soc. Reproductive Surgeons (fellowship com. 1989—), Soc. for Male Reproduction and Urology (pres. 1996), Alpha Omega Alpha, N.Y. Rd. Runners Club (completed 18 N.Y.C. marathons), Brit. Mountaineering Coun. Office: NY Hosp-Cornell Med Ctr Dept Urology 525 E 68th St Dept Urology New York NY 10021-4885 E-mail: mgoldst@med.cornell.edu.

GOLDSTEIN, MARGARET FRANKS, special education educator; b. Toledo, July 3, 1940; d. Ray E. and Esther R. (Drewicz) Franks; m. William D. Goldstein, July 30, 1961; children: Sheldon, Benjamin, Marshall, Rochelle. BS in Edn., Bowling Green (Ohio) State U., 1975; MEd, U. Toledo, 1984. Cert. spl. edn. and indsl. arts educator. Tchr. indsl. arts Toledo Pub. Schs., 1970-77, tchr. devel. handicapped/behavior disordered, 1980-86, tchr. devel. handicapped/transitional tchr., 1986—99, severe behavior disability career ladder tchr., 1987—2000, mem. state supt.'s spl. edn. adv. coun., 1988—, chair, 1999—. Mem. state supt.'s task force for preparing spl. educators Toledo Pub. Schs., 1986—. Mem. Am. Fedn. Tchrs. (conv. del.), Ohio Fedn. Tchrs. (exec. coun., publicity and svcs. com., elections com., chmn., conv. del.), Toledo Fedn. Tchrs. (bd. dirs.), NW Ohio Spl. Edn. Assn. Office: McTigue Jr HS 5557 Hill Ave Toledo OH 43615-4699

GOLDSTEIN, MELVYN C. anthropologist, educator; b. N.Y.C., Feb. 8, 1938; s. Harold and Rae (Binen) G.; 1 son, Andre. BA, U. Mich., 1959, MA, 1960; PhD, U. Wash., 1968. Asst. prof. Case Western Res. U., Cleve., 1968—71, assoc. prof., 1971—76, prof. anthropology, 1976—2002, chmn, dept. anthropology, 1976—2002, dir. ctr. rsch. on Tibet, 1987—, J.R. Harkness prof., 1991—. Author: Modern Spoken Tibetan, 1970, Modern Literary Tibetan: A Grammar and Reader, 1973, Tibetan English Dictionary of Modern Tibetan, 1975, Tibetan for Travellers and Beginners, 1980, English-Tibetan Dictionary of Modern Tibetan, 1984, Tibet Phrasebook, 1987, A History of Modern Tibet, 1913-1951: The Demise of the Lamist State, 1989, 2d edit., 1991, Nomads of Western Tibet, The Survival of a Way of Life, 1990, Essentials of Modern Literary Tibetan: A Reading Course and Reference Grammar, 1991, The Changing World of Mongolian Nomads, 1994, The Struggle for Modern Tibet: The Autobiography of Tashi Tsering, 1997, The Snow Lion and the Dragon: China, Tibet and the Dalai Lama, 1997, Buddhism in Contemporary Tibet: Religious Revival and Cultural Identity (with Matthew Kapstein), 1998, The New Tibetan-English Dictionary of Modern Tibetan, 2001; editor Jour. Cross-Cultural Gerontology; contbr. articles to profl. jours. Grantee Am. Council Learned Socs., 1973-74, NIH, 1976-77, 80-82, NEH, 1980-82, 84-85, 89-97, 2000-03, Dept. Edn., 1980-82, Smithsonian Instn., 1981-83, Nat. Geographic Soc., 1980-81, Nat. Inst. Child Health and Human Devel., 1981-83, NSF, 1982-83, Com. for Scholarly Exchange with People's Republic China, 1985-86, 87-88, Nat. Geog. Soc., 1986-88, 90, 91-93, 96-97, Dept. of Edn., 1986-87, 94-96, IREX, 1990-92, Henry Luce Found., 1997-2000, 2001—. Mem. Assn. Asian Studies, Am. Anthropol. Assn., Soc. Applied Anthropology, Soc. Med. Anthropology, Assn. for Anthropology and Gerontology. Home: 50 E 252d St Euclid OH 44132-3901 Office: Case Western Res Univ 241 Mather Memorial Cleveland OH 44106

GOLDSTEIN, PAUL, lawyer, educator; b. Mount Vernon, N.Y., Jan. 14, 1943; s. Martin and Hannah Goldstein; m. Jan Thompson, Aug. 28, 1977. BA, Brandeis U., 1964; LL.B. Columbia U., 1967. Bar: N.Y. 1968, Calif. 1978. Asst. prof. law SUNY-Buffalo, 1967-69, assoc. prof., 1969-71, prof., 1972-75; vis. assoc. prof. Stanford U., Calif., 1972-73, prof. law, 1975—, Stella W. and Ira S. Lillick prof. law, 1985—; of counsel Morrison and Foerster, San Francisco, 1988—. Author: Changing the American Schoolbook--Law, Politics and Technology, 1978, Real Estate Transactions--Cases and Materials on Land Transfer, Development and Finance, 1980, 3d edit. (with G. Korngold), 1993, Real Property, 1984, Copyright, 4 vols., 2d edit., 1996, Copyright, Patent, Trademark and Related State Doctrines--Cases and Materials on the Law of Intellectual Property, 5th edit., 2002, Copyright's Highway: From Gutenberg to the Celestial Jukebox, 1995, revised edit., 2003, International Copyright Law, 2001, International Intellectual Property Law, 2001. Mem. Assn. Litteraire et Artistique Internationale, Copyright Soc. U.S.A. Office: Stanford U Law Sch Nathan Abbott Way Stanford CA 94305 E-mail: paulgold@stanford.edu.

GOLDSTEIN, PHYLLIS ANN, art historian, educator; b. Chgo., Apr. 27, 1926; d. Frederick and Belle Florence (Hirsch) Jacoby; m. Seymour Goldstein, Nov. 19, 1947 (dec. 1980); children: Arthur Bruce, Kathy Susan Goldstein Maultasch. BA, Hunter Coll., 1948; MA, Hofstra U., 1985. Tchr. home econs. Cin. Pub. Schs., 1948-50; nutrition instr. Brandeis U. Nat. Women's Com., Westbury, N.Y., 1975-78, instr. art history, 1984-91; lectr. art history Brandeis U./Nat. Women's Com., Westbury, N.Y., 1985-92; instr. art history Herricks Adult Cmty. Edn. Program, 1990-91. Camp counselor, troop leader Girl Scouts U.S., N.Y.C., Cin., 1942-51; cub leader Boy Scouts Am., Westbury, 1963-64; active Sisterhood of Temple Beth Avodah, Westbury, 1958-80, pres. 1964-65; active Sisterhood of Temple of Beth Am., Merrick, N.Y., 1980-91; life mem. Brandeis U. Nat. Women's Com., lectr. art history, 1992—, Meadowbrook chpt. pres., 1985-87, South Dade chpt., 1996-98, mem. Fla. regional bd., 1998-99; vol. Fairchild Tropical Gardens, 1994—. Mem. Williamsburg Mus., Mus. Art Ft. Lauderdale, Met. Mus. Art N.Y., Hadassah (life). Democrat. Avocations: sewing, swimming, needlework, quilting, travel.

GOLDSTEIN, RICHARD JAY, mechanical engineer, educator; b. NYC, Mar. 27, 1928; s. Henry and Rose (Steierman) G.; m. Barbara Goldstein; children: Arthur Sander, Jonathan Jacob, Benjamin Samuel, Naomi Sarith. BME, Cornell U., 1948; MS in Mech. Engring., U. Minn., 1950, MS in Physics, 1951, PhD in Mech. Engring., 1959; DSc (hon.), Israel Inst. Tech., 1994; Dr. honoris causa, U. Lisbon, 1996; hon. doctorate, A.V. Luikov Heat and Mass Transfer Inst., Minsk, Belarus, 1997. Instr. U. Minn., Mpls., 1948-51, instr., rsch. fellow, 1956-58, mem. faculty, 1961—, prof. mech. engring., 1965—, head dept., 1977-97, James J. Ryan prof., 1989—, Regents' prof., 1990—; devel. rsch. engr. Oak Ridge Nat. Lab., 1951-54; sr. engr. Lockheed Aircraft, 1956; asst. prof. Brown U., 1959-61. Vis. prof. Technion, Israel, 1976, Imperial Coll., Eng., 1984; cons. in field, 1956—; chmn. Midwest U. Energy Consortium; chmn. Coun. Energy Engring. Rsch.; NSF sr. postdoctoral fellow, vis. prof. Cambridge (Eng.) U., 1971-72; Prince lectr., 1983, William Gurley lectr., 1988, Hawkins Meml. lectr., 1991; disting. lectr. Pa. State U., 1992; mem. acad. com. internat. bd. govs. Technion; hon. mem. sci. bd. A.V. Luikov Heat and Mass Transfer Inst., Minsk, 1997. Mem. editl. bd. Experiments in Fluids, Heat Transfer-Japanese Rsch., Heat Transfer-Soviet Rsch., Bull of the Internat. Centre for Heat and Mass Transfer, Internat. Archives of Heat and Mass Transfer; hon. editl. adv. bd. Internat. J. Heat and Mass Transfer, Internat. Comms. in Heat and Mass Transfer. 1st U.S. Army lt. AUS, 1954-55. Recipient NASA award for tech. innovation, 1977, MUEC Dist. Svc. award, 1986, NAE, 1985, George Taylor Alumni Soc. award, 1988, A.V. Lykov medal, 1990, Max Jakob Meml. award ASME/AICE, 1990, Nusselt-Reynolds prize, 1993, Dr. Scientiarum Honoris Causa award Technion-Israel Inst. Tech., 1994, Thermal Engring. Internat. award Japan Soc. Mech. Engring.; NATO fellow, Paris, 1960-61, Lady Davis fellow Technion, Israel, 1976. Fellow AAAS, ASME (hon., BEG v.p. 1984-88, sr. v.p. 1989-93, BOG 1993-97, pres. 1996-97, sr. v.p. COE 1988-92, Heat Transfer Meml. award 1978, Svc. award 1978, Centennial medal 1980, 50th anniv. award of heat transfer divsn. 1988, Dedicated Svc. award 2001, Long Term Mem. award 2002-03), Royal Acad. Engring. (fgn.), Am. Soc. Engring. Edn., Assembly for Internat. Heat Transfer Confs. (pres. 1986-90), Internat. Ctr. for Heat and Mass Transfer (exec. com. 1985—, chmn. 1992, pres. 1998-2002), Am. Phys. Soc., Japan Soc. Promotion of Sci., Royal Acad. Engring. (fgn.); mem. Minn. Acad. Sci., Nat. Acad. Engring., Nat. Acad. Engring.-Mex. (corr. 1991), Golden Key Nat. Honor Soc., Sigma Xi, Tau Beta Pi, Pi Tau Sigma. Achievements include research in thermodynamics, fluid mechanics, heat transfer, optical measuring techniques. Home: 4241 Bassett Creek Dr Golden Valley MN 55422-4257 Office: U Minn Dept Mech Engring 111 Church St SE Minneapolis MN 55455-0150

GOLDSTEIN, SHARON LOUISE, elementary education educator; b. Gettysburg, Pa., Aug. 27, 1951; d. Ray Ernest and Geraldine Mildred (Shetter) Moose; m. Edward James Reaver (div. Dec. 1989); 1 child, Sara; m. Marshall Bernie Goldstein, Dec. 24, 1989; 1 child, Todd. BS, Shippensburg (Pa.), 1972, MEd, 1977; postgrad., Pa. State U., 1990-91, 93, U. Alaska S.E., Carlow Coll., 1992-93, Seattle Pacific U., 1993-94, Wilkes U., 1994, Millersville U., 2003. Cert. elem. edn. tchr., Pa. Tchr. gifted 4th grade Littlestown (Pa.) Area Sch. Dist., 1973-82, tchr. 3d grade, 1984-94, 2001—, on sabbatical, 1990-91, tchr. people skills/gifted edn., 1994—2001. Deacon Christ United Ch. of Christ. 2001-02; sec., treas., pres. Hanover (Pa.) Area Jaycettes, 1970; mem. YWCA, YWCA Pixie Gymnastic Parents, pres., 1992-93; asst. sec. Women's Guild of Christ United Ch. in Christ, 1970-03, mem. choir, 1971-80, celebration choir, 1997-99; mem. Seahorse Swim Parents Club, 1993-95. Mem. ASCD, NEA, Pa. State Edn. Assn., Pa. Assn. for Gifted Edn., Littlestown Edn. Assn., Internat. Assn. for Study of Coop. in Edn., South Western High Sch. Band and Athletic Boosters, 1997—. Republican. Avocations: cross stitching, reading, painting, crewel. Home: 628 W Middle St Hanover PA 17331-3743

GOLDSTICK, THOMAS KARL, biomedical engineering educator; b. Toronto, Ont., Can., Aug. 21, 1934; came to U.S., 1955, naturalized. s. David and Iva Sarah (Kaplan) G.; m. Marcia Adrienne Jenkins, July 4, 1982. BS, MIT, 1957, MS, 1959; PhD, U. Calif., Berkeley, 1966, U. Calif., San Francisco, 1966-67. Asst. prof. Northwestern U., Evanston, Ill., 1967-71, assoc. prof. chem. engring. and biol. sci., 1971-81, prof. chem. engring., neurobiology and physiology, 1981-85, prof. chem. engring., biomed. engring., neurobiology and physiology, 1985-99, prof. emeritus, 1999—. Adj. prof. ophthalmology U. Ill., Chgo., 1981-91. Editor: Oxygen Transport to Tissue V, 1983, VII, 1985, X, 1988, XI, 1989, XII, 1990, XIII, 1992. Rsch. grantee NIH, 1968—; Spl. Rsch. fellow U. Calif., San Diego, LaJolla, 1971-73. Mem. Internat. Soc. Oxygen Transport to Tissue (sec. 1980-86, exec. com. 1986-93), Biomed. Engring. Soc. (bd. dirs. 1983-86, chmn. publs. bd. 1985-86). Home: 2025 Sherman Ave Apt 504 Evanston IL 60201-3269 Office: Chem Engring Dept Northwestern U Evanston IL 60208-3120 E-mail: t-goldstick@northwestern.edu.

GOLEMBIEWSKI, GAE S. gifted education educator; b. Erie, Pa., Nov. 13, 1951; d. Richard Leroy and Leona Louise (Volgstadt) Anderson; m. Wlater T. Golembiewski; 1 child, Leeanna Louise. BE, Edinboro (Pa.) U., 1973, MEd, 1977; EdD, U. Pitts., 1992. Cert. early childhood edn. tchr., elem. tchr., prin. Tchr., computer coord. Millcreek (Pa.) Twp. Sch. Dist., 1973-79, gifted specialist, 1979-89; headmistress Erie Day Sch., 1989-90; instr. U. Pitts., 1990-92; assoc. prof., coord. gifted programs Norfolk (Va.) State U., 1992—. Co-dir. Project eSS, 1992-97; advisor Olympian Soc., Norfolk State U., 1993—. Contbr. articles to profl. jours. Pres. Coun. Giftedness, Erie; past pres. Erie Summer Festival of Arts. Recipient Exec. Acad. Computer award Pa. Dept. Edn., 1991, Hollingworth award Intertel Found., 1994; Alumni scholar U. Pitts., 1993. Mem. NAGC (chair creativity divsn. 1997—). Avocations: travel, gardening, writing. Home: 2901 River Breeze Cv Virginia Beach VA 23452-7113 Office: Norfolk U # 204 Education Bldg Norfolk VA 23504

GOLIAN-LUI, LINDA MARIE, librarian; b. Woodbridge, N.J., Mar. 27, 1962; d. Joseph John Golian and Mary Grace (Juba) Rodriguez; m. Gary S. Lui, Oct. 6, 1988; 1 child, Katherine Jana Lui-Golian. BA, U. Miami, 1986; MLIS, Fla. State, 1988; EdS, Fla. Atlantic U., 1995, EdD, 1998; postgrad., Fla. Gulf Coast U., 1999—2002. Libr. tech. asst. U. Miami, 1981-86; serials control libr. U. Miami Law Sch., 1986-89; serials dept. head Fla. Atlantic U., Boca Raton, 1990-97; univ. libr. Fla. Gulf Coast U., Ft. Myers, 1997—2002, adj. instr. Coll. Arts and Scis., 1999—2002; dir. U. Hawaii, Hilo, 2002—. Adj. instr. Fla. Atlantic U. Coll. Continuing & Distance Edn., 1993-97, U. So. Fla. Coll. Libr. Sci., 1995-2002; program specialist Marriott Statford Ctr. Sr. Living Cmty., Boca Raton, 1994-96. Vol. storyteller Aid to Victims of Domestic Assault, Delray Beach, Fla., 1994-96. Mem. NOW, AAUW, NAFE, NLA, Spl. Libr. Assn., N.Am. Serials Interest Group (co-chair mentoring com. 1996-97), ASCD, Southeastern Libr. Assn., Assn. Libr. and Info. Sci. Educators, Am. Libr. Assn., Assn. Libr. Collection & Tech. Svcs., Libr., Adminstrn. & Mgmt. Assn., Reference & User Svcs. Assn. (continuing libr. edn. network & exch. round table, intellectual freedom round table, libr. instruction round table, new members round table, staff orgn. round table, women's studies sect. comm. com. 1994—, serials nomination com. 1993, Miami local arrangements com. 1994, chair libr. sch. outreach 1994—, pres. 1998-99, 3M profl. devel. grantee 1995), Assn. Coll. Rsch. Libr. (Lazerow rsch. fellow 1997), Laubach Literary Vols. of Am., Am. Assn. Adult and Continuing Edn., Fla. Libr. Assn. (serials libr. or yr. 1994, grantee 1987). Roman Catholic. Avocations: reading, fishing, ceramics, tennis. Office: U HI Hilo Edwin H Mookini Lib & Graphic Ser 200 W Kawili St Hilo HI 96720-4091

GOLL, PAULETTE SUSAN, education educator; b. Cleve., June 5, 1947; d. Ferdinand Paul and Lillian Clarice (Mehalko) G. BA in English, Cleve. State U., 1969, MEd, 1974; MA in English, U. Bridgeport, Conn., 1979; PhD in English, Case Western Res. U., 1987. Cert. secondary tchr., English tchr., asst. supr., secondary prin., Ohio. Part-time instr. U. Bridgeport, 1978-79, Case Western Res. U., Cleve., 1985-87; tchr. English, Cleve. Pub. Schs., 1969—99, chmn. dept., coord. Ohio Proficiency Test, 1991—96; regional dir. Summer Inst. for Gifted Midwest Region, Granville, Ohio, 2000—02; lectr. Case Western Reserve U., Cleve., 2002—. Adj. instr. English Case Western Reserve U., Cleve. State U., 1999—2000; vis. assoc. prof. edn. Dickinson Coll., Carlisle, Pa., 2000; advisor Students Against Drunk Drivers, 1985—86; coord project success Lincoln West H.S., Cleve., 1987—90; ACT vis. tchr., 1999; external reviewer Bedford/St. Martins, 2003. Co-author: Shakespearean Comedies, 1985; external reviewer Reading Critically, Writing Well, textbook cons. textbook cons. McDougal Littel, 1999—2000, Bedford St. Martin, 2003. Mem. com. on human rels. Cleve. Partnerships, 1989-92; co-chmn. High Schs. for Future, 1985-86; liaison MetroHealth/Lincoln-West Partnership, 1989-92. Named Master Tchr., Martha Holden Jennings Found., 1988; recipient Congl. Commendation Mary Rose Oaker, 1988, Award of Excellence, Rotary, 1989, British Petroleum Tchr. of Year, 1997; NEH fellow, 1985, NEH Ind. Studies in Humanities fellow, 1993; Jennings scholar, 1985, 88. Mem. ASCD (presenter), Nat. Assn. Gifted (presenter 2001), North Ctrl. Assn. (chair vis. team 1991, 93), Phi Delta Kappa (v.p. programs 1993). Republican. Roman Catholic. Avocations: travel, music, needlepoint, writing fiction, camping. Home: 11366 Clarke Rd Columbia Station OH 44028-9626 Personal E-mail: psg3ecwru.edu.

GOLLAND, JEFFREY H. psychologist, psychoanalyst, educator; b. Bklyn., Apr. 28, 1941; s. Gerald Edward and Rose Alice (Finkelstein) G.; m. Patricia Elaine Yeager, July 14, 1969 (div. July 1991); children: David Hamilton, Richard Morris; m. Marcia Bergson, June 27, 1993. AB cum laude, Brandeis U., 1961; AM, NYU, 1962, PhD, 1969; Cert. in Psychoanalysis, N.Y. Freudian Soc., Inc., 1973. Lic. psychologist, N.Y. From psychologist to chief of psychology Brooke Gen. Hosp., San Antonio, 1966-68; psychologist-in-charge outpatient clinic Bellevue Psychiat. Hosp., N.Y.C., 1968-70; instr. psychiatry NYU Med. Ctr., 1968-70; asst. prof. edn. Baruch Coll., CUNY, 1970-75, chmn. dept., 1974-79, 96-98, assoc. prof. edn., 1975—98, assoc. prof. psychology, 1998—2000; prof. edn. York Coll., CUNY, 2000—01; vis. prof. edn. Lehman Coll., CUNY, 2001—; solo practice psychoanalysis and psychology N.Y.C., 1968—. Field supr. psychotherapy Rutgers Grad. Sch. Psychology, Piscataway, N.J., 1975-85; with faculty Am. Inst. for Psychoanalysis and Psychotherapy, N.Y.C., 1976-84, N.Y. Freudian Soc., 1984—. Author book chpts. and revs.; contbr. articles to profl. jours. Trustee Brandeis U., Waltham, Mass., 1985-89, The Village Temple, N.Y.C., 1984-92; pres. emeritus 145 Fourth Ave. Tenants Assn., N.Y.C., 1977—. Served to capt. U.S. Army Res., 1966-68. Recipient Founders Day award NYU, 1967. Fellow APA (pres. sect. 1 divsn. 39, 1995); mem. Psychologists Interested in Study of Psychoanalysis (pres. 1997-99), N.Y. Freudian Soc. (treas. 1984-90, v.p. 2001-03), Brandeis U. Alumni Assn. (bd. dirs. 1976-91, pres. 1985-89), Phi Delta Kappa. Democrat. Jewish. Avocations: tennis, running, skiing. Home: 145 4th Ave New York NY 10003-4906 Office: CUNY Lehman Coll ECCE Bedford Park Blvd W Bronx NY 10468

GOLTZ, ROBERT WILLIAM, physician, educator; b. St. Paul, Sept. 21, 1923; s. Edward Victor and Clare (O'Neill) G.; m. Patricia Ann Sweeney, Sept. 27, 1945; children: Leni, Paul Robert. BS, U. Minn., 1943, MD, 1945. Diplomate: Am. Bd. Dermatology (pres. 1975-76). Intern Ancker Hosp., St. Paul, 1944-45; resident in dermatology Mpls. Gen. Hosp., 1945-46, 48-49, U. Minn. Hosp., 1949-50; practice medicine specializing in dermatology Mpls., 1950-65; clin. instr. U. Minn. Grad. Sch., 1950-58, clin. asst. prof., 1958-60, clin. assoc. prof., 1960-65, prof., head dept. dermatology, 1971-85; prof. medicine and dermatology U. Calif., San Diego, 1985—, acting chair divsn. dermatology, 1995-97; prof. dermatology, head div. dermatology U. Colo. Med. Sch., Denver, 1965-71. Former editorial bd.: Archives of Dermatology; editor: Dermatology Digest. Served from 1st lt. to capt., M.C. U.S. Army, 1946-48. Mem. Assn. Am. Physicians, Am. Dermatol. Assn. (dir. 1976-79, pres. 1985-86), Am. Soc. Dermatopathology (pres. 1981), Am. Dermatologic Soc. Allergy and Immunology (pres. 1981), AMA (chmn. sect. on dermatology 1973-75), Dermatology Found. (past dir.), Minn. Dermatol. Soc., Soc. Investigative Dermatology (pres. 1972-73, hon. 1988), Histochem. Soc., Am. Acad. Dermatology (pres. 1978-79, past dir.) (hon.), Brit. Assn. Dermatology (hon.), Chilean Dermatology Soc. (hon.), Colombian Dermatol. Soc. (corr. mem.), Can. Dermatol. Soc. (hon. mem.), German Dermatol. Soc. (hon.), Pacific Dermatol. Soc. (hon.-mem.), S. African Dermatol. Soc. (hon. mem.), N.Am. Clin. Dermatol. Soc., Assn. Profs. Dermatology (sec.-treas. 1970-72, pres. 1973-74), West Assn. Physicians. Home: 6097 Avenida Chamnez La Jolla CA 92037-7404 Office: U Calif San Diego Med Ctr Divsn Dermatology H-8420 200 W Arbor Dr San Diego CA 92103-1911

GOLTZMAN, DAVID, endocrinologist, educator, researcher; b. Montreal, Que., Can., Sept. 22, 1944; s. Jack and Lily (Roth) G.; m. Naomi Lyon, Dec. 29, 1968; children: Jonathan, Rebecca, Daniel. BSc, McGill U., 1966, MD, 1968. Diplomate Am. Bd. Internal Medicine, Am. Bd. Endocrinology and Metabolism. Med. intern Royal Victoria Hosp., Montreal, 1968-69; med. resident Columbia U. Coll. Physicians and Surgeons, N.Y.C., 1969-71; clin. and rsch. fellow in endocrinology Mass. Gen. Hosp., Boston, 1971-75; instr. medicine Harvard Med. Sch., Boston, 1974-75; asst. prof. medicine McGill U., Montreal, 1976-78, assoc. prof., 1978-83, prof., 1983—, chmn. physiology, 1988-93, dir. calcium rsch. lab., 1981—, hosmer prof. physiology, 1992-93, Massabki prof. medicine, 1994—; chmn. medicine, 1994—. Sr. physician dept. medicine Royal Victoria Hosp., 1987-94, physician-in-chief, 1994-98; physician-in chief, McGill U. Hlth. Ctr., 1998—; chmn. exptl. medicine com. Med. Rsch. Coun. Can., Ottawa, Ont., 1984-88; mem. gen. medicine B study sect., NIH, Bethesda, Md., 1987-91; active Exec. Med. Rsch. Coun. Can., 1993—. Author: (with others) Principles of Bone Biology, 2001, Primer of Metabolic Bone Disease and Disorders of Mineral Metabolism, 1996, 1989, Primer of Osteoporosis, 2000, Principles and Practice of Endocrinology and Metabolism, 2001; editl. bd. Endocrinology Jour., 1985-90, Jour. Bone Mineral rsch., 1985-90, Bone and Mineral, 1991-94, Osteoporosis Internat., 1991-94, Assoc. Edn. Bone, 1989-94; assoc. editor: Jur. Bone Mineral research, 1995-2002; contbr. numerous articles to profl. jours. Recipient Chercheur Boursier award Que. Med. Rsch. Coun., 1980-83, Scientist award Med. Rsch. Coun. Can., 1983-88, Andre Lichtwitz prize Nat. Inst. for Med. Rsch., France, 1987; named officer Order of Can., 2000—. Fellow Royal Coll. Physicians and Surgeons, Royal Soc. Canada; mem. Can. Soc. Endocrinology and Metabolism (pres. 1990-92), Am. Soc. for Bone and Mineral Rsch. (chmn. program com. 1989-90, pres. 1999-00), Am. Assn. Physicians, Endocrine Soc. (program com. 1989-91), Can. Soc. Clin. Investigation (councillor 1986-89, pres. 1998-99) Am. Soc. Clin. Investigation, Canadian Assn. Profs. of Medicine (pres. 1998-99). Avocations: classical music, gardening, tennis. Office: Royal Victoria Hosp 687 Pine Ave W Montreal QC Canada H3A 1A1 E-mail: david.goltzman@mcgill.ca.

GOMER, EDITH ANNE, special education educator; b. Norfolk, Va., Jan. 12, 1956; d. Owen Russell Jr. and Edith Walker Gomer. BS in Edn., Old Dominion U., 1978, MS in Edn., 1983. Faculty mem. Deep Creek Jr. High Sch., Chesapeake, Va., 1980-89; faculty mem., dept. chmn. spl. edn., chair child study team Great Bridge Middle Sch. North, 1990—. With First Presbyn. Ch., Norfolk. Recipient Thomas R. Terry Music award Brewbaker Acad., 1974, Tchr. of Yr. Hickory Middle Sch., 1996-97. Mem. Old Dominion (chpt. #100, worthy matron 1985-86), Order of Ea. Star (asst. lectr., grand rep. of Ohio in Va. 1994-96), Va. Edn. Assn. (lobbiest 1994), Chesapeake Edn. Assn. (bldg. rep. 1992-94). Presbyterian. Avocations: needlecraft, piano, reading. Home: 3860 Weems Rd Norfolk VA 23502-3336 Office: Chesapeake Pub Schs 369 Battlefield Blvd S Chesapeake VA 23322-5311

GOMEZ, FABIOLA, university official; b. Chgo., June 23, 1974; d. Ruben Gómez and Carmen Carmona. Cert. practique, U. Upper Brittany, Rennes, France, 1994; BA, Beloit Coll., 1996. Spanish tutor Learning Resource Ctr., Beloit (Wis.) Coll., 1993-95, office clk. Acctg. Office, 1994-95, telemarketer Office Admissions, 1995-96; Hispanic recruiter, admission counselor Office Admissions, Roosevelt U., Chgo., 1996—. Rsch. assoc. Cmty. Rsch. and Policy Studies Ctr., Beloit, 1996; tchr.'s and libr. aide Inst. Franco-Am., Rennes, 1994; presenter 10th Ann. Nat. Conf. for Undergrad. Rsch., 1996. Minority scholar Assoc. Colls. Midwest, 1995. Mem. Ill. Assn. for Coll. Admissions Counseling, Ill. Latino Coun. on Higher Edn., Profls. for Latino Recruitment in Higher Edn. Office: Roosevelt U 430 S Michigan Ave Chicago IL 60605-1394

GOMEZ, LOUIS M. computer scientist, educator; BA in Psychology, SUNY, Stony Brook, 1974; PhD in Cognitive Psychology, U. Calif., Berkeley, 1979. Dir. Human Computer Sys. Rsch. Bellcore, Morristown, NJ; Aon prof. learning sci. and computer sci. Northwestern U., Evanston, Ill., 2000—, co-dir. The Learning Through Collaborative Visualization Project. Co-dir. Ctr. for Learning Techs. in Urban Schs.; chair vis. panel rsch. Ednl. Testing Svc. Contbr. articles to profl. jours. Recipient Mentorship award, Spencer Found. Mem.: Carnegie Found. for Advancement of Tchg. (bd. mem.). Office: Northwestern Univ Sch Edn Annenberg Hall Rm 337 2120 Campus Dr Evanston IL 60208*

GOMEZ, MARY ALICE, bilingual elementary educator; b. San Antonio, June 1, 1953; d. José I. and Alicia R. (Martinez) Lara; m. Pete F. Gómez, Aug. 21, 1976; children: Christina, Lindsey Michelle, Peter Joseph. BS in Home Econs., Our Lady of Lake U., 1975; cert. tchr., U. Tex., San Antonio, 1991. Cert. tchr. bilingual edn., elem. tchr., Tex. Nutritionist W.I.C. program San Antonio Met. Health Dist., 1981-89; elem. bilingual tchr. Edgewood Ind. Sch. Dist., San Antonio, 1989-92, Northside Ind. Sch. Dist., San Antonio, 1992—2001, Northeast Ind. Sch. Dist., San Antonio, 2001—. Roman Catholic. Home: 6742 Spring Rose St San Antonio TX 78249-2943 Office: Colonial Hills Elem 2627 Kerrybrook San Antonio TX 78230-4534

GOMEZ, TERRINE, school director; b. Trivandrum, India, Jan. 29, 1928; came to U.S., 1977; Tchr. Tng. Degree, Trinity Coll. Music, London, 1949; BA in History of Music, U. Ill., 1982. Licentiate in violin; assoc. in voice; Rolland specialist. Head dept. music Internat. Sch., India, 1959-72; head string dept. Am. Internat. Sch., India, 1972-77; asst. to artistic dir. Nat. Acad. of Arts and Conservatory of Champaign, Ill., 1983-89; major instr. violin CCI assisting Ian Hobson, 1983-89; dir. Young Artists' Studio, Champaign, 1989—. Condr. nat. and internat. workshops in preparation for Rolland Specialist category, Cambridge, Eng., 1976, Chichester, Eng. and Lausanne, Switzerland, 1977, Laval U., Que., 1981. Author: The Young Violinist (in 3 parts), 1985. Mem. European String Tchrs. Assn., Am. String Tchrs. Assn., Soc. Am. Musicians, Chamber Music Am. (Heidi Castleman award 1994). Roman Catholic. Avocations: languages, history, art, literature, shih-tzu dogs. Office: Young Artists Studio 1305 Mayfair Rd Champaign IL 61821-5023

GOMEZ LANCE, BETTY RITA, sciences and foreign language educator, writer; b. San Jose, Costa Rica, Aug. 28, 1923; came to U.S., 1942; d. Joaquín Gómez-Fernández and Blanca Castillo-Salazar De Gómez; children: Edward T., Harold Elliott. BS, Ctrl. Mo. State U., 1944; MA, U. Mo., 1947; PhD, Washington U., St. Louis, 1959. Cert. tchr., Costa Rica, Mo. Rsch. asst. U. Mo., Columbia, 1944-47; tchg. asst. Washington U., 1955-59; asst. prof. U. Ill., Urbana, 1959-61; prof. Kalamazoo (Mich.) Coll., 1961-88, prof. emeritus, 1988—. Author short stories and poetry. Mem. Friends of Libr., Kalamazoo, 1961—, Kalamazoo Inst. Arts, 1961—, Nature Ctr., Kalamazoo, 1961—, Environ. Concerns Com., Kalamazoo, 1988—. Mem. Poets and Writers Am., Am. Assn. Tchrs. Spanish and Portuguese, Assn. Prometeo De Poesía, Assn. Iberoamericana De Poesía, Assn. De Escritores Costarricenses, and others. Avocations: hiking, nature activities, knitting. Home: 1562 Spruce Dr Kalamazoo MI 49008-2227

GOMOPOULOS, MARY, elementary school educator; b. Vatera, Lesbos, Greece, Oct. 13, 1946; came to U.S., 1962; d. Nick and Irene (Psoma) Tsakyris; m. Nick Gomopoulos, Oct. 26, 1969; children: Peter, Paul. BA, Roosevelt U., 1977; MEd, U. Ill., Chgo., 1993. Cert. elem. tchr., secondary French tchr., ESL tchr., Ill. Montessori tchr. Children's House, Chgo., 1978-80; English tutor Athens, Greece, 1980-82; ESL tchr., part time adminstr. Campion Internat. Sch., Athens, 1980-85; ESL tchr. Waterbury Elem. Sch., Roselle, Ill., 1988—. Greek tchr. evening sch. St. Dimitrios Cmty. Sch., Elmhurst, Ill., 1986—; mem. parents' adv. com. KIM Project, Medinah, Ill., 1992-93. Mem. Soc. of Mytilene (sec. 1990—). Avocations: summering on greek islands, reading, writing short stories, children, swimming. Office: Waterbury Sch 355 Rodenburg Rd Roselle IL 60172-1646

GONDER, SHARON, special education educator; b. Princeton, Mo., Aug. 1, 1943; d. Raymond Dale and V. Juanita (Wharton) Hagan; m. Glen William Gonder, Oct. 18, 1985; 1 child, Patricia; stepchildren: Gil, Gailen, Gary, Geoffrey, Gregory, Douglas. BS in Edn., U. Mo., 1968, MEd in Spl. Edn., 1971; MEd in Counseling, Lincoln U., Jefferson City, Mo., 1978. Cert. elem. edn., behavioral disorders, learning disabilities, mentally handicapped, orthopedic handicapped, counseling, psychol. exam., adaptive phys. edn.. Instr. Mental Health Ctr., Columbia, Mo., 1969-71; diagnostician staffing coord. Non-Pub. By-Pass Program, Jefferson City, 1976-89; psychol. examiner Disabilities Determ, Dept. Elem. and Sec. Edn., Jefferson

City, 1981-84; coord. Project Lift-Up Lincoln U., Jefferson City, 1984-86; diagnostician Metro Bus. Coll., Jefferson City, 1987-89; tchr., psychol. examiner Jefferson City Pub. Schs., 1968-97. Program cons. Lincoln U., Jefferson City, 1980-99, adj. prof., 1985-99; sec., spl. programming cons. Osage Bend Pub. Co., 1989—; bd. dirs. Ednl. Resources Info. Ctr.; cons. for establishing vol. programs, 2000—; developer policies for reporting child abuse/neglect for vols., 2002—; presenter workshops in field. Leader 4-H, Jefferson City, 1978-81; non-registered lobbyist Mo. State Tchrs. Assn., 1987-97; deacon, tchr. Sunday sch. First Christian Ch., 1985—, elder; mem. task force to establish area at risk programs Jefferson City C. of C., 1993-97. Named Mo. State Spl. Edn. Tchr. of Yr., Mo. Fedn. Coun. for Exceptional Children, 1991. Mem. Coun. for Exceptional Children (legis. chmn., sec.-treas., pres. subdivsns. learning disabilities and mentally retarded and pioneers 1988—, bd. rep. Mo. coun. 1973-88, state fedn. pres. 1984-86, internat. del. 1974, 85, non-registered lobbyist 1983—, profl. devel. standing com. internat. coun. 1997-2001, Internat. Spl. Edn. Tchr. of the Yr. 1992), Learning Disabilities Assn. (chpt. pres., exec. bd. dirs. 1975-91), Gen. Fedn. Women's Clubs (1st v.p.), Delta Kappa Gamma (spkr. nat. circuit 1991-99), author nat. publs. 1992—, bd. dirs. Ednl. Resource Info. Ctr. 1993-2000). Avocations: traveling, camping, crafts, gardening, volunteer tutoring. Office: Osage Bend Pub Co Inc 213 Belair Dr Jefferson City MO 65109-0703 E-mail: obpc@socket.net.

GONG, MAMIE POGGIO, elementary education educator; b. San Francisco, June 26, 1951; d. Louis and Mary Lee (Lum) G.; m. Andy Anthony Poggio. BA, U. Calif., Berkeley, 1973, postgrad., 1981-83, MEd, 1982. Tchr. Oakland (Calif.) Unified Sch. Dist., 1974-84, Palo Alto (Calif.) Unified Sch. Dist., 1984-91. Cons., writer Nat. Clearinghouse for Bilingual Edn., Washington, 1984; cons. ARC Assocs., Oakland, 1983; rsch. asst. dept. edn. Stanford U., 1987-89. Co-author: Promising Practices: A Teacher Resource, 1984. Recipient Kearney Found. award, 1969, others. Mem. Tchrs. English to Speakers Other Langs. (presenter 1990 conf.), Calif. Assn. Tchrs. English to Speakers Other Langs. Democrat. Office: Palo Alto Unified Sch Dist 25 Churchill Ave Palo Alto CA 94306-1099

GONGWER, CAROLYN JANE, human factors engineer; b. Mishawaka, Ind., July 9, 1936; d. Walter Bryan and Mary Saxton (Blocher) G.; 1 child, Yen Yaing. BS, Purdue U., 1958; student, Ill. State U., 1969-79, George Mason U., 1990, U. Md., 1990. Cert. Fed. Contracting U.Va. Svc. sales engr. Ctl. Ill. Light Co., Peoria, Ill., 1958-69; coll. instr. Bradley U., Peoria, Ill., 1962-63, Ill. Ctl. Coll., E. Peoria, Ill., 1971-73; ESL instr. YMCA, Kaohsiung, Taiwan, 1971; ESL ednl. coord. CSS Govt. Contract, Peoria, Ill., 1979-83; asst. human resources mgr. Foster & Gallagher, Peoria, Ill., 1984-87; tech. trainer, instr. tech. NYMA FAA Traffic Mgmt. Sys. Contract, Greenbelt, Md., 1988-94; pres. Trident Tech. Tng. SYs. & Human-Tech. Interface Evaluations, Crofton, Md., 1992—. Adv. Talon Prints, Crofton, Md., 1992—. Bd. mem. Home Owner's Assn., Crofton Meadown, Md., 1990-94; mem. Md. Save Our Streams, Glen Burnie, Md., 1990—, League of Women Voters, Annapolis, Md., 1992—. Grantee Travel Study, Ill. State U., Taiwan, 1971. Mem. ACM, APA (divsn. applied exptl. and engring. psychologists), NAFE, Human Factors Soc., Nat. Soc. Performance and Instrn., Software Psychol. Soc., Sig Computer-Human Interaction. Avocations: travel, art history, archeology, gardening, nature hiking. Home and Office: Trident Tech Tng Sys 1713 Jones Falls Ct Crofton MD 21114-1836

GONSALVES, MARGARET LEBOY, elementary school educator; b. Paia, Maui, Hawaii, Feb. 10, 1935; d. John Algarin and Antonia (Leboy) G. BS in Edn., Marylhurst U., 1959; elem. tchr. cert., U. Hawaii, 1971. Cert. elem. tchr., Hawaii. Nurses' aide St. Vincent Hosp., Portland, Oreg., 1956; office clk. Bur. Med. Econs., Honolulu, 1959; tchr. State of Hawaii Dept. Edn., Honolulu, 1959—, Benjamin Park Sch., Kaneohe, Hawaii, 1966-92. Tchr. ESEA-Title I Chpt. I reading and math. fed. program, 1979-92, coord. Parker Sch. Chpt. 1 reading and math. program. Vol. Am. Cancer Soc., Honolulu, 1979, Am. Diabetes Assn., Honolulu, 1992; reporter Nat. Data Corp.-Price Waterhouse, Springfield, Va., 1991-2002. Mem. NEA, Internat. Reading Assn., Hawaii State Tchrs. Assn. (faculty rep. 1960-62, 87-89, Golden Heart cert., 2003), Sigma Delta Pi. Roman Catholic. Avocations: reading, sweepstakes, fishing, gardening, traveling. Home: 1328 Maalahi St Honolulu HI 96819-1727

GONSHER, WENDY, educational administrator; b. N.Y.C., Oct. 9, 1951; d. Bernard and Nora (Eisen) G.; m. John Thomas Holmes, Oct. 7, 1989; 1 child, Amanda Holmes. BA, CUNY, 1972; MA, Columbia U., 1974; Adminstr./Supr., Fla. Atlantic U., 1984. Cert. supr. instrn., tchr., hearing disabilities, adminstrn., supr Coun. on Edn. of Deaf, Fla. Tchr. Sch. Bd. of Broward County, Ft. Lauderdale, Fla., 1974-78, program monitor, 1978-87, curriculum supr., 1987—. Sec. Conv. Am. Inst. Deaf, Rochester, N.Y., 1991-93; cons. Broward County Pub. Defenders Office, Ft. Lauderdale, 1991-93, Rotary Club Internat., Plantation, Fla., 1986-88. Contbr. articles to profl. jours. Fla. whole lang. grantee Fla. Dept. Edn., Tallahassee, 1990. Mem. A.G. Bell Assn. Deaf, Conv. Am. Instrs. Deaf (sec. 1991-93), Conf. Ednl. Adminstrs. Serving the Deaf, Inc., Fla. Educators of Deaf (pres. 1981-83), Fla. Lang., Speech and Hearing Assn., Rotary. Avocations: boating, travel. Office: Exceptional Student Edn 600 SE 3rd Ave Fl 9 Fort Lauderdale FL 33301-3125

GONZALES, ELOISE A. elementary education educator; b. Rawlins, Wyo., Sept. 12, 1956; d. Leo Gerald and Pauline Mary (Sanchez) Gonzales. BA in Edn., U. Wyo., 1979; MA in Edn. Adminstrn., Northeastern State U., 1990. Bus. mgr. Wyute Paving Co., Rawlins, 1981-82; elem. tchr. St. Joseph's Sch. and Rawlins Pub. Sch., Rawlins, 1987-87; substitute tchr. Sapulpa (Okla.) Sch., 1987-88; elem. tchr. Berryhill (Okla.) Sch., 1988-89, Broken Arrow (Okla.) Sch., 1989—96; bus. owner, 1997—. Coach volleyball, basketball, softball, Rawlins Schs. Senator U. Wyo., Laramie, 1978. Mem. Toastmasters. Democrat. Roman Catholic. Avocations: golf, reading. Home: 1713 Gates Ave Kingman AZ 86401-4072

GONZALES, JUDITH ANNE, retired elementary school educator; b. Hoboken, N.J., Mar. 11, 1945; d. Angelo Julius and Margaret Mary (Egan) Mai; m. Thomas Gonzales, Apr. 6, 1968; children: Ian Thomas, Katelyn Marbeth. BA, Jersey City State Coll., 1966. Cert. elem. tchr., N.J.; cert. ESL. Elem. tchr. Hoboken Bd. Edn., 1966, Hackettstown (N.J.) Bd. Edn., 1966-67, Union City (N.J.) Bd. Edn., 1967—2003, peer training, 1987-90, grade chmn., 1988-90, faculty counsel, 2000—02, ret., 2003. Property mistress Our Lady of Grace Theater Group, Hoboken, 1974-76, Holy Family Players, Nutley, N.J., 1977. Mem. NEA, N.J. Edn. Assn., Union City Edn. Assn. Roman Catholic. Avocations: music, poetry, writing.

GONZALES, RICHARD ROBERT, counselor; b. Palo Alto, Calif., Jan. 12, 1945; s. Pedro and Virginia (Ramos) G.; m. Jennifer Ayres; children: Lisa Dianne, Jeffrey Ayres. AA, Foothill Coll., 1966; BA, San Jose (Calif.) State U., 1969; MA, Calif. Poly. State U., San Luis Obispo, 1971; grad., Def. Info. Sch., Def. Equal Opportunity Mgmt. Inst. Lic. marriage family child counselor, Calif.; cert. counselor Nat. Bd. Cert. Counselors. Counselor student activities Calif. Poly. State U., San Luis Obispo, 1969-71, instr. ethnic studies, 1970-71; counselor Ohlone Coll., Fremont, Calif., 1971-72, coord. coll. readiness, 1971; counselor De Anza Coll., Cupertino, Calif., 1972-78, mem. cmty. spkrs. bur., 1975-78; counselor Foothill Coll., Los Altos Hills, Calif., 1978—, mem. cmty. spkrs. bur., 1978—. Instr. Def. Equal Opportunity Mgmt. Inst., 1984-96; mem. U. Calif. C.C. Counselor Adv. Com., 1998—. Mem. master plan com. Los Altos (Calif.) Sch. Dist., 1975-76; vol. worker, Chicano cmtys., Calif.; active mem. Woodside (Calif.) Recreation Commn. Commd. officer Calif. Army N.G., now ret. Adj. Gen. Corps, USAR. Masters and Johnson fellow. Mem. ACA, Am. Coll. Counseling Assn., Calif. Assn. Marriage and Family Therapists, Calif. C.C. Counselor Assn. (former pres.), Calif. Assn. Counseling and Devel. (former pres. Hispanic Caucus, former pres.), Calif. Assn. for Humanistic Edn. and Devel. (former pres.), Calif. Assn. for Multi-Cultural Counseling, Res. Officers Assn., La Raza Faculty Assn. Calif. C.C., Nat. Career Devel. Assn., Phi Delta Kappa, Chi Sigma Iota. Republican. E-mail: rrgincal@aol.com.

GONZALEZ, ELEANOR MORODO, secondary educator; b. Havana, Cuba, Apr. 4, 1948; came to U.S., 1950; d. Julian Rodriguez and Angelita (Morodo) G. BA, Simmons Coll., 1967; MA, Brown U., 1968. Cert. secondary tchr., Conn. Instr. English, U. Autonoma, Madrid, 1972-74; tchr. Spanish, Wilton (Conn.) High Sch., 1968-72, 74—, foreign lang. dept. chairperson, 1986—. Faculty cons. A.P. Lang. Spanish Exams Ednl. Testing Svc., 1992, 1993. Author: (workbook) Destinos, 1992. Lector coord., eucharistic minister, Holy Family Ch., Fairfield, Conn. Fellow Quincentennial Com., Spain, 1989. Mem. NEA, Am. Coun. on Teaching Fgn. Langs., Am. Assn. Tchrs. Spanish and Portuguese, Conn. Edn. Assn., Conn. Coun. Lang. Tchrs., Delta Kappa Gamma. Avocations: travel, reading, theater. Office: Wilton High Sch 395 Danbury Rd Wilton CT 06897-2093

GONZALEZ, OLGA ESTELA, special education educator; b. Rio Grande City, Tex., Feb. 3, 1947; d. Filemon and Guadalupe (Trimble) Garza; m. Enrique Gonzãlez, Oct. 23, 1971; 1 child, Maria Luana. BS, Pan Am. U., 1977; MS, Tex. A&I U., 1990. Cert. tchr. Eng., forensics, ESL, special edn., Tex. Tchr. K-1 for seasonal migrants, Lakota, Ohio, 1984-88; tchr. special edn. Robstown (Tex.) Ind. Sch. Dist., 1987-89, Rio Grande City Consolidated Ind. Sch. Dist., 1989—. Curriculum rschr. Robstown Ind. Sch. Dist., 1987-89; mem. site base decision com., special edn. site base team, Rio Grande City CISD, 1990—; liaison press, media Ringgold Intermediate Campus, Rio Grande City, 1989—. Editor Recipes, children's poetry, calendar. Biling Edn. scholar Findlay U., Ohio, 1981-82. Mem. Tex. State Tchrs. Assn., Coun. for Exceptional Children, Florence J. Scott Study Club, Phi Beta Kappa, Sociedad Guadalupana de St. Joseph (treas. 1988-89). Democrat. Roman Catholic. Avocations: reading, writing, cooking, traveling. Home: 404 W 4th St Rio Grande City TX 78582-3206 Office: Ringgold Intermediate Sch Ft Ringgold Campus Rio Grande City TX 78582

GONZALEZ, RICARDO, surgeon, educator; b. Buenos Aires, June 26, 1943; s. Salvador Maria and Clyde Alcira (Prevettoni) G.; children: Diego Andres, Carlos Ricardo. BA, Coll. Nat. San Isidro, Buenos Aires, 1959; MD, U. Buenos Aires, 1965. Diplomate Am. Bd. Urology. Resident in surgery Hosp. Militar Cent., Buenos Aires, 1966-68; intern in surgery U. Minn., 1969-70, resident (med. fellow) in urologic surgery, 1970-74, from instr. to prof. urology, 1974-85, prof. urology, 1985-94, prof. pediat., 1993-94; chief, pediat. urology Children's Hosp. of Mich., Detroit, 1994; prof. urology Wayne State U., Detroit, 1995-99; prof. urology and pediat., chief pediat. urology divsn. U. Miami /Jackson Meml. Hosp., Fla., 1999—2002; dir. pediatric urology fellowship A1 DuPont Hosp. for children, Wilmington, Del., 2002—; prof. urology Thomas Jefferson U., Phila., 2002—, pres., 2002. Pres. Pediat. Urology P.C., Detroit, 1995-2000; vis. prof. Harvard U., Cambridge, Mass., 1994, Johns Hopkins U., Balt., 1995, U. Washington, Seattle, 1995, U. Calif., San Francisco, 1996, Cornell U., NY, 1998, U. Montreal, 2000, Thomas Jefferson U., 2000, McGill U., 2000, U. Vienna, Austria, 2003, Chinese U. Hong Kong, 2003, State U. N.Y. Upstate Med. Coll., Syracuse, 2003; presenter in field. Contbr. over 200 articles to profl. jours., over 50 chpts. to books; editor 2 books. Am. Acad. Pediat. fellow, 1981, Nat. Kidney Found. rsch. fellow 1974-76; co-prin. investigator USPHS cancer grant 1976-78. Fellow Am. Acad. Pediat. (mem. exec. sect. on urology com. 1995-98); mem. Am. Urologic Assn., Mex. Coll. Urology (hon.), Venezuelan Soc. for Spina Bifida, Argentine Confedn. Urology, Societé Internat. d'Urologie, Ibero-Am. Soc. Pediat. Urology (pres. 1995-98, Medal of Merit 2000), Soc. for Pediatric Urol. Surgeons (by invitation), European Soc. Paediat. Urology (hon.). Avocations: opera, music, language, reading, writing. Office: AI duPont Hosp for Children Dept Urology 1600 Rockland Rd Wilmington DE 19899 E-mail: rgonzale@nemours.org.

GONZALEZ, ROLANDO NOEL, secondary school educator, religion educator, photographer; b. Rio Grande City, Tex., Sept. 10, 1947; s. Ubaldo and Beulah (Gutierrez) G. BA, U. Tex., 1968; MA, Tex. A & I U., 1972. Cert. tchr. all scis., guidance and counseling. Tchr., head sci. dept. Roma (Tex.) Jr. High Sch., 1968-71; migrant/Title I counselor Roma Elem. and Roma Jr. High Sch., 1972-76; head sci. dept. Rio Grande High Sch., Rio Grande City, Tex., 1976-78; tchr., head sci. dept. Ringgold Jr. High Sch., Rio Grande City, 1982-83, Pharr-San Juan-Alamo High Sch., Pharr, Tex., 1986—; seminarian Diocese of Brownsville, San Antonio, 1979-82; pastoral asst. Our Lady, Queen of Angels Ch., La Joya, Tex., 1982-83; coord., lay ministries Brownsville Diocese, McAllen, Tex., 1983-85; lectr., tchr. on scripture Perpetual Help Ch., McAllen, 1986-88, Holy Spirit Ch., McAllen, 1989—; tchr. psychology South Tex. C.C., 2003—. Instr. history of chemistry U. Tex.-Pan Am., Edinburg, 1990; wedding and portrait photographer, 1973—; psychology tchr., South Tex. C.C., 2003—. Contbr. articles to profl. jours. Tchr. scripture, lectr. Sts. Mary and Margaret Ch., Pharr, Tex., 1988, Sacred Heart Ch., Mercedes, Tex., 1990; tchr. scripture Holy Spirit Parish, McAllen, Tex., 1992—. Recipient Appreciation award Sacred Heart Ch., 1990, Tchr. of Yr. award Rio Grande Valley Sci. Assn., 1996-97, Holy Spirit Parish Vol. award, 2000. Home: 2800 W Iris Ave Mcallen TX 78501-6200

GONZALEZ-DEL-VALLE, LUIS TOMAS, Spanish language educator; b. Nov. 19, 1946; BA in Spanish cum laude, Wilmington Coll.-U. N.C., Wilmington, 1968; MA in Spanish and Spanish-Am. Lits., U. Mass., 1972; Phd in Spanish and Spanish-Am. Lits. five coll. coop. program, Amherst Coll., Hampshire Coll., Mt. Holyoke Coll., Smith Coll., U. Mass., 1972. Asst. prof. modern langs. Kans. State U., 1972-75, assoc. prof. modern langs., 1975-77; assoc. prof. modern langs. and lits. U. Nebr., Lincoln, 1977-79, prof. modern langs. and lits., 1979-86; prof. Spanish and Portuguese U. Colo., Boulder, 1986—, chmn. dept. Spanish and Portuguese, 1986-98, assoc. chair for grad. studies, 2003—. Reading cons. South-Western Pub. Co., Inc., 1974, Eliseo Torres & Sons, 1974; dir. Ibero-Latin Am. Studies Ctr., 1987—; lectr. in field. Author: La nueva ficcion hispanoamericana a traves de M.A. Asturias y G. Garcia Marquez, 1972, La ficcion breve de Valle Inclán, 1990, El Canon: Reflexiones Sobre la Recepcion Literaria-Teatral, 1993, La canonización del Diablo: Baudelaire y la estética moderna en España, 2002, Bauelaire y la estetica moderna en Espana, 2002; co-author: Luis Romero, 1979; gen. editor Anales de la literatura española contemporánea, 1975—, Siglo XX/20th Century, 1985—; editor: Jour. Spanish Studies: 20th Century, 1972—80, Studies in 20th Century Lit., 1975—79, Annual Bibliography of Post-Civil War Spanish Fiction, 1977—82, Ecos de Cuba, 1997; co-editor: La generacion de 1898 ante España, 1997; contbr. articles, essays, book revs. to profl. jours. Recipient Postdoctoral Rsch. award Coun. for Internat. Exch. Scholars, 1984, 500th Rsch. Award Spanish Fgn. Ministry, 1992, Silver Medal of Honor Galician Govt., 2000; grantee Coun. on Rsch. and Creative Work, U. Colo., 1986-87, Com. for Ednl. & Cultural Affairs, U. Nebr.-Lincoln, Chancellor's Rsch. Initiation Fund, U. Nebr.-Lincoln, 1980-81, Rsch. Coun., U. Nebr.-Lincoln, 1978, 79; Sr. Faculty Summer Rsch. fellow Rsch. Coun., U. Nebr.-Lincoln, 1978, Woodrow Wilson Dissertation fellow, 1971-72, Univ. fellow U. Mass., 1968-69, 70-72, Grad. fellow, 1969-70. Mem.: MLA, Nebr. Fgn. Lang. Assn., Cervantes Soc. Am., Cir. de Cultura Panamericano (exec. coun. 1972), 20th Century Spanish Assn. (exec. sec. 1982—), Soc. Spanish and Spanish-Am. Studies (bd. dirs. 1975—), Am. Assn. Tchrs. Spanish and Portuguese (Excellence in Tchg. award Colo. chpt. 1996), Assn. Europea de Profesores de Espanol, Fgn. Lang. Adminstrs. of Colo., Assn. de Escritores y Artistas Espanoles (U.S. rep.), Assn. Colegial de Escritores (spl. rep. to U.S., v.p.), Spain's Pen Club (founding 1984), Conf. Editors of Learned Jours. (bd. dirs. 1987—), N.Am. Acad. Spanish Lang. (corr.), Castilian Assn. Writers (hon.), others, Phi Kappa Phi. Home: 1875 Del Rosa Ct Boulder CO 80304-1800 Office: U Colo Dept Spanish Portuguese Boulder CO 80309-0001

GONZALEZ PINO, BARBARA, foreign languages educator; b. San Antonio, May 13, 1941; d. Alton William and Ottillie Jane (Baetge) Vordenbaum; m. Frank Pino, Jr. BA in Spanish, English, French, U. Tex., 1963, MA in Fgn. Lang. Edn., Spanish, French, 1964, PhD in Fgn. Lang. Edn., Spanish, French, 1971. Tchr. San Antonio Ind. Sch. Dist., 1964-66; instr. U. Tex., Austin, 1966-67, 69-70; asst. prof. S.W. Tex. State U., San Marcos, 1967-69; tchr., adminstr. Bexar County Sch. Dist., San Antonio, 1970-73; instr. St. Philip's Coll., San Antonio, 1973-75; lectr. Incarnate Word Coll., San Antonio, 1973-75; from lectr. to asst. prof. edn., bilingual studies, Spanish U. Tex., San Antonio, 1974-81, assoc. prof., 1981—. Mem. com. on internat. issues Tex. Commr. Higher Edn., 1991-97; presenter, lectr. numerous workshops and confs. in field; chief rater, Tex. Oral Proficiency Test of Spanish, 1992—. Contbr. numerous articles and papers to profl. publs. Past mem. exec. bd. San Antonio Literacy Coun.; past pres. El Patronato de la Cultural Hispano-Americana; past pres. Sembradoras de Amistad. Grantee Coord. Bd. TCUS, 1986, 87, 87-88, 88-89, Tex. Edn. Agy., 1986, 87, 88-89, 94, 97. Mem. MLA, South Cen. MLA (past sect. chair, sec.), Am. Coun. Teaching Fgn. Langs. (past exec. bd.), S.W. Conf. Lang. Teaching (past chmn., mem. adv. coun., Founders award 1987, 2003), Tex. Fgn. Lang. Assn. (past pres.), Am. Assn. Tchrs. Spanish and Portuguese, So. Conf. Lang. Teaching (past exec. bd.), Univ. Roundtable (sec., pres. 2003), Tex. Assn. Coll. and Univ. Lang. Suprs. (pres. 1990—), Kappa Delta Pi, Phi Delta Kappa. Methodist. Avocations: reading, travel, antiques, hand-made houses. Office: U Tex San Antonio Dept Interdisciplinary Studies San Antonio TX 78249

GONZALEZ-VALES, LUIS ERNESTO, historian, educational administrator; b. May 11, 1930; s. Ernesto and Carmen (Vales) G.; m. Hilda González, July 16, 1952; children: Carmen L., Luis E., Antonio S., Maria G., Rosa Maria, Gerardo, Rosario, Hildita. BA with honors, U. P.R., 1952; MA, Columbia U., 1957; doctorate (hon.), Pontifical Cath. U. P.R., 1995. From instr. humanities to assoc. prof. U. P.R., Rió Piedras, 1955—67, assoc. prof. history, 1967, prof. history, 1983, from asst. dean faculty gen. studies to assoc. dean, 1960-67. Author: Alejandro Ramirez: La Vida de un Intendente Liberal, 1972, Gabriel Gutierrez de Riva: Essays on 18th Century Puerto Rico History, 1990; editor: 1898: Enfoques y Perspectivas, 1998; contbg. author Puerto Rico: A Political and Cultural History, 1983; contbr. articles to profl. jours.; mem. editl. bd. Revista Historia, 1960-67. Dir. P.R. Acad. History, 1992—; exec. sec. Coun. on Higher Edn., 1967-83, Commonwealth Post Secondary Commn., 1973-83; chancellor P.R. Jr. Coll., 1985-87; bd. dirs. Inst. Puerto Rican Culture, 1993-2001; bd. trustees U. P.R., 1997-2001; collegiate ednl. adv. panel cadet command U.S. Army, 1986-96. 1st lt. inf. U.S. Army, 1952-55, adj. gen. P.R. N.G., 1983-85, ret. maj. gen. U.S. Army, 1990. Decorated Gran Cruz del Merito Militar con Distintivo Blanco Spain; named Ofcl. Historian of P.R., P.R. Legislature and Gov., 1997, Humanist of Yr., P.R. Humanities Found., 1998. Mem. Am. Hist. Assn., P.R. Acad. History, Latin Am. Studies Assn., Assn. U.S. Army, N.G. Assn., Mil. Order World Wars, Res. Officers Assn., P.R. Acad. of Arts and Scis., Phi Alpha Theta (pres. 1962-63). Roman Catholic.

GOOCH, AUDREY SMITH, retired education educator; b. St. Louis, July 7, 1925; d. James Irving and Mabel Dorthea (Higgins) Smith; m. Robert Thomas Gooch; children: Keith Ewing, Robert Kenneth. BA, Stowe Tchrs. Coll., 1947; MA in Tchg., Webster U., 1971. Cert. elem. tchr., reading specialist, coll. instr., child care. Elem. tchr. St. Louis Pub. Schs., 1947-66; edn. dir. Project Head Start, St. Louis, 1966-69, project dir., 1969-72; dir. Right to Read, St. Louis, 1972-74, Forest Park C.C., St. Louis, 1974-79; coord. Family Support Svcs., St. Louis, 1979-84; dir. Early Childhood Edn. Unit, St. Louis, 1984-90. Adj. faculty Harris Tchrs. Coll., St. Louis, 1972, Forest Park C.C., 1973; adv. bd. Learning Tree Day Care Ctr., St. Louis, 1991-97; cons. St. Louis Urban League, Right to Read Nat. Office, Washington, 1974, Mo. Vol. Accredition EOC, Jefferson City, 1989-90. Author: (booklet) A Guideline For Head Start Curriculum, 1967, Read On, 1973, Handbook for Reading Tutors, 1974. Mem. collections com. Mo. History Mus., St. Louis; mem. scholarship com. U. Mo., St. Louis; vice chmn. Kirkwood (Mo.) Human Rights Commn.; v.p. Kirkwood Hist. Soc., 2000; Oasis tutor Kirkwood Pub. Schs. Recipient Gateway medal City of St. Louis, 1972, Outstanding Vol. Svc. award at Mo. Hist. Soc., Union Electric and City of St. Louis, 1996, Woman of Achievement award St. Louis Globe Dem., 1985, Disting. Alumni award Harris-Stowe State Coll., 1992. Mem. Mo. Assn. for Edn. of Young Children (sec.), Gideon Internat. Aux. (v.p. 1993), Links Inc. (fin. sec. 1994), Delta Sigma Theta. Lutheran. Avocations: reading, volunteering. Home: 302 W Rose Hill Ave Saint Louis MO 63122-5942

GOOD, IRVING JOHN, statistics educator, mathematician, philosopher of science; b. London, Dec. 9, 1916; arrived in US, 1967; s. Morris Edward and Sophia (Polikoff) G. ScD, Cambridge (Eng.) U., 1963; DSc, Oxford (Eng.) U., 1964. Scientific officer Fgn. Office, Bletchley, Eng., 1941-45; lectr. math. and electronic computing Manchester (Eng.) U., 1945-48; sr. prin. sci. officer Govt. Communications Hdqrs., Cheltenham, Eng., 1948-59; spl. merit dep. chief sci. officer Admiralty Rsch. Lab., Teddington, Middlesex, Eng., 1959-62; sr. rsch. fellow Trinity Coll., Oxford U. and Atlas Computer Lab., Didcot, Berkshire, Eng., 1964-67; Univ. disting. prof. stats, adj. prof. philosophy Va. Poly. Inst. and State U., Blacksburg, 1967—; prof. emeritus. Adj. prof. Ctr. Study of Sci. in Society; mem. comm. theory com. Ministry Supply, London, 1953-56; mem. comm. com. electronics rsch. com. Ministry Aviation, London, 1960-62; mem. rsch. sect. com. Royal Statis. Soc., London, 1965-67. Author: Probability and the Weighing of Evidence, 1950, The Estimation of Probabilities, 1965, Good Thinking, 1983; gen. editor: The Scientist Speculates, 1962 (also French and German translations); chpt. in The Codebreakers, 1994; also 5 chpts. in Festschriften; contbr. over 900 articles to profl. jours. Grantee NIH, 1970-89; recipient Smith's prize, Cambridge, Eng., 1940. Fellow Am. Acad. Arts and Scis., Va. Acad. Scis., Inst. Math. Stats., Am. Statis. Assn.; mem. IEEE Computer Soc. (Pioneer award 1998), Internat. Statis. Inst. (hon.), Internat. Order Merit. Home: 1309 Lynn Dr Blacksburg VA 24060-3001 Office: Va Poly Inst and State U Dept Stats Blacksburg VA 24061-0439

GOOD, JOANNA CHRISTINA, retired secondary education educator; b. Chambersburg, Pa., Nov. 27, 1947; d. Merle Abram and Mary Susan (Meyers) Frey; m. Kenneth Eugene Good, June 20, 1970; 1 child, Amy Elizabeth. BS in Math., Elizabethtown Coll., 1969. Cert. tchr., Pa. Math. tchr. grade 7 Ctrl. Jr. High, Chambersburg, Pa., 1969-70; math. tchr. grade 8 Garden Spot Middle Sch., New Holland, Pa., 1970—2003. Mem. NEA, Pa. State Edn. Assn., Nat. Coun. Tchrs. Math., Ea. Lancaster County Edn. Assn. Avocations: bridge, needlework, watching ice hockey, reading, spectator sports. Home: 159 Skyline Dr New Holland PA 17557-9353 Office: Garden Spot Middle Sch PO Box 609 669 E Main St New Holland PA 17557-1409

GOOD, LINDA LOU, elementary education educator; b. Zanesville, Ohio, May 30, 1941; d. John Robert and Alice Laura (Fulkerson) Moore; m. Larry Alvin Good, Jan. 11, 1964; children: Jason (dec.) Alicia and Tricia (twins), Amy Jo. BS in Elem. Edn., Ohio U., 1964. Tchr. West Muskingum Sch. Dist., 1962-64; 1st grade tchr. Bellevue, Ohio, 1964-68; 2nd grade tchr. Zanesville Sch. Sys., 1970—, head tchr., 1981—89. Head tchr. Munson Sch., Zanesville. Co-chmn. Zane Trace Commemoration; pres. Munson-Garfield Schs. PTA; mem. Trinity Presbyn. Ch. Scholar Jennings scholar, 1997—98. Mem. NEA, Ohio Edn. Assn., Zanesville Edn. Assn., Ea. Ohio Tchrs. Assn. Presbyterian.

GOOD, MARTHA GAIL, educational administrator; b. Great Bend, Kans., Dec. 12, 1943; d. John F. and Keeta E. (Strong) Stoskopf; m. Jack R. Good, Aug. 23, 1965; children: Tereasa D., Catherine D. BS in Elem. Edn. magna cum laude, Troy State U., 1977; M in Adminstrn., Okla. U., 1990. Cert. adminstrn., tchr., Kans., Okla. Airline stewardess Am. Airlines, Nashville, 1963-65; sec. Am. Life Inst., Lexington, Ky., 1965-67; registrar Boston U., Bremerhaven, Germany, 1977-80; tchr. Nativity Blessed Virgin Mary, Biloxi, Miss., 1980-83, Truman & Dunbar Elem. Sch., Oklahoma City, 1983-89; adminstrv. intern Eugene Field Elem. Sch., Oklahoma City, 1989-90; administr. Danforth Prin. Preparation Program, 1988-89; adminstr. Westwood Elem. Sch., Junction City, Kans., 1990-92, Auburn Elem. Sch., Auburn-Washburn Sch. Dist., Topeka, Kans., 1992-95. Mem. Effective Schs. Cadre with Unified Sch. Dist. 437, Topeka, 1994-95. Presented at Nat. Conv. of Am. Assn. Sch. Adminstrs., 1994, United Sch. Adminstrs. Conf., 1994. Mem. United Sch. Adminstrs., Pi Beta Phi, Phi Delta Kappa, Delta Kappa Gamma. Avocations: traveling, sewing, cooking. Office: Auburn Elem Sch PO Box 9 810 Commercial St Auburn KS 66402-9346

GOOD, MARY MARTHA, special education educator; b. Garden City, Kans., Dec. 14, 1954; d. Robert E. and Mary U. (Gerber) Schreiber; m. W. Kyle Good, June 17, 1988; children: Meredith R., Milton R. BSE, Pittsburg State U., 1978; M in Ednl. Psychology, Wichita State U., 1994. Sales mgr. Schreiber Motors, Inc., Garden City, 1978-85, Western Lease Svcs. Inc., Garden City, 1985-88; spl. edn. tchr. Unified Sch. Dist. # 490, El Dorado, Kans., 1989—; coord. Towanda Elem. Sch., 1998—2000, Jefferson Elem Sch., El Dorado, 2000—. Mem. Leadership Kans., 1985—; bd. dirs. Leadership Butler, 1996—. Named Outstanding Young Kansan Kansas Jaycees 1985. Mem. NEA, Am. Coun. of Learning Disabilities, Kans. Edn. Assn. Republican. Roman Catholic. Avocations: walking, cross-stitch. Home: PO Box 1243 El Dorado KS 67042-1243

GOOD, STEPHEN HANSCOM, academic administrator; b. Columbus, Nebr., July 19, 1942; s. William Stanley and Cleora Eleanor (Hanscom) G.; m. Judith Ann Schroetlin, Sept. 1, 1963; children: Jennifer, Catherine, William. BA with distinction, Nebr. Wesleyan U., 1964; MA, U. Pitts., 1965, PhD, 1972. English instr. U. Nebr., Lincoln, 1966-68; prof., chmn. dept. English, Mt. St. Mary's Coll., Emmitsburg, Md., 1968-79; v.p. for acad. affairs Westmar Coll., LeMars, Iowa, 1979-83, Drury U., Springfield, Mo., 1983—. Cons. Coun. Ind. Colls. Nat. Cons. Network, Washington, 1980—. Editor and introduction: The Virgin Unmask'e, 1975, A Treatise of the Hypochondriack and Hysterick Diseases, 1976, Free Thoughts on Religon, 1988. Mem. adminstrv. lay bd. Wesley United Meth. Ch., Springfield, 1983-88; mem. adv. bd. S.W. Mo. Assn. Talented and Gifted, Springfield, 1983-88; mem. Springfield Commn. on Excellence in Edn., 1983-85; pres. Ozarks Sci. and Engring. Fair Found., 1990-94; pres. coun. fin. and adminstrn. Mo. West Conf., United Meth. Ch., 1992-96, mem. gen. bd. for higher edn. and ministry, 1996—; bd. dirs. Sister Cities Assn., 1987-95, treas., 1991-95; bd. dirs. Sta. KOZK Pub. TV, 1991-95. Recipient Dean's award Coun. Ind. Colls., 1994. Mem. Am. Conf. Acd. Deans, Am. Assn. Higher Edn., Am. Soc. for 18th Century Studies (pres. Eastern Ctrl. Conf. 1976-77), Assn. N.W. Am. Colls. (v.p. coord. coun. 1999—), Higher Learning Commn. N.C. Assn. (cons./evaluator 1990—, mem. instnl. actions coun. 2003—). Home: 1134 W Highpoint St Springfield MO 65810-2522 Office: Drury U 900 N Benton Ave Springfield MO 65802-3712 E-mail: sgood@drury.edu.

GOODAKER, DIANNE MCCRYSTAL, language educator; b. Harrodsburg, Ky., Jan. 2, 1948; d. Garnett A. and Lois M. (Gibson) McCrystal; m. Gary R. Goodaker, June 14, 1969; children: Thomas A., Ann M. BA, McNeese State U., 1983, MEd, 1988; postgrad., 1996. Cert. tchr. English. Tchr. English Washington-Marion H.S., Lake Charles, La., 1984-89, A.M. Barbe H.S., Lake Charles, 1989—. Humanities tchr. Gov.'s Program for Gifted Children, Lake Charles, 1991—; cons. McNeese Writing Project, Lake Charles, 1990—. Mem. NEA, Nat. Assn. Secondary Sch. Prins., Nat. Coun. Tchrs. English, Calcasieu Assn. Educators, Phi Delta Kappa. Democrat. Roman Catholic. Home: 516 Central Pky Lake Charles LA 70605-6236 Office: A M Barbe H S 2200 W Mcneese St Lake Charles LA 70605-4114

GOODART, NAN L. lawyer, educator; b. San Francisco, Apr. 4, 1938; BA, San Jose State U., 1959, MA, 1965; JD, U. of the Pacific, 1980. Bar: Calif. 1980, U.S. Dist. Ct. (ea. dist.) Calif. 1981. Tchr. Eastside Union High Sch., San Jose, Calif., 1960-65; counselor San Jose City Coll., 1965-75; atty. Sacramento, 1981—. Speaker numerous seminars throughout no. Calif. and other western states, 1988—. Author: Who Will It Hurt When I Die? A Primer on the Living Trust, 1992 (Nat. Mature Media award 1993), The Truth About Living Trusts, 1995 (Nat. Mature Media award 1996). Judge pro tem Sacramento County Small Claims Ct., 1988-96; instr. continuing edn. of bar Am.'s Legal Ctr., Sacramento, 1992—. Mem. Nat. Acad. Elder Law Attys., Calif. State Bar Assn., Sacramento County Bar Assn. Office: 7230 S Land Park Dr Ste 121 Sacramento CA 95831-3658

GOODBERRY, DIANE JEAN (DIANE OBERKIRCHER), mathematics educator, tax accountant; b. Buffalo, June 24, 1950; d. Ralph Arthur and Muriel Carol (Glaeser) O.; m. Lawrence D. Goodberry, Sr. BS in Math. Edn., State Univ. Coll., Brockport, N.Y., 1972, MS in Ednl. Adminstrn., 1974; grad., Nat.Tax Tng. Sch., Monsey, N.Y., 2000. Cert. in secondary math. edn., N.Y. Uni-Pay clk. Marine Midland Bank, Buffalo, 1968-72; asst. registrar State Univ. Coll., Brockport, 1972-74; home instrn. tutor Clarence Ctrl. Sr. H.S., Sweet Home Sr. H.S., NY, 1974-75; part-time inst. Erie C.C., Buffalo, 1975-86; instr. math. Ednl. Testing Methods, Buffalo, 1984-90, Buffalo Pub. Sch. System, 1974—. Mem. curriculum devel. com. Buffalo Pub. Schs., 1988, 92—, yearbook advisor 1994—, math. intervention coord., 2002—; cooperating tchr. BRIET-U. Buffalo, 1990-96; owner Taxes by Diane; CEO, Larry's GrassRoots Landscaping Inc.; cons. Nat. Tax Tng. Sch., 1999—; AIS coord., Buffalo Pub. Sch. Sys., 2002—. Vol., World Univ. Games, Buffalo, 1993. Mem. AAUW, Nat. Assn. of Female Execs., Women Tchrs. Assn. (bd. dirs., v.p. 1993-94, pres. 1994-96, rec. sec. 1996-98, treas. 1998), Assn. Math. Tchrs. N.Y. State (conf. spkr.), Theodore Roosevelt Rough Riders, Nat. Coun. Math. (conf. spkr.), Assn. Curriculum Devel. and Supervision (Top 2000 scholar of 20th Century award, named one of 2000 Outstanding Scholars of 20th Century Winner in Math). Republican. Methodist. Avocations: crafts, reading, travel, sports. Home: 10644 Crump Rd Holland NY 14080-9303 Office: South Park HS 150 Southside Pkwy Buffalo NY 14220-1552

GOODE, ANNE, early childhood education administrator; b. Whitakers, N.C., Jan. 7, 1951; d. Buddy and Pauline (Reynolds) Johnson; m. Robert E. Goode, Oct. 7, 1977; children: Earl, Hassan, Robert II, Gavin. BS, Marymount Manhattan Coll., N.Y.C., 1976; MS in Elem. Edn., Dowling Coll., 1989. Dir. Econ. Opportunity Coun. Suffolk, Patchogue, N.Y., 1977-85; dep. dir. L.I. Head Start Child Devel. Svcs., Patchogue, 1986-90; speech therapist L.I. Group Homes, Center Moricher, N.Y., 1988-89; exec. dir. Takoma Park (Md.) Child Devel., 1990—. Cons. interpretation of fed. regulations regarding sch. attendance United Planning Ordn., Washington, 1989-90; rev. panelist Agy. for Children, Youth and Families, HHS, Washington, 1989-92; mem. Working Parents Assn. Program, Rockville, Md., 1991—; participant, presenter profl. confs. Chairperson Freedom Fund, NAACP, Suffolk County, N.Y., 1985-87; pres. Suffolk County Head Start Dirs., 1978-81; active Suffolk County coun. Girl Scouts U.S. Recipient Outstanding Women award Suffolk County coun. Girl Scouts U.S., 1987. Mem. ASCD, NAFE, Nat. Assn. Child Care Profls., Orgn. for Child Care Dirs., Nat. Assn. for Edn. of Young Children. Baptist. Avocations: reading, swimming, dancing. Office: Takoma Park Child Devel 310 Tulip Ave Takoma Park MD 20912-4339

GOODE, B. ERICH, sociologist, educator, retired criminologist; b. Austin, Tex., Sept. 21, 1938; s. William Josiah and Josephine Mary (Cannizzo) Goode; m. Alice N. Neufeld, Dec. 23, 1968 (div.); m. Barbara S. Weinstein, Mar. 23, 1984; children: Sarah Rachel, Lawrence Daniel. BA, Oberlin Coll., 1960; PhD, Columbia U., 1966. Asst. prof. NYU, N.Y.C., 1965-67; asst. prof. sociology SUNY, Stony Brook, 1967-70, assoc. prof., 1970-81, prof., 1981-2000; vis. prof. U. Md., College Park, 2000—03, ret., 2003. Vis. assoc. prof. U. N.C., Chapel Hill, 1977—2003; Lady Davis vis. prof. Hebrew U., Jerusalem, 1993. Author: (book) The Marijuana Smokers, 1970, Drugs in American Society, 1972, 1999, Deviant Behavior, 1978, 2001, Paranormal Beliefs, 2000, Deviance in Everyday Life, 2002. Recipient Chancellors award for excellence in tchg., SUNY, 1997; grantee, NIMH, 1968; Guggenheim fellow, 1975—76. Office: U Md Dept Criminal and Criminal Justice Le Frak Hall College Park MD 20742 E-mail: egoode2001@comcast.net.

GOODE, BOBBY CLAUDE, retired secondary education educator, writer; b. Celeste, Tex., Dec. 10, 1940; s. Claude Elmer and Clarice Edna G.; m. Jean Helen Ames, June 9, 1963; children: James Lonnie, Joel Dietrich, John Shalom. BS, MIT, 1963; MA, Andover Newton Sem., Newton Centre, Mass., 1968; MS, Rensselaer Poly. Inst., 1972. Cert. tchr. sci. and math. Tchr. math. Lawrence D. Bell High Sch., Hurst, Tex., 1966-67; tchr. physics and chemistry Grapevine (Tex.) High Sch., 1967-70; tchr. advanced physics, advanced chemistry, advanced biology South Plainfield (N.J.) High Sch., 1970-96, ret., 1996. Sci. tchr. Princeton (N.J.) U., 1983, Disting. Secondary Sch. Tchg. finalist, 1983. Author: (booklets) Lap Physics, 1973, Stars, Planets, People, 1980, Atoms and Molecules, 1980, Physics Problem Solutions, 1980. Mem. Civil Rights Commn., Piscataway, N.J., 1977, Sr. Citizens Housing Com., Piscataway, 1975; ch. sch. tchr. First Bapt. Ch. of New Market, 1970-96. Named Outstanding Sci. Tchr., Sigma Xi, 1986. Mem. NEA, N.J. Edn. Assn., Am. Assn. Physics Tchrs., Nat. Sci. Tchrs. Assn. (recipient Exemplary Secondary Sci. Tchr. Nat. award 1980). Democrat. Avocations: family, travel, writing, sports. Home: 129 Stonegate S Boerne TX 78006-3411 E-mail: bobgoode@gvtc.com.

GOODE, JAMES CLEVELAND, educational administrator; b. McKinney, Tex., Aug. 21, 1944; s. James Haskell and Helen Marie (Russell) G.; m. Rhonda Kay Balch, July 2, 1977; children: Corey, Robbie. AS in Biology, Cooke County Jr. Coll., 1967; BS in Biology, East Tex. State U., 1970, MSc in Biology, 1979, MEd in Ednl. Adminstrn., 1985. Cert. tchr., Tex. Varsity coach Honey Grove (Tex.) Ind. Sch. Dist., 1969-70, Malakoff (Tex.) Ind. Sch. Dist., 1970-72, Terrell (Tex.) Ind. Sch. Dist., 1972-73, Lake Worth Ind. Sch. Dist., Ft. Worth, 1973-75; dir. driver edn. McKinney (Tex.) Job Corps, 1975-77; supervising tchr. driver edn. Region X Edn. Svc. Ctr., Richardson, Tex., 1977-89; area supr. driver edn. Region IV Edn. Svc. Ctr., Houston, 1989—. Contbg. author Drive Right Text Book; contbr. articles to profl. jours. Mem. Tex. Driver and Traffic Safety Assn. (regional pres. 1985-86, regional rep. 1986-87, state bd. dirs. 1987-93, pres. 1994-95, Tchr. of Yr. award 1987), Am. Driver and Traffic Safety Assn. Avocations: guitar, physical fitness. Home: 3826 Shadycreek Dr Garland TX 75042-4746 Office: Region IV Edn Svc Ctr 7145 Tidwell Rd Houston TX 77016-4827

GOODE, JANET WEISS, elementary school educator; b. Chattanooga, Tenn., Sept. 3, 1935; d. Albert H. and Dorothy E. (Crandall) Weiss; m. Gene G. Goode, June 11, 1961; children: Jennifer E., Amy V. BS in Biology, Carson-Newman Coll., 1957; MA in Botany, Vanderbilt U., 1959; MEd, Lynchburg Coll., 1980. Cert. postgrad. profl. tchr., Va. Instr. gen. biology, botany, zoology, animal ecology Carson-Newman Coll., Tenn., 1959-61; tchr. biology, chemistry Salem Acad., Winston-Salem, N.C., 1961-64; tchr. chemistry Wade Hampton High Sch., Greenville, S.C., 1964-65; tchr. sci. Va. Treatment Ctr. for Children, Richmond, 1966; tchr. biology Quantico (Va.) H.S., 1969-70; pvt. tutor Madison Heights, Va., 1980-85, James River Day Sch. and Seven Hills Sch., Lynchburg, Va., 1980-85; reading specialist Title I reading program Monelison Mid. Sch., Madison Heights, 1985-93; reading specialist Amherst County Adult Basic Edn. Program, 1992-94, 95—; reading specialist Title I reading and Reading Recovery Pleasant View Elem. Sch., Monroe, Va., 1993-96, Madison Heights (Va.) Elem. Sch., 1996—. Vis. instr. U. Chattanooga, summer 1960; mem. learning disabilities del. to Russia and Lithuania, Citizen Amb. Program, 1993; mem. mentor tchr. program Amherst County Pub. Schs., 1999-2000. Editor: (newsletter) Topics for Title I; author: Can You Read a Baseball Card?; co-author: Transitional Intervention Program. Sponsor sch. lit. mag. Monelison Mid. Sch., Pleasant View Elem. Sch.; organist, newsletter editor for Ptnr. Ch. com. First Unitarian Ch.; mem. Friends of Libr., Madison Heights Br. Libr., helper ann. book sale. Recipient Reading Tchr. of the Year Piedmont Va. Area Reading Coun., 1993-94. Mem. NEA, Nat. Coun. Tchrs. of English, Va. Edn. Assn., Amherst Edn. Assn., Internat. Dyslexia Assn., Piedmont Area Reading Coun. (past newletter editor, past treas.), Va. State Reading Assn., Internat. Reading Assn., Lynchburg Stamp Club. E-mail: jwgoode@worldnet.att.net.

GOODE, PAUL, psychologist, educator, consultant; b. Bklyn., Nov. 14, 1937; s. Arthur and Bertha (Rose) G.; m. Judith Granich, June 22, 1960; children: Lawrence J., Andrew P., Joshua S. BA in Psychology, Bklyn. Coll., 1959; MA in Sch. Psychology (rsch. asst.), Syracuse U., 1962; EdD in Sch. Psychology (doctoral fellow), Temple U., 1972. Unemployment ins. claims examiner N.Y. State Employment Svc., Cortland, 1961-62; sch. psychologist Steuben County Bd. Coop. Ednl. Svcs., Bath, N.Y., 1962-66, Camden (N.J.) Bd. Edn., 1966-67, Delaware County Bd. Sch. Dirs., Media, Pa., 1967-68, intern psychologist, 1968-69; sch. psychologist specialist Phila. Non-Pub. Elem. Schs., 1969-70; assocs. dir. clin. ednl. svcs. project King of Prussia (Pa.) Intermediate Unit #23, 1970-73; coord. suburban unit Nat. Regional Resource Ctr. of Pa., King of Prussia, 1971-74, assoc. dir., 1974-75; dir. Pa. Area Learning Resources Ctr., Doylestown, 1975-77; dir. IEP devel. program Bucks County (Pa.) Intermediate Unit #22, Doylestown, 1977-79, coord. fed. programs in spl. edn., 1979-81, acting dir. spl. edn., 1980-81, asst. exec. dir., dir. spl. edn., 1981-93; pvt. practice Melrose Park, Pa., 1993—. Vis. prof. U. de Antioquia, Colombia, 1964-65; part-time instr. Corning (N.Y.) C.C., 1965-66, Cabrini Coll., Radnor, Pa., 1972; instr. diagnosis of ednl. disabilities Pa. State U., Ogontz, 1972-84; adj. prof. faculty Temple U., Phila., 1988—. Assoc. editor : Archives, newsletter Nat. Regional Resource Ctr. Pa., 1970—72. Treas. Cub Scout Pack 190, 1970—80; mgr. Old York Rd. Little League, 1970—80. Recipient Alumni award Temple U., 1980. Fellow Pa. Psychol. Assn. (editor divsn. newsletter 1975-77, pres. sch. psychology divsn. 1978-79, pres. 1981-82); mem. APA (divsn. 16), Coun. Exceptional Children, Coun. Orgn. Edn. (pres. 1989-90), Pa. Assn. Sch. Adminstrs., Pa. Assn. Pupil Pers. Adminstrs., Phi Delta Kappa. Home and Office: 7610 Montgomery Ave Elkins Park PA 19027-2901 E-mail: pgoode3@comcast.net.

GOODEN, BENNY L. school system administrator; Supt. Ft. Smith (Ark.) Pub. Schs. State finalist Nat. Supt. Yr. award, 1993; recipient Phoebe Apperson Hearst Outstanding Educator award Nat. PTA, 1999. Office: Ft Smith Pub Schs 3205 Jenny Lind Rd Fort Smith AR 72901-7101

GOODENBERGER, MARY ELLEN, English educator; b. Trenton, Nebr., Aug. 4, 1923; d. George Andrew and Ida May (Stewart) Marshall; m. Marvin Eugene Goodenberger, Aug. 9, 1947; children: Daniel Marvin, Beverly Jane, Marshall Eric. BSEd, U. Nebr., 1947, MEd, 1963, PhD, 1976. Elem. tchr. Culbertson (Nebr.) Pub. Schs., 1940-41, 43-44; prin., tchr. English, libr. Trenton (Nebr.) Pub. Sch., 1957-58, 60-66; cons. in English Nebr. Dept. Edn., Lincoln, 1968-72; K-12 dir. instrn. McCook (Nebr.) Pub. Schs., 1973-80; coll. instr. U. Nebr. at Kearney, Lincoln, 1967-68, 80-85; county supt. Hitchcock County Schs., Trenton, 1984-90. Author: (books) Ida May's Real People, 1985, Of Mice and Birds, 1986, Aedith's Fables, 1987, (curriculum) Breakthrough in English, I, II, III, 1969-71. County chair Rep. Party, Red Willow County, 1950-54; Sunday sch. tchr. Youth Fellowship, leader, choir mem. local ch., McCook, Trenton, 1950-66; 4-H leader, Trenton, 1956-66; mem. Women's Fellowship, Trenton, 1980-90, pres. 1988-90. Regents scholar U. Nebr., Lincoln, 1940, 42, grad. study scholar Delta Kappa Gamma, Nebr., 1968, Disting. Educator award U. Nebr. at Omaha, 1980. Mem. Nebr. State Edn. Assn. (pres.-elect McCook and Holdrege 1966), Nebr. Coun. Tchrs. of English (pres. 1973), Nebr. Assn. for Supervision and Curriculum Devel. (bd. dirs. 1973-78), Nebr. Schoolmasters Club (pres. 1977), Delta Kappa Gamma (various offices), Phi Beta Kappa, Pi Lambda Theta. Methodist. Home: HC 2 Box 123 Trenton NE 69044-9744

GOODHUE, PETER AMES, obstetrician and gynecologist, educator; b. Ft. Fairfield, Maine, Feb. 26, 1931; s. Lawrence and Zylpha (Ames) G.; m. Edith Ann Helfenstein, June 21, 1958; children: Lisa Grace, Scott Ames. BA, Amherst Coll., 1954; MD, U. Vt., 1958. Diplomate Am. Bd. Ob-Gyn. Intern Bellevue Hosp., N.Y.C., 1958-59; resident Yale-New Haven Med. Ctr., 1959-62; practice medicine specializing in ob-gyn. Stamford, Conn., 1964—. Assoc. clin. prof. ob-gyn. N.Y. Med. Coll., 1984—98; asst. clin. prof. ob-gyn. Columbia Presbyn. Hosp., 1999—. Contbr. articles to profl. jours. Served to capt. USAF, 1962-64. Recipient Carbee prize U. Vt., 1958. Fellow ACOG (chmn. Conn. sect. 1976, pres. Conn. sect. 1973-76), ACS, Am. Fertility Soc., Am. Soc. for Colposcopy and Cervical Pathology, Am. Assn. Gynecologic Laproscopists; mem. Conn. Med. Soc., Conn. Soc. Am. Bd. Obstetricians and Gynecologists (pres. 1973-76), Fairfield County Med. Soc., Fairfield County Gynecol. and Obstet. Soc., Stamford Med. Soc. (pres. 1989-90). Republican. Episcopalian. Office: Stamford Gynecology PC 70 Mill River St Stamford CT 06902-3725

GOODINE, ISAAC THOMAS, development executive, educator; b. Hazeldean, N.B., Can., Apr. 11, 1932; s. Lewis Ambrose and Beatrice Ann (Babineau) G.; m. Sandra Jean Campbell, May 3, 1958 (div. 1981); children: Darlene Lynn, Sharon Ann, Catherine Elizabeth; m. Gloria Ann Whiting, Aug. 3, 1981; 1 child, Claudia Ann. BS, Mt. Allison U., Sackville, N.B., 1956, Cert. in Engring., 1957, BE, 1960. Instr. N.B. Inst. Tech., Moncton, 1961-65, vice prin., 1965-66, prin., 1966-70, Zambia Inst. Tech., Kitwe, 1970-72; dep. dir. Dept. Tech. Edn. and Vocat. Tng., Lusaka, Zambia, 1972-73; dir., 1973-74; policy analyst N.B. Community Coll., Fredericton, 1974-75; dir. Kenya Tech. Tch's Coll., Nairobi, 1975-78; sr. tech. educator The World Bank, Washington, 1978-88; sr. devel. officer Can. Internat. Devel. Agy., 1988-91; dir. tech. edn. Colombo Plan Staff Coll., Manila, 1991-92; first sec. Can. High Commn., Barbados, 1992-94; mng. dir. Knowledge Devel. Inst., Barbados, 1994—96. Sec. Nat. Com. on Physics for Insts. Tech. in Can., 1955-58, Coordinating Com. on Tech. Tchr. Edn. for Ea. Africa, Nairobi, 1975-78; co-chmn. Working Party on Coun. for Higher Edn. in Zambia, Lusaka, 1973-74; bd. dirs. Greater Moncton Community Chest, 1968-69, Moncton Family YMCA, 1966-69, Colombo Plan Staff Coll. for Technician Edn., 1988-90. Mem. Internat. Vocat. Edn. and Tng. Assn., Am. Vocat. Assn., Can. Vocat. Assn., Royal Can. Armoured Corps Assn. Mem. United Ch. Lodge: Rotary (Moncton, Kitwe, Nairobi clubs). Address: 902, 27 Henderosn Ave Ottawa ON Canada K1N 7P3 E-mail: itgoodine@rogers.com.

GOODLAD, JOHN INKSTER, education educator, writer; b. North Vancouver, B.C., Can., 1920; s. William James and Mary Goodlad; m. Evalene M. Pearson, Aug. 23, 1945; children: Stephen John, Mary Paula. Teaching certificate, Vancouver Normal Sch., 1939; BA, U. B.C., 1945, MA, 1946; PhD, U. Chgo., 1949; DPS (hon.), Brigham Young U., 1995; LHD (hon.), Nat. Coll. Edn., 1967, U. Louisville, 1968, So. Ill. U., 1982, Bank Street Coll. Edn., 1984, Niagara U., 1989, SUNY Coll. Brockport, 1991, Miami U., 1991, Linfield Coll., 1993, W.Va. U., 1998; LLD (hon.), Kent State U., 1974, Pepperdine U., 1976, Simon Fraser U., 1983, U. Man., 1992; DEd (hon.), Eastern Mich. U., 1982, U. Victoria, 1998; LittD (hon.), Montclair State U., 1992; PedD (hon.), Doane Coll., 1995; LHD (hon.), U. Nebr., Lincoln, 1999, U. So. Maine, 2001. Tchr. Surrey Schs., B.C., 1939-41, prin., 1941-42; dir. edn. Provincial Sch. For Boys, B.C., 1942-46; cons. curriculum Atlanta Area Tchr. Edn. Service, 1947-49; assoc. prof. Emory U., 1949-50; prof., dir. div. tchr. edn. Agnes Scott Coll. and Emory U., 1950-56; prof., dir. U. Chgo. Center Tchr. Edn., 1956-60; prof., dir. Univ. Elem. Sch. UCLA, 1960-85, dean Grad. Sch. Edn., 1967-83; prof. U. Wash., Seattle, 1985-91; prof. emeritus, 1991—; dir. Ctr. for Ednl. Renewal U. Wash., Seattle, 1986-2000; pres. Inst. for Ednl. Inquiry, Seattle, 1992—. Chmn. Coun. on Coop. Tchr. Edn., Am. Coun. Edn., 1959-62; dir. rsch. Inst. for Devel. of Ednl. Activities, 1966-82; mem. governing bd. UNESCO Inst. for Edn., 1971-79. Author: (with others) The Elementary School, 1956, Educational Leadership and the Elementary School Principal, 1956, (with Robert H. Anderson) The Nongraded Elementary School, 1959, rev. edit., 1963, reprinted, 1987, (with others) Computers and Information Systems in Education, 1966, Looking Behind the Classroom Door, 1970, rev. edit., 1974, Toward a Mankind School, 1974, The Conventional and the Alternative in Education, 1975, Curriculum Inquiry: The Study of Curriculum Practice, 1979, Planning and Organizing for Teaching, 1963, School Curriculum Reform, 1964, The Changing School Curriculum, 1966, School, Curriculum and the Individual, 1966, The Dynamics of Educational Change, 1975, Facing the Future, 1976, What Schools Are For, 1979, A Place Called School, 1983, Teachers for Our Nation's Schools, 1990, Educational Renewal: Better Teachers, Better Schools, 1994, In Praise of Education, 1997; author, editor: The Changing American School, 1966, (with Harold S. Shane) The Elementary School in the United States, 1973, (with M. Frances Klein and Jerrold M. Novotney) Early Schooling in the United States, 1973, (with Norma Feshback and Alvima Lombard) Early Schooling in England and Israel, 1973, (with Gary Fenstermacher) Individual Differences and the Common Curriculum, 1983, The Ecology of School Renewal, 1987, (with Kenneth A. Sirotnik) School-University Partnerships in Action, 1988, (with Pamela Keating) Access to Knowledge, 1990, (with others) The Moral Dimensions of Teaching, 1990, Places Where Teachers Are Taught, 1990, (with Thomas C. Lovitt) Integrating General and Special Education, 1992, (with Timothy J. McMannon) The Public Purpose of Education and Schooling, 1997, (with Roger Soder and Timothy J. McMannon) Developing Democratic Character in the Young, 2001, (with Timothy J. Mannon) The Teaching Career; mem. bd. editors Sch. Rev, 1956-58, Jour. Tchr. Edn, 1958-60; contbg. editor: Progressive Edn, 1955-58; mem. editorial adv. bd. Child's World, 1952-80; chmn. editorial adv. bd. New Standard Ency, 1953— ; chmn. ednl. adv. bd. Ency. Brit. Ednl. Corp, 1966-69; contbr. chpts. to books, articles to profl. jours. Recipient Disting. Svc. medal Tchrs. Coll., Columbia U., 1983, Outstanding Book award Am. Ednl. Rsch. Assn., 1985, Disting. Contbns. to Ednl. Rsch. award 1993; named Faculty Rsch. Lectr. U. Wash., 1987-88, faculty of High Distinction, UCLA, 1987; Edward C. Pomeroy award, Amer. Assn. of Coll. for Teacher Edn., 1995, Disting. Svc. award Coun. Chief State Sch. Officials, 1997, Harold W. McGraw, Jr. Prize in Edn., 1999, Edn. Commn. State James Bryant Conant award, 2000, Brock Internat. prize in edn., 2002, N.Y. Acad. of Edn. medal, 2003. Fellow Internat. Inst. Arts and Letters; mem. Nat. Acad. Edn. (charter; sec.-treas.), Am. Ednl. Rsch. Assn. (past pres., award for Disting. Contbns. to Ednl. Rsch. 1993), Nat. Soc. Coll. Tchrs. Edn. (past pres.), Nat. Soc. for Study of Edn. (dir.), Am. Assn. Colls. for Tchr. Edn. (pres. 1989-90). Office: U Wash Coll Edn PO Box 353600 Seattle WA 98195-3600

GOODMAN, ELLEN, elementary education educator; b. Starkville, Miss., Dec. 27, 1958; d. Arthur Louis Jr. and Grace W. (Henry) G. BS, Miss. State U., 1981, MEd, 1982, 93. Cert. nursery, kindergarten, K-3 elem. tchr., elem. adminstr., Miss. Tchr. kindergarten and remedial reading Magnolia Heights Sch., Senatobia, Miss., 1982-83; tchr. Aiken Village Presch., Mississippi State, Miss., 1983-84, dir., 1984-86; tchr. kindergarten Starkville Sch. Dist., 1986—. Recipient Excellence in Tchg. award Miss. Power Found., 1990, Tchr. of Month award Starkville Exch. Club, 1993, Tchr. of Yr. award

Starkville Sch. Dist., 1993. Mem. NAESP, Miss. Early Childhood Assn. (local pres. 1991-92), Pilot Club (pres. 1989-90), Phi Delta Kappa (sec. 1992-94, Outstanding Pub. Sch. Tchr. award 1989), Delta Kappa Gamma (sec. 1994-95, v.p. 1995-97, pres. 1998—). Presbyterian. Avocations: college baseball fan, flutist. Home: 2103 Douglas MacArthur Dr Starkville MS 39759 Office: Sudduth Elem Sch 101 Greenfield St Starkville MS 39759-2222 E-mail: egoo1227@aol.com.

GOODMAN, ERIK DAVID, engineering educator; b. Palo Alto, Calif., Feb. 14, 1944; s. Harold Orbeck and Shirley Mae (Lillie) G.; m. Denise Rowand Dyktor, Aug. 10, 1968 (div. 1976); m. Cheryl Diane Barris, Aug. 27, 1978; 1 child, David Richard. BS in Math., Mich. State U., 1966, MS in Systems Sci., 1968; PhD in Computer Communication Sci., U. Mich., 1972; Hon. Doctorate, Dneprodzerzhinsk State Tech U., Ukraine, 1996. Asst. prof. elec. engring. Mich. State U., East Lansing, 1972-77, assoc. prof. elec. engring., 1977-84, dir. case ctr. for computer aided engring. and mfg., 1983—2002, prof. elec. engring., dir., 1984—, prof. mech. engring., 1992—. Dir. Mich. State U. Mfg. Rsch. Consortium, 1993—; v.p. Red Cedar Tech., Inc., East Lansing, Mich., 1999-; pres. Tech. Gateway, Inc., East Lansing; cons. Chinese Computer Comms., Inc., Lansing, 1988—; gen. chair First Internat. Conf. on Evolutionary Computation and its Applications, Moscow, 1996, Seventh Internat Conf. on Genetic Algorithms, 1997, Genetic and Evolutionary Computation Conf., 2001; gen. co-chmn. Internat. Computer Graphics Conf., Detroit, 1986; adv. prof. Tongji U., Shanghai, China, 2002-. Author: (with others) SYSKIT: Linear Systems Toolkit, 1986; patentee in field. Academician, Internat. Informatization Acad. (Russia), 1993—. Mem. AIAA (chair rsch. and future dirs., subcom. CAD/CAM tech. com. 1987-89, Outstanding Svc. 1990), IEEE Computer Soc., Soc. Mfg. Engrs., Aircraft Owners and Pilots Assn., Acad. Engring. Scis. Ukraine, Internat. Soc. for Genetic and Evolutionary Computation (exec. com. 2001—, chair 2001-). Avocations: musician, tennis, studying chinese. Office: Mich State U Dept Elec & Computer Engring 2308M Engineering Bldg East Lansing MI 48824 E-mail: goodman@egr.msu.edu., e.goodman@redcedartech.com.

GOODMAN, JOSEPH WILFRED, electrical engineering educator; b. Boston, Feb. 8, 1936; s. Joseph and Doris (Ryan) G.; m. Hon Mai Lam, Dec. 5, 1962; 1 dau., Michele Ann. BA, Harvard U., 1958; MS in E.E., Stanford U., 1960, PhD, 1963; DSc (hon.), U. Ala., 1996. Postdoctoral fellow Norwegian Def. Rsch. Establishment, Oslo, 1962-63; rsch. assoc. Stanford U., 1963-67, asst. prof., 1967-69, assoc. prof., 1969-72, prof. elec. engring., 1972-99; vis. prof. Univ. Paris XI, Orsay, France, 1973-74; dir. Info. Sys. Lab. Elec. Engring. Stanford U., 1981-83, chmn. dept. of elec. engring., 1988-96, William E. Ayer prof. elec. engring., 1988-99, sr. assoc. dean engring., 1996-98, acting dean engring., 1999, prof. emeritus, 2000—. Cons. to govt. and industry, 1965—; v.p. Internat. Comm. for Optics, 1985-87, pres., 1988-90, past pres., 1991-93. Author: Introduction to Fourier Optics, 1968, 2nd edit. 1996, Statistical Optics, 1985, (with R. Gray) Fourier Transforms: An Introduction for Engineers; editor: International Trends in Optics, 1991; contbr. articles to profl. jours. Recipient F.E. Terman award Am. Soc. Engring. Edn., 1971, Frederic Ives Medal, 1990, Optical Soc. Am., Ester Hoffman Beller award Optical Soc. of Am., 1995. Fellow AAAS, Optical Soc. Am. (dir. 1977-83, editor jour. 1978-83, Max Born award 1983, Frederick Ives award 1990, Esther Hoffman Beller medal 1995, v.p. 1990, pres.-elect 1991, pres. 1992, past pres. 1993), IEEE (edn. medal 1987), Soc. Photo-optical Instrumentation Engrs. (bd. govs. 1979-82, 88-90, Dennis Gabor award 1987), Am. Acad. Arts & Scis.; mem. NAE, Electromagnetics Acad. Home: 570 University Ter Los Altos CA 94022-3523 Office: Stanford U Dept Elec Engring Stanford CA 94305 E-mail: goodman@ee.stanford.edu.

GOODMAN, MARK, journalist, educator; B in Journalism with honors, U. Mo., 1982; JD, Duke U., 1985. Lectr. U. Md. Univ. Coll., College Park, 1987-88; exec. dir. Student Press Law Ctr., Washington, 1985—. Mem. faculty Inst. Study Ednl. Policy, U. Wash., Seattle, 1987; instr. summer journalism workshops Ball State U., Muncie, Ind., 1988, U. Iowa, Iowa City, 1991, 92, 93, 94, Mich. State U., East Lansing, 1991, 93; adj. guest lectr. Sch. Mass Comm., Bowling Green (Ohio) State U., 1990; mem. faculty coll. newspaper advisers seminar Poynter Inst. Media Studies, St. Petersburg, Fla., 1989, 90, 92; media law com. Coll. Media Advisers, Inc.; panelist Danforth Found., 1988, 89, Assn. Edn. in Journalism and Mass Comm., 1987, 88; guest lectr. Sch. Comm. Am. U., Washington, 1989, 90, 94. Contbr. articles to profl. jours. Recipient Golden Quill award Garden State Scholastic Press Assn., 1987, Disting. Svc. award Mich. Interscholastic Press Assn., 1987, Ind. Scholastic Journalism award Ball State U., 1988, Disting. Svc. award So. Interscholastic Press Assn., 1988, Presdl. citations Coll. Media Advisers, Inc., 1987, 88, 89, Disting. Svc. award Fla. C.C. Press Assn., 1989, Knight award, Earl English Scholastic Journalism award Mo. Interscholastic Press Assn./Mo. Journalism Edn. Assn., 1992, Cert. of Merit, Soc. Collegiate Journalists, 1989, Gold Key award Columbia U. Scholastic Press Assn., 1988, Carl Towley award Journalism Edn. Assn., 1992. Mem. Kappa Tau Alpha. Office: Student Press Law Ctr 1815 Fort Myer Dr Ste 900 Arlington VA 22209-1817 E-mail: director@splc.org.

GOODMAN, MICHAEL B(ARRY), communications educator; b. Dallas, July 10, 1949; s. Harold A. and Dora (Einhorn) G.; m. Karen E. Kailenta, June 4, 1977; children: 1 stepchild, Craig Cook, 1 child, John David. BA, U. Tex., 1971; MA, SUNY, Stony Brook, 1972, PhD, 1979. Adj. instr. SUNY, Old Westbury, 1976-79; adj. asst. prof. N.Y. Inst. Tech., N.Y.C., 1976-82, N.Y.U., 1979-81; asst. prof. SUNY, Stony Brook, 1979-81, Northea. U., Boston, 1982-86; prof., dir. MA in Corp. Comm. program Fairleigh Dickinson U., Madison, NJ, 1986—2002; founder, dir. Corp. Comms. Inst., 1999—. Cons. in communications to numerous orgns. in U.S.; conducts seminars and workshops on written communication, 1979—; conf. chmn. Internat. Profl. Communication Conf., Phila., 1993, New Orleans, 1999; lectr. Moscow, 1992, U. Alaska, 1996; founder Ann. Conf. on Corp. Comm., 1988-98. Author: William S. Burroughs: An Annotated Bibliography, 1975, Contemporary Literary Censorship: The Case History of Burroughs Naked Lunch, 1981, Write to the Point: Effective Communication in the Workplace, 1984, William S. Burroughs: A Research Guide, 1990, Corporate Communication: Theory and Practice, 1994, Working in a Global Environment—Understanding, Communicating, and Managing Transnationally, 1995, Corporate Communications for Executives, 1998; contbr. articles and revs. to profl. jours., encys. and lit. mags.; assoc. editor Issues in Corp. Comm., IEEE Transactions on Profl. Comm., 1990-99; editl. bd. mem. N.J. Jour. Comm.; mem. editl. adv. bd. Corp. Comms. An Internat. Jour., 1999—; cons. reader for Coll. English. V.p. Friends Sem. PTA, N.Y.C., 1990-91. Named to Resident Faculty Nat. Faculty Excellence in Teaching English Program, Vassar Coll., 1984. Fellow Royal Soc. Encouragement Arts, Mfrs. & Commerce (London), Soc. Tech. Comm. (assoc.); mem. Profl. Comm. Soc. of IEEE (sr., mem. adminstrv. com., Alfred Goldsmith award 1994), MLA, Nat. Coun. Tchrs. of English, Am. Mgmt. Assn., Assn. for Bus. Comm., Authors Guild, Authors League, Arthur W. Page Soc. Avocations: hiking, skiing, running, cycling. Home: 28 W 38th St Apt 11W New York NY 10018-6287 Office: Fairleigh Dickinson U 285 Madison Ave Madison NJ 07940-1099

GOODMAN, MYRNA MARCIA, school nurse; b. Bklyn., Mar. 5, 1936; d. Louis and Anna R. (Bernowitz) Sheinberg; m. Stanley M. Goodman, June 30, 1957; children: Farrell Jay, Blayne Barrie, Devin Josh, Danica Janine. Diploma, L.I. Coll. Hosp., Bklyn., 1956; B in Elected Studies, Thomas More Coll., 1980; postgrad., Xavier U., 1984-86. Cert. sch. nurse, Ohio. Sch. nurse, supr. health and wellness svcs. L.I. Coll. Hosp., 1956-58; nurse, office mgr. Pediatric Assocs. of Fairfield (Ohio), Inc., 1962-72; nurse Fairfield City Sch. Dist., 1972-89, dir. health svcs., 1989-92, supr. health and wellness svcs., 1992-96, ret., 1996, sch. nurse Kindergarten Ctr., 1995. Sec. Fairfield City Safety Coun., 1987-90; mem. Intervention Team for At-Risk Students, 1987-90, 95-96, Del. to Study Sch. Health, Australia, 1989, Mentor Program at Fairfield West Elem. Sch., 2002-; keynote spkr. Ohio Comprehensive Sch. Health Conf., 1991; conf. spkr. Ohio Assn. Health, Phys. Edn., Recreation and Dance, 1990, Nat. Sch. Bds. Assn., 1993; mem. Butler Behavioral Health Svcs. Bd., 1997-2003, sec.-treas., 2002. Mem. adv. coun. on drug free schs. and cmty. Butler County Mental Health Assn., 1988; mentor Fairfield W. Elem. Sch., 2002; chmn. sch. site com. Am. Heart Assn., 1981—, coord. heart-at-work program, co-pres. Hamilton-Fairfield divsn., 1995, bd. dirs., chmn. employee wellness com., spkr. del. assembly Ohio affiliate, 1992, pres., 1995, mem. adv. com. for county practical nurse program, 1994-95; pres. Fairfield Tempo Club, 1976; com. mem. Fairfield Sister City Program; mem. Modern Music Masters, 1976; mem. adv. coun. Daytime Ctr. for Girls; bd. dirs. Greater Hamilton Safety Coun., 1988; mem. adv. com. Fairfield Pub. Presch.; chmn. adv. com. Fairfield Schs. Food Svc.; co-founder B'nai Tikvah Congregation, 1998, svc. chair, 1999—, mem. ritual and worship com., chair. Recipient Outstanding Svc. award Fairfield Cen. Sch., 1974, 77, 78, 89, Letters of Recognition for Outstanding Svc. to Fairfield Sch. Dist. Supt., 1980, 86, 89, 90, March of Dimes, Am. Lung Assn., 1980, Am. Heart Assn., 1988, 89, 90, Hall of Fame award Am. Heart Assn., 1992, co-recipient Cert. of Appreciation, Am. Heart Assn. Sch. Site Task Force, 1992. Mem. NEA, ASCD, Ohio Edn. Assn., Ohio Assn. Sch. Nurses (conf. speaker 1993), S.W. Ohio Sch. Nurses Assn. (sec. 1987-90), Am. Sch. Health Assn., Nat. Assn. Sch. Nurses, Parents and Tchrs. for Children, Ohio Assn. Secondary Sch. Adminstrs., Nat. Assn. Secondary Sch. Adminstrs., Butler County Ret. Tchrs. Assn., Ohio Ret. Tchrs. Assn. (life). Home: 5180 Suwannee Dr Fairfield OH 45014-2482

GOODMAN, SAM RICHARD, electronics company executive; b. N.Y.C., May 23, 1930; s. Morris and Virginia (Gross) G.; m. Beatrice Bettencourt, Sept. 15, 1957; children: Mark Stuart, Stephen Manuel, Christopher Bettencourt. BBA, CCNY, 1951; MBA, NYU, 1957, PhD, 1968. Chief acct. John C. Valentine Co., N.Y.C., 1957-60; mgr. budgets and analysis Gen. Foods. Corp., White Plains, N.Y., 1960-63; budget dir. Crowell Collier Pub. Co., N.Y.C., 1963-64; v.p., chief fin. officer Nestle Co., Inc., White Plains, 1964; chief fin. officer Aileen, Inc., N.Y.C., 1973-74, Ampex Corp., 1974-76; exec. v.p. fin. and adminstrn. Baker & Taylor Co. div. W.R. Grace Co., N.Y.C., 1976-79, Magnuson Computer Systems, Inc., San Jose, Calif., 1979-81; v.p., chief fin. officer Datamac Computer Systems, Sunnyvale, Calif., 1981; pres. Nutritional Foods Inc., San Francisco, 1983-84; chmn., chief exec. officer CMX Corp., Santa Clara, Calif., 1984-88; dir., sr. v.p. Masstor Systems Corp., Santa Clara, 1988—; pvt. cons. Atherton, Calif., 1990—; sr. mgmt. cons. Durkee/Sharlit, 1991—; pres. Mayfair Packing Co., 1991—; mng. dir. Quincy Pacific Ptnrs., L.P., 1992—; pres., CEO Mayfair Packing Co., San Jose, Calif., 1991-94; pvt. cons. BMG Assocs., 1994—. Lectr. NYU Inst. Mgmt., 1965-67; asst. prof. mktg. Iona Coll. Grad. Sch. Adminstrn., 1967-69; prof. Golden Gate U., 1974—; prof. fin. and mktg. Pace U. Grad. Sch. Bus. Adminstrn., 1969-79. Author 7 books, including Controller's Handbook; contbr. articles to jours. Lt. (j.g.) USNR, 1951-55. Lt. jg USN, 1951—55. Decorated Korean Occupation Svc. medal Armed Forces Svc., Nat. Def. Svc. medal. Mem. Fin. Execs. Inst., Nat. Assn. Accts., Am. Statis. Assn., Am. Econs. Assn., Planning Execs. Inst., Am. Arbitration Assn., Turnaround Mgmt. Assn. Home and Office: 60 Shearer Dr Atherton CA 94027-3957 E-mail: bgoodman@cbnorcal.com.

GOODPASTER-TROYER, SHEILA ROGERS, elementary education educator; b. Campbellsville, Ky., Jan. 02; d. Herman Short and Nell Lee (Tarter) Rogers; m. Mitchell G. Goodpaster, Aug. 12 (div. 1974); 1 child, Shawn Cody; m. Stuart R. Troyer, Dec. 20, 1980. AA, Lindsey Wilson Coll., 1974; BS, Campbellsville Coll., 1975; MEd, U. Louisville, 1978, student, 1980. Cert. tchr. and cons., Ky. Tchr. Evangel Schs., Louisville, Ky., 1975-77, Adair County Bd. Edn., Columbia, Ky., 1977-80, Jefferson County Pub. Schs., Louisville, 1980-91, Ky. Edn. Reform Act facilitator, 1991—. Trainer Ky. Tchr. Internship Program U. Louisville, 1988—. Contbr. articles to profl. jours. Bd. dirs. mother's day out Fern Creek United Meth. Ch., Louisville. Mem. NEA, ASCD, Ky. Edn. Assn., Ky. Acad. Sch. Execs., Ky. Assn. for Children Under Six, Jefferson County Tchrs. Assn. (bldg. rep. 1978-79), Women in Sch. Adminstrn., Delta Kappa Gamma, Kappa Delta Pi. Democrat. Avocation: reading. Office: Jefferson County Pub Schs 5001 Garden Green Way Louisville KY 40218-4111 Address: 4604 Fox Chase Dr Shepherdsville KY 40165-9438

GOODRICH, ISAAC, neurosurgeon, educator; b. Milledgeville, Ga., Sept. 19, 1939; s. Ellis and Frieda (Bergman) G.; m. Dianne L. Brittain, Aug. 28, 1965; children: Mindy Anne, Scott David, Jennifer Gale. AA, Ga. Mil. Coll., 1959; BS, U. Ga., 1961; MD, Med. Coll. Ga., 1964. Cert. Am. Bd. Neurol. Surgery. Intern Columbia-Presbyn. Med. Ctr., N.Y.C., 1964-65; resident in neurosurgery Yale-New Haven Med. Ctr., 1967-71; practice medicine specializing in neurosurgery New Haven, 1971—. Instr. neurosurgery, Yale U. Med. Sch., 1970-71, asst. clin. prof., 1978-86; assoc. clin. prof., 1986—; attending neurosurgeon Yale-New Haven Hosp., 1973—, Hosp. St. Raphael, 1971—; mem. courtesy staff Milford Hosp., 1986—; cons. staff Midstate Med. Ctr., 1986—, VA Hosp., West Haven, 1990—, Griffin Hosp., 1992-99, St. Mary's Hosp., 1995-99, courtesy staff, 1999—. Contbr. articles to profl. jours. Capt. U.S. Army, 1965-67. Decorated Bronze Star, Air Medal; recipient Disting. Alumni award Ga. Mil. Coll., 1980; named Hon. Citizen, Boys Town, Nebr., 1971. Fellow: ACS, Royal Soc. Medicine, Internat. Coll. Surgeons; mem.: AAAS, AMA (Physicians Recognition awards for Continuing Med. Edn.), N.Y. Acad. Scis., New Haven County Med. Assn. (pres. 1998—99), Conn. State Med. Soc. (v.p. 2000—01, pres.-elect 2001—02, pres. 2002—03), Conn. State Neurosurg. Soc. (pres. 2001—03), Am. Assn. Neurol. Surgeons, Soc. Med. Cons. to Armed Forces, Pan Pacific Surg. Assn., New Eng. Neurosurg. Soc. (pres. 1997—99), Congress Neurol. Surgeons, Veterans of Fgn. Wars, New Haven City Med. Assn. (pres. 1989—90), 28th Inf. Assn., Soc. 1st Inf. Divsn., Am. Legion. Jewish. Home: 264 Rimmon Rd Woodbridge CT 06525-1847 Office: 330 Orchard St Ste 316 New Haven CT 06511-4430

GOODRUM, MARLENE ROACH, secondary school educator; b. Mason, W.Va., July 24, 1946; d. James Rankin and Irma Rose (Ord) Roach; m. David Elliott Goodrum, June 1, 1968; children: Rachel Diane Goodrum Wall, Richard Warfield. BA in Math. and Art, Marshall U., 1968. Math. and art tchr. Stonewall Jackson H.S., Mt. Jackson, Va., 1968-71; math. tchr. Berkeley (Mo.) Jr. H.S., 1971-72; kindergarten tchr. Covenant Christian Sch., Smyrna, Ga., 1977-80, 95-98, primary grades tchr., 1980-86; math. and English tchr. Chalcedon Christian Sch., Dunwoody, Ga., 1986-90; mid. grades tchr. Cherokee Christian Sch., Woodstock, Ga., 1990—, schedule organizer, 1991—, yearbooks dir., 1984—; learning disabilities therapist and tchr. Fellowship Christian Schs., Roswell, Ga., 1999—2003; math. tchr. Marietta (Ga.) Mid. Sch., 2003—. Republican. Presbyterian. Home: 3032 Hacienda Ct Marietta GA 30066-4016

GOODSPEED, KATHRYN ANN, pre-school educator; b. Elgin, Ill., Oct. 2, 1939; d. Earle Muller and Ruby Vera Curtiss; m. Robert Harrison Goodspeed, Feb. 4, 1961; children: Julie, Jill, Jerry, Jeff, Jennifer. BS, No. Ill. U., 1961. Tchr. spl. edn. Sch. of Hope, Rockford, Ill., 1962—65; home day care provider, 1971—78; tchr. presch., dir. Melrose DayCare Ctr., Iowa City, 1978—89; tchr. Blind Children's Learning Ctr., Santa Ana, Calif., 1989—92, dir. early childhood ctr., 1992—2001, asst. exec. dir., 2001—. Bd. pres. So. Calif. Network Serving Infants and Preschool Children with Visual Impairments, 1998. Co-treas. Joint Action Com. Visually Impaired, Calif., 1997—; co-chair Infant Vendor Com., Santa Ana, 2000; edn. commn. head Yorba Linda United Meth. Ch., 1998—2002. Named Laywoman of Yr., Yorba Linda United Meth. Ch., 2000. Mem.: Family Support Ntetwork Bd., Assn. for Edn. and Rehab. Blind and Visually Impaired, Coun. Exceptional Children, Calif. Transcribers & Educators Multihandicapped Specialist, Calif. First Chance Consortium (bd. dir., family support network com., mem. camp TLC). Avocations: reading, cooking, travel. Home: 856 Amber Ln Anaheim CA 92807

GOODWIN, BECKY K. educational technology resource educator; Sci. tchr. USD 233 Sch. Dist., Olathe, Kans. Christa McAuliffe fellowship grantee State of Kans., 1992, 94, 97; named Kans. Tchr. of Yr., 1995; recipient Presdl. award for Excellence in Sci. and Math. Secondary Sci. for Kans., 1992, Outstanding Biology Tchr. award Nat. Assn. Biology Tchrs., 1992, Sci. Teaching Achievement Recognition Star award NSTA, 1993, Milken Nat. Educator award, 1995, Tandy Tech. Tchr. award, 1998. Office: USD 233 14160 Black Bob Rd Olathe KS 66063

GOODWIN, BRUCE KESSELI, retired geology educator, researcher; b. Providence, Oct. 14, 1931; s. Thomas William and Lizetta Christina (Kesseli) G.; m. Joan Marilyn Horton, June 9, 1956; children: Stephen Bruce, Susan Joan, Jennifer Anne. AB, U. Pa., 1953; MS, Lehigh U., 1957, PhD, 1959. Grad. asst. Lehigh U., Bethlehem, Pa., 1956-59; geologist Vt. Geol. Survey, Burlington, 1956-58; instr. U. Pa., Phila., 1959-63; asst. prof. geology Coll. William and Mary, Williamsburg, Va., 1963-66, assoc. prof. geology, 1966-71, prof. geology, 1971-96, chmn. dept. geology, 1970-76, 82-88, 92-96; tchr. geology Math.-Sci. Ctr., Richmond, Va., 1968-70. With Va. Bd. Geology, 1982-88, chair, 1983; mem. Va. Geologic Mapping Adv. Com., 1993—. Contbr. articles to profl. jours. Pres. Lafayette Ednl. Fund, Inc., Williamsburg, Va., 1976-79, Lafayette High Sch. PTA, Williamsburg, Bruton Heights PTA, Williamsburg; mem. com. Va. Jr. Acad. Sci., 1971-73. Recipient Thomas Jefferson Teaching award Coll. William and Mary, 1971; cert. of merit Math.-Sci. Ctr. Fellow Geol. Soc. Am. (edn. com. 1994-96); mem. AAAS, Nat. Assn. Geology Tchrs. (pres. eastern sect. 1982), Va. Acad. Sci. (chmn. geology sect. 1970, 98), Am. Inst. Profl. Geologists (sec., treas. Va. sect. 1989, pres. Va. sect. 1990), St. Andrews Soc., Coun. on Undergrad. Rsch (geology councilor 1988-94), Kiwanis, Delta Upsilon, Sigma Xi. Republican. Presbyterian. Avocations: fishing, sailing, geology, travel, ballroom dancing. Home: 103 Wakerobin Rd Williamsburg VA 23185-4441

GOODWIN, CHARLES HUGH, technology education educator; b. Cortland, NY, Feb. 2, 1945; s. Arthur George and Elizabeth Sarah (Pratt) G.; m. Frances Margaret Dunkle, Aug. 18, 1967 (div. June 1979); 1 child, Chad Conlin; m. Barbara Louetta Milan, Aug. 16, 1980. BS, SUNY, Oswego, 1967, MS in Edn., 1973. Cert. tech. tchr. trainer, N.Y. Indsl. arts tchr. Worcester (N.Y.) Ctrl. Schs., 1967-69, Endicott (N.Y.) Ctrl. Schs., 1969-86, tech. edn. tchr., 1986—; chairperson tech. and mgmt. sci. dept. Union-Endicott (N.Y.) Ctrl. Schs., 1996—. Applied physics tchr. Broome C.C., Binghamton, N.Y., 1994—; curriculum writer N.Y. State Edn. Dept., Albany, 1983-88, test writer, evaluator, 1978—, tchr. trainer, 1986-92, sch. quality reviewer, 1992—; higher edn. com. N.Y. State Strategic Systemic Initiative, 1995; mem. Endicott Sch. Dist. Planning Team, 1992-03; N.Y. State Edn. Assn. adv. coun. chair, 2002-03. Contbr. articles to profl. publs. Merit badge counselor Boy Scouts Am., Endicott, 1984—; mem. com., planner Endicott Tech. Ctr., 1993—. Named N.Y. State Tech. Tchr. of Yr., Internat. Tech. Edn. Assn., 1986; named Disting. Alumnus, SUNY, Oswego, 1986; named to Elmira Southside H.S. Sports Hall of Fame, 1997; recipient Tech. in Edn. award 8 N.Y. County Tech. Rsch. Com., 1997, Outstanding Educator award N.Y. State Tech. Prep. Conf., 1998, 2003, Citizen of Yr. award N.Y. State Soc. Profl. Engrs., 1999. Mem.: N.Y. State Congress Parents and Tchrs. (hon. life), So. Tier Tech. Educators' Assn. (pres. 1974—75, Tchr. of Yr. 1984), Soc. Plastics Engrs. (pres. 1991—92, editor newsletter Perspective, Mem. of Yr. 1991—92, Past Pres. award 1992), N.Y. State Tech. Edn. Assn. (pres. 1992—93, polit. action chmn. 1991—96, authentic assessment chmn. 1994—, co-chair statewide adv. coun. 2002—03, Outstanding Svc. award 1996, Recognition award 2003), Epsilon Pi Tau. Avocations: running, hunting, woodworking, dancing. Home: 12 Tudor Dr Endicott NY 13760-4332 Office: Union-Endicott Ctrl Schs 1200 E Main St Endicott NY 13760-5220 E-mail: cgnystea@aol.com., cgoodwin@uegw.stier.org.

GOODWIN, JOHN ROBERT, lawyer, law educator, author; b. Morgantown, W.Va., Nov. 3, 1929; s. John Emory and Ruby Iona Goodwin; m. Betty Lou Wilson, June 2, 1952; children: John R., Elizabeth Ann Paugh, Mark Edward, Luke Jackson, Matthew Emory. BS, W.Va. U., 1952, LLB, 1964, JD, 1970. Bar: W.Va., U.S. Supreme Ct. Formerly city atty., county commr., spl. pros. atty.; then mayor City of Morgantown; prof. bus. law W.Va. U., Morgantown, 1964—80; prof. hotel and casino law U. Nev., Las Vegas, 1980—93, prof. emeritus, 1994—; pvt. practice, Morgantown, 1964—. Author: Legal Primer for Artists, Craftspersons, 1987, Hotel Law, Principles and Cases, 1987, Twenty Feet from Glory, 1970, Bus. Law, 3d edit., 1976, High Points of Legal History, 1982, Travel and Lodging Law, 1980, Desert Adventure, Gaming Control Law, 1985; editor Hotel and Casino Letter; past editor Bus. Law Rev., Bus. Law Letter. 1st lt. U.S. Army, Korean War. Named Outstanding West Virginian, State of W.Va.; named Hon. Gen. Gov. of W.Va., 1970. Democrat. Home: Casa Linda 48 5250 E Lake Mead Blvd Las Vegas NV 89156-6751 also: Goodwin Bldg 2d Fl Morgantown WV 26505

GOODWIN, LESLIE DIANE, elementary education educator; b. Des Moines, Jan. 28, 1949; d. John J. and Phyllis A. (Jensen) Goeders; m. Glenn Anspach, July 31, 1970 (div. 1975); 1 child, Dana M.; other children: Diana L. Goodwin, Jacob D. Goodwin. BA, U. Iowa, 1974; MA in Teaching, Webster U., 1992; postgrad., St. Louis U., St. Louis, 1997—. Cert. tchr., Mo., Fla., Iowa. Tchr., reading specialist Cedar Rapids (Iowa) Community Sch. Dist., 1974-79; reading specialist Kirkwood (Mo.) Community Sch. Dist., 1980-84, Pattonville Sch. Dist., Maryland Heights, Mo., 1984-85, Osceola County Sch. Dist., Kissimmee, Fla., 1985-88; tchr. pre-kindergarten reading readiness Lea's Learning Lair, St. Petersburg, Fla., 1989; reading specialist Holy Family Schs., St. Louis, 1989-90, Webster Groves (Mo.) Sch. Dist., 1990-91, Ft. Zumwalt Sch. Dist., O'Fallon, Mo., 1991—. Presenter workshops; presenter at profl. confs.; curriculum writer Metcalf Group Youth Divsn., St. Louis, 1996-97. Author curriculum materials. Mem. ASCD, NEA (rep. to nat. conv. 1997), MLA, Cedar Rapids Edn. Assn. (exec. bd.), Mo. State Edn. Assn., Internat. Reading Assn., Mo. Mid. Sch. Assn., Phi Delta Kappa, Pi Lambda Theta. Avocations: barbershop quartet singing, guitar, drawing, painting, writing poetry and lyrics. Office: Dubray Middle Sch 100 Dubray Dr Saint Peters MO 63376-2170

GOODWIN, MARY MCGINNIS, secondary education educator; b. Clovis, N.Mex., Nov. 18, 1947; d. Fredrick and Virginia (Neal) McGinnis; m. Roger Dawson Goodwin, Aug 20, 1980; children: Roger, Jon, Kim. AA, Gulf Park Jr. Coll. Women, 1967; BFA, So. Meth. U., 1969; MS, Tex. A&M, Corpus Christi, 1989. Cert. tchr., Tex., mid-mgmt., Tex., tchr. gifted and talented, Tex. Tchr. gifted and talented Port Aransas (Tex.) Ind. Sch. Dist., 1987—, tchr. history, 1991—. Pres. dist. wide edn. implovement com. Gov.'s Task Force in Edn., Austin, 1994-95; mem. delegation Gifted and Talented Educators to China, 1989, 91; edn. curriculum developer Tex. State Aquarium, 1996. Mem. NEA, Tex. State Tchrs. Assn., Tex. Assn. Gifted and Talented Edn. Republican. Presbyterian. Avocations: archaeology, walking. Home: PO Box 958 Port Aransas TX 78373-0958

GOODWIN, SHARON ANN, academic administrator; b. Little Rock, May 19, 1949; d. Jimmy Lee and Eddie DeLois (Cluck) G.; m. Mitchell Shayne Mick, May 4, 1968 (div. Mar. 1973); 1 child, Heather Michelle; m. Raymond Eugene Vaclavik, June 24, 1974 (div. Aug. 1982); 1 child, Tasha Rae Vaclavik. BA in Psychology, U. Houston-Clear Lake, 1980; MEd in Higher Edn. Adminstrn., U. Houston, 1990. Various clerical positions Gen. Telephone Co., Dickinson, Tex., 1969-80; state dir. Challenge, Inc., Oklahoma City, 1980-82; gen. mgr. Mr. Fix It, Houston, 1982-85; assoc. dir.

admissions U. Houston, Tex., 1985-92; adminstr. Inst. for the Med. Humanities U. Tex. Med. Br., Galveston, 1992—. Contbr. poetry to World of Poetry Anthology, 1986, 87, 90, 91, Nat. Libr. of Poetry Anthology, 1997, SOL Mag., 1997-2000, Lucidity Jour., 1997, New Winds Jour., 1997, Galveston Writers Anthology, 1998-99, Nat. Poetry Guild Anthology, 1998; author (poetry exhibited) Moody Med. Libr., UTMB, 2003. Mem. legis. com. Comm. Workers, Dickinson and Austin, 1975; mem. centennial choir U. Tex. Med. Br., Galveston, 1992—; vol. Dickens on the Strand, Galveston, 1993—. Recipient award of merit World of Poetry Anthology, 1986, 91, Golden Poet award, 1987, Silver Poet award, 1990, rd 1990, Golden Poet award, 1991, hon. mention SOL Mag., 1997, 98, 1st pl., 1998, 2d pl., 1998; named to Internat. Poetry Hall of Fame, 1997. Mem. AAUW, Assn. of Am. Med. Colls.-Group on Institutional Planning. Avocations: travel, music, sports, books, movies. Office: Univ Tex Med Br Inst for the Med Humanities 301 University Blvd Galveston TX 77555-1311 Home: PO Box 1346 League City TX 77574

GORAL, JUDITH ANN, educator; b. Cleve., July 12, 1947; d. Chester and Elenore (Majka) C. BA, Cleve. State U., 1969; postgrad., Inst. Am., Guadalajara, Jalisco, Mex.; MAT, Marygrove Coll., 1998. Cert. Spanish, Eng. tchr., Ohio. Tchr. Spanish Wiley Mid. Schs., Cleveland Heights, Ohio; advanced courses coord. Inst. Cultural Mexicano Norteamericano de Jai, Guadalajara, tchr., bus.; tchr. Colegio Victoria, Guadalajara; tchr., Spanish Brecksville (Ohio) Sr. High Sch. Mem. Am. Assn. Tchrs. Spanish and Portuguese, MEs. Assn. Tchrs. Eng. to Speakers of Other Langs. (2d v.p. acad. programs and events 1985-86, pres. 1986-87), Ohio Fgn. Lang. Assn., Phi Beta Omicron. Office: Wiley Middle Sch 2155 Miramar Blvd University Heights OH 44118

GORDAN, DENNIS STUART, physiatrist, educator; b. N.Y.C., Sept. 24, 1945; s. Harold Bernard and Helen (Marberg) G.; m. Miriam Laufer, Sept. 5, 1971; children: Michael Noah, Rachel, Israel Moses. BS, Union Coll., Schenectady, 1967; MD, Union U., Albany, N.Y., 1971. Diplomate Am. Bd. Internal Medicine, Am. Bd. Phys. Medicine and Rehab., Am. Bd. Electrodiagnostic Medicine, Nat. Bd. Med. Examiners. Resident Albany Med. Ctr. Hosp., 1972-73, 75-78; intern Albany med. Ctr. Hosp., 1971-72, resident internal medicine, 1972-73, 75-76, resident phys. med. and rehab., 1976-78; instr. rehab. medicine U. Wash. Med. Sch., Seattle, 1978-80; asst. prof. rehab. and internal medicine Tufts U. Sch. Medicine, Boston, 1980-89, clin. asst. prof. rehab. medicine, 1989—2000; med. dir. Weldon Ctr. for Rehab., Mercy Hosp., Springfield, Mass., 1989-98; physiatrist Hampden County Physician Assocs., 1998—2000; med. dir. Mass. Mut. Fin. Group, Hartford, Conn., 2000—. Chief rehab. medicine svc. VA Med. Ctr., Boston, 1986-89; pres. We. Health Svcs., Inc., P.C., Springfield, 1989-98; manuscript reviewer Archives Phys. Medicine and Rehab., Chgo. Contbg. author: The Practical Management of Spasticity in Children and Adults, 1990. Bd. dirs. Temple Beth El, Springfield, 1993-98, Jewish Family Svcs., Springfield, 1995—, v.p. 1997-2001. Maj. M.C., USAF, 1973-75. Fellow Am. Acad. Phys. Medicine and Rehab., Am. Assn. Electrodiagnostic Medicine; mem. Assn. Acad. Physiatrists, New Eng. Soc. Phys. Medicine and Rehab. (pres. 1986), Mass. Med. Soc., Hampden Dist. Med. Soc. (co-editor Hampden Hippocrat 1995, pres. 2002-2003). Avocations: singing, community theater, model railroading. Office: Mass Mut Fin Group 140 Garden St Hartford CT 06154

GORDENKER, LEON, political sciences educator; b. Detroit, Oct. 7, 1923; s. Samuel and Anna (Posalsky) G.; m. Belia Emilie Strootman, Aug. 16, 1956 (dec. Apr. 1984); children: Robert Jan Mario, Hendrik Willem Paul, Emilie Elise Saskia. AB, U. Mich., 1943; student, Inst. d'Etudes Politiques, Paris, 1951-52; MA, Columbia U., 1954, PhD, 1958; postgrad., Acad. Internat. Law, Hague, The Netherlands, 1958. Journalist AP, 1943, Detroit Free Press, 1944-45; info. officer Nat. War Labor Bd., 1945; pub. info. officer UN, 1945-53; instr. Dartmouth Coll., 1956-58; mem. faculty Princeton U., 1958—, prof. politics, 1966-86, faculty assoc. Ctr. Internat. Studies, 1963—, prof. emeritus, 1986—, sr. rsch. polit. scientist, 1990-94; prof. Institut Universitaire de Hautes Internationales, Geneva, 1986-89, vis. prof., 1979-80; dir. Centre de Recherches sur les Institutions Internationales, Geneva, 1986-89. Vis. prof. Columbia U., 1961, 67, Makerere U., Uganda, 1969-70, U. Pa., 1971, 74, U. Witwatersrand, South Africa, 1976, Leiden U., 1984-85, 93, Erasmus U., 1985, CUNY, 1989, 90, 92, 95, Inst. Social Studies, The Hague, 1993-97. Author: The United Nations and the Peaceful Unification of Korea, 1959, The UN Secretary-General and the Maintenance of Peace, 1967, The United Nations in the International System, 1971, International Aid and National Decisions, 1976, The International Executive, 1978, (with W.P. Davison) Resolving Nationality Conflicts, 1980, (with P.R. Baehr) The United Nations: Reality and Ideal, 1984, Refugees in International Politics, 1987, (with T.G. Weiss) Soldiers, Peacekeepers and Disasters, 1991, (with P.R. Baehr) The United Nations in the 1990s, 1992, 94, De Verenigde Naties: Werkelijkheid en Ideaal, 1992, 94, 96, (with Benjamin Rivlin) The Challenging Role of the UN Secretary-General, 1993, (with others) International Cooperation in Response to AIDS, 1995, (with T.G. Weiss) NGOs, The UN and Global Governance, 1996, (with P.R. Baehr) The United Nations at the End of the 1990s, 1999; mem. editl. bd. Acta Politica, Global Governance. Fellow The Netherlands Inst. Advanced Study, 1972-73, 96-97. Mem. Acad. Coun. on UN, Princeton Club of N.Y. Office: Princeton U Ctr Internat Studies Princeton NJ 08544-0001

GORDIS, DAVID MOSES, academic administrator, rabbi; b. N.Y.C., June 4, 1940; s. Robert and Fannie (Jacobson) G.; m. Felice Witztum, Sept. 3, 1962; children: Lisa, Elana. BA, Columbia U., 1960, MA, 1966; MHL, Jewish Theol. Sem., 1962, PhD, 1980. Ordained rabbi, 1964. Dean of students Tchrs. Inst., Jewish Theol. Sem., N.Y.C., 1966-72; exec. dir. Found. for Conservative Judaism, 1981-84; assoc. prof., v.p. U. of Judaism, L.A., 1972-84; v.p. Jewish Theol. Sem., N.Y.C., 1981-84; exec. v.p. Am. Jewish Com., N.Y.C., 1984-87; v.p. U. Judaism, L.A., 1988-92, dir. Wilstein Inst. of Jewish Policy Studies, 1988—, adj. assoc. prof. Talmud, 1988-92, dir. inst. rsch.; pres. Hebrew Coll., 1993—. Mem. editl. bd.: Tikkun. Pres., prof. rabbinics Hebrew Coll., 1993—; exec. com. Am. Found. for Polish-Jewish Studies, 1988—; trustee Am. Jewish Hist. Soc., 1993—, vice-chair Archives for Hist. Documentation, 1995—; chair United Synagogue Coun. on Jewish Edn., 1973-82. Mem. Rabbinical Assembly Am., Assn. Colls. of Jewish Studies. Avocation: cello. E-mail: dgordis@hebrewcollege.edu.

GORDON, ALICE JEANNETTE IRWIN, secondary and elementary education educator; b. Detroit, Mar. 18, 1934; d. Manley Elwood and Jeannette (Coffron) Irwin; m. Edgar George Gordon, Feb. 4, 1967; children: David Alexander, John Scott. BA in Elem. Edn., Mich. State U., 1956; MA in Child Devel., U. Mich., 1959, EdS in Ednl. Psychology, 1967, MA in Reading, 1990; postgrad., Western Mich. U., 1990-97. Cert. K-12 tchr., Mich.; cert. K-12 reading specialist. Elem. tchr. Detroit Pub. Schs., 1956-67, reading tchr., 1967-68; secondary tchr. English and reading Parchment Pub. Schs., 1989-94; secondary reading specialist Kalamazoo Pub. Schs., 1994-96; jr. high reading specialist South Middle Sch., Kalamazoo, 1996-99; tchr. Milwood Elem. Sch., Mich., 1999-2001; ret. Reading therapist Western Mich. U., Kalamazoo, 1992-97; participant Ednl. Leadership Acad., 1998-99; bd. dir. U. Mich. Coll. Edn. Mem. alumni bd. Mich. State U. Coll. Edn., 1992-96; chmn. Century Ball, Nazareth Coll., Kalamazoo, 1987; co-chmn. Evening of Nte, Kalamazoo Symphony, 1989; precinct del. Kalamazoo Rep. Com., 1989, 92, 96, 99—; mem. Mich. Adult Edn. Practitioner Inquiry Project, 1994, 95, 96; docent Kalamazoo Inst. Art, 2002; bd. mem. Ready to Read, 2002, Literacy Coun., 2002; bd. dirs. U. Mich. Coll. Edn., 2003—, alumni bd. Coll. Edn., 2003—; bd. dirs. Ready to Read, 1998-2003, Kalamazoo Literacy Coun., 2002—; mentor, tutor Cmty. in Schs. Americorps, 2002—03; docent Kalamazoo Inst. Arts, 2003. Recipient Crystal Apple award Mich. a., 1990, Excellence in Edn. grantee, 1997, Kalamazoo Pub. Edn. Found. grantee, 1997, 98, Arts Coun. Greater Kalamazoo mini-grantee, 1997, 2000, State Dept. Arts grantee, 1997, Kalamazoo Pub. Edn. Found., 1998; Third Coast Writing fellow, 1998; MLPP grantee, 2001. Mem. Internat. Reading Assn., Mich. Reading Assn., Homer Carter Reading Assn., P.E.O. (pres. 2003—), Jr. League, Lawyers Wives Aux. (bd. dirs. 2002—, pres. 2003—), Phi Delta Kappa (pres. 1998-01, bd. dirs. 2002—), Alpha Omega Pi, Delta Kappa Gamma (bd. dirs. 2002—). Presbyterian. Avocations: miniatures, antiques, reading, genealogy, public education. Home: 4339 Lakeside Dr Kalamazoo MI 49008-2802

GORDON, AUDREY KRAMEN, healthcare educator; b. Chgo., Nov. 18, 1935; d. Edward J. and Anne (Levin) Kramen; children: Bradley, Dale, Holly. BS with highest distinction, Northwestern U., 1965, MA, 1967, postgrad., 1971; MA, U. Chgo., 1970; PhD, U. Ill., Chgo., 1991. Cert. in clin. pastoral edn. Lectr. Northwestern U., Evanston, Ill., 1966-74; vis. asst. prof. Beloit (Wis.) Coll., 1974-75; research specialist U. Ill., Chgo., 1983-86, dir. continuing edn. Sch. Pub. Health, 1986-91, lectr. cmty. health scis., 1988-91, dir. coll. advancement Sch. Pub. Health, 1991-92, asst. prof., 1992—, sr. rsch. specialist Health Rsch. and Policy Ctr., 1992-2001, dir. instnl. rev. bd., 1998—, dir. human subjects rsch. Health Rsch. Policy Ctrs., 2001—; coord., counselor Jewish Hospice, Chgo., 1984-89. Lectr. Loyola U. Stritch Sch. Medicine, Maywood, Ill., 1982—90; pres. Rainbow Hospice Orgn., 1984—88, cons., 1988—92, rsch. cons., 2001—; project dir. S.E. Lake County Faith in Action Program, Highland Pk., 2003—. Co-author: (book) They Need to Know: How to Teach Children About Death, 1979; co-editor: Hospice and Cultural Diversity, 1995. Bd. dirs. AIDS Pastoral Care Network, 1999—2001. Recipient Merit award, Northwestern U. Alumni, 1993, Heart of Hospice award, Nat. Coun. Hospice Profls., 1997. Mem.: APHA, Nat. Hospice Orgn. (mem. ethics com. 1997—2000), Ill. Hospice Orgn. (pres. 1989—90, v.p. 1997—98), Ill. Pub. Health Assn., Delta Omega, Alpha Kappa Lambda, Alpha Sigma Lambda.

GORDON, CRAIG JEFFREY, oncologist, educator; b. Detroit, Feb. 10, 1953; s. Maury Allen and Shirley Phoebe (Jacoby) G.; m. Susan Ann Blase, Aug. 3, 1980; children: Sari, Scott, Brittany. BS, Oakland U., 1978; DO, U. Osteo. Med. and Health Scis, Des Moines, 1983. Diplomate Am. Bd. Internal Medicine, Am. Bd. Med. Oncology. Intern-chief Botsford Gen. Hosp., Farmington Hills, Mich., 1983-84, resident, 1984-87; fellow in hematology and oncology Wayne State Univ. (affiliated Hosp.'s Prog.), Detroit, 1987-90, fellow-chief, 1989-90; clin. asst. prof. dept. medicine Wayne State U., Detroit, 1990—; dir. divsn. hematology and oncology Botsford Hosp., Livonia, Mich., 1992—; med. dir. Angela Hospice, 1993—98, Weisberg Cancer Ctr., Karmanos Cancer Inst., 2000—. Mem. extrarenal transplantation com. Mich. Dept. Pub. Health; physician advisor Gilda's Club Mich., 1993—2001; mem. Greater Detroit Area Health Care Coun. on Cancer Care. Contbr. articles to profl. jours. Named Intern of the Yr. Botsford Hosp. Staff, 1984, Resident of the Yr., 1985-87; clin. fellow Am. Cancer Soc., 1987-90. Fellow Am. Coll. Osteo. Internists; mem. Am. Osteo. Assn., Mich. Assn. Osteo. Physicians and Surgeons, Mich. Soc. Hematology and Oncology, Assn. Cancer Execs., S.W. Oncology Group, Am. Soc. Clin. Oncologists, Oakland County Osteo. Assn. Avocations: sports, popular music, astronomy, electronics. Office: 31995 Northwestern Hwy Farmington MI 48334-1625

GORDON, EDMUND WYATT, psychologist, educator; b. Goldsboro, N.C., June 13, 1921; s. Edmund Tayloe and Mabel (Ellison) G.; m. Susan Elizabeth Gitt, Nov. 6, 1948; children: Edmund T., Christopher W., Jessica G., Johanna S. BS, Howard U., 1942, BD, 1945, LHD (hon.), 1997; MA, Am. U., 1950; EdD, Columbia U., 1957; DS, Mt. Holyoke Coll., 1994; MA (hon.), Yale U., 1979; LHD (hon.), Yeshiva U., N.Y.C., 1986, Brown U., 1989, Bank St. Coll., 1992; DS, Mt. Holyoke Coll., 1994; DHL (hon.), Howard U., 1996. Asst. dean men Howard U., Washington, 1946-50; from assoc. prof. to prof. Yeshiva U., N.Y.C., 1961-68; prof., chmn. dept. guidance Columbia U., N.Y.C., 1968-78, Richard March Hoe prof. psychology and edn., 1978-79; John M. Musser prof. of psychology Yale U., New Haven, 1979-91, John M. Musser prof. of psychology emeritus, 1991; disting. prof. ednl. psychology CUNY, N.Y.C., 1992-96; interim dean, v.p. acad. affairs Tchrs. Coll. Columbia U. Author: Compensatory Education for the Disadvantaged: Programs and Practices, 1966; editor: Equality of Educational Opportunity: Handbook for Research, 1974, Human Diversity and Pedagogy, 1989; editor Am. Jour. Orthopsychiatry, 1978-83, Rev. of Rsch. in Edn., 1983-85, Ednl. Resilience in Inner City America, 1994; contbr. articles to Am. Jour. Orthopsychiatry, Am. Jour. Mental Deficiency, Am. Zoologist, Jour. of Genetic Psychology, Am. Child, others. Pres. Rockland County NAACP. Fellow AAAS, APA, Am. Orthopsychiatric Assn., Am. Psychol. Soc.; mem. Am. Ednl. Rsch. Assn., Nat. Assn. Black Psychologists, Nat. Acad. Edn., N.Y. Acad. Sci. Achievements include research in human diversity, cultural hegemony, culture and cognitive development, and education of low status populations; responsible for and one of the founders and the 1st director of research for Project Head Start, 1965-67. Home and Office: 3 Cooper Morris Dr Pomona NY 10970-3309

GORDON, EDWARD HARRISON, choral conductor, educator; b. N.Y.C., Aug. 24, 1946; s. James Sumter and Marguerite Catherine (Thomas) G.; m. Marilyn Clarke, Oct. 21, 1967; children: Harrison, Eva. BA, Bklyn. Coll., 1972; MA, Columbia U., 1977, MEd, 1983. Choir dir. various area jr. high schs., N.Y.C., 1972-84; choir dir., coord. music Boys and Girls H.S., Bklyn., 1984-88; choir dir., coord. Carnasie H.S., Bklyn., 1988-94; choir dir. Thomas Jefferson H.S., Bklyn., 1994-98, John Dewey H.S., Bklyn., 1998—; affiliate music dept. L.I. U., Bklyn., 2000—. Pres. Nubian Conservatory Music, Bklyn., 1977—, mem. chancellor's music com. Author: Black Classical Musicians, 1978; condr. A Collection of Afro-American Spirituals, 1978, also others. Treas. Winthrop St Block Assn., Bklyn., 1991; appt. chancellor Music Comm., 1998; apptd. cultural com. Cmty. Planning Bd., 1998. With U.S. Army, 1967-69, Vietnam. Mem. Assn. Supervision and Curriculum Devel., United Fedn. Tchrs., Kappa Delta Pi. Presbyterian. Avocations: archery, chess. Home: 233 Winthrop St Brooklyn NY 11225-3811 Office: John Dewey H S 50 Avenue X Brooklyn NY 11223-5799

GORDON, ELLA DEAN, health and nurse educator, women's health and orthopedic nurse; b. Chgo., Jan. 19, 1947; d. Ed and Mozelle (Jordan) Hall; m. Starling Alexander Gordon, Aug. 2, 1969; children: Gerald Alexander, Dana Rolean. Diploma, Grady Meml. Hosp., 1968; student, Ga. State U., 1969-75; BSN, Med. Coll. Ga., 1976; M in Health Sci., Armstrong State Coll., 1983. RN, Ga., Tex. Charge nurse pediatrics evenings Grady Meml. Hosp., Atlanta, 1968-71; staff nurse pediatrics Dr.'s Meml. Hosp., Atlanta, 1971; charge nurse Pediatricians Office, Decatur, Ga., 1971-72; staff nurse VA Hosp., Atlanta, 1972-76, nurse primary care med. ICU San Antonio, 1983; charge nurse, army nurse corps Eisenhower Army Med. Ctr., Ft. Gordon, Ga., 1976-79; staff nurse obstet. Noble Army Hosp., Ft. McClellan, Ala., 1984; instr. clin. nursing Jacksonville (Ala.) State Coll. Nursing, 1984-85; clin. nurse obstet. Gorgas Army Hosp., Republic of Panama, 1987-89; charge nurse oncology days Eisenhower Army Med. Ctr., Ft. Gordon, Ga., 1989-90; charge nurse obstet. Brooke Army Med. Ctr., Ft. Sam Houston, Tex., 1990-96; mem. labor & delivery Wilford Hall Air Force Med. Ctr., Lackland AFB, Tex., 1996; charge nurse orthopedics Brooke Army Med. Ctr., Ft. Sam Houston, Tex., 1996-99, health/nurse educator Health Promotion Ctr., 2000—. Cons. health edn. ETOWAH County Clinics, Gadsden, Ala, 1985; health educator Cardiovascular Coun. of Savannah, Ga., 1983, Parent/Child Devel. Svcs., Savannah, 1982. Contbr. articles to profl. jours. Instr. ARC, Ft. McClellan, 1985-86, chmn., vols., 1986-87. Capt. U.S. Army, 1976-79; col. USAR, 1991, ret., 1998. Named One of Outstanding Young Women in Am., 1979, 83. Mem. Ret. Army Nurse Corps Assn., Orthopaedic Nurses Assn., Officers Wives Club (publicity chmn. 1982-83), Sigma Theta Tau. Democrat. Avocations: cross-stitching, bowling, reading, ceramics. Home: 12810 El Marro St San Antonio TX 78233-5832 Office: Brooke Army Med Ctr Fort Sam Houston TX 78234 E-mail: satxella33@hotmail.com.

GORDON, ERLINE SCHECTER, educational administrator; b. El Paso, Tex., Apr. 7, 1956; d. Irving and Jean (Lapowski) Schecter; m. Bruce L. Gordon. BA in Elem. Edn., U. Ariz., Tucson, 1978; MEd, Lesley Coll., 1988; postgrad., Sul Ross State U., 1990. Cert. mid-mgmt., Tex. Tchr. Dept. Def. Dependent Schs., Iwakuni, Japan, 1980-83; elem. tchr. El Paso Ind. Sch. Dist., 1978-80, 83-85, tchr. computers, 1985-92, staff devel., 1992-96, asst. dir. tech. tng. programs, staff devel., 1996-97, facilitator region 1, 1997-2000, facilitator curriculum, instrn., & assessment, 2000-01, facilitator career and tech. edn. program, 2001—. Cons. Region XIX Edn. Svc. Ctr., El Paso, 1985-88, Norton Bros. Computer Ctr., El Paso, 1984-86, Ector County Ind. Sch. Dist., 1989-90. Chairperson Border Ednl. Tech. Conf., 1996-98. Mem. AAUW, ASCD, Tex. Computer Edn. Assn. (treas.1990-94, Area II dir. 1986-90, electronic editor 1994-95, scholarship chairperson 1996-97), Internat. Soc. for Tech. in Edn., Nat. Coun. Jewish Women, Alpha Epsilon Phi, Phi Delta Kappa. Avocations: needlework, computers, reading. Office: El Paso Ind Sch Dist 6531 Boeing Dr El Paso TX 79925-1008

GORDON, FLORENCE SHANFIELD, mathematics educator; b. Montreal, Que., Can., Mar. 11, 1942; came to U.S., 1968; d. Morris and Jean (Rubacha) Shanfield; m. Sheldon P. Gordon, June 27, 1965; children: Craig, Kenneth. BSc with honours in Math., McGill U., Montreal, 1963, MSc in Math. Stats., 1964, PhD in Math. Stats., 1968. Asst. prof. C.W. Post Coll., L.I. U., Greenvale, N.Y., 1968-71, Adelphi U., Garden City, N.Y., 1982-83; prof. math. N.Y. Inst. Tech., Old Westbury, 1983—. Precalculus reform project NSF, 1991—96. Author: (book and software) Contemporary Statistics: A Computer Approach, 1994; co-author: Functioning in the Real World: A Precalculus Experience, 2004; co-editor: Statistics for the Twenty First Century, 1986, A Fresh Start for Collegiate Mathematics: Rethinking the Courses Below Calculus, 2003; contbr. articles to profl. jours. Mem. Math. Assn. Am., Am. Statis. Assn., Am. Math. Assn. for Two Yr. Colls. Home: 61 Cedar Rd East Northport NY 11731-4128 Office: NY Inst Tech Dept Math Old Westbury NY 11568

GORDON, HELEN HEIGHTSMAN, English language educator, writer, publisher; b. Salt Lake City, Sept. 7, 1932; d. Fred C. and Florence Isabel Heightsman; m. Norman C. Winn, Aug. 10, 1950 (div. Sept. 1972); children: Bruce Vernon Winn, Brent Terry Winn, Holly Winn Willner; m. Clifton Beverly Gordon, Feb. 17, 1974. Student, U. Utah, 1959-62; BA in English and Edn., Calif. State U., Sacramento, 1964, MA in English, 1967; EdD, Nova U., 1979. Cert. tchr., Calif.; lic. counselor, Calif. Stenographer, payroll clk. Associated Food Stores, Inc., Salt Lake City, 1951-59; part-time instr. in remedial English U. Utah, Salt Lake City, 1960-61; tchr. high sch. Rio Americano H.S., Sacramento, 1965-66; assoc. prof., counselor Porterville (Calif.) Coll., 1967-74; prof., counselor Bakersfield (Calif.) Coll., 1974-95; editor, tech. writer dept. computer engring. U. Calif., Santa Barbara, 1999—. Chair lang. arts divsn. Porterville Coll., 1971-74; coord. women's studies Bakersfield Coll., 1977-78, adminstrv. intern, 1982-83; dir. region V, English Coun. of Calif. Two Yr. Colls., 1990-92; articulation coord. Bakersfield Coll., 1992-93; pres., pub. Anacade Internat. Ednl. Books and Games, 1998—. Author: (textbook) From Copying to Creating, 2d edit., 1983, Developing College Writing, 1989, Wordforms, Book I & II, 2d edit., 1990, Interplay: Sentence Skills in Context, 1991, (novel) Voice of the Vanquished: The Story of the Slave Marina and Hernan Cortes, 1995 (memoirs) First Captured, Last Freed: Memoirs of a P.O.W. in World War II Guam and Japan, 1995; pub.: (game) Anagrabber, the Word Game for All Ages, 1998 (poetry book) Life, Love and Laughter, 1998, (game book) Anagrams, Anagrabber and Other Word Games, 1999, (poetry book) Love Lyrics in Light and Shadow, 1999, (humor book) Age is a Laughing Matter: How to Laugh Through the Second Half of Your Life, 1999. Founder, 1st pres. Writers of Kern, Bakersfield, 1993; guest mem. editl. bd. Bakersfield Californian Newspaper, 1988; past pres. Unitarian Fellowship of Kern County, Bakersfield, 1976-78. Calif. Fund for Instrn. grantee, 1978; U. Utah scholar, 1959-62. Mem. NEA, AAUW (pres. Santa Barbara chpt. 1997-98), Am. Assn. Women in Cmty. and Jr. Colls. (founder Bakersfield chpt., pres., program chair 1988-91), Nat. Coun. Tchrs. of English, Faculty Assn. Calif. Cmty. Coll., Text and Acad. Authors Assn. (charter, columnist Acad. Author 1996—), LWV (pres. Bakersfield chpt. 1981-83, 89-90), Calif. Writers Club, Pi Lambda Theta. Democrat. Avocations: poetry, personal computer, travel, bowling, theatre. Home: 3775 Modoc Rd Apt 135 Santa Barbara CA 93105-4462

GORDON, JEFFREY NEIL, law educator; b. Richmond, Va., June 18, 1949; s. Irving Leonard and Viola Anne (Clayman) G. BA, Yale U., 1971; JD, Harvard U., 1975. Bar: N.Y. 1977, U.S. Dist. Ct. (so. and ea. dists.) N.Y. 1978, U.S. Ct. Appeals (2nd cir.) 1979, D.C. 1981. Reporter Rocky Mount News, Denver, 1971-72; law clk. to judge U.S. Ct. Appeals (10th cir.), Denver, 1975-76; assoc. Cleary, Gottlieb, Steen & Hamilton, N.Y.C., 1976-78; spl. asst. to gen. counsel, atty. advisor U.S. Treasury, Washington, 1978-81; prof. law NYU, N.Y.C., 1982-88, Columbia U., N.Y.C., 1988—, Alfred W. Bressler prof., 1998—. Co-dir. Ctr. Law and Econ. Studies, Columbia U. Contbr. articles to profl. jours. Recipient Exceptional Svc. award U.S. Dept. Energy, 1982. Mem. ABA, Am. Law Inst., Assn. of Bar of City of N.Y., Harvard Club, Phi Beta Kappa. Democrat. Jewish. Home: 410 Riverside Dr Apt 81 New York NY 10025-7923 Office: Columbia Law Sch Ctr Law Econ Studies 435 W 116th St New York NY 10027-7297

GORDON, JOHN L., JR., historian, educator; b. Elizabethtown, Ky., July 14, 1942; s. John L. and Rose (Kemph) G.; m. Susan L. Cooper, Sept. 1963; 1 child, Sarah Elizabeth. AB History and Mathematics, Western Ky. U., 1963; MA, Vanderbilt U., 1965, PhD, 1972. From instr. to assoc. prof. history U. Richmond, Va., 1967-90, prof. history, 1990—, interim v.p., provost, 1983, interim dean faculty arts and scis., 1981-82, assoc. dean faculty arts and scis., 1980-87, dean grad. studies, 1980-87, chair dept. history, 1989—. Spkr. in field; rschr. in field, England, Ireland, Can. Contbr. numerous articles to profl. jours. Grantee Can. Studies Faculty Enrichment Program, 1987; Duke Alberta Rsch. fellow, 1984; faculty summer rsch. fellow, grantee U. Richmond, 1977, 88, 95. Mem. Am. Hist. Assn., Assn. Can. Studies in U.S., Can. Hist. Assn., Carolinas Symposium Brit. Studies, N.Am. Conf. Brit. Studies, S.E. Coun. Can. Studies (exec. com., pres. 1993-96), So. Conf. Brit. Studies (exec. coun., program chair 1993, 94), So. Hist. Assn., Omicron Delta Kappa, Phi Alpha Theta. Home: 4 Bostwick Ln Richmond VA 23226-3107 Office: U Richmond Ryland Hall Richmond VA 23173

GORDON, JOYCE ANNE, elementary education educator; b. West Memphis, Ark., Nov. 16, 1955; d. James Jr. and Helen Jean (Mullins) G. BS in Edn., Ark. State U., 1990, MS in Edn., 1995. 2d-11th grade reading tchr. Bethel Acad., Amory, Miss., 1981-82, 1st grade tchr., 1982-83; customer svc. rep. Walmart, Amory, 1983-87; upper elem. sci. tchr. Cotter (Ark.) Elem. Sch., 1990—. Mem. gifted edn. adv. bd., computers in edn. bd. Cotter Sch. Dist. 60, 1994-95; owner Gordon's Bulletin Boards and Supplies. Leader, organizer After Sch. Study Club, 1990—. Mem. Kappa Delta Pi. Avocation: international sign language. Office: Cotter Sch Dist 60 PO Box 70 Cotter AR 72626-0070

GORDON, LARRY DEAN, elementary education educator; b. Greentop, Mo., Oct. 24, 1938; s. Aubrey T. and Oletha F. (Lay) G.; m. Dolores M. Overstreet, Aug. 23, 1959; children: Sheila, David, Shelly. BSE, N.E. Mo. State U., 1959, MA, 1962; EdS, George Peabody Coll., 1968; EdD, Mo. U., 1971. Tchr. Riverview Gardens Sch. Dist., St. Louis, 1959—; instr. grad. program N.E. Mo. State U., Kirksville, 1974—. Pres. Nat. Edn. Assn.

Riverview Gardens, St. Louis, 1978. Mem. Phi Epsilon Kappa (Disting. Svc. award, pres. 1975-76, 90-91), Phi Delta Kappa. Avocations: reading, traveling, music, sports. Office: Glasgow Sch 10560 Renfrew Dr Saint Louis MO 63137-3896

GORDON, LAWRENCE ALLAN, accounting educator; b. Bklyn., Apr. 15, 1943; s. Seymour and Jessie G.; m. Hedy Hellen Ambrozy, Nov. 23, 1968; children: Lauren Allison, Marc Elliot. BS, SUNY, Albany, 1966, MBA, 1967; PhD, Rensselaer Poly. Inst., 1973. Asst. prof. acctg. Clarkson Coll. Tech., 1971-72, McGill U., Montreal, Can., 1972-74, assoc. prof. acctg., 1974-76, U. Kans., Lawrence, 1976-79, prof. acctg., 1979-80, U. Md., College Park, 1980-81, Ernst & Young Alumni prof. managerial acctg. and info. assurance, 1981. Coord. PhD program in acctg. U. Md., 1980-96, dir. PhD program Coll. Bus. and Mgmt., 1996—, chairperson acctg. faculty, 1982-87, chairperson numerous univ. and profl. coms., 1972—; cons. IBM, 1984-91, U.S. Dept. Labor, 1985-87, U.S. Gen. Acctg. Office, 1978-84, N.Y. State Tchr.'s Retirement System, 1968-69; mgmt. acctg. cons./lectr. Dept. of Supplies and Svcs., Ottawa, Can., 1974-79; mem. audit staff Peat, Marwick, Mitchell & Co., N.Y.C., 1966; presenter in field. Co-editor Jour. Acctg. and Pub. Policy, 1982—; assoc. editor Jour. Bus. Fin. and Acctg., 1991—; editorial bd. mem. Acctg. Rev., 1981-82, Mgmt. Internat. Rev., 1982—, Contemporary Acctg. Rsch., 1984-92; ad-hoc reviewer Jour. Fin. and Quantitative Analysis, Acctg., Orgns. and Soc., Acctg. Rev., Jour. Bus. and Econ. Stats.; author: (with others) Improving Capital Budgeting: A Decision Support System Approach, 1984, The Pricing Decision, 1981, others; author: Managerial Accounting: Concepts and Empirical Evidence, 2000 (5th edit.); author articles. Rsch. grantee U. Md. Coll. Bus. and Mgmt., 1980—, Am. Acctg. Assn., 1976, summer rsch. grantee U. Kans., 1977, grantee Arthur Andersen & Co., 1977, Nat. Assn. Accts. and the Soc. Mgmt. Accts., 1976-80, McGill U., 1975, 75-76, U. Western Ont., 1974, expense grantee for rsch. McGill U., 1973, grantee (with others) U.S. Dept. Labor, 1978-80. Mem. Am. Acctg. Assn., Inst. Mgmt. Accts. Office: Robert H Smith Sch Bus U Md College Park College Park MD 20742-0001

GORDON, LEE DIANE, school librarian, educator; b. Lafayette, Ind., Oct. 30, 1948; d. Henry Charles and Leonora (Brower) G.; m. James J. Thomas, Aug. 27, 1977 (div. Feb. 1994); m. Daniel L. Weber, July 10, 1999. BA, Calif. State U., Long Beach, 1970; MEd, U. Nev., Las Vegas, 1980. Cert. tchr., Nev., Calif.; cert. libr., Nev. Tchr. Carmenita Jr. High Sch., Cerritos, Calif., 1971-77, Jim Bridger Jr. High Sch., North Las Vegas, Nev., 1977-79, libr., 1979-84, Eldorado High Sch., Las Vegas, 1984—2001, Sierra Vista H.S., Las Vegas, 2001—. Adj. faculty U. Nev.-Las Vegas, 1997—. Co-author: The Overworked Teacher's Bulletin Board Book, 1981; filmstrips, 1983; author: World Historical Fiction Guide for Young Adults, 1996; contbr. articles to profl. jours. Mem. Am. Assn. Sch. Librs. (affiliate del., various coms. 1987—; dir. Region VII 1999-2001), Nev. Assn. Sch. Librs. (chair 1987), Clark County Sch. Librs. Assn. (pres. 1987-88), Delta Kappa Gamma (Iota chpt. pres. 1990-92). Office: Sierra Vista High Sch 8100 W Robindale Rd Las Vegas NV 89113

GORDON, LEONARD H(ERMAN) D(AVID), history educator; b. N.Y.C., Aug. 8, 1928; s. Herman and Ray (Keidan) G.; m. Marjorie J(osephine) Hunt, June 11, 1951; children: Herman, David. BA, Ind. U., 1950, MA, 1953; PhD, U. Mich., 1961. Far Eastern diplomatic historian U.S. Dept. State, Washington, 1961-63; asst. prof. East Asian history U. Wis., Madison, 1963-67; assoc. prof. Chinese history Purdue U., West Lafayette, Ind., 1967-94, chmn. Asian studies program, 1992-94, prof. emeritus Chinese history, 1994—. Mem. preliminary screening com. Am. Coun. Learned Socs., N.Y.C., 1971-72, nat. com., 1972-74. Editor: Taiwan: Studies in Chinese Local History, 1970; co-editor: Doctoral Dissertations on China, A Bibliography of Studies in Western Languages, 1945-70, 1972, Bibliography of Sun Yat-Sen in China's Republican Revolution, 1985-1925, 1991, 2d edit., 1998; co-author: All Under Heaven: Sun Yat-Sen and His Revolutionary Thought, 1991. With U.S. Army, 1953-56. Faculty grantee U. Wis., 1963, 64, Faculty grantee Purdue U., 1968, grantee Am. Philos. Soc., 1963, 67, 80; Fulbright Rsch. fellow, Tokyo, 1959-60; Inter-Univ. fellow for Field Tng. in Chinese, Taipei, 1958-59. Mem. Assn. for Asian Studies (publs. com. 1968-71, editor newsletter). Office: Dept of History Purdue U West Lafayette IN 47907-1358 E-mail: lhdgordon@alumni.indiana.edu.

GORDON, MARGARET LOUISE, former education educator; b. Norfolk, Va. d. Daniel D. and Mary E. (Giddings) G. BS, Va. State U., 1938; MA, Howard U., 1944. Asst. prof. edn. Va. State U., Petersburg; elem. tchr. Norfolk City Sch. Bd.; prin. Jacox Jr. High Sch., 1957-67; jr. high sch. prin. Norfolk City Sch. Bd.; assoc. prof. secondary edn. Norfolk State U., 1967-76. Recipient Disting. Svc. award Howard U., award Omega Psi Phi. Mem. ASCD, Nat. Assn. Secondary Sch. Prins., Alpha Kappa Alpha.

GORDON, MARJORIE, lyric coloratura soprano, opera producer, teacher; b. N.Y.C. d. Theodore and Minnie (Glantz) Fishberg; m. Nathan Gordon; children: Maxine, Peter Jon. BA cum laude, Hunter Coll. Nat. cert. voice tchr. Prof. voice Duquesne U., 1957-59, Wayne State U., 1961-91, Nat. Music Camp, Interlochen, 1963-65, Meadowbrook Sch. Music, 1966-71, U. Mich., 1970, Mich. State U., 1971; soloist, tchr. Am. U.-Wolf Trap Program, Washington, 1973. Spl. edn. cons. Detroit Grand Opera Assn.; adj. prof. Oakland (Mich.) U.; pres., gen. dir. Piccolo Opera Co., Inc. Solo debut N.Y. Philharm. Symphony, 1950, soprano soloist, N.Y.C. Opera, 1955-57, Chautauqua Opera Co., 1949-61, Pitts. Opera, 1956; dir. Detroit Opera Theatre, 1960-72, Piccolo Opera Co., 1961—; soloist with orchs., opera cos., summer stock, on radio and TV; recitals U.S., Greece, Europe, Can., Israel; editor: Opera Study Guide, 1968—. Mem. music adv. panel Mich. Arts Coun.; mem. Palm Beach County Cultural Coun.; opera producer Blue Lake Fine Arts Camp, 1993—. Recipient resolution honoring 25th Anniversary Piccolo Opera Co., Mich. Senate; established voice scholarship in perpetuity Nat. Opera Assn. Mem.: AFTRA, Nat. Assn. Tchrs. Singing, Met. Opera Guild, Ctrl. Opera Svc., Nat. Opera Assn., Music Tchrs. Nat. Assn., Am. Guild Mus. Artists, Mich. Music Tchrs. Assn. (voice chmn. 1970—76), Fla. Music Tchrs. Assn., Boca Delray Music Soc., Broward County Music Club, Mu Phi Epsilon. Avocations: handcrafts, swimming, reading, sketching. Fax: 561-394-0520. E-mail: leejon51@msn.com.

GORDON, MARSHALL, former university president; b. LaCenter, Ky., Sept. 1, 1937; s. Ollie James and Dora Ellen (Everett) G; m. Annette Waters, Mar. 17, 1962; 1 child, Mary Ann. BA, Murray (Ky.) State U., 1959; PhD, Vanderbilt U., 1963. Instr. Murray State U., summer 1959; teaching asst. Vanderbilt U., Nashville, 1959-63; rsch. chemist E.I. duPont de Nemours & Co., Inc., Chattanooga, summer 1961; from asst. prof. to prof. chemistry Murray (Ky.) State U., 1963-75, dean, 1975-77, v.p. for univ. svcs., 1977-83, pres., 1981, S.W. Mo. State U., Springfield, 1983-92; mgmt. cons., 1992—. Cons. in field. Contbr. articles to profl. jours. Bd. dirs. Lester E. Cox Med. Ctr., Springfield, 1985—, Hammons Heart Inst. Reg. Adv. Bd., Springfield, 1983—. Mem. ACS (sec.-treas. 1968-70), Am. Assn. State Colls. and U. (com. on agr. and rural devel.), Springfield C. of C. (bd. dirs. 1983-86), Rotary. Avocation: various outdoor activities. Home: PO Box 3691 Springfield MO 65808-3691

GORDON, MARTIN ELI, physician, educator; b. Kiev, Russia, Aug. 15, 1921; came to U.S., 1922; s. Isadore and Belle Gordon; m. Evelyn E. Gordon, Mar. 17, 1946; children: Jeffrey I., Judy I. Dienstag. BS, Kent State U., 1943; MD, Yale U., 1946. Diplomate Am. Bd. Internal Medicine, Nat. Med. Bds. Intern U. Chgo. Clinics, 1946-47; jr. to chief med. resident VA Hosp., Newington, Conn., 1949-51, acting chief to chief gastroenterology sect. West Haven, Conn., 1953-54; cons. gastroenterologist dept. univ. health Yale Univ., New Haven, 1954-72; clin. instr. to clin. prof. medicine Yale Sch. Medicine, New Haven, 1951—; pvt. cons. gastroenterologist various hosps., Conn., 1955-91; cons. practice in gastroenterology New Haven, 1955-91; pres. Med. Films, Inc., New Haven, 1956—. Assoc. fellow Pierson Coll., Yale U., 1979—; sem. chmn., exhibitor 1st and 2nd Internat. Conf. Travel Medicine, Zurich, Atlanta, Paris, 1988, 91, 93; trustee Yale Med. Libr., 1989—; internat. jury judge various film festivals. Author, producer, dir. various med. ednl. films, 1971—; contbr. articles to profl. jours. Med. advisor Am. Cancer Soc., Conn., 1967, 90, Experimental Five Yr. BA Internat. Program, Yale U., 1966-67; chair bd. trustees Assocs. Cushing Whitney Libr. Yale U., 1994—. Sr. asst. surgeon USPHS, 1947-49. Recipient Svc. award Am. Cancer Soc., Conn., 1967, 71. Fellow AAAS, ACP (Laureate award 1991 Conn. chpt., audiovisual and sci. coms.), Am. Coll. Gastroenterology (archives com. 1991-93); mem. AMA (div. ednl. devel.), Am. Gastroenterologic Assn., Am. Fedn. Clin. Rsch., Am. Soc. Gastrointestinal Endoscopy (past chmn. archives and sci. coms.), Am. Soc. Tropical Medicine and Hygiene (ad hoc com. on tng. aids), Yale Alumni Assn. (del. to nat. 1989-94, Disting. Svc. award 2000), Sigma Xi. Avocations: woodworking, casual photography, swimming. Office: Med Films Inc PO Box 288 North Branford CT 06471-0288

GORDON, MILTON PAUL, biochemist, educator; b. St. Paul, Feb. 8, 1930; s. Abraham and Rebecca (Ryan) G.; m. Elaine Travis, Jan. 1, 1955; children— David, Karen, Nancy, Peter. BA summa cum laude, U. Minn., 1950; PhD, U. Ill., 1953. Upjohn Co. fellow U. Ill., 1950-51; Am. Cancer Inst. fellow Sloan-Kettering Inst. for Cancer Research, N.Y.C., 1953-55, research asst., 1955-57; lectr. Bklyn. Coll., 1955-57; asst. research biochemist Virus Lab., U. Calif. at Berkeley, 1957-59; mem. faculty U. Wash., Seattle, 1959—, prof., 1966—, acting chmn., 1984-85. Sec., treas. Pacific Slope Biochem. Conf., 1964-68, pres., 1968; vis. scholar Max Planck Inst., Tübingen, Fed. Republic Germany, 1975; sci. adv. bd. Ctr. forExcellence in Molecular Biology, Lahore, Pakistan; founding organizer Verdant Technologies.; mem. adv. bd. Calgene, Biolex, Caisson Labs., SynGene Biotech., Inc. Assoc. editor Biochemistry, 1960-91. Mem. Am. Chem. Soc., AAAS, Am. Soc. Biol. Chemists, Am. Acad. Microbiology. Rsch. and publs. on plant tumorogenesis and plant transformation, research on phytoremediation. Home: 7111 Linden Ave N Apt 404 Seattle WA 98103-5169 E-mail: miltong@u.washington.edu.

GORDON, PAUL, metallurgical educator; b. Hartford, Conn., Jan. 1, 1918; s. Charles Dana and Anne Mabel (Hirshberg) Gordon; m. Evelyn Rubin, Oct. 16, 1941; children: Dana Charles, Jane Ellen. Student, Wesleyan U., 1935—37; BS in Metallurgy, MIT, 1939, MS, 1940, ScD, 1949. Rsch. assoc. metallurgy MIT, 1941—42; group leader Manhattan Project, 1942—47; faculty Ill. Inst. Tech., 1949—50, 1954—57, prof. metall. engring., from 1957, chmn. dept., 1966-76; asst. prof. Inst. Study Metals, U. Chgo., 1951—54. Author: Principles of Phase Diagrams in Materials Systems, 1968; contbr. articles to profl. jours., chpts. to books. Recipient Albert Easton White Disting. Tchr. award, ASM Internat., 1993. Fellow: Am. Soc. for Metals; mem.: AAAS, Am. Soc. for Testing and Materials, Engrs. Council Profl. Devel., Am. Soc. Engring. Edn., Inst. Metals, Am. Inst. Mining and Metall. Engrs. (Mathewson Gold medal 1957), Sigma Xi. Home: Highland Park, Ill. Died June 7, 2001.

GORDON, ROBERT JAMES, economics educator; b. Boston, Sept. 3, 1940; s. Robert Aaron and Margaret (Shaughnessy) G.; m. Julie S. Peyton, June 22, 1963. AB, Harvard U., 1962; MA, Oxford U., Eng., 1969; PhD, MIT, 1967. Asst. prof. econs. Harvard U., 1967-68; asst. prof. U. Chgo., 1968-73; prof. econs. Northwestern U., Evanston, Ill., 1973—, Stanley G. Harris prof. social scis., 1987—, chair econs. dept., 1992-96. Rsch. assoc. Nat. Bur. Econ Rsch., 1968—; mem. Brookings Panel Econ. Activity, 1970—; co-chmn. Internat. Seminar Macroecons., 1978-94; mem. exec. com. Conf. Rsch., Income and Wealth, 1978-83; mem. panel rev. productivity measures NAS, 1977-79; cons. bd. govs. Fed. Res. Sys., 1973-83, U.S. Dept. Treasury, 1967-80, U.S. Congl. Budget Office, 1996—, U.S. Bur. Econ. Analysis, 1999—; mem. Nat. Commn. on Consumer Price Index, 1995-97. Author: Macroeconomics, 1978, 9th edit., 2003, Milton Friedman's Monetary Framework, 1974, Challenges to Interdependent Economies, 1979, The American Business Cycle: Continuity and Change, 1986, The Measurement of Durable Goods Prices, 1990, International Volatility and Economic Growth, 1991, The Economics of New Goods, 1997; editor Jour. Polit. Economy, 1970-73. Recipient Lustrum prize Erasmus U., 1999; Marshall fellow, 1962-64; fellow Ford Found., 1966-67; grantee NSF, 1971—; fellow Guggenheim Meml. Found., 1980-81; rsch. fellow German Marshall Fund, 1985-86. Fellow AAAS, Econometric Soc. (treas. 1975—); mem. Am. Econ. Assn. (bd. editors 1975-77, mem. exec. com. 1981-83), Phi Beta Kappa Office: Northwestern U Dept Econs Evanston IL 60208-0001 E-mail: rjg@northwestern.edu.

GORDON, ROY GERALD, chemistry educator; b. Akron, Ohio, Jan. 11, 1940; s. Nathan Gold and Frances (Teitel) G.; m. Myra Sheila Miller, Dec. 24, 1961; children: Avra Karen, Emily Francine, Steven Eric. AB summa cum laude, Harvard, 1961, A.M. in Physics, 1962, PhD in Chem. Physics, 1964. Jr. fellow Soc. of Fellows, Harvard, 1964-66, mem. faculty, 1966—, prof., 1969—. Sloan Found. fellow, 1966-69, Einstein fellow, Israel, 1985. Fellow Am. Phys. Soc.; mem. Am. Chem. Soc. (award in pure chemistry 1972, Baekeland award 1979, Esselen award 1996) R & D award 1991, Faraday Soc., Union of Concerned Scientists, NAS, Am. Acad. Arts and Scis., Phi Beta Kappa, Sigma Xi. Achievements include inventions in solar energy, energy conservation and microelectronics, theoretical research discovering forms of forces between molecules, the way molecules collide with each other, motion of molecules in liquids and solids. Office: Harvard U Dept Chemistry 12 Oxford St Cambridge MA 02138-2902 E-mail: gordon@chemistry.harvard.edu.

GORDON, SHARON J. special education educator; b. Calif., 1972; m. Ted H. Gordon, 1972; 1 child, Matthew. BA, San Jose State U., 1969, MA, 1973. Cert. tchr., Calif. Speech lang. pathologist Walnut Creek (Calif.) Elem. Sch. Dist., 1969, San Ramon Unified Sch. Dist., Danville, Calif., 1969-75, Cotati-Rohnert Park (Calif.) Sch. Dist., 1975-80, spl. edn. educator lang. handicapped students, 1980-92, spl. edn. educator, 1992—. Mem. leadership team Waldo Rohnert Sch., 1993—. Pres. Congregation Rodef Sholom, San Rafael, Calif., 1989-91; social action chair no. Calif. Union Am. Hebrew Congregations, San Francisco, 1985-88; chair Jewish Cmty. Rels. Coun., San Rafael, 1992-94. Named Woman of Yr. ORT, 1991. Mem. Am. Speech Lang. Hearing Assn., Calif. Speech Lang. Hearing Assn., Calif. Tchrs. Assn. Avocation: community service projects. Office: Waldo Rohnert Sch 550 Bonnie Ave Rohnert Park CA 94928-3897

GORDON, SUSAN MARQUIS, researcher; b. Orange, NJ, Feb. 20, 1937; d. Bryon St. Croix and Pauline Ruth (Deibert) Marquis; m. Gerald Arnold Gordon; Dec. 17, 1966; children: David Bryon, Janet Ellen. BA, Western Coll., Ohio, 1959; MA, Hunter Coll., N.Y.C., 1965; PhD, U. Chgo., 1972. Rsch. asst. U. Chgo., Ill., 1962-67; rsch. assoc. Cornell U., Ithaca, NY, 1967-71; asst. prof. SUNY, Binghamton, 1969-71, Ithaca Coll., NY, 1972-76; program dir., asst. prof. Boston U., 1976—83; core programs evaluation team dir. Boston Pub. Sch., 1987—89; cons. SMG Cons., Beverly, Mass., 1983-93; prin. Ctr. for Informed Practice, Policy and Rsch., 1993—; project dir. Edn. Devel. Ctr., Newton, Mass., 1989-94; faculty mentor Fielding Graduate Inst., 2000—; State Adv. Coun. for Spl. Ed. Monitor's Report Beverly Solid Waste Mgmt. Comm., 2002. Chair Regional Adv. Coun. for Spl. Edn., 1985-87; vice chair State Adv. Coun. for Spl. Edn., Boston, 1987-88; bd. dirs. Ptnrs. for Youth with Disabilities, 1991-93. Sec. Beverly Garden Club, Mass., 1989-92. Schering Found. fellow, 1971-73; HEW grantee, 1974-76, DOE-OSEP grantee, 1994-96. Mem. Coun. for Exceptional Children, Learning Disabilities Assn., Beverly LWV (sec.). Avocations: swimming, gardening. E-mail: suemgordon@fielding.edu.

GORE, CAROLYN WILLIAMS GARDNER, special education educator, reading specialist; b. Shreveport, La., Dec. 29, 1948; d. Jack Franklin and Kathleen Florence (Hicks) Williams; m. Bruce Lee Gardner, Mar. 9, 1969 (div. Jan. 1990); m. James Thomas Gore, Jan. 11, 2000. BA in Speech Therapy, La. Tech, 1970; MEd, La. State U., Shreveport, 1992, EdS, 1994, PhD, 2002. Cert. tchr., reading specialist, speech therapist, La. Tchr. spl. edn. Caddo Parish Sch. Bd., Shreveport, 1989—94, tchr., lang. enrichment, 1994—97, dyslexia tchr., 1997—. Tchr., cons. Nat. Writing Project, Shreveport, 1991—. Leader Girl Scouts, Shreveport, 1979-89. Mem.: ASCD, LASE, Internat. Dyslexia Assn., Internat. Reading Assn., Coun. Exceptional Children, Phi Delta Kappa. Republican. Methodist. Avocations: camping, bluegrass music.

GORE, PATRICIA W. federal agency administrator; b. 1949; B, U. DC, 1973; grad. study, George Washington U. Dir. tchr. quality programs US Dept. Edn., Innovation and Improvement, Wash., 2002—; sr. exec. fellow Kennedy Sch. Govt., Harvard U., 1999. Office: US Dept Edn Off Innovation and Improvement 400 Maryland Ave SW Rm 5E121 Washington DC 20202*

GORELICK, ELLEN CATHERINE, museum director, curator, artist, educator, civic volunteer; b. Chgo., Jan. 2, 1946; d. Martin Francis and Doris Harriet (Adams) Heckmann; m. Walter Lee Gorelick, Dec. 19, 1970. AA cum laude, Coll. of Sequoias, 1976; BA cum laude, Calif. State U., Fresno, 1979, MA in Art, 1982. Book divsn. corr. Time, Inc., Chgo., 1964-68; accounts receivable supr. Tab Products Co., San Francisco, 1968-69; exec. sec. Foremost-McKesson, Inc., San Francisco, 1969-71, McCarthy Land Co., Visalia, Calif., 1972-74; adminstrv. dir. Creative Ctr. for Handicapped, Visalia, 1979-80; curator Tulare (Calif.) Hist. Mus., 1984-87, dir., curator, 1994—; mem. adj. faculty Coll. of Sequoias, Visalia, 1985-96; gallery dir. Calif. State U., Fresno, 1997—, adj. faculty, 1998—. Bd. dirs. Tulare-Kings Regional Arts Coun., pres., 1989-90; bd. dirs. Tulare County Art League, pres., 1977-78; bd. dirs. Leadership Tulare, founding CORE com., 1991-93, alumni chair, 1992-93; bd. dirs. Tulare County U. Calif. Campus Expansion task force, Visalia, 1988-91, Tulare City Sch. Dist. Classrooms for Kids Campaign, co-chair, 1989; mem. Tulare City Hist. Soc. long range planning com., 1995; mem. Tulare County Symphony Assn., 1992-95, sec., 1993—; founding bd. dirs., v.p., program chair Tulare Cultural Arts Found., 1997—. Named Artist of Yr., Tulare-Kings County Arts Coun., 1988; recipient cert. of appreciation City of Tulare, 1989, Tulare County Bd. Suprs., 1991, Woman of Distinction award Soroptimists, Tulare, 1994. Mem. Tulare Palette Club (pres. 1984-85, Artist of Yr. award 1985). Democrat. Roman Catholic. Avocations: photography, travel, gourmet cooking. Office: Tulare Hist Mus 444 W Tulare Ave Tulare CA 93274-3831

GORELICK, MOLLY CHERNOW, psychologist, educator; b. N.Y.C., Sept. 17, 1920; d. Morris and Jean Chernow; m. Leon Gorelick, Apr. 12, 1941; children: Walter, Peter. AB, UCLA, 1948, MA, 1955, EdD, 1962. Tchr., counselor Los Angeles City Bd. Edn., 1948-61; instr., chief guidance svcs. Exceptional Children's Found., Los Angeles, 1963-70; prof. Calif. State U., Northridge, 1970-91, prof. emeritus, 1991—; research project dir. Vocat. Rehab. Adminstrn. HEW, Los Angeles, 1964-66. Owner, dir. Hi-Ho Day Camp, 1950-57; cons. Riverside County Schs., 1962-70, Kennedy Child Study Ctr., 1975-79; rschr., project dir. Preschool Integration of Children with Handicaps, 1971-75; co-project dir. Establishing Nutritious Food Practices in Early Childhood, USDA-Food and Nutrition Svc., 1979-81; invited lectr. on mental retardation, Eng., Uruguay, Mex., Argentina, China, Poland and Brazil. Co-author: Rescue series, 5 vols., 1967-68; contbr. articles to profl. jours. Former mem. adv. bd. Calif. State Regional Diagnostic Ctr. Children's Hosp., Mirman Sch. Gifted Children, Calif. Ednl. Ctr., Friendship Day Camp; adv. bd. UCLA Sch. Social Welfare. Mem. APA, Western Psychol. Assn., NEA, Coun. Exceptional Children, Am. Assn. Mental Retardation, Phi Beta Kappa, Pi Lambda Theta, Pi Gamma Mu, Phi Kappa Phi.

GORELIK, ALLA, piano educator; b. Chernobyl, Ukraine, Oct. 9, 1949; came to U.S., 1992; d. Simon and Eugena (Ben) Tsoiref; m. Roman Gorelik, June 16, 1971 (div. Apr. 1978); m. Valentin Stadnik, Dec. 26, 1979; children: Regina, Vladislav. BA, State Mus. Coll., Kiev, Ukraine, 1970. Piano and theory tchr. Music Sch. #5, Kiev, 1970-91; accompanist Fort Myers, Fla., 1992—; organist Temple Beth El, Fort Myers, 1993—; music instr. Learning Tree, Fort Myers, 1994—; piano and theory tchr. Fort Myers, 1992—. Children musical program dir. North Shore Child Care, Fort Myers, 1993-95; youth art dir. Music Sch. #5, Kiev, 1986-90. Vol., performer Jewish Fedn., Fort Myers, 1992—, Hadassah, Fort Myers, 1993—; vol., accompanist Temples Beth-El and Judea, Fort Myers, 1992—. Recipient Labor Merit medal Ministry of Culture, 1990. Mem. Nat. Music Tchrs. Assn. Avocations: travel, cooking, reading. Home: 18257 Huckleberry Rd Fort Myers FL 33912-5234

GORENSTEIN, DAVID G. chemistry and biochemistry educator; b. Oct. 6, 1945; s. Ben and Shirley (Adelberg) G.; m. Deborah H. Joseph, June 11, 1967; 1 child, Jennifer. BS in Chemistry, M.I.T., 1966; MA in Chemistry, Harvard U., 1967, PhD in Chemistry, 1969. Asst. prof. U. Ill., Chgo., 1969-73, assoc. prof., 1973-76, prof., 1976-85; prof. chemistry Purdue Univ., West Lafayette, Ind., 1985-94; dir. Purdue Biochem. MRI Lab., West Lafayette, Ind., 1985-94, NSF Nat. Biol. Facilities Ctr., West Lafayette, 1987-93, NMR and Structural Biology Cores, West Lafayette, 1988-94; dep. dir. NIH Designated AIDS Rsch. Ctr., West Lafayette, 1993-94; prof. human biol. chemistry and genetics U. Tex. Med. Sch., Galveston, 1994—; sr. investigator Sealy Ctr. Molecular Sci. U. Tex. Med. Br., Galveston, 1994—; dir. Nuclear Magnetic Resonance Ctr. U. Tex. Med. Br., Galveston, dir. Sealy Ctr. for Structural Biology, 1995—2002, dep. dir. NIEHS Ctr., 1996—, Charles Marc Pomerat Disting. Prof. of biology, 1997—, vice chmn. human biol. chem. genetics, 1999—2002, assoc. dean rsch., 2002—. Dir. Gulf Coast NMR Consortium; vis. assoc. prof. U. Wis., Madison, 1975; vis. prof. Oxford U., 1977-78, U. Calif., San Francisco, 1986; adj. prof. Biomed. Engring. U. Tex., Austin, 1996—; cons. Baxter Travenol, 1985-95, Merck and Co., 1988, Eli Lilly, 1987-89, Ill. Tool Works, 1973-85, Chronomatic Inc., 1973-85, U.S. Dept. of Labor, 1975, Continental Group, Inc., 1982-84, Abbott Corp., 2001- Abbott Diagnostics, 2002; active numerous univ. coms.; lectr. in field. Editor Bull. of Magnetic Resonance, 1982-99; mem. editorial bd. Magnetic Resonance Revs., 1983-93, Jour. Magnetic Resonance, 1992-99, Biophys. Jour., 1992-98; pub. abstracts; contbr. articles to profl. jours. Grantee: NSF, 1987-93, NIH, 1970—, Eli Lilly, 1988-94 and numerous others; tchg. fellow Harvard U., 1966-69, trainee summer fellow NSF, 1966, predoctoral fellow NIH, 1967-69, Alfred P. Sloan fellow 1975-79, Sr. Rsch. fellow Fulbright, 1977-78, Guggenheim fellow, 1986; recipient Internat. Lectr. award Fulbright, 1978. Fellow AAAS; mem. Am. Soc. for Biochemistry and Molecular Biology, Am. Chem. Soc. (program chmn. divsn. biol. chemistry 1985-87, vice chmn. Purdue sect. 1990-91, chmn. 1991-92), Biophys. Soc., Protein Soc., Sigma Xi, Phi Lambda Upsilon. Achievements include patents in process for Preparing Dithiophosphate Oligonucleotide Analogs via Nucleoside Thiophosphoramidite Intermediates and in vivo selection of aptamers; research in proteomics and applications of NMR spectroscopy and other physical techniques to biological systems, theoretical bio-organic chemistry, biomolecular design; cancer and anti-viral drugs development. Address: 3922 Crown Ridge Ct Houston TX 77059-3711 Office: U Tex Med Br Sch Medicine Galveston TX 77555-1157

GORIN, ROBERT MURRAY, JR., history educator; b. Oct. 29, 1948; s. Robert Murray and Vivian Margaret (Schleider) Gorin. AB, MA, Xavier U., 1970; MS in Edn., Hofstra U., 1974; MA, Fordham U., 1978; PhD, St. Louis U., 1980; MS, Johns Hopkins U., 1992; postgrad., Yale U., Harvard U., Civil War Inst., Gettburg Coll., U. Calif., Berkeley, Oxford U. Cert. N.Y.

State Edn. Dept. Tchr. social studies Bellmore-Merrick (N.Y.) Ctrl. H.S. Dist., 1974—77, 1978—83, Rockville Centre (N.Y.) Union Free Sch. Dist., 1977—78, Manhasset (N.Y.) Pub. Sch., 1983—. Adj. asst. prof. history Hofstra U., 1986—. Mem. N.Y. Pub. Libr. With USAR, 1968—69. Fellow, Robert A. Taft Inst. Govt., 1976, Soc. Values in Higher Edn. Mem.: Moral Edn. Assn., Nat. Coun History Edn. Assn. for Preservation of Civil War Sites, Civil War Soc., Soc. Civil War Historians, N.Y. Hist. Soc., N.Y. State Coun. Social Studies, L.I. Coun. Social Studies, Nat. Coun. Social Studies, Soc. History Edn., Ctr. for Study Presidency, Orgn. History Edn., Orgn. Am. Historians, So. Hist. Assn., Am. Hist. Assn., Am. Mus. Natural History, Civil War Round Table N.Y., Worcester Coll. Assocs., Am. Friends of Bodleian Libr., Taft Assocs., Friends of Nat. Pks. Gettysburg, Am. Friends of Rowley House, Oxford, Met. Mus. Art, Met. Opera Guild, ASCD, Phi Alpha Theta. Republican. Roman Catholic. Home: 51 Somerset Ave Garden City NY 11530-1145

GORNEY, RODERIC, psychiatry educator; b. Grand Rapids, Mich., Aug. 13, 1924; s. Abraham Jacob Gorney and Edelaine (Roden) Harburg; m. Carol Ann Sobel, Apr. 13, 1986. BS, Stanford U., 1948, MD, 1949; PhD in Psychoanalysis, So. Calif. Psychoanalytic Inst., 1977. Diplomate Am. Bd. Psychiatry and Neurology. Pvt. practice psychiatry, San Francisco, 1952-62; asst. prof. UCLA, 1962-71, assoc. prof., 1971-73, prof. psychiatry, 1980—, dir. psychosocial adaptation and the future program, 1971—. Faculty So. Calif. Psychoanalytic Inst. Author: The Human Agenda, 1972. Served with USAF, 1943-46. Fellow AAAS, Acad. Psychoanalysis, Am. Psychoanalytic Assn., Internat. Psychoanalytic Assn., Am. Psychiatric Assn. (essay prize 1971), Group for Advancement of Psychiatry. Avocation: music. Office: UCLA Neuropsychiatric Inst 760 Westwood Plz Los Angeles CA 90095-8353 E-mail: preadapt@ucla.edu.

GORON, MARA J. social studies educator, assistant principal; b. Jackson Heights, N.Y., Apr. 9, 1968; d. Stuart Platt and Joan (Arkin) Scolnick. BA, The George Washington U., 1990, MA, 1992; MEd, U. Md., 1995. Cert. secondary social studies and spl. edn. adminstrn. Resident asst., adminstr., supr. The George Washington U., Washington, 1989-92; tchr. religion Temple Sinai, Washington, 1990-96; peer tutoring coord. The George Washington U., 1991-92; adult edn. tchr. Montgomery County Pub., Rockville, Md., 1992; spl. edn. tchr. Alexandria (Va.) Pub. Schs., 1992, Prince Georges Pub. Schs., Upper Marlboro, Md., 1992-93; tutor Lab Sch. Washington, 1992—2002; spl. edn. tchr. Howard County Pub. Schs., Ellicott City, Md., 1993-96, social studies tchr., 1996-99; asst. prin. Centennial H.S., Ellicott City, 1999—2001; inaugural asst. prin. Reservoir H.S., 2001—02; asst. prin. Spanish River Cmty. H.S., Boca Raton, Fla., 2002—. Adviser Howard County Assn. Student Couns., 1997—99; pres. Howard County Coun. for Social Studies, 1997—99; adj. prof. Towson U., 1998, 99. Troop leader Girl Scouts of Am., 1994-95. Mem. ASCD, NAFE, Nat. Assn. Secondary Sch. Prins., Pi Kappa Phi, Omicron Delta Kappa. Avocations: walking, hiking, knitting, reading, going to movies. E-mail: goronm@palmbeach.k12.fl.us.

GORR, ELAINE GRAY, therapist, elementary education educator; b. Pitts., Oct. 3, 1949; d. Elmer and Elizabeth Gray; m. Joseph Charles Bonasorte, June 20, 1969 (div. 1972); 1 child, Leah Christine Bonasorte; m. Arthur Richard Gorr, Aug. 12, 1983; children: Arthur, Stephen, Ellen, Bruce, Matthew, Leah, Carl. BS in Psychology, U. Pitts., 1972; MA in Counseling/Psychology, Norwich U., 1993; PhD in Clin. Psychology, Walden U., 2000. Cert. elem. sch. counselor, Pa., elem. tchr., Pa. Tchr. Pitts. Pub. Schs., 1973-89; outpatient therapist Mercy Behavioral Health, Pitts., 1999—; pvt. practice clin. therapist Pitts., 1992—. Nat. bd. dirs. Children and Adults with Attention Deficit Disorders., 1997-2001. Mem. APA, PPA, Nat. Assn. Cognitive Behavioral Therapists, Greater Pitts. Psychol. Assn. Office: 615 Washington Rd Ste 302 Pittsburgh PA 15228

GORSALITZ, JEANNINE LIANE, elementary school educator; b. Appleton, Wis., Sept. 22, 1939; d. Gustav Herman and Viola Rachel (Wiedenhaupt) G. BS, Dr. Martin Luther Coll., 1961; MA, U. Wis., Oshkosh, 1969; PhD, U. Wis., Madison, 1980. Cert. elem. tchr., Wis. Tchr. Palos Luth. Sch., Palos Heights, Ill., 1959-60; tchr., prin. St. Peter's Luth. Sch., Freedom, Wis., 1960-65; tchr. Grace Luth. Sch., Neenah, Wis., 1965—69, Gegan Elem. Sch., Menasha, Wis., 1969—93, Butte des Morts Elem. Sch., Menasha, 1993—; coord. elem. social studies Menasha Schs., 1988—. Advisor Wis. Coun. for Local History, Madison, 1987—; lectr. Sch. Edn., U. Wis. Author/co-author ednl. curriculum (various awards). Vol. First Responder, Ellington, Wis., 1981—86; tchr. translator Hmong Outreach, 1985—; block capt. Neighborhood Watch, Neenah, 1989—; mem. Victim Crisis Responders, 1998—; organizer Spanish ESL Outreach, 1999; active State Hist. Soc. Wis., Madison. Recipient Outstanding Contbn. award State Hist. Soc., 1980, Excellence in Edn. award U.S. Sec. Edn., Washington, 1989, Excellence award Nat. Coun. Econs., N.Y.C., 1990. Mem. Nat. Fedn. Tchrs., Nat. Coun. for Social Studies, Wis. Fedn. Tchrs., Wis. Coun. for Social Studies, Wis. Coun. for Environ. Edn., Wis. Coun. for Econ. Edn., Kiwanis, Attrasa Internat. Lutheran. Avocations: travel, geography and history of state of wisconsin. Home and Office: 440 E Peckham St Neenah WI 54956-4168

GORSKI, NANCY ANNE, elementary education educator; b. Chgo., Aug. 8, 1932; d. Frank Adam and Bernice Dolores (Bukala) Glusack; m. Joseph Edward Gorski, June 27, 1953; children: Gregory Francis, Loren Walter. BS in Elem. Edn., Phys. Edn., Chgo. Tchrs. Coll., 1954. Cert. tchr., Ill. Phys. edn. tchr. Beidler and Skinner Elem. Schs., Chgo., 1954-55, Wadsworth Elem. Sch., Chgo., 1955-56, Beale Elem. Sch., Chgo., 1956-57, Parker Elem. Sch., Chgo., 1955-57, Joseph E. Gary Elem. Sch., Chgo., 1960—. Administered practical exam in dance for phys. edn. certification, Chgo. Pub. Schs., 1969-74, 81-87, presenter phys. edn. workshops, 1970-73, 77. Author phys. edn. curriculum Chgo. Pub. Schs., 1977-78; profl. dancer convs. and indsl. shows; choreographer ch. prodns., 1972-82. Mem. Am. Alliance for Health, Phys. Edn., Recreation and Dance, Ill. Assn. for Health, Phys. Edn., Recreation and Dance (Quarter Century award 1992, Outstanding Elem. Phys. Educator 1992), Henry Suder Club. Roman Catholic. Avocations: grandchildren, ballet, tap, jazz, swimming. Home: 418 Ruby St Clarendon Hills IL 60514-2710

GORZKA, MARGARET ROSE, elementary education educator; b. Akron, Ohio, Sept. 2, 1945; d. Alfonso Sebastian and Hannah Jean (Morris) Brown; m. Joseph Frank Gorzka Sr., Nov. 24, 1966; children: Joseph Frank Jr., Julie-Anne. BS in Elem. Edn., Akron U., 1968; MS in Elem. Edn., Nazareth Coll., 1986. Permanent cert. N-6. Tchr. 1st grade # 3 Sch. Rochester (N.Y.) City Schs., 1967-68, St. John the Evangelist, Rochester, 1968-70, Mother of Sorrows, Rochester, 1971-72; tchr. kindergarten St. John's Sch., Spencerport, N.Y., spring 1978; tchr. 1st, 2d, 3d grades St. Rita's, West Webster, N.Y., 1978-79; tchr. 1st grade St. Anne's, Rochester, 1979-81, St. Jerome's, East Rochester, N.Y., 1981-86; tchr. kindergarten, 1st grade East Rochester Union Free Schs., East Rochester, 1986-91; tchr. 1st grade Fairport (N.Y.) Ctrl. Schs., 1991—2001, kindergarten tchr., 2001—. Geselle trainer East Rochester Union Free Schs., 1987—, essential elements of effective instrn. trainer, 1987-91, clin. supervision trainer, 1987-91; cons. and presenter in field. Mem. fundraising com. Advent House, Fairport, 1993—; PTA chair for Parent Edn., 1995-96; mem. staff devel. Fairport Cen. Sch. Dist., 1996-2002; mem. policy bd. Fairport Tch. Ctr., 1999—; chair Daffodil Day, 1994—. Grantee Sci. Wizards at Work, 1994; recipient Disting. Svc. award East Rochester PTA, 1986, Crystal Apple award, 1995, PASE award, 1995, 98, Team Performance Recognition award for Fairport Cen. Sch. dist., 1993-94, Phoebe Apperson Hearst Outstanding Edn. Excellence award 1996. Mem. AAUW, N.Y. State United Tchrs., Fairport Edn. Assn., Phi Mu Alumnae (v.p. 1970s). Republican. Roman Catholic. Home: 1 Cobblestone Dr Fairport NY 14450-3152

GOSLIN, GERALD HUGH, concert pianist, educator; b. Detroit, Jan. 7, 1947; s. Hugh Jennings and Helen Margaret (Senauit) Goslin. Student, Wayne State U., Detroit, 1966-69. Music tchr. Peralta Music, Farmington, Mich., 1965—80, Hammell Music, Livonia, 1980—83; prof. music Oakland CC, Farmington Hills, 1983—; host The Piano Hour Sta. WHND-AM, Oak Park, 1995; recitalist Allen, Rodgers and Baldwin Organs, Detroit, 1975—90; prof. voice, theory and piano Livonia Conservatory, 1998—. Judge Leontyne Price Vocal Competition, 1986—2003, Verdi Opera Assn. Vocal Competition, 1995—96. Block capt. Rogers Park Residents Assn., Redford, Mich., 1995—2002; choirmaster, organist Bushnell Congl. Ch., Detroit, 2000—. Mem.: Am. Guild Organists, Am. Choir Dir. Assn., Detroit Fedn. Musicians Local # 5. Home and Office: 22600 Middlebelt Rd C-10 Farmington Hills MI 48336-3672

GOSS, PATRICIA ELIZABETH, secondary education educator; b. Cheyenne, Wyo., June 6, 1958; d. Alan Robert and Donna Jean (Hirst) G.; m. Michael Holland Argall, Nov. 6, 1993. BA, Colo. Women's Coll., 1979; MA, U. Denver, 1980; postgrad., U. Colo., 1986. Cert. secondary tchr., Colo. Exec. dir. Denver Dem. Com., 1980-82; coord. 3d Congl. dist. Mondale for Pres. Campaign, Colo., 1984; tchr. mid. sch. gifted and talented Denver Pub. Schs., 1988-90, tchr. history, 1991—. Supr. student tchrs. Regis Coll., Denver, 1996. Contbr. articles to profl. jours. Chmn. precinct com. Denver Dem. Com., 1980—, mem. exec. com., 1980-86. Mem. NEA (congl. contact team 1993—, rep. assembly del. 1993, 96), Colo. Edn. Assn. (legis. action team 1991—, bd. dirs. 1992—), Denver Classroom Tchrs. Assn. (dir. govtl. rels. 1991—), DAR, Order Ea. Star, Alpha Delta Kappa. Presbyterian. Avocations: travel, photography, cooking, miniature dollhouses. Home: 328 Croton Dr Maitland FL 32751-3114 Office: George Washington HS 655 S Monaco Pkwy Denver CO 80224-1228

GOSSETT, JANINE LEE, middle school educator; b. Carlsbad, N.Mex., Jan. 22, 1950; d. William Adair and Anita Jeanne (Hilty) G. BS, N.Mex. State U., 1974, MA, 1992. Tchr., dir. Sunshine Sch., Parker, Ariz.; tchr. spl. edn. Lubbock (Tex.) State Sch.; tchr. regular and accelerated lang. arts Carlsbad Mcpl. Schs.; tchr. 7th & 8th gr. advanced ednl. placement Carlsbad Mcp. Schs. Mem. Nat. Coun. Tchrs. English, Nat. Mid. Sch. Assn., N.Mex. Coun. Tchrs. English (past treas., directory/membership chair). Office: 408 N Canyon St Carlsbad NM 88220-5812

GOSSETT, KATHRYN MYERS, language professional, educator; b. Baltimore, Ohio; d. Charles Edgar and Vera Mae (Good) Myers; m. William Thomas Gossett, June 30, 1984. BA summa cum laude, Ohio U., 1931, MA, 1936. Cert. tchr., Ohio, Pa., Mich. Latin and English tchr. Beccaria Twp. High Sch., Coalport, Pa., 1931-32; French, Latin and English tchr. Buford (Ohio) High Sch., 1932-36; tchr. fgn. langs. Oak Hill (Ohio) High Sch., 1936-42; critic tchr. Ohio U. and Athens High Sch., 1942-43; English and Spanish tchr. Eastern High Sch., Lansing, Mich., 1943-45; French tchr. Kingswood/Cranbrook Pvt. Sch., Bloomfield Hills, Mich., 1945-55, chmn. fgn. lang., 1955-75. Fulbright tchr. Lycée de Jeunes Filles, Annecy, France, 1953-54. Contbr. articles to profl. jours. Decorated chevalier des Palmes Academiques (France); recipient Cranbrook Founders medal, 1976; U. Besancon (France) scholar. Mem. AAUW, Am. Assn. Ret. Persons, Eastern Star, Bloomfield Hills Country Club, The Ocean Club of Fla. (Ocean Ridge), The Little Club (Gulf Stream, Fla.), The Village Club (Bloomfield Hills), Phi Beta Kappa. Republican. Episcopalian. Avocations: art, music, history. Home: 1276 Covington Rd Bloomfield Hills MI 48301-2365

GOSSMAN, JANE MCMINN, school system administrator; b. Omaha, Dec. 31, 1955; d. H. Samuel and Beverly Jane (Haarmann) McMinn; m. Charles Craig Moyer, June 27, 1981 (div. Nov. 1992); children: Charles Scott, Thomas McMinn; m. John D. Gossman, Nov. 13, 1999. BS in Edn., U. Nebr., 1978; MA in Ednl. Adminstrn., Kearney State Coll., 1985. Cert. adminstr., secondary sch. prin. type D, Colo.; cert. adminstr., supr. secondary endorsed English tchr., reading and mildy-moderately handicapped 7-12, Nebr. Tchr. Omaha Pub. Sch., summers 1978/81, Waverly Pub. Sch., Nebr., 1978-79, Millard Pub. Sch., Omaha, 1979-82, Grand Island Pub. Sch., Nebr., 1982-93; asst. prin. Grand Junction HS, Colo., 1993-94, Widefield HS, Colo. Springs, 1994—2000; prin. Sunrise Elem. Sch., Colo. Springs, 2000—02, asst. dir. curriculum and instrn., 2002—. Bd. dir. Cen. Nebr. Coun. Alcoholism, Grand Island, 1989-93, sec. 1990-91; bd. dir. First Presbyn. Ch. Pre-Sch., Grand Island, 1990-93; mem. Grand Island Edn. 2000 Commn., Grand Island Pub. Sch., 1992-93. Mem. Nat. Assn. Secondary Sch. Prin., Colo. Assn. Sch. Exec., Nebr. Assn. Mid. Level Edn. (pres. elect 1993, mem. chmn. 1991-93, bd. dir. 1991-93), Phi Delta Kappa, Kappa Kappa Gamma (area rush chmn. Nebr. chpt. 1978-93). Republican. Lutheran. Avocations: music, needlework, reading, travel, sports. Home: 7835 Fawn Meadow Vw Colorado Springs CO 80919-3897 Office: Widefield Administrn Bldg 1820 Main St Colorado Springs CO 80911-1839

GOTSCH, AUDREY ROSE, environmental health sciences educator, researcher; b. Milw., May 30, 1939; d. Carlos Louis and Florence Olga (Clausing) Grandy; m. Thomas Gotsch, June 20, 1959; children: Christine Anne Robinson, Allison Lorraine. BS, Ind. U., 1963; MPH, U. Mich., 1966; DrPH, CHES, Columbia U., 1976. Pvt. practice as dental hygienist, Lafayette, Ind., 1962-63, Springfield, Ill., 1963-65; health educator Ill. Dept. Health, Springfield, 1966-67, N.J. State Dept. Health, Trenton, 1968; from assoc. prof., chief dept. environ. and cmty. medicine to prof. U. Medicine and Dentistry N.J. Robert Wood Johnson Med. Sch., Piscataway, 1978—2001, prof. Dept. Environ. and Cmty. Medicine, 2001—; dean Sch. Pub. Health U. Medicine and Dentistry of N.J., New Brunswick, 2001—; dir. pub. edn. and risk com. divsn. Environ. and Occupational Health Scis. Inst., 2001—, prof. (coterminous), 2001—. Cons. Nat. Hospice Demonstration Programs, 1980, Hospice of Ctrl. N.Y., Syracuse, 1980, Nat. Cancer Inst., 1981—, Fox Chase Cancer Ctr., Phila., 1983, Medcom, Inc., Calif., 1985, NIH, Heart, Lung and Blood Inst., Bethesda, Md., 1985—, and others; assoc. mem. grad. faculty, Rutgers U., New Brunswick, N.J., 1984—; mem. Outreach Task Force, The Cancer Inst. N.J., 1991—; assoc. mem. Inst. for Health, Health Care Policy and Aging Rsch., Rutgers, 1992; councilor, Coun. on Edn. for Pub. Health, 1990-96, pres. 1993-96; chair ednl. programs com. Environ. Health Found., 1995—; mem. steering com. Cmty. Environ. Health Assessment, NACCHO and Nat. Ctr. Environ. Health, CDC, 1995—; chair sch. health edn. com. Nat. Ctr. for Health Edn., 1997; mem. adv. bd. Joint NIEHS/NIH Office of Sci. Edn. Project. Author: (with others) Communication of Risk, 1992, Education for Health: Strategies for Change, 1978, The Environment and the Community: Environmental Health Lessons for Grades 10-12, 1990, Occupational Health Awareness: Lessons for Vocational Students in Secondary Schools, 1990, Healthy Environment--Healthy Me for Kindergarten-Sixth Grade, 1991, 92, Environmental Decision Making, 1995, Advanced Decision Making: Solid Waste Issues in Businesses, Schools and the Community, 1996, and others; mem. editl. bd. Health Edn. Quar., 1986-89; editor-in-chief INFOletter: Environmental and Occupational Health Briefs, 1988-96; contbr. reports, articles and abstracts to profl. jours. and newspapers; videos Alexandria's Clean-Up Fix-Up Parade, 1988, Alu-man the Can, 1987 (Sci. Commendation Cath. Audio Visual Educators 1991), A Breath of Fresh Air: Improving Air Quality in Your Office, 1989, Take Charge! Jobs or Health: A Town's Dilemma, 1989, Safety Sense, 1989, Sam's Safety Star Award, 1988, Down the Drain, 1989, Keeping the Lid on Air Pollution, 1989 (Cable award Programming Excellence CTN NJ. 1990), Inside Story on Air Pollution, 1990, What To Do With All Our Garbage?, 1990, PEOSH & RTK: What's It All About?, 1990, Talkin' Trash, 1992, Enviro-Decisions: Solid Waste, 1996, Environ-Decisions: Living with Toxins, 1997, ToxRAP: Toxicology, Risk Assessment and Air Pollution, 1998 (Nat. Environ. Edn. Achievement award 1997); bd. of assoc. editors: Am. Assn. for Health Edn., 1997-2001; contbr. numerous articles to profl. jours. Mem. N.J. Pub. Health Coun., Trenton, 1987—, sec., 1992-94, 2001-02, vice chair, 1994-96, chair, 1996-98; task force Gov.'s Conf. on Aging, 1980-81; mem. State Health Planning Bd., 1996—; bd. govs. Sch. Pub. Health Alumni Soc., U. Mich., 1996—; bd. dirs. Nat. Ctr. for Health Edn., 1996—. Recipient sec.'s award HHS, 1988, 94, statewide faculty recognition award N.J. Bd. Higher Edn., 1989, Spl. Recognition award Commr. N.J. Dept. Health and Sr. Svcs., 1998, Virginia S. DeHaan Lecture award on Health Promotion and Edn., Rollins Sch. Pub. Health, Emory U., 1998, Harry R.H. Nicholas award N.J. Environ. Health Assn., 2001, Salute to the Policy Makers award Exec. Women of N.J., 2002; named Woman of Distinction World of Environment Del.-Raritan Girl Scout Coun., 2000; USPHS fellow, 1965-66, 72-74; grantee Nat. Inst. Environ. Health Scis., 1987—, NSF, 1991-95, N.J. Bus. Roundtable, 1989-92, N.J. Dept. Edn., 1991-92, EPA, 1991-96, N.J. Dept. Environ. Protection and Energy, 1991-92, numerous others; C.V. Mosby scholar, 1962. Mem. APHA (pres.-elect 1998-99, Disting. Career award 1996, Recognition award for leadership to APHA's First Satellite Broadcast 2000), Assn. for Social Scis. in Health, Assn. Tchrs. Preventive Medicine, Soc. for Pub. Health Edn. (subcom. on environ. outreach and svc. Greater N.Y. and N.J. chpts.), Internat. Union for Health Edn., Soc. Toxicology (Pub. Comm. award 1997), Nat. Hospice Orgn., N.J. Hospice Orgn. (bd. trustees 1980-82), N.J. Pub. Health Assn. (state health planning bd. 1996—, Dennis J. Sullivan award 1997), Soc. for Risk Analysis, Royal Soc. Health (hon.), Sigma Xi, Sigma Phi Alpha. Lutheran. Avocations: sailing, tennis, swimming, church choir, theater. Office: UMDNJ-Sch Pub Health 335 George St Libert Plaza Ste 2200 New Brunswick NJ 08903 E-mail: perc@eohsi.rutgers.edu.

GOTT, MARJORIE EDA CROSBY, conservationist, former educator; b. Louisville; d. Alva Baird and Nellie (Jones) Crosby; m. John Richard Gott, Jr., Mar. 12, 1946 (dec. Sept. 1993); 1 child, J. Richard III. AB in Math., U. Louisville, 1934; postgrad., U. Ky., 1938-42. Nationally accredited flower show judge, landscape design critic and judge. Underwriter Commonwealth Life Ins. Co., Louisville, 1934-37; tchr. English Hikes Sch., Buechel, Ky., 1937-43; civilian chief stats. control unit Materiel Command, Army Air Force, Dayton, Ohio, 1943-46; tchr. psychology Bapt. Hosp. and Gen. Hosp., Louisville, 1950-52. Dedicated Ky.'s Floral Clock to All Kentuckians Who Take Pride in the Beauty of Their State Commonwealth of Ky.,1961. Author: (booklet) How a Garden Club Beautifies a City, 1967. Pres. Young Women's Rep. Club of Louisville and Jefferson County, 1938-40; pres. Beautification League Louisville and Jefferson County, 1963-64; co-chair Keep Ky. Cleaner-Greener, 1963-68; bd. dirs. Scenic Ky., Inc., 1989—, Nat. Coun. State Garden Clubs, 1961-83. Recipient Conservation award of merit Commonwealth of Ky., 1963, Landscape Design Critics award Nat. Coun. State Garden Clubs, 1979. Mem. Woman's Club of Louisville (pres. 1973-75, hon. 1991—), Garden Club of Ky. (pres. 1961-63), Nat. Assn. Parliamentarians (founder, pres. Louisville unit 1961-63), Louisville Astron. Soc. (hon.). Presbyterian. Avocations: travel, bridge, cooking. Home: 136 Indian Hills Trl Louisville KY 40207-1541

GOTT, WESLEY ATLAS, art educator; b. Buffalo, Mar. 6, 1942; s. Raymond and Rowena (Pettitt) G.; m. Alice Blalock, May 26, 1972; children— Andrew, Deidre. BS, S.W. Mo. State U., 1965; M of Ch. Music, Southwestern Theol. Sem., 1969; MFA, George Washington U., 1975; postgrad. Nova U. Tchr. ceramic classes Springfield Art Mus., Mo., 1964-66; minister of music Terrace Acres Bapt. Ch., Ft. Worth, Tex., 1966-70; minister music and youth First Bapt. Ch. Wheaton, Md., 1970-75; asst. prof. art S.W. Bapt. U., Bolivar, Mo., 1975-79, assoc. prof., chmn. dept. art, 1979— ; judge art contests for High Schs., 1978—. Artist christmas sculpture with lights, 1981-84. Mem. Coll. Art Assn. Am., Mid-Am. Coll. Art Assn., Smithsonian Assocs., Nat. Trust for Historic Preservation, Community Concert Assn., Alpha Gamma Theta, Phi Mu Alpha. Baptist. Avocations: hunting; fishing; boating; tennis; golf. Home: 127 W Maupin St Bolivar MO 65613-1946 Office: SW Bapt U 1600 University Ave Bolivar MO 65613-2597 Business E-Mail: wgott@sbuniv.edu.

GOTTA, ALEXANDER WALTER, anesthesiologist, educator; b. Bklyn., Apr. 10, 1935; s. A. Walter and Helen C. (Bruskewic) G.; m. Colleen A. Sullivan, July 17, 1965; 1 child, Nancy C. BS summa cum laude, St. John's U., 1956; MD, NYU, 1960. Diplomate Am. Bd. Anesthesiology, Am. Bd. Med. Examiners. Intern U. Chgo., 1960-61; resident in surgery Boston City Hosp., 1961-62; resident in anesthesiology N.Y. Hosp.-Cornell U., N.Y.C., 1962-64; instr. anesthesiology Cornell U., 1965-66; adj. prof. St. John's U., 1977—79; dir. anesthesia St. Mary's Hosp., Bklyn., 1968-78; from asst. prof. to prof. SUNY, Bklyn., 1968—97; prof. emeritus, 1997—. Dir. anesthesia L.I. Coll. Hosp., Bklyn., 1983-90, Kings County Hosp. Ctr., 1990-97; spkr. in field. Editor: Anesthesiology Clinics Trauma, 1996; contbr. articles to profl. jours. Capt. U.S. Army, 1966-68, Vietnam. Fellow N.Y. Acad. Medicine (chmn. anesthesia sect. 1990, recognition for svc. to urban medicine 1997), Am. Coll. Anesthesiologists, Am. Soc. Anesthesiologists (ho. dels. 1986-97, chmn. refresher course com. 1995); mem. N.Y. Soc. Anesthesiologists (bd. dirs. 1983-97, chmn. sci. program com. 1991-93, chmn. PGA 1994-96, v.p. 1994, pres.-elect 1995, pres. 1996), N.Y. Soc. Critical Care Medicine (pres. 1985), Assn. Univ. Anesthesiologists, Acad. Anesthesia. Republican. Roman Catholic. Home: 29 Ascot Ridge Rd Great Neck NY 11021-2912 Office: Kings County Hosp Ctr 451 Clarkson Ave Brooklyn NY 11203-2097 E-mail: alexwg@optonline.net.

GOTTESMAN, IRVING ISADORE, psychology educator; b. Cleve., Dec. 29, 1930; s. Bernard and Virginia (Weitzner) G.; m. Carol Applen, Dec. 23, 1970; children— Adam M., David B. BS, Ill. Inst. Tech., 1953; PhD, U. Minn., 1960. Diplomate in clin. psychology and psychol. assessment; lic. psychologist Calif., Va. Intern clin. psychology VA Hosp., Mpls., 1959-60; lectr. dept. social relations Harvard U., 1960-63; USPHS fellow in psychiat. genetics Inst. Psychiatry, London, 1963-64; assoc. prof. psychiat. & genetics, dept. psychiatry U. N.C., 1964-66; prof. dept. psychology, psychiatry and genetics U. Minn., 1966-80; prof. dept. psychiatry and genetics Washington U., St. Louis, 1980-85; Commonwealth prof. psychology U. Va., Charlottesville, 1985-94, Sherrell J. Aston prof. psychology, prof. clin. pediats., 1994-2001, prof. emeritus, 2001—; sr. fellow, Drs. Irving and Dorothy Bernstein prof. adult psychiatry U. Minn., 2001—. Cons. NIMH, Washington, 1975-79, 92-96, NIMH Nat. Plan for Schizophrenia, 1988-89; mem. Pres.'s Commn. on Huntington Disease, 1977; tng. cons. VA, Washington, 1968-85, 2001—; fellow Ctr. for Advanced Studies in the Behavioral Scis., Stanford, Calif., 1987-88; Inst. of Medicine Com. cons. Vietnam War Experience Study, 1987-88, Med. Follow-Up Agy., 2000—; NRC cons. Workshop on Schizophrenia, 1995-96; cons. human rights Equal Opportunities Commn., Hong Kong, 1999-2003; mem. Inst. Medicine Follow-up Agy., 2000—; chair twins com. Inst. Medicine, 2000—. Author: Schizophrenia and Genetics, 1972 (Hofheimer prize), Schizophrenia The Epigenetic Puzzle, 1982, Schizophrenia Genesis: The Origins of Madness, 1991 (transl. into Japanese and German, William James Book award, Phi Beta Kappa U. Va. Book award 1992), Schizophrenia and Genetic Risks, 1992, 3d edit., 1999, Schizophrenia and Manic Depressive Disorder: Biological Roots of Mental Illness Revealed by Study of Identical Twins, 1994, transl. into Japanese, 1998, Seminars in Psychiatric Genetics, 1994, 2d edit., 2004, Psychiatric Genetics and Genomics, 2002; editor: Man, Mind and Heredity, 1971, Vital Statistics, Demography and Schizophrenia, 1989. Served with USNR, 1949-53, 56-61; USN, 1953-56. Guggenheim fellow U. Copenhagen, 1972; recipient R. Thornton Wilson prize Ea. Psychiat. Rsch. Assn., 1965, Stanley Dean award Am. Coll. Psychiatrists, 1988, Eric Stromgren medal Danish Psychiat. Soc., 1991, Kurt Schneider prize, Bonn, 1992, Alexander Gralnick prize Am. Assn. Suicidology, 1992, Jonathan Logan award Nat. Alliance for Mentally Ill, 1995; David C. Wilson lectr. U. Va. Sch. Medicine, 1967, Lifetime Achievement award Internat. Soc. for Psychiat. Genetics, 1997; Parker lectr. Ohio State U. Sch. Medicine, 1983, 93, others. Fellow APA (Disting. Scientist award divsn. 12, sect. 3 1994, Disting. Sci. Contbns. award 2001),

AAAS, Am. Psychopathol. Assn., Royal Coll. Psychiatrists (hon.), Am. Psychol. Soc. (human capital initiative task force for psychopathology rsch. agenda 1993-96); mem. Minn. Human Genetics League (v.p. 1969-71), Soc. Study Social Biology (v.p. 1976-80), Behavior Genetics Assn. (pres. 1976-77, T. Dobzhansky award 1990), Am. Soc. Human Genetics (editl. bd. 1967-72), Soc. Rsch. in Psychopathology (pres. 1993, Joseph Zubin award 2001), Japanese Soc. Biol. Psychiatry (spl. lecture award 2001), Inst. of Psychiatry (14th Eliot Slater Lectr., 2002). Home: 5823 Vernon Ln Edina MN 55436 E-mail: gotte003@umn.edu.

GOTTHEIMER, GEORGE MALCOLM, JR., insurance executive, educator; b. Orange, N.J., Mar. 26, 1933; s. George Malcolm Sr. and Rosalie Kahn Zugsmith; m. Patricia Ann Savarese, Apr. 30, 1966; children: Nancy Lorraine, Kerry Suzannne. BSBA, Edison State Coll., Princeton, N.J., 1978; MBA, St. John's U., N.Y.C., 1980; PhD, Calif. Coast U., 1983. Cert. assoc. in reinsurance. Sec. Am. Internat. Group, N.Y.C., 1958-66; pres. Reinsurance Agy. Mgmt. Corp., Bala Cynwyd, Pa., 1966-69; v.p. Occidental Life Ins. Co., Raleigh, N.C., 1969-72, Midland Ins. Co., N.Y.C., 1972-77; exec. v.p. John D. Ryan & Co. Inc., N.Y.C., 1977-82; v.p. Gen. Re Group, 1982-84; sr. v.p. Pro Re of Am., Inc., N.Y.C., 1984-86; pres. Kernan Assocs., Inc., Berkeley Heights, N.J., 1986—. Adj. asst. prof. ins., reinsurance mgmt. St. John's U., N.Y.C., 1972-80, adj. assoc. prof., 1980-97, assoc. prof., 1997—; adj. prof. Baruch Coll. CUNY. Contbr. articles to profl. jours. Research fellow Harry J. Loman Found., Malvern, Pa., 1982. Mem. Chartered Property Casualty Underwriters (cert. 1957, nat. dir. 1983-86, regional v.p. 1985-86, pres. N.Y. chpt. 1980-81, Eugene A. Toale Meml. award 1985), CLU's (cert. 1973). Home: 6 Oechsner Ct Berkeley Heights NJ 07922-1731 E-mail: ggottheimer@kernanassoc.com.

GOTTO, ANTONIO MARION, JR., internist, educator; b. Nashville, Tenn., Oct. 10, 1935; s. Antonio M. and Reather (Gray) Gotto; m. Anita Louise Safford, July 21, 1959; children: Jennifer, Gillian, Teresa. BA magna cum laude, Vanderbilt U., 1957, MD, 1965; DPhil, Oxford (Eng.) U., 1961; LLD (hon.), Abilene Christian U., 1979; MD (hon.), U. Bologna, 1982. Diplomate Am. Bd. Internal Medicine. Intern Mass. Gen. Hosp., Boston, 1965—66, resident, 1966—67; practice medicine specializing in internal medicine, 1967—; head molecular disease br. Nat. Heart and Lung Inst. NIH, Bethesda, Md., 1969—71; dir. and prin. investigator Lipid Research Clinic, Houston, 1971—77; prof. medicine, chief dir., arteriosclerosis and lipoprotein rsch. Baylor Coll. Medicine, Houston, 1971—96; dir., prin. investigator specialized center rsch in arteriosclerosis Nat. Heart, Lung and Blood Inst., 1971—96; dir., prin. investigator Spl. Ctr. Rsch. Arteriosclerosis Nat. Heart, Lung, and Blood Inst., 1971—96; J.S. Abercrombie prof. Baylor Coll. Medicine, 1976—96, Disting. Service prof., 1985—96; sci. dir. Meth. Hosp. and Baylor Nat. Rsch. and Demonstration Ctr., 1974—83, 1987—90; Bob and Vivian Smith prof. and chmn. dept. medicine Baylor Coll. Medicine, 1977—96; chief internal medicine svcs. The Meth. Hosp., 1977—96; dean Weill Med. Coll., Cornell U., 1997—; provost med. affairs Cornell U., 1997—. Hon. guest lectr. various med. socs., schs. and hosps., 1972—; mem. nat. diabetes adv. bd. HEW (now HHS), 1977—84; mem. steering com. Italian-Am. com. on cardiovascular disease NIH, 1978—; mem. adv. coun. Nat. Heart, Lung and Blood Inst., 1987—91; hon. prof. U. Buenos Aires, 1985. Author (with Michael E. DeBakey): The Living Heart, 1977; author: The Living Heart Diet, 1984, The New Living Heart Diet, 1996, The New Living Heart, 1997; editor: Current Atherosclerosis Reports, 1998—, Current Practice of Medicine, 1999—; co-editor: Atherosclerosis Rev. Series, 1976—92, Jour. Cardiovasc. Risk, 1994—; mem. editl. bd.: Jour. Biol. Chemistry, 1976—81, Advanced in Lipid Rsch., 1973—78, Am. Heart Jour., 1981—, Arteriosclerosis, 1981—89, Circulation Rsch., 1974—79, Cardiovascular Rsch. Ctr. Bull., 1972—; contbr. articles on biochem. and cardiovascular rsch. to profl. publs. Mem. sci. adv. bd. Fondation Cardiologique Princesse Liliane, Brussels, 1976—, Lorenzini Found., Milan, Fritz Thyssen Found., Cologne, Germany; mem. Mission of Houston Econ. Devel. Coun., 1985; walkathon chmn. Juvenile Diabetes Found., 1986. With USPHS, 1967—69. Decorated knight Order of Merit, Italy, Order of the Lion Finland; named hon. cons., Adm. Bristol Hosp., Istanbul, Turkey, Houston Internat. Exec. Yr., 1987; recipient Albert Weinstein award, 1965, Laurea ad Honorem, U. Bologna, Seale Harris award, So. Med. Assn., 1995; grantee, John A. Hartford Found., 1971—75. Fellow: Am. Coll. Cardiology; mem.: Am. Longevity Assn., Am. Assn. Rhodes Scholars, Am. Bd. Internal Medicine, Am. Heart Assn. (pres. 1983—84, past pres. 1984—86, Paul Ledbetter award for disting. svc., Paul Dudley White award for outstanding contbns., Gold Heart award 1989), Am. Diabetes Assn., Am. Soc. Biol. Chemists, Am. Assn. Physicians, Internat. Soc. Atherosclerosis (pres. 1985—, Achievement award 1982), So. Soc. Clin. Investigation, Am. Soc. Clin. Investigation (v.p. 1980—81), Inst. Medicine of NAS, River Oaks Country Club, Alpha Omega Alpha. Presbyterian. Home: 435 E 70th St Apt 31 J K New York NY 10021-5351 Office: Weill Med of Cornell U 1300 York Ave Rm F 105 New York NY 10021-4805

GOTTSCHALK, ALFRED, retired college chancellor, museum executive; b. Oberwesel, Germany, Mar. 7, 1930; came to U.S., 1939, naturalized, 1945; s. Max and Erna (Trum-Gerson) G.; m. Deanna Zeff, 1977; children by previous marriage: Marc Hillel, Rachel Lisa. AB, Bklyn. Coll., 1952; MA with honors, Hebrew Union Coll.-Jewish Inst. Religion, 1957; PhD, U. So. Calif., 1965, STD (hon.), 1968, LLD (hon.), 1976, U. Cin., 1976, Xavier U., 1981, Mt. St. Joseph Coll., 1995, No. Ky. U., 1996; DHL (hon.), U. Judaism, 1971, Jewish Theol. Sem., 1986, Bklyn. Coll., 1991, Trinity Coll., 1996; LittD (hon.), Dropsie U., 1974, St. Thomas Inst., 1982; D Religious Edn. (hon.), Loyola-Marymount U., 1977; DD (hon.), NYU, 1985. Ordained rabbi, 1957. Dir. Hebrew Union Coll., Jewish Inst. Religion, L.A., 1957-59, dean, 1959-71, prof. Bible and Jewish intellectual history, 1965—; pres., 1971-95, chancellor, 1996—2000, chancellor emeritus, disting. prof. emeritus of Jewish Intellectual History, 1995—; pres. Mus. of Jewish Heritage, N.Y.C., 1999—2001. Hon. fellow Hebrew U., Jerusalem, 1972, Oxford Ctr. for Hebrew and Jewish Studies, 1994. Author: Your Future as a Rabbi-A Calling that Counts, 1967, (translator) Hesed in the Bible, 1967, The Man Must be the Message, 1968, Jewish Ecumenism and Jewish Survival, 1968, Ahad Ha-Am, Maimonides and Spinoza, 1969, Ahad Ha-Am as Bible Critic, 1971, A Jubilee of the Spirit, 1972, Israel and the Diaspora: A New Look, 1974, Limits of Ecumenicity, 1979, Israel and Reform Judaism: A Zionist Perspective, 1979, Ahad Ha-Am and Leopold Zunz: Two Perspectives on the Wissenschaft Des Judentums, 1980, Hebrew Union College and Its Impact on World Progressive Judaism, 1980, Diaspora Zionism: Achievements and Problems, 1980, What Ecumenism Means to a Jew, 1981, Introduction: Religion in a Post-Holocaust World, 1982, Problematics in the Future of American Jewish Community, 1982, Introduction to the American Synagogue in the Nineteenth Century, 1982, A Strategy for Non-Orthodox Judaism in Israel, 1982, Our problems and Our Future: Jews and America, 1983, From the Kingdom of Night to the Kingdom of God: Jewish Christian Relations and the Search for Religious Authenticity after the Holocaust, 1983, The Making of a Contemporary Reform Rabbi, 1984, Is Yom Kippur Obsolete?, 1985, Ahad Ha-am: Confronting the Plight of Judaism, 1987, To Learn and To Teach, Your Future as a Rabbi, 1988, Preface to Gezer V: The Field I Caves, 1988, The American Reform Rabbinate Retrospect and Prospect, A Personal View, 1988, The German Pogrom of November 1938 and the Reaction of American Jewry, 1988, Building Unity in Diversity 1989, Ahad Ha'am and the Jewish National Spirit (Hebrew), 1992; contbr. to Studies in Jewish Bibliography, History, and Literature, 1971, The Yom Kippur War: Israel and the Jewish People, 1974, The Image of Man in Genesis and the Ancient Near East, 1976, The Public Function of the Jewish Scholar, 1978, The Reform Movement and Israel: A New Perspective, 1978, The Use of Reason in Maimonides--An Evaluation by Ahad Ha-Am, 1993, Reform Judaism of the New Millenium: A Challenge, 2001, Israel and America: Beyond Survival and Philanthropy, 2000; also numerous articles to profl. jours. Mem. Pres. Johnson's Com. on EEO, 1964-66, Gov.'s Poverty Support Corps Program, 1964-66, Pres.'s Commn. on Holocaust, 1979, U.S. Holocaust Meml. Coun., 1980-92, 96-01 (exec. com., 1980-87, 96—, chmn. edn. com., 1986-88, chmn. acad. com., 1988-96, com. on conscience, 1996—); chmn. N.Am. Assoc. Internat. Ctr. Univ. Teaching of Jewish Civilization, 1982-93; bd. trustees Am. Sch. Oriental Rsch., Albright Inst. Archaeol. Rsch., 1972-95; sr. fellow Mus. of Jewish Heritage, N.Y.C., 2001—; bd. govs. Oxford Ctr. for Hebrew and Jewish Studies, 1995—; bd. trustees Mus. Jewish Heritage, N.Y.C., 2001-; exec. com. Nat. Underground Railroad Freedom Ctr., 1997-2000, Nat. Adv. Bd., Nat. Underground Freedom Ctr., 1996—; mem. coun. World Union Jewish Studies, 1997. Recipient award for contbns. to edn. L.A. City Coun., 1971, Human Relations award Am. Jewish Com., 1971, Tower of David award for cultural contbn. to Israel and Am., 1972, Gold medallion Jewish Nat. Fund, 1972, Alumnus of Yr. award Bklyn. Coll., 1972, Myrtle Wreath award Hadassah, 1977, Brandeis award Z.O.A., 1977, Nat. Brotherhood award NCCJ, 1979, Alfred Gottschalk Chair in Communal Svc. HUC, 1979, Jerusalem City of Peace award 1988, Defender of Jerusalem award honoree, 1990, Isaac M. Wise award, 1991, Heritage award Jewish Club of 1933, 1991, Nat. award NCCJ, 1994, Shanghai Acad. Social Scis. award, 1994, others, Xavier Medallion, Xavier U., 1996, Elie Wiesel Holocaust Rememerance award, State of Israel bonds, 2001; grantee State Dept./Smithsonian Instn., 1963, 67.; honoree Assn. Hebrew Union Coll., 1996; recipient Award Svc. to City, Cin. City Council, 2001. Mem. AAUP, NEA, Union Am. Hebrew Congregations and Ctrl. Conf. Am. Rabbis (exec. com., bd. govs. Hebrew Union Coll.), Soc. Study Religion, Am. Acad. Religion, Soc. Bibl. Lit. and Exegesis, Internat. Conf. Jewish Communal Svc., Israel Exploration Soc., So. Calif. Assn. Liberal Rabbis (past pres.), So. Calif. Jewish Hist. Soc. (hon. pres.), World Union Jewish Studies (internat. coun.), World Union Progressive Judaism (gov. bd.), Coun. for Initiatives in Jewish Edn. (bd. dirs.). Office: Hebrew Union Coll Jewish Inst of Religion One W 4th St New York NY 10012-1186

GOUGEON, LEN GIRARD, literature educator; b. Northampton, Mass., Aug. 8, 1947; s. William Louis and Helen Ann Gougeon; m. Deborah Jean Zagorski, Feb. 21, 1980; children: Elliott, Nadia, Wesley. BA, St. Mary's U., Halifax, N.S., Can., 1969; MA, U. Mass., 1972, PhD, 1974. Asst. prof. Am. lit. U. Scranton, Pa., 1974-78, assoc. prof. Am. lit., 1978-82, prof. Am. lit., 1982—. Author: Virtue's Hero: Emerson, Antislavery and Reform, 1990; editor: Emerson's Antislavery Writings, 1995; contbr. essays to collections The Emerson Dilemma, 2001, Emersonian Circles, 1997; contbr. articles to lit. publs. NEH fellow, 1981, grantee, 1996, 2000. Mem. MLA, Am. Lit. Assn., Ralph Waldo Emerson Soc. (pres.), Thoreau Soc. Office: Univ Scranton Dept English Scranton PA 18510

GOUGHER, RONALD LEE, foreign language educator and administrator; b. Allentown, Pa., July 27, 1939; s. Samuel Franklin and Beatrice Dorothy (Shanaberger) G.; 1 child, Robert. BA, Muhlenberg Coll., 1961; MA, Lehigh U., 1964; postgrad., Albright Coll., 1962, Stanford U., 1963, Harvard U., 1964, U. Pa., 1964-75; advanced cert., Goethe Inst., Munich, 1969. Chmn. fgn. lang. dept. Parkland H.S., Allentown, Pa., 1961-65; tchr. German Moravian Sem. for Girls, 1965-69; instr. German Lehigh U., 1965-69; assoc. prof. German West Chester (Pa.) U., 1969—, coord. German studies, 1972-2001, dir. internat. edn., 1974-83, chmn. dept. fgn. langs., 1977-96, campus dir. Expt. in Internat. Living, 1972-92, coord. German studies, 1972—. Treas. Pa. Consortium Internat. Edn., 1978-83, pres., 1983-86, World Learning Inc., 1992—; coord.-chairperson Assn. Depts. Fgn. Langs., State Sys. Higher Edn., Pa., 1984-88, del. First Joint Conf. Chinese and Am. Edn. Great Hall of People, Beijing, 1992; citizen amb. Linguistics del. to China, 1991, 92, lectr. in field, cons. Franklin Mint, 1992—; cons., program dir. Chester Conty Intermediate Unit; guest lectr. Ufa, Ivanova, Russia, 1993, Czestochowa, Poland, Ufa, Russia, Sendai, Japan, Jurmala, Riga, Valmiera, Latvia, 1994-96, Kaunus, Lithuania, 1995; participant Hungarian Parliament Sessions, Budapest, 1994; dir. Am.-European studies program, West Chester U. and Soros Found., Latvia, Lithuania, Czech Republic, Slovakia, Hungary, Romania, Yugoslavia, Bulgaria, Croatia, Slovenia, Macedonia, 1994, Moldova, 1995, Estonia, 1996, Albania, Bosnia, Kyrgystan, Mongolia, 1997—, Kazakhstan, 1998—, Azerbaijan, 1999, Kosovo, 2001-02, Georgia, 2003; dir. Internat. Sch.-U. Partnership Program, West Chester U. and Chester County Intermediate Unit, 1988—. Co-editor, Individualization Fgn. Lang. Learning in Am., 1970-75; author numerous publs. in German lang. and lit., individualizing instrn. in fgn. langs. Bd. dirs. Peters Valley Crafts Ctr., U.S. Info. Agy., 1988-95; active Congress-Bundestag Youth Exch. Program, 1988-96, Citizen Amb. Program, China, 1991, 92. Fulbright travel grantee, 1963, 69, Soros Found., 1990-94; travel and study grantee, Finland and Leningrad, USSR, 1990; travel grantee to Poland, Slovakia, Romania, 1991-92, Russia, 1993, 95, Bulgaria, Slovenia, 1994, Kagoshima, Japan and Taipei, Taiwan, 1996, Croatia, Latvia, Lithuania, Slovenia, 1996, Hungary, Bulgaria, Macedonia, 1999, Mongolia, 1999; Fed. Fgn. Lang. Assistance Act grantee, 1992-96, dir. Internat. Sch.-U. Ptnrs. program Chester County Intermediate Unit and West Chester U., 1991-97, Soros Found. grantee internat. program devel. Latvia, Lithuania, Czech Republic, Slovakia, Hungary, Slovenia, Yugoslavia, Romania, Bulgaria, Macedonia, Moldova, Estonia, Mongolia, Kyrgystan, Bosnia, Albania, 1994—; Open Soc. grantee, 1994-2003, others; recipient Chapel of Four Chaplains award, 1981. Mem. Am. Assn. Tchrs. German, Am. Coun. Tchg. Fgn. Langs., N.E. Conf. Tchg. Fgn. Langs., Internat. Platform Assn., Smithsonian Instn., Ruffed Grouse Soc., Trout Unlimited, Ducks Unlimited. Republican. Lutheran. Home: 3309 Windsor Ln Thorndale PA 19372-1038 Office: West Chester U Dept Fgn Langs West Chester PA 19380

GOUKE, CECIL GRANVILLE, economist, educator; b. Bklyn., Dec. 5, 1928; s. Joseph and Etheline (Grant) G.; m. Mary Noel, June 19, 1964; 1 son, Cecil Granville. BA, CCNY, 1956; MA, N.Y. U., 1958, PhD, 1967. Instr. econs. Fisk U., 1958-60; asst. prof. Grambling Coll., 1962-64, asso. prof., 1964-67; prof., chmn. Hampton (Va.) Inst., 1967-73; prof. Ohio State U., 1973—. Vis. assoc. prof. UCLA., 1969, fulbright prof. U. of Dar es Salaam, Tanzania, 1979-80, vis. prof. Ohio U., 1981, Disting. vis. prof. Atlanta U., 1982, vis. prof. U. Vt., 1984; cons. U.S. Treasury Dept., 1973 Author: Amalgamated Clothing Workers of America, 1940-66, 1972, Blacks and the American Economy, 1987; assoc. editor: Jour. Behavioral and Social Scis, 1974-84. Vestryman St. Cyprians Episcopal Ch., 1968-71. Served with U.S. Army, 1947-49, 50-51. Recipient Founders Day award N.Y. U., 1967; sr. Fulbright scholar, 1979-80 Mem. Am. Econ. Assn., Am. Fin. Assn., Am. Statis. Assn., Indsl. Relations Research Assn., Western Econ. Assn., Nat. Econ. Assn., Hampton NAACP (exec. bd. 1968-70), Ohio Assn. Econs. and Polit. Sci. (v.p. 1986-87, pres. 1987-88), Phi Beta Sigma. Republican. Episcopalian. Avocations: art, music. Home: 1788 Kenwick Rd Columbus OH 43209-3249 Office: Ohio State U Dept Econs 410 Arps Hall 1945 N High St Columbus OH 43210

GOULART, JANELL ANN, elementary education educator; b. Merced, Calif., July 29, 1936; d. James Riddoch and Rowena Janell (Futrell) Mitchell; m. Frank Goulart, May 19, 1956; children: Robert, Frank, Sharon. BA, Fresno (Calif.) State U., 1972, postgrad., Fresno Pacific Coll., Irvine U. Cert. elem. sci. tchr., Calif.; cert. Calif. Assn. for Gifted. Tchr. Royal Oaks Sch., Visalia, Calif., 1972—; sci. staff developer, K-12 alliance staff developer Calif. Sci. Implementation Network, Irvine, Calif., 1989-2001. Trainer Calif. Learning Assessment System state testing; sci. and math mentor for Visalia Unified Sch. Dist. Mem. Nat. Sci. Tchrs. Assn., Calif. Sci. Tchrs. Assn., Ctrl. Calif. Sci. Tchrs. Assn., Tulare County Reading Coun., Kappa Delta Pi. Home: 1546 River Way Dr Visalia CA 93291-9212 Office: Royal Oaks Sch 1323 S Clover St Visalia CA 93277-4299

GOULD, ALAN BRANT, academic administrator; b. Aug. 2, 1938; m. Mary Nell; children: Adam, Charles, Christopher. BA in History cum laude, Marshall U., 1961, MA in History, 1962; PhD in Am. History, W.Va. U., 1969. Grad. instr., dept. history W.Va. U., Morgantown, 1962-65; instr., dept. history D.C. Tchrs. Coll., 1965-66; asst. prof. history No. Va. Community Coll., 1966-69; prof., dept. history Marshall U., Huntington, W.Va., 1969—, sr. v.p., 1988-89, provost, 1989-92, interim pres., 1990-91, v.p. for acad. affairs, 1991-94, dean Coll. Liberal Arts, 1980-88, acting v.p. acad. affairs, 1984-86, asst. to pres. for spl. projects, 1986, chmn. dept. history, 1977-80, asst. to v.p. acad. affairs, 1976-77, coord. Regents BA degree program, 1976-80, 86-94; exec. dir. John Deaver Drinko Acad., 1994—. Adj. prof. history W.Va. Coll. Grad. Studies, 1976-86; lectr. Ohio U., Ironton, 1970-74; vis. lectr. for Project Newgate, Fed. Youth Correction Inst., Summit, Ky., fall 1970. Contbr. articles to hist. jours, also conf. papers. Chmn. Cabell County Hist. Landmark Commn., 1983-92; trustee Huntington Mus. Art, 1983-93, chmn. edn. com., mem. exec. com.; pres. River Cities Cultural Coun., 1985-91; bd. dirs. W.Va. Humanities Coun., 1986-90, v.p., 1989-91, pres., 1991-94, W.Va. Coalways, Inc., 1987—; mem. Mayor of Huntington's Main St. Project, 1987-92, Marshall U. Rsch. Corp., 1988, mem., 1982-86; mem. W.Va. Antiquities Commn., 1975-77, Cabell County Commn. on Crime, Delinquency and Corrections, 1982-86, statewide steering com. Ideas That Built Am., 1985-86, Carter G. Woodson Meml. Commn., 1986—; mem. steering com. Ethics W.Va. Program, 1983-84, chmn. Great Books Program; mem. affirmative action bd. City of Huntington, 1989-91, mem. Cabell County (W.Va.) hist. landmark commn., 1989-91, 94—; trustee W. Va. Ednl. Found., Inc., 1993-2001; mem. W.Va. Libr. Commn., 1997—. Inducted into Huntington East High Sch. Hall of Fame, Class of 1986, City of Huntington (W.Va.) Wall of Fame, 1997; recipient Charles Daugherty Humanities award W.Va. Humanities Coun., 1996. Mem. Am. Hist. Assn. (com. on status of history in schs. 1974-76), Orgn. Am. Historians (state rep.), W.Va. Hist. Assn. (sec. 1974, v.p. 1975, pres. 1976), W.Va. Assn. Acad. Deans (mem. exec. bd. 1982-86). W.Va. Bd. Regents (univ. rep., acad. affairs adv. com. 1984-86), Soc. Yeager Scholars (steering com. 1986-87), W.Va. Humanities Ctr. (exec. com. 1987—), Gamma Theta Upsilon, Omicron Delta Kappa, Phi Alpha Theta, Phi Eta Sigma, Pi Sigma Alpha. Avocations: tennis, travel. Office: Marshall U John Deaver Drinko Acad One John Marshall Dr Huntington WV 25755-0003

GOULD, BETTY CHAIKIN, elementary school educator; b. Bklyn., Apr. 19, 1928; d. Julius and Jeannette (Lipkin) C.; m. Joseph Gould, Dec. 9, 1951; children: Nancy Marla, Jodie Ellen. BA, L.I. U., 1950; MA, Columbia U., 1954. Lic. guidance counselor. Tchr. Yorktown Cen. Sch. Dist., Yorktown Heights, N.Y. Recipient Edgar Lilien Meml. award. Mem. N.Y. LWV. Home: 1471 Old Logging Rd Yorktown Heights NY 10598-6242

GOULD, HARRY J., III, neurology educator; b. Columbus, Ohio, Mar. 1, 1947; s. Harry J. Jr. and Madeline (Folger) G.; m. Anne Marie Thompson, Jan. 30, 1971; children: Trevor Nicholas, Laura Nicole. BS, SUNY, Stony Brook, 1969; PhD, Brown U., 1974; MD, La. State U., 1990. Asst. prof. Med. Sch. U. Cin., 1974-80; asst. prof. Med. Sch., La. State U., New Orleans, 1980-86, assoc. prof., 1986, resident in neurology, 1990-94; asst. prof. med. sch. La. State U., New Orleans, 1994-98, assoc. prof. neurology, 1998—, Tom Benson prof. neurology, dir. Multidisciplinary Pain Ctr. Contbr. articles to profl. jours. With USAR, 1970-76. NSF grantee, 1986-89. Mem. Internat. Assn. for the Study Pain, Soc. for Neurosci., Am. Acad. Neurology, Am. Pain Soc., Am. Acad. Pain Medicine. Republican. Methodist. Avocations: songwriting, banjo, guitar. Home: 104 Paradise Pt Slidell LA 70461-3225 Office: La State U Med Ctr Dept of Neurology 1542 Tulane Ave New Orleans LA 70112-2825

GOULD, HELEN JANE, special education educator; b. N.Y.C., Apr. 25, 1949; d. David Edward and Celia Zelda (Sandek) Gould; children: Rachel Beth, Jason Scott. BA in Psychology, Hofstra U., Hempstead, N.Y., 1972, MS in Elem./Spl. Edn., 1976. Cert. tchr. elem. edn. K-6, spl. edn. N-12, edn. of orthopedically impaired and learning disabled, N.Y. Learning disabilities cons. Hauppauge (N.Y.) Sch. Dist., 1977-78; tchr. Middle Country Sch. Dist., Centereach, N.Y., 1979; tchr./chair Island Trees Mid. Sch., Levittown, N.Y., 1979—, team leader grade 7, 1993-94, tchr. mem. com. on spl. edn., 1992—. Mem. ASCD, United Tchrs. Island Trees, Nassau Reading Coun., PTA, Island Trees Spl. Edn. PTA. Avocations: piano playing, reading, travel, computers. Office: Island Trees Middle School 45 Wantagh Ave S Levittown NY 11756 E-mail: eliza@spec.net.

GOULD, JAMES L. biology educator; b. Tulsa, July 31, 1945; s. James L. and Doris Mae (Frazier) G.; m. Carol Holly Grant, June 6, 1970; children: Grant Frazier, Clare Holly. BS, Calif. Inst. Tech., 1970; PhD, Rockefeller U., 1975. Asst. prof. Princeton (N.J.) U., 1975-80, assoc. prof., 1980-84, prof. biology, 1984—. Author: Ethology, 1982, Biological Science, rev. edit., 1996, The Honey Bee, 1988, Sexual Selection, 1989, The Animal Mind, 1994, Biostats Basics, 2001; contbr. more than 100 articles to profl. jours. With U.S. Army, 1967-68. Guggenheim Found. fellow, 1987, AAAS fellow, 1988, Animal Behavior Soc. fellow, 1992; grantee NSF, 1976, 79, 82, 85, NIH, 1976, Nat. Geogrphic Soc., 1984; named Prof. of Yr. Carnegie Found. N.J., 1996, Tchr. of Yr. Animal Behavior Soc., 1997. Presbyterian. Achievements include research in animal behavior. Office: Princeton U Dept Ecol Evol Biology Princeton NJ 08544-0001 E-mail: gould@princeton.edu.

GOULD, JAY WILLIAM, III, management development educator, lecturer, author, international consultant; b. Glencoe, Minn., Oct. 30, 1930; m. May-Lun Lum, Apr. 5, 1989. Student, U. Minn., 1948-49; BS, U.S. Mil. Acad., 1954; postgrad., U. Denver, 1959-60; MS in Systems Mgmt., U. So. Calif., 1990, MPA, DPA, U. So. Calif., 1995. Cert. level III program mgr., level III rsch. devel. and engring., level III mfg. mgr., level III test and evaluation; cert. acquisition profl.; charter cert. Myers Briggs type indicator profl. Commd. 2d lt. U.S. Army, 1954; served as USAF liason officer, tng. officer, war game umpire; missile officer U.S. Army, Ft. Bliss, Tex., 1954, advanced guided missile officer, 1st lt., 1957, ranger, airborne jump master Ft. Benning, Ga., 1955, resigned, 1957; program engr., project office Martin Marietta Corp., Denver, 1957-64; sr. bus. systems analyst Honeywell, Inc., Mpls., 1964-66; project engr., new products devel. 3M Co., St. Paul, 1966-80; program mgr. HiMilage Corp., 1980-81; chief engr., procurement officer, project mgr. Litton Microwave Cooking, Plymouth, Minn., 1981-83; mgr. engring. Enercon Data Corp., Mpls., 1983-85; systems engr. Dept. Def. Logistics Agy., St. Louis, 1985-87; missile deployment program mgr. USAF Ballistic Missile Office, Norton AFB, Calif., 1987-90; prof. test and evaluation, course dir. Def. Acquisition U., Ft. Belvoir, Va., 1990—, prof. level IV, 1998—. Mem. Office of Sec. of Def. Detailed Operational Test and Evaluation, Live Fire Test, Pentagon, 1998—2002; actionand ethics officer indsl. com. for operational test and eval. Nat. Def. Indsl. Assn.; participant Paradigm Mastery Series U. Tex., Austin, 1999, cons., 2000—. Contbg. author: Deming: The Way We Knew Him; former columnist Jour. Mgmt. History, Eng., Dod's Acquisition Review Quarterly Jour.; inventor ferrule, bullet clip, non-lethal bullet, non-welded microwave oven cavity and safety door interlocks. Past scoutmaster, dist. chmn. Boy Scouts Am.; past pres. Assoc. Bloomington (Minn.) Schs. PTA's; eucharistic lay min. Episc. Chs., 1968—81, 1998—2001; bd. dirs. Bloomington YMCA. Served USAR, 1954—62. Named Outstanding Grad. USAF Air War Coll., 1989; recipient personal commendation for conservation Sec. Interior Morris Udall, numerous community awards. Office: Def Acquisition U 9820 Belvoir Rd Ste G38 Fort Belvoir VA 22060-5565 E-mail: jay.gould@dau.mil.

GOULD, RICHARD ALLAN, anthropologist, archaeologist, educator; b. Newton, Mass., Oct. 22, 1939; s. Samuel Brookner and Laura Johanna (Ohman) G.; m. Elizabeth Barber, Dec. 22, 1962. BA cum laude, Harvard U., 1961; PhD, U. Calif., Berkeley, 1965. Asst. curator N. Am. archaeology

Am. Mus. Natural History, N.Y.C., 1965-71, research asso., 1971—; asso. prof. anthropology U. Hawaii, Honolulu, 1971-76, prof., 1976-80, Brown U., Providence, R.I., 1980—; rsch. assoc. anthropology Western Australian Mus., Perth, 1995—. Cons. in charge of planning exhibits Wattis Hall of Man, Calif. Acad. Scis., San Francisco, 1975-76, cons. for research design on U.S.S. Monitor for NOAA, 1985-86; cons. for shipwreck rsch. at Dry Tortugas Nat. Park, Fla. for Nat. Park Svc., 1990-95; organizer, team leader Forensic Archaeology Recovery, World Trade Ctr. site, 2001-02, The Station, Nightclub Fire scene, West Warwick, R.I., 2003; forensic anthropologist Nat. Disaster Mortuary Ops. Team. Author: The Archaeology of the Point St. George Site and Tolowa Prehistory, 1966, Yiwara, Foragers of the Australian Desert, 1969, Man's Many Ways, 1973, Puntutjarpa Rockshelter and the Australian Desert Culture, 1977, Explorations in Ethnoarchaeology, 1978, Living Archaeology, 1980, Modern Material Culture: The Archaeology of Us, 1981, Shipwreck Anthropology, 1983, Recovering the Past, 1990, Archaeology and the Social History of Ships, 2000. Served with U.S. Army, 1961-62. Australian Nat. U. vis. fellow, 1977; Social Sci. Rsch. Coun. rsch. grantee, 1966-67, F.G. Voss rsch. grantee Am. Mus. Natural History, 1969-70, NSF rsch. grantee, 1973-74, 80-81, Earthwatch grantee, 1986-92, 99-2000. Fellow AAAS (chmn. sect. H-anthropology 1984-86), Am. Anthrop. Assn.; mem. Soc. Am. Archaeology, Australian Inst. Aboriginal Studies, Australasian Inst. Maritime Studies. Office: Brown Univ Dept Anthropology PO Box 1921 Providence RI 02912-1921

GOULD, SANDRA JOYCE, elementary education educator; b. Springfield, Mo., Oct. 31, 1946; d. John Jackson and Sarah Hazel (Hass) Hume; m. Bruce Dana Gould, June 7, 1969; children: Vicki Lynn, Lisa Michelle. BA, U. Mo., 1968; MA, Tex. Woman's U., 1986. Cert. tchr., Mo., Tex. Elem. tchr. Jefferson City (Mo.) Pub. Schs., 1968-69, Guam Pub. Schs., Agana, 1969-70, Pensacola (Fla.) Pub. Schs., 1971-72; substitute tchr. Peoria, Ill., 1972-73; tchr.'s aid Ft. Zumwalt (Mo.) Schs., 1974-75; chpt. I tchr. reading Lake Dallas (Tex.) Ind. Sch. Dist., 1981-90; chpt. I tchr. reading and math. Decatur (Tex.) Ind. Sch. Dist., 1990-91, elem. tchr. spl. edn., 1992, tchr. at risk students, 1991—, 1st grade tchr., 1994—99; 2nd grade tchr. DeLeon, Tex., 1999—2000; 1st grade tchr. Katy ISD-James William Elem., 2001—. Sunday sch. tchr. So. Bapt. chs., 1969-92; pres. Lake Dallas H.S. Band Boosters, 1987-89; vol. Laubach Literacy, 1991-93. Mem.: ATPE, Tex. Classroom Tchrs. Assn. Avocations: cooking, reading, snow skiing. Home: RR 1 Box 164 De Leon TX 76444-9646 Office: James Williams Elem 3900 S Peek Rd Katy TX 77450-4403

GOULD, STEPHEN JAY, paleontologist, educator; b. N.Y.C., N.Y., Sept. 10, 1941; s. Leonard and Eleanor (Rosenberg) G.; m. Deborah Ann Lee, Oct. 3, 1965; children: Jesse, Ethan. AB in Geology, Antioch Coll., Yellow Springs, Ohio, 1963; PhD, Columbia U., 1967; DHL (hon.), Marlboro Coll., 1982; DSc (hon.), Bucknell U., 1982; LLD (hon.), Antioch Coll., 1983; LHD (hon.), Colgate U., 1984, Pace U., 1984, Suffolk U., 1984, New Sch. for Social Rsch., 1986, Hofstra U., 1987, Bank Street Coll. of Edn., 1988, Westfield State Coll., 1989, Miami U., Oxford, Ohio, 1992; DSc (hon.), Bucknell U., 1982, MacAlester Coll., 1983, Denison U., 1984, U. Md., 1984, Williams Coll., 1985, Bard Coll., 1986, Kalamazoo U., 1986, SUNY, 1986, L.I. U., 1986, Union Coll., 1987, Rutgers U., 1987, Bates Coll., 1987, Pomona U., 1988, Dickinson Coll., 1988, Duke U., 1989, U. Mo., Saint Louis, 1990, Clark U., 1990, Am. U., 1991, Ripon Coll., 1991, U. Pa., 1991, Wheaton Coll., 1992, CUNY, 1992, Leeds U., England, 1992. Asst. prof. geology, asst. curator Invertebrate Paleontology Harvard U., Cambridge, Mass., 1967-71, assoc. prof. geology, assoc. curator Invertebrate Paleontology, 1971-73, prof. geology, from 1973, curator Invertebrate Paleontology Mus. Comparative Zoology, from 1973, Alexander Agassiz prof. zoology, from 1982, mem. com. profs. dept. biology, adj. mem. dept. history sci., from 1973. Tanner lectr. Cambridge U., 1984, Stanford U., 1989; Terry lectr. Yale U., 1986; Mila Manfield lectr., Tokyo, 1989; inaugural lectr. for Isaiah Berlin annual lectureship, Wolfson Coll., Oxford U., England; mem. Smithsonian Council, 1976—; bd. dirs. biol. scis. curriculum study, 1976-79; adv. bd. Children's TV Workshop, 1978-81; adv. bd. TV program NOVA, 1980—. Author: Ontogeny and Phylogeny, 1977, Ever Since Darwin, 1977, The Panda's Thumb, 1980 (Am. Book award Sci. 1981, Nat. Book award for sci., 1981), The Mismeasure of Man, 1981 (1981 Nat. Book Critics Circle award for gen. non-fiction 1982, Outstanding Book award Am. Ednl. Rsch. Assn. 1983, Iglesias prize for Italian transl., 1991), rev. edit., 1995, (with S.E. Luria and S. Singer) A View of Life, 1981, Hen's Teeth and Horse's Toes, 1983 (Phi Beta Kappa Book award in Sci. 1983), The Flamingo's Smile, 1985, Illuminations, A Bestiary, 1986, Time's Arrow, Time's Cycle, 1987, An Urchin in the Storm, 1987, Wonderful Life, 1989 (Forkosch award for best book on humanistic subject, 1990, Phi Beta Kappa book award in sci., 1990, Rhone-Poulenc prize, 1991), Bully for Brontosaurus, 1991, (with R.W. Purcell) Finders, Keepers, 1992, Eight Little Piggies, 1993, Dinosaur in a Haystack, 1995, Full House, 1996, Questioning the Millenium, 1997; gen. editor, preface The Book of Life, 1993; assoc. editor Evolution, 1970-72; editorial bd. Systematic Zoology, 1970-72, Paleobiology, 1974-76, Am. Naturalist, 1977-80; bd. editors Science mag.; also numerous articles, mo. col. This View of Life (Nat. Mag. award 1980), others. Mem. coun. Nat. Portrait Gallery, Washington, 1989—; mem. NASA Space Exploration Coun., 1989-91; bd. dirs. British Mus. Internat. Found., 1992—. Recipient Scientist of Yr. award Discover Mag., 1981, Medal of Excellence Columbia U., 1982, F.V. Haydn medal Phila. Acad. Scis., 1982, J. Priestley award and medal Dickinson Coll., 1983, Neil Miner award for excellence in teaching Nat. Assn. Geology Tchrs., 1983, Disting. Service award Am. Humanists' Assn., 1984, Silver medal Zool. Soc. London, 1984, Founders Coun. award of merit Field Mus. of Natural History, chgo., 1984, Meritorious Service award Am. Assn. Systematics Collections, 1984, Bradford Washburn award and Gold medal Mus. Sci. Boston, 1984, John and Samuel Bard award in Medicine and Sci. Bard Coll., 1984, Creative Arts award Brandeis U., 1986, Glenn T. Seaborg award for contribution to public interest in sci. Internat. Platform Assn., 1986, In Praise Of Reason award CSICOP, 1986, H.D. Vursell award AAAL for recent writing in book form that merits recognition for quality of prose, 1987, Anthropology in Media award Am. Anthrop. Assn., 1987, History of Geology award Geol. Soc. Am., 1988, T.N. George medal U. Glasgow, Scotland, 1989, Sue T. Friedman medal Geol. Soc. London, 1989, Disting. Svc. award Am. Inst. Profl. Geologists, 1989, Edinburgh medal City of Edinburgh, 1990, Britannica award and gold medal, 1990, Disting. Svc. award Nat. Assn. Biology Tchrs., 1991, Homer Smith medal NYU Sch. Medicine, 1992, Disting. Svc. medal Tchrs, James H. Shea awd., Nat. Assn. of Geology Teachers, 1992. Coll. Columbia U., 1992, UCLA medal, 1992, 1st recipient Commonwealth award State of Mass., 1993, J.P. McGovern award and medal in sci. Cosmos Club, 1993, Public Svc. award, Geological Soc. of Am., 1999); named Humanist Laureate Acad. of Humanism, 1983; Buwalda lectr. Calif. Inst. Tech., 1985; McArthur Found. prize fellow 1981-86; subject of film profile for TV program NOVA, 1985 (Westinghouse Sci. Film award to producers 1985); prin. investigator numerous grants NSF, 1969—; NSF fellow, Woodrow Wilson hon. fellow, Columbia U. hon. fellow, 1963-67, Lilly lectr. Royal Coll. Physicians, London, 1993; Human Talk lectr. Muratec, Kyoto, Japan, 1993. Fellow Am. Acad. Arts and Scis., European Union Geosciences (hon.), AAAS (mem. council 1974-76, com. council affairs 1976-77), Royal Soc. Edinburgh, European Union Geoscis. (hon. fgn.); mem. NAS, Paleontol. Soc. (pres. 1985—, Schuchert award for excellence in paleontol. research (under age 40) 1975), Soc. Study Evolution (v.p. 1975), Soc. Systematic Zoology, Am. Soc. Naturalists (pres. 1977-80), Paleontol. Soc. U.K., Soc. Vertebrate Paleontology, Linnean Soc. (Silver medal 1992), History of Sci. Soc., Soc. for Study Evolution (pres. 1990), Soc. Am. Baseball Rsch., Soc. Study Sports History, Bermuda Biological Station (trustee 1988—), Galerie de l'Evolution Mus. d'Histoire Naturelle, Paris (internat. bd. advisors 1989—), Sigma Xi (sec. treas. Harvard-Radcliffe chpt. 1968-70). Died May 20, 2002.

GOULDER, DEBRA KRIEGSMAN, elementary education educator; b. Winston-Salem, N.C., Apr. 14, 1961; d. Robert Marvin and Rascha Sarah (Sklut) Kriegsman; m. Gerald Polster Goulder, July 28, 1990. BS in Edn., Univ. N.C., Greensboro, 1983. Cert. tchr. N.C. Tchr. Greensboro Pub. Schs., N.C., 1984—. Vol. Jr. League, Greensboro, 1987—. Mem. N.C. Assn. Educators, Assn. Supervision and Curriculum Devel. Avocations: knitting, gardening. Home: 1006 N Holden Rd Greensboro NC 27410-4826

GOUMNEROVA, LILIANA CHRISTOVA, physician, neurosurgeon, educator; b. Jakarta, Indonesia, Sept. 27, 1956; came to U.S., 1988; d. Christo Todorov and Jeanne Dimitrova (Petkova) G. BSc, Faculty of Medicine, Sofia, Bulgaria, 1977; MD, U. Toronto, 1980. Intern U. Toronto, 1980-81; resident in neurosurgery U. Ottawa, Can., 1981-86; fellow in pediatric neurosurgery Hosp. Sick Children, Toronto, 1987-88, assoc. staff neurosurgeon, 1987-88; assoc. staff surgeon Ottawa (Can.) Civic Hosp., 1986-87; Dana fellow in neurosurgery U. Pa., Phila., 1988-90; assoc. in neurosurgery Children's Hosp., Boston, 1990—, dir. clin. pediat. neurosurg. oncology, 1999—; assoc. in neurosurgery Brigham & Women's Hosp., Boston, 1990—; cons. neurosurgeon Dana Farber Cancer Inst., Boston, 1990—, dir. clin. pediat. neurosurg. oncology; asst. prof. surgery Sch. Medicine Harvard U., Boston, 1990—. Mem. Am. Assn. Neurol. Surgeons (Young Investigator award 1996). Office: Childrens Hosp 300 Longwood Ave Boston MA 02115-5737

GOURLEY, MARY E. education educator; b. Yonkers, N.Y., Apr. 20, 1934; d. Rivers W. and Elizabeth (Johnston) Best; m. Robert N. Gourley, July 25, 1970; children: Janice, Christine, Gail, Lynn, Brooke, James. BA in Elem. Edn., Davis and Elkins (W.Va.) Coll., 1957; MS in Supervision, Portland State U., 1970; postgrad., U. So. Calif.; EdD, U. Sarasota, 1994. Cert. prin., adminstr., Oreg. Asst. prof. Portland (Oreg.) State U.; staff specialist NW Regional Edn. Lab., Portland; program dir. spl. edn. N.H. Dept. Edn., Concord; cons., evaluator Western Mich. U., Kalamazoo; ednl. cons., chief exec. officer Gourley Assoc., Inc., 1991-94; assoc. prof. U. Sarasota, Fla., 1994—. Author: Inservice Education, 1977, Staff Evaluation Training Manual, 1978, Evaluation Criteria for the Assessment of Vocational and Technical Education, 1989, Kellogg Youth Initiatives Program Final Report, 1994. Spl. fellow IDEA, 1984. Mem. ASCD, Am. Assn. Sch. Adminstrs., Phi Delta Kappa. Office: U Sarasota 5250 17th St Sarasota FL 34235-8242 Home: 71386 Northshore Dr Birkenfeld OR 97016

GOURLEY, PAULA MARIE, art educator, artist, designer bookbinder, writer, publisher; b. Carmel, Calif., Apr. 29, 1948; d. Raymond Serge Voronkoff and Frances Eliseyvna (Kovtynovich) G.; m. David Clark Willard, Feb. 10, 1972 (div. Oct. 1973). AA, Monterey (Calif.) Peninsula Coll., 1971; BA, Goddard Coll., 1978; MFA, U. Ala., 1987; pvt. bookbinding study with, Donald Glaister, Roger Arnoult, Paule Ameline, Michelene de Bellefroid, Francoise Bausart, Sun Evrard, James Brockman. Radiologic technologist Cen. Med. Clinic, Pacific Grove, Calif., 1970-71, Community Hosp. of Monterey, 1972-75, Duke U. Med. Ctr., Durham, N.C., 1975-77; dept. head, ultrasound technologist Middlesex Meml. Hosp., Middletown, Conn., 1977-79; asst. prof. U. Ala., Tuscaloosa, 1985-93, assoc. prof., 1993-98. Established Pelegaya Press and Paperworks, 1978, Lilyhouse Studio Editions, 1999; asst. dir. Inst. for Book Arts U. Ala., 1985—88, coord., 1988—94, co-dir. MFA program in the book arts, 1994—97; U.S. rep. Les Amis de la Reliure d'Art, Toulousee, France, 1989—; founding dir. Southeastern chpt. Guild of BookWorkers, 1995—99; guest artist Marriott Library. Book Arts Program U. Utah, 1999—; contbr. journalist for U.S. to Art et Metiers du Livre Revue Internat., Paris; adj. faculty Lane Micro Bus./Lane C.C., resource and edn. coord., 2002—; Saturday Market resource coord., Eugene, Oreg., 2001—; bd. dirs. Eugene (Oreg.) Saturday Mkt., Oreg. Micro Enterprise Network, Oreg. Coun. Bus. Edn. Editor First Impressions (newsletter), 1988-97; contbr. articles to profl. jours.; numerous nat. and internat. bookbinding exhbns., 1978—; contbr. editor Resource Corner, Saturday Market Newletter. Vol. PLUS Literacy Program, Tuscaloosa, 1991-96. U. Ala. grantee, 1988, 89, 90, 92; recipient Diplome of honneur Atelier d'Arts Appliques, France, 1986, Craft fellowship Ala. State Coun. on Arts, 1993-94. Mem. Am. Registry Radiologic Technologists, Am. Registry Diagnostic Med. Sonographers, Guild of Bookworkers (founder and bd. dirs. Southeastern regional chpt., editor, pub. newsletter True Grits, mem. exec. com.), Hand Bookbinders Calif., Bookbinders Internat. (v.p. U.S. 1989-92), Pacific Ctr. for the Book Arts, Am. Craft Coun., Ala. Craft Coun., Can. Bookbinders and Book Artists Guild, Nat. Mus. Women in Arts, Willamette Jazz Soc. (founding mem.). Avocations: photography, quilting, reading, cuisine, travel. Studio: 1936 W 34th Ave Eugene OR 97405-1709

GOUTERMAN, MARTIN PAUL, chemistry educator; b. Phila., Dec. 26, 1931; s. Bernard and Melba (Buxbaum) G.; 1 child, Mikaelin BlueSpruce. BA, U. Chgo., 1951, MS, 1955, PhD in Physics (NSF Predoctoral fellow), 1958. Faculty Harvard U., Cambridge, Mass., 1958-66, postdoctoral fellow to asst. prof. chemistry dept.; mem. faculty U. Wash., Seattle, 1966—, prof. chemistry, 1968-99, prof. emeritus, 2000—. Fellow Am. Inst. Physics; mem. Am. Chem. Soc., Sigma Xi. Achievements include research and publications in spectroscopy and quantum chemistry of porphyrins and their use as luminescence sensors for biomedical and aeronautical application, in particular pressure sensitive paint; developed BS degree program in biochemistry and a chemistry minors program. Office: U Wash Chemistry Box 351700 Seattle WA 98195-1700

GOUTI, SAMMY YASIN, psychologist, educator, television talk show host, psychotherapist, writer; b. Gaza, Jordan, June 19, 1963; arrived in U.S., 1981, naturalized, 1994; s. Yasin Ahmed and Helala Yossef (Abomarie) Gouti; m. Inna Annatolievna, 1998; 1 child, Chelsey Ann. AS, San Jacinto Coll., Pasadena, Tex., 1984; BS with honors, U. Houston-Ctrl., 1987; MA, U. Houston-Clear Lake, 1989, postgrad., 1993-95; Cert. Massage Therapy, Phoenix Sch. Massage, Houston, 1992; student, TVI Actors Studios, Hollywood, Calif., 1995; cert. in acting, The Mayo Hill Sch., 1994; postgrad., Sam Houston State U., 1995; cert. in filming and directing, Access Houston TV, 1998. Lic. profl. counselor-intern. Asst. tchr. presch. U. Houston Human Lab. Sch., 1986-87; social sci. instr. George I. Sanchez High Sch., Houston, 1989-90; psychotherapist Life Resource-A Mental Health Ctr., Beaumont, Tex., 1990-91; psychology instr. Lamar U., Orange, Tex., 1991; assoc. clin. psychologist Tex. Dept. Mental Health and Mental Retardation, Beaumont, 1991-92; counseling program Sam Houston State U., 1995; massage therapist The Houstonian Health Club, 1993-95; prof. psychology U. Houston System, 1992—2000; prof. Houston C.C. System, 1998—; pub., CEO Profiles & Portraits mag., 2000—02. Founder The Ctr. for Stress Release, Houston, 1992, The SHUMS World Magic Ctr., Houston, 1992; creator Psychotherapeutic Massage, and Psychobodynalysis, 1996, 97; adj. prof. psychology Kingwood Coll., 1996-98, San Jacinto Coll., 1996-98, U. Houston, Clear Lake, 1997-99; Dem. Nat. Com. rep. State of Tex., 1995—; CEO, founder Crescent Moon Entertainment TV & Film Prodns., 1998—. Trade Mark (TM) Super Human Universal Monkeys, 1992, The SHUMS, 1992, The SHUMS Adventures, 1992; appeared in music videos with Clay Walker, Clinton Gregory, 1995; appeared on John Bradshaw TV Talk Show, 1996; guest appearance on The Bradshaw Difference, 1996; featured in 6 Hollywood films including Tin Cup, Rocket Man, Killing the Badge, The Evening Star, Apollo 11, Cable TV, Rough Riders; featured on mag. cover AMOCO's; TV host Arab-Am. TV and TV Houston, 1996-98; founder, prodr., host of weekly show Arab Broadcasting Network (ABN), 1998-2000; prodr., host (weekly talk show) Profile and Portraits, 1998—, ABN with Sammy Gouti, 1998—; spl. corr. Jordan TV, 1998—, ANA Radio and Satellite Net TV, 1998—; guest host: HCCTV: Author Showcase, 1999; host, prodr.: The Sammy Gouti Show, 1999—(AEGIS award for excellence in TV prodn., 2003, Top Hohors award for programming excellence, 2003), (TV program) Greetings with Love, 1998, Greetings with Love, Part II, 2000, (TV spl.) H.M. King Hussein of Jordan, First Memorial, 2000, King Abdullah II of Jordan, 2002; author: (poems) The Shums, 1993, The Encounter, 1994, Princess, 1995; co-writer, co-prodr., co-host: (TV programs) The Life Contentment Inventory: A Psychological Test, 1992, The Life Priority Questionnaire, 1992, Peace Talks The Palestinian Israeli & American Perspectives, 1997, Jordan: A Special Program, 2001; author: A Multidimensional Approach to the Treatment of Stress: Psychology, Psychiatry and Massage Therapy, 1997, Massage Methods, 1996, Psychotherapeutic Massage and Psychobodyanalysis, 1997; editor, writer Almaraya newspaper, 1998-99; freelance reporter El Dia newspaper, 1999-2002; contbr. articles to profl. jours. Rep. Dem. Nat. Com., 1995—; mem. The Carter Ctr., 1997-99, Juvenile Diabetes Found., 2000—. Recipient Editor's Choice award Nat. Libr. Poetry, 1993, 94, 95, Pres. Clinton's Leadership Recognition award, 1997, Letter of Appreciation, Pres. Clinton, 2000; U. Houston scholar, 1986-87, 88-89, Award of Appreciation Al Gore, 1998. Fellow Royal Soc. New Zealand; mem. AACC, Arab Am. Cultural Cmty. Ctr. (dir. media 1998-2000) Am. Screenwriters Assn., N.Am. Assn. Masters in Psychology, Royal Inst. Linguistics and Anthropology, New Zealand Stats. Assn., Stats. Soc. Australia, Sci. Fiction and Fantasy Writers Am., Am. Film Inst., Internat. Soc. Poets (life), Assn. for Humanistic Psychology, Jordanian Am. Assn. (media cons. 1999-2001), Inst. Noetic Scis., Nat. Guild Hypnotists, Nat. Geographic Soc., The Carter Center, Assn. for Body and Massage Profls., Am.-Palestinian C. of C. (dir. media 1998-2000), Nat. Scholars Honor Soc. (Award of Recognition 2001), Golden Key, Psi Chi, Alpha Epsilon Delta. Avocations: pencil drawing, poetry, photography, writing, calligraphy, pencil drawing, poetry, writing, photography, calligraphy. Mailing: PO Box 631693 Houston TX 77263 E-mail: sammygouti@yahoo.com.

GOUTMAN, LOIS CLAIR, retired drama educator; b. Clairton, Pa., Apr. 14, 1923; m. Dolya Goutman, Mar. 10, 1947; children: Andrew, Christopher, Thomas. BFA in Drama, Carnegie-Mellon U., 1944. Tchr., head drama dept. Baldwin Sch., Bryn Mawr, Pa.; ret. Dir. St. Thomas Players, Circle Theatre, L.A., Carnegie Tech. Drama Sch.; asst. dir. Actors' Lab., L.A., Arlington Films; presenter workshops in field; instr. theatre studies program Rosemont Coll. Forum, Pa. Appeared in various theatrical prodns., including The Tempest; writer, performer of one woman play Edith Wharton; dir. play reading group of srs. Surrey Sr. Svcs., Berwyn, Pa. Stanford U. fellow, Nat. Theatre Conf. alt. fellow, 1947; recipient Olmsted prize Williams Coll., Williamstown, Mass., 1992; holder first Rosamond Cross Chair in Teaching, The Baldwin Sch., 1991; teaching chair endowed in her honor Baldwin Sch. Mem. Am. Edn. Theatre Assn., Am. Alliance for Theatre and Edn., Theatre Edn. Assn., Actors' Equity. Avocations: theatre, concerts, reading, art exhibitions. Home: 314 Williams Rd Bryn Mawr PA 19010-1214

GOUX, CLARAJANE TEAL, retired special services director, educator; b. Seattle, Oct. 9, 1939; d. John Wesley and Marjorie Newkirk (Robertson) Teal; m. Robert William Goux, Aug. 30, 1958; children: John Augustine, Marjorie Marie, Benjamin Julian. BA, Coll. of the Pacific, 1961; MEd, Seattle Pacific U., 1971. Cert. adminstr. Tchr. Lincoln Sch. Dist., Stockton, Calif., 1960-62, Claremont (Calif.) Sch. Dist., 1962-63, Edmonds (Wash.) Sch. Dist., 1964-65, Bremerton (Wash.) Sch. Dist., 1965-73, remediation specialist, 1973-82, elem. prin., 1982-83, coord. compensatory edn., 1983-94, 95-97, dir. spl. svcs., 1994-95, retired, 1997. Bd. mem. Wash. Assn. Grants Mgrs., Seattle, 1990-94; chairperson Wash. State Chpt. 1 Practitioners' Com., Olympia, Wash., 1991-93. State conv. del. Rep. Party, Tacoma, 1988. Recipient Secondary cert. merit U.S. Dept. Edn., 1987, Elem. cert. merit U.S. Dept. Edn., 1988, sch.-wide programs, 1996. Mem. Internat. Reading Assn. (presenter 1987, 89, 97, hon. coun. 1990-93), Wash. Orgn. for Reading Devel., Bremerton Reading Coun. (pres.-elect., pres. 1992-94), Alpha Delta Kappa (pres. 1980-82, treas. 1994—, S.W. Wash. regional pres. 1982-84). Methodist. Avocations: needlework, gardening, reading, traveling. Home: 276 Sylvan Way Bremerton WA 98310-2144

GOVE, PETER CHARLES, special education educator; b. St. Louis, Oct. 13, 1954; s. Clem Charles and Adelaide (Bockhorst) G. AS, George Washington U., 1992; BS in Edn. cum laude, Lincoln U., 1994. Laborer Kingsford Charcoal Co., Belle, Mo., 1973; x-ray aide Charles E. Still, Jefferson City, 1974-76; substitute tchr. Linn (Mo.) RII H.S., 1993, East Elem. Sch., Waynesville, Mo., 1994, South Callaway RII Sch., Mokane, Mo., 1994, tchr. H.S. learning disabled, 1994—; asst. audio visual Lincoln U., Jefferson City, Mo., 1994. Troop leader Boy Scouts Am., Beaufort, S.C., 1986-89. With USN, 1977-89. Mem. Coun. for Exceptional Children, Disabled Am. Vets, Nat. Order Trench Rats, Am. Legion, Phi Alpha Theta. Avocations: reading, woodworking, camping, gardening, cooking. Home: PO Box 79 1114 E Jefferson St Linn MO 65051-9704

GOVERN, FRANK STANLEY, health facility administrator, consultant, healthcare educator, writer; b. Plainfield, NJ, May 18, 1951; s. Fred John and Jane Louise (Schweitzer) Govern; m. Patricia Loretta Hermanns, Aug. 19, 1972; children: Jason, Heather. AAS, Middlesex County Coll., 1973; BA, Salem State Coll., 1979; MAS, Johns Hopkins U., 1981; PhD in law, policy, and soc., Northeastern U., 1997. Asst. adminstr. Circle Terrace Hosp., Alexandria, Va., 1981-84; CEO Tyrone (Pa.) Hosp., 1984—85; pres., CEO Charles River Hosp., Wellesley, Mass., 1985—86; COO Joint Ctr. Radiation Therapy, Boston, 1986—98; dep. dir. radiation oncology scis. program, chief oncology outreach, radiation rsch. Nat. Cancer Inst., Bethesda, Md., 1998—. Sr. instr. Northeastern U., Boston, 1986—98; instr. Harvard Med. Sch., Boston, 1986—98. Author: U.S. Health Policy and Problem Definition: A Policy Process Adrift, 2000; contbr. chapters to books, articles to profl. jours. Founder, pres. Cmty. for Ednl. Excellence, Beverly, Mass., 1991. Capt. USAF, 1974—76. Avocations: cycling, reading, writing, skiing. Home: 11908 Bristol Manor Ct North Bethesda MD 20852-5804 Office: NCI Exec Plz N 6130 Exec Blvd Ste 6020 Bethesda MD 20892

GOVIL, NARENDRA KUMAR, mathematics educator; b. Aligarh, India, Jan. 5, 1940; arrived in U.S., 1983; s. Panna Lal and Kamla Devi (Agrawal) G.; m. Urmila Agrawal, Feb. 1, 1964; children: Sanjay, Sandeep. BSc, Agra (India) U., 1957; MSc, Aligarh (India) U., 1959; PhD, U. Montreal, Que., Can., 1968. Lectr. Concordia U., Montreal, 1967-68, asst. prof., 1968-70, Indian Inst. Tech., New Delhi, 1970-78, assoc. prof., 1978-80, prof., 1980-85; assoc. prof. Auburn (Ala.) U., 1985-86, prof., 1986—. Vis. scientist Dalhousie U., Halifax, Canada, 1980; vis. prof. U. Alberta, Edmonton, Canada, 1981, Auburn U., 1983—85; mem. exec. com. Forum Interdisciplinary Math, Delhi, 1989—91; reviewer Math. Reviews; mem. editl. bd. Archives of Inequalities and Applications, Internat. Jour. Math. and Math. Sci., Internat. Jour. Nonlinear Differential Equations, Pan-Am. Math. Jour., 1994—98, Jour. Inequalities and Applications, 2000—02. Co-editor 2 books; contbr. articles to profl. jours. Mem. exec. India Cultural Assn. East Ala., Auburn, 1986, 96-97. Fellow: Nat. Acad. Scis. India (life); mem.: Indian Math Soc. (life), India Cultural Assn. East Ala. (pres. Auburn 1991). Avocations: music, reading. Home: 523 Owens Rd Auburn AL 36830-2513 Office: Auburn Univ Dept Math Auburn AL 36849 E-mail: govilnk@auburn.edu.

GOVINDJEE, biophysics, biochemistry, and biology educator; b. Allahabad, India, Oct. 24, 1933; came to U.S., 1956, naturalized, 1972; s. Vishveshwar Prasad and Savitri Devi Asthana; m. Rajni Varma, Oct. 24, 1957; children: Anita Govindjee, Sanjay Govindjee. BSc, U. Allahabad, 1952, MSc, 1954; PhD, U. Ill., 1960. Lectr. botany U. Allahabad, 1954-56; grad. fellow U. Ill., Urbana, 1956-58, research asst., 1958-60, USPHS postdoctoral trainee biophysics, 1960-61, mem. faculty, 1961—, assoc. prof. botany and biophysics, 1965-69, prof. biophysics and plant biology, 1969-99, disting. lectr. Sch. Life Scis., 1978, emeritus prof. biophysics, plant biology and biochemistry, 1999—. Author (with E. Rabinowitch): Photosynthesis, 1969; editor: Bioenergetics of Photosynthesis, 1975, Photosynthesis: Energy Conversion by Plants and Bacteria Carbon Assimilation and Plant Productivity, 2 vols., 1982 (Russian transl. 1987); co-editor: The Oxygen Evolving System of Photosynthesis, 1983, Light Emission by Plants and Bacteria, 1986, Excitation Energy and Electron Transfer in Photosynthesis, 1989, Molecular Biology of Photosynthesis, 1989, Photosynthesis: From Photoreactions to Productivity, 1993, Concepts in Photobiology: Photosynthesis and Photomorphogenesis, 1999; editor Hist. Corner: Photosynthesis Rsch., 1989—; guest editor spl. issue Biophys. Jour., 1972, Photochemistry and Photobiology, 1978, Photosynthesis Research, 1993, 96, 2002-04; editor-in-chief Photosynthesis Rsch., 1985-88; series editor: Advances in Photosynthesis and Respiration, vol. 1, 1994, vol. 2, 1995, vols. 3, 4 and 5, 1996, vols. 6 and 7, 1998, vol. 8, 1999, vol. 9, 2000, vols. 10 and 11, 2001, vol. 12, 2002, vol. 13, 2003; contbr. articles to profl. jour., also Sci. Am. Fulbright scholar, 1956-61, 96-97. Fellow AAAS, NAS (India); mem. Am. Soc. Plant Biologists, Biophys. Soc. Am., Am. Soc. Photobiology (coun. 1976, pres. 1981), Internat. Photosynthesis Soc. (exec. com., publ. com. 1995-01), Sigma Xi (emeritus). Home: 2401 Boudreau Dr Urbana IL 61801-6655 E-mail: gov@uiuc.edu.

GOWEN, RICHARD JOSEPH, electrical engineering educator, academic administrator; b. New Brunswick, N.J., July 6, 1935; s. Charles David and Esther Ann (Hughes) G.; m. Nancy A. Applegate, Dec. 28, 1955; children: Jeff, Cindy, Betsy, Susan, Kerry. BS in Elec. Engring., Rutgers U., 1957; MS, Iowa State U., 1961, PhD, 1962. Registered profl. engr., Colo. Rsch. engr. RCA Labs., Princeton, N.J., 1957; commd. USAF; ground electronics officer Yaak AFB, Mont., 1957-59; instr. USAF Acad., 1962-63, rsch. assoc., 1963-64, asst. prof., 1964-65, assoc. prof., 1965-66, tenured assoc. prof. elec. engring., 1966-70, tenured prof., 1971-77, dir., prin. investigator NASA instrumentation group for cardiovascular studies, 1968-77; mem. launch and recovery med. team Johnson Space Ctr., NASA, 1971-77; v.p., dean engring., prof. S.D. Sch. Mines and Tech., Rapid City, 1977-84, pres., 1987—, Dakota State U., Madison, 1984-87. Prin. investigator program in support space cardiovascular studies NASA, 1977-81; co-chmn. Joint Industry, Nuclear Regulatory IEEE, Am. Nuclear Soc. Probabilistic Risk Assessment Guidelines for Nuclear Power Plants Project, 1980-83; mem. Dept. Def. Software Engring. Inst. Panel, 1983; mem. Congl. Web-based Edn. Commn., 1999—. Contbr. articles to profl. jours.; patentee in field. Bd. dirs. St. Martins Acad., Rapid City, S.D., Journey Mus., 1998—, Greater Rapid City Econ. Devel. Partnership, 1991—, Rapid City C. of C., 1998—; mem. U.S. Web Edn. Commn., 1999—. Fellow IEEE (Centennial Internat. pres. 1984, bd. dirs., 1976-75), USAB/IEEE Disting. Contbns. to Engring. Professionalism award 1986); mem. Am. Assn. Engring. Socs. (bd. dirs., 1983-87, chmn. 1988), Rapid City C. of C. (bd. dirs. 1998—), Rotary, Sigma Xi, Phi Kappa Phi, Tau Beta Phi, Eta Kappa Nu (bd. dirs., 1994, pres. 1998—) Pi Mu Epsilon. Roman Catholic. Home: 1609 Palo Verde Dr Rapid City SD 57701-4461 Office: SD Sch Mines & Tech Office of Pres Rapid City SD 57701

GOZEMBA, PATRICA ANDREA, women's studies and English language educator, writer; b. Medford, Mass., Nov. 30, 1940; d. John Charles and Mary Margaret (Sampey) Curran; m. Gary M. Gozemba, Sept. 4, 1967 (div. Feb. 1975). BA, Emmanuel Coll., Boston, 1962; MA, U. Iowa, 1963; EdD, Boston U., 1975. Tchr. Waltham (Mass.) H.S., 1963-64; prof. Salem (Mass.) State Coll., 1964—. Vis. fellow East-West Ctr., 1995; vis. prof. U. Hawaii, 1997-98; co-chair The History Project, Boston, 2000—; bd. dirs. Healthlink. Editor: New England Women's Studies, 1977—87; mem. editl. bd.: Thought and Action, 1990—93; contbr. articles to profl. jours.; author: Pockets of Hope: How Students and Teachers Change the World, 2002. Bd. dirs. Salem Alliance for the Environment, 2003—. Mem. NEA (standing com. 1982-93), NOW, NAACP, Nat. Women's Studies Assn. (gov. bd. 1977-89), Nat. Coun. Tchrs. English, Nat. Gay and Lesbian Task Force, Mass. State Coll. Assn. (editor 1982-90, 92-97), Herb Soc. Am. Democrat. Avocations: walking, tennis, gardening, photography. Home and Office: 17 Sutton Ave Salem MA 01970-5728

GRABILL, JAMES R., JR., education educator, editor, writer; b. Bowling Green, Ohio, Nov. 29, 1949; s. James R. Sr. and Bette L. (Baker) G.; ptnr. Marilyn Burki. BFA, Bowling Green State U., 1974; MA, Colo. State U., 1984, MFA, 1988. Poet, writer, 1968—; instr. Colo. State U., Ft. Collins, Colo., 1985-87, CCC, PCC, OWW, Portland, Oreg., 1990—. Editor, pub. Leaping Mountain Press, Ft. Collins, 1985-86; editor: The Banyan, 2002—; author: (poems) Poem Rising Out of the Earth, 1995 (Oreg. Book Award), Listening to the Leaves Form, 1997, (poems and essays) Through the Green Fire, 1995, An Indigo Scent After the Rain, 2003; contbr. numerous poems and essays to lit. publs. Coord. readings Power Plant Arts Ctr., Ft. Collins, 1984-86. Grad. fellow Colo. State U., 1981-83, 87-88, Nat. Presbyn. fellow, 1967-70. Avocations: art, drawing, reading, running.

GRABILL, VIRGINIA LOWELL, retired English educator; b. Hastings, Minn., Apr. 20, 1919; d. Charles S. and Dora May (Parker) Lowell; m. Paul E. Grabill, June 14, 1952 (dec. Feb. 1980); 1 child, Cynthia Maud. BA summa cum laude, Wheaton (Ill.) Coll., 1941; PhD, U. Ill., 1947. Asst. prof. English, Western Ill State Coll., Macomb, 1947-51; prof., head English dept. Taylor U., Upland, Ind., 1951, Bethel Coll., St. Paul, Ind., 1951-57; asst. prof. English and journalism Evansville Coll. (now U. of Evansville), Ind., from 1957; prof. English, women's counselor U. Evansville, 1957-89; ombudsman; chmn. senate, 1976-86; prof. Henderson (Ky.) Jr. Coll., 1990-92; ret., 1992. Named Hon. Alumna of Yr., U. Evansville, 1994. Mem. Delta Kappa Gamma. Avocations: tutoring through literacy center, shopping, eating, reading. Home: 905 S Spring St Evansville IN 47714

GRABOIS, NEIL ROBERT, foundation administrator, former college president; b. N.Y.C., Dec. 11, 1935; s. Lazarus Lawrence and Florence (Graber) G.; m. Miriam Blau, Aug. 19, 1956; children: Adam, Daniel. BA, Swarthmore Coll., 1957; MA, U. Pa., 1959, PhD, 1963; LLD (hon.), Williams Coll., 1988; LHD (hon.), Colgate U., 1999. Asst. instr. math. U. Pa., Phila., 1957-61; instr. math. Lafayette Coll., Easton, Pa., 1961-63; mem. faculty Williams Coll., Williamstown, Mass., 1963-88, prof. math., 1972-88, dean coll., dean faculty, then provost, 1970-80, chmn. dept. math. scis., 1981-83, provost, 1983-88; pres. Colgate U., Hamilton, N.Y., 1988-99; v.p. for strategic planning, program coord. Carnegie Corp. N.Y., N.Y.C., 1999—. Treas. Roper Ctr., Storrs, Conn., 1979-88. Co-author: Linear Algebra and Multivariable Calculus, 1970. Chmn. edn. subcom. Gov.'s Task Force for No. Berkshires, North Adams, Mass., 1985-87; trustee Swarthmore Coll., 1991—, L.I.U., 2002—. Mem. Am. Math. Soc., Math. Assn. Am. (vis. lectr. 1971), AAAS, N.Y. Acad. Scis. Democrat. Avocations: squash, tennis, clarinet, recorder. Office: Carnegie Corp NY 437 Madison Ave New York NY 10022-7001 E-mail: nrg@carnegie.org.

GRABOW, BEVERLY, learning disability therapist; b. Chgo, Aug. 21, 1929; d. Meyer and Sara (Winograd) Segal; m. Leonard Williams, June 25, 1950; children: Bonnie Williams Mincu, Larry Williams; m. Jack Grabow, Dec. 21, 1974. BA, U. Chgo., 1950; MA, N.E. Ill. U., 1971. Tchr. learning disabled Bd. Edn. Dist. 108, Highland Park, Ill., 1968-93; pvt. practice edn. therapist, Glencoe, Ill., 1975—. Author: Your Child Has A Learning Disability...What Is It?, 1971; contbr. articles to profl. jours. Pres. South Shore Valley Community Orgn., Chgo., 1960-62; mem. Chgo. Drug Task Force, 1980-85. Mem. Profls. in Learning Disabilities (bd. dirs.). Avocations: writing, bridge, tennis. Home and Office: 1162 Carol Ln Glencoe IL 60022-1103

GRACE, JOHN ROSS, chemical engineering educator; b. London, Ont., Can., June 8, 1943; s. Archibald John and Mary Kathleen (Disney) G.; m. Sherrill Elizabeth Perley, Dec. 20, 1964; children— Elizabeth, Malcolm. BESc, U. Western Ont., 1965, DSc (hon.), 2003; PhD, Cambridge (Eng.) U., 1968. From asst. prof. to prof. chem. engring. McGill U., Montreal, Que., 1968-79; sr. research engr. Surveyor Nenniger & Chenevert Inc., 1974-75; prof. chem. engring. U. B.C., Vancouver, 1979—, head dept. chem. engrin., 1979-87, dean faculty grad. studies, 1990-96, prof. chem. and biol. engring., 2000—, Can. rsch. chair, 2001—; pres., CEO Membrane Reactor Techs. Ltd., 1998—2003. Cons. in field. Co-author: Bubbles, Drops and Particles, 1978; co-editor: Fluidization, 1980, Fluidization VI, 1989, Circulating Fluidized Beds, 1997, Circulating Fluidized Bed Technology VII, 2002; editor: Chem. Engring. Sci., 1984—90; contbr. articles to profl. jours. NRC sr. indsl. fellow; Athlone fellow; Can. Coun. Killam Res. fellow, 1999. Fellow Royal Soc. Can., Can. Acad. Engring., Chem. Inst. Can. (v.p. 1994-95, pres. 1995-96); mem. Can. Soc. Chem. Engring. (pres. 1989-90, Erco award, R.S. Jane award), Assn. Profl. Engrs. B.C., Instn. Chem. Engrs. Office: 2216 Main Mall Vancouver BC Canada V6T 1Z4 E-mail: jgrace@chml.ubc.ca.

GRACE, RICHARD EDWARD, engineering educator; b. Chgo., June 26, 1930; s. Richard Edward and Louise (Koko) G.; m. Consuela Cummings Fotos, Jan. 29, 1955; children: Virginia Louise, Richard Cummings (dec.). BS in Metall. Engring., Purdue U., 1951; PhD, Carnegie Inst. Tech., 1954. Asst. prof. Purdue U., West Lafayette, Ind., 1954-58, assoc. prof., 1958-62, prof., 1962-2000, head sch. materials sci. and metall. engring., 1965-72, head div. interdisciplinary engring. studies, 1970-82, head freshman engring. dept., asst. dean engring., 1981-87, v.p. for student services, 1987-95, dir. undergrad. studies program, 1995-2000, prof. emeritus, v.p. emeritus, 2000—. Cons. to Midwest industries. Author: When Every Day Is Saturday, 2002; contbr. articles to profl. jours. Pres. Lafayette Symphony Found. Bd., 1993-95. Named Sagamore of Wabash, Gov. of Ind., 1995. Fellow Am. Soc. Metals (tchr. award 1962), Am. Soc. Engring. Edn. (Centennial medallion 1993), Accreditation Bd. Engring. and Tech. (past dir. and officer engring. edn. and accreditation com., related engring. com., Grinter award 1989); mem. Minerals, Metals and Materials Soc. (bd. dirs. 1987-90), Lafayette Country Club, Rotary, Elks, Sigma Xi, Tau Beta Pi, Omicron Delta Kappa, Phi Gamma Delta. Home: 2175 Tecumseh Park Ln West Lafayette IN 47906-2118 Office: Purdue U 501 Northwestern Ave West Lafayette IN 47907-2036

GRACIA, JORGE JESUS EMILIANO, philosopher, educator; b. Camaguey, Cuba, July 18, 1942; s. Ignacio Jesus Loreto and Leonila (Otero) G.; m. Norma Elida Silva, Sept. 3, 1966; children: Leticia Isabel, Clarisa Raquel. BA, Wheaton Coll., Ill., 1965; MA, U. Chgo., 1966; MSL, Pontifical Inst. Mediaeval Studies, Toronto, 1970; PhD, U. Toronto, 1971. From asst. prof. to prof. SUNY, Buffalo, 1971-95, Disting. prof., 1995—, assoc. chmn. dept. philosophy, 1974-76, chmn. dept., 1980-85, acting chmn., 1988-89, Samuel P. Capen chair philosophy, 1998—. Magister Schola Lullistica Maioricensis, Palma de Mallorca, 1976-96. Author: Suárez on Individuation, 1982, Introduction to the Problem of Individuation, 1984, 2d edit., 1986, Individuality: An Essay in the Foundations of Metaphysics, 1988, Philosophy and Its History: Issues in Philosophical Historiography, 1991, A Theory of Textuality: The Logic and Epistemology, 1995, Texts: Ontological Status, Identity, Author, Audience, 1996, Metaphysics and Its Task: The Search for the Categorial Foundation of Knowledge, 1999, Filosofía hispánica: Concepto, origen y foco hisforiográfico, 1998, Hispanic/Latino Identity: A Philosophical Perspective, 2000, How Can We Know What God Means: The Interpretation of Revelation, 2001, Que' son las categorias?, 2002, Old Wine in New Skins: The Role of Tradition in Communication, Knowledge, and Group Identity, 2003; editor: Man and His Conduct, 1980, El Hombre y los valores, 1975, Com Usar Be de Beure e Menjar, 1977; (with others) Philosophical Analysis in Latin America, 1984, Latin American Philosophy in the XXth Century, 1986, Risieri Frondizi: Ensayos Filosoficos, 1986, Filosofia e Identidad Cultural, 1987, The Metaphysics of Good and Evil, 1989, Philosophy and Literature in Latin America, 1989, Directory of Latin American Philosophers, 1988, Social Sciences in Latin America, 1989, Latin American Philosophy Today, 1989, Individuation in Scholasticism, 1994; (with K. Barber) Individuation and Identity in Early Modern Philosophy, 1994, Concepciones de la Metafisica, 1998, Hispanics/Latinos in the United States: Identity, Race, and Rights, 2000; (with T. Noone) Blackwell Companion to Philosophy in the Middle Ages, 2003; (with G. Reichberg and B. Shoumacher) The Classics of Western Philosophy, 2003; (with J. Yu) Rationality and Happiness: From the Ancients to the Early Medievals, 2003. NEH grantee, 1981-82, N.Y. Coun. for Humanities, 1987, John N. Findlay prize Metaphysical Soc. Am., 1992. Mem. Am. Philos. Assn. (com. internat. cooperation 1981-84, chmn. com. for Hispanics in philosophy 1991-95, chmn. prog. com. 1993-94, exec. com. 1996-2000, Am. Cath. Philos. Assn. (exec. com. 1983-86, chmn. program com. 1987, v.p. 1996-97. pres. 1997-98), Soc. for Iberian and Latin Am. Thought (exec. com. 1982—, v.p. 1984-85, pres. 1986-88), Soc. for Medieval and Renaissance Philosophy (exec. com. 1986-97, chmn. program com. 1989-91, v.p. 1989-91, pres. 1991-93, chmn. nominating com. 1993-95), Soc. de Filosofia Iberoamericana (exec. com. 1985—), Internat. Fedn. Latin Am. and Caribbean Studies (pres. 1987-89), Metaphy. Soc. Am. (program com. 1992-93, councillor 1995—, chmn. Findlay prize com. 1995, v.p. 1999—, pres. 2000), Soc. Internat. pour Etude de Philos. Medievale (orgn. com. 1992, program com. 1996), Internat. Fedn. Philos. Socs. (program com. 1994-98). Home: 420 Berryman Dr Buffalo NY 14226-4640 Office: Univ at Buffalo Dept Philos 123 Park Hall Buffalo NY 14260-1000 E-mail: gracia@acsu.buffalo.edu.

GRAD, FRANK PAUL, law educator, lawyer; b. Vienna, May 2, 1924; came to U.S., 1939, naturalized, 1943; s. Morris and Clara Sophie (Scher) G.; m. Lisa Szilagyi, Dec. 6, 1946; children: David Anthony, Catharine Ann. BA magna cum laude, Bklyn. Coll., 1947; LLB, Columbia U., 1949. Bar: N.Y. 1949. Assoc. in law Columbia U. Law Sch., N.Y.C., 1949-50, asst. dir. Legis. Drafting Research Fund, 1953-55, assoc. dir., 1956-68, dir., 1969-95, faculty, 1954-69, prof., 1969—, Joseph P. Chamberlain prof. legis., 1982-95, Joseph P. Chamberlain prof. emeritus legis. and spl. lectr., 1995—; legal adv. com. U.S. Council Environ. Quality, 1970-73; mem. N.Y. Deptl. Com. Ct. Adminstrn., Appellate Div., 1st Dept., 1970-74; counsel N.Y. State Spl. Adv. Panel Med. Malpractice, 1975; legal counsel Nat. Mcpl. League, 1967-88. Cons. in field; reporter U.S. Superfund Study group, 1981-82; dir. rsch. N.Y.C. Charter Revision Commn., 1982-83, N.Y. State-City Commn. on Integrity in Govt., 1986. Author: Public Health Law Manual, 1st edit., 1965, 2d rev. edit., 1990, The Drafting of State Constitutions, 1963, Environmental law: Sources and Problems, 3d edit., 1985, 4th edit. (with Joel Mintz), 2000, Treatise on Environmental Law, 8 vols., 1973—; co-author other legal reports; contbr. articles to profl. jours.; draftsman mcpl. codes and state legislation. With AUS, 1943-46. 10th Horace E. Read Meml. lectr. Dalhousie Law Sch., 1984. Mem. ABA, APHA, Assn. of Bar of City of N.Y., N.Y. Bar Assn., Am. Law Inst., Am. Soc. Law and Medicine, World Conservation Union (commn. on environ. law 1991—), Human Genome Orgn., Internat. Coun. Environ. Law, N.Y.. Soc. Med. Jurisprudence. Office: Columbia U Sch Law 435 W 116th St New York NY 10027-7297 E-mail: fgrad@law.columbia.edu.

GRADELESS, DONALD EUGENE, secondary education educator; b. Warsaw, Ind., Apr. 17, 1949; s. Harmon Willard and Donna Maxine (Mort) G. BS in Acctg., U. Wis., Stevens Point, 1972; MS in Teaching, U. Wis., Eau Claire, 1975; PhD in Edn., Pacific Western U., 1988. Cert. in data edn. Tchr. high schs., Racine, Wis., 1972-77; mgr. constrn. Computer Control Corp., Milw., 1977; indsl. engr. Weatherhead div. Dana Corp., Columbia City, Ind., 1977-78; instr. bus. edn. Elmbrook pub. schs., Brookfield, Wis., 1978—. Coordinator instructional data processing Racine Unified Schs., 1973-77. Author geneal. books. Recipient Cmty. Svc. award, DAR, 1998. Fellow Am. Coll. Genealogists; mem. NEA, NRA (life, golden eagles), SAR (sec., host. 1977, registrar 1975-76, publs. chmn. 1975-77, pres. 1976-77, 95-96, Nat. Soc. Mem. awards 1976-78, Silver Good Citizenship medal 1978, mem. Ind. soc.), S.R. (chmn. 1975-79, pres. 1979-83, registrar 1979-82, 84-87, sec. 1983—, gen. v.p. 2000—, various state bds. mgrs., Gen. Pres.'s Spl. Commendation award 1985, 2000, 02, Outstanding Svc. award 1982), Nat. Bus. Edn. Assn., Wis. Bus. Edn. Assn., Children Am. Revolution (sr. registrar 1976-77, 80-83, sr. v.p. 1984-86, sr. pres. 1986-90, hon. sr. state pres. 1990—), Sons and Daus. of Pilgrims (counselor 1979-80, 2d dep. govs. 1989-90, 1st dep. gov. 1990-92, gov. 1992-98), Soc. Am. Colonists (state pres. 1997—), Soc. Colonial Wars (dep. sec. Wis. chpt. 1978-79, registrar 1994-96, lt. gov. 1975-77), Studebaker Family Nat. Assn. (life), Soc. of the War of 1812 (life, v.p. 1994-95, pres. 1995—, gen. v.p. 2000—), Huguenot Soc. (registrar 1975-77, chaplain 1993-96, treas. 2003), Wis. State Old Cemetery Soc., U.S. Postal Svcs. Racine (customer adv. com. 1992—), Mensa, Whitley County Hist. Soc. (Pres. award 2002), Soc. Ind. Pioneers, Sons of Union Vets of Civil War, Children Am. Revolution, Genealogical Soc. Whitley County, Nat. Officers Club (patron award 1993), Sons of Am. Colonists (gov. 1996—), Delta Phi Epsilon. Lodges: Masons (32 degree), K.T. Home: 2655 Fairview Ln Brookfield WI 53045-4117 Office: Brookfield East High Sch 3305 Lilly Rd Brookfield WI 53005 Office Fax: 262-781-3500. E-mail: DrG@execpc.com.

GRADIE, CHARLOTTE MAY, history educator; b. Putnam, Conn., Nov. 7, 1949; d. Robert Richmond and Avis Leonia (Gregg) Gradie; m. Frank Palmer Hendrick, Dec. 30, 1978; children: Rachel May Hendrick, Emily Rose Hendrick, Adam Palmer Hendrick. BA, U. Conn., 1973, MA, 1975, PhD, 1990. Prof. history Sacred Heart U., Fairfield, Conn., 1990—. Cons. Conn. Humanities Coun., Middletown, 1993—; cons. scholar So. Conn. Libr. coun., Hamden, 1992—. Contbr. articles to profl. jours. Bd. dirs. Haddam (Conn.) Hist. Soc. Andrew W. Mellon grantee, 1994; Sacred Heart U. rsch. grantee, 1993-94. Mem. Phi Alpha Theta. Methodist.

GRADO-WOLYNIES, EVELYN (EVELYN WOLYNIES), clinical nurse specialist, educator; b. N.Y.C., Apr. 2, 1944; d. Joseph Frederick and Evelyn Marie (Ronning) Grado; m. Jon Gordon Wolynies, July 12, 1964; children: Jon Andrew, Kristine Elisabeth; m. Brian Bereika, 1999. AAS, Burlington County Coll., 1990; AS, Camden C.C., 1990; BSN cum laude, Thomas Jefferson U., 1991, MSN summa cum laude, 1992; postgrad., Johns Hopkins U., 1993-95. RN N.J., Pa. Charge nurse Hampton Hosp., Westampton, N.J., 1990-92; adjunct clin. instr. psychiat. nursing Burlington County Coll., Pemberton, N.J., 1992-93; project leader Alzheimer's disease clin. drug study Olsten Health Care, Cherry Hill, N.J., 1992-95, psychiat. case mgr., 1992-94; CNS neuropsych in Huntingtons Disease Dr. Allen Rubin, Camden, N.J., 1992; psychiat. case mgr. Moorestown (N.J.) Vis. Nurses Assn., 1992; charge nurse, group therapist, rschr. Friends Hosp., Phila., 1994-99; clin. mgr. The Caring Link partial geriatric outpatient program Frankford Hosp., Phila., 1996-99; psychotherapist Penn Friends, Marlton, NJ, 2000—02. Pvt. practice hypnotherapy/psychotherapy; cons. psychiat. care, Alzheimer's Disease, RN/home health aide instr. Olsten-Kimberly Home Care; clin. preceptor U. Pa. Sch. NSG, MSN, GNP and Adult Mental CS Programs. Contbr. articles to nursing jours. Mem. Burlington County Coll. Alumni Bd.; founder, dir. Support Group for Adult Children with Aging Parents; Developed music therapy/exercise program for Geriatric Psych patients. Recipient Juanita Wilson award, 1991, Farber fellowship, 1991-92.; Nurse in Washington intern, 1992; named to Burlington County Coll. Hall of Fame, 1994 Mem. Am. Assn. of Neuroscience Nurses, Am. Psychiat. Nurses Assn., N.J. State Nurses Assn., Sigma Theta Tau (Delta Rho chpt.), Phi Theta Kappa. Home: PO Box 3604 Cherry Hill NJ 08034-0550

GRAF, JOHN CHRISTIAN, JR., secondary education educator; b. Lancaster, Pa., Apr. 25, 1948; s. John C. and F. June (Hauer) G.; m. Karen S. Felter, Aug. 21, 1971; children: John C. III, Kimberly R. BS, Franklin and Marshall Coll., 1970; MA, Montclair State Coll., 1976. Cert. supr., prin., N.J. Tchr. Pequannock Twp. High Sch., Pompton Plains, N.J., 1970—, supr. social studies, 1982—. Field cons. N.J. Coun. for Econ. Edn., Trenton, 1989—; advanced placement U.S. history exam. reader, 2000—. Mem. Vernon Twp. Bd. Edn., 1991—, v.p., 1994—. Recipient DEEP Dist. award Nat. Coun. on Econ. Edn., 1989, Exemplary Grade Level Econ. Program award Nat. Coun. on Econ. Edn., 1990, 91, 92, N.J. Exemplary Coord. award Econs. USA, 1992, Educator of Yr. award Lakeland Hills YMCA, 1993, The Coll. of NJ Outstanding Educators Program, 2001, 03. Mem. Nat. Coun. for Social Studies, Pequannock Twp. Adminstrs. Assn. (pres. 1985-91). Avocations: skiing, model trains, home building. Home: 3 Evergreen Rd Sussex NJ 07461-4702 Office: Pequannock Twp High Sch Pompton Plains NJ 07444 E-mail: graf4@wawick.net.

GRAFF, HENRY FRANKLIN, historian, educator; b. NYC, Aug. 11, 1921; s. Samuel F. and Florence Babette (Morris) G.; m. Edith Krantz, June 16, 1946; children: Iris Joan (Mrs. Andrew R. Morse), Ellen Toby (Mrs. Martin A. Fox). BSS magna cum laude, Coll. City N.Y., 1941; MA, Columbia, 1942, PhD, 1949. Fellow history Coll. City N.Y., 1941-42, tutor history, 1946; lectr. history Columbia U., N.Y.C., 1946-47, instr. to asso. prof., 1946-61, prof. history, 1961-91, prof. emeritus, 1991—, chmn. dept. history, 1961-64; sr. fellow Freedom Forum Media Studies Ctr., N.Y.C., 1991-92; disting. lectr. Med. Sch. Columbia U., N.Y.C., 1992. Lectr. Vassar Coll., 1953; chmn. advanced placement com. Am. History Coll. Entrance Exam. Bd., 1959-63; presdl. appointee Nat. Hist. Publs. Commn., 1965-71; mem. hist. adv. com. to sec. Air Force, 1972-80; acad. cons. Gen. Learning Corp., Time-Life Books; cons. editor Alfred A. Knopf, Inc.; hist. adviser to CBS for Bicentennial TV Series The American Parade, 1973-76, Presdl. Portraits, 1987-88; disting. spkr. U.S. Air Force Acad., 1980; hist. adviser to ABC for TV series Our World, 1986-87, 20th Century Project, 1993-99; presdl. appointee J.F.K. Assassination Records Rev. Bd., 1993-98; humanities lectr. Med. Sch. Yale U., 1993; Richard W. Cooper lectr. Phi Beta Kappa Assocs., 1996. Author: Bluejackets with Perry in Japan, 1952; author: (with Jacques Barzun) The Modern Researcher, 1962; author: (with Clifford Lord) American Themes, 1963; author: (with John A. Krout) The Adventure of the American People, 3d edit., 1973; author: The Free and the Brave, 4th edit., 1980, Thomas Jefferson, 1968, American Imperialism and the Philippine Insurrection, 1969, The Tuesday Cabinet, 1970; author: (with Paul J. Bohannan) The Call of Freedom, 1978; author: The Promise of Democracy, 1978, This Great Nation, 1983, The Presidents: A Reference History, 1984, 2d edit., 1996, paperback, 1997, 3d edit., 2002, America: The Glorious Republic, 1985, rev. edit., 1990, Grover Cleveland, 2002; cons. editor Life's History of the United States, 1963—64; contbr. articles to profl. jours. 1st lt. AUS, 1942-46. Recipient citation War Dept., Townsend Harris medal CCNY, 1966, Mark Van Doren award Columbia U., 1981, Gt. Tchr. award Columbia U., 1982, Kidger award New Eng. History Tchrs. Assn., 1990; Am. Coun. Learned Socs. fellow, 1942, Presdl. medal George Washington U., 1997, James Madison award ALA, 1999, Disting. Author award Westchester C.C. Found., 2000. Mem. Orgn. Am. Historians, Am. Hist. Assn., Coun. Fgn. Rels., Author's Guild, P.E.N., Soc. Am. Historians, Soc. Historians Am. Fgn. Rels., Mass. Hist. Soc. (corr.), Century Assn. (N.Y.C.), Sunningdale Country Club, Phi Beta Kappa (former pres. Gamma chpt.), Phi Beta Assocs. (hon.). Home: 47 Andrea Ln Scarsdale NY 10583-3115

GRAFF, PAT STUEVER, secondary education educator; b. Tulsa, Mar. 24, 1955; d. Joseph H., Sr. and Joann (Schneider) Stuever; m. Mark A. Rumsey; children: Earl, Jr., Jeremy. BS in Secondary Edn., Okla. State U., 1976; postgrad., U. N.M., 1976-87. Cert. tchr. lang. arts, social studies, journalism, French, N.Mex. Substitute tchr. Albuquerque Pub. Schs., 1976-78; tchr. Cleveland Mid. Sch., Albuquerque, 1978-86, La Cueva H.S., Albuquerque, 1986—, co-chair English dept., 1996—, chair sch. restructuring coun., 1999-2001. Adviser award winning lit. mag. El Tesoro, sch. newspapers The Edition, Huellas del Oso; instr. journalism workshops, N.Mex. Press Assn., Ind. U., Bloomington, Nat. Scholastic Press, Mpls., Kans. State U., Manhattan, Interscholastic Press League, Austin, Tex., St. Mary's U., San Antonio, Ala. Scholastic Press Assn., Wash.; keynote spkr. at numerous confs. in Ohio, Ind., Kans., S.C., Utah, La., Okla., Ala., N.Mex., Tex., Wash., Idaho, and N.Y.; reviewer of lang. and textbooks for several cos.; instr. Dial-A-Tchr., N.Mex., 1991—; textook evaluator Holt

Pub., Inc., 1991; nat. bd. cert. tchr. adolescent/young adult English lang. arts, 2001—; mem. N.Mex. Network of Nat. Bd. Cert. Tchrs., 2002—, 2d v.p., 2003—; bd. dirs. N.Mex. Coun. for the Social Studies, 1999—, chair state conf., 2001, state pres., 2002-03. Comm. coord. ABC Tchrs. Fed. 2003- rep. 2001- Author: Journalism Text, 1983; contbg. author: Communication Skills Resource Text, 1987, Classroom Publishing/Literacy, 1992; contbr. articles to profl. jours. Troop leader Girl Scouts U.S., 1979—90, coord. various programs, asst. program com. chmn. Chaparral Coun., 1988—89, chmn. adult recognition task force, 1991—96, bd. dirs., 1991—98; active PTA Gov. Bent Elem. Sch., 1983—86, v.p., 1985—86, Osuna Elem. Sch., 1986—92, N.Mex. PTA, 1994—2000; pub. various children's lit. mags., 1987—; pub. parent's newsletter, 1986—; newsletter layout editor Albuquerque Youth Soccer Orgn., 1985—88; active YMCA youth and govt. model legis.; faculty advisor La Cueva del., 1986—2002, press corps advisor, 1987—2001, asst. state dir., 2001—; asst. den. leader Boy Scouts Am., 1987—88, den leader, 1988—91; mem. N.Mex. Coun. for Social Studies, 1998—2003, state bd. dirs., 1998—, state pres., 2002—03. Recipient Innovative Teaching award Bus. Week mag., 1990, Svc. commendatin Coll. Edn. Alumni Assn., Okla. State U., 1990, Alumni Recognition award, 1993, Mem. Yr. Svc. award Bernalillo County Coun. Internat. Reading Assn., Thanks to Tchrs. award Apple Computers, 1990, Spl. Recognition Albuquerque C. of C., 1992; named Spotlighted Mem. Phi Delta Kappa, 1990, Spl. Recognition Advisor Dow Jones Newspaper Fund, 1990, Nat. H.S. Journalism Tchr. of Yr., 1995, Disting. Advisor, 1991, U.S. West Tchr. Yr. finalist, 1991, N.Mex. Pubs. Adviser of Yr., 1991, N.Mex. State Tchr. of Yr., 1993, finalist Nat. Tchr. Yr., 1993, finalist Am. Tchr. Awards, Disney, 1998; named USA Today All-Am. Tchr., 1999; grantee Phi Delta Kappa 1989, 91, Geraldine R. Dodge Found., 1990, 92, 95-97, Learn and Serve Am., 1999. Mem.: AAUW (chpt. newsletter editor 1995—2001, local v.p. 1997—99, state program v.p. 1997—99, state media chair 2000—), ASCD (editor newsletter 1991—92, focus on excellence awards com. 1992—94, state bd. dirs. 2002—, Focus on Excellence award 1990), N Mex. Coun. for Social Studies (mem. bd. 1999—, state vice- pres 2001—02, pres. 2002—03), N. Mex. World Class Tchr. Network (state vice-pres. 2002—), N.Mex. Goals 2000 (panel mem. 1994—97), Quill & Scroll (adv. La Cueva chpt. 1986—, judge nat. newspaper rating contest 1988—97), Albuquerque Press Women (v.p. 1994, pres. 1995, Communicator of Achievement award 1993), N.Mex. Press Women (state scholarship chair 1994, publicity chair 1995—96, state treas. 1996—98, state v.p. 1998—99), N.Mex. Scholastic Press Assn. (state v.p. 1985—89, coord. workshop 1986, editor newsletter 1986—89, asst. chair state conf. 1988, 1989, state bd. dirs. 1991—2000, state v.p. 1992—95), N.Mex. Coun. Tchrs. English (regional coord. Albuquerque 1983—86, chair state confs. 1985—87, editl. bd. N.Mex. English Jour. 1986—88, state pres. 1987—88, chair facilities for Fall conf. 1988—93, chair English Humanities expo com. 1988—99, adv. mgr. 1989—90, editor N.Mex. English Jour. 1999—, Svc. award 1989, Outstanding H.S. English Tchr. N.Mex. 1991), Journalism Edn. Assn., Journalism Edn. Assn. (judge nat. contests 1988—, mem. nat. cert. bd. 1989—99, presenter nat. convs. 1989—, cert. journalism educator 1990, nat. bd. 1991—2002), Nat. Fedn. Press Women, Nat. Sch. Pub. Rels. Assn. (issues seminar planning com. 1990, master journalism educator 1991, chair 1991, nat. conf. chmn. 1997—99, Zia chpt., contest winner 1991—94, Pres.'s award 1993), Nat. Coun. Tchrs. English (nat. chair com. English Tchrs. and Pubs. 1988—91, standing com. affiliates 1991—94, nat. chair 1995—98, Secondary Sect. Com. 1999—, nat. exec. com. 2001—, chair English Humanities expo com. 2001—, nat. chair assembly for advisors of student pubs., regional rep. Tex., La., N.Mex.), Nat. Alliance High Schs. (tchr. rep. 1997—2000), Nat. Assn. Secondary Sch. Prins. (Breaking Ranks tchr. rep.), Phi Delta Kappa (pres. U. N.Mex. br. 2002—), Delta Kappa Gamma, Pi Lambda Theta (Ethel Mary Moore award Outstanding Educator 1993). Roman Catholic. Avocations: soccer, running, hiking, travel, skiing. Home: 8101 Krim Dr NE Albuquerque NM 87109-5223 Office: La Cueva H S 7801 Wilshire Ave NE Albuquerque NM 87122-2807 Fax: 505-797-2250. E-mail: pgraff@aol.com.

GRAFFEO, MARY THÉRÈSE, music educator, performer; b. Mineola, N.Y., Jan. 20, 1949; d. Michael Joseph and Florence Marie (Lonette) G. BA in Music Edn., Adelphi U., 1972; MusM in Vocal Performance, Kent State U., 1982. Cert. music tchr. N.Y. Tchr., therapist Nassau County Bd. Coop. Ednl. Svcs., Westbury, NY, 1972-85; tchr. music, developer curricula Great Neck (N.Y.) Pub. Schs., 1985-87; tchr. music Syosset (N.Y.) Pub. Schs., 1987-88, 89-90, Jericho (N.Y.) Pub. Schs., 1988-89; tchr. music, developer creative programs Lawrence (N.Y.) Pub. Schs., 1990-92; tchr. music Herricks Pub. Schs., New Hyde Park, N.Y., 1992-93, Hempstead (N.Y.) Pub. Schs., 1993—. Music dir. summer programs Friends Acad., Locust Valley, N.Y., 1989-95. Author: Creative Enrichment Programs/America: The First 300 Years in Song, 1990, (curriculum) Music for the Trainable Mentally Retarded, 1973, Music for the Early Childhood Center of Hempstead Public Schools, 2002; co-author: The Remediation of Learning Discrepancies Through Music, 1980; composer: (mus. play) Red Riding Hood's Day, 1993, The Bell of Atri, The Children's Song, 1995. Cultural adv. bd. Lawrence Pub. Schs., 1990-92, Hempstead Pub. Schs., 1993—; founding mem. United We Stand Am., Dallas, 1992-93. Scholar Adelphi U., 1968-72, Blossom Festival Sch., Kent, Ohio, 1978-79. Mem. NEA, Am. Fedn. Tchrs., Music Educators Nat. Conf., N.Y. State United Tchrs., N.Y. State Sch. Music Assn., Nassau Music Educators Assn. Democrat. Roman Catholic. Avocations: aviculture, needlework, travel, photography, concerts. Home: 18 Osborne Ln Greenvale NY 11548-1140 Office: Early Childhood Ctr 436 Front St Hempstead NY 11550-4212 E-mail: mgraffeo@optonline.net.

GRAFFIUS, RICHARD STEWART, II, middle school educator; b. Punxsutawney, Pa., May 27, 1948; s. Richard S. and Adeline L. (Piquet) G.; m. Rose M. Ingham, Apr. 13, 1974; children: Alissa, Lindsay, Emily. BS in Elem. Edn., Ind. U. Pa., 1970; MEd in Ednl. Adminstrn., Pa. State U., 1975, EdD in Ednl. Adminstrn., 1993. Cert. elem. tchr., elem. and secondary prin., supt., Pa. Sci. tchr. Punxsutawney (Pa.) Area Middle Sch., 1970—. Author (coloring book) The Official Punxsutawney Phil Coloring Book, 1978. Councilman, v.p. Borough of Punxsutawney, 1981-85; consistory mem. St. Peter's United Ch. of Christ, Punxsutawney, 1993-96. Mem. NEA, ASCD, Pa. State Edn. Assn., Punxsutawney Area Ednl. Assn. Avocations: skiing, hunting, fishing, antique and classic car restoration. Home: 136 Wayne Rd Punxsutawney PA 15767

GRAFFMAN, GARY, pianist, music educator; b. N.Y.C., Oct. 14, 1928; s. Vladimir and Nadia (Margolin) G.; m. Naomi Helfman, Dec. 5, 1952. Student, Curtis Inst. Music, 1936-46, Columbia U., 1947-48; studied with Vladimir Horowitz, Rudolf Serkin, Isabelle Vengerova; MusD (hon.), Trinity Coll., 1986, Juilliard Sch., 1993, Moravian Coll., 1995, St. Josephs U., 1996, Univ. Pa., 1997, New Eng. Conservatory Music, 2003. Dir. Curtis Inst. Music, Phila., 1986-95, pres., dir., 1995—. Soloist debut, Phila. Orch, 1947; first tours U.S., 1951, S.Am., 1955, Europe, 1956, Asia-Australia, 1958, South Africa, 1961; solo appearances with N.Y. Philharmonic, Boston, Chgo., Cleve., San Francisco, Los Angeles, London, Cape Town symphony orchs., Philharmonia London, Halle Orch. of Manchester, Royal Liverpool, Berlin, Lisbon, Oslo, Warsaw philharmonic orchs., Johannesburg, Sydney, Melbourne orchs., others; rec. artist with N.Y., Phila., Boston, Cleve., Chgo., San Francisco orchs., also solo recs.; author: I Really Should Be Practicing, 1981. Fulbright scholar, 1950; Ford Found. fellow, 1962; recipient Rachmaninoff Fund. spl. award, 1948, Leventritt award, 1949, Pa. Gov. Excellence in Arts award, 1991. Office: Curtis Inst Music Office of Director 1726 Locust St Philadelphia PA 19103-6187 also: ICM Artists Ltd 40 W 57th St Fl 16 New York NY 10019-4001

GRAHAM, ALBERT DARLINGTON, JR., educational administrator; b. Camden, N.J., July 28, 1948; s. Albert Darlington and Betty Jane (Belancin) g.; m. Susan K. Tomarchio, July 30, 1994; children: Jason Carl, Jayme Lynn. BS cum laude, Union Coll., Barbourville, Ky., 1970, MA, 1973; EdM, Johns Hopkins U., 1977; EdD, Calif. Western U., 1980; MA, Rowan U., 1991; PhD, LaSalle U., 1992; postgrad., Rutgers U., 2003. Cert. supt., prin., supr., sch. bus. adminstr., secondary social studies tchr., in student personnel svcs., N.J. Tchr. social studies Penns Grove (N.J.) Mid. Sch., 1970-82, coord. career edn., 1974-75, chmn. social studies dept., 1978-82; athletic dir. Penns Grove H.S., Carneys Point, N.J., 1983-85, coord. gifted and talented program, 1986-87, dir. guidance, vice prin. in charge curriculum, fin.-instrn., 1982-92, dir. spl. projects, 1992—, dir. early childhood and fed./state programs, 2001—. Adj. prof. Sch. Law Wilmington Coll., 2002—, LaSalle U., 2002—. Mem. Carneys Point Twp., 1979-84, 91—; mayor Carneys Point Twp., 1992, 96, 99, 2000; mem. Salem County (N.J.) Bd. Chosen Freeholders, 1985-87, N.J. Gov.'s Coun. on Phys. Fitness and Sports, 1986—; chmn. Carneys Point Sewerage Authority, 1981-85, 91—; pres. Salem County Selective Svc. Bd., 1982-2002; pres. Salem County Assn. Local Govt., 1983-84, Village Arms Sr. Citizens Complex, Carneys Point, 1984—; pres. Carneys Point Rep. Club, 1981-84; trustee Salem C.C., 1987-91, Union Coll., 1992—. Recipient Gov. James D. Black Sr. award for acad. excellence, Balckwell Meml. award in polit. sci., medal for excellence in ednl. adminstrn., Disting. Cmty. Svc. award Carneys Point Twp. Com., 1983, Disting. Leadership award Salem County Assn. Local Govt., 1986, Salem County recognition award Salem County Bd. Chosen Freholders, 1987, Citizen of Yr. Penns Grove VFW, 1993; named to Personal Achievement Hall of Fame, Penns Grove H.S., 1994, Educators Hall of Fame, Union Coll., 1998, Selective Svc. medal, 2002. Mem. ASCD, N.J. Pins. and Suprs. Assn. (svc. and leadership award 1984), N.J. League Municipalities (svc. and leadership award 1984), South Jersey Assn. Freeholders (svc. and leadership award 1985), Penns Grove High Sch. Alumni Assn. (treas. 1975—, Selective Svc. medal 2002, Personal Achievement Hall of Fame 1994), Penns Grove Exch. Club (pres. Penns Grove 1984-85, Exchangite of Yr. 1984, Cmty. Svc. award 1985), Masons (32d degree), Elks (leading knight Penns Grove 1986-87), Mensa, Phi Delta Kappa, Iota Sigma Nu, Gamma Beta Phi, Phi Delta Gamma. Roman Catholic. Avocations: reading, sports, coin collecting, working on 1929 mercedes. Home: 58 N Norman Ave Carneys Point NJ 08069-1546 Office: Penns Grove-Carneys Point Sch Dist Adminstrv Offices 100 Iona Ave Penns Grove NJ 08069-1322 E-mail: agraham@pennsgrove.k12.nj.us.

GRAHAM, ANNA REGINA, pathologist, educator; b. Phila., Nov. 1, 1947; d. Eugene Nelson and Anna Beatrice (McGovern) Chadwick; m. Larry L. Graham, June 29, 1973; 1 child, Jason. BS in Chemistry, Ariz. State U., 1969, BS in Zoology, 1970; MD, U. Ariz., 1974. Diplomate Am. Bd. Pathology. With Coll. Medicine U. Ariz., Tucson, 1974—, asst. prof. pathology, 1978-84, assoc. prof. pathology, 1984-90, prof. Pathology, 1990—. Fellow Am. Soc. Clin. Pathologists (bd. dirs. Chgo. chpt. 1993—, sec. 1995-99, v.p. 1999-2000, pres.-elect 2000-2001, pres. 2001-02), Internat. Acad. Pathology, Internat. Acad. Telemedicine, Coll. Am. Pathologists; mem. AMA (alt. del. Chgo. chpt. 1992-99, del. Chgo. chpt. 1999—), Ariz. Soc. Pathologists (pres. Phoenix chpt. 1989-91), Ariz. Med. Assn. (treas. Phoenix chpt. 1995-97). Republican. Baptist. Avocations: motorcycles, piano, choir. Office: Ariz Health Scis Ctr Dept Pathology Tucson AZ 85724-5108

GRAHAM, DENIS DAVID, marriage and family therapist, educational consultant; b. Santa Rosa, Calif., Oct. 21, 1941; s. Elbert Eldon and Mildred Bethana (Dyson) G.; m. Margaret Katherine Coughlan, Aug. 31, 1968; children: Kathleen Ann, Todd Cameron (dec.). BS in Edn., U. Nev., 1964, MEd, 1973, MA, 1982. Cert. for ednl. pers.; lic. marriage and family therapist, Nev. Tchr. vocat. bus. edn. Earl Wooster H.S., Reno, 1964-66, chmn. dept. bus. edn., 1966-67; stare supr. bus. and office edn. Nev. Dept. Edn., Carson City, 1967-70, adminstr. vocat. edn. field svcs., 1970-74, asst. dir., 1974-78, vocat. edn. cons., 1978-85; edn. curriculum specialist Washoe County Sch. Dist., Reno, 1985-89, curriculum coord., 1989-94, ret., 1994; pres. Midpoint Inc., 1995—. Marriage and family counselor Severance & Assocs., Carson City, 1983-85, Mountain Psychiat. Assocs., 1985-87; mem. tng. and youth employment coun. S.W. Regional Lab. for Ednl. R&D, Los Alamitos, Calif., 1982, mem. career edn. coun., 1980-81. Editor Coun. of Chief State Sch. Officers' Report: Staffing the Nation's Schools: A National Emergency, 1984; contbr. articles to profl. jours. Bd. dirs. U. Nev.-Reno Campus Christian Assn., 1988-90, 97-99; mem. adv. com. Truckee Meadows C.C., Reno, 1988-94; mem. Gov.'s Crime Prevention Com., Carson City, 1979-83, Atty. Gen.'s Anti-Shoplifting Com., Carson City, 1974-78, Gov.'s Devel. Disabilities Planning Coun., Carson City, 1977-79; bd. dirs. Jr. Achievement No. Nev., 1989-92, sec., mem. exec. com., 1990-91; bd. dirs. Friends of the Coll. of Edn., U. Nev., Reno, 1995-99. Recipient award for svc. Bus. Edn. Assn. No. Nev., 1973, Svc. award YMCA, 1962, 63, Helping Hand award Procter R. Hug H.S., 1993-94. Mem. ACA, Am. Vocat. Assn., Nat. Assn. Vocat. Edn. Spl. Needs Pers. (Outstanding Svc. award Region V 1982), Am. Assn. Marriage and Family Therapy, Nev. Vocat. Assn. (Outstanding Svc. award 1991, Bill Trabert Meml. award Excellence in Occup. Edn. 1994), Internat. Assn. Marriage and Family Counselors, U. Nev. Reno Alumni Assn. (exec. com. 1971-75), Phi Delta Kappa, Phi Kappa Phi. Democrat. Methodist. Home: 3056 Bramble Dr Reno NV 89509-6901 Office: PO Box 33034 Reno NV 89533-3034 E-mail: denisg2348@aol.com.

GRAHAM, GEORGE J., JR., political scientist, educator; b. Dayton, Ohio, Nov. 12, 1938; s. George J. and Mary Elizabeth (McBride) G.; m. Scarlett Gower, Sept. 10, 1966 (div. 1991); 1 child, Carmen Michelle. BA in History, Wabash Coll., 1960; PhD, Ind. U., 1965. Instr. Vanderbilt U., Nashville, 1963-64, asst. prof., 1965-71, assoc. prof., 1971-77, prof. polit. sci., 1977—, assoc. dean, 1986-88, 97-00, chair dept. polit. sci., 1988-92. Series editor Chatham (N.J.) House Pub., 1978—; Fulbright John Marshall chair Budapest U. of Econ. Studies, 1995-96. Author: Methodological Foundations, 1971; author, editor: Post-Behavioral Era, 1972, Founding Principles, 1977; contbr. articles to profl. jours. Chair Mt. Juliet (Tenn.) Sewer Commn., 1985-86; sec. Zoning Commn., Mt. Juliet, 1988-89. Guggenheim fellow, 1973-74, NEH fellow New Haven Nat. Humanities Inst., 1976-77; Fulbright John Marshall chair in Budapest, Hungary, 1995-96. Mem. Am. Polit. Sci. Assn. (founder Found. Polit. Theory sect. 1975—), So. Polit. Sci. Assn. (mem. coun. 1987-90), Midwest Polit. Sci. Assn., Internat. Polit. Sci. Assn., Com. Conceptual Analysis (chair). Avocations: painting, guitar, travel, bicycling. Office: Vanderbilt U PO Box 1814-B Nashville TN 37235-1814 Business E-Mail: grahamgj@trvax.vanderiblt.edu.

GRAHAM, HUGH DAVIS, history educator; b. Little Rock, Sept. 2, 1936; s. Otis L. and Lois (Patterson) G.; m. Ann Clary, June 11, 1966 (div. 1976); children: Hugh Patterson (dec.), Holter Ford; m. Janet Gorman, Feb. 5, 1978. BA magna cum laude, Yale U., 1958; MA, Stanford U., 1961, PhD, 1964. Instr. history Foothill Coll., Los Altos, Calif., 1962-64; asst. prof. San Jose State Coll., Calif., 1964-65; tng. officer, regional dir. Peace Corps, Washington, 1965-66; vis. asst. prof. history Stanford U., 1966-67; assoc. prof. history, assoc. dir. Inst. So. History Johns Hopkins U., Balt., 1967-71, acting dir. Inst. So. History, 1969-70; assoc. prof. History, chmn. divsn. social scis. U. Md.-Baltimore County, 1971-72, prof. History, 1972-91, dean div. social scis., 1972-77, dean grad. studies and rsch., 1982-85; Holland N. McTyeire prof. history Vanderbilt U., Nashville, from 1991, chmn. dept. history, 1994-97. Reporter Nashville Tennessean, 1960. Author: Crisis in Print, 1967 (Award of Merit 1968), Since 1954: Desegregation, 1972, (with Numan V. Bartley) Southern Politics and The Second Reconstruction, 1975 (V.O. Key award 1976), The Uncertain Triumph, 1984, The Civil Rights Era, 1990 (jury nominee Pulitzer prize 1991), Civil Rights and the Presidency, 1992, (with Nancy Diamond) the Rise of American Research Universities, 1997; co-editor: Violence in America, 1969, rev. edit., 1979, Southern Elections, 1978, The Carter Presidency, 1998; editor: Huey Long, 1970, Violence, 1971, American Politics and Government, 1975, Civil Rights in the United States, 1994. Co-dir. history task force Nat. Com. on Causes and Prevention of Violence, 1968-69; commr. Howard County Commn. Human Rights, Md., 1980-83. Served to 1st lt., arty. USMCR, 1958-60. Woodrow Wilson fellow, 1960-61, 63-64, Guggenheim fellow, 1970-71; recipient Merit award Am. Assn. State and Local History, 1968; V.O. Key award for best book on So. politics So. Polit. Sci. Assn., 1975; Wilson Ctr. fellow Smithsonian Instn., 1985-86; Sr. fellow NEH, 1989-90. Mem. Am. Hist. Assn., Am. Polit. Sci. Assn., So. Hist. Assn., Orgn. Am. Historians., Phi Beta Kappa. Home: Santa Barbara, Calif. Died Mar. 26, 2002.

GRAHAM, JAMES HENRY, computer science and engineering educator, consultant; b. Indpls., July 23, 1950; s. Raymond and Rosemary H. (Kiefner) G.; m. Cheryl L. Lovell, May 8, 1976; 1 child, David. BS, Rose Hulman Inst. Tech., 1972; MS, Purdue U., 1978, PhD, 1980. Registered profl. engr., Ind. Product design engr. GM, Anderson, Ind., 1972-76; grad. rsch. asst. Purdue U., West Lafayette, Ind., 1977-80, vis. asst. prof., 1980-81; asst. prof. Rensselaer Poly. Inst., Troy, N.Y., 1981-85; assoc. prof. U. Louisville, 1985-90, prof., 1990-91, Henry Vogt endowed prof., 1991—. Cons. GE, Schenectady, N.Y., 1983-85, TPX, Inc., Louisville, 1988-92, EAS, Inc., Louisville, 1991-93, Sci. Engring. Svcs., Inc., Burtonsville, Md., 2002-03. Editor: Computer Architectures for Robotics and Automation, 1987, Safety, Reliability and Human Factors in Robotic Systems, 1991. Mem. IEEE (sr. mem.), Assn. Computing Machinery, Am. Assn. Artificial Intelligence. Methodist. Avocations: camping, racquetball, tennis, reading. Office: Univ of Louisville Speed Sch-CECS Louisville KY 40292

GRAHAM, JOHN BORDEN, pathologist, writer, educator; b. Goldsboro, N.C., Jan. 26, 1918; s. Ernest Heap and Mary (Borden) G.; m. Ruby Barrett, Mar. 23, 1943; children: Charles Barrett, Virginia Borden, Thomas Wentworth. BS, Davidson Coll., 1938, D.Sc. (hon.), 1984; MD, Cornell U., 1942. Asst. Cornell U., 1943-44; medical corps U.S. Army, 1944-46; mem. faculty U. N.C., Chapel Hill, 1946—, Alumni Disting. prof. pathology, 1966—, chmn. genetics curriculum, 1963-85, assoc. dean medicine for basic scis., 1968-70, coordinator interdisciplinary grad. programs in biology, 1968—, dir. hemostasis program, 1974-87. Vis. prof. haematology St. Thomas's Hosp. Med. Sch., London, 1972; vis. prof. Teikyo U. Med. Sch., Tokyo, 1976; mem. selection com. NIH research career awards, 1959-62; genetics tng. com. USPHS, 1962-66, chmn., 1967-71; mem. genetic basis of disease com. Nat. Inst. Gen. Med. Scis., 1977-80; mem. pathology test com. Nat. Bd. Med. Examiners, 1963-67; mem. research adv. com. U. Colo. Inst. Behavioral Genetics, 1967-71; mem. Internat. Com. Haemostasis and Thrombosis, 1963-67; chmn. bd. U. N.C. Population Program, 1964-67; sec. policy bd. Carolina Population Center, 1972-78; cons. Environ. Health Center, USPHS, WHO, Bolt, Beranek & Newman, Inc.; mem. med. and sci. adv. council Nat. Hemophilia Found., 1972-76; hon. cons. in genetics Margaret Pyke Centre, London, 1972— Author: Sand in the Gears, 1992, 2d edit., 1998, How It Was, 1896-1973, 1996, Coping with Old Age: An Odyssey, 1998, Southeastern Cookery, 2000, Memories and Reflections, 2002; mem. editl. bd.: NC Med. Jour., 1949—66, Am. Jour. Human Genetics, 1958—61, Soc. Exptl. Biology and Medicine, 1959—62, Human Genetics Abstracts, 1962—72, Haemostasis, 1975—80, Christian Scholar, 1958—60. Recipient O. Max Gardner award U. N.C., 1968, Disting. Svc. award U. N.C. Med. Sch., 1992; Markle scholar in med. sci., 1949-54. Mem. AMA, AAAS, Elisha Mitchell Sci. Soc. (pres. 1963), AAUP, Soc. Exptl. Biology and Medicine, Am. Soc. Exptl. Pathology, Assn. Univ. Pathologists, Am. Assn. Pathologists and Bacteriologists, Am. Soc. Human Genetics (sec. 1964-67, pres. 1972), Genetics Soc. Am., Internat. Soc. Hematology, Am. Inst. Biol. Sci., Royal Soc. Medicine (London), Med. Soc. N.C., Mayflower Soc., Cosmos Club, Sigma Xi. Democrat. Presbyterian. Achievements include publs. on blood clotting, inherited diseases in humans including x-linked vitamin D resistant richets, human population dynamics, medical history; co-discoverer blood coagulant Factor X (Stuart factor). Home: 108 Glendale Dr Chapel Hill NC 27514-5910

GRAHAM, JUDITH KAY, principal; b. Three Hills, Alberta, Can., Oct. 22, 1951; came to U.S., 1967; d. Jay Gordon and Norma Jean (Bertrand) Dykstерhouse; m. Chapman, May 29, 1971 (div. Nov. 1987); m. Michael Louis Graham, July 16, 1988; children: Sara, Jonathan, Daniel, Paul. BA, We. Mich. U., 1973; MA, Grand Valley State U., 1978; EdS, U. Denver, 1987. Resource tchr. Grand Rapids (Mich.) Pub. Schs., 1975-76, instructional coord., 1976-78; bilingual tchr. Milw. Pub. Schs., 1978-81; curriculum specialist, tchr. Mapleton Pub. Sch., Denver, 1981-84, bilingual dir., 1984-89, elem. sch. prin., 1989—. Office: Mapleton Pub Schs 591 E 80th Ave Denver CO 80229-5806

GRAHAM, KENNETH ROBERT, psychologist, educator; b. Phila., June 5, 1943; s. Edgar and Margit (Leafgreen) Graham; m. Michele Carolyn Monroe, Aug. 10, 1968; children: Mark Andrew, Richard Alan. BA, U. Pa., 1964; PhD, Stanford U., 1969. Lic. psychologist, Pa. Asst. prof. Muhlenberg Coll., Allentown, Pa., 1970-77, assoc. prof., 1977-84, prof., 1984-99, emeritus prof., 1999—, head psychology dept., 1984-93; rsch. psychologist Unit for Exptl. Psychiatry Inst. of Pa. Hosp., Phila., 1969-70; adj. asst. prof. U. Pa., Phila., 1969-70. Cons. smoking cessation various hosps., 1985-1999. Author: (text) Psychological Research, 1977; asst. editor Am. Jour. Clin. Hypnosis, 1974-95; contbr. over 30 articles to profl. and sci. jours. Bd. dirs., pres. Lehigh Valley Child Care, Allentown, 1979-85; advisor Pathways (Conf. of Chs.), Allentown, 1989-98, N.E. Pa. Synod Luth. Ch. in Am., Wescosville, Pa., 1989-93. Mem. APA (pres. divsn. psychol. hypnosis 1980-81), European Soc. Hypnosis in Psychotherapy and Psychosomatic Medicine, Kiwanis (pres. Allentown chpt. 1991-92, lt. gov. Pa. dist. 1994-95). Democrat. Avocations: swimming, collecting glass paperweights and signatures of 19th century explorers. Office: Muhlenberg Coll Psychology Dept Allentown PA 18104 E-mail: krg6543@aol.com.

GRAHAM, KIRSTEN RAE, computer scientist, educator; b. Inglewood, Calif., July 20, 1946; d. Ray Selmer and Ella Louise (Carter) Newbury. BS, U. Wis., Oshkosh, 1971; MS, U. Colo., 1980; postgrad., Army War Coll., 1987; EdD in Adult and Higher Edn., EdD, Mont. State U., 1998. Cert. flight instr. FAA. Chief info. svc. Mont. State Dept. Labor and Industry, Helena; dir., personal property and bus. lic. div. County of Fairfax, Va.; analyst officer U.S. Army Pentagon, Washington; battalion commdr. U.S. Army, Frankfurt, Germany, assoc. prof. West Point, NY; tchr. computer tech. Helena Coll. Tech., U. Mont., chmn. computer electronics tech. dept., 2002—03. Adj. prof. Western Mont. Coll., U. Mont.; del. People-to-People Women Computer Sci. Profls. program, China; coord. 1st statewide program for instrs. new to 2-yr. coll. sys.; faculty practitioner U. Phoenix; faculty fellow for svc. learning Mont. Campus Compact, 1999—2000, mentoring fellow, 2001—03. Del. to China Citizen's Amb. Program, 1993. Lt. col. U.S. Army, 1964—88. Faculty fellow, Mont. Campus Compact, 1999—2000, Mentoring fellow, 2001—02. Mem.: Am. Fedn. Tchrs., Assn. Computing Machinery.

GRAHAM, OTIS LIVINGSTON, JR., history educator; b. Little Rock, Ark., June 24, 1935; s. Otis Livingstone and Lois (Patterson) G.; m. Ann Zemke, Sept. 5, 1959 (div. 1981); children— Ann Kathryn Lakin, Wade Livingston; m. Delores Yochum, Apr. 24, 1982 BA, Yale U., New Haven, 1957; MA, Columbia U., N.Y.C., 1961, PhD, 1966. Asst. prof. history Mt. Vernon Coll, Washington, 1962-64, Calif. State U., Hayward, 1965-66; prof. history U. Calif., Santa Barbara, 1966-80, 89-95; disting. univ. prof. history U. N.C., Chapel Hill, NC, 1980-89, disting. vis. prof. Wilmington, 1995—. Mem. editl. bd. U. Calif. Press, 1991-95; disting. Fulbright lectr. U. Bologna, 2002. Author: An Encore for Reform: The Old Progressives and the New Deal, 1967; The Great Campaigns: Reform and War in America 1900-1928, 1971; The New Deal: The Critical Issues, 1971; Toward a Planned Society: From Roosevelt to Nixon, 1977, Losing Ground: The Industrial Policy Debate, 1992, A Limited Bounty: The U.S. Since World War II, 1996; editor The Pub. Historian, 1989-97; contbr. chpts. to books, articles to profl. jours. Chair policy bd. Ctr. for Immigration Studies. Served with USMC, 1957-60. Am. Philos. Soc. grantee, 1966; NEH sr. fellow, 1972; Guggenheim fellow, 1977; Woodrow Wilson Internat. Ctr. for Scholars fellow, 1983; recipient Robert Kelley award Nat. Coun. Pub. History, 1999. Fellow Soc. Am. Historians, Ctr. for Advanced Study in the Behavioral Scis.; mem. Am. Hist. Assn., Orgn. Am. Historians (program chmn. 1977, nominating bd. 1993-95), Ctr. Study Democratic Instns. (assoc. 1975—, program dir. 1976-79), Fedn. Am. Immigration Reform (nat. bd. dirs. 1978-2001), NEH, Woodrow Wilson Ctr., Soc. Am. Historians (chmn. Parkman prize com. 1974, 80). Avocation: sailing. Office: U NC 601 S College Rd Wilmington NC 28403-3297 E-mail: graham@history.ucsb.edu.

GRAHAM, PATRICIA ALBJERG, education educator; b. Lafayette, Ind., Feb. 9, 1935; d. Victor L. and Marguerite (Hall) Albjerg; m. Loren R. Graham, Sept. 6, 1955; 1 child, Marguerite Elizabeth. BS, Purdue U., 1955, MS, 1957, DLett (hon.), 1980; PhD, Columbia U., 1964; MA (hon.), Harvard U., 1974; DHL (hon.), Manhattanville Coll., 1976; LLD (hon.), Beloit Coll., 1977, Clark U., 1978; DPA (hon.), Suffolk U., 1978, Ind. U., 1980; DLitt (hon.), St. Norbert Coll., 1980; DH (hon.), Emmanuel Coll., 1983; DHL (hon.), No. Mich. U., 1987, York Coll. of Pa., 1989, Kenyon Coll., 1991, Bank St. Coll. Edn., 1993; LLD (hon.), Radcliffe Coll., 1994, Salem State Coll., 1998. Tchr. high sch., Norfolk, Va., 1955-56, 57-58, N.Y.C., 1958-60; lectr., asst. prof. Ind. U., 1964-66; asst. prof. history of edn. Barnard Coll. and Columbia Tchrs. Coll., N.Y.C., 1965-68, assoc. prof., 1968-72, prof., 1972-74; dean Radcliffe Inst., 1974-77; also v.p. Radcliffe Coll., Cambridge, Mass., 1976-77; prof. Harvard U., Cambridge, Mass., 1974-79, Warren prof., 1979—2001, Warren Rsch. prof., 2001—; dean Grad. Sch. Edn., 1982-91; pres. Spencer Found., Chgo., 1991-2000. Author: Progressive Education: From Arcady to Academe, 1967, Community and Class in American Education: 1865-1918, 1974, S.O.S. Sustain Our Schools, 1992. Bd. dirs. Dalton Sch., 1973-76, Josiah Macy, Jr. Found., 1976-77, 79—; trustee Beloit Coll., 1976-77, 79-82, Northwestern Mut. Life, 1980—, Found. for Teaching Econs., 1980-87; bd. dirs. Spencer Found., 1983-2000, Johnson Found., 1983-2001, Hitachi Found., 1985—, Carnegie Found. for Advancement of Tchg., 1984-92, Ctrl. European U., Budapest, 2002—, Apache, 2002—. Mem.: AAAS (coun. 1993—96, v.p. 1998—2001), Ctr. for Advanced Study in the Behavioral Scis. (bd. dirs. 2001—), Am. Philos. Soc., Am. Hist. Assn. (v.p. 1985—89), Nat. Acad. Edn. (pres. 1984—89), Sci. Rsch. Assocs. (dir. 1980—89), Phi Beta Kappa. Episcopalian. Office: Harvard U Grad Sch Edn Cambridge MA 02138

GRAHAM, ROGER JOHN, photography and journalism educator; b. Phila., Feb. 16; s. William K. and Peggy E. (Owens) G.; divorced; children: John Roger, Robb Curt; m. Debbie Kenyon, Dec. 28, 1991. AA, Los Angeles Valley Coll., 1961; BA, Calif. State U., Fresno, 1962, MA, 1967; postgrad, UCLA, 1976. Cert. in elem., jr. high, high sch., cmty. coll., counseling and adminstrn. Tchr. Riverdale (Calif.) Sch., 1963, Raisin City (Calif.) Sch., 1964; tchr., counselor Calif. State Prison, Jamestown, 1966; tchr. trainer UCLA's Western Ctr. War on Poverty, 1967; chmn. media arts dept. Los Angeles Valley Coll., Van Nuys, Calif., 1968—, prof. emeritus, 1999—. Vis. prof. Pepperdine U., Malibu, Calif., 1976, Calif. Luth. Coll., Thousand Oaks, 1973, South Africa, 1997; vis. prof. Chapman U., Orange, Calif., 1996, GAIN prof., 1998; del. Calif. Fedn. Tchrs. Conv., 1997; dir. Photography Seminar, Spain, summer 1990. Author: Observations on the Mass Media, 1976, Our Lives in Bits and Pieces, 1998, Patchwork of Life, 2001, L.A. to Philly - Looking Back, 2002; co-author: We Remember WW II, 2003; author: (jour.) Jr. Coll. Jour., 1972; photo illustrator: The San Fernando Valley, 1980, display advertiser: Turlock (Calif.) jour., 1962, Fresno Guide, 1963; contbr. articles to profl. jours. Mem. Tom Hayden's Com. for Schs., Santa Monica, Calif., 1984; pres. Pacific Palisades Dem. Club, 1992; rep. to 41st assembly dist. Calif. Dem. Party State Ctrl. Com., 1993, sec. srs. caucus, 1993—. With USN, 1957. NEH scholar 1981; recipient Mayor's Outstanding Citizen award Los Angeles Mayor's Office, 1974, Extraordinary Service award UCLA, 1971; named one of Outstanding Young Men Am., 1971. Mem. C.C. Journalism Assn. (nat. pres. 1978—, Nat. Dedication Journalism award 1972-76), Journalism Assn. C.C. (pres. Calif. sect. 1972—), Calif. Srs. Caucus (state sec. 1993—), L.A. Profs. Club, Dem. Club Pacific Palisades (pres. 1992-93), Patrons Assn. (bd. dirs. 2000—), L.A. Valley Coll. Retirees Assn. (Outstanding Alumnus award 1999, pres. 1999), Am. Legion (sgt. at arms 1986—, Palisades chpt. adminstrv. officer 1996—), Patrons Assn. (bd. dirs. 2000), Sons of the Desert, SR, Sigma Delta Xi, Phi Delta Kappa, Pi Lambda Theta. Avocation: hiking. Home: 7878 Naylor Ave Los Angeles CA 90045-2909 Office: Los Angeles Valley Coll 5800 Fulton Ave Van Nuys CA 91401-4062

GRAHAM, SUSETTE RYAN, retired English educator; b. Plattsburgh, N.Y., Aug. 31, 1929; d. Andrew Warren Ryan and Lillian Grace MacDougall; m. James H. Graham, July 1, 1950; children: Marguerite, Andrea, James Jr., Martha, Amy, Matthew. BA, Wellesley Coll., 1950; MA, U. Rochester, 1967, PhD, 1987. Prof. English Nazareth Coll., Rochester, N.Y., 1963-93, prof. emerita, 1993; ret. Contbr. articles, revs. to profl. jours. Fulbright sr. lectr., Poland, 1992-93. Mem. AAUW, MLA, Am. Acad. Poets. Democrat. Avocations: travel, reading, genealogical research. Home: 10 Arbor Ct Fairport NY 14450-1602 also: 603 Pipers Ln Surfside Beach SC 29575-5846 E-mail: jamesgraham@sc.rr.com.

GRAHAM, SYLVIA SWORDS, secondary school educator, retired; b. Atlanta, Nov. 15, 1935; d. Metz Jona and Christine (Gurley) Swords; m. Thomas A. Graham, Nov. 29, 1958 (div. 1970). BA, Mary Washington Coll., Fredericksburg, Va., 1957; MEd, W. Ga. Coll., Carrollton, 1980; SEd, W. Ga. Coll., 1981; postgrad., Coll. William and Mary, 1964-67. Tchr. Atlanta pub. schs., 1957-58, Newark County pub. schs., Newark, Calif., 1960-61; tchr. history Virginia Beach (Va.) pub. schs., 1964-75, Paulding County pub. schs., Dallas, Ga., 1976-97, ret., 1997. Tour dir. Paulding High Sch. trips, Far East, 1985, USSR, 1989, Australia, 1988-89. County chmn. Rep. Party, 1987-89, county chmn. for re-election of Newt Gingrich, 1982; mem. Gingrich edn. com., 1983, 88; 1st vice chmn. 6th Congl. Dist., 1989-90, chmn. 1989-90; chmn. 7th Congl. Dist., 1992-95; del. Nat. Rep. Conv., 1992. Named Star Tchr., Paulding County C. of C., Dallas, Ga., 1989, 97. Mem. Dallas Woman's Club (pres. 1982-84, 1st v.p. 1986-88, pub. affairs chmn. 1986—, treas. for Civic Ctr. fund 1984—), Phi Kappa Phi. Republican. Baptist. Avocations: travel, reading, piano, bridge. E-mail: maxitaxi2@earthlink.net.

GRAHAM, WILLIAM ALBERT, religion educator, history educator; b. Raleigh, NC, Aug. 16, 1943; s. William Albert and Evelyn (Powell) G.; m. Barbara Stecconi, Aug. 26, 1983; 1 child, Powell Louis. Student, U. Goettingen, Fed. Republic Germany, 1964-65; BA summa cum laude, U. N.C., 1966; AM, Harvard U., 1970, PhD, 1973. Lectr. Islamic religion Harvard U., Cambridge, Mass., 1973-74, asst. prof., 1974-79, Allston Burr sr. tutor, 1975-77, assoc. prof., 1979-81, sr. lectr. history of religion, 1981-85, prof. history of religion and Islamic studies, 1985—2001, chmn. Study of Religion, 1987-90, Murray A. Albertson prof. Middle Eastern studies, 2001—, dir. Ctr. for Middle Eastern Studies, 1990-96, chmn. Near Eastern Langs. and Civilizations, 1997—2002; master Currier House Harvard Coll., 1991—; dean and John Lord O'Brian prof. divinity Harvard Div. Sch., 2002—. Chmn. Coun. on Grad. Studies in Religion, 1993-96; vis. lectr. Friedrich-Wilhelms U., Bonn, 1982-83. Author: Divine Word and Prophetic Word in Early Islam, 1977 (Am. Coun. Learned Socs. book prize 1978), Beyond the Written Word, 1987, 93; co-author: Heritage of World Civilizations, 1986, 6th edit., 2003, Three Faiths, One God, 2002; co-editor: Islamfiche: Readings from Islamic Primary Sources, 1987; mem. editl. bd. jours. and ency.; contbr. articles to profl. jours. Woodrow Wilson Found. grad. fellow Harvard U., 1966-67, Danforth Found. grad. fellow Harvard U., 1966-73, John Simon Guggenheim Found. fellow, Germany, India, 1982-83, Alexander von Humboldt Found. fellow, Germany, 1982-83, IRCICA quinquinnial award for excellence in rsch. Islamic Studies, Orgn. of the Islamic Conf., 2000; Keller vis. Scholar in religion, HighPoint U., 2001. Mem. Am. Soc. for Study of Religion, Am. Acad. Religion, Middle East Studies Assn., Am. Oriental Soc., Am. Alpine Club, Phi Beta Kappa. Democrat. Avocation: tech. mountaineering. Home: 44 Francis Ave Cambridge MA 02138 Office: Harvard Divinity Sch 45 Francis Ave Cambridge MA 02138

GRAMES-LYRA, JUDITH ELLEN, retired artist, building plans examiner; b. Inglewood, Calif, Feb. 7, 1938; d. Glover Victor and Dorothy Margaret (Burton-Bellingham) Hendrickson and Carolyne Marie Carrick Hendrickson (stepmother); children: Nansea Ellen Ryan, Amber Jeanne Shelley-Harris, Carolyn Jane Angel Longmire, Susan Elaine Gomez, Robert Derek Shallenberger; m. Jon Robert Lyra, Feb. 14, 1997. Cert in journalism, Newspaper Inst. Am., N.Y.C., 1960; AA, Santa Barbara City Coll., 1971; BA, U. Calif., Santa Barbara, 1978, cert. in teaching, 1979. Cert. bldg. inspector, plumbing inspector, Calif. Editor, reporter, photographer Goleta Valley Sun Newspaper, Santa Barbara, 1968-71; editor, team asst. Bur. of Ednl. Rsch. Devel., Santa Barbara, 1971; bus. writer, graphics cons. Santa Barbara, 1971-77; art and prodn. dir. Bedell Advt. Selling Improvement Corp., Santa Barbara, 1979-81; secondary sch. tchr. Coalinga Unified Sch. Dist., Calif., 1981-83; bldg. insp. aide Santa Barbara County, Lompoc, 1983-88, from bldg. engrng. inspector I to III, 1988-99, asst. plans examiner, 1999—2003. Exhibited in group shows at Foley's Frameworks and Interiors, 1984, Grossman Gallery, 1984, 98, Lompoc Valley Art Assn., 1984— (numerous awards including Best of Show 1985, 1st place 1984, 94, 2002, 2d place 1984, 86, 88, 96, 97, 99, 3d place 1987, 89, 97, Hon. Mention 1986, 90, 91, 97, 99, 2001), Brushes and Blues Invitational, 1998; featured artist Harvest Arts Festival, 1989, Cypress Gallery, 1994; contbr. poetry to anthologies. Mem. disaster response team Calif. Bldg. Ofcl., 1992-2003; exec. bd. dir. Lompoc Mural Soc., 1991—. Delta Kappa Gamma scholar. Mem. NOW, Nat. Abortion Rights Action League, Nat. Mus. of Women in the Arts (charter), Internat. Conf. Bldg. Ofcl., Engr. and Tech. Assn., Lompoc Valley Art Assn. (bd. mem.), Toastmasters Internat. (Outstanding Speaker awards 1991-93). Avocations: painting, stained glass, home improvement activities, illustrating note cards, writing children's stories.

GRANAT, RICHARD STUART, lawyer, educator; b. N.Y.C., Nov. 11, 1940; s. George and Judith G.; m. Nancy Ruth Wruble, Dec. 23, 1962; children: Lisa, Hilary, Peter, David. BA, Lehigh U., 1962; JD (Harlan Fiske Stone scholar), Columbia U., 1965. Bar: Md. 1966, D.C. 1977. Asst. counsel U.S. OEO, Washington, 1965-67, dir. housing programs, 1967-78; asst. dir. Model Cities Agy. Office of Mayor, Balt., 1968-69; dir. Cmty. Planning and Evaluation Inst., Balt., 1970-71; pres. Univ. Rsch. Corp. Mgmt. Svcs. Corp., Balt., 1970-77; pvt. practice Washington and Md., 1969—. Pres. Automated Lagal Systems, Inc., Phila., 1984—89; dir. MA in Legal Studies Program, Antioch Sch. Law, 1979—83; pres., chmn. bd. Ctr. for Legal Studies, Washington, 1979—89; chmn. bd. dirs. Ctr. Sch., Rockville, Md.; pres. Inst. Paralegal Tng., Inc., Phila., 1982—89, The Phila. Inst., 1987—89, Inst. for Employee Benefits Tng., 1986—89, The Inst. for Law and Tech., Phila., 1990—92, Interactive Legal Media, Inc., 1992—96; instr. Rutgers Sch. Law, Camden, NJ, 1992—94, Sch. Lang., U. Balt., 1995—; adj. prof. Sch. Law, U. Md., 1994—, dir. Ctr. for Law Practice Tech., 1994—, dir. Peoples Law Libr., 1996—2000, dir. Ctr. for On-Line Mediation, Inc., 1996—2000; pres. The Granat Group, LLC, Am. Law On Line, Inc., 2001—. Mem. ABA, Md. Bar Assn., D.C. Bar Assn. Home: 320 Morgause Pl N Baltimore MD 21208-1430 Office: 9141 Reisterstown Rd Owings Mills MD 21117 E-mail: richard@granat.com.

GRANDY, RICHARD E. philosophy educator; b. Dec. 6, 1942; s. Richard Stanley and Sarah Elizabeth (Greiner) G.; m. Janice D. Bordeaux, June 21, 1980; children: Gwynn, Bryan. BS in Math., U. Pitts., 1963; MA, Princeton U., 1968. NSF postdoctoral fellow, 1970-71; asst. prof. Princeton (N.J.) U., 1967-74; assoc. prof. U. N.C., Chapel Hill, 1974-79, prof., 1979-80, Rice U., Houston, 1980—, chmn., 1982-88, 1992, dir. cognitive sci. program, 1989-93, Carolyn and Fred McManis prof. philosophy, 1993—; Harrison Wray disting. prof. Washington U., St. Louis, 2001. Vis. asst. prof. Columbia U., 1969, U. Calif. Berkeley, 1972, vis. assoc. prof. Stanford U., 1977; dir. Mellon Workshop, 1981; dir. NEH Summer Seminar, 1979, 82. Author: Advanced Logic for Applications, 1977, 2d edit. 1989; editor: Theories and Observation in Science, 1973, (with Richard Warner) Philosophical Grounds of Rationality: Intentions, Categories, Ends, 1986, (with B. Brody) Readings in the Philosophy of Science, 1989; mng. editor Linguistics and Philosophy, 1980-88, Vols. 3-10; contbr. numerous articles to profl. jours. ACLS Study fellow, 1976, Rsch. fellow, 1980, NEH Summer Rsch. fellow, 1986. Mem. Am. Philosophical Assn. Philosophy Sci. Assn., Assn. Symbolic Logic, Am. Edn. Rsch. Assn. Office: Rice U MS14 Humanities Bldg Rm 206 6100 Main St Houston TX 77005-1892

GRANDY, WALTER THOMAS, JR., physicist, educator; b. Phila., June 1, 1933; s. Walter Thomas and Margaret Mary (Hayes) G.; m. Patricia Josephine Langan, Dec. 27, 1955; children: Christopher, Neal, Mary, Jeanne. BS, U. Colo., 1960, PhD, 1964. Physicist Nat. Bur. Standards, Boulder, Colo., 1958-63; mem. faculty U. Wyo., Laramie, 1963—, prof. physics, 1969-98, head dept., 1971-78; prof. emeritus, 1998—. Fulbright lectr. U. Sao Paulo, Brazil, 1966-67, vis. prof., 1982; vis. prof. U. Tubingen, W. Germany, 1978-79, U. Sydney, Australia, 1988. Author: Introduction to Electrodynamics and Radiation, 1970, Foundations of Statistical Mechanics: Volume I, Equilibrium Theory, 1987, Vol. II, Nonequilibrium Phenomena, 1988, Relativistic Quantum Mechanics of Leptons and Fields, 1991, Scattering of Waves from Spherical Targets, 2000. Served with USNR, 1953-57. Fellow AAAS; mem. Am. Phys. Soc., Brasilian Phys. Soc., Am. Assn. Physics Tchrs., Sigma Xi, Sigma Pi Sigma. Achievements include rsch. on statis. mechanics, electrodynamics, quantum theory. Home: 604 S 18th St Laramie WY 82070-4304 E-mail: wtg@uwyo.edu.

GRANT, ALFRED DAVID, orthopaedic surgeon, educator; b. N.Y.C., June 12, 1933; s. Charles Meyer and Lillie (Eigen) G.; m. Ellen M. Michels, Apr. 16, 1961; children: Susan, Michele, Laura. BA, Emory U., 1952; MD, Chgo. Medical, 1957. Cert. Nat. Bd. Medical Examiners. Intern 4th surg. divsn. Bellevue Hosp, N.Y., 1957-58; resident gen. surgery Montefiore Hosp, Bronx, N.Y., 1958-59; resident orthopaedic surgery Hosp. for Joint Diseases/Orthopaedic Inst., N.Y., 1959-62; instr., prosecutor gross anatomy Chgo. Medical Sch., 1954-57; assoc. orthopaedic surgery Tulane Medical Sch., 1962-64; pvt. practice orthopaedic surgery, 1964—; with Hosp. Joint Diseases/Orthopaedic Inst., N.Y.C., 1964—, emeritus chief neuromuscular sect. dept. orthopaedics, 1973—, emeritus med. dir. first chance child devel. sch., 1974—, med. dir. Muscular Dystrophy clinic, 1974—, emeritus dir. ctr. neuromuscular and devel. disorders, 1979—97, assoc. dir. orthopaedic surgery, 1982—; clin. asst. prof. orthopaedic surgery Albert Einstein Coll., 1970-79; asst. prof. orthopaedic surgery Mt. Sinai Sch. of Medicine, 1981—; clin. prof. orthopedic surgery NYU Sch. Medicine, 1987-95; clin. prof., 1995—. Vis. surgeon Boston Children's Hosp., 1989, Shriner's Hosp., Springfield, Mass., 1989; asst. attending Montefiore Hosp., 1964—66, Morrisania Hosp., Bronx, NY, 1964—66, Albert Einstein Coll. Hosp., 1969—73; chief orthopaedic surgery United Hosp., Port Chester, NY, 1964—81, cons., 1981—; orthopaedic cons. St. Vincent's Hosp. Westchester Divsn., 1966—, Rye Psychiat. Hosp., 1968—83, Staten Island (N.Y.) Devel. Ctr., 1976—89, Osborne Meml. Home, Rye, 1973—89; attending orthopaedist Rose Kennedy Ctr. Human Devel. and Retardation, Bronx, 1970—73; attending orthopaedics and birth defects clinic Albert Einstein Coll. Hosp., 1969—93; dept. surgery, orthopaedics sect. Beth Israel Hosp., NY, 1979—98. Edit. bd. Bulletin Hosp. Joint Diseases/Orthopaedic Inst.; lectr., presenter numerous courses, papers, symposia in field, U.S., Eur.; contbr. articles, chpts. profl. jours. Bd. trustees United Cerebral Palsy of Westchester, 1982—. HEW grant, 1974-77. Fellow N.Y. Acad. Medicine; mem. AMA, Am. Bd. Orthopaedic Surgery (examiner 1984—), N.Y. Med. Soc., Am. Soc. Surgery Foot and Ankle, Am. Ortho. Assn., Am. Acad. Orthopaedic Surgery (rehab. com. 1984-87), Am. Coll. Surgeons (trauma com. Westchester chpt. 1973-76), Am. Acad. Cerebral Palsy and Devel. Medicine (credential's com. 1987—, sci. program com., 1986-88, rsch. and awards com., 1995—), Pediatric Orthopaedic Club of N.Y. (pres. 1988-89, sec. 1986-87, pres.-elect 1987-88), N.Y. County Med. Soc., Internat. Soc. Prosthetics and Orthotics, N.Y. State Soc. Orthopaedic Surgeons, Pediatric Orthopaedic Soc. No. Am., No. Am. Assn. Study and Application of Methods of Ilizarov, Israel Ortho. Assn. (hon.). Office: Hosp Joint Diseases Orthopaedic Inst 301 E 17th St New York NY 10003-3804

GRANT, J. KIRKLAND, law educator, lawyer; b. Monroe, Mich., Feb. 14, 1943; s. Stanley Gordon and Neva Alene (Piper) G.; 1 child, Alexandra. BBA, U. Mich., 1965, JD cum laude, 1967. Bar: Mich. 1968, N.Y. 1970, S.C. 1975, U.S. Supreme Ct. 1979. Acct. Peat Marwick Mitchell, Detroit, 1964-65; asst. prof. Ga. State U., 1967-70, U. Toledo, 1970-71; assoc. coun. Sullivan & Cromwell, N.Y.C., 1970-72; prof. U. S.C., 1972-80; dean, prof. law Del. Law Sch., Wilmington, 1980-83; assoc. counsel Bingham, Dana & Gould, Boston, 1983-84; prof. of law Touro Law Ctr., Huntington, N.Y., 1984—, academic dean, 1984-85; pvt. practice Charleston, SC, 1987—, Huntington, NY, 1111. Vis. scholar Columbia U., 1980, Harvard U.,1982-83; chair com. on legal edn. N.Y. State Bar, Albany, 1992-95; cons. in the field; comml. and securities arbitrator; arbitrator, mediator U.S. Dist. Ct. Author: Securities Arbitration, 1994; reporter Revision of S.C. Bus. Corp. Law, 1981; contbr. articles to profl. jours. Mem. ABA, Am. Law Inst., Scribes, Alexander Hamilton Inn of Ct. (pres. 1998-2000, 2002—), Harvard Club (N.Y.), Sand Dollar Club (Folly Beach). Office: Touro Law Ctr 300 Nassau Rd Huntington NY 11743-4342

GRANT, KAY LALLIER, early childhood education educator; b. Leavenworth, Kans., Oct. 22, 1951; d. Leon Ernest and Retha Pearl (Poos) Lallier; m. Cary Benson Grant, Aug. 12, 1972; children: Shannon, Ryan. BA in Psychology, Human Devel. & Family Life, U. Kans., 1973; MA in Spl. Edn., U. Tulsa, 1982; EdD in Curriculum & Instrn., Okla. State U., 1990. Cert. early childhood and spl. edn.-mental retardation tchr. Kindergarten tchr. Muskogee (Okla.) Day Nursery, 1973; presch. tchr. Children's House Montessori Sch., Muskogee, 1974; kindergarten tchr. Haskell (Okla.) Pub. Schs., 1974-75; dir., tchr. presch. for handicapped Muskogee Pub. Schs., 1975-78; dir. child care ctr. Muskogee Gen. Hosp., 1982-84; instr. early childhood edn., field svc. coord. Northeastern State U., Tahlequah, Okla., 1985-88, program chair early childhood edn., 1988—92, asst. prof. early childhood Coll. of Edn., 1990—92; dir. early childhood edn. Muskogee Pub. Schs., 1992—99; asst. dean coll. edn. Northeastern State U., 1999—2001, interim dean, 2001—03, dean, 2003—. Reviewer Music and Child Devel., 1988, Total Learning: Curriculum for Young Child, 1987, The Boy Who Would Be a Helicopter, 1990; contbr. articles to profl. jours. Elder Bethany Presbyn. Ch., Muskogee, 1991—99. Recipient scholarship award Okla. Assn. on Children Under Six, 1988, Faculty Rsch. grant Northeastern State U., 1989. Mem. Okla. Assn. Childhood Edn. Internat. (pres. 1991-1999), Nat. Assn. Edn. Young Children, Okla. Assn. Early Childhood Tchr. Educators, So. Early Childhood Assn., Okla. Inst. Child Advocacy (bd. dirs. 1999-2001), Internat. Reading Assn., Phi Delta Kappa, Delta Kappa Gamma, Kappa Delta Phi, Okla. Assoc. Colls. Edn. Office: Northeastern State U Coll Edn Tahlequah OK 74464 E-mail: grantk1@nsuok.edu.

GRANT, LEONARD TYDINGS, clergyman; b. Lakewood, N.J., May 8, 1930; s. Allaire Harrison and Edith Dorothy (MacEntee) Grant; m. Nancy Elisabeth MacKerell, June 21, 1958; children: Scott Alexander, Elisabeth Tydings, Constance Allaire. BA, Rutgers U., 1952; BD, Princeton Theol. Sem., 1955; STM, Temple U., 1958; PhD, U. Edinburgh, 1961; LHD (hon.), Elmira Coll., 1987. Ordained Presbyn. Ch. U.S.A., 1955. Pastor 4th Presbyn. Ch., Camden, N.J., 1955-58, Meml. Presbyn. Ch., Wenonah, N.J., 1961-65; instr. Rutgers U., 1956-58; lectr. Conwell Sch. Theology, Phila., 1962-65; prof. history Indpls. Univ., 1965-76; grad. dean Indpls. U., 1966-76, acad. dean, 1974-76; pres. Elmira (N.Y.) Coll., 1976-87; pres. emeritus, 1987—; pres. Independent Coll. Fund N.Y., 1987-95; interim assoc. pastor Presbyn. Ch., Westfield, NJ, 1995-97; assoc. pastor Ctrl. Presbyn. Ch., Summit, NJ, 1997—2002, dir. planned giving, 2003—. Author: Prayers and Devotions of Richard Baxter, 1965; contbr. articles on edn., history and religion to jours. Former mem. adv. com. Am. Inst. Banking, Arnot-Ogden Hosp., Coun. Ind. Coll., Ind. Coll. Fund N.Y.; former mem. adv. com. Sullivan Trail Coun. Boy Scouts Am.; former mem. adv. com. Coun. Elizabeth Presbytery, Found. for Ind. Higher Edn.; trustee Elizabeth Presbytery. Mem.: Princeton Club N.Y.C., Rotary, Phi Delta Kappa, Phi Alpha Theta, Alpha Sigma Lambda. Presbyterian.

GRANT, MARILYNN PATTERSON, secondary educator; b. Washington, Oct. 26, 1952; d. Rossie Lee and Mattie (Pringle) Patterson; m. David Michael Grant, Oct. 11, 1980; children; Karissa Joy, Jared David Michael. BA in History, U. Rochester, 1975, MS in Edn., 1982, postgrad; Cert. advanced studies, SUNY, Brockport, 1987. Cert. tchr., sch. adminstr., supr., N.Y. Jr. high coord. Rochester (N.Y.) City Sch. Dist., 1980-81, team tchr., 1981-83, skills cluster tchr., 1983-85, jr. high tchr., 1985-86, alternative to suspension, 1986-87, 89-90, dean of students, 1987-88, curriculum coord., 1988-89, acting house adminstr., 1990-91, social studies tchr., 1991—96, dir. of social Studies & multicultral edn., 1996—2002; prin. Joseph C. Wilson HS, Rochester, 2002—. Bd. dirs., allocations com. Rochester Monroe County Youth Bd., 1990-92; active Mt. Olivet Bapt. Ch., 1990—. Named one of Outstanding Young Women Am., 1984; recipient Volunteerism award Mayor of Rochester, 1991, Jack & Jill of Rochester Disting. Mother, 2000-01, RCSD Staff excellance award, 2001. Mem. Christian Visitor's Com. (chmn. 1990—), Rochester Urban League Guild (v.p. 1982-83), Jack & Jill of Am. (corr. sec. 1991-92, group leader 1992-93), Zeta Phi Beta (pres. 1985-87, parliamentarian 1985-87), Kappa Delta Pi. Democrat. Avocations: event planning, singing, drama, reading, writing. Home: 227 Genesee Park Blvd Rochester NY 14619-2459

GRANT, MICHAEL ERNEST, educational administrator, institutional management educator; b. L.A., June 6, 1952; s. Ernest Grant and Shirley Ruth (George) G. BA in Spanish, Calif. State U., Long Beach, 1974, MA in Edn. Adminstrn., 1978; EdD, Pepperdine U., 1984. Cert. elem., secondary, and community coll. tchr., bilingual and cross-cultural edn., adminstr. Tchr. kindergarten through adult edn. Long Beach Unified Sch. Dist., 1975-83, tchr. 5th grade, 1975, tchr. 6th grade, 1975-76, bilingual multicultural specialist, 1976-78, tchr. 6th, 7th and 8th grades, 1978-79, mgmt. program specialist, 1979-80, adminstr., program specialist, 1980-81, vice prin., 1981-83; asst. prof. tchr. edn. Calif. State U., San Bernardino, 1986-88, prin. dir. IMPACT/TEACH, assoc. prof. ednl. psychology and adminstrn. Long Beach, 1988-91; pres., founder Mykulphone-An Empowerment Through Edn. Project, Beverly Hills, 1991—; Spanish instr. Calif. Disting. Sch., Beverly Hills, 1993—. Asst. part-time instr. tchr. edn. Grad. Sch. Edn., Calif. State U., Long Beach, 1983-86; pres., CEO Mykulphone, Real Estate Developer, 999—; lectr. in field. Exec. prodr., dancer, singer, songwriter (animated music video) The Flashy Dancer, 2003; contbr. articles to profl. jours. Pepperdine U. scholar, 1983-84; Calif. State U. grantee, 1988-89, 89-90, 89-91. Mem. NEA, Assn. Calif. Sch. Adminstrs., Nat. Assn. Tchr. Educators, Nat. Coun. States In-Svc. Edn., Nat. Black Congress Faculty, Calif. Faculty Assn., Calif. State Intersegmental Coordination Coun., Calif. Black Faculty and Staff Assn., Calif. Assn. Tchr. Educators, Calif. Edn. Rsch. Assn., Intersegmental Coordinating Coun. Democrat. Baptist. Avocations: shotokon karate (black belt), acting, dancing, singing, songwriting. Home and Office: No 1220 270 N Canon Dr Beverly Hills CA 90210-9999

GRANT, MICHELE BYRD, educator; b. Kansas City, Mo., Oct. 30, 1926; d. Ernest Louis and Violetta (Wallace) Byrd. B.S., Lincoln U., 1952; M.S. in Sci. Edn., U. Ill., 1955, advanced cert., 1964. Tchr., Unit 4, Champaign, Ill., 1956-66; tchr. sci. St. Louis Pub. Schs., 1966—, dept. head, 1978—, Mo. Outstanding Biology Tchrs. program dir., 1974— ; participant NSF Summer Inst., CCNY, 1968-69; instr. Webster Coll. Upward Bound Program, 1969-70; judge Monsanto-St. Louis Post Dispatch Sci. Fair, 1970— . Developer, edn. dir. Adventures in Medicine and Sci., 1992; coord., co-develpper Vashon Interdisciplinary Project for Edn. Reform, 1999-2000. Mem. Cath. Sch. Bd., St. Louis, 1982-83; mem. life aux. Barnes Hosp., 1968— ; trustee Meml. and Planned Funeral Soc., 1980. Recipient Mo. Outstanding Biology Tchr. award, Nat. Biology Tchrs. Assn., 1974, One of 50 Nationwide Unsung Heroes award Newsweek, 1987, Excellence in Leadership award Lincoln U., 1987, Newsweek Mag. Unsung Hero Satte Mo., 1987, Monsanto Sci. Tchg. award, 2001; named STARS Tchr., Solutia-NSF, 1999. Mem. ASCD, Nat. Sci. Tchrs. Assn., Nat. Assn. Biology Tchrs., Biology Tchrs. Assn., Mo. Sci. Tchrs. Assn., Mo. Acad. Sci., Alpha Kappa Alpha, Kappa Delta Pi. Roman Catholic. Office: 3405 Bell Ave Saint Louis MO 63106-1604

GRANT, MIRIAM ROSENBLOUM, secondary school educator, journalist; b. Collinsville, Ala. d. Harry M. and Rae (Rosenberg) Rosenbloum; m. Morton A. Grant, Nov. 17, 1952 (dec. 1967). AB, U. Ala., 1935; postgrad., U. Miami, 1968-69, Fla. Internat. U. Cert. tchr., Fla. Reporter Chattanooga Free Press., 1936-41, Birmingham (Ala.) Post, 1942; reporter, movie editor, drama critic Chattanooga News-Free Press, 1943-49; tchr., head journalism dept., newspaper and yearbook adviser North Miami (Fla.) Sr. High Sch., 1969-89. Pres. Curling Iron Club, 1943. Recipient Disting. Svc. award Chattanooga Little Theater, 1949, Golden Medallion Fla. Scholastic Press Assn., 1987, named life member, 1990, service award Coll. Fraternity Editors Assn., 1989, (1st recipient) Woman of Achievement award Study Club, Collinsville, Ala., 1999. Mem. AAUW, U. Ala. Nat. Alumni Assn. (coun. mem.-at-large 1960-61), Ceramic League Miami (Corr. sec. 1963-64), Women's Panhellenic Assn. Miami (Sec. 1992-93), nat. Panhellenic Editors Conf. (vice chmn. 1986-87, chmn. 1987-89), Sigma Delta Tau (nat. pres. 1950-54, editor The Torch mag. 1968-98, honor key 1988, scholarship named in her honor as 1st mem. to serve 50 yrs. on sorority nat. coun. 1991, archivist 1992—, devel. com. 1996—, CFEA recognition award as editor 1993, granted life membership for past outstanding svc. 1997, recipient Gold Key award for over 50 yrs. outstanding svc., 1998), Theta Sigma Phi, Phi Lambda Pi, Rho Lambda, Sigma Delta Chi.

GRANT, PAULA DIMEO, lawyer, nursing educator, mediator; b. Bridgeport, Conn., Aug. 3, 1943; d. Samuel Peter and Emilie Alyce (DiChiera) DiMeo; m. James Mullett Grant, Nov. 26, 1975. AS in Nursing, U. Bridgeport, 1973; BSN cum laude, Boston Coll., 1975; JD, No. Va. U., 1982; MA in Nursing, NYU, 1994. Bar: D.C. 1985, U.S. Ct. Appeals (D.C.) 1985, U.S. Dist. Ct. D.C. 1985, U.S. Supreme Ct. 1989, U.S. Dist. Ct. Md. 1995. RN, Conn. Coronary care nurse Cornell Med. Ctr., N.Y.C., 1969-70; with Trans World Airlines, Chgo. and N.Y.C., 1980—84; pvt. practice, Washington, 1986-98; of counsel Ross & Hardies, Washington, 1998—. Mediator Superior Ct. D.C., 1991—2003; clin. asst. prof. cmty. and preventive medicine N.Y. Med. Coll., 1992—96; adj. prof. dept. nursing Columbia U. Tchrs. Coll., N.Y.C., 1993, 94; adj. asst. prof. nursing Sacred Heart U., Fairfield, Conn., 1998—99, mem. adv. coun., 1998—2000; co-chair Annual TAANA Conf., Washington, 2003. Mem. task force for women Boston Coll., 2003. Mem. ABA, ATLA, D.C. Bar Assn., Am. Assn. Nurses Attys. (co-chmn. legis. affairs com. 1987-91, bd. dirs. N.Y. Met. chpt. 1986-88, sec. 1986-87, nat. bd. dirs. 1996-2000, pres. Found. 1998-99), Conn. Nurses Assn. (chmn. cabinet on econ. and gen. welfare 1985-88), Nurse Atty. Resource Group, Inc. (co-founder), Task Force for Women are Boston Coll., Sigma Theta Tau. Roman Catholic. Avocations: reading, theater, music. Office: Ross and Hardies 65 E 55th St 31st Fl New York NY 10022

GRANT, PAULINE LARRY, retired daycare center director, consultant; b. Thonotosassa, Fla., Feb. 19, 1930; d. Raymond Leland and Bell Beatrice (Jennings) Larry; m. Albert C. Brown, 1951 (div. 1966); children: Paulette Beatrice, Alya Joyce. Student, U. So. Fla., 1965-70. Lic. practical nurse, Fla. Dir. Hidgon's Day Nursery, Thonotosassa, 1963-65; tchr. aide Hillsboro County (Fla.) Sch. System, Tampa, 1965-70; office mgr. Kompleat Enterprises, Inc., Haines City, Fla., 1970-74; nutrition technician Hillsboro County Bd. County Commrs., Tampa, 1977-78, licensing inspector, 1977-87; adminstr. Priority One Learning Ctr., Inc., Temple Terrace, Fla., 1988-91; owner-dir. Complete Child Care, Thonotosassa, 1988—. Cons. day care industry, 1991—, Account Svcs., Tampa, 1992—. Sec. Democrat. Women's Club, Tampa, 1986; membership chair Nat. Coun. Negro Women, Tampa, 1993; membership com. NAACP, Tampa, 1993; active Thonotosassa Civ. Orgn., Thonotosassa/Seffner. Named Unsung Hero, Tampa Orgn. Black Affairs, 1984. Mem. ASCD, NAFE, NAACP (life), Fla. Assn. Children Under Six, Hillsboro Assn. Children Under Six, Nat. Assn. Edn. Young Child, NCNW Inc. (life). Avocations: gardening, sewing, baking, volunteering, reading. Home and Office: PO Box 181 Thonotosassa FL 33592-0181

GRANT, PETER RAYMOND, biologist, researcher, educator; b. London, Oct. 26, 1936; came to U.S., 1978; m. B. Rosemary Matchett, Jan. 4, 1962; children: Nicola, Thalia. BA with honors, Cambridge U., England, 1960; PhD, U. B.C., Vancouver, Can., 1964; PhD (hon.), U. Uppsala, 1986; DSc (hon.), McGill U., 2000. Prof. McGill U., Montreal, 1965-78, U. Mich., Ann Arbor, 1978-85, Princeton (N.J.) U., 1985—. Author: Ecology and Evolution of Darwin's Finches, 1986, 99; co-author: Evolutionary Dynamics of a National Population, 1989; editor: Evolution on Islands, 1998; co-editor: Molecules, Molds and Metazoa, 1992. Fellow AAAS, Am. Acad. Arts and Scis., Royal Soc. London, Royal Soc. Can.; mem. Am. Philos.l Soc. Office: Princeton U Dept Ecol Evol Biology Princeton NJ 08544-1003

GRANT, SANDRA KAY, adult education educator; b. Honolulu, Hawaii, Sept. 1, 1948; d. Wallace Everett and Setsuko (Shiozawa) G.; m. Ageel Moin Chishty, Jan. 1, 1983 (div. May 1989). BS, Weber State U., 1974. Cert. tchr. level 4 math., Utah. Tchr. N. Davis Jr. High Sch., Clearfield, Utah, 1973, Bonniville High Sch., Riverdale, Utah, 1973, Roy (Utah) High Sch., 1974; lectr. Weber State U., Ogden, Utah, 1974-87; instr. Ogden-Weber Applied Tech. Ctr., Ogden, 1987—. Initiated first statewide Light on Literacy conf., 1992. Author, compiler: ATC Cook Book, 1989; author: Applied Mathematics, 1990. Grantee Utah State Office of Edn., 1990, 92, 93. Mem. ASCD, Am. Assn. Adult Edn., Am. Vocat. Assn., Nat. Coun. Tchrs. Math., Utah Vocat. Assn., Utah Coun. Tchrs. Math., Utah State Ednl. Resource Libr. (adv. 1992—), Utah State Adult Edn. Suprs., Utah Assn. Adult, Community and Continuing Edn. (bd. dirs. 1992-95, pres.-elect), Utah Literacy and Adult Edn. Coalition (bd. dirs. 1991——), N. Utah Literacy Coalition (co-chmn. 1992—), Mountain Plains Adult Edn. Assn. Avocations: arts and crafts, floral arrangements, walking, swimming, cooking. Office: Ogden-Weber Applied Tech Ct 559 Avc Ln Ogden UT 84404-6704 Home: 3223 Taylor Ave Ogden UT 84403-1359

GRANTUSKAS, PATRICIA MARY, elementary education educator; b. Irvington, N.J., Jan. 17, 1952; d. Albert L. and Mary D. (Gradeckis) G. BA summa cum laude, Kean Coll., Union, N.J., 1973, MA, 1977 and 1993, supr.'s cert., 1980. Cert. prin. supr., tchr., reading specialist, elem. tchr. Reading clinician Reading Inst., Kean Coll., 1977-80; instr. reading Newark Acad., Livingston, N.J., 1983—; reading specialist, test and basic skills coord. Garwood (N.J.) Bd. Edn., 1977-89; reading instr. Summer Clinic Pingry Sch., N.J., 1977-82; reading specialist, coord. basic skills Harrington Park (N.J.) Bd. Edn., 1989-2001, lead tchr., 1999-2001, program dir., 2001—; remedial reading tchr. Garwood (N.J.) Pub. Schs., 1973-77. Pvt. tutor; reading specialist, basic skills coord. Garwood Pub. Schs., N.J., 1978-89. Mem. YMCA. Chairperson award of Excellence. Mem. ASCD, N.J. ASCD, Nat. Coun. Tchrs. English, Internat. Reading Assn. (hon. coun., Pres.'s Club), N.J. Edn. Assn., N.J. Reading Assn. (bd. dirs. 1991-94, sec. bd. dirs. 1989-90), Garwood Tchrs. Assn., Harrington Park Edn. Assn., Suburban Reading Coun. (past pres., bd. dirs.), Delta Kappa Gamma, Kappa Delta Pi, Phi Kappa Phi. Office: Harrington Park Sch 191 Harriot Ave Harrington Park NJ 07640-1400

GRASELA, JAMES WALTER, librarian; b. Acushnet, Mass., Jan. 6, 1952; s. Joseph Walter and Elsie Alta (Wing) G.; m. Corron Elizabeth Brierley, Apr. 16, 1983; children: Ryan, Victoria, Michael. BA in History, U. Mass., North Dartmouth, 1974; postgrad., Bridgewater State Coll., 1978-84; M in Libr. and Info. Studies, U. R.I., 1994. Cert. sch. libr., unified media specialist, profl. libr. Media tech. Apponequet Regional High Sch., Lakeville, Mass., 1977-85, sch. libr. media specialist, 1985—. Part-time reference libr. So. New Eng. Sch. Law, North Dartmouth, 1993—. Pres. Fort Taber Hist. Assn., New Bedford, Mass., 1974-82. Mem. Am. Libr. Assn., Am. Assn. Sch. Librs., Mass. Sch. Libr. Media Assn., Mass. Assn. Student Couns., Nat. Assn. Student Activity Advisors, Phi Kappa Phi, Beta Phi Mu. Democrat. Roman Catholic. Home: 41 Dana St New Bedford MA 02745-1002 Office: Apponequet High Sch Libr 100 Howland Rd Lakeville MA 02347-2230

GRASER, BERNICE ERCKERT, elementary school principal, educational consultant, psychologist; b. Buffalo, May 5, 1933; d. George Snead Sr. and Ada Louise (Sheasley) Erckert; m. Stanley Richard Graser, May 8, 1953; children: Deberah Dawn Walvoord Rogers. BA magna cum laude, Coll. Gordon & Barrington, 1963; MA, R.I. Coll., 1965; postgrad., Boston U., 1969-71. Cert. elem., pre-sch.-high sch. handicapped tchr.; cert. spl. edn. adminstr.; cert. sch. psychologist. Spl. edn. instr. United Coll. Gordon (Mass.) & Barrington; prin. Pleasant View Sch. for Handicapped Children, Providence; spl. edn. supr. Meeting Street Sch., East Providence; prin. Wm. D'Abate Meml. Elem. Sch., Providence. Established State Model Child Opportunity Zone at Wm. D'Abate Sch.; cons. on ednl. reform; spkr. on critical ednl. issues; presenter workshops and confs.; cons. and lectr. in field. Producer TV broadcast Internat. Celebrations of Cultures; contbr. articles to profl. jours. Named Sch. Adminstr. of Yr., State of R.I., 1993; grantee: U.S. Govt. Dept. Edn.1971—, 1991-93; Very Spl. Arts, State of R.I., 1985-87. Avocations: world travel, photography, videography, business economics, volunteer church work. Home: 45 Clarke Rd Barrington RI 02806-4037

GRASMICK, NANCY S. school system administrator; b. Balt. m. Louis J. Grasmick. BS in Elem. Edn., Towson State U., 1961; MS in Deaf Edn., Gallaudet U., 1965; PhD in Communicative Scis. with distinction, Johns Hopkins U., 1979; LHD (hon.), Towson State U., 1992, Goucher Coll., 1992, U. Balt., 1996, Villa Julie Coll., 1998. Tchr. deaf William S. Baer Sch., Balt., 1961-64; tchr. hearing and lang. impaired children Woodvale Sch., Balt., 1964-68; supr. Office Spl. Edn. Balt. County Pub. Schs., 1968-74; prin. Chatsworth Sch., Balt., 1974-78; asst. supt. Balt. County Pub. Schs., 1978-85, assoc. supt., 1985-89; sec. juvenile svcs. Dept. Juvenile Svc., Balt., 1991; spl. sec. children, youth and families Gov.'s Exec. Office, Balt., 1989-94; supt. schs. Md. Dept. Edn., Balt., 1991—. Mem., chmn. interagy. com. on sch. constrn. Gov.'s Subcabinet for Children, Youth and Families; mem. Gov.'s Workforce Investment Bd.; mem. profl. stds. and tchr. edn. bd. Md. Assocs. for Dyslexic Adults and Youth; mem. State Bd. Edn. profl. adv. bd. Met. Balt. Assn. Learning Disabled Children. Trustee Md. Retirement and Pension Sys.; active Women Execs. in State Govt.; mem. adv. coun. Scholastic, Inc. Recipient Medallion award Jimmy Swartz Found., 1989, Louise B. Makofsky Meml. award Md. Conf. Social Concern, 1990, Child Advocacy award Am. Acad. Pediat., 1990, Humanitarian award March of Dimes, 1990, Disting. Citizen's award Md. Assn. Non-pub. Spl. Edn. Facilities, 1991, Women of Excellence award Nat. Assn. Women Bus. Owners, 1991, Andrew White medal Loyola Coll., 1992, Nat. Edn. Adminstr. of Yr. award Nat. Assn. Ednl. Office Profls., 1992, Nat. award computing to asst. persons with disabilities Johns Hopkins U., 1992, Vernon E. Anderson Disting. Lecture award for outstanding leadership in edn. Coll. Edn., U. Md., 1992, DuBois Circle Award of Honor, 1992, Disting. Alumna of Yr. award Johns Hopkins U., 1992, Pub. Affairs award Md. C. of C., 1994, Educator of the Yr. award Am. Coun. on Rural Spl. Edn., Profl. Legal Excellence-Advancement of Pub. Understanding of Law award Md. Bar Found., Inc., Pressley Ridge award, Victorine Q. Adams Humanitarian award; named Communicator of Yr. by Speech and Hearing Agy., 1990, Marylander of Yr. by Advt. and Profl. Club of Balt., 1990, Marylander of Yr. by The Balt. Sun, 1997, Most Disting. Woman Girl Scouts Ctrl. Md., 1994, Cmty. Honoree 9th Ann. Heartfest Johns Hopkins Hosp., 1999; selected as one of Md.'s Top 100 Women, Warfields Bus. Record, 1996, 98. Fellow Nat. Assn. Pub. Adminstrs.; mem. Phi Delta Kappa (Excellence in Edn. award), Pi Lambda Theta. Office: Md Dept Edn 200 W Baltimore St Baltimore MD 21201-2595*

GRAUPNER, SHERYLL ANN, elementary education educator; b. Independence, Mo., Sept. 19, 1947; d. Horace Alvin and Estelle (LeJeune) G. BS in Edn., Ctrl. Mo. State U., 1969; MEd, U. Mo., Kansas City, 1972. Tchr. Independence Pub. Schs., 1969—; head tchr. Procter Sch., Independence, 1995—. Chmn. Procter Sch. North Ctrl., Independence, 1982, 97, co-chmn., 1989; tchr. math. connection Mo. Ednl. Incentive Grant, Independence, 1987, 94. Mem. NEA, Internat. Reading Assn., Nat. Congress Parents and Tchrs.

GRAVELIN, JANESY SWARTZ, elementary education educator; b. Cleve., Mar. 28, 1952; d. Jesse Franklin and Adele Myra (Pesek) Swartz; m. Christopher James Hof, June 15, 1974 (div. May 1988); 1 child, Zachary Christopher Hof; m. David Paul Gravelin, June 6, 1991. BS in Edn., Bowling Green State U., 1974; MEd, U. South Fla., Ft. Myers, 1985. Cert. elem., spl. edn. tchr., adminstr., supr., Fla., Ohio. Infant stimulation tchr. Wood Lane Sch., Bowling Green, 1974-76, developmentally delayed tchr., 1976-77; 1st grade tchr. Peace River Elem. Sch., Charlotte Harbor, Fla., 1978-85, 3rd grade tchr., 1985-90, computer edn. tchr., 1990-98, ESE liaison, 1998—. Yearbook advisor Peace River Elem. Sch., 1991-96; com. mem. So. Assn. Colls. and Schs., 1989. Recipient Fla. Merit Tchr. award State of Fla., 1984. Mem. Coun. for Exceptional Children, Mensa, Phi Delta Kappa (v.p. 1994-96). Avocations: reading, travel, crosswords. Home: 18749 Ackerman Ave Port Charlotte FL 33948-9463 Office: 18749 Ackerman Ave Port Charlotte FL 33948-9463

GRAVELLE, JOHN DAVID, secondary education educator; Tchr. math, Eng. grades 10-12 Merrill (Wis.) High Sch., to 1997, technology coord., 1997—. Recipient State Tchr. of Yr. Math/Eng. award Wis., 1992. Office: Merrill High Sch 120 N Sales St Merrill WI 54452-2648

GRAVEN, STANLEY NORMAN, pediatrician, educator; b. Greene, Iowa, May 20, 1932; s. Henry Norman and Helen T. (Davis) G.; m. Mavis Nadine Johnson, Aug. 21, 1954; children: Nadine E., Michael A., Kendall E., Douglas B. Student, St. Olaf Coll., 1951-52; BS, Wartburg Coll., 1955; MD, U. Iowa, 1956; postgrad., U. Wis., 1964-66. Diplomate Am. Bd. Pediatrics, Am. Bd. Neonatal-Perinatal Medicine. Chief pediatrics USAF, Spokane, Wash., 1960-62, dir. nurseries San Antonio, 1962-64; asst. prof. dept. pediatrics U. Wis., Madison, 1966-69, assoc. prof. dept. pediatrics, 1969-72, prof. dept. pediatrics, 1972-76, U. S.D., Sioux Falls, 1976-80, U. Mo., Columbia, 1980-84; prof. Coll. of Pub. Health, U. So. Fla., Tampa, 1984-86; prof., chmn. U. So. Fla., Tampa, 1986-93, dir. divsn. child devel., prof. dept. pediatrics, 1993-99, dir. Lawton and Rhea Chiles Ctr., 1999—2003, dean Coll. Pub. Health, 2003—. Chmn. Neonatal-Perinatal Medicine Bd., 1974-76; project dir. Egyptian Newborn Care Program, Cairo, 1978-85; sr. program cons. Robert Wood Johnson Found., Princeton, N.J., 1978-85. Contbr. articles to profl. jours. Capt. USAF, 1956-64. Recipient Borden Undergrad. Rsch. award U. Iowa, 1956, Stanley Graven award Nat. Perinatal Assn., 1988; named John & Mary Markle scholar, 1968. Fellow Am. Acad. Pediatrics; mem. Am. Pub. Health Assn. (gov.'s coun. 1986-90), Soc. Pediatric Rsch., Am. Pediatric Soc., Fla. Perinatal Assn., Nat. Perinatal Assn., Fla. Pediatric Soc., Fla. Med. Assn. Democrat. Lutheran. Avocations: woodworking, building.

GRAVER, JACK EDWARD, mathematics educator; b. Cin., Apr. 13, 1935; s. Harold John and Rose Lucille (Miller) G.; m. Yana Regina Hanus, June 3, 1961; children: Juliet Rose, Yana-Maria, Paul Christopher. BA in Math., Miami U., Oxford, Ohio, 1958; MA in Math., Ind. U., 1961, PhD in Math., 1964. Instr. Ind. U., Bloomington, 1964; John Wesley Young Rsch. instr. Dartmouth Coll., Hanover, N.H., 1964-66; asst. prof. math. Syracuse (N.Y.) U., 1966-69, assoc. prof., 1969-76; vis. prof. U. Nottingham (Eng.), 1971-72; prof. math. Syracuse U., 1976—, chmn. dept. math., 1979-82. Co-author: (books) (with M. Watkins) Combinatorics with Emphasis on Graph Theory, 1977, Locally Finite, Planar, Edge-Transitive Graphs, 1997, (with J. Baglivo) Incidence and Symmetry in Design and Architecture, 1982, (with B. and H. Servatius) Combinatorial Rigidity, 1993, Counting on Frameworks, 2001; contbr. articles to profl. jours. With USN, 1953-55. Fellow Inst. Combinatorics and its Applications; mem. Soc. Indsl. and Applied Math., Nat. Coun. Tchrs. of Math., Assn. Math. Tchrs. N.Y. State, Math. Assn. Am. (bd. govs. 1985-88, Seaway sect. chair 1995-97), Am. Math. Soc. Home: 871 Livingston Ave Syracuse NY 13210-2935 Office: Syracuse Univ Dept Math Syracuse NY 13244-1150 E-mail: jegraver@syr.edu.

GRAVER, LAWRENCE STANLEY, English language professional; b. N.Y.C., Dec. 6, 1931; s. Louis and Rose (Pearlstein) G.; m. Suzanne Levy, Jan. 28, 1960; children— Ruth, Elizabeth. BA, CCNY, 1954; MA, U. Calif., Berkeley, 1959, PhD, 1961. Asst. prof. English UCLA, 1961-64; asst. prof. English, Williams Coll., Williamstown, Mass., 1964-67; assoc. prof. English Williams Coll., 1967-72, prof. English, 1972—; William R. Kenan, Jr. prof. English, Williams Coll., 1977-81, John H. Roberts prof., 1981-97, Roberts prof. emeritus, 1997—. Author: Conrad's Short Fiction, 1969, Carson McCullers, 1969; editor: Mastering the Film, 1977, Samuel Beckett, 1979, (Landmarks of World Lit. series) Waiting for Godot, 1989, An Obsession With Anne Frank: Meyer Levin and the Diary, 1995; asst. editor: Columbia Companion to the Twentieth Century American Short Story, 2001. Served with U.S. Army, 1954-56. Nat. Endowment for Humanities fellow, 1980-81 Mem. MLA, AAUP. Democrat. Home: 117 Forest Rd Williamstown MA 01267-2028 Office: Williams Coll Dept English Williamstown MA 01267 E-mail: lgraver@williams.edu.

GRAVER, SUZANNE LEVY, English literature educator; b. N.Y.C., Aug. 17, 1936; BA summa cum laude, CUNY, 1958; MA, U. Calif., Berkeley, 1960; PhD, U. Mass., 1976. Tchr. English Berkeley High Sch., 1960-61, Culver City High Sch., 1961-62; asst. prof. Berkshire Community Coll., 1966-72; vis. asst. prof. Tufts U., 1976-78; assoc. ind. study Empire State Coll., SUNY, 1978; lectr. Williams Coll., Williamstown, Mass., 1976, 78-82, coord. writing workshop, 1981-85, asst. prof., 1983-87, chair dept. women's studies, 1988-89, assoc. prof. English, 1988-91, assoc. dean faculty, 1990-91, prof., 1991—2002, John Hawley Roberts prof. English prof. emerita, 2002—, dean of faculty, 1991-94. Manuscript reader Ind. U. Press, Victorian Studiesm, A Victorian Periodicals Review, PMLA; fellowship and grants application reader NEH, Nat. Humanities Ctr., The Grad. Ctr., CUNY. Author: George Eliot and Community : A Study in Social Theory and Fictional Form, 1984, and numerous essays and revs. in Victorian lit. and culture. NEH fellow, 1985, 95, U. fellow U. Mass., Amherst, 1974-76, Am. Coun. Learned Socs. fellow, 1985-86, 89-90, Nat. Humanities Ctr. fellow, 1989-90. Fellow NEH; mem. AAUP, ACLU, NOW, Modern Lang. Assn. (rep. to del. assembly 1988-91), Amnesty Internat., Wilderness Soc., Northeast Modern Lang. Assn. (chair English novel sect. 1980). Office: Williams Coll Stetson Hall Williamstown MA 01267-0141

GRAVES, DANA LOUISE, elementary school educator; b. Takoma Park, Md., Mar. 15, 1948; d. John William and Patricia Eloise (langdon) Perkins; m. George William Graves, Nov. 7, 1977; 1 child, Jennifer; 1 stepchild, Michael. BA, Elon Coll., N.C., 1970. Cert. tchr. elem. edn., Va. Tchr. 5th grade Hope Valley Sch., Durham, N.C., 1971, tchr. 2d grade, 1971-72; tchr. 4th grade Alanton Elem. Sch., Virginia Beach, Va., 1972-73, tchr. 2d grade, 1973-77; tchr. 3d grade North Springfield Elem. Sch., 1978; tchr. 2d grade Hunt Valley Sch., Fairfax, Va., 1985-86, 1987—. Parent mem./helper Girl Scouts U.S., Fairfax, 1987—. Tchr. of Yr. at Alanton Elem. Sch., Virginia Beach Pub. Schs., 1976-77, Cert. of Appreciation for outstanding contbn., dedication and commitment Children and Adults with Attention Deficit Disorders of No. Va., 1994. Mem. NEA, Va. Edn. Assn., Fairfax Edn. Assn., Virginia Beach Edn. Assn., Nat. Coun. Tchrs. English, Nat. Sci. Tchrs. Assn., Greater Washington Reading Coun., Internat. Reading Assn., Va. State Reading Assn. (co-chmn. sch. plan com., sci. lead tchr., colleague lead tchr., mainstream tchr. lng. disabled and autistic). Roman Catholic. Avocations: crafts, aerobics. Home: 5023 Dequincy Dr Fairfax VA 22032-2432

GRAVES, KAREN LEE, counselor; b. Twin Falls, Idaho, Dec. 9, 1948; d. Isaac Mason and Agnes Popplewell; m. Frederick Ray Graves, Apr. 2, 1987 (dec. Dec. 2001). BA, Idaho State U., 1971; MEd, Coll. of Idaho, 1978. Cert. tchr. secondary edn., english 7-12, vocat. home econs. 7-12, pupil pers. svcs. K-12, Idaho. Tchr. Filer (Idaho) Sch. Dist., 1971-74, 76-80, Twin Falls (Idaho) Sch. Dist., 1974-76; counselor Mountain Home (Idaho) Sch. Dist., 1980—, dept. chairperson, dir. Mem. NEA, ACA, ASCD, Am. Sch. Counseling Assn., Idaho Counseling Assn., Idaho Sch. Counseling Assn., Idaho Edn. Assn., Idaho Affiliation Supervision and Curriculum Devel., Mountain Home Edn. Assn. Avocations: painting ceramics, crafting, stamping, reading, crossword puzzles. Home: 1105 Maple Dr Mountain Home ID 83647-2027 Office: Mountain Home H S 300 S 11th E Mountain Home ID 83647-3235 E-mail: graves_kp@sd193.k12.id.us.

GRAVES, MELISSA JUNE, elementary school educator; b. Gt. Lakes, Ill., Mar. 7, 1956; d. Robert Eugene and Bettyelou G. BA, Calif. State U., Fresno, 1979, BA; postgrad., Fresno Pacific Coll., Chapman Coll. Cert. life elem. Ryan Act teaching credential, Calif., lang. devel. specialist. Elem. tchr. Columbine Elem. Sch., Delano, Calif., 1980-88, St. James Cathedral Sch., Fresno, 1988-89; tchr. Mayfair Elem. Sch., Fresno Unified Sch. Dist., 1989—. Calif. State scholar, 1974-79. Mem. Calif. Tchrs. Assn. (del., sch. site rep. 2002-03, ngeotation team, 2003—), Mu Phi Epsilon (internat. chmn.). Office: Mayfair Elem Sch 3305 E Home Ave Fresno CA 93703-4044

GRAVES, MICHAEL, architect, educator; b. Indpls., July 9, 1934; s. Thomas Browning and Erma Sanderson (Lowe) Graves; children from previous marriage: Sarah Browning, Adam Daimhinstepchildren: Anne Gilbert, Liza Gilbert. BS in Architecture, U. Cin., 1958, DFA (hon.), 1982; MArch, Harvard U., 1959; postgrad. (Acad. fellow), Am. Acad. in Rome, 1960—62; PhD (hon.), U. Cin., 1982; LHD (hon.), Boston U., 1984; HHD (hon.), Savannah Coll. Art and Design, 1986; DFA (hon.), RISD, 1990, N.J. Inst. Tech., 1991; LHD (hon.), Rutgers U., 1994, U. Colo., 1995; PhD (hon.), Internat. Fine Arts Coll., 1996, Pratt Inst., 1996, Drexel U., 2000. Lectr. architecture Princeton (N.J.) U., 1962—67, assoc. prof., 1967—72, Schirmer prof. architecture, 1972—2001, emeritus, 2001—; pres. Michael Graves & Assocs., Princeton, 1964—. Arch. in residence Am. Acad. in Rome, 1979. Exhibited in group shows including Mus. Modern Art, N.Y.C., 1967, 68, 75, 78, 79, 80, 81, 84, Cooper-Hewitt Mus., 1976, 78, 79, 80, 82, 85, 87, Triennale, Milan, Italy, 1973, 85, Roma Interrotta, Rome, 1978, Venice Biennale, Italy, 1980, Met. Mus. Art, 1985, 86, 87, Emory U. Mus. Art and Archaeology, Atlanta, 1985, Denver (Colo.) Art Mus., 2002; one-man shows include U. So. Calif., 1981, No. Ill. U., 1982, Inst. for

Architecture and Urban Studies, N.Y.C., 1982, Colby Coll., Maine, 1982, Moore Coll. Art, Phila., 1983, Fla. Internat. U., Miami, 1983, Pa. State U., University Park, 1984, Royal Inst. Brit. Archs., Heinz Gallery, London, 1984, Wadsworth Athenaeum, Hartford, Conn., 1984, Carleton Coll., Northfield, Minn., 1986, W.Va. U., 1986, Hamilton Coll., Clinton, NY, 1987, Archivolto Gallery, Milan, Italy, 1987, U. Va., Charlottesville, 1987, U. Md., College Park, 1988, Duke U. Mus. Art, Durham, NC, 1988, Butler Inst. Art, Youngstown, Ohio, 1989, 1989, Deutsches Architekturmuseum, Frankfurt, German Dem. Republic, 1989, Washington Design Ctr., 1989, Syracuse U. Sch. Architecture, 1990, Kunstemes Hus, Oslo, 1990, Mikimoto Hall, Tokyo, 1992, Pitts. Cultural Trust, 1993, Richard Stockton Coll., 1993, Clark County Libr., 1994, Thessaloniki Design Mus., Greece, 1996, The Min. Bldg., Seoul, Korea, 1996, Princeton Arts Coun., 1996, 99, U. Conn. Aronoff Ctr. Design and Art, 1996, NJ Sch. Arch., NJ Inst. Tech., 2000; prin. works include Hanselmann House, 1967 (AIA Nat. Honor award, 1975), Newark (NJ) Mus., 1968, Rockefeller House, 1969 (Progressive Architecture Design award, 1970), Gunwyn Ventures Office, 1971 (AIA Nat. Honor award, 1979), Snyderman House, 1972, Crooks House, 1976 (Progressive Architecture Design award, 1977), Schulman House, 1976, (AIA Nat. Honor award, 1982), Fargo-Moorhead Cultural Ctr., 1977-79 (Progressive Architecture Design award, 1978), Plocek House, 1978 (Progressive Architecture Design award, 1979), pvt. residence in Green Brook, NJ, 1978 (Progressive Architecture Design award, 1980), Sunar showrooms N.Y.C., 1979, 81 (Interiors award, 1981), Chgo., 1979, Houston, 1980, LA, 1980, London, 1985, Loveladies Beach House, 1979 (Progressive Architecture Design award, 1979) Environ. Edn. Ctr., 1980 (Progressive Architecture award, 1983), Portland (Oreg.) Bldg., 1980 (AIA Nat. Honor award, 1983), San Juan Capistrano Pub. Libr., Calif., 1980 (AIA Nat. Honor award, 1985), Newark Mus. Master Plan and Renovation, 1982 (AIA Nat. Honor award, 1992), Human Bldg., Louisville, 1982 (Interiors award, 1985, AIA NAt. Honor award, 1987), Emory U. Mus. Art and Archaeology, 1982 (Interiors award 1985, AIA Nat. Honor award, 1987), Riverbend Music Ctr., 1983, Whitney Mus. Am. art, N.Y.C., 1984, Diane Von Furstenburg Boutique, 1984, Clos Pegase Winery, Calif., 1984 (AIA Nat. Honor award, 1990), Sotheby's Tower, N.Y.C., 1985, Warehouse Renovation (Graves House), 1985 (Progressive Architecture Design award, 1978), Aventine Devel., La Jolla, Calif., 1985, Shiseido Health Club, Tokyo, 1985, Disney Co. Corp. Office Bldg., Burbank, Calif., 1985, Crown Am. Hdqs., Johnston, Pa., 1985, Walt Disney World Dolphin and Walt Disney World Swan hotels, Fla., 1986 (Progressive Architecture award, 1989), Youngston (Ohio) Hist. Ctr. Industry and Labor, 1986 (Progressive Architecture Design award, 1987), 10 Peachtree Pl., Atlanta, 1987, Henry House, Rhinebeck, NY, 1987 (Progressive ARchitecture award, 1989), U. Va. Arts. and Scis. Bldg., Charlottesville, 1987, Portside Dist. Condominium Tower, Yokohama, Japan, 1987, Momochi Dist. Apt. Bldg., Fukuoka, Japan, 1987, Metropolis Master Plan LA, 1988, stores and galleries for Lenox, Tysons Corner, Va., 1988, Palm Beach, 1988, N.Y.C., 1988, Mpls., 1988, Costa Mesa, 1989, Frankfurt, 1989, Phila., 1989, Nashville, 1989, Midousuji Minami Office Bldg., Osaka, 1988, Tajima Office Bldg., Tokyo, 1988, Hotel NY, 1988, Euro Disneyland, France, 1988, Inst. for Theoretical Physics, U. Calif., Santa Barbara, 1989, Detroit Inst. of Arts Master Plan, 1989, Indpls. Art Ctr., 1989, Emory U. Mus. Art and Archaeology Addition, 1989, Fukuoka Internat. Office Project, 1990, Kasumi Group Rsch. and Tng. Ctr., Tsukaba City, Japan, 1990, Clark County Libr., Las Vegas, 1990, U. Cin. Sci. and Engring. Rsch. Ctr., 1990, Richard Stockton Coll. Arts and Scis. Bldg., Pomoma, NJ, 1991, Denver Ctrl. Libr., 1991 (AIA-NJ Design award, 1992, 95, AIA Nat. Honor award for Interior Architecture, 1998, AIA and Am. Libr. Assn. Excellence award, 2001), Astrid Park Plz. Hotel and Bus. Ctr., Antwerp, Belgium, 1992, Thomson Consumer Electronics Hdqs., Indpls., 1992 (AIA-NJ Design award, 1994), Rome Reborn Vatican Exhibit, Libr. Congress, 1992 (Casebook award Print Mag., 1993), Pitts. Cultural Trust Theater and Office Bldg., 1992, Taiwan Mus. Pre-History, Taipei, 1993 (AIA-NJ Design award, 1994), Archdiocesan Ctr., Newark, 1993, Internat. Fin. Corp. Hdqs., Washington, 1993 (AIA-NJ Design award, 1997), 1500 Ocean Dr. Condominiums, Miami, 1994, Del. River Port Authority Hdqs., Camden, NJ, 1994 (AIA-NJ Design award, 1998), St. Martin's Coll. Libr., Lacey, Wash., 1994, Topeka (Kans.) and Shawnee County Pub. Libr., 1995, Miramar Hotel, Egypt, 1995 (AIA-NJ Design award, 1996), NJ Inst. Tech. Residence Hall, 1995, Jiang-to Blvd. Master Plan, Xiamen, China, 1995, Alexandria (Va.) Ctrl. Libr., 1996, U.S. Courthouse Annex, Washington, 1996, Life Mag. Dream House, 1996, Lake Hills country Club, Seoul, Korea, 1996, World Trade Exch., Manila, 1996, new residence Hall, Drexel U., Phila., 1997, Miele Appliances Americas Hdqs. Bldg., Princeton, 1997 (AIA-NJ Design award, 2002), NovaCare Sports Training Facility, 1997 (AIA-NJ Design award, 2002), El Gourna Golf Villas, Egypt, 1997 (AIA-NJ Design award, 2002), French Inst. Libr, N.Y.C., 1997, Hyatt Regency Taba Heights Hotel, Egypt, 1997, St. Mary's Ch., Rockledge, Fla., 1998, Rice U. Master Plan, Houston, 1998, The Impala Bldg., N.Y.C., 1998, Wash. Monument Restoration Scaffolding, 1998 (AIA-NJ Design award, 1998), Rolex Watch Technicum training and Svc. Ctr., Lancaster county, Pa., 1999, Theater Square: Pitts. Cultural Trust Svc. Ctr., 1999, Mus. Shenandoah Valley, Winchester, Va., 1999, 425 Fifth Ave. Tower, N.Y.C., 2000, Mahler IV Mixed-Use Bldg., Amsterdam, 2000, Fed. Res. Bank Dallas: Houston Br., 2000, Famillr-Tsukishima Bldg., Tokyo, 2000, U.S. Embassy, Seoul, 2000, Dept. Transp. Hdqs., Washington, 2001, Detroit Inst. Arts, 2001, St. Coletta's Sch., Washington, 2002, NJ City U. Arts and Scis. Bldg., 2002, Nat. Automobile Mus., The Netherlands, 2003, U.S. Courthouse, Nashville, 2003; designer furniture, artifacts, textiles, and consumer products, V'Soske, 1979-80, Sunar, 1980-83, Alessi, 1981—Baldinger Archtl. Lighting, 1983—, Swid Powell, 1985—, Steuben, 1986—, Munari, 1986—Tajima, 1987-88, WMF, 1987—, Atelier Internat., 1987—Vorwerk, 1987—, Lenox Inc., 1988—, Markuse Corp., 1989—, Dunbar Furniture, 1989—, Arkitektura, 1989—, Moeller Internat. Design, 1992—, Target Stores, 1997—, Glen Eden Wool Carpet, 2002—, Delta Faucets, 2003—; monographs include: Five Architects, 1972, Michael Graves, Academy Editions, 1979, Michael Graves: Buildings and Projects 1966-1981, 1981, Michael Graves: Buildings and Projects 1982-1989, 1990, Michael Graves: Buildings and Projects 1990-1994, 1995, The Master Architect Series III: Michael Graves: Selected and Current Works, 1999, Michael Graves:Buildings and Projects 1995-2002, 2003. Named Designer Yr., Interiors, 1981; recipient Arnold W. Brunner Meml. prize in Architect., 1981, 61 awards, N.J. Soc. Architects, Euster award, 1984, Ind. Arts award, 1984, Henry Hering Meml. medal, Am. Sculpture Soc., 1986, profile Best Architects and Designers Working Today, Architectural Digest, 1990, 1995, 2000, Nat. Medal Arts, Nat. Endowment Arts, 1999, Frank Annuzio award, 2001, AIA Gold medal, Sigma Tau Delta, 2003. Fellow: AIA (Gold medal, 2001); mem.: N.Y. Sch. Interior Design (bd. trustees), Mus. Arts and Design (bd. trustees), Am. Acad. in Rome (bd. trustees, Rome prize 1960—62), Am. Acad. Arts and Letters. Office: Michael Graves & Assoc 341 Nassau St Princeton NJ 08540 also: Michael Graves & Assocs 560 Broadway Ste 401 New York NY 10012 Office Fax: 609-924-1795. E-mail: info@michaelgraves.com.

GRAVES, NADA PROCTOR, retired elementary school educator; b. Kewaunee, Wis., Oct. 9, 1933; d. John and Martha Proctor; m. Harmon Sheldon Graves III, Dec. 28, 1958; children: Jessica, Gemont. BS, U. Wis., 1956. With TWA, Chgo., 1956-58; tchr. Denver Pub. Schs., 1959-61, Cherry Creek Schs., Englewood, Colo., 1980—99. Membership chmn. Denver Art Mus., 1966-68; treas. Glenmoor Homeowners, 1991-92; mem./vol. D.A.M., Mus. Nat. History, Ctrl. City Guild, The Guild Diabetes, Denver Lyric Opera Guild, Gathering Place., P.E.O., D. of the King Home: 17 Glenmoor Cir Englewood CO 80110-7121

GRAVES, ROBERT JOHN, industrial engineering educator; b. Buffalo, Sept. 25, 1945; s. Paul Frederick and Ann (Mayer) G.; m. Virginia Jane Burry, June 8, 1968; children: Peter F., Anna K., Christopher J. BS Indsl. Engring., Syracuse U., 1967; MS Indsl. Engring., SUNY, Buffalo, 1969, PhD, 1974. Instr. indsl. engring. SUNY, Buffalo, 1973-74; asst. prof. sch. indsl. and sys. engring. Ga. Tech., Atlanta, 1974-79; assoc. prof. indsl. engring. U. Mass., Amherst, 1979-80, prof. indsl. engring., 1988-91, Rensselaer Poly. Inst., Troy, NY, 1991—2003; Krehbiel chaired prof. engring. Thayer Sch. Engring. Dartmouth Coll., 2003—; program dir. Agile Mfg. Rsch. Inst., 1994—. Pres. Coll. Industry Coun. on Material Handling Edn., Charlotte, N.C., 1990-92. Editor: Material Handling of the 90's, 1991, Progress in Material Handling Research, 1992; U.S. editor Internat. Jour. Prodn. Planning and Control, 1992-99; contbr. articles to profl. jours. Mem. sch. com. Town of Pelham, Mass., 1985-86, mem. planning bd., 1987-95. Recipient David Baker Outstanding Rsch. award IIE, 1997; grantee Mass. Ctrs. Excellence Corp., 1987-90, NSF, 1989-91, NSF/ATT 1994-99, MHI's Reed Apple award, 2002. Fellow Soc. Mfg. Engrs., Inst. Indsl. Engrs. (sr., faculty divsn. rsch. chair 1980-81, program chair 1981-82, editor newsletter 1990-91, dir. divsn. 1991-92, Spl. Citation award 1985) Achievements include research in flexible assembly systems scheduling, printed circuit board assembly, electronics agile manufacturing. Office: Dartmouth Coll Thayer Sch Engring 8000 Cummings Hall Hanover NH 03755-8000 E-mail: graver@rpi.edu.

GRAVES, RUTH PARKER, educational executive, educator; b. Port Arthur, Tex., Oct. 19, 1934; d. Thomas B. and Eunice Parker; m. Glenn R. Graves, Aug. 8, 1956; 1 child, Christopher. BA, Baylor U., 1956; MA, U. Tex., 1961; postgrad., George Washington U., 1963-64. Migrant labor advisor Tex. State AFL-CIO, Austin, 1959-61; pub. info. officer Pres.'s Com. on EEO, Washington, 1961-63; tchg. fellow George Washington U., Washington, 1963-64; labor desk coord. Dem. Nat. Conv., Washington, 1965-67; program analyst U.S. OEO, Washington, 1965-67, dir. migrant divsn., 1967-72; pres. emerita Reading is Fundamental, Inc., Washington, 1998. Nat. adv. coun. Ctr. for the Book, Libr. of Congress, 1977-97; adv. bd. Kidwave Radio Network, Phila., 1990-97; bd. advisors Ednl. Pub. Group, 1994-97; faculty Salzburg Seminar, 1998—; lectr. in field. Mem. editl. bd. Child Mag., N.Y.C., 1989-97; adv. coun. Ednl. Pub. Group, 1994-97; editor: The RIF Guide to Encouraging Young Readers, 1987; contbr. articles to profl. jours. Recipient William A. Jump award, U.S. Govt., 1971, Jeremiah Ludington Literacy Leadership award Ednl. Paperback Assn., 1982, Manhattan Literacy Coun. award, 1986, Internat. Reading Assn. Literacy award, 1987, As They Grow award Parents Mag., 1991; named Bookwoman of the Yr. Woman's Nat. Book Assn., 1987. Avocations: reading, theater, design and production of craft items.

GRAVES, VIRGINIA BETH, elementary education educator; b. Oceanside, Calif., Sept. 19, 1950; d. Joe Howard and Bertha Elizabeth (Denney) Long; children: Betsy Lynn, John Howard. BS in Edn. with distinction, U. Okla., 1972; M in Reading, UCO, 1996. Cert. in elem. edn., Okla. Tchr. 5th grade Oklahoma City Pub. Schs., 1972-75; tchr. 1st grade Westminster Day Sch., Oklahoma City, 1989-94, tchr. 2d grade, co-chair lang. arts curriculum, 1994-97, reading recovery tchr., 1997-2000, reading recovery tchr. leader, 2000—. Mem. Jr. League Oklahome City, 1985-89, 92-95. Mem. Internat. Reading Assn. Presbyterian. Home: 1605 Brighton Ave Oklahoma City OK 73120 Office: Putnam City Schs 5401 NW 40th St Oklahoma City OK 73122 E-mail: vgraves1@cox.net.

GRAVING, RICHARD JOHN, law educator; b. Duluth, Minn., Aug. 24, 1929; s. Lawrence Richard and Laura Magdalene (Loucks) G.; m. Florence Sara Semel; children: Daniel, Sarah. BA, U. Minn., 1950; JD, Harvard U., 1953; postgrad., Nat. U. Mex., 1964-66. Bar: Minn. 1953, N.Y. 1956, U.S. Dist. Ct. (so. dist.) N.Y. 1956, Pa. 1968, U.S. Dist. Ct. (we. dist.) Pa. 1968, Tex. 1982, U.S. Dist. Ct. (so. dist.) Tex. 1982. Assoc. Reid & Priest, N.Y.C., 1955-61, Mexico City, 1961-66; v.p. Am. & Fgn. Power Co., Inc., Mexico City, 1966-68; atty. Gulf Oil Corp., Pitts., 1968-69, Madrid, 1969-73, London, 1973-80, Houston, 1980—82; pvt. practice London, 1982—84; prof. law South Tex. Coll., Houston, 1983—; prof. Bush Grad. Sch.. Tex. A&M U., Coll. Sta., 2001—. With U.S. Army, 1953-55. Mem. Am. Soc. Internat. Law. Home: 8515 Ariel St Houston TX 77074-2806 Office: 1303 San Jacinto St Houston TX 77002-7000

GRAY, ARTHUR MICHAEL, elementary principal; b. Owensboro, Ky., Aug. 10, 1950; s. Arthur M. Gray and Mildred (Marksberry) Crowe; m. Rhonda Houston Vanmilligen, Dec. 26, 1969 (div. Feb. 1982); children: Stephanie, Natalie Gray, Matt Ross; m. Mary Pat Swift, Apr. 8, 1984. BS, Western Ky. U., 1975, MS, 1980, rank I, 1982. Cert. tchr., elem. and secondary prin., supr., supt., Ky. Tchr. Burns Mid. Sch. Daviess County Schs., Owensboro, 1976-80, asst. prin. Daviess County Mid. Sch., 1980-82, prin. Burns Elem. Sch., 1982-84, pres. Tamarack Elem. Sch., 1984—. Pres. elect., v.p., treas., bd. dirs. Ky. Coalition Sch. Age Child Care, Frankfort, Ky., 1988—. With USAR, 1969-75. Democrat. Avocations: tennis, boating, swimming, travel, reading. Office: Tamarack Elem Sch 1733 Tamarack Rd Owensboro KY 42301-6865

GRAY, AUDREY NESBITT, elementary education educator; b. Kalamazoo, Mich., Feb. 5, 1920; d. Walter Hale and Hazel Violet (Wriglesworth) Nesbitt; m. Llewellyn Wallace Gray, Apr. 22, 1943; children: Susan Nesbitt Moffitt, Deborah Llewellyn Gray-Olker, Gretchen Clarke Shannon. BS, Western Mich. U., 1943. Cert. elem. edn. tchr., Mich. Tchr. Three Rivers (Mich.) Pub. Schs., 1943-45; tchr. music Schoolcraft (Mich.) Pub. Schs., 1945-46; tchr. Comstock (Mich.) Pub. Schs., 1963-83, ret., 1983. Bd. dirs. Mich. In Action for Drug Free Youth; mem. cons. team Drug Edn. Curriculum Guide, 1971, adv. com. Gov. Conf. Drug Free Schs. and Communities, 1990, steering com. for Med., Ednl., Legal Law Enforcement, State Bar Mich., 1991—, Mich alliance Drug Free Schs. and Communities, 1990-91; innovator, dir., advisor cmty. story hour program Juvenile Detention Facilities, Mich., 1993. Mem. Forum for Kalamazoo County, 1986—, Greater Kalamazoo Consortium, 1990—; mem. steering com. Nat. Issues Forum, Kalamazoo, 1989—; bd. dirs. Kalamazoo Area Families in Action, 1986-87; mem. State Bar of Mich. Task Force on Substance Abuse, 1991—; dir. Cmty. Story Hour Program, Kalamazoo County Juv. Home, 1993—. Recipient Top Tchr. award Grade Tchr. Mag., 1967, First Tchr. Appreciation award Nat. Honor Soc. Comstock High Sch., 1990. Mem. AAUW, Am. Lawyers Aux. (chair drug awareness com. 1990—, coun. state affiliates 1989-90, 91—, 2d v.p., 1991, pres., 1993), Gov.'s Conf. on Drug Free Schs. and Communities (adv. mem.), Mich. Lawyers Aux. (pres. 1987-88, drug awareness chair, 1989, co-chair statewide No Drug Use rally 1989), Kalamazoo Lawyers Aux. (pres., 1970-71, 88-89), Republican. Presbyterian. Avocations: 18th century antiques, genealogy, music, gardening. Home: 1442 Prospect Hl Kalamazoo MI 49006-4446

GRAY, BRADFORD HITCH, health policy researcher; b. Greenwich, Conn., Dec. 31, 1942; s. John Bradford and Joyce (Hitch) G.; m. Anne Morgan, Aug. 6, 1966 (div. 1980); children: Carrie Elizabeth, Joshua Bradford; m. Helen Darling, Jan. 15, 1983. BS, Okla. State U., 1964; PhD, Yale U., 1973. Asst. prof. U. N.C., Chapel Hill, 1971-74; staff sociologist Nat. Commn. for the Protection of Human Subjects of Rsch., Washington, 1975-77; study dir. Inst. of Medicine NAS, Washington, 1977-88; prof. pub. health Yale Sch. Medicine, New Haven, 1989-96; exec. dir. Program on Non-Profit Orgns. Yale U., New Haven, 1989-96, dir. Inst. for Social and Policy Studies, 1992-96; dir. divsn. health and sci. policy N.Y. Acad. Medicine, N.Y.C., 1996—. Author: Human Subjects in Medical Experimentation, 1975, The Profit Motive and Patient Care, 1991; editor: New Health Care for Profit, 1983, For-Profit Enterprise in Health Care, 1986. Grantee Lilly Endowment, Indpls., 1990, Ford Found., N.Y., 1989, Rockefeller Bros. Fund, N.Y., 1989, Robert Wood Johnson Found., 1989, 93, 96, Commonwealth Fund, 1997. Mem.: Inst. of Medicine, Grolier Club, Yale Club of N.Y. Home: 93 Buttery Rd New Canaan CT 06840-5002 Office: 2500 Virginia Ave NW #407-S Washington DC 20037

GRAY, CHRIS HABLES, adult education educator, writer; b. Bishop, Calif., Aug. 23, 1953; s. George Edward and Edna Benita (Hables) G.; m. Jane Lovett Wilson, Mar. 3, 1986; children: Corey Alexander Grayson, Zackary Hables Grayson. BA, Stanford U., 1975; PhD in the History of Consciousness, U. Calif. (Santa Cruz), 1991. Cons. various computer firms, Oreg., Calif., 1984-94; tech. asst. U. Calif. (Santa Cruz), 1987-90, lectr., 1989-91; vis. prof. Ore. State U., Corvallis, 1992-95, Musaryk U., Brno, Czech Republic, 1995; assoc. faculty Goddard Coll., Plainfield, Mass., 1994—; assoc. prof. U. Great Falls (Mont.), 1996—; faculty mem. Grad. Coll. Union Inst. and Univ., Cin., 2000—. Student rep. History Consciousness Bd., U. Calif. (Santa Cruz), 1989-90; mem. History Consciousness Bd. Admissions Com., 1990; panel organizer Soc. Lit. Sci. conf., 1990, Soc. Social Studies Sci. meeting, 1994; chmn. Internet Com., U. Great Falls, 1996-98; mem. faculty devel. com., U. Great Falls, 1997-98, Accreditation Self-Study Com., U. Great Falls, 1997-98; spkr. numerous colls. and univs. Author: Power-Learning: Developing Effective Study Skills, 1992, Postmodern War: The New Politics of Conflict, 1997 (also Turkish and Chinese edits.), Cyborg Citizen, 2001 (also German and Spanish edits.); editor: The Cyborg Handbook, 1995, Technohistory: Using the History of American Technology in Interdisciplinary Research, 1996; contbr. over 70 articles to profl. jours. Active mem. Columbae, Stanford, Calif., 1977-83; organizer Abalone Alliance, Calif., 1981-90; del. 5th Internat. Student Pugwash Conf., 1987, soccer coach Ayso, Mini-Bolts, Thunderbolts, Corvallis, Great Falls, 1994—; treas., bd. dirs. Guardians ad Litem, Cascade County, Mont., 1997-99. Recipient U. Calif. Regents fellow, 1986, 91, Smithsonian Instn. summer fellow, Washington, 1990, NEH summer fellow, Cleve., 1992, Ore. State U. fellow, 1992-94, NASA History fellow, Washington, 1993-94, Eisenhower Found. fellow, Czech Republic, 1995, Silicon Valley Rsch. Group grantee, 1986, IGCC Rsch. grantee, 1987-88. Mem. Am. Studies Assn., Computer Profls. Social Responsibility, Assn. Advancement Computing Edn., Soc. History Tech., History Sci. Tech., Soc. Social Studies Sci., Cultural Studies Sci. Tech. Rsch. Group, Circus Numicus. Avocations: gardening, writing, soccer. Home: 606 5th Ave N Great Falls MT 59401-2334 Office: University of Great Falls 1301 20th St S Great Falls MT 59405-4934 E-mail: cgray@ugf.edu.

GRAY, CLARENCE JONES, foreign language educator, dean emeritus; b. June 21, 1908; s. Clarence J. Sr. and Elsie (Megill) G.; m. Jane Love Little, Aug. 25, 1934 (dec. June 1998); children: Frances Gray Adams (dec. Nov. 1997), Kenneth Stewart. BA, U. Richmond, 1933; MA, Columbia U., 1934; postgrad., Centro de Estudios Historicos, Madrid, summer 1935; EdD, U. Va., 1962; LLD, U. Richmond, 1979. Underwriter Aetna Life and Casualty, 1925-30; instr. Spanish Columbia U., 1934-38; gen. sec., mem. exec. council Instituto de las Espanas en los Estados Unidos, 1934-39; instr., sec. dept. Romance langs. Queens Coll., N.Y.C., 1938-46; (on mil. leave 1943-46); dean students U. Richmond, Va., 1946-68, assoc. prof. modern langs., 1946-62, prof., 1962-79, emeritus, 1979—, dean adminstrv. svcs., 1968-73, exec. asst. to pres., 1971-79, dean adminstrn., 1973-79, emeritus, 1979—, spl. cons. to pres., 1979-91, spl. cons. to chancellor, 1991—. Editor bull., 1968-74, moderator U. Richmond-WRNL Radio Scholarship Quiz program, mem. bd. Univ. Assos. Cons., Commn. on Coll., So. Assn. Coll. and Schs. Trustee Inst. Mediterranean Studies. Contbr. articles to profl. jours. Served from lt. to lt. comdr., USNR, 1943-46. Recipient Nat. Alumni award for disting. svc. U. Richmond. Mem. MLA, NEA, Am. Assn. Tchrs. Spanish, Am. Assn. for Higher Edn., Newcomen Soc. N. Am., Inst. Internat. Edn. (cert. meritorious svc.), English-Speaking Union, Legion of Honor, Order of De Molay, Country Club of Va., Colonnade Club, Masons, Rotary, Phi Beta Kappa (Epsilon chpt. sec. emeritus, historian), Phi Delta Kappa, Kappa Delta Pi, Omicron Delta Kappa (nat. sec. gen. council 1966-72, Disting. Svc. key 1968, nat. chmn. scholarship awards 1972-78), Alpha Psi Omega, Phi Gamma Delta (award for disting. and exceptional svc.), Alpha Phi Omega, Phi Beta Kappa Assocs. (life).

GRAY, DENISE DEANNE, elementary school educator; b. Shelton, Wash., Dec. 22, 1951; d. Robert Bertin and Myrtle Louise G.; children: Jason Gray, Michelle Leanne. BA, Graceland Coll., Lamoni, Iowa; MEd, U. Nebr.; EdD, Boston U., 1985. Cert, K-8 tchr., spl. subject supr., reading, K-12 reading specialist, basic skills-reading, Ariz. Teaching fellow, asst. dir. ednl. clinic Boston U. Sch. Edn., 1983-85; reading specialist Arlington (Va.) County Schs., Arlington, No. Va., 1986-91; reading instr. Glendale C.C., 1992-96; elem. lang. arts curriculum specialist Peoria (Ariz.) Unified Sch. Dist., 1997—2002; dist. lit. coord. LIberty Sch. Dist., Buckeye, Ariz., 2003—. Adj. faculty No. Ariz. U. Ctr. for Excellence in Edn., Ariz. State U. West. Bd. dirs. Reading Is Fundamental. Mem. ASCD, NEA, Nat. Coun. Tchrs. English, Internat. Reading Assn.

GRAY, DONALD DWIGHT, civil engineering educator; b. New Orleans, July 1, 1946; s. Edward Morris and Jeanne (Saucier) G.; m. Kay Ann Hess, June 1, 1968; children: Donald Douglas, Benjamin David, Michael Joseph. BSE in Mech. Engring., Tulane U., 1968; MSE, Purdue U., 1969, PhD, 1974. Registerd profl. engr., Ind. Rsch. assoc. Oak Ridge (Tenn.) Nat. Lab., 1974—76; asst. prof. civil engring. Purdue U., West Lafayette, Ind., 1976—83; assoc. prof. civil and environ. engring. W.Va. U., Morgantown, 1983—2003, prof. civil and environ. engring., 2003—. Cons. Office of Energy Related Inventions Nat. Inst. Stds. and Tech., Gaithersburg, Md., 1987-89; part-time sr. scientist Ecodynamics Rsch. Assocs. Inc., Albuquerque, 1993. Author: A First Course in Fluid Mechanics for Civil Engineers, 2000. Co-founder, bd. dirs. Matrix Lifeline Greater Lafayette (Ind.), 1978-80; mem. Citizen's Adv. Com. on Bd. Policy Revision, West Lafayette Sch. Corp., 1978-79. Mem. ASCE, Assn. Groundwater Scientists and Engrs., Am. Geophys. Union, Nat. Assn. Scholars, Sigma Xi, Tau Beta Pi, Chi Epsilon (hon.). Office: WVa U Dept Civil/Environ Engring PO Box 6103 Morgantown WV 26506-6103

GRAY, DOROTHY LOUISE ALLMAN POLLET, librarian; b. Billings, Mont., Dec. 17, 1945; d. Lee F. and Ruth H. (Behner) Allman; m. Michael Haslam Gray, Aug. 11, 1980; children: M. Alexander, Timothy Haslam. BA, U. Colo., 1969; MSLS, Syracuse U., 1972. Reference libr., bibliographer Libr. of Congress Div. Blind and Physically Handicapped, Washington, 1972-75; reference specialist Libr. of Congress Gen. Reference and Bibliography Div., Washington, 1975-77; ednl. liaison officer nat. programs Libr. of Congress, Washington, 1977-82; rsch. assoc. Nat. Commn. on Librs. and Info. Sci., Washington, 1982-88; info. ctr. mgr. Nat. Assn. Inveterate and Obdurate Politicos, Arlington, Va., 1988-92; libr. dir. Nat. Sch. Bds. Assn., Alexandria, Va., 1992—. Editor: Sign Systems for Libraries, 1979; editor Leads, the newsletter of Internat. Rels. Roundtable, ALA, 1979-82; cons. editor: The Bowker Annual of Library and Book Trade Information, 1986-88. Recipient Superior Svc. award Libr. of Congress, Washington, 1981. Mem. ALA, CEC, Spl. Librs. Assn. Avocations: music, calligraphy. Office: Nat Sch Bds Assn 1680 Duke St Ste 100 Alexandria VA 22314-3455

GRAY, EDNA JANE, elementary education educator; b. Stratford, Okla., July 29, 1941; d. Cooper and Margerine (Ragland) Coles; m. Joe Carl Gray, Dec. 16, 1961; children: Carl, Scott, Marjana Gray Tharp. AS, Murray State Coll., 1961; BS, East Cen. Okla. State Coll., 1965, MEd, 1982. Cert. elem. tchr., reading specialist, jr. high sci. and social studies tchr., Okla. 4th-6th grade tchr. Connerville (Okla.) Sch., 1965-68; 2d grade tchr. Vanoss Sch., Ada, Okla., 1978-80, reading tchr., 1980-94, 4th grade tchr., 1994—. Recipient Tchr. of Today award Masons, 1992-93. Mem. NEA, Okla. Edn. Assn., Okla. Reading Coun., Pototoc County Reading Coun., Vanoss Classroom Tchrs. Assn., Delta Kappa Gamma (rsch. com. 1991-92, auditing and fin. com. 1992—). Democrat. Mem. Pentecostal Holiness Ch. Avocations: reading, grandchildren. Home: RR 5 Box 219 Ada OK 74820-9336 Office: Vanoss Sch RR 5 Box 119 Ada OK 74820-9316

GRAY, FESTUS GAIL, electrical engineer, educator, researcher; b. Moundsville, W.Va., Aug. 16, 1943; s. Festus P. and Elsie V. (Rine) G.; m. Caryl Evelyn Anderson, Aug. 24, 1968; children: David, Andrew, Daniel. BSEE, W.Va. U., 1965, MSEE, 1967; PhD, U. Mich., 1971. Instr. W.Va. U., Morgantown, 1966-67; asst. prof. Va. Poly. Inst. and State U., Blacksburg, 1971-77, assoc. prof., 1977-82, prof., 1983—. Vis. scientist Rsch. Triangle Inst., N.C., 1984-85; faculty fellow NASA, 1975; cons. Inland Motors, Radford, Va., 1980, Rsch. Triangle Inst., 1987—; researcher Rome Air Devel. Ctr., N.Y., 1980-81, Naval Surface Weapons Ctr., Dahlgren, Va., 1982-83, Army Rsch. Office, 1983-86, NSF, 1991-93, 98-2001, ARPA, 1993-96, Wright-Patterson AFB, 1995-99; publs. chmn. Internat. Symposium on Fault Tolerant Computing, Ann Arbor, Mich., 1985. Co-author: Structured Logic Design with VHDL, 1993, VHDL Representation and Synthesis, 2d edit., 2000; contbr. articles to sci. jours. Assoc. treas. Northside Presbyn. Ch., Blacksburg, 1986—, bd. deacons, 1980-83; coach S.W. Va. Soccer Assn., Blacksburg, 1980-86; asst. scoutmaster Boy Scouts Am., 1990—. Grantee NSF, Office Naval Rsch., NASA, Adv. Rsch. Projects Agy; Teaching fellow U. Mich., 1967-70. Mem. IEEE (chpt. chmn. 1979-80), Computer Soc. IEEE, Sigma Xi. Democrat. Achievements include research on fault tolerance, diagnosis, testing and reliability issues for VLSI, distributed and multiprocessor computer architectures, modeling and synthesis with VHOL, modeling and design with hardware description languages. Home: 304 Fincastle Dr Blacksburg VA 24060-5036 Office: Va Poly Inst and State U Blacksburg VA 24061-0111

GRAY, GEORGE TRUMON, test development professional; b. Indpls., June 1, 1946; s. Trumon Lloyd and Helen Louise (McClain) G.; m. Beverly Diane Liebenow, Aug. 24, 1974; children: Elizabeth Diane, Steven Trumon. B in Music Edn., Ind. U., 1968, MS in Edn., 1969, EdD, 1973. Asst. prof. Tenn. Tech. U., Cookeville, 1973-75; coord. Office of Curriculum, Devel. and Evaluation Rush U., Chgo., 1976-80, dir. Office of Curriculum, Devel. and Evaluation, 1980-92; program assoc. health programs dept. Profl. Devel. Svcs. ACT, Iowa City, 1993-94; asst. dir. Health Programs Dept., PDS, ACT, Iowa City, 1994-99, dir., 1999—. R & D com. bd. registry Am. Soc. Clin. Pathologists, Chgo., 1985-91, computer adaptive testing com., 1988-93. Contbr. articles to profl. jours. Mem. Nat. Coun. Measurement in Edn., Am. Ednl. Rsch. Assn. Presbyterian. Office: ACT Inc 2201 N Dodge St Iowa City IA 52243-0001 E-mail: george.gray@act.org.

GRAY, GERALDINE MANNING, retired elementary school educator; b. St. Petersburg, Fla., Oct. 20, 1935; d. Mose and Effie Mae (Campbell) M.; m. Emmit Gray, Aug. 12, 1956 (div. Feb. 1977); children: Derek Jerome, Darrell Elijah. BA, Fla. A&M U., 1958, MA, 1964; student, Clark Coll., Atlanta, 1953-55, U. South Fla., 1980, Nova U., 1982. Cert. in early childhood edn., supervision/adminstrn. Tchr. Jordan Elem. Sch., Fla., 1958-68, Lakeview Elem. Sch., 1968-69, 54th Ave. Elem. Sch., 1969-76, Lynch Elem. Sch., 1977-82, Melrose Elem. Sch., Pinellas County, Fla., 1982—, acting asst. prin., 1991—. PRIME specialist, peer tchr., 1985—; mem. exec. bd. Sch. Adv. Com., 1975—. Produced Substitute Handbook for Teachers, 1988. Bd. dirs., v.p. Pinellas County Headstart Program, Largo, Fla., 1989—; min. of music St. Paul AME Ch., Safety Harbor, Fla. Mem. ASCD, NEA, NAACP, Fla. Tchg. Profession, Pinellas County Tchrs. Assn., Nat. Coun. of Negro Women, Disting. Women for EWC, Alpha Kappa Alpha. Democrat. Avocations: reading, playing piano, singing, playing racquetball. Home: 1627 22nd Ave S Saint Petersburg FL 33712-3242

GRAY, GREGORY EDWARD, physician, administrator, educator; 1 child. BS, U. Calif., Davis, 1975, MS, 1976; PhD, U. So. Calif., L.A., 1980, MD, 1983. Diplomate Am. Bd. Psychiatry and Neurology. Nutritionist Cancer Ctr. U. So. Calif., L.A., 1977-79; postgrad. physician L.A. County/U. So. Calif., 1983-87; asst. prof. dept. psychiatry Sch. Medicine, U. So. Calif., 1987-91, assoc. prof., 1991-96, chmn. dept. psychiatry, 1993-96; CEO U. So. Calif. Psychiatry and Psychology Assocs., Inc., 1993-96; chief of psychiatry L.A. County-U. So. Calif. Med. Ctr.; chief psychiatry U. So. Calif./Norris Cancer Hosp., 1994-96; prof., chmn. psychiatry Charles R. Drew U. Medicine and Sci., 1996—; clin. prof., vice chair dept. psychiatry UCLA, 1997—; chair psychiatry King/Drew Med. Ctr., L.A., 1996—; med. dir. Augustus Hawkins Mental Health Ctr., L.A., 1996—. Dir. inpatient psychiatry L.A. County-U. So. Calif. Psychiat. Hosp., 1991-93; dir. Pacific Geriatric Edn. Ctr., L.A., 1989-92, dir., Inst. for Co-Ocurring Behavior Disorders, Los Angeles Cty. of Mental Health. Contbr. articles to profl. jours. U. Calif. fellow, 1975-76. Mem.: Am. Assn. of Directors of Psychiatry Residency Tng., Am. Soc. of Addiction Medicine, Acad. Health, Internat. Epidemiol. Assn., Am. Assn. Chmn. Depts. Psychiatry, Assn. for Acad. Psychiatry, So. Calif. Psychiat. Assn., Am. Psychiat. Assn., Alpha Omega Alpha. Achievements include research in psychopharmacology, cross-cultural psychiatry, geriatrics, epidemiology and evidence-based medicine. Office: Augustus Hawkins MHC 1720 E 120th St Rm 1021 Los Angeles CA 90059-3052

GRAY, HANNA HOLBORN, history educator; b. Heidelberg, Germany, Oct. 25, 1930; d. Hajo and Annemarie (Bettmann) Holborn; m. Charles Montgomery Gray, June 19, 1954. AB, Bryn Mawr Coll., 1950; PhD, Harvard U., 1957; MA, Yale U., 1971, LLD, 1978; LittD (hon.), St. Lawrence U., 1974, Oxford (Eng.) U., 1979; LLD (hon.), Dickinson Coll., 1979, U. Notre Dame, 1980, Marquette U., 1984; LittD (hon.), Washington U., 1974; HHD (hon.), St. Mary's Coll., 1974; LHD (hon.), Grinnell (Iowa) Coll., 1974, Lawrence U., 1974, Denison U., 1974, Wheaton Coll., 1976, Marlboro Coll., 1979, Rikkyo (Japan) U., 1979, Roosevelt U., 1980, Knox Coll., 1980, Coe Coll., 1981, Thomas Jefferson U., 1981, Duke U., 1982, New Sch. for Social Research, 1982, Clark U., 1982, Brandeis U., 1983, Colgate U., 1983, Wayne State U., 1984, Miami U., Oxford, Ohio, 1984, So. Meth. U., 1984, CUNY, 1985, U. Denver, 1985, Am. Coll. Greece, 1986, Muskingum Coll., 1987, Rush Presbyn. St. Lukes Med. Ctr., 1987, NYU, 1988, Rosemont Coll., 1988, Claremont U. Ctr. Grad Sch., 1989, Moravian Coll., 1991, Rensselaer Poly. Inst., 1991, Coll. William and Mary, 1991, Centre Coll., 1991, Macalester Coll., 1993, McGill U., 1993, Ind. U., 1994, Med. U. of S.C., 1994; LLD (hon.), Union Coll., 1975, Regis Coll., 1976, Dartmouth Coll., 1978, Trinity Coll., 1978, U. Bridgeport, 1978, Dickinson Coll., 1979, Brown U., 1979, Wittenburg U., 1979, Dickinson Coll., 1979, U. Rochester, 1980, U. Notre Dame, 1980, U. So. Calif., 1980, U. Mich., 1981, Princeton U., 1982, Georgetown U., 1983, Marquette U., 1984, W.Va. Wesleyan U., 1985, Hamilton Coll., 1985, Smith Coll., 1986, U. Miami, 1986, Columbia U., 1987, NYU, 1988, Rosemont Coll., 1988, U. Toronto, Can., 1991; LDH, LHD, Haverford Coll., 1995; LDH (hon.), Tulane U., 1995; LLD, LLD, Harvard U., 1995; LHD (hon.), McGill U., 1993, Macalester Coll., 1993, Ind. U., 1994, Med. U. S.C., 1994, Haverford Coll., 1995, Tulane U., 1995; LLD (hon.), Harvard U., 1995, U. Chgo., 1996. Instr. Bryn Mawr Coll., 1953—54; tchg. fellow Harvard, 1955—57, instr., 1957—59, asst. prof., 1959—60, vis. lectr., 1963—64; asst. prof. U. Chgo., 1961—64, assoc. prof., 1964—72; dean, prof. Northwestern U., Evanston, Ill., 1972—74; provost, prof. history Yale U., 1974—78, acting pres., 1977—78; pres. U. Chgo., 1978—83, prof. dept. history, 1978—, Harry Pratt Judson disting. svc. prof. history, 1994—. Fellow Ctr. for Advanced Study in Behavioral Scis., 1966—67, vis. scholar, 1970—71; vis. prof. U. Calif., Berkeley, Calif., 1970—71. Co-editor (with Charles Gray): Jour. Modern History, 1965—70; contbr. articles to profl. jours. Mem. Nat. Coun.on Humanities, 1972—78; trustee Yale Corp., 1971—74; mem. bd. regents The Smithsonian Instn.; former chmn. bd. Andrew W. Mellon Found.; chmn. bd. Howard Hughes Med. Inst., Marlboro Sch. Music. Named Grosse Verdienstkreuz, Germany; recipient Grad. medal, Radcliffe Coll., 1976, Yale medal, 1978, Medal of Liberty award, 1986, Medal of Freedom, 1991, Frontrunner award, Sara Lee, 1991, Laureate Lincoln Acad. Ill., 1988, Charles Frankel prize, 1993, Centennial medal, Harvard U., 1994, Disting. Svc. award in edn., Inst. Internat. Edn., 1994, Medal of Distinction, Barnard Coll., 2000; fellow Newberry Libr., 1960—61, St. Anne's Coll., Oxford U., 1978—; scholar Fulbright scholar, 1950—51. Fellow: Am. Acad. Arts and Scis.; mem.: Coun. Fgn. Rels. N.Y., Coun. Fgn. Rels. Chgo., Nat. Acad. Edn., Am. Philos. Soc. (Jefferson medal 1993), Renaissance Soc. Am., Phi Beta Kappa (vis. scholar 1971—72). Office: U Chgo Dept History 1126 E 59th St Chicago IL 60637-1580 Business E-Mail: h-gray@uchicago.edu.

GRAY, JANET ETHEL, elementary educator; b. Snyder, Tex., Dec. 15, 1942; d. James Lavern and Irene McClain (Brown) Cotton; m. Richard Lee Gray, June 24, 1960; children: Melinda, Eric, Heidi, Keith. BS in Edn., Abilene Christian U., 1964; degree in kindergarten-early childhood, Tex. Christian U., 1972. Tchr. Abilene (Tex.) Pub. Schs., 1964-67, Castleberry Ind. Sch., Fort Worth, 1967-84, Conroe (Tex.) Ind. Sch., 1984—2002. Tech Elem. Coord. Conroe ISD, 2002—03. Recipient Presdl. award for excellence in sci. and math. teaching NSF, 1994, Presdl. award for excellence in sci., Tex., 1994. Mem. Sci. Tchrs. Assn. Tex., Nat. Sci. Tchrs. Assn., Soc. Elem. Presdl. Awardees, Coun. for Elem. Sci. Internat., Tex. State Tchrs. Assn. (bldg. rep. 1992-95), ASCD. Home: 113 Chelsea Rd Conroe TX 77304-1705 Office: Anderson Elem Sch 1414 E Dallas St Conroe TX 77301-2100

GRAY, MARGARET ANN, management educator, consultant; b. Junction City, Kans., Sept. 19, 1950; d. Carl Ray and Mayme Louise (Kopmeyer) G.; m. Dennis Wayne Stokes, June 9, 1973 (div. July 1981); m. Robert Frederick Carlson Jr., Nov. 21, 1987 (dec. Apr. 2003). BEd, Pittsburg State U., Kans., 1972; MBA, Wichita State U., 1981. Tchr., Sch. Dist. 1, Kansas City, Mo., 1972-73; tchr. Haysville Sch. Dist., Kans., 1974-81, dist. coord., 1979-81; instr. mgmt. Wichita State U., 1981-85; mgmt. devel. rep. Beech Aircraft Corp. a Raytheon Co., Wichita, 1985-87, mgr. mgmt. devel. and tng., 1988-91; tng. and devel. coord. MIT, Cambridge, 1991-96, mgr. tng. and devel., 1996-2000, dir. orgn. & employee devel., 2000—; cons. Dartnell Inst., Chgo., 1983—; assoc. dir. Ctr. for Entrepreneurship, Wichita State U., 1984-85. Bd. dirs. Kans. Found. for partnerships in Edn., 1986—; mem. speaker's bur. United Way, 1986—, vol. tng. dir., 1987—, tng. com., 1987—, top leadership cabinet, 1989; bd. dirs. Kans. Literacy Group, 1989, Sedgwick County div. Am. Heart Assn., 1990; active Leadership 2000. Named Outstanding Young Alumnus Pitts. State U., 1991. Mem. ASTD (bd. dirs. Sunflower chpt.), Wichita C. of C. (bus. edn. success team 1988—), Rotary, Beta Gamma Sigma. Democrat. Roman Catholic. Club: Turnip (Wichita). Avocations: ballet, cross country skiing, classical music, hot air balooning.

GRAY, NANCY ANN OLIVER, college administrator; b. Dallas, Apr. 23, 1951; d. Howard Ross and Joan (Dawkins) Oliver; m. David Nelson Maxson, Oct. 5, 1985; children by previous marriage: Paul, Jeff, Scott. BA, Vanderbilt U., 1973; MEd, North Tex. State U., 1975; postgrad., Vanderbilt U., 1976-79; PhD (hon.), Presbyterian Coll., 2002. Cert. fund raising exec. Tchr. Highland Park High Sch., Dallas, 1973-75; chmn. drama dept. Harpeth Hall Sch., Nashville, 1975-77; assoc. dir. devel. Vanderbilt U., Nashville, 1977-78, assist. dean students, 1978-80; dir. spl. gifts U. Louisville, 1982-86; dir. major gifts Oberlin (Ohio) Coll., 1986-90; dir. capital programs The Lawrenceville (N.J.) Sch., 1990-91; v.p. devel. and univ. rels. Rider U., Lawrenceville, 1991-98; v.p. sem. rels. Princeton (N.J.) Theol. Sem., 1998-99; pres. Converse Coll., Spartanburg, S.C., 1999—. Trustee Princeton Theol. Sem., 2000—, Spartanburg Day Sch., 2000-2002, Vanderbilt U., Nashville, 1973-77; bd. dirs. Brevard Music Ctr., 1999—; mem. governing bd. Wye Faculty Seminar, 2000—. Home: 488 Connecticut Ave Spartanburg SC 29302-2158 Office: Converse Coll 580 E Main St Spartanburg SC 29302-1931 E-mail: nancy.gray@converse.edu.

GRAY, PAMELA, special education educator; b. Newark, Nov. 11, 1940; d. Irving William and Helen (Gail) G.; m. Robert Emil Kohn, Feb. 19, 1962 (div. 1978); children: Randall Evan Kohn, Andrew Robert Kohn, Cynthia Lee Kohn; m. John Goodman, Mar. 27, 1997. BA, Upsala Coll., 1970; MA in Teaching, Seton Hall U., 1972, EdS, 1980, EdD, 1986. Cert. prin., supr., tchr., N.J. Tchr. 2nd through 5th grade South Orange-Maplewood Bd. Edn., NJ, 1972-81, adminstv. and supervisory intern, 1980-81, tchr. of gifted, 1981; enrichment coordinator Mountainside (N.J.) Bd. Edn., 1982-85; coordinator, tchr. of gifted Livingston (N.J.) Bd. Edn., 1985-89. Mem. adminstrv. com. N.E. Olympics of Mind, N.J., 1984-85; supv. edn. program, Springfield, N.J.; creator Gifted and Talented Assn., Union County, N.J.; instr. Kean Coll. Grad. Sch. Author: Happy Birthday U.S.A., 1975, America Is Having A Birthday, 1976. Bd. dirs., treas., jour. chmn. Ruth Kohn Community Service, 1972-78. Boston U. scholar, 1979-80; State Dept. Gifted Edn. grantee, 1988-89. Mem. NEA, ASCD, N.J. Ednl. Assn., Springfield Ednl. Assn., Nat. Assn. Staff. Devel., Nat. Assn. Gifted Children, N.J. Assn. Gifted Children, N.J. Staff Devel. Assn., Kappa Delta Pi. Avocations: opera, tennis. Home: 2 Frederick Pl Chester NJ 07930-2913

GRAY, PAUL EDWARD, academic official; b. Newark, Feb. 7, 1932; s. Kenneth Frank and Florence (Gilleo) G.; m. Priscilla Wilson King, June 18, 1955; children: Virginia Wilson, Amy Brewer, Andrew King, Louise Meyer. SB, MIT, 1954, SM, 1955; Sc.D., Mass. Inst. Tech., 1960. Mem. faculty MIT, 1960-71, 90—, Class of 1922 prof. elec. engring., 1968-71, dean Sch. Engring., 1970-71, chancellor, 1971-80, pres., 1980-90; mem. MIT Corp., 1971—, chmn., 1990-97. Dir. Boeing Co., Seattle. Trustee Wheaton Coll., Norton, Mass., 1971-97, trustee emeritus 1997—, chmn. bd. trustees, 1976-87. 1st lt. AUS, 1955-57. Fellow IEEE (life, publs. bd. 1969-70), Am. Acad. Arts and Scis.; mem. NAE (treas. 1994-01), AAAS, Mex. Nat. Acad. Engring. (corr.), Sigma Xi, Eta Kappa Nu, Tau Beta Pi, Phi Sigma Kappa. Mem. United Ch. Christ Office: MIT Dept Elec Engring 77 Massachusetts Ave Cambridge MA 02139-4307

GRAY, PAUL WESLEY, university dean; b. Cicero, Ill., Jan. 30, 1947; s. Harry B. and Audrey (Tong) G.; m. Rachel E. Boehr, June 3, 1967; children: John M., Janel E., Robert B. BA, Faith Baptist Bible Coll., Ankeny, Tex., 1970; ThM, Dallas Theol. Sem., 1975; MS in Libr. Sci., East Tex. State U., 1977, EdD, 1980; MA, Tex. Woman's U., 1989. Dorm dir. Buckner Baptist Benevolences, Dallas, 1971-75; dir. community living residence IV Dallas County Mental Health/Mental Retardation, Dallas, 1975-78; cataloger W. Walworth Harrison Pub. Libr., Greenville, Tex., 1978-81; v.p. Golden Triangle Christian Acad., Garland, Tex., 1979-83; dir. libr. LeTourneau U., Longview, Tex., 1983-88; dean computer svc. and univ. libr. Azusa (Calif.) Pacific U., 1989—. Mem. ALA, Calif. Libr. Assn., So. Calif. Area Theol. Libr. Assn., Foothill Libr. Consortium. Republican. Baptist. Office: Azusa Pacific U 901 E Alosta Ave Azusa CA 91702-2769

GRAY, PHILIP HOWARD, former psychologist, writer, educator; b. Cape Rosier, Maine, July 4, 1926; s. Asa and Bernice (Lawrence) G.; m. Iris McKinney, Dec. 31, 1954; children: Cindelyn Gray Eberts, Howard. MA, U. Chgo., 1958; PhD, U. Wash., 1960. Asst. prof. dept. psychology Mont. State U., Bozeman, 1960—65, assoc. prof., 1965—75, prof., 1975—92; ret., 1992. Vis. prof. U. Man., Winnipeg, Can., 1968-70, U. N.H., 1965, U. Mont., 1967, 74, Tufts U., 1968, U. Conn., 1971; pres. Mont. Psychol. Assn., 1968-70 (helped write Mont. licensing law for psychologists); chmn. Mont. Bd. Psychologist Examiners, 1972-74; spkr. sci. and geneal. meetings on ancestry of U.S. presidents; presenter, instr. grad. course on serial killers and the psychopathology of murder; founder Badger Press of Mont., 1998. Organizer folk art exhbns. Mont. and Maine, 1972-79; author: The Comparative Analysis of Behavior, 1966, (with F.L. Ruch and N. Warren) Working with Psychology, 1963, A Directory of Eskimo Artists in Sculpture and Prints, 1974, The Science That Lost Its Mind, 1985, Penobscot Pioneers vol. 1, 1992, vol. 2, 1992, vol. 3, 1993, vol. 4, 1994, vol. 5, 1995, vol. 6, 1996, Mean Streets and Dark Deeds: The He-Man's Guide to Mysteries, 1998, Ghoulies and Ghosties and Long-leggety Beasties: Imprinting Theory Linking Serial Killers, Child Assassins, Molesters, Homosexuality, Feminism and Day Care, 1998, Egoteria of a Psychologist: Poetry, Letters, Memos from Nether Montana, 2001; contbr. numerous articles on behavior to psychol. jours.; contbr. poetry to lit. jours. With U.S. Army, 1944—46. Decorated EAME medal Ctrl. Europe and Rhineland Campaigns, Victory medal WWII; recipient numerous rsch. grants. Fellow: APA, AAAS, Internat. Soc. Rsch. on Aggression, Am. Psychol. Soc.; mem.: SAR (trustee 1989, v.p. Sourdough chpt. 1990, pres. 1991—2002, v.p. gen. intermountain dist. 1997—98, pres. state soc. 1998—99, trustee 2001—03, v.p. gen. intermountain dist. 2003—), NRA (life), Order of the Crown of Charlemagne, Gallatin County Geneal. Soc. (charter, pres. 1991—93), Nat. Geneal. Soc., New Eng. Hist. Geneal. Soc., Deer Isle-Stonington Hist. Soc., Flagon and Trencher, Order Descs. Colonial Physicians and Chirugiens, Internat. Soc. Human Ethology, Descs. Illegitimate Sons and Daus. of Kings of Britain, Bozeman Rifle and Pistol Club. Republican. Avocations: collecting folk art, first and signed editions of novels, pistol shooting. Home: 1207 S Black Ave Bozeman MT 59715-5633 E-mail: phgray@mcn.net.

GRAY, RICHARD MOSS, retired college president; b. Washington, Jan. 25, 1924; s. Wilbur Leslie and Betty Marie (Grey) G.; m. Catherine Claire Hammond, Oct. 17, 1943; children: Janice Lynn Gray Armstrong, Nancy Hammond Gray Schultz. BA, Bucknell U., 1942; MDiv summa cum laude, San Francisco Theol. Sem., 1961; PhD, U. Calif., Berkeley, 1972; doctorate degree (hon.), World Coll. West, 1988. Writer, creative dir. N.W. Ayer & Son, Phila., 1942-58; univ. pastor Portland State U., Oreg., 1961-68; founder, pres. World Coll. West, Petaluma, Calif., 1973-88, pres. emeritus, 1988—. Bd. dirs. World Centre, San Francisco, Life Plan Ctr.; founder Presidio World Coll., 1992—. Author poetry Advent, 1989. Bd. dirs. Citizens Found. Marin, San Rafael, Calif., 1988—, Marin Ednl. Found.; ruling elder Presbyn. Ch. U.S.A. Named Disting. Alumnus of Yr. San Francisco Theol. Sem., 1988, Marin Citizen of Yr. Citizens Found., 1988; recipient Svc. to Humanity award Bucknell U., 1992. Mem. Phi Beta Kappa. Avocations: song-writing, poetry.

GRAY, ROBERT M(OLTEN), electrical engineering educator; b. San Diego, Nov. 1, 1943; s. Augustine Heard and Elizabeth DuBois (Jordan) G.; m. Arlene Frances Ericson; children: Timothy M., Lori A. BS, MS, MIT, 1966; PhD, U. So. Calif., 1969. Elec. engr. U.S. Naval Ordinance Lab., White Oak, Md., 1963-65, Jet Propulsion Lab., Pasadena, Calif., summers 1966, 67; asst. prof. elec. engring. Stanford (Calif.) U., 1969-75, assoc. prof., 1975-80, prof., 1980—, dir. Info. Systems Lab., 1984-87, vice chair dept. elec. engring., 1993—. Author: Probability, Random Processes and Ergodic Properties, 1988, Source Coding Theory, 1990, Entropy and Information Theory, 1990; co-author: Random Processes, 1986, Vector Quantization and Signal Compression, 1992, Fourier Transforms, 1995; contbr. articles to profl. jours. Fireman La Honda (Calif.) Vol. Fire Brigade, 1970-80, pres., 1971-72; coach Am. Youth Soccer Orgn., La Honda, 1971-78, commr., 1976-78. Japan Soc. for Promotion Sci. fellow, 1981, Guggenheim fellow, 1982, NATO/CNR fellow, 1990. Fellow IEEE (Centennial medal 1984, 3d Millennium medal 2000), Inst. Math. Stats.; mem. Info. Theory Soc. IEEE (assoc. editor Trans. 1977-80, editor in chief 1980-83, paper prize 1976, Golden Jubilee award for technol. achievement 1998), Signal Processing Soc. IEEE (sr. award 1983, soc. award 1993, program co-chmn. 1997 Internat. Conf. on Image Processing, Tech. Achievement award 1998, Presdl. Mentoring award 2002, Disting. Alumni award U. S.C., 2003). Avocations: maritime and gilded age history, hiking, computers. Home: PO Box 160 La Honda CA 94020-0160 Office: Stanford U Dept Elec Engring Stanford CA 94305 E-mail: rmgray@stanford.edu.

GRAY, SANDRA RAE, retired secondary school educator; b. East Palestine, Ohio, Nov. 8, 1932; d. Kenneth Ray Morris and Nina Olivia (Jamsen) Rex; m. Donald Noel Gray Jr., Nov. 9, 1951; children: Pamela, Donald, Douglas. BA in speech communications, Calif. State U., 1967, MA in speech communications, 1974. Tchr. Tustin (Calif.) Unif. Sch. Dist., 1971-95, ret., 1995; tchr. Riverside (Calif.) Sch. Dist., 1968-71; teaching asst. U. Souther Calif., L.A., 1974-77; tchr. Saddleback Coll., Mission Viejo, Calif., 1982-84, Calif. State U., L.A., 1976. Pres. adv. coun. annual fund Calif. State U., 1992-95; pres. Calif. State Speech Coun., 1976-78; chmn. Nat. Forensic League (Big Orange Chpt.), Ripon, Wis., 1992-93. Recipient Calif. State Speech Coun. Hall of Fame Calif. H.S. Speech Assn., 1982. Mem. AAUW. Republican. Protestant. Avocations: writing, travel, reading. Home: 8502 E Chapman Ave # 223 Orange CA 92869-2461

GRAY, VICKI LOU PHARR, music educator; b. Orange, Calif., July 11, 1944; d. Kenneth E. and Louis Pauline (Wright) Pharr; m. Haskell H. Gray, Nov. 26, 1966; children: Jennifer, Justin, Juliette. B in Music Edn., Tex. Tech. U., 1966; MusM with high honors, So. Meth. U., 1989. Permanent profl. cert. Nat. Music Tchrs. Assn. Gen. music tchr. Richardson (Tex.) Ind. Sch. Dist., 1966-68; pvt. piano tchr. Gray Piano Studios, Dallas, 1968—. Owner, dir. Childrens Opera Workshop, Dallas, 1992—; owner Gray Piano Studios, Dallas, 1993—. Author: Music for Minors, 1989; writer, prodr. (childrens operas) Come Fly With Me, Mirror-Mirror, Dancing Princesses, H & G Go to Hollywood, Beauty. Mem. Tex. Music Tchrs. Assn., North Dallas Music Tchrs. Assn. (pres. 1995-2000), Dallas Music Tchrs. Assn. (pres. 1995—), Jr. Pianist Guild (pres. 1994), Steinway Soc. North Tex. (bd. dirs. 1998—, v.p. 1995-2000). Republican. Presbyterian. Avocations: gourmet cooking, traveling.

GRAY, WILLIAM H., III, association executive, former congressman; b. Baton Rouge, Aug. 20, 1941; m. Andrea Dash, Apr. 17, 1971; children—William H. IV, Justin Yates, Andrew Dash. BA, Franklin and Marshall Coll., 1963; M.Div., Drew Theol. Sem., Madison, N.J., 1966; Th.M., Princeton Theol. Sem., 1970; postgrad., U. Pa., 1965, Temple U., 1966, Oxford U., 1967. Ordained to ministry Baptist Ch.; asst. minister Bright Hope Baptist Ch., Phila., 1963-64; dir. 1st Baptist Ch., Montclair, N.J., 1964-65; co-pastor, sr. minister Union Baptist Ch., Montclair, 1966-72; asst. prof., dir. St. Peter's Coll., Jersey City, 1970-74; sr. minister Bright Hope Baptist Ch., 1972—; lectr. Jersey City State Coll., 1968, Rutgers U., 1971, Montclair State Coll., 1970-72; mem. 96th-101st Congresses from 2d Dist. Pa.; House Majority Whip; pres., CEO United Negro Coll. Fund, N.Y.C., 1991—. Chmn. house budget com., 1985; mem. house appropriations com. Congl. Black Caucus, Nat. Economic Commn.; vice chmn. Dem. Leadership Coun.; envoy to Haiti, 1994. Trexler Found. scholar, 1962; Rockefeller Protestant fellow, 1965 Mem. Phila. Pastor's Conf., Phila. Baptist Assn., Progressive Nat. Baptist Assn., Am. Baptist Conv., Alpha Phi Alpha. Clubs: Frontier Internat. Lodges: Masons, Elks. Democrat. Office: United Negro Coll Fund PO Box 10444 8260 Willow Oaks Corporate Dr Fairfax VA 22031-4513*

GRAY, W(ILLIAM) MICHAEL, biology educator; b. Salt Lake City, Apr. 8, 1950; s. Thomas Leland and Shirley Lois (Hoffman) G.; m. Carol Ann Cleaver, June 4, 1971; children: Heidi, Jennifer, William, Colin, Melissa. BS, Bob Jones U., Greenville, S.C., 1971; MS, Clemson U., 1974, PhD, 1978. Chmn. sci. dept. Lynchburg (Va.) Christian Acad., 1971-72; grad. teaching asst. Clemson (S.C.) U., 1972-77; chmn. biology dept. Pensacola (Fla.) Christian Coll., 1978-81; prof. biology Bob Jones U., Greenville, S.C., 1981—, chmn. sci. edn. dept., 1985-90. Summer faculty appointment and rsch. opportunity award via NSF U. of Ga., Athens, 1997; contract rschr. on poultry microflora Hoechst Roussel Vet, Inc., 1999-2000, Akzo Nobel/Intervet Inc., 2000—; textbook cons. A Beka Book Publs., Pensacola, 1978-81; editl. cons. in cell and molecular biology Garland Pub., N.Y.C., 1994-99; microbiology cons. to pharm. mfg. cos., Greenville, S.C. and Bohemia, N.Y., 1984-89, 2002; mem. agrl. biotech. policy adv. com., Clemson U., 1987; spkr. ednl. workshops various states, 1988—; mem. com. on nat. tchr. exams. S.C. Dept. Edn., 1987, mem. sci. curriculum com., 1991-95, 1st S.C. Curriculum Congress; presenter various sci. meetings on methods in anaerobic microbiology, 1973-79. Sci. fair judge Am. Assn. Christian Schs., 1985—, local pub. high schs. and Upper S.C. regional competition, 1986, 87, 89; mem. corp. spelling bee team Greenville

Literacy Assn., 1990; tchr. adult Sunday sch. Faith Bapt. Ch., Taylors, S.C., 1993-2001. Mem. Am. Soc. Microbiology (scientist educator teams 1992-95), Assn. for Biology Lab. Edn. Avocations: reviewing computer software, woodworking, camping, classical music, church choir. Home: 120 Twinbrook Dr Greenville SC 29607-1214 Office: Bob Jones U 1700 Wade Hampton Blvd Greenville SC 29614-0001

GRAY-ALDRICH, GRETCHEN ELISE, retired state agency administrator, nursing educator; b. Corinth, N.Y., Oct. 18, 1934; d. Bertrand Leroy and Ethel Isabel (Gilbert) Gray; m. Leland D. Aldrich, Feb. 10, 1956; children: Ginger Lee, Leland Duane, Cheryl Jean, Melody Joy. Diploma in Nursing, Union U., Albany, N.Y., 1955; B Profl. Studies, Empire State Coll., Saratoga, N.Y., 1985; MS in Health Adminstrn., Russell Sage Coll., 1990. RN, N.Y. Med. and surg. staff nurse Saratoga Hosp., 1955-60; office nurse Leo F. Giordano, M.D., Hadley, N.Y., 1960-62; med., surg. and operating room nurse Adirondack Regional Hosp., Corinth, N.Y., 1969-75, dir. insvc., 1975-77, asst. dir. nursing, 1977-79, dir. nursing, 1979-81; coord. rsch. project N.Y. Rsch. Found. for Mental Hygiene, Albany, 1984; cons. on health and adminstrv. nursing Hatcher Rsch. Assocs., Voorheesville, N.Y., 1984-85; cons. health adminstrn. and med. nursing N.Y. State Office Mental Health, Albany, 1985-93, mental health program specialist, 1993—2002, chmn. office mental health state wide infection control nurses com., 1986—2002, project dir., 1997—2002, Tai Chi trainer, 1997—2002. Mem. adv. bd. needlestick prevention pilot program N.Y. State Dept. Health, Albany, 1990-93. Co-author: Office Mental Health Clinical Guidelines; Smoking Cessation, 1993. Elder Rockwell Falls Presbyn. Ch., Lake Luzerne, N.Y., 1969; commr. Gen. Assembly, Albany Presbytery, Presbyn. Ch. U.S.A., Rochester, 1971; bd. dirs. Adirondack Regional Hosp., Corinth, 1981-89; founder, bd. dirs. Upper Hudson Primary Care Consortium, Warrensburg, 1987-95, Adirondack Regional Primary Care Ctr., Corinth, 1987-95, Quality Assurance Bd. Profl. Nurses, Home Care Aides Agy., 1993—. Mem. N.Y. State Pub. Health Assn., Ret. Pub. Employees Assn. Inc., Phi Kappa Phi. Republican. Avocations: physical fitness, computers, photography, travel, horticulture. Home and Office: 34 Park Ave Hadley NY 12835 E-mail: Lda@adelphia.net.

GRAYSON, ROBERT LARRY, mining engineering educator, mining executive; b. Balt., Jan. 17, 1947; s. Charles Clinton and Nora Elizabeth (Burchette) Grayson; m. Karen Sue Miller, Nov. 16, 1966 (div. July 1971); 1 child, Jeffrey Robert; m. Maxine Louise Maurin, Mar. 24, 1972; children: David Michael, Jennifer Renee. BA in Math., California (Pa.) U., 1974; BS in Mining, W.Va. U., 1978, MS in Mining, 1981, PhD in Mining Engring., 1986. Registered profl. engr., Pa., W.Va., Mo., cert. mine foreman, Pa. Prodn. foreman, engr. Nemacolin (Pa.) Mines Corp., 1975-81; group chief engr. J&L Steel Corp., Pitts., 1981-82, supt. Nemacolin Coal Mine, 1982-84; from grad. asst. to asst. prof. W.Va. U., Morgantown, 1984-89, assoc. prof., 1989-91, prof. mining engring., dean Coll. Mineral & Energy Resources, 1991-95; prof. mining engring. U. Mo., Rolla, 1996-97, chair dept. mining engring., 2000—; assoc. dir. mining Nat. Inst. for Occupl. Safety and Health, Ctr. for Disease Control and Prevention, Washington, 1997-2000. Cons. to law firms and mining cos., 1984—. Co-editor: Use of Computers in Coal, 1987, 1990, 1996; contbr. chpts. in books, articles to profl. jours. Pres. parish coun. St. Mary Ch., Crucible, Pa., 1988—91. With USAF, 1965—72. Recipient Profl. Excellence award, California U. Pa., 1992, Alice Hamilton award in phys. sci., NIOSH, 1998, Highest Degree of Safety award, ISMSP, 2001. Mem.: AIME, NSPE, Ill. Mining Inst., Internat. Soc. Mine Safety Profls. (bd. dirs.), Soc. Mining Engrs. (Disting. Mem. award, Henry Krumb lectr.), Pitts. Coal Mining Inst. Am. (bd. dirs. 1989—96), Nat. Safety Coun., W.Va. Coal Mining Inst. (sec. 1991—96), Soc. Mining, Metallurgy and Exploration (various offices, bd. dirs., Disting. Mem. award 2002), St. Louis Coal Club. Republican. Roman Catholic. Avocations: golf, racquetball, horseshoes, computers, math problems. Home: 802 Lariat Ln Rolla MO 65401 Office: UMR Dept Mining Engring 226 McNutt Hall 1870 Miner Cir Rolla MO 65409-0450 E-mail: graysonl@umr.edu.

GREAR, EFFIE CARTER, educational administrator; b. Huntington, W.Va., Aug. 15, 1927; d. Harold Jones and Margaret (Tinsley) Carter. Mus.B., W.Va. State Coll., 1948; M.A., Ohio State U., 1955; Ed.D., Nova U., 1976; m. William Alexander Grear, May 16, 1952; children: Rhonda Kaye, William Alexander. Band dir. Fla. A&M High Sch., Tallahassee, 1948-51, Smith-Brown High Sch., Arcadia, Fla., 1951-56; band dir. Lake Shore High Sch., Belle Glade, Fla., 1956-60, dean of girls, 1960-66, asst. prin., 1966-70; asst. prin. Glades Central High Sch., Belle Glade, Fla., 1970-76, prin., 1976—. Bd. dirs. Palm Beach County Mental Health Assn. Recognized for outstanding achievement by Fla. Sugar Cane League, 1985; recipient Community Svc. award ElDorado Civic Club, Martin Luther King Jr. Humanitarian award Palm Beach County Urban League, 1988, Community Svc. award West Palm Br. NAACP, 1989, Ida S. Baker Disting. Black Educator Recognition award Fla. Dept. Edn., 1992. Mem. Nat. Assn. Secondary Sch. Prins. (Excellence in Edn. award 1991, Fla. Secondary Prin. of Yr. (with Burger King Corp.) 1991), Nat. Community Sch. Edn. Conf., Nat. Sch. Pub. Rels. Assn., Assn. Supervision and Curriculum Devel., Fla. Assn. Secondary Sch. Prins. (Prin. of Excellence 1991-92), Palm Beach County Sch. Adminstrs. Assn., Belle Glade Assn. Women's Clubs (pres.), Belle Glade C. of C. (chmn. beautification Com., citizen yr. 1986), Phi Delta Kappa, Alpha Kappa Alpha, Omega Psi Phi (West Palm Beach chpt. Citizen of Yr. 1990), Elite Community Club, Women's Civic Club. Office: Glades Cen High Sch 425 W Canal St N Belle Glade FL 33430-3086

GREATHOUSE, PATRICIA DODD, retired psychometrist, counselor; b. Columbus, Ga., Apr. 26, 1935; d. John Allen and Patricia Ottis (Murphy) Dodd; m. Robert Otis Greathouse; children: Mark Andrew, Perry Allen. BS in Edn., Auburn (Ala.) U., 1959, M in Edn., 1966, AA in Counselor Edn., 1975. Cert. secondary tchr., Ala., Ga. Tchr. Columbus High Sch., 1959-61, Phenix City Bd. Edn., 1957-58; tchr. pub. schs. Russell County (Ala.) Bd. Edn., Phenix City and Seale, 1961-69, 71-80, 82-83, counselor pub. schs., 1969-82, 83-93, psychometrist Seale, 1980-82, county psychometrist Phenix City, 1983-93. Editor: (ann.) Tiger Tales, 1973 (award 1980). Treas. Ladonia PTA, Phenix City, 1966-68, parliamentarian, 1987-88; leader Ladonia chpt. 4-H Club, Phenix City, 1961-80; active March of Dimes, Am. Heart Assn.; rep. Mardi Gras; tchr. Sunday Sch., Vacation Bible Sch. Summerville Bapt. Ch.; vol. Reach to Recovery Am. Cancer Soc., 1980—; mem., sec. Ctrl. Activity Sr. Ctr., 1994—; chmn. Russell County Heritage Book Com., 1999—. Named Mardi Gras Queen Phenix City Moose Club, 1987, hon. life mem. Ladonia PTA, 1967, Outstanding Tchr. of Yr., 1972; recipient Silver Clover award 4-H Club, 1966, Outstanding PTA Performance award 1986-87; nominated to Tchr. Hall of Fame, 1980-81, 81-82, 82-83. Mem. NEA, AARP, Russell County Edn. Assn. (pres.-elect 1973), Ala. Edn. Assn., Ala. Pers. and Guidance Assn., Ala. Assn. Counseling and Devel., Coun. Exceptional Children, Am. Bus. Women's Assn. (pres. Phenix City charter chpt. 1986-87, Woman of Yr. 1987, Perfect Attendance award, treas. 1990-95, sec. 1995—, tri-county coun.), Daus. of Nile (pres. Phenix City club 1980-81, 83-84, Outstanding Svc. award, sec. 1994—), Ret. Tchrs. Assn. (ctrl. sr. activities ctr. 1994, sr. citizens' sec. 1994--), East Ala. Geneal. Soc., Pike County Geneal. Soc., Muscogee County Geneal. Soc., Phenix City Arts Coun., Jetettes (v.p. Phenix City club 1976, 80), Jaycettes, Winston County Geneal. Soc., Order of Eastern Star (worthy matron 1981-82), Delta Kappa Gamma (sec. 1979-80, pres. 1990-94), Kappa Iota. Democrat. Baptist. Avocations: stamp collecting, genealogy, painting, quilting, ceramics. Home: 1502 Nottingham Dr Phenix City AL 36867-1941

GREAVER, JOANNE HUTCHINS, mathematics educator, author; b. Louisville, Aug. 9, 1939; d. Alphonso Victor and Mary Louise (Sage) Hutchins; 1 child, Mary Elizabeth. BS in Chemistry, U. Louisville, 1961, MEd, 1971; MAT in Math., Purdue U., 1973. Cert. tchr. Pres. Math Mentors Inc., 1962—. Part-time faculty Bellarmine Coll., Louisville, 1982-2002, U. Louisville, 1985—; project reviewer NSF, 1983—; advisor Council on Higher Edn., Frankfort, Ky., 1983-86; active regional and nat. summit on assessment in math., 1991, state task force on math., assessment adv. com., Nat. Assessment Ednl. Progress standards com.; charter mem. Commonwealth Tchrs. Inst., 1984—; mem. Nat. Forum for Excellence in Edn., Indpls., 1983; metric edn. leader Fed. Metric Project, Louisville, 1979-82; mem. Ky. Ednl. Reform Task Force, Assessment Com., Nat. Framework, Nat. Assessment Ednl. Progress Rev. Com.; lectr. in field. Author: (workbook) Down Algebra Alley, 1984; co-author curriculum guides. Named Outstanding Citizen, SAR, 1984; named to Hon. Order Ky. Cols.; recipient Presdl. award for excellence in math. tchg., 1983; grantee, NSF, 1983, Louisville Cmty. Found., 1984—86. Mem. Greater Louisville Coun. Tchrs. of Math. (pres. 1977-78, 94-95, Outstanding Educator award 1987), Nat. Coun. Tchrs. of Math. (reviewer 1981—), Ky. Coun. Tchrs. of Math. (pres. 1990-91, Jefferson County Tchr. of Yr. award 1985), Math. Assn. Am., Kappa Delta Pi, Delta Kappa Gamma, Zeta Tau Alpha. Republican. Presbyterian. Avocations: tropical fish, gardening, handicrafts, travel, tennis. Home: 11513 Tazwell Dr Louisville KY 40241 E-mail: jogreaver@aol.com.

GREBSTEIN, SHELDON NORMAN, university administrator; b. Providence, Feb. 1, 1928; s. Sigmund and Sylvia (Skotkin) G.; m. Phyllis Strumar, Sept. 6, 1953; children: Jason Lyle, Gary Wade. BA cum laude, U. So. Calif., 1949; MA, Columbia U., 1950; PhD, Mich. State U., 1954. Instr. then asst. prof. English U. Ky., 1953-62; asst. prof. U. South Fla., 1962-63; mem. faculty SUNY, Binghamton, 1963-81, prof. English, 1968-81, asst. to pres., 1974-75; dean arts and scis. Harpur Coll., 1975-81; pres. SUNY, Purchase, 1981-93, univ. prof. of lit., 1993-95; dir. edn. Westchester Holocaust Edn. Ctr., 1995—. Fulbright-Hays lectr. U. Rouen, France, 1968-69; vis. lectr. Caen U., Hull U., and Edinburgh U., 1969. Author: Sinclair Lewis, 1962, John O'Hara, 1966, Hemingway's Craft, 1973; Editor: Monkey Trial, 1960, Perspectives in Contemporary Criticism, 1968, Studies in For Whom The Bell Tolls, 1971; editorial cons. univ. presses, publishers.; Contbr. articles to profl. jours. E-mail: whc@bestweb.net.

GRECO, ANTHONY JOSEPH, artist, educator, administrator; b. Cleve., Apr. 24, 1937; s. Joseph Anthony and Catherine C. (Corrao) G.; m. Astrida Paeglis, 1962 (div. July 1984); children: Joseph, Vivan, Regina; m. Elizabeth Vernon Shackelford, June 23, 1990. BFA, Cleve. Inst. Art, 1960, Kent State U., 1964, MFA, 1966. Head dept. drawing Atlanta Coll. Art, 1966-75, chmn. divsn. advanced studio, 1974-76, asst. to pres., 1975-76, acad. dean, 1976-82, acting acad. dean, 1985-86, prof. painting and drawing, 1988—2001, prof. emeritus, 2001—. Solo exhbns. include Armstrong State Coll., Savannah, Ga., 1976, Javo Gallery, Atlanta, 1978, Atlanta Coll. Art Libr., 1986, Chattahoochee Valley Art Mus., LaGrange, Ga., 1992; exhibited in group shows at Auburn U., 1987, Dekalb Coun. for Arts, 1989, U. Montevallo, Ala., 1989, Fay Gold Gallery, Atlanta, 1990, McIntosh Gallery, Atlanta, 1991, 92, 93, Spruill Ctr. Arts, Atlanta, 1999, Lazzaro Signature Gallery Fine Art, Stoughton, Wis., 1999; represented in collections at Jimmy Carter Presdl. Libr., Coca-Cola U.S.A., Atlanta, Chase Manhattan Bank, Summit Bank Corp., Atlanta, Kilpatrick and Cody Law Offices, Atlanta, Kent State U., Ga. State Art Commn., Atlanta, Butler Inst. Am. Art., King & Spalding Attys., Atlanta. Bd. dirs. Auditory Ednl. Clinic for Hearing Impaired, Atlanta, 1979-82; mem. adult programs adv. bd. High Mus. Art, Atlanta, 1985; mem. MARTA Coun. for the Arts, Atlanta, 1976-82, 85-86; mem. panel So. Arts Fedn., Visual Arts Dirs. Job-Alike Meeting, Atlanta, 1990. So. Arts Fedn./NEA regional fellow, 1988; recipient purchase awards and other awards for art. Office: Atlanta Coll Art 1280 Peachtree St NE Atlanta GA 30309-3502

GRECO, DONNA, educational administrator; b. N.Y.C., Mar. 24, 1956; d. Jack and Angelina (DiGangi) Dagnese; m. Frank Greco, Sept. 20, 1975; children: Daniel, Melissa, Matthew. BA in Econs., Coll. Staten Island, 1991; MS in Elem. Edn., St. John's U., Queens, N.Y., 1994. Tchr. presch. Alphabetland Presch., Staten Island, 1974-80, New Dorp Christian Acad., Staten Island, 1989, tchr. 2d grade, 1991-94; asst. prin. Gateway Acad., Staten Island, 1994—. With carers ministry Gateway Cathedral, Staten Island, 1992—, nursery supr., 1993-94. Presdl. scholar Coll. S.I., 1990, Scholastic All-Am., 1987, Learning Styles Seminars, 1994. Mem. ASCD, N.Y. State Reading Assn., S.I. Reading Assn., Phi Delta Kappa, Omicron Delta Epsilon. Home: 401 Jefferson Blvd Staten Island NY 10312-2330 Office: Gateway Acad 200 Boscombe Ave Staten Island NY 10309-2604

GRECO, JANICE TERESA, psychology educator; b. N.Y.C., May 14, 1948; d. Joseph Ralph and Harriett May (McArdle) G.; m. Forlano, July 29, 1969 (div. Feb. 1993); children: Christopher, Jason, Jennifer. BS, MEd, U. Houston, 1975; PhD, U. Tex., 1992. Ins. clk. John Hancock Life Ins. Co., West Islip, N.Y., 1965-69; instr. San Jacinto Jr. Coll., Houston, 1976-77; with assessment & referral divsn. Employee Assistance Program, U. Tex., Houston, 1987-88; instr. psychology Houston C.C., 1977—, head behavioral stats.; adj. prof. HFH SCh. Social Work and Coll Pharmacy. Vol. Huppotherapy Group, Galveston, Tex., 1990-91, fellowshp., Automated Lectr., Instrl. Computing, 1998, web access to statistics course, 1998. Fellow Instructional Computing, 1998, Coll. Computer Program. Mem. ACA, Tex. Assn. Counseling and Devel., Tex. Jr. Coll. Tchr. Assn., Stats. for Behavioral Scis. (rsch. com.). Avocations: horse-back riding, travel, reading, billiards, lionel collector. Home: 12219 Monticeto Ln Stafford TX 77477-1430

GRECO, JOSEPH M, parochial school educator; b. Great Neck, N.Y., May 9, 1942; s. Joseph Laurence and Estelle Josephine (Kwiecinska) G. BA, Marist Coll.; postgrad., S.B.I. Colgate. Cert. tchr. N.Y., Archdiocese of N.Y. Tchr. Marist Coll., Poughkeepsie, N.Y., 1964, Fiocese of Rockville Center, N.Y.; tchr., counselor Mount Loretto, N.Y.; tchr., dept. coord. Archdiocese of N.Y.; dir. religious edn. Diocese of Rochester, N.Y.; instr. Fordham U., N.Y.C., 1993—. Cons. adv. New York State Dept Edn., 1983—; sci. mentor New York State Dept. Edn. 1985—. Author-editor: Essentials Of Learning, 1992; author: (small booklets) Learning the Computer, 1993, Teaching Math, 1993, Teaching Science, 1993. Democrat. Roman Catholic. Avocations: playing the violin, printmaking, calligraphy.

GRECO, RALPH STEVEN, surgeon, researcher, medical educator; b. N.Y.C., May 25, 1942; s. Charles Mario and Lydia Antoinette (Barone) G.; m. Irene Leonor Wapnir, Feb. 23, 1991; children: Justin Michael, Eric Matthew, Ilana Rose. BS, Fordham U., 1964; MD, Yale U., 1968. Surgery intern and resident Yale U., New Haven, 1968—73, instr., 1972—73; asst. prof. Rutgers Med. Sch., Piscataway, NJ, 1975-79, assoc. prof., 1979-83; chief gen. surgery Robert Wood Johnson Med. Sch., New Brunswick, 1982—2000, prof., 1983-2000; chief of surgery Robert Wood Johnson Univ. Hosp. U. Medicine & Dentistry of N.J., New Brunswick, 1997-2000; J & J prof., chief divsn. gen. surgery, dir. surg. tng. Stanford U. Sch. Medicine, 2000—. Cons. Nat. Heart, Lung and Blood Inst.-NSF, Bethesda, Md., 1991. Contbr. articles to profl. jours. Maj. U.S. Army, 1973-75. NHLBI grantee, 1980-84. Fellow Am. Surg. Assn.; mem. Soc. Univ. Surgeons. Achievements include research in in antibiotic bonding, treatment of prosthetic infection and nanobiology; patents in field. Home: 773 Frenchman's Rd Stanford CA 94305 Office: Stanford U Sch Medicine 300 Pasteur Dr Stanford CA 94305 E-mail: grecors@stanford.edu.

GREDZENS, SANDRA MAY PILLSBURY, art educator; b. Mpls., Sept. 30, 1949; d. Robert Kinsey and Elizabeth Anne (Massie) Pillsbury; m. David Inesis Gredzens, Nov. 25, 1989; stepchildren: Tabatha, Alex. AA, Stephens Coll., 1971; BFA, U. Calif. Santa Cruz, 1980; MEd, Hamline U., 1995. Cert. elem. and secondary educator. Lay-out artist Monterey (Calif.) Peninsula Herald, 1973-75; tchr.'s aide spl. edn., substitute tchr. Pacific Grove (Calif.) Unified Sch. Dist., 1978-82; educator art Shattuck-St. Mary's Sch., Faribault, Minn., 1982-84; tchr. elem. Woods Acad., Maple Plain, Minn., 1986-87; tchr. elem. art, art cons. Anoka (Minn.)-Hennepin Ind. Sch. Dist., 1987-97; art tchr. Lake Superior Sch. Dist., Two Harbors, Minn., 1997—. Exhibited in group shows at Grant Marais Art Colony, 1986—98, 2001, Itasca Art Assn. Exhbn., 1996, 1999, 2001, 2003, Sally Brown Collaborative Art Exhbn., 1995, Union St. Gallery, Chicago Heights, Ill., 2000, Duluth (Minn.) Art Inst., 2002, 2003, Lake County Ct. House Atrium, 2002, Vanilla Bean Bakery and Café, 2003. Mem. Nat. Art Educators Am., Art Educators Minn., Delta Phi Delta. Republican. Lutheran. Avocations: painting, hiking, church activities, photography. Office: Two Harbors HS 405 4th Ave Two Harbors MN 55616

GREELEY, PATRICIA E. elementary school educator; b. Port Chester, N.Y. d. Horace James and Edna (Streich) G. BA, SUNY, Fredonia; MA, Fairfield (Conn.) U.; postgrad., Northeastern U. Cert. nursery, elem. and secondary English grades 7-9 tchr., N.Y. Mentor, cooperating tchr., insvc. instr. Katonah-Lewisboro (N.Y.) Sch. Dist., elem. tchr. Named to Putnam-No. Westchester Bd. Coop. Ednl. Svcs. Tchr. Talent Bank, 1990, 91. Mem. ASCD, Nat. Coun. Tchrs. English, Internat. Women's Writing Guild.

GREEN, ASA NORMAN, university president; b. Mars Hill, Maine, July 22, 1929; s. Clayton John and Annie Glenna (Shaw) G.; m. Elizabeth Jean Zirkelbach Ross, May 27, 1965; 1 son, Stephen Richard Ross. AB cum laude, Bates Coll., Lewiston, Maine, 1951; MA, U. Ala., 1955; LL.D., Jacksonville (Ala.) U., 1975. Research dir. Ala. League Municipalities, Montgomery, 1955-57; city mgr. Mountain Brook, Ala., 1957-65; exec. sec. Ala. Assn. Ins. Agts., 1965-66; dir. devel. Birmingham-So. Coll., 1966-71; dir. devel. and communications Dickinson Coll., Carlisle, Pa., 1971-73; pres. Livingston (Ala.) U., 1973-93; pres. emeritus Livingston U., 1993—. Cons. NCAA Pres.'s Commn., 1993—99; instr. polit. sci. U. Ala. Ext. Ctr., Montgomery and Birmingham, 1955—57, 1958—60. Author: Revenue for Alabama Cities, 1956. Dir. U. South Ala. Found., 1997—. Served with CIC U.S. Army, 1952—54. Grad. fellow So. Regional Tng. Program in Pub. Adminstrn., 1951 Mem.: Phi Beta Kappa. Democrat. Methodist. Office: PO Box 1620 Livingston AL 35470-1620

GREEN, BARBARA, communications educator; b. Hinsdale, Ill., May 26, 1950; d. Roger J. and Lois L. (Froehlich) Green; m. Richard A. Webb, Sept. 8, 1984; 1 child, Claire Catherine. BA, Drake U., Des Moines, 1972; MA, So. Ill. U., 1979, U. Chgo., 1998. Tech. writer Dial Fin. Corp., Des Moines, 1972-74; faculty St. Lawrence Coll., Kingston, Ont., Can., 1977-78; tech. writer Can. Dept. Def., Ottawa, Ont., 1978-79; copy editor Deltak Inc., Oak Brook, Ill., 1980-81; tng. cons., course designer Willowbrook, Ill., 1981-86; instr. composition and newswriting George Williams Coll., Downers Grove, Ill., 1983-85; instr. composition, tech. writing Benedictine U., Lisle, Ill., 1987-88, 91, Aurora (Ill.) U., 1988-90; weekly columnist Lisle Sun, 1993—; instr. writing Coll. of DuPage, Glen Ellyn, Ill., 1980-97, instr. composition, poetry, tech., creative and memoir writing, 2001—; tech. writer Lucent Technologies, Naperville, Ill., 1997, tng. mgr., 1998—99. Author, editor: (video) Peg Lehman Show, 1988; editor Rivulets 14, 2002, Rivulets 15, 2003; author numerous poems, short stories. Mem. No. Ill. Newspaper Assn., Naperville Writers Group. E-mail: barbara.l.green@worldnet.att.net.

GREEN, BERT FRANKLIN, JR., psychologist; b. Honesdale, Pa., Nov. 5, 1927; s. Bert Franklin and Emily May (Brown) G.; m. Hasseltine Beck Robinson, Apr. 29, 1961 (div. 1974); children: Malcolm, Edward. AB, Yale, 1949; MA, Princeton, 1950, PhD, 1951. Mem. psychology group Lincoln Lab., Mass. Inst. Tech., 1951-62, leader, 1958-62; cons. RAND Corp., 1961; prof. psychology Carnegie Inst. Tech., Pitts., 1962-69, head psychology dept., 1962-67; prof. psychology Johns Hopkins, Balt., 1969-98, prof. emeritus, 1998—. Author: Digital Computers in Research, 1963. Mem. Am. Psychol. Assn., Am. Statis. Assn., Psychometric Soc., Am. Edn. Rsch. Assn. Home: 311 Eastway Ct Baltimore MD 21212-4710 Personal E-mail: bfgreen@verizon.net. Business E-Mail: bfgreen@jhu.edu.

GREEN, BETTY NIELSEN, education educator, consultant; b. Copenhagen, Apr. 30, 1937; came to U.S., 1979; d. Alfred Christian Josef and Lilly Nielsen; m. Philip Irving Green, Apr. 16, 1962; children: Ruth, Erik, Nils. AA in Fgn. Langs., Daytona Beach C.C., 1981; BA in Liberal Arts, U. Ctrl. Fla., 1986; MS in TESOL, Nova Southeastern U., 1988; EdD in Curriculum and Instrn., U. Ctrl. Fla., 1994. Cert. tchr., Fla.; cert. TESOL trainer, Fla. Tchr. TESOL, program mgr. English Lang. Inst. Daytona Beach C.C., Fla., 1986-91; tchr. TESOL, fgn. lang. specialist Volusia County Schs., Daytona Beach, 1991—; tchr. trainer, facilitator Nova Southeastern U., Ft. Lauderdale, Fla., 1991—. Cons. TESOL, Ormond Beach, Fla., 1991; adj. faculty, Daytona Beach, 1997—; chair Fla. Consortium of Multilingual-Multicultural Edn., 2001--. Author, editor Teaching Assistant Manual, 1987; editor Unitarian Universalist Soc. newsletter, 1987—, religious editl. dir., 1996—; eidtor Fla. Fgn. Lang. Assn. Newsletter. Pres. Unitarian Universalists, Ormond Beach, 1982-84, N.E. Cluster Unitarian Universalists, Volusia, 1982-86; pres., v.p. S.E. Unitarian Universalists Sem. Inst., Blacksburg, Va., 1985-89. Mem. TESOL, Sunshine State TESOL (mem.-at-large 1999—, 2d v.p., 1st v.p., pres. 2003—), N.E. Fla. TESOL (pres. 1995—, editor newsletter 1998—), ASCD, Nat. Coun. Tchrs. of English, Fla. Fgn. Lang. Assn. (membership bd., editor 2002—), Fgn. Lang. Adminstrn. and Mgmt. Edn. (sec. 1995-97, pres. 1998), Fla. Assn. Bilingual Edn. Suprs. (sec. 1995), Fla. Consortium on Multicultural Edn. (chair), Phi Kappa Phi, Kappa Delta Pi, Pi Delta Kappa. Democrat. Avocations: foreign languages, research on second language and multi-cultural educations, music, travel. Home: 771 W River Oak Dr Ormond Beach FL 32174-4641 Office: Volusia County Schs 729 Loomis Ave Daytona Beach FL 32114-4723 E-mail: drtesol@philgreen.org., drtesol@philgreen.org.

GREEN, BONNIE JEAN, early childhood administrator; b. Crookston, Minn., Oct. 23, 1950; d. Francis Romain and Dorothy Marion (Boatman) Bagne; m. Steven Douglas Wedger, July 21, 1973 (div. Feb. 1985); m. Charles Edward Green Jr., June 15, 1985; stepchildren: Andrew Green, Russell Green. BS in Edn. magna cum laude, U. N.D., 1972; cert. human rels., Minn. State U., 1973; postgrad., U. Minn., 1975-83. Cert. elem./early childhood edn. adminstr. Math/reading tutor bilingual students U. N.D., Grand Forks, 1969-71; 1st grade tchr. Park Rapids (Minn.) Ind. Sch. Dist., 1972-73; asst. dir./curriculum writer, tchr. Child Devel. and Learning Ctr., Burnsville, Minn., 1973-75, dir., 1975-87; caring ministry outreach Luth. Ch. of Incarnation, Davis, Calif., 1990—. Facilitator-parent edn. program Dakota County Vo-Tech, 1973-78; advisor, cons. Dakota County Childcare Coun., 1977-83; advisor, tchr. cert. program Augsburg Coll., Mpls., 1977-78; supr. student tchrs. Coll. of St. Catherine, Augsburg, St. Paul, 1977-87; cons. Minn. Edn. for Young Children, 1978, State of Minn., 1979-81, Am. Luth. Ch., Mpls., 1981-83; cons., kindergarten curriculum Burnsville Sch. Dist., 1983; liaison coord. Head Start Program, Burnsville, 1985-87. Vol. Prince of Peace Luth. Ch., Burnsville, 1975-87 facilitator parents of divorce, 1984-87; vol. Yolo Wayfare Ctr., Woodland, Calif., 1992; bd. dirs. Riverwoods Homeowners Assn. Arch. Control, 1978-85; mem., vol. Holy Cross Luth., Wheaton, Ill., 1987-89, Luth. Ch. of Incarnation, Davis, 1989—, curriculum planner, 1989; publicity chair, bd. dirs. U. Calif. Farm Circle, Davis, 1989—; fundraiser Wheaton (Ill.) Newcomers, 1987-89; fraternal communicator Luth. Brotherhood, 1994—. Mem. Nat. Assn. for Edn. Young Children, PEO (guard, treas., sec., v.p., pres.), Pi Lambda Theta. Avocations: gardening, interior decorating, gourmet cooking, travel. Home and Office: 39648 Lupine Ct Davis CA 95616-9756

GREEN, CATHERINE GERTRUDE, retired secondary school educator, education educator; b. Indpls., Nov. 23, 1945; d. Gentry L. and Helen G. (Peters) Kirby; m. Alan E. Green, June 3, 1967 (div. May 1996); m. James G. Green, Mar. 8, 1975; 1 child, Heather Vanessa. BA, Purdue U., 1967;

MA, Northwestern U., 1970; cert. in adminstrn., No. Ill. U., 1985, EdD. Cert. tchr., assoc. status Ill. Adminstr. Acad. English and speech tchr. Wellington (Mo.)-Napoleon High Sch., 1967-68; communication and English tchr. Crystal Lake (Ill.) Cen. High Sch., 1968-85, chair English dept., 1985-86, dean of students, 1986-87; asst. prin. Cary Grove H.S., Cary, Ill., 1987-88, prin., 1988-94, curriculum dir. H.S. Dist. 155, 1994—2000, ret., 2000—; asst. prof. dept. edn. St. Mary's Coll., Notre Dame, Ind., 2003—. Speech instr. Purdue U., West Lafayette, Ind., 1974-75; speech tchr. McHenry County Coll., Crystal Lake, 1968-70; analyst, mentor, bd. trustees Ednl. Svc. Ctr. #1 Ill. State Bd. of Edn., 1991—, presenter, 1991—. Named Disting. Citizen, Crystal Lake Jaycees, 1986. 75th Anniversary Paul Harris fellow. Mem. Assn. Supervision and Curriculum Devel., Assn. Tchr. Educators, Rotary, Delta Kappa Gamma (state corr. sec. 1989-91, chpt. pres., mem. various coms.scholar 1983), Zeta Phi Eta, Alpha Omicron Pi. Avocation: rosarian. Office: 95 Madeleva Hall Saint Mary's Coll Notre Dame IN 46556

GREEN, CATHERINE L. special education educator; b. Alexandria, Va., Apr. 13, 1959; d. Russell James and Betty Joyce (Sellers) G. AA, Gulf Coast C.C., Panama City, Fla., 1980; BS in Social Sci., Fla. State U., 1991. Cert. tchr. spl. edn., emotionally handicapped. Tchr. emotionally handicapped Carabelle (Fla.) H.S., 1992, Merritt Brown Middle Sch., Panama City, Fla., 1992—, head emotionally handicapped dept., 1993—, coach girl's volleyball, 1992—, coach girl's basketball, 1993, mem. leadership team Onward Toward Excellence team, 1994—. Site supr. JTPA Work Enclave, Panama City, 1993—. Youth dir. Springfield Meth. Ch., Panama City, Fla., 1985-90. Mem. ASCD, Coun. for Exceptional Children. Democrat. Avocations: playing drums, volleyball, playing/coaching softball. Office: Merritt Brown Middle Sch 5044 Merritt Brown Way Panama City FL 32404-0800 Home: Apt 32 924 Florida Ave Panama City FL 32401-2302

GREEN, CYNTHIA DIANE, special education educator; b. Battle Creek, Mich., Feb. 7, 1958; d. LeRoy J. and Bette J. (Wright) Miller; m. Jeffrey G. Green, May 9, 1980; children: Nicole Marie, Katherine Elizabeth. BS, MA, Western Mich. U. Tchr. adult basic edn. Portage (Mich.) Pub. Schs., Kalamazoo Pub. Schs., tchr. spl. edn., dir. spel. edn., 1999—. Instr. Direct Instr. Conf.; mem. improvement team Woods Lake and Edison Schs. Grantee Project Access Computer, Kalamazoo Pub. Edn. Found., State of MIch., Excellence in Edn. Mem. Coun. for Exceptional Children, Mich. Coun. on Learning for Adults. Home: 2404 Chaparral St Kalamazoo MI 49006-1383

GREEN, DON WESLEY, chemical and petroleum engineering educator; b. Tulsa, July 8, 1932; s. Earl Leslie and Erma Pansy (Brackins) G.; m. Patricia Louise Polston, Nov. 26, 1954; children: Guy Leslie, Don Michael, Charles Patrick. BS in Petroleum Engring., U. Tulsa, 1955; MSChemE, U. Okla., 1959, PhD in Chem. Engring., 1963. Rsch. scientist Continental Oil Co., Ponca City, Okla., 1962-64; asst. to assoc. prof. U. Kans., Lawrence, 1964-71, prof. chem. and petroleum engring., 1971-82, chmn. dept. chem. and petroleum engring., 1970-74, 96-200, co-dir. Tertiary Oil Recovery project, 1974—, Conger-Gabel Disting. prof., 1982-95, Deane E. Ackers Disting. prof., 1995—. Faculty rep. to NCAA. Editor: Perry's Chemical Engineers' Handbook, 1984, 1997; co-author: Enhanced Oil Recovery, 1998; contbr. articles to profl. jours. 1st lt. USAF, 1955-57. Fellow Am. Inst. Chem. Engrs.; mem. Soc. Petroleum Engrs. (Disting. Achievement award 1983, chmn. edn. and accreditation com. 1980-81, Disting. mem. 1986, Disting. lectr. 1986). Democrat. Avocations: handball, baseball, mountain hiking. Home: 1020 Sunset Dr Lawrence KS 66044-4546 Office: U Kans Dept Chem & Petroleum Engring 4008 Learned Hall Lawrence KS 66045-7526 E-mail: dgreen@ku.edu.

GREEN, DONALD PHILIP, education educator; b. Chgo., June 23, 1961; s. Burton and Isabel (Engelhardt) G.; m. Ann Gerken, June 18, 1989; children: Aaron, Rachel. BA in Polit. Sci., UCLA, 1983; MA in Polit. Sci., U. Calif., Berkeley, 1984, PhD, 1988. From asst. to assoc. prof. dept. polit. sci. Yale U., New Haven, 1989-94, prof., 1994—, dir. Instn. for Social and Policy Studies, 1996—, A. Whitney Giswold chair, 2001. Author: Pathologies of Rational Choice Theory, 1994; contbr. articles to profl. jours.; inventor abstract strategy games. Recipient Nat. Young Investigator award NSF, 1993—. Office: Yale Univ 124 Prospect St New Haven CT 06511-3741

GREEN, EDWARD THOMAS, JR., education educator; b. Oxford, N.J., Apr. 19, 1921; s. Edward Thomas and Euphemia (Lanterman) G.; m. Margaret Evelyn Tuttle, Jan. 30, 1944; children: Marsha, Margaret, Barbara. BS cum laude, Ithaca Coll., 1942; MS, Syracuse U., 1947, EdD, 1965. Music instr. high sch., Palmyra, N.Y., 1942-50; dir. guidance, vice-prin., 1946-50; prin. Palmyra-Macedon Ctrl. Sch., 1950-54; supervising prin. New Berlin (N.Y.) Ctrl. Sch., 1954-58, Rondout Valley Ctrl. Sch., Accord, N.Y., also supt. schs., 1958-66; supt. schs. Oneida (NY) City Schs., 1966-77; prof. edn. Ga. So. U., Statesboro, 1977-87, prof. emeritus, 1987—. Pres. Mid-Hudson Sch. Study Coun., New Paltz, N.Y., 1960; vice chmn. CHE-MAD-HER-ON, Inc.; area sec. Ctrl. Sch. Study; mem. exec. com. Catskill Study on Small Sch. Design; v.p. N.Y. State Tchrs. Retirement Bd.; v.p. Rip Van Winkle coun. Boy Scouts Am., 1964-66, v.p., then pres. Madison County coun., chmn. Madison Dist., pres. Iroquois coun.; pres. Palmyra Betterment Club 1952; mem. Ulster County Cmty. Action Program; past pres. Ithaca Coll. Alumni Coun. Served with AUS, 1942-46, ETO. Mem. N.Y. State Sch. Dist. Adminstrs. (pres.), Am. Assn. Sch. Adminstrs., Assn. for Supervision and Curriculum Devel., Nat. Sch. Pub. Rels. Assn., Nat. Assn. Secondary Sch. Prins., Nat. Assn. Elem. Sch. Prins., Ga. Assn. Ednl. Leaders, So. Assn. Colls. and Schs. (Ga. sec. com. 1991-95), Ga. Accrediting Commn., Nat. Orgn. for Legal Problems in Edn., Masons, Shriners, Rotary Internat., Lions Club, Phi Delta Kappa (chpt. pres., area coord.), Phi Mu Alpha. Republican. Presbyterian. Home: 301 Bella Vista Dr Ithaca NY 14850-5774

GREEN, ELBERT P. retired university official; b. Laneview, Va., June 9, 1935; s. James H. and Levallia C. (DeLeaver) G.; m. Mary M. Green, July 6, 1961; children: Mark B., Marsha B. BS, Va. State Coll., 1957; BD, Felix Adler Meml. U., Chapel Hill, N.C., 1969; MS in Edn., Troy State U., Montgomery, Ala., 1988; MBph, Am. Bible Sch., Kansas City, Kans., 1968; PhD, S.W. U., New Orleans, 1991. Cert. tchr., Ala., cert. hypnotherapist; ordained minister. 2d lt. U.S. Army, 1958, advanced through grades to maj.; ret., 1979; dir. jr. ROTC, Indianola (Miss.) City Schs., Macon County (Ala.) Schs.; dir. residence hall Tuskegee (Ala.) U. Author: Poetry Is Soul, 1988, Poetry Is Gold, 1982, The Light of the World Is Poetry, 1995; contbr. articles to newspapers. Inductee Internat. Poetry Hall of Fame, 1997, Who Is Who of Contemporary Achievers Hall of Fame, 1997, Phi Beta Sigma Hall of Fame, 1999, Am. Biographical Inst. Hall of Fame, 2002. Mem. Internat. Soc. of Poets, Profl. Educators Orgn., Am. Legion, Lions Internat., Scabbard and Blade, Phi Beta Sigma, Phi Delta Kappa, Gamma Beta Phi. Home: 2910 W Martin L King Hwy Tuskegee AL 36083

GREEN, GAYLA MAXINE, elementary school educator; b. Gastonia, NC, Sept. 1, 1951; d. Woodrow and Mildred Louise (Cagle) G. BS, Mars Hill Coll., 1973; cert. in intermediate edn., Sacred Heart Coll., 1974; MA in Edn., Western Carolina U., 1977, EdS, 1985. Cert. elem. tchr. NC; nat. bd. cert. tchr. in early/mid. childhood phy. edn. 2002. Elem. phys. edn. tchr. Gaston County Schs., Gastonia, NC, 1974—2003; creative arts tchr. Hope Luth. Sch., 2003—. Line assoc. rides Paramount's Carowinds, Charlotte, N.C., 1992-94; adj. instr. Belmont (N.C.) Abbey Coll., 1985-87, Gaston Coll., Dallas, N.C., 1986-87, 2002—, Sacred Heart Coll., Belmont, 1980-84; games cons. Gaston Coll. Day Camp, Dallas, 1993-96; counselor, group leader Civitan Youth Camp, Bolling Springs, N.C., 1979-81. Contbr. articles to profl. jours. Coach Spl. Olympics, Gaston County, N.C., 1986—; ch. music asst. First Bapt. Ch., Gastonia, N.C., 1983-88, Covenant Bapt. Ch., Gastonia, 1988—. Named one of Outstanding Young Women of Am., 1982, 84; recipient Knight-Ridder Exemplary Tchr. award Charlotte Observer, 1996; named Tchr. of Yr. Gardner Pk. Elem. Sch., 2000-01. Mem.: ASCD, NC AAHPERD, AAHPERD, Pi Lambda Theta, Kappa Delta Pi, Phi Kappa Phi. Democrat. Avocations: harpist, solo handbell ringer. Home: 202 Dallas Bessemer City Hwy Dallas NC 28034-9476

GREEN, HARRY WESTERN, II, geology-geophysics educator; b. Orange, N.J., Mar. 13, 1940; s. Harry Buetel and Mabel (Hendrickson) G.; children from previous marriage: Mark, Stephen, Carolyn, Jennifer; m. Maria Manuela Marques Martins, May 15, 1975; children: Alice, Miguel, Maria. AB in Geology with honors, UCLA, 1963, MS in Geology and Geophysics, 1967, PhD in Geology and Geophysics with distinction, 1968. Postdoctoral research assoc. materials sci. Case Western Res. U., Cleve., 1968-70; asst. prof. geology U. Calif., Davis, 1970-74, assoc. prof., 1974-80, prof., 1980-92, chmn. dept., 1984-88, prof. geology and geophysics Riverside, 1993-99, disting. prof. geology and geophysics, 1999—, dir. Inst. Geophysics and Planetary Physics, 1993-95, 2001, dir. analytical electron microscopy facility, 1994—2000, vice chancellor for rsch., 1995-2000, dir. ctrl. facility advanced microscopy and microanalysis, 2000—. Exch. scientist U. Nantes, France, 1973, vis. prof., 1978-79; vis. prof. Monash U., Melbourne, Australia, 1984; specialist advisor World Bank Program, China U. of Geoscis., Wuhan, 1988; adj. sr. rsch. scientist Lamont-Doherty Earth Obs., Columbia U., 1989-95, Vetlesen vis. prof., 1991-92; expert advisor geophysics rev. panel NSF, 1991-94; co-founder Gordon Conf. on Rock Deformation, 1995, chmn. 2d conf., 1997; hon. faculty China U. Geoscis., Wuhan, 1998—; vis. scientist Carnegie Inst. Washington, 2000—, Abelson lectr., 2000, faculty rsch. lectr., U.C. Riverside, 2002-03. Contbr. articles to books and profl. jours. Grantee NSF, 1969—, Dept. Energy, 1988-94. Fellow AAAS, Mineral Soc. Am., Am. Geophys. Union (N.L. Bowen award 1994, Francis Birch lectr. 1995); mem. Materials Rsch. Soc., Cosmos Club (Washington), Sigma Xi. Achievements include discovery of a new mechanism of deep earthquakes and exhumation of rocks from great depth in subduction zones. Office: U Calif Inst Geophysics & Planetar Physics Riverside CA 92521-0001 E-mail: harry.green@ucr.edu.

GREEN, JERILYN D. secondary school educator; b. Detroit, Sept. 19, 1942; d. Alphonzo and Eloise (Franklin) Harrison; m. Victor E. Green, Apr. 15, 1966; children: Victor A., Christopher Todd. BA in Music, Wayne State U., 1972, MA in Music, 1974, postgrad. Cert. essential elements effective instrn.; cert. in instructional tech. Tchr. computers Detroit Bd. Edn.; pres., owner Computerese Inc. Presenter Mich. Coun. Social Studies. Recipient Spirit of Detroit award Detroit City Coun. Mem. Mich. Assn. Computer Users and Learners (presenter), Detroit Assn. Black Orgns., Delta Sigma Theta (treas. 1987-90).

GREEN, JOHN HOWARD, scouting association administrator; b. May 04; s. Howard Nathan and Ramona (Kay) G.; m. LaDonna McCarty, June 5; children: Daniel, Joshua. BS, West Tex. State U., 1972. With Boy Scouts Am., 1972—, dir. field svc., 1981-82, scout exec. Lake Charles, La., 1982-86, Albuquerque, 1986-90, nat. dir. Learning for Life program Irving, Tex., 1990—. V.p. Carrollton (Tex.) Kent Elem. PTA, 1992-93. Mem. ASCD, Nat. Assn. Elem. Sch. Prins., Nat. Assn. Secondary Sch. Prins., Nat. Sch. Bds. Assn., Am. Assn. Sch. Adminstrs., Nat. Assn. State Bds. of Edn. Methodist. Avocations: basketball, golf, snow skiing. Office: Learning for Life/BSA 1325 W Walnut Hill Ln PO Box 152079 Irving TX 75015-2079

GREEN, JONATHAN DAVID, music educator, composer, conductor; b. Batavia, NY, Apr. 26, 1964; s. Gary Martin and Justine Elaine (Ferguson) G.; m. Lynn Marie Buck, Apr. 23, 1988. MusB, SUNY, Fredonia, 1985; MusM, U. Mass., 1987; D Musical Arts, U. N.C., Greensboro, 1992. Music libr. Bennington (Vt.) Coll., 1987-88; vis. asst. prof. Hampden-Sydney (Va.) Coll., 1988-89; co-condr. Greensboro Symphony Youth Orch., 1990-93; asst. prof. music Elon Coll., N.C., 1991-96; assoc. prof. music, chmn. Sweet Briar Coll., 1996—2002, assoc. dean, 2002—03, assoc. dean and v.p. for acad. affairs, 2003—. Adjudicator Fiestival, Richmond, Va., 1992—; condr. Lee County Orch., 1995-96. Author: A Conductor's Guide to Choral Orchestral Music, vols. I and II, 1994, 98, A Bio-Bibliography of Carl Ruggles, 1995, A Conductor's Guide to the Choral-Orchestral Works of J.S. Bach, 2000, A Conductor's Guide to the Choral-Orchestral Works of Mozart and Haydn, 2002; composer 40 songs, 6 symphonies, also others; editor Jour. of the Conductors Guild, 2001—. Crandall scholar Chautauqua Instn., 1982; Ornest fellow U. Mass., 1985-87, Excellence fellow U. N.C., 1989-92. Mem. ASCAP (mem. standard panel awards 1997—), Condrs. Guild (bd. dirs.), Am. Symphony Orch. League, Am. Choral Dirs. Assn., Am. Music Ctr., Phi Mu Alpha Sinfonia (sustaining). Avocations: hiking, cooking, travel. Office: Sweet Briar Coll Office of Dean Sweet Briar VA 24595 Home: 118 Madison St Lynchburg VA 24504 E-mail: jgreen@sbc.edu.

GREEN, KAREN ANN, college administrator; b. Amarillo, Tex., Feb. 9, 1957; d. Stanley Dwight and Virginia Darlene (Milton) Bailey; children: Stephanie, Courtney. BBA in Acctg., West Tex. A&M U., 1985. Lic. real estate, Colo. Acct. Mesa Ltd. Partnership, Amarillo, 1980-90; real estate sales assoc. Edens Realty, Brighton, Colo., 1991-93; exec. v.p., contr., bd. dirs. Colo. Grease Svc., Inc., Ft. Lupton, Colo., 1990-92; loan officer The Mortgage Broker, Ltd., Englewood, 1993; pres., owner Red Hot Enterprises, Amarillo, Tex., 1993—; instructional lab. supr. II Amarillo Coll., 1996—. Mem. Grad. Realtors Inst. Republican. Avocations: snow skiing, travel. Home: 2400 S Polk St Unit 210 Amarillo TX 79109-2859 Office: Amarillo Coll PO Box 447 BB416 2201 S Washington St Amarillo TX 79109-2411

GREEN, KAY SUZANNE, school system administrator; b. Kankakee, Ill., July 17, 1943; d. Fayette and Florence Bernice (Manssen) McMullen; m. Donald Edward Green, July 3, 1965; children: Susan Michelle, Steven Michael. BS, Ill. State U., 1965, EdD, 1993; MEd, U. Ill., 1968. Cert. 6-12 English tchr., gen. adminstr., supt., Ill. English tchr. Manteno (Ill.) High Sch., 1965-67, Westview High Sch., Kankakee, Ill., 1970-71; magnet sch. program coord. Kankakee Sch. Dist., 1978-92, dir. pub. rels., 1984-93, asst. supt. competitive state and fed. programs, 1992-93, supt., 1993—. Past sec. bd. dirs. YMCA, Kankakee, 1985-99; pres. Kankakee County Hist. Soc., 1975-2002; active, past chair Stone Barn Found., Kankakee, 1989—, Kankakee Valley Symphony Orch. Found., 1989—; past pres. Kankakee Valley Symphony Orch. Assn., 1980-89; bd. dirs. Cmty. Resource Ctr., 1995-2001, Martin Luther King Found., 1995-98; bd. dirs. United Way, v.p., 2002—; bd. dirs., chair Provena St. Mary's Hosp. Found., 1998—. Named Outstanding Vol. in Kankakee County Jr. League, United Way, 1st Nat. Bank Kankakee, 1990, Adminstr. of Yr. Kankakee County Ednl. Office Pers., 1997, Athena award, 1997, Adminstrn. of Yr., Ill. Ednl. Office Pers., 1997, Jr. League Vol. of Yr., 2002. Mem. ASCD, Am. Assn. Sch. Adminstrs. (Ill. chpt.), Kankakee C. of C. (chair bus.-edn. coun. 1985—), Kiwanis, Zonta (Leadership award 1992), Kappa Delta Epsilon, Kappa Delta Pi. Home: PO Box 1702 1480 Sunset Ln Kankakee IL 60901-4543 Office: Kankakee Sch Dist No 111 240 Warren Ave Kankakee IL 60901-4319

GREEN, KENNETH CHARLES, education educator, researcher; b. N.Y.C., Feb. 2, 1951; s. Gilbert and Shirley (Milter) G.; m. Rika Rosemary van Dam, June 29, 1980; children: Aaron Hans, Mara Claire. BA, New Coll., 1973; MA, Ohio State U., 1977; PhD, UCLA, 1982. Assoc. dir., operating officer Higher Edn. Rsch. Inst., assoc. dir. Am. coun. Edn. Coop. Instl. Rsch. Program. UCLA, 1984-89; sr. rsch. assoc. James Irvine Found. Ctr. Scholarly Tech. U. So. Calif., 1989-94, dir. Ctr. Scholarly Tech., 1992-95; rschr., author Campus Computing, Nat. Survey Info. Tech. Am. Higher Edn., 1990-98; founding dir. The Campus Computing Project, 1990—. Vis. scholar Claremont Grad. (Calif.) U., 1995—; vis. prof. Case Western Res. U., 2003—; lectr., various colls. and univs.; speaker, cons. in field. Author: (with F.R. Kemerer and J.V. Baldridge) Strategies for Effective Enrollment Management, 1982, Government Support for Minority Participation in Higher Education, 1982, (with Daniel Seymour) Whose Going to Run General Motors, 1992, and numerous research publs.; reviewer Jour. Higher Edn., also monograph series; rschr.; contbr. articles to profl. jours. Recipient Edn. award for leadership in pub. policy and practice, 2002. Mem. Am. Assn. Higher Edn., Assn. for Study of Higher Edn., Am. Edn. Research Assn., Fund for Improvement of Postsecondary Edn. (reviewer), Policy Studies Orgn. Office: PO Box 261242 Encino CA 91426-1242 Fax: 818-784-8008.

GREEN, KENNETH NORTON, law educator; b. Chgo., Mar. 18, 1938; s. Martin and Sarah (Owens) G.; m. Joan Nemer, Oct. 17, 1968 (div. July 1974); 1 child, Joey. AA, Wright Jr. Coll., 1960; BA, Calif. State U., Los Angeles, 1963; postgrad. Southwestern U., 1965-67; JD, U. San Fernando Valley, 1968; Cert. (hon. teaching) Los Angeles Unified Sch. Dist., 1979. Bar: Calif. 1970, U.S. Dist. Ct. (cen. dist.) Calif. 1970, U.S. Supreme Ct. 1973. Tchr. Los Angeles, Calif., 1964-70; dep. pub. defender Los Angeles County, Calif., 1970-73, 75— ; ptnr. Green & Pirosh, Los Angeles, 1973-75; chief pub. defender, 1989; instr. Paralegal dept. U. Calif., Los Angeles, 1975— ; judge pro tem Los Angeles Mcpl. Ct., 1978. Contbr. articles to legal publs. Ex officio mem. Prison Preventers, Calif. Dept. of Parole; mayor's com. Project Heavy; bd. dirs. City of Hope; Vista Del Mar; legal adv. panel Jewish Family Service; vol. atty. for indigents UCLA Law Sch.; vol. in Parole Program, com. chmn. Research Prejudice-Pvt. Clubs (Disting. Service award 1971). Served with U.S. Army, 1957-58, Korea. Mem. Pub. Defender Assn. (dir. 1971-74, chief wage negotiator 1973-75) ABA, Los Angeles County Bar Assn. (vice chmn. drug abuse 1975, exec. com. criminal justice 1977). Democrat. Jewish. Lodge: Justice (bd. dirs. 1971-72). Office: Pub Defender Los Angeles County 210 W Temple St Los Angeles CA 90012-3210

GREEN, LINDA C. education specialist administrator, researcher; b. Memphis, Nov. 21, 1947; d. Frank Allen and Mary Elizabeth (Hankins) Green; m. John Newton Osborne, Feb. 7, 1975 (div. June 1979); 1 child, Suzanne; m. Phillip Harold James, Oct. 17, 1980 (div. Aug. 2003); 1 child, Sarah Elizabeth. BA, U. Tenn., Martin, 1970; MA, Calif. State U., Long Beach, 1975; EdD in Higher Edn., U. Memphis, 1995. Instr. Memphis State U., 1979-85, dir. Wordsmith, 1984-85; asst. prof. Jackson (Tenn.) State C.C., 1985-90; adminstrv. intern State Tech. Inst. Memphis, 1990-91; asst. dir. Mid South Quality Productivity Ctr., Memphis, 1991-92; dir. acad. devel. State Tech. Inst. Memphis, 1992-93; edn. specialist Nat. Inst. Stds. and Tech., Gaithersburg, Md., 1993-94; systems mgmt. specialist U. Tenn., Martin, 1994-95; dir. assessment State Tech. Inst. Memphis, 1995-2000; v.p. acad. affairs The Nat. Grad. Sch., 2000—01. Bd. dirs., v.p. Greater Memphis Area Award for Quality; mem. adv. com. Nat. Govs. Conf. Edn., 1994; cons. City of Memphis Dept. Planning, 1993; mem. editl. bd. CQI Newsletter, 1994—; mem. adv. coun. Total Quality Learning Sys. Am. Soc. Quality, 1995—; trainer Koalaty Kids, 1996; bd. dirs. ASQ; Koalaty Kid Alliance, 1997—; mem. adj. faculty Nat. Grad. Sch., 1997—; bd. examiners Malcolm Baldrige Nat. Quality award, 1995-98, 99. Facilitator Leadership Memphis Diversity Program, 1993; vol. Girl Scouts, N.W. Tenn., 1986-89. Recipient grant Bell-South, 1991-93, fellow Tenn. Collaborative Acad., 1990-91. Mem. Am. Assn. Higher Edn., Am. Soc. Quality Control (assoc., Memphis sect. co-chair quality forum 1992-93), Tenn Assn. Devel. Educators, Phi Delta Kappa. Home: 30 Benjamin Nyes Ln North Falmouth MA 02556

GREEN, LORA MURRAY, immunologist, researcher, educator; b. Redfield, S.D., Feb. 8, 1955; d. Everett k. and Marlene Y. (Palm) Murray; m. Timothy W. Green, Jan. 24, 1976; 1 child, Keigm W. BS in Biochemistry, U. Calif., Riverside, 1981, MS in Biochemsitry, 1982, PhD in Immunology, 1987. Fellow in immunology U. Calif., Riverside; fellow in cell biology Loma Linda (Calif.) U.; rsch. immunologist JL Pettis VA Med. Ctr., Loma Linda, 1991—. Assoc. prof. medicine Loma Linda Med. Ctr., 1996—; bd. dirs. Dept. Micro and Molecular Genetics, Loma Linda; rschr. on radiation effects of thyroid NASA. Contbr. articles to profl. jours. Grantee VA, 1991-94, Loma Linda, 1995-96. Fellow Am. Assn. Immunology, Assn. Cell Biologists. Achievements include research in the role of the target tissue in autoimmune disease. Office: Loma Linda U Radiobiology Dept 11175 Campus St Loma Linda CA 92350-1700 E-mail: lgreen@dominion.llumc.edu.

GREEN, MARJORIE JOAN, elementary education educator; b. Sacramento, Apr. 8, 1938; d. Albert Robertson and Mabel Elizabeth (Wallington) Oughton; m. Norman Everett Green, Mar. 22, 1959; children: Scott Allan, Victoria Elizabeth Green-Spicer. BA, Calif. State U., Sacramento, 1960, MA, 1981. Cert. gen. edn. tchr., lang. devel. specialist, reading specialist, adminstr., Calif. Classroom tchr., reading recovery/title I tchr. San Juan Unified Sch. Dist., Carmichael, Calif., 1967-71, 91-96, reading specialist, 1971-91. Author: (curriculum guide) On the Write Track with Spelling, 1992, Teacher to Teacher: A Professional's Handbook, 1993. Bd. dirs. Fair Oaks (Calif.) Theater Festival, 1984-89, Concert Dance Found., Carmichael, 1976-79, Capital Cadets, Sacramento, 1974-76. Mem. Internat. Reading Assn., Calif. Reading Assn., Sacramento Area Reading Assn. (rec. sec. 1986-87, bd. dirs. 1980-82). Lutheran. Avocations: singing, acting, live theater. Office: Carmichael Sch 6141 Sutter Ave Carmichael CA 95608-2738

GREEN, MAY CLAYMAN, early childhood educator and administrator; b. Bklyn., Apr. 8, 1923; d. Joseph and Anna (Steinger) Clayman; m. Jerome E. Bloom, Oct. 14, 1945 (div. May 1963); children: Jeffrey Clayman Bloom, Claudia J. Segal; m. Milton Green, May 10, 1963; stepchildren: Carol R. Green, Peter A. Green. BA, Adelphi U., 1944; MA, NYU, 1956; postgrad., C.W. Post Coll./Long Island U., 1978. Rsch. asst. Winston Pub. Co., Phila., 1953-55; various positions Roslyn (N.Y.) Jr. H.S., 1956-80; adminstrv. asst. to dir. Afro-Am. affairs NYU, 1971-72; owner, exec. adminstr. New Horizons Country Day Sch., Palm Harbor, Fla., 1984-96; pres. New Horizons Edn. Cons. Firm, Palm Harbor, 1996—; bus. mgr. Curves For Women, Chantilly, Va., 2000—, Middleburg, Va., 2002. Mem. adv. bd. St. Petersburg Jr. Coll., Tarpon Springs, Fla., 1992; pres. New Horizons Edn. Found., Palm Harbor, 1992, New Horizons in Learning-Child Care Mgmt., Tarpon Springs, 1983-88, New Horizons Rsch. Cons., New Horizons Rsch. Divsn., 2003—; validator Nat. Acad. for Early Childhood Programs; mem. adv. bd. Cmty. Sch., Tarpon Springs, 1982-85; bd. dirs. Rexall Showcase Internat., Prentice Health Care; mgr. Curves for Women, 2002; rsch. dir. to author, 2003—. Pres. L.I. Riding for the Handicapped, Brookville, N.Y., 1978-80; audience devel. Fla. Orch., Tampa, 1995; mem. adv. com. Heritage Hall, Leesburg, Va., 1998—; mem. adv. bd. Fla. Symphony, 1995—; bd. dirs. North Suncoast Fla. Symphony, 1995-96; mem. Christmas in April, 1999-2000; chairperson Middleburg Point to Point Race Com., 2003. Recipient svc. appreciation awards Nassau County Children's Mus., 1960, Nassau County Girl Scouts, 1961, Inst. Afro-Am. Affaris, NYU, 1979, Jenkins Meml. award N.Y. State PTA, 1980, Pres.'s award Hempstead Child Care Ctr., 1962. Mem. ASCD, Nat. Tchrs. Assn., Roslyn Tchrs. (Ret.) Assn., Nat. Assn. for Edn. of Young Children, Middleburg Hunting Club. Avocations: travel, reading, knitting, water aerobics, theatre and music. Office: New Horizons Edn Consulting Firm # 1122 19385 Cypress Ridge Ter Lansdowne VA 20176-5171 E-mail: mayc45@aol.com.

GREEN, MICHAEL SCOTT, history educator, columnist; b. Santa Monica, Calif., Mar. 27, 1965; s. Robert W. and Marsha (Greene) H. BA with honors, U. Nev., Las Vegas, 1986, MA, 1988; PhD, Columbia U., 2000. Tchg. asst. U. Nev., Las Vegas, 1986-88, adj. instr., 1988-91, 2001—,

C.C. So. Nev., N. Las Vegas, Nev., 1987-95; tchg. asst. Columbia U., 1989-90; instr. C.C. So. Nev., N. Las Vegas, Nev., 1995-99, prof., 1999—. Columnist Nev.'s Washington Watch, Washington, 1996—, Las Vegas Mercury, 2001—. Editor: (with Gary E. Elliott) Nevada: Readings and Perspectives, 1997; contbr. chpts. to books. Spkr. Leadership Las Vegas, 1994—; spkr., exhibit author Clark County Heritage Mus., Henderson, Nev., 1990—. Rsch. fellow The Huntington Libr., 1992, 93, Ball Bros. Found., 1992, Pres.'s fellow Columbia U., 1988. Mem. Orgn. Am. Historians, We. History Assn., Nev. Hist. Soc., Far West Popular Am. Culture Assn., Phi Kappa Phi, Phi Alpha Theta. Democrat. Avocations: baseball, animation, film, music. Office: C C So Nev 3200 E Cheyenne Ave North Las Vegas NV 89030-4228

GREEN, MILDRED SIMPSON, retired elementary school educator; b. Norfolk, Va. d. Clarence and Gertrude (Perry) Simpson; m. Wallace Green Jr., July 7, 1953; 1 child, Kendall Donnell. BS, Elizabeth City Sta. Tech. U., 1952; MS in Edn., Old Dominion U., 1976. Cert. tchr., Va. Mgr. Rosedale Dairy Stores, Tidewater, Va., 1942-53; tchr. Norfolk (Va.) City Pub. Schs., 1956-88, math. and sci. tchr., 1974-88, resource tchr. for slow students, summers 1972-88, multicultural and after sch. math. tchr., 1983-88, ret., 1988. Modern dance tchr. YWCA, Norfolk, 1952-53; group leader Girl Scouts USA, Queen St. Bapt. Ch., Norfolk, 1952-53; mem. Women's Dem. Com., Norfolk, 1985; mem. civic league Chesapeake Gardens Residence, Norfolk, 1953. Named Woman of Yr. Queen St. Bapt. Ch., 1988. Avocations: interior decorating, water aerobics.

GREEN, MONICA H. history educator; BA, Barnard Coll., 1978; MA, Princeton U., 1981; PhD in History of Sci., Princeton (N.J.) U. Fellow U. N.C., Chapel Hill; assoc. prof. history Duke U.; prof. history Ariz. State U., Tempe, 2001—. Author: (essays) Women's Helathcare and the Medieval West: Texts and Contexts, 2000; contbr. articles; editor, translator: The Trotula: A Medieval Compendium of Women's Medicine, 2001. Fellow, NEH, Inst. Advanced Study, Princeton U., Nat. Humanities Ctr., John Simon Guggenheim Meml. Found., 2003. Office: Ariz State U Dept History PO Box 872501 Tempe AZ 85287-2501*

GREEN, NANCY LOUGHRIDGE, newspaper executive; b. Lexington, Ky., Jan. 19, 1942; d. William S. and Nancy O. (Green) Loughridge. BA in Journalism, U. Ky., 1964, postgrad., 1968; MA in Journalism, Ball State U., 1971; postgrad., U. Minn., 1968; EdD, Nova Southeastern U., 2003. Tchr. English, publs. adv. Clark County H.S., Winchester, Ky., 1965-66, Pleasure Ridge Park H.S., Louisville, 1966-67, Clarksville (Ind.) H.S., 1967-68, Charleston (W.Va.) H.S., 1968-69; asst. publs., pub. info. specialist W.Va. Dept. Edn., Charleston, 1969-70; tchr. journalism, publs. dir. Elmhurst H.S., Ft. Wayne, Ind., 1970-71; adviser student publs. U. Ky., Lexington, 1971-82; gen. mgr. student publs. U. Tex., Austin, 1982-85; pres., pub. Palladium-Item, Richmond, Ind., 1985-89, News-Leader, Springfield, Mo., 1989-92; asst. to pres. newspaper divsn. Gannett Co., Inc., Washington, 1992-94; exec. dir. advancement Clayton State Coll., Morrow, Ga., 1994-96; v.p. advancement Clayton Coll. & State U., Morrow, Ga., 1996-99; v.p. comm. Ga. GLOBE U. Sys., 1999-2000; dir. circulation/distbn., sales & mktg. Lee Enterprises, Davenport, Iowa, 2000—02; v.p. circulation LEE Enterprises, 2002—. Dir. urban journalism program Harte-Hanks, 1984, various Louisville and Lexington newspaper pubs., 1976-82; pres. Media Cons., Inc., Lexington, 1980; sec. Kernel Press, Inc., 1971-82. Contbr. articles to profl. jours. Bd. dirs. Studen Press Law Ctr., 1975—, Richmond Cmty. Devel. Corp., 1987-89, United Way of the Ozarks, 1990-92, ARC, 1990-92, Springfield Arts Coun., 1990-91, Bus. Devel. Corp., 1991-92, Bus. Edn. Alliance, 1991-92, Caring Found., 1991-92, Cox Hosp. Bd., 1990-92, Springfield Schs. Found., 1991-92, Jr. League, Lexington, 1980-82, Manchester Ctr., 1978-82, pres., 1979-82; chmn. Greater Richmond Progress Com., 1986-87, bd. dirs., 1986-89; pres. Leadership Wayne County, 1986-87, bd. dirs. 1985-89; adv. bd. Ind. U. East, 1985-89, Richmond C. of C., 1987-89, Ind. Humanities Coun., 1988-89, Youth Comm. Bd., 1988-92, Opera Theatre No. Va., 1992-94, Atlanta chpt. AIWF, 1995. Recipient Coll. Media Advisers First Amendment award, 1987, Disting. Svc. award Assn. Edn. Journalism and Mass Comm., 1989; named to Ball State Journalism Hall of Fame, 1988, Coll. Media Advisers Hall of Fame, 1994. Mem. Student Press Law Ctr. (bd. dirs. 1975—, pres. 1985-87, 94-96, v.p. 1992-94), Assoc. Collegiate Press, Journalism Edn. Assn. (Carl Towley award 1988), Nat. Coun. Coll. Publs. Advs. (pres. 1979-83, Disting. Newspaper Adv. 1976, Disting. Bus. Adviser 1984), Columbia Scholastic Press Assn. (Gold Key 1980), So. Interscholastic Press Assn. (Disting. Svc. award 1983), Nat. Scholastic Press Assn. (Pioneer award 1982, diversity com. 1992-, circulation fedn. bd. 2002-, postal com. 2001-), Soc. Profl. Journalists, Internat. Newspaper Mktg. Assn. N. Am. (bd. dir., 2002—), Newspaper Assn. of Am. Circulation Fedn. (postal com., 2001—, leadership adv. group, 2002—, diversity subcom., 1991—), Clayton County C. of C. (adv. bd. 1995-99, internat. com. chmn. 1996-98). E-mail: nancy.green@lee.net.

GREEN, PATRICIA PATAKY, school system administrator, consultant; b. NYC, June 18, 1949; d. William J. and Theresa M. (DiGianni) P.; m. Stephen I. Green, Dec. 7, 1975. BS, U. Md., 1971, MEd, 1977, PhD, 1994. Tchr. Prince George's County Pub. Sch., Md., 1971-83; elem. instrnl. adminstrv. specialist Thomas Stone Sch., Mt. Ranier, Md., 1984-85, Glenridge Sch., Lanham, Md., 1984, Greenbelt Ctr. Sch., Md., 1983-84, Prince George's County Pub. Schs., 1985-91; prin. Columbia Pk. Sch., Landover, Md., 1985-91; asst. supt. Prince George's County Pub. Sch., 1991-95, assoc. supt., chief divsn. adminstr., 1995-99, assoc. supt. for pupil svc., 1999—2001, acting dep. supt. for instrn., 2000—02, fellow Broad Ctr. Supt., Bd. Found., 2002; supt. sch. North Allegheny Sch. Dist., Pitts., 2002—. Exec. dir. North Allegheny Found.; cons. nationwide sch. systems; presenter in field. Featured in numerous mag. and on TV shows; contbr. articles to profl. jour. Apptd. commr. Prince George's Commn. for Children, Youth and Families; bd. dir. Prince George's County Cmty. in Sch., 1998—2002; trustee North Allegheny Found., 2002, exec. dir., 2002—03. Recipient Nat. Sch. Recognition award US Dept. Edn., 1988, Outstanding Adminstr. award Prince George's County C. of C., 1990, Outstanding Rsch. award Md. Assn. Supervision and Curriculum Devel., 1995, Outstanding Educator award Prince George's County, 1983, Spotlight on Prevention award Md. State Atty. Gen., 1998, Disting. Achievement award North Allegheny Sch. Dist., 2002. Mem. NAESP (Excellence of Achievement award 1988), ASCD, NEA, Am. Ednl. Rsch. Assn., Phi Kappa Phi. Kappa Delta Pi. Avocations: landscape gardening, photography, reading, writing, bicycling. E-mail: pgreen@northallegheny.org.

GREEN, PAUL ALLAN, scientist, engineer, educator; b. Phila., May 28, 1950; s. Leonard Arthur and Sylvia Ruth (Reuben) G. BSME, Drexel U., 1972; MSE, U. Mich., 1974, MA in Psychology, PhD, U. Mich., 1979. Occupational safety and health engr. Sterling Lighting div. Scovill, summers 1972-73; tchg. and rsch. asst. Trans Dept. Psychology/Indsl. Ops. Engring. U. Mich. Transp. Rsch., Ann Arbor, 1972-79; lectr. dept. psychology U. Mich. Transp. Rsch. Inst., 1980, lectr. dept. indsl. and ops. engring., 1980-82, adj. asst. prof. dept. indsl. and ops. engring., 1982—, asst. rsch. scientist Human Factors divsn., 1982-93, assoc. rsch. scientist Human Factors divsn., 1988-97, sr. rsch. scientist Human Factors divsn., 1998—. Adj. assoc. prof. Dept. Indsl. and Ops. Engring. U. Mich., 1993—. Contbr. numerous articles to profl. jours. Phila. Naval Shipyard trainee, 1967-72; NSF fellow, 1972-73; Nat. Inst. Occupational Safety and Health fellow, 1974, others. Fellow Ergonomics Soc.; mem. SAE, Human Factors and Ergonomics Soc. (sec. treas. elect), ITS Am. Jewish. Avocations: volleyball, running, sailing, contra dancing. Home: 1615 Harbal Dr Ann Arbor MI 48105-1815 Office: Univ of Mich Transp Rsch Inst 2901 Baxter Rd Ann Arbor MI 48109-2150

GREEN, RACHAEL PAULETTE, librarian; b. Shreveport, La., Nov. 28, 1953; d. Harold Dayton and Carolyn Francis (Sholars) G. BA in English, La. Tech U., 1975; M in Libr. and Info. Sci., La. State U., 1986; MA in Indsl. and Orgnl. Psychology, La. Tech. U., 1993. Libr. Shreve Meml. Libr., Shreveport, 1976-78, 79-89; dept. clk. ct. Fed. Ct. House, Shreveport, 1978-79; asst. libr. La. State U., Shreveport, 1989-96; mem. acad. calendar com., 1989-90, 92; mem. Noel Meml. Libr. faculty com., mem. environ. com. La. State U., Shreveport, 1991—, mem. bldgs. and grounds com., 1991—, mem. faculty senate, 1996-97, mem. faculty R&D com., 1995-97, faculty senate exec. com., 1997, assoc. libr., 1996—, mem. student affairs com., 1999-2000, chair student affairs com., 2001—02, mem. policy and pers. com., 2002—. Author: The Argument of the Eye: A Select Bibliography of the Pre-Raphaelite Movement 1848-1914, 1995; reviewer Nat. Productivity Rev., 1994-97, 99-2000, Am. Reference Books Annual, 1995—, Libr. and Info. Sci. Ann., 1999—, Jour. Organizational Excellence, 2000—. Contbg. mem. Dem. Nat. Com., 1990—. Mem. ALA (reference and adult svcs. divsn., govt. documents round table, libr. instruction round table), APA (tchg. of psychology sect.), So. States Comm. Assn., Assn. Coll. Rsch. Libraries. Democrat. Methodist. Avocations: gardening, reading. Office: 1 University Pl Shreveport LA 71115-2301 E-mail: rgreen@pilot.lsus.edu.

GREEN, ROBERT EDWARD, JR., physicist, educator; b. Clifton Forge, Va., Jan. 17, 1932; s. Robert Edward and Hazle Hall (Smith) G.; m. Sydney Sue Truitt, Feb. 1, 1962; children: Kirsten Adair, Heather Scott. BS, Coll. William and Mary, 1953; PhD, Brown U., 1959; postgrad., Aachen (Germany) Technische Hochschule, 1959-60. Physicist underwater explosions rsch. divsn. Norfolk Naval Shipyard, Va., 1959; asst. prof. mechanics Johns Hopkins U., Balt., 1960-65, assoc. prof., 1965-70, prof., 1970—, chmn. mechanics dept., 1970-72, chmn. mechanics and materials sci. dept., 1972-73, chmn. civil engring./materials sci. and engring. dept., 1979-82, chmn. materials sci. and engring. dept., 1982-85, 91-93, dir. ctr. for nondestructive evaluation, 1985—2002. Ford Found. resident sr. engr. RCA, Lancaster, Pa., 1966-67; cons. U.S. Army Ballistic Research Labs., Aberdeen Proving Ground, Md., 1973-74; physicist Ctr. for Materials Sci., U.S. Nat. Bur. Standards, Washington, 1974-81; program mgr. Def. Advanced Research Projects Agy., 1981-82; mem. nat. materials adv. bd. Author: Ultrasonic Investigation of Mechanical Properties (Treatise on Materials Science and Technology, vol. 3), 1973; co-editor 11 books; also articles. Fulbright grantee. Mem. ASM Internat., Am. Phys. Soc., Acoustical Soc. Am.; Met. Soc. AIME, Am. Soc. Nondestructive Testing, Soc. for the Advancement of Material and Process Engring., Materials Rsch. Soc., Sigma Xi, Tau Beta Pi, Alpha Sigma Mu, Sigma Nu. Methodist. Achievements include research in recovery, recrystallization, elasticity, plasticity, crystal growth and orientation, X-ray diffraction, electro-optical systems, linear and non-linear elastic wave propagation, light-sound interactions, high-power ultrasonics, ultrasonic attenuation, dislocation damping, fatigue, acoustic emission, non-destructive testing, polymers, biomaterials, synchrotron radiation, composites, sensors and process control. Office: Johns Hopkins U Materials Sci and Engring Dept 3400 N Charles St Baltimore MD 21218-2689 E-mail: robert.green@jhu.edu.

GREEN, ROSE BASILE (MRS. RAYMOND S. GREEN), poet, author, educator; b. New Rochelle, N.Y., Dec. 19, 1914; d. Salvatore and Caroline (Galgano) Basile; m. Raymond S. Green, June 20, 1942; children: Carol-Rae Green Sadano, Raymond Ferguson St. John. BA, Coll. New Rochelle, 1935; MA, Columbia U., 1941; PhD, U. Pa., 1962; LHD (hon.), Gwynedd-Mercy Coll., 1979, Cabrini Coll., 1982. Tchr. Torrington H.S., Conn., 1936-42; writer, researcher Fed. Writers Project, 1935-36; freelance script writer Cavalcade of Am., NBC, 1940-42; assoc. prof. English, univ. registrar Tampa U., Tampa, 1942-43; spl. instr. English, Temple U., Phila., 1953-57; prof. dept. English, Cabrini Coll., Radnor, Pa., 1957-70, chmn. dept., 1957-70. Author: Cabrinian Philosophy of Education, 1967, (criticism) The Italian-American Novel, 1972, (poetry books) To Reason Why, 1971, Primo Vino, 1972, 76 for Philadelphia, 1975, Woman, The Second Coming, 1977, Lauding the American Dream, 1980, Century Four, 1981, Songs of Ourselves, 1982, (transl.) The Life of Mother Frances Cabrini, 1984, The Pennsylvania People, 1984, Challenger Countdown, 1988, Five Hundred Years of America, 1492-1992, 1992, The Distaff Side: Great Women of Am. History, 1995; editor faculty jour. A-Zimuth, 1963-70. Exec. dir. Am. Inst. Italian Studies; dir. lit. com. Phila. Art Alliance; bd. dirs., trustee Free Libr. of Phila.; v.p., dir. Nat. Italian-Am. Found.; chair Nat. Adv. Coun. Ethnic Heritage Studies; adv. bd. Women for Greater Phila.; dir. Balch Inst. Phila. Decorated cavalier Republic of Italy; named Woman of Yr. Pa. Sons of Italy, 1975, Disting. Dau. of Pa., 1978; recipient Nat. Amita award for lit., 1976, Nat. Bicentennial award for poetry DAR, 1976, other awards for contbns. to lit. and edn. Fellow Royal Soc. Arts (London); mem. AAUW (dir.-at-large), Am. Acad. Polit. and Social Sci., Acad. Am. Poets, Acad. Polit. Sci., Am. Studies Assn., Ethnic Studies Assn., Nat. Council Tchrs. English, Am.-Italy Soc. (dir. 1952—), Eastern Pa. Coll. New Rochelle Alumnae (pres. 1951-54), Cosmopolitan Club, Franklin Inn Club (Phila.), Kappa Gamma Phi. Home: 308 Manor Rd Lafayette Hill PA 19444-1741

GREEN, ROSE MARY, school system administrator; b. St. Louis, July 20, 1943; d. Lawrence Deval and Rose Amelia (Truhe) G. BA, Notre Dame Coll., 1965; MEd, U. Mo., St. Louis, 1971. Tchr. St. Peter Sch., Jefferson City, Mo., 1965-68, Ascension Sch., Normandy, Mo., 1968-75; reading specialist Normandy (Mo.) Sch. Dist., 1975-89; summer sch. prin. Normandy (Mo.) Early Childhood, 1979-89; curriculum coord. Normandy (Mo.) Sch. Dist., 1989—. Mem. ASCD, Nat. Coun. Tchrs. English, Internat. Reading Assn., Mo. State Tchrs., Greater St. Louis Tchrs. (sec. 1989-93), St. Louis Suburban Reading (membership dir. 1991—). Home: 11860 Doverhill Ct Saint Louis MO 63128-1520 Office: Normandy Sch Dist 3855 Lucas And Hunt Rd Saint Louis MO 63121-2919

GREEN, THEREASA ELLEN, elementary education educator; b. Wichita, Kans., Nov. 22, 1945; d. Ralph Elwood and Wilma Arleen (Ambler) Becker; m. Gary Joseph Fox, May 27, 1964 (dec. Dec. 1975); children: Angela Ellen, Tamara Jo; m. Bruce Green, Aug. 21, 1977 (div. 1993); 1 child, Christian Todd. BS Edn., McPherson Coll., 1968; M Elem. Edn., Wichita State U., 1987, Reading Specialist, 1990; cert. in Adminstrn., Kans. State U., 2001. Cert. tchr. elem. edn., Kans. Elem. tchr. Unified Sch Dist. 308, Hutchinson, Kans., 1969-70, 1970-72, 1972-78, 1978—; lead tchr. Unified Sch. Dist. Allen Elem., Hutchinson, 1994-98; McCandless reading specialist, 1998—2001; prin. Fairfield West Elem., Sylvia, Kans., 2001—. Cons./presenter Attention Deficit Disorder Orgn. for Parents of ADHD Children, 1994, 99; tchr. summer sch., Hutchinson, mem. curriculum coms, other coms.; ct. apptd. spl. child advocate, Reno County Kans. Cts. Author curriculum for Farm Skills for City Kids, 1986. Asst. chmn. Christian Bus. Women, Hutchinson, 1970-71; Christian edn. dir. First Christian Ch., Hutchinson, 1972-78; dir. children's ministries First Ch. of Nazarene, Hutchinson, 1993-94; Kans. self-propelled camping dir. Nat. Camper/Hikers Assn., 1978-90. Excellence grantee Southwestern Bell Telephone Co., Topeka, Kans., 1991-94; recipient scholarship Performance Learning Systems Project TEACH, 1993, others. Mem. ASCD, AAUW, Kans. Assn. Tchrs. USA Math., Internat. Reading Assn., Performance Learning Systems, Kans. Reading Assn. (sec. Reno county chpt. 1996-98), Elem. Adminstrs. of Kans., Ark Valley Reading Assn. (sec. 1996-97, 97-98, v.p. 1999—), others. Nazarene. Avocations: skiing, collecting cows and foxes, travel, working with children. Home: 602 Eldorado Dr Hutchinson KS 67502-8416 E-mail: egreen@usd310.k12.ks.us.

GREEN, VICKIE LEE, gifted and talented educator, music educator; b. Sterling, Colo., Sept. 28, 1954; d. Victor Eugene and Beth Arlene (Hunter) Hanson; m. James Harvey Green, Aug. 6, 1976; 1 child, Erich Alan. B in Music Edn., U. Denver, 1976, MA in Gifted and Talented Edn., 1988. Cert. music edn. tchr., Colo. Elem. vocal tchr. East Otero R-1 Sch. Dist., La Junta, Colo., 1976-83; tchr. music Morgan C.C., Ft. Morgan, Colo., 1983-84; mid. sch. band and vocal tchr. Sch. Dist. RE-3, Ft. Morgan, 1984-89, elem. vocal tchr., 1989-91; tchr. Weld 6, Greeley, Colo., 1991—. Cons. gifted edn. Colo. Dept. Edn., Denver, 1989-91; mem. artist-in-residence program Colo. Coun. Arts and Humanities, Denver, 1984. Mem. NEA, ASCD, Colo. Edn. Assn., Greeley Edn. Assn. Avocations: piano, flute, clarinet, reading. Home: 2318 Sunset Ln Greeley CO 80634-7608 Office: Meeker Elem Sch 2221 28th Ave Greeley CO 80634-7650 E-mail: vlhansongreen@comcast.net.

GREEN, VIVIAN LOUISE, preschool program specialist; b. Belle Glade, Fla., Apr. 8, 1949; d. George Nathenial and Jimmie Louise (Thomas) Berry; m. Ernest Green II, Aug. 28, 1971; 1 child, Ernest Green III. BS, Fla. A&M U., 1971; MA, U. West Fla., 1981, MEd, 1990. Reading tchr. Palm Beach (Fla.) County Schs., 1971-72; tchr. 2d grade Oakaloosa County Schs., Ft. Walton Beach, Fla., 1971-80, primary resource tchr., 1980-88, specialist, 1988—. Mem. NAACP (chair fund raising 1989—), Okaloosa-Walton Assn. Young Children (pres. 1991—), League of Women Voters, Phi Delta Kappa, Delta Kappa Phi, Delta Sigma Theta (pres. Okaloosa County 1984-86, 89). Democrat. Roman Catholic. Avocations: tennis, walking, reading. Home: 242 Echo Cir Fort Walton Beach FL 32548-6315

GREEN, WAYNE HUGO, psychiatrist, psychoanalyst; b. Schenectady, N.Y., July 23, 1941; s. Albert George and Mildred (Hugo) G. AB, U. Chgo., 1963; MD, NYU, 1967. Diplomate Am. Bd. Psychiatry and Neurology; cert. in Psychoanalysis, William Alanson White Inst. Psychiatry, Psychoanalysis, and Psychology, 1977. Intern Lenox Hill Hosp., N.Y.C., 1967-68; resident in psychiatry NYU-Bellevue Med. Ctr., 1970-72, fellow in child psychiatry, 1972-74; asst. dir. Children's Mental Hygiene Clinic-Bellevue Psychiat. Hosp., N.Y.C., 1974-77; unit chief Children's Psychiat. Inpatient Svc.-Bellevue Hosp., N.Y.C., 1978-86, unit chief child and adolescent outpatient clinic, 1986—2000; asst. clin. prof. psychiatry NYU, 1977—79, asst. prof. psychiatry, 1979—85, assoc. prof. clin. psychiatry, 1985—2000; chief psychiatrist Children's Aid Soc., N.Y.C., 2001—. Asst. attending psychiatry NYU Med. Ctr., U. Hosp., N.Y.C., 1974-2000; asst. attending psychiatrist Bellevue Hosp. Ctr., N.Y.C., 1974-2000; dir. tng. & edn. NYU Residency in Child and Adolescent Psychiatry, 1995-99. Author: Child and Adolescent Clinical Psychopharmacology, 3d edit., 2001; contbr. more than 50 articles to profl. jours. With USPHS, 1968-70. Fellow Am. Acad. Child Psychiatry, N.Y. Coun. Child Psychiatry. Office: Children's Aid Soc 150 E 45th St New York NY 10017

GREEN, WILLIAM, archaeologist; b. Chgo., May 30, 1953; s. David and Lillian (Kerdeman) G. AB, Grinnell Coll., 1974; MA, U. Wis., 1977, PhD, 1987. Staff archaeologist State Hist. Soc. of Wis., Madison, 1978-86; asst. prof. archaeology Western Ill. U., Macomb, 1980, 81; state archaeologist U. Iowa, Iowa City, 1988-2001, adj. asst. prof. anthropology, 1988-94, adj. assoc. prof. anthropology, 1994-2001; dir. Logan Mus. Anthropology, Beloit (Wis.) Coll., 2001—, adj. prof. anthropology, 2001—. Editor jour. The Wis. Archaeologist, 1983-88; editor: Midcontinental Jour. Archaeology, 1998-02; contbr. articles and revs. to profl. jours. Chair Johnson County Hist. Preservation Commn., Iowa, 1991-93. Grantee NSF, 1990-91, State Hist. Soc. Iowa, Leopold Ctr. for Sustainable Agr., Iowa Acad. Sci., 1988-91, 95. Fellow Am. Anthropol. Assn., Midwest Arch. Conf., Inc (pres. 2002-). Jewish. Office: Logan Mus Anthropology Beloit Coll Beloit WI 53511

GREENAWALT, ROBERT KENT, lawyer, law educator; b. Bklyn., June 25, 1936; s. Kenneth William and Martha (Sloan) G.; m. Sanja Milic, July 14, 1968 (dec. Nov. 1988); children: Robert Milic, Alexander Kent Anton, Andrei Milenko Kenneth; m. Elaine Pagels, June 1995; children: Sarah Pagels, David. AB with honors, Swarthmore Coll., 1958; Ph.B.; Keasbey fellow, Oxford (Eng.) U., 1960; LL.B.; Kent scholar, Columbia U., 1963. Bar: N.Y. 1963. Law clk. to Justice Harlan, U.S. Supreme Ct., 1963-64; spl. asst. AID, Washington, 1964-65; mem. faculty Columbia U. Law Sch., 1965—, prof. law, 1969—, Cardozo prof., 1979—, Univ. prof., 1990—. Dep. solicitor gen. U.S., 1971-72; assoc. dir. N.Y. Inst. Legal Edn., 1969; vis. prof. Stanford U. Law Sch., 1970, Northwestern U. Law Sch., 1983, Marshall-Wythe Sch. Law, 1985, N.Y.U. Law Sch., 1989-90; atty. Lawyers Com. Civil Rights, 1965, trustee, 1992; mem. staff Task Force Law Enforcement N.Y.C., 1965; vis. fellow All Souls Coll. Oxford (Eng.) U., 1979 Co-author: The Sectarian College and The Public Purse, 1970; author: Legal Protections of Privacy, 1976, Discrimination and Reverse Discrimination, 1983, Conflicts of Law and Morality, 1987, Religious Convictions and Political Choice, 1988, Speech, Crime and the Uses of Language, 1989, Law and Objectivity, 1992, Private Consciences and Public Reasons, 1995, Fighting Words, 1995, Statutory Interpretation: Twenty Questions, 1999; editor in chief Columbia U. Law Rev., 1962-63; contbr. articles to legal jours. Recipient Ivy award Swarthmore Coll., 1958; fellow Am. Council Learned Soc., 1972-73. Fellow Am. Acad. Arts and Scis.; mem. Am. Philos. Soc., Am. Law Inst., Am. Soc. Polit. and Legal Philosophy (pres. 1992-93). Office: Columbia U Law Sch 435 W 116th St New York NY 10027-7201

GREENBAUM, STUART I. economist, educator; b. N.Y.C., Oct. 7, 1936; s. Sam and Bertha (Freimark) G.; m. Margaret E. Wache, July 29, 1964; children: Regina Gail, Nathan Carl. BS, NYU, 1959; PhD, Johns Hopkins U., 1964. Fin. economist Fed. Res. Bank of Kansas City, Mo., 1962-66; sr. economist Office of the Comptroller of the Currency, Washington, 1966-67; assoc. prof. econs. U. Ky., Lexington, 1968-74, prof., 1974-76, chmn. dept. econs., 1975-76; vis. prof. fin. Kellogg Grad. Sch. Mgmt., Northwestern U., Evanston, Ill., 1974-75, prof. fin., 1976-78, Harold L. Stuart prof. banking and fin., 1978-83, Norman Strunk disting. prof. fin. instns., 1983-95, dir. Banking Research Ctr., 1976-95, assoc. dean for acad. affairs, 1988-92; dean John M. Olin Sch. of Bus. Washington U., St. Louis, 1995—, Bank of Am. prof. mgrl. leadership, John M. Olin Sch. bus., 2000—. Cons. Fed. Res. Bank Chgo., 1994-95; mem. Fed. Savs. and Loan Adv. Coun., 1986-89; vis. prof. banking and fin. Leon Recanati Grad. Sch. Bus. Adminstrn., Tel Aviv (Israel) U., 1980-81. Assoc. editor Nat. Banking Rev., 1966-67, So. Econ. Jour., 1977-79, Jour. Fin., 1977-83, Jour. Banking and Fin., 1980-92, Jour. Fin. Rsch., 1981-87, Fin. Rev., 1985-89, Managerial and Decision Econs., 1989-94, Jour. Econs., Mgmt. and Strategy, 1991-95; founding and mng. editor Jour. Fin. Intermediation, 1989-96. With U.S. Army, 1958-64. Mem. Am. Econ. Assn., Am. Fin. Assn. Office: Washington U Campus Box 1133 One Brookings Dr Saint Louis MO 63130-4899 E-mail: greenbaum@olin.wwtl.edu.

GREENBAUM, VICKY, music and English educator; b. Denver, May 17, 1957; d. Joseph and Ruth Marianne Claire (Schonfeld) G. BA, Calif. State U., Northridge, 1980; MA, Calif. State U., 1984. Cert. secondary educator, English and music. Staff summer program Meadowmount Sch. for Music, Elizabethtown, N.Y., 1980-84; grad. asst. English Calif. State U., Northridge, 1980-82; violinist Houston Grand Opera Orch., 1982-84; conducting asst. Berkeley (Calif.) Opera, 1985-88; tchr. English Newark (Calif.) and Alameda Pub. Schs., 1985-88; music dir. Morristown (N.J.) Beard Sch., 1988-89; master tchr. English Phillips Acad., Andover, Mass., 1988-90; tchr. English, music dir. Frisch Sch., Paramus, N.J., 1989-90; tchr., orch. dir. Northfield (Mass.) Mt. Hermon Sch., 1990-95; orch. dir. Menlo Sch., Atherton, Calif., 1995—. Conductor Northampton (Mass.) Cmty. Music Ctr., 1993-94; guest conductor Springfield (Mass.) Young Peoples Symphony, 1993—. Contbr. articles to profl. English jours. Vol. counselor Pacific Ctr. for Human Growth, Berkeley, 1985-87; mem. acad. com. Northfield Mt. Herman Sch., 1991-94, sec. to faculty exec. com., 1994-95. Recipient fellowship NEH, 1992, Pflug fellowship Northfield Mt. Herman Sch., 1994, named Tchr. of Yr. Rotary, 2002; grantee Northfield Mt. Herman Sch., 1993. Mem. Mensa, Hemingway Soc. Office: Menlo Sch 50 Valparaiso Ave Atherton CA 94027-4401 E-mail: vgreenbaum@menloschool.org.

GREENBERG, DAVID BERNARD, chemical engineering educator; b. Norfolk, Va., Nov. 2, 1928; s. Abraham David and Ida (Frenkil) G.; m. Helen Muriel Levine, Aug. 15, 1959 (div. Aug. 1980); children: Lisa, Jan, Jill BS in Chem. Engring., Carnegie Inst. Tech., 1952; MS in Chem. Engring., Johns Hopkins U., 1959; PhD, La. State U., 1964. Registered profl. engr., La. Process engr. U.S. Indsl. Chem. Co., Balt., 1952-55; project engr. FMC Corp., Balt., 1955-56; asst. prof. U.S. Naval Acad., Annapolis, Md., 1958-61; from instr. to prof. La. State U., Baton Rouge, 1961-74; prof. chem. engring. U. Cin., 1974—, head dept., 1974-81. Program dir. engring. divsn. NSF, Washington, 1972-73, chem. and thermal scis. divsn., 1989-90; sr. scientist Chem. Sys. Lab., Dept. Army, Edgewood, Md., 1981-83; cons. Burk & Assocs., New Orleans, 1970-78. Contbr. numerous articles on chem. engring. to profl. jours. Mem. Cin. Mayor's Energy Task Force, 1981— . Served to lt. USNR, 1947-52 Esso research fellow, 1964-65, NSF fellow, 1961 Fellow Am. Soc. for Laser Medicine and Surgery; mem. Am. Inst. Chem. Engrs., Am. Chem. Soc., Am. Soc. for Engring. Edn., Sigma Xi, Tau Beta Pi, Phi Lambda Upsilon. Jewish. Home: 8547 Wyoming Club Dr Cincinnati OH 45215-4243 Office: Univ Cin Dept Chem Engring PO Box 210012 Cincinnati OH 45221-0171 E-mail: David.Greenberg@uc.edu.

GREENBERG, DEBORAH, speech and language pathologist; b. N.Y.C., Dec. 11, 1966; d. Stanley and Annette (Kreistman) G. BA, Queens Coll., 1988; MS, Bklyn. Coll., 1990. Cert. tchr. of speech and hearing handicapped, N.Y. Speech/lang. pathologist N.Y.C. Bd. Edn., 1990—. Cons. speech-lang. pathologist Caring Profls., Lawrence, N.Y., 1994—. Mem. Am. Speech and Hearing Assn., N.Y. State Speech and Hearing Assn. Republican. Jewish. Avocations: reading, music, piano, exercise, travel. Home: 7943 Summerdale Ave Philadelphia PA 19111-2949 Office: NYC Bd Edn 65 Court St Brooklyn NY 11201-4916

GREENBERG, ELINOR MILLER, university official, consultant; b. Bklyn., Nov. 13, 1932; d. Ray and Susan (Weiss) Miller; m. Manuel Greenberg, Dec. 26, 1955; children: Andrea, Julie, Michael. BA, Mt. Holyoke Coll., 1953; MA, U. Wis.-Madison, 1954; EdD, U. No. Colo., 1981; LittD (hon.), St. Mary-of-the-Woods, Ind., 1983; LHD (hon.), Profl. Sch. Psychology, Calif., 1987. Speech pathologist, faculty mem. Arapahoe Inst. for Cmty. Devel., Littleton, Colo., 1954—69, exec. dir., 1969—71; founding dir. Univ. without Walls, Loretto Heights Coll., Denver, 1971—79, asst. acad. dean, 1982—84, asst. to pres., 1984—85; regional exec. officer Coun. for Adult and Experiential Learning, Chgo., 1979—91; founding exec. dir. US West Comm.-CWA, Pathways to the Future, 1986—91; rsch. assoc. Inst. for Rsch. on Adults in Higher Edn., U. Md., U. Coll., 1991; exec. dir. project leadership, 1986—. Project dir. Healthcare Seminars, Colo. Rural New Economy Initiative, 2000-02; pres., CEO EMG and Assocs.; sr. cons. US West Found., No. Telecom, Rose Found., Cogeoinfo., 1992-96; cons. Western Interstate Commn. on Higher Edn., 2003—; founding regional coord. Mountain and Plains Partnership, 1996-2002; adminstr. Visible Human Project-Undergrad. Edit., U. Colo. Health Scis. Ctr., 2002—; cons. NEON Project, Western Interstate Commn. for Higher Edn., 2003—; cons. in field. Co-editor, contbr.: Educating Learners of All Ages, 1980; co-author: Designing Undergraduate Education, 1981, Widening Ripples, 1986, Leading Effectively, 1987, In Our Fifties: Voices of Men and Women Reinventing Their Lives, 1993, MAPP Online Voices, 2000; editor, contbr.: New Partnerships: Higher Education and the Nonprofit Sector, 1982, Enhancing Leadership, 1989, Liberal Education Journal, 1992, Seven MAPP Studies, 2002; author: Weaving: The Fabric of a Woman's Life, 1991, Journey for Justice, 1994; guest editor Liberal Edn., 1992; gen. editor Seven MAPP Studies, 2002; feature writer Colo. Woman News, 1993-96, Women's Bus. News, 1995-96; contbr. Sculpting The Learning Organization, 1993; contbr. articles to profl. jours. Bd. dirs., exec. com. Anti Defamation League of B'nai B'rith, Denver, 1981-99, chair women's leadership com., 1991-93, bd. dirs., 1985-95; mem. Colo. State Bd. for C.C. and Occupational Edn., 1981-86, vice-chair, 1984-85; bd. dirs. Internat. Women's Forum, 1986-88, Internat. Women's Forum Leadership Found., 1991-95, Griffith Ctr., Golden, Colo., 1982-86, Colo. Bd. Continuing Legal and Jud. Edn., 1984-96; pres. Women's Forum of Colo., 1986; v.p. Women's Forum Colo. Found., 1987; adv. bd. Anchor Ctr. Blind Child, Colo. Coalition Prevention Nuclear War, Mile Hi Girl Scouts, Nat. Conf. on Edn. for Women's Devel.; cmty. adv. bd. Colo. Woman News; adv. com. Colo. Pvt. Occupl. Sch., 1990-98, Colo. Cmty. Incentive Fund; co-chair Gov.'s Women's Econ. Devel. Taskforce, Women's Econ. Devel. Coun., 1988-96; bd. visitors U. Hosp., U. Colo., 1990-91, gov. apptd. Colo. Math., Sci. and Tech. Commn., chair, 1991-93, co-telecom. adv. commn. TAC 14, chair, 1993-95; founding steering com. Colo. Women's Leadership Coalition, 1988-96; mem. interdisciplinary telecomm. program, exec. bd. U. Colo., 1992—; U.S. Dept. of Edn., mem. Tech. Panels, 1991—, mem. Expert Panel on Lifelong Learning, 1999—, Western AHEC Reg. Learning System, chair, coursework com., 1998; bd. dirs. Colo. Rural Tech. Program, 1996-2000, Housing for All/Metro Denver Fair Housing Ctr., 1999-2003, chair, 2002-03; chair Colo. Coalition for the Advancement of Telehealth, 2002—; co-chair Colo. Coun. on Telehealth, 2003—; mem. UPT Task Force on Telehealth. Named Citizen of Yr., Omega Psi Phi, Denver, 1966, Woman of Decade Littleton Ind. Newspapers, 1970; grantee W. K. Kellogg Found., 1982, Weyerhaeuser Found., 1986, Fund for Improvement of Post Secondary Edn., 1977, 80, Robert Wood Johnson Found., 1997-2002; recipient Sesquicentennial award Mt. Holyoke Coll. Alumni Assn., 1987, Minoru Yasui Cmty. Vol. award, 1991, Women of Excellence award Colo. Women's Leadership Coalition, 1996, Founding Mothers award, 1997, Woman of Dist., Mile High Girl Scouts, 1997, Martin Luther King Disting. Svc. award to Little Coun. for Human Rels., Arapahoe C.C., 2003, Arthur and Bea Branscombe Meml. award Housing for All: The Metro Denver Fair Housing Ctr., 2003. Mem. Am. Assn. for Higher Edn., Assn. for Experiential Edn. (editl. bd. 1978-80), Am. Speech, Lang. and Hearing Assn., Colo. Rural Devel. Coun., Nat. Conf. Women's Devel. Edn., Kappa Delta Pi. Democrat. Jewish. Home: 6725 S Adams Way Littleton CO 80122-1801 E-mail: ellie.greenberg@uchsc.edu.

GREENBERG, EVA MUELLER, librarian; b. Vienna, July 19, 1929; came to U.S., 1939; d. Paul and Greta (Scheuer) Mueller; m. Nathan Abraham Greenberg, June 22, 1952; children: David Stephen, Judith Helen, Lisa Pauline. AB, Harvard/Radcliffe Coll., 1951; MLS, Kent State U., 1975. Head reference McIntire Libr., Zanesville, Ohio, 1978; with Lorain (Ohio) Pub. Libr., 1978-81; head reference Elyria (Ohio) Pub. Libr., 1981-82; reference libr. adult svcs. Cuyahoga County Pub. Libr., Strongsville, Ohio, 1983-89; head adult svcs. Oberlin (Ohio) Pub. Libr., 1989—. Contbr. articles to profl. jours. Grantee Ohio Humanities Coun. for Pub. Programs; named Libr. of Yr., Ohio Support Svcs., 2000. Mem. ALA, Ohio Libr. Assn. (coord. community info. task force). Home: 34 S Cedar St Oberlin OH 44074-1520 Office: Oberlin Pub Libr 65 S Main St Oberlin OH 44074-1673

GREENBERG, HENRY MORTON, physician, educator; b. N.Y.C., Oct. 5, 1940; s. David and Flora (Budnick) G.; m. Barbara Helene Brown, June 20, 1965; children: Lisa, Jeffrey Oliver. BA, U. Pa., 1961; MD, Tufts U., 1965. Intern St. Elizabeth Hosp., Boston, 1965-66; resident St. Lukes Hosp., N.Y.C., 1968-70; fellow in cardiology Roosevelt Hosp., N.Y.C., 1970-72, dir. CCU, 1972-79; dir. coronary care unit Roosevelt site St. Lukes Roosevelt Hosp., N.Y.C., 1979—; from instr. to assoc. clin. prof. of medicine Columbia U. Coll. Physicians & Surgeons, N.Y.C., 1972-87, assoc. prof. clin. medicine, 1987—. Editor: Sudden Coronary Death, 1982, Clinical Aspects of Life Threatening Arrhythmias, 1984, Beyond the Crisis: Preserving the Capacity for Excellence in Health Care and Medical Science, 1994; contbr. articles to profl. jours. With USPHS, 1966-68, Peace Corps physician, Cameroon, West Africa. Fellow ACP, Am. Coll. Cardiology, Am. Heart Assn. (coun. clin. cardiology), N.Y. Acad. Scis. (bd. govs. 1991-99, pres. 1994-95, chmn. 1995-96). Office: St Lukes Roosevelt Hosp 428 W 59th St 1000 10th Ave New York NY 10019-1192

GREENBERG, HINDA FEIGE, library director; b. Bayreuth, Germany, Feb. 26, 1947; arrived in U.S., 1951; d. Samuel Leon and Sima (Schampagnere) F.; m. Joseph Lawrence, July 6, 1968; children: David Micah, Jacob Alexander. BA, Temple U., 1969; MLS, Rutgers U., 1981; PhD, Drexel U., 1999. Assoc. librarian Ednl. Testing Svc., Princeton, NJ, 1981-86; dir. info. ctr. Carnegie Found., Princeton, 1986-97, Robert Wood Johnson Found., Princeton, 1997—. Pres.-elect Consortium of Found. Librs. Avocation: travel.

GREENBERG, INA FLORENCE, retired elementary education educator; b. N.Y.C., May 1, 1933; d. David Samuel and Nettie (Schapiro) Grossman; m. Ira Greenberg, Dec. 24, 1966 (dec. Dec. 1991); 1 child, Charles Joseph. BS in Edn., CCNY, 1955, MS in Edn., 1958. Cert. elem. tchr., N.Y. Tchr. elem. Pub. Sch. 2 Bronx, N.Y.C., 1955-69; tchr. writing Pub. Sch. 46 Bronx, N.Y.C., 1983-95; retired, 1995. Mem. Hadassh (Bay Club chpt., pres. Orah group Yonkers chpt. 1992-93), B'nai B'rith (Bay Club unit, pres. Lincoln Pk. chpt. 1977-79), Sigma Tau Delta. Avocation: creative writing.

GREENBERG, JACK, lawyer, law educator; b. N.Y.C., Dec. 22, 1924; s. Max and Bertha (Rosenberg) G.; m. Sema Ann Tanzer, 1950 (div. 1970); children: Josiah, David, Sarah, Ezra; m. Deborah M. Cole, 1970; children: Suzanne, William Cole. AB, Columbia U., 1945, LLB, 1948, LLD, 1984, Morgan State Coll., Central State Coll., 1965, Lincoln U., 1977, John Jay Coll. Criminal Justice, 1983, De Paul U., 1994. Bar: N.Y. 1949. Rsch. asst. N.Y. State Law Revision Commn., 1949; asst. counsel NAACP Legal Def. and Ednl. Fund, 1949-61, dir.-counsel, 1961-84; argued in sch. segregation, sit-in, employment discrimination, poverty, capital punishment, other cases before U.S. Supreme Ct.; adj. prof. Columbia U. Law Sch., 1970-84, prof., vice-dean, 1984-89; dean Columbia Coll., 1989-93; prof. Columbia U. Law Sch., 1993—. Cons. Ctr. Applied Legal Studies, U. Witwatersrand, 1978; vis. lectr. Yale U. Law Sch., 1971; vis. prof. CCNY, 1977, Tokyo U., 1993-94, 99, St. Louis U. Law Sch., 1994, Lewis and Clark Law Sch., 1994-98, Princeton U., 1995, U. Munich, 1998; lectr. Harvard U. Law Sch., 1983, Shikes fellow, 1981; disting. lectr. humanities Columbia Coll. Physicians and Surgeons, 1998, U. Nurenberg-Erlangen, 1999. Author: (with H. Hill) Citizens Guide to Desegregation, 1955, Race Relations and American Law, 1959, Judicial Process and Social Change, 1976, (with James Vorenberg) Dean Cuisine or the Liberated Man's Guide to Fine Cooking, 1990, Crusaders in the Courts, 1994; contbg. author: Race, Sex and Religious Discrimination in International Law, 1981; contbr. articles to profl. jours. Bd. dirs. N.Y.C. Legal Aid Soc., Internat. League for Human Rights, Mex.-Am. Legal Def. Fund, 1968-75, Asian Am. Legal Def. Fund, 1980—, Human Rights Watch, 1978-98, NAACP Legal Def. and Ednl. Fund. Co-recipient Grenville Clark prize, 1978; hon. fellow U. Pa. Law Sch., 1975. Fellow AAAS, Am. Coll. Trial Lawyers; mem. ABA (commn. to study FTC, adv. com. to spl. com. on crime prevention, sect. on individual rights and responsibilities, Silver Gavel award, Thurgood Marshall prize, Presdl. Citizens medal 2001), N.Y. State Bar Assn. (exec. dir. spl. com. study state antitrust laws 1956), Am. Law Inst., Bar Assn. City N.Y. (Cardozo lectr. 1973) Adminstrv. Conf. U.S. Home: 118 Riverside Dr New York NY 10024-3708 Office: Columbia Law Sch 435 W 116th St New York NY 10027-7297

GREENBERG, MARC LELAND, education educator; b. LA, Nov. 9, 1961; s. Howard A. and Suzanne (Blau) G.; m. Marta Pirnat-Greenberg, July 6, 1988; children: Benjamin C., Lea H. BA, UCLA, 1983; MA, U. Chgo., 1984; PhD, U. Calif., L.A., 1990. Asst. prof. U. Kans., Lawrence, 1990-95, assoc. prof., 1995-2001, chmn. Slavic dept., 2000—, prof., 2001—. Author: A Historical Phonology of the Slovene Language, 2000; N.Am. editor Slovenski jezik/Slovene Linguistic Studies jour., Ljubljana, Slovenia, Lawrence, Kans., 1997—; contbr. articles to profl. jours. Humanities Rsch. fellow Hall Ctr., U. Kans., Lawrence, 1994; Univ. Tchrs.' fellow NEH, Washington, 1993; Tchg. fellow Am. Coun. Learned Soc., Washington, 1990; rsch. fellow Fulbright-Hayes, Washington, 1988-89; Zahvala/Gratitude award Govt. of Rep. Slovenia, Ljubljana, 1992. Mem. Soc. Slovene Studies (exec. coun. 1994-97), Am. Assn. Advancement Slavic Studies, Am. Assn. Tchrs. Slavic and East European Langs. (Best Book in Slavic Linguistics 2002), East European Anthropology Group, Assn. Study Nationalities, Phi Beta Kappa. Home: 4209 Wheat State St Lawrence KS 66049-3585 Office: U Kans Slavic Dept 1445 Jayhawk Blvd Rm 2133 Lawrence KS 66045-7590 E-mail: mlg@ku.edu.

GREENBERG, MILTON, political scientist, educator; b. Bklyn., Feb. 20, 1927; s. Samuel and Fannie (Schnell) G.; m. Sonia B. Brown, June 20, 1948; children: Anne Greenberg Bookin, Nancy R. BA, Bklyn. Coll., 1949; MA, U. Wis., 1950, PhD (univ. scholar), 1955; LLD (hon.), Am. U., 1993. Instr. polit. sci. U. Tenn., Knoxville, 1952-55; from asst. prof. to prof. Western Mich. U., Kalamazoo, 1955-64, chmn. polit. sci. dept., 1965-69; dean Coll. Arts and Scis., Ill. State U., Normal, 1969-72; v.p. acad. affairs, dean faculties Roosevelt U., Chgo., 1972-80; provost, v.p. acad. affairs Am. U., Washington, 1980-93, prof. govt., 1980-97, interim pres., provost, 1990-91, prof. emeritus, 1997—. Rsch. assoc. Cleve. Met. Svcs. Commn., 1957; cons. Citizens for Mich. (constl. reform movement), 1960; cons. Supreme Ct. Hist. Soc., 1997—, Coun. for Higher Edn. Accreditation, 1997—. Author: (companion book to PBS show) The GI Bill: The Law That Changed America, 1997, (with J.C. Plano) The American Political Dictionary, 1962, 11th edit., 2002; (with others) The Poltical Science Dictionary, 1973; contbr. to Collier's Yearbook, 1959-93, Chronicle of Higher Education Career Network, 1999-; mem. editl. bd. Ednl. Record, 1985-97, guest editor, 1994; cons. editor ASHE-ERIC Higher Edn. Reports, 1986-90; contbr. articles to profl. jours. and newspapers. Mem. Mich. Gov.'s Commn. on Legis. Apportionment, 1962, Kalamazoo Community Rels. Bd., 1964-65; mem. bd. dirs. Combined Health Appeal of Nat. Capital Area, 1982-93, v.p., 1983-85, pres., 1986-88. Social Sci. Rsch. Coun. grantee, 1959, 61. Mem. Am. Polit. Sci. Assn., Midwest Polit. Sci. Assn. (exec. coun. 1972-75), Mid. States Assn. Colls. and Schs. (cons.-evaluator 1983-97), Law and Soc. Assn., AAUP, Am. Assn. Higher Edn. (vis. scholar 1994), North Ctrl. Assn. Colls. and Schs. (commn. on instns. higher edn. 1975-80, exec. bd. 1979-80, cons.-evaluator 1975-80), Nat. Coun. Chief Acad. Officers, Am. Coun. on Edn. (exec.com. 1983-85, chmn. 1985). Office: Am U 4400 Massachusetts Ave NW Washington DC 20016-8022

GREENBERG, NATHAN ABRAHAM, retired classics educator; b. Boston, Aug. 23, 1928; s. Samuel and Jenny (Marty) G.; m. Eva Lucy Mueller, June 22, 1952; children: David S., Judith H., Lisa P. B in Jewish Edn., Hebrew Tchrs.' Coll., Boston, 1948; AB, Harvard U., 1950, MA, 1952, PhD, 1955. From instr. to prof. classics Oberlin (Ohio) Coll., 1956—97, assoc. dean, 1967-68, chmn. dept. classics, 1970-76, 86-90. Contbr. articles to profl. jours. Fulbright scholar, Italy, 1955-56; sr. research fellow, Fulbright Found., Belgium, 1969-70; fellow Rockefeller Found., 1962-63; fellow and vis. fellow Am. Council Learned Socs. and Wolfson Coll., Oxford, Eng., 1976-77. Mem. Am. Philol. Assn., Archeol. Inst. Am., Classical Assn. Middle West and South. Democrat. Jewish.

GREENBERG, RITA MOFFETT, special education educator, consultant; b. May 29, 1945; d. Joseph and Rita Marie (Clifford) Moffett; m. Morris Greenberg, Aug. 8, 1971. BA in Early Childhood Edn., Elem. Edn., Paterson State Coll., 1967; M in Spl. Edn., Learning Disabilities, William Paterson Coll. (formerly Paterson State Coll.), 1988. Cert. early childhood tchr., N.J., elem. tchr., N.J., spl. edn./learning disabilities tchr., N.J., supr. Tchr. learning disabilities, cons. child study team Waldwick (N.J.) Bd. of Edn., 1990—. Adj. on-site supr. William Paterson Coll., Wayne, N.J., 1987-90, adj. grad. extern in learning disabilities, summer 1991, 92, 97, adj. undergrad. in spl. edn., 1992-93, guest lectr., 1994; cons. Bergen County Dept. Youth and Family Guidance, 1994. Contbr. articles to profl. jours. Mem. N.J. Assn. Learning Cons. (chairperson membership com. 1990-92), Coun. for Exceptional Children (divsn. learning disabilities, Professionally Recognized Spl. Educator in Edn. Diagnosis 2001), Waldwick Edn. Assn., Orton Dyslexia Soc., N.J. Edn. Assn., Kappa Delta Pi. Avocations: baking, travel. Home: 2077 Center Ave Apt 18B Fort Lee NJ 07024-4904 Office: Waldwick Bd of Edn Spl Svcs 155 Summit Ave Waldwick NJ 07463-2133

GREENBERG, ROBERT JAY, law educator; b. N.Y.C., Nov. 22, 1959; s. Murray Louis and Jeanette (Adams) G.; m. Dafna Rena Fuerst, June 29, 1993; children: Ashira Esther, Aliza Gila, Leora Adina. BA, Yeshiva U., 1981, JD, 1984, LLM, 2000. Bar: N.Y. 1986, U.S. Dist. Ct. N.Y. (ea. and so. dists.) 1986, U.S. Supreme Ct. 1989, U.S. Ct. Appeals (2d cir.) 1998, N.J. 2000, U.S. Dist. Ct. N.Y. (no. and we. dists.) 2000, U.S. Dist. Ct. N.J. 2000, D.C. 2001, U.S. Ct. Appeals (fed. cir.) 2001, Conn. 2001, U.S. Ct. of Internat. Trade 2002, Wyo. 2003; lic. real estate broker N.Y., notary public N.Y., N.J. Asst. to judge N.Y.C. Civil Ct., Bklyn., 1982; assoc. Simon, Meyrowitz, Meyrowitz and Schlussel, N.Y.C., 1983-86; instr. Bruriah High Sch. for Girls, Elizabeth, N.J., 1985-87; lectr. Nat. Acad. for Paralegal Studies, Mahwah, N.J., 1987-88; sr. legal editor Matthew Bender and Co., Inc., N.Y.C., 1987-94. Adj. asst. prof. bus. law Yeshiva U., N.Y.C., 1994-98, asst. prof., 1998—; lectr. NYU Inst. Paralegal Studies, N.Y.C., 1994-2000, adj. assoc. prof., 2001—; instr. dept. paralegal studies Queens College CUNY, 1994—. Asst. to author: Judaism and Vegetarianism, Judaism and Global Survival. Lectr. in Jewish law Young Israel of Staten Island, 1976—93, Congregation Beth Yehuda, Staten Island, 1980—93, Young Israel of Forest Hills, Queens, 1993—2003, Queens Jewish Ctr., 2000—03, Congregation Ohr Moshe, Queens, 2003—. Recipient Disting. Svc. award Congregation Beth Yehuda, 1988, Outstanding Svc. award, 1991. Mem.: ABA, Acad. of Legal Studies in Bus., N.Y. County Lawyers Assn., N.Y. State Bar Assn. Democrat. Office: 75-27 171st St Fresh Meadows NY 11366-1416

GREENBERG, RONALD DAVID, lawyer, law educator; b. San Antonio, Sept. 9, 1939; s. Benjamin and Sylvia (Ghetlzer) G. BS, U. Tex., 1957; MBA, Harvard U., 1961, JD, 1964. Bar: N.Y., 1966, U.S. Dist. Ct. (ea. and so. dists.) N.Y. 1970, U.S. Ct. Appeals (2d cir.) 1975, U.S. Supreme Ct. 1975. Engring. lab. instr. U. Tex., 1957; engr. Redstone Arsenal, Army Ballistic Missile Agy., 1957; engr., bus. analyst Exxon Corp., N.Y.C., 1957-64; rsch. asst. Harvard Bus. Sch.; with Smithsonian Astrophys. Observatory and Ednl. Testing Svc., N.J., 1961-62; atty., engr. Allied Corp., N.Y.C., 1964-67; assoc. Arthur, Dry, Kalish, Taylor & Wood, N.Y.C., 1967-69, Valicenti, Leighton, Reid & Pine, N.Y.C., 1969-70; instr. faculty Columbia U., N.Y.C., 1972-81, adj. prof. bus. law and taxation, 1970-71, 82-98; of counsel Delson & Gordon, N.Y.C., 1973-87; sole practitioner Harrison, N.Y., 1988—. Lectr., cons. AICPA, Inst. Internal Auditors, New Haven C. of C., Citibank, Mfrs. Hanover Trust Co., Harcourt, Brace, Jovanovich, Inc., Prudential-Bache, Drexel, Burnham & Lambert, E.F. Hutton; vol. instr. vol. income tax program, Columbia U., N.Y.C., 1991-92; vis. prof. Stanford U., Palo Alto, Calif., 1978, Harvard U., Boston, 1981. Author: Business Income Tax Materials, 1994; (with others) Business Organizations: Corporations, General Practice in New York, 1998, Business/Corporate Law and Practice, 3d edit., 2001; editor: The Compleat Lawyer, 1985-88, Tax Lawyer, 1982-95; editor in chief N.Y. Internat. Law Rev., 1988-91, chair adv. bd., 1992—; editor in chief Internat. Law Practicum, 1987-91; contbr. chpts. to books, articles to profl. jours. Cons. coun. City of N.Y., 1971-72, Manhattan C.C., 1974-76. Lt. USNR, 1957-59. Recipient Outstanding Prof. award Columbia U. Grad. Sch. Bus., 1973, MIT Fellowship Mech. Engring. Dept., 1959, Harvard U., Teagle Found., 1959-61; grantee Ford Found., 1977, Columbia U. Ctr. Internat. Studies, Sch. Internat. Pub. Affairs, 1992, Columbia Bus. Sch., 1976, 92, 93, 94. Mem. AAAS, ABA (chmn. com. on taxation gen. practice sect. 1978-83, chmn. com. on corp. banking and bus. law. gen. practice sect. 1985-87, moderator, chair profl. edn. programs 1986, 87), ASME, NSPE, N.Y. State Bar Assn. (gen. practice sect., chmn. tax law com. 1983-92, chmn. bus. law com. 1985-88, internat. law & practice sect., chmn. pubs. com. 1988-91, coord. study com. on med. malpractice legislation, 1980-82), Assn. Bar City N.Y., N.Y. Acad. Scis., Mensa, Tau Beta Pi, Pi Tau Sigma, Phi Eta Sigma, Am. Assn. for the Advancement of Sci. E-mail: rdgreenberg@hotmail.com.

GREENBERGER, HOWARD LEROY, lawyer, educator; b. Pitts., July 16, 1929; s. Abraham Harry and Alice (Levine) G.; m. Bette Jo Bergad, June 15, 1959. BS magna cum laude, U. Pitts., 1951; JD cum laude, NYU, 1954; diploma in law (Fulbright scholar), Oxford (Eng.) U., 1955. Bar: Pa. 1955, D.C. 1954, N.Y. 1969, U.S. Supreme Ct. 1964. Law clk. U.S. Ct. Appeals (3d cir.), 1958-60; assoc. Kaufman & Kaufman, Pitts., 1960-61; assoc. prof. law NYU, 1961-65, prof., 1965—2001, prof. emeritus, 2001—; assoc. dean NYU Sch. Law, 1968-72; dean and dir. Practising Law Inst., 1972-75; senator NYU, 1994—. Cons. in field.; v.p. Nat. Ctr. Para-Legal Tng.; pres. Early Am. Industries Assn., 1979-82; chmn. Commn. on Fgn. Grad. Study, AALS. Author: (with G. Cole) The Meriden Experiment, 1973; Study of the Quality of Continuing Legal Education in the US, 1980; contbr. articles to legal publs.; chmn. editorial bd. Jour. Legal Edn, 1974-77. Pres. N.Y.C. chpt. Am. Jewish Com., 1977-79, nat. bd. govs., 1979-85; vice chmn., gen. counsel Coalition to Free Soviet Jews, 1977—; trustee Law Ctr. Found., 1973-91, Am. Friends of Hebrew U. Jerusalem, 1986—; chair New Amsterdam dist. Boy Scouts Am., 1990—, Ctr. on Social Welfare Policy and Law, 1991—, Blaustein Inst. on Human Rights, 1992—. Capt. JAGC, U.S. Army, 1955-58. Recipient Alumni Meritorious Svc. award NYU, 1977, Stanley Isaacs award Am. Jewish Com., 1982, Gt. Tchr. award NYU, 1993, Friendship award Govt. of Germany, 1988, Robert B. McKay Disting. Svc. award N.Y.U. Sch. of Law, 1997, Great Tchr. award 1999; Root-Tilden grantee NYU, 1954. Fellow Am. Bar Found.; mem. ABA, Assn. of Bar of City of N.Y., N.Y. County Lawyers Assn. (bd. dirs. 1990—), Am. Law Inst., Assn. Am. Law Schs., NYU Club (pres. 1981-83, Masons, Sojourners, Order of Coif, Phi Epsilon Pi. Democrat. Jewish. Home: 4 Washington Square Vlg Apt 16 New York NY 10012-1936 Office: NYU Sch Law Vand Hall 40 Washington Sq S New York NY 10012-1005

GREENBLATT, MIRIAM, writer, editor, educator; b. Berlin; d. Gregory and Shifra (Zemach) Baraks; m. Howard Greenblatt (div.). BA magna cum laude, Hunter Coll.; postgrad., U. Chgo. Editor Am. People's Ency., Chgo., 1957-58, Scott Foresman & Co., Chgo., 1958-62; pres. Creative Textbooks, Chgo., 1972—. Tchr. New Trier (Ill.) HS, 1978—81. Author (with Chu): (book) The Story of China, 1968; author: (with Cuban) Japan, 1971; author: The History of Itasca, 1976; author: (with others) The American People, 1986; author: James Knox Polk, 1988, Franklin Delano Roosevelt, 1989, John Quincy Adams, 1990; author: (with Welty) The Human Expression, 1992; author: Cambodia, 1995; author: (with Jordan and Bowes) The Americans, 1996; author: Hatshepsut and Ancient Egypt, 2000, Alexander the Great and Ancient Greece, 2000, Augustus and Imperial Rome, 2000, Peter the Great and Tsarist Russia, 2000; author: (with Lemmo) Human Heritage, 2001; author: Genghis Khan and the Mongol Empire, 2002, Elizabeth I and Tudor England, 2002, The War of 1812, 2003, Iran, 2003, Charlemagne and the Early Middle Ages, 2003, Suleyman the Magnificent and the Ottoman Empire, 2003, Lorenzo de Medici and Renaissance Italy, 2003, Afghanistan, 2003; editl. cons. Peoples and Cultures Series, 1976—78, subject area cons. World Geography and Cultures, 1994; contbg. editor: (book) A World History, 1979. Mem. nat. exec. coun. Am. Jewish Com., 1980—84, v.p. Chgo chpt., 1977—79; treas. Glencoe Youth Svcs., 1981—83. Mem.: Cliff Dwellers, Nat. Assn. Scholars. Jewish. Address: 2754 Roslyn Ln Highland Park IL 60035-1408

GREENE, ANNIE LUCILLE, artist, retired art educator; b. Waycross, Ga. d. Henry William and Ella Mae (Hall) Tarver; m. Oliver Nathaniel Greene; children: Zinta LaRecia Greene Perkins, Oliver N. Greene, Jr. BS, Albany State Coll., 1954; MA, NYU, 1961. Art tchr. Thomasville (Ga.) Sch. Sys., 1954—55, Troup County Sch. Sys., LaGrange, Ga., 1955—89; ret., 1989. Apptd. mem. Ga. Humanities Coun., 2002—. 34 one-woman art shows, 1976—, 112 group exhbns., 1962— (numerous awards). Past mem.

Neighborhood Housing Svcs. Pub. Rels. com.; Grand Marshall Sweet Land of Liberty July 4th Parade, LaGrange, 2001; pianist St. Paul African Meth. Episcopal Ch. and McGhee Chapel African Meth. Episcopal Ch., Hogansville, Ga., trustee, chmn. stewardship and fin. commn.; bd. dirs. March of Dimes, 1991—; bd. mem. Keep Troup Beautiful, 1997—2001; past bd. dirs. LaGrange Meml. Libr. Named one of Gracious Ladies of Ga., 1998; recipient Outstanding Svc., St. Paul A.M.C. Ch., 2000, Ch. Citizen of Yr. award, McGhee Chapel A.M.E. Ch., 1999. Mem.: LaGrange Symphony Guild, LaGrange Artist Guild, Chattahoochee Valley Art Mus. (past bd. mem.), Troup Ret. Tchrs. Assn. (past sect.), The Links, Inc. (Outstanding Svc. award 1987, parliamentarian 1999—2001, Presdl. award 2001, LaGrange chpt., Outstanding Svc. award 1987, Presdl. award 2001), Delta Sigma Theta (pres. 1991—93, LaGrange Alumnae chpt. Presdl. awards 1993—97, pres. 1995—97, Annie B. Singleton award 2000, fund raiser chair 2001—03, LaGrange Alumnae chpt. Presdl. awards 1993—97, Annie B. Singleton award 2000, numerous other awards). Avocations: music, crafts, reading, photography, travel. Home: 712 Pyracantha Dr Lagrange GA 30241

GREENE, EDWARD FORBES, chemistry educator; b. N.Y.C., Dec. 29, 1922; s. Roger Sherman and Kate (Brown) G.; m. Hildegarde Forbes, June 11, 1949; children: Susan Curtis, Judith Elizabeth, David Forbes, Roger Cobb. AB, Harvard U., 1943, A.M., 1947, PhD, 1949. Jr. research chemist Shell Oil Co., Wood River, Ill., 1943-44; mem. staff Los Alamos Sci. Lab., 1949; research assoc. Brown U., Providence, 1949-51, instr., 1952-53, asst. prof. chemistry, 1953-57, assoc. prof., 1957-63, prof., 1963-92, dept. chmn., 1980-83, Jesse H. and Louisa D. Sharpe Metcalf prof. chemistry, 1985-92; prof. emeritus, 1993—. Vis. prof. Tougaloo (Miss.) Coll., 1965; resident visitor Bell Labs., Murray Hill, N.J., 1976-77 Co-author: (with J.P. Toennies) Chemical Reactions in Shock Waves, 1964. Served with USN, 1944-46. NSF fellow, 1959-60, 66-67 Fellow Am. Phys. Soc.; mem. Am. Chem. Soc. Home: 229 Medway St Apt 105 Providence RI 02906-5300 E-mail: Edward_Greene@Brown.edu.

GREENE, ELINORE ASCHAH, speech and drama professional, writer; b. Springfield, Mass., Oct. 14, 1928; d. Harry Joshua and Esther Gertrude (Cohen) Ziff; m. Kermit Greene, June 29, 1947; children: Clifford M., Laura L., William L. B of Lit. Interpretation, Emerson Coll., Boston, 1949. Dramatic interpreter Margaret E. Richardson Lect. Agy., Boston, 1950s, Flora Frame Lect. Bureau, Boston, 1960s; speech tchr. Academie Moderne, Boston, early 1970s, pvt. practice, Newton, MA, 1975-87, speech cons., 1985-89; writer, dir. Newton, 1989—. Presenter in field; voice-overs radio, TV, indsl. Author: (children's stories) AIM, Lollipops, Happiness, The Communique, Players, 1970—80, (poetry) Creative Urge, Dark Starr, Dreams; reviewer books: ; contbr. voice-overs. Brandeis women's com. and aid to speech therapy Emerson Coll. Mem. Aid to Speech Therapy Found. (pres. 1970s, bd. dirs. 1960s, Advocate Rose award 1975), Mass. Comm. of Boston, Am. Fedn. Theatre-Radio-TV Assns., Nat. Writers Orgn. (sr. mem.), Orgn. for Rehab. through Tng. (life), Hadassah. Avocations: family, music, composing greeting cards, reading, theater.

GREENE, FREDERICK D., II, chemistry educator; b. Glen Ridge, N.J., July 9, 1927; s. Phillips Foster and Ruth (Altman) G.; m. Theodora Elizabeth Whatmough, June 5, 1953; children— Alan, Carol, Elizabeth, Phillips. Grad., Phillips Andover Acad., 1944; BA, Amherst Coll., 1949, D.Sc. (hon.), 1969; PhD, Harvard, 1952. Research assoc. U. Calif., Los Angeles, 1952-53; instr. dept. chemistry Mass. Inst. Tech., Cambridge, 1953-55, asst. prof., 1955-58; assoc. prof. MIT, 1958-62, prof., 1962-95; prof. emeritus, 1995—. Editor-in-chief: Jour. Organic Chemistry, 1962-88; contbr. articles to sci. jours. Served with USNR, 1945-46. Alfred P. Sloan fellow, 1958-62; NSF Sr. Postdoctoral fellow, 1965-66 Fellow AAAS; mem. Am. Chem. Soc., Royal Soc. Chem. (U.K.), Am. Acad. Arts and Scis., Phi Beta Kappa. Office: Mass Inst Tech Dept Chemistry 77 Massachusetts Ave Cambridge MA 02139-4301

GREENE, GLEN LEE, secondary school educator; b. Alexandria, La., Sept. 28, 1939; s. Glen Lee and Grace Lois (Prince) G. BA, La. Coll., 1960, U. La., Monroe, 1967; MLIS, La. State U., 1994. Tchr. Destrehan (La.) H.S., 1964—, social studies chair, 1980-99. Mem. St. Charles Parish Profl. Improvement Program Com., Luling, La., 1981-85. Mem. ALA, ASCD, Nat. Coun. for the Social Studies, Phi Kappa Phi. Democrat. Baptist. Home: PO Box 203 Oak Ridge LA 71264-0203 Office: Destrehan HS 1 Wildcat Ln Destrehan LA 70047-4001

GREENE, JAMES S., III, school administrator; b. Harlan, Ky., Nov. 10, 1943; s. James S. Jr. and Elizabeth (Howard) G.; m. Glenda Hollors, Feb. 2, 1968; children: Laurel Elizabeth, Amy Janine, James McKeehan. Postgrad., U. N.C., 1961-62; BS in Edn. French and History, U. Wis., 1965; MA in Edn., Union Coll., Barbourville, Ky., 1973; PhD in Edn., Ohio State U., 1982. Cert. tchr. secondary edn., sch. adminstrn. and supervision, Ky. Tchr. French and History Harlan H.S., 1965-83; supr. instrn. Harlan Ind. Sch. Dist., 1983—. Adj. instr. history S.E. Cmty. Coll., Cumberland, Ky., 1977-83; humanities scholar multimedia project The Lynch Legacy Project, 1987. Reviewer The History Tchr., 1973-83; contbr. (book): The Kentucky Ency., 1992. Bd. dirs. Southeastern Ky. Spl. Edn. Coop., Harlan, 1983-88; mem. adv. coun. Stokely Inst. for Liberal Arts Edn., U. Tenn., Knoxville, 1982-89; trustee Pine Mountain (Ky.) Settlement Sch., 1989—; coord. Harlan Christian Arts Festival, 1973, 76; mem. Ky. Bicentennial Commn., Frankfort, 1988-93; pres. bd. dirs. Romance of the Hills Corp., Harlan, 1992-93; elder First Presbyn. Ch., Harlan, 1968-73, 80-83, 90-95, 97-2003, organist, 1982—; mem. Ky. State Hist. Records Adv. Bd., 1996—. Recipient Award for Outstanding Contbns. to Math. Edn., Ky. Coun. Tchrs. Math., 1992; Humanities scholar So. Mountains Settlement Symposium, 1999-2000. Avocation: composing and choral arranging. Office: Harlan Ind Sch Dist 420 E Central St Harlan KY 40831-2372 E-mail: jgreene@harlan-ind.k12.ky.us.

GREENE, JAMIE CANDELARIA, special education educator; Diploma in French Lang. Studies, Aix-Marseille II U., 1975; BA in French, Calif. State U., Sacramento, 1978, MA in Spl. Edn., 1979; postgrad., U. Calif., Davis, 1979. Cert. multiple subject tchr., Calif., educationally handicapped, tchr., Colo. Tutor remedial English and ESL Delta Coll., Stockton, Calif., 1972-74; tutor, counselor N040postgrad., 1973; tchr. learning handicapped children, resident care supr. St. Elizabeth's Sch. and Home for Epileptic Children & Women, Stockton, 1974; educator L'Ecole St. Michel, Spa, Belgium, 1977; tchr. severely handicapped Nevada County Office of Edn., Grass Valley, 1982-91. Adj. prof. edn. Nat. U., Sacramento, 1988—; nurse's aide St. Blasien, Schwartzwald, Fed. Republic of Germany, 1974; featured mus. artist Cypriot Broadcasting System, Nicosia, Cyprus, 1975; mountain gorilla researcher Karisoke Rsch. Centre, Ruhengeri, Rwanda, Republic of South Africa, 1981. Guest broadcaster Sta. KVMR Pub. Radio, 1984—. Bd. dirs., coord. programs in schs. UN Assn., Grass Valley, 1984-88; sch. vol. liaison, trainer Vol. Bur. Nevada County and Regional Occupational Program of Nevada County, 1983—; mem., performer Community Players and Rainbow Theatre Group, Grass Valley, 1983—; bd. dirs. Sierra Mus. Arts Assn., 1983—. Holmes Scholar U. Calif., Berkeley, 1991-92, 92-93. Mem. AAUW, Assn. for the Developmentally Disabled, Nevada County Spl. Educators Group, Calif. Tchrs. Assn., NEA, Coun. for Exceptional Children (rsch. div.), Sierra, Optimists. Avocations: guitar, french literature, theatre, classical music. Home: 33 Beaufort Harbor Lndg Alameda CA 94502-6517

GREENE, JOHN SAMUEL, JR., art educator; b. Richmond, Va., Nov. 15, 1954; s. John Samuel and Ann Delores (Jones) G.; m. Lafonda Bridgeforth, Oct. 22, 1977; children: Alexis Patrice, Tiffany Reneé. BA in Graphic Design, Norfolk State Coll., 1977; BFA in Art Edn., Va. Commonwealth U., 1985. Cert. art tchr., Va. Art resource specialist Richmond (Va.) Pub. Schs., 1979-86, tchr., 1986—. Chief artist-in-residence 5th St. Bapt. Ch., Richmond, 1980—. Artist jour. cover illustrations Va. State NAACP, 1989-91, logo designs Bapt. Gen. Conv., 1990-92; author art curriculum materials. Mem. Forest Dale Civic Assn., Chesterfield, Va., 1990—. Mem. NNat. Art Edn. Assn., Va. Art Edn. Assn., Va. Edn. Assn., Richmond Edn. Assn., Va. High Sch. Coaches Assn., Alpha Phi Alpha, Xi Delta Lambda (Man of Yr. 1987). Democrat. Baptist. Avocations: running, tennis, fishing, singing, swimming. Home: 2021 Chevelle Dr Richmond VA 23235-5642

GREENE, KATHERINE MARGARET, secondary education educator, mathematics educator; b. Youngstown, Ohio; BA in Bus. Adminstrn. cum laude, Grove City (Pa.) Coll., 1978; BS Secondary Edn./Math. summa cum laude, Youngstown (Ohio) State U., 1991; MSc in Edn., Youngstown U., 1995. Cert. tchr. math. Coll. mktg. rep. Mademoiselle Mag., 1976-78; mdse. mgr. J.C. Penney Co, Inc., Youngstown, 1978-83; dir. sales, mdse. and tng. Watch What Develops Franchise Concepts, Inc., Youngstown, 1983-88; instr. math. Youngstown State U., 1991—; secondary math. tchr. Struthers (Ohio) High Sch., 1991—. Author manuals. Vol. recruiting rep. Grove City Coll.; advisor Jr. Achievement. Grove City Coll. acad. scholar, 1975-78; recipient Award of Excellence for Chpt. I Math. Instrn., State of Ohio, 1993. Mem. Am. Mgmt. Assn., Math. Assn., Am., Ohio Coun. Tchrs. Math., Nat. Coun. Tchrs. Math., Am. Econs. Soc., Golden Key, Phi Kappa Phi, Kappa Delta Pi, Pi Mu Epsilon. Avocations: photography, reading.

GREENE, LINDA KAY, retired secondary school educator; b. Elk City, Okla., Nov. 8, 1943; d. Granville E. and Edna (Nicholson) G. BA, U. N.Mex., 1966, MA in Teaching of English, 1970. Cert. tchr. Calif., lic. N.Mex. English tchr. Albuquerque Pub. Schs., 1971—96, English dept. chair, 1989-91; English tchr. Orange (Calif.) Unified Sch. Dist., 1970-71, Muroc Unified Sch. Dist., Edwards Air Force Base, Calif., 1966-69; ret., 1996. Mem. Sch. Restructuring Team, 1990-92; mem. Tchr. Adv. Coun., 1991-93, Supt. Tchr. Adv. Coun., 1992-93, exec. com., 1992-93, south region adv. com., 1993-94. Contbr. poems to profl. jours. (hon. mention poetry contest 1992). Named Tchr. of Yr. (twice) Harrison Jr. High Sch., 1970's, Most Improved Bowler WIBC, 1970's; recipient 3rd and 6th place N.Mex. Poet Soc. Contests, 1970's. Mem. NEA (chair, co-chair), Albuquerque Press Club. Avocations: writing, drawing, painting, bowling, swimming, reading. Home: 6107 Del Campo Pl NE Chimney Ridge Albuquerque NM 87109-2529

GREENE, LYDIA ABBI JWUAN, elementary education educator; b. La Fayette, Tenn, Sept. 20, 1963; d. Thomas and Icy (Daniel) G. BSBA, Tenn. State U., 1985, M in Elem. Edn., 1993; MLIS, Trevecca NAzarene U., 2001. Customer svc. rep. JC Penney Telemarketing Ctr., Nashville, 1986-93; tchr. Paragon Mills Elem. Sch., Nashville, 1993—. Tchr. Youth Hobby Shop Camp, Nashville, 1981-83, Met. Nashville Edn. Assn., 1994—; mem. Faculty Adv. Com.; sci. facilitator Paragon Mills Elem. Mem. NEA, Nat. Sci. Tchr. Assn., Tenn. Edn. Assn., Fed. Aviation Assn. (educator 1995—), Tenn. Reading Assn., Nashville Inst. Arts, Libr. Congress, Title I (com. 1999—), MNEA (sch. rep 1999-2000). Mem. Ch. Christ. Avocations: personal computing, reading, travel. Office: Paragon Mills Elem Sch 260 Paragon Mills Rd Nashville TN 37211-4075

GREENE, THOMAS MCLERNON, language professional, educator; b. Phila., May 17, 1926; s. George Durgin and Elizabeth (McLernon) G.; m. Liliane Massarano, May 20, 1950; children: Philip James, Christopher George, Francis Richard. BA, Yale U., 1949, PhD, 1955; student, U. Paris, 1949-51. Mem. faculty Yale U., New Haven, 1954-96, prof. English and comparative lit., 1966-96, chmn. directed studies program, 1965-68, chmn. dept. comparative lit., 1972-78, 86-88, chmn. Renaissance studies program, 1980-85, Frederick Clifford Ford prof. English and comparative lit., 1978—. Vis. prof. Sch. Criticism and Theory Dartmouth U., Hanover, N.H., 1988, Coll. de France, 1989; vis. Mellon prof. Inst. for Advanced Study, 1994-95; tchr. NEH summer seminar, 1982, NEH Summer Inst., 1991; founder, exec. dir. The Open End Theater, 1996—. Author: The Descent From Heaven: A Study in Epic Continuity, 1963, Rabelais: A Study in Comic Courage, 1970, The Light in Troy: Imitation and Discovery in Renaissance Poetry, 1982, The Vulnerable Text: Essays on Renaissance Literature, 1986, Poésie et magie, 1991, Calling from Diffusion: Hermeneutics of the Promenade, 2002; also articles.; co-editor: The Disciplines of Criticism: Studies in Literary Theory, Interpretation and History, 1968. With AUS, 1945-47. Recipient Harbison prize for disting. teaching Danforth Found., 1968, medal Coll. de France, 1989, Arts award Arts Coun. Greater New Haven, DeVane medal for tchg. and scholarship Yale Phi Beta kappa, 2002; grantee Am. Coun. Learned Socs., 1963-64, NEH, 1978-79; Guggenheim fellow, 1966-69. Fellow Am. Acad. Arts and Scis.; mem. MLA (exec. coun. 1987-90, James Russell Lowell prize 1983), Renaissance Soc. Am. (v.p. 1981-82, pres. 1982-83, Paul Oskar Kristeller Lifetime Achievement award 1999), Am. Comparative Lit. Assn. (v.p. 1980-83, pres. 1983-86, mem. adv. bd. 1971-77, Harry Levin prize 1983), Internat. Comparative Lit. Assn. (v.p. 1991-94). Home: New Haven, Conn. Died June 23, 2003.

GREENE, THOMASINA TALLEY, concert pianist, educator; b. Nashville, June 29, 1913; d. Thomas Washington and Ellen Elizabeth (Roberts) Talley; m. Lorenzo Johnston, Dec. 19, 1942 (dec. 1988); 1 child, Lorenzo Thomas. BA, Fisk U., 1929; diploma in music, Julliard Sch. of Music, 1932; EdD, Columbia U., 1942. Head music dept. St. Phillips Jr. Coll., San Antonio, 1933-34; supr. music dept. Columbia (Mo.) Pub. Schs., 1932-33, Sam Houston Coll., Austin, Tex., summer 1934; head music dept. N.C. State U., Durham, 1934-39; part-time dir. art dept. Lincoln U., Jefferson City, Mo., summer 1942, part-time prof. music, 1943-45; dir. Greene Sch. of Music, Jefferson City, 1942-89. With music program Sta. KRCG-TV, Jefferson City, 1966-81. Mem. exec. bd. Jefferson City Community Concert Assn., 1967-71; dir. project upbeat grant Md. Coun. Arts, 1978-79. Named Woman of Achievement for Jefferson City, 1963; recipient Disting. Svc. award 2d Bapt. Ch., Jefferson City, 1978, 89; fellow Julliard Sch. Music, 1929-32, Rockefeller Found., 1939-42. Mem. Nat. Soc. Lit. and Arts, Nat. Music Tchrs. Assn., Mo. Music Tchrs. Assn., Area Music Tchrs. Assn., Modern Priscilla Art and Charity Club, AAUW (bd. dirs. Jefferson City chpt., Woman of Yr. award 1963), Alpha Kappa Alpha (Regional Disting. Svc. award 1965), Kappa Delta Pi, Pi Lambda Theta. Episcopalian. Avocations: painting, china, card games, exercise. Died June 3, 2003.

GREENE, VIRGINIA ANNE, elementary education educator; b. Phila., Jan. 24, 1955; d. James F. Jr. and Lillian V. (Dechant) McGivern; m. Clarke V. Greene, June 19, 1982; 1 child, Karin Emma. B of Music Edn., Hartt Coll. of Music, 1976; Cert., Orff Institut, Salzburg, Austria, 1980; MS in Elem. Edn., Ctrl. Conn. State U., 1983. Cert. music tchr., elem. tchr., Conn. Music educator Haddam Elem. Sch., Higganum, Conn., 1979-85, classroom tchr., 1985—; counselor YMCA Camp Ingersoll, Portland, Conn., 1982, 83; piano tchr. Avon and Higganum, Conn., 1973—. Author: (with others) Music for Children vol. I, 1982. Recipient Tchr. of Yr., Haddam Elem. Sch., 1990, Presdl. Sci. award State of Conn., 1991, Award of Merit, Young Writers' Contest Found., 1990, Recognition award, 1989. Mem. NEA, Conn. Edn. Assn. (treas. 1980-81), Mu Phi Epsilon Sorority. Democrat. Avocations: comic book collecting, playing piano and guitar, sewing, bicycling. Office: Haddam Elem Sch 272 Saybrook Rd Higganum CT 06441-4103

GREENE, WENDY SEGAL, special education educator; b. New Rochelle, N.Y., Jan. 9, 1929; d. Louis Peter and Anna Henrietta (Kahan) Segal; m. Charles Edward Smith (div. 1952); m. Richard M. Greene Jr. (div. 1967); children: Christopher S., Kerry William, Karen Beth Greene Olson; m. Richard M. Greene Sr., Aug. 29, 1985 (dec. 1986). Student, Olivet Coll., 1946-48, Santa Monica Coll., 1967-70; BA in Child Devel., Calif. State U., Los Angeles, 1973, MA in Elem. Edn., 1975. Cert. tchr., Calif.; cert. Specially Designed Acad. Instrn. in English, 1999. Counselor Camp Watitoh, Becket, Mass., 1946-49; asst. tchr. Outdoor Play Group, New Rochelle, 1946-58; edn. sec. pediatrics Syracuse (N.Y.) Meml. Hosp., 1952-53; with St. John's Hosp., Santa Monica, Calif., 1962-63; head tchr. Head Start, L.A., 1966-77; tchr. spl. edn. L.A. Unified Sch. Dist., 1977—, Salvin Spl. Edn. Ctr., L.A., 1976—85, Perez Spl. Edn. Ctr., L.A., 1986-. Instr. mktg. rsch. for motivational rsch. Anderson-McConnell Agy., 1966; mentor tchr. L.A. Unified Sch. Dist., 1992-99; mem. adv. com. for spl. edn. Tustin Unified Sch. Dist. Comty., 1994—. Contbr. to house organ of St. John's Hosp.; co-editor of newspaper for Salvin Sch., L.A.; contbg. reporter El Aquilar (The Eagle), Perez. Mem. LEARN Coun., Perez, 1996—; mem. cmty. adv. com. spl. edn. Tustin Unified Sch. Dist., 1994—; bd. dirs. Tustin Area Coun. for Fine Arts, 2002—; bd. dirs. Richland Ave. Youth House, L.A., 1960-63, Emotional Health Assn., L.A., 1961-66, Richland Ave. Sch. PTA, 1959-63. Mem.: AAUW, United Tchrs. L.A., Olivet Coll. Alumni Assn., Celebration of Life Singers, Cmty. Singers Tustin, Westside Singers (L.A.), Kappa Delta Pi. Jewish. Avocations: music, writing, theater, travel, family. Home: 14291 Prospect Ave Tustin CA 92780-2316

GREENFIELD, LINDA SUE, nursing educator; b. Dover, Del., Aug. 5, 1950; d. Norman Raymond and Eleanor Henrietta (Harmon) Connell; m. Douglas Herman Greenfield, Dec. 27, 1976; children: Leah, Paige. BSN, Cath. U., 1972; MSN cum laude, Boston U., 1977; student, Met. Hosp. Sch. Nurse Anesthetists, 1979—81; postgrad., Coll. New Rochelle, 1986-88; PhD, Adelphi U., 1998. RN, N.Y. Staff nurse emergency rm. and ICU Washington Hosp. Ctr., 1974-75; operating rm. nurse Mass. Eye & Ear, Boston, 1975; ICU nurse Peter Bent Brigham Hosp., Boston, 1975-76; surg. nurse practitioner Kingsbrook Jewish Hosp., Bklyn., 1976-79; cert. registered nurse anesthetist Brookdale Hosp., Bklyn., 1981-92, Winthrop U. Hosp., Mineola, N.Y., 1992-94; adj. prof. Adelphi U., Garden City, N.Y., 1995-99; adj. prof. nursing N.Y. Inst. Tech., Old Westbury, 1998-99; clin. supr. Midtown Ctr. Complementary Care, N.Y.C., 1999-2000; clin specialist St. Francis Hosp., Roslyn, N.Y., 2000-01; asst. prof. nursing Adelphi U., 2001—. Bd. officer Manhasset Newcomers, N.Y., 1988-90; bd. dirs. Friends of Manhasset Libr., N.Y., 1990-94; mem. Make a Wish Found., Port Washington, N.Y., 1990—. Lt. U.S. Army, 1970-74. Mem.: ANA, Nat. Assn. U. Women, Nat. Assn. for Holistic Nurses, Nat. Assn. Homeopathy, Noetic Soc., Sch. Cmty. Assn., Am. Assn. Nurse Anesthetists, Sigma Theta Tau. Avocations: skiing, sailing, dancing.

GREENHILL, H. GAYLON, retired academic administrator; Chancellor U. Wis., Whitewater, 1991-99, chancellor emeritus, 1999—. Address: PO Box 507 Whitewater WI 53190-0507 E-mail: greenhig@mail.uww.edu.

GREENHUT, MELVIN LEONARD, economist, educator; b. NYC, Mar. 10, 1921; s. Ab and Lillian (Frudman) G.; m. Elmara Margaret Griffith, Mar. 24, 1944; children: Margaret Lee, Pamela Jo, John Griffith, Patricia Lynn. PhD, Washington U., 1951. Prof. econ. various univ., 1948-62; prof., head dept. econ. Tex. A&M U., Coll. Sta., 1966-69, disting. prof. econ., 1969—, alumni disting. prof. econ., 1980-85, Abell Prof. Liberal Arts, disting. prof. econ., 1986—, Abell Prof. Liberal Arts, disting. prof. econ. emeritus, 1992—, chmn. disting. prof., 1988-89. Vis. prof., lectr. in field. Co-author (with John Greenhut): (book) Sci. and God, 2002, Our Teleological Econ. World, 2002; author: 19 books; contbr. articles to profl. jour. Mem. nat. econ. policy com. and econ. adv. coun. US C. of C., 1960-63. Maj. US Army. Mem. Am. Econ. Assn., So. Econ. Assn. (past v.p.), Regional Sci. Assn. (councillor), Royal Econ. Soc., Econometric Soc., Delta Chi, Omicron Delta Gamma. Lutheran. Home: 5814 Constellation Cir Rockwall TX 75032-5770 Office: Tex A&M U Dept Econs College Station TX 77843-0001

GREENKORN, ROBERT ALBERT, chemical engineering educator; b. Oshkosh, Wis., Oct. 12, 1928; s. Frederick John and Sophie (Phillips) G.; m. Rosemary Drexler, Aug. 16, 1952; children: David Michael, Eileen Anne, Susan Marie, Nancy Joanne. Student, Oshkosh State Coll., 1951-52; BS, U. Wis., 1954, MS, 1955, PhD, 1957. Postdoctoral fellow Norwegian Tech. Inst., 1957-58; rsch. engr. Jersey Prodn. Rsch. Co., Tulsa, 1958-63; lectr. U. Tulsa, 1958-63; assoc. prof. theoretical and applied mechanics Marquette U., Milw., 1963-65; assoc. prof. chem. engring. Purdue U., Lafayette, Ind., 1965-67, prof., head chem. engring. dept., 1967-72, asst. dean engring., 1972-76, assoc. dean engring., dir. engring. expt. sta., 1976-80, v.p., assoc. provost, 1980-86; v.p. programs Purdue Rsch. Found., 1980-94, v.p. rsch., 1986-92, v.p. rsch., dean grad. sch., 1993-94, spl. asst. to the pres., 1994-2000, v.p. spl. programs, 1994-2000, R. Games Slayter disting. prof. chem. engring., 1995-2000, R. Games Slayter disting. prof. emeritus chem. engring., 2000—. Rsch. coord. Ind. Clean Mfg. and Safe Materials Inst., 1994-2000; dir. Tech. Assistance Program, 1996-2000. Author: (with D.P. Kessler) Transfer Operations, 1972, (with K.C. Chao) Thermodynamics of Fluids: An Introduction to Equilibrium Theory, 1975, (with D.P. Kessler) Modeling and Data Analysis for Engineers and Scientists, 1980, Flow Phenomena in Porous Media, 1983, Momentum, Heat and Mass Transfer Fundamentals (with D.P. Kessler), 1999; contbr. articles to profl. jours. Served with USN, 1946-51. Decorated D.F.C., Air medal with two oak leaf clusters; recipient Fellow Members awd., Am. Soc. for Engineering Education, 1992. Fellow AIChE, Am. Soc. Engring. Edn.; mem. AAAS, Soc. Petroleum Engrs., Am. Chem. Soc., Am. Geophys. Union, Sigma Xi, Phi Eta Sigma, Tau Beta Pi, Phi Gamma Delta. Roman Catholic. Achievements include patents in field. Home: 151 Knox Dr West Lafayette IN 47906-2147

GREENLAW, MARILYN JEAN, education educator, consultant, writer; b. St. Petersburg, Fla., Apr. 1, 1941; d. Hinckley and Dorothy Rebecca (Ball) G. BA, Stetson U., 1962, MA, 1965; PhD, Mich. State U., 1970. Elem. tchr. Broward County schs., Ft. Lauderdale, Fla., 1962-64; ele. cons. Harper and Row Publs., Evanston, Ill., 1965-69; from asst. to assoc. prof. U. Ga., Athens, 1970-78; from assoc. to full prof. U. North Tex., Denton, 1978-87, regents prof., 1987—. Cons. Scholastic Publs., N.Y.C., 1978-87, Houghton Mifflin Co., Boston, 1984-94, Tex. Instruments, Dallas, 1981-85, Coordinating Bd., Austin, Tex., 1987-91. Author: Ranch Dressing: The Story of Western Wear, 1993, Welcome to the Stock Show, 1997; co-author: Storybook Classrooms, 1985, Educating the Gifted, 1988; editor book rev. column Jour. Reading, 1981-84, The New Adv., 1987-94. Mem. Friends of the Libr., Denton, 1984—, pres., 1995-97; bd. dirs. Denton Libr., 1992-97, chair, 1995-96. Recipient Arbuthnot award, 1992, Disting. Svc. award Tex. State Reading Assn., 1996, Pres.'s Coun. Disting. Svc. award U. North Tex., 1996. Mem. ALA (com. chairperson 1984-85), Nat. Coun. Tchrs. of English (com. chairperson 1980—, Outstanding Leadership in Edn. award 1976), Internat. Reading Assn. (com. chairperson 1980-90, Arbuthnot award 1992), Phi Delta Kappa (pres. 1982-83, Outstanding Young Educator award 1981), Phi Kappa Phi (v.p. 1986-87). Republican. Avocations: reading, gardening, photography. Home: 2600 Sheraton Rd Denton TX 76209-8620

GREENLEAF, DIANA CRAMPTON, school media generalist; b. Boston, Feb. 8, 1952; d. Arthur William and Nancy Taylor (Buttrick) Crampton; m. Daniel Edward Greenleaf, June 26, 1971; children: Meghan Kate, Hilary Sara. BA in Elem. Edn., U. N.H., 1973. Cert. media generalist, N.H. Media assoc. New Durham (N.H.) Sch., 1985-90, media generalist, 1990-2000; K-12 dept. head libr. media Gov. Wentworth Regional Sch. Dist., Wolfeboro, N.H., 1993-2000, co-chair enabling skills curriculum com., 1993—2000, mem. commencement goals task force, 1994; dist. libr. Windham Sch. Dist., 2000—. Sec. New Durham Athletic Assn., 1989-93; mem. Ladybug Picture Book Award Com., 2003-. Mem. ALA, NEA (grantee N.H. chpt. 1989), Am. Assn. Sch. Librs., N.H. Ednl. Media Assn. (Excellence award 2000), Tech. Com, 2000-, First Tchrs. Project, 2000-, Program Evaluation and Review Com. (PERC), 2000-. Home: 660 Cilley Rd Manchester NH 03103-3701 Office: Windham Sch Dist 2 Lowell Rd Windham NH 03087

GREENLEAF, JANET ELIZABETH, principal; b. Hazleton, Pa., May 30, 1942; d. Edgar Henry and Mary Elizabeth (Rabenold) Bohstedt; m. James Albert Greenleaf, Nov. 19, 1966; children: John Edward, Jean Marie. BS, Bloomsburg (Pa.) U., 1964; MEd, Lehigh U., 1966. Cert. tchr., Pa., N.J. Tchr. Allentown (Pa.) Sch. Dist., 1964-67; remedial reading tchr. East Orange (N.J.) Sch. Dist., 1967-70; tchr. Lehigh Valley Luth. Sch., Northampton, Pa., 1984-89, prin., 1989-2000. Adj. prof. edn. Cedar Crest Coll., Allentown, 1989-90; mem. adv. bd. Safe Drug Free Schs. and Cmty's., 1992—. Author, presenter workshops; facilitator seminars. Bd. dirs. Bethlehem (Pa.) Pub. Libr., 1992—, treas. 1994—; bd. dirs. Sayre Child Ctr., Bethlehem, 1979-85, Ea. Pa. Luth. Camp Corp., 1993-99, v.p., 1996-99; sch. bd. pres. Lehigh Valley Luth. Sch., Northampton, 1982-85; pres. Jr. League of Lehigh Valley, Bethlehem, 1980-81; nominating chmn. Assn. Jr. Leagues, Washington, 1981-83; dir. Christian edn. St. Lukes Luth. Ch., Allentown, 1989-98, mem. ch. coun., 1981-83, 87-92, 2000—, v.p. 1982-83; chmn. Luth. schs. and early childhood ctrs. com. N.E. Penn Synod, 1995-99. Recipient Vol. award Jr. League of Lehigh Valley, 1979. Mem. ASCD, Evang. Luth. Edn. Assn. Democrat. Avocations: reading, gardening, golf, working with youth. Home: 309 Pine Top Trl Bethlehem PA 18017-1731 Office: Lehigh Valley Luth Sch 1335 Old Carriage Rd Northampton PA 18067-8969 E-mail: jamesgreenleaf@worldnet.att.net.

GREENOUGH, WILLIAM TALLANT, psychobiologist, educator; b. Seattle, Oct. 11, 1944; s. Harrison and Maryon C. (Whitten) G.; 1 dau., Jennifer Anne. BA, U. Oreg., 1964; MA, UCLA, 1966, PhD, 1969. Instr. U. Ill., Urbana-Champaign, 1968-69, asst. prof., 1969-73, assoc. prof., 1973-77, chair neural and behavioral biology program, 1977-87, prof. psychology, psychiatry, cell and structural biology, 1978—; assoc. dir. Beckman Inst. for Advanced Sci. and Tech., 1987-91; prof. U. Ill. Ctr. Advanced Study, 1997—, Swanlund prof. psychology, psychiatry, cell biology, bioeng., 1998—; dir. neurosci. program U. Ill., 1999—2001, dir. Ctr. Advanced Study, 2000—. Vis. prof. psychobiology U. Calif., Irvine, 1972; vis. prof. psychology U. Wash., 1975-76; program chmn. Winter Conf. on Brain Rsch., 1984-85, conf. chair, 1994-95; panel mem. integrative neural sys. NSF, 1987-91; dir. NSF Ctr. of Neurobiology of Learning and Memory, 1989-94; v.p., exec. com. Forum on Rsch. Mgmt., Fed. Behavioral, Psychol. and Cognitive Sci., 1991-93; mem. sci. adv. bd. Am. Psychol. Assn. Sci. Directorate; mem. NSF Biol. Sci. Directorate Adv. Com. Editor: (with R.N. Walsh) Environments as Therapy for Brain Dysfunction, 1976, (with J.M. Juraska) Developmental Neuropsychobiology, 1987; co-editor jour. Neurobiol. Learning and Memory, 1984—; contbr. numerous articles to profl. jour. Recipient William Rosen award for rsch. Nat. Fragile X Found., 1998; Cattell Found. fellow, 1975-76; USPHS and NSF grantee, 1969— ; U. Ill. sr. scholar, 1985-88. Fellow AAAS (chair sect. I, Psychology 2001-02), Soc. for Rsch. into child dev. (SRCD) disting. Sci. contrib. award, 2003; APA (Disting. Sci. Contbn. award 1999), Am. Psychol. Soc. (William James Fellow award, 1998), Soc. Exptl. Psychology; mem. NAS, Soc. Neurosci. (councilor 1990-94, treas.-elect 2003), Soc. Devel. Neurosci., Soc. Devel. Psychobiology (bd. dir. 1977-80), Sigma Xi. Achievements include rsch. interests in morphological plasticity of cerebellum, experience and learning-based synapse formation, molecular mechanisms of mental retardation, and plasticity of glial cells. Home: 1919 Melrose Dr Apt C Champaign IL 61820-2013 Office: U Ill Beckman Inst 405 N Mathews Ave Urbana IL 61801-2325 E-mail: wgreenou@psych.uiuc.edu.

GREENSPAN, HARVEY PHILIP, applied mathematician, educator; b. N.Y.C., Feb. 22, 1933; s. Louis and Jessie (Scholnick) G.; m. Mirian Gordon, Sept. 6, 1953; children— Elizabeth, Judith. BS, CCNY, 1953; MS, Harvard U., 1954, PhD, 1956; D Tech. (hon.), Royal Inst. Tech., Stockholm, 1991. Asst. prof. applied math. Harvard, 1957-60; faculty MIT, Cambridge, 1960—, prof. applied math., 1964—2002, prof. emeritus, 2002—. Author: Theory of Rotating Fluids, 1968, Calculus: An Introduction to Applied Mathematics, 1973; editor: Studies in Applied Mathematics, 1969; patentee centrifugal spectrometer. Home: 15 Chatham Cir Brookline MA 02446-5410 Office: Mass Inst Tech 77 Massachusetts Ave Cambridge MA 02139-4301 E-mail: hpg@math.mit.edu.

GREENSPAN, VALEDA CLAREEN, nursing educator; b. Ellsworth, Kans., Sept. 10, 1940; d. Theodore Frederick and Clara Lydia (Weinhardt) Steinle; m. Edward Phil Fabricius, June 10, 1962 (div. 1973): children; Craig Philip, Sheri Kay. BS, Ft. Hays State U., 1962; M Nursing, Ind. U., 1966; cert. in gerontology, North Tex. State U., 1980, PhD, 1982. Instr. Bartholomew County Hosp., Columbus, Ind., 1971-72; asst. prof. Ft. Hays State U., Hays, Kans., 1973-74, Tex. Woman's U., Denton, 1974-80, Minot (N.D.) State U., 1980-82, dean, 1982—99. Cons., expert witness Zuger & Bucklin, Bismarck, N.D., 1982-83; mem. N.D. adv. bd. No. States Power Co., 1989-92; treas. health bd. 1st Dist., 1994-97. Matthews fellow North Tex. State U., 1979; grantee Bush Found., 1983-84. Mem. ANA (del. 1986-87), Nat. League Nurses (bd. rev. 1992-95, baccalaureate higher degree programs site visitor 1983-1998), Nat. Gerontol Assn., N.D. Nurses Assn. (treas. dist. 2 1982-84, nominating com. 1984-85, 93-94, v.p. 1989-92, Excellence in Writing award Am. Jour. Nursing, 1987), Phi Delta Kappa, Sigma Theta Tau. Avocations: reading, camping, sewing, cooking, crafts. Home: 8465 Sevan Ct Annandale VA 22003-1160

GREENSTEIN, FRED IRWIN, political science educator; b. N.Y.C., Sept. 1, 1930; s. Arthur Aaron and Rose (Goldstein) G.; m. Barbara Elferink, July 14, 1957; children: Michael, Amy, Jessica. BA, Antioch Coll., 1953; MA, Yale U., 1956, PhD, 1960. Instr. Yale U., New Haven, 1959-62, vis. prof., 1965-68; mem. faculty Wesleyan U., Middletown, Conn., 1963-73, prof. polit. sci., 1966-73; Henry Luce prof. politics, law and society Princeton U., 1973-81, prof. politics, 1973—2000, prof. emeritus, 2000—. Vis. prof. U. Essex, Eng., 1968-69, 91. Author: The American Party System and the American People, 1970, Children and Politics, 2d edit., 1969, Personality and Politics, 2d edit., 1975; co-author: (with R.E. Lane and J.D. Barber) Introduction to Political Analysis, 2 edit., 1965, (with M. Lerner) A Source Book for the Study of Personality and Politics, 1971, (with N.W. Polsby) The Handbook of Political Science, 8 vols., (with R. Wolfinger and M. Shapiro) Dynamics and American Politics, 1976, (with L. Berman and A. Felzenberg) The Evolution of the Modern Presidency: A Bibliographical Review, 1977; author: The Hidden-Hand Presidency: Eisenhower as Leader, 1982, The Reagan Presidency: An Early Appraisal, 1983, Leadership in the Modern Presidency, 1988, How Presidents Test Reality: Decisions on Vietnam, 1954 and 1965, 1989, The Presidential Difference: Leadership Style from FDR to Clinton, 2000. Served with AUS, 1953-55. Fellow Ctr. Advanced Study Behavioral Scis., 1964-65; NSF sr. postdoctoral fellow, 1968-69 Fellow Am. Acad. Arts And Scis.; mem. Am. Polit. Sci. Assn. (editorial bd. 1968-72, sec. 1976-77), Internat. Soc. Polit. Psychology (pres. 1996-97). Home: 340 Jefferson Rd Princeton NJ 08540-3475 Office: Princeton Univ Dept Politics Princeton NJ 08544-0001

GREENSTEIN, JESSE LEONARD, astronomer, educator; b. N.Y.C., Oct. 15, 1909; s. Maurice and Leah (Feingold) G.; m. Naomi Kitay, Jan. 7, 1934; children: George Samuel, Peter Daniel. AB, Harvard U., 1929, AM, 1930, PhD, 1937; DSc (hon.), U. Ariz., 1987. Engaged in real estate and investments, 1930-34; Nat. Research fellow, 1937-39; assoc. prof. Yerkes Obs., U. Chgo., 1939-48; research assoc. McDonald Obs., U. Tex., 1939-48; mil. research under OSRD (optical design), Yerkes Obs., 1942-45; prof. Calif. Inst. Tech., 1948-70, Lee A. DuBridge prof. astrophysics, 1971-81, prof. emeritus, 1981—. Also staff mem. Hale Obs., 1949-79, Palomar Obs., 1979—, exec. officer for astronomy, 1949-72; chmn. of faculty of inst., 1965-67; mem. obs. com. Hale Observatories; mem. staff Owens Valley Radio Obs.; cons., also com. mem. NASA and NSF on astronomy and radio astronomy; chmn. astronomy survey Nat. Acad. Scis., 1969-72; spl. cons. NASA, 1978-83; vis. prof. Princeton, 1955, Inst. for Advanced Studies, 1964, 68-69, U. Hawaii, 1979, Niels Bohr Inst., 1979, NORDITA, Copenhagen, 1972, U. Del., 1981; lectr. in field; cons. Sci. Adv. Bd. USAF; former dir. Itek Corp., Hycon Corp.; chmn. bd. dirs. Assoc. Univs. Rsch. in Astronomy, 1974-77; bd. overseers Harvard, 1965-71; life trustee Pacific Asia Mus. Author sects. of treatises, 440 tech. papers; editor: Stellar Atmospheres, 1960; contbr. sci. articles to profl. jours.; author govt. reports. Named Calif. Scientist of Yr., 1964; recipient Apollo award, Disting. Public Service medal NASA, 1974, Centennial medal Harvard Grad. Sch., 1989. Mem. Royal Astron. Soc. (assoc.; Gold medal 1975), Astron. Soc. Pacific (Bruce medalist 1971), Am. Astron. Soc. (councillor 1947-50, v.p. 1955-57, Russell lectr. 1970), Internat Astron. Union (pres. commn. on spectroscopy 1952-58, chmn. U.S. delegation 1969-72), Nat. Acad. Scis. (councillor, sect. chmn. com. on sci. and pub. policy), Am. Philos. Soc., Am. Acad. Arts and Scis., Athenaeum (Pasadena), Phi Beta Kappa. Home: 1763 Royal Oaks Dr Apt B5 Bradbury CA 91010-1979

GREENSTEIN, JULIUS SYDNEY, zoology educator; b. Boston, July 13, 1927; s. Samuel and Helen (Shriber) G.; m. Joette Mason, Aug. 23, 1954; children: Gail Susan, Jodi Beth, Jay Mason, Blake Jeffrey, Joette Elise. BA, Clark U., 1948; MS, U. Ill., 1951, PhD, 1955; postgrad., Harvard U., 1966. Mem. faculty U. Mass., Amherst, 1954-59; faculty Duquesne U., Pitts., 1959-70, chmn. dept. biol. scis., 1961-70, prof., 1964-70; prof., chmn. dept. biology State SUNY, Fredonia, 1970-74, acting dean arts and scis., 1973-74; dean math. and natural scis. Shippensburg (Pa.) U., 1974-80; also dir. Ctr. for Sci. and the Citizen; pres. Ctrl. Ohio Tech. Coll., 1980-94, pres. emeritus, 1994—; dean, dir. Ohio State U., Newark, 1980-94, prof. zoology, 1980—. Vis. lectr. Am. Inst. Biol. Scis., 1966-76; disting. vis. prof. USAF Acad., 1994-95. Author: Contemporary Readings in Biology, 1971, Readings in Living Systems, 1972; spl. editor Internat. Jour. Fertility, 1958-69, Contraception, 1970-77; columnist Newark Advocate, 1981-93, Licking Countian, 1993-94; contbr. articles to profl. jours. Mem. Carnegie Civic Symphony Orch.; mem. sci. adv. bd. Human Life Found.; trustee Licking Meml. Hosp., Licking County Symphony Orch.; mem. campaign cabinet United Way Licking County; exec. bd. Cen. Ohio Rural Consortium and Pvt. Industry Coun.; mem. higher edn. panel Am. Coun. on Edn., labor com. Higher Edn. Coun. Ohio. Served in armored div. AUS, World War II. Recipient Wisdom award honor, 197O Mem. AAAS, Am. Assn. Acad. Deans, Am. Assn. Univ. Admintrs., Am. Assn. Anatomists, Am. Inst. Biol. Scis., Internat. Fertility Assn., Am. Soc. Zoologists, Am. Fertility Soc., Soc. Study Fertility (Eng.), Coun. Biol. Editors, Pa. Acad. Sci. (editorial bd. 1963-70), N.Y. State Acad. Sci., Soc. Study Devel. Biology, Ohio Assn. Regional Campuses (vice chair 1988-89, chair 1989-90, pres.), North Cen. Assn. Colls. and Schs. (cons., evaluator), Newark C. of C., Rotary, Sigma Xi. Achievements include contributions to understanding of causes and prevention of reproductive failure in mammals by studying early developmental stages of embryo, nature of male and female reproductive organs and endocrine glands; developed new techniques for staining specimens and smears; first to demonstrate that estradiol injections cause corpus luteum regression, hence early termination of pregnancy; investigated relationship of specific diseases to normal reproductive performance. Home: 1284 Howell Dr Newark OH 43055-1742 Office: Ohio State U at Newark University Dr Newark OH 43055-1797 E-mail: juliusg@peoplepc.com.

GREENWOOD, CARL MICHAEL, physical education educator; b. Ft. Campbell, Ky., Sept. 12, 1956; s. Carl Ivan and Barbara Leigh (Shawn) G. BSE, Greenville Coll., 1978; MSE, No. Ill. U., 1983; PhD, Tex. Woman's U., 1990. Cert. tchr., Ill. Tchr., coach Divernon (Ill.) Sch. Dist., 1978-80, Aptakisic-Tripp Jr. High Sch., Prairie View, Ill., 1980-81; grad. asst. No. Ill. U., DeKalb, 1981-82; mgr. Olympic Health & Racquet Club, Sycamore, Ill., 1982-83; tchr., coach Genoa (Ill.) Sch. Dist., 1983-84; asst. prof. Hardin-Simmons U., Abilene, Tex., 1984-87, 89-92; asst. prof., baseball coach Barry U., Miami Shores, Fla., 1992—. Cons. Hendrick Home for Children, Abilene, 1989-92, Tri-County Co-op, Stanford, Tex., 1989-92, Stephenville (Tex.) Ind. Sch. Dist., 1987-89. Contbr. articles to profl. jours. Mem. AAHPERD, Tex. AHPERD, Tex. Assn. Phys. Edn. (chairperson 1989-90), Tex. Program for Handicapped, Fellowship Christian Athletes, Phys. Fitness Coun., Christians United in Phys. Edn., Phi Kappa Phi. Republican. Avocations: travel, exercise, reading, movies. Office: Barry Univ 11300 NE 2nd Ave Miami FL 33161-6695

GREENWOOD, DAVID WILBUR, elementary education educator; b. Bethesda, Ohio, Aug. 25, 1948; s. Wilbur Lewis and Helen M. (Breedlove) G.; m. Jeanette Ann Cheney, Apr. 17, 1976. BS in Edn., Ohio U., 1970. Cert. tchr., Ohio. Tchr. Cambridge (Ohio) City Schs., 1970—. Mem. NEA, Ohio Edn. Assn., Cambridge Edn. Assn. Methodist. Avocation: collecting antiques. Home: 64597 Slaughter Hill Rd Cambridge OH 43725-9127 Office: Park Elem Sch 150 Highland Ave Cambridge OH 43725-2573

GREENWOOD, FRANK, information scientist, educator; b. Rio de Janeiro, Mar. 6, 1924; came to U.S., 1935; s. Heman Charles and Evelyn (Heyns) G.; m. Mary Mallas, Oct. 24, 1972; children: Margaret, Ernest, Nicholas. BA, Bucknell U., 1950; MBA, U. So. Calif., 1959; PhD, UCLA, 1963; hon. doctorate, Commonwealth Open U. Brit. VI, 1999. Cert. systems profl., project mgmt. profl. Various positions The Tex. Co., U.S., Africa and Can., 1950-60; assoc. prof. U. Ga., Athens, 1961-65; chmn. dept. computer sys. Ohio U., Athens, 1966-76; dir. computer ctr. U. Mont., Missoula, 1977-84; prof. mgmt. info. sys. Southea. Mass. U. (now U. Mass.), North Dartmouth, 1985-89, Ctrl. Mich. U., Mt. Pleasant, 1990-93; pres. Greenwood & Assocs., Ltd., Bloomfield Hills, Mich., 1993. Instr. on-line clases Jones Internat. U., Englewood, Colo., Gatlin Ednl. Svcs., Ft. Worth, Tex. Author: Casebook for Management and Business Policy: A Systems Approach, 1968, Managing the Systems Analysis Function, 1968; (with Nicolai Siemens and C.H. Marting Jr.) Operations Research: Planning, Operating and Information Systems, 1973; (with Mary Greenwood) Information Resources in the Office Tomorrow, 1980, Profitable Small Business Computing, 1982, Office Technology: Principles of Automation, 1984, Business Telecommuncations: Data Communications in the Information Age, 1988, Introduction to Computer-Integrated Manufacturing, 1990, How to Raise Office Productivity, 1991, Meeting the Challenges of Project Management: A Primer, 1998; columnist: Computerworld mag., 1972-73, The Daily Record, 1982-83, (with Mary Greenwood) Herald News, 1986, The Beacon, 1986, Morning Sun, 1990-93; contbr. monographs, articles to profl. jours. and chpts. to books. Sgt. AUS, 1943-45. UCLA Alumni scholar, 1961; Ford Found. fellow, 1962-63. Mem. Wamsutta Club (New Bedford, Mass.). Greek Orthodox. Avocation: exercise. Home and Office: 7426 Deep Run Apt 1322 Bloomfield Hills MI 48301-3844 E-mail: fgreenw617@aol.com.

GREENWOOD, SHEILA LYNN, principal, coach; b. Olney, Ill., Apr. 11, 1964; d. Sharon Ann (Hardy) G. AS, Olney Ctrl. Coll., 1984; BS, Eastern Ill. U., 1986, MS, 1995. Basketball coach Flora (Ill.) Sch. Dist., 1986; tchr., coach Athens (Ill.) Sch. Dist., 1987-88, Olney (East Richland) Dist., 1988-93, Villa Grove (Ill.) Dist., 1993-2000; prin. Moulton Mid. Sch., Shelbyville, 2000—. Camp dir., athletic dir. Villa Grove Schs., 1993-2000. Mem. Women's Basketball Coaches Assn., Ill. H.S. Assn. (mem. sportsmanship com. 1997, 98, 2000). Avocations: golf, gardening. Home: 15264 N C R 2400 E Oakland IL 61943 E-mail: bogeysmom@hotmail.com.

GREER, CYNTHIA FAYE, mediator, law educator, consultant; b. Madison, Tenn., Oct. 22, 1954; d. Leo Curtis Sr. and Vera Evelyn Greer. BA, David Lipscomb U., Nashville, 1976; MEd, Ga. State U., 1978; EdD, Pepperdine U., 1988, M in Dispute Resolution, 1997. Cert. in dispute resolution; cert. counselor and mediator. Secondary English tchr. Greater Atlanta Christian Sch., 1977-80; dir. career svcs. David Lipscomb U., Nashville, 1980-81; dir. career svcs. and alumni rels. Pepperdine Sch. Law, Malibu, Calif., 1981-82, asst. dean, 1982-92, assoc. dean instnl. advancement, 1992—98; dir., sr. mediator Calif. Acad. Mediation Profls., Encino, Calif., 1999—. Mem. faculty Straus Inst. Pepperdine Sch. Law, 1989—. Editor Pepperdine Law Quar., 1981-98. Mem. Malibu Vol. Patrol, 1994-98. Mem. ABA, Calif. State Bar (com. on continuing legal edn. 1990-93), Am. Assn. Law Schs. (sec. sects. on student svcs. 1995, exec. com. 1995), Assn. Conflict Resolution (pres. L.A. chpt. 2001-03). Office: California Acad of Mediation Professionals 16501 Ventura Blvd Ste 606 Encino CA 91436 E-mail: cgreer@mediate.com.

GREER, DAVID S. university dean, physician, educator; b. Bklyn., Oct. 12, 1925; s. Jacob and Mary (Zaslawsky) Greer; m. Marion Clarich, June 25, 1950; children: Jeffrey, Linda. BS, U. Notre Dame, 1948; MD, U. Chgo., 1953; MA (hon.), Brown U., 1975; LHD (hon.), Southeastern Mass. U., 1981. Diplomate Am. Bd. Internal Medicine. Intern Yale-New Haven Med. Center, 1953—54; resident in medicine U. Chgo. Clinics, 1954—57; instr. endocrinology and medicine U. Chgo., 1957; practice medicine specializing in internal medicine Fall River, Mass., 1957—74; chief staff dept. medicine Fall River Gen. Hosp., 1959—62; med. dir. Earle E. Hussey Hosp., Fall River, 1962—75; chief staff dept. medicine Truesdale Clinic and Truesdale Hosp., Fall River, 1971—74, pres. med. staff, 1968—70; sr. clin. instr. medicine Tufts U. Coll. Medicine, 1969—71, asst. clin. prof., 1971—78; clin. asso. prof. community health Brown U., 1973—75, dir. family practice residency program, 1975—78, prof. community health, 1975—93, prof. emeritus, 1993—, assoc. dean medicine, 1974—81, dean medicine, 1981—92, dean emeritus, 1992—, chmn. sect. community health, 1978—81. Mem. Gov.'s Task Force on Quality of Care, Medicaid Program, Commonwealth of Mass., 1969—70; del. White House Conf. Aging, 1971, 81; pres. Ind. Living Authority, State of R.I., 1975—81; mem. exec. com. Cancer Control Bd. R.I., 1975—80; mem. R.I. Gov.'s Task Force for Inst. of Mental Health, 1976—81; bd. dirs. Health Planning Coun., Inc., Providence, 1976—78; chmn. com. on aging Jewish Fedn. R.I., 1978—80; chmn. Gov.'s Commn. on Provision of Comprehensive Mental Health Svcs. in R.I., 1980—81; trustee Southeastern Mass. U., 1970—81, chmn., 1973—74, Providence Mayor's Sr. Citizens Task Force, 1975; bd. dirs. Assn. Home Health Agys. R.I., 1975—80; founding dir. Internat. Physicians for Prevention of Nuc. War, Inc., 1980—85; vis. prof. dept. medicine Georgetown U., 1992—93; scholar-in-residence Assn. Am. Med. Colls., 1992—93. Contbr. articles to profl. jours. Named Prof. of the Yr., Brown U., 1992; recipient Outstanding Svc. award, Mass. Easter Seal Soc., 1970, Outstanding Citizens award, Jewish War Vets. Aux., 1973, Disting. Svc. award, U. Chgo. Med. Alumni Assn., Cutting Found. medal, Andover Newton Theol. Sem., 1976; fellow in health, Kellogg Found. Internat., 1986—89, vis. fellow, Green Coll. Oxford U., 1985. Master: ACP; mem.: R.I. Med. Soc., Internat. Soc. Rehab. Medicine, Am. Congree Rehab. Medicine, Gerontol. Soc., Inst. Medicine. Jewish. Office: Brown U Box G Providence RI 02912 E-mail: Greer@brown.edu.

GREER, JOHN ONLY, architect, educator; b. Henderson, Tex., Oct. 21, 1933; s. Dolphus Only and Sarah Flonelle (Brison) G.; m. Wanda Faye Knight, June 5, 1954; children: Gregg Only, Valorie Ann. BArch, A&M Coll. Tex., 1957; MArch, Tex. A&M U., 1964. Registered arch., Tex. Grad. tchg. asst. Sch. Arch. Tex. A&M U., College Station, 1962-63, instr. Sch. Arch., 1963-65, asst. rsc. arch. Mgmt. Svcs. Dir., Arch. Rsch. Ctr., 1971-72, asst. prof. arch., 1972-74, assoc. prof. arch. and enrivon. design, 1974-80, head dept. environ. design, 1976-85, prof. arch. environ. design, 1980—, Wallie E. Scott Arch. Practice & Mgmt. prof., 1989, assoc. dean for devel. Coll. Arch., 1989-90, exec. assoc. dean, 1990-91, interim dean, 1991-92; arch. John Only Greer Arch., Bryan, Tex., 1972—, mem. archtl. rev. panel, 1992—. Draftsman Caudill Rowlett Scott, Archs., Bryan, 1956-57; job capt. Killebrew and Assocs., Archs. and Engrs., Wichita Falls, Tex., 1959-61; project arch. Matthews and Assoc., Archs. and Engrs., Wichita Falls, 1965-66; ptnr. Maynard and Greer, Archs., Nacogdoches, Tex., 1966-71. Prin. works include Regional Welfare Office Renovations, Tex. State Bldg Comm., Nacogdoches, Comml. Nat. Bank, Nacogdoches, Parish Hall and Sch. Bldg., Christ Episcopal Ch., Nacogdoches, Santuary and Ednl. Bldg. Addition, First Meth. Ch., Nettie Marshall Elem. Sch., Del Rentzel Regional Airport Adminstrn. Bldg., Cable TV Bldg., Tex. Cmty. Antennas, Inc., St. Joseph's Hosp., Bryan, among others; contbr. articles to profl. jours. Bd. dirs. Woodstock Condominium Homeowners Assn., College Station, 1982-97, treas., 1982-97; mem. restrictions com. North Oakwood Subdivsn., Bryan, 1981-84, treas., 1982-84; life mem. Houston Livestock Show and Rodeo, 1982—. Recipient award for disting. achievement in tchg. Coll. Arch., 1989, Tex. A&M U., 1999. Fellow AIA (bd. dirs. 1992-94, sec. Brazos chpt. 1972, dir. 1972-74, v.p. 1974, pres.-elect 1980, pres. 1981, bd. dirs. N.E. Tex. chpt. 1969-71, Richard Upjohn fellow 1994); mem. Tex. Archtl. Found. (bd. trustees 1984—, sec. 1984-86, 1990-95, treas. 1989), Tex. Soc. Archs. (AIA dir. 1992-94, pres. 1988, pres.-elect 1987, v.p. 1978, sec. 1975, chmn. nominating com. 1989, chmn. practice law com. 1989, govt. affairs com. 1989-93, Excellence in Arch. Edn. 1989, Llewelen Pitts award 1995), Tex. Bd. Arch. Examiners (chmn. 1995-2000, Am. Arbitration Assn. (constrn. panel), Constrn. Specifications Inst. (cert.), Nat. Coun. Archtl. Registration Bds. (Tex. dir. 1995-2000, invited grader design exam. 1990, grader design exam Ft. Lauderdale 1985, grade site and design exam. Chgo. 1981), Tex. Forestry Assn., Ducks Unltd., Tau Sigma Delta (Alpha Alpha chpt. Silver medal 1995). Methodist. Avocations: professional society service, travel, gardening. Home: 506 Brookside Dr E Bryan TX 77801-3703 Office: Tex A&M U Coll Arch College Station TX 77843-0001

GREER, SUSAN ANNE, educational materials writer; b. Sacramento; m. W. Thomas Greer; 2 children. BA in Biology, U. Calif., Santa Cruz, 1978; BA in Liberal Studies, San Francisco State U., 1980, MA in Edn., 1985. Cert. tchr. Rschr., writer George Lucas Ednl. Found., Fremont, Calif.; ednl. designer for software and CD/Rom prodn. The Learning Co., Fremont; evaluator video & software Calif. Dept. Edn. Editor: (tradebook) Art of Skiing, sci. textbooks. Avocations: skiing, hiking, writing, reading, painting.

GREEVER, JANET GROFF, history educator; b. Philadelphia, Sept. 12, 1921; m. William St. Clair Greever, Aug. 24, 1951; 1 child. BA, Bryn Mawr Coll., 1942, MA, 1945, Harvard U., 1951, PhD, 1954. Resident head grad. houses Radcliffe Coll., Cambridge, Mass., 1947-48; resident head undergrad. hall Bryn Mawr (Pa.) Coll., 1949-51, instr. history, 1949-50; asst. prof. history Wash. State U., Pullman, 1962-63, U. Idaho, Moscow, 1965-66; ind. rschr., lectr. history Moscow, Idaho, 1954—. Interim lectr. history Whitman Coll., Walla Walla, Wash., 1978; Idaho regional admissions cons. and interviewer Bryn Mawr COll., 1955-81. Author: Jose Ballivian y El Oriente Boliviano, 1987. Bd. dirs. U. Idaho Libr. Assocs., Moscow, 1979-81, pres. 1980-81. Pa. State scholar, 1938-42, History fellow Bryn Mawr (Pa.) Coll., 1944-45, Margaret M. Justin fellow AAUW, Washington, 1948-49; grantee Lucius N. Littauer Found., N.Y.C., 1948-49. Mem. Am. Hist. Assn. (life), Conf. on Latin. Am. History (life), Latin Am. Studies Assn., Soc. for Am. Archaeology (life), Archaeol. Inst. Am. (life), Phi Alpha Theta. Avocations: travel, photography. Home: 315 S Hayes St Moscow ID 83843-3419

GREEVER, JOHN, retired mathematics educator; b. Pulaski, Va., Jan. 30, 1934; s. John Jay Greever and Hulah Lily (Loyd) Bentley; m. Margaret LeSueur Quarles, Aug. 29, 1953; children: Catherine Patricia, Richard George, Cynthia Diane. BS in Math., U. Richmond, 1953; MA in Math., U. Va., 1956, PhD in Math., 1958. Asst. prof. math. Fla. State U., Tallahassee, 1958-61; mem. faculty Harvey Mudd Coll., Claremont, Calif., 1961-95, prof. math., 1970-95, chmn. math. dept., 1972-75, founding dir. math. clinic, 1973-75. Faculty Claremont Grad. Sch., 1962-95; vis. prof. Kyoto (Japan) U. Rsch. Inst. for Math. Sci., 1967-68, U. B.C. Inst. Animal Resource Ecology, Vancouver, 1984-85; rsch. assoc. dept. biology U. Calif., Riverside, 1975-78; vis. rsch. mathematician dept. entomology U. Calif., 1978. Author Theory and Examples of Point Set Topology, 1967; contbr. articles to profl. jours. Mem. Am. Math. Soc., Coun. on Undergrad. Rsch. (councilor 1989-95, vice-chmn. math. and computer scis. sect. 1991-92, chmn. 1992-94), Math. Assn. Am. (sec.-treas. So. Calif. sect. 1973-76, pres. 1981-82), Soc. of the Cin., Pole Pass Power Squadron (comdr. 2001), Orcas

Island Yacht Club (commodore 2002), Pi Mu Epsilon, Sigma Xi, Kappa Mu Epsilon, Phi Kappa Sigma. Avocations: boating, gardening. Home: 260 Grey Havens Loop PO Box 413 Orcas WA 98280-0413

GREEVER, MARGARET QUARLES, retired mathematics educator; b. Wilkensburg, Pa., Feb. 7, 1931; d. Lawrence Reginald and Ella Mae (LeSueur) Quarles; m. John Greever, Aug. 29, 1953; children: Catherine Patricia, Richard George, Cynthia Diane. Cert. costume design, Richmond Profl. Inst., 1952; student, U. Va., 1953-56; BA in Math., Calif. State U., L.A., 1963; MA in Math., Claremont Grad. Sch., 1968. Cert. tchr. specializing in Jr. Coll. math., Calif. Tchr. math. Chaffey Unified H.S. Dist., Alta Loma, Calif., 1963-64, L.A. Unified Sch. Dist., 1964-65, Chino (Calif.) Unified Sch. Dist., 1965-81; from asst. prof. to prof. Chaffey Coll., Rancho Cucamonga, 1981-96, phys. sci. divsn. chmn. Alta Loma, 1985-92, dean, phys., life, health sci., 1992-96. Mem. AAUW (pres. local chpt. 1998-2000), Orcas Island Garden Club (treas. 1997-2000, pres.-elect 2000, pres. 2001), Orcas Island Yacht Club, Pi Lambda Theta. Avocations: quilting, cooking, sewing, gardening.

GREFE, JEAN BUTLER, secondary education art educator; b. Denver, May 28, 1942; d. Paul Porter Butler and Nelle Montana (Stewart) Clark; divorced; children: Christopher, Frederick. BS, East Carolina U., 1963; M of Interdisciplinary Studies, Va. Commonwealth U., 2000. Cert. secondary art tchr., Va. Ptnr. Grefe & Grefe, Great Falls, Va., 1971—89; art tchr., chair dept. Fairfax (Va.) County Pub. Schs., 1981—, curriculum writer, 1993, 1994, 2003. Cons. Countryside Day Sch., Sterling, Va., 1984; life model study leader Smithsonian Instn., Washington, 1994-97; sponsor, cons. reenactment video Project Enlightenment: Corcoran Mus., 1994; mem. Disciplined Based Art Edn. seminar Getty Found., U. Cin., 1994, Advanced DBAE Getty Seminar, Cranbrook, 1995, Freer Gallery of Art Tchr. Inst., 1995; presenter workship Nat. Mus. Women in Arts, 1997, Am. Studies Nat. Conv., 1997, UAEA Conv., 2002; adj. prof. Va. Commonwealth U., 2000-01; mem. Tchr. Inst., U. No. Mich., Marquette, 2002. Exhibited photographs in solo show at The Gallery/Reston Cmty. Ctr.; group shows, 1993, 94, 95, 96, 97, 98. Named Cafritz Found. artist Nat. Endowment for Arts, 1987-90. Mem. Nat. Art Edn. Assn., Va. Art Edn. Assn. (Tchr. of Yr. 1986, 87), Am. Scandinavian Cultural Union, Wasa Drott Lodge, Delta Phi Delta. Lutheran. Avocations: travel, swedish language, photography. Home: 1514 Farsta Ct Reston VA 20190-4910 E-mail: Jean.Grefe@fcps.edu.

GREGG, KATHY KAY, school system administrator; b. Washington, N.C., Aug. 26, 1956; d. Merwin Jack and Mary Elizabeth Gregg. BS, East Carolina U., 1978; MA, Appalachian State U., 1980; MEd, U. South Fla., 1993; PhD, Union Inst., Cin., 1998. Cert. educator Fla. Dept. Edn. Guidance counselor Waycross (Ga.) H.S., 1981—82; family life educator Family Svc. Ctrs., Clearwater, Fla., 1982—84; guildance counselor Pinellas County Schs., Largo, Fla., 1984—92, full svc. sch. coord., 1992—96, sch. adminstr., 1996—. Prof. Eckerd Coll., St. Petersburg, Fla., 1994—. Grantee Challenge Ropes Course, Jr. League St. Petersburg, 1997. Mem.: Assn. Experiential Edn. Avocations: reading, writing, sports, nature photography. Office: Northeast Cmty Sch 1717 54th Ave N Saint Petersburg FL 33714

GREGG, PAULA ANN, education educator; b. Corpus Christi, Tex., Feb. 26, 1956; d. Roy Paul and Mary Faye (Smith) G. BS, Coll. of Charleston, 1978; MEd, U. S.C., 1987, postgrad.; PhD, Clemson U., 1998. Cert. elem. and mid. sch. math. tchr., S.C. Tchr. Bells Elem. Sch., Ruffin, S.C., 1979-80; tchr. math. Hanberry Mid. Sch., Blythewood, S.C., 1980-86, Northside Mid. Sch., West Columbia, S.C., 1986-92, Irmo Mid. Sch., Columbia, S.C., 1992-98; asst. prof. math. Converse Coll., Spartanburg, SC, 1998—2000; asst. prof. math. edn. U. S.C.-Aiken, 2000—. Pres. Walterboro (S.C.) Jaycee-ettes, 1979. Named Tchr. of Yr., Northside Mid. Sch., 1992. Mem. NEA, Nat. Coun. Tchrs. Math. (v.p. mid. schs. 1985), S.C. Coun. Tchrs. Math. (v.p. postsecondary edn. 2001—), Daus. of Nile. Baptist. Avocations: singing, pianist, bowling, reading, walking. Home: 200 Cody Ln Apt D Aiken SC 29803-7377 Office: U SC-Aiken 471 University Pkwy Aiken SC 29801

GREGO, LAUREN HARRIS, reading specialist; b. Kingston, Pa., Feb. 8, 1950; d. Lazarus C. and Doris (Searfoss) Harris; m. Michael F. Grego, Aug. 5, 1978; children: Paul Michael, David Harris; 1 child from previous marraige: Kimberly O'Hara Kauffman. BA in English, Wilkes Coll., Wilkes-Barre, Pa., 1974; MS in Reading Edn., Marywood Coll., Scranton, Pa., 1978. Libr. West Pittston (Pa.) Pub. Libr., 1975-77; reading tchr. Scranton Sch. Dist., 1977-78; reading specialist Mifflin County Sch. Dist., Lewistown, Pa., 1978—. Newspaper in edn. coord. The Sentinel, 1991—, early childhood action team, 2001—, portfolio assessment team, 2001—; founder off campus Master Degree program, Wilkes U., Mifflin County, 1998; rschr., cons. Performance Learning Sys., Nevada City, Calif., 1981—; co-chmn. goal team 1 Mifflin County 2000, dir. organizer county-wide jump into reading program; instr. Wilkes U., 1981—. Bd. dirs. Mifflin County 2000, Lewistown, 1994—, Juanita Mifflin Literacy Coalition, Lewistown, 1990; den leader Cub Scout Troop 7; chmn. Santa's Bookbag, 1999—. Mem. ASCD, Keystone State Reading Assn., Stone Arch Reading Coun. (v.p. 1993-95, pres. 1995-98), Internat. Reading Assn., Phi Delta Kappa. Methodist. Avocations: golf, reading, piano. Home: 265 Cornfield Cir Lewistown PA 17044-9750

GREGOIRE, SISTER THERESE GERMAINE, retired secondary education educator; b. Lowell, Mass., June 12, 1942; d. Lionel G. and Gertrude C. (Houle) G. BS in Edn., U. Mass., Lowell, 1971; postgrad., Nicholls State U., 1983-87. Cert. elem. edn., secondary math. and computers, La., elem. edn., Mass., nat. cert. Nat. Bd. Profl. Teaching Standards. 1st grade tchr. St. Joseph Sch., Haverhill, Mass., 1962-64, tchr. grades 5, 6, 1971-73; 1st and 3d grade tchr. Maltrait Meml. Sch., Kaplan, La., 1964-66, jr. high math. and sci. tchr., libr., 1973-79; tchr. grades 5, 6, libr. Notre Dame Sch., Ogdensburg, N.Y., 1966-68; tchr. grades 7-12 math. and computers Mt. Carmel Sch., New Iberia, La., 1979-88; tchr. grades 9-12 math. and computers Vermilion Cath. High Sch., Abbeville, La., 1988-98. Web site designer. Vol. tchr. Plantation Edn. Program, New Iberia, 1981; provider workshops in computer use and stamp collecting Boy Scouts of Am., Ogdensburg, 1966-68, Girl Scouts Am., New Iberia, Abbeville, 1979-90; congregation treas. for the Sisters of Mt. Carmel, Lacombe, La.; congregation archivist and webmaster. Mem. Soc. of Southwest Archivists, Soc. of Am. Archivists, Nat. Assn. of Treasurers of Religious Insts., Archivists for Congregation of Women Religious. Democrat. Roman Catholic. Avocations: stamp collecting, geneaology. E-mail: teegreg42@yahoo.com.

GREGOR, MARLENE PIERCE, primary education educator, elementary science consultant; b. Oak Park, Ill., Apr. 22, 1932; d. Kenneth Bryant and Dorothy Rose Pierce; m. G. Ray Timmons, Aug. 1, 1953 (div. 1972); children: Gregg R., Todd P., Wendy S. Timmons McGuire; m. Harold L. Gregor, 1987. BS in Elem. Edn., U. Ill., 1953; MS in Elem. Edn., Ill. State U., 1974, postgrad., 1975-91. Tchr. 2d grade Wethersfield Community Unit Schs., Kewanee, Ill., 1953-54; primary tchr. Fairbury (Ill.) Cropsey Schs., 1965-84, Prairie-Cen. Community Unit #8 Schs., Fairbury, 1984-91; ret. Prairie-Ctr. Community Unit # 8 Schs., Fairbury, 1991. Item writer Stanford Achievement Test Psychol. Corp., San Antonio, 1989, sci. assessment Ill. State Bd. Edn., Springfield, 1987-88, Ill. student achievement test Metritech Corp., 2000-01; grant reader Ctr. Sci. Literacy, Springfield, 1991-93. Author: Bark Hunters, 2000, (with others) Horizons Plus Science Stories-Grade 2, 1992, Toys That Teach Science, 1993, Celebrating Science, 1990, Award Winning Nutrition Education Lessons and Units, 1994; mem. sci. tchrs. writing team Ill. State U., 1992; contbr. articles and stories to various publs. Bd. dirs. Friends of the Arts Ill. State U., Normal, 1980-86, 92-98, v.p., 1994-96; mem. Bloomington Mayoral Downtown Commn., 1993-98, sec., 1994-98; mem. adv. bd. Children's Mus., 1993-95; mem. steering com. Downtown Heritage Festival, Bloomington, 1995, 96; mem. steering com. Ill. State U. Fell Arboretum, 1994-2001, bd. dirs. and chair sch. outreach com., 1995-2001; mem. Leadership McLean County Class of 1996; mem. fundraising cabinet Fell Arboretum, Working Forum for Vision of Downtown, 1997-98; bd. dirs., chair visual arts com. Downtown Bloomington Assn., 1998-2000, mem. downtown aesthetics com., 1999—; bd. dirs. Sr. Profls., Ill. State U., 2001—; mem. Uniquely Bloomington Downtown Commn., sec., 1999—, art chair Sesquicentennial 2000 Festival, 1999-2000; bd. dirs. Ctrl. Ill. Neurosci. Found., 2000—; pub. art chair Corn-On-The-Curb, 2000, 01; bd. dirs. Ill. Symphony Guild, 2002—. Named Outstanding Tchr. Sci. NSF-Ill. State U., 1985, Honors Sci. Tchr. Ill. State U., 1985, 86, 87; Chpt. II Mini grantee Edn. Svc. Ctr. #13, 1985-90; recipient Creative Nutrition award Nutrition and Edn. Tng. Ctr., 1989, Women of Distinction award YWCA, 1999, Jean Anderson Downtown Improvement award, 2000. Mem. NEA, Nat. Sci. Tchrs. Assn. (presenter conv. 1985, 87), Coun. for Em. Sci. Internat., Ill. Edn. Assn. (Tchr. Excellence award 1989), Ill. Ctr. Sci. Literacy (adv. mem. 1991-93), Ill. Sci. Tchrs. Assn. (sec. 1989-93, Presdl. Excellence Sci. Tchg. award 1991, State Finalist), Delta Kappa Gamma (v.p. chpt. 1990-92). Presbyterian. Avocations: art, watercolor, travel, physical fitness, golf. Home: 107 W Market St Bloomington IL 61701-3917

GREGORCHIK, LAMEECE ATALLAH, early childhood educator; b. Bethlehem, Jordan, July 21, 1955; d. Sami Isa and Dorothea (Shoffner) Atallah; m. Patrick Kelly Gregorchik, may 19, 1990; children: Emily, Ian. AA in Communication, Palm Beach Community Coll., 1982; BS in Elem. Edn., Framingham State Coll., 1985. Cert. elem., English, early childhood tchr., Mass.; cert. elem., ESOL, early childhood tchr., Fla. Tchr. Palm Beach County Sch., Fla., 1986—. Author: The Cocaine Children are Here. Grantee Ednl. Found. Palm County. Avocations: snorkeling, travel. Home: 6575 Paul Mar Dr Lake Worth FL 33462-3937

GREGORIAN, VARTAN, foundation administrator; b. Tabriz, Iran, Apr. 8, 1934; came to U.S., 1956; s. Samuel B. and Shushanik G. (Mirzaian) G.; m. Clare Russell, Mar. 25, 1960; children: Vahe, Raffi, Dareh. Grad., Coll. Armenian, 1955; BA, Stanford U., 1958, PhD, 1964; hon. degree, Boston U., 1983, Brown U., 1984, Jewish Theol. Seminary, 1984, SUNY, 1985, Johns Hopkins U., 1987, NYU, 1987, U. Pa., 1988, Dartmouth Coll., 1989, Rutgers U., 1989, CUNY, 1990, Tufts U., 1994. From instr. to assoc. prof. history San Francisco State Coll., 1962—68; assoc. prof. UCLA, 1968; from assoc. prof. to prof. U. Tex., 1968—72, dir. spl. programs, 1970—72; Tarzian prof. Armenian and Caucasian history U. Pa., Phila., 1972—80; dean U. Pa. (Faculty Arts and Scis.), 1974—78, provost, 1978—80; pres. N.Y. Pub. Libr., 1981—89; prof. New Sch. Social Rsch., N.Y.C., 1984—89; prof. History and Near Eastern studies NYU, 1984—89; pres., prof. History Brown U., Providence, 1989—97; pres. Carnegie Corp., N.Y.C., 1997—. Author: The Emergence of Modern Afghanistan, 1880-1946, 1969. Bd. dirs. Aaron Diamond Found., 1990-97, Brookings Instns., 1994-97, Inst. for Internat. Edn., 1989-95, Internat. League of Human Rights, 1984-97, Inst. for Advanced Study, 1987—, J. Paul Getty Trust, 1988—, Aga Khan U., 1995—, Human Rights Watch, 1996—; chmn. bd. visitors Grad. Sch. and Univ. Ctr., CUNY, 1984-90; bd. trustees Mus. Modern Art, 1994—. Decorated Officier de l'Ordre des Arts et Lettres (France), Grand Oficial Ordem Infante D. Henrique Portuguese Govt., 1995; recipient Danforth E.H. Harbison Teaching award 1969, Cactus Teaching award 1971, award of distinction Phi Lambda Theta and Phi Delta Kappa, 1980, Silver Cultural medal Italian Ministry Fgn. Affairs, 1977, Gold medal of honor City and Province of Vienna, Austria, 1976, 1st Disting. Humanist award Pa. Humanities Coun., 1983, Nat. Fellowship award Fellowship Commn., Phila., 1984, Gold medal Nat. Inst. Social Scis., 1985, Disting. Svc. to the Arts award Third St. Music Sch. Settlement, 1997, Disting. Svc. to Pub. Edn. award N.Y. Acad. Pub. Edn., 1998, Friends of the Arts award Town Hall, 1998; fellow Social Sci. Rsch. Coun., 1960, Ford Found. Fgn. Area Tng., 1960-62, Am. Coun. Learned Socs.-Social Sci. Rsch. Coun., 1965, John Simon Guggenheim Found., 1971-72, Social Sci. Rsch. Coun., 1971-72, Am. Coun. Edn., 1973. Fellow Acad. Arts Scis., Am. Philos. Soc.; mem. Am. Antiquarian Soc., Am. Hist. Assn. (program chmn. 1972), Am. Philos. Soc. (grantee 1965, 66), Internat. Fedn. Libr. Assns. (co-chmn. program com. 1985), Assn. Advancement Slavic Studies (program chmn. Western Slavic Conf. 1967), Mid-East Studies Assn., Coun. Fgn. Rels., Grolier Club, Round Table, Century Club, Econ. Club, Phi Beta Kappa. Office: Carnegie Corp Office of the Pres 437 Madison Ave Fl 27 New York NY 10022-7001*

GREGORY, FLAUDIE STEWART, special education educator; b. Pensacola, Fla., Nov. 6, 1938; d. Huddie Mosco and Martha Ophelia (Hattaway) Stewart; m. Alfred Quincy Gregory, June 7, 1957; children: Cynthia, Timothy, Donald, Ronald, Joan. AA, Pensacola Jr. Coll., 1970; BA, U. West Fla., 1980; MEd, U. North Fla., 1985. Cert. learning disabilities and hearing impaired tchr., Fla. Tchr. specific learning disabilities Escambia County Schs., Pensacola, 1980-82, 83—, interpreter, tutor of hearing impaired, 1983. Mem. Fla. Tribe of Eastern Creek Indians, Pensacola. Recipient Golden Apple award 1990. Mem. NEA, Coun. for Exceptional Children (exec. bd. 1986-88, treas. 1989-90), Fla. PTA, Escambia Edn. Assn., Kappa Delta Pi (treas. 1980-81, historian 1983-84). Democrat. Avocations: reading, flower gardening, needlework, travel. Home: 7000 Lindskog St Pensacola FL 32506-3848

GREGORY, JEAN WINFREY, ecologist, educator; b. Richmond, Va., Feb. 13, 1947; d. Thomas Edloe and Kathryn (McFarlane) Winfrey; m. Ronald Alfred Gregory, Dec. 13, 1973. BS in Biology, Mary Washington Coll., 1969; MS in Biology, Va. Commonwealth U., 1975, postgrad., 1982-90; MA in Environ. Sci., U. Va., 1983. Cert. fisheries sci. Lab. specialist A Cardiovascular Divsn. Med. Coll. Va., Richmond, 1969-70; pollution specialist State Water Control Bd. (now Dept. Environ. Quality), Richmond, 1970-77, pollution control specialist B, 1977-81, ecologist, 1981-85, ecology programs supr., 1985-88, environ. program mgr., 1988-2000, environ. mgr. II, 2000—. Adj. faculty Va. Commonwealth U., Richmond, 1978-93. Contbr. articles to profl. jours. Named One of Outstanding Young Women of Am., 1974; EPA fellow, Va., 1974-76. Mem. Am. Soc. Limnology and Oceanography, N.Am. Lake Mgmt. Soc., N.Am. Benthological Soc., Sisters in Crime, Assn. Trad. Hooking Artists. Democrat. Methodist. Avocations: herb gardening, walking, rug hooking, dalmation rescue. Office: Office Water Quality Programs PO Box 10009 Richmond VA 23240-0009 E-mail: jwgregory@deq.state.va.us.

GREGORY, JUDITH MARY, secondary education educator; b. Pitts., Sept. 29, 1946; d. Paul E. and Ruth Ann (Harding) McCauley; divorced; 1 child, David Paul Gregory. BS, Mt. Union Coll., 1968; MEd, U. Dayton, 1980. Tchr. Columbus (Ohio) Pub. Schs., 1968-70; tchr., volleyball coach, basketball coach Crestview Local H.S., Columbiana, Ohio, 1971—2003; ret., 2003. Coach jr. high volleyball, basketball, and track Crestview Mid. Sch., Columbiana, 1971-81; varsity coach track Crestview H.S., Columbiana, 1971-86, varsity coach basketball, 1971-97, asst. basketball coach, 1997—, varsity HS coach volleyball, 1971-2002; coach volleyball club Trumbull Volleyball Club, Hubbard, Ohio, 1993-2003. Mem. Ohio H.S. Volleyball Coaches (poll voter 1993-2002, named to Hall of Fame 1997, Coach of the Yr. 1994, 95), Ohio H.S. Basketball Coaches (dist. dir. women's N.E. 1978-95, Coach of the Yr. 1993). Methodist. Avocations: golf, swimming, reading, coaching. Home: 5330 Jimtown Rd East Palestine OH 44413-8746

GREGORY, MARIAN FRANCES, retired elementary school educator, retired principal; b. Gary, Ind., Apr. 24, 1919; d. August Robert and Agnes Mae (Sturgess) Kuhn; m. Robert Wayne Gregory. BS in Edn., Ind. U., 1941; MA in Counseling, Columbia U., 1960. Elem. tchr. Bremen (Ind.) Schs., 1941-46, Gary Pub. Schs., 1947-56, tchr. remedial reading, 1956-68; elem. prin. Spaulding and Lincoln schs., Gary, 1968-74; student tchr. cons. Ind. U., Bloomington, 1974-91; sec. Heritage Motors, Hammond, Ind., 1974; ret. Contbr. articles to profl. jours. Mem., poll watcher LWV, Hammond, 1980-95, 98; mem. Master Gardners Purdue U., Crown Point, Ind., 1977—; elder Presbyn. Ch. Mem. AAUW (pres. 1956-57), DAR, Bus. and Profl. Women's Club (pres. 1957-58), N.W. Ind. Women's Club (1st v.p. 1994-96), Delta Kappa Gamma, Kappa Kappa Kappa. Avocations: genealogy, gardening, stock market, history, swimming. Home: 2238 Ridge Rd Highland IN 46322-1562

GREGORY, MARILYN, primary school educator; b. San Marcos, Tex., Jan. 8, 1950; d. James F. and Mildred (Baker) Farmer; m. William Frederick Gregory III, June 2, 1973; children: William Frederick IV, James Patrick. BS, S.W. Tex. State U., San Marcos, 1972, MA in Edn., 1987. Kindergarten tchr. Luling (Tex.) Ind. Sch. Dist., 1972-73, Manor (Tex.) Ind. Sch. Dist., 1973-81, Lake Travis Ind. Sch. Dist., Austin, Tex., 1981—. Tchr. cons. State Seat Belt Program, Austin, 1978; student tchr. supr., tchr. tng. cons. S.W. Tex. State U., 1986. Co-author kindergarten curriculum guide and curriculum units, 1984. Vol. Am. Cancer Soc., Austin, 1992, Am. Heart Assn., Austin, 1994, Neighborhood Watch Program, Austin, 1994—, Muscular Dystrophy Assn., Austin, 1976. Recipient Sally Beth Moore award Austin Assn. Edn. of Young Chilodren, 1987; named Tchr. of Yr., Lake Travis Ednl. Found., 1987. Mem. AAUW, Am. Fedn. Tchrs., Classroom Tchrs. Assn., Tex. State Tchrs. Assn., Delta Kappa Gamma (Tex. Neurology chmn. 1997-99). Avocations: reading romantic novels, making craft items, computer, sports. Home: 11508 Quarter Horse Trl Austin TX 78750-1392

GREGORY, MYRA MAY, religious organization administrator, educator; b. N.Y.C., Sept. 21, 1912; d. Thomas and Anna (Collins) G. Diploma, Maxwell Tchrs. Tng. Sch., Bklyn., 1933; BS in Edn., Bklyn. Coll., 1940, MA in History, 1952. Cert. music tchr. Tchr. N.Y.C. Bd. Edn., Bklyn., 1943-75; social worker Berean Bapt. Ch., Bklyn., 1932-48, supr., 1932-94, fin. sec. Sunday sch., 1935-94. Bd. dirs. Berean-Vacation Bible Sch., Bklyn., 1935-86; tchr. Protestant Coun., N.Y.C., 1940-81; bd. dirs. Recreation Bedford-Stuyvesant Area Project Inc., Bklyn.; dir. seminar Christian Teaching, Bklyn., 1974-86, 1990—. Bd. mgrs. Bklyn. Sun. Sch. Union, 1974—; bd. dirs. Bklyn. Divsn. Coun. of Chs. 1935—, pres., 1984-86, bd. dirs. Bklyn. Sunday Sch. Union, 1974—. Named Tchr. of Yr. Cmty. Sch. Bd. Dist. 14 N.Y.C. Bd. Edn., Bklyn., 1973, Outstanding Tchr., Stuyvesand divsn., Bklyn. Sunday Sch. Union, 1977, Educator/Leader Berean Bapt. Ch., 1977; recipient Ecumenism citation Borough Pres.'s Office, Bklyn., 1985, Religious Educator citation Bklyn. Ch. Women United, Inc., 1993, Cmty. Svc. awrd Mayors Office, N.Y.C., 1993, Ecumenical Svc./Educator Honors Office the Coun. City of N.Y., 1994, Lifetime Achievement award Bklyn. Coll., 1995, Outstanding Svc. award Coun. Chs. the City of N.Y., 1995, Leadership/Educator Citation Borough Pres. Office, Bklyn., 1999, Educator/Svc. Citation Berean Baptist Ch., 2000. Mem. ASCD, Am. String Tchrs. Assn., Am. Viola Soc., Assn. Childhood Edn. Internat., Orgn. Am. Historians, Ctr. Study of Presidency, Music Tchrs. Nat. Assn., Nat. Orch. Assn., Schomburg Ctr. Rsch. Black Culture. Democrat. Avocations: string ensemble, drama, writing.

GREGORY, THOMAS BRADFORD, mathematics educator; b. Traverse City, Mich., Dec. 13, 1944; s. Philip Henry and Rhoda Winslow (Hathaway) G.; m. Deirdre Dianne Mason, July 15, 1995. BA, Oberlin (Ohio) Coll., 1967; MA, Yale U., 1969, M of Philosophy, 1975, PhD, 1977. Lectr. Ohio State U., Mansfield, 1977-78, asst. prof. math., 1978-84, assoc. prof. math., 1984—, pres. faculty, 2001—02. Reviewer: Math. Revs., 1984—; contbr. articles to profl. jours. Active Mansfield (Ohio) Symphony Chorus, 1977—, Presbytery Youth Ministries Com., New Philadelphia, Ohio, 1980-87, Ohio State U. Community Singers, Mansfield, 1985—; mem. Presbytery Biblical Authority task force, 1994-95; bd. dirs. Lay Acad. Religion, Wooster (Ohio) Coll., 1997—; commd. lay min. Presbytery of Muskingum Valley, New Philadelphia, Ohio, 1998—. Comdr. USNR, 1969-96. Fellow NSF, Washington, 1967; hon. fellow U. Wis., Madison, 1987-88, 92. Fellow Phi Beta Kappa; mem. Am. Math. Soc. (translator 1974-82), Ohio Coun. Tchrs. Math., Am. Soc. Naval Engrs., Res. Officers Assn., Naval Res. Assn., Navy League, Sigma Xi. Avocations: classical piano, singing. Home: 411 Overlook Rd Mansfield OH 44907-1533 Office: Ohio State U 1680 University Dr # O-15 Mansfield OH 44906-1547 E-mail: tgregory@math.ohio-state.edu.

GREINER, WILLIAM ROBERT, university administrator, educator, lawyer; b. Meriden, Conn., June 9, 1934; s. William Robert and Dolores (Quinn) G.; m. Carol A. Morrissey, Aug. 24, 1957; children: Kevin Thomas, Terrence Alan, Daniel Robert, Susan Lynn. BA, Wesleyan U., Conn., 1956; MA in Econs., Yale U., 1959, JD, 1960, LLM, 1966. Bar: Conn. 1961, N.Y. 1973. Asst. prof. Sch. Bus., U. Wash., 1960—64, assoc. prof., 1964—67, Sch. Law, SUNY, Buffalo, 1967—69, prof., 1969—, assoc. provost, 1970—74, assoc. dean, 1975—80; assoc. v.p. acad. affairs SUNY, Buffalo, 1980—83, interim v.p. acad. affairs, 1983—84, provost, 1984—91, pres., 1991—. Cons. in field. Author: (with Harold J. Berman) Nature and Functions of Law, 1966, 72, 80, 96; contbr. articles to profl. jours. Home: 889 Lebrun Rd Amherst NY 14226-4224 Office: U at Buffalo 506 Capen Hall Buffalo NY 14260-1600

GREITZER, EDWARD MARC, aeronautical engineering educator, consultant; b. N.Y.C., May 8, 1941; s. Arthur O. and Harriet G.; m. Helen Moulton, Nov. 24, 1966; children: Mary Lee, Jennifer Elizabeth. BA, Harvard U., 1962, MS, 1964, PhD, 1970. Asst. project engr. Pratt & Whitney divsn. United Techs., East Hartford, Conn., 1969-76; indsl. fellow commoner Churchill Coll., Cambridge U., Eng., 1975-76; asst. prof. MIT, Cambridge, 1977-79, assoc. prof., 1979-84, prof., dir. Gas Turbine Lab., 1984-96, H.N. Slater prof. aero. and astronautics, 1988—, assoc. head dept., 1996—2002; sr. rsch. engr. United Techs. Rsch. Ctr., East Hartford, 1976-77, dir. aeromech., chem. & fluid sys., 1996-98. Royal Soc. guest fellow, SERC vis. fellow, overseas fellow Churchill Coll., Cambridge U., 1983-84; vis. fellow Japan Soc. for Promotion of Sci., 1987, Peterhouse, Cambridge U., 1990-91; mem. aeronautics adv. com. NASA, 1990-94; mem. sci. adv. bd. USAF, 1992-96. Contbr. articles to profl. jours., handbooks. Recipient T. Bernard Hall prize Instn. Mech. Engrs., London, 1978, Exceptional Civilian Svc. award USAF, 1996. Fellow AIAA (Air Breathing Propulsion Best Paper award 1987), Nat. Acad. Engring., ASME (gas turbine award 1977, 79, 96, Freeman scholar in fluids engring. 1980, bd. dirs. Internat. Gas Turbine Inst. 1993-98, chmn. 1996-97, chmn. turbomachinery com. 1989-91, chmn. gas turbine scholar selection com. 1989-93, turbomachinery com., Best Paper award 1991, 92, 95, Aircraft Engine Tech. award 1995, Controls and Diagnostics com. Best Paper award 1998). Avocations: jogging, photography, rock climbing. Home: 77 Woodridge Rd Wayland MA 01778-3611 Office: MIT Dept Aeronautics & Astronautics Bldg 31-264 Cambridge MA 02139 E-mail: greitzer@mit.edu.

GREMBOWSKI, DAVID EMIL, educator, researcher; b. San Diego, May 26, 1951; s. Emil Dem and Delphine Joyce (Kurowski) G.; m. Mary West, June 22, 1974; children: Megan, Leda. BA, Wash. State U., Pullman, 1973, MA, 1975; PhD, U. Wash., Seattle, 1982. Rsch. analyst Stanford Rsch. Inst., Menlo Park, Calif., 1974-76; systems designer flexible intergovtl. grant project City of Tacoma, 1979-80; from rsch. instr. to prof. U. Wash., Seattle, 1981—. Prin. investigator of health svc. rsch. grants; instr. health program evaluation and health care system. Author: The Practice of Health Program Evaluation, 2001; contbr. articles to profl. jour. Mem. APHA, Internat. Assn. Dental Rsch. (officer in behavioral sci. and health svc. rsch. group 1988-94), Am. Assn. Dental Rsch., AcademyHealth, Am. Evaluation Assn., Phi Beta Kappa. Avocations: golf, travel, reading, painting. Office: U Wash Dept Health Svc Box 357660 Seattle WA 98195-0001

GREMINGER, MICHAEL LEO, secondary education educator; b. St. Louis, Nov. 12, 1948; s. Gilbert Joseph and Rita Marie (Donze) G.; m. Vicki

Leigh Oberle, Aug. 6, 1974; 1 child, Adam. BS in Secondary Edn., S.E. Mo. State U., 1971, MA in Tchg., 1980. Cert. biology tchr. grades 7-12, gen. sci. tchr. grades 7-12. Biology tchr. Mehlville Sr. H.S., St. Louis County, 1973—, sci. dept. chair, 1996—. Coll. credit H.S. class tchr. St. Louis (Mo.) U., 1991-95. Den leader Pack 472 Cub Scouts, Festus, Mo., 1992-94; asst. scoutmaster Boy Scouts, Festus, 1994—. With U.S. Army, 1971-73. Mem. NEA, Mo. Edn. Assn., Nat. Sci. Tchrs. Assn., Mehlville Cmty. Tchr. Assn. (treas. 1984-87, profl. rights chairperson 1984-87, Tchr. Adv. of Yr. 1988-89). Avocations: canoeing, camping. Home: 712 Jerome Dr Festus MO 63028-1079 Office: Mehlville Sr HS 3200 Lemay Ferry Rd Saint Louis MO 63125-4418

GRENANDER, ULF, mathematics educator; b. Våstervik, Sweden, July 23, 1923; came to U.S., 1966; s. Sven and Maria (Persson) G.; m. Emma-Stina Hallquist, Dec. 22, 1946; children: Sven, Angela, Charlotte. Fil. Dr., U. Stockholm, Sweden, 1950; DSc (hon.), U. Chgo. Prof. U. Stockholm, 1958-66, Brown U., Providence, R.I., 1966—. Author: General Pattern Theory, 1993. Fellow Inst. Math. Stats., Am. Acad. Arts and Scis.; mem. Royal Swedish Acad. Sci., Royal Statis. Soc. (hon.), Nat. Acad. Sci. E-mail: ulf-grenander@cox.net.

GRENZEBACH, WILLIAM SOUTHWOOD, nuclear engineer, consultant, historian; b. Chgo., Sept. 5, 1945; s. William Southwood Sr. and Edla (Edin) G.; m. Judith Samuels, June 16, 1968 (div. Feb. 1978). BA, Grinnell Coll., 1967; MA, Brandeis U., 1970, PhD in Comparative History, 1978; MS in Engring., Boston U., 1988; MS in Indsl. Engring., Northeastern U., Boston, 1988. Cert offshore drilling rig supt., U.S. Geol. Survey; cert. in offshore rescue, Govt. of Newfoundland. Mgr. Greyhound Lines East, Boston, 1970-77; engring. technician Sylvester Assocs., Rockland, Mass., 1977-78; subsea engr. ODECO, Inc., New Orleans, 1978-81; project mgr. SEDCO, Inc., Dallas, 1981-85; rsch. assoc. dept. energy Northeastern U., 1987-89; with Applied Mgmt. Cons., Assonet, Mass., 1989-90; sr. nuclear engr. Yankee Atomic Electric Co., Bolton, Mass., 1990-92; applied mgmt. cons. Assonet, Mass., 1992-95; tech. and cert. mgr. British Stds. Instn., Reston, Va., 1995—. Cons. Palisades Nuclear Power Sta., Covert, Mich., 1989, Peach Bottom/Limerick (Pa.) Power Sta., Delta and Limerick, 1989-90, Fitzpatrick Station, Lycoming, N.Y., 1992, Indian Point III, Buchanan, N.Y., 1993, New Brunswick Power Commn., Fredricton, 1990, New Eng. Med. Ctr., 1994-95; mem. Conf. Group on Ctrl. European History. Author: Germany's Informal Empire in East-Central Europe, 1988; contbr. articles to profl. publs.; author: (computer software) Reactor Coolant Expert System, 1988 (Copywrite award 1990). Supporter Friends of Cohasset (Mass.) Libr., 1978-83; mem. Cohasset Hist. Soc., 1978-83. Fellow U. Calif., San Diego, 1967-68, Brandeis U., Waltham, Mass., 1968-71, German Acad. Exch. Svc., Bonn, West Germany, 1971-72, Inst. for European History, Mainz, West Germany, 1972-74, Brandeis U., 1974-75. Mem. AAAS, Am. Nuclear Soc., Am. Soc. Quality, Inst. Indsl. Engrs., Soc. for Risk Analysis, Marine Tech. Soc., Soc. for History of Tech., Statis. Process Control Soc. Avocations: historical writing, reading, scuba diving, horseback riding. Office: 325 Huntington Ave Boston MA 02115-4401

GRESS, EDWARD J(ULES), educator, consultant; b. Jerusalem, Jan. 11, 1940; came to U.S., 1966; s. Jules Charles and Mary (Alonzo) G.; m. Katie Lorenzo, Sept. 30, 1962; children: Albert, Richard, Alexander. BBA, Am. U. Beirut, 1961, MBA, 1964; PhD, U. Ariz., 1970. Instr. acctg. Am. U. Beirut, 1961-66; lectr. acctg. U. Ariz., Tucson, 1967-70; assoc. prof. acctg. U. Saskatchewan, Saskatoon, Can., 1970-72; vis. assoc. prof. Am. U. Cairo, 1973-74; assoc. prof. N.E. La. U., Monroe, 1972-76; prof. Canisius Coll., Buffalo, 1976-78, 81—; prof., dir. TAG Bus. Ctr., Buffalo, 1988—. Recipient Faculty award Haskins and Sells Found., 1968, George Washington Honor medal Freedoms Found., Valley Forge, 1986, 87, Outstanding Acct. of Yr. award, 1992, Disting. Prof. award, Canisius Coll., 1995; named Outstanding Prof. in MBA program at Canisius Coll., 1983, 86, Hon. Citizen, City of Tucson, 1969. Mem. Fin. Execs. Inst. (chmn. acad. rels. com.), Arab Soc. Cert. Accts., Am. Acctg. Assn., Am. Mgmt. Assn., Arab Mgmt. Soc. (founding mem., trustee, chmn. edn. com.). Republican. Roman Catholic. Avocations: cross country skiing, bicycling, swimming. Office: Canisius Coll 2001 Main St Buffalo NY 14208-1035

GRETHER, DAVID MACLAY, economics educator; b. Phila., Oct. 21, 1938; s. Ewald T. and Carrie Virginia (Maclay) G.; m. Susan Edith Clayton, Mar. 24, 1961; children: Megan Elizabeth, John Clayton. BS, U. Calif., Berkeley, 1960; PhD, Stanford U., 1969. Research staff economist Cowles Found., Yale U., 1966-70; lectr. econs. Yale U., 1966-68, asst. prof., 1968-70; assoc. prof. econs. Calif. Inst. Tech., Pasadena, 1970-75, prof. econs., 1975—, exec. officer for social scis., 1978-82, chmn. Humanities and Social Scis. div., 1982-92. Author: (with M. Nerlove and J.L. Carvalho) Analysis of Economic Time Series: A Synthesis, 1979; contbr. articles to profl. jours. Mem. Econometric Soc., Am. Statis. Assn., Am. Econ. Assn. Home: 2116 N Craig Ave Altadena CA 91001-3519 Office: Calif Inst Tech Divsn Humanities Socia Pasadena CA 91125-0001

GREVE, SALLY DOANE, English educator; b. Detroit, June 2, 1934; d. Haven Frazelle and Keitha Maxine (Littler) Doane; m. John Henry Greve, June 21, 1956; children: John Haven, Suzanne Carol, Pamela Jean. BA, Mich. State U., 1956; MA in Tchg. English as Second Lang., Iowa State U., 1989. Adj. instr. ESL off-campus Des Moines Area C.C., Ankeny, Iowa, 1975-97, ESL cons., 1975-97, ret. Vol. tutor trainer Iowa Refugee Svc. Ctr., Des Moines, 1979-82; chmn. bldg. com. Episcopal Parish Ames, Iowa, 1972-74, supt. ch. sch., jr. warden, 1963-64, newsletter editor, 1991-2002, mem. choir, 1991—; sec., membership chair Ames Town and Gown Chamber Music Assn., 1999-2000, v.p., 2000-01, pres., 2001-02; bd. dirs. Story County Conservation Ptnrs., 1998-. Mem. TESOL, Mid-Am. TESOL (bd. dirs. 1985-91, pres. 1989-90), Missouri Valley Adult Edn. Assn., Iowa Assn. for Lifelong Learning, AVMA Aux., Internat. Hon. for Leadership in Univ. Apt. Cmtys. (hon.), Omega Tau Sigma (hon.). Avocation: church activities.

GREVER, JEAN KEMPEL, business education and adminstrative services educator; b. Pearl City, Ill., Nov. 7, 1926; d. Fred Lorenze and Alma Christina (Althof) K.; m. Richard Murphy, Aug. 8, 1949 (dec. Sept. 1956); children: Mark, Richard, Daniel, Donald; m. Glenn Grever, June 12, 1965 (dec. June 1992). BS in Bus. Edn., Ill. State U., 1949, MS in Bus. Edn., 1963; EdD in Bus. Edn., No. Ill. U., 1975. Tchr. Donovan (Ill.) High Sch., 1949-52, Woodland High Sch., Streator, Ill., 1957-62, Streator Twp. High Sch., 1962-63, Univ. High Sch., Normal, Ill., 1963—69; chairperson Ill. State U. Bd. Edn. Dept., Normal, 1963-65; prof. bus. edn. Ill. State U., Normal, 1965—93. Contbr. over 40 articles to profl. jours. Grantee Ill. State U., 1976-77, 80, 83, 84-89. Mem. Internat. Soc. Bus. Edn. (pres. elect 1990-91, pres. 1991-92), Ill. Bus. Edn. Assn. (bd. dirs., awards chairperson 1985-87, 1st v.p., program chairperson 1986-87, pres. 1987-89), Delta Pi Epsilon, Beta Gamma Sigma, Phi Delta Kappa. Avocations: collecting antique pattern glasses, collecting stamps. Home: 5 Ellen Way Normal IL 61761-2356

GREVILLE, FLORENCE NUSIM, secondary school educator, mathematician; b. Lynn, Mass., Nov. 19, 1913; d. Melach Joseph Nusim and Lillian Montrose; m. Thomas N.G. Greville (dec. Feb. 18, 1998). AB, Cornell U., 1935; MA, Columbia U., 1947. Sub. tchr Wis. Pub. Schs., Madison, 1975—80; tchr. math. Madison Area Tech. Coll., 1980—81; lectr. math. Piedmont C.C., Charlottesville, Va., 1982—84; sub. tchr. Charlottesville Pub. Schs., 1987—99. Instr. in math Oswego State Coll., 1947—48; tchr. Am. sch., Rio de Janeiro, 1953—54; program dir. AAUW, Monona, Wis., 1966—68, Charlottesville, Va., 2001—02. Author: (book) Computer Oriented Basic Math, 1970, Breafeast Gems, 2002. Fellow: AAAS; mem.: Math. Assn. Am. Avocation: playing classical piano. Home: 505 Pebble Hill Ct Charlottesville VA 22903-7873

GREW, PRISCILLA CROSWELL, university official, geology educator; b. Glens Falls, NY, Oct. 26, 1940; d. James Croswell and Evangeline Pearl (Beougher) Perkins; m. Edward Sturgis Grew, June 14, 1975. BA magna cum laude, Bryn Mawr Coll., 1962; PhD, U. Calif., Berkeley, 1967. Instr. dept. geology Boston Coll., 1967-68, asst. prof., 1968-72; asst. rsch. geologist UCLA, 1972-77, adj. asst. prof. environ. sci. and engring., 1975-76; dir. Calif. Dept. Conservation, 1977-81; commr. Calif. Pub. Utilities Commn., San Francisco, 1981-86; dir. Minn. Geol. Survey, St. Paul, 1986-93; prof. dept. geology U. Minn., Mpls., 1986-93; vice chancellor for rsch. U. Nebr., Lincoln, 1993-99, prof. dept. geoscis., 1993—, prof. conservation/survey divsn. Inst. Agr., 1993—, dir. U. Nebr. State Mus., 2003—; coord. Native Am. Graves Protection and Repatriation Act, 1998—. Vis. asst. prof. geology U. Calif., Davis, 1973-74; chmn. Calif. State Mining and Geology Bd., Sacramento, 1976-77; exec. sec., editor Lake Powell Rsch. Project, 1971-77; cons., vis. staff Los Alamos (N.Mex.) Nat. Lab., 1972-77; com. on minority participation in earth sci. and mineral engring. Dept. Interior, 1972-75; chmn. Calif. Geothermal Resource Task Force, 1977, Calif. Geothermal Resources Bd., 1977-81; earthquake studies adv. panel US Geol. Survey, 1979-83, adv. com., 1982-86; adv. coun. Gas Rsch. Inst., 1982-86, rsch. coord. coun., 1987-98, vice-chmn., 1994-96, chmn., 1996-98, sci. and tech. coun., 1998-2001; bd. on global change rsch. NAS, 1995-99, subcom. on earthquake rsch., 1985-88, bd. on earth scis. and resources, 1986-91, bd. on mineral and energy resources, 1982-88, Minn. Minerals Coord. Com., 1986-93, US nat. com. for internat. union of geological scis. (IUGS), 1985-93, US nat. com. for the internat. union of geodesy and geophysics 2001—, chmn., 2003—; mem. US Nat. Com. on Diversitas, 2000—; adv. bd. Stanford U. Sch. Earth Scis., 1989—, Sec. of Energy Adv. Bd., 1995-97; com. on equal opportunities in sci. and tech. NSF, 1985-86, adv. com. on earth scis., 1987-91, adv. com. on sci. and tech. ctrs. devel., 1987-91, adv. com. on sci. and tech. ctrs., 1996, adv. com. on geoscis., 1994-97; mem. State-Fed. Tech. Partnership Task Force, 1995-99, Fed. Coun. for Continental Sci. Drilling, 1992-98, Gt. Plains Partnership Coun., 1995-99; trustee Am. Geol. Inst. Found., 1988— (Ian Campbell medlist 1999). Contbr. articles to profl. jours. Bd. dirs. Abendmusik:Lincoln, 1995-97; trustee 1st Plymouth Congl. Ch., Lincoln, 1997-2000. Fellow NSF, 1962-66. Fellow AAAS (chmn. electorate nominating com. sect. E 1980-84, mem.-at-large 1987-91, chmn.-elect 1994, chmn. 1995, coun. del. 1997-98), Geol. Soc. Am. (nominations com. 1974, chmn. com. on geology and pub. policy 1981-84, audit com. 1988-90, chair 1990, com. on coms. 1986-87, 91-92, chmn. com. on coms. 1995, chair Day medal com. 1990, councilor 1987-91), Mineral. Soc. Am. (mem. Roebling medal com. 1999—), Geol. Assn. Can.; mem. Am. Geophys. Union (chmn. com. pub. affairs 1984-89), Soc. Mayflower Descs., Nat. Parks and Conservation Assn. (trustee 1982-86), Nat. Assn. Regulatory Utility Commrs. (com. on gas 1982-86, exec. com. 1984-86, com. on energy conservation 1983-84), Interstate Oil and Gas Compact Commn. (mem. Petroleum Profls. Task Force, 2001-03), Cosmos Club, Country Club of Lincoln. Congregationalist. Office: U Nebr State Mus 307 Morrill Hall Lincoln NE 68588-0338 Office Fax: 402-472-8899.

GREWAL, PARWINDER S. biologist, educator; b. Dharour, Punjab, India, May 26, 1961; came to U.S., 1991; s. Joginder S. and Amarjit K. (Sekhon) G.; m. Sukhbir K. Battu, Feb. 22, 1987; children: Parbir, Sharanbir. BS with honors, Punjab Agrl. U., Ludhiana, India, 1981, MS in Nematology, 1983; PhD in Zoology, U. London, 1990; DIC Nematology, Imperial Coll., London, 1990. Scientist Indian Coun. Agrl. Rsch., Solan, 1984-87; higher sci. officer Horticulture Rsch. Internat., Littlehampton, Eng., 1987-91; postdoctoral rsch. assoc. Rutgers U., New Brunswick, N.J., 1991-93; mgr. nematode rsch. Biosys, Inc., Palo Alto, Calif., 1993-95, rsch. leader Columbia, Md., 1995-97; asst. prof. Ohio State U., Wooster, 1997—2002, assoc. prof., 2002—. Contbr. chpts. to books, over 100 articles to profl. jours. Recipient Team award for Environ. Achievement, Her Majesty the Queen, 1993, Young Scientist of Yr. award U.K. Mushroom Growers Assn., 1991, Lindbergh award 1999, Disting. Jr. Faculty award Ohio Agr. Rsch. and Devel. Ctr., 2002, Syngenta Crop Protection award 2002, Award of Excellance in Intergrated Pest Mgmt., 2003. Mem. AAAS, Soc. Nematologists, European Soc. Nematologists, Entomol. Soc. Am., Assn. Applied Biologists, Afro-Asian Soc. Nematologists (exec. bd. 1990—, editorial bd. 1990—). Avocations: running, travel, gardening. Office: Dept Entomology Ohio State U 1680 Madison Ave Wooster OH 44691-4114

GREY EAGLE, SANDRA LEE, special education educator; b. Sidney, Mont., Sept. 22, 1952; d. Donald Merl and June Dorothy (Burman) Radke; m. Benedict Matthew Grey Eagle, Sept. 19, 1978; children: Jason Wade, Justin Michael. BS cum laude, Black Hills State Coll., Spearfish, S.D., 1973; MA, Goddard Coll., Plainfield, Vt., 1979. Tchr. Sky Ranch (S.D.) for Boys, 1974, learning disabilities specialist, 1974-78, acting prin., 1978, dir. spl. edn., 1980-89; spl. educator/house parent Vision Quest Program, Tucson, Ariz., 1978; ednl. diagnostian Cheyenne River Sioux Tribe, Eagle Butte, S.D., 1978-79; spl. educator Timber Lake (S.D.) Pub. Sch., 1979-80; dir. spl. edn. N.W. Area Schs. Edn. Coop., Lemmon, S.D., 1989—; ednl. specialist Office Spl. Edn., Pierre, S.D., 1989—. Mediator ednl. disputes Office Spl. Edn., Pierre, 1989—; mem. adv. bd. State Wide Systems Change, Pierre, 1991—; cons. Collaborative Effective Edn. Design, 1991-93; bd. dirs. Am. Coun. on Rural Spl. Edn., 1996—. Chmn. Harding County Horse Show, Camp Crook, S.D., 1984-91, Dakota Family Horse Club Show, Haynes, N.D., 1992—; conf. chmn. Correctional Edn. Assn., Balt., 1988, dir. correctional edn. region IV, 1986; bd. mem. Live Ctr. Adjustment Tng. Ctr. for Developmentally Disabled, 1995. Mem. Coun. for Exceptional Children (Outstanding Adminstrs. S.D. fedn. 1994), Am. Coun. Rural Spl. Edn. Avocations: family, raising and training paints and quarter horses, crafts. Home: HC 5 Box 308 Haynes ND 58639-8768 Office: NW Area Schs Ednl Coop 11 4th St E Lemmon SD 57638-1524

GRIBBEN, ALAN, English language educator, research consultant; b. Parsons, Kans., Nov. 21, 1941; s. J.S. and Ruth E. (North) G.; m. Irene Wong, Feb. 14, 1974; children: Walter Blake, Valerie Janet. BA in English, U. Kans., 1964; MA, U. Oreg., 1966; PhD, U. Calif., Berkeley, 1974. Rsrch. editor Mark Twain Papers, Bancroft Libr. U. Calif., Berkeley, 1967-74, instr. dept. English, 1972-73; asst. prof. dept. English, U. Tex., Austin, 1974-80, assoc. prof., 1980-88, prof., 1988-91, chmn. grad. studies dept. English, 1984-88; head dept. English and philosophy Auburn U. Montgomery, Ala., 1991—; disting. rsch. prof. Auburn U., 1998, pres. Heads Coun., 2002—. Mem. State Graduation Requirements Task Force, 1995-96; spl. cons. Mark Twain Libr. Assn., 1981; co-chair nat. conf. The State of Mark Twain Studies, 1993, nat. conf. Cotton: The Fiber, The Land, The People, 1994. Author: Am. Literary Scholarship: An Annual, 1995—, Mark Twain's Library: A Reconstruction, 1980; editor: Mark Twain's Rubaiyat, 1983; co-editor: Overland with Mark Twain: James B. Pond's Photographs and Jour. of the North American Lecture Tour of 1895, 1992; mem. editl. bd. Studies in Am. Fiction, 1988-97, U. Miss. Studies in English, 1986-96, Studies in Am. Humor, 1982—, Western Am. Lit., 1991-98, Am. Literary Realism, 2003—; nat. panel juror NEH, 1990-94; assoc. editor Librs. and Culture, 1980-91; contbr. articles to profl. jours. Recipient President's Assocs. Tchg. Excellence award U. Tex., 1983, Henry Nash Smith fellow Ctr. for Mark Twain Studies, Elmira Coll., 1997, Jervis Langdon Jr. fellow Ctr. for Mark Twain Studies, Elmira Coll., 1990. Mem. South Atlantic MLA, Mark Twain Cir. of Am. (hon. life, pres. 1987-89), Am. Lit. Assn. (exec. bd. 1989-96), Am. Humor Studies Assn., Western Am. Lit. Assn., Phi Kappa Phi. Avocations: bicycling, tennis, record and cd collecting (bands of 1930s and 1940s), rare book collecting, gardening. Home: 308 Arrowhead Dr Montgomery AL 36117-4108 Office: Auburn U Montgomery Dept English and Philosophy PO Box 244023 Montgomery AL 36124-4023 E-mail: agribben@mail.aum.edu.

GRIBLER, JEFFERY LYNN, secondary education educator; b. Van Wert, Ohio, Apr. 21, 1966; s. Larry John and Anne Louise (Keihl) G.; m. Catherine K. Gibson, Sept. 15, 1990. BS, Defiance Coll., 1989. Cert. tchr., Ohio. Sub. tchr. various schs., 1991—; home instr. Tiffin (Ohio) Columbian, 1993—; social studies tchr. Napoleon (Ohio) H.S., 1993-94. Summer sch. tchr. Tiffin Columbian, 1992; tutor Bettsville (Ohio) Sch., 1992; mem. review com. Kids Link, Atlanta, 1994. Campaign worker Bush/Quayle Campaign, Napoleon, 1988. Mem. NEA, Ohio Edn. Assn. Republican. Methodist. Avocations: collecting radio show tapes, milk bottles and historical items, following politics, working with teens. Home and Office: 1070 Willard St Napoleon OH 43545-1115

GRIBSCHAW, VICTORIA MARIE, social sciences educator, department chairman; b. Pitts., Aug. 18, 1942; d. James S. and Elizabeth M. Gribschaw. BA, Seton Hill U., 1970; MS, W.Va. U., 1974; PhD, Ohio State U., 1985. Cert. Family and Consumer Scis. Upper elementary sci. and math tchr. Pitts. Cath. Schs., 1960—72; grad. tchg. asst. W.Va. U., Divsn. of Family Resources, Coll. of Human Resources and Edn., Morgantown, 1972—74; instr. home econs. Seton Hill Coll., Greensburg, Pa., 1974—78; rschr. Ohio Agrl. R&D Ctr. Ohio State U., Columbus, 1982—83; grad. rsch. assoc. Ohio Agrl. R&D Ctr. and Dept. of Home Mgmt. and Housing Ohio State U., Columbus, 1983—84; asst. prof. home econs. Seton Hill Coll., Greensburg, Pa., 1978—88, assoc. prof. home econs., dir. family studies, 1988—91, assoc. prof. home econs. with tenure, dir. family studies, 1991—93, assoc. prof. human ecology with tenure, dir. family studies, 1993—95, assoc. prof. family and consumer scis. with tenure, chair family and consumer scis. dept., dir. family studies, 1995—97, assoc. prof. of family and consumer scis. with tenure, chair divsn. mgmt., family and consumer scis., 1997—2002, chair divsn. social scis., 2002—. Editor: (proceedings) 1994 Conf. Proceedings Eastern Family Econs. and Resource Mgmt. Assn., 1994; contbr. articles to profl. jours. Mem. commn. on global mission and internationality Sisters of Charity of Seton Hill, Greensburg, 2000—01; mem. investment adv. bd. Sisters of Charity, Greensburg, 1999—2003; mem. fin. adv. bd. Sisters of Charity of Seton Hill, Greensburg, 1992—99; v.p. bd. dirs. Pregnant Adolescent Childcare Tng., Greensburg, 2001—; sec. bd. trustees Mercy Jeannette Hosp. (formerly Jeannette Dist. Meml. Hosp.), 1998—2001; trustee Mercy Jeannette Hosp., 1986—2003, chair med. and clin. affairs com., 2001—, mem. fin. com. bd. trustees, 1990—2003; treas. bd. dirs. JDMH HealthNet, Jeannette, 1996—2001; mem. Pregnant Adolescent Childcare Tng., Greensburg, 1988—2001; v.p. bd. dirs. Pregnant Adolescent Childcare Tng. Program, Greensburg, 2001—; sec. Pregnant Adolescent Childcare Tng., Greensburg, 1999—2001, 1989—94; active Ctrl. Westmoreland Unemployment Steeering Com., Greensburg, 1988—90. Mem.: Am. Assn. Family Consumer Sci., Am. Assn. of Housing Educators, Nat. Coun. on Family Rels., Am. Coun. on Consumer Interests, Eastern Family Econs. and Resource Mgmt. Assn., Pa. Assn. of Family and Consumer Scis. (Western area v.p. 1998—2001, pres.-elect 2002—03, pres. 2003—), Alpha Sigma Lambda, Kappa Omicron Nu (leadership acad. scholarship 2000). Democrat. Roman Catholic. Office: Seton Hill Univ Seton Hill Box 307 Greensburg PA 15601-1599

GRIER, DOROTHY ANN PRIDGEN, secondary education specialist; b. Pitts, Jan. 14, 1936; d. Jay Lawrence and Myra (Morgan) Pridgen; m. Robert Warren Grier, Mar. 27, 1959; children: Cassandra Ann, Robert Warren Jr. BS, U. Pitts., 1959, MEd, 1981, PhD, 1989. Tchr. Pitts. Pub. Sch., 1960-63, 72-75, reading specialist, 1975-84, program specialist, 1984-85, supervisory instrl. specialist, 1985—. State evaluator Dept. Edn. State of Pa., Harrisburg, 1988—; mem. tech. com. strategic plan Pitts. Pub. Schs., 1995—; invited speaker 4th No. Am. Conf. on Adolescent/Adult Literacy, Washington, 1996; presenter in field, Internat. Reading Assoc. Adol. Lit. Comm.,"Adolescent Promising Practices", 2000; Nat. Mid. Sh. Urban Conf., Pitts., Pa., " Lit. Plus", 2001; Internat. Read. Assoc. Inst., Sa Francesco, Calif., "Lit. Improvement for Adolescents takes Collaboration at all Levels", 2002; Internat. Reading Assoc. Adolescent Lit. Comm., 2002. Mem. Strategic Planning Com. for Sewickley (Pa.) Acad., 1988-91; trustee Pine Richland Sch. Dist. Opportunities, Inc., 1994—. Mem. Internat. Reading Assn. (exec. com. Pitts.-Three Rivers coun. 1990-93, invited spkr. adolescent literacy commn. 2000, 2001-, 2002), Internat. Assn. Secondary Reading Interest Group (pres.-elect 1992, pres. 1994-96, com. media awards for broadcast and print 1998, 99—), Secondary Reading Interest Group (chmn. 1990-94, v.p. Pa. Keystone State coun. 1991—), Pitts. Women's Missionary Circle, Harty Bible Sch. Alumni Assn. (pres. 1992—), No. Allegheny County C. of C. (tchr. excellence award selection com. 1996, Pa. framework for reading, writing and talking across the curriculum com. 2000-), Nat. Mid. Sch. Urban Conf. (invited spkr. 2001). Avocations: walking, knitting, reading, golf.

GRIER, JAMES WILLIAM, zoology educator; b. Waterloo, Iowa, Sept. 15, 1943; s. Perry H. and Frances W. (Williams) G.; m. Joyce C. Petersen, June 5, 1965; children: Karlene K. Froehling, Dean G. BA, U. No. Iowa, 1965; MS, U. Wis., 1968; PhD, Cornell U., 1975. Asst. prof. zoology N.D. State U., Fargo, 1973-78, assoc. prof. zoology, 1978-83, prof. zoology, 1983—. Team leader No. States Bald Eagle Recovery Team, 1978-93. Author: Biology of Animal Behavior, 2 edits., 1984, 92; contbr. numerous articles to profl. jours. Recipient several awards and grants. Mem. several profl. orgns. Lutheran. Achievements include being first to breed eagles in captivity using artificial insemination. Office: Dept Biol Sci ND State Univ Fargo ND 58105-5517

GRIESÉ, JOHN WILLIAM, III, astronomer, educator, mental health advocate; b. Norwalk, Conn., Sept. 27, 1955; s. John William Jr. and Celia (Bolté) G. Student, Franklin and Marshall Coll., 1974-77, U. Bridgeport, 1977-78; diploma, Morse Sch. Bus., 1986; student, U. Conn., 1991-95, Trinity Coll., 1995-97, Wesleyan U., 1995-96; BS with honors, Charter Oak State Coll., 2003. Observer Stamford (Conn.) Obs., 1973, asst. dir., 1978—; observer Van Vleck Obs., Middletown, Conn., 1986, asst. astrometry program, 1992-99; user Perkin-Elmer PDS, Yale U., New Haven, 1992-99, rsch. asst., 1993-99; rsch. asst. astrometry-photometry group Wesleyan U., Middletown, 1997—2001; asst. editor Hartford Lit. mag. U. Conn., 1991-95; founder Morse Tutoring Svc., 1985. Tutor Math. Ctr., Trinity Coll., 1995-96; lectr. Stamford Mus., 1985-2001; presenter and lectr. in field, 1996—; adj. instr. Middlesex Cmty. Tech. Coll., Conn., 1996-99; course asst. Wesleyan U., 1998-2001, instr. adult edn., 1998—; alt. consumer rep. Nat. Alliance for Mentally Ill-CT (NAMI-CT), 1998-99, spkrs. bur., 2000—. Contbr. articles to Jour. Am. Assn. Variable Star Obs., Deep Sky Mag., The Astronomical Jour.; observations of variable stars pub. on circulars of Cen. Bur. for Astron. Telegrams, Internat. Astron. Union, Smithsonian Astrophys. Obs. Mem. consumer support coun. Conn. Alliance for Mentally Ill., Hartford, 1997-98; mem. Friends of the Ctr. for the History of Physics. Named one of Outstanding Young Man of Am., 1987. Mem.: Friends of the Ctr. for the History of Physics, Astron. Soc. Coonabarabran (NSW, Australia), Riverside Astron. Soc., Westport Astron. Soc., Astron. League (long range planning com. 1992—94), Astron. Soc. Greater Hartford (pres. 1992—93), Fairfield County Astron. Soc. (treas. 1985—88, pres. 1988—94, v.p. 1994—96, acting treas. 1996—99, pres. 1996—99, v.p. 1999—2003, v.p., treas. 2003—), L.A. Astron. Soc., We. Observatorium (bd. dirs. 1994—2000), Internat. Dark Sky Assn., Mt. Wilson Obs. Assn., Astron. Soc. Pacific, Hungarian Astron. Assn., Royal Astron. Soc. Can., Am. Astron. Soc., Am. Assn. Variable Star Observers (coun. 1985—90, liaison and rep. to mems. in Hungary, contbr. Variable Star Atlas, edits. I and II, preliminary charts com., supernova search com., telescopes com., Observer award 1994), Nat. Alliance Mentally Ill-Conn.,

Mental Health Assn. Conn. (facilitator self-help support groups and adv. com. 1998—), We. Amateur Astronomers (pub. info. coord. 1989—90, v.p., acting pres. 1992, v.p. 1992—94, Caroline Herschel Astronomy project award 1988), Phi Beta Lambda (pres. local chpt. 1985), Golden Key.

GRIEVE, WILLIAM ROY, psychologist, educator, educational administrator, researcher; b. N.Y.C., Mar. 15, 1917; s. Walter Stuart and Grace (Buttendorf) G.; m. Harriet Bush, Mar. 30, 1978; children: Leslie Lynne Grieve Bainbridge, Davelyn Anne Grieve Sandhowe. Student, SUNY, Oswego, 1934-35; BS, NYU, 1937, MA, 1938; EdD, Rutgers U., 1954. Tchr. secondary edn., N.Y.C., 1938-48; rsch. fellow Ohio State U., 1942; ind. arts editor High Point Mag. N.Y.C. Bd. Edn., 1948-65, textbook and instnl. materials com., 1954-65, curriculum specialist N.Y.C. Bur. Curriculum Rsch., 1948-50, supr., adminstr. secondary edn., 1950-65; prof. NYU, 1965-72, ombudsman Sch. Edn., 1969-71; prof. grad. program NYU/U. PR, N.Y., 1966-67; rsch. predictive testing specialist in vocat./tech. edn. NYU; ESSA, ESAA, and ESEA evaluation studies in reading, math., ESL and indsl. edn. N.Y., N.J., Conn., Mass., Md., 1970-83; assoc. dir. evaluation studies divsn. Psychol. Corp., 1972-75; dir. Ednl. Planning and Rsch. Inc., Boston, 1975-83, pres. Glencove, N.Y. and Stuart, Fla., 1983—. Asst. examiner ind. edn., supervision, guidance lics., N.Y.C. Bd. Edn., 1950-72; chmn. ind. edn. standing com. Bd. Supts., N.Y.C., 1960-65; adj. prof. psychology L.I. U., Bklyn., 1965-70; adj. prof. edn. N.Y. Inst. Tech., Westbury, N.Y., 1981-86, SUNY, Westbury, 1986-89; cons. N.Y. C.C. orthotics and prosthetics, 1966, N.C. State U., 1968, Pub. Edn. Assn./Nat. Alliance Businessmen, N.Y., 1968-72, Citibank, P.R., 1970, Met. Mus. Art (The Art of Black Africa), N.Y.C., 1970, Sta. UFT-TV, N.Y., 1970; Young and Rubicam, N.Y., 1974; cons. Cautaulds Internat., Mobile, Ala., 1975, Rheem Mfg., Chgo., 1975, Bankers Trust, N.Y.C., 1975, Republic Steel, Akron and Canton, Ohio, 1977, S.W. Regional Lab., Calif., 1980, N.Y. State Dept. Edn., 1985—, job and task analysis, equal opportunity test devel., alt. edn. programs, coop. edn., work study, career edn., work study, career edn., tng. and devel., 1990—; prof., U. Puerto Rico, Rio Piedras, 1966-67, rsch. predictive specialist, 1970-83. Author rsch. and evaluation reports, curriculum, testing programs and other pubs., 1985—; contbr. articles to profl. jours. Bd. mgrs. Prospect Park YMCA, Bklyn., 1960-65; adviser desegregation measures Boston Pub. Schs., 1976-81. With U.S. Army, 1944-45. Mem.: Am. Psychol. and Guidance Assn., Am. Assn. Tchr. Educators, Am. Vocat. Assn., Am. Vocat. Ednl. Rsch. Assn. (charter), N.Y. Schoolmasters Club, Masons, Kappa Delta Pi, Kappa Phi Kappa, Epsilon Pi Tau, Phi Delta Kappa. Home: 59 Longfellow Ave Staten Island NY 10301 Home (Summer): 5684 SE Riverboat Dr Stuart FL 34997

GRIFFEY, KAREN ROSE, special education educator; b. Phila., May 15, 1955; d. Arnold and Jacqueline (Wasserman) Salaman; m. Kenneth Paul Griffey, June 18, 1988; 1 child, Jessica; stepchildren: Kristina, Joseph. BS in Elem. Edn., W. Chester U., Pa., 1977; cert. Paralegal Studies, Nat. Ctr. Paralegal Tng., Atlanta, 1986; M in Edn., U. Ga., 1994. Adult habilitation program Jewish Vocat. Svc., Phila., 1977-79; instr. Phila. Sch. Sys., 1979-81; tchr. 3rd grade Fla. Sch. Sys., Fort Myers, 1981-86; paralegal Atlanta, 1986-89; tchr. Interrelated Sharp Middle Sch., Covington, Ga., 1989-91; tchr. Spl. Kindergarten Rorterdale and Fairview Elem., Covington, Ga., 1991-96; spl. edn. tchr. Hickory Flat Elem. Sch., 1997-99; interrelated resource tchr., spl. ed. chair Meml. Middle Sch., 1999—. Tchr., liaison, bd. mem., PAC rep., bldg. rep. Tchrs. Assn. Lee County, Fort Myers, Fla., 1981-86. Tchr. liaison Senators and Reps. in Fla. Legis., Tallahassee, 1981-86; PAC bd., 1981-86; exec. bd. mem. Leadership Team. of Tchrs. Assn. Lee County, Ft. Myers, Fla., 1981-86; Bargaining Team mdm. Tchrs. Assn. Lee County, Ft. Myers, Fla., 1981-86. Recipient Svc. award for working with handicapped, Phila. Sch. Sys., 1973; Phila scholarship Phils Sch. Sys., Mayor's Sch., Phila., 1973; NEA Svc. award in Edn., NEA, Ft. Myers, Fla., 1980. Mem. Coun. for Exceptional Children, Nat. Mus. of Women in the Arts, B'Nai B'rith, Spl. Olympics, Nat. Multiple Sclerosis Soc., Kappa Delta Pi. Democrat. Jewish. Avocations: reading, sewing, classical and jazz music, writing, arts and crafts. Home: 2580 Highland Dr Conyers GA 30013-1908 Office: Meml Middle Sch 3205 Underwood Rd SE Conyers GA 30013-2309

GRIFFIN, BARBARA CONLEY, reading educator; b. Valdosta, Ga., Mar. 29, 1955; d. Paul and Sarah Elizabeth (Ganas) Conley; children: Stephanie E., Paul E. AA in Art, Middle Ga. Coll., Cochran, 1975; EdB, Mercer U., 1977, MEd in Early Childhood, 1986. Cert. elem. tchr. support specialist Ga. Kindergarten tchr. Houston County Bd. Edn., Perry, Ga., 1978-80, 1st grade tchr. Bonaire, Ga., 1980-87, kindergarten tchr., 1987-99, faculty advisor student coun. and tchr. empowerment com., 1991-95, tchr. empowerment chmn., 1992-94; reading recovery tchr.; devel. reading tchr. Middle Ga. Tech., 1998-99; assoc. mgr. Eddie Bauer, Macon, Ga.; literacy coach Pearl Stephens Elem., 1999—. Owner Timeless Treasures Antiques and Collectibles, Bonaire, Ga., 1995—; presenter in field. Mem. PTO, 1980-99, Parents Assisting With Students, 1989-99; tchr. Shirley Hills Bapt. Ch.-Tng. Union, Warner Robins, Ga., 1987-91; summer missionary Inst. Caribbean Missions, Jamaica, 1992; mem. Shirley Hills Baptist Church. Recipient Exemplary Svc. award Pilot Club of Houston County, Warner Robins, Ga., 1990, Tchr. of Yr. award Bonaire Elem. Sch., 1990. Mem. PAGE (state and local chpts.), Internat. Reading Assn. (state and local chpts., v.p. and pres. HOPE reading coun. 1993-95), Bonaire/Kathleen Jaycettes (sec. 1979-81, Outstanding Young Woman of the Year award 1981), Warner Robins Jr. Womens Club (co-chair spl. projects 1991, corr. sec. 1993). Republican. Mem. Southern Baptist Ch. Avocations: swimming, entertaining, travel, walking, gardening. Home: 202 Williams Dr Bonaire GA 31005-3825

GRIFFIN, BETTY JO, elementary school educator; b. Monroe, La., Jan. 12, 1947; d. Julia Odell (Foster) Calhoun; divorced; 1 child, James Odell Griffin, Jr. BA, So. U., 1969; MA, San Francisco State U., 1975; PhD, LaSalle U., 2000. Cert. elem. tchr., Calif. Tchr. lang. arts Oakland (Calif.) Unified Sch. Dist., 1970-73, Garfield Elem. Sch., 1973-77, 1977-96; splty. prep. libr. and lang. arts tchr. Webster Acad., 1996—. Trustee Allen Temple Bapt. Ch., Oakland, Calif., 1987—; lit. tutor Delta Sigma Theta, Oakland, 1990—; chairperson African Am. Chain Read In, 1995—. Recipient Libr. Protection Fund award State Dept. Edn., 1997, Leadership award Dem. Nat. Com., 1997. Mem. NAACP, NEA, Oakland Edn. Assn. (bd. dirs.), Calif. Tchrs. Assn. (coun. of edn. 1996), Nat. Alliance Black Sch. Educators, Delta Sigma Theta, Phi Delta Kappa. Democrat. Avocations: reading, helping others, public speaking. Home: 2559 Oliver Ave Oakland CA 94605-4820 E-mail: BettyJGri@aol.com.

GRIFFIN, BETTY LOU, not-for-profit developer, educator; d. Julius Craven and Rachel Idell Best; m. Jack Wayne Griffin, May 28, 1960; children: Cheryle Louann, Melanie Lynn Young, Penelope. BS in Elem. Edn. magna cum laude, Campbell U., 1967; ME in Adult and Cmty. Coll. Edn., N.C. State U., 1974; ME in Adminstrn. and Supervision, Fayetteville State U., 1995. Tchr. Sampson County Schs., Clinton, NC, 1965-67, Clinton City Schs., 1967-87; founder, exec. dir. U Care Inc., Sampson County Domestic Violence Program, Clinton, 1996—; CEO, bd. dirs., exec. dir. On Track Youth Svcs., Clinton, 2000—02. Evening bus. math. instr. Sampson CC, 1973—75, instr., 1975—77; notary pub. State of N.C., 1995—. Author: (poems) Poetry Collection, 1997, Rhyme in Time, 1999. Founder, dir. Sampson County Women's Assembly, 1994, 1996, 1998; legis. chmn., monitor chmn. Youth Adv. Coun., Sampson, 1994—98; founder, pres., exec. dir. Sampson County Coun. Women, 1995—. Named N.C. Dem. Women Poet Laureate, 1997, Sampson County Disting. Woman of the Yr., Sampson County Coun. Women, 1998; recipient Carpathian award, N.C. Equity, 1996. Mem.: DAR, N.C. Dem. Women (pres. exec. bd. 1995—99, 1st poet laureate 1997—), Sampson County Dem. Women (v.p. 1993, 2d v.p. 1996—97, 2000—03, pres. 1994—95, 1998—99), Order of Eastern Star, Delta Kappa Gamma. Democrat. Methodist. Avocations: reading, creative writing, arts and crafts, hunting, fishing. Home and Office: 2535 Rosebory Hwy Clinton NC 28328

GRIFFIN, CONNIE MAY, school system administrator; b. Canton, Ohio, Apr. 23, 1957; d. Carl Robert and Mary Elizabeth (Hawkins) Pearson; m. Eric Steven Griffin, Aug. 4, 1984; children: Anthony Michael, Julie Christine. BS, Kent State U., 1979; MEd, Ashland U., 1991. Cert. tchr., prin., Ohio. Substitute tchr. Tuscarawas County Schs., Dover, Ohio, 1979-80; coach, tchr. health, phys. edn. Fairless Local Schs., Navarre, Ohio, 1980-91; prin. Beach City (Ohio) Elem. Sch., 1991-92; dir. programs and ops. Fairless Local Schs., Navarre, Ohio, 1992-94; supr., coord. early childhood edn. supr. Stark County Sch. Dist., 1994—. Profl. adv. com. Spina Bifida Assn., Canton, 1990—, v.p., 1991-92. Mem. ASCD, Ohio Assn. Elem. Sch. Adminstrs., Ohio Assn. Edn. Young Children, Buckeye Assn. Sch. Adminstrs., Fairless Edn. Assn. (v.p, 1986-88), Coun. Exceptional Children, Phi Delta Kappa. Republican. Lutheran. Avocations: reading, music, sports, travel, fine cuisine. Home: 5 Cherokee Trl Malvern OH 44644-9615 Office: Stark County Sch Dist 2100 38th St NW Canton OH 44709-2312

GRIFFIN, GLADYS BOGUES, critical care nurse, educator; b. Elizabeth City, N.C., July 18, 1937; d. Matthew Boques and Lucy Griffin Boques Eason; m. Oct. 21, 1957 (div.); children: Terry, Lucy, Misty, Derrick. AAS, Nassau (N.Y.) Community Coll., 1972. RN, N.C.; cert. ACLS. Nurse Long Beach (N.Y.) Meml. Hosp., 1968-70, staff nurse team leader, 1972-75, head nurse, 1975-76; staff nurse Critical Care Unit Albemarle Hosp., Elizabeth City, 1976-78, staff nurse Surg. Intensive Care Unit then coord., 1978—; BLS instr., head nurse surg. intensive care —, 1981-87. Pub. speaker health related topics, Long Beach and Elizabeth City. Featurered Life Styles of Elizabeth City. Recipient Glowing Lamp for the Nurse award Chi Eta Phi, 2000; named one of Disting. Women N.C., 1989. Mem. Am. Assn. Critical Care Nurses, ARC Nurses, Soc. Notary Pub., NAFE, N.Y. Nurses Assn. Democrat. Avocations: reading, bowling, playing guitar, Bingo. Home: 616 Crooked Run Rd Elizabeth City NC 27909-7538

GRIFFIN, GLORIA JEAN, retired elementary school educator; b. Emmett, Idaho, Sept. 10, 1946; d. Archie and Marguerite (Johnson) G. AA, Boise (Idaho) Jr. Coll., 1966; BA, Boise Coll., 1968; MA in Elem. Curriculum, Boise State U., 1975. Cert. advanced elem. tchr., Idaho. Tchr. music, tutor, Boise, Idaho; sec. Edward A. Johnson, atty., Boise, Idaho; tchr. Head Start, Boise, Idaho; elem. tchr. Meridian Sch. Dist., Idaho, 1968—2002, ret., 2002. Developer multi-modality individualized spelling program; co-developer program for adapting curriculum to student's individual differences. Author: The Culture and Customs of the Argentine People As Applied to a Sixth Grade Social Studies Unit. Sec. PTA. Named Tchr. of Yr., Meridian Sch. Dist., 1981. Mem. Actor's Guild, Alpha Delta Kappa (rec. sec.).

GRIFFIN, HENRY CLAUDE, chemistry educator; b. Greenville, S.C., Feb. 14, 1937; s. Arthur Gwynn and Christa Lou (Wilson) G.; m. Barbara Jean Pierson, Sept. 3, 1960; children: Gwen Meredith Van Ark, Lyle Deborah Warshauer. BS, Davidson Coll., 1958; PhD, MIT, 1962. Instr. math. New Prep. Sch., Cambridge, Mass., 1960-61; rsch. assoc. Argonne Nat. Lab., Lemont, Ill., 1962-64, guest scientist, 1964-70; asst. prof. chemistry U. Mich., Ann Arbor, 1964-70, assoc. prof., 1970-89, prof., 1989—. Vis. scientist Swiss Fed. Reactor Inst., Wurenlingen, 1971-72; vis. rsch. engr. U. Calif., Berkeley, 1978-79; chairperson senate assembly U. Mich., 1993-94; dir. nuc. studies Environ. Rsch. Group, Ann Arbor, 1980-81. Inventor process for separation of Na-22. Mem. AAAS, Am. Chem. Soc. (chairperson steering com. Ctrl. region 1994-95), Am. Phys. Soc. Home: 1410 Harbrooke Ave Ann Arbor MI 48103-3618 Office: Univ Mich Dept Chemistry 930 N University Ave Ann Arbor MI 48109-1055

GRIFFIN, KIRSTEN BERTELSEN, nursing educator; b. Oakland, Calif., Mar. 23, 1940; d. Elmer V. and Helen E. (Hansen) Bertelsen; children: Colleen Hime Risvold, Sean W., Patrick C.; m. John R. Griffin. Diploma, Samuel Merritt Coll. Nursing, 1961; BA, U. Redlands, 1982; A in Bus., Advantage-Health Edn., 1992. Pvt. practice cons./stress trainer, San Jacinto, Calif.; cons. Calif. State Dept. Edn., Sacramento, 1979—; program dir. nursing asst. program Riverside (Calif.) County Office Edn., 1984—. Part-time instr. Mt. San Jacinto (Calif.) Coll., 1989; part-time staff nurse acute psychiat. unit Hemet (Calif.) Med. Ctr.-Behavioral Health; advisor, judge Health Occupation Students Am., 1990—; rater Nurse Asst. Tng. Assessment Program, 1992—. Youth advisor, judge Vocat. Indsl. Clubs Am., 1977-88; instr. ARC, Am. Heart Assn. Recipient Women Helping Women award Soroptimists, 1989. Mem. Calif. Assn. Health Career Educators (pres.-elect 1984-85, pres. 1985-86), Beta Sigma Phi (Order of Rose award, Laureate 1995). Home: 3109 La Travesia Dr Fullerton CA 92835-1421

GRIFFIN, LAURA MAE, retired elementary and secondary school educator; b. Woodland, Calif., Aug. 14, 1925; d. George Everette Ramsey and Bertha (Storz) Ramsey Lowe; m. Roy J. Griffin, Nov. 19, 1944; children: Robert Eugene, Dennis Charles, Kathleen Ann. AA in Social Sci., Sacramento City Coll., 1969; BA in Geography, Calif. State U., Sacramento, 1972. Cert. elem. and secondary tchr., Calif.; Master Gardener. Sec. Alameda Naval Air, Alameda, Calif., 1944-45, Cal-Western Life Ins., Sacramento, 1945-47, Pacific Sch. Dist., Sacramento, 1956-57; substitute tchr. Sacramento Unified Sch. Dist., 1974-75; tchr. Mt. Diablo Unified Sch. Dist., Concord, Calif., 1976-91; ret., 1991. Dir. Heather Farm Garden Ctr., Walnut Creek, Calif., 1985-86, edn. chmn., 1986-87, pres., 1987-88, fin. sec., 1993-94; sec. investment group AAUW, Walnut Creek, 1978-79. Guardian Jobs Daus.-Bethel 325, Walnut Creek, 1978-79; leader Girl Scouts Am., Sacramento, 1971-72; den mother Boy Scouts Am., Sacramento, 1957-60; publicity chmn. membership Northgate Music Boosters, Walnut Creek, 1976-77. Recipient Bert A. Bertolero Gardening award, 1996. Mem. Calif. Garden Clubs (life), Heather Farm Garden Club (pres. 1987-88, Outstanding Svc. award 1995), Walnut Creek Garden Club (pres. 1983-84, civic project chmn. 1994-95, 95-96), Order Ea. Star. Republican. Avocations: reading, travel, bowling, golf, music, gardening.

GRIFFIN, LEAH G. art specialist; b. Nebraska City, Nebr., May 24, 1942; d. Leigh Addison and Ferne Gwendolyn (Ferguson) Sharp; m. Kenyon Neal Griffin, Mar. 2, 1962; children: Karol René, Shari Lené. Student, U. Nebr., 1960-61, U. Kans., 1964; BA, U. Wyo., 1981. Cert. in art K-12, elem. edn. K-6, Wyo. Teaching asst. Albany County Sch. Dist. 1, Laramie, Wyo., 1971-80, art specialist, 1981—2001. Instr. U. Wyo., 1993-94; panelist Wyo. Coun. on the Arts, 1985-92. Exhibited lithographs, etchings, woodcuts and silkscreen art in various shows, 1981—. Leader, camp dir. Camp Fire Girls, Laramie, 1971-84. Recipient Gov.'s Art award Wyo. Coun. on Arts, 1991; USIS acad. specialist grantee, United Arab Emirates, 1990; Fulbright Meml. fellowship, Japan, 1998. Mem. NEA, Nat. Art Edn. Assn., Colo. Art Edn. Assn., Albany County Edn. Assn. (Tchr. of Yr. 1985-86), PTA (life; v.p., pres.), Clowns of Am. Democrat. Episcopalian. Avocations: horseback riding, clowning, skiing, rollerblading, art. Home: 1808 Beaufort St Laramie WY 82072-1940

GRIFFIN, LINDA LOUISE, English language and speech educator; b. Yale, Mich., Dec. 23, 1942; d. Benjamin and Ruth (Steenbergh) Hinton; m. James Griffin, Nov. 23, 1980. BA, U. Mich., 1965, MA, 1967; postgrad., Bowling Green (Ohio) State U., 1975, U. N.C., 1985; PhD, U. South Fla., 1996. Tchr. English and speech Sandusky (Mich.) H.S.; instr. Jackson (Mich.) C.C., Terra Tech. Coll., Fremont, Ohio, Edison C.C., Naples, Fla. Frequent speaker and presenter, including harp lecture programs; mem. NEH Shakespeare Seminar, 1985; keynote speaker Collier County Tchrs. Assn. Conf., 1987. Recipient Edison C.C. Excellence in Teaching award and endowed chair in comms.; Fulbright award winner No. Ireland. Mem. MLA, South Atlantic MLA, S.E. Medieval Assn., Medieval Inst., S.C. Renaissance Assn., Nat. Coun. Tchrs. English, Folger Shakespeare Libr., So. State Comm. Assn., Fla. Comm. Assn. (pres. 1989-90), Phi Kappa Phi. Home: 2292 Piccadilly Circus Naples FL 34112-3659 Office: 7007 Lely Cultural Pkwy Naples FL 34113-8976

GRIFFIN, MARY JANE RAGSDALE, educational consultant, writer, small business owner; b. Crawfordsville, Ind., Aug. 15, 1927; d. Ira Vincent and Sophronia Burdetti (Thompson) Ragsdale; m. Walter Wanzel Griffin, Jan. 20, 1951; children: Walter Vincent, Glenn Edwin, Edwin Wanzel. BS, U. Tenn., 1949, MS, 1970, doctoral student (hon.), 1975, EdS, 1976, EdD, 1980. Cert. math., sci., physics, chemistry, computer programming, elem. tchr., secondary and elem. adminstr., Tenn. Instr. physics lab., pianist, accompanist modern dance class U. Chattanooga (Tenn.), 1945-47; pvt. tchr. piano and violin Knoxville, Tenn., 1947-50; honorary captain airforce cadet, mil. sponsor Com. I U. Tenn., Knoxville, 1948-49; asst. dir. Sunshine Schoolette, Knoxville, 1954-69; tchr. sci. and math. Knox County Schs., Knoxville, 1970-74; tchr. math. methods U. Tenn., Knoxville, 1975-76; tchr. math. and computer programming Knox County Schs., Knoxville, 1977-88; freelance writer Knoxville, 1970—; real estate investor and mgr., 1975—; owner, pres. MJRG Enterprises, Knoxville, 1976—; freelance edn. cons. Knoxville, 1988—. Student asst. physics dept. head U. Chattanooga, 1945-47; asst. treas., historian, music chmn. U. Chattanooga, 1946-47; orientation leader U. Tenn., 1948; graduate asst. U. Tenn., Knoxville, 1975-76. Contbr. articles to various publs.; writer curriculum guides. Violinist Chattanooga Symphony, 1944-47; officer bd. dirs. Ossoli Circle, Knoxville, 1954-64, 89-90; poetry contest chmn. Fontinalis, 1993-96, fine arts chair, 1995-96; officer, bd. dirs. Girls Club Knoxville, Inc., 1962-70, charter signer, 1962; mem. Fountain City Town Hall, 1985—, Knoxville Symphony League, 1990—; tchr. adult Sunday sch., 1988-92; mem. chancel choir 1st Christian Ch., Knoxville, 1949-85, bd. dirs., 1982-85; mem. chancel choir Fountain City United Meth. Ch., Knoxville, 1985-91, bd. dirs., 1993-97, cert. 50 yr. mem.; pres. United Meth. Women, 1993-97, v.p. Knoxville Dist., 1996-98; mem. steering com. Just Older Youth, Fountain City, Tenn., 1998—. U. Chattanooga scholar, 1947; U. Tenn. fellow, 1968-70. Mem. NEA, ASCD, AAUW, DAR, Nat. Coun. Tchrs. Math. (life), Tenn. Edn. Assn. (workshop presenter 1980-88), East Tenn. Edn. Assn., Knox County Edn. Assn. (rep. 1980-85), East Tenn. Hist. Soc. (life), Ind. Hist. Soc. (life), Ky. Hist. Soc. (life), Va. Hist. Soc., Montgomery County (Ind.) Hist. Soc., Boone County (Ind.) Hist. Soc., Union County (Tenn.) Hist. Soc., Gen. Fedn. Womens Clubs, Tenn. Fedn. Womens Clubs, Appalachian Zool. Soc. (life), Soc. for Preservation Tenn. Antiquities (life), Nat. Corvette Mus., First Families of Tenn., U. Tenn. President's Club (life), Smoky Mountain Z-Car Club, Optimists (life, local bd. dirs. 1990-92, Tenn. dist. essay contest chmn. 1990-91, 1992-93, 1993-94, Tenn. dist. 1st lady 1990-91), Sigma Phi Sigma (life, chpt. pres. U. Chattanooga 1945-47), Nat. Corvette Mus., Delta Kappa Gamma (fin. com. 1980-91), Phi Delta Theta, Kappa Delta Pi (internat. voting del. 1982, 84, 86, conf. presenter 1982), Kappa Delta (life), Women's Athletic Assn. U. Chattanoga, Coed Colillion U. Chattanoga, Home Econs. Club U. Tenn., Women's Student Govt. Assn. U. Tenn. Avocations: nature walks and study, travel, photography, reading, public speaking. Home: 5213 Haynes Sterchi Rd Knoxville TN 37912-2816

GRIFFIN, PAUL, JR., navy officer, engineer, educator; b. Aiken, S.C., Mar. 13, 1961; s. Paul and Mamie Lou (Curry) G. AS, Fla. Keys C.C., 1985; BS, Fla. A&M U., 1986, MEd, M in Applied Social Sci., 1993. Asst. produce mgr. Winn-Dixie Store, Goose Creek, S.C., 1977-79; enlisted USN, 1979—, commd. ensign, 1986, advanced through grades to lt. comdr., 1990, data systems technician, 1979-86; electrical officer, asst. safety officer USS Leyte Gulf, Mayport, Fla., 1986-88; anti-submarine officer USN, Mayport, Fla., 1988-90; asst. prof. Fla. A&M U./USN, Tallahassee, 1990-93; quality assurance officer, 1993-97; chief engr. USS Stump, 1993-97; master tng. specialist USN, 1992—, dept. head, engr. officer, 1993-97, chmn. cash verification bd., 1993-97; 1st lt. USS Enterprise (CVN 65), 1997-99, 99-2000; comdr., gen. staff coll. Staff Coll., 2000—02; dir. quota mgmt. Navy EnlistedQuota Mgmt. Office, 2000—; asst. dir. Navy Selection and Classification Mgmt. Office, 2001—02; registrar Tng. Quality Performance Transp. Adminstrn., 2002—; dep. dir. distributed learning and tng. support Transp. Security Adminstrn., 2002—. Project handclasp and cmty. rels. coord. La Guardia, Salvador, Rio de Janeiro, Puerto Ingeniero White, Valparaiso, S. Am., 1994; propulsion and control sys. analyst Comdr. Naval Surface Forces Atlantic, 1997; chmn. Integrated Tng. Requirements and Planning Databases Configuration Control Bd., 2000-2002. Mentor Griffin Mid. Sch., Tallahassee, 1990-92; asst. coord. Family Support Group for Desert Storm, Tallahassee, 1991; spkr., vol. Hugh O'Brien Youth Leadership Program, Tallahassee, 1991; judge Capital Regional Sci. and Engring. Fair, Tallahassee, 1992; advisor City of Tallahassee Examination of Drug and Crime Activity Project, 1992; vol., spkr. Gadsden County GED and Dropout Prevention Program, 1992-93; vol. Riley Elem. Sch. Say No To Drug's Program; founder, coord. Men of Faith Support Group 1st Missionary Bapt. Ch., 1999-2000; chmn. tech. rsch. com. Command and Gen. Staff Coll. 2000 LLC, 1999-2002; others. Delores Auzenne fellow, 1992. Mem. 100 Black Men of Am., Fla. A&M U. Nat. Alumni Assn. (life), Nat. Naval Officers Assn. (life). Democrat. Baptist. Avocations: photography, chess, tennis. Home: 8402 Deegan Ct Clinton MD 20735-2999 Office: Chief Naval Ops # 2 FOB Navy Annex Washington DC 20370 E-mail: n132e@bupers.navy.mil.

GRIFFIN, SHANNON, middle school principal; b. Northfield, Minn., Mar. 27, 1937; d. Burnett Harrison and Beulah Theodora (Forstrom) Voss; m. Bromley Griffin, Dec. 15, 1959 (div. July 1984); children: Hayley, Kyle Bromley. BA, Carleton Coll., 1959; postgrad., St. Cloud State U., 1983, U. Minn., 1983. Cert. tchr. English 7-12, math. 7-12, cert. h.s. prin., supt., Minn. Tchr. math., Wausau, Wis., 1959-60; remedial math. tchr. Wackernheim, Germany, 1960-61; tchr. math. and English, St. Anthony Village H.S., 1961-66; tchr., supr., coord. Onamia Ind. Sch. Dist., 1967-68, 78-86; asst. prin. Sanford Jr. H.S., 1986-90, Roosevelt H.S., 1990-91, Washburn H.S., 1991-94, Edison H.S., 1991-95; prin. Olson Mid. Sch., 1995—2002; ret. Contbr. to editl. page Star Tribune. Named Mpls. Secondary Prin. of Yr., 1998, Carleton Coll. Disting. Alumni, 1999; scholar U. Minn. Coffman Alumni scholar, 1986. Mem. ASCD, Nat. Assn. Secondary Sch. Prins., Phi Kappa Phi. Mem. Dem. Farmer Labor Party. Mem. United Ch. of Christ. Avocations: golf, walking, weight lifting, tennis, gardening. Office: Olson Mid Sch 1607 51st Ave N Minneapolis MN 55430-3433 E-mail: sgriffin@olson.mpls.k12.mn.us.

GRIFFIN, SYLVIA GAIL, reading specialist; b. Portland, Oreg., Dec. 13, 1935; d. Archie and Marguerite (Johnson) G. AA, Boise Jr. Coll., 1955; BS, Brigham Young U., 1957, MEd, 1967. Cert. advanced teaching, Idaho. Classroom tchr. Boise Pub. Sch., Idaho, 1957-59, 61-66, 67-69, reading specialist, 1969-90, 91-95, 98-2001, inclusion specialist, 1995-98, early childhood specialist, 1990-91. Tchr. evening Spanish classes for adults, 1987-88; lectr. in field; mem. cons. pool US Office Juvenile Justice and Delinquency Prevention, 1991—. Author: Procedures Used by First Grade Teachers for Teaching Experience Readiness for Reading Comprehension; The Short Story of Vowels; A Note Worthy Way to Teach Reading; The Little Black Schoolhouse; Hellside Elementary School; Reading, Righting, and Revenge, Memorandum: Murder. Advisor in developing a program for dyslexics Scottish Rite Masons of Idaho, Boise. Mem.: NEA, Actor's Guild, Idaho Edn. Assn. (pub. rels. dir. 1970—72), Boise Edn. Assn. (pub. rels. dir. 1969—72, bd. dirs. ednl. polit. involvement com. 1983—89), Alpha Delta Kappa. Avocations: music, creative writing. Home: 9948 W Sleepy Hollow Ln Boise ID 83714-3665

GRIFFIN, WALTER ROLAND, college president, historian, educator; b. Carbondale, Pa., Nov. 20, 1942; s. Walter Joseph and Maud Loftus (Boland) G.; m. Mary Eleanor Armstrong, Aug. 16, 1961 (div. 1980); children: Rebecca, Kathleen, Shawn; m. Penni Susan Oncken, Dec. 6, 1980; 1 child, Megan. BA, Loyola Coll., Balt., 1963; MA, U. Cin., 1964, PhD, 1988. Lectr. history Xavier U., Cin., 1965-66; asst. prof. history Mt. St. Mary's Coll., Emmitsburg, Md., 1967-68, Upper Iowa U., Fayette, 1966-67, 68-84, chmn. dept., chmn. div. social sci. and bus. adminstrn., 1969-78, assoc. acad. dean, 1977-78, assoc. prof., 1984-89, head coach men's and women's tennis, 1979-88, dir. off-campus programs, 1981-89; assoc. dean Union Inst., Cin., 1989-92; pres. Limestone Coll., Gaffney, S.C., 1992—. Contbr. articles to profl. jours. Councilman City of Fayette, 1971-76; chmn. Fayette County (Iowa) Dems., West Union, 1972-77, 79-80; mem. Iowa State Dem. Ctrl. Com., Des Moines, 1974-78; del. Dem. Nat. Conv., N.Y.C., 1976; Dem. candidate for Iowa Sec. of State, 1978; mem. S.C. Higher Edn. Tuition Grants Commn., 1992-95, 99-2000, Crustbreakers, 1997—; bd. dirs. Cherokee County Boys and Girls Club, 1993-98; pres. Carolinas-Va. Athletic Conf., 2002—. Recipient Community Svc. award Fayette Jaycees, 1973, Appreciation award Iowa Democratic Party, 1974, 78, Cert. Appreciation, Iowa N.G., Camp Dodge, 1985; named Coach of Yr. in Men's Tennis, Iowa Intercollegiate Athletic Conf., Waverly, 1985; Taft Teaching fellow U. Cin., 1963-64; Paul Harris fellow 2002. Mem. Phi Alpha Theta, Pi Gamma Mu, Rotary. Avocations: tennis, traveling. Home: 1008 College Dr Gaffney SC 29340-3708 Office: Limestone Coll 1115 College Dr Gaffney SC 29340-3778 E-mail: wgriffin@limestone.edu.

GRIFFIN-BURRILL, KATHLEEN R. F. See BURRILL, KATHLEEN R. F.

GRIFFING, GEORGE THOMAS, medical educator, endocrinologist; b. Lawrence, Kans., Apr. 3, 1950; s. George W. and Roberta J. (Brown) G.; m. Bonnie Anne Brennen, June 14, 1985; children: Nathaniel, Samuel, Emily. Student, U. Utah, 1971; MD, Wayne State U., 1975. From instr. medicine to asst. prof. medicine Boston U. Med. Sch., 1980-87, mem. dept. physiology, assoc. prof. medicine, 1987-92; prof. medicine U. Mo., Columbia, 1992-99, St. Louis U., 1999—. Asst. vis. physician Boston City Hosp., 1981-92; dir. Cosmo Internat. Diabetes Ctr./U. Mo., Columbia, 1992-99; dir. divsn. endocrinology/metabolism Sch. Medicine, U. Mo., Columbia, 1992-99, dir. divsn. gen. internal medicine St. Louis U., 1999-2001, dir. divsn. endocrinology, diabetes and metabolism, 2001—; vis. scientist dept. biochemistry Tufts U. Health Sci. Ctr., Boston, 1986-92; mem. Problem Based Learning Task Force, Columbia, 1995-99; chmn. admissions com. Sch. Medicine, U. Mo., 1994-99; chmn. activities com. Mo. regional chpt. Am. Coll. Medicine, 1994—. Author: (jours.) Jour. Clin. Endocrine, New Eng. Jour. Medicine. Mem. Cosmopolitan Internat., Columbia, 1992. Named New Investigator, NIH, 1983-86, Phi Zeta hon. lectr. U. Mo. Vet. Sch., 1994. Fellow Coun. for High Blood Pressure, ACP (dir. sub-splty. update regional meeting 1994—); mem. Am. Fedn. Clin. Rsch., Endocrine Soc. Achievements include investigation of new drug application for intranasal insulin. Home: 4 Cedar Crest Saint Louis MO 63132-4205 Office: St Louis U Fdt-12S 1402 S Grand Blvd-Univ Saint Louis MO 63104

GRIFFITH, B(EZALEEL) HEROLD, physician, educator, plastic surgeon; b. N.Y.C., Aug. 24, 1925; s. Bezaleel Davies and Henrietta (Herold) G.; m. Jeanne B. Lethbridge, 1948; children: Susan, Tristan. BA, Johns Hopkins U., 1992; MD, Yale U., 1948. Diplomate: Am. Bd. Plastic Surgery (dir. 1976-82, chmn. 1981-82). Asst. in anatomy Yale U., New Haven, 1947—48, asst. in surgery, 1948—49; intern Grace New Haven Cmty. Hosp.-Yale U., 1948-49; resident in surgery VA Hosp., Newington, Conn., 1949-50; asst. resident in surgery 2d (Cornell) Surg. Divsn., Bellevue Hosp., N.Y.C., 1952-53; instr. surgery Cornell U., 1956; resident in plastic surgery VA Hosp., Bronx, 1953-55; resident (sr. registrar) in plastic surgery U. Glasgow, Scotland, 1955; chief resident in plastic surgery N.Y. Hosp. Cornell Med. Ctr., N.Y.C., 1956; rsch. fellow in plastic surgery Cornell U. Med. Coll., 1956-57; pvt. practice specializing in plastic surgery Chgo., 1957-96; attending plastic surgeon Northwestern Meml., Children's Meml., VA Lakeside hosps., Rehab. Inst. Chgo.; instr. surgery Northwestern U., 1957-59, assoc. in surgery, 1959-62, asst. prof. surgery, 1962-67, assoc. prof., 1967-71, prof., 1971-96, prof. emeritus, 1996, chief divsn. plastic surgery, 1970-91; chief plastic surgery Shriners Hosp. for Crippled Children, Chgo., 1994-96; retired. Assoc. editor: Plastic and Reconstructive Surgery, 1972-78; contbr. articles to profl. jours. Lt. M.C., USNR, 1950-52. Fellow ACS, Am. Assn. Plastic Surgeons, Chgo. Surg. Soc., Royal Soc. Medicine; mem. AAAS, AMA, Am. Soc. Plastic and Reconstructive Surgeons (sec. 1972-74), Brit. Assn. Plastic Surgeons, Plastic Surgery Rsch. Coun. (chmn. 1969), Am. Cleft Palate Assn., N.Y. Acad. Scis., Ill., Chgo. Med. Socs., Midwestern Assn. Plastic Surgeons, Soc. Head and Neck Surgeons, Ill., Chgo. Hist. Socs., Civil War Round Table, Evanston Hist. Soc. (trustee 1974-78), Sigma Xi (pres. Northwestern U. 1986-87, 94-95). Clubs: Yale (Chgo.). Lodges: Masons. Achievements include research in transplantation, skin tumors, cleft palate, paraplegia.

GRIFFITH, DANIEL ALVA, geography educator; b. Pitts., Nov. 15, 1948; s. Donald Sanford and Mary Jane (McClain) G.; m. Diane Elaine Swartz, Jan. 3, 1970; children: Darren Lee, Michele Renee. BS, Indiana U. of Pa., 1970, MA, 1972; MS, Pa. State U., 1985; PhD, U. Toronto, Ont., Can., 1978. Instr. Ryerson Polytech. U., Toronto, 1975-78; from asst. prof. to full prof. SUNY, Buffalo, 1978-88; prof. geography Syracuse (N.Y.) U., 1988—, dir. stats. program, 1991-92, 93-95, chair, 1995-97; adj. prof. Coll. Environ. Sci. and Forestry, 1992—. Vis. EPA/EMAP rsch. affiliate stats. dept. Oreg. State U., Corvallis, 1990, 91, 92, 93; vis. rsch. prof. Erasmus U., Rotterdam, 1992, U. Rome, 1995; dep. dir. N.Y. State program in geographic info. and analysis Syracuse U., 1989-90; ASI dir. NATO Sci. Affairs, Brussels, 1979-80, 81-82, 85, cons. Peru Minister Edn., 2000-01; Leverhulme vis. prof. Cambridge U., 2004. Author: Spatial Autocorrelation, 1987, Advanced Spatial Statistics, 1988, Statistical Analysis for Geographers, 1991, Spatial Regression Analysis on the PC, 1993, Multivariate Statistical Analysis for Geographers, 1997, A Casebook for Spatial Statistical Data Analysis, 1999; editor books; contbr. articles to profl. jours. NSF grantee, 1981, 83-84, 85, 88-90, 92-93, 95-97, 99, 2002—; Fulbright fellow, 1992-93, rsch. fellow ASA/USDA-NASS, 1999, Guggenheim fellow, 2001-02; recipient Award Pa. Geog. Soc., 1999. Fellow N.Y. Acad. Scis.; mem. Am. Statis. Assn., Regional Sci. Assn. (pres. 1996-97), Assn. Am. Geographers (chair 1987-88, Nystrom Dissertation award 1980, Pub. Domain Computer Software award 1994, 97), Sigma Xi (Syracuse chpt. pres. 1999-2000). Democrat. Methodist. Avocation: traveling. Home: 5270 Wethersfield Rd Jamesville NY 13078-9727 Office: Syracuse U Geography Dept Syracuse NY 13244-1020

GRIFFITH, JERRY LYNN, physical education educator; b. Chattanooga, July 24, 1954; s. Marvin Joy and Nerine (Greer) G.; m. Dianne Gooslby, June 11, 1977; children: Matthew, Coleman. AS, Cleveland (Tenn.) State U., 1974; BS, David Lipscomb Coll., Nashville, 1976; MS, Mid. Tenn. State U., Murfreesboro, 1980, D of Arts, 1990. Tchr., basketball coach Boyd-Buchanan H.S., Chattanooga, 1977, Ezell-Harding H.S., Antioch, Tenn., 1977-80; coll. tchr., coach David Lipscomb U., Nashville, 1980—, dir. tennis camp, 1984-93. Adj. tchr. Free Will Bible Coll., Nashville, 1994—2001; profl. tennis tchr. Sequoia Club, Nashville, 1980—82, West Meade Club, Nashville, 1983—84. Author: Tennis Manual, 1991, also articles. Youth baseball coach Crieve Hall Youth Athletic Assn., Nashville, 1987—, Jr. Pro, Nashville, 1988, 94. Named Tennis Coach of Yr., Tenn. Collegiate Athletic Conf., 1981, 1982, 1984, 1985, 1991, NCAA Divsn 1 Ind. Tennis Coach of Yr., 2002; named to Outstanding Young Men of Am., 1982. Mem.: U.S. Profl. Tennis Registry. Mem. Ch. of Christ. Avocations: biking, tennis, swimming, strength training. Home: 4029 Outer Dr Nashville TN 37204-4025 Office: David Lipscomb U 3901 Granny White Pike Nashville TN 37204-3903 E-mail: lynn.griffith@lipscomb.edu.

GRIFFITH, JOHN SCOTT, secondary school educator; b. New Castle, Ind., July 1, 1951; s. Harold Elsworth and Oleta Marie (Riggs) G. AB in Math. magna cum laude, Ind. U., 1973; MA in Secondary Edn., Ball State U., 1976. Cert. tchr. secondary math. Tchr. math. Parkview Jr. H.S., New Castle, 1973-89, chair dept. math., asst. athletic dir., 1990—. Prodr. video tapes: Something New at Parkview -- The Math Lab Concept, Paperwad Math. Mem. Human Rights Commn., New Castle, 1978. Recipient Ind. U. Found. award, 1973. Mem. NEA (del. conv. 1984), Nat. Coun. Tchrs. Math., Phi Beta Kappa, Pi Mu Epsilon (hon.). Home: 279 N Pleasantview Dr New Castle IN 47362-1322 Office: Parkview Jr High Sch 601 Parkview Dr New Castle IN 47362-2947

GRIFFITH, PETER, mechanical engineering educator, researcher; b. London, Sept. 23, 1927; came to U.S., 1930; s. Sanford and Katherine (Bennett) G.; m. Sylvia Biorn-Hansen, June 10, 1954 (dec. Sept. 1981); children: Sonja, Katherine; m. Kathleen Mayo, July 23, 1983. MSME, U. Mich., 1952; DSc, MIT, 1956. Rsch. asst. MIT, Cambridge, 1952, instr. mech. engrng., 1954-56, asst. prof., 1956-59, assoc. prof., 1959-63, prof., 1963—. Cons. on heat transfer and two-phase flow, 1956—. Cpl. USAF, 1946-47. Fellow ASME. Home: 107 Louise Rd Belmont MA 02478-3968 Office: MIT 77 Massachusetts Ave Cambridge MA 02139-4307

GRIFFITH, PHILIP ARTHUR, elementary school educator; b. N.Y.C., Nov. 13, 1934; s. Jesse Lloyd and Anna (McGovern) G.; m. Nancy Sullivan, June 18, 1960; children: Philip, Margaret. BA, Hunter Coll., 1960; MS, CUNY, 1963. Cert. edn. Tchr. 6th grade N.Y.C. Pub. Schs., 1960-64; tchr. Central Islip (N.Y.) Pub. Schs., 1964—. Instr. Dowling Coll., Oakdale, N.Y., 1970-75; supr. N.Y.C. (N.Y.) Bureau of Cmty. Edn., 1970-80. Author: The History of Infant Jesus Parish; contbr. articles to profl. publs. Hockey coach Cath. Youth Orgn., Central Islip, 1976-82, St. Anthony's H.S., 1986-87; baseball coach Police Athletic League, Central Islip, 1976-86; del. L.I. Fedn. Labor, Mineola, N.Y., 1976-90; N.Y. state del. N.Y. State AFL-CIO, Albany, 1976-95, N.Y. Com. Health and Safety, N.Y.C., 1988-95; N.Y. State Tenure Hearing Panelist, Albany, 1978-99; mem. parents coun. Boston Coll., Chestnut Hill, Mass., 1990-92. Cpl. U.S. Army, 1954-56. Recipient N.Y. State PTA Jenkins award Charles Mulligan Sch. PTA, Central Islip, 1978, Leadership award United Way, L.I., 1978, Pride in the Union award Am. Fedn. Tchrs., 1990, 92, Influential Tchr. award MIT, Cambridge, 1980. Mem. Am. Fedn. Tchrs. (del. 1972-95), Ctrl. Islip Tchrs. Assn. (pres. 1976-95), N.Y. State United Tchrs. (del. 1970-95), N.Y. State Tchrs. Retirement Sys. (del. 1974-95), U.S. Golf Assn., Port Jefferson Country Club, Port Jefferson Hist. Soc. (editor The Echoes of Port), Port Jefferson Civic Assn. (editor Jeffersonian), Nat. Geographic Soc., L.I. Pres. Coun. (dist. dir.), Indsl. Rels. Rsch. Assn., Chmn. Infrant Jesus R.C. Ch. History Comm.,Smithsonian Inst., Am. Legion. Democrat. Roman Catholic. Avocations: golf, folk art, irish history, theatre, travel. Home: 14 Cove Ln Port Jefferson NY 11777-1103 Office: Central Islip Tchrs Assn Central Islip NY 11722

GRIFFITH, ROBERT CHARLES, allergist, educator, planter; b. Shreveport, La., Jan. 9, 1939; s. Charles Parsons and Madelon (Jenkins) G.; m. Loretta Dean Secrist, July 15, 1969; children: Charles Randall, Cameron Stuart, Ann Marie. BS, Centenary Coll., 1961; MD, La. State U., 1965. Intern, Confederate Meml. Med. Ctr., Shreveport, 1965-66, resident in internal medicine, 1966-68; fellow in allergy and chest disease, instr. U. Va. Med. Sch. Hosp., Charlottesville, 1968-70; practice medicine specializing in allergies, Alexandria, La., 1970-72, The Allergy Clinic, Shreveport, 1972; pres. Griffith Allergy Clinic, Shreveport, 1973—; faculty internal medicine La. State U., 1972—; owner, planter Riverpoint Plantation, Caddo Parish, La. and Miller and Lafayette Counties, Ark. Bd. dirs. Caddo-Bossier Assn. Retarded Citizens, 1977-84, Access (fomerly Child Devel. Ctr.), Shreveport, 1979-85; mem. (life) NRA, med. adv. com., spl. edn. adv. com. Caddo Parish Sch. Bd., 1977-89; mem. commission on missions and social concerns First Methodist Ch., 1981-84, mem. adminstrv. bd., 1981-84; mem. med. panel for transfer Caddo Parish Sch. Bd., 1974-94; mem. adopt a flag program Confederate Meml. Mus. New Orleans; co-chair Loyola Fund Drive, 1994-95. Served to maj. M.C., U.S. Army, 1965-71. Recipient Physician of the Yr. award Shreveport-Bossier Med. Assts., 1984. Fellow Am. Coll. Asthma, Allergy and Immunology, Am. Coll. Chest Physicians (assoc.), Am. Thoracic Soc.; mem. AMA, SAR (chpt. surgeon 1994—), Am. Acad. Allergy, Asthma and Immunology, Am. Legion, Jamestowne Soc., So. Med. Assn., La. Med. Soc., Shreveport Med. Soc. (allergy sposkesman 1984—), La. Allergy Soc. (charter; past pres.), U. Va. Med. Alumni Assn. (life), Pace Soc. Am., La. State U. Med. Alumni Assn., Confederate Soc. Am., Heritage Preservation Assn., League of the South (charter, sustainer), League of the South La. (bd. dirs.), Legion South, Am. Legion (Viet Nam), Mil. Order Stars and Bars, Order of So. Cross, Shreveport C. of C., Kappa Alpha, Methodist. Lodges: Masons (32 degree). Clubs: Shreveport Country, Petroleum of Shreveport, Shreveport, Ambs., Cotillion, Royal, Plantation, Shriners (El Kahruba Temple), Jesters, Les Bon Temps., Demoiselle Club. Home: 7112 E Ridge Dr Shreveport LA 71106-4749 also: Riverpoint Plantation Ida LA 71044

GRIFFITHS, ROBERT BUDINGTON, physics educator; b. Etah, India, Feb. 25, 1937; s. Walter Denison and Margaret (Hamilton) H. AB, Princeton U., 1957; MS, Stanford U., 1958, PhD, 1962. Postdoctoral fellow U. Calif. at San Diego, 1962-64; asst. prof. Carnegie-Mellon U., Pitts., 1964-67, assoc. prof., 1967-69, prof. physics, 1969—, Otto Stern prof., 1979—, univ. prof., 1998—. NSF fellow, 1962-64, Alfred P. Sloan Rsch. fellow, 1966-68, J.S. Guggenheim fellow, 1973; recipient Sr. Scientist award Humboldt Found., 1973, A. Cressy Morrison award Acad. Scis., N.Y., 1981, Dannie Heineman prize for math. physics, 1984. Mem. Am. Phys. Soc., Am. Sci. Affiliation, U.S. Nat. Acad. Scis., Phi Beta Kappa, Sigma Xi. Presbyterian. Achievements include research in statistical and quantum mechanics. Office: Carnegie-Mellon U Dept of Physics Pittsburgh PA 15213 E-mail: rgrif@cmu.edu.

GRIFFITH-THOMPSON, SARA LYNN, resource reading educator; b. Kansas City, Mo., July 27, 1965; d. Hugh Wallace and Mary Elizabeth (Mullinix) Griffith; m. Joey Lee Thompson, May 30, 1992; 2 children. BS in Edn., Ctrl. Mo. State U., 1986, MS in Reading, 1992. Tchr. grade 4 East Lynne (Mo.) Sch. Dist., 1987-88, Pleasant Lea Elem., Lee's Summit, Mo., 1988-93; tchr. grade 4 resource reading K-6 Trailridge Elem., Lee's Summit, 1993—. Pres. Internat. Reading Assn.; asst. After Sch. Group, Lees Summit, 1993—94; mem. Tchr. Expectation Student Achievement, Lees Summit, 1992; sponsor Student Coun., Lees Summit, 1994—96; supr. Student Tchrs., Lees Summit, 1992. Pres. Lee's Summit Reading Coun., 2001-02. Recipient Excellence in Tchg. award Lee's Summit C. of C., 1992. Mem. Internat. Reading Assn. (bldg. rep. 1994-98, presenter Plains regional 1995, state conf. 1996), Mo. State Tchr. Assn., PEO, Grand Cross, Optimist Club (super friends), Phi Delta Kappa. Office: Trailridge Elem 3651 SW Windemere Dr Lees Summit MO 64082-4412

GRIGG, EDDIE GARMAN, minister, educator; b. Shelby, N.C., Feb. 20, 1957; s. Gaston Theodore and Sylvia Evlyn (Davis) G.; m. Susan Wanda Ray, May 28, 1977; children: Mark Zolton, Jamie Ray, Steven Russell. BA, Gardner-Webb Coll., 1980; MDiv, Southeastern Bapt. Theol. Sem., 1985; D Ministry, Emmanuel Bapt. U., 1994, DRE, 1995; DD (hon.), New Life U., 1998. Ordained to ministry So. Bapt. Conv., 1976. Pastor Victory Bapt. Ch., Kings Mountain, N.C., 1975-79, Christian Freedom Bapt. Ch., Kings Mountain, 1979-81, Sanford Meml. Bapt. Ch., Brodnax, Va., 1981-85, Pleasant Hill Bapt. Ch., Shelby, N.C., 1985-89; sr. min. Wilson Grove Bapt. Ch., Charlotte, N.C., 1989-93; founder, pastor New Life Bapt. Ch., Charlotte, 1993—; co-founder, pres. New Life Theological Seminary, 1996—. Mem. Bapt. Metrolina Ministries Pastor's Conf. (pres. 1995-97), Bapt. Metrolina Ministries Assn. (evangelism com. 1990-93, urban ch. com. 1990-94). Republican. Office: New Life Theol Sem PO Box 790166 Charlotte NC 28206

GRIGG, KATHY AUSTELL, elementary education educator; b. Shelby, N.C., Sept. 22, 1952; d. Joseph Forest and Katherine (Bailey) Austell; m. James Richard Grigg, Jr., Jan. 20, 1977. BS, Appalachian State U., 1973; MA, Appalachian State Coll., 1976; AA, Cleveland Community Coll., 1980, 83. Cert. Tchr. N.C. Tchr. Cleveland County Schs., Shelby, 1974—2002. Pres. Cleveland-Rutherford Kidney Assn., Shelby, 1990, treas., 1993—. Named Vol. of Yr. Cleveland-Rutherford Kidney Assn., 1992, 2002, named Vol. of Yr. Shelby Lions Club, 2003. Mem. NEA, N.C. Assn. Educators, Nat. Coun. Tchrs. Math. (presenter 1985, 86, 89, Outstanding Elem. Math. Tchr. 1985), N.C. Coun. Tchr. Math., N.C. Sci. Tchrs. Assn. ret, 2002. Baptist. Avocations: reading, walking, crafts, traveling. Home: 3214 Yates Rd Shelby NC 28150-8837

GRIGGS, GARY BRUCE, science administrator, oceanographer, geologist, educator; b. Pasadena, Calif., Sept. 25, 1943; s. Dean Brayton and Barbara Jayne (Farmer) G.; m. Venetia Gina Bradfield, Jan. 11, 1980; children: Joel, Amy, Shannon, Callie, Cody. BA in Geology, U. Calif., Santa Barbara, 1965; PhD in Oceanography, Oreg. State U., 1968. Registered geologist, Calif.; cert. engr. geologist, Calif. Rsch. asst., NSF grad. fellow in oceanography Oreg. State U., 1965-68; from asst. prof. to prof. earth scis. U. Calif., Santa Cruz, 1969—; Fulbright fellow Inst. for Ocean & Fishing Rsch., Athens, Greece, 1974-75; oceanographer Joint U.S.A.-N.Z. Rsch. Program, 1980-81; chair earth scis. U. Calif., Santa Cruz, 1981-84, assoc. dean natural scis., 1992-95; dir. Inst. of Marine Scis., 1991—2002. Vis. prof. Semester at Sea program U. Pitts., 1984-96; guest lectr. World Explorer Cruises, 1987; chair marine coun. U. Calif., 1999-02; bd. govs. Consortium for Oceanographic Rsch. and Edn., 1995—. Author: (with others) Geologic Hazards, Resources and Environmental Planning, 1983, Living with the California Coast, 1985, Coastal Protection Structures, 1986, California's Coastal Hazards, 1992; mem. editl. bd. Jour. of Coastal Rsch., Geology; contbr. numerous articles to profl. jours. Mem. Am. Geophys. Union, Am. Geol. Inst., Coastal Found. Achievements include research in coastal processes; coastal erosion and protection; coastal engineering and hazards; sediment yield, transport and dispersal; geologic hazards and land use. Office: U Calif Inst Marine Scis Santa Cruz CA 95064 E-mail: griggs@emerald.ucsc.edu.

GRIGORIADIS, KAROLOS MICHAIL, mechanical engineering educator; b. Athens, Greece, Sept. 4, 1964; Diploma in Mech. Engring., Nat. Tech. U., Athens, 1987; MS in Aerospace Engring., Va. Poly. Inst., 1989; MS in Maths., Purdue U., 1993, PhD in Aerospace Engring., 1994. Rsch. asst. Va. Poly. Inst. & State U., Blacksburg, 1987-89, Purdue U., West Lafayette, Ind., 1989-94; asst. prof. U. Houston, 1994-99, assoc. prof., 1999—, dir. aero. engring. program, 2000—. Contbr. articles to profl. jours. and confs. Recipient NSF Career award, 1997, SAE Ralph R. Teetor Ednl. award, 1998. Mem. AIAA, IEEE, ASME, ASCE. Achievements include development of a unified algebraic approach for linear control design with applications to mechancal and aerospace systems. Office: U Houston Mech Engring Dept 4800 Calhoun Rd Houston TX 77004-2610 E-mail: karolos@uh.edu.

GRILLO, ISAAC ADETAYO, surgery educator, consultant; b. Lagos City, Nigeria, Jan. 15, 1931; s. Jeremiah Aina and Rachel Oni (Aluko) G.; m. Elizabeth Arinade Adejunmobi, July 18, 1957; children: Adewale, Adedayo, Adebola, Aderonke, Adeola, Adebusola, Adedamola, Adegboyega, Adedunmoye, Adebukola, Adeboye, Adejoke. BS cum laude, BA in Edn./Psychology, McPherson (Kans.) Coll., 1955, DSc (honoris causa), 1987; MD, U. Kans., 1960. Diplomate Am. Bd. Gen. Surgery, Am. Bd. Thoracic Surgery. Intern Menorah Med. Ctr., Kans. City, Mo., 1960-61; resident in gen. surgery Homer G. Phillips Hosp., St. Louis, 1961-65; resident in cardiothoracic surgery Olive View Hosp., Calif., 1965-66, Highland-Alameda County Hosp., Oakland, Calif., 1966-67; physician II Fairmont Hosp., San Leandro, Calif., 1967-68; from lectr. to prof. U. Ibadan, Nigeria, 1968-89; cons. to chief cons. U. Coll. Hosp. Ibadan, 1968-89; head dept. surgery U. Ibadan and U. Coll. Hosp. Ibadan, 1985-88; chief cons., head of surgery King Fahad Ctrl. Hosp., Gizan, Saudi Arabia, 1988-90; sr. cons. cardiothoracic surgery Assir Ctrl. Hosp., Abha, Saudi Arabia, 1990-99; prof. cardiothoracic surgery Coll. of Medicine, King Saud U., Abha, 1991-98, King Khalid U., Abha, 1998-99; physician and surgeon Salinas Valley State Prison, Calif. Dept. Correction, Soledad, 2000—. Cons. surgeon, (1971-88) acting med. supt (1971) Ogbomosho (Nigeria) Bapt. Hosp. Contbr. articles to profl. jour. Active choir McPherson Coll. Chapel and Ch. of the Brethren, McPherson, 1952-55, Ch. of the Brethren, Kansas City, Kans., 1956-60; active choir, violinist Orita Mefa Bapt. Ch., Ibadan, 1968—, New Haven Bapt. Ch., Ibadan, 1990—. Lt. col. Nigerian Army MC, 1969. Chemistry and Fgn. Students scholar McPherson Coll., 1952-55, Japanese Overseas Cooperation Agy. scholar Japanese Govt., 1971; Fulbright-Hayes fellow in cardiothoracic surgery U.S. Govt., 1977. Fellow ACS, Am. Coll. Angiology, Internat. Coll. Surgeons, Coll. Chest Physicians, West African Coll. Surgeons, Nigeria Med. Coun. Surgery. Avocations: playing music, writing poetry. Office: PO Box 4095 UI Post Office Ibadan Nigeria also: PO Box 367 Soledad CA 93960-0367 E-mail: isaacgrillo@aol.com.

GRIM, ELLEN TOWNSEND, artist, retired art educator; b. Boone County, Ind., Nov. 1, 1921; d. Horace Wright and Sibyl Conklin (Lindley) Townsend; m. Robert Little Grim, Apr. 5, 1952; children: Nancy Ellen Grim Garcia, Howard Robert. Student, Our Lady of the Lake U., 1939-41, U. Tex., 1941-42; BA in Art, U. Wash., 1946; MA in Art, UCLA, 1950; postgrad., Otis Art Inst., L.A., 1970-71. Cert. secondary tchr., Calif. Art tchr., chairperson secondary Calif. and L.A. Unified Sch. Dist., 1947—82; retired, 1982; artist, 1975—. Guest speaker on art TV and cable, L.A., 1993. One-woman shows include Ventura County Mus. Art, 1982, Riverside Mcpl. Mus., 1984, Craft and Folk Art Mus., L.A., 1986, S.W. Mus., L.A., 1987, Calif. Heritage Mus., 1991, Brand Art Ctr., Glendale, 1996, Wurdermann Gallery, L.A., 1997, others; exhibited in more than 100 group shows. 1st lt. USMC, 1943-45. Recipient Purchase prize Gardena Fine Arts Collection, 1982, Watercolor West award San Diego Watercolor Soc. Internat., 1983, N.Mex. Watercolor Soc. award, 1989, 1st pl. award Fine Arts Fedn., 1987, 1st pl. award Art Educators L.A., 1988, 89, 1st pl. award Collage Artists Am., 1995, 2002, Brand Art Ctr. Watercolor West award, 1999, Painting award Valley Inst. of Visual Art, San Fernando Valley, 1999, 2001, Long Beach Arts painting award, 1999, 2000. Mem.: Alliance of Women Vets., Women Marines Assn., Collage Artists Am. (1st Place award 1995, 2002), Pasadena Soc. Artists (Painting award 1986, 1988, 1990, 1992, 1993, 1999, 2001, 2002), L.A. Art Assn. (bd. dirs. 1993—95), Women Painters West (membership chair, mem.-at-large 1983—89, Painting award 1985, 1986, 1989, 1992, 1993, 1995, 1999, Best of Show award 2000, Painting award 2000, 2001), Nat. Watercolor Soc. (historian 1989—90, Painting award 1984, 1999, 2000), Women in Mil Svc. for Am., Pi Lambda Theta, Alpha Phi. Avocations: Native American and Latin American culture, travel, Southwestern history.

GRIM, SAMUEL ORAM, chemistry educator; b. Landisburg, Pa., Mar. 11, 1935; s. Oram Michael and Esther Blanche (Gable) G.; m. Faith H. Rojahn, June 8, 1957 (div. 1982); children: Stephen W., Amy R., Lucy G.; m. Caren L. Klarman, Mar. 11, 1983 (div. 1993); 1 child, Christina K.; m. Rebecca A. Allen, Aug. 11, 2001. BS, Franklin and Marshall Coll., 1956; PhD, MIT, 1960. Faculty U. Md., College Park, 1960—, prof. chemistry, 1968—, chmn. inorganic chemistry divsn., 1970-77, 80-86, 1995—96, assoc. chmn., chemistry dept., 1996-98. Program officer in inorganic chemistry NSF, 1988-90. Contbr. articles to profl. jours. Union Carbide Co.

scholar, 1954-56; NSF fellow, 1958-60; summer teaching fellow, 1960; research fellow Imperial Coll., London, 1961-62; Sir John Cass's Found. sr. research fellow City of London Poly., 1979-80 Fellow AAAS, Am. Inst. Chemists, Royal Soc. Chemistry (London); mem. Am. Chem. Soc., N.Y. Acad. Scis., Internat. Union Pure and Applied Chemistry, Internat. Coun. Main Group Chemistry, Chem. Soc. Washington, Phi Beta Kappa, Sigma Xi (Sci. Achievement award 1983), Phi Lambda Upsilon, Alpha Chi Sigma. Clubs: Terrapin (College Park). Republican. Home: 14219 Greenview Dr Laurel MD 20708-3215 Office: U Md Dept Chemistry College Park MD 20742-2021

GRIMES, CRAIG ALAN, electrical engineering educator; b. Ann Arbor, Mich., Nov. 6, 1956; s. Dale Mills and Janet LaVonne (Moore) G.; m. Elizabeth Carol Dickey, 1998; children: Keltin Maxwell, Kyra Megan. BS in Physics, BSEE, Pa. State U., 1984; MS, U. Tex., 1985, PhD, 1990. Engr. Applied Rsch. Labs., Austin, Tex., 1981-83; pres. Crale, Inc., Austin, 1985-90; rsch. scientist Lockeed Rsch. Labs., Palo Alto, Calif., 1990-92; dir. advanced materials lab. Southwall Techs., Palo Alto, Calif., 1992-94; asst. prof. dept. elec. engring. U. Ky., Lexington, 1994-98, assoc. prof., 1998-2000, Frank J. Derbyshire prof., 2000-01, dir. Ctr. for Micro-Magnetic and Electronic Devices, 2000-01; assoc. prof. dept. elec. engring. Pa. State U. and Materials Rsch. Inst., 2001—; pres. Sentechbiomed Corp., 1999—. Rsch. asst. U. Tex., Austin, 1985-88, teaching asst., 1987-90; cons. Eastman Kodak, San Diego, 1989, Storage Tech., Boulder, Colo., 1989, Read-Rite, Fremont, Calif., 1994, AT&T Bell Labs., Murray Hill, N.J., 1995; mem. Clark County Rural Electric Coop.; founder, pres. Sentech Biomed Corp., 1999—. Co-author: Essays on the Formal Aspects of E&M Theory, 1992, Advanced Electromagnetism: Foundation, Theory and Applications, 1995, The Electromagnetic Origin of Quantum Theory and Light, 2002; editor-in-chief: Sensor Letters, 2003—; contbr. articles to profl. jours. Active Nature Conservancy, 1988-95, Austin Triathletes, 1987-90. Mem.: IEEE, AAAS, Bluegrass Masters. Achievements include 6 patents, 8 pending in field; development and manufacture of permeameters, magnetic measurement tools for high frequency permeability measurements; development of size independent antennae. Home: 615 Windmill Rd Boalsburg PA 16827 Office: PSU 217 Materials Rsch Lab University Park PA 16802-4801 E-mail: cgrimes@engr.psu.edu.

GRIMES, PAMELA RAE, retired elementary school educator; b. Cumberland, Md., Dec. 30, 1943; d. Robert Elmer and Mary Evelyn (Hill) McFarland; m. George Edward Grimes, Feb. 9, 1962; children: George Edward Jr., Robert Eric, Jonathon William, David James, Richard Allen. AA, American River Coll., 1965; BA, MA, Calif. State U., Sacramento, 1975, adminstrv. credential, 1999; cert. in computer literacy, Sacramento Unified Sch. Dist., 1981. Cert. elem. tchr., Calif.; cert. adminstrv. credential. Tchr. aide O.W. Erlewine Elem. Sch., Sacramento, 1965-67, elem. gate tchr., 1969-71; tchr. aide Cohen Elem. Sch., Sacramento, 1967-69; libr., tchr. 1st through 6th grades Golden Empire Elem. Sch., Sacramento, 1979-89; tchr. Hubert Bancroft Elem. Sch., Sacramento, 1989-95; staff tng. specialist Literacy Curriculum & Instrn. Dept., 1995-97; reading coach Sacramento Unified Sch. Dist., 1998—2002; ret., 2002. Mentor tchr. Sacramento City Unified Sch. Dist., 1985-95; fellow, mem. Calif. History/Social Sci. course of study, 1991; mem. libr./lit. course of study, 1975, mem. CORE lit. com., 1979, mem. lang. arts assessment com., 1990—, mem. CLAS adv. com., 1993-94, mem. literacy task force, 1995-97, mem. adv. com. on assessment testing, 1995, co-chairperson 20-1 class size reduction program, mem. Young Authors program, mem. curriculum alignment project; literacy leader, facilitator CSIN, 1995—; No. Calif. coord. Ottawa U., 1991—; mem. lang. arts/literacy/ ELD Task Force, 1996-97. Ednl. cons. Children's Mus. Com., 1985—, Sacramento History Ctr., 1985. Fellow Calif. Lit. Project, 1989, Area III Writing Project, 1988, Calif. Social Studies Inst., 1990. Fellow Calif. Geog. Inst., East Asian Humanities Inst.; mem. NEA, ASCD, SARA, CRA, IRA, Nat. Coun. Tchrs. English, Geography Inst. (mem. social studies project. stds. com. 1991), Calif. Alliance Elem. Edn., Calif. English Tchrs. Assn., Calif. Tchrs. Assn. Democrat. Methodist. Avocations: reading, writing, gardening, grandchildren. Home: 9005 Harvest Way Sacramento CA 95826-2203

GRIMES, RICHARD ALLEN, economics educator; b. Toledo, Ohio, Apr. 24, 1929; s. Robert Howell and Mary Mildred Grimes; m. Helen Ann Schaeffer, Aug. 25, 1951; children: Gregory Allen, Julianne, Frank Edwin, Mary Ann. BS major in Chemistry, U. Ga., 1951; MS in Mgmt., Ga. Inst. Tech., 1959; postgrad., Ga. State U., 1979. Commd. lt. U.S. Army, 1951, advanced through grades to lt. col., ret. 1971; asst. prof. econs. Clayton State Univ., Morrow, Ga., 1971-74; assoc. prof. econs. Ga. Perimeter Coll., Decatur, 1974-97. Adj. prof. Jacksonville State U., 1959—63, Va. Commonwealth U., 1964—67, Ga. Mil. Coll., 1979—91, Ctrl. Tex. Coll., 1997—2001, Gordon Coll., 1998—; ednl. cons.; real estate broker, instr. Author: (book) Economics and Finance Study Guide, 2000; reviewer: Economics, 1979—99. Organizing dir. Cmty. Bank, 2001—; umpire Atlanta Area Football Ofcsl. Assn., treas., 1971—95; evaluator Ga. H.S. Football Ofcls., 1996—; active Spl. Olympics, Atlanta, 1971—; founding pres. Rex Civic Assn., 1973; sec.-treas. Villages Homeowners Assn., 1994—95; tax cons., instr. AARP, 2001—. Decorated Soldier's medal for valor Vietnam; named Rotarian of the Yr., 1976, Football Ofcl. of the Yr., Atlanta area, 1980; recipient Eagle Scout award, 1944. Mem.: AAUP (pres. Ga. Perimeter Coll.chpt. 1987—97), VFW (life), Mil. Officers Assn. Am., Nat. Soc. Pub. Acctgs., Ga. Assn. Acctg. Profls. (past pres.), Ga. Assn. Econs. and Fin. (past pres.), Am. Acctg. Assn., So. Econ. Assn., U. Ga. Varsity Letterman, South Atlanta U. Ga. Alumni Club, So. Metro. Ga. Tech. Alumni Club (sec., scholarship chmn.), Am. Legion, Delta Pi Epsilon. Presbyterian. Avocations: football, golf, camping, swimming. Home: Eagles Landing 118 Carron Ln Stockbridge GA 30281-6302 E-mail: r_grimes@bellsouth.net.

GRIMES, TRESMAINE JUDITH RUBAIN, psychology educator; b. N.Y.C., Aug. 3, 1959; d. Judith May (McIntosh) Rubain; m. Clarence Grimes, Jr., Dec. 22, 1984; children: Elena Joanna, Elijah Jeremy. BA, Yale U., 1980; MA, New Sch. for Social Rsch., 1982; MPhil, PhD, Columbia U., 1990. Advanced tchg. fellow Jewish Bd. Family and Childrens Svcs., N.Y.C., 1980-82; tchg./rsch. asst. Columbia U. Tchrs. Coll., N.Y.C., 1983—84; rschr., historian Youth Action Program, N.Y.C., 1984-86; psychologist Hale House for Infants, N.Y.C., 1986-89; asst. rschr. Bank St. Coll., N.Y.C., 1988; addiction program adminstr. Harlem Hosp. Ctr., N.Y.C., 1989-91; asst. prof. psychology S.C. State U., Orangeburg, 1991-96, assoc. prof., 1996—2000, chmn. dept. psychology, 1998—2000, chmn. psychology & sociology, 1998-2000; asst. prof. psychology Iona Coll., 2001—02, assoc. prof., 2002—. Adj. prof. psychology Tchrs. Coll., Columbia U., N.Y.C., 1990-91; adj. prof. Iona Coll., New Rochelle, N.Y., 2000-01. Named one of Outstanding Young Women of Am., 1981. Mem.: APA, Soc. for Tchg. of Psychology, Assn. Black Psychologists, Ea. Psychol. Assn., Psi Chi, Kappa Delta Pi, Delta Sigma Theta. Democrat. Avocations: singing, drama. Office: Iona Coll 715 North Ave New Rochelle NY 10801 E-mail: newgrimes@yahoo.com.

GRIMES, WILLIAM GAYLORD, adult education educator; b. El Paso, Tex., Sept. 21, 1943; s. William Lawrence and Norma Sue (Miller) G.; div. 1988; 1 child, Sean Weston; m. Gloria L. Grimes, 1995. BA in English, History, U. Tex., El Paso, 1966; MA in Ednl. Psychology, Calif. State U., Northridge, 1972, MA in English, 1978. Tchr. English Thousand Oaks (Calif.) H.S., 1967-81; psychotherapist Lincoln County Mental Health Ctr., Ruidoso, N.Mex., 1981-82; tchr. ESL, tchr. grad. equivalency program San Jacinto Adult Learning Ctr., El Paso, 1984-95; mgr. comprehensive competencies program El Paso Ind. Sch. Dist., 1984-95; vocat. counselor Tex. Dept. Criminal Justice, Windham Sch. Sys., 1996—. Interagy. adv. subcom. on testing El Paso Dept. Human Svcs., 1992; pres. Tex. Basic Skills Investment Corp. Office: Windham Sch Rogelio Sanchez State Jail 3901 State Jail Rd El Paso TX 79938-8465

GRIMLEY, JUDITH LEE, speech and language pathologist; b. Bklyn., Dec. 15, 1939; d. Harold H. and Pauline (Flecker) Rosenblum; m. Philip M. Grimley, June 24, 1962; children: Daniel, David, Ben. Student, Pa. State U., 1957-59; BS, Boston U., 1961; MA, U. Md., 1983. Tchr. Wantagh (N.Y.) Pub. Sch., 1961-62, San Mateo (Calif.) Pub. Sch., 1962-63; speech-lang. pathologist Montgomery County Pub. Schs., Rockville, Md., 1982—. Presenter Brain Injury Assn. Am., 2001. Pres. Kehila Chadasha Congregation, Rockville, 1990-92, program chairperson, 1988-90, edn. co-chair, 1984-86; mem. supporting screens test for Tay Sachs disease com. Nat. Capital Tay Sachs Found., 1972-78. Recipient scholarship N.Y. State, 1957. Mem.: Speech and Hearing Discussion Group, Md. State Tchrs. Assn., Md. Speech Lang. Hearing Assn., Montgomery County Edn. Assn. (co-chair speech lang. liaison com. 1992—94), Am. Speech-Hearing Assn. (presenter 1985, 1991, 1993, mem. pub. rels. adv. group 2003, cert.), Pi Lambda Theta. Home: Five Lakenheath Ct Potomac MD 20854

GRIMM, NANCY JO See MCCLAIN, SYLVIA

GRIMME, A. JEANNETTE, retired educator, community activist; b. Eaton, Ohio, Jan. 13, 1921; d. Charles H. and Nelle L. (Scott) G. BA, Ohio Wesleyan U., 1943; MA, Oberlin Sch. Theology, 1953. Tchr. Eaton Pub. Sch., 1943-47, Zanesville (Ohio) Religious Edn. Coun., 1947-49; dir., tchr. Findlay (Ohio) Religious Edn. Coun., 1949-64; tchr. Findlay Pub. Schs., 1964-65, Consol. Dist. 2, Mo., 1965-83; dir. Christian edn. Unity of Independence, 1983-85. Co-owner Bess's Tea Room, Independence, 1996-98. Author: What is the Church, 1953; editor: Mutant Message Downunder, 1991; contbr. chpt. to book and articles to profl. jours. Program coord. Shepherd's Ctr. of Independence, 1987—, pres., 2000—. Mem. AAUW, Mission Work Area, Edn. Work Area, Raytown Ret. Tchrs. (pres. 1989-90), Delta Kappa Gamma. Meth. Avocations: travel, clown ministry.

GRIMMER, DENNIS L. principal; b. Belleville, Ill., Apr. 23, 1949; s. Paul P. and Margaret C. (Hoercher) G.; m. Mary E. Stolte, Aug. 23, 1969; children: Edwin P., Amy E. BS, So. Ill. U., 1971, MS, 1975, Adminstrv. Cert., 1978. Social studies tchr./coach Berkeley (Mo.) H.S., 1971-73; football/track coach O'Fallon Twp. (Ill.) H.S., 1973-94, social studies tchr., 1973-94, chair dept. social studies, 1978-94, athletic dir., 1993-94, prin., 1994—. Alderman, Ward 1, O'Fallon, 1978-94, mem. planning commn., 1976-78, mem. libr. bd., 1995—. Named Tchr. of the Yr., O'Fallon Twp. H.S. Student Coun., 1981, 85, 86, 87, Social Studies Tchr. of the Yr., So. Ill. U., 1990. Mem. ASCD, Nat. Assn. Secondary Sch. Prins., Ill. Prins. Assn., O'Fallon Sportsman's Club, O'Fallon Booster Club, O'Fallon KC. Roman Catholic. Home: 413 W Madison St O Fallon IL 62269-1180 Office: O'Fallon Township High Sch 600 S Smiley St O Fallon IL 62269-2399 E-mail: grimmer@oths.k12.il.us.

GRIMMET, ALEX J. clergyman, school administrator, elementary and secondary education educator; b. July 17, 1928; s. Alex A. and Edna Mae (Boyd) Grimmet; m. Lois Jean Grimmet, June 24, 1949; children: Larry Bruce, Raven Alexis. AB, Ky. Christian Coll., 1949; MEd, U. Cin., 1964; postgrad. in math., Washburn U., 1967, U. Cin., 1968—69, Georgetown U., 1968. Ordained to ministry Ch. of Christ, 48. Elem. tchr. Highland County schs., Hillsboro, Ohio, 1957—62; tchr. math. Warren County, Morrow, Ohio, 1964—67, Lebanon H.S., Ohio, 1967—85, head dept., 1969—84; student min. Olympia Christian Ch., Owensville, Ky.; min. Choatville Christian Ch., Frankfort, Ky., 1949—51, Evang. Mountains Ky. and W.Va., Pike County, Ky., Mingo County, W.Va., 1951—52, Jefferson and Capella Chs. of Christ near Winston Salem, NC, 1952—57, Danville Ch. of Christ, Hillsboro, Ohio, 1957—62, Loveland (Ohio) Ch. of Christ, 1962—66, Lerado Ch. of Christ, 1966—. Adminstr. Christian Schs. of Greater Cin., 1991—96; chmn. math. curriculum revision com. Lebanon City Schs., 1969—70, 1982—85, chmn. competency based edn. program for math., 1982—85; with IRS, 1986—89; sub. tchr. Cin. Hills Ch. Sch., 1996—. Vol. math. instr. GED program Loveland Lit. Program, 1986—, Adult Literacy Program, 1996; sub. tchr. Cin. Hills Christian Acad., Loveland; precinct exec. Dems. Hamilton County, Loveland, 1980—. Mem.: NEA, Lebanon Tchrs. Assn. (mem. liaison com.), Ohio Coun. Tchrs. Math. (dist. dir. 1981—84, v.p. 1984—87, conv. program chmn. 1986), Ohio Edn. Assn., Kiwanis (sec. local chpt., sec.-treas. 8th Ohio divsn.). Home: 848 Kenmar Dr Loveland OH 45140-2819

GRIMSHAW, JAMES ALBERT, JR., English language educator; b. Kingsville, Tex., Dec. 10, 1940; s. James A. and John Maurine (Haley) G.; m. Glenda Darlene Hargett, June 10, 1961; children: Courtney Anne, James A. IV. BA in English, Tex. Tech. U., 1962, MA in English, 1968; PhD in English, La. State U., 1972. Commd. 2d lt. USAF, 1962, advanced through grades to lt. col., ret., 1983; instr. in English USAF Acad., Colorado Springs, 1968-70, asst. prof., 1970-74, assoc. prof., 1974-80, prof., 1980-83; prof. and dept. head Tex. A&M U. (formerly East Tex. State U.), Commerce, 1983-90, prof., 1990—2003, regent's prof., 1995—2003. Pres. Northeast Tex. Orgn. of Lang. Educators, Commerce, 1984-85, S. Cen. Assn. Depts. English, 1984-85, Tex. Assn. Depts. English, Commerce, 1988-89; chmn. Robert Penn Warren Adv. Group, Bowling Green, Ky., 1990-98; pres. Robert Penn Warren Circle, Durham, N.C., 1991-93. Author: The Flannery O'Connor Companion, 1981, Understanding Robert Penn Warren, 2001; compiler: Robert Penn Warren: A Descriptive Bibliography, 1981; editor: Cleanth Brooks at the United States Air Force Academy, 1980, Robert Penn Warren's A Brother to Dragons, 1983, Time's Glory: Original Essays on Robert Penn Warren, 1986, The Paul Wells Barrus Lectures, 1983-89, 1990, Friends of Their Youth: Cleanth Brooks and Robert Penn Warren, 1993, Cleanth Brooks and Robert Penn Warren: A Literary Correspondence, 1998, (with James A. Perkins) Robert Penn Warren's All the King's Men: Three Stage Rersions, 2000. Mem. vestry Epiphany Episcopal Ch., Commerce, Tex., 1989-91, sr. warden, 95-96. Decorated Bronze Star medal USAF, Vietnam, 1965-66; recipient Disting. Faculty award, Faculty Senate East Tex. State U., Commerce, 1988, 95, East Tex. State U. Honors Prof. of Yr. award, 1993, Tex. Assn. of Coll. Tchrs. Disting. Faculty Tchg. award, 1992-93; named to the Flannery O'Connor Vis. Professorship, Ga. Coll., Milledgeville, 1977, vis. fellow in bibliography, Beinecke Rare Book & Manuscript Libr., Yale U., New Haven, Conn., 1979-80. Mem. Am. Lit. Assn., Nat. Bison Assn., Assn. of Literary Scholars and Critics, Soc. for Study of So. Lit., Bibliog. Soc. U. Va. Avocations: swimming, gardening, cross-country skiing, chess, 5-string banjo, raising bison and peafowl. Home: 248 County Rd 4101 Greenville TX 75401-4799 Office: Tex A&M U-Commerce Dept of Lit & Langs Commerce TX 75429 E-mail: james_grimshaw@tamu-commerce.edu.

GRIMSLEY, BESSIE BELLE GATES, retired special education educator; b. Iola, Kans., Feb. 22, 1938; d. Dwight Leonard and Ruth Bebee (Colwell) Gates; m. Dale Dee Grimsley, Feb. 14, 1959; 1 child, Lendi Lea Grimsley Bland. BS in Edn., Emporia State U., 1962, MS in Edn., 1970. Music tchr., Hamilton, Kans., 1957-58; music tchr. Belle Plaine, Kans., 1958-59; 3rd grade tchr. Johnson, Kans., 1959-61; mid. sch. tchr. Kendall, Kans., 1961-63-68; kindergarten tchr. Alma, Kans., 1968-69; music, reading, phys. edn., math. tchr. Council Grove, Kans., 1969-94; Title I reading and math tchr., 1994-2000. Polit. chmn. USD #417 Tchr.'s Orgn., Council Grove, 1992-94, pres., 1987-89, uniserve rep., 1987-93, sec., 1997-2000; adv. prof. Emporia State U., 2003. Vice chmn. Lyon County Dem. com., 1988-94; mem. planning bd. Americus, Kans. zoning commn., 1985-97; mem. Americus Fall Festival com., parade chmn., 1992-94, 97; pres. WKDC, 1997-98; chmn. Americus Days, 1997-2000. Mem. Americus C. of C. (pres. 1993-95, 97-99), Emporia Antique Auto Club (sec.-treas. 1993-94, pres. 2001-2003), 4-H Alumni, VFW Aux., Am. Legion Aux., Woman's Kans. Day Club (2d v.p. 1994, state pres. 1997-98), Delta Kappa Gamma (pres. 2000-2002). Presbyterian. Avocations: tennis, tap dancing, running, softball, bowling. Home: PO Box 147 Americus KS 66835-0147

GRINAGE, DEBRA L. secondary education educator; d. Samuel and Bertha Rogers; m. Theron E. Grinage; children: Theron Jr., Kindale. BA in Govt. and Pub. Adminstrn., John Jay Coll. Criminal Justic, 1983; MS in Reading, Adelphi U., 1989; profl. diploma ednl. adminstrn., Long Island U., 1992. Cert. tchr., sch. dist. adminstr., sch. adminstr. supervision, N.Y. Various positions Uniondale (NY) H.S., Pub. Sch., South Ozone Park, N.Y., 1985-90; reading specialist Lawrence Road Jr. High Sch., Uniondale, N.Y., 1990—, adminstrv. asst. summer sch., 1992—; interim acting asst. prin. Grand Avenue Sch., No. Parkway Sch., North Baldwin, Uniondale, N.Y., 1992—. Asst. prin. summer sch., 1993; mem. Ctr. for Ednl. Leadership, N.Y.C., 1987-90; coord.-advisor student mediation alternative resolution team Lawrence Road Jr. High Sch., 1990—; adj. Queensboro C.C. Pres. 132-114 Block Assn., South Ozone Park, 1982-86; active Fedn. Laurelton (N.Y.) Block Assn., 1986—; vacation Bible sch. tchr. Bethel Gospel Tabernacle, Jamaica, N.Y. Grantee N.Y. State Edn. Dept., 1987, Diamond Found., 1990. Mem. Nat. Coun. Negro Women, Nassau Reading Coun., Internat. Reading Assn., ASCD, Nat. Assn. Secondary Sch. Prins., Delta Kappa Gamma. Avocations: family activities, church activities, reading, travel. Office: Uniondale HS 50 Lawrence Rd Hempstead NY 11550-7599

GRINARML, SANDI MOLNAR, elementary education educator; b. Tyrone, Pa., Oct. 18, 1950; d. John Francis and Helen (Chalan) Molnar; m. Robert Grinarml, July 20, 1974; children: Jason, Beth Ann. BS in Art Edn., Edinboro U., 1972, BS in Elem. Edn., 1974. Masters equivalency, 1980. Tchr. elem. art Berwick (Pa.) Schs., 1972-74; subs. tchr. Penncrest Schs., Cambridge Springs, Pa., 1974-75, tchr. 5th grade, 1975—. Developer, coord. coach Odyssey of Minds, Cambridge Springs, 1985-90. Leader, program developer Cub Scouts, Cambridge Springs, 1983-88; leader Brownies, Cambridge Springs, 1990-92; chair community beautification project, 1980, repairing Youth Activity Bldgs., 1993; coach Odyssey of the Mind, 1993—. Home: 19531 Skeltontown Rd Cambridge Springs PA 16403-2153

GRINBERG, MEYER STEWART, educational institute executive; b. New Brunswick, N.J., Aug. 31, 1944; s. Allen Lewis and Edith (Bart) G.; children: David, Lee, Benjamin. BA, Franklin and Marshall Coll., 1965; JD, U. Pa., 1968; MBA, George Washington U., 1973. Bar: Pa., U.S. Ct. Claims, U.S. Customs Ct., U.S. Ct. Internat. Trade, U.S. Ct. Mil. Appeals, U.S. Supreme Ct.; CPA, Pa. Tax acct. Arthur Andersen & Co., Pitts., 1973-77; v.p., co-owner Buy-Wise, Inc., Pitts., 1977-91; exec. dir. Jewish Edn. Inst. Pitts., 1991—. Chmn. Maccabi Culture and Edn. com., JCCA. Exec. v.p. Cong. B'nai Israel, Pitts., 1982—; v.p. western Pa. region United Synagogues Am., Pitts., 1984—, mem. nat. adv. bd., 1986—; v.p. Sch. Advanced Studies, Pitts., 1983—; pres. Community Day Sch., 1988—, past v.p.; bd. dirs. Solomon Schechter Nat. Day Sch. Assn.; co-founder Solomon Schechter Day Sch., Pitts.; bd. dirs. Forward-Shady Housing Project, United Synagogue of Conservative Judaism-Israel Affairs Com.; chmn. Pitts. delegation to the Maccabai Games of Israel; mem. Israel Bond Cabinet, Jewish Com. Ctr. (Rogal-Ruslander award, Pitts. 1990), coach Little League; chmn. health and phys. edn. com. Jewish Community Ctr.; gen. chmn. Invitational Maccabi Youth Games, 1989; mem. N.Am. Youth-Maccabar Games Com.; bd. dirs. Hebrew Inst. of Pitts.; mem. wish com. Make-A-Wish Found., Pitts.; chair Nat. Maccabi Culture and Edn. Com. Lt. USCG, 1968-73. Recipient Latterman Vol. Mitzuah award, 1988, JWB New Leadership award, 1990, Rogal-Ruslander Leadership award Jewish Community Ctr., 1990; named Outstanding Citizen of Pitts., Sta. WQEX, Pitts. Post-Gazette, 1989. Mem. Am. Inst. CPA's, Pa. Inst. CPA's, Pa. Bar Assn., Commn. on Jewish Edn. Lodges: Kiwanis. Democrat. Avocations: jogging, photography. Address: Jewish Education Institute 2740 Beechwood Blvd Pittsburgh PA 15217-2521

GRINDER, MARYJO I. elementary education educator; b. New Castle, Pa., Oct. 31, 1955; d. Patsy C. and Mary Jane (Frengel) Iovanella; m. John F. Grinder III, June 30, 1979; 1 child, Melanie Lynne. BS in Elem. edn., spl. Edn., Slippery Rock (Pa.) U., 1977, MEd, 1981. Itinerant tchr. of learning disabled Hampshire County Schs., Romney, W.Va., 1977-78; tchr. of non-publ. sch. spl. svcs. Intermediate Unit 4, Grove City, Pa., 1978-81; spl. edn. tchr. Butler (Pa.) Area Sch. Dist., 1981-91, 4th grade tchr., 1991—2002; lang. support tchr. Ctr. Twp. Elem., 2002—. Mem. gifted adv. com., Butler, 1993-94, strategic planning com., 1995—. Mem. Butler Little Theatre, 1982—, Musical Theatre Guild, 1994—. Mem. NEA, ASCD, Pa. State Edn. Assn., Butler Edn. Assn., GFWC Intermediate League of Butler. Avocations: community theatre, travel, reading, vocal music. Home: 112 Rembrandt Dr Butler PA 16002-7558 Office: Ctr Twp Elem 338 N Washington St Butler PA 16001-5242

GRINDLAY, JONATHAN ELLIS, astrophysics educator; b. Richmond, Va., Nov. 9, 1944; s. John Happer and Elizabeth (Ellis) G.; m. Sandra Kay Smyrski, Oct. 10, 1970; children: Graham Charles, Kathryn Jane. AB, Dartmouth Coll., 1966; MA, Harvard U., 1969, PhD, 1971. Jr. fellow Harvard U., Cambridge, Mass., 1971-74, asst. prof., 1976-81, prof. astronomy, 1981—2001, Paine prof. astronomy, 2001—, chmn. dept. astronomy, 1985—90, 2001—03; astrophysicist Smithsonian Obs., 1974—76. Cons. MIT Lincoln Lab., Bedford, Mass., 1982—; mem. vis. com. astronomy U. Chgo., 1983, Astrophys. Lab. Saclay, France, 1988—, NASA/Goddard Space Flight Ctr., 1995—96; mem. vis. com. dept. physics Columbia U., 1998; chmn. NASA/Goddard Space Flight Ctr., 1997; mem. vis. com. Naval Rsch. Lab., 1998; mem. vis. com. dept. astronomy and space physics Rice U., 1999; mem. users com. Cerro Tololo Interam. Obs., La Serena, Chile, 1981—84; mem. Aspen Ctr. for Physics, Colo., 1991—2001, trustee, 1989—90; chmn. high energy astrophysics mgmt. ops. group NASA, 1986—88; mem. users com. Compton Gamma Ray Obs., 1992—94; chair users com. NASA High Energy Astrophysics Sci. Archive Ctr., 2000—02; mem. space sci. bd. NAS, 1986—89; mem. com. astronomy and astrophysics NRC, 1992—98, mem. com. on internat. programs, 1996—98, mem. high energy astronomy forum space panel, 1998—99; mem. Space Telescope Inst. Coun., 1993—96, 1989—90, Space Telescope Ind. Sci. Rev. Com., 1996—97; chmn. binary panel Space Telescope Cycle 7 Time Allocation Commn.; chmn. space sci. working group AAU, 1990—92; mem. sci. orgn. com. for numerous internat. mtgs. Contbr. articles to profl. jours. and books. Recipient Bart J. Bok prize dept. astronomy Harvard U., 1976; NSF and NASA rsch. grantee, 1978—; Guggenheim fellow, 1991-93, Sloan fellow, 1981-84. Fellow: AAAS, Am. Astron. Soc. (high energy divsn. nat. sec.-treas. 1982—84, councilor 1989—90, nat. v.p. 1994—97, nat. vice chair 2000—01, nat. chair 2002—), Am. Phys. Soc. (chair divsn. astrophysics 1998—99); mem.: Internat. Astron. Union (pres. commn. 6 1991—94, organizing com. 1997—). Home: 195 Lincoln Rd Lincoln MA 01773-4102 Office: Harvard Coll Obs 60 Garden St Cambridge MA 02138-1516 E-mail: josh@cfa.harvard.edu.

GRINE, FLORENCE MAY, secondary education educator; b. Sycamore, Ohio, Apr. 21, 1927; d. Murray J. and Ethel (Kingseed) G. BS, Bowling Green State U., 1949, MEd, 1966. Cert. tchr., Ohio. Bus. tchr. McCutchenville (Ohio) Sch., 1949-51, Fostoria (Ohio) High Sch., 1951-60, Tiffin (Ohio)-Columbian High Sch., 1960-90. Mem. NEA, AAUW, Nat. Bus. Edn. Assn., Ohio Edn. Assn., N.W. Ohio Edn. Assn., Ohio Vocat. Assn., Ohio Bus. Tchrs. Assn., Tiffin Edn. Assn. (pres. 1965-66), Tiffin Bus. and Profl. Women (pres. 1955, 63, Woman of Yr. award 1987), Delta Kappa Gamma (chpt. pres. 1970-72, state pres. 1989-91). Republican. Presbyterian. Avocations: travel, gardening.

GRING, STEPHEN ROBERT, educational administrator; b. Reading, Pa., Jan. 28, 1951; s. Paul R. and Edna (Culp) G.; m. Mary Ann Geise, Nov. 18, 1978. BS in Math. Edn. magna cum laude, Millersville (Pa.) U., 1972; MS in Edn., Temple U., 1975; EdD in Curriculum and Instrn., U. Pa., 1979; postgrad., West Chester (Pa.) U., 1981-83. Cert. math. tchr., secondary prin., supervision curriculum and instrn., Pa. Tchr. math., team leader Penn Manor

Sch. Dist., Millersville, 1972-79; curriculum coord. Phoenixville (Pa.) Area Sch. Dist., 1979-86; asst. supt. schs. Unionville (Pa.)-Chadds Ford Sch. Dist., 1986—. Teaching fellow, supr. student tchrs. U. Pa., Phila., 1976-78; asst. prof. math. Delaware County C.C., Media, Pa., 1982-83. Contbr. articles to profl. publs. Pa. Senatorial scholar U. Pa., 1977-78. Mem. ASCD, Pa. ASCD, Phi Delta Kappa. Avocations: swimming, tennis, piano music. Home: 286 Steeplechase Dr Exton PA 19341-3120 Office: Unionville-Chadds Ford Sch Dist Adminstrv Office 740 Unionville Rd Kennett Square PA 19348-1531

GRINNELL, ALAN DALE, neurobiologist, educator, researcher; b. Mpls., Nov. 11, 1936; s. John Erle and Swanhild Constance (Friswold) G.; m. Verity Rich, Sept. 30, 1962 (div. 1975); m. Feelie Lee, Dec. 23, 1996. BA, Harvard U., 1958, PhD, 1962. Jr. fellow Harvard U., 1959-62; research assoc. biophysics dept. Univ. Coll. London, 1962-64; asst. research zoologist UCLA, 1964-65, from asst. prof. to prof. dept. biology, 1965-78, prof. physiology, 1972—; dir. Jerry Lewis Neuromuscular Research Ctr. UCLA Sch. Medicine, 1978—2003; head Ahmanson Lab. Cellular Neurobiology UCLA Brain Research Inst, 1977—; dir. tng. grant in cellular neurobiology UCLA, 1968—, rsch. assoc. Fowler Mus. Cultural History, 1990—, chmn. dept. physiol. sci., 1997—2001. Author: Calcium and Ion Channel Modulation, 1988, Physiology of Excitable Cells, 1983, Regulation of Muscle Contraction, 1981, Introduction to Nervous Systems, 1977, others; contbr. editorial revs. to profl. jours., pub. houses, fed. granting agys. Guggenheim fellow, 1986; recipient Sr. Scientist award Alexander von Humboldt Stiftung, 1975, 79, Jacob Javits award NIH, 1986. Mem. AAAS (mem.-at-large neurosci. steering group 1998-2002), Muscular Dystrophy Assn. (mem. med. adv. com. L.A. chpt. 1980-92), Soc. for Neurosci. (councilor 1982-86), Am. Physiol. Soc. (mem. neurophysiol. steering com. 1981-84), Soc. Fellow, Phi Beta Kappa, Sigma Xi, others. Avocations: music, anthropology, archaeology, travel. Home: 510 E Rustic Rd Santa Monica CA 90402-1116 Office: UCLA Sch Medicine Dept Physiology Los Angeles CA 90095-0001 E-mail: adg@ucla.edu.

GRINOLS, EARL LEROY, III, economist, educator; b. Bemidji, Minn., May 2, 1951; s. Earl Leroy and Betty Annette (Wolfe) G.; m. Anne Dudley Bradstreet, Feb. 2, 1978; children: Kimberly Anne, Lindsay Elizabeth, Daniel Stephen. BS in Econs., BA in Math. summa cum laude, U. Minn., 1973; PhD in Econs., MIT, 1977. Asst. prof. econs. Cornell U., Ithaca, N.Y., 1977-84; assoc. prof. U. Ill., Champaign, 1984-87, prof., 1988—; sr. economist Coun. of Econ. Advisers, Washington, 1987-88; vis. prof. U. Chgo., 1991. Cons. Dept. Labor, Washington, 1985-86. Author: Uncertainty and the Theory of International Trade, 1987, Microeconomics, 1994. Grad. fellow NSF, 1973-76. Mem. Am. Econ. Assn., Econometric Soc., Assn. Christian Economists, Royal Econ. Soc., Phi Beta Kappa. Home: 1104 Galen Dr Champaign IL 61821-6913 Office: U Ill 1206 S 6th St Champaign IL 61820-6978

GRISÉ, CATHERINE, French educator; b. Toronto, Ont., Can., Apr. 30, 1936; d. Frederick Didace and Mary (D'Aoust) Grisé; m. Cameron Tolton, Aug. 15, 1970; 1 child, Caroline Tolton. B.A., U. Toronto, 1959, M.A., 1960, Ph.D., 1964. Asst prof. French U. Toronto, 1965—70, assoc. prof., 1970—77, prof., 1977—. Author: Cognitive Space and Structures of Deceit in La Fontaine's Contes, 1998, Le Conte en vers gaillard, 2000, Rencontres avec la poésie, 2002; editor: Tristan L'Hermite, Vers Héroiques, 1967, Tristan L'Hermite, Lettres Meslees, 1972; contbr. articles to profl. publs. Mem.: MLA. Roman Catholic. Office: French Dept Univ Toronto St Michaels Coll 81 St Mary St Toronto ON Canada M5S 1J4 E-mail: catherine.grise@utoronto.ca.

GRISH, MARILYN KAY, speech educator; b. Detroit, Jan. 20, 1951; d. George and Olga (Yanowsky) G.; 1 child, Christina Kay. BS, Ea. Mich. U., 1973, MA, 1974; EdD, Nova U., 1985. Speech pathologist Sch. Bd. Broward County, Ft. Lauderdale, Fla., 1974-90, adminstr., 1990—. Instr. Nova Southeastern U., Ft. Lauderdale, 1990—, grant writer, 1992—; adv. bd. mem. Family and Sch. Ctr., Ft. Lauderdale, 1992-94. Supporter Broward Edn. Found., Ft. Lauderdale, 1994—, United Way, Ft. Lauderdale, 1990—, Orthodox Ch. Am., 1974—, Nova Southeastern U. Sch. & Parents Assn., 1994—. Grantee Title II Math. Sci. Project, 1992-93. Mem. Am. Speech and Hearing Assn. (hospitality com. nat. conv. 1994), Fla. ASCD (tech. jour. editor 1992—), Fla. Speech, Lang. and Hearing Assn. (publicity chairperson state conv. 1986). Democrat. Avocations: fitness, tennis, sailing. Office: Nova Southeastern U 3301 College Ave Fort Lauderdale FL 33314-7796

GRISHAM, GEORGE ROBERT, mathematics educator; b. Wheeler, Miss., Nov. 30, 1930; s. George B. and Maggie (Oakley) G.; m. Garnette S. Swinney, May 28, 1955; children: Deborah K. Grisham O'Neal, Jennifer L. Grisham Rochford. BS, Miss. State U., 1952, MEd, 1956. Cert math. tchr., K-14 gen. supervision, Ill.; cert. math. tchr., Tex. Tchr. Streator (Ill.) Twp. High Sch., 1956-68; prof. math. Ill. Cen. Coll., East Peoria, Ill., 1968-86, chmn. dept., 1981-86; tchr. N.E. Ind. Sch. Dist., San Antonio, 1986-87; asst. prof. Bradley U., Peoria, Ill., 1987-92; ret., 1992. Author algebra study guides; editor The Math Connexion, 1972-75. Bd. dirs. Am. Field Svc., Morton, Ill., 1972. With USN, 1952-54, Korea, comdr. USNR, ret. Named Tchr. of Yr., Peoria Savs. and Loan Assn., 1972. Mem. ACLU, Math. Assn. Am., Nat. Coun. Tchrs. Math. (conv. chmn. Peoria 1980), Ill. Coun. Tchrs. Math. (pres. 1976, co-chmn. conv. 1989), Interfaith Alliance, Ill. Math. Assn. C.C.'s (life, pres. 1981), Mil. Officers Assn. (life), Moose, Elks. Democrat. Unitarian Universalist. Avocations: reading, gardening, ballroom dancing, genealogy. Home: 22 Maple Ridge Dr Morton IL 61550-1152 E-mail: gg@insightbb.com.

GRISMORE, ROGER, physics educator, researcher; b. Ann Arbor, Mich., July 12, 1924; s. Grover Cleveland and May Aileen (White) G.; m. Marilynn Ann McNinch, Sept. 15, 1950; 1 child, Carol Ann. BS, U. Mich., 1947, MS, 1948, PhD, 1957; BS in Computer Sci., Coleman Coll., 1979. From asst. to assoc. physicist Argonne (Ill.) Nat. Lab., 1956-62; assoc. prof. physics Lehigh U., Bethlehem, Pa., 1962-67; specialist in physics Scripps Inst. Oceanography, La Jolla, Calif., 1967-71, 75-78; prof. physics Ind. State U., Terre Haute, 1971-74; from mem. staff to sr. scientist JAYCOR, San Diego, 1979-84; lectr. Calif. Poly. State U., San Luis Obispo, 1984-92, rsch. prof., 1992—, lunar sample investigator, 1994—. Contbr. numerous articles to profl. jours. Served as ensign USNR, 1945-46, PTO. Mem. Am. Phys. Soc., Am. Geophys. Union, N.Y. Acad. Scis., Sigma Xi. Achievements include co-discovery of the radioisotope silver-108m in the general marine environment, and development of the technique of radiosilver dating. Home: 535 Cameo Way Arroyo Grande CA 93420-5574 Office: Calif Poly State U Dept Physics San Luis Obispo CA 93407

GRISSOM, ROBERT JESSE, SR., criminal justice educator; b. Little Rock, June 4, 1927; s. Robert Clarence and Eva Snowden (Downs) G.; m. Mildred Louise Cossey, Aug. 29, 1966; children: Robert Jesse, Eva Dawn, Sybile Louise. BS, U. Ctrl. Ark., 1951; MA, Harding U., 1958; EdS, Pittsburg State U., 1972; EdD, U. Fla., 1977, PhD, 1997. Tchr. pub. schs., Ark., 1951-52, 56-60, 1962-68; vocat. rehab. counselor Mo. Dept. Edn., Farmington, 1968-71; tng. officer Fla. Divsn. Youth Svcs., Ocala, 1972-73; state supr. rsch. and planning Ark. Dept. Corrections, Pine Bluff, 1978-79; state dir. corrections data Ala. Dept. Corrections, Montgomery, 1979-80; prof. criminal justice Ctrl. Fla. C.C., Ocala, 1980-87. Cons., rsch. in field. Served with USN, 1952-56. Recipient J. Edgar Hoover commendation, 1954, Nat. Jaycee award, 1980, Ark. Traveler award Gov. Bill Clinton, 1985. Mem. Internat. Platform Assn., Kiwanis Internat., Lions Internat., Alpha Kappa Delta, Alpha Psi Omega, Kappa Delta Pi, Phi Kappa Phi. Home and Office: 720 NE 45th St Ocala FL 34479-1918

GRITTS, GERALD LEE, home health nurse, AIDS care nurse, AIDS educator; b. Tulsa, Okla., May 14, 1956; s. Arlie Lee and Kathleen Joyce (Thomas) G. A in Nursing Sci., Greenville (S.C.) Tech. Coll., 1993. RN, Colo. With Preferred Mobile Nurses, Greeley, Colo., 1993-94; grad. RN Fair Acres Manor, Greeley, Colo., 1993-94, Quality Home Healthcare Svcs., Greeley, Colo., 1994—99, dir. nursing, 1996-99; subacute care coord. Fair Acres Manor, 1999-2000, staff devel., nursing assessment coord., 2000-01; hospice nurse for homecare and inpatient unit Hospice and Palliative Care No. Colo., 2000—. Advisor/cons. HIV services Quality Infusion Services, 1994—99; adj. instr. nursing U. No. Colo., 1996—; adj. instr. death, dying, grief Colo. State U., 1993—. Author: (pamphlets) Losing a Loved One to AIDS, 1994, When Your Partner Has AIDS, 1994; author, co-editor, co-producer: (videos) Tears, Smiles and Remembrances, 1993, Healthcare and AIDS: The PWA, Family, and Medical Professionals, 1996. Co-founder, advisor, media chairperson AIDS Pub. Edn. League, Ft. Collins, Colo., 1994-96; cons. HIV vols.; cons. student HIV svcs. Colo. State U., Ft. Collins, 1993—; vol. HIV patients No. Colo. AIDS Project, Ft. Collins, 1993—, bd. dirs., 1995-2002, sec., 1997—; vol. Parents, Friends of Lesbians and Gays, Denver, 1986—, Friends of the Names Project Quilt, 1994—. Recipient AIDS Health Educator award Straight, But Not Narrow Group, Ft. Collins, 1994, Profls. for AIDS Edn. award AIDS Pub. Edn. League, Ft. Collins, 1994, award of merit Wednesday Noon Moms Group for AIDS Care of Children, Adolescents and Adults, 1995. Mem. Assn. Nurses in AIDS Care, No. Colo. Aids Project (bd. dirs. 1995-2002, mem. speakers bur. 1994—), Grief and Loss Task Force of Weld County. Avocations: outdoors, travel, reading, music. Office: Hospice of No Colo 2726 W 11th St Rd Greeley CO 80634

GRIVNA, DORIS M. elementary education educator; b. Rochester, Pa., Feb. 22, 1947; d. Lloyd F. and D. Emily (Agnew) Miller; m. Drew Grivna, Apr. 20, 1974; children: Marc A., Aaron J. BE, Clarion U., 1969. Tchr. elem. Potter Schs., Monaca, Pa., 1969-72, Ctr. Area Sch., Monaca, 1972—. Residential camp dir. ARC Beaver County, Monaca, 1991-00. Mem. Marion Guild, Beaver, Pa., 1984—, Assn. for Retarded Citizens, Beaver County, 1974—. Mem. NEA, Internat. Reading Assn., Pa. Edn. Assn., Keystone State Reading Coun., Ctr. Area Ednl. Assn., Leotta C. Hawthorne Coun., Am. Camping Assn. Roman Catholic. Avocations: stamping, travel, hockey. Home: 109 Hill Dr Beaver PA 15009-1205 Office: Todd Lane Elem Sch 113 Todd Ln Monaca PA 15061

GROAH, LINDA KAY, nursing administrator, educator; b. Cedar Rapids, Iowa, Oct. 5, 1942; d. Joseph David and Irma Josephine (Zitek) Rozek; m. Patrick Andrew Groah, Mar. 20, 1975; 1 child, Kimberly; stepchildren: Nadine, Maureen, Patrick, Marcus. Diploma, St. Luke's Sch. Nursing, Cedar Rapids, 1963; student, San Francisco City Coll., 1976-77; BA, St. Mary's Coll., Moraga, Calif., 1978; BSN, Calif. State U., 1986; MSN, U. Calif., 1989. Staff nurse to head nurse U. Iowa, 1963-67; clin. supr., dir. oper. and recovery rm. Michael Reese Hosp., Chgo., 1967-73; dir. oper. rms. Med. Ctr. Ctrl. Ga., Macon, 1973-74; dir. oper. and recovery rms. U. Calif. Hosps. and Clinics, San Francisco, 1974-90, asst. dir. hosps. and clinics, 1982-86; v.p. patient care svcs., dir. hosp. ops. Kaiser Found. Hosp., San Francisco, 1990—. Asst. clin. prof. U. Calif. Sch. Nursing, San Francisco, 1975—; cons. to oper. room suprs., to div. ednl. resources and programs Assn. Am. Med. Colls., 1976—; condr. seminars. Author: Perioperative Nursing Practice, 1983, 3d edit., 1996; contbr. articles to project jours. and textbooks; author, prodr. audio-visual presentations; author computer software. Mem. San Francisco C. of C. Fellow Am. Acad. Nursing; mem. ANA (vice chmn. oper. rm. conf. group 1974-76), Assn. Oper. Rm. Nurses (com. on nominations 1979-84, treas. 1985-87, 93-95, bd. dirs. 1991-93, pres.-elect 1995-96, pres. 1996-97, found. bd. trustees 1995-97, pres. found. 1992-95, Excellence award in Preoperative Nursing 1989), Nat. League for Nurses, Ctr. for Study Dem. Instns., San Francisco C. of C. Home: 5 Mateo Dr Belvedere Tiburon CA 94920-1071 Office: 3020 Bridgeway Ste 399 Sausalito CA 94965-2839 E-mail: lindag1005@aol.com.

GROER, CONNIE JEAN, accounting educator; b. Annapolis, Md., Jan. 8, 1957; d. Donald Duncan Daugherty and Doris Irene Bolles Long; m. John L. Groer, Aug. 17, 1984. BS in Acctg., Frostburg (Md.) State U., 1980, MBA, 1982. CPA, Md. Staff acct. Faw, Casson & Co., CPAs, Annapolis, Md., 1982-84; supr. Hammond & Heim, Chartered, Annapolis, 1984-87; vis. lectr. Frostburg State U., 1987-90, asst. prof., chair, 1990-94, assoc. prof. acctg., 1994—, asst. dean Coll. Bus., 2000-01, interim dean Coll. Bus., 2001—03, assoc. dean Coll. Bus., 2003—. VITA Site 212 coord. IRS, Balt., 1988-2003. Mem. Md. Assn. CPAs (Outstanding Md. Acctg. Tchg. award 1993), Am. Acctg. Assn. Republican. Avocations: reading, cross-stitch, gardening. Office: Frostburg State U Guild Center 231 Frostburg MD 21532 E-mail: cgroer@frostburg.edu.

GROFF, CHARLOTTE VIRGINIA, elementary education educator; b. Hinsdale, Ill., Aug. 9, 1932; d. Robert Earle and Virginia Fairchild (Boone) G. BA with hons., Emmanuel Missionary Coll., 1954; MA summa cum laude, Andrews U., 1965, PhD, 1986. Cert. elem educator (permanent), Mich. Elem. educator Coloma Cmty. Schs., Mich., 1956-68, head bldg., 1968-74, reading specialist, 1975—, summer migrant tchr., 1968-85, summer migrant resource tchr., 1986—, tchr. reading recovery, 2001—. Author: (short story) in Youth's Instr. Mag., 1954 (Grand prize 1954), (novel) Glory, Ashes, and Love for Job and Dinah, 2001; editor: (units of study) Coloma Career Units K-6, 1975. Asst. head deaconess Pioneer Meml. Seventh-day Adventist Ch., 1989—. Mem. Mich. Reading Assn., Internat. Reading Assn., Tri County Reading Coun. (past treas.), Alden Kindred of American (life), Colonial Dames SVII Century, Soc. Mayflower Descendants in Mich. (life), Algonquin chpt. DAR (chair Am. History 1974—, three nat. winners, 1992, 93, 99), Phi Delta Kappa, Phi Kappa Phi Hon. Frat. Seventh day Adventist. Avocation: genealogist. Home: 624 N Cass St Berrien Springs MI 49103-1047 Office: Coloma Elem Sch 262 S West St Coloma MI 49038-9511

GROGAN, STANLEY JOSEPH, educational and security consultant; b. N.Y.C., Jan. 14, 1925; s. Stanley Joseph and Marie (Di Giorgio) G.; m. Mary Margaret Skroch, Sept. 20, 1954; 1 child, Mary Maureen. AA, Am. U., 1949, BS, 1950, MA, 1955; grad., Fed. Emergency Mgmt. Agy. Staff Coll., 1970; degree, Indsl. Coll. Armed Forces Air War Coll., 1972; MS, Calif. State Coll., Hayward, 1973; EdD, Nat. Christian U., 1974. Cert. Protection Profl. Personal asst., recruitment asst. CIA, Washington, 1954-56; disting. grad. acad. instr., allied officer course Air Command and Staff Coll., Maxwell AFB, Ala., 1962; asst. prof. air sci. U. Calif., Berkeley, 1963-64, Chabot Coll., 1964-70, Oakland Unified Sch. Dist., 1962-83, Hayward Unified Sch. Dist., 1965-68; instr. ednl. methods, edn. rsch. methods instrn. Nat. Christian U., 1975—, Nat. U. Grad. Studies, Belize, 1975—. Pres. SJG Enterprises, Inc., cons., 1963—; cons. pub. rels., 1963—; bd. dirs. We T.I.P., Inc., 1974. Contbr. articles to profl. jours. and newspapers. Asst. dir. Nat. Ednl. Film Festival, 1971. With AUS, 1945; lt. col. USAFR, 1948-76; col. Calif. State Mil. Res. Decorated Air medal with oak leaf cluster, Korean Svc. medal with four battle stars, Cold War medal; named to Hon. Order Ky. Cols., Commonwealth of Ky., 1970; recipient Air Force Commendation medal (2), UN Svc. medal, citation, Korea, RCVP Korean Vets. Assn. medal, 1994. Fellow: Internat. Inst. Security and Safety Mgmt. (vice chmn., mem. bd. dirs. 2001—, Vet. of Millennium award 2000); mem.: DAV (life), VFW (life), NRA (life), Nat. Def. Exec. Res./FEMA, Am. Soc. Indsl. Security, Res. Officers Assn. (life), Air Force Assn. (life), Night Fighter Assn. (nat. publicity chmn. 1967), Assn. Nat. Def. and Emergency Resources (bd. dirs. 1995—98), Am. Def. Preparedness Assn. (life), Marines Meml. Home: 2585 Moraga Dr Pinole CA 94564-1236

GROLLMAN, SIGMUND SIDNEY, physiology educator; b. Stevensville, Md., Feb. 12, 1923; s. Ellis Phillip and Rachel Naomi (Krystal) G. BS, U. Md., 1947, MS, 1949, PhD, 1952. Cert. biochem. physiology. Teaching asst. U. Md. Zoology Dept., College Park, 1947-49, instr., 1949-51, asst. prof., 1952-55, assoc. prof., 1955-58, prof., 1958-84, chair div. physiology, 1966-73, dir. grad. studies, 1973-83, prof. emeritus, 1984; pres. Sigmund Grollman Ltd., Balt., 1970—. Author: (textbook) The Human Body--Its Structure and Function, 1964, 4th rev. edit., 1984, (manual) Anatomy and Physiology, 1960-84, Experimental Mammilian Physiology, 1971-83; contbr. articles to profl. jours. Sgt. U.S. Army, 1940-43, ETO. Fellow Am. Coll. Sports Medicine; mem. Soc. Exptl. Biology and Medicine, N.Y. Acad. Sci., Sigma Xi. Home: 4001 N Charles St Baltimore MD 21218-1749

GROMOSIAK, PAUL, historian, consultant, writer, science and math educator; b. Niagara Falls, N.Y., Aug. 21, 1942; s. John and Anna (Rimanosky) G. BS in Chemistry, Niagara U., 1964. Chemist Eastman Kodak, Rochester, N.Y., 1965, Durez Plastics div. Occidental, North Tonawanda, N.Y., 1966-68; tchr. Niagara Falls Bd. Edn., 1969-89; author Western N.Y. Wares, Inc., Buffalo, 1990—. Guest lectr. Ctr. of Renewal, Stella Niagara, N.Y., 1991—. Author: Soaring Gulls and Bowing Trees, 1990, Answers to the 100 Most Common Questions About Niagara Falls, 1990, Zany Niagara, 1992, Sensing the Wonders of Niagara, 1994, Water Over the Falls, 1996, Daring Niagara, 1998, Nature's Niagara, 2000, Owahonton, Maid of the Mist, 2002, Goat Island, Niagara's Scenic Retreat, 2003. Vol. historian Schoellkopf Geol. Mus., Niagara Falls, 1984-90. Mem. Old Fort Niagara Assn. (life). Avocations: public speaking, gardening, hiking. Home: 5819 Grauer Rd Niagara Falls NY 14305-1455

GRONICK, PATRICIA ANN JACOBSEN, school system administrator; b. Madison, S.D., May 1, 1930; d. Jay C. and Lauretta (Lynch) Jacobsen; m. Joseph Gronick, Aug. 12, 1950; 1 child, Joseph Patrick Michael. BS, Pa. State U., 1952; MEd, Kent State U., 1970; postgrad., John Carroll U., 1972—. Home economist to dir. regional home econs. West Pa. Power Co., Pitts., 1952-61; dir. nat. home econs. Cleve. Range Co., 1961-70; coord. mktg. edn. Beachwood, Mayfield, Richmond Heights, Orange, Chagrin Falls, West Geauga, Aurora and Solon Sch. Systems, Ohio, 1969—; coord. distributive edn. Mayfield, Richmond Heights, Orange, Bratenahl, and Beachwood Sch. Systems, Ohio, 1970—. Cons. photog. food layouts, 1960-61. Recipient Excel award, 1968-93, Mktg. award Ohio State Dept., 1983, 88, 93 Svc. award, Voc. Ednl. Plannint Dist., Mayfield, 1988, Award for Ednl. Excellence, 1988, VIP award, 1988, Consortium award of Appreciation, 1993. Mem. Cleve. Social Health and Welfare Assn., Am. Home Econs. Assn., AAUW, Elec. Women's Round Table, Internat. Fedn. Univ. Women, Cath. Daus. Am., Home Economists in Bus., Woman's Club (rec. sec. Cleve. 1962, parliamentarian 1965-66), Isabella Guild (officer 1985-89), Delta Kappa Gamma. Home: 880 Haywood Dr Cleveland OH 44121-3404 Office: Beachwood High Sch 25100 Fairmount Blvd Cleveland OH 44122-2299

GRONKA, M(ARTIN) STEVEN, educational association executive, film and television producer; b. Westchester, Pa., Apr. 30, 1952; s. Martin Joseph and Dorothy Elizabeth (Snyder) G. BA in Arts and Scis., U. Del., 1974, MBA, postgrad. in econs., U. Del., 1982; postgrad. in div., Westminster Theol. Sem., 1976. Prodr., dir. Synthetic Imagery, Princeton, N.J., 1987-90, Masterworks Prodns., Newark, Del., 1989—; vice chmn., CEO Found. Against Smoking & Tobacco, Newark, 1988—; exec. dir. Americape, 1988—; chmn., pres. Advance Am. Found., Cape May Court House, N.J., 1989—; U.S. nat. sales rep. Natural Environment Recovery, Inc., Toronto, Ont., Can., 1993—; exec. dir. Americape, 1988—; U.S. nat. sales cons. Earth Care Systems, Inc., Lincoln, Ark., 1993—; v.p. Sail U.S.A. Inc., 1993—. Cons. pub. rels. Cape May (N.J.) Harbor Marine & Resort, 1990-93; bd. dirs. Reggie Brown, Inc., Couture Womens Apparel, Unusual Villas and Islands; chmn., prodr., dir. Hobie 16 Open Nat. Sailing Championships, U.S.A., 1986, Hobie 16 Women's World Championships, 1986; fo-founder, prodr., dir., mgr. 1st all women's sailing team allowed into an all men's sailing event The Hog's Breath 1,000 Internat. Sailing Challenge, 1987; chmn., prodr., dir. Hobie 17 Nat. Sailing Championship, U.S.A., 1988; prodr., dir. largest exhibit of Magna Charta on Am. Express; tour for Bicentennial Commn., 1988; dir. advt. and promotions Domino's World Pizza Record, Wildwood, N.J., 1988; author 1st Rap radio comml. Domino's Pizza World Record Rap, 1988; founder See Kids in Action family of programs, Sea Quest Kids Boat Bldg., Fish Tales Anglers Club, Sea Post Times and Mighty Mates Safety Club, 1998—; pres., bd. dirs. Heartlight Ministries Ch. Without Walls, Children's Outreach for Jesus Christ, 1998—; chief adminstr. Hearts of Fire Christ Fest, Internat. Christian Family Conf., 1997—; founder, adminstr. Latino Migrant Farm Workers MIssions, 1998—; founder See Kids In Action Family of Programs, Sea Quest Kids Boat Bldg., Fish Tales Anglers Club, Sea Post Times, Mighty Mites Safety Club, 1998—. Prodr., art dir. 3-D computer-animated opening Am.'s Cup Opening, 1988; co-prodr. SUSA Cup and TV show, 1993; (music video, film) Please Save Us the World, UN Global Youth Forum, 1992; exec. prodr. (ednl. children's shows) Chessie Kids, Chessie Build a Boat and Water Safety Program, Huckleberry Finn Fishing and Water Safety Program, 1993—, Water Safety Primer, 1994; author rap radio comml. Domino's Pizza World Record Rap, 1988; restorer Civil War Battleship model Merrimack for Valentine Mus., Richmond, Va., 1993; exec. prodr., dir. (video) How to Build a Chessie Boat, 1996. Bd. dirs. Cape May Ctr. Pub. Policy, 1989-97; com. 100 to Honor Law Enforcement Officers, Cape May, 1991; pres., chmn. Advance Am. Found.; dir. TV and video prodn. Faith City Family Ch., 1996-97; bd. dirs., pres. Heartlight Ministries, Children's Outreach for Jesus Christ, 1998—; chief adminstr. Heart of Fire Christ Fest, Internat. Christian Family Conf., 1997—; founder Latino Migrant Farm Workers Missions, 1998—; dir. Boat Bldg. for Spl. Olympics Athletes, Spl. Olympics World Games, 1995, 99—, State of N.J., The Call DC, Youth for Fasting and Prayer for Jesus, Washington, 2000; prodr. Advance Am., Am.'s Cup Campaign, 1984-91. Mem. U. Del. Bus. and Econ. Alumni Assn. (founding 1000), Stone Harbor Hobie Cat Sailors Assn. (commodore), Internat. Platform Assn., Les Ami Du Vin Internation Wine Club (life). Presbyterian. Avocations: sailing, physical fitness, gemology, the arts, horticulture. Home: 6 S Dillwyn Rd Newark DE 19711-5544

GROPPER, DANIEL MICHAEL, college assistant dean, business educator; b. Takoma Park, Md., June 3, 1959; s. Bernard Adolph and Roberta Gropper; m. Sareen Stepnick, July 31, 1982; children: Michelle Lauren, Michael James. BA, U. Md., 1981; MS, Fla. State U., 1985, PhD, 1989. Planning/rsch. economist Fla. Pub. Svc. Com., Tallahassee, 1984; economist Econ. Rsch. Svc. (ERS) Inc., Tallahassee, 1985-88; from instr. to asst. prof. Auburn (Ala.) U., 1988-94, assoc. prof., 1994—, dir. MBA programs, 1995-99, asst. dean, exec. dir. MBA program, 1999—. Cons. Conn. Atty. Gen., Hartford, 1995-96, Sabel & Sabel, LLP, Montgomery, Ala., 1995-96, Ala. Power Co., Birmingham, 1990. Contbr. articles to profl. jours. Recipient Outstanding Prof. award Auburn Panhellenic Coun., 1995; Fed. Home Loan Bank grantee, 1989-90; Richard Weaver fellow Intercoll. Studies, Wilmington, Del., 1985-86. Mem. Assn. Grad. Bus. Dirs. (sec., v.p. 1995-97), Am. Econ. Assn., So. Fin. Assn., Phi Kappa Phi, Beta Gamma Sigma, Mensa. Republican. Avocations: golf, fishing. Office: Auburn U Coll Bus 415 W Magnolia Ste 503 Auburn AL 36849

GROSE, ELINOR RUTH, retired elementary education educator; b. Honolulu, Apr. 23, 1928; d. Dwight Hatsuichi and Edith (Yamamoto) Uyeno; m. George Benedict Grose, Oct. 19, 1951; children: Heidi Diane Hill, Mary Porter, John Tracy, Nina Evangeline. AA, Briarcliff Jr. Coll., 1948; postgrad., Long Beach State U., 1954-55; BS in Edn., Wheelock Coll., Boston, 1956; MA in Edn., Whittier Coll., 1976. Cert. tchr., Mass., N.Y., Calif. Reading tchr. Cumberland Head Sch., Plattsburgh, N.Y., 1968-70; master tchr. Broadoaks Sch., Whittier (Calif.) Coll., 1971; reading tchr. Phelan/Washington Schs., Whittier, 1971-73; elem. tchr. Christian

Sorensen Sch., Whittier, 1977-94, ret., 1994. Cons. Nat. Writing Projet, 1987—, South Basin Writing Project, Long Beach, 1987—; team tchr. first Young Writers' Camp, Long Beach State U., 1988. Author: Primarily Yours, 1987, Angel Orchid Watercolor, 1994. First v.p. Women's League of Physicians Hosp., Plattsburgh, 1970; photo historian of Acad. for Judaic, Christian and Islamic Studies at 6th Assembly World Coun. of Churches, Vancouver 1983, UCLA, 1994—, MIT, 1999—, Abraham Symposium, Istanbul, Turkey, 2000. Named Companion of the Order of Abraham, 1987. Mem. AAUW (assoc. in dialogue 1996—), NEA, Calif. Tchrs. Assn., Whittier Elem. Tchrs. Assn., English Coun. of Long Beach, Acad. Judaic, Christian and Islamic Studies (named companion Order of Abraham 1987), Orange County Soc. Calligraphy. Presbyterian. Avocations: travel, painting, gardening, gym. Home: Museum Heights 171 N Church Ln # 619 Los Angeles CA 90049-2000

GROSECLOSE, WANDA WESTMAN, retired elementary school educator; b. Clarks, Nebr., Oct. 5, 1933; m. B. Clark Groseclose; children: D. Kim, Byron C. Jr., Eric P., A. Glenn. B degree, Brigham Young U., 1976; M in Tchg., St. Mary's Coll., Moraga, Calif., 1981. Cert. tchr., Calif. 5th grade tchr. Brentwood (Calif.) Union Sch. Dist., 1977-97; ret. Art tchr., mentor tchr. Contra Costa County Program of Excellence. Author: American Music in Time, 1992, In the Shadow of Our Ancestors, 2003, The Lees of Southwest Virginia, 2003. Human rels. bd. dirs. City of Livermore, 1968—70. Republican. Mem. Lds Ch. Avocations: oil painting, sewing, gardening, genealogy. Home: 83 Payne Ave Brentwood CA 94513-4701 E-mail: grosclose@ecis.com.

GROSKIN, SHEILA MARIE LESSEN, primary school educator; b. Syracuse, N.Y., Sept. 18, 1946; d. Saul and Juliette (Port) Lessen; m. Lawrence J. Groskin, Nov. 23, 1967; children: Stefanie, Elissa, David. BA, SUNY, Buffalo, 1968, MA, 1971. 3d grade tchr. Maryvale East Elem. Sch., Cheektowaga, N.Y., 1968-71; pre-sch. tchr. ABC Nursery Group, Spring Valley, N.Y., 1972-74; pres., ceo Ambrosia, Tuxedo Park, N.Y., 1979-83; tchr. Monroe (N.Y.) Sch. Dist., 1983-87; 2d grade tchr. Tuxedo Park Sch., 1987—. Pres. bd. edn. Reform Temple of Suffern, N.Y., 1984-94, trustee, 1984-94. Mem. panel of educators assessing sch. accreditation for the N.Y. State Assn. Ind. Schs., 1995, 99. Recipient Reform Temple of Suffern annual award of Appreciation for Commitment, 1990. Mem. Internat. Reading Assn., Orton Dyslexia Soc. Avocations: cross-country skiing, knitting, reading, travel. Office: Tuxedo Park Sch Mountain Farm Rd Tuxedo Park NY 10987

GROS LOUIS, KENNETH RICHARD RUSSELL, humanities educator; b. Nashua, N.H., Dec. 18, 1936; s. Albert W. and Jeannette Evelyn (Richards) Gros L.; m. Dolores K. Winandy, Aug. 28, 1965; children: Amy Katherine, Julie Jeannette. BA, Columbia U., 1959, MA, 1960; PhD (Knapp fellow), U. Wis., 1964. Asst. prof. Ind. U., Bloomington, 1964—67, assoc. prof. English and comparative lit., 1967—73, prof., 1973—, assoc. chmn. comparative lit. dept., 1967—69, assoc. dean arts and scis., 1970—73, chmn. dept. English, 1973—78, dean arts and scis., 1978—80, v.p., 1980—88, chancellor, 1988—2001, v.p. acad. affairs, 1994—2001, trustee prof., 2001—. Bd. dirs. Anthem, Inc.; exec. coun. acad. affairs Nat. Assn. Univ. and Land Grant Colls., 1986-97, bd. dirs. Bd. dirs. Editor Yearbook of Comparative and Gen. Lit., 1968—, Vol. I: Literary Interpretations of Biblical Narratives, 1974, Vol. II, 1982; contbr. articles to profl. jours. Bd. dirs. Assoc. Group, 1983-95, Anthem Blue Cross and Blue Shield, 1995—; mem. Ind. Com. Humanities, chmn., 1980-81; chmn. Com. on Instnl. Coop., 1986-2000; mem. Nat. Commn. on Libr. Preservation and Access, 1986-93; vice chmn., bd. dirs. Ctr. for Rsch. Librs., 1986—, chmn. bd. dirs., 1987-88. Recipient Disting. Teaching award Ind. U., 1970 Mem. MLA, Nat. Coun. Tchrs. English, AAUP, Phi Beta Kappa. Home: 4965 E Heritage Woods Rd Bloomington IN 47401-9313 Office: Ind U Wylie Hall Bloomington IN 47405 E-mail: grosloui@indiana.edu.*

GROSS, ARIELA JULIE, law educator; b. San Francisco, Sept. 22, 1965; d. David Jonathan and Shulamith Pia Gross; m. Jon Edward Goldman, Sept. 2, 1990; children: Raphaela, Sophia. BA, Harvard U., 1987; JD, Stanford U., 1994, PhD, 1996. Bar: Calif. 1995. Acting asst. prof. law Stanford (Calif.) Law Sch., 1996; asst. prof. law U. So. Calif. Law Sch., LA, 1996—98, assoc. prof. law, 1998—2001, prof. law and history, 2001—. Steering com. Ctr. for Law, History & Culture, LA, 1999—; juror Frederick Douglass Book prize Gilder Lehman Ctr., 2002—03. Author: Double Character: Slavery & Mastery in the Antebellum Southern Courtroom, 2000 (Phi Kappa Phi award, 2001); contbr. articles to profl. jours. Grantee Fgn. Lang. Area Studies scholar, US Dept. Edn., 1993; Littleton-Griswold grant, Am. Hist. Assn., 1995, Zumberge Rsch. Innovation grant, U. S.C., 1997—98, Guggenheim fellow, 2003—, Huntington fellow, NEH, 2003—, Burkhardt fellow, Am. Coun. Learned Socs., 2003—. Mem.: Law and Soc. Assn. (Willard Hurst prize com. 1999—), Am. Soc. Legal History (exec. com., bd. dirs., program chair 2001—). Office: Univ SC Law Sch Los Angeles CA 90089 Business E-Mail: agross@law.usc.edu.

GROSS, CATHERINE MARY (KATE GROSS), writer, educator; b. Seattle, Jan. 21, 1931; d. Daniel Bergin Hutchings and Eleanor Paris (Miller) Bold. Student, Northwestern U., Evanston, Ill., 1958; BA, U. Wash., 1962, postgrad, 1984, cert. fiction grad., 1996. Cert. vocat. tchr. Copywriter Pacific Nat. Advt., Seattle, 1963; prodn. coord. Sta KRON-TV, San Francisco, 1963-65, acting program mgr., 1965; chief copywriter, TV and radio producer Teawell-Shoemaker Advt., San Diego, 1966-68; asst. pub. rels. dir. San Diego Zoo, 1968-70; pub. relations dir. Univ. Village, Seattle, 1975-77; pub. rels. dir. Seattle/King County Bd. Realtors, 1978; adj. instr. bus. Seattle Pacific U., 1980-89; instr. ASUW Exptl. Coll., 1980—; instr. humanities Heritage Inst. Antioch U., 1991—; instr. humanities Bellevue C.C., 1992-96; instr. U. Wash. Exptl. Coll., 1985—. Instr. Wonder Sch. Art, 1998; instr. writing by formula Women's Ctr. of U. Wash.; cons. in field. Author: Advertising for a Small Business, 1984, Fund Raising Magic, 1984, Conversations With Writers, 1993, Sunshine the Magician's Rabbit, 1996 (juvenile fiction award Wash. Press Assn. 1996, 2d place best book Rocky Mountain Outdoor Writers 1996, creative nonfiction award Klondike Centennial Anthology 1997); author, pub. Mary, The Mouse and the Coal Mine, 1999; editor: Hiking and Bushwalking in Papua, New Guinea, 1987; tech. editor oceanography and medicine U. Wash., 1974-75; contbr. short stories to Compass and Sea Classics, 1982. Vol. sponsor Big Sisters of Puget Sound, Seattle, 1978-87, Seattle Parks; vol. coordinator World Affairs Council, Seattle, 1986; bd. dirs. Seattle Aquarium, 1985-87. Recipient Non-Fiction Book award Pacific Northwest Writers' Conf., 1979, Juvenile Story award Pacific Northwest Writers' Conf., 1984, Short Story award Fictioneers, 1993, Juv. Fiction award Washington Press Assn., 1997, Writers Digest award for Secrets of the Whispering Waters, 2002. Mem. AAUW (internat. rep. 1988), Seattle Freelance Writers Assn., Wash. Press Assn., Wash. Ornithol. Soc., Rocky Mountain Outdoor Writers, Mountaineers, Issaquah Alps Trails Club, Audubon Soc. Republican. Avocation: hiking. Office: Kate Finegan Books Box 381 117 E Louisa St Seattle WA 98102-3203

GROSS, CHARLES WAYNE, physician, educator; b. Covington, Va., Nov. 9, 1930; s. Charles Calvin and Frances Hattie (Field) G.; m. Catherine McCombs; children: Charles Edward, William Elsworth, Alice Carey, Nicholas Fleming, Catherine Elizabeth. BS, U. Ky., 1953; MD, U. Va., 1961. Diplomate: Am. Bd. Otolaryngology. Instr. Midway (Ky.) Jr. Coll., 1956-57; intern U. Va. Hosp., Charlottesville, 1961-62; surgery resident Buckley (W.Va.) Meml. Hosp., 1962-63; otolaryngology resident Mass. Eye and Ear Infirmary, Boston, 1963-66; teaching fellow, then asst. otolaryngology Harvard Med. Sch., 1966-67; asst. prof. U. Cin. Med. Sch., 1967-68; prof., chmn. dept. otolaryngology and maxillofacial surgery U. Tenn. Med. Sch., 1970-77; chief of staff La Bonhuer Children's Med. Ctr., 1987-89; prof. dept. head and neck surgery and otolaryngology, prof. dept. pediatrics U. Va. Health Sci. Ctr., Charlottesville, 1989—. Past chmn. advisory bd., v.p. Better Hearing Inst.; past pres. bd. regents Hearing Instruments Inst. Contbr. articles to profl. jours. Bd. dirs. The Covenant Sch., 1991—, chmn., 1993-96. Lt. USNR, 1953-56. Mem. AMA (ho. of dels. 1979-83), Am. Acad. Otolaryngology Head and Neck Surgery (pres. 1984), Am. Acad. Facial Plastic and Reconstructive Surgeons (dir., chmn. edn. com. 1975-82), Am. Coll. Surgeons (otolaryngology program rep. trauma com. 1977-83), Memphis Soc. Otolaryngology (pres. 1979-81), Am. Cancer Soc., Am. Coun. Otolaryngology (past nat. mem. chmn.), Triological Soc. (coun. 1984-85, treas. 1989-94, pres. 2000), Am. Soc. Head and Neck Surgery, Am. Laryngol. Assn., Am. Broncho-Esophogeal Assn., Va. Soc. Otolaryngology Head and Neck Surgery, Albermarle Med. Soc., Am. Rhinol. Assn. (bd. dirs., 2d v.p. 1995-96, pres. 2000), Am. Soc. Pediatric Otolaryngologists, U. Va. Med. Alumni Assn. (bd. dirs. 1995-2000, treas. 2003). Home: PO Box 318 Ivy VA 22945-0318 Office: U Va Health Sci Ctr Dept ORL-HNS PO Box 430 Charlottesville VA 22902-0430

GROSS, DOROTHY-ELLEN, library director, dean; b. Buffalo, June 13, 1949; d. William Paul and Elizabeth Grace (Hough) Gross. BA, Westminster Coll., 1971; MLS, Benedictine U., 1975; MDiv, McCormick Theol. Sem., 1975. Jr. cataloger McCormick Theol. Sem., Chgo., 1972-75; head tech. svcs. Barat Coll., Lake Forest, Ill., 1975-79, head libr., 1980-82; dir. coll. libr. North Park Coll. and Theol. Sem., Chgo., 1982-87, dir. coll. and sem. librs., 1987-96, assoc. dean, 1990-96, prof., 1991—. Cons. acad. librs.; spkr. various profl. meetings and confs. Author (with Karsten): From Real Life to Reel Life, 1993; editor: LIBRAS Handbook and Directory, 1982—96; co-editor: North Park Faculty Publs. and Creative Works, 1992; contbr. chpt. in book, articles, book reviews to profl. jours. Dir. rsch. United Way, Chgo., 1996—99; bd. dirs. Eldredge Libr., 2000—. Recipient Melvin R. George award, 1996. Mem.: LIBRAS (pres. 1983—85), ALA, Pvt. Acad. Librs. Ill. (pres. 1981—83, 1994—95, newsletter editor, contbr.), Assn. Coll. and Rsch. Librs. Presbyterian. E-mail: dgross@northpark.edu.

GROSS, FELIKS, writer; b. Cracow, Poland, June 17, 1906; came to U.S., 1941; s. Adolf and Augusta (Alexander) G.; m. Priva Baidaff, July 25, 1937; 1 child, Eva Helena Gross Friedman. LLM, Jagiellonian U., 1930; LLD, Jagiellanian U., 1931. Bar: Poland 1937. Sec., gen. Cen. Ea. European Planning Bd., 1941-45; editor New Europe and World Reconstrn. jour., N.Y.C., 1942-45; prof. sociology and anthropology grad. ctr. Bklyn. Coll., N.Y.C., 1946-77, prof. emeritus, 1977—, resident prof. CUNY grad. ctr., 1988—. Vis. prof. NYU, 1945-68; vis. prof., dir. Inst. Internat. Affairs, U. Wyo., Laramie, summers 1945-52; vis. prof. Woodrow Wilson Sch. Fgn. Affairs, U. Va., Charlottesville, 1951, 54-56, U. Vt., Burlington, 1957; sr. Fulbright sr. lectr. U. Rome, 1957-58, 64-65, 74; lectr. other European, Am. univs.; mem. rsch. coun. Fgn. Policy Rsch. Inst., Phila., 1966—; vis. prof. Columbia U., N.Y.C., 1973; lectr. U. Florence, 1977, Italian Fgn. Office, Rome; cons. Nat. Com. on Causes and Prevention of Violence, 1968. Pres., Taraknath Das Found., N.Y., 1965; hon. pres. CUNY Acad. Humanities and Scis., 1985; co-founder, bd. dirs. Non-Profit Coordinating Com. N.Y., 1984-86. Author: Nomadism, 1936; Polish Worker, 1945; Foreign Policy Analysis, 1954; Seizure of Political Power, 1957; Valori Sociali e Struttura, 1967; World Politics and Tension Areas, 1967; Violence in Politics, 1973; Il Paese, Values and Social Change in an Italian Village, 1974; The Revolutionary Party, 1974; Ethnics in the Borderland, 1979; Ideologies, Goals and Values, 1986; Working Class and Culture (in Polish), 1986, Toleration and Pluralism (in Polish), 1992, European Federation & Confederations, Origin and Visions (in Polish), 1994, The Civic and the Tribal State, 1998, Citizenship and Ethnicity, 1999, The Civic and Tribal State, 1998, others; contbr. numerous articles to profl. jours. Decorated Golden Cross of Phoenix (Greece); Order Polonia Restituta (Poland); Carnegie scholar, Paris, 1931, Pub. Affairs Found. NYU, 1962-63; recipient Ethnic New Yorker award N.Y.C., 1987, Alfred Jurzykowski Price award for scholarship contbn., Polish Nat. Archives award, 1995, award Polish Ministry Culture and Art, 1995, N.Y.C. commendation for serving the Polish-Am. Cmty., 1998; ILO/League of Nations scholar, Geneva, 1930, Carnegie Scholarship, 1931; grantee Sloan Found., 1963, City U. Rsch. Found., 1971-74, NSF, 1972, Rockefeller Found., 1974; Fulbright grantee, 1956-57, 64-65, 74. Fellow Polish Inst Arts and Scis. (pres. E-7 1988-99); mem. Internat. League Rights of Man (dir. 1960-88), Am. Sociol. Assn., Acad. Polit. Sci., N.Y. Acad. Scis., Polish Acad. Scis. (fgn.), Polish Sociology Soc. (hon.), Sigma Xi. Home: 310 W 85th St New York NY 10024-3819 Office: CUNY Acad for Human and Science 365 Fifth Ave New York NY 10016-4309

GROSS, HARRIET P. MARCUS, religious studies and writing educator; b. Pitts., July 15, 1934; d. Joseph William and Rose (Roth) Pincus; children: Sol Benjamin, Devra Lynn. AB magna cum laude, U. Pitts., 1954; cert. in religious tchg., Spertus Coll. of Judaica, Chgo., 1962; MA, U. Tex., Dallas, 1990, postgrad., 1998—. Assoc. editor Jewish Criterion of Pitts., 1955-56; publs. writer B'nai B'rith Vocat. Svc., 1956-57; group leader Jewish Cmty. Ctrs. Met. Chgo., 1958-63; columnist Star Publs., Chicago Heights, Ill., 1964-80; pub. info. specialist Operation ABLE, Chgo., 1980-81; dir. religious sch. Temple Emanu-El, Dallas, 1983-86; freelance writer, 1986—; columnist Dallas Jewish Life Monthly, 1992-96, Dallas Jewish Week, 2000—. Lectr. U. Tex., Dallas, 1994-98; tchr. writing Homewood-Flossmoor (Ill.) Park Dist., Brookhaven Jr. Coll., Dallas; advisor journalism program Prairie State Coll., Chicago Heights, 1978-80; mem. adv. bd. The Creative Woman Quar. Publ., Gov.'s State U., Governors Park, Ill., The Mercury U. Tex., Dallas. Bd. dirs., sec. Family Svc. and Mental Health Ctr. of South Cook County, Ill., 1965-71; active Park Forest (Ill.) Commn. on Human Rels., 1969-80, chmn., 1974-76; bd. dirs. Ill. Theatre Ctr., 1977-80, Jewish Family Svc. of Dallas, 1982-95, Dallas Jewish Hist. Soc., 1995—; mem. Dallas Jewish Edn. Com., 1992-95. Recipient Humanitarian Achievements award Fellowship for Action, 1974, Honor award Anti-Defamation League of B'nai B'rith, 1978, Cmty. Svc. award Dr. Charles E. Gavin Found., 1978, 1st Ann. Leadership award Jewish Family Svc., 1990, Katie award Dallas Press Club, 1995; inducted into Park Forest (Ill.) Hall of Fame, 2000, Tex. Press Women State Writing award, 2003. Mem. Nat. Fedn. Press Women, Tex. Press Women, Ill. Woman's Press Assn. (named Woman of Yr. 1978), Intertel (pres. Gateway Forum of Dallas 1984-85), Nat. Assn. Temple Educators, Mensa, Soc. Profl. Journalists, Dallas Press Club, Nat. Soc. of Newspaper Columnists, Am. Jewish Press Assn., Phi Sigma Sigma. Jewish. Achievements include development of 1st community newspaper action line column, 1966. Office: 8560 Park Ln Apt 23 Dallas TX 75231-6312 E-mail: hgross@utdallas.edu.

GROSS, JONATHAN LIGHT, computer scientist, mathematician, educator; b. Phila., June 11, 1941; s. Nathan K. and Henrietta E. (Light) G.; m. Susan Fay Kodner, Aug. 29, 1976; children: Aaron, Jessica, Joshua, Rena Lea, Alisa Sharon BS, M.I.T., 1964; MA, Dartmouth Coll., 1966, PhD, 1968. Instr. math. Princeton (N.J.) U., 1968-69; asst. prof. math. stats. Columbia U., N.Y.C., 1969-72, assoc. prof., 1973-78, prof. computer sci., math. and stats., 1978—, vice-chmn. dept. computer sci., 1982-89; dir. edn. Ctr. for Advanced Tech., 1989-93. Cons. Russell Sage Found., Inst. Def. Analyses., AT&T Bell Labs., Alfred P. Sloan Found., IBM, Oak Ridge Nat. Lab.; vis. scientist Carnegie-Mellon U., Pitts., 1984-85. Co-author: Fundamental Programming Concepts, 1972, FORTRAN 77 Programming, 1978, Introduction to Computer Programming, 1979, Pascal Programming, 1982, Measuring Culture, 1985, PASCAL, 1984 FORTRAN 77 Fundamentals and Style, 1985, Topological Graph Theory, 1987, WATFIV-S Fundamental Style, 1986, Graph Theory and Its Applications, 1999; editor: Handbook of Discrete and Combinatorial Mathematics, 2000; adv. editor: Columbia U. Press, Jour. Graph Theory, Computers and Electronics, CRC Press; contbr. articles to profl. jours. IBM postdoctoral fellow, 1972-73; Sloan fellow in math., 1973-75; rsch. grantee NSF, Office of Naval Rsch., Exxon Found., ARCO Found., Mellon Found., Russell Sage Found., N.Y. State Sci. and Tech. Found., Citicorp. Mem. Am. Math. Soc., Assn. Computing Machinery, Soc. Indsl. and Applied Math. (sec. discrete math. 1994-96), Jewish Ctr. of Princeton (v.p. 1997-99, pres. 2000—). Jewish. Home: 3 Stuart Ln W Princeton Junction NJ 08550-1844 Office: Columbia U Dept Computer Sci New York NY 10027

GROSS, LILLIAN, psychiatrist, educator; b. N.Y.C., Aug. 18, 1932; m. Harold Ratner, Feb. 4, 1961; children: Sanford Miles, Marcia Ellen. BA, Barnard Coll., 1953; postgrad., U. Lausanne, Switzerland, 1954-56; MD, Duke U., 1959. Diplomate Bd. Pediatrics, Am. Bd. Psychiatry and Neurology, Am. Bd. Child Psychiatry. Intern Kings County Hosp., Bklyn., 1959-60, resident, 1967-70, psychiatrist devel. evaluation clinic, 1970-72; resident Jewish Hosp., Bklyn., 1960-62; physician in charge pediatric psychiat. clinic Greenpoint (N.Y.) Hosp., 1964-67; pvt. practice pvt. practice, Great Neck, N.Y., 1970—. Clin. instr. psychiatry Downstate Med. Ctr., Bklyn., 1970-74, clin. asst. prof., 1974-99; lectr. in psychiatry Columbia U., 1974-99; psychiat. cons. N.Y.C. Bd. Edn., 1972-75, Queens Children's Hosp., 1975-96; mem. med. bd. Saras Ctr., Great Neck, N.Y., 1977—. Child psychiatry fellow Kings County Hosp., 1969-70, pediatric psychiatry fellow, 1962-63. Fellow Am. Acad. Pediatrics, Am. Acad. Child Psychiatry, Am. Psychiat. Assn. (life), N.Y. Soc. Clin. Hypnosis (pres.); mem. AMA, Nassau Pediatric Socs., Soc. Adolscent Psychiatry, N.Y. Coun. Child Psychiatry, Am. Med. Women's Assn. (Nassau, pres. 1985-86, 95-96), N.Y. Med. Socs., Internat. Soc. Study of Multiple Personality and Dissociation (founder, pres. L.I. component study group), Greater Long Island Psychiat. Soc. Home and Office: 55 Blue Bird Dr Great Neck NY 11023-1001 E-mail: drlillian@aol.com.

GROSS, LINDA MARIA, secondary school educator; b. Washington; d. Leroy Raymond Holmes and Williemae Hammond Crenshaw; children: Derek, Michael. BA, U. Md., 1979. Tchr. English and Film Arts Atholton H.S., Columbia, Md., 1979—. Ch. sch. supt. Good Hope United Meth. Ch., Silver Spring, Md., 1990-94, youth coord., 1990-93; vol. Prince Georges County Art Coun., Riverdale, Md., 1994; vol. tutor Oasis Enrichment Ctr. Recipient Cert. of Merit, NAACP, 1990; named Outstanding Tchr., Students of Atholton High Sch., 1990. Avocations: photography, writing poetry and short stories, collecting movie memorabilia, tennis, singing in choir. Home: 979 Saint Michaels Dr Mitchellville MD 20721-1984 Office: Atholton High School 6520 Freetown Rd Columbia MD 21044-4099

GROSS, MELISSA KAY, elementary education educator; b. Red Bud, Ill., Sept. 22, 1957; d. Jackie Bevo and Kay Frances (Siegfried) Bivens; m. William Joseph Gross, June 14, 1980; children: Meredith Kay, Morgan Kristine. BS, McKendree Coll., 1979; MS, So. Ill. U., 1989. Cert. elem. tchr., Ill. Tchr. grade 1 St. Mary's Sch., Chester, Ill., 1979-81; tchr. grades 5, 6 Chester Pub. Schs., 1981-82; tchr., gifted counselor Prarie du Rocher (Ill.) Community Unit, 1982-89; tchr. grade 3 Steeleville (Ill.) Elem. Sch., 1989-91; tchr. grades 5-8 St. John's Luth. Sch., Chester, Ill., 1991-92; ednl. gifted cons. Chester Community Grade Sch., 1992—, 7th grade lang. arts tchrs. Bd. trustees Chester Libr., 1986-91; svc. unit leader, dir. Girls Scouts of U.S., Chester, 1988—; asst. supt. St. John Sunday Sch., Chester, 1990-92. Mem. St. John Parent-Tchr. League, Chester Grade Sch. Parent-Tchr. Soc. (pres. 1994—), Chester Swim Club (v.p. 1991), Delta Kappa Gamma (sec.), Xi Mu Delta Beta Sigma Phi (pres., Woman of Yr. 1984, '86). Republican. Lutheran. Avocations: reading, skiing, sewing. Home: 1212 George St Chester IL 62233-1430 Office: Chester Pub Grade Sch Opdyke St Chester IL 62233

GROSS, MILTON DAVID, internist, educator, nuclear medicine physician; b. Highland Park, Mich., July 19, 1948; s. Samuel David and Rhoda (Gurvis) G.; m. Susan M. Kleiman, July 6, 1971; children: Daniel Stephan, Jennifer Beth. BS, U. Mich., 1970, MD, 1974. Diplomate Am. Bd. Internal Medicine, Am. Bd. Nuclear Medicine. Intern U. Mich. Med. Ctr., 1974-75, resident in internal medicine, 1975-77, fellow in nuclear medicine and endo-metabolism, 1977-80, asst. prof. internal medicine, 1980-84, assoc. prof. internal medicine, 1984-88, prof. internal medicine, 1988—. Chief nuclear med. svcs. Dept. Vets. Affairs Med. Ctr., Ann Arbor, 1980—, dir. nuclear med. svcs., Washington, 1990—. Contbr. numerous articles to profl. jours. and chpts. to books; co-editor: Endocrine Imaging, 1992. Fellow Am. Coll. Internal Medicine, Am. Coll. Nuclear Physicians; mem. Nat. Assn. VA Chiefs Nuclear Medicine (pres. 1988-89). Office: Dept Vets Affairs Med Ctr Nuclear Medicine Svc 115 2215 Fuller Rd Ann Arbor MI 48105-2300

GROSS, THEODORE LAWRENCE, university administrator, author; b. Bklyn., Dec. 4, 1930; s. David and Anna (Weisbrod) G.; m. Selma Bell, Aug. 27, 1955 (dec. 1991); children: Donna, Jonathan; m. Joellen Gross, 2001. BA, U. Maine, 1952; MA, Columbia U., 1957, PhD, 1960. Prof. English CCNY, 1958-78, chmn. dept., 1970-72, assoc. dean and dean humanities, 1972-78, v.p. instl. advancement, 1976-77; provost Capitol Campus, Pa. State U., Middletown, 1979-83; dean Sch. Letters and Sci. SUNY Coll., Purchase, 1983-88; chmn. SUNY-Purchase Westchester Sch. Partnership, 1984-88; pres. Roosevelt U., Chgo., 1988—2002, chancellor, 2002—03. Vis. prof., Fulbright scholar, Nancy, France, 1964-65, 68-69, Dept. State lectr., Nigeria, Israel, Japan, Austria. Author: Albion W. Tourgée, 1964, Thomas Nelson Page, 1967, Hawthorne, Melville, Crane: A Critical Bibliography, 1971, The Heroic Ideal in American Literature, 1971, Academic Turmoil: The Reality and Promise of Open Education, 1980, Partners in Education: How Colleges Can Work with Schools to Improve Teaching and Learning, 1988, Roosevelt University: From Vision to Reality, 2002; also essays, revs.; editor: Fiction, 1967, Dark Symphony: Negro Literature in America, 1968, Representative Men, 1969, A Nation of Nations, 1971, The Literature of American Jews, 1973; gen. editor: Studies in Language and Literature, 1974, America in Literature, 1978. With AUS, 1952-54. Grantee, Rockefeller Found., 1976-77, Am. Coun. Learned Socs. Mem. MLA, PEN, Nat. Coun. Tchrs. of English (chmn. lit. com.), Century Assn., Univ. Club, Chgo. Club. Home: 1100 N Lake Shore Dr Chicago IL 60611-1070 E-mail: tgross@roosevelt.edu.

GROSS ALVAREZ, CYNTHIA MARIE, bilingual education coordinator; b. Aquadilla, P.R., Dec. 30, 1951; d. James Louis and Emma Antonia (Alvarez) G. BS in Edn., Duquesne U., 1973; MEd, Temple U., 1979, EdD, 1983. Tchr. Phila. Bd. Edn., 1973-79, 82-83, 90-91; asst. to dean Fairleigh Dickinson U., Teaneck, N.J.; dir. office bilingual edn. issues N.J. Dept. Higher Edn., Trenton; supr. bilingual program Passaic (N.J.) Bd. Edn.; coord. office edn. for Latino students Phils. Sch. Dist., 1994—. Vis. instr. West Chester (Ohio) U., 1994—, Kean Coll., Union, N.J., 1990—, LaSalle U., 1996; summer program evaluator Migrant Edn., Harrisburg, Pa., 1994—. Apptd. commr. Mayor's Commn. on Latino Affairs, Phila., 1994; apptd. Gov.'s adv. coun. edn. subcom. Bd. Edn., Harrisburg, 1991—; apptd. mem. adv. coun. Hispanic Schs. Fund, Phila., 1994. Mem. ASCD, Nat. Assn. Bilingual Edn., Pa. Assn. Bilingual Edn., Phi Delta Kappa. Democrat. Roman Catholic. Avocations: tennis, reading, piano, dance, art collecting. Office: Phila Sch Dist Office Edn Latino Students 21st And The Pky Rm 607 Philadelphia PA 19103-1031

GROSSENBACHER, KATHERINE ANN, elementary education educator; b. Guantanamo Bay, Cuba, Nov. 20, 1947; (parents Am. citizens); d. John Daniel and Dorothy Helen (Collins) Collins; m. John Joseph Grossenbacher, Apr. 24, 1971; children: Michael Joseph, Heidi Kristin. AA in Liberal Studies with distinction, San Marcos-Palomar Coll., 1988; BS in Edn. with distinction, George Mason U., 1991. Cert. NK-4 collegiate profl. tchr., Va. Adminstrv. asst. CIA, Washington and McLean, Va., 1968-71; tchr. kindergarten Westmore Elem. Sch., Fairfax City, Va., 1991-92; tchr. Kempsville Meadows Elem. Sch., Va. Beach, 1992-94, White Oaks Elem. Sch., Burke, Va., 1994-96. Mem. ASCD, NEA, Assn. for Childhood Edn. Internat., Fairfax Edn. Assn., Golden Key, Alpha Chi, Kappa Delta Pi. Avocations: all genres of children's literature, cooking, travel. Home: care COMSUB Psc 810 Box 16 Fpo AE 09619-0810

GROSSMAN, ALLEN, III, educational administrator; b. Aug. 11, 1943; m. Jane Grossman; children: John, Matt. BS, U. Pa., 1965. V.p. Grossman Paper Co, 1965-75; chmn. bd., 1975-88; regional chief exec. Albert Fisher PLC, 1988-90; CEO, Outdoor Bound USA, Garrison, N.Y., 1991-97. Exec. dir. IK Info. Sys., 1974-80; mem. Businessman's Coun. to create consumer affairs dept. as ind. agy. at cabinet level, 1978; pres. bd. Neighborhood Playhouse Repertory Co., 1980-82; bd. dirs. Search for Common Ground, 1987-88, pres. bd., 1988-91; mem. Am. bd. African Med. and Rsch. Found., Nairobi, Kenya, 1988-90, mem. exec. com., 1990—; mng. ptnr. PARTNERS, 1990-92; treas. South-North Devel. Initiative, 1990—; mem. N.Y.C. Mayor's Vol. Action Coun., 1990-91. Office: South North Development Initiative 866 UN Plz Ste 4016 New York NY 10017*

GROSSMAN, HERSCHEL I. economics educator; b. Phila., Mar. 6, 1939; BA with highest honors, U. Va., 1960; BPhil, U. Oxford, Eng., 1962; PhD, Johns Hopkins U., 1965. Asst. prof. econs. Brown U., Providence, R.I., 1964-69, assoc. prof. econs., 1969-73, prof. econs., 1973—, Merton P. Stoltz prof. social scis., 1980—, chmn. dept. econs., 1982-85, 86-91. Rsch. assoc. Nat. Bur. Econ. Rsch., 1979—; faculty rep. NCAA, 1985-90; vis. scholar Russell Sage Found., 2000-01. Author: Money, Employment and Inflation, 1976, Chinese translation, 1981, Japanese translation, 1982, Italian translation, 1982; mem. editl. bd. European Jour. Polit. Economy, 2000—, Econ. of Governance, 1997—, Jour. Monetary Econs., 1977-83, rev. editor, 1984-91; bd. editors Am. Econ. Rev., 1980-83; contbr. numerous articles to profl. jours. John Simon Guggenheim Meml. Found. fellow, 1979-80; grantee NSF, 1969, 72, 76, 78, 82, 84, U.S. Dept. Labor, 1974, 80, Social Sci. Rsch. Coun., 1982: IRIS scholar, 1991. Office: Brown U Dept Econs Box B Providence RI 02912-9079 E-mail: Herschel_Grossman@Brown.edu.

GROSSMAN, LAWRENCE I. molecular biology educator; b. N.Y.C., Nov. 15, 1939; s. David Morris and Dora (Turkenich) G.; m. Andrea Auerbach (div.); m. Esta Paula Shaftel, Dec. 27, 1970; 1 child, Daniel Alan. BS, CCNY, 1961; PhD, Albert Einstein Coll. Medicine, Bronx, N.Y., 1970. Rsch. fellow in biology Calif. Inst. Tech., Pasadena, 1970-74; asst. prof. biochemistry Wayne State U., Detroit, 1974-78; asst. prof. biology U. Mich., Ann Arbor, 1978-85; sr. editor Sci. Mag., Washington, 1985-86; vis. scientist NIH, Bethesda, Md., 1985-86; assoc. prof. molecular biology and genetics Wayne State U. Sch. Medicine, Detroit, 1986-91, prof., 1991-94; chmn., 1992; assoc. chmn. Wayne State U. Sch. Medicine, Detroit, 1992-94; prof., assoc. dir. Ctr. Molecular Medicine and Genetics, 1994—2003, interim dir., 1993—. Contbg. editor Sci. Mag., 1986-94; assoc. editor Applied and Theoretical Electrophoresis, 1989-93, Mitochondria, 1999—; mem. editl. bd. Biochim. Biophys. Acta, 2000—; consulting editor: McGraw Hill Encyclopedia of Science and Technology, 1989—; contbr. numerous papers and book chpts. on molecular biology. Rsch. grantee NSF, NIH, Muscular Dystrophy Assn. Mem. The Internat. Electrophoresis Soc. (treas. 1989—), Am. Soc. for Biochemistry and Molecular Biology, Sigma Xi. Achievements include research in mitochondrial genes, nuclear-mitochondrial evolution and interaction and molecular biology of ischemic reperfusion injury. Office: Wayne State U Sch Medicine 540 E Canfield St Detroit MI 48201-1928

GROSSMAN, MARY MARGARET, elementary education educator; b. East Cleveland, Ohio, Sept. 26, 1946; d. Frank Anthony and Margaret Mary (Buda) G. Student, Kent State Univ., 1965-67; BS in Elem. Edn. cum laude, Cleveland State Univ., 1971; postgrad, Lake Erie Coll., 1974-77, John Carroll Univ., 1978, 81, 82, 83, 85, Cleveland State Univ., 1985. Cert. elem. sch. tchr. grades 1 to 8, Ohio; cert. data processing, Ohio. Tchr. Cleve. Catholic Diocese, Cleve., Ohio, 1971-72, Willoughby-Eastlake Sch. Dist., Willoughby, Ohio, 1972—. Participant Nat. Econ. Edn. Conf., Richmond, Va., 1995. Eucharistic min. St. Christine's Ch., Euclid, 1988—, mem. parish pastoral coun., 1995-00. Recipient Samuel H. Elliott Econ. Leadership award, 1986-87, Consumer Educator award N.E. Ohio Region, 1986, 1st pl. award for excellence in tchg. Tchrs. in Am. Enterprise, 1984-85, 89-90; Martha Holden Jennings scholar, 1984-85. Mem. NEA, Ohio Edn. Assn. (human rels. award 1986-87, cert. merit 1987-88), N.E. Ohio Edn. Assn. (Positive Tchr. Image award 1988). Roman Catholic. Avocations: racquetball, softball, walking, tennis, bicycling. Home: 944 E 225th St Cleveland OH 44123-3308 Office: McKinley Elem Sch 1200 Lost Nation Rd Willoughby OH 44094-7324

GROSSMAN, PAMELA LYNN, education educator; d. Moses and Verle Anne Grossman; m. David Ezra Kahn; children: Ben Grossman-Kahn, Rebecca Grossman-Kahn, Sarah Grossman-Kahn. BA, Yale U., 1975; MA, U. of Calif., Berkeley, 1981; PhD, Stanford U., 1988. Boeing prof. of tchr. edn. U. of Wash., Seattle, 1996—2000; prof. English Edn. Stanford (Calif.) U., 2000—. Author: The Making of a Teacher: Teacher Knowledge and Teacher Education, 1990 (CEE Richard A. Meade Award for Disting. Rsch. in English Edn., 1991). Fellow Dissertation, The Spencer Found., Postdoctoral. Mem.: Am. Edn. Rsch. Assn. (v.p. divsn. K 2002—). Office: Stanford U Sch of Edn 485 Lasuen Mall Stanford CA 94305

GROTH, IZYDOR PAWEL, agricultural studies educator; s. Antoni and Tekla Groth; m. Zofia Wielgosz, Oct. 10, 1993; children: Mariusz Hubert children: Daniel Artur. Degree in agrl. engring., U. Agr., Olsztyn, Poland, 1959, MS, 1963, DAgr, 1971. Asst. U. Agr., Olsztyn, 1961—71, reader, 1971—2002. Cons. Main Tech. Orgn., Olsztyn, 1971—2002. Author: Cattle Breeding, 1988, Fundamentals of Cattle Breeding, 1998. Mem.: AAAS, Internat. Soc. Food Physicists, Polish Soc. Animal Prodn. Roman Catholic. Avocation: tennis. Office: U Warmia and Mazury Oczapowskiego 5 Olsztyn 10-957 Poland Office Fax: +(48) (089) 5234413. E-mail: groth@uwm.edu.pl.

GROTJAN, ELIZABETH GAYLE, special education educator; b. Marshall, Mo., Feb. 14, 1948; d. Ledru Clarence and Esther Irene (Vogelsmeier) Kothe; children: Scott Edward, Allison Rae. BS in Edn., U. Mo., 1971; postgrad., U. Mo., Kansas City, 1973-74, U. Houston, 1977; MA in Edn., U. S.D., 1985, EdD, 1988. Cert. tchr. elem. edn. and physically handicapped, Mo., Tex.; tchr. elem. edn. with spl. edn. endorsement, S.D. Spl. edn. tchr. Marshall (Mo.) State Sch., 1971, Kansas City (Mo.) Pub. Schs., 1971-75, Houston Ind. Sch. Dist., 1975-83, Vermillion (S.D.) Pub. Schs., 1983-85; instr. edn. U. S.D., Vermillion, 1985-88; asst. prof. edn. Concordia Coll., Seward, Nebr., 1988—97; prof., dean sch. edn. Concordia U., Ann Arbor, Mich., 1997—2002; regional dir. Luth. Spl. Edn. Ministries, Dallas, 2002—. Cons. Seward Pub. Schs., 1991-97, Waverly (Nebr.) Pub. Schs., 1991-92, Plattsmouth (Nebr.) Pub. Schs., 1992-95, Bellwood (Nebr.) Pub. Schs., 1995-97. Editor newsletter Teaching Exceptional Learners in Luth. Schs., 1991-97. Mem. ASCD, Coun. for Exceptional Children (chpt. pres. 1984-85), Learning Disabilities Assn., Phi Delta Kappa (v.p. 1986-87). Office: 6121 E Lovers Ln Dallas TX 75214 E-mail: ggrotjan@luthsped.org.

GROTTANELLI, PAMALA N. nursing administrator, educator; b. Corinth, Miss. d. William Robert and Estelle (Carter) Stewart; m. Richard Grottanelli. ASN, Miss. Univ. Women, 1975, BSN, 1980; MSN, U. Ala., Birmingham, 1983. RN Miss. Asst. dir. staff devel. Golden Triangle Regional Med. Ctr., Columbus, Miss., 1980-81, staff/charge nurse ICU, 1981-82; nursing instr. Auburn U., Montgomery, Ala., 1983-84, La. State U., New Orleans, 1984-85; staff nurse ICU East Jefferson Gen. Hosp., Metairie, La., 1984-85; nursing instr. Itawamba CC, Fulton, Miss., 1985-86, 90-92; varied hourly critical care nurse U. Colo. Health Scis. Ctr., Denver, 1986-87; mgr. nursing systems U. Community Hosp., Tampa, Fla., 1987-89; critical care float Northside Hosp., Atlanta, 1989-90, N.E. Miss. CC, Corinth, 1992-95; nurse educator Valparaiso U., 1995; dir. profl. divsn. Horizon Career Coll., 1995-96; dir. Hope Hospice House, 1998—. Malpractice cons. to various law firms, 1978—; dir. nursing and curriculum devel. GREC, 1996—98; spkr. Miss. Student Nurses Assn., Biloxi, 1991. Affiliate faculty Am. Heart Assn., Miss., 1982—86. Alumnae scholar, Alcorn County MSCW Alumnae, 1973. Mem.: ANA, AACN, Emergency Nurses Assn., Nat. League Nursing, Sigma Theta Tau. Avocations: genealogy, cooking. Home: 7499 Barrancas Ave Bokeelia FL 33922-3808

GROTZINGER, LAUREL ANN, librarian, educator; b. Truman, Minn., Apr. 15, 1935; d. Edward F. and Marian Gertrude (Greeley) G. BA, Carleton Coll., 1957; MS, U. Ill., 1958, PhD, 1964. Instr., asst. libr. Ill. State U., 1958-62; asst. prof. Western Mich. U., Kalamazoo, 1964-66, assoc. prof., 1966-68, prof., 1968—, asst. dir. Sch. Librarianship, 1965-72, chief rsch. officer, 1979-86, interim dir. Sch. Libr. and Info. Sci., 1982-86, dean grad. coll., 1979-92, prof. univ. libr., 1993—. Author: The Power and the Dignity, 1966; mem. editl. bd. Jour. Edn. for Librarianship, 1973-77, Dictionary Am. Libr. Biography, 1975-77, Mich. Academician, 1990—; contbr. articles to profl. jours., books. Trustee Kalamazoo Pub. Libr., 1991-93, v.p., 1991-92, pres., 1992-93; pres. Kalamazoo Bach Festival, 1996-97, bd. dirs. 1992-98, exec. com. 1996-98. Mem. ALA (sec.-treas. Libr. History Round Table 1973-74, vice chmn., chmn-elect 1983-84, chmn. 1984-85, mem.-at-large 1991-93), Spl. Librs. Assn., Assn. Libr. Info. Sci. Edn., Mich. acad. Sci., Arts and Letters (mem.-at-large, exec. com. 1980-86, pres. 1983-85, exec. com. 1990-94, pres. 1991-93, vice chmn. libr./info. scis. 1996-97, chair 1997-98), Internat. Assn. Torch Clubs (v.p. Kalamazoo chpt. 1992-93, pres. 1993-94, exec. com. 1989-95), Soc. Collegiate Journalists, Phi Beta Kappa (pres. S.W. Mich. chpt. 1977-78, sec. 1994-97, pres. 1997-99), Beta Phi Mu, Alpha Beta Alpha, Delta Kappa Gamma (pres. Alpha Psi chpt. 1988-92), Phi Kappa Phi. Home: 2729 Mockingbird Dr Kalamazoo MI 49008-1626 E-mail: grotzinger@wmich.edu.

GROUT, CORAL MAY, school system administrator, consultant; b. Winchendon, Mass., May 2, 1953; d. Charles Edward and Rachel Alberta (Laplante) G. AB, Mt. Holyoke Coll., 1975; MEd, Boston Coll., 1976; EdD, U. Mass., 1990. Tchr. Winchendon Pub. Schs., 1976-85, asst. prin., 1985-86; curriculum coord. Narragansett Regional Sch. Dist., Otter River, Mass., 1986-93; supt. of schs. Winchendon (Mass.) Pub. Schs., 1993-94; asst. supt. of schs. Athol-Royalston Regional Sch. Dist., Athol, Mass., 1994—. Pvt. practice cons., Winchendon, 1990—. Mem. bingo com. Am. Legion, Winchendon, 1979—; chmn. Winchendon Hist. Commn., 1986-89. Named Citizen of the Yr., Colonial Dames 17th Century, 1985. Mem. ASCD, Am. Assn. Sch. Adminstrs., Ctrl. Mass. Curriculum Assn. (treas. 1988-92), Am. Legion Aux. (Mass. pres. 1991-93, vice chmn. nat. exec. com. and nat. edn. 1992-95), DAR (regent Mary Varnum Platts chpt. 1985), Phi Delta Kappa (life). Republican. Roman Catholic. Avocations: vexillology, golf, traveling, voice, crocheting. Home: 464 Central St Winchendon MA 01475-1207 Office: Athol-Royalston Regional Sch Dist 1062 Pleasant St Athol MA 01331

GROVE, GEOFFREY ERIC, emergency medical technician, educator; b. L.A., Aug. 4, 1976; Student, Brandeis U., 1994-98, Harvard U., 1998—2000. Cert. EMT Mass., Calif. Prodn. asst. Am. Sports Radio Network, Colorado Springs, Colo., 1990-91; asst. securities asst. Merrill Lynch, L.A., 1991-94; intern Mass. Gen. Hosp., Boston, 1994—; instr. in ACLS Boston, 1997—. Rschr. infectious disease unit Mass. Gen. Hosp., Boston, 1998; rschr. molecular biology Harvard Inst. Medicine, 1998—; intern Paramount Capital, 2001; rschr. Harvard Inst. of Medicine, 1998—; sr. v.p. world wide mktg. Grove Comms. Co., Mass., 2002—; biotech. cons. Vol. firefighter/EMT L.A. City Fire Dept., 1994-97. Mem.: AAAS, Nat. Kidney Found., Internat. Soc. Nephrology, N.Y. Acad. Scis. Home: 453 Washington St 8A Boston MA 02111

GROVE, MYRNA JEAN, elementary education educator; b. Bryan, Ohio, Oct. 24, 1949; d. Kedric Durward and N. Florence (Stombaugh) G. Student, Bowling Green State U., 1970-71; BA in Edn., Manchester Coll., 1971; postgrad., U. No. Colo., 1974-76, Purdue U., 1977, St. Francis Coll., Ft. Wayne, Ind., 1986, Coll. Mount St. Joseph, Ohio, 1986; MLS, Kent State U., 1999. Cert. elem. tchr., Ohio, 1971, permanent cert., 1999. Tchr. elem. sch. Bryan City Schs., 1972—. Author: Asbestos Cancer: One Man's Experience, 1995, Legacy of One-Room Schools, 1999; editor newspaper column Education Today, 1975-82, newsletter N.W. Ohio Emphasis, 1981-83 (award 1981). Dir., violinist Bryan String Ensemble, 1981—; organist Trinity Episc. Ch., Bryan, 1979-89; active Lancaster Mennonite Hist. Soc., Hans Herr Found.; trustee Bryan Area Cultural Assn., 1984-89; bd. dirs. Williams County Cmty. Concerts; sec. Black Swamp Arts Coun., 2001—. Jennings scholar Martha Holden Jennings Found., Bowling Green State U., 1982-83. Mem. ALA, NEA (Ohio del., state contact 1986-87), Am. Booksellers Assn. (assoc. mem.), Ohio Edn. Assn. (presenter 1984, del. global issues 1986, sec. N.W. Ohio Tchrs. Uniserv. 1975-78), Bus. and Profl. Women Ohio (individual devel. com. 1986-90, speaking skills cert. 1987), Ohio Libr. Coun., Ohioana Libr. Assn., N.W. Ohio Manchester Coll. Alumni Assn. (past pres.), Bryan Edn. Assn. (exec. com., pres. 1985-86), Williams County Geneal. Soc., Williams County Hist. Assn., P. Buckley Moss Soc., Trees of Life (v.p. 1994-2001, region moss docent), Alpha Delta Kappa (pres. 1996-98), Alpha Mu. Avocations: collecting dolls, playing piano, organ and violin, reading, travel.

GROVER-MOORES, MARY LEA, elementary music education educator; b. Natick, Mass., Apr. 18, 1953; d. John Taylor and Mildred Hazel (Main) G.; m. Leslie Raymond Moores, June 24, 1989. MusB cum laude, Lowell (Mass.) State Coll., 1975; cert. Orff-Schulwerk, Lowell State Coll., 1979; MA in Edn., Am. Internat. Coll., Springfield, Mass., 1981; cert. in music therapy, Ball State U. in Vienna, Austria, 1982; cert., Orff-Inst., Salzburg, Austria, 1987. Cert. elem. and secondary music tchr. Tchr. piano, recorder, and children's choir Nantucket (Mass.) Chamber Music Ctr., 1989—; elem. music specialist Nantucket Pub. Schs., 1975—; mem. Orff Ensemble. Mem. NEA, Am. Orff-Schulwerk Assn., New Eng. Orff-Schulwerk Assn. (pres.), Music Educators Nat. Conf. (nat. registered), Mass. Music Educators Assn., Mass. Tchrs. Assn., Nantucket Tchrs. Assn. (treas.). Office: Nantucket Elem Sch 30 Surfside Rd Nantucket MA 02554-2887

GROVES, BERNICE ANN, elementary school educator; b. Bklyn., Feb. 5, 1928; d. Charles and Mary (Silverman) Lichtenstein; m. Stuart Weiss, June 5, 1949 (div. June 1978); children: Joel Weiss, Patricia Weiss Levy; m. Sidney Groves, July 30, 1978 (dec. May 2000). MA, Adelphi U., 1971; MS in Edn., Coll. of New Rochelle, 1975. Cert. adminstr., supr., N.Y. K-6th grade tchr., reading tchr. Ossining (N.Y.) Schs., Byram Hills Schs., Armonk, NY, Bedford (N.Y.) Schs., 1964-84; reading specialist The Hallen Sch., Mamaroneck, NY, 1984-88, coord. testing and curriculum New Rochelle, NY, 1988—2001; ret., 2002. Mgr. nutrition ctr. GNC, Scarsdale, NY, 1981—82; mem. curriculum adv. coun. Lower Westchester BOCES, 1988—2001. Pres. Mineola (N.Y.) Elem. Sch. PTA, 1962-63. Mem. ASCD, Lower Hudson Coun. Adminstrv. Women in Edn., Westchester Reading Coun., Orton Dyslexia Soc., Am. Mensa Ltd. Avocations: tennis, U.S.T.A., gourmet cooking, nutrition.

GROVES, JOHN TAYLOR, III, chemist, educator; b. New Rochelle, N.Y., Mar. 27, 1943; s. John Taylor and Frances (Gaylor) G.; m. Karen Joan Morrison, Apr. 15, 1967; children: Jay, Kevin. BS, M.I.T., 1965; PhD, Columbia U., 1969. Asst. prof. U. Mich., Ann Arbor, 1969-76, assoc. prof., 1976-79, prof. organic chemistry, 1979-85; prof. organic and inorganic chemistry Princeton (N.J.) U., 1985—, chmn. dept. chemistry, 1988-93, Hugh Stott Taylor prof. chemistry, 1991—. Morris S. Kharasch Vis. Prof. U. Chgo., 1993; cons. in field; dir. Mich. Center for Catalytic and Surface Scis., Ann Arbor, 1981-85 Bd. editors: Bioorganic Chemistry, 1984—, Bioorganic and Medicinal Chemistry, 1994—, Bioorganic and Medicinal Chemistry Letters, 1994—; mem. editl. bd.: Reaction Kinetics and Catalysis Letters, 1989—, Jour. of Biol. Inorganic Chemistry, 1995—; contbr. articles to profl. jours.; mem. adv. bd. Inorganic Chemistry, 1995-97. Recipient Phi Lambda Upsilon award for outstanding teaching and leadership, 1978, NSF Extension award, 1990-92. Fellow AAAS, Am. Acad. Arts and Scis.; mem. Am. Chem. Soc. (Arthur C. Cope Scholar award 1991, Alfred Bader award in bio-organic and bioinorganic chemistry 1996), N.Y. Acad. Sci., Sigma Xi. Office: Princeton U Dept Chemistry 203 Hoyt Lab Princeton NJ 08544-0001

GROVES, NORALENE KATHERINE, elementary school educator; b. Tecumseh, Okla., Oct. 14, 1941; d. Lee Edward and Clota Meryl (Bolding) Andrews; m. Douglas M. Stewart, Jan. 27, 1962 (div. May 1975); children: Diana, Kathy, Ginger; m. Glen Wesley, Dec. 19, 1975. BS in elem. edn., East Ctrl. U., 1973, MS in learning disabilities, 1976. Cert. elem. edn. tchr., Okla. Elem. tchr. Centrahoma (Okla.) Sch., 1973-76; spl. edn. tchr. Vanoss Sch., Ada, Okla., 1976-91, elem. tchr., 1991—, chmn. staff devel., 1989-96. Pres., v.p. Ctr. Woman's Aux., Ctr. Free Will Bapt. Ch., Ada, 1986-92, women's tchr., 1987—; study chmn. Dist. Woman's Aux., Ctr. Dist., 1988-90, 94-96, 5th and 6th grade Sunday sch. tchr., 1995—; coord. spelling bee, 1992—. Recipient Controlling Worry award Dale Carnegie Inst., 1991, Dicus' Jan. Tchr. of Month, 1995. Mem. Okla. Edn. Assn., Reading Coun., Delta Kappa Gamma (rsch. com. 1992-93, 2d v.p.). Republican. Avocations: reading, walking, interior decorating, weightlifting. Home: RR 5 Box 87 Ada OK 74820-9310

GROVES, SHARON SUE, elementary education educator; b. Springfield, Mo., Apr. 25, 1944; d. William Orin Jr. and Ruth M. (Jones) Hodge; m. Donald L. Groves, July 20, 1963. BA, Drury Coll., 1966, MEd, 1969. Cert. life elem. tchg.; Psychol. Examiners Cert. Adminstrn. Elem. tchr. Springfield Pub. Schs., 1966-96; asst. instr. individual testing Drury Coll., Springfield, 1969-76; asst. instr. enhancing math. S.W. Mo. State U., Springfield, 1991-94; parent resource educator Springfield Pub. Schs., 1998—. Sr. leader MAP 2000 (Mo. Assessment Project) Class I. Author: Modeling Effective Practices: Geometry and Computation. Active Springfield's Curriculum Coun.; mem. Tchg. Cadre, Strategic Planning Team; hon. life mem. PTA; chmn. adminstrv. coun. Hood United Meth. Ch.; children's coord., math. workshops.; sr. leader Mo. Assessment Project, 1993—. Recipient Extra Mile award, 1989; named Fremont Tchr. of the Yr., 1988, 93. Mem. ASCD, Internat. Reading Assn., Assn. for Childhood Edn., Nat. Coun. Tchrs. Math., Mo. Coun. Tchrs. Math., Mo. State Tchrs. Assn. (pres. S.W. dist. 1994-95, Educator of Yr. 1989), Springfield Edn. Assn. (pres. 1989-90, 93-96, Leader of Yr. 1990, pres. Scholarship corp. 1998-2000), Delta Kappa Gamma (1st v.p., pres. 2000-2002). Home: 8076 W Farm Road 144 Springfield MO 65802-8782

GRSKOVIC, JANICE ANN, special education educator; b. Gary, Ind., Oct. 17, 1952; d. James August and Marian (Thompson) Johnson; m. Jerome D. Grskovic, Aug. 3, 1974; children: Jasmine, Jerome, Jessie. BS, Ind. U., 1974; MS in Spl. Edn., Purdue U., Lafayette, 1990; PhD, Purdue U., 2000. Cert. tchr., Ind. Program dir. Portage (Ind.) Twp. YMCA, 1974-78; tchr. phys. edn. St. Paul Sch., Valparaiso, Ind., 1980-81; tchr. Valparaiso Sch. Corp., 1987-90; itinerant tchr. seriously emotionally handicapped N.W. Ind. Spl. Edn. Coop., 1990-92; prof. spl. edn. Ind. U. N.W., Gary, 1998—. Rschr. in field. Contbr. articles to profl. jours. Mem. Hayes-Leonard PTA, Valparaiso, 1988. Anne Rhodes Rsch. scholar, 1995. Mem.: AAUW, Coun. for Exceptional Children, Assn. Behavior Analysis. Roman Catholic. Avocation: ethnic dance. Home: 2351 Marshall Dr Valparaiso IN 46385-5431

GRUBBS, DONALD RAY, educational director, educator, welder; b. Houston, Tex, Oct. 22, 1947; s. J. W. and Imo Gene (Williams) G.; Glenda Carol Nowell, Nov. 27, 1967; 1 child, Sean Lynn. EdB, Lamar U., 1974, AAS, 1983. Welder Bethlehem Steel, Beaumont, Tex., 1968-73; pipefitter, welder Pipefitters Local 195, Beaumont, 1973-86; regents instr. Lamar U., Beaumont, 1973-87, placement dir. tech. arts, 1986-87; chief instr. Am. Welding Soc., Miami, Fla., 1987—, dir. qualification and cert., 1988-92; welding quality mgr. Base Line Data Inc., Portland, Tex., 1993-95; dir. edn. Am. Welding Soc., Miami, Fla., 1992—; v.p. Guardian NDT, Corpus Christi, Tex., 1995—; edn. dir. Base Line Data, Portland, Tex., 1996-98; sr. insp. Longview Inspection, Tex., 1998—. Cons. in field. Scoutmaster Boy Scouts Am., Beaumont, 1978-86. Served with USMC, 1968-70, Vietnam. Mem. Am. Welding Soc. (chmn. 1983-84, dir. edn. Miami chpt. 1992—), Tex. Jr. Coll. Tchrs. Assn. (chmn. 1980-83), Placement Assn. Tex., Lamar Ex-Students Assn. Democrat. Mem. Christian Ch. (Disciples Of Christ). Avocation: outdoor sports. Home: PMB 498 1137 E 42nd St Odessa TX 79765 Office: Longview Inspection 12410 W Hwy 80E Odessa TX 79765

GRUBE, LINDA LOUISE, elementary education educator; b. Indpls., June 4, 1949; d. Dallas Wilson Carpenter and Olga McKinnon (Blank) Jones; m. Kenneth William Grube, June 10, 1972; children: Amanda Rose, Andrea Rae. BS, Ball State U., 1971, MA, 1974. 1st grade tchr. Mount Vernon Community Schs., Fortville, Ind., 1971—. Grantee Ind. Dept. Edn. Mem. Am. Bus. Women Assn. (sec., treas. 1992-95), Damar Guild (fundraiser co-chair 1992-93), Alpha Delta Kappa (sec. 1991-92, sgt.-at-arms 1993-94). Methodist. Avocations: traveling, antiques, childrens books. Home: 9780 Wild Cherry Ln Indianapolis IN 46280-1866

GRUBER, DONALD DAVID, secondary education educator, graphic artist; b. Decatur, Ill., July 13, 1947; m. Debra Sue Gibson, July 17, 1977; children: Lindsey Ryan Gibson-Gruber, Evan Donald. BFA, Millikin U., Decatur, 1975; MA, U. Ill., Springfield, 1990; EdD, Ill. State U., Normal, 1998. Cert. tchr. art, ednl. adminstr., Ill. Visual arts instr. Decatur Pub. Schs. Dist. 61, 1975-82; tng. supr. Baldwin Assocs., Clinton, Ill., 1982-85; art dir. C. Bendsen Co., Decatur, 1985-88; visual arts instr. Clinton (Ill.) Cmty. Unit Schs. 15, 1988—. Mem. art tchr. edn. adv. bd. Ill. State U., 1994—; owner Design Graphics, Clinton, 1974—; bd. experts Traditional Parent Mag., columnist. Contbr. articles to profl. jours. Sgt. USAF, 1966-70. Mary Packwood grad. scholar, 1992; recipient numerous grants, 1976—. Mem. NEA, ASCD, Nat. Art Edn. Assn., Ill. Art Edn. Assn. (bd. dirs. 1991—, newsletter co-editor, Jr. High Art Tchr. of Yr. 1996), Phi Delta Kappa (pres. chpt. 2002—). Avocations: writing, painting, woodworking, gardening. Office: Clinton Cmty Unit Schs Dist 15 220 N Monroe St Clinton IL 61727-1327

GRUBER, SHARON DORIS, former secondary education educator; b. Buffalo, June 2, 1942; d. Adam Michael and Helen Mary (Donovan) G. BS, SUNY, Geneseo, 1963; MEd in English, Kent State U., 1968; MEd in Adminstrn., Cleve. State U., 1988. Cert. secondary English tchr., Ohio. Tchr. English, John Adams High Sch., Cleve., 1963-65, John F. Kennedy High Sch., Cleve., 1965-93. Democrat. Roman Catholic.

GRUEN, GERALD ELMER, psychologist, educator; b. Granite City, Ill., July 19, 1937; s. Elmer George and Velma Pearl G.; m. Karol Jane Selvidge, Mar. 20, 1960; children— Tami Jane, Christy Lynn. BA, So. Ill. U., 1959; MA, U. Ill., 1963, PhD, 1964. Postdoctoral fellow Heinz Werner Inst. of Developmental Psychology, Clark U. and Worcester (Mass.) State Hosp., 1964-66; asst. prof. dept. psychol. scis. Purdue U., West Lafayette, Ind., 1966-69, assoc. prof., 1969-74, prof., 1974—, head dept. psychol. scis., 1987-97. Author: (with T. Wachs) Early Experience and Human Development; contbr. chpt. to The Structuring of Experience, 1977; contbr. articles to profl. jours. Deacon Calvary Baptist Ch., West Lafayette. Recipient USPHS rsch. awards, 1968-71, Nat. Rsch. Svc. award NIMH, 1976-80, Research award Nat. Insts. Child Health and Human Devel., 1981—; recipient Ind. Psychol. Assn. Gordon Barrows award for disting. career contbns., 2000. Fellow APA, Am. Psychol. Soc. (charter mem.); mem.

Midwestern Psychol. Assn., Soc. for Rsch. in Child Devel., Sigma Xi. Home: 3738 Westlake Ct West Lafayette IN 47906 Office: Purdue U Psychology Dept West Lafayette IN 47907 E-mail: gruen@psych.purdue.edu.

GRUENWALD, BARBARA SAVAGE, secondary school art educator, art coordinator; b. Washington, Nov. 12; d. Robert Arnold and Betty Lois Savage; m. Kirk Rodger Gruenwald, 1 child, Kent Thomas. Student, U. Conn., 1970-73; BFA, Ea. Mich. U., 1976; MPA, Wayne State U., 1984; postgrad.; Ed Specialist in Edn. Leadership, Wayne State U., 1995. Cert. elem. and mid. sch. tchr., cert. tchr. elem. and secondary art; cert. tchr. secondary social scis. and polit. sci. Client cost control coord. Young & Rubicam, Detroit, 1974; layout artist Crowley Milner & Co., Detroit, 1977; tchr. art Grosse Pointe (Mich.) Pub. Sch. System, 1977-87, secondary art dept. chair, 1987—. Ad hoc com. h.s. of future, 1986; Grosse Pointe Pub. Sch. Sys. tchr. rep. Idea Conf., Seattle, 1989; mem. tchr. adv. group, Grosse Pointe, 1985-87; juror Grosse Pointe Artists Assn., 1980, The Art Studio, Detroit, 1992, Art on the Pointe, 1993, 94, mem. h.s. restructuring team, 1993. Artist posters and advt. materials. Mem. Founders' Soc., Detroit Inst. Art; asst. Cub den leader Boy Scouts Am., 1987. Presdl. Mgmt. Internship finalist Office Pers. Mgmt., U.S. Govt., Washington, 1985. Mem. ASCD, AAUW, Mich. Edn. Assn., Delta Kappa Gamm (scholarship chairperson 1994-96). Avocations: reading, painting, travel, textiles, exercise. Office: Grosse Pointe Pub Sch System 11 Grosse Pointe Blvd Grosse Pointe MI 48236-3711

GRUENWALD, RENEE, special education educator; b. Bklyn., Oct. 8, 1948; d. Isidor and Monia (Kaczanowska) Oshinsky; m. Laurence David Gruenwald, June 22, 1969; children: Kate, Sara. BA, Brandeis U., 1969; MA, Kean Coll., 1983. Cert. elem., spl. edn., learning disabilities tchr., cons. supervision and adminstrn. Tchr. Marlboro (Mass.) Pub. Schs., 1969-71, Colegio Anglo-Mexicano, Guadalajara, Mex., 1971-73, So. Orange/Maplewood (N.J.) Pub. Schs., 1981—. Mem. N.J. Edn. Assn. (negotiations cons. 1993-97), South Orange-Maplewood Edn. Assn. (v.p. 1984-86, pres. 1986-88, negotiations chair 1991-94, grievance chair 1994-96, grievance com. 1999—), N.J. Assn. Learning Cons., Kappa Delta Pi. Home: 364 Redmond Rd South Orange NJ 07079-1505 Office: South Orange Middle Sch 70 N Ridgewood Rd South Orange NJ 07079-1518 E-mail: rgru@infioline.net.

GRUFFERMAN, SEYMOUR, medical educator, researcher; b. N.Y.C., Nov. 29, 1937; s. Leo and Claire (Eisdorfer) G.; m. Sue Young Sook Kimm, Dec. 23, 1967. BS, CUNY, 1960; MD, SUNY, Syracuse, 1964; MPH, Harvard U., 1968, MS, 1974, DrPH, 1979. Diplomate Nat. Bd. Med. Examiners, Am. Bd. Pediatrics. Intern U. Ill. Research and Ednl. Hosps., Chgo., 1964-65; resident in pediatrics N.Y. Hosp.-Cornell Med. Ctr., N.Y.C., 1965-67; asst. prof., head Dept. Pub. Health, Gondar (Ethiopia) Pub. Health Coll. Haile Selassie I U., 1971-73; epidemiologist Mgmt. Scis. for Health, Cambridge, Mass., 1973-74; teaching fellow, Dept. Epidemiology Harvard Sch. Pub. Health, Boston, 1975-76; asst. prof. pediatrics Duke U. Med. Ctr., Durham, N.C., 1976-81, assoc. prof., 1981-87, asst. prof. Dept. Medicine, chief Clin. Epidemiol. Div. Dept. Pediatrics, 1984-87; dir. Epidemiology and Biostats. Unit Comprehensive Cancer Ctr. Duke U., 1976-87, dir. Cancer Prevention and Control Program, also exec. com., 1981-87; attending pediatrician Duke U. Hosp., 1976-87; dir. epidemiology study program Sch. Medicine Duke U., 1978-87; prof. dept. epidemiology grad. sch. pub. health U. Pitts., 1987-88; prof., chmn. dept. family medicine and clin. epidemiology U. Pitts. Sch. Medicine, 1988—98; dir. family medicine divsn. Children's Hosp. of Pitts., 1993—98; pres. Univ. Family Practice Assocs., 1994—98; prof. dept. family medicine and clin. epidemiology U. Pitts. Sch. Medicine, 1998—. Adj. assoc. prof. dept. epidemiology Sch. Pub. Health, mem. grad. faculty U. N.C., Chapel Hill, 1982-87; mem. admissions com. Harvard Sch. Pub. Health, 1974-76, search com. for dir. internat. health program, 1975; mem. 3d yr. curriculum com. Sch. Medicine, Duke U., 1976-78; med. records com. Duke U. Med. Ctr., 1977-87, clin. cancer edn. program com., 1978-87, Intergroup Rhabdomyosarcoma Study com., 1978-95; mem. commn. on cancer N.C. Sec. Human Resources, 1979-81; pub. edn. com. N.C. divsn. Am. Cancer Soc., 1984-87, sci. adv. com. on clin. investigations III, 1987-91; mem. sci. com. Nat. Com. on Radiation Protection and Measurements, 1985-89; ad hoc mem. Epidemiology and Disease Control Study Sect. NIH, 1978, chmn. epidemiology and tech. transfer subcom. on AIDS rsch. rev. com., 1987-91; mem. cancer ctr. support rev. com. Nat. Cancer Inst., 1979-83, mem. cancer manpower and tng. subcom., 1997-2003; mem. numerous spl. rev. and ad hoc coms., participant workshops, confs. Nat. Cancer Inst., NIH, reviewers reserve, 1991-95; mem. com. to review health effects in Vietnam vets. of exposure to herbicides Inst. Medicine of Nat. Acad. Scis., 1995-96; cons. Rsch. Triangle Inst., N.C., 1977-78, Burroughs Wellcome Co., 1979-87, Internat. Agy. for Rsch. on Cancer worldwide, 1981-90, tropical disease rsch. program WHO, 1981, Rockfeller Found., 1982, Plough, Inc., Memphis, 1985-93, European Inst. Oncology, Milan, 1993-2000; invited lectr. Assn. Tchrs. Preventive Medicine, 1992, M.D. Anderson Hosp. and Tumor Inst., Houston, 1982, Leukemia Soc. Am., 1984—, Agy. for Toxic Substances and Disease Reporting, 1994—, Johns Hopkins Med. Instns., 2001, 2002, U. N.Mex., 2001-2002, Nat. Cancer Inst., 2000-02, U. Manchester, Eng., 2003; bd. dirs. Tri-State Health Sys., 1996-98; cons. and lectr. in field. Reviewer Jour. Clin. Epidemiology, Jour. Nat. Cancer Inst., Am. Jour. Epidemiology, New Eng. Jour. Medicine, others; editl. bd. Jour. Epidemiology and Biostats., 1995-2001; contbr. articles to profl. jours. Served to maj. USAF, 1968-71. Grantee NIH, 1974-75, 77-79, 77-80, 80-83, 80-85, 83-85, 86-88, 87-93, 88-92, 94—, Dept. HHS, 1989-92, Am. Family Corp., 1980-85, A.W. Mellon Found., 1981-84, 85-87; Individual Rsch. fellow NIH; recipient Preventive Oncology Acad. award Nat. Cancer Inst., 1980-85. Fellow AAAS, Am. Coll. Epidemiology; mem. Am. Assn. Cancer Rsch., Children's Oncology Group, Dandie Dinmont Terrier of Am. Achievements include contributions to knowledge of the epidemiology of Hodgkin's disease, non-Hodgkin's Lymphomo, multiple myeloma, and of childhood cancer. Avocations: raising orchids, collecting decorative arts. Home: 432 Morewood Ave Pittsburgh PA 15213-1814 Office: U Pitts Sch Medicine Dept Family Medicine and Clin Epidemiolo 3518 5th Ave Pittsburgh PA 15261-0001

GRUHL, ANDREA MORRIS, librarian; b. Ponca City, Okla., Dec. 9, 1939; d. Luther Oscar and Hazel Evangeline (Anderson) Morris; m. Werner Mann Gruhl, July 10, 1965; children: Sonja Krista, Diana Krista. BA, Wesleyan Coll., 1961; MLS, U. Md., 1968; postgrad., Johns Hopkins U., 1970-71, U. Md., 1968, 71-73, Oxford U., 1996. Tchr. Broward County, Fla., U.S. Dept. Def. Montgomery County, Md., 1961-66; libr. Prince Georges County (Md.) Pub. Libr., 1966-68, 81-83, U. Md., College Park, 1970-72; art. history rschr. Joseph Alsop, Washington, 1972-74; libr. Howard County Pub. Libr., Columbia, Md., 1969-70, 74-79; European exch. staff Libr. of Congress, Washington, 1982-86; cataloger fed. documents GPO, Washington, 1986-93, supervisory libr., 1993—2001. Women's program adv. com., processing dept. rep. Libr. of Congress, 1983-86, mem. ofcl. Libr. of Congress delegation to Internat. Fedn. Libr. Assn. ann. conf., Munich, 1983, Chgo., 1985; state del. White House Conf. on Librs., 1978, 90. Indexer, editor: Learning Vacations, 3d edit., 1980; editor: Federal Librarian, 1994-99; LCPA Index to Libr. of Congress Info. Bull., 1984. Trustee Howard County (Md.) C.C., 1989-95, Howard County Pub. Libr., Columbia, Md., 1979-87; publ. chmn. LWV Howard County, 1974, bd. dirs., 1996-97, sec., 2002—; bd. dirs. LWV Nat. Capital Area, 2002—; chair Homeland Security Com., 2003—; citizens rep. Howard County, exec. bd. Balt. Regional Planning Coun. Libr. com., 1976-79; Friends of Libr., Howard County, pres., 1976; vol. Nat. Gallery Art Libr., Washington, 1978-80. Mem. ALA (councilor 1997-2001, co-chair coun. caucus 2000-01, fed. libr. round table 1988—, IFLA rep. 1996-2003, v.p. 1997-98, pres. 1998-99, editor 1994-99, govt. documents roundtable 1986—), Libr. Adminstrn. and Mgmt. Assn. (planning and evaluation libr. svcs. 1996-97), D.C. Libr. Assn. (co-chair mgmt. interest group 1996-97, v.p. 2001-02, pres. 2002-03), Assn. Coll. and Rsch. Librs., Internat. Fedn. Libr. Assns. and Instns. (sect. on cataloging, internat. std. bibliographic description/cartographic materials working group 1999-2001), UN Assn. (Nat. Capital area chpt., membership com., Md. telephone chair 1992-94), Art Librs. Soc. N.Am. (coord. mems.' publ. exhbn. 1980-82), Libr. Congress Profl. Assn. (coord. ann. staff art shows 1982-83, chair libr. sci. interest group 1985-87), Libr. Congress Am. Fedn. State County and Mcpl. Employees Union (program chair 1984-86), Md. Libr. Assn. (pres. trustee divsn. 1982-83), Md. Assn. C.C. Trustees (sec. 1991-92, bd. dirs. 1992-93), Md. Assn. C.C. (bd. dirs. 1992-95), Oxford Univ. Soc., Fed. and Armed Forces Librs. Round Table (chmn. constn. and bylaws com. 2001—, Disting. Svc. award 2001), Beta Phi Mu. Democrat. Lutheran. Home: 5990 Jacobs Ladder Columbia MD 21045-3817

GRUNBERG, ROBERT LEON WILLY, nephrologist, educator; b. Bucharest, Romania, July 23, 1940; came to U.S., 1972, naturalized, 1977; s. William A. and Isabelle L. (Rosen) G.; m. Donna M. Fishman, Oct. 19, 1975; children: Wendie I., Andrea B. MD, U. Orleans-Tours, France, 1969. Diplomate Am. Bd. Internal Medicine, Am. Bd. Nephrology; cert. hypertension specialist in clin. hypertension. Intern, then resident in cardiology Vichy (France) Hosp., 1968-72; resident in internal medicine Albert Einstein Med. Ctr., Phila., 1972-74; fellow in nephrology-hypertension Hahnemann Univ. Hosp., Phila., 1974-76, sr. clin. instr. then asst. clin. prof. div. nephrology, 1976; pvt. practice medicine specializing in nephrology Allentown, Pa., 1976—. Attending physician St. Luke's Hosp., Bethlehem, Pa., Lehigh Valley Ctr. (now Lehigh Valley Hosp.), Allentown; attending charge divsn. nephrology Easton (Pa.) Hosp.; courtesy staff Hahnemann Univ. Hosp.; dir. Renal Dialysis Ctr. at Easton (Pa.) Hosp., 1989; chief dialysis Warren Hosp., Phillipsburg, N.J., 1999. Fellow ACP; mem. AMA (Physician's Recognition award 1975, 79, 82, 85, 88, 89-92, 92-95, 95-98, 2001), Pa. Med. Soc., Am. Soc. Nephrology, Am. Soc. Artificial Internal Organs, Internat. Soc. Hypertension, Am. Soc. for Parenteral and Enteral Nutrition, Internat. Soc. for Artificial Organs, Internat. Soc. Nephrology, Assn. for Advancement of Med. Instrumentation, Internat. Soc. for Peritoneal Dialysis, Nat. Kidney Found., N.Y. Acad. Scis. Office: 50 S 18th St Easton PA 18042-3912 also: 401 N 17th St Allentown PA 18104-5034

GRUNDLER, MARY JANE LANG, business education educator; b. Wentworth, Mo., Oct. 26, 1919; d. Charles Fremont and Angeline Rose (Baker) Lang; m. Francis Edward Grundler, Dec. 26, 1963. BS in Edn., U. Mo., 1944, MEd, 1947, EdD, 1960. Tchr. Shiloh Sch., Carthage, Mo., 1940-41, Duenweg (Mo.) Elem. Sch., 1941-42; bus. tchr. Duenweg High Sch., 1942-43, Seneca (Mo.) High Sch., 1943-45, Lindenwood Coll., St. Charles, Mo., 1945-47; instr. bus. tchr. edn. U. Mo., Columbia, 1947-60, asst. prof., 1960-67, assoc. prof., 1967-76, prof., 1976-85, prof. emeritus, 1985—. Coord. bus. edn. Coll. Edn. U. Mo., Columbia, 1968-80. Contbr. articles to profl. bus. edn. jours. and yearbooks. Bd. dirs. Koinonia House, Columbia, 1988—. Recipient Disting. Svc. award U. Mo. Alumni Assn., 1986, Outstanding Alumnus award Mo. So. State Coll., Joplin, 1988. Mem. AAUW (state treas. 1988-90), Am. Vocat. Assn. (Outstanding Svc. cert. Divsn. Bus. Edn. 1980), Nat. Assn. Tchr. Educators Bus. Edn. (Recognition award 1984), Nat. Bus. Edn. Assn., Ret. Tchrs. Assn. Mo. (newsletter editor 1988-90), Mo. State Tchrs. Assn., Mo. Vocat. Assn., Mo. Bus. Edn. Assn. (Outstanding Bus. Educator 1979, Disting. Svc. award 1985, past pres., v.p., sec., charter inductee Who's Who in Mo., Bus. Edn. 1992), U. Mo. Alumni Assn. (life, sec. bd. dirs. 1972-86, historian 1994—), Pi Lambda Theta (sponsor Alpha chpt. 1989—, mem. nat. nominating com. 1992-93), Delta Kappa Gamma. Roman Catholic. Avocations: reading, music. Home: 106 E Stewart Rd Columbia MO 65203-4206

GRUNER, GEORGE RICHARD, retired secondary education educator; b. Springfield, Mo., Apr. 6, 1940; s. George Fredrick and Elsie Rachel (Souders) G.; m. Grayce Anne Hartman, Mar. 29, 1957 (div. June 1977); children: Mark Randall, Stephen Eric; m. Rita Marie Torres, May 31, 1982; children: Gregory Lee, Dawn Marie. BA in History, Lincoln U. of Mo., 1961; tchg. credentials, U. Puget Sound, 1965; MS in Edn., Calif. State U., Fullerton, 1972; postgrad., U.S. Army War Coll., Carlisle, Pa., 1986. Cert. tchr. Calif. History tchr. Huntington Beach (Calif.) High Sch., 1965-69; tchr., coord. for gifted/talented edn. Edison High Sch., Huntington Beach, 1969-81, English tchr., 1983-90, chmn. English dept., 1991-98, chmn. site restructuring com., 1992-97, cross-curricular integration mentor, 1993-95; commandant Calif. Mil. Acad., Sacramento, Calif., 1986-90; dep. dir. Nat. Interagy. Counterdrug Inst., San Luis Obispo, Calif., 1991; lectr., student tchr. supr. Calif. Poly. State U., San Luis Obispo, 2001—. Acad. bd. dirs. Calif. Mil. Acad., Sacramento, 1986-91; mem., nat. rep. State Mil. Acad. Adv. Coun., Region VII, Calif., Nev., Utah, Ariz., Hawaii, 1986-90; cons. Calif. Army Nat. Guard, L.A., 1992—; mem. Orange County Vital Link Assessment Com., 1993-98; adminstrv. coord. Ctr. for Internat. Bus. and Comm. Studies, 1994-99. Contbr. articles to regional and nat. jours., author publs. in field. Exec. bd. PTA Edison High Sch., 1971-75; adult leader, cubmaster Boy Scouts Am., Huntington Beach, 1967-74; mem. Huntington Beach Dist. Tech. Coun., 1994-95, Action Planning Com., 1993-95; steering com. CIBACS Found., 1995-99; dir. Ret. and Sr. Vols. Program, San Luis Obispo County, 2001—; exec. dir. Lifespan Found. for Human Svcs., 2003; bd. dirs. Camp Roberts Mil. Mus.; commr. at large San Luis Obispo County Commn. on Aging, 2003—; adv. coun. Ctrl. Coast Commn. Sr. Citizens. Col. U.S. Army, 1962-92. Decorated Legion of Merit, Order of Calif., 1992; grantee AST Rsch. Corp., 1993, Calif. Dept. Edn., 1994-98; recipient Hon. Svc. award Calif. Congress of Parents, Tchrs. and Students, 1995. Mem. AARP (cmty. presence team), Dist. Educators Assn. (faculty rep.), Calif. Tchrs. Assn., NEA, Nat. Coun. Tchrs. English, Nat. Guard Assn. U.S. and Calif., Am. Legion, Mil. Officers Assn. Am. (sec. Ctrl. Coast chpt.), So. Calif. RSVP Dirs. Assn., Calif. Ret. Tchrs. Assn. (exec. bd. divsn. 86), Lions Club, Audubon Soc., Nature Conservancy. Avocations: hiking, camping, nature study. Home: 1535 Via Arroyo Paso Robles CA 93446 E-mail: rgruner@tcsn.net.

GRUNERT, DAVID LLOYD, school administrator; b. Vancouver, B.C., Can., Oct. 1, 1949; s. Wilfred Erwin Leslie and Phyllis Helen (Toews) G.; m. Cynthia A. McManus, Mar. 21, 1981; children: Joh, Michaela, Timothy. BA, Master's Coll., 1971; MDiv, L.A. Bapt. Theol. Sem., 1974; postgrad., U. Calif., Berkeley, 1975-77, Oreg. State U., 1984-86. Tchr. Berean Christian High Sch., Walnut Creek, Calif., 1974-77, Albany (Oreg.) Christian Sch., 1977-87, Apple Valley (Calif.) Christian Sch., 1987-88, tchr./prin., 1988-90, prin., 1990-91, adminstr., 1991—. Mem. ASCD, Nat. Geog. Soc., Internat. Fellowship of Christian Sch. Adminstrs., High Desert Prins. Roundtable. Office: Apple Valley Christian Sch 22434 Nisqually Rd Apple Valley CA 92308-6577

GRYDE, CAROL JOAN, occupational therapy educator, administrator; b. Walsh County, N.D., July 9, 1940; d. Edwin Gryde and Myrtle Christopherson. BS, San Jose State U., 1963; MA, Columbia U., 1975; postgrad., U. Memphis, 1989—. Supr. occupational therapy Conn. Mental Health Ctr., New Haven, 1968-69; chief occupational therapy Fordham Hosp., Bronx, N.Y., 1969-73, Jacobi Hosp.-Albert Einstein, Bronx, 1973-76; asst. prof. occupational therapy U. N.H., Durham, 1976-81; exec. Ctr. for the Study of Sensory Integrative Dysfunction, Pasadena, Calif., 1981-84; dir. occupational therapy Burke Rehab. Ctr., White Plains, N.Y., 1984-86; cons., sr. therapist St. Agnes Hosp. Rehab. Ctr., White Plains, 1986-88; asst. prof. program in occupational therapy U. Tenn., Memphis, 1988-99, interim chair dept. occupational therapy, 1993-95; pvt. practice Memphis, 1999-2001. Cons. summer sch. program Bd. Coop. Ednl. Svcs., White Plains, 1986; cons. Bronx Devel. Svcs., 1973-76; presenter occupl. therapy confs., state, regional, nat. and internat. locations. Chair screening com. Memphis Works program United Cerebral Palsy, Memphis, 1991-2000. Named Outstanding Vol., UCP Nat., 1999 Mem. Am. Occupl. Therapy Assn. (rep. 1986-88, alt. rep. 1991-95, apptd. individual disability act-idea, Cadre, Aota, 2000—, liaison to world Occupl. Therapy Assn. 1997-2001, registered and cert.), Tenn. Occupational Therapy Assn. (award of recognition 1994, award for leadership 1996, award for rsch. 1998), Sensory Integration Internat. (cert.), Alpha Eta, Kappa Delta Pi. Office: Pacific Univ Occupl Therapy 2043 College Way Forest Grove OR 97116 E-mail: cjgryde@aol.com.

GU, KEQIN, mechanical engineering educator; b. Lanxi, China, Nov. 23, 1957; came to U.S., 1985; s. Lijian Gu and Jieping Jiang; m. Xinxin Zhu, Apr. 20, 1985; children: Siyao, Patrick. BS, Zhejiang U., 1982, MS, 1985; PhD, Ga. Tech. Inst., 1988. Instr. Zhejiang U., China, 1985; rsch. asst. Ga. Tech. Inst., Atlanta, 1985-88; rsch. assoc. Oakland U., Rochester, Mich., 1989-90; from asst. prof. to prof. So. Ill. U., Edwardsville, 1990—, grad. program dir., 1998—2002, acting chair, 2003—. Faculty advisor Siue Me Club, Edwardsville, 1990-91; co-organizer NSF-CNRS Workshop on Advances in Time-delay Systems, 2003; program com. mem. Conf. on Decision and Control, 2001-03. Contbr. articles to profl. jours.; assoc. editor IEEE Transactions on Automatic Control, 2000-02; program editor IFAC Workshop on Time-delay Systems, 2001. Mem. IEEE, ASME, Am. Soc. Engrng. Edn., Control Sys. Soc. (conf. assoc. editor 1995-99). Achievements include research in time-delay systems, robust control theory, robotics, nonlinear dynamics. Office: So Ill U Dept ME/IE Edwardsville IL 62026

GUADAGNO, MARY ANN NOECKER, social scientist, consultant; b. Springville, N.Y., Sept. 21, 1952; d. Francis Casimer and Josephine Lucille (Fricano) Noecker; m. Robert George Guadagno, Aug. 29, 1970 (div. Mar. 1981). BS in Edn. cum laude, SUNY, Buffalo, 1974; MS, Ohio State U., 1977, PhD, 1978. Grad. teaching assoc. Ohio State U., Columbus, 1974-77, grad. rsch. assoc., 1977-78; asst. prof. U. Minn., St. Paul, 1978-83; cons. Nationwide Ins. Co., Columbus, 1982-83, rsch. assoc. Corp. Rsch., 1983-86, product devel. assoc., Office of Mktg., 1986-89; adjunct prof. Coll. Bus. & Pub. Adminstrn. Franklin U., Columbus, Ohio, 1985-89; lectr. Coll. Bus. Adminstrn. and Econ. Ohio Dominican Coll., Columbus, 1986-89; scientist family econ. rsch. group USDA, Washington, 1989-93; survey statistician Nat. Ctr. for Health Stats., HHS, Washington, 1993—. Chair Women's Coun., DHHS, Hyattsville, Md., 1993-96; mem. women in sci., 1991-93; health scientist adminstr. Nat Inst. Health, Nat. Inst. Aging DDHS, Washington. Author: Family Inventory of Money Management, 1982, Family Inventory, 1982; contbr. articles to profl. jours., 1978—. Com. mem. United Way, Mkt. Rsch. Info. Exchange, Columbus, Ohio. Recipient Spl. Recognition award Ohio House Reps., 1987, Cert. Grad. award Columbus Area Leadership Program, 1987, Cert. Appreciation award Am. Mktg. Assn., 1987, Cert. Merit award U.S. Dept. Agr., 1991. Mem. Columbus Area Leadership Program, Ohio State U. Coll. Human Ecology Alumni. Republican. Roman Catholic. Avocations: horseback riding, classical music, eastern philosophy, gardening. Home: 4853 Cordell Ave Apt 921 Bethesda MD 20814-3024 Office: Nat Inst Health Ctr for Sci Rev 6701 Rockledge Dr Bethesda MD 20817 E-mail: guadagma@csr.nih.gov.

GUAJARDO, ELISA, counselor, educator; b. Roswell, N. Mex., Nov. 13, 1932; d. Alejo Najar and Hortensia (Jiminez) Garcia; m. David Roberto Guajardo, Oct. 15, 1950; 1 child, Elsie Edith. BS, Our Lady of the Lake U., 1962, MEd, 1971; MA, Chapman U., 1977. Cert. tchr., adminstr., counselor, Calif. Elem. tchr. San Antonio (Tex.) Sch. Dist., 1962-63; tchr. social sci. Newport Mesa Sch. Dist., Costa Mesa, Calif., 1963-67, Orange (Calif.) Unified Sch. Dist., 1967-70, project dir., 1970-71, tchr. English, 1972-73, counselor, 1973—. Pres. Bilingual, Bicultural Parent Adv. Bd., Orange, Calif., 1971-72; reader bilingual projects Calif. State Dept. Edn., Orange, 1971-72; vis. lectr. We. Wash. Univ., Bellingham, 1972-73; mem. curriculum and placement couns., Orange Unified Sch. Dist., 1973-78, 95-96. Author: (Able)Adaptations of Bilingual/Bicultural Edn, Fed. Project Proposal. Mem. NEA, AAUW, Calif. Tchrs. Assn., Orange Unified Edn. Assn, Hon., Alpha Chi, Our Lady of Lake U., Tex. chpt. Democrat. Mem. Assemblies of God Church. Avocations: choir and solo singing, piano, marimba, organ. Home: 335 E Jackson Ave Orange CA 92867-5743 Office: Canyon HS 220 S Imperial Hwy Anaheim CA 92807-3945 E-mail: davielisa2@juno.com.

GUARD, PATRICIA J. federal agency administrator; b. Lafayette, Ind., June 9, 1948; BS, MS, Purdue U. Therapist speech, lang. and hearing Logansport Area Joint Spl. Svcs. Coop., 1974-76, supr. speech dept., 1976-78; dir. spl. edn. Boone-Clinton-NW Hendricks Count Joint Svcs. Spl. Edn. Coop., 1978-81; rsch. asst. U.S. Ho. of Reps., 1981-82; legis. specialist Office Legis. and Pub. Affairs, 1983-84; acting dir. Office Spl. Edn. Programs Dept. Edn., 1985-86, deputy dir. Office Spl. Edn. Programs, 1984-85, 86-87, sr. legis. analyst Office Legis. and Pub. Affairs, 1987-90, dir. policy and planning staff Office Spl. Edn. and Rehabilitative Svcs., 1990-92, dep. dir. Office Spl. Edn., 1992-93, acting dir. Office Spl. Edn. Programs, 1993-94; mem. sr. exec. svc. Office Edn. Programs, Washington, 1994—. Vice chmn., trustee Arlington Cmty. Residence, Inc., 1993, bd. dirs., 1989—. Fellow Inst. Ednl. Leadership, 1981; recipient Disting. Alumni award Purdue U., 1989, Mentor award Dept. Edn., 1994. Office: Spl Edn Programs 330 C St SW Washington DC 20201-0001

GUARINO, ANTHONY MICHAEL, pharmacologist, educator, consultant, counselor; b. Framingham, Mass., Dec. 11, 1934; s. Alfred V. and Nellie L. (Beatrice) G.; m. Aida Iris Gerena, Nov. 9, 1957; children: Theresa, Elizabeth, Barbara, Cathy, Tom, Gregory, Paula, Phil, Richard, Paul. BS in Chemistry, Boston Coll., 1956; MS in Chemistry, U. R.I., 1963, PhD in Pharmacology and Toxicology, 1966; MA in Counseling, Liberty U., 1993. Lic. profl. counselor. Lt. comdr. USPHS, 1966, advanced through grades to capt., 1979; staff fellow pharmacology-toxicology rsch. assoc. program Nat. Heart Inst., NIH, Bethesda, Md., 1966-68; rsch. pharmacologist NCI Nat. Cancer Inst., NIH, Bethesda, Md., 1968-73, chief lab. toxicology, 1973-80; regulatory pharmacologist Ctr. for Drugs and Biologics-FDA, Md., 1980-84; lab. dir. fishery rsch. br. FDA, Dauphin Island, Ala., 1984-93. Adj. prof. U. South Ala. Coll. Medicine, Mobile, 1984—, U. South Ala. Coll. Allied Health Professions, Mobile, 1996—; marriage and family counselor Cath. Social Svcs., Mobile, 1993—; vice chmn. com. on animals as monitors in environ. hazards NAS. Contbg. author: Handbook of Experimental Pharmacology—Concepts in Biochemical Pharmacology, 1971, Handbook of Experimental Pharmacology, Antineoplastic and Immunosuppressive Agents, 1974, Methods in Cancer Research, 1979, Pesticides and Xenobiotics Metabolism in Aquatic Organisms, 1979, Pesticides and Xenobiotics Metabolism in Aquatic Organisms, 1979, Cisplatin—Current Status and New Developments, 1980, Modern Pharmacology, 1982; contbr. 106 articles to profl. jours. Mem. Am. Soc. Pharmacology and Exptl. Thearapeutics, Soc. Toxicology, Am. Chem. Soc., Am. Assn. Christian Counselors. Roman Catholic. Home: 968 Westbury Dr Mobile AL 36609-3332 Office: U So Ala Coll Medicine Dept Pharmacology Msb 3130 Mobile AL 36688-0001 E-mail: amguarino@cssmobile.org.

GUAY, GORDON HAY, federal agency administrator, marketing educator, consultant; b. Hong Kong, Aug. 1, 1948; came to U.S., 1956; s. Daniel Bock and Ping Gin (Ong) G. AA, Sacramento City Coll., 1974; BS, Calif. State U., Sacramento, 1976, MBA, 1977; postgrad., U. of the Pacific, 1978; PhD, U. So. Calif., 1981. Mgmt. assoc. U.S. Postal Svc., Sacramento, 1980-82, br. mgr., 1982-83, fin. mgr., 1983-84, mgr. quality control, 1984-86, mgr. tech. sales and svcs. divsn., 1986-91, dir. mktg. and comm., 1991-95, postmaster, 1996—. Prof. bus. adminstrn., mktg. and mgmt. Calif. State U., Sacramento, 1981-85; prof. mktg. Nat. U., San Diego, 1984—; pres. Gordon Guay and Assocs., Sacramento, 1979—; cons. Mgmt. Cons. Assocs., Sacramento, 1977-79. Author: Marketing: Issues and Perspectives, 1983; also articles to profl. jours. With U.S. Army, 1968-70. Recipient Patriotic Svc. award U.S. Treasury Dept., San Francisco, 1985. Fellow

Acad. Mktg. Sci.; mem. NEA, AAUP, Am. Mgmt. Assn., Am. Mktg. Assn. (Outstanding Mktg. Educator award 1989), Am. Soc. Pub. Adminstrn., Soc. Advancement Mgmt. (Outstanding Mem. 1976), Assn. MBA Execs. Democrat. Avocations: teaching, golf, tennis, fishing, camping.

GUAZZALOCA, EDWARD FRANCIS, elementary school educator; b. Cambridge, Mass., Feb. 18, 1961; s. William A. and Virginia M. (Lewis) G.; m. Kathleen Anne Stamatis, June 24, 1989; children: Krystina Anne, Emily Danielle. BS in Elem. Edn., Salem State Coll., 1985; MEd in Reading and Literacy, Endicott Coll., 1998. Cert. elem. tchr., Mass. Tchr. grades 7 and 8 Immaculate Conception Sch., Cambridge, 1985-86; tchr. grades 5 and 6 Spofford Pond Sch., Boxford, Mass., 1986—. Editor: Laughable Limericks from Room 13, 1991, Laughable Limericks from Room 16Vol. I, 1992, Vol. II, 1993 Mem. Reading (Mass.) Town Meeting, 1980-83; assoc. mem. Reading Dem. Town Com., 1989-95; del. Dem. State Conv., 1994; coord. confirmation St. Agnes Parish, Reading, 1992-93. Recipient Golden Apple award Salem (Mass.) Evening News, 1992. Mem. Mass. Tchrs. Assn., Boxford Tchrs. Assn. (treas. 1989-90, v.p. 1990-96). Roman Catholic. Avocations: hockey, softball, reading. Office: Spofford Pond Sch 31 Spofford Rd Boxford MA 01921-1501

GUDNITZ, ORA M. COFEY, secondary education educator; b. Crawforddsville, Ark., Jan. 24, 1934; d. Daniel S. and Mary (Oglesby) Cofey; children: Ingrid M. Hunt, Carl Erik, Katrina Beatrice. BA, Lane Coll., Jackson, Tenn., 1955; MEd, Temple U., 1969; student, U. Copenhagen, 1957; MA in Theol. Studies, Ea. Bapt. Theol. Sem., Pa., 1995, Eastern Bapt. Theol. Sem., 1995. Cert. permanent English, social studies and French tchr., Pa. Tchr. English, chmn. dept. Sayre Jr. High Sch., Phila.; tchr. English, Overbrook High Sch., Phila. Founder, exec. dir. Young Communicators Workshop, Inc.; lectr., Denmark. Contbr. articles to newspapers, poetry to anthologies. Recipient award Chapel of Four Chaplains, 1976, Women in Edn. award, 1988; grantee Haas Found., 1977, also others. Mem. Nat. Coun. Tchrs. English, Assn. for Ednl. Communication and Tech., Phi Delta Kappa, Delta Sigma Theta.

GUENTER, HELEN MARIE GIESSEN, librarian, reading specialist; b. El Dorado, Ark., Dec. 21, 1944; d. Charles Henry and Thelma (Fish) G.; m. James Claude Burson, June 3, 1967 (div. 1982); children: Laura Marie, Alicia Zillana; m. Joseph Martin Guenter, June 20, 1992. BA in English, Centenary Coll., 1966; MA in Reading, La. Tech. U., 1980; MLS, U. So. Miss., 1986. Cert. tchr., Ark., La. Libr. researcher, editor, tutor for pvt. clients, Houston, also Minden, La., 1967-79; libr. asst. Shreveport (La.) Meml. Pub. Libr., 1966-67; libr. Dubberly and Heflin (La.) Elem. Schs., 1979-80, Glenbrook Sch., Minden, La., 1980-82; full-time cons. S.E. Ark. Ednl. Coop. Media Ctr., Monticello, Ark., 1982; serials and reference libr. U. Ark., Monticello, 1982—. Tchr. Caddo-Bossier Parishes Headstart, Shreveport, 1966-67; part-time tchr. Webster Parish Schs., Minden, 1977-80; asst. libr. Phillips Lab. Sch., Rustin, La., 1980; reading diagnostician, clinican Reading Ctr. La. Tech. U., Ruston, 1980; coll. reading instr. U. Ark., Monticello, 1986, 89, mem. coun. assessment of student acad. achievement, 1994—, sec. faculty assembly, 1995-96, honors coun., 1995—. Column editor Ark. Librs., 1991—; contr. articles to profl. publs. Mem. founders' grant com. Webster Parish Hist. Mus., Minden, 1976-79; mem. organizational com. Drew County Lit. Coun., Monticello, 1986-87; mem. grants com. Drew Hist. Soc., Monticello, 1986—; press. rep. S.E. Ark. Dist., Monticello chpt. Nat. Fedn. Music Clubs, 1986—, S.E. dist. sec., 1991—; mem. commn. archives and history LIttle Rock Conf. United Meth. Ch., 2002—. Anderson Acad. scholar Centenary Coll., La., 1962-66; Wilson scholar Sch. Libr. Svc., U. So. Miss., 1986; U. Ark. Monticello faculty devel. grantee, 1986—. Mem. ALA, AAUW, Assn. Coll. and Rsch. Librs. (nat. adv. com. 1991-95, sec. Ark. chpt. 1988-90), Ark. Libr. Assn. (intellectual freedom com. 1989-93, ALA scholar 1985, publs. com. 1994—), Ark. Assn. for Instrnl. Media, Monticello Book Club, Internat. Reading Assn., Ark. Tchr. Educators of Reading (honor status com. 1989), Beta Phi Mu. Methodist. Avocations: cats, choir handbells and piano, needlework, reading, travel. Home: 315 Glenwood Dr Monticello AR 71655-5525 Office: U Ark Monticello PO Box 3599 Monticello AR 71656-3599

GUESS, AUNDREA KAY, accounting educator; b. Seth, W.Va., Feb. 7, 1953; d. Hobert and Inez Elizabeth (Howell) Adams; children: Renae, Rhonda. BBA, Baylor U., Waco, Tex., 1988; MBA, Auburn U., 1989; PhD, U. North Tex., 1993. CPA, Ala., Fla. Co-owner Stevenson (Ala.) All-Mart, 1967-94; grad. rsch. asst. Auburn (Ala.) U., 1988-89; teaching fellow U. North Tex., Denton, 1989-90, lectr., 1990-93; prof., dir. acctg. program Samford U., Birmingham, Ala., 1993—97, dir. new masters of acctg. degree program; prof. U. Tex., 1997—; dir. acctg. MBA profram St. Edwards U., Austin, Tex., 1998—. Cons. Kay Guess Cons., Birmingham, 1993—, activity based costing Coca-Cola; presenter Southwestern Bus. Adminstrn. Conf., 1994; discussant, 1995 track chair for acctg. and fin. Southwestern Case Rsch., pres. 2003—; owner Kay's Designer Dresses, Stevenson; prof. St. Edwards U., 2003; bd. dir. N.Am. Case Rsch. Assn. Contbr. pubs. to various jours. Recipient Fin. Execs. Inst. award, 1987, 89; Rsch. grantee Samford U.Heloise Brown Canter scholar Am. Women's Soc. CPA and Am. Soc. Women Accts., 1992. Mem. AICPA, Am. Acctg. Assn., Am. Soc. Women CPAs (South Birmingham chpt., Laurel scholar 1992, scholar 1989), Fla. Inst. CPAs, Inst. Mgmt. Accts. (bd. dirs. 1994—, dir. tech. meetings 1994—), Acad. Acctg. Historians, Inst. Internal Auditing, Phi Theta Kappa, Alpha Kappa Psi, Beta Alpah Psi (treas. Auburn chpt. 1989), Phi Kappa Phi, Beta Gamma Sigma. Baptist. Avocations: sewing, cake decorating, running. Home: 651 Martin Rd Dripping Springs TX 78620-3506

GUEST, JAMES DONALD, elementary education educator; b. Chgo., Dec. 7, 1961; s. Donald Arthur and Arlene Marie (Burghardt) G.; m. Laurie Lynn Kunasek, May 29, 1993. AA, Coll. of DuPage, 1983; BS in Phys. Edn., U. Wis., LaCrosse, 1985; MS in Phys. Edn., Chgo. State U., 1990. Phys. edn. tchr. Pewaukee (Wis.) Pub. High Sch., 1985; elem. phys. edn. tchr. Minooka (Ill.) Community Grade Sch., 1985-86, Sch. Dist. Unit 46, Elgin, Ill., 1986—. Asst. girls gymnastic coach, Ill. High Sch. Assn., Streamwood, Ill., 1986—, head boys cross country coach, Elgin, Ill., 1986-91, asst. boys track coach, Elgin, 1987, 88, asst. boys gymnastic coach, Carol Stream, Ill., 1991—. Mem. NEA, Ill. Edn. Assn., AAHPERD, Ill. Assn. Health, Phys. Edn., Recreation. Avocations: 12 inch softball, weight training, jogging, reading, biking. Home: 3750 Winston Dr Schaumburg IL 60195-1844 Office: 1701 Greenbrook Blvd Hanover Park IL 60133-5338

GUEST, LINDA SAND, education educator; b. Ft. Morgan, Colo., Sept. 9, 1945; d. Robert E. and Leona Mae (Prettyman) Sand; m. Richard E. Guest, June 5, 1966; children: Elise M., Gregory D. BA, Colo. State U., 1967, MEd, 1983; EdD, Harvard U., 1990. Ednl. cons. Nat. Office for Rural Edn., Ft. Collins, Colo.; tchr. Denver Pub. Schs., East Maine Sch. Dist. 63, Niles, Ill., Poudre R-1 Sch. Dist., Ft. Collins, 1979-91; asst. prof. curriculum and instrn. U. Denver Sch. Edn., 1991-94; project coord. Rocky Mountain Tchr. Edn. Collaborative, Greeley, Colo., 1994-98; dir. curriculum Am. Honda Eagle Rock Sch. and Profl. Devel. Ctr., Estes Park, Colo., 1998—. Adj. faculty mem. Sch. Edn. Colo. State U., 1997—. Mem. ASCD, Am. Ednl. Rsch. Assn., Phi Delta Kappa. Office: Eagle Rock Sch PO Box 1770 Estes Park CO 80517-1770

GUEST, SUZANNE MARY, adult education educator, artist; b. Monroe, Mich., Sept. 24, 1935; d. Hubert George Guest and Lola Viola Anne Pfeffer. BA, Marygrove Coll., 1957; MFA, U. Notre Dame, 1969. Chmn. art dept. Marian H.S., Birmingham, Mich., 1960—66, St. Mary H.S., Akron, Ohio, 1966—68, Am. Sch., London, 1971—91; adult educator Wordens World of Art, Pompano, Fla., 1994—, Ft. Lauderdale (Fla.) H.S., 1994—, First Presbyn. Ch., Pompano, 1999—; mem. sisterhood Immaculate Heart of Mary, Detroit, 1957—69. Freelance artist Alan Kent Design Group, London, 1970; presenter workshops in field; calligraphy sabbatical Oreg. Sch. Arts and Crafts, Portland, 1988—89. Author: Calligraphy for Those Who Are Young at Heart, 1988; contbr. Ency. Calligraphy Techniques, 1990; exhibitions include various schs., restaurants, art stores, chs. Recipient Outstanding Svc. in Secondary Edn. award, European Coun. Internat. Schs., London, 1977—90, Calligraphy award, Soc. Scribes and Illuminators, London, 1991. Mem.: So. Fla. Watercolor Soc., Mus. for Women in Arts, Humane Soc. Democrat. Roman Catholic. Avocations: music, meditation, watercolor. Home: 3051 NE 48th St Apt 104 Fort Lauderdale FL 33308-4903

GUETTNER, PAMELA REA, elementary school educator; b. Corpus Christi, Tex., Dec. 10, 1953; d. Glen Burleson and Bertha Marie (Cook) Brewer; m. Anthony Wayne Guettner, Dec. 28, 1974; children: Anchen Nichole, Amber Kirsten. BS in Edn., Southwest Tex. State U., 1977, MEd, 1992. Cert. tchr., Tex. Tchr. Wonderland Sch., San Marcos, Tex., 1981-86, San Marcos Consol. Ind. Sch. Dist., 1986-93, instrnl. coord., 1993—. Cons. Tex. DARE Inst., San Marcos, 1991-93; presenter at profl. confs. Co-author: Text for DARE Police Training, 1993. Mem. ASCD, Tex. Classroom Tchrs. Assn., San Marcos High Sch. Band Boosters Club, San Marcos High Sch. Girls Athletic Boosters Club, Phi Delta Kappa. Avocations: skiing, reading, water skiing. Home: 4124 Day Dr San Marcos TX 78666-9540 Office: San Marcos Consol Ind Schs PO Box 2340 San Marcos TX 78667-2340

GUFFEY, BARBARA BRADEN, elementary education educator; b. Pitts., Pa., Aug. 10, 1948; d. James Arthur and Dorothy (Barrett) Braden; 1 child, William Butler Guffey III. BA in Elem. Edn., Westminster Coll., New Wilmington, Pa., 1970; MEd in Elem. Edn., Slippery Rock State Coll., 1973; postgrad., U. Pitts., Duquesne U., Westminster Coll. Cert. tchr., elem. and secondary history and govt. edn, elem. prin. Tchr. Shaler Area Sch. Dist., Glenshaw, Pa., 1970—, lang. arts area specialist, 1988—91, 1992—93, grad. level chmn., 1991—92, curriculum support math./sci., 1994—, mem. instrnl. support team, 1995—. Mem. Shaler Area Stretegic Planning Core Team, 1992—; mem. A.S.S.E.T. Leadership Team, 1995—; condr. seminars and workshops in field. Pres. alumni coun. Westminster Coll., 1996—97, v.p., 1995—96, chmn. homecoming all-alumni luncheon, 1991—93, chmn. homecoming, 1995—96, trustee, 1999—, mem. sesquicentennial com., 2002, mem. enrollment mgmt., ednl. policy and student affairs com. institut. advancement, vice chmn. instl. advancement com., 2003—; chairperson Westminster Fund; active Burchfield Elem. Sch. PTA; chmn. publicity Shaler Area Choir Parents Assn., 1996—2000; vice chmn. Dist. Adv.; mem. Child Care Adv. Bd.; elder, chair Christian edn. com. Glenshaw Presbyn. Ch., 1995—2001, mem. Presbyn. Women. Mem.: NEA, Shaler Area Edn. Assn. (mem. at large, negotiator, former rec. sec., v.p., bldg. rep., editor newsletter), Pa. Edn. Assn., Nat. Geneal. Soc. (local arrangements chair Pitts. conf. 2003), Armstrong County Hist. and Mus. Soc., Ind. County Geneal. and Hist. Soc., Western Pa. Geneal. Soc. (bd. dirs. 1992—, chair 25th Anniversary 1999, pres. 1999—2000, publicity 2000—03, pres. 2002—03), Perry Historians, Juniata County Hist. Soc., First Families of Western Pa. (charter mem.), Westminster Coll. Women's Club Pitts. (pres. 1975—76, treas. 1994—99, pres. 2001—03, v.p., sec., chair ways and means), Kappa Delta Pi. Office: Burchfield Elem Sch 1500 Burchfield Rd Allison Park PA 15101-4099

GUFFIN, JAN ARLEN, secondary education educator; b. Rush County, Ind., May 11, 1938; s. James Lowell and Helen Lorene (Whitinger) G. BS in Edn., Ind. U., 1963, MAT in English, 1966; PhD, Duke U., 1975. Cert. in English and edn., Ind. Adminstrv. trainee Am. Fletcher Nat. Bank, Indpls., 1957-62; tchr. English Shortridge H.S., Indpls., 1964-65, North Ctrl. H.S., Indpls., 1966-86, chmn. dept., 1977-89, coord. internat. baccalaureate, 1986-94, curriculum coord., 1989-94; chmn. dept. English, coord. global scholars program Park Tudor Sch., Indpls., 1994—2003. Chair Advanced Placement test devel. com. The Coll. Bd., N.Y.C., 1975-77, chair English adv. bd., 1977-79; seminar leader Coll. Bd. and U.S. Dept. State, Taipei, Taiwan and U.S., 1980-90; cons. dept. English, Culver (Ind.) Mil. Acad., 1992; cons. Spoleto (Italy) Study Abroad, 1997, instr., 1998-2000; mem. ISSACS accreditation team Summit Country Day Sch., Cin., 1998. Cons. editor The Clearinghouse, 1979&; asst. editor Jour. of Teaching Writing, 1980—; author articles. Mem. edn. bd. North United Meth. Ch., Indpls., 1980-83; mem. adv. bd. Arts, Ind., Indpls., 1993—, Gov.'s Scholar Acad., Indpls., 1985-86; external examiner Internat. Baccalaureate, N.Y.C., 1994-97. Recipient E.H. Kemper-McComb award Ind. Coun. Tchrs. English, 1986. Mem. ASCD, Nat. Coun. Tchrs. English, Ind. Tchrs. of Writing (exec. bd. 1976-79, treas. 1977-79), Ind. Commn. for Humanities, Phi Beta Kappa, Phi Delta Kappa. Democrat. Avocations: gardening, reading, drawing. Office: Park Tudor Sch 7200 N College Ave Indianapolis IN 46240-3016

GUGGENHEIM, MARTIN FRANKLIN, law educator, lawyer; b. N.Y.C., May 29, 1946; s. Werner and Fanny (Monatt) G.; m. Denise Silverman, May 29, 1969; children: Jamie, Courtney, Lesley. BA, SUNY, Buffalo, 1968; JD, NYU, 1971. Bar: N.Y. 1972, U.S. Dist. Ct. (so. dist. and ea. dist.) N.Y. 1973, U.S. Ct. Appeals (2d cir.) 1974, U.S. Ct. Appeals (3d cir.) 1979, U.S. Ct. Appeals (6th cir.) 1977, U.S. Supreme Ct. 1976. Staff atty. Legal Aid Soc., N.Y.C., 1971-72, dir. spl. litig. unit, juvenile rights divsn., 1972-73; clin. instr. NYU Sch. Law, N.Y.C., 1973-75; staff atty. juvnile rights project ACLU, N.Y.C., 1975-79, acting dir., 1976-77; asst. prof. clin. law NYU, N.Y.C., 1975-77, assoc. prof. clin. law, 1977-79, prof. clin. law, 1980—; of counsel Mayerson & Stutman LLP, N.Y.C., 2001—. Exec. dir. Washington Sq. Legal Svcs., Inc., N.Y.C., 1986-2000; pres. Nat. Coalition for Child Protection Reform, 2000—; pres., founding dir. Family Def. Law Project, Inc., N.Y.C., 1992-2000; advisor program for children Edna McConnell Clark Found., 1993-2001; dir. clin. and advocacy programs NYU, 1989-2002; founding dir. Ctr. for Family Representation, N.Y.C., 2002–; cons. juvenile justice stds. project ABA/Inst. Jud. Adminstrn., 1979-81; acting dir. Clin. Advocacy Programs, Sch. of Law NYU, 1988-89. Author: (with Alan Sussman) The Rights of Parents, 1980, Abuse and Neglect Volume, 1982, The Rights of Young People, 2d edit., 1985, (with Anthony G. Amsterdam and Randy Hertz) Trial Manual for Defense Attorneys in Juvenile Court, 1991, (with Alexandra Lowe and Diane Curtis) The Rights of Families, 1996. Dir. William J. Brennan Ctr. NYU, 1995-2000; mem. adv. bd. N.Y.C. Adminstrn. Children, 1997—; pres. Nat. Coalition for Child Protection Reform, 2000—. Arthur Garfield Hays Civil Liberties fellow, 1970-71, Criminal Law Edn. and Rsch. fellow, 1969-70; Kathryn A. McDonald award Assn. of the Bar of the City of N.Y., 2000. Mem. ABA, Am. Assn. Law Schs., Assn. of Bar of City of N.Y. Office: NYU Sch Law 161 Ave of the Americas New York NY 10013 E-mail: martin.guggenheim@nyu.edu.

GUGLIELMINO, LUCY MARGARET MADSEN, education educator, researcher, consultant; b. Charleston, S.C., Feb. 20, 1944; d. Robert Allen and Margaret Webb (Rodgers) Madsen; m. Paul Joseph Guglielmino, July 31, 1965; children: Joseph Allen, Margaret Rose. BA in English magna cum laude, Furman U., 1965; MEd in English and Edn., Savannah Grad. Ctr., 1973; EdD in Adult Edn., U. Ga., 1977. Tchr. English various pub. schs., Mass., 1965-72; vis. asst. prof. adult and cmty. edn. Fla. Atlantic U., Boca Raton, 1978-87, asst. prof., 1987-88, assoc. prof., 1988-90, prof., 1991—, chmn. dept. ednl. leadership, 1991-94, dir. Melby Cmty. Edn. Ctr., 1994—2000. Cons. AT&T, Motorola, Westvaco, S.E. banks, 1979—; bd. dirs. South Fla. Ctr. for Ednl. Leaders. Author: Adult ESL Instruction: A Sourcebook, 1991, Community Education and Florida's Future: Proceedings of the Commissioner's Summit, 1997; co-author: Administering Programs for Adults, 1997; author: (adult form) Self-Directed Leaning Readiness Scale, 1978, 3 other forms and translations into 17 other langs., 1979—94, Learning Preference Assessment (self-scoring format for business), 1991; editor: Florida GED Teachers' Handbook, 1999, 2001, Florida GED Teachers' Lesson Bank, 2001; co-editor: Internat. Jour. Self-Directed Learning, 2003—; contbr. over 90 articles to profl. jours., chapters to books. Mem. Fla. Literacy Coalition, 1990—. Recipient Tchr. of Yr. award Coll. Edn., Fla. Atlantic U., 1990, Outstanding Achievement award 1991, Presdl. Merit award, 1993, Profl. Excellence award, 1998, Malcolm Knowles Meml. award for outstanding lifelong contbn. to rsch. in self directed learning, 2002; named to Fla. Adult and Cmty. Edn. Hall of Fame, Fla. Adminstrs. Adult and Cmty. Edn., 1992; numerous grants, 1979—. Mem. AAUW, Nat. Cmty. Edn. Assn., Am. Assn. for Adult and Continuing Edn., Commn. Profs. Adult Edn. (chmn. self-directed learning task force 1987-88, 90-91), Fla. Adult Edn. Assn. (bd. dirs. 1989-90), Phi Kappa Phi, Phi Delta Kappa. Episcopalian. Avocations: reading, swimming, biking, flower arranging, gardening. Home: 7339 Reserve Creek Dr Port Saint Lucie FL 34986 Office: Fla Atlantic U CO 113 500 NW California Blvd Port Saint Lucie FL 34986 E-mail: lguglie@fau.edu.

GUGLIOTTI, ROBERT ANTHONY, sports publishing and media relations specialist; b. Youngstown, Ohio, Mar. 7, 1960; s. Joseph Guy and JoAnn Marie (Haschak) G. BA in Speech and Comm./Journalism, Youngstown State U., 1983; postgrad., Kent State U. Asst. student sports info. dir. Youngstown State U., 1980-83; local sports media liaison for Austintown area, 1984—; athletic events corr. Phoenix Publs., Inc., Niles, Ohio, 1984-93; head statis., league sec. Steel Valley Conf., Youngstown, 1987-94; adminstrv. asst., data sys. entry specialist Compass Enterprises/Falcon Transport Inc., Youngstown, Ohio, 1993-95; participating mentor 8th grade gifted/accelerated program Austintown Mid. Sch., 1995—. Assoc. dir. media/press/publicity rels. Youngstown Pride, World Basketball League, 1990-92, pub. address announcer, 1991-92, asso./assoc. media info. rels. dir., 1991-92; statistician of football, basketball and baseball teams and pub. address announcer various athletic events Austintown-Fitch H.S., 1987—; pub. address announcer Youngstown Class B Sandlot Amateur Baseball League, 1995; studio co-host Falcon Focus, Armstrong Cable Co., 1994—, also co-prodr. Editor, copy proofreader The 1990 Youngstown Pride Post-Season Media Guide--A Championship Season in Review; co-editor: World Basketball League Media Guide, 1992; editor, data rschr. team media info. guides Youngstown Pride, 1990-91. Co-host, producer, creator (cmty. TV) Falcon Focus, 1994—. Mem. Coll. Sports Info. Dirs. Am., Alpha Epsilon Rho. Roman Catholic. Avocations: reading, writing, jogging, bicycling, sports. Home: 4711 Driftwood Ln Youngstown OH 44515-4834 Office: Austintown-Fitch HS Dept Athletics 4560 Falcon Dr Austintown OH 44515-3701

GUIDRY, GAYE CHERAMIE, elementary education educator; b. Thibodaux, La., Sept. 1, 1963; d. Raymond Michael and Norma Marie (Jambon) Cheramie; m. Rickey Joseph Guidry, Aug. 27, 1984. BA, Nicholls State U., 1984, MEd, 1992. Cert. tchr., La. Tchr. Golden Meadow (La.) Upper Elem. Sch., 1985, Larose (La.) Lower Sch., 1985-88, Golden Meadow Lower Elem. Sch., 1988—. Dyslexic coord. Golden Meadow Lower, 1992—. Recipient Tchr. of Yr. award Golden Meadow Lower Sch., 1991-92. Mem. Associated Profl. Educators of La., Nicholls Reading Coun., Delta Kappa Gamma. Roman Catholic. Avocations: reading, scuba diving, swimming. Office: Golden Meadow Lower Sch 2617 Alcide St Golden Meadow LA 70357-2301

GUILMET, GEORGE MICHAEL, cultural anthropologist, educator; b. Seattle, Feb. 8, 1947; s. Michael D. and Avis M. (Degerness) G.; m. Glenda J. Black, May 24, 1980; children: Michelle R., Douglas J. BS in Metallurg. Enging., U. Wash., Seattle, 1969, MA in Anthropology, 1973; PhD in Anthropology, UCLA, 1976. Lectr. anthropology Calif. State U., Bakersfield, 1976-77, program dir. urban anthropology internship program, 1977-78; asst. prof. comparative sociology U. Puget Sound, Tacoma, 1977-82, assoc. prof., 1982-88, prof., 1988—2002, prof. emeritus, 1992—. Reader dept. anthropology UCLA, 1974-75; rsch. cons. dept. psychiatry UCLA, 1975-76; rsch. assoc. Nat. Ctr. Am. Indian Alaska Native Mental Health Rsch., U. Colo., 1986—; disting. vis. prof. anthropology San Diego State U., 1991; grant reviewer NIMH, Bethesda, 1991, 92; spkr. in field. Author, co-author: (chpts.) Research in Philosophy and Technology, vol. 8, 1985, Technology and Responsibility: Philosophy and Technology, vol. 3, 1987, Behavioral Health Issues among American Indians and Alaska Natives: Explorations on the Frontiers of the Biobehavioral Sciences, 1988, Native America in the Twentieth Century: An Encyclopedia, 1994, (rsch. monograph) The People Who Give More, 1989; contbr. articles to profl. jours.; keyboardist, vocals Brave New World; singles released include It's Tomorrow, 1967. Evaluation cons. Chief Leschi Sch., Puyallup Tribe Indians, Tacoma, 1989, 96—, vol. musician Puyallup Tribe Indians, Tacoma, 1996, 97, cultural needs assessment cons., 1996-97, juvenile justice program cons., 1997-98. Kaiser Aluminum Chem. Corp. scholar, 1968-69; grantee Carnegie Found., 1974, U. Puget Sound, 1977-79, 83-84, 86, 88, 89, 91, 93, 2001. Fellow Am. Anthrop. Assn. (bd. dirs. coun. anthropology edn. 1983-85, anthropology and environ. sect.); mem. Soc. Philosophy Tech., Fedn. Small Anthropology Programs, Pacific N.W. Historians Guild. Home and Office: 652 Old Blyn Hwy Sequim WA 98382-9695 E-mail: guilmet@ups.edu.

GUINN, MARY ANN, elementary education educator; b. Jackson, Tenn., Nov. 23, 1968; d. Dan McCain and Ann (Averitt) G. BS in Health and Phys. Edn., BS in Sports and Fitness Mgmt., Freed-Hardeman U., 1992, postgrad, 1992—. Tchr. East Chester Elem. Sch., Henderson, Tenn., 1992—. Mem. nationally-ranked Lady Lions Varsity Tennis Team, Henderson, Tenn., 1987-91; head counselor Freed-Hardeman U. Tennis Camp, Henderson, 1986-90. Vol. Spl. Olympics, Jackson, 1987, 90. Recipient athletic awards Tenn. Collegiate Athletic Conf., 1987-91, Outstanding Phys. Edn. award, Nat. Assn. for Sports and Phys. Edn., 1991, Tennis All-Conf. award NAIA Dist. 24, 1987-88, 89, 90-91, others. Mem. Student Nat. Edn. Assn., Freed-Hardeman U. Honors Assn., Phi Epsilon, Sigma Rho. Mem. Ch. of Christ. Avocations: tennis, photography, travel. Home: 1038 Norchester Dr Henderson TN 38340-7631

GUINTHER, CHRISTINE LOUISE, special education educator; b. Chgo., Oct. 27, 1949; d. William Joseph and Olga (Sandul) Bacha; m. Paul H. Demper, July 22, 1972 (div. 1987); m. William Robert Guinther, June 25, 1988. BS in Edn., Ill. State U., 1971; MA in Exceptional Child Edn., Ohio State U., 1974. Cert. tchr., Mo. Resource tchr. for learning disabled students Palatine (Ill.) Community Consol. Sch. Dist. #15, 1971-72, Scioto-Darby City Schs., Hilliard, Ohio, 1972-76, Francis Howell Sch. Dist., St. Charles, Mo., 1976—. Mem. NEA (human rels. com. 1987-93, bd. dirs. 1993—), ACLU, ASCD, Nat. Staf devel. Coun., AAUW, Mo. NEA (bd. dirs. 1985-91, human rels. com. 1983—, exec. com. 1993—), Francis Howell Edn. Assn. (pres. 1981-82), NMSA, Delta Kappa Gamma. Methodist. Avocations: walking, music, needlework, reading, Scrabble. Home: 161 Castlewood Rd Ballwin MO 63021-7217

GULGOWSKI, PAUL WILLIAM, German language, social science, and history educator; b. Oberhausen, Germany, July 4, 1940; s. Paul and Katharina (van Look) G.; m. Heide Anna Maria Hegenscheidt, July 6, 1989; children: Audrey-Annette, Paul William. BSc, U. Tex., El Paso, 1970; MA, Marquette U., 1992; PhD, U. Bremen, Germany, 1981. Cert. tchr., social sci., German and history. Commd. 2d lt. U.S. Army, 1970, advanced through grades to maj., 1981; gen. staff officer, comdr. combat and support forces U.S. Army, worldwide, 1970-80; polit. advisor, forces comdr. U.S. Army, Germany, 1980-82; prof. German U.S. Mil. Acad., West Point, N.Y., 1982-85; personal rep. of NATO Land Forces comdr., Heidelberg, Germany, 1985-87; ret. U.S. Army, 1987; lectr. German and fgn. lang. study methodology U. Wis., Whitewater, 1993—. Author: U.S. Military Government in Germany, 1983, Flucht aus Ostpreussen, 1986, Die unglaubliche

Story des Peter V., 2001; author articles. Chief historian USCG Aux., Washington, 1992-94; comdr. northwestern USCG 9th, 1994—; v.p. Wis. Profl. Edn. & Info. Coun., 1997-99, pres., 2000—. Decorated D.S.M. with four oak leaf clusters; comdr.'s cross German Order of Merit. Mem. Phi Kappa Phi. Roman Catholic. Avocations: classical music, literature, skiing, boating, travel. Home: PO Box 180347 Delafield WI 53018-0347 E-mail: phgulgow@milwpc.com.

GULLEDGE, KAREN STONE, educational administrator; b. Fayetteville, N.C., Feb. 3, 1941; d. Malcolm Clarence and Clara (Davis) Stone; m. Parker Lee Gulledge Jr, Oct. 17, 1964. BA, St. Andrews Presbyn. Coll., Laurinburg, N.C., 1963; MA, East Carolina U., 1979; EdD, Nova U., 1986. Social worker Lee County, Sanford, N.C., 1963-64; tchr. Asheboro (N.C.) City Schs., 1964-67, Winston-Salem (N.C.)/Forsyth County Schs., 1967-70; research analyst N.C. Dept. Pub. Instrn., Raleigh, 1971-76, sch. planning cons., 1976-89, dir. sch. planning, 1989-95; dir. ednl. svcs. Peterson Assocs., Raleigh, 1995-98, The Roberts Group, PA, Raleigh, 1998-99; ret. Chmn. N.C. Elem. Commn. of So. Assn. Colls. and Schs., 1995; leader profl. seminars; spkr. in field. Trustee St. Andrews Coll. Recipient Outstanding Educator award East Carolina U., 1992. Mem. Am. Biographical Assn., So. Assn. Colls. and Schs. (Distinguished Educator award 1994), Coun. Ednl. Facility Planners (pres., chmn. 1995, Disting. Ednl. Achievement award 1994, Disting. Svc. award 1996, 98), The Order of the Long Leaf Pine, Five Hundred Leaders of Infullerence, Delta Kappa Gamma. Democrat. Avocations: reading, needlework, entertaining, travel. Home and Office: 9119 Carrington Ridge Dr Raleigh NC 27615-1000

GULLIVER, JEAN K. educational association administrator; m. John W. Gulliver; children: Peter, Kate, Elizabeth, Jean. BA in History, Wheaton Coll., 1974. Loan officer Conn. Bank & Trust Co., 1974—77; real estate, 1986—94; vice chair Maine State Bd. Edn., 1998—2000, chairperson, 2000—. Chair Educator Devel. Stakeholder Group, 1998—, Maine Edn. and Tech. Adv. Coun., 1998—99; mem. Maine Sci. and Tech. Bd., 1998—, vice chair, 2001—02; mem. Info. Svcs. Policy Bd., 1999—, Maine Learning Tech. Initiative Adv. Group, 2001—. Trustee Breakwater Sch., Portland, Maine, 1983—87, chair bd. trustees, 1985—86; trustee Portland Stage Co., mem. exec. bd., 1984—87; active classroom vol., com. mem. Falmouth Sch. Sys., 1985—; co-chair sesquicentennial capital campaign Maine Wheaton Coll., 1986—87; mem. Falmouth Bd. Edn., 1990—94, chair, 1992—94; Sunday sch. tchr. St. Mary's Ch., Falmouth, 1985—. Mem.: Nat. Assn. State Bd. Edn. (chair 2001—), Wheaton Coll. Club (pres. 1982—83). Home: 27 Thornhurst Rd Falmouth ME 04105*

GULYA, AINA JULIANNA, neurotologist, surgeon, educator; b. Syracuse, N.Y., Feb. 3, 1953; d. Aladar and Sylvia E. Gulya; m. William R. Wilson, May 21, 1983. AB cum laude, Yale Coll., 1974; MD with distinction in rsch., U. Rochester, 1978. Diplomate Am. Bd. Otolaryngology. Intern, jr. resident in gen. surgery Beth Israel Hosp., Boston, 1978-80; resident in otolaryngology Mass. Eye and Ear Infirmary, Boston, 1980-83; fellow in otology/neurotology Bapt. Hosp. Ear Found., Nashville, 1983-84; asst. prof. surgery George Washington U., Washington, 1984-87, assoc. prof. surgery, 1987-90; assoc. prof. otolaryngology and head and neck surgery Georgetown U., Washington, 1990-94, prof., 1994-96; chief clin. trials br. Nat. Inst. on Deafness and other Comm. Disorders, Bethesda, Md., 1996-2000, chief clin. trials epidemiology biostatistics sect., 2000—; clin. prof. surgery, otolaryngology, head and neck surgery George Washington U., 1998—. Assoc. examiner Am. Bd. Otolaryngology, 1993-97, bd. dirs., 1997-2002, oral exam. leader for otology, 2000-02, chair neurotology sub-specialty cert. com., 2000-02. Co-author: Anatomy of the Temporal Bone With Surgical Implications, 1986, 95; assoc. editor Am. Jour. Otology, 1989-99. Bd. dirs. Deafness Rsch. Found., 1994—2001. Recipient Libr. award, Rochester Acad. Medicine, 1975, presdl. citation, Am. Otol., Rhinol. and Laryngol. Soc., 1999. Mem.: Am. Acad. Otolaryngology, Head and Neck Surgery (bd. dirs. 1995—97, Honor award 1991, Disting. Svc. award 2001), Am. Neurotology Soc. (coord. for continuing med. edn. 1990—95), Am. Otological Soc. (coun. 1993—, editor-libr. 1995—2000, trustee rsch. fund 1993—2001, pres.-elect 1999—2000, pres. 2000—01). Avocation: water skiing. Office: EPS 400D-7 6120 Executive Blvd Rockville MD 20852-4909

GUMPEL, LISELOTTE, retired language educator; b. Berlin; d. Karl and Gretchen (Philipps) G. BA summa cum laude, State U. of San Francisco, 1964; MA, Stanford (Calif.) U., 1966, PhD, 1971. Asst. prof. U. Minn., Morris, 1968-72, assoc. prof., 1972-80, full prof. in German, 1980—98, ret., 1998, prof. German lang. and lit. emerita, 1999—. Lectr. in field. Author: Concrete Poetry from East and West Germany: The Language of Exemplarism and Experimentalism, 1976, Metaphor Reexamined: A non-Aristotelian Perspective, 1985; contbr. MLA, 2000, Poetry for Today and Tomorrow, Goethe-Inst. Inter Nationes, 2002; contbr. poetry and articles to profl. jours. Nat. Endowment fellow, 1972, Helen Cam fellow Girton Coll., Cambridge, Eng., 1977. Mem. MLA (life), Am. Assn. Tchrs. German, Soc. for Internat. Germanistics, Internat. Union of Germanic Lang. and Lit., Older Women's League. Democrat. Jewish. Avocations: reading, visiting museums, libraries, theatres, concerts, writing.

GUMZ, CAROL ANN, elementary education educator; b. Oshkosh, Wis., Aug. 15, 1953; d. Harland and Marian Gumz. BS, U. Wis., Oshkosh, 1975. Tchr. St. Vincent de Paul Parish, Oshkosh, 1975-92, St. Frances Xavier Cabrini Sch., Oshkosh, 1992—. Named Elem Tchr. of the Yr. Green Bay Diocese, 1992, recipient Disting. Svc. award. Mem. ASCD, Nat. Cath. Edn. Assn., Kappa Delta Pi. Avocations: reading, needlepoint, sports. Home: 1409 Oak St Oshkosh WI 54901-3130

GUNDERSON, MARY ALICE, writer, educator; b. Sheridan, Wyo., Jan. 18, 1936; d. Bernard Graham and Leah Mary (Gilkeson) Wright; m. Edwin Donald Gunderson, July 16, 1964; 1 child, James Nelson. BA in Elem. Edn., U. Wyo., 1957, postgrad., 1971-86. Elem. tchr. Sweetwater County, Green River, Wyo., 1957-58, Natrona County Sch. Dist., Casper, Wyo., 1958-68, homebound instr., 1969-73; pub. info. officer Natrona County Libr., Casper, 1976-79; artist in residence Wyo. Arts Coun., Cheyenne, 1973-88; instr. creative writing Casper Coll., 1993-96, devel. studies in English, 1986-94; freelance writer, 1968—. Poetry editor/cons. High Plain Press, Glendo, Wyo., 1994—; mem. lit. adv. com. Casper Coll., 1988-92; grants panelist Wyo. Coun. on Arts, Cheyenne, 1988—. Author: Devils Tower: Stories in Stone, 1988 (Nat. Fedn. Presswomen award 1989), Land Marked: Collected Curry Stories, 1992 (Wyo. State Hist. Soc. award 1992); monthly columnist Casper Star Tribune, 1999-2000; contbr. essays, fiction, poetry to numerous lit. mags. (1st prize fiction Ann. Women's Voice award, InterMountain Women mag., 1997). Dir. PressWomen H.S. Journalism Contest, 1987-88; contest dir., booklet editor Wyo. Writers, Inc., 1983; bd. dirs. Cmty. Concert Assn., Casper, 1988. Recipient Fiction award, 1st Ann. Women's voice award InterMountain Woman mag., 1997; Writing and Rsch. grantee Wyo. Coun. for Humanities, 1980, Individual Artist grantee Wyo. Coun. on Arts, 1995-96, Fiction fellow Wyo. Coun. on Arts, 1987, Ucross Found. resident, 1986, others. Mem. Wyo. Alumni Assn., Am. Assn. Ret. Persons. Democrat. Presbyterian. Avocations: walking, reading, travel, photography, listening to music. Home: 318 W 14th St Casper WY 82601-4204

GUNDERSON, SARAH CHLOE (CHLOE SARAH BURNS), historian, educator; b. Owensboro, Ky., Nov. 24, 1949; d. Robert Louis and Eleanor Lucille Burns; m. Dale William Denio, June 21, 1969 (div. May 1988); children: Krista Lynn Denio, Deborah Ann Denio, Matthew Justin Denio; m. Darryl Eugene Gunderson, Oct. 18, 1992. BA, Calif. State U., Bakersfield, 1994, MA, 1996. Tchg. intern Bakersfield Coll., 1995—96, prof. history, 1996—2002; instr. Porterville (Calif.) Coll., summer, 1997; lectr. dept. history Calif. State U., Bakersvield, 2002—. Lectr., presenter in field. Author: Daughters of Juno, Chronicle One; Matilda of Argyll, 2003. Recipient Honorarium for book rev., Addison Wesley Longman Pubs., 1998. Mem.: AAUW (chmn. legal adv. fund 2000—01, v.p. ednl. found. 2001—02), Orgn. Am. Historians, Bodleian Libr., Phi Alpha Theta (del. and presenter at Oxford Roundtable 2003, 1st pl. award in CSUB local paper contest 1996, 3rd pl. award in So. Calif. regional paper contest 1996). Avocations: writing, piano, tennis, swimming, travel. Home: PO Box 20100 Bakersfield CA 93390-0100

GUNION, JOHN FRANCIS, physicist, educator; b. Washington, July 21, 1943; s. John Bowman and Katherine (Hawes) G.; m. Margaret Ann Hutchings, July 15, 1967; children: Christopher, Andrew. BS, Cornell U., 1965; Fulbright fellow, Imperial Coll., London, 1966; PhD, U. Calif., San Diego, 1970. Rsch. assoc. Stanford Linear Accelerator, Calif., 1970-72, MIT, Boston, 1972-73; assoc. prof. physics U. Pitts., 1973-74, assoc. prof., 1974-75, U. Calif., Davis, 1975-79, prof., 1979—. Participant confs. and workshops. Contbr. over 380 articles to sci. jours.; editor conf. procs. Alfred P. Sloan fellow, 1977-81; NSF grantee, 1973-74, 78—. Dept. Energy grantee, 1975—. Fellow: Am. Phys. Soc. Office: U Calif Dept Physics Davis CA 95616

GUNN, ALAN, law educator; b. Syracuse, N.Y., Apr. 8, 1940; s. Albert Dale and Helen Sherwood (Whitnall) G.; m. Bertha Ann Buchwald, 1975; 1 child, William BS, Rensselaer Poly. Inst., 1961; JD, Cornell U., 1970. Bar: D.C. 1970. Assoc. Hogan & Hartson, Washington, 1970-72; asst. prof. law Washington U., St. Louis, 1972-75, assoc. prof., 1975-76; assoc. prof. law Cornell U., Ithaca, N.Y., 1977-79, prof., 1979-84, J. duPratt White prof., 1984-89; prof. law U. Notre Dame, Ind., 1989-96, John N. Matthews prof., 1996—. Apptd. spl. advocate St. Joseph County Probate Ct., 2001—. Author: Partnership Income Taxation, 1991, 3d edit., 1999; (with Larry D. Ward) Cases, Text and Problems on Federal Income Taxation, 5th edit., 2002; (with Vincent R. Johnson) Studies in American Tort Law, 1994, 2d edit., 1999. Methodist. Office: U Notre Dame Law Sch Notre Dame IN 46556

GUNN, EDGAR LINDSEY, educational consultant; b. Forrest City, Ark., Aug. 20, 1950; s. Grover Earl and Beulah James (Lindsey) G.; m. Mary Anna Wald, Dec. 22, 1975. BA in Edn., U. Miss., 1973; MA in Bibl. Studies, Dallas Theol. Sem., 1977; MEd, U. North Tex., 1981, PhD in Higher Edn., 1988. Math. tchr. Vines H.S., 1976-79; counselor Clark H.S., 1979-81, Plano (Tex.) East Sr. H.S., 1981-83, asst. prin., 1983-85; ednl. specialist cen. adminstrn. Plano Ind. Sch. Dist., 1985-87, rsch. and planning analyst cen. adminstrn., 1987-91, dir. quality improvement ctrl. adminstrn., 1991-95; ind. cons. specializing strategic planning The Cambridge Group, Plano, 1990—. Assoc. The Cambridge Group, 1994—. Youth min. chs., Dallas, 1974-76. Recipient Ross Perot Excellence in Teaching award, 1979. Mem. Am. Assn. Sch. Adminstrs., Am. Soc. for Quality, Assn. Supervision and Curriculum Devel. Avocations: golf, college football. Home: 307 Laurel Creek Dr Sherman TX 75092-7654 Office: 307 Laurel Creek Dr Sherman TX 75092-7654 E-mail: elgunn@aol.com.

GUNN, JAMES E. English language educator; b. Kansas City, Mo., July 12, 1923; s. J. Wayne and Elsie M. (Hutchison) G.; m. Jane Frances Anderson, Feb. 6, 1947; children: Christopher Wayne, Kevin Robert. BS, U. Kans., 1947, MA, 1951. Editor Western Printing and Litho, Racine, Wis., 1951-52; asst. dir. Civil Def., Kansas City, Mo., 1953; instr. U. Kans., Lawrence, 1955, mng. editor Alumni Assn., 1956-58, adminstrv. asst. to the chancellor for univ. rels., 1958-70, lectr. English, 1970-74, prof., 1974-93, emeritus prof., 1993—. Cons. Easton Press, Norwalk, Conn., 1985-98; lectr. in field. Author: over 25 books including Station in Space, 1958, The Immortals, 1962, The End of Dreams, 1975, Alternate Worlds: The Illustrated History of Science Fiction (World Sci. Fiction Conv. Spl. award, 1976, Pilgrim award Sci. Fiction Rsch. Assn., 1976), The Listeners, 1972, The Dreamers, 1980, Isaac Asimov: The Foundations of Science Fiction, 1982 (Hugo award World Sci. Fiction Conv., 1983), The Science of Science-Fiction Writing, 2000, The Millennium Blues, 2001, Human Voices, 2002, numerous plays, screenplays, radio scripts; editor: The Road to Science Fictions, 6 vols., 1977—2002, 8 other books; contbr. 99 stories to mags.; contbr. articles. Dir. Ctr. for Study Sci. Fiction, Lawrence, 1984—. Lt. (j.g.) USN, 1943-46, PTO. Recipient Eaton award Eaton Conf., 1992, Hugo award, 1983; Mellon fellow U. Kans., 1981, 84. Mem. Author's Guild, Sci. Fiction and Fantasy Writers Am. (pres. 1971-72), Sci. Fiction Rsch. Assn. (pres. 1981-82, Pilgrim award 1976)., Avocations: golf, bridge. Home: 2215 Orchard Ln Lawrence KS 66049-2707 Office: U Kans English Dept Lawrence KS 66045-0001

GUNN, MARY ELIZABETH, retired English language educator; b. Great Bend, Kans., July 21, 1914; d. Ernest E. and Elisabeth (Wesley) Eppstein; m. Charles Leonard Gunn, Sept. 13, 1936 (dec. Apr. 1985); 1 child, Charles Douglas. AB, Ft. Hays State U., 1935, BS in Edn., 1936, MA, 1967. Tchr. English Unified Sch. Dist. 428, Great Bend, 1963-80, Barton County C.C., Great Bend, 1977-84, tchr. adult edn., 1985-87, tchr. ESL, 1988-94; ret., 1994. Conf. Am. Studies fellow De Pauw U., 1969; recipient Nat. Cmty. Svc. award DAR, 1996. Mem. AAUW (Outstanding Mem. 1991), NEA, Bus. and Profl. Women (Woman of Yr. 1974), Kans. Adult Edn. Assn. (Master Adult Educator 1986), Kans. Assn. Tchrs. English, PEO, Delta Kappa Gamma, Alpha Sigma Alpha. Democrat. Mem. United Ch. of Christ. Avocations: travel, driving, needlepoint, crossword puzzles, reading. Home: 3009 16th St Great Bend KS 67530-3705

GUNNELS, LEE O. retired finance and management educator, manufacturing/research company director, inventor; b. Huntington Park, Calif., Sept. 11, 1933; s. LeRoy O. and Marrion W. Gunnels; m. Laura Gunnels, Nov. 7, 1958; children: Cornelia, Amelia, Sarah. BA in Math./Physics, U. Hawaii, 1960; MBA, Xavier U., Cin., 1970, PhD in Edn., 1983. Nuc. physicist Battelle Meml. Inst., Columbus, Ohio; ret. assoc. prof. fin. and mgmt. Muskingum Tech. Coll., Zanesville, Ohio, past chmn. faculty senate; inventor, developer Gunnels Rsch. LLC. Contbr. articles to various publs. Home: 1849 Drugan Ct SW Reynoldsburg OH 43068-8181 also: Stoney Meadow Farms Adamsville OH 43802

GUNNERSON, DEBRA ANN, piano teacher; b. Detroit, Apr. 30, 1955; d. Robert James and Marjorie Jane (Page) Robinson; m. Gary Lee Gunnerson, May 22, 1976; children: Adam Lee, Julie Ann, Carrie Ann, Aaron Lee. BA in Piano Performance, George Mason U., 1976, MA in Piano Performance, 1991. Nat. cert. piano tchr. Music Tchrs. Nat. Assn. Pvt. tchr. piano, Chantilly, Va., 1971—. Asst. adj. prof. George Mason U., Fairfax, 1990-91; pianist Kennedy Ctr., Washington, 1973, Nat. Cathedral, Washington, 1973, McLean (Va.) Symphony, 1990. Scholar George Mason U., 1973. Mem. No. Va. Music Tchrs. (yearbook chmn. 1993-95, chmn. judged recital 1995-97, pres.-elect 1999-2001), Fairfax West Music Fellowship (historian 1996-97), Springfield Music Club (membership chmn. 1994-95, pres. 1997-99, historian 1999-2001); chmn. Chamber Music at Home Friday Morning Music Club, 1998—. Avocation: walking. Home: 4509 Hazelnut Ct Chantilly VA 20151-2415

GUNNING, MONICA OLWEN MINOTT, elementary educator; b. Jamaica, W.I., Jan. 5, 1930; came to U.S., 1948; d. Reginald Minott and Gwendolyn (Spence) Morgan; m. Elon S. Gunning, Feb. 2, 1957 (div. 1982); children: Michael Anthony, Mark Elon. BS in Edn., CUNY, 1957; M in Edn., Mount St. Mary's Coll., 1971. Elem. tchr., 1959-87; tng. tchr. UCLA, U. So. Calif., 1969-72; bilingual tchr. 10th St Sch., L.A., 1974-76; ESL tchr. Union Are Sch., L.A.; dir. vacation ch. sch. Wilshire United Meth. Ch., L.A., 1977. Spkr. in field. Author: (poetry) Not A Copper Penny in Me House, 1993 (award 1994), Under the Breadfruit Tree, 1998 (Am. Studies award), Perico Bonito and the Two Georges, 1976. Active Friends of the Libr., 1974—; mem. So. Calif. Coun. of Lit. for Children and Young People, L.A., 1990—. Recipient Meritorious award Friends of the Libr., 1974—, Christian Edn. award Wilshire Meth. Ch., 1983. Mem. Soc. of Children's Book Writers and Illustrators, Toastmasters Beverly Hills Club (pres. 1990-91 Max Damm Outstanding Toastmaster 1995). Democrat. United Methodist. Avocations: gardening, traveling, shopping flea markets, continuing education classes. Home: 30731 Paseo Del Niguel Laguna Niguel CA 92677-2306

GUNNING, ROBERT CLIFFORD, mathematician, educator; b. Longmont, Colo., Nov. 27, 1931; s. Clifford Henry and Inez (Wilhelm) G.; m. Wanda S. Holtzinger, July 9, 1966. AB, U. Colo., 1952; MA, Princeton U., 1953, PhD, 1955. NSF fellow U. Chgo., 1955-56; mem. faculty Princeton U., 1956—, prof. math., 1966—, chmn. dept., 1976-79, dean of faculty, 1989-95. Vis. prof. U. São Paulo, Brazil, 1957, U. Munich, 1967, ULCA, 1972, Oxford (Eng.) U., spring 1968, fall, 1980, 88, 95; Sloan fellow, 1958-61; asst. dir. studies, math. St. Catharines Coll., Cambridge (Eng.) U., 1959-60; mem. editl. bd. Princeton (N.J.) U. Press, 1969-73. Author: Lectures on Modular Forms, 1962, (with H. Rossi) Analytic Functions of Several Complex Variables, 1965, Lectures on Riemann Surfaces, Vol. I, 1966, Vol. II, 1967, Vol. III, 1972, Complex Analytic Varieties, Vol. I, 1970, Vol. II, 1974, Generalized Theta Functions, 1976, Uniformization of Complex Manifolds, 1978, Introduction to Holomorphic Functions of Several Variables, 3 vols., 1990; editor: Problems in Analysis, 1970, Theta Functions, 1989, Collected Papers of Salomon Bochner, 4 vols., 1991; contbr. articles to profl. jours. Fellow AAAS; mem. Am. Math. Soc., Princeton Club (N.Y.C.), Nassau Club (Princeton), Phi Beta Kappa, Sigma Xi. Episcopalian. Office: Fine Hall Washington Rd Princeton NJ 08544-1000

GUNSALUS, ROBERT PHILIP, microbiologist, educator, molecular geneticist; b. Ithaca, N.Y., Aug. 24, 1947; s. Irwin and Merle G. BS, S.D. State U., 1970; MS, U. Ill., 1972, PhD, 1977. Postdoctoral fellow Stanford (Calif.) U., 1978-80; asst. prof. microbiology UCLA, 1981-87, assoc. prof., 1987, prof., 1992—. Mem. Molecular Biology Inst. UCLA, Los Angeles, 1981—; Gauss prof. U. Göttingen, 2001. Editor FEMS Microbiology Letters, Archives Microbiology, 1996-98; mem. editl. bd. Jour. Bacteriology, 1988-2002, Molecular Microbiology, Biofactors, 1990-92, Jour. Biol. Chemistry. Chmn. Gordon Conf. on Methanogenesis, 1990. Mem. ASM (chair div. gen. microbiology 1992), AAAS, Am. Soc. Microbiology, Am. Chem. Soc., Am. Soc. Biochem. and Molecular Biologists. Office: Microbiology/Molecular Genetics Dept 1601 MSB UCLA Los Angeles CA 90095

GUNTER, DEVONA ELIZABETH (BETTY GUNTER), retired special education educator; b. Jonesboro, Ark., Jan. 25, 1933; d. Coy W. and DeVona Bethel Hiett; m. Norman Lee Gunter, Sept. 26, 1952; children: Carolyn Sue, Ronald Lee, Rickey Lynn. BEd, S.W. Mo. State U., 1972, MEd in Learning Disabilities, 1979, specialist degree in adminstrn., 1985. Cert. elem., spl. edn. tchr., prin., supt., Mo. Kindergarten, 6th grade tchr., tchr. of learning disabled Oregon-Howell R-3 Sch. Dist., Koshkonong, Mo., dir. spl. svcs., tchr.; coord. spl. svcs., tchr. Fair View R-XI Sch. Dist., West Plains, Mo., elem. prin.;, 1997; tax preparer H&R Block, West Plains, Mo. Sec., treas., bd. dirs., co-founder tng. ctr. for handicapped adults. Contbr. articles to profl. publs. Mem. ASCD, Assn. Spl. Citizens (bd. dirs., sec.-treas.), Missouri State Tchrs. Assn., Koshkonong Tchrs. Assn. (pres., sec., v.p.). Home: 3869 County Road 6340 West Plains MO 65775-6637

GUNTHER, BARBARA, artist, educator; b. Bklyn., Nov. 10, 1930; d. Benjamin and Rose (Lev) Kelsky; m. Gerald Gunther, June 22, 1949; children: Daniel Jay, Andrew James. BA, Bklyn. Coll., 1949; MA, San Jose State U., 1975. Instr. printmaking, drawing, painting Cabrillo Coll., Aptos, Calif., 1976-93. Instr. lithography Calif. State U., Hayward, 1978-79; instr. studio arts Calif. State U., San Jose, summer 1977, 78, 80; co-founder San Jose Print Workshop, 1975. One-woman shows include include Palo Alto (Calif.) Cultural Ctr., 1981, Miriam Pearlman, Inc., Chg., 1984, D.P. Fong and Spratt galleries, San Jose, 1991—93, Branner/Spangenburg Gallery, Palo Alto, 1991, U. Calif., Santa Cruz, 1991, Cabrillo Coll., 1997, Frederick Spratt Galleries, San Jose, 1996, San Francisco, 2000, Triton Mus. of Art, Santa Clara, 2001, Represented in permanent collections San Jose Art in Pub. Places Program, Triton Mus., Santa Clara, Calif., Mus. City NY, Santa Clara Law Sch., Found. Press, Chrysler Motors. Recipient Purchase award Palo Alto Cultural Ctr., 1975, Judges' Merit award Haggin Mus., 1988. Mem. Calif. Printmakers Soc., San Jose Inst. of Contemporary Art. Studio: 199 Martha St Ste 22 San Jose CA 95112-5878 E-mail: bgunther@law.stanford.edu.

GUO, PEIXUAN, molecular virology educator; b. Chaoyang, Guangdong, China, Apr. 4, 1951; s. Yongjian Guo and Huifang Zhang; m. Mar. 29, 1981; children: Yinyin, Sida, Owen. DVM, Foshan (Guangdong) U. Sci. and Tech., 1978; MS in Microbiology, South China Agr. U., Guangzhou, 1981; PhD in Microbiology and Genetics, U. Minn., 1987. Guest rschr. U. Basel, Switzerland, 1985; rsch. scientist II N.Y. State Dept. Health, Albany, 1987-88; vis. scientist NIH, Bethesda, Md., 1988-89; asst. prof. Purdue U., West Lafayette, Ind., 1990-93, assoc. prof., 1994-97, prof. molecular virology, 1998—. Ad hoc mem. study sect. on biomed. and behavioral rsch facilities, NIH, 1997; chmn. search com. for tenure-track faculty, 1994-95. Contbr. over 50 articles to profl. jours. including Sci., PNAS, Genome Letters, Jour. Molecular Biology, Jour. Virology, RNA, Molecular Cell, Gene, Nuc. Acid Rsch., Virology and Viral Genes; mem. editl. bd. Jour. Nanosci. and Nanotech.; mem. adv. bd. Actica. Bioch., Biophy. Sinica; editor seminars in virology, 1994. Recipient 1st award NIH, 1993, Pfizer Disting. Faculty award for rsch. excellence, 1995; Purdue U. faculty scholar, 1999; grantee Solvay, 1991-93, Integrated Biotech. Corp., 1991-94, NIH, 1992—, NSF, 1997—. Mem. AAAS, Am. Soc. Virology, Am. Soc. Microbiology, Am. Soc. Biochemistry and Molecular Biology, Soc. Chinese Bioscientists in Am., RNA Soc. Achievements include discovery of a small viral RNA novel and essential in viral DNA packaging leading to the opening of a new area of research; successful assembly of infectious double-stranded DNA virion of ø29 in vitro with recombinant proteins and synthetic nucleic acids; being first to demonstrate a natural RWH that binds ATP; design of a novel strategy for high efficient inhibitiion of virion assembly; development of particle vaccines, subunit vaccines with multiple gene products; development of new methods for the quantification of stoichiometry for intermediate reactions; discovery of a hexameric molecular motor composed of 6 RNA molecules. Office: Purdue U Cancer Ctr Purdue Univ HAN5B-036 Lafayette IN 47907

GUO, QIZHONG, engineering educator, researcher, consultant; b. Guangdong, China, Oct. 8, 1962; came to U.S., 1984; m. Xiaolan Wang; children: Lillian, Joshua. B of Engring., Tianjin (China) U., 1982; MS, U. Minn., 1987, PhD, 1991. Registered profl. engr., Minn. Rsch./tchg. asst. U. Minn., Mpls., 1985-91, rsch. assoc., 1991-92; R & D engr. Lemna Corp., St. Paul, 1992; asst. prof. Rutgers U., Piscataway, N.J., 1992-98, assoc. prof., 1998—. Tech. adv. steering com. Barnegat Bay Nat. Estuary Program, Trenton, N.J., 1996—; tech. adv. com. Whippany Watershed Project, Trenton, 1996—. Contbr. articles to profl. jours. Mem. ASCE, Am. Waterworks Assn., Am. Geophysical Union, Am. Water Resources Assn. (U. Minn. student chpt. pres. 1990-91), Water Environ. Fedn. Achievements include research in solutions to hydraulic problems in deep tunnel project for Greater Chicago; revealing environmental problems that may occur as a result of processing hazardous waste derived fuel in cement kilns; developing a new method for quantifying freshwater input and flushing time in estuaries. Office: Rutgers Univ 623 Bowser Rd Piscataway NJ 08854-8014 E-mail: qguo@rci.rutgers.edu.

GUOKAS, JOAN ELLEN (MRS. MATTHEW GUOKAS SR.), retired elementary educator; b. New Rochelle, N.Y., Aug. 24, 1919; d. Homer Vincent and Mary Ellen Ann (Ivory) Burnham; widowed; children: Mary Tyrrell, Matthew Jr. BS in Edn., St. Joseph U., 1961; MEd, Temple U., 1970. Elem. sch. tchr. St. Timothy's Sch., Phila., 1950-53, St. Bernard's Sch., Phila., 1953-59, Vare Elem. Sch., Phila., 1961-68, McCall Elem. Sch., Phila., 1969-81; ret., 1981. Mem. fellowship award com. Emergency Aid, 1981—; mem. alumnae bd. Chestnut Hill Coll., Phila., 1990—; mem. Jefferson Hosp. Women's Bd., 1991; mem. election day voting panel Phila. Election Bd., 1981—; vol. Ocean City's Hist. Mus.; choir mem. Frances Cabrini Roman Cath. Ch., Ocean City. Mem. AAUW. Roman Catholic. Avocations: tutoring foreign students, mentoring, church activities. Address: 812 Seacliff Rd Ocean City NJ 08226-4730

GUP, BENTON EUGENE, banking educator; b. Reading, Pa., Mar. 5, 1936; married; children: Lincoln, Andrew, Jeremy. BA, U. Cin., 1961, MBA, 1963, PhD, 1966. Economist Fed. Res. Bank of Cleve., 1967-70; prof. fin. U. of Tulsa, 1970-82, prof., chair banking, 1970-82; vis. prof., chair banking U. Va., Charlottesville, 1980-81; prof., chair banking U. Ala., Tuscaloosa, 1983—. Author: Guide to Strategic Planning, 1980, Financial Intermediaries, 2d editl, 1980, Principles of Financial Management, 1983, 2d edit., 1987, Management of Financial Institutions, 1984, The Basics of Investing, 5th edit., 1992, (with Charles Meiburg) Cases in Bank Management, 1986, Personal Investing: A Complete Handbook, 1987, Commercial Bank Management, 1989, Bank Mergers: Current Issues and Perspectives, 1989, Bank Fraud: Exposing the Hidden Threat to Financial Institutions, 1990, (with Robert Brooks) Interest Rate Risk Management, 1993, Targeting Fraud: Uncovering and Detering Fraud in Financial Institutions, 1995 (with Donald Fraser and James Kolari) Commercial Banking: The Management of Risk, 1995, The Bank Director's Handbook, 1996, Bank Failures in the Major Trading Countries of the World, 1998, International Banking Crises, 1999, The New Financial Architecture, 2000, Megamergers in a Global Economy, 2002, The Future of Banking, 2003, Investing OnLine, 2003. Served with USAF, 1954—58. Mem. Fin. Mgmt. Assn. (chmn. site selection 1975-85), Midwest Fin. Assn. (pres. 1982-83), Am. Fin. Assn., Fin. Execs. Inst., Acad. Fin. Svcs. (v.p., dir. 1988-91). Home: 1124 Forest Oaks Ln Tuscaloosa AL 35406-2673 Office: U Ala Dept Fin PO Box 870224 Tuscaloosa AL 35487-0154

GUPTA, NARENDRA KUMAR, physician, educator; b. Rishikesh, India, May 18, 1947; s. Rishi Ram and Sita Devi G.; m.; children: Deepali, Sonali. BS in Biology, Chemistry, CUNY, 1973, MS in Microbiology, 1975, PhD, 1982, MD, 1986, MPhil, MA in Biochemistry, CUNY. Diplomate Am. Bd. Internal Medicine. Intern Univ. Hosp., U. Medicine and Dentistry, N.J. Med. Sch., Newark; resident Jersey Shore Med. Ctr., UMDNJ, Robert Wood Johnson Med. Sch., Neptune, N.J.; endocrinology rsch. fellow Rutgers U., New Brunswick, N.J.; cardiology rsch. fellow UMDNJ, N.J. Med. Sch.; oncology rsch. fellow Meml. Sloan Kettering Cancer Ctr., N.Y.C.; postdoctoral fellow in biochemistry CUNY (Bklyn. Coll.); adj. assoc. prof. CUNY, L.I. U.; lectr. Columbia U., Bklyn. Coll., CUNY. Fellow ACP; mem. AMA (Physician Recognition award 1995), AAAS, Am. Soc. Internal Medicine, N.Y. Acad. Scis., Am. Heart Assn., Sigma Xi. Avocations: travel, discovering ancient med. practices, movies.

GUPTA, PARVEEN P. accounting educator, consultant, researcher; b. New Delhi, Apr. 26, 1957; came to U.S., 1980; s. Netar Prakash and Bimla (Aggarwal) G.; m. Taruna Chopra, Aug. 23, 1955; children: Jatin P., Mukul M. BCom with honors, Delhi U., 1976, LLB, 1980; MBA, U. Conn., 1983; PhD, Pa. State U., 1987. Acct. Jay Engring. Works, Delhi, 1977-80; cons. Small Bus. Devel. Ctr., Storrs, Conn., 1982-83; grad. asst. Pa. State U., State College, 1983-86; asst. prof. acctg. Lehigh U., Bethlehem, Pa., 1987—. Author: Total Quality Improvement Process and Internal Audit Function, 1995, Internal Audit Reengineering: Survey, Model and Best Practices, 2001; contbr. articles to profl. jours. Editor Hindu Temple Soc., Allentown, Pa., 1988-90, treas., 1992-94. IIARF rsch. grantee, 1986, 91, Price Waterhouse grantee, 1984, 85. Mem. Am. Acctg. Assn., Acad. Internat. Bus., Inst. Mgmt., Inst. Internat. Auditors, Acad. of Mgmt. Hindu. Avocations: music, reading, outdoors. Office: Lehigh U RBC 37 Bethlehem PA 18015

GUPTA, SURAJ NARAYAN, physicist, educator; b. Haryana, India, Dec. 1, 1924; came to U.S., 1953, naturalized, 1963; s. Lakshmi N. and Devi (Goyal) G.; m. Letty J.R. Paine, July 14, 1948; children: Paul, Ranee. MS, St. Stephen's Coll., India, 1946; PhD, U. Cambridge, Eng., 1951. Imperial Chem. Industries fellow U. Manchester, Eng., 1951-53; vis. prof. physics Purdue U., 1953-56; prof. physics Wayne State U., Detroit, 1956-61, disting. prof. physics, 1961-99, disting. prof. emeritus physics, 1999—. Researcher on high energy physics, nuclear physics, relativity and gravitation. Author: Quantum Electrodynamics, 1977. Fellow Am. Phys. Soc., Nat. Acad. Scis. of India. Achievements include quantum theory with negative probability and quantization of the electromagnetic field; flat-space interpretation of Einstein's theory of gravitation and quantization of the gravitational field; regularization and renormalization of elementary particle interactions; development of the theory of bound states in quantum electrodynamics and quantum chromodynamics; mass matrix formulation of quark mixing and CP violation in weak interactions; investigation of phenomena at supercollider energies. Home: 30001 Hickory Ln Franklin MI 48025-1566 Office: Wayne State U Dept Physics Detroit MI 48202

GURGA, ROSEMARY, secondary foreign language educator; b. New Haven, Apr. 29, 1953; d. Frederick John and Fortunata Fay (DeFelice) Torniero; m. (div.); children: Rosina-Maria Lucibello, Francesca (dec.), Michele (dec.); m. Joseph John Gurga III, Aug. 7, 1988; 1 child, Gianna Luisa. BA in Spanish, Albertus Magnus Coll., New Haven, 1975; MS in History, So. Conn. State U., New Haven, 1984. Cert. tchr., Conn. Organist, choir dir. St. Rita Ch., Hamden, Conn., 1973-77; claims adjuster Conn. Comml. Travelers Ins., New Haven, 1973-75; Spanish tchr. Foran H.S., Milford, Conn., 1975-76; Spanish tchr., master tchr. Hillhouse H.S., New Haven, 1976-77; tchr. Spanish, Italian, ESOL Wilbur Cross H.S., New Haven, 1977—, master tchr., 1983-84, 86-87. Bd. mgrs. Leila Day Nursery Sch., New Haven, 1991-94; com. mem. Spl. Olympics, 1995; mem. St. Aloysius Ch. Ladies Guild. Named Chef du Jour, Waterbury Republican-Am., 1991. Mem. Conn. Orgn. Lang. Tchrs. Avocations: cooking, baking, flower arranging, cake decorating, sewing. Home: 100 Winding Rdg Southington CT 06489-2114

GURHOLT-WIESE, VICTORIA JEAN (VICKI WIESE), special needs educator; b. Sheboygan, Wis. d. Victor Eugene and Francis Blanche (Lynch) Gurholt; m. Steven John Wiese, Oct. 14, 1978; 1 child, Brett Harvey Wiese. BS in Spl. Edn./Elem. Edn., Silver Lake Coll., 1985; M in Transitional Spl. Needs, U. Wis., Whitewater, 1991. Cert. spl. edn. learning/emotional disabilities tchr., tech. coll. system spl. needs and goal instr., goal and ESL instr., Wis. Parent involvement/social svc. coord. Head Start, Sheboygan, 1980-84; relief house parent Hearthside Group Home for Girls, Sheboygan, 1984-85; spl. edn. tchr. of emotionally disturbed Port Washington (Wis.) Mid. Sch., 1985-86, Sheboygan Pub. Schs., 1986-89, program support tchr. for emotionally disturbed, 1989; spl. needs instrnl. support/affirmative action 504 coord. Lakeshore Tech. Coll., Cleve., Wis., 1989-94. Instr., designated vocat. instr., transition adj. faculty mem. U. Whitewater, 1994-95. Mem. Internat. League of Peace/Freedom, Sheboygan, 1987—; Sunday sch. coord./tchr., 1993-94; Sunday sch. tchr., 1994—; mem. exec. bd. Sheboygan County Literacy Coun., 1994—; mem. Wis. State Leadership Sch. to Work Spl. Populations, 1994—. Mem. Am. Vocat. Assn., Nat. Assn. Vocat. Assessment in Edn., Wis. Coun. Exceptional Children (pres. profl. devel. 1992—), Phi Delta Kappa (tech. prep. spl. populations chair 1992-94). Avocations: swimming, reading, cooking. Home: 6279 S 18th St Sheboygan WI 53081-9436 Office: Lakeshore Tech Coll 1290 North Ave Cleveland WI 53015-1414

GURLEY, DEBORAH CARLENE, elementary school educator; b. Carbondale, Ill., Mar. 26, 1957; d. Carl LaRue and Mary Isabelle (Nance) Stanley; m. Rickey Lynn Gurley, Oct. 24, 1975; children: Kelly Christine, Ryan Christopher. AS, John A. Logan Jr. Coll., Carterville, Ill., 1977; BS, So. Ill. U., 1980, M in Tchr. Leadership, 2001. Tchr. 3d grade Carbondale Elem. Sch. Dist., 1981-82; tchr.'s aide 1st grade Giant City Sch. Dist. 130, Carbondale, 1982-83; libr. K-8th Unity Point Sch. Dist. 140, Carbondale, 1983-84, tchr. 6th and 3d grades, 1984—; coop. tchr. edn. So. Ill. U., Carbondale, 1990—, also tchg. fellow mentor program, mem. profl. devel. sch. program. Tchr. in newspaper edn. So. Illinoisan Newspaper, Carbondale, 1987—. Color guard/vol. Carbondale Cmty. H.S. Color Guard, 1994—; tchr. Vacation Bible Sch., 1990-97, also children's ministry coord.; participant Goal 2000, Carbondale, 1995-2001. Mem. NEA, Ill. Edn. Assn., Unity Point Edn. Assn. Avocations: canning and cooking, embroidering, church activities. Office: Unity Point School Dist 140 4033 S Ill Ave Carbondale IL 62903 E-mail: dgurley@up140.jacksn.k12.il.us.

GURNO, MARY ANN, school system administrator; b. Jourdanton, Tex., Mar. 9, 1944; d. Leonard and Annie (Simmons) Ottinger. BS, Mary Hardin-Baylor U., 1967; MEd, S.W. Tex. State U., 1975, supervision cert., 1981, mid-mgmt. cert., 1984. Tchr. Killeen (Tex.) Ind. Sch. Dist., 1967-84, Burnet (Tex.) Consol. Ind. Sch. Dist., 1984-85, dir. curriculum/instrn., 1985-88, asst. supt., 1989—. Tech. advisor Lower Colo. River Authority, Austin, Tex., 1987-89. Named Educator of Month Rotary, 1982. Mem. Tex. Assn. Sch. Adminstrs./Tex. Assn. Sch. Bds., Tex. Assn. for Supervision and Curriculum Devel., Assn. for Compensatory Educators of Tex., Kiwanis (treas. 1996), Am. Legion Aux., Phi Delta Kappa. Republican. Methodist. Avocations: reading, gardening. Office: Burnet CISD 1201 N Main St Burnet TX 78611-1340

GURR, TED ROBERT, political science educator, author; b. Spokane, Wash., Feb. 21, 1936; s. Robert Lucas and Anne (Cook) G.; m. Erika Brigitte Klie, Feb. 20, 1960 (dec. May 1980); children: Lisa Anne, Andrea Mariel; m. Barbara Harff, Jan. 14, 1981. BA, Reed Coll., 1957; postgrad., Princeton U., 1957-58; PhD, NYU, 1965, Sofia U., 2002. From asst. editor to assoc. editor Am. Behavioral Scientist, 1961-64; asst. to dir. NYU Office Research Services, N.Y.C., 1962-64; research assoc. Princeton (N.J.) U., 1965-67, asst. prof., 1967-69, assoc. dir. workshop in comparative politics, 1966-69; assoc. prof. polit. sci. Northwestern U., Evanston, Ill., 1969-72, prof., 1972-74, Payson S. Wild prof. polit sci., 1974-84, chmn. dept., 1977-80; prof. polit. sci., dir. Ctr. for Comparative Politics U. Colo., Boulder, 1985-89; prof. govt. and politics U. Md., College Park, 1989—, disting. univ. prof., 1995—. Co-dir. hist. and comparative task force Nat. Commn. Causes and Prevention of Violence, 1968-69; vis. fellow Inst. Criminology Cambridge (Eng.) U., 1976; dir. Minorities at Risk project Ctr. Internat. Devel. and Conflict Mgmt. U. Md., College Park, 1987-2002; fellow U.S. Inst. Peace, Washington, 1988-89, PIOOM fellow Leiden U., 1993, sr. cons. Task Force on State Failure, U.S. Govt., 1994—; Olof Palme vis. prof. Uppsala U., 1996-97. Author: (with A. de Grazia) American Welfare, 1961; Why Men Rebel (Woodrow Wilson Found. award 1970), 1970, Politimetrics, 1972; (with C. Ruttenberg) Cross National Studies of Civil Violence, 1969; (with H.D. Graham) Violence in America: Historical and Comparative Perspectives, 1969, rev. edit., 1979; (with H. Eckstein) Patterns of Authority, 1975; Rogues, Rebels, Reformers, 1976; (with P. Grabosky and R.C. Hula) The Politics of Urban Crime and Conflict, 1977; Handbook of Political Conflict: Theory and Research, 1980; (with D.S. King) The State and the City, 1987; Violence in America, Vol. 1: History of Crime, Vol. 2: Protest, Rebellion, Reform, 20th ann. edit., 1989; (with J.A. Goldstone and F. Moshiri) Revolutions of the Late Twentieth Century, 1991, Minorities at Risk: A Global View of Ethnopolitical Conflict, 1993; (with B. Harff) Ethnic Conflict in World Politics, 1994; (with J.L. Davies) Preventive Measures: Building Risk Assessment and Crisis Early Warning Systems, 1998, Peoples Versus States: Minorities at Risk in the New Century, 2000; (with R. Alker and K. Rupesinghe) Journeys Through Conflict: Narratives and Lessons, 2002; (with M.G. Marshall) Peace and Conflict, 2003; mem. editl. bd. World Politics, 1970-73, Comparative Polit. Studies, 1968-99, Nationalism and Ethnic Politics, 1994—; co-editor Sage Professional Papers in Comparative Politics, 1969-73; editor: Comparative Political Studies, 1979-80. Fellow Wilson Nat., 1957, Ford Found., 1970, Guggenheim, 1972-73, German Marshall Fund., 1976, Fulbright, Australia, 1981. Mem. Am. Polit. Sci. Assn. (coun. 1989-91, Lifetime Achievement award 1991), Peace Sci. Soc., Internat. Studies Assn. (chmn. profl. rights and responsibilities com. 1985-88, chmn. govtl. rels. com. 1989-91, pres. 1994-95), Phi Beta Kappa. Home: 3551 Narragansett Ave Annapolis MD 21403-4937

GUSKEY, THOMAS ROBERT, education educator; b. Johnstown, Pa., Feb. 15, 1950; s. Robert C. and Evelyn M. (Yarnick) G. BA, Thiel Coll., 1972; MEd, Boston Coll., 1975; PhD, U. Chgo., 1979. Tchr. St. Andrew's Sch., Erie, Pa., 1972-74; rsch. asst. Boston Coll., Chestnut Hill, Mass., 1974-75; teaching asst. U. Chgo., 1975-78; rsch. cons. Chgo. Bd. Edn., 1975-76, dir. R&D, 1976-78; dir. rsch. Ctr. for Improvement of Teaching, Chgo., 1980-82; asst. prof. edn. U. Ky., Lexington, 1978—81, assoc. prof., 1981—85, prof., 1985—. Chmn. dept. edn. policy studies and evaluation U. Ky., Lexington, 1995-96; vis. prof. various colls. and univs.; cons. edn. systems. Author: Implementing Mastery Learning, 1985, 2d edit., 1997, Improving Student Learning, 1988, High Stakes Performance Assessment, 1994, (with J. Block and S. Everson) School Improvement Programs, 1995, (with M. Huberman) Professional Development in Education, 1995, Communicating Student learning, 1996, (with J. Block and S. Everson) Comprehensive School Reform: A Program Perspective, 1999, Evaluating Professional Development, 2000, (with J. Bailey) Implementing Standard-Led Conferences, 2001, (with Bailey) Developing Grading and Reporting Systems for Student Learning, 2001, How's My Kid Doing? A Parents' Guide to Grades, Marks, and Report Cards, 2002; editor Elem. Sch. Jour., 1990—, Focus on Learning, 1996—, Ednl. Measurement: Issues and Practice, 1997—. Named one of Outstanding Young Men of Am., 1981, Tchr. for 21st Century, 1996; commd. Honorable Order of Ky. Cols., 1994. Mem. APA, ASCD, Am. Ednl. Rsch. Assn., Nat. Soc. for Study of Edn., Nat. Staff Devel. Coun. (Article of Yr. award 1996, 99, 2002, Book of Yr. award 1996, 2002), Nat. Coun. on Measurement in Edn., Phi Delta Kappa. Home: 2108 Shelton Rd Lexington KY 40515-1170 Office: U Ky Coll Edn 145 Taylor Edn Bldg Lexington KY 40506-0001 E-mail: guskey@uky.edu.

GUSKIN, ALAN E. university president; b. Bklyn., Mar. 22, 1937; s. David N. and Frances (Midler) G.; m. Lois La Shell, 1990; children from previous marriage: Sharon, Andrea. BA with honors, Bklyn. Coll., 1958; PhD, U. Mich., 1968; LHD (hon.), Saybrook Inst., 1989, Antioch U., 1997. Instr., Peace Corps. vol. Chulalongkorn U., Thailand, 1961-64; dir. of selection VISTA, 1964-65; asst. dir. Ctr. for Research on the Utilization of Scientific Knowledge, Inst. for Social Research, 1968-69; lectr. dept. of psychology and residential coll. U. Mich., 1968-71, dir. ednl. change team, Sch. of Edn., 1969-71, assoc. prof. edn., 1971; provost Clark U., Worcester, Mass., 1971-73, acting pres., 1973-74, prof. sociology and edn., 1973-75; chancellor, prof. edn. U. Wis.-Parkside, Kenosha, 1975-85; pres., prof. Antioch Coll. and Antioch U., Yellow Springs, Ohio, 1985-94; chancellor, Disting. univ. prof. Antioch U., 1994-97, disting. prof., 1997—. Author: (with Samuel Guskin) A Social Psychology of Education, 1970; editor New Directions on Teaching and Learning, The Administrator's Role in Effective Teaching, 1981; contbr. numerous articles and reports to profl. jours. Chmn. bd. Coun. on Adult and Experiential Learning, 1993-95. Mem. Am. Assn. Higher Edn.

GUSOFF, PATRICIA KEARNEY, retired elementary education educator; b. Phila., Jan. 25, 1951; d. William Anthony and Helen Frances (Budnik) Kearney; m. Ronald Gusoff, June 22, 1975; children: Wayne Kenneth, Howard Brandon. BS in Edn., Temple U., 1973, MEd, 1977, EdD, 1988. Cert. elem. tchr., supr., adminstr., Pa., N.J. Elem. sch. tchr. Sch. Dist. Phila., 1973—2001, elem. sci. tchr., 1989-90, basic skills tchr., 1990-96, tchr. remedial work primary grades, 1990-96; asst. facilitator, tutor William McKinley Elem. Sch., Phila., 1992-96; ret., 2001. Coord. sch. recycling Phila. Pride, 1990-96. Mem. ASCD (assoc.), Pa. ASCD, Phila. Fedn. Tchrs. Home: 1119 Hedgerow Ln Philadelphia PA 19115-4808

GUSSOW, MILTON, electrical engineer, educator; b. Newark, Sept. 19, 1924; s. Israel and Minnie (Finkelstein) G.; m. Libbie Gloria Kaye, Dec. 24, 1951; children: Myra Gussow Hamilton, Susan Gussow Vengrove. BS, U.S. Naval Acad., 1949; BSEE, Navy Postgrad. Sch., Monterey, Calif., 1956; MS, MIT, 1957. Enlisted U.S. Navy, 1943, advanced through grades to comdr., 1964, ret., 1967; sr. v.p. McGraw-Hill Book Co., Washington, 1968-78; sr. engr. prin. staff The Johns Hopkins U. Applied Physics Lab., Laurel, Md., 1978—2003. Dir. systems assessment Nat. Defense Indsl. Assn., 1989—; adj. prof. Sch. of Advanced Internat. Studies, Johns Hopkins U., Washington, 1990-93, Am. U., George Washington U., 1960-87. Author: Basic Electricity, 1983, paperback edit., 2002; author over 50 monographs in math., elec. engring.; contbr. articles to profl. jours. Recipient Cert. Merit, Nat. Security Indsl. Assn., 1983, 92, Admiral John H. Sides award, 1997. Mem. IEEE (life), Sigma Xi.

GUSTAFSON, DEBORAH LEE, educational administrator, educator; b. Boston, Dec. 17, 1948; d. Edward Michael and Patricia Frances (Curtin) Lee; m. Robert Edward Gustafson, Oct. 1, 1977; children: Lauren Elizabeth, Jared Lee. BS in Edn., Wagner Coll., 1970, MEd, 1973; cert. advanced grad. studies, Bridgewater State Coll., 1993. Tchr. Trinity Luth. Sch., Staten Island, N.Y., 1970-74, Town of Wareham, Mass., 1974—, elem. curriculum developer, 1983—, dir. acad. Olympics program, 1999-2000, core acad. lead tchr., 2000—. Chmn. com. to write statement of mission and goals Wareham Pub. Schs., 1987—89. Mem. Wareham 250th Anniversary Commn., 1987-89, Constn. Bicentennial Commn. Wareham, 1986-88; chmn. 250th Anniversary Sch. Planning Commn., Wareham, 1988-89; pres. Wareham Hist. Soc., 1989-95; tour guide Fearing Tavern Mus., Wareham, 1988—; reader Talking Infor Ctr. for the Visually Impaired, 1988—; aquatic fitness instr., 2000—. Horace Mann grantee State of Mass., 1988-89. Mem. Mass. Tchrs. Assn. (regional rep., 1995—), Plymouth County Tchrs. Assn. (honor 1985, citation 1988), Plymouth County Edn. Assn. (bd. dirs. 1989-95, 2000—, profl. recognition com. 1990-92, chmn. profl. devel. com. 2001—), Wareham Edn. Assn. (sec. 1978-83, pres. 1983-89, chmn. profl. rights and responsibilities com. 1990-2000, pres. 2000—), People to People Student Amb. Program (rch/leader 1995-99), Delta Kappa Gamma. Roman Catholic. Avocations: needlework, travel. Office: Minot Forest Sch Minot Ave Wareham MA 02571

GUSTAFSON, ROBERT PAUL, exercise science educator; b. Austin, Tex., Feb. 22, 1954; s. Robert Leonard and Mary Wanda (Taylor) G. BS, U. Tex., 1978, MEd, 1980; PhD, Tex. Woman's U., 1991. Cert. Am. Kinesiotherapy Assn. Tchr. Dallas Ind. Sch. Dist., 1980-81, Kemp (Tex.) Ind. Sch. Dist., 1981-83, Jacksboro (Tex.) Ind. Sch. Dist., 1983-85; instr. So. Ark. U., El Dorado, 1985-86; teaching asst. Tex. Woman's U., Denton, 1986-87; rsch. asst. U. Tex. S.W. Med. Ctr., Dallas, 1988-91; assoc. prof. exercise sci. Augusta (Ga.) State U., 1991—. Contbr. articles to profl. jours. Mem. Ga. Assn. for Health, Phys. Edn., Recreation and Dance, Am. Kinesiotherapy Assn. Avocation: racquet sports. Home: 249 Deerfield Ln Martinez GA 30907-2420 Office: Augusta State U Health and Phys Edn 2500 Walton Way Augusta GA 30904-4562 E-mail: rgustafs@aug.edu.

GUSTAFSON, SANDRA LYNNE, retired secondary school educator; b. Phila., Mar. 8, 1948; d. William Henry Gustafson and Ruth Blossom (Berger) Watson. BS in Edn., Temple U., 1969. Tchr. Lincoln H.S., Phila., 1969—78, Germantown H.S., Phila., 1978—85, Lincoln H.S., Phila., 1985—88, Germantown-Lankenau Motivation H.S., Phila., 1988—98, dean of discipline, 1994—96; tchr. Germantown H.S., Phila., 1998—99, Saul H.S., Phila., 1999—2003; ret., 2003. Asst. to vice prin. Lincoln H.S., Phila., 1970-78; sponsor Nat. Honor Soc., Phila., 1989-92, 93-96, Peer Counselors and Peer Tutors, Phila., 1989-98, records mgr., testing coord. Germantown-Lankenau Motivation H.S., 1997-98; chaperone on choir's trip to Europe, Lincoln H.S., 1973, coord. Freshman Orientation Program, Phila., 1993-98. Sponsor Big Brother/Big Sister Program, 1994-98. Mem. MLA, Phila. Fedn. Tchrs. (del. to state conv. 1973, del. to nat. conv. 1973, 74), Phila. Area Spanish Educators, Sigma Delta Pi, Kappa Delta Epsilon. Democrat. Jewish. Avocations: theater, music, ballet, opera, reading. Personal E-mail: slgandcats@aol.com.

GUSTAFSSON, LARS ERIK EINAR, writer, educator; b. Västerås, Sweden, May 17, 1936; came to U.S., 1983; s. Einar H. and Lotten Margaretha (Carlson) G.; m. D. Alexandra Chasnoff, 1982 (div. 2002); children: Benjamin, Karen. PhD, Uppsala (Sweden) U., 1978. Editor-in-chief Bonniers Pub. House, Stockholm, 1961-72; rsch. fellow Ctr. Advanced Studies, Bielefeld, Germany, 1980-81; Aby Warburg rsch. prof. Warburg Found. U. Hamburg, Germany, 1997-98. Bd. dirs. Svenska Dagbladet Found.; bd. regents Uppsala (Sweden) U., 1994-97; adj. prof. U. Tex., Austin, 1983—; Jamail Disting. prof., 1998—. Author numerous novels and poetry collections. John Simon Guggenheim Meml. fellow of poetry, 1993. Mem. Acad. of Arts (Berlin), Acad. Scis. and Lit. (Mainz, Germany), Royal Swedish Acad. Engring. (Stockholm), Bavarian Acad. Fine Arts (Munich). Avocation: painting. Office: U Tex Austin Dept Philosophy Austin TX 78712 E-mail: lars.gustafsson@mail.utexas.edu.

GUTENTAG, PATRICIA RICHMOND, social worker, family counselor, occupational therapist; b. Newark, Apr. 10, 1954; d. Joseph and Joan (Miller) Leflein; m. Herbert Norman Gutentag; children: Steven, Jesse. BS in Occupational Therapy, Tufts U., 1976; MSW, Boston Coll., 1979. Lic. family and marriage counselor, lic. clin. social worker, N.J.; diplomate Am. Bd. Examiners in Clin. Social Work; registered occupational therapist, N.J. Social worker Jewish Family Svc., Salem, Mass., 1979-82; pvt. practice family and marriage counselor Westfield and Red Bank, N.J., 1982—. Cons. high stress, Westfield and Red Bank, 1982—. Fellow N.J. Soc. for Clin. Social Work; mem. NASW, Am. Occupational Therapists Assn., Registered Occupational Therapists Assn., Soc. for Advancement Family Therapy in N.J., Am. Anorexia-Bulimia Assn., Am. Assn. Marriage and Family Therapy. Avocation: reading. Office: 200 Maple Ave Red Bank NJ 07701-1732

GUTFREUND, OWEN DAVID, historian, educator; b. N.Y.C., Mar. 26, 1963; s. John H. Gutfreund and Joyce Ranger (Low) Furth; m. Victoria Lammot Rhodes, June 21, 1986; children: Charlotte R., Willa M. AB, Vassar Coll., 1985; MA, Columbia U., 1990, MPhil, 1992, PhD, 1998. Assoc. Lazard Freres & Co., N.Y.C., 1985-89, v.p., 1989; dir. Keewaydin Camp, Salisbury, Vt., 1991—; instr. Barnard Coll., N.Y.C., 1993-98, asst. prof. history and urban studies, 1998—. Trustee Blythedale Children's Hosp., Valhalla, N.Y., 1990—, vice chair, 1996—; trustee Keewaydin Found., Salisbury, Vt., 1990—; mem. sch. bd. Mt. Pleasant Blythedale UFSD, Valhalla, 1991-93, pres. 1993—; bd. dirs. N.Y. Coun. for Humanities, 1998—, chmn. 2002—; bd. dirs., treas. The Skyscraper Mus., N.Y.C., 1996—. Home: One Gracie Square New York NY 10028 E-mail: gutfreund@columbia.edu.

GUTHEINZ, JOSEPH RICHARD, JR., lawyer, former politician, investigative consultant, retired army officer and NASA official, educator, author; b. Camp Lejune, N.C., Aug. 13, 1955; s. Joseph R. Sr. and Rita C. (O'Leary)

G.; m. Lori Ann Bentley, Jan. 16, 1976; children: Joseph, Christopher, Michael, Jim, Bill, Dave. AS, AA, Monterey Peninsula Coll., Calif., 1975; BA, Calif. State U., Sacramento, 1978, MA, 1979; postgrad., U. Calif., Davis, 1979-80; grad. U.S. Army Mil. Intelligence Officer Basic Course, U.S. Army Tactical Intelligence Sch., 1980; grad., U.S. Army Flight Sch., 1984; MS in Sys. Mgmt., U. So. Calif., 1985; JD, S. Tex. Coll. Law, 1996; grad. Criminal Investigators Basic Course (hon.), Fed. Law Enforcement Tng. Ctrs., 1988; grad. (disting.), Fed. Law Enforcement Tng. Ctrs. Office Inspector Gen., 1989. Bar: Tex. Supreme Ct. 1997, U.S. Dist. Ct. (so. dist.) Tex. 1997, U.S. Vets. Ct. Appeals 1998, U.S. Armed Forces Ct. Appeals 1998, U.S. Ct. Appeals (5th, 10th, 11th and fed. cirs.) 1998, U.S. Tax Ct. 1998, U.S. Supreme Ct. 2001; lic. FAA comml. pilot, cert. fraud examiner, tchr. credentials in aeronautics, mil. sci., bus. and indsl. mgmt., pub. svcs. and adminstrn., sociology and police sci. Calif. Officer U.S. Army, Kitzigen, Fed. Rep. Germany, 1980-82, capt., mil. intelligence officer Stuttgart, Fed. Rep. Germany, 1982-84, capt., aviator Ft. Polk, La., 1984-86; spl. agt. civil aviation security FAA, Oklahoma City, 1986-87; spl. agt. U.S. Dept. Transp., Denver, 1987-90; sr. spl. agt., acting sr. resident agent in charge Office Insp. Gen. NASA, Houston, 1990-2000; pvt. practice atty. Houston, 1996—; mentor, instr. organized crime U. Phoenix, 2002—. Police sci. instr. Ctrl. Tex. Coll., Nelligan, 1983; case agt. FAA Air Traffic Control Acad. Cheating Scandal, 1987, New Denver Airport Investigation, 1988—2000; case agt. in pilot match investigation FBI/FAA Pilot Match Investigation, 1989—90; case agt. in charge of investigating space shuttle temperature transducers Grounded Shuttle Fleet, 1991; task force leader Nine Agy. Fed. Omniplan, 1992—96; task force leader leaseback scheme investigation Lockheed Engrng. Sci. Corp., 1999—2000; guest spkr. Internat. Bus. Forum, 1995, Assn. Govt. Accts., 1996, NASA OIG Auditor Conf., 2000; chief NASA OIG investigator Russian Mir Space Stas. fire and collision, 1997; task force leader Bid and Proposal Investigation Rockwell Space and Ops. Co., 1996—2000; criminal def. atty., expert witness, 1997—; chief investigator and arresting agt. Jerry Whittridge the astronaut and CIA assassin impersonator, 1998, Op. Lunar Eclipse, 1998—2000; investigator Civilian Astronaut Corps., 1999—2002; task force leader Fed. Agy. Investigation Rockwell Internat./Boeing N.Am. and U.S. Alliance, 2000; task force leader Fed. Agy. Investigation, Lockheed Martin; extensively quoted on Columbia disaster, 2003. Author: The Moon Rock Con, Stealing the Dream, Is it Legal to Provately Own Space Shuttle Tiles. Pres. Calif. State U. United Students for Life, 1976—79; chairperson Calif. Rally for Life, 1980; atty./activist against San Jacinto C.C. spl. election to annex parts of Clear Lake Texas; proponent Calif. Pro-Life Initiative, 1977; organizer Morton Downey Dem. Presdl. Campaign, 1979; bd. dirs. Sea Isle Property Owners, 2001—02; briefed Pres. Yeltsin's econ. advisors, 1995. Decorated U.S. Army Meritorious Svc. medal, Army Commendation medal; recipient letter of commendation FBI Dir. Louis Freeh, 1995, Tex. Spl. Commendation U.S. Atty. Office So. Dist., 1996, NASA Exceptional Svc. medal, 2000, Pres.'s Coun. for Integrity and Efficiency Career Achievement award, 2000, Cert. of Appreciation U.S. Atty. (so. dist.) Tex., 2003, Cert. of Commendation Univ. Phoenix, 2003; named Hon. Lt. Gov. Okla., 1987; Merit scholar South Tex. Coll. Law. Mem.: Haris County Lawyers assn., Nat. Rep. Lawyers Assn., Tex. Criminal Def. Lawyers Assn., Tex. Bar Assn., Cert. Fraud Examiners. Republican. Roman Catholic. Avocations: reading, teaching, public speaking, political activism, helping the poor. Office: 205 Woodcombe Houston TX 77062 E-mail: jguteinz@sbcglobal.net.

GUTHKE, KARL SIEGFRIED, foreign language educator; b. Lingen, Germany, Feb. 17, 1933; came to U.S., 1956, naturalized, 1973; s. Karl Hermann and Helene (Beekman) G.; m. Dagmar von Nostitz, Apr. 24, 1965; 1 child, Carl Ricklef. MA, U. Tex., 1953; PhD, U. Göttingen, Germany, 1956; MA (hon.), Harvard U., 1968. Faculty U. Calif., Berkeley, 1956-65; prof. German lit. U. Calif. at Berkeley, 1962-65, U. Toronto, Ont., Can., 1965-68, Harvard U., 1968-78, Kuno Francke prof. German art and culture, 1978—. Vis. prof. U. Colo., 1963, U. Mass., 1967; vis. fellow Sidney Sussex Coll., Cambridge U., Nat. Rsch. Ctr., Wolfenbüttel, Inst. for Adv. Studies, U. Edinburgh, Humanities Rsch. Ctr., Australian Nat. U., Canberra. Author: Englische Vorromantik und deutscher Sturm und Drang, 1958, (with Hans M. Wolff) Das Leid im Werke Gerhart Hauptmanns, 1958, Geschichte und Poetik der deutschen Tragikomödie, 1961, Gerhart Hauptmann: Weltbild im Werk, 1961, rev. edit., 1980, Haller und die Literatur, 1962, Der Stand der Lessing-Forschung: Ein Bericht über die Literatur, 1932-1962, 1965, Modern Tragicomedy: An Investigation into the Nature of the Genre, 1966, Wege zur Literatur: Studien zur deutschen Dichtungs-und Geistesgeschichte, 1967, Hallers Literaturkritik, 1970, Die Mythologie der entgötterten Welt: Ein literarisches Thema von der Aufklärung bis zur Gegenwart, 1971, Das deutsche bürgerliche Trauerspiel, 1972, 5th rev. edit., 1994, G.E. Lessing, 3d edit., 1979, Literarisches Leben im 18. Jahrhundert in Deutschland und in der Schweiz, 1975, Das Abenteuer der Literatur, 1981, Haller im Halblicht, 1981, Der Mythos der Neuzeit, 1983, Erkundungen, 1983, Das Geheimnis um B. Traven entdeckt, 1984, B. Traven: Biographie eines Rätsels, 1987, The Last Frontier: Imagining Other Worlds, 1990, Letzte Worte, 1990, B. Traven: The Life Behind the Legends, 1991, Last Words, 1992, Trails in No-Man's Land, 1993, Die Entdeckung des Ich, 1993, Schillers Dramen, 1994, Ist der Tod eine Frau, 1997, The Gender of Death, 1999, Der Blick in die Fremde, 2000, Goethes Weimar und die grosse Öffnung in die weite Welt, 2001, Epitaph Culture in the West, 2003, Lessings Horizonte, 2003, also others; transl.: Die moderne Tragikomödie: Theorie und Gestalt, 1968; editor: Haller, Die Alpen, 1987; co-editor: (Hanser) Gotthold Ephraim Lessing, Werke, 1970-72, Joh. H. Füssli, Sämtliche Gedichte, 1973, B. Traven: Briefe aus Mexiko, 1992, Lessing Yearbook, Colloquia Germanica, Twentieth Century Literature, German Quar. Honored in History and Literature: Essays in Honor of Karl S. Guthke, 2000. Fellow Humanities Rsch. Ctr., Canberra Australia, Inst. Advanced Studies, Edinburgh, Scotland, Rsch. Ctr., Wolfenbuttel; mem. Lessing Soc. (past pres.), Inst. Germanic Studies (London corr. fellow). Office: Harvard U Dept German Cambridge MA 02138

GUTHRIE, FRANK ALBERT, chemistry educator; b. Madison, Ind., Feb. 16, 1927; s. Ned and Gladys (Glick) G.; m. Marcella Glee Farrar, June 12, 1955; children: Mark Alan, Bruce Bradford, Kent Andrew, Lee Farrar. AB, Hanover Coll., 1950; MS, Purdue U., 1952; PhD, Ind. U., 1962. Mem. faculty Rose-Hulman Inst. Tech., Terre Haute, Ind., 1952—, assoc. prof., 1962-67, prof. chemistry, 1967-94, prof. emeritus, 1994—, chmn. dept., 1969-72, chief health professions adviser, 1975-94. Kettering vis. lectr. U. Ill., Urbana, 1961-62; vis. prof. chemistry U.S. Mil. Acad., West Point, N.Y., 1987-88, 93-94, admissions coord., 1989—; vis. prof. chemistry Butler U., spring 2000. Mem. exec. bd. Wabash Valley coun. Boy Scouts Am., 1971-87, scoutmaster, 1979-82, adv. bd., 1988—, v.p. for scouting, 1976; selection chmn. Leadership Terre Haute, 1978-80. Served with AUS, 1945-46. Recipient Vigil Honor Order of Arrow, Wabash Valley coun. Boy Scouts Am., 1975, Wood badge, 1976, Dist. award of merit, 1976, Silver Beaver award, 1980. Fellow Ind. Acad. Sci. (treas. 1966-68, pres. 1970, chmn. acad. found. trustees 1986—); mem. Am. Chem. Soc. (sec. 1973-77, editor directory 1965-77, chmn. divsn. analytical chemistry 1979-80, chmn. 1958, counselor Wabash Valley sect. 1980—, local sect. activities com. 1982-86, nominations and elections com. 1988-94, sec. 1992-94, coun. policy com. 1995, constn. and bylaws com. 1996-2002, membership affairs com., 2003—, steering com. for Joint Ctrl.-Gt. Lakes Regional Meetings, Indpls., 1978, 91, vis. assoc. com. profl. tng. 1984—, chmn. analytical chemistry exam. inst. std. exam. 1994), Coblentz Soc., Midwest Univs. Analytical Chemistry Conf., Hanover Coll. Alumni Assn. (pres. 1974, Alumni Achievement award 1977), Masons (32 deg.), Sigma Xi (treas. Wabash Valley chpt. 1994-98), Phi Lambda Upsilon, Phi Gamma Delta, Alpha Chi Sigma (E.E. Dunlap scholarship selection com. 1986—, chmn. 1990—, dir. expansion 1995-99, profl. rep. 1997-2000). Presbyterian. Home: 120 Berkley Dr Terre Haute IN 47803-1708 Office: Rose Hulman Inst Tech 5500 Wabash Ave Terre Haute IN 47803-3999 E-mail: frank.guthrie@rose-hulman.edu., fguthrie@chilitech.com.

GUTHRIE, GLENDA EVANS, academic counselor, development specialist; b. De Funiak Springs, Fla., Aug. 10, 1945; d. Owen Clement and Vera Mae (Adams) Evans; m. Theron Asbury Guthrie Jr., June 10, 1967; children: Michael Patrick, Jennifer Leigh. BS in Elem. Edn., Samford U., 1967; MA in Elem. Edn., U. Ala., 1983; EdS in Ednl. Leadership, U. Fla., 1990. Tchr. grades 8-9 Warrington Jr. High, Pensacola, Fla., 1967; tchr. grades 4-5 Birmingham (Ala.) City Schs., 1967-69; tchr. grade 5 Faith Christian Sch., Bessemer, Ala., 1969-70; tchr. grade 4 Fairfield Highlands Christian Sch., Birmingham, 1973-74, First Bapt. Sch., Pleasant Grove, Ala., 1974-83; tchr. grade 5 Ctrl. Park Christian Sch., Birmingham, 1983-84, elem. dir., 1984-86; tchr. grades 5-6 Duval County Sch., Jacksonville, Fla., 1986-90; ednl. cons. Jostens Learning Corp., Phoenix, 1990-92, sr. ednl. cons., 1993-95; profl. devel. specialist CompassLearning, 1995—; acad. counselor U. Phoenix-Nashville Campus, 2003. Co-founder Success Unlimited Learning Ctr., Birmingham, 1985-86; judge Sci. Fair, Jacksonville, 1988-90; seminar/workshop leader; mem. elem. textbook com. Duval County Schs., 1988-89. Active Brentwood Bapt. Ch. Named Tchr. of Yr. Livingston Sch., Jacksonville, 1989, Ednl. Cons. of Yr., 1991-92. Mem. ASCD, Internat. Reading Assn., Nat. Coun. Tchrs. Math., Kappa Delta Pi. Republican. Baptist. Avocation: reading. Home and Office: 159 Carphilly Cir Franklin TN 37069

GUTIERREZ, ARTURO LUIS, school system administrator; b. Zapata, Tex., Aug. 12, 1934; s. Arturo Carlos and Josefa (Martinez) G.; m. Armandina Isabel Gonzalez, Dec. 15, 1968. Student, Laredo Jr. Coll., 1950-51; BS, North Tex. State Coll., 1953, MEd, 1961; PhD, U. Tex., Austin, 1972. Cert. profl. supt., Tex. Cons. bilingual edn. Tex. Edn. Agy., Austin, 1970-72, dir. bilingual edn., 1972-76; dep. assoc. supt. Dallas (Tex.) Ind. Sch. Dist., 1976-78; dir. instrn. svcs. Region XX-Edn. Svc. Ctr., San Antonio, 1978-83; dir. curriculum devel. Dallas (Tex.) Ind. Sch. Dist., 1983, asst. supt., 1983-86; assoc. supt. Corpus Christi (Tex.) Ind. Sch. Dist., 1986-90; supt. South San Antonio (Tex.) Ind. Sch. Dist., 1990; assoc. supt. Corpus Christi (Tex.) Ind. Sch. Dist., from 1990, interim supt., from 1992. Pres. Tex. Assn. Bilingual Edn., 1976-78; chmn. Urban Curriculum Coun., Tex., 1989-90. Author: (textbooks) Language Basics Plus, 1979, Preparate/Listo, 1980, Harper and Row English, 1982. Commr. Corpus Christi (Tex.) Housing Authority, 1988-90, vice chmn., 1991-93, chmn., 1993—; mem. Foster Grandparents Adv. Com., Corpus Christi, 1990—. Named Educator of Yr., Dallas (Tex.) Mexican C. of C., 1976-77. Mem. Tex. ASCD, Corpus Christi ASCD, Tex. Assn. Sch. Adminstrs., Tex. Edn. Assn. (chmn. subcom. devel. performance indica 1989-90, chmn. subcom. acad. excellence indicators 1990—), Phi Delta Kappa. Home: San Antonio, Tex. Died Apr. 13, 2002.

GUTIN, MYRA GAIL, communications educator; b. Paterson, N.J., Aug. 13, 1948; d. Stanley and Lillian (Edelstein) Greenberg; m. David Gutin, Sept. 5, 1971; children: Laura, Sarah, Andrew. BA, Emerson Coll., 1970, MA, 1971; PhD, U. Mich., 1983. Asst. prof. comm. Cumberland County Coll., Vineland, N.J., 1972-80, Rider U., Lawrenceville, N.J., 1981-88, prof., 1989—. Adj. instr. Essex County Coll., Newark, 1971-72, Nassau C.C., Garden City, N.Y., 1972, Trenton (N.J.) State Coll., 1981-84; adj. asst. prof. Rider U., 1981-85; lectr. in field. Author: The President's Partner The First Lady in the 20th Century, 1989; contbr. articles to profl. jours. Officer Emerson Coll. Nat. Alumni Bd., 1994—2002, pres., 1998—2000; bd. dirs. Harry B. Kellman Acad., 1999—2002, vice chair bd. dirs., 1998—2000, chair bd. dirs., 2000—02; bd. dirs. Jewish Cmty. Relations Coun., 2003—. Recipient Alumni Achievement award, Emerson Coll., Boston, 1991. Mem. Ctr. for Study of the Presidency, Nat. Comm. Assn., Ea. Comm. Assn. Avocations: travel, theatre. Home: 119 Greenvale Ct Cherry Hill NJ 08034-1701

GUTKE, JEFFREY ALAN, Spanish language educator; b. Chgo., Nov. 19, 1968; s. Earl George and Linda May (Hlavac) G. BA, No. Ill. U., 1991, MA in Spanish, 1993. Instr. No. Ill. U., DeKalb, 1991-93, Kishewaukee C.C., Malta, Ill., 1992-93; Spanish tchr. Thornton Fractional North H.S., 1993-94, Woodland Mid. Sch., 1994—. Mem. Grad. Adv. Coun., DeKalb, 1991-92. Vol. Transitional Program of Instrn., DeKalb, 1992-93. Mem. Ill. Coun. on Teaching Fgn. Langs., Sigma Delta Pi (pres. 1991-93), Phi Sigma Iota (sec. 1991-93). Avocations: reading Latin Am. short stories, foreign film, Latin Am. and European travel.

GUTMAN, HARRY LARGMAN, lawyer, educator; b. Phila., Feb. 23, 1942; s. I. Cyrus and Mildred B. (Largman) Gutman; m. Anne G. Aronsky, Aug. 28, 1971; children: Jonathan, Elizabeth. AB cum laude, Princeton U., 1963; BA, U. Coll., Oxford, Eng., 1965; LLB cum laude, Harvard U., 1965; MA (hon.), U. Pa., 1984. Bar: Mass. 1968, U.S. Tax Ct. 1969, Pa. 1989, DC 1996. Assoc. Hill & Barlow, Boston, 1968-75, ptnr., 1975-77; clin. assoc. Law Sch. Harvard U., Cambridge, Mass., 1971-77; instr. Boston Coll., 1974-77; atty.-advisor Office Tax Legis. Counsel U.S. Dept. Treasury, 1977-78, dep. tax law legis. counsel, 1978-80; assoc. prof. law U. Va., Charlottesville, 1980-84; prof. Law Sch. U. Pa., 1984-89; ptnr. Drinker Biddle & Reath, Phila., 1989-91; chief staff joint com. taxation U.S. Congress, 1991-93; ptnr. King & Spalding, Washington, 1994-99, KPMG LLP, Washington, 1999—. Cons. Office Tax Policy U.S. Dept. Treasury, 1980, Am. Law Inst., 1980—84; reporter Generation-Skipping Tax Project Arden Ho. III Conf.; vis. prof. Law Sch. U. Va., 1985—89, Ill. Inst. Tech., 1986. Author: (book) Transactions Between Partners and Partnerships, 1973, Minimizing Estate Taxes: The Effects of Inter Vivos Giving, 1975; author: (with F. Sander) Tax Aspects of Divorce and Separation, 1985; author: (with D. Lubick) Treaury's New Views on Carryover Basis, 1979, Effective Federal Tax Rates on Transfers of Wealth, 1979; author: (with others) Federal Wealth Transfer Taxes after ERTA, 1983, Reforming Federal Wealth Transfer Taxes after ERTA, 1983, A Commnet on the ABA Tax Section Task Force Report on Transfer Tax Restructuring, 1988, Where Does Congress Go From Here? Base Timing and Measurement Issues in the Transfer Tax, 1989. Trustee Washington Opera. Fellow: Am. Coll. Tax Counsel (trustee); mem.: Am. Tax Policy Inst. (trustee). Office: KPMG LLP 2001 M St NW Washington DC 20036-3310 E-mail: hgutman@kpmg.com.

GUTMAN, LUCY TONI, school social worker, educator, counselor; b. Phila., July 13, 1936; d. Milton R. and Clarissa (Silverman) G.; divorced; children: James, Laurie. BA, Wellesley Coll., 1958; MSW, Bryn Mawr Coll., 1963; MA in History, U. Ariz., 1978; MEd, Northwestern State U., 1991, MA in English, 1992; postgrad., U. So. Miss., 1992—. Cert. sch. social work specialist, Nat. Bd. Cert. Counselor; diplomate in clin. social work; cert. secondary tchr., La.; cert. counselor, La.; cert. Acad. Cert. Social Workers, La. Bd. Cert. Social Workers. Social worker Phila. Gen. Hosp., 1963-65; sr. social worker Irving Schwartz Inst. Children and Youth, 1965-66; sr. psychiat. social worker Child Study Ctr. Phila., 1966-68; chief social worker Framingham (Mass.) Ct. Clinic Juvenile Offenders, 1968-72; dir. clinic, supr. social work Tucson East Cmty. Mental Health Ctr., 1972-74; coord. spl. adoptions program Cath. Social Svcs. So. Ariz., Tucson, 1974-75; social worker Met. Ministry, 1983; supr. social work Leesville (La.) Mental Health Clinic, 1984; sch. social worker Vernon Parish Sch. Bd., Leesville, 1984—. Cons. Nashua (N.H.) Cmty. Coun., 1969-72; adj. instr. English, sociology, Am. and European history Northwestern State U., Ft. Polk, La., 1984—; part-time counselor River North Psychol. Svcs., Leesville, 1989-92; presenter La. Sch. Social Workers Conf., 1986, 87, Ann. Conf. NASW, 1987, 88, La. Spl. Edn. Conf., 1988, La. Conf. Tchrs. English, 1991, 94, So. Assn. Women Historians, 1994, Mid-Am. Conf. History, 1997, Conf. Contemporary So. Women's Lit., 1997, La. Hist. Assn. Conf., 1998. Contbr. articles to profl. jours. Nat. Soc. Colonial Dames scholar, 1978-79; fellow Pa. State, 1961-62, NIMH, 1962-63. Mem. NASW (diplomate), La. Hist. Assn., So. Hist. Assn., So. Assn. Women Historians, Gamma Beta Phi, Phi Alpha Theta, Phi Kappa Phi. Home: 2004 Allison St Leesville LA 71446-5104

GUTMANN, BARBARA LANG, nurse, educator administrator, consultant; b. Niagara Falls, N.Y. d. Frank J. and Beryl (Tennant) Lang; m. James F. Gutmann, June 25, 1960; children: Carolyn Dougherty, Bennett J. BSN cum laude, Niagara U., 1956; cert. sch. nurse tchr., Syracuse U., 1962; MSN, SUNY, Buffalo, 1975. Cert. pub. health nurse, basic CPR instr., Calif., N.Y., aids educator, Calif. Nurses Assn., 1987. Staff nurse VA Hosp., Syracuse, N.Y., 1956-58; pub. health nurse Syracuse City Health Dept., 1958-62, County Dept. Pub. Welfare, 1961-62; sch. nurse tchr. North Syracuse Ctrl. Schs., 1962-65; vol. Peace Corps, India, 1965-66; tchr. educable retarded North Syracuse Ctrl. Schs., 1966-67; staff nurse Stanford U. Hosp., Palo Alto, Calif., 1970-71; pvt. duty nurse Buffalo, 1972-74; assst. prof. nursing Niagara County C.C., Sanborn, N.Y., 1975-77; dir. nursing svcs. Homemaker Upjohn Contract Offices, Santa Barbara County, Calif., 1977-78; project dir. Upjohn Health Care Svcs., Santa Barbara, 1978; dir. nursing Sansum Med. Clinic, Santa Barbara, 1979-81; dir. inservice edn. and staff devel. Pinecrest Hosp., Santa Barbara, 1981-82; dir. edn. Meml. Rehab. Hosp., Santa Barbara, 1982-84; dir. staff devel. Beverly La Cumbre Convalescent Hosp., 1989, dir. nursing, 1990-92; asst. adminstr. health, dir. nursing Vista del Monte Retirement Cmty., 1992-96; instr. nursing, health tech. and adult edn. Santa Barbara City Coll., 1984-89, 96—, cons. health care and nursing edn., 1996—. Profl. adv. bd. upper divsn. nursing program Daemen Coll., Buffalo, 1975-77; mem. Niagara Falls Regional Hypertension Bd., 1975-77, Buffalo Quality of Life Com., 1976-77; profl. adv. com. and utilization rev. com. Niagara County Health Dept., 1976-77; home nurse educator multiple sclerosis patients ARC, 1978; adv. com. Upjohn Health Care Svcs., 1979-82; health occupations adv. com. med. assisting program Santa Barbara C.C., 1980; mem. Head Trauma Recovery Group, Santa Barbara, 1982-85; contbr. to core curriculum Assn. Rehab. Nurses, 1987. Adv. com. Friendship Ctr., Santa Barbara, 1977-79; bd. dirs. Friendship Sr. Day Care Ctr., Montecito, Calif., 1986-94, pres., 1989-91, 92-94, v.p., 1985-86, bd. dirs. emeriti, 1994—; mem. basic CPR com. Am. Heart Assn., 1982-85; bishop's com. Diocese of Syracuse, 1965; bd. dirs. Onondaga County Health Assn., 1965; edn. com. Hillbrook Detention Home, 1967-70; mem. Inner City Bd. Dirs., Syracuse, 1968-70; sec. exec. com. bd. dirs. Onondaga Pastoral Counseling Ctr., 1967-70; asst. leader Girl Scouts Am., 1976-77, Boy Scout Com., 1977-86; bd. dirs. Jodi House, 1982-85; docent Cachuma Nature Ctr., 1996—, sec., 1997-2002, pres. 2002-2003; mem. Friendship Force Santa Barbara, 2003—, v.p. 2002. Roman Catholic. Home and Office: 5474 Berkeley Rd Santa Barbara CA 93111-1614

GUTMANN, DAVID LEO, psychology educator; b. N.Y.C., Sept. 17, 1925; s. Isaac and Masha (Agronsky) G.; m. Joanna Redfield, Aug. 18, 1951; children: Stephanie, Ethan. MA, U. Chgo., 1956, PhD, 1958. Lectr. psychology Harvard U., Cambridge, Mass., 1960-62; prof. U. Mich., Ann Arbor, 1962-76, Northwestern U., Chgo., 1976-97, prof. emeritus, 1998—, chief of psychology, 1976-81, dir. older adult program, 1978-95. Vis. emeritus prof. Hebrew U., Jerusalem, 1997. Author: Reclaimed Powers: Toward a New Psychology of Men and Women in Later Life, 1987, Reclaimed Powers: Men and Women in Later Life, 1994, The Human Elder in Nature, Culture, and Society, 1997; co-author: (with Bardwick, Douvan and Horner) Feminine Personality and Conflict, 1979. With U.S. Mcht. Marine, 1943-46. Recipient Career Devel. award NIMH, 1964-74. Fellow Gerontol. Soc. Am.; mem. Am. Vets. of Israel, Nat. Assn. Scholars. Jewish. E-mail: d-gutmann@northwestern.edu., dgutmann@aol.com.

GUTMANN, KATHRYN CAROL, physical education educator; b. West Islip, N.Y., Apr. 5, 1960; d. Leonard M. and Carolyn (Kopf) G. BA, Lynchburg Coll., 1982; MA, Appalachian State U., 1988. Athletic dir., tchr. phys. edn. Notre Dame Acad., Middleburg, Va., 1983-86; instr. phys. edn., coach softball and field hockey Davis and Elkins (W.Va.) Coll., 1988-90; tchr. phys. edn. Bishop Ireton H.S., Alexandria, Va., 1991—. Umpire Amateur Softball Assn., 1990—, VHSL Varsity Softball, 1991—; field hockey ofcl. Old Dominion Athletic Conf., Balt., 1991-97; referee Cardinal Basketball Assn., Fairfax, 1991-2000; coach Fairfax Jr. Volleyball Club, 1993-96; varsity volleyball coach Oalcton H.S., 2000-02. Mem. AAHPERD, Am. Volleyball Coaches. Avocations: officiating, playing softball and volleyball. Home: 1913 N Quaker Ln Alexandria VA 22302-2105 Office: Bishop Ireton High Sch 201 Cambridge Rd Alexandria VA 22314-4809 E-mail: gutmannk@bishopireton.org.

GUTMANN, RONALD J. electrical engineering educator; b. Bklyn., Nov. 16, 1940; s. Ludwig G. and Dorothy (Levy) G.; m. Suzanne French, Aug. 27, 1967; children: David, Jennifer. BSEE, Rensselaer Poly. Inst., 1962, PhD in Electrophysics, 1970; MSEE, NYU, 1964. Mem. tech. staff Bell Telephone Labs., Whippany, N.J., 1962-66; sr. engr. Lockheed Electronics Co., Plainfield, N.J., 1966-67; rsch. asst. Rensselaer Poly. Inst., Troy, N.Y., 1967-70, asst. prof. elec. engrng., 1970-74, assoc. prof., 1974-80, prof., 1980—. Dir. Ctr. for Integrated Electronics, 1989-94; vis. mem. tech. staff Bell Labs., Whippany, 1979; program dir. NSF, Washington, 1981-83; presenter in field; cons. in field. Author, editor McGraw Hill series on continuing edn. in electonics; co-author: Chemical-Mechanical Planarization of Microelectronic Materials, 1997, Copper-Fundamental Mechanisms for Microelectronic Applications, 2000, Chemical-Mechanical Polishing of Law Dielectric Constant Polymers and Organosilicate Glasses, 2002; contbr. numerous articles to profl. jours. Recipient Disting. Svc. award NSF, 1983; engrng. fellow NASA, 1977. Fellow IEEE (chmn. awards com. 1984-85, vice chmn. awards bd. 1987-88, mem. numerous tech. program coms., fellow award for contbns. to microwave semiconductor tech.). Avocations: jogging, tennis, reading. Office: Rensselaer Poly Inst CII 6129 15th St Troy NY 12181 E-mail: gutmar@rpi.edu.

GUTTMAN, EGON, law educator; b. Neuruppin, Germany, Jan. 27, 1927; came to U.S., 1958, naturalized, 1968; s. Isaac and Blima (Liss) G.; m. Inge Weinberg, June 12, 1966; children: Geoffrey David, Leonard Jay. Student, U. Cambridge, 1945-48; LLB, U. London, London, England, 1950, LLM, 1952; post grad., Northwestern U. Sch. Law, 1958-59. Barrister: Eng. 1952. Sole practice, England, 1952-53; faculty Univ. Coll. and U. Khartoum, 1953-58; legal advisor to chief justice, 1953-58; founder, editor Sudan Law Jour. & Reports, Sudan, 1956-57; researcher, lectr. Rutgers U. Sch. Law, Newark, 1959-60; asst. prof. U. Alta., Edmonton, Canada, 1960-62; prof. Howard U. Law Sch., Washington, 1962-68, vis. adj. prof., 1968-96; adj. prof. law Washington Coll. Law, Am. U., Wash., 1964-68, Levitt Meml. Trust scholar-prof., 1968—, dir. JD-MBA joint degree program, 1990-2000; lectr. Practicing Law Inst., 1964—. Adj. prof. law Georgetown U. Law Ctr., 1972-74, Johns Hopkins U., Balt., 1973-81; vis. prof. Faculty of Law, U. Cambridge, Wolfson Coll., Eng., 1984, U. Haifa, Israel, 2000; atty.-fellow SEC, 1976-79; cons. to various U.S. agys. and spl. commns.; U.S. rep. to UNCITRAL working groups; mem. various ALI-ABA working groups on the revision of the uniform comml. code; mem. Sec. of State's Adv. Com. on Pvt. Internat. Law; arbitrator NY Stock Exch. and NASD, 1997—. Author: Crime, Cause and Treatment, 1956; author: (with A. Smith) Cases and Materials on Domestic Rels., 1962; author: Modern Securities Transfers, 3d edit., 2002, 4th edit., 2002; author: (with R.G. Vaughn) Cases and Materials on Policy and the Legal Environment, 1973, rev., 1978, 3d edit., 1980; author: Problems and Materials on Sales Under the Uniform Comm. Code and the Convention on Internat. Sale of Goods, Comm. Transactions, vol. 2, 1990; author: (with F. Miller) supplement, 1996—98; author: (with L.F. Del Duca and A.M. Squilante) Problems and Materials on Secured Transactions Under the Uniform Comm. Code, Comm. Transactions, vol. 1, 1992; author: supplement, 1997, Problems and Materials on Negotiable Instruments Under the Uniform Comm. Code and the UN Conv. on Internat. Bills of Exch. and Internat. Promissory Notes, Comm. Transactions, vol. 3,

1993, supplement, 1995; author: (with R.B. Lubic) Secured Transactions-A Simplified Guide, 1996; author: Securities Laws in the United States-A Primer for Fgn. Lawyers, 1996—99; author: (with L.F. Del Duca, F.H. Miller, P. Winship, W.H. Henning) Secured Transactions Under the Uniform Comm. Code and Internat. Commerce, 2002; contbr. numerous articles, revs., briefs to profl. lit. Howard U. rep. Fund for Edn. in World Order, 1966-68; trustee Silver Spring Jewish Ctr., Md., 1976-79; mem. exec. com. Sha'are Tzedek Hosp., Washington, 1971-72, 97—. Leverhulme scholar, 1948-51; U. London studentship, 1951-52; Ford Found. grad. fellow, 1958-59, NYU summer workshop fellow, 1960, 61, 64; Levitt Meml. Trust scholar-professor 1982—; recipient Outstanding Svc. award Student Bar Assn., Am. U., 1970, Law Rev. Outstanding Svc. award, 1981, Washington Coll. of Law Outstanding Contbn. to Acad. Program Devel. award, 1981. Mem. Am. Law Inst., ABA, Fed. Bar Assn. Assn. Trial Lawyers Am., Brit. Inst. Internat. and Comparative Law, Soc. Pub. Tchrs. Law (Eng.), Hon. Soc. Middle Temple, Hardwick Soc. of Inns of Ct., Sudan Philos. Soc., Assn. Can. Law Tchrs., Am. Soc. Internat. Law, Can. Assn. Comparative Law, B'nai Brith, Argo Lodge, Phi Alpha Delta (John Sherman Myers award 1972). Home: 14801 Pennfield Cir Silver Spring MD 20906-1580 Office: Am U Washington Coll Law 4801 Massachusetts Ave NW Washington DC 20016-8196 Fax: (202) 274-4130. E-mail: guttman@wcl.american.edu.

GUTWIRTH, MARCEL MARC, French literature educator; b. Antwerp, Belgium, Apr. 11, 1923; s. Jacob Nahum and Frieda (Willner) G.; m. Madelyn Katz, June 20, 1948; children: Eve, Sarah, Nathanael. Student, NYU, 1941-42; AB, Columbia, 1947, MA, 1948, PhD, 1950. Mem. faculty Haverford (Pa.) Coll., 1948-87, William R. Kenan, Jr. prof. French lit., 1977-82, John Whitehead prof., 1983-87; Disting. Prof. Grad. Ctr. CUNY, 1987-94, exec. officer PhD program in French, 1987-93. Vis. prof. Johns Hopkins U., 1967, Queens Coll., 1968, Bryn Mawr Coll., 1969, 76; Andrew Mellon vis. prof. humanities Tulane U., 1980; lectr. Folger Inst., 1985. Author: Molière ou l'Invention Comique, 1966, Jean Racine: Un Itinéraire Poétique, 1970, Stendhal, 1971, Michel de Montaigne ou le Pari d'Exemplarité, 1977, Un Merveilleux sans Eclat: La Fontaine ou La Poésie Exilée, 1987, Laughing Matter, 1993. Bd. dirs. Childbirth Edn. Assn. Greater Phila., 1961-64. With AUS, 1943-46, ETO. Fulbright postdoctoral fellow Paris, 1953-54, Am. Coun. Learned Socs. fellow, 1964-65, Guggenheim fellow, 1971-72, 85, Nat. Humanities Ctr. fellow, 1985-86. Mem. ACLU, MLA (mem. editl. bd. publs. 1973-76), Am. Assn. Tchrs. of French. Jewish. Home: 640 Valley View Rd Ardmore PA 19003-1029

GUYER, HEDY-ANN KLEIN, special education educator; b. Phila., Dec. 25, 1947; d. Edward Chuck Klein and Gladys Selma (Shapiro) Sussman; m. Eugene August Guyer, Aug. 24, 1980 (div. Mar. 2002). BS in Secondary Edn., St. Joseph's U., Phila., 1981; MEd in Spl. Edn., Arcadia Univ., 1996. Cert. in social studies, elem. edn., spl. edn. of mentally and/or physically handicapped, Pa. Tchr. spl. edn. Sch. Dist. Phila., 1996—. Mem. ASCD, Women in Edn., George Washington H.S. Alumni Assn., B'nai B'rith (educators unit), Coun. Exceptional Children. Home: 1033 Bloomfield Ave Philadelphia PA 19115-4829 Office: Sch Dist Phila William Penn HS Broad and Master Sts Philadelphia PA 19122-4097

GUYONNEAU, CHRISTINE HUGUETTE, librarian; b. St. Etienne, France, Jan. 20, 1948; d. Maurice Daniel and Helene Marcelle (Bossoutrot) G.; m. Thomas A. Mason, Aug. 11, 1984; 1 child, Charlotte. Lic., U. St. Etienne, 1973; MA in French Lit., U. Va., 1983; MS in Libr. and Info. Sci., U. Ill., 1984. Libr. asst. U. Va. Libr., Charlottesville, 1975-78, bibliographer, 1978-87; dir. reference svcs. U. Indpls. Libr., 1987-94, dir. pub. svc., 1994—. Pres. U. Ill. Libr. Sch. Alumni Assn., Urbana, 1993-95. Author book revs.; contbr. articles to profl. jours. Pres. Ameri-France, Indpls., 1993-95. Rsch. grantee Woodson Inst., 1986. Mem. ALA, Assn. Coll. and Rsch. Librs. (officer 1991-93), Cen. Ind. Area Libr. Svc. Authority, Ind. Online Libr. User Group (v.p./pres.-elect 1995-97), Ind. Libr. Fedn. (officer 1994—). Avocations: cooking, reading, swimming. Office: U Indpls Libr 1400 E Hanna Library Indianapolis IN 46227

GUZAK, DEBRA ANN, special education educator; b. Blue Island, Ill., Jan. 11, 1963; d. Robert Joseph and Angeline (Kozak)G. BS in Edn., Ea. Ill. U., 1985; MEd, U. Ill., 1993; postgrad., U. Wis., Whitewater, U. Manosh, Frankston, Australia. Cert. tchr., early childhood spl. edn., Ill. Spl. edn. tchr. Southwest Cook County Coop., Oak Forest, Ill., 1985; early childhood specialist Sunnybrook Sch. Dist. 171, Lansing, Ill., 1985—, intern in administrn., 1992-93. Pvt. tutor, Lansing, 1985—; track coach Heritage Mid. Sch., Lansing, 1990—. Editor: Share a Story, 1992. Vol. Little City, Paletine, Ill., 1986—, Orland Park (Ill.) Spl. Recreation; fundraiser Miserecordia/Heart of Mercy, Chgo., 1986—; steering com. Young Hearts Am. Heart Assn., Chgo., 1987-91; co-chmn. fashion show seating com. Ronald McDonald House, Chgo., 1994, 95, 97, 98, 99-. Grantee Ill. State Bd. Edn., 1990; recipient Educator of Yr. award Lansing Rotary, 1996, Educators Making a Difference award South Suburban Chgo. chpt. Children and Adults with Attention Deficit Disorders. Mem. Assn. Supervision and Curriculum Devel., Coun. Exceptional Children (divsn. early childhood, svc. award 1981-86), Ind. Order Foresters. Republican. Roman Catholic. Avocations: water sports, winter sports, golf, fine dining, theater. Home: 17555 W Quail Trl Tinley Park IL 60477

GUZMAN, ANA MARGARITA, university administrator; b. Havana, Cuba, June 12, 1947; came to U.S., 1960; d. Gabriel and Margarita (Gomez) G.; children: Sean, Ryan; m. Gilberto Sosa Ocañas, May 27, 1989. BS in Edn., Stout State U., Menomonie, Wis., 1968; MA in Sociology, Tex. So. U., 1974; EdD in Edn., U. Houston, 1979. Lic. tchr., Va., Tex., supt., Va., mid-mgmt. tchr., Tex., Va. Dir. bilingual edn. Goose Creek Ind. Sch. Dist., Houston, 1981-85, dir. program devel., 1985-86; dir. staff devel. Houston Ind. Sch. Dist., 1986-88, prin., 1988-89; dir. regional program Fairfax County Pub. Schs., Fairfax, Va., 1988-89; program officer NSF, Washington, 1990-92; fellow to chancellor, assoc. prof. edn. Tex. A&M U., Kingsville, 1992—, program dir. Alliances for Minority Participation, 1995-99; exec. v.p. Austin C.C., Cedar Park, Tex., 1993—; vice-chair President's Adv. Commn. on Ednl. Excellence for Hispanic Americans, 1994-96, Chair, 1996—. Mem. Gov.'s Commn. on Lit., Tex., 1985-87; cons. N.Y. Pub. Schs., 1990, Ednl. Devel. Corp., State Systems Inst., 1992; mem. Task Force for NSF State Systemic Initiatives. Author: Questions and Answers About Bilingual Education-Quality Education for Mentors, 1991, Science Strategies for Limited English Proficient Student, 1992. Mem. Assn. for Advancement of Mexican Americans, Houston, 1986-88, Hispanic Action Com., Washington, 1992—; mem. Supt. Minority Achievement Com., Fairfax County, 1980-92; vice-chair Mexican Am. Legal Def. Edn. Fund, L.A., 1988-92; bd. dirs. ERIC Clearinghouse, N.Y., 1991—; chair Pres. Clinton's Adv. Commn. Ednl. Excellence for Hispanic Ams., 1994—. Doctoral fellow HEW, Washington, 1975-78. Mem. Am. Ednl. Rsch. Assn., Nat. Assn. Bilingual Edn., Am. Assn. Sch. Adminstrs. Democrat. Roman Catholic. Avocations: reading, aerobics, swimming, travel.

GUZMAN-SMITH, MARILYN ELIZABETH, elementary school educator; b. N.Y.C., Sept. 28, 1953; d. Cosme Guzman and Luz Maria Molina; m. Steven Smith; children: Jermaine Steven, Camille Manuela. BA in Elem. Edn., SUNY, Stony Brook, 1975; MS in Adminstrn. and Supervision, CCNY, 1995, MS in Bilingual Edn., 1978. Bilingual tchr., bilingual coord. Bronx (N.Y.) Bd. Edn., 1975—89, bilingual coord., 1989—90; 3d grade tchr. Dorado (P.R.) Acad., 1990—91; 4th grade tchr., lang. arts coord. Baldwin (P.R.) Sch., 1991—92; AIDP facilitator P.S. - M.S. 279, Bronx, 1991—96; tchr. 3rd grade P.S. 86 Sch., Bronx, NY, 1992—97; acting asst. prin. P.S. 207, Bronx, 1996—97; asst. prin. P.S. 27 and 277, Bronx, 1997—2002; prin. P.S. 30, 2002; asst. supt. Dist. 5, N.Y.C., 2002—. Address: 110 Parkway S Mount Vernon NY 10552-2322

GUZY, MARGUERITA LINNES, middle school education educator; b. Santa Monica, Calif., Nov. 19, 1938; d. Paul William Robert and Margarete (Rodowski) Linnes; m. Stephen Paul Guzy, Aug. 25, 1962 (div. 1968); 1 child, David Paul. AA, Santa Monica Coll., 1959; student, U. Mex., 1959-60; BA, UCLA, 1966, MA, 1973; postgrad. in psychology, Pepperdine U., 1988-92; cert. bilingual competence, Calif., 1994. Cert. secondary tchr., quality review team ednl. programs, bilingual, Calif. Tchr. Inglewood (Calif.) Unified Sch. Dist., from 1967, chmn. dept., 1972-82, mentor, tchr., 1985-88; clin. instr. series Clin. Supervision Levels I, II, Ingelwood, 1986-87; clin. intern Chem. Dependency Ctr., St. John's Hosp., Santa Monica, 1988-92; lectr. chem. and codependency St. John's Hosp., Santa Monica, from 1992. Tchr. Santa Monica Coll., 1975-76; cons. bilingual edn. Inglewood Unified Sch. Dist., 1975—, lead tchr. new hope program at-risk students, 1992; cons. tchr. credentialing fgn. lang. State of Calif., 1994; sch. rep. restructuring edn. for state proposal, 1991-93; mem. Program Quality Rev. Team Pub. Edn., Calif., 1993; mem. Supt.'s Com. for Discrimination Resolution, 1994-95, tech. com. for integrating multimedia in the classroom, 1997—. Author: Elementary Education: "Pygmalion in the Classroom", 1975, English Mechanics Workbook, 1986. Recipient Teaching Excellence cert. State of Calif., 1986; named Tchr. of Yr., 1973, 88. Mem. NEA, Calif. Tchrs. Assn., Inglewood Tchrs. Assn. (local rep. 1971-72, tchr. edn. and profl. svcs. com. 1972-78), UCLA Alumnae Assn. (life), Prytanean Alumnae Assn. (bd. dirs. 1995-96, 1960's rep., 2d v.p. membership 1996-98). Republican. Avocations: reading, travel, swimming, dancing, cooking. Home: Los Angeles, Calif. Died Jan. 2, 2002.

GUZZETTI, BARBARA JEAN, education educator; b. Chgo., Nov. 15, 1948; d. Louis Earnest and Viola Genevive (Russell) G. BS, No. Ill. U., 1971, MS, 1974; PhD, U. Colo., 1982. Title I reading tchr. Harlem Consolidated Sch. Dist., Loves Park, Ill., 1971-72; elem. classroom tchr. Rockford (Ill.) Pub. Schs., 1972-77; diagnostic tchr. Denver Pub. Schs., 1977-78; secondary reading tchr. Jefferson County Pub. Schs., Lakewood, Colo., 1979-81, secondary reading specialist, 1981—82; rsch. and program assoc. Mid-Continent Regional Ednl. Lab., Aurora, Colo., 1983-84; evaluation specialist N.W. Regional Ednl. Lab., Denver, 1984-85; assoc. prof. Calif. State U., Ponoma, 1985-88; prof. Ariz. State U., Tempe, 1988—. Chair tech. com. Nat. Reading Conf., 1994—97. Author: Literacy Instruction in Content Areas, 1996, Reading, Writing and Talking Gender in Literacy Learning; editor: Perspectives on Conceptual Change, Literacy in America: An Encyclopedia of History, Theory and Practice; mem. editl. bd. The Reading Tchr., Jour. of Reading Behavior, Nat. Reading conf. Yearbook; contbr. articles to profl. jours. Mem. Am. Ednl. Rsch. Assn., Nat. Reading Conf., Internat. Reading Assn. (chair studies and rsch. grants com. 1992-95). Democrat. Lutheran. Avocations: reading, oenology, raising a pot-bellied pig, piglet. Home: 2170 E Aspen Dr Tempe AZ 85282-2953 Office: Ariz State U Coll of Edn Tempe AZ 85287-0411 E-mail: guzzetti@asu.edu.

GWALTNEY, CORBIN, editor, publishing executive; b. Balt., Apr. 16, 1922; s. Howell Corbin and Margaret (Bell) G.; m. Doris Jean Kell, July 13, 1946 (dec.); children: Margaret Kell, Jean Corbin, Thomas Stewart; m. Jean Caryl Wyckoff, June 20, 1973 (dec.). BA, Johns Hopkins U., 1943; LHD (hon.), L.I. U., 1970; DHL (hon.), Johns Hopkins U., 1998. Instr., English Johns Hopkins U., 1946; with indsl. relations dept. Western Electric Co. and Locke div. Gen. Electric Co., 1946-49; editor Johns Hopkins Mag., 1949-59; editor, exec. dir., chmn. Editorial Projects for Edn., Inc., Balt. and Washington, 1959-78; exec. editor Chronicle Higher Edn., Washington, 1966-2000, chmn., 2000—; exec. editor Chronicle of Philanthropy, 1988—, chmn., 2000—. Served with AUS, 1943-45. Recipient Robert Sibley award Am. Alumni Council, 1951, 56, 59, Disting. Service to Higher Edn. awards Columbia U. Alumni Fedn., 1964, Disting. Service to Higher Edn. awards Am. Coll. Public Relations Assn., 1971; George Polk award for edn. reporting, 1979 Home: 5104 Brookview Dr Bethesda MD 20816-1602 also: 4755 Bayfields Rd Harwood MD 20776-9576 Office: Chronicle Higher Edn 1255 23rd St NW Ste 700 Washington DC 20037-1146 E-mail: corbin@chronicle.com.

GWALTNEY, THOMAS MARION, education educator, writer; b. Sikeston, Mo., Sept. 17, 1935; s. Thomas Marion and Niva (Kem) G.; m. Dolores Doreen Barrow, Dec. 23, 1962; children: Anne Elise, Karen Lee Gwaltney Holder, Kristen Diane. BS, S.E. Mo. State U., 1957; MS, So. Ill. U., 1959, PhD, 1963; BA, Ea. Mich. U., 1979; postgrad., U. Mich., Harvard U. Cert. elem. and secondary tchr. Mich., humanities profl. Mich. Tchr. Wyatt (Mo.) Elem. Sch., 1955-56; jr. high tchr. Scott County Sch. Dist., Sikeston, 1957-58, elem. supr. Benton, 1958-60; vis. lectr. So. Ill. U., Carbondale, 1960-63; asst. prof. edn. No. Mich. U., Marquette, 1963-64; prof. Ea. Mich. U., Ypsilanti, 1964—, assoc. dean grad. sch., 1989-90, honors advisor, 1984—, cons., 1986—, coord. grad. advising, 1992—, coord. social founds. program, 1995-96, 2002—03. Ednl. cons. Computing and Ednl. System, Dallas, 1969-70, World Coll., 1986, cons., 1987-89; vis. prof. U. Autònoma Met., Mexico City, 1990—, sr. Fulbright lectr., rschr., 1990-91; vis. prof. sch. langs. and sch. sociology U. Autònoma de Querètaro, Mex., 1994; mem. Fulbright Selection Com., U.S. Embassy, Mex. City, 1990-91; rschr., tchr. edn. U.S., Russia, 1991-93; vice chair Collegium for Advanced Studies, 1992-93, chair, 1993-95, bd. dirs., 1995—; vis. prof. Escuela de Idiomas U. Autònoma de Querètaro, Mex., 1993; cons. Field-Intensive Tchr. Tng. Bilingual Program, 1988—; cons. rschr. and supr. bilingual edn. spl. transition project Ea. Mich. U., Farmington Pub. Schs., U.S. Dept. Edn., 1993-94; invited lectr. (in Spanish) Fundaciòn Gran Mariscal Ayachucho, Venezuela, 1994; vis. prof. Escuela de Idiomas and Escuela Sociology, 1994; mem. Fulbright Commn. on the Environ., 2001—; presenter in field Author: EDUSIM: Educational Simulation, 1972, Teaching Cultural Foundations, Handbook for Freshman, 1979; editor: Orientation Course, 1984, Teacher and Educational Foundations; book reviewer Houghton Mifflin Co., 1994-95; contbg. poet: Amidst the Splendor, 1996; contbr. articles to profl. jours. Active desegregation bd. Ypsilanti Pub. Schs., 1975-76, campaign organizer, 1983-84; cons. Latin-Am. Initiative, 1989-90. Recipient Disting. Faculty award Ea. Mich. U., 1984-87, award Collegium for Advanced Studies, 1986—, Excellence in Higher Edn. Tchg. award State of Mich., 1990, Alumni Assn. Excellence in Teaching award Ea. Mich. U., 1993, Excellence award Mich. Assn. Governing Bds., 1996, alumni merit award Southeast Mo. State U., 1999. Mem.: AAUW, Mich. Directories of Humanities Profls., Soc. Profl. of Edn., Mich. Assn. Bilingual. Edn. Advocates, Mich. Assn. Bilingual Edn., Mich. Assn. Staff Devel. and Sch. Improvement (exec. bd. 1992—), Coun. Grad. Schs., Spanish and Portuguese, Am. Edn. Studies Assn., Am. Assn. Tchrs., Southea. Mich. Fulbright Assn. (bd. dirs. 1993—2000, treas. 1999—, mem. Fulbright commn. of environ. 2001—, Tech. award Renaissance Group 2000—), Fulbright Assn. on the Environment, Fulbright Assn., Mich. One Rm. Sch. Assn. (exec. bd. 1993—, 2002—, trustee), Hist. Soc. Mich., Mich. Ethnic Heritage Found., Detroit Inst. Arts (founder's soc. 1982—), Internat. Assn. Poets (disting.), Kappa Delta Pi (Mich. area rep. 1990—, internat. com. 1992—, Latin Am. rep. 1992—, co-founder 1st Latin Am. chpt. in Mex. 1994, Queré taro Quo Mex. chpt. 1994, installing officer 1994, internat. constn. and bylaws com. 1994—, lectr. internat. convocation 1995, Honor Key 1992, Outstanding Counselor award 1998—2000), Phi Kappa Phi, Phi Delta Kappa. Baptist. Avocations: photography, writing, bicycling, walking, reading. Home: 6154 Eagle Trace Dr Ypsilanti MI 48197-6223 Office: Ea Mich U Dept Tchr Edn 313 W Porter Bldg Ypsilanti MI 48197-2210 E-mail: Thomas.Gwaltney@emich.edu.

GWIAZDA, CAROLINE LOUISE, school system administrator; b. Cleve., Jan. 6, 1941; d. Michael Anthony and Catherine Anna (Papciak) Skutnik; m. Stanley John Gwiazda, June 30, 1962; children: Stanley, Cheryl, Catherine, Stephen. BA, Ursuline Coll., 1978; MEd, John Carroll, 1982; EdD, U. Akron, 1988. Tchr. St. Thomas More, Brooklyn, Ohio, 1961-62, 64-65, Washington Park Sch., Newburgh Heights, Ohio, 1963-64, St. Stephen Sch., Cleve., 1976-79; reading cons. Cleve. Bd. Edn., 1979-85; asst. prin. Case Sch., Cleve., 1985-87; prin. Bolton Sch., Cleve., 1987-89; curriculum cons. Lucas County Bd. Edn., Toledo, 1989-90; prin. Revere Bd. Edn., Bath, Ohio, 1990-91; curriculum dir. Diocese of Cleve., 1991-93; gen. edn. supr. Avon Lake (Ohio) Bd. Edn., from 1993. Mem. exec. bd. Project Discovery Cleve., 1992—, John Carroll Ctr. Profl. Devel., University Heights, Ohio, 1992-94; mem. exec. bd. Cleve. Coun. Adminstrs. and Suprs.; chairperson, dist. rep. Ohio Assn. Elem. Adminstrs.; presenter in field. Mem. exec. bd. Coalition for Literacy, Cleve., 1992—, Jr. Achievement, Cleve., 1992-94; mem. adv. coun. Cancer Soc., Cleve., 1992-94; treas. Fire Safety Task Force, Cleve., 1992-94; active IDEA Acad. Fellows, 1998, Broadview Heights Planning Commn. Bd. Appeals. Effective Schs. grantee Ohio Dept. Edn., Columbus, 1992, Jennings grantee, 1992, Stocker Found. grantee, 1993, Continuous Improvement Plan grantee, 1999. Mem. ASCD, Ohio ASCD, Am. Assn. Adminstrs. and Suprs., Nat. Secondary, Elem. Sch. Adminstrs., Buckeye Assn. Sch. Adminstrs., Internat. Reading Assn. (initiated Greater Cleve. chpt. 1980), Ohio Reading Assn., Lillian Hinds Coun., Avon Lake Wellness Coun. (pres.), Phi Delta Kappa (pres. Cuyahoga Valley chpt., Disting. Kappan Svc. Key award, Outstanding Educator). Avocations: travel, reading, exercising, music, theatre. Home: Broadview Heights, Ohio. Died June 4, 2000.

GWIN, DOROTHY JEAN BIRD, psychology educator, college dean; b. Smith, Tex., June 26, 1934; d. Joseph William and Elva Gracie (Elledge) Bird; m. Clinton Dale Gwin, Nov. 21, 1964; 1 child, Clinton Bird. BBA, East Tex. State U., 1954, MS, 1955; EdD, U. Kans., 1958. Lic. psychologist, La. Tchr. Thomas Jefferson High Sch., Port Arthur, Tex., 1954—55; resident dir. U. Kans., Lawrence, 1955-57; sch. psychologist Caddo Parish Schs., Shreveport, La., 1958-67, con. psychologist, 1967-70; prof. psychol., edn. Centenary Coll., Shreveport, La., 1967-79, 1996—, dean, 1979-92, dean enrollment mgmt., 1992—96, prof. edn., psychol. and dir. alumni rels., 1992-93, prof., 1996—97; exec. dir. Cmty. Found. Shreveport-Bossier, Shreveport, La., 1997—. Bd. dirs. Vol. of Am., Shreveport, 1967-70; pres. bd. dirs. Southfield Sch., Shreveport, 1984-86, bd. dirs. 1974-87. Fulbright U.S. Ednl. Adminstrs. grantee to Germany, 1990. Mem. Am. Pers. Guidance Assn. (life). Home: 3402 Madison Park Blvd Shreveport LA 71104-4546 Personal E-mail: dbgwin@sport.rr.com.

GWIN, JOHN MICHAEL, retired education educator, consultant; b. Montgomery, Ala., June 21, 1949; s. Emmett Brindley Jr. and Irma Rebecca (Watkins) G.; m. Pamela Jane Blair, Sept. 7, 1970 (dec. Dec. 1998); children: Colin Blair, Connor Brindley. BBA, Auburn U., 1971; MBA, U. Ga., 1973; PhD, U. N.C., 1979. Fiscal officer U. Ga., Athens, 1971-73; ops. mgr. Bedsole & Gwin Inc., Fairhope, Ala., 1973-75; instr. Faulkner Coll., Bay Minette, Ala., 1975-76; rsch. asst. U. N.C., Chapel Hill, 1976-78, vis. lectr., 1978-79; asst. prof. Ind. U., Bloomington, 1979-81, U. Va., Charlottesville, 1981-83, assoc. prof., 1983-2000, mktg. area coord., 1990-93, dir. Ctr. for Entrepreneurial Studies, 1992-96, prof. emeritus, 2000—; mng. dir. QuixCinch, Inc. Fulbright prof. Trinity Coll., Dublin, Ireland, 1986-87; vis. prof., 1993; exec. educator numerous U.S. firms, 1981—; cons. numerous internat. and U.S. firms, 1983—; invited lectr. Sorbonne, U. Paris, Alsace Inst., Strasbourg, France, 1987. Inventor LaMaze Timer and audio text. Sesquicentennial Research Assoc., U. Va., 1986-87, 93-94; named Outstanding Young Man Am., U.S. Jr. C. of C., 1976. Mem. Am. Counseling Assn., Am. Psychol. Assn., Am. Mktg. Assn. (conf. coord. Cen. Va. chpt. 1986), Am. Personal Constuct Assn., Am. Soc. Bus. & Behavioral Studies, So. Mktg. Assn., Acad. Mktg. Sci. Episcopalian. Avocations: fiction writing, golf, sailing, blue-water fishing. Home: 8 Rolling Oaks Dr Fairhope AL 36532-3060 E-mail: jgwin621@aol.com., jmg4z@virginia.edu.

GYFTOPOULOS, ELIAS PANAYIOTIS, mechanical and nuclear engineering educator; b. Athens, Greece, July 4, 1927; came to U.S., 1953, naturalized, 1963; s. Panayiotis Elias and Despina (Louvaris) G.; m. Artemis S. Scalleri, Sept. 3, 1962; children: Vasso, Maro, Rena. Diploma in Mech. and Elec. Engring., Tech. U. Athens, 1953; Sc.D. in Elec. Engring., M.I.T., 1958; Dr. (hon.), Tech. U. Athens, Greece, 1992, Tech. U. Nova Scotia, Halifax, Canada, 1997, Dalhousie U. Poly., Halifax, Can., 1997, U. Patras, Greece, 2001. Registered profl. engr., Mass. Instr. MIT, Cambridge, 1955-58, asst. prof., 1958-61, assoc. prof., 1961-64, prof., 1964-70, Ford prof. engring., 1970-96; chmn. Nat. Energy Council Greece, 1975-78. Bd. dirs. Thermo Electron Corp., Waltham, Mass., Thermo Retec Corp., Waltham, ThermoLase Corp., San Diego, ThermoCardio Systems, Woburn, Mass., Thermo Spectra Corp., Waltham, Trex Med. Corp., Dunbury, Conn., others; cons. to various U.S. corps. Author: Thermionic Energy Conversion, vol. 1, 1973, vol. 2, 1979, Fuel Effectiveness in Industry, 1974; editor-in-chief 17 Energy Conservation Manuals, 1982, Thermodynamics: Foundations and Applications, 1991. Trustee Anatolia Coll., Salonika, Greece, 1971-2001; vice chmn. bd. trustees, 1988-2001. With Greek Navy, 1948-51. Fellow: ASME (James Harry Potter Gold medal 1995, Robert Henry Thurston award 2002, Edward Obert award 2001), NAE, Acad. Athens, Am. Acad. Arts and Scis., Am. Nuc. Soc. (bd. dirs. 1966—69). Greek Orthodox. Office: MIT Dept Nuclear Engring Rm 24-111 77 Mass Ave Cambridge MA 02139-4307 E-mail: epgyft@aol.com.

GYRA, FRANCIS JOSEPH, JR., artist, educator; b. Newport, R.I., Feb. 23, 1914; s. Frank Joseph and Ellen Frances (Mahoney) G.; m. Beatrice Anne Vincent, June 25, 1955; children: Maureen Ellen, Mary Frances, Barbara Ann, Michael Francis, eileen Margaret, Paul Damian, Katherine Mary, Theresa Louise. Student, Parsons Sch. Design, Paris, 1935, Italian Rsch. Sch. of Parsons, 1937, Brighton Coll. Art Inst., Eng., 1945, 48, U. Hawaii, 1951, Froebel Inst., Roehampton, Eng., 1953, McNeese State Coll., 1956; BS, Keene Tchrs. Coll., 1962; B of Art (hon.), R.I. Sch. Design, 1995. Dir. Gyra Sch. Art, Newport, R.I., 1938-39; Gyra Sch. Art, Woodstock (Vt.) Cmty. Recreation Ctr., 1947, 49; supr. art edn. Woodstock Elem. Sch., Union High and Rural Schs., 1949-69; art tchr. Woodstock Elem. Sch., 1969-84; Glyncoed Secondary Modern Sch., Ebbw Vale, Wales, 1952-53. Dir. art workshops Vt. State Dept. Edn., 1954-56, 58-62; faculty advisor in art and art edn., Aquinas Jr. Coll., Nashville, 1963; mem. design rev. bd., Woodstock, 1985-91; lectr. in field. Exhibited group shows Chgo. Art Inst., Pa. Acad. Fine Arts, Mpls. Inst. Arts, Toledo Mus. Art, Milw. Art Inst., Meml. Art Gallery, Carnegie Inst., Phila. Art Alliance, Providence Art Mus; one-man shows Art Assn. Newport, Washington Arts Club, Rundell Gallery, Parsons Sch. Design Gallery, N.Y.C., Robert C. Vose Gallery, L.D.M. Sweet Meml., Portland, Maine, Aquinas Jr. Coll., 1963, 64, Beaux Arts Gallery, Scranton, Pa., Dorado Beach Hotel Gallery, P.R., Chaffee Art Mus., Rutland, Vt.; represented in collections at Providence Art Mus., Vanderbilt U., Nashville, Checkwood, Nashville Mcpl. Gallery, Nashville. Eucharistic min. Roman Cath. Ch. Served with U.S. Army, 1942-46. Decorated Bronze Star; Fulbright fellow, 1952; Leopold Schepp Found. grantee, 19 31; named Hon. Citizen Nashville Davidson County, 1964; honorary Rotarian, Woodstock Rotary Club, 1972, Outstanding Vt. Tchr. Yr. for Windsor Ctrl. Supervisory Union, 1982; State of Vt. Tchr. of Yr. for Windsor Ctrl. Supervisory Union, 1982; recipient Award of Merit for Disting. Svcs. to the Arts in State Vt., vt. coun. Arts, 1969, New Eng. Art Edn. Conf. award for Vt., 1983, Recognition award, NEA, 1980, Eva Gehbard-Gourgaud grantee, 1963-68, 73-74. Mem. Vt. Art Tchrs. Assn. (award 1984), Red Carpet (Nashville) Kappa Delta Pi (hon.) Address: Box 540 6 Linden Hl Woodstock VT 05091-1233

HA, ANDREW KWANGHO, education educator; b. Korea, Nov. 14, 1939; s. Hyunku and Soonnam (Kim) H.; m. Jumok Lim; children: Susan, Steve, Joanna, Toby. BA, Chosun U., Kwangju, Korea, 1965; MA, Glassboro (N.J.) State Coll., 1967; EdD, Seton Hall U., 1988. Cert. elem. and secondary English and social studies tchr., guidance counselor, prin., supr., N.J. Tchr. Mantua (N.J.) Twp. Pub. Schs., Greenwich Twp. Pub. Schs., Gibbstown, N.J.; instr. ESL tchg. Passaic County C.C., Paterson, N.J.; adj. prof. English teaching Glassboro (N.J.) State Coll.; tchr. reading and English lang. arts methods Potsdam Coll., SUNY, 1991—. Author: The Key to Reading Comprehension, 1994, Get'em to Plunge into the Sea of English, 1995, Get'em to Swim in the Sea of English, 1996, Get'em to Rise in the Sea of English, 1997, Dr. Ha's English Grammar, 1998. Elected into the Internat. Ctr. for Ednl. Achievement, 1997. Mem. NEA, ASCD, N.J. Edn. Assn., Am. Fedn. Tchrs., Am. Ednl. Rsch. Assn., United Univ. Profession, Nat. Coun. Tchrs. English, Internat. Reading Assn., Tchrs. English to Speakers of Other Langs, Phi Delta Kappa, Kappa Delta Pi. Home: PO Box 873 Potsdam NY 13676-0873

HAAG, HARVEY EUGENE, physics educator; b. DuBois, Pa., July 2, 1950; s. Harvey E. and Miriam Haag; m. Janet M. Postlewait, June 9, 1973; children: Elizabeth Ann, Christian J.W. BS in Secondary Edn. Physics, Pa. State U., 1971, MEd in Curriculum and Instruction, 1979. Instr. physics and math. Moshannon Valley Schs., Houtzdale, Pa., 1971-75; tchr. physics and math. computers Clearfield (Pa.) Area Schs., 1975-83, tchr. physics and engring., 1983—; tchr. physics and computers Pa. State U., DuBois, 1979—; owner, photographer Haag's Photography Svc., Clearfield, 1974—. Borough councilman Clearfield Borough, 1993—, pres., 2000—; Rep. precinct area chmn. Rep. Party, Clearfield County, 1976-85; dist. advancement chmn. Bucktail coun. Boy Scouts Am., DuBois, Pa., 1975-98, coun. advancement chmn., 1990-98, vigil mem. Order of Arrow. Recipient Silver Beaver award Boy Scouts Am. Mem. U.S. Power Squadron, Bald Eagle Squadron (commdr. 2003), Cen. Pa. Assn. Physics Tchrs., Western Pa. Assn. Physics Tchrs., Clearfield Edn. Assn. (past pres. 1977-78), Masons (# 314, Master 1989, ednl. chmn. Grand Lodge 1990—), Lake Glendale Sailing Club (commodore 2003). Republican. Presbyterian. Avocations: sailing, woodworking, photography, camping, hunting. Home: 4 Turnpike Ave Clearfield PA 16830-1742 Office: Clearfield Area Schs PO Box 710 Clearfield PA 16830-0710

HAAK, HAROLD HOWARD, university president; b. Madison, Wis., June 1, 1935; s. Harold J. and Laura (Kittleson) H.; m. Betty L. Steiner, June 25, 1955; children— Alison Marie, Janet Christine. BA, U. Wis., 1957, MA, 1958; PhD, Princeton U., 1963. From asst. prof. to assoc. prof. polit. sci., pub. adminstrn. and urban studies San Diego State Coll., 1962-69, dean coll. profl. studies, prof. pub. adminstrn. and urban studies, 1969-71; acad. v.p. Calif. State U., Fresno, 1971-73, pres., 1980-91, pres. emeritus, 1991—, trustee prof., 1991-2000, trustee, prof., vice chancellor acad. affairs, 1992-93; v.p. U. Colo., Denver, 1973, chancellor, 1974-80; pres. Fresno Pacific U., 2000—02. Trustee William Saroyan Found., 1981-91; mem. NCAA Pres. Commn., 1987-91; bd. dirs. Fresno Econ. Devel. Corp., 1981-91, Cmty. Hosps. Ctrl. Calif., 1989-92, Pacific Luth. Theol. Sem., 1998-2002; bd. visitors Air Univ.; mem. Army adv. panel on ROTC affairs, 1988-92; vice-chair Calif. Commn. on Agr. and Higher Edn., 1993-96; pres., trustee Ctrl. Calif. br. Leukemia and Lymphoma Soc., 2002—; pres., bd. dirs. Armenian Agribus. Edn. Fund, 2002—. Recipient U. Colo. medal, 1980. Mem.: Phi Kappa Phi, Phi Beta Kappa.

HAALAND, GORDON ARTHUR, psychologist, university president; b. Bklyn., Apr. 19, 1940; s. Ole E. and Ellen R. (Hansen) H.; m. Carol E. Anderson, Jan. 19, 1963; children: Lynn, Paul. AB, Wheaton (Ill.) Coll., 1962; PhD, SUNY, Buffalo, 1966. Instr. SUNY, Buffalo, summer, 1965; asst. to assoc. prof. psychology U. N.H., Durham, 1965-74, prof., 1974-83, chmn. dept. psychology, 1970-74, v.p. for acad. affairs Coll. Arts and Scis., 1979-83, interim pres. of univ., 1983-84, pres., 1984-90; dean Coll. Arts and Scis., prof. psychology U. Maine, Orono, 1975-79; pres. Gettysburg (Pa.) Coll., 1990—. Vis. prof. U. Bergen, Norway, 1972-73; mem. New Eng. Land-Grant Univs., chmn. 1985-86; v.p. N.H. Coll. and Univ. Coun., 1985-87; bd. dirs. New Eng. Bd. Higher Edn., 1986—, chmn., 1988-90; bd. dirs. Eisenhower World Affairs Inst.; chmn. N.H. Postsecondary Edn. Commn., 1986-88; dir. Maine Coun. Econ. Edn., 1975-79; evaluator NSF CAUSE Project, U. Maine, 1980-83; bd. dirs. First N.H. Banks, Inc., 1987—, mem. First NH Investment Svcs., 1987—; corporator Bangor (Maine) Savs. Bank, 1975-79. Contbr. articles, papers to profl. publs. and confs. procs. Incorporator N.H. Charitable Fund, 1985-88, Trust for N.H. Lands, 1986—; bd. dirs. Ctr. for N.H.'s Future, 1980—, N.H. Coun. World Affairs, 1986-89; mem. Gov.'s Commn. on N.H. in 21st Century, 1989—; trustee Theater-by-the-Sea, Portsmouth, N.H., 1980-83, N.H. Higher Edn. Assistance Found., 1986—; co-dir. series pub. workshops Dickey-Lincoln and Passamaquoddy Hydroelectric Projects; chair Coun. Higher Edn. Accreditation, dir., 1997-2002. Norwegian Rsch. Coun. fellow, 1972-73; grantee NSF, NIMH, HEW, 1966-75. Mem. AAAS, AAUP, NCAA (pres. commn. 1996-2000), Council of Colls. of Arts and Scis. (bd. dirs. 1977-79), Nat. Assn. State Univs. and Land-Grant Colls. (commn. on arts and scis. 1978-81, chair exec. com. council on acad. affairs 1983, internat. affairs com. 1985-87, exec. com. 1986—, chair commn. edn. for teaching professions 1987-88), Nat. Assn., Ind. Colls. and Univs. (bd. dirs. 1993—), Am. Psychol. Assn. (div. 8 and 26, coun. of reps. N.H., Vt., Maine and R.I. 1968-71, com. on structure and function of coun. 1968-71), Eastern Psychol. Assn., N.H. Psychol. Assn. (program dir. 1971), Eisenhower World Affairs Inst. (bd. dirs. 1991—), Soc. Exptl. Social Psychology, Phi Kappa Phi, Sigma Xi. Office: Gettysburg Coll Office of Pres Gettysburg PA 17325-1486

HAAR, CHARLES MONROE, lawyer, educator; b. Dec. 3, 1920; came to U.S., 1921; s. Benjamin and Dora (Eisner) H.; children: Jeremy, Susan Eve, Jonathan. AB, N.Y.U., 1940; LLB, Harvard, 1948; MA, U. Wis., 1941; LLD, Lake Erie U., 1968, Hebrew Coll., 1988. Bar: N.Y. 1949, U.S. Dist. Ct. (so. dist.) N.Y. 1950, U.S. Supreme Ct. 1968, Mass. 1978. Practice law, N.Y.C., 1949-52; asst. prof. law Harvard, 1952-54; prof., 1954-66, 69—, Louis D. Brandeis prof. law, 1972—; disting. prof. U. Miami Law Sch., 1998—. Chmn. Joint Ctr. for Urban Studies, Mass. Inst. Tech. and Harvard, 1969—, chmn. land policy roundtable Lincoln Inst. Land Policy; dir. Charles River Assocs.l asst. sec. met. devel. Dept. Housing and Urban Devel., Washington, 1966-69. Author: Land Planning Law in a Free Society, Feeral Credit and Private Housing, 1960, Law and Land, 1964, Golden Age of American Law, 1966, The End of Innocence, 1972, Housing the Poor in Suburbia, 1973, Suburban Problems, 1973, Property and Law, 1977, 2d edit., 1985, Of Judges, Politics and Flounders: Perspectives on the Cleaning Up of Boston Harbor, 1985; (with others) The Wrong Side of the Tracks, 1986, Fairness and Justice, 1987, Land-Use Planning: A Casebook in the Use, Misuse and Re-use of Urban Land, 4th edit., 1989, Landmark Justice, 1989, Zoning and the American Dream, 1989; editor: Beacon Classics of the Law, Suburbs Under Siege, 1992; contbr. articles to profl. jours. Chief reporter Am. Land Inst. project model code land devel. 1964-66; mem. Cambridge Redevel. Authority, Met. Area Planning Coun., Mass. Gov.'s Com. on Resource Mgmt., 1974, Fin. Adv. Bd., 1978—, Uniform Commn. State Laws, 1979—, Jerusalem Com., 1970—; chmn. Pres.'s Task Force Preservation Natural Beauty, Task Force on Model Cities, on Suburban Problems; chmn. com. on met. governance RFF, 1970-72; cons. WHite House AID, HHFA, U.S. Senate state and city agys.; mem. U.S. del. to UN Conf. on Habitat, 1976; pres. Regional and Urban Planning Implementation, Onc., bd. dirs. Zelda Zinn Found.; trustee Mass. Gen. Hosp., 1979—. Lt. (j.g.) USNR, 1942-46. Fellow Urban Land Inst.; mem. Am. Acad. Arts and Scis., Am. Inst. Planners, Brit. Town Planning Inst., Am. Bar Assn., Am. Law Inst., Phi Beta Kappa. Office: Harvard Law Sch Griswold 300 Cambridge MA 02138

HAAS, CHARLES NATHAN, environmental engineering educator; b. N.Y.C., Dec. 27, 1951; s. Louis and Gertrude (Abrams) H.; m. Victoria Soderholme, June 27, 1989. BS, Ill. Inst. Tech., Chgo., 1973, MS, 1974; PhD, U. Ill., 1978. Asst. prof. Rensselaer Poly. Inst., Troy, N.Y., 1978-81, Ill. Inst. Tech., Chgo., 1981-84, assoc. prof., 1984-87, prof., 1987-90; L.D. Betz prof. environ. engring. Drexel U., Phila., 1991—. Editor Jour. Water Environ. Rsch., 1991-96. Recipient Charles Ellet award Western Soc. Engrs., 1983, Octave Chanute medal, 1984. Mem. Am. Water Works Assn., Internat. Assn. Water Quality (pres. nat. com. 1994—), Water Environment Assn. Office: Drexel U 32d & Chestnut Sts Philadelphia PA 19104

HAAS, JUNE F. special education educator, consultant; b. Burien, Wash., June 5, 1934; d. Carl Edwin and Mary Rebecca (Best) Flodquist; m. Frank M. Haas, June 21, 1958; children: Michael Edward, Katherine June Haas Dunning. BA in Elem. Edn., Psychology, U. Wash., 1956; MS in Early Childhood Edn., Oreg. Coll. Edn., 1975. Tchr. Haines (Alaska) Borough Sch. Dist., 1956-76, spl. edn. tchr., 1976-86, gifted, talented coord., 1978-87, migrant edn. tchr., 1986-87; instr. U. Alaska, Haines, 1984-85; cons. Ednl. Cons. Svcs., Haines, 1987—. Instr. World Conf. Gifted/Talented Children, Hamburg, Germany, 1985, Sydney, Australia, 1989, 2d Gifted Asian Conf. on Giftedness, Taipei, Taiwan, 1992, World Conf. Gifted/Talented Children, Toronto, Can., 1993 ; coach Alaska Future Problem Solving Program, 1982-87; del. Citizen Ambassador Program Russia, Siberia, Hungary, 1991; del./presentor U.S./Russia Joint Conf. Edn., Moscow, 1994. Pres. Bus. and Profl. Women's Clubs, Alaska, 1973-74; pres. Am. Legion Aux., Alaska, 1990-91, nat. exec. com., 1991-92, mem. nat. edn. com., 1991-92; bd. dir. Am. Cancer Soc., Alaska, 1976—; chmn. we divsn. Nat. Edn. Com., 1992-93. Mem. World Coun. Gifted/Talented Children, Coun. Exceptional Children, Bus. and Profl. Women's Club (v.p. 1972-73, Woman of Yr. 1972), Am. Legion Aux. (nat. jr. activities com., western divsn. chmn. 1993-94, mem. citizens flag alliance 1994-95), Lynn Canal Community Players (nat. drama festival com. 1983), Haines Women's Club (pres. 1988-90), Pioneers of Alaska (pres. 1990-91). Methodist. Avocations: photography, community theater, flying, bridge, travel. Home and Office: Ednl Cons Svcs PO Box 97 Haines AK 99827-0097

HAAS, KAY BUSHMAN, secondary school English educator; b. Kansas City, Mo., Aug. 28, 1951; d. Jerome Patterson and Florence Alene (Howard) Parks; m. William James Haas, Dec. 12, 1997; 1 child, Eric Jerome. BS, U. Kans., 1973, MA, 1978. Cert. English, social studies tchr., Kans. English, social studies tchr. Old Mission Jr. H.S., Shawnee Mission, Kans., 1974-80; English tchr. Ottawa (Kans.) Jr. H.S., 1980-81, Ottawa H.S., 1981-2000; instructional resource tchr. Olathe (Kans.) Dist. Schs., 2000—. Adj. lectr. U. Kans., Lawrence, 1989—; cons. Scott Foresman Pub. Co., Glenview, Ill., 1993. Co-author: Using Young Adult Literature in English Classroom, 1992, Teaching English Creatively, 1993; editor columns for English Jour., 1992-94, ALAN Rev., 1990-97. V.p. Ottawa Cmty. Theatre, 1983. Recipient Nancy Landan Kassebaum award Kans. State Bd. Edn., 1993; NEH fellow, 1983; named Kans. Master Tchr., 2000. Mem. ASCD, Nat. Coun. Tchrs. English (steering com. secondary sect., pres., mem. assembly on lit. for adolescents, exec. bd. dirs. 1995-97), Kans. Assn. Tchrs. English (bd. dirs.), Olathe Edn. Assn., Ottawa Edn. Assn. (pres. 2000). Methodist. Avocations: reading, exercise. Home: 2 E Brookside Ln Ottawa KS 66067-3616 Office: Olathe Sch Dist 14090 Blackbob Rd Olathe KS 66062 E-mail: kpbhaas@yahoo.com.

HAAS, ROBERT DONNELL, flight instructor, airline transport pilot, lawyer, retail executive, retail executive; b. Ft. Worth, Nov. 28, 1953; s. Albert Donnell and Shirley (Tucker) H.; m. Dawn Elaine Wallace, Jan. 9, 1975 (div. June 1976); m. Barbara Anne Sonnemann, July 4, 1981 (div. Mar. 1989); m. Linda Marie Roberson Shinall, July 28, 1995; 1 stepchild, Amber Dawn. Student, U. Tex., 1971-72, Tarrant County Jr. Coll., Ft. Worth, 1975-76; B of Profl. Studies, Memphis State U., 1988, JD, 1990. Bar: U.S. Dist. Ct. (we. dist.) Ky.; cert. comml. aviator. Night supr. Tex. Leisure Chair, Inc., Ft. Worth, 1972-76; prin. Memphis Parts House, Inc., Memphis, 1976-86; pilot, dir. of flight standards Exec. Charter of Memphis, 1986-88; prin. Haassong Prodn. Enterprises and Haastronix, Ltd. Corp., Ft. Worth and Memphis, 1975—; with sales dept., purchasing agt., of counsel Preferred Engine Parts, Inc., 1987—97; head acctg. exec., of counsel Weiss Auto Parts Co., Inc., Memphis, 1993—97; store mgr. Radio Shack, Bartlett, Tenn., 1997—2002; sales coord. Circuit City, 2002—. Flight instr. Metro Flying Sch., Olive Branch, Miss., 1985-90, Lazy Eight Flight Ctr., Memphis, 1985-88. Author: (poems) Songs of Feeling, 1975, Portraits of Love, 1976, Girls of My Dreams, 1987. Mem. ABA, Future Aviation Profls. Am., Aircraft Owners and Pilots Assn., World Future Soc., Assn. Trial Lawyers Am., Tenn. Trial Lawyers Assn., Tenn. Bar Assn., Sherby County Bar Assn., Phi Delta Phi. Republican. Jewish. Avocations: music, coin collecting. Address: 520 Fite Rd Atoka TN 38004-6217

HAASE, DONALD PAUL, German language, literature and culture educator; b. Cin., Mar. 20, 1950; m. Harry Paul and Evelyn Blanche Haase; m. Connie Lee Kordenbrock, Mar. 18, 1972; children: Emily Marie, Rebecca Anne, Sarah Elizabeth. BA, U. Cin., 1972, MA, 1973; PhD, U. N.C., 1979. Vis. asst. prof. Miami U., Oxford, Ohio, 1979-81; asst. prof. German, Wayne State U., Detroit, 1981-85, assoc. prof., 1985—, chmn. dept., 1989—, dir. jr. yr. in Germany programs, 1993-95. Mem. editorial bd. Wayne State U. Press, Detroit, 1989—. Editor: Reception of Grimms' Fairy Tales, 1993, English Fairy Tales and More English Fairy Tales, 2002; contbg. author: Deutsches Literatur-Lexikon, 1986; mng. editor Carolina Quar., 1974-75; editor Marvels and Tales: Jour. Fairy-Tale Studies, 1997—; mem. editl. bd. The Child and the City Series, 2000—; contbg. editor Oxford Companion to Fairy Tales, 2000; contbr. articles to profl. jours. Bd. dirs. St. Cyril Sch., Taylor, Mich., 1982; mem. strategic planning com. Livonia (Mich.) Pub. Schs., 1992. Recipient Probus award for acad. achievement Probus Club, Detroit, 1987, Pres.'s award for excellence in tchg. Wayne State U., 1985; grantee German Acad. Exch. Svc., 1976, 90, NEH, 1985, 87, 88, 90, 94. Mem. MLA (regional del. 1989-91), Brueder Grimm-Gesellschaft, Am. Assn. Tchrs. German, Am. Folklore Soc, Internat. Soc. for Folk Narrative Rsch., Phi Beta Kappa. Office: Wayne State U 443 Manoogian Hall Detroit MI 48202

HABER, LYNN BECKER, English language educator; b. River Vale, N.J., Oct. 20, 1961; d. Murray Leonard and Anita (Goodman) Becker; m. Samuel Myles Haber, Nov. 6, 1994; children: Gary, Craig. BA in Psychology, Muhlenberg Coll., 1983; MA in Teaching, Montclair State U., 1987; PhD in English Edn., NYU, 1987. Cert. elem. tchr., English tchr., N.J. Tchr. English Cedar Grove (N.J.) H.S., 1987-89; writing instr. Middlesex County Coll., Edison, N.J., 1989; instr. English Union County Coll., Cranford, N.J., 1990; teaching fellow NYU, N.Y.C., 1990-92, adj. asst. prof., 1995—; asst. prof. English So. Conn. State U., New Haven, 1995-99. Rep. NYU Grad. Student Orgn., N.Y.C., 1991-92. Mem. Nat. Coun. Tchrs. English, Kappa Delta Pi. Avocations: reading, travel, jogging, Scrabble.

HABERL, VALERIE ELIZABETH, physical education educator, company executive; b. N.Y.C., July 6, 1947; d. William Anthony and Rose Mary (Hoholecek) H. BS, So. Conn. State U., 1969, postgrad., 1979. Cert. elem. tchr., Conn. Tchr. phys. edn. West Haven (Conn.) Bd. Edn., 1969—. Pres. Creative Studio, 1992—; inventory control specialist, 1997-2001. Mem. Conn. Assn. Health, Phys. Edn., Recreation and Dance. Republican. Roman Catholic.

HABERMAN, SHELBY JOEL, statistician, educator; b. Cin., May 4, 1947; s. Jack Leon and Miriam Leah (Langberg) H.; m. Elinor Penny Levine, Feb. 18, 1979 (dec. 1996); children: Shoshanah, Chasiah, Sarah, Milcah, Boaz, Devorah. AB, Princeton U., 1968; PhD, U. Chgo., 1970. Asst. prof. to prof. U. Chgo., 1970-82; prof. Hebrew U., Jerusalem, 1982-84; prof. stats. Northwestern U., Evanston, Ill., 1984—2002, chmn. dept., 1986-88; dir. Ctr. for Statis. Theory and Practice, Ednl. Testing Svc., Princeton, NJ, 2002—. Author: Analysis of Frequency Data, 1974, Analysis of Qualitative Data, Vol. I, 1978, Vol. II, 1979, Advanced Statistics, Vol. I, 1996; contbr. articles to profl. jours. Guggenheim fellow, 1977-78. Fellow AAAS, Inst. Math. Stats., Am. Statis. Assn. Home: 414 S 4th St Highland Park NJ 08904- Office: Ednl Testing Svc Rosedale Rd 08541 Princeton NJ 08541-0001 E-mail: SHaberman@ets.org.

HABERSHAM, JANICE JOHNSON, media specialist, music educator; b. Gary, Ind., Aug. 6, 1950; d. James Richard and Margaret Ree (Washington) Johnson; m. Jerry Dean Habersham, July 11, 1987; children: Jeremy Richard Johnson, Jasmine Deanna Habersham. BS in English, Ind. U., 1972, MLS, 1974; degree in edn. specialist instrn. tech., U. Ga., 1991. Reference libr. Middle Ga. Coll., Cochran, 1975-76; media specialist Winship Elem., Macon, Ga., 1976-78; media specialist, asst. to prin. Danforth Primary, Macon, Ga., 1978—; media specialist Skyview Elem. Sch., Lizella, Ga., 2002—. Bd. dirs. James Wimberly Inst. Black Studies. Chmn. bd. dirs. Cmty. Day Care II, Macon, 1978-89; sec., v.p. Neighborhood Arts, Inc., Macon, 1995-97; mentor for teenage mother Teen Ctr., Macon, 1997—; edn. chair Tubman African Am. Mus.; active Mus. Arts and Scis.; bd. dirs. Macon Symphony Orch. Named Media Specialist of Yr., Bibb County Pub. Schs., Macon, Ga., 1992, 98-99, Dist. IX Media Specialist of Yr., 1999; recipient internat. student media festival winner Assn. for Ednl. Comm. and Tech., 1987, 94, 97-2000; Nat. Tchrs. grant Black Entertainment Network, Washington, 1995, Pub. Edn. Fund grant Peyton Annderson Found., Macon, 1995-96. Mem. NAACP, Nat. Music Tchrs.' Assn., Delta Sigma Theta, Phi Delta Kappa. Democrat. Avocations: music, sewing, crafts, storytelling. Home: 204 Glen Holly Ct Lizella GA 31052-4606 Office: Skyview Elem Sch 5400 Fulton Mill Rd Lizella GA 31052 E-mail: jhabersham@bibb.k12.ga.us.

HABICHT, JEAN PIERRE, healthcare educator, nutritionist; b. Geneva, Dec. 15, 1934; arrived in US, 1962; s. Max H. and Elizabeth (Peterson) Herzog; m. Pat Hinxman, Jan. 3, 1959 (div. Oct. 1990); children: Heidi, Christopher, Oliver; m. Gretel H. Pelto, June 13, 1997. MD, U. Zurich, 1962, MD, 1964; MPH, Harvard U., 1968; PhD, MIT, 1969. Cert. in clin. nutrition Am. Bd. Nutrition. Biochem. rsch. asst. Merck, Sharpe, and Dohme, Rahway, NJ, 1958-59; pediat. intern Children's Hosp. Med. Ctr., Boston, 1965-66; med. officer WHO, Guatemala, 1969-74; prof. maternal and child health U. San Carlos, Guatemala, 1972-74; spl. asst. Nat. Ctr. Health Stats., Washington, 1974-77; James Jamison prof. nutritional epidemiology Cornell U., Ithaca, NY, 1977—. Cons. pub. health issues nat. and internat. govt., profl. agy., 1975—; mem. expert com. nutrition WHO, Geneva, 1975—, mem. com. epidemiology and disease prevention, 1986—89, chmn., expert com. phys. status, 1991—93; me.. epidemiology and disease control study sect. NIH, Washington, 1980—83; mem. joint nutrition monitoring and evaluation com. HHS-USDA, 1982—86; mem. adv. group coordinating subcom. nutrition U.N., 1983—89, chmn., 1986—87; mem. food and nutrition bd. NAS, Washington, 1994—96, mem..com. internat. nutrition, 1994—97, mem. com. uses dietary reference intakes Inst. Medicine, 1997—2000; chmn. expert com. optimal duration exclusive breastfeeding, 2001; mem. tech. adv. com. Child and Adolescent Health and Devel., 2001—. Contbr. articles to profl. jour., chapters to books. Fellow: Soc. Internat. Nutrition Rsch. (pres. 2002—), Am. Soc. Nutritional Scis. (Atwater Meml. lectr. 1998, Kellogg prize 1994, Conrad A. Elvehjem award 1999), Am. Coll. Epidemiology; mem.: APHA, Internat. Soc. Rsch. Human Milk and Lactation (exec. com. 1995—96), Internat. Epidemiol. Assn., Soc. Epidemiologic Rsch., Am. Soc. Clin. Nutrition, Delta Omega, Gamma Sigma Delta, Sigma Xi. Office: Cornell Univ Div Nutritional Sci Savage Hall Ithaca NY 14853

HABLUTZEL, NANCY ZIMMERMAN, lawyer, educator; b. Chgo., Mar. 16, 1940; d. Arnold Fred Zimmerman and Maxine Lewison (Zimmerman) Goodman; m. Philip Norman Hablutzel, July 1, 1980; children: Margo Lynn, Robert Paul. BS, Northwestern U., 1960; MA, Northeastern Ill. U., 1972; JD, Ill. Inst. Tech. chgo.-Kent Coll. Law, 1980; PhD, Loyola U., Chgo., 1983. Bar: Ill. 1980, U.S. Dist. Ct. (no. dist.) Ill. 1980, U.S. Supreme Ct. 1995. Speech therapist various pub. schs. and hosps., Chgo. and St. Louis, 1960—63, 1965—72; audiologist U. Chgo. Hosps., 1963—65; instr. spl. edn. Chgo. State U., 1972—76; asst. prof. Loyola U., Chgo., 1981—87; adj. prof. Ill. Inst. Tech. Chgo.-Kent Coll. Law, 1982—, Lewis U., 1990—92; lectr. Loyola U., Chgo., 1990—98; legal dir. Legal Clinic for Disabled, Chgo., 1984—85, exec. dir., 1985—87; of counsel Whitted & Spain P.C., 1987—89; prin. Hablutzel & Assocs., Chgo., 1989—94, 1997—. Hearing officer Cir. Ct. of Cook County, 1994—96, supervising hearing officer, 1995—97; faculty No. Ill. U., 1997—2003; advisor Ill. Dept. Children and Family Svcs., 1997—2003; hearing officer Ill. State Bd. Edn., 1999—; asst. prof. Coll. Edn. U. St. Francis, Joliet, Ill., 2003—. Co-author (with B. McMahon): Americans with Disabilities Act: Access and Accomodations, 1992; contbg. editor: Nat. Disability Law Reporter, 1991—92. Mem. Ill. Gov.'s Com. on Handicapped, 1972—75; mem., faculty moderator student divsn. Coun. for Exceptional Children, 1982—87; mem. adv. com. for disabled Ill. Atty. Gen., 1985—; mem. adv. com. Scouting for People with Disabilities, Chgo. Area Boy Scouts Am., 1988—92. Grantee Loyola-Mellon Found. grantee, 1983. Fellow: Ill. Bar Found. (sec. fellows 1992, vice chair fellow 1993, chair 1994), Chgo. Bar Found. (life); mem.: ABA, Chgo. Hearing Soc. (bd. dirs. 1992—94, Marion Goldman award 1988), Chgo. Bar Assn. (corp. law com., exec. com. 1984—94, chmn. Divsn. IV 1988—91, sec. 1991—92, vice chair 1992—93, chair 1993—94), Ill. Bar Assn. (assoc., standing com. on juvenile justice, sec. 1986—87, vice chmn. 1987—88, chmn. 1988—89, Inst. Pub. Affairs 1985—, legis. com. 1991—, mem. juvenile justice sect. coun. 1994—), Nat. Coun. of Juvenile and Family Ct. Judges (permanency planning com., continuing jud. edn. com.). Avocations: sailing, travel, cooking, swimming. Office: 500 Wilcox Street Joliet IL 60435

HACCOUN, DAVID, electrical engineering educator; b. Bizerte, Tunisia, July 4, 1937; arrived in Can. 1957; s. Charles and Emma (Melloul) H.; m. Lyson Tobaly, Dec. 26, 1971; children— Nathalie, Laurent. B.Sc. Engring. Physics, U. Montreal, 1965; SM, MIT, 1966; PhD, McGill U., 1974. Registered profl. engr., Que. Communications engr. City of Montreal, Que., Can., 1965; research asst. MIT, Cambridge, 1965-66; prof. Ecole Polytech. U., Montreal, Que., Can., 1966—; vis. research prof. Concordia U., Montreal, Que., Can., 1984-85. Project leader Can. Inst. for Telecom. Rsch. under Nat. Ctrs. Excellence of Govt. Can., 1990-2003; vis. rsch. fellow Advanced Study Inst., U. BC, Vancouver, 1992; vis. rschr. INRIA, Paris, 1992, 1998-99; co-founder, pres. Can. Soc. Into. Theory, 1986-87; vis. rsch. prof. Higher Sch. Tech., Montreal, 1999, U. Victoria, B.C., Can., 1999; mem. exec. com. Telecom. Engring. Mgmt. Inst. Can., 1997—; cons. in field. Co-author: Digital Communications by Satellite, 1981, translated in Japanese, 1984, in Chinese, 1989, The Communications Handbook, 1997, 2001, The Encyclopedia of Telecommunications, 2002; contbr. articles to profl. jours. Mem. exec. com. Can. Jewish Congress, 1996—; bd. dirs. Comm. Rsch. Ctr., Ottawa, 1999—. Commonwealth fellow London, 1965; Grass fellow MIT, 1966, MIT scholar, 1965-66; Hydro-Que. fellow, Montreal, 1969-72. Fellow IEEE (life), 1993; mem. AAAS, 1997, Order of Engrs. of Que., 1968-, NY Acad. Scis., Sigma Xi. Avocations: photography, swimming, skiing. Office: Ecole Polytechnique PO Box 6079 Sta Centre Ville Montreal QC Canada H3C 3A7 E-mail: david.haccoun@polymtl.ca.

HACHEY, THOMAS EUGENE, British and Irish history educator, consultant; b. Lewiston, Maine, June 8, 1938; s. Leo Joseph and Margaret Mary (Johnson) H.; m. Jane Beverly Whitman, June 9, 1962. BA, St. Francis Coll., 1960; MA, Niagara U., 1961; PhD, St. John's U., 1965. Asst. prof. history Marquette U., Milw., 1964-69, assoc. prof., 1969-77, prof., 1977—, chmn. dept. history, 1979-93, dean Coll. Arts and Scis., 1993-2000; exec. dir. Irish programs, endowed chair dept. history Boston Coll., 2000—. Vis. prof. history Sch. Irish Studies, Dublin, 1977-78; cons. investments in Ireland Frost & Sullivan, N.Y.C., 1978-82; pres. Am. Conf. Irish Studies, 1983-85; dir. Bradley Inst. for Democracy and Pub. Values, 1988-99. Author: Problem of Partition: Peril to World Peace, 1972, Britain and Irish Separatism, 1977; co-author: The Irish Experience, 1988, expanded edit., 1996, Perspectives of Irish Nationalism, 1988; editor: Voices of Revolution, 1972, Confidential Despatches, 1975; contbr. over 100 articles and revs. to

Brit., Irish and Am. jours. and newspapers. Danforth assoc., 1979-85. Fellow Anglo-Am. Assocs. Roman Catholic. Home: 20 Deerpath Rd Dedham MA 02026 Office: Boston Coll Connolly House 300 Hammond St Chestnut Hill MA 02467-3930

HACK, RANDOLPH C. advocate, educator, counselor; b. N.Y.C., Feb. 14, 1947; s. Sidney and Eleanor (Bermak) Hack. BA, U. Hawaii, Honolulu, 1980. Per diem tchr. Hawaii Dept. Edn., Honolulu, 1984—92; dir. consumer adv. United Self-Help, Honolulu, 1989—95; program dir. United Self Help, Honolulu, 1992—95, exec. dir., 1995—99; consumer advisor Adult Mental Health Divsn., Honolulu, 1999—2003, acting dir. consumer affairs, 2003—. Counselor Armed Svcs. YMCA, Schofield Barracks, Hawaii, 1987—95; participant White Ho. Conf. Mental Health, Washington, 1999; bd. dirs. Statewide Ind. Living Coun. Vice chmn. State Coun. Mental Health, 1995—99; mem. Diamond Head Svc. Area Bd. Mental Health & Substance Abuse, Honolulu, 1989—92; precinct chmn. Dem. Com. Hawaii, Honolulu, 2000; bd. dirs. Mental Health Assn. Hawaii, 1984—86, Waikiki Health Ctr., 1999—, Mental Health Kokua, 1990—. Recipient Cmty. Svc. award, Mental Health Assn., 1991, Senator Daniel K. Inouye award, Hawaii Psychol. Assn., 1998. Mem.: Nat. Alliance Mentally Ill (state rep., nat. consumer coun. 1998—, bd. dirs. Hawaii 1997—, bd. dirs. Oahu 1997—). Avocation: swimming. Home: 1117 12th Ave Apt 8 Honolulu HI 96816-3747 Office: Adult Mental Health Divsn 1250 Punchbowl St Honolulu HI 96813 E-mail: rchack@mail.health.state.hi.us.

HACKAM, REUBEN, electrical engineering educator; b. Baghdad, Iraq, Feb. 18, 1936; arrived in Can., 1978; s. Yechiel and Rachel (Cohen) H.; m. Estelle Malkinson, June 7, 1964; children: Judy, David, Abby, Dan. BSc, Israel Inst. Tech., Haifa, 1960; PhD, U. Liverpool, Eng., 1964, DEng, 1988. Sr. engr. GE, Stafford, Eng., 1964-69; lectr. elec. engring. U. Sheffield, Eng., 1969-73, sr. lectr., 1973-74, reader, 1974-78; prof. U. Windsor, 1978—2001, prof. emeritus, 2001—, chmn. dept., 1981-82, 84-86. Vis. staff dept. math. Staffordshire Poly., Stafford, 1964-69, Sheffield Poly, 1970-78, Hong Kong Poly. U., 1990-91; cons. Brit. Rail, Derby, Eng., 1975-78, English Electric Co., Stafford, 1975-77, Windsor Star, 1981-91, Corp. City of Windsor, 1983-92, Green Shield Prepaid Svcs., Inc., 1982—, County of Essex Libr., 1986—, Can. Salt Co., 1988—, Windsor Real Estate Bd., 1996—; vis. prof. Kumamoto U., Japan, 1998-99. Contbr. articles to profl. jours. Cons. Windsor Bd. Edn., 1988, Essex Bd. Edn., Windsor, 1989-94. Fellow: IEEE (bd. dirs. conf. on elec. insulation and dielectric phenomena 1985—91, gaseous dielectrics tech. com. 1985—, mem. tech. program com.IEEE-CEIDP 1986—97, mem. editl. bd. IEEE Insulation Mag. 1990—98, asst. editor Digest IEEE Transactions on Dielectrics and Elec. Insulat 1990—99, mem. permanent sci. com. int. synomps. on discharges and elec. insulat 1991—2001, sec. 1992—93, fellows award com. 1993—96, vice chmn. conf. on elec. insulation and dielectric phenomena 1994—95, chmn. 1996—97, various working groups 1997—, mem. editl. bd. IEEE Insulation Mag. 1999—2001, assoc. editor 1999—2001, editor-in-chief 2002—, program com. publicity and pub. chmn., Third Millennium medal 2000, Eric O. Forster Disting. award 2000, Innuishi Meml. lecture award 1998); mem.: IEEE Dielectrics and Elec. Insulation Soc. (nominating and adv. coms. 1988—91, pub. com. 1988—96, chmn. publ. com. 1990—91, edn. com. 1990—95, asst. treas. 1991, treas. 1993—94, v.p. adminstrn. 1995—96, pres. 1997—98, mem. IEEE meetings and svcs. com. 1997—98, chair 1999—2000, treas. 1999—2001, pub. com. 1999—2001). Jewish. Office: U Windsor 401 Sunset Ave Windsor ON Canada N9B 3P4 E-mail: hackam@u.windsor.ca.

HACKLEY, CAROL ANN, public relations director, educator, consultant; b. Sacramento, Mar. 20, 1940; d. Charles Peter and Alice Marian (Schmidt) Cusick; m. William E. Hall, Sept. 1, 1966 (dec. Aug. 1991); children: Kevin Dennis, Kimberlee Marian Hall Floyd; m. T. Cole Hackley, Apr. 10, 1993. BA, Calif. State U., Sacramento, 1961; MA, Ohio State U., 1984, PhD, 1985. Pub. rels. dir., tchr. Lincoln Unified Schs., Stockton, Calif., 1961-63; advt. promotion copy writer, columnist Honolulu (Hawaii) Star-Bulletin, Hawaii Newspaper Agy., 1964; instr. U. Nebr., Lincoln, 1964-66, Ohio State U., Columbus, 1972-80, 82-85; exec. dir. Jour. Assn. Ohio Schs., Columbus, 1974-80, 82-85; asst. prof. U. Hawaii, Honolulu, 1980-82; prof. pub. rels. comm. dept. U. of the Pacific, Stockton, 1985—, chair comm. dept., 1992-94; pub. rels. cons. Hackley Ent. Inc., 1995—; owner, pub. rels. and sr. cons. Pacific Pub. Rels., 1999—. Pub. rels. cons. Hall and Hall Prescriptive Pub. Rels., Stockton, 1987-91; prof.-in-residence Edelman Pub. Rels. Worldwide, Sydney, London and San Francisco, 1990-92; dir. of mktg. and univ. rels., U. of the Pacific, Stockton, San Francisco and Sacramento, 1997-98. Co-author: Wordsmithing: The Art and Craft of Writing for Public Relations, 2003. Chmn. bd. Mountain Valley Multiple Sclerosis, Stockton, 1989-91; nat. v.p. Stockton coun. Navy League of U.S., 1997, 98, chair nat. pub. affairs com., 1997-99. Mem. Pub. Rels. Soc. Am. (accredited, internat. sect., internat. pub. rels. exec. com. 1995, v.p. Oakland/East Bay chpt. 1994, del. nat. assembly 1995-97, 2001—, pres.-elect 1997, pres. 1998, ethics officer 2001—), Internat. Comm. Assn., Assn. for Edn. in Journalism and Mass Comm., Stockton C. of C. (edn. task force 1996-99). Avocations: singing, cooking, traveling. Home: 2618 Sheridan Way Stockton CA 95207-3246 Office: Univ of the Pacific 3601 Pacific Ave Stockton CA 95211-0197

HACKMAN, ROBERT CORDELL, pathology educator, researcher; b. Maryville, Mo., Jan. 24, 1939; s. Carl Conrad and Louise Matilda (Gassmann) H.; m. Evette Marie Abraham, Dec. 1967; children: Stephanie Elizabeth Hackman Fine, Rebecca Lee Hackman Schmidt. BA in Anthropology, Oberlin Coll., 1961; MD, Stanford U., 1971. Diplomate Am. Bd. Pathology. Resident Pathology U. Wash., Seattle, 1974-78, chief resident dept of Lab. Medicine, 1975-76; rsch. microbiologist Nat. Labs., Kansas City, Kans., 1966-67; dir. tech. svs. vet. biol. div. Armour Pharm. Co., Omaha, 1967-69; instr. pathology U. Wash. Sch. Medicine, Seattle, 1978-85, asst. prof., 1985-91, assoc. prof., 1991—, assoc. prof. lab. medicine, 1994—; asst. mem. Fred Hutchinson Cancer Rsch. Ctr., Seattle, 1984-93, assoc. mem., 1993—2002, dir. clin. labs., 1991—, dir. autopsy svc., 1994—, full mem., 2002—. Co-founder Biotec Lab., Overland Park, Kans., 1967; staff physician Swedish Hosp. Med. Ctr., Seattle, 1981-2001, U. Wash. Med. Ctr., 2001-; cons. pathologist Children's Hosp. and Reg. Med. Ctr., Seattle, 2001-. Contbr. numerous articles to med. jours., chpts. to books. Fellow Am. Cancer Soc., 1981-84; Alfred P. Sloan Found. scholar, Nat. Found. Health scholar, Vivian B. Allen Found. scholar, Alice C. Steel Found. scholar. Fellow Coll. Am. Pathologists, Am. Soc. Clin. Pathologists; mem. Internat. Acad. Pathology, Binford-Dammin Soc. Infectious Disease Pathologists, Am. Soc. for Blood and Marrow Transplantation. Achievements include elucidation of pulmonary and infectious complications of bone marrow transplantation. Office: Fred Hutchinson Cancer Rsch Ctr 1100 Fairview Ave N Pathology 1 G1-300 Box 19024 Seattle WA 98109-1024 E-mail: rhackman@fhere.org.

HADAS, RACHEL, poet, educator; b. N.Y.C., Nov. 8, 1948; d. Moses and Elizabeth (Chamberlayne) H.; m. Stavros Kondilis, Nov. 7, 1970 (div. 1978); m. George Edwards, July 22, 1978; 1 child, Jonathan. BA in Classics, Radcliffe Coll., 1969; MA, Johns Hopkins, 1977; PhD, Princeton U., 1982. From adj. to assoc. prof. Rutgers U., Newark, N.J., 1981-92, prof., 1992—, Bd. Govs. Prof., 2002—; adj. prof. Columbia U., N.Y.C., 1992-93. Vis. prof. Hellenic studies program Princeton U., spring 1995. Author: (poetry) Slow Transparency, 1983, A Son From Sleep, 1987, Pass It On, 1989, Living in Time, 1990, Mirrors of Astonishment, 1992, Other Worlds Than This, 1994, The Empty Bed, 1995, The Double Legacy, 1995, Halfway Down the Hall: New and Selected Poems, 1998, Indelible, 2001. Recipient award Am. Acad. Inst. Arts and Letters, 1990; Guggenheim fellow in poetry, 1988-89. Fellow Am. Acad. Arts and Scis.; mem. MLA, Poets, Essayists and Novelists, Nat. Book Critics Cir. Democrat. Avocation: reading. Home: 838 W End Ave Apt 3A New York NY 10025-5365 Office: Rutgers U Dept English Hill St Fl 5 Newark NJ 07102-2607

HADDAD, ABRAHAM HERZL, electrical engineering educator, researcher; b. Baghdad, Iraq, Jan. 16, 1938; came to U.S., 1963; s. Moshe M. and Masuda (Cohen) H.; m. Carolyn Ann Kushner, Sept. 9, 1966; children: Benjamin, Judith, Jonathan. BSEE, Technion-Israel Inst. Tech., Haifa, 1960, MSEE, 1963; MA in Elec. Engring., Princeton U., 1964, PhD in Elec. Engring., 1966. Asst. prof. elec. engring. U. Ill., Urbana, 1966-70, assoc prof., 1970-75, prof., 1975-81; sr. staff cons. Dynamics Research Corp., Wilmington, Mass., 1979; program dir. NSF, Washington, 1979-83; prof. Ga. Inst. Tech., Atlanta, 1983-88; Dever prof., chmn. elec. engring and computer sci. dept. Northwestern U., 1988-98, Dever prof. dept. elec. and computer engring., 1996—, interim chair dept., 2001—02, dir. master info. and tech., 1998—. Dir. Computer Integrated Mfg. Sys. Program, 1987—88; adv. U.S. Army Missle Command, Huntsville, Ala., 1969—79; vis. assoc. prof. Tel Aviv U., Israel, 1972—73; cons. Lockheed-Ga. Co., 1984—88; gen chmn. Am. Control Conf., 1993; sec. Am. Automatic Control Coun., 1990—2003; chmn. policy com. Internat. Fedn. Automatic Control, 1996—2002, chmn. awards com., 2002—. Editor: Non-linear Systems, 1975; assoc. editor Control Engring. Practice, 1999—. Fellow AAAS, IEEE (editor Trans. on Automatic Control 1983-89, Centennial medal 1984, mem. awards bd. 1997-99, third millenium medal 2000); mem. Control Systems Soc. of IEEE (gen. chair 1984 Conf. on Decision and Control, Disting. mem. award 1985, v.p. fin. affairs 1989-90, pres.-elect 1991, pres. 1992, assoc. editor at large Trans. Automatic Control 1998-2003, chair Axelby award com. 2002-03). Jewish. Office: Northwestern U Dept ECE Evanston IL 60208-3118

HADDAD, GEORGE ILYAS, engineering educator, research scientist; b. Aindara, Lebanon, Apr. 7, 1935; came to U.S., 1952, naturalized, 1961; s. Elias Ferris and Fahima (Haddad) H.; m. Mary Louella Nixon, June 28, 1958; children: Theodore N., Susan Anne. BS in Elec. Engring, U. Mich., 1956, MS, 1958, PhD, 1963. Mem. faculty U. Mich., Ann Arbor, 1963—, assoc. prof., 1965-69, prof. elec. engring., 1968—, Robert J. Hiller prof., 1991—, dir. electron physics lab., 1968-75, chmn. dept. elec. engring. and computer sci., 1975-87, 91-97, dir. ctr. for high-frequency microelectronics, 1987—. Cons. to industry. Contbr. articles to profl. jours. Recipient Curtis W. McGraw research award Am. Soc. Engring. Edn., 1970, Excellence in Research award Coll. Engring., U. Mich., 1985, Disting. Faculty Achievement award U. Mich., 1985-86, S.S. Attwood award, 1991, MTT-S Disting. Educator award, 1996. Fellow IEEE (editor proc. and trans.); mem. NAE, Am. Soc. Engring. Edn., Am. Phys. Soc., Acad. Engring., Sigma Xi, Phi Kappa Phi, Eta Kappa Nu, Tau Beta Pi. Office: U Mich Dept Elec Engring & Computer Sci 2309 EECS 1301 Beal Ave Ann Arbor MI 48109-2122 E-mail: jih@umich.edu.

HADDAD, MAHMOUD MUSTAFA, management educator; b. Jerusalem, Aug. 15, 1948; s. Mustafa Mahmoud and Azizeh Abdullah (Azizeh) H.; m. Salam Ibrahim Jallad, Apr. 12, 1985; children: Suha, Mustafa, Dahlia, Nour. BA, Mankato State U., 1974, MBA, 1976; PhD, U. Ala., 1984. Tchr. Buhtary Sch., Jericho, 1968-71; mgr. Red Fez, Lansdale, Pa., 1972-74; instr. Mankato (Minn.) State U., 1975-79; acctg. supr. Am. Family Ins., Eden Prairie, Minn., 1980-81; grad., rsch. asst. U. Ala., 1981-84; asst. prof. Wayne State U., Detroit, 1984-92; assoc. prof. U. Tenn., Martin, 1993—. Contbr. articles to profl. jours. Competitive Summer Rsch. grant Wayne State U., 1985, 86, 88, 89, 90, 91; Competitive ANR Pipeline fellow., 1989. Mem. Am. Fin. Assn., Fin. Mgmt. Assn., Eastern Fin. Assn., Midwest Fin. Assn., So. Fin. Assn., Fin. Mgmt. Honor Soc. Avocations: swimming, soccer, tennis. Home: 112 Bates Cv Martin TN 38237-2320 Office: U Tenn 113 Bus Administrn Bldg Martin TN 38238-0001

HADDEN, MAYO ADDISON, chamber of commerce executive, military officer, educator; b. Norfolk, Va., Mar. 19, 1943; s. Mayo Addison Jr. and Lorain Erma (Grant) H.; m. Susan Farris Nelson, June 19, 1966; children: Tracy Noelle, Robert Addison, Terri Lynn. BA in Polit. Sci., U. Ala., 1972; MBA, Hardin Simmons U., 1981; diploma, USAF Air War Coll., Montgomery, Ala., 1985, Army War Coll., Carlisle Barracks, Pa., 1988. Commd. U.S. Army, 1964, advanced through grades to col., 1987; various assignments U.S., Germany, Iceland, Vietnam, Middle East, Latin Am., 1962-78; asst. prof. mil. sci. Hardin Simmons U., Abilene, Tex., 1978-81; dir. ops. Hdqrs. Mil. Forces, St. George, Grenada, 1983; chief of tng. 18th Airborne Corps, Fort Bragg, N.C., 1981-84, bn. comdr., 1984-85; prof. mil. sci. U. Akron, Ohio, 1985-87; comdr. 4th Brigade 2d Region, 1987-88; comdr. insp. gen. Army Infantry Ctr. and Sch., 1988-93; ret., 1993; sr. v.p. Columbus C. of C., Ga., 1993—. Asst. coach orienterring team Hardin Simmons U., 1979-81 (nat. champions 1980, 81); faculty advisor Pershing Rifles Hardin Simmons U., 1978-81, U. Akron, 1985-87; comdr. ROTC, Mich. and Tenn., 1987-88. Active Boy Scouts Am. (dist. award of merit 1984-85); active youth sports, 1979-95; pres. Westover Jr. High Sch. PTA, Fayetteville, N.C., 1983; pres. Ft. Benning Mgmt. Assn., 1991-92; pres. & CEO Columbus Aquatic Club, 1991-93; co-chair Ft. Benning Retiree Coun., 1993—; active Columbus Quality Coun. Decorated Legion of Merit, Bronze Star with V device and three oak leaf clusters, Air medal with V device and 5 oak leaf clusters, Purple Heart, numerous others; named to Inf. Officer Candidate Sch. Hall of Fame, Ft. Benning, Ga., 1988. MEM. VFW, Am. Soc. Mil. Compts., Vietnam Vets Am., Assn. U.S. Army, Kiwanis (sec. 1977-78), USA Karate Fedn., Ft. Benning Mgmt. Assn. (v.p. 1989-91, pres. 1991-92), Mil. Order of Purple Heart, Columbus Aquatic Club (v.p. 1991-92, pres., chief exec. officer), Nat. Infantryman's Assn. (exec. dir. 1994—), U. Akron Faculty Club, North Columbus Exchange Club, Nat. Eagle Scout Assn., Mil. Order World Wars. Avocations: karate, running, numismatics. Home: 6510 Mink Dr Midland GA 31820-3732

HADDOCK, FRED(ERICK) T(HEODORE), JR., astronomer, educator; b. Independence, Mo., May 31, 1919; s. Fred Theodore Sr. and Helen (Sea) H.; m. Margaret Pratt, June 24, 1941 (div. Sept. 1976); children: Thomas Frederick, Richard Marshall; m. Deborah J. Fredericks, Dec. 7, 2003. SB, MIT, 1941; MS, U. Md., 1950; DSc (hon.), Rhodes Coll., 1965, Ripon Coll., 1966. Physicist U.S. Naval Rsch. Lab., Washington, 1941-56; assoc. prof. elec. engring. and astronomy U. Mich., Ann Arbor, 1956-59, prof. elec. engring., 1959-67, prof. astronomy, 1959-88, emeritus prof., 1988—. Lectr. radio astronomy Jodrell Bank U. Manchester, Eng., 1962; vis. assoc. radio astronomy Calif. Inst. Tech., 1966; vis. lectr. Raman Inst., Bangalore, India, 1978; sr. cons. Nat. Radio Astron. Obs., W.Va., 1960-61; founder, dir. U. Mich. Radio Astron. Obs., 1961-84. Author: (chpts. in books) Space Age Astronomy, 1962, Radio Astronomy of the Solar System, 1966; contbr. articles to prof. jours. and publs. Mem. Union Radio Sci. Internat., nat. chmn. comm. on radio astronomy, 1954-57; trustee Associated Univs., Inc., 1964-68; prin. investigator, five Orbiting Geophys. Observatories, 1960-74, and Interplanetary Probe 9, 1964-77; co-investigator on Voyager planetary probes, 1970-86, NASA, Washington; mem. astronomy adv. panel NSF, Washington, 1957-60, 63-66. With USN, 1944-45. Fellow IEEE (life), Am. Astron. Soc. (v.p. 1961-63); mem. Internat. Astron. Union (commn. on radio astronomy 1948—), NAS (adv. panel astronomy facilities 1962-64), AIA (hon. mem. Huron Valley chpt. 1980—), Sigma Xi (past pres. U. Mich. chpt. 1956—). Achievements include design and development of first submarine periscope radar antenna, 1943-44; early discoveries in microwave astronomy, gaseous nebulae in 1953 and early space detection of kilometer waves from galaxy and the sun, 1962. Home: 3935 Holden Dr Ann Arbor MI 48103-9415 Office: U Mich Astronomy Dept Ann Arbor MI 48109 E-mail: fhaddock@umich.edu.

HADIARIS, MARIE ELLEN, special education educator; b. N.Y.C., July 16, 1944; d. Regis Henri and Mary (Cullen) Courtemanche; m. Daniel P. Hadiaris, May 27, 1972; 1 child, Regis. BA, Molloy Coll., 1966; MS, Canisius Coll., 1968. Cert. deaf educator, N.Y., Mich. Tchr. of hearing impaired Cath. Charities Sch. for Deaf, Westbury, N.Y., 1967-68, Mill Neck (N.Y.) Manor Sch. for Deaf, 1968-69, Grand Rapids (Mich.) Pub. Schs., 1969-72; tchr. cons. for physically impaired Muskegon (Mich.) Pub. Schs., 1972-79, tchr. of hearing impaired, 1979—. Presenter Nat. Symposium on Use of Tech. in Edn. of Deaf Nat. Tech. Inst. for Deaf Rochester (N.Y.) Inst. Tech., 1992; coord. Theater of the Deaf program Rochester Inst. Tech. Nat. Tech. Inst., Muskegon Pub. Schs., 1987-94; introduction AT&T Learning Network Computer Program, Muskegon Pub. Schs., 1990—; presenter AT&T Learning Network Program West Shore Spotlight, 1993; participant Close Up, Washington, 1997. Contbr. articles to newspapers; coord. theatrical prodn. Sunshine Too, Tech. Inst. for Deaf, Rochester, 1997 (Muskegon Cmty. Found. grantee). Grantee Mich. Dept. Edn., 1990, 92, Muskegon Cmty. Found., 1997. Mem. Conv. of Am. Instrs. of Deaf. Home: 962 Hampden Rd Muskegon MI 49441-4121 Office: Muskegon H S 80 W Southern Ave Muskegon MI 49441-2541

HADLEY, DONNA LOUISE BARNES, retired secondary education educator; b. Fort Lauderdale, Fla., Aug. 4, 1945; d. Edwin H. and Grace A. (Nagel) Barnes; m. James Richard Hadley, Feb. 16, 1974; children: Thomas Arthur, John Christopher. BS in Edn., Ohio U., 1967; MEd, Xavier U., 1985. Cert. permanent, std. and secondary tchg. Ohio. Staff Camp Glen NoWeOh Coun. Camp Fire, Findlay, Ohio, 1965, 66, 67; tchr. grades 11 and 12 Chillicothe (Ohio) H.S., 1967-68; tchr. grades 7 and 8 Princeton Jr. Sch., Cin., 1968-69; tchr. grades 9-12 Sycamore H.S., Cin., 1969-96. Rep. to Nat. Coun. Tchrs. of English Conv., Sycamore English Dept., Cin., 1988. Elder, mem. Session, Blue Ash (Ohio) Presbyn. Ch., 1978, 79, 80; sec. Session, Greenhills Cmty. Ch. (Presbyn.), 1981-82, elder, mem. Session, 1991, 92, 93, 98—; guidance adv. com. Winton Woods H.S., Forest Park, Ohio, 1993-95. Mem. Ohio Ret. Tchrs. Assn., Sycamore Edn. Assn. (bldg. rep. 1981-83, sec. 1983-84), Chillicoth Edn. Assn., Princeton Edn. Assn., Nat. Coun. Tchrs. English, Ohio Coun. Tchrs. English (grader, judge contest 1989, 90). Avocations: walking, reading, physical fitness. Home: 850 Carini Ln Cincinnati OH 45218-1512

HADLEY, JUDITH MARIE, archaeologist, educator; b. Toledo, Dec. 21, 1956; d. John Bothwell and D. Ruth (Reynolds) H. BA, Wheaton (Ill.) Coll., 1978; MA, Inst. of Holy Land Studies, Jerusalem, 1984; PhD, Cambridge U., Eng., 1989. Lectr. St. George's Coll., Jerusalem, 1981-84; field archaeologist Tel Aviv U. Excavations, various, 1979-89; supr. St. John's Coll., Cambridge, 1986-89; lectr. Cambridge (Eng.) Univ., 1987-90, Westcott House Theol. Coll., Cambridge, 1989-90; asst. prof. archaeology Villanova (Pa.) U., 1990-98, assoc. prof., 1998—. Staff archaeologist Tel Jezreel Excavations, Israel, 1990-91, Tel Megiddo Excavations, Israel, 1998—. Author: The Cult of Asherah in Ancient Israel and Judah: Evidence for a Hebrew Goddess, 2000; contbr. articles to profl. jours. Recipient overseas rsch. studentship Cambridge U., 1984, benefactor's studentship St. John's Coll., 1984, scholar, 1986, Naden Sr. Rsch. award, 1988, Crosse studentship divinity faculty, 1987. Mem. AAUP, AAUW, Am. Sch. Oriental Rsch., Internat. Orgn. for Study of Old Testament, Cath. Biblical Soc., Soc. Bibl. Lit., Soc. Old Testament Studies, U. Pa. Women in Soc. Seminar, Archaeol. Inst. Am. Avocations: singing in church choir, jigsaw puzzles, pottery restoration, word games, travel. Office: Villanova U Theology and Religious Studies Dept 800 Lancaster Ave Villanova PA 19085-1603

HADLEY, LANDON R. mathematician, educator; b. Iowa City, Jan. 28, 1969; s. Richard T. and Wynton H. (Adams) H. BA, N.C. Ctrl. U., 1992; MA in Edn., Fayetteville State U., 1993. Analyst Northern Telecom, Research Triangle Park, N.C.; instr. math. Cumberland County Sch. Sys., Fayetteville, N.C. Vice-chmn. Fayetteville Parks and Recreation, 1992-95, chmn. 1995—, mem. Cumberland County Domiciliary Home Adv. Com., 1995. Grantee Fayetteville Sunrise Legion, 1994. Mem. Inst. Managerial Accts. Avocations: tennis, reading, chess. Home: PO Box 1504 Fayetteville NC 28302-1504

HADLEY, ROBERT CLINTON, secondary art educator; b. Lancaster, Ohio, Oct. 19, 1967; s. John William and Sara Jane (Collins) Hadley; m. Nancy Jill Herman, June 12, 1993; children: Robert Clinton II, Hannah Alexandra, Annie Elizabeth, Emily Victoria. BS, U. Indpls., 1990; MS, Ind. U., 1998. Lic. tchr. including visual arts grades K-12, Ind.; lic. secondary sch. adminstr. Part-time engring. records clk. Citizens Gas and Coke Utility, Indpls., 1987-91; student tchr., substitute tchr., coach Franklin Ctrl. H.S., Indpls., 1990-91; art tchr., coach Whiteland (Ind.) Cmty. H.S., 1991—, chmn. dept. art, 1994—2003. Project dir. Gifted and Talented Art Program, Whiteland, 1992-94; sponsor Nat. Art Honor Soc., Whiteland, 1993—. Deacon Ctr. Grove Presbyn. Ch., Greenwood, Ind., 1985-87, elder, 1992-93. Recipient cert. tchg. honor Nat. Scholastic Art awards, N.Y.C., 1994. Mem. NEA, Nat. Art Edn. Assn., Ind. H.S. Wrestling Coaches Assn., Ind. H.S. Golf Coaches Assn. Avocations: golf, ceramics, wrestling, coin collecting, travel, family. Home: 1002 Sugar Maple Dr Greenwood IN 46143-7700 Office: Whiteland Cmty HS 300 Main St Whiteland IN 46184-1550 E-mail: rob.hadley@cpcsc.k12.in.us.

HADLEY, ROBERT GORDON, rehabilitation counselor educator, consultant; b. Portland, Oreg., Feb. 28, 1931; s. Howard E. Hadley and Carol (McElmurry) Hadley Bryans; m. Patricia Ann Stephan Meyer, Dec. 21, 1968; children: Vanita Spaulding, Stephanie Koza. BA, Reed Coll., 1953; MS, State U. Wash., 1955; PhD, UCLA, 1962. Psychology trainee U.S. VA, L.A., 1956-61, psychologist, 1961-65; asst. prof. Calif. State U., L.A., 1965-68, assoc. prof., 1968-73, prof., 1973-87, prof. emeritus, 1987—. Ptnr. The Empowerment Group, Culver City, Calif., 1987-2002. Author: Professional Report Writing for Counselors, 1987, revised as Professional Counselor Reporting, 1992; co-author: Counseling Research and Program Evaluation, 1995. Mem. Direction 21 Com., Culver City, 1987-88; bd. dirs. Culver City Parks and Svc. Found., sec., 1996—. Mem. APA, Phi Beta Kappa. Avocations: reading, writing, walking. Home: 11408 Diller Ave Culver City CA 90230-5176 E-mail: BobPatHadley@aol.com.

HADLEY-BANAHENE, SARA SINGLETARY, elementary education educator; b. Lake City, S.C., Feb. 26, 1956; d. Charles Carr Jr. and Dorothy Belle (Singletary) Williams; m. Eugene L. Hadley Jr., Dec. 12, 1981 (div. June 1984); 1 child, Brandon Alexander; m. Rockson O. Banahene, Apr. 11, 1988; 1 child, Arryelle Evian. BA cum laude, CCNY, 1978, MS magna cum laude, 1983; postgrad., N.Y. Law Sch., 1978-79; profl. diploma adminstrn., St. John's U., Jamaica, N.Y., 1995. Tchr. N.Y.C. Bd. Edn., Bklyn., 1981—. Mem. United Fedn. Tchrs., N.Y. Librs. Assn., N.Y. State United Tchrs. Democrat. Baptist. Office: Bd Edn City NY 175 W 166th St Bronx NY 10452-4500

HAEBERLE, ROSAMOND PAULINE, retired educator; b. Clearwater, Kans., Oct. 23, 1914; d. Albert Paul and Ella (Lough) H. BS in Music Edn., Kans. State U., 1936; MusM, Northwestern U., 1948; postgrad., Wayne State U., 1965-66. Profl. registered parliamentarian. Tchr. sch. dist., Plevna, Kans., 1936-37, Esbon, Kans., 1937-41, Frankfort, Kans., 1941-43, Garden City, Kans., 1943-44, music supr. Waterford Twp., Mich., 1944-47, tchr. Pontiac, Mich., 1947-80, ret., 1980. Pres. Pontiac Fedn. Tchrs., 1961-63. Bd. dirs. Pontiac Oakland Town Hall; adv. coun. Waterford Sr. Citizens, chmn., 1990-93; pres. Oakland County Pioneer and Hist. Soc., 1992-94. Recipient Tchrs. Day award Mich. State Fair, 1963. Mem. AAUW (pres. Pontiac br. 1970-72, founds. chair Pontiac br.), Mich. Fedn. Music Clubs (state pres. 1993-95, chmn. state bylaws and citations, chair parliamentarian 2001—, pres. Tuesday musicale of Pontiac 1984-86, pres. S.E. dist. 1986-90, chmn. Music for the Blind Northeastern region 2000), Mich. Fedn. Bus. and Profl. Womens Club (Woman of Achievement award dist. IX

1994), Mich. DARS (state parliamentarian 1985-2002), DAR (Gen. Richardson chpt., regent 1983-85, libr. and parliamentarian, Excellence in Cmty Svc. award 1995), Waterford-Clarkston Bus. and Profl. Womens Club (bylaws and parliamentarian), Pontiac Area Ret. Sch. Pers. (parliamentarian, pres. 1981-84), Mich. Assn. Retired Sch. Pers. (Disting. Svc. award 1994), Mich. Bus. and Profl. Women's Club (dir. dist. 10 1965-67), Mich. Fedn. Music Clubs (Honored Recognition award 2000, Citations award 2000), Pontiac Bus. and Profl. Women (pres. 1959-61, Woman of the Yr. award 1974), Pontiac Area Fedn. Women's Clubs (pres. 1976-78, 81-84), Mich. Registered Parliamentarians, Louise Saks Parliamentary Unit (pres. 1990-92), Bloomfield Rep. Women's Club (parliamentarian 1999-2003), Detroit Women's Club, Eastern Star, Mu Phi Epsilon, Beta Sigma Phi (life), Zeta Tau Alpha. Republican. Methodist. Avocations: travel, playing piano, reading, bell ringing, dance.

HAEFELI, LILLIAN REARDON, school administrator; b. Dunn, N.C., Apr. 11, 1925; d. John B. and Ellen (McLean) Reardon; B.A., William Paterson Coll., 1967, M.Ed., 1970, 76; Ed.D., Rutgers U., 1983; m. John Edo Haefeli, Feb. 13, 1954; children— Lillian Ruth, John Edo. Asst. engring. aide Signal Corps, U.S. Army, Fort Monmouth, N.J., 1942-44; with Allen B. DuMont Labs., East Paterson, N.J., 1949-55; elem. tchr. public schs., Clifton, N.J., 1967-72, reading specialist, 1972-73, ednl. specialist, 1973-74; head tchr. in charge, 1974-77, elem. prin., 1977-85, coordinator basic skills for K-12, 1985— . Mem. NEA, N.J. Adminstrs. and Prins. Assn., Clifton Adminstrs. Assn., Delta Kappa Gamma, Kappa Delta Pi. Methodist. Home: 306 W D St Erwin NC 28339-2526 Office: 735 Clifton Ave Clifton NJ 07013-1801

HAEFNER, DON PAUL, retired psychology educator; b. Albany, N.Y., Mar. 7, 1928; s. Carl William and Mary Theresa (Diamond) H.; m. Allegra Ouida Turner, June 11, 1951 (dec. Oct. 1981); children: Carol, Ann, Thomas; m. Cynthia Jean Stewart, May 29, 1982. AB in psychology, Clark U., 1951; PhD, U. Rochester, 1956. Chief soc. psychologist Vets. Adminstrn. Ctr., Bath, NY, 1956—57; rsch. soc. psychologist VA Hosp., Brockton, Mass., 1957—60, U.S. Pub. Health Svc., Washington, 1960—62; rsch. assoc., lectr. to prof. U. Mich. Sch. Pub. Health, Ann Arbor, 1962—93, asst. dean, 1968—84, prof. emeritus, 1993—. Vis. instr. U. Rochester, N.Y., 1956-57; lectr. psychology Boston U., 1958-60; reviewer profl. jours., 1975-94; cons. to health orgns., 1975-85. Contbr. articles to profl. jours. Fellow APHA, Soc. Pub. Health Edn.; mem. APA, Sigma Xi, Delta Omega. Unitarian Universalist. Avocations: travel, photography, choral singing. Home: 2250 Pine Grove Ct Ann Arbor MI 48103-2338

HAEMMERLIE, FRANCES MONTGOMERY, psychology educator, consultant; b. Gainsville, Fla., Feb. 2, 1948; d. Henry John and Ruth Elizabeth (Collins) H.; Robert L. Montgomery, June 16, 1979. BA, U. Fla., 1972; MS, Fla. State U., 1976, PhD, 1978. Prof. U. Mo., Rolla, 1978—. Rsch. fellow Ctr. for Applied Engring., U. Mo., Rolla, 1984-87. Contbr. articles to profl. jours, chpts. to books. Sec. Rolla Jr. High Parent-Student-Tchr. Assn., 1989-90. Recipient Teaching awards U. Mo., 1980-85, 87-94, Disting. Tchg. award, 1995, Amoco Teaching award, 1981-82, Faculty Excellence award, 1986-89, Reade Beard Faculty Excellence award, 1989-90, John Stafford Brown, 1991-92, 92-93, 93-94. Mem. APA (membership chmn. div. 12 sect. IV 1990—), Southwestern Psychol. Assn. (placement chmn. 1986, program chmn. 1988-89, coun. rep. 1994—), Psi Chi (Outstanding Advisor award 1980, 86, Profl. Svc. award 1983). Achievements include research in promoting technology development in rural settings and human adaptation to technological environments. Home: 12341 Williams Pl Rolla MO 65401-7407 Office: U Mo Dept Psychology 110 Hss Rolla MO 65401

HAEN, JOANNE LEE, English educator; b. Iola, Kans., Dec. 25, 1943; d. Wesley Ross and Virginia Lee (Sechrest) Clendenen; m. Michael Edward Haen, June 12, 1965 (dec. 1978); children: Pier Michelle, Micah Aaron, Nichole Tennille. AA, Iola Jr. Coll., 1963; BS in Edn., Emporia State Tchrs., 1965; MS, Kans. State U., 1968. English tchr. 8th-9th grade Junction City (Kans.) Sch. Sys., 1965-67; journalism instr. Kansas City (Kans.) C.C., 1968-91, English instr., 1991—. English coord. Kansas City C.C., 1992-94, instrl. cons. humanities and fine arts divsn., 1993—, honors faculty, 1994—, honors coun. chair, 1994-95, editor coll. catalog, 1991—, coord. freshman orientation, 1998-99. Asst. softball coach Girls Softball League, 1980's. Mem. NEA, Kans. Nat. Edn. Assn., Lighthouse Preservation Soc., Nat. Coun. of Tchrs. of English. Avocations: photographing lighthouses, book collector. Office: Kansas City Cmty Coll 7250 State Ave Kansas City KS 66112-3003

HAENICKE, DIETHER HANS, academic administrator emeritus, educator; b. Hagen, Germany, May 19, 1935; came to U.S., 1963, naturalized, 1972; s. Erwin Otto and Helene (Wildfang) H.; m. Carol Ann Colditz, Sept. 29, 1962; children: Jennifer Ruth, Kurt Robert. Student, U. Gottingen, 1955-56, U. Marburg, 1957-59; PhD magna cum laude in German Lit. and Philology, U. Munich, 1962; DHL (hon.), Cen. Mich. U., 1986; DHL, We. Mich. U., 1998. Asst. prof. Wayne State U., Detroit, 1963-68, assoc. prof., 1968-72, prof. German, 1972-78, resident dir. Jr. Year in Freiburg (Ger.), 1965-66, 69-70, dir. Jr. Year Abroad programs, 1970-75, chmn. dept. Romance and Germanic langs. and lits., 1971-72, assoc. dean Coll. Liberal Arts, 1972-75, provost, 1975-77, v.p., provost, 1977-78; dean Coll. Humanities Ohio State U., 1978-82, v.p. acad. affairs, provost, 1982-85; pres. Western Mich. U., Kalamazoo, 1985-98. Asst. prof. Colby Coll. Summer Sch. of Langs., 1964-65; lectr. Internationale Ferienkurse, U. Freiburg, summers 1961, 66, 67 Author: (with Horst S. Daemmrich) The Challenge of German Literature, 1971, Untersuchungen zum Versepos des 20. Jahrhunderts, 1962; editor: Liebesgeschichte der schonen Magelone, 1969, Der blonde Eckbert und andere Novellen, 1969, Franz Sternbalds Wanderungen, 1970, Wednesdays with Diether, 2003, University Governance and Humanistic Scholarship (Festschrift), 2002; contbr. articles to acad. and lit. jours. Mem. Mich. State Atty. Discipline Bd. Fulbright scholar, 1963-65 Mem. MLA, AAUP, Am. Assn. Tchrs. of German, Mich. Acad. Arts and Scis., Mich. Coun. for Arts and Cultural Affairs, Phi Beta Kappa. Office: Western Mich U 3019 Waldo Library Kalamazoo MI 49008-3804 E-mail: diether.haenicke@wmich.edu.

HAENSLY, PATRICIA ANASTACIA, psychology educator; b. Kronenwetter, Wis., Dec. 4, 1928; d. Paul Frank and Valeria (Woyak) Banach; m. William E. Haensly, 1954; children: Paul, Robert, Thomas, James, John, David, Mary, Katherine. BS, Lawrence U., 1950; MS in Genetics, Iowa State U., 1953; PhD in Ednl. & Devel. Psychology, Tex. A&M U., 1982. Histo technique specialist dept. vet. pathology Iowa State U., Ames, 1958-63; asst. prof. dept. ednl. psychology Tex. A&M U., College Station, 1982-97; instr. Blinn Jr. Coll., College Station; prin. Investigator Project Mustard Seed, U.S.D.O.E. Javits Grant, 1993-96; assoc. dir. programs Inst. for Gifted and Talented Tex. A&M U., College Station, dir. summer presch. program Minds Alive, 1987-95. Mem. adj. faculty psychology Western Wash. U., Bellingham, 1996—. Contbg. editor Roeper Rev., 1996—; contbr. articles to profl. jours., chpts. to books; mem. editl. bd. Gifted Child Quar., 1996—, Gifted Child Today, 1997—; guest editor: (spl. issue) Gifted Teachers/Teachers of Gifted Learners, Parenting the Gifted. Alt. U.S. del. World Coun. Gifted and Talented Children, 1997-99, 2001-02, del., 1999-2001; del. People to People amb. program Pacific N.W. Initiative to the People's Rep. of China., 1998. Recipient Outstanding Woman award AAUW, 1980, Govt. Rsch. Javits grante, 1993-96, Hon. Mention Hollingworth award Intertel Found., 1993. Mem. Tex. Assn. for Gifted and Talented (1st v.p. 1988, 89, editor news mag. 1988, 89), Nat. Assn. Gifted Children (co-chmn. rsch. and evaluation com. 1985-87, John Curtis Gowan Rsch. award 1981, program chair Conceptual Found. divsn. 1997-99, chair 2000-01), World Coun. for Gifted and Talented Children, Inc., Soc. for Rsch. in Child Devel., Coun. for Exceptional Children, Assn. for Childhood Edn. Internat., Am. Creativity Assn. (charter), Am. Psychol. Soc., Phi Kappa Phi. Home: 3384 Northgate Rd Bellingham WA 98226-9263 E-mail: haensly@cc.wwu.edu.

HAFFNER, ALDEN NORMAN, university official; b. Bklyn., Oct. 3, 1928; s. Irving and Irene (Gutfleisch) H. AB, Bklyn. Coll., 1948; OD, Pa. Coll. Optometry, 1952; MPA, NYU, 1960, PhD, 1964; DOS (hon.), Mass. Coll. Optometry, 1960; ScD (hon.), Pa. Coll. Optometry, 1973. Exec. dir. Optometric Center of N.Y., N.Y.C., 1957—; acting chief adminstrv. officer State Coll. Optometry, SUNY, N.Y.C., 1970-71, dean, 1971-76, pres., 1976-78; assoc. chancellor for health scis. SUNY, Albany, 1978-82, vice chancellor for research, grad. studies and profl. programs, 1982-87, pres. coll. optometry, 1987—. Pub. svc. prof. health poligy Rockefeller Coll., SUNY-Albany, 1986; chmn. N.Y. State Com. on Health Personnel and Productivity, 1990—; cons. in field. Contbr. articles in field to profl. jours. Mem. adv. com. Commn. for Blind and Visually Handicapped, State Dept. Social Services, 1966-70; mem. bd. nat. study commn. on optometry Nat. Commn. on Accrediting, 1968-70; mem. health manpower planning com. Comprehensive Health Planning Agy., N.Y.C., 1969-73; project dir. Fed. Program of Identification, Counseling, Guidance and Recruitment of Minority Students in Profession of Optometry, 1968-74; mem. Mayor's Com. for Study of Aging, N.Y.C., 1958; chmn. bd. trustees Manhattan Health Plan, Inc., 1976-81. Served to 1st lt. M.C. U.S. Army, 1953-55. Recipient Albert Fitch Meml. award, 1962; Prof. Frederick A. Woll Meml. award, 1961; Distinguished Achievement award Alumni Assn., N.Y. U. Grad. Sch. Pub. Health Adminstrn., 1974 Fellow Am. Pub. Health Assn., AAAS, Am. Sch. Health Assn., Am., N.Y. Acad. Optometry; mem. N.Y. Acad. Scis., Group Health Assn. Am., Am. Pub. Welfare Assn., Am. Soc. Pub. Adminstrn., Nat. Rehab. Assn., Illuminating Engring. Soc., Am. Optometric Assn., N.Y. State Optometric Assn., Gerontol. Soc., Am. Assn. Univ. Adminstrs., Pub. Health Assn. City of N.Y. (dir. 1967—), Nat. Assn. Land Grant Colls. and State Univs. (com. health affairs 1981), Community Family Planning Coun., Am. Coun. on Edn., Assn. Cad. Health Ctrs., Hermann Biggs Soc., Beta Sigma Kappa (Gold Medal award 1974), Home: 201 E 36th St New York NY 10016-3668 Office: SUNY Coll Optometry 33 W 42nd St New York NY 10036-8003

HAFNER-EATON, CHRIS, health services researcher, medical educator, policy analyst; b. N.Y.C., Dec. 9, 1962; d. Peter Robert and Isabelle (Freda) Hafner; m. James Michael Eaton, Aug. 9, 1986; children: Kelsey James, Tristen Lee, Wesley Sean. BA, U. Calif., San Diego, 1986; MPH, UCLA, 1988, PhD Health Svcs. Rsch./Policy Analysis, 1992. Cert. health edn. specialist; internat. bd. cert. lactation cons. Cons. dental health policy UCLA Schl. Dentistry, 1989; grad. teaching asst. UCLA Sch. Pub. Health, 1987-92; health svcs. researcher UCLA, 1987-92; cons. health policy U.S. Dept. Health & Human Svcs., Washington, 1988—; analyst health policy The RAND/UCLA Ctr. Health Policy Study, Santa Monica & L.A., 1988-94; asst. prof. health care adminstrn. Oreg. State U. Dept. Pub. Health, Corvallis, 1992-95; pres. Health Improvement Svcs. Corp., 1994—; dir. rsch. rev. La Leche League Internat., 1996-99. Adj. faculty pub. health Linn-Benton Coll., 1995—; bd. dirs. Benton County Pub. Health Bd., Healthy Start Bd.; mem. Linn-Benton Breastfeeding Task Force, Samaritan Mother-Baby Dyad Team., Am. Public Health Assn. (sect. Council Med. Care). Peer reviewer for NIH jours., others; contbr. articles to profl. jours. including JAMA, Midwifery Today, Jour. Ambulatory Care Mgmt.; other numerous lay publs. such as Mothering Mag.. Rsch. grantee numerous granting bodies, 1988—. Mem. AAUW, NOW, Internat. Lactation Cons. Assn., La Leche League Internat. (area prof. liaison for Oreg.), Am. Pub. Health Assn. (med. care sect. coun., women's caucus), Am. Assn. World Health, Oreg. Pub. Health Assn., Oreg. Health Care Assn., Assn. Health Svcs. Rsch., Soc. Pub. Health Edn., Physicians for Social Responsibility, UCLA Pub. Health Alumni Assn. (life), Pub. Health Honor Soc., Delta Omega. Home: 1807 NW Beca Ave Corvallis OR 97330-2636 E-mail: drmom@proaxis.com.

HAGANS, VALERIE MAE GEE, special education educator; b. San Antonio, Mar. 23, 1966; d. George Francis and Mae (Smith) Gee; m. Danny Franklin Hagans, June 24, 1989. Bachelors in Early Childhood Edn., Meth. Coll., 1988; MA in Edn.-Spl. Edn., Fayetteville State U., 1993. Cert. tchr., N.C. Spl. educator Cumberland County Pub. Schs., Fayetteville, N.C., 1989—. Mem. Alpha Delta Kappa (Gamma Sigma chpt.), Coun. for Exceptional Children, Omicron Delta Kappa. Methodist. Home: 5336 Westminster Dr Fayetteville NC 28311-1392 Office: Warrenwood Elem Sch 4618 Rosehill Rd Fayetteville NC 28311

HAGEMAN, RICHARD PHILIP, JR., educational administrator; b. Derby, Conn., Dec. 21, 1941; s. Richard Philip and Elizabeth (Serafinowicz) H.; m. Patricia Steele; children: Margaret Anne, Sheila Marie. BS, Cen. Conn. State U., 1964; MS, U. Bridgeport, 1968, profl. diploma, 1972. Cert. counselor Nat. Bd. Cert. Counselors; cert. tchr., Conn. Tchr. Stony Brook Sch. Stratford (Conn.) Bd. Edn., 1964—69, elem. sch. guidance counselor, 1969—81, secondary sch. guidance counselor, 1981—83; asst. prin. Stratford Acad., 1983—90; prin. Whitney Sch., 1990—95, Ctr. Sch., 1995—99; ret., 1999; univ. supr. Sacred Heart U., Fairfield, Conn. Lectr. edn. Fairfield U. Grad. Sch. Edn., 1971-93; head counselor Stratford Continuing Edn. Program, 1983-91, program facilitator, 1999—; chief examiner Gen. Ednl. Devel., 1986-91; assessor, trainer Beginning Educator Support and Tng. program Conn. State Dept. of Edn.; mem. adv. bd. counselor edn. Fairfield (Conn.) U., 1970-74; co-chmn. Stratford Juvenile Deliquency Prevention Team, 1979-81; pres. Stratford Elem. Prin. Assn., 1991-92; chief reader Conn. Adminstrs. Test, 1999—. Mem. Youth Adv. Bd. Stratford, 1981-85, chairperson, 1984-85; radio announcer Sta. WMNR, Monroe, Conn., 1982—. Mem. ACA, ASCD, NEA (life), Stratford Edn. Assn. (pres. 1978-79), New Eng. Assn. Specialists Group Work (pres. 1982-83, v.p. 1999-2003), Phi Delta Kappa. Roman Catholic. Democrat. E-mail: hagemanrandp@msn.com.

HAGEN, AGNES MARY, adult education educator, writer; b. Albany, N.Y., June 14, 1938; d. Terrence Francis and Julia Treanor Hagen. BA in English, Medaille Coll., Buffalo, 1968; MEd as Reading Specialist, U. Va., 1974. Cert. adult edn., elem. edn. and spl. edn. 1-6 Va., lic. postgrad. profl. Elem. tchr. SNJM, Albany, 1958—72; reading specialist Washington parochial schs., 1972—76; social worker St. Ambrose Housing Aid/Balt. Cath. Charities, 1976—83; adult edn. tchr. Susquehanna/Chesapeake Job Corps Ctr. U.S. Dept. Labor, Port Deposit, Md., 1983—86; adult edn. tchr. Va. Dept. Correctional Edn., Staunton, 1986—. Lectr. in field. Author: The Jack Sloan series, 2002 (Top Titles for Adult New Readers award, Pub. Libr. Assn., 2000), The Tony Jefferson series, 2001. Mem.: AARP (v.p. 2000—), Va. Assn. for Adult Continuing Edn., Va. Assn. Correctional Educators (bd. dirs. 1994—), Delta Kappa Gamma. Roman Catholic. Avocations: reading, travel, kyaking. Home: PO Box 1444 Staunton VA 24402 Office: Staunton Correctional Ctr 301 Greenville Ave Staunton VA 24401

HAGEN, DANIEL RUSSELL, physiologist, educator; b. Springfield, Ill., Sept. 29, 1952; s. Robert William and Russella Mae (Lane) H.; m. Rosemary Ellen Simonetta, Mar. 25, 1978; children: Matthew, Mark, Lane, Elise. BS, U. Ill., 1974, PhD, 1978. Rsch. assoc. Cornell U., Ithaca, N.Y., 1978; asst. prof. Pa. State U., University Park, 1978-84, assoc. prof., 1984-93, prof., 1993—. Vis. assoc. prof. U. Wis., Madison, 1988-89, interim dept. head, 1995-98. Mem. editl. bd. Jour. Animal Sci., 1983—86, 1993—96, Biology Reprodn., 1997—2000; contbr. numerous articles to profl. jours. Mem.: Soc. for Study Fertility, Soc. for Study Reprodn., Am. Soc. Animal Sci., Sigma Xi. Office: Pa State U 324 Henning Bldg University Park PA 16802-3503 E-mail: drh@psu.edu.

HAGEN, MICHAEL DALE, family physician educator; b. St. Louis, Nov. 11, 1949; s. Hubert Dale and Gwendel (Carden) Hagen; m. Barbara Carroll Keifer, Aug. 21, 1971; children: Laura Carrol, Sandra Ann. BS in Biology, Denison U., 1971; MD cum laude, U. Mo., Columbia, 1975. Cert. family practice bd. Pvt. practice Family Medicine Assocs., Aurora, Mo., 1978—81; asst. prof. dept. family practice U. Ky., Lexington, 1981—87, assoc. prof. dept. family practice, 1987—92, prof. dept. family practice, 1993—, interim chmn. dept. family practice, 1992—93, assoc. chmn. dept. family practice, 1993—97, project dir., computer-based assessment, 1996—; assoc. dir. assessment methods Am. Bd. Family Practice, 2003—. Fellow clin. decision making New Eng. Med. Ctr., Boston, 1987—89; at-large dir. Am. Bd. Family Practice, Lexington, 1991—96, pres., 1995—96; residency rev. com. family practice Accreditation Coun. for Grad. Med. Edn., Chgo., 1994—97. Author: Saunders Review Family Practice, 1992, 1997, 2002; contbr. articles to profl. jours. Mem.: AMA, Omicron Delta Kappa, Soc. for Med. Decision Making, Am. Acad. Family Physicians (clin. policies task force 1994—95), Phi Kappa Phi, Alpha Omega Alpha. Presbyterian. Avocations: amateur radio, gardening. Home: 2012 Blairmore Rd Lexington KY 40502-2435 Office: Assessment Techs Inc 2224 Young Dr Lexington KY 40505-4219 E-mail: hagenmd@prodigy.net., mhagen@assesstech.com.

HAGEN, NICHOLAS STEWARD, medical educator, consultant; b. Plentywood, Mont., Aug. 6, 1942; s. William Joseph and June Janette (Reuter) H.; m. Mary Louise Edvalson, July 26, 1969; children: Brian Geoffrey, Lisa Louise, Eric Christopher, Aaron Daniel, David Michael. BS in Chemistry, Ariz. State U., 1964; MBA in Internat. Bus., George Washington U., 1969; MD, U. Ariz., 1974. Lic. physician Ariz., Utah, Idaho.; diplomate Nat. Bd. Med. Examiners. Intern., resident Good Samaritan Hosp., Phoenix, 1974-75; pvt. practice Roy, Utah, 1975-77; dir. clin. rsch. Abbott Labs., North Chicago, Ill., 1977-84; v.p. med. affairs Rorer Group, Inc., Ft. Washington, Pa., 1984-88; clin. prof. Ariz. State U., Tempe, 1988-90. Pres. Southwestern Clin. Rsch., Tempe, 1987—, Travel Profl. Internat., Tempe, 1989-98; mem. Ariz. Bd. Med. Student Loans, 1998-2002. Author: Valproic Acid: A Review of Pharmacologic Properties and Clinical Use in Pharmacologic and Biochemical Properties of Drug Substances, 1979; contbr. articles to med. jours.; patentee in field. Bishop Ch. Jesus Christ of Latter-day Saints, Gurnee, Ill., 1981-84; various positions with local couns. Boy Scouts Am., 1988—; active Rep. campaigns, Mesa, Ariz., 1988—; 2d vice chmn. Maricopa County Rep. Assembly, 1997-99; dist. republican chmn., 1996-98; mem. governing bd. East Valley Inst. Tech., 1998-2003. Lt. comdr. USCG, 1965-69. Joan Mueller-Etter scholar Ariz. State U., 1960, Phelps-Dodge scholar Ariz. State U., 1961; NASA fellow Brigham Young U., 1964. Mem. Am. Coll. Sports Medicine, Eagle Forum, Nat. Right-to-Life Assn., Utah Hist. Soc., Nat. Geneal. Soc., Bucks County Geneal. Soc., Sons of Norway, Soc. Descendants Emigrants from Numedal, Hallingdal and Hedmark, Norway, Blue Key, Archons, Kappa Sigma (treas. Greater Phoenix alumni chpt. 1999—), Beta Beta Beta, Alpha Epsilon Delta, Phi Eta Sigma, Sophos. Republican. Mem. Lds Ch. Avocations: genealogy, swimming, philately, medieval history, art collecting. Office: 2251 N 32d St Lot 20 Mesa AZ 85213-2445

HAGENBUCH, STEPHEN LEE, principal; b. Cumberland, Md., June 12, 1948; s. Robert D. and Ruth M. (Sturtz) H.; m. Meredith Gurley, Aug. 23, 1969; children: Christopher Scott, Alison Lauren. BS in Edn., Frostburg State Coll., 1970; MA in Edn., U. Md., 1975. Sanitarian Md. State Dept. Health, Balt., 1970-71; tchr. Harford County Pub. Schs., Bel Air, Md., 1971-79, asst. prin., 1979-86, prin., 1986—. Life mem. PTA. Mem. NAESP, Md. Assn. Elem. Sch. Prins. (pres. 1992-93, nat. rep. 1994-97), Harford County Elem. Sch. Adminstrs. Assn. (pres. 1987-88, nat. rep. 1994-97), Phi Delta Kappa. Episcopalian. Office: Ring Factory 1400 Emmorton Rd Bel Air MD 21014-5580

HAGER, ANTHONY WOOD, mathematics educator; b. Marshfield, Wis., Dec. 16, 1939; s. Cyril Francis and Margaret Ruth (Wood) H.; 1 child, Amanda D. BS, Pa. State U., 1960, PhD, 1965. Rsch. scientist Leeds & Northrup Co., N. Wales, Pa., 1960-61; instr. U. Rochester, N.Y., 1965-67, asst. prof., 1967-68, Wesleyan U., Middletown, Conn., 1968-69, assoc. prof., 1969-75, prof., 1975—, chmn. dept. math., 1976-77, 88-90, 93, 95-96. Contbr. articles to profl. jours. NAS vis. rschr., Prague, 1973, 75; Italian N.C.R. vis. rschr. Padua, 1978; U. Fla. vis. rschr., Gainesville, 1995. Mem. Am. Math. Soc. Office: Wesleyan U Math Dept Middletown CT 06459-0001 E-mail: ahager@wesleyan.edu.

HAGER, JULIE-ANN, lawyer, educator; b. Kermit, Tex., Aug. 25, 1954; d. Howard Glenn and Marianne Johanne (Ratzer) H. BA magna cum laude, Baylor U., 1976; JD, U. Tex., 1979. Bar: Tex., U.S. Dist. Ct. (we. dist.) Tex., U.S. Ct. Appeals (5th cir.). Assoc. Wilson, Grosen Heider & Burns, Austin, Tex., 1979-83, ptnr., 1983-90; pvt. practice Law Offices of Julie Ann Hager, Austin, 1990—. Tchr. U. Tex. Paralegal Inst., Austin, 1990—. Vol. Austin Rape Crisis Hotline, 1988—, Austin Ctr. for Battered Women, Tex. Head Injury Assn., 1987—; vol. mediator Alternative Dispute Resolution, Austin, 1988—; speaker in field. Fellow Tex. Bar Found.; mem. ABA, ATLA, AAUW, Am. Soc. Law and Medicine, Travis County Women's Law Assn., Travis County Bar Assn. Democrat. Avocations: snow skiing, sailing, French horn. Home: 7629 Parkview Cir Austin TX 78731-1127 Office: 111 Congress Ave Ste 1060 Austin TX 78701-4244

HAGERDON, KATHY ANN (KAY HAGERDON), electric power industry executive, educator; b. Fremont, Ohio, Mar. 20, 1956; d. Willis Harold and Lillian Mae (Bahnsen) Lehmann; m. Michael Lee Hagerdon, Apr. 21, 1979; children: Patrick Michael, Robert Joseph, Andrew Richard. BSBA, Ohio State U., 1978; MBA, Ashland U., 1991. Budget analyst Small Motors divsn. Westing House, Bellefontaine, Ohio, 1978-80; fin. analyst Aerospace Elec. divsn. Westing House, Lima, Ohio, 1980-82, fin. cost analyst, 1982-85; sr. fin. analyst Elec. Sys. divsn. Westing House, Lima, 1985-91, lead profl., 1991-92; sr. fin. analyst Sund Strand Electric Power Sys., Lima, 1992-96, plant controller Phoenix, 1996-98; bus. mgr. Sund Strand Aerospace, Phoenix, 1998-99; contr. UTC, Phoenix, 1999—. Chmn. supervisory com. Westing House Credit Union, 1991-94; part-time prof. Tiffin U., Lima, 1994-96, Northwestern Bus. Coll., Lima, 1994-95. Asst. girls basketball coach, 1998-99; tchr. religious edn., 1999. Mem. Inst. Mgmt. Accts. (v.p. membership 1994-96), Toastmasters Internat. (pres. 1993-95, Com. award 1991), Neighborhood Assn. (bd. dirs. 1999). Roman Catholic. Avocations: reading, swimming, exercising. Home: 115 N Heather Hill Dr Bellefontaine OH 43311-2701

HAGERTHEY, GWENDOLYN IRENE, retired music educator; b. Sheffield, Eng., Sept. 28, 1937; arrived in U.S., 1938; d. Colin Clifford and Dorothy Abbott Oldfield; m. George Robert Hagerthey, June 23, 1962; children: Wendy Lee Hagerthey Canfield, Scot Edward. BS in Music, Trenton State Coll., 1959. Tchr. music Northfield Pub. Schs., NJ, 1959—64, 1971—74, Enfield Pub. Schs., Conn., 1974—78, Mt. Olive Twp. Pub. Schs., Budd Lake, NJ, 1978—99; ret., 1999. Organist, choir dir. various chs. including Stanhope (N.J.) Meth. Ch., 1950—98; camp music dir. Willow Lake Day Camp, Lake Hopatcong, NJ, 1985—97. Vol. Shore Meml. Hosp., Somers Pt., NJ, 1999—, Meadowview Nursing Home, Northfield, 1999—; dir. Atlantic County Hist. Soc., Somers Pt., 1999—. Named Rookie of Yr., Shore Meml. Hosp., 2000; recipient Govs. award for Outstanding Tchg., 1991. Mem.: AAUW (1st v.p. 1959—61). Home: 26 E Meyran Ave Somers Point NJ 08244

HAGGARD, GERALDINE LANGFORD, primary school educator, adult education educator, consultant; b. Wellington, Tex., Dec. 12, 1929; d. Frank and Zelma Dell (Edmondson) Langford; children: Colby, Sarah, Mary. MEd, Tex. Women's U., 1973, EdD, 1980; Cert. in Reading Recovery, Ohio State U., 1989. Elem. sch. tchr. Denton County (Tex.) Schs., 1949-62, Plano

(Tex.) Ind. Sch. Dist., 1963-69, reading tchr., reading dir., 1999-2001. Vis. prof. Tex. Woman's U. Editor and author lang. arts texts; contbr. articles to profl. jours.; author: Teaching and Assessing Comprehension Strategies, 2003. Sunday Sch. tchr. Prairie Creek Baptist Ch., Plano, 1994—; vol. facilitator Journey of Hope program for grief counseling. Named Hero Plano ISD centennial celebration, 1998. Mem. N.Am. Coun. Reading Recovery (bd. mem. 1995-99), Internat. Reading Assn., Tex. State Coun. Reading, Tex. Assn. Improvement of Reading, Coalition Reading English Suprs. Tex. (sec. 1994-97), Tex. Ret. Tchrs. Assn. (Plano chpt.), Alpha Delta Kappa, Delta Kappa Gamma, Phi Delta Kappa. Home: 2017 Meadowcreek Dr Plano TX 75074-4663

HAGGARD, VICTORIA MARIE, elementary education educator, secondary education educator; b. Denver, Nov. 7, 1951; d. Donald Eugene and Elaine Marie (Geisert) Russell; m. Robert Michael Haggard, Dec. 22, 1973; 1 child, Robert Donald. BS in Edn., Concordia Tchrs. Coll., 1973; postgrad., U. Tex., 1993; M in Ednl. Adminstrn., Our Lady of the Lake U., 2000. Cert. tchr., Colo., Okla., Tex.; cert. Dantes test specialist, gifted and talented endorsement. Elem. tchr. Bethlehem Luth Sch., Lakewood, Colo., 1973-85; idea instr., testing coord. USAF Vance AFB, Enid, Okla., 1985-87; elem. tchr. St. Thomas Moore Cath. Sch., San Antonio, 1987-89; secondary English tchr. Kirby Jr. High Judson Ind. Sch. Dist., San Antonio, 1989—, coord. gifted and talented program, 1992—, gifted and talented elective tchr., 1992—, chair lang. arts dept., 1994—, vice prin., 2000—01, 2003—, Woodlake Hills Mid. Sch., San Antonio, 2001—. Mem. Coll. Bd. for Acad. Excellence, San Antonio, 1992-93; presenter in field. Named Outstanding Tchr. Bethlehem Luth. Sch., 1983-85, Outstanding IDEA instr. USAF, 1985-87, Clearly Outstanding Tchr. Kirby Jr. High, 1990—, Dr. Helen Rook award for Gifted/Talented Educator, Judson Ind. Sch. Dist., 1992-93, Class Act Tchr. Hispanic Univs. and Coll., 1993. Mem. San Antonio Area Coun. Tchrs. English, Delta Kappa Gamma (sec. Epsilon Beta chpt. 1993, rec. sec. 1994-96), Phi Delta Kappa. Republican. Methodist. Avocations: reading, biking, hiking, board games. Home: 7827 Sun Frst San Antonio TX 78239-3224

HAGGER, BOBBIE, elementary education educator; b. Green Bay, Wis. d. Robert G. and Thelma R. (Wickman) Alwin; children: Katie, Julie. BS in Elem. Edn., Wayne State U., 1971; M of Elem. Edn., Western Mich. U., 1976. Elem. tchr. Dept. Def. Dependent Schs., Strullendorf, Germany, 1985-87, Fennville (Mich.) Pub. Schs., 1971-85, 87—. Named Tchr. of Yr., Fennville Pub. Schs., 1993. Home: 6272 126th Ave Fennville MI 49408-9650 Office: Fennville Pub Schs Memorial Dr Fennville MI 49408

HAGGERSON, NELSON LIONEL, JR., education educator; b. Silver City, N.Mex., June 11, 1927; s. Nelson L. and Gladys Lenore (Jackson) H.; m. B. Kate Baldwin, June 1, 1949 (dec. 2001); children: Patrick, Frederick, Teresa, Rebecca, Lionel, Mary; m. Catherine Rumsey, Dec. 1, 2001. BA, Vanderbilt U., 1949; MS, Western N.Mex. U., 1952; PhD, Claremont Grad. U., 1960. Cert. secondary tchr.; cert. adminstr. Dir. Exptl. Sch. Webster Coll., Webster Groves, Mo.; asst. prof. edn. Western N.Mex. U., Silver City; prin. Cobre High Sch., Bayard, N.Mex.; prof. emeritus edn. Ariz. State U., Tempe. Vis. prof. U. W.I., St. Augustine, Trinidad and Tobago, 1993-99, U. Pitts., 1982, 91, 92, R.I. Coll., 1991, Western N.Mex. U., 1988, 97, 98, 99, 2000, 01. Author: Secondary Education Today, 1967, To Dance With Joy, 1971, Naturalistic Research Paradigms: Theory and Practice, 1983, Informing Educational Policy and Practice Through Interpretive Inquiry, 1992, From Geronimo's Lookout, Growing Up and Living in the Southwest: An Autobiography, 1993, Oh Yes I Can!, A Biography of Arlena Seneca, 1994, A Celebration: The Life of Father Ramon Estivill, Renaissance Man of God, 1999, Expanding Curriculum Research and Understanding, 2000, Stories of the Academy: Learning From the Good Mother, 2002, The Mission of the Scholar: Research and Practice, A Tribute to Nelson Haggerson, 2002, also 12 book chpts.; guest editor: Education in Asia, Silver Ann Edit., World Coun. Curriculum and Instrn., Winter, 1995; contbr. over 50 articles to profl. jours. With USN, 1945-46. Fulbright fellow, 1986; recipient Award in Curriculum, MacDonald, 1986, Lifetime Achievement award Am. Biog. Inst.; named Outstanding Researcher, Coll. Edn., 1987, Outstanding Tchr., 1988; Rsch. grantee Deakin U., Victoria, Australia, 1988, The Mission of the Scholar, Research and Practice: A Tribute to Nelson Haggerson, 2002. Mem. AERA, ASCD, Profs. Curriculum, Soc. for Study of Curriculum History, World Coun. for Curriculum and Instrn. (program chmn. 1989), Order Internat. Fellowship, Phi Delta Kappa, Phi Kappa Phi, Kappa Delta Pi. Home: PO Box 24177 Tempe AZ 85285-4177

HAGLUND, THOMAS ROY, research biologist, consultant, educator; b. Beloit, Wis., Jan. 19, 1950; s. Roy Wilhelm and Marguerite Jean (Anderson) H.; m. Doris Anne Mendenhall, Oct. 22, 1988; 1 child, Victoria Tamsin. BS in Earth Sci., U. Wash., 1972; postgrad., U. Ill., Chgo., 1972-74; PhD in Biology, UCLA, 1981. Lectr., biology Calif. State Univ., L.A., 1981-83; sci. chair Windward Sch., L.A., 1983—97, 2002—; rsch. biologist UCLA, L.A., 1985—98; dir. Windward Conservation Biology Inst., 1997—. Adj. prof. biology Calif. State Poly. U., Pomona, 1991—; cons. U.S. Army C.E., L.A., 1979-80, Calif. Dept. Fish and Game, 1986—, Met. Water Dist., L.A., 1991, 93, 94, Dept. Pub. Works, Los Angeles County, 1991, 94—, U.S. Fish Wildlife Svc., 1992—, Perrier Corps of Am., 1998—; chair So. Calif. Native Fishes Working Group, 1996—. Contbr. chpt. to Historial Biogeography of North American Fish, 1991, articles to Jour. Paleontology, Evolution, Paleobiology, Biochem. Systematics Ecology, Copeia. Grantee NSF, 1978, Calif. Dept. Fish and Game, 1986, 87, 90, 91, 92, 93, 94, 99, World Bank, 1999-2001. Mem. AAAS, Am. Soc. Ichthyology and Herpetology, Am. Fisheries Soc., Desert Fishes Coun., European Ichthyological Congress. Achievements include research in systematics and population genetics of minnows, suckers and sticklebacks, conservation genetics of endangered North American fish, recovery strategies for endangered fishes; biological impacts of sediment management associated with dams. also: Windward Sch 11350 Palms Blvd Los Angeles CA 90066-2104

HAGMAN, HARLAN LAWRENCE, education educator; b. DeKalb, Ill., Sept. 8, 1911; s. Gus Carl and Emily Sophia (Peterson) H.; m. Mary Anna Cassels, May 23, 1943; children: William Gordon, Richard Harlan, Jean Cassels, Thomas Lawrence; foster children: James Evanson, Donald Jones. EdB, No. Ill. U., 1936; MA, Northwestern U., 1939, PhD, 1947. Formerly tchr. pub. schs., prin. and supt.; instr. Northwestern U., 1940-41; assoc. prof. Drake U., Des Moines, 1947-49, prof. edn., 1949-50, dean coll. edn., 1950-57; prof. edn. Wayne State U., 1957-60, dean adminstrn., 1960-72; prof. higher edn., 1972—. Moderator fgn. policy radio broadcasts, nat. network. Author: A Handbook for the Schoolboard Member, 1941, The Administration of American Public Schools, 1951, (with Alfred Schwartz) Administration in Profile for School Executives, 1955, Administration of Elementary Schools, 1956, September Campus, 1977, Bright Michigan Morning: The Years of Governor Tom Mason, 1981, The Academic Life, 1983, A Seasonal Present and Other Stories, 1989, (with Howard Snyder) Second Balcony, 1990, Nathan Hale and John Andre: Reluctant Heroes of the American Revolution, 1991; editorial cons., McGraw-Hill Book Co., Internat. City Mgrs. Assn.; editor: We Hold These Truths: The Collected Sermons of Rt. Rev. Richard Emrich; contbr. to: Am. Peoples Ency.; also contbr. to ednl. jours.. Bd. dirs. Youth for Understanding, Internat. Edn. Exchange. Served as lt. comdr. USNR, World War II. Mem. Players Club, Circumnavigators Club. Home: 1017 Kensington Ave Grosse Pointe MI 48230-1402 Office: Wayne State U Coll of Education Detroit MI 48202

HAGMANN, LILLIAN SUE, violin instructor; b. Fontana, Calif., Mar. 10, 1931; d. Riley Royston and Winifred Lillian (Humphry) Green; m. Armand P. Oueilhe, Dec. 17, 1950 (div. 1971); children: Ellen Lynne Oueilhe Keene, Karen Sue Oueilhe Stanton, A. Louis Oueilhe (dec. 1971), Gregoire Pierce Oueilhe; m. Rolf Hagmann, May 19, 1971. AA, Chaffey Coll., 1951; Travel Counselor, Internat. Travel Tng., Chgo., 1974; student, Suzuki Violin Tchr. Tng. Inst., Guelph, Can., 1992, Suzuki Violin Tchr. Tng. Inst., Forest Grove, Oreg., 1993, 97, Occidental Coll., Eagle Rock, Calif., 1994, Suzuki Violin Tchr. Tng. Inst., Stevens Point, Wis., 1995, Suzuki Violin Tchr. Tng. Inst., Aspen, Colol., 1998, Suzuki Violin Tchr. Tng. Inst., Chgo., 2000. Pricer MacNall Bldg. Materials, Santa Barbara, Calif., 1964-67; office mgr. Laguna Blanca Sch. Devel. Program, Santa Barbara, 1968; pub. rels. asst. to mgr. Goleta (Calif.) Savs. and Loan, 1969-71; travel counselor Around The World Travel, Palatine, Ill., 1974-77; travel mgr./dir. pub. rels. Newport Area Travel, Newport Beach, Calif., 1977-80; travel counselor Cresenta Valley Travel, La Crescenta, Calif., 1981; violin instr. Arise Acad. Arts, Pomona, Calif., 1989-94, U. Redlands (Calif.) Cmty. Sch. Music, 1989—2003, Arts Encounter, Rowland Heights, Calif., 1996—97. Del. 1st Stringed Instrument Edn. Del., China, 1997. Mem. The Fandango Chamber Group. Violinist Santa Barbara Symphony, 1962-70, Riverside (Calif.) City Coll. Symphony, 1990-97; judge Search for Talent contest Riverside Exch. Clubs, 2000-02; active Adams Sch. PTA, Santa Barbara, 1967—; bd. dirs. Calif. Congress PTA; organizer, pres. Assn. for Neurologically Handicapped Children, 1970-71; choir Corona Cmty. Ch., 1995-97; mem. five piece ensemble Evang. Free Ch. of Corona; organizer violin concerts for children including MC Orange County Suzuki Festival, 2002-03. Democrat. Avocations: gardening, artist. Home: 1143 Via Santiago Corona CA 92882-3950 E-mail: mrbeethoven@prodigy.net.

HAGSTEN, IB, animal scientist, livestock consultant; b. Assens, Denmark, May 18, 1943; arrived in U.S., 1971, naturalized, 1980; s. Kresten and Marie (Jakobsen) H.; m. Patricia Ellen Dettman, July 13, 1968; children: Ellen Marie, Scot (dec.), Lisa R. BS, Bygholm Landbrugskole, Horsens, Denmark, 1965; MS, Royal Danish Agr. U., Copenhagen, 1971, Purdue U., 1973, PhD, 1975. Cert. animal scientist; diplomate Am. Coll. Animal Nutrition. Farm laborer, foreman various livestock farms, Denmark, Eng., Germany, Can., 1958-65; tchg. asst. Royal Danish Agr. U., 1969-70; rsch. assoc. Nat. Danish Rsch. Found., Copenhagen, 1971; cons. nutritionist M.D. King Milling Co., Pittsfield, Ill., 1976-77; acting product mgr. Am. Hoechst Corp., Somerville, N.J., 1978, tech. specialist, 1977-83; profl. sales rep. Hoechst Roussel Agri-Vet. Co., Gladstone, Mo., 1983-89, tech. svc. specialist, 1989-90, sr. profl. svc. specialist, 1990-98; pres. Hagsten Enterprises, Internat., livestock cons. svc., Kansas City, Mo., 1999—. Cons. Shell Farm, Inc., Ørum, Denmark, 1970—71, Agri-Bus. Tng. and Devel., Inc., Roswell, Ga., 1979—95, Nat. Renderer's Assn., Hong Kong, 1989, USDA Trade Mission, Moldova, 1995, HRVet-Asia Workshop, Thailand, 1998, Hoechst Asia, Bangkok, 1998; cons. employee-tng. Ukraine and Moldova, 2000, Ukraine, Moldova and Kazakhstan, 2001, Moldova and Hungary, 2002; adj. prof. Rutgers U., New Brunswick, NJ, 1981—84, U. Mo., Columbia, 1990—97; vis. prof. Saratov State Agrarian U., Russia, 2001; pres. Personal Growth Alternatives, 1982—; cert. assessor environ. assistance program Nat. Pork Prodrs. Coun.; cert. agrl. cons., United States, 2001—, Canada, 2002—; cert. assessor environ. assistance program Environ. Mgmt. Svcs. LLC. Author: Energy Metabolism Evaluations, 1971; contbr. articles to profl. jours. and popular publs. Bd. dirs. MACOS handicapped support group, Macomb, Ill., 1976-77; co-chair Cmty. Hunger Walks (CROP), Western N.J., 1978-82; mem. family curriculum bd. Lopatcong Twp. Sch., Phillipsburg, N.J., 1982; vice moderator Pilgrim Presbyn. Ch., Phillipsburg, 1980-83, elder, 1979-83, Gashland Presbyn. Ch., Gladstone, 1990-93; regional exec. bd. mem. United Marriage Encounter, Mo., Kans., 1983-95; bd. dirs. Gashland Christian Presch., 1991-93, World-In-Need Internat., 2002- ; mem. Core of Advocates, Coll. Vet. Medicine Kans. State U.; bd. dirs. Heartland Presbyn. Pro-Life, 1993—, pres., 1999-2002; v.p. Trade Palms, a mission-funding corp., 2001—; bd. dirs. World In Need Internat., 2002--. Sgt. Danish King's Royal Guard, 1959-61. Mem.: Am. Registry Profl. Animal Scientists (chmn. ethics com. 1982—85, cert.), Nat. Feed Ingredient Assn., Am. Coll. Animal Nutrition (charter, diplomate), Am. Soc. Agrl. Cons. Internat. (charter), Am. Soc. Agrl. Cons. (bd. dirs. 1978—81, sec.-treas. 1990—2000, bd. dirs. 1992—94, chmn. ethics com. 1992—94, bd. dirs. 1995—97, v.p. 2000—01, pres. 2002—03, Disting. Svc. award 1980), Danish Soc. Animal Sci., Greater Kans. City Scandinavian Club (bd. dirs. 1992—96). Republican. Avocations: people, gardening, travel, reading. Home and Office: 7212 N Woodland Ave Kansas City MO 64118-2263 E-mail: hagsten@bww.com.

HAHN, BEVRA HANNAHS, medical educator; b. Wheeling, W.Va., Dec. 9, 1939; d. Chester Hobart and Isa May (Quillen) Hannahs; m. Theodore J. Hahn, May 3, 1964; children: Alysanne Yvonne, April Dianne. BS, Ohio State U., 1960; MD, Johns Hopkins U., 1964. Diplomate Am. Bd. Internal Medicine, Am. Bd. Rheumatology. Intern Barnes Hosp., Washington U., St. Louis, 1964-65; resident in medicine Washington U., St. Louis, 1965-66, from instr. to assoc. prof. medicine, 1969-83; fellow in rheumatology Johns Hopkins U., Balt., 1966-69; prof. medicine, chief of rheumatology UCLA, 1983—. Chmn. Immunologic Scis. Study Sect. NIH, Washington, 1983-85; mem. Nat. Arthritis Adv. Bd., U.S. Dept. Health and Human Services, Washington, 1983-85. Contbr. articles to profl. jours. Mem. Am. Coll. Rheumatology (pres.1999), Am. Soc. Clin. Investigation, Am. Assn. Immunologists, Lupus Found. Am. (med. advisor 1980—), Arthritis Found., Phi Beta Kappa, Alpha Omega Alpha. Presbyterian. Avocations: tennis, swimming, music, reading. Office: UCLA Rheumatology 37-139 1000 Veteran Ave Los Angeles CA 90024-2704

HAHN, CYNTHIA THERESE, foreign language educator; b. Berwyn, Ill., Oct. 3, 1961; d. Richard E. and Audrey M. Blaha; m. James N. Hahn, July 23, 1983 (div. Nov. 1991). BA, Rosary Coll., River Forest, Ill., 1983; MA, Purdue U., 1985; PhD, U. Ill., 1990. Translator, office asst. Perspectives Réformées, Palos Heights, Ill., 1983; asst. prof. French U. Ill., Chgo., 1989-90; prof. Lake Forest (Ill.) Coll., 1990—, assoc. dean faculty, 2002—. Adminstr. oral exam. Paris C. of C. in Chgo., 1990-92; freelance translator, Lake Forest, 1992—. Author numerous poems; contbr. articles to profl. jours.; translator 2 novels; gen. editor: Collages lit. mag. Mem. Am. Assn. Tchrs. French, Assn. for Quebec Studies in U.S., Am. Transls. Assn., Assn. Women in French. Avocations: poetry, photography, playing bass guitar. Office: Lake Forest Coll Box K1 555 N Sheridan Rd Lake Forest IL 60045-2338

HAHN, GERALD EUGENE, industrial education educator; b. Peoria, Ill., July 15, 1942; s. Earl L. and Clarice A. (Briggs) H. BS, U. Ill., 1965, MEd, 1968. Cert. indsl. edn. tchr., Ill.; ordained deacon 1988. Tchr. Thornton Twp. High Sch., Harvey, Ill., 1965-95, chmn. dept. indsl. edn., 1985-90; retired, 1995; tchr. Queen of Apostles Parish Sch., 1998—2003. Mem. Holy Name Soc. Queen of Apostles Parish, PTA (life). Mem. NEA, Ill. Edn. Assn. Lodges: KC. Roman Catholic. Avocations: swimming, stained glass crafting, canoeing, travel, music. Home: 14261 Pennsylvania Ave Apt 11 Dolton IL 60419-1160

HAHN, JOAN CHRISTENSEN, retired secondary education educator, travel agent; b. Kemmerer, Wyo., May 9, 1933; d. Roy and Bernice (Pringle) Wainwright; m. Milton Angus Christensen, Dec. 29, 1952 (div. Oct. 1 1971); children: Randall M., Carla J. Christensen Teasdale; m. Charles Henry Hahn, Nov. 15, 1972. BS, Brigham Young U., 1965. Profl. ballroom dancer, 1951-59; travel dir. E.T. World Travel, Salt Lake City, 1969—; tchr. drama Payson (Utah) H.S., 1965-71, Cottonwood H.S., Salt Lake City, 1971-95; owner Travel Passport, 1992—. Dir. performing European tours, Salt Lake City, 1969—76, Broadway theater tours, 1976—. Regional dir. dance LDS Ch., 1954—72; pres. Elder Quest, Utah divsn. Elderhostel, Utah Valley State Coll., 2002—; bd. dirs. Salem (Utah) City Days, 1965—75. Named Best Dir. H.S. Musicals, Green Sheet Newspapers, 1977, 82, 84, 91, Utah's Speech Educator of Yr., 1990, 91, to Nt. Hall of Fame, Ednl. Theatre Assn., 1991, Cottonwood H.S. Hall of Fame, 1995, Nat. Women's Hall of Fame, 1999, Ohio Thespians Hall of Fame, 2000, Outstanding Educator, Utah Ho. of Reps., 1995; recipient 1st place award Utah Drama Tournament, 1974, 77, 78, 89, 90, 91, 94, 95, Tchr. of Yr. award Cottonwood H.S., 1989-90, Limelight award, 1982, Exemplary Performance in Tchg. Theater Arts award Granite Sch. Dist., Salt Lake City, 1982; Joan C. Hahn Theatre named in her honor Cottonwood H.S., 1997. Mem. NEA, Internat. Thespian Soc. (internat. dir. 1982-84, trustee 1979-84), Utah Speech Arts Assn. (pres. 1976-78, 88-90), Utah Edn. Assn., Granite Edn. Assn., Profl. Travel Agts. Assn., Utah H.S. Activities Assn. (drama rep. 1972-76), AAUW (pres. 1972-74). Republican. Avocations: reading, travel, dancing. Home: PO Box 36 Salem UT 84653-0036 E-mail: joanhahn@juno.com.

HAHN, YOON SUN, pediatric neurosurgeon, educator; b. Seoul, Republic of Korea, Sept. 23, 1937; came to U.S., 1970; s. D..C. and Kyung S. Hahn; m. Wonjae Cho, Sept. 25, 1965; children: Susie, David, Jimmy. BS, Yonsei U., Seoul, 1958; MD, Yonsei U., 1962. Diplomate Am. Bd. Pediat. Neurosurgery, Am. Bd. Neurol. Surgery, Korean Bd. Neurol. Surgery. Chief neurosurgery 101 Evacuation Hosp., Vungtao, Vietnam, 1968-69; fellow in neurosurgery, vis. asst. prof. U. Mich., Ann Arbor, 1970-71; spl. fellow neurosurgery and craniofacial surgery Hôpital Foch U. Paris, Suresnes, France, 1976; assoc. prof. neurosurgery Yonsei U. Med. Sch., Seoul, 1976; asst. prof. neurosurgery Children's Meml. Hosp., Chgo., 1979-88; prof., chief pediat. neurosurgery Loyola U. Med. Ctr., Chgo., 1988-95; dir. pediat. neurosurgery, surgeon-in-chief Hope Children's Hosp., Oak Lawn, Ill., 1995—; prof., chief divsn. pediat. neurosurgery U. Ill. Coll. Medicine, Chgo., 1996—. Contbr. chpts. to books; inventor in field. Major Korean Army, 1967-70. Recipient Silver medal Republic of Korea Army, Vietnam, 1969. George Joost award for outstanding tchg. Northwestern U. Med. Sch., 1999; named Best Neurosurgery Resident of Yr., Northwestern U. Children's Meml. Hosp., Chgo., 1975. Fellow ACS, Am. Acad. Pediat.; mem. Am. Assn. Neurol. Surgery, Am. Soc. Pediat. Neurosurgeons, Congress of Neurol. Surgery, Internat. Soc. Pediat. Neurosurgeons. Avocations: golf, skiing, reading. Office: U Ill Coll Medicine Pediat Neurosurgery 912 S Wood St Chicago IL 60612-7329 Fax: 312-996-9018.

HAIG, FRANK RAWLE, physics educator, clergyman; b. Phila., Sept. 11, 1928; s. Alexander M. and Regina A. (Murphy) H. AB, Woodstock Coll., Md., 1952, S.T.L., 1960; Ph.L., Bellarmine Coll., Plattsburgh, N.Y., 1953; PhD, Catholic U., 1959; LHD honoris causa, SUNY, 1987. Ordained priest Roman Cath. Ch. 1960. Joined S.J., 1946; postdoctoral fellow U. Rochester, N.Y., 1962-63; asst. prof. Wheeling Coll., W.Va., 1963-66, pres., 1966-72; asst. and assoc. prof. Loyola Coll., Balt., 1972-81; pres. Le Moyne Coll., Syracuse, N.Y., 1981-87; prof. physics Loyola Coll., Balt., 1987-2000, emeritus prof., 2000—. Editor Jour. Md. Assn. Higher Edn., 1979-81; contbr. articles on nuclear physics, bibl. theology and internat. politics to profl. publs. Pres., Wheeling C. of C., 1969-71; pres. Syracuse Opera Co., 1983-85, chmn. bd., 1985-87; gen. campaign chmn. United Way Onondaga County, Syracuse, 1985-86 Recipient Mayor's Achievement award Mayor of Syracuse, 1983; Harry J. Carman award Middle States Council for Social Studies, 1985; NSF fellow, 1962-63 Mem.: AAUP (v.p. Md. Conf. 1990—92, 1995, pres. 1995—98), Charles Carroll House of Annapolis (chmn. bd. 2001—), Washington Acad. Scis. (pres. 1993—94, treas. 1999—), Am. Phys. Soc., Am. Assn. Physics Tchrs. (pres. Chesapeake sect. 1976—77, 1990—92). Republican. Roman Catholic. Office: Loyola Coll Dept Physics 4501 N Charles St Baltimore MD 21210-2699

HAIG, MONICA ELAINE NACHAJSKI, special education educator; b. Bay Shore, N.Y., Nov. 17, 1963; d. Walter Andrew and Elaine Gilda (Guerringue) Nachajski; m. Michael Haig, June 24, 1989; children: Kathleen Mary, Michael Christopher, Christina Jean. BS in Edn., SUNY, Geneseo, 1985; MS in Edn. with high honors, L.I. U., 1989. Cert. permanent spl. and elem. edn. tchr., N.Y. Tchr. spl. edn. Convalescent Hosp. for Children, Rochester, N.Y., 1985, Patchogue-Medford Sch. Dist., Patchogue, N.Y., 1985. Edn. cons., mem. Suffolk County Exec.'s Conf. on Youth, Alcohol and hwy. Safety, Ronkonkoma, N.Y., 1990; presenter internet usage in elem. sci. classroom curriculum, CEC Conv. N.Y. State, 1999; participant seminars, workshops and confs.; presenter in field. Mem. Coun. for Exceptional Children. Avocations: reading, movement therapy. Office: Oregon Mid Sch Oregon Ave Medford NY 11763

HAIGH, CHARLES, criminal justice educator; b. Paterson, N.J., Oct. 29, 1939; s. Wallace Glover and Myrtle (Lewis) H.; m. Patricia Brennan, Apr. 12, 1986; children: Michael C., Charles E. BS in Law Enforcement Adminstrn., U. New Haven, 1972, MPA, 1976; CAS in Ednl. Adminstrn./Supervision, Fairfield (Conn.) U., 1980; EdD in Ednl. Mgmt., U. Bridgeport, 1989. Dir. tng. Milford (Conn.) Police Dept., 1965-91; asst. prof., adj. prof. criminal justice/criminology program Ctrl. Conn. State U., New Britain, 1991—. Adj. prof. criminal justice program U. New Haven, West Haven, Conn., 1979—. Adv. bd. criminal justice program Housatonic C.C., Bridgeport, 1985-92; deacon First United Ch. of Christ, Congl., Milford, 1993—, chmn., 1995, cons./lectr. Milford, Conn. Police Acad., 1997—. With USN, 1957-60. Ctrl. Conn. State U. grant, 1994. Mem. Acad. Criminal Justice Scis., Northeastern Assn. Criminal Justice Scis. (Outstanding Svc. to Assn. award 1994), Elks (chmn. Most Valuable Student scholarship program 1990—), Masons (lodge historian 1998—). Democrat. Avocations: golf, biking, swimming. Home: 25 Art St Milford CT 06460-4318

HAIGH, CINDY LOU, private/parochial school physical education educator; b. Uniontown, Pa., Apr. 12, 1962; d. Benjamin Francis and Linda Karen (Amos) H. BS in Edn., Indiana U. of Pa., 1984, MS in Sport Sci., 1992. Cert. tchr., Pa. Substitute tchr. Indiana County (Pa.) Pub. Schs., 1984-85; grad. asst. softball coach Indiana U. of Pa., 1984-86; health, phys. edn. tchr. Purchase Line (Pa.) Sch. Dist., 1985-87, Diocese of Greensburg (Pa.), 1987—; demonstration site tchr. phys. edn. Learning Is for Everyone Demonstration Sch., 1989—. Asst. basketball coach Purchase Line Sch. Dist., 1985-87, Greensburg Cen. Cath. High Sch., 1987-90; head basketball coach Greensburg Cath. Mid. Sch., 1989-91; softball umpire Amateur Softball Assn., Pa., 1985—. Named Outstanding Tchr. of Yr., St. Paul Sch. Bd., 1989, 90, Phsy. Edn. Tchr. of Yr., Pa. State Assn., 1993, Alumni Amb., Coll. of Health and Human Svcs. Ind. U. Pa., 1994. Mem. AAHPERD, Pa. State Assn. Health, Phys. Edn., Recreation and Dance (Tchr. of Yr. 1993), Pa. Sch. Health Assn., Amateur Softball Assn. Roman Catholic. Avocations: swimming, golf, biking, theatre. Home: 7557 Kensington St Pittsburgh PA 15221-3223 Office: Aquinas Acad 330 N Main St Greensburg PA 15601-1811

HAILEY, KATHLEEN WILSON, elementary education educator; b. Porterville, Calif., Sept. 24, 1947; d. Kenneth Carmel and Margaret Elenor (Worthen) Wilson; m. John David Hailey, Feb. 7, 1970; children: Jonathan David, Carolyn Elizabeth. AA, Porterville Coll., 1967; BA, St. Mary's Coll. of Calif., Moraga, 1979. Profl. clear teaching credential. 2nd grade tchr. Terra Bella (Calif.) Union Sch. Dist., 1968-69; 1st grade tchr. Hughson (Calif.) Elem. Sch. Dist., 1984-85, 2nd grade tchr., 1985-88, 5th grade tchr., 1988-89, 6th grade tchr. Emilie J. Ross Mid. Sch., 1989—. Adult sch. night tchr. Ceres (Calif.) Adult Sch., 1985-94; program quality rev. team Stanislaus County Schs., Modesto, Calif., 1992—; mem. Stanislaus UniServ Bd., 1996—, sec., 1997-98, treas., 1998-2000, v.p., 2000, pres., 2001; treas. Hughson Elem. Educator/CTA, 1991-94, pres., 1995-2001, chief negotiator, 1996—; trainer, Calif. Arts Project, 1999—, I Can Do It Trainer, 2001; trainer I Can Do It/I Have Done It, CTA, 2001—. Editor: (anthologies) Thoughts Beneath the Tower, 1993, Facts, Faces, Fiction and Fantasy, 1995; contbr. Micro Computers in Education, 1988. Mem. Persephone Guild, Ceres, 1994-95; bd. dirs., den leader cub scouts, Boy Scouts Am., 1981-84; bd. dirs. Ceres Cmty. Found., 1995-96. Named Mentor Tchr. Hughson Elem. Sch. Dist., 1994. Mem. Internat. Order Job's Daus. (dep. grand guardian 1992—, Bethel guardian 1990-95, Cert. of Appreciation

1994, Grand 2d Messenger 2000). Democrat. Bah'a'i. Avocations: sailing, sewing, reading, travel. Home: 2817 Joy Ave Ceres CA 95307-2810 Office: Emilie J Ross Mid Sch PO Box 189 Hughson CA 95326-0189 E-mail: ladykat000@aol.com.

HAIMAN, FRANKLYN SAUL, author, communications educator; b. Cleve., June 23, 1921; s. Alfred Wilfred and Stella (Weiss) H.; m. Louise Goble, June 11, 1955; children— Mark David, Eric Saul. BA, Case Western Res. U., 1942; MA, Northwestern U., 1946, PhD, 1948. Mem. faculty Northwestern U., Evanston, Ill., 1948—, chmn. dept. communication studies, 1964-75, prof. communication studies, 1970-88, John Evans prof. communication studies, 1988-91, John Evans prof. emeritus, 1991—. Adj. prof. U. of San Francisco, 1992—. Author: Group Leadership and Democratic Action, 1951, Freedom of Speech: Issues and Cases, 1965, Freedom of Speech, 1976, Speech and Law in a Free Society, 1981, "Speech Acts" and the First Amendment, 1993, Freedom, Democracy, and Responsibility: The Selected Works of Franklyn S. Haiman, 2000, Religious Expression and the American Constitution, 2003; co-author: The Dynamics of Discussion, 1960, 2d edit., 1980; editor: (book series) To Protect These Rights, 1976-77; contbr. articles to profl. jours. Pres. ACLU of Ill., 1964-75, nat. bd. dirs., 1965-96, nat. corp. sec., 1976-82, nat. v.p., 1987-96, vice chair nat. adv. coun., 1996—. With USAAF, 1942-45. Mem. ACLU, Nat. Comm. Assn., Am. Psychol. Assn., AAUP, Phi Beta Kappa. Home: 5283 Broadway Ter Apt 4-b Oakland CA 94618-1491

HAIMES, YACOV YOSSEPH, systems and civil engineering educator, consultant; b. Baghdad, Iraq, June 18, 1936; came to U.S., 1965, naturalized, 1972; s. Yosseph and Rose (Elani) H.; m. Sonia E. Jamison, June 16, 1968; children: Yosef, Michelle. BS, Hebrew U., Jerusalem, 1964; MS, U. Calif., 1967, PhD with distinction, 1970. Jr. petroleum engr. Ministry of Devel., Jerusalem, 1962-65; asst. prof. engring. Case-Western Reserve U., Cleve., 1970-71, assoc. prof. systems engring., 1971-76, dir. grad. program water resources and systems engring., 1972-87, prof. systems engring. and civil engring., 1976-87, dir. Center for Large Scale Systems and Policy Analysis, 1980-84, chmn. systems engring. dept., 1983-86; Lawrence R. Quarles Prof. of Engring. and Applied Sci. U. Va., Charlottesville, 1987—; dir. Ctr. for Risk Mgmt. of Engring. Systems, U. Va., Charlottesville, 1987—. Pres. Environ. Systems Mgmt. Inc., Ohio, 1974—; mem. staff Office of Sci. and Tech. Policy, Exec. Office of President, 1977, Com. on Sci. and Tech., Ho. of Reps., 1978; cons. in field.; chmn. UNESCO Working Group on Water Resources Planning, 1980-87; mem. bd. on water sci. and tech. NRC, 1982-84; chmn. tech. adv. com. Internat. Ground Water Modeling Ctr. Holcomb Research Inst., 1985-88, mem. 1983-88; cons. Congl. Office of Tech. Assessment, 1977-89; cons. Sci. Adv. Bd. U.S. EPA, 1986-96, Oil and Gas Regulatory Commn. State of Ohio, 1986-87, chmn. regulatory com., 1986-87. Author: (with W.A. Hall and H.T. Freedman) Multiobjective Optimization in Water Resources Systems, 1975; Hierarchical Analyses of Water Resources Systems, 1977; (with V. Chankong) Multiobjective Decision Making: Theory and Methodology, 1983; (with J. Pet-Edwards, V. Chankong, H. Rosenkranz and F. Ennever) Risk Assessment and Decisionmaking Using Test Results: The Carcinogenicity Prediction and Battery Selection (CPBS) Approach, 1989; (with K. Tarvainen, T. Shima and J. Thadathil) Hierarchical Multiobjective Analysis of Large-Scale Systems, 1990; (with V. Chankong) Multiobjective Problems: Theory and Methods, 1996; Risk Modeling, Assessment, and Management, 1998; editor: Scientific, Technological and Institutional Aspects of Water Resource Policy, 1980; (with P. Laconte) Water Resources and Land Use Planning, 1982; Energy Auditing and Conservation, 1980; Risk/Benefit Analysis in Water Resources Planning and Management, 1981: Large Scale Systems, 1982; (with D. Allee) Multiobjective Analysis in Water Resources, 1984; (with V. Chankong) Decision Making with Multiple Objectives, 1985; (with J.H. Snyder) Groundwater Contamination, 1986; (with E.Z. Stakhiv) Risk-Based Decision Making in Water Resources, 1986; (with J. Kindler and E. Plate) The Process of Water Resources Planning: A Systems Approach, 1987; (with D. Baumann) Water Resources Planning and Management: The Role of the Social Sciences, 1988; (with E. Stakhiv) Risk Analysis and Management of Natural and Man-Made Hazards, 1989; (with J. Bear, F. Walters and G. Jousma) Modeling of Groundwater Contamination, 1989: (with E.Z. Stakhiv) Risk-Based Decision Making in Water Resources, 1990; (with E.Z. Stakhiv and D. Moser) Risk-Based Decision Making in Water Resources, 1992; (with E.Z. Stakhiv and D. Moser), Risk Based Decision Making in Water Resources VI, 1994, (with E.Z. Stakhiv and D. Moser), Risk Based Decision Making in Water Resources, VII, 1996, (with E.Z. Stakhiv and D. Moser) Risk Based Decision Making in Water Resources VIII, 1998, (with E.Z. Stakhiv and D. Moser) Risk Based Decision Making in Water Resources IX, 2001; assoc. editor IEEE Trans. on Systems, Man and Cybernetics, 1979-2001, Automatica, 1981-92, Large Scale Systems: Theory and Applications, 1981-88, Jour. Control, Theory and Advanced Tech., 1985-92, Info. and Decision Techs., 1988-91, Reliability Engring. and Systems Safety, 1990—, Risk Analysis Internat. Jour., 1991—. Mem. UNESCO IHP IV Panel Water Resources, 1991-97. Case Centennial Scholar Case Inst. Tech., Case Western Res. U., 1980. Fellow IEEE, AAAS, ASCE (com. on water resources systems 1975-80, outstanding rsch. paper award 1990), Am. Water Resources Assn. (pres. Ohio sect. 1974-75), Internat. Water Resources Assn., Soc. Risk Analysis, Internat. Coun. Engring. Sys., IEEE Systems, Man and Cybernetics Soc. (v.p. for tech. activities 1990-91, v.p. for publs. 1992-93, Norbert Weiner award 2001), Univs. Council on Water Resources (chmn. com. on environ. quality 1977-79, dir. 1979-85, v.p. 1983-84, pres. 1984-85, Pub. Svc. award 1991, Warren A. Hall medal 1997), Internat. Fedn. Automatic Control (chmn. working group on water resources 1973-87, vice-chmn. systems engring. com. 1987-90), Am. Automatic Control Council (vice-chmn. systems engring. com. 1976-79), Am. Geophys. Union (com. on water resources systems 1970-74, chmn. water resource environ. mgmt. com. 1980-82), Ops. Rsch. Soc. Am., Soc. for Risk Analysis (chmn. com. on confs. and workshops 1989-91, Disting. Achievement award 2000), Multiple Criteria Decision Making Soc. (exec. com. 1984-98), Sigma Xi (past pres. local chpt.), Tau Beta Pi. Home: 3160 Waverly Dr Charlottesville VA 22901-9576 Office: U Va Olsson Hall Rm 112 Dept Systems and Info Engring Charlottesville VA 22903

HAINES, CHARLES WILLS, mathematics and mechanical engineering educator; b. Phila., Apr. 14, 1939; s. J. Edward and Ella Green (Peck) H.; m. Carolyn Hanna Anderson, June 17, 1961; children: Marie Jeanette, Karen Louise. AB in Math. and Physics, Earlham Coll., 1961; MS in Applied Math., Rensselaer Poly. Inst., 1963, PhD, 1965. Math. instr. Rensselaer Poly. Inst., Troy, N.Y., 1965-66; asst. prof. Clarkson U., Potsdam, N.Y., 1966-71; assoc. prof. Rochester (N.Y.) Inst. Tech., 1971-86, asst. provost, 1973-82, math. dept. chmn., 1973, assoc. dean, 1982-90, prof. mech. engring. and math., 1986—, acting dean, 1989-90, dept. head of mech. engring., 1990-95, assoc. dept. head mech. engring., 1999—. Summer rsch. fellow NASA Langley Rsch. Ctr., Newport News, Va., 1967-68; cons. Xerox Corp., Rochester, 1976-84. Author: Analysis for Engineers, 1974, Differential Equation Solutions Manual, 1986, 92, 96, 2001, Calculus Solutions Manual, 1988. Mem. allocations com. United Way, Rochester, 1984-90, steering com., 1988-92; trustee Allendale Columbia Sch., Rochester, 1977-86. Fellow Am. Soc. for Engring. Edn. (v.p. bd. 1991-95, Centennial medallion 1993); mem. ASME (treas. local sect. 1987-96), Soc. for Indsl. and Applied Math., Math. Assn. Am. Avocations: tennis, racquetball, skiing. Office: Rochester Inst Tech 76 Lomb Memorial Dr Rochester NY 14623-5604 E-mail: cwheme@rit.edu.

HAINES, JACQUELINE IRENE, institute director; b. Denver, June 26, 1933; d. Carl James and Elsie Irene (Hurt) H. Bachelor's degree, U. No. Colo., 1955. Tchr. Aurora (Colo.) Pub. Schs., 1955-67, guidance counselor, 1967-69; rsch. asst. Gesell Inst., New Haven, 1969-75, coord. clin. svc., 1975-80, dir. clin. svc., 1980-86, lectr., dir., 1978—, dir. devel. dept., 1980-88, sr. devel. specialist, 1988-90. Co-author: School Readiness, 1978, The Child From 1 to 6, 1979, Gesell Pre-school Assessment test manual, 1980. Active Women's Internat. League Peace and Freedom, New Haven, 1982—. Recipient Outstanding Tchr. of Yr. award Univ. No. Colo., Greeley, 1980. Mem. NEA, Nat. Assn. Edn. Young Children, Assn. Childhood Edn. Internat., Delta Kappa Gamma. Office: Gesell Inst 310 Prospect St New Haven CT 06511-2188

HAINES, JOYBELLE, retired elementary school educator; b. Geronomo, Okla., Oct. 20, 1930; d. William Tommie and Ruby Dell Heffington; m. Meredith C. Haines, Aug. 22, 1953; children: Cynthia Elaine, Stephen Michael, Lisa Joy. Grad., Asbury Coll., Wilmore, Ky.; postgrad., Ball State Tchrs. Coll., Calif. State U. Missionary tchr., Seoul, Republic of Korea, 1954—56; tchr. Hartford City, Ind., 1956—65, Muncie, Ind., 1965—66, Stockton (Calif.) Unified Sch. Dist., 1966—2000; ret., 2001. Cons. new tchrs., tutor, Stockton, 1999—. Mem.: AAUW, Rep. Women's Club. Baptist. Home: 9530 Springfield Way Stockton CA 95212

HAINES, LISA ANN, secondary education educator; b. Camden, N.J., Dec. 14, 1966; d. Sonia Joan (Kiriluk) F. BA, Rutgers U., Camden, 1990; postgrad., Rutgers U., 1993—; MA in English. Cert. tchr. K-12, N.J. Tchr. Pennsauken (N.J.) Bd. of Edn., 1990—. Mem. Pennsauken H.S. scholarship com., 1994-96, mem. prin.'s adv. com., 1996-97, Gold Card com., 1996-98, Century III Scholarship com., curriculum co-chair departmental in-svc. group, mem. faculty discipline com., prop mistress sch. show, faculty vol., co-editor The Looking Glass, co-adviser yearbook. Mem. Nat. Coun. Tchrs. of English, N.E. MLA, Kappa Delta Pi. Avocations: writing, poetry, travel, theater, rollerblading. Home: 1304 Wharton Rd Mount Laurel NJ 08054-5296

HAIRALD, MARY PAYNE, vocational education educator, coordinator; b. Tupelo, Miss., Feb. 25, 1936; d. Will Burney and Ivey Lee (Berryhill) Payne; m. Leroy Utley Hairald, May 31, 1958; 1 child, Burney LeShawn. BS in Commerce, U. Miss., 1957, M in Bus. Edn., 1963; postgrad., Miss. Coll., 1964, Miss. State U., 1970, U. So. Miss., 1986-88, 90, U. Calif., Davis, summer 1997, Babson Coll., summer 1998. Bus. edn. tchr. John Rundle High Sch., Grenada, Miss., 1957-59; youth recreation leader City of Nettleton, Miss., summers 1960-61; tchr. social studies Nettleton Jr. High Sch., 1959-70; tchr.-coord. coop. vocat. edn. program Nettleton High Sch., 1970—; area mgr. World Book, Inc., Chgo., 1972-84; local coord. Am. Inst. for Fgn. Study, Stamford, Conn., 1988—. Instr. bus. Itawamba C.C., Tupelo, 1975-80; with Cmty. Coord. for Program of Acad. Exch. (PAX), 1998—; advisor DECA, Nettleton, 1985—, state officers' advisor, 1995-01; apptd. adv. coord. mem. Miss. Coop. Edn.-State Dept. Edn. Editor advisor State DECA Newsletter, 1987-92; contbr. articles on coop. edn. to newspapers. Co-organizer Nettleton Youth Recreation Booster Club; fundraiser Muscular Dystrophy Assn.; Sunday sch. tchr. coll. and career class Nettleton United Meth. Ch. Recipient 1st place Nat. Newsletter award Nat. DECA, 1988, 89, 90, 92, Excellence in Supervision award Am. Inst. for Fgn. Study, 1992; named Star Tchr., Miss. Econ. Coun., 1978, 95, Dist. II DECA Advisor of Yr., Miss. Assn. DECA, 1990, 93, 00, also State DECA Advisor of Yr., 2000, hon. lifetime mem., Alumni Mem. of Yr., 1998; Nat. DECA Hall of Fame charter mem., 1996; named tchr. of yr. Wal-Mart, 1997; recipient award for excellence Pub. Edn. Forum, 1997; award finalist Miss. Mfrs. Assn., 1997, 98, 02. Mem. AAUW (charter), Am. Vocat. Assn. (Region IV New and Related Svcs. Tchr. of Yr. 1986, 96, Region IV Mktg. Edn. Tchr. of Yr. 1988, Region IV Outstanding Vocat. Tchr. of Yr. 1996, Nat. Tchr. of the Yr. 97), Coop. Work Experience Edn. Assn., Miss. Assn. Vocat. Educators (dist. sec., pres. 2001-02), Miss. Assn. Coop. Vocat. Edn. Tchrs. (v.p. 1980-83, pres. 1983-84, Miss. Tchr. of Yr. 1984, 87, 95), Miss. Assn. Mktg. Educators (Dist. II Tchr. of Yr. 1993, 94), Mktg. Edn. Assn., Jim Bowers/DECA Found. (charter, life), Nettleton Ladies Civitan Club (charter), Phi Delta Kappa (Phi Delta Kappa Kappan of Yr. 1998, found. rep.). Democrat. Methodist. Home: PO Box 166 Nettleton MS 38858-0166 E-mail: mhairald@hotmail.com.

HAIRSTON, JAY TIMOTHY, college administrator; b. Welch, W.Va., Dec. 3, 1956; s. John Thomas and Marion Naomi (Teal) H.; m. Sylvia Marie Borden, Sept. 10, 1983; children: Jay Timothy II, Jharie Danielle, Jason Danté. BA, Ohio Wesleyan U., 1978; MS, Bowling Green State U., 1982. Asst. dir. Upward Bound/Talent Search Bowling Green (Ohio) State U., 1982-84, assoc. dir. coll. access program, 1984-85; dir. EMCEC (cultural ctr.) U. No. Iowa, Cedar Falls, 1985-88; dir. student activities/acad. and cultural events series Baldwin-Wallace Coll., Berea, Ohio, 1988-95, dir. acad. and cultural events series, 1996—, prof., 1992—. Tchr. Upward Bound program U. No. Iowa and Bowling Green State U., summers 1980-85; cons. on multiculturalism U. No. Iowa, Cedar Falls, Baldwin-Wallace Coll., Berea, Berea Pub. Schs., 1985—, It's Your Move conf. NCCJ, Cleve.; grant writer U. No. Iowa, Cedar Falls, Baldwin-Wallace Coll., Berea, 1986—; cons. gospel music workshops, guest artist Bowling Green State U., Eng., Sweden, Norway, Germany. Dir./founder (Gospel musical group) The Krooners, 1979—; artist, songwriter, musician, producer (Gospel recording-solo album) I'm Going On, 1990, 91; songwriter/vocalist (Gospel recording with choir) Jesus Never Fails, 1989; dir., artist, producer (Gospel recording with choir) We Should Pray, 1980; artist, grant writer (Gospel music demo tape) Creative Artists' Grant, 1987 (Iowa Arts Coun. award); cast mem. Glories of Gospel, 1992—; recorded with Glories of Gospel: Live, 1994. Dir. Berea Cmty. Mass Choir, 1995—; min. of music Faith Tabernacle United Holy Ch., Cleve., 1988-94; dir., musician United Faith Ch. of Christ, Cleve., 1988-92; cons., mem. presenting touring panel Ohio Arts Coun., 1991-94. Recipient Iowa Bus. and Profl. award Minority Leadership Agenda Com., Cedar Falls/Waterloo, 1988, Outstanding Adminstr. award Omicron Delta Kappa, 1991, Faculty Excellence award Student Senate, 1990, Adminstrv. Excellence award Student Senate, 1994; grantee Gospel Music Workshops, U. No. Iowa and Baldwin-Wallace Coll.; named Outstanding Young Man Am., Jaycees, 1981, 86, 92; artist's grantee Ohio Arts Coun., 1996. Mem. Am. Coll. Pers. Assn., Nat. Assn. Campus Activities, Nat. Hairston Clan, Inc., Ohio Coll. Pers. Assn, Kappa Alpha Psi (treas. 1985-86). Holiness. Avocations: songwriting, playing piano, most sports, singing. Home: 137 Jacob St Berea OH 44017-2013 Office: Baldwin Wallace Coll ACES Office 275 Eastland Rd Berea OH 44017-2005

HAIRSTON, NELSON GEORGE, JR., ecologist, educator; b. Asheville, NC, Sept. 26, 1949; s. Nelson George and Martha Turner (Patton) H.; m. Deborah Susan (Whitaker)Hairston, Nov. 30, 1974; 1 child, Peter Whitaker Hairston. BS, U. Mich., 1971; PhD, U. Wash., 1977. Asst. prof. U. R.I., Kingston, 1977-81, assoc. prof., 1981-85, Cornell U., Ithaca, NY, 1985-87, prof., 1988—, Frank H.T. Rhodes prof. environ. sci., 1996—, chmn. dept. ecology and evolutionary biology, 2001—. Vis. disting. ecologist U. Mich. Biol. Sta., Pelston, 1984; vis. eminent ecologist Mich. State U. Biol. Sta., Hickory Corners, 1989; cons. Westinghouse Savannah River Co., 1990-95, NSF Program in Population Biology and Physiol. Ecology, 1985-87, Swedish Nat. Rsch Coun., 1991, 99, U. Stockholm, 1996, Max Planck Inst. for Limnology, 1997, U. Uppsala, 1998; Douglas Disting. lectr. Rocky Mountain Biol. Lab, Crested Butte, Colo., 1992. Mem. editl. bd. Limnology and Oceanography, 1986-89, 2003, Ecology/Ecol. Monographs, 1989-92, 94-96; contbr. more than 75 articles and papers to sci. jours. NSF grantee, 1980, 83, 86, 88-89, 89-90, 91-92, 92-93, 95, 97, 99, 2000; EPA grantee, 1997, 2001; Andrew Mellon Found. grantee, 1997,2003. Mem. Ecol. Soc. Am. (coun. reps. 1990-93, chair awards com. 1992-95, governing bd. 1996-99, 2001-2004), Internat. Assn. Theoretical and Applied Limnology (nat. rep. 1992-95, 2002—). Avocations: boating, skiing, reading. Home: 6125 Perry City Rd Trumansburg NY 14886-9011 Office: Cornell U Dept Ecology and Evolutionary Biology Ithaca NY 14853 E-mail: NGH1@cornell.edu.

HAJEK, ELOISE, educational consultant, educator; b. Ft. Worth, Feb. 28, 1952; d. William John Hajek and Ammie May (Childress) Kruzick; m. Rod Schmidt, May 27, 1978; 1 child, Katherine Hajek Schmidt stepchildren: Jack Schmidt, Bret Schmidt, Heather Schmidt Nakagawa. BA, U. Tex., 1980; MA, U. Tex., Arlington, 1993; PhD, Tex. Woman's U., 2000. Program adminstr. North Ctrl. Tex. Coun. Govts., Arlington, 1976-80; neighborhood edn. coord. Holy Cross Parish, Dallas, 1980-84; program dir. Brookhaven Coll., Dallas, 1984-91, ESL amnesty dir., 1989-91. Vis. lectr. Tex. Woman's U., Denton, 1993-95, adj. prof., 1991-93, 95—; ednl. cons., 1992—. Chair Dallas Women's Coalition, 1988-89, 94, steering com., 1990-95; mem. Dallas Women's Found., 1989-91. Mem. AAUW, Nat. Reading Confs., Internat. Reading Assn., Tchrs. English Spkrs. Other Langs., Pi Lambda Theta (scholar 1996), Phi Kappa Phi. Office: 1008 Wilson Rd Lancaster TX 75146-5521

HAKANSSON, NILS HEMMING, financial economics and accounting educator; b. Marby, Sweden, June 2, 1937; came to U.S., 1956; s. Nils and Anna (Nilsson) H.; m. Joyce Beth Kates, Aug. 28, 1960; children— Carolyn Ann, Nils Alexander BS with honors, U. Oreg., 1958; MBA, UCLA, 1960, PhD, 1966; D. of Econs. (hon.), Stockholm Sch. Econs., 1984. C.P.A., Calif. Staff acct., cons. Arthur Young & Co., L.A., 1960-63; asst. prof. UCLA, 1966-67, Yale U., New Haven, 1967-69; assoc. prof. U. Calif.-Berkeley, 1969-71, prof., 1971-77, Sylvan C. Coleman prof. fin. and acctg., 1977—, chmn. fin., 1976-79. Cons. Rand Corp., Santa Monica, Calif., 1965-71, Bell Labs., Murray Hill, N.J., 1974, 79-81; chmn. bd. dirs. Anna och Nils Hakanssons Stiftelse; bd. dirs. Berkeley Fin. Found., AXA-Rosenberg Mut. Funds. Editorial cons. Acctg. Rev., 1977-80; cons. editor Jour. Acctg. and Econs., 1978-81; contbr. articles to profl. jours. Served with Royal Swedish Corps Engrs., 1956 Recipient Graham and Dodd award Fin. Analysts Fedn., 1976, 82; Ford Found. fellow UCLA, 1963-66; Hoover fellow U. New South Wales, 1975 Fellow Acctg. Rschrs. Internat. Assn.; mem. AICPA, Fin. Economists Roundtable, Econometric Soc., Am. Fin. Assn., Western Fin. Assn. (pres. 1983-84), Am. Acctg. Assn., Soc. for Promotion Fin. Studies (founding). Office: U Calif Sch Bus Berkeley CA 94720-0001 E-mail: hakansso@haas-berkeley.edu.

HAKIMI, S. LOUIS, electrical and computer engineering educator; b. Meshed, Iran, Dec. 16, 1932; came to U.S., 1952, naturalized, 1967; s. A. Moshe and Miriam (Nabavian) H.; m. Mary Yomtob, Aug. 22, 1965; children: Alan, Carol, Diane. BS in Elec. Engring., U. Ill., Urbana, 1955, MS in Elec. Engring., 1957, PhD in Elec. Engring., 1959. Asst. prof. elec. engring. U. Ill., 1959-61; assoc. prof. Northwestern U., Evanston, Ill., 1961-66, prof., 1966-86, chmn. dept. elec. engring., 1972-77; prof. U. Calif., Davis, 1986—2001, chmn. elec. and computer engring., 1986-96, prof. emeritus, 2001—. Assoc. editor Networks, 1975-90, adv. editor, 1990—; assoc. editor IEEE Transactions on Circuits and Systems, 1975-77; bd. adv. editors Transp. Sci., 1985—. Fellow IEEE (life); mem. Soc. Indsl. and Applied Math., Sigma Xi, Tau Beta Pi, Phi Kappa Phi. Home: 27017 E El Macero Dr El Macero CA 95618-1008 Office: U Calif Dept Elec & Computer Engring Davis CA 95616 E-mail: SLHakimi@ece.ucdavis.edu.

HALAR, EUGEN MARIAN, physiatrist, educator; came to the U.S., 1965; m. Olga Katarina Svete, Aug. 19, 1961; children: Zeljko, Eugene. MD, Zagreb (Croatia) U., 1959. Diplomate Am. Bd. Phys. Medicine and Rehab. Intern Gen. Hosp. Karlovac, Croatia; resident in phys. medicine and rehab. Zagreb (Croatia) U., 1965, 1965—68, NYU, 1968—71; attending physician Univ. Hosp., 1968-69, Harborview Med. Ctr., 1971—97; chief svc. rehab. medicine VA Hosp., 1971-97; phys. medicine and rehab. attending physician Puget Sound Healthcare Sys., 1997-99, co-dir. cardiac rehab. program, 1997—99, prof. emeritus, 1999—. Prof. rehab. medicine U. Wash., Seattle, 1986—. Guest editor: Cardiac Rehabilitation, 1995, Stroke Mgmt. and Rehab., 1999. Fellow Am. Acad. Phys. Medicine and Rehab.; mem. Assn. Acad. Physiatrist, King County Med. Soc. Avocations: skiing, tennis, travel. Home: 817 179th Ct NE Bellevue WA 98008-4241 Office: U Wash Hsb Dept Rehab Medicine Ctr Seattle WA 98195-0001 E-mail: Halarem@msn.com.

HALASI-KUN, GEORGE JOSEPH, hydrologist, educator; b. Zagreb, Austria-Hungary, July 28, 1916; came to U.S., 1958, naturalized, 1963; s. Tibor and Priscilla (Tholt) Halasi-K.; m. Elisabeth Christina Szorad., Mar. 10, 1945; children: Beatrice, Georgie. BA summa cum laude, Coll. of Budapest, 1934; MS in Civil Engring. summa cum laude, Inst. Tech., Budapest, 1938; C.E., Slovak Tech. U., Bratislava, Czechoslovakia, 1949; Dr.Eng.Sci., Tech. U., Braunschweig, Germany, 1968; DSc (hon.), U. J.P Pécs, Hungary, 1993, Agr. U. Budapest, 1995. Registered profl. engr., Conn., N.J. registered profl. hydrologist. Dir. water engring., assoc. prof. Tech. U.; also prof. Coll. Water Engring., Kosice, Czechoslovakia, 1948-53; mgr.-chief engr. Pozemne Stavby Constrn. Co., Kosice, 1954-57; project mgr., assoc. Columbia U., N.Y.C., 1958-71, chmn. seminar water resources, 1967—; research assoc. Tech. U., Braunschweig, 1969-71; adj. prof. N.Y. Inst. Tech., 1971-76; vis. prof. Rutgers U., 1976-79; adj. prof. Fairleigh Dickinson U., 1979-84; state topographic engr. N.J. Environ. Protection Dept., 1971-91. Author: Hydrology, 1949, Water Economy, 1952, Water in Agricultural Engineering, 1954, Analysis of Maximum Flood in Smaller Watershed Area-Computations, 1968, Hydrogeological Aspects of Pollution and Water Resources in Urbanized and Industrialized Areas, 1971, Ground Water Computations in New Jersey, 1974, Land Oriented Water Resources Data System in New Jersey, 1978, Waste Site Assessment in Land Use, 1985, Ottoman map of N.J., New England from 17th Century, 1987, Hazardous Waste, 1990, Solid Waste and Recycling, 1990, Environmental Protection Strategy of New East Central Europe after 1989 - Global View, 1991, Removal of Hazardous Materials: Decontamination, 1992, Organization of Environmental Oriented Data Bank in Hungary, 1993, Water supply of Szigetköz (West Hungary) From Danube-Lajta Channel in Austria, 1995, Hydrographic Description of Drave River, 1998, Water Level of the Lake Balaton in XVI-XVIII Centuries, 1999; editor: publs. Columbia U. Seminar on Pollution and Water Resources. NAS fellow, 1977, 82, 84; Fulbright scholar, 1990-94. Fellow ASCE, Hungarian Acad. Scis., Ukrainian Acad. Sci., Geol. Soc. Am., Croatian Hungarian Soc. of Scis. and Art; mem. AAAS, AAUP, Internat. Water Resources Assn., Am. Water Resources Assn., Am. Congress Surveying and Mapping, Am. Inst. Hydrology, N.J. Acad. Sci., Société des Ingénieurs et Scientifiques de France, Croatian-Hungarian Soc. Scis. and Arts. Home: 31 Knowles St Pennington NJ 08534-1410

HALASKA, THOMAS EDWARD, academic administrator, director, engineer; b. Childress, Tex., Aug. 4, 1945; s. Howard Edward and Ruth Marie (Reinders) H.; m. Marilyn Jean Walenta, June 7, 1969; 1 child, Jean Ellen. BSEE, Milw. Sch. Engring., 1969; MBA, Ga. State U., 1975; EdD, U. Ga., 1992. Plant engr. Tom's divsn. Gen. Mills, Inc., Columbus, Ga., 1969-74; dir. mfg. Stuckey Stores div. Pet, Inc., Eastman, Ga., 1974-82; dir. mgmt. info. systems Mid. Ga. Coll., Cochran, 1982-87, dir. instnl. rsch., 1987—, CIO, 1992—. Mem. Soc. Coll. and Univ. Planning, Assn. for Instnl. Rsch., Univ. System Computer Network (regents adminstrv. com. info. tech.), Rotary (bd. dirs. Cochran chpt. 1986—). Republican. Roman Catholic. Avocation: pilot. Home: 2696 Chester Hwy Eastman GA 31023 Office: Mid Ga Coll 1100 2nd St SE Cochran GA 31014-1599 E-mail: thalaska@mgc.edu.

HALBERG, F. DAVID, principal; b. Toronto, Ont., Can., Sept. 18, 1943; s. Max and Esther (Sherman) H.; m. Georgette Greenberg, June 9, 1966; children: Michael, Jason, Eric. BEd, U. Miami, Coral Gables, Fla., 1966, MEd, 1967. Cert. tchr., adminstr., supr., Fla. Tchr. Dade County Schs., Miami, 1967-80, ESE placement specialist, 1980-81, asst. prin., 1981-89; prin. Fienberg Elem. Sch., Miami Beach, Fla., 1989-90, North Beach Elem. Sch., Miami Beach, 1990-96, Gloria Floyd Elem. Sch., West Kendall, 1996—. Named Elem. Prin. of Yr., Dade County Media Specialist Assn.,

1993, Miami Beach Feeder Pattern Prin. of Yr., 1994; 1st runner-up Adminstr. of Yr., Coun. for Exceptional Children, 1999; recipient Cervantes Outstanding Educator award Nova Southea. U., 1999. Mem. Coun. for Exceptional Children, Dade County Sch. Adminstrs. Assn., ASCD, Am. Fedn. Sch. Adminstrs. Home: 16203 SW 108th Ct Miami FL 33157-2924

HALBREICH, URIEL MORAV, psychiatrist, educator; b. Jerusalem, Nov. 23, 1943; came to U.S., 1978, naturalized, 1982; s. Mordechai and Zipora (Tennenbaum) H.; m. Judith Thadine, 1987; children: Jasmine, Bethany. MD, Hebrew U., 1969. Diplomate Tel Aviv U. Psychiatry and Psychotherapy. Intern gen. medicine Hadassah U. Hosp., Jerusalem, 1968; comdr., vice-chief med. officer Israeli Navy, 1970-72, chief psychiatrist, 1977-78; resident, 2d then 1st asst. Hadassah Hosp. Hebrew U., Jerusalem, 1972-78; temp. chief physician Hadassah U. Hosp., Jerusalem, 1978; asst. prof., rsch. psychiatrist Columbia U., N.Y.C., 1978-80; assoc. prof., dir. divsn. biol. psychiatry Albert Einstein Coll. Medicine, N.Y.C., 1982-85; prof. psychiatry, dir. biobehavioral rsch. SUNY, Buffalo, 1985—, prof. ob-gyn, 1988—. Vis. prof. Harvard U., 1996-98, exec. cons. dept. psychiatry; chmn. 1st Internat. Congress on Hormones, Brain and Neuropsychopharmacology, 1993, chmn. sect. on interdisciplinary collaboration World Psychiat. Assn., 1997—, others; chmn. 2d Congress on Hormones, Brain and Neuropsychopharmacology, 2000; chmn. bd. dirs. Internat. Inst. Edn. in Mental Health and Psychopharmacology, 1997—; cons. in field. Editor: Transient Psychosis, 1983, Resistance to Treatment with Antidepressant Drugs, 1986, Hormones and Depression, 1987, Multiple Sclerosis: A Neuropsychiatric Disorder, 1992, Psychopharmacology of Women, 1996, Psychiatric Issues in Women, 1996, Training in Psychiatry and Psychopharmacology, 1998, Psychopharmacology of Mood Anxiety and Cognition, 2000, Psychiatry and the Law in Eastern Europe, 2000, Womens Mental Health, 2002; contbr. articles to profl. jours., chpts. to books. Recipient Ben Gurion award Gen. Fedn. Labor, 1976, Yair Gon award Hebrew U. Hadassah Med. Sch., 1978, Nat. Rsch. Svc. award NIH, 1978, Svc. award ISCNE, 2003; grantee NIMH, 1982—. Fellow: Am. Coll. Psychiatrists, Am. Psychiat. Assn. (disting.), Coll. Internat. Neuropsychopharmacology (co-chmn. edn. com. 1994—96), Am. Coll. Neuropsychopharmacology (chmn. rules and constitution com. 1996), Am. Psychopathology Assn.; mem.: Endocine Soc., Assn. Med. Psychiatry (chmn. edn. com. 1992—96, councilor 1992—96), Soc. Biol. Psychiatry (chmn. program com. 1992—93), Am. Coll. Psychiatrists, Internat. Assn. Womens Mental Health (pres. 2001—), Internat. Soc. Psycho. Neuro. Endocrinology (chmn. 21st congress 1990, pres. 1999—2002). Jewish. Office: SUNY Sch Med & Biomed Hayes C Ste 1 3435 Main St Bldg 5 Buffalo NY 14214-3016 E-mail: urielh@acsu.buffalo.edu.

HALBROOK, ARTHUR MARSHALL, educational educator, assessment specialist; b. Monroe, La., Feb. 20, 1948; s. Louie Marshall and Helen Corene (West) H. BA in English Edn., U. La.-Monroe, 1970; MA in English Lit., La. State U., 1973, PhD in Edn., 1991. Instr. English Ouachita Parish High Sch., Monroe, La., 1973-86; teaching asst. La. State U., Baton Rouge, 1986-89; mgr. edn. program La. Dept. Edn., Baton Rouge, 1989-93; writing assessment specialist Am. Coun. Edn. (GED Testing Svc.), Washington, 1993—2001; sr. project mgr. Coun. Chief State Sch. Officers, Washington, 2001—. Mem. Smithsonian Soc., Washington, 1994—, Fulbright Assn., Washington, 1994—, La. State Soc., Washington, 1994—; bd. dirs. C/P Found., Washington, 1998-2000, Kennedy Ctr., 1996—, Wolf Trap, 1996—. Fulbright fellow, 1978; recipient La. Outstanding Young Educator La. Jaycees, 1976; named Outstanding Edn. Alumni, U. La.-Monroe, 1993. Mem. Nat. Coun. Tchrs. English, Am. Ednl. Rsch. Assn., Assembly State Coords. English Lang. Arts, Coun. State Sci. Suprs., Phi Delta Kappa, Omicron Delta Kappa. Avocations: photography, travel. Home: 4540 Raleigh Ave Apt 402 Alexandria VA 22304-6976 Office: Coun Chief State Sch Officers 1 Massachusetts Ave NW Ste 700 Washington DC 20001-1431 E-mail: arthurh@ccsso.org.

HALDAR, FRANCES LOUISE, business educator, accountant, treasurer; b. Mineola, N.Y., July 2, 1948; d. Alfred Karl and Gudrun Maria (Lucks) Loschen; m. Kali S. Haldar, Feb. 29, 1972; children: Neil Alexander, Monica Joyce. AA, The Ohio Sate U., 1985, BSBA in Acctg. summa cum laude, 1989, MBA, 1991, PhD, 1999. Adminstrv. asst. Pam Am. World Airways Inc., N.Y.C., 1968-73; acct., treas. K.S. Haldar, MD, Inc., Mansfield, Ohio, 1978—; adj. prof. to assoc. prof. bus., then assoc. prof. acctg. North Cen. State Coll., Mansfield, 1991-99; acad. advisor N. Ctrl. Tech. Coll., Mansfield, 1991-98; assoc. prof. bus. N. Ctrl. State Coll., Mansfield, 1993-96, assoc. prof. acctg., 1996-99, prof. acctg., 1999-2000; asst. dean bus., math. and tech. Cuyahoga Cmty. Coll., Highland Hills, Ohio, 2000—. Mem. Am. Assn. Higher Edn., Nat. Bus. Edn. Assn., Am. Assn. C.C., Inst. Mgmt. Accts., Golden Key, Phi Kappa Phi, Beta Gamma Sigma. Avocations: reading, travel. Office: Cuyahoga Cmty Coll 4250 Richmond Rd Highland Hills OH 44122 E-mail: fran.haldar@tri-c.cc-oh.us.

HALE, ALLEAN LEMMON, writer, educator; b. Bethany, Nebr. d. Clarence Eugene and Constance (Harlan) Lemmon; m. Mark Pendleton Hale, Dec. 31, 1936 (dec. Nov., 1977); children: Susanna, Mark Jr. AA, Columbia Coll., 1933; BA in English with Distinction, U. Mo., 1935; MA in Humanities, U. Iowa, 1962. Prodn. asst. in drama Chgo. Theol. Sem., 1941; alumni dir., editor Columbia (Mo.) Coll., 1951-56; instr. comm. U. Iowa, Iowa City, 1960-62; contract playwright Friendship Press, N.Y.C., 1960-75; instr. creative writing Adult Edn. Program, Urbana, Ill., 1965; editl. asst. Oscar Lewis Anthropologist, Urbana, 1966-69; instr. creative writing Parkland Coll., Champaign, Ill., 1979-80; editor Tenessee Williams Plays New Dirs. Publishers, N.Y.C., 1996-2000; adj. prof. in theater U. Ill., Urbana, 1996—. Editl. asst. to Lyle Leverich on Tom: The Unknown Tennessee Williams, 1986-87; mem. editl. bd. The Tennessee Williams Literary Jour., New Orleans, 1989-2000; lectr. Am. Playwrights Exhibit Humanities Rsch. Ctr., U. Tex., Austin, 1994; cons. to PBS Am. Masters Tennessee Williams: Orpheus of the American Stage, Internat. Cultural Programming, N.Y., 1995; photo cons. A&E Biography TV program Tennessee Williams, 1998; cons. French TV prodn. Blue Devils, 2001. Author: Petticoat Pioneer, 1957, 2d. rev. edit., 1968; editor: Tennessee Williams, The Notebook of Trigorin, 1997, Tennessee Williams, Not About Nightingales, 1998, Tennessee Williams, Stairs to the Roof, 1999, Tennessee Williams, Fugitive Kind, 2001; mem. editl. bd. Tennessee Williams Annual Rev., Middle Tenn. State U., 1998—; contbr. The Cambridge Companion to Tennesseee Williams, 1997, The Undiscovered Country: the Later Plays of Tennessee Williams, 2002, The Tennessee Williams Encyclopedia, 2004; playwright: The Hero (Samuel French Playwriting award 1933, Zeta Phi Eta Playwriting Contest 1st, 1933, Last Flight Over, Midwestern Intercollegiate Playwriting Contest 1st, 1935, The Red Bastard of Genesis, Mahan Story Contest, U. Mo. 1st, 1935, They Walk in Darkness, U. Mo. Dramatic Arts Contest, 1949; other plays include: Two in a Trap, 1966, The Second Coming of Mrs. C., 1971, The Battle at Liberty Courthouse, 1975; contbr. s more than 30 articles on Tennessee Williams to lit. jours., presenter in field. Mem. Krannert Art Mus. Assocs., 1980—; media chair Internat. Conf. on Women and Peace, U. Ill., 1989. Recipient 1st award best column in mag., Nat. Fedn. Presswomen, 1953, Distinguished Alumni award Columbia (Mo.) Coll., 1964. Mem. Champaign Social Sci. Club, U. Ill. Women's Club, Red Herring Fiction Workshop, Phi Beta Kappa. Democrat. Avocations: art, history, langs., aerobics. Home: 305 G H Baker Dr Urbana IL 61801-1160 Office: U Ill Dept Theatre 4-122 Krannert Ctr Pfm Arts 500 S Goodwin Ave Urbana IL 61801-3741 E-mail: ahale@uiuc.edu.

HALE, CECIL, communications educator, finance educator; b. St. Louis, Aug. 3, 1945; s. Cecil and Allean (Cunningham) H.; m. Brenda Kidd; children: Juanita, Tasha, Cecil-Jamil, Carolyn. Student, So. Ill. U., 1963-66; MA, Internat. U. of Comm., Washington, 1975; PhD, Union Inst., Cin., 1978; MPA, Harvard U., 1995. Lic. by FCC. Announcer, asst. gen. mgr. WMPP Radio, 1966—68; announcer XPRS Radio, L.A., 1972-74; announcer, asst. program/music dir. WNOV Radio, Milw., 1968-70, WVON Radio, Chgo., 1970-77; nat. dir., mgr. Phonogram/Mercury Records, Chgo., 1977-78; v.p. Capitol Records, Inc., Hollywood, Calif., 1978-81; prof. San Francisco State U., 1984-94, City Coll. San Francisco, 1986—; prof. Mass Media Inst. Stanford U., 1987-92. Cons. N.T.A., Lagos, Nigeria, 1982-83, Gallo Winery, Inc., Modesto, Calif., 1977, Capitol Records, Inc., Hollywood, 1981-82, Congl. Caucus, Washington, 1975. Author: The Music Industry, 1990; exec. producer phono records. Recipient Key to City and City Coun. Resolution, L.A., 1980, Outstanding Tchr. award Acad. Senate, City Coll. San Francisco, 1990, San Francisco State U. Faculty award, 1986; U. Calif. fellow, 1992; honored as Nat. African-Am. History Maker, 2002; fellow NATAS, 2000. Mem.: NEA, AAUP, ABA, NAACP, Kennedy Sch. Exec. Coun., Soc. Values in Higher Edn., Am. Fedn. Tchrs., Am. Fedn. TV and Radio Artists, Am. Fedn. Musicians, Nat. Acad. Recording Arts and Scis., Harvard Black Alumni Soc., Harvard Alumni Assn., Coun. Black Am. Affairs, Stanford Alumni Assn., Nat. Eagle Scout Assn., Harvard Club San Francisco (ex-officio bd. mem.), Harvard Club N.Y., Masons, Alpha Phi Alpha. Avocations: aviaton, computer science. Home: PO Box 26274 San Francisco CA 94126-2674 Office: City Coll San Francisco 50 Phelan Ave San Francisco CA 94112-1821

HALE, JANE ALISON, French and comparative literature educator; b. Washington, Sept. 29, 1948; BA in French magna cum laude, Coll. William and Mary, 1970; MST in Edn., U. Chgo., 1974; MA in French, Stanford U., 1981; postgrad., Ecole Normale Supérieure de Jeunes Filles, Paris, 1981-82; PhD with distinction, Stanford U., 1984. Student tchg. supr., counselor Peace Corps Tng. Program, Ft. Archambault, Chad, 1971; tchr. French, cross-cultural coord. Peace Corps Tng. Ctr., St. Thomas, V.I., 1972; Peace Corps vol., tchr. English as fgn. lang. Lycée Franco-Arabe, Abéché, Chad, 1970-72; tchr. 2d grade Pleasant Grove Union Elem. Sch., Burlington, N.C., 1974-77; tchg. fellow in French Stanford U., 1982-83; tchr. French Inst. Intensive French, U. Fla., 1986-88; asst. prof. French and comparative lit. Brandeis U., Waltham, Mass., 1985-91, assoc. prof. French and comparative lit., 1991—. Presenter Internat. Conf. on TV Drama at Mich. State U., 1985, Samuel Beckett at 80 at U. Stirling, Scotland, 1986, Internat. Colloquium on Raymond Queneau, Thionville, France, 1990, Internat. Vian-Queneau-Prévert Colloquium at U. Victoria, Can., 1992, Internat. Symposium on Beckett in the 1990s, The Hague, 1992, MLA, N.Y.C., 1992, West Africa Rsch. Assn. Internat. Symposium, Dakar, Senegal, 1997, African Literature Assn., Fès, Morocco, 1999, Internat. Colloquium on Feminist Rsch. in French, Dakar, Senegal, 1999. Author: The Broken Window: Beckett's Dramatic Perspective, 1987, The Lyric Encyclopedia of Raymond Queneau, 1989; contbr. chpts. to books and articles to profl. jours. French Govt. scholar, 1981-82, Fulbright Sr. scholar, Senegal, 1993-94; Whiting fellow in the humanities, 1983-84, Dana faculty fellow Brandeis U., 1985-90, Bernstein faculty fellow Brandeis U., 1989, Marion and Jasper Whiting fellow, 1994-98; NEH travel grantee, 1988, Mazer grantee for faculty rsch. Brandeis U., 1990; recipient Lerman-Neubauer prize for excellence in tchg. and counseling, 2001. Mem. Samuel Beckett Soc. (exec. bd. dirs. 1989-92), Les Amis de Valentin Brû, Phi Beta Kappa. Office: Brandeis U Dept Romance & Comp Lit MS 024 Waltham MA 02454 E-mail: jhale@brandeis.edu.

HALE, MARGARET SMITH, insurance company executive, educator; b. Browning, Mont., May 10, 1945; d. Stephen Howard and Evelyn Sarah (Beer) Smith; m. Lawrence L. Hale, Apr. 25, 1970 (div. Jan. 1984); children: Katherine Moore, Laura Ellen. BSBA, Boston U., 1967; AS in Risk Mgmt., Ins. Inst. Am., 1986. Underwriter Chubb & Son, Inc., N.Y.C., 1967-70, br. mgr., asst. v.p. Boston, 1970-80; asst. v.p., account exec. Marsh & McLennan Inc., Boston, 1980-84; sr. v.p. Frank B. Hall, Boston, 1984-87; resident v.p. Warwick Ins. Co., Needham, Mass., 1987-90; pres. Smith & Hale Assocs., Inc., South Orleans, Mass., 1990—. Lectr. Risk and Ins. Mgrs. Soc., Boston, 1975-85; mem. fin. div. Babson Coll., Wellesley, Mass., 1987—. Bd. dirs. Lupus Erythematosus Assn., Boston, 1975-78, Parker Hill Med. Ctr., Boston, 1978-80; tchr. Congl. Ch. Sch., Needham, Mass., 1982—; chmn. ins. adv. com. Town of Needham, 1982-95; pres. Interfaith Coun. for the Homeless, 1999—. Mem. Ins. Mgrs. Assn. (treas. Boston 1971-80), Ins. Library Assn. (dir. 1980-82). Home: 76 Lienau Dr Chatham MA 02633-2118 Office: Smith & Hale Assocs PO Box 136 South Orleans MA 02662-0136

HALE, NANCY ANNETTE, kindergarten educator; b. Paris, Tex., Sept. 6, 1959; d. William Richard and Ruby Lee (Davidson) Bills; m. Roy Wayne Hale, May 6, 1983; 1 child, Christopher Wayne. BA in Elem. Edn., U. Tex., San Antonio, 1986, MEd in Early Childhood Edn., 1995. Cert. elem. tchr., early childhood specialist, kindergarten team leader, supr., Tex. Presch. tchr. Adventure Presch., San Antonio, 1986-87; 1st grade tchr. Bob Hope Elem. Sch. S.W. Ind. Sch. Dist., San Antonio, 1987-89, 1st grade tchr. Hidden Cove Elem. Sch., 1989-91, kindergarten tchr. Hidden Cove Elem. Sch., 1991—. Mem. Districtwide Improvement Coun. S.W. Ind. Sch. Dist., 1990-91, instnl. coord., 1992-93, site-based mgmt. com., 1992-93, social studies instrnl. coord., 1992-93, dist. curriculum design com., 1996-98, campus improvement com., 1996-97, kindergarten team leader, 1996—, dist. curriculum designer, 1996—, mentor tchr., 1996, campus improvement com., 1996—. Mem. Neighborhood Watch, Atascosa, Tex., 1988—; sec. Macdona Heights Homeowners Assn. Mem. NEA, ASCD, ATPE, Nat. Assn. for Edn. of Young Children, Tex. Tchrs. Assn., Kindergarten Tchrs. Tex. Baptist. Avocations: reading, camping, travel, snow skiing. Home: 10925 Kelly Rd Atascosa TX 78002-3728

HALES, RALEIGH STANTON, JR., mathematics educator, academic administrator; b. Pasadena, Calif., Mar. 16, 1942; s. Raleigh Stanton and Gwendolen (Washington) Hales; m. Diane Cecilia Moore, July 8, 1967; children: Karen Gwen, Christopher Stanton. BA, Pomona Coll., 1964; MA, Harvard U., 1965, PhD, 1970. Tchg. fellow Harvard U., Cambridge, Mass., 1965—67; instr. math. Pomona Coll., Claremont, Calif., 1967—70, asst. prof., 1970—74, assoc. prof., 1974—85, prof., 1985—90, assoc. dean. coll., 1973—90; pres. Claremont Computations, 1983—90; prof. math. scis., v.p. acad. affairs Coll. Wooster, Ohio, 1990, pres., 1995—. Cons. Calif. Divsn. Savs. and Loan, 1968—70, Econs. Rsch. Assocs., L.A., 1969, Devel. Econs., L.A., 1971, Fed. Home Loan Bank Bd., Washington, 1971—72. Author: computer software; contbr. articles to profl. jours.; patentee calculator. Trustee Polytech. Sch., Pasadena, Calif., 1973—79, Foothill Country Day Sch., Claremont, 1985—90, chmn., 1989—90; coun. Internat. Badminton Fedn., 1989—99; bd. dirs. U.S. Badminton Assn., 1967—73, 1978—89, pres., 1985—88; mem. exec. bd. U.S. Olympic Com., 1989—90. Named Wig Disting. prof., Pomona Coll., 1971. Mem.: Wooster Country Club, Math. Assn. Am., Am. Math. Soc., Univ. Club N.Y., Pasadena Badminton Club (pres. 1978—85). Republican. Episcopalian. Home: 433 E University St Wooster OH 44691-2931 Office: Coll of Wooster 1189 Beall Ave Wooster OH 44691-2393

HALEY, JEANNE ACKERMAN, preschool director; b. Dayton, Ohio, June 26, 1953; d. Harold John and Florence Mary (Jacobs) Ackerman; m. James Francis Haley, Feb. 28, 1975; children: J. Michael, Jason, Jamie. AB, Miami JAcobs Jr. Coll., 1972; BBA, Ft. Lauderdale Coll. Bus., 1974. Sec. to pres. Fla. Atlantic U., Boca Raton, 1974-76; tchrs. aide Meth. Early Childhood Edn., Boca Raton, 1974-83; substitute tchr., tchrs. aide Mint Hill Presbyn. Ch. Presch., Charlotte, N.C., 1984-86; tchr. St. James Epsicopal Presch., Warrenton, Va., 1987-93; dir. St. John Presch. and Extended Care Program, Warrenton, Va., 1993-96, St. John Presch. Program and Parish Sch. of Religion Program, 1993-97; adminstrv. asst. to propertors The Inn at Little Washington (Va.), 1993. Chairperson Diocesan Com. on Extended Day Programs, Diocesan Com. on Pre-Schs., 1995-98, organizer, dir.'s com., Diocese of Arlington, Va.; leader, organizer Boy Scouts Am., Charlotte, N.C., Warrenton, 1984-86, asst. dist. commr., Warrenton, 1991-93, com. mem. troop 175, 1992-98 (Dist. award Merit 1992, Key Three award 1991); leader, organizer Girl Scouts U.S. Nat. Capital, Washington, 1991-94; v.p. Friends of Libr. Bd., Deerfield Beach, Fla., 1975-83. Roman Catholic. Avocation: promoting successful implementation of prganiozation & good business practices for the small business. Office: Office Solutions 6245 Ghadban Ct Warrenton VA 20187-7944

HALEY, JOHNETTA RANDOLPH, musician, educator, university official; b. Alton, Ill., Mar. 19; d. John a. and Willye E. (Smith) Randolph; children form previous marriage: Karen, Michael. MusB in Edn., Lincoln U., 1945; MusM, So. Ill. U., 1972. Cert. cons. 1995. Vocal and gen. music tchr. Lincoln High Sch., E. St. Louis, Ill., 1945-48; vocal music tchr., choral dir. Turner Sch., Kirkwood, Mo., 1950-55; vocal and gen. music tchr. Nipher Jr. High Sch., Kirkwood, 1955-71; prof. music Sch. Fine Arts So. Ill. U., Edwardsville, 1972—; dir. East St. Louis Campus, 1982—. Adjudicator music festivals; area music cons. Ill. Office Edn., 1977-78; prgram splst. St. Louis Human Devel. corp., 1968. Interim exec. dir. St. Louis Coun. Black People, summer, 1970; bd. dirs. YWCA, 1975-80, Artist Presentation Soc., St. Louis, 1975, United Negro Coll. Fund, 1976-78; bd. curators Lincoln U., Jefferson City, Mo., 1974-82, pres., 1978-82; chairperson Ill. Com. on Black Concerns in Higher Edn.; mem. Nat. Ministry on Urban Edn. Luth. Ch.-Mo. Synod, 1975-80; bd. dirs. Coun. Luth. Chs. Stillman Coll.; pres. congregation St. Phillips Luth. Ch.; bd. dirs. Girls, Inc.; mem. Ill. Aux. Bd., United Way; v.p. East St. Louis Cmty. Fund, Inc.; parliamentarian The Links, Inc. Recipient Cotillion de Leon award for Outstanding Cmty. Svc., 1977, Disting. Alumnae award Lincoln U., 1977, Disting. Svc. award United Negro Coll. Fund, 1979; SCLC, 1981; recipient Cmty. Svc. award St. Louis Drifters, 1979, Disting. Svc. to Arts award Sigma Gamma Rho, Nat. Negro Musicians award, 1981, Sci. awareness award, 1984-85, Tri Del Federated award, 1985, Martin Luther King Drum Maj. award, 1985, Bus. and Profl. Women's Club award, 1985-86, Fred L. McDowell award, 1986, Vol. of Yr. award Inroads Inc., 1986, Woman of Achievement in Edn. award Elks, 1987, Woman of Achievement award Suburban Newspaper of Greater St. Louis and Sta. KMOX-Radio, 1988, Love award Greeley Cmty. Ctr., Sammy Davies Jr. award in Edn., 1990, Yes I Can award in Edn., 1990, Merit award Urban League, 1994, Legacy award Nat. Coun. Negro Women, 1995, Diversity award Mo. ARC, 2001; named Disting. Citizen St. Louis Argus Newspaper, 1970, Dutchess of Paducah, 1973; the Johnetta Haley Scholars Acad. minority scholarship named in her honor So. Ill. U. Mem. AAUP, Music Educators Nat. Conf., Nat. Choral Dirs. Assn., Nat. Assn. Negro Musicians, Coll. Music Soc., Coun. Luth. Chs., Ill. Music. Educators, Jack and Jill, Inc., Women of Achievement in Edn., Friends of St. Louis Art Mus., The Links, Inc. (nat. parliamentarian, chair constnl. and by-laws com.), Las Amigas Social Club, Alpha Kappa Alpha (internat. parliamentarian, Golden soror award 1995, Grad Svcs. award 2001, nat. parliamentarian, 2002-), Mu Phi Epsilon, Pi Kappa Lambda. Lutheran. Home: 1926 Bennington Common Dr Saint Louis MO 63146-2555

HALEY, MICHAEL CABOT, English educator, researcher; b. Birmingham, Ala., Dec. 30, 1947; s. John Hendon and Margaret Reese (Beavers) H. BA, MA, U. Ala., 1969; PhD, Fla. State U., 1975. Instr. Fla. Coll., Temple Terrace, Fla., 1969-72; tchg. asst. Fla. State U., Tallahassee, Fla., 1972-75; asst. prof. North Ctrl. Coll., Naperville, Ill., 1975-79; from adj. prof. to prof. U. Alaska, Anchorage, 1979-93, prof., 1993—. Author: The Semeiosis of Poetic Metaphor, 1988, Noam Chomsky, 1994; editor: Linguistic Perspectives on Literature, 1980; mng. editor Peirce Seminar Papers, Providence, R.I., Oxford, England, N.Y.C., 1993-99. Named Moss Chair of Excellence U. Memphis, 1998. Mem. Semiotic Soc. am., S.E. Conference Linguistics, Phi Beta Kappa. Republican. Avocations: motorcycling, camping, fishing. Home: 3550 W Dimond Blvd Unit 311 Anchorage AK 99502-1556 Office: English Dept Univ AK 3211 Providence Dr Anchorage AK 99508-4614 E-mail: afmch@uaa.alaska.edu.

HALFERTY, FRANK JOSEPH, middle school music educator; b. Seattle, May 7, 1954; s. Edward A. and Eva Mae (Ellis) H.; m. Margaret A. Taylor, Mar. 17, 1979 (div. June 1991); children: Bryan W., Patrick Joseph; m. Melissa A. Rowland, July 31, 1992. BA in Music Edn., BA in Music Theory and Lit., Seattle Pacific U., 1976; MA in Music Composition, N.Mex. State U., 1982. Cert. tchr., Wash. Band and choral tchr. Raymond (Wash.) Sch. Dist., 1976-77; band and orch. tchr. Bellevue (Wash.) Sch. Dist., 1977-80; MA in Music Composition N.Mex. State U., Las Cruces, 1980-82; band tchr. Lake Washington Sch. Dist., Kirkland, Wash., 1982-93, Shoreline Sch. Dist., Seattle, 1993—, head music dept., 1994—2003, also dist. music specialist, coord., 2003—04. Mem. site-based mgmt. coun. Einstein Mid. Sch., Seattle, 1994-97; dir. Lake Washington All-Dist. Band, Kirkland, 1984-92; bd. dirs. Shoreline Arts Coun. Composer, arranger numerous musical works for band, instrumental ensembles, string orch. and choral groups. Crimson scholar, 1982; named Tchr. of Yr. by students, tchrs. and parents of Kirkland Jr. H.S., 1990; recipient Golden Acorn award Einstein Mid. Sch. PTSA, 1997. Mem. ASCAP (Writer award 1998-03), NEA, Music Educators Nat. Conf., Sno-King Music Edn. Assn. (sec. 1994-96), Shoreline Arts Coun. (bd. mem. 1997—), Phi Kappa Phi, Alpha Kappa Sigma. Avocations: camping, canoeing, woodworking, sailing. Home: 6155 NE 187th St Kenmore WA 98028-3221 Office: Einstein Mid Sch 19343 3rd Ave NW Seattle WA 98177-3012

HALFVARSON, LUCILLE ROBERTSON, music educator; b. Petersburg, Ill., May 17, 1919; d. Harris Morton and Lucille (Fox) Robertson; m. Sten Gustaf Halfvarson, Aug. 8, 1946; children: Laura, Eric, Linnea, Mary. BA, Knox Coll., 1941; MusM, Am. Conservatory, 1969; DHL (hon.), Aurora U., 2000. Cert. tchr., Ill. Tchr. music and speech Freeman Elem. Sch., Aurora, Ill., 1941-44; choral dir. Galesburg (Ill.) Sr. H.S., 1944-46; dir. of music Our Savior Luth. Ch., Aurora, Ill., 1950-63; oratorio soloist, 1952-67; dir. of music Westminster Presbyn. Ch., Aurora, 1963-84; vocal instr. Merit Music Program, Chgo., 1982-93; ret., 1993. Choir dir. 1st Meth. Ch., Galesburg, 1944-46; choral-vocal instr. Waubonsee C.C., Sugar Grove, Ill., 1967-79; organizer Jr. Coll. Music Festival, Waubonsee Coll., Sugar Grove, 1972-73; pvt. vocal instrn., Aurora, 1979—. Conductor Messiah Concert Waubonsee Coll., Paramount Arts Ctr., 1968—, 25th Concert, 1992. Co-chair Citizens Adv. Com. Paramount Arts. Ctr., Aurora, 1977-78; founder United Arts Bd. Fox Valley, pres., 1977-82, Fox Valley Arts Hall of Fame, 2001; chair Paramount Celebration Arts, 1985-86; residency dir. Met. Life Affiliate Artist, Aurora, 1982-83; bd. dirs. YWCA, 1984-91, chair corp. award com., 1994-95; dir. New Eng. Congl. Ch. Bell Choir, 1997-99. Recipient Disting. Svc. award Cosmopolitan Club, Aurora, Ill., 1983; named Woman of Year YWCA, Aurora, 1976, Disting. Alumni Knox Coll., Galesburg, Ill., 1984; Paul Harris fellow Rotary Found. of Rotary Internat., 1999. Mem. AAUW, DAR, PEO, Music Educators Nat. Conf., Am. Choral Dirs. Assn., Aurora C. of C. (Image Maker 1992), Phi Beta Kappa. Avocations: needlecrafts, gardening, fishing, reading. Home: 1105 W Downer Pl Aurora IL 60506-4821

HALGREN, LEE A. academic administrator; Pres., v.p. acad. and student affairs State Coll. Colo., Denver, 1995—. Office: The State Coll Colo 1580 Lincoln St Ste 750 Denver CO 80203-1505 E-mail: halgrenl@mscd.edu.

HALKIAS, CHRISTOS CONSTANTINE, electronics educator; b. Monastiraki, Doridos, Greece, Aug. 23, 1933; s. Constantine C. and Alexandra V. (Papapostoloy) H.; m. Demetra Saras, Jan. 22, 1961; children: Alexandra, Helen-Joanna. BSEE, CCNY, 1957; MSEE, Columbia U., 1958, PhD, 1962. Prof. elec. engrng. Columbia U., N.Y.C., 1962-73; prof. electronics Nat. Tech. U. Athens, Greece, 1973—2000. Fulbright vis. prof. Nat. Tech. U. Athens, 1969, dir. informatics divsn., 1983-86; dir. Nat. Rsch. Found., Athens, 1983-87; mem. BOD INTRACOM, 2000-. Author: Electronic Devices and Circuits, 1967, Integrated Electronics, 1972, Electronic Fundamentals and Applications, 1976, Design of Electronic Filters, 1988;

contbr. articles to profl. jours. Recipient D.B. Steinman award CCNY, 1956; Higgins fellow Columbia U., 1958. Mem. IEEE (sr. mem., chmn. Greek sect. 1982-86, Centennial medal 1984), European Unions Info. Soc. (tech. adv. group 1999—), Info. Soc. Techs. Adv. Group, Sigma Xi. Home: 4 Kosti Palama St Paleo Psyhico 15452 Athens Greece Office: Nat Tech U Athens Zographou 15773 Athens Greece E-mail: halkias@cs.ntua.gr.

HALL, BRAD BAILEY, orthopaedic surgeon, health care administrator; b. Lubbock, Tex., Nov. 16, 1951; s. John Robert and Anna Ruth Hall; m. Carol Lynn Martin, Dec. 20, 1975; children: Clint Berkeley, Kathryn Lynn. Student, Ariz. State U., 1970-72; MD, Tex. Tech U., 1977; MS in Healthcare Adminstrn., U. Colo., 1996. Diplomate Am. Bd. Orthopaedic Surgery. Resident in orthopaedic surgery Mayo Clinic, Rochester, Minn., 1977-82, cons. in orthopaedic surgery, 1982-83; spine fellow U. Toronto, Ont., Can., 1982; pvt. practice, San Antonio, 1983-97; sr. v.p. quality Bapt. Health Sys., San Antonio, 1997-98, v.p. med. mgmt., 1998—; med. dir. Bapt. Health Network, San Antonio, 1998—. Clin. assoc. prof. U. Tex. Health Sci. Ctr., San Antonio, 1984—, med. dir. orthopaedic clinic, 1996-97; orthopaedic staff physician Audie L. Murphy Meml. VA Hosp., San Antonio, 1985—; chmn. dept. orthopaedics St. Luke's Luth. Hosp., San Antonio, 1986-88, dir. residency, 1987-94, chief of staff, bd. dirs., mem. fin. com., chmn. exec. staff com., 1992—; pres., bd. dirs. Musculoskeletal Assocs. So. Tex., P.A., 1994-97; presenter in field. Contbr. articles and abstracts to med. jours., chpts. to books. Grantee Orthopaedic Rsch. and Edn. Found., 1979; scholar Mayo Found., 1982. Mem. AMA (physicians recognition award 1984-87, 88-96), Orthopaedic Rsch. Soc., Am. Acad. Orthopaedic Surgeons, Mid-Am. Orthopaedic Assn., N.Am. Spine Soc., Clin. Orthopaedic Soc., Western Orthopaedic Assn., Tex. Spine Soc. (bd. dirs., pres. 1994-95), Tex. Med. Assn., Tex. Orthopaedic Assn., Bexar County Med. Soc., San Antonio Orthopaedic Assn. (pres.), Am. Coll. Physician Execs. Office: Bapt Health Sys 660 N Main Ave Ste 325 San Antonio TX 78205-1209

HALL, CAROL ANN, music educator; b. Lamar, Colo., Dec. 22, 1952; d. Raymond Dewey and Hazel Vera Morrow; m. Charlie Merle Hall, Apr. 21, 1979 (dec. Oct. 10, 2001); 1 child, Charlie Walter. AA, Lamar C.C., 1972; BA in Elem. Edn., BA in Music Edn. K-12, Adams State Coll., Alamosa, Colo., 1974. 4th grade tchr. Springfield Elem. Sch., 1974—75, tchr. K-6 music, 1990—; tchr. K-6 music Parkview Elem. Sch., Lamar, 1975—78; tchr. K-12 music Vilas Sch., 1986—88. Piano tchr., Vilas, 1986—88; voice tchr., Pritchett, Vilas and Springfield, Colo.; performer, recorded composed song Goldband records, 2002—03. Music leader, mem. Tri Ch. Trio Springfield Bapt. Chapel. Recipient award, Am. Women of Who's Who, 2002—03. Mem.: Springfield Elem. Tchrs. Assn., Music Educators Nat. Conf. Baptist. Avocations: bowling, composing. Home: 429 Monroe Box 85 Pritchett CO 81064

HALL, CAROL BETH, elementary school educator; b. Joliet, Ill., Jan. 9, 1947; d. Ellis Hugh and Elizabeth Edna (Corrigan) Jones; m. Alan Shelby Hall, June 8, 1969; children: Kevin William, Scott Ellis, Brian Patrick. BS in Edn., Ill. State U., 1970. Cert. Tchr. Ill. Tchr., Lisbon, Ill., 1969—71, Christian Learn & Care, Loves Park, Ill., 1981, Forrestville Valley Dist. 221, Leaf River, Ill., 1984—. Author: Autopsied Poems, 1996, Know Missteakes, 1999. Mem. Highland C.C. Chorale, Freeport, Ill., 1995—. Recipient 1st Place award, Phidian Art Club, 1992. Mem.: NEA, Northwest Writer's Assn., Nat. Assn. Music Edn., Internat. Educators Assn., Soc. Mayflower Descendants of Ill. Republican. Lutheran. Avocations: horseback riding, antiques, crocheting, knitting, singing. Home: 8602 W NW Rd Mount Morris IL 61054 Office: Forrestville Valley Sch Dist #221 PO Box 665 Forreston IL 61030

HALL, CHARLES WORTH LEO, college administrator; b. Louisville, Ky., Dec. 18, 1946; s. Worth Leroy and Gertrude Omega (Greenwell) H.; m. Judelyn Lumbab Montebon, Jan. 26, 1990; children: Evelyn, Nghia, Hanh, Wanda, Charlotte, Shenandoah, Michelle, Annamarie, Andre, Angelyn, Bernadette. AA, Hartnell Coll., 1975; BS, U. So. Miss., 1976; MEd, U. Louisville, 1978; EdS, U. So. Miss., 1982; postgrad., Walden U., 1982—, Vanderbilt U., 1984-86. Cert. tchr., Tenn., Ind., Calif., counselor; LPC, Tex., La., Miss., Tenn. Commd. capt. U.S. Army, 1963, tchr., 1972-73, advanced through grades to maj., 1988, career counselor, 1976-77; fin. aid counselor Ind. State U., New Albany, 1978; admissions officer Ind. Vocat. Tech. Coll., Sellersburg, 1979-81, asst. dir. student svcs., 1979-81; profl. devel. coord. U. So. Miss., Hattiesburg, 1981-83, asst. registrar, 1981-83; v.p. student affairs Excel Bus. Coll., Madisonville, Tenn., 1984; military personnel officer Camp Shelby, Miss., 1984-86; tng. adminstr. USDA, New Orleans, 1986-92; dir. Internat. Bus. Coll., Agana, Guam, 1992—. Pres. Personnel Svc. Orgn., Jackson, Miss., 1977-78; dir. Marquis Adv. Bd., Hattiesburg, Miss., 1978-82; chmn. Franklin (Tenn.) Battlefield Restoration, 1983-92; exec. dir. New Horizons Devel. Co., Louisville, 1988—. Author: Professional Development, 1981, Needs Assessment for Professional Development, 1982, Professional Development Procedural Guide, 1982, Professional Development Bibliography, 1982. Dist. commr. Pine Burr Coun., Boy Scouts Am., Hattiesburg, 1968-83. Monterey Bay Coun., Salinas Calif., 1972-73; senator U. So. Miss. Student Govt. Assn., Hattiesburg, 1974-75; pres. U. So. Miss. Young Dems., Hattiesburg, 1975-76; SMF social case worker ARC, Hattiesburg, 1975-76; active Foster Parent Plan. Major USAR, 1963-90, major AGC USAR, 1963—. Decorated Army Commendation medal, Army Achievement medal, Army Reserve Achievement medal, Vietnam Cross Gallantry with bronze palm; recipient Scouters Training award, Commissioner's Key award, Order of Arrow; Walden Inst. Advanced Studies fellow, Acad. Mgmt. fellow Pa. State U. Mem. ASTD, AACD, ASPA, KC. (treas. 4th patriotic degree 1975-76), VFW, (surgeon 1991-92), AASECT, AAGC, Philippine-Am. Guardian Assn., Internat. Scout Assn., Ind. Personnel and Guidance Assn. (pres. 1979-80), Order Battle Flag, Am. Assn. Philippines, Children Internat., Confederate Alliance, Friends Confederate Soc., Mensa, Career Coll. Assn., Nat. Bus. End. Assn., Am. Legion, Vets. Vietnam War, Order Vietnam Republic of Cross of Gallantry, Mil. Order World Wars, Reserve Officers Assn., Adjutant Gen. Regimental Assn., Order So. Cross, Hon. Order Ky. Cols., Hub City Kiwanis Club (bd. dirs. 1982-83), Omicron Delta Kappa, Phi Kappa Phi, Alpha Phi Omega (pres. 1976-77, disting. svc. key), Phi Gamma Mu (v.p. 1975-76), Phi Delta Kappa, Phi Tau Chi, Psi Chi, Delta Tau Kappa, Epsilon Delta Chi. Roman Catholic. Avocations internat. youth work, internat. Boy Scout Movement. Office: care R Taylor PO Box 3783 Hagatna GU 96932-3783

HALL, DAVID MCKENZIE, business and management educator; b. Gary, Ind., June 21, 1928; s. Alfred McKenzie and Grace Elizabeth (Crimiel) H.; m. Jaqueline Virginia Branch, Apr. 30, 1960; children: Glen D., Gary D. BA, Howard U., 1951; MS, N.C. Agrl. Tech. State U., 1966; PhD, Kennedy Western U., 2002. Enlisted USAF, 1951; advanced through grades to brig. gen.; chief social actions Hdqrs. Mil. Airlift Command, Scott AFB, Il., 1972-1974; dep. base comdr. 375th Air Base Group, Scott AFB, 1974-75, base comdr., 1975-76; dir. data processing Air Force Logistics Command, Wright-Patterson AFB, Ohio, 1976-77, comptr., 1977-83; ret. USAF, 1983; dir. data processing Delco-Remy div. GM, Anderson, Ind., 1983-85; regional mgr. Electronic Data Systems, Anderson, 1985-88, Saginaw, Mich., 1988-93; prof. mgmt. and mktg. Northwood Univ., Midland, Mich., 1993-97; exec. in residence Saginaw Valley State U., University Center, Mich., 1997—. Brig. gen. USAF, 1951—83. Recipient Hon. Citizenship East St. Louis, Ill., 1975, Key to City Gary Ind., 1981, spirit of Saginaw award, 1999, Sagimore of the Wabash, 1999. Mem. NAACP, Saginaw Cmty. Found., Cmty. Affairs Com., Prince Hall Masons, Kappa Alpha Psi. Methodist. Avocations: reading, woodworking. Home: 49 W Hannum Blvd Saginaw MI 48602-1938 Office: Saginaw Valley State U Curtiss Hall 7400 Bay Rd University Center MI 48710 E-mail: dhall@svsu.edu.

HALL, DORIS SPOONER, music educator; b. New Orleans, Dec. 27, 1949; d. Henry and Geneva (Battley) Spooner; m. Morris D. Hall, Aug. 4, 1973; 1 child, Amy Evon. B of Music Edn., La. State U., 1971, M of Music Edn., 1972, postgrad., ALA A&M U., 1991. Cert. tchr. Ala., La. Band dir. Shreveport (La.) City Schs., 1972-73; asst. band dir. Ala. A&M U., Normal, 1973-74, asst. prof. music, 1974-79, aux. coord. marching units, 1979-87, prof. music, 1980—. Lectr. music U. Ala., Huntsville, 1980-89, Oakwood Coll., Huntsville, 1980-90; clinician Ala. Sch. System, Birmingham, 1989-92; cons. in field. Active Huntsville Sympjony Orch., 1975-79, 86-92; recitals U. Ala. and Ala. A&M U., 1990-92. Named Outstanding Young Women, 1982; recipient Outstanding Achievers awards, 1983. Mem. AAUP, Nat. Flute Assn., Nat. Woodwinds Assn., Music Educators Nat. Conf., Ala. Edn. Assn., Tau Beta Sigma, ALpha Kappa Alpha. Roman Catholic. Avocations: dancing, reading, skating. Home: 12000 Bell Mountain Dr SW Huntsville AL 35803-3406 Office: Ala A&M U PO Box 258 Normal AL 35762-0258

HALL, DOROTHY LOUISE PARZYK, academic administrator; b. Worcester, Mass., Nov. 23, 1943; d. Francis Stephen and Jeanne Anita (Mathieu) Parzyk; m. Michael Stephen Hall, June 30, 1967; children: Michelle Stephanie, Suzanne Marie. BS in Edn., Worcester State Coll., 1965; MEd, U. N.C., Greensboro, 1983, CAS, 1986, EdD, 1991. Cert. tchr., Mass.; cert. tchr., reading specialist, curriculum specialist, N.C. Tchr. 1st grade Town of Holden, Mass., 1965-67; tchr. 1st and 2d grades Old Richmond Elem. Sch. Winston-Salem (N.C.)-Forsyth County Schs., 1967-71, tchr. 1st grade Old Town Elem. Sch., 1971-83, reading/curriculum coord., 1986—99; dir. Four Blocks Ctr. Wake Forest U., Winston-Salem, 1999—. Vis. instr. Wake Forest U., Winston-Salem, 1983—86; cons. schs., NC, SC, Va., Ga., Mo., Wis., Ohio, Ky., Mich., Del., NY, Ill., Ind., Utah, Tex., Okla., NH, Conn., Pa., Wash., Oreg., Calif., Ariz., Kans., Miss., Canada, Mexico. Author: Making Words, 1994, Making Big Words, 1994, Making More Words, 1997, Making More Big Words, 1997, Reading and Writing in Kindergarten, 1997, Month by Month Phonics for First Grade, 1997, Second Grade, 1998, Third Grade, 1998, Upper Grades, 1998, The Teachers' Guide to the Four Blocks, 1998, Guided Reading the Four Blocks Way, 1999, Teachers Guide to Building Blocks, 2000, True Stories From Four Blocks Classrooms, 2001, Self-Selected Reading, 2002, Writing Mini-Lessons for First Grade, 2002, Second Grade, 2002, Kindergarten, 2003, Upper Grades, 2003, others; contbr. articles to profl. jours., chapters to books. Mem. Internat. Reading Assn. (local pres. 1993-94), Phi Delta Kappa, Delta Kappa Gamma (local pres. 1996—). Roman Catholic. Home: 3060 Minart Dr Winston Salem NC 27106-2613 Office: Edn Dept Wake Forest U Winston Salem NC E-mail: halldp@wfu.edu.

HALL, DOROTHY MARIE REYNOLDS, dental educator; b. Columbus, Ohio, Dec. 22, 1925; d. Thomas Franklin and Nellie May (Nail) R.; m. Grant Forrest Hall; children: Stacy L., Cynthia Kay Hall Henderson, Mark Kevin. Student, Ohio State U., 1973-79, Sinclair C.C., 1976. Cert. Dental Asst.; lic. dental radiographer, Ohio. Dental asst., office mgr. dental offices in Westerville, Ohio, 1954-68, Columbus, Ohio, 1968-70; dental asst., staff supr. dental aux. utilization, clinic in Good Samaritan Dental Clinic, Columbus, 1970; instr., staff supr., clinic instr. Ohio State U. Coll. Dentistry, 1970-72; instr. adult edn. Eastland Vocat. Ctr., Groveport, Ohio, 1969; expanded function duty asst., 1977; instr. dental assisting Eastland Career Ctr., 1972-91; ret., 1991. Substitute tchr., Ohio, 1992-99; examiner, mem. trustee Ohio Commn. on Dental Testing, Inc., 1979—, Commn. Ohio Dental Assts. Testing, Inc., 1977—, chief examiner, 1977-81, examiner, 1981—; mem. 12th grade competency exam. reviewer com. Ohio Vocat. Edn. Rsch. Lab., 1993. Author profl. publs.; developer, artist: A Manual of Lesson Plans for Teaching for the Ohio Vocat. Edn. Dental Asst. Programs, 1981. Sr. leadership group coord., Delaware, Morrow Counties Vol. Ctr., Connections. Mem. Columbus Dental Assts. Soc. (pres. 1968-69, Dental Asst. of Yr. 1980), Ohio Dental Assts. Assn. (pres. 1978-79, 80-81), Ohio Dental Assts. Assn. (pres. 1978-79, 80-81), Am. Dental Assts. Assn. (cert. AQP dental asst., life mem.), Eastland Edn. Assn., Eastland Vocat. Assn. (pres. 1981-82), Ohio Vocat. Assn. (Dental Assisting Tchr. of Yr. award 1991), Nat. Ret. Tchrs. Assn. (life), Ohio Vocat. Tchrs. Assn. (chairperson S.E. sect. 1986-91), Ohio Vocat. Asst. Tchrs. SE Region, Order Eastern Star, Iota Lambda Sigma. Mem. Reformed Ch. Am. Home: 4676 Big Walnut Rd Galena OH 43021-9330 Office: 4465 S Hamilton Rd Groveport OH 43125-9333

HALL, DOUGLAS LEE, computer science educator; b. San Antonio, Feb. 5, 1947; s. Robert Arthur and Thelma (Stischer). AA in Foreign Lang., San Antonio Coll., 1967; BA in Spanish, U. Tex., 1969; MEd in Bilingual Edn., Pan Am. U., 1977; PhD, N. Tex. State U., 1987. Tchr. Edgewood Ind. Sch. Dist., San Antonio, 1969-73, Brownsville (Tex.) Ind. Sch. Dist., 1973-74, 76-78; precious metals specialist Nu-Metals, Inc., Dallas, 1974; tchr. DPC Am. Sch., Dubai, UAE, 1975-76; tng. dir. ABDick, San Antonio, 1978-79; bilingual tchr. Dallas Ind. Sch. Dist., 1979-82; computer cons. Taylor Mgmt. Systems, Dallas, 1982-83; lectr. in field N.Tex. State U., Denton, 1984-86; grad. advisor St. Mary's U., San Antonio, 1986—, chair dept. computer sci., 1990—2003, pres. faculty senate, 1992-93. Dir. Deutscher Volkstanzverein, San Antonio, 1987—; asst. dir. San Antonio Folk Dance Fest, 1986—; advisor St. Mary's U. Chpt. Assn. for Computing Machinery, 1989—; CEO Athens Solutions, 2000—, Xarism Multi Media, 2000—. Contbr. articles to profl. jours. Docent Inst. Texan Cultures, San Antonio, 1989—; pres. Crown Hill Pk. Homeowners, San Antonio, 1986-89; del. 1st U.S.-Japan Grassroots Summit, 1991. Named Tchr. of Yr., Brownsville Ind. Sch. Dist., 1974, 1977, Outstanding Elem. Tchr., 1974, Disting. Grad. Faculty Mem., U. North Tex., 1991—92, Disting. Computer Sci. Alumnus, 1998; recipient Disting. Alumnus award, San Antonio Coll., 2000, Tex. Folk Dance award, 2002. Mem. NEA, IEEE, ACM, Tex. State Tchrs. Assn., Am. Assn. Artificial Intelligence. Avocations: theology, genealogy, foreign languages. Home: 515 Marquis St San Antonio TX 78216-5217 Office: Saint Mary's U One Camino Santa Maria San Antonio TX 78228-8524

HALL, DOUGLAS SCOTT, astronomy educator; b. Lexington, Ky., May 30, 1940; s. William Scott and Catherine (Read) H.; m. Bonnie Schumacher, June 3, 1964 (div. 1978); children: Bruce Douglas, Brandon Scott; m. Mimi Kemp, Aug. 1, 1981. BA in Chemistry, Swarthmore Coll., 1962; MA in Astronomy, Ind. U., 1964, PhD in Astronomy, 1967. Rsch. assoc. Dyer Obs., Nashville, 1967; asst. prof. Vanderbilt U., Nashville, 1967-71, assoc. prof., 1971-80, prof., 1980—. Dir. Dyer Obs., Nashville, 1986—; cons. Tenn. State U., Nashville, 1988—, adj. prof., 1991—; chair allocations com. Internat. Space Sta. Amateur Telescope, 2001--, chmn. proposal rev. com., 2001—. Co-author: Supernova 1987-A!, 1988, Photoelectric Photometry of Variable Stars, 1988; contbr. papers to profl. jours.; referee for various astron. jours. and rsch. found.; founder Internat. Amateur and Profl. Photoelectric Photometry Comms., 1980—, editor, 1984—; mem. edit. bd. Inf. Bull. Variable Stars, 1991—. Recipient U.S. Sr. Scientist award Alexander von Humbolt Found., Fed. Republic Germany, 1973-74; named Astronomer of Yr., Astron. League, 1984; rsch. grantee NSF, 1968-87, NASA, 1977-83, Rsch. Corp., 1979. Mem. Internat. Astron. Union, Am. Astron. Soc. (rsch. grantee 1988), Astron. Soc. of the Pacific (liaison), Internat. Amateur and Profl. Photoelectric Photometry (pres. 1980—), Am. Assn. Variable Star Observers (editl. bd. 1976—), Tenn. Acad. Sci. (editl. bd. 1972), S.E. Assn. for Rsch. in Astronomy (bd. dirs. 1992—), Barnard-Seyfert Astron. Soc. (bd. dirs. 1996—), Sigma Xi (pres. Vanderbilt chpt. 1987-89). Office: Arthur J Dyer Observatory Vanderbilt Univ Nashville TN 37235 E-mail: hall@astro.dyer.vanderbilt.edu.

HALL, ELTON ARTHUR, philosophy educator; b. San Fernando, Calif., Sept. 18, 1940; s. Harwood Harry and Verna Florentina (Engelhardt) H.; m. Katherine May Lennard, Aug. 27, 1961; children: Helena Louise, Anita Virya. BA, Occidental Coll., 1963; MA, U. Calif., Santa Barbara, 1965, MA, 1967. Asst. prof. philosophy Moorhead (Minn.) State U., 1967-69, Calif. State U., Fresno, 1969-75; head dep. social sci. Oxnard (Calif.) Coll., 1987-90, prof. philosophy, 1975-92, acting div. dir. arts, letters and sci., 1990-91, acting dean gen. edn., 1991-92; prof. philosophy Moorpark (Calif.) Coll., 1992—; pres. acad. senate, 1996-99. Adj. prof. sociology Calif. Luth. U., 1994; tchr. trainer Calif. Assn. Schs. Cosmetoloty, Sacramento, 1988-91, Calif. Assn. Pvt. Postsecondary Schs., 1991-93. Contbr. articles to profl. jours. Chief negotiator local 1828 Am. Fedn. Tchrs., 1996-99. Mem. Internat. Soc. Neoplatonic Studies, Muyiddin Ibn 'Arabi Soc. Avocations: religious studies, poetry, hiking. Office: Moorpark Coll 7075 Campus Rd Moorpark CA 93021-1605

HALL, GENE E. dean; PhD, Syracuse U. Faculty mem., project dir. nat. R&D Ctr. for Tchr. Edn. U. Tex., Austin, Tex.; prof. ednl. leadership U. Fla.; dean Coll. Edn. U. N.C., 1988—93; prof. ednl. leadership U. No. Colo., Colo., 1993—98; dean Coll. Edn. U. Nev., Las Vegas, 1999—. Bd. mem. WestEd Regional Edn. Lab. Author (with S.M. Hord): Implementing Change: Pattersn, Principles and Potholes, 2001; author: (with others) Introduction to the Foundations of American Education, 2002; contbr. articles to profl. jours. Office: Univ Nev Las Vegas 4505 Maryland Pkwy Las Vegas NV 89154*

HALL, GEORGANNA MAE, elementary school educator; b. St. Louis, June 4, 1951; d. George Winfred and Judith Lou (Wheatley) H. BS in Edn., Stephen F. Austin U., 1973; MS in Edn., U. Houston, 1979. Cert. elem., early childhood and kindergarten edn. tchr., Tex.; cert. mid mgmt. adminstr. Elem. educator Lamar Consol. Ind. Sch. Dist., Rosenberg, Tex., 1973-94; part-time campus coord. Houston C.C., 1994; regional dir. Sylvan Learning Ctrs. Pasadena (Tex.) Ind. Sch. Dist., 1994—. Mem. Smith Elem. Improvement Task Force, Richmond, Tex., summers 1988-90, active mem., summer 1991. Mem. choir St. John's Meth. Ch., Richmond. Mem. Tex. Classroom Tchrs. Assn., Nat. Assn. for the Edn. Young Children, Assn. Curriculum and Supervision, Celebration Ringers, Delta Kappa Gamma, Sigma Kappa. Avocations: needlework, crafts, doll collecting. Home: 4771 Sweetwater Blvd #147 Sugar Land TX 77479 Office: Sylvan Learning Ctrs 1020 E Thomas Pasadena TX 77506-2213

HALL, GERALDINE CRISTOFARO, biology educator; b. Elmira, N.Y., Dec. 27, 1941; d. Michael Dominic and Rita Marie (Stachel) Cristofaro; m. Thomas J. Hall, July 16, 1966; children: John Michael, Alexandra Marie. BS magna cum laude, Nazareth Coll., 1964; MS, Purdue U., 1967; PhD, SUNY, Binghamton, 1981. Grad. instr. biology Purdue U., Lafayette, Ind., 1964-67; rsch. assoc. U. N.H., Durham, 1967-68; part-time rsch. assoc. SUNY, Binghamton, 1978-81; instr. Elmira Coll., 1968-78, asst. prof., 1982-88, assoc. prof., 1988-98, prof. emeritus, 1998—. Contbr. articles to profl. publs. Sci. teaching workshop grantee N.Y. State Dept. Edn., Albany, 1991; recipient NSF Rsch. Opportunity award, 1984. Mem. NSTA, Internat. Assn. Blood Pattern Analysts, Beta Beta Beta. Avocations: golf, cross-country skiing, sailing, bridge.

HALL, GRACE ROSALIE, physicist, educator, writer; b. Meriden, Conn., July 15, 1921; d. George John and Grace Cleora (Gleason) White; m. Eldon Conrad Hall, July 2, 1948; children: Brent Channing, Pamela Rosalie, Craig Gleason, Gordon Timothy. Spl. student, Pembroke Coll., 1940-41; BS in Chemistry, Ea. Nazarene Coll., 1946; MA in Physics, Boston U., 1946, postgrad., 1946-53; MA in English, Simmons Coll., 1975. Bookkeeper Cherry & Webb Co., Providence, 1939-42; sec. to registrar Eastern Nazarene Coll., Quincy, Mass., 1942-44, instr. physics, chemistry, 1945-46; teaching fellow physics Boston U., 1946-49; instr. physics lab. Northeastern U., Boston, 1956-57; instr. physics Simmons Coll., Boston, 1949; asst. prof. physics Eastern Nazarene Coll., Quincy, 1957-61, asst. prof. chemistry, 1969, asst. prof. phys. sci., 1974. Instr. Shakespeare Barrington (R.I.) Coll., 1984; tchr. Westwood (Mass.) Sem., 1975; ch. sch. dir. 1st Parish, Westwood, 1977—81; chair sem. U. Louisville, 1988. Author: The Tempest as Mystery Play: Uncovering Religious Sources of Shakespeare's Most Spiritual Work, 1999; contbg. author: Webs and Wardrobes, 1987; contbr. articles to profl. jours. Bd. dirs. South County Norfolk Assn. for Retarded Citizens, 1978—79; judge H.S. Sci. Fairs, North Quincy, Mass., 1960—64, 1969—76, Regional Sci. Fairs, Bridgewater, Mass., 1960—62; chair City-Wide Bookfair, Quincy, 1962; bd. dirs. Westwood Interfaith Coun., 1985—89; pres. Ch. Women United, 1959. Named R.I. Honor Soc.; recipient Libr. Family of Yr. award, City of Quincy, 1960; scholar faculty scholarship, Ea. Nazarene Coll., 1943—45. Mem.: MLA (session participant 1978, 1984), Shakespeare Inst. (spkr. 1999), Christianity and Lit. Assn. (conf. participant 1984, 1989—90, 1995, 2001), Shakespeare Assn. Am. (seminar participant 1988—96, 2000—01), Mythopoetic Soc., New Eng. Hist. Geneal. Soc., MIT Women's League (editor activities guide and newsletter 1989—2001, adv. group 1999—2001), Internat. Soc. Poets, Clarendon Soc., Munro Soc., Phi Delta Lambda. Avocations: children's literature, recycling, snorkeling. E-mail: grwhall@aol.com.

HALL, HELENE W. retired adult education educator; b. Centralia, Ill., Sept. 17, 1926; d. James O. and Gladys (Hosman) Lawrence; m. William E. Hall, June 27, 1948; children: Ronald William, Steven Charles, Jerry Victor. BS, Emporia State U., 1966, MS, 1969, EDS, 1974. Sec., asst. Med. Physicians & Dentists, Kansas City, Mo., 1966—69; tchr. Roosevelt Lab. HS, Emporia, Kans.; coord. secondary sch. tchrs. Emporia State U., 1969—71; team leader Tchr. Corps, 1971—73; instr., coord. secretarial sci., word processing Kans. City C.C., Kans., 1973—92; instr., coord. secretarial scis., word processing Allen County C.C. Satellite Ctr., Kans., 1992—94. Mem.: Assn. Info. Systems Profls., Office Edn. Assn., Nat. Secs. Assn., Kans. Bus. Edn. Assn., Classroom Educators Adv. Com., Kans. Vocat. Assn., Am. Vocat. Assn., Nat. Bus. Edn. Assn., Delta Pi Epsilon. Baptist. Home: 603 NW Redbud Dr #B Lees Summit MO 64081-1351 Office: Kansas City Comty Coll 7250 State Ave Kansas City KS 66112-3003

HALL, JAMES ROBERT, secondary education educator; b. Salem, Ill., Dec. 24, 1947; s. James Wesley and Patricia Joyce (Ellis) H. BS, U. Ill., 1970. Cert. secondary tchr., Ill. Tchr. Murphysboro (Ill.) H.S., 1970—. Author, compiler (tng. manual) Key Club Faculty Advisors, 1975. Sunday sch tchr. United Meth. Ch., Murphysboro, 1973-76, youth dir., 1973-76, mem. coun. on ministries, 1984—, trustee, 1984—; founder, dir. Christian Lay Coun. Youth Coffeehouse, 1973-75; mem. Murphysboro Recreation Bd., 1974-76, pres. 1975-76; cmty. amb. So. Ill. U. Area Svcs., 1975—; bd. dirs. Murphysboro Heart Fund, 1973-76, co-chmn. 1975-76; chmn. Murphysboro Muscular Dystrophy Assn., 1971-74; counsellor Little Grassy Youth Ch. Camp, 1973; mem. steering com. Murphysboro Apple Festival, 1975—, exec. com., 1983—; bd. dirs. Murphysboro United Way, 1978-83, Murphysboro Sr. Citizens Coun., 1980-83, Resource Reclamation Inc., 1979-85; vice chmn. Murphysboro Swimming Pool Project Commn., 1983-84, chmn. 1984-88; active Murphysboro Tourism Commn., 1995—; chmn. Murphysboro Mainstreet Promotions Commn., 1998—. Named One of Outstanding Young Men of Am. 1975, 84; recipient Citizenship award Sta. WTAO Radio, 1983, 84, Ann. Cmty. Svc. award Modern Woodmen Am., 1982, Citizen of Yr. award Murphysboro C. of C., 1984, 2002, Disting. Educator award Phi Delta Kappa, 1991, Founder award Murphysboro Apple Festival, 2000, Joseph P. Whitehead Educator of Distinction award, 2002. Mem.: NEA, Murphysboro Edn. Assn., Ill. Edn. Assn., Key Club, Kiwanis (pres. 1977—78, chmn. spl. club svcs. Ill.-Ea. Iowa dist. 1984—85, Mid. sch. Builders Club advisor 1993—, cert. trainer 1993—, gov-elect 1995—96, Ill.-Ea. Iowa resolutions chmn. 2000—, counsellor 2001—, v.p. Internat. Conf. Key Club Adminstrs. 2003—, Kiwanis Internat. com. on Key Clubs 2003—, long range planning com. for Key Club, Target 2000, Key Club past dist. gov., Dr. Luis V. Amador medallion 1995, G. Harold Martin fellow 1996, Gerge F. Hixson fellow Diamond 2 Level I 1996—98), Key Club (advisor 1972—, lt. gov. dist. divsn. 1984—85, adminstr. Ill.-Ea. Iowa dist. 1985—96, 2002—, mem. com. of Key Clubs

2003—, I-I dist. Key Club James R. Hall achievement award named in his honor 1999). Avocations: collecting books and plates, bowling, tennis. Home: 28 Candy Ln Murphysboro IL 62966-2953 Office: Murphysboro H S 16 Blackwood Dr Murphysboro IL 62966-2937

HALL, JAMES GRANVILLE, JR., history educator; b. Phila., Aug. 22, 1917; s. James Granville and Jane Margaret (Moorehead) H.; m. Eva Mae Woodruff, June 1946; 1 child, Evelyn Alison. AB, George Washington U., 1950; cert., Georgetown U., 1951; postgrad., U. Colo., Colorado Springs, 1965-67; MA, Va. State U., 1972. Commd. 2nd lt. U.S. Army, 1943; transferred to USAF, 1948, advanced through ranks to lt. col., 1961; aircraft controller U.S. Army, Panama, U.S., 1943-50; various assignments, 1950-64; comdr. dir. staff officer, weapons staff officer NORAD, 1964-67; comdr. MDC, King Salmon, 1968, Air Def. Sector, King Salmon, Alaska, 1967-68; dir. ops. 5th Tactical Control group, comdr. 605th Tactical Control Squadron, Clark Air Base, The Philippines, 1969-71; chief control & environ. 20th Air Div., Ft. Lee, Va., 1971-72; retired USAF, 1972; faculty history and govt. Austin (Tex.) C.C., Austin, 1973-93. Participant Mid. East Seminar, Fgn. Svc. Inst., U.S. Dept. State, Washington, 1953; lectr. civic and garden clubs, Tex., 1974—. Author: Men's Garden Club Show and Judges Handbook, 1980; contbr. articles to profl. jours. Polit. worker, Austin, 1974—2000; bd. dirs. Colorado Springs Opera Assn., 1967; organizer, leader Girl Scouts Am., Opheim, 1959—60; pres. Little League, Itazuke, Japan, 1961—63; mem. Austin Lyric Opera, 1987—90; guest expert TV and radio garden shows Austin, 1976—. Decorated Meritorious Svc. medal, Joint Svcs. Commendation medal, Air Force Commendation medal, Am. Campaign medal, World War II Victory medal, Nat. Def. Svc. medal with 1 Bronze Star, Vietnam Svc. medal with 1 Bronze Star, Armed Forces Expeditionary medal, Combat Readiness medal with 1 Bronze Oak Leaf Cluster, Air Force Reserve medal, Air Force Outstanding Unit Citation, Master Weapons Dir. Badge; recipient Philippine Presidential Unit Citation for Humanitarian Svc., 1970-71. Mem.: Heritage Found., Capitol Area Chrysanthemum Soc. (pres. 1975, 2000—03), Nat. Chrysanthemum Soc. (accredited judge 1976—85, awards chmn. 1986—91, master judge 1986—), S.W. Chrysanthemum Region Soc. (organizer, pres. 1981—82), VFW (life), Claremont Inst., Men's Garden Club of Am. (accredited judge 1976—, nat. schs. and judges chmn. 1979—81, judge emeritus 2000—), Men's Garden Club (pres. 1977). Republican. Anglican. Avocations: gardening, bridge, computers. Home and Office: JE Hall Family Partnership 12317 SE 89th St Oklahoma City OK 73150

HALL, JAMES H(ERRICK), JR., philosophy educator, writer; b. Houston, Oct. 20, 1933; s. James Herrick and Loula Ben (Vining) H.; m. Bonlyn Goodwin, 1957 (div. 1977); children: Christopher Vining, Jonathan Goodwin; m. Myfanwy Seaver Monroe, 1977; 1 child, Charles Trevor. AB, Johns Hopkins U., 1955; BD, Southeastern Sem., Wake Forest, N.C., 1958, ThM, 1960; PhD, U. N.C., Chapel Hill, 1964. Instr. philosophy U. N.C., Chapel Hill, 1960-62; asst. prof. Furman U., Greenville, S.C., 1963-65; assoc. prof. U. Richmond, Va., 1965-74, chmn. dept. philosophy, 1965-89, 94-96, 99—, prof., 1974—, The Thomas chair, 1982—, univ. quest dir., 1999-2001. Author: Knowledge Belief and Transcendence, 1975, Logic Problems, 1991; (with others) Biblical and Secular Ethics, 1988, Philosophy of Religion, 2003. Mem. vestry St. Paul's Episc. Ch., Richmond, 1988-91; profl. ch. musician, Chapel Hill, Raleigh, Balt., Washington, Richmond. NamedDisting. Educator, U. Richmond, 2001; Coun. for Philosophic Studies fellow, Grand Rapids, 1973, U. Warwick fellow, Coventry, U.K., 1989-90, Kenan fellow U. N.C., 1960-61; rsch. grantee Duke Found., Durham, 1964, Mednick Trust, 1973-74. Mem. AAUP (chpt. pres. 1991-92), Am. Philos. Assn., Soc. for Philosophy of Religion, So. Soc. for Philosophy and Psychology, Omicron Delta Kappa. Democrat. Episcopalian. Avocations: choral music, camping, computers, travel. Home: 209 Wood Rd Richmond VA 23229-7538 Office: U Richmond Dept Philosophy North Ct Richmond VA 23173 E-mail: jhall@richmond.edu.

HALL, JAMES RAYFORD, III, adult educator; b. Chgo., Sept. 4, 1946; s. James Rayford and Hortense Elizabeth (Jones) H. BA, Langston U., 1968; MA, Ball State U., 1970. History tchr. Chgo. Bd. Edn., 1968-86; history instr. Joliet (Ill.) Jr. Coll., 1970-71, Kennedy-King Coll., Chgo., 1987-91; instr. Gary (Ind.) Community Schs., 1987—, at-risk specialist, 1988-89; history instr. Calumet Coll., Whiting, Ind., 1989-91; polit. sci. and sociology instr. Ivy Tech State Coll., Gary, Ind., 1996—. Precinct Capt. 17th Ward Democratic Party, Chgo., 1978-81. Fellow Polit. Socialization of Disadvantage Youth, Ball State U. Office of Edn., 1969. Mem. Nat. Tchrs. Assn., Am.Fedn. Tchrs., Am. Polit. Sci. Assn., Am. Black Polit. Scientist Assn., TransAfrica. Democrat. Baptist. Avocations: photography, writing. Home: 584 Roosevelt St Gary IN 46404-1310 Office: Interplanetary Music BMI 584 Roosevelt St Gary IN 46404-1310

HALL, J(AMES) R(OBERT), English educator; b. Rochester, N.Y., Mar. 17, 1946; s. James Robert and Helen Grace (Schauseil) H.; m. Joan Marie Wylie, Aug. 17, 1974; children: Jennifer Joy Wylie Hall, Justin James Wylie Hall. BA, St. John Fisher Coll., 1968; MA, U. Notre Dame, 1970, PhD, 1973. Vis. lectr. U. Ill., Urbana, 1973-74; instr. English St. Mary-of-Woods (Ind.) Coll., 1975; asst. prof. U. Miss., University, 1978-84, assoc. prof., 1984-90, prof., 1990—. Scholarship reviewer Old English Newsletter Western Mich. U., 1976—2001; referee scholarly manuscripts; cons. Nat. Endowment Humanities, Washington, 1990—. Contbr. essays to profl. jours. Adviser Ole Miss Coll. Reps., University, 1995—; mem. exec. com. Lafayette County Rep. Party. Am. Coun. Learned Socs. rsch. fellow, 1981-82; Harvard U. tchg.-rsch. fellow, 1983-84, NEH rsch. fellow, 1993-94; Earhart Found. rsch. fellow, 2000. Mem. Medieval Acad. Am., Internat. Soc. Anglo-Saxonists, South Atlantic Modern Lang. Assn., Am. Friends Bodleian Libr., Assn. Lit. Scholars and Critics, Nat. Assn. Scholars. Roman Catholic. Home: 1705 Johnson Ave Oxford MS 38655-4725 Office: U Miss Dept English University MS 38677-1848 E-mail: jrhall@olemiss.edu.

HALL, JAMES WILLIAM, university chancellor; b. Chester, Pa., Oct. 14, 1937; s. James William and Margaret (Crothers) H.; children: Laura, Janet, Carol. MusB, Bucknell U., 1959; M of Sacred Music, Union Theol. Sem., 1961; MA, U. Pa., 1964, PhD, 1967; DHL (hon.), Thomas Edison State Coll. N.J., 1992, U. Sys. N.H., 1994, DePaul U., 1996. Instr. Cedar Crest Coll., Allentown, Pa., 1961-66; vis. asst. prof. SUNY, Albany, 1966-71, asst. acad. personnel, sys. adminstrn., 1966-68; assoc. univ. dean univ.-wide activities, 1968-70; asst. vice chancellor policy and planning, 1970-71; pres. Empire State Coll. SUNY, Saratoga Springs, 1971-97; interim pres. SUNY Coll., Old Westbury, N.Y., 1981-82; vice-chancellor for ednl. tech. SUNY System, 1993-95; chancellor Antioch U., Yellow Springs, Ohio, 1998—2002, chancellor emeritus, 2002—. Editor: Am. Problem Series, Forging the American Character, 1971, (with B. Kevles) In Opposition to Core Curriculum: Alternative Models for Undergraduate Education, 1982, Access Through Innovation: New Colleges for New Students, 1991; contbr. articles to profl. jours. Trustee Monmouth Coll., N.J., 1981-93, U.S. Open U., 1999-02, Fielding Inst., Calif., 1990-99, chair 1995-97; bd. dirs. Saratoga Hosp., 1990-93, Nat. Commn. on Coop. Edn., 1999-02; bd. overseers Nelson A. Rockefeller Inst. Govt., SUNY, 1983-95. Danforth fellow, 1959-67 Mem. Am. Studies Assn., Soc. Values in Higher Edn., Am. Assn. Higher Edn., Assn. Am. Colls. (bd. dirs. 1986-89), Coun. for Adult and Experiential Learning (bd. dirs., chmn. 1987-88).

HALL, JEAN QUINTERO, communications and history educator; b. Manila, July 28, 1946; came to U.S., 1963; d. Evan Drake Moody and Victoria (Quintero) Bombon; m. Edward Payson Hall. BA in Comm., U. Wash., 1978; MPA, U. Del., 1984. Faculty Kapiolani C.C., Honolulu, 1984-85; cmty. developer Cath. Social Svcs., Honolulu, 1985; adminstr. City & County of Honolulu, 1985-86; faculty New River C.C., Dublin, Va., 1986-90; adminstr. Radford (Va.) U., 1987-89, faculty, 1989-92; pres. Global Soc., Radford, 1989-92; ind. cons. Silver City, N.Mex., 1992-94; faculty Western N.Mex. U., Silver City, 1994—. Spkr. in field; columnist Filipino-Am. J., Phoenix, 1999—. Author: Desiderate Melodies, 1990, Rizal - Our Beloved Beacon, 1996. Grantee Commonwealth Va., 1991. Mem. Pacific & Asian Comm. Assn., Asian Studies/Philippine Studies Group, Filipino Am. Educators Assn., Filipino Cultural Heritage Soc., Filipino Am. Assn. N.Mex., Sigma Iota Epsilon. Avocation: writing. Home: 20 Vista Grande Silver City NM 88061-6613 E-mail: lysander@cybermesa.com.

HALL, JEROME WILLIAM, research engineering educator; b. Brunswick, Ga., Dec. 1, 1943; s. William L. and Frances K. H.; m. Loretta E. Hood, Aug. 28, 1965; children: Jennifer, Bridget, Bernadette. BS in Physics, Harvey Mudd Coll., 1965; MS in Engring., U. Wash., 1968, PhDCE, 1969. Registered profl. engr., D.C., N.Mex., Va. Asst. prof. civil engring. U. Md., College Park, 1970-73, assoc. prof., 1973-77, U. N.Mex., Albuquerque, 1977-80, prof., 1980—, dir. bur. engring. research, 1981-88, asst. dean engring., 1985-88, chmn. dept. of civil engring., 1990-97. Cons. in field. Contbr. articles to profl. jours. Recipient Teetor award Soc. Automotive Engrs., 1975; Pub. Partnership award Alliance For Transportation Rsch., 1997. Fellow Inst. Transp. Engrs. (pres. N.Mex. sect. 1985, pres. western dist. 1989, internat. bd. dirs. 1993-95)); mem. Transp. Rsch. Bd. (chmn. com. 1986-92, chmn. group coun. 1992-95, panel chmn. 1990—), Am. Soc. Engring. Edn., Am. Rd. and Transp. Builders Assn. (pres. rsch. and edn. divsn. 2002-03), Nat. Assn. County Engrs. Republican. Roman Catholic. Office: Dept Civil Engring MSC01 1070 1UNM Albuquerque NM 87131-0001 E-mail: jerome@unm.edu.

HALL, JOHN FRANKLIN, classicist, educator; b. Jacksonville, Fla., Apr. 14, 1951; s. John F. and Ann B. (Lord) H.; m. Eliza Anne Lee, Dec. 11, 1998; children: John, James, Jefferson. BA, Brigham Young U., 1975; MA, U. Pa., 1978, PhD, 1983. Instr. classics Brigham Young U., Provo, Utah, 1978-83, asst. prof. classics and ancient history, 1983-89, assoc. prof. classics and ancient history, 1989-94, prof. classics and ancient history, 1994—, dept. chair humanities classics and comparative lit., 1992-96. Dir. Inst. for Study and Preservation of Ancient Religious Texts, 2000—. Author: Etruscan Italy, 1995, Masada and the World of the New Testament, 1997, Charting the New Testament, 2000, New Testament Witnesses of Christ: Peter, John, James, and Paul, 2002; contbr. articles to profl. jours. Chair Utah County Bd. Adjustment, Provo, 1990-93; pres. Highland Kiwanis Club, Highland, Utah, 1992-93. Summer fellow Vergilian Soc. Am., Rome, 1983; Faculty Rsch. grantee Brigham Young U., 1983-93. Mem. Classical Assn. Middle West and South (v.p. 1978-95, exec. sec. 1990-95, nat. pres. 1996-97, nat. dir., bd. dirs. 1987-95, chair various coms., Outstanding State V.p. award 1986), Utah Classical Assn. (chief officer, pres. 1985-88). Office: Brigham Young Univ 3010 Jhkb Provo UT 84602-1031 E-mail: John_Hall@BYU.EDU.

HALL, JOHN THOMAS, lawyer, educator; b. Phila., May 14, 1938; s. John Thomas and Florence Sara (Robinson) H.; m. Carolyn Park Currie, May 26, 1968; children: Daniel Currie, Kathleen Currie. AB, Dickinson Coll., 1960; MA, U. Md., 1963; JD, U. N.C., 1972. Bar: N.C. 1972. Chmn. dept. speech Mercersburg (Pa.) Acad., 1960-63, U. Balt., 1963-69; research asst. N.C. Ct. Appeals, Raleigh, 1972-73, dir. pre-hearing research staff, 1974-75, asst. clk., marshall, librarian, 1980-81; counsel Dorothea Dix Hosp., Raleigh, 1974; asst. dist. atty. State of N.C., Raleigh, 1975-80, 81-83; pvt. practice Raleigh, 1973-74, 83—. Mem. faculty King's Bus. Coll., Raleigh, 1973-75, N.C. Bar Assn., 1987—; undercover inmate Cen. Prison Duke Ctr. on Law and Poverty, Durham, N.C., 1970; vis. lectr. dept. comm. N.C. State U., 2000—; faculty U. Phoenix Online, 2003—. Mem. Raleigh Little Theatre, Theatre in the Park, Raleigh; charter mem. Wake County Dem. Men's Club, 1977—. Named Best Actor, Raleigh Little Theatre, 1975, 77, 80, 82, 85, 86, 93, 98. Mem.: Neuse River Valley Model R.R. (Raleigh), ABA, Wake County Acad. Criminal Trial Lawyers (v.p. 1986—87), 10th Jud. Dist. Bar Assn. (bd. dirs. 1986—89, chmn. grievance com. 1987—90), Wake County Bar Assn. (bd. dirs. 1986—89, vice chmn. exec. com. 1986—87), N.C. Bar Assn., Scottish Clan Gunn Soc. Avocations: model railroading, reading. Office: PO Box 1207 Raleigh NC 27602-1207

HALL, KENNETH RICHARD, chemical engineering educator, consultant; b. Tulsa, Okla., Nov. 5, 1939; s. Snipes Webster and Selina Rose (Scarpin) H.; m. Janet Beulah Blood, June, 1964 (div. 1975); children: Tara Marie, Deirdre Rene; m. Frieda Maria Karner, Mar. 12, 1976; children: Kent Max, Keith Anton, Krysta Maria. BS ChemE, U. Tulsa, 1962; MS, U. Calif., Berkeley, 1964; PhD, U. Okla., 1967. Registered engr., Tex. Asst. prof. U. Va., Charlottesville, 1967-70, 71-74; asst. to pres. ChemShare Corp., Norman, Okla., 1970; sr. rsch. engr. AMOCO, Tulsa, 1970-71; vis. prof. U. Louvain, Belgium, 1971-72; assoc. prof. Tex. A&M U., College Station, 1974-78, prof., 1978—, dir. Thermodynamics Rsch. Ctr., 1979-85, 97-2000, asst. dir. Tex. Engring. Experiment Sta., 1985-88, assoc. dean engring., 1987—94, 2002—, from assoc. dir. to dep. dir., 1988—94, 2002—, assoc. dep. chancellor for engring., 1990—94, 2002—, interim head petroleum engring., 1991, interim head chem. engring., 1994; dir. CTS divsn. NSF, Va., 1994-96; GPSA prof. Tex. A&M U., College Station, 1997-2000, Jack E. and Frances Brown chair, 2001—, head dept. chem. engring., 2002—. Cons. OPC Engring., Houston, 1980-85, Quantum Tech., Houston, 1981-85; cons. Precision Measurement Inc., Duncanville, Tex., 1981-90; bd. dirs. Lorax Corp., Syn Fuels. U.S. editor Flow Measurement and Instrumentation; contbr. over 200 articles to profl. jours. Recipient numerous grants for research. Mem.: Am. Inst. Chem. Engrs. (chmn. ctrl. Va. chpt. 1969, chmn. cyrogenics 1977—79, exec. position II South Tex. sect. 1991—92, bd. dirs. fuels and petrochems. divsn. 1992—94), Am. Soc. Engring. Edn., Am. Chem. Soc., ASTM (chmn. D-3 1985—91, 1994—2001). Avocations: sports, reading. Home: 1401 Millcreek Ct College Station TX 77845-8352 Office: Tex A&M U Dept Chem Engring College Station TX 77843

HALL, LAWRENCE JOHN, physics educator; b. Perivale, U.K., Sept. 9, 1955; came to U.S., 1977; s. Kenneth and Patricia Kathleen (Stock) H.; m. Paula Louise Petti, June 27, 1982; children: Geoffrey Kenneth, David Lawrence. BA, Oxford U., Eng., 1977; MA, Harvard U., 1978, PhD, 1981. Miller fellow U. Calif., Berkeley, 1981-83, from asst. prof. to prof. physics, 1986—; from asst. to assoc. prof. Harvard U., Cambridge, Mass., 1983-86. Contbr. over 150 articles in rsch. jours. Recipient Presdl. Young Investigator award NSF, 1987-92. Fellow Am. Phys. Soc. Office: Univ of Calif Dept Physics Berkeley CA 94720-0001

HALL, LINDA NORTON, principal, reading specialist; b. Houston, Oct. 7, 1947; d. Charles E. Norton and Carol (Kirkpatrick) Allen-Poulos; m. Robert William Hall, Jan. 28, 1967; children: Christoper M., Kevin M., Michelle K. Student, Tarleton State U., 1965-67; BA with distinction, San Jose State U., 1969; postgrad., U. Florence, Italy, 1970-71; MA in Edn./Reading with honors, U. Tex., Permian Basin, 1996. Cert. elem. tchr. K-9, Calif., tchr. elem. and sociology, Tex.; cert. Reading Recovery trained tchr., Tex., advanced Reading Recovery, Ohio. 4th grade math. and sci. tchr. Los Arboles Elem., San Jose, Calif., 1969; tchr. 1st and 3rd grades K.R. Smith Elem., San Jose, 1969-72; tchr. ESL Dr. Russell Elem., Garden Grove, Calif., 1972; tchr. 1st and 1st/2nd combination A. Smith Elem., Huntington Beach, Calif., 1972-75; tchr. 3rd grade Travis Elem., Midland, Tex., 1988-91; reading specialist, reading recovery tchr. Crockett Elem. Sch., Midland, 1991-99, title I lead tchr., 1995-2001, coord. staff devel., 1995-2001, asst. prin., 1999-2001; prin. Jane Long Elem. Sch., 2001—. Campus resource rep. Crockett Elem. Sch., Midland, 1991-99, compter technologist, 1992-2001, study group facilitator, 1994-97; rep., sec. sight-based mgmt. com. Campus Ednl. Improvement Coun., Midland, 1992-2001; coord./liaison Mobil Oil and Midland Ind. Sch. Dist., 1991-2000; coord., liaison Cotton, Bledsoe, Tighe & Dawson Law Firm, Midland Ind. Sch. Dist. Photographer: Balboa Island in Zoom, 1973 (1st pl. award 1970); seamstress: Child Busy Book: Orange County Fair, 1977 (1st pl. award). Study group mem. Bible Study Fellowship, Calif., Tex., 1973-85; presch. tchr./leader Cmty. Bible Study, Midland, 1985-88; swim meet timer City of Midland Swim Team, 1986-92; tchr. 8th and 11th grade Sunday Sch. First Bapt. Ch., Midland, 1986-97; liaison/coord. Ptnrs. in Edn., Midland, 1991-2001. Recipient horse tng./showing awards, 1960-65; named Parent of Yr. Midland Bapt. Schs., 1985, Tchr. of Yr. Crockett Elem., Midland C. of C., 1994; recipient Austin Meml. Tchr. Scholarship Midland PTA, 1991, Pegasus Grant awards-1st pl. Mobil Oil, Midland, 1991-94, 96-97; Mobil Found. grantee schoolwide thematic unit structures, 1994, 95. Mem. Internat. Reading Assn., Tex. State Reading Assn., Midland PTA, Midland Reading Coun. (sec. 1992-93,v.p. 1993-94), Reading Recovery Coun. N.Am., Delta Kappa Gamma, Phi Delta Kappa. Baptist. Avocations: photography, backpacking, walking, reading, horseback riding. Home: 1501 W Pine Ave Midland TX 79705-6526 Office: Jane Long Elem Sch Midland Ind Sch Dist 4200 Cedar Spring Dr Midland TX 79703

HALL, LOIS BREMER, retired educator, volunteer; b. Oak Park, Ill., July 27, 1923; d. Frederick Statler and Mabel (Forbes) Bremer; m. Bruce Hall, Sept. 9, 1955 (dec. Mar. 1981); children: Donald, Richard, Barbara. B in Music Edn., U. Mich., 1946. Cert. elem., secondary tchr. Mich., Ky.; ordained elder Presbyn. Ch. Tchr. handbell ringing Elm St. Recreation Ctr., Atlantic Recreation Ctr. Handbell ringer AARP, Osprey Village and Quality Health, Bapt. Hosp., 1st Presbyn. Ch. Fernandina Beach; dir. Amelia Handbell Choir; singer Amelia Island Chorale, Meml. United Meth. Ch., Amelia Plantation Chapel, Amelia Bapt. Ch., St. Peter's Episcopal Ch. Mem. com. Peck Ctr.; founding mem., vol. coord. CROP Walk, 1989—99; mem. exec. bd. Meml. United Meth. Ch.; vol. Church World Svc., Fernandina Beach, Synod of South Atlantic Coun., 1989; mem. Presbytery of St. Augustine Coun., 1984—97, music coord. of handbell and choral workshops, 1990—98; mem. hunger com. Presbyn. Gen. Assembly, 1992—96; vol.-in-mission New Hope Meth. Presbyn. Ch., N. Pole, Alaska, 1991—94, 1996; soloist, clarinet Ch. Choirs; bd. dirs. Amelia Arts Acad., 1994—2003, Ann. Fernandina Beach Talent Show, 2001—02. Recipient award for cultural enrichment, City of Fernandina Beach, 2001. Mem.: AARP (bd. dirs.), Woman's Club Fernandina Beach (pres. 1983—84, 1991—92, Outstanding New Mem. 1980—81, Cmty. Svc. award 1987—88), Rose Garden Club (treas. 1998—2002), Alpha Omicron Pi, Delta Omicron. Republican. Home: 607 Goldenrod Way Saint Marys GA 31558

HALL, LORENE MARY, elementary school administrator; b. Miami Beach, Fla., July 31, 1961; d. Henry Thomas and Eugenia Devene (Guidry) H. BS in Elem. Edn., Miami Christian Coll., 1984. Tchr. Asbury Christian Sch., Hialeah, Fla., 1983-84, Dade Christian Sch., Miami, Fla., 1984-89, supr., 1989—. Named Tchr. of the Yr. Dade Christian Sch., 1988. Republican. Baptist. Avocations: reading, camping, biking, swimming, crafts.

HALL, LULA, retired special education educator; b. Eastman, Ga., Oct. 11, 1942; d. Lawrence and Lizzie Jackson Hall. BS, postgrad., Tuskegee U. Cert. spl. edn. tchr. Ga. Tchr. Ga. Dept. Juvenile Justice, Eastman, Dodge County Bd. Edn., Eastman; ret., 1997. Author poetry; contbr. articles to local newspaper. Sec. United Concerned Citizens of Dodge County, Eastman, 1994—99; vol. Dodge County Hosp. Aux./Pink Ladies, 1997—; actove civil rights projects and cmty. improvement. Recipient cert. of appreciation, Dodge County chpt. NAACP, Eastman, 1990. Baptist. Home: PO Box 844 Eastman GA 31023-0844

HALL, MADELON CAROL SYVERSON, elementary education educator; b. Kerkhoven, Minn., Dec. 27, 1937; d. Reuben C. and Hattie C. (Anderson) Syverson; m. Lewis D. Hall, June 13, 1959 (dec. 1984); children: Warren L., Charmaine D. BA, Trinity Bible Coll., Chgo., 1959; MEd, U.Cin., 1973. Cert. tchr., Ohio. Dir. admissions, asst. registrar Trinity Bible Coll., 1959-62; supr. elem. music edn. Dist. 80 Cook County Schs., Norridge, Ill., 1962-65; tchr. Rockford (Ill.) City Schs., 1966-67; tchr. music elem. grades Boone County Pub. Schs., Florence, Ky., 1970-72, Oak Hills Local Sch. Dist., Cin., 1972—. Also bldg. career coord., Jr. Achievement coord., safety patrol sponsor; mem. sch. improvement team. Composer: Seven Ways to Grow for Children's Mus., 1991. Dir. Summer Safety Village Program, 1987-91, Cin. May Festival Chorus, 1991-1993. Recipient Spl. Projects award Great Oaks Career Devel., 1992; named Tchr. of Yr. Oak Hills Sch. Dist, 1990-91, Ptnr. with PTA award, 2002-03. Mem. NEA, Ohio Edn. Assn., Music Educators Nat. Conf., Career Edn. Assn. (Tchr. of Yr. Ohio unit 1989-90), The Hunger Project, Just Say No Club. Methodist. Avocations: vocal music, piano, composing. Home: 456 Happy Dr Cincinnati OH 45238-5254

HALL, MARGARET JEAN (MARGOT HALL), biochemistry educator; b. Boston, Mar. 25, 1942; d. Robert King and Margaret (Wheeler) H. AB in Chemistry, French, U. N.C., 1964; MS in Chemistry, U. Denver, 1971; PhD in Biochemistry, U. N.C., 1984. Med. technologist U. N.C., Chapel Hill, 1963-65, rsch. asst., 1965-84, postdoctoral/rsch. asst., 1984-85; asst. prof. U. So. Miss., Hattiesburg, 1985-91, assoc. prof., 1991-97, full prof., 1997—. Contbr. articles to profl. jours. Fellow Am. Inst. Chemists; mem. Am. Soc. Clin. Pathologists, Am. Assn. Clinic Chemistry, Miss. Acad. Sci. (past pres.), Royal Soc. Chemistry. Republican. Episcopalian. Home: 104 Kensington Dr Hattiesburg MS 39402-1933 Office: U So Miss PO Box 5134 Hattiesburg MS 39406-1000 E-mail: margot.hall@usm.edu.

HALL, MARIAN M. retired music educator; b. York, Pa., June 22, 1932; d. Thomas Adrian and Olive Murray Martin; m. John H. Hall, June 1, 1953; children: Debra Grey, Cindy Dolen, Michael, Daniel. BA, Western Md. Coll., 1953; M Equivalence, Towson State U., 1972. Music tchr. Balt. City Schs., 1971—95; ret., 1995. Organist, choir dir. Rocklin Meth. Ch.; with Beth Ifiloh Summer Camp, Pikesville, Md.; piano tchr. Jason's Music Store, 1990—. Mem.: Suzuki Assn., Music Educators Nat. Conf. Avocations: music, camping, hiking, boating, swimming. Home: 4600 Lincoln Dr Baltimore MD 21227

HALL, MARIE-JOYEE FAITH, Spanish and English language educator; b. Jersey City; d. Frederic Michael and Marie F. Claudia (Melè) Contey; m. Samual Xavier Conca, Sept. 6, 1947 (dec. Nov. 1964); 1 child, Marie-Joyee Abagail Holian; m. Walter Tildon Hall (dec.). AABA, Ocean County Coll., 1969; BA, Georgian Ct. Coll., 1972. Substitute tchr. Ocean County Sch., 1968—; tchr. Kavner Sch., 1971; tchr. Spanish and English N.J. State Program, Lakewood, 1978—. Author: Tapestries-An Anthology, 1988, Narda-Nymphae del Mar, 1999, Pirate Ship, 1999, Great Sea Bird, 1999, Toy Fella and Friends (Tetralogy), Tangles of Movements and Outdoor Spoken Words, Big Store, A Story of Fella, Warmhearted Lum, Fella and Sweetie, A Story of Play Fella and His Friends, Ol' Solly Guyon's Trolley Train and Aeroplane, 2000, 15 children's books, short stories, poems, Aunt Kit and the Baby Stars. Committeewoman Bricktown Dem. Club, 1978-80. Roman Catholic.

HALL, MARVIN, psychology educator, counselor; b. Elizabethtown, N.C., Nov. 5, 1948; s. Grover Cleveland and Pearl (Smith) H.; m. Virginia Christine Warren, Aug. 2, 1980. BS in Polit. Sci., A&T State U., 1971, MS in Edn., 1979; EdD, Western Mich. U., 1991. Apprentice counselor credential in substance abuse. Tchr. occupl. edn. Pub. Sch. Sys. Bladen County, Elizabethtown, N.C.; customer svc. agt. Major Airlines, Greensboro, N.C.; asst. dir. Luth. Family Svcs., Inc., Burlington, N.C.; counselor, media technician II Fayetteville State U., Fayetteville, N.C.; doctoral rsch., tchr. asst. Western Mich. U., Kalamazoo, grad. sch. chairperson grad. student adv. com.; asst. dir. Youth Opportunity Homes, Inc., Winston-

Salem, N.C.; adj. prof. psychology Winston Salem State U. Asst. prof. A & T. State U., Greensboro; adj. prof. Social Sci. Dept., Surry C.C., Greensboro, Guilford Tech. C.C., Greensboro. Mem. ASCD. Avocations: all sports, music, rev. of lit. psychology/counseling, travel, advocating for underprivileged. Address: 227 Hedrick Dr Kernersville NC 27284-2309

HALL, MARY HUGH, retired secondary school educator; b. Sumter, S.C., Apr. 15, 1937; d. Hughson Perry and Virginia Dare (Owens) Matthews; m. James Wallace Hall Sr., July 2, 1960; 1 child, James Wallace Jr. BA in Social Studies and French, Columbia Coll., 1959; postgrad., West Ga. Coll., 1975-79. Tchr. Arlington (Ga.) Schs., Inc., 1959-61; tchr., chair French dept. Douglas County H.S., Douglasville, Ga., 1965—97; ret., 1997. Mem. steering com. West Ga. Alliance, Carrollton, 1992—. Recipient Outstanding Officer award Jaycees, 1970, 71. Mem. NEA, Douglas County Assn. Educators, Ga. Assn. Educators. Avocations: dancing, reading, cooking, wood crafts. Home: 4679 Bedford Pl Douglasville GA 30135-1805

HALL, MERRILL SOUEL, III, head master; b. New Orleans, Dec. 5, 1944; s. Merrill Souel and Sylvia (Young) H.; m. Bronwen Patterson, Nov. 22, 1969; children: Aubrie, Erin. BS, La. State U., 1967, MEd, 1970; MLA, Johns Hopkins U., Balt., 1989. Cert. type A lifetime tchr., counselor, prin., supr., adminstr., La. Tchr. J.C. Ellis Pub. Sch., New Orleans, 1967-70, Metairie Park Country Sch., New Orleans, 1970-74, head lower sch., 1974-79; prin. St. John's Lower Sch., Houston, 1979-83; head master Calvert Sch., Balt., 1983—. Evaluator U.S. Dept. Edn., Washington, 1990—. Trustee Calvert Sch., 1983—; bd. dirs. Kinder-Care, Inc., Montgomery, Ala., 1988-90. Recipient Andrew White medal, Loyola Coll., Md., 2003. Mem.: Elem. Sch. Heads Assn. (pres. 2002—03), Oxford Round Table. Office: Calvert Sch 105 Tuscany Rd Baltimore MD 21210-3098 E-mail: hall@calvertschool.org.

HALL, MINA ELAINE, geriatrics nurse; b. Oakes, N.D., Sept. 22, 1953; d. Bryan J.W. Tyson and Emma Adelaide Durbin; m. Thomas Edward Hall, Feb. 23, 1979; children: John Joseph, Patrick Michael. BS, Winona State U., 1975; MS, S.D. State U., 1990; student, N.Am. Baptist Sem., 2001—03. Staff nurse, supr. Wadena (Minn.) Tri County Hosp., 1975-76; staff nurse Abbott-Northwestern Hosp., Mpls., 1976-79; lic. practice nursing instr. Worthington (Minn.) C.C., 1979-84; instr. nursing Augustana Coll., Sioux Falls, S.D., 1984-86; dir. nursing Luther Manor, Sioux Falls, 1990; instr. U. S.D., Vermillion, 1991-96; exec. dir. S.D. Nurses Assn., Sioux Falls, 1996—2001. Mem. S.D. Bd. Examiners Nursing Home Adminstrs., Sioux Falls, 1993—; assoc. project dir. Colleagues in Caring, Sioux Falls, 1998-2001. Chair S.D. Covering Kids Coalition, Sioux Falls, 2000-01. Grantee VA, 1989. Mem. S.D. Nurses Assn. (Dist. Nurse of Yr. 1989), Sioux Falls Sister Cities Assn. (pres. 1999-2001), S.D. League Women Voters (pres. 1995-99, natural resources chair 1986-91), Sioux Falls League Women Voters (pres. 1991, bd. dirs. 1992-96); Sigma Theta Tau. Avocations: reading, organic gardening, skiing, piano.

HALL, PHYLLIS CHARLENE, therapist, counselor; b. LA, Mar. 18, 1957; d. Clellan James Jr. and Yvonne Rayedith Hall. BA, Whittier Coll., 1979; MS in Phys. Edn., Calif. State U., Fullerton, 1985, MS in Counseling, 1988; PhD in Psychology, U.S. Internat. U., 1996. Cert. critical incident debriefing. Coach varsity girls basketball, softball Calif. HS, Whittier, Calif., 1979-80; counselor Rio Hondo Coll., Whittier, Calif., 1980-88; coach asst. girls varsity basketball Long Beach Wilson H.S., Calif., 1985-88; therapist intern Turning Point Counseling, Garden Grove, Calif., 1988-89; counselor Long Beach City Coll., 1988—, girls acad. advisor, 1989-94, asst. coach girls basketball, 1993-94; psychologist asst./intern Family Svc. Long Beach, 1994-98. Bd. dir. Long Beach City Coll.; mem. adv. bd. U. Calif. C.C.; exec. bd. Long Beach City Coll., 1997—2001. Author: Liberators from Planet Liberx, 1985. Mem. cmty. adv. coun. U. Calif., 1996-98; co-sponsor African Am. in Unity Long Beach City Coll., 1990-92; com. mem. 1st Annual African Am. Achievement Conf., San Diego, 1994. Recipient PhD Student Achievement award dept. marriage and family therapy USIU, 1996. Mem.: NEA, Long Beach City Coll. Counselors Assn., Calif. Tchr. Assn. (del. 2000—03), C.C. Assn., Women in Arts (founding). Avocations: reading african culture and history, basketball, racquetball, writing. Office: Long Beach City Coll 1305 E Pch Long Beach CA 90806

HALL, ROBERT ERNEST, economics educator; b. Palo Alto, Calif., Aug. 13, 1943; s. Victor Ernest and Frances Marie (Gould) H.; m. Susan E. Woodward; children: Christopher, Anne, Jonathan, Andrew. BA, U. Calif.-Berkeley, 1964; PhD, MIT, 1967. Asst. prof., acting assoc. prof. U. Calif., Berkeley, 1967-70; from assoc. prof. to prof. MIT, Cambridge, 1970-78; prof., sr. fellow Stanford U. (Calif.), 1978—, Robert and Carole McNeil joint prof. and sr. fellow, 1998. Dir. econ. fluctuation program Nat. Bur. Econ. Research, Cambridge, 1978— ; adv. com. Congl. Budget Office, Washington, 1993—. Author: Macroeconomics, 1985, 5th rev. edit., 1997, Booms and Recessions in a Noisy Economy, 1990, The Rational Consumer: Theory and Evidence, 1990, Flat Tax, 1995, Economics, 1997, 2d rev. edit., 2000, Digital Dealing, 2001; editor: Inflation, 1983. Woodrow Wilson fellow, 1964; Ford Found. faculty rsch. fellow, 1969 Fellow Econometric Soc., Am. Acad. Arts and Scis.; mem. Am. Econs. Assn., Am. Statis Assn. Democrat. Office: Stanford U Hoover Instn Stanford CA 94305 E-mail: hall@hoover.stanford.edu.

HALL, ROBERT JOSEPH, physician, medical educator; b. Buffalo, June 4, 1926; s. Joseph M. and Florence C. (Kirst) H.; m. Dorothy Nowak, Aug. 28, 1948; children: Thomas R., Kathleen A. Hall Noble, Mary J. Hall Stuart, Michael F., Steven E. Student, Canisius Coll., Buffalo, 1943-45; MD, U. Buffalo, 1948. Diplomate Am. Bd. Internal Medicine, Sub Bd. Cardiovascular Disease (mem. cardiovascular disease sect. 1969-75). Intern Mercy Hosp., Buffalo, 1948-49; commd. 1st lt. M.C. U.S. Army, 1948, advanced through grades to col., 1966; resident in internal medicine Walter Reed Gen. Hosp., Washington, 1949-52, resident in cardiovascular diseases, 1956-57; asst. cardiovascular research Walter Reed Army Inst. Research, 1957-58; service in Korea and Japan, 1952-55; chief cardiology service Brooke Gen. Hosp., Ft. Sam Houston, Tex., 1961-66, Walter Reed Gen. Hosp., 1966-69; ret., 1969; clin. assoc. prof. medicine Georgetown U. Med. Sch., 1967-69; clin. prof. medicine Baylor U. Coll. Medicine, Houston, 1969—, U. Tex. Med. Sch., Houston, 1977—; med. dir. Tex. Heart Inst., Houston, 1969-93, chmn. exec. com. profl. staff, 1969-93; dir. div. cardiology St. Luke's Episcopal Hosp., Houston, 1969-95, assoc. chief med. service, 1970-83; dir. edn., cardiology Tex. Heart Inst. Tex. Heart Inst. and St. Luke's Episcopal Hosp., 1992—2002, dir. emeritus, 2002—. Cons. Tex. Children's, VA, Brooke Gen. hosps., M.D. Anderson Hosp. and Tumor Inst.; mem. cardiovascular study sect. NIH, 1958-61; mem. phys. evaluation team Gemini project NASA, 1958-61; mem. nat. adv. heart counseil Dept. Def., 1966-69; adv. council Mended Hearts, 1970-78 Contbr. numerous articles med. jours. Mem. President's Adv. Panel Heart Disease. Decorated Legion of Merit; recipient Disting. Alumnus award Canisius Coll., 1975. Fellow A.C.P., Am. Coll. Cardiology (gov. 1968-71-74, chmn. bd. govs. and trustee 1973-74); mem. Am. Heart Assn. (fellow council clin. cardiology; pres. Houston chpt. 1974-75, advisor corp. cabinet 1980-86), Assn. Mil. Surgeons U.S., Assn. Advancement Med. Instrumentation, Pan Am. Med. Assn. (chmn. sect. cardiovascular diseases 1978-81), Assn. Univ. Cardiologists, Tex. Med. Assn., Tex. Cardiology Club, Harris County Med. Soc., Houston Cardiology Soc. (chmn. 1976-77), Houston Soc. Internal Medicine, Alpha Omega Alpha, 1948—. Home: 5504 Sturbridge Dr Houston TX 77056-1623 Office: 6624 Fannin St Ste 2480 Houston TX 77030-2309 E-mail: rjhall@wt.net.

HALL, ROGER LEE, musicologist, educator, composer; b. Glen Ridge, N.J., Nov. 13, 1942; Cert., Trinity Coll., London, 1967; BA, Rutgers U., 1970; MA, SUNY, 1972. Music cons. Nat. Geographic Soc., Washington, 1972; lectr. various colls., mus., 1974—; researcher, writer various jours., mags., 1975—; instr. Stonehill Coll., North Easton, Mass., 1979-82, Brookline (Mass.) Adult and Community Edn. Program, 1983-96; composer ASCAP, N.Y.C., 1985—; cable TV producer Pinetree Prodns., Stoughton, Mass., 1987—. Cons. Paul Revere House, Boston, 1981, The Shaker Seminar, Pittsfield, Mass., 1984-87. Editor: (music collection) The Happy Journey, 1982, Love is Little, 1992, Joy of Angels, 1995; composer: Piano Variations, 1984, Peace - A Patriotic Ode, 1989, A Little Theatre Music, 1990, Three Shaker Poems, 1996; feature writer: The World of Shaker, 1985—96; prodr., host Continental Cablevision, Stoughton, Mass., 1986; author: (pamphlet) Singing Stoughton, 1985, (booklets) Story of Simple Gifts, 1987, Music in Stoughton, 1989, The Stoughton Songster, 1991, A Guide to Film Music, 1997, 2d edit., 2002, A Guide to Shaker Music, 1997, 5th edit., 2002, New England Songster, 1997, A Guide to George Gershwin, 1998, Remembering Radio, 1998, A Guide to Christmas Music in America, 1999; radio tributes Sta. WBET-AM, 1985—93, Sta. WGBH-FM, 1981—98. Chmn. bd. Stoughton Arts Coun., 1980-84; mem. Town Hall Centennial Com., Stoughton, 1981. Served with U.S. Army, 1960-63. SUNY assistantship, 1971-72; Title IV fellow Case Western Res. U., 1972-74; Mass. Arts Lottery grantee, 1985-90. Mem.: Tune Lovers Soc. (pres. 2001—), Soc. For Am. Music, Old Stoughton Mus. Soc. (v.p. 1978—86), Shaker Study Group (pres. 1987—89). Lutheran. Avocations: collecting autographs, poetry, photography. Home and Office: 235 Prospect St Stoughton MA 02072-4163 E-mail: tunemaker3@aol.com.

HALL, SAMUEL M., JR., career educator, career development consultant; b. Saginaw, Mich., Dec. 23, 1937; s. Samuel M. and Marie Hall; m. Mary Josephine Fisher, Aug. 13, 1973; 1 child, John Anthony. AA, Ferris Inst., Big Rapids, Mich., 1962; AB, Western Mich. U., Kalamazoo, 1963; MA, Mich. State U., 1965. Coord. sch. dropout program Lansing (Mich.) Sch. System, 1964-65; dir. career devel., asst. prof. edn. Langston (Okla.) U., 1965-66; edn. advisor U.S. Office of Edn., Washington, 1966-67; dir. career planning and placement, acad. counselor Del. State Coll., Dover, 1967-70; dir. career svcs. Howard U., Washington, 1970—. Bd. dirs. Coun. Career Devel. for Minorities; editorial advisor CareerVision Mag., N.Y.C., 1988-90; feature author Black Collegian, New Orleans, 1985; mem. adv. bd. Kinexus, exec. bd. dirs. Mid. Atlantic Placement Assn., bd. govs. coll. placement coun., 1993—; chair commn. on career devel. for young adults, Nat. Voc. Guidance Assn. Author: Planning and Implementing the Careers Conference, 1975; contbr. articles to mags.; interviewed on radio and TV. Co-pres. Ind. Living for the Handicapped, Washington, 1990-91, pres.; v.p. Belmont Living for the Handicapped, Washington, 1990-91; Mayor's Youth Adv. Task Force, Washington, 1983-86; dep. dir. Summer Jobs Program, Washington, 1980; chair recognition com. Howard U., 1986-87; chair career counseling panel, 1989—. Recipient Outstanding Svc. award 1987, Middle Atlantic Placement Assn., 1985, Ed Parrish award, 1989. Mem. Alpha Phi Alpha (house mgr. 1964-65, corr. sec. 1964-65), Alpha Phi Omega Svcs. Orgn. (chpt. advisor 1968-70). Avocations: collecting antiques and afro-american paintings, cobalt blue glass and clear crystal. Home: 217 Rittenhouse St NW Washington DC 20011-1468 Office: Howard U Student Resource Ctr 6th And Bryant Sts NW Washington DC 20059-0001

HALL, SHARON GAY, retired language educator, artist; b. Centralia, Ill., Oct. 2, 1942; d. Leon Lucene and Olyve Elizabeth Hall. BS, So. Ill. U., 1966, MS, 1984; postgrad., Ea. Ill. U., 1985—90. Cert. secondary tchr. Ill. English tchr. Webber Twp. H.S., Bluford, Ill., 1966—67, Mt. Vernon (Ill.) H.S., 1967—99, ret., 1999. Artist-in-residence Cedarhurst Art Guild, Cedarhurst Mus., 1974—. Treas. bd. dirs. Bus. and Profl. Women's Club, Mt. Vernon, 1966—76; mem. Jefferson County Hist. Soc., 2000—. Recipient Recognition award, Cedarhurst Mus., 2000. Mem.: NEA, AAUW, Ill. Edn. Assn., Mt. Vernon Edn. Assn. (sec., treas., bd. dirs. 1967—99), Phi Delta Kappa, Phi Theta Kappa, Alpha Delta Kappa. Republican. Avocations: raising exotic animals, handspinner, weaver, fiber artist, seamstress. Home: 11384 E Idlewood Rd Mount Vernon IL 62864

HALL, SUSAN LAUREL, artist, educator, writer; b. Point Reyes Sta., Calif., Mar. 19, 1943; d. Earl Morris and Avis Mary (Brown) H. BFA, Calif. Coll. Arts & Crafts, Oakland, 1965; MA, U. Calif., Berkeley, 1967. Mem. faculty Sarah Lawrence Coll., Bronxville, NY, 1972—75, Sch. Visual Arts, NYC, 1981—92, Skowhegan Sch. of Painting and Sculpture, Maine, 1981, Univ. of Colo., Boulder Co., 1981, Art Inst. of Chgo., Chgo., 1981, Univ. of Tex., Austin, Tex., 1993, San Antonio, 1995, San Francisco Art Inst., San Francisco, 1996. One-woman shows include San Francisco Mus. Art, 1967, Quay Gallery, San Francisco, 1969, Phillis Kind Gallery, Chgo., 1971, 1998, 98 Greene St. Loft, N.Y.C., Whitney Mus., Henderson Mus. U. Colo., Boulder, 1973, Nancy Hoffman Gallery, N.Y.C., 1975, U. R.I. Gallery, Kingston, 1976, Harcus Krakow Rosen Sonnabend Gallery, Boston, 1976, Hal Bromm and Getler-Pall Galleries, N.Y.C., 1978, Helene Shlien Gallery, Boston, 1978, Hamilton Gallery, N.Y.C., 1978—79, 1981, 1983, Ovsey Gallery, L.A., 1981—82, 1984, 1987, 1989, 1991, Paule Anglim Gallery, San Francisco, 1975—83, Ted Greenwald Gallery, N.Y.C., 1986, Trabia Macafee Gallery, 1988—89, Wyckoff Gallery, Aspen, Colo., 1990—92, Milagros Contemporary Art, San Antonio, 1995, Brendan Walter Gallery, L.A., 1995, U. Tex., San Antonio, 1996, Jan Holloway Gallery, San Francisco, 1997, San Francisco Mus. Art Gallery, 1998, Gail Harvey Gallery, L.A., 1999, 2001, Frank Lloyd Wright Civic Ctr., San Rafael, 1999, Jernigan Wicker Gallery, San Francisco, 1999, exhibited in group shows at Whitney Mus. Am. Art, San Francisco Mus., Oakland Mus., Balt. Mus., Inst. Contemporary Art, Phila., Hudson River Mus., Bklyn. Mus., Nat. Mus. Women in the Arts, Mus. Fine Arts, Boston, Aldrich Mus. Contemporary Art, G.W. Einstein Gallery, Blum Helman Downtown, Leo Castelli Gallery Uptown, Graham Modern, N.Y.C., Kunstmus., Luzern, Switzerland, Landesmus., Bonn, Bolinas (Calif.) Mus., 2002, Represented in permanent collections pub. collections Whitney Mus., San Francisco Mus., Bklyn. Mus., Carnegie Inst., St. Louis Mus., Nat. Mus. Women in the Arts, others; author: Painting Point Reyes, 2002. Nat. Endowment Arts fellow, 1979-87, Adolph Gottleib Found. fellow, 1995; grantee: Pollack Krasner Found., N.Y. State Coun. on Arts; recipient Marin Arts Coun. Bd. Dirs. award, 1999.

HALL, SUSAN LIDDELL, elementary education educator; b. Logansport, Ind., July 5, 1951; d. Robert William and Marjorie Evelyn (Barnes) Bulmer. BS in Edn. summa cum laude, Ind. U., New Albany, 1991. Cert. tchr. K-6, Ind. Corp. officer Citizen's Fidelity Bank & Trust, Louisville, 1975-80; tchr. Morgan Elem. Sch., Palmyra, Ind., 1992—. Math., sci. tutor Floyd Cen. High Sch., Floyds Knobs, Ind., 1988—. Named to Hon. Order Ky. Cols.; Ind. U. Found. travel scholar to Egypt, 1992. Mem. Pi Lmabda Theta (v.p. 1989—, Margaret Walk and Hazel Bolen Academic scholar, 1990, Disting. Nat. Scholar award 1991), Kappa Delta Pi (pres. 1992, scholar), Kappa Kappa Kappa, Phi Delta Kappa (found. rep., 1994-95), Alpha Chi (Ind. U. Southeast Alumni Spotlight 1993, Merit scholar, State Partial Credit scholar). Avocations: tennis, bicycling, reading, piano. Home: 8504 N Valley View Dr Greenville IN 47124-9632

HALL, TELKA MOWERY ELIUM, retired educational administrator; b. Salisbury, NC, July 22, 1936; d. James Lewis and Malissa (Fielder) Mowery; m. James Richard Elium III, June 20, 1954 (div. 1961); 1 child, W. Denise Elium Carr; m. Allen Sanders Hall, Apr. 15, 1967 (div. 1977). Student, Am. Inst. Banking, 1955-57, Mary-Hardin Baylor Coll., Waco, Tex., 1957; BA, Catawba Coll., Salisbury, 1967; MEd, Miss. U. for Women, Columbus, 1973; EdS, Appalachian State U., 1975; postgrad., U. N.C., Greensboro, 1977; EdD, U. N.C., Chapel Hill, 1990; postgrad., Ind. U., 1998. Cert. early childhood, intermediate lang. arts and social studies tchr., curriculum specialist, adminstr., supr., supt., NC; notary pub., NC; cert. in CPR and first aid and safety, ARC. Bookkeeper, teller Citizens & So. Bank, Spartanburg, SC, 1955-56; bookkeeper 1st Nat. Bank, Killeen, Tex., 1956-58; bookkeeper, savs. teller Exch. Bank & Trust Co., Dallas, 1958-61; acct. Catawba Coll., 1961-65; floater teller bookkeeping and proof depts. Security Bank & Trust Co., Salisbury, 1965-68, 71; tchr. Rowan County Sch. System, Salisbury, 1967-70, 71-72, 1973-82; asst. prin. North Rowan Elem. Sch., Spencer, NC, 1982-94, Rockwell Elem. and China Grove Elem. Sch., NC, 1994-96, ret., 1996; part-time asst. prin. of curriculum China Grove Elem., 1996-99, also part-time outside observer for Ctrl. Office, 1996, asst. prin. curriculum, 1996-99, ret., 1999. Receptionist H & R Block, Salisbury, 1979-83; Chpt. I reading tchr. Nazareth Children's Home, Rockwell, NC, 1979-81. Author: The Effect of Second Language Training in Kindergarten on the Development of Listening Skills. Mem. Salisbury Cmty. Chorus, 1951—52, Hist. Salisbury Found., Inc., Salisbury Concert Choir, 1981—83; foreperson Rowan County grand jury, 1991; cons. Dial HELP, Salisbury, 1981—83; charter mem. bd. dirs. Old North Salisbury Assn., 1980—2000; past mem. Children's Literacy Guild, ARC; mem. YMCA, Am. Red Cross Harford-Dole chpt., 2002—, bd. dir., 2004—; pianist Franklin Presbyn. Ch., 1952—55, choir dir., 1975—87, past pres. Women of Ch., adult class Sunday sch. tchr., 1979—80, nursery Sunday sch. tchr., 1996—99, substitute S.S. adult class tchr., 2002—03, deacon, 1980—83, elder, 1991—92, 1996—99, 2001—03, clk. of session, 1992, 1996—98, 2002—03, choir mem., 1947—, co-moderator women of ch., 1999—2003; mem. Magnify Christian Concert Choir, 1999—. Civitan Music scholar, 1954, Kiwanis Acad. scholar, 1966, Catawba Coll. Acad. scholar, 1965-67, Mary Morrow Ednl. scholar N.C. Assn. Educators, 1966. Mem. NEA, NCAE, AARP, AAUW (v.p. 1985-87, 91-93), AARP, ARC (vol.), NC Ret. Govtl. Employees' Assn., Rowan-Salisbury Ret. Pers., Salisbury Hist. Assn., Kappa Delta Pi, Theta Phi (pres. 1992-93). Avocations: photography, genealogy, calligraphy, singing, composing poetry. Home: 105 Sharon Ct Salisbury NC 28146-7241

HALLBAUER, CELINDA, school system administrator, music educator; b. Lubbock, Tex., May 31, 1954; d. Alvin Oren and Minnie Fern (Harlan) H.; m. John Burton Messer, Aug. 5, 1972 (div. Feb. 1988); 1 child, John Burton Messer, Jr. B in music, Univ. Tex., 1974; M in music, Baylor Univ., 1977. Instr. preparatory music program Univ. Mary Hardin-Baylor, Belton, Tex., 1975-78, music faculty, dir. prep. music program, 1978-88, dir. preparatory music program, 1988-96; music faculty, dir. prep. music program Central Tex. Coll., Killeen, 1996-98, music faculty chair, 1998—. Recipient Contributor to Education award Tex. Fedn. of Music Clubs, 1984. Mem. Tex. Music Educators, Music Educators Nat. Assn., Tex. Choral Dirs. Assn., Am. Choral Dirs., Tex. Music Tchrs. Assn. (v.p. student affairs 1996-98, v.p. bus. affairs 1998-2000, coord. comm. 1995-96, asst. coord. MTNA composition, 1994-95, cert. chmn. 1986-95, trustee 1992-96, pres.-elect 2000-02, pres. 2002—). Avocations: bridge, snow skiing. Office: Central Tex Coll PO Box 1800 Killeen TX 76540-1800

HALLE, MORRIS, linguist, educator; b. Liepaja, Latvia, July 23, 1923; s. Irving and Lisa (Kahan) H.; m. Rosamond Thaxter Strong, July 2, 1955; children— David S., John G., M. Timothy. Student, CCNY, 1941-43; MA, U. Chgo., 1948, DHL (hon.), 1992; postgrad., Columbia, 1948-49; PhD, Harvard U., 1955; DSc (hon.), Brandeis U., 1989. Mem. faculty Mass. Inst. Tech., Cambridge, 1951-96, prof. modern langs. and linguistics, 1961-76, Ferrari P. Ward prof. modern langs. and linguistics, 1976-81, Inst. Prof., 1981-96, prof. emeritus, 1996—. James R. Killian, Jr. Faculty Achievement Award lectr., 1978-79 Author: (with R. Jakobson and C.G.M. Fant) Preliminaries to Speech Analysis, 1952, The Sound Pattern of Russian, 1959, (with N. Chomsky) The Sound Pattern of English, 1968, (with S.J. Keyser) English Stress: Its Form, Its Growth, and Its Use in Verse, 1971, (with G.N. Clements) Problem Book in Phonology, 1983, (with J. R. Vergnaud) An Essay on Stress, 1987, On Stress and Accent in Indo-European, 1997. Served with AUS, 1943-46. Recipient Union des Assurances de Paris Sci. prize, 1991; Guggenheim fellow, 1960-61; Am. Acad. Arts and Scis. fellow, 1963—. Mem. NAS, Linguistic Soc. Am. (v.p. 1973, pres. 1974). Home: 10 Arlington St Cambridge MA 02140-2713 Office: MIT 77 Massachusetts Ave Cambridge MA 02139-4307 E-mail: halle@mit.edu.

HALLEGUA, DAVID SAMUEL, internist, rheumatologist, educator; b. Cochin, India, Oct. 2, 1963; arrived in U.S., 1988; s. Samuel H. and Queenie S. Hallegua; m. Sayareh F. Hallegua, Nov. 26, 1995. Med. diploma, Trivandrum Med. Coll., India, 1987. Diplomate Am. Bd. Internal Medicine, Am. Bd. Rheumatology. Clin. instr. UCLA Sch. Medicine, 2001—. Bd. dirs. Spondylitis Assn. Am., Burbank, Calif. Co-author: Dubois Lupus Erythematosus, 5th edit., 2001; contbr. articles to profl. jours. Recipient Intern of Yr. award, Sinai Hosp., Detroit, 1989—90; fellow, Cedars-Sinai Hosp., L.A., 1996—98. Mem.: ACP, Am. Coll. Rheumatology. Avocations: philately, philanthropy, public speaking. Office: 8737 Beverly Blvd #203 Los Angeles CA 90048

HALL-ELLIS, SYLVIA DUNN, library science educator, consultant; b. Kewanee, Ill., June 21, 1949; d. M. Orrill and Elizabeth J. (Boase) Dunn; m. J. Theodore Ellis, Dec. 24, 1989. BA, Rockford (Ill.) Coll., 1971; MLS, U. North Tex., Denton, 1972; MA, U. Tex., San Antonio, 1976; PhD, U. Pitts., 1985. Cert. pub. libr., Tex., N.Y., Pa. Sys. coord. San Antonio Pub. Libr., 1973-76; div. libr. Corpus Christi Pub. Librs., 1976-78; asst. dir. So. Tier Libr. Sys., Corning, N.Y., 1978-81; dir. libr. devel. State Libr. of Pa., Harrisburg, 1981; devel. officer PRLC, Inc., Pitts., 1981-85; pres., owner The Blue Bear Group, Inc., Central City, Colo., 1985-92; profl. cataloger Arapahoe Libr. Dist., Littleton, Colo., 1991; head libr. Rocky Mountain Coll. Art, Denver, 1992-93; asst. prof. L.S. Sam Houston State U., Huntsville, Tex., 1993-95, adj. prof., 1995—. Devel. officer/grant proposal writer Region One Edn. Svc. Ctr., Edinburg, Tex., 1995-97; dir. devel. Mid-continent Regional Ednl. Lab., Aurora, Colo., 1997-98; spl. asst., U.S. Dept. Edn. Region VIII, 2000-01; prof. libr. sci. U. Denver, 1999—; adj. prof. libr. sci. U. Ariz., Tucson, 1995, San Jose State U., 2002—; cons. to various state govts., 1981—. Author: Grantwriting For School And Small Public Libraries, 1999, Grants for Schools, 2003; contbr. articles to profl. jours. Docent, Denver Mus. Natural History, 1992—; pres. Rocky Mountain LAN Engrs., Denver, 1993; cons., treas. Columbine Family Health Ctrs., Inc., Black Hawk, 1988-89; mem. Gilpin County Econ. Devel. Commn., Central City, 1987-89; tech. prep mem. Rio Grande Valley Inc., Tex., 1995—. Mem. ALA, Tex. Libr. Assn., Colo. Libr. Assn., Colo. Ednl. Media Assn. Office: U Denver Ste 107 2135 E Wesley Ave Denver CO 80208 Fax: (303) 756-0424. E-mail: shellis@bigplanet.com.

HALLENBECK, LINDA SUE, elementary school educator; b. Iowa, 1948; m. Theodore R. Hallenbeck; children: Robert, Elizabeth. BS, Kent State U., 1974, MEd, 1976, postgrad. Cert. tchr. K-3, K-8, computer sci., math., Ohio; Nat. bd. cert.. Grad. asst. Kent (Ohio) State U., 1974-76; 3d grade tchr. Hudson (Ohio) Elem. Sch., 1976-77; 1st grade tchr. Evamere Sch., Hudson, 1977-86; 5th grade tchr. J.P. McDowell Elem. Sch., Hudson, 1986-92, East Woods Sch., Hudson, 1992—2001; tchr. Hudson Mid. Sch., 2001—03; rsch. assoc. NSF, 2002—03. Cons. NSF, Washington, 1989-95, tchr. in residence, office of Gov. Bob Taft, 1999-2001, tchr., Presdl. Acad. for Excellence in Tchng. Mathematics at Princeton and Northwestern U., Middleschool Mathematics State Trainer, Math Acad., 2001-. Active Hudson Soccer, 1980-95. Recipient Presdl. award for excellence in teaching sci. and math. NSF, 1993, Govs. Edn. leadership award, 1998, Ohio Pioneer in Edn award, 2000. Mem. Nat. Coun. Tchrs. Math., Ohio Coun. Tchrs. Math.(pres. elect), Ohio Math. Edn. Leadership Coun., PTO, Coun. for Presdl. Awardees of Math, Govs. Commn. for student success, Exec. Bd. of Ohio Math/Sci. Coalition. Avocations: snow skiing, gardening, sewing, decorating. Home: 7615 Oxgate Ct Hudson OH 44236-1877

HALLER, ARCHIBALD ORBEN, sociologist, educator; b. San Diego, Jan. 15, 1926; s. Archie O. and Eleanor (Brizzee) Haller; m. Hazel Laura Zimmermann, Feb. 15, 1947 (dec. 1985); children: Elizabeth Ann, Stephanie Lynn Bylin, William John; m. Maria Camila Omegna Rocha, Apr. 12, 1986 (div. 1987); m. Maria Cristina Del Peloso, Sept. 16, 1989;

stepchildren: Graziella, Camila. BA magna cum laude, Hamline U., 1950; MA, U. Minn., 1951; PhD, U. Wis., 1954. Assoc. prof., then prof. sociology Mich. State U., East Lansing, 1956-65; postdoctoral rschr. U. Wis., Madison, 1954-56, vis. prof., summer 1964, prof. sociology and rural sociology, 1965-94, emeritus prof., 1994—; affiliated faculty Indsl. Rels. Rsch. Inst., U. Wis., Madison, 1975-94; faculty in Latin Am. and Iberian studies U. Wis., Madison, 1965-94; affiliated faculty Inst. Environ. Studies, U. Wis., Madison, 1990-94. Fulbright prof. sociology Rural U. of Brazil, 1962; vis. prof. sociology Brigham Young U., Provo, Utah, 1973; Fulbright prof. sociology U. Sao Paulo, 1974; Fulbright travel grantee Univ. Sao Paulo, Brasilia, Pernambuco, Paraiba and Ceara, Brazil, 1979; vis. fellow Australian Nat. U., 1981; disting. vis. prof. rural sociology Ohio State U., 1982—83; Fulbright prof. sociology U. Sao Paulo, 1987—90; cons. UNESCO, 1989; cons. on Amazonian rsch. Govt. of Brazil, 1991—95; cons. Fed. U. Pernambuco, 1994; cons. for nat. social change to Pres. of Brazil, 1994—96; cons. on Amazonian rsch. Govt. of Brazil, 1997; cons. Faculty of Agrarian Sci. of Para, 1997—98, others; vis. prof. doctoral program in sociology and polit sci. Fed. U. Minas Gerais, Brazil, 1998; cons. Ind. U., Bangladesh, 1998; organizer symposia on Brazil; cons. on Amazonian rsch. Govt. of Brazil, 1999—2000; vis. prof. doctoral program in sociology and polit sci. Fed. U. Minas Gerais, Brazil, 2000—02; fellow Nat. Rsch. Coun. Brazil, 2000—02. Author: The Occupl. Aspiration Scale: Theory, Structure and Correlates, 1963, 71, The Socioeconomic Macroregions of Brazil--1970, 1983; co-editor (with R.M. Hauser et al) Social Structure and Behavior: Essays in Honor of William Hamilton Sewell, 1982; editor spl. issues Luso-Brazilian Rev.; author rsch. monographs and tech. articles; contbr. articles to profl. jour.; contbr. to theory of societal stratification, to processes of status allocation, to the demographic structure of societal inequality, to identifying the socioeconomic develop. regions of Brazil, and to the measurement of internat. devel. Mem. Mich. Com. on Mental Health Policies, 1961-62, Nat. Exec. Res., 1959-66; mem. sociology fellowship panel Coun. on Internat. Exch. Scholars, 1977-81, chmn., 1981. Decorated Grand Officer Order of Merit of Labor, Govt. of Brazil, 1981; univ. fellow U. Wis., 1953-1954; recipient John Luddy Phalen award in Latin Am. Studies U. Wis., 2000; Ann. Haller Disting. Lecture Series named in his honor U. Wis., 2000. Fellow AAAS, Am. Sociol. Assn.; mem. Internat. Rural Sociol. Assn., Internat. Sociol. Assn., Sociol. Rsch. Assn., NY Acad. Sci., Rural Sociol. Soc. (pres. 1970-71, rep. AAAS 1973-86, Disting. Rural Sociologist 1990), Univ. Club, Sigma Xi, Gamma Sigma Delta, Phi Beta Kappa. Home: 12928 Salt Cedar Dr Oro Valley AZ 85737 Office: U Wis 350 Agriculture Hall Madison WI 53706 Fax: 520-797-8444. Business E-Mail: haller@ssc.wisc.edu.

HALLER, GARY LEE, chemical engineering educator; b. Loup City, Nebr., July 10, 1941; s. Leo Edward and Carrie Dorothy (Obermiller) H.; m. Sondra Sue Krueger, Dec. 23, 1962; children: Jared Paul, Sarah Lynn, Joshua Nathaniel. BS, U. Nebr., Kearney, 1962; PhD, Northwestern U., 1966. From mem. faculty to prof. Yale U., New Haven, 1967—90, Henry Prentiss Becton prof. engring. and applied sci., 1990—; master Jonathan Edwards Coll., 1997—. Harry Fair lectr. U. Okla., 1995; Burnell lectr. N.Am. Catalysis Soc., 1995; Lacey lectr. Calif. Inst. Tech., 1996; Ipatieff lectr. Northwestern U., 1996. Editor: Jour. Catalysis, 1988-93; mem. bd. editors Catalysis Revs.; author: (with Delgass, Lunsford and Kellerman) Spectroscopy in Heterogeneous Catalysis, 1979; contbr. articles to profl. jours. Mem. AAAS, AICE, Am. Chem. Soc. (divsn. chmn. 1982), Catalysis Soc. (v.p., fgn. sec. 1984-89, pres. 1989-93), Sigma Xi. Home: 841 Whitney Ave Hamden CT 06517-4001 Office: Yale U 9 Hillhouse Ave New Haven CT 06511-6815

HALLER, IRMA TOGNOLA, secondary education educator; b. Bainbridge, N.Y., Aug. 25, 1937; d. Tullio and Margaretha (Fuchs) Tognola; m. Hans R. Haller, July 11, 1964. BA, SUNY, Albany, 1959; MEd in Teaching of Social Studies, Boston U., 1962. Tchr. social studies Chenango Valley Jr.-Sr. High Sch., Binghamton, N.Y., 1959-64; tchr. social studies and English Sidney (N.Y.) High Sch., 1964—, chair dept. social studies, 1986—. Mem. tchr. edn. adv. bd. SUNY, Oneonta, 1983-97, chair, 1985-88, 93-94; active local sch. improvement coms. Mem. steering com. Sidney Ctrl. Schs. Bus. Edn. Cmty. Partnership, 1992—. N.Y. State Electric and Gas Corp. grantee, 1985; Catskill Regional Tchr. Ctr. grantee, 1985, 87, 89. Mem. Nat. Coun. Social Studies, N.Y. State Social Studies Coun., N.Y. State United Tchrs., Catskill Area Social Studies Coun. (newsletter editor 1989-90), Sidney Tchrs. Assn., Phi Delta Kappa. Avocations: reading, walking. Office: Sidney H S 95 W Main St Sidney NY 13838-1601

HALLETT, CHARLES ARTHUR, JR., English and humanities educator; b. New Haven, July 19, 1935; s. Charles Arthur and Bridie D. (McIntyre) H.; m. Elaine Stewartson, Nov. 7, 1958. BA, The New Sch., 1961; MA, Columbia U., 1963; DFA, Yale U., 1967. Mem. faculty Fordham U., Bronx, N.Y., 1967—, assoc. prof. English, 1971-81, prof., 1981—. Asst. project dir. NEH Shakespeare Summerfest, N.Y.C., 1981; vis. prof. U. Warwick, Eng., 1978, Loyola U., New Orleans, 1994, Dartmouth Coll., 2001-03. Author: Middleton's Cynics, 1975, The Revenger's Madness, 1981, Analyzing Shakespeare's Action, 1991; (play) Aaron Burr, also articles; contbr. to Ency. Americana. Fellow Lawrence Langner Theatre Guild Found., 1965-66; Am. Coun. Learned Socs. grantee, 1981. Home: 116 E 91st St Apt 5 New York NY 10128-1667 Office: English Dept Fordham U Bronx NY 10458

HALLIBURTON, LLOYD, Romance philology educator; b. Shreveport, La., July 31, 1934; s. Ralph Eloe and Mary Katherine (Smith) H.; m. Donna Lee Cavanagh, May 27, 1965 (div. Sept. 1976); children: Richard Lloyd, William Cavanagh de Tuite, Cristopher Lee, Manon Lee; m. María F. Sánchez, Jan. 6, 1993; children: Carlos David, Lawden Nerea. AB, Centenary Coll., 1955; MA, La. State U., 1961, PhD, 1970; C en F y L, U. de Valladolid, Spain, 1965; LittD (hon.), London Inst. for Applied Rsch., 1993. Instr. Spanish U. Notre Dame, Ind., 1962-63; asst. prof. Spanish Centenary Coll., Shreveport, 1963-66, Va. Mil. Inst., Lexington, 1966-69, assoc. prof. Spanish, 1970-80, asst. commandant, 1971-74; asst. prof. fgn. langs. La. Tech. U., Ruston, 1981-84, assoc. prof., 1984-91, prof., 1991—, dir. grad. program in romance langs., 1992-95. Vis. lectr. Romance langs. U. N.C., 1970; adj. prof. Spanish U. Va., Charlottesville, 1978—80; vis. prof. English Ga. Mil. Coll., Barksdale AFB, La., 1980—81, Grambling State U., 1986, 2001—03, U. Autonoma de Coahuila, Centro de Idiomas, Mexico, 2002; cons. USAF, U.S. Dept. Justice, Mosher Steel Co., Studebaker Internat., Irrigation Internat. de Mex., others; rsch. bd. advisors Am. Biog. Inst. Author: Colombia en la Poesía, 1967, Hendaye, 1990, Saddle Soldiers: General William Stokes and the 4th South Carolina Cavalry, 1993, The Cemaco Seed, 1996, García Lorca and Other Things Spanish: Critical Essays, 2002, John William Corrington: Reflections, 2003; contbr. articles to profl. jours. Mem. State Dem. Com., Lincoln Parish, La., 1984-94. Capt. U.S. Army, 1955-57. NDEA fellow, 1959-62; Fulbright fellow, 1965; NEH fellow, 1971; postdoctoral fellow La. State U., 1992; grantee VMI Found., La. Tech. U., 1967-92, La Tech summer rsch. grantee, Spain, 1998, 2001. Mem. Coun. for Devel. of Spanish in La., Phi Kappa Phi, Phi Sigma Iota, Sigma Tau Delta, Sigma Delta Pi, Alpha Chi, Omicron Delta Kappa. Roman Catholic. Avocations: gardening, hunting, deep-sea fishing. Office: Dept Fgn Langs La Tech U Ruston LA 71272-0001

HALLIGAN, JAMES EDMUND, university administrator, chemical engineer; b. Moorland, Iowa, June 23, 1936; s. Raymond Anthony and Margaret Ann (Crawford) H.; m. Ann Elizabeth Sorenson, June 29, 1957; children: Michael, Patrick, Christopher. MS in Chem. Engring, Iowa State U., 1962, MS, 1965, PhD, 1968. Registered profl. engr., Okla. Process engr. Humble Oil Co., 1962-64; mem. faculty Tex. Tech U., 1968-77; dean engring. U. Mo., Rolla, 1977-79, U. Ark., Fayetteville, 1979-82, vice chancellor for acad. affairs, 1982-83, interim chancellor, 1983-84; pres. N.Mex. State U., Las Cruces, 1984-94, Okla. State U., Stillwater, 1994—2003, pres. emeritus, 2003—. Mem. Gov. Tex. Energy Adv. Council, 1972-74; prof. achievement citation engr. Iowa State U. Coll. Engring., 1984. Served with USAF, 1954-58. Recipient Disting. Teaching award Tex. Tech U., 1972, Disting. Research award, 1975, 76; Disting. Teaching award U. Mo., Rolla, 1978, Disting. Achievement citation Iowa State U. Alumni Assn., 1996. Mem. AIChE, NSPE, Am. Chem. Soc., Am. Soc. Engring. Edn., Rotary, Tau Beta Pi, Phi Kappa Phi, Pi Mu Epsilon. Roman Catholic. Office: Okla State U 470 SU Stillwater OK 74078-1010

HALLINAN, MAUREEN THERESA, sociologist, educator; BA, Marymount Coll., 1961; MS, U. Notre Dame, 1968; PhD, U. Chgo., 1972. Prof. U. Wis., Madison, 1980-84; with U. Notre Dame, 1984—, now William P. and Hazel B. White prof. arts and letters, dept. sociology, dir. Ctr. for Rsch. on Ednl. Opportunity. Assoc. editor Social Forces, 1977-80; assoc. editor Sociology of Edn., 1979-81, editor, 1981-86, session organizer, 1980, 84, 89, 92; author: the Structure of Positive Setiment, 1974; editor: The Social Organization of Schools: New Conceptualizations of the Learning Process, 1987, Restructuring Schools: Promising Practices and Policies, 1995, Handbook of the Sociology of Education, 2000; co-editor: The Social Context of Instruction: Group Organization and Group Proceses, 1983, Change in Societal Institutions, 1990;co-editor Stability and Change in American Education: Structuce, Process and Outcomes, 2003; contbr. articles to profl. jours. Mem. Am. Sociol. Assn. (pres. sociology of edn. sect. 1993-94, sec.-treas. 1988-90, chairperson 1991-92, pres. 1995-96), Sociol. Rsch. Assn. (sec.-trea. 1999-2000, pres. 2000-01), Nat. Acad. of Edn., Phi Beta Kappa. Office: U Notre Dame Dept Of Sociology Notre Dame IN 46556

HALLMAN, PATRICIA ANN, music educator; b. Lincolnton, N.C., May 24, 1948; d. Glen Rodney and Tessie Juanita (Crowder) Fox; m. Larry Reeves Hallman, Aug. 24, 1969; 1 child, Jeremy Reeves. BA in Music Edn. and Sacred Music, Gardner Webb U., Boiling Springs, N.C., 1982; Orff-Schulwerk Level I Cert., Radford (Va.) U., 1984; Orff-Schulwerk Level II Cert., Hofstra U., 1985; Orff-Schulwerk Level III Cert., Memphis State U., 1987. Cert. music educator, N.C. Minister of music Oak Grove Bapt. Ch., Lincolnton, N.C., 1975-77, Reepsville Bapt. Ch., Lincolnton, N.C., 1980-83; minister youth and activities New Hope Bapt. Ch., Earle, N.C., 1983-84; minister of music Mountain View Bapt. Ch., Lincolnton, 1984-86, Boger City Bapt. Ch., Lincolnton, 1990-92; tchr. music Lincoln County Schs., Lincolnton, 1984—; minister of music Lawings Chapel Bapt. Ch., Lincolnton, 1994, Calvary Bapt. Ch., Lincolnton, 1996-98, Antioch Bapt. Ch., 1999—2000, North Brook Bapt. Ch., Cherryville, NC, 2000—. Tchr. pvt. piano and voice lessons, 1986—; conducted crusades in field, 1993, 94, 95, 96, 98. Bd. dirs. Local Chpt. N.C. State Symphony, Lincolnton, 1987-92. Mem. N.C. Assn. Educators, Am. Orff-Schulwerk Assn. (bd. dirs. 1993, composer From Us To You 1993), South-fork Bapt. Assn. (children's choir coord. 1984—). Baptist. Avocations: swimming, traveling, singing, performing, cooking. Home: 2536 Pickwick Pl Lincolnton NC 28092-7749 Office: Iron Station Elem Sch 4207 W Highway 27 Lincolnton NC 28092-0713

HALLMAN, VICTORIA STELLA, athletic director; b. Phila., May 3, 1952; d. John Betchel Hallman and Elizabeth (Rita) Di Gregorio Ford. BA, San Diego State U., 1975; MA, S.W. Tex. State U., 1981, postgrad., 1987, 91. Cert. mgmt., supt., Tex.; cert. athletic adminstr.; ASEP coaching principles trainer; NIAAA leadership trainer. Tchr., coach San Antonio Ind. Sch. Dist., 1978-82; women's track coach, instr. S.W. Tex. State U., San Marcos, 1982-83; tchr., coach Westlake H.S. Eanes Ind. Sch. Dist., Austin, Tex., 1983-90; asst. prin. Jr. H.S. Del Valle (Tex.) Ind. Sch. Dist., 1990-93, athletic dir., 1993—. Mem. rsch. com. Tex. Athletic Equality Project, Austin, 1987-88; curriculum cons. Concordia Luth. Coll., Austin, 1987-88. Mem. AIDS care team St. Austin's Cath. Ch., Austin, 1993—, mem. Landings, 1991—; self responsibility curriculum com. Del Valle Independent Sch. Dist., 1997; chmn. facilities planning com. Tex. assn. Health, Physical Edn., Recreation, Dance, 1997. Oshman's grant for girls Jr. League of Austin, 1994, 96. Mem. Tex. H.S. Coaches Assn., Tex. H.S. Women's Coaching Assn., Tex. Coun. Women Sch. Execs. (pres. local chpt. 1988-90), San Diego State U. Aztec Varsity Club, Assn. for Nat. Girls and Women Sports (mentor 1998), Nat. Fedn. of Interscholastic Adminstrs., Tex. H.S. Athletic Dirs. Assn., Phi Delta Kappa. Democrat. Avocations: sports, boating. Home: 4001 Stonecroft Dr Austin TX 78749-3165 Office: Del Valle Ind Sch Dist 5201 Ross Rd Del Valle TX 78617-2245

HALLSTROM, VICTORIA JANE, primary school educator, consultant; b. Hallock, Minn., Mar. 23, 1948; d. Anton August and Hilda Elizabeth (Streed) Baker; m. Paul Brent Hallstrom, Feb. 8, 1969; children: Tina, Jennifer, Kjell. Cert. in religious studies, Golden Valley Luth. Coll., 1968; AA in Pre-Edn., San Bernardino Valley Coll., 1974; BA in Liberal Studies, Calif. State U., San Bernardino, 1985; MA in Edn. and Adminstrn., Azusa Pacific U., 1991. Cert. tchr., Fla., Calif. Tchr. Highland Ave. Luth. Ch., San Bernardino, 1982-84, Valley Christian Sch., San Bernardino, 1984-86, Fontana (Calif.) Unified Sch. Dist., 1986-91, mentor tchr., mem. staff devel., 1989-91, mentor tchr. Calif. New Tchr. Project, 1990; primary tchr. Seminole County Schs., Oviedo, Fla., 1992—. Nat. cons. The Math. Learning Ctr., Portland, Oreg., 1985—. Recipient Outstanding Reading Tchr. Arrowhead Reading Coun., Calif. State U., 1990, Teacherific award Walt Disney World Co., 1993, named Elem. Math Tchr. of the Year Seminole County, 1995. Mem. NEA, Fla. Edn. Assn., Seminole Edn. Assn., Internat. Reading Assn., Fla. Reading Assn., Seminole Reading Assn., Nat. Coun. Tchrs. Math., Seminole Coun. Tchrs. Math. Avocations: traveling, reading, antiques, family, arts and crafts. Home: 853 Lullwater Dr Oviedo FL 32765-8513 Office: partin Elem Sch 1500 Twin Rivers Blvd Oviedo FL 32766-5061

HALM, NANCYE STUDD, retired private school administrator; b. Jamestown, N.Y., Mar. 26, 1932; d. Thomas Howerton and Margaret Hazel (LeRoy) Neathery; m. David Philip Mack, Aug. 25, 1951 (div. 1972); children: Margaret, Jennifer, Geoffrey, Peter; m. Loris L. Studd, July 6, 1974; m. James Richard Halm, Aug. 30, 1991. BS in Edn., SUNY, Fredonia, 1954, postgrad., St. Bonaventure U. Tchr. Morning Sun (Iowa) Consolidated Schs., 1956-57, Panama (N.Y.) Cen. Schs., 1958-65, Jamestown (N.Y.) Pub. Schs., 1967-69, Olean (N.Y.) Pub. Schs., 1969-72, Jamestown Pub. Schs., 1972-73; pers. mgr. F.W. Woolworth Co., Lakewood, N.Y., 1972-79; dir. Nat. Conf. Christians & Jews, Jamestown, 1979-86; counselor N.Y. State Div. for Youth, Jamestown, 1979-89; exec. rep. Am. Bapt. Found., Valley Forge, Pa., 1989-94; adminstr. New Castle Christian Acad., 1996—2002; ret., 2002. Pastor West Pitts. United Meth. Ch., 2003—. V.p. Chautauqua County Am. Bapt. Women, 1981—90; pres. Falconer Bapt. Women, 1986—90; love gift chmn. Pitts. Bapt. Assn., 1990—91; trustee, chair endowment fund Chautauqua Bapt. Union at Chautauqua Inst., 1982—; pres. ch. coun. Wesley United Meth. Ch., 2001—; pastor W. Pitts. United Meth. Ch., 2003—; mem. nat. bd. dirs. Am. Bapt. Chs. U.S.A., Valley Forge, Pa., 1988—89. Recipient Cert. of Merit Cassadaga Job Corp, 1984. Mem. Rebekah. Democrat. Avocations: quilting, reading, crafts. Home: 1702 W Washington St New Castle PA 16101-1360

HALMOS, PAUL RICHARD, mathematician, educator; b. Budapest, Hungary, Mar. 3, 1916; came to U.S., 1929; s. Alexander Charles and Paula (Rosenberg) H.; m. Dorothy Moyer, Jan. 1, 1934 (div. Mar. 1945); m. Virginia Templeton Pritchett, Apr. 7, 1945. BS, U. Ill., 1934, MS, 1935, PhD, 1938; DSc (hon.), U. St. Andrews, Scotland, 1984; D Math. (hon.), U. Waterloo, Can., 1990. Instr. U. Ill., Urbana, 1938-39, assoc., 1942-43; fellow, asst. Inst. for Advanced Study, Princeton, N.J., 1939-42; asst. prof. Syracuse (N.Y.) U., 1943-46; from asst. prof. to prof. U. Chgo., 1946-61; prof. U. Mich., Ann Arbor, 1961-68; prof., chmn. dept. U. Hawaii, Honolulu, 1968-69; prof., then Disting. prof. Ind. U., Bloomington, 1969-85; prof. Santa Clara (Calif.) U., 1985-96, prof. emeritus, 1996—. Author: Finite Dimensional Vector Spaces, 1942, Measure Theory, 1950, A Hilbert Space Problem Book, 1967, I Want to Be a Mathematician, 1985, others. Mem. Math. Assn. Am. (Haimo award for Dist. Coll. & Univ. Teaching of Mat., 1994), Am. Math. Soc., others. Avocations: photography, walking. Home: 110 Wood Rd Apt I-203 Los Gatos CA 95030-6720 Office: Santa Clara U Dept Math Santa Clara CA 95053-0001

HALPERN, DAVID RODION, special education administrator; b. Ann Arbor, Mich., Mar. 29, 1951; s. Werner Israel and Edith (Winograd) H.; m. Noreen Danzo, May 28, 1972; children: Aaron Benjamin, Joseph Morris. BS, SUNY, Buffalo, 1973; MS, Nazareth Coll., 1977; cert. advanced study, SUNY, Brockport, 1985. Tchr. emotionally disturbed Rochester (N.Y.) Mental Health Ctr., 1973-78, program coord., 1981-88; tchr. emotionally disturbed Rochester City Sch. Dist., 1978-81; prin. alternative high sch. Monroe 1 Bd. Coop. Ednl. Svcs., Fairport, NY, 1988-98, prin. alternative edn. dept., 1998—2003; spl. edn. coord. Greater Rochester Sch. Support Ctr., 2003—. Cons. Monroe #2 Bd. Coop. Ednl. Svcs., Rochester; mem. alternative edn. steering com. N.Y. State Dept. Edn.; mem. Reclaiming Youth Work Group Monroe County Interagy. Coun.; adj. faculty Grad. Sch. Edn., Nazareth Coll., 1994—. Photographer: A Brand Plucked From the Fire, 1986. Mem. N.Y. State Educators of the Emotionally Dist., Jewish Fedn. Bd. Dirs., Bur. Jewish Edn. (pres. 1993-95), N.Y. State Alt. Edn. Assn. (pres.-elect 1999-2001, pres. 2001-03). Avocations: fishing, photography, reading science fiction and fantasy. Office: Foreman Ctr 41 Oconnor Rd Fairport NY 14450-1327 E-mail: david_halpern@boces.monroe.edu.

HALPERN, JACK, chemist, educator; b. Poland, Jan. 19, 1925; came to U.S., 1962, naturalized; s. Philip and Anna (Sass) H.; m. Helen Peritz, June 30, 1949; children: Janice Henry, Nina Phyllis. BS, McGill U., 1946, PhD, 1949, DSc (hon.), 1997, U. B.C., 1986. NRC postdoc. overseas fellow U. Manchester, England, 1949-50; instr. chemistry U. B.C., 1950, prof., 1961-62; Nuffield Found. traveling fellow Cambridge (Eng.) U., 1959-60; prof. chemistry U. Chgo., 1962-71, Louis Block prof. chemistry, 1971-83, Louis Block Disting. Svc. prof., 1983—. Vis. prof. U. Minn., 1962, Harvard, 1966-67, Calif. Inst. Tech., 1968-69, Princeton U., 1970-71, Max. Planck Institut, Mulheim, Fed. Republic Germany, 1983—, U. Copenhagen, 1978; Sherman Fairchild Disting. scholar Calif. Inst. Tech., 1979; guest scholar Kyoto U., 1981; Firth vis. prof. U. Sheffield, 1982, Phi Beta Kappa vis. scholar, 1990; R.B. Woodward vis. prof. Harvard U., 1991; numerous guest lectureships; cons. editor Macmillan Co., 1963-65, Oxford U. Press; cons. Am. Oil Co., Monsanto Co., Argonne Nat. Lab., IBM, Air Products Co., Enimont, Rohm and Haas; mem. adv. panel on chemistry NSF, 1967-70; mem. adv. bd. Am. Chem. Soc. Petroleum Rsch. Fund, 1972-74, Trans Atlantic Sci. and Humanities Program, 2001--; mem. medicinal chemistry sect. NIH, 1975-78, chmn., 1976-78; mem. chemistry adv. coun. Princeton U., 1982—; mem. univ. adv. com. Ency. Brit., 1985—; mem. chemistry vis. com. Calif. Inst. Tech., 1991—; chmn. German-Am. Acad. Coun., 1993-96, chmn. bd. trustees, 1996—. Assoc. editor: Inorganica Chimica Acta, Jour. Am. Chem. Soc.; co-editor: Collected Accounts of Transition Metal Chemistry, vol. 1, 1973, vol. 2, 1977; assoc. editor Procs. NAS; mem. editl. adv. bd. Oxford Univ. Press, Internat. Series Monographs on Chemistry; mem. editl. bd. Jour. Organometallic Chemistry, Accounts Chem. Rsch., Catalysis Revs., Jour. Catalysis, Jour. Molecular Catalysis, Jour. Coord. Chemistry, Gazzetta Chimica Italiana, Organometallics, Catalysis Letters, Kinetics and Catalysis Letters; contbr. articles to Ency. Britannica, rsch. jours. Trustee Gordon Rsch. Confs., 1968-70; bd. govs. David and Arthur Smart Mus., U. Chgo., 1988—; bd. dirs. Ct. Theatre. Recipient Young Author's prize Electrochem. Soc., 1953, award in catalysis Noble Metals Chem. Soc., London, 1976, Humboldt award, 1977, Richard Kokes award Johns Hopkins U., 1978, Willard Gibbs medal, 1986, Bailar medal U. Ill., 1986, Wilhelm von Hoffman medal German Chem. Soc., 1988, Chem. Pioneer's award Am. Inst. Chemists, 1991, Paracelsus prize Swiss Chem. Soc., 1992, Basolo Medal, Northwestern U., 1993, Robert A. Welch award, 1994, Henry J. Albert award Internat. Precious Metals Inst., 1995, award in Organometallic Chem. Am. Chem. Soc., 1995, Order of Merit Federal Republic of Germany, 1996. Fellow AAAS, Royal Soc. London, Am. Acad. Arts and Scis., Chem. Inst. Can., Royal Soc. Chemistry London (hon.), N.Y. Acad. Scis., Japan Soc. for Promotion Sci.; mem. NAS (fgn. assoc. 1984-85, mem. coun. 1990—, chmn. chemistry sect. 1991-93, v.p. 1993—, assoc. editor Proceedings NAS), Am. Chem. Soc. (editl. bd. Advances in Chemistry series 1963-65, 78-81, chmn. inorganic chemistry 1985, award in inorganic chemistry 1968, award for disting. svc. in advancement of inorganic chemistry 1985, award in organometallic chemistry 1995), Max Planck Soc. (sci. mem. 1983—), Art Inst. Chgo., Renaissance Soc. (bd. dirs.), New Swiss Chem. Soc. (Paracelsus prize 1992), Am. Friends of the Royal Soc. (bd. dirs.), Sigma Xi. Home: 5801 S Dorchester Ave Apt 4A Chicago IL 60637 Office: U Chgo Dept Chemistry Chicago IL 60637 E-mail: jhjh@midway.uchicago.edu.

HALPERN, MARTIN BRENT, physics educator; b. Newark, Aug. 26, 1939; s. Melvin M. and Blanche B. (Friedman) H.; m. Penelope J. Dutton, June 2, 1988; 1 child, Tamar Lillian. BSc, U. Ariz., 1960; PhD, Harvard U., 1964. Postdoctoral fellow CERN, Geneva, 1964—65, U. Calif., Berkeley, 1965—66, prof. physics, 1967—; postdoctoral fellow Inst. Advanced Study, Princeton, NJ, 1966—67. Office: U Calif 366 Le Conte Hall Berkeley CA 94720-7303

HALSEY, MARTHA TALIAFERRO, Spanish language educator; b. Richmond, Va., May 5, 1932; d. James Dillard and Martha (Taliaferro) H. AB, Goucher Coll., 1954; MA, U. Iowa, 1956; PhD, Ohio State U., 1964. Asst. prof. Spanish, Pa. State U., Univ. Pk., 1964-70, assoc. prof., 1970-79, prof., 1979-95, prof. emeritus, 1995—. Vis. Olive B. O'Connor prof. lit. Colgate U., Hamilton, NY, 1983. Author: Antonio Buero Vallejo, 1973, Dictatorship to Democracy: the Recent Plays of Buero Vallejo (La Fundación to Música cercana), 1994; editor: Madrugada, 1969, Hoy es fiesta, 1978, Los inocentes de la Moncloa, 1980, El engaño, Caballos desbocaos, 1981, (with Phyllis Zatlin) The Contemporary Spanish Theater: A Collection of Critical Essays, 1988, Entre actos: Diálogos sobre teatro español entre siglos, 1999, Estreno, 1992-98; gen. editor Estreno Contemporary Spanish Plays, 1992-98, Estreno Studies in Contemporary Spanish Theater, 1998—; mem. editl bd. Modern Internat. Drama, 1968-75, Ky. Romance Quar., 1970-76, Annals Contemporary Spanish Lit., 1991—, Tesserae: Jour. Iberian and Latin Am. Studies, 1997—; contbr. articles to profl. jours. Grantee Am. Philos. Soc., 1970, 78, Inst. for Arts and Humanistic Studies, 1977, Program Cultural Coop. Between Spanish Ministry Culture and U.S. Univs., 1992, 94-95. Fellow Hispanic Soc. Am. (hon.); mem. MLA, N.E. MLA, Am. Assn. Tchrs. Spanish and Portuguese, Fellowship of Reconciliation, War Resisters League, Phi Beta Kappa, Phi Sigma Iota, Sigma Delta Pi. Democrat. Episcopalian. Home: 500 E Marylyn Ave Apt I 140 State College PA 16801-5248 Office: Pa State U Dept Spanish University Park PA 16802

HALVERSTADT, DONALD BRUCE, urologist, educator; b. Cleve., July 6, 1934; s. Lauren Oscar and Lillian Frances (Jones) H.; m. Margaret Ann Marcy, Aug. 4, 1956; children: Donna, Jeffrey, Amy. BA magna cum laude, Princeton U., 1956; MD cum laude, Harvard U., 1960. Diplomate Am. Bd. Urology. Intern, then resident in surgery Mass. Gen. Hosp., Boston, 1960-62, resident in urology, 1964-67; pvt. practice medicine specializing in urology Oklahoma City, 1967—; chief pediatric urology svc. Okla. Children's Meml. Hosp., Oklahoma City, 1967—, chief staff, 1974-79; clin. prof. urology and pediatrics U. Okla. Med. Sch., 1970—, vice chair dept. urology, 1982—; interim provost U. Okla. for Health Scis., Oklahoma City, 1979-80; spl. asst. to pres. for hosp. affairs Oklahoma U., 1980-84; CEO State of Okla. Teaching Hosps., 1980-83, also bd. dirs.; CEO State Regents for Higher Edn., 1988-93. Mem. U. Okla. Bd. Regents, 1993-2000, chmn. 1999; founder, vice chmn., dir. Lincoln Nat. Bank, Oklahoma City; vice chair bd. govs. Okla. Med. Ctr. Hosp. Sys., 1998—; bd. dirs. Triad Hosps.,

Inc., chair compliance com., 2000—, nominating com. Contbr. articles to med. jours. Vice chair bd. govs. Univ. Health Ptnrs.; pres., chmn. bd. Okla. Ind. Phys. Svcs. Corp., 1986-96; trustee Columbia Presbyn. Hosp., 1990-96, chmn., 1995-96; bd. dirs. Nat. Assn. Basketball Coaches FDTN; athletic dir. adv. coun. U. Okla., 2003. Fellow ACS; mem. AMA (physicians recognition award 1969, 72, 79, 82, 85, 91, 94, 96, 99, 2002), Am. Urol. Assn., Am. Acad. Pediat., Soc. Pediat. Urology, Am. Soc. Nephrology, Soc. Univ. Urologists, So. Med. Assn., Okla. Med. Assn., Oklahoma County Med. Soc., Okla. State Regents for Higher Edn., Am. Coll. Physician Execs., Assn. Governing Bds. Colls. and Univs. (bd. dirs., sec. 1996-97, treas. 1997-98). Presbyterian. Home: 2932 Lamp Post Ln Oklahoma City OK 73120-6105 Office: # 707 711 Stanton L Young Blvd Oklahoma City OK 73104-5023

HALVORSON, JUDITH ANNE (JUDITH ANNE DEVAUD), elementary education educator; b. Bethesda, Md., Apr. 28, 1943; d. Henri J. and Mary L. (Baumgart) Devaud; m. Peter L. Halvorson, Feb. 4, 1964; 1 child, Peter Chase. BS in Edn., U. Cin., 1965; MA in Edn., U. Conn., 1974, Cert. Advanced Grad. Study in Edn., 1980, postgrad. in French, 2003—. Tchr. Greenhills-Forest Park (Ohio) City Schs., 1965-67, Weld County Schs., Greeley, Colo., 1969-70, Chaplin (Conn.) Elem. Sch., 1970-2000; ret., 2000. Mentor Beginning Educator Support program State of Conn. and Chaplin Elem. Sch., 1988-2000; supr. student tchrs. East Conn. State U., U. Conn., U. No. Colo., 1969-2000. Past vice-chmn., past chmn., past sec. Coventry (Conn.) Bd. Edn., 1981-95; chmn. Coventry Sch. Bldg. com., 1981-92, Coventry Parks and Recreation Com., 1980-82, chmn., 1982; mem. Dem. Town Com. Coventry, 1973-98. Grantee, Nat. Sci. Edn. project, 1977-78; named Outstanding Elem. Tchr. Am., 1974; recipient Citation for Cmty. Leadership, Nat. Women's History Month, 1991; recognized for svc. to pub. edn. in Conn., Conn. Assn. Bds. of Edn., 1993, 94, 95, for contbns. to Conn., Beginning Educator Support and Tng. program Conn. State Dept. Edn., 1991-93, for svc. to cooperating tchr. programs Ea. Conn. State U., 1993, 95, for Outstanding Svc. to Pub. Edn., State of Conn., 1995. Mem. NEA (life), Conn. Edn. Assn. (life), Chaplin Edn. Assn. (past pres., v.p., chmn. negotiations 1970-2000), Assn. Ret. Tchrs. Conn., Pi Lambda Theta (past pres., v.p., chmn. membership Beta Sigma chpt. 1974—), Phi Delta Kappa. Episcopalian. Avocations: swimming, skiing, golf, leisure travel, French language and culture. Home: 90 David Dr Coventry CT 06238-1320 E-mail: jandphalvorson@msn.com.

HALVORSON, MARY ELLEN, education educator, writer; b. Salem, Ohio, Apr. 23, 1950; d. Robert J. and Betty June (Bear) Batzli; m. Thomas Henry Halvorson, June 10, 1972; children: Christine Lynn, Matthew Thomas, Rebecca Lynn. BS in Edn. with distinction, No. Ariz. U., 1972, postgrad., 1973-92, U. Ariz., 1974-76, Ariz. State U., 1975-76, U. Phoenix, 1989-90; PhD in Edn., Calif. Coast U., 2001. Cert. Supt. Ariz., 2001, elem. tchr. libr. Ariz. Tchr. Prescott (Ariz.) Unified Schs., 1972-77, dir. community nature ctr., 1978, reading tutor, 1985-88, family math. tchr., 1989-90, part-time libr., 1991-92; dir. Prescott Study Ctr., 1987-90; writer ednl. materials Herald House, Independence, Mo., 1994—; instr. Yavapai C.C., 1994-96; edn. coord. Yavapai Prescott Indian Tribe, 1996-98; tchr. Prescott Unified Sch. Dist., 1998—99; supt. Tri-City Prep. H.S., 1999—. Guest speaker Abia Judd Young Authors, Prescott, 1992; math. enthusiast instr. Ariz. Dept. Edn., Prescott, 1989-92; asst. instr. outdoor edn. Ariz. State U., Prescott, 1977-78; tutor English grammar No. Ariz. U., Flagstaff, 1971-72; presenter, U. Oxford (Eng.) Round Table, 2003. Co-author: Arizona Bicentenial Resource Manual, 1975; contbr. book rev. column to Prescott Courier, 1993, also articles to profl. pubs. Cert. adult instr. Temple Sch., Independence, Mo., 1985—; sec., bd. dirs. Whispering Pines, Prescott, 1989-93; music docent Prescott Symphony Guild, 1982-85; state Christian edn. dir. Cmty. of Christ. Ch., Ariz., 1977-82, elder, counselor to pastor, 1993—; spokesperson Franklin Heights Homeowners, Prescott, 1985; leader Prescott Pioneers 4-H Club, 1989—, Christian Youth Group, 1985—; fundraiser Graceland Coll., 1993; craft demonstrator Sharlott Hall Mus.; master of ceremonies Prescott Summer Pops Symphony, 1995, 97. Recipient 4-H Silver Clover Svc. award, 1995; named Outstanding Young Educator, Prescott Jaycees, 1976, Outstanding Young Women of Am., 1985. Mem. Phi Kappa Phi, Kappa Delta Pi, Sigma Epsilon Sigma. Avocations: teaching piano, sewing costumes for school musical groups, oil painting. Home: 2965 Pleasant Valley Dr Prescott AZ 86305-7116

HAM, CLARENCE EDWARD, university administrator; b. Wink, Tex., Dec. 27, 1936; s. Clarence Joseph and Edwina Olive (Brantley) H.; m. Joyce Suzella Travis, Apr. 20, 1962; children: Patricia Lynn, John Joseph, Duane Michael, Christina Diane. BA, Baylor U., 1959; MEd, Tex. Technol. Coll., 1965; PhD, U. Tex., Austin, 1969. Cert. supt., prin., secondary tchr. Elem. prin. Perrin (Tex.) County Line Sch. Dist., 1960-62; h.s. prin. Cotton Ctr. (Tex.) Ind. Sch. Dist., 1962-66; supt. schs. Orange (Tex.) Common Sch. Dist. #1, 1967-68, Bay City (Tex.) Ind. Sch. Dist., 1969-74, Killeen (Tex.) Ind. Sch. Dist., 1974-88; dep. supt. for instrn. Fort Bend Ind. Sch. Dist., Sugar Land, Tex., 1989-92; dean sch. edn. U. Mary Hardin-Baylor, Belton, Tex., 1992—. Contbr. articles to profl. jours. Named Outstanding Adminstr. of Yr. Tex. Classroom Tchrs. Assn., 1984. Mem. Nat. Assn. of Federally Impacted Schs. (pres. 1987-88, area v.p., bd. dirs. 1980-87), Am. Assn. Sch. Adminstrs., Tex. Assn. Sch. Adminstrs., Assn. of Tchr. Educators, Tex. Assn. Colls. for Tchr. Edn. (pres. 1999-2000), Consortium of State Orgns. Tex. Tchr. Educators (chair 2000-01), Phi Delta Kappa (pres. Ctrl. Tex. chpt. 1981-82, Educator of Yr. 1984, Kappan of Yr. 1995-96). Baptist. Home: 2220 Red Rock Dr Belton TX 76513-1346 Office: Univ of Mary Hardin-Baylor Sta UMHB Sta Box 8017 Belton TX 76513 Personal E-mail: ham@stonemedia.com. Business E-Mail: cham@umhb.edu.

HAM, GEORGE ELDON, soil microbiologist, educator; b. Ft. Dodge, Iowa, May 22, 1939; s. Eldon Henry and Thelma (Ham) H.; m. Alice Susan Bormann, Jan. 11, 1964; children: Philip, David, Steven. BS, Iowa State U., 1961, MS, 1963, PhD, 1967. Asst. prof. dept soil sci. U. Minn., St. Paul, 1967-71, assoc. prof., 1971-77, prof., 1977-80; prof., head dept. agronomy Kans. State U., Manhattan, 1980-89; assoc. dean Coll. Agr., assoc. dir. Kans. Agr. Expt. Sta., 1989-2001, ret., 2001; bd. dirs. Kans. Crop Improvement Assn., Manhattan, Kans. Fertilizer and Chem. Inst., Topeka, Kans. Crops and Soils Industry Coun., Manhattan; cons. Internat. Atomic Energy Agy., Vienna, Austria, 1973-79. Assoc. editor Agronomy Jour., 1979-84. Contbr. articles to profl. jours. and biol. nitrogen fixation rsch. Asst. scoutmaster Indianhead coun. Boy Scouts Am., St. Paul, 1977-80; pres. North Star Little League, St. Paul, 1979-80. Sgt. U.S. Army, 1963-69. Fellow AAAS, Am. Soc. Agronomy, Soil Sci. Soc. Am.; mem. Crop Sci. Soc. Am. Sigma Xi, Gamma Sigma Delta, Phi Kappa Phi. Home: 2957 Nevada St Manhattan KS 66502-2355

HAMADA, ROBERT S(EIJI), educator, economist, entrepreneur; b. San Francisco, Aug. 17, 1937; s. Horace T. and Maki G. Hamada; m. Anne Marcus, June 16, 1962; children: Matthew, Janet. BE, Yale U., 1959; SM, MIT, 1961, PhD, 1969. Economist Sun Oil Co., Phila., 1961—63; instr. U. Chgo., 1966—68, asst. prof. fin., 1968—71, assoc. prof., 1971—77, prof., 1977—89, Edward Eagle Brown prof., 1989—93, Edward Eagle Brown Disting. Svc. prof., 1993—, dir. Ctr. for Rsch. in Security Prices, 1980—85, dir. Ctr. Internat. Bus. Edn. and Rsch., 1992—94, dep. dean for faculty Grad Sch. Bus., 1985—90, dean, 1993—2001; CEO, dir. Merchants' Exchange, 2001—02. Vis. prof. univs. including London Bus. Sch., 1973, 79-80, UCLA, 1971, U. Wash., Seattle, 1971-72, U. B.C., Vancouver, Can., 1976; bd. dirs. A.M. Castle & Co., Fleming Cos., Inc., No. Trust Corp.; pub. dir. Chgo. Bd. Trade, 1989-2000; cons. numerous fin. instns., banks, mfg., mgmt. cons., acctg. and law firms. Past assoc. editor Jour. Fin., Jour. Fin. and Quantitative Analysis, Jour. Applied Corp. Fin.; cons. editor Scott, Foresman & Co. fin. series; contbr. numerous articles to profl. jours. Bd. dirs. numerous non-profit orgns., including Hyde Park Neighborhood Club, Chgo., Harper Ct. Found., Chgo., Hyde Park Co-op, U. Chgo. Lab. Schs., Window to the World Comms., Inc. (WTTW-TV), Terra Found. for the Arts. Named to 8 Outstanding Bus. Sch. Profs., fortune Mag., 1982; recipient 1st Outstanding Tchr. award, Grad. Sch. Bus., U. Chgo., 1970, McKinsey Tchg. prize, 1981; Sloan Found. fellow, 1959—61, Ford Found. fellow, 1963—65, Standard Oil Found. fellow, 1965—66, MIT scholar, 1959—61, Yale scholar, 1955—59. Mem. Am. Fin. Assn. (bd. dirs. 1982-85), Econometric Soc., Nat. Bur. Econ. Rsch. (bd. dirs., mem. investment and exec. coms.), Am. Econ. Assn. (investment com.), Inst. Mgmt. Scis. (investment com.), Tau Beta Pi. Office: U Chgo Grad Sch Bus 1101 E 58th St Chicago IL 60637-1511

HAMALAINEN, PEKKA KALEVI, historian, educator; b. Finland, Dec. 28, 1938; s. Olavi Simeon and Aili Aliisa (Laiho) H.; children: Kim Ilkka, Leija-Lee Louise Aili, Timothy Pekka Olavi, Kai Kalevi Edward. AB, Ind. U., 1961, PhD, 1966. Acting asst. prof. history U. Calif., Santa Barbara, 1965-66, asst. prof. history, 1966-70; assoc. prof. history U. Wis., Madison, 1970-76, prof., 1976—2001, prof. emeritus, 2001—, chmn. Western European area studies program, 1977—. Nat. screening com. Scandinavian area Inst. Internat. Edn., Fulbright Hays Program; cons. Dept. State., Washington, 1991—; chair grad. edn. coun. U. Wis., 1996—, Vilas assoc. Author: Kielitaistelu Suomessa 1917-1939, 1968, Nationalitetskampen och sprakstriden i Finland 1917-1939, 1969, In Time of Storm: Revolution, Civil War and the Ethnolinguistic Issue in Finland, 1978, Luokka ja Kieli Vallankumouksen Suomessa, 1978, Uniting Germany: Actions and Reactions, 1994; contbr. articles to profl. publs. and jours. Served to lt. Finnish Navy, 1957-58. Faculty research grantee U. Calif., 1966-69; faculty summer fellow, 1969; Ford Found. grantee, 1967; faculty research grantee U. Wis., Madison, 1970— ; Am. Philos. Soc. research grantee, 1973; Am. Council Learned Socs. fellow, 1976; research grantee, 1978 Mem. AAUP, Am. Hist. Assn., German Studies Assn., Soc. Advancement Scandinavian Study (adv. com. exec. coun.), Fin. Hist. Assn. (corr. emem.), Coun. European Studies, Paasikivi Seura, Ind. U. Alumni Assn. Office: U Wis 3211 Humanities 455 N Park St Madison WI 53706-1405

HAMAMOTO, PATRICIA, school system administrator, educator; BA in History, profl. tchg. diploma, Calif. State Coll., Long Beach, 1967; education administrator's cert., U. Hawaii M, 1985. Social studies tchr. Fountain Valley (Calif.) H.S., 1967—72; social studies tchr., dept. chair Liima Intermediate Sch., Ewa Beach, Hawaii, 1976—81; tchg. grad. asst. geography dept. UHM, 1981—83; tchr. guidance/math. Pearl City H.S., Hawaii, 1985; vice prin. Maui H.S., Kahlui, Hawaii, 1983—85, Nanakul H.S. and Intermediate Sch, Waianae, Hawaii, 1985—87; prin. Pearl City Highlands Elem. Sch, Hawaii, 1987—89; pers. specialist ii Office Personnel Svcs. Contract Adminstrn., Honolulu, 1989—91; prin. Pres. William McKinley H.S., Honolulu, 1992—99; dep. supt. Hawaii Dept. Edn., Honolulu, 1999—2001, interim supt., 2001; supt. Hawaii Dept Edn., Honolulu, 2001—. Mem.: ASCD. Avocations: golf, reading, travel, walking. Office: Hawaiian Dept Edn 1390 Miller St #307 Honolulu HI 96813

HAMBLEN, KAREN, art educator; PhD, U. Oreg., 1981. Prof. art edn. La. State U., Baton Rouge, 1985—; vis. scholar Getty Mus. and Found., 1996-97. Vice chmn. art com. Nat. Bd. Profl. Tchg. Stds., 1990—; reviewer, cons. Getty Ctr. for Edn. in Arts, 1991-94. Sr. editor Studies in Art Edn., 1991-93; contbr. articles to profl. jours. Recipient Art Edn. Jour. award, 1996, Rsch. Studies award, 1997. Mem. NAEA (Manuel Barkan award 1984, Mary Rouse award 1985, June McFee award 1995, Lecture Aestetics award 1998). E-mail: khambl@lsu.edu.

HAMEKA, HENDRIK FREDERIK, chemist, educator; b. Rotterdam, Holland, May 25, 1931; came to U.S., 1960, naturalized, 1963; s. Dirk C. and Johanna (Mannebeck) H.; m. Charlotte C. Procacci, Aug. 3, 1972. Drs., U. Leiden, The Netherlands, 1953, DSc cum laude, 1956; MA (hon.), U. Pa., 1971. Rsch. assoc. U. Rome, Italy, 1956-57; fellow Carnegie Inst. Tech., 1957-58; rsch. physicist N. V. Philips Lamps, Eindhoven, The Netherlands, 1958-60; asst. prof. chemistry Johns Hopkins, 1960-62; assoc. prof. chemistry U. Pa., 1962-67, prof. chemistry, 1967—. Disting. vis. rsch. prof. USAF Acad., 1986-87. Author: Advanced Quantum Chemistry, 1965, Introductory Quantum Theory, 1967, Physical Chemistry, 1977, Chemistry, Fundamentals and Applications, 2002; contbr. numerous articles to sci. jours. Recipient Alexander von Humboldt prize, 1981; Alfred P. Sloan Research fellow, 1963-67. Achievements include research on theory of molecular structure and optical and magnetic properties of molecules; calculations of spin-orbit and spin-spin coupling; theory of resonance optical rotation, spectral predictions. Home: 1503 Argyle Rd Berwyn PA 19312-1905 Office: U Pa Dept Chemistry Philadelphia PA 19104

HAMEL, REGINALD, history educator; b. Frampton (Beauce-Nord), Que., Can., Feb. 14, 1931; s. Come and Helena (Chevalier-Welsh) H.; m. Pierrette Methe, Oct. 26, 1957; children— Julie, Sonia. BA, U. Ottawa, Ont., Can., 1956; MA, U. Ottawa, 1961; PhD, U. Montréal, Que., 1971. Lectr. history U. Ottawa, 1959-61; lectr. history U. Montréal, 1964-69, asst. prof., 1969-71, assoc. prof., 1971-82, full prof., 1982-94, prof. honoraire, 1994—. Advisor Nat. Mus. of Can., Ottawa, 1957; curator Pub. Archives Mus., Ottawa, 1958-61, rsch. ctr., U. Montréal, 1964-69; vis. prof. U. Sorbonne, Paris, 1972, U. Birmingham, Eng., 1972-73, Haifa U., Tel Aviv, Beercheva U., Jerusalem, 1978, Nanjing U., China, 1992—; lit. critic for radio and TV, 1951-89. Author: Cahiers bibliographiques des lettres québécoises, 1966-69, La litterature et l'érotisme, 1967, Correspondence of Charles Gill, 1969, (with others) Dictionnaire pratique des auteurs québécois, 1976, Gaètane de Montreuil (1867-1951), 1976, Alexandre Dumas (père), bibliographie, chronologie et index des personages, 1979, 1990-2003, La Louisiane Créole, Litteraire, Politique et Sociale, 1762-1900, 1984, Soixante minutes avec Dumas insolite, 1987, L'Habitation St-Ybars de Mercier, 1987, Dictionnaire des auteurs de langue française en Amérique du Nord, 1988, Dumas insolite, 1988, Introduction a la francophonie, 1989, Dictionnaire Dumas, 1990, Jules Faubert, le roi du papier de Paquin, 1991, L'Image de la Révolution française au Québec, 1789-92, Charles Gill, poésies completes, 1995, Guy Fregault, Histoire de la Litterature (1860-1920), 1996—, Louis-Moreau Gottschalk (1829-1869), Histoire du "Devoir" Littéraire 1994, Biographie de Charles Gill, 1997, Panorama de la littératures québécoise contemporaine, 1997, Québec 2000+ (1534-1999), 1999, Dictionnaire Des Poètes Dici, 2001, Johnelle de Mercier, 2003, Les Voleurs d'Or de Dumas, 2003, Les deux Faria, 2003. Sec. Dept. Transport, Ottawa, 1962. Served to lt. Can. Army, 1952-55 Decorated Chevalier de l'Ordre des Palmes Académiques, France, 1991; recipient Gold medal Renaissance française, 1998; Ottawa Dept. Edn. scholar, 1962-64. Mem. Assn. of Lit. (v.p. 1974-75), Assn. Profs. of French of Que. Home: 219 Springdale St Pointe-Claire QC Canada H9R 2R4 Office: U Montreal 2900 Blvd Edouard Montpetit Montreal QC Canada H3C 3J7

HAMELINK, JERRY LEE, environmental research scientist, educator; b. Grand Rapids, Mich., May 23, 1941; s. John William and Jane (Jelsma) H.; m. Mary Jill Bolich, Dec. 28, 1964; children: John, Jason. BS, Mich. State U., 1963, PhD, 1969. Cert. fisheries scientist. Fisheries assoc. Mich. Dept. Conservation, Lansing, 1963-69; asst. prof. Purdue U., West Lafayette, Ind., 1969-74; instr. Butler Coll., Indpls., 1975-76; sr. toxicologist Eli Lilly & Co., Greenfield, Ind., 1974-79, rsch. scientist, 1979-88; assoc. rsch. scientist Dow Corning, Midland, Mich., 1988-93; prof. chemistry Aquinas Coll., Grand Rapids, Mich., 1994-95; prof. math. and stats. Grand Valley State U., 1995-96. Adj. prof. fisheries Mich. State U., East Lansing, Mich., 1989-92, environ. healt sci. U. Mich., Ann Arbor, 1991-2002; 1st peer review panel U.S. EPA Ops. Lab., Pensacola, Fla., 1991. Editor: Aquatic Toxicology and Hazard Evaluation, 1977, (and chair) Bioavailability: Physical, Chemical and Biological Interactions, 1994; contbr. articles to profl. jours. Bd. dirs. Mich. Head Injury Alliance, Brighton, 1992-95; bd. dirs., organization Unitarian Universalist Ch. of Indpls., 1980-81. Named vol. of the quarter Midland Vols. for Recycling, 1993. Mem. Soc. Environ. Toxicology and Chemistry (bd. dirs. 1989-92, BCF symposium in honor 1994), Internat. Assn. Gt. Lakes Rsch., Ind. Aquaculture Assn. (sec., treas. 1987-88). Democrat. Unitarian Universalist. Achievements include origination of concept of bioconcentration--direct uptake from water controlled dynamics of DDT in experimental ponds; designed duck cages which permitted testing with pairs; recognized and led use of fluridone as aquatic herbicide. Home: 4209 Blair St Hudsonville MI 49426-9343

HAMES, CARL MARTIN, educational administrator, art dealer, consultant; b. Birmingham, Ala., July 12, 1938; s. William Geda and Mary Anna (Martin) H. BA, Birmingham So. Coll., 1958; MA, Samford U., 1971, MS, 1980. Cert. tchr. in English, History and Spanish; cert. sch. adminstr. Tchr. Birmingham Pub. Schs., 1958-64, Birmingham U. Sch., 1964-69, asst. headmaster, 1969-75; coll. counselor The Altamont Sch., Birmingham, 1975-91, dean of students, 1975-89, asst. headmaster, 1989-91, headmaster, 1991—2002, headmaster emeritus, 2002—. Dir. Town Hall Gallery, Birmingham, 1965—; chmn. Birmingham Nat. Coll. Fair, 1995, 96, 97; Chenoweth lectr. Birmingham Mus. Art, 2000. Writer poetry. Ethnic heritage chmn. Birmingham Hist. Soc., 1989—, co-editor Twentieth Century Painters; active Birmingham Mus. Art, 1958-92; com. ann. meeting Am. Hort. Soc., 1991; chmn. visual arts com. Arts Coun. Birmingham So. Coll., 1995—, founder, chmn. "Writing Today" Writers' Conf., 1980; featured spkr. Ind. Presbyn. Ch./Ind. Arts Festival, 1998; dist. dir. Ala. Penman Contest, 1999, 2000—; co-chmn. Nat. Conf. Opera for Youth, 2000; bd. dirs., chmn. edn. com. Alys Robinson Stephens Ctr. for Performing Arts, U. Ala. Birmingham, 2001; bd. dirs. Collectors Cir. Photography Guild; bd. dirs. Ala. Kidney Found. Recipient Silver Bowl awards in drama, visual arts Birmingham Festival of Arts, Disting. Alumnus award Birmingham-So. Coll., 1993, 1st Pl. Hackney prize for poetry State of Ala., 1996, 2d Pl. Hackney, 2001, Citation for tchg. creative writing Ala. Sch. Fine Arts, 2000, Cmty. Arts Vol. of Yr. award Women's Com. of 100, 2001-02; named Barton Hill Head Instr. in the Humanities the Altamont Sch., 1986, Gem of Birmingham, Black & White newspaper, 1996. Mem. Nat. Coun. Tchrs. English, Ala. Assn. Ind. Schs. (bd. dirs. 1991—, chmn. biennial conf. 1994, v.p. 1997-99, pres. 1999-2001), Nat. Assn. Coll. Admissions Counselors (chmn. Nat. Coll. Fair Sept. 1995, 96, 97), So. Assn. Coll. Admissions Counselors (chmn. Coll. Fair 1994), Birmingham Bot. Soc., Birmingham Art Assn. (editor), Nat. Soc. of Arts and Letters (co-hmn. lit. competition 1998), Birmingham Mus. Art (editor, juror. lectr. 2002, Energen Art competition 2001), Birmingham Hist. Soc., Garden Conservancy (vol. 1998, 99), Newcomen Soc. N.Am., Birmingham Inst. Aesthetic Edn., The Club, Rotary Club of Birmingham, Phi Delta Kappa. Democrat. Roman Catholic. Avocations: collecting art, travel, gardening. Home: 4260 Mountaindale Rd Birmingham AL 35213-2724 Office: The Altamont Sch PO Box 131429 Birmingham AL 35213-6429

HAMIDZADEH, HAMID REZA, mechanical engineer, educator, consultant; b. Tehran, Iran, July 22, 1952; came to U.S., 1982; s. Khodadad and Nosrat (Fassieh) H.; m. Azar Mofid, July 2, 1987; children: Cyrus, Archer. BSc, Arya Meher U. of Tehran, 1974; MSc, Imperial Coll. U. London, 1975, PhD, 1978. Postdoctoral rsch. asst. Imperial Coll., London, 1978-82; lectr., assoc. mem. grad. sch. U. Md., College Park, 1982-83; asst. prof. U. So. Colo., Pueblo, 1983-86; assoc. prof. S.D. State U., Brookings, 1986-90, prof., 1990—, prin. investigator mech. engring., 1994-96. Sr. design cons. Cummins Engine Co., Columbus, Ind., 1995; organizer numerous tech. confs.; rev. manuscripts of tech. books for pubs. Contbr. more than 67 articles to profl. jours. including Jour. Shock and Vibration, ASME, among others. Recipient numerous grants. Mem. ASME (sr. del NSSC com. 1988-93, regional chair bd. minority and women 1989-92, profl. devel. com. 1993-96, Faculty Advisor of Yr. 1991). Avocations: swimming, poetry. Home: 6015 S Mustang Ave Sioux Falls SD 57108-3800 Office: SD State U Dept Mech Engring 214 Crothers Engring Hl Brookings SD 57007-0001

HAMIL, LYNN RAY, secondary education educator; b. Kingsley, Iowa, May 28, 1952; s. Veryl D. and Fern C. (Meister) H.; m. Lori A. Leekley, Mar. 28, 1981; children: James, Steven. BS, Morningside Coll., 1974, tchr. certification, 1984. Cert. tchr., Iowa. Tchr. chemistry, physics, advanced biology, applied physics, Remsen-Union Cmty. Sch., Remsen, Iowa, 1994—. Mem. Iowa State Ednl. Assn. Office: Remsen-Union High Sch 511 Roosevelt St Remsen IA 51050

HAMILTON, AMELIA WENTZ (AMY WENTZ), elementary school educator; b. Elizabethtown, Ky., Mar. 31, 1970; d. Willard Mason and Judith Parr Wentz; m. Brian Joseph Hamilton; children: Clinton, Levi, Samuel Jewell. B in Music Edn., Morehead State U., 1993, BA in Edn., 1994; MA in Edn., Western Ky. U., 1997. Rank I in edn. adminstrn. (elem. principalship). Music tchr. Flaherty Elem. Sch., Ekron, Ky., 1995—, extended sch. svc. tchr., 1995—. Testing cons. Ky. Instrnl. Results Info. Sys. Stewart Pepper Mid. Sch., Brandenburg, Ky., 1995; substitute tchr. Meade County Bd. Edn., Brandenburg, 1995; test scoring Ky. Instrnl. Results Info. Sys. Advanced Sys., Lexington, 1993—94; mem. scholarship com. Flaherty Elem. PTO, Ekron, 2001—. Named to All-Collegiate Band, Ky. Music Educators Nat. Conv., 1992, 1993; recipient 18 Outstanding Salesperson awards, The Castle, 1993—95. Mem.: Mothers of Preschoolers, Am. Orff-Schulwerk Assn., Meade County Edn. Assn., Ky. Edn. Assn., Ky. Music Educators Nat. Conf., Ky. Orff-Schulwerk Assn., Meade County Women's Dem. Club, Pi Kappa Phi, Gamma Beta Phi, Sigma Alpha Iota (life), Chi Omega (life). Baptist. Avocations: vocal music, reading. Home: 326 Homeview Dr Brandenburg KY 40108 Office: Flaherty Elem Sch 2615 Flaherty Rd Ekron KY 40117 Personal E-mail: brianamy@bbtel.com.

HAMILTON, BARBARA, secondary school educator; b. Port Chester, N.Y., Feb. 11, 1949; d. Joseph A. and Laura P. (Marcocilli) Santoro; m. Tom T. Hamilton, July 9, 1977; 1 child, Sean. BA, Boston U., 1971; MA, Columbia U., 1972; 6th Yr. Diploma, U. Bridgeport, Conn., 1978. Cert. tchr. social studies, guidance counselor. Tchr. Port Chester Pub. Schs., 1973-83; tchr. social studies Bronxville (N.Y.) Sch., 1983—, dept. chair, 1989—. Named Outstanding Tchr., U. Richmond, Va., 1994. Office: Bronxcville Sch 177 Pondfield Rd Bronxville NY 10708-4829

HAMILTON, CARL HULET, retired academic administrator; b. Morris, Okla., Sept. 30, 1934; s. Alva H. and Olah E. (Pryor) H.; m. Gloria Joyce Gore, Sept. 3, 1954; children: Ray, Carla Jo, Deanna Jean. ThB, Southwestern Coll., 1956; BA, Oklahoma City U., 1957; MA, U. Tulsa, 1962; PhD, U. Ark., 1968. English tchr. Southwestern Coll., Oklahoma City, 1957-60; editor Oral Roberts Evangelistic Assn., Tulsa, 1960-62; English tchr., editor Oral Roberts U., Tulsa, 1966-68; acad. dean, 1968-75; provost Oral Roberts U., Tulsa, 1975-84; adminstr. World Evangelism, San Diego, 1984-86; chief of staff Feed the Children, Oklahoma City, 1986-88; provost, chief acad. officer Oral Roberts U., 1989-98; ret., 2001. Min. of adminstrn. First United Meth. Ch., 1999-2001. Republican. Methodist. Avocations: fishing, water sports, motorcycling. Home: PO Box 488 Disney OK 74340-0488 E-mail: piscatore@brightok.net.

HAMILTON, DAGMAR STRANDBERG, lawyer, educator; b. Phila., Jan. 10, 1932; d. Eric Wilhelm and Anna Elizabeth (Sjöström) Strandberg; m. Robert W. Hamilton, June 26, 1953; children: Eric Clark, Robert Andrew Hale, Meredith Hope. AB, Swarthmore Coll., 1953; JD, U. Chgo. Law Sch., 1956, Am. U., 1961. Bar: Tex. 1972. Atty. civil rights divsn. U.S. Dept Justice, Washington, 1965-66; asst. instr. govt. U. Tex., Austin, 1966-71; lectr. Law Sch. U. Ariz., Tucson, 1971-72; editor, rschr. Assoc. William O. Douglas U.S. Supreme Ct., Washington, 1962-73, 75-76; editor, rschr. Douglas autobiography Random House Co., 1972-73; staff counsel Judiciary Com. U.S. Ho. of Reps., 1973-74; asst. prof. L.B. Johnson Sch. Pub. Affairs U. Tex., Austin, 1974-77, assoc. prof., 1977-83, prof., 1983—, assoc. dean., 1983-87. Interdisciplinary prof. U. Tex. Law Sch., 1983—; vis. prof. Washington U. Law Sch., St. Louis, 1982, U. Maine, Portland,

1992; Godfrey Disting. vis. prof. U. Maine Law Sch., 2002; vis. fellow U. London, QMW Sch. Law, 1987—88; vis. prof. U. Maine, Portland, 2002; vis. fellow U. Oxford Inst. European & Comparative Law, 1998. Contbr. to various publs. Mem. Tex. State Bar Assn., Am. Law Inst., Assn. Pub. Policy Analysis and Mgmt., Swarthmore Coll. Alumni Coun. (rep.), Kappa Beta Phi (hon.), Phi Kappa Phi (hon.). Democrat. Mem. Soc. Of Friends. Home: 403 Allegro Ln Austin TX 78746-4301 Office: U Tex LBJ Sch Pub Affairs Austin TX 78713 E-mail: dagmar.hamilton@mail.utexas.edu.

HAMILTON, DONNA MARTHA, secondary education educator; b. Paden, Okla., Feb. 14, 1944; d. Raymond George and Emma Veneda (Rogers) Van Zant; m. Jimmie Joe Hamilton, Oct. 5, 1962. MA, St. Mary's Coll. Md., 1973; MEd, U. Okla., 1978. Tchr. George Washington Carver Middle Sch., Lexington Park, Md., 1973, Spring Ridge (Md.) Middle Sch., 1973-74, Norman (Okla.) High Sch., 1975—. Exec. officer Close Up Okla., Oklahoma City, 1980—. Mem. APA, NEA, Okla. Edn. Assn., Okla. Coun. for Social Studies. Avocations: running, weight lifting, physical fitness. Office: Norman High Sch 911 W Main St Norman OK 73069-6997

HAMILTON, GEORGE WESLEY, agronomist, educator; b. Williamsport, Pa., May 29, 1961; s. George Wesley and Sarah Jane (Stryker) H.; m. Rebecca Sue Renn, July 16, 1983; children: Natalie Jane, Julia Louise. BS, Pa. State U., 1983, MS, 1990, PhD, 2001. Rsch. technologist Pa. State U., University Park, 1983-86, sr. rsch. aide, 1986-90, supr., 1990-91, instr., 1991—, sr. lectr., 1996—2002, asst. prof., 2002—. Author: Fate and Significance of Pesticides in Urban Environments, 1992, Science and Golf II, 1994. Named Innovator of Yr., N.E. Weed Sci. Soc., 1994, 97. Mem. Am. Soc. Agronomy, Soil Sci. Soc. Am., Crop Sci. Soc. Am. Achievements include patents for calibration for granular broadcast spreaders and pelletized mulch for turfgrass establishment. Home: 2467 Oak Leaf Ct State College PA 16803-3336 Office: Pa State U 116 ASI Bldg University Park PA 16802

HAMILTON, JEAN See CHAUDOIR, JEAN

HAMILTON, JOHN MAXWELL, university dean, writer; b. Evanston, Ill., Mar. 28, 1947; s. Maxwell Millings and Elizabeth Curran (Carlson) H.; m. Regina Frances Nalewajek, Aug. 19, 1975; 1 child, Maxwell Janek. BA in Journalism, Marquette U., Milw., 1969; postgrad., U. N.H., 1971-73; MS in Journalism, Boston U., 1974; PhD in Am. Civilization, George Washington U., 1983. Reporter Milw. Jour., 1967-69; free-lance journalist Washington, 1973-75; fgn. corres., 1976-78; spl. asst., asst. adminstr. Agy. for Internat. Devel., Washington, 1978-81; staff assoc. House Fgn. Affairs Subcom. Internat. Econ. Policy/Trade, Washington, 1981-82; chief U.S. fgn. policy corres. Internat. Reporting Info. Sys., Washington, 1982-83; dir. Main St. Am. and the Third World, Washington, 1985-87; sr. counselor World Bank, Washington, 1983-85, 87-92; dean and prof. Manship Sch. Mass. Comm. La. State U., Baton Rouge, 1992—, Hopkins Breazeale found. prof., 1998; commentator MarketPlace Pub. Radio Internat., 1991—. Bd. dirs., treas. Internat. Ctr. for Journalists; bd. dirs. Pub. Affairs Rsch. Coun., Lamar Advt. Corp.; guest lectr. U.S. Info. Svc., Brazil, 1993, Pulitzer prize juror, 1999-2000; chair Roy W. Howard Award Jury, 2001; fellow Shorenstein Ctr. for the Press, Politics and Pub. Affairs, Kennedy Sch., Harvard U., 2002. Author: Main Street America and the Third World, 1986, 2d edit., 1989, Edgar Snow: A Biography, 1988, revised, 2003 (Critics Choice, L.A. Times, Frank Luther Mott-Kappa Tau Alpha Rsch. award 1988), Entangling Alliances: How the Third World Shapes Our Lives, 1990; co-author: (with George Krimsky) Hold the Press: The Inside Story on Newspapers, 1996, Casanova Was A Book Lover: And Other Naked Facts and Provocative Curiosities About Reading, Writing and Publishing, 2000; author chpts. in books; contbr. numerous articles to profl. jours. including Atlanta Constn., Balt. Sun, Bull. of Atomic Scientists, Boston Globe, Chgo. Tribune, Christian Sci. Monitor, Columbia Journalism Rev., Jour. Commerce, L.A. Times, N.Y. Times, The Nation, others. Officer USMC, 1969-73. Grantee Ford Found., Carnegie Inst., US AID, others, 1985-94; recipient By-Line award Marquette Coll. Journalism, 1993; named Journalism Adminstr. of the Yr., Freedom Forum, 2003. Mem. Assn. of Schs. of Journalism and Mass Comm. (chair task force on alliances 1992-94), Soc. Profl. Journalists. Democrat. Home: 3 Hidden Oak Ln Baton Rouge LA 70810 Office: La State Univ Manship Sch Mass Cmn Baton Rouge LA 70803-0001 E-mail: jhamilt@lsu.edu.

HAMILTON, JOSEPH HANTS, JR., physicist, educator; b. Ferriday, La., Aug. 14, 1932; s. Joseph Hants and Letha (Gibson) H.; m. Jannelle Jauree Landrum, Aug. 5, 1960; children: Melissa Claire, Christopher Landrum. BS, Miss. Coll., 1954, D.Sc. (hon.), 1982; MS, Ind. U., 1956, PhD, 1958; PhD (hon.), Nat. U., Frankfurt, 1992, U. Bucharest, 1999, U. St. Petersburg, 2001. Mem. faculty Vanderbilt U., Nashville, 1958—, prof. physics, 1966—, Landon C. Garland prof. physics, 1981-92, Landon C. Garland disting. prof. physics, 1992—, chmn. dept., 1979-85; adj. prof. Tsinghua U., China, 1986—. Hon. adv. prof. Fudan U., People's Republic of China, 1988—; NSF postdoctoral fellow U. Uppsala, Sweden, 1958-59; rsch. fellow Inst. Nuclear Studies, Amsterdam, 1962; vis. prof. U. Frankfurt, 1979-80, 90, 98, U. Louis Pasteur, Strasbourg, France, 1991; mem. adv. panel Nat. Heavy Ion Labs., 1971-73; mem. nat. policy bd. Holifield Heavy Ion Facility, 1974-84; organizer, chmn. exec. com., prin. investigator Univ. Isotope Separator, Oak Ridge, 1970-95; organizer Univ. Radioactive Ion Beam Consortium, 1996; cons. Oak Ridge Nat. Lab., 1972—; mem. coun. Oak Ridge Assoc. Univs., 1974-80, bd. dirs., 1995-97; organizer, dir. Joint Inst. for Heavy Ion Rsch., Oak Ridge, 1980—; mem. Oak Ridge Health Agreement Steering Panel for State of Tenn., 1993-2000; sci. and tech. advisor coun. for State of Tenn., 1994-2001; chmn. Internat. Conf. Internal Conversion Processes, 1965, Internat. Conf. Radioactivity in Nuclear Spectroscopy, 1969, Internat. Conf. Future Directions in Studies Nuclei far from Stability, 1979, Internat. Conf. Dirs. Nuclear Structure Rsch., 1984; co-chmn. Internat. Workshop Physics with a Recoil Mass Spectrometer, 1986; chmn. Internat. Symposium on Reflections and Directions in Low Energy Heavy Ion Physics, 1991, Internat. Conf. on Fission and Properties of Neutron Rich Nuclei, 1997, Internat. Symposium Perspectives in Nuclear Physics, 1998; co-chair Second Internat. Conf. on Fission and Properties of Neutron Rich Nuclei, 1999; chair third Internat. Conf., on fission and properties neutron rich nuclei, 2002; dir. Vanderbilt Summer Sci. Collaborative for High Sch. Students and Tchrs., 1991—; vis. disting. lab. fellow Oak Ridge Nat. Lab., 2000—. Co-author: Science: Faith and Learning, 1972, ORAU from the Beginning, 1980, Graphical Representation of K-shell and Total Internal Conversion Coefficients from Z=30-104, 1984, Modern Atomic and Nuclear Physics, 1996; co-author, editor: Internal Conversion Processes, 1966, Radioactivity in Nuclear Spectroscopy, 1972, Reactions Between Complex Nuclei, 1974, Future Directions in Studies of Nuclear Far from Stability, 1980, Microscopic Models in Nuclear Structure Physics, 1989, Reflections and Directions in Low Energy Heavy Ion Physics, 1993, Structure of the Vacuum and Elementary Matter, 1997, Fission and Properties of Neutron Rich Nuclei, 1998, Perspectives in Nuclear Physics, 1999, Fission and Properties of Neutron Rich Nuclei, 2000; Third Internat. Conf. Fission and properties of Neutron Rich Nuclei, 2003. assoc. editor Jour. Physics G: Nuc. Physics, 1984-87; internat. advisor nuc. physics World Sci. Pub. Corp., 1986-91, Jour. Modern Physics Letters A, 1986-91; mem. editl. bd. Progress in Particle and Nuc. Physics, 1993-98; contbr. articles to profl. jours., chpts. in books. Mem. Mayor Nashville Citizens Adv. Com. Housing, 1970-74; bd. dirs. Vineyard Conf. Center, Louisville, 1972-77, Danforth assoc., 1965-86, So. Bapt. Conv. Hist. Commn., 1983-91. Recipient Harvie Branscomb Disting. Prof. award Vanderbilt U., 1983-84, Sutherland prize for rsch., 1988, Guy and Rebecca Forman award for outstanding physics tchg., 1990, Thomas Jefferson award for svc. in univ. couns., 1995, Jeffrey Nordhaus award for excellence in undergrad. tchg., 1996, Outstanding Sci. Tchr. award, Tenn., 1998, Humbolt prize W. Germany, 1979, Order Golden Arrow Outstanding Alumni award Miss. Coll., 1985; named State of Tenn. Outstanding Prof. of Yr. Coun. for Advancement and Support Edn., 1991; honored by Internat. Symposium on Nuc. Physics of Our Times, 1992, D. Ilkovic Gold medal Slovak Acad. Sci., 2002; Internat. Sci. and Tech. Cooperation award, Peoples Republic China 2002, GN. Flerov Prize Russia 2003. NSF grantee, 1959-76, ERDA-Dept. Energy grantee, 1975—, First Outstanding Svc. award Oak Ridge Associated U., 2000. Fellow AAAS (Internat. Cooperation award 1996), Am. Phys. Soc. (vice chmn. Southeastern sect. 1972-73, chmn. 1973-74, mem. coun. 1994—, Jesse Beams Gold medal for rsch. 1975, George Peagram Gold medal for tchg. 1988, Francis Slack gold medal for Svc. 2000); mem. Am. Assn. Physics Tchrs., Sigma Xi (chpt. pres. 1970). Home: 305 Mountainside Dr Nashville TN 37215-4324

HAMILTON, LOIS ANN, math educator, consultant; b. Bonners Ferry, Idaho, Oct. 29, 1939; d. Harry Powers and Wilma Eileen (Magart) Copeland; m. John Alexander Hamilton Jr., July 21, 1956 (div. Aug. 1987); foster children: Linda Singer, Theodore Alan Osterhout. BA, Wilkes U., 1969; MS, Elmira Coll., 1974; postgrad., Cornell U., 1976-77, SUNY, Cortland, 1991-92. Cert. nursery and elem. tchr. Sec. to Rev. John A. Hamilton Jr., Pa., N.Y., 1963-70; elem. tchr. Watkins Glen (N.Y.) Cen. Schs., 1969-71; summer sch. tchr. Odessa-Montour N.Y. Sch. Dist., 1970, 71; transition elem. tchr. Addison (N.Y.) Cen. Sch., 1971-74, elem. tchr., 1974-80, kindergarten tchr., 1980-81, remedial math. tchr., 1981-94, tchr. fun with math, ret., 1994—. Tchr. Fun with Math. Addison Community Sch., 1989, 90, 91; co-chmn. A.C.T.I.O.N. Grant Com., Alfred, N.Y., 1988-89; advisor math clubs, Addison, 1987-89, 5th and 6th Grade Math. Clubs, 1987-92; coord. 3rd and 4th Grad. Math. Clubs, 1990-92, writer, bound 3rd and 6th grade, P.E.P. Test Analyses, Addison Ctrl. Sch., 1983-93; chmn. Student of Month Com., 1987-92; cons. in field; lectr. in field. Caretaker elderly person Horseheads, N.Y., 1991-95, vol. 1995-; vol. Red Cross, Elmira, N.Y., 1972, design, print certs. and signs, 1995-, Baptist Christian Sch. Assn. N.Y. State, 2000-; vol. sec. Pastor Sidney S. Aldrich, Horseheads, N.Y., 1994-. Mem. Nat. Coun. Tchrs. Math., Assn. Math. Tchrs. N.Y. State (presenter summer workshop 1989, mem. program com. and presenter 10th ann. meeting 1990, presenter major strand summer workshop 1991), Oreg. Coun. Tchrs. Math., Conceptually Oriented Sci./Math. Integrated Curriculum Inst. (pilot tchr. 1991-92). Republican. Baptist. Avocations: singing, church visitation, reading, helping children. Home: 151 Matthew Cir Horseheads NY 14845-1939

HAMILTON, PENNY RAFFERTY, research executive, writer, educator; b. Altoona, Pa., Feb. 18, 1948; d. William E. and Lois B. Rafferty; m. William A. Hamilton, Dec. 21, 1971. AA, Temple U., 1968; BA, Columbia (Mo.) Coll., 1976; MA, U. Nebr., 1978, PhD, 1981; postdoctoral studies, Menninger Found., Topeka, 1984. Community educator U.S. Forces in Europe, Fulda, Fed. Republic of Germany, 1972-74; health educator Nebr. State Govt., Lincoln, 1974-84; v.p. Advanced Rsch. Inst., Granby, Colo., 1984—. Spl. features editor, newspaper columnist Sun Newspapers/Capital Times, Lincoln, 1982-91; dir. pub. affairs Sta. KHAT-KMXA, Lincoln, 1986-92. Bd. dirs. Grand County Pet Pals, 1992—, Grand County Aviation Assn., 1992—, Friends of Granby Airport, 1992—. Set world and nat. aviation speed record, 1991. Home: PO Box 2001 Granby CO 80446-2001 Office: Advanced Rsch Inst PO Box 2 Granby CO 80446-0002

HAMILTON, RHODA LILLIAN ROSÉN, guidance counselor, language educator, consultant; b. Chgo., May 8, 1915; d. Reinhold August and Olga (Peterson) Rosén; m. Douglas Edward Hamilton, Jan. 23, 1936 (div. Feb. 1952); remarried, Aug. 1995 (dec. 1997); children: Perry Douglas, John Richard Hamilton. Grad., Moser Coll., Chgo., 1932-33; BS in Edn., U. Wis., 1953, postgrad., 1976; MAT, Rollins Coll., 1967; postgrad., Ohio State U., 1959-60; postgrad. in clin. psychology, Mich. State U., 1971, 76, 79, 80; postgrad., Yale U., 1972, Loma Linda U., 1972; postgrad. in computer mgmt. sys., U. Okla., 1976; postgrad. in edn., U. Calif., Berkeley, 1980. Exec. sect. to pres. Ansul Chem. Co., Marinette, Wis., 1934-36; pers. counselor Burneice Larson's Med. Bur., Chgo., 1954-56; adminstrv. asst. to Ernst C. Schmidt Lake Geneva, Wis., 1956-58; assoc. prof. fin. aid Ohio State U., 1958-60; tchr. English to spkrs. of other langs. Istanbul, Turkey, 1960-65; counselor Groveland (Fla.) H.S., 1965-68; guidance counselor, psychol. cons. early childhood edn. Dept. Def. Overseas Dependents Sch., Okinawa, 1968-85; instr./lectr. early childhood Lake Sumter Jr. Coll., Leesburg, Fla., 1986-88; pres. Hamilton Assocs., Groveland, Fla., Frederick, Md., 1986—. Vis. lectr. Okla. State U., 1980; co-owner plumbing, heating bus., Marinette, 1943-49; journalist Rockford (Ill.) Morning Star, 1956-58, Istanbul AP, 1960; lectr. Lake Sumter C.C., 1989—, Lake Sumter Jr. Coll., 1989. Author poetry on Middle East, 1959-64; Career Awareness, 1978; Listen Up, 1997-98. Vol. instr. U.S. citizenship classes, Okinawa, 1971-72; judge Gold Scholarships Okinawa Christian Schs., 1983, 84. Mem. Am. Fedn. Govt. Employees, Fla. Retired Educators, Order Ea. Star (organist; life mem. Shuri One in Okinawa and Trillium 208 in Wis.), Marinette Woman's Club (Wis., pres. 1949-51), Groveland Woman's Club (Fla.), Phi Delta Gamma. Episcopalian. Home: 2408 Ellsworth Way Apt 1A Frederick MD 21702-3124

HAMILTON, RICHARD, Greek language educator; b. Bryn Mawr, Pa., Dec. 19, 1943; s. Charles and Elizabeth Hamilton; m. Lucinda Pantaleoni, Aug. 14, 1965; children: Sarah Elizabeth, Ellen Emma. AB, Harvard U., 1965; PhD, U. Mich., 1971. From asst. prof. to prof. Bryn Mawr Coll., 1971—. Author: Epinikion, 1974, Architecture of Hesiod, 1989, Choes and Anthesteria, 1992, Treasure Map, 2000. Home: 708 Pennstone Rd Bryn Mawr PA 19010-2913 Office: Bryn Mawr Coll Dept Greek 101 N Merion Ave Bryn Mawr PA 19010-2859

HAMILTON, ROBERT WOODRUFF, law educator; b. Syracuse, N.Y., Mar. 4, 1931; s. Walton Hale and Irene (Till) H.; m. Dagmar S. Strandberg, June 2, 1953; children: Eric Clark, Robert Andrew, Meredith Hope. BA, Swarthmore Coll., 1952; JD, U. Chgo., 1955. Bar: D.C. 1956, U.S. Ct. Appeals (D.C. cir.) 1960, U.S. Supreme Ct. 1965. Law clk. to justice Tom Clark U.S. Supreme Ct., Washington, 1955-56; assoc. Gardner, Morrison & Rogers, Washington, 1956-64; assoc. prof. law U. Tex., Austin, 1964-67, prof., 1967—2004, Minerva House Drysdale Regents chair in law. Rsch. dir. U.S. Admin. Conf., Washington, 1972-73; vis. prof. U. Pa., U. Minn., Washington U., St. Louis, others; mem. rev. panel on new drugs HEW, Washington, 1974-77. Author (with Robert Ragazzo and Elizabeth Miller): Texas Practice, vols. 19 and 20, 1973; author: (with Jonathan Macey) Cases on Corporations, 1975; author: 8th rev. edit., 2003, Cases on Contracts, 1984, 2d rev. edit., 1992, Nutshell on Corporations, 1980, 5th rev. edit., 2000, Cases on Corporate Finance, 1984, 2d rev. edit., 1989, Fundamentals of Modern Business, 1990, Money Management for Lawyers and Clients, 1993, Business Organizations: Unincorporated Businesses and Closely Held Corporations, 1996; author: (with Richard Booth) Business Basics for Law Students, 2d edit., 1998; author: 3d edit., 2002. Chmn. bd. dirs. U. Coop. Soc., Austin, 1989-2002; elected mem. Westlake Hills (Tex.) City Coun., 1969-72; chmn. zoning commn. Westlake Hills, 1983-87. Rsch. grantee U. Tex., 1970, 84, 92, 97. Mem. ABA (reporter), Am. Law Inst., Tex. Bar Assn. (partnership com., corp. laws com.), Tex. Bus. Law Found., Order of Coif. Democrat. Office: U Tex Law Sch 727 E Dean Keeton St Austin TX 78705-3224

HAMILTON, SHARON (SAROS), secondary education English educator; b. Detroit, June 6, 1943; d. Spiro George and Rose Mary (Giardina) Saros; m. Robert Morse Hamilton, Aug. 20, 1966 (deceased); children; Emily, Kate, Abigail. BA in English, U. Mich., 1965; MA in English, U. Wis., 1966; PhD in English, U. Ill., 1976. Instr. in English Eastern Mich. U., Ypsilanti, Mich., 1966-67; lectr. in English Hunter Coll., NYC, 1967-68, Lehman Coll., Bronx, 1970-71; tchg. asst. U. Ill., Urbana, Ill., 1972-73; lectr. in English Baylor U., Waco, Tex., 1975-77; instr. in English Phillips Exeter (NH) Acad., 1977-82, Sch. Yr. Abroad, Rennes, France, 1981-82; chair English dept. Buckingham Browne & Nichols Sch., Cambridge, Mass., 1983—. Instr. Exeter Shakespeare Conf., 2002; cons. AP English lit., instr. Taft Edn. Ctr., 2002, 03. Author: Shakespeare: A Teaching Guide, 1993, Solving Common Writing Problems, Solving More Common Writing Problems, 2003, Shakespeare's Daughters, 2003 contbr. articles to profl. jours. Spkr. Secondary Sch. Tchr. Workshop, Folger Libr., Washington, 1983, 84; panelist Exeter Symposium on Poetry, 1983; spkr. New Eng. Theatre Conf., Providence, 1988, Assn. Ind. Schs. of New Eng., Providence, 1994. Recipient Woodrow Wilson fellowship, 1966, Tchr.-Scholar grant NEH, 1992-93; named Ind. Study Summer fellow NEH, 1986, Summer Seminar participant NEH, 1987. Mem. Nat. Coun. Tchrs. English, Internat. Shakespeare Assn. Home: 30 Everett Ave Watertown MA 02472-1882 Office: Buckingham Browne & Nichols Sch Gerry's Landing Rd Cambridge MA 02138 E-mail: sharon_hamilton@bbns.org.

HAMILTON, VIRGINIA MAE, mathematics educator, consultant; b. Winchester, Indiana, Apr. 15, 1946; d. Charles and Mildred Alene (Horseman) Campbell; m. William Earl Hamilton, Dec. 27, 1974; 1 child, Michelle Annette. BS in math., Ball State U., Muncie, Ind., 1968, MA in math., 1974. Math. tchr. Osborn High Sch., Manassas, Va., 1968-71; grad. asst., math. Ball State U., Muncie, Ind., 1971-74; math. tchr. Wes Del High Sch., Gaston, Ind., 1974-76, Ball State U., Muncie, Ind., 1977-87, dir. testing and placement, dir. math learning ctr., 1984-87; math. prof. Shawnee State U., Portsmouth, Ohio, 1987—. Cons. assessment, Fla. and Ohio 2000-; faculty devel. mentor, ACCLAIM NSF project 2002-; assessor, Ohio Dept. of Edn.1999-; NCTM and NCATE Program coord.for Ohio Dept. of Edn., 2001-; cons. placement testing several universities., Calif., Ind., Ohio, 1986—; cons. in svc. Scioto County Schs., Portsmouth, Ohio, 1989—; mentor-tchr. Minority Edn. Advs., Muncie, Ind., 1985-87; presenter, Ohio Acad. Sci., Portsmouth, Ohio, 1988—; assessment chair nat. project to reform Devel. Math., 1992—1998; bd. dirs., Project Discovery South Region, 1993-98, mem. steering com., 1994-98; spkr. at various conf. on math. and assessment; facilitator, Devel. Edn. math. workshop, 1997; assessment presentations at nat. and state conf.; mem. Ohio Faculty Coun., 1998—, exec. bd. dirs., 1999—. Chair, 1999-2002; mem. of a twenty five person people to people math edn. del. to mainland China to advise Chinese Educators on revision of their math edn program in Oct. 2000; author: Testbank for Fundamentals of Mathematics, 1989, Testbank for Elementary Algebra, 1989, Testbank for Intermediate Algebra, 1990, Prepared Tests for Elementary Algebra, 1990, (computer software) Dose Calc, 1984, Arithmetic Skill Builder, 1987, Instructors Manual and Testbank for Intermediate Algebra, 1995; editor: (testbanks) Keedy-Bittinger Worktext Trilogy, 1986, Intermediate Algebra, 1986. Mem. NEA, Nat. Coun. Tchrs. Math., Nat. Assn. Devel. Educators (chmn. com. on math. placement 1990—1998, co-chair math. SPIN 1994-97), Math. Assn. Am., Ohio Coun. Tchrs. Math., South Ctrl. Ohio Coun. Tchrs. Math. (bd. dirs. 1993-97), Ohio Assn. Devel. Educators (chmn. spl. interest group 1989—1999, treas., 1992-97, Svc. award 1992), Ohio Edn. Assn., Am. Math. Assn. 2-Yr. Colls., Am. Assn. Higher Edn., Assn. Supr. Curriculum Devel., ATE. Avocations: crochet, plaster craft. Office: Shawnee State U 940 2nd St Portsmouth OH 45662-4347 E-mail: ghamilton@shawnee.edu.

HAMIN, AMY LYNN, speech and language pathologist; b. Stevens Point, Wis., Nov. 6, 1961; d. David John and Marilyn C. (Dorn) Jacobs; m. Jody Arthur Hamin, July 13, 1985; 1 child, Cody Jacob. BS, U. Wis., Stevens Point, 1984, MS, 1985. Cert. in speech and lang. pathology; cert. Hanen Parent trainer. Speech/lang. pathologist Marshfield (Wis.) Sch. Dist., 1986-92, Wisconsin Rapids (Wis.) Pub. Schs., 1992—. Varsity cheerleader coach John Edwards H.S., Port Edwards, Wis., 1995-98; evaluator, diagnostician, cons. Augmentative Comm. Tech. Team, Wisconsin Rapids, 1992—; provider speech/lang. svcs. Mem. Am. Speech/Lang./Hearing Assn. Lutheran. Avocations: shopping, collecting and refinishing antiques, fishing, reading. Home: 1454 A County JJ Nekoosa WI 54457

HAMLER, SHELLEY JEFFERSON, administrator; b. Cin., Oct. 22, 1951; d. Browne Elliott and Elizabeth Sanfré (Showes) Jefferson. BS in Edn., Ohio State U., 1972; MEd, Xavier U., 1974; EdD, U. Cin., 1995. Tchr. Cutter Jr. High Sch., Cin., 1972-76, Woodward High Sch., Cin., 1976-82; coord. Cin. Pub. Schs., 1982-86, local sch. evaluator, 1986, asst. prin., 1986-88, prin., 1988-94, dir. career paths, 1994-98; asst. supt. Princeton City Schs., 1998—2002, ret., 2002; project dir. Warren County Edn. Svc. Ctr., 2002—. Asst. prof. Univ. Ctr. Named Prin. of Yr. State of Ohio, 1994-95. Mem. NAACP (life), Nat. Alliance of Black Sch. Educators (life), Urban League, The Links Inc. (Cin. chpt.), Delta Sigma Theta (life), Delta Kappa Gamma (scholar 1994-95).

HAMLIN, WILFRID GARDINER, retired literature and philosophy educator; b. N.Y.C. s. Talbot Faulkner and Hilda Blanche Hamlin; m. Elizabeth Brett Hamlin, June 11, 1944 (dec. Apr. 1968); 1 child, Christopher Stone. BA, Wayne U.; MA, Antioch Coll., Yellow Springs, Ohio; PhD, Union Inst., Cin. Test psychologist Johnson O'Connor Rsch. Found., N.Y.C., 1940-42, 44-46, Adjutant Gen.'s Office, N.Y.C., 1945-46; mem. faculty Goddard Coll., Plainfield, Vt., 1948-99, coll. editor, 1975-98, mem. emeritus faculty, 1998—; student, asst. Black Mt. Coll. (N.C.), 1940—42. Edn. cons., 1950's and 60's. Author: To Start a School, 1971; editor: Teacher/School/Child, 1964. Avocations: photography, reading, theater, films, classical music. Home: PO Box 263 Plainfield VT 05667-0263

HAMM, GEORGE ARDEIL, retired secondary education educator, hypnotherapist, consultant; b. San Diego, Aug. 13, 1934; s. Charles Ardeil and Vada Lillian (Sharrah) H.; m. Marilyn Kay Nichols, July 1, 1972; children: Robert Barry, Charles Ardeil II, patricia Ann. BS in Music, No. Ariz. U., 1958, MA in Music Edn., 1961; MA in Ednl. Adminstrn., Calif. Lutheran Coll., 1978, MS in Guidance and Counseling, 1981; PhD, U. Mass., 1998. Cert. secondary sch. tchr., adminstr. pupil pers. svcs., Calif., clin. hypnotherapist. Tchr. music Needles (Calif.) H.S., 1958-61; music sociology, psychology tchr., counselor Hueneme H.S., Oxnard, Calif., 1961-93; ret. Dean instrn. U. Martial Arts and Scis.; founder Nat. Judo Inst., Colorado Springs, Colo., Coll. Sport Sci., Nat. Judo Inst.; cons. applied sport hypnotherapy; creator tchg. program. Contbr. numerous articles to nat. and internat. Judo jours. Served with USMC, 1953-55, Korea. Mem. Am. Fedn. Tchrs., Am. Coun. Hypnotist Examiners, U.S. Judo Assn. Inc. (7th degree black belt of Judo, 8th degrees black belt of Ju Ji Tsu, master level coach of Judo, 1980, cert. sr. rank examiner), Phi Delta Kappa, Kappa Delta Pi. Republican. Mem. Lds Ch. Pioneer ednl. hypnosis. Home: 2560 Ruby Dr Oxnard CA 93030-8607

HAMM, THOMAS DOUGLAS, archivist, history educator; b. New Castle, Ind., Jan. 8, 1957; s. James Stewart and Lois Diane (Knotts) H.; m. Mary Louise Reynolds, May 12, 1984. BA, Butler U., 1979; MA, Ind. U., 1981, PhD, 1985. Editorial asst. Jour. Am. History, Bloomington, Ind., 1981-84; vis. asst. prof. Ind. U., Indpls., 1985-87; archivist, asst. and assoc. prof. history Earlham Coll., Richmond, Ind., 1987-2000, prof., 2000—. Cons. Conner Prairie, Noblesville, Ind., 1990—, Henry County Hist. Soc., New Castle, 1985—. Author: Transformation of American Quakerism, 1988 (Brewer prize 1987), Earlham College: A History, 1997, God's Government Begun, 1995, The Quakers in America, 2003; editorial bd. Ind. Mag. of History, 1990-93; book rev. editor Quaker History, 1990—; contbr. articles to profl. jours. Mem. exec. com. Ind. Yearly Meeting of Friends, Muncie, 1992—93, 2002—; chmn. geneal. pub. com. Ind. Hist. Soc., Indpls., 1992—95, mem. libr. com., 1995—2001. Recipient O'Kell Teaching prize Ind. U., 1981; Butler U. scholar, 1978; Phi Kappa Phi grad. fellow, 1979; Ind. Hist. Soc. rsch. fellow, 1982. Mem. Orgn. Am. Historians, Am. Hist. Assn., Am. Soc. Ch. History, Conf. of Quaker Historians and Archivists (convener 1988-90, 2000—), Ind. Assn. Historians (exec. bd. 1990-92, pres.-elect 1995, pres. 1995-96), Soc. Ind. Archivists (pres. 1994-95), Ind.

Libr. and Hist. Bd. (pres. 1999—). Democrat. Mem. Soc. Of Friends. Avocations: genealogy, reading, antiques. E-mail. Home: PO Box 410 Spiceland IN 47385-0410 Office: Earlham Coll Library Richmond IN 47374 E-mail: tomh@earlham.edu.

HAMMACK, GLADYS LORENE MANN, reading specialist, educator; b. Corsicana, Tex., Nov. 15, 1923; d. John Elisha and Maude (Kelly) Mann; m. Charles Joseph Hammack; Sept. 4, 1949;children: Charles Randall, Cynthia Lorain, Kelly Joseph. B in Journalism, U. Tex., 1953; elem. tchr. cert., U. Houston, 1970, MEd, cert. reading specialist, U. Houston, 1974. Cert. profl. reading specialist, Tex. Tchr. Zion Luth. Sch., Pasadena, Tex., 1964-68, Housman Elem. Sch., Houston, 1970-74, Pine Shadows Elem. Sch., Houston, 1975-76; reading lab. tchr. Spring Br. High Sch., Houston, 1976-82; tchr. St. Mark Luth. Sch., Houston, 1982-88, pvt. tutor and homework study hall tchr., 1988—. Mem. Spring Br. Ind. Sch. Dist. Textbook Selection Com., Houston, 1973; field rep. to. student tchrs., U. Houston, 1974; presenter reading workshop, U. Tex., Austin, 1983. Author: (guide) Evaluation of Textbooks, 1974. Del. Tex. Dem. Conv., Austin, 1960. Recipient scholarship, U. Tex. Sports Assn., Austin, 1947. Mem. Tex. State Tchrs. Assn., Tex. Ret. Tchrs. Assn. Lutheran. Avocations: collector shells, foreign dolls, travel, reading. Home: 8926 Theysen Dr Houston TX 77080-3023

HAMMEL, ERNEST MARTIN, medical educator, academic administrator; b. Ashtabula, Ohio, May 2, 1939; s. Eugene Christian and Etna Maria (Costas) H.; m. Martha Lorene Hertzer, Dec. 16, 1961; children: Eric John, James Martin. BS, Heidelberg Coll., 1962; MPH, U. Mich., 1966; PhD, 1976. Program develper Mich. Assn. Regional Programs, East Lansing, 1973-74; asst. dir. ops., 1975-76; exec. dir. OHEP Ctr. Med. Edn., Southfield, Mich., 1976—2002, dir. emeritus, 2002—. Adj. asst. dean Wayne State U. Sch. Medicine, Detroit, 1993-2002; adj. faculty health svcs. adminstr. extended degree programs Ctrl. Mich. U., Mt. Pleasant, 1980-99; adj. asst. prof. of cmty. and family medicine, Wayne State U. Sch. of Medicine, 1993—; co-dir. SAVE 100 Pharmacy Initiative of WSU-OHEP Consortium Quality, Cost-Effective Med. Care Program, 1995—; mem. task force Mich. Antibiotic Resistance Reduction Program, 1998-2002; task groups coord. OHEP Resource Ctr. on Gen. Competencies, 2002—. Editor several med. care orgns. publs. Contbr. articles to profl. jours. Trustee Kenny Mich. Rehab. Found., Rochester Hills, 1984-88; chmn. program consultation and cont. med. edn. devel. CME Accreditation com. Mich. State Med. Soc., Lansing, 1989—. Behavioral Sci. fellow U. Mich., 1969-70, Behavioral Sci. rsch. fellow, 1971-72; grad. student rsch. grantee Rackham Sch. Grad. Studies, U. Mich., 1972; Pub. Health svc. trainee U. Mich., 1965-66, 70-71, 72-73; contract Nat. Ctr. Health Svcs. R & D, 1973. Mem.: APHA, Mich. Pub. Health Assn., Mich. Assn. Med. Edn. (pres. 1995—97), Assn. Hosp. Med. Edn. (chmn. coun. med. edn. consortia 1997—99), U. Mich. Alumni Assn., Heidelberg Fellows. Office: OHEP Ctr for Med Edn 21415 Civic Center Dr Ste 301 Southfield MI 48076-3954

HAMMEL, HAROLD THEODORE, physiology and biophysics educator, researcher; b. Huntington, Ind., May 8, 1921; s. Audry Harold and Ferne Jane (Wiles) H.; m. Dorothy King, Dec. 29, 1948; children: Nannette, Heidi. BS in Physics, Purdue U., 1943; MS in Physics, Cornell U., 1950, PhD in Zoology, 1953; DSc (hon.), Huntington Coll., 1999. Jr. physicist Los Alamos (N.Mex.) Lab., 1944-46, staff physicist, 1948-49; from instr. to asst. prof. U. Pa., Phila., 1953-61; assoc. prof., fellow John B. Pierce Lab. Yale U., New Haven, 1961-68; prof. Scripps Instn. of Oceanography U. Calif., San Diego, 1968-88, emeritus prof., 1988—. Adj. prof. physiology and biophysics Ind. U., Bloomington, 1989—; fgn. sci. mem. Max Planck Inst. for Physiol. and Clin. Rsch., 1978—; U.S. sr. scientist Alexander von Humboldt Found., 1981. Author: (with Scholander) Osmosis and Tensile Solvent, 1976; contbr. over 200 articles to profl. jours. Fellow AAAS; mem. Am. Phys. Soc., Am. Chem. Soc., Am. Physiol. Soc. (Fifth August Krogh Disting. lectureship 1998, Honor award Environ. and Exercize sect. 1996), Am. Soc. Mammalogy, Norwegian Acad. Sci. and Letters. Democrat. Achievements include first measurement of phloem sap, and of xylem sap pressure in higher plants; research in osmosis and fluid transport in plants; thermal and metabolic responses to moderate cold exposure in Australian Aborigine, Kalahari Bushmen, Innuit, Alacalut Indians; explanation of freezing without cavitation in evergreen plants; extension and application of kinetic theory to Hulett's theory of solvent tension and to osmotic force in Starling's experiment; research in theory of adjustable set point and gain for regulation of body temperature in vertebrates, research in control of salt gland function in birds. Home: 1605 Ridgeway Dr Ellettsville IN 47429-9474 Office: Ind U Med Scis Program Bloomington IN 47405 E-mail: hhammel@indiana.edu.

HAMMER, JOYCE MAE, gifted and talented education educator; b. Milw., May 21, 1933; d. George and Sara (Arne) Leviton; children: Deborah, Lori. BS, U. Ill., 1954; MA, Northwestern U., 1958, postgrad., 1974-78, Nat. Coll. Edn., Evanston, Ill., 1986-89, Aurora U., 1990-92, 95. Tchr. math. Fairview Sch., Skokie, Ill., 1957-65, Arie Crown Sch., 1967-72, Fairview South Sch., 1972-77, elem. tchr. gifted math. edn., coord. gifted edn., designer sch. gifted program, 1978—. Recipient Those Who Excel award; grantee. Mem. Nat. Coun. Tchrs. Math., Ill. Coun. Tchrs. Math., Ill. Assn. for Gifted Children, Phi Delta Kappa.

HAMMER, RICHARD LEE, music educator; b. Huron, S.D., July 8, 1953; s. Gilmore Albert and Neva Grace (Eckmann) H.; m. Teresa Marie Lathrop, June 18, 1991; children: Kimberly Lea Shuffield, Cody William. BA in Music Edn., East Tex. State U., 1977. Cert. secondary tchr., Tex. Band dir. Hughes Springs (Tex.) High Sch., 1977-80, Rains High Schs., Emory, Tex., 1980-81, Redwater (Tex.) High Sch., 1984—. Owner, gen. mgr. Winnsboro (Tex.) Broadcasting Corp., 1979-84. Mem. Four States Bandmasters Assn. (pres. 1991-92, 97-98, exec. sec. 1992-96), Tex. Bandmasters Assn., Tex. Music Educators Assn., Phi Mu Alpha Sinfonia (pres. Pi Psi chpt. 1975-77, rep. to nat. conv. 1976). Republican. Methodist. Avocations: fishing, golf, tennis. Office: Redwater Ind Sch Dist PO Box 347 Redwater TX 75573-0347

HAMMERLE, HOLLY ANN, health and physical education educator; b. San Antonio, Dec. 22, 1945; d. Clarence B. and Pearl A. (Webb) H. BS, Pa. State U., 1967; MEd, Colo. State U., 1970. Cert. health, driver edn., phys. edn. and biology tchr., Va. Health and phys. edn. instr. Falls Church H.S., Fairfax County, Va., 1967-72, Chantilly H.S., Fairfax County, 1972—, coach field hockey, softball and track, 1967-88, head mens gymnastics coach, 1989-98. Grad. asst. Colo. State U., Ft. Collins, 1969-70. Bd. dirs. Newgate Forest Homeowners Assn., Centreville, Va., 1980-92; v.p. West Fairfax County Citizens Assn., Centreville, 1986-95; mem. Land Use Com., Centreville, 1990-95. Mem. NEA, Va. Edn. Assn., Fairfax Edn. Assn., Am. Assn. Health, Phys. Edn., Recreation and Dance, Izaak Walton League of Am., USA Gymnastics Profl. Avocations: dog showing, dog agility and obedience, outdoor activities, reading. Office: Chantilly HS 4201 Stringfellow Rd Chantilly VA 20151-2622

HAMMON, KATHLEEN CAMPBELL, health science association administrator, educator; b. Rocky Mountain, N.C., June 21, 1950; d. Walker Aylett and Sarah Davis Campbell; m. Gordon Lee Hammon, June 21, 1978 (dec. Sept. 1991); children: Anna Lee, Gordon Lee, Walker Lee. BA in Sociology, N.C. State U., 1973, MEd in Guidance and Pers. Scis., 1976. Cert. elem. sch. counselor. Instr. Wake Tech. C.C., Raleigh, N.C., 1976-77; owner, mgr. Coll. Exxon, Raleigh, 1978-92; coord. Christmas Events Artspace, Raleigh, 1993; curator Joel Lane Hist. House, Raleigh, 1994-95; project mgr. Cortium Info. Tech., N.C. State U., 1995; aerobics instr. City of Raleigh Parks and Recreation Dept., 1996; family support coord. Brain Injury Assn. N.C., Raleigh, 1996—. Named Outstanding Citizen and Leader, Bus. Leader Mag., Raleigh, 1996, 97, NC TBI Task Force, 2003, Plmstead Project Access Coord., 2002. Bd. dirs. Life Experiences, Cary, N.C., 1993—; adminstrv. bd. Fairmont Meth., Raleigh, 1993-96; vol., announcer N.C. Spl. Olympics Summer Games, Raleigh, 1996-98; mem. Raleigh and N.C. task force ACCESS, Brain Injury Resources. Mem. Cardinal Singers of Raleigh, Adv. Coun., Carolina's Med Traumatic Barin Injury Rsch. Coun., 2001, Penn Life Adv. Coun., 2002. Methodist. Office: Brain Injury Assn NC 133 Fayetteville Street Mall Raleigh NC 27601-1356

HAMMOND, CHARLES BESSELLIEU, obstetrician, gynecologist, educator; b. Ft. Leavenworth, Kans., July 24, 1936; s. Claude G. and Alice (Sims) H.; m. Peggy A. Hammond, June 21, 1958; children: Sharon L., Charles B. BS, The Citadel, 1957, Duke U., 1961. Diplomate Am. Bd. Ob-Gyn. Intern in surgery Duke U., 1961-62, resident in ob-gyn, 1962-63, 66-69, fellow in reproductive endocrinology, 1963-64, asst. prof. dept. ob-gyn, 1969-73, asso. prof., 1973-78, prof., 1978-81, E.C. Hamblen prof., 1981—, chmn., 1980—2002. Contbr. in field. Served with USPHS, 1964-66. Fellow (hon.) Royal Coll. Ob-gyn. (ad eundeum), Soc. Ob-gyn. Can. (hon.); mem. AMA, Am. Fertility Soc. (pres. 1985), ACOG (chmn. dist. IV 1997-2000, pres. 2002), Am. Assn. Ob-Gyn. Found. (pres. 1996-2002), Assn. Profs. Obstetrics and Gynecology, Am. Gynecol. and Obstet. Soc. (pres. 1993-94), Soc. Gynecol. Investigation, Am. Gynecol. Soc., Am. Assn. Obstet. and Gynecology, N.C. Med. Soc., N.C. Soc. Obstetricians and Gynecologists (pres. 1985), Am. Gynecol. Club (pres. 1994), Inst. of Medicine. Presbyterian. Home: 2827 McDowell Rd Durham NC 27705-5604 Office: Duke U Med Ctr PO Box 3853 Durham NC 27710 E-mail: hammo005@mc.duke.edu.

HAMMOND, CHARLES ROBERT, astronomer, educator; b. Table Grove, Ill., Nov. 7, 1915; s. Thomas Arthur and Julia Berniece (Parmenter) H.; m. Jean Marguerite Jones, Nov. 16, 1946; children: Robert Arthur, Philip Warner. AB in Astronomy, UCLA, 1938. Tchg. asst. astronomy UCLA, 1936-38; co-dir. La Crescenta (Calif.) Obs., 1938-40; organizer, libr., edn. dept. Lockheed Aircraft Corp., Burbank, Calif., 1940-41; chief libr. Vega Aircraft Corp. (subs. Lockheed), Burbank, Calif., 1941-42; contract technicist, assoc. physicist, chief libr. divsn. Naval Ordnance Lab., Washington, Silver Spring, Md., 1942-46; mgr. tech. publs., mgr. office svcs., libr. Hartford-Empire Co. (Emhart Corp.), various cities, Conn., 1946-78; instr. and lectr. astronomy U. Hartford (Hillyer Coll.), Conn., 1957-72. Instr., lectr. astronomy St. Joseph Coll., West Hartford, Conn., Tunxis C.C., Bristol, Conn., and Ctrl. Conn. State U., New Britain, 1960-82; adj. prof. astronomy Trinity Coll., Hartford, 1981—. Contbr. sect. on chem. elements to Chem. Rubber Co. Handbook of Chemistry and Physics, 46th-85th edits., 1964-; contbr. articles to profl. jours. Historian First Ch. Christ Congl., West Hartford, 1982-92. Mem. Soc. for Rsch. on Meteorites, Meteoritical Soc., Astron. Soc. of Pacific, Brit. Astron. Assn., Royal Astron. Soc. Can., Astron. Soc. Greater Hartford (hon., former pres., Astronomer of Yr. 1993), Civitan Club Hartford (former pres.), Sigma Xi. Achievements include being first to identify positively both meteorites that fell in Wethersfield, Conn., 1971, 82. Home: 17 Greystone Rd West Hartford CT 06107-3728 Office: Trinity Coll Physics and Astronomy Dept Hartford CT 06106 also: East Hartland Astron Obs East Hartland CT 06027

HAMMOND, DAVID ALAN, stage director, educator; b. NYC, June 3, 1948; s. Jack and Elizabeth Alida (Furno) H. BA magna cum laude, Harvard U., 1970; M.F.A., Carnegie-Mellon U., 1972. Mem. faculty Juilliard Theatre Center, N.Y.C., 1972-74; asst. conservatory dir. Am. Conservatory Theatre, San Francisco, 1974-81, assoc. stage dir., 1974-78; dir. Summer Tng. Congress, 1976-80, resident stage dir., 1979-81. Adj. assoc. prof. acting and directing Yale Sch. Drama, New Haven, 1981—85; adj. prof. dept. dramatic art U. N.C., Chapel Hill, 1985—88, prof., 1988—; artistic dir. PlayMakers Repertory Co., Chapel Hill, 1985—92, 1999—, assoc. producing dir., 1992—99; guest artist Pacific Conservatory Performing Arts, 1976, U. Wash., 1977, SUNY, Purchase, 1979, Tisch Sch. Arts/NYU, NYC, 1999—2003; guest dir. Aspen (Colo.) Music Festival, 1974—75, San Francisco Opera, 1978, Carmel (Calif.) Bach Festival, 1979—80, Sherwood Shakespeare Festival, Oxnard, Calif., 1981, Roundabout Theatre, N.Y.C., 1983, Valley Shakespeare Festival, Saratoga, Calif., 1984, 86, 88, Shakespeare Festival of Dallas, 1990, Teatro Alianza, Montevideo, 1992, Teatro Ailanza, Montevideo, 1994, Teatro Alianza, Montevideo, Uruguay, 1997, Inst. Teatral El Galpun, Montevideo, 1995, Opera Co. N.C., 1998—99; resident dir. Yale Repertory Theatre, New Haven, 1981—85; Arts Am. cultural specialist U.S. Info. Svc., 1992, 94; guest prof. Escuela Mcpl. de Arte Dramatico, 2003, Escuela de Espresion Teatral Anglo-o.m.b.u., 2003, El Univ. del Plata, Montevideo, Uruguay, 2003. Recipient Drama-Logue Critics award, L.A., 1980, 81, Florencio award, Montevideo, Uruguay, 1992. Mem. Soc. Stage Dirs. and Choreographers, Actors' Equity, Am. Guild Mus. Artists, Dramatists' Guild, Nat. Theater Conf., Assn. for Theatre in Higher Edn. Office: PlayMakers Repertory Co Ctr For Dramatic Art cb 3235 Chapel Hill NC 27599-0001 E-mail: dhammond@email.unc.edu.

HAMMOND, DEBORAH E. special education educator, consultant; b. Jackson, Mich., May 9, 1955; d. Robert E. and Elaine (Spicer) Finn; m. Dusty S. Hammond, May 28, 1983; children: Crystal Lynn, April Renae. BS in Elem. Edn., hearing impaired K-12, Ea. Mich. U., 1980; MS in Learning Disabilities, Kans. State U., 1992. Itinerant spl. edn. tchr., cons. Twin Lakes Ednl. Coop., Clay Ctr., Kans., 1981-89; spl. edn. tchr. Ctrl. Kans. Coop., Salina, Kans., 1990—. Supt., tchr. Bethel United Meth. Ch., Longford, Kans., 1983-90; dean, counselor United Meth. Ch. Camps, Abilene, Kans., 1995; parade coord. Longford (Kans.) Rodeo Club, 1984—. Mem. Alexander Graham Bell Coun. for Exceptional Children (childrens rights coord. for hearing impaired, 1985—, in state of Kans., 1993—). Republican. Avocations: reading, cooking, horseback riding, violin, piano. Home: 999 2nd Rd Longford KS 67458-9425 Office: Ctrl Kans Coop Ctrl HS 650 E Crawford St Salina KS 67401-5119

HAMMOND, EDWARD H. university president; b. McAllen, Tex., May 4, 1944; s. Will J. and Bergit A. (Lund) H.; m. Vivian hammeke, Aug. 26, 1967; children: Kelly Edvidge, Lance Edward, Julie Marie. BS in Speech, Kans. State Tchrs. Coll., 1966, MS, 1967; PhD, U. MO., 1971. Asst. dir. of field svcs. Kans. State Tchrs. Coll., Emporia, 1966-67; dir. student affairs Purdue U. North Cen. campus, Westville, Ind., 1967-68; counselor housing office U. Mo., Columbia, 1969-70; asst. dean of students So. Ill. U., Carbondale, 1970, asst. to pres. for student rels., 1970-73; v.p. student affairs Seton Hall U., S. Orange, N.J., 1973-76, U. Louisville, 1976-87; pres. Fort Hays State U., Hays, Kans., 1987—. Chair bd. trustees Boost Alcohol Consciousness Concerning the Health of U. Students of the U.S. Inc., 1987-93; trustee The Lincoln Found., 1979-87; mem. Inter-Assn. Task Force on Coll. Alcohol Abuse and Misuse, 1984—; vis. faculty mem. Ind. U., Bloomington, 1972-83; cons. in field. Contbr. articles to profl. jours. NDEA fellow U. Mo., 1968-70; named to Mid-Am. Edn. Hall of Fame, 1997. Mem. Am. Coun. on Edn., Am. Assn. State Colls. and Univs., Am. Assn. Univ. Adminstrs., Nat. Assn. Student Pers. Adminstrs. (nat. pres. 1983, John Jones award 1986), Kans. C. of C. and Industry (bd. dirs. 1990—), Pi Kappa Delta, Sigma Phi Epsilon. Avocations: golf, racquetball, water sports, tennis. Office: Fort Hays State U 600 Park St Bldg 1 Hays KS 67601-4099 E-mail: ehammond@fhsu.edu.

HAMMOND, HAROLD LOGAN, pathology educator, oral and maxillofacial pathologist; b. Hillsboro, Ill., Mar. 18, 1934; s. Harold Thomas and Lillian (Carlson) H.; m. Sharon Bunton, Aug. 1, 1954 (dec. 1974); 1 child, Connie; m. Pat J. Palmer, June 3, 1986. Student Millikin U., 1953-57, Roosevelt U., Chgo., 1957-58; DDS, Loyola U., Chgo., 1962; MS, U. Chgo., 1967. Diplomate Am. Bd. Oral and Maxillofacial Pathology. Intern, U. Chgo. Hosps., Chgo., 1962-63, resident, 1963-66, chief resident in oral pathology, 1966-67; asst. prof. oral pathology U. Iowa, Iowa City, 1967-72, assoc. prof., 1972-80, assoc. prof., dir. surg. oral pathology, 1980-83, prof., dir., 1983—; cons. pathologist Hosp. Gen. de Managua, Nicaragua, 1970-90, VA Hosp., Iowa City, 1977—. Cons. editor: Revista de la Asociation de Nicaragua, 1970-71, Revista de la Federacion Odontologica de Centroamerica y Panama, 1971-77. Contbr. articles to sci. jours. Recipient Mosby Pub. Co. Scholarship award, 1962. Fellow AAAS, Am. Acad. Oral and Maxillofacial Pathology; mem. Am. Men and Women of Sci., N.Y. Acad. Scis., AAUP, Internat. Assn. Oral Pathologists, Internat. Assn. Dental Rsch., N.Am. Soc. Head and Neck Pathologists, Am. Dental Assn., Am. Assn. for Dental Rsch. Avocations: collecting antique clocks, collecting gambling paraphernalia, collecting toys. Home: 1732 Brown Deer Rd Coralville IA 52241-1157 Office: U Iowa Dental Sci Bldg Iowa City IA 52242-1001

HAMMOND, JANE LAURA, retired law librarian, lawyer; b. nr. Nashua, Iowa; d. Frank D. and Pauline Hammond. BA, U. Dubuque, 1950; MS, Columbia U., 1952; JD, Villanova U., 1965, LHD, 1993. Bar: Pa. 1965. Cataloguer Harvard Law Libr., 1952-54; asst. libr. Sch. Law Villanova (Pa.) U., 1954-62; libr. Sch. Law, Villanova (Pa.) U., 1962-76; prof. law Sch. Law Villanova (Pa.) U., 1965-76; law libr., prof. law Cornell U., Ithaca, N.Y., 1976-93. Adj. prof. Drexel U., 1971-74; mem. depository libr. coun. to pub. printer U.S. Govt. Printing Office, 1975-78; cons. Nat. Law Libr., Monrovia, Liberia, 1989. Fellow ALA; mem. ABA (coun. sect. legal edn. 1984-90, mem. com. on accreditation 1982-87, mem. com. on stds. rev. 1987-95), PEO, Coun. Nat. Libr. Assn. (sec.-treas. 1971-72, chmn. 1979-80), Am. Assn. Law Librs. (sec. 1965-70, pres. 1975-76). Episcopalian. Office: Cornell U Sch Law Myron Taylor Hall Ithaca NY 14853

HAMMOND, MARY SAYER, art educator; b. Bellingham, Wash., Oct. 1, 1946; d. Boyd James and Jacqueline Anna (Thurston) Sayer; m. Lester Wayne Hammond, Aug. 26, 1967 (div. Feb. 1972); m. Wiley Devere Sanderson, Jan. 13, 1983. BFA in Art Edn., U. Ga., 1967, MFA in Photo Design, 1977; PhD in History of Photo/Art Edn., Ohio State U., 1986. Art supr. Madison County Pub. Schs., Danielsville, Ga., 1968-71; art instr. U. Ga., Athens, 1971-73, instr. photo design, 1975-76; instr. in art edn. North Ga. Coll., Dalonega, 1975; instr. in art Valdosta (Ga.) State Coll., 1976-77, asst. prof. art, 1979-80; asst. prof. art, Am. Studies George Mason U., Fairfax, Va., 1980-87, assoc. prof. art, Am. Studies, 1987-94, prof. art, Am. studies, 1995-98, dir. divsn. art studio. Adminstrv. assoc. Ohio State U., Columbus, 1978-79, tchg. assoc., 1977-78; co-dir. Saturday program U. Ga., 1966-76, tchg. asst., 1974. Photographs represented in permanent collections at Ctr. for Creative Photography, Ariz., Internat. Mus. Photography, Rochester, N.Y., Nat. Gallery of Art, Washington, Nat. Mus. Women in Arts, Washington. Treas. Faculty Senate of Va., 1991-96. Grantee Fulbright Hays Commn., 1973-74; travel grantee Samuel H. Kress Found., 1986, George Mason U., 1991, 93, 96-98; photographer's fellow NEA, 1982-84. Mem. Soc. Photo Edn. (mid-Atlantic bd. dirs. 1990-98), Phi Kappa Phi (hon.). E-mail: mshammond@earthlink.net.

HAMMOND, MICHAEL, linguistics educator; b. L.A., Mar. 30, 1957; s. John and Felicia Florence (Giganti) H.; m. Linda Ann Rousos, Jan. 2, 1987 (div. 1992); 1 child, Joseph Rousos-Hammond; m. Diane Kathleen Ohala, Mar. 13, 1999. BA, UCLA, 1979, MA, 1981, CPhil, 1982, PhD, 1984. Vis. asst. prof. U. Minn., Mpls., 1983-84; asst. prof. U. Wis., Milw., 1984-88; asst. prof. linguistics U. Ariz., Tucson, 1988-92, assoc. prof., 1992-99, prof., 1999—, head dept. linguistics, 2001—. Mem. faculty senate U. Wis., Milw., 1987-88, U. Ariz., Tucson, 1992-94. Author: Constraining Metrical Theory, 1988, Phonology of English, 2000, Programming for Linguists: Java Technology for Language Researchers, 2002, Programming for Linguists: Perl Programming for Language Researchers, 2003. Fogarty sr. internat. fellow NIH, Paris, 1992-94. Mem. Linguistic Soc. Am. Avocations: hiking, bridge. Office: U Ariz Dept Linguistics Tucson AZ 85721-0001 E-mail: hammond@u.arizona.edu.

HAMMOND, NORMAN DAVID CURLE, archaeology educator, researcher; b. Brighton, Eng., July 10, 1944; BA, U. Cambridge, Eng., 1966, Diploma in Classical Archaeology, 1967, MA, 1970, PhD, 1972, ScD, 1987, DSc (hon.), 1999. Rsch. faculty Cambridge U., Eng., 1967-75; faculty Bradford U., Eng., 1975-77; vis. prof. Rutgers U., 1977-78, faculty, 1978-88, assoc. prof., 1978-84, prof., 1984-88; member staff Peabody Mus., Harvard U., 1988—, Willey lectr., 2000; prof. archaeology Boston U., 1988—. Vis. prof. U. Calif., Berkeley, 1977, Jilin U., China, 1981, Calif. Acad. Sci., 1984-85, U. Paris, 1987, Acad. Scis., USSR, 1991, U. Bonn, 1994; vis. faculty U. Cambridge, 1981-82, 91, 96-97, U. Oxford, 1989, 2004; archaeology corr. The Times, London (Press award, Brit. Archaeol. Awards 1994, 98), 1967—; field work in North Africa, Afghanistan, Greece, Guatemala, Belize, Ecuador, Spain; disting. lectr. Montana State U., 1996, Bushnell lectr. Cambridge U., 1997, Stone lectr. AIA, 1998, 2004, Brush lectr. AIA, 2001, Armand Brunswick disting. lectr. Met. Mus. Art, 2001. Author: (with F.R. Allchin) The Archaeology of Afghanistan, 1977, (with G.R. Willey) Maya Archaeology and Ethnohistory, 1979, Ancient Maya Civilization, 1982, 5th edit., 1994, various foreign edits., Cuello: An Early Maya Community in Belize, 1991; numerous monographs on excavations in No. Belize, 1973, 75, 76, Lubaantun, 1975, Nohmul, 1985; gen. editor: Procs., 44th Internat. Congress of Americanists, 1982-84. Dumbarton Oaks fellow, 1988; Rockefeller Found. scholar, 1997. Fellow Soc. Antiquaries London (medallist 2001), Brit. Acad. Office: Boston Univ Dept Archaeology 675 Commonwealth Ave Boston MA 02215-1406

HAMMOND, VERNON FRANCIS, school administrator; b. Grand Rapids, Mich., Sept. 27, 1931; s. Rodney Clyve and Wylida Helen (Bonner) H.; m. Anne Louise Seeley, Dec. 10, 1954; children; Michelle, Milissa, Milanie, Michael. BA, Bob Jones U., 1959, MA, 1960; postgrad., Butler U., 1968-69, Pepperdine U., 1969-72; MEd, Lynchburg Coll., 1975. Cert. ednl. adminstrn. Tchr., coach, vice prin. Cen. Bapt. Schs., Anaheim, Calif., 1963-68; tchr. Indpls. Christian Acad., 1968-69; tchr., coach Faith Bapt. Schs., Canoga Park, Calif., 1969-72; prin. Lynchburg (Va.) Christian Acad., 1972-75, Bethany Christian Sch., Troy, Mich., 1975-84, Heart to Heart Christian Acad., Phoenix, 1984-88; adminstr. Temple Christian Schs., Lakeland, Fla., 1989-97. Girls head basketball coach Temple Christian Sch., 1990-97; instr. Ind. Bapt. Coll., Indpls., 1968-69, Lynchburg Bapt. Coll., 1973-75; sec.-treas. Mich. Assn. Christian Schs., Troy, 1982-83; bd. dirs. Western Fellowship Christian Schs., Phoenix, 1985-88; conv. spkr. Christian Edn. Assn., S.E., Pensacola, Fla.; founder, pres. V and A Enterprises, 1994—. Del. Mich. Rep. Conv., 1980, 82; precinct del. Mich. Rep. Party, Troy, 1980-84; precinct leader Ariz. Rep. Party, Phoenix, 1986-89; bd. dirs. Bethany Villa, Troy, 1975-84. With USN, 1951-55. Coach of Fla. Christian Girls Conf. State Championship Basketball Team, 1993-94. Mem. adv. bd. Sketch Erickson Nat. Ministries, Lakeland, Fla., 1995—. Avocations: reading, gardening, woodworking, coaching.

HAMMONDS, JAY A. retired secondary education educator, administrator; b. Conshohocken, Pa., July 18, 1943; s. Sidney E. and Grace E. Hammonds; m. Susan A. Earl, June 25, 1966; 1 child, Elizabeth A. BS in Edn., West Chester State Coll., 1965, MEd, 1971; postgrad. in Edn., U. Del., 1980—. Cert. social studies tchr. Del. Tchr. social studies Felton (Del.) Pub. Schs., 1965-67, P.S. du Pont High Sch., Wilmington, Del., 1967-78, Glasgow High Sch., Newark, Del., 1978-96, dept. chair, 1980-96; G.H.S. restructuring com. Network Adminstr. (MAC). Tchr. clin. studies coop. U. Del., Newark, 1985—86, curriculum cons., 1989. Author (multimedia software): Historic Atlas of South Asia, Historic Atlas of East Asia. Merit badge counselor Chester County Coun. Boy Scouts Am., West Chester, 1963—70, neighborhood commr., 1970—73; asst. coord. Amateur Radio Emergency Svc., Chester County, 1980—89; Del. rep. Internat. Credit Assn., Edn. Found. Seminar, 1992. Named G.H.S. Tchr. of Yr., 1987, Christina Dist. H.S. Tchr. of Yr., 1987, Del. Tchr.-Historian of Yr., 1992; Am. Studies fellow, Ea. Coll., 1987, Robert A. Taft fellow, U. Del., 1989,

Dewitt Wallace-Reader's Digest fellow, Woodrow Wilson Inst., Princeton, 1991, Keizai Koho Ctr. fellow, Japan, 1992. Avocations: amateur radio, photography, genealogy, computing. Home: 1314 Sherwood Dr West Chester PA 19380-1607

HAMNER, EUGENIE LAMBERT, English educator; b. Darlington, Ala, May 24, 1936; d. Robert Eugene Jr. and Helen (Burford) Lambert; m. Gustavus O. Hamner, 1966 (div. 1988); children: Helen Gaussen, Nicholas Feagin. BA in English & history, Huntingdon Coll., 1958; MA in English, U. N.C., 1959, PhD in English, 1965. Instr. English, Winthrop Coll., Rock Hill, SC, 1959-60; instr. U. NC, Chapel Hill, NC, 1963-64; asst. prof. Huntingdon Coll., Montgomery, Ala., 1964-65, U. Ga., Athens, Ga., 1965-66; from asst. prof. to prof. U. So. Ala., Mobile, Ala., 1969-96, prof. emeritus, 1996. Co-editor: Ways of Knowing: Essays on Marge Piercy, 1991, (children's book) A Kitten for Julie and Christopher, 1997. Bd. dir. Mobile Mus. Art, 1984-88; mem. Mobile Hist. Devel. Commn., 1987-92; elem. sch. vol. Rolling Readers USA. Alpha Beta scholar, 1958, Sigma Sigma Sigma scholar, 1958. Mem. South Atlantic Modern Lang. Assn., Habitat for Humanity (pres.'s cir.), Mobile Opera Guild, Nat. Soc. Colonial Dames of Am., Omicron Delta Kappa. Democrat. Episcopalian. Avocations: reading, gardening, travel, children. Home: 3764 Mordecai Ln Mobile AL 36608-2007

HAMOND, KAREN MARIE KOCH, secondary education educator; b. Arlington, Mass., Dec. 12, 1954; d. James Walter and Dorothy Mary (Buchanan) Koch; m. Norman Roy Hamond, Oct. 9, 1976; children: Jeremy Michael, Jason Matthew, Jillian Marie, Jennifer Margaret. BA, Salem (Mass.) State Coll., 1976; MS, Lowell (Mass.) U., 1983; Cert. Advanced Studies, Harvard U., 1992. Cert. secondary math. tchr. Mass., secondary maths. tchr. N.H. Tchr. St. Mary's High Sch., Lawrence, Mass., 1976-77, Peabody (Mass.) Vets. Meml. High Sch., 1977-78, Triton Regional High Sch., Byfield, Mass., 1978—99, math. team advisor, 1980-91; prof. math. Western New Eng. Coll., Springfield, Mass., 1992—99; head math. dept. Timberlane Regional HS, Plaistow, NH, 1999—2001; head math. and bus. dept., head math./tech. dept. Everett (Mass.) HS, 2001—; math dept. coord., 1995—99. Tchr. summer sch. Gov. Dummer Acad., Byfield, Mass., 1993-99. Mem ASCD, Nat. Coun. Tchrs. of Maths., Math. Assn. Am., NEA, Mass. Tchrs. Assn.. Am. Math. Soc. Avocations: camping, skiing, travel. Home: 14 Riverview Dr Newbury MA 01951-1807

HAMP-LANE, SANDRA N. special education educator; b. Buffalo, July 21, 1953; d. Norman J. and Irene M. (Szczepanski) Luczak; m. D. Jay Lane; 1 child, Timothy Jay. BS summa cum laude, SUNY, Buffalo, 1992. Cert. elem. and exceptional edn. tchr., N.Y. Leisure edn. specialist Community Svcs., Buffalo, 1991—. Scholar Order of Alahambra, 1991, 92. Mem. Coun. for Exceptional Children, N.Y. State Coun. for Exceptional Children (regional rep. 1991-92), Kappa Delta Pi. Avocations: travel, calligraphy, roller skating, quilling. Home: 7954 Transit Rd Ste 328 Williamsville NY 14221-4117

HAMPLE, JUDY G. academic administrator; BA in Speech Comm. and Secondary Edn./French, David Lipscomb U.; MA and PhD in Comm., Ohio State U. Univ. fellow, asst. dir. intercollegiate debate Ohio State U.; faculty dept. speech comm. U. Ill., Champaign-Urbana; divsn. dir. dept. comm. arts and scis. Western Ill. U., assoc. dean for budget and pers. Coll. Arts and Scis.; dean Coll. Liberal Arts and Scis. Emporia (Kans.) State U., 1983—86; dean Coll. Arts and Scis. Ind. State U., 1986—93; sr. v.p. acad. affairs U. Toledo, 1993; chancellor Pa. State Sys. of Higher Edn., Harrisburg, 2001—. Cons.-evaluator North Cen. Accreditation Assn.; pub. cons.-evaluator ABA. Co-editor: Teaching in the Middle Ages, 3 vols.; editor: Studies in Medieval and Renaissance Teaching. Office: Pa State Sys of Higher Edn Dixon Univ Ctr 2986 N 2d St Harrisburg PA 17110*

HAMPTON, CAROL MCDONALD, priest, educator, historian; b. Oklahoma City, Sept. 18, 1935; d. Denzil Vincent and Mildred Juanita (Cussen) McDonald; m. James Wilburn Hampton, Feb. 22, 1958; children: Jaime, Clayton, Diana, Neal. BA, U. Okla., 1957, MA, 1973, PhD, 1984; cert. individual theol. study, Episcopal Theol. Sem. of S.W., 1998; MDiv summa cum laude, Phillips Theol. Sem., 1999. Ordained to Episcopal Transitional Diaconate, 1999, ordained priest, 1999. Tchg. asst. U. Okla., Norman, 1976—81; instr. U. Sci. and Arts Okla., Chickasha, 1981—84; coord. Consortium for Grad. Opportunities for Am. Indians U. Calif., Berkeley, 1985—86; trustee Ctr. of Am. Indian, Oklahoma City, 1981. Vice chmn. Nat. Com. on Indian Work, Episc. Ch., 1986; field officer Native Am. Ministry of Episc. Ch. (Nat.), 1986-94, sec., co-chmn., advising elder, prin. elder coun., 1994-96; field officer for Congl. Ministries of Episc. Ch. (Nat.), 1994-97; mem. nat. coun. Chs. Racial Justice Working Group, 1990-97, co-convenor, 1991-93, convenor, 1993-95; officer Multicultural Ministries of Episc. Ch. (Nat.), 1994-97. Mem. editl. bd.: First Peoples Theology Jour.; contbr. articles to profl. jours. Trustee Western History Collections, U. Okla., Okla. Found. for the Humanities, 1983-86; mem. bd. regents U. Sci. and Arts Okla., 1989-95; bd. dirs. Okla. State Regents for Higher Edn., mem. adv. com. on social justice; mem. World Coun. of Chs. Program to Combat Racism, Geneva, 1985-91; bd. dirs. Caddo Tribal Coun., Okla., 1976-82; accredited observer Anglican Consultative Coun. UN 4th World Conf. on Women, 1995; v.p. Nat. Conf. Cmty. Justice, 1999-2002; bd. dirs. Ctrl. Okla. Human Rights Alliance, 1999—, Planned Parenthood, Oklahoma City, 2002—. Recipient Okla. State Human Rights awatrd, 1987; Francis C. Allen fellow Ctr. for the History of Am. Indian, 1983. Mem.: Okla. Conf. Chs. (bd. dirs. 2000—), Indigenous Theol. Tng. Inst. (bd. dirs. 2000—), Jr. League (Oklahoma City), Am. Assn. Indian Historians (founding mem. 1981—), Okla. Hist. Soc., Am. Hist. Assn., Orgn. Am. Historians, Western Social Sci. Assn., Western History Assn. Democrat. Episcopalian. Avocation: travel. Home: 1414 N Hudson Ave Oklahoma City OK 73103-3721 E-mail: cjchampton@aol.com., champton@stpaulscathedralokc.org.

HAMPTON, MARGARET ANN BARNES, elementary education educator; b. Blakely, Ga., Aug. 15, 1963; d. Ernest Owen and Jessie Carole (Scarborough) Barnes; m. Kenneth Michael Hampton, June 15, 1984; children: Michael Aaron, Nicholas Edward, Rachel Leigh. BS in Music and Bible, Free Will Bapt. Coll., Nashville, 1986, BS in Elem. Edn., 1996; BS in Music Edn., Free Wil Bapt. Coll., 2002. Asst. tchr. Westminster Mother's Day Out, Nashville, 1987-88; preschool tchr. Clouse Acad., Nashville, 1990-91; substitute tchr. Metro Bd. Edn., Nashville, 1992-96; tchr. kindergarten Woodbine Christian Acad., 1996-98, Tom Joy Elem. Sch., Nashville, 1998—2001, tchr. music, 2001—. Libr. supr. Free Will Bapt. Bible Coll., Nashville, 1987-96. Republican. Avocations: piano, camping, reading. Home: 1010 Keystone Dr Pleasant View TN 37146-8059

HAMPTON, SHELLEY LYNN, hearing impaired educator; b. Muskegon, Mich., Nov. 27, 1951; d. Donald Henry and Ruth Marie (Heinanen) Tamblyn; m. John Pershing Hampton Jr., Aug. 10, 1985; 1 child, Sarah Elizabeth. BA, Mich. State U., 1973, MA, 1978. Cert. tchr., Wash., Mich., N.Y. Tchr. presch. thru 3d grade N.Y. State Sch. for Deaf, Rome, 1973-78; cons. Ingham Intermediate Sch. Dist., Lansing, Mich., 1978-81; hearing impaired coord. Shoreline Sch. Dist., Seattle, 1981—. N.W. rep. Bur. of Edn. Handicapped, N.Y.C., 1978; N.Y. del. Humanities in Edn., 1977; adv. bd. State Libr. for the Blind, Lansing, 1980-81; adj. prof. Mich. State U., 1979-81, Seattle Pacific U., 1984-86; participant World Cong. Edn. and Tech., Vancouver, B.C., 1986; computer resource technician Spl. Programs, 1988-92, collegial team leader, 1992-95; rep. Site-Based Mgmt. Coun., Seattle, 1992-95. Writer: Social/Emotional Aspects of Deafness, 1983-84. Del. N.Y. State Assn. for Edn. of Deaf, N.Y.C., 1974-78; N.Y. del. Humanities in Edn., 1977; mem. bd. Plymouth Congl. Ch., Seattle, 1983-87; coord., Kids on the Block puppet troupe, 1999-2003. Recipient Gov.'s Plaque of Commendable Svc., State of Mich., 1981; grantee State of Wash., 1979, 82, Very Spl. Arts Festival, 1979-81; recipient Outstanding Svc. award Mich. Sch. for the Blind, 1980. Mem. NEA, Wash. State Edn. Assn., Shoreline Edn. Assn., Alexander Graham Bell Assn., Regional Hearing Impaired Coop. for Edn., Internat. Orgn. Educators of the Hearing Impaired, Auditory-Verbal Internat., U.S. Pub. Sch. Caucus, Conf. Ednl. Adminstrs. Serving the Deaf. Home: 14723 62nd Dr SE Everett WA 98208-9383 Office: Shoreline Hearing Program 16516 10th Ave NE Seattle WA 98155-5904

HAMROCK, MARGARET MARY, retired educator, writer; d. Louis Francis and Mary (Augustin) H. BS in Edn., Kent State U., 1946. Tchr. Campbell (Ohio) Bd. Edn., 1927-75; ret., 1975. Author: Tell Me I'm Somebody, 1994; composer of songs; over 100 letters to editor pub. in Cleve. Plain Dealer, Youngstown Vindicator, nat. mags. Mem. Ohio Ret. Tchrs. Assn. (life), Kent State U. Alumni Assn. Avocations: reading, writing.

HAMWI, RICHARD ALEXANDER, art educator; b. Bklyn., June 11, 1947; s. Alexander and Yvonne (Traboulsi) H. BA in Art, CUNY, Queens, 1970; MA in Drawing, U. N.Mex., 1973; MFA in Painting, U. Calif., Santa Barbara, 1974; PhD in Art Edn., Pa. State U., 1978. Lic. tchr. art, N.Y.C. Tchr. art St. Athanasius Sch., Bklyn., 1970-71; teaching asst. U. N.Mex., Albuquerque, 1971-73, U. Calif., Santa Barbara, 1973-74; asst. prof. Pa. State U., State College, 1978-87; assoc. prof. Cumberland Coll., Williamsburg, Ky., 1987-95, Mansfield (Pa.) U., 1995-99; art edn. program dir. Mercyhurst Coll., Erie, Pa., 1999—. Juror painting exhibits Ctrl. Pa. Festival of the Arts, State College; juror drawing and watercolor exhibits Ind. State Fair, Indpls. Artist (drawing) Ky. Graphics, 1988 (jurors' award for excellence 1988), (drawings and paintings) Exhbn. at Prince St. Gallery, N.Y.C., 1993; represented in permanent collections at The Phillips Collection, Washington, 1982, Nat. Mus. Am. Art, Smithsonian Inst., 1983. Recipient Meml. award Chantaugau (N.Y.) Nat. Exhibit, 1981; James Still fellow U. Ky., Lexington, 1988, 94. Mem. Nat. Art Edn. Assn., Coll. Art Assn. Am. Avocations: drawing, painting, walking, bicycling. Home: 1299 Ponderosa Dr Erie PA 16509-4801 E-mail: rhamwi@mercyhurst.edu.

HAN, CHINGPING JIM, industrial engineer, educator; b. Shanghai, People's Republic China, Aug. 24, 1957; came to U.S., 1983; s. Bao-San Zhang and Xiao-xian Han; m. Marie Han; children: George, Elaine. PRC, BSME, Dalian Inst. Tech., Dalian, 1982; MS in Indsl. Engring., Pa. State U., 1985, PhD, 1988. Asst. prof. mfg. systems engring. Fla. Atlantic U., Boca Raton, 1988-93, assoc. prof. and assoc. dir. mfg. systems engring., 1993-2000, prof. computer sci., 2001—. Contbr. articles to profl. jours., procs. Avocations: classical music, travel. Home: 20208 Back Nine Dr Boca Raton FL 33498 Office: Fla Atlantic Univ Dept Computer Sci and Engring 777 Glades Rd Boca Raton FL 33431-6498 E-mail: han@fau.edu.

HAN, JIAWEI, computer scientist, educator; b. Shanghai, Aug. 10, 1949; came to U.S., 1979; arrived in Can., 1987; s. Yu-chang Han and Jia-zhi Wang; m. Yandong Cai, July 3, 1979; 1 child, Lawrence. BSc, USTC, Beijing, China, 1979; MSc, U. Wis., 1981, PhD, 1985. Asst. prof. Northwestern U., Evanston, Ill., 1986-87, Simon Fraser U., Burnaby, B.C., Can., 1987-91, assoc. prof., 1991-95, prof., 1995-2001, U. Ill., Urbana-Champaign, 2001—. Editor Jour. Intelligent Info. Sys., Jour. of Knowledge Discovery and Data Mining; author: Data Mining: Concepts and Techniques, 2001. Mem. IEEE, ACM, Spl. Interest Group on Mgmt. of Data, Spl. Interest Group on Knowledge of Discovery and Data Mining. Office: U Ill Dept Computer Sci Urbana IL 61801

HANAN, PATRICK DEWES, foreign language professional, educator; b. New Zealand, Jan. 4, 1927; s. Frederick Arthur and Ida Helen (Dewes) H.; m. Anneliese Drube, July 1951; 1 son, Rupert Guy. BA, Auckland U., 1948, MA, 1949; BA, U. London, 1953, PhD, 1960. Lectr. Sch. Oriental and African Studies, 1954-63; assoc. prof., then prof. Stanford U., 1963-68; prof. Chinese lit. Harvard U., Cambridge, Mass., 1968-89, Victor S. Thomas prof. Chinese lit., 1989-98, Victor S. Thomas rsch. prof. Chinese lit., 1998—. Dir. Harvard-Yenching Inst., 1987-95. Author: The Chinese Short Story, 1973, The Chinese Vernacular Story, 1981, The Invention of Li Yu, 1988; transl.: The Carnal Prayer Mat, 1990, Silent Operas, 1990, A Tower for the Summer Heat, 1995, The Sea of Regret, 1995, The Money Demon, 1999. Named Officer of New Zealand Order of Merit. Fellow Am. Council Learned Socs., Guggenheim Found.; Mem. Am. Acad. Arts and Scis. Office: 2 Divinity Ave Cambridge MA 02138-2020

HANAWALT, PHILIP COURTLAND, biology educator, researcher; b. Akron, Ohio, Aug. 25, 1931; s. Joseph Donald and Lenore (Smith) H.; m. Joanna Thomas, Nov. 2, 1957 (div. Oct. 1977); children: David, Steven; m. Graciela Spivak, Sept. 10, 1978; children: Alex, Lisa. Student, Deep Springs Coll., 1949-50; BA, Oberlin Coll., 1954; MS, Yale U., 1955, PhD, 1959; ScD (hon.), Oberlin Coll., 1997. Postdoctoral fellow U. Copenhagen, Denmark, 1958-60, Calif. Inst. Tech., Pasadena, 1960-61; rsch. biophysicist, lectr. Stanford U., Calif., 1961-65, assoc. prof., 1965-70, prof., 1970—, Howard H. and Jessie T. Watkins univ. prof., 1997—, chmn. dept. biol. scis., 1982-89; faculty dept. dermatology Stanford Med. Sch., 1979—. Mem. physiol. chemistry study sect. NIH, Bethesda, Md., 1966—70, mem. chem. pathology study sect., 1981—84; mem. sci. adv. com. Am. Cancer Soc., N.Y.C., 1972—76, Coun. for Extramural Grants, 1998—2001; chmn. 2d ad hoc senate com. on professoriate Stanford U., 1985—90; mem. NSF fellowship rev. panel, 1985; mem. carcinogen identification com. Calif. EPA, 1995—98; mem. toxicology adv. com. Burroughs-Welcome Fund, 1995—2001, chmn., 1997—2000; mem. sci. adv. bd. Fogarty Internat. Ctr., NIH, 1995—99; chmn. Gordon Conf. on Mutagenesis, 1996, Gordon Conf. on Mammalian DNA Repair, 1999; mem. bd. on radiation effects rschr. NAS Commn. on Life Scis., 1996—98; trustee Oberlin Coll., 1998—; Sonnebonn lectr. Ind. U., 2002. Author: Molecular Photobiology, 1969; author, editor: DNA Repair: Techniques, 1981, 83, 88, Molecular Basis of Life, 1968, Molecules to Living Cells, 1980; mng. editor DNA Repair Jour., 1982-93; sr. editor Cancer Rsch., 2003—; assoc. editor Jour. Cancer Rsch., Molecular Carcinogenesis, Environ. Health Perspectives, Biotechniques; bd. rev. editors Sci.; mem. editl. bd. Procs. of NAS, 2003—; contbr. more than 400 articles to profl. jours. Recipient Outstanding Investigator award Nat. Cancer Inst., 1987-2001, Excellence in Tchg. award No. Calif. Phi Beta Kappa, 1991, Environ. Mutagen Soc. Ann. Rsch. award, 1992, Peter and Helen Bing award for Disting. Tchg., 1992, Am. Soc. for Photobiology Rsch. award, 1996, Internat. Mutation Rsch. award, 1997, Ellison Found. Sr. scholar award, 2001—, John B. Little award in radiation scis. Harvard Sch. Pub. Health, 2002; Hans Falk lectr. Nat. Inst. Environ. Health Scis., 1990, Severo Ochoa Meml. Hons. lectr. NYU, 1996, IBM-Princess Takamatsu lectr. Japan, 1999; Fogarty sr. rsch. fellow, 1993. Fellow: AAAS, Am. Acad. Microbiology; mem.: NAS, European Molecular Biology Orgn. (fgn. assoc.), Radiation Rsch. Soc., Environ. Mutagen Soc. (pres. 1993—94, Student Mentoring award 2001), Am. Soc. Biochemistry and Molecular Biology, German DNA Repair Network (hon.), Biophys. Soc. (exec. bd. 1969—71), Genetics Soc., Am. Soc. for Photobiology, Am. Assn. Cancer Rsch. (bd. dirs. 1994—97), Radiation Rsch. Soc. Achievements include co-discovery of DNA excision-repair and transcription-coupled DNA repair; research on role of DNA change in human genetic disease and aging. Home: 317 Shasta Dr Palo Alto CA 94306-4542 Office: Stanford U Dept Biol Scis Herrin Biology Labs 371 Serra Mall Stanford CA 94305-5020

HANBURY, RAYMOND FRANCIS, JR., psychologist, consultant; b. Jersey City, Mar. 28, 1945; s. Raymond Francis and Rose Ann (Doorley) H.; m. Patricia Ann Delaney, Mar. 9, 1974; children: Amy, Kim, BS, St. Peter's Coll., 1967; MA, Seton Hall U., 1969; PhD, NYU, 1980. Lic. psychologist, N.J.; diplomate Am. Bd. Psychol. Specialties, Am. Bd. Forensic Examiners; cert. addictions specialist. Adj. asst. prof. dept. psychiatry Mt. Sinai Sch. Medicine, N.Y.C., 1980—; pvt. practice Manasquan, N.J., 1989; dir. clin. svcs. Mt. Sinai Med. Ctr., N.Y.C., 1970-90; dir. rehab. psychology dept. JFK Med Ctr., Johnson Rehab Inst., Edison, NJ, 1990-97. Adj. asst. prof. dept. phys. medicine and rehab., dept. psychiatry UMDNJ-Robert Wood Johnson Med. Sch., 1992—; adj. asst. prof. dept. psychiatry Mt. Sinai Sch. Medicine; assoc. prof. neurosci. Seton Hall, 1996-; adj. asst. prof. psychology Pace U., White Plains, N.Y., 1980-82; police psychologist Spring Lake Heights (N.J.) Police Dept., 1989—, VA Med. Ctr., Bronx, N.Y., 1978-79, Spring Lake (N.J.) Police Dept., 1993—; crisis intervention specialist Mid-Bergen Cmty. Mental Health Ctr., Paramus, N.Y., 1980-89; state clin. dir. Critical Incident Stress Mgmt. Network N.J., 1989. Assoc. editor Psychology Addictive Behaviors, 1987-1991; mem. edtl. bd. Jour. Addictive Diseases, 1990—; contbr. articles to profl. jours. Mem. ARC, Disaster Mental Health Svcs., 1993—. Fellow Rehab. Svcs. Adminstrn., 1967-69; named Disting. Practitioner in Psychology, Nat. Academies of Practice, 1994. Fellow APA (pres. divsn. addictions 1994-95); mem. Am. Bd. Med. Psychotherapists and Psychodiagnosticians (fellow, diplomate), Am. Acad. Experts in Traumatic Stress (diplomate), N.J. Psychol. Assn., N.J.(pres. 2000) Acad. Psychology (pres. 1996), Soc. Psychologists in Addictive Behaviors (pres. 1989-91, newsletter editor 1989-94), Am. Acad. Health Care Providers in Addictive Disorders (internat. adv. bd. 1990—), Internat. Critical Incident Stress Found. Roman Catholic. Avocations: tennis, biking, reading, music. Office: Brielle Hills Profl Park Bldg 7-a 2640 Highway 70 Ste 7A Manasquan NJ 08736-2611

HANBY, DONNA M. WEISS, gifted/talented education educator; b. Hamilton, Ohio, Apr. 29, 1951; d. Donald R. and Alnes E. (Fildes) Weiss; m. Donald G. Hanby, June 15, 1974 (div. Feb. 1981); 1 child, Christopher Ryan. BS, Ohio State U., 1973; MEd, Miami U., 1993. Cert. gifted edn., elem. edn. tchr. Elem. tchr. Fairfield (Ohio) City Sch. Dist., 1973-78, tchr. of gifted and talented edn., 1978—. Evaluator asst. of spectra art program, Hamilton/Fairfield Arts Coun., 1992—; dir. evaluation study, Fairfield City Schs. Dist., 1992-94; participant and presenter Ohio Classroom of the Future, Columbus, Ohio, 1991; presenter Confs. of Tchg. and Learning, Columbus, 1992, Ohio Social Studies Conf., Columbus, 1992; trained facilitator Support Emotional Needs of Gifted, Fairborn, Ohio, 1993; rsch. asst. W. Miami U., 1992—; presenter in field. Author: (book) Fairfield City School District's Gifted and Talented Program: A Collaborative Evaluation Study (1978-1994), 1994; contbr. articles to profl. jours. Grantee Ohio Dept. Edn., 1977, Staff Devel. award, 1991. Mem. ASCD, NEA, Ohio Edn. Assn., Fairfield City Tchr.'s Assn., Ohio Assn. for Gifted Children (regional rep. 1979-80), Odyssey of the Mind (regional dir. 1988-90), Phi Delta Kappa. Methodist. Avocations: cross stitch, fabric painting, computers, reading, action rsch. Home: 621 Vinnedge Ave Fairfield OH 45014-1723 Office: Fairfield South Elem 5460 Bibury Dr Fairfield OH 45014-3610

HANCOCK, CHARLES R. education educator; BA in Edn., MA in Secondary Edn., La. State U.; attended, Fondation Franco-Américaine, Paris; student, Ohio State U. Assoc. supt. divsn. secondary, vocation, adult and community edn. Balt. City Pub. Schs.; coord. of foreign lang. Montgomery County Pub. Schs., 1984-85; assoc. prof. Dept. Edn. Ohio State Univ. Pres. Am. Coun. Teaching Foreign Lang., 1984-85, Md. Foreign Lang. Assn., 1990-91, Ohio Foreign Lang. Assn., 1990-91. Recipient Anthony Papalia award for Excellence in Tchr. Edn., 1992, Florence Steiner award for Leadership in Foreign Lang., 1980.*

HANCOCK, NANNETTE BEATRICE FINLEY, mental health educator, consultant; b. Birmingham, Ala., Aug. 24, 1937; d. James L. and Minnie (Mason) Finley; m. Frank J. Hancock Jr., Dec. 27, 1958 (div. May 1976); children: Andria Denise, Frank J. III, Cheryl René. BSN, Dillard U., 1958; MPH in Pub. Health, U. Calif., Berkeley, 1970; PhD in Psychology, Western Colo. U., 1977; MA in Clin. Psychology, John F. Kennedy U., 1991. Lic. marriage, family and child therapist. 2d lt. staff nurse U.S. Army Nurse's Corp, Denver, 1958-59; staff nurse, head nurse St. Francis Hosp., Evanston, Ill., 1960-64, Richmond (Calif.) Hosp., 1964-65; sch. nurse Richmond Unified Sch. Dist., 1965-69; prof. Contra Costa Coll., San Pablo, Calif., 1970—; pvt. practice mental health cons. Richmond, 1977—; founder, owner Nannette's Beauty and Figure Salon, 1982-86. Mem. Social Heritage Group, 1964—, human rels. com., 1966—70, Easter Hill Meth. Ch., 1964—. Col. Army Nurse's Corp. USAR, 1978—95. Mem. Calif. Assn. Marriage and Family Therapy, Calif. Nurse's Assn., Bay Area Assn. Black Psychologists, Res. Officer's Assn. Avocations: water skiing, opera, symphony, theatre, reading. Office: 4801 Reece Ct Richmond CA 94804-3444

HANCOCK, PRISCILLA TEDESCO, retired education educator; b. Farmingdale, N.Y., Aug. 25, 1938; d. Peter John and Lillian (Guando) Tedesco; m. Robert G. Hancock, Aug. 6, 1960; children: Gregory, Kimberly, Glenn. BS, SUNY, Cortland, 1960. Cert. tchr. kindergarten through grade 8. Instr. arts and crafts Farmingdale Youth Coun., 1956-63; tchr. Farmingdale Pub. Schs., 1960-63, Bay Shore (N.Y.) Schs., 1982-94. Tchr. in-svc. courses to tchrs. Bay Shore Schs., 1986-87. Mem. Student Fin. Aid Fund, Bay Shore, 1974-75, Bay Shore Hist. Soc., 1985—, Friends for L.I. Heritage, 1986—; organized student exhibits Bay Shore Garden Club Shows, 1985-87; co-founder mother's aux. Boy Scouts Am., Bay Shore, 1976. Recipient Citizenship awards DAR, 1956. Mem. N.Y. State United Tchrs. Assn., Bay Shore Classroom Tchrs. Assn., AAUW (life, tchr. needlework workshops L.I. 1967-79, v.p., treas. membership bd. 1966-76), Music Sponsors of Bay Shore, Bay Shore Hist. Soc. (v.p., creator rsch. libr., membership chairperson, Disting. Svc. Award, Islip Township, 2002), Summit Coun. Bay Shore/Brightwaters.

HANCOCK, SANDRA OLIVIA, secondary school educator, elementary school educator; b. Jackson, Tenn., Oct. 22, 1947; d. Carthel Leon and Thelma (Thompson) Smith; m. Jerome Hancock, Aug. 1, 1969; children: Casey Colman, Mandy Maria. BS, U. Tenn., 1969, MS, 1973; grad. safety seminar, Universal Cheerleaders Assn., 1989. Cert. educator. Educator Lexington (Tenn.) H.S., 1969-70, Clarksburg (Tenn.) H.S., 1970-78, 83-90, Dresden (Tenn.) Jr. H.S., 1994-95; instr. Camden (Tenn.) Elem. Sch., 1995—. Instr. Very Spl. Arts Festival, Carroll County, Tenn., 1994; GED instr. Contbr. poetry to various publs. Cub scout leader Boy Scouts Am., Clarksburg, 1982—84; assoc. mem. St. Labre Indian Sch. and Home Arrow Club, Ashland, Mont., 1988—89; vol. March of Dimes, Leukemia Soc. Am.; mem. fund raising com. Project Graduation Huntingdon H.S., 1992—95; art edn. asst. Huntingdon Spl. Sch. Dist., 1993—94; sec. Harbor Town Property Owners' Assn., 2001—; dir. presch. 1st United Meth. Ch., Huntingdon, 1992—93. Recipient various poetry awards. Mem.: NEA, Tenn. Reading Assn., Haiku Soc. Am., Benton County Tenn. Arts Coun., Poetry Soc. Tenn. (rec. sec. 1993—94, spkr. 1994), Am. Assn. Cheerleading Coaches and Advisors, Nat. Cheerleaders Assn. (Superior Advisor Performance award 1988), U.S. Olympic Assn., Tenn. Writers' Alliance, Nat. Fedn. State Poetry Socs., Benton County Reading Assn., Benton County Edn. Assn., Tenn. Edn. Assn., Phi Delta Kappa (N.W. Tenn. chpt. sec. 1993—94). Republican. Avocations: travelling, water skiing, snorkeling. Home and Office: 250 Branch Loop Rd Big Sandy TN 38221 also: Camden Elem Sch 208 Washington Ave Camden TN 38320-1130

HAND, HERBERT HENSLEY, finance educator, writer, entrepreneur; b. Hamilton, Ohio, July 11, 1931; s. Herbert Lawrence and Berta Elizabeth (Hensley) H.; m. Katharine Harris Gucker, July 26, 1952; children: Stephen Harris, Herbert Gucker. BS, Ind. U., 1953; MSEE, ABT, MIT, 1955; MBA, U. Miami, 1966; PhD, Pa. State U., 1969. V.p. Hand Oil Co., 1955-65; instr. Pa. State U., 1968-69; asst. and assoc. prof. Ind. U., Bloomington, 1969-73, assoc. prof., 1973-76; disting. prof. entrepreneurship U. S.C. Coll. Bus. Adminstrn., Columbia, 1976-95. State dir. Small Bus. Devel. Ctr. S.C., 1968-69; exec. v.p. Carter-Miot Engring. Co., Columbia, S.C., 1981, also bd. dirs.; pres. Carolina Consultants, 1973-84; chmn., CEO, pres. Phronesis, Inc., 1985-92, Alternative Control Sys. Corp., 1993-99; cons. to numerous cos., 1973—. Author: (with H.P. Sims, Jr.) Managerial Decision Making in the Business Firm-A Systems Approach, 1972, The Profit Center Simulation, 1975; (with A.T. Hollingsworth) A Guide to Small Business Management, 1979, Practical Readings in Small Business, 1979; contbr. over 90 research articles and papers in field to profl. jours.; mem. editorial bd. Bus. Horizons, 1971-73, Acad. of Mgmt. Review, 1975-79; holder numerous U.S. and fgn. patents in field of biotech. Served to 1st lt. USAF, 1953-55. Recipient Western Electric award for most innovative bus. course, 1971, 23 other teaching awards; Small Bus. Inst. Regional award SBA, 1976, 80, 81, Small Bus. Inst. Nat. award, 1980; Office Naval Research grantee, 1976, 77, 78. Mem. Acad. Mgmt., So. Mgmt. Assn., Am. Inst. Decision Scis., Internat. Coun. for Small Bus., Rotary. Presbyterian. E-mail: hekat@bellsouth.net.

HANDFORD, H. ALLEN, retired psychiatrist, educator; b. Des Moines, July 1, 1930; s. Harvey Eugene and Lenore (Allen) H.; m. Sandra Lee Betz, Sept. 3, 1955 (div.); children: Lee Allen, Christiana Lenore, Jennifer Miriam, Alice Faith; m. Laura Jane Diller, May 2, 1970 (div. AB, Harvard U., 1953; MD, State U. Iowa, 1957. Intern Broadlawns, Des Moines, 1957-58; fellow in psychiatry Pa. Hosp. Inst., 1958-60; fellow child psychiatry St. Christopher's Hosp., Phila., 1960-62; dir. rsch. unit autistic children Ea. State Sch. and Hosp., Phila., 1962-73; dir. children's unit Haverford (Pa.) State Hosp., 1973-74; dir. children and youth programs mental Pa. Dept. Pub. Welfare, 1976-79; clin. asst. prof. psychiatry and human behavior Jefferson Med. Coll., Phila., 1974-78; assoc. prof. psychiatry Coll. Medicine, Pa. State U., Hershey, 1978—2000, also past dir. divsn. child psychiatry residency tng.; ret., 2000. Dir. psychiatry/psychology Univ. Hosp. Rehab. Ctr., 1979-84; dir. psychosocial program Hemophilia Ctr. Cen. Pa., 1979-96; past mem. mental health com. Nat. Hemophilia Found. Contbr. articles to med. jours. Bd. dirs. Dauphin County Mental Health/Mental Retardation. Mem. AMA, Am. Psychiat. Assn., Am. Acad. Child and Adolescent Psychiatry, Pa. Med. Soc., Pa. Psychiat. Soc., Regional Coun. Child Psychiatry, Coll. Physicians Phila. Rsch. on childhood autism, psychosocial aspects of hemophilia, childhood depression, child and parent reaction to Three Mile Island nuclear accident, sleep disorders of childhood, eating disorders of childhood.

HANDLEY, SUE ANN, professional quiltmaker, educator; b. Decatur, Ill., Feb. 22, 1955; d. Max Gail and Virginia Ellen (Paul) Handley; m. Gregory Alan Poteat, June 28, 1975 (div. 1992); children: Brian, Zachary. Student, Antelope Valley Jr. Coll., Lancaster, Calif., 1983-85. Tchr. quilting Sr. Citizen Ctr., Lancaster, 1984-85, House of Fabrics, Palmdale, Calif., 1984-88; lectr. quilting Palmdale Sch. Dist., 1984-88; vol. St. Andrew's Priory, Valyermo, Calif., 1983—. Quiltmaker MGM Studios, Hollywood, Calif., 1990; banner maker So. Calif. Renewal Communities, Anaheim, 1986; lectr. First Presbyn. Ch., Palmdale, 1991, Palmdale Elks Lodge, 1991, othrs. Completed more than 700 quilts; contbr. to Quilter's Newsletter; exhibited in Mus. Am. Quilters Soc., 1992. Recipient 1st place award Inland Empire Quilt Guild, Riverside, Calif., 1990, 3d place award Smoky Mountain Quilt Competition, 1982, Best of Show award Antelope Valley Fair, Lancaster, 1978; Calif. State champion Calif. State Fair Bd., Sacramento, 1979. Mem. Am. Quilters Soc. (included in calendar 1994). Democrat. Roman Catholic. Avocations: sewing, costumes, raquetball, crafts, nfl football. Home and Office: Sue's Custom Quilting 38563 Jacklin Ave Palmdale CA 93550-4019

HANDLY-JOHNSON, PATRICIA, school administrator, school psychologist, educational consultant; b. Bryn Mawr, Pa., Feb. 20, 1950; d. Robert Shanaman and Raye (Piland) Handly; m. Michael Lane Johnson, Sept. 14, 1991. BA in Child Devel., Conn. Coll., 1972; MA in Clin. Psychology, George Mason U., 1979. Cert. profl. tchr., sch. psychologist, Va., elem. prin., Pa. Elem. tchr St. Agnes Sch., Alexandria, Va., 1972-74; tchr. Lordswood Jr. Mixed Sch., Chatham, Eng., summer 1973; elem. tchr. Fairfax County (Va.) Pub. Schs., 1974-78, sch. psychologist, 1978-84; lectr. in psychology No. Va. C.C., Woodbridge, 1978-84; sch. psychologist The Carol Morgan Sch., Santo Domingo, Dominican Republic, 1984-88, elem. sch. prin., 1988-91; ednl. cons. Houghton Mifflin Co., Boston, 1992; asst. prin. St. John's Sch., San Juan, P.R., 1992-96; adminstr. and co-trainer Prin.'s Tng. Ctr. for Internat. Leadership, summers 1994-96; co-prin. Escuela Campo Alegre, Caracas, Venezuela, 1996. Adv. bd. Instructor mag., N.Y.C., 1980-81; presenter in field. Vice pres. bd. dirs. Sacred Music Soc., Santo Domingo, 1985-88; mem. Coro Sinfonico de Puerto Rico, Newcomers Club, Puerto Rico. Recipient acad. scholarship Conn. Coll., 1971-72. Mem. ASCD, Internat. Reading Assn., Sailing Assn. (sgt.-at-arms 1984-89). Episcopalian. Avocations: photography, windsurfing, music.

HANDY, F. PHILIP, investment company executive, educational association administrator; BA in Econs. cum laude, Princeton U.; MBA, Harvard U. Securities analyst Fidelity Mgmt. and Rsch., Boston, 1968—70; v.p. investment banking Donaldson, Lufkin & Jenrette, Inc., N.Y.C., 1970—76; CEO ComBanks Corp.; founder, owner Winter Park Capital Co., 1980—97; CEO Strategic Industries, LLC, 2001—. Bd. dirs. Anixter Internat., Inc., iDine Rewards Network, Inc., Wink Comm., Inc., WCI Cmtys., Inc. Chmn. Fla. State Bd. Edn., 2001—; active Edn. Governance Reorganization Task Force, 2000—; trustee, treas., mem. exec. com. Northfield Mount Hermon Sch.; mem. bd. overseers Rollins Coll. Crummer Grad. Sch. Bus.; mem., pres. bd. trustees Orlando Mus. Art; active Govs. Commn. on the Future of Fla. Environment, 1989—90; bd. dirs. PRIDE (Prison Rehabilitative Industries and Diversified Enterprises, Inc.) of Fla., 1989, chmn. bd.; bd. dirs. Govs. Fla. Coun. of 1000. With USAR, 1966—73. Mem.: Chief Execs. Orgn. Avocations: long distance running, mountain biking. Office: Fla Dept Edn Office Commr Ste 1514 325 W Gaines St Tallahassee FL 32399*

HANEKE, DIANNE MYERS, retired education educator; b. San Francisco, Feb. 23, 1941; d. Wayne and Dorothy (Johnson) Myers; m. John Paul Haneke, Apr. 10, 1965; children: Mark, Debra, Julie. BA in Social Sci., Edn., So. Calif. Coll., 1964; MS in Edn., SUNY, Albany, 1971, cert. advanced studies, 1990, PhD in Reading, 1998. Cert. elem., social studies and reading tchr. N.Y. Reading specialist Greenville (N.Y.) Elem. Sch., 1971-72, 84-85, Durham (N.Y.) Elem. Sch., 1972-74, Cairo (N.Y.) Durham Schs., 1979-82, 86-89; counselor Capital Area Christian Counseling, Delmar, NY, 1980-81; instr. psychology Columbia Greene CC, Hudson, NY, 1982-83; reading specialist Hunter (N.Y.)-Tannersville Schs., 1985-86; instr. edn. and reading Mt. St. Mary Coll., Newburgh, NY, 1990-92; assoc. prof. reading edn. Concordia U., Austin, Tex., 1993—2001, dir. field work experiences, 1993—2001, prof. emeritus, 2001—. Author: A Woman After God's Own Heart, 1982, A View From the Inside: An Action Plan for Gender Equity in New York State Educational Administration, 1990, Improve Your Writing: A Workshop and Desktop Reference, 2001. Instr. water safety ARC, 1978—91; host parents Youth for Understanding, 1984—85, 1988—89; leader, resource person Girl Scouts U.S., 1978—90. Recipient Alumnus of the Yr. award, So. Calif. Coll., 1979, Disting. Contbr. award, 1988, Disting. Svc. award, So. Calif. Coll. Alumni Assn., 1994; Myers-Haneke Edn. endowed scholar, So. Calif. Coll., 1971—. Mem.: ASCD, Tex. State Reading Assn., Internat. Coun. Tchrs. English, Nat. Reading Conf., Coll. Reading Assn., Christian Educators Assn. Internat., Capital Area Reading Coun., Assn. Tchr. Educators, Am. Ednl. Rsch. Assn., Phi Delta Kappa, Delta Kappa Gamma. Republican. Avocations: swimming, tennis, music, travel, Special Olympics. E-mail: d.haneke@prodigy.net.

HANES, SANDRA JEAN, secondary education educator; b. St. Marys, Pa., Jan. 29, 1954; d. Alfred Anthony and Gertrude Helen DiDonato; m. Robert William Hanes, May 15, 1976. BS in Edn., Indiana U. of Pa., 1975; Master's equivalent, Pa. dept. of Edn., 1992. Cert. in Spanish edn., Pa. Tchr. Ridgway (Pa.) Area Sch. Dist., 1976—. Cheerleader coach Ridgway H.S.; student coun. advisor Ridgway H.S. Student Coun. Mem. Pa. Action Com. for Edn., Harrisburg, 1985. Sch.-to-work grantee North Cen. Regional Planning and Devel. Coun., 1997, 98. Mem. Pa. State Tchrs. Assn. (pres. 1976—), Delta Kappa Gamma (past pres. 1988—). Democrat. Roman Catholic. Avocations: reading, skiing, aerobics, baking. Office: Ridgway Area Sch Dist 1403 Hill St Ridgway PA 15853-2399 Fax: 814-776-4247. E-mail: sjhanes@hotmail.com.

HANEY, EDWARD FRANCIS, social studies educator, educator; b. Pitts., Mar. 24, 1947; BS, Ind. (Pa.) U., 1969; MEd, Duquesne U., 1976. Cert. Tchr. Pa., Mediator. Tchr. Pitts. Pub. Schs., 1969—, also peer coach coord. Design team New Am. Schs. Team-Oliver, Pitts., 1995—; team leader Personalize Academic Learning Strategies Team-Oliver, Pitts., 1989-95; curriculum chmn. Brentwood Sch. Dist., health, safety & transp. chair; vol. Meals on Wheels; peer coach facilitator Oliver High.; fgn. exch. student host 15 times. Vol. CCD instr., ch. coun. mem., pastoral coun., Pitts.; committeeman Boro of Brentwood, Pa., inspector of Elections; v.p. Threnhauser Civic Assn., Brentwood, market day vol.; dir. Brentwood Sch. Dist., 1996-97; active New Am. Schs. Com., Parent Tchr. Student Orgn., Crime Watch. Recipient vol. cert. USAF Recruiting, 1985-86, Vol. Svc. award Jr. Achievement, Pitts., 1987-93, Nat. Bronze Leadership award Jr. Achievement, 1998, Educator of Yr. award S.W. Pa., 1999, Tchr. Excellence award, 1999, Tchr. of Distinction S.W. Pa. award, 2000, Thanks to Tchr. Impact award, 2000-01, Innovation award Jr. Achievement of S.W. Pa., 2001. Mem. Pa. Fedn. Tchrs., Pitts. Fedn. Tchrs., World Affairs Coun. (Pitts. Recogntion award 2002). Democrat. Roman Catholic. Avocations: travel, reading. Home: 247 Wainwright Ave Pittsburgh PA 15227-3324

HANEY, MARLENE CAROL, music educator; b. Spokane, Wash., Dec. 10, 1952; d. Edward Nishan and Myrtle Anne (Jenkins) Getoor; m. Dennis Lee Haney, June 14, 1975; children: Mark Phillip, Stephanie Ann. BA, Whitworth Coll., 1975. Cert. Music Tchrs. Nat. Assn., 97, Wash. State Music Tchrs. Assn., 1998. Prin., owner Grand M Studio, Spokane, 1980—. Adv. bd. Music Fest N.W., Spokane, 1995—; adjudicator sonatina/sonata festival Ctrl. Wash. U., 2003. Adjudicator Sonatina/Sonatina Festival Ctrl. Wash. U., 2003. Mem.: Spokane Music Tchrs. Assn. (pres. 1995—97), Wash. State Music Tchrs. Assn., Music Tchrs. Nat. Assn., Mu Phi Epsilon. Nazarene. Avocations: rose gardening, travel.

HANKERSON, CHARLIE EDWARD, JR., music educator; b. Ft. Lauderdale, Fla., Oct. 16, 1934; s. Charlie Edward Sr. and Pearl Lee (Patterson) H.; m. Orcenia Rookard, Oct. 14, 1962 (div. Feb. 1985); children: Anita Lynn, Leslie Arnetta, Charles III; m. Gwendolyn Araminta Betancourt, Apr. 6, 1985. BS in Instrumental Music, Fla. A&M U., 1956; MusM in Edn., Cath. U. Am., 1971. Commd. 2d lt. U.S. Army, 1956; advanced through grades to col. USAR, 1987; counselor Dist. Tng. Sch., Laurel, Md., 1961-62; music tchr. Loudoun County Schs., Leesburg, Va., 1962-67, D.C. Pub. Schs., Washington, 1968-94. Bd. dirs. South Potomac Citizens Assn., Ft. Washington, Md., 1990-91. Recipient Army Commendation medal Dept. Army, 1975, Army Achievement medal, Sec. of Army, 1983, Cert. of Appreciation, Chief USAR, 1987, Meritorious Svc. medal Dept. Army, 1987. Mem. Omega Psi Phi. Avocations: fishing, sports. Home: 9715 Traverse Way Fort Washington MD 20744-5745

HANKIN, JOSEPH NATHAN, college president; b. N.Y.C., Apr. 6, 1940; s. Harry and Beatrice H.; m. Carole G. Hankin, Aug. 20, 1960; children—Marc, Laura, Brian. BA in Social Scis. (N.Y. State Regents scholar), CCNY, 1961; MA in History, Columbia U., 1962, Ed.D. in Adminstrn. Higher Edn. (Kellogg fellow), 1967; postgrad. seminar, Harvard U. Grad. Sch. Bus., 1979; Litt.D. (hon.), Mercy Coll., 1979; DHL (hon.), Coll. New Rochelle, 1996; D Pedagogy (hon.), Manhattan Coll., 2000; DHL (hon.), Lehman Coll., 2002. Cert. large complex case arbitrator Am. Arbitration Assn. N.Y. State Regents coll. teaching fellow, 1961-63; fellow dept. history CCNY, 1962-63, lectr., 1963-65; lectr. history Bklyn. Coll. CUNY, summer 1963, lectr. history Queens Coll., summer 1964; course asst. dept. higher and adult edn. Tchrs. Coll., Columbia U., spring 1965, occasional lectr., 1965—, adj. prof. higher and adult edn., 1976—; dir. evening div. and summer session Harford Jr. Coll., Bel Air, Md., 1965-66, dean continuing edn. and summer session, 1966-67, pres., 1967-71, Westchester C.C., Valhalla, N.Y., 1971—. Mem. vis. team Md. State Bd. Cmty. Colls., Annapolis, 1976; bd. dirs. Mut. Funds Trust, 1988—; mem. task force on study higher edn. in D.C., 1966-67; spkr., panelist and cons. in field; condr. workshops and seminars. Contbr. articles and revs. to profl. publs. and newspapers. Mem. adv. com. Columbia U. Tchrs. Coll. C.C. Ctr., 1970—; bd. dirs., mem. exec. com. Westchester C.C. Found., 1971—; mem. Tri-State Coll. Consortium (now Eastern Ednl. Consortium), 1975—, pres., 1977-89, fin. com., 1982-87; mem. adv. com. SUNY Ednl. Opportunity Ctr., 1975—; mem. Coun. for Arts in Westchester, N.Y., 1971—, mem. coll. adv. com., 1971, mem. arts action plan for Westchester com., 1974-75, mem. Friends of Arts, 1976—, mem. benefit com., 1983-86, trustee, 1983-85; mem. Westchester Rockland Newspapers Lend-A-Hand Adv. Bd., 1974-90; mem. Friends Harrison Pub. Libr., 1980—, Friends Neuberger Mus., 1979—; bd. advisors Hudson River Mus., 1985—; mem. adv. bd. Westchester County Hist. Soc., 1981-84; trustee Westchester Econ. Understanding Found., 1979, Hartford Family Found., 1984—. Recipient Disting. Service award Bel Air (Md.) Jaycees, 1968, Brotherhood award Westchester region NCCJ, 1975, Arabic Soc. plaque, 1977, Plaque Pres. Ea. Ednl. Consortium, 1978, Championship of Youth award Youth Services div. B'nai B'rith, 1978, Community Svc. award Soc. Italian-Am. Orgns., 1986, plaque Alpha Beta Gamma and Drucker Mgmt. Soc., 1983, plaque Italian Club, 1984, plaque French Club, 1977, Honor award AIA, 1983, Cert. Vol. Services United Way Westchester, 1986, Cert. Appreciation Westchester 2000, 1988; Kellog fellow in C.C. adminstrn. Columbia U., 1965. Mem. Am. Assn. Jr. Colls. (v.p. 1971-74, bd. dirs. 1971-74, pres.'s acad. 1976—, various coms., Cert. Recognition 1981), Am. Assn. Higher Edn. (charter, life), Assn. Pres.'s Public C.C.s (legis. com. 1974-76, 86—, exec. com., mem.-at-large 1987-88), Faculty Student Assn. Westchester C.C. (dir. 1971—), Coll. Consortium for Internat. Studies (exec. com. 1974-88, sec.-treas. 1984-88, mem. ad hoc com. on by-laws 1983), Middle States Assn. Colls. and Schs. (ad hoc com. centennial celebration 1985—, pres. 1999) N.Y. State Assn. Jr. Colls., Young Presidents Orgn. (pres.'s forum 1979-90, founding dir. 1979-80, 84-85, day chairperson 1977-89), CEO Orgn., World Pres. Orgn., Westchester County C. of C. (bd. dirs. 1981-85, chmn. 1988, reaccreditation task force com. on staff 1982-83, chmn. nomination com. 1983-85), Phi Delta Kappa, Alpha Beta Gamma (hon.), Phi Theta Kappa. Home: 4 Merion Dr Purchase NY 10577-1302 Office: Westchester Community Coll 75 Grasslands Rd Valhalla NY 10595-1636 E-mail: joseph.hankin@sunywcc.edu.

HANKINS, MARY DENMAN, elementary school educator; b. Roane County, Tenn., Jan. 31, 1930; d. Elmer Hoyle and Lela Emiline (Cox) Denman; m. Charles Russell Hankins, Mar. 23, 1951; children: Jennifer, Susan, Charles Thomas, Amy. BS, Montreat (N.C.) Coll., 1950; postgrad., East Tenn. State U., Tusculum Coll., Greeneville, Tenn. Cert. elem. tchr., Tex., Tenn. Tchr. elem. Greene County (Tenn.) Schs., 1955-87; tchr. adult basic edn. Greeneville (Tenn.) Schs., 1978-85; elem. tchr. Cedar Hill (Tex.) Ind. Sch. Dist., 1987-95. Contbg. author of sci. and math. home activities for children for textbook cos. Vol. tutor local schs. Mem. NEA, Tenn. Edn. Assn., Tenn. Tchrs. Study Coun., Greene County Edn. Assn. (past editor newsletter), Delta Kappa Gamma.

HANKO, MARY ELLEN, elementary education educator; b. Milw., Aug. 13, 1967; d. John Anthony and Ellen Anne Hanko. BS in Edn., Alverno Coll., Milw., 1992. Lic. tchr., Wis. Early childhood and elem. substitute tchr. Milw. Pub. Schs., 1992—; summer sch. tchr. Mukwonago (Mich.) Pub. Schs., Mukwonago, 1992—; kindergarten tchr. Waukesha Pub. Sch. Dist., 1994—. Nursery leader Bethany-Calvary Ch., Wauwatosa, Wis., 1988-93. Mem. Milw. Kindergarten Assn. Roman Catholic. Avocations: writing poetry, children's stories. Home: 1011 Guthrie Rd # 4-5 Waukesha WI 53186-6996

HANLEY, ROBERTA LYNN, alternative education coordinator, educator; b. Gary, Ind., May 4, 1953; BA, Purdue U., 1975; MS, Ind. U., Gary, 1982. Substitute tchr. Hobart (Ind.) High Sch., 1974-77, social studies tchr., 1977—, sophmore gifted/talented tchr., future problem solving coach, 1985-89, 90-91, coord./tchr. Challenge Program, Alternative Edn. Program, 1991-94; coord. Hobart (Ind.) Challenge Sch., 1994—. Faculty advisor Hobart Jr. High Sch. yearbook, 1978-80, 81-84. Choir libr. Hobart Presbyn. Ch., 1980-93, Sunday sch. sec., 1987-93, ch. historian, 1988-93. Recipient Tchr. of Yr. award Hobart Rotary Club, 1988, Tchr. of Yr. award Inland Steel-Ryerson Found., 1992. Mem. Nat. Coun. Social Studies, Ind. Coun. Social Studies. Office: Sch City Hobart 32 E 7th St Hobart IN 46342-5154

HANLEY, THOMAS RICHARD, engineering educator; b. Logan, W.Va., July 26, 1945; s. Thomas Jesse and Dorothy Louise (Hay) H.; m. Norma Kathryn Decker, Dec. 27, 1979; children: Thomas Jeffrey, Alan Michael, Andrew Richard, Caitlin Marisa. BSChemE, Va. Poly. Inst., 1967; MSChemE, Va. Poly. Inst. and State U., 1971, PhDChemE, 1972; MBA in Mgmt., Wright State U., 1975. Registered profl. engr., Ky. Devel. engr. AF Materials Lab., Wright Patterson AFB, Ohio, 1972-75; asst. prof. Tulane U., New Orleans, 1975-79; assoc. prof. Rose-Hulman Inst. Tech., 1979-83; prof., dept. head La. Tech. U., Ruston, 1983-85; prof., chmn. dept. Fla. State U., Fla. A&M U., Tallahassee, 1985-91; dean Speed Sci. Sch. U. Louisville, 1991—. Bd. dirs. Plasticolors, Ashtabula, Ohio; divsn. advisor NSF, Washington, 1987-93; presenter at numerous nat. and internat. profl. confs. Contbr. articles to profl. jours. Capt. USAF, 1972-75. Recipient award Soc. Am. Mil. Engrs., 1966, 67, Acad. award Am. Legion, 1967, Ralph R. Teetor Ednl. award SAE, 1989, Outstanding Engr. in Edn. award Ky. Soc. Profl. Engrs., 1994; grantee NSF, Nat. Renewable Energy Lab., GE, Colgate-Palmolive, United Catalysts, IKA Works, Swan Biomass, Toro, Olin, Stone and Webster. Fellow AIChE (profl. devel. recognition cert. 1980, student chpt. advisor award 1979); mem. Am. Soc. Engring. Edn., Nat. Assn. Basketball Coaches, Sigma Xi, Phi Kappa Phi, Tau Beta Pi, Phi Lambda Upsilon, Omega Chi Epsilon. Office: U Louisville Speed Sci School Louisville KY 40292-0001 E-mail: tom.hanley@louisville.edu.

HANLON, C. ROLLINS, physician, educator; b. Balt., Feb. 8, 1915; s. Bernard and Harriet (Rollins) H.; m. Margaret M. Hammond, May 28, 1949; children: Philip, Paul, Richard, Christine, Thomas, Mary, Martha, Sarah. AB, Loyola Coll., Balt., 1934; MD, Johns Hopkins U., 1938; D.Sc. (hon.), Georgetown U., 1976, U. Ill., 1986, St. Louis U., 1986. Diplomate Am. Bd. Surgery (chmn. 1966-67). Intern John Hopkins Hosp., 1938-39, W.S. Halsted fellow in surgery, 1939-40, instr. surgery, 1946-48, asst. prof., 1948-50, assoc. prof., 1950; asst. resident, resident in surgery Cin. Gen. Hosp., 1940-41, 43-44; exchange fellow surgery U. Calif., 1941-42; prof. surgery, chmn. dept. St. Louis U., 1950-69; prof. surgery Northwestern U. Med. Sch., 1969-85, prof. emeritus, 1985—. Chmn. surgery study sect. NIH, 1965-66; pres. Council Med. Specialty Socs., 1974-75; chmn. Coordinating Council on Med. Edn., 1976-77 Contbr. articles to profl. jours. Served to lt. (j.g.) M.C. USNR, 1944-46, CBI. Recipient Fleur-de-lis award St. Louis U., 1969; Statesmen in Medicine award Airlie Found., 1974 Founder group Am. Bd. Thoracic Surgery (1948); fellow ACS (gov., regent 1967-69, exec. dir. 1969-86, pres. elect 1986-87, pres. 1987-88), Royal Australasian Coll. Surgeons (hon.), Royal Coll. Surgeons of Eng. (hon.), Royal Coll. Surgeons in Ireland (hon.), Royal Coll. Surgeons of Can. (hon.), Am. Assn. Surgery of Trauma (hon.), Am. Urol. Assn. (hon.), Am. Hosp. Assn. (hon.); mem. Internat. Cardiovascular Soc. (pres. N.Am. chpt. 1963-64), Soc. Vascular Surgery (pres. 1968), AMA, Am. Surg. Assn. (sec. 1968-69, pres. 1981-82), Western Surg. Assn., So. Surg. Assn., Soc. Thoracic Surgeons (hon.), Central Surg. Assn., Am. Assn. Thoracic Surgery (treas. 1962-68), Soc. U. Surgeons (pres. 1958), Soc. Clin. Surgery (pres. 1968-70), St. Louis Surg. Soc. (pres. 1954-55), Johns Hopkins Med. and Surg. Assn. (v.p. 1975-77), Johns Hopkins Soc. Scholars, Cosmos Club, Alpha Omega Alpha. Roman Catholic. Address: 633 N Saint Clair St Chicago IL 60611-3211

HANLON, MARY JO, special education educator, early intervention specialist; b. Pitts., Jan. 19, 1959; d. William John and JoAnn Margery (Strobel) H. BA, Hiram Coll., 1980; MEd, Kent State U., 1987, postgrad. Cert. elem. edn. 1-8, spl. edn., learning disabilities, behavior disabilities, moderate-severe-profoundly handicapped 1-12, ednl. supr., neurodevel. treatment. Prevocat. tchr. Clark County Bd. Mental Retardation, Springfield, Ohio, 1980-81; tchr. of severely handicapped Crestwood Local Schs., Mantua, Ohio, 1981-83, William Harvey Sch., London, 1983-84, Hornsey Trust, London, 1985-87; tchr. severely/profoundly handicapped Green Devel. Ctr., Warrensville, Ohio, 1987-88; early intervention specialist Cuyahoga County Bd. Mental Retardation Devel. Delays, Cleve., 1988—; mentor Cuyahoga County Bd. Mental Retardation/DD, Cleve., 1993-94. Presenter state conf. Ohio Perinatal Network, 1992; presenter nat. conf. Assn. for Severe Handicaps, 1982, mem., 1982-89; mem. Staff Devel. Com., 1987-88, 92-94. Fulbright scholar U.S. Dept. Info., London, 1983-84. Mem. Coun. for Exceptional Children, Fulbright Alumni Assn., Cuyahoga County Early Intention Collaborative Group. Roman Catholic. Avocations: travel, reading, camping. Home: 26 Borton Ave Akron OH 44302-1012 Office: Cuyahoga County Bd MRDD Fifty Public Sq 1050 Terminal Tower Cleveland OH 44113-2207

HANNA, JOHN, JR., lawyer, educator, arbitrator, mediator; b. Dec. 19, 1934; m. Jane Merchant, Dec. 27, 1958; children: Elizabeth Hanna Morss, Katharine Hanna Morgan, John M. AB, Princeton U., 1956; LLB, Harvard U., 1959. Bar: N.Y. 1960, Mass. 1964, U.S. Dist. Ct. Mass. 1965, U.S. Dist. Ct. (ea. and so. dists.) N.Y. 1963, U.S. Dist. Ct. (no. dist.) N.Y. 1976, U.S. Dist. Ct. (we. dist.) N.Y. 1983, U.S. Ct. Appeals (1st and 2d cirs.) 1963. Assoc. Root, Barrett, Cohen, Knapp & Smith, N.Y.C., 1959-61; asst. U.S. atty. So. Dist. N.Y., 1961-63; assoc. Ropes & Gray, Boston, 1963-69; counsel N.Y. State Office Employee Rels. Govs. Office, Albany, 1969-73; dep. commr., gen. counsel N.Y. State Dept. Environ. Conservation, Albany, 1973-75; ptnr. Whiteman, Osterman & Hanna, Albany, 1975—. Adj. prof. Rensselaer Poly. Inst., Troy, NY, 1988—98; adj. prof. internat. environ. law John Marshall Law Sch., 2001—; NY panel disting. neutrals CPR Inst. Alternative Dispute Resolution, 2003—; mem. adv. bd. Inst. Transnat. Arbitration. Co-author: New York State Bar Association Environmental Handbook, 1987, New York Treatise on Environmental Law, 1992. Adv. bd. Inst. for Transnat. Arbitration; active Town of Chatham Planning Bd., NY, 1976—, Princeton U. Alumni Schs. Comm. No. NY, 1982—, co-chmn., 1982—2003; treas., trustee Shaker Mus. Found., Old Chatham, NY, 1978—96; trustee ea. N.Y. chpt. The Nature Conservancy, 1994—2002, chair conservation com., 1996—2002; trustee N.Y. State Archives Partnership Trust, 1995—, chair, 1996—; trustee Olana Partnership, 2002—; mem. commn. on environ. law Internat. Union for Conservation of Nature, 1999—; vol. arbitrator VIS Internat. Comml. Moot, Pace U. Law Sch., 1998—2000; adv. coun. Ctr. for Internat. Bus. and Trade Law, John Marshall Law Sch. Mem.: ABA (internat. law sect., practice sect., natural resources and environ. sect.), N.Y. State Bar Assn. (1st vice chmn. 1981—83, chmn. 1983—84, ho. of dels. 1984—85, 2003—), Cert. Inst. of Arbitrators London. Office: Whiteman Osterman & Hanna One Commerce Plz Albany NY 12260 E-mail: jhanna@woh.com.

HANNA, MARY ANN, education educator; b. Sumter, S.C., Apr. 16, 1947; d. Ernest Lee and Lucile (Horton) Kluttz; m. Dixon Boyce Hanna, June 21, 1994; children: Patrick D., Nathon Lee. BA, Furman U., Greenville, S.C., 1969; MA, Va. Tech., Blacksburg, 1975; PhD, 1979. Lic. prof. counselor, Va.; cert. mental health counselor. 1st grade tchr. N.C. Pub. Schs., Gastonia, Raleigh, N.C., 1969-70; kindergarten tchr. Pitts. Pub. Schs., 1970-71; lead tchr., program coord. A. Leo Weil Elem. Sch., Pitts., 1971-72; curriculum supr. Montgomery County Schs., Christiansburg, Va., 1974-76; ednl. cons. pvt. practice, 1979-91; asst. prof. Coll. Human Resources Va. Tech., Blacksburg, 1978-80; counselor dept. psychology Radford (Va.) U., 1992;

specialist assessment Dept. Edn. Commonwealth of Va., 1992-93; asst. prof. Coll. Edn. Radford U., Va., 1993—. Cons., instr. U. Va., Charlottesville, 1976-78; cons. Neonatal Assessment Roanoke (Va.) Meml. Hosp., 1980-92; cons. Assessment CTB/McGraw Hill, Monterey, Calif., 1993—; cons., asst. prof. Continuing Edn. Va. Tech., Blacksburg, 1994—. Author: The Open Classroom: A Practical Guide for the Elementary School teacher, 1974, Your Child's Development Scrapbook, 1986; contbr. articles to profl. jours. Bd. dirs. NRV Childcare Program Dublin, Va., 1982-84; Sunday Sch. tchr. Lutheran Meml. Ch., Blacksburg, Va., 1991—; vol. Gilbert Linkous Elem. Sch. Blacksburg, Va., 1988-92. Named Outstanding Student Tchr. Furman U., Greensville, S.C., 1969. Fellow Orthopsychiatry; mem. ACA, Va. Assn. Counselors, Educators, Suprs. (pres. 1996-97). Lutheran. Home: 3700 W Ridge Dr Blacksburg VA 24060-8564 Office: Radford University PO Box 6994 Radford VA 24142-6994

HANNA, SAMI A. education educator; b. Fayoum, Egypt, Oct. 3, 1927; s. Ayad and Balsam H.; m. Nadia Ayad, Dec. 29, 1981; children: Lisa, Mark, Michael. BA, Cairo U., 1948; Higher Diploma of Edn., Ein Shaws U., Cairo, 1950; MS, Hunter Coll., 1956; MA, Columbia U., 1958; PhD, U. Utah, 1964. Asst. dir. Mid. East Ctr., U. Utah, Salt Lake City, 1969-73; prof. U. Bahrain, 1983-93; dean Senior Univ., B.C., Can., 1993—; pres., founder Am. Coptic Studies Assn., Portland, 1996—. Vis. prof. coptic studies Pa. State U., 1993—. Author: Dictionary of Modern Linguistics, 1997; contbr. articles to profl. jours.; editor-in-chief Am. Jour. Arabic Studies, Am. Jour. Coptic Studies. Fulbright award Washington, 1997-98. Mem. Mid. East Studies Assoc., Brit. Mid. East Studies Assn., Am. Bahrain Friendship Assoc., Arab Gulf Studies Soc., Phi Delta Kappa, Phi Kappa Phi. Avocations: fishing, painting, cinematography, music, writing. Home: 2625 SE Market St Portland OR 97214-4946 Fax: 503-231-1296. E-mail: cfsh@pdx.edu.

HANNA, SHERMAN DAVIE, financial planning educator; b. Los Angeles, Dec. 24, 1946; s. Pat Hanna and Joan (Oberly) Haviland; m. Suzanne Lindamood, Jan. 20, 1972; 1 child, Emily Jane. BS, MIT, 1968; PhD, Cornell U., 1974. Asst. prof. So. Ill. U., Carbondale, 1973-74, Auburn (Ala.) U., 1974-77; asst. prof., assoc. prof. Kans. State U., Manhattan., 1977-84, prof., acting dept. head, 1983-85; prof., chmn. family resource mgmt. dept. Ohio State U., Columbus, 1986-94, prof. consumer and textile scis., 1994—. Author: Housing, Society and Consumers, 1979; co-editor Housing Educators Jour./Housing and Soc., 1973-77; mem. editorial bd. Jour. Consumer Affairs, 1979-89; contbr. articles to profl. jours. Mem. Am. Coun. Consumer Interests, Am. Econ. Assn., Assn. Fin. Counseling and Planning Educators (com. chmn. 1987-90, editor Fin. Counseling and Planning 1990—2002). Home: 2161 Arlington Ave Columbus OH 43221-4225 E-mail: hanna.1@osu.edu.

HANNAFORD, KARLA, college official; b. Kansas City, Mo., Sept. 19, 1944; d. Jim and Margaret (Stephens) Allison; m. Buddy Hannaford, July 27, 1968. BSE, Mo. Valley Coll., 1966. Cert. tchr., Mo. Tchr. Smithton (Mo.) Sch. Dist., 1966-68, Adrian (Mo.) Sch. Dist., 1968-69, Gallatin (Mo.) Sch. Dist., 1970-73; faculty sec. North Ctrl. Mo. Coll., Trenton, 1973—. Rschr.: Camp Counseling, 5th edit., 1977. Recipient Key to the City of Trenton City Coun., 1987. Mem. AAUW, Mo. C.C. Assn. Avocations: fishing, outdoor activities. Office: North Ctrl Mo Coll 1301 Main St Trenton MO 64683-1824

HANNAH, BARBARA ANN, nurse, educator; b. Pawnee, Okla., Sept. 25, 1943; d. Harold Ray and Betty Jean (Newport) Norris; m. Charles Bush Hannah, Mar. 25, 1971; children: Charles Douglas, Harry William. AS, Rogers State Coll., Claremore, Okla., 1974; BS in nursing, Tulsa U., 1976; MS, Okla U., 1985; EdD, Okla. State U., 1998. RN, Okla.; cert. BLS, ACLS, PALS. Nurse St. Francis Hosp., Tulsa, 1968-77, edn. specialist, 1986-90, clin. mgr. post-anesthesia care unit, 1991-96, critical care edn. coord., 1996—2001; dir. clin. prodn. CSI Prodns. for Medcom Inc., Tulsa, 1977-86; asst. adminstr. nursing Cleveland (Okla.) Area Hosp., 1990-91; dir. edn. Okla. Cmty. Healthcare Alliance, Tulsa, 2001—. Cons. St. Anthony Hosp., Oklahoma City, 1985; mem. affiliate faculty, chmn. emergency cardiac care com. Am. Heart Assn., 1986, mem. nat. faculty, 1990—, chmn. bd. Okla. affiliate, 1996-98; bd. dirs. Citizen CPR, 1986-91, chmn. comprehensive monitoring com., 1990-91. Producer audio-visual programs for nursing edn., 1977-86. Mem. Food & Refreshment Com. Channel 8 fund raising drive, Tulsa, 1985, 86. Recipient spl. awards and honors All Heart Vol., 1988, Lifetime Achievement award Am. Heart Assn.; named Woman of Yr., 1998. Mem. NAFE, Acute Care Nurses Assn. (seminar dir., treas. Greater Tulsa area chpt.), Okla. Nurses Assn. (dist. 2 com. on profl. practice), Am. Heart Assn. (v.p. program com. 1990—, chmn. faculty BLS task force Woman of Yr., Okla. affiliate 1993, 97, chmn. Okla. affiliate 1994, 95-96, Lifetime Achievement award 1998), Am. Soc. Post Anesthesia Nurses (1st pl. poster award Nat. Ann. Conf. 1993, alt. del. from Okla. 1994), Okla. Soc. Post Anesthesia Nurses (pres. Tulsa chpt. 1993), Okla. Perioanesthesia Nurses Assn. (pres. 1999-2000), Am. Soc. Peri Anesthesia Nurses (Okla. del. to bd. 1996—, mem. stds., guidelinse and practice com. 1998-2000, rsch. com. 1999-2000, chairperson cont. edn. approver ctr. 2000), Sigma Theta Tau. Avocations: biking, hiking, quilting, travel. Home: PO Box 112 Skiatook OK 74070-0112 Office: OOkla Cmty Health Care Alliance Bldg 11 Ste 150 4504 E 67th St Tulsa OK 74136

HANNAH, JUDY CHALLENGER, private education tutor; b. Balt., Oct. 8, 1948; d. John Thomas and Doris Rose (Etherington) Diehl; m. Brian Challenger, Apr. 15, 1968 (div. Dec. 1994); children: John Joseph, Jennifer Elizabeth; m. W. P. Hannah, Oct. 6, 2001. AA, Arlington Bible Coll., 1985; BS, Liberty U., 1991; M in Edn., Mt. St. Mary's Coll., 1996; Diploma, Inst. of Children's Lit., 1997. Cert. elem. tchr., Md., 1996. Tchr., K-4 Mill Valley Sch., Owing Mills, Md., 1984-85, Arlington Bapt. Sch., Balt., 1985-86, Mill Valley Sch., 1986-87; bookkeeper, sec. Challenger Engr., Inc., Finksburg, 1987-92; dir. B/A child care ABC Care Inc., 1992-95; tchr. internship Thurmont Elem. Sch., Md., 1995-96; tutor/office mgr. Learning Resources, Westminster, Md., 1996-97; pvt. tutor, owner A Lesson Learned, Inc., Union Bridge, Md., 1997—. Mem. delegation People to People Amb. Programs, China, 2001. Vol. Crisis Hotline, Balt., 1972, leader/tchr. Pioneer Girls Internat., Arlington Bapt. Ch., 1975-78; mem. profl. women's adv. bd. Am. Biog. Inst. Mem. Md. Emmaus, Internat. Dyslexia Assn., Smithsonian Inst., Vol. in Missions, Pi Lamba Theta, People To People Internat. Republican. Avocations: writing, hiking. Home: 48 Bucher John Rd Union Bridge MD 21791-9527

HANNAM-OOSTERBAAN, MARIA GERTRUDE, educator; b. The Netherlands, July 28, 1916;, U.S., 1948,arrived in U.S., 1948; d. Jan and Anna Geertruida (Vanderweg) O.; m. Aug 12, 1940. Tchr. Degree, Christian Coll., Amsterdam, 1936; Bachelor, Whittier Coll., 1953. Elem. tchr. Batavia Christian Sch. Dist., Java, Indonesia, 1937-38; tchr. Palembang, Sumatra, Indonesia, 1938-41; clandestine tchr. Concentration Camp, Semarang, Indonesia, 1942—46; tchr. Ranchito Sch. Dist., Pico., Calif., 1953—55, L.A. City Sch. Dist., 1955-77. Mem. Westminster Presbyn. Ch. Mem. AAUW, Calif. Ret. Tchrs. Assn., Order Eastern Star. Presbyn. Home: # G222 710 W 13th Ave Escondido CA 92025-5511

HANNEMAN, DARLENE MARIE, elementary school educator; b. Chgo., June 27, 1950; d. Robert and Gilda (Hasmeyer) Culler; m. Dennis F. Hanneman, June 24, 1972; children: Tamara, Beth, Eric, Angela. BS in Edn., Bowling Green U., 1971, MS in Edn. in Reading, MS in Reading Specialization, Bowling Green U., 1977. Elem. sch. tchr. Ottoville (Ohio) Local Schs., 1972—. Mem. writer, author com. Putnam County Schs., 1989—; mem. com. for selection of reading and math. pupil performance objectives for Ohio State Schs., Putnam, 1990—. Active local Altar and Rosary Soc.; pres. Am. Legion Aux., Ottawa, 1990—; publicity chair, score tally person Putnam County Soccer Assn.; advisor 4-H, Ottawa, 1972— Mem. Ohio Edn. Assn. (3 times past pres.), Ohio English Assn., Internat. Reading Assn. (3 times past pres.), Sci. Educator Assn. Democrat. Roman Catholic. Avocations: reading, collecting picture books, swimming, baking, children. Home: 15290 Road 15M Columbus Grove OH 45830-9772 Office: Ottoville Local Sch PO Box 248 Ottoville OH 45876-0248

HANNEWALD, NORMAN EUGENE, secondary school educator; b. Stockbridge, Mich., Aug. 4, 1945; s. Martin Carl and Helen Pauline (Archenbronn) H.; m. Penny Lynn Boyer, Jan. 28, 1967; children: Marcia, Gregory, Mark. BS, Ea. Mich. U., 1967, MS, 1972. Sci. tchr. mid. sch. Northville (Mich.) Pub. Schs., mem. after sch. gifted sci. program. Mem. Nat. Sci. Tchrs. Assn., Mich. Sci. Tchrs. Assn.

HANNS, CHRISTIAN ALEXANDER, vocational and educational consultant; b. Elizabeth, N.J., Sept. 12, 1948; s. Christian Julius and Elizabeth (Branch) Hanns. BA, Kean Coll., Union, N.J., 1972; MA in Social Scis. and English Edn., Kean Coll., 1973. Cert. vocational evaluation specialist Assn. Adult Edn. N.J., work adjustment specialist Assn. Adult Edn. N.J., internat. cert. drug and alcohol counselor Assn. Adult Edn. N.J. Dir. counseling and testing Union Coll., Cranford, NJ, 1972—76; dir. counseling, curriculum and devel. Ednl. Resource Inst., Elizabeth, 1974—76; coord. coll. level. exam. program preparation and course devel., instr., counselor Watchung Hills Adult Sch., Warren, Lakewood (N.J.) Cmty. Schs., 1975—85; project coord. human svcs. delivery sys. assessment Union County Coalition, 1976—77; coord. career, vocat. counseling and placement Integrity House, Inc., Berkeley Heights, NJ, 1978; cons. employment, ednl. vocat. counseling N.J. State Dept. Health, 1978—84; dir. rsch. and devel. Spectrum Health Care, Inc., 1984—88. Adj. faculty Montclair State U., Hudson County C.C., Essex County C.C., Kean U.; faculty mem. N.J. Summer Sch. of Alcohol & Drug Studies, Rutgers U. Ctr. of Alcohol Studies, 1984—, Old Bridge Adult Sch., 1984—; clin. dir. Damon House Inc., New Brunswick, NJ, 1988—92, clin. cons., 1992—; cons. N.J. Coll. of Medicine and Dentistry Cmty. Mental Health Ctr., 1986—98, AT&T, Bedminster, NJ, 1986—99, TKR, Piscataway, NJ, 1986—92, Thomas A. Edison State Coll., 1986—; cons., dir. life skills edn. East Orange (N.J.) Bd. Edn., 1979; cons., condr. workshops. Active March of Dimes; chmn. pastor-parish relations com. Linden United Meth. Ch.; No. regional rep. Met. Ecumenical Ministry; mem. exec. bd. dirs. Eastern Union County chpt. ARC, chmn. spl. projects, fund raising and public rels.; chmn. bd. dirs. Clara Barton Aux.; sec. bd. dirs. Union County Psychiat. Clinic; chmn. welfare/social svc. com. Salvation Army. Served with AUS, 1966—69. Recipient various pub. service awards. Mem.: Middlesex County Coun. Drug & Alcohol, Nat. Coun. Tchrs. English, Nat. Cmty. Edn. Assn., Internat. Platform Assn., Speech Assn. N.J., Assn. Cmty. Edn. (sec.), Assn. Adult Edn. N.J. (co-chmn. counseling). Democrat. Methodist. Home: 31 Louis St Parlin NJ 08859-1919

HANOVER, R(AYMOND) SCOTT, tennis management professional; b. Des Moines, June 10, 1964; s. Norman E. and Jo Ann (Taylor) H.; m. Marla J. Boicourt, Apr. 23, 1988. BA, Grand View Coll., 1986. Staff writer, news asst. Des Moines Register, 1985-90; sch. dir. Missouri Valley sect. U.S. Tennis Assn., Kansas City, Mo., 1990-96; mgr. Plaza Tennis Ctr., Kansas City, Mo., 1996—. Dir. 73d Nat. Pub. Parks Tennis Championships, 1999, USTA Men's Futures Profl. Tournament, 1998-00; mem. exec. com. Big 12 Collegiate Tennis Conf. Championships, 2000, 03; mem. USTA Mo. Valley bd. dirs., 2000-02, NCAA Divsn. II nat. exec. com., 2002. Editor U.S. Profl. Tennis Assn. Missouri Valley divsn. newsletter, 1992-95. Dir. Heart of Am. Dist. Tennis., 1996-98, sec., 1999-2000, pres., 2000-02; co-founder, bd. dirs. Kansas City Met. Tennis Assn., sec., 2000—. Recipient Svc. award Nebr. AHPERD, 1991, Missouri Valley Tennis Assn. and Heart of Am. Tennis Assn. Facility of Yr. award, 1997; named U.S.A. Sch. Clinician of Yr., 2002. Mem. U.S. Tennis Assn. (NRPA Excellence in Tennis award, life, referee 1997—, liaison to Club Mgrs. Assn. 1998—, Mo. Valley nominating com. 1998, nat. com. USA Sch. Tennis 2001-02, nat. SERV com. 2003—, nat. com. cmty. tennis 2001—, Outstanding Pub. Facility award 1998, Heart of Am. Orgn. of Yr. award 1998, dir. Heart of Am. Tournament of Yr. 1999, 2001), Missouri Valley Tennis Assn. (chmn. pub. rels. com. 1989-90, chmn. cmty. devel. com. 1996-98), U.S. Profl. Tennis Registry, Grand View Alumni Coun. (pres. 1988-90). Office: Kansas City Parks/Recreation 4747 JC Nichols Pkwy Kansas City MO 64112-1627

HANSBURY, VIVIEN HOLMES, elementary and secondary school educator, consultant; b. Richmond, Va., Feb. 5, 1927; d. Arthur Jefferson and Mary (Spain) Holmes; m. Horace Trent, Dec. 24, 1942 (div. Feb. 1958); children: Sandra, Horace Jr., Vernard; m. Leonard Andrew Hansbury, Oct. 28, 1962. Cert. elem., spl. edn. tchr., elem. sch. prin., Pa. Fiscal acct. VA, Phila., 1950-62; intermediate unit tchr. Delaware County (Pa.) Pub. Schs., 1966-68, supr. spl. edn., 1968-69; counselor, instr. Pa. State U., Ogontz, 1969-74; spl. edn. tchr. Phila. Schs., 1974-76, program mgr., 1976-78, instrnl. advisor, 1978-84, resource tchr., cons., 1984-92; retired, 1992. Ednl. cons. NIA Psychol. Assocs., Phila., 1982—; Pa. coordinator Assault on Illiteracy, 1983—, Northeastern sectional dir., 1988—; tutor Mayor's Commn. on Literacy, Phila., 1984-90. Den mother Boy Scouts Am., Phila., 1957; dir. adult basic edn. Pinn Meml. Bapt. Ch., Phila., 1985-91; pres. Phila. chpt. Pan-Hellenic Council, 1982; exec. bd. Phila. Opportunities for Industrialization Ctr., 1984—, Wynnefield Residents Assn., 1992. Recipient numerous community service awards; named Tchr. of Yr. Sch. Dist. Phila., 1988. Mem. Northeastern Fedn. Women (recording sec. Phila. 1987), Phila. Coalition Federated Women (pres. 1988-90), Pa. Fedn. Women's Clubs (fin. sec. 1986-90, Disting. Svc. award 1987), Nat. Assn. Univ. Women, Nat. Assn. of Colored Women's Club (exec. bd., del. to U.N.), Top Ladies of Distinction (organizer and pres. Phila. chpt. 1988-93, Dedicated Svc. awards 1991, 92), Sigma Pi Epsilon Delta, Kappa Omega Zeta, Zeta Phi Beta, Phil Delta Kappa (v.p. Phila. chpt., editor newsletter 1990-93). Clubs: Monday Evening (pres. 1984-90), Thirty Clusters (pres. 1985-87). Democrat.

HANSEL, JAMES GORDON, engineer, educator; b. N.Y.C., Oct. 17, 1937; s. Gordon Franklin and Edith (Bradshaw) H.; m. Sarah Elizabeth Martin, Dec. 27, 1964; 1 child, Claire E. BS in Engring. with high honors, Stevens Inst. Tech., 1959, MSME, 1960, ScD, 1964. Mem. rsch. faculty Princeton (N.J.) U., Guggenheim Labs., 1964-69; rsch. engr. Exxon Rsch., Linden, N.J., 1969-72; mgr. new catalyst devel. Engelhard Corp., Menlo Park, N.J., 1972-81; sr. engring. assoc. Air Products and Chems., Inc., Allentown, Pa., 1981—. Adj. assoc. prof. Columbia U., N.Y.C., 1976-80; vis. lectr. mech. engring. Stevens Inst. Tech. Hoboken, N.J., 1970-76; cons. on engring. safety to major corps., 1987—; adj. prof. chem./mech. engring. Pa. State U., State Coll., 1992-2000. Author: Theory of Experiments, 1967; contbr. author Book of Knowledge encyc., 1979, Encyclopedia of Chemical Technology, 1994; contbr. articles to profl. jours. Bd. dirs. Am. on Wheels Mus., 1998—; indsl. and profl. adv. coun. Pa. State U., Coll. of Engring., 1998—. Mem. Am. Inst. Chem. Engrs. (tech. com. on reactive chems.), Internat. Standards Orgn. (tech. com. on hydrogen vehicles), N.Y. Acad. Sci., Sigma Xi, Tau Beta Pi. Achievements include patents for on applications of oxygen; development of Three Way Conversion catalyst and automotive engine control system used in over 400 million automobiles worldwide; safety practices for hydrogen powered vehicles. Home: 829 Frank Dr Emmaus PA 18049-1505 Office: Air Products & Chems Inc 7201 Hamilton Blvd Allentown PA 18195-1526 E-mail: hanseljg@acpi.com.

HANSEL, WILLIAM, biology educator; b. Vale Summit, Md., Sept. 16, 1918; s. John W. and Helen M. (Sperlein) H.; m. Milbrey Downey, Aug. 16, 1942; children: Barbara, Kay. MS, Cornell U., 1947, PhD, 1949. Asst. prof. Cornell U., Ithaca, N.Y., 1949-52, assoc. prof., 1952-61, prof., 1961-90, Liberty Hyde Bailey prof., 1983-90, chmn. physiology dept., 1978-83; Gordon D. Cain prof. La. State U., Baton Rouge, 1990—. Scientific adv. Merck, Sharp and Dohme, Rahway, 1980-85, Smith, Kline, Beecham, Westchester, Pa., 1986-91. Author: Genetic Engineering of Animals, 1990, Nutrition and Reproduction, 1998; contbr. over 300 articles to profl. jours. Maj. U.S. Army, 1941-46, ETO. Recipient 13 nat. or internat. rsch. and svc. awards including first Pharmacia and Upjohn Internat. award for life time rsch. in ruminant reproduction, 1998. Fellow AAAS; mem. Soc. Study Reprodn. (pres. 1976), Am. Physiol. Soc., Endocrine Soc., Soc. Exptl. Biology and Medicine (treas. 1975), Gamma Sigma Delta, Sigma Xi, Phi Kappa Phi. Achievements include isolation and identification of cusative agent of bovine x-disease; development of successful technique for estrous cycle regulation in cattle; pioneered development of assays for hormones in blood of animals; discovery of control mechanisms for corpus luteum function in cattle; demonstrated the relationships between nutrition and reproduction in cattle; development of successful targeted treatment for human prostate and breast cell tumors grown in test mice. Office: Pennington Biomed Rsch Ctr 6400 Perkins Rd # B1047 Baton Rouge LA 70808-4124 E-mail: hanselw@mhs.pbrc.edu.

HANSELL, PHYLLIS SHANLEY, nursing educator, administrator, researcher, consultant; b. N.Y.C., Jan. 3, 1947; s. Peter James and Jewell Mae (Altis) S.; m. Robert Lewis Hansell, June 16, 1984; children: Benjamin, Christopher. BS, Fairleigh Dickinson U., 1972; MEd, Columbia U., 1975, EdD, 1981. RN. Staff nurse Mountainside Hosp., Montclair, N.J., 1967-69; head nurse N.Y. Med. Coll., N.Y.C., 1970-72, clin. instr., 1972-75; instr. Seton Hall U., South Orange, 1975-77, asst. prof., 1977-79, prof. nursing, 1986-94, 96—, dir. nursing rsch., 1986-94, dept. chair, 1996-99, acting dean, 1999-2000, dean Coll. Nursing, 2000—; dir. nursing rsch. Meml. Sloan-Kettering, N.Y.C., 1984-86; dean, prof. Coll. Nursing Seton Hall U., 2000. Chair N.J. Assn. of Baccalaureate and Higher Degree Programs in Nursing. Contbr. articles to profl. jours., chpt. to book. Bd. dirs. Jr. League, Montclair, 1992-94, chair grants and corp. devel., chair Newark Teen Arts Festival, Montclair and Newark, 1994-95. Recipient Gov.'s merit award Gov. N.J., 1994. Fellow: Am. Acad. Nursing; mem.: ANA (chair rsch., Gov.'s award 1994), N.J. State Nurses Assn. (mem. coun., rsch. award 1994), Am. Acad. Practice (Disting. Practitioner 2000), Sigma Theta Tau (v.p. Gamma Nu chpt. 1994—96, rsch. award 1983). Avocations: opera, ballet, skiing, tennis, golf. Office: Seton Hall U 400 S Orange Ave South Orange NJ 07079-2697

HANSEN, ANNE KATHERINE, poet, retired elementary education educator; b. Coulter, Iowa, Oct. 29, 1928; d. Carl Christian and Else Katherine (Paulsen) H. BA, Chapman U., 1958; MA, U. Redlands, 1971. Life credential, Calif. Elem. tchr. Bloomington (Calif.) Schs., 1958-60, San Bernardino (Calif.) Unified Sch. Dist., 1960-87; ret., 1987. Contbr. poetry to anthologies. Recipient Golden Poet award World of Poetry, 1988, 89, 90, 91, 92, Poet of Merit award Internat. Soc. Poets, plaque, 1993, 94, 96, medallion, 1996. Home: 1632 Sepulveda Ave San Bernardino CA 92404-4702

HANSEN, CHERRY A. FISHER, special education educator; b. Jackson, Minn., Nov. 9, 1951; d. Marlo Argene and Mary Ellen (Walsh) Fisher; m. Paul Herbert Hansen, June 26, 1977; children: Angela, Rachel. BA, U. No. Iowa, 1974; MS, Drake U., 1994. Cert. tchr., Iowa, cons. endorsement behavior disorders. Tchr. of emotionally disturbed Pottawattamie County Agy., Council Bluffs, Iowa, 1974-76; behavior disorders tchr. Council Bluffs (Iowa) Cmty. Schs., 1974-78, 87-91; adult edn. tchr. Iowa Western C.C., Council Bluffs, 1984-86; behavior disorders tchr. Area Edn. Agy. # 13, Council Bluffs, 1991-98, lead tchr., 1994-99. Mem. state para conv. com. Area Edn. Agy., summer 1997—, spl. edn. cons., 1998—. Mem. altar guild, com. head, Bible sch. St. John's Luth. Ch., Honey Creek, Iowa; treas. LWML Evening Group, 1997; del., rep. Camp Okoboji; bd. dirs. Human Care, St. John's Presch.; mem. Phase III and SPARC Com., 1999—. Mem. ASCD, Mdilands Reading, Iowa Cons. Group, Phi Delta Kappa. Avocations: antiquing, sewing, stained glass, crafts, cooking. Home: 30063 Coldwater Ave Honey Creek IA 51542-4187

HANSEN, ELAINE T. academic administrator; AB with greatest distinction cum laude, Mt. Holyoke Coll., 1969; MA, U. Minn., 1972; PhD, U. Wash., 1975. Asst. editor Mid. English dictionary U. Mich., 1975-77, assoc. rsch. editor, 1977—78; asst. prof. Haverford (Pa.) Coll., 1978—80, assoc. prof., 1980—90, dept. chair, 1989-92, prof. dept. English, 1991—, provost, 1995—2002; pres. Bates Coll., 2002—. Lectr. in field. Author: The Solomon Complex: Reading Wisdom in Old English Poetry, 1988, Chaucer and the Fictions of Gender, 1992, Mother Without Child: Contemporary Fiction and the Crisis of Motherhood, 1997; mem. editl. bd. Coll. Lit.; reader manuscripts for jours. and univ. presses; contbr. articles to profl. jours., also revs. and papers. NEH Summer stipendee, 1981; Mellon grantee for faculty devel. in humanities, 1983-84, Whitehead grantee for faculty in the humanities, 1987-88; Am. Coun. Learned Socs. fellow, 1993-94. Mem. MLA (mem. Chaucer divsn. exec. com. 1995-99, divsn. rep. to del. assembly 1996-99, com. on acad. freedom and profl. rights and responsibilities 1997-2000), Am. Coun. Learned Socs. (prescreener Cen. Fellowship Program), Medieval Acad., New Chaucer Soc., Nat. Women's Studies Assn., Soc. for Feminist Medieval Scholarship (pres. 1993-95). Office: Bates College Office of the Pres Lane Hall Rm 204 Lewiston ME 04240 E-mail: president@bates.edu.

HANSEN, HAROLD B., JR., principal; b. Sewickley, Pa., July 3, 1955; s. Harold B. and Mary Clara (VanderVort) H.; m. Patty Jo Gabhart, Sept. 19, 1976; children: Jeremiah James, Joshua Andrew, Esther Beth, Christopher Seth. BA in Elem. Edn., Purdue U., 1980; MA in Sch. Adminstrn., Western N.Mex. U., 1987. Cert. secondary lang. arts and spl. edn. tchr., TESL tchr., instrnl. leader, sch. adminstr., elem. tchr., coach, N.Mex. Resource rm. tchr. Flossmoor/Homewood (Ill.) Pub. Schs., 1981, Newcomb (N.Mex.) H.S., 1981-82; tchr. self-contained spl. edn. Chester (Mont.) Pub. Schs., 1982-84; adminstr., prin., tchr. Bennett (Colo.) Bapt. Ch. Sch., 1984; propr., tutor Hemispheric Learning Tutorial Svcs., 1982—; tchr. resource room, coach cross county, wrestling, track and field Gallup-McKinley County Pub. Schs., Tohatchi/Navajo Reserv., N.Mex., 1985-90, elem. tchr. phys. edn. and health, at-risk tchr. Tohatchi Elem. Sch. Tohatchi, 1990-98, 5th grade track & field head coach, 1991-98, 5th grade boys' and girls' basketball asst. coach, 1995-98; prin. Smith Lake Elem. Sch., Gallup-McKinley County Pub. Schs., 1998—. Mem. various sch. coms. Gallup-McKinley County Pub. Schs., 1990—98, 2001—; seminar leader on hemispherecity; dep. registration officer McKinley County, N.Mex., 1986—98; mem. Prins.' Leadership Inst. with RE: Learning NM, Prins.' Leadership Acad. with Success for All Found. Past pres. Village of Hope, substance abuse tng. ctr.; co-founder, past bd. dirs. Christian Home Educators Assn.; dir. Approved Workmen Are Not Ashamed; past coord. Jump Rope for Heart, Am. Heart Assn.; past mem. Coun. for Curricular Excellence, McKinley County; pst TESOL rep. for Western N.Mex. U.'s Gallup Grad. Ctr.'s Advd. Coun., 1997—99. Named to Outstanding Young Men of Am., 1987. Mem. N.Mex. Assn. Health, Phys. Edn., Recreation and Dance, Christian HomeEducators Assn., Aesthetic Realism Found. Home: PO Box 100 Smith Lake NM 87365-0100 Fax: 888-391-4847; 505-786-5542. E-mail: hbchansen@citilink.net., chansen@sle.gmcs.k12.nm.us.

HANSEN, JAMES EDWARD, medical educator, researcher; b. Green Bay, Wis., Sept. 4, 1926; s. James Christian and Helen Dorothy (Terp) H.; m. Beverly May Kapke, June 5, 1948; children: Barbara Parry, Patricia Begley, Linda DeGroot, James H. Student, St. Norbert's Coll., 1942-43, U. Wis., 1943-44, Marquette U., 1944-45; MD, Johns Hopkins U., 1945-49. Diplomate Am. Bd. Internal Medicine. Intern, then resident Letterman Army Med. Ctr., San Francisco, 1949-53; commd. 1st lt. U.S. Army, 1949, advanced through grades to col., 1975, physician, 1950-62; chief physiology div. U.S. Army Med. Rsch. and Nutrition Lab., Denver, 1962-65; sci. dir. U.S. Army Rsch. Inst. Environ. Medicine, Natick, Mass., 1965-71; chief clin. investigation svcs. Tripler Army Med. Ctr., Honolulu, 1971-75; assoc.

prof. dept. medicine UCLA, Torrance, 1976-78, prof. dept. medicine, 1978-86, emeritus prof. dept. medicine, 1986—. Instr., asst. prof. U. Colo., 1961-65; liaison mem. applied physiology study sect. NIH, 1965-71; cons. environ. medicine U.S. Army Surgeon Gen., Washington, 1965-73; lectr. environ. medicine Johns Hopkins U., Balt., 1966-71; clin. prof. physiology U. Hawaii, 1972-75. Co-author: Principles of Exercise Testing and Interpretation, 1986, 3d rev. edit., 1999; contbr. numerous articles to profl. jours. Chmn. congregation St. Matthew's Luth. Ch., Aurora, Colo., 1962-64, Gloria Dei Luth. Ch., Pearl City, Hawaii, 1972-74; sch. supt. Luth. Ch., Natick, 1967-69; elder, mission com. chmn. St. Peter's By the Sea Presbyn. Ch., Rancho Palos Verdes, Calif., 1992-95. Pulmonary fellow Fitzsimons Army Med. Ctr., 1960, UCLA Ctr. Health Scis., 1975-76; recipient Sustaining Membership award Assn. Mil. Surgeons, 1970, Calif. medal Am. Lung Assn., 1996 Fellow ACP, Am. Coll. Chest Physicians; mem. Am. Physiol. Soc., Am. Thoracic Soc. (sci. adv. bd. 1983—), Calif. Thoracic Soc. (pulmonary chmn. 1980-83, physiology com). Avocations: piano, tennis. Home: 1692 Morse Dr San Pedro CA 90732-4336 Office: Harbor-UCLA Med Ctr PO Box 405 1000 W Carson St Torrance CA 90502-2004

HANSEN, JAMES VERNON, computer science, information systems educator; b. Idaho Falls, May 31, 1936; s. Heber Lorenzo and Myrtle Jane (Simmons) H.; m. Diane Lynne Bradbury, Sept. 18, 1963; children: Tamsin, Jeffrey, Dale, Peter. BS, Brigham Young U., 1963; PhD, U. Wash., 1973. Systems analyst TRW, Redondo Beach, Calif., 1966-69; sr. rsch. scientist Battelle Meml. Inst., Richland, Wash., 1972-74, also cons.; asst. prof. Ind. U., Bloomington, 1974-77, assoc. prof., 1977-81; Glen Ardis prof. Brigham Young U., Provo, Utah, 1982—. Instr. EDI Group, Chgo., 1987-91. Author: Controls in Microcomputer Systems, 1984, Data Communications: Concepts and Controls, 1987, Database Management and Design, 1992, 2d edit., 1995, Machine Learning and Multiagent Systems. Served with U.S. Army, 1959-62. Grantee Peat, Marwick, Mitchell Found., 1982, 83, 84. Mem. Assn. Computing Machinery, Inst. for Ops. Rsch. and Mgmt. Sci., IEEE Computer Soc., Am. Assn. Artificial Intelligence, Sierra Club. Mem. Lds Ch. Office: Brigham Young U Dept Comp Sci Provo UT 84602

HANSEN, JEAN MARIE, math and computer educator; b. Detroit, Mar. 8, 1937; d. Harvey Francis and Ida Marie (Hay) Chapman; m. Donald Edward Hansen, Aug. 29, 1968; children: Jennifer Lynn, John Francis. BA, U. Mich., 1959, MA, 1960. Cert. Secondary Sch. Tchr. Tchr. Detroit Pub. Schs., 1959-60, Newark (Calif.) Sch. Dist., 1960-65, Dept. Def., Zweibruken, Germany, 1965-67, Livonia (Mich.) Pub. Schs., 1967-69; instr. Ford Livonia Transmission Plant, 1990—. Trustee/pres. Northville (Mich.) Bd. Edn., 1981-97; trustee Northville Dist. Libr., 1999—, pres. bd., 2003. Author: California People and Their Government, 1965, Voices of Government, 1969-70. Named Disting. Bd. Mem., Mich. Assn. Sch. Bds., 1991, Citizen of Yr., Northville C. of C., 1991. Mem. AAUW (v.p. Northville bd. 1982-86, pres. 1987-89, Mich. chpt. Agt. of Change award, edn. area 1985), LWV, Kiwanis, Northville Women's Club. Republican. Avocations: weaving, basket weaving, skiing, golf, travel. Home: 229 Linden St Northville MI 48167-1426 E-mail: jhansen@comcast.net.

HANSEN, JO-IDA CHARLOTTE, psychology educator, researcher; b. Washington, Oct. 2, 1947; d. Gordon Henry and Charlotte Lorraine (Helgeson) H.; m. John Paul Campbell. BA, U. Minn., 1969, MA, 1971, PhD, 1974. Asst. prof. psychology U. Minn., Mpls., 1974-78, assoc. prof., 1978-84, prof., 1984—, dir. Ctr. for Interest Measurement Rsch., 1974—, dir. counseling psychology program, 1987—, dir. Vocat. Assessment Clinic, 1997—, prof. human resources and indsl. rels., 1997—. Author: User's Guide for the SII, 1984, 2d edit., 1992, Manual for the SII, 1985 2d edit. 1994; editor: Measurement and Evaluation in Counseling and Development, 1993-2000; editor Jour. Counselling Psychology, 1999—; contbr. numerous articles to profl. jours., chpts. to books. Recipient early career award U. Minn., 1982, E.K. Strong, Jr. gold medal, 1984. Fellow APA (coun. reps. 1990-93, 97-99, pres. divsn. counseling psychology 1993-94, chmn. joint com. testing practices 1989-93, com. to revise APA/Am. Ednl. Rsch. Assn. nat. coun. measurement evalation testing stds. 1993-99, exam. com. Assn. State Provincial Psychology Bds. 1996-99, bd. sci. affairs, 2003-05, chair coun. of editors 2003-04; Leona Tyler award for rsch. and profl. svc. 1996); mem. ACA (extended rsch. award 1990, disting. rsch. award 1996), Assn. for Measurement and Evaluation (pres. 1988-89, Exemplary Practice award 1987, 90). Avocations: golf, theater, music, water and downhill skiing, spectator sports. Office: U Minn Dept Psychology Ctr Interest Measurement 75 E River Rd Minneapolis MN 55455-0280

HANSEN, MEREDITH JANE, physician assistant educator; b. Fresno, California, June 7, 1955; d. William Bruce and Isabelle Ione (Misenheimer) H.; m. David Keith Watkins, June 15, 1991; children: David, Taylor. Student, U. Okla., San Antonio, 1983-85; BS summa cum laude, U. Okla., Norman, 1989; MPH, U. Tex. Health Sci. Ctr., 1995. Lic. physician asst., cert. EMT, Tex. Enlisted U.S. Army, 1975, advanced through grades to capt., 1992, pharmacy technician, 1976-83, physician asst. Fort Bragg, N.C., 1985-91, San Antonio, 1991-95; asst. prof. U. Tex. Health Sci. Ctr., San Antonio, 1995—. Author: Clinical Preceptors Handbooks, 1996; co-author: (with others) Primary Care for Physician Assistants, 1998; editor videotape Examination of the Musculoskeletal, 1993, The Neurological Examination, 1994. Decorated Bronze Star; recipient Saudi Arabian Military Med. Excellence award Saudi Arabian Dept. Defense, 1990, Young Faculty award Upjohn, 1995; grantee Area Health Edn. Ctr. of So. Tex., 1997. Mem. AAUW, Am. Acad. Physician Assts., Assn. Physician Assts. Programs, Tex. Assn. Allied Health Profls., Tex. Acad. Physician Assts., Tex. Public Health Assn. Republican. Avocations: gardening, reading, volunteer work.

HANSEN, PAULA J. academic administrator; b. Manitowoc, Wis., July 2, 1951; d. Paul and Anne (Reedy) H.; children: Megan, Benjamin, Molly. BS, U. Wis., 1972, MS, 1977, Adminstrv. Leadership Specialist, 1990. Title I adminstrv. asst. Coop. Svc. Agy. #9, Green Bay, Wis., 1974-75; dir. govt. programs West Bend (Wis.) Joint Sch. Dist., 1976-89; asst. supt. Sch. Dist. Rhinelander, Wis., 1989—. Evaluator Head Start program rev. U.S. Dept. HHS Region V, Dayton, Ohio, 1982; mem. com. pupil svcs. planning meeting Wis. Dept. Pub. Instrn., Madison, 1995; evaluator pub. sch. dist. consortium Sch. Edn. Consortium Rev. Sch. Dist., 1989. Contbr. articles to profl. jours. Active ad hoc zoning com. County of Oneida, Wis., 1997; bd. dirs., officer Lake Thompson Assn., Rhinelander, 1995—, Devel. Disabilities Svcs., Inc., Washington County, Wis., 1980-83; foster care parent Washington County Foster Care Program, 1982-85. Mem. Assn. Wis. Sch. Adminstrs., Assn. Sch. Dist. Rhinelander Adminstrs. (sec., exec. bd. 1995-97), Wis. Head Start Dirs. Assn. (sec. 1980-84), Wis. Coun. for Gifted and Talented, Rotary (pres., mem. exec. bd. 1990—), Lake Thompson Assn. Roman Catholic. Avocations: alpine and nordic skiing, sailing, playing various musical instruments. Office: Sch Dist Rhinelander 315 S Oneida Ave Rhinelander WI 54501-3422

HANSEN, ROBERT DENNIS, educational administrator; b. San Francisco, July 17, 1945; s. Eiler Cunnard and Muriel Lenore (Morrison) H.; BA, U. San Francisco, 1967, MA in Counseling and Guidance, 1971, MA in Supervision and Adminstrn., 1973; EdD, U. La Verne, 1988; children from a previous marriage: April Michelle, Alison Nicole, Andrew Warren. Tchr., dept. chmn., counselor, dir. student affairs, attendance officer South San Francisco Unified Sch. Dist., 1968-74, coord., asst. prin. Jurupa Unified Sch. Dist., Riverside, Calif., 1974-78; prin., asst. supt. San Gabriel (Calif.) Sch. Dist., 1978-91; supt. Rosemead (Calif.) Sch. Dist., 1991—; adj. prof. U. La Verne, Calif., 1988—. Mem. exec. bd. South San Francisco PTA, 1968-74; bd. dirs. West San Gabriel YMCA; mem. parade formation com. Pasadena (Calif.) Tournament of Roses. Recipient Hon. Svc. award Calif. State PTA. Mem. U. San Francisco Edn. Alumni Soc. (pres. 1972-73), Nat. Assn. Year-Round Edn., U. San Francisco Alumni Assn., ASCD, Am. Assn. Sch. Adminstrs., Assn. Calif. Sch. Adminstrs., Phi Delta Kappa. Republican. Presbyterian. Masons (32 degree). Office: Rosemead Sch Dist 3907 Rosemead Blvd # 213 Rosemead CA 91770-1951

HANSEN, SALLY JO, educational consultant; b. San Fernando, Calif., Sept. 8, 1937; d. Kenneth Morris Sr. and Carmen (Woods) High; m. Mark Herman Hansen, June 14, 1958; children: Laurie Jo, Mark. BA, U. Redlands, 1959. Cert. lang. devel. specialist, Calif., cert. crosscultural lang. and acad. devel. specialist, Calif. Tchr. remedial reading Newport-Mesa Unified Sch. Dist., Newport Beach, Calif., 1965-80, tchr. ESL, 1980-88, title VII coord., 1988-97, ESL bilingual project coord., 1990-97, coord. Healthy Start, 1990-97, coord. staff devel., 1992—97; ednl. cons. Costa Mesa, Calif., 1997—; external evaluator Sch. Reform, State of Calif., 2001—. Mem. Sch. Intervention Audit team State of Calif.; adj. prof. tchr. tng. program U. Calif., Irvine, 2001—; presenter and staff trainer in field. Author and editor: ESL Guide for Classroom Teachers, 1992. Pres. PTA, Newport Beach/Costa Mesa, 1965-70 (bd. dirs. 1965-80); legis. rep. Orange County Tchr. of Speakers of Other Langs., 1985-87. Mem. Nat. Assn. Bilingual Edn., Calif. Assn. Bilingual Edn., Nat. Charity League (officer), Rep. Women, U. Redlands Alumni Assn., Assistance League Newport-Mesa (officer). Presbyterian. Avocations: travel, reading, camping, fishing.

HANSEN, WILLIAM, educational consultant; b. Pocatello, Idaho; BS in Econs., George Mason U. Legis. asst. Dept. Edn., Washington, 1981, acting asst. sec. legis. and congl. affairs, dep. asst. sec. elem. and secondary edn., acting dep. under sec. for planning, budget, and evaluation, 1990—91, asst. sec. mgmt. and budget, CFO, 1991—93; dep. dir. pub. affairs Dept. Commerce; head Office Intergovtl. and Industry Affairs Dept. Energy; pres., CEO Edn. Fin. Coun., 1993—2001; dep. sec. edn. Dept. Edn., Washington, 2001—03; sr. ofcl. Affiliated Computer Svcs. (ACS), Dallas, 2003—. Mem. nat. bds. and commns. on sch. reform; mem. Nat. Commn. on Cost of Higher Edn. Office: ACS 2828 N Haskell Bldg 1 Dallas TX 75204*

HANSEN-KYLE, LINDA L, managed health care nurse, nursing educator; b. Selma, Calif, Aug. 24, 1947; d. Ernest L. and Mary Hansen; m. Kenton L. Kyle, Feb. 16, 1974. BA in History summa cum laude, Humboldt State, 1969, MA in Psychology, 1972; ASN, Saddleback Coll., 1976; MS in Human Resources and Mgmt. Devel., Chapman U., 1993; MSN, Calif. State U., Dominguez Hills, 2000; postgrad. in nursing, U. San Diego, 2001—. Cert. case mgr.; RN Calif. ICU nurse supr. Scripps Clinic and Rsch., San Diego, 1978-81; asst. dir. nursing Maric Coll., San Diego, 1980-85; mgr. of ops. United Healthcare, San Diego, 1985—97; adj. instr. nursing Grossmont CC, 1999—. Mem.: ANA, ASTD, Cas Mgmt. Soc. Am., Phi Kappa Phi, Sigma Theta Tau.

HANSMANN, HENRY BAETHKE, law educator; b. Highland Park, Ill., Oct. 5, 1945; s. Elwood Hansmann and Louise Frances (Baethke) Moore; m. Marina Santilli, 1992; 1 child, Lisa Santilli. BA, Brown U., 1967; JD, Yale U., 1974, PhD, 1978. Asst. prof. law U. Pa. Law Sch., Phila., 1975-81, assoc. prof. law, econs. and pub. policy, 1981-83; prof. law Yale U., New Haven, 1983-88, Harris prof., 1988—2003; prof. law NYU, N.Y.C., 2003—. Author: The Ownership of Enterprise, 1996. John Simon Guggenheim Found. fellow, 1985-86. Mem. Am. Econs. Assn., Am. Law and Econ. Assn. Home: 240 Mercer St # 1603 New York NY 10012-1507 Office: NYU Sch Law 40 Washington Sq S New York NY 10012 E-mail: henry.hansmann@nyu.edu.

HANSON, BARBARA JEAN, education educator; b. Pawtucket, R.I., June 4, 1940; d. Joseph Leo and Gladys May (Knowles) Wahl; m. Donald Roland Hanson, June 16, 1962 (div. 1996); children: Erika, Jake. B in Edn., R.I. Coll., 1962; MEd, Bridgewater State Coll., 1993. Tchr. Attleboro (Mass.) Sch. Sys., 1962-65, 68—, Pattonville (Mo.) Sch., 1965-67. Lectr. in field. Tchr. leader Ptnrs. for the Advancement Math and Sci. Mass. Tchr. fellow. Mem. NEA, Attleboro Tchrs. Assn., Attleboro Hist. and Preservation Soc., Order Eastern Star, Alpha Delta Kappa. Avocations: nature, arts, singing, crafts. Home: 41 Deerfield Rd Apt 13 South Attleboro MA 02703-7871

HANSON, CAROL HALL, elementary school educator; b. Greenwood, S.C., Sept. 19, 1941; children: Jay, Wendy, Patrick. AA, Brewton-Parker Coll., 1980; BS, Tift Coll., 1981. Tchr. Milan (Ga.) Elem., 1981-85, Lumber City (Ga.) Elem., 1985-88, C.B. Greer Elem., Brunswick, Ga., 1988-89, McIntosh County Middle Sch., Darien, Ga., 1989—96, Todd Grant Elem., Darien, 1996—. Mem. Profl. Assn. Telfair Educators (pres. 1982-83), Profl. Assn. Ga. Educators. Methodist. Home: 203 S Teakwood Ct Brunswick GA 31525-8417

HANSON, DAVID JUSTIN, sociology educator, researcher; b. Orlando, Fla., Aug. 10, 1941; s. George Dewey and Clair (Cameron) H.; m. Carol Ann Wenger, Aug. 1,1 964; 1 child, Cynthia Denice. BA cum laude, Fla. State U., 1963; MA, Syracuse U., 1967, PhD, 1972. Asst. prof. sociology SUNY Coll Arts & Sci., Potsdam, 1968-76, assoc. prof., 1976-82, chair dept. sociology, 1977-85, prof. sociology, 1982—, dir. MA program in human svc., 1983-88, dir. of assessment, 1989-95. Alcohol and alcohol abuse cons. for 3d edit. Books for Coll. Librs., ALA, Chgo., 1985-86; alcohol cons. Health Can., Ottawa, 1996. Author: Preventing Alcohol Abuse: Alcohol, Culture and Control, 1995, Alcohol Education: What We Must Do, 1996; editor: Current Social Research, 1993; contbr. articles to profl. jours. V.p. Alcohol and Substance Abuse Coun. of St. Lawrence County, Inc., Canton, N.Y., 1987-95. Recipient Award for Excellence, N.Y. State Sociol. Assn., 1987; grantee Rsch. Found. of SUNY, Albany, 1984. Mem. Phi Kappa Phi (pres. Potsdam chpt. 1991—), Alpha Kappa Delta, Phi Eta Sigma. Office: SUNY Potsdam Coll of Arts & Scis Pierrepont Ave Potsdam NY 13676 Home: 112 Breckenridge Pl Chapel Hill NC 27514-3253 E-mail: hansondj@potsdam.edu.

HANSON, EILEEN, principal; b. Camden, N.J., Mar. 3, 1948; d. Thomas Edward and Rita Theresa (Madison) Bannan; m. Kenneth Wesley Hanson, Mar. 22, 1975; 1 child, Michelle Eileen. BA, San Diego State U., 1970; teaching cert., Calif. State U., Dominguez Hills, 1974, cert. adminstr., 1976. Cert. tchr., adminstr., Calif.; cert. mediator, Calif. Prin. St. Anthony Sch., El Segundo, Calif., 1976-80; dir. St. Charles Catechetical Program, San Diego, 1980-87; prin. Holy Family Sch., San Diego, 1987-92, St. Pius X Sch., Chula Vista, Calif., 1992—. Grant project coord. for Cath. Schs. San Diego, 1992-94; trained mediator. Mem. edn. adv. com. U. Phoenix, 2001—. Mem. ASCD, Nat. Cath. Educators Assn., Greater Math. Assn., San Diego Child Care and Devel. Com., Western Cath. Ednl. Assn., Western Assn. Schs. and Colls. Home: 942 Grove Ave Imperial Beach CA 91932-3347 Office: 37 E Emerson St Chula Vista CA 91911-3507

HANSON, HAROLD PALMER, physicist, government official, editor, academic administrator; b. Virginia, Minn., Dec. 27, 1921; s. Martin Bernhard and Elvida Elaine (Paulsen) H.; m. Mary Jean Stevenson, June 22, 1944; children: Steven Bernard, Barbara Jean. BS, Superior (Wis.) State Coll., 1942; MS, U. Wis., 1944, PhD, 1948. Mem. faculty U. Fla., 1948-54, dean grad. sch., 1969-71, v.p. acad. affairs, 1971-74, exec. v.p., 1974-78, exec. v.p. emeritus, 1990—; mem. faculty U. Tex., Austin, 1954-69, prof. physics, 1961-69, chmn. dept., 1962-69; provost Boston U., 1978-79; exec. dir. Com. on Sci. and Tech., U.S. Ho. of Reps., Washington, 1979-82, 84-90; provost Wayne State U., Detroit, 1982-84. Summer rsch. physicist Lincoln Labs., MIT, 1953, Gen. Atomic Co., San Diego, 1964; summer vis. lectr. U. Wis., 1957; Fulbright rsch. scholar, Norway, 1960-61. Editor DELOS, 1991—. Bd. dirs. N. Central Fla. Health Planning Coun.; mem. steering com. Fla. Ednl. Computer Network. With USNR, 1944-46. Decorated St. Olav's medal Norway, Order of North Star 1st class Sweden; U. Fla. presdl. scholar, 1976 Fellow Am. Phys. Soc.; mem. Sigma Xi, Sigma Pi Sigma, Omicron Delta Kappa. Clubs: Town and Gown (Austin); Rotary. Office: U Fla 118 440 2346 NPB Gainesville FL 32611-2085 E-mail: hanson@phys.ufl.edu.

HANSON, JOHN M. civil engineering and construction educator; b. Brookings, S.D., Nov. 16, 1932; m. Mary Josephson, Jan. 16, 1960 (dec. 1999). BSCE, S.D. State U., 1949; MS in Structural Engring., Iowa State U., 1957; PhD in Civil Engring., Lehigh U., 1964. Profl. engr. Ill., N.C., Colo., Oreg., Mich. Structural engr. J.T. Banner & Assoc., Laramie, Wyo., 1957-58, Phillips, Carter, Osborn, Denver, 1958-60; research inst. prof. Lehigh U., Bethlehem, Pa., 1960-65; engr., asst. mgr. structural devel. Portland Cement Assn., Skokie, Ill., 1965-72; rsch. dir., v.p., pres. Wiss, Janney, Elstner Assocs., Northbrook, Ill., 1972-92; disting. prof. civil engring. and constrn. N.C. State U., Raleigh, 1993-2000, cons. engr., 2000—. Contbr. articles to profl. jours. Served to lt. USAF, 1953-55, Korea Recipient Disting. Engr. award S.D. State U., 1979; Profl. Achievement citation Iowa State U., 1980 Fellow Prestressed Concrete Inst. (bd. dirs. 1977-80, 93-95, Korn award 1978); mem. ASCE (hon., State of Art award 1974, Reese award 1976, 88, T.Y. Lin award 1979, Boase award 1995, Forensic Engring. award 1999), Am. Concrete Inst. (hon., bd. dirs. 1981-84, 88-94, v.p. 1988-89, pres. 1990, Bloem award 1976, Henry Crown award Ill. chpt. 1993), Internat. Assn. Bridge and Structural Engring. (hon., pres. 1993-97), Internat. Concrete Repair Inst. Lutheran. E-mail: jmhanson@nc.rr.com.

HANSON, KAREN, philosopher, educator; b. Lincoln, Nebr., Apr. 11, 1947; d. Lester Eugene and Gladys (Diessner) H.; m. Dennis Michael Senchuk, Aug. 22, 1970; children: Tia Elizabeth, Chloe Miranda. BA summa cum laude, U. Minn., 1970; MA, PhD, Harvard U., 1980. Lectr. to assoc. prof. Ind. U., Bloomington, 1976-91, prof. philosophy, 1991—, Rudy prof., 2001—, adj. prof. Am. studies, gender studies & comparative lit., 1991—, chair philosophy, 1997—2002, dean Honors Coll., 2002—. Mem. governing bd. Ind. U. Inst. for Advanced Study, Bloomington, 1992-95, Ind. U. Soc. for Advanced Study, 2001-02; mem. editl. bd. Peirce Edition Project, Indpls., 1982-89, 90—. Author: The Self Imagined, 1986; co-editor: Romantic Revolutions, 1990; assoc. editor Jour. Social Philosophy, 1982-86; mem. editl. bd. Philosophy of Music Edn. Rev., 1992—, Notre Dame Philosophical Reviews, 2001-, Essays in Philosophy, 2000-, Symploke, 1998-; editl. cons. Am. Philos. Quar., 1995-99; contbr. articles to profl. books and jours. Del. Am. Coun. Learned Socs., 1993-98 (exec. com., 1994-98); officer John Dewey Found., 1989—. Scholar Disting. scholar, Office Women's Affairs, 1995. Mem. Am. Philos. Assn. (exec. officer 1986-91, 2000-03, program com. 1984-91, nominating com. 1993-94, 95-96, chair com. priorities and problems 1998-2000), Am. Soc. for Aesthetics (program com. 1989-90, 98-2000, trustee 1997-2000), Soc. for Women in Philosophy, Phi Beta Kappa (exec. com. Gamma of Ind. chpt. 1993-97, 2002—, officer 1995-97, 2002—, pres. 1996-97). Home: 1606 S Woodruff Ln Bloomington IN 47401-4448 Office: Ind U Dept of Philosophy Sycamore 026 Bloomington IN 47405

HANSON, ROBERT DUANE, civil engineering educator; b. Albert Lea., Minn., July 27, 1935; s. James Edwin and Gertie Hanson; m. Kaye Lynn Nielsen, June 7, 1959; children: Craig Robert, Eric Neil. Student, St. Olaf Coll., Northfield, Minn., 1953-54; BSE, U. Minn., 1957, MS in Civil Engring., 1958; PhD, Calif. Inst. Tech., Pasadena, 1965. Registered profl. engr., Mich., N.D. Design engr. Pitts.-Des Moines Stel, Des Moines, 1958-59; asst. prof. U. N.D., Grand Forks, 1959-61; rsch. engr. Calif. Inst. Tech., 1965; asst. prof. U. Calif.-Davis, 1965-66; from asst. prof. to prof. civil engring. U. Mich., Ann Arbor, 1966—2001, prof. emeritus, 2001—, chmn. dept. civil engring., 1976-84; sr. earthquake engr. Fed. Emergency Mgmt. Agy., 1994-2000. Vis. prof., dir. Earthquake Engring. Rsch. Ctr., U. Calif., Berkeley, 1991; dir. BCS divsn. NSF, Washington, 1989-90; cons. NSF, 1979-88, 92-94; cons. Bechtel Corp., Ann Arbor, 1976-87, Sensei Engrs., Ann Arbor, 1977-90, Bldg. Seismic Safety Coun., 1988-94, Fed. Emergency Mgmt. Agy., 1992-94, 2000—. Contbr. articles to profl. jours. Recipient Reese Rsch. award ASCE, 1980; recipient Disting. Svc. award U. Mich., 1969; tchg. award Chi Epsilon, 1985, Attwood Engr. Excellence award, 1986. Mem. NAE, ASCE (life; com. chmn. 1975-94), Earthquake Engring. Rsch. Inst. (hon., v.p. 1977-79, bd. dirs. 1976-79, 88-92, pres.-elect 1988, pres. 1989-91, past pres. 1991-92). Lutheran. Home: 2926 Saklan Indian Dr Walnut Creek CA 94595-3911 E-mail: rdhanson2@aol.com.

HANSON, TRUDY L. speech professional, educator; b. Magnolia, Miss., June 12, 1950; d. Truett Carr and Marie (Green) Lewis; m. Michael D. Hanson, Aug. 19, 1972; children: Leah, Chad, Ashley, Tori. BS in Speech/English Edn., La. State U., 1971, MA Speech, 1973; EdD Higher Edn., Tex. Tech U., 1994. Tchg. asst. La. State U., Baton Rouge, 1971-73; prof. West Tex. A&M, Canyon, 1989—. Instr. Thomas Nelson C.C., Hampton Roads, Va., 1974, Amarillo Coll., 1981-89. Dir. West Tex. A&M U. Storytelling Festival, 1991—; parent chair Amarillo Coll. Suzuki Strings, 1985—, Amarillo Coll. Symphony Youth Orch., 1993-96, Amarillo Symphony Youth Orch., 1993-96. Mem. Nat. Comm. Assn., So. States Comm. Assn. (pres. 2000-01), Tex. Speech Comm. Assn. (pres. 1998), Tejas Storytelling Assn., Tex. Assn. Comm. Adminstrn. (pres. 1994-95), Storytellers of the High Plains (pres. 2000—). Democrat. Mem. Lds Ch. Home: 6209 Estacado Ln Amarillo TX 79109-6922 Office: WTAMU Box 60747 ACT Dept Canyon TX 79016

HANSTINE, BARBARA ANN, reading specialist; b. Middletown, N.Y., Nov. 17, 1940; d. John Norton and E. Belle (Price) Botens; m. John Forest Mason, Nov. 24, 1963 (div. Aug. 1973); m. William Griffin Hanstine, Oct. 3, 1975; children: John Norton Mason, Barbara Irene Mason Worobey, Regina Catherine Mason O'Boyle. BS in Edn., SUNY, Oneonta, 1979, MS in Edn., 1982. Cert. reading K-12, cert. elem. tchr. N-6; ordained Episcopalian deacon, 1989. Elem. libr., remedial math Hancock (N.Y.) Ctrl. Sch., 1979-80, reading tchr., 1980-81, 2d grade tchr., 1981-82, reading specialist, 1982-84, Deposit (N.Y.) Ctrl. Sch., 1984—. Presenter in field. Coord. aspirants program Episcopal Diocese of Albany, 1990—; family ministry cord. Episcopal Deanery of the Susquehanna, 1985—; vacation bible sch. tchr. Christ Ch., Deposit, 1994, Deposit Coun. of Chs., 1990-93. Democrat. Avocations: russian icons, collecting antiques. Home: 18 W Main St Hancock NY 13783-1139 Office: Deposit Ctrl Sch 171 2nd St Deposit NY 13754-1188

HANUSHEK, ERIC ALAN, economics educator; b. Lakewood, Ohio, May 22, 1943; s. Vernon F. and Ruth (Hostetler) H.; m. Nancy L. Keleher, June 11, 1965 (div.); children: Eric Alan, Megan E. BS, U.S. Air Force Acad., 1965; PhD in Econs., MIT, 1968. Sr. staff economist Coun. Econ. Advisers, Washington, 1971-72; assoc. prof. USAF Acad., Colo., 1972-73; sr. economist Cost of Living Coun., Washington, 1973-74; assoc. prof. econs. Yale U., New Haven, 1975-78; dir. pub. policy analysis U. Rochester, N.Y., 1978-83, prof. econs. and polit. sci., 1978-2000, chmn. dept. econs., 1982-87, 88-90, dir. W. Allen Wallis Inst. Polit. Economy, 1992-99; rsch. assoc. Nat. Bur. Econ. Rsch., 1996—; Hanna sr. fellow Hoover Instn. Stanford (Calif.) U., 2000—; sr. rsch. fellow Green Ctr. U. Tex., Dallas, 2000—. Dep. dir. Congl. Budget Office, Washington, 1984-85; mem. com. nat. stats. Nat. Rsch. Coun., 1992-98, adv. coun. on Edn. Statistics, 2002; cons. World Bank 1984-95, U.S. Com. on Civil Rights, 1986-89. Author: Education and Race, 1972, (with J. Jackson) Statistical Methods for Social Scientists 1977, (with C. Citro) Improving Information for Social Policy Decisions, 1991, (with R. Harbison) Education Performance of the Poor, 1992, Making Schools Work, 1994, (with J. Banks) Modern Political Economy, 1995, (with N. Maritato) Assessing Knowledge of Retirement Behavior, 1996, (with Dale W. Jorgenson) Improving America's Schools, 1996, (with Constance F. Citro) Assessing Policies for Retirement Income,

1997, The Economics of Schooling and School Quality, 2003. Served to capt. USAF, 1965-74. Disting. vis. fellow Hoover Instn., Stanford U., 1999-2000. Fellow Internat. Acad. Edn. (bd. dirs. 2002—), Assn. Pub. Policy Analysis and Mgmt. (v.p. 1986-87, pres. 1988-89), Am. Econ. Assn., Econometric Soc., Soc. Labor Economists. E-mail: hanushek@hoover.stanford.edu.

HAQUE, MOHAMMED SHAHIDUL, electrical engineer, educator; b. Dhaka, Bangladesh, May 12, 1965; came to U.S., 1991; s. Shamsul and Hafiza H.; m. Aynun Naher, June 14, 1994; children: Afsara, Sakib. BSEE, Bangladesh U. Engring. & Tech., Dhaka, 1989; MSEE, U. Ark., 1992, PhD, 1997. Tchg. asst., dept. elec. engr. Bangladesh U. Engring. and Tech., 1990; rsch. asst., dept. elec. engr. U. Ark., Fayetteville, 1991-92, sr. rsch. asst., 1993-97, rsch. asst. prof., 1997; process devel. engr. Novellus Systems Inc., San Jose, 1997-99, process mgr. 300 mm PECVD program, 2000—. Lectr. in field. Contbr. articles to Jour. Applied Physics, Solar Energy Materials and solar Cells, Jour. Elec. Materials, others. Mem. IEEE, Electrochemical Soc. Islamic. Achievements include research in microelectronic materials for solar cell applications and multichip module packaging technology; invention of a low temperature silicon solar cell fabrication process; contribution to understanding and quality improvement of chemical vapor deposited silicon dioxide and diamond dielectric films. Office: Novellus Sys Inc 3970 N 1st St San Jose CA 95134-1501 Home: 1346 Elkwood Dr Milpitas CA 95035-2422

HARADER, DANA L. behavior consultant; b. Wichita, Kans., Jan. 11, 1963; d. Wayne Richard and Dorothy Louise (Heeney) H. BA in French, U. Tex., Arlington, 1987; MEd in Special Edn, U. North Tex., 1991, PhD in Spl. Edn., 1995. Cert. elem. edn., Fr. edn., severe emotional disturbances/behavior disorders autism, generic spl. edn., Tex. Receptionist Decorating Den, Arlington, 1987; tchr. 3rd grade Arlington Ind. Sch. Dist., 1987-88; milieu therapist Children's Med. Ctr., Dallas, 1988-89; hosp. tchr. Bedford Meadows Psychiat. Hosp., Bedford, Tex., 1989-91; resource 3 tchr. Hurst-Euless-Bedford Ind. Sch. Dist., Bedford, 1991-93; doctoral intern, profl. devel. dept. Coun. for Exceptional Children, 1994; cons. emotional/behavioral disorders West Ky. Ednl. Coop., 1995—. Tchr. Coun. Exceptional Children, Coun. Children with Behavioral Disorders, Tex.; active PTA, Tex. Spl. Edn. PTA. Aetna scholar; grantee U. Tex., 1988-91, 92-95.

HARBAUGH, JOHN WARVELLE, geologist, educator; b. Madison, Wis., Aug. 6, 1926; s. Marion Dwight and Marjorie (Warvelle) H.; m. Josephine Taylor, Nov. 24, 1951 (dec. Dec. 25, 1985); children: Robert, Dwight, Richard; m. Audrey Wegst, Oct. 21, 2000. BS, U. Kans., 1948, MS, 1950; PhD, U. Wis., 1955. Prodn. geologist Carter Oil Co., Tulsa, 1951-53; prof. geol. sci. Stanford U., 1955-99, prof. emeritus, 1999—. Author: (with G. Bonham Carter) Computer Simulation in Geology, 1970, (with D.M. Tezlaff) Simulating Clastic Sedimentation, 1989, (with P. Martinez) Simulating Nearshore Environments, 1993, (with R. Slingerland and K. Furlong) Simulating Clastic Sedimentary Basins, 1994, (with J.C. Davis and J. Wendebourg) Computing Risk for Oil Prospects: Principles and Programs, 1995, (with J. Wendebourg) Simulating Oil Entrapment in Clastic Sequences, 1997. Recipient Haworth Disting. Alumni award U. Kans., 1968, Krumbein medal Internat. Assn. Math. Geologists, 1986, U. Wis.-Madison Disting. Alumni award, 2003. Fellow Geol. Soc. Am.; mem. Am. Assn. Petroleum Geologists (Levorsen award 1970, Disting. Svc. award 1987, Disting. Edn. award Pacific sect. 1999, 2001, Disting. alumni award, U. Wis. 2003). Republican. Home: 683 Salvatierra St Stanford CA 94305-8539 E-mail: harbaugh@pangea.stanford.edu.

HARBAUGH, LOIS JENSEN, secondary education educator; b. Elmhurst, Ill., Sept. 16, 1942; d. G. E. and Dorothy G. (Madsen) Jensen; m. Lou L. W. Harbaugh Jr., Aug. 8, 1964; children: Michelle, Bill. BA, Wheaton Coll., 1964; MAT in Sci. Edn., U. Tex., Dallas, 1978. Cert. composite secondary sci. tchr., Tex. Tchr. Troy Mills (Iowa) Sch., 1965-66, Richardson (Tex.) Jr. High Sch., 1969-71; tchr., chair sci. First Bapt. Acad., Dallas, 1975-81, Lake Highlands Jr. High Sch., Richardson, 1981-98; tchr. advanced placement physics, acad. decathlon coach Woodrow Wilson H.S., Dallas, 1998—. Mem. Tex. State Textbook Com., Tex. Edn. Agy., 1990, 94, 97. Bd. dirs.Pregnancy Resource Ctr., Dallas, 1983-88; bd. dirs. and educators Found. for Thought and Ethics, Richardson, 1988—. Christa McAuliffe fellow Dept. Edn., 1988; grantee Recognizing Innovation for Student Edn. (RISE) Found., 1989; recipient Nat. Radio Astronomy Observatory (NRAO) Inst. award NSF, 1988, Newmast award NASA, 1989, Tchr. Cons. award Tex. Instruments, 1991. Mem. Nat. Sci. Tchrs. Assn., Nat. Sci. Suprs. Assn. (sec. 1988-92), Sci. Tchrs. Assn. Tex., Richardson Assn. Tex. Profl. Educators (pres. 1994-96), Assn. Tex. Profl. Edn. (region X sec. 1996-98), Tex. Earth Sci. Tchrs. Assn., Mensa. Achievements include amateur radio. Office: Woodrow Wilson HS 100 S Glasgow Dr Dallas TX 75214-4598

HARBIN, MICHAEL ALLEN, religion educator, writer; b. Vincennes, Ind., May 24, 1947; s. Hugh Allen and Norma June (Palmer) H.; m. Esther Marie Rinas, May 31, 1971; children: Athena Colleen, Heidi Elizabeth, Douglas Allen. BS, U.S. Naval Acad., 1969; ThM, Dallas Theol. Sem., 1980, ThD, 1988; MA, Calif. State U., Carson, 1993. Instr. Dallas Bible Coll., 1984-86; freelance writer Garland, Tex., 1986-93; prof. Taylor U., Upland, Ind., 1993—, chair biblical studies, 1999—. Mem. elder bd. South Garland Bible Ch., Garland, Tex., 1981-93, chmn. elder bd., 1982-86; mem. elder bd. Upland Cmty. Ch., 1995—; del. nat. conv. Evangel. Mennonite Ch., 1996, 99, 2002, 03. Author: To Serve Other Gods, 1994, The Promise and the Blessing, 2003; contbr. articles to profl. jours. Del. 16th Senatorial Dist. Rep. Conv., Dallas, 1990, 92; alt. del. State Rep. Conv., Ft. Worth, 1990. Capt. USNR, ret. Fellow Inst. of Bibl. Rsch.; mem. Soc. Bibl. Lit., Bibl. Archaeol. Soc., Evang. Theol. Soc., Near Ea. Archaeol. Soc. Home: 629 W South St Upland IN 46989-0673

HARBIN, THOMAS SHELOR, JR., ophthalmologist, educator; b. Annapolis, Md., May 31, 1945; s. Thomas Shelor and Margaret (Troutman) H.; m. Ellen Gregson, June 6, 1970; children: Katherine, Tom. BA magna cum laude, Vanderbilt U., 1966; MD, Cornell U., N.Y.C., 1970; MBA, Ga. State U., 1991. Diplomate Am. Bd. Ophthalmology. Intern U. Wash. Affiliated Hosp., Seattle, 1970-71; resident in ophthalmology Wilmer Inst. Johns Hopkins Hosp., Balt., 1971-74; fellow glaucoma ctr. Barnes Hosp., Washington U. Sch. Medicine, St. Louis, 1974-75; pvt. practice Atlanta, 1976—; sr. v.p., dir. Prime Vision Health, Inc., 1996-99; pres., CEO Accountable Eye Care, Inc., 1994—96. Clin. prof. Emory U., Atlanta, 1976-97, emeritus clin. prof, 1997—; chief ophthalmology staff Piedmont Hosp., Atlanta, 1984-94, vice-chmn., 1995-99; chmn. bd. Piedmont Hosp., 1999-2003; chmn. Ctr. for Visually Impaired, 1979-80; med. adv. bd. Ga. Soc. to Prevent Blindness, 1977-95, chmn. 1980, pres., 1987-89. Mem. editl. rev. bd. Rev. Ophthalmology, 1994—. Participant Leadership Ga., 1983; dir. med. campaign United Way, Ga., 1984. Mem. AMA, Am. Acad. Ophthalmology (quality care com. 1989-94, state affairs com. 1991-94, trustee 1994-96, chmn. young ophthalmologists com. 1994-95, chmn. membership adv. com., exec. com. 1996, mem. managed care advocacy com. 1994-96, Honor award 1985, Sr. Honor award 1997), Med. Assn. Ga., Am. Glaucoma Soc. (founding), Ga. Soc. Ophthalmology (legis. com. 1977-85, chmn. 1978-91, pres. 1982-83), Atlanta Ophthal. Soc. (pres. 1982), Wilmer Residents Assn., Phi Beta Kappa. Avocations: fishing, hunting, birdwatching. Home: 3888 Tuxedo Rd NW Atlanta GA 30342-4034 Office: Eye Cons Atlanta MD's PC 95 Collier Rd NW Ste 3000 Atlanta GA 30309-1721

HARCOURT, ROBERT NEFF, educational administrator, journalist, genealogist; b. East Orange, N.J., Oct. 19, 1932; s. Stanton Hinde and Mary Elizabeth (Neff) H. BA, Gettysburg Coll., 1958; MA, Columbia U., 1961. Cert guidance, secondary edn., career and vocational guidance, N.Mex. Social case worker N.J. State Bd. Child Welfare, Newark and Morristown, 1958-61; asst. registrar Hofstra U., 1961-62; asst. to evening dean of students CCNY, 1961-62; housing staff U. Denver, 1962-64; fin. aid and placement dir. Inst. Am. Indian Arts (IAIA), Santa Fe, 1965-95, contract cons., 1999, apptd. by coll. pres. to steering com., 2000, nat. capital campaign steering com.; appointed by corp. pres. to adv. bd. Genre Ltd. Art Pubs., L.A., 1986—; nat. color ad participant The Bradford Exchange, Chgo., 1986—. Truman scholar coord. Donor Am. Indian Lib. collection Gettysburg (Pa.) Coll., active Santa Fe Civic Chorus, 1977-78, art judge, 3d and 4th ann. Aspen Fundraiser Nat. Mus. Am. Indian, 1993, 94, vol. Inst. for Preservation Original Langs. Am. (IPOLA). With U.S.Army, 1954-56. Decorated Nat. Def. medal, 1970; named Hon. Okie, Gov. Dewey F. Bartlett; postmasters fellow U. Denver, 1962-64, col. a.d.c. to N.Mex. Gov. David F. Cargo, 1970; recipient disting. Alumni award Gettysburg Coll. Alumni Assn., 1995. Mem. Am. Contract Bridge League (exec. bd., Santa Fe unit, life master, ACBL dist. 17 rep.), SAR, Santa Fe Coun. Internat. Rels., Am. Assn. Counseling and Devel., New England Historic Geneal. Soc., Assn. Specialists in Group Work (charter), Adult Student Pers. Assn. (charter), Southwestern Assn. Indian Affairs, Neff Family Hist. Soc., St. Andrew Scottish Soc. of N.Mex., Gen. Soc. Mayflower Descs. (bd. assts. N.Mex. chpt.), Pilgrim John Howland Soc., Upson Family Assn., Order of the Founders and Patriots of Am. (regional counselor), Mil. Order of the Loyal Legion of the U.S., Mil. Order Fgn. Wars of U.S., Gen. Soc. of War of 1812, Nat. Soc. Sons and Daus. of the Pilgrims, Soc. Descs. Washington's Army at Valley Forge, Presdl. Families Am. (charter, N.Mex. regent), Decs. Colonial Physicians and Chirurgiens, Phi Delta Kappa (past mem. exec. bd. local chpt.), Alpha Tau Omega, Alpha Phi Omega, Safari Club Internat. Home: 2980 Viaje Pavo Real Santa Fe NM 87505-5344

HARCUM, LOUISE MARY DAVIS, retired elementary education educator; b. Salisbury, Md., May 1, 1927; d. E. Linwood and Dora Ellen (Shockley) Davis; m. W. Blan Harcum, Sr., Sept. 5, 1944; children: W. Blan, Jr., Angie E., Lee P., R. Linwood. BS, Salisbury State U., 1962, MEd, 1969; grad., Inst. Children's Lit., 1995. Cert. tchr. 9-10 English, Md. Tchr. Wicomico County Bd. Edn., Salisbury, Md., 1962—93, subs. tchr., 1994—96; tchr. English evening H.S. Bd. Edn. Salisbury, Md., 1995—. Columnist Daily Times, 1985-87; tchr. cons. Eastern Shore Md. Writing Project; ptnr., owner Beechnut Farms, Md. Co-author: Wicomico County History, 1981; author: Behavior Modification, 1989-92. Co-coord. Rep. Party Campaign, Wicomico County, Md., 1992; vice chmn. Zoning Appeals Bd.; pres. Wicomico County Farm Bur. Women, 1993, leader Olympians-Mardela 4-H Club, 1994-1997; mem. New Cmty. Singers, 1975-95, Sen. Richard Colburn's Scholarship Com., Wicomico County; chmn. senatorial com. for Colburn, 1996-2003. Mem. AAUW (pres. 1970-72, pres. Salisbury Branch 1994-96), Third Time Around-Salisbury Studio of Dance, County Rep. Women's Club (chmn. 1999-2001, state cmty. chmn. 2001, Rep. Fedn. 2000 Caring for Am. com. 1999-2001, established Cmty. Tutorial Ctr. in San Domingo 1998), Wicomico County Rep. Women (pres. 1998-2000), Wicomico Rep. Club, Ret. Tchrs. Wicomico County (pres. 1996-98). Republican. Methodist. Avocations: gardening, writing, dancing. Home: 10720 Snethen Church Rd Mardela Springs MD 21837-2246

HARDACRE, HELEN, university professor; b. Nashville, May 20, 1949; d. Paul Hoswell and Gracia Louise (Manspeaker) H. BA, Vanderbilt U., 1971, MA, 1972; PhD, U. Chgo., 1980. Asst. prof. Dept. of Religion Princeton (N.J.) U., 1980-86, assoc. prof. Dept. of Religion, 1986—. Prof. Japanese studies Griffith U., Australia, 1990-92; prof. Reischauer Inst. Japanese Religions & Soc. Harvard U., 1992—; asst. editor (Japan) Jour. Asian Studies, 1986-89; assoc. editor Jour. of Am. Acad. of Religion, 1986-89. Author: (books) The Religion of Japan's Korean Minority, 1984, Lay Buddhism in Contemporary Japan, 1984, Kuroyumiko and the New Religions of Japan, 1984, Shinto and the State, 1868-1988, 1989. Recipient Fulbright Hays Diss Grant, 1976-77, Social Sci. Rsch. Coun. Grant, 1988, Japan Found. Fellowship, 1982-83. Mem. Am. Soc. for the Study of Religion, Am. Academy of Religion, Assn. for Asian Studies. Office: Harvard U Inst Japanese Studies 1737 Cambridge St Cambridge MA 02138-3016

HARDAGE, PAGE TAYLOR, elementary education educator; b. Richmond, Va., June 27, 1944; d. George Peterson and Gladys Odell (Gordon) Taylor; 1 child, Taylor Brantley. AA, Va. Intermont Coll., Bristol, 1964; BS, Richmond Profl. Inst., 1966; MPA, Va. Commonwealth U., Richmond, 1982. Cert. tchr., Va. Competent toastmaster, dir. play therapy svcs. Med. Coll. Va. Hosps., Va. Commonwealth U., Richmond, 1970-90; dir. Inst. Women's Issues, Va. Commonwealth U., U. Va., Richmond, 1986-91; adminstr. Scottish Rite Childhood Lang. Ctr. at Richmond, Inc., 1991-99. Bd. dirs. Richmond Bus. Coun. Math. and Sci. Ctr. Found., Richmond, Emergency Med. Svcs. Adv. Bd., Richmond. Treas. Richmond Black Student Found., 1989—90, Leadership Metro Richmond Alumni Assn.; group chmn. United Way Greater Richmond, 1987; bd. dirs. Maggie L. Walker Hist. Found., Richmond YWCA, 1989—91, Capital Area Health Adv. Coun.; commr. Mayors Commn. of Concerns of Women, City of Richmond. Mem.: ASPA, NAFE, Va. Assn. Fund Raising Execs., Va. Recreation and Park Soc. (bd. dirs.), Internat. Mgmt. Coun. (exec. com.), Adminstrv. Mgmt. Soc., Rotary Club of Hanover. Unitarian Universalist. Avocations: bridge, target shooting, aerobics, pub. speaking.

HARDESTY, DAVID CARTER, JR., university president; b. Philadelphia, Miss., Sept. 20, 1945; m. Susan B. Hardesty, 1968; children: Ashley, D(avid) Carter III. AB, W.Va. U., 1967; MA, Oxford (Eng.) U., 1969; JD, Harvard U., 1973. Bar: W.Va. 1973. Tax commr., sec. Econ. Devel. Authority, State of W.Va., Charleston, 1977-80, chmn. Mcpl. Bond Commn., 1977-80; assoc. Bowles Rice McDavid Graff & Love, Charleston, 1973-77, ptnr., 1981-95; pres. W.Va. U., Morgantown, 1995—. Chmn. W.Va. Tax Study Commn., 1982-84; mem. W.Va. Asian Trade Missions, 1978-79, 95; chmn. W.Va. Roundtable, Inc., 1994-95; frequent speaker at bus. group meetings. Chancellor United Meth. Ch., W.Va., 1986-95; trustee Univ. Sys., 1989-95, 1st chmn., 1989-91; trustee W.Va. Wesleyan Coll., 1986-94, Nat. 4-H Coun., 2000--; mem. Gov.'s Energy Task Force, 2001--; mem. W.Va. Rhodes Scholar Selection Com., 1980-2000, sec., 1991-98; bd. advisors W.Va. U., 1980-89, chmn. bd. advisors, 1987-89; bd. dirs. United Meth. Charities W.Va., 1978-94; bd. dirs. Greater Kanawha Valley Found., 1980-89, chmn., 1988-90. Rhodes scholar, 1969. Mem.: ABA, Nat. Assn. State Univs. and Land Grant Colls., Nat. Assn. Coll. and Univ. Attys., Am. Coun. on Edn., 4th Cir. Jud. Conf., W.Va. Bar Assn. Office: WVa U Office of Pres PO Box 6201 Morgantown WV 26506-6201 E-mail: dhardest@wvu.edu.

HARDESTY, STEPHEN DON, secondary education educator; b. Oak Park, Ill., Feb. 23, 1945; s. Donald A. and Corinne M. (Wilson) H.; m. Linda C. Shafer, Aug. 2, 1968; 1 child, Heather Anne. BA in Geology, U. South Fla., 1967; postgrad., U. Mo., 1968; MS in Bus., Rollins Coll., 1977. Cert. tchr., Fla. Tchr. earth sci. and math. Maitland (Fla.) Jr. H.S., 1968-69; tchr. earth, life and physical scis., geography Conway Jr. H.S., Orlando, 1969-87, chmn. sci. dept., 1981-87; adj. instr. earth sci., astronomy, meteorology Valencia C.C., 1977—; tchr. earth and environ. sci., astronomy, dual enrollment geology Dr. Phillips Sr. H.S., Orlando, 1987—. Tchr. for tchr. inservice insts. in earth scis. Orange County Schs./Valencia C.C., 1982-88; instr. summer inst. in oceanography/hist. geology Valencia C.C., 1982-88; mem. earth/space scis. middle/jr. sect. State Ednl. Frameworks Com., 1985; chmn. earth/space scis. State Ednl. Materials Coun., 1986-88; mem. earth/space scis. sr. high and middle/jr. sects. State Course Performance Standards Com., 1986-87; mem. earth/space sci. sect. State Tchr. Cert. Writing Team, U. South Fla., 1987-89, State Tchr. Cert. Specialization Validation Team, 1987-88, mem. State Minimum Performance Standards in Sci. Writing and Review Coms., 1987-88; mem. State Tchr. Cert.-Passing Score Com. Earth Sci., U. Ctrl. Fla., 1989; mem. student performace test writing team Fla. State U., 1989-90; owner, tartan weaving instr. Caithness Shuttle Crafts. Past pres. Greenview Homeowners Assn., Orlando. Mem. Nat. Assn. Geology Tchrs. (Fla. Earth Sci. Tchr. of Yr. 1992), Nat. Earth Sci. Tchrs. Assn., Soc. Econ. Paleontologists and Mineralogists, Fla. Assn. Sci. Tchrs., Fla. Earth Scis. Tchrs. Assn., St. Andrews Soc. Ctrl. Fla. (past pres.), Scottish-Am. Soc. Ctrl. Fla. (past chmn. bd.), Clan Gunn Soc. North Am. (past pres.). Republican. Office: Dr Phillips HS 6500 Turkey Lake Rd Orlando FL 32819-4718

HARDIN, DAWN THOMLEY, education leadership educator; b. Ruston, La., Sept. 6, 1957; d. Louise (Humble) Terracina; m. James O. Hardin, Aug. 8, 1988. BA in English Edn., La. Tech. U., 1978; MEd in Ednl. Adminstrn. & Supervision, N.E. La. U., 1990; PhD in Ednl. Adminstrn., U. So. Miss., 1993. Tchr. Monroe (La.) City Sch. System, 1985-90; adminstrv. intern to dean N.E. La. U., Monroe, 1990-91; rsch. asst. U. So. Miss., Hattiesburg, Miss., 1991-93; asst. prof. N.E. La. U., Monroe, 1993—. Cons. Ednl. TV Network Study, Jackson, Miss., 1993, West Carroll Parish Feasibility Study, Monroe, 1993, Union Parish Feasibility Study, 1993; primary rsch. investigator Sch. Prin. and Climate Evaluation Project, Monroe, 1994-95. Contbr. articles to profl. jours. Mem. ASCD, Am. Ednl. Rsch. Assn., Mid-South Ednl. Rsch. Assn. S.W. Ednl. Rsch. Assn., Mensa, Phi Kappa Phi, Gamma Beta Phi, Phi Delta Kappa, Kappa Delta Pi. Republican. Avocations: reading, movies, travel. Office: NE La U Strauss Hl # 306 Monroe LA 71209-0001

HARDIN, ELIZABETH ANN, academic administrator; b. Charlotte, N.C., Nov. 21, 1959; d. William Gregg and Ann (Astin) H. BBA magna cum laude, U. Ga., 1981; MBA, Harvard U., 1985. Spl. project coord. NCNB Corp., Charlotte, 1981-82, investment officer, 1982-83; cons. Booz, Allen & Hamilton, Atlanta, 1985-86; asst. placement dir. Harvard U. Bus. Sch., Boston, 1986-87, dir. MBA program adminstrn., 1987-89, acting placement dir., 1988-89; mgr. employment Sara Lee Hosiery, Winston-Salem, N.C., 1990-92, mfg. mgr., 1992-93, dir. product devel., 1993-94; mng. cons. Info. Sci. Assocs., Charlotte, N.C., 1994-95; assoc. vice chancellor for bus. planning U. N.C., Charlotte, 1995—2002; exec. dir. Charlotte Inst. for Tech. Innovation, 2000—02, spl. asst. to chancellor, 2002—03; v.p. adminstrn. U. Wyoming, 2003—. Cons., developer adminstrv. policy guide Chelsea (Mass.) Pub. Schs., 1989-90. Mem. adv. bd. Harvard Non-Profit Fellowship, 1986—; chmn. Harvard Non-Profit Mgmt. Fellowship, 1989-96; active AIDS Action Com. Mass., Holy Comforter, Charlotte; mem. total quality edn. task force N.C. Bus. Com. on Edn., 1992-93; troop leader Girl Scouts U.S.A.; mem. Leadership Charlotte, 1996—. Leadership N.C., 1999-2000; mem. grant panel Arts and Scis. Coun., 1998, 99. Named one of 40 under 40, Charlotte Bus. Jour.; fellow State Farm Co. Found., 1980, Delta Gamma Found., 1983. Mem. Assn. for Corp. Growth (bd. advisors 1996-99), Harvard Bus. Sch. Assn., Phi Kappa Phi, Delta Gamma (pres. alumnae Charlotte 1982-83). Republican. Avocations: reading, writing, public policy, photography. Office: U of NC at Charlotte Charlotte NC 28223

HARDIN, GLENDA KENDRICK, retired special education educator; b. Clanton, Ala., Sept. 9, 1946; d. James Luther and Glennie Roberta (Mims) Kendrick; m. Billy Ray Smith, Feb. 10, 1968 (div. Mar. 1979); children: Mark Stephen, Michael William; m. Gary Eugene Hardin, Mar. 12, 1988. Student, U. Ala., 1963-65; BS, U. Montevallo, 1978; MEd, U. Ala., 1980. Tchr. Chilton County Bd. Edn., Clanton, Ala., 1966-67, tchr., learning disabilities, 1979-88; tchr. Montgomery (Ala.) Pub. Schs., 1988—2002; ret., 2002. Tchr., spl. class learning disabilities First United Meth. Ch., Clanton, 1981-84, Frazer United Meth. Ch., 1988—. Recipient Tchr. of Week award, WCOV-TV, 1992, Excellence in Tchg. award, Montgomery County, 2001. Mem. Learning Disabilities Assn. Avocations: walking, Rainbows for children. Home: 4007 Faunsdale Dr Montgomery AL 36109-2424

HARDIN, PAUL, III, law educator; b. Charlotte, NC, June 11, 1931; s. Paul and Dorothy (Reel) Hardin; m. Barbara Russell, June 8, 1954; children: Paul Russell, Sandra Mikush, Dorothy Holmes. AB, Duke U., 1952, JD, 1954; LHD (hon.), Clemson U., 1970, Coker Coll., 1972; LittD (hon.), Nebr. Wesleyan U., 1978; LLD (hon.), Adrian Coll., 1987, Monmouth Coll., 1988; HHD (hon.), Wofford Coll., 1989; LLD (hon.), Rider Coll., 1990; LHD (hon.), Duke U., 1994. Bar: Ala. 1954. Practiced in, Birmingham, 1954, 1956—58; asst. prof. Duke Law Sch., 1958—61, assoc. prof., 1961—63, prof., 1963—68, univ. trustee, 1969—74, 1995—2001; pres. Wofford Coll., Spartanburg, SC, 1968—72, So. Methodist U., Dallas, 1972—74, Drew U., Madison, NJ, 1975—88; chancellor U. NC, Chapel Hill, NC, 1988—95, chancellor emeritus, prof. law, 1995—; interim pres. U. Ala., Birmingham, Ala., 1997. Vis. prof. U. Tex., 1960, U. Pa., 1962—63, U. Va., 1974; dir. Smith Barney mut. funds. Author (with Sullivan, others): The Administration of Criminal Justice, 1966; author: (with Sullivan) Evidence, Cases and Materials, 1968; contbr. articles to profl. jours., law revs. Chmn. Human Rels. Com., Durham, NC, 1961—62; pres. Nat. Assn. Schs. and Coll. of United Meth. Ch., 1984; mem. gen. conf. United Meth. Ch., 1968, 1976, 1980, 1984; chmn. Nat. Commn. on United Meth. Higher Edn., 1975—77. Served with CIC U.S. Army, 1954—56. Mem.: Order of Coif, Carnegie Found. for Advancement Tchg. (bd. dirs. 1990—98), Phi Beta Kappa. Office: University of North Carolina School of Law Chapel Hill NC 27599-3380 E-mail: phardin1@bellsouth.net.

HARDIN, SHERYL DAWN, elementary education educator; b. Austin, Tex., Sept. 12, 1963; d. James West and Emma Heaner (Larison) Shelton; 1 child, Matthew Doyle. BS in Edn., U. Tex., 1986, MEd, 1997. Cert. tchr., Tex. Primary tchr., reading specialist Austin (Tex.) Ind. Sch. Dist., 1987—. Facilitator Early Literacy Insvc. Course, 1994—. Mem. Nat. Coun. Tchrs. Math., Ctrl. Tex. Whole Lang. Network (membership dir. 1992-95). Home: 309 Brentwood St Austin TX 78752-4101 Office: Gullett Elem Sch 6310 Treadwell Blvd Austin TX 78757-4399 E-mail: shhardin@austin.ids.tenet.edu.

HARDING, F(RED) VICTOR, fitness consultant; b. San Juan, P.R., May 7, 1954; s. Warren G. and Martha Lee (Pinkston) H.; m. Linda Ruth Yocum, June 11, 1977; children: James Matthew, Bryan David, Rachael Christine. BA, Azusa Pacific U., 1980; Ma, U. So. Calif., 1985. Cert. fire fitness coord., ARA human factors; cert. health/fitness dir. and instr. Asst. football coach Azusa (Calif.) Pacific U., 1982, 1984-85; grad. teaching asst. U. So. Calif., L.A., 1981-84; instr. Calif. State U., Fullerton, 1984-86, 88; instr., asst. football coach Citrus Coll., Glendora, Calif., 1986-89, asst. football coach, 1990; instr. PACE program, asst. football coach L.A. Harbor Coll., Wilmington, Calif., 1989; dir. fitness programs and rsch. Fortanasce & Assoc. Physical Therapy/Sports Medicine, 1992—. Presenter in field; rschr. in field; cons. corp. fitness Bally's Nautilus/Aerobics Plus; instr. fitness preparation Valley Fire Edn. Assn., Ventura, Calif. Mem. AAHPERD, Am. Coll. Sports Medicine, Nat. Strength and Conditioning Assn. Republican. Baptist. Avocations: basketball, softball, weight lifting, building models. E-mail: vharding@prodigy.net.

HARDING, ILO-MAI, program director; b. Parnu, Estonia, Apr. 4, 1944; d. Ants and Aino (Liidak) Soots; m. Imre Lipping (div.); children: Arno Timo, Mark Eero, Tuuli Mai; m. Jordan Lee Harding, Oct. 21, 1986. BA, U. Toronto, 1966. Program asst. Office of Symposia and Seminars Smithsonian Instn., Washington, 1979-80, Nat. Mus. Am. Art, Washington, 1980-81; internat. radio broadcaster (Estonian svc.) Voice of Am., Washington, 1981-84; internat. visitor exch. specialist USIA, Washington, 1984-85, acad. exch. specialist, 1985-88, sr. program officer Fulbright Tchr. Exchange office acad. programs, 1988—. Vol. Am. Cancer Soc., Chevy Chase, Md. Avocations: teaching, counseling. Home: 4719 Merivale Rd Chevy Chase MD 20815-3705 Office: USIA Office Acad Programs Bur Ednl And Cultural Affai Washington DC 20547-0001

HARDISTY, WILLIAM LEE, English language educator; b. Creston, Iowa, Feb. 14, 1946; s. Ernest Dale and Velda Marie (Schaffer) H.; m. Bernadine Maxine Reimers, July 30, 1967; children: Lance William, Chad Eugene. AA, Creston (Iowa) C.C., 1965; BS, N.W. Mo. State U., Maryville, 1967, MA, 1972; postgrad., U. No. Iowa, Cedar Falls, 2003. Cert. tchr., Iowa, Mo. Instr. Iowa Western Coll., Council Bluffs, 1987—; chmn. lang. arts A-H-S-T H.S., Avoca, Iowa, 1967—; drama dir. A-S-T High Sch., Avoca, Iowa, 1967-92; instr. U. No. Iowa Workshops. Presenter Iowa Tchrs. English, Des Moines, 1991-95, Iowa Conservation Edn. Coun., Ames, 1995, Iowa State Edn. Assn., 1982-99, others. Contbr. articles to profl. and popular publs. Dist. chmn. Mid-Am. coun. Boy Scouts Am., 1984-2000, trustee; chmn. Rep. Party Knox Twp., Avoca, 1988—; pres. Iowa Assn. County Conservation Bds., Des Moines, 1990; pres. Pott count R.E.A.P. Bd. Council Bluffs, 1992; elder Presbyn. Ch., 1969—; mem. Sheriff's Dept. Citizens Adv. Bd., 1994—. Mem. NRA (life), NEA (life), Nat. Coun. Tchrs. English (life), Pheasants Forever (bd. dirs. 1990-91), Iowa State Edn. Assn., Southwest Uniserv Unit (exec. bd. 1994—, UNIeiicadre 1998—), Phi Delta Kappa. Avocations: writing, hunting, hiking, canoeing, travel. Home: 317 E Jaycee St Avoca IA 51521-5104 Office: A-H-S-T High Sch 768 S Maple Avoca IA 51521

HARDMAN, CORLISTA HELENA, school system administrator, educator; b. Charleston, W.Va., Feb. 5, 1948; d. Curtis Thomas and Maelena Hardman; 1 child, Bruce. BS in Edn., W.Va. State Coll., 1969; MEd, Baldwin-Wallace Coll., 1977. CErt. tchr., Ohio. Tchr. Cleve. City Schs., 1969—; supr. Cleve. State U., 1981—. Adj. prof. John Carroll U., 1996. Fin. sec. Everlasting Bapt. Ch., Cleve., 1978—; leader Lake Erie coun. Girl Scouts U.S., 1989—. Martha Holden Jennings scholar, 1985; named Tchr. in Excellence Nat. Coun. Negro Women, 1992; recipient Presdl. award elem. sci., 1997. Mem. Nat. Sci. Tchrs. Am., Ohio Coun. Tchrs. English and Lang. Arts, Cleve. Tchrs. Union, Cleve. Regional Coun. Sci. Tchrs. (co-pres. 1998), Ctr. City Profl. Devel. (chair 1986—), Alpha Kappa Alpha (Excellence in Sci. and Math. Tchg. 1997). Avocations: reading, aerobics. Office: Cleve Mcpl Sch Dist 1380 E 6th St Cleveland OH 44114-1606

HARDY, DUANE HORACE, retired federal agency administrator, educator; b. Ogden, Utah, June 8, 1931; s. Willis and Julia Mary (Garder) H.; m. Janet Myrnel Slater, Aug. 3, 1951; children: Rochelle Anne Leishman, Leslie Kaye Woolston, Kathy Korinne Davis. AA, Weber State Coll., 1951. Cert. EEO investigator/counselor. Ordained Mormon bishop, 1987. Enlisted U.S. Army, 1951, advanced through grades to lt. col., 1967, ret., 1971; EEO investigator U.S. Postal Svc., San Bruno, Calif., 1978-96, EEO instr., 1982-96; ret., 1996. Mem. EEO civic council, Salt Lake City, 1978—. Mem.: Kiwanis. Republican. Mem. Lds Ch. Avocations: watch, clock and jewelry making, engraving. Home: 120 W 5200 S Ogden UT 84405-6627

HARDY, HENRY REGINALD, JR., physicist, educator; b. Ottawa, Ont., Can., Aug. 19, 1931; came to U.S., 1966; s. Henry Reginald Sr. and Lois Irene (Moreland) H.; m. Margaret Mary Lytle, June 5, 1954; children: William Reginald, David Alexander. BS, McGill U., 1953; MS, Ottawa U., 1962; PhD, Va. Poly. Inst. and State U., 1965. Sci. officer Can. Dept. Energy, Mines and Resources, Ottawa, 1953-60, rsch. scientist, 1960-66; assoc. prof. mining Pa. State U., University Park, 1966-70, prof., 1970—2001, chmn. geomechanics sect., 1976-90, prof. emeritus, 2001—. Dir. Mining and Mineral Resources Rsch. Inst., 1990—2001; cons. UN, Ankara, Turkey, 1984; vis. prof. U. Nottingham, 1973, U. Aachen, Germany, 1980; sr. vis. fellow Tohoku U., Japan, 1986. Editor: procs. 6 internat. confs. on acoustic emission, 5 internat. confs. on salt mechanics, 1975—91; author: Acoustic Emission/Microseismic Activity, Vol. 1, Principles, Techniques and Geotechnical Applications, 2003. Mem. ASTM, Am. Geophys. Union, Can. Assn. Physicists, Internat. Soc. Rock Mechanics, Am. Soc. Nondestructive Testing, Acoustic Emission Working Group. Avocations: antiques, sport cars, travel. Office: Pa State U Hosler Bldg Rm 121 University Park PA 16802-5000

HARDY, JANE ELIZABETH, communications educator; b. Fenelon Falls, Ont., Can., Mar. 27, 1930; came to U.S., 1956, naturalized, 1976; d. Charles Edward and Augusta Miriam (Lang) Little; m. Ernest E. Hardy, Sept. 3, 1955; children: Edward Harold, Robert Ernest. BS with distinction, Cornell U., 1953. Garden editor and writer Can. Homes Mag., Maclean-Hunter Pub. Co., Ltd., Toronto, Ont., 1954-55, 56-62; contbg. editor Can. Homes, Southam Pub. Co., Toronto, Ont., 1962-66; instr. Cornell U., 1966-73, sr. lectr. in comm., 1979-96. Mem. Cornell U. Provost's Adv. Com. on Status of Women, 1977—81; lectr., condr. workshops on writing. Author: Writing for Practical Purposes, 1996; editor pro-tem Cornell Plantations Quar., 1981-82; author numerous publs. including brochures, slide set scripts, contbr. numerous articles in mags. Mem. coun. Cornell U., 2003—; chmn. bd. dirs. Matrix Found, 1998—2003, bd. dirs., 1998—. Mem.: Cornell U. Coun., Assn. Women Comms. (nat. bd. dirs. 1997—2000), Women in Comms., Inc. (faculy adv. 1977—95, liaison 1986—94, chair, adv. mem. 1988—90), Ithaca Women's Club, Ithaca Garden Club, Royal Hort. Soc., Alpha Omicron Pi, Phi Kappa Phi, Pi Alpha Xi. Home: 215 Enfield Falls Rd Ithaca NY 14850-8797

HARDY, JOEL ALLEN, microbiologist, educator; b. L.A., Dec. 1, 1952; s. Allen Williams and Ina Carolyn (Cobia) H.; m. Vicki Lynn Nickens, Dec. 20, 1974; children: Thomas Joel, Lucas Allen, Janna Marie, Jonica Anne. BS, Weber State Coll., 1977; MS, Idaho State U., 1979. Chemist Firestone Tire & Rubber Co., Salinas, 1980-82; microbiologist Internat. Shellfish Enterprises, Moss Landing, Calif., 1980-82; rsch. specialist U. Utah Sch. Medicine, Salt Lake City, Gull Labs, Salt Lake City, 1984-89, Bio-Rad Labs., Hercules, Calif., 1989—. Grantee Idaho State U., 1979. Mem. AAAS, Am. Soc. for Microbiology, Sigma Xi. Republican. Mem. Lds Ch. Home: 355 Woodhaven Dr Vacaville CA 95687-5955 Office: Bio-Rad Labs 4000 Alfred Nobel Hercules CA 94547

HARDY, JOY MILLER, academic administrator, consultant; b. Memphis, Oct. 30, 1947; d. Clifford Jasper and Lucille (Branch) Miller; m. Wade Randolph Hardy, Dec. 21, 1974; 1 child, Summer Beatrice Hardy. BA in Humanities, LeMoyne-Owen Coll., Memphis, 1969; MS in Linguistics, Ill. Inst. Tech., Chgo., 1971; PhD, U. Miss., Oxford. Cert. in Edn. Adminstrn. and Supervision, Tenn. Asst. prof. English LeMoyne-Owen Coll., Memphis, 1972-78; tchr. Memphis City Schs., 1979-90; program dir. Health Sci. Ctr. U. Tenn., Memphis, 1990—2001; exec. dir. Southwest Tenn. C.C., 2001—. Bd. dirs. Young Women's Christian Assn., Memphis, 1979-80. Mem. Coll. Lang. Assn., Nat. Coun. Tchrs. English, NEA, ASCD, Delta Sigma Theta. Avocations: crafts, reading. Home: 2092 Jamie Dr Memphis TN 38116-8124 Office: Workforce Devel Ctr 3523 Lamar Ave Memphis TN 38116

HARDY, LINDA LEA STERLOCK, media specialist; b. Balt., Aug. 15, 1947; d. George Allen and Dorothy Lea (Briggs) Sterlock; m. John Edward Hardy III, Apr. 25, 1970; 1 child, Roger Wayne. BA in History, N.C. Wesleyan Coll., 1969; MEd in History, East Carolina U., 1972, MLS, 1990. Cert. tchr., N.C. History tchr. Halifax (N.C.) County Schs., 1972-83, learning lab tchr., 1983-91, computer lab tchr., 1990-95; media specialist Nash-Rocky Mount (N.C.) Schs., 1995—. Part-time history instr. Nash C.C., 1993. Mem. AAUW (pres. Rocky Mount br. 1993-95, sec. 1997-99, Named Gift award 1987), Bus. and Profl. Women (pres. Rocky Mount chpt. 1986-87, 90-91, 2003—, treas. 1992-97, 2000-03, sec.-treas. dist X 1989-90, state election chmn. 1989-90, 93-95, state credentials chmn. 1997-98, sec.-treas. dist. 6 1997-98, Girl Friday award 1981, 98, Woman of Yr. award 1986, 97, 2002, state found. fin. chair 1996-97, state treas. 1999-2001, state sec. 2001-02, dist. VI dir. 2002-03, state membership chair 2003—, trustee 2003—), Nat. Assn. Educators, N.C. Assn. Educators, Nash/Rocky Mount Assn. Educators (faculty rep. 1995—), Phi Delta Kappa, Pi Gamma Mu. Methodist. Avocations: reading, travel, needlepoint, computers. Office: Red Oak Middle School 3170 Red Oak Battleboro Rd Battleboro NC 27809-9284 E-mail: llshardy@netscape.net.

HARDY, MARGARET ANTOINETTE KUMKO, science educator; b. Grand Rapids, Mich., Apr. 17, 1949; d. Edward Joseph and Marie Elizabeth (Tomasunas) Kumko; m. Thomas J. Hardy, July 27, 1973; children: Brian T., Kevin E., Cullen P. BS, Western Mich. U., 1971; MS, Med. Coll. Va., 1979. Cert. Med. Technologist. Med. technolgist various orgns., 1971-77; dir. microbiology Braddock Gen. Hosp., Pitts., 1977-79; sci. tchr. Sacred Heart Sch., Danville, Va., 1985-87, Carlisle Sch., Martinsville, Va., 1987—; prin., owner Harrington House, LLC, 2002—. Bd. dirs. Carlisle Sch. Curriculum Com., Martinsville, 1988-92, 2000—, sci. dept. chair 2000—. Religious educator, program dir., Sacred Heart Ch., Danville, 1981-92. Recipient Va. Assn. Ind. Schs. Excellence in Edn. award, 1991. Mem. Nat. Sci. Tchr. Assn., Am. Soc. Clin. Pathologists. Roman Catholic. Avocations: antiques, horticulture, reading, golf. Home: 285 Hawthorne Dr Danville VA 24541-3619 Office: Carlisle Sch PO Box 5388 Martinsville VA 24115-5388

HARDY, PATTI SANDERS, school system administrator; b. High Point, N.C., Aug. 6, 1954; d. Freager R. and Gladys (Ross) Sanders; m. Robert Harvey (div. 1984); 1 child, Robert Eugene III; m. James Hardy, 2000. BS, Winston Salem (N.C.) State U., 1976; MA in Edn., East Carolina U., 1988, postgrad. Tchr. Harnett County Schs., Angier, N.C., 1976-77, New Bern (N.C.) City Schs., 1978-79, Los Angeles Community Coll., Iwakuni, Japan, 1979-81, Manassas Park (Va.) City Schs., 1981-83, Greenville (N.C.) City Schs., 1984-85, Pitt County Schs., Greenville, 1985-89, asst. prin., 1989-90; prin. Halifax (N.C.) County Schs., 1990-92; instructional specialist III N.C. Dept. Pub. Instruction, 1992—; prin. Washington County Schs., 1997-99. Participant N.C. Ctr. for Advancement of Teaching, 1986, prin.'s exec. program U. N.C., Chapel Hill, 1992; mem. adv. bd. J.H. Rose H.S.; project tchr. recruiter N.C. State Employees Assn. Active E.B. Aycock PTA, Brawley Middle Sch. PTSO. Mem. Halifax County Prins. Assn., Winston-Salem State U. Alumni Assn. (pres. 1986), Phi Delta Kappa, Delta Sigma Theta (Wilson Alumnae chpt., v.p.). Democrat. Roman Catholic. Avocations: watching movies, recording music, collecting elephants and anything wicker. Home: 200 Ravenwood Dr Greenville NC 27834-6737 Office: Wilson County Schs PO Box 2048 Wilson NC 27894-2048

HARDY, RALPH W. F. biochemist, biotechnology executive; b. Lindsay, Ont., Can., July 27, 1934; s. Wilbur and Elsie H.; m. Jacqueline M. Thayer, Dec. 26, 1954; children: Steven, Chris, Barbara, Ralph (dec.), Jon. BSA, U. Toronto, 1956; MS, U. Wis.-Madison, 1958, PhD, 1959; DSc (hon.), U. Guelph, 1997. Asst. prof. U. Guelph, Ont., Can., 1960-63; research biochemist DuPont deNemours & Co., Wilmington, Del., 1963-67, research supr., 1967-74, assoc. dir., 1974-79, dir. life scis., 1979-84; pres. Bio Technica Internat., Inc., Cambridge, Mass., 1984-86; pres., CEO Boyce Thompson Inst., Inc., Ithaca, NY, 1986-95, pres. emeritus, 2000—; dep. chmn. Bio Technica Internat., Inc., 1986-90, cons., bd. dirs., 1990-99; pres. Nat. Agrl. Biotech. Coun., Ithaca, 1996—. Mem. exec. com. bd. agr. NRC, 1982—88, mem. commn. life scis., 1984—90, bd. biology, 1984—90, mem. com. on biotech., 1988—95, chmn. com., 1993—94, bd. sci. technol. internat. devel., 1990—93, chmn. com. on biol. control, 1992—95, chmn. com. on biol. nitrogen fixation, 1992—94, chmn. com. on natural products, 1996—97; mem. com. genetic experimentation Internat. Coun. Sci. Union, 1981—95; chmn., founder Nat. Agrl. Biotech. Coun., 1988—93; mem. sci. adv. com. U.S. Dept. Energy, 1991—95; mem. alt. agr. rsch. comml. bd. USDA, 1992—96, mem. and corp. sec. alt. agrl. rsch. comml. corp., 1996—2000; mem. Can. reallocations com. NSERC, 1997—98; mem. sci. adv. bd. Foragen, Guelph, Ont., Canada, 1999—; bd. dirs. BioCap, Canada, BioProducts, Can. Author: Nitrogen Fixation, 1975, A Treatise on Dinitrogen Fixation, 3 vols., 1977-79; contbr. over 150 articles to sci. jours. Mem. biotech. exec. bd. Cornell U., 1986-95, adv. coun. Vet. Coll., 1989-96; mem. gov. bd. Cornell Ctr. for Environment, 1991-95. Recipient Gov. Gen.'s Silver medal, 1956, Sterling Henricks award 1986; WARF fellow, 1956-58; DuPont fellow, 1958-59 Mem. Indsl. Biotech. Assn. (bd. dirs. 1986-89), Agr. Rsch. Inst. (bd. govs. 1988-91), Am. Chem. Soc. (exec. com. biol. chemistry divsn. 1978-81, Del. award 1969), Am. Soc. Biol. Chemists and Molecular Biologists, Am. Soc. Plant Biology (exec. com., treas. 1974-77), Am. Soc. Agronomy, Am. Soc. Microbiology. Episcopalian.

HARDY, RICHARD EARL, rehabilitation counseling educator; b. Victoria, Va., Oct. 11, 1938; s. Clifford E. and Louise (Hamilton) H.; 1 son, Jason Elliott. BS, Va. Poly. Inst. and State U., 1960, MS, 1962, EdD, 1966. Rehab. counselor State of Va., Richmond, 1961-63; rehab. advisor HHS, Washington, 1964-66; chief psychologist S.C. Dept. Rehab., Columbia, 1966-68; prof. chmn. dept. rehab. counseling Med. Coll. Va., Richmond, 1968-96, chmn., prof. emeritus, 1996—. Former bd. mem. S.C. State Bd. Psychology, former ABPP candidate examiner; internat. cons. to numerous countries including Turkey, Iraq, Peru, Uruguay, South Africa, Brazil, Thailand Author, editor: International Rehabilitation: Approaches and Programs, Hemingway: A Psychological Portrait, 1988, Gestalt Psychotherapy, 1991, Hispaniola Episode: A Mental Health Allegory, 1992, (with J.G. Cull) The Brass Chalice: Drug Prevention Stories and Information for Children and Youth, 1994, Counseling in the Rehabilitation Process, 1999, Woodpeckers Don't Get Headaches: The Psychology of Stress, Relationships, and Addiction, 2001, numerous others. Recipient Nat. award Nat. Rehab. Assn., 1976; recipient Nat. award Am. Assn. Workers for Blind, 1976, Outstanding Grad. award Med. Coll. Va./Va. Commonwealth U., Dept. Rehab. Counseling, 1997, Richard E. Hardy endowed scholarship Med. Coll. Va., 1998. Fellow Am. Psychol. Soc., Assn. Allied & Preventive Psychology; mem. Am. Assn. Vol. Action Scholars, Phi Kappa Phi. Office: Va Commonwealth U 6962 Forest Hill Ave Richmond VA 23225 E-mail: richardehardy@cs.com.

HARDY, VICKI, elementary school principal; b. Dallas, Dec. 12, 1949; d. Charles Preston and Bertha Frances (Wynne) Sheldon; m. Howard Lawrence Hardy, Jan. 22, 1972; children: Shane, Travis, Erin. BS, U. Tex., 1971; MEd, U. North Tex., 1977, 81. Tchr. Pearland (Tex.) Ind. Sch. Dist., 1972-73; tchr., asst. prin. Hurst Euless Bedford Ind. Sch. Dist., Bedford, Tex., 1973-86; curriculum cons. Irving (Tex.) Ind. Sch. Dist., 1986-89; prin. Schertz-Cibolo-Universal City Sch. Dist., Schertz, Tex., 1989-92, Cedar Hill (Tex.) Ind. Sch. Dist., 1992-96, Northwest Ind. Sch. Dist., Trophy Club, Tex., 1996—. Evaluator So. Assn. of Schs., 1987; TSII mem. Tex. Edn. Agy., Austin, 1990—. Mem. ASCD, Internat. Reading Assn., Nat. Coun. Tchrs. English, Tex. Elem. Prins. and Suprs. Assn., Ex-Students Assn. of U. Tex., Women in the Major Leagues, Delta Kappa Gamma (v.p. 1985-86, Friendship award 1985), Phi Delta Kappa (2d v.p. 1988-89, pres. 1989-90) Avocations: travel, crafts, sports, photography, sewing. Office: Lakeview Elem Sch 100 Village Trl Trophy Club TX 76262-5201 E-mail: vhardynisd@yahoo.com.

HARDY, VICTORIA ELIZABETH, management educator; b. Marion, N.C., Feb. 26, 1947; d. Milton Victor Roth and Bertha Jean (Norris) R.; m. Michael Carrington Hardy, June 19, 1983 (div. 1993); 1 child, Christopher. BS in Edn., U. Mo., 1970; postgrad., So. Ill. U., 1974-75; postgrad. Mgmt. Devel. Program, Stanford U., 1980-81; MA in Mgmt., Aquinas Coll., 1999. Cert. facility mgr. Pub. sch. tchr. English and Theater, 1970-75; gen. mgr. Miss. River Festival, Edwardsville, Ill., 1975-77; dir. events and svcs. Stanford (Calif.) U., 1977-83; exec. dir. Meadowlands Ctr. for the Arts, Rutherford, N.J., 1983-87; pres., chief exec. officer Music Hall Ctr. for the Arts, Detroit, 1987-89; prin. AMS Planning & Rsch., Conn., 1989-94; 2003prof. facility mgmt. Ferris State U., Big Rapids, Mich., 1994; acad. dept. head Wentworth Inst. Tech., 2003—. Mem. faculty CUNY, 1986-88. Contbr. to various publs. Mem. USICA study team to China, 1981; state bd. dirs. Arts Found., Mich., 1987-95; bd. dirs. Internat. Facility Mgmt. Assn., 1994-97, standing coms. recognition and profl. devel.; mem. People to People facilities del. to Australia and New Zealand, 1996; bd. dirs., chair IFMA Found., 1998—. Named Disting. Educator of Yr., IFMA, 2001; named to Creativity in Business Doubleday, 1986; recipient Gold medal for Cmty. Programs, Coun. for Advancement and Support of Edn., Stanford, 1985. Mem. League of Hist. Am. Theaters (pres. bd. dirs. 1987-89), Arts Presenter Assn. (exec. bd. dirs. 1977-83). Democrat. Avocations: skiing, gardening. Office: Ferris State Univ Coll of Tech Swan 312 915 Campus Dr Big Rapids MI 49307-2291

HARE, ELEANOR O'MEARA, computer science educator; b. Charlottesville, Va., Apr. 6, 1936; d. Edward King and Eleanor Worthington (Selden) O'Meara; m. John Leonard Ging, Feb. 4, 1961 (div. 1972); 1 child, Catherine Eleanor Ging Huddle; m. William Ray Hare, Jr., May 24, 1973. BA, Hollins Coll., 1958; MS, Clemson U., 1973, PhD, 1989. Rsch. asst. cancer rsch. U. Va. Hosp., Charlottesville, 1957-58; rsch. specialist rsch. labs. engring. sci. U. Va., Charlottesville, 1959-64; tchr. Pendleton (S.C.) High Sch., 1964-65; vis. instr. dept. math. sci. Clemson (S.C.) U., 1974-79, instr. dept. computer sci., 1979-83, lectr. dept. computer sci., 1983-90, asst. prof. dept. computer sci., 1990-98, assoc. prof. dept. computer sci., 1998—. Contbr. articles to profl. jours. Bd. dirs. LWV of the Clemson Area, 1988-96; chmn. nursing home study LWV of S.C., 1988-92; oboe and English horn player Anderson (S.C.) Symphony, 1980—. Fellow Inst. Combinatorics and its Applications; mem. AAUP. Office: Clemson U Dept Computer Sci Clemson SC 29634-0001

HARE, PETER HEWITT, philosophy educator; b. N.Y.C., Mar. 12, 1935; s. Michael Meredith and Jane Perry (Jopling) H.; m. Daphne Joan Kean, May 30, 1959 (dec. Aug. 1995); children: Clare Kean, Gwendolyn Meigs; m. Susan Howe, Nov. 1, 2000. BA, Yale U., 1957; MA, Columbia U., 1962, PhD, 1965. Lectr. philosophy SUNY, Buffalo, 1962-65, from asst. prof. to prof., 1965-97, disting. svc. prof., 1997—, asst. chmn. dept., 1965-68, chmn. dept., 1971-75, 85-94, assoc. dean divsn. undergrad. edn., 1980-82, prof. emeritus, 2001—. Vis. prof. Moscow State U., 1989; bd. advisors, Peirce Edition Project, Ind. U./Purdue U., 1998—. Author: A Woman's Quest for Science, 1985; (with others) Evil and the Concept of God, 1968, Causing, Perceiving and Believng, 1975; editor: Doing Philosophy Historically, 1988, (with others) History, Religion and Spiritual Democacy, 1980, Naturalism and Rationality, 1986, (series) Frontiers of Philosophy, Prometheus Books, 1986—; photo illustrations in Susan Howe, Kidnapped, 2002, The Midnight, 2003; mem. editl. bd. Am. Philos. Quar., 1978-87, Jour. Speculative Philosophy, 1987—. Mem. Am. Philos. Assn. (nominating com. ea. divsn. 1990-92, program com. 1993-95, chmn. program com. 1994-95, mem. nat. bd. officers 1996-99, chmn. com. career opportunities, 1996-99, ombudsman 1996-99, chair Romanell lectr. com. 2000-2001), Peirce Soc. (editor Transactions 1974—), pres. 1975-76), N.Y. State Philos. Assn. (pres. 1975-77), Soc. for Advancement Am. Philosophy (exec. com. 1977-80, pres. 1988-90, Herbert W. Schneider award 1996), Josiah Royce Soc. (mem. exec. com. 2003—), Elizabethan Club. Home: 115 New Quarry Rd Guilford CT 06437-1621 Office: SUNY Dept Philosophy Park Hall Buffalo NY 14260 E-mail: phhare@acsu.buffalo.edu.

HARGITAI, PETER J. English language educator; b. Budapest, Hungary, Jan. 28, 1947; came to U.S., 1957; s. Gaspar and Margit (Barna) H.; m. Dianne M. Kress, June 24, 1967; children: Suzanna, Peter. BA, Cleve. State U., 1970, MA, 1975; MFA, U. Mass., 1988. Tchr. Cleve. Cath. Diocesan Schs., 1969-71; instr. Whiting (Ohio) Coll., 1971-74; tchr. Mentor (Ohio) High Sch., 1974-78, Telshe Yeshiva Jewish Sch., Ohio, 1977-78; instr. U. Miami, Fla., 1978-86; teaching asst. U. Mass., Amherst, 1986-88; lectr. Broward C.C., Fla., 1988-90; instr. Fla. Internat. U., Miami, 1990—. Author: Perched on Nothing's Branch, 1986 (Am. Acad. Arts Translation award 1988), Budapest to Bellevue, 1988, Magyar Tales, 1989; co-author Fodor's Budget Zion, 1991; editor: Forum: 10 Poets of the Western Reserve, 1976. Grantee Martha-Holden Jennings Found., 1976, Fulbright-Hayes Found., Washington, 1988; recipient Fiction award, Fla. Arts Coun., 1990. Mem. AAUP, P.E.N. Internat., Poets and Writers, Inc., Hungarian Am. Educators Assn. Democrat. Roman Catholic. Avocations: war games, bore rifle, modern pentathlon. Office: Fla Internat U University Park Miami FL 33199-0001

HARGREAVES, MARY-WILMA MASSEY, retired history educator; b. Erie, Pa., Mar. 1, 1914; d. Albert Edward and Bess (Childs) Massey; m. Herbert Walter Hargreaves, Aug. 24, 1940. BA, Bucknell U., 1935; MA, Radcliffe Coll./Harvard U., 1936, PhD, 1951. Rsch. editor Harvard U. Grad. Sch. Bus. Adminstrn., Cambridge, Mass., 1937-39; fellow Brookings Inst., Washington, 1939-40; assoc. editor Clay Papers U. Ky., Lexington, 1952-74, co-editor, project dir. Clay Papers, 1974-79, asst. prof. history, 1964-69, assoc. prof., 1969-73, prof., 1973-84, Hallam prof. history, 1973-75, prof. emerita, 1984—. Mem. adv. bd. Henry Clay Found., 1995—. Author: Dry Farming in the Northern Great Plains, 1900-1925, 1957, Presidency of John Quincy Adams, 1985, Dry Farming in the Northern Great Plains, Years of Readjustment, 1920-1990, 1993; assoc. editor, co-editor: The Papers of Henry Clay, 6 vols., 1959-81; mem. editl. bd. Great Plains Quar., 1986-88; contbg. editor Miller Ctr. of Pub. Affairs, U. Va., 2003. Recipient Saloutos Book award in Agrl. History, 1994. Mem. Am. Hist. Assn. (com. chmn.), Orgn. of Am. Historians (com. chmn.), Agrl. History Soc. (pres. 1975-76, com. chmn.), So. Hist. Assn. (com. chmn.), Econ. History Assn., Soc. Early Am. History, Ky. Hist. Soc., Mont. Hist. Soc., Phi Beta Kappa, Sigma Tau Delta, Phi Alpha Theta. Democrat. Methodist. Avocations: reading, gardening, classical music. Home: 237 Cassidy Ave Lexington KY 40502-2303 Office: U Ky History Dept 1719 Patterson Office Tower Lexington KY 40506-0027

HARING-SMITH, TORI, academic administrator; b. Chgo., Jan. 1, 1953; d. Philip Smyth and Jacqueline (Kolle) Haring; m. Robert Henry Smith, June 1, 1974; 1 child, Whitney Patrick Haring-Smith. BA, Swarthmore Coll., 1974; MA, U. Ill., 1977, PhD, 1980. Teaching asst. U. Ill., Urbana, 1975-80; asst. prof. Brown U., Providence, 1980-86, assoc. prof. English, 1986—, assoc. prof. theatre, 1987—, dir. writing fellows program, 1982-91. Freelance ednl. cons., Providence, 1981—; theatre dir., Providence, 1986—; artistic dir. Wallace Theatre, Cairo, 1996—99; chair dept. performing and visual arts Am. U., Cairo, 1996—99; exec. dir. Thomas J. Watson Found., Providence, 1999—2001; dean coll. liberal arts Willamette U., Salem, Oreg., 2001—02, v.p. ednl. affairs, 2002—. Author: A.A. Milne, 1982, A Guide to Writing Programs, 1984, From Farce to Melodrama, 1985, Learning Together, 1992, Writing Together, 1993, Monologues for Women by Women, 1994, (translation) Napoli Milionaria, 1995, More Monologues for Women by Women, 1996, Scenes for Women by Women, 1998, also numerous on pedagogy, lit. and theatre. Recipient sr. class citation Brown U., 1984, 85, 86; fellow Watson Found., 1974, Lilly Found., 1981, Wriston fellow Brown U., 1984. Mem.: Assn. Am. Colls. and Univs., Am. Coun. Acad. Deans., Assn. for Theatre in Higher Edn. Office: Willamette U VP Ednl Affairs Salem OR 97301 E-mail: tharings@willamette.edu.

HARIRI, V. M. arbitrator, mediator, lawyer, educator; BS, Wayne State U.; JD, Detroit Coll. Law; LLM, London Sch. Econs. and Polit.Sci.; diploma arbitration, Reading (Eng.) U. Pvt. practice internat. and U.S. bus. law, Detroit. Drafting com. Republic of Kazakhstan Code on Arbitration Procedure, Free Econ. Zone Legislation, Republic of Belarus; instr. internat. comml. arbitration Chartered Inst. Arbitrators, Am. Arbitration Assn. Fellow Chartered Inst. Arbitrators (exec. com. N.Am. br., founding com. and expert advisor); mem. ABA, Internat. Bar Assn., Am. Soc. Internat. Law, Am. Arbitration Assn., London Ct. Internat. Arbitration, World Jurist Assn., Mich. Trial Lawyers Assn. Office: 143 Cadycentre Ste 352 Northville MI 48167-1244

HARITON, JO ROSENBERG, psychotherapist, educator; b. Albany, N.Y., June 12, 1948; d. Irving H. and Madeline P. Rosenberg; m. Frank J. Hariton; 2 children. BA, Goucher Coll., Towson, Md., 1970; MS, Columbia U., 1973; PhD, NYU, 1992; postgrad., Postgrad. Ctr. Mental Health, N.Y.C., 1979. Cert. psychoanalyst. With maternal and child health dept. Bronx (N.Y.) Mcpl. Hosp. Ctr., 1973-76, coord. emergency svcs. children's dept. child psychiatry, 1976-79; field work instr. NYU Sch. Social Work, 1977-79; sr. psychiat social worker divsn. child and adol. psychiatry Westchester divsn. N.Y. Hosp.-Cornell Med. Ctr., White Plains, N.Y., 1979-82, social work coord., 1982-98; mem. faculty Cornell U. Med. Sch., 1982—; pvt. practice psychoanalysis and psychotherapy N.Y.C. Co-head ADHD Svc. Line, 1996—. Contbr. articles on group therapy to profl. jours. Fellow N.Y. State Soc. Clin. Social Work Psychotherapists; mem. NASW, Acad. Cert. Social Workers, Am. Orthopsychiat. Assn., Am. Group Psychotherapy Assn. Home: 1065 Dobbs Ferry Rd White Plains NY 10607-2212 Office: NY Presby Hosp Westchester Divsn 21 Bloomingdale Rd White Plains NY 10605-1596 E-mail: jhariton@med.cornell.edu.

HARITOS, GEORGE KONSTANTINOS, engineer, educator, military officer; b. Athens, Greece, Nov. 29, 1947; came to the U.S., 1964; naturalized, 1970; s. Konstantinos G. and Maria K. (Yiakoumakis) H.; m. Mary Jeannette Martell, June 20, 1971; children: Konstantinos, Marika. BS in Engring., U. Ill., Chgo., 1969, MS in Mechanics and Materials, 1970; PhD in Structural Mechanics, Northwestern U., 1978. Commd. 2d lt. USAF, 1971, advanced through grades to col., 1993; ret., 2001; aero. structures engr. aero. systems divsn. USAF, Dayton, Ohio, 1971-75; asst. prof. engring. mechanics USAF Acad., Colorado Springs, 1978-82; assoc. prof. engring. mechanics Air Force Inst. Tech., Dayton, 1982-85; program mgr. mechanics of materials Air Force Office Scientific Rsch., Washington, 1986-89, dir. aerospace scis., 1989-90, assoc. dir., 1990-91, dep. dir. and comdr., 1993-95; chief flight vehicles divsn. Hdqrs. Air Force Systems Command, Washington, 1991-92; chief air vehicles br. Hdqrs. Air Force Materiel Command, Dayton, 1992-93; assoc. dean Grad. Sch. Engring. Air Force Inst. Tech., Dayton, Ohio, 1995-98, vice comdt., 1998-99, comdt., 1999—2001, prof. engring. mechanics, 2001—03; dean, prof. Coll. Engring. U. Akron, 2003—. Mem. Def. Com. on Rsch., Washington, 1993-95, OSR Rsch. Coun., Washington, 1993-95. Editor: Damage Mechanics in Composites, 1987, Smart Structures and Materials, 1991; assoc. editor: Internat. Jour. Damage Mechanics, 1990—; contbr. articles to profl. jours. Decorated Legion of Merit, Meritorious Svc. medal with five oak leaf clusters, Air Force Commendation medal with oak leaf cluster, nat. def. svc. medal with svc. star; Walter P. Murphy fellow Northwestern U., 1975. Fellow AIAA (assoc.); mem. Am. Acad. Mechanics, Am. Soc. for Engring. Edn., ASME (materials and structures com. 1986—). Achievements include research in fracture mechanics; fatigue at elevated temperature; engineering mechanics and materials; initiated international research thrusts in mesomechanics for connecting the behavior of materials to their microstructural makeup, and in biomimetics for synthesizing multifunctional materials that imitate biological materials. Office: U Akron Auburn Sci & Engr Center 201 Akron OH 44325-3901

HARKAVY, ROBERTA SUSAN, retired humanities educator; b. NYC, Apr. 4, 1935; d. Daniel and Ruth (Wool) Firsty; m. Ira Baer Harkavy, Aug. 11, 1957; children: Steven, Daniel, Elliot. AB, Hunter Coll., 1956, MS, 1964; postgrad., Bklyn. Coll., 1963, 67, 78-82, Adelphi U., 1983—, MA, 1989. Lic. tchr., N.Y. Tchr. NYC Bd. Edn., 1956—2001; ret., 2001. Asst. Bklyn. Coll., 1977—. Active Midwood Devel. Corp., Bklyn., 1981-82, Madison Civic Assn., Bklyn, 1985—. Hunter Coll. scholar, 1956, N.Y. State Dept. Edn. fellow, 1987. Mem. N.Y. Pub. Sch. Early Childhood Assn., United Fedn. Tchrs., Nat. Council, Tchrs. English, Bklyn. Reading Council Internat. Reading. Assn., Tchrs English to Speakers Other Languages, LWV, B'nai B'rith (v.p. local 1959—, exec. bd. local 1957—, columnist, editor Horizons 1961, 67), Schs. Unit. Democrat. Jewish. Avocations: photography, writing. Home: 1784 E 29th St Brooklyn NY 11229-2517

HARKIN, ANN WINIFRED, elementary school educator, psychotherapist; b. Glasgow, Scotland, Oct. 14, 1951; came to US, 1956; d. John Joseph and Mary W. Leavy H.; 1 child, Julia A. Wilkinson. BA in Psychology cum laude, Immaculata Coll., 1973, MA in Counseling Psychology summa cum laude, 1999. Instrnl. II permanent cert. elem., secondary sch. tchr., Pa. Tchr. grade 3 St. Anastasia, Newtown Square, Pa., 1973-78; tchr. grade 1 Mother of Divine Providence, King of Prussia, 1979-89, St. Aloysius Acad., Bryn Mawr, Pa., 1989—; legal asst. Elizabeth R. Howard, Esquire, 2001—. Counselor Paoli Addictions Ctr., Pa. Mem. APA, ACA, Nat. Cath. Educators Assn., Diamond Rock Schoolhouse Assn., Donegal Soc. Phila., Chi Sigma Iota. Avocations: horticulture, animals, hiking, swimming, drawing. Home: 738 Cedar Dr Phoenixville PA 19460-3606

HARKNESS, BRUCE, English language educator; b. Beaver Dam, Wis., Apr. 16, 1923; s. Reuben Elmore Ernest and Ruth (Thomas) H.; m. Barbara McNutt White, Oct. 29, 1967; 1 child, Mark Andrew Joseph; children by previous marriage: Stephen W., Marguerite, Laura C., Jonathan C., Michael B. Student, Kalamazoo Coll., 1941-42, Swarthmore Coll., 1942-42; MA in English, U. Chgo., 1948, PhD, 1950. From instr. English to prof. U. Ill., 1950-63, 64-66, assoc. dean liberal arts and scis., 1964-66; prof. English, chmn. dept. So. Ill. U., 1963-64; dean arts and scis. Kent (Ohio) State U., 1966-74, prof. English, 1974-93; prof. emeritus, 1993—. Author: Bibliography and Novelistic Fallacy, 1959, Secret of the Secret Sharer Bared, 1965; editor: Heart of Darkness (Conrad), 1960, Secret Sharer (Conrad), 1962, Secret Agent (Conrad), 1990; adv. editor: College English, 1964-70; founding editor, gen. editor: Cambridge edit. Works of Joseph Conrad, 1977-95. With USAAF, 1942-45. Carnegie fellow, 1949-50; Guggenheim fellow, 1957-58; Beinecke Libr. vis. fellow, 1990. Mem. MLA (exec. bd. Midwest sect. 1961-64), Nat. Coun. Tchrs. English (dir.-at-large 1964-68), Joseph Conrad Soc. Am. (pres. 1995-99). Home: 1295 Lake Martin Dr Kent OH 44240-6263

HARL, NEIL EUGENE, economist, lawyer, educator; b. Appanoose County, Iowa, Oct. 9, 1933; s. Herbert Peter and Bertha Catherine (Bonner) H.; m. Darlene Ramona Harris, Sept. 7, 1952; children: James Brent, Rodney Scott. BS, Iowa State U., 1955, PhD, 1965; JD, U. Iowa, 1961. Bar: Iowa 1961. Field editor Wallace's Farmer, 1957-58; research assoc. U.S. Dept. Agr., Iowa City and Ames, Iowa, 1958-64; assoc. prof. econs. Iowa State U., Ames, 1964-67, prof., 1967—, Charles F. Curtiss Disting. prof., 1976—, dir. Ctr. Internat. Agrl. Fin., 1990—. Mem. adv. group to commr. IRS, 1979-80; mem. adv. com. Heckerling Inst. on Estate Planning, Miami, Fla., 1983-96; mem. adv. com. Office Tech. Assessment, U.S. Congress, 1988-95, vice chair, 1992-93, chair, 1993-94; mem. exec. bd. U.S. West Comms., Iowa, 1989-90; mem. adv. com. on agrl. biotech. USDA, 2000-02; mem. Fed. Commn. on Payment Limitations, 2002-03; lectr. in field. Author: Farm Estate and Business Planning, 1973, Farm Estate and Business Planning, 15th edit., 2001, Legal and Tax Guide for Agricultural Lenders, 1984, Legal and Tax Guide for Agricultural Lenders, supplement, 1987, Agricultural Law, 15 vols., 1980—81, Agricultural Law Manual, 1985, rev. edit., 2003, The Farm Debt Crisis of the 1980s, 1990; co-author: Farmland, 1982, Principles of Agricultural Law, 1997, 3d edit., 2003, Taxation of Cooperatives, 1999, Reporting Farm Income, 2000, Family Owned Business Deduction, 2001, Arrogance and Power: The Saga of WOI-TV, 2001, The Law of the Land, 2002; author, actor films and videotape programs; contbr. articles to profl. jours. Trustee Iowa State U. Agrl. Found., 1969-85. 1st lt. AUS, 1955-57. 1st lt. U.S. Army, 1955—57. Recipient Outstanding Tchr. award Iowa State U., 1973, Disting Svc. to Agr. award Am. Soc. Farm Mgrs. and Rural Appraisers, 1977, Iowa sect. 1996, Faculty Svc. award Nat. Univ. Ext. Assn., 1980, Disting. Svc. award Am. Agrl. Editors Assn., 1984, Disting. Achievement citation Iowa State U., 1985, Disting. Svc. to State Govt. award Nat. Gov.'s Assn., 1986, Disting. Svc. award Iowa State U., 1986, Farm Leader of Yr. award Des Moines Register, 1986, Henry A. Wallace award, 1987, Superior Svc. award USDA, 1987, Disting. Svc. to Iowa Agr. award Iowa Farm Bur., 1992, Faculty Excellence award, Iowa Bd. Regents, 1993, Charles A. Black award Coun. Agrl. Sci. Tech., 1997, Excellence in Internat. Agr. award Iowa State U., 1999, Disting. Svc. to Agr. award Chgo. Farmers Club, 1999, Exceptional Svc. to Agr. award Iowa Master Farmers, Wallaces Farmer, 2000, Pres.'s award for disting. svc. Iowa State U., 2002, Lifetime Achievement award Iowa Farmers Union, 2003; named Seminar Leader of Yr. Nat. Assn. Accts., 2000. Fellow Am. Coll. Trusts and Estates Counsel, Am. Agrl. Econs. Assn. (exec. bd. 1979-85, pres. 1983-84), Am. Agrl. Econs. Found. pres. 1993-94, Outstanding Ext. Program award 1970, Excellence in Communicating Rsch. Results award 1975, Disting. Undergrad. Tchr. award 1976), ABA Rsch. Found., Iowa State Bar Found.; mem. ABA, Iowa Bar Assn. (Pres. award 1991), Am. Agrl. Law Assn. (pres. 1980-81, Disting. Svc. award 1984); bd. dirs. Iowa Barn Found. (v.p. 1999-2001). Home: 2821 Duff Ave Ames IA 50010-4709 also: 3001 Kanaloa 78-261 Manukai St Kailua Kona HI 96740 Office: Iowa State U Dept Econs Ames IA 50011-1070 E-mail: harl@iastate.edu.

HARLAND, BARBARA FERGUSON, nutritionist, educator; b. Chgo., Apr. 16, 1925; d. Frank Cleveland and Dorothy Sargent (Brown) Ferguson; m. James Wallace Harland, Sept. 6, 1947; children: Joseph A., Jane, Janet. BS, Iowa State U., 1946; MS, U. Wash., 1949; PhD, U. Md., 1971. Registered dietitian, lic. dietitian, lic. nutritionist. Chief dietitian Lakeview Meml. Hosp., Stillwater, Minn., 1946-47; dietitian U. Wash., Seattle, 1947-49; nutrition instr. Ind. U. S.E., New Albany, 1964-65; math., sci. substitute tchr. Montgomery County High Schs., Md., 1966-67; nutrition instr. U. Md., College Park, 1967-70; rsch. biologist nutrition div. FDA, Washington, 1971-84; prof. nutrition and food Coll. Allied Health Scis. Howard U., Washington, 1984—. Referee for Phytate Assn. Official Analytical Chemists, Washington, 1980—; mem. Howard U. Instl. Animal Care and Use Com., Washington, 1984—. Author: Minerals: Nutrition and Metabolism, 1999; sr. author: (book chpt.) World Review of Nutrition and Diets, 1987; contbr. articles to profl. jours. Chmn. adminstrv. coun. Concord-St. Andrews United Meth. Ch., Bethesda, Md., 1977-83, 91-96, vice chmn., 1988-91, mem. planning com., 1984-88, peace advocacy com., 1984-88. Faculty and corp. rsch. grantee Howard U., Washington, 1985-87, rsch. grantee Proctor & Gamble, Cin., 1988, USDA, 1995; named Outstanding Scholar-Researcher Coll. Allied Health Scis., 1996-97, 98-99, 99-2000. Mem. Am. Soc. Nutritional Sci., Am. Dietetic Assn., Am. Chem. Soc., Am. Soc. Clin. Nutrition, Soc. Exptl. Biology and Medicine, Soc. Nutrition Edn., Congl. Country Club (chmn. tennis com. 1982-92, chmn. paddle tennis com. 1988-97). Republican. Methodist. Avocations: tennis, paddle tennis, skiing, ice skating. Home: 7929 Robison Rd Bethesda MD 20817-6928 Office: Howard U Coll Pharmacy Nursing Allied Health Scis Dept Nutritional Scis Washington DC 20059-0001 E-mail: bharland@howard.edu.

HARLEY, ROBISON DOOLING, JR., lawyer, educator; b. Ancon, Panama, July 6, 1946; s. Robison Dooling and Loyde Hazel (Goehenauer) Harley; m. Suzanne Purviance Bendel, Aug. 9, 1975; children: Arianne Erin, Lauren Loyde. BA, Brown U., 1968; JD, Temple U., 1971; LLM, U. San Diego, 1985. Cert.: Calif. Bd. Legal Specialization (criminal law specialist since 1981) 1981, Nat. Bd. Trial Advocacy (criminal trial adv. since 1981) 1982, bar: Pa. 1971, Calif. 1976, NJ 1977, DC 1981, US Dist. Ct. (cen. and so. dists.) Calif. 1976, US Dist. Ct. NJ 1977, US Dist. Ct. (ea. dist.) Pa. 1987, US Ct. Appeals (9th cir.) 1982, US Ct. Appeals (3rd cir.) 1986, US Supreme Ct. 1980, US Ct. Mil. Appeals 1972. Asst. agy. dir. Safeco Title Ins. Co., LA, 1975—77; ptnr. Cohen, Stokke & Davis, Santa Ana, Calif., 1977—85; prin. prin. Harley Law Offices, Santa Ana, 1985—. Adj. prof. Orange County Coll. Trial Advocacy; adj. prof. paralegal program U. Calif.; instr. trial adv. programs US Army, USN, USAF, USMC; judge pro-tem Orange County Cts. Author: Orange County Trial Lawyers Drunk Driving Syllabus; contbr. articles to profl. jours. Trial counsel, def. counsel, mil. judge, asst. staff judge adv. USMC, 1971—75, regional def. counsel Western Region, 1986—90; bd. dirs. Orange County Legal Aid Soc. Lt. col. JAGC USMCR. Decorated Nat. Def. Svc. medal, Res. medal. Mem.: ATLA, ABA, Orange County Criminal Lawyers Assn. (found. com.), Orange County Trial Lawyers Assn., Orange County Bar Assn. (judiciary com., criminal law sect., adminstrn. of justice com.), Assn. Specialized Criminal Def. Advs., Nat. Assn. for Criminal Def. Attys., Calif. Pub. Defenders Assn., Calif. Attys. for Criminal Justice, Calif. Trial Lawyers Assn., Marine Corps Assn., Marine Corps Res. Officers Assn., Res. Officers Assn. Republican. Avocations: sports, physical fitness, reading. Home: 31211 Paseo Miraloma San Juan Capistrano CA 92675-5505 Office: Harley Law Offices 825 N Ross St Santa Ana CA 92701-3419

HARLEY, RUTH, artist, educator; b. Phila. children: Peter Wells Bressler, Victoria Angela. Student, Pa. State U., 1941; BFA, Phila. Coll. Art, 1945; postgrad., U. N.H., 1971, Hampshire Coll., 1970. Former instr. Phila. Mus. Art, 1946-59; former art supt. Ventnor (N.J.) City Bd. Edn., 1959-61. Art tchr. The Print Club, Phila., Allens Lane Art Ctr., Phila., Suburban Ctr. Arts, Lower Merion, Pa., Radner (Pa.) Twp. Adult Ctr., 1949-59, Atlantic City Adult Ctr., 1959-60. One-woman shows include Dubin-Lush Galleries, Phila., 1956, Contemporary Art Assn., Phila., 1957, Vernon Art Exhbns., Germantown, Pa., 1958, Detroit Inst. Arts, 1958, Phila. Mus. Art, 1957, 59, Moore Inst., Phila., 1962-68, Greenhill Galleries, Phila., 1974, Phila. Civic Ctr., 1978, Natal Rio Grande du Norte, Brazil, 1979, Galerie Novel Esprit, Tampa, Fla., 1992-95, Mind's Eye Gallery, St. Petersburg, Fla., 1993, Ga. Tech. Art Ctr., 1998, Robert Ferst Ctr. for the Arts Ga. Inst. Tech., 1998-99; exhibited in group shows, including Group 55, Phila., 1955, Print Club, Phila., 1955, Nat. Tours 1956-59, Pa. Acad. Fine Arts, 1957, Vernon Art Exhbns., 1958, Detroit Inst. Arts, 1958, Phila. Mus. Art, 1959, Moore Inst., 1962, Phila. Civic Ctr. Mus., 1975, Galerie Nouvel Esprit Assemblage Russe, 1992, Kenneth Raymond Gallery, Boca Raton, 1992-93, Mind's Eye Gallery, 1993, Polk Mus. Art, Lakeland, Fla., 1993, Don Roll Gallery, Sarasota, Fla., 1994-95, Las Vegas (Nev.) Internat. Art Expo, 1994, Heim Am. Gallery, Fisher Island, Fla., 1996, McLean Gallery, Malibu, Calif., 1997, 98, 99, Robert Ferst Ctr. Arts, Ga. Tech. U., 1998, 99, Christina Gallery, Atlanta, 1999, 2000, Adrian Howard Gallery, St. Petersburg, 2000, 2001, 2002, Melrose Bay Art Gallery, Melrose, Fla., 2001, Red River Valley Mus., Vernon, Tex., 2001, Kirkpatrick Mus., Okla., 2001, Airport, Gainesville, Fla., 2001; represented in permanent collections at U. Villanova (Pa.) Mus., TemplU. Law Sch., Pa., Woodmere Mus., Phila.; included in Art in America Ann. Guide, 2000-01, 2002; photo sculpture commd. through Phila. Re-Devel. Authority. Contbr. art prize to Ventnor N.J. Sch. Sys. Address: PO Box 433 Melrose FL 32666-0433 E-mail: harleyruth@aol.com.

HARLOW, ELIZABETH MARY, retired music educator; b. Boston; d. William Joseph and Elizabeth Frieda (Binnig) H.; 1 child, William Harlow Gunn. MusB, Danbury State Tchrs. Coll., Conn., 1959. Music tchr. Guilford Bd. Edn., Conn., 1959-62, North Haven Bd. Edn., Conn., 1962-65, Hamden Bd. Edn., Conn., 1976-99; ret., 1999. Mem. Conn. Ednl. Assn., Nat. Music Educators, Am. Choral Dirs. Assn. Hamden Edn. Assn.

HARLOW, JUDITH LEIGH, educational institute executive, consultant; b. Denver, Aug. 11, 1943; d. Roy Afton and Virginia Lee (Whitehead) H. BA in Secondary Edn., U. N.Mex., 1966, MA in Counseling, 1973. Cert. in guidance and counseling, ednl. adminstrn., N.Mex.; lic. ednl. diagnostician, mediator. Tchr. Albuquerque Pub. Schs., 1966-79, ednl. diagnostician, 1979-80, adminstr. spl. edn., 1980-87, asst. prin., 1987-95; dir. Inst. for Behavior Intervention in the Schs. Ednl. Assessment Systems, Inc., Albuquerque, 1997—. Mem. adv. bd. Desert Hills Residential Treatment Ctr., Albuquerque, 1998—. Vol. N.Mex. Ctr. for Dispute Resolution, Albuquerque. Mem. Coun. for Exceptional Children (Disting. Svc. award N.Mex. 1992). Democrat. Avocations: golf, tennis. Home: 10920 Central Park Dr NE Albuquerque NM 87123-5426 Office: Inst for Behavior Intervention in the Schs 5200 Copper Ave NE Albuquerque NM 87108-1473

HARMAN, GILBERT HELMS, philosophy educator; b. East Orange, NJ, May 26, 1938; s. William Henry and Marguerite Variel (Page) H.; m. Lucy Newman, Aug. 14, 1970; children: Elizabeth, Olivia. BA, Swarthmore Coll., 1960; PhD, Harvard U., 1964. With dept. philosophy Princeton (N.J.) U., 1963—, prof., 1971—, acting chair, 2001—02, chair cognitive studies program, 1992-97. Author: Thought, 1973, The Nature of Morality, 1977, Change in View, 1986, Skepticism and the Definition of Knowledge, 1990, (with Judith Jarvis Thomson) Moral Relativism and Moral Objectivity, 1996, Reasoning, Meaning, and Mind, 1999, Explaining Value and Other Essays in Moral Philosophy, 2000; editor: On Noam Chomsky, 1974, (with Donald Davidson) Semantics of Natural Language, 1971, (with Donald Davidson) The Logic of Grammar, 1975, Conceptions of the Human Mind, 1993. Mem.: Philosophy Sci. Soc., Am. Psychol. Soc., Cognitive Sci. Soc., Am. Philos. Assn. Home: 106 Broadmead St Princeton NJ 08540-7216 Office: Princeton Univ Dept Philosophy Princeton NJ 08544-1006 E-mail: harman@princeton.edu.

HARMAN, LISA ELAINE, special education educator; b. Harrisburg, Pa., May 28, 1965; d. Marlin Chester and Jean Elaine (Mentzer) H. BS in Edn., Lock Haven (Pa.) U., 1987. Elementary LD tchr. Harrisburg (Pa.) Sch. Dist., 1987—88; lng. support tchr. Dauphin County Tech. Sch., Harrisburg, 1988—. Mem. NEA, Pa. State Edn. Assn., DCTSEA. Home: 213 B Enola St Enola PA 17025-2603

HARMAN, NANCY JUNE, elementary education educator, principal; b. WaKeeney, Kans., June 23, 1954; d. Don Raymond and Ida Berdena (Hildebrand) Legere; m. Roger Dean Harman, May 24, 1975; children: Michael James, Jennifer Legere. BS in Elem. Edn., Ft. Hays State U., 1975, MS in Edn. Adminstrn., 1993. Cert. early childhood, elem. tchr., elem. adminstr., Kans., cert. early childhood generalist Nat. Bd. Cert. Tchrs. Tchr. Catherine Elem. Sch., Hays, Kans., 1975-76, Dodge Elem. Sch., Wichita, Kans., 1977-80, Franklin Elem. Sch., Wichita, 1981-82, Felten Mid. Sch., Hays, 1987-90; prin. O'Loughlin Elem. Sch., Hays, 1990-98, 1998—. Mem. nat. leadership team Operation Primary Phys. Sci., 1996—. Mem. com. Sternberg Discovery Rm., Hays, 1993-94; mem. Hays Book Guild, 1987—; past mem. bd. dirs. Hays Arts Coun. Recipient Presdl. award for excellence in math. and sci. tchg., 1997, Gov.'s award for tchg. excellence, 2000. Mem. ASCD, PEO, Nat. Coun. Tchrs. English, Kans. Reading Assn., Kans. Assn. Tchrs. English (state bd. dirs. 1993-96), Kans. Comm. Arts (stds. writers com.), Kans. Assn. Tchrs. Math., Phi Delta Kappa (pres. 1997—), Alpha Delta Kappa (pres. 1988-93). Presbyterian. Avocations: running, reading, collecting antiques. Home: 2306 Plum St Hays KS 67601-3035 Office: O Loughlin Elem Sch 1401 Hall St Hays KS 67601-3753

HARMAN, WILLARD NELSON, malacologist, educator; b. Geneva, NY, Apr. 20, 1937; s. Samuel Willard and Mary Nelson (Covert) H.; m. Susan Beth Mead, June 12, 1968 (div. 1980); children: Rebecca Mary, Willard Wade; m. Barbara Ann Stong, June 8, 1981; children: Jessica Mary, Samuel Willard. Student, Hobart Coll., 1954-55; BS, Coll. Environ. Sci. and Forestry, SUNY, 1965; PhD, Cornell U., 1968; postgrad., Marine Biol. Lab., Woods Hole, Mass., 1968. Asst. prof. SUNY, Oneonta, 1968-69, assoc. prof., 1969-76, prof. biology, 1976—2002, chmn. dept. biology, 1981-89, dir. Biol. Field Sta., 1989—, disting. svc. prof., 2002—. Resource advisor N.Y. State Dept. Environ. Conservation, Albany, 1980—. Contbr. articles to profl. jours. Rep. Otsego County Republican Com., N.Y., 1973-76; chmn. planning bd., Springfield, N.Y., 1984-96. Served with USN, 1956-61. Recipient Chancellor's award SUNY, 1974-75, Quality award EPA, 1989, Excellence award SUNY, 1990. Mem. Soc. Limnology and Oceanography, N.Am. Benthological Soc., Soc. for Exptl. and Descriptive Malacology, Am. Malacological Union, Otsego County Conservation Assn. (bd. dirs. 1970—, pres. 1974-78, 80-81, chmn. lake com. 1981—). Episcopalian. Avocations: sailing, fishing, scuba diving, skiing. Home: RR 2 Box 829 Cooperstown NY 13326-9327 Office: Biol Field Sta 5838 St Hwy 80 Cooperstown NY 13326-9330

HARMON, GEORGE MARION, academic administrator; b. Memphis, Aug. 12, 1934; s. George Marion and Madie P. (Foster) H.; m. Bessie W. Porter, Dec. 27, 1958; children: Nancy R., Mary K., Elizabeth T., George Marion III. BA, Rhodes Coll., 1956; MBA, Emory U., 1957; DBA, Harvard U., 1963. Market rsch. analyst Continental Oil Co., Houston, 1957; rsch. assoc. Harvard U., 1960-63; asst. prof. Coll. Bus. Adminstrn., dir. Salzberg Meml. Transp. Program Syracuse U., N.Y., 1963-66; sr. assoc. sys. econs. divsn. Planning Rsch. Corp., Washington, 1966-67; prof., chmn. dept econs. and bus. adminstrn., dir. continuing edn. program in econs. and bus. adminstrn. Rhodes Coll. (formerly Southwestern at Memphis), Memphis, 1967-74; prof., dean divsn. bus. and mgmt. W.Va. Coll. Grad. Studies, Charleston, 1974-75; prof., dean Sch. Bus. and Mgmt. Saginaw Valley State Coll., University Center, Mich., 1975-78; pres. Millsaps Coll., Jackson, Miss., 1978-2000, pres. emeritus, sr. counsel spl. projects, 2000—; mem. faculty fin. Sch. Banking of the South, La. State U., 1968-72; dir. Audio Visual Sys., Inc., Tenn., 1970-72; v.p., treas. Allen Industries, Inc., Tenn., 1970-72; co-founder, v.p. Computer Survey Sys., Inc., Tenn., 1972-73. Bd. dirs., chmn. exec. compensation com. MacCarty Farms, Inc., Magee, Miss., 1982-95; bd. dirs. Entex, Inc., Houston, 1981-99; mem. So. Regional Edn. Bd., Atlanta, 1994-98; bd. dirs. Union Planters Bank of Miss. Contbr. articles on bus. adminstrn. to profl. jours. Bd. dirs. Fayetteville-Manlius Cen. Sch. Dist., N.Y., 1961-63, John Houston Wear Found., Jackson, 1979-2000, Endora Welty Found., 1999—; trustee, chmn. pers. and labor rels. com. Saginaw Osteo. Hosp., 1977-78; bd. dirs. Jackson Symphony Orch. Assn., 1981-85, Miss. Opera Assn., 1981-86; chmn. So. Colls. and Univs. Union, 1983-88, Miss. Found. Ind. Colls., 1982; univ. senate United Meth. Ch., 1990-2000; comm. and sec. Jackson Internat. Airport Authority, 1991-97; chmn., bd. dirs. Jackson Med. Edn. Dist., 1998-2000; bd. dirs. Cath. Charities of Miss., 2002—, Madison County Libr. Found., 2002—, St. Catherine's Village Retirement Ctr. Found., 2002—. Mem. NCAA (coun. 1986-92), Jackson C. of C. (bd. dirs. 1981-84), Newcomen Soc. Miss. (pres. 2001-, chmn. 2001-), Soc. Internat. Bus. Fellows, Jackson Country Club, Univ. Club, Capitol City Club, Harvard Club (N.Y.C.), Rotary, Phi Beta Kappa, Beta Gamma Sigma, Omicron Delta Kappa, Kappa Sigma (Pres.'s Commn. 2000—). Roman Catholic. Home: 104 Adderbury Ct Ridgeland MS 39157-8709 Office: 210 E Capitol St Ste 1088 Jackson MS 39201-2306 Fax: 601-914-3783. E-mail: harmon@millsaps.edu.

HARMON, HEATHER CATHARINE, elementary school educator; b. Pottstown, Pa., May 29, 1967; d. John David and Rebekah Ann (Voll) Keeney; m. Timothy James Harmon, Oct. 28, 1989; 1 child, Shawn Keeney. AA, Southea. C.C., Keokuk, Iowa, 1987; BA, U. No. Iowa, 1989, 92. Lead tchr. Aliber Child Devel. Ctr., Des Moines, 1989-90; lang. arts instr./tutor U. No. Iowa for Urban Edn., Waterloo, Iowa, 1990-91; student asst./processor U. No. Iowa Curriculum Lab., Cedar Falls, Iowa, 1991-92; substitute tchr. Mid-Cen. Coop., Platte, S.D., 1992-93; tchr. 5th grade St. Joseph's Indian Sch., Chamberlain, S.D., 1993—. Student govt. rep. Southea. C.C., 1986-87. Mem. Nat. Coun. Social Studies, Nat. Mid. Sch. Assn. Mem. United Ch. of Christ. Avocations: travel, studying other cultures, reading, art, family activities. Office: St Joseph's Indian Sch PO Box 89 Chamberlain SD 57325-0089 Home: PO Box 400 Kimball SD 57355-0400

HARMON, KAY YVONNE, elementary education educator; b. Albert Lea, Minn., Dec. 12, 1942; d. Melvin Harold and Bertha Loretta (Sorensen) Vogelsang; m. Perry Dean Harmon, Aug. 14, 1971; children: Kristine Kay, Phillip Dean. BA, Luther Coll., 1963; BS, U. Minn., 1966. Tchr. elem. Grand Meadow (Minn.) Pub. Sch., 1963-65; tchr. secondary art edn. Little

Falls (Minn.) Pub. Sch., 1966-68; secondary art tchr. Robinsdale Pub. Sch., New Hope, Minn., 1968-73; arts and crafts leader Crystal (Minn.) Park and Recreation, summer 1969; dir. chpt. I, art secondary tchr. Ulen (Minn.)-Hitterdal Pub. Sch., 1982—. Instr. Community Edn., Ulen, 1986-88, Hawley, Minn., 1987-88, 91. Adult leader Eglon Hawks 4-H Club, 1984-93; mem. Hawley Art Show Com., 1987—, treas., 1999—; mem. Hawley Friends of Fine Arts, 1989-99, sec.-treas., 1991-96. Mem. ASCD, NEA, Nat. Art Educators Assn., Minn. Edn. Assn., Art Educators Minn., Minn. Alliance for Arts, Ulen-Hitterdal Edn. Assn. (pres. 1990, treas. 1996—, membership chair 1997—), Alpha Delta Kappa (chpt. chaplain 1996-98, chpt. rec. sec. 1994-96). Methodist. Avocations: reading, drawing, bowling, golf, painting. Home: 26258 28th Ave S Hawley MN 56549-9161 Office: Ulen-Hitterdal Pub Sch PO Box 389 Ulen MN 56585-0389

HARMON, LELIA TODD, elementary school educator; b. Phenix City, Ala., Oct. 16, 1948; d. Joe Nathan and Lillie (Mitchell) Todd; m. Robert Joseph Harmon, June 10, 1972; children: Jahbaree Atu, Ajani Jaha, Akilah Jaha, Jendayi Atu, Adeleke Jaha. BS in Elem. Edn., Morris Brown Coll., Atlanta, 1972; MS in Elem. Edn., NYU, 9176. Cert. tchr., Ga. Lead tchr. Tremont Crotona DAy CAre, Bronx, N.Y., 1972-76; elem. tchr. Atlanta Pub. Schs., 1978—. Sunday sch. mem. Cascade United Meth. Ch., Atlanta, mem. gospel choir. Named Tchr. of Yr., E.L. Connally Elem. Sch., Atlanta, 1985, Mother of Yr. award Southlake Mall, Morrow, Ga., 1986. Mem. Am. Fedn. Tchrs., Ga. Fedn. Tchrs., Atlanta Fedn. Tchrs. Democrat. Avocations: sewing, bicycling, jogging, reading, crafts. Home: 115 Princeton Trce Fayetteville GA 30214-3440

HARMON, NANCY JEAN, elementary school educator; b. Rockford, Ill., Apr. 21, 1946; d. Wayne Walter and Cecilia Marie (Wasileski) Crotzer; m. John Edmund Harmon, June 13, 1970. BA, Monmouth Coll., 1968; cert., Nat. Coll. Edn., 1974; MA, Roosevelt U., 1985. Tchr. 4th grade Sch. Dist. #54, Schaumburg, Ill., 1968—. Leader Girl Scouts Am., Schaumburg, 1968-70; chmn. Crusade of Mercy, Schaumburg, 1980-92. Recipient Outstanding Educator award Schaumburg Jaycees, 1972; named Tchr. of Yr., Aldrin Sch. PTA, 1993. Mem. NEA, Coun. for Exceptional Children, Schaumburg Ednl. Assn., Delta Kappa Gamma. Avocations: stained glass artist, race walker, calligraphy artist. Home: 496 Sheridan Ln Schaumburg IL 60193-2928 Office: Sch Dist 54 524 E Schaumburg Rd Schaumburg IL 60194-3597

HARMON, PATRICIA MARIE, special education educator; b. Bklyn., May 16, 1942; d. Richard Francis and Rita Ann (Baker) Sullivan; m. James Floyd Harmon Jr., June 30, 1984. BS, Molloy Coll. for Women, 1972; cert. in spl. edn., SUNY, Brookville, 1978. Cert. tchr., spl. edn. tchr., N.Y., Va. Tchr. Long Beach (N.Y.) Cath. Sch., 1960-65, St. Martin's Parish Sch., Amityville, N.Y., 1965-70, St. Ignatius Parish Sch., Hicksville, N.Y., 1970-75; adminstr. St. Joseph Parish, Monticello, N.Y., 1975-76, Holy Redeemer Parish, Freeport, N.Y., 1976-77; reading specialist Smithtown (N.Y.) Reading Clinic, 1977-78; tchr. spl. edn. St. Christopher's Home, Sea Cliff, N.Y., 1978-79, Buckingham Sch., Bayside, N.Y., 1979-81, Northampton (Va.) Pub. Schs., 1981—, Accomack County (Va.) Pub. Schs., 1987—. Presenter programs Rockville Centre Diocese, N.Y., 1970-75, religious cons. Girl Scouts, 1974. Coun. mem. Local Adv. Com., Nassau County, N.Y., 1970-73; phone counselor Birthright, Levittown, N.Y., 1975; founder Ea. Shore Va. chpt. Big Bros./Big Sisters, Belle Haven, 19860-91; active Right to Life Accomac County, 1988; mem. Richmond Diocese Pastoral Coun., 1984-86; mem. social action com. St. Peter's Ch., 1989—, parish sacristan, 1991—, mem. parish coun., 1992-94, retreat coord., 1999—, Bible study facilitator, 2000-, alt. presider, 2003-. Grantee Va. Dept. Social Svcs., 1989, Ea. Shore Soil and Conservation, Accomac, 1990, 91, 92, Delmarva Power, 1991. Mem. NEA, Va. Edn. Assn., Coun. Excpetional Children, Va. Coun. Learning Disabilities, Women's Aglow Fellowship (corr. sec.1991, v.p. 1993, pres. 1995—). Avocations: reading, sewing, gardening, canning, doll collecting. Office: Pungoteague Elem Sch RR 1 Box 409 Melfa VA 23410-9801

HARMON, WILLIAM FRANCIS, principal; b. Mpls., Jan. 17, 1947; s. Thomas Paul and Alta (Miller) H.; m. Marcia Braun Harmon, Aug. 15, 1968; children: William C., Eric P. BA, St. Thomas U., 1970; MS, Winona State U., 1978; EdD, Tex. A&M U., 1988. Cert. tchr., supt., Tex. English tchr. Bethlehem Acad., 1970-74, Cochrane-Fountain City Ind. Sch. Dist., 1974-78; libr. Medina Valley Ind. Sch. Dist., 1978-81, vice prin., 1984-88, prin., 1992-95; reading tchr. San Antonio Ind. Sch. Dist., 1982-84; vice prin. Schertz-Cibolo Consol. Ind. Sch. Dist., 1988-92; prin. alternative campus S.W. Ind. Sch. Dist., San Antonio, 1995—. Aquatics cons. City of Fairbault, Minn., 1970-74, City of Winona, Minn., 1974-78; speaker in field. Mem. Fiesta San Antonio Commn., 1984-92; vol. Am. Herat Assn., San Antonio, 1990—; Multiple Sclerosis Soc., San Antonio, 1983-86; block capt. Neighborhood Watch, San Antonio, 1990—; mem. dist. wide adv. com. Medine Valley Ind. Sch. Dist.; mem. Texas State Inprovement Initiatives. Recipient Appreciation plaque Office Edn. Assn. of Tex., 1981, Target 90/Goals for San Antonio, 1987, chpt. founder plaque Alamo City Rugby Football Club, 1983; U.S. Fed. Govt. grantee, 1978. Mem. Nat. Assn. Secondary Sch. Prins., Tex. Assn. Secondary Sch. Prins. (vice prin. of yr. 1990), Tex. Soc. Rugby Referees, South Tex. Mid. Sch. League, Harp & Shamrock Soc. (parade commr. 1984—), Police Activities League. Republican. Roman Catholic. Avocation: playing and refereeing rugby. Home: 7811 Braun Cir San Antonio TX 78250-2665 Office: SW Ind Sch Dist 11914 Dragon Ln San Antonio TX 78252-2612

HARMOND, RICHARD PETER, historian, educator; b. NYC, Mar. 19, 1929; s. William and Violet (Makein) H. BA, Fordham U., 1951; MA, Columbia U., 1954, PhD, 1966. Assoc. prof. history St. John's U., N.Y.C., 1957—. Co-author: Long Island as America, 1977, A History of Memorial Day: Unity, Discord and the Pursuit of Happiness, 2002; co-editor: Technology in the 20th Century, 1983, Biographical Dictionary of American and Canadian Naturalists and Environmentalists, 1997; assoc. editor L.I. Hist. Jour., 1989—2003, mem. editl. bd., 2003—; contbr. articles to profl. jours. With U.S. Army, 1951-53. Mem. Orgn. Am. Historians, Soc. History of Tech., Theodore Roosevelt Assn. (trustee 1994-97), Phi Alpha Theta (paper prize com. 1994-97). Office: St John's U Hist Dept Jamaica NY 11439-0001

HARNER, JAMES LOWELL, English language educator; b. Washington, Ind., Mar. 24, 1946; s. Thomas Lloyd and Ruth Ellen (Clark) H.; m. Darinda Jane Wilson, Aug. 26, 1967; 1 child, Lenée Francais. BS magna cum laude, Ind. State U., 1968; MA, U. Ill., 1970, PhD, 1972. Prof. English Bowling Green (Ohio) State U., 1971-88, Tex. A&M U., College Station, 1988—. Author: Literary research Guide, 1989 (Choice Mag. Outstanding Acad. Book 1990), 4th edit., 2002, English Renaissance Prose Fiction, 1978, 3d edit., 1992, On Compiling an Annotated Bibliography, 1983-2000, Samuel Daniel and Michael Drayton, 1980, Directory of Scholarly Presses, 1991, (online database) World Shakespeare Bibliography Online, 1996—, (Besterman medal 1997, Besterman/McColvin medal, 2001); editor World Shakespeare Bibliography, 1988—, Essential Bibliographies Series, 1985-96; mem. editl. bd. Seventeenth-Century News, 1973—, Lit. Rsch., 1984—, Shakespeare Yearbook, 1992—, Shakespeare Quar., 1993—. Mem. MLA, The Bibliog. Soc., Shakespeare Assn. of Am., Internat. Shakespeare Assn., Bibliog. Soc. of Am. Democrat. Presbyterian. Avocations: book collecting, travel, manuscript collecting. Home: 4736 Stonebriar Cir College Station TX 77845 Office: World Shakespeare Bibliog Tex A&m U Dept English College Station TX 77843-4227

HARNER, MICHAEL JAMES, anthropologist, educator, author; b. Washington, Apr. 27, 1929; s. Charles Emory and Virginia (Paxton) H.; m. June Knight (Kocher), 1951; children: Teresa J., James E.; m. Sandra Ferial (Dickey), 1966. AB, U. Calif., Berkeley, 1953, PhD, 1963, Calif. Inst. of Integral Studies, 2003. Asst. prof. Ariz. State U., 1958—61; from sr. mus. anthropologist to assoc. rsch. anthropologist and asst. dir., Hearst Mus. Anthropology U. Calif., Berkeley, 1961—66; from vis. assoc. prof. to assoc. prof. Columbia U., N.Y.C., 1966—70; from assoc. prof. to prof. grad. faculty New Sch. Social Rsch., N.Y.C., 1970—87, chmn. dept. anthropology, 1973—77; internat. tchr. shamanism, 1977—; founder, dir. Ctr. for Shamanic Studies, Norwalk, Conn., 1979—87; founder, pres., trustee Found. for Shamanic Studies, Mill Valley, Calif., 1985—. Field rsch. Harvard U. Upper Gila expdn., 1948, Upper Amazon Basin, 1956-57, 60-61, 64, 69, 73, Western North Am., 1951-53, 59, 65, 76, 78, Lapland, 1983, 84, Can. Arctic, 1987; vis. assoc. prof. U. Calif., Berkeley, 1971, 72, vis. prof., 1975; vis. assoc. prof. Yale U., 1970; co-organizer first Internat. Congress on Shamanism, Moscow, 1999. Author: Population Pressure and the Social Evolution of Agriculturalists, 1970, The Jivaro: People of the Sacred Waterfalls, 1972, 2d edit., 1984, Music of the Jivaro of Ecuador, 1972, The Ecological Basis for Aztec Sacrifice, 1977, The Way of the Shaman, 1980, 3d edit., 1990; co-author: Cannibal, 1979, Core Practices in the Shamanic Treatment of Illness, 1999; editor: Hallucinogens and Shamanism, 1973. Fellow Social Sci. Rsch. Coun., Doherty Found., Am. Mus. Nat. History fellow. Fellow AAAS, Am. Anthrop. Assn., Royal Anthrop. Inst. G.B. and Ireland; fellow N.Y. Acad. Scis. (life, co-chmn. anthropology sect. 1980-81); mem. Am. Ethnol. Soc., Soc. Am. Archaeology, Soc. Ethnohistory, Internat. Transpersonal Assn. (bd. dirs. 1982-85, 89-91), Assn. for the Anthropology of Consciousness, Xat Medicine Men's Soc., Inst. Andean Studies, Explorers Club. Office: Found Shamanic Studies PO Box 1939 Mill Valley CA 94942-1939 E-mail: michaelharner@shamanism.org.

HARP, ROSE MARIE, secondary education educator; b. Austin, Tex., Dec. 25, 1937; d. William Bryan and Regina Mary (Korioth) Cullen; m. Andrew Howell Bone, Jan. 19, 1957 (div. Jan. 1971); 1 child, Wylie Andrew; m. James Franklin Harp, Feb. 18, 1971. BS, No. Mich. U., 1961; MAIS, U. Tex., 1980. Sec. Dept. of Def., Nouasseur AB, Morocco, 1957-59; tchr. St. Xavier's Sch., Denison, Tex., 1962-63, Sumter (S.C.) Ind. Sch. Dist., 1963-66, Dept. of Def., Kadena, Okinawa, 1967-68; tchr. H.S., dept. chair Richardson (Tex.) Ind. Sch. Dist., 1976—. Mock trial sponsor Richardson Ind. Sch. Dist., 1979—, pre law club sponsor, 1979—. Mem. LWV, Richardson, 1988—. Recipient First Peace Inst. award, 1992, Leon Jaworski award State Bar Tex., 1994; named Most Influential Tchr., 1991, 96, 97. Mem. Nat. Coun. for Social Studies, Tex. Coun. for Social Studies (bd. dirs.), Richardson Coun. for Social Studies (pres. 1991-92). Roman Catholic. Avocations: ikebana, biking. Home: 7315 Larchview Dr Dallas TX 75254-2726 Office: Richardson Ind Sch Dist 300 S Greenville Ave Richardson TX 75081-4105

HARPER, BARBARA CLARA, counselor, educational program administrator, counselor; b. NYC, Aug. 9, 1932; d. James Gullins and Irene Christine (Robinson) H.; m. William C. Booth, Apr. 24, 1951 (div. 1958); 1 child, James Alan; m. Washington Mays, Jan. 1, 1959 (div. 1987). AA, Mattaluck Community Coll., 1978; BS, N.H. Coll., 1987, MS, 1989. Cert. profl. counselors inc. Conn. Bd., lic. profl. counselor, foster mother. Gen. office staff Avnet Electronics, Bronx, NY, 1955-59; sec., gen office staff PHA, Waterbury, Conn., 1959-64; pers. interviewer Scovill Mfg. Co., Waterbury, 1964-66; caseworker, ctr. dir. New Opportunities for Waterbury, 1966-68; coord. Waterbury Cmty. Sch., 1969-94; clinician Child Guidance Clinic Greater Waterbury, Inc., 1963—. Part-time instr. Displaced Housewives and Work Incentive Programs, 1975-80; mem. clerical staff Mattaluck C.C., Waterbury, 1974-80. Mem. Drug Free Sch., 1984; vol. leader Coop. Ext. Svc., USDA 4-H, 1984-91; com. leader Boy Scouts Am., 1974-76, Girl Scouts, 1962; sec. Northeastern Heights Coun., 1971, The Promoters Club of Wilson Sch., 1980; bd. dir. NOW Inc., 1964; vol. organist, choir dir. St. Cecilia's Ch., 1960. With USAF, 1950-52. Recipient Silver Clover award Coop. Extension Svc., U. Conn. 1989, Cert. of Appreciation award Youth Svc. Bur., Dedicated Svc. Appreciation award Boy Scouts of Am. Troop 223, 1975. Mem.: Conn. Assn. Marriage and Family Counselors (sec. 1998—99, pres. 2001—02), Nat. Polit. Congress of Black Women (sec. 1998—99, pres.-elect 1999—2001, pres. 2001—02), Long Hill Cmty. Club (sec.), Waterbury Black Dem. Club. Democrat. Home and Office: 165 Traverse St Waterbury CT 06704-3229

HARPER, DOROTHY GLEN, education educator; b. San Antonio, June 25, 1927; d. Jack Wallace and Bess Mae (Hopkins) Douglas; children: Nancy Gail, John Douglas; m. Orville Earl Harper, Apr. 2, 1975. A.A., Cisco Jr. Coll., 1978; Ed.B., Hardin-Simmons U., 1981, MEd, 1983. Cert. tchr., Tex. Mem. faculty Hardin Simmons U., Abilene, Tex., 1981-98. Vice pres. Taylor-Jones Haskell Counties Med. Aux., Abilene, 1978, treas., 1980, mem. nominating com., 1985, chmn. scholarship com., 1987-92; active Abilene Met. Ballet, 1980-83; co-chair Southwestern Regional Ballet Assn. Festival, 1993; bd. dirs. Abilene Ballet Theatre. Mem. Museums of Abilene (charter), Alpha Chi, Kappa Delta Pi, Pi Gamma Mu, Phi Delta Kappa. Republican. Methodist. Avocations: horseback riding, swimming, reading. Home: 38 Lytle Pl Abilene TX 79602-7424 Office: Hardin-Simmons Univ Abilene TX 79698

HARPER, JANE WALKER, educational administrator; b. Warren, Ohio, Aug. 10, 1946; d. Thomas C. and Julia M. (Reyes) Walker; m. Elmer A. Harper, June 20, 1970; children: Allison, Kasie, Timothy. BA, Stetson U., 1968; MA, Rollins Coll., 1976; EdS, Stetson U., 1994. Cert. elem tchr., guidance counselor, reading tchr., ednl. leadership. Tchr. Lake County Schs., Tavares, Fla., program specialist. Presenter in field. Mem. ASCD, Internat. Reading Assn., Fla. Reading Assn., Fla. Assn. State and Fed. Ednl. Program Adminstrs., Reading Suprs. Fla., Lake County Reading Assn., Phi Delta Kappa. Home: 27839 Lisa Dr Tavares FL 32778-9706

HARPER, JANET SUTHERLIN LANE, retired educational administrator, writer; b. La Grange, Ga., Apr. 2, 1940; d. Clarence Wilner and Imogene (Thompson); m. William Sterling Lane, June 28, 1964, (div. Jan. 1981); children: David Alan, Jennifer Ruth; m. John F. Harper, June 9, 1990. BA in English and Applied Music, LaGrange Coll., 1961; postgrad., Auburn U., 1963; MA in Journalism, U. Ga., Athens, 1979. Music and drama critic The Brunswick News, Brunswick, Ga., 1979-99; info. asst. Glynn County Schs., Brunswick, 1979-82; adj. prof. Brunswick Coll., Ga., 1981-87; dir. pub. info. and publs. Glynn County Schs., Brunswick, 1982-99, dir. grant writing and rsch., 1999-2000; ret., 2000. Contbg. editor Ga. Jour., 1981-84; editor, writer GAEL Conf. Jours., 1987-89. Mem. Golden Isles Arts and Humanities Bd., 1997—2000, sec., 1998—2000; organist St. Simons United Meth. Ch., 1981—; bd. dirs. Jekyll Island Music Theatre, 1994—2001, pres., 1994—97; bd. dirs. Am. Cancer Soc., 1998—2001. Recipient award of excellence in sch. and cmty. rels. Ga. Bd. Edn., 1984, 92, Edn. Leadership award, Ga., 1989, disting. svc. award Ga. Sch. Pub. Rels. Assn., 1991. Mem.: Ga. Sch. Pub. Rels. Assn. (exec. bd. 1981—87, pres. 1985—86, exec. bd. 1996—2000), Brunswick Press-Advt. Club (award of excellence in pub. rels. 1992), Ga. Assn. Ednl. Leaders (media rels. 1983—2001), Nat. Sch. Pub. Rels. Assn. (Golden Achievement award 1985, 2 awards 1988, 1990, 3 awards 1991, 1992, 1994, 1998), Mozart Soc. E-mail: harperss@bellsouth.net.

HARPER, KAREN BEIDELMAN, secondary special education educator; b. Des Moines, June 27, 1952; d. Oliver Jason and Luana Margery (Wills) Beidelman; m. Doyle Ray Harper, Aug. 6, 1977; children: Jenny, Abby. B in music edn., Drake U., 1974; MM in Music Therapy, Loyola U., 1977; cert. in elem. edn., U. Iowa, 1990; cert. in spl. edn., Iowa State U., 1998. Cert. tchr. Iowa; cert. music tchr. Iowa; cert. spl. edn. tchr.; registered music therapist; cert. infant edn. and massage therapist. Elem. tchr. J.J. Finley Elem. Sch., Gainesville, Fla., 1977-78, W.H. Beasley Mid. Sch., Palatka, Fla., 1978-79, Lincoln Elem. Sch., Iowa City, 1991, Community Edn. Ctr. Secondary Sch., Iowa City, 1991-92, St. Anthony Sch., Des Moines, 1992-95; substitute tchr., 1996-97; spl. edn. tchr. grades 6-8 Panorama (Iowa) Cmty. Schs., Panora, Iowa, 1997—2003, Des Moines Pub. Schs., 2003—. Child life specialist Schoitz Med. Ctr., Waterloo, Iowa, 1980-83; activity coord. The Carney Hosp., Boston, 1984-85; child life coord. South Shore Hosp., Weymouth, Mass., 1985-88; infant massage instr. Infant Sensory Enrichment Edn., Grimes, Iowa, 1984—, parent-infant instr., 1984—. Recipient Outstanding Svc. award Beta Phi Zeta, 1974. Mem. Internat. Assn. Reading, Nat. Mid. Sch. Assn., Pi Lambda Theta, Mu Phi Epsilon (sec., historian 1973-74). Avocations: reading, playing piano, sewing, cooking. Home: 716 Dolan Dr Grimes IA 50111-1085

HARPER, SANDRA STECHER, university administrator; b. Dallas, Sept. 21, 1952; d. Lee Roy and Carmen (Crespo) Stecher; m. Dave Harper, July 6, 1974; children: Justin, Jonathan. BS in Edn., Tex. Tech. U., 1974; MS, U. N. Tex., 1979, PhD, 1985; grad. mgmt. devel. program, Harvard U., 1992. Speech/reading tchr. Nazareth (Tex.) High Sch., 1974-75; speech/English tchr. Collinsville (Tex.) High Sch., 1975-77, Pottsboro (Tex.) High Sch., 1977-79; instr. comm. Austin Coll., Sherman, Tex., 1980-82; rsch. asst. U. N. Tex., Denton, 1982-84; vis. instr. comm. Austin Coll., Sherman, 1985; from asst. prof. to assoc. prof. comms. McMurry Coll., Abilene, Tex., 1985-95; dean Coll. Arts and Scis. McMurry U., Abilene, Tex., 1990-95; v.p. for acad. affairs Oklahoma City U., 1995-98; asst. dir. NEH univ. core curriculum project McMurry U., Abilene, Tex.; provost, v.p. for acad. affairs Tex. A&M, Corpus Christi, 1998—, prof. comms., 1998—. CIES mentor for Russian adminstr. from Moscow State U., Ulyanovsk, 1995-96; mem. adv. bd. Coll. Am. Indian Devel., 1995-98; critic judge Univ. Interscholastic League, Austin, 1980-93; mem. adv. bd. Univ. Rsch. Consortium, Abilene, 1990-95; mem. formula adv. com., mem. instrn. and operation formula study com. Tex. Higher Edn. Coordinating Bd., 1999—, mem. adv. com. AA in Tchg., 2003—; mem. working group Am. Assn. State Colls. and Univs. Am. Democracy Project, 2002—. Contbr. articles to profl. jours.; author: To Serve the Present Age, 1990; co-author U.S. Dept. Edn. Title III Grant; editl. bd. Soc. for the Advancement of Mgmt. Jour., 1999—. Planner TEAM Abilene, 1991; del. Tex. Commn. for Libr. and Info. Svcs., Austin, 1991; chair Abilene Children Today: Life and Cmty. Skills Task Force, 1994-95; del. Oklahoma City Ednl. TV Consortium, 1997-98; bd. dirs. South Tex. Pub. Broadcasting, 1998—, Leadership Corpus Christi; mem. gov.'s exec. devel. program Class XVIII, LBJ Sch. Pub. Affairs, U. Tex., Austin, 1999, S. Tex. Regional Leaders Forum, 2001-02. Named Outstanding Faculty Mem., McMurry U., 1988, Outstanding Adminstr., 1993; Media Rsch. scholar Ctr. for Population Options, 1989; recipient Corpus Christi YWCA Women in Careers Secondary Edn. award, 2000. Mem. Nat. Comm. Assn., Am. Assn. Higher Edn., Tex. Pub. Univ. Chief Acad. Officers Assn. (v.p. 2003—). Democrat. Roman Catholic. Office: Tex A&M 6300 Ocean Dr Corpus Christi TX 78412-5503 E-mail: sharper@falcon.tamucc.edu.

HARPER, SHERYL ANN, music educator; b. Fernandina, Fla., Dec. 2, 1956; d. Willis Austin and Betty Sue (Bryant) Boyett; m. Mark Elliott Harper, Feb. 18, 1979; 1 child, Alicia. BA in Music, Palm Beach Atlantic Coll., 1978; postgrad. studies in music edn., U. N. Fla., 1980-83. Cert. music tchr., Fla. Music tchr. Nassau County Sch. Bd., Fernandina, Fla., 1980—. Music dir. N. 14th St. Bapt. Ch., Fernandina, 1980-87; children's choir coord.,Springhill Bapt. Ch., Fernandina, 1987—, choir, soloist, ensemble dir., 1987—; dir. alumni madrigal Fernandina Beach H.S., Fla., 1993. Mem. Nassau County Music Educators (chairperson 1988—). Democrat. Baptist. Avocations: mothering, teaching singing, sewing, cooking, singing. Home: 1335 Greenberry Rd Fernandina Beach FL 32034-7256 Office: PO Box 48 Yulee FL 32041-0048

HARPER, SHIRLEY FAY, nutritionist, educator, consultant, lecturer; b. Auburn, Ky., Apr. 23, 1943; d. Charles Henry and Annabelle (Gregory) Belcher; m. Robert Vance Harper, May 19, 1973 (dec. Mar. 2000); children: Glenda, Debra, Teresa, Suzanna, Cynthia. BS, Western Ky. U., 1966, MS, 1982. Cert. nutritionist and lic. dietitian, Ky. Dir. dietetics Logan County Hosp., Russellville, Ky., 1965-80; cons. Western State Hosp., Hopkinsville, Ky., 1983-84, instnl. dietetic adminstr., 1984-88; dietitian Rivendell Children's Psychiat. Hosp., Bowling Green, Ky., 1988-90; instr. nutrition Western Ky. U., Bowling Green, 1990-92. Cons. Auburn (Ky.) Nursing Ctr., 1976-95, Belle Meade Home, Greenville, Ky., 1980—, Brookfield Manor, Hopkinsville, Ky., 1983—, Sparks Nursing Ctr., Central City, Ky., 1983—, Muhlenberg Cmty. Hosp., Greenville, 1989-2000, Russellville (Ky.) Health Care Manor, 1978-83, 92—, Westlake Cumberland Hosp., Columbia, Ky., 1993—, Franklin-Simpson Meml. Hosp., Franklin, Ky., 1993—, Lakeview Health Care Ctr., Morgantown, Ky., 2001—, Trigg County Personal Care Home, Cadiz, 2002—, Gainsville Manor, Hopkinsville, 2002—; nutrition instr. Madisonville (Ky.) Cmty. Coll., 1995-98. Mem. regional bd. dirs. ARC of Ky., Frankfort, 1990-96; vice chair ARC of Logan County, 1992-93, chmn., 1993-96, 97—; bd. dirs. Logan County ARC United Way, 1993—; co-chair adv. coun. devel. disabilities Lifeskills, 1992-93, adv. coun. Lifeskills Residential Living Group Home, 1993-2000, human rights adv. coun., 1994-2000; chair Let's Build our Future Campaign; nutrition del. Citizen Am. Program to USSR, 1990; adv. chair for vocat. edn., Russellville; mem. adv. coun. for home econs. and family living, We. Ky. U., 1990-93; bd. dirs. ARC of Logan County for United Way, 1993—; del. 24th Internat. Congress on Arts and Comm., Oxford (Eng.) U., 1997. Recipient Outstanding Svc. award Am. Dietetic Assn. Found., 1993, Outstanding Svc. award Barren River Mental Health-Mental Retardation Bd., 1987, Svc. Appreciation award Logan-Russellville Assn. for Retarded Citizens, 1987, Internat. Woman of Yr. award for contribution to Nutrition and Humanity, Internat. Biographical Assn., 1993-94, World Lifetime Achievement award Am. Biographical Inst., 1995; inaugurated Lifetime Dep. Gov., Am. Biographical Rsch. Bd., 1995, Pres.'s award ARC of Logan County, 1996, award of excellence Oxford, Eng. Internat. Congress on Arts and Comm., Internat. Sash of Acad., Am. Biograph. Inst., 1997. Mem. Am. Dietetic Assn., Nat. Nutrition Network, Ky. Dietetic Assn. (pres. Western dist. 1976-77, Outstanding Dietitian award 1984), Bowling Green-Warren County Nutrition Coun., Nat. Ctr. for Nutrition and Dietetics (charter), Ky. Nutrition Coun., Logan County Home Economist Club (sec. 1994-95, 1999-2000, v.p. 1995-96, 2000-01, pres. 1996-97, 2001—), Internat. Biog. Assn., Internat. Platform Assn., Diabetes Care and Edn., Dietitians in Nutrition Support, Cons. Dietitians in Health Care, Phi Upsilon Omicron (pres. Beta Delta alumni chpt. 1994-96, Outstanding Alumni award 1997). Avocations: music, drawing and art, poetry, reading, cake decorating. Home and Office: 443 Hopkinsville Rd Russellville KY 42276-1286 E-mail: harp299@bellsouth.net.

HARPHAM, EDWARD JOHN, political science educator, dean, writer, research; b. Montreal, Que., Can., June 16, 1951; arrived in U.S.A., 1952, naturalized, 1957; s. John and Jean Harpham; m. Wendy Schlessel, Oct. 18, 1954; children: Rebecca, Jessica, William. BA in Polit. Sci., Pa. State U., 1973; MA in Govt., Cornell U., 1976, PhD in Govt., 1980. Vis. asst. prof. polit. sci. U. Houston, 1978-81; asst. prof. govt. and polit. economy U. Tex. at Dallas, Richardson, 1981-86, coll. master Sch. Social Scis., 1986-89, assoc. prof. govt. and polit. economy, 1986-2001, prof., 2001—. Dir. Collegium V Honors Program, U. Tex. at Dallas, 1998—, assoc. dean undergrad. edn., 1998—, Andrew R. Cecil lectr., 1994. Author: Disenchanted Realists, 1985, Rhythms of American Politics, 1998, We the People: Texas Edition, 2001, 2d edit., 2003; editor: Political Economy of Public Policy, 1982, Attack on the Welfare State, 1984, Texas at the Crossroads, 1987, John Locke's Two Treatises of Government: New Interpretations, 1992, Texas Politics: A Reader, 1997, 2d edit., 1998; contbr. articles to profl. jours. Coach youth soccer Dallas North Soccer Assn., Richardson, 1992-98; coach youth softball Spring Valley Athletic Assn., Richardson, 1993-2000, coach youth basketball, 1995-98; coach youth volleyball Garland Volleyball Assn., 2003. Fellow Ctr. for Study of Am. Polit. Economy, 1977, resident fellow Inst. for Humane Studies, 1977-78.

Mem. Am. Polit. Sci. Assn., History of Econ. Thought Soc., David Hume Soc., Southwestern Polit. Sci. Assn. (v.p. 1993-94, pres. 2001-02), Golden Key (hon.), Phi Eta Sigma, Phi Kappa Phi, Phi Beta Kappa. Avocations: music, history. Office: U Tex-Dallas PO Box 830688 Richardson TX 75083-0688

HARR, ALMA ELIZABETH TAGLIABUE, nursing educator; b. Glen Cove, N.Y., Apr. 11, 1927; d. Frederick Edwin and Lillian T. (Spittel) Tagliabue; (widowed 1981); m. Kenneth E. Harr, Nov. 21, 1962; 1 child, Kendal Elizabeth; stepchildren: Rose Marie Torreano, Kathleen Dobson. Student, Renssalaer Poly. Inst., 1947; RN, N.Y. Hosp. Sch. Nursing, 1950; BSN, Cornell U., 1950; MA, Columbia U., 1955; cert. in maternal nutrition, U. N.C., 1982. Cert. pub. health nurse, sch. nurse tchr., childbirth educator. Asst. head nurse Cornell U.-N.Y. Hosp., N.Y.C., 1950-51, head nurse, 1951-52; asst. DON, dir. nursing and patient edn. Trudeau Sanitorium, N.Y., 1952-54; instr. Bklyn. Coll., 1955-63, lectr., 1963-65, asst. divsn. chmn. dept. nursing, 1961-65; assoc. prof. Nassau Community Coll., Garden City, N.Y., 1965-69, prof., 1969-91, prof. emerita, 1991—. Contbr. articles to profl. jours. Mem. nurses adv. com. March of Dimes, 1969-91, chmn. nurses adv. com., 1981-88, mem. profl. com., 1981-88. Mem. ANA, Am. Soc. Psychoprophylactic Obstetrics, Nassau Community Coll. Fedn. Tchrs., Nat. League Nursing, Pi Lambda Theta, Kappa Delta Pi, Sigma Theta Tau. Republican. Episcopalian. Avocations: reading, swimming, walking, knitting, needlepoint, crocheting. Home: Shell Point Island 1106-1108 Cameo Ct Fort Myers FL 33908-1601

HARRE, ALAN FREDERICK, academic administrator; b. Nashville, Ill., June 12, 1940; s. Adolph Henry and Hilda (Vogt) Harre; m. Diane Carole Mack, Aug. 9, 1964; children: Andrea Lyn, Jennifer Leigh, Eric Stephen. BA, Concordia Sr. Coll., 1962; MDiv, Concordia Sem., St. Louis, 1966; MA, Presbyn. Sch. Christian Edn., Richmond, Va., 1967; PhD, Wayne State U., 1976. Ordained to ministry Luth. Ch. Asst. pastor St. James Luth. Ch. Grosse Pointe, Grosse Pointe Farms, Mich., 1967-73; asst. prof. theology Concordia Tchrs. Coll., Seward, Nebr., 1973-78, assoc. prof., 1978-84, asst. to pres., 1981, dean student affairs, 1982-84, acting pres., 1984; pres. Concordia Coll., St. Paul, 1984-88, Valparaiso (Ind.) U., 1988—. Author: (book) Close the Back Door, 1984. Bd. dirs. Associated New Am. Colls., Cmty. Found. N.W. Ind., Inc., N.W. Ind. Forum, Ind. Campus Compact, Independent Coll. Ind. Found., Luth. Ednl. Conf. Am., Luther Inst., Christmas in April, Porter County Cmty. Foun., Cmty. Devel. Corp., Quality Life Coun., Gary Accord; mem. adv. bd. YMCA; mem. Pres.'s Coun. Mid-Continent Conf. Recipient Disting. Cmty. Leader award, 1998, Sam Walton Bus. Leader award, 1999, Crystal Globe award, 1999. Mem.: Ind. Soc. Chgo., Ind. Conf. Higher Edn., Am. Assn. Higher Edn., Union League Club Chgo. Home: 3900 Hemlock Dr Valparaiso IN 46383-1814 Office: Valparaiso U Office of the President Valparaiso IN 46383-9978 E-mail: alan.harre@valpo.edu.

HARRELL, CONSTANCE LORESS, elementary education educator; b. N.Y.C., Aug. 27, 1949; d. Clearance Carter and Dorethea (Branch) Thomas; m. Robert Harrell, Sr., Oct. 25, 1969; children: Robert Jr., Terrance, Justin. BA, William Paterson Coll., 1972; MA, Montclair State U., 1985. Cert. elem. edn., tchr. handicapped, learning disabilities tchr. cons. Tchr. elem. Pub. Sch. No. 25, Paterson, N.J., 1972-80, basic skills instr., 1980-84; supplementary instr. Pub. Sch. No. 2, 9, 12, 24 and Rosa Parks, Paterson, N.J., 1984-88; tchr. cons. learning disabilities Eastside High Sch., Paterson, N.J., 1988—. Learning cons. Dept. of Corrections, N.J., 1991—; chair N.J. Pub. Health Com. of Secondary & Elem. Schs. Pers. chairperson YWCA, Paterson, 1990—; sec. 4-Ward Alliance, Paterson, 1991—; bd. dirs. TLP Performing Arts Ctr., Gilmore Meml. Learning Ctr. Mem. ASCD, N.J. Assn. Learning Cons., Orton Dyslexia Soc., PTA of Rosa Parks (treas. 1989-91). Avocations: needlepoint, reading, arts and crafts. Home: 560 Broadway Paterson NJ 07514-2518 Office: Eastside High Sch 150 Park Ave Paterson NJ 07501-2355

HARRELL, FLORENCE LOUISE, elementary education educator; b. Eure, N.C., Mar. 24, 1954; d. Lillian and Florence (Nowell Morings; m. Robert Leon Harrell Jr., Aug. 15, 1977; 1 child, Kenya LaCole. BS, Norfolk State U., Va., 1976; MEd, U. Va., 1987. Tchr. Gates County Schs., Gatesville, N.C., 1976-79, Hertford County Schs., Ahoskie, N.C., 1979-82, Suffolk (Va.) City Schs., 1982—. Bd. dirs. Vacation Bible Sch., Drum Hill, N.C., 1986. Mem. Edn. Assn. of Suffolk (bldg. rep. 1987—). Democrat. Pentacostal Ch. Avocations: reading the bible, cooking, tropical fish. Home: 410 White Oak Rd Eure NC 27935-9731 Office: Robertson Elem Sch 132 Robertson St Suffolk VA 23438-9705

HARRELSON, CLYDE LEE, retired secondary school educator; b. Baton Rouge, Nov. 20, 1946; s. Hezzie Clyde and Marguerite Lucille (Tucker) Harrelson. BA, Southeastern La. U., 1968; MA, La. State U., 1974, EdS, 1980, postgrad., 1981, So. U., 1982. Cert. social studies and English tchr., prin., supr. La. Tchr. English East Baton Rouge Parish Sch. Bd., 1970—2003, McKinley Mid. Magnet Sch., Baton Rouge, 1982—2001, dean of students, 1998—2001; tchr. social studies Ctrl. HS, 2002—03; ret., 2003. Mem. Arts Coun. Greater Baton Rouge, Found. Hist. La., La. Preservation Alliance, Nat. Trust Hist. Preservation, Colonial Williamsburg Found., NCCJ, La. Dem. Com., Nat. Dem. Com.; mem. exec. com. East Baton Rouge Parish Dems., 1981—85, 1996—. Mem.: Smithsonian Instn., Mus. Modern Art, Met. Mus. Art, New Orleans Mus. Art, Baton Rouge Gallery, La. Endowment for the Humanities, Old State Capitol Assocs., La. Arts and Sci. Ctr., La. State U. Mus. Art, Kiwanis, Phi Delta Kappa. Episcopalian. Home: 12418 Lake Sherwood Ave S Baton Rouge LA 70816-4454

HARRIES, KARSTEN, philosophy educator, researcher; b. Jena, Thuringia, Germany, Jan. 25, 1937; came to U.S., 1951; s. Wolfgang and Ilse (Grossmann) H.; m. Elizabeth Wanning, July 4, 1959; children: Lisa, Peter, Martin; 2d m., Elizabeth L. Langhorne, Mar. 14, 1991. BA, Yale U., 1958, PhD, 1962. Instr. Yale U., New Haven, 1961-63, asst. prof. philosophy, 1965-66, assoc. prof., 1966-70, prof., 1970—, Mellon prof., 1986-91; asst. prof. U. Tex., Austin, 1963-65. Lectr. U. Bonn, Fed. Republic Germany, winters 1965-66, 68-69. Author: The Meaning of Modern Art, 1967, The Bavarian Rococo Church, 1983, The Broken Frame, 1989, The Ethical Function of Architecture, 1996 (Winner of 8th Ann. AIA Internat. Architecture Book award for criticism), Infinity and Perspective, 2001; editor: (with Christoph Jamme) Martin Heidegger: Kunst, Politik, Technik, 1992, Martin Heidegger: Politics, Art, and Technology, 1994; contbr. numerous articles and revs. to profl. jours. Recipient Disting. Teaching Effectiveness award U. Tex., 1964; Morse fellow Yale U., 1965-66, Guggenheim fellow, N.Y.C., 1971-72. Mem. Am. Philos. Assn., Soc. for Eighteenth Century Studies, Cusanus Soc. Home: 16 Morris St Hamden CT 06517-3423 Office: Yale U Dept Philosophy New Haven CT 06520 E-mail: karsten.harries@yale.edu.

HARRIGAN, ROSANNE CAROL, medical educator; b. Miami, Feb. 24, 1945; d. John H. and Rose (Hnatow) Harrigan; children: Dennis, Michael, John. BS, St. Xavier Coll., 1965; MS in Nursing, Ind. U., 1974, EdD in Nursing and Edn., 1979. Staff nurse, recovery rm. Mercy Hosp., Chgo., 1965, evening charge nurse, 1965-66; head nurse Chgo. State Hosp., 1966-67; nurse practitioner Health and Hosp. Corp. Marion County, Indpls., 1975-80; assoc. prof. Ind. U. Sch. Nursing, Indpls., 1978-82; nurse practitioner devel. follow-up program Riley Hosp. for Children, Indpls., 1980-85; chief nursing sect. Riley Hosp. Child Devel. Ctr., Indpls., 1982-85; prof. Ind. U. Sch. Nursing, Indpls., 1982-85; chmn., prof. maternal child health Loyola U. Niehoff Sch. Nursing, Chgo., 1985-92; dean Sch. Nursing U. Hawaii, Honolulu, 1992—2002; nurse practitioner Waimanalo (Hawaii) Health Ctr., 1998—; chair complementary and alternative medicine dept. John A. Burns Sch. Medicine, 2002—; prof. pediat. Frances A. Matsuda Chair, Women's Health, 2000—, JABSOM, 2003—. Lecturer Ind. U. Sch. Nursing, 1974-75, chmn. dept. pediatrics, family and women's health, 1980-85; adj. prof. of pediatrics Ind. U. Sch. Med., 1982-85; editorial bd. Jour. Maternal Child Health Nursing, 1984-86, Jour. Perinatal Neonatal, 1985—, Jour. Perinatology, 1989—, Loyola U. Press, 1988-92; adv. bd. Symposia Medicus, 1982-84, Proctor and Gamble Rsch. Adv. Com. Blue Ribbon Panel; scientific review panel NIH, 1985; mem. NIH nat. adv. coun. nursing rsch., 2000-, ; cons. in field. Contbr. articles to profl. jours. Bd. dirs. March of Dimes Cen. Ind. Chpt., 1974-76, med. adv., 1979-85; med. and rsch. adv. March of Dimes Nat. Found., 1985—, chmn. Task Force on Rsch. Named Nat. Nurse of Yr. March of Dimes, 1983; faculty research grantee Ind. U., 1978, Pediatric Pulmonary Nursing Tng. grant Am. Lung Assn., 1982-85, Attitudes, Interests and Competence of Ob-Gyn Nurses Rsch. grant Nurses Assn. Am. Coll. Ob-Gyn., 1986, Attitudes, Interests and Priorities of Neonatal Nurses Rsch. grant Nat. Assn. Neonatal Nurses, 1987, Biomedical Rsch. Support grant, 1988; Doctoral fellow Am. Lung Assn. Ind. Tng. Program, 1981-86. Mem. AAAS, ANA (Maternal Child Nurse of Yr. 1983), Assn. Women's Health, Obstetrical and Neonatal Nursing (chmn. com. on rsch. 1983-86), Am. Nurses Found., Nat. Assn. Neonatal Nurses, Nat. Perinatal Assn. (bd. dirs. 1978-85, rsch. com. 1986), Midwest Nursing Rsch. Soc. (theory devel. sect.), Ill. Nurses Assn. (commn. rsch. chmn. 1990-91), Ind. Nurses Assn., Hawaii Nurses Assn., Ind. Perinatal Assn. (pres. 1981-83), N.Y. Acad. Sci., Ind U. Alumni Assn. (Disting. Alumni 1985), Sigma Xi, Pi Lambda Theta, Sigma Theta Tau (chpt. pres. 1988-90).

HARRIMAN, RICHARD LEE, performing arts administrator, educator; b. Independence, Mo., Sept. 10, 1932; s. Walter S. and M. Eloise (Faulkner) H.; AB, William Jewell Coll., 1953, LittD (hon.), 1983. MA, Stanford U., 1959. Instr., asst. prof. English U. Dubuque, Iowa, 1960-62; asst. prof. English, William Jewell Coll., Liberty, Mo., 1962, acting head English dept., 1965-69, dir. fine arts program, 1965—, asso. prof., 1966—. Treas. Kansas City Arts Council, 1980, sec., 1981; sec. Kansas City Am. Arts Festival, 1988-89. Served with, AUS, 1953-55. Woodrow Wilson fellow, 1957. Mem. MLA, AAUP, Internatl. Soc. of Performing Arts, Shakespeare Assn. Am., Assn. Performing Arts Presenters (nat. exec. bd. 1975-78), Lambda Chi Alpha, Sigma Tau Delta, Alpha Psi Omega. Methodist. Home: 1043 E Highway H Apt 3 Liberty MO 64068-4303

HARRINGTON, ANTHONY ROSS, radio announcer, educator; b. Sanford, N.C., Feb. 18, 1958; s. Refus Roy and Pauline (Kelly) H. Diploma, Cen. Carolina Tech. Coll., 1977; AGE, Cen. Carolina C.C., 1983; BS summa cum laude, Campbell U., 1985, MEd, 1988, EdS, 1993; EdD, N.C. State U., 1995-2000. Cert. tchr., N.C.; lic. FCC radiotelephone operator. News announcer Sandhills Community Broadcasters, Southern Pines, N.C., 1977-78; announcer, engr. Harnett Broadcast, Inc., Lillington, N.C., 1978-88; bus driver Harnett County Schs., Lillington, 1974-76, instr. social studies, 1985—; mgr. radio sta., instr. radio-TV, mem. transfer adv. bd. Ctrl. Carolina C.C., 1988-99, lead history instr., 1999—, chmn. dept. pub. svcs., 2000. Campus rep. Ctrl. Carolina C.C. Found., 2002—. Mem. Cen. Carolina C.C. Tri-County English Alliance, 1989—; support N.C. Dems., Raleigh, 1986—; pres. Campbell U. Friends of Libr., 2003—. Pres.'s scholar Campbell U., 1983-85, Coates-Rodgers History scholar Campbell U., 1983-85. Mem. ASCD, NEA, Nat. Assn. Secondary Sch. Prins., N.C. Assn. Educators, N.C. C.C. Faculty Assn., N.C. Assn. Historians, N.C. Distance Learning Assn., N.C. Assn. Broadcasters, Nat. Coun. Social Studies, Century Club (N.C.), Campbell U. Century Club, Masons (chaplain 1983, jr. steward 1984, sr. steward 1990, sec. 1991-97), Ctrl. Carolina C.C. Century Club, Profl. Educators of N.C., Masons, Shriners. Presbyterian. Avocations: photography, singing popular and religious music. Home: 4224 Mount Pisgah Church Rd Broadway NC 27505-8506 Office: Ctrl Carolina CC 1105 Kelly Dr Sanford NC 27330-9059

HARRINGTON, DONALD JAMES, university president; b. Bklyn., Oct. 2, 1945; s. John Joseph and Ruth Mary (Cummings) H. BA, Mary Immaculate Sem., Northampton, Pa., 1969, MDiv, 1972, ThM, 1973; LLD (hon.), St. John's U., 1985; postgrad., U. Toronto, 1980-82; PhD (hon.), Fu Jen U., Taipei, Taiwan, 1994; DHum (hon.), Am. U. Rome, 1994, Dowling Coll., 1996; D of Pedagogy (hon.), St. Thomas Aquinas Coll., Sparkhill, N.Y.; STD (hon.), Niagara U., 2000. Ordained priest Roman Catholic Ch., 1973. Instr. Niagara U., Niagara University, N.Y., 1973-80, dir. student activities, 1974-77, dean student activities, 1977-80, exec. v.p., 1981-84, pres., 1984-89, St. John's U., Jamaica, N.Y., 1989—. Bd. dirs. The Bear Stearns Cos., Inc., 1993—, Commn. Ind. Colls. and Univs., Albany, N.Y., 1987-89; mem. bd. cath. edn. Diocese of Buffalo, 1987-89. Trustee Niagara U., 1984—, St. John's U., 1986—, DePaul U., 1988-91, Sem. Immaculate Conception, 1990-97, Res. Group, 1988—, Sisters Hosp., Buffalo, 1988-89; chair adv. com. Love Canal Land Use, 1988-89; bd. dirs., mem. exec. com. Commn. Ind. Colls. and Univs., 1991—; chair Big East Athletic Conf., 1994-97; mem. sanctity of life com. Diocese of Bklyn., 1990-96; chair Western N.Y. Consortium for Higher Edn., 1988-89, mem. exec. com., 1985-89; mem. adv. bd. New Yorkers Caring for N.Y.-N.Y. Med. Coll., 1998—; mem. Commr.'s Coun. on Higher Edn., 1998—. Recipient Pro Ecclesia et Pontifice, Pope John Paul II, 1989. Mem. Assn. Cath. Colls. and Univs. (bd. dirs. 1997—). Office: St John's U Office of Pres 800 Utopia Pkway, Newman Hall Rm 318 Jamaica NY 11439-0001*

HARRINGTON, JAMES L., JR., elementary school educator; b. San Luis Obispo, Calif., Feb. 12, 1946; s. James L. Sr. and Irene V. (Rusca) H.; m. Terri A. Prather, Apr. 4, 1971; children: Matthew, Andrew. BA, U. Calif., Santa Barbara, 1967; MA, U. Santa Clara, 1973. Cert. tchr., Calif. Tchr. Alum Rock Sch. Dist., San Jose, Calif., 1970-74; tchr., tech. coord. Grants Pass (Oreg.) Sch. Dist., 1974—. Student teaching seminar asst. U. Santa Clara, Calif., 1973; master tchr. So. Oreg. State Coll., Ashland, 1980; family math. instr. N.W. Equals, Portland, Oreg., 1982. Bd. dirs. Headstart, Josephine County, Oreg., 1977-80; asst. scoutmaster Boys Scouts Am., Grants Pass, 1986-92. Sgt. Signal corps, U.S. Army, 1968-70. Democrat. Methodist.

HARRINGTON, JOHN NORRIS, ophthalmic plastic and reconstructive surgeon, educator; b. Dallas, Oct. 1, 1939; s. Marion Thomas and Ruth Evelyn (Norris) H.; m. Elizabeth Hunt, June 20, 1964; children: Thomas Wesley, Clinton Hunt. BA, Tex. A&M U., 196l, BS, 1964; MD, U. Tenn., Memphis, 1966. Diplomate Am. Bd. Ophthalmology. Intern Letterman Gen. Hosp., San Francisco, 1966-67; resident in ophthalmology Scott and White Clinic, Temple, Tex., 1970-73; fellow in ophthalmic plastic and reconstructive surgery U. Calif., San Francisco, 1973-74; plastic and reconstructive surgeon Tex. Ophthal. Plastic, Reconstructive & Orbital Surg. Assoc., Dallas, 1974—. Clin. prof. ophthalmic plastic and reconstructive surgery U. Tex. Southwestern Med. Ctr., Dallas, 1974—, chair faculty svc. bd., 2003; chief staff Mary Shiels Hosp., Dallas, 1986-88; active staff, dir. ophthalmic plastic and reconstructive surgery Baylor U. Med. Ctr., Dallas; active staff dept. oncology Baylor-Sammons Cancer Ctr.; team physician NHL Dallas Stars, NBA Dallas Mavericks. Mem. editl. bd. Ophthalmic Plastic and Reconstructive Surgery Jour.; contbr. chpts. to textbooks, articles to med. jours. Mem. Univ. Park Citizens League, Dallas, 1976-82; pres. Highland Park High Sch. Dads Club, Dallas, 1982-83; sec. bd. deacons Park Cities Bapt. Ch., Dallas, 1981. Maj. M.C., U.S. Army, 1966-70, Vietnam. Decorated Bronze Star. Fellow ACS, Am. Soc. Ophthalmic Plastic and Reconstructive Surgery (sec. 1991-93, v.p. 1994, pres.-elect 1995, pres. 1996, del. to AMA 1995—), Am. Acad. Ophthalmology (bd. counselors 1991-94, Honor award 1989, Sr. Achievement award 2003); mem. AMA (house of dels. 1995—), Tex. Med. Assn., Dallas Acad. Ophthalmology (pres. 1986). Avocations: music, skiing, water sports. Office: 2731 Lemmon Ave E Ste 304 Dallas TX 75204-2866 E-mail: jnhoplsurg@aol.com.

HARRINGTON, JOSEPH FRANCIS, educational company executive, history educator; b. Boston, Oct. 24, 1938; s. Joseph Francis and Mary Virginia (Lynch) H.; m. Brenda Marie Crowley, Sept. 3, 1966; children: Megan Marie, Christopher Joseph John. BS, Boston Coll., 1960; MA, Georgetown U., 1963, PhD, 1971. Instr. Framingham (Mass.) State Coll., 1966-68, asst. prof., 1968-70, assoc. prof., 1970-72, prof., 1972—2003, bd. chmn. dept. history, 1972—82; pres. Learning, Inc., Stoughton, 1979—2003, bd. dirs.; pres. J.C. Ednl. Enterprises, 2003—. Treas. The East European Rsch. Ctr., 1990—. Author: Masters of War, Makers of Peace, 1985, Powers, Pawns and Parleys, 1978, Tweaking the Nose of the Russians: American-Romanian Relations, 1940-90; editorial bd. dirs. New England Jour. of History, 1991—, editor, 1995—; editor: The Creative Child and Adult Quarterly, 1991-94; contbr. articles to profl. jours. Mem. Stoughton, Mass. Sch. Com., 1971-77, 82-87, 91-94. With U.S. Army, 1962-65. Tchg. fellow Georgetown U., Washington, 1960-62, 65-66, hon. fellow Kennedy Presdl. Libr., 1986-93. Mem. Mass. Assn. for Advancement of Individual Potential (bd. dirs., pres. 1987-89, 90-92, v.p. for R&D 1989), Nat. Assn. Creative Children and Adults (bd. dirs. 1985-92, editor The Creative Child and Adult Quar. 1991-93), New Eng. Slavic Assn. (v.p. 1990-91, treas. 1991-98), Soc. for Romanian Studies (pres. 1994-97, bd. dirs. 1997-2000), Kennedy Libr. Acad. Adv. Coun. Roman Catholic. Avocations: reading, racquetball. Home: 119 Holmes Ave Stoughton MA 02072-1926 Office: Framingham State Coll State St Framingham MA 01701

HARRINGTON, LUCIA MARIE, elementary education educator; b. Marquette, Mich., May 19, 1947; d. Eugene and Saima (Bentti) Latvala; m. Warren Henry Harrington, June 21, 1969; children: Robert Joseph, Christen Marie. BS with high honors, No. Mich. U., 1969. Cert. tchr., Mich. Tchr. Marquette Area Pub. Schs., 1969-70, 71-73, 75-76, 82-95, Ysleta Ind. Schs., El Paso, Tex., 1970-71; substitute tchr. Schaumburg (Ill.) and Clear Lake (Iowa) Schs., 1973-75; tchr. 2d grade Whitman Elem. Sch., Marquette, 1996—. Instr. Aerobic Dancing, Inc., Marquette, 1980-82; participant Gessell Sch. Readines and Devel. Placement, 1985, Mich. Model Comprehensive Sch. Health Edn., 1987—, Essential Elements Effective Instrn., 1988, Lions/Quest Skills for Growing, 1990, Dyslexia Outreach Program Seminar, 1992; supr. student tchrs. 1988-96; mem. Marquette-Alger Reading Coun.; introduced Foreign Language Program Whitman Elem. Sch., 1996-97; mem. Rotarion Group Study Exchange to Norway, 1997; evaluator Tchr.'s Choice Awards, Internat. Pen Pal Projects; state presenter, trainer writing workshops. Lake Superior Cmty. Partnership, Edn. Human Svcs. Com. Rep.,1998. Named Elem. Tchr. of Yr., Kiwanis, 1991, Marquette Area Pub. Schs. Outstanding Educator, 1994; Collaborative Practices Inquiries grantee, 1997. Mem. ASCD, NEA, Internat. Reading Assn., Mich. Edn. Assn. (cert. of merit), Mich. Coun. Tchrs. of Math., Mich. Coun. Tchrs. English, Upper Peninsula Reading Assn. (hospitality chair 1990-97), Mich. Reading Assn., Coop. Team Learning Initiative Group, Internat. Platform Assn., Mich. English Lang. Arts Framework Project (presenter), No. Mich. U. Alumni, Marquette City Edn. Assn., Phi Delta Kappa. Lutheran. Avocations: piano, water skiing, music, walking. Home: 1705 West Ave Marquette MI 49855-1555 Office: Marquette Area Pub Schs Whitman Elem Sch 1400 Norway Ave Marquette MI 49855-2651

HARRINGTON, MARY EVELINA PAULSON (POLLY HARRINGTON), religious journalist, writer, educator; b. Chgo. d. Henry Thomas and Evelina (Belden) Paulson; m. Gordon Keith Harrington, Sept. 7, 1957; children: Jonathan Henry, Charles Scranton. BA, Oberlin Coll., 1946; postgrad., Northwestern U., Evanston, Ill., Chgo., 1946-49, Weber State U., Ogden, Utah, 1970s, 80s; MA, U. Chgo.-Chgo. Theol. Sem., 1956. Publicist Nat. Coun. Chs., N.Y.C., 1950-51; mem. press staff 2d assembly World Coun. Chs., Evanston, Chgo., 1954; mgr. Midwest Office Communication, United Ch. of Christ, Chgo., 1955-59; staff writer United Ch. Herald, N.Y.C., St. Louis, 1959-61; affiliate missionary to Asia, United Ch. Bd. for World Ministries, N.Y.C., 1978-79; freelance writer and lectr., 1961—; corr. Religious News Svc., 1962—. Prin. lectr. Women & Family Life in Asia series to numerous librs., Utah, 1981, 1981—82; pub. rels. coord. Utah Energy Conservation/Energy Mgmt. Program, 1984—85; tchr. writing Ogden Cmty. Schs., 1985—89; adj. instr. writing for publs. Weber State U., 1986—; instr. Acad. Lifelong Learning, Ogden, 1992—95, Eccles Cmty. Art Ctr., Ogden, 1993—94; dir. comm. Shared Ministry, Salt Lake City, 1983—97; chmn. comm. Intermountain Conf., Rocky Mountain Conf. Utah Assn. United Ch. of Christ, 1970—78, 1982—, Ind. Coun. Chs., 1960—63, United Ch. of Christ, Ogden, 1971—; dir. comm. United Chs., 1971—78, Christ Congl., Ogden,, 1980—; chmn. comm. Ch. Women United Utah, 1974—78, Ogden rep., 1980—, hostess Northern Utah, 1998. Editor: Sunshine and Moonscapes: An Anthology of Essays, Poems, Short Stories, 1994, (booklet) Family Counseling Service: Thirty Years of Service to Northern Utah, 1996; contbr. numerous articles and essays to religious and other publs. Pres. T.O. Smith Sch. PTA, 1976-78, Ogden City Coun. PTA, 1983-85; assoc. dir. Region II, Utah PTA, Salt Lake City, 1981-83, mem. State Edn. Commn., 1982-87; chmn. state internat. hospitality and aid Utah Fedn. Women's Clubs, 1982-86; v.p. Ogden dist., 1990-92, pres. Ogden dist., 1992-96, state resolutions com., 1996—; trustee Family Counseling Svc. No. Utah, Ogden, 1983-95, emeritus trustee, 1995—; Utah rep. to nat. bd. Challenger Films, Inc., 1986—; state pres. Rocky Mountain Conf. Women in Mission, United Ch. of Christ, 1974-77, sec., 1981-84, vice moderator Utah Assn., 1992-94; chair pastor-parish rels. com. United Ch. of Christ Congl., Ogden, 1999-2003, chmn. search com., 1995-96, Mission com., 2002-. Recipient Ecumenical Svc. citation Ind. Coun. Chs., 1962, Outstanding Local Pres. award Utah PTA, 1978, Outstanding Latchkey Child Project award, 1985, Cmty. Svc. award City of Ogden, 1980, 81, 82, Celebration of Gifts of Lay Woman Nat. award United Ch. of Christ, 1987, Excellence in the Arts in Art Edn. award Ogden City Arts Commn., 1993, Spirit of Am. Woman in Arts and Humanities award Your Cmty. Connection, Ogden, 1994, Heart and Hand award United Ch. of Christ, Ogden, 2001; Utah Endowment for Humanities grantee, 1981, 81-82. Mem. Nat. League Am. Penwomen (chmn. Utah conv. 1973, 11 awards for articles and essays 1987-95, 1st pl. news award 1992, 1st pl. short stories 1997, 3d pl. articles 1997), AAUW (state edn. rep. 1982-86, parliamentarian Ogden br. 1997—, membership v.p. Ogden br. 2003—), League of Utah Writers (Publ. Quill award 1998). Democrat. Avocation: building miniature world of peace each Christmas by family in the home. Home and Office: 722 Boughton St Ogden UT 84403-1152 E-mail: gkHarrington1@comcast.net.

HARRIOTT, WENDY A. special education educator; b. Sellersville, Pa., Aug. 18, 1959; d. Robert L. and Marjorie R. (Fleetman) Godshall; m. Guy S. Harriott, Apr. 7, 1990. BS cum laude, Bloomsburg U., 1981; grad., Shippensburg (Pa.) U., 1984; MS, Marywood Coll., 1988; PhD, Pa. State U., 2001; supr. cert., East Stroudsburg U., 1993; secondary prin. cert., Pa. State U., 1998. Tchr. spl. edn. Lincoln Intermediate Unit, Chambersburg, Pa., 1981-84, Colonial Northampton Intermediate Unit, Milford, Pa., 1984-90, ednl. cons., 1990-91; tchr. spl. edn. Delaware Valley Sch. Dist., Milford, 1991-94; grad. asst. spl. edn. Pa. State U., University Park, 1994-97; instr. State U. West Ga., 1998-2000; asst. prof. Sch. Edn., Monmouth U., West Long Branch, N.J., 2000—. Coord. Spl. Olympics, Delaware Valley Sch. Dist., 1991-94, mentor, tchr., 1988, 92-93. Advisor Am. Field Svc. Club, Chambersburg, 1982-84. Mem. NEA, Pa. State Edn. Assn., Coun. Exceptional Children, Assn. Supervision and Curriculum Devel., Phi Delta Kappa, Phi Kappa Phi, Theta Tau Omega (rep. exec. bd. 1980-81). Avocations: skiing, step aerobics, reading. Home: 422 Monmouth Rd West Long Branch NJ 07764 E-mail: wharriot@monmouth.edu.

HARRIS, ALICE CARMICHAEL, linguist, educator; b. Columbus, Ga., Nov. 23, 1947; d. Joseph Clarence and Georgia (Walker) H.; m. James Vaughan Staros, Aug. 7, 1976; children: Joseph Vaughan, Alice Carmichael. BA, Randolph-Macon Woman's Coll., 1969; MA, U. Essex (Eng.), 1972; PhD, Harvard U., 1976. Tchg. fellow linguistics Harvard U., Cambridge,

Mass., 1972-74, 75-76, lectr. linguistics, 1976-77, rsch. fellow linguistics, 1977-79; rsch. asst. prof. linguistics Vanderbilt U., Nashville, 1979-84, assoc. prof. linguistics, 1985-91, assoc. prof. anthropology, 1986-92, prof. linguistics, 1991—2002, prof. anthropology, 1992—2002, chair dept. Germanic, Slavic langs., 1993—2002; prof. linguistics SUNY, Stony Brook, 2002—. Chair faculty coun. Coll. Arts and Scis., 1995-96; vice chair grad. faculty coun., 1993-94, sec. faculty senate, 1993-94; assoc. rsch. U. Tbilisi, USSR, 1974-75; tutor linguistics Dunster House, Harvard U., Cambridge, 1975-77; cons. to Simon and Schuster; Erskine vis. prof. U. of Canterbury, Christchurch, New Zealand, 1999. Author: (book) Georgian Syntax, 1981, Diachronic Syntax, 1985, The Indigenous Languages of the Caucasus, 1991, Endoclitics and the Origins of Udi Morphosyntax, 2002; co-author: Historical Syntax in Cross-Linguistic Perspective, 1995 (Leonard Bloomfield book award, 1998); mem. editl. bd. (book) Natural Language and Linguistic Theory, 1987—90, assoc. editor (jour.) Language, 1988—89, mem. editl. bd. Diachronica, 1994—, mem. adv. com. Publs. MLA, 1995—98; contbr. articles to profl. jours. Sinclair Kennedy fellow Harvard U., 1974-75, NSF Nat. Needs Postdoctoral fellow, 1978-79; grantee Internat. Rsch. and Exch. Bd., 1973, 74-75, 77, 81, 89, 92, Linguistic Soc. Am., 1981, NSF 1980-83, 81-83, 83-85, 85-89, 97-99, 2001-03, NEH, 1990-91, Deutscher Adademischer Austausch Dienst, 1994; scholar Harvard U. 1972-73, Georgetown U., 1973; recipient Mellon Found. Regional Faculty Devel. award 1981, ACLS travel award, 1988, venture fund Vanderbilt U., 1987, 92, 94. Mem. Internat. Soc. Hist. Linguistics (mem. exec. com. 1995-01), Linguistic Soc. Am. (cons., com. status women in linguistics, nominating com.), Southeastern Conf. Linguistics, Soc. for Study of Caucasia (exec. coun. 1990-98), Societas Caucasologica Europaea (v.p. 1990-92, exec. com. 1992-94, 1994-2000), Phi Beta Kappa (Earl Sutherland prize for rsch. Vanderbilt U. 1998). Office: SUNY Dept Linguistics Stony Brook NY 11794-4376

HARRIS, ANN, elementary school teacher; b. Eden, Miss., Aug. 20, 1946; d. Tommie L. and Rosetta (Tolbert) H. BS in Edn., Jackson (Miss.) State Coll., 1968, MS, 1972, EdS, 1974; EdD, Ind. U., 1983. Cert. elem. tchr., Miss. Elem. tchr. Jackson Pub. Schs.; asst. prof. edn. Ky. State U., Frankfort, Western Ky. U., Bowling Green; elem. tchr. Atlanta Pub. Schs. Guest lectr. home econs. dept. Indiana U., Bloomington, 1982-83; elem. tchr. Atlant Pub. Schs. Former leadership team chairperson E.L. Connally Sch., Olympics Com.; chair Red Cross and March of Dimes; rep. Am. Heart Fund; mem. PTA. Fundraiser chairperson, program chairperson Tchr.'s Awards Banquet, 1998, 99, 2000; v.p. Wesley Sunday Sch. Class, Atlanta First United Meth. Ch., 2001. Recipient Outstanding Elem. Tchr. Am. award, 1975, Finer Womanhood award Nat. Coun. Negro Women, 1980, Disting. Svc. citation United Negro Coll. Fund, 1979-80, Ky. Amb. Goodwill award, 1986, Atlanta Asssn. Educators cert. for Tchr. of Yr., 1996-97, Achievement cert. Atlanta Fedn. Tchrs., 1996-97, Spl. Congrl. Recognition for Edn. cert. Rep. John Lewis, 1997, Spl. Recognition in Edn. cert. Phi Delta Kappa, 1997, John Herkiotz award for outstanding contbns. of tchg. democracy for work in mock election NASSP, 1997, Cert. of Appreciation Am. Red Cross Mem. Enrollment Campaign, 1997-98, Rotary Red Apple for Reading award Apple Corps, 2002; named Tchr. of Yr., Connally Elem. Sch., 1996-97, Coca-Cola, 1996-97; cert. Red Cross, 1997-98, 99-2000; named to Hon. Order Ky. Cols., 2001. Mem. NEA, Ga. Assn. Educators, Atlanta Assn. Educators.

HARRIS, AUDREY LEONHARDT, middle school educator; b. Morganton, N.C., Feb. 9, 1959; d. Ervin Dewey and Faye Lois (Branch) Leonhardt; m. Kenneth Douglas Harris, June 16, 1984; 1 child, Kevin Douglas. AA, Western Piedmont C.C., 1979; BS, MA, Gardner-Webb Coll., 1982. Cert. health edn., phys. edn., gen. sci., earth sci. tchr., N.C. Tchr. healthful living Kings Mountain (N.C. Dist. Schs., 1982—. Mem. health coun. Kings Mountain Dist. Schs., 1994—; presenter at workshops in field. Recipient N.C. Intramural Program of Yr. award N.C. Assn. for Intramurals and Recreation, 1994-95; named Young Educator of Yr. Kings Mountain Jaycees, 1984, N.C. Secondary Health Educator of Yr. N.C. Assn. for Advancement of Health Edn., 1992-93. Mem. AAHPERD, N.C. Alliance Health, Phys. Edn., Recreation and Dance. Democrat. Baptist. Avocations: tennis, aerobics, crafts, collecting. Home: 145 Winchester Acres Dallas NC 28034-8609 Office: Kings Mountain Mid Sch 1000 Phifer Rd Kings Mountain NC 28086-3750

HARRIS, CHARLES UPCHURCH, seminary president, clergyman; b. Raleigh, N.C., May 2, 1914; s. Charles Upchurch and Saidee (Robbins) H.; m. Janet Jeffrey Carlile, June 17, 1940; children: John C., Diana Jeffrey (Mrs. Melvin). BA, Wake Forest Coll., 1935, DHL (hon.), 1979; BD, Va. Theol. Sem., 1938, DD (hon.), 1958; postgrad., Union Theol. Sem., 1939-40; DCL (hon.), Seabury-Western Sem., 1972. Ordained deacon P.E. Ch., 1938, priest, 1939; rector All Saints Ch., Roanoke Rapids, N.C., 1938-39; asst. rector St. Bartholomew's Ch., N.Y.C., 1939-40; rector Trinity Ch., Roslyn, L.I., 1940-46, Highland Park, Ill., 1946-57; pres., dean Seabury-Western Theol. Sem., Evanston, Ill., 1957-72, pres., dean emeritus, 1972—; dean Lake Shore Deanery; vicar St. John's Ch., Harbor Springs, Mich., 1969-85, vicar emeritus, 1985—; founder St. Gregory's Ch., Deerfield, Ill.; hon. canon St. James Cathedral, Chgo., 1975-82; pres. Episc. Theol. Sch., Claremont, Calif., 1977-82. Trustee Sch. of Theology, Claremont, 1979-82; chmn. exam. chaplains 5th and 6th provinces Episcopal Ch.; cons. nat. dept. Christian edn.; pres. Chgo. Inst. Advanced Theol. Studies, 1968-70; sec. Drafting Com. on Holy Eucharist, 1970-79; pres. Chgo. Inter-Sem. Faculties Union, 1971-72; vice chmn. N. Am. com. St. George's Coll., Jerusalem, 1981-83, pres, 1985-91; pres. Cyprus-Am. Archaeol. Inst., 1985-91, chmn., 1991, 98—; mem. exec. com. Nat. Cathedral, Washington, 1978-84, 95; v.p. Chgo. Inst. Advanced Theol. Studies, 1967-72; mem. Anglican Theol. Rev. Bd., 1959—, editor, 1971-72, pres., 1968-85, v.p., 1985—, pres. emeritus, 1991; mem. Am. Schs. Oriental Rsch., 1959—, trustee, 1969-72, 76-78, treas., 1984-87, chmn., CEO, 1992-94; hon. chmn. Inst. Christianity & Antiquities, Calif., 1996—; hon. pres. Cyprus Am. Archaeol. Rsch. Inst., 1997-98, chmn., 1998—. Author: (with A. LeCroy) Harris-Lecroy Report, 1975; contbr.: Sermons on Death and Dying, 1975; asst. editor Anglican Theol. Rev., 1958-71, editor, 1971-72. Trustee Little Traverse Conservancy, 1986; mem. bd. visitors Wake Forest U., 1979-94, Div. Sch. U. Chgo.; mem. bd. coun. Am. Rsch. Ctrs. Overseas, 1989-94, treas., 1991-95; mem. adv. com. Inst. for Antiquity and Christianity, 1987-94; mem. Com. of 40, Va. Theol. Sem., 1988-92. Mem. Am. Theol. Soc., Am. Acad. Religion, Soc. Bibl. Lit., Soc. Colonial Warriors, SAR, Conf. of Anglican Theologians. Clubs: University, Wequetonsing Golf (Harbor Springs); Little Sturgeon Trout; Desert Forest (Carefree, Ariz.). Home: Chicago, Ill. Died Sept. 16, 2001.

HARRIS, CHAUNCY DENNISON, geographer, educator; b. Logan, Utah, Jan. 31, 1914; s. Franklin Stewart and Estella (Spilsbury) H.; m. Edith Young, Sept. 5, 1940; 1 child, Margaret (Mrs. Philip A. Straus, Jr.). AB, Brigham Young U., 1933; BA, Oxford U., 1936, MA, 1943, DLitt, 1973; postgrad., London Sch. Econs., 1936-37; PhD, U. Chgo., 1940; DEcon (honoris causa), Catholic U., Chile, 1956; LLD (honoris causa), Ind. U., 1979; DSc (honoris causa), Bonn U., 1991, U. Wis., Milw., 1991. Instr. in geography Ind. U., 1939-41; asst. prof. geography U. Nebr., 1941-43, U. Chgo., 1943-46, assoc. prof., 1946-47, prof., 1947-84, prof. emeritus, 1984—, dean social scis., 1955-60, chmn. non western area programs and internat. studies, 1960-66, dir. ctr. for internat. studies, 1966-84, chmn. dept. geography, 1967-69, Samuel N. Harper Disting. Svc. prof., 1969-84, spl. asst. to pres., 1973-75, v.p. acad. resources, 1975-78. Del. Internat. Geog. Congress, Lisbon, 1949, Washington, 1952, Rio de Janeiro, 1956, Stockholm, 1960, London, 1964, New Delhi, 1968, Montreal, 1972, Moscow, 1976, Tokyo, 1980, Paris, 1984, Sydney, Australia, 1988, Washington, 1992, The Hague, 1996; v.p. Internat. Geog. Union, 1956-64, sec.-treas., 1968-76; mem. adv. com. for internat. orgns. and programs Nat. Acad. Scis., 1969-73, mem. bd. internat. orgns. and programs, 1973-76; U.S. del. 17th Gen. Conf. UNESCO, Paris, 1972; exec. com. div. behavioral scis. NRC, 1967-70; hon. cons. geography Libr. of Congress, 1974-80, mem. coun. of scholars, 1980-83, Conseil de la Bibliographie Géographique Internationale, 1986-94. Author: Cities of the Soviet Union, 1970; editor: Economic Geography of the U.S.S.R, 1949, International List of Geographical Serials, 1960, 71, 80, Annotated World List of Selected Current Geographical Serials, 1960, 64, 71, 80, Soviet Geography: Accomplishments and Tasks, 1962, Guide to Geographical Bibliographies and Reference Works in Russian or on the Soviet Union, 1975, Bibliography of Geography, Part I, Introduction to General Aids, 1976, Part 2, Regional, vol. 1, U.S., 1984, A Geographical Bibliography for American Libraries, 1985, Directory of Soviet Geographers 1946-87, 1988; contbr. Sources of Information in the Social Sciences, 1973, 86, Encyclopedia Britannica, 1989, Columbia Gazetteer of the World, 1998; contbg. editor: The Geog. Rev., 1960-73, Soviet Geography, 1987-91, Post-Soviet Geography and Economics, 1992-99, emeritus 2000—; hon. editor Urban Geography, 1984—; contbr. articles to profl. jours. Life mem. vis. com. U. Chgo. Libr.; pres. coun. Residents Assn., Montgomery Place, Chgo., 2000-01. Recipient Alexander Csoma de Körösi Meml. medal Hungarian Geog. Soc., 1971, Lauréat d'Honneur Internat. Geog. Union, 1976; Alexander von Humboldt Gold Medal Gesellschaft für Erdkunde zu Berlin, 1978; spl. award Utah Geog. Soc., 1985; Rhodes scholar, 1934-37. Fellow Japan Soc. Promotion of Sci.; mem. Assn. Am. Geographers (sec. 1946-48, v.p. 1956, pres. 1957, Honors award 1976), Am. Geog. Soc. (coun. 1962-74, v.p. 1969-74; Cullum Geog. medal 1985), Am. Assn. Advancement Slavic Studies (pres. 1962, award for disting. contbns. 1978), Am. Acad. Arts and Scis., Social Sci. Rsch. Coun. (bd. dir. 1959-70, vice-chmn. 1963-65, exec. com. 1967-70), Internat. Coun. Sci. Unions (exec. com. 1969-76), Internat. Rsch. and Exchs. Bd. (exec. com. 1968-71), Nat. Coun. Soviet and East European Rsch. (bd. dir. 1977-83), Nat. Coun. for Geog. Edn. (Master Tchr. award 1986); hon. mem. Royal Geog. Soc. (Victoria medal 1987), Geog. Socs. Berlin, Frankfurt, Rome, Florence, Paris, Warsaw, Belgrade, Japan, Chgo. (Disting. Svc. award 1965, bd. dir. 1954-69, 82-90), Polish Acad. Scis. (fgn. mem.). Home: 5550 S South Shore Dr Apt 906 Chicago IL 60637-5033 Office: U Chgo Com on Geog Studies 5828 S University Ave Chicago IL 60637-1583

HARRIS, COLIN CYRIL, mineral engineer, educator; b. Leeds, Eng., 1928; came to U.S., 1960; m. Sylvia Glonstein, Apr. 16, 1964 (dec. Oct. 1979). B.Sc. in Math. and Physics (Brit. Govt. scholar), London U., 1952; PhD in Mineral Engring. and Coal Preparation, Leeds (Eng.) U., 1959. Chartered engr., Gt. Britain. Rsch. asst. Leeds U., 1952-57; lectr. in coal preparation and mineral processing, 1957-60, 61-63; vis. asst. prof. mineral engring. Columbia U., 1960-61, assoc. prof. mineral engring., 1963-70, prof., 1970—98, prof. emeritus mineral engring., 1998—. Adv. on faculty appointments, research and grad. programs to U.S. and fgn. univs.; external examiner fgn. univs.; adv. on research proposals to govt. funding agys.; adv., cons. to mining, research and mfg. cos.; mem. organizing coms. for several internat. confs. on mineral processing. Contbr. numerous articles on theory of mineral processing ops. to profl. publs.; editor: Symposium on Coal Preparation, 1957; assoc. editor: Internat. Jour. Mineral Processing, 1973-86 ; mem. editorial bd. Mineral Processing and Extractive Metallurgy Rev.— An Internat. Jour., Minerals and Metall. Processing; adv. to internat. jours. Served as sgt. Brit. Armed Forces, 1946-49. Nat. Coal Bd. Rsch. grantee, 1957-60, 62-63, Clean Coal Rsch. grantee U.S. Dept. Energy, U.S. Bur. Mines, Comm. Ctr., others. Mem. AIME (past chmn. publs. com., mem. awards. com., student affairs com.), AIME Soc. for Mining, Metallurgy and Exploration (A.M. Gaudin award and lectr. 1990), Operational Rsch. Soc. (London), Assn. Univs. Tchrs. (Gt. Brit.), Instn. Mining and Metallurgy (London), Inst. Materials, Minerals and Mining, Leeds U. Record Club (libr. 1954-59). Office: Columbia U Sch Mines 907 Engring Ctr New York NY 10027

HARRIS, CYNTHIA VIOLA, principal; b. San Francisco, Aug. 18, 1948; d. Gilbert and Mary Lee (barnes) H. BA in Speech, San Francisco State U., 1970, MA in Counseling, 1975; EdD, Nova U., 1987. Cert. tchr., adminstr., Calif. Tchr. Martin L. King Elem. Sch., Oakland, Calif., 1971-74; tchg. v.p. Peratta Yr. Round Sch., Oakland, 1974-80, prin., 1980-86, coord. staff devel., 1986-90, dir. staff devel., 1990-91, coord. recruitment, 1991—, asst. coord. to supt. cmty., parents, bus. ptnrships, 1992—; prin. Nystrom Magnet Sch., 2003—. Mgmt. cons. year-round educ., leadership; guest lectr. Mills Coll., LaVerne U; coord. Community, Parents and Bus. Partnership; coord. coaches West Contra Costa Unified Sch. Dist., 2002-03; devel. dir. Help Other People Evolve; mem. Head Start commn. panel City of Oakland. Author: (tchg. manual) All About Us, 1980. Bd. dirs. Wiley Manuel Law Found., Charles Harrison Mason Scholarships; chair minority caucus New Oakland Com. Nominated Outstanding Woman of Am., Alpha Kappa Alpha, 1981; recipient Capwell's Networker award, 1985; named Outstanding Youth Leader, Nat. Bus. and Profl. Bd., 1981; named to Alameda Edn. Hall of Fame, 2001. Mem. Nat. Assn. Female Execs., Nat. Assn. Prins., Nat. Ch. of God in Christ Bus. and Profl. Women, United Adminstrs. Oakland, Alliance Black Educators, Black Summit (internat. enrollment mgr.), Glamor Working Women's Panel, Coalition of 100 Black Women, Phi Delta Kappa. Democrat. Mem. Pentacostal Ch.

HARRIS, DANIEL FREDERICK, biomechanical analyst, educator; b. Pitts., Nov. 11, 1944; s. Frederick C. and Elizabeth May (Donley) H. BA, W.Va. U., 1966, MA, 1972, postgrad., 1986, Yale U., 1990. Instr. photographic and computer graphics Greenville (S.C.), 1987-96; clin. researcher in motion analysis St. Francis Hosp., Greenville, 1991-95, clin. and indsl. rsch. in applied ergonomics, human factors and motion analysis, 1993—; instr. photography Greenville Tech. Coll., 1992, dept. head Visual Arts Inst., 1995—. Adj. instr. art history U. S.C., Spartanburg, 1987-91; mem. S.C. Curriculum Congress, 1991—; cons. Motion Analysis Corp., Calif., 1991—; presenter in field. Named Tchr. of Yr. Monongalia County, W.Va., 1981. Mem. Phi Delta Kappa. Presbyterian. Avocations: racing, hiking, photography, water sports. Home: 205 Springvale Dr Mauldin SC 29662-1622

HARRIS, DAVID THOMAS, immunology educator; b. Jonesboro, Ark, May 9, 1956; s. Marm Melton and Lucille Luretha (Buck) H.; m. Francoise Jacqueline Besencon, June 24, 1989; children: Alexandre M., Stefanie L., Leticia M. BS in Biology, Math. and Psychology, Wake Forest U., 1978, MS, 1980, PhD in Microbiology and Immunology, 1982. Fellow Ludwig Inst. Cancer Rsch., Lausanne, Switzerland, 1982-85; rsch. asst. prof. U. N.C., Chapel Hill, 1985-89; assoc. prof. U. Ariz., Tucson, 1989-96, prof., 1996—. Cons. Teltech, Inc. Mpls., 1990—, Advanced Biosci. Resources, 1994-95; bd. sci. advisors Cryo-Cell Internat., 1992-95; bd. dir. Ageria, Inc., Tuscon; dir. Cord Blood Stem Cell Bank, 1992—; mem. Ariz. Cancer Ctr., Steele Meml. Children's Rsch. Ctr., Ariz. Arthritis Ctr. Program, sci. adv. bd. Cord Blood Registry, Inc., chief sci. div. Cord Blood Registry, Inc.; founder ImmuneRegen BioScis., Inc., 2002. Co-author chpts. to sci. books, articles to profls. jour.; reviewer sci. jour.; co-holder 7 scientific patents. Grantee numerous grants, 1988—. Mem. AAAS, Am. Assn. Immunologists, Reticuloendothelial Soc., Internat. Soc. Hematotherapy and Graft Engring., Internat. Soc. Devel. and Comparative Immunology, Scandanavian Soc. Immunology, Sigma Xi, Democrat. Mem. Ch. of Christ. Avocations: tennis, hiking, jogging, skiing, travel. Office: U Ariz Dept Microbiology Bldg 90 Tucson AZ 85721-0001 E-mail: davidh@U.Arizona.edu.

HARRIS, DELMARIE JONES, elementary education educator; b. New Orleans, Mar. 16, 1947; d. Ralph and Ruth Lena (Ackerson) Jones; m. Hosey W. Williams (div. 1974); children: Hosey Willie, Sabrena Michelle; m. Ronald Andrew Harris, Mar. 7, 1978; 1 child, Rene Andrea. Student, Southern U., New Orleans, 1967-70; BA, Southern U., 1971. Tchr. St. Mary of Angels, New Orleans, La., 1971-73, J.F. Gauthier Elem. Sch., Poydras, La., 1973—. Grade chmn. J.F. Gauthier steering com. bull. 741, 1987, language arts textbook adoption rep., 1992-93; recorder St. Bernard Parish Discipline Dress Code Adoption Com., 1988-90, math. rep., 1990, primary tchr.; mem. com. to rewrite curriculum for math. State of La., 1996. Mem. NEA, Nat. Coun. Tchrs. Math., Internat. Reading Assn., La. Assn. Educators, St. Bernard Assn. Educators. Democrat. Roman Catholic. Avocations: interior decorating, dancing.

HARRIS, DOLORES M. retired academic administrator; b. Camden, N.J., Aug. 5, 1930; d. Roland Henry, Sr. and Frances Anna (Gatewood) Ellis; m. Morris E. Harris, Sr., 1948 (div. 1987); children: Morris E. Jr., Sheila Davis, Gregory M. Sr. BS, Glassboro (N.J.) State Coll., 1959, MA, 1966; EdD, Rutgers U., 1983. Tchr., reading specialist Glassboro Bd. Edn., 1958-68, dir. aux. svcs., 1968-70; supr. adult edn. Camden Welfare Bd., summer 1968; head state dir. Glassboro SCOPE, summer 1969-70; assoc. dir. Jersey City State Coll., summer 1971; dir. adult edn. Glassboro State Coll., 1970-74, dir. continuing edn. dept., 1989-90, acting assoc. v.p. acad. affairs, 1989-91; ret., 1991. Cons. Mich. State Dept. Edn., Lansing, 1973; examiner N.Y. State Civil Svc. Commn., 1976—; chmn. adv. bd. Women's Ednl. Equity Comm. Network Project, San Francisco, 1977—78; cons. crossroads project Temple U., Phila., 1977; bd. dirs. Mgmt. Inst. Glassboro State Coll.; cons. corrections project Va. Commonwealth U., Richmond; mem., vice-chmn. comm. Accrediting Coun. Continuing Edn. and Tng., Richmond, 1985—89, chmn., 1989—; workshop/seminar chair Ea. Montgomery County chpt. SCORE, 1991—. Author: (book) How to Establish ABE Programs, 1972; author: (with others) Black Studies for ABE and GED Programs in Correction, 1975; founding editor: newsletter For Adults Only, 1970; contbr. articles to profl. jours. Founder, trustee, chair bd. trustees Glassboro Child Devel. Ctr., 1974—87; bd. dirs. Gloucester County United Way, NJ, 1977—, sec. bd. dirs., 1980, pres. bd. dirs., 1983—85; charter mem., bd. dirs. Glassboro Glass Mus., 1979—87; vice chair, chair, mem. Gloucester County Commn. Women, NJ, 1983—87; trustee Frederick Douglas Meml. and Hist. Assn., 2000—. Named Woman of the Yr., Gloucester County Bus. and Profl. Women's Club, 1985, Woman of Achievement, Gloucester County Commn. Women, 1987; named one of Outstanding Citizens, Holly Shores Girl Scouts U.S., 1987, 100 Most Influential Black Ams., Ebony Mag., 1989; named to Legion of Honor, Chapel of Four Chaplains, 1983; recipient Disting. Alumnae award, Glassboro State Coll., 1971, Disting. Svc. award, Camden County, 1974, N.J. Woman of Achievement award, 1991, Disting. Svc. award, Holly Shores Girl Scouts U.S., 1979. Mem.: AAUW (v.p. membership com. Gloucester County chpt. 1986—87), NEA, Montgomery County SCORE (chair seminars, workshop programs 2001—), N.J. Edn. Assn., Svc. Corps Ret. Execs., Women Greater Phila. (bd. dirs.), N.J. Assn. (life; pres. 1973—74), Soc. Docta (bd. dirs. 1987—), Links Club, Nat. Assn. Colored Women's Clubs, Inc. (pres. 1988—92), Northeastern Fedn. Women's Clubs (v.p.-at-large 1983—85, parliamentarian 1985—), N.J. State Fedn. Colored Women's Clubs (pres. 1976—80). Presbyterian. Avocations: reading, fitness exercises.

HARRIS, EMILY LOUISE, special education educator; b. New London, Conn., Nov. 16, 1932; d. Frank Sr. and Tanzatter (McCleese) Brown; m. John Everett Harris Sr., Sept. 10, 1955; children: John Everett Jr., Jocelyn E. (dec.). BS, U. Conn., 1955; MEd, Northeastern U., 1969. Cert. tchr. elem. spl. subject sci., Mass., spl. subject reading, secondary prin., elem. prin. Tchr. New Haven Sch. Dept., 1957-59, Boston Sch. Dept., 1966-68, Natick (Mass.) Sch. Dept., 1969-72; cert. nurse's asst. The Hebrew Rehab. Ctr., Roslindale, Mass., 1973-75; spl. edn. educator Boston Sch. Dept., 1975-76, 78—, support tchr., 1976-78. Site coord. Tchr. Corps., 1977-81; leader, co-leader Harvard U. Student Tchrs. at Dorchester H.S. Sem., 1995—; tchr. adviser Future Educators Am. Dorchester H.S. Editor, compiler: Cooking With the Stars, 1989. Mem.-del. Mass. Fedn. Tchrs., Boston, 1993-96; elected rep. AFL-CIO (Boston Tchrs. Union), 1986-96; registrar of voters Dorchester (Mass.) H.S., 1986—; adv. bd. New England Assn. Schs. and Colls., 1980-93; 1st v.p., bd. dirs. League of Women for Comty. Svcs., Boston, 1976-80, Cynthia Sickle-Cell Anemia Fund, Boston, 1976-80. Recipient Tchg. award Urban League Guild Mass., 1993. Mem. AAUW, Zeta Phi Beta (Zeta of Yr. 1994), Alpha Delta Kappa, Kappa Delta Pi, Order Ea. Star (past worthy matron Prince Hall chpt. 1983-84), Delta Omicron Zeta, Phi Delta Kappa. Baptist. Avocations: reading, sewing. Home: 36 Dietz Rd Hyde Park MA 02136-1134

HARRIS, FREDERICK HOLLADAY DEBROSCHE, business educator; b. Durham, NC, Feb. 16, 1949; s. Frederick Holladay and Rose (deBrosche) H.; m. Nancy Taylor Steed, Sept. 12, 1970; children: Taylor Drake, Sarah Elizabeth. AB, Dartmouth Coll., 1971; PhD, U. Va., 1981. From asst. to assoc. prof. econs. U. Tex., Dallas-Fort Worth, 1982—90; assoc. dean of faculty affairs, McKinnon prof. econ. and fin. Babcock Sch., Wake Forest U., Winston-Salem, NC, 1991—. Cons. in field. Contbr. articles to profl. jours.; assoc. editor Jour. Indsl. Econs., 1988-93. Mem. Am. Econ. Assn., Fin. Mgmt. Assn., Am. Fin. Assn. Office: Babcock Grad Sch Mgmt PO Box 7659 Winston Salem NC 27109-7659 E-mail: rick.harris@mba.wfu.edu.

HARRIS, GRANT WARREN, principal; b. Bath, Maine, Oct. 25, 1931; s. Grant Monroe and Margaret Ellen (Holland) H.; m. Donna Yardley Fisher, Dec. 24, 1955 (div. Nov. 1975); children: Grant, Scott, Lauren, Keith, Ellen; m. Patricia Ann Guyhn, Mar. 23, 1976; children: Edward, Pamela. BA, U. Conn., 1953; MS, Ea. Conn. State U., Willimantic, 1962; cert. in advance grad. study, U. Hartford, 1964. Cert. tchr., prin., supt. Tchr. grade 6 Noank Sch., Groton, Conn., 1957-58; tchr. grade 7 scis. and math. West Side Jr. H.S., Groton, 1958-61; tchr. 7th and 8th grade math. Hartford (Conn.) Bd. Edn., 1961-62; tchr., prin. Union (Conn.) Elem. Sch., 1962-63; asst. prin. Green Achres Sch., North Haven, Conn., 1963-64; prin. Flanders Sch., East Lyme, Conn., 1965-85, Lake Way Elem. Sch., Littleton, N.H., 1985-90, Walpole (N.H.) Sch., 1990—. Dir. gifted and talented program East Lyme Pub. Schs., Niantic, Conn., 1968-72. Author: The Principal Award System, 1975. Chmn. Guidance Clinic West, Niantic, 1975; supt. Ch. Sch., Niantic, 1973. 1st lt. U.S. Army, 1953-57. Named Outstanding Tchr. Noank (Conn.) PTA, 1957, Outstanding Citizen Niantic C. of C., 1975, Outstanding Vol. Student Coun., Walpole, N.H., 1994; recipient Citation Conn. Legis. Assembly, Hartford, 1984. Mem. NAESP, ASCD, N.H. Elem. Sch. Prins., U.S. Merchant Marines, St. John's Lodge, Phi Delta Kappa. Episcopalian. Avocation: captain passenger vessels. Home and Office: Walpole Sch PO Box 721 Walpole NH 03608-0721

HARRIS, HARRIETT SMITHERMAN, retired elementary school educator; b. Centreville, Ala., Apr. 28, 1932; d. Burl Herbert and Adelaide Helen (Parker) Smitherman; m. Winton Walter Harris, June 3, 1955. BS, U. Chattanooga, 1956; postgrad., Cumberland U., Lebanon, Tenn., 1990. Profl. career ladder III cert., Tenn. Tchr. 5th grade Eastdale/Woodmore Elem. Sch., Hamilton County, Tenn., 1954-56; tchr. 4th and 5th grades Spring Creek Elem. Sch., Hamilton County, Tenn., 1956-59, Anna B. Lacey Elem. Sch., Hamilton County, Tenn., 1959-85, East Ridge Elem. Sch., Chattanooga, 1985-94; retired from tchg., June 1994. Homework hotline tchr. Hamilton County Bd. Edn., 1988—; chmn. Sci. and Health Textbook Adoptionk, Chattanooga, 1991, Hamilton County Zone Spelling Bee, 1991; coord. for sch. Acad. Olympics, Chattanooga State Tech. C.C., 1991-93; mentor Gov.'s Sch. for Prospective Tchrs., U. Tenn. Chattanooga Campus, 1992; mentor Pub. Edn. Found., 1992-94, grade level chairperson 1992-94; mem. Site-Based Decision Making Coun., 1992-94, adv. coun. PACE, 1992-94; judge Tenn. Dept. Edn. Mini-Grants, 1993; sch. rep. Southeast Region Teacher's Study Coun., 1989-94; judge Hamilton County and SE Dist. Co-author: Write On, Hamilton County, 1986. Membership v.p. Freedoms Found., Chattanooga, 1990-92, pres. chpt., 1992-94, v.p. edn., 1995—; vol. Media Ctr., 1995; docent Chattanooga Symphony and Opera Guild, 1995—. AAUW grantee, 1976; recipient Master Tchr. award East Ridge Elem Sch., 1990, Disting. Citizen of the Yr. award Hamilton County, Ind. Bd. Commrs., 1991; named Tchr. of Yr. (grades. 5-8), Hamilton County

Sch. System, 1991, S.E. Dist. Tchr. of the Yr., Tenn. Dept. Edn., 1991, Tenn. Tchr. of Yr., 1992, Hamilton County Edn. Assn. (bd. dirs. 1992); nominee Walt Disney Am. Tchr. awards, 1992. Mem. NEA, PTA (life), AAUW (corr. sec. Tenn. div. 1988-89), Nat. Ret. Tchrs. Assn., Tenn. Edn. Assn., Hamilton County Edn. Assn. (chmn. 1990—), Tenn. Mid. Schs. Assn., Internat. Reading Assn. (chair comms. com. 1995—), Internat. Speakers Platform Assn., Delta Kappa Gamma (membership chmn. chpt. 1990-91), Phi Mu (v.p. chpt. 1953-54). Baptist. Avocations: writing poetry, reading, interior decorating, music, visiting historical sites. Home: 4101 Wiley Ave Chattanooga TN 37412-2635 Office: East Ridge Elem Sch 1014 John Ross Rd Chattanooga TN 37412-1620

HARRIS, IRA STEPHEN, secondary education educator, administrator; b. Bklyn., July 13, 1945; s. Simon and Vera (Vichness) H.; m. Arlene Cramer, Dec. 25, 1971; children: Elliot, David, Sara. BS, Fairleigh Dickinson U., 1968; MS, L.I. U., 1970, Profl. Diploma magna cum laude, 1978. Sci. educator 158Q Marie Curie H.S., Bayside, N.Y., 1968-76; tchr. math., sci. and social studies, media specialist Campbell Jr. H.S. 218Q, Flushing, N.Y., 1976-79, Beard Jr. H.S. 189Q, Flushing, 1979-86; tech. specialist Carson Intermediate Sch. 237Q, Flushing, 1986—; asst. prin. Carr Jr. H.S. 194Q, Flushing, 1995-2001; ret. Commodore Newbridge Boat Club, Bellmore, N.Y.; v.p., edn. chmn. Bellmore Jewish Ctr.; pres. East Bay Civic Assn., Bellmore. Mem. N.Y. Acad. Scis. (judge sci. fair N.Y.C. 1985—). Republican. Home: 2729 Claudia Ct Bellmore NY 11710-4740 E-mail: captainira@aol.com.

HARRIS, JAMES FRANKLIN, philosophy educator; b. Nashville, June 30, 1941; s. James F. and Martha Belle (Elder) H.; 1 child, James F. BA, U. Ga., 1962, MA, 1964; PhD, Vanderbilt U., 1966. Asst. prof. philosophy Transylvania Coll., Lexington, Ky., 1966-67, U. Ga., Athens, 1967-73; assoc. prof. philosophy Coll. William and Mary, Williamsburg, Va., 1974-80, prof., 1980—, Haserot prof. of philosophy, 1984—, chmn. dept., 1989—. Vis. instr. Inst. Higher Edn., U. Ga., Athens, 1967, 68; cons. Nat. Ctr. for State Cts., Williamsburg, 1978 Editor: Analyticity, 1970, Logic, God and Metaphysics, 1992; author: Against Relativism: A Philosophical Defense of Method, 1992, Single Malt Whiskies of Scotland, 1992, Philosophy at 33 1/3 rpm: Themes of Classic Rock Music, 1993, The Book of Classic American Whiskeys, 1995, Analytic Philosophy of Religion, 2002. Fellow Am. Council Learned Soc. Mem. AAUP, Am. Philos. Assn., So. Soc. for Philosophy and Psychology (Jr. award 1969, pres. 1992-93), Soc. for Philosophy of Religion, Phi Beta Kappa. Home: PO Box 447 White Marsh VA 23183-0447 Office: Coll William and Mary Dept Philosophy Williamsburg VA 23168

HARRIS, JAMES HAROLD, III, lawyer, educator; b. Texarkana, Tex., Apr. 26, 1943; s. James Harold Jr. and Mildred (Freeman) H. BA, Dartmouth Coll., 1964; JD, Vanderbilt U., 1967. Bar: Tenn. 1967, U.S. Dist. Ct. (mid. dist.) Tenn. 1972, U.S. Ct. Appeals (6th cir.) 1972. Asst. dean Vanderbilt U. Sch. Law, Nashville, 1971; atty. Met. Govt. Nashville, Nashville, 1972-75; ptnr. Harris & Leach, Nashville, 1975-87, Harris & Baydoun, Nashville, 1987-90; counsel Wyatt, Tarrant, Combs, Gilbert & Milom, Nashville, 1990-93, Gordon, Martin, Jones & Harris, Nashville, 1994—. Capt. USNR, 1967-92. Mem. ABA, Copyright Soc. U.S., Tenn. Bar Assn., Nashville Bar Assn. Home: 103 Burlington Ct Nashville TN 37215-1843 Office: Gordon Martin Jones & Harris 49 Music Sq W Ste 600 Nashville TN 37203-3231 E-mail: j3@lawyer.com.

HARRIS, JAMES HERMAN, pathologist, neuropathologist, consultant, educator; b. Fayetteville, Ga., Oct. 19, 1942; s. Frank J. and Gladys N. (White) H.; m. Judy K. Hutchinson, Jan. 30, 1965; children: Jeffrey William, John Michael, James Herman. BS, Carson-Newman Coll., 1964; PhD, U. Tenn.-Memphis, 1969, MD, 1972. Diplomate Am. Bd. Pathology; sub-cert. in anatomic pathology and neuropathology. Resident, fellow NYU-Bellevue Med. Ctr., N.Y.C., 1973-75; adj. asst. prof. pathology NYU, N.Y.C., 1975-83; asst. prof. pathology and neuroscis. Med. Coll. Ohio, Toledo, 1975-78, assoc. prof., 1978-82, dir. neuropathology and electron microscopy lab., 1975-82; cons. Toledo Hosp., 1979-82, assoc. pathologist/neuropathologist, dir. electron microscopy pathology lab., 1983-91, mem. courtesy staff, 1991—, mem. overview com., credentials com., appropriations subcom. medisgroup, interqual task force. Chmn. clin. support svcs. com., vice chmn. med. staff quality rev. com. Toledo Hosp.; cons. neuropathologist Mercy Hosp., 1976—93, mem. courtesy staff, 1993—; cons. neuropathologist U. Mich. Dept. Pathology, 1984—93; cons. med. malpractice in pathology and neuropathology; mem. AMA Physician Rsch. and Evaluation panel; mem. ednl. and profl. affairs commn., exec. coun. Acad. Medicine; mem. children's cancer study group Ohio State U. Satellite; chmn. tech. and issues subcom. of adv. com. Blue Cross; mem. Task Force on Cost Effectiveness N.W. Ohio; chmn. med. necessity appeals com. Blue Cross/Blue Shield; adv. bd. PIE Mut. Ins. Co. Author med., sci. papers; reviewer Jour. Neuropathology and Exptl. Neurology. Chmn. fin. com., dir. bldg. fund campaign First Bapt. Ch., Perrysburg, Ohio; chmn. steering com. Pack 198 Boy Scouts Am.; faculty chmn. Med. Col. Ohio United Way Campaign; mem. adv. com. Multiple Sclerosis Soc. N.W. Ohio; chmn. alumni scholarship fund Carson-Newman Coll., 1994—95; alumni exec. com. Truett McConnell Coll., 1995—2001; chmn. Loyalty Fund Campaign for 50th Ann., 1996—98. Recipient Outstanding Tchr. award Med. Coll. Ohio, 1980; named to Outstanding Young Men Am., U.S. Jaycees, 1973; USPHS trainee, 1964-69, postdoctoral trainee, 1973-75; grantee Am. Cancer Soc., 1977-78, Warner Lambert Pharm. Co., 1978-79, Miniger Found., 1980, Toledo Hosp. Found., 1985, Promedica Health Care Found., 1986. Mem. Am. Profl. Practice Assn., Am. Pathology Found., Am. Soc. Law and Medicine, Am. Coll. Physician Execs., Lucas County Acad. Medicine (bar acad. liaison com.), Ohio State Med. Assn. (fed. key contact), Med. Assn. Ga., Am. Assn. Neuropathologists (profl. affairs com., awards com., program com., constn. com.), Internat. Acad. Pathologists, Ohio Soc. Pathologists, Truett McConnell Coll. Alumni Assn. (pres. 1998-2001, mem. steering com. capital campaign), EM Soc. Am., Sigma Xi. Republican. Avocations: tennis, real estate rehabilitation, building developer, gardening, white water rafting. Home and Office: 9105 Nesbit Lakes Dr Alpharetta GA 30022-4028

HARRIS, JOSEPH C. education educator; b. Columbus, Ga., Sept. 18, 1940; s. Joseph Clarence and Georgia (Walker) H.; m. Nancy Flowers; children: Alice Kittrell, Elizabeth Whiting Flowers; m. Monika Maria Totten; 1 child, Sonja Sophia Totten-Harris. BA, U. Ga., 1961; BA with honors, Cambridge (Eng.) U., 1967; MA, Harvard U., 1963, PhD, 1969. Asst. prof. Harvard U., Cambridge, Mass., 1969-72, prof., 1985—; from asst. prof. to prof. Stanford (Calif.) U., 1972-82; prof. Cornell U., Ithaca, N.Y., 1982-85. Vis. prof. Bonn U., 1992. Editor: The Ballad & Oral Literature, 1991; contbr. articles to profl. jours. Jr. fellow Soc. for the Humanities, 1971-72, Guggenheim Found. fellow, 1985-87, Am. Coun. Learned Soc. fellow, 1975-76; recipient Elliott prize Medieval Acad., 1972. Office: Harvard Univ Dept English 12 Quincy St Cambridge MA 02138-3902

HARRIS, JOSEPHINE STEVENSON, health educator; b. Jackson, Miss., Sept. 19, 1947; d. Arvesta and Addie Boddie (Davis) Kelly; m. Lee Stevenson, June 17, 1976 (div. 1986); children: George A., Michael Lawrence; m. Johny L. Harris, Apr. 1995. BS in Health, Phys. Edn., Jackson State U., 1971, MS in Health Edn., 1974, cert. edn. adminstrn., 1994. Instr. phys. edn. Langston (Okla.) U., 1971-73; instr. health edn. Ctrl. H.S., St. Paul, Minn., 1974-77; instr. health, coll. prep. MS Jobs Corps Ctr., Crystal Springs, Miss., 1977-79; instr. phys. edn. Lanier H.S., Jackson, Miss., 1979-80, asst. prin., 1996—; instr. health edn., dept. chmn. Blackburn Middle Sch., Jackson, Miss., 1980-96. Trainer C.O.A. U. So. Miss.; mem. adv. bd. J.C.P.T.S.A., Jackson, 1994-95; choreographer Cotillion Links, Debutantes Ball. Mem. Women for Progress of Miss., Jackson; dir. sanctuary choir Pine Grove Bapt. Ch., Jackson, 1991—; designer beautification circle, 1984—. Mem. NEA, AAUW, AAHPERD, Miss. Edn. Assn., Delta Sigma Theta. Democrat. Baptist. Avocations: arts and crafts, singing. Home: 251 Valley Ridge Dr Jackson MS 39206-3160 Office: Blackburn Middle Sch 1311 W Pearl St Jackson MS 39203-2841

HARRIS, LINDA JEAN, principal; b. Tyler, Tex., Nov. 8, 1949; d. Bernardo Navarro and Lavada (Land) H.; divorced; children: Darryl Nickerson, Nathan Jay Nickerson. BA in Lang. Arts and English, Marylhurst Coll., 1971; MS in Edn. and Psychology, Portland State U., 1983. Cert. tchr., adminstr., Oreg. 6th grade tchr. Whitaker Mid. Sch., Portland, Oreg., 1971-76, adminstr. asst., 1983-84; adv. specialist area supt.'s office Office of Staff Devel. and Community Rels., Portland, 1976-82; adminstr. asst. Boise Sch., Portland, 1983-84, Boise-Eliot Sch., Portland, 1984-88; prin. Woodlawn Sch., Portland, 1988—. Bd. dirs. Portland Tchrs. Credit Union. Author: (poems) Voices of Kuumba, Vol. 1, 1990, Vol. II, 1991, Vol. III, 1992; contbr. poems to profl. publs. Bd. dirs. I Have A Dream Found., Portland, 1992—, prin. program; mem. adv. bd. Woodlawn Children of Promise, Portland, 1991—, Woodlawn Initiative for Success and Empowerment, Portland, 1991—, Inner/N.E. YMCA, Portland, 1990-92. Named Vol. of Yr., YMCA, 1991; Edn. Policy Program fellow, 1990; recipient cert. of appreciation Portland Assn. Tchrs., 1991. Mem. Nat. Assn. Elem. Sch. Prins., Oreg. Alliance Black Sch. Adminstr. (sec. 1984, v.p. 1990, cert. of appreciation 1992), N.W. African Am. Writers Workshop (editor 1988-90, award 1992), Portland Elem. Prins. Assn., Confedn. Oreg. Sch. Adminstrs., The Links, Inc. (Portland chpt.), Portland Assn. Pub. Sch. Adminstrs., Delta Sigma Theta (sec.), Delta Kappa Gamma, Phi Delta Kappa. Democrat. Roman Catholic. Avocations: poetry, cinema, reading, bridge, board games. Office: PO Box 3107 Portland OR 97208-3107

HARRIS, MARIA LOSCUTOFF, special education educator, consultant; b. Rahmet Abad, Iran, Jan. 25, 1940; came to U.S., 1949; d. Vasiliy Vasilivitch and Esfir Alexsevna (Samadouroff) Loscutoff; m. Bernard Harris, Sept. 30, 1972; children: William, Richard, Lynn, Clifford, Robert, Bernard, Peter, Steven, Barbara. AA, Sierra Coll., Rocklin, Calif., 1960; BS, San Francisco State U., 1963; MS, Manhattan Coll., 1985. Cert. in spl. edn. and field of dyslexia, N.Y., Calif. Tchr. bus. edn. Westmoor H.S., Daly City, Calif., 1963-66, Coll. San Mateo, Calif., 1964, 65, Amador Sch. Dist., Pleasanton, Calif., 1967-69; adminstrv. asst. LTV, Inc., Anaheim, Calif., 1969-71; office mgr. Western div. Ocean & Atmospheric Sci. Inc., Santa Ana, Calif., 1971-72, office mgr., asst. to adminstr. Dobbs Ferry, N.Y., 1972-79; officer mgr., adminstr. Harris Sci. Svcs., Dobbs Ferry, 1979-84; reading and classroom tchr. Windward Sch., White Plains, N.Y., 1984-88; learning specialist Irvington (N.Y.) Union Free Sch. Dist., 1988—. Cons., tutor Harris Sci. Svcs., Dobbs Ferry, 1993—; mem. Westchester Reading coun. Supporter, contbr. Midnight Run for Homeless, 1985—; vol. Census Bur., 1990, Dobbs Ferry, 1989. Mem. Orton Dyslexia Soc., Internat. Reading Assn., Kappa Delta Pi. Avocations: reading, cooking, travel, volunteer work. Home: 15 Overlook Rd Dobbs Ferry NY 10522-3209 Office: Irvington Union Free Schs 6 Dows Ln Irvington NY 10533-2102

HARRIS, MARQUITA BOLDEN, school librarian; b. Jackson, Tenn., Feb. 21, 1939; d. Freda Bolden and Gracie Mae (Goodrich) Hurst; m. Thomas Alphonso Harris, Jr., Aug. 6, 1961; children: Cheryl Marquita, Stephanie Virginia, Grace Michelle. B in Elem. Edn., Knoxville Coll., 1961; M in Supervision and Adminstrn., Trevecca Coll., 1989. Cert. libr. sci., Tenn. Classroom tchr. Chattanooga (Tenn.) City Schs., 1964-86, libr., 1986—. Bd. dirs. Chattanooga Children's Advocacy Ctr., 1989—. Bd. dirs. Friendship Haven, Chattanooga, 1984—. Mem. Links, Inc. (Chattanooga chpt.), Carats, Inc. (Chattanooga chpt.), Alpha Kappa Alpha. Baptist. Avocation: jazz enth. Home: 3001 Brunswick Cir Hampton Cove AL 35763-8452

HARRIS, MARVIN DEWITT, special education educator; b. Baton Rouge, Sept. 19, 1964; s. Willie Harris and Cherrie (Woodlief) Seales. BA in Spl. Edn., So. U., Baton Rouge, 1988. Cert. tchr., La. Spl. edn. tchr. East Baton Rouge Parish Sch. Bd., 1989-96, dean students, 1996—. Grant writer in field. Mem. com. Boy Scouts Am., Baton Rouge, 1991-92; vol. coach Spl. Olympics, Park Elem. Sch., chmn. "I Care", 1995; coord. edn. Park Clinic/Park Elem. Connection, 1995. Acad. Distinction Fund grantee, 1994-95. Mem. La. Fedn. Tchr.-AFT. Democrat. Seventh Day Adventist. Avocations: photography, music, computers, reading, art. Home: 5576 Asphodel Dr Baton Rouge LA 70806-3552 Office: Park Elem Sch 2700 Fuqua St Baton Rouge LA 70802-2697

HARRIS, MATTHEW NATHAN, surgeon, educator; b. N.Y.C., Dec. 20, 1931; s. Saul and Deborah (Moskowitz) H.; m. Frances Wicentowski, June 27, 1954; children: Amy Rachel, Julie Rebecca, Daniel Charles. BA, NYU, 1952; MD, Chgo. Med. Sch., 1956. Diplomate Am. Bd. Surgery, Nat. Bd. Med. Examiners; lic. physician, N.Y. Intern Bellevue Hosp. Ctr., N.Y.C., 1956-57, resident in gen. surgery, 1957-58, 60-63; sr. clin. trainee in cancer USPHS, N.Y.C., 1963-64; instr. anatomy NYU, N.Y.C., 1966-68, dir. elective surg. anatomy, 1973-74; prof. surgery, dir. surg. oncology NYU Sch. Medicine, N.Y.C., 1979—. Vis. surgeon Bellevue Hosp. Ctr.; attending surgeon Tisch Hosp.; cons. and lectr. in field.; cons. surgeon Manhattan V.A. Hosp. Contbr. articles to Jour. ACS, Breast Disease, Cancer, Annals Surgery, Radiology, N.Y. State Jour. Medicine, Cancer Rsch., Surgery, Jour. Lab. Investigations, others. Capt. USAR, 1958-60, Korea. Chgo. Med. Sch. scholar, 1955. Fellow ACS (cancer liaison fellow, N.Y. state chmn.); mem. AMA, Am. Soc. Clin. Oncology, Am. Assn. Clin. Anatomists, Am. Radium Soc., N.Y. Cancer Soc., N.Y. Surg. Soc. (pres. 1991-92), N.Y. Med. Soc., N.Y. Met. Breast Cancer Group, Soc. Surg. Oncology, N.Y. Cancer Programs Assn., Inc., Pan-Am. Med. Soc., Soc. Cons. Armed Forces, 38th Parallel Med. Soc. (Korea), Pan Pacific Surg. Assn., Internat. Pigment Cell Soc., Assn. Cancer Edn., Assn. Academic Surgery, So. Alumni Bellevue Hosp., Chgo. Med. Sch. Alumni Assn., Alpha Omega Alpha, Sigma Xi, Beta Lambda Sigma. Achievements include research in cytologic evaluation breast diseases by stereoactic aspiration, malignant melanoma vaccine, primary surgical management malignant melanoma. Office: NYU Med Ctr 530 1st Ave New York NY 10016-6402

HARRIS, MELBA IRIS, elementary education educator, secondary school educator, state agency administrator; b. Cullman, Ala., Aug. 8, 1945; d. Karl and Leona Christine (McDowell) Budweg; m. James Allen Harris, Apr. 17, 1965 (div. June 1981); 1 child, James Allen II. BS in Home Econs., U. Ala., 1970, MA in Elem. Edn., 1977, EdS, 1982; BS in Elem. Edn. magna cum laude, St. Bernard Coll., 1975. Instr. Cullman (Ala.) City Schs., 1966-68, Ft. Payne (Ala.) City Schs., 1974-99; curriculum developer Ala. State Dept. Edn., Montgomery, 1987-89; aerospace edn. coordinator Ala. State Dept. Aeronautics, Montgomery, 1987-89; instr. Gwinnett County (Ga.) Schs., 1999—. V.p. Ft. Payne Civettes, 1979. Recipient commendations Ala. Gov. George C. Wallace, 1985, 86, Gov. Guy Hunt, 1987, Ft. Payne City Coun., 1987, Ft. Payne City Bd. Edn., 1987, Civil Air Patrol Albertville Composite Squadron, 1987, Ala. State Bd. Edn., 1987, Ala. State Excellence in Edn. award Fed. Aviation Adminstrn., 1987, Stewart G. Potter award Nat. Aircraft Distbrs. and Mfrs. Assn., 1988, Nat. Frank G. Brewer Meml. Aerospace Edn. award Civil Air Patrol, 1989, Aviation Edn. Excellence award Nat. Gen. Aviation Mfrs. Assn., 1989, NEWEST award NASA, 1995, Achievement in Edn. award Optimist Club, 1999, Tchrs. as Leaders Inc. award, Gwinnett County Bd. Edn., 2001; named A. Scott Crossfield Nat. Aerospace Educator of Yr., 1987, The Nat. Aerospace Edn. Tchr. of Yr., 1987; Christa McAuliffe fellow, 1987, Tchr. of Yr. Meml. award, 1991; named to Ala. Aviation Hall of Fame, 1991. Mem. NEA, NSTA, Ala. Edn. Assn. (state aerospace edn. coord. 1992—), Ft. Payne Edn. Assn. (pres. 1985-86), Air Force Assn. (life), Ala. Aviation Assn., Exptl. Aircraft Internat. (maj. achievement award 1988), Exptl. Aircraft Chpt. 683 (sec., treas. 1987, pres. 1988), Internat. Ninety-Nines, Inc., Kappa Delta Pi. Home: PO Box 681174 Fort Payne AL 35968-1613 Office: Bethesda Sch 525 Bethesda School Rd Lawrenceville GA 30044-3509 E-mail: fflight@peoplepc.com.

HARRIS, MICALYN SHAFER, lawyer, educator, arbitrator, mediator; b. Chgo., Oct. 31, 1941; d. Erwin and Dorothy (Sampson) Shafer. AB, Wellesley Coll., 1963; JD, U. Chgo., 1966. Bar: Ill. 1966, Mo. 1967, U.S. Dist. Ct. (ea. dist.) Mo. 1967, U.S. Supreme Ct. 1972, U.S. Ct. Appeals (8th cir.), 1974, N.Y. 1981, N.J. 1988, U.S. Dist. Ct. N.J., U.S. Ct. Appeals (3d cir.) 1993. Law clk. U.S. Dist. Ct., Mo., 1967-68; atty. The May Dept. Stores, St. Louis, 1968-70, Ralston-Purina Co., St. Louis, 1970-72; atty., asst. sec. Chromalloy Am. Corp., St. Louis, 1972-76; pvt. practice St. Louis, 1976-78; atty. CPC Internat., Inc., 1978-80; divsn. counsel CPC N.Am., 1980-84, asst. sec., 1981-88; gen. counsel S.B. Thomas, Inc., 1983-87; corp. counsel CPC Internat., Englewood Cliffs, NJ, 1984-88; assoc. counsel Weil, Gotshal & Manges, N.Y.C., 1988-90; pvt. practice, 1991; v.p., sec., gen. counsel Winpro, Inc., 1991—. Arbitrator Am., Arbitration Assn., NYSE, NASD; adj. prof. Lubin Sch. Bus. Pace U.; mediator. Mem.: ABA (Ctr. Profl. Responsibility, bus. law sect., past chair corp. counsel com., past chair subcom. counseling the mktg. function, mem. securities law com., tender offers and proxy statements subcom., chair task force on e-mail privacy, task force on electronic contracting, task force on conflicts of interest, ad hoc com. on tech., profl. responsibility com.), Am. Law Inst. (mem. consultative groups, restatement of agy. 3d, UCC Arts. 1 & 2, internat. jurisdiction & judgements projects), Computer Law Assn., N.J. Gen. Coun., Am. Corp. Counsel Assn. N.Y. (mergers and acquisitions com., corp. law com.), Mo. Bar Assn. (past chmn. internat. law com.), Bar Assn. Metro St. Louis (past chair TV com.), Assn. Bar City N.Y., N.J. Bar Assn. (computer law com.), N.Y. State Bar Assn. (exec. com. bus. law sect., securities regulation com., chair internet and technology law com., past chair subcom. on licensing, task force on shrink-wrap licensing, electronic comm. task force). Address: 625 N Monroe St Ridgewood NJ 07450-1206

HARRIS, MICHAEL GENE, optometrist, educator, lawyer; b. San Francisco, Calif., Sept. 20, 1942; s. Morry and Gertrude Alice (Epstein) H.; m. Dawn Block; children: Matthew Benjamin, Daniel Evan, Ashley Beth, Lindsay Meredith. BS, U. Calif., 1964, M in Optometry, 1965, D in Optometry, 1966, MS, 1968; JD, John F. Kennedy U., 1985. Bar: Calif., U.S. Dist. Ct. (no. dist.) Calif. Assoc. practice optometry, Oakland, Calif., 1965-66, San Francisco, 1966-68; instr., coord. contact lens clinic Ohio State U., 1968-69; asst. clin. prof. optometry U. Calif., Berkeley, 1969-73, dir. contact lens extended care clinic, 1969-83, chief contact lens clinic, 1983—, assoc. clin. prof., 1973-76, asst. chief, then assoc. chief contact lens svc., 1970—, lectr., then sr. lectr., 1978—, vice chmn. faculty Sch. Optometry, 1983-85, 95—, prof. clin. optometry, 1984-86, clin. prof., 1986—, dir. residency program, 1993-95, asst. dean, 1994-95, assoc. dean, 1995—, acting dean, 2000, dir. policy and planning, 2003—; lectr. Peter's Meml. U. Calif. Sch. Optometry, 2000. Peter's Meml. lectr. U. Calif. Sch. Optometry, 2000; vis. prof. City U., London, 1984; vis. rsch. fellow U. NSW, Sydney, Australia, 1989; sr. vis. rsch. scholar U. Melbourne, Victoria, Australia, 1989, Victoria, 92; mem. ophthalmic devices panel med. device adv. com. FDA, 1990—, interim chmn., 1994; lectr., cons. in field; mem. regulation rev. com. Calif. Bd. Optometry; cons. hypnosis Calif. Optometric Assn., Am. Optometric Assn.; cons. Nat. Bd. Examiners in Optometry, Soflens divsn. Bausch & Lomb, 1973—, Barnes-Hind Hydrocurve Soft Lenses, Inc., 1974—87, Pilkinton-Barnes Hind, 1987—94, Contact Lens Co., 1977—2001, Palo Alto, Va., 1980, Primarius Corp., Cooper Vision Optics, 1979—, Alcon, 1980—, CIBA, 1976—, Vistakon, 1980—2000; co-founder Morton D. Sarver Rsch. Lab., 1986. Editor current comments sect. Am. Jour. Optometry, 1974-77; editor Eye Contact, 1984-86; assoc. editor The Video Jour. Clin. Optometry, 1988-92; cons. editor Contact Lens Spectrum, 1988—; author: Contact Lenses: Treatment Options for Ocular Disease, Contact Lenses for Pre & Post-Surgery; editor: Problems in Optometry, Special Contact Lens Procedures; Contact Lenses in Ocular Disease, 1990; mem. editl. bd. Contact Lens and Anterior Eye Jour.; contbr. chpts. to books, articles to profl. jours. Planning commnr. Town of Moraga, Calif., 1986, vice-chmn., 1987—88, chmn., 1988—90; mem. Town Coun., Moraga, 1992—96; mem. adv. planning commn. Medi-Cal., 1993—95, chmn., 1994—96, with managed care commn., 1995—, chmn. managed care commn., 1996—98; life mem. Bay Area Coun. for Rescue & Recovery, 1976—; grantor Michael G. Harris Family Endowment Fund U. Calif., Dr. Michael G. Harris Tchg. award U. Calif.; commr. Sunday Football League Contra Costa County, 1974—78; planner, fin. advisor College Pk. HS Track Project; mem. Pleasant Hill C. of C., Friends of Rodgers Ranch, Friends of Libr.; vice-mayor Town Coun., Moraga, 1994—95; city county rels. com. Contra Costa County, Calif.; planning commr. City of Pleasant Hill, Calif., 1999—2002, coun. mem., 2002—; vice chair Redevel. Agy., Pleasant Hill, 2002—; founding mem. Young Adults divsn. Jewish Welfare Fedn., 1965—69, chmn., 1967—68; charter mem. Jewish Cmty. Ctr. Contra Costa County; founding mem. Jewish Cmty. Mus. San Francisco, 1984; pararabinnic Temple Isaiah, Lafayette, Calif., 1987, bd. dirs., 1990, Jewish Cmty. Rels. Coun. Greater East Bay, 1979—83, Campolindo Homeowners Assn., 1981—85. Named Alumnus of Yr., U. Calif. Sch. Optometry, 1999; U. Calif. fellow, 1971; Calif. Optometric Assn. scholar, 1965, George Schneider meml. scholar, 1964. Fellow: AAAS, Prentice Soc. (pres.-elect 1994—96, pres. 1996—98), Assn. Schs. and Colls. Optometry (coun. on acad. affairs), British Contact Lens Assn., Am. Acad. Optometry (diplomate cornea and contact lens sect., chmn. contact lens papers, mem. contact lens com. 1974—, vice-chmn. contact lens sect. 1980—82, chmn. sect. 1982—84, immediate past chmn. 1984—86, chmn.jud. com. 1989—2001, chmn. bylaws com. 1989—, ethics taskforce 1999—, Eminent Svc. award 2003); mem.: ABA, Contra Costa Bar Assn., Calif. Acad. Sci., Calif. State Bd. Optometry (regulation rev. com.), Internat. Soc. Contact Lens Rsch., Mex. Soc. Contactology (hon.), Nat. Coun. on Contact Lens Compliance, Am. Optometric Found., Internat. Assn. Contact Lens Educators, Assn. Optometric Contact Lens Educators, Calif. Optometric Assn., Am. Optometric Assn. (proctor 1969—79, cons. on hypnosis, mem. contact lens sect., position papers com., mem. com. on opthalmic stds., subcom. on testing and certification, cons. editor Jour.), Internat. Assn. Contact Lens Educators, Robert Gordon Sproul Assn. U. Calif., Mensa, Benjamin Ide Wheeler Soc. U. Calif., JFK U. Sch. Law Alumni Assn., U. Calif. Optometry Alumni Assn. (life), Pleasant Hill C. of C. Democrat. Office: U Calif Sch Optometry Berkeley CA 94720-0001 E-mail: mharris@uclink.berkeley.edu.

HARRIS, MICHAEL HATHERLY, educational administrator; b. Indpls., Sept. 8, 1940; s. John Edward and Bessie (Hatherly) H.; children: Christopher, Erik, Megan. BA, Macalester Coll., 1966; MA, U. Denver, 1970; postgrad., Portland State U., 1999—. Acct. exec. Benson Optical Co., Mpls., 1966-70; tchr. Adams County Sch. Dist. 14, Commerce City, Colo., 1970-75, dir. student svcs., 1975-80; prin. Portland (Oreg.) Pub. Schs., 1980-99; coord. Multnomah County Cmty. Schs., 1999—2000; prin. Kelly Creek Elem. Sch. Gresham (Oreg.) Barlow Sch. Dist., 2001—. Active Met. Youth Commn., Portland; chmn. bd. Brentwood/Darlington Cmty. Ctr. Recipient Vol. of Yr. award Multnomah County Commrs., Mayor's Spirit of Portland award, 1995; Dept. Commerce grant, 1995. Mem. Oreg. Assn. for Alternative Edn. (pres. 1988, lobbyist, Spl. Svc. award 1993, treas. 1994, 96), Portland Assn. Med. Sch. Prins. (pres. 1994-95). Avocations: flying, skiing, biking, computers. Office: Kelly Creek Elem Sch 2400 SE Baker Way Gresham OR 97080 Home: 11028 SE Troina Ave Portland OR 97236

HARRIS, MILDRED CLOPTON, clergy member, educator; b. Chgo., May 27, 1936; d. Jordan and Willa Mildred Clopton; m. Herbert Curlee Harris, Feb. 4, 1928. BA, DePaul U., 1957; MA, Columbia U., 1963, Governors State U., 1975; MPS, Loyola U., Chgo., 1985; D in Min., Bible Inst. Sem., Plymouth, Fla., 1985. Ordained to ministry Ind. Assemblies of God. Tchr. Gary (Ind.) Pub. Schs., 1957-93; founder, pres. God First

Ministries, Chgo., 1978—. Organizer Chgo. March for Jesus, 1995-97. Author: Traits of an Intercessor, 1991, Educating Your Child God's Way, 1991, The Productive Prayer Guide, 1991; exec. prodr. (cassette) tribe of Judah En Danse, 1995-96 (ASCAP award); host (TV show) Born Again, (radio show) WYCA 92.3, WCFJ 1470 AM. Bd. dirs. Midwestern U., Chgo., 1989-97, Goodman Theater, Chgo., 1994—, Make a Wish Found., Chgo., 1994-97, Windows of Opportunity, Chgo., 1997—; mem. exec. adv. com. Chgo. Housing Authority, 1995-99, commr., 1999—; overseer Gary (Ind.) Educators for Art, 1990—. Recipient CHANCE award Chgo. Housing Authority, 1998, Seniors-Gladys Reed award, 1998; Mary Herrick scholar Du Sable H.S. Alumni, 1998. Mem. ASCAP, Nat. Soc. Fundraising Execs., Religious Conf. Mgmt. Assn., Nat. Coun. Negro Women (life), Union League Club Chgo., Chgo. Ill. Links Inc. Avocations: traveling, interior decorating. Home: 7246 S Luella Ave Chicago IL 60649-2514

HARRIS, PAMELA MAIZE, journalism educator; b. Topeka, Aug. 14, 1952; d. Oliver Loren and Patricia (Kuhnke) Maize; m. Allen Dortch Harris, May 30, 1976. BA, So. Coll., 1975; MLS, Vanderbilt U., 1979; PhD, U. Tenn., 1994. English, speech and journalism tchr. Madison Acad., Nashville, 1975-79; English tchr., pub. info. officer Forest Lake Acad., Orlando, Fla., 1979-83; asst. editor Classic Chevy World Mag., 1983-84; mng. editor E. Tex. Farm and Ranch News, 1984; editor, corp. comm. Blue Cross and Blue Shield of Tenn., Chattanooga, 1986-88; prof. journalism So. Adventist U., Collegedale, Tenn., 1989-2000, chair journalism and comm. dept., 1994-2000; chair comm. Walla Walla Coll., College Place, Wash., 2001—. Recipient East Tex. Addy and Pradd award, 1985, Award of Merit, Assoc. Ch. Press, 1991, Partnership Rsch. award Coun. for Advancement and Support of Edn., 1992, Mark Excellence award Soc. Profl. Journalists Dist. III, 1992, Grad. Rsch. award U. Tenn. Coll. Comm., 1992-93, Doctoral Forum award Am. Soc. for Info. Sci., 1995. Mem. Assn. Educators Journalism and Mass Comm. (newspaper divsn. McDougal award 1993), Soc. Profl. Journalists, Pub. Rels. Soc. Am., (accredited), Soc. Adventist Communicators (pres. 2001), Beta Phi Mu, Phi Kappa Phi, Kappa Tau Alpha. Office: 204 S College Ave College Place WA 99324 E-mail: harrpa@wwc.edu.

HARRIS, PAULETTE COLLIER, pre-school administrator, educator; b. Nashville, Nov. 5, 1956; d. Rogers Rayfield Collier and Lillie Elois (Waltower) Shannon; m. James Erwin Harris, June 17, 1989; children: Kenyada Shannon, James Jr. BA in Behavioral Sci., Shaw U., 1978. Cert. child devel. assoc. Replacement 5tchr. J. Enos Ray Elem. Sch., Takoma Park, Md., 1978; office mgr. Hawkins & Shannon Constrn., Bloomingdale, Ga., 1979-89; shift mgr. Eastern Airlines, Atlanta, 1989-91; bookkeeper Hair Palace Salon, Atlanta, 1989-91; tchr. Kindercare, Atlanta, 1991-94, Clark Atlanta U. Head-Start, 1994—, mem. adv. bd., 1995-96. Co-author curriculum materials. Mem. NAACP, Order of Ea. Star (Electra award 1997). Democrat. Baptist. Avocations: walking, reading, singing. Home: 381 Pine Valley Rd SW Mableton GA 30126-1621

HARRIS, PENELOPE CLAIRE, preschool, daycare administrator, consultant; b. Martinez, Calif., Aug. 20, 1952; d. John R. and Watrine (Spencer) H.; children: Sara A. Davidson, Rachel L. Harris. AA, Diablo Valley Coll., Pleasant Hill, Calif., 1973; BA, San Francisco State U., 1975; MA, Calif. State U., Hayward, 1993. Tchg. credential, cmty. colls. instr. credential, Calif. Tchr. spinning Albany (Calif.) Adult Sch., 1976; guest instr. U. Calif. Extension, Berkeley, 1978; tchr. Martinez Early Childhood Ctr., 1981-83, YWCA Child Care Ctr., Pacheco, Calif., 1986-87; co-dir. Martinez Parent Coop. Nursery Sch., 1983-87; program dir. YWCA of Contra Costa County, Pacheco, 1987-90; assoc. Internat. Child Resource Inst., Berkeley, 1988-92; dir. Escondido Children's Ctr., Stanford, Calif., 1990-92; coord. Sch. Age Parenting and Infant Devel. Program, Hayward, Calif., 1992—; teen pregnancy prevention coord. Helen Turner Children's Ctr., Hayward, Calif., 1995—, latchkey coord., 1998—. Textile arts cons. Judy Chicago's Through the Flower Corp., Benecia, Calif., 1986-87; instr. Chabot Coll., Hayward, Calif., 1996-97. Bd. dirs. Through the Flower, Belen, N.Mex., 1999—. Mem. AAUW, Calif. Assn. Concerned with Sch. Age Parents, Calif. School-Age Consortium, Delta Kappa Gamma. Office: Helen Turner Children's Ctr 23640 Reed Way Hayward CA 94541-7326

HARRIS, RANDY JAY, university official, finance executive; b. Provo, Utah, Nov. 6, 1946; s. Robert Jay and Odessa Webster (Hill) H.; m. Donna Clara Dodge, Aug. 29, 1969; children: Chad Randy, Tiffiny Lyn, Kimberly Dawn, Christopher Jay, Matthew Scott, Heather Anne. BS, Brigham Young U., 1971, MPA, 1988. CPA; cert. real estate appraiser; ordained bishop LDS Ch. Tax acct. Price Waterhouse & Co., CPA's, L.A., San Diego, 1971-72; tax mgr. Dodge & Dodge, CPA's, Orem, Utah, 1972-73; from sr. auditor to fin. mgr. Latter Day Saints Ch., Salt Lake City, 1973—79, fin. mgr., 1979—80; contr. Weber State U., Ogden, Utah, 1980-90; mng. ptnr. Dodge, Evans & Harris CPA, P.C., Orem, Utah, 1990-92; contr., CFO, asst. v.p. fin. Fla. State U., Tallahassee, 1992-95; assoc. v.p. for fin. U. Mich., Ann Arbor, 1995-97; pres. Veritas Ins. Co., Burlington, Vt., 1995-97; vice chancellor adminstrn. and fin. U. Houston Sys., 1997—2002; v.p. adminstrn. and fin. U. Houston, 1997—2002; pres. Guatamala Norte mission The Ch. of Jesus Christ of Latter Day Saints, 2002—. Instr. pub. mgmt. Grad. Sch. Bus., Brigham Young U., 1988-91; adj. instr. acctg. Weber State U., 1980-90; chmn. bd. Screendesign, Inc., 2000-01. Councilman City of Layton, Utah, 1973-81; bd. dirs. Heritage Mus., Layton, 1984-86, Utah Children's Aid Soc., 1991-92, Ann Arbor Summer Festival, 1996-97; bd. dirs. Humana Hosp. Davis North, Layton, chmn., 1987-92; mem. Layton Parks and Recreation Commn., 1973-75, Utah Layton and Recreation Comm., Layton, 1974-76; mem. exec. com. Western Assn. Coll. and Univ. Bus. Officers, 1989-90; bd. suprs. Latter-Day Saints Credit Union; treas. Bonneville coun. Boy Scouts Am., 1984-85, v.p. Suwannee River Area Coun., 1994-95; Davis County Reps., 1984-85. Mem. AICPA, Nat. Assn. Coll. and Univ. Bus. Officers, Utah Assn. CPAs (chmn. strategic planning com. 1989-92, pres. No. chpt. Ogden 1984-85, chmn. ann. conv. cpm., vice-chmn. practice rev. com. 1982-83, chmn. personal fin. planning com. 1984-85), Ctrl. Assn. Coll. and Univ. Bus. Officers, Fin. Affairs Tax Com. (chmn. Fla. interinstitutional coun. 1992-95), U. Mich. Musical Soc. (bd. dirs. 1997), Nat. Assn. of State Univs. and Land-Grant Colls. (coun. on bus. affairs 1998—, pres. 2000-01). Avocations: marathon running, cross country skiing. Home: 382 West 1750 South Kaysville UT 84037 Office: 5a Avenida 5-55 Edificio Euro Plaza Torre 2 15 Nivel Oficina 1504 Zona 14 Guatemala City Guatemala E-mail: rjharrisd@hotmail.com.

HARRIS, RICHARD JOHN, social sciences educator; b. Belgrade, Minn., Apr. 5, 1948; s. Johnny Lee and Marjorie (Meyers) H.; m. Carolyn Besser (div. 1993); children: Karl, Mark; m. Juanita M. Gillette Firestone, Apr. 18, 1994. BA, Macalester Coll., 1971; MA, Cornell U., 1974, PhD, 1976. From asst. to full prof. U. Tex., San Antonio, 1976—. Project dir. Alamo Area Cmty. Info. Sys., 2000—; vis. prof. Univ. Klagenfurt, Austria, 2002. Contbr. articles to profl. jours.; editor: The Politics of San Antonio: Community Progress and Power, 1983. Active Odyssey of the Mind, San Antonio Sch. Sys., 1994-95; mem. faculty adv. com. U. Tex. Sys., Austin, 1994-96; sec. gen. faculty U. Tex., 1991-96. Staff sgt. USAFR, 1969-74. Recipient cert. of achievement Black Legis. Caucus, U.S. Congress, 1996; postdoctoral fellow U. So. Calif., 1980-82. Mem. Am. Sociol. Assn., Population Assn. of Am., Am. Acad. Polit. and Social Scis., Southwestern Social Sci. Assn., Tex. Econ. and Demographic Assn. (bd. dirs.), Alpha Kappa Delta. Office: U Tex San Antonio Dept Sociology San Antonio TX 78249

HARRIS, RUTH HORTENSE COLES, retired accounting educator; b. Charlottesville, Va., Sept. 26, 1928; d. Bernard Albert and Ruth Hortense (Wyatt) Coles; m. John Benjamin Harris, Sept. 2, 1950; children: John Benjamin Jr., Vita Michelle. BS, Va. State U., 1948; MBA, NYU, 1949; cert. advanced study, EdD, Coll. William and Mary, 1977; LHD, Va. Union U., 1998. CPA, Va. Instr. commerce dept. Va. Union U., Richmond, 1949-53, asst prof., 1953-64; head dept., 1956-69; assoc. prof., head dept. Va. Union U., Richmond, 1964-69, prof., dir. div. commerce, 1969-73, dir. Sydney Lewis Sch. Bus. Adminstrn., 1973-81, prof. acctg., 1981-85, 87—, chmn. dept., 1987-97, mem. mgmt. team Sch. Bus., 1985-87, disting. prof. emeritus, 1997. Bd. dirs. Am. Assembly Collegiate Schs. Bus., St. Louis, 1976-79; mem. adv. bd. Intercollegiate Case Clearing House, 1976-79; mem. state adv. coun. Cmty. Svc. and Continuing Edn. (Title I) Agy., Charlottesville, 1977-81. Chmn. Interdeptl. Com. on Rate-Setting for Children's Facilities, Richmond, 1983-85; bd. dirs. Richmond Urban League; mem. agy. evaluation comn. United Way Greater Richmond; mem. fin. sec. Va. Commonwealth chpt. Nat. Coalition 100 Black Women; participant Va. Heroes, Inc., Richmond, 1991-94, 96. Recipient tchg. excellence award Sears Roebuck Found., 1990, Outstanding Faculty award Va. Coun. for Higher Edn., 1992, Eboné Image award No. Va. chpt. Nat. Coalition of 100 Black Women, 1993, Serwa award Va. Commonwealth chpt., Nat. Coalition 100 Black Women, 1989, Tenneco Excellence in Tchg. award United Negro Coll. Fund, 1995; named Belle Ringer of Richmond—1992 Richmond br. Nat. Assn. Univ. Women. Mem. AICPA (Outstanding Va. Educator award), Va. Soc. CPA's (com. mem., Outstanding Va. Educator award, Disting. Career in Acctg. Edn. award). Baptist. Avocations: ringing handbells, reading, playing piano. Home: 2816 Edgewood Ave Richmond VA 23222-3518 E-mail: hortense2@aol.com.

HARRIS, SHIRLEY, elementary, secondary and adult education educator; b. Chgo., Aug. 14, 1945; BA in Behavioral Sci., Nat. Louis U., 1985; MS in Edn., Chgo. State U., 1993. Cert. in curriculum and instr. Legal sec. Friedman/Rochester, Chgo. and Portland, Oreg., 1974; supr., clerical positions Model Cities, Chgo. and Portland, Oreg., 1973-75; bd. sec. Portland Comm., 1976-78; tchr., clerical positions Portland O.I.C., 1975-76; tchr., juvenile/youth counselor Yaun Youth Ctr., Portland, 1978-80; pres. Flexible Temps, Chgo., 1980—. Part-time prof. Wright Jr. Coll., 1999, Northeastern Ill. U., 1999—, Robert Morris Coll., 2000, DeVry Inst. Tech., 2000; cons. in field, Chgo., 1983; typing tchr., Chgo., 1983; pers. recruiter, Chgo., 1974-75. Contbr. poetry to anthologies. Bd. dirs. Operation Probe, Chgo., 1990-93. Mem. NAFE, ASCD, Internat. Platform Assn. Baptist. Home: 28 E Jackson Blvd Ste 1023-580 Chicago IL 60604

HARRIS, STEPHEN ERNEST, electrical engineering and applied physics educator; b. Bklyn., Nov. 29, 1936; s. Henry and Anne (Alpern) H.; m. Frances Joan Greene, June 7, 1959; children: Hilary Ayn, Craig Henry. BS, Rensselaer Poly. Inst., 1959; MS, Stanford U., 1961, PhD, 1963. Mem. tech. staff Bell Telephone Labs., Murray Hill, N.J., 1959-60; coop. student Sylvania Electric Systems, Mountain View, Calif., 1961-63; prof. elec. engring. Stanford U., Calif., 1963-79, prof. elec. engring. and applied physics, 1979—, dir. Edward L. Ginzton Lab., 1983-88, Kenneth and Barbara Oshman prof., 1988—. Chair Dept. Applied Physics, Stanford U., 1993-96. Recipient Alfred Noble prize ASCE, 1965, Curtis McGraw rsch. award Am. Soc. Engring. Edn., 1973, Davies medal for engring. achievement Rensselaer Poly. Inst., 1984, Einstein prize, 1991, Optical Soc. Am. Teaching award, 1992, Frederic Ives medal Optical Soc. Am., 1999, IEEE/LEOS Quantum Electronics award, 1994. Fellow: IEEE (David Sarnoff award 1978), AAAS (Arthur L. Schawlow prize in laser sci. 2002), Am. Phys. Soc., Optical Soc. Am. (Charles Hard Townes award 1985), Am. Acad. Arts and Scis.; mem.: Nat. Acad. Scis., Nat. Acad. Engring. Office: Stanford Univ Edward L Ginzton Lab 450 Via Palou Mall Stanford CA 94305-4085

HARRIS, VALERIE COLEMAN, office assistant; b. King William, Va., June 5, 1957; d. James Edward Sr. and Maude Ellen (Taylor) Coleman; m. Ronald Stevenson Harris Sr., Aug. 1, 1981; 1 child, Ronald Steven Harris Jr. Student, Va. Commonwealth U., 1982-88, J. Sargeant Rey Coll., 1978-86. Adminstr. Med. Coll. Va., Richmond, 1981-90; office asst. CSX Corp., Richmond, 1991—. Mem. NAFE. Home: 3404 Hollow Ridge Ct Chesterfield VA 23832-8560

HARRIS, VIRGINIA SYDNESS, religious studies educator; b. Fargo, N.D., Oct. 24, 1945; d. Kenneth Jeffries and Jeanette Lucille Sydness; m. Granville Reed Harris, Dec. 29, 1966; children: G. Richard, Donald Thomas, Steven Jeffrey. BS in Polit. Sci. and Edn., Moorhead State U., 1967; CSB (hon.), Mass. Metaphysical Coll., 1982; postgrad., Principia Coll., Elsah, Ill., Mills Coll. Owner Edgewater Inn & Marina, Detroit Lakes, Minn., 1966-70; asst. to presdl. interpreter U.S. Dept. State, Washington, 1967-68; sec. sch. tchr. Fargo (N.D.) Pub. Schs., 1968-70; TV host, prodr. Pub. Broadcast Sys., Fargo, 1968-70; Christian Sci. tchr., 1982—; Christian Sci. lectr., 1983-89. Faculty mem. Healing & Spirituality Symposium Harvard Med. Sch. and New Eng. Deaconess Hosp., Boston, 1995—. Contbr. articles to profl. jours.; spkr. in field. Bd. dirs. LWV, 1968-73, YWCA, 1969-73; clk. Christian Sci. Ch., Boston, 1986-90, bd. dirs., chair, 1990—; treas., bd. dirs. Nat. Found. Women Legislators, Inc., Washington, 1994—. Mem. AAUW, PEO, Jr. League Boston, Wellesley Coll. Club, City Club Washington. Avocations: jogging, skiing, reading, needlepoint. Home: 111 Bogle St Weston MA 02493-1056 Office: The First Ch of Christ Scientist 175 Huntington Ave # A253 Boston MA 02115-3117

HARRIS, WALTER EDGAR, chemistry educator; b. Wetaskiwin, Alta., Can., June 9, 1915; s. William Ernest and Emma Louise (Humbke) H.; m. Phyllis Pangburn, June 14, 1942; children: Margaret Anne, William Edgar. BS, U. Alta., 1938, MS, 1939; PhD, U. Minn., 1944; DSc (hon.), U. Waterloo, 1987, U. Alta., 1991. Research fellow U. Minn., 1943-46; prof. analytical chemistry U. Alta., Edmonton, 1946-80, chmn. dept. chemistry, 1974-79, chmn. Pres.'s Adv. Com. on Campus Revs., 1980-90. Author: (with H.W. Habgood) Programmed Temperature Gas Chromatography, 1965, (with B. Kratchovil) Chemical Separations and Measurements, 1974, Teaching Introductory Analytical Chemistry, 1974, An Introduction to Chemical Analysis, 1981, Risk Assessment, 1997, (with H.A. Laitinen) Chemical Analysis, 1975; contbr. numerous articles to profl. jours. Decorated Order of Can., 1998; recipient Outstanding Achievement award U. Minn., 1973; Govt. Alta. Achievement award, 1974 Fellow AAAS, Royal Soc. Can., Chem. Inst. Can. (hon., Fisher Sci. Lecture award 1969, Chem. Edn. award 1975, hon. fellow, 2001); mem. Am. Chem. Soc., Sigma Xi. Home: Ste 515 11148-84 Ave Edmonton AB Canada T6G 0V8 Office: U Alta Dept Chem Edmonton AB Canada T6G 2G2 E-mail: Walter.Harris@ualberta.ca.

HARRIS-OLAYINKA, VERDA (LORRAINE HARRIS-OLAYINKA), health agency administrator, cultural consultant; b. Bklyn., Jan. 19, 1949; d. Warren Linwood and Mattie (Noonan) Harris; m. Ade Olayinka, July 16, 1988; children: Khalebo Harris, Khalim Harris. BA, Bklyn. Coll., 1975; M of Profl. Studies, Cornell U., 1985. Coord., supr. FAMUS Artists-St. Petersburg (Fla.) Arts Comsn., 1977-78; project dir. NAACP-APETS, St. Petersburg, 1978-79; intake coord. Vocat. Found., Inc., N.Y.C., 1979-80; job developer Westside Cluster Ctrs. and Settlements, Inc., N.Y.C., 1980-82; instr. continuing edn. York Coll., Jamaica, N.Y., 1984-86; project dir. Paul Robeson Theatre, Bklyn., 1987; program dir. Latimer-Woods Econ. Devel. Assn., Bklyn., 1987-89; cultural cons. Rsch. and Devel., Bklyn., 1989—; rsch. coord. East Fulton Street Group, Bklyn., 1991-92; project coord. HEALTH WATCH Info. and Promotion Svcs., Inc., Bklyn., 1992—96; city rsch. scientist III N.Y.C. Dept. Pub. Health, 1996—2001, pres., dir. office correction AIDS prevention, 2001—. Bd. dirs. 40 Greene Avenue Cultural Ctr., Inc., Bklyn., 1988-90, East Fulton Street Group, 1991-97; facilitator Nat. Conf. Artists, N.Y.C., 1987, Ednl. Summit: Linking Culture and Edn., N.Y.C., 1992. Author: (booklet) African American Studies for the Adult Basic Reader, 1986; (book) Advancing the Mission of Education, 1992, AIDS & African-Americans: It's Time for Action, 1996, Internat. Jour. Africana Studies, 2000. Grantee CUNY/Mcpl. Assistance Corp./Adult Edn. Act literacy project. Avocations: classical piano, blues/jazz bassoon, traditional african flutes, expounding african culture and the arts. Home: 400 Marion St Brooklyn NY 11233-2716

HARRISON, ALICE KATHLEEN, retired elementary educator; b. Lafayette, Ind., Dec. 4, 1937; d. Robert Ellsworth and Stella Martha (Cisan) Van Voorst; m. George William Harrison, Apr. 6, 1960 (div. 1978); children: Martha Jo, Wesley Todd. BA, Ball State U., 1960, postgrad., 1987-88, 91; MA, Jersey City State Coll., 1984. Cert. tchr., supr., reading specialist, N.J. Tchr. Midland Park (N.J.) Pub. Schs., 1960-61, Cresskill (N.J.) Pub. Schs., 1962-65, Byram Twp. Pub. Schs., Stanhope, N.J., 1967-69, Sparta (N.J.) Pub. Schs., 1969-94, mem. curriculum coun., 1989-94, ret., 1994, presenter in-svc. edn. programs, 1990. Mem. music com. Sparta United Meth. Ch., 1982-87; coach Sparta Soccer Club, 1982-86; coord. Sparta area Boy Scouts Am., 1984-87, unit commr. Morris-Sussex coun., 1988—; leader 4-H Club, Sparta, 1985-86; broom maker, tour guide Hist. Waterloo Village, Stanhope, N.J., 1995—; chair edn. curriculum Com. at Waterloo Found. for Arts. Recipient Scouter's Key award Morris-Sussex coun. Boy Scouts Am., 1987. Mem. N.J. Ret. Educators Assn., Sussex County Ret. Educators Assn. (mem. com. scholarship philantropic fund, Am. Legion Aux., Alpha Omicron Pi. Avocations: writing children's literature, stamp collecting, backpacking, gardening. Home: 92 Glenside Trl Sparta NJ 07871-1230

HARRISON, ARTHURLYN CAROL, special education educator; b. San Angelo, Tex., Aug. 10, 1948; d. James Lawrence and Jacquelyn (Brown) Anderson; m. Ronald Lea Harrison, Sept. 5, 1969; children: Clinton Lea, Jeremy James. BA, Angelo State U., 1972, MEd, 1974. Cert. English tchr., learning disabilities tchr., supr., Tex. Gifted & talented, spl. edn. educator San Angelo Ind. Sch. Dist., dir. spl. programs, 1997-98. Adv. bd. mem. Region Svc. Ctr., San Angelo, 1991, Community Action Coun., Mental Health Mental Retardation, San Angelo; dir. United Way, San Angelo, 1990., Coordinated Resource Cmty. Group Concho Valley. Named one of Outstanding Young Women Am., 1980. Mem. Tex. Coun. Adminstrs. Spl. Edn., Alpha Delta Kappa, Phi Delta Kappa. Home: PO Box 3214 San Angelo TX 76902-3214 Office: San Angelo Ind Sch Dist 1621 University Ave San Angelo TX 76904-5164

HARRISON, CARLA ISLEY, secondary education educator; b. Burlington, N.C., Dec. 13, 1948; d. Frederick Palmer and Elizabeth (Phillips) Isley; m. William Glenn Harrison III, June 17, 1973; children: Allison Palmer, William Glenn IV. BS, Atlantic Christian Coll., 1971; MEd, Elon Coll., 1989. Tchr. Chatham County Schs., Pittsboro, N.C., 1971-74, Alamance County Schs., Graham, N.C., 1974—; tchr. trainer Tchr. Effectiveness Program Alamance County Schs., 1986-87; mem. support team ICP Tchrs., 1988; mentor tchr. 1988— Treas. Haw River Elementary PTA, N.C., 1981-82, mem. 1990-93; mem. Alamance County Arts Assn., Graham, N.C., 1982-86, Woodlawn Mid. PTA, 1990-93; precinct official Alamance County Bd. Elections, Graham, 1982-84; hon. mem. Service League Alamance County, Burlington, N.C., 1980; chmn. Haw River Sch. Site Based Decision Making Tchr. Team, 1989—; rep. staff devel. team Haw River Elem., 1992-93; del. to conv. N.C. Reading Assn., 1993; instr. N.C. Tchr. Acad., 1994-95; named to Haw River Elem. Crisis Intervention Team, 1992—, Alamance County Adminstrv. Leadership Intern Program, 1994—. 1st runner up Tchr. of Yr. Alamance County, 1989; recipient Elem. Sci. Teaching award ctrl. chpt. Am. Chem. Soc., 1990, Excellence in Edn. Teaching award Alamance County C. of C., 1993. Mem. NEA, N.C. Assn. Sci. Tchrs. (presenter conv. 1986), NAFE, N.C. Assn. Educators (rep. Haw River 1989-90, 91-92, 92-93), Smithsonian Inst. (assoc.), Internat. Reading Assn. (presenter 1988), Alpha Delta Kappa, Phi Mu. Democrat. Methodist. Clubs: Burlington Jr. Women's (chmn. child identification project 1986, winner 1st and 3d place Alamance County Women's Club arts competition) (N.C.); Brownies (food and entertainment dir. 1985-86) (Graham, N.C.), Quarry Hills Country (Graham). Lodge: Moose. Office: Alamance County Schs Haw River Elem RR 1 Box 1 Haw River NC 27258-9801

HARRISON, DENNIS I. archivist; b. Cleve., May 26, 1941; s. Irven W. and Doris B. (Rieger) H.; m. Patricia J. Yeskulsky, June 1980; 1 child, Thomas A. AB cum laude, Heidelberg Coll., 1965; MA, Western Res. U., 1967; PhD, Case Western Res. U., 1975. Manuscripts processor Western Res. Hist. Soc., Cleve., 1967-68, asst. curator of manuscripts, 1968-69, curator of manuscripts, 1970-85; univ. archivist Case Western Res. U., Cleve., 1985—. Pres. Soc. Ohio Archivists, 1975-77, 89-91; mem. Ohio Hist. Records Adv. Bd., 1977-97. Author: Working History, 1984. Consumers League grantee Hist. Hist. Record and Publs. Commn., U.S. Govt., 1979, Fedn. for Com. Planning Planning grantee Nat. Hist. Record and Publs. Commn., U.S. Govt., 1981, New Med. Curriculum Archival Project, Culpeper and Cleve. Found., 1994. Mem. Soc. Am. Archivists (coun. mem. 1998-2001), Soc. Ohio Archivists (v.p., pres., coun. mem.). Democrat. Episcopalian. Office: Case Western Res Univ 10900 Euclid Ave Cleveland OH 44106-4901

HARRISON, EARL GRANT, JR., educational administrator; b. Media, Pa., Oct. 10, 1932; s. Earl Grant and Carol Rogers (Sensenig) H.; m. Jean Spencer Young, July 6, 1957; children: Colin Young, Dana How. BA, Haverford Coll., 1954, LLD (hon.), 1991; BDiv, Yale U., 1959; MA in Social and Philos. Founds. Edn., Columbia U., 1965. Instr. Religion and Philosophy Antioch Coll., 1956-58; dir. Coun. Religion Ind. Schs., N.Y.C., 1959-64; tchr. Bklyn. Friends Sch., 1964-65; dir. religious edn. William Penn Charter Sch., Phila., 1965-68; headmaster Westtown (Pa.) Sch., 1968-78; head of sch. Sidwell Friends Sch., Washington, 1978-98. Interim exec. dir. Friends Coun. on Edn., Phila., 2000-01; bd. mgrs. Haverford Coll., 1973-85; mem. instl. rev. bd. Nat. Eye Inst., 1987—03; trustee The Kendal Corp., 1999—. Trustee Good Hope Sch., St. Croix, 1974-80, 82-88. Mem. The Headmasters Assn. (v.p. 1986-87), Country Day Headmasters Assn. (pres. 1992-93), Assn. Ind. Schs. Greater Washington (pres. 1989-90). Democrat. Avocations: tennis, travel.

HARRISON, EDWARD MATTHEW, retired industrial educator; b. Baton Rouge, Mar. 19, 1943; s. Nicholas Samuel and Sadie (Kelly) H. BS, So. U., 1964, MEd, 1970; PhD, Kans. State U., 1977; postgrad., Harvard U., 1984. Tchr. Houston Sch. Sys., 1965, Buena Vista Sch. Dist., Saginaw, Mich., 1965-72; asst. prof. indsl. edn. So. U., Baton Rouge, 1972-80; prof., head dept. indsl. and engring. tech. Grambling State U., La., 1980—2002, dir. vocat. edn. and tech. edn., 1980—2002, dir. Title III Activity, 1987-99. Mem. Am. Vocat. Assn., Internat. Tech. Edn. Assn., Nat. Assn. Indsl. Tech., Am. Coun. Indsl. Arts Tchr. Edn., Lions (treas. 1982-84), Masons, Phi Delta Kappa, Phi Beta Sigma. Democrat. Baptist. Avocations: sports cars, fishing, reading, wood and plastic crafts. Home: PO Box 228 Grambling LA 71245-0228

HARRISON, HELEN RAY GRIFFIN, elementary school educator, volunteer; b. Enterprise, Ala., Oct. 13, 1936; d. A. D. and Ethel (Hitchcock) Griffin; m. Burt P. Redmon, June 3, 1956 (div.); children: John Patrick, Michael Lee; m. Dan Albert Harrison, Nov. 19, 1982 BS in Edn., Troy State U., 1975, MS in Elem. Edn., 1979. Tchr. Enterprise (Ala.) Pub. Schs., 1975-97. Facilitator current missions group Bapt. Women; raise puppies for Southeastern Guide Dogs, Inc., area coord. for Wiregrass puppy raisers. Vol. disaster relief Coffee County chpt. ARC. Mem. NEA, Ala. Edn. Assn., Enterprise Edn. Assn., Ala. Ret. Tchrs. Assn., Lions Club Baptist. Avocations: church, needlework, tolepainting, reading, family. Home: 115 Kate St Enterprise AL 36330-3745

HARRISON, JONATHAN, philosophy educator; b. West Derby, Liverpool, Eng., Sept. 22, 1924; s. Edward Albert and Dorothy Marshall (Williams) H.; m. Jean Bradbury (dec. 1969); children: Roger Marshall,

Kate Elizabeth, Timothy James, John Edward; m. Antonia Gransden, 1978. BA in Politics, Philosophy and Econs., Corpus Christi Coll./Oxford U., 1945, MA, 1952. Lectr. in philosophy U. Durham, Eng., 1947-59; sr. lectr. in philosophy U. Edinburgh, 1959-64; prof. philosophy U. Nottingham, Eng., 1964-88. Prof. philosophy Northwestern U., Chgo., 1968. Author: Our Knowledge of Right and Wrong, 1971, reprinted, 1993, Hume's Moral Epistemology, 1976, Hume's Theory of Justice, 1981, A Philosopher's Nightmare and Other Stories, 1985, Time-Travel for Beginners and Other Stories, 1988, Ethical Essays, Vols. I, II, III, 1993-95, Essays in Metaphysics and the Theory of Knowledge, Vols. I, II, 1995-96, God, Freedom and Immortality, 1999; editor, introduction and top notes Challenges to Morality, 1993; contbr. numerous articles to profl. jours. Mem. Mind Assn. (past pres.), Royal Inst. Philosophy (mem. coun.). Avocations: walking, reading, music. Home: 10 Halifax Rd Cambridge CB4 3PX England

HARRISON, LOIS SMITH, hospital executive, educator; b. Frederick, Md., May 13, 1924; d. Richard Paul and Henrietta Foust (Menges) Smith; m. Richard Lee Harrison, June 23, 1951; children: Elizabeth Lee Boyce, Margaret Louise Wade, Richard Paul. BA, Hood Coll., 1945, MA, 1993, Columbia U.; LHD (hon.), Hood Coll., 1993. Counselor CCNY, 1945-46; founding adminstr., counselor, instr. psychology and sociology Hagerstown (Md.) Jr. Coll., 1946-51, registrar, 1946-51, 53-54, instr. psychology and orienta, 1954-56; registrar, instr. psychology, Balt. Jr. Coll., 1951-54; bus. mgr., acct. for pvt. med. practice Hagerstown, 1953-2000; trustee Washington County Hosp., Hagerstown, 1975-97, chmn. bd., 1986-88, 95—; mem. bd. Washington Couty Health Sys. Inc., 1997—. Chmn. Home Fed. Savs. Bank, Hagerstown, 1997-99; chmn. acute care Health Sys. Bd., 1997—; chmn. bd. dirs. Home Fed. Savs. Bank, 1998-2000, emeritus, 2001—; spkr. ednl. panels, convs. hosp. panels and seminars. Author: The Church Woman, 1960-65. Trustee Hood Coll., Frederick, 1972—, chmn. bd., 1979-95; mem. Md. Gov.'s Commn. to Study Structure and Ednl. Devel. Commn., 1971-75; pres. Washington County Coun. Ch. Women, 1970-72; appointee Econ. Devel. Commn., County Impact Study Commn. Bd.; bd. dirs. Md. Hosp. Assn., 1988-98, Md. Chs. United, 1975—; chmn. bd. dirs. Md. Hosp. Edn. Inst., 1978-98; mem. Christ's Reformed Ch., 1935—; pres. Ch. Consistory; chmn. Chesapeake Healthcare Forum, 1995-97. Recipient Alumnae Achievement award Hood Coll., 1975, Washington County Woman of Yr. award, AAUW, 1984, Md. Woman of Yr. award, 1984, Md. Woman of Yr. award Francis Scott Key Commn. for Md.'s 350th Anniversary, 1984; named one of top 10 women Tri-State area, Herald-Mail Tri-State newspaper, 1990, Zonta Internat. Woman of Yr., 1994, Outstanding Woman of the Yr., Woman At the Table award, 2002. Mem. Hagerstown C. of C. Republican. Home: 12835 Fountain Head Rd Hagerstown MD 21742-2748 Office: Washington Cty Hosp Off Chmn Bd Hagerstown MD 21740 E-mail: lorichco@aol.com.

HARRISON, VALERIE E. English language educator; b. Orangeburg, S.C., Nov. 12, 1954; d. Brantley Edward Sr. and Josephine (Robinson) Evans; m. Gerald Harrison Sr., Dec. 30, 1978; children: Gerald Jr., Gerrin. BA in english Edn., S.C. State Coll., 1976, MEd in English, 1984; postgrad., U. S.C., 1989-91, Francis Marion Coll., 1989-91. Cert. tchr., S.C. Tchr. Florence Sch. Dist., 1976-80; tchr. Rosenwald High Sch. Darlington (S.C.) County Sch. Dist., 1980-82, tchr. St. John's High Sch., 1982-89, chair English dept. St. John's High Sch., 1988-89, dist. curriculum/secondary coord., 1989—, chpt. 1 parent involvement coord., 1989. Mem. state writing improvement coord. coun., mem. 1992 evaluating and rating com. for lit., mem. nat. writing standards collaboration state delegation, mem. state exit exam. writing com. S.C. State Dept. Edn.; mem. writing team S.C. Lang. Arts Framework, 1993—; presenter in field. Sec. ladies guild St. Ann's Cath. Ch. Grantee S.C. State Dept. Edn. Mem. ASCD, NEA, S.C. Edn. Assn., Darlington County Edn. Assn., Am. Assn. Sch. Adminstrs., S.C. Assn. Sch. Adminstrs., S.C. Lang. Arts Coords. Assn., S.C. ASCD, S.C. Internat. Reading Assn., S.C. Coun. Tchrs. English, S.C. State Coll. Alumni Assn., Phi Delta Kappa. Avocations: reading, writing, football, exercise. Home: 120 Wildwood Dr Quinby SC 29506-7234 Office: Darlington County Sch Dist 102 Park St Darlington SC 29532-3124

HARRISON, WALTER ASHLEY, physicist, educator; b. Flushing, N.Y., Apr. 26, 1930; s. Charles Allison and Gertrude (Ashley) H.; m. Lucille Prince Carley, July 17, 1954; children: Richard Knight, John Carley, William Ashley, Robert Walter. B. Engring. Physics, Cornell U., 1953; MS, U. Ill., 1954, PhD, 1956. Physicist Gen. Elec. Research Labs., Schenectady, 1956-65; prof. applied physics Stanford (Calif.) U., 1965-2001, prof. emeritus, 2001—, chmn. applied physics dept., 1989-93, prof. emeritus, 2001—. Scientific adv. bd. Max Planck Inst., Stuttgart, Germany, 1989-92. Author: Pseudopotentials in the Theory of Metals, 1966, Solid State Theory, 1970, Electronic Structure and the Properties of Solids, 1980, Elementary Electronic Structure, 1999, Applied Quantum Mechanics, 2000; editor: the Fermi Surface, 1960, Proceedings of the International Conference on the Physics of Semiconductors, 1985, Proceedings of the International Conference on Materials and Mechanisms of High-Temperature Superconductivity, 1989. Guggenheim fellow, 1970-71; recipient von Humboldt sr. U.S. scientist award, 1981, 89, 94; vis. fellow Clare Hall, Cambridge U., 1970-71. Fellow Am. Phys. Soc. Home: 817 San Francisco Ct Stanford CA 94305-1021 Office: Stanford U Dept Applied Physics Stanford CA 94305-4045 E-mail: walt@stanford.edu.

HARRISON, WENDY JANE MERRILL, insurance company executive; b. Waterbury, Conn., Dec. 4, 1961; d. David Kenneth and Jane Joy (Nevius) Merrill; m. Aidan T. Harrison (div. Nov. 1998); children: Christopher, Charlotte, Ryan; m. Michael G. Kelly, Oct. 2, 1999. BA in Journalism, George Washington U., Washington, 1981; MBA in mgmt., Cornell U., 1992. Intern in edn. HEW, Washington, summer 1978, writer, summer 1979; rsch. asst. dep. health svcs. adminstrn. George Washington U., Washington, 1979-81; sec. Nat. Assn. Beverage Importers, Washington, 1981; account exec. Staff Design, Washington, 1982; adminstrv. aide Internat. Food Policy Rsch. Inst., Washington, 1983-86; program assoc. Acad. for Ednl. Devel., Washington, 1986-87; pvt. practice cons. Washington, 1987-88; adminstrv. mgr. food and nutrition policy program Cornell U., Ithaca, 1988-92; cons. in mgmt. of med. practices Med. Bus. Mgmt., Ithaca, 1994-95; realtor Century 21 Alpha, 1995-97; compensation mgr. Santa Clara (Calif.) U., 1996-98; sr. compensation analyst Stanford (Calif.) U., 1998-99; human resources cons. Siemens Info. and Comm. Networks, 2000; compensation and benefits mgr. Kana Comms., 2000-2001; U.S. compensation mgr. KLA-Tencor, 2001—02; pres. The Benefits Source Ins. Svcs. Inc., Calif., 2003—. Cons., editor George Washington U., 1986; cons., rapporteur Internat. Food Policy Restaurant Inst., Washington and Copenhagen, Denmark, 1987; cons., adminstr. Hansell & Post, Washington, 1987-88, Cornell U., Washington and Ithaca, 1988; pvt. practice cons., 2001—. Sponsor Worldvision, Tanzania, 1988-91. George Washington U. scholar, 1979-81. Mem. AMA, Soc. for Human Resources Mgmt., Sigma Delta Xi (scholar 1980). Democrat. Episcopalian. Avocations: piano, hiking, swimming. Home: 39 Starlite Ct Mountain View CA 94043-1937 E-mail: wendy@benefits-source.org.

HARRISON-SCOTT, SHARLENE MARIE, elementary school educator; b. Fresno, Calif., Dec. 5, 1949; d. Philip B. and Geraldine Marie (Doucette) German; m. Russell Albert Harrison, Aug. 29, 1970 (div. June 1991); children: Nicholas Benjamin, Christopher Ryan; m. Jeffrey Brian Scott, Dec. 11, 1993. BA, Calif. State U., Fresno, 1971; cert. in libr. media tchg., Fresno Pacific Coll., 1996. Tchr. kindergarten Modesto (Calif.) City Schs., 1972-90, tchr., libr. K-6th grades, 1991—. Master tchr. Demonstration Sch. for Calif. State, Stanislaus, 1974-76; instr. Fresno Pacific Coll., 1985-91, Ottowa U., Phoenix, 1990; cons. Archdiocese L.A., 1986-91; mem. recommended reading lit. list revision com. Calif. Dept. Edn. Author: Bear Necessities, 1987-93. Recipient Disting. Educator in Tech. award Computer Using Educators Region VI, 1998, Profl. Svc. award Calif. Sch. Libr. Assn., 2001, Disting. Sch. award winner, 1999. Mem. ALA, Calif. Reading Assn. (symposia spkr. 1989-93), Calif. Sch. Libr. Assn. (pres. 1997-98, chair sch. libr. stds. for K-6 info. skills sect. 2002—), Phi Delta Kappa, Omega Nu. Democrat. Roman Catholic. Avocations: gardening, decorating, antique collecting, reading. Home: 3501 Sagewood Ct Modesto CA 95356-1724 E-mail: bks4me@thevision.net.

HARRIS-WARRICK, RONALD MORGAN, education educator; b. Berkeley, Calif., July 28, 1949; s. Morgan and Marjorie Ruth (Mason) H.; m. Rebecca Lamar Warrick, Apr. 5, 1975; children: Sheridan, Thomas. BA, Stanford U., 1970, PhD, 1976, Postdoctoral fellow, 1978, Harvard Med. Sch., Boston, 1980. Asst. prof. Cornell U., Ithaca, N.Y., 1980-86, assoc. prof., 1986-92, prof., 1992—. Vis. scientist Ecole Normale Superieure, Paris, 1986-87; vis. prof. Stanford Med. Sch., 1994, Karolinska Inst., Stockholm, Sweden, 2001-02; chmn. dept. neurobiology and behavior Cornell U., 2002—. Editor: Dynamic Biological Networks, 1992; assoc. editor Jour. Neurophysiology; contbr. articles to profl. jours; assoc. editor Jour. Neurophysiology. Asst. scoutmaster Boy Scouts of Am., Ithaca, N.Y., 1992—. Recipient Stephen Fox Meml. award Stanford U., 1970, Guggenheim fellowship, 1985. Mem. AAAS, Internat. Soc. for Neuroethology, Soc. for Neurosci., Phi Beta Kappa. Avocations: skiing, camping, hiking, music. Office: Cornell U Sect Neurobiology/Behavior Seeley G Muld Hall Ithaca NY 14853 E-mail: rmh4@cornell.edu.

HARROLD, MERRY ELLENOR, retired secondary education educator; b. New Phila., Ohio, Oct. 27, 1937; d. Paul Davis and Ellenor Adella (Close) Geis; m. Richard Max Harrold, Aug. 29, 1958; 1 child, Lee Ellen Harrold Hollingsworth. BS in Math., Chemistry, Music, Ctrl. Mich. U., 1959, MA in Math., 1963. Cert. secondary permanent credential, Mich., gen. secondary credential, Calif., adminstrv. svc. credential, Calif. Tchr. math., chair dept. Pinconning (Mich.) H.S., 1959-61; tchr. math., physics, music Rapid River (Mich.) H.S., 1961-62; tchr. math., chair dept. Gladwin (Mich.) H.S., 1962-63, Escalon (Calif.) H.S., 1963-67; tchr. math. Modesto (Calif.) H.S., 1967-74, Fred C. Beyer H.S., Modesto, 1974-76; tchr. math., chair dept. Thomas Downey H.S., Modesto, 1976—97; ret., 1997. Dir. Ctrl. Calif. Math. Project, Calif. State U., Stanislaus, Turlock, 1983-84; cons. Calif. State Dept. Edn., Sacramento, 1976-92. Mem. NEA, Nat. Coun. Tchrs. Math. (del. 1975-96), Calif. Math. Coun. (life, editor newsletter Communicator 1982-85, Polya award 1993), Stanislaus Math. Coun. (v.p., pres., treas., life), Calif. Tchrs. Assn., Modesto Tchrs. Assn., Calif. Math. Coun. (ctrl. v.p., sec., life, pres. elect 1996-97, pres. 1998-99). Republican. Presbyterian. Avocations: travel, reading, needlecraft. Home: 1363 S 800 W Preston ID 83263-5445

HARRYMAN, RHONDA L. education educator; b. Perry, Okla., Apr. 1, 1954; d. Otis Issac Jr. and Jeanette Roberta (Creacy) Shelley; m. Gilbert Wayne Harryman, Mar. 19, 1978. BS in Edn. cum laude, U. Ctrl. Okla., 1975, M in Spl. Edn., 1979; postgrad., Okla. State U., 1992—. Cert. learning disabilities, mentally handicapped, physically handicapped, emotional disturbance, elem. sch. adminstrs., Okla. Asst. workshop coord. for trainable mentally handicapped, physically handicapped Edmond (Okla.) ARC, 1974-76; instr. educable mentally handicapped, physically handicapped, emotionally disabled Edmond Pub. Schs., 1976-77, instr. spl. edn., emotionally disabled, educable mentally handicapped, physically handicapped, visually and hearing impaired, 1977-91; univ. coord., supr. practicums, instr. spl. edn. U. Ctrl. Okla., Edmond, 1992—. Edn. advisor tchrs. undrepresented populations in Shawnee, Okla. Three Feathers Assn., Norman, Okla. 1983; pvt. teaching, parent counseling learning disabilities, 1982-87; instr. spl. edn. Okla. Christian U., 1992—, mem. tchr. edn. adv. coun.; co-moderator New Eng. Joint Conf. Specific Learning Disabilities, Boston, 1991; edn. rep. Okla. Joint Conf. Juvenile Justice; edn. del. Okla. Japan-Am. Grassroots Coun., Tokyo, 1991; conducted workshops, presented insvcs., speaker in field. Editorial rev. bd. Teaching Resources, Dayton, Ohio. Counselor Edmond Youth Advocacy Bd.; mem. Gov.'s Round Table on Edn. and Bus., Edmond Juvenile Crime Commn.; sponsor Ala-Teen, Boys Ranch Town. Named Okla. Tchr. of Yr. by Okla. State Dept. Edn., 1992. Mem. Orton Dyslexia Soc., Coun. Exceptional Child, Kappa Delta Pi. Home: 3816 Deason Dr Edmond OK 73013-7742 Office: U Ctrl Okla Dept Spl Svcs 100 N University Dr Edmond OK 73034-5207

HARSHMAN, THOMAS RINGWOOD, writer; b. N.Y.C., Feb. 27, 1961; s. Richard Renville and Mary Ashley Cooper (Hewitt) H. AB cum laude, Princeton U., 1985; AM, Brown U., 1987, PhD, 1995. Instr. Brown U., Providence, R.I., 1988-91; investor, 1982—. Author of music revs. Vol. Keep Providence Beautiful, 1991-92. Princeton U. scholar, 1983-85, fellow, 1991. Mem. Dark Shadows. Episcopalian. Avocations: classical and jazz piano, sketching, tennis, french lit. Home: 11 S Angell St Providence RI 02906-5206 Office: 11 S Angell St Providence RI 02906-5206

HART, ANN WEAVER, educational administration educator; b. Salt Lake City, Nov. 6, 1948; d. Ted Lionel and Sylvia (Moray) Weaver; m. Randy Bret Hart, Sept. 12, 1968; children: Kimberly, Liza, Emily, Allyson. BS in History, U. Utah, 1970, MA in History, 1981, PhD in Ednl. Adminstrn., 1983. Tchr. pub. schs., Salt Lake City, 1970-73, 80-81; jr. high sch. prin. Provo (Utah) Pub. Schs., 1983-84; prof. ednl. adminstrn. U. Utah, Salt Lake City, 1984—98, assoc. dean Grad. Sch. Edn., 1991-93, dean Grad. Sch., 1993—98; provost, v.p. acad. affairs Claremont Grad. U., Calif., 1998—2002; pres. U. N.H., Durham, 2002—. Cons. various sch. dists., 1983—, regional ednl. labs., 1986—; bd. dirs. Citizens Bank N.H. Author: Principal Succession: Establishing Leadership in Schools, 1993, The Principalship, 1996, Designing and Conducting Research, 1996; editor: Ednl. Adminstrn. Quar., 1990-92; contbr. articles to profl. jours. Grantee U. Utah, State of Utah, U.S. Dept. Edn. Mem. Am. Ednl. Rsch. Assn., Am. Coun. on Edn., Phi Beta Kappa, Phi Kappa Phi. Avocations: skiing, backpacking, hiking, kayaking, bicycling. Office: Univ of New Hampshire Pres Office 201 Thompson Hall Durham NH 03824

HART, BRENDA REBECCA, retired gifted and talented educator; b. West Point, Ga., Aug. 29, 1941; d. Howard William Godfrey, Sarah Will Clegg; m. William Samuel Hart, Mar. 26, 1961 (dec. Oct. 1971); 1 child, Keith Samuel. BA in Social Studies, La Grange Coll., 1977, MEd in History, 1979. Tchr. gifted and talented State Dept. Edn., Atlanta, 1998—2003, ret., 2003. Collector data State Dept. Edn., Atlanta, 1985—, advance placement, 1998—. Home: 1702 Rosemont Ave West Point GA 31823

HART, CLAIRE-MARIE, educator; b. Lawrence, Mass., Dec. 6, 1942; d. Roderick P. and M. Claire (Sullivan) H. BS in Edn., Bridgewater State Coll., 1964; MA, U. R.I., 1968; MAT, Salem State Coll., 1985. Tchr. English B.M.C. Durfee High Sch., Fall River, Mass., 1964-68, Beverly (Mass.) High Sch., 1968—. Adj. prof. English No. Shore C.C., Danvers, Mass., 1970—, Endicott Coll., Beverly, 1997—; mentor cons. Beverly Sch. Dist., 1996—; cons., presenter in field. Mem. subcom. Beverly Sch. Com., 1998-2000; mem. Local Religious Ch. Orgn., Beverly, 1978—, Dem. City Com., Beverly, 1978—. Recipient Outstanding Educator award, Harvard U., Cambridge, Mass., 2000; NEH grantee, 1986, 88. Mem. NEA, MLA, Nat. Coun. Tchrs. English, Dante Soc. Am., New Eng. Assn. Tchrs. English, Mass. Tchrs. Assn. Roman Catholic. Avocations: reading, antiques, gardening, theatre. Home: 5 Cornell Rd Beverly MA 01915-1611 Office: Beverly High Sch 100 Sohier Rd Beverly MA 01915 E-mail: cmhdante@aol.com.

HART, CYNTHIA FAYE, elementary education educator; b. Orange, N.J., July 26, 1938; d. James Benjamin and Elizabeth (Massey) Kelly; m. Lionel DePau Hart, June 18, 1960 (div. Oct. 1975); 1 child, Kevin Blair. BS, Fairleigh Dickinson U., 1961; MA in Early Childhood, Kean Coll., 1996. Cert. elem. tchr., N.J. Tchr. Newark Bd. Edn., 1963—. Mentor Camden St. Sch., Newark, 1994-95. V.p. Martin Luther King Jr. Civic, N.J., 1994—; lifetime mem. NAACP, Urban League. Recipient Recognition Resolution award City Coun. City Newark, 1992, 2d place Newark Bd. Edn. Math. Fair, 1992; named Outstanding Tchr. Martin L. King Jr. Civic, 1992. Mem. ASCD, ACEI, Assn. for Childhood Edn. Internat., Nat. Edn. Assn., Nat. Assn. of Colored Women's Clubs, Inc., N.J. State Fed. of Colored Women's Clubs, Inc., N.J. Chpt. Nat. Com. for Prevention of Child Abuse, Newark Early Childhood Educators Assn., N.J. Edn. Assn., Newark Tchrs' Assn., Federated Clubs Am., Kappa Delta Pi. Avocations: writing, poetry, childrens books. Home: 55 Hillcrest Ter East Orange NJ 07018-2357

HART, DENISE MARIE, adult education educator, director; b. Perth Amboy, N.J., Jan. 22, 1951; d. Dennis Kardos and Maryann Edith Lippay; m. Stirling Hugh Hart, June 3, 1973 (div. Dec. 1984). AA in Dental Hygiene, Fairleigh Dickinson U., 1970, BS, 1972; MS, Columbia U., 1973; EdD, Rutgers U., 1984. Registered dental hygienist. Dental hygiene supr. Fairleigh Dickinson U., Hackensack, N.J., 1973-79, dental hygiene faculty, 1973-86, invited faculty, sociology dept. Teaneck, N.J., univ. dir. adult edn. Rutherford, N.J., 1985-94, univ. dir., adult ednl. svcs. Teaneck, N.J., 1994-95, prof. sch. edn., 1995—, coord. women's studies, 1994—, dir. adult edn., 1999—. Cons. U. North Tex., Denton, 1970, Caldwell (N.J.) Coll., 1992, Hudson County C.C., 1996, Westbrook Coll., 1996; mem. Nat. Commn. on Orthotic and Prosthetic Edn., 1998, UGA, 1999. Author: Guidelines for Prior Learning Assessment, 1994; contbr. articles to profl. jours. Mem. adv. bd. Teaneck Women Train & Work, 1994—; co-chairperson Swim Across, ARC, North Bergen, N.J., 1980; legis. contact dist. 38 N.J. Dental Hygiene Assn., 1974-75; endl. con. N.J. Charter Sch. Resource Ctr., 1999—. Recipient USPHS grant, 1972-73. Mem. Coun. for Adult and Experiential Learning (chair mktg. com. 1993-94, state rep. 1991—, co-chairperson commn. learning assessemnt, 1998), Assn. for Continuing Higher Edn. (chair region III 1994-95, sec.-treas. 1992-93, chair emeritus 1995-96, chair media com. 1995-98, tri-regional conf. planning com. 1996, nat. conf. planning com. 1996, 97, mem. membership devel. and svc. com. 1994—, program site selection com. 1997—, bd. dirs. 1999—), Nat. Coalition Sex Equity Edn., NJDOE (gender equity adv. com. 1998—). Office: Fairleigh Dickinson U 1000 River Rd Teaneck NJ 07666-1996

HART, GARY CHARLES, secondary school educator; b. Tiffin, Ohio, July 25, 1967; s. Michael John and Joyce Barbara (Elchert) H. B degree, Bowling Green State U., 1989; MA in Edn., Heidelberg Coll., 2002. Cert. tchr., Ohio. Social studies tchr. Calvert H.S., Tiffin, 1989-97, Mt. Gilead H.S., 1997-98, Columbian H.S., 1998—. Roman Catholic. Avocations: reading, running. Home: 118 Ann St Tiffin OH 44883-3014 Office: Columbian HS 300 S Monroe St Tiffin OH 44883

HART, JAMES WARREN, retired academic administrator, retired football player; b. Evanston, Ill., Apr. 29, 1944; s. George Ezrie and Marjorie Helen (Karsten) H.; m. Mary Elizabeth Mueller, June 17, 1967; children: Bradley James and Suzanne Elizabeth (twins), Kathryn Anne. BS, So. Ill. U., 1967. Quarterback St. Louis Cardinals Profl. Football Team, 1966—83, Washington Redskins Profl. Football Team, 1984; radio sports personality Sta. KMOX, 1975—84, Sta. KXOK, 1985—86; sports analyst Sta. WGN Radio, Chgo., 1985—89; athletics dir. So. Ill. U., Carbondale, 1988—99, assoc. chancellor for external affairs, 1999—2000; head coach So. Ill. Spl. Olympics, 1973—90, Mo. Spl. Olympics, 1976—78; co-owner Dierdorf & Hart's Steak House (2 locations), St. Louis; spl. asst. to vice chancellor for instnl. devel. So. Ill. U., 1999—2002. Co-author: The Jim Hart Story, 1977. Gen. campaign chmn. St. Louis Heart Assn., 1974-88; hon. chmn. St. Louis Sr. Olympics, 1986-88. Named Most Valuable Player in Nat. Football Conf., 1974, Most Valuable Player with St. Louis Cardinals, 1973, 1975, 1978, Man of Yr., St. Louis Dodge Dealers, 1975—76, Miller High Life, 1980; named to So. Ill. U. Sports Hall of Fame, 1978, Mo. Sports Hall of Fame, 1998, Mo. Valley Conf. Hall of Fame, 2001, Chicagoland Sports Hall of Fame, 2003. Mem.: AFTRA, NFL Players Assn. (Brian Piccolo Nat. YMCA award 1980, Byron Whizzer White award 1976, Brian Piccolo Nat. YMCA Humanitarian award 1980), Fellowship Christian Athletes. Republican.

HART, MARIAN GRIFFITH, retired reading educator; b. Bates City, Mo., Feb. 5, 1929; d. George Thomas Leon and Beulah Winiferd (Hackley) Griffith; m. Ashley Bruce Hart, Dec. 23, 1951; children: Ashley Bruce Hart II, Pamela Cherie Hart Gates. BS, Ctrl. Mo. State Coll., 1951; MA, No. Ariz. U., 1976. Title I-chpt. I reading dir. Page (Ariz.) Sch. Dist.; Title I dir. Johnson O'Malley Preschool; dist. reading dir. Page Sch. Dist.; ret. Bd. dirs. Lake Powell Inst. Behavioral Health Svcs., sec., 1993-95, chmn. fin. com., 1995-96. Contbr. articles to profl. jours., childrens mags. Vol., organizer, mgr., instr. Page Cmty. Adult Literacy Program, 1986-91, Marian's Literacy Program, 1991-95; lifetime mem. Friends of Page Pub. Libr., sec. bd., 1990-91. Mem. Delta Kappa Gamma (pres. chpt. 1986-90, historian 1990-92, Omicron state coms., scholarship 1988-89, nominations 1991, Omicron State Comms. com. 1995-99, Tau chpt. nominations com. chair 1998), Beta Sigma Phi (pres. chpt., v.p. chpt., pvt. reading tutor 1997-2000). Home and Office: 66 S Navajo Dr PO Box 763 Page AZ 86040-0763

HART, MICHAEL ALLEN, educator, counselor; b. Providence, Aug. 25, 1966; s. John R. and Marian A. (DePastine) H. AA, C.C. R.I., 1986; BS, U. Maine, Ft. Kent, 1988. Cert. tchr., R.I. Tchr. St. Aloysius Sch., Smithfield, R.I., 1988—; counselor at-risk youths St. Aloysius Home, Smithfield, 1988—. Coach, referee Smithfield Youth Basketball Assn., 1980-92. Grantee Providence Jour. Bull., 1991-92. Mem. ASCD, Nat. Geographic Soc., Nat. Fraternal Order Police, Nat. Fedn. High Sch. Coaches, Nat. Whole Lang. Assn., Readers Digest Assn. Democrat. Roman Catholic. Avocations: basketball, football, psychology, reading. Home: 63 Federal Rd Barrington RI 02806-2407

HART, PHILIP RAY, religion educator, minister; b. Dendron, Va., Oct. 4, 1925; s. Edward Lee and Sarah Oceana (West) H.; m. Nancy Jean Padgett, Sept. 12, 1953; children: John Philip, Stephen Anson. BA, U. Richmond, 1945; BD, So. Bapt. Theol. Sem, Louisville, 1948; MA, Columbia U., 1952; PhD, U. Edinburgh, 1962. Ordained to ministry So. Bapt. Conv., 1948. Asst. pastor Tabernacle Bapt. Ch., Richmond, Va., 1948-51; prof. religion U. Richmond, 1956-91, prof. emeritus, 1991—. Bd. dirs. Va. Bapt. Mins.' Relief Fund. Contbr. articles to religious jours. Friend Va. Bapt. Hist. Soc., 1987—. Capt. USAF, 1953—55. Mem. Am. Acad. Religion, Theta Alpha Kappa (pres. 1992-96). Home: 6801 Lakewood Dr Richmond VA 23229-6930

HART, RUSS ALLEN, telecommunications educator; b. Seguin, Tex., June 30, 1946; s. Bevelly D. and Hattie V. (Reh) H.; m. Judith Harwood, 1984 (div. 1986); m. Patricia Barrios, Mar. 22, 1987. BA, Tex. Tech. U., 1968; MA, U. Ariz., 1976; PhD, U. Wyo., 1984. Chief cinematographer, producer-dir. dept. med-TV-film, health sci. ctr. U. Ariz., Tucson, 1973-77; instr., coord. ednl. TV and cinematography U. Wyo., Laramie, 1977-81; assoc. prof., dir. biomed. communication Mercer U., Macon, Ga., 1981-84; prof., dir. instructional telecommunications Calif. State U., Fresno, 1984-92, prof., assoc. dir. computing, comm. and media svcs., 1992-95, prof., assoc. dir. Acad. Innovation Ctr., 1995-98, prof. mass comm., 1998—2002, dir. grad. program, 2000—02. Coord. ednl. confs.; tech. cons. for distance edn. Contbr. articles to profl. jours. Served to capt. USAF, 1968-73. Recipient Cert. Merit, Chgo. Internat. Film Festival, 1975, 1st pl. INDY Indsl. Photography award, 1976, 2d pl. INDY Indsl. Photography award, 1975, Silver plaque Chgo. Internat. Film Festival, 1978, Winner of case study competition Internat. Radio and TV Soc., 1989, Bronze Telly award, 1992-93, 95, Crystal Shooting Star award, 1993, 94, Cine Golden Eagle award, 1994. Mem. Assn. for Ednl. Comms. and Tech. (rsch. session chmn. 1983), Am. Assn. Adult and Continuing Educators (mem. eval. task force 1986), Broadcast Edn. Assn., Health Sci. Comms. Assn. (mem. continuing edn. subcom. 1983), Biol. Photog. Assn. (film judge 1975), Alliance for Distance Edn. in Calif. (founding mem. 1991), Ednl. Telecom. Consortium of Ctrl. Calif. (founding mem. 1993), Phi Delta Kappa, Phi Kappa Phi. Office: Calif State U Mass Comm & Journalism 2225 E San Ramon Ave MF10 Fresno CA 93740-8029 E-mail: Russ_Hart@csufresno.edu.

HART, VIRGINIA WADE, elementary education educator; b. Rolla, Mo., Nov. 20, 1943; d. Clifford Neil and Nellie Z. (Jaggers) Wade; m. Edward F. Hart, Oct. 12, 1968 (div. June 1994); children: Edward S., Clifford T., James R., Deborah J., Sarah E. BA in Sociology, Mary Washington Coll., Fredricksburg, Va., 1965; MA in Elem. Edn., Adelphi U., Garden City, N.Y., 1973; MA in Reading, U. Ala., Birmingham, 1988, student, 1990. Cert. in elem. edn., reading, early childhood edn., Ala. Tchr. 1st grade Nassakegg Elem. Sch., Setauket, N.Y., 1966-68, Blue Point (N.Y.)-Bayport Schs., 1968-69; ednl. outreach Discovery Place Children's Mus., Birmingham, 1986-87; tchr. developmental kindergarten Hall Kent Elem. Sch., Birmingham, 1989-90, tchr. kindergarten, 1990-91, tchr. 2d grade, 1991—. Clin. master tchr. U. Ala., Tuscaloosa, 1993—; mem. curriculum adv. com. Hoover Pub. Sch., 1989-91. Bd. dirs. Grace House Ministries, Fairfield, Ala., 1993-96. Mem. Internat. Reading Assn., Nat. Coun. Tchrs. English, Kappa Delta Pi, Delta Kappa Gamma Soc. Internat. Baptist. Office: Hall Kent Elem Sch 213 Hall Ave Homewood AL 35209-6530

HARTE, SANDRA WISWELL, principal; b. Chgo., Feb. 29, 1944; d. Robert Howard and Virginia Ailleene (Lawrence) W.; m. Charles R. Harte III, Aug. 6, 1966; children: Laurence, Brian, Andrew. BS in Edn., Miami U., Oxford, Ohio, 1965; MEd, Xavier U., Cin., 1981. Cert. elem. tchr. 1-8, counselor K-12, gifted edn. tchr. K-12, supr. K-12, elem. prin., Ohio. Tchr. 5th grade Hammond (Ind.) Pub. Schs., 1965-66, Stoneham (Mass) Pub. Schs., 1966-67; homebound instr. K-8 Green Bay (Wis.) Pub. Schs., 1970-77; tchr. 4th grade, sch. counselor Yavneh Day Sch., Cin., 1978-80; tchr. gifted edn., counselor Indian Hill Exempted Village Schs., Cin., 1980-97; prin. Indian Hill Primary Sch., 1997—. Chair bd. dirs. Montgomery Nursery Sch., Cin.; instr. thinking skills Profl. Growth Coun., Cin., 1988-91. Presdl. finalist elem. math. tchr. State of Ohio, 1990; recipient Ashland Oil Golden Apple Achiever award, 1996. Mem. ASCD, OSCA, NAGC, NAESP, OAESP, Phi Delta Kappa. Methodist. Avocations: pets, needlework, reading. Home: 8363 Shadowpoint Ct Cincinnati OH 45242-3401 Office: Indian Hill Village Schs 6845 Drake Rd Cincinnati OH 45243-2737

HARTER, CAROL CLANCEY, university president, English language educator; m. Michael T. Harter, June 24, 1961; children: Michael R., Sean P. BA, SUNY, Binghamton, 1964, MA, 1967, PhD, 1970; LHD, Ohio U., 1989. Instr. SUNY, Binghamton, 1969-70; asst. prof. Ohio U., Athens, 1970-74, ombudsman, 1974-76, v.p., dean students, 1976-82, v.p. for adminstrn., assoc. prof., 1982-89; pres., prof. English SUNY, Geneseo, 1989-95; pres. U. Nev., Las Vegas, 1995—. Co-author: (with James R. Thompson) John Irving, 1986, E.L. Doctorow, 1990; author dozens of presentations and news columns; contbr. articles to profl. jours. Bd. dirs., mem. exec. com. NCAA, 2000—; mem. exec. com. Nev. Devel. Authority, 2001—; bd. dirs. Nev. Test Site Devel. Corp., 2000—; trustee Associated Western Univs., 2001—. Office: U Nev Office Pres 4505 S Maryland Pkwy # 1001 Las Vegas NV 89154-1001 E-mail: harter@ccmail.nevada.edu.

HARTINGER, PATRICIA BERNARDINE, elementary school educator; b. Monterey, Calif., Sept. 16, 1935; d. John George and Myra Hall Curran; m. Walter Hartinger, Nov. 14, 1959; children: Maureen, John. AA with honor, Monterey Peninsula Coll., 1955; BA with great distinction, San Jose State U., 1958; postgrad., U. Calif., Santa Cruz, U. Santa Clara. Cert. life sch. libr., jr. high sch., child devel. Libr. San Jose (Calif.) State Coll., 1956-58, Milpitas (Calif.) Sch. Dist., 1960-62, Alma Coll., Los Gatos, Calif., 1963-65, Santa Clara (Calif.) Pub. Libr., 1966-69; tchr. Westerner Schs., Los Gatos, 1975-82, Town & Country Pre-Sch., San Jose, Calif., 1982-83, St. Frances Cabrini Sch., San Jose, 1983-85, St. Lucy Sch., Campbell, Calif., 1985-93, St. Lawrence The Martyr Sch., Santa Clara, Calif., 1993-94; substitute tchr. Diocese of San Jose, 1994—. Curriculum writer in field; spkr. in field. Author: Earthquake of Apr. 18, 1906 in the Santa Clara Valley, 1973 (cash award), History of Santa Clara Valley Handweavers Guild, 1988; contbr. articles on Peace Edn. to various pubs., recipes to Sunset Mag. Vol. tchr. Lyceum of Santa Clar County for Gifted Children, San Jose, 1974-80; vol. libr. Santa Clara Valley Med. Ctr., San Jose, 1962-63, Los Gatos Elem. Sch. Dist., 1968-75; tchr. of religion pre-sch. Diocese of San Jose, 1971-80; mem. N.D. Lewis and Clark Bicentennial Foun. Scholar Kiwanis Club, 1956, Delta Delta Delta Sorority, 1957-58, Angel Island Immigration Sta., 2001-02, Found. Tchrs. Fellows Program, 2001-02. Mem. Calif. Coun. Social Studies, Santa Clara County Reading Coun., Lewis and Clark Trail Heritage Found., Inc., Santa Clara Valley Handweavers (founding), mem. Nat. Audubon Soc., Nature Conservancy, San Jose State U. Key Club, Phi Alpha Theta, Phi Kappa Phi. Democrat. Avocations: weaving, reading, travel. Home: 16155 Jacaranda Way Los Gatos CA 95032-3627 E-mail: shadowcat16155@yahoo.com.

HART-KEPLER, VIRGINIA LYNN, nurse, educator; b. Chico, Calif., Dec. 17, 1953; d. Lloyd G. and Patricia B. Hart; m. William Edward Kepler, Mar. 21, 1987. AA, Pasadena City Coll., 1976; BSN, Calif. State U., L.A., 1980; FNP, UCLA, 1986, M in Nursing, 1987. Cert. family nurse practitioner. Lectr. primary care sect. family nurse practitioner program UCLA Sch. Nursing, 1987—99; mem. clin. lab. faculty Azusa Pacific U. Sch. Nursing, 1999—, adj. clin. faculty, 1999—. Nurse practitioner Project Achieve Health Clinic, El Monte, Calif., Pomona Valley Med. Ctr. Ambulatory Care Clinic, 2003—. Active in cmty. working with homeless and underprivileged. Recipient Audrienne H. Moseley Rsch. Fund award. Mem. Am. Acad. Nurse Practitioners, Calif. Assn. Nurse Practitioners, Assn. Christian Therapists, Sigma Theta Tau.

HARTLEY, CORINNE, painter, sculptor, educator; b. L.A., July 24, 1924; d. George D. and Marjorie (Fansher) Parr; m. Thomas L. West, Sept. 3, 1944 (div. 1970); children: Thomas West III, Tori West, Trent West; m. Clabe M. Hartley, Aug. 27, 1973 (div. 1997). Attended, Chouinard Art Inst., L.A., 1942-44, Pasadena (Calif.) Sch. Fine Arts, 1952-54. Paste up artist Advt. Agy., L.A., 1944; fashion illustrator May Co., L.A., 1944-45; freelance fashion illustrator Bullock's, L.A., 1946-76. Art tchr. Pasadena Sch. Fine Arts, 1965—69; pvt. art tchr., owner studio, Venice, Calif., 1970—2000, Newport Beach, Calif., 2000—; presenter art workshops; works pub. and distributed by Art in Motion, Prints and Cards, Vancouver, B.C., Canada, 1990—. Gallery representation includes Dassin Gallery, L.A., 1981—, Legacy Gallery, Scottsdale, Ariz., 1989—, G. Stanton Gallery, Dallas, 1990—, Coda Gallery, Palm Desert, Calif., 1993—, Huntsman Gallery, Aspen, Colo., 1995—, Carol Kavanaugh Gallery, Des Moines, 1996—, Jones & Terwilliger Gallery, Carmel, Calif., 1997—, Lee Youngman Gallery, Calistoga, Calif., 1997—, Mountain Trails Gallery, Park City, Utah, 2000, Terbush Gallery, Santa Fe, 1997—. Recipient Purchase award Nat. Orange Show, San Bernardino, Honor award All City Art Festival, Barnsdall Park, L.A., Best of Show award Clumer Mus. Wash., 3d pl. award still life Calif. Art Club, award of excellence Oil Painters Am./Springville Mus., Utah, N.Mex.; others. Mem. Calif. Art Club, Oil Painters Am. Republican. Avocation: singing in church choir.

HARTLEY, HELEN ROSANNA, business educator; b. Hannibal, Mo., May 6, 1947; d. Roger Chase and Rose Evelyn (Peterson) Higgins; m. William Clarence Hartley, Aug. 17, 1969; children: Nathan William, Andrew Chase. BS in Edn., Ctrl. Mo. State U., 1969; MA, Appalachian State U., 1988. Cert. tchr., N.C., Mo. Instr. Spanish, Ctrl. H.S., Argyle, Iowa, 1969-70; tchr. modern langs. Burke County Pub. Schs., Morganton, N.C., 1974-81; instr. ednl. computing Appalachian State U., Boone, N.C., 1988-91; instr. info. sys./internet techs. Western Piedmont C.C., Morganton, 1990—, chmn. faculty and staff coun., 1998-99, Sterling R. Collett endowed tchg. chair, 2000. Mem. N.C. Virtual Learning Cmty., 1999-2001; mem. tech. adv. com. Burke County, N.C., 1991-93, mem. chpt. II adv. com., 1992-94; sponsor computer club Salem Elem. Sch., Burke County, 1989-91; mem. Info. Tech. Task Force, 1995—, N.C. Curriculum Improvement Project, 1994-96. Contbr. articles to profl. jours. Mem., treas. Burke Soccer Assn., 1989-97; mem. past officer Morgan Jr. Woman's Club, 1975-86; advisor Explorer Scout Post, Morganton, 1990-93. Mem. State Employees Assn. N.C., Computer Instrs. Assn. (treas. 1998-2002). Avocations: hiking, sewing, painting, reading. Office: Western Piedmont CC 1001 Burkemont Ave Morganton NC 28655-4504 E-mail: rhartley@wpcc.edu.

HARTMAN, ELIZABETH DIANE, retired elementary education educator; b. Berlin Center, Ohio, Feb. 25, 1937; d. Keith Gayle and Edna Elizabeth (Blymiller) Renick; m. Lowell Lloyd Hartman, June 29, 1956; children: Deborah Kay, Dennis Lowell, Kathrine Sue. BS in Edn., Bowling Green State U., 1970, MEd, 1978. Cert. edn. profl. Substitute tchr. Genoa Area & Oak Harbor Schs., Ohio, 1966-70; dir. migrant sch. Genoa Area Schs., Clay Center, Ohio, 1969, elem. tchr., 1970-95; ret., 1995. Rep. career edn. Penta County Vocat. Sch., 1980-90; prin.'s adv. bd. Allen Elem. Curtice, Ohio, 1989-94; adv. bd. educators Toledo Blade, 1992-93. Author poem. Organist, jr. choir dir. St. John Luth. Ch., Williston, Ohio, 1957-80, dir. bell choir, 1986-96; delivery person Mobile Meals, Genoa, 1988-94. Recipient Tchrs.'s in Am. Enterprise award Sohio, 1982-83; Educator of Yr., Consumer Econ. Edn. Assn. Ohio, 1989. Mem. Internat. Reading Assn. (vacationland coun., pres. 1982-83), Allenettes (past officer 1970—, chairperson United Way 1989-90), Delta Kappa Gamma (music chmn. 1990-94). Democrat. Lutheran. Avocations: music, golfing, boating, fishing, traveling.

HARTMAN, GEOFFREY H. language professional, educator; b. Germany, Aug. 11, 1929; came to U.S., 1946, naturalized, 1946; s. Albert and Agnes (Heumann) H.; m. Renee Gross, Oct. 21, 1956; children: David, Elizabeth. BA, Queens Coll., N.Y.C., 1949, LHD (hon.), 1990; PhD, Yale U., 1953; LHD (hon.), Hebrew Union Coll./Inst. Religion, 2003. Mem. faculty Yale U., 1955-62; assoc. prof. English U. Iowa, Iowa City, 1962-64, prof. English, 1964-65, Cornell U., Ithaca, N.Y., 1965-67; prof. English and comparative lit. Yale U., 1967—, Karl Young Prof., 1974-94, Sterling prof., 1994-97, prof. emeritus, 1997—; disting. vis. scholar George Washington U., 1998-2000; disting. prof. New Sch. U., 2001-03. Vis. lectr. and/or prof. U. Chgo., U. Wash., Hebrew U., Jerusalem, U. Zurich, Switzerland, Princeton U., NYU, Tel Aviv U., U. Konstanz, Germany; Clark lectr. Trinity Coll., Cambridge, 1983; Tamblyn lectr. U. Western Ont., 1983; Wellek lectr. U. Calif., Irvine, 1992, Tanner lectr. U. Utah, 1999; dir. Sch. Theory and Criticism, Dartmouth Coll., 1982-87, also sr. fellow; Haskins lectr. ACLS, 2000. Author: The Unmediated Vision, 1954, Andre Malraux, 1960, Wordsworth's Poetry, 1964 (Christian Gauss award Phi Beta Kappa 1965), Beyond Formalism, 1970, The Fate of Reading, 1975, Akiba's Children, 1978, Criticism in the Wildernes, 1980, Saving the Text, 1981, Easy Pieces, 1985, The Unremarkable Wordsworth, 1987, Minor Prophecies, 1991, The Longest Shadow, 1996, The Fateful Question of Culture, 1997, A Critic's Journey, 1999, Scars of the Spirit, 2002; editor: Hopkins: A Collection of Critical Essays, 1966, Selected Poetry and Prose of William Wordsworth, 1970, Romanticism: Vistas, Instances, Continuities, 1973, Psychoanalysis and the Question of the Text, 1978, Shakespeare and the Questions of Theory, 1985, Bitburg in Moral and Political Perspective, 1986, Midrash and Literature, 1986, Holocaust Remembrance: The Shapes of Memory, 1993. Trustee English Inst., 1978-85; Revson project dir. Video Archive Holocaust Testimonies, Yale, 1982—. Served with AUS, 1953-55. Decorated chevalier Order of Arts and Letters govt. of France, 1997; recipient Disting. Alumnus award Queens Coll. CUNY, 1971, award Nat. Found. Jewish Culture, 1997, René Wellek prize Am. Assn. Comparative Lit., 1998, Disting. Scholar award Keats-Shelley Assn., 1998; Fulbright fellow U. Dijon, France, 1951-52, study fellow Am. Coun. Learned Socs., 1963, 79, Guggenheim fellow, 1969, 86, fellow Humanities Ctr. Wesleyan U., 1972, NEH, 1975, Inst. Advanced Studies Hebrew U., 1986, Inst. Humanities U. Calif., Irvine, 1989, Woodrow Wilson Internat. Ctr., 1995, Sackler Inst., U. Tel Aviv, 1997, Wissenschafts Coll., Berlin, 1998; assoc. fellow Ctr. Rsch. Philosophy and Lit. U. Warwick, Eng., 1993; Gauss seminarist Princeton U., 1968; Fulbright Disting. lectr., 1986, 87; corr. fellow British Acad. Mem. Modern Lang. Assn. (exec. council 1977-80), Am. Acad. Arts and Scis. Home: 260 Everit St New Haven CT 06511-1309

HARTMAN, LEE ANN WALRAFF, educator; b. Milw., Apr. 21, 1945; d. Emil Adolph and Mabelle Carolyn (Goetter) Walraff; m. Patrick James Hartman, Oct. 5, 1968; children: Elizabeth Marie, Suzanne Carolyn. BS, U. Wis., 1967; postgrad., U. R.I., 1972—73, Johns Hopkins U., 1990, Trinity Coll., 1996. Cert. tchr., Wis., Md. Secondary educator Port Wash. Bd. Edn., Wis., 1967-68; instr. ballet YWCA, Wilmington, Del., 1977-78; tutor Md. Study Skills Inst., Columbia, 1984-86; tchr. Howard County Bd. Edn., Columbia, 1985—. Contbr. articles to profl. jours. Bd. dirs. Columbia United Christian Ch., 1980-83; mem. Gifted and Talented Com., Columbia, 1980—, Lang. Arts Com., 1985—, USCG Officers Wives Club, 1970-72, Hosp. Aux. Bay St. Louis, 1970-72; troop leader Girl Scouts U.S., Columbia, 1980-91, Hospice; exec. bd. PTA, 1990-2000. Recipient Life Achievement award, Internat. Biog. Ctr., 1994, Woman of Yr. award, Am. Biog. Inst., 1994, Shirley Mullinex Tchr. of Yr. award, 1997, State of Md. Home/Hosp. Tchr. of Yr. award, 2001—02. Mem.: NAFE, AAUW (exec. bd. 1985—, v.p. Howard County br. 1990—92, pres. Howard County br. 1998—2000, chair membership 2003—), Internat. Platform Assn. (mem. citizen's adv. com. 1995—), Home Hosp. Tchrs. Assn. Md. (chair pub. rels., sec. 1994—98, v.p. 1998—99, pres. 1999—2002), Beaverbrook Homemakers Assn. (pres. 1995—97). Avocations: reading, swimming, skiing, ballet. Home: 5070 Durham Rd W Columbia MD 21044-1445 Office: Howard County Bd Edn Rte 108 Columbia MD 21044

HARTMAN, MARILYN D. English and art educator; b. Denver, May 2, 1927; d. Leland DeForest Henshaw and Evelyn Wyman Henshaw; m. James Hartman, Oct. 7, 1949 (dec. Dec. 1989); children: Charles, Alice, Mary Hale. Student, U. Denver, 1947; BA, U. Colo., 1958; MA, UCLA, 1965, EdD in English Edn., 1972. Calif. life std. tchg. credential English and art, Colo. secondary English and art. Tchr. Denver Pub. Schs., 1959—65; asst. prof. San Fernando Valley State U., Northridge, Calif., 1970—72, San Diego State U. Mem., presenter Am. Ednl. Rsch. Assn., L.A., 1965-72; mem. Nat. Coun. Tchrs. English, L.A., 1965-72; officer Pi Lambda Theta-Alpha Delta chpt., L.A., 1970-72; with Ctr. for the Study Dem. Instns., L.A., 1970-72; tchg. asst., 1964, discussion leader linguistics; tchr. evaluator UCLA, 1970-72, Iliff Sch. Theology, Denver U.; cons. Dept Edn., Riley, 1992-2000, State Dept., 1992-2000, to Pres. Clinton, 1992-2000. Author: Linguistic Approach to Teaching English, 1965, Two Letters and Some Thoughts, 1968, Sound and Meaning of BE Speech, 1969, Teaching a Dialect, 1970, Contrastive Analysis: BE and SE Teaching, 1972, Touch the Windy Finger, 1980, Under the Hand of God, 2000; author: (with Bill Kirton) (short stories) O God, 1970, On Her Own: To Know and Not Know, 2002; author: The Luckiest People, 2002. Chmn. Denver Metro Area Food Drive, 1985, Interfaith Alliance; mem. Dem. Nat. Com., 1992—2002. Mem.: VFW, NOW, AAUW, Women in the Arts, Interfaith Alliance, Nat. Philatelic Soc., Am. Philatelic Assn., Common Cause, Sierra Club, Franciscan Missions, Natural Resources Def. Coun., Kempe Children's Found., Colo. Fedn. Dem. Women's Clubs, Inc. (officer 2001). Avocations: singing, painting, writing, teaching, counseling.

HARTMAN, MARY S. historian, educator; b. Mpls., June 25, 1941; married. BA, Swarthmore Coll., 1963; MA, Columbia U., 1964, PhD, 1970. From instr. to asst. prof. Rutgers U., 1968-75; from assoc. prof. to prof. history Douglass Coll., Rutgers U., 1975—; dean Douglass Coll. Rutgers U., 1982-94; dir. Inst. for Women's Leadership Douglass Coll., 1994—; prof. Rutgers U., 1994—. Author: Clio's Consciousness Raised, 1974, Victorian Murderesses, 1978; editor: Talking Leadership: Conversations with Powerful Women, 1999, The Household and the Making of History: A Subversive View of the Western Past, 2003. Office: 162 Ryders Ln New Brunswick NJ 08901-8555

HARTMAN, PATRICIA JEANNE, lawyer, educator; b. Redding, Calif., Apr. 24, 1956; d. Gary Mac and Rosemary Catherine (Aldrich) H. BS in Bus. Adminstrn., BA in Econs., Calif. State U., Sacramento, 1978, MBA with honors, 1979; JD with distinction, U. of Pacific, Sacramento, 1983. Bar: Calif. 1983, U.S. Dist. Ct. (ea. dist.) Calif. 1983. Adminstrv. analyst Dist. Attys. Office, Sacramento, 1976-80; assoc. prof. Calif. State U., Sacramento, 1979—; assoc. Van Camp & Johnson, Sacramento, 1983-85, Diepenbrock, Wulff, Plant & Hannegan, LLP, Sacramento, 1985-89, ptnr., 1989—98, Hunter, Richey, DiBenedetto & Eisenbeis, LLP, Sacramento, 1999—. Mem. County Bar Sects., Sacramento, 1983—. Contbr. articles to profl. jours. Trustee Sutter Hosps. Found., Sacramento, 1988-2002. Fellow AAUW; mem. ABA, LWV (steering com. 1994), Calif. State Bar, Women Lawyers of Sacramento, Med.Group Mgmt. Assn., Sacramento C. of C. Avocations: running, skiing, weightlifting, hiking. Office: Hunter Richey DiBenedetto & Eisenbeis LLP 801 K St Ste 2300 Sacramento CA 95814-3500

HARTMAN, ROSEMARY JANE, retired special education educator; b. Gainesville, Fla., Aug. 24, 1944; d. John Leslie and Irene (Bowen) Goddard; m. Alan Lynn Gerber, Feb. 1, 1964 (div. 1982); children: Sean Alan, Dawn Julianne Silva, Lance Goddard; m. Perry Hartman, June 27, 1992. BA, Immaculate Heart Coll., 1967; MA, Loyola U., 1974. Cert. resource specialist. Tchr. L.A. Unified Schs., 1968-78; resource specialist Desert Sands Unified Sch. Dist., Palm Desert, 1978-83, Palm Springs Unified Schs., 1983-99, ret., 1999. Co-author: The Twelve Steps of Phobics Anonymous, 1989, One Day At A Time in Phobics Victorious, 1992, The Twelve Steps of Phobics Victorious, 1993; founder Phobics Victorious, 1992. Mem. Am. Assn. Christian Counselors (charter), Nat. Assn. of Christian Recovery, Anxiety Disorders Assn. Am. Office: Phobics Victorious PO Box 695 Palm Springs CA 92263-0695 E-mail: rosemary_jane@earthlink.net.

HARTMAN, RUTH CAMPBELL, director, educator; b. Galion, Ohio, Aug. 18, 1938; d. Richard Lewis and Florence Evelyn (Ireland) Campbell; m. Richard Louis Hartman, Jan. 14, 1956; children: Jeffery Lee, Marsha Elaine, Jerry Steven. BS, Ohio State U., 1970; MEd, U. LaVerne, 1976, postgrad., 1985—, U. Akron, 1977-85. cert. tchr., Ohio. Tchr. Willard (Ohio) City Schs., 1964-65; educator Mansfield (Ohio) City Schs., 1966—, home tutor, 1971-81, educator, 1977—, faculty advisory com., 1990-2001, young authors coord., 1991-92, co-coord. career edn., 1991-97; owner, dir. Hope Sch., Plymouth, Ohio, 2002—. Cons. Ohio State U., Ashland (Ohio) Coll., Mt. Vernon (Ohio) Nazarene Coll., 1976—. Co-author: Handbook for Student Teachers, 1983; contbr. to Norde News. Dir. of contruction Hope School. Mem NEA, Ohio Edn. Assn., North Cen. Ohio Tchrs. Assn., Mansfield Edn. Assn. Republican. Methodist. Avocations: reading, traveling, tennis, music. Home: RR 1 Plymouth OH 44865-9801 Office: Hope School 4200≧ Opdyke Rd Plymouth OH 44865-

HARTMAN-ABRAMSON, ILENE, adult education educator; b. Detroit, Nov. 8, 1950; d. Stuart Lester and Freda Vivian (Nash) Hartman; m. Victor Nikolai Abramson, Oct. 24, 1941. BA, U. Mich., 1972; MEd, Wayne State U., 1980, PhD in Higher Edn., 1990. Cert. continuing secondary tchr., Mich. Program developer and instr. William Beaumont Hosp., Royal Oak, Mich., 1972—74; vocat. counselor for emigres Jewish Vocat. Svc. and Cmty. Workshop, Detroit, 1974—81; program developer and cons. Detroit Psychiat. Inst., 1982; instr. for foreign students Oakland C.C., Farmington Hills, Mich., 1983-99. Mem. adv. bd. Mich. Dept. Edn., Detroit, 1981; lectr. Internat. Conf. Tchrs. English to Speakers of Other Langs., 1981; guest presenter Wayne State U., Lawrence Tech. U., 1991, U. Mich. Anxiety Disorders Program, 1993; presenter rsch. presentations Nat. Coalition for Sex Equity in Edn., Ann Arbor, Mich.; presenter at seminar on learning anxiety Interdisciplinary Studies program Wayne State U., 1995; chair profl. stds. and measures com. Mich. Devel. Edn. Consortium, editor newsletter, 1997; mem. rehab. adv. coun. State of Mich.; guest lectr. med. edn./residency tng. initiatives Detroit Med. Ctr. Hutzel Hosp., Providence Hosp., Beaumont Hosp., Detroit Med. Ctr., Harper Hosp.; adj. faculty Wayne State U., 2000; adj. prof. internat. comms. Lawrence Tech. U., 2000—. Mem. editl. bd. Mensa Rsch. Jour.; contbr. articles to prof. jours. Mem. Am. Acad. on Physician and Patient, Am. Mensa (rsch. rev. com.). Jewish. Avocations: self-defense for women, Karate. Office: Lawrence Tech U 21000 W Ten Mile Rd Southfield MI 48075-1058 E-mail: ah2574@wayne.edu., ihabramson@aol.com.

HARTMAN-IRWIN, MARY FRANCES, retired language professional; b. Portland, Oreg., Oct. 18, 1925; d. Curtiss Henry Sabisch and Gladys Frances (Giles) Strand; m. Harry Elmer Hartman, Sept. 6, 1946 (div. June 1970); children: Evelyn Frances, Laura Elyce, Andrea Candace; m. Thomas Floyd Irwin, Apr. 11, 1971. BA, U. Wash., 1964-68; postgrad., Seattle Pacific, 1977-79, Antioch U., Seattle, Wash., 1987, Heritage Inst., 1987. Lang. educator Kennewick (Wash.) Dist. # 17, 1970-88. Guide Summer Study Tours of Europe, 1971-88. Sec. Bahai Faith, 1971-99, libr., 2000, Pasco, Washington, 1985-88; trustee Mid. Columbia coun. Girl Scouts U.S. Fulbright scholar, 1968. Mem. NEA, Wash. Edn. Assn., Kennewick Edn. Assn., Nat. Fgn. Lang. Assn., Wash. Fgn. Lang. Assn., Literacy Coun. (literacy tutor Tillamook Bay C.C.). Avocations: painting, sewing, writing essays and short stories. Home: PO Box 247 Netarts OR 97143-0247 E-mail: maryi@oregoncoast.com.

HARTMANN, DENNIS LEE, atmospheric science educator; b. Salem, Oreg., Apr. 23, 1949; s. Alfred R. and Angeline K. Hartmann. BS, U. Portland, 1971; PhD, Princeton U., 1975. Rsch. assoc. McGill U., Montreal, Que., Can., 1975-76; vis. scientist Nat. Ctr. Atmospheric Rsch., Boulder, Colo., 1976-77; asst. prof. U. Wash., Seattle, 1977-83, assoc. prof. atmospheric sci., 1983-88, prof. atmospheric sci., 1988—, chair dept. atmospheric sci., 2002—. Mem. MAP panel NRC, 1981-87; mem. steering com. GEWEX Sci., 1995—. Author: Global Physical Climatology, 1994; ssoc. editor Jour. Atmospheric Scis., 1983-93, Jour. Geophys. Rsch., 1985-88; mem. editl. bd., contbr. Atmospheric Physics; mem. bd. reviewing editors Sci., 2002—; contbr. articles to sci. jours. Recipient Editors award Am. Geophys. Union, 1994; Aldo Leopold Leadership fellow, 1999. Fellow AAAS (chmn.-elect atmospheric and hydrospheric scis. sect. 1997—), Am. Geophys. Union; mem. Joint Inst. for Study of Atmosphere and Ocean (sr.), Am. Meteorol. Soc. (mem. com. upper atmosphere 1978-83, chmn. com. 1980-82, com. undergrad. awards 1983-85, com. climate variations, 1993—, Editors award 1993, 96, 98), NAS (space sci. bd. com. on earth scis. 1987-90, U.S. Toga panel 1990-95, climate rsch. com. 2001—), Internat. Commn. Dynamic Meterology. Office: U Wash PO Box 351640 Dept Atmospheric Scis Seattle WA 98195-1640

HARTMANN, RUTH ANNEMARIE, health care education specialist; b. Naumburg, Saale, Germany, Mar. 16, 1936; came to U.S., 1957; d. Kurt and Anna (Jöesch) H.; m. Karl-Heinz Falatyk (div. 1983); children: Ulrich, Ute; m. Franklin J. Herzberg, 1987. Diploma in nursing, Medizinische Fachschule, Potsdam, German Dem. Republic, 1956; BA in German summa cum laude, U. Wis., Milw., 1978, MLS, 1979; EdD in Adult Edn., Nova U., 1987. Info. specialist Fluid Power Assn., Milw., 1980-81; asst. librarian Miller Brewing Co., Milw., 1979-82; patient edn. librarian VA Med. Ctr., Milw., 1982-85, health care edn. specialist, 1986—. Adj. prof. (part-time) grad. health-care scis. Cardinal Stritch Coll. Mem. editl. bd. Jour. Health-care Edn. and Tng., 1993-95; contbr. articles to profl. jours. Bd. dirs. Concord Chamber Orch., Milw., 1982-91; vol. Cancer Soc., Milw., 1985—; reviewing bd. for program certification Am. Diabetes Assn., 1990-94;

chairperson pub. edn. com. Am. Cancer Soc., 1993-94, mem. exec. bd. dirs., editl. bd. Jour. Healthcare Edn. and Tng. Mem. Am. Assn. Adult Continuing Edn., Am. Soc. Healthcare Edn. and Tng., Spl. Libr. Assn. (treas. 1981-83), Libr. Community Milw., Area Coun. Health Educators (chairperson 1986-88), Nat. Wellness Coun., U. Wis. Alumni Assn., Phi Kappa Phi. Avocations: skiing, biking, classical music, writing.

HARTNETT, GINA ANN, elementary education educator; b. Kansas City, Mo., July 22, 1957; d. George Anthony and Karen Frances (Kirch) Z.; m. Robert Neil Hartnett, Aug. 2, 1980; children: Erin Regina, Kevin Robert. BS in Edn., Cen. Mo. State U., 1979; MS in Edn., U. Kans., 1983. Math tchr. Raymore-Peculiar (Mo.) H.S., 1979, Pleasant Lea Jr. H.S., Lee's Summit, Mo., 1979-92, BC Campbell Mid. Sch., Lee's Summit, Mo., 1992—. Tchr. facilitator BC Campbell Mid. Sch., Lee's Summit, 1993—. Mem. NEA, Nat. Coun. Tchrs. Math., Delta Kappa Gamma. Roman Catholic. Home: 508 SE Adobe Dr Lees Summit MO 64063-4484

HARTNETT, KATHLEEN MARY, coordinator special education; b. Flushing, N.Y., Aug. 15, 1955; d. Timothy Lawrence and Patricia Marie (Degnan) H. BA in Elem. Spl. Edn., Mount St. Mary Coll., Newburgh, N.Y., 1977; MS in Spl. Edn., Adelphi Univ., 1981; profl. diploma, Long Island U., 1989. Cert. tchr., N.Y. Dean of students North Babylon High Sch UFSD, North Babylon, N.Y., 1989—; spl. edn. tchr. North Babylon High Sch. UFSD, North Babylon, N.Y., 1978—, coord. spl. edn., 1993—. Coach girls basketball North Babylon UFSD, N.Y., 1981—, girls softball coach, 1981—; coach Suffolk County Girls Basketball Coaches Assn. Mem. N.Y. State United Tchrs., North Babylon Coun. Chairpersons and Coords. (sec. 1993-94), Phi Delta Kappan.

HART-NOLAN, ELSIE FAYE, elementary education educator; b. Shelbyville, Ill., Oct. 15, 1920; d. James Ray and Maude May (Allison) Cain; m. Harold Delbert Bible, June 15, 1941 (div. Apr. 1948); children: Gary H., Rex. E. (dec.); m. Frederick Christopher Hart, July 28, 1950 (dec. Dec. 1994); children: Susan Hart Eichman, Pamela L.; m. Jerome F. Nolan, May 1, 1999. Elem. teaching cert., Ea. Ill. U., 1942; BS in Edn., No. Ill. U., 1968; postgrad., Rockford Coll., 1972-73. Cert. elem. tchr., Ill. Tchr. Findlay (Ill.) Elem. Sch., 1942-47; tchr. Winnebago County Schs., Rockford, Ill., 1948-52, Rockford Parochial Schs., 1957-63, Rockford Pub. Schs., 1964-82, substitute tchr., 1982—. Author: The On and the Under Dog, 1992; contbr. articles to profl. jours. Vol. tchr. Rockford Parochial schs. Recipient Cert. of Commendation in recognition of meritorious svc. Ill. Supt. Pub. Instrn., 1974; nominated Ill. Retired Tchrs. Hall of Fame. Mem. AAUW (historian Rockford chpt. 1970—), Ill. Ret. Tchrs. Assn., Winnebago/Boone Ret. Tchrs. Assn., Women of the Moose, Holy Family Women's Guild, Rockford Women's Club (sec. 1970, publicity com. 1971, membership com. 1972, ways/means com. 1988-91, bd. dirs. 1993-94, long-range planning com. 1994—, program com. 1994-95, dir. 1995-98), Nat. Women's Hall of Fame. Republican. Roman Catholic. Avocations: dancing, swimming, golf, volunteer teaching, fundraising. Home: 3611 Pinecrest Rd Rockford IL 61107-1307

HARTSHORN, BRENDA BEAN, elementary education educator; b. Randolph, Vt., June 23, 1962; d. David Anthony and Reta Mae (Jones) Bean; children: Tyler Anthony, Caitlyn Elizabeth. BA, Vt. Coll., 1985; MEd, St. Michael's Coll., 1990. Teaching prin. aide Moretown (Vt.) Elem. Sch., 1984-85, 1-3 grade tchr., 1985—. Cons. math. & assessment, Waitsfield, Vt., 1993—; assoc. in math. Inst. for Math. Mania, Montpelier, Vt., 1994—, specialist for Vt. Dept. Edn. and Univ. of Vt., Early Literacy Intervention, 1999-2001. Contbr. articles to jours. Forums with state legis., Vt. NEA, 1985—; Justice of the Peace, 1998-. Recipient Sallie Mae Outstanding First Yr. Tchr. award Sallie Mae, 1985-86, Outstanding Tchr. of Yr. award, 1993-94, Presdl. award in Math. Nat. Sci. Found., 1994-95. Mem. NEA, Nat. Coun. of Tchrs. Math., Vt. Coun. on Reading, Assn. Supervision & Curriculum Devel. Democrat. Avocations: quilting, reading, writing, outdoor sports, travelling. Home: 1192 Crossett Hill Waterbury VT 05676 Office: Moretown Elem Sch Rt 100B Moretown VT 05660

HARTSTEIN, HAROLD HERMAN, psychology educator, consultant; b. N.Y.C., Jan. 9, 1921; s. Samuel and Margaret Amanda (Wussow) H.; m. Marion Elizabeth Shea, Apr. 11, 1953; children: Marion Farnham Korzec, Margaret Ann. BGS, U. Nebr.-Omaha, 1971; MA, U. South Fla., 1972; EdD, Nova U., 1978. Enlisted U.S. Army, 1942, commd. 2d lt., 1948, advanced through grades to lt. col., 1967, served in ETO, 1944-45, 1949-50, 1950-51, 1955-57, 1960-61; with 3d Inf. Honor Guard, Washington, 1951-54; comdg. officer Signal Battalion, Korat, Thailand, 1967-68; gen. staff officer Hdqrs., U.S. Army Strategic Comm. Commd., Ft. Huachua, Ariz., 1968-70; ret., 1970; prof. psychology Hillsborough C.C., Tampa, Fla., 1973-91; ret., 1991. Cons. textbook pubs. Decorated Legion of Merit, Bronze Star medal, Army Commendation medal. Mem. NEA, VFW, Ret. Officers Assn., Am. Assn. Ret. Persons, Am. Legion, Common Cause, U. Nebr. at Omaha Alumni Assn., U. South Fla. Alumni Assn., Nova U. Alumni Assn., Friends of Tampa Mus. Art. Democrat. Mem. United Ch. of Christ.

HARTSTEIN, SAM, public relations professional; b. N.Y.C., Aug. 6, 1921; m. Rachel Zimmerman, June 23, 1963; children: Gila, Jonathan. Tchrs. Diploma, Yeshiva U., 1941, BA, 1943, LHD (hon.), 1994; postgrad., New Sch. Social Rsch. Dir. pub. rels. Yeshiva U., N.Y.C., 1943-94, cons., 1994—. Writer, producer films including: Faith and Learning, The Story of Yeshiva U.; vis. lectr. to various schs., profl. meetings, nat. orgns. Past pres. Met. Coll. Pub. Rels. Coun. Author: A Guide to Public Relations, 1970, Yeshiva U. Centennial film Building an American Tradition: Yeshiva University—The First Century, 1987 (Bronze medal, CASE); contbr. numerous articles to various publs. Past pub. rels. chmn. Jewish Cmty. Coun. Washington Heights-Inwood; mem. bd. edn. Yeshiva Rabbi Moses Soloveitchik; bd. dirs. YM & YWHA Washington Heights and Inwood. Mem. CASE (Seasoned Sage award 1970, Gold Medal award 1987), Nat. Sch. Pub. Rels. Assn., Coll. Sports Info. Dirs. Am., Am. Jewish Pub. Rels. Soc. Home: 66 Overlook Terr New York NY 10040-3824 Office: Yeshiva U 500 W 185th St New York NY 10033-3201

HARTZELL, KARL DREW, retired university dean, historian; b. Chgo., Jan. 17, 1906; s. Morton C. and Bertha V. (Drew) H.; m. Anne Lomas, Sept. 7, 1935; children: Karl Drew, Richard Lomas, Julian Crane; m. Elizabeth Farnum Guibord, Oct. 2, 1993. PhB cum laude, Wesleyan U., 1927; AM, Harvard U., 1928, PhD, 1934. Mem. faculty European history and Western civilization Carleton Coll., 1930-31; mem. faculty European history and western civilization dept. Ga. Sch. Tech., 1935-40; with SUNY, Geneseo, 1940-47; historian N.Y. State War Coun., 1945-46; adminstrv. officer Brookhaven Nat. lab., 1947-52; dean Cornell Coll., Iowa, 1952-56, Bucknell U., 1956-62; acting chief adminstrv. officer SUNY, Stony Brook, 1962-65, adminstrv. officer, 1965-71; libr. Inst. Advanced Studies of World Religions, cons. Author: The Empire State at War: World War II, 1949, Opportunities in Atomic Energy, 1950, A Philosophy for Science Teaching, 1957; editor: The Upperclass Student and His Curriculum, 1955; co-editor: The Study of Religion on the Campus of Today, 1967. Wilbur Fisk scholar, Wesleyan U. Fellow Soc. for Values in Higher Edn. (sr. mem.); mem. Soc. Christian Ethics, Phi Beta Kappa. Republican. Home: Elstead #210 1000 Vicars Landing Way Ponte Vedra Beach FL 32082 Home (Summer): PO Box 166 Shelter Island Heights NY 11965-0166

HARTZLER, GENEVIEVE LUCILLE, physical education educator; b. Hammond, Ind., June 19, 1921; d. Lewis Garvin and Effie May (Orton) H. BS in Edn., Ind. U., 1944; MEd, U. Minn., 1948. Tchr. phys. edn. Griffith (Ind.) Pub. Schs., 1944-45, Northrup Collegiate Sch., Mpls., 1945-47; supr. student tchrs., 1947-79; tchr. phys. edn. Marquette (Mich.) Pub. Schs., 1948-50, Albion (Mich.) Pub. Schs., 1951-56, Jackson (Mich.) Pub. Schs., 1957-79, coord., project dir., tchr., coach, 1979-83. Chair equity workshop Jackson Pub. Schs., 1979-83; chair various convs., 1964-70. Mem. Am. Heart Assn., Jackson, 1977-83; mem., chair Women in Mgmt., Jackson, 1981-83; mem. Bus. and Profl. Women, Jackson, 1980-90. Recipient Honor awards Young Woman's Christian Assn. and Mich. Divsn. Girls and Women's Sports. Mem. AAHPERD, NEA, Mich. Assn. Health, Phys. Edn. and Recreation (Honor award), Mich. Edn. Assn. (Women's Cultural award), Delta Kappa Gamma (Woman of Distinction award). Avocations: golf, swimming, travel, reading. Home: 703 Bay Meadows Cir Lady Lake FL 32159-2285 E-mail: genhar621@webtv.net.

HARVARD, MARY RUTH, special education educator; b. Americus, Ga., Mar. 6, 1950; d. Brenton Brooks and Ruth (Methvin) McCarty; m. Donovan Ruis Harvard, Aug. 21, 1971; children: Donovan Markus, Augustus Blake. BS in Elem. Edn., Ga. Southwestern Coll., 1968; EdM, U. South Ala., 1980. Elem. tchr. A.C. Moore Sch., Atmore, Ala., 1971-77; specific learning disabilities tchr. Gables Acad., Mobile, Ala., 1977-78, Semmes (Ala.) Middle Sch., 1978-81; tchr. educably mentally handicapped Elvin Hill Elem. Sch., Columbiana, Ala., 1981; specific learning disabilities tchr. Montevallo (Ala.) High Sch., 1981-85, Tuscaloosa (Ala.) County High Sch., 1985-88, B.B. Comer Meml. High Sch., Sylacauga, Ala., 1988—96, dept. chairperson, 1990—96, Sylacauga (Ala.) HS, 1996—. Sponsor student coun. B.B. Comer Sch., Sylacauga, 1990-92. Rep. United Way, Sylacauga, 1990-95. Named Tchr. of the Yr., Nat. Jr. Honor Soc., Semmes Middle Sch., 1979; recipient Stutz-Bearcat grant Stutz-Bearcat/Talladega (Ala.) Coll., 1992. Mem. ASCD, NEA, Ala. Edn. Assn., Sylacauga City Edn. Assn., Coun. for Exceptional Childre, Coun. for Learning Disabilities. Methodist. Avocations: reading, cross-stitching. Home: 320 Cross Creek Ln Alpine AL 35014-5181 Office: Sylacauga HS 704 N Broadway Ave Sylacauga AL 35150

HARVEY, CAROL SAMMONS, educator; b. Tulsa, Mar. 20, 1945; d. Virgil Carl and Virginia (Whittredge) Sammons; m. Lee Murphey Coleman, Dec. 17, 1966 (div. Aug. 1975); m. David Freal Harvey, Aug. 13, 1978. BA, Ga. State Coll., 1967; MEd, U. Ala., 1972; EdS, U. Ga., 1975. Cert. tchr., pupil personnel, sch. psychology, Calif. Tchr. Tuscaloosa (Ala.) County Schs., 1967-68, Tuscumbia (Ala.) City Schs., 1968-70, Advent Episcopal Day Sch., Birmingham, Ala., 1970-72, Oconee County Schs., Watsonville, Ga., 1972-73, Clarke County Schs., Athens, Ga., 1973-75; sch. psychologist Jefferson County Schs., Birmingham, 1975-77, Cupertino (Calif.) Union Sch. Dist., 1977-78; resource tchr., projects specialist Gilroy (Calif.) Unified Schs., 1979-81; sch. psychologist, cons. Humboldt County Office Edn., Eureka, Calif., 1982-87; tchr. Pacific Union Sch. Dist., Arcata, Calif., 1987-95; Title I coord. Eureka City Schs., 1995—. Cons. program rev. State of Calif. Dept. Edn., 1979-81, Humboldt County Office Edn., 1984-87. V.p. Humboldt Handweavers and Spinners Guild., Eureka. State of Ga. Regents scholar, 1963-67. Mem. NEA, Nat. Assn. for Edn. of Young Children, Internat. Reading Assn., Calif. Tchrs. Assn., Calif. Kindergarten Assn., Crimson Key Honor Soc., Phi Kappa Phi, Delta Kappa Gamma Soc. Internat. Democrat. Episcopalian. Avocations: weaving, wearable art, travel, folk and ballroom dancing, reading. Office: Eureka City Schs 3200 Walford Ave Eureka CA 95503-4828

HARVEY, DENISE ELAINE, secondary education educator; b. Marceline, Mo., Aug. 26, 1959; d. Wayne Lee and Karen Beth (Jones) Drake; m. Timothy Edward Harvey, July 25, 1981; children; Joshua Timothy, Cierra Denise. BS in English Edn., N.E. Mo. State U., 1981, MA, 1986. Cert. tchr. and libr., Mo. Tchr. LaPlata (Mo.) High Sch., 1981-82, Macon (Mo.) R-I High Sch., 1982-98, Shelby County R-IV Schs., Shelbina, Mo., 1998—. Instr. Moberly Area (Mo.) C.C., 1992—; libr. Macon Elem. Sch., 1992, 94. Active tchr., youth sponsor Clarence (Mo.) Christian Ch., 1982—, dir. vacation Bible sch., 1990-91. Named one of Outstanding Young Women Am., 1984; recipient Tchr. Appreciation award Mo. Scholars Acad., 1994. Mem. Nat. Coun. Tchrs. English, Mo. Coun. Tchrs. English, Mo. State Tchrs. Assn., South Shelby Tchrs. Assn., Delta Kappa Gamma. Republican. Avocations: water skiing, crafts, reading, writing. Home: 208 N Center St # 125 Clarence MO 63437 Office: South Shelby High Sch Hwy 36 W Shelbina MO 63468

HARVEY, DONALD LEROY, secondary education educator; b. Ashland, Ky., Oct. 5, 1950; s. George Leroy and Ruby Jean (Sparks) H.; m. Shirley Dawn Habada, Sept. 6, 1970; children: Tammra Michelle, Kevin Michael, Ana Maria. AS, Kettering Coll. Med. Arts, 1970; BS, Walla Walla Coll., 1973; MS, Andrews U., 1982. Sci./math. tchr. Reading (Pa.) Jr. Acad., 1973-77, Greater Balt. (Md.) Jr. Acad., 1977-83; sci. dept. chmn. Bass Meml. Acad., Lumberton, Miss., 1983—2001, Madison (Tenn.) Acad., 2001—. Mem. curriculum com., acad. standards com., libr. com. Bass Meml. Acad., Lumberton, 1985—; tchr., facilitator Miss. Literacy Program, Lumberton, 1988. Recipient Thomas and Violet Zapara Award of Recognition for Excellence in Tchg., Office of Edn. of the Gen. Conf. of Seventh-day Adventists, 1989, Star Tchr. award Miss. Econ. Coun., Jackson, 1989-90. Mem. AAAS, Nat. Sci. Tchrs. Assn. (tchr. cert. in biology 1993), Nat. Assn. Biology Tchrs. Avocations: sports, scuba diving, flying, photography. Home: 625 Vanoke Drive Madison TN 37115 Office: Madison Academy 100 Academy Drive Madison TN 37115

HARVEY, EDITH M. federal agency administrator; Bachelors Degree, Kans. State U.; M in Edn. Adminstrn. and Supervision, U. Nebr. Mgr., program specialist, contracting officer's rep. U.S. Dept. Edn., Washington, dir. improvement programs Office Innovation and Improvement. Office: US Dept Edn FOB-6 Rm 3E106 400 Maryland Ave SW Washington DC 20202*

HARVEY, GLEN H. educational association administrator; BA in Psychology and Sociology, MA in Social and Philos. Founds. of Edn., U. Ky.; AM in Philosophy, PhD in Philosophy of Edn., Stanford U. With The NETWORK, Inc., Nat. Inst. Edn.; exec. dir. Learning Innovations WestEd and the Regional Lab. for Ednl. Improvement of the N.E. and Islands; CEO WestEd Regional Edn. Lab., 1997—. Office: WestEd 730 Harrison St San Francisco CA 94107-1242*

HARVEY, HILDA RUTH, special education educator; b. Kingsville, Tex., Sept. 6, 1950; d. Nicolas Guerra and Maria de Jesus (Sanchez) Montalvo; m. Steve Allen Harvey, Oct. 20, 1978 (div. Nov. 1991); children: John, Kristy. BA, Tex. Wesleyan Univ., 1982; cert., Univ. Mary Hardin Baylor, 1985. Cert. secondary edn. educator. Tchr. adult edn. Ctrl. Tex. Coll., Killeen, 1985-86; tchr. homebound Fort Worth Ind. Sch. Dist., 1986-87, psychoednl. instr., 1987-91, adult ESL instr., 1988-90; spl. educator Killeen (Tex.) Ind. Sch. Dist., 1991—; fgn. lang. chmn. Manor Mid. Sch., Killeen, Tex., 1995—. Cons. Fort Worth Ind. Sch. Dist., 1990-91. With USAF, USAFR, U.S. Army Res., 1975-96. Recipient Outstanding Coach-Girls Softball Dependent Youth Activity Ctr., 1983. Fellow ASCD; mem. AAUW, Tex. State Tchrs. Assn., Disabled Am. Vets., Century Club, Sigma Delta Pi. Republican. Southern Baptist. Office: Manor Mid Sch 1700 S W S Young Dr Killeen TX 76543-5097

HARVEY, JAMES GERALD, educational counselor, consultant, researcher; b. California, Mo., July 15, 1934; s. William Walter and Exie Marie (Lindley) H. BA Amherst Coll., 1956; MAT (fellow), Harvard U., 1958, MEd, 1962. Asst. to dean grad. sch. edn. Harvard U., Cambridge, Mass., 1962-66, dir. admissions, fin. aid, 1966-69; dir. counseling service U. Calif., Irvine, 1970-72; ednl. cons., Los Angeles, 1972—. Author: (ednl. materials) HARVOCAB Vocabulary Program, 1985—. 1st lt. USAF, 1958-61. Amherst Mayo-Smith grantee, 1956-57; UCLA Adminstrv. fellow, 1969-70. Mem. Am. Ednl. Research Assn., Nat. Council Measurement in Edn. Address: 1845 Glendon Ave Los Angeles CA 90025-4653

HARVEY, JOANN MARIE, physical education specialist; b. Lapwai, Idaho, Feb. 4, 1938; d. Jesse and Anna (Jackson) H.; children: Bradley, Jeffrey, Joel (dec.), Jennifer, Rosalyn. BA in Edn., Phys. Edn., Natural Sci., Ea. Wash. U., 1978; M in Orgnl. Leadership, Gonzaga U., 1993. Fitness dir. YMCA, Coeurd Alene, Idaho, 1973-81; owner, mgr. Fitness Ctr., Hayden, Idaho, 1981-86; phys. edn. specialist Coeur d'Alene Sch. Dist., Dalton, 1986—. Wellness cons. hosp. and sch., Coeur d'Alene, 1981-86. Author poetry. Mem. human & civil rights Idaho Edn. Assn., 1995—; bd. dirs. Kootenai County Task Force on Human Rels.; mem. North Idaho Dem. Party, Coeur d'Alene, 1994—; candidate, House Rep., 2000, Senate, 2002. Mem. NEA (Am. Indian/Ala. native caucus chmn., 2001-03, exec. com., 2002-03, bd. dirs., 2002-03), Idaho Edn. Assn. (mem. del. assembly 1994—), Coeur d'Alene Edn. Assn. (human/civil rights chair 1994-95, region 1 chair 2000—, pres. 2000-03), Idaho Coun. Cath. Women (bd. dirs. 1991-95, past pres.). Avocations: outdoor activities, aerobics, Karate, tang soo do (1st dan), animals. Home: 6015 N Mount Carrol St Coeur D Alene ID 83815-9606 E-mail: jharvey@imbris.com.

HARVEY, JUDITH GOOTKIN, elementary school educator, real estate agent; b. Boston, May 29, 1944; d. Myer and Ruth Augusta (Goldstein) Gootkin; m. Robert Gordon Harvey, Aug. 3, 1968; children: Jonathan Michael, Alexander Shaw. BS in Edn., Lesley Coll., Cambridge, Mass., 1966; MS in Edn., Nazareth Coll., Rochester, NY, 1987. Kindergarten tchr. Williams Sch., Chelsea, Mass., 1966-69; owner, tchr. Island Presch., Eleuthera, The Bahamas, 1969-70; substitute tchr. Brighton Cen. Sch., Rochester, NY, 1985-95; agt. Prudential Rochester Realty, Pittsford, NY, 1994—98. Author, dir. : (plays) The Parrot Perch, 1991. Bd. dir. in charge pub. rels. George Eastman Ho. Coun., mem. award steering com. honoring Lauren Bacall, 1990, chmn. gala celebration honoring Audrey Hepburn, 1992, mem. steering com. honoring Ken Burns, 1995; mem. art in bloom steering com. for fashion show Meml. Art Gallery, 1994; co-chmn. Fashionata, Rochester Philharm. Orch., 1990; mem. steering com. of realtors Ambs. to Arts; mem. Parrot Players Acting Group, 1990—; mem. steering com. Reels and Wheels Antique Car Festival, 1995, 1996; bd. dir. Birmingham Bloomfield Newcomers, 2000—03, in charge spl. events, 2000—02; com. mem. Birmingham Antiques Festival, 2000—02; co-chair World of James Bond Gala and the Spring Fashion Show, 2001, Saturday Night Fever...Live It! Gala and Spring Fashion Show, 2002; historian Birmingham Bloomfield Newcomers, 2002—03. Mem.: Multimillion Dollar Prodr.'s Club, Genesee Valley Club, Chatterbox Club. Avocations: acting, directing, gardening, writing, bridge.

HARVEY, KARON LEE, secondary education educator; b. Leavenworth, Kans., July 20, 1943; d. Charles F. and Coyla Mae (Lesher) Nutter; m. Dean Kent Harvey, May 21, 1966; children: Kim, Kirk, Kif. BS in Edn., Chadron State Coll., 1966; MA in English, U. No. Colo., 1972. Life cert. in secondary English, Nebr. Tchr. English Chadron (Nebr.) High Sch., 1966-67, Gering (Nebr.) Jr. High Sch., 1967-86, media dir., 1986—. Adj. faculty Nebr. Western Coll., Scottsbluff, 1979-80. Mem. adv. bd. Scottsbluff Pub. Libr., 1974-86, bd. dir. 1994—; commr. Nebr. Libr. Commn., Lincoln, 1986-89; bd. dirs. Campfire, 1989-94. Recipient Svc. award City of Scottsbluff, 1986, Admiralty in Nebr. Navy Office of Gov., Lincoln, 1989. Mem. NEA, Nebr. State Edn. Assn., Nebr. Libr. Assn., Nebr. Edn./Media Assn. Roman Catholic. Avocation: travel. Home: 2101 3rd Ave Scottsbluff NE 69361-2030 Office: Gering Jr High Sch 800 Q St Gering NE 69341-2972

HARVEY, NANCY MELISSA, media specialist, art teacher; b. Atlanta, Mar. 31, 1934; d. Alfred Alonzo and Helen Rosella (Puntney) Ettinger; m. Dale Gene Harvey, Aug. 23, 1957; children: Howard Russell, Andrew Dale, Renee Jeannine. BA, U. Mont., 1957; M in Human Svcs., Coll. of Gt. Falls, Mont., 1987. Cert. tchr., Mont. Media specialist, libr. Flathead H.S., Kalispell, Mont., 1971-79; libr., art tchr. Cut Bank (Mont.) H.S., 1979-94. Author: (poetry collection) Bluffs, 2000; contbr. poetry to Arts in Mont., Mont. Arts mag., Poetry Today quar., Today's Poets anthology. Recipient Mary Brennan Clapp Poetry awrd Mont. Arts Found., 1973; grantee Mont. Com. for the Humanities, 1985, 87. Mem. AAUW (life), Mont. Genealogy Soc. (treas. Tangled Roots chpt. 1990—), Delta Kappa Gamma (chpt. pres. 1994-96), Phi Kappa Phi. Democrat. Presbyterian. Avocations: music, painting, creative writing, photography.

HARVEY, PATRICIA JEAN, special education administrator, retired; b. Newman, Calif., Oct. 27, 1931; d. Willard Monroe and Marjorie (Greenlee) Clougher; m. Richard Blake Harvey, Aug. 29, 1965; children: G. Scott Floden, Timothy P. BA, Whittier Coll., 1966, MA, 1971. Resource specialist Monte Vista High Sch. and Whittier (Calif.) High Sch., 1977-98; dept. chair spl. edn. Whittier (Calif.) High Sch., 1982-94; ret., 1998. Author: (tchrs. manual) The Dynamics of California Government and Politics, 1970, 90; co-author: Meeting The Needs of Special High School Students in Regular Education Classrooms, 1988. Active Whittier Fair Housing Com., 1972; pres. Women's Aux. Whittier Coll., 1972-73, sec., 1971-72; historian Docian Soc. Whittier Coll., 1963-64, pres. 1965-66. Democrat. Episcopalian. Home: 424 E Avocado Crest Rd La Habra Heights CA 90631-8128 Office: The Learning Advantage Ctr 13710 Whittier Blvd Ste 206 Whittier CA 90605-4407

HARVEY, TAMARA MAUREEN, English literature and women's studies educator; b. Pullman, Wash., Mar. 14, 1966; d. Robert Gordon and Linda Mae (McInturf) H.; m. Douglas Boulton Stewart, July 2, 2000; child: Daniel Gordon Stewart. AB in Hist. and Lit., Harvard U. & Radcliffe Coll., 1988; MA in English, U. Wis., 1989; PhD in English, U. Calif., Irvine, 1998. Tchg. asst. U. Wis., Madison, 1988-91; tchg. assoc., lectr. U. Calif., 1992-98; asst. prof. English U. So. Miss., Hattiesburg, 1998—. One of top 40 Westinghouse Sci. Talent Search, 1984; Univ. scholar U. Wis, 1988-91, Nat. Merit scholar, 1984, NCR Centennial scholar, 1984, Chancellor's fellow U. Calif., Irvine, 1992-96. Mem. MLA, Soc. Early Americanists. Office: U So Miss Dept English Hattiesburg MS 39406 E-mail: tamara.harvey@usm.edu.

HARVILL, MELBA SHERWOOD, retired university librarian; b. Bryson, Tex., Jan. 22, 1933; d. William Henry and Delta Verlin (Brawner) Sherwood; m. L. E. Harvill Jr., Feb. 2, 1968; children: Sherman T., Mark Roling. BA, North Tex. State Coll., 1954; MA, North Tex. State U., 1968, MLS, 1973, PhD, 1984. Tchr. Graham (Tex.) Ind. Sch. Dist., 1966-68; reference libr. Midwestern U., Wichita Falls, 1968—73; dir. librs. Midwestern State U., Wichita Falls, 1973-2000. Presenter in field. Vol. Boy Scouts Am., Wichita Falls, 1969—74, Wichita Falls Sr.-Jr. Forum, 1978—2000, mem. exec. bd. girls club, ways and means com., sec., asst. treas.; chmn. United Way Midwestern State U., 1975—76; mem. talent coordinating com. Wichita Falls Centennial Celebration; vol. Conv. and Vis. Bur., Lone Stars, 1993—; grad. Leadership Wichita Falls, 1990; pres. Southside Girls Club, 1997—98; auditor, budget com. chair Woman's Forum, 1997—99; ednl. programming chair Wichita Falls Arts Coun., 2001—; mem. U. North Tex. Advancement Adv. Coun.; bd. dirs. YWCA Wichita Falls, 1987—94, pres. bd. dirs., 1989—91, 1994—95; bd. dirs. River Bend Nature Works. Recipient Svc. award Sr.-Jr. Forum, Wichita Falls United Way Community Svc. award, 1975, Svc. award YWCA Bd. Dirs., 1991; named Met. BPW Woman of Yr., 1980. Mem. ALA, LWV (program v.p., pres. 1991-92), Tex. Libr. Assn. (mem. planning com., mem. membership com., mem. legis. com., mem. rsch. and grants com., chairperson dist VII, chairperson adminstrn. round table), Tex. Coun. State U. Librs. (sec.-treas. 1990-92), Wichita Falls Rotary North (sec. 1993-96), U. North Tex. Alumni Assn. (bd. dirs. 1992-94, 97-2002), Phi Alpha Theta, Pi Sigma Alpha, Phi Delta Phi, Gamma Theta Upsilon, Alpha Chi, Beta Phi Mu. Democrat. Avocations:

spectator sports, swimming, music, reading, travel. Home: 4428 BUS 287J Iowa Park TX 76367 E-mail: mharvill33@aol.com.

HARVILLE, MARTHA LOUISE, special education educator; b. Detroit, Sept. 28, 1958; d. Henry and Emma Jean (Campbell) H.; m. Russell Smith, May 1, 1993; children: David-Akem, Russell Timothy. BA in Edn., Queens Coll., 1981, MS in Edn., 1986; D in Curriculum and Tchg., Columbia U., 2000. Cert. tchr. spl. edn., elem. tchr. N-6, sch. dist. adminstr., N.Y.; lic. asst. prin., N.Y. Caseworker Bur. of Child Welfare, Jamaica, N.Y., 1981-82; tchr. spl. edn. Pub. Sch. 46Q, Bayside Queens, N.Y., 1982-83, Pub. Sch. 213Q, Bayside Queens, N.Y., 1983-85; Pub. Sch. 153, Maspeth, 1986; gen. indsl. arts tchr. Ind. Sch. 227Q/Louis Armstrong East, Elmhurst, N.Y., 1985-89; spl. edn. tchr. Pub. Sch. 153, Bayside Queens, 1986; tchr. technology Ind. Sch. 227Q/Louis Armstrong East, Elmhurst, N.Y., 1990-91, 93-94; staff devel. specialist Cen. Bd. Edn., Bklyn., 1989-90; rsch. asst. Columbia U. Tchr.'s Coll., N.Y.C., 1991—, curriculum instructional specialist of tech., 2003—; rsch. asst., intern Ctr. Adaptive Tech., N.Y.C., 1991—; tech. cons. CSTIP project Tchrs. Coll. Columbia U. IUME Ctr. Computer tchr. Bd. Edn. Dist. 26, Bayside Queens, 1983-85; software evaluator, Bd. Edn., Bklyn., 1988-89; yearbook adv. Ind. Sch. 227Q, 1986-89; adj. lectr. Big Buddy Program at Queens Coll., Flushing, N.Y., 1989-90; owner Harville's. Inventor in field; contbr. articles to profl. jours. Mem. exec. bd. Reach for Cultural Heights, 1992—; mem. Lincoln Ctr. Inst., 1984—; del. Citizen Amb. Program, Spokane, Wash., 1995; dep. gov. Am. Biog. Rsch. Inst., 1995—; coach 1st Lego League. Recipient Svc. award Girl Scouts US., Jamaica, 1980. Mem. Queens Coll. Alumni, Edn. Adminstrn. Orgn. Columbia U., Queens Coll. Grad. Student Assn. (pres. 1988), Kappa Delta Pi. Avocations: theatre, drawing, reading, hobbies.

HARVIN, KAY KERCE, elementary school educator; b. Arcadia, Fla., Mar. 9, 1947; d. Woodrow and Mary Lillian (Durrance) Kerce; m. Wesley Reid Harvin Sr., Aug. 22, 1964; 1 child, Wesley Reid II. BA, Fla. State U., 1967; MA, U. South Fla., 1974, EdS, 2001. Tchr. Hillsborough County, Tampa, Fla., 1967-71, Leon County, Tallahassee, Fla., 1971-73, Pinellas County, St. Petersburg, Fla., 1973-76, Martin County, Stuart, Fla., 1977—. ESOL trainer, 1996—;adj. instr. IRCC, 1996—; presenter in field. Contbr. to Anthology of Treasured Poems, 1995, 96, 97, 98. Mem. Jr. Women's Club, 1969-80; mem. Rep. Exec. Com., Martin County, 1979-81; vol. Polit. Campaigns, Martin County, 1978, 80, 82, 84, 92, 94. Methodist. Avocations: reading, writing. Home: 3959 SW Marlin Dr Palm City FL 34990-3817 Office: Martin County Schs 500 E Ocean Bvld Stuart FL 34994

HARWICK, BETTY CORINNE BURNS, sociology educator; b. L.A., Jan. 22, 1926; d. Henry Wayne Burns and Dorothy Elizabeth (Menzies) Routhier; m. Burton Thomas Harwick, June 20, 1947; children: Wayne Thomas, Burton Terence, Bonnie Christine, Beverly Anne Carroll. Student, Biola, 1942-45, Summer Inst. Linguistics, 1945, U. Calif., Berkeley, 1945-52; BA, Calif. State U., Northridge, 1961, MA, 1965; postgrad., MIT, 1991. Prof. sociology Pierce Coll., Woodland Hills, Calif., 1966-95, pres. acad. senate, 1976-77, pres. faculty assn., 1990-91, chmn. dept. for philosophy and sociology, 1990-95, co-creator, faculty advisor interdisciplinary program religious studies, 1988-95. Chmn. for sociology L.A. C.C. Dist., 1993-95; occasional cmty. guest lectr. religious studies and sociology, 1995—. Author: (with others) Introducing Sociology, 1977; author: Workbook for Introducing Sociology, 1978. Faculty rep. Calif. C.C. Assn., 1977-80. Alt. fellow NEH, 1978. Mem. Am. Acad. Religion, Soc. Bibl. Lit., Am. Sociol. Assn. Presbyterian. Home: 19044 Superior St Northridge CA 91324-1845

HARWOOD, VIRGINIA ANN, retired nursing educator; b. Lawrenceville, Ohio, Nov. 5, 1925; d. Warren Leslie and Ruth Ann (Wilson) H.; m. Kenneth Dale Juillerat, Dec. 21, 1946 (div. 1972); children: Rozanne Augsburger, Vicki Anderson, Carol Mann, Karen Albaugh. RN, City Hosp. Sch. Nursing, Springfield, Ohio, 1946; BSN, Ind. U., 1968; MS in Edn., Purdue U., 1973, PhD, 1982. Cert. psychiat./mental health nurse, ANA. Staff nurse various hosps., 1946-60; pub. health nursing supr. Whitley County Health Dept., Columbia City, Ind., 1960-65; nursing supr., coordinator staff devel. Ft. Wayne (Ind.) State Hosp., 1965-69; faculty sch. nursing Parkview Hosp., Ft. Wayne, 1969-74; faculty dept. nursing Ball State U., Muncie, Ind., 1974-77; dir. nursing program Thomas More Coll., Ft. Mitchell, Ky., 1977-79; faculty sch. nursing Purdue U., West Lafayette, Ind., 1979-80; dean sch. nursing Ashland (Ohio) Coll., 1980-83; retired, 1983-86; charge nurse admission psychiat. unit VA Med. Ctr., Marion, Ind., 1986-93, ret., 1994—. Active Rep. Nat. Com., 1978—, U.S. Senatorial Club, 1984—, Rep. Pres. Task Force, 1982—; mem. ch. coun. Grace Luth. Ch., Gas City, Ind., 1993-96; bd. dirs. Luth. Ctr., Ball State U., Muncie, Ind., 1994-96; bd. mgrs. Covington Creek Condominium Assn., 1997-2001; vol. Foellinger-Freeman Bot. Conservatory, 1993—. Mem. Am. Nurses Found., Ohio State Nurses Assn. (pres. Mohican dist. 1981-83), Mensa, Intertel, Sigma Theta Tau, U.S. Amateur Ballroom Dancing Assn. (bd. dirs. Ft. Wayne chpt. 1998—, v.p. 2000, pres. 2001), Ft. Wayne Woman's Club. Avocations: travel, reading, dancing, orchid culture. Home: 6611 Quail Ridge Ln Fort Wayne IN 46804-2875

HASKELL, THOMAS LANGDON, history educator; b. Washington, May 26, 1939; s. Anthony Porter and Martha Averill (Bullock) H.; m. Dorothy Ann Wyatt, Aug. 27, 1966; children: Alexander Bullock, Susan Wyatt. BA, Princeton U., 1961; PhD, Stanford U., 1973. From instr. to prof. Rice U., Houston, 1970—, Samuel G. McCann prof. history, 1987—. Vis. mem. Inst. Advanced Study, Princeton, N.J., 1978-79. Author: Emergence of Professional Social Science, 1977, 2d edit. 2001, Objectivity is Not Neutrality, 1998; editor: The Authority of Experts, 1984; co-editor: (with Richard Teichgraeber) The Culture of Capitalism, 1993; mem. bd. editors Jour. Am. History, 1983-86, Am. Hist. Rev., 1988-91; contbr. articles to profl. jours. Lt. USN, 1961-65. Guggenheim Found. fellow, 1986-87; fellow NEH, Rockefeller Found., Mellon Found., Am. Coun. Learned Socs. Fellow Ctr. Advanced Study in Behavioral Scis.; mem. Orgn. Am Historians, Am. Hist. Assn. Office: Rice U Dept History Houston TX 77005-1892

HASKINS, JAMES LESLIE, mathematics educator; b. St. Louis, Aug. 10, 1947; s. Delbert George and Betty Ann (Reese) H.; m. Jane T. Barnard; children: Todd M., Nathan E., Elizabeth M. BS in Applied Math. and Computer Sci., Washington U., St. Louis, 1969, MBA, 1983; MAT, Webster U., 1971; postgrad., St. Louis U., 1995—. Tchr. math. Desmet Jesuit H.S., St. Louis, 1969-70, John Burroughs Sch., St. Louis, 1970—. Adj. prof. Washington U., St. Louis, 1982-2000, St. Louis U., 1994-97; traveling team mem. Woodrow Wilson Found., Princeton, N.J., 1991-95; instr. Command and Gen. Staff Officer Course USAR, St. Louis, 1991-94; bd. dirs. Martha Rounds Acad., St. Louis. Author: Algebra, 1990. Bd. dirs. Forsyth Sch., St. Louis, 1986-91, bldgs./grounds com., 1986-92; credit com. chmn. Credit Union, St. Louis, 1989-96. Woodrow Wilson fellow, 1990. Mem. Nat. Coun. Tchrs. of Math., Mo. Coun. Tchrs. Math., Math. Educators Greater St. Louis (exec. bd. 1991—, pres. 1997), Beta Tau Sigma. Democrat. Roman Catholic. Avocations: travel, sports, antiques. Home: 2857 Laclede Station Rd Saint Louis MO 63143-2809 Office: John Burroughs Sch 755 S Price Rd Saint Louis MO 63124-1899 E-mail: jhaskins@jburroughs.org.

HASKVITZ, ALAN PAUL, elementary education educator, consultant; b. Mpls., Sept. 7, 1942; s. Harry and Rose (Portugal) H.; married, Apr. 1, 1970; children: Anna, Maxwell Harry. AA, Chaffey Coll., 1963; MS, Calif. State U., 1965; BE, Meml. Coll., St. John's, Newfoundland, 1972; MA, Calif. State U., L.A., 1970. Cert. secondary tchr., adminstr., Calif.; cert. tchr., Ont., Newfoundland, N.Y.; cert. cmty. coll. instr., Calif.; cert. audio-visual. Tchr. Cornwall (Ont.) Sch. Bd., Can., 1970-78; vice prin. Quest School for the Gifted, Oshawa, Ont., 1978-80; tchr. Corono (Calif.) Sch. Sys., 1980-81, Walnut (Calif.) Sch. Dist., 1987—; cons. Edn. Strategies, Alta Loma, Calif., 1981—. Lectr. U. Calif., 1970—89, Calif. Poly., 1970—89, Western Wash. U., 2000; pres.-elect Nat. Coun. for the Social Scis.; mem. Nat. Critical Thinking Com., Coun. of Chief State Sch. Officers, Nat. Assessment of Ednl. Progress, Nat. Responder Com. on Tchrs. and Schs., Constl. Rights Found., Western States Accreditation Commn., Cal Poly Master Tchr. Com. on Student Tng. Programs; evaluator Nat. Coun. for Accreditation of Tchr. Edn.; spkr. to numerous orgns., meetings and confs.; sr. Olympian weightlifter. Author: Resources for Social Studies Educators; syndicated automobile journalist: The Car Family; contbr. numerous articles to profl. jours.; features in: Futures videos, Project citizen video, Time, Newsweek, CNN, ABC, CBS, NBC, NPR, numerous textbooks. Commr. City of Rancho Cucamonga, 1986—; pres. United Counties Sports, Cornwall, 1980-84; bd. advisors Americans All. Named USA Today All Am. Educator, 2000; named one of 100 Most Influential Educators in Am.; named to Nat. Tchrs. Hall of Fame, 1997; recipient Am.'s Profl. Best Tchr. award, Learning mag., 1989, Heroes in Edn. award, Reader's Digest, George Washington medal, Freedom Found., 1992, Spirit of Edn. award, NBC, 1997, Nat. Bicentennial Tchg. award, Bicentennial Com., 1993, Presdl. award for environ. edn., 1988, Calif. Dept. Water Agencies, Cmty. award, Walnut Valley Water Dist., 1989, Outstanding Citizen award, L.A. County Supr., 1994, Outstanding Tchr. award, Christa McAuliffe award, 1996, Nat. Coun. for Social Studies, 1992, Nation's Best Program, 1994, Nation's Outstanding Mid. Sch. Tchr., 1996, Agr. Tchr. of Yr., Nat. Coun. for Social Studies, 1995, Baylor U., Calif. Agr. in Classroom, Robert Cherry Internat. Tchr. of Yr., 1997, Campbell's Tchrs. in Am. award, Disney Regional Winner, Busch Environ. award, 1996, Nat. Garden award, Leavey award for pvt. enterprise edn., 1998, Freedom Found., Calif. Water Environ. Edn. award, Calif., 1995, Agy. for Water Edn., Calif. History Tchrs. of Yr., Daus. of Am. Colonies, 1999, Crystal Apple award, NBC, 1998, Bell award, Calif. Sch. Bd. Assn., 1987, 1997, numerous awards for sch. programs. Achievements include devel. of Reach Every Child and the Children's Speed Reading Record Holders. Home: 9655 Carrari Ct Alta Loma CA 91737-1653 E-mail: freealan@yahoo.com.

HASSAN, AFTAB SYED, education specialist, author, editor; b. Lahore, Punjab, Pakistan, Apr. 20, 1952; came to U.S., 1976; s. Maqsud Syed and Saliha Akhtar Hassan. BSCE with distinction, U. Engring. and Tech., Lahore, 1973; postgrad. in aerodyns., Colo. State U., 1976; MS, George Washington U., 1977; PhD, Columbia Pacific U., 1985. Scientist in ocean, coastal and environ. engring. George Washington U., 1977-84, grad. tchg. asst., 1979-84, asst. prof., 1980-85; chmn. math. and sci. Emerson Prep. Inst., Washington, 1979-89; acad. coord. Ctr. for Minority Student Affairs Georgetown U. Med. Sch., Washington, 1983-87; v.p. Met. Acctg. Assocs., Washington, 1987-88; acctg. mgr. Washington Info. Group, 1988-91; owner Met. Acctg. and Rsch., Washington, 1988-91; sr. tech. editor and author Betz Pub. Co., Rockville, Md., 1991-94, designer new products, dir. sci. rsch., 1991-94, v.p. acad. devel. Williams and Wilkins Ednl. Svcs. div., 1994-96, v.p. acad. devel. Betz Sci. Rsch. div., 1994-96; v.p. acad. devel., strategic planning Metro Acad. Rsch., Washington, 1996—. Adj. prof., clin. coord. Harlem Hosp. Ctr. Physicians Asst. program, The Sophie Dairs Sch. Biomed. Edn., 1998—. Author, dir. sci. rsch.: A Complete Preparation for the MCAT, 7th edit., 1996, Preparing for the D.A.T., 1992, Dental Admission Test--The Betz Guide, 1993, Optometry Admission Test--The Betz Guide, 1993, Problem Solving Software for the MCAT-Biological Sciences and Physical Sciences, 1994, Pharmacy College Admission Test--The Betz Guide, 1994, Allied Health Professions Admission Test--The Betz Guide, 1994, Veterinary Entrance Tests--The Betz Guide, 1995. Bd. dirs. Ctr. for Edn. Achievement, Charles R. Drew U. Medicine and Sci., Ebon Internat. Acad., Forsythe, Ga.; ednl. specialist Am. Physician Asst. Programs; curriculum advisor statewide programs for minority health professions State of Pa.; curriculum and ednl. specialist for ACCESS, statewide program at Priarie View (Tex.) A&M U. Recipient Merit award Nat. Assn. Chiefs of Police, Leaders in Cmty. Svc. award Am. Biog. Inst. 1990, Bell award Nat. Assn. Black Sch. Educators Found. Mem. ASCE, NSPE, Am. Soc. Engring. Edn., Am. Inst. Profl. Bookkeepers, Soc. Am. Mil. Engrs., Nat. Soc. Tax Profls., Nat. Coun. for Testing and Measurement, Nat. Law Enforcement Acad. (hon.), Nat. Assn. Advisors for Health Professions, Nat. Assn. Fgn. Student Advisors, Nat. Sci. Tchrs. Assn., Nat. Assn. Profl. Educators, Nat. Assn. Minority Med. Educators, Am. Ednl. Rsch. Assn., Soc. Tchrs. Family Medicine, N.Y. Acad. Scis., Soc. Competitive Intelligence Profls., Assn. Am. Med. Colls. (assoc.), Acad. Physician Assts. (assoc.). Avocations: exotic cooking, swimming, collecting currency. Address: American Soc Landscape Asso 636 I St NW Washington DC 20001-3736

HASSAN, HOSNI MOUSTAFA, microbiologist, biochemist, toxicologist and food scientist, educator; b. Alexandria, Egypt, Sept. 3, 1937; came to U.S., 1961; s. Moustafa Hosni and Sania M. (El-Hariri) H.; children: Jehan, Suzanne, Nora Elizabeth. BSc, Ain Shams U., Cairo, 1959; PhD, U. Calif., Davis, 1967. Asst. prof. Cairo High Polytech. Inst., 1968-70, U. Alexandria, 1970-72; vis. prof. McGill U., Montreal, 1972-74; rsch. asst. prof. U. Maine, Orono, 1974-76; rsch. assoc. biochemistry Duke U. Med. Ctr., Durham, N.C., 1976-79; assoc. prof. McGill U. Med. Sch., Montreal, 1979-80, N.C. State U., Raleigh, 1980-84, prof., 1984-93, prof., head microbiology dept., 1993—, head dept. microbiology, interim head toxicology dept., 1999-2001. Mem. editl. bd. Free Radicals in Biology and Medicine, 1984—; author: (chpts.) Enzymatic Basis of Toxicology, 1980, Biological Role of Copper, 1980, Advances in Genetics, 1989, Stress Responses in Plants, 1990, FEMS Microbiol. Reviews, 1994, Lung Biology Series, Vol. 15, 1997, others; author/co-author over 100 rsch. publs. Fellow NIH, 1967, Fulbright sr. fellow, Paris, 1987-88; NIH-NSF grantee N.C. State U., 1982, 83-93. Fellow Am. Inst. Chemists, Sigma Xi; mem. Am. Soc. Biol. Chemists and Molecular Biology, Am. Soc. for Microbiology (pres.-elect and pres. N.C. chpt. 1993-95). Democrat. Achievements include discovery of the toxicity and mutagenicity of oxygen free radicals and the protective role of the antioxidant enzymes superoxide dismutases and hydroperoxidases; the mechanism of regulation of the synthesis of the enzyme Mn-superoxide dismutase and catelases in bacteria. Home: 2637 Freestone Ln Raleigh NC 27603-3950 Office: NC State U Microbiology Dept PO Box 7615 Raleigh NC 27695-7615 E-mail: hosni_hassan@ncsu.edu.

HASSEL, RUDOLPH CHRISTOPHER, English educator; b. Richmond, Va., Nov. 16, 1939; s. Rudolph Christopher and Helen Elizabeth (Poehler) H.; m. Sedley Louise Hotchkiss, June 16, 1962; children: Bryan Christopher, Paul Sedley. BA, U. Richmond, 1961; MA, U. N.C., 1962; PhD, Emory U., 1968. English instr. Mercer U., Macon, Ga., 1962-65; asst. prof. Vanderbilt U., Nashville, 1968-73, assoc. prof., 1973-85, prof., 1985—. Dir. grad. studies English dept. Vanderbilt U., 1974-81, dir. undergrad. studies, 1991, 99-00; mem. exec. com. Folger Inst., Washington, 1986-95; cons. State of Tenn., Nashville, 1987-93; cons. for various univ. presses and profl. jours. Author: Renaissance Drama and the English Church Year, 1979, Faith and Folly in Shakespeare's Romantic Comedies, 1980, Songs of Death, 1987; contbr. articles to Shakespeare Quar., Shakespeare Jahrbuch, Comparative Drama, Studies in Philology, and others and poems to Vanderbilt Rev. and Arts and Letters. Mem. choir Christ Episcopal Ch., Nashville, 1974-95, outreach vol., 1974—, vestryman, 1980-83; vol. United Way, Vanderbilt U., 1980—, Habitat for Humanity. Woodrow Wilson Found. fellow, 1962; Emory U. fellow, 1965; Folger Libr. fellow, 1976; Am. Philol. Soc. fellow, 1986. Mem. MLA, Internat. Shakespeare Assn., Shakespeare Assn. Am., Malone Soc. New Variorum Editor (Richard 3 vol.), Omicron Delta Kappa. Avocations: biking, hiking, tennis, gardening, woodcrafting. Home: 107 Pembroke Ave Nashville TN 37205-3728 Office: PO Box 129B Nashville TN 37202-0129 E-mail: r.chris.hassel@vanderbilt.edu.

HASSELMO, NILS, academic administrator, linguistics educator; b. Kola, Sweden, July 2, 1931; arrived in U.S., 1958; s. A. Wilner and Anna Helena (Backlund) Hasselmo; m. Patricia June Tillberg, Oct. 25, 1958; children: Nils Peter, Michael Erik, Anna Patricia. Fil. mag., Uppsala U., 1956, Fil. lic., 1962, PhD (hon.), 1979; BA, Augustana Coll., Ill., 1957, DHL (hon.), 1995; PhD, Harvard U., 1961; LHD (hon.), North Park Coll. Theol. Sem., 1992. Asst. prof. Swedish Augustana Coll., Rock Island, Ill., 1958—59, 1961—62; from assoc. prof. to prof. Scandinavian langs. and lit. U. Minn., Mpls., 1965—83, 1988—2001, chmn. Scandinavian langs. and lit., 1970—73; dir. U. Minn. Ctr. for N.W. European Langs. and Area Studies, Mpls., 1970—73; assoc. dean U. Minn. Coll. Liberal Arts, Mpls., 1973—78; v.p. for adminstrn. and planning U. Minn., Mpls., 1980—83; sr. v.p. acad. affairs, provost U. Ariz., Tucson, 1983—88, prof. English and linguistics, 1983—88; pres. U. Minn., Mpls., 1988—97, Assn. Am. Univs., Washington, 1998—. Vis. com. dept. Germanic langs. and lit. Harvard U., Cambridge, Mass., 1981—86; trustee Nat. Merit Scholarship Corp., 1992—97. Author: Amerikasvenska, 1974, Swedish America: An Introduction, 1976; editor: Perspectives on Swedish Immigration, 1978. Active Gov.'s Task Force on Technology and Improvement of Employment, Minn., 1982—83; trustee Am. Scandinavian Found., 1992—; bd. dirs. Swedish Coun. Am., 1978—, chmn. bd., 1999—2001; bd. dirs. Walker Art Ctr., 1989—95; bd. overseers Mpls. Coll. Art and Design, 1982—83; bd. dirs. Carnegie Found. for Advancement of Tchg., 2002—. Sgt. Royal Signal Corps Swedish Army, 1951—54. Decorated Royal Order of North Star Sweden; named Swedish-Am. of Yr., Swedish Govt. and Vasa Order Am., 1991; recipient King Carl XVI Gustaf's Bicentennial medal in Gold, Sweden, 1976, Ellis Island medal of honor, 1993; fellow Fulbright-Hays fellow, 1968. Mem.: MLA, Univ. Rsch. Assn. (trustee 1993—97), Nat. Assn. State Univs. and Land Grant Colls. (exec. com. acad. affairs coun. 1986—88, chmn. coun. pres. and chancellors 1992—93, chair bd. 1994—95), Swedish-Am. Hist. Soc. (chmn. bd. 1984—86), Royal Gustavus Adolphus Acad., Vetenskaps-Soc., Linguistic Soc. Am., Soc. for Advancement Scandinavian Study (pres. 1971—73).*

HASSENBOEHLER, DONALYN, principal; Prin. McMain Magnet Secondary Sch. Evaluator FIRST grants U.S. Dept. Edn. Recipient U.S. Dept. Edn. Blue Ribbon award, 1990-91. Office: McMain Magnet Secondary Sch 5712 S Claiborne Ave New Orleans LA 70125-4908

HASSLER, DONALD MACKEY, II, English language educator, writer; b. Akron, Ohio, Jan. 3, 1937; s. Donald Mackey and Frances Elizabeth (Parsons) H.; m. Diana Cain, Oct. 8, 1960 (dec. Sept. 1976); children: Donald, David; m. Sue Smith, Sept. 13, 1977; children: Shelly, Heather. BA (Sloan fellow), Williams Coll., 1959; MA (Woodrow Wilson fellow), Columbia U., 1960, PhD, 1967. Instr. U. Montreal, 1961-65; instr. English Kent (Ohio) State U., 1965-67, asst. prof., 1967-71, assoc. prof., 1971-76, prof., 1977—, acting dean honors and exptl. coll., 1979-81, dir., 1973-83, coord. writing cert. program, 1986-91, chmn. undergrad. studies, 1987-91, dir. Wick Poetry Competition, 1987-91, coord. grad. studies, 1991-94; sec. faculty senate Kent (Ohio State U., 1996—, coord. maj. program, 1998—. Author: Erasmus Darwin, 1974, The Comedian as the Letter D: Erasmus Darwin's Comic Materialism, 1973, Asimov's Golden Age: The Ordering of an Art, 1977, Hal Clement, 1982, Comic Tones in Science Fiction, 1982, Patterns of the Fantastic, 1983, Patterns of the Fantastic II, 1984, Death and the Serpent, 1985, Isaac Asimov, 1991; mng. editor Jour. Extrapolation, 1986-87, co-editor, 1987-89, editor, 1990-2001, exec. editor, 2002—; co-editor (with Sue Hassler) Letters of Arthur Machen and Montgomery Evans, 1923-1947, 1993, (with Clyde Wilcox) Political Science Fiction, 1997; adv. editl. bd. Hellas, 1988—; editl. bd. Paradoxa, 1994—. Co-chmn. Kent Am. Revolution Bicentennial Commn., 1974-77; deacon Presbyn. Ch., 1971-74, elder, 1974-77; sec. Kent State Faculty Senate, 1996—, chancellor's faculty adv. com., 1996—, univ. priorities and budget adv. coun., 1998—; spkr. Smithsonian Yesterday's Tomorrow's exhibit, 2003. Recipient J. Lloyd Eaton award, Eaton Libr. Collection U. Calif., Riverside, 1993. Mem. Sci. Fiction Rsch. Assn. (treas. 1983-84, pres. 1985-86, Thomas D. Clareson award 2001), Kiwanis (bd. dirs. 1974-76), Phi Beta Kappa (pres. 1983-84). Home: 1226 Woodhill Dr Kent OH 44240-2832 E-mail: extrap@kent.edu.

HASTINGS, EVELYN GRACE, retired elementary school educator; b. Seguin, Tex., May 25, 1938; d. Ed Howard Coleman and Mae Stella (King) Haywood; m. Marvin Hastings, Oct. 9, 1982. BS, Tex. Luth. Coll., 1960; MA, U. Tex., San Antonio, 1985. Cert. tchr., Tex. Tchr. Seguin (Tex.) Ind. Sch. Dist., 1962-94, Vogel Elem. Sch., Seguin, 1991-94; retired, 1994. Sec. Guadalupe County Tchr.'s Meeting, Seguin, 1962-65, Juan Seguin Sch. PTA, 1969. Historian, corr. sec. Tex. Women's Conv. Ch. of our Lord Jesus Christ, 1961-69, internat. treas. IFAE; treas. Tex. Armor Bears Young Peoples Union, 1960-63, pres., 1963-65, 68-70; sec. Tex. Sunday Sch. Assn., 1960-63, asst. supt., 1968-70, state supt., 1970-74; local missionary pres., fin. sec. Rufuge Ch.; state supr. Tex. Jr. Conv., 1970—; Sunday supr. Lighthouse Ch., 1975—; state missionary v.p. Tex.-Okla. Conv. Ch. of Our Lord Jesus Christ of Apostolic Faith. Recipient Cert. of Outstanding Svc. Nat. Youth Congress Ch. of Our Lord Jesus Christ, 1968, Cert. of Appreciation, Tex.-Okla. Conv. of the Ch. of Our Lord Jesus Christ of The Apostolic Faith, 1989, Outstanding Svc. Plaque, 1981, Tchr. of Yr. Plaque Seguin-Guadalupe County C. of C., 1990; inducted into The Internat. Sunday Sch. Hall of Fame of the Ch. of Our Lord Jesus Christ of the Apostolic Faith, 1990. Mem. AAUW (sec. 1968-70), NEA, Tex. State Tchrs. Assn. (minority del. 1982) Seguin Educators Assn. Democrat. Avocations: reading, sewing, needlcraft. Home: 950 Elsik St Seguin TX 78155-6756

HASTINGS, JOHN WOODLAND, biologist, educator; b. Salisbury, Md., Mar. 24, 1927; s. Vaughan Archelaus and Kathrine (Stevens) H.; m. Hanna Machlup, June 6, 1953; children: Jennifer, David, Laura, Karen. BA, Swarthmore Coll., 1947; MA, Princeton U., 1950, PhD, 1951; MA, Harvard U., 1966. AEC postdoctoral fellow Johns Hopkins, 1951-53; instr. to asst. prof. biol. scis. Northwestern U., 1953-57; from asst. prof. to prof. biochemistry U. Ill. at Urbana, 1957-66; prof. biology Harvard, 1966-87, Paul C. Mangelsdorf prof. natural scis., 1987—; master Pforzheimer House, 1976-96. Summer rsch. participant Oak Ridge Nat. Lab., 1958; vis. lectr. biochemistry Sheffield (Eng.) U., 1961-62; instr. physiology Marine Biol. Lab., Woods Hole, Mass., 1961-66, dir., 1962-66, dir. marine ecology, 1989-91, mem. corp., 1961, trustee, 1966-74, exec. com., 1968-74; guest prof. Rockefeller U., 1965-66, Inst. Biol. Phys. Chemistry Paris, 1972-73, U. Konstanz, Ger., 1979-80, Nat. Biology Inst., Okazaki, Japan, 1986, U. Munich, 1993; Disting. vis. scientist Calif. Inst. Tech., 2000, Jet Propulsion Lab., 2000--; mem. panel molecular biology NSF, 1963-66, mem. adv. com. biology and medicine, 1968-71; com. postdoctoral fellowships chemistry Nat. Acad. Scis., 1965-67, com. photobiology, 1965-71, com. on phototherapy, 1971-73, com. on low frequency radiation, 1975-77; mem. Commn. Undergrad. Edn. in Biol. Scis., 1965-66; space biology com. NASA, 1966-71; biochemistry tng. com. Nat. Inst. Gen. Med. Scis., 1968-72; a founding mem., mem. internat. adv. bd. Marine Biol. Lab., Eilat, Israel, 1968—; faculty assoc. Calif. Inst. Tech., 2000. Contbr. profl. jours. Served with USNR, 1944-45. Guggenheim fellow, 1965-66, NIH fellow, 1972-73, Yamada Found. fellow, Osaka, Japan, 1986; recipient Alexander von Humboldt prize, 1979, Humboldt fellow, 1993. Fellow AAAS, NAS, Am. Soc. Biol. Chemists, Biophys. Soc., Soc. Am. Microbiologists, Am. Soc. Photobiology (pres. 1999-2001), Soc. Gen. Physiology (pres. 1963-65), Am. Acad. Arts and Scis., Soc. Chemi- and Bio-luminescence (founding pres. 1994-98), Pierian Found. (pres. 1999—), Johns Hopkins Soc. Scholars. Home: 14 Concord Ave Cambridge MA 02138-2356 Office: 16 Divinity Ave Cambridge MA 02138-2020 E-mail: hastings@fas.harvard.edu.

HASTINGS, LAWRENCE VAETH, lawyer, physician, educator; b. Flushing, N.Y., Nov. 23, 1919; m. Doris Lorraine Erickson, Dec. 11, 1971. Student, Columbia U., 1939-40, student Law Sch., 1949-50; student, U. Mich. Engring. Sch., 1942-43, Washington U., 1943-44, U. Vt., 1943; MD,

Johns Hopkins U., 1948; JD, U. Miami, 1953. Bar: Fla. 1954, U.S. Supreme Ct. 1960, D.C. 1976; cert. Am. Bd. Legal Medicine. Intern U.S. Marine Hosp., S.I., N.Y., 1948-49; asst. surgeon, sr. asst. surgeon USPHS, 1949-52; asst. resident surgery Bellevue Hosp. Med. Ctr., 1951; med. legal cons., trial atty. Miami, Fla., 1953—; ptnr. Lawrence V. Hastings, P.A.; asst. prof. medicine U. Miami, 1964-70, lectr. law, 1966; past adj. prof. St. Thomas U. Law Sch., Miami, Fla. Contbr. articles to profl. publs. Bd. dirs. Miami Heart Inst.; past trustee Barry U., Miami; trustee Fla. Internat. U., 1979-82. Served with AUS, 1943-46. Fellow Acad. Fla. Trial Lawyers, Am. Coll. Legal Medicine, Law-Sci. Acad. Found. Am.; mem. ABA, AMA, ATLA, Fla. Bar Assn., Dade County Bar Assn., Am. Acad. Forensic Scis., Fla. Med. Assn., Dade County Med. Assn., Fla. Bar (vice chmn. med. legal com. 1957, vice chmn. trial tactics com. 1963-65, chmn. steering com. trial tactics and basic anatomy seminars), Pitts. Inst. Legal Medicine, Johns Hopkins Med. and Surg. Assn., Pithotomy Club, Assn. Mil. Surgeons, U. Miami Law Alumni Assn. (pres. 1967), Acad. Psychosomatic Medicine, Fairbanks Ranch Country Club (Rancho Santa Fe, Calif.), Alpha Delta Phi, Phi Eta Sigma, Phi Alpha Delta. Clubs: Surf (bd. govs. 1976—, chmn. bd. 1980-82, pres. 1978-80), Com. 100, Indian Creek Country, Miami Beach, River of Jacksonville; N.Y. Athletic, Metropolitan, Princeton (N.Y.C.). Roman Catholic. Achievements include first to institute jury verdict lawsuit of Green vs. Am. Tobacco in 1960 resulting in 1964 Surgeon Gen.'s report that cigarettes are hazardous to health. Address: Palm Beach Towers 44 Cocoanut Row Palm Beach FL 33480

HASTINGS, LEE L. secondary education educator; Secondary educator Westlake High Sch. Recipient Tchr. Excellence award Internat. Tech. Edn. Assn., 1992. Office: Westlake High Sch 3300 Middletown Rd Waldorf MD 20603-3705

HASTINGS, REED, film company executive, educational association administrator; Bachelors Degree, Bowdoin Coll.; M in Computer Sci., Stanford U. Founder Pure Software, 1990; co-founder, CEO Netflix, Inc., LosGatos, Calif., 1998—. Pres. Calif. State Bd. Edn., 2000—; founding mem. NewSchools.org, Aspire Pub. Schs., Pacific Collegiate Sch., Ed-Voice.net; CEO Technology Network; vol. Peace Corps, Swaziland, 1983—86. Office: NetFlix com Inc 970 University Ave Los Gatos CA 95032*

HASTINGS-BISHOP, SUSAN JANE, education educator, educator; b. Ogdensburg, N.Y., May 26, 1951; d. Arthur Clement and Harriet McSwan (Clark) Hastings; m. Glen R. Bishop, May 26, 1985; 1 child, Ann. BS in Phys. Edn., SUNY, Brockport, 1973; MA in Recreation, U. No. Colo., 1976; PhD, Tex. A&M U., 1993. Cert. tchr., N.Y. Community ctr. dir. Salvation Army, Watertown, N.Y., 1974-75; coord. Indian Creek Nature Ctr., Canton, N.Y., 1976-77; youth svcs. and recreation dir. Villiage/Town, Canton, 1977-78; asst prof. Dean Jr. Coll., Franklin, Mass., 1978-82; recreation curriculum coord. U. So. Colo., Pueblo, 1982-84; assoc. prof. Ferris State U., Big Rapids, Mich., 1988—. Adv. U.S. Forest Svcs., Huron, Manistee, Mich., 1989—; coun. mem. St. Lawrence Environ. Coun., Canton, 1977-78; assoc. prof., program coord. recreation, leadership and mgmt. Dept. Leisure Studies and Wellness. Membership del. rep. Columbine Girl Scout Coun., Pueblo, 1983-84; bd. dirs. YWCA, Pueblo, 1983-84. Timme Instrnl. Assistance grantee Ferris State U., 1989-90, 91-92, Coll. Edn. Innovative Teaching grantee, 1990-91. Mem. Nat. Recreation and Parks Assn., Mich. Recreation and Park Assn., Mich. Alliance for Environ. and Outdoor Edn. Avocations: llama packing, backpacking, canoeing.

HATCH, D. PATRICIA P. principal; Prin. Naubuc Sch. Recipient U.S. Dept. Edn. Elem. Sch. Recognition award, 1989-90, Women of the Year award Glastonbury Profl. Women. Office: Naubuc Sch 84 Griswold St Glastonbury CT 06033-1006

HATCH, NATHAN ORR, university administrator; b. May 17, 1946; m. Julia Gregg; 3 children. AB summa cum laude, Wheaton Coll., 1968; AM, Washington U., 1972, PhD, 1974. Postdoctoral fellow Johns Hopkins U., 1974-75; from asst. prof. to prof. history U. Notre Dame, Ind., 1975-88, dir. grad. studies dept. history, 1980-83, assoc. dean Coll. Arts and Letters, dir. Inst. for Scholarship in the Liberal Arts, 1983-89, acting dean Coll. Arts and Letters, 1988-89, v.p. for grad. studies and rsch., 1989-96, prof., 1989, provost, 1996—, Andrew V. Tackes prof. history, 1999—. Author: The Sacred Cause of Liberty: Republican Thought and the Millennium in Revolutionary New England, 1977, The Democratization of American Christianity, 1989 (Albert C. Outler prize Am. Soc. Ch. History 1989, 1989 Book prize Soc. for Historians of Early Am. Republic, co-winner John Hope Franklin Publ. prize Yale U. Press 1990); also articles; editor: The Professions in American History, 1988; co-editor: The Bible in America: Essays in Cultural History, 1982, Jonathan Edwards and the American Experience, 1988. Bd. dirs. United Way St. Joseph County, Ind., 1987-92; trustee St. Joseph's Med. Ctr., 1994, chair bd. trustees, 1997-99; mem. nat. adv. bd. Salvation Army, 1997-99; trustee Fuller Theol. Sem., 1998—; mem. Nat. Coun. Humanities, 2000—. Recipient Paul Fenlon Teaching award U. Notre Dame, 1981; Am. Coun. Learned Socs. fellow, 1976, Fred Harris Daniels fellow Am. Antiquarian Soc., 1977, Charles Warren fellow Harvard U., 1977-78; grantee Lilly Endowment, 1979, Ind. Com. for the Humanities, 1981-82, NEH, 1981-85. Mem. Johns Hopkins Soc. Scholars, Am. Soc. Ch. Hist. (pres. 1993), Phi Beta Kappa. Office: U Notre Dame Office of the Provost Notre Dame IN 46556

HATCH, ROBERTA ANNE, lawyer, educator; children: William Henry IV, Robert Malcolm, Mary Ashley. BA, Wheaton Coll., 1963; MA, NYU, 1968; JD, U. Bridgeport, 1987; LLM, NYU, 1994. Bar: Conn. 1987, U.S. Dist. Ct. Conn. 1988. Assoc. Cummings & Luckwood, Stamford, Conn., 1987-92; Meyers Breiner & Neufeld, LLP, Fairfield, Conn., 1994-97; v.p., trust officer JP Morgan Chase Bank, New Canaan, Conn., 1997—. Adj. prof. Quinnipiac Coll. Sch. Law, Hamden, Conn., 1996-2000. Office: JP Morgan Chase Bank 122 Main ST New Canaan CT 06840 E-mail: roberta.hatch@chase.com.

HATCHER, LUCILLE ROBINSON, science educator; b. Prairie Point, Miss., July 28, 1951; d. Eddie D. and Lucille (White) Robinson; m. Levi Mark Hatcher, Dec. 27, 1994; children: Christopher, Ayatti, Lavetta. BSBA, Alcorn State U., 1973; BS in Secondary Sci., Miss. State U., 1976, BS in Biology, 1992. Data processor Sparatus Corp., Louisville, Miss., 1973-74; tchr. gen. sci., earth sci., biology, bus. math. Noxubee County Schs., Macon, Miss., 1974—. Co-owner Pineywood Quik Shop, Macon, 1985-90, Airport Food Mart, Macon, 1987—, Corner Quick Stop, 1987-92, Our Restaurant, 1995—; coord. reading and GED program, 1992-93. Advisor, editor: (newsletter) The Energy Educators, 1988 (1st pl. award 1988). Mem. NAACP, Jackson, Miss., 1987; del. Young Dems. of Miss., Jackson, 1979, Young Dems. of Am., St. Louis, 1980; scout leader Girl Scouts Am., Macon, 1976; ch. adminstr. Fellowship of Hope Comty. Ch., 1990-94. Recipient Miss. State award of excellence Miss. Dept. of Energy, 1987, Miss. Gov.'s award, 1988; grantee Noxubee County Edn. Fund, 1987-91. Mem. Nat. Assn. Biology Tchrs., Nat. Mid. Sch. Tchrs., Miss. Sci. Tchrs. Assn., Miss. Assn. Edn. and Nat. Dels., Noxubee County Assn. Edn. Pres. (past pres.). Avocations: helping abused children and women, supporting black males and black liberty, senior citizens. Home: 202 E North St Macon MS 39341-2810

HATFIELD, JAMES ALLEN, theater arts educator, administrator; b. Marion, Ind., May 1, 1953; s. Frederick Marion and Mary Josephine (Murray) H.; 1 child, Edward Everett. BS, Ball State U., 1974, MA, 1975; PhD, Wayne State U., 1981. Asst. prof. Oakland U., Rochester, Mich., 1978-83; assoc. prof. Jackson (Miss.) State U., 1983-86; assoc. prof., chmn. theater dept. Butler U., Indpls., 1986-90; prof., dir. theater dept. U. Tex., Tyler, 1990—. Bd. dirs. Opera South, 1984-86; mem. Performance evaluation com. Miss. Arts Commn., Jackson, 1983-86; vice-chair Tex. Kennedy Ctr./Am. Coll. Theatre Festival, 1992-95, state chair, 1996-99. Dir., designer: (operas) Lost in the Stars, 1987, The Marriage of Figaro, 1988, The Merry Widow, 1989, The Great Soap Opera, 1990; (plays) My Sister in This House, 1988 (Am. Coll. Theatre Festival nomination), Another Antigone, 1991 (Am. Coll. Theatre Festival N.E. Tex. Cert. of Excellence), The Doctor in Spite of Himself, 1991, Thymus Vulgaris, 1991, Antigone, 1992, Habeas Corpus, 1992, The Norman Conquests, 1992, Getting Married, 1993, Anatol, 1993, Old Times, 1993, La Ronde, 1994, As You Like It, 1994, You Never Can Tell, 1994, Oleanna (Am. Coll. Theatre Festival Critics Choice Cert. of Excellence), 1994, Oleanna, 1995, KC/ACTF Region VI Production, Later Life, 1995 The Heiress, 1995, 3 Courtelines, 1995, Lettice & Lovage, 1995, Best of Friends, 1996, Phaedra, 1996, Octavia, 1996, Mrs. Klein, 1996, A Midsummer Night's Dream, 1997, Love Letters, Ravenscroft, 1998, The School for Wives, 1998, Love Letters, 1998, Mandrake, 1999, Molly Sweeney, 1999, Indiscretions, 1999, Mandrake, 1999, Love, Shakespeare to Coward, 2000, Coriolanus, 2000, Blithe Spirit, 2001, Comic Potential, 2001, Othello, 2003; (mus. theater prodns.) Candide, 1987, Sunday in the P George, 1988, Marry Me a Little, 1989 (Am. Coll. Theatre Festival Nomination), Two by Two, 1993, Candide, 1998, Kismet, 2000, My Fair Lady, 2001, The Sound of Music, 2002, The Fantasticks, 2002, Annie, 2003; (dir., playwright) Rosalis, 2002, She's Shakespeare Loving, 2002. State chmn. Kennedy Ctr./Am. Coll. Theatre Festival, 1996-99; bd. govs. The Assn. for Theatre in Higher Edn., 1997-99. Recipient medal of excellence in lighting Am. Coll. Theatre Festival, 1978, Outstanding Tchg. award U. Tex. Chancellor's Coun., 1993, KC/ACTF Bronze medal for excellence in theatre, 1999, 2000, 01. Mem. Am. Fedn. Musicians, Assn. for Theatre in Higher Edn. (governing coun.), Speech Communication Assn., Assn. Communication Adminstrn., Soc. Stage Dirs. and Choreographers, Tex. Ednl. Theatre Assn., Am. Alliance for Theatre and Edn., South West Theatre Assn. Avocations: photography, graphic design, sailing. Office: U Tex Dept Theater PO Box 8152 Tyler TX 75711-8152

HATFIELD, JANICE LEE (FORD), secondary education educator; b. Washington, Jan. 23, 1941; m. William F. Hatfield. BS, Concord Coll., Athens, W.Va., 1962; MA in English, Bowling Green State U., 1964; postgrad., W.Va. U., 1977-80. Cert. journalism educator Pa. Tchr. Alderson HS, W.Va., 1963-64, Beverly HS, W.Va., 1964-65, Charles Town Sch., W.Va., 1965-67; instr. W.Va. U., Morgantown, W.Va., 1967-69, Marshall U., Huntington, W.Va., 1969-70, King's Coll., Raleigh, NC, 1974-75, NC State U., Raleigh, NC, 1975-76; teaching fellow W.Va. U., W.Va., 1977-80; tchr. English W Greene HS, Waynesburg, Pa., 1981—. We. Pa. Writing Project fellow, 1993. Mem. Journalism Edn. Assn., Nat. Coun. Tchrs. English, We. Pa. Coun. Tchrs. English., Pa. Scholastic Press Assn. (bd. dirs. state exec. coun., State treas., co-dir. Scholastic Art-Writing awards of Southwestern Pa.). Home: PO Box 353 Mount Morris PA 15349-0353 Office: West Greene Schs 1352 Hargus Creek Rd Waynesburg PA 15370-8600

HATGIL, PAUL PETER, artist, sculptor, educator; b. Manchester, N.H., Feb. 18, 1921; s. Peter and Katina (Karkadou) H.; m. Katherine Haritos. BS, Mass. Coll. of Art, 1950; MFA, Columbia U., 1951. Instr. art U. Tex., Austin, 1951-54, asst. prof., 1954-56, assoc. prof., 1956-67, prof., 1967-85, prof. emeritus, 1985—, design curator Archer M. Huntington Gallery Mus., 1965-68. Vis. instr. Columbia U. (summer) 1958; designed and installed Tex. Pavilion Exhbn., N.Y. World's Fair; coord. for Gov. John Connolly's Exhbn. of Art and Conf. on the Arts; aux. edn. officer Dist. 8 U.S. Coast Guard, 1965-74; bd. dirs. AHEPA Nat. Ednl. Found., 2003—. Author: Establishing Residency in Greece. 1988, (autobiography) Apostolos, The Immigrant's Son, 1990; (book) Contemporary Encaustic Painting, 1994; contbr. numerous articles and papers to profl. jours. One-Woman shows include Baylor U. Gallery, Bass Concert Hall, U. Tex.; exhbns. include: 42 annual faculty exhbns. U. Tex., Austin, 2d, 3d, 4th Internat. Invitational Exhbn. of Ceramic Art Smithsonian Mus., Washington, 2d, 3d and 7th Nat. Decorative Arts Exhbns., Wichita, Kans., Internat. Invitational Exhbn. of Ceramic Art Iowa State U., Ceder Rapids, Flatbed Print Gallery, 1985-2003, St. Stephen's Emeriti Exhbn., Tex., Austin (Tex.) Mus. Fine Arts; pvt. collections including St. Paul's Luth. Ch., U. Tex. Bus. Adminstrn. Bldg., Huston Tillotson Coll., Seguin Luth. Coll., U. Tex. Faculty Club, U. Tex. Coll. Fine Arts, Woodlands Corp., Houston, Zapata Corp., Houston, Warren Cravens Corp., Houston, U.S. Mil. Ins. Corp., Harry Litwin Industries, Wichita, Kans., Coopers & Lybrand Corp., Houston, Cesar Design Inc., Cleve., Abilne (Tex.) 1st Nat. Bank, Tchr. Retirement Sys., Austin, FAA, Panama C.Z., Austin (Tex.) Mus. Art, Fox Collection, Austin, Tex., Voutsinas Collection, Elgin, Tex., Iatrou Collection, Austin, Tex.; videos collections include Ceramic History 1951-1976, Baylor U. Archives, Art in Texas - 1951-2000, Baylor U.; work featured in Encaustic Painting, 2000. With USAAF, 1943-45, PTO. Recipient Estelle Grey Meml. prize in art, Margaret Flowers prize in art, White Mus., San Antonio, Wolff and Marx prize in art, Dallas Mus. of Fine Arts; purchase prizes Dallas Mus. of Art, Laguan Gloria Mus. Austin; grantee U. Tex. Mem. Am. Hellenic Ednl. and Progressive Assn. (pres. Stephen F. Austin chpt. 312, dist. gov., 1999-2002, nat. ednl. found. bd. mem.). Home: 2203 Onion Creek Pky Unit 7 Austin TX 78747-1648

HATHAWAY, KATHERINE JANE, special education educator; b. Salida, Colo., Jan. 16, 1968; d. William E. Hathaway and Patricia R. Sloan. BSE, John Brown U., Siloam Springs, Ark., 1989; MA, PhD, Columbia State U., 1997. Tchr. Seriously Emotionally Disturbed children Oak Grove Inst., Murrieta, Calif., 1990-91; tchr. Learning Handicapped children Moreno Valley (Calif.) Unified Sch. Dist., 1991-97, resource specialist, 1997—. Advisor Pub. Edn. for Everyone in Regular Schs., Moreno Valley, Calif., 1991—; advisor, cons. Inclusion Model Pilot Program, Moreno Valley, 1991—. Dep. registrar Office to Register Voters, Siloam Springs, Ark., 1987-88. Mem. DAR (honor award 1985). Avocations: painting, needlework, camping, travel. Office: Moreno Valley Unified Sch Dist Seneca Sch 11615 Wordsworth Rd Moreno Valley CA 92557-8451

HATHAWAY, RICHARD DEAN, retired language educator; b. Chillicothe, Ohio, Aug. 8, 1927; s. Dale and Edith (Hart) H.; m. Viola Hale, Apr. 16, 1978; children by previous marriage: Linda Hathaway Ellis, Bruce. AB summa cum laude, Oberlin Coll., 1949; AM, Harvard U., 1952; PhD, Western Res. U., 1964. Instr. English Oberlin Jr. H.S., 1949-50; chief interviewer U.S. Bur. of Census, Boston, 1952-53; exec. sec. New Eng. Fellowship of Reconciliation, Boston, 1953-55; instr. in English, Rensselaer Poly. Inst., Troy, N.Y., 1957-62; from asst. prof. to assoc. prof. SUNY, New Paltz, 1962-69, prof., 1970—2001; ret., 2001. Assoc. prof. Millsaps Coll., Jackson, Miss., 1965-66. Author: Sylvester Judd's New England, 1981, The Henry James Scholar's Guide to Web Sites, 1997; (computer software) Text: A Program About Literature, 1990; contbr. articles to profl. jours. Chair legis. com. SCLC Poor People's Campaign, 1968. Served with USNR, 1945-46. Mem. MLA. Mem. Religious Soc. of Friends. Home: 11 Crescent Ln New Paltz NY 12561-2809

HATLEY, AMY BELL, elementary education educator, broadcast journalist; b. Concord, N.C., May 5, 1940; d. Austin H. and Frances Louise (Norris) Bell; m. Wayne Douglas Hatley, Aug. 27, 1961; 1 child, Adam Douglas. BA, Meredith Coll., 1962; MEd, Converse Coll., 1986. Cert. tchr. N.C., S.C. Tchr. grades 1-3 Thomasboro Elem., Charlotte, N.C., 1962-67, tchr. grade 3, 1968-71; tchr. grade 2 Allenbrook Elem., Charlotte, 1966-67, Charlotte (N.C.) Latin, 1971-72, Carmel Acad., Charlotte, 1972-75, Spartanburg (S.C.) Day Sch., 1977-95; producer, broadcast journalist, assignment editor WSPA AM-FM Radio & TV, CBS Affiliate, Spartanburg, 1984—. Author, producer: (broadcast documentary series) The Unraveling of the American Teacher, 1989 (1st pl. award AP 1989), Standardized Testing: Has It Failed the Grade?, 1990 (1st pl. award AP 1990), Illiteracy: S.C.'s Abiding Legacy, 1991 (1st pl. award AP 1991). Com. chmn. Bd. Spartanburg (S.C.) Little Theater, 1990; mem. pub. rels. com. United Way of the Piedmont, Spartanburg, 1991-94; bd. regents Leadership Spartanburg, 1992-94; bd. dirs. Spartanburg County Literacy Orgn.; edn. com. Spartanburg CCounty Consensus Project, 1991-94; strategy com. Spartanburg County Am. 2000 Project, 1992-94. Mem. Nat. Press Fedn., Palmetto Assn. Ind. Schs., Spartanburg Speakers Bur., S.C. Media Women. Methodist. Avocations: writing, hist. rsch., hist. restoration. Home: 624 Gramercy Blvd Spartanburg SC 29301-6157 Office: WSPA-TV Communications Park Spartanburg SC 29304

HATLEY, PATRICIA RUTH, business/education partnership coordinator; b. Norborne, Mo., Sept. 8, 1945; d. William Bernard and Bessie (Evans) Henks; m. Richard V. Hatley, Aug. 17, 1985; children: Timothy Wilde, Kent Wilde; stepchildren: Christine, Angela. BS in Edn., Ctrl Mo. State U., 1966, MA, 1968; Ednl. Specialist, U. Mo., 1980, EdD, 1991. Cert. supt., prin., tchr., Mo. Tchr. English William Chrisman H.S., Independence, Mo., 1968-80, asst. prin., 1980-87; asst. prin. for curriculum Blue Valley North H.S., Overland Park, Kans., 1987-88; dir. secondary edn. Blue Springs (Mo.) R IV Schs., 1988-97; coord. Ea. Jackson County Bus./Edn. Partnership, 1997—. Chair lang. arts dept. Independence Pub. Schs., 1975-80; adv. bd. Ea. Jackson County H.S., Blue Springs, 1988-91, minority student summer program U. Mo., Columbia, 1991—; instr. Cen. Mo. State U. Grad. Sch., 1997—. Active Planning and Zoning Commn., Blue Springs, 1976-80; mem. Mo. U. Alumni Bd., 1993-95; pres. St. Mary's Hosp. Aux., 1998-99; mem. governing bd. U. Mo. Partnership, 1995—. Recipient State Media award Mo. State Tchrs. Assn., 1988-89, 91, named Adminstr. of Yr., 1990. Mem. ASCD, Nat. Assn. Secondary Sch. Prins., Nat. Sch. Pub. Rels. Assn. (pres. Mo. chpt. 1995-96), Nat. Tech. Prep. Network, Mo. Assn. Sch. Adminstrs., Mo. Assn. Supervision and Curriculum Devel., Mo. Assn. Secondary Sch. Prins., Greater Kansas City Prins. Assn., Kansas City Network Women in Sch. Adminstrn. (pres. 1991-93), Mo. Network Women in Sch. Adminstrn. (chair exec. bd. 1995-96), Internat. Orgn. Women Edn., Internat. Reading Assn., C. of C., Phi Delta Kappa, Delta Kappa Gamma, Beta Sigma Phi (pres. 1979-80). Democrat. Roman Catholic. Avocations: bridge, golf, reading, travel. Office: 601 NW Jefferson St Ste 3 Blue Springs MO 64014-2290

HATLEY, RICHARD V(ON), education educator; b. Goodnight, Tex., Oct. 19, 1936; s. R.V. and Rula Belle (Evans) H.; m. Patricia Ruth Henks, Aug. 17, 1985; children: Christine L., Angela K.; stepchildren: Timothy A. Wilde, Kent C. Wilde. BA, Ea. N.Mex. U., 1959, MA, 1967, EdS, 1968; EdD, U. N.Mex., 1970. Cert. tchr., prin., sch. supt., Mo. Tchr. English Borger (Tex.) Ind. Sch. Dist., 1963-65, Amarillo (Tex.) Ind. Sch. Dist., 1965-67; adminstrv. intern Portales (N.Mex.) Mcpl. Schs., 1967-68; fin. cons. N.Mex. Dept. Edn., Santa Fe, 1968; grad. asst. U. N.Mex., Albuquerque, 1968-70; asst. prof., then assoc. prof. U. Kans., Lawrence, 1970-76; chair dept. ednl. adminstrn. U. Mo., Columbia, 1976-86, prof. ednl. leadership and policy analysis, 1976—; assoc. dir. Univ. Coun. for Ednl. Adminstration, 1996—. Fin. cons. to Republic of Nicaragua, U.S. AID, Managua, 1971; salary cons. Platte County Schs., Platte City, Mo., 1980; reorgn. cons. St. Joseph (Mo.) Pub. Schs., 1982; referendum strategy cons. Jefferson City (Mo.) Pub. Schs., 1984, Ft. Osage (Mo.) Pub. Schs., 1991-92. Contbr. articles, revs. to profl. publs.; author reports, monographs. Active Blue Springs (Mo.) Schs. Citizens Adv. Com., 1988—. Grantee U.S. Office Edn., 1972, U.S. Dept. Edn., 1982-85. Mem. ASCD, Am. Ednl. Rsch. Assn. (program chairperson 1983), Univ. Coun. Ednl. Adminstrn (mem. exec. bd. 1983-89, pres. 1986-87, assoc. dir. 1996—), Masons, Phi Delta Kappa. Democrat. Avocations: reading, writing, fiction, travel, computers. Office: U Mo Dept Ednl Leadership and Policy Analysis 211 Hill Hall Columbia MO 65211-2190

HATT, BARBARA ANN, elementary and secondary school educator; b. Wood River, Ill., Aug. 22, 1952; d. Mayo Louis and Virgel Myrle Hutchens; children: Corey Lee Kraushaar, Neil Eugene Kraushaar. BA, Ill. Coll., 1974; MA, So. Ill. U., 1981; BA in French, Portland State U., 2000. Cert. elem. and secondary educator, lang. arts, Oreg., Ill. Tchr. Washington Elem. Sch., Jacksonville, Ill., 1974-76, Columbia Christian Schs., Portland, Oreg., 1982-84; sub. tchr. Portland Pub. Schs., 1985; tchr. Centennial Sch. Dist., Portland, 1985—; tchr. English and French Centennial High Sch., Gresham, Oreg., 1990—97. Mem. NEA, Oreg. Edn. Assn., Centennial Edn. Assn. Republican. Avocations: reading, quilting. Home: 2812 SE 120th Ave Portland OR 97266-1023

HATTAR, MICHAEL MIZYED, mathematics educator; b. El-Salt, Jordan, Mar. 17, 1934; came to U.S., 1954; s. Mizyed Zedan and Rif'a (Naber) H.; m. Helen Jean Sharbrough, June 30, 1962; children: Mai Michelle, Amiel Michael, Khalid Mikhail, Muna Michelle. BA, Greenville (Ill.) Coll., 1958; MS, Western Wash. State U., 1968; postgrad., Oxford U., 1989. Tchr. Don Bosco Tech. Inst., Rosemead, Calif., 1962-76, 95—, chmn., 1968-76; part-time tchr. Rio Hondo Coll., 1983—; tchr. Mt. Sac Coll., 1969—, Ontario (Calif.) High Sch., 1976-92, Rancho Cucamonga (Calif.) High Sch., 1992-95; with Don Bosco Tech. Inst., Rosemead, Calif., 1995—. Speaker math. confs. Participant U.S./Russian Joint Conf. on Math. Edn., Moscow, 1993. Recipient Tchr. of Yr. award Industry Edn. Coun. San Gabriel Valley, 1970, Award of Excellence, U.S. Orgn. Med. and Edn. Needs South Bay chpt., 1975, Citation, Assn. Arab-Am. Univ. Grads., 1977, Man of Yr. award Am. Arab Soc., 1978, Commendation, Olympic Neighbor Program, 1984, Tchr. of Yr. award Ontario H.S., 1987-88, Award of Excellence, U.S. Orgn. Med. and Edn.; named Tchr. of Yr. Inland Valley, Calif., 1991, 95. Mem. ASCD, Nat. Coun. Tchrs. of Math., Calif. Math. Coun., San Bernardino County Math. Coun. (Tchr. of Yr. award 1991, pres. 1992-93). Home: 1247 E Dore St West Covina CA 91792-1313 Office: Don Bosco Tech Inst 1151 San Gabriel Blvd Rosemead CA 91770-4251

HATTAWAY, LINDA, special education educator; b. Durant, Miss., Dec. 6, 1955; d. Coyle McGee and Lora Ruth (Mitchell) McCreary; m. Orrin Edd Hattaway. BS, Miss. State U., 1977, MS, 1978, EdS, 1984. Spl. edn. tchr. Starkville (Miss.) Pub. Schs., 1978-80; spl. edn. supr. Clay County Schs., Montpelliar, Miss., 1980-82; spl. edn. tchr. Starkville Sch., 1982—. Adj. instr. Miss. State U., 1986—. Mem. Coun. for Exceptional Children, Miss. Profl. Educators.

HATTON, BRENDA NAFZINGER, secondary education educator; b. Lewistown, Pa., Mar. 15, 1946; d. J. David and Nedra (Yoder) Nafzinger; 1 child, Jenny W. Shapiro. BS, Bloomsburg (Pa.) U., 1968; EdM, Boston U., 1974. Cert. secondary sch. tchr., Pa. Math. tchr. Neshaminy Schs., Langhorne, Pa., 1968-69, Milton (Mass.) Pub. Schs., 1969-72, Endicott (N.Y.) Schs., 1972-74, New Berlin (N.Y.) Cen. Schs., 1977-80, Whitney Point (N.Y.) Schs., 1980-81, Abington Heights Sch. Dist., Clarks Summit, Pa., 1982—. Pvt. tutor; faculty mem. ACT 178 Com.; student coun. advisor, 1995-97; advisor Nat. Honor Soc., 1991-2002; judge Pa. Jr. Acad. Sci., 1995—; cons. Geometry. Leader, cons., trainer Scranton (Pa.) Pocono Girl Scouts, 1982—; active Clarks Summit (Pa.) United Meth. Ch.; vol. WVIA; cons. geometry; mem. alumni bd. Bloomsburg U.; mem. student aid bd. Abington Heights. Mem. Nat. Coun. Tchrs. Math., Pa. Coun. Tchrs. Math., Northeastern Pa. Coun. Tchrs. Math. (exec. bd., historian), NEA, Abington Heights Edn. Assn. (mem. coord., treas. 1990-95), Pa. State Edn. Assn. Avocations: gardening, tennis, travel, music, sports. Home: 547 Deerfield Dr Clarks Summit PA 18411-1312

HATTON, JANIE R. HILL, principal; Formerly prin. Milw. Trade and Tech. H.S.; cmty. supt. Milw. Pub. Schs., 1989-91; dir. Dept. Leadership Svcs., 1996-97; dep. supt. Leadership Svcs., Milw., 1997-99; prin. Pulaski H.S., Milw., 1999—2001, N. Div. H.S., Milw., 2001—. Recipient Milw. Prin. Yr. award Alexander Hamilton H.S., 1986, Nat. Principal of the Year award Nat. Assn. Secondary Sch. Principals and Met. Life Ins. Co., 1993,

It Takes a Whole Village Leadership award, 1999. Mem. Milw. Links Inc., Delta Sigma Theta. Office: 1011 W Center St Milwaukee WI 53206-3299*

HAUBRICH, ROBERT RICE, biology educator; b. Claremont, N.H., May 4, 1923; s. Frederick William and Marion Norma (Rice) H. BS in Forestry, Mich. State U., 1949, MS in Zoology, 1952; PhD in Biology, U. Fla., 1957. Asst. prof. biology East Carolina U., Greenville, N.C., 1957-61, Oberlin (Ohio) Coll., 1961-62, Denison U., Granville, Ohio, 1962-64, assoc. prof. biology, 1964-67, prof. biology, 1968-88, chair dept. biology, 1968-69, alumni chair, 1983-89, prof. emeritus, 1988—. Assoc. dir. Earlham Coll. Biol. Sta., Syracuse, Ind., 1967-72; mem. marine sci. edn. consortium Duke Marine Lab., Beaufort, N.C., 1983-88; libr. reader Marine Biol. Lab., Woods Hole, Mass., 1965—. Contbr. articles to profl. publs. Sgt. USAF, 1943-46. Fellow AAAS, Ohio Acad. Sci.; mem. Internat. Soc. History, Philosophy and Social Studies. Avocations: swimming, hiking. Home and Office: Denison U Dept Biology Granville OH 43023

HAUCH, VALERIE CATHERINE, historian, educator; b. Washington, May 20, 1949; d. Charles Christian and Ruthadele Bertha (LaTourrette) H.; life ptnr. Jacquelyn Farrow. BA in History, Kalamazoo Coll., 1971; MA in Medieval Studies, Western Mich. U., 1977; grad. cert. C.C. Teaching, U. St. Thomas, St. Paul, 1995. Social sci. analyst congl. rsch. svc. Libr. Congress, Washington, 1971-72; ind. contractor Minn. Hist. Soc., St. Paul, 1987-88, adminstrv. asst., 1990—; cmty. edn. tchr. Mpls. Pub. Schs., 1990—; instr. Fla. Com. Coll., 2003. Instr. Minn. Sch. Bus., 1999—, Fla. C.C., Jacksonville, 2003—. Mem. Am. Hist. Assn., Am. Assn. Mus., Phi Beta Kappa. Home: 3540 33rd Ave S Minneapolis MN 55406-2725

HAUG, EDWARD JOSEPH, JR., retired mechanical engineering educator, simulation research engineer; b. Bonne Terre, Mo., Sept. 15, 1940; s. Edward Joseph and Thelma (Harrison) H.; m. Carol Jean Todd, July 1, 1979; 1 child, Kirk Anthony. BSME, U. Mo., Rolla, 1962; MS in Applied Mechanics, Kans. State U., 1964, PhD in Applied Mechanics, 1966. Rsch. engr. Army Armaments Command, Rock Island, Ill., 1969; chief sys. analysis Army Weapons Command, Rock Island, Ill., 1970, chief sys. rsch., 1971-72, chief concepts and tech., 1973-76; prof. U. Iowa, Iowa City, 1976—2003, Carver Disting. prof., 1990—2003, dir. Ctr. for Computer Aided Design, 1983-95; dir. Nat. Advanced Driving Simulator and Simulation Ctr., 1992-98. Author 9 books on computer aided design and dynamics; editor 5 books; contbr. numerous papers to profl. jours. Capt. U.S. Army, 1966-68. Recipient Innovative Info. Tech. award Computerworld/Smithsonian Instn., 1989, Colwell Merit award Soc. Automotive Engrs., 1989. Fellow ASME (Design Automation award 1991, Machine Design award 1992), Am. Acad. Mechanics. Achievements include patents for Constant Recoil Automatic Cannon, and for Real-Time Simulation System. Home: 2440 County Rd 500 Bayfield CO 81122-8729 E-mail: haug@nads-sc.uiowa.edu.

HAUG, JAMES CHARLES, business and management educator; b. Nashua, N.H., Dec. 3, 1948; s. Charles Louis and Doris A. (Lynch) H.; m. Mary Theresa Dowley, Dec. 19, 1970; children: Michele, Emily, Brian, Matthew, Jonathan, Mary Louise. Student, Manhattan Coll., Bronx, 1966-68; BS, Columbia U., 1970; MBA, U. Calif., Berkeley, 1971; DBA, George Washington U., 1981. Registered profl. engr., Calif. Commd. ensign USN, 1971, advanced through grades to lt. comdr, 1981; activity customer engr Navy Pub. Wks. Ctr, Oakland, Calif, 1974-75; asst. pub. wks. officer Naval Rsch. Lab., Washington, 1975-77; facilities planning officer Naval Data Automation Command, Washington, 1977-80; pub. wks. officer Naval Air Sta, South Weymouth, Mass., 1980-82; facilities planning instr. Naval Civil Engrng. Officer Sch, Port Hueneme, Calif, 1982-85; dir. contracts group Naval Air Sta, Pensacola, Fla., 1985-88; asst. officer in chg Navy Broadway Complex Project, San Diego, 1988-91; ret; asst. prof. Troy State U., Pensacola, 1991-92. Coord. MS in Mgmt. program Troy State U., Norfolk, Va., 1992—, assoc. prof., 1997—; vis. prof. U. San Diego, 1991-92; mem. adv. com. San Diego ext. U. Calif., 1989-91. Contbr. articles to profl. jours. Chmn. adv. bd. on spl. edn. Hampton (Va.) City Schs., 1994-96; scoutmaster Boy Scouts Am., San Diego, 1991; treas. Early Childhood Ctr., Alexandria, Va., 1978-80. Mem. Alpha Pi Mu, Tau Beta Pi, Beta Gamma Sigma. Roman Catholic. Avocation: jogging. Home: 60 Chowning Dr Hampton VA 23664-1755 Office: Troy State Univ PO Box 15218 Norfolk VA 23511-0218

HAUGELAND, JOHN, philosophy educator; BS in Physics, Harvey Mudd Coll., 1966; PhD, U. Calif., Berkeley, 1976. Instr. U. Pitts.; prof. philosophy U. Chgo., 1999—. Author, Artificial Intelligence: The Very Idea, 1986, Having Thought, 1998; editor: Mind Design, 1981, 2d edit., 1997; co-editor: The Road Since Structure, 2000. Fellow, John Simon Guggenheim Meml. Found., 2003. Office: U Chgo Dept Philosophy 1010 E 59th St Chicago IL 60637*

HAUGH, JOYCE EILEEN GALLAGHER, education educator, volunteer; b. Ironton, Ohio, Sept. 3, 1937; d. Lawrence James and Frances Irene (Wilson) Gallagher; m. Charles R. Haugh, July 29, 1978; children: Kevin Charles, Maria Frances, Kateri Lynn. BS, Coll. St. Teresa, Winona, Minn., 1967; MEd, Ohio U., 1969; PhD, Loyola U. Chgo., 1975; ME/PD, U. Wis.-LaCrosse, 1984. Tchr. various schs., various locations, 1958-68; instr. psychology Coll. St. Teresa, Winona, Minn., 1969-72, v.p. student affairs, dean students, 1975-76; assoc. prof psychology St. Mary's Coll., Winona, 1976-82, assoc. prof. edn., 1982-86, prof. edn., 1986-95; prof. emeritus, 1995—; ind. beauty cons., edn. cons., 1995-2000; real estate cons. Edina Realty, 1997—2002, leadership circle, 2000-01; handler of therapy dogs Therapy Dogs Internat., Inc., 2002—. Co-chmn. dept. edn. St. Mary's Coll., 1986-87, dir. grad. program in counseling and psychol. svcs., 1986-87, dir. grad. program in pastoral svc., 1986-88, others; adj. prof. U. Wis.-LaCrosse, 1985, Winona State U., 1988; therapy dog handler, 2002—; mem. Cath. Schs. Acreditation Visitation Team, 1988; NAEYC validator, 1988-99; bd. dirs. Family Svcs., Winona. Franciscan cojourner, 1985—; chmn. continuing edn. com. Birthright, 1981, mem., 1980-99; eucharistic min. Cathedral of the Sacred Heart, 1981—2003, Sacred Heart Ch., 2003— others; bd. dirs. Winona Day Care, Inc., 1991-95, Family Svcs. of Winona, 2001—. NDEA fellow, 1968-69. Mem. Nat. Assn. for Edn. Young Children, Nat. Assn. Realtors, Minn. Assn. Realtors, Psi Chi, Phi Delta Kappa, Kappa Delta Pi (counselor 1989-95), Delta Epsilon Sigma (pres. 1993-95). Roman Catholic. Home: 48891 Noline Place Palm Desert CA 92260 E-mail: eileenhaugh@edinarealty.com.

HAUGLAND, SUSAN WARRELL, education educator, consultant; b. Portland, Oreg., Aug. 29, 1950; d. George William and Commery Wallace (Coleman) Warrell; children from previous marriage: Charles, Michael. BS in Child Devel., Oreg. State U., 1972; PhD in Psychology, Saybrook Inst., 1976. Cert. family and consumer scis. Dir., head tchr. Lafayette Co-op Nursery Sch., Detroit, 1973-75; handicapped svcs. coord. OutWayne County Head Start, Wayne, Mich., 1975-76; asst. prof. child devel. Va. Poly. Inst. and State U., Blacksburg, 1976-79; prof. emeritus child devel. S.E. Mo. State U., Cape Girardeau, 1979-99, prof. emeritus, 1999—; pres. K.I.D.S. & Computers, Inc., Cape Girardeau, 1999—; prof. early childhood edn. The Met. State Coll. of Denver, 2000—. Dir. Ctr. for Child Studies, Cape Girardeau, 1979-99, Kids Interacting with Devel. Software, Cape Girardeau, 1985—; chair Human-Environ. Studies, Cape Girardeau, 1990-93; judge Developmental Software Awards, 1991—, Child Mag. Awards, 1992-99. Author: Helping Young Children Grow, 1980, Developmental Evaluations of Software for Young Children, 1990, Young Children and Technology: A World of Discovery, 1997, Haugland Developmental Software Scale, 1997, Haugland/Gertzog Developmental Scale for Web Sites, 1998; dept. editor Early Childhood Education Jour., 1992—; contbr. numerous articles to profl. jours. Grantee numerous orgns.; recipient Gov.'s award for Teaching Excellence, 1996. Mem. Assn. for Childhood Edn. Internat., Nat. Assn. for Edn. Young Children, Nat. Assn. for Early Childhood Tchr. Educators, Tech. and Young Children Caucus, Omicron Nu. Democrat. Methodist. Avocations: reading, travel, cooking, bicycling. E-mail: susanhaugland@hotmail.com.

HAUKE, RICHARD LOUIS, retired science educator; b. Detroit, Apr. 28, 1930; s. Henry George and Eleanor Anne (Duquette) H.; m. Kathleen Armstrong, Sept. 20, 1958; children: Katherine Emma Jane, Nellie Maura, Andrew Martin De Porres, Henry John La Farge. BS, U. Mich., 1952; MA, U. Calif., Berkeley, 1954; PhD, U. Mich., 1960. Instr. U. R.I., Kingston, 1959-60, from asst. prof. to assoc. prof., 1960-69, prof., 1969-89; part-time instr. Ga. State U., Atlanta, 1990—99. With U.S. Army, 1954-56. Mem. Am. Fern Soc. (pres., sec., treas., v.p.). Roman Catholic.

HAUPIN, ELIZABETH CAROL, retired secondary school educator; b. East Orange, N.J., June 10, 1929; d. Edward M. and Edna (Wolverton) Bohsen; m. George W. Haupin, June 9, 1951; children: George, Linda, James, Robert. BA, Douglass Coll., Rutgers U., 1951; elem. cert., Newark State Coll., 1952; postgrad., Trenton (N.J.) State Coll. Cert. permanent English and Latin tchr., elem. endorsement, N.J. Elem. tchr. Bloomfield (N.J.) Bd. Edn., 1951-53; home tchr., East Brunswick, N.J.; elem. tchr. Pub. sch., Milltown, N.J., 1957-58; tchr. lang. arts Milltown (N.J.) Bd. Edn., 1970-92. Past moderator, bd. deacons, deacon Trinity Presbyn. Ch., East Brunswick, N.J., elder session, 1998; active local ch.; formerly active Girl Scouts USA; past pres., rec. sec. PTA. Recipient Outstanding Elem. Tchr. award, 1974. Mem. NEA, N.J. Edn. Assn., Middlesex County Ret. Educators Assn., Phi Beta Kappa (rep. Douglass alumnae coun.). Home: 32 Ellwood Rd East Brunswick NJ 08816-3003

HAUPT, PATRICIA A. principal; Diplome du premier cycle, U. Strasbourg, France, 1969; dipome des etudes superieures, U. Montpellier, France, 1971; BA summa cum laude, St. Francis Coll., 1972; MA in French summa cum laude, Middlebury Coll., 1976; prin.'s cert. summa cum laude, Western Md. Coll., 1984; EdD in Adminstrn. and Leadership summa cum laude, Temple U., 1986. Cert. instrnl. II Pa., prin. Pa., asst. supt.'s letter of eligibility Pa., supt.'s letter of eligibility Pa. Die casting machine operator Doehler-Jarvis Internat., Pottstown, Pa., 1972—74; tchr. French Palmyra (Pa.) Area H.S., 1973—84; real estate agt. Jack Gaughen Realtor, Hershey, Pa., 1979—84; dir. pupil pers. svcs. K-12 So. Lehigh Sch. Dist., 1985—89; asst. prin. So. Lehigh Mid. Sch., 1984—89; prin. Fleetwood Area Mid. Sch., 1989—92, Bala Cynwyd (Pa.) Mid. Sch., Bala Cynwyd, 1992—. Lectr. and presenter in field; co-facilitator Lang. Immersion Program; coord. Tri-Dist. Consortium; mem. Gov.'s Task Force for Fgn. Langs.; ednl. liaison Kutztown Area C. of C. Recipient Leadership award, Am. Legion, ednl. scholarship for study abroad. Mem.: ASCD, Nat. Mid. Schs. Assn., Pa. Sch. Bds. Assn., Nat. Assn. Secondary Sch. Prins., Am. Assn. Sch. Adminstrs., Delta Epsilon Sigma, Delta Kappa Gamma (pres. Delta chpt.). Avocations: playing classical organ and piano, reading, swimming.*

HAUPTMAN, LAURENCE MARC, history educator; b. New Paltz, New York, May 18, 1945; s. David and Frieda (Landesman) H.; m. Ruth (Jacobs), May 23, 1970; children: Beth, Eric. BA, N.Y. Univ., 1966, MA, 1968, PhD, 1971. From instr. to assoc. prof. State Univ. of N.Y., New Paltz, NY, 1971-82, prof., 1982-99, disting. prof. History, 1999—. Hist. cons. for Am. Indian nations including Cayuga Nation, Mashantucket Pequot Tribal Nation of Conn., Oneida Nation of Wis., Seneca Nation of Indians, N.Y.; expert witness Senate select com. on Indian Affairs, U.S. Congress, 1990, House subcom. on interior and insular affairs, 1990, Cayuga Indian land claims, 2000; Alexander Flick lectr. in N.Y. history N.Y. State History conf., 1998. Author: The Iroquois and the New Deal, 1981, The Iroquois Struggle for Survival, 1986 (Notable Book of Yr. Choice mag.), Formulating Am. Indian Policy in N.Y. State, 1988, The Iroquois Indians in the Civil War: From Battlefield to Reservation, 1993, Tribes & Tribulations, 1995, Between Two Fires: Am. Indians in the Civil War, 1995 (Notable Book of Yr., Choice mag.), Conspiracy of Interests: The Iroquois Dispossession and the Rise of N.Y. State, 1999 (John Ben Snow Book prize), Chief Daniel Bread and the Oneida Nation of Indians of Wisconsin, 2002; editor: Neighbors and Intruders, 1978, The Oneida Indian Experience: Two Perspectives, 1988, The Pequots in Southern New England, 1990, A Seneca Indian Sgt. in the Civil War, 1995, The Oneida Indian Journey: from N.Y. to Wisconsin, 1999. Recipient: Peter Doctor Meml. Award, Peter Doctor Fellowship Found. of Iroquois Indians, 1987, 98, NYS-UUP Award for Excellence in Teaching, 1991, Excellence in Rsch. Award N.Y. State Bd. of Regents, 1992, book prize State Hist. Soc. Wis., 1999. Mem.; Am. Hist. Assn., Orgn. Am. Historians, Western History Assn., Am. Soc. for Ethnohistory, N.Y. State Hist. Assn. Avocations: golf, travel. Home: 2 Sarafian Rd New Paltz NY 12561-3816

HAUSE, EDITH COLLINS, college administrator; b. Rock Hill, SC, Dec. 11, 1933; d. Ernest O. and Violet (Smith) Collins; m. James Luke Hause, Sept. 3, 1955; children: Stephen Mark, Felicia Gaye Hause Friesen. BA, Columbia Coll., SC, 1956; postgrad., U. NC, Greensboro, 1967, U. SC, 1971—75. Tchr. Richland Dist. II, Columbia, 1971—74; dir. alumnae affairs Columbia Coll., 1974—82, v.p. alumnae affairs, 1989—99, ret., 1999. Named Outstanding Tchr. of Yr., Richland Dist. II, 1974; recipient Disting. Svc. award, Columbia Coll. Alumae Assn., 2003, Columbia Coll. Medallion, 2003. Mem.: Nat. Soc. Fund Raising Execs., Coun. for Advancement and Support Edn., Columbia Network for Female Execs., SC Advocates for Women on Bds. and Commrs. (bd. dirs.), SC Assn. Alumni Dirs. (pres. 1996—98). Republican. Methodist. Home: 92 Mariners Pointe Rd Prosperity SC 29127-7674

HAUSEMAN, ROSEMARY, secondary education educator; b. Pottstown, Pa., June 4, 1943; d. Irvin K. and M. Catherine Hauseman; 1 child, Jennifer L. BA, Elizabethtown Coll., 1965; MA, Kutztown U., 1978. Permanent tchg. cert., Pa. Tchr. Elizabethtown (Pa.) Sr. H.S., 1965-66, Boyertown (Pa.) Area Sr. H.S., 1967-72; tchr., dept. chair Exeter Twp. Sr. H.S., Reading, Pa., 1976—; tchr. Reading Area C.C. Tchr. cons. Pa. Writing Project, West Chester. Mem. NEA, NOW, Pa. State Edn. Assn. Avocations: reading, travel, friends and family.

HAUSER, DENNIS JAMES, technology educator; b. New Ulm, Minn., May 12, 1958; s. James Henry and Lorjean Bernice (Abram) H.; m. Anna Marie Nichols, Dec. 10, 1988; children: Laura, Julie, Christina. BS in Edn., Mankato State U., 1989; MEd, City U., Bellevue, Wash., 1994. Edn. dir. Minn. Trapper Assn., Melrose, Minn., 1986-88; with Carpenter Ptnr.'s Inc., Vancouver, Wash., 1988-90; tech. tchr. Roy Jr. H.S. Evergreen Sch. Dist., 1990—. Mem. Sight-Base Com., Vancouver, Wash., Vocat. Steering Com., Vancouver, Tech. Com., Vancouver; sec. Vocat. Adv. Com., Vancouver. Cub master Boy Scouts Am., Vancouver, 1989, scout master, 1990-93, varsity team coach, 1993-95. Grantee Evergreen Sch. Dist. 114, 1994, Evergreen Vocat. Dept., 1994. Mem. Ch. of Jesus Christ of LDS. Avocations: hunting, fishing, hiking, camping. E-mail: dennis.hauser@cache.k12.ut.us.

HAUSLER, SARA FINCHAM, learning disabilities specialist, educator; b. Pratt, Kans., Aug. 3, 1940; d. Donald Arthur and Lois (Figge) Farmer; m. Robert Kent Fincham, Sept. 2, 1962 (div. Aug. 1978); children: Amy Lynn Fincham Keller, Anne Elisabeth Fincham Marshall, Sara Kimberly Fincham Lambeth; m. William Hausler, June 29, 1991. BS in Secondary Edn., Kans. U., 1962; MEd, Wichita State U., 1985. Cert. learning disabilities, French, social studies tchr. French, civics tchr. Richlands (N.C.) H.S., 1965-66; substitute tchr. Wichita (Kans.) Pub. Schs., 1967-72; learning disabilities resource tchr. Newton (Kans.) H.S., 1980-81; substitute tchr. Wichita Pub. Schs., 1981-82; learning disabilities resource tchr. Horace Mann Mid. Sch., Wichita, 1982, Derby (Kans.) 7-8 Ctr., 1982-83, Valley Center (Kans.) H.S., 1983-93; substitute tchr. Wichita Pub. Schs., 1993-94; learning support tchr. Wichita Collegiate Sch., 1994-96; substitute tchr. Wichita Pub. Schs., 1997—. Mem. Eastminster Presbyn. Ch. Women's Circle, Wichita, 1984-91; home room mother Andover (Kans.) Elem. Sch., 1974-78; laymem. gifted com. Andover H.S., 1976. Recipient Big Sister award Kans. U., 1959. Mem. Learning Disabilities Assn., Kans. U. Alumni, Wichita State U. Alumni, Kappa Alpha Theta (editor, sec. 1966—), Phi Kappa Phi. Avocations: reading, gardening, decorating, tennis.

HAVENS, PAMELA ANN, college official; b. Plattsburgh, N.Y., Nov. 30, 1956; d. Thomas L. and MaryAnn (Zalen) Romeo; m. Stephen L. Havens, Aug. 9, 1986; children: Stephanie Leigh, Skylar Lucas. BA, Eisenhower Coll., 1978; MA summa cum laude, SUNY, Plattsburgh, 1987; AAS summa cum laude, Cayuga C.C., 1999. VISTA vol. Retired Sr. Vol. Program, Plattsburgh, 1978-79; copywriter, newsperson Stas. WEAV-AM/WGFB-FM, Plattsburgh, 1979-83; traffic clk. Sta. WCFE-TV, Plattsburgh, 1983-84, pub. info. coord., 1984-85; coll. rels. officer Clinton Cmty. Coll., Plattsburgh, 1985-89; dir. publs. and comm. Cayuga C.C., Auburn, N.Y., 1989-2001; dir. stewardship Hamilton Coll., Clinton, N.Y., 2001—. Mem. adv. bd., vice-chair St. Mary's Sch. PTA, Clinton, NY, 2002—. Mem. adv. com. Cayuga C.C. Presch. Ctr., 1999-2001. Named Young Careerist Alternate Bus. and Profl. Women's Club, 1986; recipient award ACC/CCC Alumni Assn., 2000. Mem.: CASE, AAUW, Nat. Coun. Mktg. and Pub. Rels. (Pro Devel. award 1999, Disting. Svc. award 2000), Eisenhower Coll. Aumni Assn. (bd. dirs. 1990—97, chmn. bd. 1992—95), Phi Theta Kappa. Avocations: fiction and poetry writing, doll and bear collecting, olympic pin collecting, tap dancing. Office: Hamilton Coll 198 College Hill Rd Clinton NY 13323 E-mail: phavens@hamilton.edu.

HAVILAND, KAY LYNN (KADE HAVILAND), English literature educator; b. Deer Lodge, Mont., July 16, 1952; d. Jackson C. and Juanita Maxine (Voelkel) Price; children: Jesse Jean, Kelsey Ann, Molly Claire. MA in Guidance and Counseling, Adams State Coll., 1994. Cert. addictions counselor, counseling psychologist Arapahoe House Denver Outpatient Clinic, Denver, 1996—. Asst. therapist, CORE obesity project, Weight Choice Program dept. pediatrics U. Colo., 1998—2001; asst. therapist State of Colo. Alcohol Drug Abuse Division; treatment trainer Denver Health Hosp., 2001—. Author, editor: (mag.) Human Interest, 1987-88 (1st place award 1989); contbr. articles to profl. jours. Mem. ACA, Colo. Counselors Assn. Avocations: calligraphy, cross-country skiing, reading.

HAVILAND, MARLITA CHRISTINE, elementary school educator; b. Moses Lake, Wash., Sept. 4, 1952; d. Marvin Curtis and Delita F. (Grout) McCully; m. James A Haviland, June 18, 1971. BS in Edn., So. Nazarene U., Bethany, Okla., 1973; MA in Edn., No. Ariz. U., 1987. Cert. elem. tchr., Ariz., Colo., ESL, basic edn., spl. edn. tchr., c.c., Ariz., early childhood edn., Colo.; cert. libr./media specialist. Elem. tchr. St. Paul (Ark.) Pu. Sch., Twin Wells Indian Sch., Sun Valley, Ariz., Navajo Gospel Mission, Kykotsmovi, Ariz., Shonto (Ariz.) Boarding Sch. (now Shonto Prep Sch.). Instr. Northland Pioneer Coll., Diné Coll.; coord. Sch. Wide Book Fair.; coach Accelerated Schs. Coord. Children Inc., Shonto; local chair, North Ctrl. Assn., amb. Mem. Nat. Fedn. Fed. Employees (past pres., sec.-treas., steward), Am. Lit. Assn., Internat. Reading Assn., Alpha Nu, Phi Kappa Phi. Home: PO Box 7427 Shonto AZ 86054-7427 E-mail: mchaviland@yahoo.com.

HAVLIN, JOHN LEROY, soil scientist, educator; b. Chgo., May 8, 1950; s. Joseph Leroy and Dorothy Jean (Williams) H.; 1 child, Jonathon Cary. MS, Colo. State U., 1980, PhD, 1983. Asst. prof. U. Nebr., Scottbluff, 1983-85, Kans. State U., Manhattan, 1985-90, prof. dept. agronomy, 1990-96; prof. N.C. State U., Raleigh, 1996—. Author: Soil Fertility and Fertilizers; contbr. articles articles to profl. pubs., chapters to books. Named Researcher of Yr., Nat. Fertilizer Solutuions Assn., 1989; recipient Werner L. Nelson Rsch. award, 1991, R.E. Wagner award, 2003; fellow Tchr. fellow, Nat. Assn. Coll. Tchrs. of Agr., 1994. Fellow: Soil Sci. Soc. Am. (Edn. award 2002), Am. Soc. Agronomy; mem.: Soil and Water Conservation Soc., Phi Kappa Phi, Sigma Xi, Gamma Sigma Delta (Outstanding Tchr. award 1992). Republican. Presbyterian. Achievements include research in advancement of dryland soil and crop managment technologies to improve productivity and profitability; crop rotation and tillage effects on soil organic matter and productivity; dryland fertilizer managment and precision farming. Home: 8709 Bluff Pointe Ct Raleigh NC 27615-4195 Office: NC State U Dept Soil Sci Raleigh NC 27695-0001 E-mail: havlin@ncsu.edu.

HAVNER, KERRY SHUFORD, civil engineering and solid mechanics educator; b. Huntington, W.Va., Feb. 20, 1934; s. Alfred Sidney and Jessie May (Fowler) H.; m. Roberta Lee Rider, Aug. 28, 1954; children: Karen Elese Smith, Clark Alan, Kris Sidney. BSCE, Okla. State U., 1955, MS, 1956, PhD, 1959. Registered prof. engr., Okla. Stress analyst Douglas Aircraft Co., Tulsa, 1956; from instr. to asst. prof. civil engrng. Okla. State U., Stillwater, 1957-62; sr. stress and vibration engr. Garrett Corp., Phoenix, 1962-63; sect. chief solid mechs. rsch. missile/space systems divsn. McDonnell-Douglas Corp., Santa Monica, Calif., 1963-68; lectr. civil engrng. U. So. Calif., L.A., 1965-68; from assoc. prof. to prof. civil engrng. N.C. State U., Raleigh, 1968-82, prof. civil engrng. and materials sci., 1982-99, prof. emeritus, 1999—. Sr. vis. dept. applied math. and theoretical physics U. Cambridge, 1981, 89. Author: Finite Plastic Deformation of Crystalline Solids, 1992; contbg. author: Mechanics of Solids, The Rodney Hill 60th Anniversary Volume, 1982; contbr. articles to Jour. Applied Math. and Physics, Jour. of Mechs. and Physics of Solids, Acta Mechanica, Procs. and Phil. Trans. Royal Soc., others; hon. sci. adv. bd. Mechs. of Materials; editl. adv. bd. Internat. Jour. Plasticity. 2d lt. U.S. Army, 1961, 1st lt. USAR, 1962. Rsch. grantee NSF, 1971, 74, 76, 78, 81, 83, 87, 91, 94; vis. fellow Clare Hall, 1981; recipient Melvin R. Lohmann medal Okla. State U., 1994. Fellow ASCE (sec. engrng. mechs. divsn. 1983-85, chmn. 1987-88, chmn. engrng. mechs. adv. bd. 1990-91, chmn. TAC-CERF awards com. 1991-94; assoc. editor Jour. Engrng. Mechs. 1981-83), Am. Acad. Mechanics (assoc. editor Mechanics, 1991-97); mem. ASME, Soc. Engrng. Sci., Soc. Indsl. and Applied Math., Sigma Xi. Democrat. Methodist. Achievements include research in theories and analyses of anisotropic hardening and finite deformation in crystalline materials, particularly metals. Home: 3331 Thomas Rd Raleigh NC 27607-6743 Office: NC State U PO Box 7908 Raleigh NC 27695-7908 E-mail: havner@eos.ncsu.edu.

HAVRAN, MARTIN JOSEPH, historian, educator, author; b. Windsor, Ont., Can., Nov. 12, 1929; came to U.S., 1956; s. Joseph W. and Helen (Bachinger) H.; m. Clara L. Kovacs, Aug. 30, 1958; 1 child, Justin M. PhB, U. Detroit, 1951; MA, Wayne State U., 1953; PhD, Case Western Res. U., 1957. Instr. history Kent (Ohio) State U., 1957-60, asst. prof., 1960-64, assoc. prof., 1964-68; assoc. prof. history U. Va., Charlottesville, 1968-72, prof. history, 1972-99, chmn. dept. history, 1974-79, dir. Self-Study Program, 1984-86, sec. of gen. faculty, 1994-99, prof. history emeritus, from 1999. Vis. assoc. prof. history Northwestern U., Evanston, Ill., 1967-68. Author: Catholics in Caroline England, 1962, England: Prehistory to Present, 1968, Life of Lord Cottington, 1973; editor: Readings in English History, 1967. Recipient Whittaker History prize Mich. Hist. Commn., 1953; Social Sci. Rsch. Coun. fellow, 1956-57; Govt. of Can. grantee, 1984. Fellow Royal Hist. Soc.; mem. Am. Cath. Hist. Assn. (pres. 1982), N.Am. Conf. on Brit. Studies (pres. 1979-81), Royal Stuart Soc., Ch. of Eng. Record Soc., Multicultural History Soc. Ont., Raven Soc., Torch Club (pres. 1993-94). Roman Catholic. Avocations: classical music, walking, gardening. Home: Charlottesvle, Va. Died July 22, 2000.

HAVRILCSAK, GREGORY MICHAEL, history educator; b. Uniontown, Pa., Feb. 18, 1951; s. Michael and Geneveve Anne (Satterfield) H.; m. Laura Ann Hart; 1 child, Karen Elizabeth. BA, U. Mich., Flint, 1978; MA,

Oakland U., 1989; postgrad., U. Va., 1995. Instr. history St. Mary's Sch., Swartz Creek, Mich., 1978-79, Riverside Mil. Acad., Gainesville, Ga., 1979-85, Notre Dame High Sch., Harper Woods, Mich., 1985-88, East Detroit Cmty. Schs., Eastpointe, Mich., 1986-91, Notre Dame High Sch., Harper Woods, Mich., 1991—, chmn. dept. social sci., 1996, debate and forensics coach, 1998—. Dir. social studies learning ctr. correctional edn. divsn. L'Anse-Creuse Cmty. Schs., Mt. Clemens, Mich., 1986-89; adj. instr. history Monroe (Mich.) County C.C., 1988-94, Oakland C.C., Auburn Hills, Mich., 1989-2000; adj. lectr. in history Coll. Arts and Scis., U. Mich., Flint, 2000—; Monticello-Stratford Hall Plantation Summer Seminar for Tchrs., 1995; with Inst. on the Tchg. of Advanced Placement European History, St. Johnsbury Acad., Vt., 1992, Internat. Symposium on the War of 1812 on the Great Lakes, U. Windsor, 1988; radio host Havrilcsak's History, WSDS AM 1480, 1998-99. Vol. Big Bros./Big Sisters, Macomb County, Mich., 1987—89; pres. Ventura Condominium Homeowners Assn., 1999—2001. With USN, 1969—71. Named Outstanding Young Men of Am., U.S. Jaycees, 1980. Mem. Mich. Hist. Soc., Oakland U. Alumni Assn., U. Mich. Alumni Assn., Orgn. Am. Historians, Mich. C.C. History Assn., Ctr. Tchg. Mich. History, Phi Alpha Theta. Avocations: photography, travel. Home: 15744 Charles R Ave Eastpointe MI 48021 Office: Notre Dame High Sch 20254 Kelly Rd Harper Woods MI 48225-1287 E-mail: greghav@umflint.edu.

HAVRILLA, JOHN WILLIAM, middle school educator; b. Hermitage, Pa., Jan. 18, 1945; s. Francis and Anna Louise (Kisegy) H.; m. Mary Justine Olshavsky, Aug. 27, 1966; 1 child, John-Michael. BS in Edn., Youngstown State U., 1966; MA in Elem. Adminstrn., Westminster Coll., 1970. Cert. tchr., adminstr., Pa. Tchr. West Middlesex (Pa.) Sch. Dist., 1966-69, Hermitage (Pa.) Sch. Dist., 1969-72, 77—, prin., 1972-77. Mem. Phi Delta Kappa. Republican. Roman Catholic. Home: 814 Dogwood Ln Hermitage PA 16148-2438

HAWES, NANCY ELIZABETH, mathematics educator; b. Phila., Oct. 28, 1944; d. Charles E. and Margaret M. (Cassel) H. BS in Edn., Millersville (Pa.) State Coll., 1966; MAT, Purdue U., 1970; M.Div., Ea. Bapt. Theol. Sem., Phila., 1979. Ordained deacon A.M.E. Zion Ch., 1978, elder, 1980. Tchr. math. Penncrest High Sch./Rose Tree Media (Pa.) Sch. Dist., 1966-68; asst. pastor Wesley A.M.E. Zion Ch., Phila., 1975-82; pastor St. John A.M.E. Zion Ch., Bethlehem, Pa., 1982-88, Mt. Tabor A.M.E. Zion Ch., Avondale, Pa., 1988-90; assoc. pastor Wesley A.M.E. Zion Ch., Phila., 1990—; tchr. math. Upper Merion Area Sch. Dist., King of Prussia, Pa., 1968—. Sponsor, Upper Merion Area High Sch. Math. Team, 1987—. Mem. Nat. Coun. Tchrs. Math., Math. Assn. Am., Pa. Coun. Tchrs. Math., Assn. Tchrs. Math. of Phila. and Vicinity. A.M.E. Zion Ch. Office: Upper Merion Area High Sch 435 Crossfield Rd King Of Prussia PA 19406-2363

HAWK, DAWN DAVAH, secondary education educator; b. Dodge, Nebr., Apr. 14, 1945; d. Fred John and Marcella Martha (Kunes) Lerch; m. Floyd Russell Hawk, June 14, 1969. BAE, Wayne State Coll., 1967. Cert. tchr., Nebr., Iowa, Ariz. English tchr. Tekamah (Nebr.) Pub. Sch., 1967-69, West Lyon Community Schs., Inwood, Iowa, 1970-74, Norfolk (Nebr.) Cath. Schs., 1974-85; English tchr., libr. Beemer (Nebr.) Pub. Schs., 1969-70; English and reading tchr. San Manuel (Ariz.) Sch. Dist., 1986—. Chair dept. adaptive edn. San Manuel H.S., 1992—2003; tutor in field. Active Catalina Luth. Ch., Tucson. Recipient Cooper Found. award for excellence in teaching U. Nebr., 1983, Fan award to study at Gilder/Lehrman Inst. Am. History, Radcliffe Inst. for Advanced Study at Harvard, 2002; NEH edn. grantee, 1987, 89, 91, 95; Ariz. Reading Assn. grad. scholar, 1995; Michael Jordan Fundamentals grantee, 2002. Mem. NEA, Nat. Coun. Tchrs. English, Internat. Reading Assn., Ea. Pinal Lit. Coun., Ariz. English Tchrs. Assn., Tucson Area Reading Coun. (bd. advisors), San Manuel Tchrs. Assn. Avocations: reading, writing poetry, travelling, visiting museums, golf. Home: 3950 E Hawser St 5 Tucson AZ 85739-9537 Office: San Manuel HS PO Box 406 San Manuel AZ 85631-0406 E-mail: azhawks@att.net.

HAWK, FLOYD RUSSELL, secondary school educator; b. Fresno, Calif., Oct. 7, 1945; s. Floyd Edward and Velma Irene (Lyon) H.; m. Dawn Davah Lerch, June 14, 1969. BA in Bus., Wayne State Coll., 1971. Cert. tchr. Ariz. Tchr. W. Lyon Pub. Schs., Inwood, Iowa, 1970-74, Norfolk (Nebr.) Cath. Schs., 1974-76, Madison (Nebr.) Pub. Schs., 1977-85, Young (Ariz.) Pub. Schs., 1985-86, San Manuel (Ariz.) High Sch., 1986--. State rep. Nat. Coaches Assn., Madison, Nebr., 1980-82; bd. dirs. Pinal County Adult Literacy, San Manuel. Mem. adv. bd. Multiple Sclerosis Soc.; commd. deacon Catalina Luth. NEH grantee, 1995. Mem. NEA, Ariz. Edn. Assn., Ariz. Bus. Edn. Assn., Ariz. Hist. Soc., Optimist Club (pres. 1972, lt. gov. 1973). Lutheran. Avocations: baseball, reading, teaching, church work. Office: San Manuel HS PO Box 406 San Manuel AZ 85631-0406

HAWK, PAULETTA BROWNING, student elementary school educator; b. Gilbert, W.Va., Aug. 10, 1952; d. Walter Browning and Gracie (Johnson) Tyner; children: Clifford Thompson III, Angie Thompson. AA, Cen. Fla. Community Coll., Ocala, 1988; BS in Elem. Edn., U. Cen. Fla., 1991; MEd in Curriculum and Instrn., Nat. Louis U., 1996. Med. receptionist Bluefield (W.Va.) Clinic, 1975-76; ins. clk. Bristol (Tenn.) Meml. Hosp., 1976-78; med. sec. Inter-Mountain Pathology Assn., Bristol, Tenn., 1978-80; substitute tchr. Citrus County Sch. Bd., Inverness, Fla., 1980-81, guidance sec., 1981-85, acct. I (on profl. leave of absence), 1990-91; office mgr. Victor Nothnagel, O.D., Inverness, 1985-87; tchr. Inverness Primary, 1991—99, Banyan Elem., Sunrise, Fla., 1999—2002; 'tchr. Brooksville (Fla.) Elem., 2002—. Vol. Nat. Arthritis Found., 1988-89, Inverness Primary Sch., Citrus County Sch. Bd., 1989. Mem. Phi Theta Kappa. Democrat. Baptist. Avocations: reading, swimming, cycling, gardening, clay modeling. Home: 415 Tulip Ln Inverness FL 34452

HAWKEN, PATTY LYNN, retired nursing educator, dean of faculty; b. Wheaton, Ill., July 13, 1932; d. Leonard William and Betty (Stock) H. BSN, U. Mich., 1956; MSN, Case Western Res. U., 1962, PhD, 1970. Instr. U. Mich., Ann Arbor, 1956-57, Highland Hosp., Oakland, Calif., 1957-59; from instr. to assoc. prof., assoc. in adminstrn. Case Western Res. U., Cleve., 1960-71; assoc. prof. Emory U., Atlanta, 1971-72, prof., dir., 1972-74; dean, prof. U. Tex. Health Sci. Ctr. Sch. Nursing, San Antonio, 1974-97, ret., 1997. Contbr. articles to profl. jours. Bd. dirs. Wesley Cmty. Ctr., San Antonio, 1986, 89; mem. United Way Allocation Com., San Antonio, 1987; adv. com. Trinity U. Health Care Adminstrn., San Antonio, 1984-97, VA Dean's Com., San antonio, 1982-97. Recipient Nurse of Yr. award Tex. Nursing Assn., San Antonio chpt., 1985, Disting. Alumni award Case Western Res. U., 1991, U. Mich., 1995; named to Women's Hall of Fame. Mem. ANA (cabinet on edn. 1986-88), Nat. League Nursing (pres. 1989-91, Disting. Svc. award 1991), Am. Assn. Colls. of Nursing (com. on edn. 1986-88), Commns. Grads. Fgn. Nursing Schs. (trustee, pres. 1983-85), Am. Acad. Nursing (bd. govs. 1994-97), San Antonio 100 Club, Internat. Women's Forum (San Antonio pres. celebration, Hall of Fame 1994-97). Avocations: snorkeling, swimming. Home: 1826 Fallow Run San Antonio TX 78248-2000

HAWKINS, CALVIN MAE, secondary education educator; b. Emporia, Va., Nov. 5, 1941; d. James and Virginia (Ridley) Pegram; m. Benjamin Hawkins, June 10, 1966; children: Sabrina, Jason. BS, Va. State Coll., 1964. Cert. bus. edn. tchr., Va., N.J. Bus. tchr. Luther H. Foster H.S., Nottowa, Va., 1965-68; dir. bus. dept. Jersey City (N.J.) Job Corps, 1969-76; bus. tchr. Franklin Twp. Pub. Schs., 1976—. Advisor nat. honor soc. Franklin H.S., 1990—, advisor future bus. leaders of Am., 1976—; owner Cal's Typing Svc., Highland Park, 1986—. Poll clk. Dist. 13, Highland Park, 1983—; ch. clk. Zion Hill Bapt. Ch., Piscataway, N.J., 1990—; mem. adv. com. Realizing Equity in Edn. for Children in Highland Park, 1988—. Named Queen for a Day, Betty L. Hodges Cmty. Girls Club, 1995. Mem. NEA, N.J. Edn. Assn., Franklin Edn. Assn. Democrat. Baptist. Avocation: computers. Home: 10C Bartle Ct Highland Park NJ 08904-2003

HAWKINS, CHRISTINE MARGUERITE, special education educator; b. Chgo., Jan. 18, 1952; d. Arthur Charles and Marian Lee Hawkins. BA, Calif. Western Sch., 1974; credential in learning handicaps, Calif. State U.-Northridge, 1980; MS, Calif. Luth. Coll., 1985. Cert. tchr., learning handicaps tchr., resource specialist, Calif. Tchr. spl. edn. West Valley Ctr. (name now Parkhill), Canoga Park, Calif., 1977-85, ednl. therapist, 1977-85; resource specialist San Jose (Calif.) Unified Sch. Dist., 1985-90, dist. trainer coop. learning, 1987-89, tchr. spl. day class, 1990-94; resource specialist, 1994—. Active PTA. Recipient Ed Press award, 1988. Mem. AAUW (dir. San Jose br. 1988, area rep. edn. 1986-87, v.p. edn. found. 1990, program v.p. 1991, pres. 1993-94, com. women's history project 1994-2000), Assn. Ednl. Therapists (membership com. 1982-85), Orton Soc. (treas., bd. dirs. 1982-85). Avocations: reading, painting, music, sitting at beach.

HAWKINS, CYNTHIA, artist, educator; b. N.Y.C., Jan. 29, 1950; d. Robert D. Hawkins and Elease Coger; m. Steven J. Chaiken, Feb. 5, 1977 (div. Aug. 1985); m. John Edward Owen, Aug. 24, 1985; children: Ianna, Zachary. BA, Queens Coll., 1977; MFA, Md. Inst. Coll. Art, 1992. Tchg. asst. Md. Inst. Coll. of Art, Balt., 1990-92; adj. instr. Rockland C.C., Suffern, N.Y., 1993-96, Parsons Sch. Design, N.Y.C., 1996, The Coll. at New Paltz, SUNY, 1996-98, Ramapo Coll. of N.J., 1998-99; dir. galleries Cedar Crest Coll., Allentown, Pa., 2000—03; curator Rush Art Gallery, 2003—; ind. curator Lore Regenstein Gallery, 2003—. Mentor Empire State Coll., Nyack, N.Y., 1994; artist-in-residence The Studio Mus. Harlem, N.Y., 1987-88, Va. Ctr. for Creative Arts, Sweet Briar, Va., 1995-96; vis. artist Round House Press, Hartwick Coll., Oneonta, N.Y., 1994; curator Rockland Ctr. for Arts, art dept. Rockland C.C., Nyack, 1994-95, The Rotunda, 1994-95; vis. lectr. Forman Gallery, Hartwick Coll., Oneonta, 1994, Rockland C.C., Suffern, 1994-95; presenter in field. One-woman shows include, Paul Klapper Libr., Queens Coll., N.Y., 1974, Just Above Midtown/Downtown Gallery, N.Y.C., 1981, Frances Wolfson Art Ctr., Miami (Fla.)-Dade C.C., 1986, Cinque Gallery, N.Y.C., 1989, Essex (Md.) C.C., 1991, Queens Coll. Art Ctr., Benjamin S. Rosenthal Libr., Queens Coll., CUNY, Trinity Luth. Ch., New Milford, Conn., 1993, exhibited in group shows, Queens Coll. Gallery, N.Y.C., 1973, Emily Lowe Gallery, Hempstead, N.Y., 1979, Jamie Szoke Gallery, N.Y.C., 1984, Grace Borgenicht Gallery, N.Y.C., 1986, Aljira Gallery, Newark, 1989, Dome Gallery, N.Y.C., 1990, Decker Gallery, Balt., 1991, Kromah Gallery, Balt., 1992, Arts Alliance Haverstraw, N.Y., 1993, Nabisco Gallery, East Hanover, N.J., 1994, Artist Space, N.Y.C., 1993, Bronx Mus. Arts, 1994, U. Notre Dame at Balt., 1995, No. Westchester Ctr. for Arts, Mt. Kisco, N.Y., 1996, Hopper House, Nyack, 1996, Rush Art Gallery, N.Y., 1999, Foxglove Gallery, Stroudsburg, Pa., 2002, Represented in permanent collections, The Bronx Mus. of Arts, N.Y.C., Trinity Luth. Ch., New Milford, Dept. of State, Washington, The Printmaking Workshop, Chevron Corp., Calif., Cameron and Colby, N.Y.C., C.D. Walsh Assocs., Conn., Brooks Sausage Co., Kenosha, Wis., The Habitat Co., Chgo., Brown Mgmt., Balt.; art works featured in pubs. including N.Y. Times, Village Voice, 25 Years of African American Women Artist, Home Mag. Mem. com. Art in Pub. Places, Rockland County, 1999—2001. Recipient 2d pl. award for mixed media Atlanta Life Ins. Co. exhbn. and competition, 1984; fellow Va. Ctr. for Creative Arts, 1996, The Studio Mus. in Harlem, 1987-88, Patricia Robert Harris fellow U.S. Dept. Edn., 1990-92. Democrat. Episcopalian. E-mail: chawkins@cedarcrest.edu.

HAWKINS, DALE CICERO, aviator, educator, engineer; b. Topeka, June 17, 1958; s. Dale R. Coleman and Linda C. (Parks) Meiergerd; m. Patricia Bermudez, Nov. 20, 1982; 1 child, Athena C. AS in Electronic Engring. Tech. with honors, Cleve. Inst. Electronics, 1987, BS in Electronic Engring. Tech. summa cum laude, 1993, MS in Engring. and Tech. Mgmt. summa cum laude, 1998; doctoral candidate, Northcentral U. Cert. quality engr., regulatory affairs cert.; cert. comml. pilot, flight instr. Electronic engring. technician Litton G & CS, L.A., 1979—82; sr. electronics technician Cedars-Sinai Med. Ctr., L.A., 1982—85; svc. engr. Litton AMS, San Diego, 1985—86; elect. engr. tech. IMED Corp. R & D, San Diego, 1987—93, regulatory affairs engr., 1993—98; mgr. regulatory affairs Laborie Med. Technologies, Williston, Vt., 1998—2000; flight instr. Daniel Webster Coll., Nashua, NH, 2001—02; CMD post controller, safety & tng. mgr. Vt. Air N.G., 2001—02; exec. dir. SFR Valuations, LA, 2003—. Participant Space Life Scis. mission Space Sta. Freedom, NASA; project mgr. Internat. Space Sta. Infusion Pump Project, 1995-98; adj. prof. engring. and tech. mgmt. So. Calif. U. for Profl. Studies, 1999-2000. Co-author: The Art of Hsin Hsing Yee Ti Kenpo Kung Fu, 1991; contbr. articles to profl. jours. Active UN Assn., 1979—, bd. dirs., 1994-98; sr. officer USCG Aux., 1980—2001, aviator, flotilla comdr., 1994-95; USCG liaison U.S. Naval Sea Cadet Corps., NAS Miramar, 1985-98; officer USAF Aux., 2000—. With USN, 1976-79. Numerous US Navy, Coast Guard, and Air Force citations and svc. awards; named Outstanding Citizen Exch. Club, 1989. Mem. IEEE, Nat. Assn. Flight Instrs., Am. Soc. for Quality, Airline Pilots Assn., Alpha Beta Kappa. Achievements include contributions to patents for improved switching power supply and medical device interunit interface connector system; research in H2 generation of reversed biased capacitors, and in lead-acid battery life prolongation. Home and Office: 20401 Soledad Canyon Rd #225 Canyon Country CA 91351

HAWKINS, DAVID ROLLO, SR., psychiatrist, educator; b. Springfield, Mass., Sept. 22, 1923; s. James Alexander and Janet (Rollo) H.; m. Elizabeth G. Wilson, June 8, 1946; children: David Rollo Jr., Robert Wilson, John Bruce, William Alexander. BA, Amherst Coll., 1945; MD, U. Rochester, N.Y., 1946. Intern Strong Meml. Hosp., Rochester, 1946-48; Commonwealth Fund fellow in psychiatry and medicine U. Rochester, 1950-52; instr. psychiatry U. N.C. Sch. Medicine, 1952-53, asst. prof., 1953-57, asso. prof. psychiatry, 1957-62, prof., 1962-67; prof., chmn. dept. psychiatry U. Va. Sch. Medicine, 1967-77, Alumni prof. psychiatry, 1967-79, asso. dean, 1969-70; psychiatrist-in-chief U. Va. Hosp., 1967-77; prof. psychiatry Pritzker Sch. Medicine, U. Chgo., 1979-90, U. Ill., 1990—; clin. prof. psychiatry U. N.C., Chapel Hill, 1992—. Dir. liaison and consultation svcs. dept. psychiatry Michael Reese Hosp., Chgo., 1979-87, chmn., 1987-92; assoc. attending physician N.C. Meml. Hosp., Chapel Hill, 1952-62, attending physician, 1962-67; cons. Watts Hosp., Durham, 1952-67, VA Hosp., Fayetteville, N.C., 1956-67, Eastern State Hosp., Williamsburg, Va., 1971—, VA Hosp., Salem. Va., 1969-79, mem. deans com., 1971-77; spl. rsch. fellow Inst. Psychiatry, U. London, 1963-64, Fogarty internat. rsch. fellow, 1976-77, U.S.-USSR and Romania health exch. fellow, 1978. Rev. editor Psychosomatic Medicine, 1958-70; assoc. editor Psychiatry, 1970-92. Mem. small grants com. NIMH, 1958-62; mem. nursing rsch. study sect. NIH, 1965-67; mem. Gov.'s Commn. Mental, Indigent and Geriatric Patients, 1968-72; mem. rsch. evaluation com. Va. Dept. Mental Hygiene and Hosps., 1970-73; mem. behavioral sci. test com. Nat. Bd. Med. Examiners, 1970-73. Served as capt. M.C., AUS, 1948-50. Fellow Am. Coll. Psychoanalysts (charter bd. regents 1979-81, treas. 1989-91, pres.-elect 1992, pres. 1994), Am. Psychiat. Assn.; mem. AAUP, Am. Psychosomatic Soc. (mem. coun. 1959), AMA, Group for Advancement Psychiatry (bd. dirs. 1987-89), Assn. Am. Med. Colls. (coun. acad. socs. 1973-78), Am. Psychoanalytic Assn., Am. Coll. Psychiatrists, AAAS, Va. Psychoanalytic Soc., Washington Psychoanalytic Soc., Chgo. Psychoanalytic Soc., N.C. Psychoanalytic Soc., Ill. Psychiat. Soc. (coun. 1981-82, pres.-elect 1987, pres. 1988-90), Soc. Neurosci., Am. Assn. Chmn. Depts. Psychiatry (sec.-treas. 1971-73, pres. 1974-75), Sleep Rsch. Soc., Nat. Bd. Med. Examiners (exam. com. 1983-87), Phi Beta Kappa, Sigma Xi, Alpha Omega Alpha. Address: 405 Deming Rd Chapel Hill NC 27514-3207

HAWKINS, ELEANOR CARROLL, veterinary educator; b. Balt., Apr. 18, 1957; d. Elbert Stewart and Elizabeth Eleanor (Howard) H. BS, U. Md., 1978; DVM, Ohio State U., 1982. Diplomate Am. Coll. Vet. Internal Medicine. Intern small animal medicine and surgery Animal Med. Ctr., N.Y.C., 1982-83; resident small animal medicine U. Calif., Davis, 1983-85; asst. prof. internal medicine Purdue U., West Lafayette, Ind., 1985-91, assoc. prof. internal medicine, 1991; asst. prof. small animal medicine N.C. State U., Raleigh, 1991-93, assoc. prof. small animal medicine, 1993—2000, prof. small animal medicine, 2000—. Author: (with others) Current Veterinary Therapy X, 1989, Current Veterinary Therapy XI, 1992, Current Veterinary Therapy XII, 1995, Textbook of Veterinary Internal Medicine, 1989, 3d edit., 1995, 4th edit., Small Animal Internal Medicine, 1992, 2d edit., 1998, others; sect. editor The 5 Minute Veterinary Consult, 2d edit., 1998; contbr. articles to profl. jours. Mem. AVMA, Am. Coll. Vet. Internal Medicine (cert. exam. com. 1994-98, chair 1998, pres. splty. of internal medicine 2003—), Comparative Respiratory Soc. (bd. dirs. 1991-94), Phi Beta Kappa, Phi Zeta. Achievements include research in techniques to perform bronchoalveolar lavage in cats and dogs with minimal equipment needs; characterization of BAL cytology in cats and dogs in health and disease; educational video of abnormal breathing patterns in dogs. Office: NC State U Coll Vet Medicine 4700 Hillsborough St Raleigh NC 27606-1428

HAWKINS, FRANCES PAM, finance educator; b. Woodland, Ala., Dec. 2, 1945; d. Lowell M. and Bernice E. Mcmanus; children: Scott Cummings, Veronica Lovvorn. AS in Bus., Southern Union C.C., 1989; BS in Bus. Edn., Auburn U., 1990, MEd, 1992. Ptnr. C & S Pharmacy, Roanoke, Ala., 1974—90; bus. office tech. instr. West Ga. Tech. Coll., Lagrange, Ga., 1991—. Bus. tech., divsn. chair West Ga. Tech. Coll., Lagrange, 1999—, bus. office tech. adv. com. mem., 1992—, chairperson libr. com., 2001—; mem. tech. in edn. com. Ga. Dept. Edn., Atlanta, 2001—. Team leader March of Dimes, LaGrange, 1998—. Mem.: Ga. Bus. Edn. Assn., So. Bus. Edn. Assn., Nat. Bus. Edn. Assn. (com. mem. 2001), Auburn Alumni Assn., Phi Beta Lambda (sec. 1997—2001, nat. bd. dirs. future bus. leaders Am. 2001—, local advisor 1992—, state advisor 1999—, pres. Ga. Found. Inc. 1998—). Methodist. Office: West Ga Tech Coll 303 Fort Dr Lagrange GA 30240 Office Fax: 706-845-4339. Business E-Mail: phawkins@westgatech.edu.

HAWKINS, IDA FAYE, elementary school educator; b. Ft. Worth, Dec. 28, 1928; d. Christopher Columbus and Nanie Idella (Hughes) Hall; m. Gene Hamilton Hawkins, Dec. 22, 1952; children: Gene Agner, Jane Hall. Student, Midwestern U., 1946-48; BS, North Tex. State U., 1951; postgrad., Lamar U., 1968-70; MS, McNeese State U., 1973. Tchr. DeQueen Elem. Sch., Port Arthur, Tex., 1950-54, Tyrrell Elem. Sch., Port Arthur, Tex., 1955-56, Roy Hatton Elem. Sch., Bridge City, Tex., 1967-68, Oak Forest Elem. sch., Vidor, Tex., 1968-91; ret., 1991. Elementary school educator; b. Ft. Worth, Dec. 28, 1928; d. Christopher Columbus and Nannie Idella (Hughes) Hall; m. Gene Hamilton Hawkins, Dec. 22, 1952; children: Gene Agner, Jane Hall. Student Midwestern U., 1946-48; BS, N. Tex. State U., 1951; student Lamar U., 1968-70; MS, McNeese State U., 1973. Tchr. DeQueen Elem. Sch., Port Arthur, Tex., 1950-54, Tyrrell Elem. Sch., Port Arthur, 1955-56, Roy Hatton Elem. Sch., Bridge City, Tex., 1967-68, Oak Forest Elem. Sch., Vidor, Tex., 1968-91, ret. 2d v.p. Travis Elem. PTA, 1965-66, 1st v.p., 1966-67; corr. sec. Port Arthur City coun. PTA, 1966-67; Sunday sch. tchr. Presbyn. Ch., 1951-53, 60-66. Named Tchr. of Yr., Oak Forest Elem., 1984-85. Mem. NEA, Tex. State Tchrs. Assn. 2d v.p. Travis Elem. PTA, 1965-66, 1st v.p., 1966-67; corr. sec. Port Arthur City Coun. PTA, 1966-67; Sunday sch. tchr. Presbyn. Ch., 1951-53, 60-66. Named Tchr. of Yr., Oak Forest Elem., 1984-85. Mem. NEA, Tex. State Tchrs. Assn. Home: 6315 Central City Blvd #611 Galveston TX 77551-3806

HAWKINS, JACQUELYN, elementary and secondary education educator; b. Russell Springs, Ky., Apr. 30, 1943; d. J.T. Hawkins and Maudie Bell Crew. BS, Andrews U., 1969; MEd, Xavier U., 1976. Cert. elem. tchr., Ohio, reading tchr. elem. and high sch., Ohio. Tchr. Cin. Pub. Schs., 1969-99, Cummins Sch., Cin., 1971-81, Windsor Sch., Cin., 1982-83, 1983-89, acting contact tchr. chpt. 1 reading program, 1989-93, reading recovery tchr., 1993-99; ret., 1999; child care worker, 2002—. Rep. Cin. Coun. Educators, 1986-89, 91-92, 92-93, mem. book com.; mem. sch. improvement program Windsor Sch., 1982-84; mem. Sch. Improvement Program Cin. Chairperson United Way at Windsor Sch. Cin., 1986-89, 90-92, United Negro Coll. Fund Cin., 1986-89, ARC, Windsor Sch., Cin., 1986-89, 90-92; rep. Fine Arts Fund Cin., 1986-88; co-leader 4-H Club, Cin., 1987-88; leader Girl Scouts U.S., Cin., 1988-93; tutor Tabernacle Bapt. Ch., 1989; co-chairperson Windsor ARC, 1991-92. Recipient Cert. Achievement Cummins Sch. Cin., 1978 Democrat. Avocations: travel, reading, needlework.

HAWKINS, LAWRENCE CHARLES, management consultant, educator; b. Greenville County, S.C., Mar. 20, 1919; s. Wayman and Etta (Brockman) H.; m. Earline Thompson, Apr. 29, 1943; children: Lawrence Charles Jr., Wendell Earl. BA, U. Cin., 1941, BEd, 1942, MEd, 1951, EdD, 1970; AA (hon.), Wilmington Coll., 1979; LittD (hon.), Cin. Tech. and C.C.; LHD (hon.), Mt. St. Joseph Coll. Cert. sch. supt. Ohio. Elem./secondary tchr. Cin. Pub. Schs., 1945-52, sch. prin./dir., 1952-67, asst. supt., 1967-69; dean U. Cin., 1969-75, v.p., 1975-77, sr. v.p., 1977-83; vis. asst. prof. Eastern Mich. U., Ypsilanti, summers 1955-60; mem. Cincinnatus Assn., 1971-87. Vice chair Student Loan Funding Corp., 1982-98; mem. cmty. rels. panel Cin. Mayors, 1979—, others; cons. U.S. Dept. Justice, Dept. Edn.; bd. dirs. We. and So. Fin. Group. Bd. dirs. exec. com. Ohio Citizens Coun. Health and Welfare, 1966-73; vice chair Ohio Valley Regional Med. Program, 1972-77, bd. trustees Cmty. Chest and Coun. Cin. Area Inc., 1970-72; bd. dirs. Wilmington (Ohio) Coll., 1980-90, Bethesda Hosp., Cin., 1980-90; trustee Children's Home of Cin., 1978-90, Coll. Mt. St. Joseph, 1989-93; pres., CEO Omni-Man, Inc., 1981-96; bd. dirs. Nat. Underground R.R. Freedom Ctr., 1994-98; owner The L.C.H. Resource; vice chmn. Greater Cin. TV Ednl. Found., WCET-TV, 1983; co-chmn. Cin. area NCCJ 1980-87; nat. bd. dirs. Inroads, 1982-87; bd. trustees Knowledge Wroks Found., 1999—. Served to lt. USAAF, 1943-45 (an original Tuskegee Airman). Recipient award of Merit, Cin. Area United Appeal, 1955, 73, cert. Pres.'s Coun. on Youth Opportunity, 1968, City Cin., 1968, Disting. Svc. citation Greater Cin. NCCJ, 1988; named Great Living Cincinnatian, Greater Cin. C. of C., 1989. Mem. NEA (life), ASCD, Am. Assn. Sch. Adminstrs. (conv.), Nat. Congress Parents and Tchrs. (hon. life; chmn. com.), Phi Delta Kappa, Kappa Delta Pi, Kappa Alpha Psi, Sigma Pi Phi. Home: 3544 Sherbrooke Dr Cincinnati OH 45241-3831

HAWKINS, LINDA PARROTT, school system administrator; b. Florence, SC, June 23, 1947; d. Obie Lindberg Parrott and Mary Francis (Lee) Evans; m. Larry Eugene Hawkins, Jan. 5, 1946; 1 child, Heather Nichole. BS, U. S.C., 1969; MS, Francis Marion Coll., 1978; EdS in Adminstrn., U. S.C., 1994, PhD in Ednl. Adminstrn., 2002. Tchr. J.C. Lynch HS, Coward, SC, 1973—80; tchr., chair bus. dept. Lake City (SC) HS, 1980—89, assoc. prin., 1989—98; dir. Florence County Sch. Dist. 3, 1998—2003, sr. dir. accountability, 1980—89. Mem. Williamsburg Tech. Adv. Coun., Kingstree, S.C., 1985-90; adv. coun. Florence-Darlington (S.C.) Tech., 1981-87; co-chair Pee Dee Tech Prep consortia steering com.; co-chmn. allied health adv. com., 1990-93; spkr., presenter in field. Editor: Parliamentary Procedure Made Easy, 1983; contbr. articles to profl. jours. State advisor Future Bus. Leaders of Am., Columbia, S.C., 1978-86; treas. S.C. State Women's Aux., 1983-93; sec.-treas. J.C. Lynch Elem. Sch. PTO. Named Outstanding Advisor S.C. Future Bus. Leaders of Am., 1985, Tchr. of Yr., S.C. Bus. Edn. Assn., 1988-89, Secondary Tchr. of Yr., Nat. Bus. Edn. Assn., 1989-90, Educator of Yr. S.C. Trade & Indsl. Edn. Assn., 1993, S.C. Asst. Prin. of Yr., 1995, 2020 Vision Dist. Adminstr. award, 2000; Mary Eva Hite scholar, 2001. Mem. Profl. Secs. Internat., Nat. Bus. Assn. (S.C. chpt. membership dir. 1986-89, so. region membership dir. 1989-92, secondary program dept. dir. 1991-92), S.C. Bus. Edn. Assn. (jour. editor 1985-86, v.p. for membership 1986-87, treas. 1987-88, pres. elect 1988-89, pres. 1989-90), Am. Vocat. Assn., S.C. Vocat. Assn. (parliamentarian 1985-86, v.p. 1989-90, treas. 1991-92), Internat. Soc. Bus. Educators, Lake City C. of C., Kappa Kappa Iota, Delta Kappa Gamma. Democrat. Baptist. Avocations: cross-stitching, reading, softball. Office: Florence County Sch Dist 3 PO Box 1389 Lake City SC 29560-1389 E-mail: lhawkins@florence3.k12.sc.us.

HAWKINS, LORETTA ANN, retired secondary school educator, playwright; b. Winston-Salem, N.C., Jan. 1, 1942; d. John Henry and Laurine (Hines) Sanders; m. Joseph Hawkins, Dec. 10, 1962; children: Robin, Dionne, Sherri. BS in Edn., Chgo. State U., 1965; MA in Lit., Governor's State U., 1977, MA in African Cultures, 1978; MLA in Humanities, U. Chgo., 1998. Cert. tchr., Ill. Tchr. Chgo. Bd. Edn., 1968—2002; lectr. Chgo. City Colls., 1987-89; tchr. English, Gage Park H.S., Chgo., 1988—2002; ret., 2002. Mem. steering com. Mellon Seminar U. Chgo., 1990; tchr. adv. com. Goodman Theatre, Chgo., 1992, mem. cmty. adv. coun., 1996—; spkr. in field; creator 5-4-3-2-1- Essay Writing Method, 1997. Author: (reading workbook) Contemporary Black Heroes, 1992, (plays) Of Quiet Birds, 1993 (James H. Wilson award 1993), Above the Line, 1994, Good Morning, Miss Alex; contbr. poetry, articles to profl. publs.; featured WYCC-TV-Educate, 1996. Mem. Chgo. Tchg. Connections Network, DePaul U. Ctr. Urban Edn., 2001; mem. Chgo. Pub. Schs. Mentoring and Induction of New Tchrs. Program. Fellow Santa Fe Pacific Found., 1988, Lloyd Fry Found. 1989, Andrew W. Mellon Found., 1991, Ill. Arts Coun., 1993; grantee Cmty. Arts Assistance Program Award, Chgo. Dept. Cultural Affairs; recipient Feminist Writers 3d pl. award NOW, 1993, Zora Neale Hurston-Bessie Head Fiction award Black Writer's Conf., 1993, Suave Tchr. Plus award, 2002; numerous others. Mem. AAUW, Nat. Coun. Tchrs. English (spkr. conv.), Am. Fedn. Tchrs., Women's Theatre Alliance, Dramatists Guild of Am., Internat. Women's Writing Guild. Achievements include invention of 5-4-3-2-1 essay writing method. Avocations: films, coins, reading, walking. Home: 8928 S Oglesby Ave Chicago IL 60617-3047

HAWKINS, RALPH G(ERALD), university media administrator, educator; b. Lilbourn, Mo., June 12, 1930; s. Ralph N. and Marguriete (Landreum) H.; m. Dorothy Case, Aug. 6, 1955; children— Randy, Kim, Michael, Christopher. BSMA Kans. State Coll., 1958, MS in Edn., 1967; EdD, U. Ark., 1979. Lab. asst. Kans. State Coll., 1955-58; photo and editor, newspaper, Portageville, Mo., 1959-61; editor, pub. weekly newspapers, Clarkton and Gideon, Mo., 1962-64; dir. photography Kans. State Coll., Pittsburg, 1965-67; dir. graphics No. Ill. U., DeKalb, 1967-69; dir. ednl. media S.W. Mo. State U., Springfield, 1969—, prof. curriculum and instrns. dept., 1969—, supr. Media Ctr., 1983—. Author multi-media show: Ed Media 2001, 1978; contbr. articles to numerous publs. Deacon Presbyterian Ch., Springfield; mem. adv. bd. Springfield Cable TV. Served with USAF, 1951-55; Korea. Mem. Assn. Ednl. Comm. Tech., Mo. Assn. Ednl. Tech., Univ. Club (pres., Springfield), Elks, Kiwanis, Phi Delta Kappa, Tau Kappa Epsilon. Home: 2020 S Oak Grove Ave Springfield MO 65804-2706

HAWKINS-SNEED, JANET LYNN, school psychologist, human resources administrator, small business owner; b. July 3, 1956; d. James Crawford Jr. and Oberia (Aiken) H. BS in Spanish and Psychology, Furman U., 1978; MEd in Secondary Edn., Converse Coll., 1981; EdS in Counseling and Sch. Psychology, Wichita State U., 1986. Tchr. Spartanburg Sch. Dist. 5, Duncan, S.C., 1979-80, Wichita (Kans.) Sch. Dist., 1982-85; psychology intern Mulvane (Kans.) Sch. Dist., 1985-86; sch. psychologist Sch. Dist. Greenville (S.C.) County, 1986-93; with Dyslexia Resource Ctr., Greenville; with benefits dept. Suitt Constrn. Co., Greenville, 1997—98, human resources coord., 1998—99; owner, CEO Mystic Gifts, Williamston, SC. Presenter at profl. confs. Chancellor, Upstate S.C. Ch. of Wicca. Mem. NOW, Coun. Exceptional Children, Nat. Assn. Sch. Psychologists, Sierra Club, Nat. Wildlife Fedn., Phi Kappa Phi. Avocations: music, art, nature, equestrian, breeder of beagles. Home: 305 HI Taylor RD Williamston SC 29697 Office: PO Box 455 Williamston SC 29697

HAWKLAND, WILLIAM DENNIS, law educator; b. Willmar, Minn., Nov. 25, 1920; s. Douglas F. and Lola (Johnston) H.; m. Rosemary Neal, Aug. 27, 1949; children: William Dennis, Stephen D. BS, U. Minn., 1942, JD, 1947, LLD (hon.), 2001; LLM, Columbia U., 1949; docteur honoris causa, France, docteur honoris causa, 1992. Bar: Minn. 1947, Ill. 1961, N.Y. 1970. Asst. prof. U. Tenn. Law Sch., 1949-50; from asst. prof. to prof. Temple U. Law Sch., 1950-56; prof. Rutgers U. Law Sch., 1956-60, Faculté Internat. Pour L'Enseignement Du Droit Compar#250, Strasbourg, France, 1970, U. Ill. Law Sch., 1960-64, 70-79; dean, prof. SUNY Buffalo Law Sch., 1964-67, prof., provost, 1968-70; adv. Dept. State; chancellor, prof. La. State U. Law Ctr., 1979-89, chancellor emeritus, 1989—; prof. univ.-wide Boyd U., 1989—. Vis. prof. UCLA Law Sch., 1956, U. Minn., 1974-75, Tulane U., 1987, Louvain, Belgium, 1988; vis. summer lectr. NYU, 1957, Tex. Law Sch., 1961. Author: (with George Bogert and William Britton) Sales and Security, 1962, A Transactional Guide to the Commercial Code, 1964, Commercial Paper and Bank Deposits and Collections, 1966, Bills and Notes, 1956, Sales an dBulk Sales Under the Uniform Commercial Code, 2d edit., 1959, (with Marion Benfield) Sales, 1979, (with Pierre Loiseaux) Debtor-Creditor Relations, 1979, Commercial Paper and Banking, 1995, Uniform Commercial Code Series, 17 vols., 1986; also articles; permanent editl. bd. Uniform Commercial Code. Bd. dirs. Am. Arbitration Assn.; vice chmn. Rep. com. to elect Senator Kenneth Keating, 1964; advisor revision of P.R. Comml. laws, 1989—. Lt. USNR, 1942-46. Mem. ABA, N.Y. Bar Assn., Minn. Bar Assn., Ill. Bar Assn., Erie County Bar Assn., Am. Law Inst., Order of Coif. Home: 3651 S Lakeshore Dr Baton Rouge LA 70808-3631 Office: La State U Paul M Herbert Law Ctr Baton Rouge LA 70803-0001

HAWKS, JANE ESTHER HOKANSON, nursing educator; b. Sac City, Iowa, Apr. 8, 1955; d. Charles Wesley and Esther Pearl (Langbein) Hokanson; m. Edward Harold Hawks, May 24, 1980; 1 child, Jennifer Jane. BSN magna cum laude, St. Olaf Coll., 1977; postgrad., Iowa State U., 1978-79; MSN magna cum laude, U. Nebr., 1981; D in Nursing Sci. summa cum laude, Widener U., 1993. RN, Iowa; cert. med.-surg. nurse ANA. Nurse Rochester (Minn.) Meth. Hosp., 1976, 77-78; instr. Morningside Coll., Sioux City, Iowa, 1978-79, Jennie Edmundson Sch. Nursing, Council Bluffs, Iowa, 1979-81; instr., asst. prof. Coll. Nursing U. Nebr., Omaha, 1981-86; supr. pvt. duty nursing Family Home Care, Omaha, 1986; instr. Jennie Edmundson Sch. Nursing, Council Bluffs, 1986-88; instr. NCLEX rev. course Stanley H. Kaplan Ednl. Ctr., Omaha, 1986-89; asst. prof. nursing Clarkson Coll., Omaha, 1988-91, assoc. prof., 1991-92; asst. prof. nursing Midland Luth. Coll., Fremont, Nebr., 1992-98, assoc. prof. nursing, 1998—. Mem. Senator Harkin's Nursing Adv. Com., 1989—; mem. edn. com. Omaha Hospice Orgn., 1985-86; bd. dirs. Health Fair Midlands, 1988-95, vice chmn., 1992-94, chmn., 1994-95. Mem. editl. com.: Urologic Nursing, 1988—90, asst. editor:, 1990—95, assoc. editor:, 1995—2000; editor, 2000—, co-author several books, book chpts.; contbr. articles to profl. jours. Bd. dirs. Midwest ARC Regional Blood Svcs., 1992—, sec.-treas., 1995-99, mem. nominations com. 1991-94, tissue donor, med. adv. exec. and fin. coms., 1993—; mem. Iowa Gov.'s Task Force on Long Term Care, 1984-85; bd. dirs. Pottawattamie County chpt. ARC, 1987-93, chmn., 1991-92, AIDS edn. speaker, 1988-93, mem. exec. com., 1991-93, mem. steering com., 1991-93, chmn. nursing and health com., 1988-93, facilitator bd. retreat, 1990. Recipient pub. awareness award Pottawattamie County chpt. ARC, 1988, Vol. of Yr. award Council Bluffs, 1989; scholar Evang. Luth. Ch. Am. div. Higher Edn., 1993, Am. Legion 40 and 8, 1991-92, Nurses Ednl. Funds, Inc., N.Y.C., 1991-92; nursing diagnosis rsch. grantee Midwest Nursing Diagnosis Task Force, 1989. Mem.: AACN, ANA, Iowa Nurses Assn. (state ethics com. 1985—86, state nursing edn. commn. 1989—93, chmn. state nursing rsch. com. 1994—96, profession devel. commn. mem. and chmn. 1996—98, bd. dirs. dist. 9 1985—91, 9th Dist. Nurse of Yr. award 1983, Teresa Christy award 1999), Iowa Nurses Found. (bd. dirs., v.p. 1985—90, grant reviewer 1987—90), Soc. Urologic Nurses and Assocs. (Pres.'s Trophy 2002), Sigma Theta Tau (faculty counselor Theta Omega chpt., Leadership award 1996, Mentor award 2001). Lutheran. Avocations: playing piano, swimming, walking. Home: 514 North St Underwood IA 51576-5026 Office: Midland Luth Coll 900 N Clarkson St Fremont NE 68025-4254

HAWLEY, CHERIE, reading and language arts educator; b. Boise, Idaho, Dec. 19, 1947; d. Jack McCartney Marley and Marilyn (Carlock) Cunningham; 1 child, Brienne DeJong. BS, San Diego State U., 1971; MA, U. Calif., Santa Barbara, 1979, PhD, 1989. Supr. tchr. edn. reading clinic U. Calif., Santa Barbara, 1982-88; from asst. prof. to prof. Calif. State U., L.A., 1989—2001, prof., 2001—, chmn. Dept. Curriculum, 2002—. Contbr. articles to profl. jours. Bd. dirs. So. Calif. chpt., Reading is Fundamental, L.A., 1990-98. Mem. ASCD, Internat. Reading Assn., Am. Ednl. Rsch. Assn., Calif. Reading Assn. (pres. Santa Barbara chpt. 1986-89), Kappa Delta Pi (counselor Iota Phi chpt. 1992-99). Home: 401 Deep Hill Rd Diamond Bar CA 91765-1204 Office: Calif State U LA Charter Coll Edn 5151 State University Dr Los Angeles CA 90032-4226 E-mail: chawley@calstatela.edu.

HAWLEY, ELLIS WAYNE, historian, educator; b. Cambridge, Kans., June 2, 1929; s. Pearl Washington and Gladys Laura (Logsdon) H.; m. Sofia Koltun, Sept. 2, 1953; children— Arnold Jay, Agnes Fay. BA, U. Wichita, 1950; MA, U. Kans., 1951; PhD (research fellow), U. Wis., 1959. Instr. to prof. history North Tex. State U., 1957-68; prof. history Ohio State U., 1968-69, U. Iowa, 1969-94, prof. emeritus, 1994—, chmn. dept. history, 1986-89. Hist. cons. Pub. Papers of the Presidents: Hoover, 1974-78. Author: The New Deal and the Problem of Monopoly, 1966, The Great War and the Search for a Modern Order, 1979, (with others) Herbert Hoover and the Crisis of American Capitalism, 1973, Herbert Hoover as Secretary of Commerce, 1981, Federal Social Policy, 1988, Herbert Hoover and the Historians, 1989; contbr. articles to profl. jours., essays to books Investigator Project to Study Hist. in Iowa Pub. Schs., Iowa City, 1978-79; cons. Quad Cities hist. project Putnam Mus., Davenport, 1978-79. Served to 1st lt. inf. AUS, 1951-53 North Tex. State U. Faculty Devel. grantee, 1967-68, U. Iowa, 1975-76. Mem. Am. Hist. Assn., Orgn. Am. Historians, So. Hist. Assn., AAUP (mem. exec. coun. Iowa chapt. 1982-84), Iowa Hist. Soc. Democrat. Home: 2524 E Washington St Iowa City IA 52245-3724 E-mail: e-hawley@worldnet.att.net.

HAWLEY, HAROLD PATRICK, educational consultant; b. Paducah, Ky., Jan. 8, 1945; s. Mathew Mark and Mae (Herndon) H.; m. Ann Dunbar, 1971 (dec. 1982); Lucrecia Thomas, Aug. 27, 1983; children: Cherise, Charlotte. AA, Paducah Jr. Coll., 1965; BA, U. Ky., 1968; MS, Ind. U., New Albany, 1974; EdD, Ind. U., Bloomington, 1977; postgrad., Mary Baldwin Coll., 1988, Ala. A&M U., 1996. Liaison to adjutant gen. 5th army U.S. Army, Ft. Carson, 1970, Bien Hoa, Vietnam, 1969-70; English tchr. Southwestern Consol. Schs., Hanover, Ind., 1971-73; asst. prin. Whitewater Consol. Sch., Lyons, Ind., 1978-80; assoc. prof., dir. secondary edn. Birmingham (Ala.)-So. Coll., 1980-86, chmn. freshman seminar, 1984-86; 1988-95 Ga. Dept. Edn., Atlanta, 1988-95; evaluator So. Assn. Schs. and Colls., 1988—; ednl. cons. Ga. Dept. Edn., Atlanta, 1988-95; chmn. Effective Sch. Rsch. Program, 1991; asst. prof. elem. edn. program Ala. A&M U., 2000—01, asst. prof. secondary edn. and multicultural edn., 2001—, advisor svc. frat., 2003; dir. Harlem Renaissance Project, Lee H.S., 2003. Adj. prof. Ind. U., Bloomington, 1975-80, Samford U., 1980-84, Auburn U., 1987, U. Ala., Gadsen, 1984-85, Brenau U., Gainesville, Ga., 1988-96, Reinhardt Coll./Brenau Coll. Collaboration, 1995—, Ala. A&M U., 1999, univ. supr., 1996—; cons. Intervarsity Beach Project, 1982—, Ford Ednl. Found., Parker H.S., Birmingham, Ala., 1981-85, Christian Acad., Cornerstone, Baton Rouge, 1983-84, FCA, 1983, Happy Valley Elem., Fairview Elem. Schoolwide Project, 1995, Walker County Curriculum Specialist, 1995-96, Nicholas Soc., 1997—; tech. advisor Polk County Schoolwide Projects, 1995; ednl. cons. Ga. Dept. Edn., Atlanta, 1988-95; coord. 9th Dist. Schs. of Excellence, Ga., 1988-92; ednl. cons. Effective Schs. Rsch./Authentic Ins.; team leader sch. improvement teams Ga. Dept. Edn., Calhoun, 1995; numerous ESEA Instrnl. Confs., Ga., 1993-94; presenter ESEA Instrnl. Conf., Statesboro, 1994, Carrolton, Ga., 1995; dir. 1st State Remedial Edn. Conf., Lafayette, Ga., 1994; dir. 1st statewide instrnl. conf. ESEA, 1995-96, Lone Oak Edn. Svcs., 1998; participant Inst. for Comm. Seminars, Birmingham So. Coll., 1983-86; tech. advisor Floyd County Schoolwide Project, 1995—, Dade County Schoolwide Project, 1996; student tchr. supr. Covenant Coll., Chattanooga, 1996—; dir. Title I Northwest Ga. Instrnl. Conf., 1996; ednl. cons. Attention Deficit Disorder/HD, 1995—; dir. Lone Oak Edn. Svcs. 1999—; rsch. asst. North Ala. Tchr. Exch., Normal, Ala., 2000—; featured presenter, Mutt Intell, 2003, ALA convention of English Tchrs., 2003; presenter in field. Author: (with Don Manlove) Classroom Climate Teacher-Student Relations, Expectancy Effects, 1976; rsch. asst. (with Floyd Coppedge) Binford Middle School Project, Bloomington, Ind., 1976, Individual Instrn. Project, 1975, Lebanon High Sch. Project, 1975-76, Katherine Hamilton Rsch. Project, New Albany, Ind., 1974 (with Carol Lewis). Bd. dirs. Boys Club of Am., Paducah, Ky., 1963-65; tech. adv. Polk County Consolidated Schs., 1995-96, Dade County Consolidated Schs., 1995. Basketball scholar, 1965, attention deficit rsch. scholar univ. supr., Ala. A&M U., 1997—; Spenser grantee, 1981, Mellon grantee, 1985; grad fellow Okla. State Sch. Supt.,1975-77, Nat. Study Sch. Evaluation fellow Ind. U., 1977. Mem. Ga. Com. Leaders Assn., Internat. Platform Assn., Phi Delta Kappa. Avocations: jogging, basketball, camping. Home: 117 Darlington Rd NE Huntsville AL 35801-1513

HAWLEY, H(ARRISON) BRADFORD, physician, educator; b. Newton, Mass., Aug. 1, 1943; s. Harry and Dorothy (LaBelle) H.; m. Christine Juno, June 5, 1971. AB, Dartmouth Coll., 1965; MD, Med. Coll. Va., 1969. Diplomate Am. Bd. Internal Medicine, Am. Bd. Infectious Diseases, Cert. Bd. Infection Control, 1983-2002. Intern, med. resident R.I. Hosp., Providence, 1969-71; infectious disease fellow U. Vt., Burlington, 1971-73; asst. prof. W.Va. U., Charleston, 1976-79; assoc. prof. Wright State U., Dayton, Ohio, 1979-87, prof., 1987-99, prof. emeritus, 1999—; dir. med. edn. Good Samaritan Hosp., Dayton, 1984-90, hosp. epidemiologist, 1987-90; med. dir. STD Clinic, Montgomery (Ohio) County, 1991-99. Bd. dirs. Certification Bd. Infection Ctr., 1997-99; chief infectious diseases Charleston div. W.Va. U., 1976-79, Wright State U., 1979-99. Assoc. editor: Clinical Medicine, 1988; (newsletter) Infectious Diseases, 1990-96; sr. editor Antimicrobics and Infectious Diseases Newsletter, 1996-2002; mem. editl. bd. Am. Jour. Infection Control, 2003-; contbr. articles to profl. jours., chpts. to books. Maj. U.S. Army, 1973-76. Fellow ACP (emeritus), Am. Coll. Chest Physicians, Infectious Diseases Soc. Am.; mem. Am. Soc. Microbiology, Soc. Hosp. Epidemiologists Am., Am. Sealyham Terrier Club (chair health com. 1995-96, 98-99). Republican. Avocations: breeding and showing dogs, photography, golf, tennis, computers. Home: 6761 Trailview Dr Dayton OH 45414-2165 Office: Miami Valley Hosp 128 E Apple St Dayton OH 45409-2902

HAWLEY, TOM, retired military officer, state agency administrator, educator; married; 3 children. BA, S.D.State U.; MA, U. No. Colo; PhD, U. Tex., Austin. Instr. various USAF Bases, 1977—97; dean Dakota State U.'s Coll. Edn, Madison, SD, 1997—. Acting sec. S.D. Dept. Edn. and Cultural Affairs., SD, 2003. Office: Dept Edn and Cultural Affairs 700 Governors Dr Pierre SD 57501 Address: Coll of Edn Office KC 149 Madison SD 57042 E-mail: Tom.Hawley@dsu.edu.

HAWN, MICAELA (MICKI HAWN), mathematics educator; b. Mobile, Ala., July 13, 1945; d. Lowell Oliver and F. Lemoine (Williams) Brummitt; 1 child, Douglas S. McKay, Jr. BS, U. South Ala., 1967, MA, 1972; EdS, Barry U., 1995. Tchr. Murphy H.S., Mobile, 1967-69; tchr., dept. chair Hillsdale Mid. Sch., Mobile, 1969-87; tchr. Deerfield Beach (Fla.) Mid. Sch., 1987-88; tchr., team leader, competitions coord. Parkway Mid. Sch., HiTech Magnet, Ft. Lauderdale, 1988-96; tchr., dept. chairperson, gifted coord. Pompano Beach (Fla.) Broadcast & Comms. Magnet Sch., 1996—. Tchr. Dauphin Way Methodist Ch., Mobile, 1970-87. Mem. ASCD, AAUW, Internat. Soc. Tech. in Edn., Nat. Coun. Tchrs. Math., Fla. Assn. Computer Educators, Mensa, Alumni Assn., Phi Delta Kappa. Methodist. Avocations: fitness, bridge, computers. Home: 1629 Coral Ridge Dr Coral Springs FL 33071-

HAWORTH, DALE KEITH, art history educator, gallery director; b. Denver, Sept. 8, 1924; s. Murle Calvin and Hildur Elizabeth (Lindquist) H.; m. Ruth Anne Cushing, July 25, 1948 (div. 1980); children: Brooke Karen, Leah Anne, Nicholas Cushing; m. Karen Friedmann Beall, Dec. 31, 1983. BS in Edn., Washington U., 1950, MA, 1951; PhD, U. Iowa, 1960. Instr. art history Washington U., St. Louis, 1951-53, fellow in charge of exhbns., 1954-56; instr. art history Beloit (Wis.) Coll., 1953-54, U. Iowa, Iowa City, 1957-60; prof. art history Carleton Coll., Northfield, Minn., 1960—77, 1979—96, dir. exhbns., 1979-96; acting chief, prints and photographs div. Libr. Congress, Washington, 1977-79; now prof. emeritus Carleton Coll., Northfield, Minn. Vis. prof. art history U. Pa., Phila., 1961, 63, U. Minn., Mpls., 1970-71, 73-74; vis. prof. humanities Internat. Christian U., Tokyo, 1990; vis. scholar art history Doshisha U., Kyoto, Japan, 1983, 94; cons. Kress Found., Ohio, 1964; mem. com. for developing advanced placement exam. in history of art Coll. Bd., 1991-93; reader, table leader art history Ednl. Testing Svc., 1990-93. Contbr. articles to profl. jours. V.p. Northfield Arts Guild, 1964-66, pres. Northfield Parents Council, 1970. Served as staff sgt. USAAF, 1943-46, PTO. Fulbright scholar, 1956-57, 1962; research grantee HEW, 1967-68; vis. scholarship U.S. Friendship Commn., 1983. Mem. Archeol. Inst. Am., Sch. Am. Rsch., Coll. Art Assn. Avocation: drawing. E-mail: kouveli@aol.com.

HAWS, ELIZABETH ANNE, education administrator, school psychologist; b. Willingboro, N.J., Mar. 30, 1970; d. William Joseph and Mary Ruth (Datko) H. BA in Edn. of the Handicapped, Kean U., 1992; MA in Sch. Psychology, Rowan U., 1998, supr. curriculum and instrn., 2000, EdS, 2001, EdD in Ednl. Leadership, 2004. Spl. edn. tchr. Willingboro Bd. Edn., NJ, 1992—98, peer mediation supr., 1994—95, peer mediation coord., 1996—98, sch. psychologist, 1998—2000; supr. Union County ESC, Westfield, NJ, 2000—03; supr. CST Eastampton Bd. Edn., NJ, 2003—. Mem.: NJPSA (N.J. Prin. and Supr. Assn.), NJASP (N.J. Assn. Sch. Psychologists), NASP (Nat. Assn. Sch. Psychologists), CEC (Coun. Exceptional Children) (chpt. 461 programming com. 1988—89, pres. 1989—91, treas. 1991—92), Burlington County Red Cross Disaster Relief Team, PADI (Profl. Assn. Dive Instructors), Cara Irish Soc., Alpha Epsilon Lambda Nat. Honor Soc. Grad. and Profl. Students, Sigma Beta Chi. Republican. Roman Catholic. Avocations: writing, bicycling, walking, travel, collecting catchy quotations. Home: 2402 Sanibel Cir Palmyra NJ 08065-2129 Office: 1 Student Dr Eastampton NJ 08060

HAX, ARNOLDO CUBILLOS, management educator, industrial engineer; b. Santiago, Chile, Aug. 9, 1936; came to U.S., 1961; s. Egon and Adela (Cubillos) H.; m. Neva Mimica, Jan. 28, 1962; children: Andrew, Neva. Degree in Indsl. Engring. with highest honors, Cath. U. Chile, Santiago, 1960; MS in Insdl. Engring., U. Mich., 1963; PhD in Ops. Rsch., U. Calif., Berkeley, 1967. Asst. prof. math. Sch. Engring., Cath. U. Chile, 1960-61, dir., assoc. prof. Ops. Rsch., 1963-65; asst. specialist Ops. Rsch. Ctr. U. Calif., Berkeley, 1965-67; mgmt. cons. ops. rsch. Arthur D. Little, Inc., Cambridge, Mass., 1976-70; lectr. Bus. Sch. Harvard U., Boston, 1970-72; assoc. prof. Sloan Sch. Mgmt., MIT, Cambridge, 1972-76, prof., 1976—, Alfred P. Sloan prof., 1985—, dep. dean, 1987-90; Thomas Henry Carroll Ford Found. vis. prof. bus. Harvard Bus. Sch., 1993-94. Indsl. engr. Chilean Inst. Steel, Santiago, 1960-61; lectr. linear programming Centro Interam. de Ensenanza de Estadistica, Santiago, 1963-65; cons. ops. rsch. and stats. CADE, Santiago, 1963-65; cons. stategic planning processes Digital Equipment Corp., Motorola, GM, Citibank, Westinghouse Electric, others in U.S., Europe, Mex., S.Am., Can.; Ford Found. vis. prof. bus. sch. Harvard U., 1993-94. Co-author: (with D. Candea) Production and Inventory Management, 1984 (Inst. Indsl. Engrs.-Joint Pubs. Book of Yr. award 1985), (with N. Majluf) The Strategy Concept and Process: A Pragmatic Approach, 1991, 2d edit., 1996, Strategic Management: An Integrative Perspective, 1984, (with D. Wilde) The Delta Project: Discovering New Sources of Profitability in a Networked Economy, 2001; author: (with others) Manuale di Gestione della Produzione, 1975, Studies in Management Science, Vol. 1, Logistics, 1975, Modern Trends in Logistics Research, 1976, Applied Mathematical Programming, 1977, Conflicting Objectives in Decisions, 1977, Handbook of Operations Research, 1978, Studies in Operations Management, 1978 (also editor), Disaggregation: Problem in Manufacturing and Service Organizations, 1979, Applications of Management Science, Vol. 1, 1981, The Management Handbook, 1981, Implementation of Stategic Planning, 1982, Production Handbook, 1987; editor: Readings in Strategic Management, 1984, Planning Strategies That Work, 1987; strategic mgmt. editor Interface jour., 1981—; former editor Ops. Rsch. jour., Naval Rsch. Logistics Quar.; contbr. numerous articles to profl. jours. and publs. Thomas Henry Carroll Ford Found. vis. prof. bus. Harvard U. Bus. Sch., Cambridge. Mem. Inst. Mgmt. Scis., Ops. Rsch. Soc., Am. Inst. Indsl. Engrs., AAAS, Am. Inst. Decision Scis., Vineyard Haven Yacht and Tennis Club, Alpha Pi Mu. Home: 242 Otis St Newton MA 02465-2525 Office: MIT Sloan Sch Mgmt 50 Memorial Dr Cambridge MA 02142-1347

HAY, GEORGE AUSTIN, actor, artist, musician, director; b. Johnstown, Pa., Dec. 25, 1915; s. George and Mary Louise (Austin) H. BS, U. Pitts., 1938; postgrad., U. Rochester, 1939; MLitt, U. Pitts., 1948; MA, Columbia U., 1948. Dir. Jr. League hosp. shows, N.Y.C., 1948-53. Producer, dir. off-Broadway prodns., 1953-55; motion picture casting dir. for Dept. Def. films, Astoria Studios, N.Y., 1955-70, motion picture producer-dir., U.S. Dept. Transp., Washington, 1973—, Office Presdl. Personnel, The White House, 1993—; group exhbns. of paintings and sculpture include, Lincoln Ctr., N.Y.C., 1965, Parrish Art Mus., Southampton, N.Y., 1969, Carnegie Inst., 1972, Duncan Galleries, N.Y.C., 1973, Bicentennial Exhbn. Am. Painters, Paris, 1976, Chevy Chase Gallery, 1979, Watergate Gallery, 1981, Le Salon des Nations a Paris, 1983; rep. permanent collections, Met. Mus. Art, N.Y.C., Library Congress, also, pvt. collections; bibliog. reference to works pub. in History of Internat. Art, 1982; author, illustrator: Seven Hops to Australia, 1945, The Moving Image, A Career in Pictures, 1990; Dir.: Bicentennial documentary Highways of History, 1976; dir.: film World Painting in Museum of Modern Art, 1972; Composer: Rhapsody in E Flat for piano and strings, 1950; writer: TV program Nat. Council Chs., 1965; Broadway appearances include: What Every Woman Knows, 1954; original Broadway run of Inherit the Wind, 1955-57; created role of Prof. Fiveash in premiere of The Acrobats, White Barn Theater, Westport, Conn., 1961; feature films include: North by Northwest, 1959, Murder, Inc., 1960, Pretty Boy Floyd, 1960, The Landlord, 1970, Child's Play, 1971, Chekhov's The Bet, 1978, Being There, 1980, No Way Out, 1986, Her Alibi, 1988, Air Force One, 1997, Guarding Tess, 1994, Contact, 1997 The Contender, 2000, Head of State, 2003; TV appearances include Am. Heritage, 1961, Americans-A Portrait in Verses, 1962, Naked City, 1962, U.S. Steel Hour, 1963, Another World, 1965, Edge of Night, 1968, As the World Turns, 1969, Love Is a Many-Splendored Thing, 1972, The Adams Chronicles, 1976, A Woman Named Jackie, 1991; piano soloist in concerts and recitals, 1937; performer Cruise Ship, Europe, 1938; author, illustrator: The Arts Scene; contbr. articles to periodicals. App. time adv. panel, pres.'s coun. Col.

William and Mary; mem. World Affairs Coun., Am. Archit. Found.; bd. govs. Home of Pres. James Monroe; trustee Home of Pres. James Monroe; mus. donor turn-of-century doctor's office from estate of surgeon father; With AUS, 1942—46; PTO; bd. dirs. Washington Film Coun. Recipient Loyal Svc. award Jr. League, 1953, St. Bartholomew's Silver Leadership award, 1966, Gold medal Accademia Italia, 1980, Smithsonian Instn. Pictorial award, 1982; Fed. Govt. Honor award in recognition 45 yrs. dedicated svc., 2000; subject of biog. work: Austin Hay, Adventures of a Christmas Child, 1970. Mem. NATAS, AFTRA, SAG, Am. Artists Profl. League, Allied Artists Am., Internat. Bach Soc., Beethoven Soc. (bd. dirs.), Nat. Soc. Arts and Letters (bd. dirs.), Music Libr. Assn., Nat. Symphony Orch. Assn., Actors Equity Assn., Nat. Trust Hist. Preservation, SAR, Nat. Parks and Conservation Assn., Shakespeare Oxford Soc., St. Andrew's Soc., Victorian Soc. (bd. dirs.), Cambria County Hist. Soc., Am. Philatelic Soc., Am. Mus. Moving Image, Jimmy Stewart Mus. (Indiana, Pa.), English Speaking Union (bd. dirs.), Nat. Arts Club (N.Y.C.), Players Club (N.Y.C.), Nat. Travel Club, Columbia U. Club, Nat. Press Club, Arts Club of Washington, Cosmos Club, Classic Car Club Am., Nat. Naval Med. Command, Sigma Chi, Phi Mu Alpha.

HAY, LEROY E. school system administrator; BA in Secondary English Edn., SUNY, Cortland, 1966; MA in Theatre, U. Conn., 1971, 6th-yr. cert. in adminstrn., 1977, PhD in Secondary Edn., 1978. Tchr. English, Marcellus (N.Y.) High Sch., 1966-68, Manchester (Conn.) High Sch., 1968-89, chmn. dept., 1983-89, interim. vice prin., 1988-89; asst. supt. schs. East Lyme (Conn.) Pub. Schs., 1989-92, acting supt., 1990; supt. schs. Windsor Locks (Conn.) Pub. Schs., 1992-93; asst. supt. schs. Wallingford (Conn.) Pub. Schs., 1993—2003; founding faculty mem. MS program in edn. innovation and tech. Walden U., 1994—; pres. ASCD, Alexandria, Va., 2000—01; dir. Conn. alt. rte. to cert. program Dept. Higher Edn., Hartford, Conn., 2003—. Adj. instr. Boston Coll., 1987—, U. Conn., Sacred Heart U., Bridgeport, Conn., Manchester C.C. cons. on English teaching Granby (Conn.) Pub. Schs., 1988; mem. English adv. bd. Conn. Dept. Edn., 1987-90; mem. adv. bd. Conn. Inst. for Tchr. Evaluation, 1987-89; mem. Presdl. Scholars Commn., 1983-84; grant reviewer U.S. Dept. Edn.; mem. nat. adv. bd. Project 6 Found., Nat. Ctr. for Innovative Ednl. Media., 1987-93. Author: (with Richard Zboray) Complete Communication Skills, 1992; contbg. author: The Shape of Things to Come: Employment and Higher Education to the Year 2000, 1988; editor: (with Arthur Roberts) Curriculum For the New Millennium, 1988, 2d edit., 1994; mem. editorial adv. bd. Edn. Digest, 1984-86; contbr. articles to profl. publs. Mem. Conn. Gov.'s Commn. on Equity and Excellence in Edn., 1984-85, Congl. Task Force on Merit Pay, 1984; judge Birmingham Internat. Ednl. Film Festival, 1984. Named Nat. Tchr. of Yr., 1983, Disting. alumnus SUNY at Cortland and U. Conn. Mem. ASCD (bd. dirs. 1990—, exec. coun. 1996-99, pres.-elect 1999—), nat. conv. adv. com. 1990-92), Conn. ASCD (bd. dirs. 1988-90, v.p. 1990-92, pres. 1992-94), World Future Soc., U. Conn. Alumni Assn., Phi Delta Kappa. Home: 33 Risley Rd Vernon CT 06066-5924 Office: Dept Higher Education 61 Woodland St Hartford CT 06105-2326*

HAYASHI, TADAO, engineering educator; b. Toyohashi, Aichi-ken, Japan; s. Yoshio and Matsue Hayashi; m. Fumi Imoto, May 15, 1950; children: Hidetaka, Fumihiko; m. Sumiko Sano, Oct. 25, 1981. BS, Tokyo U. Lit. and Sci., 1948, MS, 1950; D Engring., Tokyo Inst. Tech., 1963. Rsch. asst. Naniwa U., Osaka, Japan, 1950-52; rsch. assoc. Ohio State U., Columbus, 1952-54, U. Osaka Prefecture, 1955-63, asst. prof., 1964-68, prof. engring., 1969-86, prof. emeritus, 1986—. Co-author: Electroplating, 1980, Properties of Electrodeposits, 1986, Testbook of Electroplating, 1987. Recipient Gold medal Electrochem. Soc. Japan, 1977; Best Paper award Metal Finishing Soc. Japan, 1966, 84, Silver medal award Am. Electroplaters and Surface Finishers Soc., 1986, Sci. Achievement award, 1990. Mem. Electroplaters Tech. Assn., Electroplaters and Surface Finishers Soc. (internat. liaison rsch. bd. 1982-96), Internat. Soc. Electrochemistry, Surface Finishing Soc. Japan. Avocations: tennis, golf. Home: 4-17-17 Tezukayama-Minami Nara 631 Japan

HAYASHIDA, RALPH FRANCIS, educational publishing company executive; b. South Pasadena, Calif., Oct. 25, 1935; s. Francis Xavier and Carmen (De la Torre) H.; children: Maria, Matthew, Andrew. BS in Journalism, Marquette U., 1957. Editor Sci. Rsch. Assocs., Chgo., 1961-67; exec. editor D.C. Heath and Co., Lexington, Mass., 1968-73; editor-in-chief Merrill Pub. Co., Columbus, Ohio, 1973-76; v.p., mng. dir. J.B. Lippincott Co., Phila., 1976-78; v.p., dir. elem. pub. Ginn and Co., Lexington, 1978-84; editorial dir. Amsco Sch Publs., N.Y.C., 1985—. With U.S. Army, 1958-61. Mem. Nat. Coun. for History Edn., Nat. Coun. for Social Studies, Internat. Reading Assn. Home: 141 Grove St Apt I Stamford CT 06901-1899

HAYCOCK, CHRISTINE ELIZABETH, retired medical educator, health educator; b. Mt. Vernon, N.Y., Jan. 7, 1924; d. John B. and Madeline (Sears) H.; m. Sam Moskowitz, July 6, 1958 (dec. Apr. 1997). SB, U. Chgo., 1948; MD, SUNY, Bklyn., 1952; MA in Polit. Sci., Rutgers U., 1981. RN, N.J.; diplomate Am. Bd. Surgery. Intern Walter Reed Army Med. Ctr., Washington, 1952-53; resident in surgery St. Barnabas Med. Ctr., Newark, 1954-58, St. John's Episcopal Hosp., Bklyn., 1958-59; pvt. practice Newark, 1959-68; asst. prof. surgery, N.J. Med. Sch. U. Med. and Dentistry N.J.-N.J. Med. Sch., Newark, 1968-75; assoc. prof. surgery, N.J. Med. Sch. UMDNJ, Newark, 1975-89, prof. clin. surgery, 1989-92; prof. emeritus, 1992—. Chief GYN Svc., VA Hosp., East Orange, N.J. Trauma Soc.; pres. Med. Amature Radio Coun., 1981, bd. dirs. (Coun. award 1978); mem. editl. bd. Jour. N.J. Med. Soc., 1979-95, The Physician and Sports Medicine, 1975-98, The Main Event, 1987; adv. com. N.J. Phys. Conditioning of the Police Tng. Commn., 1984-96. Editor: Trauma and Pregnancy, 1985, Sports Medicine for the Athletic Female, 1980; contbr. articles to profl. jours. Chmn. bd. Essex County chpt. Am. Cancer Soc., West Orange, N.J., 1978-79, bd. mgrs., Livingston, N.J., 1962—, hon. life mem., 1992. With U.S. Army, 1947-86, col. Res. ret. Recipient Outstanding Alumnae award Bloomfield Coll., 1971, Res. Forces Achievement award, 1974, Distinguished Lecturer award Downstate Med. Ctr., 1976, Dr. Frank L. Babbott Meml. award SUNY Alumni Assn., 1982, Pres. Honor citation, N.J. Assn. Phys. Edn. and Health Tchrs., 1982, Commendation medal, 1982, Meritorious Svc. medal, 1986, Presdl. Citation, N.J. Assn. for Health, Phys. Edn. and Recreation, 1984, Med. Bd. Svc. award Newark City Hosp., 1986, Bertha Van Hoosen award Am. Med. Women's Assn., 1997; grantee Abbott Labs, 1981-82. Fellow ACS (hon., life, N.J. com. on trauma 1970-91), Am. Coll. Sports Medicine (trustee 1978-80), Photog. Soc. Am. (chmn. video/motion picture divsn. 1993-95; Silver medal jour. award 2000, 02); mem. AMA, Am. Med. Women's Assn. (bd. dirs. 1976-86, pres. 1980, hosp. assn. com. 1985—, Silver Medallion award 1980), Zonta Internat., Assn. Women Surgeons (treas. 1989-91, chair found. com. 1991-95, sec. 1995-99, Disting. Surgeon award 1990), N.J. Women's Assn. (pres. 1976, treas. 1989-92, Woman of Yr. 1987), Amateur Radio Relay League. Republican. Avocations: photography, dog training and showing, sports, collecting elephants, amateur radio. Home: 361 Roseville Ave Newark NJ 07107-1721

HAYCOCK, KENNETH ROY, education educator, sonsultant, administrator; b. Hamilton, Ont., Can., Feb. 15, 1948; s. Bruce Frederick T. and Doris Marion P. (Downham) H.; m. Sheila Tripp, Jan. 28, 1990. BA, U. Western Ont., 1968, diploma in edn., 1969; specialist cert., U. Toronto, Can., 1971; MEd, U. Ottawa, Can., 1973; AMLS, U. Mich., 1974; EdD, Brigham Young U., 1991. Tchr., dept. head Glebe Collegiate Inst., Ottawa, 1969-70, Col. By Secondary Sch., Ottawa, 1970-72; cons. Wellington County Bd. Edn., Guelph, Ont., 1972-76; coord. libr. svcs., supr. instrn. Vancouver (B.C.) Sch. Bd., Canada, 1976-84, acting mgr., elem./secondary edn., 1984-85, dir. instrn., head program svcs., 1985-89, 91-92; prin. Waverley Elem. Sch., 1989-91; prof. Sch. Libr., Archival and Info. Studies U. B.C., Vancouver, 1992—, dir., 1992—2002. Instr. univs. and colls.; pres. Ken Haycock and Assocs., Inc. Editor Tchr. Libr.; author various books; contbr. articles to profl. and scholarly jours. Trustee Guelph Pub. Libr., 1975-76; trustee West Vancouver Sch. Bd., 1993-99, chair, 1994-97, councilor Dist. of West Vancouver, 1999-2002; trustee West Vancouver Pub. Libr., 1999-2001. Recipient award Beta Phi Mu, 1976, Queen Elizabeth Silver Jubilee medal, 1977. Fellow: Can. Coll. Tchrs.; mem.: ASCD (urban curriculum leaders 1985—92, internat. panel 1990—94), ALA (coun. 1995—99, exec. bd. 1999—2003, Herbert and Virginia White Advocacy award 2001), Coun. for Can. Learning Resources (pres. 1995—98), Internat. Assn. Sch. Librarianship (dir. N.Am. 1993—95, exec. dir. 1995—2000, Ken Haycock Leadership Devel. award named in his honor 2001), B.C. Libr. Assn. (Ken Haycock Student Conf. award named in his honor 1999), Assn. for Libr. and Info. Sci. Edn. (sec. coun. dean and dirs. 1993—96), Ont. Libr. Assn., Can. Libr. Assn. (life; pres. 1977—78, Outstanding Svc. award 1991), B.C. Sch. Libr. Assn. (Ken Haycock Profl. Devel. award named in his honor 1984, Disting. Svc. award 1989), Can. Sch. Libr. Assn. (pres. 1974—75, Margaret B. Scott award of merit 1979, rsch. award 1984, Disting. Sch. Adminstr. award 1989, rsch. award 1995), Am. Assn. Sch. Librs. (pres. 1997—98, Baker and Taylor Disting. Svc. award 1996), Internat. Fedn. Libr. Assns. and Instns. (sect. on Edn. and Tng. 1997—, chair 1999—2001), Phi Delta Kappa (Young Leader in Edn. award). Home: 5118 Meadfeild Rd West Vancouver BC Canada V7W 3G2 Office: U BC Sch Libr Arch & Info 854C-1956 Main Mall Vancouver BC Canada V6T 1Z1 E-mail: ken.haycock@ubc.ca.

HAYDEN, COLLEEN, advanced placement secondary school educator; b. Delano, Minn., June 13, 1940; d. F. Milton and Frances (Pianko) H. BA, Coll. St. Catherine, 1962. Tchr. Bloomington (Minn.) Pub. Schs., Xavier H.S., Appleton, Wis.; chair social studies dept. Jefferson H.S., Bloomington. Adult edn. tchr. SHAPE, 1978—. Dep. edn. state literacy trainer Literacy Minn.; mem. several coms., past-chairperson coun. adminstrn. and edn. Ch. of St. Joseph. Cert. tchr., Minn. Mem. ASCD, Nat. Coun. Social Studies, Minn. Coun. Social Studies, Minn. Hist. Soc., Pi Gamma Mu.

HAYDEN, DOLORES, author, architect, educator; b. N.Y.C., Mar. 15, 1945; d. J. Francis and Katharine (McCabe) H.; m. Peter Horsey Marris, May 18, 1975; 1 child, Laura Hayden Marris. BA, Mt. Holyoke Coll., 1966; diploma in English studies, Cambridge (Eng.) U., 1967; LHD (hon.), Mt. Holyoke Coll., 1987; MArch, Harvard U., 1972; MA (hon.), Yale U., 1991. Registered architect. Lectr. U. Calif., Berkeley, 1973; assoc. prof. MIT, Cambridge, 1973-79; prof. UCLA, 1979-91, Yale U., New Haven, 1991—. Author: Seven American Utopias, 1976, The Grand Domestic Revolution, 1981, Redesigning the American Dream, 1984 (notable book award ALA, 1984, award for outstanding publ. in urban planning Assn. Collegiate Schs. of Planning 1986), rev. edit., 2002, The Power of Place: Urban Landscapes as Public History, 1995 (Assn. Am. Pubs. award), Playing House, 1998, Line Dance, 2001, Building Suburbia, 2003; also articles (Best Feature Article award Jour. Am. Planning Assn. 1994). Guggenheim fellow, 1981, Rockefeller Humanities fellow, 1980, ACLS/Ford fellow, 1989, Nat. Endowment for the Humanities fellow; recipient Radcliffe Grad. Soc. medal, 1991, Preservation award L.A. Conservancy, 1986, Vesta award Woman's Bldg., L.A., 1985, Design Rsch. award Nat. Endowment for the Arts, Feminist scholarship in the arts. Mem. Am. Studies Assn., Orgn. Am. Historians, Am. Planning Assn. (Diana Donald award 1987, various awards L.A. and Calif. chpts.), Urban History Assn. (dir. 1991-93). Avocations: travel, poetry. Office: Yale Univ Sch Architecture PO Box 208242 180 York St New Haven CT 06520-8242 E-mail: dolores.hayden@yale.edu.

HAYDEN, LINDA C. librarian, educator; b. Hazard, Ky. d. Walter H. and Nancy Catherine (Gott) Combs. BA, Coll. of William and Mary, 1966; MA in Teaching, Spalding U., 1976, postgrad., 1987; MSLS, U. Ky., 2002. Cert. elem. and early childhood edn. tchr., Ky., cert. public mgr., Governmental Svc. Ctr., Ky. Tchr. York County Pub. Schs., Poquoson, Va., 1966-67; asst. coord. children's svcs. Louisville Free Pub. Libr., 1969-74; tchr. Ursuline Spl. Edn. Ctr., Louisville, 1975-79; tchr., owner Multi-Handicapped Tutoring, Louisville, 1979-80; tchr. J-Town Presch., Inc., Jeffersontown, Ky., 1983-84; therapist Pine Tree Villa Nursing Home, Louisville, 1982-84; asst. prin., tchr. Brown's Lane Acad., Louisville, 1984-86; tchr. Jefferson County Pub. Schs., Louisville, 1986-94; access svcs. libr., reference adn interlibr. loan libr., acad. libr., asst. prof. Ky. State U., 1994—. Part-time pub. rels. and outreach asst. Ky. Commn. on Cmty. Volunteerism and Svc., 1998-99. Vol. tutor ESL with refugees, 1990-91. Mem.: ALA, Leadership Edn. Alumni Assn., Internat. Soc. for Tech. in Edn., Amnesty Internat., Pi Lambda Theta. Democrat. Avocations: music, sports, outdoors, cooking, computers.

HAYDUK, JOHN MATTHEW, English and journalism educator; b. Gary, Ind., Oct. 2, 1953; s. Michael and Dorothy Hayduk; m. Patricia Ann Cook, Nov. 5, 1977. BS in Edn., Ind. U., Gary, 1988, MS in Edn., 1996. Lic. tchr., Ind. Electrician U.S. Steel, Gary, 1974-85; tchr. Sch. City East Chgo., Ind., 1989-91, Duneland Sch. Corp., Chesterton, Ind., 1991—. Named Most Influential Tchr., 5% Club, 1993, 95, 96, 98, 99, 2002, 03. Mem. NEA, Ind. State Tchrs. Assn., Duneland Tchrs. Assn., Ind. U. Alumni Assn., Ind. U. N.W. Alumni Assn., Columbia Scholastic Press Advisers Assn., Nat. Parks Conservation Assn., Kappa Delta Pi. Roman Catholic. Avocations: classic automobiles, reading, astronomy, music. Home: 2009 Chamblee Dr Valparaiso IN 46383-3801 Office: Chesterton HS 2125 S 11th St Chesterton IN 46304-8934 E-mail: john.hayduk@duneland.k12.in.us.

HAYES, ALICE BOURKE, academic administrator, biologist, educator; b. Chgo., Dec. 31, 1937; d. William Joseph and Mary Alice (Cawley) Bourke; m. John J. Hayes, Sept. 2, 1961 (dec. July 1981). BS, Mundelein Coll., Chgo., 1959; MS, U. Ill., 1960; PhD, Northwestern U., 1972; DSc (honoris causa), Loyola U., Chgo., 1994; HHD (honoris causa), Fontbonne Coll., 1994; LHD (honoris causa), Mount St. Mary Coll., 1998; DSc (hon.), St. Louis U., 2002. Rschr. Mcpl. Tb San., Chgo., 1960-62; faculty Loyola U., Chgo., 1962-87, chmn. dept., 1968-77, dean natural scis. div., 1977-80, assoc. acad. v.p., 1980-87, v.p. acad. affairs, 1987-89; provost, exec. v.p. St. Louis U., 1989-95; pres. U. San Diego, 1995—2003, pres. emerita, 2003—. Mem. space biology program NASA, 1980—86; mem. adv. panel NSF, 1977—81, Parmly Hearing Inst., 1986—89; del. Bot. Del. to South Africa, 1984, to People's Republic of China, 1988, to USSR, 1990; reviewer Coll. Bd. and Mellon Found. Nat. Hispanic Scholar Awards, 1985—86; bd. dirs. Pulitzer Pub. Co., Loyola U. Chgo., San Diego Found., Jack-in-the-Box, ConAgra. Co-author books; contbr. articles to profl. publs. Campaign mem. Mental Health Assn. Ill., Chgo., 1973-89; trustee Chgo.-No. Ill. divsn. Nat. Multiple Sclerosis Soc., 1981-89, bd. dirs., 1988-88, com. chmn., sec. to bd. dirs., vice chmn. bd. dirs.; trustee Regina Dominican Acad., 1984-89, Civitas Dei Found., 1987-92, Rockhurst Coll., Loyola U., Chgo., San Diego Found.; trustee St. Ignatius Coll. Prep. Sch., bd. dirs., 1984-89, sec., vice chmn.; bd. dirs. Urban League Met. St. Louis, St. Louis Sci. Ctr., 1991-95, Cath. Charities St. Louis, 1992-95, St. Louis County Hist. Soc., 1992-95, Cath. Charities San Diego, 1996—, San Diego Hist. Soc., 1996—, Old Globe Theater, 1996—, also trustee. Named to Teachers' Hall of Fame Blue Key Soc.; fellow in botany U. Ill., 1959-60; fellow in botany NSF, 1969-71; grantee Am. Orchid Soc., 1967; grantee HEW, 1969, 76; grantee NSF, 1975; grantee NASA, 1980-85. Mem. AAAS, AAUP (corp. rep. 1980-85), Am. Assn. for Higher Edn., Am. Assn. Univ. Adminstrs. (mem. program com. nat. meeting 1988), Am. Soc. Gravitational and Space Biology, Assn. Midwest Coll. Biology Teachers, Am. Soc. Plant Physiology, Bot. Soc. Am., Am. Inst. Biol. Scis. Acad., Chgo. Network, Soc. Ill. Microbiologists (edn. com. 1969-70, Pasteur award com. 1975, pub. rels. com. 1974, chair speakers' bur. 1974-79), Chgo. Assn. Tech. Socs. (acad. liaison 1982-85, awards com. 1984-89), Am. Coun. on Edn. (corp. rep. higher edn. panel), Ctr. Rsch. Librs. (nominating com. 1986), North Ctrl. Assn. Colls. and Schs. (cons., evaluator Commn. on Higher Edn. 1984-95, commr.-at-large 1988-94), Mo. Women's Forum Club, Sigma Xi, Delta Sigma Rho, Sigma Delta Epsilon, Phi Beta Kappa, Alpha Sigma Nu. Roman Catholic. Home: 6801 N Loron Chicago IL 60646

HAYES, CAROL JEANNE, physical education educator; b. Cambridge, Mass., Apr. 18, 1942; d. Joseph Raymond and Gertrude Marie (Poitras) Boudreau; m. James Anthony Hayes, Oct. 24, 1964 (wid. Mar. 1978); children: James Anthony, Sharon Marie. BSEd, Boston State Coll., 1963, MEd, 1978, postgrad., 1980, Boston State Coll./Salem State, 1986—. Cert. CPR and first aid provider. Phys. edn./health instr. Wilmington (Mass.) Pub. Schs., 1963-65, 72—; part-time phys. edn. tchr. Concord (Mass.) Pub. Schs., 1968-69. Trainer Spl. Olympics participants, Wilmington, 1983-86; Little League mgr., Lexington, 1974-76; bike safety com. Wilmington Police Dept., 1983-85; coord. After Sch. Tournaments, North Intermediate Sch., Wilmington, 1986-91; mem. adv. coun. Woburn St. Sch., 1992—, mem. crisis team, 1993—; peer mediation trainer, 1997—. Author: (curriculum) Elementary/Adaptive/Kindergarten, 1986. Badge counselor Boy Scouts Am., Lexington, 1978-84; vol./minister of comfort St. Brigid, 1978—, care eucharistic minister, 1993—; mem. Lexington Hist. Soc.; coord. Heart Week Activities for Intermediate Students, 1990—; others. Mem. AAHPERD, NEA, MAHPERD, MTA, Wilmington Tchrs. Assn. (exec. bd. 1972, bargaining team 1992, greivance com. 1991, pres. 1995—), Mass. Tchrs. Assn., Mass./AHPERD. Roman Catholic. Avocations: travel, reading, golf, swimming. Home: 9 Farmcrest Ave Lexington MA 02421-7112 Office: Wilmington Pub Schs Wilmington MA 01887

HAYES, DENNIS EDWARD, geophysicist, educator; b. St. Joseph, Mo., Oct. 3, 1938; s. William Franklin and Gertrude Margaret (Lorson) H.; m. Leslie Eve Price, May 17, 1978; children—Jennifer, Katharine, Elizabeth, Élan. BSE. summa cum laude, Kans. U., 1961; PhD, Columbia U., 1966. Research asso. Columbia U., 1966-71, sr. research asso., 1971-74, asso. prof., 1974-77, prof. geophysics, 1977—, chmn. dept. geol. scis., 1989—94, 1997—2002; chmn. exec. com. Arts and Scis. faculty, 1994-96; assoc. dir. Lamont-Doherty Geol. Obs., 1978—2002; deputy dir. edn. Lamont-Doherty Obs. Columbia U., 1998—2002. Mem. ocean scis. bd. and polar rsch. bd. NAS; mem. adv. panel to earth scis. divsn. NSF, polar programs divsn., ocean scis. divsn.; vis. prof. Stanford U., 1981, vis. prof., Ecole Normal Superior (ENS), Paris, 2002; mem. IOC Commn. on Non-living Resources, Joint Oceanographic Insts. for Deep Earth Sampling Planning Commn., 1977-87; mem. Univ. Nat. Oceanog. Lab. Sys. coun., 1991—. Editor books including Antarctic Oceanology II, 1972, Marine Geophysics of S.E. Asia, I and II, 1978, 83, Marine Geology/Geophysics of the Circum-Antarctic, 1991; contbr. numerous articles to profl. jours. Recipient Haworth Disting. Alumni Honors in Geology Kans. U., 1977; NSF fellow, 1961-65; John Simon Guggenheim fellow, 1980-81 Fellow Am. Geophys. Union, Geol. Soc. Am.; mem. Soc. Exploration Geophysicists, Am. Assn. Petroleum Geologists, Tau Beta Pi. Home: 6 Century Rd Palisades NY 10964-1503 Office: Lamont-Doherty Geol Obs Palisades NY 10964 E-mail: deph@ldeo.columbia.edu.

HAYES, DIANE ELIZABETH, principal; b. East Liverpool, Ohio, Oct. 16, 1943; d. Daniel Paulovich and Elizabeth (Lozzi) Paulovich; m. H. Stuart Hayes, Mar. 24, 1963; children: Stuart, Darin, Elizabeth, Alyson. BA in English, Geneva Coll., 1973; MA in Edn. magna cum laude, Regent U., 1988. Tchr. English, substitute tchr. Western Beaver, Industry, Pa., 1967-74; prin., tchr. biblical studies Rhema Christian Sch., Coraopolis, Pa., 1986—. Tng. dir. SASCO, Dallas, 1983-85, conf. speaker. Feature editor Western Advertiser, Beaver Falls, Pa., 1972-80. Mem. ASCD, His Schs. Assn. (speaker edn. conf. 1988-92), Lambda Iota Tau. Lit. Honors Soc. Republican. Home: 3034 Estate Dr Oakdale PA 15071-1025 Office: Rhema Christian Sch 1301 Coraopolis Heights Rd Moon Township PA 15108-2920

HAYES, DONALD PAUL, JR., elementary and secondary education educator; b. Boston, Aug. 30, 1947; s. Donald P. and Grace E. (Moore) H.; m. Deborah J. Moore, July 15, 1978 (div. 2001); children: Erin Eliza, Heather Alice, Jill Melina. AB, Salem State Coll., 1969; MEd with high distinction, Rivier Coll., 1992. Cert. tchr., prin., Mass. Tchr. Lowell (Mass.) Pub. Schs., 1969—. Author, coord., developer Micro-Soc. Pub. Strand Curriculum, 1981-95; author: Locke Family Genealogy Supplement I, 1979, Historic Andover, 1971, Guide to Andover History, 1976, Locke Family Genealogy Supplement II, 2002; mem. adv. bd. Equity, Choice, 1986-94, New Schools, New Communities, 1994-96; co-author: The Micro-Society School, 1992, Piscataqua Pioneers, 2000, Locke General Supplement II, 2002; editor Locke Sickle and Sword, 1972—. Sec. Locke Family Assn., Rye, N.H., 1971—; asst. dir. Samuel Parris Archaeol. Excavation, 1970-73; active Andover (Mass.) Hist. Commn., 1974-78; pres. Andover Hist. Soc., 1976-78, 1st Parish Unitarian Universalist Ch., Chelmsford, Mass., 1992-93; 1st sgt. Danvers Alarm List Co., Danvers, Mass., 2000—. Recipient Award of Appreciation, Airflow Club of Ami, 1998, Locke Family Assn., 1980, 97, Andover Hist. Soc., 1978, Town of Andover, 1976, 78. Mem. Airflow Club Am. (v.p. 1994-98, nat. dir. 2001—), Piscataqua Pioneers (chaplain 1995-96, v.p. 1996-2002, sec. 2002—, 1st sgt. Danvers Alarm List Co. 2000—), New England Hist. Geneal. Soc., Soc. Automotive Historians, Sons Union Vets. Civil War, SAR. Mem. Unitarian Universalist Ch. Avocations: antique cars, historical research. Home: 90 Swan St U202 Lowell MA 01852 Office: Lowell High Sch 50 Father Morissette Blvd Lowell MA 01852-1050 E-mail: donald.hayes@comcast.net.

HAYES, ELIZABETH ROTHS, retired dance educator; b. Ithaca, N.Y., July 3, 1911; d. Leslie David and Emilie Christine (Roths) H. AB, W.Va. U., 1932; MS, U. Wis., 1935; EdD, Stanford U., 1949. Instr. various colls., W.Va. and Ill., 1936-40; asst. prof. U. Wis., 1945; asst. prof. dept. modern dance U. Utah, Salt Lake City, 1941-44, 46-49, assoc. prof., 1954-88, prof. emerita, 1988—. Tchrs. summers Chico (Calif.) Tchrs. Coll., 1951, West Va. U., 1952, U. Mich., 1957, U. Iowa, 1965; founder Modern Dance Maj. Program, U. Utah; spkr. in field; cons. univs. Dancer, choreographer over 40 dances; dir. over 35 dance concerts and prodns.; contbg. editor Design for Arts In Edn., 1980-85; contbr. numerous articles to profl. publs.; author: Introduction to the Teaching of Dance, 1964, Dance Composition and Production, 2d edit., 1993. Fellow Utah Acad. Sci., Arts, & Letters, 2002; recipient Hon. Disting. Alumnus award, U. Utah, 1993, Sch. Edn. Alumni Achievement award, U. Wis., 1993; univ. faculty rsch. grantee U. Utah, 1986-87. Mem. Nat. Dance Assn. (mem. various coms., chair 1969-71, Dance Heritage award 1977, Honor award 1981), Am. Dance Guild, Am. Acad. Phys. Edn., Nat. Dance Edn. Orgn. (founder, Lifetime Achievement award 2002), Coun. Dance Adminstrs. (founder, recipient Alma Hawkins Award for Excellence in Adminstr. Leadership, 2003), Phi Beta Kappa. Home: 130 S 13th E Apt 801 Salt Lake City UT 84102-1783

HAYES, JOHN THOMPSON, biology educator, educational administrator; b. Newton, Mass., Sept. 10, 1940; s. William Danforth Jr. and Charlotte Matilda (Thompson) H.; m. Nancy Jean VanDyke, Jan. 30, 1965 (div. Aug. 1978); children: Jonathan VanDyke, Dianne Jellesma; m. Patricia Anne Lynch, Aug. 23, 1980; 1 child, Robert Brennan. BA cum laude, Amherst Coll., 1962; MS, Cornell U., 1966, PhD, 1968. Postdoctoral fellow U. Ga. Savannah River Ecology Lab., Aiken, S.C., 1967-69; mem. faculty Paine Coll., Augusta, Ga., 1969—, prof. biology, 1976—; mgr. for computer-based edn. Med. Coll. Ga., Augusta, 1984-85. Contbr. articles to profl. jours. Mem. Assn. for Ednl. Communications and Tech., Extramural Assocs. NIH, Ga. Acad. Sci., Ga. Assn. for Instructional Tech., Ecol. Soc. Am., S.C. Entomol. Soc., Sigma Xi, Phi Kappa Phi. Unitarian-Universalist. Avocations: photography, travel, distance running, singing, hiking. Home: 2409 Persimmon Rd Augusta GA 30904-3354 Office: Paine Coll 1235 15th St Augusta GA 30901-3182

HAYES, JOYCE MERRIWEATHER, secondary education educator; b. Bay City, Tex., Aug. 29, 1943; d. Calvin and Alonia (Harris) Merriweather. BS, Wiley Coll., Tex., 1967; postgrad., U. N.Y., Stony Brook, 1968; MS in Guidence Counseling, Ea. Mich. U., 1974; postgrad., Mercy Coll., 1991-92, Ea. Mich. U., 1991-92; MEd, U. Detroit, 1992. English tchr. Terrance Manor Mid. Sch., Augusta, Ga., 1968-69, Longfellow Jr. H.S., Flint, Mich., 1969-81, No. H.S., Flint, 1981—2002, chmn. English dept., 1992—2002; edn. cons. Ventures Edn. Systems Corp., N.Y.C., 2000—. English and speech tchr. Jordan Coll., Flint, 1989-91; adult edn. tchr. Mott Adult H.S., Flint, 1978-80, on-state content stds. com.; presenter workshops in field.; motivational spkr. Composer 3 gospel songs. Vol. Second Ward City Coun., Flint, 1989, Cmty. Coun., Flint, 1992-93, Cmty. Wide Assn. Coun., Flint, 1993; intercessory prayer warrior, 1995—; area dir. Home Ministry new mem. class tchr., Grace Emmanuel Bapt. Ch., co-coord. spl. svc. for Nat. Coun. Tchr. of Eng. Conv. Detroit, 1997. Named Saginaw Valley Tchr. of Yr., 2001, No. Alumni Tchr. of Yr., 2001. Mem. NEA, Nat. Coun. Tchrs. English (chair workshops 1992-93, mem. nominating com. 1994), Mich. Edn. Assn., United Tchrs. of Flint (in-svc. com., Flares-English tchrs.), Phi Delta Kappa (Xinos advisor, del. to conf. 1999, past pres., textbook selection com.). Home: 621 Thomson St Flint MI 48503-1942 Office: Ventures Edn Sys Corp 245 Fifth Ave Ste 802 New York NY 10016 E-mail: silverfoxhayes@aol.com.

HAYES, JUDITH, psychotherapist, educator; b. Lumberton, N.C., June 28, 1950; d. Eugene Lennon and Ada Margaret (Regan) Hayes; m. Jonathan Lafayette II Cutrell (div. Jan. 1979); 1 child, Jonathan L. Cutrell III; m. William Evans Hannon. BA, Augusta Coll., 1973; MA summa cum laude, U. N.C., Charlotte, 1996. Cert. tchr. midl sch. exceptional children. Tchr. Horry County (S.C.) Schs., 1973-77, Alexander County Schs., Taylorsville, N.C., 1978-83, Iredell County Schs., Statesville, N.C., 1983-94; with Charter Pines Behavioral Health, Charlotte, N.C., 1996-97; counselor Brawley Mid. Sch., Mooresville, N.C., 1997—. Bd. dirs. Statesville Dogwood Festival, 1981-82; ch. organist Fair Bluff (N.C.) Bapt., 1974-78. Fellow Phi Kappa Phi; mem. ACA (rep. N.C. Assn. Educators 1993-94), Mu Tau Beta chpt. Chi Sigma Iota. Avocations: reading, music, research.

HAYES, KARLA RENE, special education educator; b. Columbus, Ohio, Nov. 22, 1967; d. Carl Glenn and Linda Lou (Diamond) H. BS, Ohio State U., 1990. Cert. spl. edn. tchr. grades K-12, Ohio; cert. developmental handicaps and specific learning disabilities. Preschool tchr. Little Sch. in the Prairie, Columbus, summer 1987; spl. edn. vol. J. W. Reason Elem. Sch., Hilliard, Ohio, 1987-90; spl. edn. tchr. Madison-Plains Middle Sch., London, Ohio, 1990-93, Grandview Heights Mid. Sch., Columbus, Ohio, 1993—. Vol. Spl. Olympics, Columbus, 1989-91; leader, co-dir. Fellowship of Christian Students, 1991-92. Named Best Christian Athlete, Heritage Christian Sch., 1986. Mem. Coun. for Exceptional Children. Republican. Baptist. Avocations: teaching Sunday sch., photography, guitar, sports, reading. Home: 1520 Cole Rd Columbus OH 43228-9706

HAYES, MARY ANN, social studies educator; b. Princeton, Ind., Sept. 25, 1941; d. John W. and Mozelle Scott; m. Donald L. Hayes, Aug. 18, 1963; 1 child, Elizabeth Ann. BA, U. Evansville, Ind., 1963; MLS, Ind. U., 1968. Tchr. Greater Jasper (Ind.) Schs., 1963-99, dept. chair social studies, 1990-99. Alt. del. Rep. Nat. Conv., Kansas City, Mo., 1976; treas. North Dubois, Raintree Girl Scout Coun., 1995-98; pres. Dubois County Hist. Soc., 1997—; troop leader Girl Scouts, 1991-99; v.p. Dubois County Mus. Inc., 1998—. Recipient Appreciation award Raintree Girl Scout Coun., Evansville, 1996. Mem. NEA, Ind. State Tchrs. Assn., Jasper Classroom Tchrs. Assn., Jasper Bus. and Profl. Women's Club (Woman of Yr. 1979), Jasper Bus. and Profl. Women's Club (pres. 1974-76, Woman of Yr. 1979), Dubois County Hist. Soc. (v.p. 1979-97), Psi Iota Xi (pres. 1971-72, pres. Aux. 1982-84). Republican. Presbyterian. Avocations: history, archaeology.

HAYES, MARY JOANNE, special education educator; b. Bloomington, Ind., Feb. 3, 1944; d. John and Marie (Van Buskirk) Reeves; m. Jack Lee Hayes, June 25, 1983. BA, Olivet U., Kankakee, Ill., 1968; MA, Ind. U., 1972; postgrad., Ind. U., South Bend, 1987, Ind. State U., 1989. Lic. tchr., Ind. Tchr. 3rd grade Saulk View Sch., Steger, Ind., 1968-69; tchr. 1st grade Break-O-Day Sch., New Whiteland, Ind., 1969-83; tchr. emotionally handicapped David Turnham Edn. Ctr., Dale, Ind., 1987—. Mem. Coun. Exceptional Children, Coun. Behavorial Disorders, Ind. Reading Coun. Home: PO Box 191 Dale IN 47523-0191 Office: David Turnham Ednl Ctr Dale IN 47523

HAYES, PATRICIA ANN, health facility administrator; b. Binghamton, N.Y., Jan. 14, 1944; d. Robert L. and Gertrude (Congdon) H. BA in English, Coll. of St. Rose, 1968; PhD in Philosophy, Georgetown U., 1974. Tchr. Cardinal McCloskey High Sch., Albany, N.Y., 1966-68; teaching asst. Georgetown U., Washington, 1968-71; instr. philosophy Coll. of St. Rose, Albany, 1973-75, instr. bus., spring 1981, adminstrv. intern to acad. v.p., 1973-74, dir. admissions, 1974-78, dir. adminstrn. and planning, 1978-81, v.p. adminstrn. and fin., treas., 1981-84; pres. St. Edward's U., Austin, Tex., 1984-98; exec. v.p., COO Seton Healthcare Network, Austin, 1998—2001, 2003—, interim pres., CEO, 2001—02. Trustee RGK Found.; bd. dirs. Topfer Family Found.; exec. bd. Austin Idea Network. Roman Catholic. Office: Seton Med Ctr 1201 W 38th St Austin TX 78705-1006

HAYES, STEPHEN MATTHEW, librarian; b. Detroit, Sept. 30, 1950; s. Matthew Cleary and Evelyn Mary (Warren) H. BS in Psychology, Mich. State U., 1972; MLS, Western Mich. U., 1974; MS in Adminstrn., U. Notre Dame, 1979. Cons. Western Mich. U., Kalamazoo, 1974; libr. U. Notre Dame, Ind., 1974-76, ref. and pub. documents libr., 1976-94; libr. Bus. Svcs. Libr., 1994—. Adv. bd. Ebsco's Bus. Sch., 2003—. Author/contbr.: What is Written Remains: Historical Essays on the Libraries of Notre Dame, 1994; editor: Environmental Concerns, 1975; contbr.: Depository Library Use of Technology: A Practitioner's Perspective, 1993. Apptd. mem. Depository Libr. Coun. to Pub. Printer, 1994—97. Recipient Rev. Paul J. Foik award, 1998. Mem. AAUP, ALA (govt. documents roundtable 1978—, chair 1987-88, chair pubs. com. 1989-91, coord. com. on access to info. 1989-90, 93-95, exec. bd. dirs. 1988-91, awards com. 1991-93, chair Godort orgn. com. 1991-93, Godort legis. com., 1999-2002, bus. ref. and svc. sect. 1994—, bus. & adult ref. roundtable 1995—, edn. com. 1996-98, resolution com. 1997-99, task force or restrictions on access to govt. info. 2002-03), Assn. Pub. Data Users (census com., steering com. 1987-96), Indigo (fed. rec. commn. chair 1992-93). Roman Catholic. Avocations: horseback riding, quilting, gardening. Home: PO Box 6032 South Bend IN 46660-6032 Office: U Notre Dame L012 Mendoza Coll Of Business Notre Dame IN 46556-5646 E-mail: stephen.m.hayes.2@nd.edu.

HAYES, WILBUR FRANK, retired biology educator; b. Rhinelander, Wis., Nov. 10, 1936; s. Wilbur Mead and Evelyn (Stritesky) H.; m. Dawn Olivia Waldorf, July 21, 1979 (div. Feb. 1991); stepchildren: Lynn, Robert, Dana, Richard, Gary, Kevin. BA, Colby Coll., 1959; MS, Lehigh U., 1961, PhD, 1965. Postdoctoral fellow Yale U., New Haven, 1965-67; asst. prof. biology Wilkes Coll., Wilkes-Barre, Pa., 1967-71, assoc. prof., 1971-99, assoc. prof. emeritus, 2000—. Vis. prof. Northeastern U., Boston, 1987-88. Contbr. articles to profl. jours. Chmn. bd. dirs. Northea. Pa. chpt. Am. Heart Assn., Wilkes-Barre, 1986-87. Mem. Soc. for Integrative and Comparative Biology, Pa. Acad. Sci., Microscopy Soc. Am., Sigma Xi (pres. Wilkes Coll. chpt. 1976-77, sec.-treas. 1984-87, 88-91). Republican. Congregationalist. Avocations: downhill skiing, photography, travel, colonial american history. Home: 47 Stanley St Wilkes Barre PA 18702-2308 Office: Wilkes U Dept Biology Wilkes Barre PA 18766

HAYES, WILLIS BOYD, academic program director; b. Long Beach, Calif., Aug. 23, 1942; s. Willis B. and Leona S. (Sewell) H.; m. Wendy Sue Lamb, May 25, 1995. BA in Biol. Sci., Stanford U., 1963; PhD in Oceanography, U. Calif., San Diego, 1969; MA in Buddhist Studies, Naropa Inst., Boulder, Colo., 1994. Rsch. asst. Scripps Inst. Oceanography, San Diego, 1963-69; rsch. ecologist Inst. Marine Resources, San Diego, 1969-70; asst. prof. biology Am. U. Beirut, 1970-73; rsch. assoc. zoology U. Ga., Athens, 1973-76, rsch. assoc. geology, 1976-92; adj. instr. environ. studies Naropa Inst., Boulder, 1992-94; dir. univ. honors program U. So. Maine, Portland, 1994—97; dir. interdisciplinary studies Valdosta (Ga.) State U., 1998—99; dir. marine edn. ctr. and aquarium U. Ga., Savannah, 1999—. Contbr. articles to Jour. Foram Rsch., Jour. Geol. Edn., Ecology, Pacific Sci., Chem. Geology, Computers and Geosci., Environ. Pollution, Nat. Honors Report. Reader Recording for the Blind, Athens, 1988-92, Denver, 1992-94. Mem. AAAS, Nat. Collegiate Honors Coun. (exec. bd.), Nat. Assn. Geology Tchrs., Phi Kappa Phi. Home: 102 Dogwood Dr Rincon GA 31326-5454 Office: U Ga Marine Edn Ctr Aquarium 30 Ocean Sci Cir Savannah GA 31411

HAYMAN, MARTIN ARTHUR, psychiatrist, educator; b. N.Y.C., Dec. 5, 1929; s. Louis and Cecelia (Klatzkin) H.; m. Traude E. Sighartner, June 9, 1957; children: Douglas, Kenneth. BA cum laude, NYU, 1951, MD, 1955. Diplomate Am. Bd. Psychiatry and Neurology, Nat. Bd. Med. Examiners. Intern Meadowbrook Hosp., East Meadow, N.Y., 1955-56; pvt. practice Nassau County, N.Y., 1959-73; sr. physician VA Med. Ctr., Northport, N.Y., 1973; resident in psychiatry SUNY Med. Ctr., Stony Brook, 1974-77, asst. prof. clin. psychiatry, 1977—. Dir. psychiatry South Brookhaven Health Ctr., Patchogue, N.Y., 1977-91; attending physician Brookhaven Meml. Hosp. Med. Ctr., Patchogue, 1977-91. Reviewer jour.; contbr. articles to profl. jours. Mem. ad hoc com. Helping Older People Emotionally, Suffolk County, 1981-82. Capt. M.C., USAF, 1956-58. Fellow Acad. Psychosomatic Medicine; mem. AMA (Physician's Recognition awards 1970—), Am. Psychiat. Assn., Med. Soc. N.Y., Suffolk County Med. Soc., Phi Beta Kappa, Beta Lambda Sigma (vice chancellor 1951). Home and Office: PO Box 626 20 Redwood Dr Great River NY 11739-0626 E-mail: mhayman@pol.net.

HAYNES, BARBARA JUDITH, language educator; b. Trenton, N.J., Apr. 6, 1942; d. Harry G. and Doris M. (Leigh) Horne; m. Joseph A. Haynes, Dec. 11, 1965; children: Joseph III, Jennifer, Charles R. III. Student, Douglass Coll., 1960-62; diploma propeudétique, U. Paris, 1965; MAT, Fairleigh Dickinson U., 1979. Cert French, ESL, elem. tchr., supervision, N.J. ESL tchr. Magnet Ctr., Orange, N.J., 1979-86, River Edge (N.J.) Bd. Edn., 1986—, world lang. facilitator, 1999—. ESL/bilingual stds. com. Nat. Bd. for Profl. Teaching Stds., 1994-99; presenter in field; cons. in field. Author: Prentice Hall Regents ESL, Newcomer Program Grades K-2, 1996; co-author: Classroom Teacher's E.S.L. Survival Kit 1, 1994, Classroom Teacher's E.S.L. Survival Kit 2, 1995, Newcomer Program Grades 3-6, 1997; content editor everything esl.net., 1998—. Pres. Bergan County ESL/Bilingual Tchrs., Paramus, N.J., 1990-93. Recipient Best Practices award State of N.J., 2002; N.J. Govs. Tchr. grant, 1989. Mem. TESOL (elem. spl. interest group sec. 1994-96, nominations com. 1996, assoc. chair elem. interest sect. 2000, Newbury House award for excellence in tchg. 1994), N.J. TESOL-BE (bd. dirs., chmn. elem. spl. interest group rep. 1994-96, rep.-at-large 1996-98, editor newsletter 1997—, ESL Tchr. of Yr. award 1993). Avocations: reading, travel. Home: 709 Stonewall Ct Wyckoff NJ 07481 Office: River Edge Bd Edn 410 Bogert Rd River Edge NJ 07661-1813

HAYNES, EILEEN B. secondary school art and photography educator; b. Dickson, Tenn., June 30, 1946; d. Francis Elmer and Mary Louise (Edwards) Brown; m. Donald Ray Haynes, Mar. 17, 1966; children: Christopher, Cynthia. BS, Mid. Tenn. State U., 1980. Cert. art and history tchr., Tenn. Art and photography tchr. Waldron Jr. H.S., LaVergne, Tenn., 1980-89; art and photography tchr., dept. chmn. Oakland H.S., Murfreesboro, Tenn., 1989—. Chmn. County Campaign for Gov., Rutherford, 1978. Recipient Mayor's award for Outstanding Contbn., LaVergne, 1983, Bus./Edn. Partnership award Rutherford County C. of C., 1993. Mem. Nat. Art Edn. Assn., Tenn. Edn. Assn., Photo Imaging Edn. Assn., Kappa Delta Phi. Baptist. Avocations: photography, printmaking, waterskiing, gardening, painting.

HAYNES, MARILYN MAE, accountant, educator; b. Fond du Lac, Wis., Apr. 30, 1933; d. Clinton Charles and Addie May (Pavey) Ehrhardt; m. Ivan R. Haynes, Aug. 13, 1960. Jr. Acctg. diploma, Madison Bus. Coll., 1952; BE, Wis. State U., Whitewater, 1959; postgrad., U. Wis., 1975-77. Bookkeeper Gas Mags., Inc., Madison, Wis., 1952-55; various positions Wis., summers 1956-60; bus. edn. tchr. Sheboygan (Wis.) Sch. Vocat. and Adult Edn., 1959-60, Edgerton (Wis.) High Sch., 1960-61; acct. Graber Mfg. Co., Middleton, Wis., 1961-71; bookkeeper Alexander Grant and Co., Madison, 1971-79; night sch. bus. edn. instr. Stoughton (Wis.) Vocat.-Adult Ctr., 1961-82, Madison Area Tech. Coll., 1961—; acct. Dane County Housing Authority, Madison, 1979—. Chmn. ch. coun. United Meth. Ch., Stoughton, 1970-72, com. chmn., 1972-76, officer ch. cir., 1970-72, handbell ringer, choir mem., Monona, Wis., 1983—. Mem. Inst. Mgmt. Accts., Order of Ea. Star. Avocations: handbell ringer, horseback rider, square dancer. Address: Dane Co Housing Authority 2001 W Broadway Madison WI 53713-3707

HAYNES, MICHAEL SCOTT, SR., resource specialist; b. Hancock, Mich., Feb. 16, 1948; s. Russell L. and Hildegard Eleanor (Habel) H.; m. Joan Loree Donaldson, July 25, 1968; children: Michael Jr., Andrew Lloyd, Gregory Alan. BA in History, Calif. Luth. U., 1970; MS in Spl. Edn., Learning Disabled, Calif. State U., Long Beach, 1993. Cert. tchr. elem. edn., Calif., cert. resource specialist tchr., handicapped specialist, Calif. Tchr. elem. edn. Rio Lindo Sch., El Rio, Calif., 1970-71, Trinity Luth. Day Sch., Hawthorne, Calif., 1973-82, L.A. Unified Sch. Dist., 1982—, learning handicapped specialist, 1988-90, resource specialist tchr., 1990—. Tchr. chair Am. Luth. Edn. Assn., 1979-82; trustee L.A. Edn. Alliance Restructuring, 1992—; sec. sch. site United Tchrs. L.A., 1991-94; chpt. chair, 1998—. Scoutmaster Boy Scouts Am., 1983-90. With USCG, 1975-85. Recipient Wood badge Boy Scouts Am., 1983. Mem. Calif. Assn. Resource Specialists (univ. liaison 1991-92), So. Calif. Chihuahua Club, Inc. (sec. 1992-94, 96-98, v.p., 1995), Orange Empire Dog Club, Kappa Delta Pi, Phi Delta Kappa. Avocations: baroque recorder, hiking.

HAYNIE, BETTY JO GILLMORE, personal property appraiser, antiques dealer; b. Jackson, Ala., July 3, 1937; d. Joe McVey and Mary Elizabeth (Bolen) Gillmore; m. William T. Haynie Jr., Aug. 21, 1960; children: Virginia Elizabeth, Mary Allison. BA, U. Ala., 1959, MA, 1960, postgrad., U. So. Miss., U. Ala., Birmingham; grad. Paris program, Parsons Sch. Design, 1992; grad., Winter Inst., Winterthur, Del., 1994. Tchr. Demopolis (Ala.) Elem. Sch., 1960-61; instr. in history U. Livingston, Ala., 1961-64; tchr. history for jr. high Brooke Hill Sch. for Girls, Birmingham, Ala., 1965; instr. in history Jefferson State Jr. Coll., Birmingham, 1965-67; tchr. history and govt. Mt. Brook High Sch., Birmingham, 1970-71; instr. history U. Ala., Birmingham, 1971-72, Jefferson Davis Jr. Coll., Gulfport, Miss., 1978-81, Faulkner Jr. Coll., Fairhope, Ala., 1983-86; instr. spl. courses U. South Ala., Mobile, 1988—2003, instr. Elderhostel programs, 1990—99. Owner Crown and Colony Antiques, Fairhope, Ala., 1982—92, Antiques and Fine Art, Fairhope, Ala., 1997—; co-owner Gillmore Plantation, Jackson, Ala., Ala., 1987—, and other properties. Contbr. articles to historical mags. Mem.: DAR, Internat. Soc. Appraisers, Clarke County Hist. Soc., Nat. Trust for Hist. Preservation. Presbyterian. Avocations: tennis, creative writing, traveling. Home: PO Box 485 Montrose AL 36559-0485

HAYNSWORTH, HARRY JAY, IV, lawyer, educator; b. Greensboro, N.C., Apr. 9, 1938; s. Harry J. Jr. and Ruth (Eberhardt) H. AB, Duke U., 1961, JD, 1964; postgrad., U. Denver Law Center, 1972; MAR, Luth. Theol. So. Sem., 1989. Bar: S.C. 1965. Assoc. Haynsworth, Perry, Bryant, Marion & Johnstone, Greenville, S.C., 1964-69, ptnr., 69-71; assoc. prof. law U. of S.C., 1971-74, prof., 1974-90, assoc. dean, 1975-76, 85-86, acting dean, 1976-77; of counsel Nexson, Pruet, Jacobs & Pollard, Columbia, S.C., 1986-90; dean., prof. law So. Ill. U., Carbondale, 1990-95; dean, pres. William Mitchell Coll. of Law, St. Paul, 1995—. Vis. prof. U. Leeds, Eng., 1978-79; commr. Nat. Conf. Commrs. on Uniform State Laws, 1992—; mem. S.C. Legis. Consumer Law Com., 1975-80 Author: Comments, S.C. Consumer Protection Code, 1983, 2d edit. 1990, Organizing a Small Business Entity, 1986, Marketing and Legal Ethics: The Rules and Risks, 1990, others; contbr. articles to profl. jours.; mem. editorial bd.: Am. Bar Assn. Jour, 1977-83, chmn. editorial bd., 1982-83. Chmn. bd. S.C. Commn. for Blind, 1973-75; bd. dirs. Greenville County (S.C.) Housing Commn., 1970-71; v.p., dir. United Speech and Hearing Center, Greenville, 1970-71; trustee Heathwood Hall, 1976-86, Randolph-Macon Women's Coll., Lynchburg, Va., 1970-75. Mem. ABA (small bus. com., spl. cons. corp. laws com. 1978-82, coun. sect. bus. law 1988-92), S.C. Bar Assn. (vice chmn. consumer and comml. law com. 1975-78, sec., exec. com. 1972-75, exec. dir. 1971-72), Minn. State Bar Assn., Ramsey County Bar Assn., Hennepin County Bar Assn., Am. Law Inst., 4th Cir. Jud. Conf. Office: 875 Summit Ave Saint Paul MN 55105-3030

HAYS, ANNETTE ARLENE, secondary school educator; b. Dallas, Jan. 22, 1951; d. Ogle Winifred and Loretta Lavelle Hatfield; m. William Ned Hays, Aug. 7, 1971; children: Quincy Merritt, Gretchen Laurel. BS in Home Econ. Edn., U. Ark., Fayetteville, 1973. Office asst. dept. entomology U. Ark., Fayetteville, 1970—71; sales assoc. Hunt's Dept. Store, Fayetteville, 1971—72, Singer Sewing Co., Joplin, Mo., 1972—76, instr., 1974—76; home econ. tchr. Parkwood HS, Joplin, 1976—80; family & consumer sci. tchr. Acorn Sch., Mena, Ark., 1988—. Owner Hatfield, Honey & Sorghum, Pine Ridge, Ark., 1980—; Family, Career and Cmty. Leaders Am. advisor Acorn Sch., 1988—, mem. personnel policy com., developer tech-prep/transition program; trainer Ark. Workplace Readiness, 1993—; apptd. by gov. Ark. Workforce Commn., 1997—98; grantwriter; spkr. in field; bd. dirs., chair Healthy Connections, Mena, Ark., 2001—. Mem. Oden Sch. Bd., 1986—98, past sec., past v.p.; choir mem First Presbyn. Ch., Mena, del. to Peacemaking Conf., 1996. Recipient Tchr. of Yr., Ark. Assn. Family & Consumer Scis., 2003. Mem.: Ark. Assn. Family Consumer Scis. (bd. dirs. 2001—), Ark. Assn. Career and Tech. Educators (bd. dirs. 1999—2001), Asn. Career & Tech. Educators, Ark. Assn. Tchrs. Family & Consumer Scis. (pres. elect 1999—2000, pres. 2000—01, past pres. 2001—02, Polk County Tchr. of Yr. 2002, Tchr. of the Yr. 2003), Delta Kappa Gamma. Presbyterian. Avocations: hiking, reading, landscaping. Home: 38 Honey Bear Ln Pine Ridge AR 71966

HAYS, KATHY ANN, elementary education educator; b. Council Bluffs, Iowa, Sept. 29, 1955; d. Leo P. and Monica G. (Schwery) Kenkel; m. Dan P. Hays, Aug. 20, 1988; children: Caitlin Leigh, Patrick Joseph. BS in Elem. Edn., Creighton U., 1977, MS in Elem. Edn., 1984. Cert. elem. tchr., Nebr. 6th grade tchr. Treynor (Iowa) Pub. Schs., 1977-79; from 6th grade tchr. to gifted cons. Ralston (Nebr.) Pub. Schs., 1979-86, 5th grade tchr., 1986-88, Blue Valley Pub. Schs., Overland Park, Kans., 1988-91, Elkhorn (Nebr.) Pub. Schs., 1991—. Lang. arts chair Elkhorn Pub. Schs., 1994—; leadership acad. Blue Valley Pub. Schs., Overland Park, 1991-92; presenter in field. Cantor St. Vincent De Paul Ch., Omaha, 1991—. Named Educator of Yr. Ralston Pub. Schs., 1988. Mem.: Internat. Reading Assn., Nat. Coun. Tchrs. English, Nebr. Assn. Gifted Children, Phi Delta Kappa. Democrat. Roman Catholic. Avocations: music, theatre. Home: 519 S 215th St Elkhorn NE 68022-2058 Office: Elkhorn Pub Schs 400 S 210th St Elkhorn NE 68022-2166

HAYS, KAY ANN, elementary counselor, educational diagnostician; b. Dallas, June 5, 1949; d. John Gilford and Billie Grace (Minter) Reynolds; m. Thomas Michael Hays, Sr., Dec. 28, 1975; children: Allison Ann, Thomas Michael. BS, East Tex. State U., Commerce, 1971, MEd, 1974; student, Tex. Woman's U., Denton, 1982-88. Cert. edn. counselor, ednl. diagnostician, Tex.; lic. prof. counselor, lic. marriage and family therapist, Tex. Tchr. Yantis (Tex.) Ind. Sch. Dist., 1971-72, Duncanville (Tex.) Pub. Schs., 1972-74, Birdville Ind. Sch. Dist., Ft. Worth, 1974-79, counselor, 1979-84, counselor, ednl. diagnostician, 1984-95, counselor, 1995-2000. Mem. Tex. Counseling Assn. (presenter 1993, 94, 95), Tex. Tchrs. Assn., Women's Club Ft. Worth, Pi Kappa Phi, DAR, AAUW, TSTA, Birdville Assn. for Adminstrs. Counselors, Cons. and Diagnosticians (past chmn., vice chmn., sec.), TCA, TSCA, Alpha Delta Pi (past pres., treas., mem. chmn.), Delta Kappa Gamma. Democrat. Methodist. Avocations: travel, snow skiing, water skiing. E-mail: khays@studenttravelamerica.com.

HAYS, SANDRA LYNN, gifted education educator; b. North Canton, Ohio, Jan. 10, 1954; d. James Lancaster and Susan Carol (Saint) Thorley; m. Jesse Ray Hays, Mar. 13, 1982; 1 child, Megan Lee. BA in Elem. Edn. cum laude, Ariz. State U., 1977. Cert. tchr. elem. edn., Ariz. Tchr. Westwood Trad. Sch., Phoenix, 1985-86, Heritage Elem. Sch., Glendale, Ariz., 1986-89, Copperwood Elem. Sch., Glendale, 1989-90, Ira A. Murphy Elem. Sch., Peoria, Ariz., 1990-91, Canyon Elem. Sch., Glendale, 1991-92, Peoria Unified Sch. Dist., 1992—. Mem design team. elem. sci. curriculum Peoria Unified Sch. Dist., 1988-92, elem. sci. acad., 1992, secondary sci. acad., 1992; cons. Glendale Libr. System, 1989—; chair curriculum Minority Sci. Math. Camp, Tempe, 1992. Appointee State Environ. Task Force, Phoenix. Recipient Heritage Environ. award Ariz. Game and Fish, 1992; named Facilitator of Yr., Ariz. Game and Fish, 1991. Mem. ASCD, Nat. Sci. Tchrs. Assn. (presenter 1990), Ariz. Sci. Tchrs. Assn., Ariz. Alliance for Learning In and About the Environment. Democrat. Lutheran. Office: Canyon Sch 5490 W Paradise Ln Glendale AZ 85306-2535

HAYS, SUZANNE RYAN, family resource center care worker; b. Lexington, Ky., Mar. 14, 1959; d. James Henry and Sarah (May) Ryan; m. Danny Elbert Hays, Mar. 2, 1991. BS in Elem. Edn. and Learning Disorders, U. Ky., 1982, MSW, 1991. Cert. social worker, Ky. Spl. edn. tchr. Winburn Jr. High Sch., Lexington, Ky., 1983-85, Tates Creek Sr. High Sch., Lexington, Ky., 1985-89, spl. edn. dept. chair, 1987-89; learning strategies program adminstr. Ky. Dept. Edn., Frankfort, Ky., 1989-90, nat. learning strategies trainer, 1987—; founder, dir. RYSAN Ednl. Support Svcs., Lexington, 1987—; intensive care worker Family Resource Ctr., Owensboro, Ky., 1991—. Adv. bd. Ky. Coalition for Career and Leisure Devel., Lexington, 1982-86; cons. Ky. Dept. Edn., Frankfort, 1992—; behavior specialist Protection and Advocacy, Frankfort, 1992—. Patentee in field; author: Study Skills, 1989. Adult leader Fayette County 4-H, Lexington, 1983-87. Recipient Instructional Assistance grant United Way, 1992. Mem. NASW, Leadership Edn. of Lexington, Coun. for Exceptional Children, Learning Disabilities Assn., Coun. for Children with Behavioral Disorders, Children with Attention Deficit Disorders. Republican. Roman Catholic. Avocations: boating, snow skiing. Home: 1539 Miller Ct Owensboro KY 42301-3643 Office: Foust Family Resource Ctr 601 Foust Ave Owensboro KY 42301-1961

HAYTHE, WINSTON MCDONALD, lawyer, educator, consultant, real estate investor; b. Reidsville, NC, Oct. 10, 1940; s. McDonald Swann and Henrietta Elizabeth (East) H.; m. Glenann Leigh Rogers, Aug. 17, 1963 (div. 1977); children: Sheila Elaine, Kevin McDonald, Rhonda Leigh. BS, S.W. Mo. State U., 1963; JD, Coll. William and Mary, 1967; postgrad., U. Va., 1968—69; grad., Command and Gen. Staff Sch., Ft. Leavenworth, Kans., 1982, U.S. Def. U., 1984; LLM, U.S. Army JAG Sch., 1976. Bar: Va. 1967, D.C. 1969. Assoc. Rhyne & Rhyne, Washington, 1969-72; sr. trial atty. AEC, Washington, 1972-73; asst. gen counsel, sr. atty. Consumer Produce Safety Commn., Washington, 1973-82; staff dir. legal office EPA, Washington, 1982-83, sr. atty. for enforcement policy, 1985-91, sr. atty. Nat.

Enforcement Tng. Inst., 1991-94, asst. dir., 1994-96, sr. legal counsel, 1996-2001; sr. counsel Office of Criminal Enforcement, Forensics and Tng., 2001—. Legis. fellow U.S. Senate, Washington, 1983-85; adv. com. paralegal studies U. Md., 1980-95, chmn., 1992-95; adj. prof. law, 1978-94; law faculty U.S. Army Judge Adv. Gen.'s Sch., Charlottesville, Va., 1969-94, Nat. Advocacy Ctr. U.S. Dept. Justice, Columbia, S.C., 1999—; cons. Barrister Ent., Washington, 1978—; elected mem. undergrad. programs adv. coun. U. Md., 1993-95; guest lectr. George Washington U. Sch. Law, 1999-2002, adj. prof. law, 2002-. Trustee Georgetown Presbyn. Ch., 1995-98, v.p. trustees, 1996, pres. trustees, 1997-98, elder, mem. session, 2000-03, clk. of session, 2003—. Col. JAGC, USAR, 1967-94, ret. Fellow: Found. Fed. Bar Assn. (life); mem.: Found. of the Fed. Bar (sustaining life), The Social List of Washington, Fed. Bar Assn. (fed. career svcs. divsn. 1974—90, nat. coun. 1998—), DC Bar Assn., Va. State Bar Assn., Coll. William and Mary Law Sch. Assn. (bd. dirs. 1988—95), Cosmos Club, Knights Templar, Kappa Mu Epsilon. Presbyterian. Avocations: playing organ, piano, theater, concerts, reading. Home: 2141 P St NW Apt 402 Washington DC 20037-1031 Office: EPA (MC-2235A) 1200 Pennsylvania Ave NW Washington DC 20460-0001 E-mail: whaythe@hotmail.com.

HAZEL, MARY BELLE, university administrator; b. Orange, N.J., May 30, 1932; d. Morris M. Sr. and Robena (Brinkley) Thomas; m. James H. Hazel, Sept. 28, 1958 (div. Sept. 1976); children: Sharon Marie Hazel-Griggs, James Thomas. BS in Bus. Adminstrn., Seton Hall U., South Orange, N.J., 1992, MA in Edn. cum laude, 1998. Publs. asst. advt. and pub. rels. dept. Foster Wheeler Corp., N.Y.C., 1969-87; ind. contractor, 1987-92; adminstrv coord. dean's office UMDNJ Sch. Health Related Professions, Newark, 1992—. Elder Elmwood United Presbyn. Ch. Mem. AAUW, NAFE, Smithsonian Nat. Assn., Soc. Allied Health Professions N.J., Spinal Cord Injured-Family Support Group-Kessler Inst. Rehab.

HAZELIP, HERBERT HAROLD, academic administrator; b. Bowling Green, Ky., Aug. 3, 1930; s. Herbert and Maggie Marie (Ferguson) H.; m. Helen Frances Royalty, Mar. 23, 1956; children: Patrick Harold, Jeffrey Alan. AA, Freed-Hardeman Coll., Henderson, Tenn., 1948; BA, David Lipscomb Coll., Nashville, 1950; MDiv, So. Bapt. Theol. Sem., 1958; PhD, U. Iowa, 1967. Ordained to ministry Ch. of Christ, 1947. Min. Cen. Ch. Christ, Owensboro, Ky., 1950-53, Taylor Blvd. Ch. Christ, Louisville, 1954-64, Cen. Ch. Christ, Cedar Rapids, Iowa, 1964-67, Highland St. Ch. Christ, Memphis, 1967-86; dean, prof. Harding U. Grad. Sch. Religion, Memphis, 1967-86; pres. Lipscomb U., Nashville, 1986-97, chancellor, 1997—. Author: Discipleship, 1977, A Devotional Guide to Bible Lands, 1979, Anchors in Troubled Waters, 1981, Lord, Help Me When I'm Hurting, 1984, Happiness in the Home, 1985, Questions People Ask Ministers Most, 1986, Jesus: Our Mentor and Model, 1987, Becoming Persons of Integrity, 1988, Anchors for the Asking, 1989. Mem. Rotary. Avocations: travel, reading. Office: David Lipscomb U 3901 Granny White Pike Nashville TN 37204-3903 E-mail: harold.hazelip@lipscomb.edu.

HAZELTINE, BARRETT, electrical engineer, educator; b. Paris, Nov. 7, 1931; came to U.S., 1932; s. L. Alan and Elizabeth (Barrett) H.; m. Mary Frances Fenn, Aug. 25, 1956; children: Michael B., Alice W., Patricia F. BSE, Princeton U., 1953, MSE, 1956; PhD, U. Mich., 1962; ScD (hon.), SUNY, Stony Brook, 1988. Registered profl. engr., R.I. Asst. prof. engring. Brown U., 1959-66, assoc. prof., 1966-72, prof., 1972—; asst. to dean Brown U. (The Coll.), 1962-63, asst. dean, 1968-74, assoc. dean, 1974-93; Robert Foster Cherry chair for disting. teaching Baylor U., 1991-92; prof. U. Botswana, 1993. Lectr., vis. prof. U. Zambia, Lusaka, 1970-71; -76-77; vis. prof. U. Malawi-Poly., Blantyre, 1980-81, 83-84, 88-89, Africa U. Mutare, Zimbabwe, 1996-97, 2000; asst. to mgr. rsch. labs., space and info. sys. divsn. Raytheon Co., 1964-65, cons., 1965-67; cons. R.I. Utilities Commn., 1977-80, others. Author: Introduction to Electronic Circuits and Applications, 1980, Appropriate Technology: Tools, Choice and Implications, 1998, Field Guide to Appropriate Technology, 2003; editor: The Weaver, 1982—90. Trustee Stevens Inst. Tech. Recipient award for excellence in instrn. Western Electric, 1968; grantee NSF, Dept. Edn.; grantee Met. Life Ins. Ednl. Found.; Fulbright fellow 1988-89, 93. Mem. IEEE (sr., chmn. Providence sect. 1971-72), Providence Engring. Soc. (pres. 1977-78), Am. Soc. Engring. Edn., Sigma Xi, Tau Beta Pi. Congregationalist (deacon). Clubs: Providence Art, Providence Review. Achievements include patents for color recognition system. Home: 60 Barnes St Providence RI 02906-1502 Office: Brown U Div Engring Providence RI 02912-0001 E-mail: Barrett_Hazeltine@brown.edu.

HAZELTON, PENNY ANN, law librarian, educator; b. Yakima, Wash., Sept. 24, 1947; d. Fred Robert and Margaret (McLeod) Pease; m. Norris J. Hazelton, Sept. 12, 1971; 1 child, Victoria MacLeod. BA cum laude, Linfield Coll., 1969; JD, Lewis and Clark Law Sch., 1975; M in Law Librarianship, U. Wash., 1976. Bar: Wash. 1976, U.S. Supreme Ct. 1982. Assoc. law libr., assoc. prof. U. Maine, 1976-78, law libr., assoc. prof., 1978-81; asst. libr. for rsch. svcs. U.S. Supreme Ct., Washington, 1981-85, law libr., 1985, U. Wash., Seattle, 1985—, prof. law, assoc. dean libr. and computing svcs., 1985—. Tchr. legal rsch., law librarianship, Indian law; cons. Maine Adv. Com. on County Law Librs., Nat. U. Sch. Law, San Diego, 1985-88, Lawyers Cooperative Pub., 1993-94, Marquette u. Sch. Law, 2002. Author: Computer Assisted Legal Research: The Basics, 1993; author: (with others) Washington Legal Researcher's Deskbook, 3d edit., 2002; contbr. articles to legal jours.; gen. editor Specialized Legal Rsch. (Aspen). Recipient Disting. Alumni award U. Wash., 1992. Mem. ABA (sect. legal edn. and admissions to bar, chair com. on librs. 1993-94, vice chair 1992-93, 94-95, com. on law sch. facilities 1998—), Am. Assn. Law Schs. (com. law librs. 1991-94), Law Librs. New Eng. (sec. 1977-79, pres. 1979-81), Am. Assn. Law Librs. (program chmn. ann. meeting 1984, exec. bd. 1984-87, v.p. 1989-90, pres. 1990-91, program co-chair Insts. 1983, 95), Law Librs. Soc. Washington (exec. bd. 1983-84, v.p., pres. elect 1984-85), Law Librs. Puget Sound, Wash. State Bar Assn. (chair editl. adv. bd.), Wash. Adv. Coun. on Librs., Westpac. Office: U Wash Marian Gould Gallagher Law Libr 1100 NE Campus Pkwy Seattle WA 98105-6605

HAZEN, ELIZABETH FRANCES, retired special education educator; b. Lamar, Colo., May 27, 1925; d. Otis Garfield and Cora B. (Baker) McDowell; children: H. Ray, Bobby D., Anita K. Iezza, Gloria G. Gill. AA, Lamar Jr. Coll., 1946; BS in Edn., Southwestern Okla. U., 1967, MS in Edn., 1969; postgrad., Ea. Ky. U., 1983. Cert. speech-hearing therapist, reading specialist, learning and behavior disorders, Ky. Elem. tchr. Granada (Colo.) Sch., 1946-51, South Ctrl. Elem. Sch., Lamar, Colo., 1951-52; lead tchr. Tom Thumb Pre-Sch., Ellsworth AFB, S.D., 1961-62; math. and sci. tchr. Elk City (Okla.) Elem. Sch., 1966-67; beginning speech tchr. Sayer Jr. Coll., Okla., 1967-68; speech and hearing therapist Burns Flat (Okla.) Schs., 1967-69, Maconaqueh Sch. Corp., Bunker Hill, Ind., 1969-72; reading specialist Myers Mid. Sch., Louisville, Ky., 1972-76; tchr. Core Westport Jr. H.S., Louisville, 1977-79, chmn. Core dept., 1978-79; learning disabled resource tchr. Jeffersontown H.S., Louisville, 1979-80, Waggoner Mid. Sch., Louisville, 1980-81, Westport Mid. Sch., Louisville, 1981-94; ret., 1994. Chmn. exceptional children's edn. dept. Westport Mid. Sch., Louisville, 1983-91; speech and hearing therapist Burns Flat (Okla.) Bd. Edn., 1967-69. Bd. dirs. Westport Middle Schs. PTA/Student Assn., 1989-90. Named Outstanding Tchr. of Disadvantaged, State of Okla., 1969. Mem. NEA (ret.), Ky. Mid. Sch. Assn., Ky. Edn. Assn. (ret.), Ky. Ret. Tchrs. Assn., Jefferson County Tchrs. Assn. Home: 1207 McVey Rd Sedalia MO 65301-8869

HAZLEHURST, FRANKLIN HAMILTON, fine arts educator; b. Spartansburg, N.C., Nov. 6, 1925; s. Robert Purviance and Lottie Lee (Nicholls) H.; m. Carol Foord, Aug. 26, 1950; children: Franklin Hamilton, Robert P. II, Mary Hadley, Abigail Norris. Student, Princeton U., 1943-44, BA cum laude, 1949; student, Ecole de Louvre, France, 1949-50; MFA cum laude, Princeton U., 1952, PhD, 1956. Asst. instr. dept. art and archaeology Princeton (N.J.) U., 1951-53, instr., 1954-56; lectr. and rsch. asst. The Frick collection, N.Y.C., 1956-57; assoc. prof. art history U. Ga., 1957-63; assoc. prof. fine arts Vanderbilt U., Nashville, 1963-65, prof. fine arts, 1965-95, prof. fine arts emeritus, 1995—. Lectr. Princeton Theol. Sem., 1956-57; chmn. fine arts dept. Vanderbilt U., 1963-90; invited lectr. in field. Author: Jacques Boyceau and the French Formal Garden, 1966, Gardens of Illusion: The Genius of André Le Nostre, 1980, revised 2d edit., 1982 (Alice Davis Hitchcock award 1982), revised 3d edit., 1986; contbr. numerous articles to profl. jours. and encys. Staff sgt. U.S. Army, 1944-46, ETO. Fulbright fellow PhD Rsch., Paris, 1953-54; Charlotte Elizabeth Proctor fellow Princeton U., 1954-55; Sarah H. Moss rsch. fellow Paris, 1961-62; grantee ACLS, 1967, Am. Philosophical Soc., 1967, 83; recipient Madison Sarratt prize Excellence in Undergrad. Teaching, 1970. Mem. Am. Archaeol. Soc., Coll. Art Assn. Am. (grantee Millard Meiss publ. fund 1979), Southeastern Coll. Art Conf. (pres. 1973-74), Société de l'histoire de l'art francais, Soc. Archtl. Historians. Office: Vanderbilt U Dept Fine Arts 2305 W End Ave Nashville TN 37203-1700

HE, XIAOHONG, finance educator; b. Beijing, May 15, 1953; came to the U.S., 1984; d. DongChang He and Zhuobao Li; m. Ping Su, June 29, 1949; 1 child, Xiaowei Su. MA in Internat. Bus., U. Tex., Dallas, 1986, MS in Fin., 1989, PhD in Internat. Mgmt., 1991. Engr., rschr. China's Nat. Acad. Agr. Mechanization Scis., Beijing, 1977-84; rsch. assoc. Hass Bus. Sch. U. Calif., Berkeley, 1984-85; mgmt. cons. Greyhound Lines & China Auto Import Co., Dallas, 1985-89; v.p. China Auto Import Co., Dallas, 1989-91; dir. Far East Econ. Devel. Greyhound Lines, Dallas, 1989-91; dir. Internat. Bus. ExchangeProg. Quinnipiac U., Hamden, Conn., 1991-93, prof., chair internat. bus. and mktg. dept., 1997—2000, dir. Internat. Bus. Rsch., 1993-94, chair internat. bus., 2001—. Contbr. articles to profl. jours., chpts. to books. Recipient Outstanding R&D Award, China's Machine Building Min., 2d Prize, 1983, 3rd Prize 1979-81, Citation of Excellence award ANBAR Electronic Intelligence, U.K., 1998, Literati Club award for excellence, MCB Univ. Press, U.K., 1999. Fellow Soc. Global Bus. Edn.; mem. Internat. Mgmt. Devel. Assn., Assn. Global Bus., Acad. Mgmt., Assn. Internat. Trade and Fin., Acad. Internat. Bus. (Best Paper award N.E. chpt. 1992). Office: Quinnipiac U Sch Bus 275 Mount Carmel Ave Hamden CT 06518-1961 E-mail: Xiaohong.He@quinnipiac.edu.

HEACKER, THELMA WEAKS, retired elementary school educator; b. Lakeland, Fla., Nov. 27, 1927; d. Andrew Lee and Stella Dicy (Hodges) Weaks; m. Howard V. Heacker, Aug. 21, 1947; children: Victor, Patricia, Paula, Jonathan, Johannah; m. V.L. Brown, Mar. 31, 1991. BA, Carson-Newman Coll., Jefferson City, Tenn., 1949; MA, Tenn. Technol. U., 1980; postgrad., U. Tenn. Cert. elem. and secondary tchr., Tenn.; cert. secondary tchr., Ga. Elem. tchr. Hamblen County Pub. Schs., Morristown, Tenn., 1949; secondary tchr. Morgan County-Coalfield High Sch., Coalfield, Tenn., 1986-87, Roane County-O. Springs High Sch., Oliver Springs, Tenn., 1949-71; elem. tchr. Morgan County-Petros-Joyner Sch., Oliver Springs, 1975-93. Vol. Keystone Elder Day Care, 2000—. Named Tchr. of Yr., 1986. Mem. NEA, Tenn. Edn. Assn., Ea. Tenn. Edn. Assn., Morgan County Edn. Assn., RCTA, HCTA Home: 102 Ulena Ln Oak Ridge TN 37830-5237 Office: Petros Joyner Elem Sch Petros-Joyner Rd Oliver Springs TN 37840-9700

HEAD, ANITA NIX, secondary educator; b. Ft. Worth, Dec. 20, 1943; d. J. Ray and Vanita Louise (Cooper) Nix; m. James Luther Head, June 4, 1966; children: Chantelle, Michelle, Christie Joy. BA, Tex. Christian U., 1966; MEd, Tenn. State U., 1985, D in Edn., 1996. Tchr. Nashville Met. Pub. Schs., Denton (Tex.) Pub. Schs., Ft. Worth Pub. Schs. Mem. NEA, (hi Delta Kappa. Home: 900 S Lane Ct Brentwood TN 37027-7645

HEAD, LILLIE JEWEL, secondary physical education educator; b. Tuskegee, Ala., July 28, 1944; d. Freddie Lee and Johnnie Mae (Neal) Tyson; m. Wilbert Head, Mar. 1, 1969; children: Wilbert Earl, Mark Fredric, Carmen Jewel. BS, Tuskegee Inst., 1969; MEd, So. Conn. State U., New Haven, 1976; EdS, U. Bridgeport, Conn., 1994. Telephone operator SNET, Waterbury, Conn., 1964-68; posting clk. Timex Corp., Middlebury, Conn., 1966-68; thcr. phys. edn. Waterbury Bd. Edn., 1969—. Mid. sch. leadership dir. YWCA, Waterbury, 1988-93; mem. adv. bd. Conn. BEST Mentor Program, New Haven, 1991-92, Sacred Heart H.S., Waterbury, 1992—. Author brochures. Mem. adv. bd., rec. sec. Mt. Olive Sr. Ctr., Waterbury, 1989—; active NAACP. Recipient Woman in Leadership award YWCA, 1992, Tchr. of Yr. award Wilby H.S., Waterbury, 1992-93. Mem. NEA, Conn. Tchrs. Assn., Waterbury Tchrs. Assn. (union rep.), Conn. Coaches Assn., Nat. Assn. Negro Bus. and Profl. Women's Clubs (1st v.p. Waterbury club 1971—, Sojourner Truth award 1992), Phi Kappa Phi. Democrat. Roman Catholic. Avocations: travel, meeting new people, reading, swimming, organizing activities. Home: 945 Hamilton Ave Watertown CT 06795-2306 Office: Wilby HS 460 Bucks Hill Rd Waterbury CT 06704-1225

HEAD, MARY MAE, elementary education educator; b. Branson, Mo., Apr. 9, 1963; d. Thomas Edwin and Evelyn Jean (Hazell) H. BS in Computer Sci., Sch. of Ozarks, Point Lookout, Mo., 1989. Asst. computer lab., libr. aide Hollister (Mo.) Elem. Sch., 1989—. Sunday sch. tchr. Hollister Presbyn. Ch., 1979-2001. Avocations: reading christian literature, needlework, photography. Office: Hollister Elem Sch 1794 State Hwy BB Hollister MO 65672-5461

HEAD, WILLIAM PACE, historian, educator; b. Miami, Oct. 15, 1949; s. Downer Pace and Ella Marguerite (Crittenden) H.; m. Randee Lynne Geiger, June 6, 1975; children: Matthew Brian, Evan Zachery. AS Bus., Miami-Dade C.C., 1969; PhD History, Fla. State U., 1980, BA History, 1971; MA History, U. Miami, 1974. Asst. prof. history U. Ala., Huntsville, 1981-84; historian USAF, Robins AFB, Ga., 1984—, chief Office of History WR-ALC, 1996—. Adj. prof. history Fla. State U., Tallahassee, 1980-81, Macon (Ga.) State Coll., 1985—, Mercer U., 1985-92, Ga. Mil. Coll., 1986-94; site dir. Ala. Heritage Festival, Ala. Humanities Coun., Huntsville, 1981; hist. advisor WMAZ-TV Robins at Fifty, 1991, Ga. Pub. TV, The State of War: Ga. in WWII, Atlanta, 1994. Author: America's China Sojourn, 1983, Reworking the Workhorse: The C-141B, 1984 (Best in AF 1985), Yenan, 1985, Every Inch a Soldier, 1995 (Best in AF 1996), War From Above the Cloud, 2002; co-author, editor: Plotting a True Course: Reflections on Strategic Attack Theory and Doctrine, the Post-World War II Experience, 2003; co-author: Time Capsule: A History of Robins AFB, 1936-96, 1997; editor Tet Offensive, 1996, Looking Back at the Vietnam War, 1993, Eagle in the Desert, 1996, Weaving A New Tapestry: Asia In The Post Cold War World, 1999, War From Above the Clouds: B-52 Operations During the Second Indo China War, 2002; mem. editl. bd. Asia, Jour. Third World Studies, 1985-98. Mem. Houston County Dem. Com. Coun., Warner Robins, Ga., 1990—; active little league baseball and basketball, Warner Robins City League, 1992—; hist. judge, Ga. Hist. Day/Ga. Humanities Coun., Atlanta, 1988—. Recipient Spl. Commendation award Ala. State Senate, Huntsville, 1986, Air Force Spl. Achievements award, 1994; Fla. State U. grad. fellow, 1977. Mem. Assn. Third World Studies (nom. com. chmn. 1989-98, exec. coun. post 1 1999-2002, pres. 2003), Ga. Assn. Historians (pubs. com. 1984-99), Assn. Asian Studies (program chmn. 2003), Soc. Mil. History, Soc. Hist. Fed. Govt., Phi Kappa Phi. Democrat. Methodist. Avocations: golf, travel, tennis, sports. Home: 111 Chantilly Dr Warner Robins GA 31088-6329 Office: USAF-Warner Robins ALC 955 Robins Pky Robins A F B GA 31098-2423 E-mail: pamccall@webtv.net.

HEAD-HAMMOND, ANNA LUCILLE, retired secondary education educator; b. Providence, Ky., Dec. 16, 1924; d. Nathaniel A. and Nora D. (Martin) Rinehammer; m. Robert F. Head, Oct. 24, 1940 (wid. Apr. 1981); 1 child, Robert N. Head; m. Arthur G. Hammond, Aug. 24, 1995. BS, Oakland City U., Ind., 1955; MS, Ind. State Coll., 1964. Tchr. Princeton (Ind.) H.S., 1955-64; instr.. Oakland City U., 1964-77; owner, operator mobile home ct., Providence, 1973-78; real estate salesperson, appraiser Ball Real Estate, Providence, 1973-89; appraiser Frontier Properties, Okeechobee, Fla., 1973-89. Elected mem. Providence City Coun., 1972-73; adv. coun. Gulfstream Agy. on Aging, West Palm Beach, 1986-87; coun. mem. Cen. Fla. Regional Planning Coun., 1988-89. Mem. AAUW, Elks, Habitat for Humanity, Hospice, Alpha Phi Gamma. Republican. Presbyterian. Avocations: swimming, golf, walking. Home: 622 Delgado Ave Lady Lake FL 32159-8768

HEADRICK, DANIEL RICHARD, history and social sciences educator; b. Bay Shore, N.Y., Aug. 2, 1941; s. William Cecil and Edith (Finkelstein) H.; m. Rita Koplowitz, June 20, 1965 (dec. 1988); children: Isabelle, Juliet, Matthew; m. Kate Ezra, Aug. 23, 1992. B, Lycée de Garçons, Metz, France, 1959; BA, Swarthmore Coll., 1962; MA, Johns Hopkins U., 1964; PhD, Princeton U., 1971. Instr. history Tuskegee (Ala.) Inst., 1968-71, asst. prof., 1971-73, assoc. prof., 1973-75; assoc. prof. social scis. Roosevelt U., Chgo., 1975-82, prof., 1982—. Vis. NEH scholar Hawaii Pacific U., 2000. Author: Ejercito y Politica, 1981, The Tools of Empire, 1981, Tentacles of Progress, 1988, The Invisible Weapon, 1991, The Earth and Its Peoples, 1997, When Information Came of Age, 2000. Coll. Tchrs. fellow NEH, 1983-84, 88-89, Guggenheim fellow, 1994, Sloan fellow, 1998; recipient Faculty Achievement award Burlington No. Found., 1988, 92. Mem. Am. Hist. Assn., World History Assn. (exec. com. 1991—), Soc. for History Tech. (exec. com. 1992—). Home: 5483 S Hyde Park Blvd Chicago IL 60615-5827 Office: Roosevelt U Univ Coll 430 S Michigan Ave Chicago IL 60605-1394 E-mail: dan.headrick@att.net.

HEAL, GEOFFREY MARTIN, economics and business educator; b. Bangor, Wales, Apr. 9, 1944; s. Thomas John and Gwen Margaret (Owen) H.; m. Felicity Chandler, 1967 (div. 1979); m. Ann Marie Biafore, 2000; children: Bridget, Marie, Natasha. BA first class, Cambridge U., 1966, PhD, 1969. Dir. studies Christs Coll., Cambridge U., 1967-73; prof. econs. Sussex U., Brighton, Eng., 1973-81, head dept. econs., 1976-81; mng. editor Rev. Econ. Studies, London, 1973-78; dir. Economists Adv. Group, London, 1975-80; prof. Essex U., Colchester, Eng., 1981-83; exec. dir. Fin. Telecommunications, London, 1984-89; prof. Grad. Sch. Bus., Columbia U., N.Y.C., 1983—, sr. vice dean Grad. Sch. Bus., 1991-94; Fulbright prof. U. Siena, Italy, 1997; Paul Garret prof. pub. policy and corp. responsibility Columbia U., N.Y.C., 1995—, prof. Sch. Internat. and Pub. Affairs, 2002—. Cons. U.K. Dept. Energy, London, 1973-76, U.S. Dept. Energy, Washington, 1976-78, OPEC Sec. Gen., Vienna, Austria, 1979-81, OECD, Paris, 1994, Global Environ. Facility, World Bank, 1994, Internat. Brotherhood of Teamsters, 1995-2000, United Mineworkers of Am., 1990-98; mem. Pew Oceans Commn.; dir. Beijer Inst., Royal Swedish Acad. Scis, 2001—; chair Nat. Rsch. Coun. Com. on Valuing Svcs. of Aquatic Ecosystems, 2002-2003. Author: The Theory of Economic Planning, 1973, Public Policy and the Tax System, 1976, Economic Theory and Exhaustible Resources, 1979, Linear Algebra and Linear Economics, 1980, The Evolving International Economy, 1987, Oil in the International Economy, 1991, The Economics of Exhaustible Resources, 1993, Sustainability: Dynamics and Uncertainty, 1998, Valuing the Future, 1998, Topological Methods in Social Choice, 1998, The Economics of Increasing Returns, 1999, Environmental Markets, 2000, Nature and the Marketplace, 2000. Grantee NSF, NOAA, Sloan Found. Fellow: Royal Soc. Arts, Econometric Soc.; mem.: Union of Concerned Scientists (dir.). Home: 800 W End Ave # 13E New York NY 10025-5467 Office: Columbia Univ Bus Sch Uris Hall New York NY 10027 E-mail: gmh1@columbia.edu.

HEALD, DEBORAH ANN, special education educator, counselor; b. Wilmington, Del., Nov. 14, 1950; d. Paul M. and Roselda K. (Cloud) H. BS in Elem. and Spl. Edn., Del. State Coll., 1986; BRE, Bapt. Bible Coll., Springfield, Mo., 1972; MEd, MA in Spl. Edn., Del. State U., 1996. Elem. tchr. Elkton (Md.) Christian Sch., 1972-73, Fairwinds Christian Sch., Bear, Del., 1975-76; tchr. spl. edn. and reading Colonial Sch. Dist., New Castle, Del., 1986-88; at risk counselor Gunning Bedford Mid. Sch., Delaware City, Del., 1988-90; spl. edn. tchr. Herperia (Calif.) Jr. High Sch., 1990-93, George Read Middle Sch., New Castle, Del., 1993-94, Bancroft Acad., Wilmington, Del., 1994-97, Drew/Pyle Comm. Arts Traditional Sch., Wilmington, 1997-99, Pulaski Elem. Sch. World Langs., Wilmington, 1999—. Mem. NEA, Del. State Edn. Assn., Coun. for Exceptional Children. Home: PO Box 10211 Wilmington DE 19850-0211

HEALE, DARRYL RHAWN, elementary and secondary education educator; b. Toms River, N.J., Apr. 21, 1969; s. Christopher Michael and Judith Ann (Anders) H. AS, Ocean County Coll., Toms River, 1989; BS in Edn. with honors, West Chester U., 1992; cert. guidance counselor, Georgian Ct. Coll., Lakewood, N.J., 1996. Cer. tchr. health and phys. edn. grades K-12, N.J. Tchr. adaptive phys. edn. and health Manchester (N.J.) Regional Schs., 1992—; health/phys. edn. tchr. Manchester H.S. Coach area high sch. soccer team, 1991; softball coach Manchester H.S., 1994. Mem. AAHPERD, Pa. Alliance for Health, Phys. Edn., Recreation and Dance, Delta Kappa Pi. Methodist. Avocations: weight training, surfing, skiing, travel. Home: 746 Northstream Dr Toms River NJ 08753-4421 Office: Regional Day Sch Manchester High School Manchester NJ 03301

HEALEY, DEBORAH LYNN, education administrator; b. Columbus, Ohio, Sept. 15, 1952; d. James Henry and Marjorie Jean Healey; 1 child, Jesse Healey Winterowd. BA in German/Religion, Queen's U., 1974; MA in Linguistics, U. Oreg., 1976, PhD in Edn., 1993. Instr. Lane C.C., Eugene, Oreg., 1976-77; instr., materials developer Rogue C.C., Ashland, Oreg., 1977-79; instr. Chemeketa C.C., Salem, Oreg., 1979-80; instr., computer ops. English Lang. Inst. Oreg. State U., Corvallis, 1979-85, 88-93; instr., computer ops. Yemen-Am. Lang. Inst., Sana'a, Yemen, 1985-88; programmer, cons. Internat. Soc. for Tech. in Edn., Eugene, 1989-91; coord. instr. English Lang. Inst. Oreg. State U., Corvallis, 1993-95, tech. coord., 1995-99, dir., 1999—; acad. specialist U.S. Dept. State, Thailand, 2000, Brazil, 1995, Qatar, Oman, 2002. Macintosh support Computer-Enhanced Lang. Instrn. Archive, 1993—; computer cons. in field. Author: (book) Something To Do On Tuesday, 1995; co-author: (chpts.) A Handbook for Language Program Administrators, 1997, CALL Environments Research, Practice and Critical Issues, 1999; editor, author Computer-Assisted English Lang. Learning Jour., 1990-98; co-editor (ann. publ.) CALL Interest Sect. Software List, 1990—; co-author (software) The House, At The Zoo, 1993. Recipient D. Scott Enright TESOL Interest Sect. Svc. award, 2001. Mem. TESOL (interest sect. chair 1992-92), Oreg. TESOL (newsletter editor 1981-84), Nat. Assn. Fgn. Student Advisors-Assn. Internat. Educators, Am. Ednl. Rsch. Assn., Computer Assn. Lang. Instrn. Consortium. Avocations: language learning, traveling, music, reading. Office: ELI Oreg State Univ 301 Snell Hall Corvallis OR 97331-8515

HEALEY, ROBERT WILLIAM, school system administrator; b. Charleston, Ill., Sept. 29, 1947; s. William Albert and Ruth M. (Wiedenhoeft) H.; m. Sharon Barbara Grande, Aug. 7, 1982; children: William Robert, Steven Anthony. BS in Elem. Edn., Ea. Ill. U., 1970, MS in Ednl. Adminstrn., 1972; EdD in Curriculum and Supervision, No. Ill. U., 1977. Cert. elem. teaching K-9, gen. adminstrv. K-12, Ill. Prin. Glidden Elem. Sch., De Kalb, Ill., 1972-74, Lincoln Elem. Sch., De Kalb, 1974-83, Littlejohn Elem. Sch., De Kalb, 1983-84, Littlejohn and Cortland Elem. Schs., De Kalb, 1984-85; prin., dist. coord. testing and evaluation Jefferson Elem. Sch., De Kalb, 1986-96; dir. personnel DeKalb Sch. Dist., 1996—98, dir. HR, 1999—2001, asst. to supt., 2001—03; interim prin. Brooks Elem. Sch., DeKalb, 2002. Dir. Title I Elem. and Secondary Edn. Act., Pre-Sch. Base Line Program, 1972-74; dir. gifted edn. Bd. Edn. Negotiating Team, 1974-81, coordinator dist. testing and evaluation, 1981-84, coordinator spl. edn., 1984-86; mem. adv. bd. Evanston (Ill.) Educators Computer Software,

1983—; dir. testing DeKalb Sch. Dist. 428, 1986—; treas. No. Ill. Commn. for Gifted Edn., Oakbrook, 1980-82; mem. various elem. sch. planning and program councils, De Kalb, 1973-2003; coordinator numerous sch. programs, De Kalb, 1973-2003; leader numerous workshops DeKalb, 1976-85; sec. De Kalb Sch. Bd. Study com. on sch. lunch programs, 1976-77; cons. Scholastic Testing Service, 1980-83; chmn. dist. reading com., De Kalb, 1986—; mem. bd. edn. collective bargaining team, 2001—. Coordinator 10 yr. study of student achievement in DeKalb Schs., 1980-83; author numerous presentations, 1975-84; co-author: DeKalb School District Parent Handbook, 1986; contbr. articles to profl. jours; inventor multi-purpose table and stage. Chmn. Task Force I DeKalb Sch. Dist., 1973-75; treas. No. Ill. Planning Commn., 1980-82; active Supts. Task Force on Spl. Edn., DeKalb, 1976-79, Mayor's Commn. DeKalb Planning Commn. for Yr. of Child, DeKalb, 1979, Dist. Computer Com., DeKalb, 1980-83, Dist. Revenue and Donations Com., 1980-83, Ill. PTA. Recipient Disting. Program award Nat. Assn. for Tchr. Educators, Chgo., 1978; named Citizen of Day, Sta. WLBK, De Kalb, 1983; Reading is Fundamental grantee Lincoln Sch., 1980-83, Ill. Ctr., 1980-83, Ill. Arts Coun., Littlejohn Sch., 1984, Jefferson Sch., 1986; named master, Ill. Adminstrs. Acad., 1995. Mem. NEA (life), ASCD, NAESP (Nat. Disting. Prin. award representing Ill. 1995), Ill. Prins. Assn. (Prin. of Yr. award 1995, Herman Graves award 1998), Ill. Assn. for Supervsion and Curriculum Devel., Soc. Am. Inventors, Ill. Coun. Gifted Edn. Avocations: swimming, computer, home. Office: De Kalb Cmty Unit Sch Dist 901 S 4th St Dekalb IL 60115-4411

HEALY, DANIEL THOMAS, secondary education educator; b. Wenona, Ill., May 25, 1930; s. Timothy John and Helen Ann (Duller) H.; m. Beverly Ann Imm, Oct. 1, 1966; 1 child, Owen Jay. AA, Fresno (Calif.) City Coll., 1972; BS, Calif. State U., Fresno, 1974; MA, Azusa (Calif.) Pacific U., 1980. Farmer, Wenona, 1948—58; mgr. Garfield Grain Elevator, Wenona, 1958—66; supt. Cargill Inc., San Joaquin, Calif., 1966—69; educator Redlands (Calif.) Unified Sch. Dist., 1974—92, Orangewood H.S., Redlands, 1992—. Advisor Future Farmers of Am., Redlands High Sch., 1974-88; leader Osage Livewires 4-H Club, Wenona, 1950-55. Performer on nat. TV, movies including Hero and Hot Shots II, appearances as Pres. Bush celebrity look-alike, 1990—. Sgt. U.S. Army, 1953-54. Fellow Am. Legion (life mem.), Elks (life). Roman Catholic. Office: Orangewood High Sch 515 Texas St Redlands CA 92374-3071

HEALY, JULIA SCHMITT, artist, educator; b. Elmhurst, Ill., Mar. 28, 1947; d. Albert Leo and Louise Anne (Tilly) Schmitt; m. Richard Healy, Apr. 6, 1973 (div. Aug. 1990); children: Patrick, Katharine. BFA, Sch. of the Art Inst. Chgo., 1970, MFA, 1972; student, U. Chgo., Yale U., Dalhousie U., NYU; SDA, SUNY, Stony Brook, 2003. Dir. Eye Level Gallery, Halifax, N.C., 1974-76; artist, tchr. Studio in a Sch., N.Y.C., 1989-94; tchr. Valley Stream Sch. Dist. 13, 1994—. Adj. prof. Sch. of the Art Inst. Chgo., 1970-72, Ocean County Coll., Toms River, N.J., 1979-81, Pratt Inst., Bklyn., 1991-93, CUNY/CSI, 1998—; art adv. bd. Chancellor's Bd., N.Y.C. Pub. Schs.; edn. com. Snug Harbor Cultural Ctr., Staten Island, N.Y., 1991—; dir. Art Lab, Staten Island, 1990-93, Alice Austen House, Staten Island, 1990-99. Columnist: (syndicated) Artmakers, 1990—; exhbns. include Staten Island Mus., 1989, Newhouse Ctr. for Contemporary Art, 1987, Soho 20, Sch. Art Inst. Chgo.; over 50 group exhbns., three maj. pub. commns.; pub. art installation Von Briesen Park, NYC, Faber Park. Mem. Community Bd. Waterfront Com., Staten Island, 199—; vol. Project Hospitality, Staten Island, 1989—. Recipient artist's grant Staten Island Coun. on the Arts, 1987, 91, Can. Coun., Ottawa, 1976-78, fellowship Yale Summer Sch. of Music and Art, 1969, Weissglass award Staten Island Mus. Mem. Artists Space, New Mus., Tibetan Mus., Mudlane Soc., Soc. for Art Religion and Contemporary Culture (bd. dirs. 2003). Home: 63 E 9th St 14R New York NY 10003

HEALY-SOVA, PHYLLIS M. CORDASCO, school social worker; b. Newark, Oct. 2, 1939; d. Carl and Mae (Seritella) Cordasco; m. James B. Healy, Dec. 22, 1966 (widowed); m. Peter J. Sova, Aug. 15, 2001. BA, Caldwell Coll., 1978; MS, Columbia U. Sch. Social Work, 1981; MA, Fairleigh Dickinson U., 1989. Cert. social worker, N.Y.; sch. social work specialist; diplomate in clin. social work; qualified clin. social worker; lic. clin. social worker, N.J. Social worker United Cerebral Palsy of North Jersey, East Orange, 1982-84, Cerebral Palsy Assn. Middlesex County, Edison, N.J., 1984-85; sch. social worker, mem. presch. child study team Newark Bd. Edn., 1985-92, social svcs. coord. N.J. Goodstarts prog. curr. svcs., 1992-96; sch. social work specialist Newark Bd. Edn., Office of Early Childhood, 1996—. Cons. in field. Founding mem. sr. citizen ctr. Borough of Caldwell, mem., past chair rent review bd. Recipient Alumna of Yr. award Caldwell Coll., 1985-86, Marion award, 1991, Veritas award, 1999. Mem. AAUW (legis. chair 1982-84), NASW, Nat. Assn. for the Edn. of Young Children, Acad. Cert. Social Workers, Coun. for Exceptional Children (N.J. divsn. early childhood pres. 1992-94, Mideast regional coord. for the internat. divsn. for early childhood 1994-98), Caldwell Coll. Alumni Assn. (scholar chair 1982-87), Columbia U. Alumni Assn. Roman Catholic. Office: Newark Pub Schs 2 Cedar St Newark NJ 07102-3015 Home: 12 Harkey Ct Roseland NJ 07068 E-mail: pandp12horkey@aol.com.

HEANEY, SEAMUS JUSTIN, poet, educator; b. Mossbawn, County Derry, No. Ireland, Apr. 13, 1939; s. Patrick and Margaret H.; m. Marie Devlin, 1965; children: Michael, Christopher, Catherine. BA, Queen's U., Belfast, 1961; postgrad., St. Joseph's Coll., Belfast, 1961-62; PhD (hon.), Queen's U., Belfast. Tchr. St. Thomas's Secondary Sch., Belfast, No. Ireland, 1962-63; lectr. St. Joseph's Coll. Edn., Belfast, 1963-66, Queen's U., Belfast, 1966-72; free-lance writer, 1972-75; lectr. Carysfort Coll., 1975-81; Boylston visiting prof. rhetoric and oratory Harvard U., 1982—96, Ralph Waldo Emerson poet-in-residence, 1996—; prof. poetry Oxford U., 1989-94. Author: Eleven Poems, 1965, Door into the Dark, 1969, Death of a Naturalist, 1966 (Somerset Maugham award 1967, Cholmondeley award 1968), Wintering Out, 1972, North, 1975 (W.H. Smith award, Duff Copper prize), Stations, 1975, Bog Poems, 1975, Field Work, 1979, Poems: 1965-75, 1980, Preoccupations: Selected Prose 1968-78, 1980, Sweeney Astray: A Version from the Irish, 1984, Station Island, 1984, The Haw Lantern, 1987 (Whitbead award), The Government of the Tongue, 1988, The Place of Writing, 1990, New Selected Poems, 1966-78, 1990, (play) The Cure at Troy (A Version of Sophocles' Philoctetes), 1991, Seeing Things, 1991, (Oxford lectures) The Redress of Poetry, 1995, The Spirit Level, 1996; ed. poetry anthologies., Beowulf, A New Verse Translation, 1999, Electric Light, 2001, Finders Keepers: Selected Prose, 2002. Recipient Eric Gregory award, 1966, Faber Meml. prize, 1968, Irish Acad. Letters award, 1971, Denis Devlin Meml. award, 1973, Am.-Irish Found. award, 1975, E.M.Forster award Nat. Inst. Arts and Letters, 1975, Bennett Award, 1982, Premio Mondello (Internat. Poetry prize) Mondello Found., Palermo, Sicily, 1993, Nobel Prize for Literature, 1995. Mem. Royal Dublin Soc. (hon. life), Am. Acad. Arts and Letters (fgn. hon.), Am. Acad. Arts and Scis. (hon. life), Irish Acad. Letters. Office: Harvard U Dept English Cambridge MA 02138

HEAP, SUZANNE RUNDIO, elementary school educator; b. Long Beach, Calif., June 10, 1935; d. George Lionel and Jennie Bolton (Rundio) Heap; children: Katharine Trent, Cecily Gullett. BA, Mary Washington Coll., Fredericsburg, Va., 1957; MA in Edn., Azua-Pacific U., 1978; student, Calif. Western-USIU, San Diego, 1970. Cert. elem. tchr. K-8, Calif., Level I Orff-Schulwerk nat. cert; cert. in master gardening, Calif. Tchr. 5th and 6th grades Chula Vista (Calif.) Elem. Sch. Dist., kindergarten tchr., ret., 1991. Cons. bargaining team Chula Vista Edn. Assn. Vol. with U. Calif. Cooperative Extension/U.S. Dept. Agr. Vol. numerous civic orgns.; past exec. com. bd., recording sec. U. Calif. Coop. Ext. Master Gardener, San Diego County. Recipient Instruction grant, ORFF Instrumentarium, We Honor Ours award San Diego county svc. ctr. coun. Calif. Tchrs. Assn., 1991. Mem. Calif. Ret. Tchrs. Assn., NSF Math. Inst. Univ. Calif. San Diego, Am. ORFF-Schulwerk Assn. (bd. sec. San Diego chpt. 1991-93), Crown Garden Club (rec. sec., past pres.), San Diego Floral Assn. (bd. dirs.), Coronado Floral Assn. (sec.), San Diego Horticulture Soc. Home: 620 1st St Coronado CA 92118-1202 Fax: (619) 437-4762.

HEAP, SYLVIA STUBER, educator; b. Clifton Springs, N.Y., Sept. 25, 1929; d. Stanley Irving and Helen (Hill) Stuber; m. Walker Ratcliffe Heap, June 9, 1951; children: Heidi Anne, Cynthia Joan, Walker Ratcliffe III. BA cum laude, Bates Coll., 1950; postgrad., U. Conn. Sch. Social Work, 1952-54, Boston U. Sch. Social Work, 1953-54, SUNY, Brockport, 1979, SUNY, Potsdam, 1980; MS in Adult Edn., Syracuse U., 1989. Dir. Y-Teens YWCA, Holyoke, Mass., 1950-51; social group worker West Haven (Conn.) Cmty. House, 1951-54; program dir. YWCA, Ann Arbor, 1954-55, part-time, 1955-59; mem. adv. bd. divsn. continuing edn. Jefferson C.C., 1965—, chmn. adv. bd., 1968-98. Pres. Jefferson County Med. Soc. Aux., 1971-72; bd. dirs. St. Lawrence Valley Ednl. TV, 1973-83, sec., 1976-80, treas., 1980-82; v.p., 1982-83, dir. Chem. People Project, 1983; bd. dirs. Watertown Lyric Theatre, 1973-83; bd. dirs. N.Y. State Med. Soc. Aux., 1974-85, 2d v.p. bd., 1979-80; fitness instr. Jefferson Community Coll., Watertown, 1977-86; chmn. health projects N.Y. State Med. Soc. Aux., 1981-85. Named Citizen of Yr., Greater Watertown C. of C., 1975, Friend of C.C., N.Y. State Bd. Trustees, 1988. Mem. AAUW, Bates Key, Alliance with the Jefferson County Med. Soc., Phi Beta Kappa. Unitarian Universalist (UN office envoy 1978—, St. Lawrence dist. envoy 1992—).

HEAPHY, LESLIE ANNE, history educator; b. Liberty, N.Y., Dec. 4, 1964; d. James Richard and Jean Isabel (Thomson) H. BA, Siena Coll., Loudonville, N.Y., 1987; MA, U. Toledo, 1989, PhD, 1995. Grad. asst. U. Toledo, 1987-93, instr., 1994-95; small group dir. Collingwood Presbyn. Ch., Toledo, 1993-95; asst. prof. Kent State U., 1995—. Speaker in field. Prodr.: The Negro Leagues, 1869-1960, 2003; contbr. articles and revs. Mem. Soc. for Am. Baseball Rsch. (chair com. women in baseball 1993-98), Phi Alpha Theta. Presbyterian. Avocations: running, reading, collecting baseball cards. Home: 135 Hillcrest Ave North Canton OH 44720 E-mail: lheaphy@stark.kent.edu.

HEARN, BEVERLY JEAN, secondary education educator, librarian; b. Lexington, Tenn., Sept. 10, 1953; d. James Lawrence and Marie (Sparks) Kee; m. Larry Joseph Hearn, June 15, 1973; children: Matthew Joseph, David Andrew. BA, Union U., 1974; MLS, George Peabody Coll. for Tchrs., 1975; EdD, Memphis State U., 1991. Acqusitions librarian Union U., Jackson, Tenn., 1975-80, reference librarian, 1980-86; tchr. Madison County Bd. Edn., Jackson, 1986—. Instr. Memphis State U., 1990-95, Jackson State C.C., 1992-97; freelance cataloger, 1978-86. Mem. TESOL, NEA, Internat. Reading Assn., Assn. for Curriculum Devel. Democrat. Baptist. Home: 558 Wallace Rd Jackson TN 38305-2839

HEARN, THOMAS K., JR., university president; b. Opp, Ala., July 5, 1937; s. Thomas H. Hearn; m. Laura Walter; children: Thomas K., William Neely, Lindsay. BA summa cum laude, Birmingham-So. Coll., 1959; BD, Baptist Theol. Sem., 1963; PhD (NDEA fellow), Vanderbilt U., 1965. Instr. Birmingham-So. Coll., 1964—65; asst. prof. Coll. William and Mary, 1965—68, assoc. prof., 1968—74; prof. philosophy U. Ala., Birmingham, 1974—83, chmn. dept. philosophy, 1974—76; dean U. Ala. Sch. Humanities, Birmingham, 1976—78; v.p. U. Ala. Univ. Coll., Birmingham, 1978—83; pres. Wake Forest U., Winston-Salem, NC, 1983—. Contbr. articles to profl. jours. Recipient Thomas Jefferson Teaching award, 1970; fellow, Council Philos. Studies, 1968, Coop. Program in Humanities, 1969—70; grantee, Nat. Found. Humanities, 1967, Faculty Summer grant, Coll. William and Mary, 1970, 1972—73. Mem.: AAUP, Newcomen Soc. N.Am., David Hume Soc., Am. Philos. Assn., Soc. Philosophy Religion (pres. 1974—75), So. Soc. Philosophy, Psychology (exec. council 1974—77, Jr. award), Phi Kappa Phi, Omicron Delta Kappa, Phi Beta Kappa. Home: 1000 Kearns Ave Winston Salem NC 27106-5824 Office: Wake Forest U Office of Pres PO Box 7226 Winston Salem NC 27109 E-mail: tkh@wfu.edu.

HEARNE, GEORGE ARCHER, academic administrator; b. Tampa, Fla., Oct. 31, 1934; s. William Duncan and Marguerite Estelle (Archer) H.; m. Jean May Helmstadter, June 9, 1956; children: Diana Leslie, George Harrison. BA, Bethany Coll., 1955; MDiv, Yale U., 1958; MA, Ill. State U., 1968; HHD (hon.), Culver-Stockton Coll., 1986; LLD, Bethany Coll., 1997. Min. Arlington Christian Ch., Jacksonville, Fla., 1958-59; dir. admissions Eureka (Ill.) Coll., 1960-70, v.p. student devel., 1970-73, dean admissions and student devel., 1973-77, dean admissions and coll. rels., 1977-82, v.p. coll. rels., 1982-84, exec. v.p., 1984-85, pres., 1985—. Bd. dirs. Christian Ch., Ill., Wis. and Ind., 1985—, Higher Edn. divsn. Christian Ch., St. Louis, 1985—; pres. Eureka Bd. Edn., 1967-76; active various cmty. drives. Mem. Assoc. Colls. Ill. (bd. dirs. 1985—), Fedn. Ill. Ind. Colls. and Univs. (bd. dirs. 1985—, exec. com. 2000—), Coun. for Advancement and Support of Edn., Coun. Ind. Colls., Coun. of Pres. (higher edn. div.). Lodges: Rotary. Avocations: reading, music, antiques, golf. Office: Eureka Coll 300 E College Ave Eureka IL 61530-1562 E-mail: ghearne@eureka.edu.

HEARRON, PATRICIA FOLINO, child development specialist, educator; b. Cleve., July 30, 1943; d. Paul John and Dorothy Helen (Langford) Folino; m. William Thomas Hearron, Oct. 27, 1968. AB, Ohio U., 1966; MA, Mich. State U., 1977, PhD, 1992. Cert. elem. tchr., Mich., N.C. Caseworker Maternal & Infant Health Project, Buffalo, 1969-71; social work assoc. Children and Youth Project, Washington, 1972-73; presch. dir. St. John's Episcopal Presch., Saginaw, Mich., 1974-78; licensing cons. divsn. child daycare licensing Mich. Dept. Social Svcs., Saginaw, 1978-94; prof. child devel. Appalachian State U., Boone, N.C., 1994—. Adj. prof. Ctrl. Mich. U., Saginaw Valley State U., Mich. State U., 1981-94; edn. cons. Bay City (Mich.) Pub. Schs., 1993-94, N.C. Dept. Pub. Instrn., Raleigh, 1996—. Author (textbook): Management of Child Development Centers, 1997, 2d edit., 2003, Guiding Young Children, 1999. Bd. sec. Watauga County Childrens Coun., Boone, 1997. Paolucci meml. scholar Mich. State U., 1989, Marie Dye fellow, 1990. Mem. Nat. Assn. Edn. Young Children, Assn. Childhood Edn. Internat. (mem. publs. com. 1997—), Early Childhood Coun. for Exceptional Children (N.C. divsn. sec. 1996—), N.C. Assn. Edn. Young Children (mem. governing bd. 1997-99). Avocation: travel. Office: Family & Consumer Scis LS Dougherty Bldg Appalachian State U Boone NC 28608-0001

HEART, SANDY See HORNER, SANDRA

HEATER, WILLIAM HENDERSON, retired psychology educator; b. Webster Groves, Mo., May 12, 1928; s. Elsor and Mary Eliza (Henderson) H.; m. Mary Ellen Fischbach, Jan. 22, 1955; children: John William, Susan Elizabeth Salinas, David Julius. BA, Denison U., 1950; MDiv, Union Theol. Sem., 1953; PhD, Mich. State U., 1967. Asst. min. Fort Street Presbyn. Ch., Detroit, 1953-56; min. 1st Bapt. Ch., Nitro, W.Va., 1956-59, Owosso, Mich., 1959-64; instr. psychology Lansing (Mich.) C.C., 1966-69, chmn. social sci. dept., 1969-86, prof., 1986-93. Vis. scholar U. Mich., 1991. Mem. Lansing Bd. Edn., 1978-89, v.p., 1979, 80, 88, pres., 1981, 86, 87; bd. dirs. Haven House, East Lansing. Recipient Excellence in Tchg. award United Ch. of Christ Gen. Synod, 1989. Mem. Torch Club Internat., Greater Lansing UN Assn. (pres. 2001-02). Democrat. Mem. United Church of Christ. Avocations: travel, hiking, stained glass, gardening, numismatics. Home: 2025 Cogswell Dr Lansing MI 48906-3610 E-mail: bheater@tir.com.

HEATH, DAVID CLAY, mathematics educator, consultant; b. Oak Park, Ill., Dec. 23, 1942; s. Wilbur Curtis and Margaret Helen (Wasson) H.; m. Judith Ellen Simonson, June 13, 1964; children: Kelley Dianne, Michael David, Susan Kathleen. AB, Kalamazoo (Mich.) Coll., 1964; MA, U. Ill., 1965, PhD, 1969. Asst. prof. Sch. Math. U. Minn., Mpls., 1969-75; asst. prof. Cornell U., Ithaca, N.Y., 1975-78, assoc. prof., 1978-88, prof., 1988-96, Merrill Lynch prof. fin. engrg., 1996—; prof. dept. math. scis. Carnegie Mellon U., Pitts., 1997-99; Hoch prof. math. scis., 1999—. Vis. asst. prof. sch. stats. U. Calif., Berkeley, 1977-78; vis. assoc. prof. sch. math. and stats. U. Minn., 1983-84; vis. prof. U. Strasbourg, France, 1990, 92-93; cons. Galton-Gauss Ptnrs., Berkeley, 1978-81, IBM Corp., Endicott, N.Y., 1981-84, The Options Group, N.Y.C., 1984-87, U.S. Army C.E., 1987-88, Quaker Oats, 1990, Credit Suisse, 1993, Morgan Stanley, 1994, Falcon Asset Mgmt., 1997; bd. dirs. Lehman Bros. Fin. Products, Lehman Bros. Derivative Products. Mem. Am. Math. Soc., Inst. for Math. Statistics, Informs. Avocations: music, scuba, photography. Office: Carnegie Mellon Univ Dept Math Scis Pittsburgh PA 15213-3890

HEATH, DWIGHT BRALEY, anthropologist, educator; b. Hartford, Conn., Nov. 19, 1930; s. Percy Leonard and Luise (Hosp) H.; 1 child, David Braley (dec.). AB in Social Rels., Harvard U., 1952; PhD in Anthropology, Yale U., 1959. Mem. faculty Brown U., 1959—, prof. anthropology, 1970—. Dir. Ctr. for Latin Am. Studies, 1984-87, 88-89; vis. prof., U.S. and abroad, cons. in field. Author: A Journal of the Pilgrims at Plymouth, 1963, 86, Land Reform and Social Revolution in Bolivia, 1969, Historical Dictionary of Bolivia, 1972, Contemporary Cultures and Societies of Latin America, 1965, 74, 3d edit., 2002, Cross-Cultural Approaches to the Study of Alcohol, 1976, Alcohol Use and World Cultures, 1980, Cultural Factors in Alcohol Research and Treatment of Drinking Problems, 1981, International Handbook on Alcohol and Cultures, 1995, Drinking Occasions, 2000; contbr. articles to profl. jours. With AUS, 1952-54. Grantee Nat. Acad. Scis., 1974, Am. Philos. Soc., 1972, Social Sci. Research Council, 1958, Doherty Found., 1956-57, Nat. Inst. Alcohol Abuse and Alcoholism, 1976-81. Mem. AAAS, Am. Anthrop. Assn., Am. Ethnol. Soc., Am. Soc. Ethnohistory, Royal Anthrop. Inst., L.Am. Studies Assn. Office: Brown U Dept Anthropology PO Box 1921 Providence RI 02912-1921

HEATH, LINDA A. gifted and talented educator; b. Milw., Sept. 4, 1952; d. Jack Aaron and Thelma Lillian (Olsen) H.; m. Leo J. Summers, Oct. 9, 1976 (div. June 1988). BA in Biology and English, Kent State U., 1973, BS in Edn., 1978; MS in Biology, U. Akron, 1987; cert. in adminstrn., Ashland U.; cert. in gifted education, Kent State Univ. Cert. tchr. biology, English 7-12, gifted K-12, Ohio. Clk., typist MB Oil & Gas Co., Canton, Ohio, 1973-74; park ranger U.S. Army Corps of Engrs., Deerfield, Ohio, 1974-77; tchr. biology Tallmadge (Ohio) H.S., 1978—85; tchr. gifted edn. Tallmadge City Schs., 1985-86, Plain Local Schs., Canton, 1986-87; tchr. English, biology, ecology, and field biology Hoban H.S., Akron, Ohio, 1987-91; tchr. gifted edn. Lucas County Office of Edn., Toledo, 1991-92, Marlington Mid. Sch., Alliance, Ohio, 1992-95, Lake Mid. Sch., Hartville, Ohio, 1992-95, Davey Mid. Sch., 1994-95; coord. gifted edn. Waterloo Local Schs., Atwater, Ohio, 1992-95, Portage County Ednl. Svc. Ctr., Ravenna, Ohio, 1995—99; gifted coord. Ednl. Svc. Ctr. Cuyahoga County, Valley View, Ohio, 1999—2001; supr. gifted svcs. Parma (Ohio) City Schs., 2001—03, Berea (Ohio) City Schs., 2003—. Edn. chair Greater Akron Audubon, 1984-88; chair youth theater Weathervane Women's Bd., Akron, 1991-92, asst. treas., 1993-96. Vol. Quail Hollow State Park, Hartville, Ohio, 1993—, Lyceum Programs, Cuyahoga Valley Nat. Recreation Area, Peninsula, Ohio, 1995, Akron (Ohio) Art Mus. Jennings scholar M.H. Jennings Found., 1981-82, Wildlife Camp scholarship Greater Akron Audubon, 1984. Mem.: Consortium Ohio Coords. for Gifted (treas. 2001—03), Ohio Assn. Gifted Children (Educator of Yr. award 1998), Environ. Edn. Coun. Ohio (life), N.Am. Assn. Environ. Edn. (life), Phi Delta Kappa, Delta Kappa Gamma (newsletter editor 2002—, founds. chmn. 2001—). Avocations: reading, traveling, gardening, bicycling, theater. Home: 8481 Acadia Dr Northfield OH 44067-3215

HEATHCOCK, CLAYTON HOWELL, chemistry educator, researcher; b. San Antonio, Tex., July 21, 1936; s. Clayton H. and Frances E. (Lay) H.; m. Mabel Ruth Sims, Sept. 6, 1957 (div. 1972); children: Cheryl Lynn, Barbara Sue, Steven Wayne, Rebecca Ann; m. Cheri R. Hadley, Nov. 28, 1980. BSc, Abilene Christian Coll., Tex., 1958; PhD, U. Colo., 1963. Supr. chem. analysis group Champion Paper and Fiber Co., Pasadena, Tex., 1958-60; asst. prof. chemistry U. Calif.-Berkeley, 1964-70, assoc. prof., 1970-75, prof., 1975—, chmn., 1986-89, dean Coll. of Chemistry, 1999—. Chmn. Medicinal Chemistry Study Sect., NIH, Washington, 1981-83; mem. sci. adv. coun. Abbott Labs., 1986-97. Author: Introduction to Organic Chemistry, 1976; editor-in chief Organic Syntheses, 1985-86, Jour. Organic Chemistry, 1989-99; contbr. numerous articles to profl. jours. Recipient Alexander von Humboldt U.S. Scientist, 1978, Allan R. Day award, 1989, Prelog medal, 1991, Centenary medal Royal Soc. Chemistry, 1995. Mem. AAAS, Am. Acad. Arts and Scis., Am. Chem. Soc. (chmn. divsn. organic chemistry 1985, Ernest Guenther award 1986, award for creative work in synthetic organic chemistry 1990, A.C. Cope scholar 1990, H.C. Brown medal 2002), Nat. Acad. Scis. (H.C. Brown award 2002), Royal Soc. Chemistry (Centenary medal 1995), Am. Soc. Pharmacology. Home: 5235 Alhambra Valley Rd Martinez CA 94553-9765 Office: U Calif Dept Chemistry Berkeley CA 94720-1460 E-mail: heathcock@cchem.berkeley.edu.

HEATON, JEAN M. early childhood educator; b. Equality, Ill., Feb. 27, 1933; d. Lytle and Loretta (Drone) Mossman; m. Fred T. Heaton, June 10, 1954 (div. Dec. 1979); children: Fred T., Laura, Sheri; m. Michael Marticorena, Mar. 14, 1987. BS in Home Econs., Southern Ill. U., 1955, MS in Edn., 1958; PhD in Child Devel., Early Childhood Edn, Fla. State U., 1971. Cert. secondary educator Ill., Fla., Calif. Tchr. Corham (Ill.) High Sch., 1955-57; rsch. asst. Southern Ill. U., Carbondale, 1957-58; tchr. Jefferson High Sch., Tampa, Fla., 1958-60, Hamilton Jr. High Sch., Oakland, Calif., 1960-61; prof. San Francisco State U., 1961-94. Ednl. cons. Dept. Home and Cmty. Devel., U. Monrovia, Liberia, 1982, Calif. State Dept. Edn., 1974-76; mem. adv. bd. Skyline Coll., 1973—, coord. Study Tours; presenter at profl. confs. Recipient Meritorious Performance award SFSU, 1986 and 1989. Mem. Infant/Toddler Consortium San Francisco Bay Area (exec. com. 1988-93), San Francisco/San Mateo Child Care Consortium (exec. com. 1987-93), Calif. Coun. on Children and Youth (exec. com. Region II 1982-90), San Francisco Assn. for Edn. Young Children (pres. 1990-92), AAUW (exec. com. San Mateo br. 1981-83, exec. bd. San Carlos br. 1996-2000), Child Care Coord. Coun. of San Mateo County (adv. com. 1995-2000, bd. dirs. 1997—, exec. com. 1997-2000), Family Forum (chair planning com. 1996), Pi Lambda Theta, Omicron Nu.

HEBENSTREIT, JEAN ESTILL STARK, religion educator, practitioner; d. Charles Dickey and Blanche (Hervey) Stark; m. William J. Hebenstreit, Sept. 4, 1942; children: James B., Mark W. Student Conservatory of Music, U. Mo. at Kansas City, 1933-34; AB, U. Kans., 1936. Authorized C.S. practitioner, Kansas City, 1955—; bd. dirs. 3d Ch., Kansas City, 1952-55, chmn. bd., 1955, reader, 1959-62; authorized C.S. tchr. C.S.B., 1964—; chmn. bd. dirs. First Ch. of Christ Scientist, Boston, 1977-83. Mem. Christian Sci. Bd. of Lectureship, Christian Sci. Bd. Edn.; bd. trustees The Christian Sci. Pub. Soc., bd. dirs. First Ch. Christ.Scientist, 1977-83, chmn., 1981-82. Contbr. articles to C.S. lit. Pres. Mother Ch., The First Ch. of Christ, Scientist, 1999, bd. dirs., 1977-83, chmn., 1981-82. Mem. Art of Assembly Parliamentarians (charter, 1st pres.), Pi Epsilon Delta, Alpha Chi Omega (past pres.), Carriage Club. Home: 310 W 49th St Ste A-2 Kansas City MO 64112-2425 Office: 310 W 49th St Apt A-3 Kansas City MO 64112-2425

HEBERLEIN, ALICE LATOURRETTE, healthcare educator, physical education educator, coach; b. L.A., Mar. 7, 1963; d. Louis and Jean Marie LaTourrette; m. Dave Heberlein, Mar. 20, 1993. BA, Idaho State U., 1985, MA, 1987. Tchr., coach Pocatello (Idaho) H.S., 1985—93; head women's volleyball coach Idaho State U., Pocatello, 1993—95; tchr., coach Pocatello H.S., 1995—99, Century H.S., Pocatello, 1999—, chair health dept., 2001—, chair phys. edn. dept., 2003—. Mem. nursing adv. bd. Vo-Tech H.S., Pocatello, 1995—2001; bd. dirs. Idaho Tennis Assn., Boise, 1998—99. Named Coach of Yr., Idaho H.S. Activity Assn., 1990—91, Jour. Coach of Yr., Idaho State Jour., 1999, Region 5 Coach of Yr., 1986—87, 1989—90, 1991—2000, Region 4-5-6 Coach of Yr., 2001. Mem.: Pocatello Edn. Assn. Achievements include coaching volleyball teams, 1989, H.S. state champions, 1990, 4th pl. State of Idaho, 2000, 2d pl. State of Idaho, 2001. Avocations: cross country skiing, hiking, tennis, snow shoeing, skate skiing. Home: 2934 Silverwood Pl Pocatello ID 83201 Office: Century HS 7801 Diamondback Dr Pocatello ID 83204

HEBERT, CHRISTINE ANNE, elementary education educator; b. Waltham, Mass., Aug. 31, 1953; d. Alfred Lionel and Virginia Eugenia (Nogas) Mellor; m. Dennis Armand Hebert, Dec. 18, 1976; 1 child, Kirsten Erica. BS in Early Childhood Edn., Wheelock Coll., Boston, 1975; MS in Spl. Edn., Coll. William and Mary, Williamsburg, Va., 1985; postgrad., Old Dominion U., 1996-99. Cert. elem. tchr., learning disabled, emotional disturbances. Title I aide Fryeburg (Maine) Pub. Schs., 1975-76; title I tutor Conway (N.H.) Pub. Schs., 1976-77; presch. tchr. Elmendorf AFB, Anchorage, 1978-80; counselor, caregiver Intermission/Parent Resource Ctr., Anchorage, 1980-81; residential counselor Group Home for MR Adults, Bridton, Maine, 1983-84; tchr. learning disabled Norfolk (Va.) Pub. Schs., 1985-90, tchr. elem., 1990—, lead tchr. sci., 1992—, tchr. magnet sch. math. and sci., 1995—, sci. tchr. specialist, 1998-99, elem. tchr., 1999—. Tutor Learning Resource Ctr., Virginia Beach, Va., 1986-89; inclusion tchr., 1993-95, 2000—; mem. NASA Tchr. Enhancement Inst., summers 1994, 97; nat. instrnl. leader Activities for Integration of Math. and Sci., 1997-2000. Recipient Norfolk Sch. Bell award, 1994-95; faculty scholar Coll. William and Mary, 1984-85; AT&T fellow Va. Sci. Mus., 1997. Mem. ASCD, Internat. Reading Assn., Nat. Coun. for Tchrs. English, Optimists (pres. Bayside chpt. 1996-97), Kappa Delta Pi. E-mail: chebe@cox.net.

HEBERT, MARY SCHROLLER KORDISCH (MRS. DOUGLAS HEBERT), retired zoology educator, genetic consultant; b. Marysville, Kans., Jan. 23, 1921; d. Rudolph Frank and Ida Theresa Schroller; children: Sherry, Terry, Foster C., Stanley R., Steven A. BS, Kans. State U., 1943, MS, 1944; postgrad., Fort Hays State Tchrs. Coll., 1953, U. Houston, 1965, La. State U., 1968, McNeese State U., 1975. Cert. realtor, notary public. Tchr. pub. schs., Marysville, 1937-40; instr. zoology Kans. State U., Manhattan, 1940-44; elem. tchr. Maplewood, La., 1953-55, LaCrosse, Kans., 1955-56, Lake Charles, La., 1956-57; mem. faculty McNeese State U., Lake Charles, La., 1957-85, assoc. prof. zoology, 1974-85, ret., 1985. Genetic cons., 1985-94; substitute tchr. Calcasieu Parish; instr. Acadiana Tech. Coll., 1990; Grad. Realtor Inst. realtor, notary pub. Co-author zoology and anatomy manuals. Active St. Luke's Simpon Meth. Ch.; past mem. First Christian Ch. Mem. AAAS, VFW, ARTA, La. Ret. Tchrs. Assn., Am. Assn. Ret. Persons (pres.), Am. Bus. Women Assn. (Woman of Yr. award 1981), Order of Ea. Star, Rebekah, Diggers and Weeders Garden Club, Sigma Xi, Phi Alpha Mu, Phi Lambda Chi.

HEBERT, ROBERT D. academic administrator; b. Abbeville, La., Nov. 14, 1938; married. BA, U. Southwestern La., 1959; MA, Fla. State U., 1961, PhD, 1966. Asst. prof. history Miss. State U., 1962-69, assoc. prof. history, 1969-76; prof. McNeese State U., 1976—, v.p. acad. affairs, 1980-87, pres., 1987—. Office: McNeese State U Office Pres Lake Charles LA 70609-0001

HECHLER, ELLEN ELISSA, elementary education educator; b. Detroit, May 20, 1954; d. Mark and Rose (Rifkin) H. BS, Wayne State U., 1976, MEd, 1980, EdD in Curriculum and Instrn., 1995. Math. tchr. Detroit Pub. Schs., 1977—. Presenter workshops in field. Author: (book) A Mathematical Word Search Puzzle Book, 1996, Real-Life Experiences Using Classified Ads, 1997, (card game) Mental Math, 1991, Mental Math Series II, 1992, mental math elem. series, 1997, mental math Spanish edit., 1997; developer in field. Bd. dirs. Orgn. for Rehab. Through Tng., Southfield, 1980—. Recipient scholarship Stephen Bufton Meml. Educators Fund, 1992-93. Mem. ASCD, Detroit Area Coun. Tchrs. of Math. (pres. 1988-89), Mich. Coun. Tchrs. of Math. (exec. bd. dirs. 1980-90, presenter workshops), Nat. Coun. Tchrs. of Math. (presenter workshops), Nat. Coun. Suprs. Math., Mich. Assn. Computer Users in Learning, Southwest Ont. Math. Educators (presenter workshops), Am. Bus. Women's Assn. Avocations: ceramics, taking videos, craft shows. Office: MidMath PO Box 2892 Farmington Hills MI 48333-2892

HECHLER, KEN, former state official, former congressman, political science educator, writer; b. Roslyn, N.Y., Sept. 20, 1914; s. Charles Henry and Catherine Elizabeth (Hauhart) H. BA, Swarthmore Coll., 1935; AM, Columbia U., 1936, PhD, 1940; LittD (hon.), U. Charleston, 1988; HHD (hon.), W. Va. Inst. Tech., 1988, LLD (hon.), 2001. Lectr. govt. Barnard Coll., Columbia Coll., N.Y.C., 1937-41; rsch. asst. to Judge Samuel I. Rosenman, 1939-50; rsch. asst. on Pres. Roosevelt's pub. papers, 1939-50; sect. chief Bur. Census, 1940; pers. technician Office Emergency Mgmt., 1941; adminstrv. analyst Bur. of Budget, 1941-42, 46-47; spl. asst. to Pres. Harry S. Truman, 1949-53; rsch. dir. Stevenson-Kefauver campaign, 1956; adminstrv. aide Senator Carroll of Colo., 1957; mem. 86th-94th Congresses from 4th W.Va. dist., 1959-77; sec. of state State of W.Va., 1985-2001. Sci. and tech. com. 86th to 94th Congresses from 4th W.Va. Dist., chmn. Energy (Fossil Fuels) Subcom.; mem. Joint Com. on Orgn. of Congress, 1965-66, NASA Oversight Subcom. (U.S. Congress); asst. prof. politics Princeton U., 1947-49; prof. polit. sci. Marshall U., Huntington, W.Va., 1957, 82-84, 2001-2003; sci. cons. U.S. House Com. on Sci. and Tech., 1978-80; radio, TV commentator Sta. WHTN, Huntington, 1957-58, Sta. WWHY, 1978; adj. prof. polit. sci. U. Charleston (W.Va.), 1981; keynote spkr. Harry Truman lecture ser. USAF Acad., 1995; lectr. Harry S. Truman Libr., George C. Marshall Found., Washington & Lee U. Law Sch., 1996, Harry S. Truman Coll. of Chgo., 1997, Southern Ilinois Univ., 1998, Mid. Ga. Coll., Appalachian State U., Ill. Wesleyan, Ill. State U., 1999, U. Va., 2000., Central Mich. U. 2000, Yale U. Law Sch., 2001, Duquesne U. Sch. Law, 2002, U. No. Fla., 2003, U. Mich., Flint, 2003, Ea. Mich. U., 2003; panelist, Truman Symposium, Key West, Fla., 2003; disting. vis. scholar, W. Va. State Coll., Inst., W. Va., 2001, Truman Legacy Symposium, Key West, Fla., 2003, Bowling Green State U., 2003. Author: Insurgency: Personalities and Politics of the Taft Era, 1940, The Bridge at Remagen, 1957, rev. edit.,tech. advisor of motion picture based on book, 1969, 1998, West Virginia Memories of President Kennedy, 1965, Toward the Endless Frontier, 1980, The Endless Space Frontier, 1982, Working with Truman, 1982, 3d edit., 2001; weekly columnist Cabell Record, Hampshire Rev., Elk River and Little Kananha News, W.Va. Hillbilly, 1990-2000. Bd. dirs. W.Va. Humanities Coun., 1982-84; del. Dem. Nat. Conv., 1964, 68, 72, 80, 84; mem. W.Va. State Dem. Exec. Com., 1998-99. Served to maj. AUS, 1942-46; served to col. Res. Adm. Nebr. Navy, 1995. Decorated Bronze Star; named W.Va. Son of Yr., W.Va. State Soc. of D.C., 1969, W.Va. Speaker of Yr., W.Va. U., 1970, Grand Marshal, Annual Martin Luther King Parade, Huntington, 2003, Mountaineer of the Yr., Graffiti Mag., 2003; recipient Conservation award Nat. Audubon Soc., 1973, Mother Jones award W.Va. Environ. Coun., 1995, Civil and Human Rights award Martin Luther King Commn. W.Va., 2001; subject of biography by Dr. Charles H. Moffat, Ken Hechler: Maverick Public Servant, 1987; Smithsonian Instn. lectr. on 50th Anniversary of Pres. Truman, 1985; Harry S Truman award for Pub. Svc., 2002; Marshall Univ. student senate, Prof. of the Year, 2002. Mem. Am. Polit. Sci. Assn. (assoc. dir. 1953-56), Civitan, Am. Legion, VFW, DAV, Judson Welliver Soc. of Presdl. Speech-Writers, Elks, Hon. mem. Golden Key Internat. hon. soc., 2002. Democrat. Episcopalian. Walked 530 miles with Granny D on behalf of campaign reform. Home: 101B Greenbrier St Charleston WV 25311-2130

HECHT, IRENE, artist, educator; b. N.Y.C., Dec. 1, 1949; d. Seymour and Rhoda (Ginsberg) H. BA, Case Western Res. U., Cleve., 1971. Artist Portraits, Inc., N.Y.C., 1976—, Grand Cen. Galleries, N.Y.C., 1985—; tchr. Del. Mus. Sch. Art, Wilmington, 1984-87. Portraits include Louis Nizer, 1982, Arthur Krim, 1983, Charles Scribner IV, 1984, Isaac Stern, 1988, Martin Bookspan, 1989, Zubin Mehta, 1990, Kathleen Battle, 1995, Nobel Laureate Eugene Wigner, 1991, Bill Bradley, 1998, Emanuel Ax, 1999, Itzak Perlman, 1999, Robert M. Morganthau, 2003, others; represented in permanent collection Nat. Arts Club, Princeton U., Lotos Club. Mem. Nat. Arts Club, Artists Fellowship, Lotos Club.

HECHT, SYLVIA LILLIAN, pianist, educator; b. Jacksonville, Fla., Feb. 2, 1920; d. Samuel and Florence (Rabinowitz) Haimowitz; m. Erwin Hecht, June 18, 1945 (div. 1950); 1 child, Francia De Beer. BMus, Rollins Coll., 1942; student with Carl Friedberg, Julliard Sch., 1940; student with Isidor Philipp, Paris Conservatory, N.Y.C., 1942-44. Mem. piano faculty N.Y. Coll. Music, N.Y.C., 1943-69, chmn. preparatory divs., 1967-69; dir. Sci. Devel. Programs Inc. Bank St. Coll., N.Y.C., 1976-78, Fordham U., N.Y.C., 1978—; vendor ESEA Title II Eisenhower Profl. Devel. Program N.Y. Bd. Edn., Bklyn., 1990—. Cons. after sch. sci. programs pub. and ind. schs., N.Y.C., 1976—; piano cons. La Guardia H.S. Performing Arts, N.Y.C., 1980—. Active sci. scholarships to Fordham U. programs N.Y.C. Pub. Schs., 1978—, free in-house sci. programs and auditoriums Inner City Pub. Schs. of Manhattan, 1986—. Recipient Young Artists award Nat. Fedn. Music Clubs, L.A., 1941; grantee Richard Lounsbery Found., 1987-89, Chase Manhattan Bank, 1992-95, Citibank, Chem. Bank, others. Mem. Assoc. Music Tchrs. League of N.Y. (bd. dirs. 1977-80), Phi Beta, Pi Kappa Lambda. Democrat. Jewish. Avocations: concerts, theater, travel, chess, science lectures.

HECK, CHARLES RALPH, university dean; b. Dec. 13, 1948; MBA, Embry-Riddle U., 1988; EdD, Nova U., Ft. Lauderdale, Fla., 1992. Instr., pers. mgr. Dept. of Defense, Fort Rucker, Rome, Ga.; asst. prof. bus. Floyd Coll., Rome; chair dept. bus. Alderson-Broaddus Coll., Phillipi, W.Va.; divsn. dean Marshall U., Huntington, Camden C.C., Blackwood, N.J.; prof. aeronautics Dept. Def., Ctr. Aviation, Ft. Rucker, Ala. Home: 6138 County Rd 708 Enterprise AL 36330 E-mail: drflyboy@aol.com.

HEDAHL, GORDEN ORLIN, theatre educator, university dean; b. Minot, N.D., Jan. 2, 1946; s. Chester Owen and Delores May (Johnson) H.; m. Kathleen Josephine Sawin, Sept. 2, 1967 (div.); children: Marc Oscar, Melissa Ann; m. Jean Louise Loudon, Dec. 31, 1983. BS, U. N.D., 1968, MA, 1972; PhD, U. Minn., 1980. Postdoctoral fellow Purdue U., West Lafayette, Ind., 1981-82; prof. theater U. Wis., Whitewater, 1970-92, chair dept. theatre and dance, 1986-89, assoc. dean Coll. Arts, 1989-90, acting assoc. vice chancellor, 1991-92, dean Coll. Arts. and Scis. River Falls, 1998—; dean Coll. Liberal Arts U. Alaska, Fairbanks, 1993-98; acad. planner U. Wis. System, 1990-91. Author: (plays) Tall Tales and True, 1976, The Brothers Grimm, 1977, Land of the Rising Sun, 1979, Trolls and Other Fjord Folk, 1983, Andersen's Storybook, 1986, The Magic of Oz, 1987, African Folk Tales, 1989, Tell Me a Story, 1992; assoc. editor: Guide to Curriculum Planning in Classroom Drama and Theatre, 1989. Recipient Roseman Excellence in Teaching award U. Wis., Whitewater, U. Wis. Mem. Am. Coun. of Colls. of Arts and Scis., Am. Alliance for Theatre and Edn., Internat. Coun. of Fine Arts Deans, Theatre in Higher Edn., Rotary. Lutheran. Office: U Wis Coll Arts and Scis 410 S 3d St River Falls WI 54022-5001 E-mail: gorden.o.hedahl@uwrf.edu.

HEDDEN, DEBRA GORDON, music educator; b. Clinton, Iowa, Apr. 5, 1951; d. Otto Edward and Edna Firm (Griffin) Bruhn; m. Steven K. Hedden, Aug. 16, 2002. BA in Music Edn., U. Iowa, 1973; MA in Music Edn., U. No. Iowa, 1985, EdD in Curriculum and Instrn., 1997. Cert. music tchr. Elem. music tchr. Lincoln Community Schs., Mechanicsville, Iowa, 1973-76; elem. music tchr., German tchr. Hudson (Iowa) Community Schs., 1976-93; assoc. prof. music edn., chair music edn. U. No. Iowa, 1993—. Mem. North Ctrl. Accredidation Team, 1980—; clinician, presenter at various convs., 1977—; mem. musician's del. to China and Kazakhstan, 1992; condr. Iowa Opus Concert, 1996, various choral festivals; master tchr. Heartland Choral Festivals, Des Moines, 1996, 98; presenter Internat. Music Edn. Symposium, Tasmania, 1999. Contbr. to Teaching Examples: Ideas for Music Educators, 1994, Strategies for Teaching K-4 General Music, 1996; contbr. articles to profl. publs., including Tchg. Music, Contbns. to Music Edn., Music Edn. Rsch., Music Educators Jour. and Gen. Music Today. Grantee Iowa Dept. Edn., 1985, 87. Mem. Iowa Music Educators (bd. dirs., exec. sec. 1984—), Am. Choral Dirs. Assn., Phi Delta Kappa, Pi Kappa Lambda. Democrat. Avocations: sewing, painting. Office: U No Iowa 42 6BPAC Cedar Falls IA 50614-0802

HEDGES, NORMA ANN, retired secondary education educator; b. Depue, Ill., May 21, 1941; d. Memford Euing and Louise Gertrude (Krueger) H. BA, Knox Coll., 1963; MEd, U. Ill., 1973. Camp sec. Pilgrim Park Camp, Princeton, Ill., 1961-64; English tchr., counselor Malden (Ill.) H.S., 1963-78, Morris (Ill.) H.S., 1978-93; ret., 1993. History of Depue, Illinois, 1976. Vol. Morris Hosp. Gift Shop, 1993—; driver We Care, 1993—2003. Mem. Grundy County Retired Tchrs.(regional dir., 2001—), Delta Kappa Gamma (state scholarship com., 2001—). Republican. Congregationalist. Avocations: reading, antiques, genealogy, travel.

HEDKE, RICHARD ALVIN, retired gifted education educator; b. Evanston, Ill., Aug. 27, 1940; s. Alvin C. and Leona Amanda (Kieper) H.; m. Carol Ann Bormet, July 21, 1962; children: Deborah, Kristen. BS in Elem. Edn., Concordia U., 1968, MA in Curriculum and Instrn., 1975; postgrad., No. Ill. U., 1980—2002, Nat. Lewis U., 1980—2002, Gov.'s State U., 1980—2002. Cert. K-9 tchr., Ill. Classroom tchr., athletic dir. Immanuel Luth. Sch., Kingston, N.Y., 1962-65, St. Paul Luth. Sch., Addison, Ill., 1965-67, St. Peter Luth. Sch., Schaumburg, 1967-74; classroom tchr. Schaumburg Twp. Dist. 54 Schs., 1974—79, 1997—2002, tchr. gifted students, 1979-97. Vis. summer sch. instr. High Sch. Dist. 214, Ill., 1983-86, gifted students math. and sci. Dist. 20, 1987; mem. grad. adv. com. Concordia U., 1984-85; dir. future studies summer program High Sch. Dist. 214; presenter various confs. including Nuts 'N Bolts Confs. No. Ill. Planning Commn. for Gifted Edn., 1979-87, Ill. State Gifted Conf., 1980; adj. faculty Aurora U., 1990, 91, 92, 93. Author gifted students curriculum Dist. 54, 1979-98. Mem. long-range planning action com. Project Horizon, 1987-90; mem. sch. leadership team, 1999—. Mem. NEA, Nat. Assn. Gifted Children (mem. future studies subcom., visual and performing arts subcom., presenter Mid-Winter Conf. 1986), Nat. Coun. Tchrs. Math. (presenter various meetings), Ill. Coun. Tchrs. Math. (presenter various meetings, named Outstanding Math. Educator), Ill. Coun. Gifted, Ill. Sci. Tchrs. Assn., Ill. Edn. Assn., Schaumburg Edn. Assn., World Future Soc. Avocations: photography, community theater acting and singing, travel. Home: 36 Brookstone Dr Fredericksburg VA 22405-2794

HEDLEY-WHYTE, JOHN, anesthesiologist, educator; b. Newcastle-upon-Tyne, Eng., Nov. 25, 1933; arrived in U.S., 1960, naturalized, 1965; s. Angus and Nancy (Nettleton) H.-W.; m. Elizabeth Tessa Waller, Sept. 19, 1959. Student, Harrow Sch., 1947-52; BA (Rothschild scholar Clare Coll.), Cambridge U., 1955, MB, 1958, MA, 1959, MD, 1972; AM (hon.), Harvard U., 1967. House surgeon St. Bartholomew's Hosp., London, 1958-59; resident in anesthesia Mass. Gen. Hosp., 1960-62, hon. anesthetist, 1977—; clin. asst. anesthesia Harvard U., 1961-63, instr., 1963-65, clin. assoc., 1965-67, assoc. prof., 1967-69, prof., 1969-76, 1st David S. Sheridan prof. anaesthesia and respiratory therapy, 1976—; prof. dept. health policy and mgmt. Harvard U. Sch. Pub. Health, 1988-2000, mem. leadership coun., 2003—; chmn. faculty seminar in health and medicine Harvard U., 1975-76; anesthetist-in-chief Beth Israel Hosp., Boston, 1967-88, chmn. com. on rsch., 1976-82. Cons. in field; mem. tech. adv. bd. on med. devices tech. Am. Nat. Standards Inst., 1973-83; U.S. del. Internat. Electrotech. Commn., 1989-91, 92—; leader U.S. del. Internat. Orgn. Standardization, Geneva, 1973-89, chmn. com. TC 121, SC 3 on anaesthetic and respiratory equipment, 1978—. Author: Respiratory Care, 1965, Applied Physiology of Respiratory Care, 1976, Continuous Anesthesia Vapor Monitoring, 1990, Operating room and Intensive Care Alarms and Information Transfer, 1992; contbr. articles to profl. jours. Recipient Hichens prize St. Bartholomew's Hosp., London, 1957. Fellow ACP (life), German Soc. Anaesthesia and Intensive Care Medicine (hon., life), ASTM (hon., chmn. com. F29 1983-89, Merit award 1994, user vice chmn. 2000—), Royal Coll. Anaesthetists (hon., life); mem. Am. Physiol. Soc., Abernethian Soc. (past pres.), Am. Soc. Anesthesiologists (chmn. com. mech. equipment 1977-82, chmn. com. on equipment and standards 1982-84), Mass. Soc. Anesthesiologists (pres. 1973-74), Am. Soc. Pharmacology and Exptl. Therapeutics, Roxbury Soc. Med. Improvement (libr. 1970-88, sec.-treas. 1988—), Mass. Med. Soc. (coun. 1975-78), Fairhaven Preservation Assn. (chmn. 1990—), Boodle's Club, The Country Club, Somerset Club, Harvard Club of Boston, Vicarage Club. Democrat. Episcopalian. Achievements include discovery that human blood has a constant relative solubility for oxygen. Office: VA Med Ctr 1400 VFW Pkwy Boston MA 02132-4927

HEE, VIVIAN SANAE MITSUDA, principal; b. Honolulu, Hawaii, May 16, 1946; d. Hozumi and Kimiyo (Ueno) Mitsuda; m. Richard K.F. Hee, Aug. 24, 1968. BA in Elem. Edn., U. Hawaii, 1970, MA in Edn. Adminstrn., 1989. Cert. tchr., sch. adminstr., state edn. adminstr. Hawaii. Elem. tchr. Dept. Edn. Dist., Windward, Hawaii, 1970-77, itinerant tchr. Kaneohe, Hawaii, 1977-83; state resource tchr. Dept. Edn. State, Honolulu, Hawaii, 1983-85, state specialist gifted talented, 1985-88; vice prin. Kapunahala Elem. Sch., Kaneohe, Hawaii, 1989-89, August Ahrens Elem. Sch., Waipahu, Hawaii, 1990-91; prin. T. Jefferson Elem. Sch., Honolulu, Hawaii, 1991—. Cons. U. Hawaii, Hilo, 1989—. Consortium for Teaching Asian Pacific Children, 1989; adv. com. Tchrs. Edn. Com. for Gifted, U. Hawaii, 1986-89; mem. State Supt. Task Force, 1990-91, Diamond Head Mental Health Svc. Bd., 1993-94. Contbr. author: (book) Scope/Sequence Gifted Curr., 1988; assoc. editor: (mag.) U. Hawaii Educational Perspective, 1989; contbr. to profl. journs. and mags. Cons. Center for Gifted Native Hawaiian Children, Hilo, 1989—, Hawaii Assn. for Gifted, 1988; outreach assoc. John Hopkins Univ., Hawaii, 1990-94; judge Senator R. Bryd. Scholarship, Hawaii, 1985-88; mem. Red Cross, Hawaii, 1980—. With Naval Intelligence Reserve, 1965-70. Recipient Outstanding Svc. award Ser Teens of Hawaii, 1988, Meritorious Svc. award Hawaii Assn. for Gifted, 1988, Outstanding Svc. award Johns Hopkins U. Ctr. for Talented Youth, 1994; Masters Program scholar U. Hawaii, 1989; Grantee to China East West Center, U. Hawaii, 1989, to Japan East West Center, U. Hawaii, 1990. Mem. Assn. Supervision Curriculum Devel. (bd. dirs. 1988-95), Hawaii Assn. Supervision Curriculum Devel. (pres. 1992-93), Nat. Assn. Elementary Sch. Principals, 1989—, Alliance for Drama, East West Center Alumni Assn., Delta Kappa Gamma. Avocations: reading, writing songs, fishing, travel, gardening. Office: Jefferson Elem Sch 324 Kapahulu Ave Honolulu HI 96815-4091

HEER, DAVID MACALPINE, sociology educator; b. Chapel Hill, N.C., Apr. 15, 1930; s. Clarence and Jean Douglas (MacAlpine) H.; m. Nancy Whittier, June 29, 1957 (div. 1980); m. Kaye S. Heymann, Dec. 11, 1980 (dec. Apr. 2000); children: Douglas (dec.), Laura, Catherine. AB magna cum laude, Harvard U., 1950, MA, 1954, PhD, 1958. Statistician population div. U.S. Bur. Census, Washington, 1957-61; lectr., asst. research sociologist U. Calif., Berkeley, 1961-64; asst. prof. demography Harvard U. Sch. Public Health, Boston, 1964-68, assoc. prof., 1968-72; dir. Population Rsch. Lab., U. So. Calif., L.A., 1995—2000, prof. sociology, 1972—2000, prof. sociology emeritus, 2000—; sr. fellow Ctr. Comparative Immigration Studies, U. Calif. San Diego, 2000—. Mem. population research study sect. NIH, 1971-73 Author: After Nuclear Attack: A Demographic Inquiry, 1965, Society and Population, 1968, (with Pini Herman) A Human Mosaic: An Atlas of Ethnicity in Los Angeles County, 1980-86, 1990, Undocumented Mexicans in the United States, 1990, Immigration in America's Future: Social Science Findings and the Policy Debate, 1996; editor: Readings on Population, 1968, Social Statistics and the City, 1968. Mem. Population Assn. Am. (dir. 1970-73), Internat. Union Sci. Study Population. Home: 3890 Nobel Dr Unit 1002 San Diego CA 92122-5782

HEESTAND, DIANE ELISSA, education educator, medical educator; b. Boston, Oct. 9, 1945; d. Glenn Wilson and Elizabeth (Martin) Heestand. BA, Allegheny Coll., 1967; MA, U. Wyo., 1968; edn. specialist, Ind. U., 1971, EdD, 1979. Asst. prof. communication Clarion (Pa.) State Coll., 1971; asst. prof. learning resources Indiana U. of Pa., 1971-72; asst. prof. communication U. Nebr. Med. Ctr., Omaha, 1972-74; assoc. prof. learning resources Tidewater Community Coll., Virginia Beach, Va., 1975-78; ednl. cons. U. Ala. Sch. Medicine, Birmingham, 1978-81; dir. learning resources, assoc. prof. med. edn. Mercer U. Sch. Medicine, Macon, Ga., 1981-88; asst. dean ednl. devel. and resources Ohio U. Coll. Osteopathic Medicine, 1989-90; assoc. prof. clin. med. edn., dir. biomed. communications U. So. Calif. Sch. Medicine, L.A., 1990-95, acting chair dept. med. edn., 1992-95; prof., dir. office ednl. devel. U. Ark. for Med. Scis., Little Rock, 1995—. Cons. Lincoln (Pa.) U., summer, 1975; vis. fellow Project Hope/China, Millwood, Va., summer, 1986. Author (teleplay) Yes, 1968 (award World Law Fund 1968); producer, dir. (slide tape) Finding a Way, 1980 (1st Pl. award HESCA 1981, Susan Eastman award 1981). Rsch. sect. chair So. Group on Ednl. Affairs, 1998-2000. Grantee, Porter Found., 1984, Ark. Dept. Higher Edn., 1996—97, UAMS Spl. Devel., 1997—99; Family and Preventive Medicine fellow, Health Resources and Svcs. Adminstrn., 2003—. Mem. Health Scis. Comm. Assn. (bd. dirs. 1982-86, pres.-elect 1987-88, pres. 1988-89, Spl. Svc. award 1990), Assn. Ednl. Comm. and Tech. (pres. media design and prodn. div. 1985-86), Assn. Biomed. Comm. Dirs. (bd. dirs. 1993-95), Soc. of Dirs. of Rsch. in Med. Edn. (steering com. 2000—, chair-elect 2002, chair 2003), Generalists in Med. Edn. (steering com. 1998-2001, chmn. 1999-2000). Democrat. Presbyterian. Avocations: tennis, gardening, golf.

HEETER, NORMA JEAN, secondary school educator; b. Dayton, Ohio, Nov. 18, 1943; d. Virgil Nelson and Grace Margaret Roser Hayes; m. Paul Richard Heeter, June 17, 1967; children: Lesli Lynn Miller. BS in Edn., Ohio State U., 1966; MS in Edn., U. Dayton, 1983; postgrad., U. Calif., San Diego, 1985-98, San Diego State U. Spanish tchr. Milton Union Sch. Dist., West Milton, Ohio, 1966-69; Spanish/Speech tchr. Huber Heights (Ohio) City Schs., 1969-84; Spanish tchr. San Diego Unified City Schs., 1984—2002, peer asst., rev. cons. tchr., 2002—. Mentor tchr. San Diego Unified City Schs., 1994-97. Recipient Abel award for Excellence in Edn., George Abel Found., 1998, Excellence in Edn. award, Point Loma Rotary Club, 1989. Mem.: NEA (del. nat. conv. 1976—2003), San Diego Edn. Assn. (bd. dirs. 1997—2001, sec. 2002—), Calif. Tchrs. Assn., Phi Delta Kappa. Democrat. Avocations: reading, corvette club activities, high school spectator sports, traveling, dining out. Home: PO Box 462245 Escondido CA 92046-2245 Office: Tchr Preparation and Support IMC Bldg A 2441 Cardinal Ln San Diego CA 92123

HEFFELFINGER, KARAN ANNICE, home economics educator; b. Dallas, May 4, 1950; d. Willie Hilbert and Elsie (Mandel) Lentz; m. Elmer Walter Heffelfinger, June 6, 1970; 1 child, Matthew Allen. AA in Liberal Arts, Canal Zone Coll., Panama, 1971; BA in Vocat. Home Econs., N.W. Nazarene Coll., 1973; MA in Mgmt. and Supervision, Cen. Mich. U., 1975;

MEd, East Stroudsburg U., 1996; DEd, Columbia U., 1998. Cert. vocat. home econs. tchr., Pa., Idaho, comml. food svc. instr., N.J. Home econs. tchr. Willingboro (N.J.) Sch. Dist., 1974-75, comml. food svc. instr., 1975-76; therapeutic dietitian St. Mary's Hosp., Passaic, N.J., 1976-77; comml. food svc. instr. Piscataway (N.J.) Sch. Dist., 1978-79; home econs. tchr. Panther Valley Sch. Dist., Lansford, Pa., 1979—; instr. adult continuing edn. program Carbon County Vocat.-Tech. Sch., Jim Thorpe, Pa., 1980—; parent edn. coord. and trainer Panther Valley Sch. Dist., Lansford, Pa., 1986-89. Owner Catering Creative Dimensions, Lansford, 1984—; food svc. mgmt. instr. Carbon-Lehigh Intermediate Unit, Schnecksville, Pa., 1983-84; food svc. coord., instr. Carbon County Vocat. Tech., Jim Thorpe, summer 1984. Editor newsletter Taking Control, 1991-93 (cert. 1992); contbr. articles to profl. publs. Leader, advisor Mahoning Valley 4-H Club, Lehighton, Pa., 1980—, Future Homemakers of Am., Lansford, 1983—; vol. Am. Cancer Soc., March of Dimes, ARC, Lansford; pub. rels. cons. Hawk Mountain coun. Boy Scouts Am., Reading, Pa., 1989—, Eastern Regional Pa. Home Econs., 1989—; Sunday sch. tchr. St. Paul's Luth. Ch. Grantee Carbon-Lehigh Intermediate Unit, Carl Perkins Fed. Vocat. Funds, 1981—. Mem. NEA, Pa. Edn. Assn. (pres. vocat. and practical art-home econs. sect. adv. bd. 1988—), Panther Valley Edn. Assn., Am. Home Econs. Assn. (nat. vice chair elem., secondary and adult edn. 1989-92), Pa. Home Econs. Assn. (pub. rels. com. 1986-92, cert.), Western Pocono Home Econs. Assn. (vice chair, pres., cert.), Lehigh Valley Home Econs. Assn., Am. Vocat. Assn., Pa. Vocat. Assn. Republican. Avocation: cake decorating. Home: 114 W Kline Ave Lansford PA 18232-1916 Office: Panther Valley Sch Dist PO Box 40 Lansford PA 18232-0040

HEFFELMIRE, VIRGINIA ANN, school nurse; b. Cin., June 20, 1953; d. Henry Geiger and Mary Bess (Barrott) Nanz; m. Steven Ray Heffelmire, Dec. 6, 1975; 1 child, Sarah Jane. BS in Psychology, No. Ky. U., 1980; diploma in nursing, Deaconess Sch. Nursing, 1987. RN, Ind. Nurse asst. Dearborn County Hosp., Lawrenceburg, Ind., 1971-74, nurse, 1987-88, South Dearborn Sch. Corp., Aurora, Ind., 1988—; mgr. Paint Pot, Lawrenceburg, 1975-78. Mem. AIDS adv. bd. South Dearborn Sch., Aurora, 1988-92; pvt. counselor, Lawrenceburg, 1988-92; informational educator Kids A Fair, 1991-92. Campaign mgr. mayoral campaign, Lawrenceburg, 1979-81; leader 4-H, Dillsboro, Ind., 1991-92. Mem. ANA, Zool. Soc., Ind. Sch. Nurse Assn., Phi Beta Phi. Republican. Presbyterian. Avocations: walking, needlepoint, cooking, crafts.

HEFFERNAN, JAMES ANTHONY WALSH, language and literature educator; b. Boston, Apr. 22, 1939; s. Roy Joseph and Kathleen (Walsh) H.; m. Nancy Coffey, June 27, 1964; children: Virginia, Andrew. AB cum laude, Georgetown U., 1960; PhD, Princeton U., 1964. Instr. English U. Va., 1963-65; asst. prof. English Dartmouth Coll., Hanover, N.H., 1965-70, assoc. prof., 1970-76, prof., 1976—, chmn. dept. English, 1978-81, Frederick Sessions Beebe prof. in art of writing, 1997—. Cons. Mt. Holyoke, 1986, PMLA, 1986-87, Johns Hopkins U., 1987, NYU, 1987, 89, U. Press New Eng., 1987, U. Press Chgo., 1988, NEH, 1988, 90, Rutgers U., 1988, U. Md., 1988, Vanderbilt U., 1989, Barnard Coll., 1992; dir. summer seminar English romantic lit. and visual arts NEH/Dartmouth Coll., Hanover, 1987, 89; spkr. various seminars; lectures on James Joyce's Ulysses videotaped for The Teaching Co., 2001. Author: Wordsworth's Theory of Poetry: The Transforming Imagination, 1969, The Re-Creation of Landscape: A Study of Wordsworth, Coleridge, Constable and Turner, 1985, Museum of Words: The Poetics of Ekphrasis from Homer to Ashbery, 1993; co-author: Writing: A College Handbook, 5th edit., 2000, Writing: A Concise College Handbook, 1st edit., 1996; editor: Space, Time, Image, Sign: Essays on Literature and the Visual Arts, 1987, Representing the French Revolution: Literature, Historiography and Art, 1992; contbr. articles to profl. jours. Trustee Vermont Acad., 1992-2001. Woodrow Wilson fellow, 1960-61, Franklin Murphy, Jr. fellow, 1961-62, R.K. Root fellow, 1962-63, Dartmouth Coll., 1968-69, NEH fellow, 1991; grantee Dartmouth Coll., 1971, 74, 87, NEH, 1984, 87, 89. Mem. MLA (evaluator essays, presenter, del. various convs.), Assn. Literary Scholars and Critics (coun. 1996-99). Office: English Dept Dartmouth College Hanover NH 03755 E-mail: jamesheff@dartmouth.edu.

HEFLER, WILLIAM LOUIS, elementary education educator; b. New Albany, Ind. s. Louis C. and Elizabeth (Grimes) H.; divorced; children: Sarah Elizabeth, Matthew Joseph; m. Linda Gryszowka; children: Jason Michael Gryszowka, Justin Bradley Gryszowka. BS in Elem. Edn., Ind. U., 1980, MS in Elem. Edn., 1983. Tchr. 5th grade East Washington Elem. Sch., Pekin, Ind., 1980-87; tchr. 6th grade Indpls. Pub. Sch., 1987-92; asst. prin. Indpls. Pub. Schs., 1992-94, M.S.D. of Wayne Twp., 1994-98; tchr. IPS, 2001—; chmn. various coms. East Washington Elem. Sch., Pekin, Ind., 1998—; prin., chmn. performance-based accreditation East-Side Elem. Sch., Edinburgh, Ind., 1998—2001; tchr. Indpls. (Ind.) Pub. Schs., 2001—. Chmn. Indpls. Pub. Sch. sub-com. LEAP conf.; instr. Project Wild, Project Learning Tree, Ind.; safe sch. specialist, 2000-2001; mem. Ind. Prin.'s Leadership Acad., 2000-2002. Deacon Speedway Christian Ch., 1997, Cen. Christian Ch., 1984-86; coach 5th grade soccer, softball, track, E. Washington Elem. Sch., 1981-84, coach 7th grade basketball 1981-85; state reviewer textbooks in math., sci., health, 1984-86. Named one of Outstanding Men of Am., 1983, 85, 89, Outstanding History Tchr. in Washington County, DAR, 1984, Ky. Col., 1990; recipient C.L.A.S.S./I.P.L. Golden Apple award, 1992. Mem. NEA, NAESP, IASP, ASCD, Nat. Sci. Tchrs. Assn., Nat. Coun. Tchrs. English, Nat. Coun. Tchrs. Math., Nat. Coun. Social Studies, Ind. State Tchrs. Assn. (local pres. 1981-85, ins. trustee 1982-85, bd. dirs. 1986, chmn. various coms., del. various confs.), Ind. Coun. Tchrs. Math., Ind. Coun. Social Studies, Ind. Basketball Coaches Assn., Hoosier Assn. Sci. Tchrs., E. Washington Tchrs. Assn., Indpls. Edn. Assn., Indpls. Prins. Assn., Tau Kappa Epsilon, Phi Delta Kappa, Pi Lambda Theta, Kappa Delta Pi. Democrat. Home: 1549 Countryside Ln Indianapolis IN 46231-3312 Office: Carl Wilde Elem 5002 W 34th Street Indianapolis IN 46224

HEGARTY, GEORGE JOHN, university rector, English educator; b. Cape May, N.J., July 20, 1948; s. John Joseph and Gloria Anna (Bonelli) H.; m. Joy Elizabeth Schiller, June 9, 1979. Student, U. Fribourg, Switzerland, 1968-69; BA in English, LaSalle U., Phila., 1970; Cert., Coll. de la Pocatiere, Que., Can., 1970; postgrad., U. Dakar, Senegal, 1970, Case Western Res. U., 1973-74, U. N.H., 1976; MA in English, Drake U., 1977; cert., U. Iowa, 1977; DA, Drake U., 1978; Cert., UCLA, 1979, U. Pa., 1981. Tchr. English, Peace Corps vol. College d'Enseignment General de Sedhiou, Senegal, 1970-71; tchr. English Belmore Boys' and Westfields High Schs., Sydney, Australia, 1972-73; teaching fellow in English Drake U., Des Moines, 1974-76; mem. faculty English Des Moines Area Community Coll., 1976-80; assoc. prof. Am. lit. U. Yaounde, Cameroon, 1980-83; prof. Am. lit. and civilization Nat. U. Cote D'Ivoire, Abidjan, 1986-88; dir. ctr. for internat. programs and svcs. Drake U., Des Moines, 1983-91; prof. grad. program intercultural mgmt. Sch. for Internat. Tng., The Experiment in Internat. Living, Brattleboro, Vt., 1991-93; provost, prof. English Teikyo Loretto Heights U., Denver, 1992-94; pres., prof. English, Teikyo Westmar U., Le Mars, Iowa, 1994-95; program dir. Am. degree program Taylor's Coll., Malaysia, 1996-97; v.p. academic affairs, prof. English Teikyo Loretto Heights U., Denver, 1997—2001; rector Webster U., Thailand, 2002—. Acad. specialist USIA, 1983-84; workshop organizer/speaker Am. Field Svcs., 1986; cons. Coun. Internat. Ednl. Exch., 1986; evaluator Assn. des Univ. Partiellment Entierément de Langue Francais, 1987, Iowa Humanities Bd., 1990-91, USAID's Ctr. for Univ. Coop. and Devel., 1991; Fulbright lectr., rschr. Am. Lit U., 2003—; cons. in field. Book reviewer African Book Pub. Record, Oxford, Eng., 1981—, African Studies Rev., 1990—; host, creator TV show Global Perspectives, 1989-91; exhibitor of African art, 1989—; contbr. articles to profl. jours. Commr. Des Moines Sister City Commn., 1984-87, 91; bd. dirs. Iowa Sister State Com., 1988-91; pres. Chautauqua Park Nat. Hist. Dist. Neighborhood Assn., 1991; bd. dirs. Melton Found., 1994-95. Drake U. fellow, 1971-72, 74-76; Nat. Endowment for Humanities grantee, 1981; Fulbright grantee, USIA, 1980-83, 86-88. Mem. Am. Assn. Pres. Ind. Colls. and Univs., NAFSA: Assn. Internat. Educators (sectional chmn. region VI 1986-87, Vt. rep. 1992), Assn. Internat. Edn. Adminstrs., Inst. Internat. Edn. Avocations: collecting tribal art, travel, swimming, writing. Office: 2040 Antananariuo Pl Dulles VA 20189-2040 E-mail: ghegarty@aol.com.

HEGEL, PAMELA RENE, elementary school educator; b. Fargo, N.D., July 9, 1958; d. James and Delores (Fisher) Booke; m. Darwin George Hegel, Aug. 3, 1984. BA, Dickinson (N.D.) State U., 1989. Office mgr. Farmers Ins. Group, Dickinson, N.D., 1974-77, Kukowski Land Co., Dickinson, 1981-88; real estate agt. Joe LaDuke Real Estate, Dickinson, 1977-81; tchr. Banning (Calif.) Unified Schs., 1988-94, Palm Springs (Calif.) Sch. Dist., 1994—. Recipient cert. of appreciation Ednl. Testing Svc., 1991. Mem. Calif. Tchrs. Assn.

HEGER, CLAUDINE LYNN, special education educator; b. Bklyn., Mar. 18, 1968; d. Ronald and Joyce (Hochman) Fields; m. Ian Michael Heger. BS in Psychology, SUNY, Buffalo, 1991; MS in Elem. Edn., Hofstra U., Hempstead, N.Y., 1992, MS in Spl. Edn., 1993. Cert. tchr. elem., spl. edn., N.Y. Group leader Camp Shane, Inc., Ferndale, N.Y., summers 1989-90; home healthcare attendant Bklyn., 1990-92; group leader Kutsher's, Monticello, N.Y., summers 1991-92; divsn. head Camp Lokanda, Glen Spey, N.Y., summer 1993; student tchr. John F. Kennedy Sch., Great Neck, N.Y., 1992-93; tchr. spl. edn. J. Lewis Aimes, Nassau BOCES, Massapequa, N.Y., 1993; spl. edn. tchr. Rosemary Kennedy Ctr., Wantagh, N.Y., 1993—. Mem. Coun. for Exceptional Children, People for the Ethical Treatment of Animals, Alpha Epsilon Phi (social chairperson/alumni chairperson). Avocations: theatre, music, poetry, horseback riding. Home: 1033 E 102nd St Brooklyn NY 11236-4419

HEGER, HERBERT KRUEGER, education educator; b. Cin., June 15, 1937; s. J. Herbert and Leona (Krueger) H.; m. Thyra Cleek. AS, Ohio Mechanics Inst., 1956; BS, Miami U., 1962, MEd, 1965; PhD, Ohio State U., 1969. Tchr. Marshall Jr. High Sch., Pomona, Calif., 1962-63; tchr. math. Mt. Healthy High Sch., Ohio, 1963-66; grad. asst., grad. assoc. Miami U.-Ohio State U., 1966-69; dir. Environ. Studies Center Central State U., Wilberforce, Ohio, 1968-69; asst. prof. U. Ky., 1969-75; assoc. dir. Louisville Urban Edn. Center, 1971-75; vis. prof. Sch. Profl. Studies, Pepperdine U., 1975-78; dir. student teaching U. Tex., San Antonio, 1975-77, coordinator curriculum and instrn., 1977-78; assoc. prof. edn. Whitworth Coll., Spokane, Wash., 1978-82, chmn. dept., 1978-79, dean Grad. Sch., 1979-82; prof. edn. U. Tex., El Paso, 1982-99, prof. emeritus, 1999—. Cons. in field Contbr. articles to profl. jours. Mem. Am. Ednl. Rsch. Assn., Nat. Soc. Study Edn., Phi Delta Kappa. Republican. Mem. Christian Ch. (Disciples Of Christ). Home: 2495 Tiffany Dr Las Cruces NM 88011-2008

HEGGERS, JOHN PAUL, surgery, immunology, microbiology educator; b. Bklyn., Feb. 8, 1933; s. John and May (Hass) H.; m. Rosemarie Niklas, July 30, 1977; children: Arn M., Ronald R., Laurel M., Gary R., Renee L., Annette M. BA in Bacteriology, Mont. State U. now U. Mont., 1958; MS in Microbiology, U. Md., 1965; PhD in Bacteriology and Pub. Health, Wash. State U., 1972. Diplomate Am. Bd. Bioanalysis. Med. technologist U.S. Naval Hosp., St. Albans, N.Y., 1951-53; bacteriologist Hahnemann Hosp., Worcester, Mass., 1958-59; commd. 2d lt. U.S. Army, 1959, advanced through grades to lt. col., 1975; mem. staff dept. bacteriology 1st U.S. Army Med. Lab., N.Y.C., 1959-60; chief clin. lab., food svc. divsn. & diet kitchen U.S. Army Hosp., Verdun, France, 1960-63; chief virology and rickettsiology div. dept. microbiology 3d U.S. Army Med. Lab., Ft. McPherson, Ga., 1965-66; instr. bacteriology Basic Lab. Sch., Ft. McPherson, 1965-66; chief diagnostic bacteriology 9th Med. Lab., Saigon, Vietnam, 1966-67; chief microbiology div. dept. pathology Brooke Gen. Hosp., Ft. Sam Houston, Tex., 1967-69; chmn. dept. microbiology U.S. Army Sch. Med. Tech., Ft. Sam Houston, 1967-69; instr. bacteriology evening div. San Antonio Jr. Coll., 1969; lab. scis. officer Office Surgeon Gen., Washington, 1972-74; microbiologist spl. mycobacterial disease br. div. geog. pathology Armed Forces Inst. Pathology, Washington, 1973, spl. asst. to dir., 1973-74; chief clin. rsch. lab. clin. rsch. svc. Madigan Army Med. Ctr., Tacoma, 1974-76, asst. chief clin. investigation svc., 1976-77; instr. immunology, parasitology and mycology Clover Park Vocat. Tech. Inst., 1976-77; ret., 1977; assoc. prof. dept. surgery U. Chgo., 1977-80, prof., 1980-83; prof. surgery Wayne State U., Detroit, 1983-88; prof. surgery and assoc. microbiology and immunology U. Tex. Med. Br., 1988—. Dir. clin. microbiology Shriners Burn Hosp., Galveston, Tex., 1988—. Author: Current Problems in Surgery, 1973, Quantitative Bacteriology, 1991; contbr. articles to profl. jours.; contbg. editor: Jour. Am. Med. Tech., 1972—. Pres. Aloe Rsch. Found., 1989-92, vice-chmn. 1992-95. Decorated Bronze Star; Legion of Merit; recipient cert. of appreciation A.C.S., 1969, cert. appreciation Armed Forces Inst. Pathology, 1974, Valley Forge Honor cert. Freedoms Found., 1974 Fisher award in med. tech., Fisher Scientific, Am. Med. Techs., 1968, 82, Gerard B. Lambert award, 1973, Ednl. Found. Rsch. award Am. Soc. Plastic and Reconstructive Surgery, 1978, Alumni Achievement award Wash. State Univ., 1993, Disting. Alumni award U. Mont., 1994. Fellow N.Y. Acad. Sci., Am. Acad. Microbiology, Royal Soc. Tropical Medicine and Hygiene, Am. Geriat. Soc.; mem. Nat. Registry Microbiologists (chmn. exec. coun. 1976-79), Am. Soc. Microbiology (chmn. com. tellers 1974-75), Wash. Soc. Am. Med. Technologists (pres. 1975-77), Wash. Soc. Med. Tech. (chmn. sect. microbiology sci. assembly, dir. 1975-77), Assn. Mil. Surgeons U.S. (life), Am. Soc. Clin. Pathologists (assoc.), Am. Med. Technologists (disting. svc. award 1975, exceptional merit award 1976, nat. dir. 1979-80, nat. sec. 1980-82, nat. v.p. 1982-84, Technologist of Yr. 1983), Am. Burn Assn. (chmn. rsch. com., 2d v.p. bd. trustees 2002), Pres.'s continuing edn. award 1981, At Large award 1986, Robert B. Lindberg award 1991, 92, Curtis P. Artz Disting. Svc. award 1996), Plastic Surgery Rsch. Coun., Surg. Infection Soc. (charter), Ill. State Soc. Med. Technologists (v.p. 1979), Internat. Soc. for Burn Injuries, Vietnam Vets. Assn. (life), Masons (32d degree, knight comdr. Ct. Honor), Shriners, Sigma Xi. Office: Shriners Hosp for Children Burns Hosp 815 Market St Galveston TX 77550-2725

HEGSTROM, WILLIAM JEAN, mathematics educator; b. Macomb, Ill., Oct. 21, 1923; s. Carl William and Thelma (Canavit) H. Student Western Ill. U., 1941-42; B.Sc., Rutgers U., 1949, Ed.M. 1952; MA in Teaching, Purdue U., 1964; postgrad. U. Fla., 1961, Fla. Atlantic U., 1965-68; EdD, U. Miami, 1971; m. Grace Ann Paladino, May 3, 1944; children: Elizabeth Louise, William Jean II, Jean (Mrs. Carl Zimbro). Tchr. jr. h.s., South Plainfield, N.J., 1949-52, high sch., Bernardsville, N.J. 1952-54, Oak St. Sch., Bernard's Twp., N.J., 1954-55, high sch., Summit, N.J., 1955-58, jr. h.s., Delray Beach, Fla, 1958-65; chmn. math. dept. John I. Leonard H.S., Lake Worth, Fla., 1965-68, dir. Palm Beach County rsch. project, 1966-68; adj. prof. Fla. Atlantic U., 1965-69, assoc. prof., 1969-70; counselor coord. John Leonard Adult Ctr., Lake Worth, 1965-68; supr. rsch. and evaluation Palm Beach County Sch. Bd., West Palm Beach, Fla., 1970-74; adj. prof. Palm Beach Jr. Coll., 1981-88, Palm Beach Atlantic Coll., 1984-86, asst. prof., 1986-87; Palm Beach Atlantic Coll., 1984-87; cons. math. prof. Palm Beach County Sch. Bd., 1985-87, ret., 1987. With USAAF, 1942-46. Mem. NEA, Nat. Assn. Investors Corp., Am. Assn. Individual Investors, Phi Delta Kappa. Contbr. articles to profl. jours. Home: 225 NE 22nd St Delray Beach FL 33444-4221

HEHIR, THOMAS F. educational administrator; b. Worcester, Mass., Feb. 2, 1950; s. Leo and Elizabeth Hehir. BA in Psychology, Coll. of Holy Cross, 1972; MS in Spl. Edn., Syracuse U., 1973; EdD in Adminstrn., Harvard U., 1990. Program devel. specialist Mass. Dept. Edn., Boston, 1976-78, program devel. specialist vocat. spl. needs, 1978-80, sr. advisor H.S. spl. edn., 1980-83; mgr. dept. student support svcs. Boston Pub. Schs., 1983-87; assoc. supt. Chgo. Pub. Schs., 1990-93; dir. Office Spl. Edn. Programs U.S. Dept. Edn., Washington, 1993—99, dir. sch. leadership program, 1999—; lectr. edn. Grad. Sch. Edn. Harvard U., Cambridge, Mass., 1999—. Contbr. articles to profl. publs. Fellow in mental retardation; recipient award Am. Ednl. Rsch. Assn., 1990. Mem. Coun. for Exceptional Children. Roman Catholic. Office: Harvard U Grad Sch Edn Gutman 414 Cambridge MA 02138*

HEIDEN, SUSAN JANE, elementary education educator; b. La Porte, Ind., Mar. 8, 1942; d. Benno Henry and Helen Frances (Rollins) Bargholz; m. Ronald William Heiden, Sept. 28, 1963; children: Gregory Scott, David Patrick, Katrina Jane. BS in EEdn., Ind. U., Bloomington, 1964; MS in Edn., Purdue U., Westville, Ind., 1976; postgrad., Ind. U., South Bend, 1989-90. lic. in real estate, Ind. Elem. tchr. La Porte Community Sch. Corp., 1964-98, parenting trainer, 1986; elem. tchr. Michigan City (Ind.) Area Schs., 1964—. Bd. dirs. La Porte Fed. Credit Union, Michigan City, 1989-95, La Porte County Literacy Coalition, 1994-98; owner, operator pvt. tutoring svc., 1993—. Mem. adv. com. 4-H Club, La Porte, 1980-85; scholarship chair PTA. Mem. Am. Fedn. Tchrs. (ednl. rsch. and dissemination linker 1986-98), Ind. U. Alumni Assn. (Write-on Hoosiers Writing award 1994), Purdue U. Alumni Assn., Purdue North Ctrl. Alumni Assn. Avocations: writing, reading, flower gardening, sewing, spending time by ocean. Home: 2065 N 100 W La Porte IN 46350-7856 Office: Hailmann Elem Sch 1001 Ohio St La Porte IN 46350-4301

HEIDER, ANNE HARRINGTON, music educator; BA, Wellesley Coll., 1963; MA, NYU, 1965; DMA, Stanford U., 1981. Assoc. prof., resident choral condr. Roosevelt U.; artistic dir. Bella Voce Profl. Chamber Choir. Recipient Tempo All-Prof. Team, Humanities award, 1993. Office: Roosevelt U Coll Performing Arts 430 S Michigan Ave Chicago IL 60605

HEIDT-DUNWELL, DEBRA SUE, vocational education educator; b. Liberty, N.Y., Oct. 28, 1952; d. Charles William and Lillian Lorraine (Ball) H. AA, Sullivan County Community Coll., Lock Sheldrake, N.Y., 1972; BS, SUNY, Oneonta, 1974, MS in Edn., 1979. Cert. permanent math. tchr., provisional elem. tchr., N.Y. High sch. tchr. math. Downsville (N.Y.) Cen. Sch., 1980-83, Oneonta Cen. Sch., 1984-85; tutor Sullivan County Community Coll., 1985; cons. tchr. related skills for vocat. programs Sullivan County Career and Tech. Edn. Ctr., Liberty, 1985—, fin. aid adminstr. LPN program, 1995—. Conf. presenter in field; rschr. Hudson Valley Faculty Portfolio Assessment. Contbr. poetry to various publs. Recipient Golden Poet award World of Poetry Press, 1986-91. Mem. ASCD, AAUW, AMTNYS, AMS, SSMA, Sullivan Reading Coun., Nat. Coun. Tchrs. Math., Am. Career and Tech. Educators, Nat. Coun. Tchrs. English, Internat. Reading Assn., Am. Poetry Assn. (Poet of Merit award 1989), Kappa Delta Pi., Delta Kappa Gamma (Tau chpt).

HEIER, MARILYN KAY, retired elementary school educator; b. Oakley, Kans., Nov. 22, 1939; d. Vincent M. and Ferne (Beckman) Dickman; m. Linus B. Heier, June 15, 1961; children: Donita Bozarth, Michael, Beverly Birney, Christina Shaheen, Lawrence. BS in Home Econs., Marymount Coll., Salina, Kans., 1960; MS in Elem. Edn., Ft. Hays State U., Hays, Kans., 1980. Cert. in elem. and secondary edn., Kans. Tchr. home econs., English and phys. edn. Bethune (Colo.) Pub. Schs., 1960-62; tchr. 5th grade Unified Sch. Dist. 291, Grinnell, Kans., 1974—99, head tchr., 1990—99; ret., 1999. Mem. Quality Performance Edn. Com., Grinnell, 1992-95; mem. Profl. Devel. Coun., Grinnell, 1990-95. Mem. St. Mary's Altar Soc., Immaculate Conception Ch. Jennibelle Watson scholar, 1979. Mem. NEA, Kans. Edn. Assn., Grinnell Tchrs. Assn. (pres. 1984-86, head negotiator 1994-95), Delta Kappa Gamma (pres 1988-90), Phi Delta Kappa. Democrat. Roman Catholic. Avocations: reading, sewing, travel, gardening, knitting. Home: Box 291 206 S Harrison Ave Grinnell KS 67738 Office: USD 291 of Grinnell PO Box 126 202 S Monroe Grinnell KS 67738

HEIFETS, LEONID, microbiologist, educator; b. Russia, Jan. 5, 1926; came to U.S., 1979; s. Boris and Luba Heifets; m. Seraphima Apsit, Jan. 1955 (div. July 1978); children: Michael, Herman. MD, Med. Inst., Moscow, 1947, PhD, 1953; DSc, Acad. Med. Scis., Moscow. Asst. prof. Med. Inst., Arkhangelsk, Russia, 1950-54, assoc. prof., 1954-57; lab. dir. Mechnikov Rsch. Inst., Moscow, 1957-69; sr. rschr. Inst. for Tb, Moscow, 1969-78; rsch. fellow Nat. Jewish Hosp., Denver, 1979-80; lab. dir. Nat. Jewish Ctr., Denver, 1980—; asst. prof. Colo. U., Denver, 1980-86, assoc. prof., 1986-92, prof. microbiology, 1992—. Mem. com. on bacteriology Internat. Union Against Tb, Paris, 1986—. Author: Effectiveness of Vaccination, 1968, Clinical Mycobaceriology (Clinics in Laboratory Medicine), 1996; author, editor: Drug Susceptibility, 1991; assoc. editor Internat. Jour. Tuberculosis; contbr. articles to profl. jours. Mem. Am. Soc. Microbiology. Avocations: hiking, snowshoeing, photography, history. Office: Nat Jewish Med Rsch Ctr 1400 Jackson St Denver CO 80206-2761 E-mail: heifetsl@njc.org.

HEIFNER, CAROL JOAN, social work educator; b. Sioux Falls, SD, July 10, 1940; d. Cecil Leonard Byg and Violet Irene (Miller) Noller; m. Dennis Roy Heifner, June 3, 1960; children: Janine, Renee, Denise. AA, S.D. State U., 1960; BSW, Briar Cliff Coll., 1978; MSW, U. Iowa, 1980; PhD, Case Western Res. U., 1999. County coord. Upper Des Moines Opportunity, Emmetsburg, Iowa, 1974-75; caseworker, family therapist Harmony Youth Home, Orange City, Iowa, 1980; coord. Woodbury County Ct. Referral Svc., Sioux City, Iowa, 1977; outside evaluator Florence Crittendon Home, Sioux City, 1980-81; sch. social worker Area Edn. Agy. 4, Sioux Center, 1980-87; instr. Dordt Coll., Sioux Center, 1987-91. Team evaluator Area Edn. Agy. 3, Cylinder, Iowa, 1984; co-tchr. in teen conflict N.W. Iowa Tech. Coll., Sheldon, Iowa, 1989; grant co-author REACH Team, Sioux Center, 1984, 85; mem. workshop Nursing Home Activity Dirs., N.W. Iowa, 1989; part-time instr. St. Mary's Coll. of Minn., Winona, 1991, Mandel Sch. Applied Social Scis./Case Western Res. U., 1991-93; cons. for curriculum devel. Babes-Bolyai U. Club-Napoca, Romania, 1993; lectr. U. Wis. LaCrosse, 1998-99, adj. faculty, 1999; part-time instr. sociology Viterbo Coll., LaCrosse, 1999; Fulbright lectr. U. Ion Cuza, Iasi, Romania; curriculum cons. clin. pastoral edn. program Franciscan Skemp Med. Ctr., 2001; ind. rschr.; facilitator Conflict Resolution Workshop. Founding mem. Sioux County Multidisciplinary Tream, Orange City, 1980-83; founding bd. dirs. Children's World Day Care Ctr., Sheldon, 1974; founding bd. dirs., chair Domestic Violence Aid Ctr., Inc., Sioux Center, 1982-86; bd. dirs. Plains Area Mental Health, LeMars, Iowa, 1978-80. Mem.: Soc. for Romanian Studies. Avocations: sewing, painting, furniture refinishing, reading, music.

HEILES, CARL EUGENE, astronomer, educator; b. Toledo, Sept. 22, 1939; children: Tod Scott, Katrina Marie. B in Engring. Physics, Cornell U., 1962; PhD in Astronomy, Princeton U., 1966. Asst. prof., then assoc. prof. U. Calif., Berkeley, 1966-69, astronomy prof., 1970—; rsch. astronomer Arecibo (P.R.) Obs., 1969-70. Vis. fellow Joint Inst. for Lab. Astrophysics, Boulder, Colo., 1989-90. Recipient Dannie Heineman prize in astrophysics Am. Astron. Soc., 1989. Mem. NAS, Am. Acad. Scis., Calif. Acad. Scis. Office: U Calif Dept Astronomy Berkeley CA 94720-0001

HEILMAN, E. BRUCE, academic administrator; b. La Grange, Ky., July 16, 1926; s. Earl Bernard and Nellie (Sanders) H.; m. Betty June Dobbins, Aug. 27, 1948; children: Bobbie Lynn, Nancy Jo, Terry Lee, Sandra June, Timothy Bruce. BS, Vanderbilt U., 1950, MA, 1951; PhD, Peabody Coll., 1961; postgrad., U. Tenn., U. Omaha, U. Ky.; LLD (hon.), Wake Forest U., 1967, Ky. Wesleyan Coll., 1980, James Madison U., 1986, U. Richmond, 1986; DHum. (hon.), Campbell Coll., 1971; LLD; LHD (hon.), Bridgewater Coll., 1991; DHL, DPS, Campbellsville Coll., 1995. Instr. bus. Peabody Coll., Vanderbilt U., 1950—51, bursar, 1957—60, adminstrv. v.p.,

1963—66; instr. accounting Belmont Coll., Nashville, 1951—52; auditor Albert Maloney Co., Nashville, 1951—52; asst. prof. accounting, bus. mgr. Ky. Wesleyan Coll., 1952—54; treas. Georgetown (Ky.) Coll., 1954—57, Georgetown (Ky.) Coll. (Louisville Housing Project), 1954—57; coordinator higher edn. and spl. schs. Tenn., 1960—61; v.p., dean Ky. So. Coll., Louisville, 1961—63; prof. edn1. adminstrn. Peabody Coll. Vanderbilt U., Nashville, 1963—66; pres. Meredith Coll., Raleigh, 1966—71, U. Richmond, Va., 1971—86, chancellor, 1966—2002, chancellor, interim chief exec. officer, 1987—88, chancellor emeritus, 2002—. Bd. dirs. Cooperating Raleigh Colls., 1967-71; cons. indsl. studies in edn. and adminstrn., 1954—; dir., cons. long range planning confs. Fund Advancement Edn., 1960—; cons. acad. Ednl. Study Task, 1964-65; mem. Wake County-Raleigh City Sh. Merger Study Com., 1969; adv. com. N.C. Dept. Pub. Instrn., 1970; bd. dirs. Fidelity Bankers Life Ins. Co., A.H. Robins Co., Richmond, Ctrl. Fidelity Bank, Fidelity Fed. Savs. Bank, Bapt. Theol. Sem., Richmond; mem. adv. bd. Sta. WLEE Radio-TV; chmn. Cardinal Savs. and Loan Assn., Fast Fox, Inc., Office Am., Richmond, Direct Med. Inc., Cordell Med., Va. Escrow & Title co. The Phoenix Corp.; trustee, chmn. bd. advisors, mem. exec. com., devel. coms. Campbellsville (Ky.) Coll; instnl. cons. adv. bd. Paine Webber, Inc. Author: (with others) Sixty College Study, 1954; also booklets and articles. Chmn. blood com. for edn. ARC, 1971; mem. Nashville Urban Renewal Coordinating Com., 1965-66; ann. giving chmn. for N.C. Peabody Coll. Vanderbilt, U., 1970-72; mem. Friends of HOME, 1974—; chmn. trustee orientation com. N.C. Bapt. Conv., 1961; mem. edn. commn. So. Bapt. Conv.; mem. bd. advisors Bapt. Hosp. Sch. Nursing, Nashville, 1956-60, 64—; mem. com. Met. Gen. Hosp. Sch. Nursing, 1965-68; mem. Federated Arts Coun. Richmond, 1975—, Robert Lee coun. Boy Scouts Am., 1975—; mem. devel. adv. bd. Va. Ctr. Performing Arts, 1980; bd. dirs. Bill Wilkerson Speech and Hearing Ctr., Nashville, 1963-64, Bapt. Theology Sem., Richmond, 1964, N.C. Symphony, United Fund Wake County, 1968-71, N.C. Mental Health Assn., 1969-71, Wake County Mental Health Assn., 1969-71, Va. Thanksgiving Festival, 1972, Richmond Pub. Libr., Richmond chpt. NCCJ, Ba. Inst. Sci. Rsch., 1971—, Leadership Metro Richmond, 1980—, Maymont Found., 1996—, Metro Bank, 1996—, chmn. of bd., 1997—; hon. dir. Richmond Ballet, 1971; bd. govs. United Givers Fund Richmond, 1971; trustee Inst. Mediterranean Studies, 1972—, E.R. Patterson Ednl. Found., 1972—, U. Richmond, 1973-86; bd. govs. Marine Corps. Assn., 1990; pres. Marine Mil. Acad., 1964, exec. v.p. bd., 1979—, chmn. bd. trustees, 1994, chmn. bd. trustees, 1994—, bd. dirs. USMC Def. Bat., Chairman, Marine Corps. U. bd. of trustees, Quantico, Va., Nat. Def. Univ. Found., So. Sem. Found., Bapt. Theol. Sem., Richmond, Va.; mem. adv. bd., chmn. devel. com., bd. dirs. Marine Hist. Found.. Served with USMCR, 1944-47. Served with U.S. Army, 1944—47. Recipient award Owensboro (Ky.) Jr. C. of C., 1953; Agrl. and Industry Service award U. Nashville, 1961; Outstanding Civic and Ednl. award Raleigh, 1970; Distinguished Salesman award Richmond, 1972, Disting. Alumni award Campbellsville Coll. and Peabody Coll. Vanderbilt U., Distinguished Citizen of Oldham County (Ky.) award, Va. Assn. Future Farmers Am. award, 1976, Disting. Citizen award Meredith Coll., 1977; named Ky. Col., 1969; Paul Harris Rotary fellow, 1970; Reverse Exchange Eisenhower fellow to Peoples Rep. of China, 1987; named Hon. Pres. Sino-Am. Cultural Soc., 1988. Mem. Internat. Assn. Univ. Pres.'s (N. Am. council 1976—), Nat. Fedn. Bus. Officers, Nat. Fedn. Bus. Officers Cons. Service, So. Assn. Colls. Women (pres. 1969), Nat. Soc. Lit. and the Arts, So. Univ. Conf., Sino Am. Soc. (hon. pres.), Am. Council Edn., Tenn. Edn. Assn., Ky. Ednl. Buyers Assn., Am. Assn. Pres.'s Ind. Colls. and Univs., Ky. Assn. Acad. Deans, Peabody Alumni Assn. Vanderbilt U. (exec. com), Nat., So. assns. coll. and univ. bus. officers, Assn. Governing Bds. Univs. and Colls., Coll. and Univ. Personnel Assn., Internat. Platform Assn., Nashville, Raleigh, Richmond, Va. chambers commerce, Nat. Assn. Ind. Colls. and Univs., Navy League U.S., Marine Corps League, Council Ind. Colls. in Va. (pres. 1974-76), Va. Found. Ind. Colls., Assn. Va. Colls., Assn. So. Bapt. Colls. and Schs. (pres. 1976), N.C. Found. Ch.-Related Colls., Assn. Am. Colls., So. Assn. Colls. and Schs. (trustee 1977), Phi Beta Kappa, Pi Omega Pi, Kappa Phi Kappa, Kappa Delta Pi, Delta Pi Epsilon, Omicron Delta Kappa, Beta Gamma Sigma, Lambda Chi Alpha (Achiever award 1993), Va. Bapt. Hist. Soc., English-Speaking Union, Newcomen Soc. N. Am. Democrat. Baptist (deacon). Clubs: Rotary (Raleigh) (bd. advisers Raleigh 1966-71), Execs. (Raleigh) (v.p., dir. 1971), City (Raleigh); Downtown (Richmond); The Club, Forum. Home: 4700 Cary Street Rd Richmond VA 23226-1703 Office: Chancellor's Office University of Richmond Richmond VA 23173

HEILMAN, MARY JOANNE, gifted education educator; b. Kansas City, Mo., Sept. 11, 1955; d. Norris Alger and Mary Jane (Brewster) Smith; m. James Heilman, Apr. 19, 1997; children: Jennifer Caruso, Angelia. AA, Miss. County Coll., 1985; BA, Gov.'s State U., University Park, Ill., 1988, MA in English, 1992. Cert. tchr, Ill., gifted students tchr., Ill. Tchr. Sch. Dist. #160, Country Club Hills, 1989-94; tchr., coord. gifted program Sch. Dist. #159, Mokena, Ill., 1994-96, Carroll County Middle Sch., Carrollton, Ky., 1997—, team leader, cluster leader writing portfolios, mem. middle sch. site based coun. Instr. Mississippi County C.C., summers 1993-96; instr. Joliet Jr. Coll., 1993-96, MOMS program; adj. instr. Jefferson C.C., 1997—; team leader, English dept. cluster leader; mem. site based decision making coun. Active NOW. Mem. NEA, Internat. Platform Assn. Avocation: reading. Home: 1 Wilson Way Carrollton KY 41008-9648

HEIM, WERNER G(EORGE), biology educator; b. Muhlheim Ruhr, Germany, Apr. 7, 1929; came to U.S., 1940, naturalized, 1946; s. Fred and Recha (Hirsch) H.; m. Julie I. Blumenthal, June 25, 1961; children: Susan L., David L.; m. Suzanne M. Levine, June 24, 1973; children: Elise B. Ginsburg, Lynn A. Ginsburg. BA in Zoology, UCLA, 1950, MA in Zoology, 1952, PhD in Zoology, 1954. Instr. Brown U., Providence, 1956-57; asst. prof. biology Wayne State U., Detroit, 1957-63, assoc. prof. biology, 1963-67, vice chmn. dept. biology, 1961-62, planning coord. biology bldg. program, 1964-67; mem. faculty Colo. Coll., Colorado Springs, 1967-94, prof. biology, 1967—91, prof. biology spl. sr. status, 1991-94, prof. emeritus, 1994—, chmn. dept biology, 1971-76, 87-90. Vis. prof. biophysics and genetics dept. U. Colo. Sch. Medicine, 1978, 86; cons., geneticist divsn. genetic svcs. Children's Hosp., Denver, 1978-2001. Contbr. book revs. and sci. articles to profl. publs. Del., Republican State Conv., Denver, 1982, 84, 86, alt., 1990, 92, 96. USPHS-Nat. Cancer Inst. fellow, 1952-54; grantee NIH, 1958-67, NSF, 1963-70, Am. Cancer Soc., 1963-65, Colo. Coll., 1979-83. Fellow AAAS; mem. Soc. Integrative Biology, Internat. Soc. Devel. Biologists, Colo.-Wyo. Acad. Sci. (v.p. 1968-69), Am. Soc. Human Genetics, Sigma Xi. Office: Colo Coll Dept Biology Colorado Springs CO 80903

HEIMANN-HAST, SYBIL DOROTHEA, language arts and literature educator; b. Shanghai, May 8, 1924; came to U.S., 1941; d. Paul Heinrich and Elisabeth (Halle) Heimann; m. David G. Hast, Jan. 11, 1948 (div. 1959); children: Thomas David Hast, Dorothea Elizabeth Hast-Scott. BA in French, Smith Coll., 1946; MA in French Lang. and Lit., U. Pitts., 1963; MA in German Lang. and Lit., UCLA, 1966; diploma in Spanish, U. Barcelona, Spain, 1972. Cert. German, French and Spanish tchr., Calif. Assoc. in German lang. UCLA, 1966-70; asst. prof. German Calif. State U., L.A., 1970-71; lectr. German Mt. St. Mary's Coll., Brentwood, Calif., 1974-75; instr. French and German, diction coach Calif. Inst. of Arts, Valencia, 1977-78; coach lang. and diction UCLA Opera Theater, 1973-93, ret., 1993, lectr. dept. music, 1973-93; interviewer, researcher oral history program UCLA, 1986-93; dir., founder ISTMO, Santa Monica, Calif., 1975—. Cons. interpreter/translator L.A. Music Ctr., U.S. Supreme Ct., L.A., J. Paul Getty Mus., Malibu, Calif., Warner New Media, Panorama Internat. Prodn., Sony Records, 1986—; voice-over artist; founder, artistic dir. Westside Opera Workshop, 1986-94. Author of poems. Mem. KCET Founder Soc. UCLA grantee, 1990-91. Mem. AAUP, MLA, SAG, AFTRA, KCET Founder Soc., Sunset Succulent Soc. (v.p., bd. dirs., reporter, annual show chmn.), German Am. C. of C., L.A. Avocations: performing arts, literature, history, plants, designing and knitting sweaters. Home and Office: River's Edge 111 Dekoven Dr Apt 606 Middletown CT 06457-3463

HEIMBERG, MURRAY, pharmacologist, biochemist, physician, educator; b. Bklyn., Jan. 5, 1925; s. Gustav and Fannie (Geller) H.; children by previous marriage: Richard G., Steven A.; m. Anna Frances Langlois Knox, July 12, 1964; stepchildren: Larry M. Knox, David S. Knox. BS, Cornell U., Ithaca, N.Y., 1948, MNS, 1949; PhD in Biochemistry (NIH fellow), Duke, 1952; MD, Vanderbilt U., 1959. NIH Postdoctoral fellow in biochemistry Med. Sch. Washington U., St. Louis, 1952-54; research asso. physiology Med. Sch. Vanderbilt U., 1954-59, asst. prof. to prof. pharmacology, and asst. prof. medicine, 1959-74; prof., chmn. dept. pharmacology, prof. medicine U. Mo., 1974-81; prof. and chmn. dept. pharmacology, prof. medicine, endocrinology and metabolism U. Tenn., Health Sci. Ctr., Memphis, 1981-96; Van Vleet prof. pharmacology U. Tenn., Memphis, 1986-96, Disting. prof. pharmacology and medicine, 1996-99, disting. prof. pharmacology and medicine emeritus, 2000—. Cons. NSF, NIH; cons., established investigator Am. Heart Assn.; attending physician U. Tenn. Hosps. and Memphis VA Hosp.; dir. lipid metabolism clinic U. Tenn. Med. Group. Contbr. articles to profl. jours. Served with inf., AUS, 1943-45, ETO. Decorated Purple Heart, Bronze Star; recipient Lederle Med. Faculty award; research grantee. Fellow AAAS, Am. Coll. Clin. Pharmacology, Am. Heart Assn.; mem. Am. Soc. Biol. Chemistry and Molecular Biology, Am. Soc. Pharmacology and Exptl. Therapeutics, Endocrine Soc., Am. Diabetes Assn., So. Soc. Clin. Investigation. Home: 105 Devon Way Memphis TN 38111-7711 E-mail: mheimberg@utmem.edu., mheimber@midsouth.rr.com.

HEIMBOLD, MARGARET BYRNE, publisher, educator, consultant; came to U.S., 1966, naturalized, 1973; d. John Christopher and Anne (Troy) Byrne; m. Arthur Heimbold, Feb. 26, 1984; children: Eric Thomas Gordon, Victoria Byrne Heimbol. BA, Queens Coll.; cert., Dale Carnegie, 1977, Psychol. Corp. Am., 1981, Wharton Sch., 1983, Stanford U., 1989; MA in Libr. Sci., Georgetown U., 2003. Group advt. mgr. N.Y. Times, N.Y.C., 1978-85; pub. Am. Film, Washington, 1985-86; v.p., pub. Nat. Trust for Hist. Preservation, Washington, 1986-90; pres. Summerville Press, Inc., Washington, 1990—. Pub. Metro Golf, 1992—; advisor Mag. Pubs.; mentor Women's Ctr. Va.; judge various publ. competitions; judge various mags. awards programs. Trustee Nat. Mus. Women in Arts, Choral Arts Soc. Washington.

HEIMES, CHARMAINE MARIE, elementary school educator, poet, writer; b. Detroit, June 28, 1960; d. Charles M. and Mary Patricia (Allen) H. BA, Olivet Coll., 1982. Cert. tchr. Tex., nat. cert. abstinence educator. Substitute tchr. Charlotte (Mich.) Pub. Schs., 1982-84; coach jr. varsity volleyball Charlotte High Sch., 1983-84, coach jr. varsity softball, 1984; tcrh. phys. edn., coach Cigarroa Mid. Sch., Laredo, Tex., 1984—, head phys. edn. dept., 1988—. Asst. field hockey coach Olivet (Mich.) Coll., 1982-83; abstinenece master tchr. 1999-. Avocations: collecting coins, plates, poetry, writing, Elvis memorabilia. Office: Cigarroa Mid Sch 2600 Palo Blanco St Laredo TX 78046-8232

HEINER, DOUGLAS CRAGUN, pediatrician, educator, immunologist, allergist; b. Salt Lake City, July 27, 1925; s. Spencer and Eva Lillian (Cragun) H.; m. Joy Luana Wiest, Jan. 8, 1946; children: Susan, Craig, Joseph, Marianne, James, David, Andrew, Carolee, Pauli. BS, Idaho State U., 1946; MD, U. Pa., 1950; PhD, McGill U., 1969. Intern Hosp. U. Pa., Phila., 1950-51; resident, fellow Children's Med. Ctr., Boston, 1953-56; asst. prof. pediatrics U. Ark. Med. Ctr., Little Rock, 1956-60; assoc. prof. pediatrics U. Utah Med. Ctr., Salt Lake City, 1960-66; fellow in immunology McGill U., Montreal, 1966-69; prof. of pediatrics Harbor-UCLA Med. Ctr., Torrance, 1969-94; disting. prof. of pediatrics UCLA Sch. Medicine, 1985-94, prof. emeritus, 1994—; med. specialist Russia Latter-day Saints Missions, 1997-99. Author: Allergies to Milk, 1980; mem. editl. bd. Jour. Allergy and Clin. Immunology, 1975-79, Allergy, 1981-88, Jour. Clin. Immunology, 1981-87, Pediat. Asthma, Allergy and Immunology, 1986-94; contbr. over 150 original articles to profl. jours. and chpts. to books. Scoutmaster Boy Scouts Am., Salt Lake City, 1963; com. chmn. Rancho Palos Verdes, 1979-81; high coun. mem. LDS Ch., Rancho Palos Verdes, 1983-86. with U.S. Army, 1952-53, Korea. Recipient Disting. Alumnus award Idaho State U., 1987. Fellow: Am. Coll. Allergy, Asthma and Immunology (Disting. fellow 1996), Am. Acad. Allergy and Immunology (food allergy com. 1981—94), Am. Pediatric Soc.; mem.: Am. Acad. Pediatrics, Clin Immunology Soc., Am. Assn. Immunologists, Western Soc. for Pediatric Rsch. (Ross award 1961), Soc. for Pediatric Rsch. Republican. Avocations: gardening, tennis, fishing. E-mail: dheiner@mobileblue.com.

HEINLEN, DANIEL LEE, alumni organization administrator; b. Columbus, Ohio, Nov. 16, 1937; s. Calvin Xenophon and Charlotte Elizabeth (Lanman) H.; m. Roberta Bishop, Mar. 20, 1966 (div. 1975); m. Gelene Vogel Kozlowski, June 17, 1978; children: Stephanie Heinlen, Kate Kozlowski Isler, Amy. BS in Social Work, Ohio State U., 1960. Youth program dir., extension dir. YMCA, Pitts., 1960-65; field dir. Alumni Assn., Ohio State U., Columbus, 1965-67, assoc. dir., 1967-73, dir. alumni affairs, 1973-92; pres., CEO Ohio State U. Alumni Assn., Inc., Columbus, 1992—; sec. Alumni Assn. Bd., Columbus, 1973—; pub. mag. Alumni Assn., Ohio State U., 1973—. Ex-officio trustee Ohio State U. Found.; presdl. search com. Ohio State U., 1990, 97, 2002; trustee Coun. for Advancement and Support of Higher Edn., Washington, 1986-88, 90-94, chmn., 1992-93; chmn. 75th anniversary Colloquium, Columbus, 1988, chmn. ann. assembly alumni track, 1988, chmn. ann. assembly, 1990; chmn. Mgmt. Inst. for Alumni Assn. Execs., Chgo., 1996, pres., 1994-96, bd. dirs., 1988-96; founding bd. Coun. Alumni Assn. Execs. 1989-96, pres. 1992-93; chmn. Univ. ProNet, Inc., Palo Alto, Calif., 1996-99, chmn. alumni dirs. Big Ten, 1973, 84, 93; mem. Ohio State U. Pres.'s Coun., 1991-98; bd. dirs. River Road Hotel Corp.; founding chmn. Self-Governing Alumni Forum, 2000—; chmn. task force on alumni advocacy Inter Univ. Coun., 2002. Author chpts. in books. Exec. com. NW Ordinance U.S. Constn. Bicentennial Commn., Ohio, 1986-88; bd. dir. Non-profit Mailers Fedn., Wash., 1985-88; mem. OSU Com. on Student Fin. Aids, Columbus, 1973-99, exec. com. Acad. Disting. Tchg., 1995—, Newcomen Soc. N.Am., 1975-90, 93—. Recipient Ohio State U. Coll. of Social Work Disting. Svc. award, 1996; named Hon. Trustee Easter Seal Rehab. Ctr. of Ctrl. Ohio, Columbus, 1988-92; D.L. Heinlen award for univ. advocacy named in his honor Ohio Sate U. Alumni Assn., Inc., 1995. Mem. Rotary (bd. dirs. Columbus Club 1986, v.p. 1987-89, pres. 1989-90), Univ. Club (bd. dirs., 2nd v.p. 1985-88, 94-95, 1st v.p. 1996), Faculty Club (mem. bd. control 1978-80, pres.-elect 1999, pres. 2000-01), Kit Kat (exec. com. 1999-2002, sec. 2001—), Golden Key Nat. Honor Soc. (hon. mem.), Sphinx Coun. Avocations: tennis, sporting clays. Home: 2981 E Powell Rd Lewis Center OH 43035-9517 Office: Ohio State U Alumni Assn Inc 2200 Olentangy River Rd Columbus OH 43210-1035 E-mail: heinlen.4@osu.edu.

HEINRICH, CARL CHESTER, retired physical education educator; b. Norwich, Conn., Aug. 26, 1952; s. Chester Edgar and Elaine Pitcher (Lawrence) H. BS, Barrington Coll. (now Gordon), 1980; MA, U. Conn., 1986. Machinist Elec. Boat div. Gen. Dynamics, Groton, Conn., 1974-77; tchr. St. Thomas More Sch., Montville, Conn., 1980-81, First Assembly Christian Sch., Memphis, 1981-84; tchr. phys. edn. Norwich (Conn.) Pub. Schs., 1984-2000, ret., 2000. Patentee double jump rope skipping apparatus. Mem. United Congl. Ch., Norwich, Conn. Mem. Masons, Order of Eastern Star. Avocations: community theater acting, astronomy, music (soloist), computers. Home: 5 Elaine St # 131 Bozrah CT 06334-1102 E-mail: cch84@aol.com.

HEINS, SISTER MARY FRANCES, private school educator, nun; b. Galveston, Tex., Nov. 12, 1927; d. George and Rosella (Eckenfels) H. BA, Dominican Coll., 1954; MEd, Lamar U., 1973. Joined Dominican Sisters, Roman Cath. Ch., 1946. Tchr. parochial schs., Tex. and Calif., 1948-68; tchr., head sci. dept., asst. prin. Kelly H.S., Beaumont, Tex., 1968-80; co-prin., then prin. St. Pius X H.S., Houston, 1980-84; tchr., head sci. dept. O'Connell Jr. H.S., Galveston, 1984-86; prin. O'Connell H.S., Galveston, 1989-97; tchr., adminstrv. asst., computer coord., sci. fair coord. Galveston Cath. Sch., 1986-89, tchr. sci., 1997—2003; tchr. theology O'Connell HS, Galveston, Tex., 2003—. Mem. Goals for Beaumont Edn. task force Beaumont C. of C., 1979-80. Mem. interfaith com. Galveston Hist. Found., 1990; mem. ch. involvement com. City-wide Conf. on Youth Violence; participant Galveston Historical Foundations Annual Home Tours, Annual Home and Garden Show benefitting the Animal Shelter. Recipient Outstanding Tchr. award Beaumont A&M Club, 1971, O'Connell Booster of Yr. award, 1995-96; named One of Top 50 Tchrs. in the City, 1998; grantee NSF. Mem. Nat. Cath. Edn. Assn., Nat. Assn. Tchrs. Math., Lamar U. Alumni Assn., World Future Soc., Sci. Tchrs. Assn. Tex. (Outstanding Tchr. 1980), Galveston C. of C. (mem. edn. com. 1990-91), Galveston Garden Club (rec. sec. 2000-04), Delta Kappa Gamma (pres. Eta chpt. 1978-80, Omicron chpt. 1988-90, rec. sec. 1998-2000, historian 2002—, Chpt. Achievement award 1990, 97). Democrat. Roman Catholic. Avocations: needlepoint, word puzzles, reading, collecting owls, collecting apples. Home: 4420 Ave L Galveston TX 77550 Office: O'Connell HS 1320 Tremont Galveston TX 77550 E-mail: smfheins@aol.com.

HEINTZ, CAROLINEA CABANISS, retired home economics educator; b. Roanoke, Va., Jan. 19, 1920; d. Luther Bertie and Emblyn Bird (Jennings) Cabaniss; m. Howard Elmer Smith, Dec. 19, 1942 (div. Aug. 1975); children: Emblyn Davis, Cynthia Shannon, Cheryl Peterson, Melyssa Sexton; m. Raymond Walter Heintz, May 21, 1977; 1 stepchild, James. BS in Home Econ. Edn., U. Ala., Tuscaloosa, 1941; vocat. home econ. degree, Montevallo Coll., 1941. Cert. vocat. home econs. tchr. Swimming instr. Camp Mudjekeewis, Centerlovel, Maine, summer 1940; home econs. tchr. Roanoke Pub. Schs., 1941-43; dietitian U. Va., Charlottesville, 1943; nutrition edn. specialist Liberty Health Ctr. Svcs., Liberty Center, Ohio, 1974-80; home economist Dayton Hudson Dept. Store, Toledo, 1980-84; splty . food instr., continuing edn. U. Toledo, 1984-85. Pres., mem. Greater Toledo Nutrition Coun., 1966-98; bd. dirs. Sunset House Aux., pres. 1999-2001. Co-editor ch. cookbook Loaves and Fishes and Other Dishes, 2000. Spkr. United Way, Toledo, 1965-90; founder, pres. Mobile Meals Toledo, Inc., 1968-71, mem. adv. bd., 1988-95, 2001-03, bd. dirs., chmn. pub. rels., 1997-99, nominating com., 2000-03, Spirit of Mobile Meals award, 1998; affiliate mem. Arts Commn., Toledo, 1976-77; chmn. Saphire Ball, Toledo Symphony Orch., Toledo Opera, 1978; adminstrv. coord. Feed Your Neighbor program Met. Chs. United, Toledo, 1979-86; deacon Collingwood Presbyn. Ch., 1969-71, elder, 1972-74, 77-79, 97-99, 2001-03, trustee, 1984-86, elder, clk. of session, 1991-94, stewardship chmn., 1996-97, del. to Maumee Valley Presbytery, 1991-99; mem. steering com. Interfaith Hospitality Network, 1992-94, bd. dirs., 1993-94; alt. del. Gen. Assembly Presbyn. Ch. U.S.A., 1993, del.-commr., 1994. Recipient Woman of Toledo award St. Vincent Hosp. and Med. Ctr. Guild, 1967, 80, Outstanding Community Svc. award United Way, 1987, Henry Morse vol. award, Greater Toledo award United Way, 1998, runner-up Nat. Vol. of the Year award Project Meal Found., Reynolds Metal Co., 1998. Mem. AAUW (bd. dirs. 1974-76, 94-96, 97-98, chmn. mem. gourmet group 1966-99, 2001, 03, edn. found. chmn. 1994-96, book sale chmn. 1998, nominating com. chmn.), Ohio Med. Aux. (1st v.p. 1973-74), Aux. Acad. Medicine (pres. 1967-68, chmn. edn. gourmet group 1966-99, 2001-03, Health Care award 1974), Indian Trails Garden Club (pres. 1997-98), Sigma Kappa (various alumni offices). Republican. Avocations: volunteering, gourmet cooking, traveling, entertaining, bridge. Home: # 108 4030 Indian Rd Toledo OH 43606-2225

HEINY, ROBERT WAYNE, special education educator; b. Oakland, Calif., Jan. 28, 1936; s. Edwin Wayne and Martha Mary (Wilkinson) H.; m. Joan Marie Umscheid, Dec. 28, 1956; children: Lawrence Wayne, Leanne Lynn, Loren Charles, Layne Pahl, Lora Joy. BA, U. LaVerne, 1960; MA, Calif. State U., L.A., 1964; PhD, U. Ill., 1969. Passenger agt. United Airlines, San Francisco, 1957-59; tchr. Azusa (Calif.) Unified Sch. Dist., 1960-63; instr. in spl. edn. U. Ill., Champaign, 1967-68; assoc. prof. edn. U. N.C., Chapel Hill, 1968-70; assoc. prof. spl. edn. George Peabody Coll., Nashville, 1970-75; dir. edn. and tng. Wassaic (N.Y.) Devel. Ctr., 1975-76; sr. rsch. assoc. Brandeis U., Waltham, Mass., 1976-80; asst. to pres. and other titles U. LaVerne, Calif., Calif., 1981-87; spl. cons. to pres. Am. Armenian Internat. Coll., LaVerne, 1984-87; assoc. prof. spl. edn. Ill. State U., Normal, 1989-93; dir. Mont. Ctr. on Disabilities, Billings, 1993-94; prof. spl. edn. and ednl. founds. Mont. State U., Billings, 1993—. Sr. ptnr. Robert Heiny Assocs., 1978-89. Editor spl. feature issues Peabody Jour. Edn., 1972; contbr. articles to profl. jours., chpts. to books. Bd. dirs. Ill. Spl. Olympics, Normal, 1992-93, MARC Ctr., Bloomington, Ill., 1992-93, Mashdots Coll., Pasadena, Calif., 1992—; legis. liaison Ill. Spl. Edn. Coalition, Springfield, 1991-92. Recipient Bronze medal Coun. for Advancement and Support of Edn., 1985. Mem. ASCD, Coun. for Exceptional Children, Am. Assn. on Mental Retardation. Mem. Ch. of the Brethren. Address: 1745 Eldena Way Modesto CA 95350-3568 also: 1745 Eldena Way Modesto CA 95350-3568

HEINZ, JOHN PETER, lawyer, educator; b. Carlinville, Ill., Aug. 6, 1936; s. William Henry and Margaret Louise (Denby) H.; m. Anne Murray, Jan. 14, 1967; children: Katherine Reynolds, Peter Lindley Murray. AB, Washington U., St. Louis, 1958; LLB, Yale U., 1962. Bar: D.C. 1962, Ill. 1966, U.S. Supreme Ct. 1967. Teaching asst. polit. sci. Washington U., St. Louis, 1958-59, instr., 1960; asst. prof. Northwestern U. Sch. Law, Chgo., 1965-68, assoc. prof., 1968-71, prof., 1971-88, Owen L. Coon prof., 1988—, dir. program law and social scis., 1968-70, dir. rsch., 1973-74, prof. sociology, 1987—. Affiliated scholar Am. Bar Found., Chgo., 1974—, vis. scholar, 1975-76, exec. dir., 1982-86, disting. research fellow, 1987—. Author: (with A. Gordon) Public Access to Information, 1979, (with E. Laumann) Chicago Lawyers, 1982, rev. edit., 1994, (with E. Laumann, R. Nelson, R. Salisbury) The Hollow Core, 1993; contbr. articles to profl. jours. Served to capt. USAF, 1962-65 Grantee NIMH, 1970-72, NSF, 1970, 78-81, 84-86, 94-97, CNA Found., 1972, Am. Bar Found., 1974—, Russell Sage Found., 1978-80. Fellow: Am. Bar Found.; mem.: ABA, Chgo. Coun. Lawyers, Law and Soc. Assn. (Harry Kalven prize for disting. rsch. 1987). Home: 525 Judson Ave Evanston IL 60202-3083 Office: Northwestern U Sch Law 357 E Chicago Ave Chicago IL 60611-3059 E-mail: j-heinz@law.northwestern.edu.

HEISER, CHARLES BIXLER, JR., botany educator; b. Cynthiana, Ind., Oct. 5, 1920; s. Charles Bixler and Inez (Metcalf) H.; m. Dorothy Gaebler, Aug. 19, 1944; children— Lynn Marie, Cynthia Ann, Charles Bixler III. AB, Washington U., St. Louis, 1943, MA, 1944; PhD, U. Calif. at Berkeley, 1947. Instr. Washington U., St. Louis, 1944-45; assoc. botany U. Calif. at Davis, 1946-47; mem. faculty Ind. U., Bloomington, 1947—, prof. botany, 1957—, Disting. prof., 1979-86, disting. prof. emeritus, 1986—. Author: Nightshades, The Paradoxical Plants, 1969, Seed to Civilization, The Story of Man's Food, 1973, The Sunflower, 1976, The Gourd Book, 1979, Of Plants and People, 1985, Weeds in my Garden, 2003. Guggenheim fellow, 1953; NSF Sr. Postdoctoral fellow, 1962; recipient Pustovoit award Internat. Sunflower Assn., 1985, Raven Outreach award, 2002. Mem. Am. Soc. Plant Taxonomists (pres. 1967, Asa Gray award 1988, Raven Outreach award 2002), Bot. Soc. Am. (Merit award 1972, pres. 1980), Soc. Study Evolution (pres. 1974), Soc. Econ. Botany (pres. 1978, Disting. Econ. Botanist 1984), Nat. Acad. Scis., Phi Beta Kappa, Sigma Xi. Achievements include research and numerous publications on systematics flowering plants, natural and artificial hybridization, origin cultivated plants. Home: 605 Bell Trace Ct Bloomington IN 47408-4410 E-mail: cbheiser@bio.indiana.edu.

HEISER, WALTER CHARLES, librarian, priest, educator; b. Milw., Mar. 16, 1922; s. Walter Matthew and Lauretta Katherine (Kopmeier) H. AB, St. Louis U., 1945, AM, 1947, STL, 1955; MSLS, Cath. U. Am., 1959. Joined S.J., Roman Cath. Ch., 1940, ordained priest, 1953. Latin tchr. St. Louis U. High Sch., 1947-50; divinity libr. Saint Louis U., St. Louis, 1955—; mem. faculty dogmatic and systematic theology St. Louis U. Div. Sch., 1966-92; ret. Cons. catalog Cath. supplement Wilson Sr. High Sch. Libr., 1968-77. Rev. editor Theology Digest, 1963—. Mem. Cath. Libr. Assn. Home: 3601 Lindell Blvd Saint Louis MO 63108-3301 Office: 3650 Lindell Blvd Saint Louis MO 63108-3302

HEISERMAN, RUSSELL LEE, electronics educator; b. Oklahoma City, Dec. 25, 1930; s. Mack Russell Heiserman and Helen Fay (Sills) Landon; m. Alberta Elizabeth Nardi, Aug. 17, 1956 (div. June 1990); children: Thomas Scott, Alan Steven (dec.), Mary Christa. Cert. in electronics tech., Okla. A&M U., 1954; BS in Physics, Okla. State U., 1960, MS in Physics, 1962, EdD in Tech. Edn., 1978. Cert. sr. electronics engring. technician, Nat. Inst. for Certification. Sr. R & D technician Airpax, Inc., 1954-56; electronics technician Labko Sci., Stillwater, Okla., 1956-58, 59; physicist Naval Ordnance Lab., White Oak, Md., summer 1960; rsch. assoc. dept. physics, NDEA grad. fellow Okla. State U., Stillwater, 1960-62, asst. prof., head electronics dept. Tech. Inst., 1962-66; pres. sch. divsn., v.p. Hickok Tchg. Sys., Boston, 1966-74; prof. electronics and computer tech. Okla. State U., Stillwater, 1984-90; assoc. prof. tech. dept. McNeese State U., Lake Charles, La., 1990—. Mem. faculty coun. Coll. Engring., Architecture and Tech., Okla. State U., 1982-84, chmn., sec., 1983-84; pres. QTEK, Inc., 1981-90; mem. adv. coun. Seminole (Okla.) Jr. Coll., 1976-83; regional project coord. Am. Coun. Edn., Washington, 1971-91; tech. writer, ednl. product developer Interplex Electronics, Inc., New Haven, 1983-88; programs advisor assigned to ADNOC Career Devel. Ctr., Internat. Gas Tech., Abu Dhabi, United Arab Emirates, 1988-90; cons. in field. Author: Electronics Curriculum Guide, 1963, Introduction to Electrochemical Systems, 1981, Basic Electricity, 1982, Microcomputer Troubleshooting, 1984, (with Thomas Scott Heiserman) Introduction to Microcomputers, 1986; (co-author: Introduction to Amplifiers, 1968, Introduction to Electronic Devices, 1968, Digital Electronics, 1987; contbg. author entry on electronics Career Opportunities Ency., 1969; contbg. author Energy Management Handbook, 1982; tech. editor, project mgr. John Wiley & Sons Pubs., 1982-83; cons. editor McGraw Hill Book Co., 1966-76; reviewer SRA Pubs., 1975-84; contbr. articles to profl. publs. With U.S. Army, 1950-52, Japan and Korea. Mem. Am. Soc. Engring. Edn. (tech. edn. sect., session chmn. joint nat. conv. with Coll. and Industry Edn. Conf. 1986), Okla. Tech. Soc. (life, bd. dirs. 1976-80, editor jour. 1976-80, cons./presenter workshops on early identification of drop-outs 1978-80),Phi Kappa Phi (mem. membership com. Okla. State U. chpt. 1980-88), Sigma Pi Sigma (pres. physics honor soc. 1958-59), Tau Iota Epsilon (pres. Sch. Tech.'s honor soc. Okla. State U. chpt. 1953-54). Avocations: photography, sailing, scuba diving. Home: 216 Aqua Dr Lake Charles LA 70605-4462 Office: McNeese State Univ Dept Tech PO Box 91780 Lake Charles LA 70609-0001

HEISLER, BARBARA SCHMITTER, sociology educator; b. Heidelberg, Germany, Dec. 17, 1940; came to U.S., 1961; d. Bernhard and Gudrun (Löffler) Epple; m. Philippe C. Schmitter, May 6, 1962 (div. 1979); children: Monika Schmitter, Marc Schmitter; m. Martin Heisler. PhD, U. Chgo., 1979. Postdoctoral fellow Duke U., Durham, N.C., 1979-80; asst. prof. sociology SUNY, Buffalo, 1980-81; assoc. prof. sociology Cleve. State U., 1982-89; prof. sociology Gettysburg (Pa.) Coll., 1989—. Contbr. articles to profl. jours. Rsch. fellow German Marshall Fund, Washington, 1990, Am. Acad. fellow, Berlin, 1999; rsch. grantee Evang. Luth. Ch. Am., 1995. Mem. Am. Sociol. Assn. (officer polit. sociology sect. 1996—). Avocations: tennis, skiing. Office: Gettysburg College Dept Sociology Gettysburg PA 17325

HEISS, FREDERICK WILLIAM, public administrator and policy researcher, political scientist, educator; b. Kansas City, Mo., Mar. 3, 1932; s. William and Sophia Else (Schmid) H.; m. Patricia Jane Stark, June 19, 1958 (div. May 1982); children: William Frederick, Scott Evan, Kerrel Kae; m. Carol Mae Knox, Jan. 9, 1983; 1 child, Brac Seaton. BSBA, U. Denver, 1958; MPA, U. Colo., 1968, PhD, 1973. Adminstr. City and County Denver, 1958-70; asst. prof. U. Colo., Boulder, 1973-78, assoc. prof., 1978-85, dir. Denver Urban Obs. Denver, 1970-82, dir. MPA grad. program, 1982-85; chmn. dpet. pub. adminstrn. Va. Commonwealth U., Richmond, 1985-91, prof., 1991—. Dir. met. study Nat. Acad. Pub. Adminstrn., Washington, 1974-76; dir. sci. tech. NSF, Denver, 1976-78, nat. chmn. sci. and tech. transfer, 1977-78; cons. U.S. Civil Svc. Commn., Utah, 1975; dir. Capital Area Study and Program, Richmond, 1987-93; vis. prof. Huanghe U., Henan, China, 1989. Author: Urban Research and Urban Policy, 1975; contbr. articles to profl. jours. Keynote speaker League of Women Voters, Denver 1975, Pres. Carters Urban Conf., Denver, 1977; dir. regional governance Capital Area Assembly, Richmond, 1990-94. With Air Corps, USN, 1953-55, Korea. Grantee HUD, 1972-83, Dept. of Energy, 1979-82. Fellow Beta Theta Pi; mem. ASPA. Avocations: sailing, skiing, fishing. Home: 14198 Mill Creek Dr Montpelier VA 23192-2837 Office: Va Commonwealth U Dept Polit Sci & Pub Admin 923 W Franklin St Richmond VA 23284-9008

HEISS, JAMES EDWARD, university administrator, accountant; b. Ft. Smith, Ark., Sept. 7, 1944; s. Fred William and Mary Kathryn (Hall) H.; m. Jennifer Catherine Haycox, Dec. 15, 1970; children: Jason Haycox, Janet Kathryn. BS, Calif. State U., L.A., 1970. CPA, Calif., Oreg. Cashier, stockman Yutterman's Market, Ft. Smith, Ark., 1959-65; property contr. TRW, Inc., Redondo Beach, Calif., 1965-66; sr. acct. Deloitte & Touche, CPAs, L.A., 1970-74; assoc. dir. bus. affairs U. Oreg., Eugene, 1974—, mem. mgmt. adv. coun., 1996. Bd. dirs. U LaneO Credit Union, Eugene, 1991-98, cmty. svc. com., 1990—; creator U. Oreg. student loan program, 1998 (pres. awawrd 1990, 99). Editor Diese Heiss Zeit, 1995—. Cubmaster pack 117 Cub Scouts Am., Goshen, Oreg., 1982-85; scoutmaster troop 179 Boy Scouts Am., Springfield, Oreg., 1986-91, dist. eagle bd., 1990—; mem. budget com. Goshen (Oreg.) Vol. Fire Dist., 1987-97; pres. St. Anne's Acad., 1959-63. With USN, 1966-68, Vietnam. Named Scoutmaster of Yr. Boy Scouts Am., Eugene, 1991. Mem. AICPA, Roundtable of Eugene (treas. 2003—), Oreg. Club, Alumni Assn. Beta Alpha Psi (pres. 1972-73). Democrat. Roman Catholic. Avocations: travel, fishing, oregon football, rving. Home: 86057 Drummond Dr Eugene OR 97405-9641 Office: U Oreg PO Box 3237 Eugene OR 97403-0237 E-mail: jimheiss@callatg.com.

HEITSMITH, WILLIAM RICHARD, educational consultant; b. Colo. Springs, Colo., May 26, 1939; s. Richard Howe and Faye (Knox) H.; m. Marjorie Kay Wilkinson June 9, 1963; children: Richard David, Jonathan Howe; m. Janet Ruth Hilton, June 20, 1981. BA in Social Sci., U. No. Colo., 1963, MA in Social Sci., 1965; EdD in Adminstrn., Curriculum, U. Colo., 1984. Cert. adminstr., ctrl. admistr., elem., secondary prin. Pres. and cons. edn., bus., govt. Orgnl. Systems Consulting, Inc., 1976-92; high sch. tchr. Englewood (Colo.) Schools, 1966-72, coord. of curriculum, 1973-76, staff devel., 1980-82, high sch. tchr., 1977-91, program coord., 1987-91. Bd. dirs. Englewood Sch's. Accountability Com., 1968-71; legis. commn. Arapahoe Ct., Colo., 1968-72; bus. cons. several sch. dists. State of Colo., 1980-92; pres. Englewood Edn. Found., 1996-97. Author, editor: The OSC Letter, Foundation Happenings, 1992-97, Fastrack, 1993. Legis. liaison Colo. Edn. Assn., 1971-73; elder Presbyn. Ch., mem. stewardship, and fin., Green Mt. Presbyn., 1990—; sch.-to-career adv. bd., Englewood. Grantee Leadership Inst. Stanford Univ., 1974. Mem. ACA, ASTD, Assn. Supervision & Curriculum Devel., Nat. Career Devel. Assn., Phi Delta Kappa, Phi Alpha Theta. Home: 2605 S Harlan Ct Lakewood CO 80227-4018

HEITZENRODER, WENDY ROBERTA, elementary school educator; b. Erie, Pa., Nov. 14, 1948; d. Robert Walfred and Ruth Wilhelmena (Sandberg) Gustavson; m. Frederick Charles Heitzenroder, June 20, 1970; 1 child, Matthew Frederick. BA, Thiel Coll., Greenville, Pa., 1970; MA, W.Va. U., 1980, EdD, 1988. Caseworker Philadelphia County, Phila., 1970-71; spl. edn. tchr. John E. Davis Sch., East. Pa. Psychiat. Inst., Phila., 1971-77, Marion County Schs., Fairmont, W.Va., 1977-90, Fox Chapel Area Schs., Pitts., 1990—. Instr. spl. edn. W.Va. U., Morgantown, 1989-90; cons. Marion County Bd. Edn., Fairmont, 1989-90. Mem. Jr. League of Fairmont, 1980s; mem. choir Salem Luth. Ch., 1990—, mem. bell choir, 1990—. Jr. League of Fairmont grantee, 1989; Excellence for Edn. grantee, Pitts., 1991, 92; Thanks to Tchrs. finalist Giant Eagle award, 1994-95; recipient, Silver award Tchr. Excellence Found., 2001, 2002. Mem. Phi Delta Kappa. Avocations: reading, swimming, tennis, needlework. Home: RR 9 Box 543 Greensburg PA 15601-9255 Office: Fox Chapel Area Sch Dist 611 Field Club Rd Pittsburgh PA 15238-2406

HEITZMANN, WM. RAY, education educator, coach; b. Hoboken, NJ, Feb. 12, 1948; s. William Henry and Mary B. (Tolland) H.; m. Kathleen Heitzmann (div.); children: Richard, Mary. BS, Villanova U.; MAT, U. Chgo.; PhD, U. Del. Cert. tchr., N.Y., Ill. Pvt. practice cons. various pub. and pvt. schs. and bus.; prof. Villanova (Pa.) U. Dir. grad. tchr. edn., dir. Writing for Pub. workshops Villanova U.; basketball, baseball and football coach, NJ, Ill., Pa. NY. Author numerous pubs. including 50 Political Cartoons for Teaching U.S. History, 1975, American Jewish Political Behavior: History and Analysis, 1975, Educational Games and Simulations, 1987, Opportunities in Marine and Maritime Careers, 1988, Opportunities in Sports and Athletics, 1992, Opportunities in Sports Medicine, 1993, Careers for Sports Nuts and Other Athletic Types, 1997, 2d edit., 2003, Super Study Skills for Success, 1997, 2d edit., 98, Opportunities in Sports and Fitness Careers, 2003. Recipient Outstanding Alumnus award Sch. Edn., U. Del., 1988. Mem. Nat. Coun. Social Studies (Outstanding Svc. award 1980), Mid. States Coun. for the Social Studies (Outstanding Rsch. award 1989, Carman award 2000), Nat. Coun. for History Edn. Office: Villanova U Dept Edn Human Svcs Villanova PA 19085

HEJTMANCIK, MILTON RUDOLPH, medical educator; b. Caldwell, Tex., Sept. 27, 1919; s. Rudolph Joseph and Millie (Jurcak) H.; B.A., U. Tex., 1939, M.D., 1943; m. Myrtle Lou Erwin, Aug. 21, 1943; children: Kelly Erwin, Milton Rudolph, Peggy Lou; m. 2d, Myrtle M. McCormick, Nov. 27, 1976. Resident in internal medicine U. Tex., 1946-49, instr. internal medicine, 1949-51, asst. prof., 1951-54, assoc. prof., 1954-65, prof. internal medicine, 1965-80, dir. heart clinic, 1949-80, dir. heart sta., 1965-80; chief of staff John Sealy Hosp., 1957-58; chief staff U. Tex. Hosps., 1977-79; prof. medicine Tex. A&M Coll. Medicine, 1981-82; cardiologist Olin E. Teague VA Hosp., Temple, Tex., 1981-82, VA Clinic, Beaumont, Tex., 1982-86. Served from 1st lt. to capt., M.C., AUS, 1944-46; ETO. Recipient Ashbel Smith Outstanding Alumnus award U.Tex. Med.Br., 1991, Titus Harris Disting. Svc award, 1992. Diplomate in cardiovascular diseases Am. Bd. Internal Medicine. Fellow ACP, Am. Coll. Chest Physicians, Am. Coll. Cardiology; mem. Am. (fellow council clin. cardiology), Tex. (pres. 1979-80), Galveston Dist. (pres. 1956) heart assns., AMA (Billing's Gold medal 1973), Am. Fedn. Clin. Research, AAAS, Tex. Acad. Internal Medicine (gov. 1971-73, v.p. 1973-74, pres. 1976-77), N.Y. Acad. Scis., Tex. Club Cardiology (pres. 1972), Galveston County (pres. 1971), Tex. (del. 1972-80) med. assns., Am. Heart Assn. (pres. Tex. affiliate 1979-80), Phi Beta Kappa, Sigma Xi, Alpha Omega Alpha, Phi Eta Sigma, Mu Delta, Phi Rho Sigma. Contbr. articles to profl. jours. Home: 500 N Spruce St Hammond LA 70401-2549

HELBERG, SHIRLEY ADELAIDE HOLDEN, artist, educator; b. Solvay, NY; d. Isaac Edgar and Gladys Evelyn (Tucker) Holden; m. Burton Edward Helberg; children: Keir Holm, Kristin Vaughan, Kecia Tucker Lau, Kandace Holden Mead, Kraig Brownlee. BE, Johns Hopkins U., 1969; MFA, Md. Inst. Art, 1975. Tchr. Norris Dam Govt. Sch., Tenn., 1945—46, various schs., N.J., Pa., N.Y., Bergenfield, Manchester (Pa.) Pub. Schs., 1965-84, Balt. City Schs., 1988-96; demonstration tchr. Balt. City Schs., O'Donnell Heights Sch., 1992. One-woman shows include U. Va. Charlottesville, 1974, Cayuga Mus. Art and History, Auburn, N.Y., 1974, Hist. Soc. York Mus., Pa., 1977, York Coll., 1984, Country Club York; represented in permanent collections Pres. Richard Nixon; author: (poetry) Chosen Few, 1998; author, illustrator: The Kitty Cat Who Wanted to Fly, 1999, The Jumping Frog of Calaveras County, 1999. Bd. dirs. York (Pa.) Arts Coun., 1964—66. Named Outstanding Tchr. Northeastern Sch. Dist. Bd. Edn. Mem. NEA, DAR, AAUW, Daus. of Union Vets., Nat. League Am. Pen Women (Pa. State art chmn. 1972-74, pres. Pa. orgn. 1974-76, nat. scholarship chair 1976-98, registrar 1986-88, 5th v.p. 1988-90, Disting. Svc. award 1978, 80, 82, 84, 86, 88, 90, 92, Disting. Achievement award 1988, 94), Pa. State Edn. Assn., Internat. Platform Assn., Harrisburg Art Assn., York Art Assn., Pa. Watercolor Soc., Johns Hopkins Faculty Club. Republican. Methodist. Home: 5433 Pigeon Hill Rd Spring Grove PA 17362-8854 also: 727 S Ann St Baltimore MD 21231-3402 Home: 727 S Ann St Baltimore MD 21231

HELFANT, MARIANN THERESA, school administrator; b. N.Y.C., Apr. 4, 1946; d. Nicholas J. and Anna (Cortese) Scardino; m. Rex John Helfant, Sept. 19, 1965; children: John, Matthew, Ann. BS, U. Conn., 1969; MA, Kean Coll., 1980, Seton Hall U., 1992. Cert. elem. tchr., supr., prin., N.J. Basic skills tchr. Union (N.J.) Twp. Schs., 1974-86; 7th-8th grade lang. arts tchr. Clinton Twp. Schs., Annandale, N.J., 1988-93; vice prin. Franklin Twp. Schs., Quakertown, N.J., 1993-95; prin. Salt Brook Sch., New Providence, N.J., 1995-97, Shongun Sch., Randolph, N.J., 1997—. Cons. in coop. learning. Mem. ASCD, NJASCD, N.J. Prins. and Suprs. Assn., Nat. Coun. Tchrs. English, Nat. Staff Devel. Coun., Phi Delta Kappa, Kappa Delta Pi. Home: 6 Timber Ridge Dr Annandale NJ 08801-2023 Office: Shongum Sch 9 Arrow Pl Randolph NJ 07869-4701 E-mail: k2am@earthlink.net., mhelfa@rtnj.org.

HELFERT, ERICH ANTON, management consultant, writer, educator; b. Aussig/Elbe, Sudetenland, May 29, 1931; came to U.S., 1950; s. Julius and Anna Maria (Wilde) H.; m. Anne Langley, Jan. 1, 1983; children: Claire L., Amanda L. BS, U. Nev., 1954; MBA with distinction, Harvard U., 1956, DBA, 1958. Newspaper reporter, corr., Neuburg, Germany, 1948—52; rsch. asst. Harvard U., 1956-57; asst. prof. bus. policy San Francisco State U., 1958-59; asst. prof. fin. and control Grad. Sch. Bus. Adminstrn. Harvard U., 1959-65; internal cons., then asst. to pres., dir. corp. planning Crown Zellerbach Corp., San Francisco, 1965-78, asst. to chmn., dir. corp. planning, 1978-82, v.p. corp. planning, 1982-85; mgmt. cons. San Francisco, 1985—. Co-founding dir., chmn. Modernsoft, Inc.; mem. Dean's adv. coun. San Francisco State Bus. Sch., sch. fin. Golden Gate U.; bd. dirs., past chmn. and pres. Harvard U. Bus. Sch. No. Calif.; trustee Saybrook Inst. Author: Techniques of Financial Analysis, 1963, 11th edit., 2003, Valuation, 1966, Valley of the Shadow, 1997, (with others) Case Book on Finance, 1963, Controllership, 1965; contbr. articles to profl. jours. Exch. student fellow U.S. Inst. Internat. Edn., 1950, Ford Found. doctoral fellow, 1956. Mem. Assn. Corp. Growth (past pres., bd. dirs. San Francisco chpt.), Inst. Mgmt. Cons., Commonwealth Club, Phi Kappa Phi. Roman Catholic. Home: 111 St Matthews Ave No 307 San Mateo CA 94401-4519 E-mail: heleassoc@rcn.com.

HELFFERICH, FRIEDRICH G. chemical engineer, educator; b. Berlin, Aug. 1, 1922; s. Karl and Anna Clara Johanna (von Siemens) H.; m. Barbara Schlubach, July, 1947; children: Christiane, Cornelia.; m. Hana M. Konecna, Feb., 1961; 1 child, Stefanie. BS, U. Hamburg, 1949, MS, 1952; PhD, U. Goettingen, 1955. Rsch. asst. Max Planck Inst., 1951-56, MIT, 1954, Calif. Inst. Tech., 1956-58; vis. scientist Max-Planck Inst., 1958; sr. rsch. assoc. Shell Devel. Co., 1958-79; lectr. U. Calif., Berkeley, 1962-63; vis. prof., lectr. U. Houston, Rice U., U. Tex., 1980, East China U. Chem. Tech., Shanghai, 1987; prof. chem. engring. Pa. State U., 1980-90, prof. emeritus, 1990—. Chmn. Gordon Rsch. Confs. on Ion Exch., 1967, on Separation and Purification, 1994; co-dir. NATO Sch. on Migration and Fate of Pollutants, 1992; cons. in field. Author: E'lon Exchange, 1962, Multicomponent Chromatography, 1970, Kinetics of Homogeneous Multistep Reactions, 2001; editor: Fire and Movement mag., 1978-84, Reactive Polymers, 1981-91; contbr. articles to profl. jours. Recipient award Am. Soc. Engring. Edn., 1985, Am. Chem. Soc., 1987, AIChE, 1989, Gold and Silver medals in race walking state and internat. Sr. Games, 1993-97; Fulbright scholar, 1954. Fellow AIChE, Am. Inst. Chemists (emeritus). Home: 1845 Woodledge Dr State College PA 16803-1858 Office: Pa State Univ Dept Chem Engring University Park PA 16802

HELFGOTT, ROY B. economist, educator; b. Bklyn., Oct. 27, 1925; s. Moses N. and Dorothy A. (Levine) H.; m. Gloria Wolff, July 4, 1948; 1 son, Daniel Andrew. BS in Social Sci, City Coll., N.Y., 1948; MA, Columbia U., 1949; PhD, New Sch., 1957. Rsch. dir. N.Y. coat bd. Internat. Ladies Garment Workers Union, N.Y.C., 1949-57; indsl. rels. analyst Wage Stblzn. Bd., N.Y.C., 1952; economist N.Y. Met. Regional Study, 1957-58; asst. prof. econs. Pa. State U., University Park, 1958-60; rsch. dir. Indsl. Rels. Counselors, N.Y.C., 1960-66, 67-68; adj. assoc. prof. Baruch Coll., 1961-68; indsl. devel. officer UN, N.Y.C., 1966-67; head UN mission, Lower Mekong Basin, 1967; disting. prof. econs. N.J. Inst. Tech., Newark, 1968-93, disting. prof. econs. emeritus, 1993—. Cons. Orgn. Resources Counselors, Inc., N.Y.C., 1968—; pres. Indsl. Rels. Counselors, Inc., N.Y.C. Author: Computerized Manufacturing and Human Resources, 1988, Labor Economics, 1974, 2d edit., 1980; co-author: Industrial Planning, 1969, Management, Automation and People, 1964, Made in New York, 1959; co-editor: Industrial Relations to Human Resources and Beyond, 2003; editor IR Concepts, 1993—. Served with AUS, 1944-46, ETO. Decorated Bronze Star with Oak Leaf Cluster, Combat Inf. badge; fellow Inter-Univ. Inst. Social Gerontology, Berkeley, Calif., 1959; sr. Fulbright rsch. scholar U.K., 1955-56. Mem. Am. Econ. Assn., Indsl. Rels. Rsch. Assn., Met. Econ. Assn. (pres. 1978-79), Phi Beta Kappa.

HELGASON, SIGURDUR, mathematician, educator; b. Akureyri, Iceland, Sept. 30, 1927; came to U.S., 1952; s. Helgi and Kara (Briem) Skulason; m. Artie Gianopulos, June 9, 1957; children: Thor Helgi, Anna Loa. Student, U. Iceland, 1946, D honoris causa, 1986; MS, U. Copenhagen, 1952, D honoris causa, 1988; PhD, Princeton U., 1954; D honoris causa, Uppsala U., 1996. C.L.E. Moore instr. MIT, Cambridge, 1954-56, asst. prof. math., 1960-61, assoc. prof. math., 1961-65, prof. math., 1965—; lectr. Princeton (N.J.) U., 1956-57; Louis Block asst. prof. math. U. Chgo., 1957-59; asst. prof. Columbia U., 1959-60. Vis. mem. Inst. Advanced Study, Princeton, 1964-66, 74-75, 83-84, 98, Mittag-Leffler Inst., 1970-71, 95. Author: Differential Geometry and Symmetric Spaces, 1962, Differential Geometry, Lie Groups and Symmetric Spaces, 1978, Groups and Geometric Analysis, 1984, Geometric Analysis on Symmetric Spaces, 1994, Radon Transform, 1999; editor Progress in Math., 1980-86, Perspectives in Math. Academic Press, Cambridge, 1985—; contbr. articles to profl. jours. Decorated Major Knight's Cross of Icelandic Falcon, 1991; recipient Jessen diploma Danish Math. Soc., 1982, Gold medal U. Copenhagen, 1951; Guggenheim fellow, 1964-65. Mem. Am. Acad. Arts and Scis., Royal Danish Acad. Scis. and Letters, Icelandic Acad. Scis., Am. Math. Soc. (Steele prize 1988). Avocations: music, photography. Office: MIT 77 Massachusetts Ave Dept Math Cambridge MA 02139-4307

HELGERT, MARK JAMES, music educator; b. Waukesha, Wis., Feb. 10, 1955; s. Edward Joseph and Elsie Josephine (Olsen) H.; m. Gwenda Lynn Noah, July 1, 1978. BA, Carroll Coll., 1977. Dir. of bands Butler Mid. Sch., Waukesha, Wis., 1977—; lectr. saxophone Carroll Coll., Waukesha, Wis., 1977-96. Conductor, music dir. Waukesha Area Jazz Ensemble, 1978—. Composer Portals of Xanth, 1991, Nightingales Wept in Tiananmen Square, 1992, Cornerstone of Liberty, 1993. Avocations: chess, cinema, philately. Home: 705 S Grandview Blvd Waukesha WI 53188-4749 Office: Butler Mid Sch 310 N Hine Ave Waukesha WI 53188-4320

HELGESON, JOHN PAUL, plant physiologist, researcher; b. Barberton, Ohio, July 25, 1935; s. Earl Adrian and Marguerite (Dutcher) H.; m. Sarah Frances Slater, June 10, 1957; children: Daniel, Susan, James. AB, Oberlin Coll., 1957; PhD, U. Wis., 1964. NSF postdoctoral fellow dept. chemistry U. Ill., Urbana, 1964-66; from asst. to prof. botany and plant pathology U. Wis., Madison, 1996—2002, prof. emeritus, 2003—. Plant physiologist USDA Argl. Rsch. Svc. plant disease resistance unit, Madison, 1966-90, rsch. leader, 1990-2003; program dir. USDA, Washington, 1982-83; vis. scientist Lab. of Cell Biology, Versailles, France, 1985-86. Lt. USAF, 1957-60. Mem. Bot. Soc. Am., Am. Phytopathol. Soc., Internat. Soc. Plant Molecular Biologists, Am. Soc. Plant Physiologists. Achievements include development of tissue culture procedures for studying interactions of plants and fungi, of somatic hybridizations to obtain new disease resistances in plants. E-mail: jph@plantpath.wisc.edu.

HELIE, ROBERT ALDEN, secondary education educator; b. Alexandria, Minn., May 18, 1947; s. Lawrence Joseph and Jean Lucille (Springer) H.; m. Lorelie Kay Hedin, Mar. 14, 1970; children: Aaron Layne, Benjamin Joe, Christopher Jon, Susanna Jean. BS, St. Cloud State U., 1975. Cert. tchr., Minn., Okla. Tchr. English and indsl. arts Foley (Minn.) High Sch., 1975-82; tchr. indsl. arts Ctrl. Mid-High Sch., Edmond, Okla., 1983-86; instr. El Reno (Okla.) Jr. Coll., 1986-88; tchr. tech. edn. North Mid-High Sch., Edmond, 1989—. Sales cons. Promotional Advt., Edmond, 1987—. Baseball coach Edmond (Okla.) All Sports Assn., 1989—. With U.S. Army, 1968-69, Vietnam. Recipient Rowley grant award Edmond (Okla.) Ednl. Endowment, 1991. Mem. NEA, Okla. Vocat. Assn. Republican. Avocations: wood creations, reading, coaching recreational baseball. Office: Edmond North High Sch 215 W Danforth Rd Edmond OK 73003-5206

HELINSKI, DONALD RAYMOND, biologist, educator; b. Balt., July 7, 1933; s. George L. and Marie M. (Naparstek) H.; m. Patricia G. Doherty, Mar. 4, 1962; children: Matthew T., Maureen G. BS, U. Md., 1954; PhD in Biochemistry, Western Res. U., 1960; postdoctoral fellow, Stanford U., 1960-62. Asst. prof. Princeton (N.J.) U., 1962-65; mem. faculty U. Calif., San Diego, 1965—, prof. biology, 1970—, chmn. dept., 1979-81, dir. Ctr. for Molecular Genetics, 1984-95, assoc. dean Natural Scis., 1994-97. Mem. com. guidelines for recombinant DNA research NIH, 1975-78 Author papers in field. Mem. Am. Soc. Biol. Chemists, Am. Soc. Microbiology, AAAS, Am. Acad. of Arts and Scis., Am. Acad. Microbiology, Nat. Acad. Scis., European Molecular Biology Orgn. (assoc.). Office: Bonner Hall 9500 Gilman Dr La Jolla CA 92093-0322 E-mail: dhelinski@ucsd.edu.

HELLE, STEVEN JAMES, journalism educator, lawyer; b. Manchester, Iowa, Nov. 9, 1954; s. Roger John and Mary Anna Helle; m. Susan Hanes. BS, U. Iowa, 1976, MA, JD, U. Iowa, 1979. Bar: Iowa 1979, Ill. 1980. Prof. journalism and advt. U. Ill., Urbana, 1979—, head dept. journalism, 1988-97. Contbr. articles to legal jours. Recipient Freedom Forum Journalism Tchr. of the Yr. award, 1998, IPA James C. Craven Freedom of the Press award, 2001; U. Ill. at Urbana tchr./scholar, 2002-. Mem. Assn. for Edn. in Journalism and Mass Comm. (head law divsn. 1984-85). Office: Univ Ill 810 S Wright St Ste 119 Urbana IL 61801-3645

HELLER, BEVERLY BUXBAUM, elementary education educator; b. Bklyn., Dec. 24, 1941; d. Arnold and Ruth (Schauer) Buxbaum; m. David Allan Heller, Jan. 26, 1964; children: Aimee Kim, Mandee-Jo, Cheree-Su. BBA, CUNY, 1964; MS, Hunter Coll., 1969. Cert. tchr., ednl. leadership. Tchr. N.Y. Pub. Schs., 1961-70, Beth Sholom, Miami Beach, Fla., 1975-86, Dade County Pub. Schs., Miami Beach, 1986—. Gifted area rep. PTA, Dade County, Fla., 1985-92; chair, sec. Magnet Adv., Miami, 1986-92; area rep., v.p. Dade County Dist. Citizen's Adv., Miami, 1986-92; chairperson Gifted Adv., Miami, 1987-92; vice chair Acad. Adv., Miami, 1988-92. Bd. dirs. JCC, 1985-93, J. Family Svc., 1985-90; legis. chair Dade County Dist. Citizen's Adv., Fla., 1989—; campaign coord. Betsy Kaplan Sch. Bd., Fla., 1992, David Williams Sch. Bd., Fla., 1992, Paul Steinberg Legislator, Fla., 1992. Recipient Recognition of Outstanding Svc., Dade County Sch. Bd., Fla., 1990, PTA, Fla., 1990, Jewish Community Ctr., Miami Beach, 1990, Magnet Adv., Fla., 1991, 92, 93, Citizen's Adv., Fla., 1991, 92. Mem. AAUW, United Tchr. Dade (designated steward 1991—), Women's Bus. and Profl. Assn., Kappa Delta Pi, Phi Delta Kappa, CUNY Alumni Assn., Miami Beach C. of C. (feeder patt. rep. 1989—). Avocations: organizing, politics, children/parents, reading. Home: 5916 Lagorce Dr Miami FL 33140-2115

HELLER, FRANCIS H(OWARD), law and political science educator emeritus; b. Vienna, Aug. 24, 1917; came to U.S., 1938, naturalized, 1943; s. Charles A. and Lily (Grunwald) H.; m. Donna Munn, Sept. 3, 1949 (dec. Dec. 1990); 1 child, Denis Wayne. Student, U. Vienna, 1935-37; JD, MA, U. Va., 1941, PhD, 1948; DHL (hon.), Benedictine Coll., 1988. Asst. prof. govt. Coll. William and Mary, 1947; asst. prof. polit. sci. U. Kans., Lawrence, 1948-51, assoc. prof., 1951-56, prof., 1956-72, Roy A. Roberts prof. law and polit. sci., 1972-88, prof. emeritus, 1988—, assoc. dean Coll. Liberal Arts and Scis., 1957-66, assoc. dean of faculties, 1966-67, dean, 1967-70, vice chancellor for acad. affairs, 1970-72. Vis. prof. Inst. Advanced Studies, Vienna, 1965, U. Vienna Law Sch., 1985, 97, Trinity U., Tex., 1992. Author: Introduction to American Constitutional Law, 1952, The Presidency: A Modern Perspective, 1960, The Korean War: A 25-Year Perspective, 1977, The Truman White House, 1980, Economics and the Truman Administration, 1982, USA: Verfassung und Politik, 1987, NATO: The Founding of the Alliance and the Integration of Europe, 1992, The Kansas State Constitution: A Reference Guide, 1992, The United States and the Integration of Europe, 1996. Mem. Kans. Commn. on Constl. Revision, 1957-61, Lawrence City Planning Commn., 1957-63, ednl. adv. commn. U.S. Army Command and Gen. Staff Coll., 1969-72; bd. dirs. Harry S. Truman Libr. Inst., 1958-96, v.p., 1962-96; bd. dirs. Benedictine Coll., chmn., 1971-79; mem. nat. adv. coun. Ctr. for Study of Presidency, 1991-97. Pvt. to 1st lt. arty. AUS, 1942-47, capt. 1951-52, maj. USAR, ret. Decorated Silver Star, Bronze Star with cluster; recipient Career Teaching award Chancellor's Club, 1986, Silver Angel award Kans. Cath. Conf., 1987, Disting. Svc. citation U. Kans., 1998. Mem. Am. Polit. Sci. Assn. (exec. council 1958-60), Order of Coif, Phi Beta Kappa, Pi Sigma Alpha (mem. nat. council 1958-60) Home: 3419 Seminole Dr Lawrence KS 66047-1622 Office: U Kans Sch Law Green Hall 1535 W 15th St Lawrence KS 66045-7577 E-mail: fheller@ku.edu.

HELLER, GEORGE NORMAN, music educator; b. Ypsilanti, Mich., Dec. 19, 1941; s. Julius G. and Norma (Smith) H.; m. Judy A. Watkins, Mar. 14, 1987; children: Scott B. Thompson, Jennifer L., David P. BMus, U. Mich., 1963, MMus, 1969, PhD, 1973. Organist/choirmaster St. Andrews Ch., Dexter, Mich., 1961-63; tchr. music Summerfield Schs., Petersburg, Mich., 1963-64, Haslett (Mich.) Pub. Schs., 1964-66, Farmington (Mich.) H.S., 1969-71; teaching fellow U. Mich., Ann Arbor, 1971-73; instr. Eastern Mich. U., 1972—73; prof. music edn. U. Kans., Lawrence, 1973—2002, prof. emeritus, 2002—. With U.S. Army, 1966-68. Named to Kans. Music Educators Assn. Hall of Fame, 2003. Mem. Music Educators Nat. Conf., Coll. Music Soc., Soc. for Am. Music, Kans. Music Educators Assn. (named to Hall of Fame 2003), Soc. for Ethnomusicology, Music Libr. Assn.

HELLER, JULES, artist, writer, educator; b. N.Y.C., Nov. 16, 1919; s. Jacob Kenneth and Goldie (Lassar) H.; m. Gloria Spiegel, June 11, 1947; children: Nancy Gale, Jill Kay. AB, Ariz. State Coll., 1939; AM, Columbia U., 1940; PhD, U. So. Calif., 1948; DLitt, York U., 1985. Spl. art instr. 8th St. Sch., Tempe, Ariz., 1938-39; dir. art and music Union Neighborhood House, Auburn, N.Y., 1940-41; prof. fine arts, head dept. U. So. Calif., 1946-61; vis. asso. prof. fine arts Pa. State U., summers 1955, 57; dir. Pa. State U. (Sch. Arts), 1961-63; founding dean Pa. State U. (Coll. Arts and Architecture), 1963-68; founding dean Faculty Fine Arts York U., Toronto, 1968-73; prof. fine arts Faculty of Fine Arts, York U., 1973-76; dean Coll. Fine Arts, Ariz. State U., Tempe, 1976-85, prof. art, 1985-90; prof. emeritus, dean emeritus, 1990—. Vis. prof. Silpakorn U., Bangkok, Thailand, 1974, Coll. Fine Arts, Colombo, Sri Lanka, 1974, U. Nacional de Tucumán, Argentina, 1990, U. Nacional de Cuyo, Mendoza, Argentina, 1990; lectr., art juror; Cons. Open Studio, 1975-76; mem. vis. com. on fine arts Fisk U., Nashville, 1974; co-curator Leopoldo Méndez exhbn. Ariz. State U., Tempe, 1999. Printmaker; exhibited one man shows, Gallery Pascal, Toronto, U. Alaska, Fairbanks, Alaskaland Bear Gallery, Visual Arts Center, Anchorage, Ariz. State U., Tempe, Lisa Sette Gallery, 1990, Centro Cultural de Tucumán, San Miguel de Tucumán, 1990; retrospective exhbn. Ariz. State U., Tempe, 1999, Town Hall, Paradise Valley, Ariz., 1999-2000; exhibited numerous group shows including Canadian Printmaker's Showcase, Pollack Gallery, Toronto, Mazelow Gallery, Toronto, Santa Monica Art Gallery, L.A. County Mus., Phila. Print Club, Seattle Art Mus., Landau Gallery, Kennedy & Co. Gallery, Bklyn. Mus., Cin. Art Mus., Dallas Mus. Fine Arts, Butler Art Inst., Oakland Art Mus., Pa. Acad. Fine Arts, Santa Barbara Mus. Art, San Diego Gallery Fine Arts, Martha Jackson Gallery, N.Y.C., Yuma Fine Arts Assn., Ariz., Toronto Dominion Centre, Amerika Haus, Hannover, Fed. Rep. Germany, U. Md., Smith-Andersen Galleries, Palo Alto, Calif., Grunewald Ctr. Graphic Arts, L.A., Steel Pavilion, Phoenix, 2003, Univ. So. Fla., Tampa, Sheldon Meml. Gallery, Lincoln, Nebr., Santa Cruz (Calif.) Mus., Drake U., Iowa, Bradley U., Ill., Del Bello Gallery, Toronto, Honolulu Acad. Fine Arts, New Orleans Mus. Art, Steel Pavilion, Phoenix, 2003; represented in permanent collections, Nat. Mus. Am. Art Smithsonian Instn., Washington, Long Beach Mus. Art, Library of Congress, York U., Allan R. Hite Inst. of U. Louisville, Ariz. State U., Tamarind Inst., U. N.Mex., Zimmerli Mus. Rutgers U., N.J., Can. Council Visual Arts Bank, also pvt. collections; author: Problems in Art Judgment, 1946, Printmaking Today, 1958, revised, 1972, Papermaking, 1978, 79; co-editor: North American Women Artists of the Twentieth Century, 1995, Codex Méndez, 1999; contbg. artist: Prints by California Artists, 1954, Estampas de la Revolución Mexicana, 1948; illustrator: Canciónes de Mexico, 1948; author numerous articles. Adv. bd. Continental affairs com. Americas Soc., 1983-86. With USAAF, 1941-45. Can. Coun. grantee; Landsdowne scholar U. Victoria; Fulbright scholar, Argentina, 1990. Mem. Coll. Art Assn. (Disting. Teaching of Art award 1995), Authors Guild, Internat. Assn. Hand Papermakers (steering com. 1986—), Nat. Found. Advancement in the Arts (visual arts panelist 1986-90, panel chmn. 1989, 90), Internat. Assn. Paper Historians, Internat. Coun. Fine Arts Deans (pres. 1968-69), So. Graphics Coun. (printmaker emeritus award 1999). E-mail: jules.heller@asu.edu.

HELLER, LOIS JANE, physiologist, educator, researcher; b. Detroit, Jan. 4, 1942; d. John and Lona Elizabeth (Stockmeyer) Skagerberg; m. Robert Eugene Heller, May 21, 1966; children: John Robert, Suzanne Elizabeth. BA, Albion Coll., 1964; MS, U. Mich., 1966; PhD, U. Ill., Chgo., 1970. Instr. med ctr. U. Ill., Chgo., 1969-70, asst. prof., 1970-71, U. Minn., Duluth, 1972-77, assoc. prof., 1977-89, prof., 1989—. Author: Cardiovascular Physiology, 5th edit., 2003; contbr. numerous articles to profl. jours. Mem. Am. Physiol. Soc., Am. Heart Assn., Soc. Exptl. Biology and Medicine, Internat. Soc. Heart Rsch., Sigma Xi. Avocation: birding. Home: 9129 Congdon Blvd Duluth MN 55804-0005 Office: Univ Minn Sch of Medicine Duluth MN 55812

HELLER, MARYELLEN, special education educator; b. Mt. Kisco, N.Y., Apr. 9, 1957; d. Michael Joseph and Ellen Agnes (O'Grady) Romano; m. Robert Edward Heller, Dec. 22, 1979; children: Kerry, Rob, Kathleen. BA Psychology, Elem. Edn., Spl. Edn., Coll. of New Rochelle, 1979; MS Reading, Western Conn., 1989. Second grade tchr. St. Patrick's Grammar Sch., Yorktown, N.Y., 1979-82; art instr. Newtown (Conn.) Continuing Edn., summer 1992; resource rm. tchr. City Hill Mid. Sch., Naugatuck, Conn., 1992-93, spl. edn. tutor, 1993; reading cons. Community Sch., Prospect, Conn., 1993-94; reading specialist Broadview Mid. Sch., Danbury, Conn., 1994—; lang. arts specialist Roberts Ave. Sch., Danbury, Conn., 1995—. Art instr. Southbury (Conn.) Parks and Recreation, 1992; dried flower instr. for adults, Newtown Adult Edn., 1992; profl. devel. instr. Community Sch., Prospect, Conn., 1994, Danbury Schs., Conn., 1995; reading cons. Broadview Mid. Sch., 1996-97; resource room tchr. Danbury H.S., 1997-98, reading specialist, 1999—. Pageant dir. Sacred Heart Ch., Southbury, 1991-94, CCD tchr., 1992-94; PTA program dir. Pomperaug Elem. Sch., Southbury, 1991-92; com. to select a site for group home for mentally retarded adults, Town Bd. of Somers, N.Y., 1978-79. Mem. Conn. Edn. Assn., Danbury Tchrs. Assn., ACES Alternat. Edn. Ctr. Avocations: watercolors, pen and ink drawing, arts and crafts, jogging, stenciling, reading. Home: 75 Stonegate Dr Southbury CT 06488-2671 Office: Danbury High Sch Clapboard Ridge Rd Danbury CT 06810-6021 E-mail: pawling@aol.com.

HELLIE, RICHARD, Russian history educator, researcher; b. Waterloo, Iowa, May 8, 1937; s. Ole Ingeman and Mary Elizabeth (Larsen) H.; children: Benjamin, Michael; m. Shujie Yu, Feb. 26, 1998. BA, U. Chgo., 1958, MA, 1960, PhD, 1965; postgrad., U. Moscow, 1963-64. Asst. prof. Rutgers U., 1965-66; asst. prof. Russian history U. Chgo., 1966-71, assoc. prof., 1971-80, prof., 1980-2001, dir. Ctr. for East European, Russian and Eurasian Studies, 1997—, Thomas E. Donnelley prof., 2001—. Author: Muscovite Society, 1967, Enserfment and Military Change in Muscovy, 1971 (Am. Hist. Assn. Adams prize 1972), Slavery in Russia 1450-1725, 1982 (Laing prize U. Chgo. Press 1985, Russian translation with new post-Soviet foreword Kholopstvo v Rossii, 1450-1725, 1998), 1982, The Russian Law Code (Ulozhenie) of 1649, 1988, The Economy and Material Culture of Russia 1600-1725, 1999; editor: The Plow, the Hammer and the Knout: An Economic History of Eighteenth Century Russia, 1985, Ivan the Terrible: A Quarcentenary Celebration of His Death, 1987, The Frontier in Russian History, 1993, The Soviet Global Impact 1945-1991, 2003; editor quar. jour. Russian History;, 1988 contbr. numerous articles to profl. jours. Fgn. area tng. fellow Ford Found., 1962-65, Guggenheim fellow, 1973-74, fellow NEH, 1978-79; grantee NEH, 1982-83, summer, 1988, NSF, 1988-90, Bradley Found., 1988-91. Mem. PEN, Nat. Hist. Soc., Am. Soc. Legal History (program com. for ann. meetings 1976), Am. Assn. Advancement Slavic Studies (editorial bd. Slavic Rev. 1979-81), Econ. History Assn., Assn. for Comparative Econ. Studies, Nat. Assn. Scholars, Jean Bodin Soc. for Comparative Instl. History, Chgo. Consortium Slavic and East European Studies (pres. 1990-92), Nat. Hist. Soc. (founding, bd. govs. 1999-2002). Home: 5807 S Dorchester Ave Apt 13E Chicago IL 60637-1729 Office: U Chgo Dept History 1126 E 59th St # 78 Chicago IL 60637-1580 E-mail: hell@midway.uchicago.edu.

HELLIWELL, THOMAS MCCAFFREE, physicist, educator; b. Minneapolis, Minn., June 8, 1936; s. George Plummer and Eleanor (McCaffree) H.; m. Bernadette Egan Busenberg, Aug. 9, 1997. BA, Pomona Coll., 1958; PhD, Calif. Inst. Tech., 1963. Asst. prof. physics Harvey Mudd Coll., Claremont, Calif., 1962-67, assoc. prof., 1967-73, prof., 1973—, chmn. dept. physics, 1981-89, chair of faculty, 1990-93, Burton Bettingen prof. physics, 1990—. Author: Introduction to Special Relativity, 1966; author papers in field of cosmology, gen. relativity and quantum theory. Sci. faculty fellow NSF, 1968. Mem.: AAAS, Am. Phys. Soc., Am. Assn. Physics Tchrs. Avocations: music, hiking. Office: Harvey Mudd Coll Dept Physics 301 E 12th St Claremont CA 91711-5901

HELLMAN, ARTHUR DAVID, law educator, consultant; b. NYC, Dec. 9, 1942; s. Charles and Florence (Cohen) H. BA magna cum laude, Harvard U., 1963; JD, Yale U., 1966. Bar: Minn. 1967, U.S. Ct. Appeals (3d cir.) 1976, U.S. Ct. Appeals (9th cir.) 1979, U.S. Supreme Ct. 1980, Pa., 1985. Law clk. to assoc. justice Minn. Supreme Ct., 1966-67; asst. prof. William Mitchell Coll. Law, St. Paul, 1967-70, U. Conn. Sch. Law, West Hartford, 1970-72; vis. asst. prof. U. Ill. Coll. Law, Champaign, 1972-73; dep. exec. dir. Commn. on Revision Fed. Ct. Appellate System, Washington, 1973-75; assoc. prof. U. Pitts. Sch. Law, 1975-80, prof., 1980—. Supervising staff atty. U.S. Ct. Appeals 9th cir., San Francisco, 1977-79, evaluation com., 1999-2001; vis. assoc. prof. U. Pa. Sch. Law, Phila., 1979; faculty Practicing Law Inst. Program on Fed. Appellate Practice, N.Y.C., 1984, Fed. Jud. Ctr. Nat. Workshop for Judges of U.S. Cts. of Appeals, 1993; planner Nat. Conf. Empirical Rsch. in Judicial Adminstrn., Tempe, Ariz., 1988; gen. editor U.S. Ct. Appeals 9th Cir. Project Improvements in Judicial Adminstrn., 1987-91; prin. investigator intercir. conflicts study Fed. Jud. Ctr., 1990; lectr., cons. and expert witness in field. Author: Laws Against Marijuana-The Price We Pay, 1975, Restructuring Justice-The Innovations of the Ninth Circuit and the Future of the Federal Courts, 1990; editor: Major Cases in First Amendment Law: Freedom of Speech, the Press, and Assembly, 1984; bus. editor: Yale U. Law Jour. Mem. liaison task panel on psychoactive drug use/misuse Pres.'s Commn. on Mental Health, 1977-78; conferee Pound Conf., 1976, The Future and the Courts Conf., 1990; conferee Nat. Conf. on State-Fed. Jud. Relationships, 1992; adv. bd. Western Legal History, 2001—. Recipient Chancellor's Disting. Rsch. award, U. Pitts., 2002; U. Pitts. Sch. Law disting. faculty scholar, 2001—. Fellow Am. Bar Found.; mem. ABA (subcom. on stds. of com. appellate staff attys., jud. adminstrn. divsn., future of cts. com. 1992—, conferee Nat. Conf. on State-Fed. Jud. Rels. 1992, conferee summit on civil justice improvements 1990), Pa. Bar Assn. (discovery rules com. 1995—), Am. Law Inst., Supreme Ct. Hist. Soc., Am. Judicature Soc. (drafting com. project on jud. election campaigns, bd. dirs. 1985-89, justice reform com. 1992-95, chair civil justice reform subcom. 1993-95, chair civil justice reform com. 1995-97, invited witness, hearings of the Subcommittee on Cts., the Internet and Intellectual Property of the US House Judiciary Com. on: Final Report of the Commn. on Structural Alternatives for the Fed. Cts. of Appeals (1999); Fed. Judicial Discipline (2001); unpublished judicial opinions (2002); The Federal Judiciary: Is There a Need for Additional Judges? (2003). Office: U Pitts Law Sch Pittsburgh PA 15260

HELLMAN, SAMUEL, radiologist, physician, educator; b. N.Y.C., July 23, 1934; s. Henry Sidney and Anna (Egar) Hellman; m. Marcia Sherman, June 30, 1957; children: Jeffrey, Richard, Deborah Susan. BS magna cum laude, Allegheny Coll., 1955, DSc (hon.), 1984; MD cum laude, SUNY, Syracuse, 1959, DSc (hon.), 1993; MS (hon.), Harvard U., 1968. Med. intern Beth Israel Hosp., Boston, 1959—60; asst. resident radiology Yale Sch. Medicine and Grace-New Haven Hosp., 1960—62, postdoctoral fellow radiotherapy and cancer research, 1962—64; postdoctoral fellow Inst. Cancer Research and Royal Marsden Hosp., London, 1965—66; asst. prof. radiology Yale Sch. Medicine, 1966—68; assoc. prof. radiology Harvard Med. Sch., 1968—70; dir. Joint Center for Radiation Therapy, 1968—83, assoc. prof., chmn. dept. radiation therapy, 1971, prof., chmn. dept., 1971—83, also Alvan T. and Viola D. Fuller-Am. Cancer Soc. prof.; physician-in-chief Meml. Sloan Kettering Cancer Ctr., 1983—88, Benno Schmidt chair in clin. oncology, 1983—88; dean div. biol. sci. and Pritzker Sch. Medicine, v.p. for Med. Ctr. U. Chgo., 1988—93, Pritzker Prof., 1988—93, Pritzker Disting. Svc. Prof., 1993—. Chmn. bd. sci. counselors divsn. cancer treatment Nat. Cancer Inst., 1980—84; bd. govs. Argonne Nat. Lab., 1990—93; trustee Brookings Inst., 1992—; bd. dirs. Varian Med. Systems Inc., Insightec; mem. sci. adv. bd. Ludwig Inst. for Cancer Rsch. Contbr. numerous articles to med. jours. Trustee Allegheny Coll., 1979—98, chmn. bd. trustees, 1987—93. Recipient Rosenthal award for cancer rsch., 1980, medal, City of Paris, 1986, award for Outstanding Contbns. to Cancer Care, Assn. Cmty. Cancer Ctrs., 1993. Fellow: AAAS; mem.: N.Y. Acad. Scis., Soc. Chmn. Acad. Radiology Depts., Inst. Medicine NAS, Assn. Am. Physicians, Am. Cancer Soc., Am. Soc. Hematology, Am. Assn. Cancer Rsch., Am. Soc. Clin. Oncology (pres. 1986, David A. Karnovsky lectr. 1994), Assn. Univ. Radiologists, Am. Coll. Radiology (gold medal 2003), Am. Soc. Therapeutic Radiologists (pres. 1983, Gold medal 1991), Am. Radium Soc., Alpha Omega Alpha, Sigma Xi, Phi Beta Kappa. Home: 4950 S Chicago Beach Dr Chicago IL 60615-3207 Office: U Chgo Divsn Biol Scis 5841 S Maryland Ave Chicago IL 60637-1463 E-mail: s-hellman@uchicago.edu.

HELLMER, LYNNE BEBERMAN, education educator; b. Nome, Alaska, Sept. 26, 1947; d. Max and Elizabeth Forrer (Chapman) Beberman; m. William T. Fillman, Nov. 8, 2003; children: Joshua Max, Lucas Andrew. BS, Eastern Illinois U., 1970; MEd, U. Ill., 1997. Tchr. Effingham (Ill.) Schs., 1970-72; personnel officer U. Ill., Urbana, 1972-81, tng. dir., 1981-93, dir. human resource devel., 1993-2000; sr. dir. systemwide profl. devel. Calif. State U., 2000—. Pres. Univ. Clearinghouse, Champaign, 1992—; founder Biennial Conf. for Working Women, 1984-2000. Bd. dirs. Coll. and Univ. Pers. Assn. Found., 1998-2000. Recipient Nat. Achievement award for creativity Coll. and Univ. Pers. Assn., 1985-86, Outstanding Svc. and Leadership award Coll. and Univ. Pers. Assn. Midwest, 1991, Optimas award Workforce mag., 1996; named Most Valuable Cmty. Leader, Ill., Student Soc. for Pers., 1989. Mem. Coll. and Univ. Pers. Assn. (sec., treas. Midwest region 1988-89; editor Midwest News 1988-92, chair 1993-94, Creative Achievement and Publ. award 1998). Avocation: musician. Office: Office of the Chancellor Calif State U 401 Golden Shore St Fl 4 Long Beach CA 90802-4275 E-mail: lhellmer@calstate.edu.

HELLUM, PERRY K. school system administrator; b. Stoughton, Wis., Nov. 16, 1941; s. Wilbur Eugene and Christine Sophia (Breingsness) H.; m. Pat L. Carlson, Dec. 28, 1983; children: Erik, Donald, Suzanne, Brian. BEd, U. Wis., Whitewater, 1963; MA, No. Mich. U., 1968, EdS, 1977; PhD, Columbia Pacific U., 1982. Cert. tchr., prin., supt., Wis. Tchr. Neenah (Wis.) Sch. Dist., 1963-68; supt. Joint Sch. Dist. # 1 Silver Lake, Wis., 1968—; prof. U. Wis., Madison, 1982—. Cons. various sch. bds., 1982—. Author: Role of Teacher Aides in the Public Schools, 1982; contbr. articles to profl. jours. Recipient citation Wis. Legislature, 1986; recipient Celebrate Literacy award Internat. Reading Assn., 1986; named to top 100 N.Am. sch. supts. Wis. Assn. Sch. Adminstrs., 1986. Mem. Am. Assn. Sch. Adminstrs., Wis. Assn. Dist. Adminstrs., Westosha Sch. Adminstrs. Assn., Phi Delta Kappa, Lambda Chi Alpha. Lutheran. Avocations: reading, motorhome travel, golf, baseball memorabilia. Office: Joint Dist 1 Silver Lake 300 E Prosser St Silver Lake WI 53170-1409

HELLWEGE, NANCY CAROL, special education educator; b. Bridgeport, Conn., Dec. 28, 1933; d. Emil and Dorothy Alma (Sell) Rosenoch; children: Michael, Christie, Patricia. BS with distinction, Ind. U., Ft. Wayne, 1972, MS, 1977; EdS, Ball State U., 1984. Tchr. 1st grade Luth. Schs., Ft. Wayne, 1962-66; coord. Head Start, Ft. Wayne, 1967-68; kindergarten tchr. Luth. Schs., Ft. Wayne, 1968-78; resource rm. tchr. East Allen County Schs., New Haven, Ind., 1978-81; cons. N.E. Colo. BOCES, Haxtun, 1982-84; strategist South Cen. BOCES, Pueblo, Colo., 1984-86; supr. Mt. BOCES, Leadville, Colo., 1986-87; coord. Broward Cunty Schs., Ft. Lauderdale, Fla., 1987-88; pres. Learning Power, Inc., 1988—; prin., owner Christi Acad., Sch. for learning disabled, 2000—. Author handbooks: Helping Children Reach Their Potential, 1991, Different Strokes/Different Folks, 1990. Mem.: NAFE, Phi Delta Kappa. Avocations: swimming, reading, camping. Office: Learning Power Inc PO Box 770253 Pompano Beach FL 33077-0253

HELMAN, IRIS BARCA, elementary school educator, consultant; b. Kenosha, Wis., May 21, 1930; d. Alphonse and Rosalie (Russo) Barca; divorced; 1 child, Gabriel Heidi. BS in Edn., U. Wis., 1955; MS in Edn., U. Wis., Milw., 1971; Student, U. Wis., Kenosha, 1980-82, Carthage Coll., 1972-74. Cert. elem. tchr. Wis. Sec. USN, Great Lakes, Ill., 1950-53; tchr. Kenosha Unified Sch. Dist. #1, 1955—92; student tchr. supr. U. Wis. Sys. Cons. in field. Author: Now What Do I Do?, 1980, Primer on Gifted Education, 1982; co-author: Shapers of Wisconsin, 1998; contbr. articles to profl. jours. Chmn. Democratic Com., Kenosha, 1977; legisl. chmn. City of Kenosha, 1979-80, harbor commr., 1987-90; pres. Wis. Orgn. for Gifted and Talented, 1977-79; chmn. Wis. Coun. for Gifted and Talented, 1979-80; bd. dirs. AFL-CIO Coun., Kenosha, 1980—; vice-chmn. City Plan Commn., 1992-98, 2000—. Named Outstanding Labor Person, City of Kenosha, 1989, County of Kenosha, 1989. Democrat. Roman Catholic. Avocations: reading, skiing, sailing, tennis, politics. Home: 6207 7th Ave Apt 22 Kenosha WI 53143-4565

HELMAR-SALASOO, ESTER ANETTE, literacy educator, researcher; b. Subiaco, W.A., Australia, Oct. 26, 1956; came to U.S., 1987; d. Harald R. and Liana M. (Kikas) H.; m. Lembit Salasoo, Jan. 2, 1988; children: Imbi, Markus, Kristjan. BA, U. W. Australia, Perth, Australia, 1977; Diploma in Edn., U. W. Australia, Perth, 1978; MS, SUNY, Albany, 1988, PhD in Edn., 2001. Tchr. English, lit. Pub. Schs. W. Australia, 1978-85; ESL tchr. Tuart Coll., W. Australia, 1986; teaching asst. SUNY, Albany, 1988, rsch. asst., 1989-90. Cons. Nat. Javits Project for Lang. Arts Rsch., Washington, 1992. Author: (reports) A National Study of States' Roles in Choosing Reading and Literature for Second Language Learning, 1993, (with Kahn S.) Collegial Support and Networks Invigorate Teaching: The Case of the Marsha Slater, 1999. Home: 2280 Berkley Ave Schenectady NY 12309-2726

HELMHOLZ, R(ICHARD) H(ENRY), law educator; b. Pasadena, Calif., July 1, 1940; s. Lindsay and Alice (Bean) H.; m. Marilyn P. Helmholz. AB, Princeton U., 1962; JD, Harvard U., 1965; PhD, U. Calif., Berkeley, 1970; LLD, Trinity Coll., Dublin, 1992. Bar: Mo. 1965. Prof. law and hist. Washington U., St. Louis, 1970-81; prof. law U. Chgo., 1981—. Maitland lectr. Cambridge U., 1987; Goodhart prof. Cambridge U., 2000-01. Author: Marriage Litigation, 1975, Select Cases on Defamation, 1985, Canon Law and the Law of England, 1987, Roman Canon Law in Reformation England, 1990, Spirit of Classical Canon Law, 1996, The Ius Commune in England: Four Studies, 2001. Guggenheim fellow, 1986; recipient Von Humboldt rsch. prize, 1992. Fellow Brit. Acad. (corr.), Am. Acad. Arts and Scis., Am. Law Inst., Medieval Acad. Am.; mem. ABA, Am. Soc. Legal History (pres. 1992-94), Selden Soc. (v.p. 1984-87), Univ. Club, Reform Club. Home: 5757 S Kimbark Ave Chicago IL 60637-1614 Office: U Chgo Law Sch 1111 E 60th St Chicago IL 60637-2776 E-mail: dick_helmholz@law.uchicago.edu.

HELMICK, GAYLE JOHNSTON, elementary education educator; b. Beaver Falls, Pa., July 22, 1936; d. Dwight Edward and Helen Ruth (Reed) Johnston; m. Wayne W. Helmick, Sept. 26, 1959; children: Susan, Kristen Helmick-Nelson, Kathleen. BS in Edn., Geneva Coll., 1961; M in Reading, Slippery Rock State U., 1983. Cert. reading specialist, Pa. Tchr. 5th grade Rochester (Pa.) Area Schs., 1960-61; reading specialist, learning advisor Beaver (Pa.) Area Schs., 1977—. Team mem. Devel. Thinking Presentation Team of Beaver Schs., Beaver, 1986—; fellow Wester. Pa. Writing Project, Pitts., 1990—. Active Cmty. Bible Study; past pres. Beaver Jr. Women's Club. Mem.: MENSA, NEA, Keystone State Reading Assn., Pa. State Edn. Assn., Internat. Reading Assn., Beaver Area Ret. Tchrs. Assn., Pa. State Ret. Tchrs. Assn., Beaver Area Heritage Soc., Leotta Hawthorne Reading Coun.

(v.p. 1992—93, pres. 1993—94), Delta Kappa Gamma (sec. Zeta chpt. 1992—). Episcopalian. Avocations: reading, remodeling house, collecting signed first editions of books, childrens literature. Home: 440 Wayne Sq Beaver PA 15009-2701

HELMING, SCOTT BRYON, principal; b. Lemars, Iowa, Oct. 22, 1953; s. Warren H. and Darlene A. (Lorenz) H.; m. Lynne K. Onderdonk, July 17, 1976; children: Stacy, Gretal, Lindsay. BA in Edn., English, Concordia Coll., 1975; postgrad., SUNY, Buffalo, 1982-84; MS in Edn., Coll. New Rochelle, 1988. Cert. sch. adminstr., Lutheran tchr., N.Y. State. Tchr., athletic dir. Queens Lutheran Sch., L.I. City, N.Y., 1975-78; prin., tchr. Calvary Lutheran Sch., Havertown, Pa., 1978-81; princ., tchr. St. Mark Lutheran Sch., North Tonawanda, N.Y., 1981-84; prin. The Chapel Sch., Bronxville, N.Y., 1984-91, Holy Cross Luth. Sch., Jacksonville, Fla., 1991-92, Trinity Luth. Sch., Lansing, Ill., 1992—. Treas. East Coast Luth. Educators Conf., Buffalo, 1984-91; mem. ch. workers task force Atlantic Dist., LC-MS, Bronxville, 1988-91; adj. instr. in edn. Condordia Coll., Bronxville, fall 1989; non-public rep. TF Cooperative, 1992—; chairperson No. Ill. Dist., Luth. Ch.-Mo. Synod, 1993—97, bd. dirs.; mem. Lansing Ednl. Access to Cable TV, 1994—; chmn. Tchrs. Conf., 2001-02. Mem. Dept. Tchr. Consortium, Bronxville, 1986-91, AIDS Taskforce, Bronxville Schs., 1988-91. Named Disting. Student Coll. New Rochelle, 1988. Mem. ASCD, Luth. Edn. Assn., Luth. Schs. Assn. (regional coord. 1984-91), Nat. Assn. Elem. Sch. Prins. Avocations: photography, videotaping, woodworking, furniture refinishing, gardening. Home: 18340 Oakwood Ave Lansing IL 60438-2906 Office: Trinity Luth Sch 18144 Glen Ter Lansing IL 60438-2152

HELMREICH, HELAINE GEWIRTZ, speech pathology professional; b. Bklyn., Jan. 15, 1947; d. Harry and Dorothy (Friedman) Gewirtz; m. William B. Helmreich, June 28, 1970; children: Jeffrey, Alan, Joseph, Deborah. BA in Speech and Theater, CUNY, Bklyn., 1968; MS in Speech and Hearing, CUNY, 1972. Cert. of clin. competence in speech/lang. pathology. Lang. and speech therapist Ctrl. and Midwestern Region Ednl. Lab., St. Louis, 1970-71; lang. and speech therapist Atlanta Pub. Schs., 1971-72; adj. lectr., speech and drama N.Y. Inst. Tech., N.Y.C., 1976-77; lang. and speech therapist Hebrew Inst. for the Deaf, Bklyn., 1977-82, Richmond Meml. Hosp., Staten Island, N.Y., 1987-89, Marathon Childhood Ctr., Whitestone, N.Y., 1992-94, lang. and speech supr., 1994-98; speech pathologist Young Adults Inst., NY League for Early Learning, Clearview Sch., Whitestone, 1998—. Cons. Comprehensive Counseling, Bklyn., 1991-93. Author: The Chimney Tree, 2000; poet: Electronic News, 1994. Mem. bd. edn. North Shore Hebrew Acad., Great Neck, N.Y., 1992—. Honored for Outstanding Svcs. McDonough St. Head Start, Bklyn., 1989; recipient Vocat. and Rehab. Svcs. assistantship Bklyn. Coll. Grad. Ctr., Dept. Speech, 1968. Mem. Am. Speech/Lang./Hearing Assn. Avocations: writing, drawing. Office: YAI-NYL Clearview Sch 1650 Utopia Pkwy Whitestone NY 11357

HELMS, BYRON ELDON, academic administrator; b. Pitts., June 2, 1951; s. John Donald and Evelyn Marie (Wilson) H.; m. Gale Ann Barbarine Helms, Jan, 23, 1976 (div. Mar. 13. 1978); m. Shari Elisa Besterman Helms, Sept. 16, 1978; children: Brandon, Thomas, Nicholas. Ba in English, Duquesne U., Pitts., 1974. Field underwriter N.Y. Life Ins., Pitts., 1974; asst. legal adminstr. Eckert, Seamans, Cherin & Mellott, Pitts., 1974-77; legal adminstr. Hayward, Cooper, Straub & Cramer, Toledo, 1977-78; adminstr., Cell Biology and Physiology U. Pitts. Sch. Medicine, 1978-95; dir. ORS pre-award contracts U. Ill. at Chicago, Chgo., 1995—. P-30 adminstr. Nat. Inst. Child Health and Human Devel., Washington, 1978-94; dir., treas., bd. govs. Faculty Club U. Pitts., 1985-94; charter mem., officer Duquesne U. Arts and Sci. Alumni Assn., Pitts., 1992-94; dir., bd. mgmt. South Hills YMCA, Pitts., 1994-97; tax acct. H&R Block, 1995—. Editor: University of Pittsburgh Financial System Overview, 1986. Longhouse officer YMCA Indian Guide Program. Pitts., 1987-93; mgmt. officer YMCA Trailblazer Program, Pitts., 1991-96; unit coord. United Way, Pitts., 1978-94; mgr., coach Mt. Lebanon (Pa.) Baseball Assn., 1989-94. Recipient Honor award, 1993 Sy Lerner Meml. award, 1994, South Hills YMCA, Pitts., Cmty. Svc. award United Way, Pitts., 1994, Chancellor's Acd. Profl. award for Excellence, U. Ill. Chgo., 2002. Mem. Soc. Rsch. Adminstrs., Nat. Coun. Univ. Rsch. Adminstrs. (treas. Region IV, 2001-03), Am. Mgmt. Assn., Islam Grotto Mystic Order of Veiled Prophets of Enchanted Realm, Grand Lodge of Pa., Crafton Lodge. Republican. Lutheran. Avocations: manage and coach baseball, soccer, football, basketball. Home: 912 Royal Blackheath Ct Naperville IL 60563-2304 Office: Univ of Illinois at Chicago ORS Pre-award Contracts 1737 W Polk St Chicago IL 60612-7227 E-mail: bhelms@uic.edu.

HELMS, CAROL DOROTHY, elementary educator; b. Yankton, S.D., Sept. 8, 1959; d. Joseph F. and Marcella M. (Schramm) Kotalik; m. John W. Helms, June 18, 1983; children: Tiffany M., J.W. BS in Elem. Edn., No. State Coll., Aberdeen, S.D., 1981. Tchr. 4th-8th grades Harding County Sch., Buffalo, S.D., tchr. 4th grade, tchr. 2d grade; tchr. Title I, 3-5 Reva Sch.; tchr. 1st-3d grades Camp Crook Sch. Mem. Internat. Reading Assn. Home: PO Box 143 Buffalo SD 57720-0143

HELSER, TERRY LEE, biochemistry educator; b. Indpls., Dec. 23, 1944; s. Lester Freeman and Frances Elizabeth (Arnold) H.; m. Wanda Joan Ralston, Aug. 11, 1968; children: Aron Trent, Janelle Lynn. BA, Manchester Coll., 1967; PhD, U. Wis., 1972. Postdoctoral fellow U. Calif., Irvine, 1972-75; rsch. fellow Brown U., Providence, 1975-77; vis. prof. Hershey (Pa.) Med. Ctr., Penn State U., 1980; asst. prof. Millersville (Pa.) State Coll., 1977-80; NSF fellow SUNY, Albany, 1984; vis. prof. U. N.C., Chapel Hill, 1986-87; prof. SUNY, Oneonta, 2000—. Chmn. Com. on Rsch. of Faculty Senate, Oneonta, 1988-91. Contbr. over 40 articles to profl. jours. Head judge Odyssey of the Mind Problems, 1988-96; judge CASSC Sci. Fair, Oneonta, 1988, Sci. Olympiad, Oneonta, 1990. Named Disting. Biologist, Hartwick Co., 1990; grantee W.B. Ford Found., 1989, NSF, 1984, 80, Rsch. Corp., 1982-84. Democrat. Achievements include devel. of two ednl. card games "The Gene Expression Game" for the lactose operon and "The Elemental Chemistry Game" for introductory chemistry courses, numerous word puzzles. Office: Dept Chemistry & Biochemistry SUNY Coll Oneonta NY 13820-4015

HELSTEDT, GLADYS MARDELL, vocational education educator; b. Forest City, Iowa, May 7, 1926; d. Gordon Ingeman and Pearl Gertrude (Hauan) Field; m. Lowell Lars Helstedt, Aug. 26, 1950; children: Mardell Lynn, David Lowell, Marilee Pearl, Marcia Kay. AA, Waldorf Coll., 1945; BS, Mankato State U., 1969. Bus. tchr. Crystal Lake (Iowa) H.S., Crystal Lake, Iowa, 1945-47; parish sec. St. Paul's Lutheran Ch., Mpls., 1949-51; bus. tchr. Sioux Valley High Sch., Lake Park, Iowa, 1969-70, Radcliffe (Iowa) High Sch., 1970-76; activity dir. Marinuka Manor Care Ctr., Galesville, Wis., 1976-79; bus. tchr. Galesville High Sch., 1979-80; asst. dir. Ret. Sr. Vol. Program, Whitehall, Wis., 1981-83; coord., instr. Western Wis. Tech. Inst., La Crosse, 1984; sr. instr. Tex. State Tech. Coll., Sweetwater, 1985-92; ret., 1992. Dir. music Salem Luth. Ch., Roscoe, Tex., 1985-90. Mem. Philos. Edn. Orgn. (pres. 1982-84), Tex. State Tech. Coll. Women (sec. 1991-92), Bus. Profls. Am. (advisor 1986-92). Avocations: plants, dolls, music, travel, knitting. Home: 570 Quant Ave N Lakeland MN 55043-9545

HELTON, LUCILLE HENRY HANRATTIE, academic administrator; b. Ft. Worth, Mar. 2, 1942; d. P.D. and Virginia (Clark) Henry; m. Wayne Hanrattie, June 26, 1965 (div. Apr. 1986); children: Clark, Chris; m. William M. Helton, Jr., Mar. 19, 1988. BA, So. Meth. U., 1964; MEd, U. Pitts., 1968; cert. in adminstrn., William Paterson Coll., 1984; cert. in mid-mgmt., Tex. Christian U., 1987. Cert. elem. tchr. N.J., Pa., Tex. Nat. field sec. Kappa Kappa Gamma Sorority, Columbus, Ohio, 1964-65; elem. tchr. Pitts. Bd. Edn., 1965-69; co-dir, chmn. dept. maths. Assn. Children with Learning Disabilities Sch., Pitts., 1969-72; tchr. elem., secondary, gifted and remedial and home instrn. programs West Milford (N.J.) Bd. Edn., 1976-84; prin., exec. dir. Hill Sch., Ft. Worth, 1984-2001, exec. dir. Learning Ctr. North Tex., 2001—. Mem. exec. bd. Tex. Assn. Non-pub. Schs. Mem. ASCD, Tex. Ind. Sch. Consortium, Learning Disabilities Assn. Am., Leadership Tex., Coalition for Spl. Needs Students, Orton Dyslexia Soc., Forum Ft. Worth. Democrat. Methodist. Avocations: reading, biking, traveling, nature. Office: The Learning Ctr 1701 River Run Ste 710 Fort Worth TX 76107

HELTON, NORMA JEAN, special education educator; b. Mentor, Tenn., Dec. 26, 1930; d. Carlyle and Mildred Nancy (Clemens) Robbins; m. Albert Layman Helton Jr., Dec. 29, 1950; children: Stanley Joseph, Patricia Faith Helton Ross, Anthony Lyndon. AA in Social Studies, Antelope Valley Coll., 1958; BS in Edn., Athens Coll., 1965, MAT, 1970; EdD in Curriculum and Instrn., Highland U., 1975. Cert. tchr., Ala., Tenn. English and bus. edn. tchr. Huntsville (Ala.) City Schs., 1965-70; spl. edn. tchr. Jackson County Schs., Scottsboro, Ala., 1971-72, Hollywood, Ala., 1975-77, adult edn. tchr., 1975-77, spl. edn. supr., 1977—91, mental retardation svc. dir., 1992—93; tchr. corps team leader Ala. A&M U., Normal, 1972-74; spl. edn. tchr. Blount County Schs., Maryville, Tenn., 1974-75. Min. United Meth. Ch., Ala., 1987—97. Mem. Coun. for Exceptional Children, Ala. Edn. Assn., NEA, Ret. Tchrs. Assn. Democrat. Avocations: playing piano, accompanying quartet, writing. Home: 117 Stacy Cir Huntsville AL 35811-9653

HELTON, THELMA ANN, elementary education educator; b. Miami, Fla., Feb. 18, 1935; d. Aaron and rita (Dempsey) Rossman; m. Victor Helton, June 22, 1957; children: Annamarie, Joseph. BA, Rollins Coll., 1984. Cert. tchr., Fla. Tchr. 1st grade St. Charles Sch., Orlando, Fla., 1980—. Mem. Nat. Cath. Edn. Assn., Nature Conservancy, Audubon Soc., Nat. Alliance for Mentally Ill. Avocations: reading, shell collecting, bird watching, hiking.

HEMBERGER, GLEN JAMES, university band director, music educator; b. Boulder, Colo., Jan. 18, 1962; s. James Frank and Jacqueline Ann (Kent) H.; m. Linda Dawn Thomas, June 3, 1989. BME, U. Colo., 1985, MMus, 1989; DMA, U. North Tex., 2001. Dir. bands Thornton (Colo.) Sr. High Sch., 1985-87; grad. asst. U. Colo. Bands, Boulder, 1987-89; assoc. dir. bands, mem. music edn. faculty U. R.I., Kingston, 1989-92; assoc. dir. bands Okla. State U., Stillwater, 1992-97; doctoral conducting assoc. U. North Tex., 1997-99; dir. bands Southeastern La. U., 1999—. Clinician R.I. Music Educators' State Conv., 1992, La. Music Educators State Conv., 2000, 2002, summer music camp U. Wis., 1993, 99, Chinese Armed Police Band, Beijing, 1996, 97, Melbourne, Brisbane & Sydney, Australia, 1997, Nat. Taiwan U. Wind Orch., Taipei and Hong Kong, 1996, Beijing Band Dirs. Assn., 1996, 97; guest condr. high schs., honor bands, clinics, 1984—, USCG Band, Okla. Mozart Internat. Music Festival, 1995, 96, Norwegian Band Championships, Hamar, 1999, Trondheim, 2000; founder So. New Eng. H.S. Honor Band, 1991; CD prodr. Drake U. Wind Symphony, 2001; condr., Assn. for Music in Internat. Schs. Internat. Honor Band, The Hague, Netherlands, 2003. Contbr. articles to profl. jours.; presenter in field. Mem. Olympic All-Am. Marching Band, L.A., 1984. Mem. Coll. Band Dirs. Nat. Assn. (mem. jour. staff, nat. athletic band adv. coun., clinician nat. conv. 1995, 97), Internat. Assn. Jazz Educators, Music Educators Nat. Conf., World Assn. for Symphonic Bands and Ensembles, Okla. Music Educators Assn. (clinician state conv. 1995, jazz ensemble performance 1997), Phi Mu Alpha Sinfonia, Kappa Kappa Psi, Tau Beta Sigma, Pi Kappa Lambda, Phi Beta Mu. Home: 3011 Willow Ln Madisonville LA 70447-9125 Office: Southeastern La Univ PO Box 10815 Hammond LA 70402-0815

HEMENWAY, MARY KAY, astronomer, educator; b. Akron, Ohio, Nov. 20, 1943; d. Ralph Elwood and Esther (Keegan) Meacham; m. Paul D. Hemenway, June 1, 1968 (div. 1993; children: Anne, Sara. BS, Notre Dame of Ohio, Cleve., 1965; PhD, U. Va, 1971. Lectr. Mary Baldwin Coll., Staunton, Va., 1970-71; lectr. in astronomy U. Tex., Austin, 1974-87, sr. lectr. in astronomy, 1987—; assoc. dir. U. Tex. Inst. Math and Sci. Edn., 1993-97. Cons. Edn. Svc. Ctr. Tex. sch. dists., 1981—, U. Houston, Victori, 1986-89. Co-author: Modern Astronomy: An Activities Approach, 1982, rev. edit. 1991; contbr. articles to RR Lyrae Stars and Astronomy Edn. Named Friend of Earth Sci. Tchrs. Assn. Tex., 1990; named to Tex. Hall of Fame for Sci., Math. and Tech., 2003. Fellow Am. Astron. Soc. (elected edn. officer 1991-97); mem. Nat. Coalition for Earth Sci. Edn. (dir. 1995), Internat. Astron. Union, Astron. Soc. of the Pacific (sec. to bd. 1999—), Sci. Tchrs. Assn. Tex. (hon.), Sigma Xi. Roman Catholic. Achievements include research on distances and motions of RR Lyrae stars.

HEMINGWAY, RICHARD WILLIAM, law educator; b. Detroit, Nov. 24, 1927; s. William Oswald and Iva Catherine (Wildfang) H.; m. Vera Cecilia Eck, Sept. 12, 1947; children: Margaret Catherine, Carol Elizabeth, Richard Albert. BS in Bus, U. Colo., 1950; JD magna cum laude (J. Woodall Rogers Sr. Gold medal 1955), So. Meth. U., 1955; LL.M. (William S. Cook fellow 1968), U. Mich., 1969. Bar: Tex. 1955, Okla. 1981. Assoc. Fulbright, Crooker, Freeman, Bates & Jaworski, Houston, 1955-60; lectr. Bates Sch. Law, U. Houston, 1960; assoc. prof. law Baylor U. Law Sch., Waco, Tex., 1960-65; vis. assoc. prof. So. Meth. U. Law Sch., 1965-68; prof. law Tex. Tech U. Law Sch., Lubbock, 1968-71, Paul W. Horn prof., 1972-81, acting dean, 1974-75, dean ad interim, 1980-81; prof. law U. Okla., Norman, 1981-83, Eugene Kuntz prof. oil, gas and natural resources law, 1983-92, Eugne Kuntz prof. emeritus oil, gas & natural resources law, 1992—. Author: The Law of Oil and Gas, 1971, 2d edit., 1983, lawyer's edit., 1983, 3d edit., 1991, West's Texas Forms (Mines and Minerals), 1977, 2d edit., 1991; contbg. editor various law reports, cases and materials. Served with USAAF, 1945-47. Mem. Tex. Bar Assn., Scribes, Order of Coif (faculty), Beta Gamma Sigma. Lutheran. Home: Apt 1024 5000 Old Shepard Pl Plano TX 75093

HEMPHILL, JEAN HARGETT, college dean; b. Pollocksville, N.C., Aug. 21, 1936; d. Robert Franklin and Frances (Hill) Hargett; m. Raymond Arthur Hemphill, Feb. 28, 1964; 1 child: Gerald Franklin. BS, East Carolina U., 1958; MEd, U. Nev., Las Vegas, 1968; student, N.C. State U., 1993. Sec.-treas. Five Points Milling Co., Inc., New Bern, N.C., 1968-77; instr. Craven C.C., New Bern, 1973-80, dean svc. techs., 1980—. Mem. mgmt. team New Bern-Craven County Coll. Tech. Prep., 1990—; mem. Craven County Schs. Sch.-to-Work Curriculum com., 1996—; internat. rep. NC Cmty. Coll. Improvment Projects, 1992—96, 2002—. Scholarship chmn. continuing edn. divsn. Woman's Club, New Bern, 1981—, treas. continuing edn. divsn., 1986—; instnl. rep. N.C. C.C. Sys. Curriculum Improvement Projects, 1992-96, 2002-2003. Achievement award Woman's Club, New Bern, 1999. Mem. N.C. Assn. C.C. Instrnl. Adminstrs., Phi Kappa Phi. Democrat. Methodist. Office: Craven Community Coll 800 College Ct New Bern NC 28562-4900

HENDERSON, ALAN SCOTT, humanities educator; b. West Palm Beach, Fla., Sept. 1, 1962; s. Clifton Russell Henderson Jr. and Mary Estelle Arnette; life ptnr. Richard Edmon Prior. BA, Fla. State U., 1984; M, Johns Hopkins U., 1985; tchr. cert., U. Va., 1986; PhD, SUNY, Buffalo, 1996. Social studies tchr. Chesapeake (Va.) City Schs., 1986—89; jr. coll. English tchr. Yamagata (Japan) Women's Jr. Coll., 1989—90; intern coord. Harry S. Truman Scholarship Found., Washington, 1990—91; asst. prof. Furman U., Greenville, SC, 1998—. Adj. prof. Furman U., Greenville, S.C., 1996-98; application evaluator Harry S. Truman Scholarship Found., Washington, 1992—; polit. cons. Parents and Taxpayers for Better Greenville Schs., 1996. Author: Housing and the Democratic Ideal: The Life and Thought of Charles Abrams, 2000; editor: Power and the Public Interest, 2002; contbr. articles to profl. jours. Bd. dirs. Greenville Concert Band, 1996—; founding bd. dirs. Friends of the Berea Libr., Greenville, 1997—; campaign cons. S.C. Demo. Com., Greenville, 1996—; ednl. cons. Greenville County Sch. Sys., 1998—. Recipient fellowship Nat. Endowment for Humanities, 1988, Harry S. Truman scholarship, 1982-86, Order of Chevalier Internat. Order of DeMolay, 1982, John Phillip Sousa award John Phillip Sousa Assn., 1980. Mem. ASCD, Japanese Assn. Lang. Tchrs. (program chair 1989-90), Orgn. Am. Historians, Urban History Assn., Soc. Am. City and Regional Planning Assn., Kappa Delta Pi, Nat. Golden Key, Phi Beta Kappa, Phi Kappa Phi, Pi Sigma Alpha, Phi Mu Alpha, Pi Gamma Mu, Omicron Delta Kappa, Omicron Delta Epsilon, Phi Alpha Theta. Democrat. Mem. Soc. Of Friends. Avocations: trumpet playing, travel, wine-making. Home: 8 Aiken Cir Greenville SC 29617 Office: Furman U 3300 Poinsett Hwy Greenville SC 29613 Fax: 864-294-3341. E-mail: scott.henderson@furman.edu.

HENDERSON, CATHERINE LYNN, retired secondary education educator, writer; b. Charleston, W.Va., Oct. 19, 1946; d. Raymond Anis Frame and Alma Madalene Green; m. W. Elliott Henderson, Apr. 12, 1978 (dec. 1985). BA in English, Morris Harvey Coll., 1968; MA in Journalism, Marshall U., 1976. Tchr. Kanawha County Bd. Edn., Charleston, W.Va., 1968—2001; ret., 2001. Stringer Offcl. Detective Group. Author: Fairs, Festivals & Funnin' in West Virginia, 1996; co-author: Essential Strategies for School Security, 2001; contbr. to Wonderful W.Va. Mag., Charleston City Mag. Mem. Nat. Writers Assn., Mystery Writers of Am., Am. Crime Writers League, Sisters in Crime, Soc. of Profl. Journalists. E-mail: murdermostfoul@charter.net.

HENDERSON, DWIGHT FRANKLIN, dean, educator; b. Austin, Tex., Aug. 14, 1937; s. Ottis Franklin and Leona (Bady) H.; m. Connie Chorlton, Dec. 24, 1966; 1 dau., Patricia Ross. BA, U. Tex., 1959, MA, 1961, PhD, 1966. Assoc. prof. Ind. U., Ft. Wayne, 1966-68, chmn. dept. history, 1968-71, assoc. prof. history, 1971-80, chmn. arts and scis., 1971-76, dean arts and letters, 1976-80, acting chancellor, 1978-79; prof. history, dean Coll. Social and Behavioral Scis. U. Tex., San Antonio, 1980-2000, acting v.p. acad. affairs, 1986-87, interim dean Coll. Engring., 2000-2001; dir. Learning Cmtys. Jour., 2003—; Fulbright lectr. East China Normal U., Shanghai, 2002; dir. Freshman Initiative, 2003—. Author: Private Journals of Georgiana Gholson Walker, 1963, Courts for a New Nation, 1971, Congress, Courts, and Criminals, 1985 Bd. dirs. Ft. Wayne Philharm. Orch., 1973-74, Pub. Transp. Corp., Ft. Wayne, 1975-77, Vis. Nurse Assn., San Antonio, 1989-94, 95-96, Vis. Nurse Assn. Hospice South Tex., 1996—, Employment Network, 1990-96. With AUS, 1962-64. Tex. Soc. Colonial Dames fellow, 1964-65, 65-66; Ind. U. fellow, 1968, 70, 72, Fulbright U.S.-German Internat. Edn. Adminstrs. Program, 1993. Mem.: Tex. Assn. Deans of Liberal Arts and Scis. (bd. dirs. 1992—98, v.p. 1994, pres. 1995—97), So. Hist. Assn., Assn. Am. Historians, Phi Alpha Theta, Delta Sigma Rho. Home: 2410 Shadow Cliff St San Antonio TX 78232-4010 Office: U Tex Dept History 6900 N Loop 1604 W San Antonio TX 78249 E-mail: dhenderson@utsa.edu.

HENDERSON, E. SUZANNE, elementary school educator; b. Champaign, Ill., Nov. 18, 1947; d. Donald Albert Fackler and Fiana B. Warfel Hardig; m. William Arthur Henderson, Aug. 17, 1968; children: Holly Janel, Rachel Eileen. BS, So. Ill. U., 1968; MEd, U. Ill., 1976. Tchr. grade 4 Pulaski County Spl. Sch. Dist., Jacksonville, Ark., 1968-70; tchr. grade 5 Tuscola Cmty. Unit Sch. Dist., Tuscola, Ill., 1970—. Recipient Presdl. Award for Excellence in Teaching of Math. and Sci., 1994. Mem. NEA, Ill. Edn. Assn., Tuscola Edn. Assn. (v.p. 1994-95), Nat. Coun. Tchrs. Math., Ill. Coun. Tchrs. Math. Avocations: flower gardening, golf. Home: 105 E Scott St Tuscola IL 61953-1834 Office: Tuscola Sch Dist 409 S Prairie St Tuscola IL 61953-1770

HENDERSON, FREDA LAVERNE, elementary education educator; b. Parker County, Tex., June 18, 1939; d. Johnnie C. and Golda Arlene (Porter) Holbrooks; m. Ronald S. Henderson, Apr. 12, 1958; children: Ronald Kevin, Kelly Doyle, Chetley Brian, Terry Dean. AA, Am. Inst. Art, 1960; BEd, U. Colo., 1991; MEd, Lesley Coll., 1997. Pvt. tchr. art, Calhan, Colo., 1981-86; elem. tchr. art Ellicott Schs., Colo., 1987-90, tchr. chpt. I, 1991-96, classroom tchr., 1996—. Sec. Ellicott Sch. PTA; chmn. High Sch. Booster Club, 1979-80; active vol. activities, 1964-79. Named Walmart Tchr. of Yr., 2002. Home: 1975 Buck Rd Calhan CO 80808-8515 Office: Ellicott Schs # 22 399 S Ellicott Hwy Calhan CO 80808-8963 E-mail: fredahenderson@hotmail.com.

HENDERSON, GERALDINE THOMAS, retired social security official, educator; b. Luling, Tex., Jan. 7, 1924; d. Cornelius Thomas and Maggie (Keyes) Thomas; m. James E. Henderson, Feb. 9, 1942 (dec. Apr. 1978); children— Geraldine, Jessica, Jennifer. BS, Fayetteville State U., 1967. Tchr. Cumberland County Schs., Fayetteville, N.C., 1966-67, Fayetteville City Schs., 1967-68; with Social Security Adminstrn., Fayetteville, 1968-87; substitute tchr. Cumberland County Sch. System, 1987—; claims rep. Pres. Fayetteville State U. Found., 1981-82; pres. NAACP, Fayetteville br., 1983-86. Deacon Coll. Heights Presbyn. Ch., 1965-79, ruling elder, 1980-91; bd. dirs. Fayetteville Art Coun., 1984—, Cumberland County United Way, 1983—, chmn. div. corp. mission Fayetteville Presbytery, 1986, mem. personnel review bd. City of Fayetteville, 1987—; inductee Nat. Black Coll. Alumni Hall of Fame, 1988; bd. dirs. Habitat for Humanity, Fayetteville, N.C., 1989, Share, Heart of the Carolinas, 1991; moderator Presbytery of Coastal Carolina, 1989; vice chair Cape Fear Food Bank, 1991. Recipient Life Membership Chmn. award NAACP Nat. Conv., Chgo., 1994, Essence of Freedom award NAACP State Conf., Goldsboro, N.C., 1995. Mem. LWV, Nat. Assn. Equal Opportunity in Higher Edn. (disting. alumni 1989), Legion Aux. (treas. 1981-83), Zeta Phi Zeta (Woman of Yr. 1984), Omega Psi Phi (Citizen of Yr. 1985). Democrat. Presbyterian. Avocations: creative dress design; gardening; travel.

HENDERSON, JANICE ELIZABETH, law librarian; b. N.Y.C., Dec. 22, 1952; d. James and Adeline M. (Fitzgerald) H. BA in Psychology, Hunter Coll., 1974; MS in Spl. Edn., CUNY, 1979; MS in Library Sci., Pratt Inst., 1980; JD, Bklyn. Law Sch., 1986. Law librarian Morgan, Lewis & Bockius, N.Y.C., 1977-83; reference librarian Weil, Gotshal & Manges, N.Y.C., 1983-85; law librarian Tenzer, Greenblatt et al, N.Y.C., 1985-86, Robinson, Silverman et al, N.Y.C., 1986-88, Kirkland & Ellis, N.Y.C., 1991-93; assoc. law libr. prof. CUNY Law Sch., N.Y.C., 1989-91; dir. libr. svcs. Epstein, Becker & Green, PC, 1993-98; dir. profl. devel. and libr. svcs. Baker & McKenzie, N.Y.C., 1998—2002; cons. law librarianship N.Y.C., 2003—. Assoc. adj. prof. Sch. Libr. and Info. Sci., St. John's U., N.Y.C., 1990-93; spkr. in field. Book reviewer Legal Info. Alert newsletter, 1984-86. Mem. Am. Assn. Law Librs., Law Libr. Assn. Greater N.Y. (advt. mgr. 1986-89, bd. dirs. 1989-90, mem. continuing legal edn. com. 1990-92, co-chair 1992-94, v.p. 1995-96, pres. 1996-97, past pres. 1997-98), Practicing Law Inst. (mng. the law libr. 1997-98, program chair 1999-2000, program co-chair 2001—). Democrat. Roman Catholic. Home: PO Box 23060 Brooklyn NY 11202-3060 E-mail: janiceehenderson@att.net.

HENDERSON, JEAN WOODBURN, retired secondary education educator; b. Portales, N.Mex., Jan. 29, 1927; d. Arthur Coffin and Willie Mae (Gilpin) Woodburn; m. Clifton Morton Henderson, Jr., Dec. 22, 1946 (dec. Apr. 1992); children: Cyrus Bruce, Walter Alan. EdB, Ea. N.Mex. U., 1948; MA in Bus. Edn., We. N.Mex. U., 1966. Instr. art appreciation We. N.Mex. U., Silver City, 1967, instr. office comm., 1977-79, instr. word processing, 1984; tchr. typing, English Cobre H.S., Bayard, N.Mex., 1968-80, office edn. and co-op coord., 1980-93, ret., 1993. Adv. Bus. Profls. Am., Bayard, 1976-93. Author: The Centennial History of the Church of the Good Shepard, 1991, Woodburn, Coffin, and Allied Nantucket Families, 1995, Descendants of Thomas Gardner, 1997; designer, creator: copper doors Ch. Good Shepherd, Silver City (award 1972), five sets of silk hangings. Mem. sick leave com. Cobre Nat. Edn. Assn., 1990-93; mem. P.E.O. (AG chpt.

Silver City), 1993—. Mem. Nat. Soc. Colonial Dames XVII Century, Daus. of Am. Colonists, Nat. Soc. Am. Revolution. Episcopalian. Avocations: travel, genealogical research, choir singing.

HENDERSON, JOHN L. academic administrator; Sr. asst. to pres. instl. devel. Cin. Tech. Coll., until 1987, v.p. instl. devel., 1987-88; pres. Wilberforce U., Ohio, 1988—. Office: Wilberforce U President's Ofc 1055 N Bickett Rd Wilberforce OH 45384-3001

HENDERSON, KATHLEEN DENISE ROSS, medical/surgical nurse, nursing educator; b. Camden, N.J., Feb. 4, 1954; r. Andrew Jr. and S. Roberta Richardson (Johnson) R.; 1 child, Thelbert (Jay) Cornish Jr. BSN, Seton Hall. U., 1978; MS, St. Joseph's U., Phila., 1990. Cert. critical care nurse, ACLS, BCLS. Staff nurse Harris Hosp., Ft. Worth, 1980-81, John Peter Smith Hosp., Ft. Worth, 1984; staff nurse, relief charge nurse Med. Plaza Hosp., Ft. Worth, 1983-84; staff nurse, med. ICU-CCU Deborah Heart and Lung Ctr., Browns Mills, N.J., 1984-88, 92—, staff devel. instr., 1988-92. Vol. AIDS Coalition So. N.J., 1993-96. Capt. USAF, 1979-83. Mem. AANC, ANA, N.J.Nurses Assn., Sigma Theta Tau. Home: PO Box 4036 Mount Holly NJ 08060-4036 Office: Deborah Heart and Lung Ctr 200 Trenton Rd Browns Mills NJ 08015-1799

HENDERSON, PAMELA MASON, elementary education educator; b. Fullerton, Calif., Feb. 26, 1947; d. Joseph Harold and Marilyn (Rogers) Mason; m. Martin D. Kobaly, June 1, 1968 (div. 1981); children: Michael Drew Kobaly, Christopher Scott Kobaly; m. Eldon Leroy Henderson, Aug. 7, 1982. AA, Coll. of the Desert, 1966; BA, Whittier Coll., 1968; MA, Pepperdine U., 1976. Tchr. Shelley (Idaho) Sch. Dist., 1969-70, Fontana (Calif.) United Sch. Dist., 1974-82, Mariposa (Calif.) County Unified Sch. Dist., 1983—, mentor, tchr. aerospace tech., 1988-89. Historian, sec. No. Mariposa County Hist. Mus., Coulterville, Calif., 1982-84. Mem. Calif. Tchrs. Assn. (rep. 1983-92), Mariposa Tchrs. Assn. (pres. 1992-94). Avocations: weaving, doll making, image consultant. Home: 2295 Golfito Way La Grange CA 95329-9625 Office: Coulterville-Greeley Sch 10326 Fiske Rd Coulterville CA 95311-9502

HENDERSON, ROBERTA MARIE, librarian, educator; b. Mosinee, Wis., July 27, 1929; d. Roy H. and Marie Helena (Dittman) H. BS, Cen. State Tchrs. Coll., Stevens Point, Wis., 1951; MS, U. Wis., 1958; MA, No. Mich. U., 1975; Cert. of Adv. Studies, U. Denver, 1980. Librarian Wiesbaden (Ger.) Am. High Sch., 1954-55, Ashland (Wis.) High Sch., 1955-56; tchr./librarian Clark AFB, Philippines, 1956-57; librarian Prescott (Ariz.) Jr. High Sch., 1958-59, Frankfurt (Ger.) Am. High Sch., 1959-63; tchr./librarian Zama Am. High Sch., Camp Zama, Japan, 1963-66; librarian Ankara (Turkey) Am. High Sch., 1966-68; tutor Nkozi Tchr. Tng. Coll., Mpigi, Uganda, 1968-70; ref. librarian/prof. No. Mich. U., Marquette, 1971-93; retired, 1993; cons. No. Mich. U. and Pub. Librs., 1993—. Coord. faculty workshops No. Mich. U., 1986-88; cons. Escanaba (Mich.) Pub. Libr., 1987, 90, 92. Author slide/tape: Locating Materials in Periodicals and Documents, 1977, Library Materials for Literature Students, 1979. Mem. libr. com. Marquette County Hist. Soc., 1981—; mem. Upper Peninsula Environ. Coalition, Houghton, 1985—; host Marquette-Japan Sister Coalition City Program, 1988. Title II-B fellow, U. Denver, 1979-80; Human Resources Dept., No. Mich. U. grantee, 1986, 87; recipient Disting Faculty award No. Mich. U., 1988. Mem. ALA, AAUP, Libr. Instrn. Roundtable, Phi Kappa Phi (chpt. treas. 1987-91). Avocations: interior decoration, gardening, hiking, cats. Home: 515 E Ridge St Marquette MI 49855-4216

HENDERSON, SHARLENE OTTESEN, special education educator; b. Salt Lake City, Sept. 9, 1954; d. Elmo Earl and Shirley Dean (Langdorf) Ottesen; m. Kim E. Henderson, Sept. 11, 1975; children: Arlo Patrick, Patience Ann. BS in Spl. Edn., U. Utah, 1986, MEd in Spl. Edn., 1993. Cert. moderate to severe disabilities, hearing impairments, and mild to moderate disabilities. Tchr. East H.S., Salt Lake City, 1985—, Children's Behavior Therapy Unit, Salt Lake City, 1989—. Asst. and family support trainer Project TURN-Autism Tchg. Home, Salt Lake City, 1984-88; cons. Autism and behavioral cons. Residential Svcs. Inc., Salt Lake City, 1989-94; cons. Autism secondary curriculum Edn. Svc. Ctr., Richardson, Tex., 1994—; cons., tutor, Salt Lake City, 1989—; pvt. tutor for hearing impaired students, 1993—. United Way coord. East H.S., 1989-94; assn. rep. Salt Lake Tchr.'s Assn., East H.S., 1994-95; mem. East H.S. Improvement Coun., 1994-95, East H.S. Comty. Coun., 1994-95. Mem. Coun. for Exceptional Children, Salt Lake Sch. Dist. Spl. Edn. Improvement Coun., Salt Lake Sch. Dist. Spl. Edn. Comty. Coun. (chair 1992—), Autism Soc. Utah. Avocations: raising and riding horses, making porcelain dolls, gardening, sewing, reading. Office: East H S 840 S 1300 E Salt Lake City UT 84102-3716

HENDERSON, STANLEY DALE, lawyer, educator; b. Monona, Iowa, June 17, 1935; s. Leon Gilbert and Iva Elizabeth H.; m. DeArliss Garretson, June 15, 1957; children: Lesli Kara, Heidi Elizabeth, Holly Ann. AB, Coe Coll., 1957; postgrad. (Woodrow Wilson fellow), Cornell U., 1957-58; postgrad., U. Chgo. Law Sch., 1958-59; JD, U. Colo., 1961. Bar: Colo. 1961, Va. 1973. Law clk. U.S. Dist. Ct., Denver, 1961-62; mem. firm Williams and Zook, Boulder, Colo., 1962-64; mem. faculty U. Wyo. Coll. Law, 1964-69; prof. law U. Va. Law Sch., Charlottesville, 1970, F.D.G. Ribble prof. law, 1976—. Vis. prof. law Ind. U., 1974, Harvard Law Sch., 1978-79, Pepperdine U., 1992-93. Author: (with Dawson and Harvey) Labor Law, (with Meltzer) Contracts; contbr. articles to profl. jours. Mem. Va. State Bar, Am. Law Inst., Am. Arbitration Assn., Order of Coif, Phi Beta Kappa, Phi Kappa Phi. Democrat. Presbyterian. Home: 1615 King Mountain Rd Charlottesville VA 22901-3003 Office: U Va Sch Law Charlottesville VA 22901 Fax: 434-924-7536. E-mail: sdh6k@virginia.edu.

HENDERSON, WILLIAM EUGENE, education educator; b. Miami, Fla., Sept. 9, 1947; s. William Bartow and Evelyn Mildred (Stansell) H. BA in Polit. Sci., Acctg., U. South Fla., 1967; MS in Guidance, Counseling, Barry U., 1971, EdS in Sch. Psychology, 1976, MBA in Mgmt., Fin., 1981; postgrad., Fla. State U., Northwestern U., U. Miami. Cert. tchr., prin., sch. psychologist, Fla. From tchr. to subject area coord. Miami-Dade County Pub. Schs., Miami, 1968—83, asst. prin., 1983-89, assoc. intern prin., 1989-2001; exec. dir. Miami Shores/Barry U. Charter Sch., 2001—03. Adj. prof. Nova U., Ft. Lauderdale, Fla., 1983-90, Barry U., Miami Shores, Fla., 1987—; assessment cons. Fla. Dept. Edn., Tallahassee, 1979-83, Ednl. Testing Svc., Princeton, N.J., 1981-82. Author: S.O.S. Sourcebook, 1985; author curriculum materials; editor, curriculum reviewer Harcourt Brace Jovanovich, Orlando, Fla., 1985-86. Named Outstanding Econs. Educator Fla. Coun. Econ. Edn., 1981, 82, 93, Outstanding Secondary Social Studies Tchr. Dade County Coun. Social Studies, 1982. Mem. Nat. Coun. Social Studies, Coun. Exceptional Children (chair region II, sec. asst. prin. 1998-2001, Oustanding Exceptional Student Edn. Adminstr. 1988), So. Assn. Schs. and Colls. (chair, facilitator 2001—), Assn. for Supervision and Curriculum Devel., dir. Fla. Consortium of Charter Schs., Phi Delta Kappa, Kappa Delta Pi, Phi Alpha Theta.

HENDREN, ROBERT LEE, JR., academic administrator; b. Reno, Oct. 10, 1925; s. Robert Lee and Aleen (Hill) H.; m. Merlyn Churchill, June 14, 1947; children: Robert Lee IV, Anne Aleen. BA magna cum laude, LLD (hon.), Coll. Idaho; postgrad., Army Univ. Ctr., Oahu, Hawaii. Owner, pres. Hendren's Inc., 1947—; pres. Albertson Coll. Idaho, Caldwell, 1987—. Bd. dirs. 1st Interstate Bank Idaho. Trustee Boise (Idaho) Ind. Sch. Dist., chmn. bd. trustees, 1966; chmn. bd. trustees Coll. Idaho, 1980-84; bd. dirs. Mountain View coun. Boy Scouts Am., Boise Retail Merchants, Boise Valley Indsl. Found., Boise Redevel. Agy., Ada County Marriage Counseling, Ada County Planning and Zoning Com.; chmn. bd. Blue Cross Idaho. Recipient Silver and Gold award U. Idaho, Nat. award Sigma Chi. Mem. Boise C. of C. (pres., bd. dirs.), Idaho Sch. Trustees Assn., Masons, KT, Shriners, Rotary (Paul Harris fellow). Home: 3504 Hillcrest Dr Boise ID 83705-4503 Office: Albertson Coll Idaho 2112 Cleveland Blvd Caldwell ID 83605-4432

HENDRICK, ZELWANDA, drama and psychology educator; b. Rusk, Tex., Nov. 28, 1925; d. Lloyd Irvin and Viola Alice (McGuire) Hendrick; A.A., Lon Morris Coll., 1945; B.S., N. Tex. U., 1947; M.A., So. Meth. U., 1958. Tchr. theatre arts Overton (Tex.) High Sch., 1947-49, Nacogdoches (Tex.) High Sch., 1949-50, Boude Storey Sch., Dallas, 1950-53, Kimball High Sch., Dallas, 1953-62; tchr. theatre arts H. Grady Spruce High Sch., Dallas, 1962-78, chmn. fine arts dept., 1963-77, ret., 1978; drama and psychology tchr. Alexander Sch., 1978— ; substitute tchr. Highland Park High Sch., Dallas, 1980— ; part-time tchr. John Robert Powers Finishing Sch., 1951— ; teaching fellow N. Tex. U., 1964-65; ptnr. Adventure II Miniature Horse Ranch, Rusk, Tex., 1985—; co-dir. Adventure II Miniature Horse Show, Lufkin, Tex., 1987—. Active, Tyler (Tex.) Civic Symphony, 1949-50, Tyler Civic Theatre, 1949-50, Dallas Theatre Center, 1960-61; guest dir. Cherokee Civic Theatre, Rusk, 1983, pres. 2002—; mem. adv. com. Smithsonian Instn., 1975; co-sponsor U.S. Inst. Tech. Theatre; del. Democratic Dist. Conv., 1980; candidate Tex. State Legislature, 1980; chmn. Dallas County Transp. Bd., 1982— ; life mem. First United Meth. Ch., Rusk. Mem. Internat. Thespians (state dir.), Tex. Speech Assn. (sec. 1973—), Am. Assn. Ednl. Theatre, Am. Miniature Horse Registry, Friends of the Railroad, Dallas Ednl. Drama Assn. (governing bd.), Tex. Tchrs. Assn., Nat. Forensic League, AAUW, Classroom Tchrs. Dallas, Internat. Platform Assn., Ednl. Arts Assn., Tex. Congress Parent Tchr. Assn. (hon. life), DAR, Daus. Republic of Tex., N. Texas Collie Club, Nat. Assn. Royalty Owners, Tex. Ind. Producers and Royalty Owners Assn., Tex. Farm Bur., Am. Miniature Horse Assn., Paws of E. Tex., Delta Kappa Gamma. Club: Order Eastern Star. Contbr. to A Guide to Student Teaching in Music, 1968-70. Home: 204 E 4th St Rusk TX 75785-1308 Office: Adventure II Miniature Horse Ranch Hwy 84 W Rusk TX

HENDRICKS, IDA ELIZABETH, mathematics educator; b. Roanoke, Va., Aug. 13, 1941; d. Samuel Jarboe and Nannie Virginia (Needy) Hodges; m. William Hampton Hendricks, Aug. 10, 1963; 1 child: William Hodges. BS in Math. & BA in Secondary Edn., Shepherd Coll., 1963; MA in Devel. Studies/Leadership Edn., Appalachian State U., 1992, cert. devel. edn. specialist, 1988. Faculty Harpers Ferry (W.Va.) High Sch., 1963-72, Jefferson High Sch., Shanandoah Junction, W.Va., 1972-78; mem. math. faculty, devel. math. specialist, adminstr. Shepherd Coll., Shepherdstown, W.Va., 1981-94; ret., 1994. Creator, implementor devel. math. program Shepherd Coll.; tutor. Contbr. articles to profl. jours. Elder, organist, supt. Sunday sch., mem. Christ Reformed Ch., Shepherdstown, 1950—; organist Shepherdstown Presbyn. Ch., 1957—. Named Outstanding Shepherdstown H.S. Alumni, 1997. Mem. AAUW (past treas.), Nat. Assn. Devel. Edn., W.Va. Assn. Devel. Edn. (sec. 1993—, v.p. 1994-95), W.Va. Coun. Tchrs. Math., Shepherdstown Hist. Soc. Avocations: music, books, travel, home, church. Home: PO Box 123 Shepherdstown WV 25443-0123

HENDRICKS, LAURA VENTURINO, special education educator; b. Pitts., May 23, 1952; d. Anthony Joseph and Eleanor Rita (Marinella) Venturino; m. Douglas Van Hendricks, Oct. 30, 1983; 1 child, Gina Marie. BS in Spl. Edn., California (Pa.) State Coll., 1974, BS in Elem. Edn., 1989. Cert. in diagnosis and treatment of autism. Elem. tchr. of learning disabled Gallipolis (Ohio) City Schs., 1974-75; elem. tchr. of educable mentally retarded Callia County Schs., Gallipolis, 1975-78; permanent substitute Pitts. City Schs., 1978-80; elem. tchr. of gifted and socially and emotionally disturbed Plum Borough Sch. Dist., Pitts., 1980-82, elem. tchr. of socially and emotionally disturbed, 1982-86, secondary tchr. of socially and emotionally disturbed, 1986-87, secondary tchr. of learning disabled, 1987-89, elem. emotional support tchr., 1989-92, instnl. suport tchr., 1992—. Home: 1721 Briarwood Ln Plum PA 15239-2045 Office: Plum Borough Sch Dist 200 School Rd Pittsburgh PA 15239-1457

HENDRICKSON, ELIZABETH ANN, retired secondary education educator; b. Bismarck, N.D., Oct. 21, 1936; d. William Earl and Hilda E. (Sauter) Hinkel; m. Roger G. Hendrickson, Apr. 18, 1960; 1 child, Wade William. BA, Jamestown Coll., 1958; postgrad., U. Calif., Davis, 1962, Calif. State U., Sacramento, 1964, U. San Diego, 1985-88, Ottawa U., 1986-88. Cert. tchr., Calif. Tchr. Napoleon (N.D.) High Sch., 1958-59, Kulm (N.D.) High Sch., 1959-61, Del Paso Jr. High Sch., Sacramento, 1961, Mills Jr. High Sch., Rancho Cordova, Calif., 1961-97; ret., 1997. Mem. sch. attendance rev. bd. Folsom-Cordova Unified Sch. Dist. Mem.: AAUW, NEA, Sacramento Area Gifted Assn., Folsom Cordova Ret. Tchrs. Assn. (sec., mem. steering com., mem. newsletter com.), Calif. Ret. Tchrs. Assn., Calif. Tchrs. Assn., Calif. Assn. for Gifted, N.G. Aux., Sgt. Maj. Assn. of Calif. Aux. Enlisted Assns., Soroptimists (news editor Rancho Cordova 1985). Democrat. Lutheran. Home: 2032 Kellogg Way Rancho Cordova CA 95670-2435

HENDRIX, BONNIE ELIZABETH LUELLAN, retired elementary school educator; b. Corry, Pa., July 21, 1942; d. Francis Wilson and Frances (Welch) Luellen. BEd, Anderson Coll., 1965; MEd, Berry Coll., 1986. 1st grade tchr. Madison County Bd. Edn., Anderson, Ind.; kindergarten tchr. Walker County Bd. Edn., LaFayette, Ga., 1994—, spl. instrn. asst., 1998—2002, spl. edn. tchr., 1999—2002, tchr. exceptional children, 1999—2000; tchr. Tiny Treasures Day Care Ctr., 2003—; presenter at confs. Mentor tchr. Continuous Quality Instructions Sys; pvt. practice piano tchr. Tchr. 4 yr. olds Tiny Treasures Day Care Ctr., active community and ch. orgns. Mem. NEA, ASCD, PAGE, Ga. Assn. Edn., Walker Assn. Edn. Home: 76 Old Trion Rd La Fayette GA 30728-3714

HENDRIX, JACQUELYN MCINTYRE, elementary music educator; b. Atlanta, Dec. 9, 1946; d. James Jackson and Stella Martha (Hinson) McIntyre; m. David Richard Hendrix, June, 4, 1966. B of Music Edn., Ga. State U., 1968, postgrad., 1976, 90—. Customer svc. rep. Ga. Power Co., Atlanta, 1965; receptionist W.M. Hinson Co., Atlanta, 1966-67; elem. music specialist Atlanta Pub. Schs., 1968-81, Gwinnett County Schs., Lawrenceville, Ga., 1982—, mid. sch. choir dir., 1981-82. Author, composer W.S.B.-TV Spl. theme song, 1995; composer Egleston Hosp. Campaign theme music, 1985; writer, editor county music curriculum Gwinnett County Elks, Lawrenceville, 1995—; contbr. articles to profl. jours. Ch. choir dir. children, youth Stewart Ave. Meth. Ch., Atlanta, 1967—, coord. children & youth, 1979—; dir.'s staff opening ceremonies Atlanta Com. Paralympic Games, 1995-96; cast asst. dir. opening ceremonies Centennial Olympic Games Atlanta Olympic Com., 1995-96; fund raiser Meth. Children's Home Aux., Decatur, Ga., 1990—; mem., co-block capt. Peachtree Hills Civic Assn., Atlanta, 1979—. Recipient Super Tchr. award Turner Broadcasting/Ga. Bus. Forum, Atlanta, 1995, Resolution Commendation Senate State Ga., Atlanta, 1993, 94, 95, Commendation award State & Nat. "Just Say No" Campaign, Ga., 1986, 88, 89, 90, 91, Gwinnett Clean & Beautiful, 1985, 90. Mem. NEA, Music Educators Nat. Conf., Ga. Citizens Arts, Ga. Assn. Educators, Ga. Music Educators Assn., Alpha Delta Kappa. Avocations: reading, travel, swimming, boating. Home: 2103 Fairhaven Cir NE Atlanta GA 30305-4314 Office: Gwinnett County Pub Schs PO Box 343 Lawrenceville GA 30046-0343

HENDRIX, JOHN EDWIN, biology educator; b. Van Nuys, Calif., Aug. 30, 1930; s. John E. and Leona (Paul) H.; m. Joan B. Haas, Apr. 10, 1954; children: Janet L., James. A. BS, Fresno (Calif.) State U., 1956, AB, 1960; MS, Ohio State U., 1963, PhD, 1967. Orchard foreman Fresno State, 1959-60; grad. asst. Ohio State U., Columbus, 1960-65, instr., 1965-67; asst. prof. plant physiology Colo. State U., Ft. Collins, 1967-72, assoc. prof., 1972-89, prof., 1989—2002, prof. emeritus, 2002—. Contbr. rsch. articles to profl. jour. Mem. AAAS, Am. Soc. Plant Physiologists (editorial bd. Plant Physiology 1982-92). Home: 3000 Tulane Dr Fort Collins CO 80525-2529 E-mail: jhndx@lamar.colostate.edu.

HENDRIX, JON RICHARD, biology educator; b. Passaic, N.J., May 4, 1938; s. William Louis and Velma Lucile (Coleman) H.; m. Janis Ruth Rouhselange, Nov. 24, 1962; children— Margaret Susan, Joann Ruth, Amy Therese BS, Ind. State U., 1960, MS, 1963; Ed.D., Ball State U., 1974. Sci. supr. Sch. Town of Highland, Ind., 1960-71; instr. Ind. U., Gary, 1968-69; assoc. prof. biology Ball State U., Muncie, 1972-80, prof., 1980-98, prof. emeritus, 1998—. Cons. Ind. Dept. Pub. Instrn., 1967-71, Ctr. for Values and Meaning, 1971— ; mem. Ind. Sci. Edn. Adv. Bd., Dept. Pub. Instrn., 1967-71 Author: The Wonder of Somehow, 1974, The Wonder of Someplace, 1974, The Wonder of Sometime, 1974, Becomings: A Parent Guidebook for In-Home Experiences with Nine to Eleven Year Olds, 1974, Becomings: A Clergy Guidebook for Experiences with Nine to Eleven Year Olds and Their Parents, 1974; contbr. articles to profl. jours. Recipient Outstanding Young Educator award Highland Jr. C. of C., 1968, Outstanding Faculty award in edn. Ind. U. N.W. Campus, 1970, Outstanding Teaching Faculty award Ball State U., 1982, Ball State U. fellowship, 1971-73, Hon. Mem. award Nat. Assn. Biology Tchrs., 1992, Outstanding Undergrad. Sci. Tchr. in Nation, Soc. of Coll. Sci. Tchrs./Kendall Mgmt., 1997; named Ind. Prof. of Yr., Coun. for Advancement and Support of Edn./Carneige, 1997. Fellow Ind. Acad. Sci.; mem. Nat. Sci. Suprs. Assn. (dir. 1969-71), Ind. Sci. Suprs. Assn. (pres. 1968-69), AAUP, Assn. Suprs. and Curriculum Devel., Nat. Biology Tchrs. Assn. (bd. dirs. 1986, 91—), Nat. Sci. Tchrs. Assn. (life), Nat. Soc. Coll. Sci. Tchrs. (undergrad. tchg. award 1997), Central Assn. Coll. Biology Tchrs., Hoosier Assn. Sci. Tchrs. Inc. (bd. dirs. 1968-71, Disting. Svc. award 1997), Ind. Assn. Tchr. Educators, Ind. Assn. Suprs. and Curriculum Devel., Ind. Biology Tchrs. Assn., Kappa Delta Pi, Phi Delta Kappa, Sigma Xi. Home: 8800 W Eucalyptus Ave Muncie IN 47304-9365 E-mail: jonh49@comcast.net.

HENEMAN, ROBERT LLOYD, management educator; b. Mpls., Jan. 17, 1955; s. Herbert G. Jr. and Jane R. Heneman; m. Renee Brausch, Sept. 9, 1989. BA, Lake Forest Coll., 1977; MA, U. Ill., 1979; PhD, Mich. State U., 1984. Personnel specialist Pacific Gas & Electric Co., San Francisco, 1979-80; assoc. prof. Mgmt. Ohio State U., Columbus, 1984—, dir. grad. programs in labor and human resources. Author: Merit Pay, 1992, Staffing Organizations, 1994, 3d edit., 2000, Business-Driven Compensation Policies, 2000, Strategic Reward Management, 2001. Mem. ch. coun. Holy Trinity Luth. Ch., Columbus. Mem. Acad. of Mgmt. (exec. com. human resource divsn. 1988-93, program chair 1992-93, divsn. chair 1994-95), Am. Compensation Assn. (rsch. com. 1992-93, edn. com. 1993-94, acad. ptnr. network, 1997—, cert. program fac., 1992—), Phi Kappa Phi, Sigma Iota Epsilon, Psi Chi. Home: 4815 Lytfield Dr Dublin OH 43017-2174

HENGELS, CHARLES FRANCIS, management consultant, educator; b. Oak Park, Ill., Sept. 4, 1948; s. Charles Leo and Vivian Marguerite (Brust) H. BS in Econs. with distinction and honors, Purdue U., 1970; BA in Polit. Sci. with distinction and honors, 1970, MS in Edn., 1976, MS in Sociology, 1978. Cert. secondary tchr. Staff resident, tchg. asst. Purdue U., West Lafayette, Ind., 1975-78; dir. Am. Med. Bldgs., Milw., 1978-80; exec. v.p. Sys. Planning Corp., Arlington, 1980—. Bd. dirs. Print Services Group, Reston, Va.; cons. Ind. Council for Econ. Edn., West Lafayette, 1976-77. Author: (poetry) America, 1971 (Freedom Found. award 1971). Regional dir. Com. for Responsible Health Care, Washington, 1978-80; dep. campaign mgr. Virginians for Zummalt U.S. Sen. campaign, Richmond, 1976. Lt. spl duty (intelligence) USN, 1970-74. Decorated Navy Achievement medal with Combat V (2), Combat Action ribbon; recipient Gen. Dynamics award Gen. Dynamics Corp., 1970, chgo. tribune award, 1970; named Disting. Naval Grad., 1970. Mem. Purdue Alumni Assn., Mensa, Kappa Delta Pi, Alpha Kappa Delta, Pi Sigma Alpha, Phi Kappa Phi, Delta Rho Kappa, Phi Eta Sigma. Republican. Roman Catholic. Avocations: athletics, writing, teaching. Home: 6135 Wellington Commons Dr Alexandria VA 22310-5307 Office: System Planning Corp 1000 Wilson Blvd Arlington VA 22209-3901

HENIKOFF, LEO M., JR., academic administrator, medical educator; b. Chgo., May 9, 1939; m. Carole E. Andersen; children from previous marriage: Leo M. III, Jamie Sue. MD with highest honors, U. Ill., Chgo., 1963. Diplomate Am. Bd. Pediat., Am. Bd. Pediat. Cardiology. Intern Presbyn.-St. Luke's Hosp., Chgo., 1963-64, resident, 1964-66, fellow in pediatric cardiology, 1966-69; clin. instr. U. Ill. Coll. Medicine, Chgo., 1964-66; clin. instr. pediatrics Georgetown U. Med. Sch., Washington, 1966-68, clin. asst. prof., 1968; asst. prof. U. Ill. Coll. Medicine, Chgo., 1968-71; asst. prof. pediat. Rush Med. Coll., Chgo., 1971-74, assoc. prof., 1974-79, asst. dean admissions, 1971-74, assoc. dean student affairs, 1974-76, assoc. dean med. scis. and svcs., 1976-79, acting dean v.p. med. affairs, 1976-78, prof. pediatrics, prof. medicine, 1984—; v.p. inter-instl. affairs Rush-Presbyn.-St. Luke's Med. Ctr., Chgo., 1978-79, pres., 1984—; pres., CEO; trustee Rush-Presbyn.-St. Luke's Med. Ctr., Chgo., 1984—; dean and v.p. med. affairs Temple U. Sch. Medicine, Phila., 1979-84, prof. pediat. and medicine, 1979-84; pres. Rush U., Chgo., 1984—. Adj. attending Presbyn.-St. Luke's Hosp., 1969, asst., 1970-72, assoc., 1973-76, sr. attending, 1977-79, 84—; staff Temple U. Hosp., 1979-84; assoc. staff St. Christopher's Hosp. for Children, 1979-84; mem. Ill. Coun. of Deans, 1977-79; vice chmn. Chgo. Tech. Pk., 1984-85, 86-87, chmn., 1985-86, 87-88; chmn. bd. dirs. Mid-Am. Health Programs, Inc., 1985—; bd. dirs. Harris Trust and Savs. Bank, Harris Bankcorp. Inc.; chmn. bd. dirs. Rush North Shore Health Svcs., 1988—, Rush/Copley Health Care Sys. Inc., 1988—. Contbr. chpts. to books, articles to profl. jours. Bd. dirs. Fishbein Found., 1975-79, Chgo. Regional Blood Program, 1977-79, Sch. Dist. 69, 1974-75, Johnston R. Bowman Health Ctr. for Elderly, 1984—; mem. bd. mgrs. St. Christopher's Hosp. for Children, 1979-84; mem. bd. govs. Temple U. Hosp., 1979-84, Heart Assn. S.E. Pa., 1979-84; trustee Episc. Hosp., 1983-84, Otho S.A. Sprague Meml. Inst., 1984—; mem. adv. bd. Univ. Village Assn., 1984—; mem. exec. com. Gov.'s Build Ill. Com., 1985—. Lt. comdr. USPHS, 1964-68, Res. 1968—. Recipient Roche Med. award, 1962, Mosby award, 1963, Raymond B. Allen Instructorship award U. Ill. Coll. Medicine, 1966, also Med. Alumni award, 1988, Phoenix award Rush Med. Coll., 1977. Fellow Am. Acad. Pediat., Inst. Medicine Chgo., Coll. Physicians Phila., Am. Coll. Physicians Execs.; mem. Assn. Am. Med. Colls. (chmn. nominating com. 1980, mem. coun. deans 1977-84, mem. audit com. 1984), Coun. Tchg. Hosps. (adminstrv. bd. 1987-90), Pa. Med. Sch. Deans Com., AMA (mem. coun. on ethical and jud. affairs 1984-88), Pa. Med. Soc., Philadelphia County Med. Soc., Assn. Acad. Health Ctrs. (bd. dirs. 1988-94, chmn.-elect 1991-92, chmn. 1992-93), Alpha Omega Alpha (chmn. nat. nominating com. 1981-90, nat. dir. 1979-90, pres. 1989-90), Omega Beta Pi, Phi Eta Sigma, Phi Kappa Phi. Office: Rush-Presbyn-St Luke's Med Ctr 1653 W Congress Pkwy Chicago IL 60612-3833

HENINGER, GEORGE ROBERT, psychiatry educator, researcher; b. L.A., Nov. 15, 1934; s. Owen P. and Rachel (Cannon) H.; m. Julie Hawkes, June 27, 1957; children: Steven, Catharine, Karen, Brian. BS, U. Utah, 1957, MD, 1960. Diplomate Am. Bd. Psychiatry and Neurology. Intern Boston City Hosp., 1960-61; resident in psychiatry Mass. Mental Health Ctr., 1961-63, chief resident, 1963-64; clin. assoc., clin. neuropharmacology rsch. ctr. St. Elizabeth's Hosp. NIMH, Washington, 1964-65, program specialist, office of dir. Bethesda, Md., 1965-66; asst. prof. psychiatry, assoc. chief rsch. ward Yale U., New Haven, 1966-71, assoc. prof., 1971-76, chief rsch. ward, 1971-78, prof. clin. psychiatry, 1976-78, prof. psychiatry, dir. Abraham Ribicoff Rsch. Facilities, 1978-93, assoc. chmn. rsch. dept. psychiatry, 1988-93, dir. lab. clin. and molecular neurobiology, 1993—. Cons. NIMH, 1975-86, 88-94, NIH, 1987, McGill U., 1989, VA, 1990-94, Nat. Rsch. Coun. Can., 1991-93, Nat. Inst. Aging, 1992-93, Wellcome Trust, 1992-94, Pfizer Inc., Merck, Sharp & Dohme, Inc., The Upjohn Co.,

Hoffman La Roche, Inc., Burroughs Wellcome Co., Bristol-Meyers Co., Squibb Corp., Kali DuPhar, Inc.; bd. sci. advisors, Neurogen Corp. REviewer manuscripts Archives Gen. Psychiatry, Am. Jour. Psychiatry, Psychiatry Rsch., Biol. Psychiatry, Jour. Affective Disorders, Jour. Clin. Psychopharmacology, Life Scis., Neurochemistry Internat., Psychiatry, Schizophrenia Bull., Psychoneuroendocrinology, Jour. AMA. Sr. asst. surgeon USPHS, 1964-66. Recipient Rsch. Sci. Devel. award Type II, NIMH, 1971, 1st prize Anna Monika Found., 1995; grantee NIMH, 1971, 74, 77, 82, 85, 89, 91. Fellow Am. Coll. Neuropsychopharmacology, Am. Psychiat. Assn.; mem. AAAS, Am. Psychopath. Assn., Soc. Neurosci., Soc. Biol. Psychiatry, Psychiat. Rsch. Soc., N.Y. Acad. Scis., Conn. Psychiat. Soc., Sigma Xi, Phi Kappa Phi, Alpha Omega Alpha. Avocation: running. Office: Yale U 34 Park St New Haven CT 06511

HENJUM, KAY DEE, elementary education educator; b. Mpls., Feb. 10, 1961; d. Richard James and Marilyn Joyce (Larson) Kennedy; m. Rand Raymond Henjum, Aug. 21, 1982; children: Eric Rand, Karen Kay, Julie Ann, Dana Raymond. BA in elem. edn./psychology, Augsburg Coll., 1982; MEd Elem. Adminstrn., Mont. State U., 1990. Kindergarten tchr. Washoe County Sch. Dist., Reno, 1982-90, tchr. mid.-sch. phys. edn., 1982-83, reading tchr. mid.-sch., 1983-84, tchr. shorthand/high sch. typing, 1982-84, tchr. 1st grade, 1990-91, program coord., 1991-92, tchr., 1992—. Chair Early Sch. Success Adv. Bd., Reno, 1991-92; co-chair No. Nev. Early Childhood Edn. Conf., Reno, 1991-92; dir. No. Nev. Writing Project, 1999-2003. Mem. ASCD, NAESP, Calif. Kindergarten Assn., Internat. Reading Assn., Nat. Assn. Edn. of Young Children.

HENKE, ANA MARI, secondary education educator; b. Albuquerque, Apr. 21, 1954; d. David Ernest and Mary Anne (Gallegos) Sanchez; m. Michael John Henke, Aug. 14, 1976; children: Kristin Mari, Michelle Lee. BA in Spl. Edn., U. N.Mex., 1976, MA in Spl. Edn., 1983. Cert. elem. and secondary spl. edn. tchr., N.Mex.; cert. elem. and secondary phys. edn. tchr., N.Mex.; cert. elem. and secondary behavior disorder tchr., N.Mex. Tchr., supr. Perceptual Motor Learning Sch. U. N.Mex., Albuquerque, 1976, 82, tchr. phys. edn., 1980-82, Nat. Youth Sports Program, Albuquerque and San Diego, 1976-82; tchr. multihandicapped Chula Vista (Calif.) Pub. Schs., 1976-77; tchr. adaptive phys. edn. San Diego City Schs., 1977-78; lab. asst. Presbyn. Hosp., Albuquerque, 1979-80; tchr. Hermosa Jr. High Sch., Farmington, N.Mex., 1983-85, Heights Jr. High Sch., Farmington, 1985—. Mem. Leadership & Risk-Taking, Nat. Summit for Hispanic Women, Albuquerque, 1989; in-svc. exercise therapist Four Corners Reg. Ednl. Conf., Farmington, 1985-86; supr. parents workshop Intervention/Awareness for Substance Abuse, Heights Jr. High Sch., 1985-86; instr. workshop Farmington Schs., 1986; active nat. youth sports prog. Leaders Are in Demand, NCAA-U. N.Mex., 1989; active progs. Bldg. Self Esteem by Taking Risks-AWAREL, 1989, Leadership/Self-Esteem Multicultural Settings workshop, dir. new tchr. tng, Wellness & Prevention, Four Corners Retirement Assn., Body Talk, Presbyn. Med. Svcs. Coord. New Educator Support Program, 1989, 90; mem. Leadership San Juan, 1990-91; commr. N.Mex. Bd. Edn., 1992—, N.Mex. State Standards, 1992—. Named Young Career Woman of San Juan County Nat. Fedn. Bus. & Profl. Women, 1988-89, Leadership award, 1990. Mem. Hispanic Women's Leadership Inst., Phi Delta Kappa (sec. 1987—, v.p. 1988-89). Republican. Roman Catholic. Avocations: tennis, racquetball, aerobics. Home: 10530 City Lights Dr NE Albuquerque NM 87111-7537

HENKE, SUSAN KAY, elementary education educator; b. Berwyn, Ill., Aug. 7, 1949; d. Henry Edward and Joan Ellen (Bangston) Roberts; 1 child, Charles Roberts Even. BS in Edn., No. Ill. U., 1971; MEd, Nat. Louis U., 1996. Cert. in elem. edn., mental retardation, behaviorally/emotionally disturbed. Tchr. jr. h.s. mentally handicapped Dekalb (Ill.) Spl. Edn., 1971-73; tchr. mentally handicapped, dir. behavioral disturbed, coord. student svcs. Speed Devel. Ctr., Chicago Heights, Ill., 1973-76; tchr. kindergarten and presch. Alpha Presch. and Kindergarten, Homewood, Ill., 1980-82; tchr. behaviorally disturbed Hoover Elem. # 157, Calumet City, Ill., 1982-89, 2003, tchr. 4th grade, sci., 1989—. Cons. Curriculum Reform Bus., Calumet City, Ill., 1996; curriculum devel./assessment chair Hoover #157 Calumet City, 1996. Docent Lincoln Park Zoo, Chgo., 1992-96; clinic instr. Olympiad Coaches, 1998-99. Adaptor grantee Ill. Math. and Sci. Acad., 1992, 93, grantee U. Calif., Berkeley, 1988-89; Mus. to Classroom grantee, 1997-98. Mem. ASCD, AAUW, Nat. Sci. Tchr. Assn., Ill. Sci. Tchrs. Assn., Ill. Fedn. Tchrs. Avocations: gardening, music, birds, motorcycling. Home: 1374 Burnham Ave Calumet City IL 60409-5924 Office: Hoover Elem Sch # 157 1259 Superior Ave Calumet City IL 60409-5703

HENKEL, CYNTHIA LEIGH, elementary education educator; b. Cape Girardeau, Mo., July 15, 1960; d. Donald Gene and Doris Jo (Keaton) Lewis; m. Robert Revere Henkel, Mar. 21, 1987. BS in Edn., U. Mo., 1982; postgrad., NOVA. Cert. elem. tchr., Mo., N.Mex., Tex. Elem. tchr. Eldon (Mo.) Sch. Dist., 1982-84, Clark County Schs., Las Vegas, Nev., 1986-89; tchr. kindergarten and elem. grades, Pyongtaek (Republic of Korea) Am. Elem. Sch., 1989-90; tchr. Osan Am. Elem. Sch., Republic of Korea, 1990-91; elem. tchr. Alamogordo, N.Mex., 1995-98, N.E. Ind. Sch. Dist., San Antonio, 1998-99, Schertz, Cibilo, Universal City Ind. Sch. Dist., 1999—. Tchr. summer sch. Muckleshoot Indian Reservation, Auburn, Wash., 1985.

HENKENIUS, CHERYL GREIMAN, educational administrator; b. Nevada, Iowa, July 10, 1959; d. Darrell Boyd and Shirley Nadine (Harrison) Greiman; m. William E. Henkenius, Mar. 19, 1994. AA, Des Moines Area C.C., Boone, Iowa, 1979; BA, U. No. Iowa, 1981; MS, Iowa State U., 1988; adminstrv. cert., Drake U., 1994, adminstrv. specialist, 2000. Sixth grade tchr., coach Carroll (Iowa) Cmty. Schs., 1981-89, Johnston (Iowa) Cmty. Schs., 1989-94, elem. prin., coord. spl. edn., 1994—. Fin. com. mem. Immanuel Meth. Ch., Des Moines, 1991-94. Mem. Sch. Adminstrs. Iowa, Iowa Coun. Tchrs. Math., Johnston Edn. Assn. (chief negotiator 1991-94). Avocations: golf, volleyball. Office: Lawson Elem Johnston Cmty Schs 5450 NW 62d Ave Johnston IA 50311 E-mail: chenkenius@johnston.k12.ia.us.

HENLEY, ERNEST MARK, physics educator, university dean emeritus; b. Frankfurt, Germany, June 10, 1924; came to U.S., 1939, naturalized, 1944; s. Fred S. and Josy (Dreyfuss) H.; m. Elaine Dimitman, Aug. 21, 1948; children: M. Bradford, Karen M. B.E.E., CCNY, 1944; PhD, U. Calif. at Berkeley, 1952. Physicist Lawrence Radiation Lab., 1950-51; research assoc. physics dept. Stanford U., 1951-52; lectr. physics Columbia U., 1952-54; mem. faculty U. Wash., Seattle, 1954—, prof. physics, 1961-95; prof. emeritus, 1995—; chmn. dept. U. Wash., 1973-76, dean Coll. Arts and Scis., 1979-87, dir. Inst. for Nuclear Theory, 1990-91; assoc. dir. Inst. for Nuclear Theory U. Wash., 1991—. Rschr., author numerous publs. on symmetries, nuclear reactions, weak interactions and high energy particle interactions; chmn. Nuclear Sci. Adv. Com., 1986-89. Author: (with W. Thirring) Elementary Quantum Field Theory, 1962, (with H. Frauenfelder) Subatomic Physics, 1974, 2nd edit. 1991, Nuclear and Particle Physics, 1975; mng. editor Jour. Modern Physics, 1992—. Bd. dirs. Pacific Sci. Ctr., 1984-87, Wash. Tech. Ctr., 1983-87; trustee Associated Univs., Inc., 1989—, chmn. bd., 1993-96. Recipient sr. Alexander von Humboldt award, 1984, T.W. Bonner prize Am. Physics Soc., 1989, Townsend Harris medal CCNY, 1989; F.B. Jewett fellow, 1952-53, NSF sr. fellow, 1958-59, Guggenheim fellow, 1967-68, NATO sr. fellow, 1976-77. Fellow AAAS (chmn. physics sect. 1989-90), Am. Phys. Soc. (chmn. div. nuclear physics 1979-80, pres. 1992, sec. treas. N.W. sect. 1999—), Am. Acad. Arts and Scis.; mem. NAS (chmn. physics sect. 1998-2001), Sigma Xi. Office: Univ Wash Physics Dept PO Box 351560 Seattle WA 98195-1560 E-mail: henley@phys.washington.edu.

HENLEY, GLORIA JANE, elementary education educator; b. Chgo., Sept. 26, 1946; d. Robert Farley and Josephine (Bryley) Niven; m. David Arthur Liedtke, Apr. 6, 1972 (dec. Mar. 1981); children: Stephen, Jeffrey, Linda; m. Richard Dar Henley, Nov. 18, 1985; children: Clay, Eric, April, Crystal, John. BSEd, Ill. State U., 1968; MS, Chgo. State U., 1980. Lic. tchr., Ill. Tchr. Kirby Sch. Dist. 140, Tinley Park, Ill., 1968—; adj. prof. Gov.'s State U., Matteson, Ill., 1991—; trainer for developmental approaches in sci., health & tech. U. Hawaii, Honolulu, 1990—. Mem. math. and sci. curriculum com. Kirby Sch. Dist. 140, Tinley Park, 1970-92, assessment task force, 1992-93. Named Master Tchr. Presentor Argonne Nat. Lab., Ill., 1991. Mem. Nat. Assn. Downs Syndrome, Ill. Sci. Tchrs. Assn., South Suburban Reading Coun. Republican. Lutheran. Avocations: fishing, crafts, travel. Home: General Delivery Vanderwagen NM 87326-9999 Office: Helen Keller Sch 7846 163rd St Tinley Park IL 60477-1299

HENLEY, ROBERT LEE, school system administrator; b. Aug. 7, 1934; m. Patricia J. Ellis; 3 children. BA, Washington U., St. Louis, 1957, MEd, 1958; EdD, U. Mo., 1967. Tchr., counselor, pers. office, bus. mgr., asst. supt. Mehlville Sch. Dist., St. Louis, 1958-75; supt. schs. Independence (Mo.) Pub. Schs., 1975-93; asst. prof. U. Mo., Kansas City, 1991—. Cons. in field; instr. various colls. & univs., St. Louis and Columbia, 1975—. Trustee Andrew Drumm Inst., Independence, 1980—; bd. dirs. Am. Cancer Soc., Independence, 1978—; adv. com. Kansas City Arts Ptnrs. Program, 1990—. Recipient Community Leader award Comprehensive Mental health Svcs., Jackson County, Mo., 1983, Disting. Svc. award Mo. chpt. Am. Assn. on Mental Deficiency, 1983, Outstanding Educator award State of Mo., 1985, Innovation in Edn. award Nat. Ctr. for Ednl. Computing, 1985-86, Exec. Educator 100 award Exec. Educator Mag., 1987, Sch. Adminstr. award Kennedy Ctr./Alliance for Arts Edn., Washington, 1988, Disting. Svc. award Am. Assn. Sch. Adminstrs., 1993; named Mo. Supt. of Yr., 1992. Mem. Am. Assn. Sch. Adminstrs., Mo. Assn. Sch. Adminstrs. (exec. com. 1988—, Robert L. Pearce award 1991, Disting. Svc. award 1993), Jackson County Sch. Adminstrs. Assn. (pres. 1981), Mid-Am. Assn. Sch. Supts., Met. Sch. Study Group (pres. 1985-86), Independence C. of C.

HENN, SHIRLEY EMILY, retired librarian; b. Cleve., May 26, 1919; d. Albert Edwin and Florence Ely (Miller) H.; AB, Hollins Coll., 1941; MS, U. N.C., 1966; m. John Van Bruggen, July 14, 1944 (div. May 1947); 1 child, Peter Albert (dec.). Libr. asst. Hollins (Va.) Coll., 1943-44, 61-64, reference libr., 1965-84, ret., 1984; advt. mgr. R.M. Kellogg Co., Three Rivers, Mich., 1946-47; exec. sec. Hollins Coll. Alumnae Assn., 1947-55; real estate salesman Fowlkes & Kefauver, Roanoke, Va., 1955-61. Pres. Soc. for Prevention Cruelty to Animals, 1959-61, 69-72, bd. dirs., 1972-81; donor Mary Williamson award in Humanities Hollins Coll., 1947—; endowed fund for purchase books children's lit. collection Fishburn Libr. Hollins Coll., 1986-93; donor, patron Women's Ctr. Hollins Coll., 1993—, Scholarship Aids, 1994, Children's Lit. Masters Program, 1993—; active Nat. Trust for Historic Preservation, 1994—, Roanoke Valley Hist. Soc., 1984—, Roanoke Valley Hist. Mus., Roanoke Valley Sci. Mus., Cystic Fibrosis Found., 1995—, Nat. Audubon Soc., 1995—, MADD, 1995—; donor Va. Tech. Found. for restoration Hotel Roanoke, 1992—; ptnr. Spl. Olympics, 1995—. Recipient Rath award, 1984, Critical Scholarship award, 1995, Creative Achievement award, 1995—. Mem. ALA, MADD, Am. Alumni Council (dir. 1952-54, dir. women's activities 1952-54), Va. Libr. Assn., Nat. DAR (libr. Nancy Christian Fleming chpt. Roanoke 1977-84, regent 1984-88, chair Good Citizenship award 1990-92, Am. Essay awards 1991—), Poetry Soc. Va. Clubs: Quota Internat. (chpt. pres. 1958-60) (Roanoke), Antique Automobile Club Am., Roanoke Valley Antique Auto Club, Roanoke Valley Mopar Club, Children's Lit. Assn., Am. Mus. Nat. History, Blue Ridge Zool. Soc., Cystic Fibrosis Found., Poetry Soc. Va., Nat. Audubon Soc. Author, illustrator: Adventures of Hooty Owl and His Friends, 1953; editor: Hollins Alumnae Bull., 1947-56. Avocations: collecting teddy bears, antique French and English plates, bells, pewter. Home: PO Box 2867 Roanoke VA 24001-2867

HENNESSY, JOHN L. academic administrator; B in Engring. in Elec. Engring., Villanova U., 1973; MS in Computer Sci., SUNY, Stony Brook, 1975, PhD in Computer Sci., 1977. Asst. prof. elec. engring. Stanford U., Calif., 1977—83, assoc. prof. elec. engring., 1983—86, prof. elec. engring. and computer sci., 1986—, chmn. dept. computer sci., 1994—96, dean Sch. Engring., 1996—99, provost, 1999—2000, pres., 2000—. Founder, chief scientist MIPS Computer Sys., 1984—92; chief arch. Silicon Graphics Computer Sys., 1992—98; founder MIPS Techs. (formerly MIPS Computer Sys.), 1998—; chmn. bd. dirs. T-span; mem. com. study internat. devels. in computer sci. and tech. NRC, 1988, mem. computer sci. and tech. bd., 1989—94, mem. com. study acad. careers for exptl. computer scientists, 1992—93, mem. statttus and direction of high performance computing and comm. initiative, 1995, mem. commn. phys. scis., math. and applications, 1998—99; mem. adv. com. computer and info. sci. and engring. NSF, 1992—96, chair oversight rev. of computer and info. sci. and engring. instnl. infrastructure program, 1992, mem. task force on future supercomputer ctrs. program, 95; tech. adv. bd. Microsoft Corp., 1992—96, Virtual Machine Works, 1995—96, Tensilica, 1998—99; strategic adv. bd. Net-Power, 1992—95; mem. fellowship sel. com. Sloan Found., 1993—96; chmn. info. sci. and tech. Def. Advances Rsch. Projects Found., 1993—96, chair, 1994—95; mem. com. study investment strategy DARPA Def. Sci. Bd., 1998—99; mem. various conf. coms.; spkr. in field. Co-author (with D.A. Patterson): Computer Organization and Design: The Hardware/Software Interface, 1993, Computer Organization and Design: The Hardware/Software Interface, 2d edit., 1998; co-author: Computer Architecture: A Quantitative Approach, 1990; contbr. articles to profl. jours. Named Profl. Young Investigator, NSF, 1984; recipient Disting. Alumnus award, SUNY, Stony Brook, 1991, J. Stanley Morehouse Meml. award, Villanova U., 1997. Fellow: IEEE (Emmanuel R. Piore award 1994, John Von Neumann medal 2000), Am. Acad. Arts and Scis., Assn. Computing Machinery; mem.: Nat. Acad. Engring. (peer selection com. computer sci. and engring. 1996—99, chair 2000), Pi Mu Epsilon, Eta Kappa Nu, Tau Beta Pi. Office: Stanford U Office of the Provost Bldg 10 Stanford CA 94305-2061 Fax: 650-724-4062. E-mail: hennessy@stanford.edu.

HENNINGS, DOROTHY GRANT (MRS. GEORGE HENNINGS), education educator; b. Paterson, N.J., Mar. 15, 1935; d. William Albert and Ethel Barbara (Moll) Grant; m. George Hennings, June 15, 1968. AB, Barnard Coll., 1956; MEd (NSF Acad. Yr. Inst. grantee), U. Va., 1959; EdD (Field Enterprise grantee), Columbia, 1965. Tchr. Pierrepont Elem. Sch., Rutherford, N.J., 1956-58, Thomas Jefferson jr. High Sch., Fair Lawn, N.J., 1959-64; prof. edn. Kean U. of N.J., Union, 1965-99, disting. prof. edn., 1999—2002, disting. prof. emeritus, 2002—. Author citation N.J. Inst. Tech., Div. Continuing Edn., 1982; author: (with B. Grant) Teacher Moves, 1971; Content and Craft: Written Expression in the Elementary School, 1973; Smiles, Nods and Pauses: Activities to Enrich Children's Communication Skills, 1974; Mastering Classroom Communication: What Interaction Analysis Tells the Teacher, 1975; (with G. Hennings) Keep Earth Clean, Blue and Green: Environmental Activities for Young People, 1976; Words, Sounds, and Thoughts: More Activities to Enrich Children's Communication Skills, 1977; Communication in Action: Teaching the Language Arts, 1978, 8th edit. 2002 (with D. Russell) Listening Aids Through the Grades, 1979; (with G. Hennings) Today's Elementary Social Studies, 1980, 2d edit., 1989; Written Expression in the Language Arts, 1981; Teaching Communication and Reading Skills in the Content Areas, 1982; (with L. Fay) Star Show, 1989, Grand Tour, 1989, Previews, 1989, Reading with Meaning: Strategies for College Reading, 1990, 5th rev. edit., 2002, Poets Journal, 1991, Beyond the Read Aloud: Learning to Read Through Listening to and Reflecting on Literature, 1992, Vocabulary Growth: Strategies for College Word Study, 2001, Words Are Wonderful: An Interactive Approach to Vocabulary, books 1 and 2, 2003; contbr. articles to Edn., The Record, Lang. Arts, Sci. Tchr., The Reading Tchr., Jour. of Adolescent & Adult Lit., Jour. of Reading, Tchr. to Tchrs., Sci. and Children, Early Years, Reading Rsch. and Instrn., New Eng. Jour. of History, Jour. Reading Edn., others. Recipient Edn. Press award, 1974, Outstanding Article award, 1999. Mem. Nat. Coun. Tchrs. English, N.J. Reading Assn. (Disting. Svc. to Reading award 1993), Internat. Reading Assn. (Outstanding Tchr. Educator in Reading award 1992), Suburban Reading Coun., Phi Beta Kappa, Phi Delta Kappa, Phi Kappa Phi, Kappa Delta Pi. Home: 21 Flintlock Dr Warren NJ 07059-5014 E-mail: hennings@verizon.net.

HENRICHS, ALBERT MAXIMINUS, classicist, educator; b. Cologne, Germany, Dec. 29, 1942; came to U.S., 1971; s. Johannes and Berti H.; m. Ingrid Ursula Schaadt, June 4, 1965 (div. Mar. 1990); children: Markus, Helen Felicitas; m. Maura Giles, June 19, 1997 (div. Apr. 2001). Student, U. Cologne, 1962-66, U. Bonn, 1962-63; Dr.phil., U. Cologne, 1966, habilitation, 1969; A.M. (hon.), Harvard U., 1972. Vis. lectr. U. Mich., Ann Arbor, 1967-69; prof. U. Cologne, 1970-71; asso. prof. classics U. Calif., Berkeley, 1971-73; prof. Greek and Latin. Harvard U., Cambridge, Mass., 1973-84, Eliot prof. Greek lit., 1984—, chmn. dept. classics, 1982-88, mem. affiliated faculty Div. Sch., 1982—90; Sather prof. classical lit. U. Calif., Berkeley, 1990. Sr. fellow Ctr. for Hellenic Studies, Washington, 1992-97. Author: Didymos der Blinde Kommentar zu Hiob (Tura-Papyrus), 2 vols., 1968, Die Phoinikika des Lollianos, 1972, Die Götter Griechenlands, 1987, Warum soll ich denn tanzen? Dionysisches im Chor der griechischen Tragödie, 1996; editor: Harvard Studies in Classical Philology, 1975-79, 2001—; adv. bd. Harvard Libr. Bull., 1981-95, Greek, Roman and Byzantine Studies, 1984—; contbr. articles on ancient Greek lit., papyrology, mythology and religion to scholarly jours. Fellow Am. Acad. Arts and Scis.; mem. Am. Philos. Soc., Am. Philol. Assn., Assn. Internationale de Papyrologues., Egypt Exploration Soc. Home: 272 Concord Ave Cambridge MA 02138-1338 Office: Harvard U Dept Classics 212 Boylston Hall Cambridge MA 02138

HENRIKSON, RAY CHARLES, retired anatomy educator; b. Worcester, Mass., May 22, 1937; s. Sigurd and Theresa (Edlin) H.; m. Katherine Pointer, Oct. 29, 1966; children: Charles A., Andrew J. BSc, U. Mass., 1959; MSc, Brown U., 1961; PhD, Boston U., 1966. Instr. Boston U. Med. Sch., 1966-67; scientist Commonwealth Sci. and Indsl. Rsch. Orgn., Australia, 1967-69; asst. prof. Columbia U., N.Y.C., 1969-76; assoc. prof. Albany (N.Y.) Med. Coll., 1976-89, prof., 1989—2002; ret., 2002. Mem. com. Nat. Bd. Med. Examiners, 1985-88. Author: Key Facts in Histology, 1986, NMS Histology, 1997, (CD-ROM) Histology Laboratory-An Interactive Review, 1999. Mem. Am. Assn. Anatomists, Am. Soc. Cell Biology. Office: Albany Med Coll Anatomy Dept (MC-135) Albany NY 12208 E-mail: rhenriks@nycap.rr.com.

HENRY, ANN RAINWATER, retired education educator; b. Okla., Nov. 2, 1939; d. George Andrew and Opal Norma (Cohea) Rainwater; m. Morriss M. Henry, Aug. 1, 1964; children: Paul, Katherine, Mark. BA, U. Ark., 1961, MA, 1964, JD, 1971. Bar: Ark. 1971. Pvt. practice law, Fayetteville, Ark., 1971-72; instr. Coll. Bus. Adminstrn. U. Ark., Fayetteville, 1976-78, asst. prof., 1978-84, assoc. prof., 1984—, asst. dean, 1984-86, assoc. dean, 1986-89, faculty chair, 1989-91. Bd. dirs. City of Fayetteville, 1977-83, 91-92, McIlroy Bd., Fayetteville, 1986—; chmn. cert. com. Ark. Tchrs. Evaluation, 1984-85; mem. Ark. Local Svcs. Adv. Bd., 1980-88, Ark. Gifted and Talented, 1989—, Ark. State Bd. Edn., 1985-86; Dem. nominee for 3d Dist. Ark. U.S. Ho. Reps., 1996. Mem. Ark. Alumni Assn. (bd. dirs., asst. treas. 1989-93), Fayetteville C. of C. (bd. dirs. 1983-85), Ark. Bar Assn. (chmn. ethics com. 1986-87). Democrat. Methodist. Avocations: reading, sailing, needlepoint, gardening. Home: 2465 Township Common Dr Fayetteville AR 72703-3568

HENRY, CYNTHIA ANN, retired gerontology nurse, educator; b. New Albany, Ind., Nov. 4, 1959; d. Walter Maxwell and Lois Velleda (Dreher) Beane; children: Christopher, David, Deborah, Micheal, Crystal; m. Johnnie Lee Henry, Feb. 27, 1998. Cert. in journalism, Newspaper Inst., 1985; cert. in med. assisting, Barton Sch., 1984; LPN, Summers County Sch. Nursing, 1988; ASN, SUNY, Albany, 1990. Tchr. health and wellness, 2002—; pvt. practice Team Wellness, 2002—. Author numerous poems. Office: 29 Zenith Rd Gap Mills WV 24941-9491 E-mail: CyndiHenry@iglide.net., CJEnterprises@iglide.net.

HENRY, ERNESTYNE ETHEL THATCH, educational administrator; b. St. Louis, July 19, 1917; d. Clarence Hardwill and Evelena (Thompson) Thatch; m. Horace McKinley Henry, Sept. 1, 1942; children: John Harvey McKinley, Joan Marcille Vernadette. U. Ark., 1938, 1936; BS, 1940; MS, U. Ill., 1950; postgrad. various colls. including, U. N.Mex., U. Colo., Colo. State U., U. Santa Clara, U. Denver, 1954-84. Tchr. Ft. Smith (Ark.) pub. schs., 1940-42; with Civil Svc., Denver, 1942-43; tchr. East St. Louis (Ill.) pub. schs., 1947-52; diagnostic and prescriptive coordinator Denver pub. schs., 1952-84; ret., 1984; asst. prin. Fairview Elem. Sch., Denver, 1961-62; founder, dir. Thatch Enterprises, Denver, 1989—. Lectr. U. Colo., summer 1959. Contbr. articles to profl. jours. Precinct com. Dem. Party, Denver, 1953-78, voter registration staff, 1952—. Mem. U. Ark. Pine Bluffs Alumni Assn. (bd. dirs. 1978—, Outstanding Alumni), AAUW (v.p. 1986-87), Nat. Coun. Negro Women (v.p.), United Teaching Profession (bldg. rep. 1980-84), Internat. Rels. Club (treas. 1970-89), Opera Colo., Top Ladies of Distinction (charter pres. 1989—), U. Ill. Alumni Assn., Lioness Club (treas. 1990), Phi Delta Kappa, Sigma Gamma Rho (bd. dirs. 1963-65, 69-75). Democrat. Methodist. Avocations: travel, drama, bridge. Office: Thatch Enterprises 1044 Downing St Apt 207 Denver CO 80218-2959

HENRY, GARY NORMAN, air force officer, astronautical engineer; b. Fort Wayne, Ind., Nov. 3, 1961; s. Norman Thomas and Elaine Cathrine (Schabb) H. BS in Astro. Engring. with distinction, USAF Acad., 1984; MS in Aero./Astronautical Engring., Stanford U., 1988; grad., USAF Test Pilot Sch., 1994, USAF Air Command & Staff Coll., 1997; student, Air War Coll., Air U., Maxwell AFB, Ala., 2002—03. CFP. Commd. 2d lt. USAF, 1984, advanced through grades to lt. col., 2000; project engr. USAF Weapons Lab., Kirtland AFB, N.Mex., 1984-87; asst. prof. astronautics USAF Acad., Colorado Springs, 1989-93; flight test engr. 418 Flight Test Squadron, Edwards AFB, Calif., 1993-94, chief flight dynamics br., 1994-95; exec. officer USAF Flight Test Ctr., Edwards, 1995-96; dep. dir. test and evaluation Airborne Laser Sys. Program Office, Kirtland AFB, N.Mex., 1997-99; lead airborne laser (PEM) Air Staff, The Pentagon, 1999-2001; dep. divsn. chief for counter air directorate global power Asst. Sec. of the Air Force, The Pentagon, 2001—02; chief advanced tech. divsn. Space Superiority Sys. Program Office, Los Angeles AFB, Calif., 2003—; sole propr. Polaris Fin. Svcs., 1987—. Editor: (textbook) Space Propulsion Analysis and Design, 1995; contbr. articles to profl. jours. Recipient sci. and engring. award USAF, 1993. Mem. AIAA (sr. mem., hybrid rocket tech. com. 1993-94, Young Engr. of Yr. Rocky Mountain region 1993), Fin. Planning Assn. Achievements include research director of 1st successful Department of Defense land-based hybrid sounding rocket flight. E-mail: gary.genry@losangeles.af.mel.

HENRY, HELGA IRMGARD, liberal arts educator; b. Soppo, Buea, Cameroon, May 30, 1915; d. Carl Jacob and Hedwig (Kloeber) Bender; m. Carl F.H. Henry, Aug. 17, 1940; children: Paul Brentwood (dec. 1993), Carol Jennifer. BA, Wheaton Coll., Ill., 1936, MA, 1937; M of Religious Edn., No. Bapt. Theol. Sem., 1945. Dean of women, instr. in German State Tchrs.' Coll., Ellendale, N.D., 1937-40; librarian, instr. in lit., religious edn. No. Bapt. Theol. Sem., Chgo., 1940-47; instr. German Wheaton Coll., 1945-47; assoc. prof. edn. Pasadena (Calif.) Coll., 1951-60; vis. instr. religious edn. Ea. Bapt. Theol. Sem., Phila., 1963-66. Chmn., treas. The Elmer Bisbee Found., 1986-91. Author: Mission on Main Street, 1955, Cameroon on a Clear Day, 1999; translator: Paulus Scharpff, History of

Evangelism, 1966. Trustee Ea. Bapt. Theol. Sem., 1971-73. Home: 1141 Hus Dr Apt 206 Watertown WI 53098-3258

HENRY, KAREN LEE, writer, lecturer; b. Grand Rapids, Mich., Feb. 20, 1944; d. Leo John and Mary Alice (Mallick) Henry. AS with high honors, Davenport Coll., 1983; BA, U. Mich., 1989. Writer Palestine Human Rights Campaign, Chgo., 1984-85; journalist Al Fajr, Jerusalem, 1985-86; dir. activities Villa Maria Retirement Cmty., Grand Rapids, Mich., 1990-93; libr. asst. Grand Rapids Pub. Libr., 1994—2000; freelance writer, lectr. Grand Rapids; exec. dir. dept. justice Weed & Seed, 2000—. Ednl. cons. on Mid. East Inst. for Global Edn., Grand Rapids, 1983—, bd. dirs., 1995—. Contbr. articles to profl. jours. Apptd. Housing Bd. Appeals, Grand Rapids, 1984; spl. projects dir. Econ. Devel. Corp., Grand Rapids, 1983; active Grand Rapids AIDS Task Force, 1986-92, Coop Am., Feminist Majority, Am. Ednl. Trust, New Jewish Agenda, Am. Arab Anti-Discrimination Com., YWCA, Nat. Humane Soc., Expressions for Women; bd. dirs. YWCA, Grand Rapids, 1996-97, Am. Friends Svc. Com. of Great Lakes Region, 1996—; pres., founding mem. Women's Action Network, Grand Rapids, 1993—; mem. pediat. oncology resource team Butterworth Hosp., 1998—, Racial Justice Inst., 1999-, Grand Rapids Inst. Info. Democracy, 1998—; chmn. task force Project Safe Neighborhood, 2002 Recipient Appreciation cert. Econ. Devel. Corp., 1983, Housing Appeal Bd., 1985, Chicago House, 1987. Mem. AAUW, Nat. Assn. Arab Am. Women, Nat. Mus. Women in Arts, Am. for Mid. East Understanding, Union Palestinian Women's Assn., Gilda's Club. Avocations: hiking, discussing books. Home and Office: 29 Wallinwood Ave NE Grand Rapids MI 49503-3719

HENRY, KILA ANN, secondary educator; b. Bethany, Mo., July 29, 1950; BS in Edn., Northwest Mo. State U., Maryville, 1972, MS in Biology, 1981. Sci. instr. South Nodaway R-IV, Barnard, Mo., 1974-80, Northeast Nodaway R-V, Ravenwood, Mo., 1980—. Sec. Ravenwood Sr. Citizens Housing, 1974-95, treas., 1983-95. Recipient Nat. Tchr. award, RadioShack, 2002, Nat. Tchr. awards, Radioshack, 2002; fellow Christa McAuliffe awardee, 1994. Mem. Community Tchrs. Assn., Chemistry Educators Assn. (pres. 1980-81), Nat. Sci. Tchrs. Assn., Mo. State Tchrs. Assn., Mo. Jr. Acad. Sci. (life), Sci. Tchrs. Mo. (life, high sch. editor 1989-90), Mo. Sci. Olympiad (exec. com. 1989—), Nat. Sci. Edn. Leadership Assn. Avocations: farming, gardening. Home: PO Box 186 Ravenwood MO 64479-0186 Office: Northeast Nodaway R-V 126 S High School Ave Ravenwood MO 64479-9174

HENRY, LETUS KAY, elementary education educator, hair designer; b. Pocola, Okla., July 29, 1942; d. Joe L. and Edna Marie (Williams) Howard; m. Thomas O. Henry, Mar. 31, 1962 (div. 1987); 1 child, Tommy Dewayne. Diploma, Millies Beauty Coll., 1961; AA, Carl Albert Jr. Coll., 1981; BS in Edn., Northea. Okla. State U., 1982, MEd, 1987. Hair designer owner Kay Styling Salon, Pocola, Okla., 1965-75; tchr. elem. Pocola Sch., 1982-95; hair designer J.C. Penney Styling Salon, Fort Smith, Ark., 1990-95; tchr. tutor, 1990-95. Tchr. cons. Northeastern State Coll., Tahlequah, Okla., 1990-91, Westark Coll., Fort Smith, Ark., 1991-93. Tchr. Am. Heart Assn., Pocola, 1991-92, chair Am. Cancer Soc., Fort Smith, 1992-95, St. Jude Children Hosp., 1992-94. Mem. NEA, Okla. Edn. Assn., Pocola Classroom Tchr. Assn., United Teaching Profession. Republican. Methodist. Avocations: tennis, swimming, painting. Home: 9700 Weddington Rd Fort Smith AR 72908-9502

HENRY, MARY LOU SMELSER, elementary education educator; b. Russellville, Ala., Mar. 2, 1953; d. Jessie Clifton and Margie Lou (Willingham) Smelser; m. Don M. Henry, Aug. 26, 1972; children: Aaron, Nathan. Student, N.W. Ala. State Jr. Coll., 1971-72; BS, Middle Tenn. State U., 1975; MA, Tenn. Tech. U., 1986, postgrad., 1998. Cert. elem. tchr., secondary tchr. history and sociology, Tenn., Ala. Substitute tchr. Warren County Bd. Edn., McMinnville, Tenn., 1979-82; tchr. LaPetite Acad., McMinnville, 1982-83; tchr. 2d grade Grundy County Bd. Edn., Altamont, Tenn., 1983—. Coord. Drug Awareness Task Force, 1990-92; mem. Grundy County Edn. Assn. Recipient Tchr. of Yr. award 1987-88, Trophy award 4H, 1988-91. Mem. NEA, Grundy County Edn. Assn. (sec. 1989-90, chmn. pub. rels. 1990-91, rep. North Elem. 1990-91, editor Tchr. Times 1989-91, pres. 1993-94, chair grievance com. 1994-95, negotiations com. 1993-99, sec. 2000-01, sec.-treas. 2001—), Tenn. Edn. Assn. (Cert. of Appreciation 1991, women status com. 1994-96). Home: 212 Forest Dr Mc Minnville TN 37110-2333

HENRY, MYRON, academic administrator; Provost Kent State U., U. So. Miss., Hattiesburg, Miss., 1999—2001, faculty senate pres., 2002—. Office: The Univ Southern Mississippi 2701 Hardy Street Hattiesburg MS 39406*

HENRY, NANCY SINCLAIR, middle school educator; b. Alexandria, Va., Aug. 4, 1940; d. John Wilson and Margaret Lucille (Bryant) Sinclair; m. James Russell Henry, June 21, 1969; 1 child, Ryan Sinclair. BA in Elem. Edn., Coll. William and Mary, 1962; MEd in Instrn. and Curriculum, Lynchburg Coll., 1997. Cert. tchr., Va. Primary tchr. Alexandria Pub. Schs., 1962-69, 70-73, Louisa County Pub. Schs., Louisa, Va., 1969-70; presch. tchr. St. Paul's Nursery and Day Sch., Alexandria, 1973-81; elem. and mid. tchr. Bedford County Pub. Schs., Bedford, Va., 1981—, math.-coop. learning cons., 1988—; cons. learning ctrs. Alexandria Pub. Schs., 1970-73. Cons. math. and coop. learning Appomattox County Schs., Appomattox, Va., 1989, 90, 91, Bedford County Schs., 1990-96, mentor, 1996—. Vol. James Earl Carter U.S. Presdl. campaign, Alexandria, 1976; pres. Bookmark Club, Bedford, 1987-88, Bedford Hist. Soc., 1989-90 (pres. 1998-2002); trustee Bedford Regional Libr., 1988-96. Named Tchr. of Yr. Bedford County Mid. Sch., 1990-91, Otter chpt. DAR, 1996-97, 97-98; grantee Va. Commn. on Fine Arts, 1989-90. Mem. NEA, Nat. Coun. Tchrs. Math., Nat. Mic. Sch. Assn., Va. Edn. Assn., Piedmont Area Reading Coun., Va. Reading Assn., Bedford County Edn. Assn. (Tchr. of Month 1991), Phi Kappa Delta, Alpha Delta Kappa, Phi Delta Phi. Episcopalian. Avocations: quilting, camping. Home: 1096 Meadowbrook Dr Bedford VA 24523-3020 Office: Bedford Mid Sch Longwood Ave Bedford VA 24523-3402 E-mail: downdogstreet@juno.com.

HENRY, NICHOLAS LLEWELLYN, public administration educator; b. Seattle, May 22, 1943; s. Samuel Houston and Ann (Connor) H.; m. Muriel Bunney; children: Adrienne Richardson, Miles Houston. BA, Centre Coll. Ky., 1965; MA, Pa. State U., 1967; M.P.A., Ind. U., 1970, PhD, 1971. Asst. to dean Coll. Arts and Scis.; instr. Ind. State U., 1967-69; vis. asst. prof. U. N.Mex., 1971-72; asst. prof. polit. sci. U. Ga., 1972-75, assoc. prof., 1975-78, prof., 1978-87, dir. Ctr. Pub. Affairs, 1975-80, dean Coll. Pub. Programs, 1980-87; prof., pres. Ga. So. U., Statesboro, 1987-98, prof. polit. sci., 1998—. Author or editor 12 books; contbr. numerous articles to profl. jours. Recipient Author of Yr. award Assn. Sci. Jours., Laverne Burchfield award ASPA, 2002; named One of 100 Most Influential People in Ga., Ga. Trend, 1994. Fellow Nat. Acad. Pub. Adminstrn.; mem. Cosmos Club (Washington). Office: Ga So U PO Box 8009 Statesboro GA 30460-1000

HENRY, PATRICIA JEAN, educational association administrator, consumer products company executive; b. Luling, Tex., Dec. 8, 1929; d. Willie Adolph and L. Belle (Streetman) Streich; m. Tommy Jo Henry, Aug. 27, 1949; children: Michael Wayne, Mark Allen, Marcia Lynn Stockwell. BA Music Edn., East Tex. Baptist U., 1951. Prin. owner, corp. officer Gibson's Discount Ctr., Tex., Okla., 1959—; bd. dirs. Nat. Congress Parents and Tchrs., 1981—; pres. Nat. Parent Tchr. Assn., Chgo., 1991-93. Bd. dirs. Okla. Acad. State Goals, 1986-90, Okla. Congress Parents and Tchrs., pres. 1981-83, various offices, coms.; bd. trustees Okla. Acad. Decathlon Inc., 1984-89; mem. Okla. Coalition Pub. Edn., 1981-83, Nat. Schs. Pub. Rels. Assn., 1986—, Horace Mann League, 1986—, So. Indsl. Devel. Coun., Pecan Grove Elem. Sch. PTA, all Okla PTA's; various past positions Nat. Congress Parents and Tchrs. Chmn. Lawton C. of C., 1986-87, 87-88 (spl. recognition to outstanding local educator, 1981-82); gov's adv. com. Ednl. Block Grants State Okla., 1981-89; Southwest Okla. Mtn. Metro Econ. Devel. Task Force, 1986-90, pres. 1988-90; mem. Gov's. Internat. adv. team, 1988-89, Commn. Reform State Govt., 1984-85, State Okla. Econ. Devel. Commn., 1981-86, Okla. adv. coun. Juvenile Justice, 1981-87, Okla. Commn. Children, Youth, Families, 1979-83; chmn. Quality Life Task Force Okla. Dept. Commerce, 1987; bd. dirs., co-founder Pathway House, 1987-90, Southwestern Hosp., 1987-90, Great Plains Area Vo-Tech Found., Lawton, Okla., 1981-89, Lawton Philharmonic Orch. Soc., Lawton/Fort Sill United Way, 1978, 83, 84, (gen. campaign chmn. 1984). Recipient Ladies in the News award Okla. Hospitality Club, 1982, Bus. in the Arts award Lawton Arts Humanities Coun., 1983, Ptnrs. Excellence in Edn. award Okla. Schs. Pub. Rels. Assn., 1984, Friends Edn. award Profl. Educators Lawton, 1984, Pub. Leadership award Higher Edn. Alumni Coun. Okla., 1985, Disting. Svc. award Cameron U., 1986, Alexis de Tocqueville Soc. award United Way Am., 1987, Artillery Order Molly Pitcher U.S. Field Artillery Assn., 1987, Citizen Humanities award Lawton Arts and Humanities Coun., 1988, Rising Above Ordinary Women of Achievement award Okla. Fedn. Bus. Profl. Women's Club, 1988, 1st Lady of Yr. award Beta Sigma Phi, 1988, medal honor DAR, 1993; Pat Henry Day proclaimed by State of Okla., 1993; Pat Henry Elem. Sch. named in her honor Bd. of Edn. Lawton, Okla., 1993; Recipient citation The State Senate of Okla., 1993. Mem. Nat. Congress Parents Tchrs. (hon. life mem., various states), Assn. U.S. Army (pres. southwest Okla. chpt. 1988-89), Comanche County Veteran's Coun. (hon. mem.). Avocations: jogging, snow skiing. also: Gibson Discount Ctr PO Box 6720 Lawton OK 73506-0720

HENRY, PAULA LOUISE (PAULA LOUISE HENRY COOVER), academic administrator; b. White Plains, NY, Mar. 5, 1947; d. Raymond Francis and Carolyn Louise (Landis) Henry; m. John David Coover, Nov. 18, 1967 (div. Jan. 1992); children: Jeffrey Darren, Robert Benson, Jennifer Danielle (dec.). AA in Psychology, Monmouth U., 1967; student, Pace U., 1972-76; BA in Psychology, Monmouth U., 1993. Chair gifted and talented com., then pres. Hunterdon County (N.J.) Coun. PTAs, 1980-86; chmn. county pres. group, nat. conv. del., gen. conv. chmn. N.J. Congress Parents & Tchrs., Trenton, 1985-87, field svc. chmn., 1985-89, pres., 1989-91, immediate past pres., 1991-93, hon. v.p., 1991—; asst. to dean Rutgers Bus. Sch., Newark and New Brunswick, 1995—2002; campus adviser Office Student Jud. Affairs, Rutgers U., Newark and New Brunswick, 1996—, sr. exec. asst. univ. rel. New Brunswick, 2002—. Sch. bd. Union Twp. Bd. Edn., N.J., 1983-86, assembly del., 1984-86, legis. chmn. 1984-86, policy chmn. 1986, edn. chmn. 1984-85; trustee Jennie M. Haver Scholarship Fund, 1984-89; active Hunterdon County Edn. Coalition, 1984-88, Child Abuse and Missing Children Com., Hunterdon, 1987-98, Hunterdon County Youth Svcs. Commn., Flemington, 1987-98, N.J. Gov.'s Commn. on Quality Edn., 1991-93; treas. Fannie B. Abbott Student Loan Found., 1985-90, trustee, 1985-80; v.p. Hunterdon County Child Assault Protection Program, 1986-90; strategic planning com. United Way of Essex and West Hudson, 1994-95; trustee Good News Home for Women, 1997-2002, sec., 1999-2002; governing bd. Quality Edn. N.J., 1998—, co-chair, 2000-02, immediate past chair 2002; bd. dirs. Recordings for the Blind and Dyslexic, NJ, 2001-02, Bus. and Edn. Partnership Somerset/Hunterdon Counties, 2002—; mem. Raritan Millstone Heritage Alliance Bd., 2002—. Democrat. Methodist. Home: PO Box 5228 Clinton NJ 08809-0228 Office: Rutgers Univ Univ Relations New Brunswick NJ 08901-1281 E-mail: pauhen@yahoo.com., phenry@oldqueens.rutgers.edu.

HENRY, RICHARD CONN, astrophysicist, educator; b. Toronto, Mar. 7, 1940; came to U.S., 1962, naturalized, 1973; s. Edwin Mackie and Jean Bonar (Conn) H.; m. Rita Mahon, May 10, 1975; children: George William, Mark Winston. B.Sc., U. Toronto, 1961, MA, 1962; PhD, Princeton U., 1967. Rsch. assoc. Inst. Advanced Study, 1967; rsch. appointee E.O. Hulburt Ctr. Space Rsch., Naval Rsch. Lab., Washington, 1967-69; research physicist E.O. Hulburt Center Space Research, Naval Research Lab., 1969-76; asst. prof. Johns Hopkins U., Balt., 1968-74, assoc. prof., 1974-77, prof., 1977—, mem. prin. profl. staff Applied Physics Lab., 1991—. Vis. staff Los Alamos Nat. Lab.; dep. dir. astrophysics divsn. NASA, 1976-78; dir. Md. Space Grant Consortium, 1989—; chair Nat. Coun. Space Grant Dirs., 1998-2000. Recipient Gold medal Royal Astron. Soc. Can., 1961; Alfred P. Sloan fellow, 1971-75 Fellow AAAS; mem. Am. Phys. Soc., Am. Astron. Soc., Internat. Astron. Union. Home: 12515 Meadowood Dr Silver Spring MD 20904-2922 Office: Johns Hopkins U Dept Physics And Astro Baltimore MD 21218 E-mail: henry@jhu.edu.

HENRY, RONALD JAMES WHYTE, university official; b. Belfast, No. Ireland, Feb. 5, 1940; came to U.S., 1965; s. William James Louis and Mary Ann (Whyte) H.; children: Norah Lynn, Andrea Marie. BSc, Queen's U., Belfast, 1961, PhD, 1964. Asst. lectr. Queen's U., 1964-65; rsch. assoc. Goddard Space Flight Ctr., Greenbelt, Md., 1965-66; asst. physicist Kitt Peak Nat. Obs., Tucson, 1966-69; assoc. prof. La. State U., Baton Rouge, 1969-73, prof., 1973-89, chmn. dept. physics and astronomy, 1976-82, dean basic scis., 1982-89; v.p. acad. affairs Auburn (Ala.) U., 1989-91; provost, exec. v.p. for acad. affairs Miami U., Oxford, Ohio, 1991-94; provost, v.p. acad. affairs Ga. State U., Atlanta, 1994—. Com. on undergrad. sci. edn. Nat. Rsch. Coun., 1998—. Fellow Am. Physics Soc. Republican. Avocation: golf. Office: Ga State U Atlanta GA 30303 E-mail: rhenry@gsu.edu.

HENRY, SALLY, assistant principal; b. Elyria, Ohio; d. Robert A. and Dorothy M. Eskins; m. James M. Henry (dec.); children: Ronald, Gregory, Mark, Tammy, Gary. A in Liberal Arts, Lorain County C.C., Elyria, 1978; B in Elem. Edn., U. Ky., 1980, M in Elem. Edn., 1981, EdD, 1987. Cert. tchg. and leadership Ky., tchg., leadership and ESOL Fla. Tchr. mid. sch. St. Peter Sch., Lexington, Ky., 1983—85; adj. instr. Lexington C.C., 1985—88; grad. asst. U. Ky., 1985—87; curriculum cons. Harcourt Brace, Orlando, Fla., 1988—89; tchr., educator Polk County Schs., Bartow, Fla., 1989—95; program specialist Collier County Schs., Naples, Fla., 1995—99, asst. prin., 1999—. Facilitator, chair Sch. Adv. Coun., Everglades City, Fla., 1995—; coord. vol. program, Everglades City, 1995—, Ptnrs. in Edn., Everglades City, 1995—. Recipient Kids Count award, First Union Bank, Naples, 1996, Environ. award, Dept. Environ. Edn., Tallahassee, Fla., 1997—2001; grantee Great Gator Reading grant, Collier County Edn. Found., Naples, 1996, Creative Writing grant, United Arts Coun., Naples, 2000. Mem.: AAUW, Fla. Reading Coun., Phi Beta Kappa. Avocations: reading, rose gardening, decorating, shopping, collecting manatee memorabilia. Home: 348 Nassau Ct Marco Island FL 34145

HENRY, STEPHEN LEWIS, lieutenant governor, orthopedic surgeon, educator; b. Owensboro, Ky., Oct. 8, 1953; s. Virgil Lewis and Wanda (Harper) Henry; m. Heather Reneé French, Oct. 27, 2000. BS, We. Ky. U., 1976; MD, U. Louisville, 1981. Diplomate Am. Bd. Orthopaedic Surgery. Intern gen. surgery U. Louisville Med. Ctr., 1981-82, resident, 1982-86, instr. orthopedic surgery, 1986—; lt. gov. Commonwealth of Ky., 1995—. Clin. investigator Richards Med. Co., Memphis, 1986—; athletic physician football teams U. Louisville, 1987—, Seneca High Sch., 1987—, Ky. State Football Championships, 1986—; commr. "A" dist. Jefferson County, 1992-95. Editor: Sports Medicine; contbr. abstracts and articles to profl. jours., chpts. to books. Treas. Louisville Tyler Park Neighborhood Assn., 1983-88, pres., 1988-89 Recipient best paper award So. Med. Assn., 1985, best clin. rsch. award U. Cin., 1986, outstanding resident rsch. award U. Louisville, 1988, Edwin G. Bovill rsch. award Orthopaedic Trauma Assn., 1989, Bell award for outstanding vol., Louisville, 1989, Presdl. recognition Nat. Vol. Week, The White House, 1989; named Outstanding Young Leader in Ky., 1988, One of 10 Outstanding Young Ams., U.S. Jaycees, 1989, Bell award, 1989, Jefferson award, 1989, Owensboro award for excellence, 1990, Lawrence-Grever award, 1990; grantee Richards Med. Co., 1986, Dept. Navy, 1989. Mem. Jefferson County Med. Soc., So. Orthopedic Assn., Ky. Med. Assn., U. Louisville House Staff Assn. (com. on health, phys. edn. and med. aspects of sports 1987—). Democrat. Home: 2550 Ransdell Ave Louisville KY 40204-1539 Office: 700 Capitol Ave Frankfort KY 40601-3410 E-mail: shenry@mail.st.ky.us.*

HENSHAW, CHRISTINE MARIE, nursing educator; b. Everett, Wash., Nov. 14, 1955; d. Robert Levi and Opal Berdelle (Mork) H. BSN, Intercollegiate Ctr. Nursing Edn., 1978; M of Nursing, U. Wash., 1987. Staff nurse, charge nurse Caldwell Health Ctr., Des Moines, Wash., 1978-81; staff nurse West Seattle Gen. Hosp., 1981-82, Riverton Hosp., Seattle, 1983-87; nursing instr. Highline C.C., Des Moines, 1984-86, 87-00; staff nurse Virginia Mason Hosp., Seattle, 1987-91; staff nurse per diem Highline Hosp., Des Moines, 1993—; asst. prof. Seattle Pacific U., 2000—. Expert witness, legal cons. in field, 1994—. Contbr. chpt. to book. Mem. King County Nurses Assn. (bd. dirs., 2d v.p. 1982-84, pres. 2001—). Avocations: reading, needlework, golf, music. Office: Seattle Pacific U 3307 3d Ave W Seattle WA 98118 E-mail: chenshaw@spu.edu.

HENSHAW, WILLIAM RALEIGH, retired middle school educator; b. Richmond, Va., Apr. 28, 1932; s. Edmund James Jr. and Dorothy Varnes (Carrier) H.; m. Joyce Winston Kuhn, Mar. 24, 1956; children: Mark Hutson, Marcia Lynne, Matthew Harrison. BA, Randolph-Macon Coll., 1957; postgrad., Va. Commonwealth U., 1964-89, Coll. William and Mary. Cert. collegiate profl. tchr. with endorsements, Va. Securities clk. Fed. Res. Bank, Richmond, 1960-62; mid. sch. tchr. Hanover County Pub. Schs., Ashland, Va., 1963-99, adviser, yearbook specialist, 1988-99; ret., 1999. Author instrnl. manuals. Vice pres., pres. Pearson's Corner Elem. Sch. PTA, Mechanicsvillle, Va., 1980-84. With U.S. Army, 1952-60, Korea. Mem. NEA, Va. Edn. Assn., Hanover Edn. Assn., Va. Assn. Sci. Tchrs. (exec. bd.), Greater Richmond Assn. Sci. Educators, U.S. Boomerang Assn. Avocations: boomerangs, making custom knives. Home: 6450 Birch Tree Trce Mechanicsville VA 23111-5306

HENSLEY, JUDITH VICTORIA, elementary school educator; b. Harlan, Ky., Dec. 4, 1951; d. Ernest and Gladys (Hamlin) Hensley; m. Don Victor Bryson, Aug. 18, 1973 (div. Aug. 1979); 1 child, Jeremy Talmadge Bryson. BA in Religious Edn., Cumberland Coll., 1974, BS in Elem. Edn., 1981, postgrad., 1981-83. Cert. elem. tchr. Acct. Chicago Heights (Ill.) Star Tribune, 1969-70; adminstrv. sec. U. Ky., Lexington, 1974-79; with job placement/counseling svcs. Cumberland Coll., Williamsburg, 1979-81; spl. edn. tchr. Harlan (Ky.) County Bd. of Edn., 1981-86, elem. tchr., 1986—. Task force mem. on edn. Harlan County Task Force, 1989—; exec. com., mem. Ea. Ky. Tchrs. Network, Hindman, 1989—; mem. Appalshop Sch. Initivative Project, Whitesburg, Ky., 1990—. Contbg. author: (spl. edn. handbook) A Handbook for Special Education, 1985-86; columnist, 1997—; contbr. articles to profl. jours. Field worker Appalachian Leadership Cmty. Outreach, Eagle, Ky., 1972, publicity mgr., Williamsburg, 1973; coord. 4th of July Cmty. Celebration, Smith, Ky., 1981-91. Foxfire Classroom grant Foxfire Tchr. Outreach Fund, 1989-90, Appalshop Video Film grant Appalshop Sch. Initiative Project, 1990-92. Mem. NEA, Ky. Edn. Assn., Harlan Edn. Assn., Harlan County Diskettes, Appalachian Writers Assn. Mem. Ch. of God. Avocations: photography, creative writing, hiking, swimming, Appalachian folklore. Home: PO Box 982 Loyall KY 40854-0982 Office: Wallins Elem Sch PO Box 10 Wallins Creek KY 40873-0010

HENSLEY, PATRICIA DRAKE, principal; BLS in Liberal Studies, MA in Edn., PhD in Edn. Adminstrn., St. Louis U., Mo. Cert. use of tech. in sch. setting Tech. Leadership Acad. Tchr. grades 7 and 8 math. and sci., 1976—82; prin. St. Mary Magdalen, St. Louis, 1982—86; vice-prin. St. Elizabeth Acad., St. Louis, 1986—91; prin. St. Francis of Assisi, St. Louis, 1991—95; acad. adviser grad. programs Webster U., St. Louis, 1990—2002; prin. Ursuline Acad., St. Louis, 1995—. Adj. instr. math. and computer sci. Webster U., St. Louis, 1986—; nat. media cons. FM radio stas.; fellow St. Louis Prin. Acad., 1994; state prin. assessor NASSP, 1994; grant reviewer U.S. Dept. Edn., 2002. Mem. Archdiocesan Com. for Rev. of H.S. Admissions, 1997—99; bd. dirs., co-chair ednl. policies com. DeSmet Jesuit H.S., 1998—; bd. dirs. Vianney H.S., 1999—.

HENSON, (BETTY) ANN, media specialist, educator; b. Tampa, Fla., Dec. 20, 1944; d. James (Jim) and Beth (Tabb) H. BA, U. South Fla., 1966; MEd, U. Fla., 1980, EdS, 1985. Cert. tchr., Fla. English tchr. Hillsborough County Schs., Tampa, 1967-68; drama tchr. Cultural Enrichment Ctr., Gainesville, Fla., 1969-70, Title II Grant, Gainesville, 1970-72; lang. arts tchr. Alachua County Schs., Gainesville, 1972-74; team leader humanities ESAA Grant Alachua County, Gainesville, 1975-82; media specialist Alachua County Schs., Gainesville, 1982—, tech. coord., 1993—2000; media specialist St. Johns County Schs., 2000—. Adj. faculty Nova U., Gainesville, 1988-96, Ctr. for Distance Learning, Ocala Ctr., St. Leo's Coll., 1994-2000; part-time libr. Alachua County Libr. Dist., asst., 1996-2000. Presenter in field; slide show prodr. (Fla. ctr. for children and youth award 1984). Mem. Gainesville City Beautification Bd., 1995—; mem. com. Kanapaha Bot. Garden Festival. Recipient First Liberty Inst. award Ams. United Rsch. Found., Washington, 1991; grantee Fla. Ctr. Tchrs. Resident Scholar, 1993; grantee in field. Mem. Profl. Assn. Libr. and Media Specialists (sec. 1991-92, 94-96), Fla. Assn. Media in Edn., Alpha Delta Pi, Delta Kappa Gamma. Avocations: reading, travel, floral arrangement. Office: Osceola Elem Sch 1605 Osceola Elementary Rd Saint Augustine FL 32084 Home: 1015 Mindello Ave Saint Augustine FL 32086-7156

HENSON, DIANA JEAN, county official; b. Evanston, Ill., Feb. 11, 1949; d. Paul J. and Mary (Norris) Roberts; m. Jim Henson; 1 child, Richard Leslie Pruyn Jr. BS in Elem. Edn., Ball State U., 1971; MS in Elem. Edn., Ind. State U., 1979; EdS in Adminstrn./Supervision, West Ga. Coll., 1985; doctoral study, U. Ga., 1986—. Cert. in adminstrn. and supervision, middle grades edn., data collection, early childhood edn., elem. tchr., Ga., Ind. Tchr. 3rd grade Blue River Valley Sch. System, Mt. Summit, Ind., 1971-73; fin. analyst Dun & Bradstreet, Indpls., 1973-74; sec. to vice chmn. mktg. dept. Glenview (Ill.) State Bank, 1974-75; tchr. 6th grade St. John's Cath. Sch., Panama City, Fla., 1976-77; tchr. 3rd to 8th grades St. Ann's Cath. Sch., Terre Haute, Ind., 1978-79; pvt. preschool and elem. prin. Learning Tree Sch., Terre Haute, 1979-81; tchr., asst. prin. Haralson County Sch. System, Buchanan, Ga., 1981-83, tchr., reading dept. chair, 1983-88; tchr. 6th grade Carroll County Sch. System, Carrollton, Ga., 1988-89, asst. prin., 1989-94; dir. compensatory edn./testing, 1994—. Active Bowdon Hist. Commn., Bowdon Planning Commn.; pres. Ga. Compensatory Edn. Leaders. Mem. Bowdon Area Hist. Soc., Phi Delta Kappa, Phi Kappa Phi, Kappa Delta Pi. Home: PO Box 277 130 W College St Bowdon GA 30108-1306

HENSON, PAMELA TAYLOR, secondary education educator; b. Mobile, Ala., Aug. 31, 1958; d. Richard Dowdy and Martha Jo (Hanson) Taylor; m. Thomas Baird Henson III, Mar. 7, 1987; 1 child, Joshua Taylor. BS in Secondary Edn./Biology, U. South Ala., 1983; MS in Secondary Edn./Biology, U. Mobile, 1989, Adminstrv. Cert., 1990; Edn. Specialist Adminstrn., Ala. State U., 1995; postgrad., U. West Fla. Cert. secondary edn. educator. Sci. tchr. Fairhope (Ala.) Middle Sch., 1984-91, Foley (Ala.) H.S., 1991-97; sci. supr., grant writer Baldwin County Schs., 1994—. Christa McAuliffe fellow State Dept. of Edn., 1994, Outstanding Biology tchr. Nat. Assn. Biology Tchrs., 1994, Outstanding Instr. in Environ. Edn., Legacy Found., 1995, Outstanding Sci. Supr. award, 2002, Mobile Bay NEP award, 2002, YWCA Woman of Profl. Achievement award, 2002; recipient Presdl. award NSTA, 1994, Melvin Paul Jones award Tuskegee U., Outstanding Svc. to Edn. award. Mem. NSTA, Nat. Assn. Biology Tchrs., Ala. Sci. Tchrs. Assn., Nat. Marine Educators Assn., Baldwin County Assn. Profl. Educators (pres. 1994—), Alpha Delta Kappa (treas. 1994-96). Republican. Baptist. Avocations: travel, walking, outdoor summer sports. Home: PO Box 1676 810 Juniper Ct Daphne AL 36526-4358

HENTON, M. LOIS SMITH, English language arts educator; b. Archer, Fla., June 26, 1947; d. Chris Smith and Cora Lee Smith (Clayton) Kennon. AA with honors, Housatonic Community Coll., Bridgeport, Conn.; BS with honors, So. Conn. State U., New Haven; MA, U. South Fla., Tampa; postgrad., U. South Fla. Counselor, fin. aid specialist and CHOICES coord. Pasco-Hernando Community Coll., Brooksville, Fla., instr. lang. arts, 1978—. Mem. staff devel. com., learning lab. com. Pasco-Hernando Community Coll., Brooksville, 1991—, minority adv. bd. dirs., 1986—, vice-chairperson ednl. support com. SACS; mem. adv. and planning com. for devel. of student internship program Southwest Fla. Water Mgmt. Dist.; mem. dist. adv. coun. Hernando County, Fla. Speaker, program developer Save Moton Sch.; organizer coord., dir. 1st Dr. Martin Luther King, Jr. Community March, Brooksville, 1989; mem. Bethlehem Progressive Bapt. Ch., Brooksville; tchr. Sunday Sch., chairperson, coord. Women's Day Program, 1985, 87, 88, 90, 91, mem. pastor's Aide Club and Benevolent Bd. Named Woman of Distinction Hernando County and State of Fla. Suncoast Girl Scout Coun. of Am., 1992. Mem. NAACP (v.p. 1988, 89 Brooksville chpt., acting v.p. 1990, 2nd v.p. 1991, life), Nat. Devel. Edn. Assn., Fla. Devel. Edn. Assn., Fla. Adult Edn. Assn., Brotherhood Orgn. of Hernando County (award 1989), Black Educators Caucus (Appreciation award) Avocations: traveling, fashion, writing short essays and poetry, designing and coordinating various programs, bridal consultant and wedding coordinator. Home: 941 Twigg St Brooksville FL 34601-4010

HEPPE, KAROL VIRGINIA, lawyer, educator; b. Vinton, Iowa, Mar. 14, 1958; d. Robert Henry and Audry Virginia (Harper) Heppe. BA in Law and Society, U. Calif., Santa Barbara, 1982; JD, People's Coll. Law, 1989. Cmty. organizer Oreg. Fair Share, Eugene, 1983; law clk. Legal Aid Found. L.A., summer 1986; devel. dir. Ctrl. Am. Refugee Ctr., L.A., 1987-89; exec. dir. Police Watch-Police Misconduct Lawyer Referral Svc., L.A., 1989-94; instr. People's Coll. Law, L.A., 1992-94; dir. alternative sentencing project Ctr. Juvenile and Criminal Justice, 1994-95; cons. Bay Area Police Watch, 1996; investigator Office Citizen Complaints City and County of San Francisco, 1998—. Vol. law clk. Legal Aid Found. L.A., 1984—86, Lane County Legal Aid Svc., Eugene, 1983. Editor: (newsletter) NLG Law Students Action, 1986, Ctrl. Am. Refugee Ctr., 1986—89, Prison Break, 1994. Mem. Coalition Human Immigrants Rights, 1991—92, So. Calif. Civil Rights Coalition, 1991—92; bd. dirs. Nat. Police Accountability Project Adv. Bd., 1999—2003, People's Coll. Law, 1985—90, Law Student Civil Rights Rsch. Coun., N.Y.C., 1986. Scholar, Kramer Found., 1984—88, Law Students' Civil Rights Rsch. Coun., 1986, Davis-Putter Found., 1988, Assn. Cmty.-Based Edn. Prudential, 1988. Avocations: reading, travel. E-mail: karol_heppe@ci.sf.ca.us.

HEPWORTH, MALCOLM THOMAS, civil engineer, educator; b. Singapore, Malaysia, Oct. 1, 1932; s. Thomas Percy and Gertrude Alice Hepworth; m. Marilyn R. Kelsy, June 15, 1957 (div. Jan. 1968); children: Allison, Marianna; m. Elouise Peck, Jan. 20, 1968; children: Edward, Todd. BS, MIT, 1954; PhD, Purdue U., 1958. Tchg. asst. Purdue U., Lafayette, Ind., 1954-58, assoc. prof., 1961-68; asst. prof. Colo. Sch. Mines, Golden, 1958-61; scientist U.S. Bur. Mines, Reno, Nev., 1968; prof. U. Denver, 1968-71, chmn. chem. engring., 1971-75; sect. supr. Amax R&D Inc., Golden, 1975-85; prof. dept. civil engring. U. Minn., Mpls., 1985-98, prof. emeritus, 1998—. Editor: Environmental Encyclopedia, 1994; contbr. articles to profl. jours. Mem. AIME. Achievements include 10 patents on waste processing and extractive metallurgy. Office: U Minn Dept Civil Engring 500 Pillsbury Dr SE Minneapolis MN 55455-0233 E-mail: hepwo001@umn.edu.

HERAKOVICH, CARL THOMAS, civil engineering, applied mechanics educator; b. East Chicago, Ind., Aug. 6, 1937; m. Marlene Vukowich, Apr. 23, 1960; children: Bradley, Douglas, Kristine, Russell. BSCE, Rose-Hulman Inst. Tech., 1959; MS in Mechanics, U. Kans., 1962; PhD in Mechanics, Ill. Inst. Tech., 1968. Registered profl. engr., Va. Prof. Va. Poly. Inst. and State U., Blacksburg, 1967-87; prof. civil engring. and applied mechanics U. Va., Charlottesville, 1987-98, Henry L. Kinnier prof. civil engring., 1990-98, prof. emeritus, 1998—, dir. applied mechanics, 1987-98; co-dir. NASA composites program Va. Poly. Inst. and State U., Blacksburg, 1974-87. Dir. Ctr. for Innovative Tech., Inst. for Materials Sci. and Engring., 1984-86, Ctr. for High Temp. Composites, 1993-98. Editor: Handbook of Composites No. 2, 1989; author: Mechanics of Fibrous Composites, 1998. Fellow ASME (chmn. com. composite materials 1989-92, exec. com. 1992-97, divsn. chair 1996-97, vp. basic engr. 2001—), ASCE, Am. Acad. Mechanics; mem. Internat. Union Theoretical and Applied Mechanics (gen. assembly 2000—), U.S. Nat. Com. on Theoretical and Applied Mechanics (sect. rep. 1996-2000, sec. 2000--), Soc. Engring. Sci. (sec. 1983-90, bd. dirs. 1989-92, v.p. 1991, pres. 1992), Soc. Exptl. Mechanics, Soc. Advancement Materials Processing and Engring.

HERALD, SANDRA JEAN, elementary education educator; b. Indpls., Aug. 3, 1950; d. Chester Lee and Mary Mae (Jeffras) H. BA, Marian Coll., Indpls., 1973; MA, Ind. U., Indpls., 1980. Dental asst. Dr. Jones, Indpls., 1969-73; instr. dance Garrison Sch. Dance, Indpls., 1968-73; elem. tchr. St. Gabriel Sch., Connersville, Ind., 1973—. Active in community theater, 1974-83. Sunday sch. tchr. Fairfax Ch., Indpls., 1966-72, East Side Meth. Ch., Connersville, 1984-86; camp counselor Meth. Ch. Summer Camp, Connersville, 1986; presiding pres. John Conner Players Bd., Connersville, 1983-84; participating staff instr. Ind. Dance Conv., Indpls., 1970-73; vol. local nursing home care ctrs.; active local gose; trio/quarter "Praise"; bd. dirs. Connersville United Way. Recipient Lavinnia Smith award John Conner Players, Connersville, 1980. Mem. Area Reading and Arts Assn. Avocations: choreography, reading, bible study, choir directing, pet care. Home: 824 Western Ave Connersville IN 47331-1601 Office: St Gabriel Sch 224 W 9th St Connersville IN 47331-2074

HERBERT, ADAM WILLIAM, JR., academic administrator, educator; b. Muskogee, Okla., Dec. 1, 1943; s. Addie (Hibler) H.; m. Karen Y. Lofty, Apr. 1980. BA, U. So. Calif., 1966, MPA, 1967; PhD, U. Pitts., 1971. Instr., asst. prof., coord. acad. programs Ctr. Urban Affairs Sch. Pub. Adminstrn., U. So. Calif., L.A., 1969-72; assoc. prof., chmn. urban affairs program div. environ. and urban systems Va. Poly. Inst. State U., Blacksburg, 1972-75, prof., dir. North Va. programs, Ctr. for Pub. Adminstrn. and Policy, 1978-79; White House fellow, spl. asst. sec. HEW, Washington, 1974-75; spl. asst. to under sec. HUD, Washington, 1975-77; prof., dean Fla. Internat. U., Miami, 1979-87, assoc. v.p. for acad. affairs, chief acad. officer North Miami campus, 1985-88, v.p., chief adminstrv. officer, 1987-88; pres. U. North Fla., Jacksonville, 1989—98; chancellor State Univ. Sys. of Fla., 1998—2001; Regents prof., exec. dir. Fla. Ctr. for Pub. Policy and Leadership U. North Fla., Jacksonville, Fla.; pres. Indiana Univ. System, Bloomington, Ind., 2003—. Office: Indiana Univ System Bloomington IN 47405*

HERBERT, AMANDA KATHRYN, special education educator; b. Cleve., Apr. 10, 1948; d. Ralph Earle and Nina Kathryn (Burkey) Herbert; m. John Davis Reeves, June 26, 1971 (div. 1978). Student, Coll. of Wooster, Ohio, 1966-68; BA, Defiance Coll., 1971; MEd, Lynchburg Coll., 1982. Cert. tchr., Va. Elem. tchr. Napoleon (Ohio) City Schs., 1970-72; substitute tchr. Juvenile Boys Correction Ctr., Maumee, Ohio, 1972-73; Title I reading tchr. Defiance City Schs., 1973-76, tchr. 4th grade, 1976-78; tchr. 4th to 6th grades Platte Valley Schs. RE3, Ovid, Colo., 1978-81; tchr. elem. and secondary spl. edn. Amherst County (Va.) Schs., 1982—. Tchr. Camp Little Indian, Defiance, 1967-77. Contbr. to book. Deacon, elder First Presbyn. Ch., Defiance, 1973-78; singer Defiance Community Choir, 1972-77; actor, singer Fine Arts Ctr., Lynchburg, Va., 1983—; mem. choir Parkland United Meth. Ch., Lynchburg, 1982—. Mem. NEA, Coun. for Exceptional Children (div. learning disabilities), Va. Edn. Assn., People to People Citizen Ambassador Program to Peoples' Rep. China, Amherst Edn. Assn., Alpha Chi. Methodist. Avocations: travel, reading, swimming, acting, instrumental and vocal performance. Office: Amherst County High Sch 139 Lancer Ln Old Rt 29 Amherst VA 24521 E-mail: aher410@aol.com.

HERBERT, JAMES DALTON, psychology educator; b. Alice, Tex., June 20, 1962; s. Jim Dalton and Gracye Lee (Cates) H.; children: Aaron J., Sylvia L., Elliott B., Joel D. BA, U. Tex., 1983; MA, U. N.C., Greensboro, 1986, PhD, 1989. Lic. psychologist, Pa. Rsch. asst. U. N.C., Greensboro, 1983-88, asst. dir. Psychology Clinic, 1987-88; psychology intern Beth Israel Med. Ctr., N.Y.C., 1988-89; asst. prof. psychiatry Med. Coll. Pa., Phila., 1989-93, co-dir. Behavior Therapy clinic, 1989-93; dir. psychol./student mental health svcs., asst. prof. Drexel U., Phila., 1993-97, assoc. prof., 1997—, pres. univ. faculty, 2002—03, dir. PhD program in clin. psychology, 2003—. Contbr. articles to profl. jours. Rsch. grantee Sigma Xi, 1988; recipient grant NIMH, 1997. Mem. Am. Psychol. Assn. (Dissertation grantee 1988), Am. Psychol. Soc., Assn. for Advancement Behavior Therapy, Am. Assn. Applied and Preventive Psychology, Phila. Behavior Therapy Assn. (mem.-at-large 1990—, exec. bd.), Phi Beta Kappa, Psi Chi. Avocations: guitar, travel, hiking, skiing, martial arts. Home: 208 Linwood Ave Ardmore PA 19003-2707 Office: Drexel U Mail Stop 988 245 N 15th St Philadelphia PA 19102-1192

HERBSTREITH, YVONNE MAE, primary education educator; b. Wayne County, Ill., Aug. 18, 1942; d. Daniel Kirby and Rizpah Esther (Harvey) Smith; m. Bobbie L. Cates, Oct. 18, 1964 (div. 1969); 1 child, Shawn L.; m. Jerry Carrol Herbstreith, Sept. 15, 1979. BS, So. Ill. U., 1964. Cert. elem. tchr., Ill. Kindergarten tchr. Beardstown (Ill.) Elem., 1964-65, Pekin (Ill.) Pub. Schs. # 108, 1966-94. V.p. Pekin Friends of 47, 1986-91, pres. 1991-93, pres. Rebecca-Sarah Cir. 1st United Meth. Ch., Pekin, 1988—; trustee Sta. WTVP-TV, Peoria, Ill., 1990-91; active PTA, 1965-94, treas. 1992-93. Recipient Louise Alloy award Sta. WTVP, 1995. Mem. NEA (life), AAUW, Ill. Edn. Assn., Pekin Edn. Assn., Pekin Friends of Libr., Tazewell County Ret. Tchrs., Alpha Delta Kappa, Alpha Theta (chpt. pres. 1986-88, state sgt. at arms 1990-92, state chaplain 1992-94, state pres.-elect 1994-96, state pres. 1996—). Democrat. Methodist. Avocations: mystery books, reading, ceramics, crafts, photography, traveling. Home: 1922 Quail Hollow Rd Pekin IL 61554-6351

HERDLEIN, RICHARD JOSEPH, III, college official and dean, educator; b. Valdosta, Ga., Dec. 8, 1944; s. Sharon L. Herdlein; 1 child, Richard J. IV. BA, St. John Fisher Coll., 1966; MA, Niagara U., 1970, MS, 1976; PhD, U. Pitts., 1985. Gen. mgr. Schmitt Sales, Inc., Amherst, NY, 1964-68; dir. residence Kent (Ohio) State U., 1969-72; dir. student ctr. D'Youville Coll., Buffalo, 1974-76; dir. student activities Eckerd Coll., St. Petersburgh, Fla., 1976-77; asst. dir. univ. ctr. Adelphi U., Garden City, NY, 1978-80; dean student affairs U. Pitts., 1980-87; v.p. Thomas More Coll., Crestview Hills, Ky., 1987-90; v.p. student affairs, dean, assoc. prof. history Medaille Coll., Buffalo, 1990-2001; assoc. prof. Grad. Sch. Higher Edn. and Student Pers. Admin. SUNY Coll. at Buffalo, 2001—. Councilman Amherst Rep. Com., 1993-96; chmn. jingle bell run Arthritis Found., Tonawanda, N.Y., 1991-95; bd. dirs., chmn. fundraising com. Leadership Buffalo, 1997—; bd. dirs. Buffalo Coun. on World Affairs; alumnus Ctr. for Entrepreneurial Leadership, SUNY, Buffalo, 1996. Sgt. USAR, 1967-73. Named Person of Yr. Adelphia U., 1980, Most Respected Dr., Ctr. for Entrepreneurial Leadership SUNY Buffalo, 1996, Adminstr. of Yr., Medaille Coll. Student Govt. Assn., 1999; named one of Outstanding Young Men of Am., 1976. Mem.: Amvets. Republican. Roman Catholic. Avocations: golf, racquetball, running, reading, arts. Office: Buffalo State Coll Bacon Hall 1300 Elmwood Ave Buffalo NY 14222 Home: 19 Sargent Dr Buffalo NY 14226-4038 E-mail: herdlerj@buffalostate.edu.

HERDMAN, SUSAN, art educator, artist; b. Yonkers, NY, May 29, 1941; d. Raymond Charles and Ellen (Saunders) Herdman; m. John C. Barker, June 12, 1965 (dec.); children: Jennifer, Carrie, John. BFA, Alfred U.; MA, U. Iowa. Artist, owner Herdman Archive, Bettendorf, Iowa, 1992—; art educator Davenport (Iowa) Cmty. Sch., 1985—, Scott C.C., Davenport, 1997—. Group shows include Quincy (Ill.) Art Ctr., 1992, Walton Art Ctr., Fayetteville, Ark., 1992, 93, Alias Gallery, Atlanta, 1992, Ga. Tech., Atlanta, 1992, Lincoln (Colo.) Art Ctr., 1992, 93, Davenport Mus. Art, 1992, Mus. Anthropology U. Calif., Chico, 1992, Red Mesa Art Gallery, Gallup, N.Mex., 1992, Putnam County Arts Coun., Mahopac, NY, 1992, Near Northwest Arts Coun., Chgo., 1993, North Platte Valley Art Guild, Scottsbluff, Nebr., 1993, U. Iowa, 1993, Chatauqua Art Assn. Galleries, 1993, Greater Harrisburg (Pa.) Arts Coun., 1993, 94, Fla. Soc. Fine Arts, Miami, Fla., 1993, Columbia Arts Ctr., Vancouver, Wash., 1993, Eiteljorg Mus. Am. Indian and Western Art, Indpls., 1994, Maude Kerns Art Center, Eugene, Oreg., 1994, Soc. Contemporary Photography, Kansas City, 1994, Mus. Northwest Colo., Craig, 1994, Fuller Mus. Art, Brockton, Mass., 1994, Perry House Galleries (Silver medal), Alexandria, Va., 1995, No. Colo. Artists Assn., Fort Collins, Colo., 1996, Photo Nat. 96 (2nd place award), Mo., 1996, Oscar Howe Art Ctr., S. Dakota, 1996; one-person show Cornell Coll., Mt. Vernon, Iowa, 1997, 2000; permanent collections include Am. Indian Art Ctr., Chgo., Mus. Anthropology U. Calif., Chico., Deere and Co., Moline, Ill, Eiteljorg Mus. Native Am. and Western Art, EverColor Corp., Wooster, Mass., Heard Mus. Libr. and Archives, Phoenix. Mem. Nat. Mus. Am. Indian, Nat. Mus. Women in Arts, Davenport Indian Parent Adv. Com., 1991-95. Recipient Best of Photography Ann. Photographers Forum Mag., 1993, Best of Show, The Camera's Eye, Mus. N.W. Colo., 1994, Photo '96, Nat. 2d Pl., S.E. Mo. Arts Coun., others; grantee Iowa Arts Coun., 1995, 99, 2000. Home: 4639 Sunset Ridge Santa Fe NM 85707

HEREFORD, PAMELA ANN, elementary school educator; b. Tacoma, Oct. 1, 1949; d. William L. and Leona A. (Leonard) Mazzoncini; m. JEffrey L. Hereford, May 24, 1980; 1 child, Katie Marie. BA, Cen. Wash. U., 1971, postgrad.; MEd, U. Portland, 1993. Cert. elem. sch. tchr. with jr. high endorcement. 6th grade tchr. Battle Ground (Wash.) Sch. Dist., 1973; tchr., jr. high sch. sci. Clover Park Sch. Dist., Lakewood, Wash., 1974—76; tchr., remedial math. Hood Canal Sch. Dist., Potlatch, Wash., 1977—. Mem. computer and math. curriculum coms., effective schs. program. City councilman City of Battle Ground, 1997—2002, dep. mayor, 1999—2001. Mem. Battle Ground Edn. Assn. (sec., treas.), Delta Kappa Gamma.

HERMAN, ELIZABETH MULLEE, elementary educator; b. N.Y.C., May 1, 1939; d. Raymond Garrett and Theresa (Lang) Mullee; m. Paul Herman, Feb. 10, 1962; children: Susan DeAlejos, Christina Cylwik, Andrew, Marianne Schell, Jane (dec.). BA, Manhattanville Coll., Purchase, N.Y., 1960; MA, Columbia U., 1962; Cert. Advanced Study, Sacred Heart U., Fairfield, Conn.; Pimms scholar, Wesleyan U., 1990-93. Tchr. Birch Wathen Sch., N.Y.C., 1960-61, Madison Jr. High Sch., Trumbull, Conn., 1978-79, Holy Rosary Sch., Bridgeport, Conn., 1979-82, St. Theresa Sch., Trumbull, 1982-88, Roosevelt Sch., Bridgeport, 1988-94, Maplewood Annex Sch., Bridgeport, 1994-99. Mem. Secular Order Franciscans. Mem. NEA, APA, Bridgeport Ret. Tchrs. Assn. Roman Catholic. Avocations: ancient ruins, swimming, sheltering abused and abandoned cats. Home: 144 Plymouth Ave Trumbull CT 06611-4152

HERMAN, MARTIN NEAL, neurologist, educator; b. Washington, July 19, 1939; m. Sydney Beryl Epstein, July 1, 1962; children: Kenneth Dayan, Heidi Felice. AA, George Washington U., 1960; BS, Northwestern U., 1961, MD, 1964. Diplomate Am. Bd. Electroencephalography, Am. Bd. Psychiatry and Neurology, Nat. Bd. Med. Examiners; lic. N.J. Intern Georgetown U./D.C. Gen. Hosp., Washington, 1964; resident psychiatry U. Rochester (N.Y.)/Strong Meml. Hosp., 1964; resident neurology U. Va., Charlottesville, 1967-70; rsch. fellow clin. neurophysiology NIH, Bethesda, Md., 1970-71; asst. prof., dir. electroencephalography N.J. Coll. Medicine and Dentistry, Newark, 1971-74; dir. neurology Monmouth Med. Ctr., Long Branch, N.J., 1974—. Asst. clin. prof. Hahnemann Med. Coll. and Hosp., 1974-91; clin. assoc. prof. Pa. U., Hahnemann U., 1991—; attending physician Martland Hosp., Newark, 1971-74, East Orange (N.J.) VA Hosp., 1971-74, Riverview Med. Ctr., Red Bank, N.J., 1983—. Contbr. chpts. to books and articles to profl. jours. Mem. AMA, Am. Acad. Neurology, Am. Med. Electroencephalographic Soc., Am. Clin. Neurophysiology Soc., N.J. Med. Soc., N.J. Acad. Medicine, Ea. Assn. Electroencephalographers, Phi Eta Sigma. E-mail: mnhermes@aol.com.

HERMANCE, BETTY JEAN, special education educator; b. Chgo., Mar. 20, 1940; d. Louis and Helen (Minnick) Matalin; m. Duane Edward Heinen, Dec. 8, 1958; children: Thadeus Heinen, Susan Heinen; m. Steven Arthur Hermance, Nov. 5, 1988. AA, Rock Valley Coll., Rockford, Ill., 1980; BS in Child Devel., Rockford Coll., 1982, postgrad., 1984; student, U. Va./Longwood Coll., 1994. Spl. educator for severely emotionally disturbed The Pines Treatment Ctr., Portsmouth, Va., 1991-94; spl. edn. tchr. Dolan Ednl. Ctr., Durand, Ill., 1994-2000, Sch. Dist. #205, Rockford, Ill., 2000—02, The Mill Residential Treatment, Rockford, 2002—.

HERMANCE, LYLE HERBERT, retired college official; b. Lincoln, Nebr., Dec. 10, 1939; s. Milo Lee Sr. and Amelia Henrietta (Schoneman) H.; m. Dorothy Kay Stanislav, June 12, 1960 (div.); children: Lane Alan, Lori Ann, Russell Joel; m. Janette Kay Sims, Oct. 11, 1986 (dec.). BS, U. Nebr., 1964, MS, 1970. Cert. agr. edn. tchr., Nebr. Tchr. vocat. agr. and indsl. arts Emerson (Nebr.)-Hubbard Pub. Schs., 1964; tchr. vocat. agr. Waverly (Nebr.) Pub. Schs., 1964-79, chmn. dept. vocat. edn., 1973-79; coord. adult agr. program area cmty. svcs. div. S.E. C.C., Lincoln, 1979—, dir. Adult Edn. Ctrs. area cmty. svcs. div., 1991—, interim dir. div., 1992-94, dir. div., 1994-96, dir. continuing edn., 1996—2002; vol. tng. engr. Folsom Children's 200 and Bot. Garden, 2003—. Rep. Nebr. Turkey Coun., 1968-72, Nebr. Grassland and Forage Coun., 1969—; nat. coord. computers in agr. demonstration contest Future Farmers Am. 1990-93; mem. adult edn. task force Nat. Coun. for Argl. Edn., 1991—; mem. adv. coun. agrl. edn. dept. U. Nebr., 1987—; mem. S.E. Rsch. and Ext. Ctr. adv. team Inst. Agr. and Natural Resources, 1992—; asst. supt. Future Farmers Am. div. sheep show Nebr. State Fair, 1988-90, supt., 1990—; pres. Nebr. Vocat. Agrl. Found., 1970-71, bd. dirs., 1991-92. Mem. Lancaster County Ext. Bd., 1990—95, pres., 1992—95; mem. Nebr. affiliate task force Am. Heart Assn., 1992—98; mem. spl. com. on agrl. edn. Nebr. Coun. Vocat. Edn., 1986—88; charter bd. dirs., advisor Nebr. Agrl. Leadership Coun., Inc., 1980—82; charter mem. Nebr. Coalition for Agrl. Fin. Mgmt. Edn., 1990—99, state co-chmn., 1991—99; bd. dirs. Nebr. Assn. Vocat. Indsl. Clubs Am., 1995—2000, state coord. leadership and skills contest, 1996—2000; Bd. dirs. Lancaster County Pub. Nursing Adv. Com., 1972—76. Recipient hon. degree Future Farmers Am., 1970, 71, 94, Nebr. Disting. Svc. award, 1994, Nebr. Lifetime Svc. award, 1996, Disting. Svc. award Nat. Farm Ranch Bus. Mgmt. Edn. Assn., 1997. Mem.: Nebr. Agrl. Educators Assn., Am. Vocat. Assn., Nat. Assn. Agrl. Educators, Assn. for Career and Tech. Edn., Nebr. Assn. for Adult Agrl. Educators ((charter, pres. 1988-89)), Nat. Farm Ranch Bus. mgmt. Edn. Assn., Nebr. Vocat. Assn., Nebr. Vocat. Agrl. Assn. ((offices: dist. chmn. 1966-67, 87-89, 97-2001, state pres. 68-69), exec. dir. 2002—), Lancaster County Agrl. Soc., Waverly Edn. Assn., Nebr. Edn. Assn., NEA, Kiwanis ((pres. elect 2001-02)). Home: 13305 N 112th St Lincoln NE 68517-9769

HERMAND, JOST, German language educator; b. Kassel, Germany, Apr. 11, 1930; came to U.S., 1958; s. Heinz and Annelies Hermand; m. Elisabeth Jagenburg, Mar. 16, 1956. Dr phil, U. Marburg, Germany, 1955, Staatsexamen, 1956. Asst. prof. German U. Wis., Madison, 1958-61, assoc. prof., 1962-63, prof., 1964-67, rsch. prof., 1968—. Mem. Saxon Acad. Sci., Leipzig, Germany, 1985; hon. prof. Humboldt U., Berlin, 2003. Author: Cultural History of Germany, 8 vols., 1959-88, A Hitler Youth in Poland, 1994, Geschichte des Germanistik, 1994. Fellow Am. Coun. Learned Socs., 1963, Internationales Kulturwissenschaftliches Institut, Vienna, 1994, 97.

HERMANN, DONALD HAROLD JAMES, lawyer, educator; b. Southgate, Ky., Apr. 6, 1943; s. Albert Joseph and Helen Marie (Snow) H. AB (George E. Gamble Honors scholar), Stanford U., 1965; JD, Columbia U., 1968; LLM, Harvard U., 1974; MA, Northwestern U., 1979, PhD, 1981; MA in Art History, Sch. Art Inst. Chgo., 1993; MLA, U. Chgo., 2001. Bar: Ariz. 1968, Wash. 1969, Ky. 1971, Ill. 1972, U.S. Supreme Ct. 1974. Mem. staff, directorate devel. plans U.S. Dept. Def., 1964-65; With Legis. Drafting Research Fund, Columbia U., 1966-68; asst. dean Columbia Coll., 1967-68; mem. faculty U. Wash., Seattle, 1968-71, U. Ky., Lexington, 1971-72, DePaul U., 1972—, prof. law and philosophy, 1978—, dir. acad. programs and interdisciplinary study, 1975-76, assoc. dean, 1975-78, dir. Health Law Inst., 1985—2000; lectr. dept. philosophy Northwestern U., 1979-81; counsel DeWolfe, Poynton & Stevens, 1984-89. Vis. prof. Washington U., St. Louis, 1974, U. Brazilia, 1976, U. P.R. Sch. Law, 1993; lectr. law Am. Soc. Found., 1975-78, Sch. Edn. Northwestern U., 1974-76, Christ Coll. Cambridge (Eng.) U., 1977, U. Athens, 1980; vis. scholar U. N.D., 1983; mem. NEH seminar on property and rights Stanford U., 1981; participant law and econs. program U. Rochester, 1974; mem. faculty summer seminar in law and humanities UCLA, 1978; Bicentennial Fellow of U.S. Constitution Claremont Coll., 1986; Law and Medicine fellow Cleve. Clinic., 1990; bd. dirs. Coun. Legal Edn. Opportunity, Ohio Valley Consortium, 1972, Ill. Bar Automated Rsch. Corp., 1975-81, Criminal Law Consortium Cook County, Ill., 1977-80; cons. Adminstrv. Office Ill. Cts., 1975-90; reporter cons. Ill. Jud. Conf., 1972-90; mem. Ctr. for Law Focused Edn., Chgo., 1977-81; faculty Instituto Superiore Internazionale Di Science Criminali, Siracusa, Italy, 1978-82; cons. Commerce Fedn., State of São Paulo, Brazil, 1975; residential scholar Christ Ch., Oxford, 1999. Editor: Jour. of Health and Hosp. Law, 1986-96, DePaul Jour. Healthcare Law, 1996—, AIDS Monograph Series, 1987—. Mem. Cook County States Atty. Task Force on Gay and Lesbian Issues, 1990—, Contemporary Arts Coun. Chgo., 1999—; bd. dirs. Ctr. Ch.-State Studies, 1982—, Horizons Cmty. Svcs., 1985—88, Chgo. Area AIDS Task Force, 1987—90, Howard Brown Health Ctr., 1994—; v.p. Inst. Genetics, Law and Ethics, Ill. Masonic Hosp., 1993—2000; trustee 860 N. Lakeshore Trust, Chgo., 1993—95; bd. visitors Oriental Inst. U. Chgo., 1995—; co-chair parity and inclusion com. Ill. HIV Prevention Cmty. Group Ill. Dept. Pub. Health; dir. Inst. Genetics, Law and Ethics, Ill. Masonic Hosp., 1993—2000; bd. dirs. Gerber-Hart Libr. and Archives, Mostly Music of Chgo., 1998—2001; mem. scholars' group ethics and med. rsch. NIH/U. Ill. Med. Sch. John Noble fellow Columbia U., 1968, Internat. fellow, NEH fellow, Law and Humanities fellow U. Chgo, 1975-76, Law and Philosophy fellow Harvard U., 1973-74, Northwestern U., 1978-82, Criticism and Theory fellow Stanford U. 1981, NEH fellow Cornell U., 1982, Judicial fellow U.S. Supreme Ct., 1983-84, U. Ill. fellow med. ethids rsch. group; Dean's scholar Columbia U., 1968, Univ. scholar Northwestern U., 1979. Mem.: ABA, Am. Inst of Ct. (Abraham Lincoln Marowitz chpt.), Chgo. Coun. Fgn. Rels., Ill. Assn. Hosp. Attys., Am. Acad. Healthcare Attys., Am. Assn. Law Schs. (del., sect. chmn., chmn. sect. on jurisprudence), Soc. Am. Law Tchrs., Internat. Penal Law Soc., Soc. Writers on Legal Subjects, Soc. Phenomenology and Existential Philosophy, Soc. Bus. Ethics, Am. Philos. Assn., Am. Judicature Soc., Nat. Health Lawyers Assn., Internat. Assn. Philosophy of Law and Soc., Am. Soc. Polit. and Legal Philosophy, Am. Soc. Law, Medicine and Ethics, Am. Law Inst., Am. Acad. Polit. and Social Sic., Chgo. Bar Assn., Ill. Bar Assn., Soc. Contemporary Art Art Inst. Chgo., Evanston Hist. Soc., Northwestern U. Alumni Assn., Chgo. Literary Soc., Quadrangle Players, Renaissance Soc. (bd. dirs. 1995—), Lawyers Club Chgo., Arts Club Chgo., Cliff Dwellers Club, Tavern Club, Quadrangle Club, University Club, Hasty Pudding Club, Signet Club Harvard. Episcopalian.

HERMES, DEAN WALTER, secondary education educator; b. Bismarck, N.D., May 8, 1944; s. Wilbert and Madeline (Mosbrucker) H.; m. Deanna Ihla, Apr. 15, 1967; children: Christopher, Allyson. BS, U. Mont., 1966, MS in Teaching, 1971. Life cert. tchr., N.D. Social studies tchr., coach Williston

(N.D.) H.S., 1967—2000. Mem. Polson Planning Bd. 1st lt. USMC, 1967-69, Viet Nam. Decorated Bronze star U.S. Army, 1968. Mem. Nat. Coun. for Social Studies, N.D. Coaches Assn. (adv. bd) 1976, N.D. Football Coach of Yr. 1980, 88, 89, N.D. Wrestling Hall of Fame 1986, Polson C. of C., Elks, Lions Club, KC. Roman Catholic. Avocations: hunting, fishing. Home and Office: 478 Rocky Point Rd Polson MT 59860-9233

HERNANDEZ, ALICIA C. elementary school educator; b. N.Y.C., Oct. 22, 1967; d. Elsie (Toro) Romero. AA, Miami (Fla.) Dade C.C., 1988; BS, Fla. Internat. U., 1991, MS, 1995. Cert. tchr., Fla.; cert. elem. edn., early childhood and ESOL endorsed. Tchr., tutor Our Lady of Charity, Hialeah, 1990, Dade County Pub. Schs., Miami, 1991—. Vol. Camillus House, Miami, 1990; peer advisor FIU Coll. Edn., Miami, 1990-91. Recipient scholarship Adolph Coors Corp., 1989; Elem. Tchr. of Yr., Ernest R. Graham, 2003. Mem. Future Educators Am., Kappa Delta Pi (pres. 1990-91, Membership award 1990), Chi Alpha Theta (pledge pres. 1990), Omicron Delta Kappa. Democrat. Roman Catholic. Avocations: aerobics, watersports. Home: 2438 Lee St Hollywood FL 33020-2053 Office: Ernest R Graham Elem Sch 7330 W 32nd Ave Hialeah FL 33018-5211

HERNANDEZ, EDWARD, JR., community college administrator; b. Sept. 11, 1944; m. Edna Jaime, Sept. 2, 1968; children: Eddie, Danny, Laura. BA in Sociology, Calif. State U., 1966; MS in Recreation, Edn., Social Svcs., Calif. State U., L.A., 1970; EdD in Community Coll. Adminstrn., Nova U., 1976. Social worker Parent/Child Guidance Ctr., L.A., 1967-68; home-sch. coord. Garvey Sch. Dist., Rosemead, Calif., 1968-69; exec. dir. Bienvenidos C.C., Rosemead, 1969-71; instr., edn. specialist Pasadena (Calif.) City Coll., 1971-74; asst. dean student activities Mt. San Antonio Coll., Walnut, Calif., 1974-77, dean continuing edn. and community svcs., 1977-89; vice chancellor student affairs and community svcs. Rancho Santiago C.C., Santa Ana, Calif., 1989-92, exec. vice chancellor, 1992—. Edn. rep. Santa Ana Pvt. Industry Coun., 1992. Vol. VISTA, 1966-67; dist. chmn. Orange County coun. Boy Scouts Am., 1991, chmn. emerging minorities com., 1992. Honoree resolutions Calif. State Senate, 1990. Mem. Assn. Mex.-Am. Educators (Outstanding Educator 1990), Calif. C.C. Chief Student Svcs. Adminstrs., So. Calif. Consortium Instrnl. TV, Calif. C.C. Coun. on Community Svcs. and Continuing Edn., Calif. Post-Secondary Edn. Com. (tech. adv. com.). Office: Rancho Santiago CC 17th St At Bristol Santa Ana CA 92706

HERNANDEZ, FLAVIA, bilingual school principal; b. Mexico, Oct. 30, 1958; came to U.S., 1962; d. P. and M. Hernandez. BA, Mundelien Coll., 1980; MS in Edn., Chgo. State U., 1984, cert. adminstrv. endorsement, 1985. Cert. tchr., adminstr., Ill. Tchr. Blessed Agnes Elem. Sch., Chgo., 1980-84, Ruben Salazar Bilingual Ctr., Chgo., 1984-87, head tchr., 1987-89, prin., 1990—. Trustee Gads Hill Ctr., Chgo., 1988—, bd. dirs. 1989—; mem. task force Pilsen Ressurrection Devel. Ctr., Chgo., 1992. Mem. Am. Assn. Sch. Adminstrs., Ill. Adminstrs. Acad. (assoc.), Ill. Assn. for Multi-lingual, Multicultural Edn., Network Hispanic Adminstrs. in Edn. (sec.). Avocations: painting, drawing, photography, gardening, travel. Office: Ruben Salazar Bilingual Ctr 160 W Wendell St Chicago IL 60610-2603

HERNANDEZ, MARY ANTONIETA, retired elementary education educator; b. San Antonio, Tex., June 13, 1933; d. Richard Peña and Flora Garza (Treviño) Gonzales; div.; children: John D., Steven M., Carole D., Stephanie M., Mark A., Mary Michelle. BS in Elem. Edn., U. Tex., Austin, 1955. Cert. bilingual edn. tchr., Tex. Tchr. Highland Park Elem. Sch., San Antonio, 1985-88, De Zavala Elem. Sch., San Antonio, 1989-90, mem. sci. adv. com., sci. coord., 1990-93; tchr. Berkeley-Ruiz Elem. Sch., 1993—. Mem. prison min. team Destiny Ch., 2003. Mem. ch. choir, San Antonio, 1988-89, tchr. Sunday sch., 1975-77; cookie chmn. San Antonio area Girl Scouts U.S., 1969-70; tchr. Sunday sch. Destiny Ch.; counselor Billy Graham Crusade, San Antonio, Tex. Mem. Am. Fedn. Tchrs., Tex. Tchrs. English to Speakers Other Langs., San Antonio Assn. Bilingual Edn. Republican. Avocations: reading, travel, fishing. Home: 119 William Classen Dr San Antonio TX 78232-1320 Office: 2311 San Luis St San Antonio TX 78207-4736

HERNANDEZ, RAMON ROBERT, retired clergyman and librarian; b. Chgo., Feb. 23, 1936; s. Eleazar Dario and Marie Helen (Stange) H.; m. Fern Ellen Muschinske, Aug. 11, 1962; children: Robert Frank, Maria Marta. BA, Elmhurst (Ill.) Coll., 1957; BD, Eden Theol. Sem., St. Louis, 1962; MA, U. Wis., 1970. Co-pastor St. Stephen United Ch. Christ, Merrill, Wis., 1960-64; dir. youth work Wis. Conf. United Ch. Christ, Madison, 1964-70; dir. T.B. Scott Free Library, Merrill, 1970-75, McMillan Meml. Library, Wisconsin Rapids, Wis., 1975-83, Ann Arbor (Mich.) Pub. Library, 1983-94; pastor Comty. Congl. Ch., Pinckney, Mich., 1994-98. Seminar leader on pub. libr. long-range planning, budgeting and handling problem patrons. Editl. com. mem. Songs of Many Nations Songbook, 1970; contbr. articles to profl. jours. Treas. Ann Arbor Homeless Coalition, 1985-88; bd. dirs., sec., v.p. Riverview Hosp. Assn., Wisconsin Rapids, 1977-83; bd. dirs. Hist. Soc. Mich., 1988-90, Ind. Living, Inc., Dame County, Wis., 2001—; bd. trustees Madison Pub. Libr, Wis., 2000—. Mem. ALA, Wis. Libr. Assn. (Leadership award 1980, pres. 1980), Rotary (pres. Merrill chpt. 1974-75, Community Svc. award 1975, pres. Ann Arbor chpt. 1990-91, Paul Harris fellow 1994).

HERNDON, CATHY CAMPBELL, artist, educator; b. Richmond, Va., Sept. 25, 1951; d. Kenneth Holcomb and Grace (Brooks) Campbell. BS in Art and Drama, Radford (Va.) U., 1973; MS in Art Edn., Va. Commonwealth U., 1980. Tchr. art Hanover County Schs., Va., 1973-76, Stafford County Schs., Va., 1976-86, Fredericksburg City Schs., 1991—; exch. tchr. Kingston U., Eng., 1995; neon mixed media constrn. artist, signmaker Fredericksburg, Va. Artist, tchr. Rappahannock Security Ctr., Fredericksburg Ctr. for Creative Arts; tchr. Inst. of Contemporary Art, Chgo. Art Inst. One-woman shows include Fredericksburg Ctr. for Creative Arts, Southside Va C.C., Art First Gallery, Fredericksburg, Shenandoah Valley Art Ctr., Geico Corp. Hdqrs., Fredericksburg, Riverby's Gallery, Frejuis, France, 1997, e.e. smith Gallery, others, exhibited in group shows at Karpathos, Greece, London, Stafford Eng., Rocquebrune and Frejuis, France, Montross Gallery, Zenith Gallery, Washington, Va. Ctr. Creative Arts, Exposure Unltd. Art Group, various murals. Mem. Fredericksburg/Frejus Sister City Assn., 1992—; pres., bd. dirs. Fredericksburg Ctr. for Creative Arts, 1984—. Named Best in Show, Hanover Arts Festival, 1995, Geico Educator of Yr., 1996, Educator of Yr., Fredericksburg Jaycees, 1998; Fulbright Meml. scholar, Japan, 2000; recipient TICA award Chgo. Art Inst., 2003. Mem.: Nat. Art Edn. Assn. Avocations: beach, travel, dancing. Home: 408 Frederick St Fredericksburg VA 22401-6028 E-mail: cherndon@cityschools.com.

HERNDON, DONNA RUTH GROGAN, educational administrator; b. Murray, Ky., Aug. 14, 1942; d. E. Leon and Virgil (Childress) Grogan; m. Clarence W. Herndon Jr., Jan. 31, 1963; children: Melissa Herndon Graves, Roger Allan (dec.). BS summa cum laude, Murray State U., 1960; MA, Western Ky. U., 1975. Tchr. biology Calloway County H.S., Murray, 1964-66, dir. project COPE, 1978-81; coord. of vols. Army Cmty. Svc., Berlin, 1972, vol. supr. Ft. Knox, Ky., 1974-75; mayor Van Voorhis Cmty., Ft. Knox, 1975-76; plant mgr. Lin-Val Garden Ctr., Penn Hills, Pa., 1977; admissions rep. Art Inst. Pitts., 1978; dir. alumni affairs Murray State U., 1981-92; coord. Family Resource Ctr., Calloway County Schs., Murray, 1992—. Bd. dirs., co-founder CHAMP, Murray, 1986-93; rep. edn. Ky. Juvenile Justice Commn., 1982-92; mem. adv. coun. dept. social work Murray State U., mem. adv. bd. Coll. Industry and Tech.; mem. rural health adv. bd. U. Ky.; bd. dirs. Murray United Way; founder, chairperson Calloway United Benevolent Svcs. Network; bd. dirs. Murray-Calloway C. of C., 1993-96, Leadership Ky. Found; mem. Ky. Primary Health Care Coalition; bd. dirs. Parents Anonymous; chair bd. dirs. Housing Auth. Murray. Recipient Recognition award Murray State U. Black Alumni, 1989, Humanitarian of Yr. award Murray Rotary Club, 1994; named Vol. of Yr., United Way of Ky., 1993; Donna Herndon scholarship established Murray State U. Student Alumni Assn., 1988; state winner Ky. Fedn. Women's Clubs Poetry Contest. Mem. Ky. Alliance for Exploited and Missing Children (bd. dirs. 1982-92), Ky. Ctr. Pub. Issues (bd. dirs. 1990-92), Nat. Coun. for Advancement and Support Edn. (achievement award 1984, bronze award 1987, Dist. III Outstanding Advisor award 1992), Nat. Assn. Parents and Tchrs. (hon. life), Leadership Ky. (bd. dirs. 1990—), Leadership Ky. Alumni Assn. (trustee 1989-95), Murray Woman's Club. Mem. Ch. of Christ. Avocations: volunteer service, music, reading, gardening. Office: Calloway County Schs Family Resource Ctr 1169 Pottertown Rd Murray KY 42071-5217

HERNDON, ELOISE J. retired elementary educator; b. Shreveport, La., Dec. 4, 1936; d. Delry M. and Allie (Hippler) Herndon; children: Kimberlyn Bowers, Kaydriene Gore. AA, Kilgore (Tex.) Jr. Coll., 1957; BS, East Tex. State U., 1959; MS, Stephen F. Austin U., Nacogdoches, Tex., 1975. Tchr. English, reading and spelling Point Comfort (Tex.) Elem. Sch., 1959; elem. tchr. Hallsville (Tex.) Ind. Sch. Dist., 1966—2001; 2d grade tchr gifted and talented Hallsville Elem. Sch., 1984-89; ret., 2001. Mem. NEA, Tex. State Tchrs. Assn., Hallsville Tchrs. Assn., Alpha Delta Kappa Internat. Hon. Sorority for Women Educators.

HERNDON, MERLE PUCKETTE, principal; b. Lynchburg, Va., Jan. 5, 1954; d. Walter William and Marion (Layne) Puckette; m. William Robertson Herndon III, June 19, 1976; children: William Robertson IV, Stuart Thomas, Caroline Whitney. BS in Elem. Edn., Averett Coll., 1974; MEd in Reading, Lynchburg Coll., 1977, EdS, 1986; EdD in Ednl. Leadership, U. Va., 1993. Cert. elem. tchr., prin., supt., reading specialist, devel. reading tchr., Va. Remedial math. and reading tchr. T. C. Miller Elem. Sch., 1974-75; remedial math. and reading tchr., reading specialist Dearington Elem. Sch.; reading specialist Linkhorne Elem. Sch., Lynchburg, Va., 1975-86, unit leader, 1984-86, staff devel. specialist, 1986-87, prin., 1987—; staff devel. specialist Lynchburg City Schs., 1986-87. Coord. partnership programs with bus. and Linkhorne Elem. Sch.; presenter in field. Mem. Madeline Hunter Inst., Williamsburg, Va., 1987; active Brookneal Elem. PTA, William Campbell Mid. Sch. PTA, Staunton River Hist. Soc.; past pres. Red Hill Garden Club; mem. adminstrv. coun. Brookneal Meth. Ch.; den leader Cub scouts Boy Scouts Am., Brookneal, 1986-89. Mem. ASCD, Piedmont Area Reading Coun., Va. Assn. Elem. Prins. (chmn. grand session 1992, mem. conf.), Nat. Assn. Elem. Prins. (Va. state del. to conv. 1992, session presider), Lynchburg Assn. Elem. Sch. Prins. (chair supt. and legislators forum 1989), Lynchburg Coll. Alumni Assn., Averett Coll. Alumni Assn., Optimist Club (chmn. youth essay contest 1988-90, project designer youth recognition program 1989—, children at risk ct. project 1988), Phi Delta Kappa, Kappa Delta Pi, Delta Kappa Gamma. Home: 7505 Old Stagecoach Rd Gladys VA 24554-9746 Office: Linkhorne Elem Sch 2501 Linkhorne Dr Lynchburg VA 24503-3398

HERNON, PETER, library science educator; b. Kansas City, Mo., Aug. 31, 1944; s. Robert M. and Ethel S. (Grazier) H.; m. Elinor Hernon, Dec. 30, 1972; children: Alison K., Linsay C. BA, U. Colo., 1966, MA, 1968, U. Denver, 1971; PhD, Ind. U., 1978. From asst. prof. to assoc. prof. Simmons Coll., Boston, 1978-83; from assoc. prof. to prof. U. Ariz., Tucson, 1983-85; prof. Simmons Coll., 1986—. Vis. prof. Victoria U., Wellington, New Zealand, 1995-96. Author: Federal Information Policies, 1987 (Best Book award 1988), Service Quality in Academic Libraries, 1996, Assessng Service Quality (Best Book award ALA), U.S. Government on the Web, 1999, 3d edit., 2003, also others; editor Govt. Info. Quar., 1984-2000, Jour. Acad. Librarianship, 1993-2002; co-editor Libr. & Info. Sci. Rsch., 1992—. Recipient Best Article award Coll. & Rsch. Libraries, 1993. Avocation: jogging. Home: 23 Westgate Rd Framingham MA 01701-8843 Office: Simmons Coll 300 Fenway Boston MA 02115-5820

HERO, BARBARA FERRELL, visual and sound artist, writer; b. LA, Jan. 3, 1925; d. Paul C. and Lucile (Evans) Ferrell; children: Alfred O. III, Barbara Ann, Michelle Claire, David Evans. BA in Art, George Washington U., 1950; EdM in Math., Boston U., 1980; cert. in techniques of computer sound Synthesis, MIT, 1981. Art tchr. Marjory Webster Jr. Coll., Washington, 1953-54; printmaker, painter, 1948—. Vis. artist, lectr. U. Mass., Amherst, 1970s, Rochester (N.Y.) Inst. Tech., 1970s, U.S. Psychotronics Assn., Chgo., 1981-89; mus. sound creator Acoustic Brain Rsch., N.C., 1989; founder, dir. Internat. Lambdoma Rsch., Wells, Maine, 1994. Inventor Lambdoma Harmonic Keybd.; exhibited in Contemporary Am. Artist series Corcoran Gallery of Art, 1950; paintings represented in collections at Chase Manhattan Bank, N.Y.C., 1960s, Miami (Fla.)-Dade U., 1960s; author: Lambdoma Unveiled (The Theory of Relationships), The Glass Bead and Knot Theory of Relationships, The Lambdoma Resonant Harmonic Scale (P, Q, R, S, T, U, V and W); contbr. articles to profl. jours. Recipient Davina Winslow Meml. prize Nat. Soc. Painters in Casein, 1964, Cert. of Achievement, Interant. Assn. Colour Healers, London, 1982, J.A. Gallimore cert. for tech. R&D in psychotronics U.S. Psychotronics Assn., Chgo., 1994. Mem. IEEE, Math. Assn. Am., U.S. Ptychotronics Assn. (v.p. 1998-2003). Office: Internat Lambdoma Rsch Inst 496 Loop Rd Wells ME 04090-7622 Business E-Mail: hero@lambdoma.com.

HEROD, CHARLES CARTERET, Afro-American studies educator; b. Florence County, S.C., Nov. 18, 1924; s. George William and Essie Lee (Johnson) H.; m. Agustina Benedicto; children: Charles-Francis, Ilona-Nora, Olivia Maria. A.B. in History and English magna cum laude, Rutgers U., 1964, A.M. in History, 1968, Ph.D. in History, 1973. Lic. tchr. N.J. Tchr. dept. social studies East Orange High Sch., N.J., 1964-66; instr. dept. history Rutgers U., New Brunswick, N.J., 1966-73; prof. Afro-Am. studies, SUNY-Plattsburgh, 1974— ; lectr. in field. Author: The Nation in the History of Marxian Thought, 1976; Afro-American Nationalism, 1986. Mem. editorial bd. Can. Rev. Studies in Nationalism, P.E.I. U., Can. Contbr. revs., articles to profl. jours. Names Hon. Squadron Comdr. 380th Bomb Wing, Plattsburgh AFB, 1978; grantee NDEA, 1966, U. Vienna, 1970-73, Ctr. for East Asian Studies, 1975; recipient Special Diplome, French Guerelme. Mem. Am. Assn. for Advancement of Slavic Studies, N.Y. State Assn. European Historians, Royal Archaeol. Inst. Great Britain and Ireland, N.Y. African Studies Assn., Univ. Coll. Honor Soc. of Rutgers U., Habsburg Discussion Group, Pi Sigma Alpha.

HEROLD, ROCHELLE SNYDER, early childhood educator; b. Bklyn., Oct. 6, 1941; d. Abe and Anna (Chazen) Snyder; m. Frederick S. Herold, May 7, 1966; children: David Marc, Caryn Michele. BA, Bklyn. Coll., 1963; MS, CCNY, 1968. Cert. tchr., N.Y.; cert. child-care provider, Fla. Tchr. N.Y.C. Pub. Schs., 1963-68; tchr., adminstr. Chanute AFB Pvt. Sch., Rantoul, Ill., 1970-72; dir. early childhood edn. Temple Solel, Hollywood, Fla., 1974-99, dir. social and ednl. programs for young couples, families and singles, 1995-99. Cons. bd. dirs. Temple Solel, 1982-99; nursery sch. com. PTO, 1982-89; lectr., coord. at tchr. seminars, parenting lecture series; freelance writer parenting mags. Author, illustrator: A Family Seder Through a Child's Eyes, 1984, Celebrating Shabbat in the Home, 1992, Choosing Chessie, 2000, Baby Bear Learns to Share, 2001, A Bear in the Brook, 2001. Mem. AMA Aux., Fla. Med. Assn. Aux., Temple Solel Sisterhood. Avocations: ventriloquism, arts and crafts, interior design, directing children's musical productions. E-mail: rsherold@aol.com.

HEROLD-JOVEN, EMMA LEE, elementary education educator; b. Marysville, Calif., July 23, 1953; d. Ambrose Leo and Evelyn Marie Herold;m. Jeffrey Lee Joven, Oct. 17, 1992. BS in Elem. Edn., North Tex. State U., 1975, MEd in Early Childhood, tchr. young children cert., North Tex. State U., 1979. Lic. tchr., ESL, Tex. Tchr. Dallas Ind. Sch. Dist., 1976—. Mem. dist. comm. com. Dallas Ind. Sch. Dist., 1990—, profl. consultation com., 1992-93; mem. staff coun. John Q. Adams Elem. Sch., Dallas, 1993. Contbr.: Leadership for Incoming Chapter Presidents Delta Kappa Gamma, 1992. Eucharistic minister, women's guild St. Bernard Cath. Ch., Dallas, 1984—, pres. parish coun., 1990, 92; worker Family Pl. Shelter, Dallas, 1990—. Mem. ASCD, Internat. Reading Assn., Assn. Early Childhood Edn., Assn. Tex. Profl. Educators (pres. Dallas 1990-92, nominee Elem. Educator of Yr. 1987), Delta Kappa Gamma (pres. Delta Rho chpt. 1988-90, Chpt. Achievement award 1991, Leadership/Mgmt. Seminar Golden Gift award 1992, state com., profl. svcs. com., 1993—). Office: John Q Adams Elem 8239 Lake June Rd Dallas TX 75217-2104

HERR, RICHARD, history educator; b. Guanajuato, Mexico, Apr. 7, 1922; s. Irving and Luella (Winship) H.; m. Elena Fernandez Mel, Mar. 2, 1946 (div. 1967); children: Charles Fernandez, Winship Richard; m. Valerie J. Jackson, Aug. 29, 1968; children: Sarah, Jane. AB, Harvard U., 1943; PhD, U. Chgo., 1954; Doctorate (hon.), U. Alcalá de Henares, Spain, 2001. Instr. Yale U., 1952-57, asst. prof., 1957-59; assoc. prof. U. Calif., Berkeley, 1960-63, prof. history, 1963-91, prof. emeritus, 1991—, chancellor's fellow, 1987-90. Directeur d'études associé, sixième sect. Ecole Pratique des Hautes Etudes, Paris, 1973; dir. Madrid Study Ctr., U. Calif., 1975-77; chair Portuguese Studies Program, U. Calif., Berkeley, 1994-98, chair Spanish Studies Program, U. Calif. Berkeley, 2002—; vis. life mem. Clare Hall, Cambridge, Eng., 1985—; vis. prof. U. Alcalá. Henares, Spain, 1991; bd. dirs. Internat. Inst. Found. in Spain, Boston, 1997-2000; fellow Ctr. for History of Freedom, Washington U., St. Louis, 1994. Author: The Eighteenth Century Revolution in Spain, 1958, Tocqueville and the Old Regime, 1962, Spain, 1971, Rural Change and Royal Finances in Spain at the End of the Old Regime, 1989 (Leo Gershoy award Am. Hist. Assn. 1990); co-author: An American Family in the Mexican Revolution, 1999; editor: Memorias del cura liberal don Juan Antonio Posse, 1984; co-editor, contbr.: Ideas in History, 1965, Iberian Identity, 1989; editor, contbr.: The New Portugal: Democracy and Europe, 1993, Themes in Rural History of the Western World, 1993; asst. editor: Jour. Modern History, 1949-50; mem. editl. bd. French Historical Studies, 1966-69, Revista de Historia Economica, 1983-91. With AUS, 1943-45. Decorated Comendador of the Orden de Isabel la Católica (Spain); recipient Bronze medal Collège de France, Paris, The Berkeley citation U. Calif., 1991; Social Sci. Rsch. Coun. grantee, 1963-64; Guggenheim fellow, 1959-60, 84-85; NEH sr. fellow, 1968-69. Fellow Am. Acad. Arts and Scis.; mem. Am. Philos. Soc., Real Academia de la Historia Madrid (corr.), Soc. for Spanish and Portuguese Hist. Studies. Office: U Calif Dept History Berkeley CA 94720-2550

HERRERA, MARY CARDENAS, education educator, music minister; b. Sugar Land, Tex., Feb. 21, 1938; d. Jose Chavez and Juanita (Lira) Cardenas; m. Saragosa Martin Herrera, Sept. 20, 1960 (dec.); children: Michael (dec.), Patricia Ann Zagrzecki, Aaron Martin Herrera, Katherine Ann Nava. Grad., Sugar Land (Tex.) High Sch., 1957, Patricia Stevens Bus. Modeling Sch., 1960; student, Houston C.C., 1991, 92. Sec. William Penn Hotel, Houston, 1959-66; payroll clk. Peakload, Inc., Houston, 1967-69; acctg. clk. Am. Gen., Inc., Houston, 1970-73; nurse asst. Ft. Bend Ind. Sch. Dist., Sugarland, Tex., 1973-88, tchr.'s asst., 1988—2001; ret., 2001. Numerous offices Holy Family Cath. Ch., Missouri City, Tex., 1981-90, Hispanic choir dir., 1981-89; Hispanic choir dir. Notre Dame Cath. Ch., 1990-91; Hispanic del. Galveston-Houston Diocese, 1987-89; regional del. Encuetro Diocesceno Conf., San Antonio, 1983, 84, 85; dir., coord. Diocesan Hispanic Choir, 1982-86, music workshops, 1982-88. Songwriter in field. Mem. Holy Family Hispanic Com.; mem. choir Iglesia del Pueblo, Pasadena, Tex., 1991, 92, asst. Sunday sch. tchr., 1992-93, coord. monthly Women's Praise Gathering, 1994-97; music min. local prayer groups Houston area, 1990—; music min. King of Kings Prison Ministry, Texas City, Tex., 2000-, Casa Oracion, South Houston, Tex., 1998-, S.E. region Texas City Women's Prison, 2000--. Mem. Women's Aglow (praise and worship music min. Pasadena chpt. 1988-90). Democrat. Avocations: jogging, playing guitar. Home and Office: 1809 Crestwood Ln Pasadena TX 77502-3233

HERRERA, ROBERT BENNETT, retired mathematics educator; b. L.A., July 24, 1913; s. Royal Robert and Rachel (Mix) H.; AA, L.A. City Coll., 1934; AB, UCLA, 1937, MA, 1939; m. Agnes Mary MacDougall, May 18, 1941; children: Leonard B., Mary Margaret, William R. Tchr. high sch., Long Beach, Calif., 1939-41; statistician U.S. Forest Survey, Berkeley, Calif., 1941-45; faculty L.A. City Coll., 1946-79, prof. math., 1966-79, chmn. math. dept., 1975-79, ret., 1979; lectr. math. UCLA, 1952-75; cons. Ednl. Testing Svc., Princeton, 1965-68, Addison Wesley Pub. Co., 1966-68, Goodyear Pub. Co., 1970-76. Mem. AAAS, Math. Assn. Am. (past sec. So. Calif. sect., past gov.), Am. Math. Soc., Internat. Oceanic Soc., Phi Beta Kappa, Pi Mu Epsilon. Democrat. Author: (with C. Bell, C. Hammond) Fundamentals of Arithmetic for Teachers, 1962. Home: Kihei, Hawaii. Died Sept. 5, 2000.

HERRICK, KRISTINE FORD, graphic design educator; b. Bryn Mawr, Pa., Feb. 7, 1947; d. Charles Burton and Leah (Bosler) Ford; m. Stephen Wickes Herrick, Oct. 11, 1969 (div. Apr. 1982); 1 child, Katharine Wickes; m. Lee M. Smith, June 6, 1987; 1 stepchild, Suzannah Stuart Smith. BS, Skidmore Coll., 1969; MFA, Temple U., 1983. Cert. art tchr., N.Y. Layout artist Capital Newspapers, Albany, N.Y., 1969-70; designer Slocum House Pub., Albany, N.Y., 1970; asst. art dir. Gen. Electric Co., Schenectady, N.Y., 1970-72; art dir. Kirkman 3 Advt., Albany, 1972-75; from instr. to asst. prof. Tyler Sch. Art Temple U., 1980-85; design cons. Springhouse (Pa.) Corp., 1983-85; asst. prof., program coordinator graphic design Coll. St. Rose, Albany, 1985-92, assoc. prof., 1992—. Author: Trademarks, A History, 1982, Trademarks, An Evolution, 1983. V.p. Ctr. Sq. Assn., Albany, 1972—; founding mem. Historic Albany Assn., 1974—; bd. dirs. Berkshire Ballet Co., Albany, 1988—. Grantee for excellence in teaching Sears Roebuck Found., 1990. Mem. Am. Inst. of The Graphic Arts, Univ. and Coll. Designers Assn., Graphic Design Edn. Assn., The Creative Club (bd. dirs. 1997—). Office: Coll St Rose 432 Western Ave Albany NY 12203-1419 E-mail: herrickk@strose.edu.

HERRIN, DAVID LESLIE, educator; b. Waycross, Ga., Aug. 15, 1955; s. Leslie Edgar and Betty Louise (Cochran) H.; m. Amy L. Schomer, May 1, 1982; children: Alex J., Joey P. BS, U. Miami, 1977; MA, U. South Fla., 1980, PhD, 1985. Rsch. assoc. U. Ga., Athens, 1985-88; asst. prof. U. Tex., Austin, 1988-94, assoc. prof., 1994—2000, prof., 2001—. Contbr. articles to profl. jours. Democrat. Avocations: golf, fishing. Office: U Tex Sch Biolog Scis Molecular Cell and Devel Biology Sect Austin TX 78713

HERRING, MARK YOUNGBLOOD, librarian, university dean; b. Dothan, Ala., Oct. 10, 1952; s. Reuben and Dorothy Lavina (McCorvey) H.; m. Brenda Carol Lane, Aug. 11, 1972; children: Adriel, Areli Allene. BA, George Peabody Coll. Tchrs., 1974; MLS, Vanderbilt U., 1978; EdD, East Tenn. State U., 1990. Libr. dir. King Coll., Bristol, Tenn., 1979-87; instr. East Tenn. State U., Johnson City, 1990; dean libr. svcs. Okla. Bapt. U., Shawnee, 1992-99; dean Winthrop U., Rock Hill, S.C., 1999—. Exec. dir. Am. 21, Bristol, Tenn., 1990-92; founder, pres. Electronic Conservative Clearinghouse Libr., Shawnee, 1998—. Author: (monographs) Controversial Issues in Librarianship, 1986, Ethics and the Professor, 1988, Organizing Friends Group, 1993, Historic Guide to the Pro-Life Pro-Choice Debate, 2003, At the Core of the Problem-Reforming Teacher Education in Oklahoma, 2001. Fellow East Tenn. State U., 1987-90; grantee Noble Found., Okla., 1999, S.C. Humanities Found. Mem. Nat. Assn. Scholars, Assn. Libr. and Learning Ctr. Dirs. (pres. 1996-97), Okla. Libr. Assn. (exec. bd. 1993-95), Okla. Assn. Scholars (pres. 1997-99). Republican. Presbyterian. Avocations: reading, running, hiking. Office: Winthrop U Dacus Libr Rock Hill SC 29733-0001 Fax: 803-323-2215. E-mail: herringm@winthrop.edu.

HERRING, MARY CORWIN, education technology educator; d. William Webb and Cora Corwin; m. Ronald Paul Herring; children: Shelly, Robert. BS in Phys. Edn., N.D. State U., 1979, MS in Edn., 1989; PhD in Edn., Iowa State U., 1997. Phys. edn. instr. Berger Mid. Sch., West Fargo, N.D., 1981-87; grad. asst. N.D. State U., Fargo, 1987-88; phys. edn. instr. West Fargo (N.D.) Mid. Sch., 1981-89; lectr. N.D. State U., Fargo, 1989-92; asst. prof. edn., dept. co-chmn. Morningside Coll., 1996-2000; asst. prof. edn., tech. divsn. coord. U. No. Iowa, 2000—. Coord. N.D. Phys. Edn. State Guidelines writing team, 1988-91. Sr. warden Gethsemane Cathedral, Fargo, 1991-92, Christian Edn. dir., 1978-80. Mem. AECT (pres., change coun., tchr. edn. divsn.), Assn. Ednl. Comm. Tech.Cen. Dist. AHPER (membership chair 1986-87, sec. 1987-88, grant 1988), N.D. AHPER (pres. 1986-88, honor 1988, newsletter editor 1986-88), Phi Kappa Phi, Phi Delta Kappa (hist. 1991-92). Episcopalian. Office: 407 SEC Cedar Falls IA 50614-0606

HERRING, SUSAN WELLER, dental educator, oral anatomist; b. Pitts., Mar. 25, 1947; d. Sol W. and Miriam (Damick) Weller; m. Norman S. Wolf, May 27, 1995. BS in Zoology, U. Chgo., 1967, PhD in Anatomy, 1971. NIH postdoctoral fellow U. Ill., Chgo., 1971-72, from asst. prof. to prof. oral anatomy and anatomy, 1972-90; prof. orthodontics U. Wash., Seattle, 1990—. Vis. assoc. prof. biol. sci. U. Mich., Ann Arbor, 1981; cons. NIH study sect., Washington, D.C., 1987-89; sci. gov. Chgo. Acad. Sci., 1982-90; mem. pub. bd. Growth Pub. Inc., Bar Harbor, Maine, 1982—. Mem. editl. bd. Cells, Tissues, Organs, 1989—, Jour. Dental Rsch., 1995-98, 2003—, Jour. Morphology, 1997—, Integrative Biology 2000—; Archives of Oral Biology, 2003-; contbr. articles to profl. jours. Predoctoral fellow NSF, 1967-71; rsch. grantee NIH, 1975-78, 81—, NSF, 1990-92, 94-95. Fellow AAAS; mem. Internat. Assn. Dental Rsch. (dir. craniofacial biology group 1994-95, v.p. 1995-96, pres.-elect 1996-97, pres. 1997-98, Craniofacial Biology Rsch. award 1999), Soc. Integrated Comp. Biol.(chmn. vertebrate zoology 1983-84, exec. com. 1986-88), Am. Soc. Biomechanics, Am. Assn. Anatomists (chmn. Basmajian com. 1988-90), Soc. Vertebrate Paleontology, Internat. Soc. Vertebrate morphology (convenor 4th congress 1994, pres. 1994-97), Sigma Xi. Avocation: semi-profl. violin. Office: U Wash Box 357446 Seattle WA 98195-7446 E-mail: herring@u.washington.edu.

HERRINGTON, JAMES PATRICK, secondary education educator; b. East St. Louis, Apr. 10, 1950; s. James Lindsey and Anna (Kotras) H.; m. Therisa Marie Hawk, July 31, 1981. BS in Math. Edn., Northwestern U., 1972; MS in Math. Edn., So. Ill. U., 1974, EdD in Instructional Process, 1980. Cert. secondary tchr., gen. adminstr., supt., Ill. Grad. rsch. asst. So. Ill. U., Edwardsville, 1972-74, 78-79; math. and sci. tchr. Pontiac Sch. Dist. #105, Fairview Heights, Ill., 1974-78; math. tchr. O'Fallon (Ill.) Twp. High Sch., 1979—, chmn. math. dept., 1986—, chmn. sci. dept., 1993-99. Contbr. articles to profl. publs. Mem. S.W. Math. Conf. (bd. dirs. 1985-98), Nat. Coun. Tchrs. Math., Ill. Coun. Tchrs. Math. (bd. dirs. 1989-92), Math. Assn. Am., Belleville Weightlifting Club (bd. dirs. 1975—), Kappa Delta Pi. Avocations: weight training, basketball. Office: O'Fallon Twp High Sch 600 S Smiley St O Fallon IL 62269-2399 E-mail: herringtonp@oths.k12.il.us.

HERRITT, DAVID R. elementary education educator; b. Canton, Ohio, Oct. 17, 1942; s. Ralph H. and Freda A. (Baker) H; m. Jean A. Quinn. BS in Edn., Malone Coll., 1969; MEd, Ashland (Ohio) Coll., 1985. Cert. tchr., Ohio. Educator, intermediate level Canton (Ohio) City Schs. Active Boy Scouts Am. Mem. NEA, Ohio Edn. Assn., ECOEA, CPEA, NESA. Home: 5535 Veldon Cir NE Canton OH 44721-3445

HERRMANN, DEBRA MCGUIRE, chemist, educator; b. Ft. Benning, Ga., Dec. 28, 1955; d. Delbert Wayne and Twyla Pauline (Moran) McGuire; m. David Read Herrmann, Aug. 2, 1980; children: Adam James, Jesse Read, Aaron Matthew. BS in chemistry, U. Tex., 1979, U. Ark., 1989. Rsch. chemist Dow Chem., Oyster Creek, Freeport, Tex., 1980-84; chemist Aluminum Co. Am., Bauxite, Ark., 1984-87; tchr. Little Rock (Ark.) Sch. Dist., 1987-90; tchr. chemistry and integrated physics and chemistry Carroll Ind. Sch. Dist., Southlake, Tex., 2002—. Pres., bd. dirs. Little Peoples Acad. Sch. Montessori, Ottumwa, Iowa, 1990-93; den leader Cub Scouts. Mem. PEO, Phi Beta Kappa. Democrat. Presbyn. Avocations: walking, watercolor, dogs, sailing, gardening. Home: 1100 Harbor Haven St Southlake TX 76092-2811

HERRMANN, JANICE RAE, remedial educator; b. Sandusky, Ohio, July 3, 1939; d. Paul Harkness Cook and Ruth Florence (Griner) Niceswanger; m. Harvey Jacob Herrmann, Aug. 3, 1963; children: Douglas Jacob, Rebecca Ruth Goodrich. BS in Edn. cum laude, Miami U., Oxford, Ohio, 1961. Cert. elem. tchr., Ohio. 7th grade English tchr. Princeton City Schs., Sharonville, Ohio, 1961-63; 7th grade English and social studies tchr. Upper Arlington (Ohio) City Schs., 1963-64; tchr. Lorain (Ohio) City Schs., 1964-65, substitute tchr., 1967-68, 79-81, learning disabilities tutor, 1973-79, remedial tchr., 1982—99. Troop leader Girl Scouts U.S., Lorain, 1977-80, sr. troop, 1984-85, jr. cons. Lakers Svc. Unit, 1979-82, day camp dir., 1981; treas. Band Parents Admiral King High Sch., 1984-85; vol. Ohio Reads, 2002—; math tutor, 2003. Mem. NEA, AAUW, Internat. Reading Assn., Ohio Edn. Assn., Faculty Wives (sec. 1967-68, treas. 1970-71, pres. 1974-75), Coaches Wives (treas. 1971-72), Rainbow Girls (mother advisor Lorain assembly 1985-87, chmn. bd. dirs. 1982-84, 91, Grand Cross of Color 1957), Order Eastern Star, White Shrine, Phi Beta Kappa, Kappa Delta Pi. Mem. Christian Ch. Avocations: travel, needle crafts, reading.

HERRON, CAROLIVIA, novelist, English educator; b. Washington, July 22, 1947; d. Oscar Smith and Georgia Carol (Johnson) H. AB in English Lit., Ea. Bapt. Coll., 1969; MA in English Lit., Villanova (Pa.) U., 1973; MA, PhD, U. Pa., 1985; student, MIT, 1995. Asst. prof. Afro-Am. studies and comparative lit. Harvard U., Cambridge, Mass., 1986-90; assoc. prof. English Mt. Holyoke Coll., South Hadley, Mass., 1990-92; asst. prof. English Calif. State U., Chico, Calif., 1998—. Bd. dirs. curriculum devel. program NEH, Cambridge, Study Group in Afro-Asiatic Roots of Classical Civilization, Cambridge; vis. fellow Folger Shakespeare Libr., Washington, 1989—; Benedict vis. prof. Carleton Coll., Northfield, Minn., 1989-90; dir. Epicenter for the Study of Epic Lit.; vis. scholar Hebrew Coll., Mass., 1994-96, Harvard Div. Sch., 1995—; tech. assoc. Harvard Grad. Sch. Edn., 1996—; dir. conf. on African-Am. Jews, Hebrew Coll., 1995—; coord. African-Am. electronic texts devel. Howard U.; vis. scholar Brandeis U., 1997-98. Author: (novel) Thereafter Johnnie, 1991, (scholarly books) Selected Works of Angelina Weld Grimke, 1991, Afrekete/The Old Lady, 1995, Beginning Anew: Jewish Women/Chamisa, 1996; (children's fiction) Nappy Hair, 1997; (feminist writing) Beginning Anew: Jewish Women/Chamisa, 1996; contbr. articles to profl. jours. Fulbright scholar, 1985-86; Bunting fellow Radcliffe Coll., 1988—. Mem. Classical Assn. New Eng. Home: 11 Dana St Revere MA 02151-3615

HERSCHBACH, DUDLEY ROBERT, chemistry educator; b. San Jose, Calif., June 18, 1932; s. Robert Dudley and Dorothy Edith (Beer) Herschbach; m. Georgene Lee Botyos, Dec. 26, 1964; children: Lisa Marie, Brenda Michele. BS in Math., Stanford U., 1954, MS in Chemistry, 1955; AM in Physics, Harvard U., 1956, PhD in Chem. Physics, 1958; DSc (hon.), U. Toronto, 1977, Cornell Coll., 1988, Framingham State Coll., 1989, Adelphi U., 1990, Dartmouth Coll., 1992, Charles U., Prague, 1993, U. Ill., Chgo., 1994, Wheaton Coll., 1995, Franklin & Marshall Coll., 1998. Jr. fellow Harvard U., Cambridge, Mass., 1957—59, prof. chemistry, 1963—76, Frank B. Baird prof. sci., 1976—2002, mem. faculty coun., 1980—83, master Currier House, 1981—86, rsch. prof., 2002—; asst. prof. U. Calif., Berkeley, 1959—62, assoc. prof., 1961—63. Cons. editor W.H. Freeman lectr. Haverford Coll., 1962; Falk-Plaut lectr. Columbia U., 1963; vis. prof. Göttingen (Germany) U., 1963, U. Calif., Santa Cruz, 1972; Harvard lectr. Yale U., 1964; Debye lectr. Cornell U., 1966; Rollefson lectr. U. Calif., Berkeley, 1969; Reilly lectr. U. Notre Dame, 1979; Phillips lectr. U. Pitts., 1971; disting. vis. prof. U. Ariz., 1971, U. Tex., 1977, U. Utah, 1978; Gordon lectr. U. Toronto, 1971; Clark lectr. San Jose State U., 1979; Hill lectr. Duke U., 1988; Priestly lectr. Pa. State U., 1990; Kaufman lectr. U. Pa., 1990; Polanyi lectr. U. N.C., 1991; Dreyfus lectr. Dartmouth Coll., 1992; Pauling lectr. Calif. Inst. Tech., 1993; Bernstein lectr. UCLA, 1994; Brown lectr. Rutgers U., 1995. Assoc. editor Jour. Phys. Chemistry, 1980—88. Named to Calif. Pub. Edn. Hall of Fame, 1987; recipient pure chemistry award, Am. Chem. Soc., 1965, Centenary medal, 1977, Pauling medal, 1978, Spiers medal, Faraday Soc., 1976, Polanyi medal, 1981, Langmuir prize, 1983, Nobel Prize in chemistry, 1986, Nat. Medal of Sci., NSF, 1991, Heyrovsky medal, 1992, Sierra Nevada Disting. Chemist award, 1993, Kosolapoff medal, 1994, William Walker prize, 1994, Council of Scientific Society President's award for support of science, 1999; fellow Guggenheim fellow, U. Freiburg, Germany, 1968, vis. fellow, Joint Inst. for Lab. Astrophysics, U. Colo., 1969, Sloan fellow, 1959—63, Exxon Faculty fellow, 1980—96, Miller fellow, U. Calif. Berkeley, 1997; scholar Fairchild Disting. scholar, Calif. Inst. Tech., 1976. Fellow: Am. Acad. Arts and Scis., Am. Phys. Soc. (chmn. chem. physics divsn. 1971—72), N.Y. Acad. Sci. (hon.; life); mem.: Am. Philos. Soc., NAS, Royal Soc. Chemistry (fgn.) (hon.), Am. Chem. Soc., AAAS, Sigma Xi, Phi Beta Kappa (orator Harvard U. 1992). Office: Harvard U Dept Chemistry Mallickrodt Lab 035 12 Oxford St Cambridge MA 02138-2902*

HERSCHER, SUSAN KAY, English language educator; b. Wisconsin Rapids, Wis., Nov. 11, 1949; d. Martin Joseph and Marian Margie (Hentz) Arnold; m. Walter Ray Herscher, June 12, 1976; children: Anne, Brian. BS in Edn., U. Wis., Stevens Point, 1971; MS in Reading Edn., U. Wis., Oshkosh, 1983. Elem. tchr. Wausaukee (Wis.) Pub. Schs., 1971-73; elem. tchr., unit leader Hortonville (Wis.) Pub. Schs., 1974-82; adult basic edn. instr., dept. chair Fox Valley Tech. Coll., Appleton, Wis., 1983—. Master tchr., facilitator for Wis. Adult Basic Edn./ESL Summer Inst., 1993; presenter in field. Recipient Quality Improvement award Fox Valley Tech. Coll., 1994. Mem. Tchrs. of English to Speakers of Other Langs., Wis. Tchrs. of English to Speakers of Other Langs., Wis. East Cen. Assn. for Vocat. Edn., Wis. Edn. Assn., NEA. Avocations: travel, reading, cross country skiing. Home: 1341 W Cloverdale Dr Appleton WI 54914-5815 Office: Fox Valley Tech Coll PO Box 2277 Appleton WI 54912-2277

HERSH, RICHARD H. academic administrator; b. N.Y.C. m. Judith C. Meyers. BA in Polit. Sci. and History, Syracuse U., 1964, MA in Social Sci. Edn., 1965; EdD, Boston U., 1969. Prof., chmn. secondary edn. Coll. Edn. U. Toledo, Ohio, 1968-75; assoc. dean tchr. edn., prof. edn. Coll. Edn. U. Oreg., 1976-80, dean grad. sch., assoc. provost rsch., 1980-83, v.p. rsch., 1983-85; v.p. acad. affairs U. N.H., Durham, 1985-89; v.p. acad. affairs, provost Drake U., Des Moines, 1989-91; pres. Hobart and William Smith Coll., Geneva, N.Y., 1991-99; dir. grants program Christian A. Johnson Endeavor Found., 1999—2000; sr. advisor C.A. Johnson Endeavor Found., New York, NY, 2000—02; sr. fellow Council for Aid to Education, 2000—02; pres. Trinity College, Hartford, Conn., 2002—03. Vis. prof., dir. moral edn. project Ont. Inst. Studies Edn. U. Toronto, 1975-76, Ctr. Moral Devel., Harvard U., Cambridge, Mass., 1975-76; vis. prof. Western Australia Inst. Tech., Perth, 1978; speaker in field. Co-author: No G.O.D.'s in the Classroom: Inquiry into Inquiry, 1972, Inquiry and Elementary Social Studies, 1972, Inquiry and Secondary Social Studies, 1972, Perspectives in Moral and Values Education, 1976, Promoting Moral Growth: From Piaget to Kohlberg, 1979, 83, Models of Values and Moral Education, 1980, The Structure of School Improvement, 1983. Stanford U. fellow, 1979, Congl. fellow, 1982-83, Ger. Acad. Exch. Svc. fellow, 1983. Avocations: skiing, tennis, rowing (mem. U.S. rowing team competed World Championships, Bled, Yugoslavia, 1966).

HERSH, STEPHEN PETER, psychiatrist, psycho-oncologist, educator; b. NYC, Aug. 11, 1940; s. Joseph Harrison and Lillian (Berk) H.; m. Jean Ann Lehrke, Apr. 10, 1969; children: Damon, Katharine, Justin, Tessa. BA, Amherst Coll., 1962; MD, NYU, 1967. Diplomate Am. Bd. Psychiatry and Neurology. Pediatric intern NYU-Bellevue Med. Ctr., N.Y.C., 1967-68, fellow in child psychiatry, 1970-72; resident in psychiatry U. Pa., Phila., 1968-70; chief Ctr. for Studies in Child and Family Mental Health, NIMH, Rockville, Md., 1972-73, spl. asst. to dir., 1973-74, asst. dir., 1975-79; dir. div. children and youth St. Elizabeths Hosp., Washington, 1981; co-founder, co-dir., chmn. bd. Med. Illness Counseling Ctr., Chevy Chase, Md., 1982-94, exec. and med. dir., 1995—; behavioral health and medicine cons. Marriott Internat., 1996—99. Clin. prof. psychiatry and pediat. George Washington U. Med. Ctr., Washington, 1989—; cons. pediat. br. Nat. Cancer Inst., Bethesda, Md., 1972-99; nat. adv. coun. Nat. Anthrop. Film Ctr., Smithsonian Instn., Washington, 1979-81; chmn. sci. adv. bd. St. Jude Children's Rsch. Hosp., Memphis, 1980-82; attending physician, 1993—; dir., prin. investigator HIV R&D project Nat. Cancer Inst., 1988—; med. staff clin. ctr., NIH, 1992-99; dir. rsch. grant J.W. and Alice S. Marriott Found., 2002—. Author: The Executive Parent, 1979, The Physician and the Mental Health of the Child, 1981, Beyond Miracles, 2000; contbg. editor Journeys, 1994-96; contbr. articles to profl. jours., chpts. to books. Mem. svcs. com. Am. Cancer Soc., Washington, 1974-79; mem. com. on traffic Somerset (Md.) Town Coun., 1975-78; bd. dirs. Barker Found., Washington, 1984-87; mem. med. bd. Lupus Found. Greater Washington, 1988—, My Image After Breast Cancer, 1995—; bd. med. advisors Multimedia Med. Sys., 1997; vol. emergency response physician Md. Dept. Health and Mental Hygiene, 2003—. Recipient spl. award Nat. Consortium for Child Mental Health Svcs., 1979. Fellow, Am. Psychiat. Assn. (disting. life, Significant Achievement award 1993); mem. AAAS, Am. Pain Soc., Internat. Assn. Study Pain. Democrat. Home: 421 Kent Square Rd Gaithersburg MD 20878-5711 Office: Med Illness Counseling Ctr 2 Wisconsin Cir Chevy Chase MD 20815-7003

HERSHEY, H(OWARD) GARLAND, JR., orthodontist, university administrator; b. Iowa City, Nov. 6, 1940; Children— Brooke Janssen, Dru Ann, Paige Marie, Alexandra Elizabeth, Howard Garland III. BS, U. Iowa, 1962, D.D.S., 1965, MS, 1971. Diplomate Am. Bd. Orthodontics; fellow Am. Coll. Dentists. Inst. dept. oral diagnosis U. Iowa, Iowa City, 1968-69, staff research asst. dept. otolaryngology, 1969-71, asst. instr. dept. orthodontics, 1970-71; asst. prof. dept. orthodontics U. N.C., Chapel Hill, 1971-74, assoc. prof., 1974-78, prof., 1978—; asst. dean acad. affairs Sch. Dentistry, U. N.C., 1975-80, assoc. dean, 1980-83, dir. grad. edn., 1975-83, vice chancellor for health affairs, 1983—, vice provost, 1988—, interim provost, 1992-93; practice dentistry specializing in orthodontics, 1971—. Mem. staff N.C. Meml. Hosp., 1973—; mem. N.C. Orthodontic Health Care Com., 1974—; mem. bd. govs. Research Triangle Inst., 1991—, mem. exec. com., 1992—; cons. on dental health to U. Alexandria, Arab Republic of Egypt, 1980— Mem. editorial cons. Am. Jour. Phys. Anthropology, 1974-80, Jour. ADA, 1975— ; mem. editorial rev. bd. Jour. Dental Edn., 1979-82, Clin. Preventive Dentistry, 1980—, Am. Jour. Orthodontics, 1986—; cons. editor Dental Student Jour., 1978— ; So. Soc. Orthodontists, 1976—, Am. Jour. Orthodontics, 1980— ; contbr. articles to profl. Jours. Bd. dirs. Chapel Hill-Carrboro United Way, 1979-82, pres., 1980-81, N.C. Meml. Hosp., 1983—, mem. Parks and Recreation Commn., Chapel Hill-Carrboro, 1980-85, vice chmn., 1983-85; bd. dirs. Triangle Univs. Ctr. for Advanced Studies, 1991—, mem. exec. com., 1994—, vice chair 1995. Capt. U.S. Army, 1965-68. Recipient Disting. Svc. award Assoc. Schs. Allied Health Professions, 1996. Fellow Internat. Coll. Dentists, Am. Coll. Dentists; mem. AAAS, APHA, ADA (cons. coun. on dental edn. 1978—, vice chmn. sect. on orthodontics and oral devel. 1978-79, chmn. 1979-80), Assn. Acad. Health Ctrs. (bd. dirs. 1992—, chair elect 1995, chair 1996), Internat. Assn. Dental Rsch., N.C. State Dental Soc., Am. Assn. Dental Schs., So. Soc. Orthodontists (edn. com.), N.C. Orthodontic Soc. (chmn. manpower evaluation 1974—), Durham-Orange Dental Soc., Am. Soc. Dentistry for Children, Internat. Assn. Dentofacial Abnormalities, Edward H. Angle Soc. Orthodontics, Charles H. Tweed Found., Assn. Am. Med. Colls., N.C. Parks and Recreation Soc., Rsch. Triangle Inst. (bd. dirs.), Order of the Golden Fleece, Delta Sigma Delta, Omicron Kappa Upsilon, Sigma Xi. Home: 722 E Franklin St Chapel Hill NC 27514-3823 Office: U NC 214 S Bldg Chapel Hill NC 27599-0001

HERSTAND, THEODORE, theatre artist, educator; b. N.Y.C., May 14, 1930; s. Max Arthur and Rose (Shyatt) H.; m. Jo Ellen Gillette, Aug. 23, 1957; children: Sarah Ellen, Michael Simpson. Cert. Advanced Studies, U. Birmingham (Eng.), 1951; BA, U. Iowa, 1953, MA, 1957; PhD, U. Ill., 1963. Instr. theatre Parsons Coll., Fairfield, Iowa, 1953-54, Eastern Ill. U., Charleston, 1957-59; asst. prof. SUNY, Plattsburgh, 1960-64, asso. prof., 1963-64; asst. prof. U. Ill., 1964-66; asso. prof. U. Minn., Mpls., 1966-70; prof., chmn. dept. theatre, drama and dance Case Western Res. U., Cleve., 1970-77, chmn. faculty senate, 1975-76; dir. Sch. Drama, U. Okla., Norman, 1977-79, prof., 1979-92; prof. emeritus U. Okla., Norman, 1992—; artistic dir., actor Okla. Profl. Theatre, 1978. Vis. prof. Mpls. Coll. Art and Design, 1969; vis. dir. Colo. Shakespeare Festival, Boulder, 1968, 82; theatre bldg. cons. Eastern Ill. U., Charleston, Ill. State U., Bloomington, Jewish Community Center Theater, Mpls.; ednl. cons. in arts; spl. contbr. Silver Burdett Music Series. Profl. actor, dir. over 70 plays; author: (plays) Sugar and Lemon, 1968; new version Oedipus, 1978, Dov, 1982, The Emigration of Adam Kurtzik, 1985, 89, It Should Be So, 1989, The Minor Matter of Cynthia Smith, 1990, Bittersweet, 1996, others; assoc. editor: Drama Survey, 1967-70; contbr. revs., articles to profl. jours.; founder Klein Nat. Playwriting award, 1974, Bliss Nat. Playwriting award, 1980. Bd. dirs. Theater-in-the-Round, Mpls., 1968, v.p., 1969; bd. dirs. Gt. Lakes Shakespeare Festival, 1970-71, Okla. Arts Inst., mem. theatre panel, 1991-2003, chair 1994-2003; chmn. bd. dirs. Okla. Hillel Found., 1981-82; trustee Karamu House, 1975-77, Temple B'nai Israel, Oklahoma City, 1989-92, 1999—; chmn. new plays program S.W. Theatre Assn., 1985-89; bd. dirs. Okla. Israel Exch., 2003—. Mem. Jewish Theatre Assn., Nat. Theatre Conf., Dramatists Guild, Omicron Delta Kappa. Home: 4418 Manchester Ct Norman OK 73072-3915

HERTEL, SUZANNE MARIE, training and development specialist; b. Hastings, Neb., Aug. 8, 1937; d. Louis C. Hertel and W. Lenore (Cross) Budd. BA, Doane Coll., Crete, Neb., 1959; MSM, Union Theol. Sem., 1961; postgrad., U. Hartford, 1966, U. Conn., 1975; MA, Merrill Palmer Inst., 1977; EdD, Boston U., 1982. Music tchr. Pub. Sch., Wethersfield, Conn., 1962-63; serials libr. Hartford (Conn.) Sem. Found., 1963-64; elem. tchr. Pub. Sch., Glastonbury, Conn., 1965-79; asst. prof. Univ. Northern Iowa, Cedar Falls, Iowa, 1979-81; training mgr. Focus Research Systems Inc., W. Hartford, Conn., 1982-89; pers. adminstr. City of Hartford, 1989-99; cons., 1999—2002. Mem. leadership educators program John F. Kennedy Sch. Govt., Harvard U., 1999; mem. Human Resource Mgmt. Del., Russia and Estonia, 1992, Initiative Edn., Sci. and Tech., South Africa, 1995. Recipient Maria Miller Stewart award, 1992. Mem.: Am. Guild Organists. Democrat. E-mail: smher82@aol.com.

HERTWECK, ALMA LOUISE, sociology and child development educator; b. Moline, Ill., Feb. 6, 1937; d. Jacob Ray and Sylvia Ethel (Whitt) Street; m. E. Romayne Hertweck, Dec. 16, 1955; 1 child, William Scott. AA, Mira Costa Coll., 1969; BA in Sociology summa cum laude, U. Calif., San Diego, 1975, MA, 1977, PhD, 1982. Cert. sociology instr., multiple subjects tchg. credential grades k-12, Calif. Staff rsch. assoc. U. Calif., San Diego, 1978-81; instr. sociology Chapman Coll., Orange, Calif., 1982-87; instr. child devel. Mira Costa Coll., Oceanside, Calif., 1983-87, 88-89; instr. sociology U.S. Internat. U., San Diego, 1985-88; exec. dir., v.p. El Camino Preschools, Inc., Oceanside, 1985—. Author: Constructing the Truth and Consequences: Educators' Attributions of Perceived Failure in School, 1982; co-author: Handicapping the Handicapped, 1985. Mem. Am. Sociol. Assn., Am. Ednl. Rsch. Assn., Nat. Coun. Family Rels., Nat. ASsn. Edn. Young Children, Alpha Gamma Sigma. Avocations: foreign travel, sailing, bicycling. Home: 2024 Oceanview Rd Oceanside CA 92056-3104 Office: El Camino Preschs Inc 2002 California St Oceanside CA 92054-5693 E-mail: ahertweck@cox.net.

HERTWECK, E. ROMAYNE, psychology educator; b. July 24, 1928; s. Garnett Perry and Nova Gladys (Chowning) H.; m. Alma Louise Street, Dec. 16, 1955; 1 child, William Scott. BA, Augustana Coll., 1962; MA, Pepperdine U., 1963; EdD, Ariz. State U., 1966; PhD, U.S. Internat. U., 1978. Cert. sch. psychologist, Calif. Night editor Rock Island (Ill.) Argus Newspaper, 1961; grad. asst. psychology dept. Pepperdine Coll., L.A., 1962; counselor VA Ariz. State U., Tempe, 1963; assoc. dir. Conciliation Ct., Phoenix, 1964; prof. Phoenix Coll., Phoenix, 1965, Mira Costa Coll., Oceanside, Calif., 1966—2003. Mem. senate coun. Mira Costa Coll., 1968-70, 85-87, 89-91, chmn. psychology-counseling dept., 1973-75, chmn. dept. behavioral sci., 1976-82, 87-88, 90-91; part-time lectr. dept. bus. adminstrn. San Diego State U., 1980-84, Sch. Human Behavior U.S. Internat. U., 1984-89; prof. psychology Chapman Coll. Mem. World Campus Afloat, 1970; pres. El Camino Preschs., Inc., Oceanside, Calif., 1985—; CEO Nutri-Cal, Inc., Oceanside, Calif., 1996-2003. Bd. dirs. Lifeline, 1969, Christian Counseling Center, Oceanside, 1970-82; mem. City of Oceanside Childcare Task Force, 1991—1992; mem. City of Oceanside Community Rels. Commn., 1991-96, vice chair, 1994; mem. steering com. Healthy Cities Project City of Oceanside, Calif., 1993-95. Mem. Am. Western, North San Diego County (v.p. 1974-75) psychol. assns., Am. Assn. for Counseling and Devel., Nat. Educators Fellowship (v.p. El Camino chpt. 1976-77), Am. Coll. Personnel Assn., Phi Delta Kappa, Kappa Delta Pi, Psi Chi, Kiwanis (charter mem. Carlsbad club, dir. 1975-77). Home: 2024 Oceanview Rd Oceanside CA 92056-3104 also: El Camino Preschs Inc 2002 California St Oceanside CA 92054-5673 Office: Mira Costa Coll 3210 Bernie Dr Oceanside CA 92056-3816 E-mail: rhertweck@cox.net.

HERWIG, JOAN EMILY, developmental education educator, researcher; b. Apr. 7, 1943; Student, Merrill-Palmer Inst., 1964; BS, U. Wis., Stout, 1965; MS, Iowa State U., 1971; PhD, Purdue U., 1978. Tchr. jr. h.s., Pt. Huron, Mich., 1965—69; dir.-tchr. Head Start, Pt. Huron, Mich., 1965—69; tchg. asst. Iowa State U., 1969—70, assoc. prof. child devel., 1971—, chmn. dept., 1983—86, faculty senate, 1997—2003. Rsch. asst. Purdue U., 1976—78; dir. Child Devel. Lab. Sch., 1993—2001; early childhood spl. edn. tchr. Licensure Com. Iowa Dept. Edn., 1993—; cons. child devel., early childhood edn.; mem. conf. U.S./China on Early Childhood Edn. to People's Republic of China, 1993. Cons. editor: Early Childhood Rsch. Quar., 1990—93, Young Children, 1990—, Jour. Family and Consumer Svcs., 1981—, mem. editl. bd.: Jour. Early Childhood Tchr. Edn., 1995—; contbr. chpts., articles to profl. jours. Named David Ross fellow, Purdue U., 1978; recipient Fulbright scholarship, India, 1991—92, Outstanding Tchr. award, Amoco, 1982—83, Disting. Alumni award, U. Wis., 1985, Outstanding Acad. Advisor award, 1982, Midwest Shirley Dean Early Childhood Educator award, 1993, Outstanding Internat. Achievement award, Coll. Family and Consumer Scis., Iowa State U., 1997, Faculty award, Iowa State U. Alumni Assn., 2002. Mem.: World Orgn. of Children, Soc. Internat. Devel., Internat. Fed. Home Econ., Am. Edn. Rsch. Assn., Nat. Assn. Early Childhood Tchrs. Educators, Am. Assn. Family and Consumer Scis. (sec.-treas. family rels. child devel. sect. 1988—90, fellowship com. 1990—91, recognition and honors com. chair 1994—96), Iowa Assn. Edn. Young Children (sec. 1979—82, v.p. 1982—83, pres. 1983—84), Iowa Assn. Early Childhood Tchr. Educators (founder), Midwestern Assn. Edn. Young Children (Iowa rep. coun. 1985—92, v.p. 1986—87, pres. 1987—90), Nat. Assn. Edn. Young Children (pres.-elect 1995—97, pres. 1997—99), Soc. Rsch. in Child Devel., Phi Beta Delta, Phi Delta Kappa, Kappa Omicron Nu. Achievements include research in cognitive development of young children's play, parent involvement and early childhood teacher education. Office: Iowa State U 2356 Palmer HDFS Bldg Ames IA 50011-4380 E-mail: jherwig@iastate.edu.

HERWIG, STEVEN ROGER, osteopathic physician, otolaryngologist, educator; b. Madison, Wis., Mar. 8, 1948; s. Roger Miles and Joyce Ivah (Mahlke) H.; m. Karen Lynn Knuteson, Aug. 30, 1960; children: Todd Steven, Paige Lynn. BS in Pharmacy with distinction, Drake U., 1971, MBA, 1999; DO, U. Osteo. Medicine-Health Sci., Des Moines, 1976. Registered pharmacist, Ill.; diplomate Am. Bd. Otolaryngology. Pharmacist Moline (Ill.) Luth. Hosp., 1971-73; intern Met. Hosp., Grand Rapids, Mich., 1976-77; resident U. Cin. Med. Ctr., 1977-81; pvt. practice, Des Moines, 1984—. Cons. Walter Reed Army Med. Ctr., Washington, 1981-84; asst. prof. surgery Uniformed Svcs. U. Health Scis., Washington, 1983-84; adj. clin. prof. Univ. Osteo. Medicine and Health Sci., 1986—; clin. asst. prof. dept. otolaryngology, head and neck surgery U. Iowa, 1998—. Contbr. articles to med. jours. Bd. govs. Walnut Creek YMCA, West Des Moines, Iowa, 1988-93; bd. chair Lakeview Surgery Ctr. Maj. M.C., USAF, 1981-84. Recipient Alter Peerless Meml. award U. Cin. Med. Ctr., 1981, pediatric recognition award Blank Children's Hosp., Des Moines, 1990. Fellow Am. Acad. Facial Plastic and Reconstructive Surgery; mem. Am. Acad. Otolaryngology, Am. Osteo. Coll. Otolaryngology (cert.), Iowa Med. Soc. (Polk County del. 1987, 90), Polk County Med. Soc., Physicians for Social Responsibility, Iowa Acad. Otolaryngology (past pres.), Sigma Sigma Phi. Avocations: cycling, scuba diving, travel. Office: The Iowa Clinic-ENT 5950 Univ Ave Ste 265 West Des Moines IA 50266

HERZOG, BARBARA JEAN, secondary school educator, administrator; b. Fond du Lac, Wis. d. Charles Victor and Helen Jean (Gutsch) H. BS in Social Studies, U. Wis., Oshkosh, 1970, MS in Teaching in History-Social Sci., 1975; PhD in Ednl. Adminstrn., U. Wis., Madison, 1984. Cert. tchr., Wis.; cert. prin., Wis. Tchr. Woodworth Jr. H.S., Fond du Lac, 1970-75, 76-81; adminstrv. intern Fond du Lac Pub. Schs., 1983, mem. insvc. edn. coun., 1978-84; grad. asst. U. Wis., Madison, 1982-83; tchr. Sabish Jr. H.S., Fond du Lac, 1981-82, 83-84, Shattuck Jr. H.S., Neenah, 1984-87; asst. prin. Neenah Jr. H.S. Dist., 1984-87; tchr., curriculum dir. Oshkosh Area Sch. Dist., 1987-97, asst. supt. instrn., 1997—. Ad hoc prof. U. Wis. Oshkosh Coll. Edn., 1977—; presenter U. Wis. Oshkosh NSF Conf., 1976, Wis. Ednl. Rsch. Assn., Milw., 1976, Nat. Coun. for the Social Studies Conf., Mpls., 1978, Tex., 1978, Wis. Coun. for the Social Studies, Oconomowoc, 1978, 83,, 84, 86, Milw. Tchrs. Edn. Assn., 1978, Great Lakes Regional Social Studies Conf., Chgo., 1979, Nat. U. Extension Assn. Region IV Conf., Kalamazoo, 1979, Wis. Edn. Assn. Coun., Milw., 1979, Assn. Tchr. Educators, Washington, 1980, San Diego, 1988, Nat. Coun. on States on Insvc. Edn., San Diego, 1980, 14th Annual Mid. and Jr. H.S. Conf., U. Wis., Oshkosh, 1986, 15th Annual Conf., 1987, Assn. Tchr. Educators Regional Spring Miniclinic, Oak Brook, Ill., 1986, Globescope Wis. 88, Oshkosh, 1988, Assn. Wis. Sch. Adminstrs., Madison, 1988, U. Wis. Oshkosh and Green Bay, 1990, 91, among others; presenter NAESP, 2003. Co-author: (with others) Programming for Staff Development: Fanning the Flame, 1990; contbr. articles to profl. jours. Mem. exec. com. Oshkosh Human Rels. Coun., 1993-96; chair, mem. faith formation com. St. Peter Cath. Ch., Oshkosh, 1993-95, communion min., 1982—; mem. South Winnebago pub. edn. com. Am. Cancer Soc., Oshkosh, 1992-96; bd. dirs. Silvercrest Girls' Group Home, Neenah, 1986-87, So. Fox Valley Child Svcs. Soc., Oshkosh 1990-96; mem. ednl. outreach subcom. Oshkosh Cmty. U. Human Rels. Coun., 1989—; alt. Oshkosh Addictions Coord. Bd., 1990-92; mem. bd. visitors Sch. Edn. U. Wis., Madison, 1997-2001; bd. dirs. Paine Art Ctr. and Gardens, 1999—; mem. adv. coun. U. Wis., Oshkosh. Recipient Advocacy award Wis. Sch. Counselors Assn., 1992, Best Overall Paper award Wis. Ednl. Rsch. Assn., 1986, Rsch. award Wis. Improvement Program, 1986, U. Wis. Sch. Edn. Alumni Achievement award, 1995, Citation award Wis. AHPERD, 1997, Adminstr. of Yr. award Oshkosh Area Sch. Dist., 1995. Mem. ASCD, Assn. Am. Sch. Adminstrs., Wis. Coun. for the Social Studies (exec. com. 1980-87), Oshkosh Area Sch. Dist. Adminstrs. Assn., TESOL, Wis. ASCD, Wis. Staff Devel. Coun., Oshkosh Area United Way, Oshkosh Southwest Rotary, Oshkosh C. of C. (edn. com. 1987-96), Phi Delta Kappa (chpt. pres. 1989-90), Delta Kappa Gamma (Helen Duling scholarship 1982). Home: 925 E Bent Ave Oshkosh WI 54901 Office: Oshkosh Area Sch Dist 215 S Eagle St Oshkosh WI 54902-5624

HERZOG, CAROL JEAN, elementary school educator; b. Huntington, Ind., Dec. 29, 1949; d. Robert Earl and Doris Mae (Goble) H. BS, Ind. Cen. Coll. (now U. Indpls.), 1972; MS, St. Francis Coll., 1976. Primary tchr. Huntington (Ind.) County Cmty. Schs., 1972—. Former 5th and 6th grade girls' basketball coach. Mem.: NEA, Huntington Classroom Tchrs. Assn., Ind. State Tchrs. Assn., Delta Kappa Gamma (state pres. 2003—).

HESBY, JOHN HOWARD, agricultural educator; b. Arlington, S.D., Oct. 25, 1943; m. Kay Hesby. BS in Animal Sci., S.D. State U., 1966; MS, Purdue U., 1969, PhD, 1971. Rsch. asst. animal nutrition Purdue U., 1966—67, tchg. asst. animal nutrition, 1967—71; from asst. prof. to prof. Tex. A&M U., Coll. Station, Tex., 1971—91, prof., 1991—. Recipient Honor Prof. award Coll. Agriculture, 1973, Outstanding Prof. award Collegiate FFA, 1974, Faculty Disting. Achievement in Teaching award Assn. Former Students Tex. A&M U., 1974, Coll. Agr. Teaching award Alpha Gamma Rho Agr. Fraternity, 1980, Teaching award Agr. Econs. Club, 1982, Faculty Disting. Achievement in Teaching award Assn. Former Students, 1982. Mem. Am. Soc. Animal Sci., Nat. Block and Bridle Club, Nat. Assn. Colls. and Tchrs. of Agr., Nat. Agri-Mktg. Assn., So. Assn. Agrl. Scientists, Tex. Assn. Coll. Tchrs., Tex. Pork Producers Assn., Nutrition Today Soc., Coun. for Agrl. Sci. and Tech., Alpha Zeta, Gamma Sigma Delta, Sigma Xi. Office: Tex A&M Univ 122 Kleberg Ctr College Station TX 77843-2471*

HESKETT, LUVINA HYLTON, retired elementary education educator; b. Floyd, Va., May 26, 1935; d. Jabe Harmon and Carsie Ella (Weeks) Hylton; m. James Edwin Heskett, June 8, 1956; children: James, Margaret, Natalie, Jeremy. BA, Bridgewater (Va.) Coll., 1957. Elem. tchr. Loudoun County Sch. Bd., Leesburg, Va., 1967-94; tchr. Lovettsville (Va.) Elem. Sch., 1967-96. Mem. NEA, Va. Edn. Assn., Loudoun Edn. Assn. (sch. rep., com.).

HESS, CHARLES EDWARD, environmental horticulture educator; b. Paterson, N.J., Dec. 20, 1931; s. Cornelius W. M. and Alice (Debruyn) H.; children: Mary, Carol, Nancy, John, Peter; m. Eva G. Carroad, Feb. 14, 1981. BS, Rutgers U., 1953; MS, Cornell U., 1954, PhD, 1957; DAgr (hon.), Purdue U., 1983; DSc (hon.), Delaware Valley Coll., Doylestown, Pa., 1992. From asst. prof. to prof. Purdue U., West Lafayette, Ind., 1958-65; rsch. prof., dept. chmn. Rutgers U., New Brunswick, N.J., 1966, assoc. dean, dir. N.J. Agrl. Exptl. Sta., 1970, acting dean Coll. Agrl. and Environ. Sci., 1971, dean Cook Coll., 1972-75; assoc. dir. Calif. Agrl. Exptl. Sta., 1975-89; asst. sec. sci. and edn. USDA, Washington, 1989-91; dean Coll. Agrl. and Environ. Scis. U. Calif., Davis, 1975-89, prof. dept. environ. horticulture, 1975-94; prof. emeritus, 1994—; dir. internat. programs Coll. Agrl. and Environ. Scis. U. Calif., Davis, 1992-98, spl. asst. to provost, 1994—2003. Cons. U.S. AID, 1965, Office Tech. Assessment, U.S. Congress, 1976-77; chmn. study team world food and nutrition study NAS, 1976; mem. Calif. State Bd. Food and Agr., 1984-89; mem. Nat. Sci. Bd., 1982-88, 92-98, vice-chmn., 1984-88; co-chmn. Joint Coun. USDA, 1987-91. Mem. West Lafayette Sch. Bd., Ind., 1963-65, sec., 1963, pres., 1964; mem. Gov.'s Commn. Blueprint for Agr., 1971-73; bd. dirs. Davis Sci. Ctr., 1992-94; trustee Internat. Svc. for Nat. Agrl. Rsch., The Hague, The Netherlands, 1992-98, bd. chmn., 1995-96. Mem. U.S. EPA (mem. biotech. sci. adv. com. 1992-96). AAAS (chmn. agriculture sect. 1989-90), Am. Soc. Hort. Sci. (pres. 1973), Internat. Plant Propagators Soc. (pres. 1973), Agrl. Rsch. Inst., Phi Beta Kappa, Sigma Xi, Alpha Zeta, Phi Kappa Phi. Office: U Calif Coll Agrl Environ Scis Dept Environ Horticulture Davis CA 95616 E-mail: cehess@ucdavis.edu.

HESS, DARLA BAKERSMITH, cardiologist, educator; b. Valparaiso, Fla., June 4, 1953; d. James Barry and Irma Marie (Baker) Bakersmith; m. Leonard Wayne Hess, July 20, 1988; 1 child, Ever Marie. BS, Birmingham So. Coll., 1975; MD, Tulane U., 1979. Diplomate Am. Bd. Internal Medicine, Am. Bd. Cardiovascular Disease. Commd. ensign USNR, 1979, advanced through grades to lt. comdr., 1988; resident in internal medicine Portsmouth (Va.) Naval Hosp., 1979-82, cardiologist, head non-invasive cardiology, 1986-88; fellow in cardiology San Diego Naval Hosp., 1982-84; cardiologist, head med. officer in charge ICU Camp Lejeune (N.C.) Naval Hosp., 1984-85; asst. prof. medicine U. Miss. Med. Ctr., Jackson, 1988-91, asst. prof. ob/gyn., 1990-91; dir. noninvasive sect. cardiology, dir. fetal echocardiography U. Mo., Columbia, 1991—99, co-dir. Adult Cogenital Heart Disease Clinic, 1991—99, assoc. prof. medicine, assoc. prof. ob/gyn., 1998—2001. Author: (with others) Obstetrics and Gynecology Clinics, 1992, Clinical Problems in Obstetrics & Gynecology, 1993, General Medical Disorders During, 1991; co-editor: Fetal Echocardiography, 1999; contbr. articles to So. Med. Jour., Ob/Gyn. Clinics N.Am., Soc. Perinatal Obs., Jour. Reproductive Medicine, others. Fellow Am. Coll. Cardiology, Fellow Am. Heart Assn. (fellow stroke coun.), Fellow Am. Soc. Echocardiography; mem. Am. Assn. Nuclear Cardiology, Phi Beta Kappa, Alpha Omega Alpha. Republican. Episcopalian. Home: 7945 Springhouse Rd New Tripoli PA 18066

HESS, DENNIS WILLIAM, chemical engineering educator; b. Reading, Pa., Mar. 1, 1947; s. John William and Dorothy E. (Miller) H.; m. Patricia Ruth Weidner, June 1, 1968; children: Amy R., Sarah E. BS in Chemistry, Albright Coll., 1968; MS in Phys. Chemistry, Lehigh U., 1970, PhD in Phys. Chemistry, 1973. Staff researcher Fairchild Semiconductor, Palo Alto, Calif., 1973-77; from asst. prof. to prof. chem. engring. U. Calif., Berkeley, 1977-91; prin. investigator Materials and Molecular Research div. Lawrence Berkeley Lab., 1978-84, Ctr. for Adv. Materials, Lawrence Berkeley Lab., 1983-85; asst. dean Coll. Chemistry U. Calif., Berkeley, 1982-87; vice chmn. dept. chem. engring U. Calif., Berkeley, 1988-91; chmn. dept. chem. engring. Lehigh U., Bethlehem, Pa., 1991-96; William W. LaRoche Jr. prof. chem. engring. Ga. Inst. Tech., Atlanta, 1996—. Contbr. articles to profl. jours. Mem. The Electrochem. Soc. (pres. 1996-97). Office: Ga Tech Sch Chem Enging 311 Ferst Dr Atlanta GA 30332-0100 E-mail: dennis.hess@che.gatech.edu.

HESS, DOLORES J. elementary education educator; b. North Charleroi, Pa., July 11, 1940; d. George and Sarah (Tatalovich) Vranges; m. Clarence K. Hess, July 29, 1961; children: Susan Elaine Nickler, Todd Isaac, Dianne Faye Dish, Scott Michael. BS, Calif. (Pa.) U., 1974, MS, 1977, reading supr. cert., 1980. Reading specialist Bethlehem Ctr. Schs., Fredericktown, Pa., 1975-78, lang. arts educator, 1978-80, reading supr., 1980-82, reading tchr., 1982-89, lang. arts tchr., 1989—. Field test participant Nat. Bd. for Profl. Tchg. Stds., Pitts., 1991-93; strategic planning mem. Bethlehem-Ctr. Schs., Fredericktown, 1991-93, presenter, 1992-93; New Zealand trip participant. Presdl. scholar Calif. (Pa.) U., 1980. Mem. AAUW, Internat. Reading Assn., Keystone State Reading Assn., Nat. Coun. Tchrs. English, Pa. State Edn. Assn. (local treas., sec., v.p., county chpt. sec.), Delta Kappa Gamma. Home: PO Box 67 Beallsville PA 15313-0067 Office: 136 Crawford Rd Fredericktown PA 15333-2012

HESS, FRANCES ELIZABETH, retired secondary school educator, retired director; b. Trenton, N.J. d. George Alfred and Frances Randall Hess. BS in Edn., Temple U., 1956, MS in Edn., 1964. Tchr. Bd. Edn., Trenton, 1956—60, Fallsington, Pa., 1960—93, aquatics dir., 1981—97; ret., 1997. Instr., trainer ARC, Levittown, Pa., 1983—2003, mem. health & safety, 1981—2003; tech. v.p. U.S. Synchronized Swimming, Indpls., 1999—2003. Named to Hall of Fame, Temple U., 1983. Avocations: swimming, jigsaw puzzles, gardening. Home: 718 S Olds Blvd Fairless Hills PA 19030

HESS, MARCIA WANDA, retired secondary school educator; b. Cin., Mar. 15, 1934; d. Edward Frederick Lipka and Rose (Wirtle) Lipka Stanley; m. Edward Emanuel Grenier, Aug. 9, 1952 (div.); m. Thomas Benton Hess, Mar. 25, 1960; children: Kathleen Ann, Cynthia Jean, Thomas Allen. Grad. high sch., Cin. Instr. asst. Cin. Pub. Schs., 1970-95, also mem. staff desegregation workshop and unified K-12 reading communication arts program staff tng. com.; ret., 1995. Contbr. tchr.-instr. asst. handbook, instr. asst. tng. film. Mem. Winton Place Vets of World War II Women's Aux. (pres. 1982-84, bd. dirs. 1982-86, 89-91, v.p. 1997-99). Republican. Roman Catholic. Avocations: travel, reading. collecting first editions, needlepoint, photography. Home: 157 Palisades Pt Apt 4 Cincinnati OH 45238-5660

HESS, MARGARET JOHNSTON, religious writer, educator; b. Ames, Iowa, Feb. 22, 1915; d. Howard Wright and Jane Edith (Stevenson) Johnston; m. Bartlett Leonard Hess, July 31, 1937; children: Daniel, Deborah, John, Janet. BA, Coe Coll., 1937. Bible tchr. Cmty. Bible Classes, Ward Presbyn. Ch., Livonia, Mich., 1959-96, Christ Ch. Cranbrook (Episcopalian), Bloomfield Hills, Mich., 1980-93, Luth. Ch. of the Redeemer, Birmingham, Mich., 1993-99. Co-author: (with B.L. Hess) How to Have a Giving Church, 1974, The Power of a Loving Church, 1977, How Does Your Marriage Grow?, 1983, Never Say Old, 1984; author: Love Knows No Barriers, 1979, Esther: Courage in Crisis, 1980, Unconventional Women, 1981, The Triumph of Love, 1987; contbr. articles to religiouos jours. Home: 15191 Ford Rd Apt 302 Dearborn MI 48126-4696

HESS, PATRICIA ALICE, nursing educator, geriatrics nurse consultant; b. N.Y.C., Apr. 25, 1938; d. Frederic and Anne (Goldman) H. BSN, Case Western Reserve U., 1961; MS, U. Colo., 1966; PhD, Walden U., 1982; cert. geriat. nurse practitioner, U. Calif., San Francisco, 1986. Cert. gerontol. nurse. Staff nurse Univ. Hosps., Cleve., 1961-62; head nurse Mt. Sinai Hosp., Cleve., 1962-65; instr. U. Mich., Ann Arbor, 1966-67; prof. nursing San Francisco State U., 1967—, U. Calif. Berkeley, 1977-85. Contbr. articles to profl. jours. Recipient Book of Yr. award Am. Jour. Nursing, 1977, 82, 86, 90, 94, 98, 2001. Mem. ANA, Gerontol. Soc. Am., Am. Soc. on Aging, Nat. Orgn. of Nurse Practitioner Faculty, Nat. Acad. Practice, Phi Beta Delta. Home: 1341 27th Ave San Francisco CA 94122-1508 Office: San Francisco State U Sch Nursing 1600 Holloway Ave San Francisco CA 94132-1722

HESS, TERRY WICHTER, music educator, composer; b. Massapequa, N.Y., Apr. 19, 1957; d. Michael and Evelyn (Epstein) W.; m. Peter Alan Hess, July 4, 1979; 1 child, Sandon Jacob. BA in Music, SUNY, 1979; postgrad., De Paul U., 1980-81. Cert. music teacher grades K-12. Music therapist Edgewater Nursing Home, Chgo., 1979-80; music edn. sec. Roosevelt U., Chgo., 1980-81; music educator Saints Faith Hope Charity, Winnetka, Ill., 1981-82, Easton (Conn.) Pub. Schs., 1986-87, Elmont (N.Y.) Pub. Schs., 1982-86, Trumbull (Conn.) Pub. Schs. and Janeryan Elementary Sch., 1988—; composer SH Prodns., 1988—. Instr. songwriting Westport (Conn.) Continuing Edn., 1990—, Wilton (Conn.) Continuing Edn., 1990—. Composer: Fire Island Lighthouse, 1986, The Children Want Peace, 1987, Desert Shield, 1991, Hole in the Wall Gang Camp, Isn't it Time, 1993, Trumbull Little League World Series Winners Theme Song; music documentary cons. The Children Want Peace; exec. prodr. Isn't it Time Radio Show, Sta. WICC AM, Conn., 1993-94, (pilot) Isn't it Time TV Show, 1994-95. Active exec. bd. Trumbull PTA, 1991—; edn. cons. Conn. Ballet Theatre, Fairfield, 1991—. Recipient Outstanding Achievement award Billboard Mag., 1991; GE grantee, Coop. Ednl. Svcs. grantee, 1993-94. Mem. Nat. Acad. Songwriters, Conn. Music Educators Nat. Conf., Broadcast Music Inc. Jewish. Avocations: sailing, cross-country skiing, windsurfing, hiking, antiques. Home: 51 Creeping Hemlock Dr Norwalk CT 06851-1017 Office: Trumbull Pub Schs Janeryan Elementary Sch Park Lane Trumbull CT 06611

HESSE, THURMAN DALE, welding and metallurgy educator, consultant; b. Plymouth, Wis., Nov. 28, 1938; s. Leonard Ferdinand and Eileen H.; m. Virginia Raynoha, Sept. 5, 1959; children: Daniel Jacob, David Tyler, Laura Alice. BS, Wis. State Coll. & Inst. Tech., 1962; MS, Stout State U., 1965; postgrad., U. Wis., 1974-75. Tchr. welding State Vocat. Tech. & Adult Edn., Madison, 1965-96, tchr. machine shop, 1966-96, tchr. welding tech., 1968-96; welding instr. indsl. div. Madison (Wis.) Area Tech. Coll., 1966-96; weld test condr. Wis. Dept. Commerce, Madison, 1976—; owner Tech. Welding Svcs. LLC, Cottage Grove, Wis., 1978—. Lectr. U. Wis. Engring. Extension, Madison, 1978-85. Producer videotape on welding career options; contbr. articles to Welding Jour. Mem. coun. St. Stephens Luth. Ch., Monona, Wis., 1982-85. Mem. ASTM, Am. Welding Soc. (cert. welding insepctor, chmn. bd. dirs. Madison-Beloit chpt., membership com. 1989-92, Howard Adkins award 1975, Dist. 12 dir. 1992-99), Am. Soc. Metals. Home and Office: Tech Welding Svc LLC 2302 Whiting Rd Cottage Grove WI 53527-8818 E-mail: thesse@mailbag.com.

HESSER, LORRAINE M, special education educator; d. Joseph V. Scolari III, Agnes E. McGovern; m. George W. Hesser III, June 1, 1979; children: Stephanie M., Matthew G. BA in Spl. Edn., Rowan U., 1996; AAS in Bus. Adminstrn., Mktg., Camden County Coll., 1977. Cert. Tchr. of Handicapped N.J., 1996, elem. tchr. N.J., 1997. Tchr. spl. edn. Vineland Pub. Schs., Vineland, NJ, 1998—, Ind. Child Study Teams, Jersey City, 1996—98. Mem. Salem County Bd. of Sch. Estimates, 2003—; chairperson Salem County Mental Health Bd., Salem, NJ, 1995—; bd. dirs. Salem County Spl. Svcs. Sch. Dist. Bd. Edn., Woodstown, NJ; parent adv. Phila. Child Guidance Ctr. Children's Hosp., 1994; organizer Girl Scouts Am., Medford, NJ, 1985—88. Mem.: NEA, Statewide Parent Adv. Network, N.J. Edn. Assn., Coun. for Exceptional Children (Learning Disabilities divsn., Culturally and Linguistically Diverse Exceptional Learners divsn., Spl. Educator award 2000). Avocations: music, travel, photography, gardening, reading. Home: 1065 Rainbow Cir Pittsgrove NJ 08318 Office: Vineland Board of Education 625 Plum St Vineland NJ 08360 Personal E-mail: lmhesser@aol.com.

HESTAD, MARSHA ANNE, educational administrator; b. Evanston, Ill., Apr. 25, 1950; d. Bjorn Mark and Florence Anne (Ragusi) H. BS, U. Ill., 1972; MEd, Nat. Coll. Edn., Evanston, Ill., 1978; postgrad., Purdue U., 1985; PhD, Loyola U., Chgo., 1991. Cert. in elem. edn., spl. reading, gifted edn., gen. adminstrn., Ill., Ind. Tchr. 5th grade Deerfield (Ill.) Sch. Dist. 109, 1972-78; head tchr. North Aegean Acad., Kavala, Greece, 1978-81; gifted resource tchr. Alief Ind. Sch. Dist., Houston, 1983-84, TeKoppel, Evansville, Ind., 1984-85; field supr. Purdue U., West Lafayette, Ind., 1987; gifted coord. MSD Mt. Vernon, Ind., 1985-88; gifted resource Libertyville (Ill.) Sch. Dist. 70, 1988-91; instr. Coll. Lake County, Grayslake, Ill., 1991; clin. prof. Loyola U., Chgo., 1991; prof. Ind. State U., Terre Haute, 1992-93; tchr. lang. arts/lit. 7th grade, co-dir./prin. summer sch. Libertyville (Ill.) Sch. Dist. 70, 1993-94; prin. Chippewa Sch., Bensenville (Ill.) Dist. 2, 1994-96, Rockland Sch., Libertyville Ill., 1996—. Adj. prof. Loyola U., Chgo., 1998-99, Lake Forest Coll., 2003—; bd. dirs. Odyssey of the Mind, Ind. and Ill.; cons. in field. Co-prodr.: Countdown Interactive (cable program), 1995—96; exec. prodr.: Blast Off (cable program), 1997—2001; contbr. articles to profl. jours. Dist. 70 coord. Learn and Serve, Am. Grant Activities. Mem. ASCD, Nat. Coun. Staff Devel., Ill. Assn. for Gifted Children (v.p. 1998, pres.-elect 1999, pres. 2000-2002, past pres. 2002-04), Phi Delta Kappa. E-mail: mhestad@d70k.12.il.us.

HESTER, DONALD DENISON, economics educator; b. Cleve., Nov. 6, 1935; s. Donald Miller and Catherine (Denison) H.; m. Karen Ann Helm, Oct. 24, 1959; children: Douglas Christopher, Karl Jonathan. BA, Yale U., 1957, MA, 1958, PhD, 1961. Asst. prof., assoc. prof. Yale U., New Haven, Conn., 1961-68; jr. vis. prof. Bombay Univ., India, 1962-63; econs. prof. U. Wis., Madison, 1968-2000, dept. chmn., 1990-93. Cons. Fed. Res., 1969-84; vis. prof. People's U. China, Beijing, 1987. Author: Indian Banks: Their Portfolios, Profits and Policy, 1964; co-author: Bank Management and Portfolio Behavior, 1975, Banking Changes in the European Monetary Union: An Italian Perspective, 2002; co-editor: Risk Aversion and Portfolio Choice, 1967; contbr. numerous articles to profl. jours. Mem. Wis. Coun. Econ. Affairs, 1983-87. Guggenheim fellow 1972, Econometric Soc. fellow, 1977; recipient faculty fellowship Ford Found., 1967, other rsch. awards. Avocations: classical music, art, hiking, traveling. Home: 2111 Kendall Ave Madison WI 53726-3915 Office: U Wis Dept Econs 1180 Observatory Dr Madison WI 53706-1320

HESTER, GERALD LEROY, retired school system administrator; b. Seattle, Aug. 6, 1928; s. Ernest Orien and Louise (Drange) Hester; m. Carol Joyce Johnston, Aug. 2, 1953; children: Mark Wyn, Sue Ann. BS, Wash. State U., 1950, EdB, 1953; EdM, Western Wash. State Coll., 1957; EdD, Columbia U., 1964. Prin. jr. high sch. Bellevue Sch. Dist., Wash., 1959—64, dir. guidance, 1964—65; supt. Vashon Sch. Dist., Wash., 1965—69, Auburn Sch. Dist., Wash., 1969—73, Vancouver Sch. Dist., Wash., 1973—80, Spokane Sch. Dist., Wash., 1980—93; exec. com. People to People, 1985—, Gov.'s High Tech Com., 1988—; mem. Provost Commn. on Tchr. Edn., Wash. State U., Pullman, 1983—84; mem. adv. bd. U. Wash. Sch. Edn., Seattle, 1974; mem. Citizens Adv. Com. Higher Edn. Consortium, Spokane, 1984; bd. mem. Wash. Coun. for Econ. Edn., Seattle, 1984. Bd. dirs. Inland Empire coun. Boy Scouts Am., 1981—89, YMCA, 1982; chmn. edn. div. United Way, Spokane, 1981—82. Served to 1st lt. U.S. Army, 1951—52. Named among Top 100 Educators, Exec. Educators Mag., 1984, 1987, 1989, 1990, Ednl. Adminstr. of Yr., Nat. Assn. Edn. Office Pers., 1989; recipient Civic Fame award, Rotary Club 21, Spokane, 1982, Alumni Achievement award, Wash. State U., 1984. Mem.: Spokance C. of C. (bd. trustees 1983—87, exec. com. 1985—88), 1st. Class Sch. Dist. Supts. (pres. 1984), Wash. Assn. Sch. Adminstrs. (exec. bd. 1971—74), Suburban Sch. Supts. (pres. 1982—83), Am. Assn. Sch. Adminstrs. (finalist nat. supt. of yr. 1990, adv. com., leadership for learning award 1992, disting. svc. award 1995), Prosperity (Spokane, Wash.) (pres. 1993), Spokane Country, Spokane, Royal Oaks Country (Vancouver, Wash.) (pres. 1979—80), Rotary, Phi Delta Kappa.

HESTER, LINDA HUNT, retired dean, counseling administrator; b. Winston-Salem, NC, June 16, 1938; d. Hanselle Lindsay and Jennie Sarepta (Hunt) H. BS with honors, U. Wis., 1960, MS, 1964; PhD, Mich. State U., 1971. Lic. ednl. counselor, Wis. Instr. health and phys. edn. for women U. Tex., Austin, 1960—62; asst. dean women U. Ill., Urbana, 1964—66; dean of women, asst. prof. sociology and phys. edn. Tex. Woman's U., Denton, 1971—73. Rsch. assoc. bur. higher edn. Mich. Dept. Edn., Lansing, 1969-70; vol. counselor Dallas Challenge and Dallas Ind. Sch. Dist., 1989-90 Stradivarious mem. Dallas Symphony, 1991—; assoc. mem. Dallas Mus. Art, 1991—; friend of Kimbell Art Mus., com. of 1000 Philharmonic Ctr. for Arts, Naples, Fla.; founder Women's Mus., Dallas; mem., donor Naples Mus. Art; bd. dirs. Dallas Opera, Dallas, 1986—; bd. dir. Disting. Svc. Registry in Counseling and Devel. Fellow coll. edn. Mich. State U., 1968. Mem. Am. Counseling Assn., Am. Coll. Pers. Assn., Nat. Assn. Women in Edn. (named one of 100 Notable Women in Tex. 2003), Brookhaven Country Club, Wyndemere Country Club, Delta Kappa Gamma, Alpha Lambda Delta. Republican. Presbyterian. Avocations: golf, reading, sailing, cooking, travel. Home: 7606 Wellcrest Dr Dallas TX 75230-4857

HETLAND, JOHN ROBERT, lawyer, educator; b. Mpls., Mar. 12, 1930; s. James L. and Evelyn (Lundgren) H.; m. Mildred Woodruff, Dec. 1951 (div.); children: Lynda Lee Catlin, Robert John, Debra Ann Allen; m. Anne Kneeland, Dec. 1972; children: Robin T. Willcox, Elizabeth J. Pickett. BSL., U. Minn., 1952, JD, 1956. Bar: Minn. 1956, Calif. 1962, U.S. Supreme Ct, 1981. Practice law, Mpls., 1956-59; prof. law U. Calif., Berkeley, 1959-91; prof. emeritus, 1991—; prin. Hetland & Kneeland, PC, Berkeley, 1959—. Vis. prof. law Stanford U., 1971, 80, U. Singapore, 1972, U. Cologne, Fed. Republic Germany, 1988. Author: California Real Property Secured Transactions, 1970, Commercial Real Estate Transactions, 1972, Secured Real Estate Transactions, 1974, 1977; co-author: California Cases on Security Transactions in Land, 2d edit., 1975, 3d edit., 1984, 4th edit., 1992; contbr. articles to legal, real estate and fin. jours. Served to lt. comdr. USNR, 1953-55. Fellow Am. Coll. Real Estate Lawyers, Am. Coll. Mortgage Attys., Am. Bar Found.; mem. ABA, State Bar Calif., State Bar Minn., Order of Coif, Phi Delta Phi. Home and Office: 20 Red Coach Ln Orinda CA 94563-1112 E-mail: hetlandj@law.berkeley.edu.

HETTCHE, L. RAYMOND, research director; b. Balt., Mar. 24, 1938; s. Leroy and Dorothy (Curtain) H.; m. Patricia Durkan, July 1965; children: Lisa, Kathleen, Matthew, Craig. BSCE, AB in Math., Bucknell U., 1961; MSCE, Carnegie-Mellon U., 1961, PhD in CE, 1965. Asst. prof. Rutgers U., New Brunswick, N.J., 1964-66; resident rsch. assoc. Nat. Bur. Standards, Washington, 1966-68; structural engr. metallurgy div. Naval Rsch. Lab., Washington, 1968-71, head thermomech. effect sect., 1971-73, head mech. br. metallurgy div., 1973-75, supt. materials sci. div., 1975-81; now, dir. Applied Rsch. Lab. Pa. State U., State College, 1981—2002, prof. engring. rsch., 2002—. Navy rep. Tech. Working Group Export Control, Washington, 1979-81; navy rep. subgroup P materials panel for metals Tech. Cooperation Program, Washington, 1977-81; session chmn. Submarine Tech. Symposium, Columbia, Md., 1990. Contbr. numerous articles to profl. jours. Tau Beta Pi Nat. fellow, 1961-63; NSF fellow, 1963; recipient Outstanding Achievement award Am. Def. Preparedness Assn., 1986. Office: Pa State U Applied Rsch Lab PO Box 30 State College PA 16804-0030

HETZLER, SUSAN ELIZABETH SAVAGE, educational administrator; b. Monticello, Iowa, Mar. 18, 1947; d. Robert Engelbert and Josephine May (Ricklefs) Savage; children: Stephanine, Michael. BS in Edn., Rockford (Ill.) Coll., 1971; 2MS in Edn., No. Ill. U., 1978, cert. advanced study, 1984; PhD, Walden U., Mpls., 1989. Cert. elem. tchr., adminstr., Ill., Iowa; supr., sociology tchr., Ill. Elem. tchr. Freeport (Ill.) Sch. Dist., 1971-86; prof. elem. edn. Iowa State U., Ames, 1986-90; dir. tchr. edn. and devel. Iowa Dept. Edn., Des Moines, 1990-96; prof. edn., dean sch. edn. Buena Vista U., Storm Lake, Iowa, 1996-99; program admin. for educator preparation Tex. State Bd. for Educator Certification, Austin, 1999—2001; dir. tchr. edn. Tex. Higher Edn. Coord. Bd., Austin, 2001—. Curriculum cons. Ames Sch. Dist., 1985-90, Des Moines Sch. Dist., 1985-90; mem. ISU adv. bd., Ames, 1991—. Author: Elementary Education Practicum Teaching, 1988, Learning Centers, 1989. Comsnr. Drug and Alcohol Prevention Project, Freeport, 1976-85; chairperson Stephenson County (Ill.) Cancer Soc., 1976-78, small bus. dvsn. United Way, Freeport, 1980-85; vol. BSA and GSA, Freeport, 1974-85. Recipient Excellence in Teaching award Iowa State U., 1989-90, Outstanding Elem. Tchrs. Am. Ill., 1974, 81. Mem. AAUP, ASCD, NEA, Iowa ASCD, Am. Assn. Colls. of Tchr. Edn., Iowa Assn. Colls. of Tchr. Edn., Iowa Ednl. Rsch. and Eval. Assn., Assn. Tchr. Educators, Tex. Tchr. Educators, Tex. Coun. Women Sch. Execs., Delta Kappa Gamma, Phi Delta Kappa, Rotary, Kiwanis. Presbyterian. Avocations: reading, skiing, tennis, piano, antiques, golf. Home: 1107 Chardonnay Crossing Leander TX 78641 Office: Tex Higher Edn Coord Bd 1200 E Anderson Ln Austin TX 78752 E-mail: susan.hetzler@thecb.state.tx.us.

HETZNER, DONALD RAYMUND, social studies educator, forensic social scientist; b. Ottawa, Ill., Jan. 1, 1938; s. James Hyatt and Thelma Margaret (Sheedy) H.; m. Coralia Josefina Lora, July 9, 1966; children: Sean, Matthew. AA, LPO Jr. Coll., 1957; BA in Social Sci., Shimer Coll., 1961; MA in Polit. Sci., No. Ill. U., 1965; EdD in Social Studies, SUNY, Buffalo, 1972. Cert. tchr. social studies, N.Y. Tchr. English, social studies Medina (N.Y.) Pub. Sch. System, 1966-68; tchr. Kenmore-Tonawanda (N.Y.) Union Free Sch. Dist. 1, 1968-69; prof. SUC, Buffalo, 1970—. Scholar in residence Am. Assn. Cmty. and Jr. Colls., Washington, 1986-87; cons. restructuring post-secondary edn. in The Acad. Namibia, Southwest Africa, 1989; founder Applecore Consulting. Co-author: Practical Methods for the Social Studies, 1977, Working in America, 1976, Historian: Building a New Nation in 1789; editor: The Social Science Record, 1975-78; contbr. articles to ednl. jours. Mem. World Assn. for Case Rsch. and Application, Nat. Coun. for Social Studies, N.Y. State Coun. for Social Studies (exec. bd. dirs. 1975-78, jour. editor), Rsch. and Planning for the Future (founder). Democrat. Avocations: travel, historical research. Home: 67 Lancaster Ave Buffalo NY 14222-1403 Office: SUC Dept History & Social Studies 1300 Elmwood Ave Buffalo NY 14222-1004

HEUER, BETH LEE, music educator, composer, arranger; b. Rockford, Ill., May 13, 1957; d. Stanton Lee and Gladys Mae Heuer. BA in Music, 1980, BFA in Music Edn., 1981, M in Music Edn., 2001. Vocal music tchr. Boylan Cath. H.S., Rockford, Ill., 1981—82, Pecatonica (Ill.) H.S., 1982—83; band dir. Boylan Cath. H.S., 1983—, chmn. dept. music, 1987—. Pvt. music tchr., Rockford, 1982—. Music arranger, composer, 1985—. Mem.: Ill. Music Educators Assn., Music Educators Nat. Conf., Internat. Jazz Educators Assn. Avocations: gardening, reading, traveling. Office: Boylan Cath HS 4000 St Francis Dr Rockford IL 61103

HEUER, MICHAEL ALEXANDER, dean, endodontist educator; b. Grand Rapids, Mich., Apr. 27, 1932; s. Harold Maynard and Gwendolyn Ruth (Kremer) H.; m. Barbara Margaret Naines, Nov. 23, 1955; children—Kristan M., Karin E., Katrina A. DDS, Northwestern U., 1956; MS, U. Mich., 1959. Pvt. practice, Chgo., 1959-86; asst. prof. Northwestern U., 1960-66; assoc. prof. Loyola U., Chgo., 1968-73; prof., chmn. dept. endodontics Northwestern U., 1974-83, assoc. dean acad affairs, 1983-88, sr. assoc. dean, 1988-93, dean, 1993-98, prof. emeritus, 1999—. Dir. Am. Bd. Endodontics, 1971-77, sec.-treas., 1973-76, pres., 1976-77; chmn. subcom. Am. Nat. Standards Inst.; mem. com. on advanced edn. Commn. on Accreditation of Dental Edn., 1974-77, endodontic cons., 1986-91, curriculum cons., 1986-92. Contbr. articles in field to profl. jours. Served with USNR, 1956-58. Recipient Northwestern U. Alumni Merit award, 2001. Fellow Am. Coll. Dentistry (life, sec.-treas. Ill. sect. 1986-92, vice chair 1992-94, chair 1994-96), Internat. Coll. Dentistry, Am. Assn. Endodontists (life; exec. coun. 1967-71, sec. 1979-84, v.p. 1984-85, pres.-elect 1985-86, pres. 1986-87); mem. AAAS, ADA (life; coun. dental materials and devices 1972-78, chmn. 1977-78, sci. coun. 1980-97), Internat. Assn. Dental Rsch., Am. Assn. Dental Schs., Chgo. Odontographic Soc. (pres. 1982-84), Edgar D. Coolidge Endodontic Soc. (life, charter sec. 1961, pres. 1964, trustee), Phi Eta Sigma, Omicron Kappa Upsilon, Chi Psi, Delta Sigma Delta. Home: 1552 Treeline Ct Naperville IL 60565-2015 E-mail: mikeaheuer@aol.com.

HEUMANN, JUDITH, bank executive; m. Jorge Pineda. BA Speech and Theatre, Long Island U., 1969; MPH, U. Calif., Berkeley, 1975. Spl. edn. and 2d grade tchr. N.Y.C. Pub. Schs., 1970-73; legis. asst. to chair Senate Com. Labor and Pub. Welfare, Washington, 1974; sr. dep. dir. Ctr. Independent Living, Berkeley, 1975-82; spl. asst. to exec. dir. State Dept. Rehab., Sacramento, 1982-83; v.p., co-founder, dir. Rsch. Tng. Ctr. Pub. Policy in Independent Living, Berkeley, Calif., 1983-93; co-founder World Inst. Disability, Berkeley, Calif.; U.S. asst. sec. U.S. Dept. Edn., Washington, 1993—2001; also chair, vice chair, bd. mem. Archtl. & Transp. Barriers Compliance Bd., Washington, 1998—2001; adv. disability and devel. World Bank, Washington, 2002—. Office: World Bank 1818 H Street NW Washington DC 20433*

HEUSEL, BARBARA STEVENS, English scholar and educator; b. Louisville, Jan. 12, 1935; d. Jay T. and Ruth L. Stevens; children: Heidi Heusel Freeman, Lisa Gillig, Gretchen Heusel. BA, Heidelberg Coll., 1957; MA, U. Louisville, 1967; PhD, U. S.C., 1983. Instr. dept. of English U. Louisville, 1965-68, Furman U., Greenville, S.C., 1968-84; vis. asst. prof. English Wake Forest U., Winston-Salem, N.C., 1985-88; lectr. in English U. N.C., Chapel Hill, 1984-85, 88-89; assoc. prof. English N.W. Mo. State U., Maryville, 1990-98, prof. English, 1998—. Dir. of curriculum The ArtSchool, Carrboro, N.C., 1988-90; cons. PENULTIMA, Chapel Hill, N.C., 1988—; lectr. in field. Author: Patterned Aimlessness: Iris Murdoch's Novels of the 1970s and 1980s, 1995, Iris Murdoch's Paradoxical Novels: Thirty Years of Critical Reception, 2001; contbr. articles to profl. jours. Mellon grant Furman U., 1979-80, grant Nat. Endowment for the Humanities, 1989. Mem. AAUW, AAUP, Iris Murdoch Soc. (founder, sec.-treas. 1986-93, pres. 1993—), MLA, James Joyce Soc., South Atlantic MLA. Avocations: traveling, aerobics, birding, canoeing, films. Office: NW Mo State U Dept English Maryville MO 64468

HEUSEL, GARY LEE, educator; b. Streator, Ill., Sept. 21, 1947; s. John Wayne and Inez Alene (Hedrick) H.; m. Karen Sue Keller, Dec. 20, 1975; 1 child, Jason Todd. BS in Agr., U. Ill., 1970, MEd, 1976, EdD, 1988. Asst. ext. advisor U. Ill. Coop. Ext., Jacksonville, 1970-72, assoc. ext. advisor Champaign, 1972-75, sr. ext. advisor Chgo., 1975-83; ext. specialist/vol. devel. U. Ga. Coop. Ext., Athens, 1983-91; owner/cons. Global Androgogical Assocs., Lincoln, Nebr., 1988—; ext. specialist Community Cares UGA Coop Ext., Athens, 1991-94; dir. Nat. 4-H Coun., Chevy Chase, Md., 1991—94; state 4-H program leader S.D. State U., Brookings, 1994—96, U. Nebr., Lincoln, 1996—2003. Mem. Exec. Devel. Inst., Dept. Agr., Washington, 1986-89; faculty Youth Developers Inst., Brasilia, Brazil, 1993—; mem. Internat. Character Counts Coalition, Marina Del Rey, Calif., 1997—; chair Coop. Curriculum Sys. U.S., 2001-03; chair U.S. 4-H Program Leaders, 2001-03, Nat. 4-H Leadership Trust, 2000-03. Author: Advisory Committees, 1987. Bd. dirs. Ptnrs. of the Ams. Atlanta and Washington, 1988—; bd. dirs. Nebr. Family Ctr., 1998—; pres. Nebr. Ptnrs. of the Ams., 2000-02; elder Good Shepherd Presbyn. Ch.; dir. Armenian Youth Programs, Yerevan, 2003—. Recipient Air Force award for Outstanding Nat. 4-H/Youth Profl., 2003. Fellow Exec. Devel. Inst.; mem. Nat. Assn. Ext. 4-H Agts. (bd. dirs. 1987-89, 2002-03, Disting. Svc. award, 1978), Partners of the Americas (fellow), Gamma Sigma Delta, Epsilon Sigma Phi. Avocations: theatre, reading, real estate speculation, travel. Home: 7640 Davies Dr Lincoln NE 68506-1757 Office: Univ Nebr 114 Agricultural Hall Lincoln NE 68583-0700

HEWES, DOROTHY WALKER, history educator; b. Milan, Ill., Apr. 15, 1922; d. Raymond Forrest and Maude Gertrude (Hull) Walker; m. David Danforth Hewes, June 11, 1949 (dec. June 2000); children: Andrew, Christopher, Rosemary, John. BS, Iowa State U., Ames, 1943; MA, Calif. State U., Northridge, 1969; PhD, Union Inst., 1974. Prof. family studies San Diego State U., 1974-92, prof. emeritus, 1992—. Chair history and archives com. Nat. Assn. for the Edn. of Young Children, Washington, 1974-78. Author: "It's the Camaraderie"-A History of Parent Cooperative Preschools, 1998, W.N. Hailman, Defender of Froebel, 2001, (with W.J. Leatherman) Early Childhood Education Administration, 1979, 5th edit., 2004,; editor: Administration: Making Programs Work, 1979; producer (video) Linkages-Preschools & Third World Parents, 1989. Staff sgt. USMC, 1942-46. Mem. Nat. Assn. Early Childhood Tchr. Educators, Orgn. Mondiale pour l'Education Prescholaire, Phi Beta Delta (charter), Delta Phi Upsilon (hon.).

HEWETT, JOYCE PARKER, educational administrator; b. Winnabow, N.C., Oct. 25, 1948; d. Leroy Sr. and Mary (McMillan) Parker; (div.); 1 child, Alvin L. Jr. Student, Graz (Austria) U., 1969; BS in Bus. Edn., Rust Coll., 1971; MA in Mgmt., Webster U., 1983. Adminstrv. asst. Inst. Modern Proc., Washington, 1971-73, Save the Children Fedn., Washington, 1973-75; fin. asst. Am.-Mideast Edn. and Tng. Svcs., Washington, 1975-77; accts. mgr. Brunswick County Hosp., Supply, N.C., 1978-81; bus. instr. Brunswick C.C., Supply, 1982-87, dir. bus. program, 1987—. Adv. mem. Brunswick County Schs., Southport, 1991— Vice chmn. Brunswick County Bd. Edn., 1998; bd. dirs. Habitat for Humanity. Recipient Leadership award Brunwick C.C. Found., 1990, C.C. Leadership award N.C. C.C., 1992, 93. Mem. NAACP (Southport chpt.), N.C. C.C. Assn. Bus. Chair and Dept. Heads, N.C. Bus. Edn. Assn., Delta Sigma Theta (pres. 1984-86, treas. 1992). Democrat. Baptist. Avocations: sewing, swimming, walking, aerobics, reading. Home: 2950 Hewett Rd SE Bolivia NC 28422-8144

HEWITT, JUNE ANN, elementary education educator; b. Excelsior Springs, Mo., July 24, 1956; d. Clarence Jr. and Norma Ann (Parman) King; m. Roger C. Hewitt, June 19, 1982 (div. Nov. 1987); 1 child, Ryan. BS in Edn., William Jewell Coll., Liberty, Mo., 1978; MEd, Webster U., 1984. Tchr. 1st and 2d grades Excelsior Springs Pub. Schs., 1978—. Named Tchr. of Yr., Excelsior Springs Sch. Dist., 1993. Mem. NEA, Mo. Edn. Assn., Excelsior Springs Edn. Assn., Beta Sigma Phi, Delta Kappa Gamma (pres. chpt. 1987-90). Baptist. Avocations: reading, walking, piano. Office: Westview Elem Sch 500 N Jesse James Rd Excelsior Springs MO 64024-3614 E-mail: appleteacher@juno.com.

HEWITT (VER HOEF), LISA CAROL, elementary education educator; b. Rock Rapids, Iowa, Oct. 7, 1963; d. Floyd Raymond and Carol Ann (Hollander) Ver Hoef; m. Douglas Ray Hewitt, July 22, 1995; 1 child, Mackenzie Ann Hewitt. BA summa cum laude, Buena Vista Coll., Storm Lake, Iowa, 1986. Cert. in elem. edn. and Spanish. Bilingual tchr. 2d grade Twombly Elem. Sch., Ft. Lupton, Colo., 1986-88; elem. tchr., technology trainer Rolling Green Elem. Sch., Urbandale, Iowa, 1988—. Jr. webmaster supr. Rolling Green Elem. Sch., 1988—, mem. bldg. assistance team, 1988—. Mem. NEA, Iowa Edn. Assn., Urbandale Edn. Assn., Iowa Jaycees (state dir. 1989-90, mgmt. v.p. 1990-91, pres. 1991-92, dist. dir. 1992-93), Iowa Jaycee (adminstrv. v.p. 1993-94, region 7 regional dir. 1994-95). Methodist. Avocations: golf, travel, reading, swimming. Home: 5143 69th St Des Moines IA 50322-6907 Office: Rolling Green Elem Sch 8100 Airline Ave Urbandale IA 50322-2446

HEWITT, PATRICIA BRADLEY, academic administrator; b. Rutherford County, N.C. d. Willard Graham Sr. and Mary (Lancaster) Bradley; children: Jody Lee, Jay Steven. BS, Gardner-Webb Coll., 1976; MEd, Appalachian State U., 1979; cert. ednl. specialist, Converse Grad. Sch., 1984; PhD, Miss. State U., 1993. Cert. tchr. N.C., S.C., Ala., Miss. Tchr. Tredell County Schs., Statesville, N.C., 1980-85, Rutherford County Schs., Rutherfordton, N.C., 1976-79, 86-90, Meridian (Miss.) City Schs., 1991-92; supr. beginning tchrs. Miss. State U., Mississippi State, 1991—. Mem. Coun. for Drug-Free Schs. and Communities, State of N.C., v.p., 1985-90; mem. N.C. Ednl. Improvement Com., 1989-91; sponsor Rutherford County cheerleading teams, 1985-90; adv. bd. Jr. Miss scholarship program, Greensboro, N.C., 1986-90; judge various local, regional, nat. and internat. sci. fairs, 1993. Contbr. to profl. publs. Mem. ARC, 1984—; adminstrv. coun. Rutherford County Boy Scouts Am., 1986-91; mem., officer Jr. Svc. League, N.C., 1980-85; mem. N.C. Fedn. Women's Club, 1980-85; tchr. Sunday sch. 1st Bapt. Ch., 1986—. Recipient Midsouth Ednl. Research award 1993. Mem. NEA, So. Assn. Schs. and Colls. (accreditation team 1986-91), So. Assn. Accreditation Team, Alpha Delta Kappa, Phi Delta Kappa, Tri Beta. Democrat. Office: Miss State U PO Box 6331 Mississippi State MS 39762-6331

HEWLETT, GLORIA LOUISE, rancher, retired educator, civic volunteer; b. Clifton, Tex., Nov. 28, 1930; d. Dock Simpson and Leona Martha (Fricke) Martin; m. Robert Eckhart Hewlett, Jr., Sept. 3, 1950; children: Robert Eckhart, III, Jeffrey Martin Hewlett. BS, Tex. A&M, Corpus Christi, 1962; MEd, Northwestern State U., Natchitoches, La., 1974; DEd, East Tex. State U., 1988. Tchr. Terrebonne Parish Sch. Dist., Houma, La., 1962-69, Natchitoches (La.) Parish Sch. Dist., 1970-76, Mesquite (Tex.) Sch. Dist., 1977-91; ret., 1991. Author: A Descriptive Study of Textbook Preparation Programs and State Level Textbook Adoption in Texas, 1988. Mem. sr. affairs commn. Dallas City Coun., 1995-97; pres. Eta Zeta chpt. of Delta Kappa Gamma, Dallas, 1992-94. Named Gift to the Ednl. Found. of AAUW, 1992-93, 94-95. Mem. AAUW (pres. Dallas br. 1991-93, v.p. Tex. 1994-96), Dallas Ret. Tchrs. Assn. (pres. 1997-99), The Women's Coun., Am. Legion Aux., Dallas County Hist. Soc. Avocations: reading, genealogy, gardening. Home and Office: 9402 Mill Hollow Dr Dallas TX 75243-6338 E-mail: gloriamh28@earthlink.com.

HEWLETT, SANDRA MARIE, clinical consultant; b. Chgo., Jan. 28, 1959; d. Stanley Vincent and Angeline Sajkiewicz. BS, Rush U., 1988, MS, 1989; postgrad., U. Ill., Chgo., 1992-95, Tex. Woman's U., 1997—. RN, Ill.; cert. BLS instr. Am. Heart Assn.; cert. breast health awareness instr.; cert. advanced oncology nurse; cert. rehab. RN and advanced cardiac life support certification. Acct., comptr. McKinsey Steel Co., Inc., Forest Park, Ill., 1976-79; exec. dir. Adolescent Youth Svcs., Village of Stone Park, Ill., 1979-81; coord. Midwest Therapeutic Assocs., Morton Grove, Ill., 1981-83, adminstr., 1983-86; in-outpatient oncology nurse Rush North Shore Med. Ctr., Skokie, Ill., 1988-89; oncology resource nurse West Suburban Hosp. Med. Ctr., Oak Park, Ill., 1989-90; oncology clin. nurse specialist Holy Family Hosp., Des Plaines, Ill., 1990-92; oncology clin. specialist, dir. autologous transplant program N.W. Oncology, Hematology S. C., Elk Grove Village, Ill., 1992-95; dir. Breast Ctr. The Dr.'s Hosp., Dallas, 1996-97; cons. Schering Plough Pharms., Mansfield, Tex., 1997—2002; dir. patient care svcs. Healthsouth Rehab. Hosp., 2002—. Asst. prof. Wright Coll., Chgo., 1990-95; mem. profl. adv. bd. Rainbow Hospice, Park Ridge, Ill., 1990-93; profl. educator Ill. Cancer Pain Initiative, N.W. Suburban Cook County, Ill., 1991—. Author: (ednl. program) AIDS-Facts & Myth, 1988, (audio cassettes-patient edn.) Chemo-Induced Sequelae, 1989, Lymphoscintigraphy and Sentinel Lymph Node Biopsy, 1999. Bd. dirs. Am. Cancer Soc. Unit 113, 1992—. Rush U. scholar, 1987-88; recipient Luther Christman award and scholarship Rush U./Rush Presbyn. St. Lukes Med. Ctr., 1988, Excellence in Gerontol Nursing award, 1988, Spl. Project award, 1988. Mem. Oncology Nursing Soc. (pres. elect local chpt., chmn. mem. com., continuing edn. approval panel bd. dirs. 1999—), Am. Cancer Soc. (mem. nurses ednl. com. 1990—, profl. educator 1990—, Grad. scholar 1988-89, bd. dirs. unit 113 1992—), Soc. Otolaryngology and Head-Neck Nurses (treas. 1990-93, legis com. 1991, editor newsletter 1991), Gamma Phi chpt. Sigma Theta Tau. Republican. Roman Catholic. Avocations: reading, writing, travel, classical and jazz music. Home and Office: 9745 Corral Dr Keller TX 76248-5522

HEY, NANCY HENSON, educational administrator; b. Cleve., Apr. 1, 1935; d. Henry Brumback Henson and Isabelle (Smock) Selverstone; m. Robert Pierpont Hey, July 4, 1959; 1 child, Julie Dean. AB, Bates Coll., 1957; MS in Edn., Bank Street Coll. Edn., 1961. Cert. advanced profl. in early childhood nursery thru grade 3, Md. Primary tchr. Concord Pub. Sch., Mass., 1958-59; tchr. The Potomac Sch., McLean, Va., 1959-60, Galloway Sch., Atlanta, 1968-69; head tchr. Beauvoir Sch. Nursery Dept., Washington, 1969-70; supr. student tchr. U. Md. Coll. Edn., Coll. Pk., Md., 1973-76, Tufts U., Medford, Mass., 1978-79; head tchr. Newton Ctr. Day Care Ctr., 1980-81, Cmty. Child Devel. Ctr., Peabody, Mass., 1981-82; dir. Greater Lawrence YWCA Children's Ctr., Mass., 1982-86; tchr. Prince George's County Pub. Sch., Md., 1986-88; dir. Child Devel. Ctr., FTC, Washington, 1988-92; dir. Chevy Chase Plz. Children's Ctr., Washington, 1992-93; assoc. dir. Ctr. for Young Children, U. Md., Md., 1994—. Supr. student tchrs. Simmons Coll., Boston, 1965-67; teaching asst. to head of lower sch.Shady Hill Sch., Cambridge, Mass., 1960-61; mem. task force com. Region III Dept. of Social Svcs., Middleton, Mass., 1984-86; bd. dirs. Greater Lawrence Coun. for Children, 1984-86. Mem. Nat. Assn. for Edn. of Young Children, Congressional and Fed. Child Care Dir. Assn. (Sec., 1990-92) Dirs. Exch., Nat. Coalition for Campus Children's Ctrs. Home: 10908 Candlelight Ln Potomac MD 20854-2756 Office: U Md Ctr for Young Children Valley Dr College Park MD 20742-0001

HEYDET, NATHALIE DURBIN, gifted and talented education educator; b. Terre Haute, Ind., Nov. 20, 1948; d. Howard Border and Hersilia (Warren) Durbin; m. Raymond Thomas Heydet, Sept. 20, 1974; 1 child, Lisa. AA in Elem. Edn., Broward C.C., Davie, Fla., 1971; BEd, Fla. Atlantic U., 1973, MEd, 1978. Cert. tchr., Fla. Tchr. Broadview Elem. Sch., Pompano, Fla., 1973-74, Tamarac (Fla.) Elem. Sch., 1974-85, tchr. gifted, 1986-88, Country Hills Elem., Coral Springs, Fla., 1988-94, Horizon Elem., Sunrise, Fla., 1994-98, Eagle Ridge Elem., 1996-98; tchr. spl. assignment in program devel. Broward County Schs., Coral Springs, Fla., 1998—2003, coord. gifted program, 2003—. Adj. English instr. Broward C.C., Coconut Creek, Fla., 1979-81; speaker in field. Mem. Coral Springs Bicentennial Com., 1991. Recipient Fla. award of Excellence, 1986, Little Red Sch. House award Fla. Prins. Assn., 1987, 90, 91; named Broward County Math. Tchr. of Yr., 1998; finalist Broward County Tchr. of Yr. Mem. Fla. Assn. of the Gifted, North Area Gifted Assn., Broward County Guild of Tchrs., Delta Kappa Gamma. Republican. Methodist. Avocations: crafts, traveling, reading. Home: 3091 NW 112th Ave Coral Springs FL 33065-3547

HEYDMAN, ABBY MARIA, academic executive; b. Des Moines, June 1, 1943; d. Frederick Edward and Zeta Margaret (Harrington) Hitchcock; m. Frank J. Heydman, Dec. 20, 1967; 1 child, Amy Lee. BS, Duchesne Coll., 1967; MN, U. Wash., 1969; PhD, U. Calif., Berkeley, 1987. Registered nurse, Calif. Staff nurse Bergan Mercy Hosp., Omaha, 1964—65; student health nurse St. Joseph's Hosp., Omaha, 1965—66, instr. sch. nursing, 1966—68; staff nurse Ballard Community Hosp., Seattle, 1968—69; instr. Creighton U., Omaha, 1969—70, asst. prof., 1970—74, acting dean, 1971—72; chairperson nursing dept. St. Mary's Coll., Moraga, Calif., 1978—85; dean nursing program Samuel Merritt-Saint Mary's Coll., Oakland and Moraga, Calif., 1985—93; acad. dean Samuel Merritt Coll., Oakland, 1989—99, acad. v.p., provost, 1999—2002, spl. asst. to pres., 2002—. Lectr. U. Calif., San Francisco, 1974-75. Contbr. articles to profl. jours. Chmn. Newman Hall Community Council, Berkeley, 1985-87; bd. dirs. Oakland YMCA, 1981-83. Mem.: ACAD, ANA, AAHE, Phi Kappa Delta, Sigma Theta Tau (chair fundraising com. Nu Xi chpt. 1998—2001, pres.-elect 2001—03, pres. 2003—). Roman Catholic. Avocations: swimming, writing, travel, reading. Home: 78629 Rainswept Way Palm Desert CA 92211 Office: Samuel Merritt Coll 450-30 St Oakland CA 94609-3108 E-mail: aheydman@samuelmerritt.edu.

HEYER, LAURA MIRIAM, special education educator; b. L.A., Jan. 6, 1967; d. William Ronald and Miriam Harriet (Muedeking) Heyer. BA, M of Tching., U. Va., 1990; EdM, George Mason U., 2001. Lic. tchr. Va. Asst. tchr. Sch. for Contemporary Edn., Annandale, Va., 1991-93, classroom tchr., 1993—2003, program supr., 2003—. Support group facilitator, Sexual Minority Youth Assistance League, Washington, 1995-96. Mem. Coun. for Children with Behavioral Disorders, Coun. for Exceptional Children. Avocation: playing sports. Office: Phillips Programs 7010 Braddock Rd Annandale VA 22003-6006

HEYMACH, GEORGE JOHN, III, physician, educator, health facility administrator, consultant; b. N.Y.C., Nov. 17, 1942; s. George John and Bertha Vina (Floerke) H.; m. Barbara Lynne Lerew, Oct. 26, 1968; children: Brooke Lerew, G. John IV, Bria Lerew. BS in Chem. Engring., CCNY, 1964; MS, U. Pa., 1966, PhD, 1969; MD, Jefferson Med. Coll., 1976; MBA,

U. Pitts., 1997. Diplomate in internal medicine, pulmonary medicine, critical care medicine, geriatrics Am. Bd. Internal Medicine. Asst. prof. chem. enging. Kans. State U., Manhattan, 1969-72; resident in medicine Thomas Jefferson U. Hosp., Phila., 1976-79; fellow in medicine Washington U., St. Louis, 1979-81; physician Pitts. Pulmonary Assn. Ltd., 1981-96; v.p. med. affairs Bapt. Med. Ctr., Kansas City, Mo., 1997-98; med. dir. Health Midwest, Kansas City, Mo., 1998—2000; sr. v.p. healthcare Fleishman-Hillard, 2000—01; pres. Physicians' Health Care Cons., 2001—. Clin. asst. prof. medicine U. Pitts., 1982-2003; adj. prof. biomed. engring. Carnegie-Mellon U., Pitts., 1982—96. Contbr. articles to profl. jours. Fire surgeon Fox Chapel (Pa.) Vol. Fire Dept., 1984-92; Tb physician Allegheny County Health Dept., Pitts., 1986-90. Served to capt. U.S. Army, 1970-72. Grantee in field. Fellow ACP, Am. Coll. Chest Physicians. Avocations: boating, travel, racketball, music. Home: 801 W 57th Ter Kansas City MO 64113-1166 Office: 801 W 57th Terr Kansas City MO 64113 Fax: 816-333-0224. E-mail: Breathdoc@aol.com.

HEYMAN, IRA MICHAEL, federal agency administrator, museum executive, law educator; b. N.Y.C., May 30, 1930; s. Harold Albert and Judith (Sobel) H.; m. Therese Helene Thau, Dec. 17, 1950; children: Stephen Thomas (dec.), James Nathaniel. AB in Govt., Dartmouth Coll., 1951; JD, Yale U., 1956; LLD (hon.), U. Pacific, 1981, Hebrew Union Coll., 1984, U. Md., 1986, SUNY, Buffalo, 1990, Dartmouth Coll., 2001. Bar: NY 1956, Calif. 1961. Legis. asst. to U.S. Senator Ives, 1950-51; assoc. Carter, Ledyard & Milburn, N.Y.C., 1956-57; law clk. to presiding justice U.S. Ct. Appeals (2d cir.), New Haven, 1957-58; chief law clk. to Supreme Ct. Justice Earl Warren, 1958-59; acting assoc. prof. law U. Calif., Berkeley, 1959-61, prof. law, 1961—93, prof. city and regional planning, 1966-93, prof. emeritus, 1993—, vice chancellor, 1974-80, chancellor, 1980-90, chancellor emeritus, 1990—; counselor to Sec. of Interior Dept. Interior, Washington, 1993-94; sec. Smithsonian Inst., Washington, 1994-99, sec. emeritus, 2000—; mem. Citizens' Stamp Adv. Com., 2000—. Vis. prof. Yale Law Sch., 1963—64, Stanford Law Sch., 1971—72; bd. dirs. Presicio Trust. Editor Yale Law Jour.; contbr. articles to profl. jours. Sec. Calif. adv. com. U.S. Commn. Civil Rights, 1962-67; trustee Dartmouth Coll., 1982-93, chmn., 1991-93; mem. Lawyers' Com. for Civil Rights under Law, 1977-95, Citizens Stamp Advisory Com., USPS, 2000-; chmn. exec. com. Nat. Assn. State Univs. and Land Grant Colls., 1986; bd. regents Smithsonian Instn., 1990-94; bd. dirs. Presidio Trust, 2000—. 1st lt. USMC, 1951-53, capt. Res. ret. Decorated chevalier Legion of Honor (France). Mem. Am. Acad. Arts and Sci. E-mail: mheyman@law.berkeley.edu.

HEYMANN, HANS PAULSEN, community college administrator; b. Luebeck, Germany, Nov. 5, 1944; came to U.S., 1953; s. Hans Gerhard and Chris (Lunge) H.; m. Jane Nichols, Mar. 10, 1968; 1 child, Amy Heymann Singleton. AB, Lenoir-Rhyne Coll., 1967; MA, Appalachian State U., 1974, MA, 1981, EdS, 1979; Cert., Duke U., 1995. Tchr. Hickory (N.C.) City Sch. System, 1968-69; asst. to bus. mgr.-treas. Lenoir-Rhyne Coll., Hickory, 1973, dir. coll. ctr. and student housing, 1973-74; extension dir. Mitchell C.C., Statesville, N.C., 1974-89, dir. new and expanding industry, 1989-95, dir. new and expanding industry and focused indsl. tng., 1995—2000; coord. customized tng. and devel. Rowan-Cabarrus Cmty. Coll., Salisbury, NC, 2000—. Mem. adj. grad. faculty Coll. Edn. Appalachian State U., Boone, N.C., 1981-86, cons. N.C. Ctr. Community Edn., 1981-86, state adv. bd., 1981-84, vice chmn. 1982-83, chmn., 1983-84, Mid-Atlantic Community Edn. Consortium, Gallaudet Coll., Washington, 1981, N.C. Assn. Arts Couns., High Point, 1982, Nat. Ctr. Community Edn., Flint, Mich., 1986; regional coord. N.C. Internat. Exchange Network, U. N.C., Charlotte and N.C. World Ctr., Raleigh, 1984-87; state liaison Nat. Coun. Community Svcs. and Continuing Edn., 1986-88; mem. N.C. Rural Econ. Devel. Ctr. Leadership Adv. Com., 1995—; mem. adv. com. Crescent Electric Membership Corp., Statesville, 1991. Mem. steering com. Iredell County Interagy. Coun., Statesville, 1978-79; core com. Iredell County Involvement Coun., Statesville, 1979-84, coun. chmn., 1982-83; mem. steering com. Iredell County Com. for Am.'s 400th Anniversary, Statesville, 1982-87; bd. dirs. Arts and Sci. Ctr., Statesville, 1992-94, v.p., 1992-93; mem. Iredell Citizens for Edn., Statesville, 1992-96, fin. chmn. steering and fin. com.; chmn. Fulbright Tchr. Exch. Com., 1994-95; co-chair adv. bd. Iredell-Statesville Schs. Youth Employment Ednl. Svcs., 1994. Staff sgt. USAF, 1969-73. Recipient Spl. Vol. Cert., Gov. N.C., 1981, Gov.'s award, 1984, Cert. Appreciation, Gov. N.C., 1986, R. D. Grier Excellence in Edn. award Mitchell C.C., 1992; Mitchell C.C. Yearbook Dedication, 1986. Mem. N.C. C. C. Adult Educators Assn. (hon.), N.C. Rural Econ. Devel. Orgn. (sec. 1996-97), Greater Statesville C. of C. (chmn. lifelong learning com. 1992-94, edn. divsn. steering com. 1995, adv. bd. commitment to excellence 1992-93, sch.-to-work initiatives com. 1995-96), Mooresville-South Iredell C. of C. (econ. devel. com. 1993). Office: Rowan-Cabarrus Cmty Coll PO Box 1595 Salisbury NC 28145-1595

HEYWOOD, JOHN BENJAMIN, mechanical engineering educator; b. Sidcup, Kent, Eng., Jan. 11, 1938; s. Harold and Frances Dora (Weaver) H.; m. Marguerite Gilkerson, Dec. 28, 1961; children: James, Stephen, Benjamin. BA, Cambridge U., 1960, DSc, 1984; MS, MIT, 1962, PhD, 1965; DTech (hon.), Chalmers U. Tech., 1999. Lectr. Northeastern U., Boston, 1963-65; rsch. assoc. mech. engring. dept. MIT, Cambridge, 1964-65, asst. prof. mech. engirg., 1968-70, assoc. prof., 1970-76, prof., 1976-92, dir. Sloan Automotive Lab., coord. transp. programs in Energy Lab., 1972—, co-dir. leaders for mfg. program, 1991-93; Sun Jae prof. mech. engring., 1992—; rsch. officer Cen. Electricity Generating Bd., Leatherhead, Eng., 1965-67, group leader, 1967-68; co-dir. Ford-MIT Alliance, 2003—. Co-dir. Ford-MIT Alliance, 2003—; cons. in field. Author, editor: (with others) Open-Cycle MHD Power Generation, 1969; author: (with others) The Automobile and the Regulation of its Impact on the Environment, 1975, Internal Engine Combustion Fundamentals, 1988, (with E. Sher) The Two-Stroke Engine, 1999; contbr. Ency. Britannica, chpts. to books, numerous articles, papers to profl. jours., confs., symposia U.S.A, Eng., Europe. Recipient Ayerton Premium Inst. Elec. Engrs., U.K., 1969; Fulbright travel scholar, 1960; Richard C. Mellon Overseas fellow Churchill Coll., Cambridge, Eng., 1976-77; recipient Nat. award for Advancement of Motor Vehicle R&D, US DOT, 1996. Fellow U.K. Instn. Mech. Engrs. (George Stephenson Internat. Lectr. 1997); mem. Soc. Automotive Engrs. (Ralph R. Teeter Outstanding Young Engr. award 1971, Arch T. Colwell Merit award 1973, 81, 89, Outstanding Oral Presentation award 1980, 2001, Horning Meml. Best Paper award 1984, Rsch. on Automotive Lubricants award 2001), ASME (Freeman scholar 1986, Honda lectr. 1990, Honda medal 1999), Nat. Acad. Engring., Am. Acad. Arts and Scis. Achievements include rsch. interests in thermodynamics, combustion, energy, power and propulsion, performance, efficiency and emissions of spark-ignition and diesel engines, control of air pollution, engine design and manufacture. Office: MIT Dept Mech Engring 77 Mass Ave # 3-340 Cambridge MA 02139-4307

HIATT, PETER, retired librarian studies educator; b. N.Y.C., Oct. 19, 1930; s. Amos and Elizabeth Hope (Derry) H.; m. Linda Rae Smith, Aug. 16, 1968; 1 child, Holly Virginia. BA, Colgate U., 1952; M.L.S., Rutgers U., 1957, PhD, 1963. Libr. intern Elizabeth (N.J.) Pub. Libr., 1955-57; head Elmora Br. Libr., Elizabeth, 1957-59; instr. Grad. Sch. Libr. Service, Rutgers U., 1960-62; libr. cons. Ind. State Libr., Indpls., 1963-70; asst. prof. Grad. Libr. Sch., Ind. U., 1963-66, assoc. prof., 1966-70; dir. Ind. Libr. Studies, Bloomington, 1967-70; dir. continuing edn. program for library pers. Western Interstate Commn. for Higher Edn., Boulder, Colo., 1970-74; dir. Grad. Sch. Libr. and Info. Sci., U. Wash., Seattle, 1974-81, prof., 1974-98; prin. investigator Career Devel. and Assessment Ctr. for Librarians, 1979-83, 90-93; dir. library insts. at various colls. and univs.; adv. projects U.S. Office Edn.-ALA, 1977-80; prof. emeritus U. Wash., 1998—. Bd. dirs. King County Libr. Sys., 1989-97, pres., 1991, 95, sec., 1993, 94; prin. investigator Career Devel. and Assessment Ctrs. for Librs.: Phase II, 1990-93. Author: (with Donald Thompson) Monroe County IN Public Library: Planning for the Future, 1966, The Public Library Needs of Delaware County, 1967, (with Henry Drennan) Public Library Services for the functionally Illiterate, 1967 (with Robert E. Lee and Lawrence A. Allen) A Plan for Developing a Regional Program of Continuing Education for Library Personnel, 1969, Public Library Branch Services for Adults of Low Education, 1964; dir., gen. editor: The Indiana Library Studies, 1970-74; author: Assessment Centers for Professional Library Leadership, 1993; mem. editorial bd. Coll. and Rsch. Librs., 1969-73; co-editor Leads: A Continuing Education Newsletter for Library Trustees, 1973-75, Octavio Noda; author chpts., articles on library continuing edn., staff devel. and libr. adult svcs. Mem. selection com. Jefferson County Pub. Libr., Washington, 2000—01; pres. Port Townsend Pub. Libr. Found., 2002—; mem. bd. dirs. Turtle Bluff Chamber Orch., Jefferson County, Wash., 2000—, mem. soloist competition jury, 2000—, mem. scholarship com., 2000—, chair spl. fundraising com., 2002—03; bd. dirs. Turtle Bluff Chamber Orch, 2000—03. Mem. ALA (officer), Pacific N.W. Libr. Assn., Assn. Libr. and Info. Sci. Educators (officer, Outstanding Svc. award 1979), ACLU. Home: 20 Sequim Pl Port Townsend WA 98368-9414 E-mail: phiatt@cablespeed.com.

HIBBS, DAWN WILCOX, elementary school educator; b. Buffalo, Sept. 30, 1940; d. Alfred and Helena Pavone; m. Leroy Wilcox, July 18, 1964 (div. June 1981); children: Brett Alan, Dana Lee; m. Harold Keith Hibbs, Dec. 27, 1986. Tchr. 5th grade North Tonawanda (N.Y.) Schs., 1961-63, Los Alamos (N.Mex.) Schs., 1963-64; tchr. 6th grade Kenmore (N.Y.) Schs., 1965-69; caseworker Erie County Dept. Social Svcs., Buffalo, 1980-84; elem. tchr. Lynwood (Calif.) Schs., 1986-88, Santa Ana (Calif.) Schs., 1988-96, intermediate tchr., 1996—2002, textbook advisor, grant writer, 1996-97. Mentor new tchrs. Santa Ana Schs., 1991-92, instr. Reading to Learn programs, 1999-2000, tchr. cabinet rep., 1998-2000, mem. sch. site coun., 2000-2001, mem. Oreg. project, 2000-02. Patentee eyewear identification labels and design. Pres. Parents Without Ptnrs., Tonawanda, 1983. Mem. AAUW (treas. 1995-96, EF fund prize chmn. 1997, membership v.p. 1997-2000, mem. membership com. Calif. 1998-2001, co-pres. Orange County Interbr. 1999—, tech. trek coord., 1999-2001, v.p. Mission Viejo-Saddleback Valley br. LAF 2000-2001, pres. 2003-), Class Act Investors (treas. 1999—).

HIBBS, ROBERT ANDREWS, analytical chemistry educator; b. Cocoa, Fla., Sept. 9, 1923; s. Charles Harold and Virginia Hibbs; m. Pauline Johnson (div. 1950); 1 child, Sally; m. Lois Elaine Boberg, May 10, 1952; children: Bruce, Laura, Ellen, Dale, Martha, James. BSA, U. Fla., 1947, MS in Agr., 1948; PhD, Wash. State U., 1951. With quality control Darigold Farms, Spokane, Wash., 1951-54; asst. prof. dairy mfg. U. Idaho, Moscow, 1954-61; dir. Hibbs Labs., Boise, Idaho, 1961-90; from asst. prof. to assoc. prof. chemistry Boise State Coll., 1965, 67; prof. analytical chemistry Boise State U., 1971-90, prof. emeritus, 1990—; tech. dir. Hibbs Analytical Labs. Inc., Boise, 1991-95; pres. Refrigerated Foods Tech. Inc., Boise, 1991—99. Adv. bd. Ctr. for Entrepreneurial and Econ. Devel., 1997—99. Contbr. articles to profl. jours. Served as sgt. Infantry, 1942-45, ETO. Decorated Bronze Star. Mem. Inst. Food Technologists (profl. emeritus 1994—, councilor 1977-89). Lodges: Masons, Shriner. Republican. Episcopalian. Avocation: hiking.

HICKEY, CATHERINE JOSEPHINE, school system administrator; b. N.Y.C., Mar. 14, 1936; d. John James and Delia Bridget (Finnegan) Tighe; m. Stephen M. Hickey, Mar. 30, 1959; children: Catherine, Marie, Joanne, Clare, Geraldine, Margaret. BS, Fordham U., 1958, PhD, 1983; MS, CUNY, 1974; LHD (hon.), Mercy Coll., 1990, Iona Coll., Kings Coll., Wilkes-Barre, Pa. Prin. Sacred Heart Sch., Dobbs Ferry, N.Y., 1977-89; instr., adj. prof. Mercy Coll., Dobbs Ferry, 1983-87, Long Island U., Dobbs Ferry, 1984-87, Fairfield (Conn.) U., 1984-87; supt. schs. Archdiocese of N.Y., N.Y.C., 1989—, sec. of edn., 2000—. Roman Catholic. Home: 415 Marlborough Rd Yonkers NY 10701-6709 Office: Archdiocese NY 1011 1st Ave New York NY 10022-4106

HICKEY, DELINA ROSE, retired education educator; b. N.Y.C., Mar. 25, 1941; d. Robert Joseph and Marie (Ripa) Hickey; m. David Andrews; 1 child, Jon Robert. BS in Edn., SUNY, Oneonta, 1963; MA, Manhattan Coll., 1967; EdD in Counselor Edn. and Psychology, U. Idaho, 1971; postgrad., Harvard U., 1995. Sch. tchr., counselor pub. schs., Westchester, NY, 1963-68; part-time instr. psychologist St. Thomas Aquinas Coll., Sparkhill, NY, 1971-72; asst. prof. edn. Nathaniel Hawthorne Coll., Antrim, NH, 1972-75; mem. faculty Keene (N.H.) State Coll., 1975—2000, assoc. prof. edn., 1978-87, prof., coord. faculty, 1987-2000, interim dean profl. studies, 1887, v.p. student affairs, 1990-2000; ret., 2000. Mem. adv. coun. Title IV, 1979—82; assoc. in edn. Harvard U., 1984—85, Inst. Ednl. Mgmt., 1995; chmn. curriculum Acad. Life Long Learning U. S.C., Aiken, SC, 2003—; presenter in field. Contbr. Bd. trustees Hist. Aiken Found., 2002—, Smart Growth Aiken, 2000—; mem. N.H. Ho. of Reps., 1981—85; trustee Big Bros.-Big Sisters, Keene, 1978—80, Family Planning Svcs. S.W. N.H., 1976—85, Monadnock Family Svcs., 1995—97, Monadnock Hospice, 1994—96, chmn. pers. com.; mem. N.H. Juvenile Conf. Com., 1976—81; bd. dirs. Cheshire Med. Ctr.; trustee Cheshire Med. Assn., 1996—2001; pres. bd. dirs. CHESCO; trustee Home Health Care, 1998—2001; CEO HMS Ednl. Cons., 2000—. Fellow, Nat. Ctr. Rsch. in Vocat. Edn., 1984—85; grantee, Marion Jasper Whitney Found. Mem.: AAUW (vice chmn. programs 2002—), N.H. Assn. Student Pers. Adminstrs. (adv. bd.), N.H. Pers. and Guidance Assn., New Eng. Rsch. Orgn., New Eng. Assn. Tchrs. and Educators, Am. Vocat. Assn., Nat. Assn. Student Pers. Adminstrs. (adv. com. region I, editor, chief Net Results electronic mag. 1997-99), N.H. Order Women Legislators. Office: HMS Ednl Cons Keene NH 03431 E-mail: dhickey@atlantic.net.

HICKEY, FRANCIS ROGER, physicist, educator; b. Troy, N.Y., June 8, 1942; s. Frank R. and Ann M. (O'Malley) H.; m. Paula Williamson, Aug. 29, 1964; children: Sharon Ann, Kevin Derus (dec.). BS, Siena Coll., 1964; MS, Clarkson U., 1967, PhD, 1970. From asst. to assoc. prof. Physics Hartwick Coll., Oneonta, N.Y., 1969-83, prof. Physics, 1983—. Adv. bd. Sci. Discovery Ctr. of Oneonta, 1989—, Oneonta Newman Found, 1988—; nat. councillor Soc. Physics Students, 1974-75. Contbr. articles to profl. jours. Founding mem. Oneonta region chpt. The Compassionate Friends. Mem. Am. Phys. Soc., Am. Assn. Physics Tchrs. Roman Catholic. Achievements include development of Physics Educational Computer Programs. Home: 117 Glen Dr Oneonta NY 13820-3553 Office: Hartwick Coll Physics Dept Oneonta NY 13820 E-mail: hickeyr@hartwick.edu.

HICKEY, HOWARD WESLEY, retired education educator; b. Bozeman, Mont., Oct. 20, 1930; s. Wesley Grandon and Frances Mildred (Howard) H.; m. Gwen Callahan, Feb. 14, 1987; children: Morris, Glenn, Griffith, Gayle; 1 child by previous marriage, Brooks. BA, Western Wash. U., 1953, M.Ed., 1958; MA, Bowdoin Coll., 1962; PhD, Mich. State U., 1968. Dir. fed. programs Puyallup (Wash.) Schs., 1962-66; asst. prof. elem. edn. Mich. State U., East Lansing, 1968-71; assoc. prof., dir. Mott Inst. for Community Improvement, Mich. State U., 1971-77, prof. higher edn., 1978-94; ret., 1994. Cons. in field. Author: (with Curt Van Voorhees) Role of the School in Community Education, 1969; assoc. editor: Community Edn. Jour, 1971-74; contbr. articles to profl. jours. NSF fellow, 1958, 61-62; Mott fellow, 1966-67 Mem. Nat. Community Edn. Assn., Rotary Club (pres. 1965-66), Phi Delta Kappa. Home: 2337 Sapphire Ln East Lansing MI 48823-7263

HICKEY, LEO J(OSEPH), museum curator, educator; b. Phila., Apr. 26, 1940; s. James J(oseph) and Helen Marie (Schwarz) H.; m. Judith McKendry, June 29, 1968; children: Geoffrey Alan, Damian Michael, Jason Alexander. BS, Villanova U., 1962; MA, Princeton U., 1964; postgrad., Rutgers U., 1963-65; PhD, Princeton U., 1967; MA (privatim), Yale U., 1983. Postdoctoral fellow NRC-Smithsonian Inst., Washington, 1966-69, assoc. curator, 1969-80; chmn. exhibits com. Natural History Mus., Smithsonian, 1973-75, curator, 1980-82; prof. geology Yale U., New Haven, 1982—; dir. Peabody Mus., Yale U., 1982-87; prof. biology Yale U., 1982-97, chair dept. geology and geophysics, 2003—; curator of paleobotany Peabody Mus. Nat. History, 1982—. Adj. prof. botany U. Md., College Park, 1981-85; adj. prof. geology U. Pa., Phila., 1982-, chmn. dept. geology and geophysics, 2003-; past pres., pres., v.p. Yellowstone-Bighorn Rsch. Assn., Red Lodge, Mont., 1979-86; dir. Mus. of Am. Theatre, New Haven, 1983-87; mem. Mars Lander Sci. Team, 1999—. Author: Stratigraphy and Paleobotany of Golden Valley Formation, 1977; co-author: The Great Dinosaur Mural, 1990; editor: (with D.W. Taylor) Origin, Early Evolution, and Phylogeny of the Flowering Plants, 1996. Recipient H.A. Gleason award NY Bot. Gardens, 1977, Best Paper award Geol. Soc. Washington, 1981, Disting. Alumnus award Villanova U., 1982, Ann. Book award Dinosaur Soc., 1992; grantee Smithsonian Rsch. Found., 1972-76, Nat. Geog. Soc., 1979, 84-85, NSF, 1984, 90, 92, 2000, 03, Bay Found., 1995-96, 2000, Nason Found., 2002. Fellow Geol. Soc. Am.; mem. AAAS, Bot. Soc. Am., Paleontol. Soc. Democrat. Roman Catholic. Office: Peabody Mus Natural History PO Box 208118 170 Whitney Ave New Haven CT 06520-8118

HICKEY, SHARON MARIE, councilman, elementary school educator, Mayoral aide; b. Leon, Iowa, Nov. 25, 1953; d. Clarence Joseph Ross and Marie Florence Page; m. Thomas Patrick Hickey, June 26, 1976; children: Melissa, Christine, Patrick, Matthew. AA, Iowa Central CC, Ft. Dodge, Iowa, 1974; BA, Buena Vista Univ., 1976. Sec. Dr. McDonald, Ft. Dodge, Iowa, 1975—76; substitute tchr. Ft. Dodge Cmty. Sch., Iowa, 1978—94; tchr. Corpus Christi, Ft. Dodge, 1994—95; substitute tchr. Ft. Dodge Cmty. Sch., 1995—2001. Sch. improvement bd. Ft.Dodge Cmty. Sch., Iowa, 2001; coun. mem. City of Ft. Dodge, Iowa, 1992—2001, mayor pro tem, 1993—2001. Recipient Gov.'s Leadership award, State of Iowa, 1991, Hillcrest Neighborhood award, 1985—2001. Roman Catholic. Home: 304 2nd St NW Fort Dodge IA 50501 E-mail: shickey@mchsi.com.

HICKEY, SHIRLEY LOUISE COWIN, elementary education educator; b. Moscow, Idaho, Nov. 20, 1950; d. George Theodore and Shirley Phyllis (Stokes) Cowin; m. Leonard Arnold Hickey, Aug. 19, 1973 (div. Sept. 1994); 1 child, Alisa Hadley; m. Stephen S. Tellari, Aug. 1, 1998. BA, Mt. Holyoke Coll., 1973; MA, Gonzaga U., Spokane, Wash., 1977. Cert. tchr., Wash. Substitute tchr. Cen. Valley Sch. Dist. and West Valley Sch. Dist., Spokane, Wash., 1973-77; svc. rep. Pacific NW Bell Telephone, Seattle, 1978-83; substitute tchr. Tahoma Sch. Dist., Maple Valley, Wash., 1983-87, St. Anthony Sch., Renton, Wash., 1983-87, St. James Sch., Kent, Wash., 1983-87; elem. tchr. Cedar Valley Sch., Kent, 1987-93, tchr., 1996—. Pvt. tchr. piano, 1983-93. Cellist Women in Music Internat., 1990-91; class agt. Mt. Holyoke Coll., South Hadley, Mass., 1972-89, co-head class agt., 2003—, class libr. chmn., 1989-92; bd. dirs. Cedar Valley PTA, Kent, 1989-90. Mem. Kent Edn. Assn. (bldg. rep. 1988-92, polit. action com. 1990-93, crisis team 1990-91, sec. 1992-93, pres. 1993-96), Music Tchrs. Nat. Assn., Wash. State Music Tchrs. Assn., Mt. Holyoke Alumnae Assn. (bd. dirs. 1990-93), Mt. Holyoke Coll. Club (western rep. 1987-90, com. chmn. 1990-93). Episcopalian. Avocation: music. Home: 12313 SE 280th St Kent WA 98031-8524

HICKMAN, HUGH V. science educator, researcher; b. Washington, June 3, 1947; s. Jack Wallis Hickman and Mary Cecelia (Regar) McCoy; m. Kayoko K. Hickman, Dec. 30, 1997; 1 child, Hugh Yamato. BSEE, U. South Fla., 1984, PhD, 1989. Entrepreneur, 1969-80; vis. prof. elec. engring. U. South Fla., Tampa, 1989-90; vis. prof. computer sci. Eckerd Coll., St. Petersburg, Fla., 1990-91; prof. physics Hillsborough CC, Tampa, Fla., 1991—2001. Contbr. articles to profl. jours. Mem. AAAS, IEEE, Am. Assn. Physics Tchrs., Am. Phys. Soc., Ye Mystic Krewe of Gasparilla, Phi Kappa Phi. Republican. Roman Catholic. Achievements include research into temporal dynamics. Home: 5010 W Dante Ave Tampa FL 33629-7513 E-mail: kayoko@tampabay.rr.com.

HICKMAN, LARRY ALLEN, philosophy educator; b. McAllen, Tex., Oct. 6, 1942; s. Roy Wilton and Vivian Russell (King) H. BA, Hardin-Simmons U., 1964; PhD, U. Tex., 1971. Asst. prof. U. Tex., Austin, 1973-74, Tex. A&M U., College Station, 1974-80, assoc. prof., 1980-89, prof., 1989-93, So. Ill. U., Carbondale, Ill., 1993—, dir. Ctr. for Dewey Studies, 1993—. Author: Modern Theories of Higher Level Predicates, 1980, John Dewey's Pragmatic Technology, 1990 (Outstanding Acad. Book, Choices mag., 1990), Philosophical Tools for Technological Culture, 2001; editor: Technology of a Human Affair, 1990, (CD-ROM) The Collected Works of John Dewey 1882-1953: The Electronic Edition, 1996, Reading Dewey, 1998, The Essential Dewey, 1998. Mem. Am. Philos. Assn., Assn. for Documentary Editing, John Dewey Soc., Soc. for the Advancement Am. Philosophy (exec. bd. dirs. 1995-98, pres. 2002—), Southwestern Philos. Soc. (pres. 1989-90), Soc. for Philosophy and Tech. (pres. 1993-95). Avocations: sailing, carpentry, gardening, travel. Office: So Ill U Ctr for Dewey Studies Carbondale IL 62901

HICKMAN, RUTH VIRGINIA, Bible educator; b. Sac City, Iowa, Oct. 15, 1931; d. Ronald Minor and Ida E. (Willcutt) Wilson; m. Charles Ray Hickman, Aug. 25, 1962; children: Ronald Everett, Lisa Michelle. BS in Home Econs., Morningside Coll., 1953. Ordained to ministry Christian Ch., 1985. Instr. Nat. Ednl. TV, 1964-76; staff coord., tchr. Life for Layman, Denver, 1974-77; founder, tchr. Abundant Word Ministries, Lakewood, Colo., 1980—; tchr. Bible Calvary Temple, Denver, 1980—; sales/trainer Hillestad Internat., Woodruff, Wis., 1978—. Women's com. Billy Graham Assn., Denver, 1986-87. Author: (book) Hope for Hurting People, 1987; spkr., instr. audio and video tape series, 1980—. Leader pilgrimages to Israel, 1984, 87, 94, 96, 98, 2001. Republican. Home: 3043 S Holly Pl Denver CO 80222-7010 Office: Abundant Word Ministries 2109 S Wadsworth Lakewood CO 80227 E-mail: RuthAbundant@c.s.com., abundant_word@hotmail.com.

HICKOK, EUGENE W. federal agency administrator; m. Katharine Pauley; 2 children. BA, Hampden-Sydney Coll., 1972; master's, U. Va., 1978, PhD, 1983. Spl. asst. Office Legal Counsel U.S. Dept. Justice, 1986—87; dir. fin. aid Hampden-Sydney Coll., Va.; assoc. dir. dept. polit. sci. Miss. State U.; instr. polit. sci. Dickinson Coll., Carlisle, Pa., 1980—, dir. Clarke Ctr. Interdisciplinary Study of Contemporary Issues; sec. edn. Commonwealth of Pa. Dept. Edn., Harrisburg, 1995—2001; under sec. edn. Dept. Edn., Washington, 2001—, acting dep. sec. edn., 2003—. Dir. Clarke Ctr. Interdisciplinary Study of Contemporary Issues. Author books; contbr. articles to profl. jours. Mem. Carlisle Area Sch. Bd. Adj. scholar Heritage Found. Office: Dept Edn Office of Under Sec 400 Maryland Ave SW Rm 7W310 Washington DC 20202-1510*

HICKOK, LEE RICHARD, obstetrician, gynecologist, educator; b. Detroit, Dec. 31, 1951; s. Durlin Walter and Charlotte Mae (Doty) H.; m. Sharon Diane Loomis, Nov. 27, 1983; children: Caitlin Mae, Molly McKenzie. BS, Mich. State U., 1975; MD, U. Wash., 1984. Diplomate Nat. Bd. Med. Examiners; bd. cert. Am. Coll. Ob-Gyn. Resident U. Wash., Seattle, 1984-88; pvt. practice Everett (Wash.) Clinic, 1988-89; reproductive endocrinology and infertility fellow, instr. Oreg. Health Scis. U., Portland, 1989-91; rsch. fellow Oreg. Regional Primate Rsch. Ctr., Beaverton, 1989-91; dir. divsn. reproductive medicine and surgery Pacific Gynecology Specialists, Seattle, 1991—. Clin. assoc. prof. dept. ob.-gyn. U. Wash., 1991-99, clin. assoc. prof., 1999—; chmn. laparoscopic surgery com. Swedish Med. Ctr., Seattle, 1994-96. Contbr. articles to profl. jours.; contbg. author: Drug Therapy in Ob/Gyn, 1991, Gynecology and Obstetrics, 1993, Current Diagnosis, 1991. Mem. AMA, Am. Soc. Reproductive

Medicine, Soc. Assisted Reproductive Tech., Pacific Coast Reproductive Soc., Seattle Gynecol. Soc. (program chmn. 1992-94, pres. 2001), Am. Coll. Ob-Gyn., Wash. State Obstetric Assn., N.Am. Menopause Soc., Pacific N.W. Ob-Gyn. Assn. pres, Soc. Reproductive Surgeons. Democrat. Avocation: flyfishing. Home: 4103 E Galer St Seattle WA 98112-3813 Office: Ste 1500 1101 Madison St Seattle WA 98104-3551

HICKOX, BARBARA NODINE, retired elementary school educator; b. Toledo, Oct. 31, 1933; d. Hubert A. Nodine and Della I. (Willis) Hickox; m. Junior W. Rowell, Sept. 10, 1949 (div. 1972); children: Teresa, Curt, Denise; m. James W. Hickox, June 25, 1976 (dec. Feb. 2002). AA, Waycross Jr. Coll., 1976; Bachelor, Valdosta State U., 1980, MEd, 1982. Cert. tchr., Ga. Tchr.'s aide Waycross Bd. Edn., 1966-78; tchr. Bacon County Bd. Edn., Alma, Ga., 1980-86, Ware County Bd. Edn., Waycross, 1986-95; ret., 1995. Vol. to vets. in nursing homes and VA hosps. Mem. AAUW (sr. v.p. Waycross br. 1997-97, pres. 1998—), Ga. Ret. Tchrs.' Assn. (life), VFW Ladies Aux. (life, # 4382 sr. v.p. 1996-97, pres. 1997-99, jr. v.p. dist. # 14 1997-98, pres. 1998-99, Voice of Democracy award), Mil. Order Cootie Ladies Aux. (# 59 pres. 1996-97, 99-2000), Am. Legion Ladies Aux. (# 10 pres. 1995-97, 2d v.p. dist. 8 1997-98), Lions (Waycross chpt. pres. 2002—). Democrat. Home: 2216 Eastover Dr Waycross GA 31501-6963

HICKROD, GEORGE ALAN KARNES WALLIS, educational administration educator; b. Fort Branch, Ind., May 16, 1930; s. Hershell Roy and Bernice Ethel (Karnes) H.; m. Ramona Dell Poole, 1952 (dec.); m. Lucy Jen Huang, 1964 (dec.); 1 stepchild, Goren Wallis Liu (dec.); m. Marcia D. Escott, 1998; stepchildren: Eric David Escott, Beth Ann Escott Newcommer. AB, Wabash Coll., 1954; MA, Harvard U., 1955, EdD, 1966. Asst. prof. ednl. and social scis. Lake Erie Coll., 1962-67; assoc. prof. ednl. adminstrn. Ill. State U., Normal, 1967-71, prof., 1971-83, disting. prof., 1983-95, emeritus disting. prof., 1995—, dir. Ctr. for Study Ednl. Fin., 1974-95. Dir. McArthur/Spencer Ill. Sch. Fin., 1987-92, Joyce Found. Sch. Fin. Study, 1990-92; pres. Coalition for Ednl. Rights Under the Constn., 1989-91, mem. ednl. rights com., 1990-98. With USMC, 1950-52, Korea. Recipient Chgo. Urban League award, 1994, Van Miller Disting. Scholar award U. Ill., 1994; State of Ill. and U.S. Govt. grantee. Mem. Am. Edn. Fin. Assn. (v.p. 1983-84, pres. 1984-85, Disting. Svc. award 1992), Scottish-Am. Soc. Ctrl. Ill. Club (past chief), Clan Wallace Internat. Royal Order of Scotland Masonic, Phi Beta Kappa, Commun Gaidhleach Am., Masons, Elks. Democrat. Unitarian Universalist. Avocations: history, genealogy, travel, cooking, gaelic (albanach) language. Home: 2 Turner Rd Normal IL 61761-4218 E-mail: AlanHickrod@aol.com.

HICKS, BILLY FERRELL, minister, educator; b. El Dorado, Ark., Aug. 12, 1930; s. Ferrell Farris and Olivia Marvell (Lookadoo) H.; m. Anna Bee Gillaspie, Jan. 25, 1952. BA, Ouachita Bapt. Coll., Arkadelphia, Ark., 1956; BS, Henderson State Coll., Arkadelphia, Ark., 1960. Ordained to ministry Bapt. Ch., 1956. Asst. hwy. engr., Ark., 1954-55; coach, tchr. Laura Connor High Sch., Augusta, Ark., 1956-57; tchr. Newport (Ark.) High Sch., 1957-59; coach, tchr. Magnolia (Ark.) Jr. High Sch., 1959-63; tchr. Dollarway High Sch., Pine Bluff, Ark., 1963-65, coach. tchr., 1967-71; head sci. dept. Smackover (Ark.) High Sch., 1965-66; tchr. L.M. Goza Jr. High, Arkadelphia, 1966-67; coach, tchr. Pine Bluff Sch. Dist., 1971-85. Tex. Refinery Corp., 1971-74; radiol. def. officer Office Emergency Svc., Clark County and State Ark., 1986-92. Minister First Bapt. Mission, Augusta, Ark., 1956-57; cons in field. Author: A Beautiful Dream and Other Poems, 1994, numerous other poems (Golden Poet award 1985-90, 91, Poet of Merit award 1990). Served to 1st lt. U.S. Army, 1952-54, Korea. Recipient Leaders in Am. Sci. award, 1962-63. Mem. Am. Assn. Ret. Persons, Ark. Ret. Tchrs. Assn., Audubon Soc., NRA, Jackson County Tchrs. Asns. (pres. 1958), Am. Legion, Kiwanis (sec. 1970), Bass Masters, N.Am. Hunting Club, Ducks Unltd. Avocations: singing, writing, gardening, hunting, fishing. Home: 2 Glendale Ct Arkadelphia AR 71923-3512

HICKS, HERALINE ELAINE, environmental health scientist, educator; b. Beaufort, S.C., Sept. 27, 1951; d. Heral and Ophelia Lillie (Albergottie) H. BA, Ohio Wesleyan U., 1973; MS, Atlanta U., 1978, PhD, 1980; postgrad., U. N.C., 1980-84. Rsch. assoc. Chapel Hill Dental Rsch. Ctr. U. N.C., 1980-81; NIH postdoctoral fellow Chapel Hill Dental Rsch. Ctr. Chapel Hill Dental Rsch. Ctr. and Dept. Surgery, 1982-84; guest scientist Naval Med. Rsch. Inst., Bethesda, Md., 1985-87; asst. prof. Chapel Hill Sch. Dentistry U. N.C., 1985-88; prof., dir. electron microscopy Morris Brown Coll., Atlanta, 1988-90; sr. environ. health scientist, dir. Cts. for Disease Control and Prevention/Agy. for Toxic Substances and Disease Registry, Atlanta, 1990—; program dir. Gt. Lakes Human Health Effects Rsch. Program, Agy. for Toxic Substances and Disease Registry. Mem. health profls. task force adv. bd. Internat. Joint Commn., Washington, 1995—. Author: (chpt.) Development and Diseases of Cartilage and Bone Matrix, 1987, Birth Defects and Reproductive Disorders, 1993; contbr. articles to profl. jours. Predoctoral traineeship NIH, 1977-79, Barnett F. Smith award for outstanding achievement Atlanta U., 1978; Acad. scholar Ohio Wesleyean U., 1969-73, Josiah Macy Jr. scholar Woods Hole Marine Biol. Lab., 1979, Tuition scholar Atlanta U., 1979-80; postdoctoral fellow NIH, 1982-84, Notable Alumnus of Clark U., 1995; named one of Outstanding Young Women of Am., 1980. Mem. Am. Soc. for Cell Biology (Young Investigator fellowship 1990), Teratology (Young Investigator fellowship 1987), Microscopy Soc. Am., Biology Honor Soc., Beta Kappa Chi. Presbyterian. Avocations: reading, exercise, playing chess. Office: Ctrs for Disease Control and Prevention Mail Stop E29 1600 Clifton Rd NE Atlanta GA 30329-4018

HICKS, JIM, secondary education educator; Tchr. Physics Barrington (Ill.) H.S. Recipient Innovative Teaching and Secondary Sch. Physics award, 1992. Office: Barrington HS 616 W Main St Barrington IL 60010-3015

HICKS, RITCHIE B. physical education educator; b. Tallahassee, Fla. d. Frank Evans and Isabella (Lawrence) Stewart; m. Eddie Jay Hicks; children: Eddie Darrell, Jay Freeman, Michele Dianne. AA, Howard Coll.; BS in Edn., Fla. A & M Univ.; MA in Secondary Sch. Adminstr., N.E. Mo. State Univ. Cert. health and phys. edn. tchr., secondary sch. adminstr. Phys. edn. tch. Scott Jr. High Sch., Savannah, Ga., Florissant Jr. High Sch., Mo.; head track coach Berkeley Sr. High Sch., Mo.; phys. edn. tchr. Airport Elem. Sch., Berkeley, Mo., Berkeley Jr. High Sch., Mo.; phys. edn. and health tchr. Ferguson Middle Sch., Mo.; basketball, volleyball and track coach McCluer North Sr. High Sch., Florissant, Mo.; chairperson, dept. phys. edn. Cross Keys Middle Sch., Florissant, Mo. Mem. sch. and dist. curriculum and instrn. coms., 1995; mem. Bldg. Improvement Com.; dir. Sch. Intramural Program, 1995. Writer guidelines for Cross Keys Mid. Sch. phys. edn. students. Apptd. to Youth Adv. Commn. City of Florissant, Mo.; coach Mo. State H.S. Basketball, Track and Field Championship Teams; bd. trustees Ward Chapel AME Ch., 1995, dir. Richard and Sarah Allen Summer Acad., 1995; coord. bldg. Ferguson-Florissant Scholarship Run/Walk Program, 1995. Recipient Tchr. of Yr. award State of Mo., 1992, Mid. Sch. Phys. Edn. Tchr. of Yr. Nat. Assn. Sport and Phys. Edn., 1993, Mo. Coach of Yr. for track and field, 1982, Salute to Am. Tchr. Walt Disney, 1993; named to Nat. Women's Hall of Fame. Mem. Nat. Edn. Assn., Am. Assn. Univ. Women, Mo. AAHPERD (middle and secondary sch. phys. educator award of 1993), AAHPERD (middle sch. phys. edn. tchr. award of 1993), Am. Running and Fitness Assn., Phi Delta Kappa. Avocations: fitness walking, reading, weight training, golf, dance.

HICKS, WILLIAM JAMES, internist, oncologist, educator; b. Columbus, Ohio, 1948; MD, U. Pitts., 1974; BS, Morehouse Coll. Diplomate Am. Bd. Internal Medicine, Am. Bd. Oncology. Intern then resident Presbyn. U. Hosp., Pitts., 1974—77; fellow in hematology, oncology Ohio State U., 1977—79; mem. staff Grant Med. Ctr., Columbus, 1979; prin. William J. Hicks, Inc., 1979—2002; prof. clin. medicine divsn. hematology and oncology James Cancer Hosp. & Solove Rsch. Inst., Columbus, 2002—. Mem. Am. Soc. Clin. Oncology, Nat. Med. Assn. Office: James Cancer Hosp & Solove Rsch Inst B402 Starling Loving Hall 320 W 10th Ave Columbus OH 43210-4372 Office Fax: 614-293-4372.

HIEMSTRA, ROGER, adult education educator, writer; b. Plainwell, Mich., Sept. 15, 1938; s. Claude and Frances (Anson) H.; m. Janet Louise Wemer, June 23, 1968; children: Nancy, David. AA, Pasadena City Coll., Calif., 1958; BS, Mich. State U., 1964; MS, Iowa State U., 1967; PhD, U. Mich., 1970. Mott Intern Flint (Mich.) Community Schs., 1968-69; program coordinator Wayne State U., Detroit, 1969-70; dept. asst. U. Mich., Ann Arbor, 1969-70; prof. adult edn. U. Nebr., Lincoln, 1970-76; prof., chmn. adult edn. Iowa State U., Ames, 1976-80; prof. adult edn., instrnl. design Syracuse (N.Y.) U., 1980—96, chmn. dept. adult edn., 1980—94, prof. emeritus, 1996—; prof., program dir. of adult edn. Elmira Coll., 1997—. Chmn. Commn. Profs. Adult Edn., Washington, 1981-83; co-dir. adult edn. resource worldwide Kellogg Project, 1986-90, dir., 1991-93. Co-author, editor: Changing Approaches to Studying Adult Education, 1980; co-author: Individualizing Instruction, 1990, Self-Direction in Adult Learning, 1991, Professional Writing, 1994, Toward Ethical Practice, 2003; author editor: Creating Environments for Effective Adult Learning, 1991; co-editor, author Overcoming Resistence to Self-Direction in Adult Learning, 1994; author: The Educative Community, 1972, Lifelong Learning, 1976; sr. editor Lifelong Learning: The Adult Years, 1980-83; editor Adult Edn. Quar., 1985-88. Mem. Commn. of Profs. of Adult Edn. With USNR, 1960-62. Named Tchr. of Yr. for Grad. Studies, Elmira Coll., 1999; inducted into Internat. Adult and Continuing Edn. Hall of Fame, 2000. Mem. Adult Edn. Assn. U.S.A. (exec. bd. 1977-82, svc. award), Am. Assn. Adult and Continuing Edn., Assn. for Continuing Higher Edn. (Nat. Leadership award 1991). Democrat. Unitarian-Universalist. Home: 318 Southfield Dr Fayetteville NY 13066-2253

HIERHOLZER, CONNIE MCARTHUR, parochial school educator; b. Vidalia, Georgia, July 21, 1943; d. Robert Stewart and Rose (Adams) McArthur; m. John Charles Hierholzer, Oct. 21, 1967; children: Jack, Karl, Mike. BS, Emory U., 1965; M in Christian edn., So. Bapt. Theol. Sem., 1995; cert. in tchg., Brewton Parker Coll., 1997. Cert. educator Ga. Lab. technologist Ctr. Disease Control, Atlanta, 1965—68, Grady Hosp., Atlanta, 1982; lab. rsch. asst. Newcastle Hosp., Australia, 1984; tchr. substitution various schs., Ga., 1997—; tchr. Internat. English Sch., 2002—03. Writer (radio ministry) Connie Hier Children's Ministry of Bible Studies, 1995—, (puppet ministry) Praise the Lord, 2001—. Mem.: Profl. Assn. Ga. Educators, Bapt. Assn., Christian Educators, Dau. Am. Colonies. Baptist. Avocations: gardening, hiking, camping, piano, sewing. Office: Connie Hier Children's Ministry PO Box 420 Uvalda GA 30473

HIGBY, GREGORY JAMES, historical association administrator, historian; s. Warren James and Gertrude H.; m. Marian Fredal, June 2, 1979. BS in Pharmacy, U. Mich., 1977; MS in Pharmacy, U. Wis., 1980, PhD in Pharmacy, 1984. Staff pharmacist Higby's Pharmacy, Bad Axe, Mich., 1977-78; asst. to dir. Am. Inst. of the History of Pharmacy, Madison, Wis., 1981-84, asst. dir., 1984-86, assoc. dir., 1986, acting dir., 1986-88, dir., 1988—; rsch. assoc. U. Wis., Madison, 1984-86. Adj. asst. prof. U. Wis., Madison, 1984-94, adj. assoc. prof., 1994-2000, adj. prof., 2000—; cons. Smithsonian Instn., Washington, 1987, Am. Soc. Hosp. Pharmacists, Bethesda, Md., 1990, U.S. Pharmacopeial Conv., 1992-95, Am. Assn. Colls. Pharmacy, 1993-99; adv. com. Fed. Drug Law Inst., Washington, 1989-90. Author: In Service to American Pharmacy: The Professional Life of William Procter, Jr., U. Ala. Press, 1992; co-author: The Spirit of Voluntarism...The United States Pharmacopeia 1820-1995, 1995; editor: One Hundred Years of the National Formulary, 1989, Pill Peddlers: Essays on the History of the Pharmaceutical Industry, 1990, Historical Hobbies for the Pharmacist, 1994, The History of Pharmacy, A Selected Annotated Bibliography, 1995, The Inside Story of Medicines, 1997, Apothecaries and the Drug Trade, 2001, 150 Years of Caring: A Pictorial History of the APHA, 2002, Drugstore Memories: American Pharmacists Recall Life Behind the Counter, 2002; author poetry; editor: Pharmacy in History Jour., 1986—; contbr. articles to profl. jours. Recipient Edward Kremers award 1995. Mem. Am. Pharm. Assn., Am. Assn. Coll. Pharm., Am. Assn. for History of Medicine, Hist. Sci. Soc., Orgn. Am. Historians, Soc. for History of Tech., Internat. Acad. History of Pharmacy. Avocations: bird watching, cycling, racquetball, musician. Office: Am Inst of the History of Pharmacy 777 Highland Ave Madison WI 53705-2222 E-mail: greghigby@aihp.org.

HIGDON, BERNICE COWAN, retired elementary education educator; b. Sylva, N.C., Feb. 26, 1918; d. Royston Duffield and Margaret Cordelia (Hall) Cowan; m. Roscoe John Higdon, Aug. 12, 1945; children: Ronald Keith, Rodrick Knox, Krista Dean. BS, Western Carolina U., 1941; cert. tchr., So. Oreg. Coll., 1967; student, Chapman Coll., 1971. Cert. tchr., Calif. Prin., tchr. Dorsey Sch., Bryson City, N.C., 1941-42; expeditor Glenn L. Martin Aircraft Co., Balt., 1942-45; tchr. elem. sch. Seneca, S.C., 1945-46, Piedmont, S.C., 1946-47, Columbia, S.C., 1950-51, Manteca, Calif., 1967-68; kindergarten tchr. 1st Bapt. Ch., Medford, Oreg., 1965-67; tchr. elem. sch. Marysville (Calif.) Unified Sch. Dist., 1968-83. Tchr. Headstart, Manteca, 1968. Past counselor Youth Svc. Bur., Yuba City, Calif.; troop leader Girl Scouts U.S.A., Medford, 1962-63; past Sunday sch. tchr. 1st Bapt. Ch., Medford; bd. dirs. Christian Assistance Network, Yuba City, 1984-85; deaconess Evang. Free Ch., Yuba City, 1991-93. Recipient cert. of appreciation Marysville Unified Sch. Dist., 1983, Christian Assistance Network, 1985; cert. of recognition Ella Elem. Sch., Marysville, 1983. Mem. Calif. Ret. Tchrs. Assn., Nat. Ret. Tchrs. Assn., Sutter Hist. Soc., AAUW, Am. Assn. Ret. Persons. Avocations: foreign traveling, photography, volunteer work, tole painting. Home: 1264 Charlotte Ave Yuba City CA 95991-2804

HIGGINBOTHAM, LARK, family and consumer sciences educator; b. Sisterville, W.Va., June 26, 1956; d. Robert Keith and Barbara Lou (Broadwater) H. AB, West Liberty State Coll., 1978; postgrad., W.Va. U., 1980, 81, Marshall U., 1984; MA, Ashland U., 1998. Cert. tchr., Ohio, W.Va. Substitute tchr. Randolph County Sch., Elkins, W.Va., 1979; vocat. tchr. Switzerland of Ohio Sch., Woodsfield, 1979; home econs. tchr. Grover Cleveland Jr. High Sch., Zanesville, Ohio, 1979-84, 87-88, Zanesville High Sch., 1986—87, family and consumer scis. tchr., 1987—. Mem. State Vocat. Planning Com., Columbus, Ohio, 1989-92. Mem. Zanesville Meml. Concert Band, 2002—. Mem.: NEA, Ohio Assn. Tchrs. Family and Consumer Scis. (bd. dirs. 1992—2002), Nat. Assn. Tchrs. Family and Consumer Scis. (nominatons chair 2001—02, legis. chair 2003—), Assn. for Career and Tech. Edn., Zanesville Edn. Assn., Ohio Edn. Assn. Methodist. Avocations: reading, sewing, cross-stitch, college basketball and football. Home: 1935 Tannehill St # A Zanesville OH 43701-2253 Office: Zanesville High Sch 1701 Blue Ave Zanesville OH 43701-2499 E-mail: goeers@y-city.net.

HIGGINS, FRANCIS EDWARD, history educator; b. Chgo., Nov. 29, 1935; s. Frank Edward and Mary Alyce (Fahey) H. BS, Loyola U., Chgo., 1959, MA, 1964; postgrad., Exeter Coll., Oxford (Eng.) U., 1962, Am. U. Beirut, 1966, McGill U., Montreal, 1967; Adminstrn. Cert., St. Xavier Coll., 1971; EdD, U. Sarasota, 1977. Tchr. Washington Jr. H.S., Chicago Heights, Ill., 1959, Chgo. Vocat. H.S., 1960-68, dept. chmn., 1964; asst. prof. social sci. Moraine Valley C.C., 1968-69; tchr. history Hillcrest H.S., Country Club Hills, Ill., 1969-93. Instr. nursing continuing edn. St. Francis Coll., 1978—. Contbr. revs. to Am. Cath. Hist. Jour., History Tchr. Jour. Mem. pres.'s coun. St. Xavier Coll., 1978—; mem. St. Germaine Sch. Bd., 1972-73, St. Alexander Sch. Bd., 1978-84; active Chgo. coun. Boy Scouts Am., 1969-77, asst. dist. commr., 1971-75, mem. dist. scout com., 1976-77; co-historian Palos Hts. Silver Jubilee Com., 1984. Recipient Disting. Svc. award Chgo. coun. Boy Scouts Am., 1974; Brit. Univ. scholar, 1962; Fulbright fellow, summer 1966; English Speaking Union fellow, 1967. Mem. Ill. Hist. Soc., Del. Hist. Soc., Am. Cath. Hist. Soc., Nat. Coun. Social Studies, Ill. Coun. Social Studies, Nat. Curriculum and Supervisory Assn., Ill. Supervisory Assn., Ill. Assn. Supervision and Curriculum Devel. (editl. rev. bd. Jour. 1984-86), Chgo. Hist. Soc., Nat. Hist. Soc., Brit. Hist. Assn., Nat. Soc. Study Edn., Phi Delta Kappa, Phi Kappa Mu. Republican. Roman Catholic. Home: 7931 W Lakeview Ct Palos Heights IL 60463-2526

HIGGINS, JANE EDGINGTON, secondary school educator; b. London, Eng., Sept. 1, 1955; came to U.S., 1966; d. John Herbert and Dorothy Ann (Bjork) Edgington; m. Brian Alton Higgins, July 1, 1975; 1 child, Devon. BA in Art Edn., Framingham State Coll., 1977; MS in art Edn., Mass. Coll. Art, 1996. Cert. tchr. art K-12, Mass. Registrar Danforth Mus. of Art, Framingham, Mass., 1979-85; head dept. art David Prouty H.S., Spencer, Mass., 1987—, set design and prodn. com. Prouty Players, 1987-94, faculty adviser sch. newspaper, 1993—, audio visual dir., 1997—. Coord. ann. portfolio art shows Spencer Art Shows, 1992-94; dir. Projects Fair and exhbns., 1995—; dir. Summer Arts, Town of West Brookfield, 1996—. Illustrator: (cover) The Onyx, 1973, Choomia Contemporary Poetry, 1977, (textbook) The Physically Handicapped Child, 1976. Recipient 1st prize Friends of Marlboro Libr. Ann. Juried Show, 1979. Home: PO Box 1011 West Brookfield MA 01585-1011 Office: David Prouty HS 302 Main St Spencer MA 01562-1841

HIGGINS, JOHN P., JR., inspector general U.S. Department of Education; m. Lucy Higgins. BS in Bus, Bethel Coll., McKenzie, Tenn. Various mgmt. positions U.S. Dept. Health, Edn. and Welfare to U.S. Dept. Edn., Washington, 1970—; chief mgmt improvement team U.S. Dept. Edn., Washington, 1994—96, dep. insp, gen, 1996—2002, insp. gen., 2002—. Office: US Dept Edn 400 Maryland Ave SW Washington DC 20202

HIGGINS, LARKIN MAUREEN, artist, poet, educator; b. Santa Monica, Calif. d. DuWayne and Mary Jean (Sampson) H. BA, Calif. State U., Long Beach, 1976; MA, Calif. State U., Fullerton, 1983; MFA, Otis Coll. Art and Design, 1995. Artist/poet resident Dorland Mountain Arts Colony, 2000, 2001, 2002; prof. art Calif. Luth. U., Thousand Oaks. Represented in numerous collections; exhibited nationally in group and one-woman shows; art reviewed/ pub. in various pubs. including L.A. Times, Artweek, The Boston Globe, Genre, Antiques & The Arts Weekly, U-TURN, others; poetry pub. in Blue Satellite, Beyond Baroque mag., Saturday Afternoon jour., others; 3 anthologies: Matchbook, Jitters: The Best of Southern California Coffee House Fiction and Poetry, So Luminous the Wildflowers: Anthology of California Poetry. Past. bd. dirs., past chairperson nat. photography exhbn. com. Westwood (Calif.) Ctr. for the Arts; past chairperson lecture com. L.A. Ctr. for Photographic Studies; founding mem. Women in Photography, L.A. Recipient cash award ASA Gallery, U. N.Mex., 1982, Purchase award Erie (Pa.) Art Mus., 1984; Hewlett Found. Ind. Artist grantee, 1987-88, Jones grantee, 1986. Mem. Coll. Art Assn., Beyond Baroque Lit. Arts Ctr., Women's Caucus Art.

HIGGINS, NANCY BRANSCOME, management and counseling educator; b. New Castle, Pa. d. Otis and Ola May (Vaughn) Branscome; m. Bernard F. Higgins, Nov. 15, 1969; 1 child, Bernard F. II. BBA, Westminster Coll., 1967, MEd, 1970, MA, Pepperdine U., 1979; EdD, Vanderbilt U., 1990. Cert. counselor; full life cmty. coll. cert. in bus. mgmt. and indsl. human resources mgmt., psychology, office svcs. and related technologies. Counselor U. Md., College Park, 1976-77, now adj. prof. bus. mgmt.; prof. part-time Hartnell Coll., Salinas, Calif., 1977-80; prof. mgmt. Monterey (Calif.) Peninsula Coll., 1977-80; coord., adminstr. Pepperdine U., Ft. Ord, Calif., 1977-80; prof. part-time Park Coll., Ft. Myer, Va., 1980-82, No. Va. C.C., Annandale, 1980-82, Prince George's Coll., Largo, Md., 1980-82; prof. mgmt. and mktg., coord. Montgomery Coll., Rockville, Md., 1982—, chmn. mgmt. dept., 1993—, mem. faculty congress, 1985-87. Mem. task force Nat. Coun. for Occupl. Edn., 1994; adj. prof. U. Md., 1998; bus. mgmt. adv. bd. U. Md. Univ. Coll., 1997—. Vol. ARC, Washington, Lakeside Hosp., Cleve., 1990; mem. WETA-Edn. TV, Fairfax, Va.; mem. bus./mgmt. adv. bd. U. Md., 1997—. Recipient Student Devel. award Montgomery Coll., 1982, Svc. award, 1982, Human Rights award Montgomery County, Md., Faculty and Counseling Excellence award, 1997, Faculty/Counseling Excellence award. Mem. AAUW, ASTD (membership com. and career devel. 1994—), Soc. Human Resources Mgmt., Nat. Soc. Exptl. Edn., Am. Assn. Women in C.C.'s, Pepperdine U. Alumni Assn., Vanderbilt U. Alumni Assn., Westminster Coll. Assn., Montgomery Coll. Alumni Assn. (50th Anniversary com. 1996, Continuing Edn. Leadership Inst. com. 1996-97, Alumni Tchr.-Counselor Excellence award 1997), Chi Omega (rush chairperson 1998—, Human Rights award, 2002). Avocation: travel. Home: 7764 Heatherton Ln Potomac MD 20854-3212

HIGGINS, ROXANNE SNELLING, educational consultant; b. Ft. Eustis, Va., Aug. 17, 1954; d. William Rodman and Anne Louise (Kurtz) Snelling; m. Vincent James Elliott, Oct. 1, 1983 (div.); children: Brian William, Lauren Elizabeth; m. Robert K. Higgins, June 16, 2001. BA, Denison U., 1976; MBA, Syracuse U., 1978. Internat. loan officer First Pa. Bank, Phila., 1978-82; ins. assoc. Ind. Sch. Mgmt., Wilmington, Del, 1982-83, dir. mgmt. insts., 1983-87, cons., exec. dir. consortium, 1984—, v.p., 1986-90, pres., 1990—. Office: Ind Sch Mgmt 1316 N Union St Wilmington DE 19806-2594

HIGHAM, ROBIN, historian, editor, publisher; b. London, June 20, 1925; came to U.S., 1940, naturalized, 1954; s. David and Margaret Anne (Stewart) H.; m. Barbara Davies, Aug. 5, 1950; children: Peter (dec.), Susan Elizabeth (dec.), Martha Anne, Carol Lee. AB cum laude, Harvard U., 1950, PhD, 1957; MA, Claremont Grad. Sch., 1953. Instr. Webb Sch. Calif., 1950-52; grad. asst. in oceanic history Harvard U., 1952-54; instr. U. Mass., 1954-57; asst. prof. U. N.C., Chapel Hill, 1957-63; assoc. prof. history Kans. State U., 1963-66, prof., 1966-98; historian Brit. Overseas Airways Corp., 1960-66, 76-78; editor Mil. Affairs, 1968-88, emeritus; editor Aerospace Historian, 1970-88, emeritus, 1989—; editor, pub. Jour. of the West, 1977—; adv. editor Tech. and Culture, 1967-85; founder, pres. Sunflower Univ. Press, 1977—; mil. adv. editor Univ. Press Ky., 1970-75. Cons. Epic of Flight, Time/Life Books, 1980-82; lectr. in field; mem. publs. com. Conf. Brit. Studies, 1965-93; advisor Core Collection for Coll. Librs., 1971-72; pres., cons. com. Revue Internat. d'Histoire Militaire, 1976-85, mem. mil. archives com., 1990—, acting pres., 1996-2000, sec. gen., 2002—; founder, organizer Conf. Historic Aviation Writers, 1982-98. Author: Britain's Imperial Air Routes, 1918-39, 1960, The British Rigid Airship, 1908-31, 1961, Armed Forces in Peacetime: Britain 1918-39, 1963, The Military Intellectuals in Britain: 1918-1939, 1966, (with David H. Zook) A Short History of Warfare, 1966, Hebrew edit., 1970, Chinese edit., 1985, The Compleat Academic (Macmillan Book Club choice), 1975, Air Power: A Concise History (selection Mil. Book Soc., History Book Club, Flying Book Club), 1973, 2d enlarged edit., 1984, 3d enlarged edit., 1988, The Bases of Air Strategy, 1998, (with Mary Cisper & Guy Dresser) A Brief Guide to Scholarly Editing, 1982, Diary of a Disaster: British Aid to Greece, 1940-41, 1986; editor: Bayonets in the Streets, 1969, 89, Civil Wars in the Twentieth Century, 1972, A Guide to the Sources of British Military History, 1971, A Guide to the Sources of U.S. Military History, 1975, (with Donald J. Mrozek) supplements, 1981, 86, 93, 99 (with Carol Brandt) The U.S. Army in Peacetime: Essays in Honor of the Bicentennial, 1975, Intervention or Abstention, 1975, (with Jacob W. Kipp) Soviet Aviation and Air Power, 1977, Garland Military History Bibliographic Series (with Jacob W. Kipp), 1978-92, Flying Combat Aircraft (with A. T. Siddall) vol. 1, 1975, (with Carol Williams) vol. 2, 1978 and vol. 3, 1981; editor (with George E. Ham) The Rise of the Wheat State: a History of Kansas Agriculture, 1861-1986, 87, (with Thanos Veremis) The Metaxas Dictatorship: Aspects of Greece, 1936-1940. (with John T. Greenwood and Von Hardesty) Russian Aviation & Air Power, 1998, A Handbook of Air Ministry Organization, 1998; ed. Writing Official Military History, 1999,

Official Military History, 2 vols., 2000, The Bases of Air Strategy, 2000, (with Frederick W. Kagan) A Military History of Russia, A Military History of the Soviet Union, 2002, (with David A. Graff) A Military History of China, 2002; sr. advisor on Ency. of U.S. Mil. History, Acad. Mil. Scis., Beijing, 1988—; advisory editor Ency. of USAF, 1988-92; mem. aviation editorial adv. bd. Smithsonian Instn. Press, 1989-92; adv. Greenwood Press, 1992—; mem. editl. bd. Defence Analysis, 1984—; cons., contbr.: Dictionary of Business Biography, 1980-86, Encyclopedia of the American Military, 1994; contbr. 100 Years of Aviation; contbr. The New Dictionary of National Biography, 1994-2002; contbr. articles to profl. jours. Trustee U.S. Commn. on Mil. History, 1993—; mem. Kans. State Aviation Adv. Com., 1986-95, sec., 1992-95. Pilot RAFVR, 1943-46. Vol. res. RAF. Named Disting. Grad., Faculty Kans. State U., 1971; recipient Victor Gondos award Am. Mil. Inst., 1983, Samuel Eliot Morison award for disting. scholarship Am. Mil. Inst., 1986, Stamey Tchg. award, 1996, Aviation Honors award Gov. Kans., 2000; Social Sci. Rsch. Coun. nat. security policy rsch. fellow, 1960-61. Mem. AIAA (standing com. history 1973—), Soc. History Tech., Am. Aviation Hist. Soc., RAF Hist. Soc., Friends of RAF Mus. (life), Burma Star Assn. (life), Air Force Hist. Found. (trustee 1984-98), Soc. Army Hist. Rsch. (corr. mem. coun. 1980-98), Am. Mil. Inst., WWII Studies Assn. (dir. 1973-75, 79-82, 83—, archivist 1977—), Am. Aviation Hist. Soc., U.S. Commn. on Mil. History, Riley County Hist. Soc. (past dir., chmn. long-range planning com. 1980-97).Hist. Book Club, 2003 Home: 2961 Nevada St Manhattan KS 66502-2355

HIGHLAND, FREDERICK, writer, humanities educator; b. Audobon, N.J., Feb. 13, 1945; s. Frederick William Sr. and Emily Barbara H.; 1 child, Sophia Angela. BA in English, Suffolk U., 1967; MA in English, U. Wis., Milw., 1971, PhD in Lit., 1983. Vol. Peace Corps, Washington, 1967-69; teaching asst. U. Wis., Milw., 1969-75; instr. Upward Bound Program, Milw., 1970-73; instr. English Bir Zeit U., West Bank, Israel, 1975-76; Pace prof. Chapman Coll., Orange, Calif., 1977-79; edn. specialist Dept. U.S. Navy, Cubi Point, Philippines, 1979-85; dir. Pace Hawaii City Colls. Chgo., Pearl Harbor, 1985-87; writer, rschr. Highland Wordsmith, Washington, 1996—. Prof. Hawaii Pacific U., 1984—95. Author: The Mystery Box, 1998, Ghost Eater, 2003. Mem. Am. Philatelic Soc., Mystery Writers Am. Home and Office: Highland Wordsmith PO Box 5961 Bellingham WA 98227-5961

HIGHLAND, MARTHA (MARTIE), retired education educator, consultant; b. Lexington, Ky., June 3, 1934; d. William Thomas and Lyda Bruce (Wilson) H.; foster children: Barbara O. Noe, Teresa O. McKenzie, Debby O. Hodges, Joseph Owens, Kathy S. Coddington. AA, Cumberland Jr. Coll., 1955; BA in Edn., U. Ky., 1958; MA in Edn., U. Louisville, 1981. Cert. tchr., Ky. Tchr. Jefferson County Bd. Edn., Louisville, 1958-59, Ft. Knox (Ky.) Dependent Schs., 1959-65, Louisville City Schs., 1965-66, reading specialist, 1966-75, Jefferson County Sch. System, Louisville, 1975-89, remedial specialist in reading and math., 1989-91; ret., 1991. Substitute tchr., vol. Jefferson County Bd. Edn., Louisville, 1991—; faculty rep. Jefferson County Tchrs. Assn., 1981-91. Nominated Disney Tchr. of Yr., 1989. Mem. ASCD, Am. Bus. Women's Assn. (sec. 1989-92, v.p. 1988-89, 92-93, Woman of Yr. 1990). Avocations: academic coaching, reading, gardening. Home: 2135 Peabody Ln Louisville KY 40218-1212

HIGHLAND, PHYLLIS ANTOINETTE, elementary education educator; b. Phila., Feb. 7, 1953; d. Melvin Jackson and Alfreda Elizabeth (Washington) Broadus. AS cum laude, Germanna C.C., Locust Grove, Va., 1973; BA, Mary Washington Coll., 1975; MEd, U. Va., 1979. Cert. tchr., Va. Tchr. 2d grade Unionville (Va.) Elem. Sch. Orange County Sch. Bd., 1977-90; clin. instr. Curry Sch. Edn., U. Va., Charlottesville, 1987—. Bd. dirs. Orange County Recreation Assn., Orange County Cancer Soc., Orange County Libr. Found. Bd.; mem., treas. Orange County You-Two Program; Sunday sch. tchr., vacation Bible sch. tchr.; sec. Shady Grove Bapt. Ch., Orange, Va.; corr. sec. Wayland Blue Ridge Bapt. Assn., 1994—; active Girl Scouts U.S. Recipient Outstanding Svc. award Va. Women in Ministry, 1987, plaque Orange Va. br. NAACP, 1988, others. Mem. Pi Gamma Mu, Sigma Omega Chi. Avocations: photography, personal computers, collecting angels. Home: 9266 Zachary Taylor Hwy Unionville VA 22567-2120 Office: Unionville Elem Sch Zachary Taylor Hwy Unionville VA 22567

HIGHTOWER, MARY LOU SWARTZ, elementary education educator; b. Galion, Ohio, May 13, 1949; d. Ralph Charles and Grace Louise (Burke) Swartz; m. William Chatman Hightower III, June 6, 1970. BS in Edn., Western Carolina U., 1971; MEd in Adminstrn., Clemson (S.C.) U., 1978; EdD, U. S.C., 1993. Lic. tchr., elem. prin., supr., art, social studies, S.C. Elem. art tchr. Spartanburg (S.C.) Dist. 6, 1971-79, art coord. kindergarten to 8th grade, tchr., 1979—; adj. prof. U. S.C., Spartanburg, 1986—. Chair, del. K-12 Arts Edn. Adv. Com., Columbia, S.C., 1988-90; del. S.C. Joint Legis. Com. for Cultural Affairs, 1987-88; bd. dirs. S.C. Tchr. Forum Steering Com., Rock Hill, 1989-90, S.C. Alliance for Arts Edn., Columbia, 1986-88; intern S.C. Gov.'s Sch. for the Arts, Greenville, 1988. Author: Masterpiece Collector, 1992 (Grant 1992). Mem. Spartanburg Arts Adv. Coun., 1973-92; chair Community Fall Arts Festival, Spartanburg Arts Ctr., 1982, Spartanburg Arts Coun. Exhbns., 1982-85. Mem. NEA, Nat. Art Edn. Assn. (southeastern dir. for arts adminstrn. 1987-91, Outstanding S.C. Art Educator 1986, Southeastern Supervision Educator 1987), S.C. Alliance for Arts Edn., Guild for S.C. Artists, Spartanburg Artist Guild, S.C. Watercolor Soc., S.C. Art Edn. Assn. (pres., past pres. 1985-89, Svc. award 1992), Phi Delta Kappa, Zeta Tau Alpha. Avocations: sports car racing, watercolor, quilting, travel. Home: 206 Thornhill Dr Spartanburg SC 29301-6419 Office: Spartanburg Sch Dist #6 1493 W O Ezell Blvd Spartanburg SC 29301-2615

HIGNITE, MICHAEL ANTHONY, computer information systems educator, researcher, writer, consultant; b. Baxter Springs, Kans., Jan. 23, 1954; s. Denver and Goldie Beatrice (Farris) H.; m. Lisa Jo Barger, May 15, 1976; 1 child, Anna. BS in Bus. Adminstrn., Okla. State U., 1976, MS in Bus., 1979; PhD in Bus. Edn., U. Mo., 1990. Computer programmer Atlantic Richfield Co., Dallas, 1979-80, 85-86, programmer, analyst Tulsa, 1980-82, systems analyst Anchorage, 1982-85, cons., 1987-88; asst. prof. S.W. Mo. State U., Springfield, 1990-95, assoc. prof., 1995—2003, prof., 2003—. Adj. prof. computer sci. Anchorage C.C., 1982-85. Mem. Am. Assn. for Higher Edn., Delta Sigma Pi, Beta Gamma Sigma. Republican. Methodist. Avocations: reading, running, collecting antiques, kayaking. Home: 4760 S Connor Ave Springfield MO 65804-7518 Office: Southwest Mo State U 901 S National Ave Springfield MO 65804-0088 E-mail: mah985f@smsu.edu

HIGUERA-PEREDA, MERCEDES, secondary education educator; b. Santiago de Cuba, Cuba, Sept. 7, 1944; d. Eustaquio and Sara (Pereda) Higuera. BA, Duchesne Coll. of The Sacred Heart, 1965; postgrad., Creighton U. Cert. tchr., Nebr., P.R. Spanish dept. coor., nat. honor soc. & student coun. advisor St. John's Sch., Santurce, P.R., tchr., Spanish. Mem. ASCD, Am. Assn. Tchrs. of Spanish and Portuguese, Nat. Assn. Student Activity Advisors, Asociacion de Maestros y Estudiantes Pro-Arte, Cum Laude Soc. Home: Cond Beach Tower Apt 1005 4327 Ave Isla Verde Carolina PR 00979-4999

HILBRINK, WILLIAM JOHN, violinist; b. Cleve., June 16, 1928; s. William and Caroline (Theil) H.; m. Patricia Anne Schultz, Aug. 6, 1955; children: Mark David, Holly Lee. B of Music Edn., Baldwin-Wallace Coll., 1955; MusM, Eastman Sch. Music, 1960. Cert. tchr. Tchr. strings, orch. Cleve. Pub. Schs., 1955-57; tchr. strings, dir. orch. MacMurray Coll., Jacksonville, Ill., 1958-62; tchr. violin, viola, string pedagogy, theory U. N.C., Greensboro, 1962-67; tchr. strings, grades 1-12, dir. orch. Fairfax (Va.) County Schs., 1967-83; asst. condr., assoc. concertmaster Fairfax Symphony Orch., 1977-84; ops. mgr. Fairfax (Va.) Symphony Orch., 1983-84; founder, 1st violinist Fairfax String Quartet, 1983—. Orch. condr. MacMurray Coll. Community Orch., Jacksonville, 1958-62; founding mem. Collegium Musicum, Jacksonville, 1960-62; concertmaster Springfield (Ill.) Symphony Orch., 1962; 1st violinist Piano Trio, String Quartet, U. N.C., Greensboro, 1962-67; freelance violinist Washington area, 1977—. Reviewer of concerts, Civic Music Assn., 1960-62; violinist in several hundred concerts and recitals, 1958—. Organizer, condr. Fairfax All-County Orch., 1977-78; organizer Washington Met. area Spl. Olympics Orch., 1979; music contractor for several choral groups, Washington; adjudicator for music festivals, Va., N.C., and Md. Recipient scholarship Eastman Sch. Music, 1957-58, Suzuki Inst., 1966. Avocations: operating and collecting O-gauge model trains, woodworking, house remodeling. Home: 5112 Forsgate Pl Fairfax VA 22030-4507 E-mail: PAHilbrink@cs.com.

HILDEBRAND, JOAN MARTIN, education educator; b. Harrisburg, Pa., Aug. 9, 1931; d. Jacob Franklin and Mary Grace (Ewing) Martin; m. Wilbur Jesse Hildebrand, Jan. 1, 1952; children: Valerie, Lannetta, Wilbur Jr., Eric. BS, Shippensburg U., 1953; MEd, U. Md., 1971, PhD, 1983. Tchr. day care ctr. Anne Arundel County Dept. Social Svcs., Annapolis, Md., 1968-71, dir. agy.-operated day care ctrs., 1971-74; day care program specialist, policy, assessment and tng. Md. Dept. Human Resources, Balt., 1974-87; adj. faculty early childhood edn. Anne Arundel C.C., Arnold, Md., 1976-88; asst. prof. Towson (Md.) State U., 1987-94, assoc. prof., from 1994, chair dept. early childhood edn., 1987-95, early childhood dept. grad. dir., from 1996. Ednl. adv. com. Balt. County/Hartford County Headstart Program, Dundalk, Md., 1986-89; adv. com. Tchr. Effectiveness Network Md. Dept. Edn., 1988-94; mem. child care task force Balt. County C. of C., 1989-90; mem. block grant proposal adv. workgroup Md. Dept. Human Resources, 1991; mem. Univ. Assessment Coun., Md. Assessment Rev., 1994—, chair majors assessment rev. subcom.; presenter at profl. confs. Editor children's book rev. column Childhood Education, 1992-96; contbr. articles Day Care and Early Edn., Child Care Quar., other publs. Elder, pres. United Ch. of Christ of Annapolis, 1987-90. Grantee HHS, 1985, Md. Dept. Human Resources, 1971-79. Mem. ASCD, OMEP, Assn. Tchr. Educators, Md. Assn. Supervision and Curriculum Devel., Md. Assn. Tchr. Educators, Nat. Assn. Edn. Young Children, Md. Assn. Edn. Young Children, Met. Washington Assn. Childhood Edn. (pres. 1991-93), Assn. Childhood Edn. Internat. (publs. com., children's book rev. editor jour.). Home: Arnold, Md. Died Nov. 26, 2001.

HILDEBRAND, JOHN FREDERICK, newspaper columnist; b. Chgo., Dec. 23, 1940; s. Paul Hedden and Harriet L. (Cummins) H.; m. Vasana Lohitkoopt, June 24, 1972; children: Marisa Cummins, Shana Victoria, Brent Daniel. B Journalism, U. Mo., 1965; MS in Journalism, Columbia U., 1966. Reporter Poplar Bluff (Mo.) Daily Am. Republic, 1963, Joplin (Mo.) Globe, 1964, AP, Jefferson City and Kansas City, Mo., 1965; fgn. svc. officer U.S. Info. Svc., Washington and Bangkok, 1966-70; reporter Newsday, Melville, N.Y., 1970-74, asst. city editor, 1974-76, edn. writer, 1976—. Adj. prof. journalism Chulalongkorn U., Bangkok, 1967; pres. Lloyd Neck (N.Y.) Holding Corp., 1988-91, bd. dirs., 1986-95. Vestryman St. John's Episcopal Ch., Cold Spring Harbor, N.Y., 1992-98. Recipient citation Adelphi U., Garden City, N.Y., 1987, citation Kappa Delta Pi, Oakdale, N.Y., 1988, citation Phi Delta Kappa Suffolk County Chpt., 1999, Newsday Pub.'s. Spl. Achievement award, 1997. Mem. Edn. Writers Assn. (1st prize opinion article 1978, 1st prize article series 1982, 97, 1st prize article package 1992), Phi Gamma Delta (sec. Chi Mu chpt. 1964). Home: 23 Target Rock Dr Huntington NY 11743-1464 Office: Newsday Inc 235 Pinelawn Rd Melville NY 11747-4250 E-mail: john.hildebrand@newsday.com.

HILDEBRAND, VERNA LEE, human ecology educator; b. Dodge City, Kans., Aug. 17, 1924; d. Carrell E. and Florence (Smyth) Butcher; m. John R. Hildebrand, June 23, 1946; children: Carol Ann, Steve Allen. BS, Kans. State U., 1945, MS, 1957; PhD, Tex. Women's U., 1970. Tchr. home econs. Dickinson County H.S., Chapman, Kans., 1945-46; tchr. early childhood Albany (Calif.) Pub. Schs., 1946-47; grad. asst. Inst. Child Welfare U. Calif., Berkeley, 1947-48; tchr. kindergarten Albany Pub. Schs., 1948-49; dietitian commons and hosp. U. Chgo., 1952-53; instr. Kans. State U., Manhattan, 1953-54, 59, Okla. State U., Stillwater, 1955-56; asst. prof. Tex. Tech U., Lubbock, 1962-67; from asst. prof. to prof. Mich. State U., East Lansing, 1967-97, prof. emeritus, 1997—. Legis. clk. Kans. Ho. of Reps., Topeka, 1955. Author: Introduction to Early Childhood Education, 1971, 6th edit., 1997, Guiding Young Children, 1975, 6th edit., 1998, Parenting and Teaching Young Children, 1981, 90, Management of Child Development Centers, 1984, 5th edit., 2002, Parenting: Rewards and Responsibilities, 1994, 2d edit., 1997, 6th edit., 2002; co-author: China's Families: Experiment in Societal Change, 1985, Knowing and Serving Diverse Families, 1996, 2d edit., 1999. Mem. Nat. Assn. for the Edn. Young Children (task force 1975-77), Am. Home Econs. Assn. (bd. dirs., Leader award 1990), Women in Internat. Devel., Nat. Assn. Early Childhood Tchr. Edn. (award for meritorious and profl. leadership 1995).

HILDEBRANDT, WILLIS HARVEY, artist, educator; b. Waverly, Iowa, Nov. 28, 1952; s. Harvey Herman and Lavera Louise (Henning) H.; m. Doris Marie O'Connell, June 11, 1954; children: Matthew Karl, Megan Elisabeth. BA, Wartburg Coll., Waverly, 1975; MA, U. No. Iowa, Cedar Falls, 1979. Cert. tchr., Iowa. Elem. art instr. Griswold (Iowa) Schs., 1975-78; high sch. art instr. East Marshall Cmty. Schs., LeGrand, Iowa, 1980—. Participant Tchr. in Contemporary Art, 2003. Exhibited paintings in shows at James and Meryl Hearst Ctr. for the Arts, 1994, Melon Ctr., Wallingford, Conn., 1994, Des Moines Art Ctr., 1994. Recipient art awards, Iowa Secondary Art Tchr. of Yr., Art Educators of Iowa, 2000. Mem. NEA, Iowa State Edn. Assn., Nat. Art Edn. Assn. (Marie Walsh Sharpe fellow 1995), Ctrl. Iowa Art Assn. (mem. bd. control 1994—, instr. high sch. summer workshop), Iowa Alliance for Arts Edn. Democrat. Roman Catholic. Home: PO Box 381 Le Grand IA 50142-0381 E-mail: hils@marshallnet.com.

HILER, MONICA JEAN, reading and sociology educator; b. Dallas, Sept. 3, 1929; d. James Absalom and Monica Constance (Farrar) Longino; m. Robert Joseph Hiler, Nov. 1, 1952; children: Robert, Deborah, Michael, Douglas, Frederick. BA, Agnes Scott Coll., Decatur, Ga., 1951; MEd, U. Ga., Athens, 1968; EdS, U. Ga., 1972, EdD, 1974. Social worker Atlanta Family and Children's Svcs., 1962-63; tchr. Hall County pub. schs., Ga., 1965-67; mem. faculty Gainesville Jr. Coll., Ga., 1968-87, prof. reading and sociology, 1975-87, chmn. devel. studies program, 1973-85, acting chmn. divsn. social scis., 1986-87, prof. emeritus reading and sociology, 1987—. Cons. So. Regional Edn. Bd., 1975-83, Gainesville Coll., 1987-95; apptd. spl. advocate Juvenile Ct. Union County, Ga., 1994-96; ch. organist, pianist, choir dir., 1964-82, 1988—. Pres. Ch. Women United, N.E. Ga., 1992-94. Named Ch. Woman of Yr, N.E. Ga., 2001, Woman of Yr., St. Francis of Assisi Ch., Blairsville, 1996. Mem. ASCD, Internat. Reading Assn., Ga. Sociol. Assn., Gainesville Music Club, Phi Beta Kappa, Phi Delta Kappa, Phi Kappa Phi. Avocations: piano, painting, sewing. E-mail: jeannbob@brmemc.net.

HILES, BARBARA LYNN, retired elementary school educator; b. Independence, Mo., Nov. 24, 1936; d. Olien Kendall and Jennie Lucinda (Bowen) Peters; m. Sylvester Scott Hiles, June 27, 1955; children: Kenneth, Ronald. BS in Edn., Cen. Mo. State U., 1975, MS in Reading, 1977, EdS, 1979. Cert. elem. edn. and reading tchr., Mo. Kindergarten tchr. Blue Springs (Mo.) R-IV Sch. Dist., 1975-76, elem. tchr., 1976-80, 1995—2000, reading tchr., 1980—95; ret., 2000; pvt. reading tutor, 2000—. Mem. Internat. Reading Assn. (pres. Mo. State Coun. 1990-91, state coord. 1997—, Literacy award 1988), Blue Springs Ret. Educators Assn. (pres. 2002-04), Delta Kappa Gamma (pres. Beta Phi chpt. 1984-88). Home: 312 Gingerbread Ln Blue Springs MO 64014-3611

HILFSTEIN, ERNA, science historian, educator; b. Krakow, Poland; arrived in U.S., 1949, naturalized, 1954; d. Leon and Anna (Schornstein) Kluger; m. Max Hilfstein; children: Leon, Simone Juliana. BA, CCNY, 1967, MA, 1971; PhD, CUNY, 1978. Tchr. secondary schs., N.Y.C., 1968-84, 86-92; collaborator Polish Acad. Scis., 1968-85. Vis. prof. Queens Coll., 1973; affiliate Grad. Sch./Univ. Ctr., CUNY. Author: Starowolski's Biographies of Copernicus, 1980; collaborator English version of Nicholas Copernicus Complete Works, vol. 1, 1972, vol. 2, 1978, vol. 3, 1985, vols. 2 and 3, 2d edit., 1992; co-translator: The Leviathan in the State Theory of Thomas Hobbes: Meaning and Failure of a Political Symbol, 1996; editor: Science and History, 1978, Copernicus and His Successors, 1995, Sebastian Petrycy, A Polish Renaissance Scholar, 1997; contbr. articles and revs. to profl. jours. Recipient Rector's medal, Univ. M. Kopernik, Torun, 1989, medal, Towarzystwo Naukowe Torun, Poland, 1990, Dom Kopernika in Torun medal, 1989, Order of Merit Silver medal, Rep. of Poland, 1991, Scholar of Polish Descent medal, 1989; grantee, NEH, 1984—85. Mem. History Sci. Soc., Polish Inst. Arts and Scis. in Am., CUNY Acad. for the Humanities and Scis., N.Y. Acad. Scis., Kosciuszko Found., United Fedn. Tchrs. (chpt. chmn. 1978-84, 86-92, del. 1980-92), Am. Mus. Nat. History, Libr. Congress,Nat. Commn. Am. Fgn. Policy, New Cracow Friendship Soc. (bd. dirs. 1998—). Home: 1523 Dwight Pl Bronx NY 10465-1121 also: Woodheaven Estate 375 Westwood Dr Hurleyville NY 12747-5506

HILGENKAMP, KATHRYN DARLINE, exercise and sport psychologist, health educator; b. Denver, Nov. 5, 1952; d. LeRoy C. and Darline L. (Callaway) Thoms; children: Jessica Erin Hoffman, Whitney Jayne Hoffman, Colton James Hilgenkamp, Devin Corinne Hilgenkamp. BS in Edn., U. Nebr., Lincoln, 1977; MS in Edn., Southern Ill. U., Carbondale, 1980; EdD, U. Nebr., Lincoln, 1987. Asst. prof. Creighton U., Omaha, 1990-93; adj. faculty U. Nebr., Omaha, 1994-95; asst. prof. La. Tech. U., Ruston, 1995-99, Coastal Carolina U., Conway, SC, 1999—2002, U. No. Colo., Greeley, Colo., 2002—. Author: Taking Charge of Your Health, 2002. CPR instr. Am. Heart Assn., ARC, Blair, Nebr., 1980-95. Recipient 2nd pl. Student Rsch. award, Soc. Prospective Med., Atlanta, 1987; Enhancement grantee La. Bd. Regents, 1997. Mem.: AAHPERD, APA, Am. Assn. Health Edn. Avocations: running, weightlifting, aerobic dance, golf, volleyball. Office: Cmty Health and Nutrition Box 93 Greeley CO 80639

HILL, ALFRED, lawyer, educator; b. N.Y.C., Nov. 7, 1917; m. Dorothy Turck, Aug. 12, 1960; 1 dau., Amelia. BS, Coll. City N.Y., 1937; LL.B., Bklyn. Law Sch., 1941, LL.D., 1986; S.J. D., Harvard U., 1957. Bar: N.Y. State bar 1943, Ill 1958. With SEC, 1943-52; prof. law So. Meth. U., 1953-56, Northwestern U., 1956-62, Columbia U., 1962-75, Simon H. Rifkind prof. law, 1975-87, Simon H. Rifkind prof. law emeritus, 1988—. Contbr. articles on torts, conflict of laws, fed. cts. constl. law to legal jours. Mem. Am. Law Inst. Home: 79 Sherwood Rd Tenafly NJ 07670-2734 Office: Columbia Law Sch New York NY 10027

HILL, ALICE LORRAINE, history, genealogy and social researcher, educator; b. Moore, Okla., Jan. 15, 1935; d. Robert Edward and Alma Alice (Fraysher) H.; children: Debra Hrboka, Pamela Spangler (dec.), Eric Shiver, Lorraine Styczinski. BS in Bus. and Acctg., Ctrl. State U., 1977; student, U. Okla., 1977-78; postgrad., Calif. Luth. U., 1988; ed. Sch. Edn., UCLA, 1990. Cert. cmty. coll. life instr. acctg., bus. and indsl. mgmt., computer and related techs., and real estate, Calif.; ordained min. Former model, 1990-95; with L.A. Unified Sch. Dist., 1990-95; tchr. mentor K-12 Asuza (Calif.) Pacific U., 2000—; active real estate broker. Founder Los Artistas for creative activities for young people, 1996. Author: America, We Love You (Congl. Record Poem, made into World's 1st Internat. Patriotic song), 1975, Land of Lands (now world's first internat. patriotic song); author: (lyrics) Come Listen to the Music, 1996, Someday John, 1996. Mem. bd. advisors Family Health Rsch., Seattle. Named hon. grad. Patricia Stevens Modeling Sch. (Fla.); recipient scholarship Leadership Enrichment Program, Okla., 1977, Hon. recognition Okla. State Bd. of Regents for Higher Edn., 1977, Presdl. citations for Pres. Ford, 1975, 76, Admired Woman of the Decade award, 1994, Life Time Achievement award, 1995, Most Gold Record award, 1995, Key award for Rsch., Internat. Cultural Diploma of Honor, 1995, Woman of Yr. award, 1995, Internat. Woman of Yr. award Order Internat. Fellowship, 1994, 95, The Alice Lorraine Hill 2003 Poet of Yr. Medallion, The Famous Poets Soc., 2003. Mem. NAFE, NEA, AAUW, Internat. Platform Assn., Internat. Poetry Soc. (disting. mem., named to internat. hall of fame, 1996, named in Best Poets of 20th Century), Ventura County Profl. Women's Networking. Home: 1646 Lime Ave Oxnard CA 93033-6897

HILL, ANITA PAMELA, secondary school administrator; b. Chgo., Sept. 17, 1952; d. Charles Edward Marston and LaVerne Grace (Fitch) Minifee; divorced; 1 child, George. BS in Edn., Ill. State U., 1974, Roosevelt U., 1976; MEd, Tex. So. U., 1985. Cert. special edn. tchr., Ill., elem. sch. tch., mid-mgmt. administr., Tex., special edn. supr., Tex., elem. tchr. 1-8, Tex., special edn. tchr. 1-12, Tex. Tchr. Ridgeway Hosp. for Adolescents Pritzker's Children's Hosp. Residential Treatment Ctr., Chgo., 1975-76; realtor Century 21 Real Estate, Houston, 1977-79; tchr. special edn. Quail Valley Middle Sch., Ft. Bend, Ind., 1980-81; tchr., dept. head special edn. Willowridge High Sch., Ft. Bend, Ind., 1981-86; asst. prin. Christa McAuliffe Middle Sch., Ft. Bend, Ind., 1986-90; assoc. prin. Missouri City Middle Sch., Sugar Land, Tex., 1990—. Prin. summer sch. McAuliffe Middle Sch., Ft. Bend, 1987, Dulles Middle Sch., Ft. Bend, 1988, First Colony Middle Sch., Ft. Bend, 1989; presenter Ft. Bend Staff Devel. and Middle Sch. Conf.; mem. Ft. Bend 5 Yr. Planning. Staff Devel. Task Force, Gifted and Talented Task Force, Ft. Bend Ind. Sch. Dist. Sponsor, com. mem. Youth Choir; exec. bd. Mo. City Middle Sch. PTO; v.p. Mzazi Parent Assn. Windsor Village United Meth. Ch.; mentor Girl's Rites of Passage program; active Boys Rites of Passage program, curriculum writer, coord.; parent coord., vol. Teen Court; active Ft. Bend County Interfaith Coun. Mem. ASCD, Tex. Assn. Secondary Sch. Prins. Avocation: computers. Office: Ft Bend Ind Sch Dist Mo City Middle Sch 200 Louisiana St Missouri City TX 77489-1120

HILL, BEVERLY ELLEN, health sciences educator; b. Albany, Calif., May 20, 1937; d. Bert E. and Catherine (Doyle) H. BA, Coll. Holy Names, 1960; MS in Edn., Dominican Coll., 1969; EdD, U. So. Calif., 1978. Producer, dir. Health Scis TV U. Calif., Davis, 1966-69, coordinator Health Scis. TV, 1969-73; asst. dir. IMS U. So. Calif., Los Angeles, 1973-76, asst. dir. continuing edn., 1976-80, dir. biocommunications, 1976-80; dir. Med. Ednl. Resources Program Ind. U. Sch. Medicine, Indpls., 1980—, acting asst. dean continuing med. edn., 1991-95. Presenter Cath. U. Nijmegen, Netherlands, 1980, 81, European Symposium on Clin. Pharmacy, Brussels, 1982, Barcelona, Spain, 1983. Contbr. articles to profl. jours. Pres. Indpls. Shakespeare Festival, 1982-83; mem. subcom. Ind. Film Commn., Indpls., 1984—. Recipient first place in rehab. category 4th Biannual J. Muir Med. Film Fest., 1980. Mem. Assn. Biomed. Communications (bd. dirs. 1985—), Health Scis. Com. Assn. (bd. dirs. 1976-79, First Place Video Festival, 1979), Assn. for Edn. Communications and Tech. Avocations: painting, travel, archeology, music, tennis, swimming. Office: Med Ednl Resources Program BR 156 1226 W Michigan St Indianapolis IN 46202-5212 Home: 849 Michigan Blvd Pasadena CA 91107-5734

HILL, BOBBY NELL, media specialist, elementary school educator; b. Dillworth, Ala., Oct. 15, 1946; d. Solon Kennedy and Hazel (Lockard) Roberts; m. Albert Wayne Hill, 1964; children: Dennis Wayne, Billy Joe. AA, Walker Coll., 1982; BA in Elem. Edn. summa cum laude, U. Ala., Birmingham, 1983, MA, 1985, EdS, 1990. Library aide Walker County (Ala.) Bd. Edn., 1977-83, tchr., 1983-84; librarian, media specialist Jefferson County (Ala.) Bd. Edn., 1984—. Workshop leader, U. Ala. Birmingham, 1989. Chmn. Leukemia Soc., 1993; vol. Am. Heart Assn., 1985; sponsor Nat. Beta Club, 1975-85. Mem. NEA, Ala. Libr. Assn., Ala. Instrnl.

Media Assn. (chpt. sec. 1989-90), Friends of Ala. Libr., Phi Theta Kappa, Kappa Delta Phi. Baptist. Avocations: quilting, antique furniture refinishing, baking, traveling. Home: 321 Garner Rd Cordova AL 35550-3223 Office: Minor HS 2285 Minor Pky Adamsville AL 35005-2532

HILL, BRUCE MARVIN, statistician, scientist, educator; b. Chgo., Mar. 13, 1935; s. Samuel and Leah (Berman) H.; m. Linda Ladd, June 18, 1958; children— Alec Michael, Russell Andrew, Gregory Bruce; m. Anne Edith Gardiner Bruce, Aug. 5, 1972. BS in Math., U. Chgo., 1956; MS in Stats., Stanford U., 1958, PhD in Stats., 1961. Mem. faculty U. Mich., Ann Arbor, 1960—, assoc. prof. stats. and probability theory, 1964-70, prof., 1970—. Vis. prof. bus. Harvard U., 1964-65; vis. prof. systems engring. U. Lancaster, U.K., 1968-69; vis. prof. stats. U. London, 1976; vis. prof. econs. U. Utah, 1979; vis. prof. math. U. Milan, U. Rome, 1989. Author: Hill Tail index estimator; editor Jour. Am. Statis. Assn., 1977-83, Jour. Bus. and Econ. Stats., 1982—; contbr. articles to profl. jours., chpts. to books on stats, encys. Grantee NSF, 1962-69, 81-86, 89—, USAF, 1971-73, 87-89. Fellow Am. Statis. Assn. (pres. Ann Arbor chpt. 1986-91), Inst. Math. Stats.; mem. AAUP, Am. Math Assn., Rsch. Club U. Mich., Psi Upsilon, Sigma Chi. Office: U Mich Dept Stats Ann Arbor MI 48109-1027 Home: 1645 Polipoli Rd Kula HI 96790-7524 E-mail: bhill@prodigy.net.

HILL, BRYCE DALE, school administrator; b. Seminole, Okla., Mar. 5, 1930; s. Charles Daniel and Ollie (Nichols) Hill; m. Wilma Dean Carter, Aug. 16, 1956; children: Bryce Anthony, Brent Dale. BS, East Ctrl. State Coll., 1952, M in Tchg., 1957; postgrad., U. Okla., 1959—70; profl. adminstrs. cert., 1969. Tchr. pub. schs., New Lima, Okla., 1952—56; supt. pub. schs., 1956—95; owner New Lima Gas Co., 1958—82. Mem. Seminole County Bd. Health, 1985—95, v.p., 1986—88, chmn., 1988—95; edn. leader com. Okla. Farmers Union, 1990—93; exec. com. Okla. Commn. for Ednl. Leadership, 1993—95; chmn. Seminole County Dem. Ctrl. Com., 1962—64, 1970—95; chmn. bd. dirs. Seminole County chpt. ARC, 1969—90; v.p. bd. dirs. Redland Cmty. Action Program, 1968—71; mem. Seminole County Rural Devel. Coun.; v.p. bd. dirs. Okla. Assn. Acad. Competition, 1991—95. Named to Seminole Jr. Coll. Hall of Fame, 1995. Mem.: NEA, Seminole County Sch. Adminstrs. Assn. (chmn. 1969—70, 1993—95), Seminole County Tchrs. Assn. (pres. 1964—65, 1971—72, 1979—80, 1990—91), Orgn. Rural Okla. Schs. (bd. dirs. 1986—92, pres. 1993—94, Pioneer award 1998), Okla. Assn. Sch. Adminstrs. (exec. com. 1976—78, 1979—81, bd. dirs. 1979—81, 1993—95, Dist. 8 Adminstr. of Yr. 1983, 1994, Lifetime Achievement award 1996), Am. Assn. Sch. Adminstrs., Okla. Edn. Assn. (Friend of Edn. award Zone 6 1996), Okla. Assn. Svc. Impact Schs. (bd. dirs. 1987—95), Seminole Hist. Soc. (v.p. 1971—73, 1974—76), Okla. Ret. Educators Assn., Seminole County Ret. Tchrs. Assn. (pres. 1996—), Legislation Steering Com., Seminole County Schoolmasters Club (pres. 1963—64, 1969—70, 1977—78). Baptist. Home: 32 Sequoyah Blvd Shawnee OK 74801-5570 Personal E-mail: bryce.wilma@charter.net.

HILL, CAROL CARD, special education educator, coordinator; b. Corpus Christi, Tex., June 28, 1949; d. Annon Melton and Frances (Holt) Card; m. James J. Hill, Aug. 29, 1978; children: George, Annie M. BA, Coll. of New Rochelle, 1976; MS in Spl. Edn., L.I. U., 1979. Cert. K-12 spl. edn., 9-12 English, N.Y., Va.; cert. K-12 spl. edn., Ga. Tchr. Pelham (N.Y.) Day Care Ctr., 1973-76; vol. coord. N.Y. State Office for Aging, R.S.V.P., Smithtown, N.Y., 1976-80; tchr., coord. spl. edn. svcs. M.D. Collins High Sch., Fulton County Pub. Schs., Atlanta, 1981-83; tchr., coord. spl. edn. svcs. South Lakes High Sch., Fairfax County Pub. Schs., Reston, Va., 1983—. Co-chair R.B.C.-S.L.H.S. sch. bus. partnership; peer observer F.C.P.S. tchr. performance evaluation program. Recipient Disting. Tchr. award Fairfax County Pub. Schs., 1991. Office: South Lakes High Sch 11400 S Lakes Dr Reston VA 20191-4199

HILL, CELIA ANN, retired education educator; b. Alpine, Tex., May 25, 1928; d. Harris Seymour and Winnie (Donald) Smith; m. Robert H. Hill, mar. 19, 1951 (div. 1969); children: Charles H. Sims, Robert N. Sims, Robbie A. Burns, Roxie L. Klinksiek, Billie M. Smith, Bettie W. Brazil, James R. Hill; m. John E. Littlejohn, May 23, 1992. BS in Bus., Sul Ross State U., 1951, MEd, 1964, postgrad., 1992. Tchr. Real County Ind. Sch. Dist., Leakey, Tex., 1951-53; sec. Tex. A&I U., Kingsville, 1954-56, asst. auditor, 1957-59; tchr. Catoosa County Ind. Sch. Dist., Ringgold, Ga., 1956-57, Banquete (Tex.) Ind. Sch. Dist., 1959-60, Buena Vista Ind. Sch. Dist., Imperial, Tex., 1960-61, Catron County Ind. Sch. Dist., Glenwood, N.Mex., 1961-63, Chaves County Ind. Sch. Dist., Roswell, N.Mex., 1963-68, Eastern N.Mex. U., Roswell, 1968-71, Roswell Ind. Sch. Dist., 1971-80, Barstow-Pecos-Toyah, Pecos, Tex., 1980-82, Terlingua (Tex.) Common Sch. Dist., 1983-87, Gadsden Ind. Sch. Dist., Anthony, N.Mex., 1987-88, Presidio (Tex.) Ind. Sch. Dist., 1989-98. Mem. TSTA (sec., treas., v.p.), Presidio Valley Women's Club (sec., treas., v.p.), Am. Legion (aux.), Kappa Delta Pi. Avocations: horseback riding, hunting arrowheads, reading, crafts. Home: HC 63 Box 2 Marfa TX 79843-9600

HILL, CHRISTINE LUCILLE, gifted and talented education educator; b. Washington, Aug. 19, 1964; d. John Henry Jr. and Carol Pearl (Halverson) Schuster; m. David Wayne Hill, June 16, 1990. AA, Iowa Lakes C.C., 1984; BS, Iowa State U., 1987; MS, U. Conn., 1996; PhD, Coll. William and Mary, 2002. 3d grade tchr. Island Paradise Sch., Honolulu, 1988-89; instr. Halawa Correctional facility, Aiea, Hawaii, 1989; 4th grade tchr. Amboy Elem. Sch., North Little Rock, Ark., 1990-92; tchr. gifted and talented Lawton (Okla.) Pub. Schs., 1990-92, facilitator gifted and talented, 1994; computer lab instr. DeRidder (La.) Jr. H.S., 1994-95; tchr. of gifted and talented East Beauregard H.S., DeRidder, La., 1995-96; grad. asst. Ctr. Gifted Edn. Coll. William and Mary, Williamsburg, Va., 1997—, Ctr. for Gifted, 1997-99; exec. intern Hampton (Va.) City Schs., 2000; cons. Skylight Profl. Devel., 1999—; asst. prof. U. La., Lafayette, 2002—. Presenter in field. Contbr. articles to profl. jours. Mem. Officer's Wives Club, 1990—, mem. scholar com., 1994; Jr. Svc. League, Lawton, 1994—. Recipient Margaret Thatcher award, 2002, 2001 sch. Edn. Excellence award, Doctoral Student award NAGC, 2000; Quality Sci. and Math. Programs La. State U. grantee, 1996; La. Assn. Educators scholar, 1995, Harry A. Passow NAGC scholar, 1996. Mem. AAUW, ASCD, NEA, NSTA, Nat. Assn. Gifted Children, Grad. Edn. Assn., Delta Kappa Gamma, Beta Sigma Phi, Pi Delta Kappa, Pi Lamba Theta, Kappa Delta Pi. Republican. Lutheran. Avocations: scuba diving, quilting, weight training, antiquing, reading. Home: 902 Charleston Pl Deridder LA 70634-2925 E-mail: chrystieh@aol.com.

HILL, EDWARD WILLIAM, economics educator, urban and regional planner; b. Derby, Conn., Jan. 4, 1952; s. John B. and Marie Louise (Wierdo) H.; mm. Karen Louise Upton, June 7, 1975; 1 child, Emma Rose. BA, U. Pa., 1973; M City Planning, MIT, 1976, PhD, 1981. Lectr. Boston U., 1978-79; v.p. Country Stores Inc., Seymour, Conn., 1980-84; asst. prof. urban studies and pub. adminstrn. Cleve. State U., 1985-90, assoc. prof., 1990-93, prof., 1993-2001, disting. prof. econ. devel., 2001—. Prin. Otter Rock Econs., 1980—; cons. to Hungarian and Russian municipalities USIA, 1991-95; non-resident sr. fellow Brookings Instn., Washington, 2000; bd. dirs. Wire-net; adv. bd. Ctr. for Regional Innovation, Coun. on Competitiveness, 2003—; adv. bd. urban divsn., local econ. devel. group World Bank, 2003—. Author: Ohio's Competitive Advantage, 2001; co-author: Banking on the Brink, 1992; co-editor: Financing Economic Development, 1990, Metropolis in Black and White, 1992, Global Perspectives on Economic Development, 1997, Financing Economic Development in the 21st Century, 2003; assoc. editor Econ. Devel. Quar., 1989-94, editor, 1994—. Chmn. Oxford (Conn.) Planning Commn., 1983-85; exec. bd. Cuyahoga County Planning Commn., Cleve., 1987-89; active Leadership Cleve., 1997, Gov.'s Urban Revitalization Task Force, 1999; trustee Cleve. (Ohio) Zoological Soc., 2000—. Recipient Comprehensive Planning award Mo. chpt. Am. Planning Assn., 1986, Robertson prize Urban Studies editors, 1994; Catherine Bauer Wurster fellow Joint Ctr. for Urban Studies, MIT, 1979-81. Mem.: Urban Affairs Assn. (bd. dirs. 1999—, treas. 2003—), Cleve. (Ohio) Zool. Soc. (trustee 2002—). Office: Coll Urban Affairs Cleve State U Cleveland OH 44115

HILL, EMITA BRADY, academic administrator, consultant; b. Balt., Jan. 31, 1936; d. Leo and Lucy McCormick (Jewett) Brady; children: Julie Beck, Christopher, Madeleine Vedel. BA, Cornell U., 1957; MA, Middlebury Coll., 1958; PhD, Harvard U., 1967. Instr. Harvard U., 1961-63; asst. prof. Western Reserve U., 1967-69; from asst. prof. to v.p. Lehman Coll. CUNY, Bronx, N.Y., 1970-91; chancellor, grad. faculty Ind. U., Kokomo, Ind., 1991-99, chancellor emerita, 1999—. Vis. advisor Salzburg Seminar Univs. Project; cons. in field. Trustee Am. U. in Kyrgyzstan; mem. Women's Forum of NY. Mem.: Internat. Assn. Univ. Pres., Phi Beta Kappa. Avocations: music, scuba diving, tennis. E-mail: ehill@indiana.edu.

HILL, EMMA LEE, education educator; b. Crane, Tex., Jan. 13, 1949; d. Howard Lee and Eddie Marie (Gill) H. BS, Hardin-Simmons. U., 1970; MEd, Abilene Christian U., 1974, postgrad., 1979. Cert. provisional elem. mentally retarded, lang./learning disabilities, bilingual tchr., profl. supr., profl. midmgmt., tchr. appraiser, Tex. Tchr. Kileen (Tex.) Ind. Sch. Dist., Harker Heights, 1970-71, Winters (Tex.) Ind. Sch. Dist., 1971-73, Abilene (Tex.) Ind. Sch. Dist., 1973—. Bldg. rep. Supt.'s Task Force on Schs. 5-Yr. Plan, Abilene, 1990-91; tchr. leader/dir. Coll. Connections, McMurray U., 1991—; sch. rep. Cleannn/Proud program. Illustrator: (book) Richard the Great, 1967. Mem. local election com. Tex. Tchrs. for Gov., Abilene, 1988; sec. Abilene PTA, 1980-82, Tex. PTA, 1980-82. Scholar Abilene C. of C., 1967-69. Mem. Assn. for Supervision and Curriculum Devel., Internat. Reading Assn., Tex. Assn. Bilingual Educators (pres. Abilene 1988-89), Tex. Classroom Tchrs. Assn., Assn. Tex. Profl. Educators (bldg. rep. 1980—, Outstanding Tchr. award 1989), AAUW, Internat. Soc. Poets (life), Nat. Honor Soc., Delta Kappa Gamma (treas. Abilene 1990-91). Avocations: watching professional sports, playing basketball and baseball, running, walking, movie classics. Home: PO Box 266 Tye TX 79563-0266 Address: 801 G Ave E Apt 3 Alpine TX

HILL, ESTHER DIANNE, business education educator; b. Maysville, Ky., Apr. 14, 1943; d. Frank Hinson and Jean Pepper (Yelton) H. BS, Ea. Ky. State Coll., 1966. Cert. bus. edn., typing and English tchr., Ohio. Tchr. Milton-Union Schs., West Milton, Ohio, 1966-68, Forest Hills Sch. Dist., Cin., 1968-96; tchr. evenings Cin. Tech. Coll., 1977-80; software verifyer South Western Pub. Co., Cin., 1982-83, ret., 1996. Writer Dist. Curriculum, Cin., 1975-96; dist. mem. County Textbook Com., Cin., 1982-96. Mem. NEA, Ohio Edn. Assn., Nat. Bus. Edn. Assn., Ohio Bus. Tchrs. Assn., Forest Hills Tchrs. Assn., Eastern Ky. U. Alumni assn. Republican. Mem. Ch. of Christ. Avocations: embroidery, travel, counted cross stitching, golf, reading. Home: 40 Bonnie Ln Fort Thomas KY 41075-2532 E-mail: dhill@fuse.net.

HILL, GEORGE JAMES, physician, educator; b. Cedar Rapids, Iowa, Oct. 7, 1932; s. Gerald Leslie and Essie Mae (Thompson) H.; m. Helene Zimmermann, July 16, 1960; children: James Warren, David Hedgcock, Sarah, Helena Rundall. AB, Yale U., 1953; MD, Harvard U., 1957; MA, Rutgers U., 1999. Intern N.Y. Hosp., 1957-58; fellow and resident in surgery Peter Bent Brigham hosp. and Harvard Med. Sch., 1958-61, 63-66; clin. assoc. NIH, Bethesda, Md., 1961-63; instr. surgery U. Colo., 1966-67, asst. prof., 1967-72, asso. prof., 1972-73; prof. Washington U., 1973-76; prof., chmn. Marshall U., 1976-81; prof., dir. surg. oncology U. of Medicine and Dentistry of N.J.-N.J. Med. Sch., Newark, 1981-96; prof. emeritus U. of Medicine and Dentistry of N.J. - N.J. Med. Sch., Newark, 1997—; Am. Cancer Soc. prof. clin. oncology U. Medicine and Dentistry N.J.-N.J. Med. Sch., Newark, 1989-92; pres. faculty N.J. Med. Sch., Newark, 1991-92; clin. prof. surgery Uniformed Svcs. U. of the Health Scis., Bethesda, Md., 1989—, Mt. Sinai Sch. Medicine, N.Y.C., 1999—; interim pres. Sterling Coll., Craftsbury Common, Vt., 1996; rsch. coord. St. Barnabas Med. Ctr., Livingston, N.J., 1997-99. Adj. prof. history Kean U., Union, N.J., 2000-2001; hon. mem. med. sch. staff St. Barnabas Med. Ctr., 1999—, chmn. clin. cancer edn. com. Nat. Cancer Inst., 1978-80; vis. fellow in molecular biology Princton U., 1988. Author: Leprosy in Five Young Men, 1970, paperback edit., 1979, Outpatient Surgery, 1973, 3d edit., 1988, Clinical Oncology, 1977; contbr. 150 articles to med. jours. Nat. dir.-at-large Am. Cancer Soc., 1989—96, mem. nat. exec. com., 1990—91, hon. life mem., 1996—; pres. Tri-State Area coun. Boy Scouts Am., Huntington, W.Va., 1980—82, v.p. Essex coun., 1983—89, commr., 1998, commr. No. N.J. Coun., 1998—2000, v.p., 2000—, chmn. nat. health careers exploring com., 1987—92; pres. W.Va. divsn. Am. Cancer Soc., 1980—81, pres. N.J. divsn., 1987—89; mem. N.J. State Commn. on Cancer Rsch., 1983—84; trustee Frost Valley YMCA, 1986—, Sterling Coll., Craftsbury Common, Vt., 1990—2002, sec., 1993—96, 1999—2002, interim pres., 1996, emeritus trustee, 2003—; pres. Hill Family Trust, 1989—; vestry Ch. of the Holy Innocents, 1994—96, 2002—. Capt. M.C. USNR, active duty USN, 1990—91, ret., 1992. Named Jerseyan of Week, Newark-Star Ledger, 1987, 1993; recipient Civic Actions medal, Republic South Vietnam, 1972, Lederle Med. Faculty award, 1970, Silver Beaver award, Boy Scouts Am., 1981, Silver Antelope award, 1998, Am. Cancer Soc. Nat. Divisional award, St. George medal, 1992, Gorgas medal, Assn. Mil. Surgeons U.S., 1991, Outstanding Svc. medal, Uniformed Svcs. U. Health Scis., 1992, Meritorious Svc. medal, USN, 1993, Nat. William Spurgeon III award, Boy Scouts Am., 1994, N.J. Disting. Svc. medal, 2001, Damon Runyon fellowship, 1973—76. Mem.: SAR (pres. N.J. Soc. 2001—02, nat. trustee 2002—03), AAUP (pres. chpt. 1988—89), ACS (com. on cancer 1987—93), N.J. Med. Club (pres. 1999—2001), Med. Soc. N.J. (chmn. com. cancer control 1985—94, sec. 1995—96), Essex County Med. Soc. (pres. 1995—96), Med. History Soc. N.J. (v.p. 2000—02), Am. Assn. Cancer Rsch., Am. Assn. Cancer Edn. (pres. 1985—86, Edwards medal 1994), Ctrl. Surg. Assn., Soc. Surg. Oncology (exec. coun. 1985—88), Soc. Univ. Surgeons, Acad. Medicine N.J. (pres. 1992—93), Oncology Nursing Soc. (hon.), Soc. War of 1812, Order Founders and Patriots of Am. (dep. gov. N.J. state soc. 2003—), Soc. of Colonial Wars (sec. N.J. state soc. 2003—), Soc. Sons of the Revolution, Soc. of the Cincinnati, Soc. Mayflower Descs. (bd. dirs. NJ state soc. 2002—), Yale Club (Ctrl. N.J.) (trustee 1986—, pres. 1991—93), Army and Navy Club, Harvard Club (N.Y.C. and Boston), Univ. Club (Denver), Explorers Club, Alpha Omega Alpha, Sigma Xi (chpt. pres. 1986—87). Republican. Episcopalian. Address: 3 Silver Spring Rd West Orange NJ 07052-4317 also: PO Box 313 South Orange NJ 07079-0313 E-mail: ghill@drew.edu.

HILL, GERRY A. special education educator, consultant; b. Vallejo, Calif., Aug. 8, 1940; d. Earl Martin and Mildred (Bogart) H. AA, San Diego City Coll., 1963; BA, San Diego State Coll., 1965; MA, U.S. Internat. U., 1970; EdD, Pacific Western U., 1981. Sec. Am. Meth. Work Team, Great Britain, 1961; trust dept. sec. 1st Nat. Bank, San Diego, 1961-63; classroom tchr. South Bay Union Sch. Dist., Imperial Beach, Calif., 1965-95, spl. edn. tchr., 1975-95. Owner Serendipity Learning Ctr., San Diego, 1991—. Vol. Muscular Dystrophy Assn., San Diego, 1975—, Habitat for Humanity, Tijuana, Mex. and San Diego, 1990, San Diego Rescue Mission, 1994—, Rolando Meth. Ch., San Diego, 1994—. Mem. Nat. Tchr. Edn., Orton Soc., San Diego Reading Assn. Republican. Methodist. Avocations: reading, travel. Office: 6161 El Cajon Blvd Ste 290 San Diego CA 92115-3922

HILL, GRACE LUCILE GARRISON, education educator, consultant; b. Gastonia, N.C., Sept. 26, 1930; d. William Moffatt and Lillian Tallulah (Tatum) Garrison; m. Leo Howard Hill, July 24, 1954; children: Lillian Lucile, Leo Howard Jr., David Garrison. BA, Erskine Coll., 1952; MA, Furman U., 1966; PhD, U. S.C., 1980. Lic. sch. psychologist, S.C. Tchr. Bible, Clinton (S.C.) Pub. Schs., 1952-53; tchr. English Parker High Sch., Greenville, S.C., 1953-55; elem. tchr. Augusta Circle Sch., Greenville, 1955-57; tchr. homebound children Greenville County Sch. Dist., Greenville, 1961-64, psychologist, 1966-77; adj. prof. grad. studies in edn. Furman U., Greenville, 1977—, U. S.C., Columbia, 1982—; ednl. cons. Ednl. Diagnostic Svcs., Greenville, 1980—. Exec. dir. Camperdown Acad., Greenville, 1986-87; cons. learning disability program Erskine Coll., Due West, S.C., 1978—; Disting. lectr. Erskine Coll., 1999. Contbr. articles to profl. jours. Pres. Lake Forest PTA, Greenville, 1970-71; pres. of Women A.R. Presbyn. Ch., Greenville, 1973-75, adult Bible tchr., 1978—; sec. bd. trustees Erskine Coll., 1982-88; bd. dirs. Children's Bur. S.C., Columbia, 1981-87, YWCA, Greenville, 1984-88; bd. advisors for adoption S.C. Dept. Social Svcs., Columbia, 1987-92. Recipient Order of the Jessamine, Greenville News award, 1994-95, Sullivan award Erskine Coll., 2000. Mem. Am. Edn. Rsch. Assn. (southeastern rep. 1982-84, editor newspaper for SIG group 1982-83), Jean Piaget Soc., Assn. for Supervision and Curriculum Devel., Orton Dyslexia Soc. (pres. Carolinas br. 1984-88), Ea. Ednl. Rsch. Assn., S.C. Psychol. Assn., Order of the Jessamine, 21st Century Learning Initiative, Delta Kappa Gamma. Democrat. Avocations: travel, writing. Home and Office: 28 Montrose Dr Greenville SC 29607-3034

HILL, IDA JOHNSON, education consultant, technologist, administrator; b. Mecklenburg, Va. d. Mack H. and Hattie H. (Hardy) Johnsn; m. Russell Langston Hill (dec.). BS, Va. State U., 1957, MS, 1962; EdD, U. Va., 1981. Cert. reading specialist. Reading cons. Richmond (Va.) Schs., 1961-68; TV tchr., specialist Sta. WCVE/WNVT-TV, Richmond, 1968-78, v.p. programming, 1978-86; dir. reading clinic Va. State U., Ettrick; instr. Va. Commonwealth U., Richmond, Va. Union Univ., Richmond, Va. State U., Petersburg; dir. of tech. Henrico County, Richmond, 1987-88; dep. supt. Va. Dept. of Edn., Richmond, 1990-94, asst. supt. for tech., 1988-97. Editl. adv. bd. Acad. Therapy/Intervention, Austin, 1985—; contbr. articles to profl. jours. Pres., bd. chair Literacy Coun. of Metro. Richmond, 1987; adv. bd. Robert E. Lee Boy Scouts, Richmond, 1997, U. Va. Continuing Edn., Charlottesville; bd. chair Richmond Cmty. H.S., 1987; bd. dirs. Richmond New Cmty. Sch., 1997. Recipient Presdl. Citation Nat. Assn. of Equal Opportunity in Higher Edn., 1991, Outstanding Accomplishments in Edn. award Zeta Phi Beta, 1997; named Outstanding Educator YWCA, 1996, Honor award Ida J. Hill Tech. Ctr. Va. Dept. Edn., 1997. Mem. ASCD, Va. Soc. for Tech. in Edn. (award for excellence in performance, hon., bd. dirs. 1987-97), Satellite Edn. Resources Consortium, (bd. dirs. 1995-97), Altrusa Club (bd. dirs. 1995-97, Ida Hill scholarship for literacy 1993). Avocations: travel, community service, reading. Home: PO Box 906 Chesterfield VA 23832-0013

HILL, IMOGENE PENTON, school administrator; b. Texarkana, Tex., July 19, 1939; d. Almor Jr. and Lennis (Hodge) P.; m. Roy Lee Samuels, Aug. 15, 1959 (div. 1963); 1 child, Rhonda Evette; m. Billy Joe Hill, July 31, 1988. BS, So. Ill. U., 1962; MS, East Tex. State U., 1972, cert. in mid. mgmt., 1986. Cert. tchr., mgr., Tex. Tchr. Washington High Sch., Texarkana, Ark., 1962-64, Dunbar High Sch., Texarkana, Tex., 1964-69, Pine St. Jr. High Sch., Texarkana, Tex., 1969-88; prin. 15th St Elem. Sch., Texarkana, Tex., 1988—. Vol., mentor Hosts Lang. Arts, Texarkana, Tex., 1992; mem. Ptnrs. in Parenting, Texarkana, Tex., 1991. Bd. dirs. Hopewell Christian Edn., Texarkana, Tex., 1965-74; mem. community rels. bd. Fed. Correctional Instn., Texarkana, Tex., 1988—. Mem. ASCD, AAUW, NAACP, PTA, Nat. Alliance Black Sch. Educators, Nat. Assn. Elem. Sch. Prins. and Suprs., Tex. Elem. Prins. and Suprs. Assn., Kappa Delta Pi. Democrat. Methodist. Avocations: fishing, reading, camping, dancing. Home: 203 Redwater Rd Wake Village TX 75501-5725 Office: 15th St Elem Sch 2600 W 15th St Texarkana TX 75501-4266

HILL, JOANNE FRANCIS, retired elementary education educator; b. Holland, Mich., Jan. 12, 1937; BA in Elem. Edn., Western Mich. U., 1961; postgrad., Mich. State U., 1961-65, Oxford U., 1965. Cert. elem. tchr. Sec. Am. Bus. Woman, Holland, 1972-74; tchr. West Ottawa Pub. Sch., Holland, 1957-97; owner std. bred horses. Former leader Camp Fire Girls, Inc., Holland; mem. Holland Cmty. Theatre, 1972-89; Sunday sch. tchr. Ref. Ch., 1970-81, mem. choir, 1972—, elder, 1981-94. Mem. ASCD, Nat. Coun. Tchrs., Nat. Coun. Tchrs. English, Mich. Edn. Assn. (pres. 1993-94, past pres. 1994-95), Area Bargaining Coun. (sec. 1992-95), Sch. Employees Coun. (sec. 1992-93), West Ottawa Edn. Assn. (sec. 1984-85, v.p. 1985-86, pres. 1986-97). Republican. Home: 1008 Bluebell Dr Holland MI 49423-6861

HILL, JOANNE MILLER, special education educator, consultant; b. Atlanta, Ill., Apr. 28, 1941; d. Euless D. and Edith L. (Pech) Miller; divorced; children: Evan, Rachel, Scot Hill. BS in Edn., Ill. State U., 1967; MA in Spl. Edn., U. Colo., Colorado Springs, 1992, MA in Gifted Edn., 1995. Cert. tchr., Tex., Colo. Tchr. Sch. Dist. 187, Springfield, Ill., 1967-68, Sch. Dist. 50 Queen Charlotte Island, B.C., Can., 1968-69, Sch. Dist. 51, Grand Junction, Colo., 1972-73; cons., tutor for learning disabled and gifted, 1973-81; dir., owner Ctr. for Individualized Edn., Anchorage, 1981-82; computer paraprofl. Sch. Dist. 20, Colorado Springs, 1990-91; tchr. spl. edn. Sch. Dist. 11, Colorado Springs, 1991-92, Dist. JE-T-23, Peyton, Colo., 1992-93, Falcon (Colo.) Sch. Dist., 1993-94; coord. supplemental svcs. U. Colo., Colorado Springs, 1995—2000; dir. disability and learning svcs. Willamette U., Salem, Oreg., 2000—. Cons. for spl. needs students, Colorado Springs, 1991—; adj. prof. U. Phoenix, Colorado Springs. Author: The Policy Book: Guidance for Disability Service Providers, 2000. Vol. Probation Ptnrs., Anchorage, 1969-70. Grantee Internat. chpt. P.E.O., 1991, State of Colo., 1991-92. Mem.: Disability Consortium, Assn. Higher Edn. and Disabilities. Avocations: reading, music, outdoor activities, volunteer public social work. Home: 777 Cottage St NE Salem OR 97301 Office: Willamette Univ 900 State St Salem OR 97301

HILL, JOHN EDWARD, school system administrator; b. Huntington, Ind., July 5, 1948; s. Guy and Helen Louise (Whittenberger) H.; m. Rebecca Sue Gast, May 23, 1970; children: Kevin, Brian, Timmothy. BS, Manchester Coll., 1970; MS, Ind. U., 1974, EdS, 1979, EdD, 1985. Cert. sch. adminstr., supt., Ind. Math. tchr., coach Sch. Dist. Wayne Twp., Indpls., 1970-74, Rochester (Ind.) Comm. Schs., 1974-76, mid. sch. prin., 1976-81; rsch. assoc. N. Cen. Assn., Bloomington, Ind., 1981-82; high sch. prin. Sunman (Ind.) - Dearborn Schs., 1982-83, Tippecanoe Valley Schs., Mentone, Ind., 1983-88; asst. supt. Whitko Community Schs., Pierceton, Ind., 1988-90, supt., 1990—. Bd. dirs. N. Cen. Spl. Edn. Coop, Warsaw; exec. bd. N.E. Ind. Svc. Ctr., South Bend; adv. bd. Ivy Tech., Warsaw. Chmn. fin. com. South Whitley (Ind.) United Meth. Ch., 1991—. Mem. Assn. Curriculum and Devel., Ins. Assn. Pub. Sch. Supts, Am. Assn. Sch. Adminstrs., Phi Delta Kappa (pres. 1991—). Office: Whitko Community Schs PO Box 114 Pierceton IN 46562-0114 Home: 14540 Olive Ln Plymouth IN 46563-9700

HILL, JOHN WALLACE, special education educator; BA in Elem. Edn. cum laude, Am. U., 1970, MEd in Spl. Edn., 1971, PhD in Edn., 1974. Dir. Learning Disabilities Clinic Meyer Children's Rehab. Inst., U. Nebr. Med. Ctr., Omaha, 1974-87; prof. spl. edn. Coll. of Edn., U. Nebr., Omaha, 1974—, acting chair dept., Regents prof., 1989-95. Adj. prof. Coll. of Pharmacy, U. Nebr. Med. Ctr., 1986-98; lectr. various univs., assns. and confs.; former mem., bd. dirs. Omaha Head Start Program, Child and Family Devel. Corp. Contbr. articles to profl. jours. Recipient Outstanding Tchg. award, U. Nebr. Omaha Alumni, 2002. Fellow Am. Acad. for Cerebral Palsy and Devel. Medicine; mem. Phi Delta Kappa, Sigma Xi. Office: Univ Nebr at Omaha Dept Spl Edn Omaha NE 68182-0001

HILL, KATHLEEN BLICKENSTAFF, lawyer, mental health nurse, nursing educator; b. Greenville, Ohio, Oct. 24, 1950; d. Donald Edward and Mary Ann (Subler) Berger; children: Benjamin Arin, Amanda Marie,

Kathryn Megan; m. David M. Hill, Sr., Sept. 27, 2002. BS, Ohio State U., 1972, MS, 1973, sch. nurse cert., 1990; JD, Capital U. Law Sch., 1998. Cert. sch. nurse grades K-12. Cons. cmty. educator S.W. Cmty. Mental Health Ctr., Columbus, 1973-77; patient and cmty. educator Daniel E. Blickenstaff, DDS, Inc., Columbus, 1977-86; staff nurse Riverside Meth. Hosp., Columbus, 1986-90; clin. instr. Columbus (Ohio) State C.C., 1989; from asst. to assoc. prof. Capital U., Columbus, 1989-2000, prof., 2000—01, adj. prof., 2001—; assoc. Porter, Wright, Morris & Arthur LLP, Columbus, 2000—. Mem. cmty. svcs. com. Mid Ohio Dist. Nurses Assn., Columbus, 1990—2001, bd. dirs., 1991—94, mem. legis. com., 2002—. Leader Girl Scouts, Grandview Heights, Ohio, 1989-93; bd. dirs. H.S. PTO, Grandview Heights (Ohio) City Schs., 1990-93, treas. H.S. PTO, 1990-92, co-chair oper. levy, 1991. Mem.: ANA, ABA, Columbus Bar Assn. (health law com.), Ohio State Bar Assn. (health and disability law com.), Ohio Nurses Assn., Am. Health Lawyers Assn., Sigma Theta Tau. Avocations: quilting, sewing, gardening. Home: 1935 Marblecliff Crossing Ct Columbus OH 43204-4968 Office: Porter Wright Morris & Arthur LLP 41 S High St Ste 2900 Columbus OH 43215-6194 E-mail: kblicken@columbus.rr.com., khill@porterwright.com.

HILL, LANSING BRENT, mathematics educator; b. Bluefield, W. Va., Mar. 16, 1960; s. Hubert Elwood and Mary Jackie (Tabor) H. BS, BA, U. Tenn., 1983; MA, U. W.Va., 1988. Cert. math. tchr. Substitute tchr. Knoxville (Tenn.) City Schs., 1983; tchr. McDowell County Schs., Welch, W.Va., 1983—. Author: Guide for Algebra I, 1989, Guide for Algebra II, 1989. Treas. Big Creek High Sch. Faculty Senate, 1990-91, pres. 1991-93. Grantee W.Va. Edn. Fund, 1984. Mem. NEA, Nat. Coun. Tchrs. Math., W. Va. Edn. Assn., McDowell County Edn. Assn., McDowell County Coun. Math. (treas. 1988—, pres. elect 1990-92, pres. 1992—), Kiwanis Club War (pres. 1991-92). Avocations: reading, attending sports events, photography, music. Office: Big Creek High Sch PO Box 278 War WV 24892-0278

HILL, LINDA MARIE PALERMO, elementary school educator; b. Newark; d. Peter and Florence (Desiderio) McCue; children: Michael, Christopher, Douglas. BA, Caldwell (N.J.) Coll., 1970; MA, Seton Hall U., 1973; postgrad., Salem (Mass.) State Coll., 1986. Cert. elem. tchr., reading specialist, project adventure instr. Tchr. Roxbury Bd. Edn., Succasunna, N.J., 1970-74; libr.-media specialist, tchr. Hopatcong (N.J.) Bd. Edn., 1983—. Founder, dir. Young Astronaut Coun. Hopatcong Borough Schs. Mem. NEA, N.J. Edn. Assn., Hopatcong Edn. Assn. Home: 14 Oklahoma Trail PO Box 905 Hopatcong NJ 07843-0905 Office: Durban Ave Sch Durban Ave Hopatcong NJ 07843-1504

HILL, MARTHA NELL, education educator; b. Clarksdale, Miss., Sept. 11, 1946; d. Edgar Hall and Virgia (Hill) McNeal. BS, LeMoyne Coll., Memphis, 1968; MEd, Trevecca Nazarene Coll., Nashville, 1987, postgrad., 1988-89. Cert. tchr. and adminstr., Tenn. Tchr., social studies dept. chmn. Memphis Bd. Edn., 1968-92; payroll clk. C.H. Hill & Son, Memphis, 1968-91; instr. LeMoyne-Owen Coll., Memphis, 1991-92. Tchr., sponsor The Close Up Found., Washington, 1981-86; mem. Prin.'s Adv. Com., Memphis, 1988-90; sponsor Whitehaven's Black History Program, Memphis, 1985-90; mem. Study Coun. for Better Schs. Program, Gov. Lamar Alexander Tenn.; mem. textbook adoption com. Memphis City Sch. System. Sponsor essay contests Whitehaven High Sch., VFW, sr. class advisor Whitehaven High Sch., 1984-90; mem. Memphis Regional Sickle Cell Coun., 1979, Facing History, 1987-89; writer curriculum on the bill of rights Memphis City Schs., 1990; mem. Career Ladder Program. Stratford scholar, 1984. Mem. NAACP, NAFE, NEA, ASCD (Leadership award 1985-90), Greenpeace, Nat. Coun. Social Studies (Tchr. of the Yr. 1984), West Tenn. Edn. Assn., Memphis Edn. Assn., Soc. of Preservation of Constn., Smithsonian Inst., Inner Circle, Black Issues in Higher Edn., Pi Lambda Theta, Pi Beta. Democrat. Baptist. Avocations: traveling, reading, cooking, poetry, music. Home: General Delivery Memphis TN 38101-9999

HILL, NANCY ELIZABETH WILSON, special education educator, journalist; b. Covington, Va., Sept. 18, 1952; d. Samuel George and Glady Oressa (Stump) Wilson; m. Charles William (Bill) Hill, June 1, 1974; children: Susan Beth, Mary Katheryn, Charles William II. AS in Secondary Edn., Potomac State Coll., 1972; BS in Journalism Edn., W.Va. U., 1974, MA in Spl. Edn., 1992; MA in Journalism, Marshall U., 1977. Lic. tchr. English/journalism, spl. edn. behavior disorders, learning disabilities, developmental and remedial reading authorization, WVU. Intern Grant County Press, Petersburg, W.Va., summer 1975; grad. asst. dept. journalism Marshall U., Huntington, W.Va., summer 1977; homebound/substitute tchr. Putnam County Schs., Winfield, W.Va., 1975-77; news editor Moorefield (W.Va.) Examiner, 1978-83; regional/local news reporter WELD-Radio Sta., Fisher, W.Va., 1978-83; substitute tchr. Grant County Bd. Edn., Petersburg, 1977-78, 83-84, Hardy County Bd. Edn., Moorefield, 1983-84, 88-89, Chapt. I reading tchr., summer 1989, reading tchr. Gov.'s Summer Youth Enhancement Program, 1990-94, spl. edn. tchr., 1989—. Mem. organizing com. ESEA Title IV Part G, Project Sch. Comm. Oriented to Occupational Preparedness, Putnam County Bd. Edn., Winfield, W.Va., 1976; participant rural behavior disorders project spl. edn. dept. W.Va. U., Morgantown, 1989-90, reflective teaching practicum project, 1990, Free the Horses: A Self-Esteem Adventure Leader Cert. workshop, Washington, 1991; respondent Potomac State Coll. Law Day, Keyser, W.Va., 1980. Co-author: Alt and Kimble Family History, 1997. Activity leader Kessel White Eagles 4-H Club, Fisher, W.Va., 1986-93, Onward Upward 4-H Club, Moorefield, W.Va., 1993—; mem. Hardy County 4-H All Stars, Moorefield, 1991—. Recipient Excellence in Photography News award W.Va. Press Assn., 2d pl. award, 1981, Interview and Page Makeup: Newspaper under 5,000 Circulation award W.Va. Press Women, 1st pl. award, 1982, photography award for newspaper other than a daily W.Va. Press Women's Comm. Contest, 1st pl. award, 1982; grantee W.Va. Dept. Edn., 1990, W.Va. Edn. Fund. Mem. AAUW, NEA, W.Va. Edn. Assn., Hardy County Edn. Assn., Hardy County 4-H Leader (5 yr. pin 1990), Moorefield Woman's Club of W.Va. Fedn. Women's Clubs (sec. 1989-93, 2d v.p. 1993-94, Club Woman of Yr., 2002), Phi Delta Kappa. Democrat. Mem. Ch. of Christ. Avocations: community theater, genealogy, camping, sign language, literacy. Home: 310 S Main St Moorefield WV 26836-1283 Office: Hardy County Bd Edn 510 Ashby St Moorefield WV 26836

HILL, PAMELA JEAN, middle school educator; b. Oxford Junction, Iowa, Jan. 6, 1964; d. Ronald Eugene and Marlene Joyce (Bright) Hansen; m. Bradley John Hill, July 25, 1987; children: Wade Alan, Ryan Thomas. BA, Luther Coll., 1986. Tchr. 5th and 6th grades Monroe (Iowa) Elem. Sch., 1986-87; tchr. 6th grade PCM Mid. Sch., Prairie City, Iowa, 1987—. Head dept. math., PCM Cmty. Schs., 1992-96, mem. instrnl. coun., 1992-96. Mem. NEA, Iowa Edn. Assn., Prairie City/Monroe Edn. Assn., PEO (chpt. BH), Delta Kappa Gamma. Democrat. Lutheran. Avocations: golf, cooking, walking, reading. Office: PCM Mid Sch PO Box 490 Prairie City IA 50228-0490

HILL, PATRICIA JO, workforce development specialist; b. Muncie, Ind., Oct. 28, 1944; d. Frederic Burnside and Elizabeth Becom (Zaring) Harbottle; widowed; 1 son, Thomas Frederic. BS, Ball State U., 1964, MA, 1978, EdS, 1981. Cert. EMT, nat. pharmacy technician. Instr., head immunology dept. Ball Meml. Hosp., Muncie, 1963-74; tchr. emotionally disturbed Indpls. Pub. Schs., 1974-75, lead tchr. severe/profound mentally retarded, 1979-84, media specialist in spl. edn., 1984-86, tchr. moderately mentally handicapped, 1986-87, tchr. mildly mentally handicapped, 1987-93, cross categorical spl. edn. tchr., 1993-2000; ret.; pharmacy technician Walgreens, Indpls., 2000—01; pvt. contractor Social Security Adminstrn. Ticket-to-Work Program. Seminar presenter Ind. State Prevent Child Abuse Conf., 1998; participant Leadership Series between C. of C. and Indpls. Pub. Schs., Area 15 Spl. Olympics Coach. Black history liaison Ind. Chpt. Prevention Child Abuse; chair Indy PAC, instnl. and profl. devel. com.; vol. first aid team, disaster team ARC; vol. Protect the Promise Coalition; med. vol. Sr. Action Coalition, 2001—; del. Ind. State Rep. Convention, Rep. Leadership conf. for Midwestern States, 1997; staff to elect 10th Dist. Rep. Congresswoman Virginia Blankenbaker, 1998; media rels. Indpls. Americans United for Separation of Ch. and State, 2001—; public rels. Angel Flight, Ctrl. Ind. Wing, Angel Flight Am., 2001—. NSF grant, 1961; Shroyer scholar Mchts. Nat. Bank Muncie, 1972, Indpls. Pub. Schs. scholar, 1981. Mem. Assn. Behavioral Analysts, Coun. Exceptional Children (med. and health problems), Ind. State Tchrs. Assn. (ret. bd. rep., spl. edn. com.), Indpls. Edn. Assn. (exec. bd., sec. 1997-2000), Greater Indpls. Rep. Women,, Indpls. C. of C., Ind. C. of C. (workforce develop com., K-12 com.), Ind. BBB, Internat. Assn. Rehab. Profls. Methodist. Home: 7330 Scarborough Blvd East Dr Indianapolis IN 46256-2053 E-mail: patricia.j.hill@att.net.

HILL, PEGGY SUE, principal; b. Roswell, N.Mex., Aug. 4, 1953; d. Cecil Vecoe and Edith Augustine (Raney) H. BS, U. Ark., 1978, MEd, 1982; EdS, 1994. Cert. elem. prin., tchr. music and libr. Music tchr., K-6 Springdale (Ark.) Schs., 1978-83, elem. prin., 1983-98, tech. coord., 1998—, coord. for curriculum, instrn., assessment and tech. Named Outstanding Young Educator Springdale Jaycees, 1983, Prin. of Ark. Exemplary Sch., Ark. Dept. Edn., 1989-90, 91-92, 93-94; recipient nat. award for teaching of econs. Joint Coun. Econ. Edn., 1990, 91, 92, 94. Mem. ASCD, Internat. Reading Assn., Ark. Assn. Edn. Adminstrs., Ark. Assn. Elem. Sch. Prins., (presenter conf. 1990), Phi Delta kappa (Outstanding Adminstr. award 1991). Office: Springdale Schs PO Box 8 Springdale AR 72765-0008

HILL, REBECCA SUE HELM, secondary education educator; b. Winchester, Ind., Sept. 8, 1955; d. Edward Arthur and Jacqueline Sue (Cassel) Helm; m. Paul Mark Hill, Dec. 29, 1977; children: Aaron Israel, Revkah Lauren, Hadassah Sue. BS, Asbury Coll., 1973; MEd, Purdue U., 1993. Cert. tchr., Ind. Tchr. N.W. Christian Acad., St. Louis, 1977-78, Monroe Ctrl. HS, Parker, Ind., 1979-80, Dayspring Acad., Parker, 1983-85; tchr. literacy and lang. McCutcheon HS, Lafayette, Ind., 1997-98, East Tipp Mid. Sch., Lafayette, Ind., 1998—; instr. Greenwood Cmty. Sch. Fine Arts, Indpls., 1990-93, Purdue U., West Lafayette, Ind., 1991-99; instr. literacy and lang. Ind. Vocat. Coll., Lafayette, 1994-97; tchr. E. Tipp Mid. Sch., Lafayette, 1998—. Bd. tchr. edn. coun. Sch. Edn. Purdue U., 1994-97; edn. supt. Stockwell (Ind.) United Meth. Ch., 1997—; adj. faculty Vincennes U., fall 2002; presenter in field. Contbr. articles to profl. publs. Performer Arts Ind. Mag., 1994, 95, 96; tchr. vol. New Cmty. Sch., Lafayette, 1995-96; mentor Curriculum and Instrn. Grad. Student Orgn., Purdue U., 1993-95. Andrews fellow, 1994-96; recipient Disting. Hoosier award Gov. of Ind., 1995. Mem. Alpha Upsilon Alpha (pres. 1994-96), Kappa Delta Pi. Avocations: family, music, outdoor activities, reading, gardening. Home: 6931 Church St PO Box 176 Stockwell IN 47983-0176 Office: E Tipp Mid Sch 7501 E 300 N Lafayette IN 47905

HILL, RONALD CHARLES, surgeon, educator; b. Parkersburg, W.Va., Sept. 4, 1948; s. Lloyd E. and Margaret (Pepper) H.; m. Lenora Jane Rexrode, June 12, 1971; children: Jeffrey, Mandy. BA, W.Va. U., 1970, MD, 1974. Diplomate Diplomate Am. Bd. Surgery, Am. Bd. Thoracic Surgery. Intern dept. of surgery Duke U. Med. Ctr., Durham, N.C., 1974-75; resident in surgery Duke U., Durham, N.C., 1974-85, rsch. assoc., 1976-79, tchg. scholar, 1984-85; asst. prof. surgery W.Va. U., Morgantown, 1985-90, assoc. prof., 1990-96, prof. surgery, 1996—, clin. prof. surgery Sch. Osteopathic Medicine, 1999—. Cons. VA Med. Ctr., Clarksburg, W.Va., 1985—; dir. surg. rsch. dept. surgery W.Va. U., 1986—88, student coord. dept. surgery, 1986—97; mem. adh hoc com. merit rev. bd. for cardiovasc. studies VA, Washington, 1988—90; mem. Surg. Edn. and Self-Assessment Program '99 Com., Surg. Edn. and Self-Assessment Program #11, Surg. Edn. and Self-Assessment Program #12; chmn. instnl. rev. bd. Protection Human Subjects, 1994—, program chmn. dept. surgery, 1998—2003. Contbr., co-contbr. numerous book chpts. and articles to profl. pubs. Mem.-at-large adminstrv. bd. Drummond Chapel United Meth. Ch., Morgantown, 1987—89, 1993—95, fin. com., 1994—96, lay del. to ann. conf., 1995—97, chmn. coun. on evangelism, 1999—2001. Recipient Lange Med. Book award, 1971, 1973, 1974, Roche Med. award, 1972, Merck Med. Book award, 1974, Sowers award, Founders Soc. Duke U., 1992. Fellow ACS (coun. W.Va. chpt. 1999-2001, sec.-treas. 2001-02, 2d v.p. 2002-03, 1st v.p. 2003—, chmn. com. on applicants dist. 1 W.Va.), Southeastern Surg. Congress, Assn. Acad. Surgery, Sabiston Soc., Am. Coll. Cardiology, Am. Coll. Chest Physicians, So. Thoracic Surg. Assn. (program chmn. 1995-96, coun. 1999-2000), Soc. Thoracic Surgeons; mem. Am. Heart Assn., (v.p., pres. elect, pres. W. Va. affiliate 1994-96), Soc. Univ. Surgeons, Am. Assn. Thoracic Surgery, Internat. Surg. Soc., Assn. Programs Dirs. in Surgery, Assn. Surg. Edn., So. Surg. Assn., W.Va. Med. Assn., Mended Hearts, Lakeview Country Club, Pines Country Club, Phi Beta Kappa, Alpha Omega Alpha, Alpha Epsilon Delta, Profl. Assn. Diving Instrs. Soc. (cert. master scuba diver). Republican. Avocations: fishing, photography, scuba diving, shell collecting. Home: 10 Flegal St Morgantown WV 26505-2240 Office: WVa U Med Ctr Dept of Surgery Medical Center Dr Morgantown WV 26506 E-mail: rhill@hsc.wvu.edu.

HILL, RUTH FOELL, language consultant; b. Houston, Sept. 13, 1931; d. Ernest William and Florence Margaret (Kane) Foell; children: Linden Ruth, Andrea Grace. Student, Principia Coll., 1950; BA, U. Calif., Berkeley, 1952; postgrad., San Diego State, 1955, Cen. Piedmont, 1981. Cert. tchr., Calif. Owner, dir. Art Gallery of Chapel Hill (N.C.), 1966-75; ecumenical bd. Campus Ministry, Charlotte; with referral svc. Charlotte (N.C.) Bed and Breakfast Registry, 1980-90; lang. cons. Berlitz Internat., Raleigh, N.C., 1988-91; ESL tchr. Albemarle Elem. Sch., 2000—. Cert. cons. Performax Internat.; rep. UN Decade for Women Conf., NGO Forum, Nairobi, Kenya, 1985, Women and Global Security Conf., 1986; rep. emerging issues forum N.C. State U., 1987-93; presenter Southeastern Women's Studies Conf. Author: (poetry) Noble House, 2003; contbr. poetry to Nat. Libr. of Poetry Internat. Hall of Fame. Bd. dirs., chmn. natural resources com. LWV; coord. USIA grant region 6, Internat. Exch. Network; mem. N.C. Leadership Forum, N.C. Citizens Assembly, 1989; chmn. Week of Edn. Pub. Forum on Energy, Union Concerned Scientists, 1990-93; bd. dirs. Nat. Women's Conf. Commn., 1994—; mem. edn. subcom. Mayor's Internat. Cabinet, 1995; mem. Congress House Spkr.'s Citizen Task Force, 1995—; mem. Rep. Platform Com. and Nat. Presdl. Task Force, 1999, Rep. Inner Cir., 1995; mem. edn. com. Charlotte/Mecklenburg Historic Properties, 1986-88; mem. groundwater subcom. Mecklenburg County Commrs., 1987. Named Outstanding Women's Athletic Assn., Woman of the Yr., Am. Biog. Inst., 1994, Internat. Poetry Hall of Fame, 1998; Hewlett Found. scholar. Mem. AAUW (v.p. membership com., bd. dirs.), Ams. for Legal Reform (adv. bd.), Am. Farm Land Trust, UN Assn. U.S.A. (chpt. pres. 1991-93, co-chair UN Day Queens Coll. 1992, N.C. divsn. sec. 1993-94, UN50 chair 1995, So. Summit Queens Coll. 2002), Am. Biog. Inst. Rsch. Assn. (nominated to bd. govs.), Am. Biog. Inst. (apptd. adv. bd.), Carolina Coun. on World Affairs, Chapel Hill-Carrboro Sch. Art Guild (pres.), Midwest Acad., World Wide Women in Environment, N.Y. Acad. Sci. Republican. Christian Scientist. Avocations: travel, environmental issues, international exchange networking. Office: PO Box 220802 Charlotte NC 28222-0802 E-mail: rhill37901@aol.com.

HILL, SANDRA KAY, secondary educator, librarian; b. Parma, Ohio, Dec. 15, 1968; d. Robert John and Joan Carol (Doering) H.; m. Brent James Broderick, Nov. 13, 1993. BS in K-12 Ednl. Media, Ohio U., 1991. Cert. tchr., Ohio. Resident asst., counselor Ohio U., Athens, 1987-89; tchr., libr., track coach, faculty mgr. Kings Jr. High Sch., Kings Mills, Ohio, 1991—. Mem. ALA, NEA, Ohio Ednl. Libr. Media Assn., Ohio Edn. Assn., Kings Edn. Assn. Democrat. Avocations: reading, fishing, dancing, roller blading, hunting. Office: Kings Jr High Sch 5620 Columbia Rd Kings Mills OH 45034

HILL, STEVEN JOHN, author, educator, political reformer, campaign manager; b. New London, Conn., June 6, 1958; s. William John and Patricia (Rogers) H. BA in Geology and Geophysics, Yale U., 1982. Freelance journalist, San Francisco, 1991—; program dir. Labor Net @ IGC, San Francisco, 1995-96; regional dir. Ctr. for Voting and Democracy, San Francisco, 1993—. Author: Fixing Elections: The Failure of America's Winner Take All Politics, 2002, co-author: Reflecting All of Us, 1999; contbr. articles to newspapers, profl. publs., and mags., including Wall St. Jour., Washington Post, Ms., Seattle Times, Am. Prospect, NY Daily News, Christian Sci. Monitor, L.A. Times, Miami Herald, San Francisco Chronicle, The Nation, others, also poetry and short fiction to small publs. Mem. steering com. LaborNet @ IGC. Avocations: hiking, bicycling, oil painting, music composition, writing novels.

HILL, VICTOR ERNST, IV, mathematics educator, musician; b. Pitts., Nov. 3, 1939; s. Victor Ernst III and Lois Kathryn (Rahenkamp) H.; m. Christi Deanne Adams, Aug. 12, 1967 (div. 1981); children: Victoria Christina Hill Resnick, Christopher Andrew Michael. BS, Carnegie-Mellon U., 1961; MA, U. Wis.-Madison, 1962; PhD, performer's cert. in harpsichord, U. Oreg., 1966. Asst. prof. math. Williams Coll., Williamstown, Mass., 1966-72, assoc. prof, 1972-78, prof., 1978-89, Thomas T. Read prof. math. Vis. prof. math. Ga. Inst. Tech., 1987-88, 91-92, artist-in-residence, 1987-88; vis. prof. music U. Oreg., 1967; concert organist, harpsichordist, 1964—; editor Tudor Choral Works Broude Bros. Author: Groups, Representations, and Characters, 1975, Groups and Characters, 2000; composer organ and choral works. Reader Rec. for Blind and Dyslexic, Inc., Williamstown, 1971—, bd. trustees Berkshire unit, 1996-99; organist-choirmaster St. John's Episcopal Ch., Williamstown, 1972-96. Mem. Math. Assn. Am., Assn. Anglican Musicians (archivist 1982—, editl. bd. 1996—, bd. review 1998—), Am. Guild Organists (dean Berkshire chpt. 1982-84, exec. bd. 1995-98), Assn. Christians in Math. Scis., Soc. of St. Margaret (assoc.). Home: PO Box 11 Williamstown MA 01267-0011 Office: Williams Coll Dept Math Williamstown MA 01267

HILL, VIRGIL LUSK, JR., academic administrator, naval officer; b. Shelby, N.C., Apr. 2, 1938; s. Virgil Lusk and Ellen (Dilling) H.; m. Mary Kimberly Jordan, Jan. 11, 1964; children: James S., Katherine E. BS in Naval Sci., U.S. Naval Acad., 1961. Commd. ensign USN, 1961, advanced through grades to rear adm. (upper half), 1989; served on USS Thomas Jefferson, Groton, Conn., 1968-70; material officer COMSUBRON 18, Charleston, S.C., 1970-73; exec. officer USS L. Mendel Rivers, Charleston, 1973-75; comdg. officer USS Hammerhead, Norfolk, Va., 1976-80; dir. spl. projects Office Chief Naval Ops., Washington, 1980-83; comdr. Submarine Devel. Squadron 12, Groton, 1983-85; dir. attack submarine divsn. Office of Chief Naval Ops., Washington, 1985-87; comdr. Submarine Group 5, San Diego, 1987-88; supt. U.S. Naval Acad., Annapolis, Md., 1988-91; comdr. operational test and evaluation forces USN, Norfolk, 1991-93; pres. Valley Forge (Pa.) Mil. Acad. and Coll., 1993-2000; sr. fellow Villanova U., 2002—. Bd. dirs. Greater Main Line br. ARC, Southeastern Pa. chpt. Decorated Distinguished Svc. medal with gold star, Legion of Merit with 3 gold stars, Meritorious Service medal with 3 gold stars, Navy Commendation medal with 1 gold star; recipient Admiral David Glasgow Farragut award Naval Order of U.S. 1996, Robert Morris award Boy Scouts Am., 1996, Order of Magna Charta, 1996. Mem. Assn. Mil. Colls. and Schs. of the U.S. (former pres.), United Svcs. Orgn. of Phila. (bd. dirs.), Assn. Ind. Colls. and Univs. Pa. (bd. dirs.), Nat. Assn. Ind. Colls. and Univs. (pub. rels. commn.), Pa. Assn. Colls. and Univs., Pa. Assn. Ind. Schs., Nat. Assn. Ind. Schs., U.S. Naval Inst., Naval Order of the U.S., Mil. Order of Fgn. Wars, U.S. Navy League, Naval Submarine League, World Affairs Coun. of Phila., Sunday Breakfast Club of Phila., Penn Club of Phila., Union League of Phila. (bd. dirs.), St. David's Golf Club (Wayne, Pa.), others. E-mail: virgilhill@aol.com.

HILL, WILLIAM VICTOR, II, retired army officer, secondary school educator; b. Carlisle, Pa., Dec. 14, 1936; s. William Victor and Frances Ellen (Swanson) H.; m. Doris Ann Cox, Nov. 11, 1961; children: William Victor III, David C., Stephanie C. Hill Trede. BBA, Tex. A&M U., 1959; MPA, U. Mo., Kansas City, 1972; diploma, Command and Gen. Staff Coll., 1969, Air War Coll., 1982. Lic. realtor. Commd. 2d lt. U.S. Army, 1959, advanced through grades to col.; tank bn. comdr. 2d Bn., 13th Armor, Ft. Knox, Ky., 1976-78; prof. mil. sci. Sam Houston State U., Huntsville, Tex., 1979-81; insp. gen. 5th U.S. Army, Ft. Sam Houston, Tex., 1982-85; ret. U.S. Army, 1986; dir. army Jr. Res. Officers Tng. Corps South San Antonio (Tex.) Ind. Sch. Dist., 1988-97; sr. Army instr. South San Antonio H.S., 1988-97, ret., 1997. Author army materials. City Coun. apptd. mem. San Antonio Cnv. Ctr. Contract Rev. Com., 1998-99; asst. crew leader Cenusus, 2000; stewardship com. United Way; ethics cons. San Antonio Ethics Com. Decorated Legion of Merit, Bronze Star medal, Combat Inf. badge, Airborne-Ranger, Silver medal Order of St. George, others. Mem. U.S. Armor Assn. Avocations: fishing, conservation activities. Home: 3208 Bent Bow Dr San Antonio TX 78209-3518 E-mail: billhillII@aol.com.

HILL, WILLIE L., JR., music educator; BS in Music Edn., Grambling State U., 1968; M in Music Edn., U. Colo., 1972, PhD in Music Edn., 1987. Instrumental music instr. Lincoln Elem. Denver Pub. Schs., 1968—71, instrumental music instr. Hill Jr. High, 1971—76, instrumental music instr. West High, 1976—81, instrumental music instr. Thomas Jefferson High, 1981—84, instrnl. cons., instrumental music supr. Music Edn. Office, 1984—88; prof. music edn. U. Colo., Boulder, 1988—99, asst. dean acad. programs Coll. Music, 1988—99; prof. U. Mass., 1999—, dir. Univ. Fine Arts Ctr., 1999—. Presenter in field; founder, dir. Rich Matteson-Telluride Jazz Acad., Rich Matteson Mile High Jazz Camp. Author: Learning to Sight-Read: Jazz, Rock, Latin, and Classical Styles, 1994, The Instrumental History of Jazz, 1997. Bd. dirs. CityStage, Springfield, Mass., Colo. Youth Symphony Orch., Young Audiences, Inc., Telluride Jazz Festival, Vail Jazz Found., Inc. Recipient Jazz Edn. Achievement award, Downbeat Mag., 2000, Lee Berk Jazz Educator of Yr. award, 2000. Mem.: Colo. Music Educators Assn. (pres.), Internat. Assn. Jazz Educators (v.p., pres.-elect, pres., past pres., Outstanding Svc. to Jazz Edn. award), Music Educators Nat. Conf. (pres.-elect), Nat. Assn. for Music Edn. (pres. 2002—).*

HILLERT, GLORIA BONNIN, anatomist, educator; b. Brownton, Minn., Jan. 25, 1930; d. Edward Henry and Lydia Magdalene (Luebker) Bonnin; m. Richard Hillert, Aug. 20, 1960; children: Kathryn, Virginia, Jonathan. BS, Valparaiso (Ind.) U., 1953; MA, U. Mich., 1958. Instr. Springfield (Ill.) Jr. Coll., 1953-57; teaching asst. U. Mich., Ann Arbor, 1957-58; instr., dept. head St. John's Coll., Winfield, Kans., 1958-59; asst. prof. Concordia Coll., River Forest, Ill., 1959-63; vis. instr. Wright Jr. Coll., Chgo., 1974-76, Ill. Benedictine Coll., Lisle, 1977-78, Rosary Coll., River Forest, 1976-81; prof. anatomy and physiology Triton Coll., River Grove, 1982-92, prof. emeritus, 1992—; vis. asst. prof. Concordia U., 1993—. Vis. instr. Wheaton (Ill.) Coll., 1988; advisor Springfield Jr. Coll. Sci. Club, 1953-57, Concordia Coll. Cultural Group, 1959-62; program dir. Triton Coll. Sci. Lectr. Series, 1983-87; participant Internat. Educators Workshop in Amazonia, 1993. Dem. campaign asst., Maywood, Ill., 1972, 88; vol. Mental Health Orgn., Chgo., 1969-73, Earthwatch, St. Croix, 1987, Costa Rica, 1989, Internat. Med. Care Team, Guatemala, 1995, Earthwatch End of Dinosaurs, 1997. Mem. AAUW, Ill. Assn. Community Coll. Biol. Tchrs., Nat. Assn. Biol. Tchrs. Lutheran. Avocation: traveling. Home: 1620 Clay Ct Melrose Park IL 60160-2419 Office: Triton Coll 2000 N 5th Ave River Grove IL 60171-1907

HILLERY, SUSIE MOORE, retired elementary school educator; b. Lunenburg County, VA, Feb. 25, 1928; d. William Edward and Sarah Anderson Moore; m. Herbert Vincent Hillery, June 17, 1956 (div. Jan. 1969); children: Vincent, Nathan. BA, Lynchburg Coll., 1950; MA, U. Ky., 1955; student, Lexington Sem., Ky.; student, U. Va., U. Tex. Youth min. Christian Ch. Disciples of Christ, Clarksville, Tenn., 1950—52; tchr.

religious edn. Martinsville (Va.) Pub. Sch., 1952—53; elem. sch. tchr. Lynchburg (Va.) Pub. Schs., 1953—54, Austin (Tex.) Pub. Schs., 1956—58, 1964—69, Henrico County Pub. Schs., Richmond, Va., 1969—91; youth min. Colonial Christian Ch., Richmond, 1983—86; pastor/min. Christian Ch., Gordonsville, Va., 1993—98, Bella Grove Christian Ch., Louisa, Va., 1998—2000; vol. chaplain Henrico Drs. Hosp., Richmond, 1999—. Rep. Interfaith Coun., 1993—; with Ch. Women United, 1998—.

HILL-HULSLANDER, JACQUELYNE L. nursing educator and consultant; b. Melrose Park, Ill., Jan. 9, 1940; d. Richard C. and Marian L. (Hamlin) Hill; m. Gale Franklin Hulslander, June 5, 1993; children: Daryl, Gary. Diploma, Evanston (Ill.) Hosp. Assn., 1961; BS, Elmhurst (Ill.) Coll., 1977, BSN, 1981; MS, Nat.-Louis U., Evanston, 1986; PhD, U. Ill., 1990. Cons. in course devel. Ill. Bell Telephone Co., Chgo.; cons. for employee devel. Glen Oaks Med. Ctr., Glendale Hts., Ill.; prof. Triton Coll., River Grove, Ill.; staff nurse OB Evanston (Ill.) Hosp. Assn., 1961-62; staff and charge nurse OB Gottlieb Mem. Hosp., Melrose Park, Ill., 1962-65; faculty OB Proviso Sch. Practical Nursing, Maywood, Ill., 1965-67; charge nurse OB Gottlieb Meml. Hosp., Melrose Park, 1970-75; grad. rsch. asst. dept. vocat. edn. U. Ill., Champaign-Urbana, Ill., 1988-89; faculty prof. basic med. surg. nursing and obstetrics Triton Coll., River Grove, Ill., 1976—, prof. emeritus. Cons. Dawson Tech. Inst., Chgo. City Coll.; cons. Engring. Systems Inc., Aurora, Ill.; presenter in field. Multicompetencies for Practical Nurses grantee, 1986, Patient Care Plans Visual Assessment Guide grantee, 1998-99. Mem. Chateau Lorraine Homeowners Assn. (sec., v.p., pres. 1992-96), U. Ill. Alumn Assn., Phi Delta Kappa, Phi Kappa Phi (life). Home: 222 Lorraine Cir Bloomingdale IL 60108-2546 Office: Triton Coll 2000 N 5th Ave River Grove IL 60171-1907

HILLIARD, CAROL SEARLS, early childhood special education consultant; b. San Mateo, Calif., Jan. 14, 1947; d. Frederick Taylor and Lydia (Churchill) Searls; m. John Marshall Hilliard, Dec. 27, 1967 (div. Sept. 1991); children: Paul Marshall, Christopher Niles. BSEd, U. Alaska, 1974; MS, Wheelock Coll., 1990. Head tchr. Lang. and Cognitive Devel. Ctr., Boston, 1990—96, cognitive devel. therapist, 1991-93, staff supr., 1993-94, program dir. early intervention, 1994-95, dir. supervision and curriculum devel., 1995—96; adj. instr. Urban Coll., 1997—, Wheelock Coll., 2001—. Cons. to Head Start and other Early Childhood Programs, 1988—, families with children with special needs, 1996—; staff devel. workshops for Early Childhood Edu. Programs, 1996—. Bd. dirs. Temporary Care Svcs. Respite Agy., Cambridge, Mass., 1989-91. Mem. Nat. Assn. Edn. Young Children, Coun. for Exceptional Children. Democrat. Episcopalian. Home: 94 Clay St # 3 Cambridge MA 02140-1710 Office: Lang & Cognitive Devel Ctr 11 Wyman St Boston MA 02130-1904

HILLIARD, DAVID CRAIG, lawyer, educator; b. Framingham, Mass., May 22, 1937; s. Walter David and Dorothy (Shortiss) H.; m. Celia Schmid, Feb. 16, 1974. BS, Tufts U., 1959; JD, U. Chgo., 1962. Bar: Ill. 1962, U.S. Supreme Ct. 1966. Mng. ptnr. Pattishall, McAuliffe, Newbury, Hilliard & Geraldson, Chgo., 1983—2002, sr. ptnr., 2003—. Adj. prof. law Northwestern U., 1971—, chmn. Symposium Intellectual Property Law and the Corp. Client, 1987—; lectr. in advanced trademark law and info. regulation U. Chgo. Law Sch., 1999—. Author: Unfair Competition and Unfair Trade Practices, 1985, Trademarks, 1987, Trademarks and Unfair Competition, 1994, 5th edit., 2002, Trademarks and Unfair Competition Deskbook, 2001, 2d edit., 2003; editor-in-chief Chgo. Bar Record, 1978-81. Trustee Art Inst. Chgo., 1980—, vice-chmn., 1998-2000, exec. com., 1994-2000, chmn. sustaining fellows, 1981-85, chmn. adv. com. dept. architecture, 1981—, pres. aux. bd., 1977-79, chmn. exhbns. com., 1993—, chmn. bd. govs. of the sch., 1997-2000; trustee Newberry Libr., 1983—, exec. com., 1987—; trustee Robert Allerton Trust, 2002—; pres. Lawyers Trust Fund Ill., 1985-88; vis. com. DePaul U. Law Sch., U. Chgo. Sch. of Law, chmn., 1987-88, Northwestern U. Assocs., 1985—; profl. adv. bd. Atty. Gen. Ill., 1982-84; mem. Ill. Commn. on Rights of Women, 1983-85; bd. dirs. Ill. Inst. Continuing Legal Edn., 1980-82; pres. Planned Parenthood Assn. Chgo., 1975-77. Lt. JAGC, USN, 1962-66. Recipient Maurice Weigle award, 1974, Chgo. Coun. Lawyers award for jud. reform, 1983. Fellow Am. Coll. Trial Lawyers (chmn. courageous adv. com. 1995-97); mem. ABA (chmn. trademark divsn. 1986-87, mem. coun. 1991-95, intellectual property law sect.), Ill. Bar Assn., Chgo. Bar Assn. (pres. 1982-83, founding chmn. young lawyers sect. 1971-72), Internat. Trademark Assn. (bd. dirs. 1989-91, ADR panel of neutrals 1994—), Arts Club, Chgo. Club, Econ. Club, Grolier Club, Lawyers Club, Legal Club (pres. 1989-90), Univ. Club, Casino, Wayfarers Club (pres. 1994-95). Home: 1320 N State Pkwy Chicago IL 60610-2118 Office: Pattishall McAuliffe Newbury Hilliard & Geraldson 311 S Wacker Dr Ste 5000 Chicago IL 60606-6631 E-mail: dhilliard@pattishall.com.

HILLIARD, LINDA WALTERS, primary education educator; b. Corning, N.Y., Dec. 11, 1947; d. Richard B. and Helen S. (Vandervort) Walters; m. John J. Cook, June 12, 1971 (div. July 1988); m. Larry Hilliard, Apr. 30, 2000. BA, Alderson-Broaddus Coll., 1971; postgrad., W.Va. U., 1972—. Cert. elem. tchr. with specialization in lang. arts, S.C. Tchr. Davis-Thomas (W.Va.) Elem. Sch., 1972-87, North Myrtle Beach (S.C.) Primary Sch., 1987—, chmn. sci. dept., 1991—, team leader strategic planning, 1994—, math. stds. pilot tchr., 1995—. Sci. mini grantee W.Va. Edn. Fund, 1985. Mem. ASCD, S.C. ASCD, S.C. Assn. Children's Sci., Palmetto State Tchrs. Orgn., S.C. Coun. Tchrs. Math., Delta Kappa Gamma (sec.). Avocations: reading, snorkeling. Office: North Myrtle Beach Primary Sch 901 11th Ave N North Myrtle Beach SC 29582-2509

HILLIS, STEPHEN KENDALL, secondary education educator; b. Hillsboro, Oreg., Jan. 5, 1942; s. Earnest Howard Hillis and Phyllis Noreen (Bagley) Gortner; m. Sharon Ione Arbogast, Aug. 5, 1967; children: Jeff Wise, Teryl Dorothy, Tonya Noreen. BA, Pacific U., 1965. Cert. Std. Oreg. Dept. Edn. H.s. tchr., Eagle Grove, Iowa, 1967-73, Madras, Oreg., 1973—2002; ret., 2002. Mem. consumer adv. coun. Oreg. Atty. Gen., 1998—. Precinct com. Jefferson County Dems., Madras, 1978-89, 2000—, chair precinct com. 1988-91,2003-, vice chair, 2001-2003; bd. dirs. Jefferson County Libr., 2000—, chair, 2003-; bd. dirs. Area Cmty. Action Team, 2002—, (regional bd.) Oreg. Cmty. Found., 2003—, Partnership, 2003; ctrl. Oreg. leadership team Oreg. Cmty. Found. With USAR, 1959—65. Mem. ASCD, NEA (human civil rights com. 1990-96, bd. dirs. 1993-2000), Oreg. Edn. Assn. (bd. dirs. 1983-2000, v.p. 1988-93). Democrat. Home: 375 NE Chestnut St Madras OR 97741-1910 E-mail: shillis@crestviewcable.com.

HILLMAN, CAROLE DOROTHY, education educator; b. Chgo., Nov. 24; d. Thomas James and Dorothy Marianne (Fritz) H.; m. Leo Frank Obriecht, Aug. 28, 1953 (dec. May 1983). BEd, Chgo. State U., 1953; MEd, U. Ill., 1959; EdD, No. Ill. U., 1985, postgrad., 1986. Learning ctr. coord. and dir. Sch. Dist. 161, Flossmoor, Ill., 1960-79; 6th grade tchr. Hollister (Mo.) Elem. Sch., 1979-80; asst. prof. edn. Coll. of the Ozarks, Pt. Lookout, Mo., 1980-82; assoc. prin., gifted coord., computer coord., libr. Butler Sch. Dist. 53, Oak Brook, Ill., 1982-95; assoc. prof. edn., dir. elem. edn. Elmhurst (Ill.) Coll., 1995—. Pvt. practice ednl. cons., Downers Grove, Ill., 1982—; spokesperson Valley Pub. Co., Appleton, Wis., 1993—. Author: Bold Beginning in Early Childhood, 1976, Learning Center/Organization an2 Implementation, 1977, Early Math Tapes, 1978, Critical Thinking Skills, 1984; appeared in film Beyond the Book, 1975 (award State of Ill.); writer Chgo. Tribune. Recipient Hon. Mention award for media program State of Ill. Bd. Edn., 1989, award for outstanding media program in U.S., Ednl. Facility Ctr., 1974. Mem. ASCD (bd. dirs. 1994-95, chair Ill. state elem. conf. 1995), Phi Delta Kappa, Kappa Delta Pi (pres. Tau Nu chpt. 1993-95, chair state 3d ann. elem. IASCD conf., editor Record). Avocations: collecting antiques, oil painting, stewarding dog shows, writing. Home: 10604 Golf Rd Orland Park IL 60462-7421 Office: Elmhurst Coll Elmhurst IL 60126

HILL-ROSATO, JANE ELIZABETH, elementary education educator; b. Newton, N.J., Nov. 21, 1958; d. Howard Russell and Gloria Frances (Clark) Hill; m. Nicholas David Rosato, Oct. 14, 1989; 1 stepchild, Domenick Patrick; 1 child, Salvator John. BS, East Stroudsburg U., 1981. Cert. tchr. elem. and early childhood, N.J., Pa. Presch. tchr. Sunrise Learning Ctr., Branchville, N.J., 1981-82; tchr. Knowlton Twp. Elem. Sch., Delaware, N.J., 1982—. Recipient Tchr. Recognition award I N.J. Gov.'s Office, Dept. Edn., Princeton,1989; invitee: Commrs. Symposium for Outstanding N.J. Tchrs., Dept. Edn., Trenton State Coll., 1989, N.J. Rural Schs. Conf. Highlighting Exemplary Programs, Practices and Resources for Rural Educators, N.J. Rural Assistance Coun., 1990; Nat. Gardening Assn. Youth Garden grantee, 1998. Mem. NEA, N.J. Edn. Assn., Monarch Tchr. Network, Knowlton Twp. Edn. Assn. Republican. Methodist. Avocations: skiing, piano, walking, reading. Home: 510 S 5th St PO Box 31 Bangor PA 18013 Office: Knowlton Twp Elem Sch Rt 46 PO Box 227 Delaware NJ 07833

HILT, BETTY MARIE, special education educator; b. Harrisburg, Ill., Jan. 17, 1927; d. Roy and Edith (Wilkins) Dixon; m. Kenneth Vinyard, June 27, 1948 (div. 1967); children: Gary Vinyard, Sara Vinyard Kyriakos; m. Alfred Hilt, Oct. 21, 1977 (dec.). AS, Blackburn U., 1946; BA in Sci., Kans. U., 1957, MA in Sci., 1969. Tchr. math. Harrisburg Pub. Schs., 1947-49, tchr. phys. edn., 1949-52; tchr. Unified Sch. Dist. 497, Lawrence, Kans., 1958-59; tchr. developmentally disabled Douglas County Assn. of Mentally Handicapped, Lawrence, 1961-65; tchr. mentally handicapped Cordley Elem. Unified Sch. Dist., Lawrence, 1965—. Mem. NEA (life), Kans. State Tchrs. Assn., Lawrence Edn. Assn., Coun. of Exceptional Children, Douglas County Assn. Retarded Citizens, Delta Kappa Gamma. Avocation: travel. Office: Cordley Elem Unified Sch Dist 1837 Vermont St Lawrence KS 66044-4183

HILTEBRANT, JANE, elementary education educator; b. New Hartford, N.Y., Apr. 9, 1940; d. Stanley and Josephine (Kwiatkowski) Zima; children from a previous marriage: Michele Isele, Kirsten Logan. BA in English, Nazareth Coll., 1962. Cert. elem. tchr. N.Y. Tchr. Utica Schs., N.Y., 1962-63, N.Y. Mills Schs., N.Y., 1968-71, Holland Patent Schs., N.Y., 1971-95, ret., 1995. Agent Better Homes and Gardens Real Estate, Old Forge, N.Y., 1986—. Sustaining mem. N.Y. State Rep. Party; founding mem. Presdl. Trust; mem. Rep. Presdl. Task Force, Nat. Rep. Com., Washington, 1991—, Old Forge Arts Guild, N.Y., 1989—, Parents as Reading Ptnrs., Holland Patent Schs., 1983-92; officer Holland Patent T.A., 1983-92; mem. Rep. Nat. Com.-Adirondack Railroad Preservation Soc., Dole for Pres., Am. Legion Aux., Nat. Rep. Congl. Com. Mem. ASCD, Am. Soc. Profl. and Exec. Women, Nat. Citizens for a Sound Economy, N.Y. Citizens for a Sound Economy, Smithsonian. Republican. Roman Catholic. Avocations: golf, writing, skiing, hiking. Home: PO Box 204 Thendara NY 13472-0204

HILTON, JEAN BULL, musician; b. Northampton County, Va., Sept. 29, 1926; d. Charles Russell and Margret Davis Bull; m. Ellis Baker Hilton Jr., July 3, 1948 (dec. Mar. 1988); children: Jeffery Allan, Ellis Baker, William Russell, Andrew Douglas. BA, Randolph-Macon Woman's Coll., 1947; MSc, Old Dominion U., 1974. Music tchr. Norfolk Pub. Schs., Norfolk, Va., 1947—48, Radford Pub. Sch., Radford, Va., 1948—49; minister of music First Luth. Ch., Portsmouth, 1951—91; tchr. Portsmouth Pub. Sch., Portsmouth, Va., 1961—68, music supr., 1969—91; minister of music First Luth. Ch., 1998—. Composer songs. Recipient 1st Place award, Va. Fedn. Music Clubs, 2000. Mem.: AAUW, Va. Gateway Ctr. for the Arts, Portsmouth Cmty. Concerts, Inc., Va. Fedn. Music Clubs, Nat. Fedn. Music Clubs, Va. Music Educators Conf., Music Educators Nat. Conf., Delta Kappa Gamma (Gamma chpt.). Lutheran. Avocations: reading, geneology, exercise.

HILTON, LINDA SUE, elementary education educator; b. Kansas City, Mo., Aug. 18; d. Arvel Leonard and Mary Lou Huston; m. John Wallace Hilton, July 19, 1975; children: Mark Christopher, Diana Lynn, Scott John. BA, William Jewell Coll., 1972; MA, U. Mo., Kansas City, 1987. Cert. elem. tchr. grades K-8, reading tchr. grades K-12, Mo. Elem. tchr. Missouri City (Mo.) Elem., 1972-87; title 1 reading tchr. Kansas City (Mo.) Sch. Dist., 1987—99, K-1 tchr., 1999—. Mem. NEA, Internat. Reading Assn., Delta Kappa Gamma (rec. sec. local chpt. 1989-92, corr. sec. 1992-94, historian 1994-96, com. chair 1996-), Pi Lambda Theta, Phi Kappa Phi. Baptist. Avocations: reading, swimming, sewing. Home: 1301 Wildbriar Dr Liberty MO 64068-4007 Office: Longfellow Arts Magnet 2830 Holmes Kansas City MO 64109

HILTON, PETER JOHN, mathematician, educator; b. London, Apr. 7, 1923; s. Mortimer and Elizabeth (Freedman) H.; m. Margaret Mostyn, Sept. 14, 1949; children: Nicholas, Timothy. MA, Oxford (Eng.) U., Eng., 1948; PhD, Oxford (Eng.) U., 1950, Cambridge (Eng.) U., Eng., 1952; HHD (hon.), No. Mich. U., 1977; DSc (hon.), Meml. U. Nfld., Can., 1983, U. Autonoma Barcelona, Spain, 1989. Lectr. Manchester U., Eng., 1948-52, sr. lectr., 1956-58; lectr. Cambridge U., 1952-55; Mason prof. pure math. Birmingham U., Eng., 1958-62; prof. math. Cornell U., 1962-71, U. Wash., 1971-73; Beaumont prof. Case Western Res. U., 1973-82; disting. prof. SUNY, Binghamton, 1982-93, emeritus, 1993—; disting. prof. U. Ctrl. Fla., Orlando, 1993—. Guest prof. Swiss Fed. Inst. Tech., Zurich, 1966—67, Zurich, 1981—82, Zurich, 1988—89, Courant Inst. Math. Scis., NYU, 1967—68, Ohio State U., 1977, U. Autonoma, Barcelona, 1989, U. Lausanne, 1996; Erskine fellow U. Canterbury, 2001, 02; Mahler lectr. Australian Math. Soc., 1997; vis. fellow Battelle Seattle Rsch. Ctr., 1970—71, fellow, 1971—; co-chmn. Cambridge Conf. on Sch. Math., 1965; chmn. com. applied math. tng. NRC, 1977—; chmn. U.S. Commn. on Math. Instrn., 1979—80; sec. Internat. Commn. Math. Instrn., 1979—82. Author: Homotopy Theory, 1953, (with S. Wylie) Homology Theory, 1960, Homotopy Theory and Duality, 1966, (with H.B. Griffiths) Classical Mathematics, 1970, General Cohomology Theory and K-Theory, 1971, (with U. Stammbach) Course in Homological Algebra, 1971, 2d edit., 1997, Le Langage des Categories, 1973, (with Y.C. Wu) Course in Modern Algebra, 1974, (with G. Mislin and J. Roitberg) Localization of Nilpotent Groups and Spaces, 1975 (with J. Pedersen) Fear No More, 1982, Nilpotente Gruppen und Nilpotente Räume, 1984, (with J. Pedersen) Build Your Own Polyhedra, 1987, (with J. Pedersen) College Preparatory Mathematics, 1992, (with D. Holton and J. Pedersen) Mathematical Reflections, 1997, (with D. Holton and J. Pedersen) Mathematical Vistas, 2002; editor: Ergebnisse der Mathematik, 1964—, Ill. Jour. Math., 1962-68, Jour. Pure and Applied Algebra, 1970-75, Topics in Modern Topology, 1968, Miscellanea Mathematica, 1991; contbr. articles to profl. jours. Recipient Silver medal U. Helsinki, Finland, 1975, Centenary medal John Carroll U., 1985. Mem. Am. Math. Soc., Math. Assn. Am. (1st v.p. 1978-80), Can. Math. Soc., Math Soc. Belgium (hon.), London Math. Soc., Cambridge Philos. Soc., Brazilian Acad. Scis. (hon.). Home: 29 Murray St Binghamton NY 13905-4504 Office: SUNY Dept Math Scis Binghamton NY 13902-6000 E-mail: marge@math.binghamton.edu.

HILTON, RONALD, international studies educator; b. Torquay, Eng., July 31, 1911; came to U.S., 1937, naturalized, 1946; s. Robert and Elizabeth Alice (Taylor) H.; m. Mary Bowie, May 1, 1939; 1 dau., Mary Alice Taylor. BA, Oxford U., Eng., 1933, MA, 1936; student, Sorbonne, Paris, 1933-34, U. Madrid, 1934-35, U. of Perugia, Italy, 1935-36. Dir. Comité Hispano-Inglés Library, Madrid, 1936; asst. prof. modern langs. U. B.C., 1939-41; assoc. prof. Romanic langs. Stanford U., 1942-49, prof., 1949-75, prof. emeritus humanities and scis., 1975—. Dir. Inst. Hispanic Am. and Luso-Brazilian studies; hon. prof. U. de San Marcos, Lima, Peru; vis. prof. U. Brazil, 1949; cultural dir. U. of Air, KGEI, San Francisco; founder, pres. World Assn. Internat. Studies; vis. fellow Hoover Instn., 1973—. Author: Campoamor, Spain and the World, 1940, Handbook of Hispanic Source Materials in the U.S, 1942, 2d edit., 1956, Four Studies in Franco-Spanish Relations, 1943, La America Latina de Ayer y de Hoy, 1970, The Scientific Institutions of Latin America, 1970, The Latin Americans, Their Heritage and Their Destiny, 1973; assoc. editor: Who's Who in America; editor: The Life of Joaquim Nabuco, 1950, The Movement Toward Latin American Unity, 1969, World Affairs Report, 1970—, Spain. From Monarchy to Civil War, 1990, La Legende Noirs, 1995. Decorated officer Cruzeiro do Sul (Brazil); Commonwealth Fund fellow U. Calif., 1937-39. Mem. Am. Assn. Tchrs. Spanish and Portuguese, Hispanic Soc. of Am., Am. Acad. Franciscan History. Office: World Assn Internat Studies Hoover Instn Stanford CA 94305-6010 E-mail: hilton@stanford.edu.

HILTON, STANLEY GOUMAS, lawyer, educator, writer; b. San Francisco, June 16, 1949; s. Loucas Stylianos and Effie (Glafkides) Goumas; m. Raquel Estrella Villalba, Feb. 25, 1996; children: Loucas, Angelika, Karmen (triplets). BA with honors, U. Chgo., 1971; JD, Duke U., 1975; MBA, Harvard U., 1979. Bar: Calif. 1975, U.S. Dist. Ct. Calif. 1975, U.S. Ct. Appeals (9th cir.) 1983, U.S. Supreme Ct. 1985. Libr. asst. Duke U. Libr., Durham, N.C., 1972-75, Harvard U. Libr., Cambridge, Mass., 1977-79; minority counsel U.S. Senator Bob Dole, Washington, 1979-80; adminstrv. asst. Calif. State Senate, Sacramento, 1980-81; pvt. practice San Francisco, 1981—; CEO Froggg, Inc., 1999—, San Francisco Landlords Union, 1999—. Adj. assoc. prof. Golden Gate U., San Francisco, 1991—; profl. spkr.; polit. writer; pres. Fair Play In the Middle East Com., 2002—; tutor Harvard U., 1978—79. Author: Bob Dole: American Political Phoenix, 1988, Senator for Sale, 1995, Glass Houses, 1998 (Best writer 1998), To Pay or Not to Pay, 2003. Pres. Com. to Stick With Candlestick Park, San Francisco, 1992-96, Value Added Tax Now, San Francisco, 1994—, Save the 4th Amendment, San Francisco, 1995—; pres., CEO Animalism, Inc., San Francisco Landlord's Union, 2001—; CEO Fountain of Youth; alt. mem. San Mateo County Dem. Ctrl. Com., 2002--; Dem. candidate for Gov. Calif. spl. recall election, 2003. Mem. Calif. State Bar, Abolish the Fed. Res. Bank Assn. (pres. 1999—), Hellenic Law Soc., Bechtel Toastmasters Club (pres.), Rhinoceros Toastmasters Club. Democrat. Avocations: philately, photography, classical music, ancient greek and roman history. Office: 580 California St Ste 500 San Francisco CA 94104-1000

HILYARD, VERONICA MARIE, education administrator; b. Phila., May 5, 1946; d. John Joseph and Antoinette M. (Gentile) H.; m. John W. Paquet, Mar. 25, 1972 (div. Feb. 1988); 1 child, Christopher Hilyard; m. Harley Mitchell Smith, Apr. 13, 1996. BS in Edn., Gwynedd Mercy coll., 1974; MA, Maryville U., 1991; postgrad., St. Louis U., 1997—. Elem. sch. rincipal Immaculate Conception Sch., Daidenne, Mo., 1982-87; tchr. Wentzville (Mo.) Mid. Sch., 1988-91; tchr. gifted Maryville University summer program, St. Louis, 1991, Rockwood Sch. Dist., Eureka, Mo., 1991-92, Clayton (Mo.) Sch. Dist., 1992-93, Northeast Ind. Sch. Dist., San Antonio, 1993-94; coord. gifted programs parkway Sch. Dist., St. Louis, 1994—. Adj. prof. Maryville U., St. Louis, 1997; mem. Mo. Improvement Team Dept. of Elem. and Secondary Edn. Mem. AAUW, NAGC, SAGE,Gifted Assn. of Mo., Women in Ednl. Leadership, St. Louis Metro Coun., Phi Delta Kappa (pres. 1997—). Avocations: music, reading, travel. Office: Parkway Sch Dit 12657 Fee Fee Rd Saint Louis MO 63146-4481

HIMBURG, SUSAN PHILLIPS, dietitian, educator; b. Norfolk, Va., May 17, 1946; d. Claude Ralph Jr. and Sarah Ann (Gilbert) Phillips; m. James Donald Himburg, Feb. 9, 1968; 1 child, Karlene Susan. BS, Fla. State U., 1968; M in Med. Sci., Emory U., 1972; PhD, U. Miami, Fla., 1979. Dietetic intern Emory U., Atlanta, 1971; clin. dietitian Emory U. Hosp., Atlanta, 1972-73; from instr. to prof. Fla. Internat. U., Miami, 1973—, dir. coordinated program in dietetics, 1979-99, dir. health scis. recruitment and retention program, 1985—, chmn. dietetics and nutrition, 1992-97, self-study dir., 1997-2000. Grant reviewer disadvantaged assistance program HHS, Rockville, Md., 1989—; site visitor So. Assn. Colls. and Schs., Atlanta, 1987—. Author: (tng. manual) ADA Self-Study, 1988, 91, 95; contbr. articles to profl. jours. Fellow Am. Dietetic Assn. (site visitor 1985—, chairperson commn. on accreditation 1992-93, medallion 1996); mem. Soc. Nutrition Edn., Fla. Dietetic Assn. (del. 1990-2000, Disting. Dietitian 1995), Miami Dietetic Assn. (mem. nominating com. 1989, Disting. Dietitian 1994), Phi Kappa Phi, Kappa Omicron Nu. Office: Fla Internat Univ Ch 201 Dietetics & Nutritio Miami FL 33199-0001 E-mail: himburgs@fiu.edu.

HIMELSTEIN, PHILIP NATHAN, psychology educator; s. Isidore and Martha H.; m. Peggy Donn, June 1, 1952; children: Steven Mark, Carol Sue, Roger Alan. AB, NYU, 1949, AM, 1950; PhD, U. Tex., 1955. Diplomate Am. Bd. Profl. Psychology. Clin. psychologist Salem (Va.) VA Hosp., 1955-56; rsch. psychologist USAF, 1956-58; mem. faculty U. Ark., Fayetteville, 1958-63; assoc. prof. N.Mex. State U., Las Cruces, 1963-65; prof. psychology U. Tex., El Paso, 1965-90, prof. emeritus, 1990—, chmn. dept., 1966-71; ret., 1990. Clin. psychologist El Paso Psychiat. Clinic, 1971-78; clin. assoc. prof. psychiatry Tex. Tech. U. Sch. Medicine, 1978-80; adj. prof. Sch. Psychology, Fla. Inst. Tech., Melbourne, 1977-90; chief psychologist El Paso State Ctr., 1995-98. Co-editor: Readings on the Exceptional Child, 1962, 2nd edit., 1972, Handbook of Gestalt Therapy, 1976. With USAAF, WWII. Mem. Fellow APA, Soc. Personality Assessment, Am. Psychol. Soc., Acad. Clin. Psychology; mem. El Paso Psychol. Assn. (pres. 1971-72), El Paso County Psychol. Soc. (pres. 1990-91), Sigma Xi, Phi Kappa Phi. Home: 331 Rainbow Cir El Paso TX 79912-3717

HIMES, BRIAN DAVID, reading educator; b. Kansas City, Mo., Jan. 13, 1960; s. William Harmon and Dorothy Mary Himes. BA in History summa cum laude, William Jewell Coll., 1982; MA in Reading Edn., U. Mo., 1989. Cert. tchr., Mo., Kans. Substitute tchr. Liberty, North Kansas City (Mo.) Schs., 1982-84, 86-89; history tchr. Breckenridge (Mo.) Pub. Schs., 1984-85; history tchr., coach Savannah (Mo.) Pub. Schs., 1985-86; chpt. 1 reading tchr. Kansas City (Kans.) Pub. Schs., 1989-92; lectr. Sch Edn. U. Mo., Kansas City, 1993; reading instr. Longview C.C., Lee's Summit, Mo., 1992—. Mem. low brass player Liberty (Mo.) Symphony Orch., 1981—; treas., elder Antioch Cmty. Ch. Mem. Nat. Assn. R.R. Passengers, Internat. Reading Assn., Phi Alpha Theta, Pi Gamma Mu, Phi Epsilon. Avocations: golf, bridge, rail travel, classical music. Office: Longview CC 500 SW Longview Rd Lees Summit MO 64081-2105

HIMES, JOHN G. biologist, educator; b. Rochester, N.Y., Nov. 14, 1973; BS, U. Miss., 1995; MS, La. State U., 1998; PhD, U. So. Miss., 2002. Field worker U. Miss., University, 1993-95; tchg. asst. La. State U., Shreveport, 1996-98; rsch. fellow La. Dept. Wildlife and Fisheries, Baton Rouge, 1996-98; tchg. asst. U. So. Miss., Hattiesburg, 1998—2002; supervising game biologist Nev. Dept. Wildlife, Las Vegas, 2002—. Office: Nev Divsn Wildlife 4747 Vegas Dr Las Vegas NV 89108

HIMES, ROSE KENDRICK, elementary school educator; b. Okolana, Miss., Jan. 13, 1942; d. John Thomas and Annie Mae (Grisby) Kendrick; m. Joseph Lex Stone, Aug. 15, 1965 (div. Sept., 1972); m. Albert Himes, Sept. 20, 1980. AA, Okolona Coll., 1962; BEd, Rust Coll., 1964; MEd, Miss. Univ. for Women, 1971. Tchr. first grade Vine Elem. Sch., Aberdeen, Miss.; tchr. fourth grade Fairview Elem. Sch., Columbus, Miss., 1971-75, Caler-man Elem., Columbus, 1975-79; tchr. Franklin Acad. Elem., Columbus, 1979—. Trustee United Meth. Ch., Columbus, Miss., 1989-94; cert. lay speaker United Meth. Ch., Miss., 1992-94. Mem. Columbus Classroom Tchrs. Assn., Columbus Reading Coun. Democrat. Avocations: reading, collecting pottery, horticulture, singing, lay speaking. Home: 225 Harris Dr Columbus MS 39705-8376

HIMMELBERG, ROBERT FRANKLIN, historian, educator; b. Kansas City, Mo., July 16, 1934; s. Alexander Franklin and Genevieve Fay (Leonard) H.; m. Josephine Ann Boone, Dec. 27, 1958; children: Thomas A., Robert A., Juliana Ruth. BA, Rockhurst Coll., 1956; MA, Creighton U., 1958; PhD, Pa. State U., 1963. Instr. Am. history Fordham U., Bronx, N.Y., 1961-63, asst. prof., 1963-68, assoc. prof., 1968-77, prof., 1977—, chmn. dept., 1969-72, pres. faculty senate, 1989-92, dean Grad. Sch. Arts and Scis., 1993-2000. Hoover Presdl. Library fellow, 1984-85, grantee, 1993. Author: The Origins of the National Recovery Administration: Business, Government and the Trade Association Issue, 1921-1933, 1976, revised edit., 1994; editor: Business and Government in America Since 1870, 1994; co-editor: Historians and Race: Autobiography and the Writing of History, 1996, The Great Depression and the New Deal, 2000; contbr. articles to profl. jours. Am. Philos. Soc. grantee, 1978. Mem.: Orgn. Am. Historians. Republican. Roman Catholic. Office: Fordham Univ Dept History Bronx NY 10458 E-mail: himmelberg@fordham.edu.

HIMMELBERGER, RICHARD CHARLES, vocational school educator; b. Reading, Pa., May 27, 1926; s. Robert Leon and Ruth Melinda (Horst) H.; m. Thelma Fay Degler, Dec. 25, 1965 (div. 1980); 1 child, Eric Christopher. Student, Wyomissing (Pa.) Inst., 1948-49, Phila. Coll. of Art, 1949-52; cert., Pa. State U., 1970; MA, Temple U., 1980. Advt. layout Glidden Paint Co., Reading, Pa., 1952-55; sign designer Superior Sign System, Elizabethtown, Pa.; lay-out adr dir. Moran Advt. Co., Shoemakersville, Pa., 1955-58; lay-out art dept. staff Kutztown (Pa.) Pub. Co. Inc., 1958-61; rep. Enameloid Sign Display Co. Inc., Reading, Pa., 1961-64; graphic printing rep. Wilt Screen Printin Co., Annville, Pa., 1964-68; mgr. art dept. Beaumont Heller Sperling AD, Reading, Pa., 1968-72; instr. Reading-Muhlenberg AVT Sch., 1972-93. Adj. instr. Reading Area C.C., 1975-76; founding mem. Challenger Ctr., Washington and Alexandria, Va., 1990—. Vol. Berks County Heritage Ctr., Phoebe-Berks Village, Inc.; active Trinity Reformed Ch. With U.S. Army, 1944-46, PTO. Mem. Nat. Wildlife Assn., Am. Assn. Retired Persons (vocat. adviser, coord. art direction expo. Pa. Vocat. Conf.), Nat. Conservatory, Libr. Congress. Republican. Avocations: gardening, swimming, horseback riding, sports, hiking. Home: 9 Reading Dr Apt 125 Wernersville PA 19565-2023

HIMMELBLAU, DAVID MAUTNER, chemical engineer; b. Chgo., Aug. 29, 1923; s. David and Roda (Mautner) H.; m. Betty H. Hartman, Sept. 1, 1948; children: Andrew, Margaret Ann. BS, MIT, 1947; MBA, Northwestern U., 1950; PhD, U. Wash., 1957. Cost engr. Internat. Harvester Co., Chgo., 1946-47; cost analyst Simpson Logging Co., Seattle, 1952-53; mgr. Excel Battery Co., Seattle, 1953-54; teaching asst., instr. U. Wash., Seattle, 1955-57; successively asst. prof., asso. prof., prof. chem. engring. U. Tex., Austin, 1957—, chmn. dept., 1973-77. Pres. RAMAD Corp.; Univ. Fed. Credit Union, 1964-68; exec officer CACHE Corp. of Mass., 1984-2000. Author: Basic Principles and Calculations in Chemical Engineering, 1962, 7th edit., 2003, Process Analysis and Simulation, 1968, Process Analysis by Statistical Methods, 1970, Applied Nonlinear Programming, 1974, Optimization of Chemical Processes, 1989, 2d edit., 2000; contbr. articles to profl. jours. Served with U.S. Army, 1943-46, 51-52. Grantee, NSF, 1953—94, NATO Sci. Com., 1969. Mem. Am. Inst. Chem. Engrs. (dir. 1973-76), Am. Chem. Soc., Am. Math. Soc., Ops. Research Soc. Am., Soc. Indsl. and Applied Mathematics, Sigma Xi, Delta Mu Delta. Clubs: Headliners (Austin). Home: 4609 Ridge Oak Dr Austin TX 78731-5211 Office: Univ Texas Coll Engring Austin TX 78712 E-mail: himmelblau@che.utexas.edu.

HINDERLING, KAREN MARIE CIANFROCCO, elementary education educator; b. Rome, N.Y., Aug. 17, 1969; d. Dominick A. and Janet L. (Clough) C. BS in Elem. Edn. cum laude, SUNY, Oswego, 1991; M in Reading, SUNY, Cortland, 1994. Cert. tchr. elem. edn. 1-6, math. ext. 7-9, nursery, kindergarten, reading tchr. Tchr. fourth grade Oriskany (N.Y.) Cen. Sch., 1991-94; 4th grade tchr. N.A. Walbran Elem. Sch., Oriskany, 1994—. Tchr. asst. spl. edn., Rome (N.Y.) Sch. Dist., 1991, tchr. TLC Day Care, Whitesboro, N.Y., 1988; mem. multiage com., Oriskany, 1992—, lang. arts com., 1991-99, tech. com., 1991-98, math. com., 1996-. Organized Explore, Discover, Connect Family Fun Night, N.A.Walbran Elem. Sch., fall 1994, 95. Recipient Beautification grant Nat. Gardening Assn., Burlington, Vt., 1993, Excellence in Tchg. award Oriskany Tchrs. Assn., 1993. Mem. PTA (treas. 1994-95). Avocations: reading, cooking, computers. Office: Oriskany Sch Dist Rte 69 Oriskany NY 13424

HINDLE, PETER GAGE, retired secodary mathematics educator; b. New Bedford, Mass., Sept. 11, 1934; s. Winston Russell and Eleanor Gage (Potter) H. AB, Amherst Coll., 1956. Tchr. math. Deerfield (Mass.) Acad., 1956-2000; ret., 2000. Author: How to Improve Your Scores on the SATs, 1959. Moderator First Ch. of Deerfield, 1975-2000, auditor, 1970-2000. Mem. Nat. Coun. Tchrs. Math., Country Club of New Bedford. Republican. Congregationalist. Avocations: golf, bridge, collecting matches. Home: 5 W Rockland Farm South Dartmouth MA 02748-3727

HINDMARSH, KENNETH WAYNE, pharmacy dean, educator; b. Grandview, Man., Can., Aug. 13, 1941; s. Frederick Joseph and Mildred Olive (Clark) H.; m. Lois Irene Dies, July 9, 1966; children: Carla Anne, Ryan James. BSP, U. Sask, Saskatoon, Can., 1964, MSc, 1965; PhD, U. Alta., Edmonton, Can., 1970. Staff pharmacist U. Hosp., Saskatoon, Can., 1965-66; lectr. U. Sask., Saskatoon, Can., 1966-67; toxicologist Royal Can. Mounted Police, Regina, Can., 1970-71; mem. faculty U. Sask. Coll. Pharmacy, 1971—, prof., 1979—, asst. dean, 1987-92; dean faculty pharmacy U. Man., 1992-98, U. Toronto, Ont., 1998—. Med. Rsch. Coun. vis. prof., Australia. Author: Nutritional Products, 1984, Drugs-What Your Kid Should Know, 1992, revised edit., 2000, Too Cool for Drugs, 1993; contbr. articles to profl. jours. Recipient Douglas M. Lucas award for excellence in forensic sci., 1999; Paul Harris fellow, 1970. Fellow Can. Soc. Forensic Sci. (pres. 1984); mem. Assn. Faculties Pharmacy of Can. (pres. 1977-78), Soc. Toxicology Can., Sask. Man. and Ont. Pharm. Assn., Can. Pharm. Assn., Can. Coun. Accreditation Pharmacy Programs (pres. 1993-95, 97-98). Baptist. Avocations: racquet sports, jogging, reading, music. Home: 801-62 Wellesley St W Toronto ON Canada M5S 2X3 Office: U Toronto Leslie Dan Faculty Pharmacy Toronto ON Canada M5S 2S2 E-mail: wayne.hindmarsh@utoronto.ca.

HINELY, BETHANY KNOLL, special education educator; b. Coshocton, Ohio, Aug. 4, 1951; d. Milton and Nora Jean (Marvin) Knoll; 1 child, Dustin Knoll. BS in Edn., Ohio State U., 1976; M in Edn. with honors, Ohio U., 1982; EdS in Sch. Adminstrn. and Supervision Ga. Southern U., 1987. Cert. in edn. and spl. edn. leadership, sch. adminstrn., supr. emotional handicaps, Fla., Ga. Tchr. spl. edn. Licking County Schs., Newark, Ohio, 1976-80; adminstr., mgmt. coord. The Knoll Group, Newark, 1980-81; spl. edn. supr.., intern Ohio U., Athens, 1982; dir. edn. and pub. relations Gallipolis Bus. Coll., Chillicothe, Ohio, 1982-83; mgr. tng. and devel. Scioto-Point Valley Mental Health Ctr., Chillicothe, 1983; dir. resource and mgmt. Comml. Hosp., Inc., Hilton Head Island, S.C., 1984; behavior mgmt. specialist, staff devel. instr., mentor tchr. Savannah-Chatham County Pub. Schs., Ga., 1985-92; spl. edn. tchr. Duval County Schs., Jacksonville, Fla., 1992—; creative design cons. Front Page Design, Savannah, Ga., 1985-86; workshop presenter. Author: Contracting for Success; presenter in field. Mem. Council for Exceptional Children, Assn. Supervision and Curriculum Devel., Phi Delta Kappa, Kappa Delta Pi. Jewish. Avocations: boating. Office: Matthew Gilbert Mid Sch 1424 Franklin St Jacksonville FL 32206-4806

HINES, CONSTANCE FAYE, elementary education educator; b. Houston, July 29, 1948; d. Charles and Trudie (Dixon) Newton; m. Kenneth Caldwell, Apr. 15, 1951 (div. June 1986; 1 child, Candace Elizabeth; m. Robert H. Hines, Nov. 26, 1992. BS, Prairie View A&M U., 1970, MEd, 1972; postgrad., Tex. So. U., 1992—. Cert. tchr., cert. in mid-mgmt. and superintendency, Tex. With North Forest Ind. Sch. Dist., Houston, 1970—; tchr. grade 3 Fonwood Elem. Sch., 1975-87; tchr. reading grade 5 Mt. Houston Elem. Sch., 1987-88, A.G. Hilliard Elem. Sch., 1988—. Curriculum writer North Forest Ind. Sch. Dist., 1988-92. Active community, sch. and ch. programs, including North Forest Community Up-Life, 1992, Knock-Out Drugs, 1988; tchr. Sunday sch. Bethel Missionary Ch., Houston, 1980-92. Named Outstanding Black Educator, Houston Area Alliance of Black Educators, 1990-91. Mem. Greater Houston Area Reading Coun., Phi Delta Kappa, Gamma Theta Upsilon. Democrat. Baptist. Avocation: reading. Home: 7913 Birmingham St Houston TX 77028-3423 Also: 7913 Birmingham St Houston TX 77028-3423

HINES, N. WILLIAM, dean, law educator, administrator; b. 1936; AB, Baker U., 1958; LLB, U. Kans., 1961; LLD, Baker U., 1999. Bar: Kans. 1961, Iowa 1965. Law clk. U.S. Ct. Appeals 10th cir., 1961-62; tchg. fellow Harvard U., 1961-62; asst. prof. law U. Iowa, 1962-65, assoc. prof., 1965-67, prof., 1967-73, disting. prof., 1973—, dean, 1976—. Vis. prof. Stanford U., 1974—75. Editor (notes and comments): Kans. Law Rev. Fellow, Harvard U., 1961—62. Fellow: Iowa State Bar Found., ABA Found.; mem.: Assn. Am. Law Schs. (exec. com. 2002—), Environ. Law Inst. (assoc.), Order of Coif, Jo. Co. Her. Trust (founder, pres.). Office: U Iowa Coll Law Iowa City IA 52242-0001

HINES, PATRICIA, social worker, educator; b. Watertown, N.Y., Nov. 4, 1947; d. Arthur and Bella (O'Neil) H. BS, SUNY, Oswego, 1969; MSW, SUNY, Buffalo, 1975; MPA, Fairleigh Dickinson U., 1982. Cert. Dr. Thomas Gordon Parent Effectiveness Trainer. Supr. social work Ocean County Bd. Social Svcs., Toms River, N.J., 1973-77, adminstrv. supr. social work, 1977-83, dep. dir., 1983-96; exec. dir. Ocean First Found., Toms River, 1996—. Social work cons. Ocean County Vis. Homemaker Svc., Inc., Toms River, 1975-80, Cmty. Meml. Hosp., Toms River, 1978-79, Manchester Manor, Bartley Manor Convalescent Ctr., Barnegat Nursing Facility, Burnt Tavern Convalescent Ctr., Logan Manor, Medicenter, Keswick Pines, Green Acres Manor, Imperial Care Center. Chmn. Ocean County Title XX Coalition, 1977-82; bd. dirs. Ocean County Family Planning Program, Toms River, 1969-73, Mental Health Bd., 1983-84; mem. exec. bd. United Way, 1983-96; mem. Aging Network Svc., 1992—. Mem. NASW (nat. register clin. social workers), Acad. Cert. Social Workers (diplomate clin. social work). Home: 13 Bay Harbor Blvd Brick NJ 08723-7303 Office: Bldg 1 1027 Hooper Ave Toms River NJ 08753-8320

HINES, VONCILE, special education educator; b. Detroit, Dec. 1, 1945; d. Raymond and Cleo (Smith) H. AA, Highland Park Community Coll., 1967; BEd, Wayne State U., 1971, MEd, 1975; MA, U. Detroit, 1978. Tchr. primary unit Detroit Bd. Edn., 1971-79, spl. educator, 1979-94; self-employed ednl. rsch. edn. co-creations. Tchr. trainee Feuerstein's Instrumental Enrichment, 1988—; cons. Queen's Community Workers, Detroit, 1977—; evaluator Teen Profl. Parenting Project, New Detroit Inc., 1986-87; guest educator, critic "Express Yourself", Sta. WQBH 1400 AM, 1989; advisor to home sch. educators. Author: I Chose Planet Earth, 1988; inventor in field. Recipient cert. of merit State of Mich., 1978, 88, cert. of appreciation Queen's Cmty. Workers, 1980, Wayne County Bd. Commrs., 1988, award of recognition Detroit City Coun., 1984, 88. Mem. Assn. for Children and Adults with Learning Disabilities, Assn. Supervision and Curriculum Devel., Nat. Thinking Skills Network, NAFE, Nat. Council Negro Women (presenter 1987), Met. Detroit Alliance of Black Sch. Educators. Democrat. Avocation: travel.

HINES-MARTIN, VICKI PATRICIA, nursing educator, researcher; b. Louisville, Aug. 18, 1951; d. William Adolphus Hines and Mary Iris Bailey; m. Kenneth Wayne Martin, Dec. 30, 1978; 1 child, Michelle Hines Martin. BSN, Spalding Coll., 1975; MA in Edn., Spalding U., 1983; MSN, U. Cin., 1986; PhD, U. Ky., 1994. Cert. clin. specialist in adult psychiat. mental. Staff nurse Norton Hosp., Louisville, 1978-81; instr. critical care Sts. Mary & Elizabeth Hosp., Louisville, 1981-82; asst. chief nursing svcs. VA Med. Ctr., Cin., 1983-85; nursing instr. Jefferson Community Coll., Louisville, 1985-87; head nurse mgr. VA Med. Ctr., Louisville, 1987-88; asst. prof. nursing Ind. U. S.E., New Albany, 1989-95, U. Ky., Lexington, 1995-98, U. Louisville, 1998—. Bd. dirs. Seven Counties Mental Health Svcs., 1995-2000; mem. steering com. on practice parameters Ky. Health Policy Bd., 1996. Contbr. articles to profl. jours. Chmn. bd. dirs. West Louisville Area Health Edn. Ctr., 1997-2000; mem. African-Am. Health Edn. Leadership Program com. Jefferson County Health Dept., 1997-98, African-Am. Health Initiative, African-Am. Strategic Planning Group, 1998-2000; bd. dirs. Ky. Nurses Found., 1998-2001. Nurses Scholar/Fellow, Lucy Zimmerman scholar, 1982, Estelle Massey Osborne Meml. scholar, 1983-84, trainee U. Cin., 1983, grad. scholar, 1983; named to Outstanding Young Women of Am., 1986; Elizabeth Carnagie scholar, 1991, Am. Nurses Found. scholar, 1992; Fellow U. Ky., 1988, grad. fellow, 1992; recipient Rsch. award Ky. Nurses Found., 1992, Nursing Excellence award Jefferson County Ky., 1995, Psychiatric Mental Health Nurse of the Year Ky. Nurses Assn., 1995, Rsch. in Minority Health award So. Nursing Rsch. Soc., 1999; postdoctoral fellow in Health Policy ANA Ethnic Minority fellowship program, 1996; Louisville Courier Jour. Forum fellow, 1997. Mem.: ANA (minority clin. fellow 1991—93, ethnic racial minority fellow 1997), Internat. Soc. Psychiat. Nurses (mem. rsch. coun.), So. Nurses Rsch. Soc., Nat. Black Nurses Assn., Kyanna Black Nurses Inc. (co-founder, past pres.), Ky. Nurses Assn. (mental health coun. sec. 1986—88, editl. bd. 1994—97), Am. Psychiat. Nurses Assn. (chair coun. African Am. nurses 2000—02), Sigma Theta Tau. Office: Univ of Louisville 3038 Bldg K 555 S Floyd St Louisville KY 40202-3801 E-mail: vphine01@louisville.edu.

HINKLE, ERIKA GALVÃO, art educator, digital artist; b. Uberlândia, Brazil, Feb. 15, 1961; d. Wilson and Ismalita César Galvão; m. Andrew Ralph Hinkle, Sept. 9, 1995. B in Art Edn., U. Federal Uberlândia, 1979, BFA, 1981; M in Art Edn., Ohio State U., 1991, PhD in Art Edn., 1995. Prof. ESEBA-U. Fed. Uberlândia, 1981-86, vis. prof., 1995-97; prof. Universidade de Uberaba, 1998—. Digital art work printed in Advocate Jour., 1990; one-woman shows include It's An Art Gallery, 1994, Barley's Restaurant, 1994, Fort Hayes Sch. Visual Arts, 1994, D'Alberto Investments Inc., 1995; contbr. articles to profl. jours. Recipient Crabbie award Calendar Mag., 1995. Avocations: reading, Tae Kwon Do. Home: 6308 Wyler Ct Dublin OH 43016-8275 Office: U Fed Uberlândia Av João Naves Avila Uberlândia 38400 Brazil E-mail: erika@nanet.com.br.

HINKLEY, NANCY EMILY ENGSTROM, foundation administrator, educator; b. St. Louis, Jan. 3, 1934; d. Sigfrid E. and Ida C. (Stenstrom) Engstrom; children: Karen Elizabeth, Christine Marie, Catherine Andrea. BA, Augustana Coll., 1955; MA, U. Fla., 1956; EdD, N.C. State U., 1975. Adult edn. specialist Nationwide Long Term Care Edn. Ctr., Raleigh, N.C., 1975-77, dir., 1977-78; owner, pres. Aging and Long Term Care Ednl. and Cons. Svcs., Raleigh, 1978-82; dir. edn. Beverly Found., South Pasadena, Calif., 1983-84; dir. tng. and mgmt. devel. Care Enterprises, Anaheim, Calif., 1984-87; pres. The Hillhaven Found., Tacoma, 1987-93; dir. employment & tng. divsn. Kitsap Cmty. Resources, 1997-99; pres. AJM Assocs., 1993—. Bd. dirs. Tacoma Community Coll. Found.; mem. editorial bd. Nursing Homes, 1988—; mem. editorial bd. Aspen Rsch. Pub. Group, 1989-93. Author: (with others) A Time and Place for Sharing: A Practical Guide for Developing Intergenerational Programs, 1984; mem. editorial bd. Jour. Univ. Programs, 1988-93; contbr. articles to profl. jours. Vol. Big Bros./Big Sisters, Tacoma, 1989-90; bd. dirs. Jessie Dyslin Boy's Ranch, Tacoma, 1988-90. Mem. ASTD, Am. Med. Dirs. Assn. (assoc.), Am. Assn. Homes for the Aging (assoc.), Am. Coll. Health Care Adminstrs. (assoc.), Am. Soc. on Aging, Gerontol. Soc. Am., Phi Kappa Phi, Phi Alpha Theta, Alpha Kappa Delta, Alpha Psi Omega, Sigma Phi Omega. Home and Office: PO Box 64190 Tacoma WA 98464-0190

HINMAN, GEORGE WHEELER, physics educator; b. Evanston, Ill., Nov. 7, 1927; s. Norman Sherman and Bess (Bryan) H.; m. Mary Louise Cauffield, June 19, 1952; children: Norman Field, Lydia Hinman, Nancy Wheeler. BS in Physics and Math., Carnegie Mellon U., 1947, MS in Physics, 1950, DSc in Physics, 1952. Asst. prof., then assoc. prof. physics Carnegie Mellon U., Pitts., 1952-63; chmn. physics Gen. Atomic Co. subs. Gulf Oil Corp., San Diego, 1963-69; prof. physics, dir. Applied Energy Studies Wash. State U., Pullman, 1983—97; dir. N.Mex. Energy Research & Devel. Inst., Santa Fe, 1982-83; chair environ. sci. & regional planning, 1989-97. Cons. Los Alamos (N.Mex.) Nat. Lab., 1976-90, GAO, 1977—, Nat. Nuclear Accreditation Bd., 1992-98. Author: Dictionary of Energy, 1983; contbr. articles to profl. jours. Grantee NSF, others. Fellow Am. Phys. Soc.; mem. Am. Nuclear Soc., AAAS, Am. Soc. Engring. Edn. Democrat. Avocation: fishing. Home: 925 SW Fountain St Pullman WA 99163-2132 Office: Wash State U Troy Hl Rm 305 Pullman WA 99164-4430

HINMAN, ROSALIND VIRGINIA, storyteller, drama educator; b. London, May 5, 1938; d. Frederick and Gladys Molly (Seabrook) Ellam; m. Richard Leslie Hinman, Sept. 23, 1967; children: Katherine, Jeremy, Adrian, Isabel. Diploma in Dramatic Art, U. London, 1958; cert. in Edn., Cen. Sch. Speech and Drama, London, 1959; MALS, Wesleyan U., Middletown, Conn., 1998. Lectr. Ministere d'Edn. Nat. U. France, Tourcoing, Albi, 1960-63, U. de Caen, France, 1960-63; domestic & overseas exhibit adminstr. The Design Coun., London, 1963-66; artist Boces, Westchester, N.Y., 1968-70, Eugene O'Neill Theater Ctr., Waterford, Conn., 1980—; freelance performer Old Lyme, Conn., 1982—. Performing artist Conntours Conn. Commn. on the Arts, Hartford, 1988—; artistic dir. Conn. Student Performing Arts Festival, Middletown, 1988-95. Author: Three Hairs From The Devil's Beard and Other Tales, 1990 (Parents' Choice Gold award 1992, ALA Notable 1992). Trustee Old Lyme (Conn.) Phoebe Griffin Noyes Libr., pres., 1992-95; mem. adv. bd. Conn. Storytelling Ctr., pres., 1994-97. Avocations: sailing, skiing, flyfishing, flytying. Home and Office: PO Box 383 Old Lyme CT 06371-0383

HINSON, ROBERT WAYNE, education educator; b. Charlotte, N.C., Oct. 24, 1949; s. Selkirt Alexander and Sally (Helms) H.; m. Sandra Rowell (div. Aug. 1988); 1 child, Jennifer AnnaBeth; m. Linda Ritchie. BA in English, U. N.C., Charlotte, 1972, MEd in English Edn., 1986, CAS in English Edn., 1989; EdS in Ednl. Adminstrn., Winthrop Coll., 1989; PhD in English, Union Grad. Sch., Cin., 1993. Cert. sch. adminstr., postgrad. in ednl. adminstrn., prin., supr., secondary tchr., S.C. Tchr. English and reading Marlboro County Sch. Dist., Bennettsville, S.C., 1981-93; Charlotte (N.C.)-Meck Schs., 1993—; writing cons. Marlboro County Sch. Dist., Bennettsville, S.C., 1986—; prof. English and writing Wingate (N.C.) Coll., 1989—. Author: (poetry) Winds of the World, 1975, Fear Years, 1978, Route Reflections, 1986, Journal of Pauley's Island, 1987, (novella) Fairfield Plantation, 1982, Individual Therapy Journal Writing, 1989. Chmn. Union County Rep. Com., 1973; chmn. steering com. campaign for N.C. gov., 1974. Ednl. Found. Pee Dee grantee, 1988. Mem. N.C. English Tchrs. Assn., S.C. English Tchrs. Assn., North and S.C. Reading Assn., Palmetto State Tchrs. Assn., Writers Workshop Asheville (co-founder). Methodist. Avocation: writing. Home: 6238 Old Monroe Rd Indian Trail NC 28079-5343

HINZE, WILLIE LEE, chemistry educator, researcher; b. Burton, Tex., Jan. 17, 1949; s. Willie Lee Hugo and Alma (Tresseler) H.; m. Wen-wen Chu, Dec. 14, 1981. AA, Blinn Coll., 1969; BS, Sam Houston State U., 1970, MS, 1972; PhD, Tex. A&M U., 1974. Instr. chemistry Blinn Coll., Brenham, Tex., 1974-75; from asst. prof. to prof. chemistry Wake Forest U., Winston Salem, N.C., 1975—, chmn., 1990-94. Lectr. Tex. A&M U., College Station, 1974-75. Co-editor: Ordered Media in Chemical Separations, 1987; mem. editl. rev. bd. Jour. Liquid Chromatography, 1990—, Analytical Letters, 1991—, Talanta, 1996—, Jour. Undergrad. Chem. Rsch., 2002—; contbr. articles to profl. jours. NIH fellow, 1974-75; grantee NSF, Rsch. Corp., Petroleum Rsch. Fund, Sigma Xi, N.C. Biotech. Ctr., N.C. Bd. Sci. and Tech., N.C. Waters Resources Rsch. Inst., NIH. Fellow Royal Soc. Chemistry; mem. Am. Chem. Soc., Am. Inst. Chemists (cert.), Assn. Ofcl. Analytical Chemists, Sigma Xi. Lutheran. Office: Wake Forest U Dept Chemistry Winston Salem NC 27109

HINZMAN, SUSAN EMMONS, retired elementary school educator; b. Balt., June 30, 1938; d. Clinton Smallwood and Marie Emmons (Lewis) Archer; m. Jerry Hinzman, Feb. 1, 1986. AA, Va. Intermont Coll., 1958; BA, Mary Washington Coll., Fredericksburg, Va., 1960; MEd, Towson State U., Balt., 1973. Cert. tchr., Va. Elem. tchr. Prince Georges County Pub. Schs., Upper Marlboro, Md., 1967-73, Harford County Pub. Schs., Bel Air, Md., 1964-67; elem. tchr. environ. sci. Fairfax County Pub. Schs., Fairfax, Va., 1974—93, lead tchr. sci., 1990—93; ret., 1993. Recipient tchr. recognition award Fairfax County, 1987; Impact II grantee. Mem. Phi Delta Kappa. Home: 9306 Fernwood Rd Bethesda MD 20817-2341

HIRASAKI, GEORGE JIRO, chemical engineer, educator; b. Beaumont, Tex., Sept. 26, 1939; s. Tokuzo and Toki (Kishi) H. BSChemE with honors, Lamar U., 1963; PhDChemE, Rice U., 1967. With Shell Devel. Co., Houston, 1967-93; A.J. Hartsook prof. in chem. engrg. Rice U., Houston, 1993—. Prof. Rice U., Houston, 1993—. Contbr. articles to profl. jours.; patentee in field. Mem. NAE, Am. Chem. Soc., AIChE, Soc. Petroleum Engrs. (Lester C. Uren award 1989), Soc. Core Analysts, SIAM. Avocations: windsurfing, skiing, mountaineering. Office: Rice U Dept Chem Engring 6100 Main St Houston TX 77005-1892

HIRATSUKA, YUJI, artist, educator; b. Osaka, Japan, Sept. 7, 1954; came to U.S., 1985; s. Toshio and Kameyo (Tsumura) H.; m. Priscilla L. Hiratsuka, Dec. 30, 1989; children: Hana Gabriella, Toshio Alan. BS, Tokyo Gakngei U., 1978; MA, N.Mex. State U., 1987; MFA, Ind. U., 1990. Vis. asst. prof. Colo. Coll., Colorado Springs, 1990-92; assoc. prof. art Oreg. State U., Corvallis, 1992—. Vis. instr. Pacific N.W. Coll. of Art, Portland, Oreg., 1994—; instr. summer workshops Sitka Ctr. Art & Ecology, Otis, Oreg., 1997—; printmaker, lectr. Recipient numerous art competition awards. Mem. Calif. Soc. Printmakers, Print Consortium. Home: 1215 NW Kline Pl Corvallis OR 97330-2914 Office: Oreg State U Dept Art Corvallis OR 97331-3702

HIRES, CLAUDIA MANIGAULT, retired elementary school educator; b. Leesburg, Fla., Dec. 29, 1947; d. Claudius J. and Lois Hettie (Wade) Manigault; m. Edison E. Hires, Aug. 2, 1969; children: Andrea D., Angela D. BS, Fla. A&M U., 1967; MEd, U. Cen. Fla., 1983. Cert. tchr., Fla. Kindergarten and elem. tchr. Lake County Sch. Bd., Tavares, Fla.; elem. tchr. Orange County Sch. Bd., Orlando, Fla., curriculum resource tchr., 1991-93; instrnl. support team tchr., early childhood Elem. Edn. Dept., Orlando, 1991-95. Support svc. coord. Catalina Elem. Sch., 1995-97; reading facilitator Success for All, 1997-2001; adminstrv. team leader and reading coord., 2002—03. Named Tchr. of Yr., Pineloch Elem. Sch., Orlando, 1988; named Tchr. of Yr., Catalina Elem. Sch., 1998-99. Mem. NEA, Fla. Teaching Profession, Orange County Tchrs. Assn., Kappa Delta Pi, Delta Sigma Theta. Home: 3521 Domino Dr Orlando FL 32805-2960 Office: Catalina Elem Sch 2510 Gulfstream Rd Orlando FL 32805

HIROKAWA, BARBARA ANNE, art educator; b. Ft. Dix, N.J., Oct. 18, 1945; d. Andrew S. and Mary Helen (Nykaza) Gall; children: Christopher Perry, Derek Perry. BS, Butler U., 1968; MA, U. Colo., 1973. Cert. tchr. art edn. K-12. Tchr. Lawrence (Ind.) Twp. Schs., 1968-71, Jefferson County Schs., Golden, Colo., 1972—2001, ret., 2002—. Mem. Colo. visual art standards task force Colo. Dept. of Edn., Denver, 1994-95; curriculum writer Jefferson County Pub. Schs., Golden, 1989. Photographic exhbns. numerous local and state juried shows, 1980—. Advisor Cherry Creek Art Festival, Denver, 1991, Denver Art Mus.-All About Art, 1993; exec. bd.

dirs. arts resource coun. Denver Pub. Schs., 1991—; sec. class of 67 St. Mary of the Woods (Ind.) Coll., 1991—. Named Colo. Art Educator of Yr., 2000, Pacific Region Art Educator of Yr., 2002; Summer Art Inst. grantee Alliance of Ind. Colls. of Art, 1986, grantee Nat. Art Edn. Found., 1990. Mem. Nat. Art Edn. Assn. (photography exhibitor Electronic Gallery 1993, Marion Quinn Div. Leadership award 1991), Colo. Art Edn. Assn. (v.p., rep. 1980-99, dir. profl. art resource team 1987-94), Photo Imaging Edn. Assn. (exec. bd. dirs., treas. 1992-95), Art Source (bd. dirs. 2000—). Home: 3144 W 26th Ave Denver CO 80211-4031 Office: Columbine H S 6201 S Pierce St Littleton CO 80123-3636 E-mail: bhirokaw@jeffco12.co.us.

HIROSE, TERUO TERRY, surgeon, educator; b. Tokyo, Jan. 20, 1926; s. Yohei and Seiko (Ogushi) H.; m. Tomiko Kodama, June 1, 1976; 1 son, George Philamore. BS, Tokyo Coll., Japan, 1944; MD, Chiba U., Japan, 1948, PhD, 1958. Diplomate Am. Bd. Surgery, Am. Bd. Thoracic Surgery. Intern Chiba U. Hosp., Japan, 1948-49, resident in surgery, 1949-52; practice medicine specializing in surgery Chiba, Japan, 1952-53; resident in surgery Am. Hosp., Chgo., 1954; resident in thoracic surgery Hahnemann Med. Coll., Phila., 1955-56; chief of surgery Tsushimi Hosp., Hagi, Japan, 1958-59; tchg. fellow surgery NY Med. Coll., NYC, 1959-60; research fellow advanced cardiovascular surgery Hahnemann Hosp., Phila., 1959; asst. prof. surgery Chiba U., Japan, 1959; instr. NY Med. Coll., NYC, 1961-62, resident in thoracic surgery, 1961-62; sr. attending surgeon St. Barnabas Hosp., NYC, 1965-81; pvt. practice NYC, 1965-89, 1965-89; chief vascular surgery Union Hosp., Bronx, NY, 1966-67; attending surgeon Flower and Fifth Ave Hosp., NYC, 1973-80; clin. prof. surgery NY Med. Coll., NY, 1974-89; dir. cardiovasc. lab. St. Barnabas Hosp., NYC, 1975-84; attending surgeon Jewish Hosp. Med. Center, Bklyn., 1976-80, St. Vincent Hosp., NYC, 1976-88, Mamonides Hosp., Bklyn., 1976-78, Passaic Gen. Hosp., 1977-88, Westchester County Hosp., NY, 1977-78, Yonkers Profl. Hosp., NY, 1978-79, Westchester Sq. Hosp., 1978-84, Yonkers Gen. Hosp., Yonkers, NY, 1980-89, St. Joseph Hosp., Yonkers, NY, 1980-89; dir. KPMG Health Care, Japan, 1997—2001; chmn., prof. dept. head, health care admin. Shumei U., Tokyo, 1999; chmn., pres. Japanese Assn. for Healthcare Adminstrs., 2002—. Author: (in Japanese) A Chaos of American Medicine, 1987, Japanese Doctor, 1987, Where American Medicine Is Going, 1988, Major Surgery Without Blood Transfusion, 1990, Problems and Solutions of American Medicine, 1991, Warning for Modern Medical Science (New Medical Ethics), 1992, Comparative Studies of Medical System in the World, 1992, The Changing Face of Geriatrics, 1994, Monologue of Japanese American Physician, 1995, Environmental Medicine, 1998, Japan! Do Not Follow American Health Care System, 1998, Quality of Life in Modern Medicine, 1998, Medicine About Life and Death, 1998, 99, Why AIDS Can Not Be Conquered, 1999, Mechanism of Human Body, 2000, Comparison of Healthcare Systems Between U.S.A. and Japan, 2000, Medicine of Death, 2000, Lifestyle Related Medicine and Cutting Edge Technique, 2001, Alternative Medicine, 2001, Thanatology, 2000, Protect Japanese Health Care System By Health Care Reform, 2002, Basic and Practice of Health Care Administration, 2002, Better Understanding of Physician and Hospital, 2003; author 10 med. monographs, 1968-80; editor Japanese Med. Planner Ltd.; contbr. over 900 articles to profl. jours. Recipient Hektoen Bronze medal AMA, 1965, Gold medal, 1971. Fellow: NY Acad. Medicine, Internat. Coll. Surgeons, Am. Coll. Cardiology, Am. Coll. Chest Physicians, Am. Coll. Angiology; mem.: Japanese Assn. Health Care Admnis. (chmn., pres.), Japan PEN Club, Am. Writers Assn., Am. Fedn. Clin. Rsch., Am. Geriatric Soc., Internat. Cardiovasc. Soc., Pan Pacific Surg. Assn., NY Soc. Thoracic Surgery, Am. Assn. Thoracic Surgery. Achievements include invention of single pass low prime oxygenator; pioneer aortocoronary direct bypass surgery, open heart surgery without blood transfusion.

HIRSCH, ANN ULLMAN, retired academic administrator; b. N.Y.C., Feb. 12, 1929; d. Julian S. and Louise (Levien) Ullman; m. James E. Galton, Aug. 22, 1948 (div. 1962); children: Beth, Jean; m. David I. Hirsch, Mar. 22, 1963; stepchildren: Peter, Amanda. BS, NYU, 1950; postgrad., Queens Coll., Flushing, N.Y., 1955-57. Music tchr. Herricks (N.Y.) Sch., 1950-52, East Meadow (N.Y.) Pub. Schs., 1952-53; exec. dir. Ea. Suffolk Sch. Music, Riverhead/Southampton, N.Y., 1977-88. Self-employed piano tchr., N.Y., 1950-95; dir. music edn. Unitarian Sunday Sch., Freeport, N.Y., 1956-63; singer Oratorio Socs., Levittown and Bridgehampton, N.Y., 1950-85, L.I. Philharm. Chorus, Westbury, N.Y., 1989—; violinist Sound Symphony, Shoreham, Wading River, N.Y., 1980—, orch. pianist, 1980—. Author: Basic Guide to the Teaching of Piano, 1974. Mem. Arts in Edn. Task Force, BOCES, Westhampton, NY, 1977—87; planning mem., panelist Nat. Guild Cmty. Schs. of the Arts, 1980—88; tchr. Literacy Vols. Am., Riverhead, Mastic, NY, 1988—91; bd. mem. LI Masterworks Chorus, Commack, NY, 1992—2000. Named East End Woman of Yr. in Edn., East End Mag., Suffolk County, N.Y., 1979. Mem.: LWV, Southampton Twp. Wildfowl Assn., Bay Area Friends of the Fine Arts, Westhampton Beach Hist. Soc., Peconic Land Trust. Avocations: reading, sewing, walking, golfing, photography. Home: PO Box 304 Remsenburg NY 11960-0304

HIRSCH, BARBARA, school administrator; b. Orange, N.J., Mar. 27, 1943; d. Lee Leon and Abby Isabel (Parker) H. BS, Fairleigh Dickinson U., Rutherford, N.J., 1965, MA, 1971. Tchr. Nutley (N.J.) Pub. Schs., 1965-71, learning cons., 1971-79, dir. spl. svcs., 1980—. Adj. prof. edn. N.J. City State U., 1969-82, Montclair State U. Author: (manuals) Math Lab - Hierarchy of Math Skills, 1975, A Modular Curriculum for Trainable Children, 1980. Bd. dirs. Nutley Family Svcs. Bur.; county committee woman Newark, N.J., 1988—; chmn. Gov.'s Mcpl. Alliance, Nutley, 1991-93. Recipient Disting. Svc. award Nutley Jaycees, 1983, Innovative Leadership award Boy Scouts Am., 1990, Handicapped Com. award Elks, 1993. Mem. AAUW, Coun. for Exceptional Children, N.J. Assn. for Gifted and Talented, N.J. Prins. and Suprs.Assn., Essex County Dirs. Spl. Svcs. (chair 1983-84, 88-90), Nutley Adminstrs. Assn. (treas.), Essec County Gifted Consortium (sec. bd. dirs.), Hadassah (life, pres. 1990-92), Rotary (sgt.-at-arms 1994-95, Rotarian of the Yr. 1993, pres. 1996). Democrat. Jewish. Avocations: reading, gardening, golf. Home: 477 Washington Ave Nutley NJ 07110-3607 Office: Nutley Public Schools 300 Franklin Ave Nutley NJ 07110-2252 E-mail: bhirsch@nutleyschools.org.

HIRSCH, BETTE G(ROSS), college administrator, foreign language educator; b. N.Y.C., May 5, 1942; d. Alfred E. and Gladys (Netburn) Gross; m. Edward Raden Silverblatt, Aug. 16, 1964 (div. Feb. 1975); children: Julia Nadine, Adam Edward; m. Joseph Ira Hirsch, Jan. 21, 1978; stepchildren: Hillary, Michelle, Michael. BA with honors, U. Rochester, 1964; MA, Case Western Res. U., 1967, PhD, 1971. Instr. and head French dept. Cabrillo Coll., Aptos, Calif., 1973-90, 2003—, divsn. chair fgn. langs. and comms. divsn., 1990-95, interim dir. student devel., 1995-96, dean of instrn., transfer and distance edn., 1996—2003. Mem. steering com. Santa Cruz County Fgn. Lang. Educators Assn., 1981-86; mem. liaison com. fgn. langs. Articulation Coun. Calif., 1982-84, sec., 1983-84, chmn., 1984-85; workshop presenter, 1982—; vis. prof. French Mills Coll., Oakland, Calif., 1983; mem. fgn. lang. model curriculum stds. adv. com. State Calif., 1984; instr. San Jose (Calif.) State U., summers 1984, 85; reader Ednl. Testing Svc. Advanced Placement French Examination, 1988, 89; peer reviewer for div. edn. programs, NEH, Washington, 1990, 91, 93; grant evaluator, NEH, 1995; mem. fgn. lang. adv. bd. The Coll. Bd., N.Y.C., 1986-91. Author: The Maxims in the Novels of Duclos, 1973; co-author (with Chantal Thompson) Ensuite, 1989, 93, 98, 2003, Moments Litteraires, 1992 (with Chantal Thompson and Elaine Phillips) Mais Oui! workbook, lab. manual, video manual, 1996, 2000; contbr. revs. and articles to profl. jours. Pres. Loma Vista Elem. Sch. PTA, Palo Alto, Calif., 1978-79; bd. dirs. United Way Stanford, Palo Alto, 1985-90, mem. allocations com., 1988, bd. dirs. Cabrillo Music Festival, 1996—, sec., 1998, v.p., 2000-2002; bd. dirs. Cmty. TV of Santa Cruz County, 1997-99, vice chair, 1997-98. Grantee NEH, 1980-81, USIA, 1992; Govt. of France scholar, 1982, 2003. Mem.: MLA (mem. adv. com. on fgn. langs. and lits. 1995—2000, chair 1999—2000, com. on info. tech. 2001—, chair 2003—), Assn. Depts. Fgn. Langs. (exec. com. 1985—88, pres. 1988), Assn. Calif. C.C. Adminstrs. Democrat. Jewish. Avocations: traveling, reading, antique collecting, gourmet eating and cooking. Home: 4149 Georgia Ave Palo Alto CA 94306-3813 Office: Cabrillo College 6500 Soquel Dr Aptos CA 95003-3194 E-mail: behirsch@cabrillo.edu.

HIRSCH, CALLIE CLARK, instructional facilitator; b. Memphis, Oct. 15, 1951; d. Wallace Jr. and Ossie Nell (Pugh) Clark; m. Arnett Sebastian Hirsch Jr. (dec. Oct. 1983); children: Wayne Morris, Sean. BS in Sociology, LeMoyne-Owen Coll., Memphis, 1976; MEd, Memphis State U., 1978. Mental health trainee N.E. Mental Health Ctr., Memphis, 1975-76; tchr. Memphis City Schs., 1978-95, instrnl. facilitator, 1995—. Program coord. Jackson Sch., Memphis, 1983-88; chairperson Leadership Coun., Memphis, 1994-95; staff devel. chairperson A.B. Hill Sch., Memphis, 1995—, lead staffer, 1997; fashion model Ebony Bridal Showcase, 1992—. Cub Scout leader Boy Scouts Am., 1997; vol. Memphis Interfaith Assn., 1992; coord. City Beautiful, Memphis, 1996; rep. Pan Hellenic Coun., Memphis, 1997. Recipient Svc. award Memphis Edn. Assn., 1987, Plaque, Jr. Achievement, Memphis, 1994; named Zeta of Yr., Zeta Phi Beta, Memphis, 1983. Mem. Tenn. Ednl. Assn. (rep. 1979—, Svc. award 1997), bd. dirs. MANDCO. Avocations: canoeing, hiking, horseback riding, reading, skeet shooting. Home: 1820 Fairmeade Ave Memphis TN 38114-5814 also: 1560 Florida St Memphis TN 38109-1902

HIRSCH, ERIC DONALD, JR., English language educator, educational reformer; b. Memphis, Mar. 22, 1928; s. Eric Donald and Leah (Aschaffenburg) H.; m. Mary Monteith Pope, June 15, 1958; children: Eric, John, Frederick, Elizabeth. BA, Cornell U., 1950; MA, Yale U., 1955, PhD (Fulbright fellow), 1957; LittD (hon.), Williams Coll., 1989, Rhodes Coll., 1993, Rollins Coll., 1994, Marietta Coll., 1997. Instr. Yale, 1956-61, asst. prof. English, 1961-64, assoc. prof., 1964-66; prof. U. Va., Charlottesville, 1966—, chmn. dept. English, 1968-71, 81-83, dir. composition, 1971—, Kenan prof. English, 1973—, Linden Kent prof. English, 1989-94, Univ. prof. edn. and humanities, 1994; founder, pres. Core Knowledge Found., Charlottesville, 1986—. Bd. dirs. U. Press; lectr. in field; supervising com. English Inst., 1972-74; mem. nat. adv. coun. N.Y. Regent's Competency Tests in Writing, 1979; advisor Nat. Coun. Ednl. Rsch., 1983; bd. dirs. Founds. Literacy Project, 1985—; pres. Cultural Literacy Found., 1987, Core Knowledge Found., 1990; dir. Albert Shanker Inst., 1997—. Author: Wordsworth and Schelling: A Typological Study of Romanticism, 1960, Innocence and Experience: An Introduction to Blake, 1964 (Explicator award), Validity in Interpretation, 1967, The Aims of Interpretation, 1976, The Philosophy of Composition, 1977, Cultural Literacy: What Every American Needs to Know, 1987; co-author: A Dictionary of Cultural Literacy, 1988; editor: A First Dictionary of Cultural Literacy, 1989, The Core Knowledge Series, Book I: What First Graders Need to Know, 1991, Book II: What Second Graders Need to Know, 1991, Book III: What Third Graders Need to Know, 1992, Book IV: What Fourth Graders Need to Know, 1992, Book V: What Fifth Graders Need to Know, 1993, Book VI: What Sixth Graders Need to Know, 1993, The Schools We Need and Why We Don't Have Them, 1996; mem. adv. bd. Jour. Basic Writing, Blake Studies, Critical Inquiry, Genre New Lit. History, Lit. in Performance; contbr. articles to profl. jours. Pres. Coalition for Core Curriculum, 1989—. Served with USNR, 1950-52. Recipient Fordham award 2003; Morse fellow, 1961-62, Guggenheim fellow, 1964-65, sr. fellow NEH, 1971, 80-81, fellow Center for Humanities Wesleyan U., 1973, fellow Council Humanities Princeton U., 1976, fellow Center for Advanced Study in Behavioral Scis., 1980-81, fellow Humanities Research Ctr., Australian Nat. U., 1982; Bateson lectr. Oxford U., 1983 Fellow Internat. Acad. Edn. in Royal Acad. Sci. Lit. and Arts (Brussels); mem. Am. Acad. Arts and Scis. (supervisory com. 1981-86), MLA, Byron Soc., Am. Fedn. Tchrs. (Biennial Quest award 1997). Home: 2006 Pine Top Rd Charlottesville VA 22903-1233 E-mail: edh9k@virginia.edu.

HIRSCH, LEDA TRESKUNOFF, elementary school educator; b. New Haven, Oct. 3, 1929; d. Abraham D. and Anna B. (Brainin) Treskunoff; m. Donald R. Hirsch, June 8, 1952; 1 child, Judith Nancy. BA, Conn. Coll., 1951, MA, 1963; PhD, U. Conn., 1981. Cert. elem. tchr., adminstr., Conn. Evaluator Priority SSch. Dist., New London, Conn.; tchr., head tchr. New London Bd. Edn. Pres. Child Guidance Clinic SE Conn. Mem. ASCD, Phi Delta Kappa, Delta Kappa Gamma. Home: 16032 Lomond Hills Tr Apt 136 Delray Beach FL 33446-3129

HIRSCH, PAUL J. orthopedist, surgeon, medical executive, educator, editor; b. Bklyn., Oct. 12, 1937; s. Morris M. and Dorothy (Wolitzer) H.; 1 child, Jeremy S. BA in English, Roanoke Coll., 1957; MD, U. Va., 1961. Diplomate Am. Bd. Orthopedic Surgery. Intern NYU-Bellevue Med. Ctr., N.Y.C., 1961-62, resident, 1964-68; chief orthop. surgery Raritan Valley Hosp., Green Brook, N.J., 1969-71; pvt. practice orthop. surgery Bridgewater, N.J., 1971—; clin. prof. orthop. surgery Seton Hall Sch. Grad. Med. Edn. Vice chmn., bd. dirs. MIIX Group, Inc.; pres., med. dir. InterMedix, Lawrenceville, N.J.; emeritus staff, orthop. svc. Somerset (N.J.) Med. Ctr.; courtesy staff Robert Wood Johnson U. Hosp., New Brunswick, N.J.; clin. asst. prof. orthop surgery Rutgers Med. Sch., 1971-79; clin. instr. orthop. surgery NYU-Bellevue Med. Ctr., 1969-79; clin. assoc. prof. orthop. surgery N.J. Med. Sch., 1980—; clin. prof. orthop. surgery Seton Hall Sch. Postgrad. Medicine; chmn., bd. trustees Jour. Bone and Joint Surgery, 1999; mem. practicing physicians adv. group Nat. Com. Quality Assurance, 1996-98. Chmn. publs. com. Jour. Med. Soc. N.J., 1980-85; contbr. articles, editor profl. jours.,; mem. editl. bd. N.J. Medicine; editor-in-chief N.J. Medicine. Chmn. N.J. Com. for Quality Orthop. Care; trustee Rutgers Prep. Sch., pres. bd. trustees, 1983—86; trustee Raritan Valley C.C., 1986—; bd. dirs. N.J. Med. Polit. Action Com., 1983—; bd. trustees Orthop. Rsch. and Edn. Found., 1989—94. Mem.: N.J. State Med. Underwriters, Inc. (bd. dirs. 1990—99, vice chmn. bd. dirs. 1991—99), Med. Inter-Ins. Exch. N.J. (bd. govs. 1987—90), Ind. Sch. Chmn. Assn., N.J. Assn. Med. Splty. Socs. (pres. 1979—80, dir. 1981—85), N.J. Hosp. Assn. (trustee 1986—89), N.J. Health Scis. Group (treas. 1982—83), Internat. Soc. Orthop. Surgery and Traumatology, Am. Trauma Soc. (pres. ctrl. Jersey unit 1977—81), Acad. Medicine of N.J. (chmn. orthop. sect. 1975—78, trustee 1978—91, pres.-elect 1982—83, pres. 1983—84), Somerset County Med. Soc. (bd. trustees), Med. Soc. N.J. (chmn. orthop. sect. 1977—78, ho. of dels. 1976—, treas. 1982—86, 2d v.p. 1986—87, 1st v.p. 1987—88, pres.-elect 1988—89, pres. 1989—90, trustee 1982—91), N.J. Orthop. Soc. (pres. 1979—80), Ea. Orthop. Assn. (trustee 1981—84), Am. Coll. Physician Execs., Am. Acad. Orthop. Surgeons (bd. councilors 1982—88), Am. Orthop. Assn., AMA, ACS. Office: Green Knoll Profl Park #720 US Hwy 202-206 Bridgewater NJ 08807-1746

HIRSCH, ROBERT W. sales executive, consultant; b. Bklyn., Aug. 15, 1939; s. Sam B. and Ruth (Kruger) H.; m. Elizabeth Louise Ziegler, Jan. 28, 1961; children: Steven Michael, Deborah Lynn (dec.), Charles Andrew. B of Chem. Engring., CCNY, 1960; postgrad., Northwestern U., 1960-61, Louis B. Allen Sch. Bus. Mgmt., 1973. Registered profl. engr., Tex. Engr. Union Carbide Corp., Tonawanda, N.Y., 1961-68, Dusseldorf, Germany, 1961-68, tech. sales rep. Houston, 1968-70, regional sales mgr. adsorbents and catalysts San Francisco, 1970-73, regional mgr. environ. systems, 1973-79, product mgr. Tonawanda, 1980; regional sales mgr. Chem. Waste Mgmt. Co., Newark, Calif., 1980-86; v.p., then sr. v.p. Chemfix Techs., Inc., Metairie, La., 1986-90; pres. Chemfix Internat. subs. Chemfix Techs., Metairie, La., 1986-90; v.p. mktg. and sales Envirosafe Mgmt. Svcs., Inc., Valley Forge, Pa., 1990-91; v.p. bus. devel. The Parsons Corp., Valley Forge, Pa., 1991-97; engring. cons., 1973-80; regional dir. mktg. Harding Lawson Assocs., 1998. Speaker, seminar presenter to Am. Inst. Chem. Engrs., ASCE, Am. Chem. Soc., Water Pollution Control Fedn., 1973-80. Contbr. articles to profl. jours. Home: 525 Brights Ln Blue Bell PA 19422-1141

HIRSCHMAN, ALBERT OTTO, political economist, educator; b. Berlin, Apr. 7, 1915; s. Carl and Hedwig (Marcuse) H.; m. Sarah Chapiro, June 22, 1941; children: Catherine Jane, Elisabeth Nicole (dec. 1999). Student, U. Sorbonne, Paris, Hautes Etudes Commerciales, London Sch. Econs., 1933-36; D in Econs. Sci., U. Trieste, 1938; hon. degree, Rutgers U., 1978, U. So. Calif., 1986, U. Turin, Italy, 1987, New Sch. for Social Rsch., 1988, Free U. of Berlin, 1988, U. Paris, 1989, U. Buenos Aires, 1989, U. Campinas, Brazil, 1990, Georgetown U., 1990, Yale U., 1990, U. Trier, Germany, 1990, Santander, Spain, 1992, U. Coimbra, Portugal, 1993, U. Paris, Nanterre, France, 1993, Williams Coll., 1993, U. Naples, 1998, U. Complutense, Madrid, 2001, Harvard U., 2002; hon. (hon.), European U. Inst., Florence, 2002. Rockefeller fellow U. Calif., Berkeley, Calif., 1941-433; Economist Fed. Res. Bd., Washington, 1946-52; fin. adviser Nat. Planning Bd., Bogotá, Colombia, 1952-54; pvt. econ. cons. Bogotá, Colombia, 1954-56; research prof. econs. Yale U., 1956-58; prof. internat. econ. relations Columbia U., 1958-64; prof. polit. economy Harvard U., 1964-74, Littauer prof. polit. economy, 1967-74; prof. Inst. for Advanced Study, Princeton, 1974-85, prof. emeritus, 1985—, chair in econs., 2000. Fellow Ctr. Advanced Study Behavioral Scis., 1968-69; mem. Inst. for Advanced Study, 1972-73; fellow Wissenschaftskolleg zu Berlin, 1990-91. Author: National Power and the Structure of Foreign Trade, 1945, The Strategy of Economic Development, 1958, Journeys Toward Progress: Studies of Economic Policy-Making in Latin America, 1963, Devlopment Projects Observed, 1967, 2d edit., 1995, Exit, Voice, and Loyalty: Responses to Decline in Firms, Organizations and States, 1970, A Bias for Hope: Essays on Development and Latin America, 1971, The Passions and the Interests: Political Arguments for Capitalism Before Its Triumph, 1977, Essays in Trespassing: Economics to Politics and Beyond, 1981, Shifting Involvements: Private Interest and Public Action, 1982, Getting Ahead Collectively: Grassroots Experiences in Latin America, 1984, Rival Views of Market Society and Other Recent Essays, 1986, 2nd edit., 1992, The Rhetoric of Reaction: Perversity, Futility, Jeopardy, 1991, A Propensity to Self-Subversion, 1995, Crossing Boundaries: Selected Writings, 1998, paperback edit. 2001; editor Latin Am. Issues-Essays and Comments, 1961; contbr. articles to profl. jours. Served with AUS, 1943-45. Decorated Orden de San Carlos (Colombia), Nacional de Cruzecro do Sul, Brazil; recipient Frank E. Seidman Disting. award in polit. economy, 1980, Talcott Parsons prize for social sci., 1983, Kalman Silvert prize L.Am. Studies Assn., 1986, 1st prize for social sci. articles Fritz Thyssen Found., 1992, Toynbee prize, 1998. Fellow Am. Econ. Assn.; mem. NAS, Council Fgn. Relations, Am. Acad. Arts and Scis., Am. Philos. Soc. (Thomas Jefferson medal 1998); fgn. mem. Brit. Acad., Accademia Nazionale dei Lincei (Rome), Acad. Scis. Berlin-Brandenburg. Address: Inst for Advanced Study Princeton NJ 08540

HIRSCHMAN, CHARLES, JR., sociologist, educator; b. Atlanta, Nov. 29, 1943; s. Charles Sr. and Mary Gertrude (Mullee) H.; m. Josephine Knight, Jan. 29, 1968; children: Andrew Charles, Sarah Lynn. BA, Miami U., Oxford, Ohio, 1965; MS, U. Wis., 1969, PhD, 1972. Vol. Peace Corps, Malaysia, 1965-67; prof. Duke U., Durham, N.C., 1972-81, Cornell U., Ithaca, N.Y., 1981-87, U. Wash., Seattle, 1987—, chair dept. sociology, 1995-98, Boeing internat. prof., 1999—. Cons. Ford Found., Malaysia, 1974-75; chair social scis. and population study sect. NIH, Washington, 1987-91; vis. scholar Russell Sage Found., 1998-99. Author: Ethnic and Social Stratification in Peninsula Malaysia, 1975; editor: The Handbook of International Migration: The American Experience, 1999; contbr. articles to profl. jours. Fellow Ctr. Advanced Study in the Behavioral Scis., Stanford, Calif., 1993-94. Fellow AAAS (chair-elect sect. K on social, econs. and polit. scis. 2003—), Am. Acad. for Arts and Scis.; mem. Assn. for Asian Studies (bd. dirs. 1987-90), Population Assn Am. (bd. dirs. 1992-94, v.p. 1997). Office: U Wash Dept Sociology PO Box 353340 Seattle WA 98195-3340 E-mail: charles@u.washington.edu.

HIRSH, CRISTY J. principal; b. Dallas, Oct. 3, 1952; d. Bernard and Johanna (Cristol) H. BS in Early Childhood and Elem. Edn., Boston U., 1974; MS in Spl. Edn., U. Tex., Dallas, 1978; MEd in Counseling and Student Svcs., U. North Tex., 1991. Cert. counselor, sch. counselor; lic. profl. counselor, Tex.; cert. tchr., Tex., Mass.; cert. prin., Tex. Dir., learning specialist Specialized Learning, Dallas, 1981-93; counselor, mem. adj. faculty Eastfield Coll., Mesquite, Tex., 1992-95; counselor Grapevine (Tex.)-Colleyville Ind. Sch. Dist., 1995-2000, alternative sch. prin., 2000—. Mem. adj. faculty Richland Coll., Dallas, 1991—92. Mem. ACA, ASCD, Am. Sch. Counselor Assn., Coun. for Exceptional Children, Coun. for Children with Behavior Disorders, Tex. Assn. for Alternative Edn., Pi Lambda Theta, Phi Delta Kappa. Avocations: travel, theater, film, cooking, reading. Office: VISTA Alternative Campus 3051 Ira E Woods Ave Grapevine TX 76051-3817

HISEY, LYDIA VEE, educational administrator; b. Memphis, Tex., July 10, 1951; d. Murray Wayne Latimer and Jane Kathryn (Grimsley) Webster; m. Gregory Lynn Hisey, Oct. 4, 1975; children: Kathryn Elizabeth, Jennifer Kay, Anna Elaine. BS in Edn., Tex. Tech U., 1974, MEd, 1990. Cert. tchr., mid-mgmt., Tex.x. Tchr. phys. edn. Lubbock (Tex.) Ind. Sch. Dist., 1975-79, tchr., 1982-91, asst. prin., 1991-95, prin., 1995-2000, assoc. H.S. prin., 2000. Recipient Way-To-Go award Lubbock Ind. Sch. Dist., 1989, Impact II grantee, 1991. Mem. Tex. Assn. Secondary Sch. Prins., Tex. Elem. Prins. and Suprs. Assn., Lubbock Elem. Prins. and Suprs. Assn. (v.p. 1997-98, pres. 1998-99), Delta Kappa Gamma, Phi Delta Kappa. Baptist. Avocation: gardening. Home: 4417 87th St Lubbock TX 79424-4231 E-mail: veehisey@lubbock.k12.tx.us.

HISKES, DOLORES G. language educator; b. Chgo. d. Leslie R. and Dagmar (Brown) Grant; m. John R. Hiskes; children: Robin Caproni, Grant. Student, U. Ill., Chgo. Tutoring programs cons.; presenter in field. Author, illustrator: Phonics Pathways, Pyramid, The Short-Vowel Dictionary; developer ednl. games: The Train Game, Blendit!, Wordworks. Mem. Assn. Am. Educators, Assn. Ednl. Therapists, Calif. Assn. of Res. Specilaists, Orton Dyslexia Soc., Learning Disabilities Assn., Nat. Right to Read Found., The Calif. Reading Assn., Pubs. Mktg. Assn., Calif. Watercolor Soc., Commonwealth Club of Calif., Bay Area Ind. Pubs. Assn. Avocations: watercolors, travel, reading, exercise. Office: Dorbooks PO Box 2588 Livermore CA 94551-2588 E-mail: dor@dorbooks.com.

HISLE, LINDA BETH See FRYE, LINDA BETH

HITCH, CHRIS DOOLEY, principal; b. Richmond, Va., June 22, 1959; s. C. Dooley and Elizabeth (Wilson) H.; m. April Metot, July 23, 1983; children: David, Sarah. BA, Austin Coll., 1981, MA, 1982; PhD, U. N.C., 1990. Tchr. Tyler (Tex.) Ind. Sch. Dist., 1982-85, Wake County Schs., Raleigh, N.C., 1985-87, math. cons., 1987-89, asst. prin., 1989-90; prin. Forsyth County Schs., Winston-Salem, N.C., 1990—. Recipient Love Teaching award, 1981; Engleman scholar AASA, 1988-89; King fellow Austin Coll., 1981. Home: 107 Lulworth Ct Apex NC 27502-6652 Office: Forsyth County Schs Speas Elem Sch 2000 Polo Rd Winston Salem NC 27106-4547

HITCHCOCK, LILLIAN DOROTHY STAW, speech and English educator, actress, artist; b. Detroit, Dec. 19, 1922; d. Charles Stawowczyk And Mary Waligora; m. Richard Elmer Hitchcock, June 28, 1952; children: Charles, Harriet, Roger, Stephen. BA in Edn., Wayne State U., 1946, MA in Interpretative Speech, 1952; postgrad., U. Wis., 1948; cert. in art, Inst. for Am. Univs., Avignon, France, 1981; cert. in French, Cath. U. Paris, 1983;

postgrad., Inst. for Am. Univs., Aix-en-Provence, France, 1991. Speech and English tchr. Lakeview High Sch., St. Claire Shores, Mich., 1947-49; speech and journalism tchr. Mercy Coll., Detroit, 1949-52; substitute tchr. in speech and English Birmingham (Mich.) Pub. Schs., 1960-88; speech and English tchr. Bloomfield Hills (Mich.) Pub. Schs., Detroit Pub. Schs., 1960-70; tchr. French, Montessori Sch., Bloomfield Hills, 1988—. Performer, dir. Civic Theatre, Wayne State U., Cath. Theatre, Detroit, 1943-46; chmn. Detroit Theatre Olympiade for World Cmty. Theatre, 1979; mem. St. Dunstan's Theatre, Bloomfield Hills; docent Cranbrook Mus. Modern Art, Bloomfield Hills, 1988—; adj. instr. speech Oakland C.C., Mich., 1998; performer Mercy Theatre, Greece, 2002. Performer Festival Original One-Act Plays, Ann Arbor, Mich., 1994, 98, Detroit film yard movie Loopholes, 1998, Rock n' Roll Lystristrata, U. Detroit-Mercy Theatre Co., 2002. Del. People to People-Health Care, China, 1984. Mem. AAUW (bd. dirs. children's theatre Birmingham 1960-80), UN rep. and del. 1970-73), Tuesday Musicale. Mem. Internat. Platform Assn. (1st Place and Silver Bowl award 1994), Birmingham Cultural coun. Roman Catholic. Home: 6140 Westmoor Rd Bloomfield Hills MI 48301-1355

HITCHCOCK, SUSAN Y. school administrator, city council member; b. South Gate, Calif., Oct. 3, 1948; d. Ralph Wayne and Evelyn Angela Hitchcock; m. David Michael Akin, July 21, 1972 (div. 1989); 1 child, David Michael Akin Jr.; m. Jerry Lee Glenn, July 1, 1995. BS in Bus. Adminstrn., Calif. State U., Sacramento, 1979; MA in Edn., U. Pacific, 1997. Cert. tchr., adminstr. Calif., adminstrv. svcs. credential Calif. Loan officer Bank of Am. NT&SA, Mountain View, Calif., 1967-74; tchr. St. Anne Sch., Lodi, Calif., 1981-92, Lodi Mid. Sch., 1992-97, Morado Middle Sch., 1997—99, vice prin., 1999—2001; prin. Clairmont Elem. Sch., Stockton, 2001—. Spkr. on urban land use planning League Calif. Cities, Sacramento, 1985-95. Mem. City Coun., City of Lodi, 1998—, planning commr., 1981-95, Mayor, 2002—; grand juror San Joaquin County, Stockton, 1979-80. Mem. AAUW (pres.). Roman Catholic. Avocation: travel. Home: 2443 Macarthur Pkwy Lodi CA 95242-3252 Office: Clairmont Elem Sch 8282 LeMans Ave Stockton CA 95210

HITCHMAN, CAL MCDONALD, SR., secondary education educator; b. Houston, July 9, 1948; s. Robert McDonald and Isabel Mary (Shugert) H.; 1 child, Cal McDonald Jr. BA, Houston Bapt. U., 1972. Cert. vocat./tech. edn. mktg. Tex. Auditor, pers. adminstr., tng. coord. Rice Food Markets, Inc., Houston, 1968-76; tchr., coord. Houston (Tex.) Ind. Sch. Dist., Sterling High Sch., 1976-80; dir. edn. Airco Tech. Inst., Houston, 1980-81; tchr., coord. Houston (Tex.) Ind. Sch. Dist., Sterling High Sch., 1981-91, Houston (Tex.) Ind. Sch. Dist., Sam Houston High Sch., 1991—. Adj. prof. U. Houston, 1997—; curriculum writer U. Tex., Austin. Named Outstanding Young Men of Am., 1975, 77. Mem. Am. Vocat. Assn., Mktg. Educators Tex., Mktg. Edn. Assn., DECA (profl. div.), DECA Tex. Assn. (dist. dir. mktg. edn. 1990—), sec., v.p. 1987-90), Metrodet, Tex. Adv. Coun. for Mktg. Edn./DECA, 1990— (chair 1995-96), Kappa Alpha Order. Methodist. Avocations: tennis, swimming, music, theatre. Home: 923 Gober St Houston TX 77017-4116 Office: Houston Ind Sch Dist Sam Houston H S 9400 Irvington Blvd Houston TX 77076-5224 E-mail: chitchmansr@aol.com.

HITE, JANET SUE, elementary education educator; b. Logansport, Ind., Feb. 22, 1948; d. Joseph William and Ruth Elizabeth (McVay) H. AA, Palomar Coll, San Marcos, Calif., 1968; BA in English, Pepperdine U., L.A., 1970; MA in Edn., Pepperdine U., Malibu, Calif., 1980. Cert. tchr. Calif., profl. adminstrv. svcs. Calif. Tchr. Graham Elem. Sch., L.A., 1971-75, 76-82, Uniontown (Ky.) Pub. Sch., 1975-76, Paseo del Rey Fundamental Magnet Sch., Playa del Rey, Calif., 1982-90, magnet sch. coord., 1990-94, magnet coord. Natural Sci. Magnet Sch., 1994-97; asst. prin. 186th St. Sch., Gardena, Calif., 1997—2001; prin. Chapman Elem. Sch., Gardena, 2001—. Master tchr. Pepperdine U., L.A., 1979-90; adj. prof. Loyola Marymount U., Westchester, Calif., 1993—; cons. program quality rev. team L.A. Unified Sch. Dist., 1993-95. Editor: Creative Writings, 1980. Co-founder, co-dir. Cultural and Urban Environ. Studies Inc., L.A., 1979-84; active San Dieguito United Meth. Ch. Grantee L.A. Ednl. Partnerships, 1983, 90, L.A. Unified Sch. Dist., 1984, City of Gardena, 2001, L.A. Unified Sch. Dist., 2001; recipient Red Apple award Tchr. Remembrance Day Found., 1972, Outstanding Tchr. of Yr. award Westchester C. of C., 1990. Mem. ASCD, Phi Delta Kappa (charter, Pepperdine chpt., newsletter editor 1979-80, treas. 1980-81, 3d v.p. 1981-82, 1st v.p. 1982-83, pres. 1983-84, advisor 1985-95), Loyola Marymount U. chpt. Kappa Delta Pi (charter). Republican. Methodist. Avocations: collecting knives, travel, camping, reading. Home: 7740 Redlands St Apt M3073 Playa Del Rey CA 90293-8452 Office: Chapman Elem Sch 1947 Marine St Gardena CA 90249

HITLIN, DAVID GEORGE, physicist, educator; b. Bklyn., Apr. 15, 1942; s. Maxwell and Martha (Lipetz) H.; m. Joan R. Abramowitz, 1966 (div. 1981); m. Abigail R. Gumbiner, 1982 (div. 1998); m. Martha Mann Slagerman, 2000. BA, Columbia U., 1963, MA, 1965, PhD, 1968. Instr. Columbia U., N.Y.C., 1967-69; research assoc. Stanford (Calif.) Linear Accelerator Ctr., 1969-72, asst. prof., 1975-79, mem. program com., 1980-82; asst. prof. Stanford U., 1972-75; assoc. prof. physics Calif. Inst. Tech., Pasadena, 1979-85, prof., 1985—. Mem. adv. panel U.S. Dept. Energy Univ. Programs, 1983; mem. program com. Fermi Nat. Accelerator Lab., Batavia, Ill., 1983—87, Newman Lab., Cornell U., Ithaca, NY, 1986—88; mem. rev. com. U. Chgo., Argonne Nat. Lab., 1985—87; chmn. Stanford Linear Accelerator Ctr. Users Orgn., 1990—93; mem. program com. Brookhaven Nat. Lab., Upton, NY, 1992—95; spokesman BABAR Collaboration, 1994—2000; mem. high energy physics adv. panel DOE/NSF, 2001—; mem. Univs. Rsch. Assn. Fermilab Bd. Overseers, 2003—. Contbr. numerous articles to profl. jours. Fellow Am. Phys. Soc. Achievements include research in elementary particle physics. Office: Calif Inst Tech Dept Physics 356-48 Lauritsen Pasadena CA 91125-0001 E-mail: hitlin@hep.caltech.edu.

HITT, ALAN BERKLEY, computer programmer, systems analyst, educator; b. El Paso, Tex., Feb. 14, 1945; s. James Kohland and Bernardine (Berkley) H.; m. Susan Stevens Ruhr, Aug. 18, 1973; children: Jason, Brian. BA in Chinese, U. Kans., 1967; MA in Edn. and East Asian Studies, Stanford U., 1972; cert. in programming, San Joaquin Delta Coll., 1981. Tchr. social studies Lincoln H.S., Stockton, Calif., 1972-82; computer programmer Sacramento (Calif.) Mcpl. Utilities Dist., 1983-85, DLH Sys., Stockton, 1985; programmer, analyst San Joaquin Delta Coll., Stockton, 1985—, instr. computer sci., 1987-90, v.p. classified senate, 1994-96, pres. classified senate, 1996—98. Coach Stockton Youth Soccer, 1986-91, coord., 1992-94; mem., trumpeter Stockton Concert Band, 1993-95. 1st lt. U.S. Army, 1967-69, Vietnam. Mem. Calif. C.C.'s, Calif. Sch. Employees Assn. (reporter 1987, 3d pl. newsletter award 1987). Democrat. Avocation: sports. Home: 2917 Estate Dr Stockton CA 95209-1157 Office: San Joaquin Delta Coll 5151 Pacific Ave Rm 131 Stockton CA 95207-6304

HIXSON, DORIS KENNEDY, retired secondary school educator; b. Sweetwater, Tenn., Mar. 24, 1944; d. Warren Harding and Orinda Eugenia (Wood) Kennedy; m. Virgil Lee Hitson, Dec. 31, 1963 (div. July 1973); m. Luther Terrell Hixson, Feb. 14, 1974; children: Rindi, Elaine, Liana. Student, Less-McRae Jr. Coll., 1962-63, Vanderbilt U., 1963-64; BA in English, Tenn. Wesleyan Coll., 1967; postgrad., U. Tenn., Chattanooga, 1983-85; MA in Liberal Studies, Hollins Coll., 1985. Cert. master gardener Charlotte County, Fla., 2002. Secondary English tchr. Cleveland (Tenn.) City Schs., 1967—99, ret., 1999. Faculty rep. United Tchg. Profession, Cleveland, 1976-86, Tchrs. Study Coun., Cleveland, 1983-87; English instr. Cleveland (Tenn.) State C.C., 1986-89; essay reader Advanced Placement Eng. Lit. Exam, 1999-2001. Bd. dirs. YMCA, Cleveland, 1978-81; pres. Bibliophillies Women's Book Club, Cleveland, 1992-94; chmn. Christian edn., 1995-98, Sunday sch. supt. Wesley Meml. Meth. Ch., Cleveland, 1994-96, tchr. Disciple Bible Study Classes, 1996-2002; co-chmn. Evangelism work area Port Charlotte United Meth. Ch., 2000-03, Lay Witness, Mission of PCUMC, 2003. Fellow in Bible Lit. NEH, Bloomington, Ind., 1977, fellow in Lit. of Alienation NEH, Hollins, 1983, fellow in English Romantics NEH, Chgo., 1987, fellow in Holocaust Lit. NEH, Boston, 1993. Mem. Nat. Coun. Tchrs. English, Tenn. Coun. Tchrs. English, United Tchg. Profession (rep. 1976-86), Delta Kappa Gamma (rec. sec. 1987-90, parliamentarian 1990-94, rep. dir. schs. adv. team 1996-98). Avocations: reading, researching holocaust literature, gardening. Home: 23161 Nancy Ave Port Charlotte FL 33952-1806

HIXSON, ELMER L. retired engineering educator; Prof. emeritus dept. elec. engring. U. Tex., Austin. Recipient Fellow Mems. award Am. Soc. Engring. Educators, 1992. Fellow Acoustical Soc. Am.; mem. IEEE (life), Inst. for Noise Control Engring. (founding mem.). Office: U Tex Dept Elec & Computer Engring Austin TX 78712 E-mail: ehixson@mail.utexas.edu.

HIXSON, STANLEY G. speech, language and computer technology educator; b. Chgo., Nov. 25, 1947; s. George Samuel and Alice Elizabeth (Domino) H.; m. Alice Jean Ray, May 25, 1975; children: Polly Alice, Jay Stanley, Christa Renee, Michael Wayne. BA, William Jewell Coll., Liberty, Mo., 1969; MS, Cen. Mich. U., 1986; postgrad., U. Kans. Dir. comm. and retail mktg. Successful Living, Inc., Mpls., 1975-78; pres. LightShine Comm., Shawnee Mission, Kans., 1979-91; editor-in-chief Successful Living, Inc., Mpls.; pub. affairs specialist U.S. Army C.E., Kansas City, Mo., 1983-84; instr. leadership, speech and lang. U.S. Army Command and Gen. Staff Coll., Ft. Leavenworth, Kans., 1984-91; sr. tng. instr. total quality leadership Naval Supply Sys. Command, Washington, 1991-92; dir. quality and process improvement Bur. of Naval Pers., Washington, 1992-94; pres. Great Ideas! in Edn., Alexandria, Va., 1994—. Adj. prof. William Jewell Coll., 1989-90; presenter computer tech., leadership, mktg. and mgmt. seminars, 1973—. Author: Research and Study Skills, 1989, Implementing Total Quality Leadership in the U.S. Navy, 1992, Professional Graphics Presentations, 1995, Intermediate and Advanced Relational Database Management Using MS Access, 1996; co-author: Effective Staff Communications, 1985, 89, Visions and Revisions, 1981, Total Quality Leadership: Customers, Teams and Tools, 1992; editor: An Application of Multiple Intelligences Theory in an Elementary Music Classroom, 1998. With USAF, 1969-73. Recipient Achievement cert. Dept. Army, 1988, Outstanding Svc. award Successful Living, Inc., 1979, 81-82, 84. Mem. Fed. Info. Coun., Washington Deming Study Group, Navy Total Quality Leadership Advocates Network, Genealogy Club (Loudon County, Va.), Assn. Philippe Du Trieux, Alpha Phi Omega (life). Home: 5211 Leeward Ln Kingstowne VA 22315-3944

HJERMSTAD, ROSLYN, elementary educator; b. Faribault, Minn., May 11, 1948; d. Sanford K. and Elaine B. (Lilleskov) Flaten; m. Robert A. Hjermstad, Feb. 25, 1984; children: Marina Lee, Raelyn Hagen, Rosalee Priem. BS in Elem. Edn., Mankato State U., 1969; MA in Curriculum and Instrn., St. Thomas U., St. Paul, 1988. Cert. tchr., Minn. 6th grade tchr. Cannon Falls (Minn.) Area Elem. Sch., 1970—. Mem. Cmty. Edn. Adv. Bd., Cannon Falls, 1986-91. Columnist Cannon Falls Beacon, Vasa Cmty. Ch. coun. Vasa Luth. Ch., 1992—95. Mem. Cannon Falls Edn. Assn. (bldg. rep. 1988-93, 97—, negotiations com. 2001—). Avocations: reading, writing, fishing, camping, genealogy. Home: 30830 Woodhaven Trl Cannon Falls MN 55009-4112 E-mail: bobnros@rconnect.com.

HLAWATI, JOYCE F. elementary education educator; b. Pitts., Aug. 23, 1948; d. Kenneth Louis and Frances Meredith (Carson) Hoerner; m. Daniel Richard Hlawati, June 12, 1971; children: Meegan P. L., Adam G. T. BA in English, St. Francis Coll., Loretta, Pa., 1970; cert. in elem. edn., Slippery Rock (Pa.) U., 1988. Cert. elem. edn. tchr., Pa. Tchr. St. Alexis Sch., Wexford, Pa., 1970-73, St. Bonaventure Sch., Huntington Beach, Calif., 1973-74; pre-sch. tchr. Young World, Pitts., 1984-86; retail clk. Sch. Days Supply, Mars, Pa., 1988-89; tchr. McKnight Elem., Pitts., 1989—2003, Peebles Elem. Sch., Pitts., 2003—. Author poems. Vol. Am. Cancer Soc., Pitts., 1976—, Leukemia Soc., Pitts., 1978—, March of Dimes, Pitts., 1979-80. Mem. Internat. Reading Assn., North Allegheny Fedn. of Tchrs., Authors and Friends, Three Rivers Reading Coun. Avocations: writing, crocheting, sewing, reading, children's literature. Home: 1570 Lenora Dr Pittsburgh PA 15237-1672

HLOUSEK, JOYCE B(ERNADETTE), school system administrator; b. Chgo., Sept. 7, 1949; d. Theodore P. and Helen J. (Pietrzak) Brewer. BSEE, DePaul U., Chgo., 1971, MA, 1976; EdD, Vanderbilt U., 1993. Cert. in elem. edn., learning disabilities, gen. adminstrn., Ill. Tchr., asst. prin. Chgo. Pub. Schs., 1970-71; tchr. Community Consol. Sch. Dist. 54, Schaumburg Twp., Ill., 1971-73, learning disabilities specialist, 1973-80, 1980-85, dir. program assessment, 1985-96, adminstr., 1996—. Instr. Ill. Adminstrv. Acd., North Cook Region, Ill., 1989-92; due process hearing officer Ill. State Bd. Edn., 1976-84. Author: The Missing Piece of Change, 1993, Understanding Your Child's Test Scores, 1982, (series) Action Mathematics, 1976; feature writer Chgo. Daily Herald and Chgo. Tribune, 1996—. Sec. Community Communicators, Schaumburg Twp., 1978-81; bd. dirs., edn. Strays Halfway House; electee Parish Religious Edn. Bd., 1997. Named Outstanding Educator, Schaumburg Jaycees, 1974. Mem. ASCD, Am. Assn. Sch. Adminstrs., Ill. Assn. for Supervision and Curriculum Devel., Inst. for Ednl. Rsch. (bd. editorial advisors), Phi Delta Kappa. Office: Schaumburg Twp Cmty Consol Sch Dist 54 Lakeview Sch 524 E Schaumburg Rd Schaumburg IL 60194-3510

HO, CHI-TANG, food chemistry educator; b. Fuzhou, Fujian, China, Dec. 26, 1944; came to U.S., 1969; s. Chia-jue and Siu (Lin) H.; m. Mary Shieh, June 29, 1974; children: Gregory, Joseph. MS, Washington U., 1971, PhD, 1974. Postdoctoral assoc. sch. chemistry Rutgers U., New Brunswick, N.J., 1975-76, postdoctoral assoc. dept. food sci., 1976-78, asst. prof. dept. food sci., 1978-83, assoc. prof., 1983-87, prof., 1987—92, prof. II, 1992. Co-editor: Thermal Generation of Aromas, 1989, Food Extrusion Science and Technology, 1991, Phenolic Compounds and Their Effects on Health, I and II, 1992, Food Phytochemicals for Cancer Prevention, I and II, 1994; contbr. over 500 articles to profl. jours. Fellow Am. Chem. Soc. (chmn. agrl. and food chemistry divsn. 1995-96); fellow Inst. Food Technologists. Achievements include patents for rosemary antioxidant and method for nutracentical screening. Home: 32 Jernee Dr East Brunswick NJ 08816-5308 Office: Rutgers U Dept Food Sci New Brunswick NJ 08901

HO, DAVID KIM HONG, education educator; b. Honolulu, Mar. 5, 1948; s. Raymond T.Y. and Ellen T.Y. (Fong) H.; m. Joan Yee, July 6, 1968 (div. Apr. 1982); 1 child, Michael J.; m. Patricia Ann McAndrews, June 25, 1983. BS in Indsl. Engring., U. So. Calif., 1970; MBA, Butler U., 1976; MS in Acctg., U. Wis., Whitewater, 1981. Cert. fellow in prodn. and inventory mgmt. Indsl. engr. FMC Corp., L.A., 1970-73, mgr. prodn. planning and inventory control Indpls., 1973-77; materials mgr. Butler Mfg. Co., Ft. Atkinson, Wis., 1977-81, systems mgr. Kansas City, Mo., 1981-82; dir. materials and systems Behlen Mfg. Co., Columbus, Nebr., 1982-84, v.p. operations, bd. dirs., 1984-86; mgr. corp. materials Lozier Corp., Omaha, 1986-90, plant mgr., 1990-91; v.p. mfg. Heatilator Inc., Mt. Pleasant, Iowa, 1991-93; prof. profl. studies Bellevue (Nebr.) U., 1993—. Instr. Met. C.C., Omaha, 1989—, Iowa Wesleyan Coll., Mt. Pleasant, 1991—92; cons., evaluator The Higher Learning Commn. of the North Ctrl. Assn., Chgo., 2001—; evaluator Assn. of Collegiate Bus. Sch. Programs, Overland Pk., Kans., bd. dirs. Mem.: Inst. Supply Mgmt., Am. Prodn. and Inventory Control Soc. Home: 11729 Fisher House Rd Bellevue NE 68123-1112 Office: Met CC PO 3777-Soc 121 Omaha NE 68103-0777 E-mail: dho@metropo.mccneb.edu.

HO, JOHN WING-SHING, biochemistry educator, researcher; b. Hong Kong, Sept. 10, 1954; came to U.S., 1979; s. Tak-Kam and Sam-Mui (Tong) H. BS in Biochemistry, U. Alberta, Can., 1979; MA in Chemistry, SUNY, Buffalo, 1982, PhD in Chemistry, 1985. Teaching asst. dept. chemistry SUNY, Buffalo, 1979-82, rsch. asst. dept. chemistry, 1982-85; chemistry lectr. Millard Fillmore Coll., SUNY, Buffalo, 1985; postdoctoral fellow SUNY, Buffalo, 1985-87; rsch. assoc. dept. chemistry U. Utah, Salt Lake City, 1987-88, rsch. faculty Ctr. for Human Toxicology, 1988—. Vis. prof. dept. applied biology and chem. tech. Hong Kong Poly., 1992; lectr. dept. biochemistry Chinese U. of Hong Kong, 1994—; spkr. seminars and confs., 1983—. Reviewer Jour. Chromatography (Biomedical Applications), 1990—; contbr. articles to profl. jours. IBR fellow Inst. Basic Rsch., 1986-88; recipient traineeship Health and Human Svcs., 1985-86. Fellow Am. Inst. Chemists; mem. AAAS, Am. Chem. Soc., N.Y. Acad. Scis., U.S. Tennis Assn.

HO, LEO CHI CHIEN, Chinese government official; b. Tai Hu, An-Wei, Republic of China, Sept. 2, 1940; came to U.S., 1964, naturalized, 1971; s. Yu Yuan and Hung (King) H.; m. Julie Yu-Ling Hou, May 11, 1967; children: Albert, Alexander. BA, Nat. Cheng Chi U., Taipei, Republic of China, 1964; MLS, Atlanta U., 1967; PhD, Wayne State U., 1975. Libr. Tex. Tech U., Lubbock, 1966-69; dir. China Sci. Pub., Taylor, Mich., 1969-77; bus. libr. Detroit Pub. Libr., 1970-75; libr. Washtenaw Community Coll., Ann Arbor, Mich., 1975-96; pres. Fin. Brokers' Exch., Farmington Hills, Mich., 1978-87, Sylvan Learning Ctr. Mich., West Bloomfield, 1987—; mem. Nat. Assembly, China, 1996—. Chmn. bd. Intellectual Svcs., Inc., 1987—; commr. Chinese Overseas Commn., China, 1989—. Mem. adv. coun. Guide to Ethnic Mus., Librs., and Archives in the U.S., 1984. Bd. govs. Internat. Inst. of Greater Met. Detroit, 1985—; v.p., commr. Mich. Gov.'s Adv. Com. on Asian Affairs, Lansing, 1986—; pres. Detroit Chinese Culture Svc. Ctr., 89—. Recipient Outstanding Svc. award Detroit Chinese Cultural Ctr., 1984, 88, Spirit of Detroit award City Coun. Detroit, 1990, 93, Pres.'s Citation award Madonna U. Livonia, Mich., 1993, Dedicated Svc. award Overseas China Commn.-Taiwan, 1995. Mem. Assn. Chinese-Ams. (v.p. 1985—, Dedicated Svc. award 1984, 88, 89), Chinese Acad. and Profl. Assn. in Mid-Am. (bd. dirs. 1987—, Outstanding Svc. award 1988), Rotary. Home: 3810 Manchester Ct Bloomfield Hills MI 48302-1239 Office: Sylvan Learning Ctr 5829 W Maple Rd # 127 West Bloomfield MI 48322-2294

HO, ROBERT EN MING, neurosurgeon, educator; b. Honolulu, Nov. 13, 1942; s. Donald Tet En Ho and Violette (Weeks) Gould; m. Edie Olsen, June 27, 1964; children: Lisa, Amy. BS cum laude, Mich. State. U., 1964; MD, Wayne State U., 1968. Diplomate Am. Bd. Neurol. Surgery. Surg. intern Detroit Gen. Hosp., 1968-69, surg. resident, 1969-70, neurosurg. resident, 1972-76; microsurg. fellow Neurochirurgische Universtatskilinik, Zurich, Switzerland, 1976; instr. dept. neurosurgery Wayne State U., Detroit, 1977-79; dir. dept. neurosurgery Gertrude Levin Pain Clinic, 1977-80; asst. prof., 1979-84; chief neurosurg. svcs. Health Care Inst., 1979-84; clin. asst. prof., 1984—. Founder, dir. Microneurosurg. Lab., 1977-89, dir. spine and spine reconstruction dept. neurosurgery med. sch., 1992-97; dir. neuroscis. intensive care unit Harper Hosp., Detroit, 1980-84, spine and spine reconstruction fellowship Wayne State Med. Sch., 1992-97; mem. audit com. Detroit Gen. Hosp., 1977-80, mem. med. device com., 1977-80, mem. credentials com, 1978-84; sec., treas. Detroit Neurosurg. Acad. Program Com., 1978-84; mem. emergency room com. Harper Hosp., 1980-84, neuroscis. intensive care unit com., 1980-84; dir. Oakland-Macomb PPO; chief neurol. sect. William Beaumont Hosp., Troy, Mich., mem. adv. bd., 1986-90; chmn. adv. com. traumatic brain injury/spinal cord injury, State Mich., 1993-96; presenter of numerous exhibits, profl. papers; organizer numerous med. meetings; lectr. in field. Contbr. articles to profl. jours. Served with U.S. Army, 1970-72, Vietnam. Recipient Intern of Yr. award Detroit Gen. Hosp., 1969. Mem. AMA, ACS, Congress Neurol. Surgeons, Detroit Neurosurg. Acad., Mich. Assn. Neurol. Surgeons (sec.-treas. 1979-82, v.p. 1982-84, pres. 1984-86, bd. dirs. 1986-90), Mich. State Med. Soc., Oakland County Med. Soc., Wayne County Med. Soc., Internat. Coll. Surgeons (U.S. sect.), Am. Assn. Neurol Surgeons (spinal disorders sec. 1981-2002, cerebrovascular surgery sect.). Office: 15520 19 Mile Rd Ste 450 Clinton Township MI 48038-6332 Office Fax: 810-263-3819.

HO, RODNEY JIN YONG, educator, medical researcher; b. Rangoon, Burma, May 21, 1959; came to U.S., 1977; s. David Shoon-Khat and Po-Kin (Paw) H.; m. Lily S. Hwang, July 10, 1988; children: Beatrice Eirene, Martin Theodore. BS, U. Calif., Davis, 1983; MS, U. Tenn., 1985, PhD, 1987. Teaching asst. U. Tenn., Knoxville, 1984-85, rsch. asst., 1985-87; post-doctoral fellow, assoc. investigator Stanford (Calif.) U. Sch. Medicine, 1987-90; asst. prof. pharmaceutics U. Wash., Seattle, 1990-96, assoc. prof. pharmaceutics Sch. Pharmacy, 1996—2002, prof., 2002—, affiliate investigator Wash. Primate Rsch. Ctr., 1996—; affiliate investigator of pharmacology Fred Hutchinson Cancer Rsch. Ctr., Seattle, 1991—. Affil. faculty, Ctr. for AIDS Rsch., U. Wash., 1991—, affil. investigator Ctr. Human Devel. & Disability. Author: Liposomes as Drug Carriers, 1988, Topics in Vaccine Adjuvant Research, 1991, Trophoblast Research, Vol. 8, 1994, Placental Toxicology, 1995, Vaccine Design: The Subunit and Adjuant Approach, 1995, Biotechnology and Biopharmaceutical: Transforming Proteins and Genes into Drugs, 2003; patentee immunoliposome assays, composition and treatment for herpes simplex; contbr. numerous articles on infectious diseases, pharmaceutical sciences, virology, AIDS, immunology and biochemistry to sci. jours. Mem. AAAS, Am. Assn. Coll. Pharmacy, Am. Assn. Pharm. Scientists, Am. Chem. Soc., Biophys. Soc., Internat. Soc. Antiviral Rsch., N.Y. Acad. Sci. Office: U Wash Sch Pharmacy Dept Pharmaceutics PO Box 357610 Seattle WA 98195-7610

HOAR, JOHN BERNARD, dean; b. Boston, Sept. 2, 1942; s. John B. and Henrietta Marie (LeBlanc) H. BA, C.W. Post Coll., 1965; MEd, Boston Coll., 1977, PhD, 1981. Instr. C.W. Post Coll., Greenvale, N.Y., 1965-66; instr., adminstrv. rep. MacArthur Mil. Acad., Mt. Freedom, N.J., 1966-70, acad. dean, 1971-75; grad. asst. adminstrv. intern Boston Coll., Chestnut Hill, Mass., 1976-80, edn. cons., lectr., 1980-82; registrar Elizabeth Seton Coll., Yonkers, N.Y., 1982-83; dean White Pines Coll., Chester, N.H., 1984—. Mem. Assn. Acad. Affairs Adminstrs. (state commr. 1987, pres.-elect 1990, pres. 1992). Roman Catholic. Avocations: musical theater, computers, pianist. Office: White Pines Coll 40 Chester St Chester NH 03036-4305

HOAR, MARY MARGRETTE, gifted education educator; b. Yonkers, NY, Dec. 28, 1948; d. Thomas Aquinas and Margaret Agnes (Delapp) H. BS, Cornell U., 1970; MS, Fordham U., 1973. Cert. tchr. early childhood edn., NY, kindergarten, NY. Tchr. elem. edn. Sch. # 12, Yonkers, NY, 1970-76, Sch. # 6, Yonkers, NY, 1976-81, tchr. gifted and talented edn., 1982-86; tchr. computer King Elem. Summer Sch., Yonkers, NY, 1986-97; tchr. early childhood gifted and talented edn. Dr. Martin Luther King Jr. Sch. Computer Sci. and High Tech., Yonkers, NY, 1986-97; prekindergarten tchr., 1997-98; literacy specialist Mark Twain Mid. Sch., 1998—2000; pre-kindergarten tchr. Scholastic Acad. Academic Excellence, 2000—. Mem. sch. improvement plan Yonkers Bd. Edn., 1987—98, United Way rep., 1974—81, mem. tchr.'s interest com., 1972—81, 1982—99, 2000—; mem. newspaper staff Yonkers Fedn. Tchrs. Svcs., 1980—, bldg. rep., 1972—81, 1987—97, 2001—; trainer Am. Fedn. Tchr.; trainer leadership effectiveness tng. workshops N.Y. State United Tchr. Officer Yonkers Jay-n-Cees, 1973—83, mem. goals com., golden age com., Outstanding Young Teenager chair; mem. Westchester exec. bd. No. Metro chpt. March of Dimes, 1974—98, walkathon coord. com., reading olympics chair, pub. affairs com., mem. Golden Gala com., 1996—98; br. chair Yonkers Red Cross Svc. Ctr., 1975—76, chair centennial com., bd. dirs., chair youth svcs.; youth coord. Senator John E. Flynn Sr. Citizens Youth Conf. Day, 1976; mem. Enrico Fermi Scholarship Breakfast com., Mayor's Cmty. Rels.

Com., 1975—, exec. chair, 1980—82, chair pub. rels. com., exec. com., salute to bus. and industry com., program com.; advisor Mayor's Youth Adv. Com., 1976—79; bd. dirs. Untermeyer Performing Arts Coun., 1976—, treas., antique show chair, chair Art in the Park, chair nominating com., chair Eileen O'Connor Performing Arts Scholarship; bd. dirs. Family Svc. Yonkers, 1978—, chair, 1987—97, mem. exec. com., chair ho. com., chair homemakers com., mem. vol. com., mem. Nearly New Shop com., mem. program com.; bd. dirs. Yonkers Hist. Soc., 1988—, 1st v.p., 1999, pres., 1999—, chair ednl. programs com.; mem. steering com. Cornell Women's Club of Westchester, Yonkers Marathon Com. Recipient Janet Hopkins Meml. award for outstanding vol. svc., 1987, Untermyer Performing Arts Coun.'s Gryphon award vol. svc., Yonkers Jay-N-Cees, 2002, N.Y. State Jay-N-Cee's Pres.'s award, Key to City of Yonkers, Mayor Angelo Martinelli, 1977; named Jay-N-Cee of Month, 1973-75. Mem. Am. Irish Assn., Cornell Women's Club of Westchester, Cornell Club Westchester. Democrat. Roman Catholic. Avocations: reading, swimming, knitting, horticulture, travel. Home: 29 Marshall Rd Yonkers NY 10705-2531 Office: Yonkers Bd Edn 77 Park Hill Ave Yonkers NY 10701

HOART, GLADYS GALLAGHER, English language educator; b. N.Y.C., June 27, 1914; d. Martin and Edna (Parker) Gallagher; m. Francis Xavier Hoart, June 25, 1939; children: Robert, Helen, Andrew. AB cum laude, NYU, 1967, MA, 1970; MA in Liberal Studies, New Sch. for Social Rsch., 1975. Cert. mem. N.Y. Stock Exchange. Adj. prof. English Nassau C.C., Garden City, N.Y., 1970—. Dir. Career Seminars for Teenage Girls, Flushing, N.Y., 1963-64; tutor Black Studies Program, Manhasset, N.Y., 1968-69. Pres., co-founder Broadway Homeowners' Assn., Flushing, N.Y., 1964-65; committeewoman Dem. Party, Manhasset, N.Y., 1970; organizer Parkchester (N.Y.) Golden Age Club, 1953; trustee Dalcroze Sch. of Music, 1998—, treas., 2001. Mem. AAUW, Alliance Floor Brokers, Musicians Club (bd. dirs. 1993—, v.p. 2001). Roman Catholic. Avocations: architecture, equitation, gardening, music.

HOBART, BILLIE, education educator, consultant; b. Pitts., Apr. 19, 1935; d. Harold James Billingsley and Rose Stephanie (Sladack) Green; m. W.C.H. Hobart, July 20, 1957 (div. 1967); 1 child, Rawson W. BA in English, U. Calif., Berkeley, 1967, EdD, 1992; MA in Psychology, Sonoma State U., 1972. Cert. tchr. Calif., Irlen screener 2003. Asst. prof. Coll. Marin, Kentfield, Calif., 1969-78; freelance cons., writer, 1969—; asst. prof. Contra Costa Coll., San Pablo, Calif., 1986-99, Santa Rosa (Calif.) Jr. Coll., 1999—. Author: (cookbook) Natural Sweet Tooth, 1974, (non-fiction) Expansion, 1972, Purposeful Self: Coherent Self, 1979, 2002, (non-fiction) Talking to Dead People, 1996, On the Subject of Prayer, 2000, (biography) Captain Granville Perry Swift, California Pioneer and Sonoma Bear, 1999, (fiction) Last Days of Gifted Light, 2000, Timethinner, 2001, Getting to Start, 2001, Clearing to Core, 2002; contbr. articles to profl. jours. Served with WAC, 1953-55. Mem. No. Calif. Coll. Reading Tchrs. Assn. (pres. 1996-98), Mensa, Commonwealth Club San Francisco, Phi Delta Kappa. Home and Office: PO Box 1542 Sonoma CA 95476-1542

HOBART, MARGERY ANNE, retired special education educator; b. Fort Dodge, Iowa, Oct. 22, 1942; d. Lawwrence John and Martha Ione (Sanders) Underberg; m. Donald John Hobart, Aug. 1, 1964; children: Patricia Ann, Duane Gilbert, David Lawrence. BS, Briar Cliff Coll., 1964; MS, Iowa State U., 1981. Chemistry and math educator Cedar Valley Community Sch., Somers, Iowa, 1969-79, multicategorical tchr. jr.-sr. high sch. Farnhamville, Iowa, 1979-88; multicategorical resource room tchr. high sch. Prairie Valley Community Sch., Gowrie, Iowa, 1988—2000; ret., 2000. Trustee Cmty. Club, Lohrville, Iowa, 2000—; Bd. trustees J.J. Hands Libr., Lohrville, Iowa, 1990—99; active Lohrville Cmty. Improvement Cmty., 2003—; aux. com. Stewart Meml. Cmty. Hosp., 1980—. Recipient County Golden Apple award. Mem.: NEA, Webster County Ret. Tchrs. Pers., Alpha Delta Kappa. Avocations: reading, exercise, gardening, travel.

HOBBS, ALTON DWAYNE, secondary education educator; b. Tifton, Ga., Oct. 19, 1954; s. A.J. Hobbs and Edna (Goodman) Blanchard; m. Teresa Deanne Lathem, Apr. 7, 1990. BS, Berry Coll., 1976. Cert. tech. educator. Tchr. Morrow (Ga.) Jr. High Sch., 1976-89, Lovejoy (Ga.) High Sch., 1989—. Editing cons. (textbook) Living with Technology, 1988. Mem. Ga. Indsl. Tech. Edn. Assn., Internat. Tech. Edn. Assn., Ga. Vocat. Assn., Am. Vocat. Assn., Epsilon Phi Tau (pres. local chpt. 1978-79). Avocations: fishing, hunting, competitive target archery. Home: 280 Quail Rd Griffin GA 30223-6809

HOBBS, CATHERINE LYNN, English language and literature educator; b. Guymon, Okla., Feb. 13, 1951; d. Dan Stewart and Betty Jean (Ray) H. m. Cecil L. Peaden, Mar. 23, 1975 (div. Feb. 15, 1994). BA in Journalism, U. Okla., 1973; MA in Modern Letters, U. Tulsa, 1983; PhD in English, Purdue U., 1989. Instr. Rogers State Coll., Tulsa, Okla., 1983-84; vis. lectr. comms. U. Tulsa, 1984-85; teaching asst. English dept. Purdue U., West Lafayette, Ind., 1985-89; asst. prof. English Ill. State U., Normal, 1989-92; asst. prof. English dept. U. Okla., Norman, 1992-95, assoc. prof., 1995—2003, prof., 2003—. Author: Rhetoric on the Margins of Modernity, 2002; editor: Nineteenth-Century Women Learn to Write, 1995; mem. editl. bd. Rhetoric and Composition Series; contbr. articles to profl. jours. NEH fellow, 1990, 93. Mem. AAUW, MLA, Am. Soc. Eighteenth Century Studies, Internat. Soc. History of Rhetoric, Nat. Coun. Tchrs. of English, Rhetoric Soc. Am., Phi Kappa Phi. Democrat. Office: U Okla English Dept Norman OK 73019-0001

HOBBS, HORTON HOLCOMBE, III, biology educator; b. Gainesville, Fla., Dec. 17, 1944; s. Horton Holcombe Jr. and Georgia Cates (Blount) H.; m. Susan Claire Krantz, Oct. 12, 1967; children: Heather H. Killion, Horton Holcombe IV. BA, U. Richmond, 1967; MS, Miss. State U., 1969; PhD, Ind. U., 1973. Instr. Christopher Newport Coll., Newport News, Va., 1973-75; asst. prof. George Mason U., Fairfax, Va., 1975-76; prof. biology Wittenberg U., Springfield, Ohio, 1976—. Com. mem. Nongame Wildlife Tech. Adv. Com., Columbus, Ohio, 1989-95; trustee Island Cave Rsch. Ctr., 1987—. Author: The Crayfishes and Shrimp of Wisconsin, 1988; life scis. editor: Nat. Speleological Soc. Bull., Huntsville, Ala., 1985-96; contbr. more than 180 articles to profl. jours. Campaign co-chair County Park Dist., Springfield, 1980. Fellow Nat. Speleological Soc. (bd. govs. 1985-88, hon. life mem.), The Explorers Club, Ohio Acad. Sci.; mem. Crustacean Soc. (coun. mem. 1980-83), Biol. Soc. Wash. (exec. coun. 1976-77), Am. Cave Conservation Assn. (bd. dirs. 1993—), Karst Waters Inst. (bd. dirs. 1999—), Cave Conservancy of the Virginias (bd. dirs. 1988—). Achievements include development of Ohio's Cave Protection Law; participation in International Speleological Expeditions to Costa Rica. Office: Wittenberg U Dept Biol Springfield OH 45501 E-mail: hhobbs@wittenberg.edu.

HOBBY, KENNETH LESTER, psychology educator; b. Searcy, Ark., Jan. 9, 1947; s. James Alvin and Georgia Alice (Pruett) H.; m. Ann Elizabeth Adair, Aug. 20, 1967; children: Anessa, Jared, Tianna, Gerren. BA, Harding U., 1969; MA, Ea. N.Mex. U., 1970, Edn. Specialist, 1971; PhD, Okla. State U., 1981. Lic. psychologist, Ark., Okla. Teaching fellow Ea. N.Mex. U., Portales, 1969-71; sch. counselor Clay County Schs., Orange Park, Fla., 1971-72, sch. psychologist Green Cove Springs, Fla., 1972-76; sch. psychometrist Regional Edn. Svc. Ctr., Grove, Okla., 1976-81; sch. psychologist Craig County Spl. Edn. Coop., Vinita, Okla., 1981-82; clin. dir., psychologist Okla. Dept. Health/Child Guidance, Jay, Okla., 1982-85; chief psychologist Grand Lake Mental Health Ctr., Nowata, Okla., 1985-89; prof. psychology Harding U., Searcy, 1989—; adj. prof. psychology for all psychology correspondence courses Ark. State U., Jonesboro, 1993—. Cons. psychologist Clearview Psychiat. Hosp., Searcy, Searcy Police Dept. and Fire Dept.; examiner for disability determination Social Security Svc., Little Rock; psychologist McPherson and Grimes Prisons, Newport, Ark., 1999-2003, S.W. Ark. Cmty. Correction Ctr., Texarkana, 2003—. Recipient Disting. Tchr. award, 1997. Mem.: Am. Psychol. Assn. Republican. Mem. Ch. of Christ. Home: 65 Mohawk Dr Searcy AR 72143-5935 Office: Harding U PO Box 12260 Searcy AR 72145-0001

HOBERG, MICHAEL DEAN, management analyst, educator; b. Pipestone, Minnesota, Feb. 27, 1955; s. Dennis Edwin and Beverly Ann (Voss) H.; 1 child, Heather; m. Janet Lee (Freeman). BS in Pk. Adminstrn., Calif. State U., Sacramento, 1977; MPA, Calif. State U., Turlock, Ca., 1982; PhD in Pub. Adminstrn., Greenwich Univ., 1993; post grad. in computer info. sys. and project mgmt., U. Calif., Berkeley, 1996—2003. Cert. govt. fin. mgr., project mgmt. profl., Internat. Pers. Mgmt. Assn. Pk. ranger Nat. Pk. Svc., State of Calif., and San Joaquin County, Calif., 1977-82; pk. svc. specialist San Joaquin County, Stockton, Calif., 1983-86, mgmt. analyst, 1986—. Adj. instr. Delta Coll., Stockton, Calif., 1987-90; dir. Hoberg Mgmt. and Consulting, Stockton, Calif., 1987—. Fencing Champion foil, No. Calif. Intercollegiate Athletic Conf., 1977; 9th Place award USFA Nat. Championships, 1988; High Jump champion, City of Stockton, 1971-73; inducted into Sacramento C. of C. Athletic Hall of Fame, 1977. Mem.: Mensa, Am. Planning Assn., Project Mgmt. Inst. Democrat. Home: 2209 Meadow Ave Stockton CA 95207-1428 Office: San Joaquin County PO Box 1810 Stockton CA 95201 E-mail: hoberg2@sbcglobal.net.

HOBGOOD, E(ARL) WADE, college chancellor; b. Wilson, N.C., June 28, 1953; s. Max Earl and Mary (Carpenter) H.; m. Dianne Bland, Apr. 24, 1977; children: Courtney, Heather. BFA, E. Carolina U., 1975, MFA, 1977; postgrad., Am. Inst. for Philanthropic Studies, 1995, Harvard U., 1997, Sashakawa Fellowship/AACSCU, 1998. Asst. prof. art Ark. State U., Jonesboro, 1977-78; design dir. and asst./assoc. prof. art Western Carolina U., Cullowhee, N.C., 1978-84; chmn., assoc. to full prof. art and design Winthrop U., Rock Hill, S.C., 1984-88, acting chmn. dept. music, 1991-92, assoc. dean and prof. Coll. Visual and Performing Arts, 1988-92; dean Coll. of Fine Arts, Stephen F. Austin State U., Nacogdoches, Tex., 1992-93; dean Coll. of Arts, Calif. State U., Long Beach, 1993-2000; chancellor N.C. Sch. of the Arts, Winston-Salem, 2000—. Sr. evaluator Nat. Assn. Schs. of Art and Design, 1987-99; bd. dirs. Rancho Los Cerritos Found., 1996-2000; presenter Global Arts Conf., New Zealand, 1999; mem. cultural planning com. City of Long Beach, 1996-2000; evaluator/cons. Arts Edn. Partnership Grants, Ky. Arts Coun., 1992; evaluator/panelist Challenge grants, NEA, 1991, correspondent/cons. Arts Edn. Rsch. Briefing, 1991; mem. bd. advisors First Wachovia Bank, 2003—. Bd. dirs. Winston-Salem Alliance, 2001--, Davidson Coll. Friends of the Arts, Brenner Children's Hosp., 2002--, Forsyth County Tourism Devel. Authority, 2002--, So. Arts Fedn., 2002—, Winston-Salem Symphony, 2002—; mem. Mayor's Task Force on Smithsonian, City of Long Beach, 1996-2000; chair bd. dirs. Kenan Inst. for the Arts, 2000—. Mem. Winston-Salem/Forsyth C. of C. (bd. dirs. 2001—). Office: NC Sch of the Arts PO Box 12189 Winston Salem NC 27117-2189 E-mail: wh@ncarts.edu.

HOCH, DAVID ALLEN, athletic director; b. Northampton, Pa., July 26, 1946; s. Sterling Palmer and Evelyn Mae (McCallister) H.; m. Diane Duffy, June 18, 1977; children: Matthew David, Jennifer Lynn. AB in German, Grove City (Pa.) Coll., 1968; MEd in Phys. Edn., The Coll. N.J., 1972; EdD in Phys. Edn., Temple U., 1989. Tchr., coach Washington Twp. H.S., Sewell, N.J., 1968-71, Upper Dublin H.S., Ft. Washington, Pa., 1972-78, Ramsey (N.J.) H.S., 1978-79, Germantown Acad., Ft. Washington, 1981-89; instr., coach Pa. State U., Altoona, 1979-80; instr. phys. edn., basketball coach U. Pitts., Bradford, 1989-93; athletic dir. Eastern Tech. H.S., Balt. County, 1994—2003, Loch Raven H.S., Balt. County, 2003—. Presenter in field. Mem. editl. adv. bd. Athletic Bus. mag., pub. com. NFHS Coaches Quar., 2002—; contbr. articles to profl. jours., chpts. in books. Mem. AAHPERD, NEA, Nat. H.S. Athletic Coaches Assn. (Regional Athletic Dir. of Yr. award 1999), Nat. Interscholastic Athletic Adminstrs. Assn. (state award of merit for Md. 2002), Nat. Fedn. Coaches Assn. (Md. state dir. 2000—),, N.Am. Soc. for Sports Mgmt., Md. State Athletic Dirs. Assn. (v.p. 1999-2003, pres. 2003, Athletic Dir. of Yr. 2000), Md. Assn. for Health, Phys. Edn., Recreation and Dance (v.p. athletics, 2000-01), Md. State Coaches Assn. (pres. 2002-03, newsletter editor and membership dir. 2001—). Presbyterian. Avocations: running, marathons, gardening, photography. Home: 1207 Peachtree Rd Fallston MD 21047-1804 Office: Loch Raven HS 1212 Cowpens Ave Towson MD 21286 E-mail: dhoch@bcps.org.

HOCHBERG, MARK STEFAN, professional society administrator, cardiac surgeon; b. Providence, Nov. 26, 1947; s. Robert and Gertrude (Meth) H.; m. Faith Shapiro, June 6, 1976; children: Alyssa T., Asher R. BA, Brown U., 1969; MD, Harvard U., 1973; MD (Honoris Causa), Chongqing Sch. Med. Sci., China, 1987. Diplomate Am. Bd. Thoracic Surgery, Am. Bd. Surgery. Chief resident cardiothoracic surgery Mass. Gen. Hosp., Boston, 1980; clin. fellow in surgery Harvard Med. Sch., Boston, 1980; attending cardiac surgeon Newark Beth Israel Med. Ctr., 1981-93, dir. cardiac surgery, 1988-93; cons. cardiac surgeon Overlook Hosp., Summit, N.J., 1983-93; asst. prof. surgery U. Medicine and Dentistry of N.J., Newark, 1981-87, assoc. prof. surgery, 1987-93; spl. asst. to pres., vis. prof. surgery George Washington U., Washington, 1993-94, dean of univ. affairs, prof. surgery, 1994-95; sr. scholar Assn. Acad. Health Ctrs., 1995-96; pres. Healthcare Found. N.J., Roseland, NJ, 1996—2002; CEO Coll. Physicians Phila., 2003—. Chmn. grant rev. com. N.J. affiliate Am. Heart Assn., New Brunswick, 1986-88, also bd. dirs.; mem. com. on med. affairs Corp. of Brown U., Providence, 1987-2002. V.p. Temple B'nai Jeshurun, Short Hills, 1988-92; trustee Coun. N.J. Grantmakers, 1997-2002, pres. 2000-02; mem. vis. com. Northeastern U. Sch. of Law. Lt. comdr. USPHS, 1975-77. Fellow ACS, Am. Coun. Edn.; diplomate Am. Bd. Surgery, Am. bd. Thoracic Surgery; mem. Soc. Thoracic Surgery, Am. Assn. Thoracic Surgery, Alpha Omega Alpha. Office: Coll Phy Phila 19 S Twenty Second St Philadelphia PA 19103-3097

HOCHMAN, NAOMI LIPSON, special education educator, consultant; b. Bklyn. d. William Lipson and Tillie Silverstein-Beech Lipson; m. Elihu Hochman (div. Mar. 1978); children: Richard, Lisa, Lauren. BA cum laude, Bklyn. Coll., 1956; MA, William Paterson U., 1973. Cert. spl. edn. tchr., N.Y., learning disability cons., N.J. Tchr. Bd. Edn., N.Y.C., 1956-58, spl. edn. tchr. Wayne, N.J., 1968-73; instr. edn. William Paterson U., Wayne, N.J., 1973-74; learning disability cons. Wayne Bd. Edn., 1973-2000; cons. Assocs. Ednl. Consulting, 2000—. Mem. Thorough & Efficient Steering Com., N.J., 1975-80, Adv. Panel Spl. Edn., 1985-93; spkr. Literacy Vols. N.J. Passaic C.C., 1991—; bd. dirs. Wayne Counseling Youth, 1987-90. Mem. LWV, Wayne, 1965-73, Wayne Arts League, 1968-72. Recipient Honors Edn. award Bklyn. Coll., 1956. Mem. N.J. Edn. Assn., Profl. Svcs. Coun. N.J., N.J. Assn. Learning Cons. (pres. 1989-91). Avocations: tennis, bldg. doll houses. Home: 201 Zeppi Ln West Orange NJ 07052-4130 Office: Assocs Ednl Cons PO Box 1829 Clifton NJ 07015-1829

HOCHMUTH, GEORGE J. horticultural educator; b. Balt., Mar. 31, 1953; married; 2 children. BS in Horticulture, U. Md., 1975; PhD in Plant Breeding and Plant Genetics, U. Wis., 1980. Staff Hochmuth Farms, Mardela Springs, Md., 1974; entomology technician U. Md. Vegetable Rsch. Farm, Salisbury, Md., 1972, summer vegetable rsch crew leader, 1973, 74; with USDA Vegetable Rsch. Lab., Beltsville, Md., 1974, 75; rsch. asst. dept. horticulture U. Wis., 1975-80; asst. prof. plant and soil scis. U. Mass., Amherst, 1980-84; asst. prof. and extension vegetable specialist, Vegetable Crops Dept. U. Fla., Gainesville, 1984-88, assoc. prof. and extension vegetable specialist, Horticultural Scis. Dept., 1988-93, prof. and extension vegetable specialist, Horticultural Scis. Dept., 1993—. Contbr. over 350 articles to scientific jours. Recipient Extension Publication award So. Region Am. Soc. for Horticultural Sci., 1989, 1994, Extension Edn. Aids award Am. Soc. for Horticultural Sci., 1994, Extension Divsn. Excellence award, 1994, Outstanding Extension Educator award, 1995. Home: 11919 SW 82nd Ave Gainesville FL 32608-5751 Office: U Fla Horticultural Scis Dept PO Box 110690 Gainesville FL 32611-0690*

HOCHSCHILD, CARROLL SHEPHERD, computer company and medical equipment executive, educator; b. Whittier, Calif., Mar. 31, 1935; d. Vernon Vero and Effie Corinne (Hollingsworth) Shepherd; m. Richard Hochschild, July 25, 1959; children: Christopher Paul, Stephen Shepherd. BA in Internat. Rels., Pomona Coll., 1956; Teaching credential, U. Calif., Berkeley, 1957; MBA, Pepperdine U., 1985; cert. in fitness instrn., U. Calif., Irvine, 1988. Cert. elem. tchr., Calif. Elem. tchr. Oakland (Calif.) Pub. Schs., 1957-58, San Lorenzo (Calif.) Pub. Schs., 1958-59, Pasadena (Calif.) Pub. Schs., 1959-60, Huntington Beach (Calif.) Pub. Schs., 1961-63, 67-68; adminstrv. asst. Microwave Instruments, Corona del Mar, Calif., 1968-74; co-owner Hoch Co., Corona del Mar, 1978—. Rep. Calif. Tchrs. Assn., Huntington Beach, 1962-63. Mem. Alta Bahia com. Orange County Philharm., 2002. Mem. AAUW, P.E.O. (projects chmn. 1990-92, corr. sec. 1992-94, 98-99, 99-2003, chpt. pres. 1994-95), NAFE, ASTD (Orange County chpt.), Internat. Dance-Exercise Assn., Assistance League Newport-Mesa, Orange County Philharm. Soc. (assoc., Alta Bahia chpt.), Toastmistress (corr. sec. 1983), Jr. Ebell Club (fine arts chmn. Newport Beach 1966-67). Republican.

HOCHSTEIN, JOHN ISAAC, mechanical engineering educator; b. Bklyn., 1953; s. Harry S. and Ruth K. Hochstein; m. Deborah Hochstein, 1976; children: David, Ann, Marie, Daniel. BE, Stevens Inst. Tech., Hoboken, N.J., 1973; MSME, Pa. State U., 1979; PhD, U. Akron, 1984. Engr. Electric Boat Divsn, Gen. Dynamics, Groton, Conn., 1975-77, Babcock & Wilcox Co., Barberton, Ohio, 1977-79; spl.lectr. U. Akron, Ohio, 1979-84; from asst. to assoc. prof. Washington U., St. Louis, 1984-91; dept. chair U. Memphis, Tenn., 1996—, assoc. prof. to prof., 1991—. Organizer 9th and 10th Space Processing Symposia, 1995, 96. Co-author: (book) Fundamentals of Fluid Mechanics, 1991; Contbr. articles to AIAA Jour. of Propulsion and Power, 1990—. Coach Little League, Creve Couer (Mo.) Athletic Assn., 1988-90, Germantown (Tenn.) Youth Athletic Assn., 1991. Grantee NASA several grants, 1984—; named Prof. of Yr. Sch. Engring., Washington U., 1991. Fellow AIAA (assoc., held several offices in different chpts., chair space processing tech. com. 1997-98); mem. ASME, Am. Soc. for Engring. Edn. Avocations: woodworking, camping. Office: The Univ of Memphis Dept Mech Engring Memphis TN 38139 E-mail: jhochstein@memphis.edu.

HOCKETT, LORNA DEE, elementary education educator; b. Portland, Oreg., Aug. 14, 1954; d. Wallace Loren and Ava Dee (Thomas) Johnson; m. John Bennett, June 15, 1975; children: Tara Dianne, Bryan Nathan, Kevin Loren. BS, Oreg. State U., 1976, MEd, 1986. Cert. elem. tchr., Oreg. Tchr. Waldport Elem. Sch., Waldport, Oreg., 1978—. Trainer, ombudsman Drug Edn. Ctr., Charlotte, N.C., 1990-92; trainer developing capable people Sunrise Assocs., Provo, Utah, 1990-95. Mem. NEA (adv. panel profl. libr., mem. task force 1992, trainer Nat. Diversity Cadre 1994—), Oreg. Edn. Assn. (del. 1984-93, chair ins. claims rev. com. 1986-92, bd. dirs. 1993—), Lincoln County Edn. Assn. (Tchr. of Yr. award 1991, treas. 1985-95, bargaining team 1992-96), Delta Kappa Gamma. Democrat. Home: PO Box 1388 Waldport OR 97394-1388 Office: Waldport Elem Sch 265 Bay St Waldport OR 97394

HODGE, KATHLEEN O'CONNELL, academic administrator; b. Balt., Dec. 26, 1948; d. William Walsh and Loretto Marie (Wittek) O'Connell; m. Vern Milton Hodge, Apr. 8, 1972; children: Shea, Ryan. BS, Calif. State U., Fullerton, 1971, MS, 1975; EdD, U. So. Calif., 2002; postgrad., U. Calif., Irvine, 1977-84. Cert. marriage and family therapist. Counselor Saddleback Coll., Mission Viejo, Calif., 1975-87, prof. of psychology, speech, 1975—2002, dean of continuing edn., cmty. svcs., dean emeritus inst., 1987-95, vice chancellor, 1995—, acting chancellor, 1998-99. Accreditation liaison officer Saddleback Coll., 1986; mem. adv. bd. Nat. Issues Forum, Calif., 1985, 87, Saddleback Coll. Community Services, 1984, Access and Aspirations U. Calif., Irvine, 1979. Author: (workbook) Assessment of Life Learning, 1978; editor emeritus: Flavors in Time Anthology of Literature, 1992. Mem. Calif. Community Coll. Counselors Assn. (region coord. 1987), Calif. Tchrs. Assn., Am. Assn. Women Community and Jr. Colls., Assn. Marriage Family Therapists, C.C. Educators of Older Adults (pres. 1990-92). Democrat. Roman Catholic. Avocations: skiing, reading, political advocacy. Home: 4011 Calle Juno San Clemente CA 92673-2616 Office: South Orange County C C Dist 28000 Marguerite Pky Mission Viejo CA 92692-3635

HODGE, MARY THOMAS, elementary education educator; b. Laramie, Wyo., Aug. 21, 1945; d. William Orvil and Olive (Williams) Thomas; m. David J. Hodge, June 6, 1966; children: Kelly, Kathy. BS, Wyoming U., 1967, MS, 1968; counseling cert., Colo. State U., 1971. Elem. phys. edn. tchr. Poudra R-1 Schs., Ft. Collins, Colo., 1969-74, elem. counselor, curriculum specialist, 1974-86, phys. edn. tchr., 1968—. Instr. Colo. State U., Ft. Collins, 1975-82, 91, 92; golf coach Poudra High Sch., 1990-93. Co-author: (workbook) 1001 Physical Education Activities, 1982-83. Golf bd. mem. City of Ft. Collins, 1991-94. Mem. AAHPERD, Colo. Assn. Health, Phys. Edn., Recreation and Dance (coord. phys. edn. 1985-86, state liaison 1991-92, state phys. edn. award 1991), Poudra Edn. Assn., Christian Woman's Club, Pi Beta Phi. Office: Werner Elem Sch 5400 Mail Creek Ln Fort Collins CO 80525-3886

HODGE, PAUL WILLIAM, astronomer, educator; b. Seattle, Nov. 8, 1934; s. Paul Hartman and Frances H.; m. Ann Uran, June 14, 1962; children: Gordon, Erik, Sandra. BS, Yale U., 1956; PhD, Harvard U., 1960. Lectr. Harvard, 1960-61; asst. prof. astronomy U. Calif. at Berkeley, 1961-65; asso. prof. U. Wash., Seattle, 1965-69, prof. astronomy, 1969—, chmn. Astronomy dept., 1987-91; fellow Mt. Wilson, Palomar Obs., Calif. Inst. Tech., Pasadena, 1960-61; physicist Smithsonian Astrophys. Obs., Cambridge, Mass., 1956-74. Author: Solar System Astrophysics, 1964, Galaxies and Cosmology, 1966, The Large Magellanic Cloud, 1967, Concepts of the Universe, 1969, Galaxies, 1972, Concepts of Contemporary Astronomy, 1974, The Small Magellanic Cloud, 1977, An Atlas of the Andromeda Galaxy, 1981, Interplanetary Dust, 1982, The Universe of Galaxies, 1985, Galaxies, 1986, The Andromeda Galaxy, 1992, Meteorite Craters and Impact Structures of the World, 1994, An Atlas of Local Group Galaxies, 1999, Higher Than Everest: An Adventurer's Guide to the Solar System, 2001, Galaxies and the Cosmic Frontier, 2003; editor: The Astron. Jour., 1984—. Mem. Am. Astron. Soc. (v.p. 1990-93), Internat. Astron. Union, Astron. Soc. Pacific (v.p. 1974-75), Korean Astron. Soc., Euro-asian Astron. Soc. (hon.). Office: U Wash Dept Astronomy Box 351580 Seattle WA 98195-1580

HODGE-CLOTMAN, ALMA R. special education educator, consultant; b. Maryland Bayou, Miss., Nov. 11, 1951; d. Lem and Johnnie Clotman; m. Marvin Hodge, Aug. 17, 1952 (div. 1985); 1 child, James. BS, Jarvis Christian Coll., 1974; MEd, Kent State U., 1986. Tchr. Cleve. Bd. Edn., 1979—, program coord., 1979-85, home instrn. cons., 1989—; tchr. Highland (Ohio) Hills Boys' Sch., 1986—. Baptist. Home: 444 Center Rd Bedford OH 44146-2224

HODGEN, MAURICE DENZIL, management consultant, retired education educator; b. Timaru, New Zealand, Aug. 7, 1929; s. William Arnold and Lindsey Frances (Neill) H.; m. Rhona Brandstater, June 20, 1951; children: Philip Denzil, Victoria Anne. Student, Avondale Coll., Cooranbong, Australia, 1948-50; BS, Pacific Union Coll., 1953; MA, Columbia U., 1956, Ed.D., 1958. Asst. prof. La Sierra Coll., Riverside, Calif., 1958-64; lectr. Solusi Coll., Bulawayo, Zimbabwe, 1964-66; dir. tchr. edn. Helderberg

Coll., Somerset W., S. Africa, 1966-68; assoc. prof. Sch. Edn., Loma Linda U., Calif., 1968—72, prof., 1972—84, dean Grad. Sch., 1978—87, coop. faculty, 1985—88; adminstr. fin. devel. Claremont (Calif.) Grad. U., 1987-93; mgmt. cons., 1999—. Exec. dir. Cmty. Found. of Riverside County, 1993-99. Served with U.S. Army, 1953-55.

HODGES, DAVID ALBERT, electrical engineering educator; b. Hackensack, N.J., Aug. 25, 1937; s. Albert R. and Katherine (Rogers) H.; m. Susan Spongberg, June 5, 1965; children: Jennifer, Alan. B.E.E., Cornell U., 1960; MS, U. Calif., Berkeley, 1961, PhD in Elec. Engring, 1966. Mem. tech. staff Bell Telephone Labs., Murray Hill, N.J., 1966-69, head system elements research dept. Holmdel, N.J., 1969-70; asso. prof. dept. elec. engring. and computer scis U. Calif., Berkeley, 1970-74, prof., 1974-98, chmn. dept., 1989-90, dean Coll. Engring., 1990-96, prof. Grad. Sch., 1998—. Contbr. articles to profl. jours.; patentee in field. Fellow AAAS, IEEE.; mem. NAE. Office: Univ Calif Coll Engring 516 Cory Hl Berkeley CA 94720-0001

HODGES, ELIZABETH SWANSON, educational consultant, tutor; b. Anoka, Minn., Apr. 7, 1924; d. Henry Otto and Louise Isabel (Holiday) Swanson; m. Allen Hodges, June 27, 1944; children: Nancy Elizabeth, Susan Kathleen, Jane Ellen, Sara Louise. BA cum laude, Regis Coll., Denver, 1966; postgrad., U. No. Colo., 1966-79, Valdosta State U., 1979-81. Cert. secondary edn., hosp./homebound, learning disabilities, Colo., Ga., Ariz. Vol. emergency St. Anthony's Hosp., Denver, 1960-64; v.p., tutor St. Elizabeth's Adult Tutorial, Denver, 1964-69; hosp./homebound tchr. Liberty County Sch. System, Hinesville, Ga., 1979-87; ednl. tutor Colo. River Indian Tribes, Parker, Ariz., 1986-87; vol. Twin Cities Community Hosp., Templeton, Calif., 1987-89, Guardian Ad Litem Cir. Ct. 5th Dist. Fla., 1992—, Munroe Regional Med. Ctr., Ocala, Fla., 1991-92; cons., tutor Sylvan Learning Ctr., Ocala, 1990—. Vol. tutor Blessed Trinity Sch., Ocala, 1996—. Democrat. Roman Catholic. Avocations: swimming, reading, sewing, piano, gardening. Home and Office: 101 Clyde Morris Blvd #221 Ormond Beach FL 32174-

HODGES, JOSEPH MARION, elementary school educator; b. Huntington, W.Va., Oct. 31, 1949; MusB, Union Coll., Barbourville, Ky., 1972; postgrad., Morehead State U., 1975-78, Georgetown Coll., 1982-84. Cert. tchr., Ky. Tchr. music Fayette County Pub. Schs., Lexington, Ky., 1974—. Pres. United Meth. Men, 1st United Meth. Ch., Lexington, 1987. Mem. NEA, Ky. Edn. Assn., Fayette County Edn. Assn. (bldg. rep. 1978-90), Ky. Music Educators Assn., Union Coll. Alumni Assn., U. Ky. Alumni Assn., Phi Delta Kappa, Phi Mu Alpha Sinfonia. Avocations: swimming, travel, football, basketball, concerts. Home: 3002 Montavesta Rd Lexington KY 40502-2908 Office: Leestown Mid Sch 2010 Leestown Rd Lexington KY 40511-1036

HODGES, VELMA QUINN, mathematics educator; b. Jackson, Miss., Nov. 17, 1944; d. Troy L. and Ethel (Finley) Quinn; m. Herman Hodges, Apr. 5, 1974; 1 child, Teri. BS, Jackson (Miss.) State U., 1967; postgrad., U. Ark., 1969, U. Nebr., 1970; MEd, Memphis State U., 1987. Tchr. Greenwood (Miss.) Pub. Schs., 1967-70, Memphis City Schs., 1970—. Chairperson governing bd. Memphis Urban Math., 1990-92; coord. summer program for mid. grades 7th and 8th Math., Sci., Computer Inst., Memphis, 1991, 92, 93; parliamentarian Community Edn. Site of Wooddale Jr. High, Memphis, 1992; mem. CLassroom Assessment in Math. project, 1992-93. Named Tchr. Excellent Rotary Club of Memphis, 1984, Outstanding Math. Tchr. Memphis City Schs. Curriculum and Inst., 1992, 93. Mem. NEA, Nat. Coun. Tchrs. math., Tenn. Edn. Assn., Tenn. Math. Tchrs. Assn., Memphis Edn. Assn., Rotary Assn. Tchr. Excellence (treas. 1991-92), Phi Delta Kappa, Delta Sigma Theta (fin. sec. 1991-94, treas. 1994-96). Democrat. Episcopalian. Avocations: tennis, reading. Home: 514 Adrian Dr Memphis TN 38122-3814

HODGESS, ERIN MARIE, statistics educator; b. Pitts., Nov. 12, 1960; d. Edwin E. and Justine J. (Plazak) H. BS in Econs., U. Dayton, 1981; MA in Econs., U. Pitts., 1987; MS in Stats., Temple U., 1989, PhD in Stats., 1995. Econ. rsch. analyst Mellon Bank, NA, Pitts., 1981-85; programmer Techalloy Co., Inc., Rahns, Pa., 1985-86; programmer analyst The Linpro Co., Berwyn, Pa., 1986-87, Jones Apparel Group, Bristol, Pa., 1987-88; programming cons. various cos., Phila., 1988-89; teaching asst. Temple U., Phila., 1990-92, adj. instr., 1992-94, group leader grad. asst. tng. workshop, 1992; asst. prof. U. Houston-Downtown, 1994—. Spkr. Temple U.-Rutgers U. Stats. Day, Brunswick, N.J., 1988; presenter Statis. Sci. Conf., Rider U. Lawrenceville, N.J., 1995. Contbr. articles to profl. jours., including Jour. Statis. Sci., Linear Algebra and Its Applications. Fellow Temple U., 1988-90, grantee, 1994. Mem. Am. Statis. Assn. (presenter winter meeting Raleigh, N.C. 1995), Soc. Indsl. and Applied Math., Inst. Math. Stats. (presenter 4th matrix workshop McGill U., Montreal Que., Can. 1995), Intertel Internat., Mensa. Democrat. Roman Catholic. Avocations: golf, ice skating, swimming. Office: U Houston-Downtown One Main St Houston TX 77002 Home: Apt 279 2475 Underwood St Houston TX 77030-3535

HODGINS, BEATRICE DAVIS, educator; b. Bangor, Maine, Dec. 8, 1932; d. Ralph Wilson and Pauline Lucille (Davis) H. BS Early Childhood Edn., Framingham State Coll., 1983. Bank bookkeeper First Nat. Bank Boston, 1950-54; tchr., co-owner Humpty Dumpty Kindergarten and Nursery Sch., Framingham, Mass., 1954-78; real estate broker Century 21, Framingham, Mass., 1978-81; pvt. home health care Newton, Mass., 1980-83; dir., tchr., owner Humpty Dumpty Kind and Nursery Sch., Framingham, 1983—. Distbr. Ecoquest Internat., 1999—. Republican. Avocation: writing fiction for children. Home and Office: 11 Warren Rd Framingham MA 01702-6344

HODNEFIELD, ELAINE MARIE, elementary education educator; b. Jackson, Minn., Mar. 21, 1948; d. Cornelius and Mildred Elaine (Olson) H. BS in Elem. Edn., Mankato State U., 1970. Cert. elem. tchr., Iowa. 3d trade tchr. Paullina (Iowa) Community Sch., 1970-72; 4th grade tchr. Kingsley-Pierson Community Sch., Pierson, Iowa, 1972-73, 5th grade tchr., 1973-82, 3d grade tchr. Kingsley, Iowa, 1982—. Vol. Jackson County (Minn.) 4-H Program, 1967-82. Recipient 4-H Alumni award Jackson County Leaders Assn., 1982. Mem. NEA, Internat. Reading Assn., Iowa Edn. Assn., Iowa Coun. Tchrs. Math., Iowa Reading Assn., Siouxland Reading Assn., Kingsley-Pierson Edn. Assn. (officer). Home: 215 Burlington St Kingsley IA 51028-5008 Office: Kingsley-Pierson Sch 90 Valley Dr Kingsley IA 51028-5034

HOEBEL, BARTLEY GORE, psychology educator; b. N.Y.C., May 29, 1935; s. Edward Adamson and Frances (Gore) H.; m. Cynthia A. Eney, June 22, 1962; children— Valerie, Carolyn, Brett. AB, Harvard, 1957; PhD, U. Pa., 1962; PhD (hon.), U. Cath. Louvain, 1991. Mem. faculty psychology dept. Princeton, 1962—, prof, 1970—. Founder Delaware River Steamboat Floating Classroom, Inc. Contbg. author: Handbook of Psychopharmacology, 1977, S.S. Stevens Handbook of Experimental Psychology, 1988, Handbook of Obesity, 1997; contbr. 120 articles to tech. jours. and books. Fellow AAAS, APA (pres. physiol. and comparative psychol. divsn. 1994), Am. Psychol. Soc.; mem. Soc. Neurosci., Soc. Study Ingestive Behavior (pres. 1995), Ea. Psychol. Assn. (pres. 1997). Unitarian Universalist. Home: 207 Hartley Ave Princeton NJ 08540-5615 Office: Dept Psychology Princeton Univ Princeton NJ 08544 E-mail: hoebel@princeton.edu.

HOEFER, MARGARET J. librarian; b. Bklyn., July 28, 1909; d. Thomas A. and Margaret Emma (Skillin) Ford. BS, Kans. State Coll., 1932; MA, Colo. State Coll., 1939; BLS, U. Denver, 1943. Tchr., Smith Ctr. High Sch., Kans., 1934-38; head English dept. Iola (Kans.) Sr. High Sch., 1939-43; head circulation dept. Topeka Pub. Libr., 1943-44; libr. Pueblo (Colo.) Jr. Coll., 1944-46; bookmobile libr. U.S. Army, Nurnberg, Germany, 1946-48; dir. SCAP Civil Info. and Edn. Libr., Osaka, Japan, 1948-50; comd. libr. PHILCOM & 13th Air Force, Clark AFB, Manila, 1950-51; staff libr. Cen. Air Def. Force, Kansas City, Mo., 1951-53; county libr., Carroll County, Md., Westminster, 1958-62; head libr. Woodlawn Jr. High Sch., Balt., 1962-63; head reference svcs. Smithtown (N.Y.) Libr., 1963-65; dir. Emma S. Clark Meml. Libr., Setauket, N.Y., 1965-67; reference libr. Nassau Community Coll., Garden City, N.Y., 1967-69; asst. prof. libr. sci. Suffolk County Community Coll., Selden, N.Y., 1969-72; libr. Golden Hills Acad., Ocala, Fla., 1972-74; reference libr. Melbourne (Fla.) Pub. Libr., part-time, 1975-78; corp. libr. Harris Corp., Melbourne, 1980-85. Mem. Palm Bay Community Assn., 1976—; v.p., membership com. Brevard Assn. for Advancement of Blind, 1975-90; archivist Sebastian Inlet Dist., Melbourne, Fla., 1977-87; mem. Brevard County Libr. Bd., 1977-81, pres., 1979; mem. Friends of the Palm Bay (Fla.) Library, 1980—, pres., 1981-82; cert. tutor Literacy, English for Speakers of Other Langs., Literacy Coun. South Brevard, 1985—; cons. librs. Brevard Art Ctr. and Mus., South Brevard Women's Ctr. Recipient 1st Ann. award for svc. to Fla. librs. Coun. for Fla. Librs., 1981. Mem. AARP, Greater Palm Bay Area Sr. Ctr. Assn., Retired Sr. Vol. Persons. Republican. Home: 2115 Palm Bay Rd NE Ste 1E Palm Bay FL 32905-2936

HOEFFER, BEVERLY, nursing educator, researcher; b. Spokane, Wash., June 14, 1944; BS, U. Wash., 1966; MS, Rutgers U., 1969; DSc in Nursing, U. Calif., San Francisco, 1979. Cert. clin. specialist adult psychiat./mental health nurse. Clin. nurse specialist Mission Community Mental Health Ctr., San Francisco, 1974-75; asst. clin. prof., dept. mental health/community nursing U. Calif., San Francisco, 1979-80; assoc. to prof., chmn. dept. mental health nursing Oreg. Health Scis. U., Portland, 1980—96, assoc. dean acad. affairs sch. of nursing, 1997—2003. Bd. govs. We. Inst. Nursing, 1999—; presenter in field. Contbr. articles to profl. jours. Recipient Geriatric Mental Health Acad. award NIMH, 1984-87, rsch. grants in field. Fellow Am. Acad. Nursing; mem. ANA (exec. com. psychiat./mental health nursing 1986-88, chmn. coun. of specialists), We. Acad. Nurses, Phi Beta Kappa.

HOEFFNER, BALBINA THECLA, retired secondary education educator; b. Montgomery, N.Y., May 19, 1946; d. George Edward and Balbina Tillie (Mazur) H. BS, SUNY, Cortland, 1968; MA, SUNY, Stony Brook, 1975; MS, U. Ill., 1969. Cert. health educator, N.Y. Tchr. health Mid. Country Sch. Dist. 11, Centereach, N.Y., 1969—, Selden Jr. High Sch., Centereach, N.Y., 1969-86; tchr. health, dir. svc. club Selden Middle Sch., Centereach, N.Y., 1987—; tchr. health Newfield (N.Y.) High Sch., 1986-87; dir. student activities Selden Middle Sch., 1983—, ret., 2001—. Coord. peer leadership Selden Mid. Sch., 1981-87. Sch. coord. walkathon March of Dimes, 1978—; instr. CPR, 1975-80, Recipient Jenkins PTA award, 1984, Vol. award Town of Bookhaven, N.Y., 1985; named Tchr. of Yr., Selden Mid. Sch., 2000; dist. mini grantee, 1977, 79, 81, 88. Mem. AAHPERD (Cert. of Achievement 1982), NEA, N.Y. Fedn. Profl. Health Educators, N.Y. State United Tchrs., Mid. County Tchrs. Assn., Am. Auto Assn., Adirondack Mt. Club (sec. 1980-82), Nat. Jr. Honor Soc. (advisor 1981-86), N.J. Honor Soc. (hon. 1984). Democrat. Roman Catholic. Avocations: hiking, sailing, wine tasting, cooking, skiing. Home: 170 Old East Neck Rd Melville NY 11747-3211 Office: Selden Mid Sch 22 Jefferson Ave Centereach NY 11720-3250

HOEFT, ROBERT GENE, agriculture educator; b. David City, Nebr., May 21, 1944; s. Otto O. Hoeft and Lula (Barlean) Pleskac; m. Nancy A. Bussen, Sept. 1, 1990; children: Jeffrey, Angela. BS, U. Nebr., 1965, MS, 1967; PhD, U. Wis., 1972. Asst. prof. S.D. State U., Rapid City, 1972-73, U. Ill., Urbana, 1973-77, assoc. prof., 1977-81, prof., 1981—. Author: Modern Corn Production, 1986, Modern Corn & Soybean Production, 2000; editor Jour. Prodn. Agr., 1986-92. Recipient Funk award U. Ill., 1990, Robert E. Wagner award Potash and Phosphate Inst., 1998. Fellow Soil Sci. Soc. Am., Am. Soc. Agronomy (pres. 2002-03, CIBA-Geigy award 1978, Agronomic Extension award, grantee 1988, Agronomic Achievement award-soils 1995, Werner Nelson award for diagnosis of yield limiting factors 1996); mem. Coun. for Sci. and Tech. Office: U Ill 1102 S Goodwin Ave Urbana IL 61801-4730

HOENIGSWALD, HENRY MAX, linguist, educator; b. Breslau, Germany, Apr. 17, 1915; s. Richard and Gertrud (Grunwald) H.; m. Gabriele Schoepflich, Dec. 26, 1944, (dec. 2001); children: Frances Gertrude, Susan Ann. Student, U. Munich, 1932-33, U. Zurich, 1933-34, U. Padua, 1934-36; DLitt, U. Florence, 1936, Perfezionamento, 1937; LHD (hon.), Swarthmore Coll., 1981, U. Pa., 1988, MA (hon.), 1971. Staff mem. Istituto Studi Etruschi, Florence, 1936-38; lectr., rsch. asst., instr. Yale U., 1939-42, 44-45. Lectr., instr. Hartford Sem. Found., 1942-43, 45-46; lectr. Hunter Coll., 1942-43, 46; lectr. charge Army specialized tng. U. Pa., Phila., 1943-44, assoc. prof., 1948-59, prof. linguistics, 1959-85, prof. emeritus, 1985—, chmn. dept. linguistics, 1963-70, co-chmn., 1978-79, cn. Caldwell Prize com., 1989-91; P-4 Fgn. Service Inst., Dept. State, 1946-47; assoc. prof. U. Tex., 1947-48; sr. linguist Deccan Coll., India, 1955; Fulbright lectr., Kiel, 1968, Oxford U., 1976-77; corp. vis. com. fgn. lits. and linguistics MIT, 1968-74; chmn. overseers com. to visit dept. linguistics Harvard U., 1978-84; vis. assoc. prof. U. Mich., 1946, 52, Princeton U., 1959-60; vis. assoc. prof. Georgetown U., 1952-53, 54, Collitz prof., 1955; vis. prof. Yale U., 1961-62, U. Mich., 1968; mem. Seminar, Columbia U., 1965—; vis. staff mem., Leuven, 1986; fellow St. John's Coll., Oxford U., 1976-77; del. Comparative Linguistics Internat. Rsch. and Exchs. Bd., 1986; cons. Etymological Dictionary of Old High German, 1980—; Poultney lectr. Johns Hopkins U., 1991; co-promotor, Leuven, 1992; mem. acad. com. Yarmouk U., 1997. Author: Spoken Hindustani, 1946-47, Language Change and Linguistic Reconstruction, 1960, Studies in Formal Historical Linguistics, 1973; editor: Am. Oriental Series, 1954-58, The European Background of American Linguistics, 1979, (with L. Wiener) Biological Metaphor and Cladistic Classification, 1987, (with M.R. Key) General and American Ethnolinguistics, 1989; assoc. editor Indian Jour. Linguistics, 1977—; cons. editor Jour. History of Ideas, 1978—; adv. bd. Lang. and Style, 1968—, Jour. Indo-European Studies, 1973—, Diachronica, 1984-94, Lynx, 1988—; csr. internat. adviser, cons. editor Internat. Ency. Linguistics, 1986-91, 2d edit., 2000—; editl. cons. Biographical Dictionary of Western Linguistics, 1994—. Am. Council Learned Socs. fellow, 1942-43, 44, Guggenheim fellow, 1950-51, Newberry Library fellow, 1956, NSF and Center Advanced Study Behavioral Scis. fellow, 1962-63, Faculty fellow Modern Langs. Coll. House, 1990-91; Festschrift in his honor, 1987. Fellow British Acad. (corr.), Am. Acad. Arts and Scis.; mem. NAS, Am. Philos. Soc. (rsch. com. 1978-84, libr. com. 1984-94, chmn. 1988-94, membership com. class IV 1984-90, chmn. 1987-90, exec. com. 1988-94, publs. com. 1994—, Henry Allen Moe prize 1991), N.Y. Acad. Scis., Linguistic Soc. Am. (pres. 1958), Am. Oriental Soc. (editor 1954-58, pres. 1966-67), Philol. Soc. (London), Linguistic Soc. India, Linguistics Assn. Gt. Britain, Internat. Soc. Hist. Linguistics, Indogermanische Gesellschaft, Am. Philol. Assn., Classical Assn. Atlantic States, Henry Sweet Soc., Studienkreis Geschichte der Sprachwissenschaft, Deutsch-polnische Gesellschaft der U. Wroclaw/Breslau, N.Am. Assn. History of Lang. Scis., Fulbright Assn., Internat. Soc. Friends of Wroclaw U., Fedn. Am. Scientists. Office: U Pa 618 Williams Hall Philadelphia PA 19104-6305 Home: 3300 Darby Rd # 3107 Haverford PA 19041-1069 E-mail: henryh@babel.ling.upenn.edu.

HOEPPNER, DAVID WILLIAM, mechanical engineering educator; b. Waukesha, Wis., Dec. 17, 1935; s. William Frank and Lillian Hulda (Rosche) H.; m. Sue Ellen McFarlane, June 13, 1959; children: Laura Anne, Lynne Susan, Amy McFarlane. BME, Marquette U., 1958; MS, PhD, U. Wis., 1963. Asst. prof. metall. engring. U. Wis., Madison, 1963-64; rsch. metallurgist Battelle Meml. Inst., Columbus, 1964-69; group leader Lockheed Calif. Co., Burbank, 1969-74; prof. U. Mo., Columbia, 1974-78; Cockburn prof. U. Toronto, Ont., Can., 1978-85; prof., chmn. dept. mech. engring. U. Utah, Salt Lake City, 1985-92, prof. mech. engring., 1992—. Cons. Rolls Royce, Derby, Eng., 1973-95, Pratt and Whitney of Can., Longueuil, Que., 1978-2003, Lockheed Aircraft (1976, 1985-2003), Boeing, 1992-95; pres. Faside Internat. Inc., Salt Lake City, 1978—. Author: (with Wallace) Case Studies in Aircraft Corrosion, 1986; editor: Effect of Environment and Complex Load History on Fatigue, 1970, Fracture Prevention, 1974, Fatigue of Weldments, 1977; co-editor: Fretting Fatigue, Current Technology and Practice, 2000, Fretting Fatigue, Advances in Basic Understanding and Applications, 2003. Internat. senator Jaycees, Santa Paula, Calif., 1973; mem. city planning commn., Santa Paula, 1972-74. Mem. AIAA, ASME, ASTM (chmn. subcom. 1969-79, co-editor fretting fatigue, 1999, 2003), Am. Soc. Metals, Am. Soc. Engring. Edn., Soc. Automotive Engrs., Sigma Xi. Avocations: gardening, reading, skiing, hiking.

HOERING, HELEN G. elementary educator; b. Liberty, N.Y., Mar. 27, 1946; d. Lewis J. and Charlotte (Huggler) Gerow Sr.; m. Rudolf O. Hoering, Dec. 23, 1968; children: Otto, Katrina. BS, SUNY, Oneonta, 1968; MSEd, SUNY, 1971. Elem. tchr. Liberty Cen. Sch. at WSS, Liberty, N.Y. Mem. N.Y. State Reading Assn., Sullivan County Reading Coun., Alpha Delta Kappa (past pres.). Home: RR 1 Box 543 Jeffersonville NY 12748-9706

HOERMANN, EDWARD RICHARD, urban planning educator; b. N.Y.C., Jan. 7, 1926; s. Karl and Ella Alma (Hunger) H.; m. Helle Banner Rasmussen, Dec. 20, 1969; 1 child, Edward Richard II. BA in Art, Okla. State U., 1951, BArch Engring., BArch, 1952; MArch, Cornell U., 1961; MArch in Urban Design, Harvard U., 1964, PhD in Urban Planning, 1984. Registered architect, N.Y., N.J., N.H., Mass., Ohio; cert. planner. Architect Charles H. Warner Jr. & Walker Field Architects, Nyack, N.Y., 1953-58; asst. prof. architecture Pa. State U., University Park, 1959-62; planning designer, architect The Architects Collaborative, Cambridge, Mass., 1964-67; head dept. urban planning and design U. Cin., 1974-77, The Architects Collaborative, Cambridge, Mass., 1974-77; prof. urban planning and design U. Cin., 1974-94, prof. urban planning and design emeritus, 1995—; acting assoc. dean acad. affairs Coll. Design, Architecture Art and Planning, 1980-81; acting dir. Sch. Planning U. Cin., 1983-84, coord. urban planning program Sch. Planning, 1988-94; assoc. dir. Sch. Planning, 1994. Treas., bd. trustees Cin. Planning Fund, 1979—; chair site visitor pool Planning Accreditation Bd., Washington, 1985—; co-dir. Cin. Urban Park Study, Univ. Cin., 1986-87; teaching fellow archtl. scis. Harvard Univ., Cambridge, Mass., 1965-67. Mem. bd. trustees German-English Alt. Sch. Found., Inc., Cin., 1979-80; treas. bd. trustees Clearview Estates Found., Cin., 1980-85; scholarship reviewer Am.-Scandinavian Found., N.Y.C., 1975-94. With USN, 1944-46, PTO. Sr. Fulbright-Hays rsch. scholar Fulbright Commn., Darmstadt, Germany, 1971-72, Stuttgart, Germany, 1977-78. Mem. Am. Inst. Cert. Planners, Am. Planning Assn., Ohio Planning Conf., Harvard Club Cin. Republican. Christian Scientist. Home: 411 Resor Ave Cincinnati OH 45220-1511 Office: U Cin Sch Planning PO Box 210073 Cincinnati OH 45221-0073

HOEVELER, DIANE LONG, English educator, researcher, writer; b. Chgo., Apr. 9, 1949; d. Vincent Leo, Jr., and Constance (Puglise) Long; m. John David Hoeveler, Jr., Jan. 29, 1972; children: John David, Emily Ann. BA, U. Ill., 1970, MA, 1972, PhD, 1976. Teaching asst. U. Ill., Urbana, 1970-72, 74-75; lectr. U. Wis.-Milw., 1972-73, 75-76; instr. Alverno Coll., Milw., 1976-78; asst. prof. English, U. Louisville, 1978-80; English tchr. King Coll. Prep., Milw., 1980-87; prof. of English, Marquette U., Milw., 1987—, coord. women's studies program, 1987—. project dir. Milw. Humanities Program, 1978-79. Author: Romantic Androgyny, 1990, Charlotte Bronte, 1997, Gothic Feminism, 1998; co-editor 6 books; contbr. book revs. and articles to publs. NEH grantee, 1978, 79, 81, 86, 87. Business E-Mail: diane.hoeveler@marquette.edu.

HOFER, CHARLES WARREN, strategic management, entrepreneurship educator, consultant; b. Phoenixville, Pa., Nov. 11, 1940; s. Charles Emil and Alice May (Howard) H.; m. Judith Racella Millner, Oct. 22, 1980. BS in Engring. Physics summa cum laude, Lehigh U., 1962; MBA in Mktg. with distinction, Harvard U., 1965, MS in Applied Math., 1966, D in Bus. Policy, 1969. Research asst. Harvard Bus. Sch., Boston, 1965-66; asst. prof. Northeastern U., Boston, 1968-69; vis. lectr. Singapore Inst. Mgmt., 1969-70; asst. prof. Northwestern U., Evanston, Ill., 1970-75, assoc. prof., 1975-76; vis. assoc. prof. Stanford (Calif.) U., 1976-77, Columbia U., N.Y.C., 1978, NYU, 1978-80; vis. prof. U. Calif., Riverside, 1980; regents prof. strategy, entrepreneurship U. Ga., Athens, 1981—. Vis. chair in entrepreneurship Rutgers U., 1988; lectr. Chgo. C. of C., 1976-78; Donald W. Riegle campaign cons., Flint, Mich., 1968-72; vis. lectr. Ga. Tech., 1993; lectr. Nova U., 1981-96, Ga. State U., 1995-99. Author: Toward a Contingency Theory of Business Strategy, 1975 (ranked 16th in world Acad. Mgmt. survey 1985), Strategy Formulation: Analytical Concepts, 1978 (ranked 30th in world Acad. Mgmt. survey 1985); co-author: Strategic Management: A Casebook in Policy and Planning, 1980, 84, Future Firms: How America's High Tech Companies Work, 1998, Creating Value through Skill-Based Strategy and Entrepreneurial Leadership, 1999; co-editor: Strategic Management: A New View of Business Policy and Planning, 1979 (ranked 6th in world Acad. Mgmt. survey 1985); editor: Strategic Planning Management, 1987-90; and others. Baker scholar Harvard U., 1965; NSF fellow, 1962-63, Ford Found. fellow, 1966-67; recipient Rsch. award U. Ga., 1990, Leavey award Freedoms Found. Valley Forge, 1991, Coleman Entrepreneurship Mentor award Acad. Mgmt., 1992, Internat. Hall Fame Entrepreneur award Inventors Club Am., 1992, Williams A. Owens Rsch. award U. Ga., 1993, Sargent Americanism award Soc. Mfg. Engrs., 1994, Robert Foster Cherry award for Gt. Tchrs., Baylor U., 2002; named MBA Tchr. of Yr., U. Ga., 2003. Fellow U.S. Assn. Small Bus. and Entrepreneurship (chair corp. entrepreneurship divsn. 1989-90, v.p. devel. 1990-92, v.p. programs 1995-96, pres. 1998, chair entrepreneurship edn. divsn. 2000, Nat. Model Entrepreneurship MBA Program award 1991, Disting. Entrepreneurship Educator of Yr. award 1992, Nat. Model Entrepreneurship PhD Program award 1998, Outstanding Entrepreneurship Edn. Pedagogy award 2000); mem. Acad. Mgmt. (chmn. policy div. 1977-78, First Outstanding Contbns. entrepreneurship divsn. award 1989, Entrepreneurship Advocate award 1999), Strategic Mgmt. Soc. (charter), Decision Scis. Inst. (chmn. policy track 1985-86), Inst. Mgmt. Scis., Am. Econ. Assn., Harvard Bus. Sch. Club Atlanta, Harvard Club Ga., Phi Beta Kappa, Phi Eta Sigma, Pi Mu Epsilon, Tau Beta Pi, Sigma Iota Epsilon, Beta Gamma Sigma. Lutheran. Avocations: chess, bridge, jogging, traveling, brandy tasting. Home: 4445 Stonington Cir Atlanta GA 30338-6621 Office: U Ga Mgmt Dept Terry Coll Bus Athens GA 30602 E-mail: chofer@uga.edu., jrmh@bellsouth.net.

HOFER, INGRID, artist, educator; b. N.Y.C., Aug. 25, 1926; d. William D. and Martha G. Kassul; m. Peter H. Hofer, Mar. 10, 1951; 1 child, Mark A. BFA, Meisterschule für Mode, Hamburg, Germany, 1949; postgrad., Traphagen Sch. Design, N.Y.C., 1949-51. Instr. Acad. Arts Trailside Mus., N.J., 1968-70, Grosse Pointe War Meml., Mich., 1974-78, Countryside Arts, Arlington Heights, Ill., 1981-93, Toledo Arts Club/Lourdes Coll., 1983-93, McCormick (S.C.) Arts Coun., 1994—2003. Represented in permanent collections Fairleigh Dickinson U., N.J., First Nat. Bank, Barrington, Ill., Good Shepherd Hosp., Ill., Lumus Co., N.J., Dana Corp., Ohio, others; exhbns. include Nat. Juried Shows, 1972-99, Union League, Chgo., 1981, Winter Sojourn, Toledo, 1987, Women Alive Ohio, 1986, 87, 89, Women on Paper, Anderson, S.C., 1996, The Arnold Gallery, Aiken, S.C., 1997, 98, Aiken Ctr. Arts, 2001-02, USCA Etherredge Art Gallery, 2002-03. Vol. John De La Howe Sch., McCormick, 1963-99, others. Fellow Am. Artist Profl. League; mem. Catharine Lorillard Wolfeart, N.J. Inst. Art, S.C. Inst. Art, Ga. Inst. Art, Ala. Inst. Art, Gertrude Herbert Inst. Art. Home: 209 Old Ferry Rd Mc Cormick SC 29835-3409

HOFF, BETTY ANN, physical education educator; b. Galesville, Wis., Nov. 18, 1938; d. Henry William and Arlene Bernice (Evenson) H. BA, Luther Coll., 1960; MS, MacMurray Coll., 1961; PhD, U. Oreg., 1970; postgrad., Ariz. State U., 1977-79. Prof. health phys. edn. Luther Coll., Decorah, Iowa, 1961—. Lectr. Sports Am., Cairo, 1987; athletic trainer Goodwill Games U.S. Team Handball Assn., Moscow, 1986, Pan Am. Games U.S. Olympic Com., Indpls., 1987. Chair divsn. 3 softball subcom. NCAA, Overland Park, Kans., 1988-93. Recipient Gold medal for 400m and 800m, Sr. Olympic Games, 2001. Mem. Nat. Athletic Trainers Assn., Nat. Softball Coaches Assn. (named to Hall of Fame 1992, 400 Victory Club award 1994, 500 Victory Club award 2000), Am. Assn. for Health, Phys. Edn., Recreation and Dance, Iowa Assn. for Health, Phys. Edn., Recreation and Dance (pres. 1973-74, Iowa Honor award 1975). Lutheran. Avocations: running, senior games participant. Home: 108 West St Decorah IA 52101-1526 Office: Luther Coll 700 College Dr Decorah IA 52101-1039

HOFF, JULIAN THEODORE, physician, educator; b. Boise, Idaho, Sept. 22, 1936; s. Harvey Orval and Helen Marie (Boraas) H.; m. Diane Shanks, June 3, 1962; children— Paul, Allison, Julia. BA, Stanford U., Calif., 1958; MD, Cornell U., N.Y.C., 1962. Diplomate Am. Bd. Neurol. Surgery. Intern N.Y. Hosp., N.Y.C., 1962-63, resident in surgery, 1963-64, resident in neurosurgery, 1966-70; asst. prof. neurosurgery U. Calif., San Francisco, assoc. prof. neurosurgery, 1974-78, prof. neurosurgery, 1978-81, U. Mich., Ann Arbor, 1981—, head sect. neurosurgery, 1981—. Sec. Am. Bd. Neurol-Surgery, 1987-91, chmn., 1991-92; mem. bd. sci. councillors Nat. Inst. Neurol. Diseases and Stroke-NIH, 1993-97, nat. adv. coun., 1999—. Editor: Practice of Neurosurgery, 1979-85; Current Surgical Management of Neurological Diseases, 1980; Neurosurgery: Diagnostic and Management Principles, 1992, Mild to Moderate Head Injury, 1989; co-editor: Neurosurgery: Scientific Basis of Clinical Practice, 1985, 3rd edit., 1999; contbr. articles to profl. jours. Served to capt. US Army, 1964-66. Recipient Tchr.-Investigator award, NIH, 1972—77, Javits Neurosci. Investigator award, 1985—99, Macy Faculty scholar, London, 1979. Fellow: ACS (2d v.p.-elect 1998—99); mem.: Soc. Neurol. Surgeons (pres. 1999—2000, Grass prize 2001), Cen. Neurosurg. Soc. (pres. 1985—86), Am. Acad. Neurosurgeons (treas. 1989—92, sec. 1992—, pres. 1996—), Congress Neurol. Surgeons (v.p. 1982—83, Honored Guest 2003), Am. Surg. Assn., Am. Assn. Neurol. Surgeons (v.p. 1991—93, pres. 1993—94, Cushing medal 2001), Inst. Medicine NAS. Republican. Presbyterian. Home: 2120 Wallingford Rd Ann Arbor MI 48104-4563 Office: U Mich Hosp TC 2128 Ann Arbor MI 48109

HOFF, SAMUEL BOYER, political science educator; b. Williamsport, Pa., June 7, 1957; s. Samuel Romberger and J. Mattie (Schultz) H.; m. Phyllis Rose Oliveto, Aug. 16, 1986. BA in Polit. Sci., Susquehanna U., 1979; MA in Polit. Sci., Am. U., 1981, SUNY, Stony Brook, 1983, PhD in Polit. Sci., 1987. Instr. SUNY, Stony Brook, 1982-86, asst. prof. Geneseo, 1987-88; asst. prof. dept. history and polit. sci. Del. State U., Dover, 1989-92, assoc. prof. dept. history and polit. sci., 1992-96, prof., 1996-99, George Washington disting. prof., 1999—, ROTC dir., 1993-99, chair dept. history and polit. sci., 2000—. Adj. instr. dept. social sci. N.Y. Inst. Tech., Old Westbury, N.Y., 1986; adj. asst. prof. Wittenberg U., Springfield, Ohio, 1987; vis. asst. prof. dept. govt. and politics Ohio Wesleyan U., Delaware, 1986-87; vis. asst. prof. Wichita (Kans.) State U., 1988-89; congl. intern U.S. Rep. Allen Ertel, Washington, 1978; mem. canvass staff Clean Water Action Project, Washington, 1980; rsch. asst. subcom. on human resources U.S. Ho. of Reps., Washington, 1980; asst. Senator Jacob Javits, Stony Brook, 1983-85. Contbr. articles to profl. jours. Committeeman Suffolk County Dems., L.I., 1984-86; presdl. candidate Dem. Party, 1988, Ind. Party, 1992, 96, 2000. Freedoms Found. scholar, 1990, 94, 2003; USMA-ROTC Mil. History fellow, 1994; Nat. Security Law fellow, 1995, Carnegie Coun. fellow, 1997, faculty fellow ExxonMobil, 2002-04. Mem. Am. Polit. Sci. Assn., Acad. Polit. Sci., Nat. Social Sci. Assn., Northeastern Polit. Sci. Assn., Midwest Polit. Sci. Assn., Western Polit. Sci. Assn., So. Polit. Sci. Assn., Social Sci. History Assn., Western Social Sci. Assn., Nat. Capital Area Polit. Sci. Assn., Pa. Polit. Sci. Assn., N.Y. Polit. Sci. Assn. Lutheran. Avocations: sports, antique collector, musician. Home: 813 Maple Pky Dover DE 19901-4238 Office: Del State Univ Dept History Polit Sci Dover DE 19901 E-mail: shoff@dsc.edu.

HOFFENBERG, MARVIN, retired political science educator, consultant; b. Buffalo, July 7, 1914; s. Harry and Jennie Pearl (Weiss) H.; m. Betty Eising Stern, July 20, 1947; children— David A., Peter H. Student, St. Bonaventure Coll., 1934-35; B.Sc., Ohio State U., 1939, MA, 1940, postgrad., 1941. Asst. chief div. interindustry econs. Bur. Labor Statistics, Dept. Labor, 1941-52; cons. U.S. Mut. Security Agy., Europe, 1952, Statistik Sentralbyra, Govt. of Norway, Oslo, 1955; dir. research, econ. cons. dept. deVegh & Co., 1956-58; economist RAND Corp., 1952-56; staff economist Com. Econ. Devel., 1958-60; project chmn. Johns Hopkins U., 1960-63; dir. cost analysis dept. Aerospace Corp., 1963-65; Research economist Inst. Govt. and Pub. Affairs, UCLA, 1965-67, prof.-in-residence polit. sci., 1967-85, prof. emeritus, 1985—; dir. M.P.A. program, co-chmn. Interdepartmental Program in Comprehensive Health Planning UCLA, 1974-76. Author: (with Kenneth J. Arrow) A Time Series Analysis of Inter-Industry Demand, 1959; editor: (with Levine, Hardt and Kaplan) Mathematics and Computers in Soviet Economics, 1967; contbr. articles to profl. jours., chpts. to books Mem. bd. advisers Sidney Stern Meml. Trust; bd. dirs. L.A. chpt. Am. Jewish Com.; foreman L.A. County Grand Jury, 1990-91; commr. L.A. County Economy and Efficiency Commn., 1991-92. C.C. Stillman scholar; Littauer fellow Harvard U., 1946; recipient Disting. service award Coll. Adminstrv. Scis., Ohio State U., 1971 Mem.: AAAS (life fellow 1957). Jewish. Home: 1365 Marinette Rd Pacific Palisades CA 90272 E-mail: hoffen@ucla.edu.

HOFFER, SHARON MARIE, secondary education educator; b. Dallas, Oct. 18, 1941; d. Bates Lowry and Marie E. (Grady) H. BA in Secondary Edn., U. Mo., Kansas City, 1971, MA in Secondary Edn. (Math), 1976; PhD in Adult and Extension Edn., Tex. A&M U., 1986. Tchr. 7th grade St. Peter's Prince Sch., San Antonio, 1962-64, St. Catherine of Siena Sch., Metairie, La., 1964-66; tchr. 7th, 8th grades Holy Trinity Sch., Kansas City, Mo., 1966-69; tchr. math., music, reading Guardian Angels Sch., Kansas City, 1969-70, St. Peter's Sch., Kansas City, 1971-77; dept. chair, tchr. math. St. Mary's High Sch., Independence, Mo., 1977-80; tchr. math. St. Teresa's Acad., Kansas City, Mo., 1980-81; instr. math. Tex. A&M U., College Station, 1982-86; curriculum-grant writer Pan-Ednl. Inst., Independence, 1987; tchr. math. East Environ. and Agribusiness Magnet High Sch., Kansas City, 1987—99, Van Horn High Sch., 1999—. Mem. Mensa. Roman Catholic. Avocations: reading, computer, games, music. Home: 2819 Campbell St Kansas City MO 64109-1125

HOFFMAN, BARBARA ANN, English language educator; b. Rochester, N.Y., Dec. 19, 1941; d. Joseph George and Lucy Rose (Voelkl) H. Student, Nazareth Coll., Rochester, N.Y., 1959-62; BA, D'Youville Coll., 1963; MA, Cath. U. Am., 1965; postgrad., Duquesne U., 1966-69. Instr. English Marywood Coll., Scranton, Pa., 1969-72, asst. prof., 1972-90, prof., 1990—. Catechist U. Scranton, 1987-92. Author (poetry) Cliffs of Fall, 1979; contbr. poetry to various publs. Student of Japanese Tea Ceremony. Recipient Excellence in Teaching award Sears Roebuck and Co., 1990; Marywood Scholarship named in her honor, 1991. Mem. AAUP, Urasenke Chanoyu Soc. Democrat. Roman Catholic. Home: 1749 Jefferson Ave Scranton PA 18509-2019 Office: Marywood Coll PO Box 814 Scranton PA 18501-0814

HOFFMAN, BARBARA JO, health and physical education educator, athletic director; b. Dayton, Ohio, Aug. 10, 1952; d. Harold Lee and Virginia May (Dafler) H. BA, Otterbein Coll., 1974; MEd, Ashland Coll., 1987. Cert. Athletic Adminstr. Tchr. Harrison Hills City Sch., Hopedale, Ohio, 1974—; coach volleyball, track, basketball Cadiz HS, Ohio, 1974-85, athletic dir., 1996—2003. Key advisor Ohio FHA/HERO, Columbus, 1990-96, mentor advisor, 1992. Recipient Golden Apple Achiever award Ashland Oil, Inc., 1989, Ohio Home Econs. Tchr. of Yr. award, 1991, Vocat. Home Econs. Program award, 1990, Pacesetter award, 1992, 93, 96, 97. Mem. NEA, AAHPERD, Nat. Interscholastic Athletic Adminstrs. Assn., Ea. Ohio Interscholastic Athletic Adminstrs. Assn. Republican. Methodist. Home: 647 Kerr Ave Cadiz OH 43907-1022 Office: Harrison Ctrl HS 440 E Market St Cadiz OH 43907-1244 E-mail: bhoffman@clover.net.

HOFFMAN, DANIEL (GERARD), literature educator, poet; b. N.Y.C., Apr. 3, 1923; s. Daniel and Frances (Beck) H.; m. Elizabeth McFarland, May 22, 1948; children: Kate, Macfarlane. BA, Columbia U., 1947, MA, 1949, PhD, 1956. Instr. English Columbia U., 1952-56; vis. prof. Am. Lit. Faculté des Lettres, Dijon, France, 1956-57; asst. prof. to prof. English Swarthmore Coll., 1957-66; prof. English U. Pa., 1966-83, poet-in-residence, 1978-93, Felix E. Schelling prof. English lit., 1983-93, prof. emeritus, 1993—. Fellow Ind. U. Sch. Letters, 1959; George Elliston lectr. poetry U. Cin., 1964; lectr. 6th Internat. Sch. Yeats Studies, Sligo, Ireland, 1965; poetry cons. Libr. of Congress, 1973-74, hon. cons. in Am. letters, 1974-77; poet-in-residence Cathedral Ch. of St. John the Divine, 1988-99; vis. prof. English, King's Coll. London, 1991-92. Author: (poetry) An Armada of Thirty Whales, 1954, A Little Geste and Other Poems, 1960, The City of Satisfactions, 1963, Striking the Stones, 1968, Broken Laws, 1970, The Center of Attention, 1974, Able Was I Ere I Saw Elba, 1977, Brotherly Love, 1981, Hang-Gliding from Helicon, 1988, Middens of the Tribe, 1995, Darkening Water, 2002, Beyond Silence: Selected Shorter Poems, 2003; (poetry transl.) A Play of Mirrors by Ruth Domino, 2002; (criticism) Paul Bunyan: Last of the Frontier Demigods, 1952, The Poetry of Stephen Crane, 1957, Form and Fable in American Fiction, 1961, Barbarous Knowledge, 1967, Poe Poe Poe Poe Poe Poe Poe, 1972, Faulkner's Country Matters, 1989, Words to Create a World, 1993; (memoir) Zone of the Interior, 2000; editor: The Red Badge of Courage, 1957, American Poetry and Poetics, 1962, Ezra Pound and William Carlos Williams, 1983; editor, contbr.: (criticism) Harvard Guide to Contemporary American Writing, 1979. Served to 1st lt. USAAF, 1943-46. Decorated Legion of Merit; recipient U. Chgo. Folklore prize, 1949, Poetry Center Introductions prize, 1951, Yale Series of Younger Poets award, 1954, Ansley prize, 1956, Lit. award Athenaeum of Phila., 1963, 83, medal for excellence Columbia U., 1964, Nat. Inst. Arts and Letters award in poetry, 1967, meml. medal Hungarian PEN, 1980, Hazlett Meml. award for lit., 1984, Paterson Poetry prize, 1989, Aiken Taylor Prize for Modern Am. Poetry, 2003; poetry grantee Ingram Merrill Found., 1971-72; fellow Am. Council Learned Socs., 1961-62, 66-67, NEH, 1975-76, Guggenheim Meml. Found., 1983-84. Mem. MLA, Assn. Literary Scholars and Critics, Acad. Am. Poets (chancellor 1973-97, chancellor emeritus 1997—), Authors Guild (council). Clubs: Century (N.Y.C.); Franklin Inn (Phila.).

HOFFMAN, DIANE MAE, special education educator; b. Camp Hill, Pa., Sept. 25, 1964; d. Edward Eugene and Ginger Mae (Benedick) H. BS in Ed., Pa. State U., 1988; cert., Millersville U., 1989. Cert. instructional 1, Pa. Ednl. paraprofl. Capital Area Intermediate Unit, Lemoyne, Pa., 1988-90; spl. edn. educator Harrisburg (Pa.) City Schs., 1990—. Swimming instr. Harrisburg Area chpt. ARC, 1973—; swimming instr., supr. West Shore YMCA, 2002-; troop leader Girl Scouts U.S. Mem.: Coun. for Exceptional Children (MHMR divsn. and behavioral disorders divsn.), York Soc. (treas., bd. mem.), Penn State Alumni Assn. Republican. Methodist. Avocations: crafts, swimming. Home: 216 E Locust St Mechanicsburg PA 17055-6523

HOFFMAN, DONALD RICHARD, pathologist, educator; b. Boston, Aug. 25, 1943; s. William Maurice and Laura (Rodman) H.; m. Valeria Anne Mossey, Oct. 24, 1971; children: Anthony Horatio, Maria Lauren, Avram Joseph. AB, Harvard, 1965; PhD, Calif. Inst. Technology, 1970. Asst. prof. pediatrics U. So. Calif. Sch. Medicine, L.A., 1971-75; assoc. prof. pathology Creighton U. Sch. Medicine, Omaha, 1975-77, East Carolina U. Sch. Medicine, Greenville, N.C., 1977-82, prof. pathology and lab. medicine, 1982—. Mem. adv. com. on allergenic products, HHS, FDA, Rockville, Md., 1990-94. Mem. editorial bd. Jour. Allergy Clin. Immunology, 1988-93, Immunochemistry, 1974-77; contbr. articles to profl. jours. Fellow Am. Acad. Allergy and Immunology; mem. Am. Assn. Immunologists, Protein Soc., N.Y. Acad. Scis., AAAS. Achievements include research isolation of insect venom allergens. Office: Brody Sch Medicine East Carolina U Dept Pathology/Lab Medicine Greenville NC 27858 E-mail: hoffmand@mail.ecu.edu.

HOFFMAN, DONNA COY, learning disabilities educator; b. Cin., Apr. 18, 1940; d. Clifford Donovan and Dorothy (Roessler) Coy; m. Donald Edward Hoffman, June 17, 1961; children: David Clifford, Dawn Susan Hoffman Osha. BS in Edn., Miami U., Oxford, Ohio, 1961; MEd, Xavier U., 1989. Cert. profl. tchr., Ohio, N.J. English tchr. Oak Hills Local Sch. Dist., Cin., 1961-62; vis. tchr. Westfield (N.J.) Sch. Dist., 1974-77; teaching staff Fair Oaks Hosp., Summit, N.J., 1974-77; learning disabilities resource tchr. Finneytown Local Sch. Dist., Cin., 1979—. Staff devel. com. Finneytown Schs., Cin., 1988-91; in-svc. com. Hamilton County Schs., Cin., 1988, 90. Deacon, chmn. Presbyn. Ch. of Wyoming, Cin., 1989-92; pres. Jr. Woman's Club Western Cin., 1966; founder, advisor Oak Hills Jr. Woman's Club, Cin., 1967. Named Outstanding Educator, Spl. Edn. Regional Resource Ctr. S.W. Ohio, 1988, Coun. for Econ. Edn., 1993. Mem. ASCD, Coun. for Exceptional Children (workshop speaker nat. meeting 1996), Orton Dyslexia Soc., Assn. on Handicapped Student Svcs. Programs in Postsecondary Edn., Transition and Comm. Consortium on Learning Disabilities (Ohio planning com. 1990-92). Republican. Avocations: music, needlework, travel. Office: Finneytown High Sch 8916 Fontainebleau Ter Cincinnati OH 45231-4898

HOFFMAN, H(OWARD) CARL, retired elementary school educator; b. Buffalo, July 2, 1942; s. Howard Carl and Thelma Elizabeth (Cox) H.; m. Gail Frances Grover, July 23, 1966 (dec. Oct. 1990); children: Kirsten Lara, Siobhan Malene; m. Darinda S. Gluc, Aug. 1, 1996; 1 stepchild, Kevin K. Gluc. Student, SUNY, Buffalo, 1961-63, Kans. State U., 1964; BS in Edn., SUNY, Geneseo, 1966, postgrad., 1966-67. Lic. lay reader Emmanuel Episc. Ch. Rsch. technician E.I. Du Pont de Nemours & Co., Tonawanda, N.Y., 1963; substitute tchr. Rochester (N.Y.) City Sch. Dist., 1966; mid. sch. tchr. Sweet Home Cen. Sch. Dist., Amherst, N.Y., 1967-98. Mem. Buffalo Schola Cantorum, 1967-70, Va. Choral Soc., 1999—, Willow Ridge Civic Assn., Amherst, N.Y., 1979-97, Morningview Homeowners Assn., 1998-, pres. 1999-2001, 2003-; supr. bid takers at annual PBS TV Auction, Buffalo, 1987-98; mem., bd. dirs. Sweet Home Fed. Credit Union, 1988-, sec. 1988-98, pres. 1998-; mem. vestry, treas. Emmanuel Episcopal Ch., 2001—. Recipient Outstanding Young Educator award Amherst Jaycees, 1976, N.Y. State United Tchrs. Leadership award, 1994. Mem. Am. Fedn. Tchrs., N.Y. State United Tchrs. (alt. del. 1984-98), Sweet Home Edn. Assn. (chmn. polit. action com. 1984-98, v.p. 1985-98). Democrat. Episcopalian.

HOFFMAN, JAMES DAVID, secondary instruction and personnel director; b. Trenton, N.J., Dec. 28, 1954; s. Walter William and Loretta Ellen (Reilly) H.; children: Allison, Christina. BA, Trenton State Coll., 1978; EdM, Rutgers U., 1986, EdD, 1993. Cert. sch. adminstr. Tchr. English and history Burlington County Vo-Tech., Mt. Holly, N.J., 1978-86; asst. prin., supr. Point Pleasant Beach (N.J.) High Sch., 1986-89; asst. prin. Lawrence Mid. Sch., Lawrenceville, N.J., 1989-93; prin. Robert Frost Elem. Sch., East Brunswick, N.J., 1993-96, Ravena (N.Y.) Coeymans Selkirk Mid. Sch., 1996—2002; dir. secondary instrn. Greater Amsterdam (N.Y.) Sch. Dist., 2002—. Adj. instr. Rutgers U., 1995-96, U. Albany, 1997—; ind. cons. in field. Contbr. articles to profl. jours. Pres., adminstrv. coun. St. Mark United Meth. Ch., Hamilton Square, N.J., 1993-97. Named to Outstanding Young Men in Am., 1988. Mem. Nat. Assn. Elem. Sch. Prins., N.J. Prins. and Supr.'s Assn., Inst. Devel. Ednl. Activities, Phi Delta Kappa (v.p. Trenton area 1993-95). Avocations: travel, music. Office: Greater Amsterdam Sch Dist II Liberty St Amsterdam NY 12010

HOFFMAN, JERRY IRWIN, retired dental educator; b. Chgo., Nov. 20, 1935; s. Irwin and Luba Hoffman; m. Sharon Lynn Seaman, Aug. 25, 1963; children: Steven Abram, Rachel Irene. Student, DePaul U., 1953-56; BS in Biology and Chemistry, Roosevelt U., 1956; DDS, Loyola U., Chgo., 1960; M of Health Care Adminstrn., Baylor U., 1972. Certificate, General Practice Residency, U.S. Army, 1978. Commd. officer U.S. Army, 1960 (served to 1962, returned 1964), advanced through grades to col., 1978, hdqrs. rep. local dental tng. confs. Europe, 1965-67; cons. to Comdg. Gen. U.S. Army Med. Research and Devel. Command, Washington, 1972-76; cons. Office of Surgeon Gen. U.S. Army, Washington, 1972-76, liaison rep. to Nat. Adv. Council and Oral Biology and Medicine Study Sessions of the Nat. Inst. Dental Research and NIH, 1973-76, resident in Gen. Practice Residency, 1976-78; comdg. officer U.S. Army Dental Activity, Fort Monmouth, N.J., 1979-82; ret., 1982; pvt. practice dentistry, 1962-64; assoc. prof. operative dentistry Loyola U. Sch. Dentistry, Maywood, Ill., 1982-93, dir. gen. practice residency, 1982-85, coordinator extramural dental resources, 1983-85, assoc. dean for clin. affairs, 1985-93; dir. sci. programs Chgo. Dental Soc., 1993—2002, ret., 2002. Staff dentist Silas B. Hayes Army Hosp., Fort Ord, Calif., 1976-79, Patterson Army Hosp., Ft. Monmouth, 1979-82; lectr., presenter seminars in field. Contbr. articles to profl. jours. Decorated Legion of Merit, Meritorious Svc. Medal with oak leaf cluster. Fellow: Am. Coll. Dentists, Internat. Coll. Dentists, Odontographic Soc.; master: Acad. Gen. Dentistry; mem. ADA, Ill. Dental Soc., Chgo. Dental Soc., Am. Assn. Dental Schs., Am. Soc. Assn. Execs., Assn. Healthcare Execs., Profl. Conv. Mgmt. Assn., Omicron Kappa Upsilon.

HOFFMAN, JOSEPH FREDERICK, physiology educator; b. Oklahoma City, Mar. 7, 1925; s. Henry Raymond and Rena Virginia (Crossman) H.; m. Elena Citkowitz. BS, U. Okla., 1947, MS, 1948; MA, Princeton U., 1951, PhD, 1952. Lectr., rsch. asst. Princeton (N.J.) U., 1952-56; physiologist, sec. Nat. Heart Inst., Bethesda, Md., 1957-65; prof. physiology Yale U. Sch. Med., New Haven, 1965-74, chmn. dept. physiology, 1973-79, Eugene Higgins prof. cellular and molecular physiology, 1974—. Fellow AAAS, Am. Acad. Arts and Scis.; mem. NAS, Biophys. Soc. (pres. 1985-86), Soc. Gen. Physiologists (pres. 1975-76), Am. Physiol. Soc., Argentine Soc. Physiol Sci. (hon.). Office: Yale U Dept Cellular & Molec Phys 333 Cedar St New Haven CT 06520-8026 E-mail: joseph.hoffman@yale.edu.

HOFFMAN, JUDY GREENBLATT, preschool director; b. Chgo., June 12, 1932; d. Edward Abraham and Clara (Morrill) Greenblatt; m. Morton Hoffman, Mar. 16, 1950 (div. Jan. 1983); children: Michael, Alan, Clare. BA summa cum laude, Met. State Coll., Denver, 1972; MA, U. No. Colo., 1976, MA in Spl. Edn. Moderate Needs, 1996. Cert. tchr., Colo. Pre-sch. dir. B.M.H. Synagogue, Denver, 1968-70, Temple Emanuel, Denver, 1970-85, Congregation Rodef Shalom, Denver, 1985-88; tchr. Denver Pub. Schs., 1988—. Bilingual tchr. adults in amnesty edn. Denver Pub. Schs., 1989-90. Author: I Live in Israel, 1979, Joseph and Me, 1980 (Gamoran award), (with others) American Spectrum Single Volume Encyclopedia, 1991. Coord. Douglas Mountain Therapeutic Riding Ctr. for Handicapped, Golden, Colo., 1985—; dir. Mountain Ranch Summer Day Camp for Denver Pub. Schs., 1989-91. Mem. Nat. Assn. Temple Educators. Democrat. Avocations: riding, writing, music. E-mail: jhoff3@earthlink.net.

HOFFMAN, JULIEN IVOR ELLIS, pediatric cardiologist, educator; b. Salisbury, South Rhodesia, July 26, 1925; arrived in U.S., 1957, naturalized, 1967. s. Bernard Isaac and Minrose (Bermant) H.; m. Kathleen (Lewis), 1986; children: Anna, Daniel. BS, U. Witwaterstrand, Johannesburg, South Africa, 1944, BSc (hon.), 1945, MB, BCh, 1949; MD, 1970. Intern, resident internal medicine, South Africa, 1950-56; research asst., postgrad. Med. Sch., London, 1956-57; fellow pediatric cardiology Boston Children's Hosp., Boston, 1957-59; fellow Cardiovasc. Rsch. Inst., San Francisco, 1959-60; asst. prof. pediat., internal medicine Albert Einstein Coll., N.Y.C., 1962-66; assoc. prof. pediat. U. Calif., San Francisco, 1966-70, prof., 1970-94, prof. physiology, 1981-88, prof. emeritus, 1994. Sr. mem. Cardiovasc. Rsch. Inst., U. Calif., San Francisco, 1966— ; mem. bd. examiners, sub-bd. pediatric cardiology Am. Bd. Pediat., 1973-78, sub-bd. pediat. intensive care, 1985-87; chmn. Louis Katz Award Com., Basic Sci. Coun., Am. Heart Assn., 1973-74; George Brown Meml. Lectr., Am. Heart Assn., 1977; George Alexander Gibson Meml. Lectr. Royal Coll. Physicians (Edinburgh), 1978; Lilly lectr. Royal Coll. Physicians (London), 1981; Isaac Starr lectr. Cardiac Systems Dynamics Soc., Eng., 1982; John Keith Lectr., 1985; Disting. Physiology Lectr. Am. Coll. Chest Physicians, 1985; Nadas Lectr. Am. Heart Assn., 1987; 1st Donald C. Fyler Lectr. Children's Hosp., Boston, 1990; First MacDonald Dick Lectr. U. Mich., Ann Arbor. Recipient Bayer Cardiovasc. Mentor Award, 1989. Fellow Royal Coll. Physicians; mem. World Congress Pediat. Cardiology and Cardiac Surgery (hon. joint pres. Paris, 1993); MacDonald Dick Lectr. U. Mich., Anabor, 2003; Am. Physiol. Soc., Am. Pediatric Soc., Soc. Pediatric Rsch. Achievements: extensive rsch. into congenital heart disease and coronary blood flow. Home: 925 Tiburon Blvd Belvedere Tiburon CA 94920-1525 Office: U Calif Med Ctr 1331 M Dept Pediat San Francisco CA 94143 E-mail: jhoffman@pedcard.ucsf.edu.

HOFFMAN, LOIS WLADIS, psychologist, educator; b. Elmira, N.Y., Mar. 25, 1929; d. Gustave and Etta (Wladis) Wladis; m. Martin Leon Hoffman, June 24, 1951 (div.); children— Amy Gabrielle, Jill Adrienne.; m. Herbert Zimiles, Oct. 25, 1981. BA cum laude, U. Buffalo, 1951; MS, Purdue U., 1953; PhD, U. Mich., 1958. Asst. study dir. Survey Rsch. Ctr., 1954—55; rsch. asst Rsch. Ctr. for Group Dynamics, 1955—56, rsch. assoc., 1956—60, cons. psychol. clinic, 1959—60; lectr. psychology, 1967-72; assoc. prof., 1972—75; prof., 1975—97; chairwoman devel. psychology, 1986-92; prof. emerita, 1997—. Author: (with F. IVan Nye) The Employed Mother in America, 1963, Working Mothers, 1974, (with S. Paris, E. Hall and R. Schell) Developmental Psychology Today, 5th edit., 1986, (with S. Paris and E. Hall) 6th edit., 1993; editor: (with Martin L. Hoffman) Review of Child Development Research, vol. 1, 1964, vol. 2, 1966 (Family Life Book award Child Study Assn. Am. 1965), (with Mednick and Tangri) Women and Achievement, (with Gandelman and Shifman) Parenting, its Causes and Consequences, Women at Work, 1999; articles. Mem. APA (pres. devel. div. 1990-91), Soc. Rsch. in Child Devel., Soc. Psychol. Study of Social Issues (pres. 1983-84), Phi Beta Kappa, Phi Kappa Phi. Address: 1307 Baldwin Ave Ann Arbor MI 48104-3623

HOFFMAN, LYNN RENEE, elementary education educator; b. Trenton, NJ, Apr. 19, 1957; d. Hugh L. and Thelma B. (Winner) H. BA in Theology, Immaculata Coll., 1983, BMus, 1985; postgrad., Gratz Coll., 1993. Joined Sisters, Servants of Immaculate Heart of Mary, 1976; lic., nationally cert. massage therapist. Elem. tchr. Diocese of Arlington, Va., 1979-80, Diocese of Allentown, Pa., 1980-82, Archdiocese Phila., 1983-86, Diocese of Trenton, NJ, 1987-95; tchr. Abrahams Hebrew Acad., Yardley, Pa., Jewish Cmty. Ctr., Belle Mead, NJ; tchr. grade 3 Univ. Sch. Nova Southeastern U., Davie, Fla., 1995-96; therapist Am. Inst. Massage Therapy, Ft. Lauderdale, 1996-97; tchr. grade 5 Guilford County Sch. Dist., Greensboro, NC, 1998—2000; tchr. St. Gregory the Gt. Cath. Sch., Plantation, Fla., 2000—03, St. John Neumann Cath. HS, Naples, 2003—. Contbr. articles to children's publs. Moderator Young Astronauts, Trenton, 1987—; mem. Phila. Task Force, 1987—. Recipient Nat. Schs. Excellence award U.S. Dept. Edn., 1988. Mem. Nat. Cath. Ednl. Assn., The Smithsonian Assocs., Nat. Assn. Female Execs. Democrat. Avocations: tennis, softball, cross stitch, swimming. Office: St John Neumann HS Greensboro FL 32330

HOFFMAN, NEIL JAMES, academic administrator; b. Buffalo, Sept. 2, 1938; s. Frederick Charles and Isabella Dias (Murchie) Hoffman; m. Sue Ellen Jeffery, Dec. 30, 1960; children: Kim, Amy, Lisa. BS, SUNY, Buffalo, 1960, MS, 1967; PhD (hon.), Otis Coll. Art & Design, 2000. Chmn. unified arts dept. Grand Island Pub. Schs., NY, 1968—69; assoc. dean, assoc. prof. Rochester Inst. Tech. Coll. Fine and Applied Art, NY, 1969—74; dir. program in artisanry Boston U., 1974—79; dean, chief adminstrv. officer Otis Art Inst., Parsons Sch. Design, L.A., 1979—83; pres. Sch. Art Inst. Chgo., 1983—85, Calif. Coll. Arts and Crafts, Oakland, 1985—93, Otis Coll. Art and Design, L.A., 1993—2000, Hoffman Cons., 2000—. Cons. to higher edn. instn. and non profit orgns. Chmn. evaluation teams Western Assn. Schs. and Colls., 1982—; chmn. cultural planning process City of Oakland, 1986—91. Mem.: Phi Delta Kappa. Avocation: photography. E-mail: neilsuehoffman@qwest.net.

HOFFMAN, REY, education educator, writer; b. Detroit, Mi., Jan. 10, 1937; s. Gerald Hoffman and Gwendolyn Barrett; m. Kathleen Richards, May 24, 1960; 1 child, Michelle. BA in Edn., 1970; MA in Ed., Whittier Coll., 1975. English prof. Western Md. Coll., 1978—90; editor Meriks Books, Paducah, Ky., 1990—. Jewish. Office: Meriks Books 3240 Lone Oak Rd #131 Paducah KY 42003-0370

HOFFMAN, SUE ELLEN, elementary education educator; b. Dayton, Ohio, Aug. 23, 1945; d. Cyril Vernon and Sarah Ellen (Sherer) Stephan; m. Lawrence Wayne Hoffman, Oct. 28, 1967. BS in Edn., U. Dayton, 1967; postgrad., Loyola Coll., 1977, Ea. Mich. U., 1980; MEd, Wright State U., 1988. Cert. reading specialist and elem. tchr., Ohio. 5th grade tchr. St. Anthony Sch., Dayton, Ohio, 1967-68, West Huntsville (Ala.) Elem. Sch., 1968-71; 6th grade tchr. Ranchland Hills Pub. Sch., El Paso, Tex., 1973-74; 3rd grade tchr. Emerson Pub. Sch., Westerville, Ohio, 1976, St. Joan of Arc Sch., Aberdeen, Md., 1976-78, Our Lady of Good Counsel, Plymouth, Mich., 1979-80; 5th grade tchr. St. Helen Sch., Dayton, 1980—2002; ret., 2002. Selected for membership Kappa Delta Pi, 1988. Mem. Internat. Reading Assn., Ohio Internat. Reading Assn., Dayton Area Internat. Reading Assn., Nat. Cath. Edn. Assn. Roman Catholic. Home: 2174 Green Springs Dr Kettering OH 45440-1120

HOFFMAN, TIMOTHY JAMES, secondary education educator; b. Bloomsburg, Pa., July 19, 1946; s. Thomas Jefferson and Ada Margaret (Foust) H.; m. Mary Sue Petrole, Sept. 4, 1971; children: Timothy James, Anthony Robert. BS in Edn., Bloomsburg State Coll., 1968; MS, Bucknell U., 1978; MA, Beaver Coll., 1988. Cert. tchr., Pa. Tchr. math and physics Upper Moreland Twp. Sch. Dist., Willow Grove, Pa., 1968—. Advisor Upper Moreland H.S. Key Club, 1976-87; mem. Mid. States Evaluating Com., Selinsgove, Pa., 1988, Olney, Pa., 1990. Mem. Hugh O'Brien Youth Leadership, 1986. Named Citizen of Week Willow Grove Guide Newspaper, 1982. Mem. NEA, Pa. Edn. Assn., Upper Moreland Edn. Assn., Am. Assn. Physics Tchrs., Nat. Sci. Tchrs. Assn., Montgomery County Sci. Tchrs. Assn., Pa. Key Club (chmn. 1995—), Old York Rd. Kiwanis Club (pres. 1986-87, 92-93; sec. 1998—; Sec. of Yr. Pa. divsn. 21 1999-2000; Internat. Found Hixson fellow). Republican. Methodist. Avocations: camping, woodworking, model trains and planes. tho719&umsd.k12.pa.edu. Office: Upper Moreland Twp Sch Dist Terwood Rd Willow Grove PA 19006 E-mail: thoffman123@home.com.

HOFFMANN, KATHRYN ANN, humanities educator; b. Rockville Centre, N.Y., Oct. 26, 1954; d. Manfred and Catherine (Nanko) H.; m. Brook Ellis, Nov. 25, 1987. BA summa cum laude, SUNY Buffalo, 1975; MA, The Johns Hopkins U., 1979, PhD, 1981. Asst. prof. French lit. and lang. U. Wis., Madison, 1981-88, U. Hawaii-Manoa, Honolulu, 1992-97, assoc. prof., 1997—2001, prof., 2001—; mng. ptnr. Yuval Design Partnership, Chgo., 1988-92. Author: Society of Pleasures: Interdisciplinary Readings in Pleasure in Power during the Reign of Louis XIV, 1997 (Aldo and Jeanne Scaglione prize for French and Francophone Studies 1998); assoc. editor Substance, 1982-87; transl. Masturbation: The History of a Great Terror, 2001; contbr. articles to profl. jours.; designer clothing accessories. Recipient Regents' medal for excellence in tchg., 1998; fellow, Inst. Rsch. in Humanities, 1984—85, Am. Coun. Learned Socs., 1984—85, Camargo Found., 1998; grantee, NEH Endowment Fund, 1993, 1995. Mem.: MLA (Aldo and Jeanne Scaglione prize for French and Francophone studies 1998), History of Sci. Soc., Soc. for Interdisciplinary Study Social Imagery, Soc. for Interdisciplinary French 17th Century Studies (exec. com. 1994—96), N.Am. Soc. for 17th Century French Lit., Am. Soc. for 18th Century Studies, Internat. Soc. for the Study of European Ideas, Phi Beta Kappa. Home: Apt M12 217 Prospect St Honolulu HI 96813-1778 Office: U Hawaii Manoa Langs & Lits Europe Ams 1890 East West Rd Rm 483 Honolulu HI 96822-2318

HOFFMANN, MARLENE ETHEL, rehabilitation administrator; b. Hibbing, Minn., Sept. 9, 1940; Student, Wis. Inst. for Med. Assts., 1958, Bus. Inst. Milw., 1958, Wis. Sch. Real Estate, 1968, Alverno Coll., 1979; BA summa cum laude, Mt. Mary Coll., 1985. Lic. real estate broker, Wis. EEG technician Mt. Sinai Hosp., Milw., 1958-59; dental asst. Grafton, Wis., 1959-61; dir. devel./pub. rels. St. Joan Antida H.S., Milw., 1985-86; pub. rels. coord. Higher Edn. Cable Consortium, Milw., 1986-88; corr. West Bend (Wis.) News, 1989-90; spl. projects coord. Cedar Haven Rehab. Agy., West Bend, 1995—. Presenter in field; mem. CESA # 1 Bd.Control; intern Dieringer Rsch. Assocs. Editor PTA Coun. Newsletter. Past mem. Gov.'s Edn. Goals and Statewide Assessment Coms., Dept. Pub. Instrn. Coms., Tchr. of Yr. Selection Com., Tchr. Educator of Yr. Selection Com., Tchr. Cert. Rules Com.; sec. Wis. PTA, 1975-77, pres., 1977-79, mem. various coms.; nat. v.p. PTA, 1979-81, mem. various coms.; past pres., v.p., sec. local PTA; bd. dirs. Germantown PTA Area Coun.; past treas. Germantown Kiwanis Club; past pres. Wis. Coun. for United Action in Pub. Edn., Wis. Action Com. for Foster Children; mem. Wis. Pupil Assessment Task Force; past mem. Wis. Immunization Initiative Coord. Com.; past mem. task force on TV critical viewing skills NSBA; mem. Parental Involvement in the Schs. Task Force; past Brownie leader Girl Scouts U.S.A.; past horse show chmn. Washington County Jr. Fair; past Sunday sch. tchr., supt.; pres. Germantown Bd. Edn. Behavioral Sci. scholar; recipient Wis. PTA Coun. and Coun. Newsletter of Yr. award. Mem. Wis. Assn. Sch. Bds. (pres., bd. dirs. region 15), Wis. Sch. Pub. Rels. Assn. (pres.), Pub. Rels. Student Soc. Am. (nat. liaison officer), Comms. Club (pres.), Alpha Kappa Delta, Delta Epsilon Sigma. Home: 2726 Maple Rd Jackson WI 53037-9720

HOFFMEISTER, ANN ELIZABETH, elementary education educator; b. Manitowoc, Wis., Mar. 27, 1957; d. William Anthony and Shirley Mary (Remiker) Gigure; m. Randal Thomas Hoffmeister, Apr. 3, 1982. BS in Spl. Edn., U. Wis., Eau Claire, 1979; MS in Curriculum and Instrn., U. Wis., Madison, 1986, MS in Ednl. Psychology, Gifted Edn., 1992. Cert. tchr., Wis.; lic. reading tchr., reading specialist. Tchr. Verona (Wis.) Area Schs., 1979—, computer coord., 1985-88, learning resource and reading coord., 1990—; whole lang. instr. U. Wis., Platteville, 1992-95, Action Rsch. instr. Plattville, 1996—; Action Rsch. site coord. Verona (Wis.) Area Schs., 1994. Cons. Wis. Writing Project, Madison, 1983-90; grad. level cons. U. Wis., Oshkosh, 1993, 94, 96; elem. curriculum specialist fo rart of teaching with multicultural arts Duquesne U., 1996. Co-author: Building Self Esteem Through Writing, 1983, Fletcher's Fabulous Folks! An Integrated Imaginative Writing, Art, and Technology Project Using the Arts Propel Model, 1996. Mem. Verona Jaycees, 1987-92. Grantee Wis. Arts Bd., 1994. Mem. ASCD, Wis. Coun. for Gifted/Talented, Wis. State Reading Assn. (Pat Bricker Meml. Rsch. award 1992, 93, 94), Wis. Edn. Assn., So. Wis. Edn. Insvc. Orgn., Internat. Reading Assn., Verona Edn. Assn. (treas. 1983-86). Avocations: golf, reading, drawing, water sports, walking. Office: Sugar Creek Elem Sch 420 Church Ave Verona WI 53593-1803

HOFFMEYER, WILLIAM FREDERICK, lawyer, educator; b. York, Pa., Dec. 20, 1936; s. Frederick W. and Mary B. (Stremmel) H.; m. Betty J. Hoffmeyer, Feb. 6, 1960 (div.); 1 child, Louise C.; m. Karen L. Semmelman, 1985. AB, Franklin and Marshall Coll., 1958; JD, Dickinson Sch. Law, 1961. Bar: Pa. 1962, U.S. Dist Ct. (mid. dist.) Pa. 1981, U.S. Supreme Ct. 1983. Pvt. practice law, 1962-81; sr. ptnr. Hoffmeyer & Semmelman, 1982—. Adj. prof. real estate law York Coll. Pa., 1980-92, real estate law, paral legal program Pa. State U., 1978-2000. Autor: Abstractor's Bible, 1981, Pennsylvania Real Estate Installment Sales Contrct Manual, 1981, Real Estate Settlement Procedures, 1982, Contracts of Sale, 1984, How to Plot a Deed Description, 1985; author, lectr., moderator and course planner numerous Pa. Bar Inst. CLE Programs. Recipient Disting. Svc. award Gen. Alumni Assn. Dickinson Sch. Law, 1993, Pa. Bar medal, 1997. Mem. ABA, Pa. Bar Assn. (co-chmn. unauthorized practice of law com.), York County Bar Assn. (chmn. continuing legal edn. com. 1992-96), Am. Coll. Real Estate Lawyers, Lions (past pres. East York club), York Area C. of C. (chair small bus. support network 1997-99), Masons, Shriners (past pres. York County). Address: 30 N George St York PA 17401-1214

HOFT, ED. D. LYNNE A. elementary and secondary school educator, differentiation specialist, educational consultant; b. Carroll, Iowa, Mar. 1, 1945; d. Norman North and Dorothy Mae (Dean) H.; 1 child, Timothy D. Cochran. BA, Briar Cliff Coll., 1971; MA in Spl. Edn., Ariz. State U., 1979; postgrad., U. Minn., 1989-92; EdD in Ednl. Leadership, U. St. Thomas, 2002. Cert. elem. and spl. edn. tchr., Ariz., Minn.; lic. prin. K-12 and spl. edn. dir.; Tchr. St. Edward Sch. Waterloo, Iowa, 1968-70, Chino Valley Sch., Ariz., 1971-77, program devel., 1974-76; spl edn. tchr. Tuba City Pub. Jr. HS, Ariz., 1978-82; spl. edn. tchr.dept. chmn. Tuba City HS, 1983-86, curriculum devel., 1984-85; recedial specialist Eagles' Nest Mid. Sch., 1986-88; spl. edn. coord. chpt. 1 Epsilon and Nexus programs Hopkins (Minn.) Pub. Sch., Hennepin County Home Sch., 1988-95, tchr. Engtlish, 1995-2001; on-line course devel./tchr., Hopkins Online Acad. MN Charter Sch., 2001-03; Short-term, modular curriculum devel., Beta Program, Henn Co. Home Sch./ Hopkins ISD270, 2003-; Owner/CEO "Back to Brilliance" Co., providing programs & materials focused on Growth Essentials Matrix. Tchr. St. Edward Sch., Waterloo, Iowa, 1968-70, Chino Valley Sch., Ariz., 1971-77, program developer, 1974-76; spl. edn. tchr. Tuba City Pub. Jr. HS, Ariz., 1978-82; spl. edn. tchr., dept. chmn. Tuba City HS, 1983-86, curriculum developer, 1984-85; remedial specialist Eagles' Nest Mid. Sch., 1986-88; spl. edn. coord. chpt. 1 Epsilon and Nexus programs Hopkins Pub. Sch., Hennepin County Home Sch., Minn., 1988-95, tchr. English, 1995—2001. Founder, pres.,Unltd. Learning Enterprises, Inc., Tuba City, 1983-85; trainer Empowering People/Positive Discipline, 1990—: trainer, mem. separate sites Minn. Dept Children, Families, Learning, 2000—; invitational cons. Aim for Excellence, Mpls., 1990-91; cons./trainer Growth Essentials Model Programs, Health Realization/Resiliency, and Program Devel., 1994—. Probation aide Waterloo Juvenile Ct., 1970-71; vol. instr. Prescott Spl. Olympics, 1977-78; local coord. Tuba City Spl. Olympics, 1978-80. Recipient US Dept. Edn. Sec. award, 1991. Mem. NEA, Minn. Edn. Assn., Hopkins Edn. Assn., Tuba City Unified Edn. Assn. (pres. 1985-86). Avocations: reading, piano, parenting. E-mail: gemprograms@aol.com., lynne_hoft@hopkins.k12.mn.us.

HOGAN, DONNA HELEN, school librarian, educator; b. Dallas, Apr. 21, 1937; d. Donald William Ross and Lillian Ethel Andrews; m. Jerry Don Hogan, June 11, 1960 (div. Jan. 29, 1986); children: Laura, Leslie, Donald. BA, U. Tulsa, 1959; MLIS, U. Okla., Norman, 1990. Cert. secondary edn. tchg. Okla., 1965. Tchr. French, Eng. Midwest City Pub. Schs., Okla., 1965—67; tchr. French Lexington Pub. Sch., Okla., 1971—72; owner Hogan's Carpets, Purcell, Okla., 1976—86; staff asst. Bilingual Edn. Multifunctional Resource Ctr., U. Okla., Norman, 1987—90; libr. Met. Libr. Sys., Oklahoma City, 1990—93, U. Ala. Librs., Tuscaloosa, 1993—98; asst. dir. pub. svcs. U. Tex. at San Antonio Libr., 1998—. Guest spkr., libr. U. Ala., Tuscaloosa, 1994—97; 2d v.p. Oklahoma Libr. Assn., Oklahoma City, 1975—93; com. chair Ala. Libr. Assn., Birmingham, 1993—98. Contbr. articles to profl. jours. Treas. Norman Cmty. Choral Soc., Norman, 1981—90; pres. Tuscaloosa Cmty. Choral Soc., 1993—98; trustee, chair Pioneer Multi-County Libr. Bd., Norman, 1975—83; pres. Friends of Librs. in Okla., Oklahoma City, 1980—82. Recipient Scholarship, Oklahoma Libr. Assn., 1988. Mem.: AAUW (Past Pres., Purcell Branch), ALA (com. chair New Mems. Roundtable 1990—2000, pres.'s program chair Reference and User Svcs. Assn. 1992—, chair mgrs. 1998—2000), Am. Soc. Engring. Edn. (mem. engring. libr. divsn.), San Antonio Choral Soc., Beta Phi Mu. Methodist. Avocations: travel, hiking, homemaking arts. Office: U Tex San Antonio Libr 6900 N Loop 1604 West San Antonio TX 78249 Office Fax: 210-458-4884. Business E-Mail: dhogan@utsa.edu.

HOGAN, JOHN DONALD, retired college dean, finance educator; b. Binghamton, N.Y., July 16, 1927; s. John D. and Edith J. (Hennessy) H.; m. Anna Craig, Nov. 26, 1976; children: Thomas P., James E. AB, Syracuse U., 1949, MA, 1950, PhD, 1952. Registered prin. Nat. Assn. Securities Dealers. Prof. econs., chmn. dept. Bates Coll., Lewiston, Maine, 1953-58; dir. edn. fin. research State of N.Y., 1959, chief mcpl. fin., 1960; staff economist, dir. research Northwestern Mut. Life Ins. Co., Milw., 1960-68; v.p. Nationwide Ins. Cos., Columbus, Ohio, 1968-76; dean Sch. Bus. Adminstrn. Central Mich. U., Mt. Pleasant, 1976-79; v.p. Am. Productivity Ctr., Houston, 1979-80; pres., chmn., chief exec. officer Variable Annuity Life Ins. Co., Houston, 1980-83; sr. v.p. Am. Gen. Corp., Houston, 1983-86; dean, prof. fin. Coll. Commerce U. Ill., Champaign, 1986-91; dean, prof. fin. and econs. Coll. Bus. Adminstrn. Ga. State U., Atlanta, 1991-97, prof. fin. and econs., 1998—2001, dean and prof. emeritus, 2002—. Bd. dirs. Sinfonia da Camera, Champaign, Ga. Coun. on Econ. Edn., Pvt. Industry Coun., World Trade Ctr., Atlanta; vis. prof. fin. Poznan (Poland) U. Econs., Caucasus Sch. Bus., Tbilisi, Georgia; cons. in field. Author: American Social Legislation, 1965, U.S. Balance of Payments and Capital Flows, 1967, School Revenue Studies, 1959, Fiscal Capacity of the State of Maine, 1958, American Social Legislation, 1973; editor: Dimensions of Productivity Research (2 vols.), 1981; contbr. articles to jours., abstracts to profl. meetings. Bd. dirs. Goodwill Industries, Columbus, 1972-76, chmn. capital fund drive, 1974-75; mem. Houston Com. on Fgn. Rels., 1980—, Chgo. Coun. on Fgn. Rels., 1986—, Chgo. com., 1987—. Served with U.S. Army, 1944-46, ETO; capt. (ret.) USAR. Maxwell fellow Syracuse U., 1950-52; recipient Best Article award Jur. Risk and Ins., Alumni Appreciation award U. Ill., 1991, 1964, Medal of Merit Poznan U., Poland, 1999; Maxwell Centennial lectr. Maxwell Grad. Sch., Syracuse U., 1970. Mem.: Inst. Rsch. in Econs. of Taxation (dir. 1984—), Nat. Tax Assn. (dir. 1981—85, treas., exec. com. 1988—2001), Nat. Assn. Bus. Economists, Inst. Mgmt. Scis., Am. Econ. Assn., Acad. Mgmt., Columbus C. of C. (chmn. econ. policy com. 1972—76), World Trade Club (Atlanta, bd. dirs. 1993—99), Columbus Athletic Club, Heritage Club (Houston), Commerce Club (Atlanta), Lincolnshire Fields Country Club (Champaign), Univ. Club (Chgo.), Beta Gamma Sigma, Phi Kappa Phi. Office: Ga State U Coll Bus Adminstrn 3892 Byrnwyck Pl NE Atlanta GA 30319

HOGAN, LINDA RAE, educator; b. Gary, Ind., Apr. 11, 1948; d. Carl Dorsey and Charlotte L. (Schreiber) Ruley; m. Charles Patrick Hogan, June 10, 1972; children: Colleen Marie, Kelly Kathleen. BS, Ind. U., 1970, postgrad., 1972, Gov.'s State U., 1986-87, Lewis U., 1987, U. Hawaii, Ind. Wesleyan U. Tchr. Crown Point (Ind.) High Sch., 1970-73; tchr. phys. edn. Solon Robinson Elem., Crown Point, 1973-74; tchr. phys. edn., coach Lowell (Ind.) Dolphins, 1978—79, AAU Swim Team, 1981-82; pvt. practice swimming tchr. Lowell, 1975-87; tchr. phys. edn. St. Edward Elem. Sch., Lowell, 1980-86; tchr. sci., health, phys. edn., biology Crete (Ill.)-Monee H.S. and Mid. Sch., 1985—99; sci. tchr. Lake Ridge Mid. Sch., Gary, 2000—. Mem.: NEA, Am. Fedn. Tchrs., Crete Monee Educators Assn., Lake Ridge Tchr. Fedn., Pi Epsilon Kappa. Roman Catholic. Home: 503 Driftwood Dr Lowell IN 46356-2516 Office: 3601 W 41st Ave Gary IN 46401

HOGAN, NANCY KAY, elementary education educator; b. Auburn, Wash., Oct. 5, 1947; d. Henry Grant and Medora Ione (Elder) Kessner; m. David Allan Hogan, June 27, 1970; children: Jeffrey Allan, Jason Patrick, Jennifer Ann. BA in Edn., Western Wash. U., 1969; postgrad., U. Wash., 1973; M Ednl. Tech., City U., 1996. Cert. K-12 tchr., Wash. Tchr. kindergarten Kent (Wash.) Sch. Dist., 1970; elem. tchr. North Thurston Sch. Dist., Lacey, Wash., 1970-73; tchr. McLane Elem. Sch., Olympia, Wash., 1986-93, McKenny Elem. Sch., Olympia, 1993-94, Hansen Elem. Sch., Olympia, 1994—2000, also mem. tchr. support team; tchr. gen. Y program Olympic Sch. Dist., 2000—01; libr. Boston Harbor Elem. Sch., Federal Way, Wash., 2001—. Mem. NEA, Internat. Reading Assn., Whole Lang. Umbrella, Wash. Edn. Assn., Olympia Edn. Assn., Dist. Inclusion Forum, Hansen Title I Team, Nat. Coun. Tchrs. English. Avocations: reading, boating, walking. Home: 29505 12th Ave SW Federal Way WA 98023

HOGAN, NEVILLE JOHN, mechanical engineering educator, consultant; b. Dublin, Feb. 11, 1949; came to U.S., 1970; s. Walter Henry and Edna Constance (Liller) H.; m. Sara Jane Seiden; children: Alexandra, Brian, Amanda, Victoria. Diploma in engring. with honors, Coll. of Tech., Dublin, 1970; MS in Mech. Engring., MIT, 1973, mech. engring. degree, 1976, PhD in Mech. Engring., 1977; D (hon.), Tech. U. Delft, 1997. Product devel. and design engr. Donnelly Mirrors Ltd., Nass, Ireland, 1977-78; prof. MIT, Cambridge, 1978—; dir. Newman Lab., 1992—. Cons. in phys. systems modeling, design and control and in biomed. engring. Contbr. numerous articles to profl. jours. TRW Found. fellow, Whitaker Health Scis. Fund fellow. Mem. AAAS, ASME, Sigma Xi.

HOGAN, ROXANNE ARNOLD, nursing consultant, risk management consultant, educator; b. Connellsville, Pa; d. Tyree Franklin Sr. and Reva Gayle (Thieler) A.; m. Patrick B. Hogan. AAS, Gloucester County Coll., 1983; BSN, Widener U., 1989. Lic. health care risk mgmt.; RN Fla., cert. operating rm. nurse. Staff devel. instr., nursing supr., cardiac care nurse Meth. Hosp., Phila., 1982-89; emergency nurse Underwood Meml. Hosp., Woodbury, NJ, 1988-89; critical care nurse Jupiter Hosp., Fla., 1989—92; emergency clin. nurse III Indian River Meml. Hosp., Vero Beach, Fla., 1990-92; EMT/paramedic instr. Indian River CC, Ft. Pierce, Fla., 1990-92; emergency asst. nurse mgr. Holmes Regional Med. Ctr., Melbourne, Fla., 1992-94; post anesthesia clin. nurse III Indian River Meml. Hosp., Vero Beach, Fla., 1994-98; surg. dir. The Rosato Plastic Surgery Ctr., Vero Beach, Fla., 1998-99; nurse mgr. pre-admissions, spl. procedures GI Lab., ambulatory infusion IV Team and Ambulatory Surgery Ctr. Indian River Meml. Hosp., Vero Beach, Fla., 1999—2001; pres. Treasure Coast Cons., Inc., 2001—02; risk mgmt. coord. HCA/St. Lucie Med. Ctr., Port St. Lucie, Fla., 2002—03; claims med. specialist S.E. Fla. Nationwide Ins., 2003—. Mem.: Fla. Soc. Healthcare Risk Mgmt., Am. Soc. Healthcare Risk Mgmt., Am. Assn. Legal Nurse Cons. (South Fla. Chpt.), Assn. of Operating Room Nurses (Platinum Coast Chpt.), Eta Beta Chpt., Sigma Theta Tau. Home: 5346 NW Rugby Dr Port Saint Lucie FL 34983-3384

HOGAN, SHEILA MAUREEN, biology educator, nurse; b. Lincoln, Ill., Mar. 20, 1958; d. Edward William and Cecilia Dolores (Shay) Krotz; children: Celia, Nicole. Cert., Practical Sch. of Nursing, 1979; AS, Richland Coll., 1983; BS, Millikin U., 1985, MS in Ednl. Adminstrn., 1998. Office nurse C.T. Johnson, Decatur, Ill., 1979-83; head nurse Community Ctr. for Developmentally Disabled, Decatur, 1981-84; lab. technician Millikin U., Decatur, 1983-85; tchr. biology Mt. Zion (Ill.) High Sch., 1985-96; pres., founder Positive Influences. Mem. Ill. Health Occupations, Ill. Vocat. Assn., Nat. Sci. Tchrs., Ill. Sci. Tchrs., Ill. Coordinating Coun. Vocat. Students (vice chmn. Springfield, Ill. chpt. 1987-96), Pi Lambda Theta. Roman Catholic. Avocations: reading, photography, needlework. Home: 17190 Poblado Ct San Diego CA 92127-1431

HOGE, GERALDINE RAJACICH, elementary education educator; b. Eveleth, Minn., Apr. 8, 1937; d. Robert and Dora (Tassi) Rajacich; m. Gregg LeRoy Hoge, Sept. 15, 1963 (div. Feb. 1972); 1 child, Sheryl Maurine. BS, U. Minn., 1959; MA with honors, Pepperdine U. Cert. elem. tchr., Calif. Tchr. Chaska (Minn.) Pub. Schs., 1959-60, Minnetonka (Minn.) Pub. Schs., 1960-62, Norwalk (Calif.) La Mirada Pub. Schs., 1962-64, Culver City (Calif.) Unified Sch. Dist., 1966—. Fellow Culver City Guidance Clinic Guild, 1981-89; mem. Calif. State Rep. Ctrl. Com., Sacramento, 1986-90, 92-94, L.A. County Rep. Ctrl. Com., 1987—; vice chmn. 49th Assembly Dist. Ctrl. Rep. Com., Culver City, 1988—; bd. dirs. Selective Svc. Sys., Culver City, 1993—. Named Tchr. of the Yr. Elks Lodge, 1982; grantee, 1988-89. Fellow Am. Fedn. Tchrs.; mem. Internat. Platform Assn., Calif. Fedn. Tchrs., Culver City Fedn. Tchrs. (v.p. 1978-79), Alpha Delta Pi (historian 1956-59), Delta Kappa Gamma. Republican. Avocations: travel, gardening, race walking. Office: Culver City Unified Sch 4034 Irving Pl Culver City CA 90232-2810

HOGEBOOM, PATRICIA ANN SCHRACK, high school guidance counselor; b. Buffalo, Feb. 17, 1937; d. Royal Elmer and Jeannette (O'Toole) Schrack; m. Willard Leroy Hogeboom, Sept. 17, 1960; children: Christopher John, Matthew Patrick. BS, Syracuse U., 1959; MS, L.I. U., 1981; profl. degree/cert. adminstrn./supervis., Coll. New Rochelle, 1995. Cert. guidance counselor. English tchr. South Park H.S., Buffalo, 1960-62, North Babylon (N.Y.) H.S., 1963-64, Islip (N.Y.) Jr. H.S., 1969-70; career counselor Suffolk County Libr., 1973-76; owner, tchr. Loaves of Love Baking Sch., Oakdale, NY, 1973-79; cons. Islip (N.Y.) Div. Sr. Citizens Svcs., 1979-84; instr. St. Joseph's Coll., Patchogue, NY, 1983—98; guidance counselor Riverhead (N.Y.) High Sch., 1986-87, McKenna Jr. H.S., Massapequa, N.Y., 1987—. Bd. dirs. Pat Hogeboom Presents Workshops in Human Devel., Specializing in Gender Equity Tng., Sexual Harrassment Issues in Edn., Oakdale, 1984—; cons. Suffolk County Office for Aging, Smithtown, N.Y., 1984-86. Contbr. articles to several publs., including Suffolk County News, Newsday, N.Y. Times, various profl. jours. Vestrymember St. Mark's Episc. Ch., Islip, 1984—, chalice bearer, lay reader. Mem. AAUW (pres. N.Y. State divsn. 1990-92, gift honoree Islip bd. 1982, Project Renew grantee 1980), ASTD, N.Y. State Counselor's Assn., Nassau County Counselor's Assn., Pers. and Guidance Assn. Avocations: boating, theatre, dance, baking. Home: 55 W Shore Rd Oakdale NY 11769-2125

HOGG, ROBERT VINCENT, JR., mathematical statistician, educator; b. Hannibal, Mo., Nov. 8, 1924; s. Robert Vincent and Isabelle Frances (Storrs) H.; m. Carolyn Joan Ladd, June 23, 1956 (dec. June 1990); children: Mary Carolyn, Barbara Jean, Allen Ladd, Robert Mason; m. Ann Burke, Oct. 15, 1994. BA, U. Ill., 1947; MS, U. Iowa, 1948, PhD, 1950. Asst. prof. math. U. Iowa, Iowa City, 1950-56, assoc. prof., 1956-62, prof., 1962-65, chmn. dept. stats., prof. stats., 1965-83, 92-93, Hanson prof. mfg. productivity, 1993-95, prof. emeritus, 2001—. Co-author: Introduction to Mathematical Statistics, 1959, 5th edit., 1995, Finite Mathematics and Calculus, 1974, Probability and Statistical Inference, 1977, 6th edit., 2000, Applied Statistics for Engineers and Physical Scientists, 1987, 2d edit., 1992; assoc. editor Am. Stats., 1971-74; contbr. articles to profl. jours. Vestryman local Episc. ch., 1958-60, 66-68, 91-92, 2001—. With USNR, 1943-46. Grantee NIH, 1966-68, 75-78, NSF, 1969-74; Disting. Alumni Award, U. Iowa, 2003. Fellow Inst. Math. Stats. (program sec., bd. bd. 1968-74), Am. Statis. Assn. (pres. Iowa sect. 1962-63, coun. 1965-66, 73-74, vis. lectr. 1965-68, 77-85, chmn. tng. sect. 1973, assoc. editor jour. 1978-80, pres.-elect 1987, pres. 1988, past pres. 1989, Founders award 1991, Noether award 2001); mem. Math. Assn. Am. (pres. Iowa sect. 1964-65, 95-96, bd. govs. 1971-74, visa. lectr. 1976-81, Outstanding Tchg.

award 1993), Internat. Statis. Inst., Rotary (pres. Iowa City 1984-85), Sigma Xi (pres. Iowa dist. chpt. 1970-71), Pi Kappa Alpha. Home: 30130 Trails End Buena Vista CO 81211 Office: U Iowa Dept Statis Acturial Sci Iowa City IA 52242 E-mail: bhogg@starband.net.

HOGGARD, LARA GULDMAR, conductor, educator; b. Kingston, Okla., Feb. 9, 1915; s. Calvin Peter and Eva Lillian (Smith) H.; m. Mildred Mae Teeter, Sept. 11, 1943; 1 dau., Susan. BA, Southea. Tchrs. Coll., 1934; MA, Columbia U., 1940, EdD, 1947. Supr. music Durant (Okla.) Pub. Schs., 1934-39; dir. choral activities, opera and oratorio U. Okla., 1940-43; assoc. founder, prin. instr. Waring Summer Choral Workshops, 1948-52; co-editor Shawnee Press, Del. Water Gap, Pa., 1946-52; dir. music and music edn. rsch. Indian Springs Sch., Ala. Edn. Found., Birmingham, 1955-60; founder Nat. Young Artist Competition, Midland-Odessa, 1962—; William Rand Kenan prof. music U. N.C., Chapel Hill, 1967-80, founder Carolina Choir, 1967—; founder N.C. Collegiate Choral Festival, 1969—; Fuller E. Callaway prof. music Columbus Coll., U. Ga., 1981-82. Condr. NBC-USN Navy Hour, 1945, assoc. condr. Waring's Pennsylvanians, 1946—52, condr., dir. (nat. touring concert group) Civic Music and Nat. Concert Artists Corp., Festival of Song, 1952—53; dir.: N.C. Summer Insts. in Choral Art, 1953—83; founder, condr., musical dir. Midland-Odessa (Tex.) Symphony Orch. and Chorale, 1962—67, condr. numerous music festivals, Am., Europe, artistic dir., prin. condr. Festival of Three Cities, Vienna-Budapest-Prague, 1973, Internat. Jugendmusikfest in Wien, 1973, 1974, guest lectr. and condr. univs. and conservatories in Am. and Europe, condr. several musical premieres, including Behold the Glory (Talmage Dean) with Louisville Orch., 1964, Light in the Wilderness (Dave Brubeck), Chapel Hill, 1968, new edit. Ein deutsches Requiem (Brahms) with N.C. Symphony, 1986, numerous others; author: Improving Music Reading, 1947, Exploring Music, 1967; editor: an oratorio Light in the Wilderness (Dave Brubeck), 1968; composer, arranger, editor 37 choral publs.; editor: new English transl. and corr. orch. score and parts Ein deutsches Requiem (Brahms), 1983—89; composer: Le Jongleur, 1951. Served to lt. (j.g.) USN, 1943-45, PTO. Recipient award for outstanding svc. to music in Ala., Ala. Fine Arts Festival, 1958, citation for outstanding svc. to fine arts in Tex., Tex. Senate and Gov., West Texan award, 1967, Tanner award U. N.C., 1972, Ten Best Profs. award, 1978, Order Long Leaf Pine Gov. N.C., 1980, Disting. Alumnus award Southeastern Okla. State U., 1981, Lara G. Hoggard endowed professorship named in his honor U. N.C., 1993. Mem. Music Educators Nat. Conf. (life; Master Builder), Am. Choral Dirs. Assn. (life, award for contbn. to music in N.C. 1976, citation for contbn. to music in Am., divsn. 5, 1986, award for excellence and lifelong commitment So. divsn. 1998), AAUP, N.C. Music Educators Assn. (hon. life), N.C. Lit. Soc. (life), Rotary, Phi Mu Alpha Sinfonia (nat. hon. life). Democrat. Presbyterian.

HOGGARD, MINNIE COLTRAIN, gifted education educator, consultant; b. Williamston, N.C. d. Joshua Herbert and Nellie Mae (Wynne) Coltrain; m. Robert Lewis Hoggard; children: Robbin Lenora Hoggard Blake, Lewis Wynne Hoggard. BS, East Carolina U., 1975, MA in Ed., 1977, curriculum instrnl. specialist, 1988, EdS, 1991. Cert. reading specialist, instrnl. specialist, academically gifted tchr., supt., prin., N.C. Draftsman, bookkeeper East Coast Surveying Svc., Windsor, N.C., 1964-75; tcchr. reading Washington County Schs., Washington, N.C., 1975; elem. tchr. Martin County Schs., Williamston, 1975-85, tchr. academically gifted, 1985-93, academically gifted specialist, coord., 1993-97, cons. academically gifted local plan, 1996-97, mentor coord., 1998—, asst. prin., 1997-98, 98-99. Supervising tchr. East Carolina U., Greenville, N.C., 1979-85; N.C. advisor Tar Heel Jr. Hist. Assn., Raleigh, 1986. Collaborating writer and tester elem. sch. curriculum in Can. for N.C. students; editor play Backwards into Time, 1986 (state award 1986). Pres. Windsor Jr. Woman's Club, 1969-71. Grantee Nat. Diffusion Network, 1986; recipient N.C. Advisor of Yr. award, 1986. Mem. Coun. for Exceptional Children, Nat. Assn. for Gifted Children. Democrat. Episcopalian. Avocations: recreational reading, walking, writing poetry, playing bridge, travel. Home: 302 Sutton Dr Windsor NC 27983-6737 Office: Martin County Schs 300 N Watts St Williamston NC 27892-2056

HOGLEN, JEWEL PAMELA, retired secondary school educator; b. Columbia, Miss., Sept. 22, 1919; d. Irvin Armstrong Blackburn and Inez Geraldine Dickens; m. Hubert J. Hoglen, Nov. 4, 1944; 1 child, Pamela J. BS, La. State Normal (now Northwestern State U. of La.), 1941; MA in Edn., Washington U., 1953. Cert. home economist, family & consumer scis. Home economist H.S., Kentwood, La., 1941—42; chmn. home economy Ward & Hanley Jr. H.S., U. City, Mo., 1947—69, Parkway N. H.S., Chesterfield, Mo., 1972—78; asst. prof. Meramec C.C., Kirkwood, Mo., 1972—75, ret., 1975. Vice chmn. profl. sect. Am. Home Econs. Assn., 1987—89; pres. Home Econs. Coun., St. Louis, 1964—65. Louis IX art mus. group Art Mus., St. Louis, 1978—. Recipient Disting. Svc. to the Profession award, Am. Home Econ. Assn., 1991—93, 50 Yrs. of Svc. award, Am. Home Econs. Assn., 1998. Mem.: AAUW, Mo. Home Econs. Assn. (pres. 1968—69, 1969—70, chmn. home economists in homemaking section, Cert. for Outstanding Contbn. & Svc. to the Profession 1985, 50 Years Dedication & Svc. to Home Econs. Profession award 1998), Am. Assn. Home (history & archives com., sec. to leader in leadership mtg.), Coll. Club of St. Louis (chmn. Centennial birthday celebration 2000, pres. 2001—03). Republican. Protestant. Avocations: tailoring, reading, horse back riding, travel. Home: 1009 Dougherty Ferry Rd Kirkwood MO 63122

HOGUE, BONNIE MARIE KIFER GOSCIMINSKI, child care educator, consultant; b. Niagara Falls, N.Y., May 31, 1947; d. Ralph Henry and Emogene Viola (Severance) Kifer; m. Conrad S. Gosciminski, Aug. 9, 1969; children: Steven, Heidi, Jason; m. William R. Hogue, Nov. 15, 1994. BEd, Mansfield (Pa.) State U., 1969; MS in Human Svcs., Murray (Ky.) State U., 1995. Tchr. Col-Mont Area Vocat. Tech., Bloomsburg, Pa., 1969-70, Coatesville (Pa.) Area Sch. Dist., 1971-72, Bradford (Pa.) Area Schs., 1972-76, Christian County Schs., Hopkinsville, Ky., 1976-82; with supply and pers. depts. U.S. Army Law Enforcement Command, Ft. Campbell, Ky., 1983-87; tng. specialist Blanchfield Army Community Hosp., Ft. Campbell, 1987-91; sch. age latch key specialist Child Devel. Svcs., Ft. Campbell, 1991-92, Family Child Care outreach Ft. Richardson, Alaska, 1992—. Officer, bd. dirs. Christian County Assn. for S.P.M.D., Hopkinsville, 1978-92; mem. Hopkinsville Human Rels. Commn., 1989-92; parent advisor Title I com. Christian County High Sch., 1989-90. Recipient Outstanding Performance award Dept. Army, 1983-92, Sustained Performance award, 1989, 93; Vol. of Yr. award Christian County Assn. Dyslexia, 1981. Mem. NAFE, NAYCC, NAEYC, AFCCA, Ky. Coalition for Sch.-Age Child Care. Home: 2200 Grizzly Bear Cir Wasilla AK 99654-2728

HOKE, EUGENA LOUISE, special education educator; b. Chgo., Feb. 26, 1949; d. Edward LaMar and Edna Lucille (Weikert) H. BS, Bowling Green State U., 1971; MEd, U. Maine, Orono, 1977. Cert. educator. Tchr. educable mentally retarded Marion Local Schs., Maria Stein, Ohio, 1971-73, Tri-Valley Local Sch., Dresden, Ohio, 1973-74; tchr. Edgewood Local Schs., Trenton, Ohio, 1974-78; learning disabilities tchr. Oak Hills Local Sch. Dist., Cin., from 1978. Mem. prin.'s adv. com. C.O. Harrison Elem. Sch., Cin., 1987-88, 92-93, mem. tchr. asst. team, 1988-90; intervention inniatives team, 1998—, tech. team Venture Capital, 1996-98. Mem. Vol. in Parks, Hamilton County, Ohio, 1981-88; vol. Cin. Symphony Assn., 1988—, Friends of Pops, 1991—, Mus. Ctr., 1991, Aronoff Ctr. for the Arts, 1995—. Mem. NEA, Ohio Edn. Assn., Oak Hill Edn. Assn., Cin. Arts. Assn. Methodist. Avocations: photography, travel, hiking. Home: Sunbury, Ohio. Died June 14, 2001.

HOKE, JUDY ANN, physical education educator; b. Mesa, Ariz., May 3, 1951; d. Jewell Juett and Margaret Lucille (Gibson) H. BA, Ariz. State U., 1973, MS, 1976. Cert. tchr. Ariz. Tchr., coach womens Tennis Tempe (Ariz.) Union High Sch. Dist., 1973—, chmn. Phys. Edn., 1978—. Former co-chmn. sch. improvement com.; chmn. East Valley Women's Tennis Region. Mem. First Christian Ch., Phoenix Zoo. Named Outstanding Secondary Phys. Edn. Tchr. Yr. State of Ariz., 1991. Mem. NEA, AAHPERD, Ariz. Alliance Health Phys. Edn. Recreation and Dance, Tempe Secondary Edn. Assn., Women's Internat. Tennis Assn., U.S. Tennis Assn. Republican. Avocation: reading. Office: Marcos de Niza High Sch 6000 S Lakeshore Dr Tempe AZ 85283-3049

HOKENSON, DAVID LEONARD, secondary school educator; b. Mpls., Nov. 9, 1950; s. Raymond Leonard and Barbara Jean (Hooker) H.; m. Cynthia Jane Luehmann, July 28, 1979. BA, St. Olaf Coll., 1972; postgrad., U. Minn., 1977, 78, 82. Lic. secondary sch. social studies and history tchr., Minn. Social studies tchr. Preston (Minn.)-Fountain Pub. Schs., 1972-93, Fillmore Ctrl. H.S., Harmony, Minn., 1993-95; Fillmore Ctrl. Mid. Sch., Preston, Minn., 1995—. Mem. team evaluation State Dept. Edn., St. Paul, 1981, 83, 91, 98. Mem. Nat. Trust for Hist. Preservation; treas. Preston-Fountain Edn. Assn., 1987—93, negotiator, 1993—94; treas. Edn. Minn. Fillmore Ctrl., 1994—; mem. evaluation team North Ctrl. Accreditation Assn., 1994; participant Project 120, 1995; mem. Minn. Hist. Soc.; precinct chair Dem.-Farmer-Labor Party, Preston, 1990—; pres. Christ Luth. Ch., 2001—02. Recipient scholarship Minn. Inst. for Advancement of Teaching, St. Paul, 1992, 97. Mem. Nat. Geog. Soc., Am. Scandinavian Found., Am.-Swedish Inst., Smithsonian Instn., Minn. Hist. Soc., Libr. of Congress. Office: Fillmore Ctrl Schs PO Box 50 Preston MN 55965-0050 E-mail: david.hokenson@isd2198.k12,mn.us., d.hokenson@mchsi.com.

HOKENSTAD, MERL CLIFFORD, JR., social work educator; b. Norfolk, Nebr., July 21, 1936; s. Merl Clifford and Flora Diane (Christian) H.; m. Dorothy Jean Tarrell, June 24, 1962; children: Alene Ann, Laura Rae, Marta Lynn. BA summa cum laude, Augustana Coll., 1958; Rotary Found. fellow, Durham (Eng.) U., 1958-59; MSW., Columbia U., 1962; PhD, Brandeis U., 1969, Inst. Ednl. Mgmt., Harvard U., 1977. With Lower East Side Neighborhood Assns., N.Y.C., 1962-64; community planning assoc. United Community Services, Sioux Falls, S.D., 1964-66; instr. Augustana Coll., Sioux Falls, 1964-66; research assoc. Ford Found. Project on Community Planning for Elderly, Brandeis U., Waltham, Mass., 1966-67; prof., dir. Sch. Social Work, Western Mich. U., Kalamazoo, 1968-74; prof., dean Sch. Applied Social Scis., Case Western Res. U., Cleve., 1974-83, Ralph and Dorothy Schmitt prof., 1983—, chmn. PhD program, 1990-94; prof. internat. health Sch. of Medicine, 1994—. Vis. prof. Inst. Sociology, Stockholm U., 1978, Fulbright lectr., 1980; vis. prof. Nat. Inst. Social Work, London, 1981, Sch. Social Work, Stockholm U., 1982-86, Eotvos Lorand U., Budapest, Hungary, 1992, 95, 96, London Sch. Econs., 1994; Fulbright rsch. scholar Inst. Applied Social Rsch., Oslo, 1989; fellow U. Canterbury, Christchurch, New Zealand, 1994; mem. UN tech. com. World Assembly on Aging, 2000-02; mem. U.S. delegation UN World Assembly on Aging, 2002. Author: Participation in Teaching and Learning: An Idea Book for Social Work Educators; editor: Meeting Human Needs: An International Annual, Vol. V, Linking Health Care and Social Services: International Perspectives; editor-in-chief Internat. Social Work Jour., 1985-87; co-editor: Profiles in Internat. Social Work, 1992, Issues in International Social Work, 1997, Models of International Exchange, 2003; (internat. issue) Jour. Gerontol. Social Work, 1988, Jour. Sociology and Social Welfare, 1990, Jour. Social Policy and Administration, 1993, Jour. Aging Internat., 1994, Jour. Applied Social Scis., 1996; contbr. articles to profl. jours., chpts. to books. Mem. alcohol tng. rev. com. Nat. Inst. Alcoholism and Alcohol Abuse, 1974-78; workshop leader Am. Assn. State Colls. and Univs., 1974; chmn. U.S. com. XVIII Internat. Congress Schs. Social Work, 1976; chmn. Kalamazoo County Cmty. Mental Health Svcs. Bd., 1971, vice chmn., 1972; mem. edn. and tng. task force Mich. Office Drug Abuse and Alcoholism, 1972-73; mem. Mich. Assn. Mental Health Bds., 1972; bd. dirs. Cleve. United Way Svcs., 1982-84, del. assembly, 1974-82, mem. periodic rev. oversight com., 1982, mem. leadership devel. com., 1978, cmty. resources com., 1988—; bd. dirs. Kalamazoo United Way, 1968-72; trustee Cleve. Internat. Program for Youth Workers and Social Workers, chmn. program com., 1985-87; mem. program devel. com. Cleve. Center on Alcoholism, 1976; trustee Alcoholism Services Cleve., Inc., 1977-86, v.p., 1982-85; trustee Cmty. Info./Vol. Action Ctr., 1982-88, chmn. leadership devel. com., 1984-86, chmn. unmet needs com., 1986-88, exec. com., 1985-88, v.p., 1986-88; exec. com. Western Reserve Geriatric Edn. Ctr., 1995—; mem. adv. com. Coun. for Internat. Exch. Scholars, 1991-93, Fedn. for Cmty. Planning Coun. on Older Persons, 1991—, chmn. caregiver support program initiative, 1995-96; mem. adv. coun. Cuyahoga County Dept. Sr. and Adult Svcs., 1998—, chair, 2001—; mem. task force of social transition in Soviet Union, U.S. State Dept. Bur. Human Rights and Humanitarian Affairs; mem. UN NGO Com. on Aging, 1996—; co-chmn. U.S. Com. for Internat. Yr. of Older Persons, 1999. Named Outstanding Alumnus, Augustana Coll., 1980, Ohio Soc. Worker of the Yr., 1992; Fulbright Research fellow; NIMH trainee, 1960-62; Vocat. Rehab. trainee, 1966; Gerontology trainee, 1967; Rotary Found. fellow, 1958-59; recipient Golden Achievement Award, Golden Age Ctr., 2003. Mem. NASW (internat. com. 1989-93, chmn. 1992-93, Found. Pioneer 2003—), Acad. Cert. Social Workers, Internat. Assn. Schs. Social Work (exec. bd. 1978-92, 98—, treas. 1978-86, v.p. N.Am. 1988-92, membership sec. 1996-2000), Internat. Coun. on Social Welfare (dir. U.S. com. 1982-92), Coun. on Social Work Edn. (del. 1972-75, 77-83, chmn. ann. program meeting 1973, chmn. com. on nat. legis. and adminstrv. policy 1975-79, nominating com. 1978-81, internat. com. 1980-86, 96—, chmn. com. 1982-84, dir. 1979-82, exec. com. 1986-89, pres. 1986-89, Lifetime Achievement award 2002), Nat. Conf. on Social Welfare (bd. dirs. 1978-80, chmn. sect. V program com. 1977-78), World Future Soc. (area coord. 1972-74), Fulbright Assn. (v.p. N.E. Ohio chpt. 1990-91), Nat. Coun. on Aging (bd. dirs. 1991-97, internat. com. 1991-97, pub. policy com. 1992-97), NASW Found. Pioneer, 2003-. Democrat. Episcopalian. Home: 2917 Weymouth Rd Cleveland OH 44120-2234 Office: Case Western Res U 10900 Euclid Ave Cleveland OH 44106-1712 E-mail: mch2@po.cwru.edu.

HOKIN, LOWELL EDWARD, biochemist, educator; b. Chgo., Sept. 20, 1924; s. Oscar E. and Helen (Manfield) H.; m. Mabel Neaverson, Dec. 1, 1952 (div. Dec. 1973); children: Linda Ann, Catherine Esther (dec.), Samuel Arthur; m. Barbara M. Gallagher, Mar. 23, 1978 (div. July 1998); 1 child, Ian Oscar. Student, U. Chgo., 1942-43, Dartmouth Coll., 1943-44, U. Louisville Sch. Medicine, 1944-46, U. Ill. Sch. Medicine, 1946-47; MD, U. Louisville, 1948; PhD, U. Sheffield, Eng., 1952. Postdoctoral fellow dept. biochemistry McGill U., 1952-54, faculty, 1954-57, asst. prof., 1955-57; mem. faculty U. Wis., Madison, 1957—, prof. physiol. chemistry, 1961-68, prof. pharmacology, 1968-99, prof., chmn. pharmacology, 1968-93, prof. emeritus, 1999—. Contbr. numerous articles to tech. jours., chpts. to numerous books on phosphoinositides, biol. transport, the pancreas, the brain and lithium in manic-depression. With USNR, 1943-45. Mem. AAAS, Am. Soc. Biochemistry and Molecular Biology, Biochem. Soc. (U.K.), Am. Soc. Pharmacology and Exptl. Therapeutics, N.Y. Acad. Scis. Achievements include discovery of phosphoinositide signaling system. Home: 4021C Monona Dr Monona WI 53716 Office: U Wis Med Sch Dept Pharm 1300 University Ave Madison WI 53706-1510 E-mail: lehokin@facstaff.wisc.edu.

HOLBROOK, JAMES ROBERT, medical technology educator, consultant; b. Encino, Calif., Aug. 10, 1956; s. Robert James and Janice Larine (Lubsen) H. Paramedic cert., Loma Linda U., 1978; B in Vocat. Edn., Calif. State U., San Bernardino, 1989, postgrad., 1989—. Cert. life time tchr. of mobile intensive care paramedics. Paramedic Courtesy Svcs., San Bernardino, 1976-80; paramedic coord. Regional Paramedic Svcs., Upland, Calif., 1980-82; paramedic educator Crafton Hills Coll., Yucaipa, Calif., 1982-84, emergency svc. prof., 1984—, dept. head emergency edn., 1988—, dir. paramedic program, 1991—. Affiliate faculty mem. Am. Heart Assn., San Bernardino, 1976—, commn. mem., 1989; chmn. prehosp. Inland Counties Emergency Agy., San Bernardino, 1986—; speakers bur. Inland AIDS Project, Riverside, Calif., 1987—; faculty advisor Gay and Lesbian Student Assn.; test writer Emergency Svc. State of Calif., Sacramento, 1987; disaster cons. Crafton Hills Coll. (chmn. planning coun.), Yucaipa, 1986—. Named Outstanding Young Man Jr. C. of C., 1986. Mem. Am. Heart Assn. (chmn. emergency cardiac subcom. 1990-92). Republican. Avocations: white water rafting, exploration, open water scuba. Home: 11686 2nd St Yucaipa CA 92399-3118 Office: Crafton Hills Coll 11711 Sand Canyon Rd Yucaipa CA 92399-1742

HOLBROOK, JOHN MILLARD, geologist, educator; b. Ashland, Ky., Dec. 20, 1963; s. James Taylor and Bernice Fern (Miller) H.; m. Camila Venita Dianis, May 31, 1986; 1 child, Zane Craig. BS, U. Ky., 1985; MS, U. N.Mex., 1988; PhD, Ind. U., 1992. Registered profl. geologist. Tchg. asst. U. N.Mex., Albuquerque, 1986-88; assoc. instr. geology Ind. U., Bloomington, 1989-92; asst. prof. geosci. S.E. Mo. State U., Cape Girardeau, 1992-96, assoc. prof. geosci., 1996—. Basin leader Western Interior Cretaceons, Global Sedimentary Geology Program, Miami, Fla., 1988—; geologic asst. Peabody Ventures, Santa Fe, summer 1988; field geologic cons. Ind. U., Bloomington, summer 1991. Contbr. articles to profl. jours. Petroleum Rsch. Fund grantee Am. Chem. Soc., 1993, 97. Mem. Am. Assn. Petroleum Geologists, Soc. for Sedimentary Geology (meeting policy com. 1995-97, K-12 earth sci. edn. com. 1995—, rsch. concepts com. 1997—, Best Paper award SEPM mid-yr. meeting 1992), Geol. Soc. Am., Am. Geophys. Union. Achievements include established relationship between low relief uplifts in Cretaceous Western Interior and Intraplate stresses with Martin Lockley; established relationship between sequence stratigraphy and track preservation on the Dinosaur Freeway; established a hierarchy for bounding surface in valley-fill deposits. Office: SE Mo State Univ Dept Geosci MS6500 Cape Girardeau MO 63701

HOLBROOK-BRYANT, JEAN CARROLL, music educator, band director; b. Lexington, Ky., July 14, 1955; d. Glenn William and Joan (Martin) Holbrook; m. William Michael Bryant, June 1, 1996. BMus, East Tex. State U., 1978, MMus, 1984. Tchr., band dir. Greenville (Tex.) Jr. H.S., 1979-84, Princeton (Tex.) Middle Sch., 1984-96, Euless (Tex.) Jr. H.S., 1996—. Adjudicator, 1988-97; guest clinician, 1988-97; guest conductor East Tex. State U., Commerce, 1995—; french horn instr. Allen, Wylie, Greenville Ind. Sch. Dist., 1984—. Mem. Tex. Music Edn. Assn. (class C honor band 1991, 1st runner up 1994), Tex. Music Adjudicator Assn., Phi Beta Mu. Avocations: computer, crafts, walking, listening to music. Office: Euless Jr High Sch 306 Airport Fwy Euless TX 76039-3667

HOLCOMB, ANNA LOUISE, physical science educator; b. Sherman, Tex., June 22, 1946; d. Louis Alvin and Louise Lorraine (Genthe) Franklin; m. Harold V. Holcomb, June 26, 1964; children: Cynthia Louise Holcomb-Wilson, John Harold. BA in Physics, U. Tex., Arlington, 1986. Cert. tchr. physics, phys. sci., English, Tex. Tchr. physics/phys. sci. Brewer H.S., Ft. Worth, 1986-91; tchr. physics, phys. sci., sci. discovery, environ. studies Ft. Worth Country Day Sch., 1991-96. Recipient Disting. Achievement award for sci. teaching DuPont Corp., Nat. Sci. Tchrs. Assn., Gen. Learning Corp., 1994, 95; 1st place winner nat. sci. competition DuPont Challenge Awards Program, 1995. Mem. Am. Assn. Physics Tchrs., Nat. Sci. Tchrs. Assn., Tex. Tchrs. Phys. Sci., Tex. Marine Edn. Assn., Associated Chemistry Tchrs. Tex. Home: 8144 Tumbleweed Trl Fort Worth TX 76108-3519 Office: Ft Worth Country Day Sch 4200 Country Day Ln Fort Worth TX 76109-4201

HOLCOMB, BEVERLY J. educational administrator; b. Springdale, Ark., Nov. 24; d. Joe Latimer and Elva M. (mcKeown) H. BA summa cum laude, John Brown U., Siloam Springs, Ark., 1950; EdM, U. Ark., 1956; MA, Brandeis U., 1965; EdD, U. Ark., 1970. Cert. in ednl. adminstrn., Spanish; cert. fundraising exec. Asst. mgr./bookkeeper Myers Variety Store, Springdale, Ark., 1944-45; traffic announcer/scriptwriter Radio Sta. KUOA, Siloam Springs, Ark., 1945-50; tchr. Spring Creek Elem. Sch., Springdale, Ark., 1945-50; linguistic rschr. Summer Inst. Linguistics, Mexico, Peru, 1950-54; co-dir. bilingual tchr. tng. inst. Peruvian Ministry of Edn., 1955-62; social/cultural anthropologist Rsch. Inst. for Study of Man, Bolivia and BWI, 1965-66; dir. counseling Opportunity Indsl. Ctr., Little Rock, 1966-68; extension specialist gerontology U. Ark. Coop. Ext. Svc., Little Rock, 1969-76; exec. dir./sch. supt. Florence Crittenton Home, Little Rock, 1976-94, exec. dir. emeritus/preventin outreach leader and cons., 1994—. Descriptive linguist Wycliffe Bible Translators, Lima, Pucallpa and Pto. Izango, Peru, 1950-55. Author: Problems of Aging in Craighead County, Ark., 1970, Annotated Bibliography on Vocational Placement of Culturally Distinct Individuals, 1969; author booklet: Educational Programs on Pregnancy and AIDS Prevention, 1994. Lay mem./alt. N.W. Conf. of United Meth. Ch., Conway, Ark., 1991—; mem. pastor/parish coun. 1st United Meth. Ch., Jacksonville, Ark., 1990-94. Inductee into Hall of Excellence, Ind. Colls. of Ark.-Statewide, 1994; named Outstanding Alumnus John Brown U., 1992, Outstanding Fundraising Exec., Nat. Soc. Fund Raising execs., 1991; Rsch. Inst. for Study of Man scholar, 1963-65, John Brown U. scholar, 1945, 48, 49, U. Nac. Mayor de San Marcos, Lima scholar, 1959, 560, Brandeis U. scholar, 1962-65. Mem. Ark. Ednl. Assn., Nat. Soc. Fund Raising Execs. (bd. dirs. 1987—), Child Welfare League of Am. (adv. coun. 1992—), Phi Delta Kappa. Avocations: reading, working corssword puzzles, driving through scenic vistas. Home: 2 Yaqui Pl North Little Rock AR 72120-3617

HOLCOMB, MINNIE IRBY, elementary educator; b. Laurens, S.C. d. Charlie and Lydia Alberta (Woody) Irby; m. Wilbert McDaniel Holcomb; children: Sabrina Wilberta, Juan Irby. BS, Tuskegee Inst., 1945; postgrad., Atlanta U., 1945-46, Bowie State U., 1980, U. D.C., 1980. Social worker Laurens County Tuberculosis Assn., 1950-60; tchr. Am. Sch., Liberia, West Africa, 1961-64, Taegu, Korea, 1966-68, Adams Elem., Washington, 1969-70, Shepherd Elem., Washington, 1970—. Demonstration tchr. on multi-cultural edn. selected students of various U.; nat. demonstration tchr. Alpha Phonics Reading Program; nat. cons. IBM Writing to Read Program; demonstration tchr. Office of Edn., Network TV, DC Pub. Schools, Washington. Cons., D.C. early childhood collaborative (devel.) proposal and traveled to Beijing, China to rsch. use of Abacus for teaching math to Kindergartners, funded by Cafritz Foundation. Mem. NAACP, Childrens Edn. Found. (adv. bd. 1989—), Jr. Citizens Corps. (adv. bd. 1985-88), Alpha Wives Club (chmn. ebony fashion show). Democrat. Home: 10913 Oakwood St Silver Spring MD 20901-4418

HOLDER, KATHLEEN, elementary education educator; b. Peoria, Ill., Jan. 19, 1942; d. Clifford B. and Margaret Anne (Bowker) Bourne; m. James Sherman Holder, Dec. 29, 1962; children: Laurie Lynn, Cheryl Anne. BS, Bradley U., 1965; MEd, Regents Coll., 1981; postgrad., SUNY, Cortland, 1990-91. Cert. elem. tchr., Ky., N.Y., Ga., Ill., Calif., tchr. birth-6 yrs., Am. Montessori Soc. Tchr. St. Philomena Sch., Peoria, Ill., 1962-63, Garfield Sch., Danville, Ill., 1964-67, St. David's Sch., Willow Grove, Pa., 1972-74, St. Austin Sch., Mpls., 1974-75, Knoxville (Tenn.) City Schs., 1977-79, Chenango Forks (N.Y.) Schs., 1985-92, Fayette County Schs., Lexington, Ky., 1992-96, Glynn County Schs., Brunswick, Ga., 1996-98; substitute tchr. Cedar Rapids, Iowa, 1999—; 1st grade tchr. Van Buren, Cedar Rapids, 1999-2000; presch. tchr. Clovis Unified, 2000—. Team coord. sci. impact project SUNY, Cortland, 1987-90, presenter tchrs. teaching tchrs., 1988, sci. insvc. workshops for tchrs. Fayette County Schs., 1994-96; team coord. Broome Tioga Boces Coop. Regional Curriculum Devel. Project. Author: Science Curriculum Resource Guide K-3, 1989. Grantee Hoyt Found., 1988, Family and Children's Svcs., 2001. Mem. Nat. Assn. for Edn. of Young Child, Calif. Assn. for Edn. of Young Child, Fresno

Assn. for Edn. of Young Child, Calif. Reading Assn., Nat. Reading Assn., Knoxville Reading Assn. (treas. 1978-79), Delta Zeta (Sec. 1977-79, Rose of Honor 1979), Sigma Alpha Iota. Lutheran. Avocations: singing, gardening, cooking, reading. Home: 29 Laurel Ave 1st flr Binghamton NY 13905 E-mail: kathybourne1@aol.com.

HOLDERNESS, SUSAN RUTHERFORD, at-risk educator; b. Cherokee, Iowa, Nov. 5, 1941; d. Parker William and Ruth Elvera (Peterson) Rutherford; m. Michael Aaron Holderness, Aug. 12, 1961; children: Lauren, Lisa, Jennifer, Joshua. BA in Edn., Wayne State U., Nebr., 1964; student, Iowa State U., 1960-61, Vocat. Cert., 1973. Tchr. various high schs. including Norwalk (Iowa) High Sch., 1968-78; tchr. South Alternative and East H.S., Des Moines, 1968-78; hist. site interpreter Salisbury House, Des Moines, 1971-78, 84-88, Minn. State Hist. Soc., St. Paul, 1978-84; cons. Profl. Match Cons., Des Moines, 1985-90; tour guide and conv. planner Des Moines Tour and Conv. Svcs., 1987-92; also dir. Christian edn. Douglas Ave. Presbyn. Ch., Des Moines; founding. mem. faculty Walnut Creek Campus H.S., 1995—. Owner gourmet food shop, 1973. V.p. fundraising Des Moines Symphony Guild, 1990-92; bd. dirs., treas., sec. playground bldg. project Greenwood Sch. PTA, Des Moines, 1986-89; co-chmn. Civic Music Assn., Des Moines, 1987; pres., v.p., tour dir. St. Paul New Residents, 1980-83, others in past; bd. dirs. Ramsey County Friends of the Libr., 1981-83, Symphony Assn., mem., steering com. showhouse and ball, fundraising v.p.; vice-chmn. Des Moines Hist. Dist. Commn., 1998—; mem. PEO, chpt. V.; pres. Des Moines Castle Club, 2002-03. Mem. Iowa Victorian Soc., Compass Club (internat. pres. 1986-87), Internat. Platform Assn., Kappa Delta Pi, Gamma Phi Beta. Republican. Congregationalist. Avocations: tennis, water sports, gourmet cooking, volunteer work, art and theater. Office: Walnut Creek Campus 815 8th St West Des Moines IA 50265-3639

HOLEN, NORMAN DEAN, art educator, artist; b. Cavalier, N.D., Sept. 16, 1937; s. Alvin C. and Norma H. Holen; m. Ilene Gronaas, Sept. 3, 1960; children: Peter John, Alisa Ilene. BA, Concordia Coll., 1959; MFA, State U. Iowa, 1962; postgrad., U. Minn., 1972. Instr. Northwestern Coll., Orange City, Iowa, 1962-63, Concordia Coll., Moorhead, Minn., 1963-64; prof. Augsburg Coll., Mpls., 1964—2002, ret., 2002. Contbr. articles to profl. jours. including The Artists mag., Pottery Making Illustrated, Clay Times, The Am. Artist; commns. including Kirchbak Gardens, Richfield, Minn., King Olav, Oslo, Norway, Augsburg Coll., Mpls., King Herald V, Norway. Mem. Artist Equity Assn. (chpt. pres., nat. exec. bd. 1974-75, v.p. Minn. chpt. 1973-74), Soc. Minn. Sculptors, Nat. Sculpture Soc. (Bronze Medal, 1980, Joel Meisner award, 1983), Allied Artists of Am. (Rachel L. Armour award, 1980, 82, In Memorium award, 1983). Republican. Lutheran. Avocations: playing classical guitar, inventing tools and splints for my physically challenged students. Home: 7332 12th Ave S Minneapolis MN 55423-3343

HOLEYFIELD, MARY ANNETTE, health and physical education educator; b. Harrison, Ark., June 20, 1955; d. Leo Dale and Etta Ruth (Petree) Borland; m. Robert Lee Holeyfield, May 18, 1974; 1 child, Ashlyn Elizabeth. BS in Health and Phys. Edn., Ark. Tech. U., Russellville, 1976, MEd in Phys. Edn., 1977; PhD in Exercise Sci., U. Ark., 1997. Cert. ARC instr. trainer. Elem. phys. edn. specialist Russellville Pub. Schs., 1979-85; instr. health and phys. edn. Ark. Tech. U., Russellville, 1985-92, asst. prof. health and phys. edn., 1992—98, assoc. prof. health and physical edn., 1998—, head dept. of health and physical edn., 1998—. Pres. Russellville Jr. Aux., 1992. Mem. AAHPERD, ASCD, SAWPASH, Ark. Assn. Health, Phys. Edn., Recreation and Dance (past chair rsch. sect.), Am. Coll. Sports Medicine, Zeta Tau Alpha (past dist. pres., past alumnae chpt. officer). Office: Ark Tech U Hull 110 1306 N El Paso Ave Russellville AR 72801 E-mail: annette.holeyfield@mail.atu.edu.

HOLGUIN, KATHRYN RAE, elementary school educator; b. Petoskey, Mich., Jan. 31, 1960; d. George and Norma (Johnston) S. BA, Albion Coll., 1982; MA, U. Tex., 1989; postgrad. studies, Mich. State U., 1989-92. Cert. tchr., Mich., Tex. Tchr. 1st grade Weslaco (Tex.) Ind. Sch. Dist., 1982-84; 5th grade and resource tchr. Seguin (Tex.) Ind. Sch. Dist., 1984-86; 2nd grade and reading resource tchr. San Antonio Ind. Sch. Dist., 1986-89; tchr. 1st grade Canutillo (Tex.) Ind. Sch. Dist., 1992—. Mem. ASCD, NEA, Tex. State Tchrs. Assn., Assn. Tex. Profl. Educators, Internat. Reading Assn.

HOLLAND, ANTONIO FREDERICK, social and behavioral science educator; b. Petersburg, Va., Dec. 5, 1943; s. Garnett George and Carmen Thersa (Kildare) H.; m. Carolyn Nolanna Turner, Nov. 26, 1975; children: Bradley Wayne, Erik Garnett. BA in History, Northeastern U., Boston, 1967, MA in History, 1969; PhD in History, U. Mo., 1984. Asst. libr. Boston Pub. Libr., Boston, 1962-65; audio-visual media asst. Northeastern U., Boston, 1965-67; instr., asst. prof. Lincoln U., Jefferson City, Mo., 1970-84, assoc., full prof. social and behavioral sci., 1984-90, head dept. social and behavioral sci., 1986—. Spkr. black history TV and radio. Author: Nathan B. Young, Black Educator, 1984, The Soldiers' Dream Continued, 1991; co-author: Missouri's Black Heritage, 1993. Chair Martin Luther King Meml. Park task force, Columbia, 1988-89; mem. Mo. Heritage Rev. Mo. Dept. Elem. and Secondary Edn., Jefferson City, Mo, 1992—; mem. adv. bd. Mo. Commn. on Hist. Preservation, 1994—. 1st lt. U.S. Army, 1968-70; Lt. Col. Mo. Army Nat. Guard, 1978-99. Nat. Tchg. fellow U.S. Dept. of Edn., 1976-77, African Travel fellow Phelps-Stokes fund, N.Y.C., Washington, 1975, Lewis Athenton fellow U. Mo., 1983, 84. Mem. NAACP, Nat. Guard Assn. of U.S., Mo. Acad. of Sci., Mo. State Hist. Soc., So. Hist. Assn., Assn. Study of Afro-Am. Life and History. Home: 306 W El Cortez Dr Columbia MO 65203-3727 Office: Lincoln U 820 Chestnut St Jefferson City MO 65101-3500 E-mail: hollanda@lincolnu.edu.

HOLLAND, DENA, ballet educator; b. Chgo., Mar. 28, 1941; d. Richard Paul and Loretto Helen (Rozak) Wachowiak; m. Harry Charles Holland, Dec. 30, 1961 (dec. 1994); children: Thomas, Daniel. Grad. high sch., Chgo.; student, Art Inst. Chgo., 1959-61. Tchr. ballet Rozak Studio of Dance, Chgo., 1956-62, Singer Learning Ctr., Monroeville, Pa., 1972-73; owner, tchr. ballet Holland Studio of Dance, Pitts., 1972-77, Irene Kaufmann Ctr., Pitts., 1973-74, Community Coll. of Allegheny County, Pitts., 1977-87, Carnegie Inst., Pitts., 1977-87, Dancespace, Pitts., 1987—, also bd. dirs. Tchr. ballet Pitts. Ctr. for the Arts, 1974, 87; tchr. folk dance Chatham Coll. Music and Arts Day Camp, summer, 1990, 91, Children's Jazz Camp: John Heinz Family Ctr., summer 1996. tchr. Hatha Yoga, Pitts. Athletic Assn., 2003— . Avocation: running. Office: Dancespace 304 5604 Solway St Pittsburgh PA 15217-1267 E-mail: dance@dancespace304.com.

HOLLAND, JEAN, elementary education educator; b. Chgo., Nov. 11, 1943; d. Robert Henry and Lillian Pauline (Matthews) Jay; m. Arnold Burns, Apr. 26, 1963 (div. July 1976); children: Anthony Scott, Leslie Denise; m. Eddie Holland, Aug. 24, 1985. AA, Chgo. Jr. Coll., 1964; BS in Ed., Chgo. State U., 1966; Math endorsement, Gov.'s State U., 1995. Tchr. Medill Elem. Sch., Chgo., 1966-68, Altgeld Elem. Sch., Chgo., 1974-81, Oglesby Elem. Sch., Chgo., 1981—. Cons. tchr. Chgo. Tchrs. Union. Gen. mem. Urban League, Chgo., Bromeliad Soc. of Greater Chgo., PUSH, Chgo. Roman Catholic. Avocations: reading, gardening. Office: Oglesby Elem Sch 7646 S Green St Chicago IL 60620-2854

HOLLAND, KATHIE KUNKEL, university official, educator; b. Lake Worth, Fla., Jan. 4, 1949; d. John Alfred and Annetta (Wellman) K.; m. James Carson Holland, Dec. 15, 1968 (div. Mar. 1987); children: J. Wesley, J. Wyatt. MBA, U. Cen. Fla., 1980, BSBA, 1978. Teller 1st Fed. Savs. and Loan, West Palm Beach, Fla., 1969-70; head teller Tallahassee Fed. Savs. and Loan, 1970-71; br. mgr. Orlando (Fla.) Fed. Savs. and Loan, 1971-75; instr. Orlando Coll., 1982-85; grad. asst. U. Cen. Fla., Orlando, 1978-80, instr., 1986—, asst. dir. Small Bus. Devel. Ctr., 1986—; dir. profl. devel. Fla. Small Bus. Devel. Ctr. Network, Orlando, 1992—. Bd. dirs. Ctr. for Continuing Edn. for Women, Orlando, 1987; co-founder Women Bus. Owners' Network, Orlando, 1988; mgmt. cons., Orlando. Co-author: Starting and Managing a Business in Central Florida, 1989, Professional Development Manual, 1994; contbr. articles to profl. jours. Com. mem. Jr. Achievement Ctr., Entrepreneur Task Force, Orlando, 1989; speaker Greater Brevard C. of C., Melbourne, Fla., 1989. Mem. ASTD, Nat. Coalition Bldg. Inst., Nat. Assn. Women Bus. Owners, Platform Speakers Assn., Women's Bus. Ednl. Coun. (bd. dirs. 1987—), Greater Orlando C. of C. (com. chmn. 1987), Inst. Mgmt. Cons., Omicron Delta Kappa. Republican. Presbyterian. Avocations: scuba diving, entertaining, reading. Office: U Cen Fla Small Bus Devel Ctr Alafaya Trl Orlando FL 32816-0001

HOLLAND, LESLIE ANN, special education educator; b. Oak Lawn, Ill., Sept. 26, 1969; d. Ronald Leo and Rosemary Seymour; m. Brian Michael Holland, Dec. 31, 1999. AA, Moraine Valley C.C., Palos Hills, Ill., 1991; BS in Edn., Ea. Ill. U., 1995. Day camp site dir. Southwest Spl. Recreation Assn., Alsip, Ill., 1996—2000, spl. edn. dept. chair Momence, Ill., 1996—; tchr., spl. edn. dept. Sylvan Learning Ctr., Tinley Park, Ill., 2001—; chair, spl. edn. dept. Momence H.S., 1996—. Home: 14600 W Aston Way Lockport IL 60441 Office: Momence Unit Sch Dist # 1 101 N Franklin Momence IL 60954

HOLLAND, MARTHA KING, primary and secondary education educator; b. Charlottesville, Va., Jan. 20, 1965; d. Frederick Conrad Jr. and Martha King (Abbott) Holland; m. Russell Frost Shipman, Aug. 7, 1993. BA Studio Art, Mt. Holyoke Coll., 1987; MA English, U. Va., 1988-90. Cert. secondary English tchr. English tchr., coach, head grades 7 and 8 The Rivers Sch., Weston, Mass., 1990-95. English and lang. arts tchr., coach Out-of-Door Acad., Sarasota, Fla., 1995—. Author poetry, (novel) The Mangrove Legacy. Named to Terrific Tchrs. Making A Difference, Edward F. Calesa Found., Mass., 1993. Mem. Nat. Coun. Tchrs. English. Avocations: writing poetry, painting, photography, soccer, basketball. Home: 1175 52nd St Sarasota FL 34234-2803 Office: The Out Of Door Acad 444 Reid St Sarasota FL 34242-1399

HOLLAND, ROBERT JAMES, special education educator; b. St. Albans, Vt., Sept. 3, 1946; s. Phillip William and Harriet Althera (Davis) H.; m. Leslie Alice Grant, Aug. 9, 1969; 1 child, Morgan Lawrence. BS Edn., Johnson State Coll., 1968; postgrad., SUNY, New Paltz, 1975, U. Maine, Orono, 1988-94, U. Maine, Portland, 1990-94. Tchr. mid. level Dover Plains (N.Y.) Elem., 1970-87; team leader U.S. Dept. Energy, Rockland, Maine, 1987-88; tchg. prin. K-8 Somerville Union 51, Coupers Mills, Maine, 1988-90; spl. edn. tchr. Eastport (Maine) Elem. Sch., 1990-95; interim spl. edn. dir., 1995. Mem. student assistance team Eastport Elem., 1991—; coach h.s. track and jr. varsity baksetball. Chmn./editor: Guide to Camp Sharparoon, 1974. Leader Boy Scouts Am., Dover Plains, 1978-84; coach Little League, 1983-84. With USNR, 1968-70. Mem. Dover Wingdale Tchrs. Assn. (pres., v.p., treas. 1971-78), Coun. for Exceptional Children, Maine Support Network for Spl. Edn., Washington Computer Consortium, Dutchess County Tchrs. Coun. (pres. 1976-77). Avocation: computers. Home: HC 35 Box 746 Tenants Harbor ME 04860-9709

HOLLANDER, JOHN, humanities educator, poet; b. NYC, Oct. 28, 1929; s. Franklin and Muriel (Kornfeld) H.; m. Anne Helen Loesser, June 15, 1953 (div. 1977); children: Martha, Elizabeth.; m. Natalie Charkow, Dec. 15, 1981. AB, Columbia U., 1950, AM, 1952; PhD, Ind. U., 1959; DLitt (hon.), Marietta Coll., 1982; LHD (hon.), Ind. U., 1990; DFA (hon.), Maine Coll. of Art, 1993; DHL (hon.), CUNY, 2001; DHL (hon.), New Sch. U., 2003. Jr. fellow Soc. Fellows, Harvard, 1954-57; lectr. English Conn. Coll., New London, 1957-59; instr. English Yale U., 1959-61; asst. prof. English, fellow Ezra Stiles Coll., 1961-64, assoc. prof., 1964-66; prof. Hunter Coll., CUNY, 1966—77; prof. English Yale U., New Haven, 1977—, A. Bartlett Giamatti prof., 1987—, Sterling prof., 1995—2002, prof. emeritus, 2002. Vis. prof. Linguistic Inst., Inc. U., 1964; faculty Salzburg Seminar in Am. Studies, 1965; Christian Gauss seminarian Princeton U., 1962; Clark lectr. Trinity Coll., Cambridge, Eng., 2000. Author: A Crackling of Thorns, 1958, The Untuning of the Sky, 1961, Movie-Going and Other Poems, 1962, Various Owls, 1963, Visions from the Ramble, 1965, The Quest of the Gole, 1966, Types of Shape, 1968, 2d edit., 1991, Images of Voice, 1970, The Night Mirror, 1971, Town and Country Matters, 1972, The Head of the Bed, 1973, Tales Told of the Fathers, 1975, Vision and Resonance, 1975, Reflections on Espionage, 1976, 2d edit., 1999, Spectral Emanations, 1978, In Place, 1978, Blue Wine, 1979, The Figure of Echo, 1981, Rhyme's Reason, 1981, 2d edit., 1989, 3rd edit., 2000, Powers of Thirteen, 1983, (with Saul Steinberg) Dal Vero, 1983, In Time and Place, 1986, Some Fugitives Take Cover, 1988, Harp Lake, 1988, Melodious Guile, 1988, Tesserae, 1993, Selected Poetry, 1993, The Gazer's Spirit, 1995, The Work of Poetry, 1997, The Poetry of Everyday Life, 1998, Figurehead and Other Poems, 1999, Picture Window, 1993; editor: Poems of Ben Jonson, 1961, (with Harold Bloom) The Wind and the Rain, 1961, (with Anthony Hecht) Jiggery-Pokery, 1966, Poems of Our Moment, 1968, Modern Poetry: Essays in Criticism, 1968, American Short Stories Since 1945, 1968, (with Frank Kermode) The Oxford Anthology of English Literature, 1973, (with Reuben A. Brower and Helen Vendler) For I.A. Richards: Essays in His Honor, 1973, (with Irving Howe and David Bromwich) Literature as Experience, 1979, The Essential Rossetti, 1990, Animal Poems, 1994, Garden Poems, 1996, Committed to Memory, 1997, Marriage Poems, 1997, War Poems, 1999, Sonnets, 2001, (with Joanna Weber) A Gallery of Poems, 2001, American Wits, 2003; contbg. editor: Harper's mag, 1969-71; mem. editorial bd. Raritan, 1981—, Art and Lit., 1985—, Lit., 1989—; assoc. for poetry Partisan Review, 1959-65; mem. poetry bd. Wesleyan U. Press, 1959-62; author numerous poems. Recipient Yale Younger Poets award, 1958, Poetry Chap Book award, 1962, award in lit. Nat. Inst. Arts and Letters, 1963, Levinson prize, 1974, Bollingen prize, 1983, Mina P. Shaughnessy award, 1963, Melville Cane award, 1990, Ambassador Book award, 1994, Gov.'s Arts award State of Conn., 1997, Robert Penn Warren-Cleanth Brooks award, 1998; Overseas fellow Churchill Coll., Cambridge (Eng.) U., 1967-68, sr. fellow NEH, 1973-74, Guggenheim fellow, 1979-80, MacArthur Found. fellow, 1990-95. Mem.: Am. Acad. Arts and Scis., Am. Acad. Arts and Letters (sec. 2000—03), Am. Assn. Lit. Scholars and Critics (pres. 2000—01), Century Assn. (N.Y.C.), Phi Beta Kappa. Office: Yale U Dept English PO Box 208302 New Haven CT 06520-8302 E-mail: john.hollander@yale.edu.

HOLLANDER, ROBERT B., JR., Romance languages educator; b. N.Y.C., July 31, 1933; s. Robert B. and Laurene (McGookey) H.; m. Jean Haberman, Apr. 23, 1964; children: Cornelia Vanness, Robert B. III. AB, Princeton U., 1955; PhD, Columbia U., 1962. Tchr. Latin and English, Collegiate Sch., N.Y.C., 1955-57; instr. English Columbia U., N.Y.C., 1958-62; mem. faculty dept. Romance langs. Princeton (N.J.) U., 1962—, prof. European lit., 1974—, chmn. comparative lit., 1994-98. Mem. Nat. Coun. on Humanities, 1974-80, 87-92, vice chmn., 1978-80; mem. N.J. Com. for Humanities, 1980-86; dir. Dartmouth Dante Project, 1982—, Princeton Dante Project, 1997—; v.p. Assn. Internat. Studi de Lingua et Lett. Italiana, 1985-94; trustee La Scuola d'Italia, N.Y.C., 1986-92, Collegiate Sch., 1990-96, vice pres. bd., 1994-96, pres. bd., 98-2001. Author: Allegory in Dante's Commedia, 1969, Boccaccio's Two Venuses, 1977, Studies in Dante, 1980, Il Virgilio dantesco, 1983, Boccaccio's Last Fiction: Il Corbaccio, 1988, Dante's Epistle to Cangrande, 1993, Boccaccio's Dante and the Shaping Force of Satire, 1997, Dante Alighieri, 2000, Dante, 2001; editor and translator: (with T. Hampton and M. Frankel) Amorosa Visione, 1986; co-editor: L'Espositione di Bernardino Daniello da Lucca sopra la Comedia di Dante, 1989, (with Jean Hollander) Dante Alighieri, Inferno, 2000, Purgatorio, 2003. Trustee Nat. Humanities Ctr., 1981—, chmn. bd. trustees, 1988-91. Guggenheim fellow, 1970-71; NEH fellow, 1974-75, 82-83; recipient Gold medal of the City of Florence for work on behalf of Dante, 1988, Bronze medal of the City of Tours, 1993, John Witherspoon award in the Humanities, Com. for the Humanities, N.J., 1988, Internat. Nicola Zingarelli prize for Dantean philology and criticism, 1999; named Disting. Alumnus, Collegiate Sch., 2003; hon. citizen Certaldo, Italy, 1997. Mem. Dante Soc. Am. (mem. council 1976-85, pres. 1980-85), Am. Boccaccio Assn. Clubs: Cosmos (Washington). Republican. Office: Princeton U Dept French and Italian E Pyne Princeton NJ 08544-0001

HOLLAWAY, LISA JEAN, secondary education educator; b. Marion, Ohio, Mar. 10, 1965; d. William Harold and Iretta Jean (Stineman) H. AA, BS, Ohio State U., 1987; MA, Marygrove Coll., Detroit, 1998. Cert. reading tchr., Ohio. Tchr. lang. arts and reading Olentangy Mid. Sch., Delaware, Ohio; tchr. English River Valley High Sch., Marion. Vol. initiative partnership coord. River Valley Sch. Dist. Mem. NEA, Ohio Edn. Assn. Home: 267 N Marion St Waldo OH 43356-9114

HOLLEMAN, VERNON DAUGHTY, physician, internist; b. Brownwood, Tex., Oct. 1, 1931; s. Vernon Edgar and Olene Nollie (Reece) H.; m. Shirley Eyvonne Roberts, April 26, 1961; children: Richard, Joel, Douglas. BA in Chemistry and Biology, Howard Payne Coll., Brownwood, 1953; MD, Baylor U., 1958. Mem. med. staff Santa Fe Meml. Hosp, 1962-83; pres. med. staff Santa Fe Meml. Hosp., 1979-83; mem. med. staff Scott and White Hosp., 1962—; asst. chief physician Santa Fe Employees Hosp. Assn., 1962-85, med. dir., 1985—; intern Scott and White Clinic and Hosp., Temple, Tex., 1958-59, resident in internal medicine, 1959-62; dir. div. gen. internal medicine Santa Fe Ctr., Temple, Tex., 1985—; assoc. prof. internal medicine Tex. A&M Coll. Medicine, Temple, 1982—. Adj. faculty clinician Ohio Coll. of Podiatric Medicine, Cleveland, 1982-86; med. dir. Consol. Assns. Railroad Employees, 1997—. Illustrator: Aesculapian, 1957, So. Bapt. Student Union Projects, 1954-58; illustrator ltd. edit. lithographs Baylor U. Lettermans Assn., 1994; contbr. photography to books, including Colorados Biggest Bucks and Bulls, Boone and Crocket Books, Awesome Antlers, Records of North American Mule Deer; author: articles on health, preventive medicine, and numerous others. Bd. dirs Santa Fe Meml. Found.; hon. chmn. physicians adv. bd. Tex. Nat. Rep. Congl. Com. Art Instrn., Inc. scholar, 1952; recipient Centennial award Santa Fe Meml. Found., 1991. Mem. AAAS, Nat. Assn. Ret. and Vet. Railway Employees (hon. life), AMA, ACP, Am. Coll. Phys. Execs., Am. Soc. Internal Medicine, Tex. Med. Assn. (Vernon D. Holleman-Lewis M. Rampy Scott and White Centennial chair gerontology 1999), Tex. Med. Found., Am. Heart Assn. (cardiopulmonary coun.), Am. Assn. Ry. Physicians, World Med. Assn., Tex. Diabetes and Endocrine Soc., N.Y. Acad. Scis., So. Med. Assn. (life), Am. Coll. Occupl. Medicine, Am. Pain Soc., Am. Acad. Pain Mgmt. (diplomate), Internat. Soc. Phys. Activity in Prevention of Osteoporosis (charter), Boone and Crockett Club, Tex. Taxidermy Assn., Nat. Safari Club (life), Alpha Chi, Phi Chi. Baptist. Avocations: medical history, art, hunting, photography, conservation. Office: Scott and White Clinic 600 S 25th St Temple TX 76504-5227

HOLLENBECK, SUE J. elementary education educator; b. Dubuque, Iowa, June 17, 1946; d. Irenaeus J. and Lois M. (Jorgensen) Timmerman; m. Michael D. Hollenbeck, July 23, 1966; children: Dean M., Dan T. 2 yr. teaching degree, Vernon County Tchrs. Coll., Viroqua, Wis., 1966; BS, U. Wis., Platteville, 1968; MS in Profl. Devel., U. Wis., La Crosse, 1988. Tchr. grades 1-7 Belmont (Wis.) Schs., 1966-67; tchr. art and music Shullsburg (Wis.) Schs., 1967-68; tchr. grade 1 Benton (Wis.) Pub. Schs., 1968-71; tchr. grades 1,2,3 DeSoto Schs., Ferryville, Wis., 1973-77, tchr. grade 1 DeSoto, 1977-81, tchr. grade 6 Stoddard, Wis., 1981-85, tchr. grade 4, 1985—; geography bee coord. DeSoto Sch. Dist., Stoddard, 1993-97. Spelling bee coord., DeSoto Sch. Dist., 1981-91, 95-97. Recipient Dist. Tchr. of Yr. award DeSoto Schs., 1981-82, Newspaper in Edn. award LaCrosse (Wis.) Tribune, 1983. Mem. NEA, ASCD, Wis. Edn. Assn., DeSoto Edn. Assn. (adv. bd. SIM 1983-95), Western Wis. Edn. Assn., Midwest Wis. Reading Coun. Avocations: reading, dancing, piano playing and singing, baking, boating. Home: W945 Trout Ln Stoddard WI 54658-9029

HOLLER, F. JAMES, chemistry educator; b. Muncie, Ind., Aug. 6, 1946; s. Lloyd H. and Phyllis Charlene (Morris) H.; m. Vicki Darlene Peirson, June 3, 1967; children: Brian J., Brad A., Scott A. BS, Ball State U., 1968, MS, 1973; PhD, Mich. State U., 1977. Tchr. chemistry, physics and math. Lincoln H.S., Cambridge City, Ind., 1968-73; asst. prof. chemistry U. Ky., Lexington, 1977-83, assoc. prof., 1983-95, prof., 1995—. Co-author: Analytical Chemistry: An Introduction, 1999, Fundamentals of Analytical Chemistry, 1995, 2d edit., 2003, Principles of Instrumental Analysis, 1998; author: Mathcad Applications for Analytical Chemistry, 1994. Named Gt. Tchr., U. Ky. Alumni Assn., 1993. Mem. Am. Chem. Soc. Avocations: woodworking, sports, golf. Office: U Ky Dept Chemistry Lexington KY 40506-0001

HOLLERAN, PRISCILLA HOOK, special education educator; b. Plainfield, N.J., June 30, 1952; d. Eugene Ray and Mary Luise (Gehan) Hook; m. Kevin J. Holleran, Apr. 7, 1990. BA in Psychol. Svcs., Hollins Coll., 1974; MEd in Spl. Edn., Temple U., 1980. Cert. tchr. mentally retarded, Pa., socially and emotionally disturbed, Pa., Fla., physically handicapped, Pa., Fla., IU program specialist, Pa., specific learning disabilities, Fla. Estates and trusts paralegal Drinker, Biddle & Reath, Phila., 1975-76; tchr. Chester County Intermediate Unit, Exton, Pa., 1977-78, Methacton Sch. Dist., Fairview Village, Pa., 1978-81, 82-84, Duval County Schs., Jacksonville, Fla., 1981-82; consulting program specialist Montgomery County Intermediate Unit # 25, Erdenheim, Pa., 1984-89; tchr. Colonial Sch. Dist., Plymouth Meeting, Pa., 1989—, master tchr., 2003—. Past pres. Jr. League Phila. Mem. Pa. State Edn. Assn., Colonial Edn. Assn. Republican. Presbyterian. Home: 323 Old Kings Hwy Downingtown PA 19335-3352 Office: Ridge Park Elem Sch 200 Karrs Ln Conshohocken PA 19428-1211

HOLLERITH, CHARLES, III, secondary school educator; b. N.Y.C., Jan. 1, 1964; s. Charles Jr. and Helen (McVey) H. BA, Beloit Coll., 1986, MA in Tchg., 1987. Cert. tchr., Ill. Social studies tchr. Hononegah H.S., Rockton, Ill., 1986—, essential schs. coord., 1994—. Mem. alumni bd. Beloit (Wis.) Coll., 1991-93, mem. Coll. Mus. com., 1994—. Named Coach of Yr., No. Ill. Conf., 1988, 89, 91, 93. Mem. ASCD, Nat. Coun. for the Social Studies, Coalition of Essential Schs., U.S. Soccer Coaches Assn., Ill. H.S. Soccer Coaches Assn. (soccer adv. bd. 1992-95, Regional Coach of Yr. 1988, 91, 93), Constl. Rights Found. Episcopalian. Avocations: soccer, gardening, boating, travel. Home: 10079 Tybow Trl Roscoe IL 61073-8562 Office: Hononegah HS 307 Salem St Rockton IL 61072-2630

HOLLEY, CHARLOTTE BUGGS, English language educator; b. Gadsden, Ala., May 1, 1949; d. Theodis Sr. and Margaret (Wright) Buggs; m. John David Holley, Aug. 9, 1975 (div. Aug. 1980); children: Kevin LeJohn, Keith LeJuan. BA, Spelman Coll., 1972; MS, Jacksonville State U., 1974; EdS, U. Ala., Tuscaloosa, 1980, PhD, 1990. Cert. tchr. secondary English, Ala. TV instr. Etowah County Bd. of Edn., Gadsden, 1972-77; tchr. English Attalla (Ala.) City Bd. of Edn., 1977-89, Faulkner U., Birmingham, 1989-93; prof. edn. U. Ala., Birmingham, 1990—. Mem. adv. bd. Jefferson County Schs., Birmingham, 1991—; adult edn. cons. Bessemer (Ala.) City Schs., 1993—; dir. lang. lab. Birmingham City Schs., 1994—; mem. honors coun. U. Ala., Birmingham, 1993. Heritage cons. Sta. WMGJ Radio, Gadsden, 1985—. Recipient Read Creative writing award Read Assn., 1970; named to Ala. Tchr. Hall of Fame, 1984. Mem. ASCD, Nat. Coun. Tchrs. English, Internat. Reading Assn., Ala. Assn. Tchr. Edn. (pres.-elect 1993-94), Phi Delta Kappa, Alpha Kappa Alpha (Lambda Eta Omega chpt. 1977, Outstanding Soror 1986). United Methodist. Avocations: creative writing, literacy tutoring, reading, singing. Home: 812 Avenue E Gadsden AL 35901-2218

HOLLIDAY, CHARLES WALTER, JR., physiology and biology educator; b. Alexandria, Va. s. Charles Walter and Eugene (Singleton) H.; m. Patricia Anne Roseman, July 26, 1971. BS in Biology, Marietta Coll., 1968; PhD in Biology, U. Oreg., 1978. Grad. teaching fellow U. Oreg., Eugene, 1973-78, instr. Oreg. Inst. Marine Biology, 1978; assoc. rsch. scientist Mt. Desert Island Biol. Lab., 1978-81; asst. prof.-in-residence U. Conn., 1981-82; asst. prof. dept. biology Lafayette Coll., Easton, Pa., 1982-87, assoc. prof., 1987-95; prof., 1995—. Mem. editorial com. Jour. Pa. Acad. Sci.; grant proposal reviewer NSF, Rsch. Corp.; presenter in field. Contbr. articles to profl. publs. Grantee Lerner Fund for Marine Rsch., 1978, NIH, 1979-81, U. Conn. Faculty Rsch. Found., 1981-82, Lafayette Coll. Com. for Advanced Study and Rsch., Rsch. Corp., 1984-85. Mem. SICB, AAAS. E-mail: hollidac@lafayette.edu.

HOLLIEN, HARRY FRANCIS, speech and communications scientist, educator; b. Brockton, Mass., July 16, 1926; s. Henry Gregory and Alice Bernice (Coolidge) H.; m. Patricia Ann Milanowski, Aug. 26, 1969; children: Karen Ann, Kevin Amory, Keith Alan, Brian Christopher, Stephanie Ann, Christine Ann. BS, Boston U., 1949, MEd, 1951; MA, U. Iowa, 1953, PhD, 1955. Asst. prof. Baylor U., 1955-58, U. Wichita, 1958-62; assoc. prof. speech U. Fla., Gainesville, 1962-68, prof., 1968-98, prof. linguistics, 1976-98, prof. criminal justice, 1979-98, assoc. dir. comm. scis. lab., 1962—65, dir. comm. scis. lab., 1968—75, dir. Inst. Advanced Study Comm. Processes, 1975—84; prof. emeritus, rsch. scientist Inst. Advanced Study of Communication Processes, 1998—, assoc. dir. linguistics, 1989-91; founding dir. Inst. Advanced Studies Comm. Processes U. Fla, 1984—98. Vis. prof. Inst. Telecomm. and Acoustics, Wroclaw Tech. U., Poland, 1974; adj. prof. Juilliard Sch. Music, N.Y.C., 1973-84; rsch. assoc. Gould Rsch. Lab., 1958; vis. sci. Speech Transmission Lab., Royal Inst. Tech., Stockholm, 1970; prof. U. Trier, Germany, 1987; fencing coach U. Iowa, 1953-55; mem. comm. sci. study sect. NIH, 1963-67; mem. neurobiology merit rev. bd. VA, 1969-74; pres. Hollien Assocs., 1966—; cons. in field. Author: Current Issues in Phonetic Sciences, 1978, Acoustics of Crime, 1990, Forensic Voice Identification, 2002; assoc. editor Jour. Speech and Hearing Rsch., 1967-69, Jour. Voice, 1987—; editor The Phonetician, 1975-92; mem. edtl. bd. Jour. Comm. Disorders, 1980-91, Jour. Rsch. in Singing, 1980-83, Jour. Phonetics, 1982-85, Studia Phonetica Posnan, 1985—, Speech, Language and the Law, 1993-2002. Chmn. bd. Unitarian Fellowship, Waco, Tex., 1956-58; chmn. bd. Wild Animal Retirement Village, 1981-90. Served with USN, 1944-46; with USNR, 1946-75. Recipient Garcia/Sandoz prize Internat. Assn. Logopedics and Phoniatrics, 1971, Gould award Wm. and Harrett Gould Found., 1975, Gutzmann medal Union European Phoniatrists, 1980, Professorial Excellence award, 1996; NIH career fellow, 1965-70, Fulbright scholar, 1987. Fellow AAAS, Am. Speech and Hearing Assn., Acoustical Soc. Am., Internat. Soc. Phonetic Scis. (pres. 1989-98, sec.-gen. 1975-89, exec. v.p. 1983-89, Kay Elemetrics prize 1987, S. Smith prize 1991, Soc. Honors 1998, hon. pres. 1999—), Am. Acad. Forensic Sci. (John R. Hunt award 1988), Inst. Acoustics; mem. SAR (pres. local chpt. 2001-03, regional v.p. 2000—, state rec. sec. 2001-03, Patriot medal, 2003), Am. Assn. Phonetic Scis. (pres. 1973-75, editor 1976-79, exec. com. 1979-82), Japan Soc. Phonetic Scis. (hon. v.p. 1989-97), World Congress Phoneticians (permanent coun.), Voice Found. (sci. bd., merit awards 1981, 93), Internat. Assn. Forensic Phonetics, Mayflower Descs. (gov. local chpt. 2002—, capt. state soc. 1999-2002), Order Found. Patriots, Sigma Xi. Republican. Achievements include patent for apparatus using radiation sensitive switch for signalling and recording data. Home: 229 SW 43rd Ter Gainesville FL 32607-2270 Office: U Fla Inst Advanced Study Comm Processes 46 Dauer Hall Gainesville FL 32611 E-mail: Hollien@Grove.ufl.edu.

HOLLINGSWORTH, JANE CANNON, art education educator; b. Elizabeth, N.J., Sept. 21, 1947; d. James Patterson and Laura Gordon (Peter) Cannon; m. Morris Elbert Hollingsworth, May 5, 1944; children: Leslie Suzanne, James Morris. BFA, U. Ga., 1968, MA in Edn., 1978. Cert. T-5 State Dept. Edn. Art tchr. Marietta (Ga.) H.S., 1968-70, Bowman H.S., Wadesboro, N.C., 1970-71, East Hall H.S., Gainesville, Ga., 1971-74, Gainesville (Ga.) Middle Sch., 1978—. Mem. Ga. Assessment Project, Ga. State U., Atlanta; pop art curriculum Brenau U., Gainesville, 1993—. Author (lesson plan) School Arts Mag., 1982. Recipient Monetary award Chromacryl Corp., N.J., 1984. Mem. Nat. Education Assn., Ga. Assn. Educators, Gainesville Assn. Educators (sec. 1992), Ga. Art Edn. Assn. (middle grades divsn. chair 1994—, Chas. McDaniel Youth Art Month award 1986, Middle Grades Art Educator of Yr. 1994-95), Phi Delta Kappa. Methodist. Avocation: painting. Home: 3727 Windy Hill Cir Gainesville GA 30504-5737 Office: Gainesville Middle Sch 715 Woodsmill Rd Gainesville GA 30501-3099

HOLLINGSWORTH, MARTHA LYNETTE, secondary school educator; b. Waco, Tex., Oct. 9, 1951; d. Willie Frederick and Georgia Cuddell (Bryant); m. Roy David Hollingsworth, Dec. 31, 1971; children: Richard Avery, Justin Brian. AA, McLennan C.C., 1972; BBA, Baylor U., 1974, MS in Ednl. Adminstrn., 1992. Tchr. Connally Ind. Sch. Dist., Waco, 1974—. With Adult Edn. Night Sch., 1974—78; chair Area III leadership conf. Vocat. Office Careers Clubs Tex., Waco, 1985—. Active Lakeview Little League Booster Club, 1985—; mem. PTA. Mem.: Assn. Tex. Profl. Educators (v.p. local chpt. 1988—90), Vocat. Office Edn. Tchrs. Assn. Tex., Tex. Future Farmers Am. (hon.), Future Homemakers Am. Area VIII (hon.), Delta Kappa Gamma. Baptist. Office: Connally Vocat Dept 715 N Rita St Waco TX 76705-1140

HOLLINGSWORTH, WILLIAM ROBERT, JR., secondary education educator; b. Greenwood, S.C., Apr. 30, 1956; s. William Robert Sr. and Verna Seal (Moss) H.; m. m. Myong Suk Paek, Mar. 9, 1985; 1 child, Victoria Caroline. BA in Secondary Edn., Clemson U., 1978; MEd, U. S.C., 1989. Cert. early childhood tchr., cert. police officer. Commd. 2d lt. U.S. Army, 1978, advanced through grades to capt., 1982, resigned, 1990; police officer Charleston and Columbia Police Dept., 1990-91; social studies tchr. Lower Richland H.S., Columbia, S.C., 1991—. Maj. U.S. Army Res., 1992—. Mem. S.C. Coun. for the Study of Social Studies, Nat. Coun. for Social Studies, Sons of Confederate Vets. (lt. comdr. 1993-94, Cert. of Appreciation 1992-94, S.C. Sharpsburg meml. monument com. chair), Descendants of Valentine Hollingsworth Sr. Soc., Res. Officers Assn., Civil Affairs Assn. Southern Baptist. Avocations: reading, physical fitness, military history, camping, backpacking. Home: 7905 Dartmoore Ln Columbia SC 29223-2546 Office: Lower Richland HS 2615 Lower Richland Blvd Hopkins SC 29061-8641

HOLLIS, LOUCILLE, risk control administrator, educator; b. Ft. Myers, Fla., Feb. 16, 1949; d. Luke Sr. and Louise (Wilcox) Black; m. Benjamin L. Hollis, Jr., Sept. 26, 1985. BS, N.Y. Inst. Tech., 1982, MBA, 1984. Staff asst. Equitable, N.Y.C., 1977-79, budget analyst, 1979-81, fin. analyst, 1981-85, mgr. operational planning, 1985-87, mgr. expense control, 1987-88; project leader L.I. R.R. Co., Jamaica, N.Y., 1988-91, asst. risk mgr., 1991-97; specialist in risk coverage Met. Transp. Authority, N.Y.C., 1997—. Comml. arbitrator Am. Arbitration Assn. Bronx fundraiser Cancer Fund Am., Knoxville, Tenn., 1991, 92; mem. bd. placement project United Way Linkage; literacy vol. Recipient Psychology award N.Y. Inst. Tech., 1981, acad. scholarship Ft. Myers Bd. Edn., 1977; honoree LIRR Women's History Celebration. Mem. NAFE, Nat. Black MBA Assn., Risk and Ins. Mgmt. Soc., RR Ins. Mgmt. Assn., Conf. Minority Transp. Ofcls., Psi Nat. Honor Soc. Democrat. Avocations: reading, personal computers, phys. fitness. Home: 19 Craig Place Bloomfield NJ 07003 Office: Met Transp Authority 347 Madison Ave New York NY 10017-3706

HOLLIS, MARY FRANCES, aerospace educator; b. Indpls., Sept. 18, 1931; d. Lucian Albert and Clara Frances Coleman; divorced; 1 child, Booker Albert Hollis. BS, Butler U., 1952, MS, 1962; postgrad., Stanford U., 1975, San Francisco State U., 1980-81. Cert. elem. tchr., Ind., Calif. Kindergarten tchr. Lockerbie Nursery Sch., Indpls., 1952, Indpls. Pub. Schs., 1952-69; tchr. K-6 San Mateo (Calif.) City Sch. Dist., 1969-91; summer sch. prin. San Mateo City Sch. dist., Foster City, Calif., 1983-91; aerospace educator, 1982—. Bd. dirs. Coun. of Math./Sci. Educators of San Mateo County, Belmont, Calif.; resident mgr. Lesley Found., Park Twrs., 1999—. Editor: San Mateo County Math./Sci. Coun. quarterly newsletter, 1988-90. Bd. dirs. Arts Coun. of San Mateo County, 1986-91, Mid-Peninsula chpt. ACLU, San Mateo, 1990—, Unitarian-Universalist Ch. San Mateo, 1996-98; bd. dirs. Peninsula Funeral and Meml. Planning Soc., 1996-2000, co-pres., 1998-99; office mgr. Roger Winston Campaign for San Mateo Union H.S. Dist. Bd. Trustees, 1993; mem. adv. com. USAF-Pacific Liaison Region-CAP, 1988-94; sr. peer counselor San Mateo County Mental Health, 1996—. Recipient Life Down to Earth award NASA, Moffet Field, Mt. View, Calif., 1985-86, Earl Sams Tchr. of Yr. award Calif. Assn. Aerospace Educators, 1989, award of merit Am. Legion, San Bruno, Calif., 1989, citation Air Force Assn., Mountain View, Calif., 1991, Aviation Summer Sch. cert. of appreciation Am. Legion Dept. Calif. Aerospace Commn., 1994. Mem. NEA (life), AAUW (bd. dirs. San Carlos chpt. 1993-95), NAACP (life), Am. Bus. Women's Assn. (rec. sec. Foster City chpt. 1985), World Aerospace Edn. Orgn. Democrat. Unitarian-Universalist. Avocations: reading, travel, music-jazz, rhythm and blues, swimming, aerospace/aviation. Office: PO Box 625 Belmont CA 94002-0625 E-mail: mfrances@pacbell.net.

HOLLIS, SUSAN TOWER, history educator; b. Boston, Mar. 17, 1939; d. James Wilson and Dorothy Parsons (Moore) Tower; m. Allen Hollis, Nov. 10, 1962 (div. Feb. 1975); children: Deborah Durfee, Harrison. AB, Smith Coll., 1962; PhD, Harvard U., 1982. Cert. C.C. instr. history and humanities. Asst. prof. Scripps Coll., Claremont, Calif., 1988-91; prof. Coll. of Undergrad. Studies The Union Inst., L.A., 1991-93; dean of the college and prof. humanities Sierra Nev. Coll.-Lake Tahoe, Incline Village, Nev., 1993-95; ind. scholar, cons. Reno, 1995-96; ctr. dir., assoc. dean Ctrl. N.Y. Ctr. Empire State Coll. of SUNY, Syracuse, 1996-99; assoc. prof. SUNY Empire State Coll., Rochester, N.Y., 1999—, coord. western region MA in Liberal Studies program, 2000—. Convener hist. studies Empire State Coll. of SUNY, 2000—, co-chair acad. policies an learning programs com., 2003—. Author: The Ancient Egyptian "Tale of Two Brothers", 1990; editor: Hymns, Prayers and Songs: Anthology of Ancient Egyptian Lyrics & Poetry (by John L. Foster), 1996; co-editor: Feminist Theory and the Study of Folklore, 1993; contbr. articles to profl. jours, encys. Music vol. Open Readings, Belmont, Mass., 1982—88; vol. Sierra Club, 1988—; problem capt. Odyssey of the Mind, Nev., 1994—95, judge, 1997—98; crew chief Tahoe Rim trail, 1994—96; active Masterworks Chorale, NY, 1996—99. Mem.: N.Y. State Network for Women Leaders in Higher Edn. (assoc. coord. 1999—2000, bd. dirs. 1997—, coord. 2000—03), N.Y. Acad. Scis., Egyptological Soc. N.Y., Soc. Bibl. Lit. (co-chair Egyptology and Ancient Israel group 1995—96, chair Egyptology and Ancient Israel group 1996—2003, convenor Ancient Near East Consortium 1998—), Soc. for Study Egyptian Antiquities, Internat. Assn. Egyptologists, Am. Rsch. Ctr. Egypt, Am. Oriental Soc., Am. Folklore Soc., Am. Assn. Higher Edn., Am. Acad. Religion, Incline Village/Crystal Bay C. of C. (sec., bd. dirs. 1994—95), Ka-na-wa-ke Canoe Club (bd. dirs. 1998—2000), Adirondack Mountain Club, Appalachian Mountain Club (co-leader 1987—88). Democrat. Home: 7 New Wickham Dr Penfield NY 14526-2703 Office: Empire State Coll of SUNY 1475 Winton Rd N Rochester NY 14609-5803 E-mail: susan.hollis@esc.edu.

HOLLOWAY, CHARLES ARTHUR, public and private management educator; b. Whittier, Calif., May 28, 1936; s. Heber H. and Theodosia S. (Stephens) H.; m. Christina Ahlm, July 11, 1959; children: Deborah, Susan, Stuart. BSEE with honors, U. Calif., Berkeley, 1959; MS, UCLA, 1963, PhD in Bus. Adminstrn. with distinction, 1969. Sr. engr. Bechtel Corp., San Francisco, 1964-65; teaching fellow UCLA, 1965-66; asst. prof. to prof. Stanford (Calif.) U., 1968—, Herbert Hoover prof. pub. and pvt. mgmt., 1980-91, assoc. dean acad. affairs Grad. Sch. Bus., 1980-87, 90-91, Kleiner Perkins Caufield and Byers prof. mgt., 1991—. Bd. dirs. Axicon, Escalate Corp., SRI Internat.; co-chair Stanford Ctr. for Entrepreneurial Studies, 1995-. Author: Decision Making Under Uncertainty: Models and Choices, 1979, Perpetual Enterprise Machine: Seven Keys to Corporate Renewal, 1994. Bd. dirs. Save Redwoods League. With USN, 1959-63. Fellow Ford Found., 1966-68 Mem. Inst. Mgmt. Sci., Ops. Rsch. Soc. Am., Stanford Integrated Mfg. Assn. (co-chair 1991-95). Home: 730 Santa Maria Ave Palo Alto CA 94305-8438 Office: Stanford U Grad Sch Bus Stanford CA 94305 E-mail: holloway_chuck@gsb.stanford.edu.

HOLLOWAY, DAVID JAMES, political science educator; b. Dublin, Oct. 13, 1943; came to U.S., 1983; s. James Joseph and Gertrude Mary (Kennedy) H.; m. Arlene Jean Smith, June 12, 1976; children: James, Ivor. MA, PhD, Cambridge (Eng.) U., 1964. Asst. lectr. U. Lancaster, Eng., 1967-69; rsch. assoc. Inst. for Strategic Studies, London, 1969—70; lectr. U. Edinburgh, Scotland, 1970—84, reader, 1984—86; prof. Stanford (Calif.) U., 1986—, co-dir. Ctr. Internat. Security and Arms Control, 1991—97, Raymond A. Spruance prof. in internat. history, 1997—, assoc. dean humanities and scis., 1997—98, dir. Inst. for Internat. Studies, 1998—. Dir. internat. rels. program Stanford U., 1989-91. Author: The Soviet Union and the Arms Race, 1983, Stalin and the Bomb, 1994; co-author: (with S. Drell and P. Farley) The Reagan Strategic Defense Initiative, 1985. Bd. dirs. Ploughshares Found., San Francisco, 1989—. Mem. Am. Polit. Sci. Assn., Am. Assn. for the Advancement of Slavic Studies. Avocations: opera, reading. Home: 710 Torreya Ct Palo Alto CA 94303-4160 Office: Stanford U Inst Internat Studies Encina Hall Stanford CA 94305-6055

HOLLOWAY, GEORGE ALLEN, JR., physician, educator; b. N.Y.C., Oct. 14, 1938; s. George Allen and Betsey (Paddock) H.; children: Mara, Brett. B.A. in Chinese Studies, Yale U., 1960; M.D., Harvard U., 1964. Diplomate Am. Bd. Internal Medicine. Fellow in pathology Mass. Gen. Hosp., Boston, 1964-65; intern, then resident I UCLA Med. Ctr., 1965-67; resident II U. Wash. Hosp., Seattle, 1967-68; USPHS fellow in nephrology U. Wash. Hosp., 1968-69; chief dept. medicine U.S. Army Hosp., Camp Zama, Japan, 1969-72; from asst. to assoc. prof. Ctr. Bioengring., U. Wash., Seattle, 1972-88; dir. vascular lab. Maricopa Med. Ctr., 1988—, pres. med. staff, 1990-92, dir. med. rsch., 1992—; cons. Nuclear Pacific/Med Pacific, Seattle, 1978—; lectr. local and nat. vascular disease and wound healing; adj. prof. of Bioengineering Ariz. State U., 1992—. Contbr. articles to profl. jours., chpts. to books. Developer laser doppler velocimeter, 1976. Med. dir. Pacific West Ski Patrol, Snoqualmie Pass, Wash., 1982-88. Served to maj. U.S. Army, 1969-72. USPHS grantee, 1976; recipient Career Devel. award USPHS, 1980-85. Mem. Wound Healing Soc. (bd. dirs. 2001-03, sec. 2002—), Biomed. Engring. Soc. (sr.), Am. Soc. Laser Medicine and Surgery, Soc. for Vascular Medicine and Biology, European Microcirculatory Soc., Western Vascular Soc., Rocky Mt. Vascular Soc. Home: 3314 E Rock Wren Rd Phoenix AZ 85044-8707 Office: Maricopa Med Center PO Box 5099 Phoenix AZ 85010-5099

HOLLOWAY, KIMBERLEY MICHELE, freelance/self-employed writer, communications executive, language educator; b. Knoxville, Tenn., Aug. 19, 1958; d. Bobby Howard and Gwendolyn Warwick Holloway; children: Jennifer Leigh Mongold, Stephanie Michele Kidd. BS in Secondary Edn. & English, Tenn. Tech. U., 1980; MA in English, East Tenn. State U., 1998. Tchr. Tri-Cities Christian Schs., Blountville, Tenn., 1985—87; freelance writer, 1997—; assoc. dir. comm., lectr. English King Coll., Bristol, Tenn., 2002—. Employee Ltd. Svc., Eastman, Kingsport, Tenn., 1994—96; grad. asst. English. dept. East Tenn. State U., Johnson City, Tenn., 1996—97, adj. instr., 1997—; lectr. in English King Coll., Bristol, Tenn., 1998—. Author: The Encyclopedia of Multiculturalism, 1998, The Sixties in America, 1999, Masterplots: Poetry Supplement, 1998, St. James Encyclopedia of Popular Culture, 1999, African American Encyclopedia, 2000, The Supreme Court, Encyclopedia of Appalachia, Encyclopedia of Great Athletes, Revised, 2001, Masterplots II: Poetry Supplement, 2002, Great Events of the Twentieth Century, 2002; editor: From a Race of Storytellers: Essays on the Ballad Novels of Sharyn McCrumb, 2003; contbr. The Business Jour., 2002, chapters to books. Prodr. ch. bull. Heritage Bapt. Ch., Johnson City, Tenn., 1989—95. Recipient George Allen Outstanding Graduate award, East Tenn. State U., 1998. Mem.: Appalachian Writers Assn. (program chmn. 2000—01, pres. 2001—02, officer-at-large 2002—03). Republican. Baptist. Avocations: reading, writing, bicycling. E-mail: kimhkidd@aol.com., khollawa@king.edu.

HOLLOWAY, RALPH LESLIE, anthropology educator; b. Phila., Feb. 6, 1935; s. Ralph L. and Marguerite (Grugan) H. BS in Geology, U. N.Mex., Albuquerque, 1959; PhD in Anthropology, U. Calif., Berkeley, 1964. Asst. prof. anthropology Columbia U., N.Y.C., 1964-69, assoc. prof., 1969-73, prof., 1973—. Editor: Primate Aggression, Territoriality and Xenophobia: A Comparative Perspective, 1974; contbr. numerous articles to profl. jours. Recipient Ctr. for Rsch. into the Anthropol. Found. Tech., Ind. U. annual award for outstanding rsch. Ctr. for Rsch. into Anthropologic. Found. of Tech., 2002, Craft award, 2002; Guggenheim Found. fellow, 1974; NSF grantee, 1984. Fellow AAAS, N.Y. Acad. Sci.; mem. Am. Anthrop. Assn., Am. Assn. Phys. Anthropologists, Soc. for Neurosci., Sigma Xi, Phi Beta Kappa. Office: Columbia U Dept Anthropology New York NY 10027 E-mail: rlh2@columbia.edu.

HOLLOWAY, SHARON KAY SOSSAMON, vocational/secondary school educator; b. Ft. Smith, Feb. 26, 1958; d. Floyd Clinton and Ruth Ann (Clemons) Sossamon; m. David Arthur Holloway, Dec. 27, 1985 (div. Aug. 1995). BS in Bus. Edn., N.E. State U., Tahlequah, Okla., 1980, MS, 1987. Cert. tchr. vocat. bus., Okla. Tchr. vocat. bus. Pawhuska Pub. Schs., Okla., 1982—2001, Sapulpa Pub. Schs., 2001—02, Pawhuska Pub. Schs., 2002—. Cons. tchr. Pawhuska Pub. Schs., 1992-93, computer tchr. community edn. program, 1988—. Recipient Tandy Tech. award for Outstanding Tchr., 1994. Mem. Nat. Bus. Assn., Am. Vocat. Assn., Okla. Bus. Assn., Pawhuska Edn. Assn., Delta Zeta Alumnae. Democrat. Baptist. Avocations: reading, crocheting, computers, computer games. Home: 316 E 14th St 1377 Pawhuska OK 74056-2214 Office: Pawhuska Pub Schs 621 E 15th St Pawhuska OK 74056-1843

HOLLOWAY, SHIRLEY J. state agency administrator; BA in Speech Pathology, Lewis and Clark Coll.; BS in Spl. Edn., Ea. Wash. U.; BS in Edn., Western Wash. U.; PhD in Ednl. Leadership, Gonzaga U. Cons. Alaska Dept. Edn., Juneau, 1971, commr. of edn., 1994—2003; spl. edn. dir. Alaska's State Operated Schs., 1972; prin., asst. supt. North Slope Borough (Alaska) Sch. Dist., 1975-90, supt., 1987-90, Nine Mile Falls Sch. Dist., Wash., 1992-94. Former speech and hearing clinician, tchr. hearing impaired students, Wash.; vis. prof. pub. sch. adminstrn. U. Alaska, Anchorage, 1990-92; past pres. Arctic Sivunmun Ilisagvik Coll., Major's Workforce Devel. Program, Barrow (Alaska), North Slope Borough. Vol. civic and profl. assns., task forces and adv. groups.*

HOLLOWAY, SUSAN MASTER, elementary education educator; b. Portsmouth, Va., June 3, 1951; d. Reuben B. and Wilbur (Gorman) Master; m. Jeffrey Carter Holloway, June 17, 1973; children: Bethany Heather, David Morris. BS, Austin Peay State U., 1973, M in Music Edn., 1974. Cert. music K-12, elem. edn. 1-8, career ladder tchr. level II, Tenn. With ins. dept. Commerce Union Bank, Nashville, 1975-77; music specialist Wilson County Schs., Mt. Juliet, Lebanon, Tenn., 1977—. Music clinician workshops various assns. Tenn., 1977—; cons., trainer, contest judge Drum Majors, Field Commdrs., Tenn., Ky., 1977—; adv. bd. music affiliated groups in music industry, 1978-80. Soloist, choir mem. Glencliff Presbyn. Ch., Nashville, 1975-90, St. Pauls United Meth. Ch. (now Grace United Meth. Ch.), Mt. Juliet, Tenn., 1990—; vol. Boy Scouts Am. pack 253, Mt. Juliet, 1991-93. Scholar music Austin Peay State U., Clarksville, Tenn., 1969-73; recipient Tchr. award Stoner Creek Elem. PTO, 1988. Mem. NEA, Music Educators Nat. Conf., Tenn. Music Educators Assn., Mid. Tenn. Vocal Assn. (rec. sec. 1985-86), Mid. Tenn. Elem. Music Educators Assn., Am. Orff Schoolwork Assn. (rec. sec. 1988-89), Tenn. Edn. Assn., Wilson County Edn. Assn. (bldg. rep. 1980-81), Sigma Alpha Iota (pres. alumnae chpt. 1976, past v.p., rec. sec., corr. sec., treas.), Soc. Gen. Music (Mid. Tenn. rep. 1984), Delta Omicron (chmn. music 1989-90). Democrat. Methodist. Home: 465 Belinda Pky Mount Juliet TN 37122-3657 Office: Stoner Creek Elementary 1035 N Mount Juliet Rd Mount Juliet TN 37122-3389

HOLLOWELL, JAN BENNETT, adult education educator; b. Valdosta, Ga., Nov. 11, 1951; d. Charles Leonard Bennett and Mitzi Brewton Driggers; m. Monte Jerry Hollowell, Nov. 19, 1972; children: Jerel Brett, Matt Jared. BS in Edn., Ouachita Bapt. U., Arkadelphia, Ark., 1973; MEd, U. Tex., El Paso, 1978. Cert. in adult edn., Ala., elem. edn., Tex., Ark.; cert. reading specialist, Ala., Ark., Tex. Elem. tchr. Pforzheim (West Germany) Elem. Sch., 1974-75; basic skills instr. Edn. Ctr., Ft. Bliss, Tex., 1978; Title I lang arts English tchr. El Paso Ind. Sch. Dist., 1978-80; GED/adult basic edn. instr. Region XIX Edn. Ctr., Wichita Falls, Tex., 1980-83; tutor The Reading Ctr., Huntsville, Ala., 1983; adult edn. instr. North Ala. Skills Ctr., Huntsville, 1984-88; mgr. Individualized Prescribed Instrn. Lab. J.F. Drake State Tech. Coll., Huntsville, 1988—. Mem. ASCD, NEA, Ala. Edn. Assn., Am. Vocat. Assn., Internat. Reading Assn., Drake Edn. Assn., Vocat. Indsl. Clubs Am. (advisor). Baptist. Avocations: reading, cross-stitch. Office: JF Drake State Tech Coll 3421 Meridian St N Huntsville AL 35811-1544

HOLLY, ELLISTINE PERKINS, music educator; b. Grenada, Miss., Aug. 12, 1934; d. Addison Lampton and Anna Pearl (Powell) Perkins; m. Donald Beall, June 10, 1960 (div. June 1966); 1 child, Donna Camille; m. Kermit Wells Holly, Jr., Dec. 23, 1979. BA in Music and Piano, Fisk U., Nashville, 1955; M Music Edn., Ind. U., 1960; MusM, U. Mich., 1972, PhD, 1978. Tchr. Middleton Sr. High Sch., Tampa, 1955-58; instr. music Mary Holmes Jr. Coll., West Point, Miss., 1960-61; tchr. Jefferson Jr. High Sch., Pontiac, Mich., 1961-68; grad. asst. U. Mich., Ann Arbor, 1972-74; counselor Sch. Music, U. Mich., Ann Arbor, 1975-76; prof. music Jackson (Miss.) State U., 1976—. Vis. lectr. U. Paris, 1989, Institut du Monde Anglophone, Universite de Paris, 1989; reviewer travel grants Nat. Endowment for Humanities, 1986-87. Performing soloist Opera South Co., Jackson State U., 1983-85, U. Mich. Chamber Choir, U.S. Cultural Team to Russia, Germany, Spoleto, Italy, Opening Ceremonies Internat. Ballet Competition, Jackson, 1986, 90; editor, compiler: Biographies of Black Composers an Songwriters, 1989; contbr. articles to prol. jours.; creator, performer: (one woman show) Miss.'s African-Am. Divas. Mem. Jackson Arts Alliance, 1985—; bd. dirs. Miss. Musicians Hall of Fame, Miss. Inst. Arts and Letters, 1997-00, Miss. Opera Assn., 1998-00. Faculty rsch. scholar NEH, Harvard U., 1982, Chgo., 1985, Newberry Libr., Chgo., 1987, Ford Found., U. Miss., Oxford, 1987. Mem. Music Educators Nat. Conf., Nat. Assn. Tchrs. Singing (pres. Miss. chpt. 1984-87), Ctr. Black Music Rsch., Nat. Links, Inc., Miss. Hist. Soc., Sonneck Soc., Coll. Music Soc. (bd. dirs. so. region), Harmonica Music Club Inc. (pres. 1983-85), Delta Sigma Theta. Home: 261 Northgate Blvd Jackson MS 39206-2618

HOLM, JOY ALICE, psychology educator, goldsmith, artist, art educator; b. Chgo., May 21, 1929; d. Alvin Herbert and Wilhelmina Eugenia (Miller) Holm. BFA, U. Ill., 1952; MS in Art Edn. Inst. Design, Ill. Inst. Tech., 1956; PhD in Edn., U. Minn., 1967. Tchr. art, Eng. West Chgo. H.S., 1952-54; instr., tchr. art J.S. Morton H.S. & Jr. Coll., Cicero, Ill., 1954-65; asst. prof. art & design Mankato (Minn.) State U., 1965-66; asst. prof. art Ill. State U., Normal, 1966-69; assoc. prof. art & design So. Ill. U., Edwardsville, 1969-71; assoc. prof. art, art edn. Winona (Minn.) State U., 1971-75; assoc. prof., chmn. dept. art St. Mary's Coll. of Notre Dame, Ind., 1975-76; assoc.

prof. art & design, secondary, continuing edn. U. Wis., Eau Claire, 1976-78; assoc. prof. art & design Sch. Art & Design Kent (Ohio) State U., 1978-80; lectr. Jungian studies C.G. Jung Inst., Chgo., 1980-82; adj. assoc. prof. art edn. Sch. Art and Design, Sch. Edn. U. Ill., Chgo., 1981-82; lectr. U. Calif. Ext., Santa Cruz, 1983—; adj. prof. art edn., design San Jose (Calif.) State U., 1983-84; owner bus. designer-goldsmith Oak Park, Ill., 1980-82, Carmel, Calif., 1982-87, Atelier XII, Winona, 1988—. Curriculum cons. North Ctrl. Assn. Accreditation Team State of Ill., Edwardsville, 1970; regional cons. Supt. Pub. Instrn., Springfield, Ill., 1970; juror exhbns.; panelist, spkr., presenter confs., meetings. Contbr., cons. Alternative Medicine: A Definitive Guide, 1994; contbg. author: Living Science, 2002; contbr. articles to profl. jours; one-woman shows: J. Sterling Morton H.S. & Jr. Coll., 1963, Russell Art Gallery, Bloomington, 1968, Owatonna (Minn.) Art Ctr., 1980, 86; exhbns. include La Grange (Ill.) Art League (Best of Show, 1st Place award prints), 1963, 64, Minn. Mus. Art, 1974, 75, Craft & Folk Art Mus., L.A., 1978, The Gallery Kent State U., 1978, 79, Saenger Nat. Small Sculpture and Jewelry Exhibit, 1978, Diamonds Internat., N.Y., 1978, Inst. Design Alumni, 1988, Internat. Biographical Ctr. Congress Exhbn., Edinburgh, Scotland, 1994, others. Fellow World Lit. Acad.; mem. AAUP, Nat. Art Edn. Assn. (rep. Wis. Women's Caucus Houston Conf. 1978, higher edn. divsn. 1961—), Am. Assn. Higher Edn., Coll. Art Assn., Soc. N.Am. Goldsmiths, Gemological Inst. Am., C.G. Jung Inst. (Chgo.), Hon. Soc. Illustrators (hon.), Internat. Soc. Study of Subtle Energies and Energy Medicine, Inst. Noetic Scis., Alpha Lambda Delta (hon.), Phi Kappa Phi (hon.). Methodist. Office: Atelier XII PO Box 183 Winona MN 55987-0183

HOLMAN, HALSTED REID, medical educator, physician; b. Cleve., Jan. 17, 1925; s. Emile Frederic and Ann Peril (Purdy) H.; m. Barbara Marie Lucas, June 26, 1949 (div. July 9, 1982); children: Michael, Andrea, Alison; m. Diana Barbara Dutton, Aug. 10, 1985; 1 child, Geoffrey. Student, Stanford U., 1942-43, UCLA, 1943-44; MD, Yale U., 1949. Med. resident Montefiore Hosp., N.Y.C., 1952-55; staff physician Rockefeller Inst., N.Y.C., 1955-60; prof. medicine Stanford (Calif.) U., 1960—, chmn. dept. medicine, 1960-71, co-chief, divsn. family and community medicine, 1987-2001, dir. clin. scholar program, 1969-97, dir. Multipurpose Arthritis Ctr., 1977-97, co-chief, divsn. immunology and rheumatology, 1997-2000, dir. Stanford Program for Mgmt. of Chronic Disease, 1997—. Pres. Midpeninsula Health Svc., Palo Alto, Calif., 1975-80; mem. adv. bd. Calif Health Facilities Commn., Sacramento, 1978-81, Office Tech. Assessment, U.S. Congress, 1979-81, Inst. Advancement of Health, N.Y.C., 1982-90; Guggenhime prof. medicine, 1960—. Author 2 books; assoc. editor Arthritis and Rheumatism, 1995-2000; contbr. articles to profl. jours. Recipient Bauer Meml. award, Arthritis and Rheumatism Found., N.Y., 1964. Master: Am. Coll. Rheumatology (Presdl. Gold medal 2001); fellow: AAAS (coun. 1974—79), ACP (Laureate award no. Calif. chpt. 1994); mem.: Improving Chronic Illness Care-R.W. Johnson Found. (Vision award 2001), Arthritis Found. (Hero Overcoming Arthritis 1998, Engalitcheff award 1999, McGuire Educator award 2000), Western Assn. Physicians (pres. 1966), Am. Soc. Clin. Investigation (pres. 1970), Assn. Am. Physicians. Democrat. Home: 747 Dolores St Stanford CA 94305-8427 Office: Stanford U Divsn Immunol and Rheumatol 1000 Welch Rd Ste 203 Palo Alto CA 94304-1808 E-mail: Holman@Stanford.edu.

HOLMES, BARBARAANN KRAJKOSKI, secondary education educator; b. Evansville, Ind., Mar. 21, 1946; d. Frank Joseph and Estella Marie (DeWeese) Krajkoski; m. David Leo Holmes, Aug. 21, 1971; 1 child, Susan Ann Sky. BS, Ind. State U., 1968, MS, 1969, specialist cert., 1976; postgrad., U. Nev., 1976-78. Acad. counselor Ind. State U., 1968-69, halls dir., 1969-73; dir. residence halls U. Utah, 1973-76; sales assoc. Fidelity Realty, Las Vegas, Nev., 1977-82; cert. analyst Nev. Dept. Edn., 1981-82; tchr. Clark County Sch. Dist., 1982-87, computer cons., adminstrv. specialist, instrnl. mgmt. sys., 1987-91, chair computer conf., 1990-92, adminstrv. specialist K-6, 1990-93; dean of student summer sch. site adminstr. Eldorado H.S., 1991-96; asst. prin. Garrett Mid. Sch., Boulder City, Nev., 1997-1999, So. Nev. Vocat. Tech. Ctr. Magnet H.S., 1999—. Mem. leadership design team Clark County Sch. Dist., 1996—98, 2001—. Named Outstanding Sr. Class Woman, Ind. State U., 1969; recipient Dir.'s award U. Utah Residence Halls, 1973, Outstanding Tchr. award, 1984, Dist. Excellence in Edn. award, 1984, 86, 87, 88. Mem. AAUW, Am. Assn. Women Deans, Adminstrs. and Counselors, Am. Pers. and Guidance Assn., Nat. Assn. Sch. Adminstrs. (Clark County sch. adminstrv. sec., 2002—), Clark County Assn. Secondary Sch. Prin. (sec. 2003—), Am. Coll. Pers. Assn., Alumnae Assn. Chi Omega (treas. Terre Haute chpt. 1971-73, pres., bd. officer Las Vegas 1977-81, state rush info. chair, 1997—), Clark County Panhellenic Alumnae Assn. (pres. 1978-79), Computer Using Educators So. Nev. (sec. 1983-86, pres.-elect 1986-87, pres. 1987-88, state chmn. 1988-89, conf. chmn. 1989-92, sec. 1994-96, Hall of Fame 1995), Job.'s Daus. Club (guardian sec. 1995-99, dir. music 1999-2001, Supreme Dep. 2001—), Order Eastern Star (worthy matron 2003—), Phi Delta Kappa (Action award 1990-96, newspaper editor 1992-93). Achievements include developing personal awareness program U. Utah, 1973-76. Home: 1227 Kover Ct Henderson NV 89015-9017 Office: So Nev Vocat Tech Magnet HS 5710 Mountain Vista St Las Vegas NV 89120-2310

HOLMES, DAVID JAMES, elementary school educator; b. Lock Haven, Pa., Sept. 8, 1947; s. Edward James and Jean Elizabeth (Taylor) H.; m. Sandra Ann Melchert, Jan. 15, 1995. BS in Edn., Lock Haven State Coll., 1969; MEd, Kutztown U., 1992. Cert. elem. and comprehensive social studies tchr., elem. prin., Pa. Elem. tchr. Tri-Valley Sch. Dist., Valley View, Pa., 1972—; ret., 2002. Adv. bd. TLC Day Care Ctr., Valley View, 1974-81; presenter in field. Mem. coun. Trinity Luth. Ch., Valley View, 1988-91, ch. sch. tchr., 1988-96; active St. Peter Luth. Ch., Mechanicsburg, Pa., 1998—. Recipient Gift of Time Tribute Am. Family Inst., 1993. Mem. Train Collectors Assn., Phi Delta Kappa (treas. Wilkes U. chpt. 1995—, Educator of Yr. 2003). Democrat. Avocations: toy trains, tennis. Home: 418 Clemens Dr Dillsburg PA 17019-1321

HOLMES, DAVID LEO, recreation and leisure educator; b. Hammond, Ind., Jan. 4, 1943; s. Leo Victor and Hannah Marget (Robertson) H.; m. Barbara Ann Krajkoski, Mar. 21, 1971; 1 child, Susan Ann Sky. AA, Vincennes U., 1967; BS, Ind. State U., 1969, MS, 1970; PhD, U. Utah, 1976. Tchr., dir. sch. recreation and outdoor edn. Rockville (Ind.) Jr. Ctr., Ind. State Dept. Corrections, 1970-72; instr. Nat. Outdoor Leadership Sch., Washington, Conn., 1972; teaching fellow U. Utah, Salt Lake City, 1973-76; from asst. to prof. program coord. sport and leisure dept. U. Nev., Las Vegas, 1976-91, prof. dept. leisure studies, 1991—. Adj. asst. prof. dept. recreation Ind. State U., Terre Haute, 1972-73; lectr. in field. Contbr. more than 125 articles to profl. jours.; author 5 monographs; editor 6 jours. Active State Comprehensive Outdoor Recreation Planning Com., Nev., 1988; planning team Clark Country Nev. Sch. Dist., 1987-88; adv. bd. Clark Country Nev. Parks and Recreation, 1979-88, vice-chmn., 1984. Officer USMCR, Desert Storm, 1990-91. Recipient Pacemaker award, Faculty Citation Vincennes U., 1990, Spl. Pres. award Nat. Assn. Country Parks & Recreation Officials, 1986; named Outstanding Alumni U. Utah, 1987; recipient Spl. Recognition award Ind. State U., 1987, Hon. Mem. Wings, Blue Parachute Team, # 1 USAF Acad., 1982; grantee various institutions. Mem. AAHPERD (life, Cmty. Svc. award 1987), Nev. Recreation and Park Soc. (Excellence award 1995), Am. Assn. for Leisure and Recreation (bd. dirs. 1981-82, v.p. recreation S.W. dist. 1981), Nev. Parks and Recreation Soc., Nev. State Parks Coop. Assn. (bd. dirs. 1991-92, 93-94), Nev. Assn. for Health, Phys. Edn. and Recreation (pres. 1979-80, Profl. of Yr. 1983-84), Armed Forces Recreation Soc. (v.p. 1998), U. Nev. Alumni Assn. (Prof. Worthy of Recognition 1995, Boyd award for svc. 2001). Methodist. Avocations: running, weightraining. Home: 1227 Kover Ct Henderson NV 89015-9017 Office: U Las Vegas Leisure Studies Program Dept Tourism/Conv Adminstrn 4505 S Maryland Pky Las Vegas NV 89154-9900 E-mail: dholmes@ccmail.nevada.

HOLMES, ERLINE MORRISON, retired educational administrator, consultant; b. Newark, Aug. 31, 1922; d. Samuel A. and Levada (Thurman) Morrison; m. William C. Holmes, Aug. 19, 1943 (dec. 1968); 1 child, William C. Jr. BS, Newark State Tchrs. Coll., 1943; MA, Seton Hall U., 1970. Cert. elem. and secondary social studies tchr., prin,. sch. adminstr., N.J. Dir. employer women and working teens YWCA, Germantown, Pa., 1943-46; elem. tchr. Orange (N.J.) Bd. Edn., 1950-64; remedial and lang. arts tchr. South Orange (N.J.) Bd. Edn., 1965-66; secondary social studies tchr. Orange H.S., 1966-69, vice prin., 1969-72, prin., 1973-75; asst. supt. Orange Bd. Edn., 1975-90, interim supt., 1990; ret., 1990. Mem. N.J. Study Commn. on Adolescent Edn., 1976-77; cons. Nat. Inst. Edn., Washington, 1982, site evaluator, cons., Paterson and Newark, N.J. Dept. Edn., Trenton, 1990-96; site evaluator N.J. Coun. on Arts, 1993. Pres., bd. dirs. YWCA of Essex and West Hudson, Orange, 1978; pres. N.J. Alliance Black Sch. Educators, 1984-86; treas. Arts Coun. Essex Area, 1986-88; v.p. Family Svc. and Child Guidance Ctr., Orange, 1992-96; Orange Bd. Adjustment, 1986-97, chmn., 1997—. Cited for Outstanding Achievement in Edn., Negro Bus. and Profl. Women, 1979; recipient Cmty. Svc. award United Way of Essex, 1983-84, 84-85. Mem. Nat. Alliance Black Sch. Educators (life), Phi Delta Kappa. Presbyterian. Avocations: bowling, travel, reading, researching family history.

HOLMES, EVERLENA MCDONALD, health science administrator, consultant, retired dean; b. Eufaula, Ala., Feb. 15, 1934; d. Oscar Lee and Carrie Belle McDonald; children: Rufus James Jr., Parvin Holmes Porsche, Gregory Warren. BS, Ky. State U., 1957; MEd, U. Houston, 1974; EdD, Va. Tech. U., 1981. Registered health info. adminstr. Chair, dept. health info. sci. Ea. Ky. U., Richmond, 1975—79; assoc. dean, Coll. Allied Health Profns. Tenn. State U., Nashville, 1982—84; dir., Helath Info. Adminstrn. George Washington U., Washington, 1984—86; dean, Sch. Health Scis. Hunter Coll., CUNY, N.Y.C., 1986—96; dean, Sch. Health Scis. and Human Performance East Stroudsburg (Pa.) U., 1996—98; dean, Coll. Allied Health Charles Drew U., L.A., 1998—2001; cons. Holmes and Assocs., Chattanooga, 2001—. Cons. developing health sci. program Project Hope, Mex., Barbados, West Indies, 1974—75; cons. evaluating health sci. program Am. Assn. State Colls. and Univs., Washington, 1984; cons. developing health sci. edn. 10 colls. and univs., various states, 1970s and 80s; cons. HEW Grant Rev. Com., NIH, VA, USPHS, HHS, 1970s and 80s. Contbr. articles to profl. jours. Mem. health and edn. brain trust Nat. Congl. Black Caucus, Washington, 1974—; program dir. Macon County/Tuskegee Model Cities Assn., Ala., 1970—73; campaign mgr. for Link Turner Freeholders' Election for Essex County, N.J., 1976. Recipient Disting. Svc. award, U. Medicine and Dentistry of N.J., 1987, Eminent Scholar award, Norfolk (Va.) State U., 1982. Mem.: NAACP, Am. Assn. Health Info. Mgmt., Nat. Soc. Allied Health Profns. (treas. 1978—81, pres. 1982—83, Outstanding Leadership award 1984), Nat. Coun. Negro Women, Phi Kappa Phi, Phi Delta Kappa. Democrat. African Methodist Episcopal. Avocation: international travel. Home and Office: Holmes & Assocs 512 Kilmer St Chattanooga TN 37404

HOLMES, GEORGE EDWARD, molecular biologist, educator; b. Chgo., May 8, 1937; m. Norreen Ruth Petersen, Mar. 12, 1967; children: George Petersen, Norreen Eliza. BS in Biology and Chemistry, Wiley Coll., 1960; MS in Natural Sci., Chgo. State U., 1967; postgrad., U. Calif., Davis, 1967-68; PhD in Molecular Biology, U. Ariz., 1973. Med. technologist DePaul Hosp., St. Louis, 1961, Chgo. Hosp., 1961-67; tchr. Chgo. Bd. of Edn., 1965-67; rsch. assoc. Rockefeller U., N.Y.C., 1973-74; asst. prof. dept. microbiology Coll. of Medicine Howard U., Washington, 1974-82, assoc. prof., 1982—. Contbr. articles to profl. jours. including Nature, Jour. Virology, Virology, Molecular and Gen. Genetics, Jour. Gerontology, Jour. Mutation Rsch. NIH fellow in molecular biology, 1968-73; grantee Nat. Inst. on Aging, 1982-87, Travel grant Am. Soc. Biol. Chemistry and Molecular Biology, 1990. Mem. AAUP (chpt. pres., chmn. faculty grievance commn. 1994—, pres. D.C. Conf.), Am. Soc. Biochemistry and Molecular Biology (invitee The Gordon Conf. on Biology of Aging 1986), Am. Soc. Virology, Am. Inst. Chemists, Am. Men and Women in Sci. and Medicine, Gerontol. Soc. Am. Lutheran. Achievements include research in molecular and general genetics, nature, mutation, virology and gerontology. Office: Howard U Coll of Medicine Dept Microbiology Washington DC 20059-0001 Fax: 410-381-0222. E-mail: gholmes@fac.howard.edu.

HOLMES, JACK EDWARD, political science educator; b. Wichita, May 16, 1941; s. Herbert Paul and Marguerite Elizabeth (Duerr) H.; m. Linda Sue Pacheco, Dec. 28, 1996; stepchildren: Valerie, Cynthia, Jacqueline, Elizabeth. BA, Knox Coll., 1963; MA, U. Denver, 1967, PhD in Internat. Studies, 1972. Asst. prof. Hope Coll., Holland, Mich., 1969-72; dist. asst. Congressman Don Brotzman, Denver, 1973-75; asst. prof. Hope Coll., Holland, 1975-76, assoc. prof., 1976-87, prof., 1987—. Chmn. polit. sci. dept. Hope Coll., 1988-95, 99—. Author: Mood/Interest Theory of American Foreign Policy, 1985; co-author: American Government Essentials and Perspectives, 1991, 94, 98. Campaign chmn. Ottawa County Reps., Holland, 1978, 82-96, chmn., 1997-2002, Ottawa County Bush for Pres, 2000; del. Rep. Nat. Conv., 2000; chmn. 2d Congl. Dist. Rep. Party, 2003—. Capt. U.S. Army, 1967-69. Named to Mich. Model UN Hall of Fame. Mem. Internat. Studies Assn., Am. Polit. Sci. Assn., Holy Cross Wilderness Def. Fund. Presbyterian. Avocations: backpacking, fishing. Home: 10 N 160th Ave Holland MI 49424-6203 Office: Hope Coll 210 Lubbers Hall Holland MI 49422-9000 E-mail: holmes@hope.edu.

HOLMES, LOIS REHDER, composer, piano and voice educator; b. Canton, Ill., Jan. 8, 1927; d. John and Elizabeth Mary Grace (Staton) Kleinsteiber; div.; 1 child, Jessica Regina. BA in Sociology, Ill. Wesleyan U., 1949, MusB in Voice, Organ & Piano, 1950; MS in Reading, Western Ill. U., 1981. Cert. tchr., Ill. Libr. worker Withers Pub. Libr., Bloomington, Ill., 1950-51; music tchr. Toledo (Ill.) Schs., 1951-52; music and art librarian Hutchinson (Kans) Pub. Libr., 1952-53; pvt. practice piano & voice tchr. various cities, Ill., 1955—. Tchr. 1st & 2d grades South Fulton Sch., Havana, Ill., 1972-81. Composer: Musical Notions, 1991, Seascape, 1993, Divertimento, 1995, Bittersweet, 1996, Buglers at Sunrise, 1997, Dream Catcher, 1998, Fourteen New Christmas Carols for the 21st Century, 1999, The Abandoned Lighthouse, 2001, Do Daisies Dream, 2003, Petals On the Pond, 2003, Dragon Mist, 2003, Giselle, The Gypsy, 2003, others. Organist/choir dir. Ctrl. Christian Ch., Havana, 1974-79; vol. March of Dimes, Chgo., 1997—, Amnesty Internat. USA, Chgo., 1993—. Mem. Nat. Guild Piano Tchrs. (adjudicator internat. piano composition contest 1996—), Phi Kappa Phi. Home: 321 Mary Alice Rd Rantoul IL 61866-2832

HOLMES, LOUIS IRA, physician assistant, educator, photojournalist; b. L.A., July 16, 1943; s. Louis Issac and Mabel Jane (Walsh) H.; m. Krystal Ladda Premchaona, Nov. 16, 1991 (separated); children: Jonathan Joseph, Kimberly Ellen, Louis Boon. AA, El Camino Coll., Torrance, Calif., 1972; cert. physician asst., U. So. Calif., 1978. Cert. Nat. Commn. Cert. Physician Assts.; cert. ACLS. Resident in surgery Norwalk Hosp.-Yale U. Sch. Medicine, 1980; nursing staff emergency dept. South Bay Dist. Hosp., Redondo Beach, Calif., 1970-75; nursing staff trauma and surg. intensive care Harbor Gen. Hosp.-UCLA Med. Ctr., Torrance, 1976-77; physician asst. Gen. Med. Corp., L.A., 1979; physician asst., divsn. thoracic surgery City of Hope Med. Ctr., Duarte, Calif., 1980-81; sr. physcian asst. thoracic and cardiovascular surgery Bert Meyer MD, et al, L.A., 1981-91; sr. physician asst. cardiothoracic surgery, instr. postgrad. cardiothoracic surgery residency program Cedars-Sinai Med. Ctr., L.A., 1991-95; asst. prof. clin. surgery and family medicine U. So. Calif., L.A., 1995—, phys. asst. in cardiothoracic surgery, 1995—. Vis. surg. instr., China; examiner Nat. Commn. on Cert. of Physician Assts., 1981—92; mem. program planning com. Masters Degree program in Health Sci. for Physician Assts., Calif. State U., Dominguez Hill, 1991—95; adj. faculty physician asst. program U. So. Calif., 1982—90, mem. adv. com., 1983—84, mem. long-range planning com., 1988—90; spkr., cons., expert witness in field; contbr. numerous color photographic images The Green Berets: Weapons and Equipment (Hans Halberstadt), 1989; bd. dirs. TV Parade Mag., 1991—2001. Contbr. articles to profl. jours. and chpts. to books; mem. editl. bd. Clinician Reviews, 1990-96, Physician Asst. Jour., 1987-90; med. tech. advisor, appeared in (feature film) City of Angles. TV program on History Channel. Instr. ACLS, Am. Heart Assn., 1980-96. With Spl. Forces, U.S. Army, 1964-70; with Calif. Army N.G., 1976-83, U.S. Army Res., 1984-91. Recipient 21 mil. decorations, including awards from U.S., Vietnam, Thailand, Outstanding Svc. award Physician Asst. Jour., 1989. Fellow Soc. Critical Care Medicine (bd. dirs. Calif. chpt. 1995), Am. Acad. Physician Assts. (ho. of dels. 1982-87, vice chair surg. coun. 1985-87, conf. planning com. 1986-88, wets. caucus chair 1986-88, advisor to bd. dirs. 1989-91), Calif. Acad. Physician Assts. (chmn. govt. affairs 1984-86, pres. 1985, Presdl. Leadership award 1986, 88), Am. Assn. Surgeons Assts. (v.p. 1988), Assn. Physician Assts. Cardiovascular Surgery (pres. 1989-91), Mil. Order World Wars, Mil. Surgeons of the U.S., VFW, Spl. Forces Assn., Spl. Ops. Assn. Republican. Buddhist. Avocations: photo journalism, running, military history. Office: Cardiothoracic Surgeons Inc 50 Bellefontaine St Ste 403 Pasadena CA 91105 Home: 24 Country Ridge Rd Pomona CA 91766-4815

HOLMES, MARGARET LESTER, school system technology coordinator; b. Clinton, Tenn., Mar. 31, 1946; d. Melford Henry Sr. and Lois Evelyn (Webber) Lester; chidlren: Scott, Leslie. BS in Edn., U. Tenn., Knoxville, 1969. Music tchr. Knoxville City Schs., 1969-71; elem. tchr. Leavenworth (Kans.) City Schs., 1971-72, Anderson County Schs., Clinton, 1973-76, Clinton City Schs., 1980-84, computer coord., 1984—. Co-author curricula. Recipient Award of Excellence Tenn. Sch. Bd. Assn., 1991. Mem. NEA, Tenn. Edn. Assn. (Disting. Classroom Tchr. of Yr. 1991-92), Clinton Edn. Assn. (pres. 1985), Tenn. Reading Assn., Phi Delta Kappa. Avocations: music, water sports. Home: 165 Terisu Cir Powell TN 37849-7151 Office: South Clifton Elem Sch 165 Terisu Cir Powell TN 37849-7151

HOLMES, RICHARD DALE, history consultant; b. Sandown, N.H., Sept. 6, 1945; s. John B. Jr. and Marjorie A. (Andrews) H.; m. Carol A. Martineau, Dec. 19, 1970; children: John B. III, Leah K. BEd, Keene (N.H.) State Coll., 1968; MA, Rivier Coll., Nashua, N.H., 1980. Cert. tchr., N.H. Tchr. social studies Pelham (N.H.) Meml. Sch., 1968-2000, chmn. dept., 1975-2000. Hist. cons., rschr. Sandown Mus., 1980-88, Chester (N.H.) Hist. Soc., 1989—. Author: View from Meeting House Hill, 1988, Derry, 1995, Chester Revisited, 1997. Pres. Old Meeting House Assn., Sandown, 1987—; dir. Derry Mus., 2001—; mem. Derry Hist. Dist. Commn., 1988—, chmn. 1998—. With U.S. Army, 1969-71, Vietnam. Decorated Cross of Gallantry with palm, Civic Action medal 1st class (Vietnam). Mem.: NEA, Derry Hist. Soc., Sandown Hist. Assn. (hist. cons., rschr. 1980—88, pres. 1986—87), N.H. Hist. Soc., Pelham Edn. Assn. (v.p. 1976—77), N.H. Guide Dog Users Assn., Nat. Fedn. Blind. Congregationalist. Avocations: collecting books, public speaking, research. Home: 33 Hillside Ave Derry NH 03038-2215 Office: Town Hall 48 E Broadway Derry NH 03038 Fax: 603-432-6131. E-mail: rholmes33@comcast.net.

HOLMES, SUSAN G. music educator; b. Kansas City, Mo., Mar. 7, 1955; d. Burton E. and Gloria A. (Spencer) H. BA, U. Kans., Lawrence, 1980. Cert. music therapy, education. Tchr. Dade County Schs., Miami, Fla.; music therapist, tchr. ESOL Miami, Fla.; tchr., music therapist The Palace Retirement Cmty.; tchr. ESOL Miami-Palmetto (Fla.) Adult Edn. Ctr., Korean cmty., Miami, Fla.; instr. writing lab. Miami Dade C.C., Miami, Fla. Tchr. ESOL to newly-arrived immigrants. Recipient Honor for TV series CBS News. Mem. Nat. Orgn. for Exec. Women. Avocations: writing, music composition.

HOLMES-BAXTER, MAUREEN OLIVIA, language arts educator; b. Burlington, N.J., May 5, 1946; d. John Edward and Verna Mae Holmes; m. Louis Edward Baxter Sr., Dec. 20, 1975; children: Louis Edward Baxter Jr., Tia Verzel Baxter. BA, Va. Union U., 1969; MA, Beaver Coll., 1977. Cert. elem. edn. and reading edn., N.J. Tchr. Burlington City Bd. Edn., 1969—. Charter mem., Black Educators Traveling Achievers group mem. Coll. Tours, N.J., 1985—; charter mem. youth achievers' com. Sci./Math Group, N.J., 1989—. Named Tchr. of Yr., N.J. Alliance Black Sch. Educators, 1992. Mem. NAACP, NEA, N.J. Edn. Assn., Jack and Jill Am., Inc. (Burlington-Willingboro chpt., past pres.), N.J. PTA (life mem.), Oliver Cromwell Soc., Alpha Kappa Alpha. Democrat. Baptist. Home: 1006 Pope St Burlington NJ 08016-2740 Office: Burlington City HS 100 Blue Devil's Way Burlington NJ 08016-2746

HOLMES-EHLERS, VALERIE LYNN, secondary school educator; b. Elgin, Ill., Feb. 23, 1969; d. Robert Dennis and Judith Lynn (Sauer) Holmes; m. David Ehlers, June 24, 1995; children: Bryce Ehlers, Lilian Ehlers. BA cum laude, Concordia Coll., 1991. English, speech and debate tchr. Ft. Dodge (Iowa) Sr. H.S., 1991-97, head debate coach, 1991—, sec. bldg. improvement sec., 1992—, mem. dist. comm. com., 1993—; speech, Eng. and theater tchr. North Tama Cmty. Schs., Traer, Iowa, 1999—. Mem. adv. bd. Newspaper In Edn., Ft. Dodge, 1994—. Leader Girl Scouts U.S., 1991-93; mem., actress Hawkeye Cmty. Theatre, 1992—; mem. bell choir, Sunday sch. tchr., mem. choir United Ch. of Christ, 1998—, sr. youth group sponsor, 1999—; mem. Christian Bd. Edn., 2002. Mem. Iowa State Edn. Assn. (del. 1994-96), Bus. and Profl. Women (pres., v.p., Iowa Young Careerist chair 1991—, Iowa Yount Careerist award 1993, Woman of Yr. 1996), Jr. Civitan (bd. dirs. 1991—, chair Minn.-Iowa 1993—, advisor 1991—, Citizenship award 1994), PEO, Delta Kappa Gamma, Omicron Delta Kappa. Address: 305 Chestnut St Reinbeck IA 50669-1107 Office: North Tama Cmty Sec Schs 605 Walnut St Traer IA 50675

HOLMGREN, JANET L, college president; b. Chgo., Dec. 1, 1948; d. Kenneth William and Virginia Ann (Rensink) H.; m. Gordon A. McKay, Sept. 7, 1968 (div. 1990); children: Elizabeth Jane, Ellen Katherine. BA in English summa cum laude, Oakland U., Rochester, Mich., 1968; MA in Linguistics, Princeton U., 1971, PhD in Linguistics, 1974. Asst. prof. English studies Federal City Coll. (now U. D.C.), Washington, 1972-76; asst. prof. English U. Md., College Park, 1976-82, asst. to chancellor, 1982-88; assoc. provost Princeton (N.J.) U., 1988-90, vice-provost, 1990-91; pres. Mills Coll., Oakland, Calif., 1991—. Mem. external adv. bd. English dept. Princeton U. Bay Area Biosci. Ctr. Author: (with Spencer Cosmos) The Story of English: Study Guide and Reader, 1986, Narration and Discourse in American Realistic Fiction, 1982; contbr. articles to profl. jours. Faculty rsch. grantee U. Md., 1978; fellow NEH, 1978, Princeton U., 1968-69, 70-72, NSF, 1969-70; recipient summer study aid Linguistic Soc. Am., Ohio State U., 1970. Mem. Assn. Ind. Caif. Colls. and Univs. (exec. com.), Nat. Assn. Ind. Colls. and Univs., Am. Coun. on Education (chair office of women in higher edn.), Calif. Acad. Sci. (coun.). Democrat. Episcopal. Avocations: traveling, swimming, reading. Office: Mills Coll Office Pres 5000 Macarthur Blvd Oakland CA 94613-1301

HOLMGREN, MYRON ROGER, social sciences educator; b. Willmar, Minn., Mar. 19, 1933; s. Alfred and Cleora Victora (Scott) H.; m. Ellen Mary Shaheen, June 9, 1957; children: Brian, Mary Jo Haas. BA, Mankato State U., 1958; MA, No. Colo. State U., 1959. Instr. Grinnell (Iowa) H.S., 1959-62, Joliet (Ill.) Jr. Coll., 1962-66; instr., fin. advisor Am. Express Fin. Advisors, Joliet, 1966-72; instr. Benedictine Coll., Atchison, Kans., 1973, Moraine Valley C.C., Palos Hills, Ill., 1974-75, Minooka (Ill.) H.S., 1974-93, dept. chmn., 1984-87, dir., coach Scholastic Bowl Team, 1976-93.

Local dir. Exrox Award in Humanities, 1988=93; chmn. philosophy and goals North Ctrl. Accreditation, 1987-88. Author: Profitable Pricing Techniques, 1973; contbr. articles to profl. jours. Block chmn. March of Dimes, Am. Cancer Soc., 1989, 92-93; treas. bd. dirs. The Family Counseling Agy. of Will and Grundy Counties, 1996-99; mem. vestry St. Edward's Episcopal Ch., 2002—. Asian Found. grant, 1962. Mem. Internat. Platform Assn. Republican. Avocations: reading, writing, travel, gourmet cooking, market analysis. Home: 1314 Douglas St Joliet IL 60435-5814

HOLQUIST, JAMES MICHAEL, Russian and comparative literature educator; b. Rockford, Ill., Dec. 20, 1935; s. Leonard and Billye Alverta (Appleby) H.; m. Lydia Landis, July 30, 1960 (div. Dec. 1972); children: Peter Isaac, Benjamin Michael, Joshua Appleby; m. Katerina Clark, Apr. 15, 1974 (div. May 1999); children: Nicholas Manning, Sebastian; m. Elise Snyder, Nov. 6, 1999. BA with highest honors, U. Ill., 1963; PhD, Yale U., 1968; PhD honoris causa, U. Stockholm, Sweden, 2001. Asst. prof. Yale U., New Haven, 1968-72, assoc. prof., 1972-75; assoc. prof., dept. chmn. U. Tex., Austin, 1976-78, prof., 1978-80; prof. Slavic langs. and lit. dept., chmn. Ind. U., Bloomington, 1981-85; prof. comparative lit., dir. lit. major Yale U., 1986-91, chmn. coun. on Russian and East European studies, 1992-98, chmn. dept. comparative lit., 1998—2003, Northrop Frye prof. lit. theory, 2000. Christian Gauss lectr. Princeton U., 1991; NEH exchangee Soviet Acad. Scis., 1983; mem. exec. com. and editl. bd. PMLA. Author: (with Kernan and Brooks) Man and His Fictions, 1973, Dostoevsky and the Novel, 1977, reprinted, 1986; editor: (co-translator) The Dialogic Imagination: Four Essays by M.M. Bakhtin, 1981, (with Katerina Clark) Mikhail Bakhtin, 1984, Dialogism: The World of Mikhail Bakhtin, 1990, 2d edit., 2003, Philosophy of the Act, 1993; editor-in-chief: Tex. Slavic Studies, 1980; co-editor: Ind. Soviet Studies, 1982; editorial bd.: Yearbook of Comparative and Gen. Lit., 1982, Slavic Rev., 1983. Served with U.S. Army, 1958-61. Rockefeller Humanities fellow, 1983; vis. scholar Phi Beta Kappa, 1984-85; grantee NEH, 1979, Morse fellow Yale U., 1970. Mem. MLA, Am. Assn. Advancement of Slavic Studies, Internat. Bakhtin Soc. (newsletter editor 1982—), Internat. Dostoevsky Soc., Am. Assn. Tchrs. Slavic and East European Langs., Grotesque Club, Mory's Assocs., Elizabethan Club. Democrat. Home: 180 Linden St Apt H3 New Haven CT 06511-2459 E-mail: michael.holquist@yale.edu.

HOLSAPPLE, CLYDE WARREN, decision and information systems educator; b. Raleigh, N.C., Nov. 1, 1950; s. Van Warren and Jeanne (Rickert) H.; m. Carol Eades; children: Christiana, Claire. BS in Math., Purdue U., 1972, MS in Computer Sci., 1975, PhD in Mgmt., 1977. From asst. prof. to assoc. prof. bus. adminstrn. U. Ill., Urbana, 1978-83; vis. asst. prof. mgmt. Purdue U., West Lafayette, Ind., 1977-78, from assoc. prof. to prof. mgmt., 1983-89; prof. decision sci. and info. systems U. Ky., Lexington, 1988—, Rosenthal endowed chair in mgmt. info. systems, 1988—, chmn. dept. decision sci. and info. systems, 1993-94. Adj. prof. U. Tex., Austin, 1989—. Co-author: Foundations of Decision Support Systems, 1981, Micro Database Management, 1984, Manager's Guide to Expert Systems, 1986, The Information Jungle, 1988, Operations Research and Artificial Intelligence, 1994, Decision Support Systems: A Knowledge-Based Approach, 1996; editor: Handbook on Knowledge Management, 2003; editor Jour. Orgnl. Computing and Electronic Commerce, Erlbaum Corp., Mahwah, N.J., 1990—; assoc. editor Mgmt. Sci., Providence, 1991-98; area editor Decision Support Systems, Amsterdam, 1992—; contbr. over 100 articles to profl. jours. Recipient Pres.'s Acad. award Purdue U., 1970, 71, 72, Computer Educator of Yr. award Internat. Assn. for Computer Info. Systems, 1993. Recipient Chancellor's award for Outstanding Tchr., 1995, R&D Excellence Program award, Ky. Sci. and Engring. Found., 2002. Mem. IEEE, Internat. Soc. for Decision Support (co-founder, co-dir. 1989—), Assn. for Computing Machinery, Inst. for Operations Rsch. Mgmt. Scis., Assn. for Info. Systems, Decision Sci. Inst., Phi Beta Kappa, Phi Kappa Phi. Office: U Ky Gatton Coll Bus & Econs Lexington KY 40506-0034

HOLSTE, JAMES CLIFTON, chemical engineering educator; b. Colby, Kansas, Feb. 8, 1945; s. Clifton John and Irene Ellen (Luedders) H.; m. Cathleen Ann Haring, June 21, 1969; children: Rachel Suzanne, Jill Cathleen. BS, Concordia Tchr.'s Coll., 1966; PhD, Iowa State U., 1973. Profl. engr., Tex. Rsch. assoc. Nat. Bur. Standards, Boulder, Colo., 1973-75; from engring. rsch. assoc. to assoc. dean engring. Tex. A&M, Coll. Sta., 1975—; asst. dir. rsch. Tex. Engring. Exp. Sta., 1995—97. Cons. Precision Measurement, Duncanville, Tex., 1984-90, Shell Devel., Houston, 1978-82, OPC Engring., Houston, 1981-83, Precision Machine Products, Dallas, 1981-84. Bd. dirs., sec. Concordia Univ. Sys., St. Louis, 1992-2001. Recipient alumnus of yr. award Concordia Coll., 1994. Mem. AAAS, AIChE, Am. Physical Soc., Am. Chem. Soc., Am. Soc. Engring. Edn. Lutheran. Avocations: music, softball. Patentee in field. Home: 3025 Hummingbird Cir Bryan TX 77807-3224 Office: Tex A&M U Chem Engring Dept 3122 TAMU 337 Zachry Engring Ctr College Station TX 77843-3122 E-mail: j-holste@tamu.edu.

HOLSTI, OLE RUDOLF, political scientist, educator; b. Geneva, Aug. 7, 1933; came to U.S., 1940, naturalized, 1954; s. Rudolf Waldemar and Liisa (Franssila) H.; m. Ann Wood, Sept. 20, 1953; children: Eric Lynn, Maija. BA with highest honors, Stanford U., 1954, PhD, 1962; MAT., Wesleyan U., Middletown, Conn., 1956. Instr., asst. prof. polit. sci., research coordinator Stanford U., 1962-67; assoc. prof. U. B.C., Vancouver, Can., 1967-71, prof., 1971-74; George V. Allen prof. polit. sci. Duke U., 1974—, chmn. dept. polit. sci., 1977-83; prof. Dept. Polit. Sci. U. Calif., Davis, 1978-79. Mem. adv. com. on hist. diplomatic documentation U.S. Dept. State, 1983-86; mem. oversight com. NSF, 1981-84; co-dir. Triangle Univs. Security Sem. Duke U., 1983-98. Co-author: Content Analysis: Handbook with Application for the Study of Internat. Crisis, 1963; author (with D.J. Finlay and R. R Fagan): Enemies in Politics, 1967; author: Analysis of Communication Content: Development in Scientific Theories and Computer Techniques, 1969, Content Analysis for Social Sciences and Humanities, 1969; co-author: International Crises, 1972; author: Crisis Escalation War, 1972, Unity and Disintegration in International Alliances: Comparative Studies, 1973, Change in the International System, 1980, American Leadership in World Affairs: The Vietnam and Breakdown of Consensus, 1984, Pub. Opinion and Am. Fgn. Policy, 1996—2004; co-author: Political Science Annual, 1975, Thought and Action in Foreign Policy, 1975, The Behavior of Nations, 1976, World Politics, 1976, Diplomacy, 1979, Challenges to America, 1979, Containment, 1986, Behavior, Society and Nuclear War, 1989, Soviet-American Relations after the Cold War, 1991, Explaining the History of American Foreign Relations, 1991, 2003—, Psychological Dimensions of War, 1991, Diplomacy, Force and Leadership, 1993; contbg. author numerous books including The United States and Human Rights, 2000; co-prodr.: American Democracy Promotion, 2000; co-author: Pondering Postinternationalism, 2000, The New International Studies Classroom, 2000; co-prodr.: Eagle Rules?: Foreign Policy and American Primacy in the 21st Century, 2001; co-author: Soldiers and Civilians: The Civil-Military Gap and American National Security, 2001, Millennial Reflections on International Studies, 2002, Encyclopedia of US Foreign Relations, 1997—; assoc editor Western Polit. Quar., 1970—79, Jour. Conflict Resolution, 1967—72, bd. editors Computer Studies in the Humanities and Verbal Behavior, 1968—76, Am. Jour. Polit. Sci, 1975—80, Internat. Interaction assoc., Am. Review of Politics, editor then bd. editors Internat. Studies Quar., 1970—, Jour. Politics, 1991—, Internat. Studies Perspectives, 1999—, adv. bd. Univ. Press Am., 1976—, corr. editor Running Jour, —, corr. Racing South, —; contbr. numerous articles to profl. jours. Served with AUS, 1956-58. Recipient Nevitt Sanford award, 1988, Disting. Tchrs. award Howard Johnson, 1990, Runner of Yr. award CGTC, 1985, Alumni Disting. Undergrad. Tchg. award, 1995, All-Am. award U.S. Masters Track & Field, 2000, 02; GE Found. Owen D. Young fellow, 1960-61, Haynes Found. Rsch. fellow, 1961-62, Can. Coun. Leave fellow, 1970-71, Ctr. Advanced Study in Behavioral Sci. fellow, 1972-73, Ford Found. Faculty Rsch. fellow, 1972-73, Guggenheim fellow, 1981-82, Pew Faculty fellow Harvard U., 1990; grantee Can. Coun. Rsch., 1969, NSF, 1975-77, 79-81, 83-85, 88-90, 92-95, 96-98; mem. Nat. Champion Cross Country Team (men 50-59), 1985, 88, champion, 1988; champion Tar Heel Running Tour, 1987, champion, Triple Crown Race, 1992-93; named Runner Yr., 1993, Carolina Godiva Track Club. Mem. Internat. Studies Assn. (pres. west region 1969-70, south region 1975-77, nat. pres. 1979-80, Tchr.-Scholar award Internat. Studies Assn. 2000), Internat. Soc. Polit. Psychology (coun. 1990-92, v.p. 1993-95, Nev. H. Sanford award 1988), Internat. Peace Sci. Soc. (pres. so. sect. 1975-76), Am. Polit. Sci. Assn. (coun. 1982-84, adminstrn. com. 1982-85, Disting. Lifetime Achievement award 1999), Can. Polit. Sci. Assn., Western Polit. Sci. Assn. (exec. coun. 1971-74), USA Track and Field (N.C. Racewalk chair 1999-2002), Phi Beta Kappa, Duke Master Runners Club, Carolina Godiva Track Club (Runner of Yr. award 1985, 93), Fleet Feet Running Club. Home: 608 Croom Ct Chapel Hill NC 27514-6706 Office: Duke U Dept Polit Sci PO Box 90204 Durham NC 27708-0204 E-mail: holsti@duke.edu.

HOLSTON, A. FRANK, retired broadcaster, communications educator; b. Balt., Feb. 25; s. Arthur F. Sr. and Sara A. Holston; m. Marianne B. Holston, Dec. 27, 1953; children: William Carroll, Sara Anne, Jeanne Marie. BS, U. Ala., 1951; MA, Mich. State U., 1962. Radio and TV broadcaster, sports dir., Balt., 1944-72; announcer ABC-TV, ESPN, N.Y.,Conn., 1974-88; prof. comm. C.C. Balt., 1956-88; ret., 1988. Chmn. faculty senate exec. com., Balt., 1969—70; gen. mgr. Liberty Campus, Balt., 1968—69, WBJC-FM, 1968—69; pres., bd. dirs. Shearwater, Inc., 1996—98; track ofcl. U.S. Naval Acad., 1998—; spkr. in field. Bd. dirs. Annapolis (Md.) Bur. Recreation, 1993—, Broadcast Edn. Assn., Washington, 1985-89, Ecumedia, Balt., 1975-76; v.p. Rep. Ctrl. Com., 1991-97, pres., 1995-97; chmn. '51 reunion U. Ala., 2001; pres. Feddayes, Boumi Temple Shrine, 1967-68. With USN, 1945, USNR. Ford Found. scholar, Northwestern U., 1958, News Am. fellow, Syracuse U., 1960. Mem.: Shriners (v.p. Annapolis club 2003—). Presbyterian. Home: 2B1 Spa Creek Landing Annapolis MD 21403

HOLT, DONALD A. agronomist, consultant, retired academic administrator; b. Minooka, Ill., Jan. 29, 1932; s. Cecil Bell and Helen (Eickoff) H.; m. Marilyn Louise Jones, Sept. 6, 1953; children: Kathryn A. Holt Stichnoth, Steven Paul, Jeffrey David, William Edwin. BS In Agrl. Sci., MS in Agronomy, U. Ill.; PhD in Agronomy, Purdue U. Farmer, Minooka, Ill., 1956-63; instr., asst. prof., assoc. prof. then prof. agronomy Purdue U., West Lafayette, Ind., 1964-82; prof., head dept. agronomy U. Ill., Urbana-Champaign, Ill., 1982-83, dir. Ill. Agr. Expt. Sta., assoc. dean Coll. Agr., 1983-96, sr. assoc. dean Coll. Agr., cons. environ. sci., 1996-2002; ret., 2002; interim dir. Nat. Soybean Rsch. Lab., 2003—03. Cons. Deere and Co., Ottumwa, Iowa, 1978, NASA, Houston, 1979, Control Data Corp., Mpls., 1978-79, EPA, Corvallis, Oreg., 1981-90. Town Bd. commr., Otterbein, Ind., 1972-76. Fellow AAAS, Am. Soc. Agronomy (pres. 1988), Crop Sci. Soc. Am.; mem. Agrl. Rsch. Inst. (pres. 1991), Am. Forage and Grassland Coun., Ill. Forage and Grassland Coun., Gamma Sigma Delta (internat. pres. 1974-76). Republican. United Methodist. Home: 1801 Moraine Dr Champaign IL 61822-5261 Office: U Ill 170 N5RC 1101 W Peabody Dr Urbana IL 61801-4723 E-mail: d-holt@uiuc.edu.

HOLT, GERALD WAYNE, retired counseling administrator; b. Woodbury, Tenn., July 17, 1935; s. Slaughter L. and Pearl (Simmons) H.; m. May Jane Neeley, Aug. 28, 1955; children: Lucinda Jane, Cheryl Kay, Beth Ann. BS, Ball State U., 1957, MA, 1959, postgrad., 1960-61. Tchr. social studies Union City (Ind.) Sch., 1957-60, Storer Jr. High Sch., Muncie, Ind., 1960-69; asst. prin. Storer Middle Sch., Muncie, 1969-78; prin. Franklin Middle Sch., Muncie, 1978-79; Christian edn. dir. Glad Tidings Ch., Muncie, 1975-78, 81-84; tchr. social studies Storer Middle Sch., Muncie, 1979-88; Christian edn. dir. Calvary Christian Ctr., Muncie, 1985-87; guidance dir. Northside Middle Sch., Muncie, 1988-99; in car driving instr. Driving Acad., 1997—2003. Bd. dirs. Sch. Employees Credit Union, Muncie, 1987-94; treas. Glad Tidings Ch., Muncie, 1961-72, trustee, 1974-83; trustee Calvary Christian Ctr., Muncie, 1984-88, 90-98. Mem. Ind. Retired Tchrs. Assn., Muncie Tchrs. Assn., Am. Assn. Counseling and Guidance, Elem. Sch. Guidance and Counseling, NEA, Ind. Tchrs. Assn., Assn. for Supervision and Curriculum Devel., Phi Delta Kappa. Assemblies of God. Avocations: golf, bowling, photography, collecting political buttons. Office: 1120 W Yale Ave Muncie IN 47304-1559 E-mail: gwh1120@aol.com.

HOLT, JANA SUE, middle school educator; b. Van Buren, Ark., Jan. 13, 1962; d. Edgar Leon and Norma Lee (Glover) Trolinder; m. William Darrin Matlock, Oct. 22, 1982 (div. Dec. 1984); m. Larry Wayne Holt, June 22, 1985; children: Cassie Marie, Jason Lee. BS in Phys. Edn., Tex. Tech. U., 1985; MS in Environ. Sci., Stepen F. Austin State U., 2000. Cert. tchr., Tex. Tchr. sci., phys. edn. Ralls (Tex.) Ind. Sch. Dist., 1989-91; tchr. sci., Quest Skills for Adolescents, coach Killeen (Tex.) Ind. Sch. Dist., 1991—. Participant Crop Walk for the Hungry, Belton, Tex., 1992; team leader Am. Heart Assn., Killeen, 1992. Avocations: boating, camping, skiing.

HOLT, KAREN ANITA YOUNG, English educator; b. Waltham, Mass., Oct. 23, 1949; d. Rexford Vernon and Linia Virginia (Duke) Young; m. Robert Jackson Holt, Dec. 30, 1974 (div. Sept. 1984). BA in English and French, Southwestern Okla. State U., 1971; MA in English, Okla. State U., 1973, postgrad., 1973-77, 86, Cen. State U., 1986. Cert. tchr., Okla. Instr. Okla. State U. Tech. Br., Oklahoma City, 1977-87; arts in edn. coord. Putnam City Schs., Oklahoma City, 1985-87; prof. Rose State Coll., Midwest City, Okla., 1987—. Dir. Righting Writing, Midwest City, 1989-91; coord. Poetry at Rose, Midwest City, 1988—, Students' Poetry, 1992—; chairperson long-range planning Cross Timbers Arts and Humanities Coun., Midwest City, 1990-91; cons. Excellence in the Arts project Kennedy Found. Sch. Bd., 1988, Okla. Writing Project, 1995. Editor: Chapbook, 1971; contbr. poetry to various publs.; poet An Evening with Oklahoma Poets, U. Okla., 1991, City Arts Conversations with the Book, 1997. Charter mem. Carpenter Sq. Theatre Vols., Oklahoma City, 1986—; mem. Rose State Coll. Speakers' Bur., Midwest City, 1990—, senator humanities divsn. faculty, 1991-94, faculty senate treas., 1993-94. Recipient honorable mention poetry award Red Dirt Press, 1988, Outstanding Prof. of Yr. award Phi Theta Kappa, 1993, keynote spkr., 1997; Adult Inst. for Arts scholar Okla. Arts Inst., 1990-92, Regents scholar, 1992-94; Project AIM grantee Nat. Endowment for Arts, 1986-87. Mem. Okla. Alliance for Arts Edn., Okla. Assn. Cmty. and Jr. Colls. (English chairperson 1989-90), Okla. Coun. Tchrs. of English, Rose State Coll. Faculty Assn., Rose State Coll. Founders Club, Okla. Arts Inst. Alumni Assn. Republican. Methodist. Avocations: reading, dance, film history, photography, flute. Home: 5800 NW 62nd St Oklahoma City OK 73122-7346 Office: Rose State Coll 6420 SE 15th St Oklahoma City OK 73110-2704

HOLT, KATHRYN SMITH, media specialist; b. Greenville, S.C., July 25, 1952; d. Thomas Lee and Celeste (Duncan) Smith; m. Roland Maxwell Holt Jr., June 22, 1974; 1 child, Richard Grady. BA, Winthrop U., 1974; MEd, Converse Coll., 1980; EdS, Converse Coll., ;, 1994. Cert. tchr., media specialist, S.C. Media specialist Inman (S.C.) Elem. Sch., 1974—. Office: Inman Elem Sch 25 Oakland Ave Inman SC 29349-1597

HOLT, LINDA FITZGERALD, elementary education educator; b. Ft. Benning, Ga., Apr. 10, 1956; d. Donald Carl and Bobbie Jane (Oliver) Fitzgerald; m. James Anthony Holt, Aug. 16, 1975 (div. June 1991); 1 child, Laura Leigh. AA, Hopkinsville (Ky.) C.C., 1976; BS, Western Ky. U., 1979; MA, Murray (Ky.) State U., 1984. Cert. elem. tchr., Ky. Math/sci. demonstration tchr. K-12 Hopkins County Schs., Madisonville, Ky., 1979-97; gifted/talented resource tchr. Caldwell County Schs., 1997—2001. Math. cons. K-12, workshop presenter Hopkins County Sch. Sys., Madisonville, 1980-97, Badgett Ctr. Ednl. Enhancement; tchr. trainer Ky. K-8 Math. Specialist Program and 4-5 Sci. Specialist Program, 1990-93. Grantee NSF, 1990, 93. Mem. Nat. Coun. Tchrs. Math. (presenter regional conf. Paducah 1993), Nat. Sci. Tchr. Assn., Internat. Reading Assn., Ky. Coun. Tchrs. Math. (conf. presider 1990), Ken-Lake Coun. Tchrs. Math., Western Ky. Math.-Sci. Alliance (bd. dirs., elem. rep.) Democrat. Baptist. Avocations: gardening, bicycling, hiking. Office: Caldwell County Bd Edn PO Box 229 Princeton KY 42445-0229

HOLT, MICHAEL KENNETH, management and finance educator, consultant, city councilman; b. Jackson, Tenn., Apr. 13, 1961; s. Kenneth Harvey and Dorothy (Price) Holt; m. Carol Lynn Walls, Aug. 13, 1983; 1 child, Mitchell Harris;1 child, Marleigh Allison. BS, Union U., 1983; MS, La. State U., 1985; postgrad, U. Memphis, 2001—. CPM. Broker First Nat. Bank of Commerce, New Orleans, 1985—86; mgr. Invest at Jackson (Tenn.) Nat. Bank, 1986—87; stock broker Merrill Lynch, Jackson, Tenn., 1987—89; prof. Union U., Jackson, Tenn., 1989—, chmn. supervisory com., 2002—. Chmn. bd. Leaders Credit Union, Jackson, Tenn., 1996-99; dir. Ctr. Bus. and Econ. Devel., 1999—; cons. Best Home Ctr., Jackson, Tenn., 1994-97, mem. regional planning commn., 1996-2001; cons. Quaker Oats, Jackson, 1991, Memphis Cablevision, Memphis, 1990; nominee bd. dirs. Fed. Res. Bank St Louis, 1997 Editor: Jour. Industry and Commerce, 1993-94, Update, 1990—; contbr. articles to profl. jours. City councilman Jackson, Tenn., 1999-2003. Recipient Instrnl. Innovation award Union U., 1995. Office: Union U 1050 Union University Dr Jackson TN 38305-3697 E-mail: kholt@uu.edu.

HOLT, MILDRED FRANCES, educator; b. Lorain, Ohio, July 30, 1932; d. William Henry and Rachel (Pierce) Daniels; B.S., U. Md., 1962, M.Ed., 1967, Ph.D., 1977; m. Maurice Lee Holt, Sept. 11, 1949 (dec.); children—Claudia, Frances, William, Rudi. Tchr. spl. edn. St. Mary's (Md.) County Public Schs., 1962-64, coordinator Felix Johnson Spl. Edn. Center, 1964-66; demonstration tchr. spl. edn. U. Md., College Park, summer 1970, instr. spl. edn. dept. Coll. Edn., 1969-73; supr. spl. edn. Calvert and St. Mary's (Md.) Counties, 1968-69; asso. prof. spl. edn. W. Liberty (W.Va.) State Coll., 1973-75; asst. prof. Eastern Ill. U., Charleston, 1975-77; supr. spl. edn. Warren County Public Schs., Front Royal, Va., 1977-85; spl. edn. tchr. Dallas Ind. Sch. Dist., 1985— . Mem. NEA, Warren County Edn. Assn., Council Exceptional Children, Assn. for Gifted, Assn. Supervision and Curriculum Devel., Va. Edn. Assn., Va. Council Exceptional Children, Blue Ridge Orgn. Gifted and Talented, Assn. Children with Learning Disabilities, Nat. Assn. Gifted Children, Phi Theta Kappa, Kappa Delta Pi. Contbr. articles to profl. jours.; author: Reach Guidebook, 1979. Home: 2916 Sidney Dr Mesquite TX 75150-2253 E-mail: mholt@texas.net.

HOLT, ROBERT RUTHERFORD, clinical psychology educator; b. Jacksonville, Fla., Dec. 27, 1917; s. Walter John Watson and Grace Lloyd Hilditch; m. Louisa C. Pinkham, Feb., 1944 (div. 1952); children: Dorothy O. Prickett, Catherine F.; m. Crusa Adelman, Dec., 1957 (dec. 1959); m. Joan Esterowitz, Aug. 2, 1963; children: Daniel W. E., Michael D. BA with highest honors, Princeton U., 1939; MA, Harvard U., 1941, PhD, 1944. Diplomate Am. Bd. Examiners in Profl. Psychology. Rsch. asst. Harvard Psychol. Clinic, Cambridge, Mass., 1941-44; study dir. divsn. program surveys B.A.E., Washington, 1944-46; instr. Am. U., Washington, 1944; clin. psychologist Winter VA Hosp., Topeka, 1946-49; clin. asst. prof. psychology U. Kans., Lawrence, 1946-50; assoc. psychologist The Menninger Found., Topeka, 1947-49, sr. psychologist rsch. dept., 1949-53; dir. psychol. staff, 1951-53; assoc. prof. psychology Grad. Sch. Arts and Sci. NYU, 1953-58, dir. Rsch. Ctr. for Mental Health, 1953-63, prof. psychology, 1958-88, prof. psychology emeritus, 1988—; with associated consortium faculty CUNY, N.Y.C., 1989-90. Tutor, teaching fellow Harvard U. and Radcliffe Coll., Cambridge, 1941-44; lectr. Topeka Inst. for Psychoanalysis, 1949-53; part-time pvt. practice of diagnostic testing, N.Y.C., 1953-60; mem. fellowship com. Founds. Fund for Rsch. in Psychiatry, 1956-61; co-dir. Rsch. Ctr. for Mental Health, NYU, 1963-69, mem. arts and sci. rsch. fund com., 1964-68, 75-76, instnl. grants com., 1970-74, Ctr. for Humanistic Studies, 1976-77, grad. curriculum com., 1982-83, dir. program in peace & global policy studies, 1985-89; fellowship rev. panel NIH-NIMH, 1963-65; vis. prof. clin. psychology Harvard U., 1967-68; bd. sci. advisors Environ. Rsch. Fund, 1971-2000; William V. Silverberg meml. lectr. Am. Acad. Psychoanalysis, 1973; Sandor Rado meml. lectr. Columbia U. Inst. Psychoanalysis, 1978; Phillips Disting. Vis. Haverford Coll., 1980; with Exploratory Project on Conditions of Peace, 1984-88, treas. 1985-86; lectr. on psychiatry Harvard Med. Sch., 1997—; cons. in field. Author: Assessing Personality, 1971, Methods of Research in Clinical Psychology, 1973, Methods in Clinical Psychology, 2 vols., 1978, Il Processo Primario nel Rorschach e nel Materiale Tematico, 1983, Freud Reappraised, 1989, Primary Process Thinking, 2 vols., 2003; co-author: (with others) Developments in the Rorschach Technique, vol. I, Technique and Theory, 1954, Personality Patterns of Psychiatrists, 2 vols., 1958, Personality, 1969, LSD: Personality and Experience, 1972, Psicoanalysi ed ermeneutica, 1996; editor: TAT Newsletter, 1946-52, Motives and Thought, 1967, Diagnostic Psychological Testing, 1968, New Horizon for Psychotherapy, 1971, Psychoanalysis and Contemporary Science, 1972, Psychoanalysis and the Philosophy of Science: The Collected Papers of Benjamin B. Rubinstein, 1997; mem. editl. bd. numerous profl. publs. including Jour. Nervous and Mental Disease, 1957-92, Psychol. Issues, 1958—, Psychoanalytic Psychology, 1983-98, Polit. Psychology, 1985-99, Psychoanalytic Books, 1988-2002, Freud Ency., 1991-2002. Mem. Village Ind. Dems., N.Y.C., 1953-88; head N.Y. chpt. Coun. for a Livable World, N.Y.C., 1958-59; mem. coun. Congress of Scientists on Survival, N.Y.C., 1962-64; chmn. Recycling Com., Truro, Mass., 1992—; mem. Bd. of Health Truro, 1994-95. Fellow NIMH 1960-61; recipient Rsch. Career award NIMH, 1962-88, Great Man award Soc. for Projective Techniques and Personality Assessment, 1969, Psychologist of Yr. award N.Y. Soc. Clin. Psychologists, 1973, Rsch. award Psychologists for Social Responsibility, 1990. Fellow APA (coun. reps. 1954-56, 61-63, pres. divsn. clin. psychology 1961-62, past pres. 1962-63, com. on nominations and elections 1948-50, 54-58, chmn. 1956-57, 62-63, exec. com. 1951-53, 54-57, 60-63, chmn. conf. orgn. com. 1961-63, awards com. 1964-65, Disting. Contbns. award 1974), AAAS, Internat. Soc. Political Psychology (bd. govs. 1988-90, awards com. 1989), Internat. Peace Rsch. Assn., Soc. for Psychol. Study of Social Issues, Fedn. Am. Scientists, Internat. Soc. for Systems Sci., Coun. Rsch. in Bibliography (pres. 1965-73), Union of Concerned Psychoanalysts and Psychotherapists, Inc. (adv. bd. 1988-1990), Phi Beta Kappa, Sigma Xi. Avocations: gardening, swimming, singing, cooking, writing poetry. Home: PO Box 1087 3 Daisy Ln Truro MA 02666

HOLT, SANDRA GRACE, middle school educator; b. Dublin, Ga., May 14, 1941; d. Wade and Grace (Wilkes) Holt Brantley. BS in Edn., Ga. So. Coll., 1963. Cert. tchr., Ga. 6th grade tchr. Charles H. Bruce Elem. Sch., Macon, Ga., 1963-65, Cen. Elem. Sch., Dublin, 1966-70; 7th grade tchr. East Laurens Sch., Dublin, 1965-66, Dublin Jr. High Sch., 1970-96. Mem. Ga. Ret. Educators Assn., Am. Legion Aux. Methodist. Avocations: piano, fishing, cooking, reading, sports.

HOLTAN, BOYD DEVERE, retired mathematics educator; b. Forest City, Iowa, Sept. 17, 1928; s. George Theodore and Marie Josephine (Haugen) H.; m. Carolyn Jane Rees, Dec. 30, 1956; children: Leslie Ann, Daniel Boyd, Rebecca Jane. AA, Waldorf Jr. Coll., Forest City, 1948; BA, St. Olaf Coll., 1950; MA, U. Iowa, 1954; EdD, U. Ill., 1963. Tchr. math. and sci. high sch., Chandler, Minn., 1950-51, tchr. math. Independence, Iowa, 1954-57, prin., tchr. math. Thompson, Iowa, 1957-59; grad. asst. U. Ill., Champaign, 1959-62; from asst. prof. to assoc. prof. math. edn. U. Fla., Gainesville, 1962-67; prof. math. edn. W.Va. U., Morgantown, 1967-96, prof. emeritus, 1997—. Vis. prof. U. Ill., summer 1965; NSF postdoctoral fellow NYU, 1971. Contbr. articles to profl. jours. With U.S. Army, 1951-53. Mem. Nat. Coun. Tchrs. Math., W.Va. Coun. Tchrs. Math., Appalachian Blacksmiths Assn. (treas. 1978—), Phi Delta Kappa. Lutheran. Avocation: blacksmithing. Home: 505 Cosgray Run Road Core WV 26529-9746 Office: WVa U PO Box 6122 Morgantown WV 26506-6122

HOLTHAUS, JOAN MARIE, elementary school educator; b. Wichita, Kans., June 3, 1964; d. Wilbur Ferdinand and Mary Teresa (Armstrong) Kruse; m. William Paul Holthaus, July 18, 1987; 1 child, Paul Thomas. BS in Edn., English, Kans. State U., 1986; Early Childhood Spl. Edn. Endorsement, Washburn U. 2nd grade and kindergarten tchr. Most Pure Heart Parochial Sch., Topeka, Kans., 1986—. Guardian Kans. Assn. Protective Svcs., 1991-98; cons. Christ the King Daycare, 1995. Author: (resource guide) Guide for Students with Diabetes (Kans. State U.), 1985. Camp dir. Am. Diabetes Assn., Rock Springs, Kans., 1990-99, chmn. bd. dirs. Shawnee County chpt., 1995-96, mem. bd. dirs. Kans., 1993-98. Named Topeka's Favorite Kindergarten Tchr., Topeka Capital Jour. Poll, 1997. Mem. Am. Mothers (Kans. Mother of Yr. 1995-96), Topeka Area Parochial Kindergarten Tchrs. (founder), Alpha Delta Pi (mem. at large alumnae assn.). Roman Catholic. Avocations: cooking, gardening, sewing, skiing, painting.

HOLTKAMP, SUSAN CHARLOTTE, elementary education educator; b. Houston, Feb. 23, 1957; d. Clarence Jules and Karyl Irene (Roberts) H. BS in Early Childhood Edn., Brigham Young U., Provo, Utah, 1979, MEd, 1982. Cert. tchr. Utah, ESL endorsement U. Utah, 2002. 2d grade tchr. Nebo Sch. Dist., Spanish Fork, Utah, 1979-84, kindergarten tchr., 1984-85; tchr. 2d grade DODDS, Mannheim, Fed. Republic Germany, 1985-86; tchr. 3d grade Jordan Sch. Dist., Salt Lake City, 1987-92, tchr. 5th grade, 1992—2002, tchr. 6th grade, 2002—. Mem. NEA, JEA, Utah Edn. Assn., ASCD.

HOLTON, SUSAN A. psychology educator; b. Columbus, Ohio, Apr. 24, 1948; d. William C. and Mary (Floyd) H.; 1 child, Christopher L. Holton-Jablonski; m. Joe Snyders, Aug. 4, 1991; stepchildren: John, Mark. BS, Miami U., Oxford, Ohio, 1970; MA, Case Western Res. U., 1973, PhD, 1976. Cert. mediator. Dir. Gabriel Ames Assocs., Taunton, Mass., 1975—; asst. to pres., asst. prof. Bridgewater (Mass.) State Coll., 1984-88, dept. chair., assoc. prof., 1988-90, prof., 1990—, asst. to pres., 1991-92. Bd. dirs. Profl. Orgn. in Higher Edn.; coord. Mass. Faculty Devel. Consortium, 1988-90; chair., nominating com. Unitarian Universalis Assn., Boston, 1987-89; cons. Alban Inst., 1989-93. Author: The Mad Madonna, 1987, Under the Influence of Life, Conflict Management in Higher Education, 1995, Mending the Cracks in the Ivory Tower: Strategies for Conflict Management in Higher Education, 1998; editor, author over 60 chpts. in books; contbr. articles to profl. jours. Dir. Ch. the Larger Fellowship, Boston, 1987-91; founder FOCUS on Gifted and Talented, Framington, Mass. Mem. Speech Communication Assn., Boston Area Assn. Psychol. Type (founder), N.E. Assn. Psychol. Type, Ea. Communications Assn., Communications Assn. Mass., Am. Assn. for Higher Edn., Assn. Conflict Resolution. Avocations: reading, writing, walking. Office: Bridgewater State Coll Maxwell Libr Bridgewater MA 02325-0001

HOLTZ, JANE KAY, special education educator; b. Ashley, N.D., Nov. 8, 1963; d. Sylvester and Florence (Feist) Meier; m. Robert A. Holtz, Nov. 13, 1993; children: Kassandra Jo, Robert Stanley. BS in Mental Retardation, Elem. Edn., Minot State U., 1986, MS in Spl. Edn., 1988. Tchr. educable mentally handicapped Denseith (N.D.) Pub. Sch., 1986-87; multiple handicapped tchr. Oliver Mercer Spl. Edn./Hazen (N.D.) Pub. Schs., 1988-91; tchr. educable mentally handicapped Oliver Mercer Spl. Edn./Beulah (N.D.) Pub. Schs., 1991-93; MSMI/MMMI/ECSE tchr. Moorhead (Minn.) Pub. Schs. #152, 1993—. Coach Minot (N.D.) Spl. Olympics, 1984—86, Hazen Spl. Olympics, 1988—91. Scholar, Dept. Pub. Instrn., 1987—88. Mem.: NEA, Coun. Exceptional Children, Kappa Delta Pi. Roman Catholic. Avocations: walking, reading, movies. Home: 1941 55th Ave S Fargo ND 58104-6368 Office: 715 11th St N Moorhead MN 56560 E-mail: rjholtz102@aol.com.

HOLTZ, NOEL, neurologist; b. N.Y.C., Sept. 13, 1943; s. Irving and Lillian H.; m. Carol Sue Smith, June 9, 1968; children: Pamela Wendy, Aaron David, Daniel Judah. BA, NYU, 1965, MD, U. Cin., 1969. Diplomate Am. Bd. Psychiatry and Neurology, Am. Bd. Sleep Medicine. Intern Cin. Gen. Hosp., 1969-70; resident in internal medicine and neurology Emory U., Atlanta, 1970-71, 73-76; pvt. practice medicine specializing in neurology, Marietta, Ga., 1977—; mem. faculty Emory U. Coll. Medicine, Atlanta, 1977—, clin. assoc. prof. dept. neurology, 1977—, assoc. prof., 1987; adj. prof. dept. nursing Kennesaw State U., 1997—; mem. staffs Kennestone Hosp.; dir. neurodiagnostics unit; mem. staff Grady Meml. Hosp.; cons. Ga. Med. Care Found. Neurology. Co-author: Conceptual Human Physiology, 1985. With USN, 1971-73. Mem. Am. Acad. Neurology, Ga. Neurol. Soc. (sec.-treas., pres. 1990-92), Alpha Omega Alpha. Office: 522 North Ave Marietta GA 30060-1125

HOLTZAPPLE, MARK THOMAS, biochemical engineer, educator; b. Enid, Okla., Nov. 16, 1956; s. Arthur Robert and Joan Carol (Persson) H.; m. Carol Ann Kamps, Jan. 11, 1992. BS, Cornell U., 1978; PhD, U. Pa., 1981. Capt. U.S. Army, Natick, Mass., 1982-85; asst. prof. Tex. A&M U., College Station, 1986-91, assoc. prof., 1991-98, prof., 1998—. Author papers on models for describing enzymatic hydrolysis of cellulose, pretreatments to enhance enzymatic digestion of cellulose; contbr. articles to profl. jours. Recipient Teaching awards Coll. Engring, 1990, Gen. Dynamics, 1990, Tenneco, 1991, Dow, 1991, Presdl. Green Chemistry Challenge award, 1996. Mem. Am. Inst. Chem. Engring. (exec. com. South Tex. sect. 1991-92). Achievements includes patents for torque monitor; orientation insensitive, high-efficiency evaporator; hermetic compressor; biomass process, high-efficiency engine and high-efficiency refrigeration. Home: 1805 Southwood Dr College Station TX 77840-4859 Office: Dept Chem Engring Tex A&M U College Station TX 77843-3122

HOLTZCLAW, DIANE SMITH, elementary education educator; b. Buffalo, May 26, 1936; d. John Nelson and Beatrice M. (Salisbury) Smith; m. John Victor Holtzclaw, June 27, 1959; children: Kathryn Diane, John Bryan. BS in Edn. magna cum laude, SUNY, Brockport, 1957, MS with honors, 1961; postgrad., SUNY, Buffalo, 1960-65, Canisus Coll., 1979, Nazareth Coll., 1981-82. Tchr. Greece Cen. Sch., Rochester, N.Y., 1957-60; supr. SUNY, Brockport, 1960-64, assoc. prof. edn., 1960-64; dir. Early Childhood Ctr., Fairport, N.Y., 1968-80; tchr. Fairport Cen. Schs., 1971—; ednl. cons. in field; specialist child devel. Ch. music dir., Rochester, N.Y., 1983—; pres. bd. dirs. Downtown Day Care Ctr., Rochester, 1974-83; mem. exec. bd. Rochester Theatre Organ Soc., 1988—. Mem. Fairport Edn. Assn. (exec. bd. 1982-83, del. 1983), N.Y. State United Tchrs., AAUW (exec. bd. 1973-74, 77-79, 83-84, pres. Fairport br. 1971-73), Internat. Platform Assn., Kappa Delta Pi. Home: 1455 Ayrault Rd Fairport NY 14450-9301 Office: Fairport Cen Schs 38 W Church St Fairport NY 14450-2130

HOLTZMAN, ROBERTA LEE, French and Spanish language educator; b. Detroit, Nov. 24, 1938; d. Paul John and Sophia (Marcus) H. AB cum laude, Wayne State U., 1959, MA, 1973, U. Mich., 1961. Fgn. lang. tchr. Birmingham (Mich.) Sch. Dist., 1959-60, Cass Tech. H.S., Detroit, 1961-64; from instr. to prof. French and Spanish, Schoolcraft Coll., Livonia, Mich., 1964-84, chmn. French and Spanish depts., 1984—. Trustee Cranbrook Music Guild, Ednl. Community, Bloomfield Hills, Mich., 1976-78. Fulbright-Hays fellow, Brazil, 1964. Mem. AAUW, NEA, MLA, Nat. Mus. Women in Arts (co-founder 1992), Am. Assn. Tchrs. of Spanish and Portuguese, Am. Assn. Tchrs. of French, Mich. Edn. Assn. Avocations: swimming, book collecting, photography, travel. Office: Schoolcraft Coll 18600 Haggerty Rd Livonia MI 45152-2696 E-mail: rholtzma@schoolcraft.edu.

HOLTZSCHUE, KARL BRESSEM, lawyer, author, educator; b. Wichita, Kans., Mar. 3, 1938; s. Bressem C. and Josephine E. (Landsittel) H.; m. Linda J. Gross, Oct. 24, 1959; children: Alison, Adam, Sara. AB, Dartmouth Coll., 1959; LLB, Columbia U., 1966. Bar: N.Y. 1967, U.S. Dist. Ct. (so. and ea. dists.) N.Y. 1968. Assoc. Webster & Sheffield, N.Y.C., 1966-73, ptnr., 1974-88; ptnr., head real estate dept. O'Melveny and Myers, N.Y.C., 1988-90; pvt. practice N.Y.C., 1990—. Adj. prof. Fordham U. Law Sch., 1990—; adj. prof. Bus. Sch., Columbia U., 1990-96, Law Sch., 1991; editl. bd. Warren's Weed N.Y. Real Property. Author: Holtzschue on Real Estate Contracts, New York Practice Guide: Real Estate, Vol. 1 on Purchase and Sale, Real Estate Transactions: Purchase and Sale of Real Property; editor: NYSBA's Res. R.E. Forms on Hot Docs. Trustee Soc. of St. Johnland, 1980-86, Ensemble Studio Theatre, 1986-88; bd. dirs. The Bridge, 1990—, pres., 1992-95; mem. alumni bd. Dartmouth Ptnrs. in Cmty. Svc., 1994—, chmn., 1994-99. Lt. (j.g.) USN, 1959-62. Mem. ABA (com. on internat. investment in real estate 1987-97, com. on legal opinions in real estate trans. 1990—), N.Y. State Bar Assn. (exec. com. real property sect. 1998—, com. on attys. opinions 1992—, com. on title and transfer 1998—, co-chmn. 1998—), Assn. Bar City N.Y. (com. on real property law 1977-80, chmn. 1987-90, 95-98, com. ctrl. and East Europe 1998-99), Am. Coll. Real Estate Lawyers (opinions com. 1989—, vice chmn. 1992-95), Tri Bar (opinions com. 1990-99). Episcopalian. E-mail: kholtzschue@nyc.rr.com.

HOLUBEC, EDYTHE JOHNSON, educational consultant; b. Muncie, Ind., July 25, 1944; d. Roger Winfield and Frances Elizabeth (Pierce) Johnson; m. James Frank Holubec, Feb. 28, 1973. BS, Ball State U., 1966; MA, U. Minn., 1976; PhD, U. Tex., 1991. VISTA vol. Vols. in Svc. to Am., N.Y.C., 1966-67; English and Reading tchr. Stevenson H.S., Livonia, Mich., 1967-69; instr., tchg. asst. U. Minn., Mpls., 1969-72; reading specialist Austin (Tex.) Ind. Sch. Dist., 1972-73, Granger (Tex.) Ind. Sch. Dist., 1976-77; English and Reading tchr. Taylor (Tex.) Ind. Sch. Dist., 1977-80; instr. U. Tex., Austin, 1981-87; ednl. cons. Coop. Learning Inst., Edina, Minn., 1987—. Co-author: Circles of Learning, 1984, 5th edit., 2002, Cooperation in the Classroom, 1984, 7th edit., 1998, Advanced Cooperative Learning, 1988, 3d edit., 1998, The Nuts and Bolts of Cooperative Learning, 1994, Cooperative Learning in the Classroom, 1994. Mem.: ASCD, Am. Ednl. Rsch. Assn., Phi Delta Kappa. American Baptist. Home and Office: PO Box 552 Taylor TX 76574-0552

HOLWAY, ELLEN TWOMBLY HAY, primary education educator; b. Summit, N.J. d. Allan and Ellen Clark (Twombly) Hay; m. William Crocker Holway III; children: Julie Ellen, Suzanne Clark, Cammy Twombly, Amy Hay, Daniel Hitchcock, Joanna Howland. AB in Psychology cum laude, Colby Coll., 1953; MEd, U. Lowell, 1975; postgrad., U. Mass., Lowell, 1987—, Boston U., 1978, Cen. New Eng. Coll., 1987. Cert. elem. tchr. and prin., perceptually handicapped, gen. supr., supt./asst.supt., Mass.; asst. psychologist, psychometrist, child welfare worker, pub. assistance caseworker, Maine. Asst. psychologist, acting dept. head Pineland Hosp. and Tng. Ctr., 1953-55; elem. tchr., specialist Odenton, Md., 1955-57; primary tchr., prof. devel. team leader Horace Mann, Maynard, Mass., 1972—; elem. asst. prin. Green Meadow Sch., 1994-97, elem. prin., 1997-99; MPS facilitator 21st century initiatives K-12, 1999—2000; freelance edn. adminstrn. cons. K-12, 2000—. Freelance edn. adminstrv. cons. K-12, 2000—; MPS facilitator 21st century initiatives K-12, 1999-2000; mem. adj. faculty dept. bus. and career edn. Boston U. Grad. Sch. Edn.; freelance editor, cons. pilot program liaison D.C. Heath Pub. Co.; developer, coord. Acton-Boxborough Student Activities Fund, numerous others; cons. Technol. R & D Corp.; mem. Mass. Math. Adv. Com., Mass. Sci. Adv. Com.; lead tchr. New Standards Project. Chmn. Acton and Acton-Boxborough Regional Sch. Com., Acton 250th Celebration; mem. MASC Assessment Com.; charter mem., bd. dirs., mem. pub. rels. com. Acton Hist. Soc.; jr. leader, coord. summer camp Girl Scouts U.S.A.; counselor citizenship badge, Eagle advisor Boy Scouts Am., Acton and Maynard; tchr., supr. ch. sch., numerous others. Mem. NEA, ASCD, Am. Ednl. Rsch. Assn., Nat. Sch. Bd. Assn., Nat. Career Edn. Assn (charter), Mass. ASCD, Mass. Assn. Sch. Coms., Mass. Tchrs. Assn., Maynard Edn. Assn., LWV (charter, v.-p., chmn. pub. rels.), Yarmouth Hist. Soc. (life), Phi Beta Kappa, Pi Lambda Theta, Pi Gamma Mu. Home: 48 Alcott St Acton MA 01720-5539 Office: Maynard Pub Schs 12 Bancroft St Maynard MA 01754-1702

HOLYER, ERNA MARIA, adult education educator, writer, artist; b. Weilheim, Bavaria, Germany, Mar. 15, 1925; d. Mathias and Anna Maria (Goldhofer) Schretter; m. Gene Wallace Holyer, Aug. 24, 1957 (dec. 1999). AA, San Jose Evening Coll., 1964; student, San Mateo Coll., 1965—67, San Jose State U., 1968—69, San Jose City Coll., 1980—81; DLitt, World U., 1984; DFA (hon.) (hon.), The London Inst. Applied Rsch, 1992. Freelance writer under pseudonym Ernie Holyer, 1960—; tchr. creative writing San Jose (Calif.) Met. Adult Edn., 1968—; artist, 1958—. Exhibited in group shows Crown Zellerbach Gallery, San Francisco, 1973, 74, 76, 77; I.B.C. Gallery, San Francisco, 1978 (medal of Congress, 1988, 89, 92, 94, Congress Challenge trophy, 1991), L.A., 1981, Cambridge, Eng., 1992, Cambridge, Mass., 1993, San Jose, Calif., 1993, Edinburgh, 1994, San Francisco, 1996. Author: Rescue at Sunrise, 1965, Steve's Night of Silence, 1966, A Cow for Hansel, 1967, At the Forest's Edge, 1969, Song of Courage, 1970, Lone Brown Gull, 1971, Shoes for Daniel, 1974, The Southern Sea Otter, 1975, Sigi's Fire Helmet, 1975, Reservoir Road Adventure, 1982, Wilderness Journey, Golden Journey, California Journey, 1997, Self-Help for Writers: Winners Show You How, 2002, Dangerous Secrets: A Young Girl's Travails Under the Nazis, 2003; contbr. articles to mags., newspapers and anthologies. Recipient Woman of Achievement Honor cert. San Jose Mercury-News, 1973, 74, 75, Lefoli award for excellence in adult edn. instr. Adult Edn. Senate, 1972, Women of Achievement awards League of Friends of Santa Clara County Commn., San Jose Mercury News, 1987, various art awards. Mem. N.L.A.P.W. Inc., World Univ Roundtable (doctoral). Home and Office: 1314 Rimrock Dr San Jose CA 95120-5611 E-mail: holyere@aol.com.

HOLZ, HANS HEINZ, philosophy educator; b. Frankfurt, Germany, Feb. 26, 1927; s. Friedrich and Martha Dorothea Berta (Kreiss) H.; m. Brigitte Klara Scheben (div. 1959); m. Silvia Elisabeth Markun, Apr. 20, 1979. PhD, U. Leipzig, 1969, U. Urbino, 2002. Freelance journalist, Frankfurt, 1945-56, Zurich, Switzerland, 1960—70; mem. editorial staff Deutsche Woche, Munich, 1957-59; chief dept. Abendstudio Hessischer Rundfunk, Frankfurt, 1962-64; prof. philosophy U. Marburg, Fed. Republic Germany, 1971-79, U. Groningen, Netherlands, 1979-97, prof. emeritus, 1997—. Founder, pres. Found. Ctr. for Philos. Studies, Sant' Abbondio. Author numerous books including Philosophische Theorie der bildenden Künste, vol. 3, 1996, Problemgeschichte der Dialektik, vol. 3, 1997, Selected Essays, 2 vols., 2003; editor: Selected Works of Leibniz, 1959-65; co-editor: Studien zur Dialektik, 33 vols., 1978-89, Dialektik, 24 vols., 1980-92, Topos, 1993—; contbr. articles to profl. jours. Recipient medal of honor, Verein Deutscher Ingenieure, 1986. Mem. Internat. Assn. for Dialectical Philosophy (pres. 1981-88, hon. pres. 1992—), Internat. Assn. for Legal and Social Philosophy (sec. 1951-54), Leibniz-Sozietaet Berlin. Home: PO Box 76 CH-6577 S Abbondio Switzerland Office: U Groningen Faculty Philosophy A-Weg 30 NL 9718 Groningen CW Netherlands

HOLZ, ROBERT KENNETH, retired geography educator; b. Kankakee, Ill., Nov. 3, 1930; s. Harry H. and Margaret (Conway) H.; m. Joyce F. Harpin, May 19, 1951; 1 child, Eric R. BA in Zoology, So. Ill. U., 1958, MA in Geography, 1959; PhD in Geography, Mich. State U., 1963. Asst. prof. U. Tex., Austin, 1962-67, assoc. prof., 1967-72, prof., 1972—, dir. ctr. for Middle Eastern Studies, 1991-99, Eric W. Zimmerman Regents prof., 1991-99, Eric W. Zimmerman Regents prof. emeritus, 1999—; ret., 1999. Cons. in field. Co-author: Mendes I, 1980; author, editor: The Surveillant Science, 2d edit., 1985. Staff sgt. USAF, 1951-55. Recipient Group Achievement award NASA, 1974, Urban Achievement award L.B.J. Sch. Pub. Affairs, 1984. Mem. Assn. Am. Geographers (chmn. remote sensing specialty group 1980-82, chmn. southwest div. 1971-72, medal for outstanding contbns. to remote sensing Remote Sensing Specialty Group 1998), Am. Soc. Photogrammetry, Tex. Assn. Coll. Tchrs., Am. Congress of Surveying and Mapping. Roman Catholic. Avocations: hunting, fishing, squash. Home: 2610 Fiset Dr Austin TX 78731-5614 Office: U Tex Dept Geography Austin TX 78712 E-mail: holzrj@aol.com.

HOLZER, MARC, public administrator educator; b. Feb. 28, 1945; s. Philip and Ann Lee (Blinder) H.; m. Madeleine Fuchs, Aug. 31, 1969; children: Matthew, Benjamin. BA in Polit. Sci., U. Rochester, 1966; MPA, U. Mich., 1967, PhD of Polit. Sci., 1971. Asst. prof. govt. and pub. adminstrn. John Jay Coll. CUNY, 1971-74, assoc. prof., 1975-79, prof., 1980-89; prof. I pub. adminstrn. Rutgers U., Newark, 1989—2002, prof. II pub. adminstrn., 2002—, chair grad. dept. pub. adminstrn., 2000—. Founder, exec. dir. Nat. Ctr. for Pub. Productivity, 1975—; founder, chmn. Internat. Productivity Network, 1988—; cons. internat. and fed. depts. agys., city, state and county agys.; dir. numerous funded projects in field; mem. Croton-Harmon Bd. Edn., 1984-87, pres. 1986-87; adv. acad. bd./bd. trustees Campus Arts & Scis., Athens. Author: (with others) Managing for Improved Productivity, 1981, (with Arie Halachmi) Public Sector Productivity, 1988, (with Virginia Cherry) Public Administration Research Guide, 1991, (with Kathe Callahan) Government at Work, 1998; editor: Productivity in Public Organizations, 1976, Public Productivity Handbook, 1991, (with K. Morris and W. Ludwin) Literature in Bureaucracy: Readings in Administrative Fiction, 1979, (with Ellen D. Rosen) Current Cases in Public Administration, 1981, (with Stuart Nagel) Productivity and Public Policy, 1984, (with Arie Halachmi) Strategic Issues in Public Sector Productivity, 1986, Competent Government, 1995, (with Vatche Gabrielian) Case Studies in Productive Public Management, 1995, (with Kathe Callahan and Joseph DeIorio) Reinventing New Jersey, 1995, Public Service: Callings, Commitments and Contributions, 2000, (with Byong-Joon Kim) Building Good Governance, 2002, (with Meng Zhong Zhang) Chinese Public Administration in Exploration, 2002; founder, editor-in-chief Public Productivity and Mgmt. Rev., 1975—, Pub. Voices, 1994—, Chinese Pub. Adminstrn. Review, 2002-, ASPA Classics Series, 1997—, (with Jay Shafritz) Selections from the International Encyclopedia of Public Adminstration, 2001; assoc. editor Internat. Ency. Pub. Policy and Adminstrn.; mem. editl. bd. Internat. Jour. Pub. Adminstrn., Pub. Adminstrn. Quar., Pub. Budgeting and Fin. Mgmt., The Pub. Mgr. (formerly The Bureaucrat), Jour. Non-Profit and Pub. Sector Mktg., Jour. Mgmt. History, Internat. Jour. Orgnl. Theory and Behavior, ASPA Classics, Internat. Rev. Pub. Adminstrn., Pub. Adminstrn. Rev., Pub. Adminstrn. and Mgmt.; contbr. numerous chpts. in books, articles to profl. jours. Founder, co-chairperson Pub. Adminstrn. Tchg. Roundtable, 1980—. Recipient Nat. Excellence in Tchg. award, Nat. Assn. Schs. Pub. Affairs & Adminstrn., 1998, Bd. Trustees award for Excellence in Rsch., Rutgers U., 2001, Southeastern Conf. Pub. Adminstrn. Sen. Peter Boorsma award, 2001, Bd. Trustees Pub. Svc. award, Rutgers U., 2002, Excellence award, Chinese Pub. Adminstrn. Soc., 2002; fellow Rockefeller Inst. Govt., 1986—87, World Acad. Productivity Sci., 2001—. Mem.: ASPA (chmn. nat. tng. com. 1981—82, 1983—84, nat. coun. 1982—85, chairperson mgmt. sci. sect 1981—82, 1989—90, pres. N.Y. Met. chpt. 1978—79, 0799—1980, chairperson sect. humanistic, artistic and reflective expression 1993—95, chair publs. com. 1993—94, nat. v.p. 1998—99, nat. pres.-elect 1999—2000, nat. pres. 2000—01, N.Y. Met. Outstanding Acad. award 1985, N.J. Outstanding Achievement award 1992, Donald C. Stone award 1994, Charles H. Levine award 2000, Mosher award Best Article (with Patricia Julnes) 2001, Wholey Disting. Scholarship award (with Patricia Julnes) 2001). Home: 4 Giglio Ct Croton On Hudson NY 10520-2005 Office: Rutgers U Hill Hall 7th Fl 360 King Blvd Newark NJ 07102-1801 E-mail: mholzer@wndromeda.rutgers.edu., mholzer@pipeline.com.

HOLZER, TAMERA LEE-PHILLIS, middle school educator; b. Chillicothe, Ohio, Apr. 8, 1961; d. William Lee and Betty Lou (Reeder) Phillis; m. Timothy John Holzer, July 1, 1989; 1 child, Jordyn Elizabeth Lee. AA, Mich. Christian, 1981; BA in Elem. Edn., Harding U., 1983; MA, The Ohio State U., 1989; degree in ednl. adminstrn. and supervision, specialist degree in ednl. adminstrn., Ga. State U., 1995. Elem. tchr. Prairie Lincoln Elem. Sch., Columbus, Ohio, 1983-89; tchr. Pinckneyville Middle Sch., Norcross, Ga., 1989-92, tchr. Quest, 1992—. County mem. Tchrs. as Leaders, Norcross, 1990—, OBE Strategic Team, Norcross, 1991-94, Tech. Subgroup, Norcross, 1992; chairperson Interdisciplinary Task Force, Norcross, 1991; freelance writer in field. Upreach leader Campus Ch. of Christ, Norcross, 1991-94. Named 1992 Coach of Yr., Gwinnett County. Mem. ASCD, Am. Ednl. Rsch. Assn. Republican. Avocations: basketball, skiing, softball, travel, biking. Home: care Kim Eagle 7936 Morris Rd Hilliard OH 43026-9713 Office: Pinckneyville Middle Sch 5440 W Jones Bridge Rd Norcross GA 30092-2021 also: 10 Wallace St Greenwich Point NSW 2065 Australia

HOLZNER, BURKART, sociologist, educator; b. Tilsit, Germany, Apr. 28, 1931; came to U.S., 1957, naturalized, 1965; s. Hans Otto and Brigitte (Prenzel) H.; children by previous marriage: Steven, Daniel, Claire; m. Leslie Salmon-Cox; stepchildren: Sara Ruth Salmon-Cox, Weir Becket Strange. Student, U. Munich, 1949-52, 53-54, U. Wis., 1952-53, postgrad., 1957-59; Diplom Psychologe, U. Bonn, 1957, Dr.Phil., 1958. Grad. asst., acting instr. U. Wis., 1958-60; asst. prof. U. Pitts., 1960-63, assoc. prof., 1963-65, prof., chmn. sociology dept., 1966-80, dir. bd. visitors field staff Learning Research and Devel. Center, 1964-66, 71-78, dir. Univ. Ctr. for Internat. Studies, 1980-2000, prof. Univ. Ctr. for Internat. Studies, 1998—, disting. svc. prof. internat. studies, 1999—2003, also sr. rsch. assoc., prof. emeritus, 2003—. Assoc. sociologist, assoc. dir. Social Sci. Rsch. Inst., U. Hawaii, 1965-66; vis. prof. sociology, dir. Social Rsch. Centre, Chinese U. of Hong Kong, 1969-70, external examiner in sociology, 1995-98; vis. prof. U. Augsburg, 1977, Chinese Acad. Social Scis., Beijing, 1979, 80; cons. Nat. Inst. Edn., Westinghouse Electric Corp.; mem. exec. com. Pa. Coun. for Internat. Edn., 1980-89, chmn., 1980-83, 88-89. Author: Amerikanische und deutsche Psychologie, 1958, Völkerpsychologie, 1960, Reality Construction in Society, rev. edit, 1972, (with John Marx) Knowledge Application: The Knowledge System in Society, 1979; editor: (with Roland Robertson) Identity and Authority, Explorations in the Theory of Society, 1980, (with Jiri Nehnevajsa) Organizing for Social Research, 1981, (with Zdenek Suda) Directions of Change: Modernization Theory, Research and Reality, 1981, (with Andrew Dinniman) Education for International Competence in Pennsylvania, 1988; co-editor Knowledge: Creation, Distribution, Utilization, 1985, Knowledge in Society, 1987-89. Mem. dist. export council U.S. Dept. Commerce. Recipient Philip R.A. May award for internat. svc., 1991; named hon. citizen of Johnstown, Pa., hon. mem. U. Augsburg, 1990. Mem. Am. Sociol. Assn., North Central Sociol. Assn., Pa. Sociol. Assn., Sociol. Rsch. Assn., Sozialwissenschaftlicher Studienkreis für Internationale Probleme, Internat. Soc. for Comparative Study of Civilizations (mem. U.S. coun., v.p. 1977-79), Assn. Internat. Edn. Adminstrs. (exec. com. 1986—, pres. 1990-91, Charles Klasek award for career achievement in internat. edn. 2000, sr. counselor 2001—), World Federalist Assn. Pitts. (pres. 1996-2001). Home: 1700 Grandview Ave Apt 801 Pittsburgh PA 15211-1006 Office: U Pitts Dept Sociology U Ctr Internat Studies 2J26 Power Hall Pittsburgh PA 15260 E-mail: holzner@ucis.pitt.edu.

HOLZSCHUH, SUSAN KAY, elementary school educator; b. Florissant, Mo., Sept. 1, 1968; d. Stephen John and Judith Ann (Huettenmeyer) Niederwimmer; m. Joseph James Holzschuh Jr., Sept. 30, 1989; children: Joseph V, Andrew, Kristina. BSE, Cen. Mo. State U., 1990; MSE, Ctrl. Mo. State Univ., 1999. Tchr. Strasburg C-3, 1994—2000, Moniteau City C-1, 2000—. Mem. Luth. Student Assn. (sec.-treas. 1987), Kappa Delta Pi. Lutheran. Avocations: reading, cooking. Home: 1604 W Main St Jefferson City MO 65109-1243

HOM, MEI LING, artist, educator; b. New Haven, Aug. 2, 1951; BA, Kirkland Coll., Clinton, N.Y., 1973; MFA, Alfred U., 1987. Asst. prof. art C.C. of Phila., 1983—2002, assoc. prof. art, 2003—. Mem. exhbn. com. Phila. Art Alliance, 1998—2002; interdisciplinary arts adv. panel Pa. Coun. Arts, Harrisburg, 1993—95, arts in edn. adv. panelist, 1995; installed Offering for Balch Inst., 1998, Golden Mountain for Phila. Mus. Art, 1998, Silkworm Grind for Japanese Am. Nat. Mus., L.A., 2001, Neuberger Mus. Art, Purchase, NY, 2001, Waxed Memory, Meguro Mus. Art, Tokyo, 2001; commd. installation Chinawedge for Pa. Conv. Ctr., Phila., 1994, Moss Ghosts, 2000. Visual artist fellow grantee Nat. Endowment for Arts, 1994, grantee for excellence Leeway Found., 1999, grantee Independence Found., 2003; fellow in visual arts Pa. Coun. on Arts, 1991, 95; creative artist exch. fellow Nat. Endowment for Arts and Japan Friendship Commn., 1996, Pew fellow, 1998. Mem. Asian Am. Arts Alliance, Asian Arts Initiative, Ctr. for Book Arts (artist mem.), Women's Studio Workshop (artist mem.), Headlands Ctr. for Arts (Marin County, Calif.), Coll. Art Assn.

HOMAN, RICHARD WARREN, neurologist, academic administrator, medical educator; b. N.Y.C., July 28, 1940; s. H. Frank and Irmgard Homan; m. Katherine Poulos, June 16, 1963; children: Gregory William, Christopher Allen. BA, Colgate U., 1962; MD, SUNY, 1966; MA, U. Tex. Med. Br., 1999-2001. Diplomate Am. Bd. Psychiatry and Neurology, Am. Bd. Clin. Neurophysiology; cert. Nat. Bd. Med. Examiners. Resident in neurology UCLA, 1970; fellow in neurophysiology Albert Einstein Coll. Medicine, Bronx, NY, 1972—74; asst. prof. neurology U. Tex., Southwestern Med. Sch. and Dallas VA Med. Ctr., 1974—82, assoc. prof. neurology, chief neurology svc., 1982—89; prof., chmn. neurology Med. Coll. Ohio, Toledo, 1989—94; chmn. neurology Tex. Tech. U. Health Sci. Ctr., Lubbock, 1994—97, prof. neuropsychiatry and behavioral medicine, pharm. practice, pharm. scis., dir. Ctr. Neuropsychiat. Studies, 1997—99; bioethics cons., 2001—; mem. bioethics faculty Southwestern Med. Sch., Dallas, 2002—. Examiner Am. Bd. Clin. Neurophysiology, 1981-94; cons. Tex. State Bd. Med. Examiners, Austin, 1995-2000. Editor (collected sci. manuscripts) Rational Polypharmacy, 1996; contbr. chpts. to books. Mem. profl. adv. bd. Dallas Epilepsy Found., 1985-87, Epilepsy Found. N.W. Ohio, Toledo, 1989-94; mediator South Plains Ctr. for Dispute Resolution, Lubbock, 1998. Fellow Am. Electroencepalographic Soc., Am. Acad. Neurology; mem. Am. Epilepsy Soc., Phi Beta Kappa. Avocations: scuba diving, playing harp. Home: 1629 Handley Dr Dallas TX 75208 E-mail: rwhoman@sbcloal.net.

HOMAN, THOMASITA, English language and literature educator; b. Pawnee City, Nebr., Aug. 7, 1938; d. Richard William and Mary Veronica Homan. BA in Edn., Mt. St. Scholastica, 1970; Reading Specialist, Cardinal Stritch Coll., 1973; MA in English, Iowa State U., 1979. Tchr. jr. high sch., Nortonville, Kans., 1969-70; tchr. Title I Atchison, Kans., 1972-77; primary coord., tchr. ACES Elem. Sch., Atchison, 1970-77; dir. campus ministry Benedictine Coll., Atchison, 1987-89, dir. alumni, 1987-89, asst. prof. English, 1979—. Mem. Assoc. Collegiate Press Evaln. Bd.; cons. in field. Poetry editor Benedictines; mem. editl. staff Atchison Benedictine Newsletter, 1983-2001, Threshold, 2001—; contbr. articles to profl. jours. Organizer Women's Day Presentation, 1980-81; mem. Atchison Art Assn., 1996-98. Mem. Phi Kappa Phi. Roman Catholic. Avocations: reading, walking, foreign travel. Home: 801 S 8th St Atchison KS 66002 Office: Benedictine Coll 1020 N 2d St Atchison KS 66002

HONEGGER, GITTA, language educator; PhD in Theater, U. Vienna, Austria. Prof. dramaturgy and dramatic criticism Yale Sch. Drama; stage dir. Yale Repertory Theatre; chair dept. drama Cath. U. Am., Washington; prof. theatre and English Ariz. State U., Tempe, Ariz. Author: Thomas Bernhard: The Making of an Austrian, 2001, Thomas Bernhard: Was ist das für ein Narr, 2002; contbg. editor Yale Theater Mag. Fellow, John Simon Guggenheim Meml. Found., 2003. Office: Ariz State U Dept English Tempe AZ 85287-0302*

HONEYCUTT, BRENDA, secondary education educator; Tchr. sci. Fort Mill (S.C.) Middle Sch.; chmn. sci. dept. Rep. Nat. Mid. Sch. Conf. Recipient hon. mention Outstanding Earth Sci. Tchr. award Nat. Assn. of Geology Teachers, 1992, S.C. Earth Sci. Tchr. Yr., 1992. Office: Fort Mill Middle Sch 200 Highway 160 Byp Fort Mill SC 29715-8746 E-mail: honeycuttb@fort-mill.k12.sc.us.

HONG, HOWARD VINCENT, library administrator, philosophy educator, editor, translator; b. Wolford, N.D., Oct. 19, 1912; BA, St. Olaf Coll., 1934; postgrad., Wash. State Coll., 1934-35; PhD, U. Minn., 1938; postgrad., U. Copenhagen, 1938-39; D.Litt. (hon.), McGill U., Montreal, 1977; D.D. (hon.), Trinity Sem., Columbus, Ohio, 1983; D.H.L. (hon.), Carleton Coll., 1987; ThD (hon.), U. Copenhagen, 1992. With English dept. Wash. State Coll., 1934-35; with Brit. Mus., 1937; mem. faculty dept. philosophy St. Olaf Coll., Northfield, Minn., 1938-78, asst. prof. philosophy, 1940-42, assoc. prof., 1942-47, prof., 1947-78, chmn. Ford Found. self-study com., 1955-56, dir. Kierkegaard Library, 1972-84. Vis. lectr. U. Minn., 1955; mem. Nat. Lutheran Council Scholarship and Grant Rev. Bd., 1958-66; lectr. Holden Village, Washington, 1963-70; mem. Minn. Colls. Grant Rev. Bd., 1970 Author, editor, contbr.: Integration in the Christian Liberal Arts College, 1956, books most recent This World and the Church, 1955; editor, contbg. author: Christian Faith and the Liberal Arts, 1960; co-editor, translator: (with Edna H. Hong) works by Gregor Malantschuk, numerous works by Soren Kierkegaard, Soren Kierkegaard's Journals and Papers, Vol. I, 1968 (Nat. Book award for transl. 1968), Søren Kierkegaard's Journals and Papers, Vol. II, 1970, Søren Kierkegaard's Journals and Papers, Vol. III-IV, 1975, Søren Kierkegaard's Journals and Papers, V-VII, 1978, The Controversial Kierkegaard (Gregor Malantschuk), 1980, Two Ages (Søren Kierkegaard), 1978, The Sickness unto Death (Søren Kierkegaard), 1980, The Corsaair Affair (Søren Kierkegaard), 1981, Fear and Trembling-Repetition, 1983, Philosophical Fragments-Johannes Climacus, 1985, Either/Or, 1987, Stages on Life's Way, 1988, The Concept of Irony, 1989, For Self-Examination and Judge for Yourself!, 1990, Eighteen Upbuilding Discourses, 1990, Practice in Christianity, 1991, Concluding Unscientific Postscript, 1992, Three Discourses on Imagined Occasions, 1993, Upbuilding Discourses in Various Spirits, 1993, Works of Love, 1995, Without Authority, 1997, Point of View, 1998, The Moment and Late Writings, 1998, The Book on Adler, 1998, The Essential Kierkegaard, 2000; gen. editor Kierkegaard's Writings, 1972—. Field sec. War Prisoners Aid, U.S., Scandinavia, and Germany, 1943-46; sr. rep. Service to Refugees, Luth. World Fedn., Germany and Austria, 1947-49; sr. field officer refugee div. World Council Chs., Germany, 1947-48; curator Kierkegaard House Foundation, 1999—. Decorated Order of Dannebrog (Denmark), Order of the Three Stars (Latvia); recipient award Minn. Humanities Commn., 1983, Minn. Forest Stewardship award DNR, 2002; fellow Am.-Scandinavian Found.-Denmark, 1938-39, Am. Council Learned Socs., 1952-53, Rockefeller Found., 1959, sr. rsch. fellow Fulbright Commn., 1959-60, 64, sr. fellow NEH, 1970-71; grantee NEH, 1972-73; publ. grantee Carlsberg Found., 1974, 86, 88, editing-translating grantee NEH, 1978-90, 95-98. Home: 5174 E 90 Old Dutch Rd Northfield MN 55057 Office: St Olaf Coll Kierkegaard Libr Northfield MN 55057

HONHART, FREDERICK LEWIS, III, academic director; b. San Diego, Oct. 29, 1943; s. Frederick Lewis Jr. and Rossiter (Hyde) H.; m. Barbara Ann Baker, Aug. 27, 1966; children: David Frederick, Stephen Charles. BA, Wayne State U., 1966; MA, Case-Western Res. U., 1968, PhD, 1972. Cert. archivist. Field rep. Ohio Hist. Soc., Columbus, 1972-73; asst. dir. univ. archives & hist. collections Mich. State U., East Lansing, 1974-79, dir., 1979—. Mem. adv. bd. Mich. Nat. Hist. Publs. & Records Commn., Lansing, 1979—; cons. in field. Creator: (microcomputer sys.), MicroMARC:amc, 1986 (Coker prize 1988), MicroMARC for Integrated Format, 1995; contbr. articles to profl. jours. Mem. Internat. Coun. Archives (steering com. sci. and univ. archives sect. 2000-2004), Soc. Am. Archivists, Mich. Archival Assn. (pres. 1984-86), Midwest Archives Conf. (chair program com. 1982, 94, chair Author Awards com. 2001). Avocations: reading, sports, flying. Office: Mich State U 101 Conrad Hall East Lansing MI 48824-1327

HONOUR, LYNDA CHARMAINE, research scientist, educator, psychotherapist; b. Orange, NJ, Aug. 9, 1949; d. John Henry, Jr. and Evelyn Helena Roberta (Pietrowski) H. BA, Boston U., 1976; MA, Calif. State U., Fullerton, 1985, UCLA, 1989; PhD, U. So. Calif., 1997. Lic. marriage, family and child psychotherapist and psychologist, Calif. Prof. psychology Pepperdine U., Malibu, Calif., 1989-95; pvt. practice mind-body behavioral medicine, including clin. psychoneuroimmunology and psychoneuroendomcrinology LaJolla, Calif., 1991—. Clin. and vis. prof. throughout so. Calif., including Calif. Sch. Profl. Psychology, Calif. State U., Long Beach, Calif. State U., Northridge, 1989—; rsch. scientist in neuroendocrinology and neurochemistry in numerous labs including 3 Nobel Prize winning rsch. teams; condr. rsch. Neuropsychiat. Inst., Brain Rsch. Inst., Mental Retardation Rsch. Ctr., UCLA, Tulane U. Med. Sch., V.A. Med. Ctr., New Orleans, Salk Inst. Biol. Studies; rsch. cons. U. Calif. Med. Ctr., Irvine; cons. in rsch. or psychotherapy, 1976—; guest expert on safety issues regarding magnetic imaging Premiere Radio Network, 2001; rsch. scientist in neuroendocrinology and neurochemistry in numerous labs.; condr. rsch. Neuropsychiat. Inst., Brain Rsch. Inst., Mental Retardation Rsch. Ctr., UCLA, Tulane U. Med. Sch., V.A. Med. Ctr., New Orleans, Salk Inst. Biol. Studies; rsch. cons. U. Calif. Med. Ctr., Irvine, Salk Inst., others; cons. Thomson Internat. Pub.; hon. chmn., Bus. Adv. Coun. Nat. Rep. Congl. Com. Contbr. articles to profl. jours. including Hosp. Practice, Peptides, Physiology and Behavior, Pharmacology, Biochemistry and Behavior, others. Hon. chair bus. adv. coun. Nat. Rep. Congl. Com. Rsch. grantee Organon Internat. Rsch. Group, The Netherlands, 1984-88. Mem. AAAS, APA, Am. Psychological Soc., Soc. for Neurosci., Internat. Behavioral Neurosci. Soc., Internat. Brain Rsch. Orgn., Calif. Assn. Marriage and Family Psychotherapists, N.Y. Acad. Scis., Sons and Daus. of Pearl Harbor Survivors, Psi Chi. Roman Catholic. Achievements include identification of a peptide which facilitates and another peptide inhibits learning and memory task performance permanently in a developmental paradigm in mice; and facilitation peptide can permanently reverse induced learning/memory deficit, with implications for mental retardation and other learning/memory deficit treatment; mem. research team which isolated and characterized corticotropic hormone releasing factor; delineated various effects of peptides on behavior including bipolar disorders, endogenous depression, mania and others; research in risks associated with MRI exposure. Avocations: professional musician, artist, mind-related issues, time-space travel involving the unified field theory, metaphysics. Office: PO Box 369 Santa Monica CA 90406-0369

HOOD, DONALD CHARLES, university administrator, psychology educator; b. Merrick, N.Y., June 2, 1942; s. David and Jessie Theresa (Vetter) H.; m. Nancy Ellen Epstein, Nov. 27, 1978. BA, Harpur Coll.-SUNY, Binghamton, 1965; MS, Brown U., 1968, PhD, 1970. Asst. prof. Columbia U., N.Y.C., 1969-73, assoc. prof., 1973-78, prof. psychology, 1978—, James F. Bender prof. psychology, 1990—, v.p. arts & sci., 1982-87, chmn. psychology dept., 1975-78. Contbr. articles to profl. jours. Trustee Smith Coll., 1989—99, vice chair, 1991—99; trustee Harry Guggenheim Found., 1996—; trustee (fellow) Brown U., 2002—. USPHS fellow, 1967-69, N.Y. State Coll. teaching fellow, 1965-67. Fellow: Optical Soc., Soc. Exptl. Psychology; mem.: Ea. Psychol. Assn., Assn. Rsch. Vision and Ophthalmology. Home: 450 Riverside Dr New York NY 10027-6801 Office: 415 Schernerhorn Hall 116th St And Broadway New York NY 10027 E-mail: dch3@columbia.edu.

HOOD, LAMARTINE FRAIN, agriculture educator, former dean; b. Johnstown, Pa., Feb. 25, 1937; s. Lamartine and Marion Camm (Frain) H.; m. Emeline Rose Harpster, June 18, 1960; children: Thomas Gregory, Christopher Michael, Sandra Beth. BS, Pa. State U., 1959, PhD, 1968; MS, U. Minn., 1963. Asst. prof. Cornell U., Ithaca, N.Y., 1968-74, assoc. prof., 1974-80, prof. food sci., 1980-86, assoc. dir. Agr. Experiment Station, 1980-83, assoc. dir. office of rsch., 1980-86, dir. N.Y. State Agr. Experiment Sta. Geneva, N.Y., 1983-86; dean Coll. Agr. Sci., dir. Agr. Expt. Sta., dir. Coop. Ext. Pa. State U., University Park, 1986-95, prof., 1986—. Mem. adv. bd. Chase Lincoln Bank, Geneva, 1984-86; chmn. bd. dirs. ADEC, 1994-95. Author/editor: Carbohydrates & Health, 1977; contbr. articles to profl. jours. and chpts. for books. Fellow Inst. Food Technologists; mem. Am. Assn. Cereal Chemists (William F. Geddes Meml. Lectureship award 1984, pres. 1987-88, chmn. bd. 1988-89), Ithaca Geneva, State Coll. Rotary Club, Gamma Sigma Delta, Phi Lambda Upsilon. Home: 1694 Princeton Dr State College PA 16803-3257 Office: Pa State U 106 Agrl Admisntn Bldg University Park PA 16802

HOOD, LEROY EDWARD, molecular biologist, educator; b. Missoula, Mont., Oct. 10, 1938; s. Thomas Edward and Myrtle Evylan (Wadsworth) H.; m. Valerie Anne Logan, Dec. 14, 1963; children: Eran William, Marqui Leigh Jennifer. BS, Calif. Inst. Tech., 1960, PhD in Biochemistry, 1968; MD, Johns Hopkins U., 1964. Med. officer USPHS, 1967-70; staff scientist Pub. Health Svc., Bethesda, Md., 1967-70; sr. investigator Nat. Cancer Inst., 1967-70; asst. prof. biology Calif. Inst. Tech., Pasadena, 1970-73, assoc. prof., 1973-75, prof., 1975-92, Bowles prof. biology, 1977-92, chmn. div. biology, 1980-89; Gates prof. molecular biotech., chmn. bd. U. Wash. Sch. Medicine, Seattle, 1992—2000; pres. Instit. for Systems Biology, 2000—. Dir. NSF Sci. and Tech. Ctr. for Molecular Biotech., 1989—2001. Author: (with others) Biochemistry, a Problems Approach, 1974, Molecular Biology of Eukaryotic Cells, 1975, Immunology, 1978, Essential Concepts of Immunology, 1978, The Code of Codes: Scientific and Social Issues in the Human Genome Project, 1992; co-editor: Advances in Immunology, 1987, Genetics: From Genes to Genomics, 1999. Co-recipient, Albert Lasker Basic Medical Research Award, 1987, recipient Scientist of the Year Award, 1993, R&D Magazine, Kyoto Prize, 2002, Lemelson prize MIT, 2003. Mem. NAS, Am. Assn. Immunologists, Am. Assn. Sci., Am. Acad. Arts and Scis., Sigma Xi, Am. Philosophical Soc. Avocations: mountaineering, rockclimbing, photography. Office: Instit for Sytems Biology 1441 34th St Seattle WA 98103

HOOD, LUANN SANDRA, special education educator; b. Bklyn., Jan. 10, 1955; d. Louie A. and Sylvia M. (Hall) Mayo; m. Stephen J. Hood. BA, St. Joseph's Coll., Bklyn., 1976; MS in Edn., Bklyn. Coll., 1979. Cert. tchr. N,K, 1-6, spl. edn., N.Y.C. lic. Edn. counselor adolescents Am. Indian Comty. House, Inc., N.Y.C., 1977-79; tchr. children with retarded mental devel. Pub. Sch. 273, Bklyn., 1979-83; tchr. early childhood Pub. Sch. 128, Bklyn., 1983-94; tchr. emotionally handicapped Pub. Sch.215, Bklyn., 1994-95; tchr. learning disabled Pub. Sch. 101, Bklyn., 1995-99, tchr. hard of hearing, 1999—. Mem. sch. leadership team, 1997—. Exec. sec. bd. trustees Am. Indian Cmty. House, Inc., N.Y.C., 1980-91. Regents scholar N.Y. State Edn. Dept., 1972; grantee Indian League of the Americas, Inc. 1972-75, Thunderbird Am. Indian Dancers, Inc., 1972-75, Internat. Order of King's Daughters and Sons, 1976. Mem. Coun. for Exceptional Children, N.Y. State Tchrs. of Handicapped. Democrat. Roman Catholic. Avocation: photography.

HOOD, MICHAEL LEE, psychologist, clinical researcher, educator; b. Springfield, Mo., July 17, 1959; s. Norvell Dennis and Beverly Anne (Vitzthum) H.; m. Rebecca Jane Apone-Hood; children: Rhonda Jo, Jody Sunshine, Robin, Randal Eric. A Gen. Studies, Ind. U.-Purdue U., Indpls., 1991; cert. psychol. testing, U. Ark., 1993; B Gen. Studies, Ind. U., Bloomington, 1996; postgrad., U. Iowa, 1992-93; MA in Psychology magna cum laude, So. Calif. U., 1999, PhD in Psychology magna cum laude, 2002. Dir. Psychol. Rsch. Assocs., Bolivar, Mo., 1991—. Tchr., facilitator Non-Traditional Edn. and Reading Svcs., Ft. Madison, Iowa, 1990-97, dir., pres., 1993-97; cons., assessor Newport, Bell & Oxley, attys., Davenport, Iowa, 1992-93. With U.S. Army, 1977—79. Mem. ASCD, Am. Psychol. Soc., Soc. for Psychol. Study Social Issues, Am. Assn. for Adult and Continuing Edn., Literacy Vols. Am. (cert. tutor and workshop leader), Inc., Am. Edn. Rsch. Assn., Ind. U. Alumni Assn., So. Calif. U. Alumni Assn., People for Ethical Treatment Animals, Toastmasters Internat. (v.p. edn. 2002, pres. 2003), Phi Theta Kappa. Native Am. Religion (Cherokee). Avocations: writing poetry, astronomy, nature walks, horseback riding, playing chess. Office: Psychol Rsch Assocs 1312 E 490th Rd Bolivar MO 65613-8159

HOODENPYLE, SANDRA KAY, elementary education educator; b. Carson City, Mich., Oct. 10, 1950; d. John Milton and Pansy E. Spohn; m. Don Lynn Hoodenpyle, June 8, 1973; children: Michael Lee, James T., Christina Marie. BS, N.W. Nazarene Coll., Nampa, Idaho, 1972; postgrad., No. Ariz. U., 1972—, U. Phoenix, 1985—, Brigham Young U., 1992. Cert. elem. edn. with endorsements in libr. sci. and ESL. Libr. Page (Ariz.) Unified Sch. Dist., 1972-74, 4th grade tchr., 1974-77, 2nd grade tchr., 1977-78, purchasing clk., 1984-90, 6th grade tchr., 1990—2002, instl. facilitator, 2002—, instr. facilitator, 2002—. Sec., mem. Lake Powell Ch. of the Nazarene, 1972—, laywoman, 1992, pres. missionary soc. Named Laywoman of Yr., Lake Powell Ch. of the Nazarene, Page, 1992; recipient Disting. Svc. award, 2003. Mem. Nat. Coun. Tchrs. English, Nat. Coun. Social Studies Tchrs. Republican. Avocations: hobbies, oil painting, cooking, reading, cross-stitching. Office: Page Middle Sch PO Box 1927 Page AZ 86040-1927 E-mail: shoodenpyle@pageud.k12.az.us.

HOOD-MINCEY, HOLLIE NANNETTE, secondary education educator; b. Chester, Pa., Dec. 16, 1963; d. William A. and Violetta (Kilson) Hood; m. David Melvin Mincey, Aug. 17, 1991. BS, Lincoln U., 1986; MS, Morgan State U., 1989. Cet. secondary tchr., Pa. Tchr. Balt. City Pub. Schs., 1987-89; psychoeducator Villa Maria Sch., Balt., 1989—. Owner, cons. Romincey's Christian Attractions, Balt., 1992—. Author: Villa Maria Music Guide, 1990. Pub. rels. Restoration Life Ch., Ellicott City, Md., 1991-93, head adminstr. Christian sch., 1992—; minister Pass the Word Ministries, Balt., 1992—. Named Outstanding Woman of Yr., 1989; faculty scholar Morgan State U., 1988, 89. Mem. Music Educators Nat. Conf., Gamma Sigma Sigma (pres. 1987-90), Mu Phi Alpha. Avocations: reading, singing, counseling, swimming, traveling. Home: 9711 Kerrigan Ct Randallstown MD 21133-2501

HOOFARD, JANE MAHAN DECKER, retired elementary school educator; b. Grand Junction, Colo., Apr. 29, 1946; d. Nat Don and Bernita Margaret (Williams) Mahan; m. William Edward Hoofard, Mar. 6, 1982; children: Lynna Kay Decker, Keith Dale. BA, Ft. Lewis Coll., 1968. Cert. tchr. Calif. Tchr. 3rd, 6th grades Shasta Lake Union Sch. Dist., Summit City, Calif., 1968-73; tchr., MGM cons., coord., brain drain writer Shasta County Schs., Redding, Calif., 1975-81; tchr. 2nd, 3rd grades Manton (Calif.) Joint Union Sch. Dist., 1987-89; elem. and mid. sch. tchr. Mineral (Calif.) Elem. Sch. Dist., 1989—2001; ret., 2001. Writer, editor, pub.: AAUW. Mem.: Calif. Ret. Tchrs. Assn. (pres. divsn. 9 Glenn/Tehama Counties 2003—). Home: 19389 Hwy 36W Red Bluff CA 96080

HOOKER, OLIVIA J. psychologist, educator; b. Muskogee, Okla., Feb. 12, 1915; d. Samuel David and Anita Juliette (Stigger) H. BS, Ohio State U., 1937; MA, Columbia U., 1947; PhD, U. Rochester, N.Y., 1962. Cert. sch. psychologist, N.Y. Elem. tchr. Columbus (Ohio) Pub. Schs., 1937-45; clin. psychologist dept. mental hygiene State of N.Y., Albion, 1948-51, Bedford Hills, 1951-57, Rochester, 1955-57, research psychologist dept. mental hygiene Letchworth Village, 1957-61; sch. psychologist Bur. Child Guidance, N.Y.C., 1951-52; psychologist Kennedy Child Studies Ctr., N.Y.C., 1961-64, dir. psychol. svcs., 1964-83; assoc. prof. Fordham U., Bronx, N.Y., 1974-85. Cons. St. Benedict's Day Care Ctr., N.Y.C., 1976—, Fred S. Keller Sch., Yonkers, N.Y., 1987-99. Trustee Terence Cardinal Cooke Health Svcs. Coun., N.Y.C., 1984-96; mem. adv. bd. Child Life program Westchester County Med. Ctr., Valhalla, N.Y., 1985-99; v.p. White Plains NAACP, 1985-87, White Plains Sr. Pers. Employment Coun., 1987-96; tutor Literacy Vols. Am., 1987—; bd. dirs. White Plains Child Day Care Assn., 1988-2000, Vis. Nurse Assn. Westchester, 1988-94; chmn. adminstrv. bd. Trinity United Meth. Ch., 1985-87. Served with women's res. USCG, 1945-46. U. Rochester fellow, 1955-56; recipient Women's award Women's History Assn., 1986. Fellow APA (div. on devel. disability), Am. Assn. Mental Retardation. Avocations: creative writing, gardening, music. Office: Fordham U Dept Psychology Bronx NY 10458

HOOKS, MARY LINDA, adult education educator; b. Albany, Ga., Apr. 22; d. Tobe Sr. and Linda (Anthony) Cain; m. Arthur Franklin Hooks; children: Angela, Darryl, Stanley, Ashia. BS, Albany (Ga.) State Coll., 1961; MS, Fla. State U., 1985. Tchr. bus. subjects, Chgo., 1961-64; course writer, instr. McNamara Skills Ctr., Detroit, 1964-74; course designer, instr. YWCA, Detroit, 1965-66; continuing edn. instr. Mary Grove Coll., Detroit, 1974-75; tchr. math. Pinetta Jr. High Sch., Madison, Fla., 1976—; tchr. media/job skills Jefferson County High Sch., Monticello, Fla., 1977-78; tchr. reading/kindergarten Jefferson Elem. Sch., Monticello, 1978-79; coord., facilitator, instr. bus. edn. and adult edn. Jefferson County Adult Sch., Monticello, 1979-98; owner MAL Found., Tallahassee, Fla., 1999—. Cons. Edwards Enterprise Sch., Albany, 1989-91; owner pvt. edn. svc., MAL Found. Inc., Tallahassee. Cons. Youth Street (television show). Judge, vol. 4-H Jefferson County, Monticello, 1985—; bd. dirs. Greenville (Fla.) Day Care Ctr., 1988-90, corr. sec., 1988-90; candidate for Supt. Pub. Schs., Monticello, 1988; mem. adv. bd. United Found., Detroit, 1969-74; vol. Youth Ctr., Greenville City Hall, 1988-90; charter mem. Fla. Adult Literacy Resource Ctr., 1993—. Recipient Dedication/Appreciation award McNamara Skills Ctr., Detroit, 1973-74, Jefferson County 4-H, 1985-91, others. Mem. LINK-Progressive Women's Club, Fla. Adult Literacy Resource Ctr. Ptnrs. (charter), Internat. Platform Assn., Kiwanis, Fla. Adult Assn. Avocations: researching herbs, collecting antiques, gardening, needlework, spectator sports. Office: Jefferson County Adult Sch 760 E Washington St Monticello FL 32344-2549

HOOKS, VANDALYN LAWRENCE, former elementary school educator; b. Dyersburg, Tenn., Feb. 26, 1935; d. James Bridges and Mary Lucille (Anderson) Lawrence; m. Floyd Lester Hooks, June 15, 1952; children: Lawrence James, Steven Lester. BA, Ky. Wesleyan U., 1967; MA, Western Ky. U., 1970, edn. specialist, 1976; postgrad., U. Tenn., 1975. Tchr. Owensboro Bd. Edn., Ky., 1967-71, adminstr., 1976-85; dir. career experience Western Ky. U., Bowling Green, 1971-73; dir. career edn., elem. tchr. Owensboro Daviess County Sch. Dist., 1967-71, elem. prin., 1974-78, 83-85, adminstr., elem. prin. dir. career experience, 1976-85; curriculum developer Career Experience Voc. Edn., Frankfort, Ky., 1971-76; cons. Motivation Workshop, Bowling Green, 1971-76, Decision and Goal Setting, 1971-76. Editor: Ky. Assn. Elem. Prin. Jour., 1977-81; editor, pub. Ednl. Alert, 1985-90, A Crash Course in Ednl. Reform, 1989, A Crash

Course in Ednl. Reform, 1989, A Dangerous Liaison A Tax Exempt Foundation and Two Teacher Unions, 1990, The Alphabet Books, 1991, Caution! Change Agents at Work, 1992, A System for Control PPBS, 1994; contbr. articles to profl. jours. Organizer, Ky. Coun. for Better Edn., Owensboro, 1984; legis. advisor Eagle Forum, leadership forum, Washington, 1985, 86-87, 88-92; Rep. legis. rschr. Recipient Presdl. award Ky. Wesleyan Coll., 1966. Mem. Pro Family Forum, Eagle Forum, Plymouth Rock Found. Republican. Baptist. Address: 3238 Peavine Rd Lakeshore Terr #109 Crossville TN 38558

HOOPER, BILLY ERNEST, retired medical association administrator; b. Pawnee City, Nebr., June 22, 1931; s. James Ernest and Beulah Edith (Thiemann) H.; m. Janice Jewell, Apr. 17, 1954; children: Roger William, Robin Suzanne. BS in Agr., DVM, U. Mo., 1961; MS, Purdue U., 1963, PhD, 1965. Diplomate Am. Coll. Vet. Pathologists. From asst. prof. to assoc. prof. Purdue U., Lafayette, Ind., 1965-68, assoc. dean, 1973-86; assoc. prof. U. Mo., Columbia, 1968-71; prof. U. Ga., Athens, 1971-73; exec. dir. Assn. Am. Vet. Med. Colls., Washington, 1986-92; assoc. dean Coll. Vet. Medicine Okla. State U., Stillwater, 1992-97; ret., 1997. Bd. dirs. Pew Nat. Vet. Edn. Program, Phila. Bd. dirs. United Way, Lafayette, 1983-86. Sgt. USMC, 1949-52. Named Alumnus of Yr. Sch. Vet. Medicine, U. Mo., 1988. Mem. AVMA (mem., chair coun. on edn., com. on animal tech. 1980-86).

HOOPER, ROBERT ALEXANDER, television producer, international educator; b. Annapolis, Md., Apr. 13, 1947; s. P. Alexander and Louise (Hickey) H.; m. Virginia L. Gordon; 1 child, Julie Alexandra. BA in Econs., U. Calif., San Diego, 1969; JD, U. Calif., Davis, 1974; MFA in Motion Picture and TV, UCLA, 1982. Bar: Calif. 1975. Film prodr. Scripps Inst. of Oceanography, La Jolla, Calif., 1978-79, EPA, Washington, 1979-81; ind. film prodr. with ABC-TV and CBC, Del Mar, Calif., 1981-84; tv prodr. Sta. KUAC-TV, Fairbanks, Alaska, 1984-86; asst. prof. comm. Boston U., 1986-87; assoc. prof. comm. Loyola Marymount U., L.A., 1987-98; exec. prodr. KPBS-TV, San Diego, 1997—2001; assoc. prof. Calif. State U., 2000—. Vis. assoc. prof. U. Calif., San Diego, 1993, 96, UCLA, 2000; cons. CBC, Toronto, 1982-83, Radio-TV Malaysia, 1998, Fiji TV, 1996; cons. Asia-Pacific Inst. for Broadcasting Devel., 1998-99, course dir., 1998—; Fulbright sr. scholar comm. program U. Sains Malaysia, Penang, 1989-90, U. South Pacific, Fiji, 1994, U. Indonesia, 2001; tng. adviser Am. Samoa Govt.-Sta. KVZK-TV, 1992—; acad. specialist U. Papua New Guinea, 1995; Eisenhower fellow, Malaysia, 1996; Fulbright sr. scholar U. Indonesia, Jakarta, 2001; Fulbright sr. specialist, Malaysia, 2002-03; spkr. in field. Prodr., dir. (documentaries) Voices From Love Canal, 1978, Decisions at 1000 Fathoms, 1981, Battle at Webber Creek, 1985 (Press Club award), Alaska's Killer Whales, 1989 (Cine Golden Eagle and Silver Apple award); segment prodr. (ABC 20/20) The Deep, 1983; exec. prodr. Nature's Classic, 1998 (Press Club award, four Emmy nominations), Afoot and Afield, 1998, The Impossible Railroad, 1999 (Press Club award, Telly award, Emmy award); op.-editor writer, L.A. Times, San Diego Union-Tribune, 1999. Recipient Hennessy trophy, Internat. Environ. Film Festival, France, 1983. Mem. NATAS, Calif. Bar Assn., Eisenhower Fellows Assn., Fulbright Sr. Specialists Roster, Sigma Delta Chi. Democrat. Avocations: underwater photography, equestrian endurance riding. E-mail: rahooper@hotmail.com.

HOOPER, WILLIAM LOYD, music educator, university administrator; b. Sedalia, Mo., Sept. 16, 1931; s. George Francis and Mary Evelyn (McNabb) H.; m. Doris Jean Wallace, Aug. 5, 1951; children: William Loyd Jr., Carol Ann. BA, William Jewell Coll., 1953; MA, U. Iowa, 1956; PhD, Vanderbilt U., 1966. Tchr. Essex (Iowa) Pub. Schs., 1953—55, Atalissa (Iowa) Pub. Schs., 1955—56; music prof. S.W. Bapt. Coll., Bolivar, Mo., 1956—60; prof., dean New Orleans Bapt. Sem., 1962—74; head dept. music Newstead Wood Sch. for Girls, London, 1974—79; chief examiner South-East Exams. Bd., Tunbridge Wells, England, 1976—80; dean fine arts S.W. Bapt. U., Bolivar, 1983—89, dir. rsch., planning and assessment, 1989—98; ret. Author: Church Music in Transition, 1963, Music Fundamentals, 1967, Ministry and Musicians, 1983, Fundamentals of Music, 1986; compositions: (cantata) Litany of Praise, (choral collection) Sing Joyfully, (cantata) Jubilee, (cantata) And He Shall Come, and over 60 anthems for church choir. Recipient citation for achievement William Jewell Coll., 1968, 1st place award Delius Composition Competition, 1973, New Times Composition Competition, 1974, Republican. Baptist. Home: 116 W Auburn St Bolivar MO 65613-2412

HOOPER-PERKINS, MARLENE, technical editor, educator; b. Jersey City, N.J., Jan. 26, 1955; d. Arthur L. and Ethel M. (Coleman) Hooper; m. James A. Perkins; children: Joy J., Samantha A. BA, Rutgers U., 1977; MS, N.J. Inst. Tech., 1994. Acct. exec. Bruno Assocs., Bloomfield, N.J., 1984-87; adj. prof. dept. humanities N.J. Inst. Tech., Newark, 1995—, technical editor, media svcs., 1987—. Pres. (consulting firm) M.H. Perkins & Assocs., Elizabeth, N.J., 1995—. Bd. dirs. YWCA of Eas. Union County, Elizabeth, N.J., 1990-92; founding mem., mentor TGIF, N.J. Inst. Tech., 1995—. Mem. Douglass Assoc. Alumnae. Avocations: electronic design, creative writing, performance enhancement training. Office: NJ Inst Tech Media Svcs 218 Central Ave Newark NJ 07103-3918

HOOPES, FARREL G. secondary education educator; Tchr. Star Valley H.S., Afton, Wyo. Recipient Tchr. Excellence award Internat. Tech. Edn. Assn., 1992. Office: Star Valley HS PO Box 8000 Afton WY 83110-8000

HOORNBEEK, LYNDA RUTH COUCH, librarian, educator; b. Springfield, Ill., July 12, 1933; d. Willard Lee and Mabel Magdalene (Forberg) Couch; m. Louis Arthur Hoornbeek, Nov. 9, 1957; children— John Arthur, David William, Mark Benjamin. B.A. in Sociology, U. Ill., 1955; M.Ed., Cornell U., 1956; M.L.S., U. So. Calif., Los Angeles, 1973. Cert. tchr. Ill., N.Y. Tchr. elem. sch. North Haven (Conn.) Pub. Schs., 1956-57; library adminstr. Winfield (Ill.) Pub. Library, 1974-77; interim library adminstr. Bloomingdale (Ill.) Pub. Library, 1977-78; ref. librarian Franklin Park (Ill.) Pub. Library, 1978-83; state literacy dir. program Literacy Vols. of Ill., Chgo., 1983—84; research coordinator Ill. Literacy Council, Office of Sec. State, 1984—85; with office libr. outreach svcs. ALA, 1985-86; adult svcs. libr. Glen Ellyn (Ill.) Pub. Libr., 1986-94; ret., 1994. Bd. dirs. YWCA, Pitts., 1957—62; vol. archivist Glen Ellyn Hist. Soc., bd. dirs. 1994—. YWCA fellow 1954; Ford Found. fellow, 1955-56; U. Ill. scholar, 1951-55. Mem. Mortar Bd., Calif. Library Assn., Ill. Library Assn., ALA, AAUW, LWV, Beta Phi Mu, Pi Lambda Theta, Alpha Phi. Congregationalist. Home: 351 N Park Blvd Glen Ellyn IL 60137-5037

HOOVER, BETTY-BRUCE HOWARD, private school educator; b. Wake County, N.C., Mar. 20, 1939; d. Bruce Ruffin and Mary Elizabeth (Brown) Howard; m. Herbert Charles Marsh Hoover, Sept. 3, 1961; children: David Andrew, Howard Webster, Lorraine Hoover Clark. BA, Wake Forest U., 1961; MA, U. South Fla., 1978. Tchr. English Greensboro (N.C.) Sr. H.S., 1961-62, Lindley Jr. H.S., Greensboro, 1963, Berkeley Prep. Sch., Tampa, Fla., 1976—2002, chmn. English dept., 1977-85, dir., upper divsn., 1984-2000, chmn. curriculum com., 1982-86, historian, 1998—2002; ret., 2000. Author: Resources in Education, 1992, Berkeley Preparatory School: A Proud Legacy, 2002. Pres., Suncoast Midshipmen Parents Club, Tampa Bay Area, 1983-84. Mem. ASCD, Nat. Coun. Tchrs. English, Sociedad Honoraira Hispanica, The Nat. Coun. States, Wake Forest U. Alumni Assn., DAR, Hillsborough County Bar Aux., Cum Laude Soc. (sec. 1981-2000), Nat. Honor Soc., Phi Beta Kappa, Phi Sigma Iota, Sigma Tau Delta, Kappa Kappa Gamma. Mem.: Thespian Soc., Quill and Scroll, Mortarboard Alumni Assn., Berkeley Blazers, Beach Pk. Garden Club, Phi Betta Kappa Alumni Assn. (v.p. membership), Kappa Kappa Gamma Almuni Assn. Republican. Episcopalian. Avocations: sewing, gardening. Home: 11902 Wandsworth Dr Tampa FL 33626-2611

HOOVER, DONNA WHITEHOUSE, math and physics educator; b. Owensboro, Ky., Nov. 16, 1954; d. Kenneth Hoover and Mary Bryant (Jarnagin) W. BS, Ky. Wesleyan Coll., 1976; MA, Western Ky. U., 1979, Rank I degree, 1981; postgrad., Amatrol Tchr. Tng. Inst., 1992-93. Cert. in teaching, guidance and vocat. adminstrn., Ky. Phlebotomist, phys. therapy asst. Owensboro-Daviess County Hosp., 1973-75; asst. chemist Peabody Coal Co., Drakesboro, Ky., 1977; biology tchr. Apollo High Sch., Owensboro, 1977-78; quality control specialist Field Packing Co., Owensboro, 1978; math. instr. Daviess County (Ky.) State Vocat.-Tech. Sch., Owensboro, 1978-88, Ky. Wesleyan Coll., Owensboro, 1982-83, Owensboro. C.C., 1988; indsl. automation tech., physics and math. instr. Ky. Tech. Owensboro, 1988—. Lifeguard youth ministry L.I.F.E. program First Bapt. Ch., Owensboro, 1992-94, rama team, 1995—, hanbell choir, 1995—, dept. sec., 1994-96, tchr. Sunday sch., percussionist ch. orch., 1996—; bd. dirs. OWensboro Concert Assn. Grantee Tex. Gas Transmission Corp., Owensboro, 1989; named Ky. Outstanding Tchr. of Yr., Ky. Workforce Devel. Cabinet, 1990, Regional Outstanding Tchr. of Yr., Vocat. Edn., Region 3, 1990; named Ky. Col. Mem. Christian Educators Assn. Internat., Vocat. Indsl. Clubs Am. (profl., robotic workcell tech. contest com. 1993). Avocations: ornithology, golf. Office: KY Tech Owensboro 1501 Frederica St Owensboro KY 42301-4806

HOPE, JAIME LYNN, foreign language educator; b. Seoul, Aug. 2, 1974; d. James Albert and Bonnie Jean (Barlow) H. BS, U. Md., College Park, 1996. Spanish tchr. U. Richmond, Va., 1993-94; mktg./advt. intern Phillips Bus. Info., Potomac, Md., 1995; mktg. intern Goodwill Industries Internat., Bethesda, Md., 1996; client rels. rep. Occupational Health & Rehab., Boston, 1996-97; asst. mgr. Macy's, Eatontown, N.J., 1997—. Mem. NAFE, Golden Key, Omicron Delta Kappa, Gamma Phi Beta (v.p. pub. rels. 1994-97), Alpha Kappa Psi. Democrat. Home: 309 Beach Front Manasquan NJ 08736-3907

HOPE, LINDA RUTH, principal; b. Kansas City, Mo., Feb. 24, 1951; d. Wilbur Emer and Ruth Karlean (Bradley) Spencer; m. John H. Hope Jr., May 29, 1977; children: Bradley, Mary Jo. BS, U. Mo., 1972; MS, U. Mo., Kansas City, 1974; EdS, U. Kans., 1980, EdD, 1993. Tchr. Independence (Mo.) Schs., 1973-81, dist. math. chmn., 1976-81; asst. prin. Olathe (Kans.) Pub. Schs., 1981-95; prin. Andover (Kans.) Mid. Sch., 1995-98; asst. prof., coord. tchr. edn. Newman U. Presenter Ednl. Excellence Cadre, Olathe, 1989-95; adv. bd. mem. U. Kans. Sch. Ednl. Leadership, 1993-95; quality performance chair Kans. Dept. Edn., Kans., 1994-95. Author: Effects of At Risk Status or a Student's Knowledge, Attitudes and Behavior Concerning Drugs, Alcohol, Self-Esteem, Peer Pressure and Sensation Seeking, 1993. Citizen rev. panel chmn. United Way, Olathe, 1986-90; pres. corp. bd. Sigma Kappa Sorority, Manhattan, Kans., 1991-95. Mem. Nat. Assn. Secondary Sch. Prins., Kans. Assn. Secondary Sch. Prins., Delta Kappa Gamma (treas.), Phi Delta Kappa. Avocation: reading. Home: 302 Lexington St Andover KS 67002-9668 Office: 115 E 2d St Hutchinson KS 67504

HOPFIELD, JOHN JOSEPH, biophysicist, educator; b. Chgo., July 15, 1933; s. John Joseph and Helen (Staff) H.; children: Alison, Jessica, Natalie; m. Mary Waltham, 1996. AB, Swarthmore Coll., 1954; PhD, Cornell U., 1958; DSc (hon.), Swarthmore Coll., 1992. Mem. tech. staff ATT Bell Labs., 1958-60, 73-89; vis. rsch. physicist Ecole Normale Superieure, Paris, 1960-61; asst. prof., then asso. prof. physics U. Calif. at Berkeley, 1961-64; prof. physics Princeton U., 1964-80, Eugene Higgins prof. physics, 1978-80; Dickinson prof. chemistry and biology Calif. Inst. Tech., Pasadena, 1980-96; Howard Prior prof. molecular biology Princeton (N.J.) U., 1997—. Trustee Battelle Meml. Inst. Guggenheim fellow, 1969, MacArthur Prize fellow, 1983; recipient Michelson-Morley prize, 1988, Wright prize, 1989, Helmholz award Internat. Neural Network Soc., 1999, Neural Net Pioneer award IEEE, 1997., Dirac medal Internat. Ctr. for Theoretical Physics, 2001, Pender award U. Pa., 2002; named Calif. Scientist of Yr., 1991. Fellow Am. Phys. Soc. (Oliver E. Buckley prize 1968, Biol. Physics prize 1985); mem. NAS, Am. Acad. Arts and Scis., Am. Philos. Soc., Phi Beta Kappa, Sigma Xi. Office: Princeton U Dept Molecular Biology Princeton NJ 08544-0001 E-mail: hopfield@princeton.edu.

HOPGOOD, JAMES F. anthropologist, educator; b. Cape Girardeau, Mo., Apr. 18, 1943; s. Finley Marshall and Marjorie Louise (Schneider) H.; m. Esther Berg, Jan. 29, 1966; 1 child, Myka Lynn. BA, U. Mo., 1965, MA, 1969; MPhil, U. Kans., 1971, PhD, 1976. Asst. prof. anthropology No. Ky. U., Highland Heights, 1973-76, assoc. prof., 1976-90, prof., 1990—2003, prof. emeritus, 2003—, chmn. dept. sociology, anthropology and philosophy, 1984-98, mem. exec. com. faculty senate, 1978-80, dir. Mus. of Anthropology, 2003—. Vis. instr. Washburn U., Topeka, 1969; vis. prof. Instituto Tecnologico y de Estudios Superiores de Monterrey, Mex., 1971, U. Monterrey, 1980; profl. assoc. Asian studies devel. program East-West Ctr. and U. Hawaii, summers, 1991, 93, 94. Author: Settlers of Bajavista: Urban Adaptation in a Mexican Squatter Settlement, 1979; editorial bd. Jour. of Third World Studies; contbr. articles, reports to profl. jours. Mem. edn. com. Cin. Mus. Natural History, 1992-94. Jewish Chautauqua Soc. scholar in residence No. Ky. U., 1988-98; recipient Sasakawa fellowship San Diego State U., summer 1996. Fellow Am. Anthrop. Assn. (mem. exec. com. 1996-98—); mem. Ky. Acad. Sci. (bd. gov. 1995-98), Ctrl. States Anthropol. Soc. (pres. 1996-97, mem. exec. bd. 1989-92, 99-01, editor CSAS Bull. 2001—), Sigma Xi, Lambda Alpha. Home: 4918 Corn Row Ct Independence KY 41051-8101 E-mail: hopgood@nku.edu.

HOPKINS, BARBARA JO GLASS, school system administrator; b. Hastings, Nebr., Aug. 14, 1951; d. William Howard and Kathryn Lucille (Sorensen) Glass; children: Ryan Lee, Jennifer Josephine. BS, U. Nebr., 1973, MEd in Reading, 1981, PhD in Adminstrn., 1992. Lang. arts tchr. 6th-8th grades, North Platte, Nebr., 1973-76; tchr. adult basic edn. Nebr. Dept. Corrections, Lincoln, 1976-77; tchr. K-6 Dist. #69, Haines Branch, Lincoln, 1977-78; tchr. jr. high English and reading Lincoln Pub. Schs., 1978—; Ventures in Partnerships coord. Lincoln Pub. Schs. and Lincoln Edn. Assn., 1987—. Lectr. and workshop leader in field. Contbr. articles, guest editorials and poetry to profl. jours. Bd. dirs., youth svcs. chmn., camp co-dir. ARC, 1980-99 . Recipient Outstanding Young Alumna award U. Nebr., 1991, Partnerships in Edn. award of Merit, 1989, 90, Cooper Found. award for sci. curriculum, 1987, Clara Barton award, 1987, First Christa McAuliffe award of teaching excellence, 1987, Vol. of Yr. award United Way, 1990, others; named Nebr. Tchr. of Yr., State Dept. Edn., 1988. Mem. NEA, Lincoln C. of C., Internat. Reading Assn. (editl. adv. bd. 1987-90), Nat. Tchrs. English, Nebr. Tchr. English, Nebr. Edn. Assn. Avocations: reading, performing arts, volunteer work. Office: Ventures in Partnerships 6800 Monterey Dr Lincoln NE 68526

HOPKINS, CATHERINE LEE, music educator; d. John James and Eleanor May (Hubert) Sanderson; m. Stephen Ernest Hopkins, June 26, 1965; children: Cheryl Lynne Hopkins Naquette, Scott Eric. MusB Edn., New Eng. Conservatory, 1961. Tchr. Nagautuck Schs., Conn., 1961—62, Attleboro Schs., Mass., 1962—68, Smithfield Schs., RI, 1982—. Parent coun. Boy Scouts Am., Smithfield, 1992—; advocate Special Olympics, Trudeau Center, 1995—, No. ARC, Woonsocket, RI, 1997—. Mem.: Am. Choral Dirs. Conf., Music Educators Nat. Conf. Home: 8 Appleseed Dr Greenville RI 02828

HOPKINS, CECILIA ANN, business educator; b. Havre, Mont., Feb. 17, 1922; d. Kost L. and Mary (Manaras) Sofos; m. Henry E. Hopkins, Sept. 7, 1944. BS, Mont. State Coll., 1944; MA, San Francisco State Coll., 1958; postgrad., Stanford U.; PhD, Calif. Western U., 1977. Bus. tchr. Havre (Mont.) H.S., Mateo, Calif., 1942-44; sec. George P. Gorham, Realtor, San Mateo, 1944-45; escrow sec. Fox & Cars, 1945-50; escrow officer Calif. Pacific Title Ins. Co., 1950-57; bus. tchr. Westmoor H.S., Daly City, Calif., 1958-59, Coll. of San Mateo, 1959-63, chmn. real estate-ins. dept., 1963-76, dir. divsn. bus., 1976-86, coord. real estate dept., 1986-91. Cons. to commr. Calif. Divsn. Real Estate, 1963-91, mem. periodic rev. exam. com.; chmn. C.C. Adv. Com., 1971-72, mem. com., 1975-91; projector direction Calif. State Chancellor's Career Awareness Consortium, mem. endowment fund adv. com., c.c. real estate edn. com., state c.c. adv. com.; mem. No. Calif. adv. bd. to Glendale Fed. Savs. and Loan Assn.; mem. bd. advisors San Mateo County Bd. Supvrs., 1981-82; mem. real estate edn. and rsch. com. to Calif. Commr. Real Estate, 1983-90; mem. edn., membership, and profl. exch. coms. Am. chpt. Internat. Real Estate Fedn., 1985-92. Co-author: California Real Estate Principles; contbr. articles to profl. jours. Recipient Citizen of Day award KABL, Outstanding Contbns. award Redwood City-San Carlos-Belmont Bd. Realtors, Nat. Real Estate Educators Assn. award emeritus, 1993; named Woman of Achievement, San Mateo-Burlingame br. Soroptimist Internat., 1979. Mem. AAUW, Calif. Assn. Real Estate Tchrs. (state pres. 1964-65, life hon. dir. 1962—, Outstanding Real Estate Educator of Yr. 1978-79), Real Estate Cert. Inst. (Disting. Merit award 1982), Calif. Bus. Edn. Assn. (cert. of commendation 1979), San Francisco State Coll., Guidance and Counseling Alumni, Calif. Real Estate Educators' Assn. (dir. emeritus, hon. dir. 1990), Real Estate Nat. Educators Assn. (award emeritus for outstanding contbns. 1993), San Mateo-Burlingame Bd. Realtors (award emeritus Outstanding Contbrs. to Membership), Alpha Delta, Pi Lambda Theta, Delta Pi Epsilon (nat. dir. interchpt. rels. 1962-65, nat. historian 1966-67, nat. sec. 1968-69), Alpha Gamma Delta. Home: 504 Colgate Way San Mateo CA 94402-3206

HOPKINS, JAMES ROY, psychology educator; b. Fieldale, Va., Dec. 7, 1944; s. Luther Edwin and Vergie Emma (Spencer) H. BA with high honors, U. Va., 1968; PhD, Harvard U., 1974. Asst. prof. Vassar Coll., Poughkeepsie, N.Y., 1974-79; assoc. prof. St. Mary's Coll., St. Mary's City, Md., 1980-85, prof., 1985—, head human devel. divsn., 1993-96, assoc. provost, 1998—2002. Cons. Child and Family Resource Program, Poughkeepsie, Head Start, Poughkeepsie. Author: (textbook) Adolescence: The Transitional Years, 1986; co-author: (textbook) Psychology, 1987, 3d edit., 1994; book rev. editor: Jour. of Adolescence, 1993-98. Bd. dirs. Assn. Retarded Citizens, St. Mary's City, 1983-86, v.p., 1985-86. Mem. APA, Soc. Rsch. in Child Devel., Soc. Rsch. in Adolescence, Soc. Psychol. Study of Social Issues, Phi Beta Kappa, Sigma Xi, Psi Chi. Office: St Mary's Coll Human Devel Divsn Saint Marys City MD 20686 E-mail: jrhopkins@smcm.edu.

HOPKINS, LAYNE VICTOR, computer science educator; b. Boone, Iowa, June 5, 1939; s. Wilson Franklin and Lucy Arlene (Stanley) H.; m. Karen Lynn Kloss, Feb. 19, 1960; 1 child, Ranae Lynn. BS, Dakota State U., 1961; MA, U. Utah, 1965; PhD, Pa. State U., 1971. Tchr. math. Springfield (Minn.) Pub. Schs., 1961-64, Bountiful (Utah) Pub. Schs., 1966-67; prof. computer sci. Mankato (Minn.) State U., 1971—. Dir. IBM-Mankato Project, Mankato, 1987—, dir. Clear With Computers-Mankato Project, Mankato, 1994—. Co-author: CAI Basic, 1984. Twp. supr. Mankato Twp., 1988-91; pres. Tech. Plus Ctr., 1998-02. Mem. Inter-Faculty Assn. Avocation: farming. Home: 21052 594th Ave Mankato MN 56001-8543

HOPKINS, ROBERT ELLIOTT, music educator; b. Greensboro, N.C., Oct. 2, 1931; s. Julian Setzer and Elizabeth Stewart (Daniel) H. MusB, U. Rochester, 1953, MusM, 1954, D Mus. Arts, 1959; postgrad., Acad. for Music, Vienna, Austria, 1959-60. Instr. Mars Hill Coll., 1954-57, 60-63; prof. music Youngstown (Ohio) State U., 1963-93; prof. emeritus, 1993—. Editor: Alexander Reinagle: The Philadelphia Sonatas, 1978; contbr. New Grove Dictionary of Music and Musicians, 1980, 2d edit., 2001, New Grove Dictionary of American Music, 1987, New Grove Dictionary of Opera, 1992. Music dir. various chs., N.C. and Ohio, 1954-81; chmn. Nat. Piano Concerto Competition, Youngstown Symphony Soc., 1986-90. Recipient Disting. Prof. award Youngstown State U., 1990; Fulbright-Hays grantee, 1959-60, rsch. grantee Youngstown State U., 1969-70, 83. Fellow Am. Guild. Organists (dean Youngstown chpt. 1968-69, 73-74, S. Lewis Elmer award 1962, 66); mem. Am. Musicological Soc., Soc. Am. Music. E-mail: dok109@zoominternet.net.

HOPKINS, SHIRLEY MAY, former educator, real estate broker; b. Detroit, Oct. 4, 1928; d. Jake Henry and Grace Mildred (Armbruster) Spiller; m. Richard Glenn Hopkins, June 7, 1949 (div. July 1955); children: Richard Reid, Leslie Lee, Scott Henry. BA, Wayne State U., 1959; MA, Calif. State U., Fullerton, 1969; PhD with honors, UCLA, 1976. Tchr. Hilltop Jr. H.S., Chula Vista, Calif., 1959-64, Santa Fe H.S., Santa Fe Springs, Calif., 1964-74; asst. prin. Fern Sch., Rosemead, Calif., 1974-76; staff adminstr. Downey (Calif.) H.S., 1976-79; realtor Creative Real Estate, Santa Barbara, Calif., 1980-84; real estate broker Allegro Realty, Santa Barbara, 1984-88. Mem. Assn. Women Sch. Adminstrs., Downey, 1976-79, Women in Ednl. Leadership, L.A., 1976-79; pres. Santa Barbara Real Estate Exchangors, 1983-84. Commr., vice-chair Santa Barbara County Affirmative Action, 1995-97; forewoman Santa Barbara County Grand Jury, 1992-93; membership dir. 1st United Meth. Ch., Santa Barbara, 1996—. Mem. AAUW, NAACP, Leadership Santa Barbara County, Golden State Mobilhome Owners, Pi Sigma Alpha, Phi Delta Kappa. Democrat. Methodist. Avocations: private pilot's license, travel, bridge, writing. Home: # A-303 6647 El Colegio Rd Goleta CA 93117-4200

HOPKINS, ZORA CLEMONS, training and development specialist; b. Burleson County, Tex., Nov. 19, 1945; d. Otto and Rubie Lee (Sams) Clemons; children: Thean, Aikia. BA in Elem. Edn., Incarnate Word Coll., San Antonio, 1968; MA in Early Childhood Edn., East Tex. State U., 1974; MEd in Ednl. Adminstrn., Prairie View A&M U., 1979. Tchr. Dallas Ind. Sch. Dist., 1968-88, staff trainer, 1988-89, specialist III, 1989-92, specialist in tng., 1992-94; vice prin. Roger Q. Mills Elem. Sch., Dallas Ind. Sch. Dist., 1994—. Curriculum writer Dallas Ind. Sch. Dist., 1987-89, monitor for sch. improvement plan, 1989-92; revision team mem. Texas Assessment Academic Skills Test State of Texas, 1992. Advisor Oratorical Club, Dallas, 1987—; counselor Ch. of Christ Youth Club, Dallas, 1970—, mem. site based decision making team, 1993; vol. tutoring program, Dallas, 1988—; organizer Neighborhood Beautification, Dallas and Cedar Hill, Tex., 1987—; mem. adv. com. infusion multicultural edn. Cedar Hill Ind. Sch. Dist. Mem. ASCD, Internat. Reading Assn., Nat. Assn. for Young Children, Nat. Staff Devel. Coun. Tex. Staff Devel. Coun., Tex. Assn. Adminstrs. and Suprs. of Programs for Young Children, Phi Delta Kappa. Avocations: reading, travel, boating, cruising/island hopping. Home: 1848A King Pl Frederick MD 21702-8210 Office: Roger Q Mills Elem Sch 1515 Lynn Haven Ave Dallas TX 75216-1362

HOPMANN, PHILIP TERRENCE, political science educator; b. St. Louis, June 25, 1942; s. Irvin Herman and Loretta (Gerlach) H.; m. Marita Raubitschek, Aug. 24, 1968; children: Alexander Irvin, Nicholas Erich. AB, Princeton U., 1964; MA, Stanford U., 1965, PhD, 1969. Rsch. asst. Stanford (Calif.) U., 1965-67, instr., 1967-68; prof. polit. sci. U. Minn., Mpls., 1968-85, Brown U., Providence, 1985—, dir. program on global security Watson Inst. Internat. Studies, 1993—, dir. Internat. Rels. program, 1985-94. Cons. U.S. Inst. of Peace, 1998—; chmn. faculty exec. com. Brown U., Providence, 1994-95. Author: Unity and Disintegration in International Alliances, 1973, 84, The Negotiation Process and the Resolution of International Conflicts, 1996. Fulbright-Hays fellow Coun. Internat. Ednl. Exch., Belgium, 1975-76, 82-83, Jennings Randolph sr. fellow U.S. Inst. Peace, 1997-98, Fulbright fellow Orgn. Security and Cooperation in Europe, Austria, 1998. Mem. Internat. Studies Assn. (editor 1980-85, v.p. 1991-92), Internat. Polit. Sci. Assn., Arms Control Assn., Am. Polit. Sci. Assn. Democrat. Home: 23 Valerian Ct Rockville MD 20852 Office: Brown U Watson Inst/Internat Studies PO Box 1970 Providence RI 02912-1970

HOPPE, LEA ANN, elementary education educator; b. Birmingham, Ala., Mar. 20, 1959; d. George Carson and Annie Merle (Carleton) Jones; m.

David Thomas Hoppe, Nov. 21, 1983; children: Kathryn Ann, Emily Louise. BS in Edn., Samford U., Birmingham, 1981; MA in Edn., U. Ala., Tuscaloosa, 1986. Cert. tchr., Ala. Reading tutor Pearson's Reading & Math. Ctr., Birmingham, 1979-81; kindergarten tchr. Scottsboro (Ala.) City Schs.-Brownwood, 1981-86; pre-kindergarten tchr., ctr. dir. First Bapt. Learning Ctr., Scottsboro, 1986-89; kindergarten tchr. Covenant Weekday Kindergarten, Huntsville, Ala., 1990-95, Randolph Sch., Huntsville, 1995—. Chmn. bd. dirs. First Bapt. Child Devel. Ctr., Huntsville, 1992-96; conf. leader Samford U., Birmingham, 1993, Farley Elem. Parents Orgn., Huntsville, 1994. Author: (children's activity books) A Child For All Seasons: Volume 1, 1994, Volume 2, 1994. Children's choir dir. First Bapt. Ch., Huntsville, 1991—, children's Sunday Sch. tchr., 1993—. Mem. Nat. Assn. Edn. Young Children, Orgn. Am. Kodaly Educators, Music Educators Nat. Conf., Music Educators Nat. Assn., So. Early Childhood Assn., Ala. Assn. Young Children, Delta Omicron (life), Kappa Delta Pi, Kappa Delta Epsilon, Pi Gamma Mu, Omicron Delta Kappa. Republican. Baptist. Avocations: singing, playing the trombone, children's literature. Home: 2911 Barcody Rd SE Huntsville AL 35801-2218 Office: Randolph Sch 1005 Drake Ave SE Huntsville AL 35802-1099 E-mail: lhoppe@randolphschool.net.

HOPPER, MARGARET SUE, academic administrator, educational diagnostician, consultant; b. New Gulf, Tex., Feb. 8, 1937; d. Thomas Clinton and Margaret Evelyn (McDaniel) Letts; m. Rufus Denman Hopper Jr., Apr. 7, 1955; children: Lloyd Wade, Nancy Marie. BS, Sam Houston State U., 1960, MEd, 1973. Cert. reading specialist, ednl. diagnostician, tchr. of mentally retarded and learning disabled elem. students, elem. edn. tchr. Tchr. Jarrell (Tex.) Ind. Sch. Dist., 1960-67; tchr. Lohn (Tex.) Ind. Sch. Dist., 1967-68, Brady (Tex.) Ind. Sch. Dist., 1968-70, Huntsville (Tex.) Ind. Sch. Dist., 1970-78, spl. edn. tchr., 1978, edn. diagnostician, 1978-80; pre-lab. student tchr. Sam Houston State U., 1971-78; edn. diagnostician Carrollton (Tex.)-Farmers Branch Ind. Sch. Dist., 1980-85, instructional diagnostician, 1985-88, instructional facilitator, 1988-91, edn. diagnostician, 1991-92; pvt. practice as ednl. cons., diagnostician, tchr. appraiser, 1992-94; inclusion specialist, 1994-95; supr. student tchrs. Sam Houston State U., 1995-97. Mem. Bd. Registry-Diagnostician #0522, Houston, 1984-2002. Mem. Tex. Ednl. Diagnosticians Assn., Tex. State Tchrs. Assn., Tex. Ret. Tchrs. Assn. (legis. com. 1995-2002, state leadership tng. team 2003), Alpha Chi. Methodist. Avocation: water sports. Home and Office: PO Box 1536 Huntsville TX 77342-1536

HOPPES, GARY JON, vocational educator, management consultant; b. Davenport, Iowa, Oct. 9, 1946; s. James William and Viola Pearl (Johnson) H.; m. Donna Rochelle Silver, Nov. 5, 1971. BA in Indsl. Edn., U. No. Iowa, 1973; MS in Indsl. Vocat./Tech. Edn., Iowa State U., 1976; PhD in Vocat. Edn. Adminstrn.. Instr., coordinator vocat. programs Lakenheath Am. High Sch., RAF Lakenheath, Eng., 1973-74; tech. writer, tng. dept. Cherry Burrell Co., Cedar Rapids, Iowa, 1974-75; grad. research asst., spl. needs Iowa State U., 1975; program coordinator Alternative Edn. Ctr., Marion (Iowa) Ind. Sch., 1976-78; instr., coordinator collision repair program Kirkwood C.C., 1978-86; assoc. dean., Dodge City (Kans.) C.C., 1986-88; adj. prof. mfg., 1988-90; vis. prof. indsl. tech., Ohio U., Athens, 1990-91; assoc. prof. indsl. tech. U. No. Iowa, Cedar Falls, Iowa, 1991-93; mfg. process and computer integration cons. TransTec Internat., Ely, Iowa, 1988—; vocat. cons. to trade and indsl. programs. Served with USN, 1965-69; Vietnam. Decorated service medal with 5 Bronze Stars, Navy Achievement medal with 1 Bronze Star; recipient Order of Arrow award Boy Scouts Am., 1961, Life Scout award, 1963. Mem. Soc. Mfg. Engrs, Coun. Vocat. Edn., Am. Vocat. Assn., Iowa Vocat. Assn., Nat. Assn. Indsl. and Tech. Tchr. Educators, Vocat. Indsl. Clubs Am., Epsilon Pi Tau. Lutheran. Author: Working Papers Special Needs Population, 1976, The Administrator's Role in Establishing and Maintaining A Vocational Cooperative Education Program, 1976, Photojournalism, A Guide, 1978, Vocational Professional/Technical Updating Needs of Trade and Industry/Technical Post-Secondary Educators, 1990. Home: 2075 Banner Valley Rd Ely IA 52227-9754 also: TransTec Internat PO Box 220 Ely IA 52227-0220 Office: Univ Arkansas 5210 Grand Ave PO Box 2649 Fort Smith AR 72913-3649 Home: R1 box 136A Spiro OK 74959

HOPPING, JANET MELINDA, principal; b. Washington, Dec. 27, 1943; d. Russell Leroy and Janet L. (Cloud) H. B.S., Tex. Christian U., 1965; M.Ed., Ga. State U., 1977. Edn. cert., Ga. Tchr., Littleton, Colo., 1965-68, East Point, Ga., 1969, Atlanta, 1969-78; Title IVc coordinator Fulton County Schs., Atlanta, 1978-81, middle sch. project coordinator, 1981-82; asst. prin. West Middle Sch., East Point, 1982-83; prin. Holcomb Bridge Middle Sch., Alpharetta, Ga., 1983-91, Crabapple Middle Sch., Roswell, Ga., 1991—; cons., trainer various sch. systems. Mem. ASCD, Am. Soc. Assn. Execs., Nat. Middle Sch. Assn. (bd. trustees 1989-91), Ga. Middle Sch. Assn. (pres. 1984-85, exec. dir. 1991—), Nat. Assn. Secondary Sch. Prins., Prins. Inst. (adv. bd.), Atlanta Hist. Soc., Atlanta Com. for the Olympic Games (edn. task force mem. 1990—, Olympic Day in Schs. steering com. 1989—), Delta Kappa Gamma, Pi Beta Phi. Republican. Roman Catholic. Avocations: golf, tennis. Home: 6106 Kayron Dr NE Atlanta GA 30328-4112 Office: 10700 Crabapple Rd Roswell GA 30075-3029

HORACEK, CONSTANCE HELLER, graphic designer, educator; b. Campbell, Nebr., Nov. 07; d. Roy B. and Mildred Bernadine (Holt) Heller; m. Michael Jay Horacek, Aug. 18, 1963 (div. Oct. 1983); children: Kachina Leigh, Marika Sian. BS in Edn., Midland Luth. Coll., 1963; MA in Ceramic Sculpture, Western Ill. U., 1977, postgrad., 1978—, U. Kans., 1974-75, Arrowmont Sch. Arts and Crafts, 1978, 79, 81, 82; MFA, Md. Inst. Art, Balt., 1986. Tchr. Ottawa (Kans.) Jr. High Sch., 1964-68, Bardolph (Ill.) Elem. Sch., 1970; mem. faculty Western Ill. U. Lab. Sch., Macomb, 1970-73, instr. clothing textile design dept. home econs., 1975-80; asst. prof. clothing/textiles Albright Coll., Reading, Pa., 1980-86, assoc. prof. fashion merchandising/design, 1986—, chairperson visual arts and design, 1992—. Acting dir. Freedman Gallery, summer 1981; instr. part-time extension campus Spoon River Jr. Coll., Macomb, 1980; graphic designer for workshops, seminars, and local bus. firms, 1975-80; ptnr. Images Unltd., Macomb, 1980; cons. visual prodn., 1975—; project dir. Outreach program, summer 1981; design cons. Tandy Leather Co., Ft. Worth; chmn. Human Ecology, Visual Arts and Design Dept., Albright Coll., 1989—. Bd. dirs. Kashahasia, Western Ill. U., 1978-80, Downtown Up (now Penn Square Commn.), sec. 1986—. Mem. Am. Crafts Council, Am. Home Econs. Assn., Pa. Home Econs. Assn., Surface Design, Kappa Omicron Phi, Kappa Pi, Alpha Psi Omega. Office: Albright Coll PO Box 15234 Reading PA 19612-5234

HORD, PAULINE JONES, primary school educator, educator; b. Memphis, Apr. 18, 1907; d. Samuel Anderson and Loretta (Hall) Jones; m. Andrew Frank Hord, Mar. 30, 1940 (div. Oct. 1946). BA, Southwestern Coll., Memphis, 1929; EdD (hon.), Crichton Coll., Memphis, 1991, Rhodes Coll., 1999. Tchr. Memphis City Sch. System, 1929-67; nat. cons. Phonovisual Products, Inc., Bethesda, Md., 1967-77; freelance cons., workshop dir. Memphis, 1978-87; dir. sing spell read and write model Memphis Sch. System, 1987-95. Dir. TV Lit. Program WKNO-TV, Memphis, 1955-60; acting dir. Primary Day Sch., Bethesda, Md., 1960-61; lit. TV Specialist with Peace Corps., Colombia, S. Am., 1963-64; dir. Heads Up Lit. Program, State Correctional Inst., Parchman, Miss., 1986-96. Author: Praying for the President, 2003, The Master Design, 2003. Lit. tchr. Heads Up Lit. Program, Parchman Penetentiary, 1987-92; bd. mem. Second Chance Prison Min., Tenn., Miss., 1988-92. Recipient Leadership Adult Edn. award Ford Found., 1958, Disting. Col. Christian Svc. award Miss. State Penetentiary, Parchman, 1987, Memphis Comml. Appeal award, 1989, 95th Daily Point of Light award, 1990, Person of Vision award Alliance for the Blind and Visually Impaired, 1993, Disting. Alumni award Rhodes Coll., 1998; named one of Outstanding Bus. Women of Yr., Women's Exec. Coun., Memphis, 1959, Sr. Citizen of Yr., Shelby County Coun. on Aging, 1988. Republican. Mem. United Meth. Avocations: reading, creating educational games, leading prayer groups. Home: 475 S Perkins Rd Apt 601 Memphis TN 38117-3926

HORE, JOHN EDWARD, commodity futures educator; b. Dec. 13, 1929; s. Ernest and Doris Kathleen (Horton) H.; m. Diana King, May 3, 1958; children: Edward John Bruce, Celia Kathleen Hore Milne, Timothy Frank. BA with honors, King's Coll., Cambridge, Eng., 1952, MA, 1957. Chartered fin. analyst. Asst. sales mgr. Borthwicks, London, 1952-54; security analyst Dominion Securities, Toronto, Ont., Can., 1955-57; asst. mktg. mgr. Rio Algom, Toronto, 1957-61; dir. Bell, Gouinlock & Co., Toronto, 1961-75; v.p., dir. futures Can. Securities Inst., Toronto, 1979-94, seminar leader, 1980-2000. Investment edn. cons., 1995—; cons. Can. Dept. Agr., 1993; founding sec. Can. Nuclear Assn.; past v.p. Brit. Can. Trade Assn.; chmn. 1st Can. Internat. Futures Rsch. Seminar, 1985, also editor Proc., 2 vols., 1986; spkr. Can.-Am. Inst. Conf. on Fin. Svcs. at Detroit-Windsor, 1989, compliance seminar Futures Industry Assn. at Alexandria, Va., 1990; chmn. Can. Futures Conf., 1986; chmn. 3d, 4th, 5th and 6th Can. Internat. Futures Conf. and Rsch. Seminars, 1987, 88, 89, 90, mng. editor Selected Papers 1988-91. Author: Trading on Canadian Futures Markets, 1984, 5th edit., 1993; co-author: Association for Investment Management and Research Standards of Practice Handbook, 1982 (Pres. Reagan Citation 1984); co-editor: Canadian Securities Course, 1980-94. Gov. Montcrest Sch., 1970-73; mem. Commodity Futures Adv. Bd., Ont., 1989-95; apptd. mem. internat. com. Futures Industry Assn., Washington, 1988-91, rowing com. Upper Can. Coll., Toronto, 1982-86; pres. St. George's Soc. Toronto, 1978-80, chmn. edn. com., 1987. With Royal Army Ednl. Corps, 1948-49, Singapore. Mem. Toronto Soc. Fin. Analysts (bd. dirs. 1968-71), Assn. for Investment Mgmt. and Rsch. (formerly Fin. Analysts Fedn., bd. dirs. investment analysis stds. 1974-85, emeritus 1985), Univ. Club Toronto (bd. dirs. 1980-83), Arts and Letters Club Toronto (exec. com. 2000, treas. 2001—), Leander Club (assoc.) (Henley-on-Thames), Hurlingham Club (London), Royal Overseas League (pres. Ont. chpt.), Toronto Round Table (pres. 1999-2001). Anglican. Avocations: historical research, squash, choral music, poetry. Office: 185 Carlton St Toronto ON Canada M5A 2K7 E-mail: johnhore@aol.com.

HORLICK, GARY NORMAN, lawyer, legal educator; b. Washington, Mar. 12, 1947; s. Reuben S. and Gertrude V. (Cooper) H.; m. Kathryn L. Mann, June 1, 1986. AB, Dartmouth Coll., 1968; BA, MA, Diploma in Internat. Law, Cambridge (Eng.) U., 1970; JD, Yale U., 1973. Bar: Conn. 1974, U.S. Ct. Appeals (D.C. cir.) 1975), D.C. 1977, U.S. Supreme Ct. 1977, U.S. Ct. Internat. Trade 1979, U.S. Ct. Customs and Patent Appeals 1980. Asst. to rep. Ford Found., Santiago, Chile, 1973-74, asst. rep. Bogota, Colombia, 1974-76; assoc. Steptoe & Johnson, Washington, 1976-80; internat. trade counsel U.S. Senate Fin. Com., Washington, 1981; dep. asst. sec. U.S. Dept. Commerce, Washington, 1981-83; ptnr. O'Melveny & Myers, Washington, 1983—2002, Wilmer, Cutler & Pickering, Washington, 2002—. Lectr. law Yale U., New Haven, 1983-86, 2001—, World Trade Inst., U. Berne, 2000—; adj. prof. Georgetown U. Law Ctr., Washington, 1986—, World Trade Inst. U. Rome; lectr. various orgns.; adv. com. U.S. Ct. Internat. Trade, 1993-97; mem. permanent group of experts World Trade Orgn., 1996-2001, chmn., 1996-97. Author: WTO and NAFTA Rules and Dispute Resolution, 2003. Mem. ABA (chmn. standing com. on customs law 1993), Coun. Fgn. Rels., Internat. Law Assn. (mem. exec. coun. Am. br. 1983—), Internat. Bar Assn. (vice chmn. antitrust and trade law 1987-89), D.C. Bar Assn. (chmn. internat. divsn. 1984-85), Am. Soc. of Internat. Law (exec. coun. 1998-99). Office: Wilmer Cutler & Pickering 2455 M St NW Washington DC 20037- E-mail: gary.horlick@wilmer.com.

HORMAN, KAREN LOEB, elementary education educator; b. Norfolk, Va., July 26, 1947; d. Joseph Arthur and Ruth Helen (Goldstein) Loeb; m. Neil Paul Rosenthal, Dec. 16, 1967 (div. 1984); children: Josh Scott, Karen; m. Richard Elliot Horman, Oct. 27, 1985 (dec.). BS, U. Md., 1969. Tchr. Brown Sta. Elem. Sch., 1969-72, Cold Spring Elem. Sch., Potomac, Md., 1972-73, Montgomery County Pub. Schs./Fallsmead Elem. Sch., Rockville, Md., 1973-93, Brown Sta. Elem. Sch., 1969-72, Thurgood Marshall Elem. Sch., Gaithersburg, Md., 1993—. Tchr. math. Montgomery County Pub. Schs., Md., 1980-86. Bd. dirs. Tourette's Syndrome of Am., Bayside, N.Y., 1988-90; antique dealer Frederick, Md. Jewish. Avocations: travel, antiques. Office: Thurgood Marshal Elem Sch McDonald Chapel Way Gaithersburg MD 20878

HORN, PATRICIA SOLOMON, technology coordinator; b. Quincy, Fla., Oct. 17, 1944; d. Thomas William and Mary Margaret (Lecky) Solomon; m. Phillip W. Horn Jr., May 14, 1965; children: Phillip W. III, Thomas W. BA, Jacksonville U., 1965; MEd, U. North Fla., 1988-91, EdD, 1997. Cert. elem. tchr., Fla. Tchr. 2d and 3d grades Newberry (Fla.) Sch., 1965-68; tchr. kindergarten Dept. of Def. Schs. Overseas, Madrid, Spain, 1969-79, Lackawanna Elem. Sch., Jacksonville, Fla., 1979-85; tchr. kindergarten, sch. improvement chair Webster Sch., St. Augustine, Fla., 1987-93; facilitator for integrated curriculum and tech. St. Johns County Sch. Dist., St. Augustine, Fla., 1993—. Technology cons. Fulbright Commn., Egyptian Ministry Edn., 1996. Co-author: to Handbook of Literacy Assessment and Evaluation, 1996, and articles to profl. jours. Den leader Cub Scouts Am., Jacksonville, Fla., 1978-84; bd. dirs. Boy Scouts Am., Jacksonville, 1979-84; pres., sec. St. Johns County Med. Aux., 1987-94; bd. dirs. Childbirth and Parenting Edn. Assn. (1991-94), mem. Tech. Resource Com. for Fla. Accountability Commn., Tallahassee, 1994. Mem. ACSD (Tech. Futures Commn. 1994-95), Fla. League Tchrs. (charter, adv. bd. 1992—), Fla. Assn. Computers in Edn. (Fla. Instrnl. Tech. Tchr. of Yr. award 1994), Internat. Reading Assn., Internat. Soc. for Tech. in Edn. (Internat. Tech. Tchr. of Yr. award 1994), cons. to Fulbright Commn. of the Middle East and Egyptian Ministry of Edn. 1996), Fla. Edn. Standards Commn., Alpha Delta Kappa, Phi Kappa Phi. Democrat. Roman Catholic. Avocations: creating thematic clothing, writing children's books. Home: 6 Versaggi Dr Saint Augustine FL 32080-6926 Office: Saint Johns County Sch Dist 40 Orange St Saint Augustine FL 32084-3633

HORN, SHARON K. government agency administrator; B in Bus. and Econs., U. Ga.; EdM, Tex. A&M U.; PhD in Higher Edn. and Curriculum, U. Tex. Legis. fellow labor and human resources com. U.S. Senate; secondary sch. tchr. of bus., econs. and polit. sci. Ga.; tchr. U. Tex., Tyler, S.W. Tex. STate U.; assoc. dir. Program on Ednl. Policy and Orgn. Nat. Inst. Edn., 1982; dir. info. svcs. Office Ednl. Rsch. and Improvement U.S. Dept. Edn., Washington, program officer, dir. Nat. Awards Program for Model Profl. Devel., dir. evaluation and dissemination Office Innovation and Improvement. Office: US Dept Edn FOB-6 Rm 4W332 400 Maryland Ave SW Washington DC 20202*

HORNE, JAMES, school system administrator; b. Orange Park, Fla., Jan. 20, 1959; m. Lori McArdle; children: Ashley, Laura, John David, Katherine. BS in Acctg., Fla. State U., 1980. CPA. Tax mgr. Price Waterhouse, Jacksonville, Fla.; mem. Fla. Senate from 6th dist., Tallahassee, 1994—2001; Fla. secy. of edn., 2001—. Mem. criminal justice com., edn. com., jud. com., rules and calendar com., ways and means com., joint legis. com. on intergovtl. rels., vice chmn. commerce and econ. opportunities com., chmn. edn. subcom. Fla. State Senate, 1996-98. Bd. dirs. Keep Clay Beautiful; mem. Clay County Transit Authority; co-founder Clay County Edn. Found. Mem. Clay County C. of C. (chmn. edn. com., bd. dirs., pres. 1992), Rotary. Republican. Baptist. Avocations: running, golf. Office: Fla Dept Edn Office of the Commr Turlington Bldg Ste 1514 325 W Gaines St Tallahassee FL 32399 Office Fax: 850-245-9667. Business E-Mail: commissioner@fldoe.org.

HORNE, THOMAS CHARLES, school system administrator; b. Montreal, Que., Can., Mar. 28, 1945; s. George Marcus and Ludwika (Tom) H.; m. Martha Louise Presbry, June 25, 1972; children: Susan Christine, Mary Alice, David Charles, Mark Walter. BA magna cum laude, Harvard U., 1967, JD with honors, 1970. Bar: Mass. 1970, Ariz. 1972, U.S. Supreme Ct. 1974. Assoc. Donovan, Leisure, Newton & Irvine, NYC; sr. ptnr. Lewis & Roca, Phoenix; mng. ptnr. Horne, Duncan, Lorona & Slaton, Phoenix. Author: Arizona Construction Law, 1978. Mem. Ariz. Ho. of Reps., 1997—2001; chmn. Ariz. Air Pollution Control Hearing Bd., Phoenix, 1976—78; mem. Paradise Valley (Ariz.) Sch. Bd., 1978—, pres., 1981—83, 1985—88, 1990—91, 1994; supt. of pub. instrn. Ariz. Dept. Edn., 2003—. Mem. Ariz. Bar Assn. (former chmn. constrn. law com. litigation sect.). Republican. Jewish. Office: Dept Ed 1535 W Jefferson Phoenix AZ 85007-4497 E-mail: thorne@ade.az.gov.com.

HORNER, ELAINE EVELYN, secondary education educator; b. Portales, N.Mex., Feb. 26, 1941; d. Carlton James and Clara C. (Roberson) Carmichael; m. Bill G. Horner, Feb. 2, 1959; children: Billy G. Jr., Frances E. Moreau, Aaron J. BA, Ea. N.Mex. U., 1973, MEd, 1978. Tchr. Artesia (N.Mex.) Jr. High Sch., 1973-98, ret., 1998. Recipient Honor of Excellence award Navajo Refining, 1993. Mem. NEA, Nat. Coun. Tchrs. Math., N.Mex. Coun. Tchrs. Math., Artesia Edn. Assn. (v.p. 1987-88), Delta Kappa Gamma (treas. 1988—). Democrat. Baptist. Avocations: reading, golf. Home: 2406 N Haldeman Rd Artesia NM 88210-9435

HORNER, MICHELLE, elementary school educator, principal; b. Burbank, Calif., Aug. 9, 1954; d. George Albert Phillips and Geraldine Lou (Anderson) Notman; children: Jesse Daniel, Molly Anne. BA in Liberal Studies, Calif. State U., Fresno, 1976; M in Adminstrn., adminstrv. svcs. credential, Fresno Pacific Coll., 1993; PhD in Religous Studies, Emerson Inst., 1999. Tchr. Coarsegold (Calif.) Sch., 1977-81; tchg. prin. Wawona (Calif.) Sch., 1981—. Mem. Calif. State Multiage Task Force, Sacramento, 1994-95; mem. info. literacy task force Calif. Tech. Assistance Program, Fresno, Calif., 1996-98. Contbr. unit to: Teachers Make A Difference (Susan Kovalik), 1986. Mgr. Wawona Sch. Recycling Ctr., 1988-98. Recipient Cmty. Svc. award Nat. Pk. Svc., Yosemite, Calif., 1993; named Disting. Sch. Prin., Calif. Dept. Edn., Anaheim, 1995. Mem. ASCD, AAUW, Assn. for Calif. Sch. Adminstrs., Calif. Alliance for Elem. Edn. (founding, mem. planning com. for conf. 1995). Avocations: doll collecting, reading, travel. Home: PO Box 2014 Wawona CA 95389 Office: Wawona Sch PO Box 2068 Wawona CA 95389-2068

HORNER, SANDRA MARIE GROCE (SANDY HEART), educator, poet, songwriter, lyricist; b. Dallas; d. Larnell and Lee Ella (Lacy) Groce; divorced; 1 child, Danielle Marie. BA in Sociol./Philosophy with honors, Calif. State U., Dominguez Hills, 1980; postgrad., UCLA, 1978, 82-83, Consumnes River Coll., 1987, Nat. U., 1991, So. Utah U., 1993. Cert. elem. edn. K-8, Nev., K-A Occ. Std.: Bus. and Office Occupations; cert. instr. credential Calif.; cert. lifetime tchg. credential bus., Calif. Prodn. asst., sec. Paramount Pictures Corp., Hollywood, Calif., 1968-74; instr. LA C.C. Dist., 1976-78; tchr. Verbum Dei HS, LA, 1977-79; tchr., dept. chair LA Unified Sch. Dist., Calif., 1975-83; tchr. Sacramento City Unified Sch. Dist., Calif., 1985-87; editor, pub. Multi-Family Publ., Sacramento, 1986-89; tchr. Clark County Sch. Dist., Las Vegas, Nev., 1991—2003. Adj. instr. C.C. So. Nev., Las Vegas, 1988-95; radio broadcast interview Poetry Today with Ken Lerch WRTN 93.5 FM, NYC, 1997. Editor: (books/newsletters) Groce Family Newsletter, 1986; recording contracts Hilltop Records, 1996, 97, AME Record Recording Co., 1997, Hollywood Artists Record Co., 1997; author numerous poems; albums include America, Hill Top Country, Star Route USA, Music of Am. Recipient Nat. History recognition award Soc. History Rsch. and Preservation, 1989, Editor's Choice awards Nat. Libr. of Poetry, 1996; inducted into Internat. Poetry Hall of Fame, 1996. Mem. Internat. Soc. Poets (Disting. Mem.), Internat. Platform Assn. Democrat. Avocations: literature, music, history, art, antiques. Office: PO Box 34325 Las Vegas NV 89133-4325 E-mail: sheart1writer@aol.com.

HORNICK, SUSAN FLORENCE STEGMULLER, secondary education educator, fine arts educator, curriculum specialist, artist; b. Aug. 29, 1947; d. August George and Florence Maybell (Meisinger) Stegmuller; m. Jesse Allan Hornick, July 20, 1974. BA, Queens Coll., 1969, MS in Art Edn., 1973; permanent N.Y. State reading cert., Hunter Coll., 1984, advanced cert. ednl. supervn./adminstrn. summa cum laude, 1996. Lic. tchr. fine arts, N.Y.C.; permanent cert. tchr. art, N.Y.; cert. in ednl. adminstrn. and supervision, N.Y.; permanent cert. sch. dist. adminstr., N.Y. Fine arts tchr. Hillcrest H.S., Jamaica, N.Y., 1973-74, Ea. Dist. H.S., Bklyn., 1974-75, Tottenville H.S., S.I., N.Y., 1975-76; fine arts tchr., title 1 reading tchr. Prospect Heights H.S., Bklyn., 1976-78; fine arts tchr. Grover Cleveland H.S., Ridgewood, NY, 1978—2003, dept. coord., 1986-98. Tchr. reading. English and reading improvement through art, Grover Cleveland H.S., 1980—85, tchr. ecol. awareness, 1995—, yearbook advisor, 1979; cooperating tchr., trainer art tchrs. Queens Coll., Flushing, NY, 1991, 2000; tchr. "bridge" ESL and math. Newcomers Summer H.S., Long Island City, NY, 2000, ESL tchr., mem. Saturday lit. program, 2000—01; conceptual art tchr., conceptual facilitator reading, writing and artistic skills with written and visual exemplification, 2000—03; conceptual facilitator reading, writing and artistic skills with written and visual exemplification, 2000—. Exhbns. include U.S. Capitol, Washington, 1982, 86, 88, U.S. Capitol, Washington, Lever House Exhibit, 1984-97, City Hall, N.Y.C., 1984, Queensborough C.C. Art Gallery, Bayside, N.Y., 1984-94, N.Y.C. Transit Mus., 1987-99, Queens Borough Hall, Kew Gardens, N.Y., 1992, Sotheby's, 1992, Internat. Arrivals bldg. JFK Kennedy Airport (award winning mural by Joanna Kadlubowska, 1992), Queens Theater in the Park, Flushing, N.Y., 1993, 97, Nat. Mus. Am. Indian, Smithsonian Inst., 1992, 93, Mus. of City of N.Y., 1998, Grover Cleveland H.S., Ridgewood, N.Y., 1998-2003, N.Y. Joint Bd. Unite, N.Y.C., 2000-01 Named Internat. Educator of Yr. award, Internat. Biographical Ctr. Cambridge, England, 2003; recipient Medal for Superior Performance, N.Y.C. Transit Authority, 1996, Cert. of Appreciation for Outstanding Performance as Art Educator in N.Y.C. Pub. Schs., N.Y.C. Bd. Edn., 1985, Cert. of Recognition for Accomplishments as Outstanding Tchr., Nat. Tchrs. Hall of Fame, 2000. Mem. ASCD, N.Y.C. Art Tchrs. Assn., United Fedn. Tchrs., Hunter Coll. Alumni Assn., Nat. Mus. Women in Arts (charter), Colonial Williamsburg Duke of Gloucester Soc., N.Am. Fishing Club (life), Downsville Women's Club. Home and Office: P O Bos 482 Downsville NY 13755

HORNSTEIN, PAMELA KATHLEEN, educational administrator, educator; b. Olympia, Wash., Sept. 22, 1950; d. Frank P. and Aileen H. (Shields) Butler; m. Anthony G. Hornstein, Nov. 2, 1992; children by previous marriage: Megan, Mia and Marcus Meinhold. BA, Ctrl. Wash. U., 1971; MA, Mich. State U., 1977. Cert. elem. tchr., spl. edn. tchr., elem. prin., Wash. Spl. edn. tchr. Kelso (Wash.) Sch. Dist., 1973-75; learning disabilities specialist Dept. Def. Dependent Schs., Byrd Sch., Yokohama, Japan, 1975-77; spl. end. tchr., spl. edn. adminstr. Zillah (Wash.) Sch. Dist., 1977-80; tchr., administr. spl. edn. Mattawa (Wash.) Schs., 1980-82; prof. English Korean Mil. Acad., Yeongchun, South Korea, 1982-84; prof. English, cons. S.D.A. Acad., Taegu, South Korea, 1982-88; tchr. kindergarten and 1st grade Dept. Def. Dependent Schs., Taegu, 1984-87; prin., tchr. kindergarten-6th grade D.H.M.S. Pvt. Sch., Taegu, 1987-88; 21st Century Outcomes Driven Devel. Model tchr. coord. Yakima (Wash.) Pub. Schs., 1988—. Co-author 3 books and videos English Through Songs, 1982-83, 93-94, 84-85, 2 books, tapes, videos Olympic English, 1986-88. Roman Catholic. Avocations: photography, writing, travel. Home: 5308 Webster Ct Yakima WA 98908-3653

HORNUNG, HANS GEORG, aeronautical engineering educator, science facility administrator; b. Jaffa, Israel, Dec. 26, 1934; came to U.S., 1987; s. Friedrich Gottlieb and Helene Wilhelmine (Wagner) H.; m. Gretl Charlotte

Frank, Jan. 29, 1960; children: Ingrid, Karl, Lisa, Jenny. BMechE with honors, U. Melbourne, Australia, 1960, M in Engring. Sci. with honors, 1962; PhD in Aeros., U. London, 1965. Rsch. scientist Aero. Rsch. Labs., Melbourne, 1962-67; lectr., sr. lectr. then reader Australian Nat. U., Canberra, 1967-80; dir., mem. senate com. for sci. and tech. Inst. Exptl. Fluid Mechanics (DLR), Göttingen, Germany, 1980-87; dir. Grad. Aero. Labs. and Clarence Johnson prof. aero. Calif. Inst. Tech., Pasadena, 1987—. Mem. fluid dynamics panel Adv. Group. Aerospace R & D, 1983-88; mem. adv. com. Internat. Shock Tube Symposia, 1979-95; chmn. adv. com. von Kármán Inst. for Fluid Dynamics, 1984-85; mem. German del. Internat. Union Theoretical and Applied Mechanics, 1984-87; Lanchester Meml. lectr. Royal Aero. Soc., London, 1988; hon. prof. U. Göttingen; Prandtl mem. lectr. Ges. Angew. Math. and Mech., Vienna, 1988. Mem. editl. adv. bd. Zeitschrift für Flugwissenschaften und Weltraumforschung, 1984-96, Experiments in Fluids jour., 1987—, Physics of Fluids, 1988-91, Ing. Archiv, 1989-96; contbr. numerous articles to profl. jours. Recipient von Karman award and medal for internat. coop. in aero. Internat. Coun. Aero. Scis.; Humboldt fellow Tech. U., Darmstadt, Germany, 1974-75. Fellow Royal Aero. Soc.; mem. Nat. Acad. of Engring.(fgn. assoc.), Sci. mem. of bd. DLR Germany, Australian Inst. Physics, Deutsche Gesellschaft für Luft-und Raumfahrt, Gesellschaft für angewandte Mathematik und Mechanik, Am. Phys. Soc., AIAA, Royal Swedish Acad. Engring. Scis., Ludwig Prandtl Ring German Soc. Aerospace Sci. Achievements include making important contbns. in hypersonic flow theory, exptl. methods and results in real-gas flows, Mach reflection and three-dimensional separation. Office: Calif Inst Tech 1201 E California Blvd Pasadena CA 91125-0001 E-mail: hans@galcit.caltech.edu.

HOROWITZ, DONALD LEONARD, lawyer, educator, researcher, political scientist, arbitrator; b. N.Y.C., June 27, 1939; s. Morris and Yetta (Hibscher) H.; m. Judith Anne Present, Sept. 4, 1960; children: Marshall, Karen, Bruce. AB, Syracuse U., 1959, LLB, 1961; LLM, Harvard U., 1962, AM, 1965, PhD, 1968. Bar: N.Y. 1962, D.C. 1979, U.S. Ct. Appeals (D.C., 6th, 7th and 10th cirs.) 1970, U.S. Supreme Ct. 1969. Law clk. U.S. Dist. Ct. (ea. dist.), Pa., 1965-66; rsch. assoc. Harvard U. Ctr. Internat. Affairs, 1967-69; atty. Dept. Justice, Washington, 1969-71; fellow Coun. on Fgn. Rels./Woodrow Wilson Internat. Ctr. Scholars, Washington, 1971-72; rsch. assoc. Brookings Instn., Washington, 1972-75; sr. fellow Rsch. Inst. on Immigration and Ethnic Studies/Smithsonian, Washington, 1975-81; prof. law and polit. sci. Duke U., Durham, N.C., 1980—, Charles S. Murphy Prof., 1988-93, James B. Duke prof., 1994—. Vis. prof. Charles J. Merriam scholar U. Chgo. Law Sch., 1988; vis. fellow Cambridge U., Eng., 1988; Sticerd Disting. visitor London Sch. Econs., 1998-2000, Centennial prof., 2001; vis. scholar Universiti Kebangsaan Malaysia Law Faculty, 1991; Fulbright sr. specialist, 2002; cons. Ford Found., 1977-82; mem. internat. adv. com. Office of the High Rep., Bosnia, 1998-99; McDonald-Currie Meml. lectr. McGill U., Montreal, 1980; mem. Coun. on Role of Cts., 1978-83; Opsahl lectr. Queen's U., Belfast, 2000. Author: The Courts and Social Policy (Nat. Acad. Public Adminstrn. Louis Brownlow prize for best book in pub. adminstrn. 1977), 1977; The Jurocracy: Government Lawyers, Agency Programs and Judicial Decisions, 1977; Coup Theories and Officers' Motives, 1980, Ethnic Groups in Conflict, 1985, A Democratic South Africa? Constitutional Engineering in a Divided Soc., 1991 (Am. Polit. Sci. Assn. Ralph J. Bunche award for best book in ethnic and cultural pluralism, 1992), The Deadly Ethnic Riot, 2001; mem. editl. bd. Ethnicity, 1974-82, Law and Contemporary Problems, 1983-84, 89-2000, Jour. Democracy, 1993—. Guggenheim fellow, 1980-81; Nat. Humanities Ctr. fellow, 1984; Carnegie scholar, 2001-2002. Fellow Am. Acad. Arts and Scis. Office: Duke University School Law Durham NC 27708-0360

HOROWITZ, FRANCES DEGEN, academic administrator, psychology educator; b. Bronx, NY, May 5, 1932; d. Irving and Elaine (Moinester) Degen; m. Floyd Ross Horowitz, June 23, 1953; children: Jason Degen, Benjamin Meyer Levi. BA, Antioch Coll., 1954; EdM, Goucher Coll., 1954; PhD, U. Iowa, 1959. Tchr. elem. sch., Iowa City, 1954-56; grad. rsch. asst. Iowa Child Welfare Sta., U. Iowa, 1956-59; asst. prof. psychology So. Oreg. Coll., Ashland, 1959-61; asst. prof. home econs. U. Kans., Lawrence, 1961-62, USHPS rsch. fellow, 1962-63, assoc. prof. dept. human devel. and family life, 1964-69, prof. dept. human devel. and family life, psychology, 1969—, chmn. dept., 1969-75, rsch. assoc., 1964-75, assoc. dean, 1975-78, vice chancellor rsch., grad. studies and pub. svc., also dean grad. sch., 1978-91, dir. Infant Rsch. Lab., 1964-91; pres. Grad. Sch. and Univ. Ctr. CUNY, 1991—. Bd. dirs. Feminist Press; guest rsch. assoc. Bur. Child Rsch. U. Kans., and Parsons (Kans.) State Hosp. and Tng. Ctr., summer 1960; vis. prof. dept. psychology Tel Aviv U., 1973—74; guest rschr. dept. pediat. Kaplan Hosp., Rehovot, Israel, 1973—74; vis. lectr. dept. psychology Hebrew U., Jerusalem, 1976, cons. rsch. programs in early edn., 1980—; pres. Ctr. for Rsch., Inc., Lawrence, 1978—91; cons. OAS, 1971, U.S. Office Edn., 1969—73, NIMH, 1979; cons. to early infant stimulation program, Caracas, Venezuela, 76; lectr. infant devel., day care to local and regional cmty. groups, 1966—; adv. com. Carolina Inst. on Early Edn. of the Handicapped, 1978—83; reviewer NSF, 1978—91; mem. U. Kans. del. to Peoples Republic China, 1980; exch. scholar Chinese Acad. Scis., China, 1982; mem. Office Sci. Integrity Rev. Adv. Com. PHS, 1991—93; nominating com. Weizmann Women in Sci. award Am. Com. Weizmann Inst. Sci., 1994; mem. Nat. Task Force Grad. Edn., 1994—; workforce devel. subcom. N.Y.C. Partnership, 1994—; mem. U.S. Nat. Com. for the Internat. Union of Psychol. Sci., 1995—97; mem. overseers' com. to visit dept. psychology Harvard U.; mem., founding adv. bd. Sackler Inst. for Human Brain Devel., 1998—; bd. dirs. Nat. Coun. for Rsch. on Women; adv. coun. Nat. Inst. Child Health and Human Devel., 1999—; chair nat. adv. bd. Office Child Devel., U. Pitts.; lectr. in field. Editor Memoir Essay, 2002; co-editor science watch sect. Am. Psychologist, 1993—; mem. editl. bd. Jour. Devel. Psychology, 1969-75, Early Childhood Edn. Quar., 1974—, Devel. Rev., 1981—, Infant Behaviour and Devel., 1984—, Contemporary Psychology, 1986-1991; contbr. articles to profl. jours.; TV host Women to Women, 1994—. Trustee Antioch Coll., 1987-91, L.I. Univ., 1992—; bd. dirs. Cmty. Children's Ctr., 1965-68, Douglas County Vis. Nurse Assn., 1968-69; mem. workforce devel. subcom., N.Y.C. Partnership; mem. coun. advisors, Nat. Ctr. for Children in Poverty; mem. commn. on women in higher edn. Am. Coun. on Edn. Recipient Trustees award medal Cherry Lawn Sch., Conn., 1971, Outstanding Educator of Am. award, 1973, Disting. Psychologist in Mgmt. award Soc. for Psychologists in Mgmt., 1993, Rebecca Rice Alumni award Antioch Coll., 1996, Sue Rosenberg Zalk award The Feminist Press, 2003; named to Women's Hall of Fame U. Kans., 1974; Ford Found. fellow, 1954, Ctr. for Advanced Studies Behavioral Scis. fellow, Stanford U., 1983-84; Spl. Commendation NYC comptroller's office, 1997, NY Women's Agenda Star award, 2002. Fellow APA (pres. divsn. devel. psychology 1977-78, mem. publs. bd. 1985-91, chief sci. adviser 1989-93, pres. 1991-94, Centennial award 1992), AAAS, N.Y. Acad. Scis.; mem. Soc. Rsch. in Child Devel. (editor monographs 1976-83, pres. 1997-2002), Jewish Cmty. Rels. Coun. (mem. bd. 1999—), Hebrew Free Loan Soc. (mem. bd. 2000—), Am. Assn. on Mental Deficiency, North Ctrl. Accrediting Assn. (bd. commrs. 1977-80), Am. Psychol. Found. (pres. 1991-94), Coun. Rsch. Polic and Grad. Edn. (chair, mem. exec. com.), Assn. Grad. Schs. (mem. exec. com.), N.Y. Women's Forum (bd. dirs. 1995—), Nat. Assn. of State Univs. and Lnd-Grant Colls. (past chair commn. on human resources and social change, bd. dirs. 1999-2002), Sigma Xi, Phi Beta Kappa (hon.). Home: 145 Central Park W Apt 4A New York NY 10023-2004 Office: CUNY Grad Ctr 365 5th Ave New York NY 10016-4309 E-mail: pres@gc.cuny.edu.

HOROWITZ, IRA R. gynecologic oncologist, educator; b. Bklyn., Dec. 17, 1954; s. Benjamin and Frieda Horowitz; m. Julie A. Wood; children: Andrea, Rebecah. BA in Biology, U. Rochester, 1976; MD, Baylor U., 1980. Diplomate Am. Bd. Ob/Gyn. From resident to chief resident ob-gyn. Baylor Coll. Medicine, Houston, 1980-84; fellow in gynecologic oncology Johns Hopkins Med. Inst., Balt., 1985-87; clin. instr. ob-gyn. Baylor Coll. Medicine, 1984-85; instr. ob-gyn. Johns Hopkins U. Sch. Med., 1985-87, asst. prof. ob-gyn. and oncology, 1987-92; prof. ob-gyn. Emory U. Sch. Medicine, Atlanta, 1992-99, Willaford Ransom Leach prof., vice chmn. dept. ob/gyn., med. dir. divsn. gyncol. oncology; mem. Winship Cancer Inst., 1999—. Co-editor: Plantao em ginecologia e obstetricia, 1995, Obstetrics & Gynecology On Call, 1st edit., 1993, Advances in Obstetrics and Gynecology, vol. 3, 1996, Advances in Obstetrics & Gynecology, vol. 4, 1997. Fellow ACOG, ASCO, ISSVD, SAAOG, Soc. Gynecologic Oncologists; mem. Soc. Gynecologic Surgeons, Soc. Surg. Oncology, MAG, World Endomeriosis Soc., Internat. Gynecologic Cancer Soc. Avocations: camping, travel. Office: Emory U Sch Medicine GYN/OB 1639 Pierce Dr Atlanta GA 30322-0001 E-mail: ihorowit@emory.edu.

HOROWITZ, IRVING LOUIS, publisher, educator; b. N.Y.C., Sept. 25, 1929; s. Louis and Esther (Tepper) H.; m. Ruth Lenore Horowitz, 1950 (div. 1964); children: Carl Frederick, David Dennis; m. Mary Curtis Horowitz, 1979. BSS, CCNY, 1951; MA, Columbia U., 1952; PhD, Buenos Aires U., 1957; fellow, Brandeis U., 1958-59. Asst. prof. sociology Bard Coll., 1960; assoc. prof. social theory Buenos Aires U., 1955-58; chmn. dept. sociology Hobart and William Smith Colls., 1960-63; from assoc. prof. to prof. sociology Washington U., St. Louis, 1963-69; chmn. dept. sociology Livingston Coll., Rutgers U., 1969-73; prof. sociology grad. faculty Rutgers U., 1969—, Hannah Arendt prof. social and polit. theory, 1979—, Bacardi chair Cuban studies, 1992—. Vis. prof. sociology U. Caracas, Venezuela, 1957, Buenos Aires U., 1959, 61, 63, SUNY, Buffalo, 1960, Syracuse U., 1961, U. Rochester, fall 1962, U. Calif., Davis, 1966, U. Wis., Madison, 1967, Stanford U., 1968-69, Am. U., 1972, Queen's U., Can., 1973, Princeton U., 1976, U. Miami, 1992; vis. lectr. London Sch. Econs. and Polit. Sci., 1962; prin. investigator for numerous sci. and rsch. projects; chmn. bd. dirs., editor-in-chief Transaction/Soc. Author: Idea of War and Peace in Contemporary Philosophy, 1957, Philosophy, Science and the Sociology of Knowledge, 1960, Radicalism and the Revolt Against Reason: The Social Theories of Georges Sorel, 2d edit., 1968, The war Game; Studies of the New Civilian Militarists, 1963, Historia y Elementos de la Sociologia del Connocimento, 1963, Professing Sociology: The Life Cycle of a Social Science, 1963, The New Sociology: Essays in Social Science and Social Values in Honor of C. Wright Mills, 1964, Revolution in Brazil: Politics and Society in a Developing Nation, 1964, The Rise and Fall of Project Camelot, 1967, rev. edit., 1976, Three Worlds of Development: The Theory and Practice of International Stratification, 1966, rev. edit., 1972, Latin American Radicalism: A Documentary Report on Nationalist and Left Movements, 1969, Sociological Self-Images, 1969, The Knowledge Factory: Masses in Latin America, 1970, Cuban Communism, 1970, 11th edit., 2003, Foundations of Political Sociology, 1972, Social Science and Public Policy in the United States, 1977, Dialogues on American Politics, 1979, Taking Lives: Genocide and State Power, 1979, 5th edit., 2001, Beyond Empire and Revolution, 1982, C. Wright Mills: An American Utopian, 1983, Winners and Losers, 1985, Communicating Ideas, 1987, Daydreams and Nightmares, 1990 (winner best biography Nat. Jewish Book Award), The Decomposition of Sociology, 1993, Behemoth: Main Currents in the History and Theory of Political Sociology, 1999, Veblen's Century: A Collective Portrait, 2002. Chmn. bd. Hubert H. Humphrey Inst. Ben Gurion U.; bd. mem. Alexis DeTocqueville Inst., 2003—. Recipient Harold D. Lasswell award Policy Sci. Orgn., Lifetime Achievement award Inter-Univ. Seminar on Armed Forces and Society. Fellow AAAS; founding mem, AAAS Sci and Human Rights Program; mem. AAUP, USIA (bd. advisors), Am. Polit. Sci. Assn., Nat. Assn. Scholars (bd. dirs.), Authors Guild, Ctr. for Study The Presidency, Coun. Fgn. Rels., Internat. Soc. Polit. Psychology (founder), Soc. Internat. Devel., U.S. Gen. Acctg. Office (exec. adv. bd.), U.S. Info. Agy. (exec. adv. bd. Radio and TV Marti), Nat. Assn. Scholars (bd. dirs.), Inst. for a Free Cuba. Achievements include Subject of Festschrift: The Democratic Imagination, 1994. Home: 1247 State Rd # Rt206 Princeton NJ 08540-1619 Office: Rutgers U Transaction Pubs Bldg 4051 New Brunswick NJ 08903 Fax: 732-445-3138. E-mail: ihorowitz@transactionpub.com.

HOROWITZ, ROBERT AARON, art educator, researcher, music educator; b. Queens, NY, July 1, 1951; s. Israel and Mildred Horowitz; m. Amy Kleiman, Sept. 8, 1985. BA, Rutgers U., New Brunswick, NJ, 1986; MA, Columbia U., N.Y.C., 1990, Ed.M., 1992, Ed.D., 1994. Cert. tchr. HS music, social studies NY. Assoc. dir. Ctr. for Arts Edn. Rsch., Teachers Coll., Columbia U., N.Y.C., 1998—. Cons. Various edni. orgns., 1994—. Author: Champions of Change: The Impact of Arts on Learning, 1999; contbr. Learning, 2002, Critical Links: Leanring in the Arts and Student Academic and Social Development, 2002. Recipient Manuel Barkan Meml. award, Nat. Art Edn. Assn., 2001. Mem.: Coll. Music Soc., Music Educators Nat. Conf., Am. Ednl. Rsch. Assn. Office: Robert Horowitz 540 Fort Washington Ave #5F New York NY 10033 E-mail: artsresearch@aol.com.

HOROWITZ, ROSALIND, education educator, researcher; b. St. Paul, Aug. 24, 1946; d. Cantor Louis and Fannie (Hartman) H. BS, U. Minn., 1968, MA, 1973, PhD, 1982; postgrad., Harvard U., 1968, Hebrew U., Jerusalem, 1971. Tchr. English Marshall-Univ. High Sch., Mpls., 1969-70; instr. edn. U. Minn., Mpls., 1970-75, supr. of student tchrs., 1972-75, adminstrv. fellow for assoc. dean Coll. Edn., 1975-81, research coordinator edn. planning and devel. office, 1975-81; affiliate mem. Ctr. for Research in Human Learning, 1979-81; prin. tchr. Hebrew and Judaic studies program Adath Jeshurun Religious Sch., Mpls., 1972-76; asst. prof. reading, edn. Coll. Social and Behavioral Scis. U. Tex., San Antonio, 1981-85, assoc. prof., 1986-95, prof. reading and literacy edn., 1995—, prof. edn. Coll. Soc. and Behavioral Scis., 1995—. Rsch. coord. Coll. Social and Behavioral Scis., 1991-93; lectr. in field; rschr. text processing, text linguistics, discourse analysis; cons. in field; participant Bryn Mawr Summer Inst. for Women in Higher Edn. Adminstrn., 1992; vis. scholar Ont. Inst. Studies in Edn., U. Toronto, Can., 2003; dir. Hillel at U. Tex. San Antonio, 1987—. Contbr. 10 chpts. to books, 60 articles to profl. jours. including Harvard Ednl. Review, Australian Jour. Remedial Edn., Jour. of Reading, The Reading Tchr., Instrnl. Sci., Jour. Reading, The Reading Behavior, Nat. Reading Conf. Yearbook, Ednl. Rschr. and Contemporary Psychology, Nat. Assn. Bilingual Edn. Jour., Lang. Learning, Jour. Adolescent and Adult Reading, Hispanic Jour. Behavioral Scis., Jour. of Reading, Jour. Ednl. Rsch.; editor: Talking Texts: Knowing the World Through Instructional Discourse, 2000; co-editor: Comprehending Oral and Written Language, 1987; spl. editor (text) Studies of Orality and Literacy, 1991; guest editor Jour. of Reading, Classroom Talk about Text, 1994; reviewer: Applied Psycholinguistics Child Development, Jour. Ednl. Psychology, Reading Research Quar., Jour. Reading Behavior, Jour. of Reading, Rsch. in the Tchg. of English, Jour. of Reading; editl. adv. bd. Nat. Reading Conf. Yearbook, 1984—; mem. editl. bd. Discourse Prosesses, Written Comm. Rsch. in Tchg. of English, 1979—, Nat. Reading Conf. Yearbook, 2002-03; acquisition editor AERA, Reading and Literacy; co-author: (chpts.) Beliefs about Text and Instruction with Text, 1994, Composing Social Identity in Written Language, 1995, (with D. Olson) Texts that talk: The special and peculiar nature of classroom discourse, 2003, What Should Teachers Know About Bilingual Learners and the Reading Process? (with A. Cohen), 2002. Mpls. Coun. PTA Scholar, 1964; U. Minn. Nicholson Bookstore Scholar, 1965; HEW-U. Minn. grantee 1966, 67; Harvard U. Scholar, 1968; selected to visit Russia and Ukraine Nat. Security Edn. Program, 1998; Wesley E. Peik scholar, U. Minn., 1979; Doctoral Dissertation Spl. grantee, 1979; U. Tex. rsch. grantee, 1984; Spencer fellow Nat. Acad. grantee, 1984; Spencer fellow Nat. Acad. Edn., 1985-88; Tex. Assn. Gifted and Talented fellow, 1993; Soref Fund grantee Hillel Found., 1998, Leader Fund grantee, 1998; recipient Gender and Equity Recognition award Am. Assn. Colls. Tchr. Edn., 1994, Outstanding Alumni, Gordon M.A. Mork award Coll. Edn. U. Minn., 2002. Mem. Internat. Assn. Applied Linguistics, Nat. Coun. Tchrs. English (Promising Rsch. 1983, Student Govt. award 1995), Am. Assn. Higher Edn., Am. Edn. Rsch. Assn. (sec.-treas. lang. and social processes 1990, pres. chair, chair basic rsch. and reading literacy 1991-94, chair Russian contbns. to literacy learning and human devel., 1994-95, program chair divsn. chair learning and instrn. 1999—, assoc. chair spl. interest group basic rsch. in reading and literacy 1997-98, chmn. reunion contbns. to literacy and learning), Internat. Reading Assn. (Outstanding Dissertation award 1983), Nat. Reading Conf., Soc. Text and Discourse (exec. bd.), Soc. for Sci. Study of Reading, N.Y. Acad. Scis. (linguistics divsn.). Office: U Tex Coll Edn and Human Devel Downtn Campus 501 Durango Blvd DB 3 224 San Antonio TX 78207 E-mail: rhorowitz@utsa.edu.

HORSELY, WILLIE WOODRUFF, educational administrator; b. Newnan, Ga., Aug. 26, 1940; d. Albert and Gussie (Malcolm) Huff; m. Harvey L. Horsely (dec. Dec. 1986); children: Harvietta Horsely Dixon, Victor. BS, Cen. State U., Wilberforce, Ohio, 1967; MEd, U. Cin., 1970; postgrad., Xavier U., Cin., 1974; EdS, U. Mo., Kansas City, 1991. Cert. tchr., adminstr., Ohio, Mo. With Kansas city Sch. Dist.; appointed to the advisory council State Mo. Adv. Coun. Vocational Edn., 1992—. Seminar and workshop presenter. With U.S. Army, 1958-61; active Big Bros. and Big Sisters. Mem. Am. Vocat. Assn. (pres.-elect, chmn. nominating com. 1990-91), Mo. Vocat. Assn. (bd. dirs. 1980-82), Nat. Assn. Vocat. Spl. Needs Pers. (bd. dirs. 1982-86, policy and legis. com. 1985-86), Mo. Vocat. Spl. Needs Assn. (membership chmn. 1980-81, pres. 1980-81, leadership award 1981), Mo. Indsl. Tech. Edn. Assn. (bd. dirs. 1988—), Indsl. Tech. Edn. Assn. (planning com.), Nat. Assn. Blacks in Vocational Edn. (program com. 1986-87), Kansas City Sch. Adminstrv. Assn. (pres. 1986-88), Nat. Assn. Vocational Edn. Special Needs Personel (regional v.p. 1983-85, pres. 1985-87, svc. award 1988). Democrat. Baptist. Avocations: gardening, photography, woodworking. Home: 26332 Riding Trl South Bend IN 46619-3932 Office: 1215 E Truman Rd Kansas City MO 64106-3152

HORSMAN, LENORE LYNDE (ELEANORA LYNDE), soprano, educator, actress; b. Saginaw, Mich., Apr. 21, 1931; d. George Clark and Gwendolyn (Steele) McNabb; m. Reginald Horsman, Sept. 3, 1955; children: John, Janine, Mara. BS in Music and Piano, Ind. U., 1956, MA in Theatre-Opera, 1958. profl. certs. in voice, Villa Schifanoia, Florence, Accademia Musicale Chigiana, Siena, Accademia Di Virgiliana, Mantua, Mozarteum, Salzburg. Tchrs: Tito Gobbi, Ettore Campogalliani. Dir. Mt. Clemens Studio of Music, Mich., 1950; tchr. voice, piano and acting for singers Milw. Conservatory of Music, 1964-65; dir., tchr. pvt. voice studio, 1965—; founder, dir., designer Milw. Opera Theater, 1966; vocal coach dept. opera U. Wis., Madison, 1969-70. Dir., performer Cameo Prodn., Milw., 1974, Opera for Two, Milw., 1975, Mu Phi Epsilon Sch. Music, Chgo., 1976-81; dir., tchr. pvt. voice studio, Chgo., 1976-92; voice coach Theatre X, Milw., 1977; tchr. of acting Northshore Theatre, Milw., 1978-80. More than 33 leading roles in opera, operetta, musicals and plays; performances and concerts in US and Italy. Pres. Wis. Women in the Arts, 1973-76; bd. dir. Internat. Women's Yr. Festival, Milw., 1975. Named Women of the Yr., Milw. Panhellenic Assn., 1975; recipient Career Achievement award, 1978, Singers medal of honor Amici della Lirica, Mantua, Italy, 1981, Palcoscenico Music Vocal Silver Stage award, 1981. Mem. AAUW (v.p. 1999-2000), Nat. Assn. Tchr. Singing, Nat. Opera Assn., Wis. Music Tchr. Assn., Mu Phi Epsilon, Theta Alpha Phi. Avocations: theater, opera, oil painting, writing poetry.

HORSTMANN, JAMES DOUGLAS, college official; b. Davenport, Iowa, Oct. 2, 1933; s. Leonard A. and Agnes A. (Erhke) H.; m. Carol H. Griffiths, Sept. 8, 1956; children: Kent, Karen, Diane. BA, Augustana Coll., 1955. C.P.A., Ill., Wis. Staff acct., auditor Arthur Andersen & Co., Chgo., 1955-61; v.p., controller Harry S. Manchester, Inc., Madison, Wis., 1961-65; sr. v.p. fin., treas. H. C. Prange Co., Sheboygan, Wis., 1965-83, also dir.; dir. planned giving Augustana Coll., Rock Island, Ill., 1983-85, v.p. for devel., 1985-93, v.p. planned giving, 1993-98, v.p. emeritus, 1998—; pres. Schonstedt Instrument Co., 1993-95. Chmn. Wis. Mchts. Fedn.; dir. First Wis. Nat. Bank, Fond du Lac. Chmn. Sheboygan County (Wis.) Rep. Party, 1969-70; vice-chmn. Wis. 6th Congl. Dist., 1972-73, Rock Island County Reps., 2000-02; del. Nat. Rep. Conv., 1976; campaign chmn. Sheboygan United Way, 1977, treas., 1973-75, v.p., 1975-78, pres., 1978-79; bd. dirs. Public Expenditure Survey Wis., 1981-83, Rock Island YMCA, 1986-87, Franciscan Health Care Systems, 1988-92, Christ Luth. H.S. Found., 2000-03, Alternatives for the Older Adult, 2001—, Marriage and Family Counseling, 2003—, Thrivent for Lutherans, 2003; v.p. Sheboygan Arts Found., 1973-75; v.p., bd. dirs. Sheboygan Retirement Home, 1977-83; bd. dirs. Franciscan Mental Health Ctr., 1984-94, pres., 1985-88; trustee Friendship Manor, 1993-2003, pres., 2000-02; trustee Jr. Achievement Found., 2003—; trustee Coun. on Children at Risk, 1989—, Franciscan Med. Ctr., 1990-92, Cmty. Found. of the Great River Bend, 2002—, vice-chair, 2003; trustee Villa Montessori Sch., 1999—, pres. 2000—; v.p. German Am. Heritage Ctr., 2000—; treas. Vis. Nurse/Homemakers Assn., 2001, Pathway Hospice, 2001. With USN, 1955-57. Named Outstanding Fund Raising Exec. Nat. Soc. Fund Raising Execs., 1992; recipient Outstanding Svc. award Augustana Coll., 1979, Jr. Achievement Free Enterprise Found., 2003. Mem. Am. Heart Assn. (bd. dirs. Quad City chpt. 1999—, pres. 2002-), Am. Cancer Soc. (bd. dirs. Rock Island unit 1992-2001), Wis. Inst. CPAs, Ill. Soc. CPAs, Sheboygan County Assn. CPAs, Fin. Execs. Inst. (dir.), Quad-City Estate Planning Coun., Augustana Hist. Soc. (bd. dirs. 1999—), Augustana Coll. Alumni Assn. (pres. 1970-71), Econ. Club Sheboygan (pres. 1976-77), Kiwanis. Lutheran. Home: 1245 36th Ave Rock Island IL 61201-6022 Office: Augustana Coll 639 38th St Rock Island IL 61201-2210

HORSTMANN, JANE KRISTI, elementary school educator; b. Washington, Mo., Dec. 18, 1962; d. Calvin Oscar and Rita Ann (Piezuch) H. AA, East Cen. Coll., Union, Mo., 1983; BS in Elem. Edn., Maryville Coll., St. Louis, 1985. Cert. elem. educator. Summer staff tchr. Boys Town of Mo., St. James, 1985-89; elem. tchr. 2d grade Gerald (Mo.) Elem. Sch., 1985-89, tchr. 5th grade, 1989-91; tchr. 6th grade Owensville (Mo.) Mid. Sch., 1991—94; tchr. 5th grade Gerald Elem. Sch., 1994—99, Camdenton R-II Schs., Osage Beach Elem. Sch., Mo., 1999—. Coach Tri-County Volleyball Club, U.S. Volleyball Assn., Union, Mo., 1990-91; asst. volleyball coach Owensville High Sch., 1991-93; head volleyball coach Owensville High Sch., 1994-95, 7th grade volleyball coach, 1997-99. Mem. Community Tchrs. Assn. (sec.-treas. 1988-89), Mo. State Tchrs. Assn., Profl. Devel. Com. (chmn. 1993-94), Mo. High Sch. Volleyball Coaches Assn. Roman Catholic. Avocations: volleyball, photography, sewing.

HORTMAN, DAVID JONES, secondary education educator; b. Washington, Aug. 12, 1954; s. Jack Doyle and Elizabeth (Jones) H.; m. Ellen Shea Johnston, Aug. 28, 1976; children: Melissa, Gregory, Jeffrey. BS, Millersville U., 1976. Tchr. Kennard Dale H.S., Fawn Grove, Pa., 1976-79; designer Gichner Mobile Sys., Dallastown, Pa., 1979-81; tchr. York (Pa.) County Vocat.-Tech. Sch., 1981, Susquehannock H.S., Glen Rock, Pa., 1982-99, York (Pa.) Tech. Inst., 1988-91; tchr. tech. edn. Milton Hershey Sch., Hershey, Pa., 1999—. Cons. in field. Pres. Dallastown (Pa.) Jaycees, 1983-84, active, 1982-85. Recipient Tchr. Excellence for Pa. award Internat. Tech. Edn. Assn., 1992. Mem. Internat. Tech. Edn. Assn. (Tchr. Excellence award 1993), Tech. Edn. Assn. Pa. (Tchr. Excellence award 1992-93), York County Tech. Edn. Assn. (pres. 1991-92). Republican. Methodist. Avocations: gardening, sports, travel. Home: 264 W High St Red Lion PA 17356-1528 Office: Mitlon Hershey Sch PO Box 830 Hershey PA 17033-0830

HORTON, FRANK ELBA, university official, geography educator; b. Chgo., Aug. 19, 1939; s. Elba Earl and Mae Pauline (Prohaska) H.; m. Nancy Yocom, Aug. 26, 1960; children: Kimberly, Pamela, Amy, Kelly. BA, Western Ill. U., 1963; MS, Northwestern U., 1964, PhD, 1966. Faculty U. Iowa, Iowa City, 1966-75, prof. geography, 1966-75; dir. Inst. Urban and

Regional Research, 1968-72, dean advanced studies, 1972-75; v.p. acad. affairs, research So. Ill. U., Carbondale, 1975-80; prof. geography and urban affairs, chancellor U. Wis., Milw., 1980-85; prof. geography, pres. U. Okla., Norman, 1985-88; prof. geography, higher edn. adminstrn., pres. U. Toledo, 1988-98, pres. emeritus, 1999—; prin. Horton & Assocs., Denver, 1999—; interim pres. So. Ill. U., 2000. Mem. commn. on leadership devel. and acad. adminstrn. Am. Coun. on Edn., 1983-85; mem. presdl. adv. com. Assn. on Governing Bds., 1986-98; dir. 1st Wis. Nat. Bank of Milw., 1980-85, Liberty Nat. Bank, Oklahoma City, 1986-89, Trustcorp. Bank, 1989-90; bd. dirs. Interstate Bakeries, GAC Corp. Author, editor: (with B.J.L. Berry) Geographic Perspectives on Urban Systems - With Integrated Readings, 1970, Urban Environmental Management - Planning for Pollution Control, 1974; editor: (with B.J.L. Berry) Geographical Perspectives on Contemporary Urban Problems, 1973; editorial adv. bd.: (with B.J.L. Berry) Transportation, 1971-78. Co-chmn. Goals for Milw. 2000, 1981-85, Greater Milw. Com., 1980; mem. bus. devel. sub-com. Okla. Coun. Sci. and Tech., 1985-88; mem. Harry S. Truman Library Inst., 1985-88, William Rockhill Nelson Trust, 1985-88; bd. govs. Am. Heart Assn., Wis., 1980-85, Ohio Supercomputer Ctr., 1993-97; mem. exec. com. Okla. Acad. State Goals, 1986-88; trustee Toledo Symphony Orch., 1989-96, Toledo Hosp., 1989-97, Pub. Broadcasting Found. Northwest Ohio, 1989-93, Key Bank, 1990-2000, Ohio Aerospace Inst., 1990-97; chair Inter-Univ. Coun. Pres. of Ohio Public Univs., 1992-93; mem. exec. com. Com. of 100, Toledo, 1989-92. Served with AUS, 1957-60. Mem. AAAs (nat. coun. 1976-78), Assn. Governing Bds. (mem. presdl. adv. commn. 1986-95), Assn. Am. Geographers, nat. Assn. State Univs. and Land Grant Colls. (chair urban affairs div. 1983-85, chmn. Coun. of Pres. 1987-88, exec. com. 1983-88), Nat. Hwy. Rsch. Soc., Okla. Coun. on Sci. and Tech., MidAm. State Univs. Assn. (pres. 1987-88), Ohio Supercomputer Ctr. (bd. govs. 1993), Ohio Aerospace Inst. (trustee 1990—), Okla. Acad. State Goals (pres. 1987-88), Okla. State C. of C. and Industry (v.p. 1987-88), Toledo Area C. of C. (vice chmn. bd. dirs. 1991-93). Home: 288 River Ranch Cir Bayfield CO 81122-8774 Office: Horton & Associates 825 E Speer Blvd Ste 300H Denver CO 80218-3719*

HORTON, JOSEPH JULIAN, JR., economics and finance educator; b. Memphis, Tenn., Nov. 7, 1936; s. Joseph Julian and Nina (Williams) H.; m. Linda Anne Langley, May 30, 1964; children: Joseph Julian, Anne Adele, David Douglas. AA, Lon Morris Jr. Coll., 1955; BA, N.Mex. State U., 1958; MA, So. Meth. U., 1965, PhD, 1968; postgrad., Harvard U., 1970-71. Claims examiner Social Security Adminstrn., Kansas City, Mo., 1958-60, claims authorizer, 1960-61; with FDIC, Washington, 1967-71, fin. economist, 1967-69, coord. merger analysis, 1969-71; prof., chmn. dept. econs. and bus. Slippery Rock (Pa.) State Coll., 1971-81; vis. fin. economist Fed. Home Loan Bank Bd., Washington, 1978-79; prof., chmn. commerce divsn. Bellarmine (Ky.) Coll., 1981-82, dean W. Fielding Rubel Sch. Bus., 1982-86; dean Sch. Mgmt. U. Scranton, Pa., 1986-96; prof. Coll. Bus. Adminstrn. U. Ctrl. Ark., Conway, 1996—2001, prof. econ. and fin., 2001—. Asst. prof. George Washington U., Washington, 1968-69, U. Md., College Park, 1969-70; pres. Pa. Conf. Economists, Internat. Acad. Bus. Disciplines, Congress of Polit. Economists, U.S.A. Bd. editors Ea. Econ. Jour.; contbr. articles to profl. jours. Recipient Cokesbury award So. Meth. U., 1965; NSF Grad. fellow, 1964-66, Ford Found. Dissertation fellow, 1966-67, Harvard U. Rsch. fellow, 1970-71, Bank Adminstrn. Inst. Clarence Lichtfeldt fellow, 1981, Burk fellow. Mem. Am. Econ. Assn., Am. Fin. Assn., Internat. Acad. Bus. Disciplines (pres.), N.Am. Econs. and Fin. Assn. (bd. dirs., v.p., pres.), Ea. Econ. Assn. (v.p.). Office: U Cen Ark Dept Econ and Fin Coll Bus Adminstrn Conway AR 72035-0001 E-mail: jhorton@mail.uca.edu.

HORTON, NADINE ROSE, school system administrator; b. Kauai, Hawaii, Nov. 10, 1944; d. Alfred and Myrtle (Silva) Fernandes; m. Michael G. Sigman, Jan. 5, 1991; children: Debra J., Benjamin J. BA, Coll. Idaho, 1966, MA, 1972; postgrad., U. Idaho, 1990. Tchr. elem. sch. Parma (Idaho) Sch. Dist., 1996-70, Nampa (Idaho) Sch. Dist., 1970-72, Pinedale (Wyo.) Sch. Dist., 1972-73, New Plymouth (IDaho) Sch. Dist., 1974-75, prin. elem. sch., 1975—. Coord. Joint Coun. Econ. Edn., Boise, 1988; mem. goals and testing commn. State Dept. Edn., Boise, 1991-94. Named Celebrity of Yr. Am. Legion Aux., New Plymouth, 1986, Adminstr. of Yr. Idaho Assn. Ednl. Officer Pers., Boise, 1988, Outstanding Elem. Tchr. Am., 1975, Exec. Educator 100, 1986, Prins. of Leadership, 1987. Mem. ASCD (assocs.), Nat. Sch. Pub. Rels. Assn., Nat. Assn. Elem. Sch. Prins. (state rep. 1988-89, fed. rels. coord. 1989—, folio reviewer 1991—, nominating com. rep. 1990, Nat. Disting. Prin. 1989), Idaho Assn. Elem. Sch. Prins. (state pres. 1986), Internat. Reading Assn. (presenter), Phi Delta Kappa. Roman Catholic. Avocations: travel, reading, bowling. Home: 819 S Plymouth Ave # 193 New Plymouth ID 83655-5289

HORTON-WRIGHT, ALMA IRENE, retired elementary school educator; b. Austin, Tex., July 05; d. Ollon and Willie; m. Henry S. Wright, June 25; children: Sheila, Stanley, Gregory, Gerry. AA in Liberal Arts, San Bernardino Valley Coll., Calif., 1976; AA, Western Okla. State U., Altus, 1984; BA, Calif. State U., San Bernardino, 1979, postgrad.; MA in edn., Prairie View A&M U., 1993. Cert. tchr., Calif., life credential, Tex. Tchr. speed reading, edn. office Altus (Okla.) AFB; tchr. adult edn. Altus Sch. Dist.; elem. tchr. Rialto (Calif.) Unified Sch. Dist., Austin Ind. Sch. Dist. Named Tchr.of Yr., 2001-02. Mem. NEA, Tex. State Tchrs. Assn., Calif. State U. Almuni Assn., Edn. Austin, Phi Delta Kappa. Austin Ret. Tchrs. Assn., Tex. Ret. Tchrs. Assn. Avocations: travel, reading, art activities.

HORVATH, CSABA, chemical engineering educator, researcher; b. Szolnok, Hungary, Jan. 25, 1930; came to U.S., 1963; s. Gyula and Róza (Lányi) H.; children: Donatella, Katalin. Diploma in Chem. Engring., U. Tech. Scis., Budapest, Hungary, 1952, Dr. (hon.), 1986; PhD, J.W. Goethe U., Frankfurt-Main, Germany, 1963; MA (hon.), Yale U., 1979. Asst. in chem. tech. U. Tech. Scis., Budapest, 1952-56; chem. engr. Hoechst AG, Frankfurt am Main, 1956-61; research fellow Harvard U., Cambridge, Mass., 1963-64; research assoc. Yale U. Sch. Medicine, New Haven, 1964-69, assoc. prof., 1970-79, prof. chem. engring., 1979—, chmn. dept. chem. engring., 1987-93. Prof. chem. engring. Llewellyn West Jones Jr., 1993-98, Roberto C. Goizueta, 1998—; organizing chmn. Internat. Symposium on Column Liquid Chromatography, N.Y.C., 1984; organizing co-chmn. Internat. Symposium on Capillary Electrochromatography, San Francisco, 1997-2000; organizing co-chmn. 1st internat. symposium on capillary electrochromatography, San Francisco; chmn. Gordon conf. ion exchangers and reactive polymers. Co-author: Introduction to Separation Science, 1973; assoc. editor: Encyclopedia of Bioprocess Technology, 1999; editor: Series High Performance Liquid Chromatography, 1981—, Capillary Electrochromatography (spl. issue of Jour. of Chromatography), 2000; mem. editl. bd. 9 sci. periodicals; contbr. more than 300 rsch. papers and articles to sci. publs. Organizing chmn. 8th Internat. Symposium on Column Liquid Chromatography, N.Y.C., 1984; organizing co-chmn. Internat. Symposia on Capillary Electrochromatography, San Francisco, 1997-2000. Recipient S. Dal Nogare award Delaware Valley Chromatography Forum, 1978, Tswett medal 15th Internat. Symposium on Advances in Chromatography, 1979, Humboldt sr. U.S. scientist award Humboldt Found., Fed. Republic of Germany, 1982, EAS Chromatography award, 1986, Van Slyke award N.Y. Metro Sect. Am. Assn. Clin. Chemists, 1992, A.J.P. Martin award Chromatography Soc. U.K., 1994, Disting. Contbn. in Separation Sci. award Calif. Separation Sci. Soc., 1995, Nat. award N.E. Region Chromatography Discussion Group, 1997, Halász medal award Hungarian Soc. for Separation Sci., 1997, Golay award 21st Internat. Symposium on Capillary Chromatography and Electrophoresis, 1999, M. Widmer award The New Swiss Chem. Soc., 2000, medal Conn. Separation Sci. Coun., 2000, award Assn. Biomolecular Resource Facilities, 2001, Austrian Ehrenkreuz for Sci. and Art 1st class, 2002, Tobern Bergman medal Swedish Chem. Soc., 2003. Fellow AIChE, Am. Inst. Med. and Biomed. Engrs. (founding); mem. AAAS, Deutsche Gesellschaft fuer Chemisches Apparatewesen, Chemische Technik und Biotechnologie e.v., Am. Chem. Soc. (nat. chromatography award 1983, nat. separation sci. and tech. award 2001), Am. Ceramic Soc., Hungarian Chem. Soc. (hon.), Hungarian Acad. Scis. (external), Hungarian Soc. Separation Sci. (hon.), Conn. Acad. Sci. and Engring., Conn. Acad. Arts and Scis., Inst. Food Technologists, Sigma Xi. Home: PO Box 605 41 Temple Ct New Haven CT 06503-0605 Office: Yale U PO Box 208286 9 Hillhouse Ave New Haven CT 06511-6815 E-mail: csaba.horvath@yale.edu.

HORVITZ, SUSAN SMITH, educator; b. Fall River, Mass., Feb. 19, 1953; d. Henry Edward and Ann Frances (Lilley) Smith; m. Stewart Marc Horvitz, Apr. 4, 1976; children: Andrew, Sarah, Emily. BA, Skidmore Coll., 1974; MEd, R.I. Coll., 1983; postgrad., Bridgewater State Coll., 1990—99. Cert. tchr., Mass. Tchr. bilingual edn. Fall River (Mass.) Pub. Schs., 1974-76, tchr. French, Spanish, 1976-80, tchr. reading, 1980-85, curriculum resource tchr., 1985—2000; instr. U. Mass., Dartmouth, 1997—2001; K-12 social studies curriculum dir. Fall River Pub. Schs., 2000—. Mem. Mass. Ednl. Assessment Program Curriculum Adv. Com.-Social Studies, 1992-96: mem. Mass. History Assessment Devel. com., 2001—; mem. Systemwide Curriculum Coun. and Curriculum Framework Leadership Teams, 1998—; presenter at profl. confs. Author: (monograph) Interdisciplinary Units, 1991; contbr. articles to profl. jours. Pres. BMC Durfee High Sch. Class of 1971, Fall River, 1971—; v.p. Somerset (Mass.) Jr. High Sch. PTO, 1990-91, pres. 1991-93; active Supts.' Parents' Adv. Coun., Somerset, 1991-93; mem. Southeast Regional Reading Coun., 1996—. Grantee Project Dir. Tchg. Am. History, 2002—05. ASCD, Nat. Coun. Tchrs. Social Studies, SE Regional Coun. Social Studies, Delta Kappa Gamma (pres. Beta chpt. 1994-98). Avocations: horseback riding, skiing, swimming, reading, cooking. Home: 10 Brewster Dr Somerset MA 02726-4709 Office: Fall River Pub Schs Fall River MA 02720

HORWEGE, RONALD EUGENE, foreign language educator; b. St. Francis, Kans., Mar. 5, 1944; s. Lynn Arthur and Lois Vivien (Hurlock) H.; m. Sandra Jean Srella, Oct. 17, 1970; children: Christopher Matthew, Monika Kristin. BA cum laude, U. Kans., 1966; MA, Ind. U., 1968, PhD, 1971; postgrad., Free U., Berlin, 1969-70. Asst. prof. German, Sweet Briar (Va.) Coll., 1971-78, assoc. prof. German, 1978-85, prof. German, 1985—. Asst. dir. Münster summer program Sweet Briar (Va.) Coll., 1990—91, 1994, 98, 2002. Scoutmaster Boy Scouts Am., Amherst, Va., 1988-95, dist. tng. chair, Lynchburg, 1985—; bd. dirs. Va. Skyline coun. Girl Scouts U.S., Salem, 1993-97; acad. judge Jr. Miss Competition, Lynchurg, Va., 1982—. Recipient Silver Beaver award Boy Scouts Am., 1992, Vigil Hon., 1992, Cert. of Merit AATG-Goethe Inst., 2003; Fulbright fellow, 1976. Mem. Am. Assn. Tchrs. German (Va. chpt. pres. 1978-80, 92-94, 2000—), Fgn. Lang. Assn. Va. (pres. 1994-95), Am. Coun. for Study of Austrian Lit., KC, Beta Theta Pi, Phi Beta Kappa, Delta Phi Alpha. Roman Catholic. Avocations: camping, hiking, stamp collecting, book collecting, travel. Home: 292 Grandview Dr Amherst VA 24521-3122 Office: Sweet Briar College PO Box 35 Sweet Briar VA 24595-0035 E-mail: horwege@sbc.edu.

HORWITZ, BARBARA ANN, physiologist, educator, consultant; b. Chgo., Sept. 26, 1940; d. Martin Horwitz and Lillian Bloom; m. John M. Horowitz, Aug. 17, 1970. BS, U. Fla., 1961, MS, 1962; PhD, Emory U., 1966. Asst. rsch. physiologist U. Calif., Davis, 1968-72, asst. prof. physiology, 1972-75, assoc. prof., 1975-78, prof., 1978—, chair animal physiology, 1991-93, chmn. neurobiology, physiology and behavior dept., 1993-98, vice provost acad. personnel, 2001—. Cons. Am. Inst. Behavioral Rsch., Palo Alto, Calif., 1980, Am. Inst. Rsch., Washington, 1993-99, NSF, Washington, 1981-84, NIH, Washington, 1995-99. Contbr. articles to profl. jours. Named Arthur C. Guyton Physiology Tchr. of the Yr., 1996, postdoctoral fellow, USPHS, 1966—68; recipient Disting. Tchg. award, 1982, U. Calif.-Davis prize for Tchg. and Scholarly Achievement, 1991, Pres.'s award for excellence in fostering undergrad. rsch., 1995. Fellow: AAAS; mem.: Phi Sigma (v.p. Davis chpt. 1983—, nat. v.p. 1989—), Phi Kappa Pi, Soc. Exptl. Biology and Medicine (exec. coun. 1990—94, pres.-elect 1999—2001, pres. 2001—03, past pres. 2003—), N.Am. Assn. for Study of Obesity (exec. coun. 1988—92), N.Y. Acad. Scis., Am. Physiology Soc. (edn. and program coms. coun. 1993—96, pres.-elect 2001—02, pres. 2002—03, past pres. 2003—), Sigma Xi (pres. Davis chpt. 1980—81), Phi Beta Kappa (pres. Davis chpt. 1991—92, 2000—02). Office: U Calif Dept Neurobiology Phys Davis CA 95616 E-mail: bahorwitz@ucdavis.edu.

HOSANG, ROBERT ANTHONY, obstetrician-gynecologist, educator; b. Kingston, Jamaica, Apr. 6, 1950; arrived in U.S., 1985; s. Hugh Anthony and Iris (Shim) H.; m. Joyce Yap, Oct. 20, 1984; children: Craig, Mark. BSc, McGill U., Montreal, Can., 1971; MB, BChir, U. West Indies, Kingston, 1976; MPH, U. Calif., Berkeley, 1985, MBA, 1995. Diplomate Am. Bd. Ob-Gyn. Medical intern U. West Indies, Nassau, Bahamas, Kingston, 1976-77, lectr. Kingston, 1980-84; resident ob-gyn. Boston City Hosp., 1977-80; sr. physician Permanente Med. Group, Hayward, Calif., 1986—; lectr. Sch. Pub. Health U. Calif., Berkeley, 1989—. Med. cons. U.S. Agy. Internat. Devel., Washington, 1985-86, Assn. Voluntary Surg. Contraception, N.Y.C., 1991-94. Co-author book chpt.; contbr. articles to med. jours. Scoutmaster Boy Scouts of Jamaica, 1980-84. Fellow Am. Coll. Ob-Gyn., Royal Coll. Obstetricians & Gynecologists. Avocations: fishing, cricket. Office: Kaiser Permanente Med Group 27400 Hesperian Blvd Hayward CA 94545-4235

HOSEY, SHERYL LYNN MILLER, editor, educator, theater director; b. Phila., May 15, 1968; d. Roger Lee and Janice Catherine (Myers) M.; m. John William Hosey, July 8, 1994. AA, Bucks County C.C., Newtown, Pa., 1989; BFA summa cum laude, Va. Commonwealth U., 1992, MA, 1997; cert. in editing, Temple U., 1999. Cert. secondary sch. tchr., Pa. Instr. drama Va. Commonwealth U., Richmond, 1989-92; program support technician Va. Commonwealth U./Med. Coll. Va., Richmond, 1992-97; editl. svcs. adminstr. Meniscus Ltd., Bala Cynwyd, Pa., 1998-99; tchr., drama dir. Council Rock H.S. South, Holland, Pa., 1999—. Proofreader, editor. Fellow Nat. Writing Project Pa. chpt. West Chester U., 2000. Mem. Nat. Coun. Tchrs. English, Ednl. Theatre Assn., Phi Kappa Phi, Phi Delta Kappa. Avocations: acting, singing, reading, designing and making clothes, attending plays, symphony and ballet. Office: Council Rock High Sch South 2002 Rock Way Holland PA 18966 E-mail: mh@millerhosey.com.

HOSHAW, LLOYD, retired historian, educator; b. Benton, Ind., May 9, 1924; s. Walter and Gladys Ethel (Blue) H.; m. Evelyn F. Tyler, Dec. 24, 1954; children: Linda, John, James, Walter, David, Paul. BA, Goshen Coll., 1949; MA, Ind. U., 1951. Tchr. Winamac (Ind.) High Sch., 1952-55; instr. LaSalle(Ill.)-Peru-Oglesby Jr. Coll., 1955-65; history prof., dept. chair Rock Valley Coll., Rockford, Ill., 1965-88, history prof., 1988—2001; ret., 2001. Bd. dirs. Rock River Christian Coll. Author: A History of Eastern Civilizations, Vol I., 1994, Vol. II, 1995, 2d edit., 2001. With USN, 1944-45. Mem. VFW (life), Archeol. Inst. Am. (Rockford chpt.), Ill. State Hist. Soc., Rockford Hist. Soc. Baptist. Avocations: photography, travel. Home: 1860 Charlotte Dr Rockford IL 61108-6508

HOSIER, LINDA GRUBE, educator; b. Somerville, N.J., Mar. 15, 1948; d. Louis S. and Linda Julia (Braun) Grube; m. David Keith Short, Aug. 1, 1970 (div. Apr. 1986); children: Kristi Elizabeth, Andrew Alan; m. Robb R. Hosier, July 25, 1998; children: Robb R. Jr., Scott J., Timothy I., James E., Sherry H. BA, Pfeiffer Coll., 1970; MEd, U. N.C., 1973. Ordained min. of gospel Impact Worship Ctr., High Point, N.C., 1999, Internat. Fellowship New Testament Chs., Greensboro, N.C., 2002. Tchr. English Lexington (N.C.) City Schs., 1970-71; tchr. lang. arts, social studies Kannapolis (N.C.) City Schs., 1971-73; tchr. English, history Franklinton (N.C.) City Schs., 1973-74; tchr. English Bristol (Tenn.) City Schs., 1976-77; tchr. lang. arts, social studies High Point (N.C.) City Schs., 1983; tchr. acad. gifted lit., math. Stokes County Schs., Danbury, N.C., 1983-95; tchr. lang. arts and social studies Guilford County Schs., 1995-99, tchr. academically gifted, advanced learner curriculum specialist, 1999—. Coord. childrens ministries Cathedral of Praise Ch., Greensboro, NC, 1993—99; missionary to Haiti, The Sioux Indian Nation, Impact Worship Ctr., High Point, NC, 1999—2001; children's pastor, Sunday sch. supt. Emmaus Way Ch., Kernersville, NC, 2000—; missionettes coord. Emmaus Way Ch., Kernersville, NC, 2002—. Mem. NEA, N.C. Edn. Assn., N.C. Assn. of Gifted, N.C. Tchrs. of English. Avocations: reading, traveling, writing, gardening, singing. Home: 9027 Ambridge Ln Kernersville NC 27284-9267 E-mail: hosierl@guilford.k12.nc.us.

HOSKINS, MABLE ROSE, secondary education educator, English language educator; b. Natchez, Miss., May 23, 1945; d. Johnny and Josephine (Jones) Reynolds; m. Charles Hoskins, Dec. 23, 1973 (div. Dec. 5, 1989). BA in English, Jackson State Coll., 1967; MED, Miss. State U., 1979, Ednl. Specialist, 1982. Tchr. English Natchez (Miss.) Pub. Schs., 1968-70, Quitman (Miss.) Consol. Schs., 1971-81, Meridian (Miss.) Schs., 1981—. Bd. dirs. Pub. Employee's Retirement Sys., Jackson, 1988-92, Meridian Bonita Lakes Authority. Co-author: (teaching units) Miss. Writers Teaching Units for Secondary English, 1988; consulting editor: (book) Mississippi Writers-An Anthology, 1991. Newsletter editor, co-editor Assn. of Meridian Educators, 1988-92; mistress of ceremonies Alpha Kappa Alpha Sorority, Meridian, 1985-90; Children's Discovery, vol. coord. Meridian Coun. for the Arts, 1990. Named S.T.A.R. tchr. Miss. Econ. Coun., 1980, Tchr. of Yr., Meridian Pub. Schs., 1988, 94, finalist Miss. Hall of Master Tchrs., 1994. Mem. NEA, Miss. Assn. Educators (Mem. of Yr. 1988, bd. dirs. 1990-93), Miss. Coun. Tchrs. English, Nat. Coun. Tchrs. English, Phi Kappa Phi, Phi Delta Kappa. Baptist. Avocations: reading, listening to music. Home: 1402 39th Ave Meridian MS 39307-6001 Office: Meridian H S 2320 32nd St Meridian MS 39305-4657

HOSKINS, WILLIAM JOHN, obstetrician, gynecologist, educator; b. Harlan, Ky., May 10, 1940; s. Lonnie S. and Joanne (Huff) H.; m. Betty Jean Gay, Sept. 10, 1960 (div. 1985); children: Tonya J., William John Jr.; m. Iffath Abbasi Ahson, Nov. 9, 1985; children: Ahad A., Mariya A. BA, U. Tenn., Knoxville, 1962; MD, U. Tenn., Memphis, 1965. Diplomate Am. Bd. Ob-Gyn., Am. Bd. Gynecol. Oncology. Commd. lt. USN, 1966, advanced through grades to capt.; intern Jacksonville (Fla.) Naval Hosp., 1966-67; med. officer Destroyer Squadron 8 USN, Mayport, Fla., 1967-68; resident in ob-gyn Oakland (Calif.) Naval Hosp., 1968-71; staff dept. ob -gyn Pensacola (Fla.) Naval Hosp., 1971—74; fellow in gynecol. oncology U. Miami, Fla., 1974-76; dir. gynecol. oncology Nat. Naval Med. Ctr., Bethesda, Md., 1976—86; assoc. prof. ob-gyn Uniformed Svcs. U., Bethesda, 1976-86; ret. USN, 1986; assoc. chief gynecology svc. Meml. Sloan-Kettering Cancer Ctr., N.Y.C., 1988-90, chief gynecology svc., 1990—, 1990—; assoc. prof. ob-gyn Cornell U. Med. Ctr., N.Y.C., 1986-90; prof. ob-gyn. Cornell U. Med. Coll., N.Y.C., 1990-94, vice chmn. protocol com. gynecol. oncology group, 1993-94, vice chmn. gynecolgic oncology group, 1993—2002; Avon chair gynecologic oncology rsch. Meml. Sloan-Kettering Cancer Ctr., N.Y.C., 1995-96, dep. physician in chief disease mgmt. teams, 1996—; dir. Curtis & Elizabeth Anderson Cancer Ctr. at Memorial Health U. Med. Ctr., Savannah, Ga., 2001—; prof. ob-gyn. Mercer Med. Coll., Macon, Ga., 2001—. Chmn. ovarian com. Gynecol. Oncology Group, Phila., 1984-89. Editor: Principles and Practice of Gynecology and Oncology, 1992, 3d edit., 2000, Cancer of the Ovary, 1993, Cervical Cancer and Perinvasive Peoplasia, 1996, Cancer Management: A Multidisciplinary Approach, 1996, Handbook of Gynecologic Oncology, 2000, 2d edit., 2002, Atlas of Procedures in Gynecologic Oncology, 2003; contbr. over 224 articles to profl. jours., chpts. to books. Fellow Am. Coll. Obstetricians and Gynecologists (v.p. Navy sect. 1982-83), ACS; mem. Am. Gynecol. and Obstet. Soc., Soc. Gynecol. Oncologists (sec.-treas. elect 1992, sec.-treas. 1994—, coun. mem. 1988-91, pres. 1999), Soc. Gynecol. Surgeons, Internat. Gynecol. Cancer Soc., Am. Radium Soc., Am. Assn Cancer rsch., 1996—. Republican. Moslem. Office: Anderson Cancer Inst at Meml Health Univ Med Ctr 4700 Waters Ave Savannah GA 31404 Office Fax: 912-350-8199.

HOSKINSON, CAROL ROWE, middle school educator; b. Toledo, Mar. 10, 1947; d. Webster Russell and Alice Mae (Miller) Rowe; m. C. Richard Hoskinson, June 8, 1969; 1 child, Leah Nicole. BS in Edn., Ohio State U., 1968; MEd, Ga. State U., 1972. Tchr. Whitehall City Sch., Columbus, Ohio, 1968-69; tchr. DeKalb County Sch., Decatur, Ga., 1969-74, Mt. Olive Twp. Sch., NJ, 1974-75, DeKalb County Sch., Decatur, 1975-79, Fulton County Sch., Atlanta, 1991—. Substitute tchr. DeKalb County Schs., Decatur, 1980-91, Fulton County Sch., Atlanta, 1989-91. Pres. Esther Jackson PTA, Roswell, Ga., 1988-89; treas. Women of the Ch., Roswell, 1983-84; chairperson local sch. adv. Esther Jackson, Roswell, 1989-91; del. Women and Constn. Conv., Atlanta, 1988; mem. Supt.'s Adv. Com.; corr. sec. Chattahoochee HS PTSA, 1997-98; VIP dedicated hostess Olympic Games, Atlanta, 1996; treas. Chattahoochee Cotillion Club, 2000, 01; mem. leadership team Holcomb Bridge Mid. Sch., 1999-2004. Named Vol. of Yr. Fulton County Schs., 1988-89. Mem. AAUW (v.p. Atlanta chpt. 1970-89, edn. scholarship honoree 1984, 86), Atlanta Lawn Tennis Assn., Roswell Hist. Soc., Roswell Hist. Preservation Com., Nat. Mid. Sch. Assn., Zoo Atlanta, High Mus. Art, Ga. PTA, Ohio State Alumni Assn., Ga. State Alumni Assn., Profl. Assn. Ga. Educators. Democrat. Presbyterian. Avocations: tennis, reading, education-related activities. Home: 1670 Branch Valley Dr Roswell GA 30076-3007

HOSMAN, SHARON, elementary education educator; b. Springfield, Mo., May 20, 1939; d. Charles E. and Jewell A. (Allgood) Beckerdite; m. Ralph W. Hosman, Jan. 1, 1980; children: Kevin Cook, Melissa Cook, Shawn Cook. BS, SW Mo. State U., 1964, MS, 1980. Tchr. music Pleasant Hope (Mo.) Sch., 1964-66; elem. tchr. Willard (Mo.) Pub. Schs., 1966-93. Mem. Internat. Reading Assn., Am. Fedn. Tchrs. Methodist. Home: HC 80 Box 782 Camdenton MO 65020-8612

HOSMAN, SHARON LEE, music educator; b. Bisbee, Ariz., Nov. 2, 1943; d. Roy Lee and Virginia Baldwin (Bandel) H. BA, Loretto Heights Coll., 1965; MA, U. No. Colo., 1979. Tchr. Livermore (Calif.) Sch. Dist., 1965-66, Jefferson County Pub. Schs., Golden, Colo., 1966-97. Faculty rep. North Area Citizens Adv. Com., Arvada, Colo., 1979-81, S.I.P.C., Arvada, 1982-83, North Area Sch. Improvement Process Com., Arvada, 1984-91, North Area Accountability com., 1991-92. Piano accompanist for sch. groups, 1965-97. Mem. NEA, DAR, Jefferson County Edn. Assn., Colo. Edn. Assn., Music Tchrs. Nat. Assn., Colo. State Music Tchrs. Assn., Denver Area Music Tchrs. Assn., Musicians' Soc. Denver, Am. Guild Organists, Hereditary Order of First Families of Mass., Smithsonian, Denver Rescue Mission, Denver Dumb Friends League, St. Luke's Hosp. Aux. (life). Republican. Episcopalian. Avocations: art, music, drama, reading, gardening.

HOSSLER, DAVID JOSEPH, lawyer, law educator; b. Mesa, Ariz., Oct. 18, 1940; s. Carl Joseph and Elizabeth Ruth (Bills) H.; m. Gretchen Anne, Mar. 2, 1945; 1 child, Devon Annagret. BA, U. Ariz., 1969, JD, 1972. Bar: Ariz. 1972, U.S. Dist. Ct. Ariz. 1972, U.S. Supreme Ct. 1977. Legal intern to chmn. FCC, summer 1971; law clk. to chief justice Ariz. Supreme Ct., 1972-73; chief dep. county atty. Yuma County (Ariz.), 1973-74; ptnr. Hunt, Kenworthy, Meerchaum and Hossler, Yuma, Ariz., 1974—. Instr. in law and banking, law and real estate Ariz. Western Coll.; instr. in bus. law, mktg., ethics Webster U.; instr. agrl. law U. Ariz.; co-chmn. fee arbitration com. Ariz. State Bar, 1990—; instr. employee/employer law U. Phoenix. Editor-in-chief Ariz. Adv., 1971-72. Mem. precinct com. Yuma County Rep. Ctrl. Com., 1974-2000, vice chmn., 1982; chmn. region II Acad. Decathalon competition, 1989; bd. dirs. Yuma County Ednl. Found. (Hall of Fame 2000), Yuma County Assn. Behavior Health Svcs., also pres., 1981; coach

Yuma H.S. mock ct. team, 1987-94; bd. dirs. friends of U. Med. Ctr. With USN. Recipient Man and Boy award, Boys Clubs Am., 1979, Freedoms Found. award, Yuma chpt., 1988, Demolay Legion of Honor, 1991, Francis Woodward award, Ariz. Pub. Svc., 2000, named Vol. of Yr., Yuma County, 1981—82, Heart of Yuma award, 2000, voted Yuma's Best (atty.), 2001—02. Mem. ATLA, Am. Judicature Soc., Yuma County Bar Assn. (pres. 1975-76), Navy League, VFW, Am. Legion, U. Ariz. Alumni Assn. (nat. bd. dirs., past pres., hon. bobcat 1996, Disting. Citizen award 1997), Rotary (pres. Yuma club 1987-88, dist. gov. rep. 1989, dist. gov. 1992-93, findings com. 1996, dist. found. chair 1996-2000, co-chmn. internat. membership retention 2000-01, John Van Houton Look Beyond Yourself award 1995, Roy Slayton Share Rotary Share People award 1996, Al Face You Are the Key award 1997, Ted Day Let Svc. Light the Way award 1998, Rotary Found. citation for meritorious svc., Internat. Svc. Above Self award, Cliff Doctorman Real Happiness is Helping Others award, Disting. Svc. award). Episcopalian (vestry 1978-82). Home: 2802 S Fern Dr Yuma AZ 85364-2919 Office: Hunt Kenworthy Meerchaum and Hossler 330 W 24th St Yuma AZ 85364-6455 also: PO Box 2919 Yuma AZ 85366-2919 E-mail: dhossler@mindspring.com.

HOSTLER, SHARON LEE, pediatrics educator, rehabilitation center executive; b. Rutland, Vt., Oct. 24, 1939; d. John Gerald and Irene Adelaide (Whitney) H.; m. Alan Duane Dimock, Dec. 29, 1965 (dec. Sept. 1974); children: Kathleen Ann Dimock, Dylan Alan Dimock; stepchildren: Timothy Dimock, Gioia L. Dimock, Dorothy Dimock McNamara, Adam Dimock; m. Joseph Boardman, May 17, 1987. AB, Middlebury Coll., 1961; MD, U. Vt., 1965. Resident, fellow U. Va., Charlottesville, 1965-70, asst. prof. pediat., 1970-76, assoc. prof., 1976-87, prof., 1986, chief divsn. devel. pediat., 1978—, med. dir. Children and Youth Project, 1970-74, med. dir. Children's Rehab. Ctr., 1974—, chair Med. Sch. com. on women, 1989—, McLemore Birdsong chair Pediat., 1991—, assoc. chair dept. pediat., 1999—. Vis. prof. Hadassah Hosp. Ben Gurion U., Jerusalem, 1983-84; cons. Project Hope, Krakow, Poland, 1981-83; active Kluge/UCP Rsch. Project, Family Autonomy Project, MCH; mem. exec. com. U. Va. Health Svcs. Found. Contbr. articles to profl. jours. Bd. dirs. Ctrl. Va. Child Devel. Assn., Charlottesville, 1972-76; mem. Gov.'s Com. on Handicapped Child, Richmond, Va., 1972-78; founder Task Force on Ventilator Dependent Children, Richmond, 1986-89; cons. pub. schs., 1972-78; mem. Children's Med. Ctr. Cmty. Bd.; chmn. bldg. com. Kluge Children's Rehab. Ctr.'s Outpatient Dept., chair com. on women Sch. Medicine; mem. task force on women U. Va., mem. permanent com. on women's concerns. Recipient Innovative Project award Am. Assn. Children's Health, 1986, Outstanding Alumni award U. Vt., 1993, Outstanding Women of Yr. award U. Va., Women's Profl. and Leadership Assn., 1993, Lectr. award Am. Assn. Children's Health, 1994, Leadership Devel. award Women in Medicine, 1995, Middlebury Coll. Alumni Achievement award, 1999; Gould Found. scholar, 1957-61. Fellow Am. Acad. Pediatrics (sect. adolescent medicine); mem. Am. Acad. Cerebral Palsy/Devel. Neurology, Soc. Adolescent Medicine, Am. Med. Women's Assn. (bd. dirs., chpt. pres. 1987, regional gov. 1988-90), Assn. Am. Med. Colls., Boars Head Sports Club, Alpha Omega Alpha. Home: 1340 Wendover Dr Charlottesville VA 22901-7713 Office: Kluge Childrens Rehab Ctr 2270 Ivy Rd Charlottesville VA 22903-4977

HOSTON, GERMAINE ANNETTE, political science educator; b. Trenton, NJ; d. Walter Lee and Veretta Louise H. AB in Politics summa cum laude, Princeton U., 1975; MA in Govt., Harvard U., 1978, PhD in Govt., 1981. Rsch. asst. Princeton U., NJ, 1973-75; tchg. asst. Harvard U., Cambridge, Mass., 1977-78; asst. prof. polit. sci. Johns Hopkins U., Balt., 1980-86, assoc. prof. polit. sci., 1986-92; prof. polit. sci. U. Calif., San Diego, 1992—, dir. Ctr. for Democratization and Econ. Devel., 1993-99; founder, pres. Inst. Trans Pacific Studies in Values, Culture and Politics, 1999—. Vis. prof. L'Ecole des Hautes Etudes en Sci. Sociales, Paris, 1986, Osaka City U., Japan, 1990, U. Tokyo, 1991; faculty advisor Chinese lang. program Johns Hopkins U., 1981-92, undergrad. ethics bd., 1980-83, pub. interest investment adv. com., 1982-85, undergrad. admissions com., 1983-84, 86-89, pres.'s human climate task force, 1987, dir. undergrad. program, 1987, 88-89, mem. com. undergrad. studies, 1987-91, organizer comparative politics colloquium, 1987-89, dept. colloquium, 1987-89, 91-92; Japanese studies program com. U. Calif., San Diego, 1992—, Chinese studies program, 1994—, field coord. comparative politics, 1994—95, dir. grad. studies comparative politics, 1997-98; bd. dir. Inst. East-West Security Studies, NYC, 1990-97; Am. adv. com. Japan Found., 1992—; edn. abroad program com. U. Calif., 1996—; adv. com. Calif. Ctr. Asia Soc.; mem. com. tech. comms. Inst. East West Security Studies, 1997—; participant numerous workshops and seminars; lectr. in field. Author: Marxism and the Crisis of Development in Prewar Japan: The Debate on Japanese Capitalism, 1986, The State, Identity, and the National Question in China and Japan, 1994, (with others) The Biographical Dictionary of Neo-Marxism, 1985, The Biographical Dictionary of Marxism, 1986, Culture and Identity: Japanese Intellectuals During the Interwar Years, 1990, The Routledge Dictionary of Twentieth-Century Political Thinkers, 1992; mem. editl. bd. Jour. Politics, 1997—2001; contbr. articles to profl. jours. Active Md. Food Com., 1983-92, program concepts subcom. CROSS ROADS Com., Diocese of Md., 1987-88, outreach com. St. David's Episcopal Ch., Balt., standing commn. human affairs Gen. Conv. of the Episcopal Ch., 1991-97; chair peace and justice commn. Episcopal Diocese Md., 1984-87, co-chair companion diocese com., 1987-92, chair CROSS ROADS program bd., 1988-92; exec. bd. dir. Balt. Clergy and Laity Concerned, 1985-86; alternate, regular lay del. 69th Gen. Conv. of The Episcopal Ch., Detroit, 1988; trustee Va. Theol. Sem., 1988-2000; lay del. 70th Gen. Conv. of The Episcopal Ch., Phoenix, Ariz., 1991; dep. Nat. Conv. Episcopal Ch., 1988-93. Am. Legion Aux. scholar, 1972, Am. Logistical Assn. scholar, 1972-76; fellow Harvard U., 1975-77, NSF, 1975-77; Lehman fellow Harvard U., 1978-79, Fgn. Lang. and Area Studies fellow, 1978-79; fellow Am. Assn. Univ. Women Ednl. Found., 1979-80; Fgn. Rsch. scholar U. Tokyo, 1979, 82, 84, 85, 86, 91; Travel grantee Assn. Asian Studies, Japan-U.S. Friendship Commn., 1981; Internat. fellow Internat. Fedn. Univ. Women, 1982, 83; Postdoctoral grantee Social Sci. Rsch. Coun., 1983; fellow NEH, 1983; Kenan Endowment grantee Johns Hopkins U., 1984-85; fellow Rockefeller Found. Internat. Rels., 1985-88; Travel grantee Assn. Asian Studies, 1991; grantee Japan-US Friendship Commn., 1997; rsch. grantee Acad. Senate Com. on Rsch., 1996. Mem. Asia Soc. (trustee 1994—2000), Am. Polit. Sci. Assn. (mem. coun. 1991-93, mem. com. on internat. polit. sci. 1997—2003, v.p. 1998—), Assn. Asian Studies (mem. N.E. Asia coun. 1992-95, vice-chair N.E. Asia coun. 1993—94, nominated editor Jour. Asian Studies 1994, mem. coun. on fgn. rels. 1990—), Internat. Platform Assn., Pacific Coun. on Internat. Policy, Women's Fgn. Policy Group. Democrat. Episcopalian. Avocations: reading, cooking, sailing, tennis, working out. Office: 9921 Carmel Mountain Rd Ste 323 San Diego CA 92129 E-mail: ghoston@myesa.com.

HOTCHKISS, BILL, author, educator; b. New London, Conn., Oct. 17, 1936; s. William H. and Merle B. (Stambaugh) H. BA in English, U. Calif., Berkeley, 1959; MA in English, San Francisco State U., 1960; MFA in Creative Writing, U. Oreg., 1964, DA in English, 1971, PhD in English, 1974. Tchr. English Colfax H.S., 1960-62; instr. English Sierra Coll., Rocklin, Calif., 1963-79, 84-85, prof. English, 1988—; instr. English Shasta Coll., 1980-81, Rogue C.C., 1985-88, 90. Author: (textbook) Tilting at Windmills, 1966; (novels) The Medicine Calf, 1981, reissue, 1987, Crow Warriors, 1981, Soldier Wolf, 1982, Ammahabas, 1983, Spirit Mountain, 1984, Mountain Lamb, 1985, People of the Sacred Oak, 1986, Fire Woman, 1987, Dance of the Coyote, To Fell the Giants, 1991, Sierra Santa Cruz, 1992, Yosemite, 1995, (vols. of poetry) Steephollow Poems, 1966, The Graces of Fire, 1974, Fever in the Earth, 1977, Climb To The High Country, 1978, Middle Fork Canyon, 1979, Great Upheaval, 1990, Who Drinks the Wine, 2000, I Hear the Coyote, 2003, others, (criticism) Jeffers: The Sivaistic Vision, 1975, Poet from the San Joaquin, 1978; author numerous poems; co-author: Shoshone Thunder, 1983, Pawnee Medicine, 1983, McLaffertys, 1986, Desert Moon, 1987, (handbook) Sancho's Guide to Uncommon Literacy, 1990, 93, 95; editor: Sierra Jour., 1965-78, 88-90, 95-96, 2003; editor, book designer, printer, publ. Blue Oak Press; book designer, text editor Castle Peak Edits., 1966—; co-editor: Perspectives on William Everson, 1992, William Everson's The Residual Years, 1997, The Internal Years, 2000, Jeffers, The Double Axe, 1977; typesetter, book design adv. Dustbooks, Quintessence, Story Line, Blue Oak Press, Castle Peak Edits.; contbr. to programmed instructional software, filmstrips. Home: 3460 Cedar Flat Rd Williams OR 97544-9605 Office: Sierra Coll NCC 250 Sierra College Dr Grass Valley CA 95945-5726

HOTELLING, HAROLD, law and economics educator; b. N.Y.C., Dec. 26, 1945; s. Harold and Susanna Porter (Edmondson) H.; m. Barbara M. Anthony, May 4, 1974; children: Harold, George, James, Claire, Charles. AB, Columbia U., 1966; JD, U. N.C., 1972; MA, Duke U., 1975, PhD, 1982. Bar: N.C. 1973. Legal advisor U. N.C., Chapel Hill, 1972-73; instr. bus. law U. Ky., Lexington, 1977-79, asst. prof., 1980-84; asst. prof. dept. econs. Oakland U., Rochester, Mich., 1984-89; assoc. prof. econs. Lawrence Technol. U., Southfield, Mich., 1989—, chmn. dept. humanities social scis. and comm., 1994-99. Contbr. articles to profl. jours. Episcopalian. Home: 2112 Bretton Dr S Rochester Hills MI 48309-2952 Office: Lawrence Technol U Dept Humanities Southfield MI 48075 E-mail: hotelling@ltu.edu.

HOTH, STEVEN SERGEY, lawyer, educator; b. Jan. 30, 1941; s. Donald Leroy and Ina Dorothy (Barr) H.; m. JoEllen Maly, July 29, 1967; children: Andrew Steven, Peter Lindsey. AB, Grinnell Coll., 1962; JD, U. Iowa, 1966; postgrad., U. Pa., 1968, Oxford (Eng.) U., 1973. Bar: US Ct. Appeals (8th cir.) 1966, US Tax Ct. 1967, US Ct. Claims 1967, US Dist. Ct. Iowa 1968, US Dist. Ct. ND 1968, US Dist. Ct. SD 1968, US Supreme Ct. 1973, US Ct. Appeals (7th cir.) 1982. Law clk. to chief justice (Lord of Foleshill) US Ct. Appeals (8th cir.), Fargo, ND, 1967-68; assoc. Hirsch, Adams, Hoth & Krekel, Burlington, Iowa, 1968-72, ptnr., 1972-91; pvt. practice Burlington, 1992—. Asst. atty. Des Moines County, Burlington, 1968-72, atty., 1972-83; alt. mcpl. judge, Burlington, 1968-69; lectr. criminal law Southeastern C.C., West Burlington, 1972-82; assoc. prof. polit. sci. Iowa Wesleyan Coll., Mt. Pleasant, 1981-82; Pres. of Amerail, Inc., Iowa Truck Rail, Amerial, Inc.; pres. Burlington Truck Rail, Burlington Short Line RR. Inc., Iowa Internat. Investments, Burlington Storage and Transfer; sec. Burlington Loading Co. Contbr. numerous articles to profl. jours. Chmn. Des Moines County Civil Svc. Commn.; trustee Charles H. Rand Lecture Trust; mem. Des Moines County Conf. Com., Des Moines County Conf. Bd.; dir. Burlington Med. Ctr. Staff Found.; moderator 1st Congl. Ch., Burlington; bd. dir. UN Assn.; clk. Burlington North Bottoms Levy and Drainage Dist.; bd. mem., pres. Burlington Cmty. Sch. Dist. Bd. Edn., chmn. commn. on ministry, mem. exec. com. Nat. Assn. Congl. Christian Chs., moderator; treas. 1st dist. Dem. Com.; bd. dir. Legal Aid Soc. Planned Parenthood Des Moines County. Recipient Chmn.'s award ARC, 1980; Reginald Heber Smith fellow in legal aid Cheyenne River Indian Reservation, Eagle Butte, SD, 1967-68. Mem. Missionary Soc.-Nat. Assn. Congl. Christian Chs., ABA (internat. sect., tax sect.), Iowa State Bar Assn. (liaison to Iowa Med. Soc.), Des Moines County Bar Assn., Am. Judicature Soc., Agrl. Law Com., Iowa Def. Coun., Iowa Archaeol. Soc., Soc. for German Am. Studies, Manorial Soc. Gt. Britain, Grinnell Coll. Alumni Assn. (bd. dir.), Malawi Soc., Burlington-West Burlington C. of C. (bd. dir.), Nat. Assn. Congrl. Christian Ch., Burlington Golf Club, New Crystal Lake Club (pres.), Elks, Eagles, Masons, Rotary. Office: PO Box 982 Hoth Bldg 200 Jefferson St Burlington IA 52601

HOTTENDORF, DIANE V. dance educator; b. New London, Conn., May 17, 1947; d. Henry August and Frances D. (Babrowicz) Hottendorf. BS magna cum laude, Calif. State U., Northridge, 1970; MA summa cum laude, U. So. Calif., L.A., 1972, PhD, 1976. Teaching asst. U. So. Calif., L.A., 1972-74; asst. prof. Calif. State U., Northridge, 1973-76; head dance program Moorpark (Calif.) Coll., 1976-77; cruise staff mem. teen program Royal Caribbean Cruise Line, 1976-77; dance cons. Dept. Parks, Alexandria, Va., 1980-81; prof. dance Gallaudet U., Washington, 1981—. Vis. asst. prof. World Campus Afloat, Seaboard Edn., Chapman Coll., Fall 1975; lectr. in field. Co-prodr.: (video tape) Fundamental Dance Signs, 1989, Sign 'n Sweat, 1987, Celebration of Deaf Dance, 1996 (Telly award, 3 Emmy awards 1996); contbr. articles to profl. jours. Sponsor AA, Falls Church, Va., 1995—. Recipient Performing Arts award in dance Cultural and Fine Arts, Oxnard, 1988; grantee Gannett Found., 1983, 87, Delta Zeta and Rotary Club, 1983, May's Scholarship Fund, 1984, Delta Zeta, 1991, Psi Xota Xi, 1993; NDEA fellow, 1972-76. Mem. AAHPERD, NOW, Am. Dance Guild, Nat. Dance Assn., Sacred Dance Guild, Friends of Nat. Zoo, Nat. Mus. of Women in the Arts. Democrat. Avocations: sailing, walking, swimming, travel. Home: 3705 S George Mason Dr Falls Church VA 22041-3759 Office: Gallaudet Univ 800 Florida Ave NE Washington DC 20002-3660

HOUCK, CAROLYN MARIE KUMPF, special education educator; b. Brazil, Ind., Aug. 20, 1945; d. Paul Melvin and Dorothy Evadean (Welch) Kumpf; m. Robert Mercer (div. 1970); children: Judith E., Cynthia D.; m. David Jome Houck, Aug. 1, 1977; 1 child, Andrew. BS, Ind. State U., 1968, MS, 1975, postgrad., 1978-79. Speech therapist Indpls. Pub. Schs., 1968-70, Child Adult Resources Svcs., Inc., Rockville, Ind., 1970-72; lang. specialist Porter County Spl. Edn. Coop., Valparaiso, Ind., 1972-73; speech and lang. specialist Child-Adult Resource Svcs., Inc., Rockville, Ind., 1973-78; tchr. learning disabilities Greencastle (Ind.) H.S., 1979—, chmn. spl. edn. dept., 1997—. Precinct committeewoman Dem. Party, Greencastle, 1992-95; mem. Cloverdale (Ind.) United Meth. Ch. Mem. NEA, PEO (sisterhood), Ind. State Tchrs. Assn., Delta Kappa Gamma (Epsilon chpt. Alpha Epsilon state orgn.). Home: 610 Highwood Ave Greencastle IN 46135-1339 Office: Greencastle High Sch Washington St Greencastle IN 46135

HOUCK, JOHN DUDLEY, investment adviser, educator; b. Detroit, May 5, 1939; s. Horace Alonzo and Mae Edward (Snyder) H.; m. Carol Kay Houck, July 16, 1958; children: Sallie Mae Williams, Cheryl Ann Richard, Jonathan Matthew, Rebecca Cyrene Myers, James Timothy. AA, L.A. Valley Coll., 1964; BS in Bus. Econs., Pacific Western U., 1982; MS in Mgmt., Am. Coll. for Fin. Scis., 1994; MA in History, Gulf So. U., 1993; PhD in Edn., LaSalle U., 2002. Pres., CFO Western Pacific Fin. Svcs., Inc., L.A., 1976—. Adj. prof. U. Phoenix, Trinity Coll. Mem. Lds Ch. Avocations: golf, fishing, history. Office: Western Pacific Fin Svcs Inc c/o CEO 1036 E Avenue J # 212 Lancaster CA 93535-3840 E-mail: jdhouck@email.uophx.edu.

HOUGH, CYNTHIA DENISE COOK, middle school educator; b. Detroit, Nov. 20, 1954; d. Freddie Lee and Ernestine (King) Cook; 1 child, Courtney Denise Hough. BS, Ea. Mich. U., 1976; MS, Wayne State U., 1982; SpA, Ea. Mich. U., 1993. Cert. middle sch. adminstrv. cert. tchr., vocat. tchr., Mich.; licensed manicurist, Mich. Tchr. home econs. Ruddiman Middle Sch., Detroit Bd. Edn., 1976—. Recipient grants in field. Mem. NAACP, ASCD, Am. Home Econs. Assn., Mich. Occupational Edn. Assn., Venereal Disease Action Coalition, Am. Vocat. Assn., Eastern Mich. U. Alumni Assn., Eastern Mich. U. Black Alumni Assn. (past pres.), Phi Delta Kappa. Avocations: collectibles, clothing construction and design, family activities. Home: 17180 Huntington Rd Detroit MI 48219-3548

HOUGH, J. MARIE, realtor; b. Trenton, N.J., Oct. 15, 1940; d. Michael J. and Evelyn M. (Klink) Mazur; m. Gary T.M. Hough, Apr. 7, 1990. Degree in bus. adminstrn., Rider Bus. Coll., 1964; AA, L.A. City Coll., 1967; BEd, Cin. Coll., 1970; MEd, Azusa Pacific U., 1982. Cert. tchr., Calif. Vocat. tchr. Papua New Guinea Inst., 1972-80; asst. The Papers of Woodrow Wilson Princeton U., NJ, 1980-82; bus. instr. Criss Coll., Anaheim, Calif., 1983-87; instr. office occupations Regional Occupational Program, Santa Ana, Calif., 1987-90; bus. instr. Somos Hermandas Unidas, Anaheim, 1991-92; office tech. instr. United Cambodian Community Vocat. Ctr., Long Beach, Calif., 1992-93; bus. mgr. Hough Enterprises, San Clemente, Calif., 1993-95; realtor First Team Real Estate, Mission Viejo, Calif., 1995, The Prudential Calif. Realty, Mission Viejo, 1995-96, Prudential-Jon Douglas Realty Co., Laguna Niguel, Calif., 1996-97, The Prudential Calif. Realty, San Clemente, 1997-98, Del Mar Realty, San Clemente, 1998-99, Profl. Real Estate/Better Homes & Gardens, San Juan Capistrano, Calif., 1999-2000. Singer Capistrano Chorale, San Juan Capistrano, Calif., Performing Arts Club, Palm Desert, Calif., 2000—02; participated in Ms. Sr. Am. Pageant, 2000. Mem. Am. Vocat. Assn., Cameo Club, Laguna Vista Players. Avocations: aquadynamics, singing, photography, travel. Home: 276 N El Camino Real # 268 Oceanside CA 92054 E-mail: MHSuccess@aol.com.

HOUGHTON, DAVID DREW, meteorologist, educator; b. Phila., Apr. 26, 1938; s. Willard Fairchild and Sara Nancy (Holmes) H.; m. Barbara Flora Coan, June 22, 1963; children: Eric Brian, Karen Jeanette, Steven Andrew. BS, Pa. State U., 1959; MS, U. Wash., 1961, PhD, 1963. Rsch. scientist Nat. Ctr. Atmospheric Rsch., Boulder, Colo., 1963-68; exch. scientist USSR Acad. Scis., Moscow, 1966; vis. scientist Courant Inst. Math. Scis., N.Y.C., 1966; asst. prof. dept. meteorology U. Wis., Madison, 1968-69, assoc. prof., 1969-72, prof., 1972-2001, chmn. dept., 1976-79, 91-94, prof. emeritus, 2001—. Scientist Internat. Sci. and Mgmt. Group for Global Atmospheric Rsch. Program, Bracknell, Eng., 1972-73; lectr. Nanjing U., People's Republic of China, 1980; vis. sr. scientist Nat. Meteorol. Ctr., Washington, 1988, Inst. Atmospheric Physics, Acad. Scis., Beijing, 2002; vis. scientist Inst. of Atmospheric Physics, Acad. of Scis., Beijing and Nanjing U., Nanjing, China, 1989; vis. cons. World Meteorol. Orgn., Geneva, 1997; vis. prof. Clark Atlanta U., 1998; trustee Univ. Corp. for Atmospheric Rsch., 1999-02. Contbr. articles to profl. jours.; editor-in-chief: Handbook of Applied Meteorology, 1985. Vice chmn. Planning Commn., Town of Dunn, Wis., 1977-81. NSF fellow, 1960-63. Fellow AAAS, Am. Meteorol. Soc. (chmn. edn. and human resources commn. 1987-93, pres. 1995-96); mem. Phi Beta Kappa, Sigma Xi, Phi Kappa Phi. Mem. Rel. Soc. Of Friends. Office: U Wis Dept Atmos and Ocean Sci Madison WI 53706 E-mail: ddhought@facstaff.wisc.edu.

HOUGHTON, RAYMOND CARL, JR., education educator; b. Greenfield, Mass., May 26, 1947; s. Raymond Carl and Phyllis Irene (Richason) H.; m. Jan Marie Laws, Sept. 22, 1973; children: Raymond James, April Monica, Amy Rose. BS in Math., Norwich U., 1969; MS in Computer Sci., George Washington U., 1975; MSEE, Johns Hopkins U., 1980; PhD in Computer Sci., Duke U., 1991. Computer operator Norwich U., Northfield, Vt., 1967-69; specialist programmer power transformer dept. GE Co., Pittsfield, Mass., 1969-70, mathematician armament dept. Burlington, Vt., 1972-73; mem. tech. staff Computer Scis. Corp., Silver Spring, Md., 1974-75; data systems analyst computer security applications div. Nat. Security Agy., Ft. Meade, Md., 1975-78; computer scientist Inst. Computer Scis. and Tech./Nat. Bur. Standards, Gaithersburg, Md., 1978-83; instrnl. rsch. asst. dept. computer sci. Duke U., Durham, N.C., 1984-91; assoc. prof. dept. math. and computer sci. Augusta (Ga.) State U., 1987—93; lectr. Skidmore (N.Y.) Coll., 1993-95; pres. Cyber Haus Learning Ctrs., Delmar, NY, 1995—99. Bd. advisers, columnist Software Engring: Tools, Techniques, Practice, 1990-94, info. sys. delegate, Peoples Rep. China, 2000; adj. prof. SUNY Sch. Bus., Albany, 1997-2000; mission in understanding del. People to People Amb. Programs, Vietnam, 2002; spkr. in field. Contbr. articles to profl. jours. 1st lt. U.S. Army, 1971-72, Vietnam. Decorated Purple Heart; recipient Certs. of Recognition, U.S. Dept. Commerce, 1981, 83, Letter of Appreciation, Def. Comms. Agy., 1976. Mem.: IEEE, Assn. Computing Machinery, 101st Airborne Divsn. Assn., People to People Internat. Lutheran. Office: Cyber Haus 159 Delaware Ave #145 Delmar NY 12054-1369 E-mail: cyhous@msn.com.

HOUGHTON, ROBERT CHARLES, secondary education educator; b. Dover, N.H., Apr. 12, 1958; s. Raymond David and Barbara Jean Houghton. Student, USCG Acad., New London, Conn., 1976-77; BA with honors, U. Calif., Riverside, 1987, postgrad., 1987-89; MA in Ednl. Adminstrn., Chapman U., 1999. Teaching credential, Calif.; adminstrv. credential. Various teaching positions, 1977-80; pharmacy technician Anaheim (Calif.) Meml./Brea (Calif.) Cmty., 1980-85; teaching asst. U. Calif., Riverside, 1988-90; instr. Mt. San Jacinto (Calif.) Coll., 1989-90; tchr. Desert Sands Unified, Indio, Calif., 1990—, interim asst. prin., 1997-98, creator P.R.I.D.E. curriculum. Counselor Chem. Awareness Network, Indio, Calif., 1990—; computer cons. Desert Sands Unified Sch. Dist., Indio, 1994—; resident tchr. Calif. State U., San Bernardino, 1994—95; asst. tour dir. Lakeland Tours, Washington, 1991—2001. Mem. NEA, Nat. Coun. Social Studies, Nat. Geographic Soc., Calif. Tchrs. Assn., Nat. Trust Historic Preservation, Civil War Trust. Republican. Avocations: travel, photography, reading, hiking, camping. Home: 79320 Port Royal Ave Indio CA 92201-1262 Office: 81195 Miles Ave Indio CA 92201-2807

HOUK, JAMES CHARLES, physiologist, educator; b. Northville, Mich., June 3, 1939; s. James Charles and Elowene (Tower) H.; m. Antoinette Iacuzio, Dec. 28, 1963; children: Philip, Nadia, Peter. BSEE, Mich. Tech. U., 1961; MSEE, MIT, 1963; PhD, Harvard U., 1966. Instr. Harvard U. Med. Sch., 1967-69, asst. prof., 1969-73; lectr. MIT, 1971-73; assoc. prof. Johns Hopkins U. Med. Sch., 1973-78; adj. assoc. prof. U. N.C., 1975; prof. physiology Northwestern U. Med. Sch., 1978—, chair dept. physiology, 1978—2001. Co-author: Medical Physiology 14th edit., 1980, Handbook of Physiology--The Nervous System II, 1981, Encyclopedia of Neuroscience, 1987, Models of Information Processing in the Basal Ganglia, 1995; contbr. chpts. to books. Recipient Javits award NIH, 1984-92. Mem. IEEE, AAAS, Soc. for Neurosci., Am. Physiol. Soc., European Neurosci. Assn., Assn. Chmn. Depts. Physiology, Internat. Neural Network Soc. Office: Northwestern U 303 E Chicago Ave Chicago IL 60611-3093

HOUNSELL, JILLANN CUSICK, secondary education educator; b. Ridley Pk., Pa., Aug. 23, 1943; d. John Thomas and Ellen Lenore (Bauer) Cusick; m. Thomas Sidney Hounsell, Aug. 5, 1967; children: Dana Jeanne, Jillann Irene, Tamryn JoyEllen, Thomas Sidney Jr. BA, Westminster Coll., 1965; MEd, U. Del., 1969; EdD, Wilmington Coll., 2000. Sci. tchr. Newark Spl. Sch. Dist., 1965-67, planetarium dir., 1968-69, Alexis I. duPont Spl. Sch. Dist., Greenville, Del., 1969-79; sci. instr. Red Clay Consol. Sch. Dist., Wilmington, Del., 1980—. Assoc. dir. State Sci. Olympiad, Dover, Del., 1998-2003; adj. sci. instr. U. Del., Newark, 1999; field tester for properties of matter Smithsonian Nat. Sci. Resources Ctr.. Pres. PTA, Wilmington, 1982-84, Hockessin, Del., 1988-90; v.p. Del. State PTA, Dover, 1986-88; choir dir. Hockessin United Meth. Ch., 1992-96. Recipient Nat. Presdl. award for excellence in sci. and math. tchg., 1999, Environ. Educator or Yr. award, 2002. Mem. NEA, Del. State Edn. Assn., Del. Dept. Edn. (tchr. mem. state assessment com., state stds. com. 1998-00), Del. Tch rs. Sci., Del. Assn. Biology Tchrs. Republican. Avocations: stained glass, shell collection & identification, painting. Home: 735 Montgomery Woods Dr Hockessin DE 19707-9324 Office: H B duPont Mid Sch 735 Meeting House Rd Hockessin DE 19707-8508

HOUPT, JEFFREY LYLE, dean, psychiatrist, educator; b. Phila., Aug. 13, 1941; s. H. Lyle and Elizabeth (McAlpine) Houpt; m. Corinne A. Anderson, Dec. 28, 1964; children: Brian Jeffrey, Eric Robert. BS in Zoology, Wheaton Coll., 1963; MD, Baylor Coll. Medicine, 1967. Diplomate Am. Bd. Psychiatry and Neurology. Intern Boston City Hosp., 1967-68; resident in psychiatry Yale U., New Haven, 1968-71; staff med. officer Oak Knoll Naval Hosp., Oakland, Calif., 1971-73; adj. asst. prof. psychiatry Presbyn. Hosp., San Francisco, 1973-75; asst. prof. to prof. psychiatry Duke Med. Ctr., Durham, N.C., 1975-83; prof. psychiatry, chmn. dept. Emory U. Sch. Medicine, Atlanta, 1983-90; dean Sch. Medicine

Emory U., Atlanta, 1988-96; dean Sch. Medicine, vice chancellor for med. affairs U. N.C., Chapel Hill, 1997—; CEO U. N.C. Health Sys., Chapel Hill, 1998—. Author: The Importance of Mental Health Services for General Health Care, 1979; contbr. articles to med. jours. Lt. comdr. USN, 1971-73 Fellow Am. Coll. Psychiatry (pres.), Am. Psychiat. Assn. Home: 51319 Eastchurch Chapel Hill NC 27517-8302 Office: U NC at Chapel Hill CB # 7000 Chapel Hill NC 27599-7000

HOUSE, JAMES STEPHEN, social psychologist, educator; b. Phila., Jan. 27, 1944; s. James Jr. and Virginia Miller (Sturgis) H.; m. Wendy Fisher, May 13, 1967; children: Jeff, Erin. BA, Haverford Coll., 1965; PhD, U. Mich., 1972. From. instr. to assoc. prof. sociology Duke U., Durham, N.C., 1970-78; assoc. prof. sociology/assoc. rsch. scientist Survey Rsch. U. Mich., Ann Arbor, 1978-82, assoc. chair dept. sociology, 1981-84, prof. sociology, sr. rsch. scientist Survey Rsch. Ctr., 1982—, chair dept. sociology, 1986-90, dir. Survey Rsch. Ctr., Inst. Social Rsch., 1991-2001. Author: Work Stress and Social Support, 1981; co-editor: Sociological Perspectives on Social Psychology, 1995; assoc. editor Social Psychology Quar., 1988-91, Jour. Health & Social Behavior, 1997-2000, Internat. Ency. of the Social and Behavioral Scis., 2001; contbr. chpts. to books and articles to profl. jours. Guggenheim fellow, 1986-87. Fellow: AAAS, Soc. Behavioral Medicine, Am. Acad. Arts and Scis.; mem.: Soc. for Epidemiol. Rsch., Soc. for Psychol. Study of Social Issues, Acad. Behavioral Medicine Rsch., Am. Sociol. Assn., Inst. Medicine of NAS. Office: Univ Mich Inst Social Rsch PO Box 1248 Ann Arbor MI 48106-1248 E-mail: jimhouse@umich.edu.

HOUSE, ROBERT WILLIAM, music educator; b. Bristow, Okla., Nov. 28, 1920; s. Richard Morton and Elizabeth (Swartz) H.; m. Esther Jean Hawkins, June 5, 1943 (dec. Oct. 1977); children: R. Edmund, Richard M., Russell L., Kathryn M.; m. Mary Elaine Thornton Wallace, Mar. 12, 1979. BFA, Okla. State U., 1941; MusM, Eastman Sch. Music, 1942; EdD, U. Ill., 1954. Asst. prof. band, cello, wind instruments Nebr. State Coll., Kearney, 1946-55; prof. orch., cello and music edn., chmn. music dept. U. Minn., Duluth, 1955-67; dir. Sch. Music, So. Ill. U., Carbondale, 1967-76; head music dept. East Tex. State U., 1976-84, orch. dir., 1984-89. Cons. Ednl. Testing Service, 1962-66 Prin. cellist, Duluth Symphony, 1955-67, Mesquite Symphony, 1987—, N.E. Tex. Symphony Orch., 1989-98; author: (with Charles Leonhard) Foundations and Principles of Music Education, 1959, rev., 1972, Instrumental Music for Today's Schools, 1965, Administration in Music Education, 1973; mem. editorial bd.: Jour. of Research in Music Edn, 1958-70; mng. editor: The Ill. Music Educator, 1975-76. Served with AUS, 1942-46, ETO. Mem. Nat. Assn. Schs. Music (panel evaluators 1966-76, chmn. com. on tchr. edn. in music 1963-67, chmn. com. on ethics 1970-72, com. on research and pubs. 1973-75, chmn. com. nominations 1980-81), Music Educators Research Council (nat. chmn. 1958-60), Music Educators Nat. Conf. (mem. pubis. planning com. 1972-82, chmn. 1976-82, pres.-elect North Central div. 1974-76, mem. com. for advancement music edn. 1976-80), Am. String Tchrs. Assn. (sec. Tex. unit 1978-80) Home: 3106 Lakeside Dr Rockwall TX 75087-5319

HOUSEMAN, ANN ELIZABETH LORD, educational administrator, state official; b. New Orleans, Mar. 21, 1936; d. Noah Louis and Florence Marguerite (Coyle) Lord; m. Evan Kenny Houseman, June 25, 1960; children: Adrienne Ann, Jeannette Louise, Yvonne Elizabeth. BA, Barnard Coll., 1957; MA, Columbia U., 1962; PhD, U. Del., 1969. State supr. reading Dept. Pub. Instrn., Del., 1977-79; prin. M.L. King Jr. Elem. Sch., Wilmington, Del., 1979-80; adminstr., exec. dir. Del. State Arts Coun., Wilmington, 1980-84; acting dir. Divsn. Hist. and Cultural Affairs State of Del., Wilmington, 1983-84; prin. P.S. du Pont Intermediate Sch., Wilmington, 1984-91; dir. Mid.-Atlantic States Arts Consortium, Balt., 1980-84. Mem. adv. bd. Rockwood Mus., Wilmington, 1981-94; bd. dirs. Opera Del., Inc., Wilmington, 1984-97, pres., 1991-93, dir. devel., 1994-95, coord. adv. bd., 1996; bd. dirs. Del. Theatre Co., Wilmington, 1984-90; bd. dirs. Aux. of Alfred I. duPont Hosp. for Children, 1997—, pres., 2000-01. Mem. Phi Delta Kappa. Republican. Presbyterian. E-mail: houseman@udel.edu.

HOUSER, CHERYL ANN, elementary education educator; b. Amarillo, Tex., Jan. 15, 1946; d. Earl Joseph and Mary Louise (Stanley) Grimes; m. John Harlie, June 10, 1967; children: Christy, Jeremy. BS in Elem. Edn., West Tex. State U., 1969; MA in Elem. Edn., Middle Sch. Edn., U. No. Colo., 1988, Type D Adminstrv. Cert., 1993. Tchr. 1st grade Sch. Dist. #11, Colorado Springs, Colo., 1969-73; tchr. 4th grade Littleton (Colo.) Pub. Schs., 1980-90, tchr. 5th grade, 1991-94; prin. Lewis Ames Elem., Littleton, 1994-96. Lectr. in field. V.p. High Sch. Boosters Club, Littleton, 1989-91; active PTO; coord. Swim Team, Littleton, 1983-87; active St. James Presbyn. Ch., cmty. orgns. Littleton Pub. Schs. IDEA grantee, 1991, 92. Mem. ASCD, NEA, Colo. Edn. Assn., Littleton Edn. Assn. Avocations: golf, tennis, bridge. Home: 6082 S Adams Dr Littleton CO 80121-3004 Office: Lewis Ames 73005 S Clermont Littleton CO 80122

HOUSER, DONALD RUSSELL, mechanical engineering educator, consultant; b. River Falls, Wis., Sept. 2, 1941; s. Elmont Ellsworth and Helen (Bunker) H.; m. Colleen Marie Collins, Dec. 30, 1967; children: Kelle, Kerri, Joshua. BS, U. Wis., 1964, MS, 1965, PhD, 1969. Registered profl. engr., Ohio. Instr. U. Wis., Madison, 1967-68; from asst. prof. to prof. Ohio State U., Columbus, 1968—2003, emeritus prof., 2003—, dir. Gear Dynamics and Gear Noise Rsch. Lab., 1979—, dir. Ctr. for Automotive Rsch., 1994-99. V.p. Gear Rsch. Inst., State Coll., Pa., 1990-99. Author: Gear Noise, 1991; contbg. editor Sound and Vibration mag., 1988-96; assoc. editor Jour. Mech. Design, 1993-94; mem. adv. bd. JSME Internat. Jour., 1996-2000; contbr. articles to profl. jours. Elder St. Andrews Presbyn. Ch., Columbus, 1972-75. Fellow ASME (legis. liaison Ohio coun. 1976-80, Century II medallion 1980); mem. Am. Gear Mfrs. Assn. (acad.), Soc. Automotive Engrs., Am. Helicopter Soc., Inst. Noise Control Engrs. Roman Catholic. Achievements include development of technology for measuring gear transmission error under load. Office: Ohio State U 206 W 18th Ave Columbus OH 43210-1189 E-mail: houser.4@osu.edu.

HOUSEWRIGHT, WILEY LEE, music educator; b. Wylie, Tex., Oct. 17, 1913; s. Jick and Lillie (Townsend) H.; m. Lucilla Elizabeth Gumm, Dec. 27, 1939. BS, U. North Tex., 1934; MA, Columbia, 1938; Ed.D., N.Y. U., 1943. Dir. music pub. schs., Tex., N.Y., 1934-41; lectr. music NYU, 1942-43; asst. prof. U. Tex., 1946-47; faculty Fla. State U., Tallahassee, 1947—, prof. music, 1948-79, prof. emeritus, 1980—, Disting. prof., 1961-62, dean Sch. Music, 1966-79. Vis. summer prof. U. Mich., 1960, U. Ind., 1955; Fulbright scholar, Japan, 1956-57; Mem. U.S. nat. com. for UNESCO, 1958; music adv. panel internat. cultural presentations program State Dept., 1958-79 Author: A History of Music and Dance in Florida, 1565-1865, 1991; co-editor: Birchard Music Series, 6 vols., editor: An Anthology of Misic in Early Florida, 1999. Adv. bd. humanities and arts Ford Found., 1958— . Served to 1st lt. AUS, 1943-46. Decorated Disting. Svc. citation; recipient Disting. Alumni citation U. North Tex., 1967; Ford Found. grantee, 1966-68. Mem. Music Educators Nat. Conf. (pres. 1968-70), Am. Musicological Soc., Music Tchrs. Nat. Assn., Internat. Soc. Music Edn., Music Libr. Assn., Sonneck Soc., Am. Choral Dirs. Assn., Fla. Econ. Club, Capital City Country Club, Govs. Club, Rotary, Pi Kappa Lambda, Phi Delta Kappa, Phi Mu Alpha, Lambda Chi Alpha, Omicron Delta Kappa, Kappa Kappa Psi. Home: 515 S Ride Tallahassee FL 32303-5134

HOUSHIAR, BOBBIE KAY, language arts educator; b. Fort Smith, Ark., Nov. 28; d. Ernest and Virgil Straham. BA, Saginaw Valley State U., 1973; MA in Elem. Edn. Adminstrn., Cen. Mich. U., 1975, Cert. Gen. Edn. Adminstrn., 1978. Elem. tchr. Saginaw (Mich.) Pub. Schs., 1973-74, jr. high tchr., 1975-76, tchr. middle sch., 1983—; learning ctr. coord. Saginaw Valley State U., University Center, Mich., 1974-75, instr. reading, 1974-75; tchr. ESL Refugee Ctr. of Saginaw, 1982-83. Instr. ind. study Cen. Mich. U., Saginaw, 1988-90; tutor bilingual students Delta Coll., Saginaw, 1987-96; supr./student tchrs. Saginaw Pub. Schs., 1988—; oratorical/writing instr. Saginaw Pub. Schs., 1983—. Editor: Young Writers in Michigan, 1989. Vol. Saginaw County chpt. ARC, 1996-99; mem./vol. League of Cath. Women, Saginaw, 1976—. Recipient Recognition award Saginaw Infant Mortality Coalition award, Saginaw Cooperative Hosp., 1998, Educator of Yr. award, Saginaw Coop. Hosp., 1999, Excellence in Tchg. English Writing Skills award, Saginaw Bd. Edn., 2002, Accent on Achievement award, Saginaw Pub. Sch. Bd. of Edn., 2002, others. Mem. NEA, Saginaw Edn. Assn., Mich. Edn. Assn., Nat. Coun. Tchrs. of English, ASCD, Mich. Mid. Sch. Assn., Delta Sigma Theta. Democrat. Roman Catholic. Avocations: reading, student mentor, tennis, swimming, horses. Office: South Middle Sch 224 N Elm St Saginaw MI 48602-2651 Personal E-mail: Siamak67@cs.com. Business E-Mail: BHoushiar@spsd.net.

HOUSINGER, MARGARET MARY, math and computer science educator; b. Hammond, Ind., Jan. 10, 1948; d. John Joseph and Cecilia Mary (Okray) U; m. Warren D. Housinger, Aug. 20,1994. BA in Math., St. Joseph's Coll., East Chicago, Ind., 1968; MS in Math., U. Ill., Chgo., 1969. Cert. secondary edn. tchr., Ill. Math. and computer sci. tchr. Elizabeth Seton High Sch., South Holland, Ill., 1969-70, Thornton Fractional North High Sch., Calumet City, Ill., 1970—. Tchr. math. and computer sci. St. Francis Coll., Ft. Wayne, Ind., 1986-87, Calumet Coll. St. Joseph, Whiting, Ind., 1974—, Purdue U. Calumet, Hammond, 1980—, South Suburban Coll., South Holland, 1986—; bd. dirs., sec. A.C. Jaacks Credit Union, Calumet City; speaker at confs. Contbr., reviewer, referee articles for Math. Tchr. jour. Mem. Nat. Coun. Tchrs. Math., Ill. Coun. Tchrs. Math. (state math. contest-question-writing com. 1990), South Inter-Conf. Assn. (mathlete contest all-conf. com. and oral com. 1975—), Nat. Honor Soc. (faculty coun.). Roman Catholic. Avocations: nature study, gardening, crafts, reading. Home: 541 154th Pl Calumet City IL 60409-4505 Office: Thornton Fractional North High Sch 755 Pulaski Rd Calumet City IL 60409-4030

HOUSMAN, B. JANE, secondary education educator; b. N.Y.C., Oct. 15, 1937; BS, Syracuse U., 1959, MA in Edn., 1961; postgrad., C.W. Post coll., 1985; EdD, Hofstra U., 1991. Cert. elem. edn. tchr., tchr. math., sch. dist. adminstr., sch. adminstr. and supr., N.Y. Tchr. math./computer Roosevelt Jr./Sr. H.S., 2000—01, staff devel. facilitator, presenter, 2000—01. Grant writer, presenter in field. Mem. West Islip (N.Y.) Bd. Edn., 1978-81; mem. Family Svc. League, West Islip, 1990-93. Mem. ASCD, Internat. Soc. for Tech. in Edn., N.Y. State Assn. for Computers and Tech. in Edn., Nat. Coun. Tchrs. Math., Nassau-Suffolk Coun. Adminstrv. Women in Edn., Nassau Reading Coun., Phi Delta Kappa (v.p. membership 1992—). Home: 15 Barberry Rd West Islip NY 11795-3910

HOUSTON, GLORIA, author, educator, consultant; b. Marion, N.C., Nov. 24; d. James Myron and Ruth Houston; children: M. Diane Gainforth, Julie Ann Floen. BS, Appalachian State, 1963; MEd., U. S.Fla., 1983, PhD, 1989. Lit., writing cons. various orgns., 1979—; founding coord. Suncoast Young Authors Conf. Coll. Edn., U. So. Fla., Tampa, 1985-94, adjunct instr., 1982-87, vis. asst. prof., author-in-residence, 1989—; author-in-residence Western Carolina U., Cullowhee, NC, 1994—2002. Cons. IBM/Goodhousekeeping Tell Me a Story Project, 1989; lectr. in field; presenter workshops nationwide. Author: (juvenile and young adult) The Year of the Perfect Christmas Tree, 1988 (Pubs. Weekly best seller list, other commendations), Littlejim, 1990, My Great Aunt Arizona, 1991, Littlejim's Gift, 1994, Mountain Valor, 1995, Littlejim's Dreams, 1997, Bright Freedom's Song, 1998, How Writing Works, 2003, Miss Dorothy and Her Bookmobile, 2003; pub. numerous books; contbr. articles to various publs. and mags. Fla. Endowment for the Humanities scholar, 1988-89; recipient Disting. Alumnae award Appalachian State U., Excellence in Edn. award for Literacy from Partnerships in Edn., 1990. Mem. Authors Guild, Internat. Reading Assn. (Disting. Educator), Soc. Children's Book Writers. Avocations: travel, reading, folklore.

HOUSTON, PAUL DAVID, school association administrator; b. Springfield, Ohio, Apr. 10, 1944; s. Paul Doran and Irene Almeda (Sansom) H.; m. Marilyn Kay Bowyer, Aug. 27, 1966 (div. July 1986); children: Lisa Lenore, Suzanne Elizabeth, Caroline Michelle; m. Jovel Kane, June 27, 1988 (div. Aug. 1997). BA, Ohio State U., 1966; MAT, U. N.C., 1968; cert. advanced study, Harvard U., 1971, EdD, 1973; D (hon.), Duquesne U., 1997. Tchr. Chapel Hill (N.C.) City Schs., 1968-70; prin. Summit (N.J.) City Schs., 1972-74; asst. supt. Birmingham (Ala.) City Schs., 1974-77; supt. Princeton (N.J.) Regional Schs., 1977-86, Tucson Unified Sch. Dist., 1986-91, Riverside (Calif.) Unified Schs., 1991-94; exec. dir. Am. Assn. Sch. Adminstrs., Arlington, Va., 1994—. Vis. prof. Brigham Young U., Princeton U.; pres. S.W. Regional Labs. Bd., 1989-90. Author: Articles of Faith and Hope for Public Education, 1997; co-author: Exploding the Myths, 1993; contbr. articles to profl. jours. Pres. N.J. Interscholastic Assn.; bd. dirs. Princeton and Tucson Libr., 1977-87, YMCA, 1977-87. Finis E. Engleman scholar, 1972; recipient Richard Green Leadership award Coun. of Great City Schs., 1991; named Exec. Educator of the Month Exec. Educator, 1985, 100 Outstanding Exec. Educators in N.Am., 1984, 93. Mem. Rotary (pres. 1983-84), Phi Delta Kappa. Home: 136 N Union St Alexandria VA 22314-3247 Office: Am Assn Sch Adminstrs 1801 N Moore St Arlington VA 22209-1813*

HOUSTON, TRACY ANNE, secondary education educator; b. Phila., June 25, 1961; d. Henry Joseph Jr. and Delores Maria (Basmajian) H. BS in Secondary Edn., Pa. State U., 1983; MEd in Curriculum and Instrn., Kutztown U., 1991. Lic. secondary tchr., Pa. Tchr. English Pennridge Sch. Dist., Perkasie, Pa., 1983-85; tng. specialist Commonwealth Fed. Savs. & Loans, Norristown, Pa., 1985-87; tchr. English Quakertown (Pa.) Sch. Dist., 1987—. Head field hockey coach Pennridge Sch. Dist., Perkasie, 1984-86; asst. field hockey coach Quakertown Sch. Dist., 1988-90, 96—, 9th, 10th grade gifted mentorship program advisor, 1990—. Recipient Pa. Writing Project fellow, 1993. Mem. NEA, Nat. Coun. Tchrs. English, Pa. State Edn. Assn., Quakertown Community Edn. Assn. (union rep. 1990—). Avocations: reading, running, walking. Home: 6832 Ridge Rd Zionsville PA 18092-2340 Office: Quakertown Sch Dist 600 Park Ave Quakertown PA 18951-1541

HOVEL, ESTHER HARRISON, art educator; b. San Antonio, Tex., Jan. 12, 1917; d. Randolph Williamson and Carrie Esther (Clements) Harrison; m. Elliott Logan Hovel, Sept. 30, 1935; children: Richard Elliott, Dorothy Auverne. BA, Incarnate Word Coll., 1935; postgrad., Oxford U., 1979, British Inst. Art, Florence, Italy, 1980. Civil svc. auditor U.S. Govt. Office of Price Adminstrn., San Antonio, 1942-44; interior decorator Parkway Interior Design Studio, El Paso, Tex., 1968-72; instr. stained glass and sculpture El Paso Mus. Art, 1972-78; tchr. sculpture Albuquerque Sr. Ctrs., 1983-85. Docent El Paso Mus. Art, 1972-82. Exhibited sculpture Museo De Artes, Juarez, Mexico, 1981 (1st place 1981). Bd. dirs. YMCA, Albuquerque, 1963-64 (plaque 1964); charter mem. and bd. dirs. Contact Lifeline Internat., Albuquerque, 1982-92 (2 plaques 1986, 90); mem. Com. on Bicentennial of U.S. Constitution, Washington and N.M., 1987-89. Recipient 2 medals Exxon Corp., 1986, 89, Medal of Merit Pres. Ronald Reagan, 1987; grantee Exxon Corp., 1986, 90. Mem. Jr. League Internat. (various offices 1948-97, emeritus mem.), Rotary "Anns" (various offices). Republican. Mem. Christian Ch. Avocations: sculpture, stained glass, oil painting, travel, volunteerism. Home: 7524 Bear Canyon Rd NE Albuquerque NM 87109-3847

HOWARD, AUGHTUM SMITH, retired mathematics educator; b. Almo, Ky., Nov. 10, 1906; d. Leander E. and Anna (Wright) Smith; m. Noel Judson Howard, Jan. 6, 1929; children: Carl Eugene, Robert Alvin. BA, Georgetown Coll., 1926; postgrad., U. Mich., 1927; MS, U. Ky., 1938, PhD, 1942. Lab technician Parke Davis Drug Co., Detroit, 1926-27; tchr. Marshall County High Sch., 1927-29; grad. asst. math. dept. U. Ky., 1936-41, fellow, 1941-42; assoc. prof. math. Ky. Wesleyan Coll., 1942-46, prof., 1946-58; assoc prof. Eastern Ky. State Coll., Richmond, 1958-62, prof., 1962-73. Mem. curriculum study com.; commn. on pub. edn., State of Ky., 1961. Tchr. adult Sunday sch. class Richmond 1st Christian Ch., 1971-78, deacon, 1986-87, elder, 1989. Mem. AAUP, Math Assn. Am. (chmn. Ky. sect. 1944-46, lectr. 1953-55, sec.-treas. 1949-51, 69-71, cert. of meritorious svc. 1988), Richmond Women's Club, Sigma Xi. Home: 2351 Egremont Dr Orange Park FL 32073-5343

HOWARD, BERNARD EUFINGER, mathematics and computer science educator; b. Ludlow, Vt., Sept. 22, 1920; s. Charles Rawson and Ethel (Kearney) H.; m. Ruth Belknap, Mar. 29, 1942. Student Middlebury Coll., 1938-40; B.S., MIT, 1944; M.S., U. Ill., 1947, Ph.D., 1951. Staff mem. Radiation Lab, MIT, Cambridge, 1942-45; asst. math. U. Ill., Champaign-Urbana, 1945-49; sr. mathematician Inst. Air Weapons Rsch., U. Chgo., 1951, asst. to dir. Inst. for Systems Rsch., 1952-56, assoc. dir., 1956-60, assoc. dir. Labs. for Applied Sci., 1958-60; dir. Sci. Computing Ctr. U. Miami, Coral Gables, Fla., 1960-64, prof. math. and computer sci., 1960-91, prof. emeritus, 1991—, assoc. faculty Grad. Sch. of Internat. Studies, 1996—; chmn. bd. dirs. Sociocybernetics, Inc.; exec. sec. Air Force Adv. Bd. Simulation, 1951-54; cons. Systems Rsch. Labs, Inc., Dayton, Ohio, 1963-67, acting dir. math. scis. div., 1965; cons. Variety Children's Rsch. Found., Miami, 1964-66, Fla. Power & Light Co., Miami, 1968, Shaw & Assocs., 1964-75; vis. fellow Dartmouth Coll., Hanover, N.H., 1976; co-investigator Positron Emission Tomography Ctr., U. Miami Dept. Neurology/Mt. Sinai Med. Ctr., 1981-84. Creator Parabolic-Earth Radar Coverage Chart, 1944; co-creator: (with Henry W. Kunce) Sociocybernetics, 1971, Optimum Curvature, 1964, Optimum Torsion, 1974, (with J.F.B. Shaw) Principles in Highway Routing, (with James M. Syck) Twisted Splines, 1992. Chmn. bd. dirs. Blue Lake Assn., Inc., Miami, 1969-96, chmn. emeritus 1996—. Am. Soc. Engrng. Edn.-Office of Naval Research fellow Naval Underwater Systems Ctr., 1981, 82. Mem. Am. Math. Soc., Soc. Indsl. and Applied Math. (treas. S.E. sect. 1964), Am. Phys. Soc., Assn. Computing Machinery (chpt. chmn. 1969-70), IEEE, AAUP (chpt. sec. 1974-91), Sigma Xi, Phi Kappa Phi, Pi Mu Epsilon, Alpha Sigma Phi, Alpha Epsilon Lambda. Home: 7320 Miller Dr Miami FL 33155-5504 Office: U Miami Sci Computing Ctr Coral Gables FL 33124

HOWARD, CAROL SPENCER, librarian, journalist; b. Great Bend, Kans., 1944; d. Thomas Glendon and Margaret Merle (Jackson) Spencer; m. William Neal Howard, Dec. 31, 1977 (div. July 1987); 1 child, Morgan William. BA in Journalism, English and Edn., Baylor U., 1967; MLS, U. Tex., 1974. Cert. libr. City desk reporter Waco (Tex.) News-Tribune, 1965-67; guest editor Mademoiselle mag., N.Y.C., 1966; womens' news reporter Houston Post, 1969; libr. Austin Ind. Sch. Dist., 1974—86, 1991—97, San Antonio Ind. Sch. Dist., 1989-90, Del Valle (Tex.) Ind. Sch. Dist., 1990-91; children's book reviewer Austin Am. Statesman, 1984-90. Freelance journalist, children's lit. cons. Contbr. articles to profl. jours. Fellow U. Tex., 1973-74. Home: PO Box 302019 Austin TX 78703-0034

HOWARD, DAVID, educational administrator; b. Delaware, Ohio, Sept. 24, 1929; s. Dale David and Clarine (Morehouse) H. BA, Ohio Wesleyan U., 1953; student, Columbia U, 1961-62, 86, NYU, 1985-86. Lic. tchr., attendance coordinator, N.Y. News writer Australian Broadcasting Co., Sydney, 1955; editl. asst. N.Y. Times, N.Y.C., 1956-58; tchr. social studies N.Y.C. Bd. of Edn., 1958-82, hotel and shelter ednl. coord., 1982-89; asst. supr. N.Y.C. Truancy Patrol Teams, 1989—. Author: Night Lights Went Out, 1966, Casa Alhambra, 1968, Picker of the Kingdom, 1999, Springtime for Kelly, 2001. Reservist FEMA, N.Y.C., 1980—. Lt. col. USAFR, 1953-75. Mem. Mystery Writers of Am., English Speaking Union. Republican. Protestant. N.Y.C. Anchor & Saber. Home: 324 E 61st St Apt 20 New York NY 10021-8709

HOWARD, DORIS MARIE, fine arts educator; b. Oyster Bay, N.Y., Feb. 24, 1946; d. Henry Seymore and Marie Mildred (Hsapray) Duncan; m. Andrew Joseph Howard, Sept. 10, 1988, 1 child, Emily Elizabeth. BFA, Syracuse U., 1968; MFA, Boston U., 1975. Cert. art tchr. Summer art dir. Thayer Acad., Braintree, Mass., 1969; art tchr. Norwood (Mass.) Schs., 1969—, adult edn. program instr., 1970-78, 80, pupil pers. svc. instr. Project Enhance, 1988-89; fine arts dept. head Norwood Jr. H.S., 1980—. Artist in residence instr. Ariz. Western Coll., Yuma, 1978; bd. dirs. Mass. Cultural Coun., Norwood. Illustrator portraits, 1980—; sculpture exhbns. include Cooper and French Gallery, Newport, R.I., 1977, Brockton (Mass.) Arts Ctr., MTA Fine Arts Festival, Boston, 1978, 79, Brockton (Mass.) Cmty. Schs., 1979, Worcester (Mass.) Crafts Ctr., 1979, Ten Members Show of New Works, Boston, 1980, Artisan's Gallery, Great Neck, N.Y., 1980, Brockton Art Mus., 1988-92. Dir., designer town mural Norwood Jr. H.S., 1981, 94, pool mural Beautification Com., Norwood, 1993; initiator, dir. Japan Internat. Intern Program, Norwood, 1993-94. Recipient 1st and 2d place awards New Eng. Ceramic League, 1977, Outstanding Tchr. award Mass. Alliance for Arts Edn., 1989, Gov.'s citation for ednl. excellence Gov. Michael Dukakis, Boston, 1989. Mem. Mass. Cultural Coun., Nat. Art Edn. Assn., Mass. Alliance for Arts Edn., Mus. Fine Arts, Broctton Fuller Mus. (mems. exhibit purchase 1989). Episcopalian. Avocations: artist, writer, interior designer, travel, exercise. Home: 103 Maple St Norwood MA 02062-2027 Office: Norwood Jr HS Endean Park Norwood MA 02062

HOWARD, G. DANIEL, university administrator; b. Yonkers, N.Y., Nov. 29, 1949; s. Gordon Francis and Margaret Elanore (Connors) H.; m. Anne M. Tournquist, Aug. 20, 1988. MS with honors, Ind. U., 1974, MPH with honors, 1975, Dr Health and Safety, 1976, PhD in Higher Edn. Adminstrn., 1993. Asst. prof. SUNY, Cortland, 1976-79, asst. v.p. acad. affairs inst. tech. Utica, 1987-90, acting v.p. acad. affairs, 1989-90; assoc. prof., chair Ind. U., Bloomington, 1979-85, postdoctoral fellow, 1990-92; dir. grants and devel. Ind. State U., Terre Haute, 1985-87; v.p. univ. advancement, dean rsch., asst. to pres. U. North Ala., Florence, 1997—2000, v.p. univ. advancement and adminstrn., 2000—, acting dean enrollment mgmt., 1993-95. Author, editor Rsch. & Creative Expression, 1987-90. Mem. Gov.'s Commn. Voluntary & Community Svc., Montgomery, Ala., 1993—; dir. DYS Youth Home Project, Florence, Ala., 1993—. With U.S. Army, 1971-73, Vietnam. Mem. Nat. Soc. Fund Raising Execs., Bd. Cert. Safety Profls., Am. Mensa, Ltd., Exch. Club. Avocations: hiking, swimming, skiing, reading, philanthrophy. Home: 310 Cypress Cv Florence AL 35634-2243 Office: U North Alabama Bibb Graves Hl Rm 110 Florence AL 35632-0001

HOWARD, HERBERT HOOVER, broadcasting and communications educator; b. Johnson City, Tenn., Nov. 7, 1928; s. Bonnie Robert and Laura Elizabeth (Crumley) H.; m. Alpha Sells Day, Nov. 16, 1956; 1 child, Joseph David. BS, E. Tenn. State U., Johnson City, 1952, MS, 1955; cert., U. N.C., 1959; PhD in Mass Comm., Ohio U., 1973. Announcer, program dir. Sta. WJHL-AM-FM-TV, Johnson City, 1951-58; writer, announcer Sta. WCHL & WUNC-TV, Chapel Hill, N.C., 1958-59; from instr. to radio network mgr. U. Tenn., 1959-70, from asst. to assoc. prof. communications, 1970-80, prof. broadcasting, 1980-99, prof. emeritus, 1999—, asst. dean Coll. Communications, 1981-93, acting dean, 1990-91; assoc. dean, 1993-99. Mem. cmty. adv. bd. WSJK-WKOP Pub. TV, 1995—; pres. Tazewell TV Corp., 1996—. Author: Multiple Ownership in Television and Broadcasting, 1979, (textbook) Radio, TV, and Cable Programming, 1984, 94, Broadcast Advertising, 1979, 88, 91; contbr. articles to profl. jours. Mem. Soc. Profl. Journalists, Assn. Edn. in Journalism and Mass Comms., Broadcast Edn. Assn. (Disting. Edn. Svc. award 2000), Optimists (So. Knoxville v.p. 1972—, pres. 1974, lt. gov. Tenn. dist. internat. chpt. 1976). Republican. Presbyterian. Avocations: traveling, stamp collecting. Home: 1724 S Hills Dr Knoxville TN 37920-2937 Office: U Tenn 333 Communications Bldg Knoxville TN 37996-0001 E-mail: herbhoward1@att.net.

HOWARD, J. WOODFORD, JR., political science educator; b. Ashland, Ky., July 5, 1931; s. J. Woodford and Florence Alberta (Stephens) H.; m. Valerie Hope Barclay, Apr. 10, 1960; 1 child, Elaine Howard Christ. BA summa cum laude, Duke U., 1952; M.P.A., Princeton U., 1954, MA, 1955, PhD, 1959. Instr. Lafayette Coll., Easton, Pa., 1958-59; postdoctoral fellow Harvard Law Sch., 1961-62; asst. prof. Lafayette Coll., 1959-62, Duke U., 1962-66, assoc. prof., 1966-67, Johns Hopkins U., 1967-69, prof. polit. sci., 1969-75, Thomas P. Stran prof., 1975-96, Thomas P. Stran prof. emeritus, 1996—, chmn. dept., 1973-75. Author: Mr. Justice Murphy: A Political Biography, 1968, Courts of Appeals in the Federal Judicial System, 1981 (cert. merit ABA 1982); mem. editl. bd. Law and Soc. Rev., 1975-76, 78-82, Am. Polit. Sci. Rev., 1977-81, Jour. Politics, 1979-93, Johns Hopkins U. Press, 1991-93; subject of essay in The Pioneers of Judicial Behavior, edited by Nancy Maveety, 2003; contbr. articles to profl. jours. Mem. history program adv. com. Fed. Jud. Ctr., 1989-95; trustee Balt. Mus. Art; mem. music com. Balt. Symphony Orch.; bd. dirs. Shriver Hall Concert Series; vestryman Ch. of Redeemer, Balt., 1988-90. Lt. USAF, 1955-57. Named to Hall of Fame, Floyd Co., Ky., 1957; recipient Outstanding Tchr. awards and citations, Lafayette Coll., 1960, Duke U., 1966, Johns Hopkins U., 1969, 1970, 1993, Pub. award, Harcourt Coll., 2001. Mem.: Law and Soc. Assn., Am. Judicature Soc., Nat. Capitol Area Polit. Sci. Assn. (coun. 1986—89), So. Polit. Sci. Assn., Am. Polit. Sci. Assn., Filson Hist. Soc., Supreme Ct. Hist. Soc., Princeton Club (N.Y.C.), 14 Hamilton St. Club (Balt.), Phi Beta Kappa, Omicron Delta Kappa. Office: Johns Hopkins U Dept Polit Sci Baltimore MD 21218-2685

HOWARD, JACK BENNY, chemical engineer, educator, researcher; b. Tompkinsville, Ky., Oct. 16, 1937; s. Harley Hugh and Opal Mae (Branstetter) H.; m. Carolyn Butler, Jan. 4, 1969; children: Courtenay Bine, Jonathan David. BS, U. Ky., 1960, MS, 1961; PhD, Pa. State U., 1965. Asst. prof. MIT, Cambridge, 1965-72, assoc. prof., 1972-75, prof., 1975—. Wilhelm lectr. Princeton U., 1977; Oblad lectr. U. Utah, 1989. Author: New Energy Technology, 1971; contbr. numerous articles to profl. jours.; patentee in field. Mem. Govt. Panels on Energy Tech., Washington, 1970—. Mem. AAAS, Am. Chem. Soc. (chair fuel chemistry div. 1983-84, Storch award 1983), Am. Inst. Chem. Engrs., Combustion Inst. (program chair 1982, Silver medal 1984, Bernard Lewis Gold medal 1992). Office: MIT 77 Massachusetts Ave Rm 66-454 Cambridge MA 02139-4307 E-mail: jbhoward@mit.edu.

HOWARD, JAMES KENTON, academic administrator, journalist; b. June 30, 1943; s. Arthur R. and Dora G. (Utt) H.; m. Lynn M. Marsh, Sept. 23, 1982; children: Lara L., James M. BA, U. Okla., 1965, MA, 1979; Inst. Ednl. Mgmt., Harvard U., 1991. Asst. dean students U. Okla., Norman, 1965-67, asst. to pres., 1967-68, asst. to v.p. for univ. rels. and devel., 1978; editor Northland Press, Flagstaff, Ariz., 1972-77; cons. Okla. Dept. Public Safety, Oklahoma City, 1977; asst. dean student affairs Northeastern State U., Tahlequah, Okla., 1978-79, dir. univ. svcs., 1979-82, asst. prof. journalism, 1979—, v.p. adminstrn., 1982-91, v.p. bus. and devel., 1991—, trustee NSU Found., 1981-90, 92—. Mem. Coun. Bus. Officers, Okla. State Regents for Higher Edn., 1982—; adv. dir. BancFirst, 1995—. Author: Ten Years With the Cowboy Artists of America, 1976. Bd. dirs. Friends of Mus. No. Ariz., 1974-77; chmn. No. Ariz. campaign March of Dimes, 1973-74; founding chmn. Cherokee County Cmty. Sentencing Coun., 1997—; No. Ariz. coord. Babbit for Atty. Gen. Campaign, 1974; trustee Flagstaff-Coconino County Pub. Libr., 1976-77, chmn. bd. trustees, 1976-77; pres. Indian Nations Soccer Coun., 1981-82; bd. dirs. Indian Nations coun. Boy Scouts Am., 1990-94, Okla. Found. for Excellence, 1996—; trustee Tahlequah Pub. Schs. Found., 1990-2000, founding chair, 1990-98; bd. dirs., exec. com. Leadership Okla., 1990-98, pres., 1994-95, mem. Class II, 1988-89; bd. dirs. Okla. Assn. of Coll. and Univ. Bus. Officers, 1993-98, pres., 1996-97; bd. dirs. Okla. Acad. for State Goals, 1993—, chair, 1999-2000; founding pres. Boys and Girls Club of Tahlequah, 1996-2000; pres., Coll. Assn. Liability Mgmt., 1996-98, 2002—; bd. dirs. Okla. Arts Inst., 1997—, Okla. Music Hall of Fame, 2000—, Communities Found. Okla., 2000-02. With USAF, 1968-72. Recipient Eason Book Collection award, 1965, Book Design award Rounce and Coffin Club of L.A., 1974-75, Citation of Profl. Merit Northeastern State U., 1991, Excellence in Okla. Leadership award, 1995, Disting. leadership award Nat. Assn. Cmty. Leadership, 1995-96. Mem. U. Okla. Assn. (life), Nat. Cowboy Hall of Fame and Western Heritage Ctr. (life), Tahlequah Area C. of C. (bd. dirs. 1985-88), Mensa, Rotary (past pres., Paul Harris fellow), Sigma Delta Chi, Kappa Tau Alpha, Lambda Chi Alpha. Office: Northeastern State U Adminstrn Bldg Ste 109 Tahlequah OK 74464

HOWARD, JANET, elementary education educator; b. Marion, Ala. d. James H. and Marie (Russell) H.; divorced; children: Stratford Howard, Reginald Antoine. AA, Loop Jr. Coll., Chgo., 1975; BS, Chgo. State U., 1979; MA, Nat. Coll. Edn., 1982; postgrad., Roosevelt U., 1995—. Dental asst. Dental Ofice Dr. Max Newsome, Chgo., 1970-72, Michael Reese Hosp., Chgo., 1972-75; tchr. spl. edn., bd. mem. for spl. people students South Met. Assn., Dalton, Ill., 1979-84; tchr. Chgo. Bd. Edn., 1985—. Union del. Langston Hughes Sch., Chgo., 1996—. Author: A Leader's Guide To Developing a Coherent Curriculum, 1996. Democrat. Baptist. Home: 9616 S Leavitt St Chicago IL 60643-1637 Office: Langston Hughes Sch 224 W 104th St Chicago IL 60628-2510

HOWARD, JEAN ELIZABETH, English educator; b. Houlton, Maine, Oct. 20, 1948; d. Ralph Woodrow and Eleanor (Ross) H.; m. James M. Baker, Sept. 30, 1972; children: Katherine Howard, Caleb Howard. BA, Brown U., 1970; MPhil, U. London, 1972; PhD, Yale U., 1975. Asst. prof. Syracuse (N.Y.) U., 1975-81, assoc. prof., 1981-88; prof. English, Columbia U., N.Y.C., 1988—. Author: Shakespeare's Art of Orchestration, 1984, The State and Social Struggle in Early Modern England, 1994; co-author: Shakespeare Reproduced, 1987, The Norton Shakespeare, 1997, Marxist Shakespeares, 2000, Engendering a Nation, 1997; (plays) Shakespeare Quar., (mem. editl. bd. Shakespeare studies), Renaissance Drama; co-author: Blackwell Companion to Shakespeare Vol 4, 2003. Folger fellow Folger Shakespeare Libr., 1996, Guggenheim fellow, 1999; sr. scholar NEH, 1997. Mem. MLA (exec. com. Shakespeare divsn. 1995-00), Shakespeare Assn. Am. (pres. 1999-00). Home: 430 W 116th St Apt 7C New York NY 10027-7220 Office: Columbia U Dept English 602 Philosophy Hall New York NY 10027 E-mail: jfh5@columbia.edu.

HOWARD, KATHY, secondary education educator; b. Buffalo, Apr. 21, 1953; d. Alfred Ralph and Joyce Loretta (Huffman) Sherry; m. James E. Howard, Jr., Aug. 13, 1977; 1 child, Kelly Lynn. BA, Canisius Coll., 1975; MEd, Valdosta (Ga.) State Coll., 1990; 5 Leadership cert., Valdosta State U., 1995. Tchr. English Jeff Davis H.S., Hazlehurst, Ga., 1976—. Home: 10 Kelly St Hazlehurst GA 31539-2020 Office: Jeff Davis High School 156 Collins St Hazlehurst GA 31539

HOWARD, KENNETH LEE, university official, consultant; b. Washington, Jan. 5, 1945; s. Clyde E. and Gladys E. (Williams) H.; m. Ava Campbell, Nov. 22, 1972 (div. Dec., 1981). BA, Howard U., 1967. Grad. asst. Howard U., Washington, 1967-68, residence hall counselor, 1968-70; from fin. aid officer to dir. fin. aid office Washington (D.C.) Tech. Inst., 1970-73; dep. dir. fin. aid. office Fed. City Coll., Washington, 1973-76; dir. fin. aid office D.C. Tchrs. Coll., Washington, 1976-78; dep. dir. fin. aid office U. D.C., Washington, 1978-79, 79-83, acting dir. fin. aid office, 1979, 1984-89, acting dir. ctr. for fin. assistance, 1983-84, dir. Fin. Aid Office, 1989—. Mem. by Congl. appointment Nat Belmont Guaranteed Student Loan Task Force, 1988, 1993; mem. by U.S. Dept. Edn. appointment Nat. Negotiation Rulemaking Group, 1993—, Nat. Direct Lending Adv. Com., 1993—. Contbr. articles to profl. jours. Recipient Dedicated Svc. cert. D.C. Pub. Schs., Washington, 1989, Appreciation cert. U.S. Drug Enforcement Adminstrn., 1991. Mem. Del.-D.C.-Md. Assn. Student Fin. Aid Adminstrs. (D.C. rep. 1975-78, pres. 1985-86, Outstanding Svc. 1988), Nat. Assn. Student Fin. Aid Adminstrs., Ea. Assn. of Student Fin. Aid Adminstrs. (Cert. Appreciation 1986, 91), Phi Delta Kappa (Cert. Recognition 1988). Roman Catholic. Avocations: motorcycles, audio and video enthusiast, gun collector. Home: PO Box 6712 Columbia MD 21045-6712 Office: U DC 4200 Connecticut Ave NW Bldg 39 Washington DC 20008-1176

HOWARD, LOU DEAN GRAHAM, elementary education educator; b. Conway, Ark., Aug. 11, 1935; d. Nathan Eldridge and Martha Regina (Sutherland) Graham; m. Robert Hunt Howard, June 4, 1961; 1 child, Kenneth Paul. BSE, U. Cen. Ark., 1957; MA, Vanderbilt U., 1960. Cert. sch. adminstr., prin./supr., curriculum specialist, mentor, grad. elem. Elem. tchr. Hughes (Ark.) Pub. Schs., 1957-59; supervisory tchr. Peabody Demonstration Sch., Nashville, 1959-61; elem. tchr. Orange County Pub. Schs., Orlando, Fla., 1965-68; elem. tchr., K-5 adminstr. Westchester Acad., High Point, N.C., 1968-77; tchr. alternative learning ctr.-mid. sch. Randolph County Pub. Schs., Archdale-Trinity, 1978; elem. tchr. Greensboro (N.C.) Pub. Schs., 1978-93, Guilford County Schs., High Point, N.C., 1993-97, ret., 1997. Contbr. articles to newspapers and AAUW Bull. Active Stephen Ministry, commnd. Stephen Leader, 2002; citizen ambassador program of People to People Internat. del. to U.S./China Joint Conf. on Women's Issues, Beijing, 1995; precinct chmn. county exec. com., state exec. com. of Dem. Party; mem. High Point (N.C.) Racial Justice Task Force. Mem.: AAUW (pres. N.C. state 1982—84, assn. nominating com. 1985—87, pres. High Point br. 1988—90, co-pres. 1998—2002, N.C. state parliamentarian 2002—, Gift honoree Ednl. Found.), NEA (sch. rep., mem. instrnl. and profl. devel. com.), ASCD, Clan Graham Soc. (sec. 1982—2002, Disting. Svc. award), N.C. Women's Orgns., Peabody Coll. Elem. Coun. (sec.), Ind. Schs. Assn., Assn. Childhood Edn. Internat. (past pres.), Order of The Golden Thistle (charter), Phi Delta Kappa, Delta Kappa Gamma (rsch. chair 1998—2000). Methodist. Home: 1228 Kensington Dr High Point NC 27262-7316

HOWARD, MARILYN, school system administrator; BA in Edn., U. Idaho, 1960, MSc in Edn., 1965; EdD, Brigham Young U., 1986; postgrad., Idaho State U. adj. faculty Idaho State U., U. Idaho. Prin. Moscow West Park Elementary Sch., 1988—99; supervisor, devel. pre-school Moscow sch. dists., 1996—99; supt. pub. instrn. Idaho State Dept. Edn., Boise, Idaho, 1999—. Past state pres. Internat. Reading Assn., nat. rsch. and studies com; bd. dirs. State Bd. Edn., State Land Bd., Northwest Regional Edn. Lab. Office: Idaho State Dept Edn 650 W State St PO Box 83720 Boise ID 83720-0027 E-mail: mhoward@sde.state.id.us.*

HOWARTH, WILLIAM (LOUIS HOWARTH), education educator, writer; b. Mpls., Nov. 26, 1940; s. Nelson Oliver and Mary Watson (Prindiville) H. BA with highest distinction, U. Ill., 1962; MA, U. Va., 1963, PhD, 1967. Instr. Princeton (N.J.) U., 1966-68, asst. prof., 1968-73, assoc. prof., 1973-81, prof. English, 1981—. Mem. exec. com. Princeton Environ. Inst.; advisor Program in Environ. Studies, Program in Am. Studies Princeton (N.J.) U.; cons. Ctr. for Edits. of Am. Authors, 1974, Rockefeller Bros. Fund, 1976, Geraldine W. Dodge Found., 1981, Nat. Geog. Soc., 1984, Corp. for Pub. Broadcasting, 1986, NEH, 1987, Nat. Rural Studies Coun., 1988, Atlantic Ctr. for Arts, 1990, Santa Fe Environ. Coun., 1991, ALA, 1993, Assn. for the Study of Lit. and Environment, 1994, Kellogg Found., 1995, Arthur Vining Davis Found., 1998, AAAS, 2000. Author: Nature in American Life, 1972, The John McPhee Reader, 1976, The Book of Concord, 1982, Thoreau in the Mountains, 1982, Traveling the Trans-Canada, 1987, Mountaineering in the Sierra Nevada, 1989, Walking with Thoreau, 2001; author book chpts.; editor-in-chief: The Writings of Henry D. Thoreau, 1972-80; mem. numerous editl. bds.; editl. adviser numerous jours. and publs.; contbr. articles to profl. jours. Woodrow Wilson Found. fellow, 1966, Henry E. Huntington Libr. fellow, 1968, NEH fellow, 1977, John E. Annan BiCentennial Preceptor, Princeton, 1973, Pew and Templeton Founds. fellow, 2000. Mem. MLA, Am. Studies Assn., Thoreau Soc. Am. (pres. 1975-76), Am. Soc. Environ. History, Am. Lit. Assn., Nat. Geographic Soc. (contract writer 1978—), Nat. Rural Studies Coun. (assoc.), Assn. for the Study of Lit. and Environ. (adv. bd.), Am. Soc. Environ. History (adv. bd.), Ctr. for Am. Places (chmn. bd. dirs.), Phi Beta Kappa. Office: Princeton U 22 McCosh Hall Princeton NJ 08544-1607

HOWATT, SISTER HELEN CLARE, former human services director, former college library director; b. San Francisco, Apr. 5, 1927; d. Edward Bell and Helen Margaret (Kenney) H. BA, Holy Names Coll., 1949; MS in Libr. Sci., U. So. Calif., 1972; cert. advanced studies, Our Lady of Lake U., 1966. Joined Order Sisters of the Holy Names, Roman Cath. Ch., 1945. Life tchg. credential, life spl. svcs. credential, prin. St. Monica Sch., Santa Monica, Calif., 1957-60, St. Mary Sch., L.A., 1960-63; tchr. jr. high sch. St. Augustine Sch., Oakland, Calif., 1964-69; tchr. jr. high math St. Monica Sch., San Francisco, 1969-71, St. Cecilia Sch., San Francisco, 1971-77; libr. dir. Holy Names Coll., Oakland, Calif., 1977-94; Spanish instr. Collins Ctr. Sr. Svcs., 1994-99; acct. St. Monica Sch., San Francisco, 1999—2002; libr. St. Martin de Porres Sch., Oakland, 2003—. Contbr. math. curriculum San Francisco Unified Sch. Dist., Cum Notis Variorum, publ. Music Libr., U. Calif., Berkeley. Contbr. articles to profl. jours. Recipient NSF grantee, 1966, NDEA grantee, 1966. Mem. Cath. Libr. Assn. (chmn. No. Calif. elem. schs. 1971-72). Home and Office: 4660 Harbord Dr Oakland CA 94618-2211

HOWE, JOHN PRENTICE, III, health science center executive, physician; b. Jackson, Tenn., Mar. 7, 1943; s. John Prentice and Phyllis (MacDonald) H.; m. Tyrrell Flawn; children: Lindsey Warren, Brooke Olmsted, John Prentice IV. BA, Amherst Coll., 1965; MD, Boston U., 1969. Diplomate Am. Bd. Internal Medicine, internal medicine and cardiovascular disease. Research assoc. cellular physiology Amherst Coll., 1963-64; research assoc. cardiovascular physiology Boston U. Sch. of Medicine, 1966-67; lectr. medicine Boston U. Sch. Medicine, 1972-73; intern Boston City Hosp., 1969-70, asst. resident, 1970-71; rsch. fellow in medicine Harvard U., 1971-73, Peter Bent Brigham Hosp., 1971-73; survey physician Framingham Cardiovascular Disease Study, Nat. Heart and Lung Inst., 1971; asst. clin. prof. medicine U. Hawaii, 1973-75; from asst. prof. medicine to assoc. prof. U. Mass., 1975-85, assoc. prof., 1977-85, vice-chmn. dept. medicine, 1975-78, asst. dean continuing edn. for physicians, 1976-78, assoc. dean profl. affairs and continuing edn., 1978-80, acad. dean, 1980-85, vice chancellor, 1980-85, acting chmn. dept. anatomy, 1982-85; pres. U. Tex. Health Scis. Ctr., San Antonio, 1985-2000; pres., CEO Project Hope, Millwood, Va., 2001—. Prof. medicine, U. Tex. Health Sci. Ctr., San Antonio, 1985—; chief of staff, U. Mass. Hosp., 1978-80. Mem. editl. bd. Archives Internal Medicine, 1991—; contbr. articles to profl. jours., chpts. to books. Trustee S.W. Found. for Biomed. Rsch., San Antonio Med. Found., S.W. Rsch. Inst. Maj. M.C, U.S. Army, 1973-75. Alfred P. Sloan scholar Amherst Coll., 1962-65; recipient Ruth Hunter Johnson award Boston U. Sch. of Medicine, 1969 Fellow: Am. Coll. Chest Physicians, Am. Coll. Cardiology, ACP; mem.: Bexar County Med. Soc. (exec. com. 1985—2000, 1985—2000, pres. 1996), Tex. Soc. Biomed. Rsch. (past pres.), Tex. Med. Soc. (coun. med. edn. 1986—2001, ho. of dels. 1989—2001, pres.-elect 1997—98, pres. 1998—99), Am. Heart Assn. (fellow coun. clin. cardiology), AMA (coun. on sci. affairs 1993—2001, del. ho. dels. 1995—2001), Omicron Kappa Epsilon, Alpha Omega Alpha. Avocations: tennis, skiing. E-mail: jhowe@projecthope.org.

HOWE, JOHN THOMAS, film director, emeritus educator; b. Toronto, Ont., Can., Aug. 30, 1926; s. Thomas and Margret Ogilvy (Manzie) H.; m. Beverley Jean Luchuck, Oct. 23, 1974; children: Natalie Elaine, Nicholas Thomas (dec.). BA, U. Toronto, 1950. Freelance radio, TV staff producer Can. Broadcasting Corp., 1945-55; staff mem. Can. Repertory theatre, 1950-51; dir., producer Nat. Film Bd. Can., 1955-83; prof. dept. cinema-TV U. So. Calif., L.A., 1983-96, emeritus prof. cinema, 1996—. Dir., composer feature film Why Rock the Boat?, 1974; producer, dir., editor, composer feature film A Choice of Two, 1981; dir., producer numerous feature documentaries, theatrical shorts, TV dramas, others. Capt. Royal Can. Arty., 1944-46, ETO. Mem. Assn. Can. TV and Radio Artists, Dir.'s Guild Am., Soc. Filmmakers (past pres.), Soc. Composers, Authors, and Music Pubs. Can., Can. Coun. Film Orgns. (past pres.), Syndicat Gen. Cinema (past pres.). Office: Sch Cinema Univ So Calif University Park Los Angeles CA 90007 E-mail: howe@iamnow.net.

HOWE, LINDA ARLENE, nursing educator, writer; b. Pitts., Dec. 12, 1948; d. Alfred Robert and Zella Jane (Lintner) Somerhalder; m. John Joseph Howe, Dec. 7, 1968; 1 child, Thomas Patrick. Diploma in nursing, Columbia Hosp., 1969; Assoc. in English, Richland Coll., 1981; BSN, U. Tex., Arlington, 1982; MS in Nursing, Tex. Woman's U., 1988; MAE in English, The Citadel, 1992; PhD in Higher Edn. Adminstrn., U. S.C., 1997. RN, Pa., S.C.; cert. BCLS, ACLS. Staff nurse Columbia Hosp., Pitts., 1969-70; staff nurse ICU Brownsville (Pa.) Hosp., 1970-72; charge nurse ICU Kennestone Hosp., Marietta, Ga., 1972-73; staff devel. dir. Autumn Breeze N.H., Austell, Ga., 1973-74; dir. nursing Hideaway Hills N.H., Austell, 1974-76; mgmt. cons. Unicare Svcs., Dallas, 1976-79; supr. ICU Meml. Hosp. of Garland, Tex., 1979-84; dir. edn. Montgomery Gen. Hosp., Olney, Md., 1984-89; dir. Roper Hosp. Sch. Nursing, Charleston, S.C., 1989-95; nurse Richland Meml. Hosp, Columbia, S.C., 1995-96; dir. Olsten Home Health Svcs., Eugene, Oreg., 1996-98; dir. critical care Valley Hosp., Santa Maria, Calif., 1998; educator St. Francis Health System, Greenville, SC, 1998—99; asst. prof. Clemson U. Sch. Nursing, 1999—. Instr. U. Md., College Park, 1985-89; instr. English Trident Tech. Coll., Charleston, 1992-95; speaker and presenter in field. Author: Passion and Persistance: A Biography of Mary Adelaide Nutting, 1997. Leader Girl Scouts USA, Marietta, 1974-76; cub scout den mother Boy Scouts Am., Dallas, 1977-80, counselor, Dallas and Olney, 1981-88; Sunday sch. tchr. Holy Comforter Luth. Ch., 1994-96, congregational coun. sec., 1994-96; bd. dirs. Pickens County ARC. Recipient Outstanding Advisor award Student Nurses Assn. S.C., 2002, Faculty Excellence award Clemson U. Bd. Trustees, 2003; named Instr. of Yr. Nat. Fedn. LPNs, 1990, 92. Mem. ANA (chair Hall of Fame com.), Nat. League for Nursing, S.C. League Nurses (pres.-elect), S.C. Nurse Educators (treas. 1991-93), Am. Assn. Nurse Historians, Am. Assn. Critical Care Nurses, Sigma Theta Tau, Phi Delta Kappa. Avocations: needlecraft, gardening, music, writing. Home: 103 Hollingsworth Dr Easley SC 29640-2612

HOWE, ROBERT WILSON, education educator; b. Klamath Falls, Oreg., July 9, 1932; s. Fred Phillip and Adelaide Alice H.; m. Alma Ann Felton, Mar. 1955; children: Jeanine Adele, Jeffrey Philip. BA, Willamette U., 1954; MS, Oreg. State U., 1962, EdD, 1964. Tchr., counselor Arlington (Wash.) pub. schs., 1955-60; instr. Oreg. State U., 1961-63; asst. prof. Ohio State U., 1963-66, assoc. prof., 1967-70, prof., 1970-91, prof. emeritus, 1991—, chmn. dept. sci. and math edn., 1969-77. Dir. ERIC Clearinghouse, 1968-90, EQ/IRC, 1977-91; spl. chair Nat. Taiwan Normal U., Taipei, 1993, 95-97; cons. fed. agys., schs. state and fgn. govts. Author, co-author books; mem. editl. bd. Jour. Sci. Edn., 1970-93; contbr. articles to profl. jours.; mem. internat. editl. adv. bd. Procs. Nat. Sci. Coun., Republic of China: Math., Sci. and Tech. Edn., 1996—. Trustees Ctr. Sci. and Industry, Columbus, Ohio. NSF fellow, 1959, 60, 61; EPA grantee, 1977-84, 87, 90; vis. scholar Nat. Rsch. Coun. Republic of China, 1989. Fellow Ohio Acad. Sci.; mem. Nat. Assn. Rsch. Sci. Tchg. (hon. life), Nat. Sci. Tchrs. Assn., Assn. Educators Tchg. of Sci.(hon. life), Phi Delta Kappa, Sigma Alpha Epsilon. Methodist. Home and Office: 4099 NW Sierra Dr Camas WA 98607-8518

HOWE, ROGER EVANS, mathematician, educator; b. Chgo., May 23, 1945; s. John Perry and Marilyn (Leilani) (Evans) H.; m. Carolyn (Rutter) Read Howe, Sept. 9, 1967; Nicholas Read, Katherine Joanna. BA, Harvard Coll., 1966; PhD in Math., U. Calif., Berkeley, 1969. Asst. prof. SUNY, Stony Brook, 1969-72, assoc. prof., 1972-74; prof. Yale U., New Haven, 1974—. Vis. mem. Inst. for Advanced Study, Princeton, NJ, 1971—72; guest prof. U. Bonn, Germany, 1973—74; vis. prof. Oxford (Eng.) U., 1978, Rutgers U., New Brunswick, NJ, 1989—90, U. Paris VII, 1996, Nat. U. Singapore, 1999, Hong Kong U. Sci. & Tech., 2002; fellow Inst. for Advanced Studies, Hebrew U. of Jerusalem, 1988; panel on math. learning NRC, 1999—2001; sci. adv. bd. Singapore Inst. Math. Scis., 2001—; math. portfolio rev. panel NSF, 2003—; steering com., undergrad. program coord. Park City Math. Inst., 2001—. Co-author: Non-abelian Harmonic Analysis, 1992; advisor Jour. die reine und angewandte Mathematik, 1985-97; editor Bull. Am. Math. Soc., 1988-90; mem. editl. bd. Math. Rsch. Letters, Hong Kong, 1993-96, Advances in Math., 1995-99, Transformation Groups, 1995-2001, Jour. Functional Analysis, 2000—; contbr. articles to profl. jours. Study panel RAND Math., 2000—03; steering com. CBMS Math. Edn. of Tchr. Report, 1998—2001. Guggenheim Found. fellow, 1983, Japan Soc. Promotion of Sci., Tokyo, 1993. Fellow Am. Acad. Arts and Scis., Conn. Acad. Sci. and Engring., Nat. Acad. Sci.; mem. Am. Math. Soc. (editor 1989-92, chair com. on edn. 2000—), Math. Assn. Am. (co-Lester R. Ford award), Nat. Coun. Tchrs. Math. Office: Yale U PO Box 208283 New Haven CT 06520-8283

HOWELL, ALVIN HAROLD, engineer, company executive, educator; b. Sedgwick, Kans., Feb. 5, 1908; s. George Alfred and Gertie (Johnson) H.; m. Helen Whitney, Sept. 7, 1934; children: Elizabeth, Alvin Harold, John Arthur, Gordon Howard. BS, U. Kans., 1929; student, Union Coll., Schenectady, 1929-30; MS, Mich. Coll. Mining and Tech., 1934; Sc.D., Mass. Inst. Tech., 1938. Registered profl. engr., Mass. Test engr. Gen. Electric Co., Schenectady, 1929-30; instr. Mich. Coll. Mining and Tech., 1931-34, research geophys. prospecting methods, summers 1931-34; research assoc. MIT, Cambridge, 1939-40; vis. prof., adminstrv. officer Radar Sch., 1942-43; asst. prof. elec. engring. Tufts U., Medford, Mass., 1940-41, assoc. prof., head dept. elec. engring., 1941-43, prof., head dept. elec. engring., dir. research, 1943-70, prof., dir. Balloon Astronomy Lab., 1970-78, emeritus prof., 1978—; devel. rocket and balloon type instrumentation; dir. Doble Engring. Co., 1960—, v.p., 1961-63, chmn. exec. com., 1969—, chmn. bd., 1979—. Mem. NRC; cons. on tethered and free floating balloon systems Air Force Geophysics Lab. Author: (with others) Principles of Radar, 1944; Contbr. (with others) articles to profl. publs. Recipient Exceptional Service award USAF, 1955; Distinguished Service award Tufts U., 1973; Tufts Service citation Tufts U. Alumni Assn., 1974; lab. named in his honor Tufts U., 1984. Mem. IEEE, Am. Phys. Soc., AAAS, AAUP, Sci. Ballooning Assn. (v.p. 1975-78), Am. Soc. Engring. Edn., Sigma Xi, Eta Kappa Nu, Tau Beta Pi. Baptist. Achievements include development of balloon-borne telescope for tracking planets and stars and balloon-borne payload for precisely pointing at ground targets to permit radiometric and interferometric measurements at IR wave lengths. Home: 990 Massachusetts Ave Arlington MA 02476-4532 Office: Tufts U Dept Elec Engring Medford MA 02155

HOWELL, BENJAMIN FRANKLIN, JR., geophysicist, educator; b. Princeton, N.J., June 12, 1917; s. Benjamin Franklin and Claire M. (Mead) H.; m. Constance M. Benson, June 30, 1943 (dec.); children: Barbara Carolyn, Catherine Ann (dec.), Bonnie Andrea, James Benjamin. AB, Princeton U., 1939; MS, Calif. Inst. Tech., 1942, Ph. D., 1949. Research engr. div. war research U. Calif. at San Diego, 1942-45; geophysicist United Geophys. Co., 1946-49; faculty Pa. State U., 1949—, prof. geophysics, 1953—, head dept. geophysics and geochemistry, 1949-63; asst. dean Grad. Sch. Pa. State U., 1968-70, assoc. dean, 1970-82, assoc. dean emeritus, 1982—. Chief cons. seismologist Vibratech Engring. Co., Hazleton, Pa., 1955-69 Author: Introduction to Geophysics, 1959, Earth and Universe, 1972, Introduction to Seismological Research: History and Development, 1990; Editor: Contributions in Geophysics in Honor of Beno Gutenberg, 1958. Fellow Am. Geophys. Union (sec. sect. tectonophysics 1956-59, sect.

seismology 1959-63), Geol. Soc. Am.; mem. soc. Exploration Geophysics, Seismol. Soc. Am. (pres. 1963-64), Phi Beta Kappa, Sigma Xi. Baptist. Home: 1143 Smithfield Cir State College PA 16801-6424 Office: 406 Deike Bldg University Park PA 16802-2713 E-mail: howellbf@aol.com.

HOWELL, BRADLEY SUE, librarian; b. McKinney, Tex., July 15, 1933; d. Jessie Leonard and Carrie Pearl (Nickerson) LaFon; m. Richard Dunn Howell, May 18, 1957; children: Mark Richard, Celeste Ella, Jane Elizabeth. BS in Edn., So. Meth. U., 1955; MS in Libr. Sci., East Tex. State U., 1968. Tchr. J.B. Hood Jr. High Sch., Dallas, 1955-56, Mineral Wells (Tex.) Jr. High Sch., 1957-58; libr. Ascher Silberstein Sch., Dallas, 1963, San Jacinto Sch., Dallas, 1960-62, 65-81, Woodrow Wilson High Sch., Dallas, 1981—. Pres. Tex. United Meth. Hist. Soc., 1980—84, v.p., 2000—; sec. South Ctr. Jurisdiction Archives and history of United Meth. Ch., 1980—88; v.p. local ch. sect. The United Meth. Hist. Soc., 1989—95, chmn., 1995—99; pres. PTA Woodrow Wilson H.S., 1983—84; leader Camp Fire, Inc., 1970—; v.p. South Ctrl. Jurisdiction, Archives and History The United Meth. Ch., 2000—04. Recipient Wakan award Camp Fire, Inc., 1976, Hilteni award, 19782, Sawnequas award, 1988, Gulick Vol. award, 1998, Terrific Tchr. award Tex. PTA, 1984, Jim Collins Outstanding award, 1986, Honor award Nat. Sch. Pub. Relation Assn., 1986, Dallas Positive Parents award, 1987, Golden Flame award, 1990; elected Woodrow Wilson H.S. Hall of Fame, 1999. Mem.: Am. Libr. Svcs. to Children (Newbery com. 1980), Tex. Libr. Assn. (chmn. archives and history roundtable 1990—92), Tex. Assn. Sch. Librs., Dallas Assn. Sch. Librs. (pres. 1975—76), Freedoms Found. and Valley Forge (pres. Dallas chpt. 1997—99, v.p. edn. 2003—), Pi Lambda Theta (Alpha Sigma chpt. pres. 1997—2002), Delta Psi Kappa, Phi Delta Kappa, Alpha Delta Pi, Delta Kappa Gamma (state achievement award 1988, Golden Gift Leadership Mgmt. award 1985). Democrat. Home: 722 Ridgeway St Dallas TX 75214-4453 Office: Woodrow Wilson High Sch 100 S Glasgow Dr Dallas TX 75214-4598

HOWELL, DONALD JAMES, vocational school administrator; b. Bonners Ferry, Idaho, Aug. 14, 1955; s. Leslie Anthony and Roberta Jean (Baker) H.; m. Pamela Yvonne Bryant, Oct. 19, 1973 (div. 1995); children: Cynthia Marie, Anthony Daun. AA in Liberal Arts, AA in Pre-Edn., Craven C.C., Newbern, N.C., 1983; BA in Theology, Twin Cities U., 1984, MA in Edn. Adminstrn., 1986. Cert. tchr., Wash.; cert. state vocat. dir. Enlisted USMC, 1972, advanced through grades to staff sgt., 1978, resigned, 1980; electronics technician Howell Electronics, Jackson, Tenn., 1980-87; vocat. instr. Lake Washington Tech. Coll., Kirkland, Wash., 1987-92; tchr. Juanita H.S., Kirkland, 1991-92; adminstr. Lake Washington Tech. Coll., Kirkland, 1992-93; asst. dir. Tri-Tech Skills Ctr., Kennewick, Wash., 1993—. Apptd. mem. new coll. planning com. State Bd. Cmty. and Tech. Colls., 1991; apptd. Gov. Blue Ribbon Com. on Assoc. in Tech. Arts, 1992. Mem. ASCD, Wash. Vocat. Assn. (exec. bd. dirs. 1992—, sec. 1993-95, Instr. of Yr. 1991), Am. Vocat. Assn., Electronics Technicians Assn. (dir. certification 1991—, vice chmn. 1989-90, chmn. 1990-91, Technician of Yr. 1992, Pres.'s award 1990), Kennewick C. of C., Lions Club (treas. 1994-95), Rotary (Columbia Ctr.). Republican. Avocations: running, hiking, mountain biking, dancing, theatre. Office: c/o Spokane Skills Ctr 4141 N Regal St Spokane WA 99207-5878

HOWELL, ELIZABETH ADELL, elementary and junior high school education educator; b. Berkeley, Calif., Apr. 2, 1944; d. Edwin Anderson and Anna Adell (Carlton) Hunt; m. John Robert Howell, Nov. 1, 1968; children: Robert, Phillip. BA in History, Ariz. State U., 1966; MA in Phys. Edn., No. Ariz. U., 1971. Cert. tchr., Ariz. Tchr. 8th grade, Holbrook, Ariz., 1966-68; tchr. phys. edn. Holbrook, Phoenix, 1968-71; tchr. English, reading Holbrook, 1980-84; tchr. 7th grade English, 1984-86; tchr. 6th grade, 1986-90; tchr. 6th/7th grade social studies and English, 1990-92; tchr. phys. edn., 1991-92; tchr. 7th grade English, 1992—99; tchr. 8th grade English, 1999—. Den mother Cub Scouts, 1980-82; asst. mother advisor Internat. Order of Rainbow for Girls, Holbrook, 1994-97, Character Counts! Coalition, 1997—. Mem. NEA, Lady Elks (bulletin editor 1993, Woman of Yr. 1980), Ariz. Ednl. Assn. Avocations: music, painting.

HOWELL, KAREN JANE, private school educator; b. Mpls., Apr. 24, 1946; d. John and Lorraine (Quale) Borgen; m. John Morris Howell; children: Laura, John. AS in Math. and Sci., Cottey Jr. Coll., Nevada, Mo., 1966; BS in Elem. Edn. Sci. and Math., U. No. Colo., Greeley, 1968; MS Science & Gifted Education, University Of Virginia, Alexandria, Va, 1980—83. Cert. 5/6th Grade Team Tchr. 1968, 6th Grade Gifted Tchr. 1971, K-6th Gifted Program Tchr. 1983. Team tchr. John Adams and Carver Elem. Schs., Colorado Springs, Colo., 1968—73; tchr. gifted 3-6th grade Math. and Sci. Washington Mill and Stratford Landing Elem. Schs., Alexandria, Va., 1973—83; tchr. gifted program Tokeneke Elem. Sch., Darien, Conn., 1983—85; 5-8th science, 1-8 art teacher Hillel Academy, Fairfield, Ct, 1985—. Art / science docent Smithsonian Instn. and Am. Mus. Nat. History, Washington, 1974—82; guide Discovery Mus., Bridgeport, Conn., 1985—. Author: (various workshops, teaching modules) Using Art Properties With Mus. Tours, 1980-1990, 1990, (teacher's guide) Motivational Techniques, Math Manipulatives, 1988,1992, 1994. Chairperson, bd. dirs. Fairfield (Conn.) Internat. Dance Co., 1990—2002; judge Conn. State Invention Conv., Hartford, 1983—87. Recipient Presdl. award for Excellence in Sci. Tchg., State of Conn., 1989, Presdl. award for Excellence in Math. Tchg., 1989, First Sci. Tchr. award, State Sci. Fair Conn., 1996, 1st Place, Middle Schs., Conn. State Sci. Fair, 1995, 1996, 1997, 1998, 1999. Mem.: NEA, Am. Chem. Soc., Nat. Math. Tchrs. Assn., Conn.. Earth Tchrs. Assn., Conn. Sci. Tchrs. Assn. (Conn. Sci. Tchr. of Yr. award 2002), Nat. Sci. Tchrs. Assn., Audubon Soc., Am. Mensa, Am. Ballet Theater (assoc.). Methodist. Avocations: ballet, jazz, dancing. Office: Hillel Academy 1571 Stratfield Rd Fairfield CT 06432 Personal E-mail: j.howell@comsoc.org

HOWELL, LYNNETTE, elementary school principal; b. Chgo., Mar. 8, 1950; d. Samuel and Betty Jane (Scherff) H. BS, Northeastern Ill. U., 1972; MS, Nat.-Louis U., 1987, MS, Cert. in Advanced Study, 1993. Tchr. jr. high St. Matthias Sch., Chgo., 1972-74; tchr., chair dept. jr. high math. Our Lady of Lourdes Sch., Chgo., 1974-95; prin. St. Pascal Sch., Chgo., 1995—. Grantwriter St. Pascal Sch., 1995—, Our Lady of Lourdes Sch., 1990-94, Archdiocese of Chgo., 1996—. Named Outstanding Tchr. St. Scholastica H.S., 1991, 93; nat. nominee Outstanding Tchr. Math., 1992. Mem. Nat. Assn. Secondary Sch. Prins., Nat. Cath. Educators Assn., Nat. Coun. Tchrs. Math., Ill. Coun. Tchrs. Math., Ill. Computer Educators, Internat. Soc. Tech. Educators, Nat. Mid. Sch. Assn. Avocations: travel, photography, reading, graphic arts, cycling. Office: St Pascal Sch 6143 W Irving Park Rd Chicago IL 60634-2598

HOWELL, MARIA DELANE, elementary physical education educator; b. Smithfield, N.C., Nov. 13, 1956; d. Pablo Vasquez Gonzales and Mary Gladys (Jordan) Gaynor; m. Dwight Thomas Howell, Nov. 12, 1988; 1 child, Hamilton Paul. AA, Peace Coll., 1977; BA in Edn., Atlantic Christian Coll., 1979. Interim elem. phys. edn. tchr. Wilson (N.C.) County Schs., 1979, elem. phys. edn. tchr., 1979—. Summer camp counselor YWCA, Raleigh, N.C., 1976, 77, Learning Tree, Raleigh, 1978, 79; girls tennis coach Beddingfield H.S., Wilson, 1979-90. Mem. AAHPERD, N.C. Assn. Health, Phys. Edn., Recreation and Dance (Ea. regional rep. Phys. Edn. Assn. 1989-91), Profl. Educators N.C., Wilson (N.C.) Area Shag Assn. Democrat. Methodist. Home: 3507 Berkshire Dr NW Wilson NC 27896-1499 Office: Rock Ridge Elem Sch 6605 Rock Ridge School Rd Wilson NC 27893-7756

HOWELL, MARY ELLEN HELMS, nursing educator, neonatal nurse; b. Florence, S.C., Jan. 13, 1960; d. Ernest Little Jr. and Sara (Amaryllis) Helms; m. David Alexander Howell; 1 child, Sara Ashley. BSN, Clemson U., 1982; M in Nursing, U. S.C., 1987; cert. Transcultural Nursing, U. No. Colo., 2001; postgrad., U. Aberdeen. RN, S.C. Nursing intern McLeod Regional Med. Ctr., Florence, 1982, staff nurse I in neonatal ICU, 1982-83, staff nurse II in neonatal ICU, 1983-87, asst. head nurse neonatal ICU, 1987; nursing instr. Florence(S.C.)-Darlington Tech. Coll., 1987-91; unit dir. newborn and spl. care nursery The Women's Ctr., 1992-93; mem. faculty nursing Florence Darlington Tech. Coll., 1993-98; nursing instr. Med. U. S.C. Instr. Am. Lung Assn. on Asthma Awareness, McLeod's Women's Resource Ctr. on Sibling Preparation Classes and Infant Care; nursing instr. Med. U. S.C.; mem. infant mortality task force, 1992—. Mem. NAACOG (cert. in high risk neonatal nursing 1989), Nat. League of Nursing, S.C. Perinatal Assn., Latta Jr. Charity League, Dillon Med. Aux., Sigma Theta Tau, Alpha Xi. Baptist.

HOWELL, PAMELA CATHERINE, vocal music educator; b. St. Louis, Oct. 15, 1949; d. Murrel Greer and Maenaskus (Hill) Freeman; m. Wayne Everette Howell, Mar. 6, 1986. MusB, Roosevelt U., Chgo., 1973. Cert. Vocal Music K-12, Ill. Bursar's office Roosevelt U., Chgo., 1970-73; grade 2 tchr. Bethune Sch., Chgo., 1973-74, 4-8 music tchr., 1973-75, K-3 libr. tchr., 1973-75; kindergarten, 6-8 music tchr. Fermi Sch., Chgo., 1975-77; K-8 music tchr. Clissold Sch., Chgo., 1977-80, 83-92; music tchr. Price Sch., Chgo., 1980-82; K-8 music tchr. Chopin Sch., Chgo., 1982-83; assoc. conductor All-City Elem. Youth Chorus, Chgo., 1982—. Vocal music K-8 tchr. Kellogg Sch., Chgo., 1992—, Cassell Sch., Chgo., 1992—; solo vocalist 1969—; instr. pvt. voice class, 1976-82; dir, pianist T.E. Brown Children Choir, 1982-87; 1st asst. dir. Adult Sanctuary Choir, 1971—; dir. Glee Chorus, 1969-71. Charter mem., soloist soprano, sect. leader community Renewal Chorus, Chgo., 1970-91; Active Progressive Bapt. Ch., Chgo., 1957-90; dir. women's ministry, treas., min. music Christ's Way Bible Ch., Chgo., 1992—. Mem. Music Educators Nat. Conf., Ill. Music Educators Assn., Ill. Arts Alliance. Baptist. Avocations: singing, cooking, reading, interior decorating. Home: PO Box 42998 Evergreen Park IL 60805-0998 Office: Chicago Board of Education 1819 W Pershing Rd Chicago IL 60609-2300

HOWELL, RICHARD C. secondary education educator; b. Lafayette, Ind., Feb. 25, 1948; s. Truman C. and Gertrude I. (McKee) H. BA in Social Studies, Purdue U., 1970, MA in History, 1971, MS in Phys. Edn., 1982. Cert. history, phys. edn. and math. tchr. Ind., math., history and phys. edn. tchr. Tex. Tchr. history and phys. edn. Frankfort (Ind.) Jr. H.S., 1971-72; tchr. history and govt. West Lafayette (Ind.) H.S., 1975; tennis coach, tchr. math. Victoria (Tex.) H.S., 1984-85; tennis coach, tchr. history Thomas C. Clark H.S., San Antonio, 1985-89; tchr. social studies Sul Ross Mid. Sch., San Antonio, 1989-98; tchr. algebra II Southside H.S., San Antonio, summer 1999; tchr. algebra I and math. models Poteet (Tex.) H.S., 1999—2000; U.S. history instr. St. Philip's Coll., San Antonio, 1999; tchr. algebra, 7th grade math. and Tex. history S.W. Enrichment Ctr., San Antonio, 2000—01; tchr.. math models, asst. tennis coach Jack C. Hays H.S., Buda, Tex., 2001—. Tennis profl. Park Dept., Lafayette, Ind., 1980-83; asst. tennis profl. Lafayette Tennis Club, 1982-83, Northside Acad. Stds. Com., 1997-98, others. Peer reviewer Strategies: A Journal for Physical and Sport Educators, 1994-96. Mem. acad. stds. com. 8th grade U.S. history Northside Ind. Sch. Dist., 1997-98. Recipient Acad. award in history Phi Alphta Theta, 1971. Mem.: U.S. Profl. Tennis Assn., U.S. Profl. Tennis Registry (San Antonio area rep. Tex. divsn. 1991), U.S. Tennis Assn., Tex. Tennis Coaches Assn., Western History Assn. Avocations: tennis, travel, reading, music. Office: Jack C Hays HS 4800 Jack C Hays Trail Buda TX 78610 Business E-mail: howellr@hayscisd.net.

HOWELL, SHARON S. retired librarian; b. Vincennes, Ind., June 8, 1947; d. Francis Ellis and Virginia Ruth (Cooper) Folck; m. Ronald Vance Howell, Sept. 1, 1973 (wid. Aug. 1990); 1 child, Alexandrea Morgaine. BS in Edn., Ind. U., 1970; MLS, Ball State U., 1974. Cert. tchr. libr./audiovisual svcs., Ind. Libr. Cmty. Unit Sch. Dist. #300, Carpentersville, Ind., 1970, Clark-Pleasant Cmty. Sch. Dist., Whiteland, Ind., 1970-2000, ret., 2000. Reviewer: The Book Report, 1982-96. Mem. NEA, Clark-Pleasant Edn. Assn. (discussion sec. 1993-99), Ind. State Tchrs. Assn., Assn. Ind. Media Educators, Ind. Geneal. Soc., Geneal. Group of Johnson County (sec. 1993-94). Avocations: counted cross-stitch, genealogy, gen. crafts. E-mail: sshowell@indy.net.

HOWELLS, WILLIAM WHITE, anthropology educator; b. N.Y.C., Nov. 27, 1908; s. John Mead and Abby MacDougall (White) H.; m. Muriel Gurdon Seabury, June 15, 1929; children— Gurdon Howells Metz, William Dean SB, Harvard U., 1930, PhD, 1934; DSc (hon.), Beloit Coll., 1975, U. Witwatersrand, 1985. From asst. prof. to prof. anthropology U. Wis., 1939-54, prof. integrated liberal studies, 1948-54; prof. anthropology Harvard U., 1954-74, prof. emeritus, 1974—. Hon. fellow Sch. Am. Research, 1975 Author: Mankind So Far, 1944, The Heathens, 1948, Back of History, 1954, Mankind in the Making, 1959, rev. edit., 1967, The Pacific Islanders, 1973, Cranial Variation in Man, 1973, Evolution of the Genus Homo, 1973, Skull Shapes and The Map, 1989, Getting Here: The Story of Human Evolution, 1993, Who's Who in Skulls, 1995; editor: Early Man in the Far East, 1949, Ideas on Human Evolution, 1962, Paleoanthropology in the People's Republic of China, 1977, Am. Jour. Phys. Anthropology, 1949-54; assoc. editor Human Biology, 1955-74. Served as lt. USNR, 1943-46 Recipient Viking Fund medal in phys. anthropology, 1954 Fellow AAAS, Indian Anthrop. Assn. (fgn.), Am. Acad. Arts and Scis., Am. Anthrop. Assn. (pres. 1951, Disting. Service award 1978), Soc. Antiquaries London; mem. NAS, Austrian Acad. Scis., Mass. Hist. Soc., Am. Assn. of Physical Anthropologists (sec., treas. 1939-41, Charles R. Darwin Lifetime Achievement award 1992); corr. mem. Geog. Soc. Lisbon, Anthrop. Soc. Paris (Broca prix du Centenaire 1980), Anthrop. Soc. Vienna, Royal Soc. South Africa (fgn.), Soc. for Biol. Anthropology Spain (corr.), Tavern Club (Boston); Harvard Faculty Club. Home: 11 Lawrence Ln Kittery Point ME 03905-5104

HOWLAND, JOAN SIDNEY, law librarian, law educator; b. Eureka, Calif., Apr. 9, 1951; d. Robert Sidney and Ruth Mary Howland. BA, U. Calif., Davis, 1971; MA, U. Tex., 1973; MLS, Calif. State U., San Jose, 1975; JD, Santa Clara (Calif.) U., 1983; MBA, U. Minn., 1997. Assoc. librarian for pub. svcs. Stanford (Calif.) U. Law Library, 1975-83, Harvard U. Law Library, Cambridge, Mass., 1983-86; dep. dir. U. Calif. Law Library, Berkeley, 1986-92; dir. law libr., Roger F. Noreen prof. law U. Minn. Sch. of Law, 1992—, assoc. dean info. tech., 2001—. Questions and answers column editor Law Libr. Jour., 1986-91; memt. column editor Trends in Law Libr. Mgmt. & Tech., 1987-94. Mem. ALA, ABA (com. on accreditation 2001—), Am. Assn. Law Librs., Am. Assn. Law Schs., Am. Indian Libr. Assn. (treas. 1992—), Am. Law Inst. Office: U Minn Law Sch 229 19th Ave S Minneapolis MN 55455-0400

HOWLAND, PETER MCKINNON, academic administrator; b. Corvallis, Oreg., Apr. 2, 1956; s. James Chase and Ruth Louise (Meisenhelder) H. BA, Linfield Coll., 1978; postgrad., Boise State U., 1981-82; MA in Interdisciplinary Studies, Oreg. State U., 1985. Travel agt. Sather Tours and Travel, Salem, Oreg., 1979-81; office asst. then devel. asst. Linfield Coll., McMinnville, Oreg., 1985-90, devel. asst. for rsch., 1990-94, dir. of rsch. and records, 1994—. Mem. Pi Sigma Alpha. Lds. Avocations: reading, travel, stamp collecting. Office: Linfield Coll Office Coll Rels 900 SE Baker St Mcminnville OR 97128-6808

HOWLE, MARTHA ALICE TURNER, retired art educator; b. Union, Miss., Sept. 10, 1934; d. Rush Lamar and Essie Alice (Parker) Turner; m. Charles Keith Howle, Feb. 29, 1932; 1 child, Emily Alice Howle Ganzerla. BFA, Miss. U. for Women, 1956; MEd, Miss. Coll., 1980. Cert. art tchr., Miss. Interior designer Kennington's Dept. Store, Jackson, Miss., 1956-56; art instr. East Ctrl. C.C., Decatur, Miss., 1958-59; art tchr. Chastain Jr. High Sch., Jackson, Miss., 1959-65, Callaway High Sch., Jackson, 1966-67, Cancel Manhattan Sch., Jackson, 1969-71, Woodland Hills Elem. Sch., Jackson, 1977-78; art/tech. drawing tchr. Jackson Prep. Sch., 1978-84; art tchr., dept. head N.W. Rankin Attendance Ctr., Brandon, Miss., 1984-93. Interior design cons., Jackson, 1994. Mem. Nat. Art Edn. Assn., Miss. Art Edn. Assn., Kappa l, Theta Kappa Pi. Methodist. Home: 5339 Saratoga Dr Jackson MS 39211-4112

HOWLETT, PHYLLIS LOU, retired athletics conference administrator; b. Indianola, Iowa, Oct. 23, 1932; d. James Clarence and Mabel L. (Fisher) Hickman; m. Jerry H. Howlett, Jan. 2, 1955 (dec. June 1972); children: Timothy A., Jane A. Field; m. Ronlin Royer, Dec. 30, 1977. BA, Simpson Coll., 1954. Tchr. phys. edn. Oskaloosa (Iowa) H.S., 1954-55; psychometrist Drake U., Des Moines, 1956-57, asst. to men's athletics dir., 1974-79; asst. dir. athletics U. Kans., Lawrence, 1979-82; asst. commr. Big Ten Conf., Inc., Park Ridge, Ill., 1982-97. Football TV com. NCAA, 1980-87, women's golf com., 1983-89, chmn. com. on women's athletics, 1987-94, spl. com. women's basketball TV, 1989-90, chair com. for women's corp. mktg., 1990-94, divsn. I championship com., 1990-95, exec. com., 1990-97, chair task force on gender equity, 1992-94, exec. dir. search com., 1993, spl. com. divsn. I football playoff, adminstrv. com., 1995-97, joint policy bd., sec.-treas., 1995-97; NACDA Exec. com., 1986-90, NCAA Coun., 1995-97, NCAA Fin. com., chair, 1995-97, NCAA Found. bd., 1995-97. Editor yearbook Simpson Coll., 1953-54. Chair Iowa Commn. Status of Women, 1976-79; pres. Vol. Bus. of Greater Des Moines, 1969-70; chair Arts and Recreation Coun. of Greater Des Moines, 1975; pres. Iowa Children's and Family Svcs., 1973; nat. pres. Assn. Vol. Bus. Am., Inc., 1972-73. Named to, Simpson Coll. Hall of Fame, 1985, Indianola H.S. Hall of Fame, 1997, NACDA Hall of Fame, 2000; recipient Alumni Achievement award, Simpson Coll., 1988, Adminstrv. Achievement award, NACDA, 1995, Honda award of Merit, 1997, Spl. award, All-Am. Football Found., 1998, Lifetime Achievement award, Ind. Sports Corp., 1997, NACWAA, 2000, Svc. award, Assn. Vol. Mem. Nat. Assn. Coll. Women's Athletics Adminstrs., Pi Beta Phi (pres., Iowa Beta chpt. 1953-54). Home: PO Box 1117 Abiquiu NM 87510-1117

HOWREY, EUGENE PHILIP, economics educator, consultant; b. Geneva, Ill., Dec. 1, 1937; s. Eugene Edgar and Ellen Pauline (Boord) H.; children: Patricia Marie, Richard Philip, Margaret Ellen, Mark McCall. AB, Drake U., 1959; PhD, U. N.C., 1964; MA (hon.), U. Pa., 1972. Asst. prof. econs. Princeton U., N.J., 1963-69; assoc. prof. econs. U. Pa., Phila., 1969-73; prof. econs. U. Mich., Ann Arbor, 1973—, prof. stats., 1978—. Cons. Mathematica, Inc., Princeton, 1965-75; guest lectr. Inst. Advanced Studies, Vienna, 1974, 76. Contbr. articles to profl. jours. Research grantee NSF, 1975, 79, 84 Mem. Ann Arbor Velo Club, Ann Arbor Bicycle Touring Club (pres. 1979-80), Phi Beta Kappa. Democrat. Roman Catholic. Avocation: bicycling. Home: 2152 Overlook Ct Ann Arbor MI 48103-2336 Office: U Mich Dept Econs Ann Arbor MI 48109 E-mail: eph@umich.edu.

HOWSARE, GALEN GLENN, school system administrator; b. Mt. Pleasant, Iowa, Nov. 10, 1949; s. Gerald Raymond and Ada Marie Howsare; m. Katherine Ann Van Roekel, Apr. 18, 1981; children: Anne Marie, Mark Jason. BA in Secondary Edn. and Math., U. No. Iowa, 1972; MA in Secondary Edn. Adminstrn., U. Iowa, 1978. Registered sch. bus. adminstr. Jr. high math. tchr. Ctrl. Jr. High, Rock Island, Ill., 1972-73; math./computer tchr. Wilton (Iowa) High Sch., 1973-77, North Scott Community Schs., Eldridge, Iowa, 1977-86, computer coord., 1986-88; exec. dir. adminstrv. svc. Lewis Ctrl. Community Schs., Council Bluffs, Iowa, 1988—. Keynote speaker Iowa Assn. Sch. Bds. Impasse Workshop, Des Moines, 1990. Co-author: Algebra and Trigonometry Structure and Method Book 2, 1982, 86, Karel the Robot - University of Iowa Courseware Critique, 1983. Vol. arbitrator Quad City Better Bus. Bur., 1986-88; mem. Council Bluffs Leadership, 1990. Recipient State Presdl. award for excellence in Sci./Math. Tchrs., 1985, 86. Mem. ASCD, Assn. Sch. Bus. Ofcls., Internat. Soc. Tech. in Edn., Sch. Adminstrs. Iowa, Iowa Assn. Sch. Bus. Ofcls. (pres.-elect 1993, pres. 1994), Sertoma, Phi Delta Kappa. Methodist. Avocations: sports, biking, photography. Home: 5204 Pommel Pl West Des Moines IA 50265-2744 Office: Lewis Ctrl Community Schs 1600 E South Omaha Bridge Rd Council Bluffs IA 51503-7820

HOWSE, W. FRANCES, academic administrator; b. Nashville, Aug. 20, 1947; s. Willie Frank and Betty Augusta (Davis) Lewis; children: Lynelle V., Allen, LaChelle L. BS with highest honors, Ten. State U., 1978; MA in Sociology, U. Pitts., 1980. Agy. liasion specialist Project Plan Allegheny Intermed. Unit, Pitts., 1980-81; instr. Careers, Inc., Pitts., 1982-83; coord., transfer svcs. La Roche Coll., Pitts., 1983-85; asst. dir. Homewood-Brushton Br. Community Coll. Allegheny, Pitts., 1985-86, asst. to v.p., exec. dean, 1986-89, dean, 1989—. Mem. Homewood-Brushton Revitalization and Devel. Corp., former sec., bd. dirs. Mem. Panel Am. Heritage; founding chairperson Youth Build, Pitts.; chmn., bd. dirs. YouthBuild Pitts.; founding bd. mem., chair East Liberty Arts Coun.; bd. dirs. Bethesda Ctr., Inc.; co-chair United Way Field of Svc. for Family Support. Fellow Nat. Sci. Found., 1978-80. Mem. Nat. Coun. Resource Devel. Republican. Baptist. Avocations: acting, writing, reading, dancing. Office: CCAC Homewood Brushton Br 701 N Homewood Ave Pittsburgh PA 15208-1806

HOXIE, RALPH GORDON, educational administrator, author; b. Waterloo, Iowa, Mar. 18, 1919; s. Charles Ray and Ada May (Little) H.; m. Louise Lobitz, Dec. 23, 1953 (dec. 1992); m. Ada B. Edgerton, June 21, 1997. BA, U. No. Iowa, 1940; MA, U. Wis., 1941; PhD, Columbia, 1950; LLD (hon.), Chung-ang U., 1965; LittD (hon.), D'Youville Coll., 1966; grad., Air War Coll., 1971; LHD (hon.), Gannon U., 1988, Wesley Coll., 1989, U. No. Iowa, 1990, Shepherd Coll., 1992, Teikyo Post U., 1994, Long Island U., 1995, Fitchburg State Coll., 1997. Roberts fellow Columbia, 1946-47, Roberts travelling fellow, 1947-48, asst. to provost, 1948-49; asst. prof. history, gen. editor Social Sci. Found.; asst. to chancellor U. Denver, 1950-53; project asso. Columbia Bicentennial History, 1953-54; dean Coll. Liberal Arts and Scis., L.I. U., 1954-55; acting dean C. W. Post Coll., 1954-55, dean, 1955-60, provost, 1960-62, pres., 1962-68; chancellor L.I. U., 1964-68, cons., 1968-69; pres. Center for Study of Presidency, 1969-95; chmn. Ctr. for Study of Presidency, 1995-96, pres., chmn. emeritus, 1997—. Pub. mem. Fgn. Svc. officer selection bd. U.S. Dept. State; vis. lectr. U. Ala., U. Calif., Irvine, Columbia U., U. Colo., Colo. State U., U. Wyo., Chapman Coll., U. No. Colo., Colo. Coll., Gannon U., Gettysburg Coll., Heidelberg Coll., U. Kans., Kans. State U., Muskingum Coll., Post Coll., St. Francis Coll. N.Y., USAF Acad., Naval War Coll., Nat. Archives, Nat. War Coll., Oglethorpe U., U. Genoa, Italy, U. Pitts., U. Tex., El Paso, U Wis., Northwestern U., U. No. Iowa; bd. govs. Banque Continentale br. Franklin Nat. Bank. Author: John W. Burgess, American Scholar, 1950, Command Decision and the Presidency, 1977, (with others) A History of The Faculty of Political Science, Columbia University, 1955, Organizing and Staffing the Presidency, 1980; editor: Frontiers for Freedom, 1952, The White House: Organization and Operations, 1971, The Presidency of the 1970's, 1973, The Presidency and Information Policy, 1981, The Presidency and National Security Policy, 1984 ; editor Presdl. Studies Quar., 1970-95; contbg. author: (with others) Freedom and Authority in Our Time, 1953, The Coattailless Landslide, 1974, Power and the Presidency, 1976, Classics of the American Presidency, 1980, The Blessings of Liberty, 1987, Popular Images of American Presidents, 1988, Rating Game in American Politics, 1988, Science and Technology Advice to the President, Congress, and Judiciary, 1988, The American Presidency: Historical and Contemporary Perspectives, 1988, Points of View, 1988, The Presidency in Transition, 1989, Dictionary of American History, 1996, Points of View, 1998, Moral Authority of Government, 1999; contbr. articles to profl. jours. and encys. Bd. dirs. United Fund L.I., Bklyn. Inst. Arts and Scis., Tibetan Found., L.I. Coun. Alcoholism, Bklyn. chpt. ARC Greater N.Y.; chmn., pres. bd. dirs. Am. Friends Chung-ang U.; pres. Pub. Mems. Assn. Fgn. Svc.; trustee Air Force Hist. Found., U. No. Iowa Found., Nat. Inst. Social Scis., Kosciuszko

Found. N.Y., Mackinac Coll., North Shore chpt. Am. Assn. UN, Downtown Bklyn. Assn., Coun. Higher Ednl. Instns. N.Y.C.; mem. adv. bd. L.I. Air res. Ctr.; co-founder, mem. adv. coun. Robert A. Taft Inst. Govt.; sec. Nassau County Commn. on Govt. Revision; co-chmn. Nassau-Suffolk Conf. Christians and Jews; dir., pres. Great-N.Y. Coun. Fgn. Students; bd. govs. Human Resources Ctr., N.Y. Korean Vets. Meml. Commn. Served to capt. USAAF, 1942-46; brig. gen. USAF ret. Decorated Meritorious Svc. medal, Legion of Merit, Korean Cultural medal, numerous other medals; recipient Disting. Svc. medal City N.Y., 1965, Alumni Achievement award U. No. Iowa, 1965, Alumni Achievement award Columbia U., 1997, Columbia award for Disting. Achievment, 1997; named Man of Yr. Paderewski Found., 1966, Man of Yr. Eloy Alfaro Found., 1966. Fellow Am. Studies Assn. Met. N.Y.; mem. Am. Hist. Assn., Internat. Assn. Univ. Pres., Am. Polit. Sci. Assn., Acad. of Polit. Sci., Navy League, Air Force Assn., Res. Officers Assn. (pres. Mitchel chpt.), V.F.W., Am. Legion, L.I. Assn. (dir.), Am. Polar Soc., Kappa Delta Pi, Pi Gamma Mu, Alpha Sigma Lambda, Delta Sigma Pi, Gamma Theta Upsilon. Clubs: Century Assn., Met., Columbia Univ. Faculty House (N.Y.C.); Met. (Washington); Bklyn., Montauk (Bklyn.); Old Westbury Golf and Country and Mill River (hon.). Episcopalian. Home: PO Box 248 Oyster Bay NY 11771-0248 Office: PO Box 248 Oyster Bay NY 11771-0248 E-mail: rghoxie@aol.com.

HOYER, MARY LOUISE, social worker, educator; b. Wausau, Wis., Dec. 4, 1925; d. Jacob and Julia (Anderson) Stuhlfauth; m. William Henriksen Hoyer, June 30, 1948; children: Mark Charles, Gail Maren. BS in Biochemistry, U. Minn., 1948; MSW, Cath. U., 1985, D of Clin. Social Work, 1994. Lic. cert. clin. social worker, Md.; bd. cert. diplomate in clin. social work. Rsch. biochemist NIH, Bethesda, Md., 1948-50; dir. Teller Tng. Ctr. Internat. Telephone and Telegraph, Washington, 1967-69; specialist employee devel. Civil Svc. Commn., Washington, 1969-75, supr. sys. sect., 1975-78; mgr. agy. assistance divsn. Office Pers. Mgmt., Washington, 1978-82; vol. counselor Comty. Crisis Ctr., Bethesda, 1980-82; classroom and field instr. Cath. U., Washington, 1986-91; clin. social worker St. Francis Ctr., Washington, 1985-88; pvt. practice as clin. social worker Bethesda, 1987—. Dep. exec. dir. task force on exec. devel. in sr. exec. svc.: Policy Initiatives for Reform of Civil Svc., Office of Pers. Mgmt., Washington, 1978-79. Contbr. rsch. articles to profl. jours. Precinct chairperson Dem. Action Group, Bethesda, 1962-66; fin. cons. Sch. Bd., Hamilton, Mont., 1950-54; cons. Internat. Visitors Info. Svc., Washington, 1962-66; vol. Md. Fair Housing, Bethesda, 1962-66. Legis. fellow U.S. Congress, Washington, 1980. Mem. NASW, Greater Washington Soc. Clin. Social Workers. Democrat. Lutheran. Home and Office: 5901 Lone Oak Dr Bethesda MD 20814-1845

HOYT, ELLEN, artist, educator; b. Bklyn., Nov. 8, 1933; d. Martin and Estelle (Rabinowitz) Reiss; m. Jack Hoyt, July 1, 1954; children: Elyse, Laurence. Student, N.Y. State Tech. Coll., 1951. Tchr. art Kingsway Acad., Bklyn., 1963-77, Studio Dragonette, Bklyn., 1977-84, El Art Studio, Bklyn., 1984—. Art cons. Salute to Israel Parade, N.Y.C., 1973-78; art juror All Cmtys. Art, Bklyn., 1988-90; art dir. Salt Marsh Nature Ctr., Bklyn.; art demonstrator, lectr. and tchr. in field, 1985—. One-woman shows include St. Francis Coll., 2002, Snug Harbor Cult. Ctr., NY; exhibited in group shows Washington Square, N.Y.C., 1979—, Bklyn. Mus., 1981, 83, Met. Mus., N.Y.C., 1979, Stohr Mus., Nebr., 1985, Pa. State, 1986, Snug Harbor Cultural Ctr., 1989, Salmagundi Club, 1982-83, Henry Howells Gallery, 1992, Pan Am. Bldg., N.Y.C., 1991, Vista Hotel, N.Y.C., 1991, Nat. Arts Club, N.Y.C., others; solo exhibits include Ethical Culture, N.Y.C., 1985, N.Y.C. Librs., 1980, 85, 86, 91, Belanthi Gallery, N.Y.C., 1982, Nat. Arts Club, N.Y.C., Cultural Ctr. at Snug Harbor, S.I., N.Y., 1997, Libr. at Cornell Med. Ctr., 1997, Dag Hammerkjold Tower Condominium, N.Y.C., 1998, Unibank Gallery, N.Y.C., 1998, Adelphi U. Gallery, SoHo, 1998, Mauro Gallery, S.I., N.Y., Watercolor Gallery, Laguna Beach, Calif.; permanent collections include Health and Hosp. Corp., N.Y.C., FAB Steel Corp., L.A., Minigrip Ltd., N.Y.C., Gateway Nat. Park, N.Y.C., Grant Koo Cons. Group, Staten Island Botanic Garden, Bklyn. Botanic Gardens, Prudent Pub., Met. Geriatric Ctr., 2001. Active Sierra Club, N.Y.C., 1980—. Recipient Best in Show award Bklyn. Mus., 1983; scholar Washington Square Outdoor Art Exhibit, 1979. Mem. Am. Watercolor Soc., Nat. Arts League, Nat. Artists Profl. League, Bklyn. Watercolor Soc. (demonstrator 1970—, sec., historian 1978—, membership chairperson), Salamagund Club. Avocations: tennis, travel, reading, nature, people. Home: 1551 E 29th St Brooklyn NY 11229-1846 E-mail: jacel@juno.com.

HRABOWSKI, FREEMAN ALPHONSA, III, university president; b. Birmingham, Ala., Aug. 13, 1950; s. Freeman A. II and Maggie (Geeter) H.; m. Jacqueline Coleman, Aug. 29, 1970; 1 child, Eric. BA, Hampton (Va.) Inst., 1970; MA, U. Ill., 1971, PhD, 1975. Asst. dean student svcs., vis. asst. prof. U. Ill., Champaign-Urbana, 1974-76; assoc. dean grad. studies Ala. A&M U., Normal, 1976-77; v.p. for acad. affairs, dean arts and scis. Coppin State Coll., Balt., 1977-87; exec. v.p. U. Md. Baltimore County, Balt., 1987-92, interim pres., 1992-93, dir. Meyerhoff scholarship program, 1989-93, pres., 1993—. Bd. dirs. Mercantile Safe Deposit & Trust Co., McCormick & Co. Co-author: Beating the Odds, 1998, Overcoming the Odds, 2002. Active Md. Gov.'s Commn. on State Taxes and Tax Structure, Annapolis, 1990, co-chair Md. Gov.'s Transition Policy Group on Edn., 1994-95, Gov.'s Commn. on Devel. of Advanced Tech. Bus., 2003—; chair Md. Humanities Coun., Balt., 1991; bd. dirs. U. Md. Med. Sys., Balt. Mus. Art, Carnegie Instn. Washington, France/Merrick Found., Marguerite Casey Found., Md. Acad. Scis., Balt. Cmty. Found., Constellation Energy Group, Inc., Corvis Corp., Balt. Equitable Soc. Recipient 20 Yr. Outstanding Alumnus award Hampton U., 1990. Baptist. Home: 18 Aston Ct Owings Mills MD 21117-1439 Office: U Md Balt County Office of President 1000 Hilltop Cir Baltimore MD 21250-0001 E-mail: hrabowski@umbc.edu.

HRIBAL, C. J. language educator; b. Chgo. m. Krystyna Hribal; children: Tosh, Roman, Hania. BA, St. Norbert Coll.; MA in Creative Writing, Syracuse U., 1982. Instr. MFA program U. Memphis; mem. fiction faculty MFA program for writers Warren Wilson Coll., Asheville, NC, 1989—; prof. English Marquette U., Milw., 1990—. Author: Matty's Heart (selected for New Voices award), American Beauty, 1987, (introduction) The Boundaries of Twilight: Czecho-Slovak Writing from the New World, 1991; editor, 1991; author: (short stories) The Clouds in Memphis, 2000 (Assoc. Writing Programs award in short fiction, 1999), And That's the Name of That Tune (Sternig award for short fiction). Recipient award for short fiction, AWP; fellow, NEA, Bush Found., Loft-Mentor fellow, fellow, John Simon Guggenheim Meml. Found., 2003. Office: Marquette U English Dept PO Box 1881 Milwaukee WI 53201-1881*

HRNA, DANIEL JOSEPH, pharmacist, lawyer; b. Taylor, Tex., March 19, 1940; s. Stephan Peter and Anna Ludmilla (Baran) H.; BS, U. Houston, 1963, JD, 1970; m. Velma Isobel Lesson, Sept. 3, 1963 (dec. Jan. 1994); children: Anna Marie, Daniel Steven, Brian Keith. Bar: Tex. 1972. In mgmt., Gunning-Casteel Co., El Paso, Tex., 1963-65; dir. pharmacy svcs. Tex. Inst. Rehab. & Rsch., Houston, 1966-79; dir. pharmacy Alief Gen. Hosp., Belhaven Hosp., Houston, 1979-85, West Houston Med. Ctr., 1985-88; mem. faculty Baylor U. Coll. Medicine, 1977-79, Sharpstown Gen. Hosp., 1988-94; with Owen Healthcare, Inc. at Sharpstown Gen. Hosp., 1990-94; pvt. practice, 1994—; pres. Rx-IBR Corp. Mem. ABA, Am. Pharm. Assn., Tex. Pharmacy Assn., State Bar Tex., Tex. Soc. Hosp. Pharmacists, Am. Soc. Pharmacy Law, Am. Hosp. Assn., Harris County Pharm. Assn., Houston Bar Assn., Galveston-Houston Pharm. Hosp. Assn., Czech Heritage Soc. Tex. (legal adv., trustee), Profl. Photographers Guild Houston (hon.), Delta Theta Phi, Kappa Psi, Phi Delta Chi. Roman Catholic. Office: 11920 Beechnut St Houston TX 77072-4034

HRONES, STEPHEN BAYLIS, lawyer, educator; b. Boston, Jan. 20, 1942; s. John Anthony and Margaret (Baylis) H.; m. Anneliese Zion, Sept. 11, 1970; children: Christopher, Katja. BA cum laude, Harvard U., 1964; postgrad., U. Sorbonne, Paris, 1964-65; JD, U. Mich., 1968. Bar: Iowa 1969, Mass. 1972, U.S. Dist. Ct. Mass. 1973, U.S. Ct. Appeals (1st cir.) 1979, U.S. Tax Ct. 1985, U.S. Supreme Ct. 1991. Pvt. practice, Heidelberg, Germany, 1970-72; pvt. practice Boston, 1973-86; ptnr. Hrones and Harwood, Boston, 1986-90, Hrones and Garrity, Boston, 1990—. Clin. assoc. Suffolk U. Law Sch., Boston, 1979-82; faculty adv. Harvard Law Sch., 1988—; instr. Northeastern Law Sch., 1998, Mass. Continuing Legal Edn. Programs, 1988—. Author: How To Try a Criminal Case, 1982, Criminal Practice Handbook, 1995, 2d edit., 1999, Massachusetts Jury (Criminal) Instructions, 2d edit., 1999; contbr. articles to profl. jours. Trustee Orgn. for Assabet River, 1990-99; schs. and scholarship com. Harvard U.; fundraiser Harvard Coll. Fund, 1985—. Recipient Edward J. Duggan Pvt. Counsel award for zealous advocacy and outstanding legal svcs. to the poor Com. for Pub. Counsel Svcs., 2000; Fulbright scholar, 1968-69. Mem. ABA, ACLU, Nat. Assn. Criminal Def. Lawyers, Mass. Assn. Criminal Def. Lawyers, Mass. Bar Assn., Boston Bar Assn., Nat. Lawyers Guild, Fulbright Assn. Democrat. Avocations: squash, skiing, wind-surfing, vegetable gardening, reading. Home: 39 Winslow St Concord MA 01742-3817 Office: Hrones and Garrity Lewis Wharf Bay 232 Boston MA 02110 Fax: 617-227-3908. E-mail: sbhlaw@comcast.net.

HRYCIW, ROMAN D. civil engineering educator; b. Phila., Sept. 23, 1958; s. Theodosij and Lucia (Stojkewycz) H.; m. Olena M. Prasicky, Dec. 26, 1981; children: Dmytri, Demyan. BS, Drexel U., 1981; MS, Northwestern U., 1984, PhD, 1986. Engr. in tng. Environ. technician Roy F. Weston Cons., West Chester, Pa., 1977-78; geotech. technician U.S. Army Engrs., Phila., 1978-79; geotech. lab. technician Woodward-Clyde Cons., Plymouth Meeting, Pa., 1980; rsch. asst. Northwestern U., Evanston, Ill., 1981-86; asst. prof. U. Mich., Ann Arbor, 1986-92, assoc. prof., 1992-98, prof., 1998—. Bd. dirs. U.S. Univs. Coun. Geotech. Engring.; cons. Egyptian Antiquities Orgn., Cairo, 1992, Dow Chem., U.S. Bur. Reclamation, Pitts. & Midway Coal Co., Martin Marietta, Mich. Atty. Office, others. Contbr. more than 60 articles to jours. Scoutmaster, bd. dirs. Plast Scouting Orgn., 1973-; prin. Ukrainian Lang. Sch. Ridna Shkola, Warren, Mich., 1998—. Fellow Woodward-Clyde, 1981, Water P. Murphy fellow Northwestern U., 1981. Mem. ASCE (editor-in-chief ASCE Jour. Geotechnical and Geoenvironmental Engring., Arthur Casagrande Profl. Devel. award 1993, Thomas A. Middlebrooks award 1999), Internat. Soc. Soil Mechs. and Found. Engrs., Chi Epsilon (James M. Robbins Excellence in Teaching award 1990). Achievements include rsch. in soil dynamics and earthquake engring., soil improvement, soil testing and in-site investigation, soil mechs. and slope stabilization. Home: 1118 Ferdon Rd Ann Arbor MI 48104-3633 Office: U Mich Dept Civil Environ Eng Ann Arbor MI 48109

HSIAO, JAMES CHINGNU, economics educator; b. Hunan, China, Feb. 4, 1934; came to U.S., 1961; m. Jean Wang, Feb. 19, 1966; children: Eugne Hsiao, Huey Hsiao. MS, Mich. State U., 1964; PhD, U. Conn., 1967. Chmn. Econs. Dept. So. Conn. State U., New Haven, 1976-80, dean Sch. Bus., 1984-86, prof. Econs. Dept., 1989—. Author: Working With Economics: Cases/Applications, 1976, Management Science, 1982. Recipient commendation Gen. Assembly State of Conn., 1985, bd. trustees Conn. State U., 1984. Home: 9 Mansfield Rd North Haven CT 06473-1212 Office: So Conn State U 501 Crescent St New Haven CT 06515-1330

HSIEH, DIN-YU, applied mathematics educator; b. Jiangsu, Peoples Republic of China, Mar. 25, 1933; arrived in the U.S., 1955; s. K.S. and C. (Wei) H.; m. Lily Kwang-Fei Chow, Dec. 26, 1958; children: Paul, Daniel. BS, Nat. Taiwan U., 1954; MS, Brown U., Providence, 1957; PhD, Calif. Inst. Tech., Pasadena, 1960. Rsch. fellow Calif. Inst. Tech., 1960-63, asst. prof., 1963-68; assoc. prof. Brown U., 1968-78, prof., 1978-2000; prof., head dept. math. Hong Kong U. Sci. & Tech., 1990-96, acting dean sci., 1990-91, 92. Cons. Jet Propulsion Lab. Pasadena, 1963-67; advisor Ningbo (Peoples Republic of China) U., 1986—. Author: Asymptotic Methods, 1983, Fluid Dynamics, 1987, America, America, 1990, Amid Hills, by the Lake, 1991, Contemplating China, 1991, Wave and Stability in Fluids, 1994, Swallow Flying, 1998. Mem. Am. Phys. Soc., Hong Kong Math. Soc., Edn. and Sci. Soc. (pres. 1987-90), Hong Kong Soc. Theoretical and Applied Mechanics (founding pres. 1996-97). Avocation: swimming. Office: Brown U Divsn Applied Maths Providence RI 02912-0001 E-mail: mahsieh@ust.hk.

HSIEH, HAZEL TSENG, retired elementary and secondary educator; b. Beijing, Nov. 4, 1934; came to U.S., 1947; naturalized, 1968; d. Hung-tu and Man-lone (Huang) Tseng; m. Hsueh Ying Hsieh, July 1, 1961; children: Durwynne, Timothy. Student, Adelphi U., 1954-56; BS, Tufts U., 1958; postgrad., Harvard U., 1959, U. Hartford, 1962-64; MA, Columbia U., 1977. Cert. tchr., N.Y. Tchr., asst. dir. Parents Nursery Sch., Cambridge, Mass., 1957; tchr. Sch. for Young Children, St. Joseph Coll., West Hartford, Conn., 1958-63; dir. Ctr. Nursery Sch., Yorktown Heights, N.Y., 1967-68; tchr. Yorktown Ctrl. Schs., Yorktown Heights, 1968-97; ret., 1997. Substitute Virginia Day Nursery, N.Y.C., summer 1953-57; co-chair adv. com. Lakeland-Yorktown BOCES Mass Comm. Project, Yorktown Heights, 1982-87; mem. Internat. Faculty, Challenger Ctr. Space Sci. Edn., Alexandria, Va., 1990—. Author: Living in Families, 1991; editor: Honor Society Competition Directory of Nominations, 1985-89. Past mem. Yorktown Schs. Dist. Mission State Com.; mem. Dist. Acad. Stds. Com., 1994-97, Dist. Task Force on Gifted and Talented Edn., 1995-97, Mohansic Shared Decision Making Coun., Yorktown Heights, 1992-97, Mohansic Literacy Com. 1992-96, Tech. Sci. Coms., 1992-97, Wee Deliver Com., 1993-94, Dem. Party; curriculum coord. Ch. Good Shepherd, Granite Springs, N.Y., 1967-69; organizer Parent Orgn. for Arlington Symphony Orch., 1982-84, Mohansic Space Day, 1993, 97; tchr. rep. PTA, 1977-78; founder Internat. Young Astronaut chpt 27796, 1990, leader, 1990-97; coord. project Marsville, Hudson Valley, 1992—; vol. crafts, space sci. workshops, 1990—. Recipient Kohl Internat. Teaching award, Wilmette, Ill., 1991; Challenger Seven fellow, 1990; Challenger Ctr. Internat. Faculty, 1990—; grantee NASA, 1989, N.Y. State Electric and Gas Co., 1987, PTA, 1987, No. Westchester Tchr. Ctr., 1988, Pi Lambda Theta, 1991, IBM, 1992, Readers Digest Found. and Westchester Edn. Coalition, 1995-97. Mem. Am. Fedn. Tchrs., Yorktown Congress Tchrs. (sr. bldg. rep. 1977-78), Union Concerned Scientists, Save the Redwoods League, Nature Conservancy, Sierra Club, Pi Lambda Theta (chair curriculum innovation award com. Westchester Area chpt. 1985-93, chpt. pres. 1991-95, 1st v.p. 1989-91, 2d v.p. 1987-89, corr. sec. 1983-87, advisor 1995—, region 1 sec. and exec. bd. 1996-98, mem. region 1 awards com. 1992-98, chair 1994-96, region 1 comm. chair 1998—, Westchester area chpt. comm. chair 1998—, grantee 1991, Outstanding Chpt. 1991-92). Avocations: downhill skiing, tennis, chinese culture and crafts. Home: 22 Mountain Pass Rd Hopewell Junction NY 12533-5331

HSU, CHO-YUN, history educator; b. Amoy, China, July 10, 1930; came to U.S., 1970; s. Feng-chao and Ying (Tsang) H.; m. Man-li Sun, Feb. 9, 1969; 1 child, Leo BA, Nat. Taiwan U., 1953, MA, 1956; PhD, U. Chgo., 1962; D of Humanities, U. Khust, 2000. Asst. rsch. fellow, 1956-62; assoc. research fellow Academia Sinica, Taiwan, 1962-67; rsch. fellow Inst. History and Philology, Academia Sinica, Taiwan, 1967-70; assoc. prof. Nat. Taiwan U., 1962-65, prof., 1965-70, chmn., 1963-70; prof. history and sociology U. Pitts., 1970-83, Univ. prof., 1983-98, univ. prof. emeritus, 1999—; Weilun chair, prof. hist. Chinese U. of Hong Kong, 1991-98, hon. prof., 1998—. John Burns prof. U. Hawaii, 1996; Semans vis. prof. Duke U., 1999—; disting. chair Academia Sinica, 1999-2000; Y.K. Pao Yak chair, prof. Hong Kong U. Sci. and Tech., 2001. Author: Introduction to Historical Research, 1965, Anthology of Studies in Ancient China, 1967, Ancient China in Transition, 1968, Han Agriculture, 1980, History of Western Chou Period, 1984, Western Chou Civilization, 1988; columnist various newspapers; contbr. articles to profl. jours. Bd. dirs. Chiang Ching-Kuo Found., 1989—, Hwanying Found., 1998—. Recipient Asian Studies Program award UCIS, U. Pitts., 1977; Fulbright-Hays Rsch. fellow, 1978 Mem. Academia Sinica Taiwan (academician), Coun. Academie Sinica, Assn. Asian Studies, Am. Assn. Chinese Studies (pres. 1985-87), Phi Beta Kappa. Avocation: reading. Office: U Pitts Dept History 3M36 Forbes Quad Pittsburgh PA 15260

HSU, DONALD KUNG-HSING, education educator, management consultant; b. Shanghai, People's Republic China, Apr. 17, 1947; came to U.S., 1970; s. Kuo Chung and Ching Hwa (Yang) H.; m. Salome Yu-Ching Hsiao, Mar. 18, 1972; 1 child, Douglas. BS, Nat. Cheng King U., Tainan, Taiwan, 1969; PhD, Fordham U., 1975. Rsch. assoc. Princeton U., 1975, Columbia U., 1976; instr. chemistry N.J. Inst. Tech., Newark, 1977-78; v.p. TCK Industries Inc., Bklyn., 1977-81; instr. data processing NYU, N.Y.C., 1980-82; asst. prof. physics and computer sci. St. Peter's Coll., Jersey City, 1978-83; coord. computer sci. program Felician Coll., Lodi, N.J., 1983-88; tech. instr. Dun and Bradstreet, Basking Ridge, N.J., 1988; assoc. prof. Dominican Coll., Orangeburg, N.Y., 1988—, dir. bus. adminstrn., 1990-96. Mktg. cons. Otsubo Internat., Ft. Lee, NJ, 1984—94, Yuasa Realty, Ft. Lee, 1995—; tech. project dir.computer grants Felician Coll., 1985—88; dir. mktg. TCT Fin., N.Y.C., 1995—2002, Fulton Group, NYC, 2002—; cons. in field. Contbr. articles to profl. jours. Sec., mem. exec. council Chinese Am. Acad. and Profl. Assn., N.Y.C., 1981-84. NASA fellow, 1975; NSF fellow, 1976, grantee, 1982-83. Mem. AAUP, IEEE (officer 1983-84), Assn. for Computing Machinery, Nat. Assn. Realtors, United Socs. of Engring. and Sci. of N.J. (pres. 1991-94), Cheng Kung U. Alumni Assn. Greater N.Y., Inc. (vice chmn.), Shanghai Tiffin Club (N.Y.C.; v.p. 1999—), World League Freedom and Democracy (pres. Greater N.Y. chpt. 1991—). Republican. Office: Dominican Coll Western Hwy Orangeburg NY 10962 E-mail: yanyou@hotmail.com.

HSU, JOHN YU-SHENG, computer scientist, educator; b. Republic of China, Mar. 17, 1938; came to US, 1962; s. James and Margaret (Yen) H.; m. Sheryl L. Hsu, Dec. 18, 1965; children: Mary, David. BSEE, Nat. Taiwan U., 1959; MSEE, U. Calif., Berkeley, 1964, PhD, 1969. Cons. Ames Rsch. Ctr., Mountain View, Calif., 1973-74, Federic Electric/ITT, Vandenberg, Calif., 1971-79, Inst. for Info. Industry, Taipei, 1979-80, Control Data Corp., Campbell, Calif., 1981-82, IBM Corp., San Jose, Calif., 1987-89; prof. Calif. Poly., San Luis Obispo, Calif., 1970—. Author: Computer Networks: Architecture, Protocols and Software, 1996, (book) Computer Arch.: Software Aspects, Coding and Hardware, 2001, Computer Logic: Design Prin. and Applications, 2002. Mem. IEEE (sr.), Assn. for Computing Machinery. Office: Calif Poly San Luis Obispo CA 93407

HSU, KATHARINE HAN KUANG, pediatrics educator; b. Foochow, Fukien, China, Feb. 12, 1914; came to U.S., 1948; d. Wen Chen and Shu Fong (Huang) H.; m. T.L. Hsu, Apr. 26, 1941 (dec. Apr. 1990). BS, Yenching U., Beijing, 1935; MD, Peking Union Med. Coll., 1939. Intern Peking Union Med. Coll., 1938-39, resident, 1939-41; asst. prof. Baylor Coll. Medicine, Houston, 1953-60, assoc. prof., 1960-69, prof. pediatrics, 1970-79, prof. emeritus, 1979-94; ret., 1994. Recipient Disting. Achievement award Am. Thoracic Soc., 1994; named Internat. Woman Yr. Internat. Biog. Ctr., 1996-97. Avocation: photography. Home: 9427 Denbury Way Houston TX 77025-4036

HSU, KYLIE, language educator, researcher, linguist; BA, U. Mich., 1980; MA, Calif. State U., Northridge, 1994; PhD, UCLA, 1996. Lang. and math. instr. U. Mich., Ann Arbor, 1976-80; asst. to pres. Am. GNC Corp., Chatsworth, Calif., 1980-86, exec. v.p., 1986-93; instr. in Chinese UCLA, 1994-95; dir. Lang. Inst. Pacific States U., L.A., 1996-97; asst. prof. Calif. State U., L.A., 1997—2002, assoc. prof., 2002—, assoc. chair dept. modern lang. and lit., 2003, assoc. dir. Chinese Studies Ctr., 1999—, assoc. chair dept. modern lang. lit., 2003. Conf. chair Eng. Lang. Tchg. Conf., L.A., 1996; editor-in-chief Pacific States U. Newsletter, 1997; judge Chinese Poetry Recital Contest, L.A., 1997; manual evaluator Edwin Mellen Press, Lewiston, NY, 1998—; com. chair Chinese Studies Scholarships, 1999—. Author: (book) Discourse Analysis, 1998, Selected Issues in Mandarin Chinese Word Structure Analysis, 2002; assoc. editor: Multimedia Ednl. Resource Learning and Online Tchg., 2000—; contbr. articles to profl. jours. Named one of 2000 Oustanding Scholars of 20th Century, 2000; recipient Hon. Sci. award, Bausch & Lomb, 1976; fellow, State of Calif., 1996—97; Olive M. Roosenraad Meml. scholar, 1976—80, Vieta Vogt Woodlock scholar, 1976—80, Lit., Sci. and Arts scholar, U. Mich., 1977—80, Alumnae Coun. scholar, 1976—80, Martin Luther King scholar, 1977—80, W. K. Kellog Found. scholar, 1977—78, James B. Angell scholar, 1979—80, Presdl. fellow/Rsch. grantee, U. Calif., Berkeley, 1996—97, Advanced Rsch. Lang. Acquisition grantee, U. Minn., Mpls., 2001, Regents-Alumni scholar, 1976—77. Mem.: IEEE (exhibits chair 1993), Assn. Linguistic Typology (scholar 1995), Am. Assn. Applied Linguistics (session chair 1995), Am. Coun. Tchg. Fgn. Langs. (panel chair 1997), Chinese Lang. Tchrs. Assn., Linguistic Assn. S.W. (organizer 31st ann. meeting), Phi Beta Kappa, Phi Kappa Phi. Office: Calif State U LA 5151 State University Dr Los Angeles CA 90032-8112 E-mail: kyliehsu@msn.com.

HSU, MING-YU, engineering educator; b. Kweiyang, Kweichow, China, Dec. 4, 1925; s. Pei-Kung and Wan-Ju (Hsiao) H.; m. Chih-Ju Yao, Jan. 1, 1952; children: Chi-Hsing, Chi-Yun, Chi-En, Chi-Che, Chi-Cheng. BE, Nat. Kweichow U., 1948; Dipl.Engr., Delft Tech. U., The Netherlands, 1959. Registered profl. engr., Ill., Ga., Fla., S.C. Prof. Cheng-Kung U., Tainan, Taiwan, 1960-68; dir. Land Devel. Commn., Taipei, 1960-68; engring. cons. Ministry of Housing & Utilities, Sebha, Libya, 1968-71; sr. engr. Philipp Holzmann Ag., Hamburg, Fed. Republic of Germany, 1971-74, Weber, Griffith & Mellican, Galesburg, Ill., 1974-80; chief engr. Chatham Engring. Co., Savannah, Ga., 1980-82; sr. cons. Hussey, Gay, Bell & DeYoung, Inc., Savannah, 1982—; prof. Savannah Coll. of Art and Design, 1986—. Designed and constructed numerous indsl. office, apt. and comml. bldgs., marine structures including docks, loading platforms, marinas, shipyards and water and waste water treatment structures. Contbr. articles on structural engring. to profl. jours. Mem. Nat. Soc. Profl. Engrs., ASCE. Home: 1115 Wilmington Island Rd Savannah GA 31410-4508 Office: Hussey Gay Bell & DeYoung 329 Commercial Dr Savannah GA 31406-3630

HSU, PATRICK KUO-HENG, retired languages educator, librarian; b. Hefei, Anhui, China, July 3, 1936; came to U.S., 1965; s. Hsiang-Chang and Yi-Yun (Tan) H.; m. You-Wei Gina Wang, Feb. 1, 1962; children: David Shing, Jim Chi. BA, Nat. Cheng-Chi U., Mucha, Taipei, Taiwan, 1960; MSLS, Western Mich. U., 1968. Asst. libr. Ripon (Wis.) Coll., 1968-77, assoc. libr., 1977-85, libr., 1985; assoc. prof., libr. dir. Tex. Luth. U., Seguin, 1985-91, prof., univ. libr., dir. info. svc., 1991—2002. Dir. Univ. Students in Am. from Taiwan Consortium, Seguin, 1990-96. Translator, editor: A Selection of Modern One-Act-Plays, 1971; translator: Theory of Literature, 1976. Dir. Chinese Sch. San Antonio, 1989-95; mem. World Affairs Coun. San Antonio, 1993—, San Antonio Chinese Cult. Inst. (chmn. bd.), 1994-95; advisor Overseas Chinese Affairs Commn., Republic of China, 1994-96. Mem. ALA, MLA, Assn. Asian Studies, Chinese Lang. Tchrs. Assn., Tex. Libr. Assn., Seguin Lions. Avocations: travel, photography, chinese art collecting.

HU, CHENMING, electrical engineering educator; b. Beijing, July 12, 1947; came to U.S., 1969; m. Margaret Hu, Feb. 14, 1972; children: Raymond, Jason. BS, Nat. Taiwan U., Taipei, 1968; MS, U. Calif., Berkeley, 1970, PhD, 1973. Asst. prof. MIT, 1973-76; prof. U. Calif., Berkeley, 1976—, Chancellor's prof., 1998-2000, Taiwan Semicondr. Mfg.

Corp. Disting. prof. microelectronics, 2000—. Mgr. nonvilatile memory devel. Nat. Semicondr., Santa Clara, 1980-81; hon. prof. Beijing U., 1988, Tsing Hwa U., 1991, Chinese Acad. Sci., 1991; dir. Joint Svcs. Electronics Program, 1989-92, Indsl. Liaison Program, 1992-95; founder, chmn. BTA Tech. Inc., 1995—. Co-author: Solar Cells, 1983, Advanced MOS Device Physics, 1989, Nonvolatile Semiconductor Memory, 1991, MOSFET Modeling, 1999; patentee solid state devices and tech.; contbr. over 500 articles to profl. jours. Chmn. bd. East Bay Chinese Sch., Oakland, Calif., 1989-91. Recipient Design News Excellence in Design award, 1991, Semiconductor Rsch. Corp. Tech. Excellence award, 1992, Outstanding Inventor award, 1993, R&D 100 award, 1996, Monie Ferst award Sigma Xi, 1998, W.Y. Pang Found. award for rsch. excellence, 1999. Fellow IEEE (editl. bd. Trans. on Electronic Devices 1986-88, Jack Morton award 1997), NAE., Inst. Physics. Office: U Calif Dept Elec Engring Computer Sci Berkeley CA 94720-0001

HU, MARY LEE, artist, educator; b. Lakewood, Ohio, Apr. 13, 1943; d. Dana Willis and Virginia Haines (Bennett) Lee; m. Tah-Kai Hu, Sept. 9, 1967 (dec. May 1972). Student, Miami U., Oxford, Ohio, 1961-63; BFA, Cranbrook Acad. Arts, Bloomfield Hills, Mich., 1965; MFA, So. Ill. U., 1967. Instr. So. Ill. U., Carbondale, 1968-69; freelance artist various locations, 1969-75; lectr. U. Wis., Madison, 1976-77; asst. prof. art Mich. State U., East Lansing, 1977-80; assoc. prof. U. Wash., Seattle, 1980-86, prof., 1986—. Vis. artist U. Iowa, Iowa City, fall 1975; instr. Kans. State U., Manhattan, summer 1976; dep. v.p. for North Am. World Crafts Coun., N.Y.C., 1982-84. Represented in permanent collections: Columbus (Ohio) Mus. Art, 1975, Am. Craft Mus., N.Y.C., 1985, Renwick Gallery, Washington, 1985, The Art Inst., Chgo., 1989, The Victoria & Albert Mus., London, 1991, Mus. Fine Arts, Boston, 1996. Bd. dirs. Wing Luke Asian Mus., Seattle, 1984-88. Fellow Nat. Endowment Arts, 1976, 84, 92; recipient Flintridge Found. award Flintridge Found., Pasadena, Calif., 2001-2002. Fellow Am. Crafts Coun. (sec. 1982-83, trustee 1980-84); mem. Soc. N.Am. Goldsmiths (disting., v.p. 1976-77, pres. 1977-80), Artist Blacksmith Assn. N.Am., N.W. Designer Craftsmen, Seattle Metals Guild, N.W. Bead Soc., James Renwick Alliance, The Am. Soc. Jewelry Historians, The Soc. Jewellery Historians. Avocations: fgn. travel, cooking, gardening. Office: U Wash PO Box 353440 Seattle WA 98195-3440

HU, STEVE SENG-CHIU, scientific research company executive, academic administrator; b. Yangchou City, China, Mar. 16, 1922; s. Yubin and Shuchang (Lee) H.; m. Lily Li-Wan Liu, Oct. 2, 1977; children: April, Yendo, Victor. MS, Rensselaer Poly. Inst., 1940; PhD, MIT, 1942; postgrad., UCLA, 1964-66. Postdoctoral vis. rsch. fellow Calif. Inst. Tech., Pasadena, 1942-44; pres., mng. tech. dir. China Aircraft, China Motor Corp., Douglas Aircraft, various locations, 1943-48, Kelly Mining and Engring. Corp., Ariz., N.Mex. and N.Y., 1949-54; sys. engr., meteorol. sci. dir. RCA, Ariz., 1955-58; rsch. specialist Aerojet Gen., Calif., 1958-60; rsch. scientist Jet Propulsion Lab., Calif., 1960-61; mng. tech. dir. Huntsville divsn. Northrop Corp., Calif. and Ala., 1961-72; pres. Century Rsch., Inc. Scientific research company executive, academic administrator; b. Yangchou City, Kiangsu Province, Peoples Republic of China, Mar. 16, 1922; s. Yubin and Shuchang (Lee) H.; m. Lily Li-Wan Liu, Oct. 2, 1977; children: April, Yendo, Victor. MS, Rensselaer Poly. Inst., 1940; PhD, MIT, 1942; postgrad., UCLA, 1964-66. Postdoctoral vis. rsch. fellow Calif. Inst. Tech., Pasadena, 1942-44; pres., mng. tech. dir. China Aircraft Corp., China Motor Corp., Douglas Aircraft Corp's China Programs, Calif. and N.J. and N.Y., 1943-48, Kelly Mining and Engring. Corp., Ariz., N.Mex. and N.Y., 1949-54; systems engr., meteorol. sci. dir. R.C.A., Ariz., 1955-58; rsch. specialist Aerojet Gen., Calif., 1958-60; rsch. scientist Jet Propulsion Lab., Calif., 1960-61; mng. tech. dir. Huntsville div. Northrop Corp., Calif. and Ala., 1961-72; pres. Century Rsch., Inc.; bd. dirs. Am. Tech. Coll., pres., U. Am. United Rsch. Inst., Gardena, San Bernardino, Calif., 1973—; pres. U. Am. Found. and U. Am. Rsch. Found., Calif. and Taiwan, Republic of China, 1981—; bd. dirs., exec. v.p. Am. Astronautical Soc., Wash., 1963-70; cons. Hsin-Hwa Nuclear Reactor Program, Taiwan, 1954-58; prof. Auburn (Ala.) U., U. Ala., U. Ariz., U. So. Calif., L.A., 1957-73. Recipient Cert. of Merit and Cash award Commn. Aeronautical Affairs, Republic of China, 1945. Mem. Am. Astronautical Soc., AIAA, Nat. Assn. Tech. Schs., Shanghai Commerce/Industry Soc. (China, hon. chmn. 1991—). Recipient Cert. of Merit and Cash award Commn. Aeronautical Affairs, Republic of China, 1945. Mem. AIAA, Am. Atronautical Soc., Nat. Assn. Tech. Schs., Shanghai Commerce/Industry Soc. (china: hon. chmn. 1991—). Office: Office Sect Century Rsch Bldg 16935 S Vermont Ave Gardena CA 90247-5630

HU, SUE KING, elementary and middle school educator; b. Prince Frederick, Md., Nov. 7, 1938; d. James Elliott and Anna Irene (Hutchins) King; m. Richard Chee Chung Hu, July 2, 1960; children: Stephen Tse Wen, Sharon Yen Mei. BS, Towson (Md.) State U., 1960; MA, Marymount U., Arlington, Va., 1987. Cert. tchr., Va. Elem. tchr. Arlington (Va.) County Pub. Schs., 1977-90, elem. sch. rep., 1986-90, tchr. sci. mid. sch., 1990-94; environ. edn. cons., instr. Phoebe Knipling Outdoor Edn. Lab., Broad Run, Va., 1994—. Workshop presenter Nat. Wildlife Fedn., Vienna, Va., 1989, 90; ednl. cons. Greenhouse Crisis Found., Washington, 1989-91; adj. prof. George Mason U., 1991, 94-95, instr. in environ. sci. Audubon Naturalist Soc., Chevy Chase, Md., 1990—; presenter children's workshops Fairfax County Schs., 1990—. Writer children's newspaper Sci. Weekly, 1990-91. Chair edn. com. Fairfax (Va.) Audubon Soc., 1987-92, bd. dirs., 1988-92, v.p. natural history and edn., 1990-92. Recipient cert. of accomplishment Arlington County Pub. Schs., 1989, svc. award Fairfax Aududon Soc., 1992; named Notable Woman of Arlington, Arlington Commn. on the Status of Women, 1993. Mem. ASCD, Nat. Assn. Biology Tchrs. (elem.-mid. sch. chair 1988-89, presenter conf. 1986-89), Nat. Sci. Tchrs. Assn. (presenter conf. 1988-89), Coun. Elem. Sci. Internat.,, Va. Assn. Sci. Tchrs., Delta Epsilon Sigma, Kappa Delta Pi. Democrat. Methodist. Avocations: hiking, birdwatching, cooking. Home: 2524 Leeds Rd Oakton VA 22124-1406

HUANG, ENG-SHANG, virology educator, biomedical engineer; b. Chia-Yi, Taiwan, Republic of China, Mar. 17, 1940; came to U.S., 1968; s. Juong-Sun and King-fa (Ong) H.; m. Shu-Mei Huong, Dec. 26, 1965; children: David Y., Benjamin Y. BS, Nat. Taiwan U., Taipei, Taiwan, 1962, MPH, 1964; PhD, U. N.C., 1971. Asst. prof. U. N.C., Chapel Hill, 1973-78, assoc. prof., 1978-86, prof., 1986—; virology program leader Cancer Rsch. Ctr., Chapel Hill, 1979-91. Mem. virology study sect. DRG/NIH, Bethesda, Md., 1978-82; mem. AIDS basic rsch. rev. com. Nat. Inst. Allergy & Infectious Diseases/NIH, 1988-90; chmn. Internat. Sci. Promotion Com., U.S. chpt., 1988—. Contbr. articles to Molecular Biology of Human Cytomegalovirus, Devel. Abnormality Induced by Cytomegalovirus Infection, Interaction between Cytomegalovirus and Human Immunodeficiency Virus. Chmn. membership com. Soc. Chinese Bioscientists in Am., Washington, 1988-89, coun. mem., 1993-96. Lt. ROTC, 1964-65. NIH fellow, 1971-73, Rsch. Career Devel. award NIAID, NIH, 1978-83; grantee in field. Mem. AAAS, Am. Soc. Microbiology, N.Y. Acad. Sci., Am. Assn. Cancer Rsch. Democrat. Achievements include development of mouse model to study the developmental abnormality induced by cytomegalovirus infection in humans; research in inhibition of human cytomegalovirus DNA replication by ganciclovir (DHPG). Office: U NC CB#7295 Lineberger Cancer Ctr Chapel Hill NC 27599-0001 E-mail: eshuang@med.unc.edu.

HUANG, GUIYOU, English studies educator, writer; b. Xinjiang, China, Dec. 24, 1961; came to U.S., 1989; s. Huang Honglai and Dong Xiuqin; m. Yufeng Qian; 1 child, George Ian. BA in English, Qufu Tchrs. U., 1983; MA in English, Peking U., 1989; PhD in English, Tex. A&M U., 1993. Instr. Qufu Tchrs. U., 1983-86; tchg. asst. Peking U., 1986-89; editl. asst. South Ctrl. Rev. Tex. A&M U., College Station, 1989-93, lectr., 1993-95; asst. prof. Kutztown U., Pa., 1995-2000, assoc. prof., 2000—03, prof., 2003—, dir. univ. honors program, 2000—, chair dept. English, 2002—. Author: Whitmanism, Imagism, and Modernism in China and America, 1997; editor: Asian American Autobiographers, 2001, Asian American Poets, 2002; contbr. articles to profl. jours. Recipient Profl. Devel. awards State Sys. Higher Edn. Pa., 1997-98, 2003. Mem. MLA, Am. Lit. Assn., Am. Studies Assn., South Cen. MLA, Frederick Douglass Inst. (founding mem.), Assn. for Asian Am. Studies. Avocations: swimming, travel, cooking, fishing, conversation. Home: 312 Susquehanna Trl Allentown PA 18104 E-mail: huang@kutztown.edu.

HUANG, KAI-LOO, religion educator emeritus; b. Indonesia, 1909; came to U.S., 1935 and 1964; BA, Tsinghua, Beijing, 1934; MA, U. Wis., 1936, PhD, 1938. Vis. prof. emeritus Moravian Coll., Bethlehem, Pa., 1965-84, Univ. Wisc. Lectr. comparative religions, Chinese religions. Contbr. articles to profl. jours. Home: PO Box 55788 Riverside CA 92517-0788

HUANG, KERSON, physics educator; b. Nan Ning, Kwangsi, Peoples Republic of China, Mar. 15, 1928; came to U.S., 1947; s. Horton T. and Shi (Ng) H.; m. Julia M. Sheng, Sept. 9, 1956 (div. 1971); m. Rosemary E. Verducci, May 19, 1979; 1 child, Kathryn Camille. SB, MIT, 1950, PhD, 1953. Instr. MIT, Cambridge, 1953-55, asst. prof. physics, 1957-61, assoc. prof., 1961-66, prof., 1966—99, prof. emeritus, 1999—; fellow Inst. for Advanced Study, Princeton, N.J., 1955-57; hon. prof. Fudan U., Shanghai, Peoples Republic of China, 1980. Author: Quarks, Leptons and Guage Field, 1982, Statistical Mechanics, 1987, I Ching, 1987, Quantum Field Theory, 1998, Introduction to Statistical Physics, 2001; cons. editor: World Sci. Pub., Singapore, 1981—. Fellow Alfred P. Sloan Found., 1961-62, Guggenheim Found., Geneva, 1962, sr. fellow Fulbright Founf., Santiago, Chile, 1974. Fellow Am. Acad. Arts and Scis., Am. Phys. Soc. Office: MIT 77 Massachusetts Ave Rm 6309 Cambridge MA 02139-4307

HUANG, MEI QING, physics educator, researcher; b. Wuhan, Hubei, People's Republic China, Jan. 20, 1942; came to U.S., 1988; parents Gong Li and Hui Qin Xia Huang; m. Jin Song Chen, Jan. 6, 1938; children: Qun Chen, Li Chen. Grad. dept. physics, U. Sci. and Tech. China, Beijing, 1964. Asst. prof. dept. physics U. Sci. and Tech. China, 1964-70, 1970-78, instr., 1978-87, assoc. prof., 1987—, head div. magnetism, 1986-88; rsch. assoc. dept. MEMS Carnegie-Mellon U., Pitts., 1983-85, 88-91, rsch. scientist in advanced materials, 1991—. Participant Chinese-Am. coop program in atomic, molecular and condensed matter physics Chinese Acad. Sci. and Am. Physics Soc., 1988; presenter 5th, 6th, 30th, 34th-38th, 40th-47th Ann. Conf. on Magnetism and Magnetic Materials, Internat. Conf. on Rare Earth Applications and Devels., 11th, 12th, 17th Internat. Workshop on Rare Earth Magnets and Their Applications. Contbr. articles to Physica, Jour. Appleid Physics, Jour. Magnetism and Magnetic Materials, Jour. Less Common Metals. Recipient 3d prize of sci. and tech. Acad. Sci. China, 1988. Mem. Chinese Phys. Soc., Am. Phys. Soc. Achievements include patents pending for Cerium-free Mischmetal Fe-B-o Permanent Magnets; research in magnetic properties and structure of magnetic recording powder using magnetic measurements; electron microscopic investigation and Mossbauer spectrum analysis, magnetic properties and structure of rare earth intermetallic properties using X-ray diffraction and magnetic measurement; influence of hydrogen on the magnetic characteristics ofR2Fe14B system; magnetic and structural properties of R2Fe17Nx, R2(Fe, Co)17Nx, (Sm, R)Fe17Nx nitrides, Fe16N2, RC013-xSix, RCo7-xZrx; sintering studies of permanent magent materials, metal bonded Sm2Fe17Nx type magnets, synthesis and characterize structure and magnetic properties of Fe-Co alloy nanoparticles. Home: 2408 Hemlock Dr Dayton OH 45431-3407 Office: Air Force Rsch Lab Universal Energy Sys Inc 4401 Dayton-Xenia Rd Dayton OH 45432

HUANG, THERESA C. librarian; b. Nanking, China; m. Theodore S. Huang, Dec. 25, 1959. BA, Nat. Taiwan U., 1955; MLS, Syracuse U., 1958. Cataloger, Harvard U., Cambridge, Mass., 1958-60; with Bklyn. Pub. Library, 1960-78, regional librarian, 1978-96; editor Dragon Horse Press, 1997—. Joint compiler bibliography: Asia: A Guide to Books for Children, 1966; Nuclear Awareness, 1983; The U.S.A. through Children's Books, 1986, 88. Mem. ALA, Assn. Library Service to Children, Pub. Library Assn., Chinese Am. Librarians Assn. (pres. Northeast chpt. 1998-99), Asia Pacific Am. Librarians Assn. Office: PO Box 401 Teaneck NJ 07666-0401

HUBAND, FRANK LOUIS, educational association executive; b. Washington, July 12, 1938; m. Carol Singer. BS, Cornell U., 1961, PhD, 1967; JD, Yale U., 1975. Bar: D.C. 1975, U.S. Patent Office, 1977; registered prof. engr., Tex. Asst. prof. elec. engring. and math. scis. Rice U., Houston, 1966-72; owner, pres. Engring. Systems, Houston, 1972-73; atty., advisor FEA, Washington, 1975-76; div. dir. NSF, Washington, 1976-90; exec. dir. Am. Soc. for Engring. Edn., Washington, 1990—; sec. gen. IACEE, 2002—. Cons. Tex. Instrument, 1968-75; lectr. George Mason U., Fairfax, Va., George Washington U. Author: Protection of Computer Systems and Software, 1986. Mem. IEEE, ABA, NSPE, Am. Chem. Soc., Am. Inst. Physics, Internat. Assn. for Continuing Engring. Edn. (sec. gen.). Office: Am Soc for Engring Edn 1818 N St NW Ste 600 Washington DC 20036-2476 E-mail: f.huband@asee.org.

HUBBARD, DEAN LEON, university president; b. Nyssa, Oreg., June 17, 1939; s. Gaileon and Rhodene (Barton) H.; m. Aleta Ann Thornton, July 12, 1959; children: Melody Ann, Dean Paul John, Joy Marie BA, Andrews U., 1961, MA, 1962; diploma in Korean Lang., Yunsei U., Seoul, Korea, 1968; PhD, Stanford U., 1979. Dir. English Lang. Schs., Seoul, 1966-71; asst. to pres. Loma Linda U., Calif., 1974-76; acad. dean Union Coll., Lincoln, Nebr., 1976-80, pres., 1980-84, NW Mo. State U., Maryville, 1984—. Chair Acad. Quality Consortium, 1993-96; examiner Malcolm Baldridge Nat. Quality Award, 1993-96; judges panel Mo. Quality Award, 1994-96; adv. coun. edn. statistics U.S. Dept. Edn., 1997-99. Mem. ACE Leadership Devel. Coun., 1996—. Avocation: classical music. Office: NW Mo State U Office of President AD143 800 University Dr Maryville MO 64468-6001

HUBBARD, JOHN LEWIS, chemist, educator, researcher; b. Kingsport, Tenn., June 16, 1947; s. Sherman Halifax and Nettie Frances (Lewis) H.; m. Jeanne Marie Delaney, May 7, 1978; children: Elizabeth Delaney, Matthew Lewis. BS in Chemistry, U. N.C., 1969; PhD, Purdue U., 1976. Vis. asst. prof. Purdue U., West Lafayette, Ind., 1976-77, rsch. assoc., 1977-78; asst. prof. Marshall U., Huntington, W.Va., 1978-84, assoc. prof., 1984-90, prof., 1990—. Reviewer and Contbr. of manuscripts for profl. jours. Cottrell Rsch. Corp. grantee, 1980. Mem. Am. Chem. Soc. (alt. councilor Ctrl. Ohio Valley sect.), W.Va. Acad. Scis., Sigma Xi (pres. Marshall U. Club 1982-83). Democrat. Episcopalian. Avocations: birding, music (organist, choral singer), wine, racquetball. Home: 333 11th Ave W Huntington WV 25701-3027 Office: Marshall U Dept Chemistry Huntington WV 25755-2520

HUBBELL, DAVID SMITH, surgeon, educator; b. Dallas, Aug. 29, 1922; s. Jay Broadus and Lucinda (Smith) H.; m. Barbara Baynard, July 3, 1947; children: Katherine, Lawrence, Daniel. AB, Duke U., 1943, MD, 1946. Diplomate Am. Bd. Surgery, Am. Bd. Thoracic Surgery. Pathologist U.S. Army Tripler Hosp., Honolulu, 1947-49; resident and Am. Cancer Soc. fellow in surgery Yale U. Hosp., New Haven, 1949-54; attending surgeon Bayfront and St. Anthony's Hosp., St. Petersburg, Fla., 1955-85; prof. depts. surgery and anatomy U. So. Fla., Tampa, 1985—, prof. emeritus, 2000—. Capt. M.C., U.S. Army, 1947-49. Recipient award for outstanding rsch. Moffitt Cancer Ctr., Tampa, 1994. Fellow Am. Cancer Soc. (life mem.); mem. ACS (pres. Fla. chpt. 1973-74), Fla. Assn. Thoracic Surgeons (pres. 1980-81), Pinellas County Med. Soc. (pres. 1969-70), Rotary. Republican. Presbyterian. Achievements include research in medical education, control of pain, chest tumors. Office: Moffitt Cancer Ctr 12902 Magnolia Dr Tampa FL 33612-9416

HUBER, DAVID LAWRENCE, physicist, educator; b. New Brunswick, N.J., July 31, 1937; s. Howard Frederick and Katherine Teresa (Smith) H.; m. Virginia Hullinger, Sept. 8, 1962; children: Laura Theresa, Johanna Jean, Amy Louise, William Hullinger. BA, Princeton U., 1959; MA, Harvard U., 1960, PhD, 1964. Instr. U. Wis., Madison, 1964-65, asst. prof., 1965-67, assoc. prof., 1967-69, prof., 1969—. Dir. Synchrotron Radiation Ctr., 1985-97, Phys. Scis. Lab, Stoughton, Wis., 1992—; disting. vis. prof. U. Mo., Kansas City, 1988. A.P. Sloan fellow, 1965-67, Guggenheim fellow, 1972-73, Nat. Assn. State Univs. and Land Grant Colls. fellow Office of Sci. and Tech. Policy, 1990-91. Fellow Am. Phys. Soc.; mem. AAAS, Sigma Xi. Office: Univ Wis Phys Scis Lab 3725 Schneider Dr Stoughton WI 53589-3034 also: U Wis Dept Physics 1150 University Ave Madison WI 53706-1302

HUBER, FRITZ GODFREY, physical education educator, excercise physiologist; b. Wauseon, Ohio, Nov. 24, 1955; BEd, U. Toledo, 1978; MS, U. Okla., 1985; EdD, U. No. Colo., 1991. Head coach Am. Turners, Toledo, 1976-78; tchr., coach St. Wendelin Sch., Fostoria, Ohio, 1978-79; head gymnastics coach Sally Stanley Acad., Perry, Ga., 1980-83, Gymnest Sch. Gymnastics, Macon, Ga., 1985-87; grad. asst. U. Okla., Norman, 1983-85, U. No. Colo., Greeley, 1987-88; prof. phys. edn. Oral Roberts U., Tulsa, 1988—. Chmn. health, phys. edn. and recreation dept., Oral Roberts U., chairperson U. Faculty Rsch. com.; clinic adviser Am. Running and Fitness Assn., Bethesda, Md., 1991—; coach, referee Spl. Olympics, Tulsa, 1988, 89, 90. Mem. AAHPERD, Am. Coll. Sports Medicine, Okla. Assn. Health, Phys. Edn., Recreation and Dance, Nat. Strength and Conditioning Assn. (cert.), U.S. Gymnastic Fedn., Am. Running and Fitness Assn. Office: Oral Roberts U 7777 S Lewis Ave Tulsa OK 74171-0001

HUBER, JOAN ALTHAUS, sociology educator; b. Bluffton, Ohio, Oct. 17, 1925; d. Lawrence Lester and Hallie (Althaus) H.; ; m. William Form, Feb. 5, 1971; children: Nancy Rytina, Steven Rytina. BA, Pa. State U., 1945; MA, Western Mich. U., 1963; PhD, Mich. State U., 1967. Asst. prof. sociology U. Notre Dame, Ind., 1967-71; asst. prof. sociology U. Ill., Urbana-Champaign, 1971-73, assoc. prof., 1973-78, prof., 1978-83, head dept., 1979-83; dean Coll. Social and Behavioral Sci., Ohio State U., Columbus, 1984-92; coordinating dean Coll. Arts and Sciences, Ohio State University, Columbus, 1987-92, provost, 1992-93; sr. v.p., provost emeritus prof. Sociology emeritus, 1994. Author: (with William Form) Income and Ideology, 1973, (with Glenna Spitze) Sex Stratification, 1983. Editor: Changing Women in a Changing Society, 1973, (with Paul Chalfant) The Sociology of Poverty, 1974, Macro-Micro Linkages in Sociology, 1991. NSF research awardee, 1978-81 Mem. Am. Sociol. Assn. (v.p. 1981-83, pres. 1987-90), Midwest Sociol. Soc. (pres. 1979-80). Home: 2880 N Star Rd Columbus OH 43221-2959 Office: Ohio State U Dept Sociology 300 Bricker Hall 190 N Oval Mall Columbus OH 43210-1321 E-mail: huber.3@osu.edu.

HUBER, MARY SUSAN, music educator; b. Buffalo, Feb. 14, 1946; d. Floyd M. Zaepfel and Thelma Zaeptel; m. David Conrad Huber, Dec. 27, 1971; children: David Conrad Jr., Kevin Michael. BS in Music, Daemen Coll., 1969; MEd in Music, State U. Buffalo, 1971; M in Ednl. Leadership, U. North Fla., 1991. Elem. music tchr. Maryvale Sch. Sys., Buffalo, 1969—74, Lakeland Prep, Orlando, Fla., 1980—81, North Shore Elem., Jacksonville, Fla., 1981—85, Loretto Elem., Jacksonville, 1985—89, Mandarin Oaks Elem., Jacksonville, 1989—90; mid. sch. choral dir. Mandarin Mid. Sch., Jacksonville, 1990—. Contbr. articles to mags. and newsletters. Mem. citizens opinion rsch. forum County of Duval, Jacksonville, 1987; life mem. Duval County PTA, 1987—; mem. choir St. Joseph Cath. Ch., 1999—2002. Named Educator of Yr., Jaycee's, Jacksonville, 1987, Tchr. of Yr., Rotary, Mandarin, 1998. Mem.: Duval County Elem. Tchrs. Assn. (past elem. pres.). Republican. Roman Catholic. Home: 11068 Great Western Ln W Jacksonville FL 32257

HUBER, MELBA STEWART, dance educator and historian, dance studio owner, retailer; b. Tex., Oct. 1, 1927; d. Carl E. and Melba (Holt) Stewart; m. William C. Kinsolving Jr.; children: William Carey, Keith Brian; m. James M. Huber (dec.); 1 child, Melba Laurin. AA, Lamar Coll., 1946; student, U. Tex. Establisher, owner Melba's, Inc., McAllen, Tex., 1958—; founder McAllen (Tex.) Dance Theatre Co., 1970; tchr. Black Cmty. at Huston-Tillotson Coll., 1948—49. Columnist, regional rep. Internat. Tap Assn.; regional rep. Gus Giordano's Jazz Dance World Congress. Columnist Tap Talk Dance and the Arts mag., 1988-97; tap columnist Dancer Pages/Dance and the Arts mag., 1998—. Recipient Plaudit award Nat. Dance Assn. Am. Alliance for Health, Physical Edn. and Recreation, 1970, Flo-Bert award N.Y. Com. to Celebrate Nat. Tap Dance Day, 1996, Savion Glover award St. Louis Tap Festival, 1998, Preservation of Our Heritage in American Dance award, Oklahoma City U., 1999, Women of Distinction award Detroit Tap Festival, 2000; named for Life Achievement in the Art of Dance and Gymnastics, presented Tex. Flag Tex. State Senate, 1997. Mem. Tex. Assn. Tchrs. Dancing (pres. 1973-74, honoree 1997), South Tex. Dance Masters Assn. (Mem. of Yr. 1989). Home: PO Box 3664 Mcallen TX 78502-3664 E-mail: Melhuber@swbell.net.

HUBER, PAUL WILLIAM, biochemistry educator, researcher; b. Medford, Mass., July 23, 1951; s. William Francis and Catherine (Sheridan) H. BS, Boston Coll., 1973; PhD, Purdue U., 1978. NIH postdoctoral fellow U. Chgo., 1979-81, rsch. assoc., 1982-85; asst. prof. U. Notre Dame, Ind., 1985-92, assoc. prof., 1992—2003, assoc. chmn., 1993-97, prof., 2003—. Vis. fellow Yale U., 1997. Contbr. articles to profl. jours. Recipient John A. Kaneb award for undergrad. tchg., U. Notre Dame, 2001. Mem. AAAS, Am. Soc. Biochemistry and Molecular Biology. Home: 1215 E Irvington Ave South Bend IN 46614-1417 Office: U Notre Dame Dept Chemistry/Biochemistry Notre Dame IN 46556 Business E-Mail: huber.1@nd.edu.

HUBER, RICHARD GREGORY, lawyer, educator; b. Indpls., June 29, 1919; s. Hugh Joseph and Laura Marie (Becker) H.; m. Katherine Elizabeth McDonald, June 21, 1950 (dec.); children: Katherine, Richard, Mary, Elizabeth, Stephen, Mark. BS, U.S. Naval Acad, 1942; JD, U. Iowa, 1950; LLM, Harvard U., 1951; LLD (hon.), New England Sch. Law, 1985, Northeastern U., 1987, Roger Williams U., 1996. Instr. law U. Iowa, 1950; assoc. prof. law U. S.C., 1952-54; assoc. prof. Tulane U., 1954-57, Boston Coll., 1957-59, prof., 1959-90, dean, 1970-85; disting. prof. Roger Williams U., Bristol, R.I., 1993-95; prof. New England Sch. Law, Newton, Mass., 1995-99. Adj. faculty Boston Coll., 1999—. Contbr. articles and book revs. to profl. jours. Past chairperson pers. and fin. coms. Mass. chpt. Multiple Sclerosis Soc.; past pres. bd. trustees Beaver Country Day Sch. With USN, 1941-47, 51-52. Mem. ABA (del., mem. coun. legal edn. 1981-85, trustee law sch. admissions coun 1983-85), Soc. Am. Law Tchrs., Assn. Am. Law Schs. (pres. 1988-89), Coun. Legal Edn. Opportunity (pres. 1975-79), Am. Judicature Soc., Mass. Bar Assn., Mass. Bar Found. Democrat. Roman Catholic. Home: 406 Woodward St Waban MA 02468-1523 Office: 885 Centre St Newton MA 02459-1148 E-mail: richard.huber1@worldnet.att.net., huber@monet.bc.edu.

HUBERT, SHELBY ANN, speech/language pathologist; b. Holbrook, Ariz., Jan. 5, 1962; d. Bradford Jay and Margaret Mary (Mense) Sweeney; m. David Eugene Hubert, July 15, 1983; children: Whitney, Lindsey, Hannah. B in Textile Mktg., Kans. State U., 1983; M in Speech-Lang. Pathology, Ft. Hays State U., 1992. Cert. clin. speech-lang. pathologist,

Kans. Speech-lang. pathologist N.W. Kans. Ednl. Svc. Ctr., Oakley, 1992—. Health adv. bd. dirs. Headstart, Oakley; mem. state com. Kans. Speech-Lang.-Hearing Pub. Rels.; mem. external adv. coun. Fort Hays State U. Speech-lang. scholar Ft. Hays State U., 1991. Mem. NEA, Am. Speech-Lang.-Hearing Assn., Kans. NEA, Kans. Speech-Lang.-Hearing Assn. (pub. rels. com. 1994), Gamma Pi Alpha (sec., pres., v.p.). Roman Catholic. Avocations: reading, needlework. Home: 510 Maple Ave Oakley KS 67748-1226 Office: NW Kans Ednl Svc Ctr 703 W 2nd St Oakley KS 67748-1258

HUBKABA, NANCY PLETTS, special education educator; b. Bath, Maine, Mar. 30, 1947; d. gilbert Oliver and Mary (Anderson) Pletts; m. Aaron Alexander Huckaba, Dec. 27, 1983; 1 child, Jennifer Cole. AA, Miami Dade Jr. Coll., 1967; BA, Fla. Atlantic U., 1970; MEd in Elem. Disturbance, U. Miami, Orono, Maine, 1974. Cert. elem. tchr., Fla. Tchr. Broward County Schs., Pompano Beach, Fla., 1970-71, Deerfield Beach, Fla., 1971-72; tchr., prin. Isleford (Maine) Grammar Sch., 1972-73; tchr. Brewer (Maine) Jr. High Sch., 1974-75, Washington Schs., Brewer, 1975-81, Polk County Schs., Winter Haven, Fla., 1981-89, LAke Wales, Fla., 1989-92, Lakeland, Fla., 1992—. Contbr. articles to profl. jours. Leader Girl Scouts Am., Pompano Beach, 1970-71. Kodak grantee, 1982. Mem. NEA, PEA, CEC, Phi Theta Kappa. Republican. Mem. Christian Ch. Avocations: sports, bicycling, arts and crafts, children's literature. Office: Polk County Sch Bd Floral Ave Bartow FL 33830

HUCHRA, JOHN PETER, astronomer, educator; b. Jersey City, N.J., Dec. 23, 1948; s. Mieczyslaw Piotr and Helen Ann Huchra; m. Rebecca M. Henderson; 1 child, Harry Matthew. BS, MIT, 1970; PhD, Calif. Inst. Tech., 1976. Ctr. fellow Ctr. for Astrophysics, Cambridge, Mass., 1976-78; astronomer Smithsonian Astrophys. Obs., Cambridge, Mass., 1978-89, sr. astronomer, 1989—; lectr. dept. astronomy Harvard U., Cambridge, Mass., 1979-84, prof. dept. astronomy, 1984—2002, Robert O. and Holly Thomis Doyle prof. cosmology, 2002—; assoc. dir. Ctr. for Astrophysics, Cambridge, Mass., 1989—98; dir. F.L. Whipple Observatory, 1994-98. Mem. coun. Space Telescope Sci. Inst., Balt., 1987-95; chmn. working group on galaxy radial velocities Internat. Astron. Union, Paris, 1988—; chmn. large astron. data base working group NASA/IPAC, Washington, 1988-92; mem. astronomy and astrophysics survey Optical Panel, NAS, NRC, 1989-90; adv. bd. and vis. com. Arecibo Obs., Ithaca, N.Y., 1989-92; users com. Cerro Tololo Inter-Am. Obs., La Serena, Chile, 1989-91; vis. com. ESO, 1993-97; mem. NRC Com. on Astronomy and Astrophysics, 1994-2001, co-chmn. 1997-2001; mem. AURA, bd. dirs., 1995-, chair, 2001—; mem. NRC bd. on physics and astronomy, 1997-2003, chair, 2000-03; chair NOAO Future Directions Com., 1998-99. Contbr. chapters to books to profl. jours. Rsch. grantee, NASA, 1979—, Smithsonian Inst., 1980, NSF, 1984-89, 99—. Fellow AAAS (Newcomb Cleve. award 1990), Am. Phys. Soc. AIP (pub. policy com. 1988-95); mem. NAS, Am. Acad. Arts and Scis., Am. Astron. Soc. (pub. bd. chmn., 1986-88, councilor 1998-2001, sci. editor Astrophys. Jour. 1998-2003), Royal Astron. Soc., Astron. Soc. of the Pacific, Am. Phys. Soc. Astrophysics Divsn. (exec. com. 1996-97), Nat. Environ. Leadership Coun., Wilderness Soc., Nat. Audubon Soc., Mass. Audubon Soc., Union of Concerned Scientists, Nature Conservancy, Trustees of Reservations, Appalachian Trail Conf., Am. Contract Bridge League, Greenpeace, Green Mtn. Club, Appalachian Mtn. Club, Sierra Club, Sigma Xi, Gamma Nu. Achievements include discovery of Comet Huchra, of nearest gravitational lens; revision of cosmic distance scale; completion of first and second Center for Astrophysics Redshift Survey; measurement of infall of our Milky Way Galaxy into the Virgo Cluster; discovery of Great Wall of galaxies, 2 Micron All Sky Survey. Office: Harvard-Smithsonian Ctr Astrophysics 60 Garden St Cambridge MA 02138-1516 E-mail: huchra@cfa.harvard.edu.

HUCKEBA, EMILY CAUSEY, retired elementary school educator; b. Carrollton, Ga., Aug. 26, 1941; d. Edward Clark and Audie Farmer Causey; m. Dale Malloy Huckeba, Aug. 27, 1961; 1 child, Catherine Nan. BS Elem. Edn., West Ga. Coll., 1962, M Edn., 1977. 2nd grade tchr. Whitesburg (Ga.) Elem. Sch., 1962—63; 1st grade tchr. Ctrl. Elem. Sch., Carrollton, Ga., 1963—68, Roopville (Ga.) Elem. Sch., 1968—96, music tchr., 1996—98, substitute tchr., 1998—2001. Mem. alumni coun. West Ga. Coll., Carrollton, 1991—93; pilot tchr. Whole Lang. Program Roopville (Ga.) Elem. Sch., 1993—95. Charter mem. Roopville Hist. Soc., 1984—; organist, pianist Roopville Bapt. Ch., 1960—. Mem.: NEA, Ga. Music Educators Assn., Carroll Heard Ret. Tchrs., Ga. Assn. Educators, Alpha Delta Kappa. Baptist. Home: 1135 S Hwy 27 Roopville GA 30170-2516

HUCKSHOLD, WAYNE WILLIAM, elementary education educator; b. St. Louis, Mar. 5, 1952; s. Albert Clarence and Jane Martha (Stewart) Huckshold; m. Paula Louise Ransin, June 14, 1977 (div. Apr. 1982); 1 child, Kristen Louise. BS in Edn., U. Mo., 1976, MEd, 1977. Cert. elem. edn. K-8, phys. edn. K-9, health edn. K-12, sci. 7-9, Mo.; Nat. Coun. Accreditation of Tchr. Edn.; cert. personal trainer Am. Coun. Exercise. Tchr. grade 3 Camdenton (Mo.) R-III, 1977-81, coach football, track and cross country, 1978-81; fitness instr., athletic trainer Columbia (Mo.) Sports Medicine, 1981-84; student athletic trainer U. Mo., Columbia, 1983-84, grad. tchg. asst., 1984-85; elem. tchr. Francis Howell Sch. Dist., St. Charles, Mo., 1985-91, elem. tchr. phys. edn., 1991—, mem. supt.'s comm. coun., 1992-93. Master's swim coach West County YMCA, Chesterfield, Mo., 1991—, personal trainer, 1992—; level 2 swim coach Am. Swimming Coaches Assn., 1997—; head women's varsity swim coach Francis Howell H.S., 1998—99; asst. head coach U.S.S. Swim Team, St. Peter's Rec-Plex, 1997—2000; new tchr. mentor Francis Howell Sch. Dist., 1996—. Olympic Torch relay runner Winter Olympic Games, Columbia, Mo., 2002. Named YMCA Endurance Athlete of Yr., YMCA, St. Louis, 1990; grantee Union Electric Co., St. Louis, 1989; fellow Tchrs. Acad. Class 1994, Network for Ednl. Devel., Danforth Found., 1993-94. Mem. NEA, AAHPERD, Mo. Edn. Assn., Francis Howell Edn. Assn., Mo. Alliance for Health, Phys. Edn., Recreation and Dance, U.S. Phys. Edn. Assn., Nat. Assn. for Sport and Phys. Edn., Assn. for Advancement Health Edn. Avocations: running, swimming, biking, triathlons, spending time with family and friends. Home: 1549 Milbridge Dr Chesterfield MO 63017-4611 Office: Francis Howell Sch Dist Warren Elem Sch 141 Weiss Rd Saint Peters MO 63376 E-mail: whuckshold@yahoo.com.

HUDAK, SHARON ANN. elementary education educator; b. Pitts., Mar. 22, 1942; d. Fred W. and Lillian M. (Huwalt) Kroll; m. Francis J. Hudak, Aug. 28, 1965; children: Leslie M., Nicole K., Kristen A. Hudak. BS in Art Edn., Edinboro (Pa.) State Coll., 1965; MEd in Art Edn., SUNY, Buffalo, 1969. Cert. elem., art edn. tchr., reading specialist, Pa. Jr. & sr. H.S. art tchr. Smethport (Pa.) Area Sch. Dist., 1965-68; art tchr. Beatty Jr. H.S., Warren, Pa., 1969; instr., supr. stds. tchr. Edinboro State Coll., 1969-70; art tchr., grades 5-8 Gen. McLane Sch. Dist., Edinboro, 1970-74, developmental reading tchr., grades 7, 8, 1981-82; art tchr., grades 1-7 Escuela Campo Alegre, Caracas, Venezuela, 1982-84; TELLS reading tchr., chpt. I reading specialist N.W. Intermediate Unit #5, Edinboro, 1985, 86-87; reading specialist Penncrest Sch. Dist., Saegertown, Pa., 1985-86; TELLS reading tchr., chpt. I reading specialist Girard (Pa.) H.S., 1987, 87-91; art tchr., grades K-4 Elk Valley Elem. Sch., Girard Sch. Dist., Lake City, Pa., 1991—. Mem. parent's adv. coun., Title I Edinboro Spl. Edn. Assn., 1985-86. Mem. Am. Fedn. Tchrs., Pa. Art Edn. Assn., Nat. Art Edn. Assn. Avocations: drawing, painting, reading, travel. Home: 207 Granada Dr Edinboro PA 16412-2363 Office: Elk Valley Elem Sch 2556 Maple Ave Lake City PA 16423-1515

HUDDLESTON, JOHN FRANKLIN, obstetrics and gynecology educator; b. Jacksonville, Fla., June 26, 1942; s. Paul Mc Kisson and Mary Rebecca (Robinson) H.; m. Kathryn Ann Welch, Dec. 30, 1982; children: Suzanne Marie, Edward Ryan, John Stuart, Mary Kathryn, Ryan Mc Kisson. BS, U. Fla., Gainesville, 1963; MD, Duke U., 1967. Diplomate Am. Bd. Ob-Gyn, Am. Bd. Maternal-Fetal Medicine. Dir. maternal-fetal medicine Sch. of Medicine, U. Ala., Birmingham, Ala., 1963-86; pvt. practice Jacksonville, Fla., 1986-89; prof., dir. maternal-fetal medicine Sch. of Medicine, Emory U., Atlanta, 1989-96, Coll. of Medicine, U. Fla. Sch. of Medicine, Jacksonville, 1997—. Contbr. to profl. jours., articles, and book chpts. Surgeon USPHS, 1969-71. Mem. Ctrl. Assn. Obstetricians and Gynecologists, Am. Gynecologic and Obstetrics Soc., Soc. Maternal-Fetal Medicine, South Atlantic Assn. Obstetricians and Gynecologists. Avocations: computers, skiing, camping, canoeing. Office: U Fla Health Scis Ctr Dept Ob/Gyn 653-1 W 8th St Jacksonville FL 32209-6511

HUDEL, CHESTELLA ALVIS, athletics educator; b. Temple, Okla., Jan. 13, 1931; d. James Chester and Jewel (McCain) Alvis; m. William August Hudel, June 14, 1952 (dec. June 1962); children: Mary Hudel Rinne, Nancy Hudel Parten, Joan Hudel Patrick. BS in Child Devel., Tex. Women's U., 1950. Tchr. Port Arthur (Tex.) Ind. Sch., 1950-53, Ridgewood Park Pre-Sch., Dallas, 1962-86; trainer Red Cross, Dallas, 1975—; adapted aquatics dir. YWCA, Dallas, 1975—. Trainer water safety instrs. Red Cross, Dallas, 1975-96; coach Spl. Olympics, 1993-98; educator Down's Syndrome Guild/Dallas Ind. Sch. Dist., 1994-96; counselor for breast cancer survivors Encore YWCA/Komen Found., Dallas, 1995-98. Elder Northridge Presbyn. Ch., Dallas, 1979-98; com. on adminstrn. YWCA, Dallas, 1980-86; mem. Northridge Learning Ctr. Bd., Northridge Presbyn. Ch., Dallas, 1987-97; swim program leader Light House for the Blind, 1986-90, Tom Landry Ctr. Baylor Hosp., 2003—; resource person Parent to Parent, 1993. Recipient Golden Rule award J.C. Penny, Dallas, 1983, Extra Step award Red Cross, Dallas, 1989, Spirit of Red Cross award, 1990, GM Vol. Spirit award GM, Dallas, 1992, George Washington medal of honor Freedom Found. Valley Forge, Dallas, 1997; named Vol. of the Yr., Helping Agys. Serving Richardson, Tex., 1990. Mem. Assn. for Retarded Citizens. Avocations: journal and scrapbook making, piano, bridge, bible study. Home: 6015 Sandhurst Ln Apt A Dallas TX 75206-4726

HUDGINS, HERBERT CORNELIUS, JR., education educator, department chairman; b. Trotville, N.C., Oct. 9, 1932; s. Herbert Cornelius and Lucille Dixie (Simpson) H. AB, High Point Coll., 1954; MEd, U. N.C., Chapel Hill, 1959; EdD, Duke U., 1966. Cert. tchr., prin., N.C. Tchr. Thomasville (N.C.) City Schs., 1954-59, 1959-64; asst. prof. U. N.C., Greensboro, 1966-69, prof., 1985-88; assoc. prof. Temple U., Phila., 1969-74, prof., 1974-80, No. Ill. U., DeKalb, 1980-85; prof. edn., chmn. dept. ednl. leadership East Carolina U., Greenville, N.C., 1988-94. Author: The Warren Court and the Public Schools, 1970; co-author: Law and Education, 1979, 3d edit., 1991, 4th edit., 1995, Liability of School Officials and Administrators for Civil Rights Torts, 1982. Recipient Lindback teaching award Temple U., 1975, Benjamin Rosner teaching award, 1977. Mem. Nat. Orgn. on Legal Problems Edn. (E.C. Bolmeier award 1989), Nat. Assn. Secondary Sch. Prins., N.C. Profs. Ednl. Leadership, Kappa Delta Pi, Phi Delta Kappa. Democrat. Methodist. Avocations: gardening, refinishing furniture, trivia. Home: 1745 Beaumont Cir Greenville NC 27858-4615

HUDGINS, LOUISE NAN, art educator; b. Ft. Worth; d. Joe Wallace and Lillian Frances (Taylor) H. BA, U. North Tex., 1960, postgrad., 1965. Cert. tchr. art, Tex. Fine arts supr. Dallas Ind. Sch. Dist., 1981-82; tchr. art Lida Hooe Elem. Sch., Dallas, 1966-81, Greiner Arts Acad., Dallas, 1982-86, Hotchkiss Montessori Acad., Dallas, 1986-94, Dealey Montessori Acad., Dallas, 1994—. State textbook com. Tex. Edn. Agy., Austin, 1981-82, com. mem., cons., 1984-85, workshop presenter U. Tex., 1989-91, Montessori Certification Program, Dallas, 1992-95, Pine Bluff, Ark., 1995, 98, Pensacola, Fla., 1998; mem. com. Tex. Art Assessments Study, Richardson, 1993; mem. faculty U.S. Dept. Edn. Blue Ribbon Sch., 2001-02. Co-author: (tchr. textbook) Through Their Eyes, 1989; contbg. author: (student textbooks) Inside Art, 1992. Named Elem. Tchr. of Yr. Oak Cliff C. of C., Dallas, 1980. Mem. ASCD, Nat. Art Edn. Assn., Tex. Art Edn. Assn. (chair elem. divsn. 1983-84, rep. assembly 1987-89, Elem. Art Educator of Yr. 1988), Dallas Art Edn. Assn. (pres. 1988-89). Home: 1451 Winding Brook Cir Dallas TX 75208-2926

HUDIAK, DAVID MICHAEL, academic administrator; b. Darby, Pa., June 27, 1953; s. Michael Paul and Sophie Marie (Glowaski) H.; m. Veronica Ann Barbone, Aug. 28, 1982; children: David Michael, Christopher Andrew, Jonathan Joseph. BA, Haverford Coll., 1975; JD, U. Pa., 1978. Bar: Pa. 1979, U.S. Dist. Ct. (ea. dist.) Pa. 1979, NJ 1981, U.S. Dist. Ct. NJ 1981. Assoc. Jerome H. Ellis, Phila., 1978-79, Berson, Fineman & Bernstein, Phila., 1979-80; pvt. practice Aldan, Pa., 1980-81; dir. tng. paralegal program PJA Sch., Upper Darby, Pa., 1982—, acting dir., 1983-89, dir., 1989—; v.p. The PJA Sch., Inc., 1989—, bd. dirs.; v.p., sec.-treas., bd. dirs. 7900 West Chester Pike Corp., 1994—. Mem. staff Nat. Ctr. Ednl. Testing, Phila., 1982-87; instr. Villanova (Pa.) U., 1985. Mem. Havertown Choristers; active U. Pa. Light Opera Co., 1977—84; mem. 10th Synod Archdiocese of Phila., 2002; active mem., parish coun., lector, cantor St. Eugene Parish. Mem. ABA, Pa. Bar Assn., Founders Club Haverford Coll. Office: PJA Sch 7900 W Chester Pike Upper Darby PA 19082-1917

HUDIK, MARTIN FRANCIS, hospital administrator, educator, consultant, writer; b. Chgo., Mar. 27, 1949; s. Joseph and Rose (Ricker) H.; m. Eileen Hudik; 1 child, Theresa Margaret. BS in Mech. and Aerospace Engring., Ill. Inst. Tech., 1971; BPA, Jackson State U., 1974; MBA, Loyola U., 1975; postgrad., U. Sarasota, 1975-76; AAS in Engring., Morton Coll., 1969. Cert. health care safety mgr., hazard control mgr., hazardous materials mgr., OSHA hazardous materials response instr., hazardous materials incident comdr., disaster coord., police instr., Ill., security cert. instr., Ill. With Ill. Masonic Med. Ctr., Chgo., 1969-94, dir. risk mgmt., 1974-79, asst. adminstr., 1979-94; facilities engring. mgr. Bethany/Adv. Hosp., 1997-98; health care cons., 2000—; bus. mgr. St. Bernadine Parish, 2001—. Capt. tng. divsn. Cicero (Ill.) Police Dept., tng. and internal affairs divsn., aux. divsn., 1971-99, U.S. Dept. Commerce, 2000, ind. cons., 2000; instr. Nat. Safety Coun. Safety Tng. Inst., Chgo., 1977-85; cons. mem. Coun. Tech. users Consumer Products, Underwriters Labs., Chgo., 1977-96; instr., lt. U.S. Def. Civil Preparedness Agy. Staff Coll., Battle Creek, Mich., 1977-85; liaison officer to Cook County Emergency Svcs.; asst. dir. Emergency Svcs. and disaster Agy. Town of Cicero, 1988-97; pres. Cook County Emergency Mgmt. Coun., 1991-92; exec. bd., pres. U.S. Postal Svc. Postal Customer Adv. Coun., Cicero, 1996-99; mem. exec. bd. Chicagoland Postal Adv. Coun., 1994—; exec. bd. advisor Cicero PCAC, 1998—. Pres. sch. bd. Mary Queen of Heaven Sch., Cicero, 1977-79, 84-86, Mary Queen of Heaven Ch. Coun., 1979-81, 83-86, St. Leonard Parish Coun., 1998-2001, I.M.M.C. Employee Club, 1983-86; co-chmn. Archdiocese of Chicago Deanery IV-C, 1999-2003; mem. Cath. Edn. Com., 2000-2003, Archdiocese of Chgo. Pastoral Coun., 2000-2003. Recipient Presdl. Sports award, Amateur Athletic Union, 1978, 1980, 1981, 2000, Meritorious Svc. award, Town of Cicero, 1990, Spl. Svc. award Underwriters Lab., 1992, medal of Merit, 1996, Emergency Svcs. Achievement award, 1997, Police Achievement award, 1998, Spl. Svc. award, Cook County Sheriffs Dept., 1993, Excellence in Svc. award, U.S. Postal Svc., 1997, Outstanding Effort award, 1998, Outstanding Svcs. award, Cicero Postal Coun., 1998, Svc. Recognition award, 1999, Outstanding Performance award, 2001, Volunteerism award, U.S. Postal Svc., 2002, Svc. Recognition award, Archdiocese of Chgo., 2003; scholar state scholar, Ill., 1969—71. Mem. Am. Coll. Healthcare Execs., Am. Soc. Hosp. Risk Mgmt., Nat. Fire Protection Assn., Am. Soc. SafetyEngrs. (profl.), Am. Soc. Law and Medicine, Ill. Hosp. Security and Safety Assn. (co-founder 1976, founding pres. 1976-77, hon. dir. 1977-82), Cath. Alumni Club Chgo. (bd. dirs. 1983-84, 86), Mensa, Masons (Berwyn, Ill. chpt.), KC (mem. 4th degree cardinal coun., Svc. award 2002), Pi Tau Sigma, Tau Beta Pi, Alpha Sigma Nu. Republican. Roman Catholic. Home: 2116 S 51st Ct Cicero IL 60804-2345 Office: 6845 Riverside Dr Berwyn IL 60402-2231

HUDLER, GEORGE, plant pathologist, educator; BS, U. Minn., 1970, MS, 1973; PhD, Colo. State U., 1976. From extension assoc. to prof. Cornell U., Ithaca, NY, 1976—97, prof. plant pathology, 1997—. Author: Magical Mushrooms, Mischievious Molds, 1998; contbr. articles to profl. jours. Recipient Outstanding New Extension Pub. award, N.Y. State Assn. County Agrl. Agents, 1995. Mem.: Mycological Soc. Am., N.Y. State Christmas Tree Grower's Assn., N.Y. State Arborists Assn. (Rsch. award 1996, 1997, 1998), Internat. Soc. Arboriculture, Am. Phytopathological Soc. (Excellence in Tchg. award 1992). Office: Cornell U 319 Plant Science Building Ithaca NY 14853-5904*

HUDSON, BRADFORD TAYLOR, management educator; b. Ithaca, NY, Dec. 17, 1962; s. John Boswell and Sandra Lee (Chermak) H. BA, U. Pa., 1984; M in Profl. Studies, Cornell U., 1993. Sr. cons. TQM Group, Boston, 1993-94; pres. Hudson Cons., 1994—2001; asst. prof. Boston U., 1995-96, 2002—; CEO Bay Tower, Inc., Boston, 1998-2000. CEO Brandpoint.com, Cambridge, 1996-98, chmn., 1998-2001; guest lectr. Harvard U., Cambridge, 1998-99. Contbr. articles to profl. publ. Page to spkr. US Ho. Reps., Washington, 1980; aide Presdl. Inaugural Com., Washington, 1981. Lt. (O-3) USN, 1984-89. Decorated Navy Achievement medal and Battle "E" commendation USN, 1989; named among Top 100 Ind. Restaurant Co. in USA, Restaurants and Instns. Mag., 1999-2000. Episcopalian. Office: Boston Univ Ste 200 808 Commonwealth Ave Boston MA 02215 E-mail: bhudson@bu.edu.

HUDSON, CAROLYN BRAUER, application developer, educator; b. Durham, NC, Dec. 17, 1945; d. Alfred Theodor and Hildegard Wolf Brauer; children: Paul Benjamin, Joel Stephen. BS in Math., U. N.C., 1967; MA in Forestry, Duke U., 1969; MS in Geology, U. S.C., 1979, PhD in Geology, 1995. Assoc. dir. office rsch. and evaluation, asst. prof. N.C. Ctrl. U., Durham, 1970—72; rsch. assoc. Nat. Lab. for Higher Edn., Durham, 1971—72; tchg. assoc. U. S.C., Columbia, 1973—74, tchg. asst., 1990—92, tchg. assoc., 1993—, programmer, 1999—; vis. scientist Geol. Survey of Can., Ottawa, 1979—82; statistician S.C. State Govt., Columbia, 1997—98. Mem. S.C. Gov's Nuclear Adv. Coun., Columbia, 2001—; tech. coord. profl. women on campus U. S.C., Columbia, 2000—. Contbr. articles to profl. jours. Vol. area pub. sch., 1978—93; Leader Boy Scouts of Am./Scouts Can., 1979—95; vol. Congaree Swamp Nat. Monument, Hopkins, SC, 1999—. Recipient Dist. Merit award, Boy Scouts of Am., 1988, Silver Beaver award, 1991, Shofar award, 1993, Profl. Devel. award, Profl. Women on Campus, 2000. Mem.: U. N.C. Alumni Assn. (life), Friends of Congaree Swamp (edn. com. 1996—), Women of Reform Judaism (v.p. 1975—76), Audubon, Sierra Club (nuclear affairs subcom. 2001—, computer chair 2003—), Hadassah (life; bd. dirs. 1983—84), LWV. Jewish. Avocations: hiking, music, travel, reading. Business E-Mail: hudson-carolyn@sc.edu.

HUDSON, CELESTE NUTTING, education educator, reading clinic administrator, consultant; b. Nashville, Sept. 18, 1927; d. John Winthrop Chandler and Hilda Bass (Alexander) Nutting; m. Frank Alden Hudson III, Dec. 30, 1948 (dec.); m. Robert Daniel Quartell, June 3, 1989; children: Frank Alden Hudson IV (dec.), Jo Ann Hudson Algermissen, Celeste Jane Hudson Norman, Jack Winthrop N. Hudson. BS, Oreg. Coll. Edn., 1952; MS, So. Ill. U., 1963, PhD, 1973. Cert. tchr., Tenn., Oreg., Mo. Iowa. Tchr. pub. schs., Crossville, Tenn., 1949-51, Salem, Oreg., 1952-53, West Walnut Manor, Mo., 1953-54, Normandy Sch. Dist., St. Louis County, Mo., 1954-66; reading coord. Sikeston (Mo.) Pub. Schs., 1966-69, Charleston, Mo., 1969-72; traveling cons. Ednl. Devel. Labs., Huntington, N.Y., 1970-71; mem. clin. staff So. Ill. U. Reading Ctr., 1972; asst. prof. edn. St. Ambrose Coll., 1972-75, U. Tenn., Chattanooga, 1975-76; project dir. Learning Skills Ctr. St. Ambrose U. (formerly St. Ambrose Coll.), 1976-80, asst. prof. edn., 1976-78, assoc. prof., 1979-86, prof., 1986-94, prof. emeritus, 1995—. Dir. elem. edn. St. Ambrose U., 1972-94, chmn. dept. edn., 1980-84, divsn. chmn., 1984-87, faculty vice-chair, 1989-90, faculty chair, 1990-91; cons. in field. Author: Handbook for Remedial Reading, 1967, Cognitive Listening and the Reading of Second Grade Children, 1973, The Effect of Visual Fatigue on Reading, 1990, Longitudinal Study of Children in Clinical Reading, 1994. Mem. Kimberly Village Bd., Davenport, Iowa, 1979-83; chmn. worship com., Asbury Meth. Ch., 1985-90, choir, 1978-98, mem. bell choir, 1995-97; co-chmn. Sarah Cir., 1996-99; mem. Trinity Hosp. Aux., 2001—. Mem.: AARP, DAR (Hist. Soc., real granddaughter), AAUW (Lit. club), AAUP, Normandy Ret. Tchrs. Assn., Orgn. Tchr. Educators Reading, Davenport Area Ret. Tchrs. Assn., Assn. Tchrs. Educators, Internat. Reading Assn. (Scott County coun.), Iowa Assn. Colls. Tchr. Edn. (exec. bd. 1989—92), United Daus. of the Confederacy (3rd v.p. 1966—70), New Eng. Women (pres.-elect 1994—95, pres. 1996—2003), Renaissance Dance Club, Real Granddaughter Club, Quad City Women's Investment Club (treas. 2001—), Original Music Students Club (corr. sec. 1995—96), Bettendorf Lionels (treas. 1998—2002), Phi Delta Kappa, Kappa Delta Pi (sponsor 1974—96), Alpha Delta Kappa (past pres.). Address: St Ambrose U Box E 140 518 W Locust St Davenport IA 52803-2829

HUDSON, ELIZABETH MAE, elementary education educator; b. Evergreen Park, Ill., Aug. 27, 1949; d. Edward Henry and Virginia (Crask) Sumner; m. Daniel W. Hudson, Nov. 16, 1968; 1 child: Elizabeth V. BA in Edn., Aurora Coll., 1971; MS in Spl. Edn., No. Ill. U., 1979, MS in Edn. Adminstrn., 1989. Cert. elem. edn., spl. edn., learning disabilities, behavior disorders, social studies, lang. arts, adminstrn. Tchr. Aurora (Ill.) Sch. Dist. 131, 1972—; tchr. 4th and 5th grades. Mem. Am. Fedn. Tchrs., PTA.

HUDSON, JERRY E. foundation administrator; b. Chattanooga, Mar. 3, 1938; s. Clarence E. and Laura (Campbell) H.; m. Myra Ann Jared, June 11, 1957; children: Judith, Laura, Janet, Angela. BA, David Lipscomb Coll., 1959; MA, Tulane U., 1961, PhD, 1965; LL.D. (hon.), Pepperdine U., 1983; D of Comm. (hon.), Tokyo Internat. U., 1997; LHD (hon.), U. Portland, 1997, Willamette U., 1997. Systems engr. IBM, Atlanta, 1961; prof. Coll. Arts and Scis., Pepperdine U., 1962-75; provost, dean Coll. Arts and Scis., Malibu Campus, Pepperdine U., 1971-75; pres. Hamline U., St. Paul, 1975-80, Willamette U., Salem, Oreg., 1980-97; exec. v.p. Collins Found., Portland, Oreg., 1997—. Dir. Portland Gen. Co., E.I.I.A. Bd. dirs. PGE/Enron Found. Mem. Nat. Assn. Ind. Colls. (bd. dirs.), Phi Alpha Theta. Office: Collins Found 1618 SW 1st Ave Portland OR 97201-5752 E-mail: jhudson@collinsfoundation.org.*

HUDSON, JOHN BOSWELL, sociologist, educator; b. Decatur, Ill., Dec. 1, 1930; s. George Taylor and Margaret Shirley (Boswell) H.; m. Sandra Lee Cermak, Mar. 16, 1957; children: Scott Martin, Bradford Taylor. Student, Reed Coll., 1948-51; BA, U. Oreg., 1952; MA, U. Wash., 1956; postgrad., Cornell U., 1957-60, PhD, 1963. Asst. prof. sociology Humboldt State U., Arcata, Calif., 1960-61, Cornell U., Ithaca, N.Y., 1961-64, Lehigh U., Bethlehem, Pa., 1964-65, Syracuse (N.Y.) U., 1965-66; rsch. assoc. Harvard U., 1966-67; rsch. sociologist Mass. Dept. Mental Health, Boston, 1967-68; sr. sociologist Abt Assocs., Inc., Cambridge, Mass., 1968-69; prof. sociology Trent U., Peterborough, Ont., Can., 1969-73; asst. adminstr. Brockton (Mass.) Multi-Svc. Ctr., 1973-74; lectr. bus. adminstrn. Northeastern U., Boston, 1974-76; cons. Cambridge, 1976-78; pres., treas. Cambridge Condominium Collaborative, Inc., 1978-86, chmn., treas., 1986-93; dir. edn. and tng. DeWolfe New Eng., 1994, v.p. for organizational devel., 1995-97. Vis. scientist dept. behavioral scis. Harvard Sch. Pub. Health, summers 1971, 72, winter-spring, 1973; lectr. real estate Boston U., 1988-90. Author: Creativity and Innovation, 1966, Functional Analysis as a Strategy for Studying Social Change and Stability, 1967, Policy-Oriented Basic Research, 1969, Social Policy and Theoretical Sociology, 1970, An Empirical Validation of Hypothesis-Generating Strategies, 1970, Social Structure and Culture: A Conceptual Analysis, 1971, Perspectives on Offender Rehabilitation, 1971, The Structure of Innovation, 1971, A

Proposal for a Center of Innovation, 1971, Nursing Education in Transition, 1972, Residential Care for the Mentally Retarded, 1972, The Interface Between Theory and Practice, 1979, Theory, Practice, and Paradigm Shifts, 1992. Mem. mgmt. com. Sch. Nursing, Peterborough Civic Hosp., 1970-72; bd. dirs. Brockton Area Assn. for Retarded Citizens, 1974-75; mem. City Mgr.'s Cable TV Adv. Com., Cambridge, 1979-85; chmn. Cambridge Condominium Network, 1979-86; docent U. Iowa Mus. Art, 1998—; bd. dirs. Coun. Internat. Visitors to Iowa Cities, 1999-2000, Iowa Arts Coun., 2002--; elected del. Imagine Iowa 2010, 2001. Social Sci. Rsch. Coun. fellow Stanford U., summer 1964; Recipient award of merit Peterborough Assn. for Mentally Retarded, 1972; named Cambridge Realtor of Yr., Greater Boston Real Estate Bd., 1993. Mem. Nat. Assn. Realtors (cert. real estate brokerage mgr. 1989, cert. internat. property specialist 1994, cert. residential specialist 1994, chair internat. adv. group 1997, mem. internat. ops. com. 1997-98), Cmty. Assns. Inst. (named Colleague of Yr. New Eng. chpt. 1985), New Eng. Sociol. Assn. (treas. 1979-82, v.p. 1987-90, pres.-elect 1990-91, pres. 1991-92, Pioneer award 1991). Home: 782 Westside Dr Iowa City IA 52246-4341 E-mail: John.B.Hudson@att.net.

HUDSON, JOHN LESTER, chemical engineering educator; b. Chgo., 1937; s. John Jones and Linda Madeline (Panozzo) H.; m. Janette Glenore Caton, June 29, 1963; children: Ann, Barbara, Sarah. BS, U. Ill., 1959; MS in Engring., Princeton U., 1960; PhD, Northwestern U., 1962. Registered profl. engr., Ill. Asst. prof. chm. engring. U. Ill.-Urbana, 1963-69, assoc. prof., 1969-75; prof., chmn. dept. chem. engring. U. Va., Charlottesville, 1975-85, mem. Ctr Advanced Studies, 1985-86, prof., 1986-88, Wills Johnson prof., 1988—. Mgr. Ill. Div. Air Pollution Control, Springfield, 1974-75; cons. to various industires and govt. agys., 1966— Contbr. articles to profl. jours. Recipient sr. Humboldt prize, 1989; NSF fellow, 1962, Fulbright fellow, 1961-63, 82-83. Mem. AIChE (Wilhelm award 1991), Am. Chem. Soc. Home: 1920 Thomson Rd Charlottesville VA 22903-2419 Office: U Va Dept Chem Engring 102 Engineers Wy Box 400741 Charlottesville VA 22904-4741 E-mail: hudson@virginia.edu.

HUDSON, JOY NUCKOLS, retired elementary school educator; b. Dumas, Ark., May 17, 1930; d. Walter Jennings and Katie Lee (Burrus) Nuckols; m. Charles Fred Hudson, Aug. 22, 1952; children: Donna Nelson, Hollis Gaston, Adrienne Willett. AA, City Coll. San Francisco, 1950; BA, U. Ark., 1951. Cert. classroom tchr., Ark. Classroom tchr. Dumas Pub. Schs., 1952-55, 66-86. Mem. Ark. Art Tchrs. Assn., Little Rock, 1975-82; treas. Ark. Assn. Spanish Tchrs., Little Rock, 1972-86. Mem., pres. PTA, Dumas, 1965-69, Hosp. Aux., Dumas, 1962-66; chair Desha County March of Dimes, 1960-66; bd. dirs., pres. Friends of the Libr., 1994—; mem. Meth. Choir, 1952—, U. Ark.-Little Rock Flute Ensemble, 1989-90; Sunday sch. tchr. United Meth. Ch.-Dumas, 1952-56. Named Woman of Yr., Dumas C. of C., 1994; named Choir Mem. of Yr., United Meth. Ch. Choir, 1995, Vol. of Yr., Trinity Village/Retirement Village, 1995; NDEA grantee. Mem. NEA, Ark. Edn. Assn., Dumas Edn. Assn., Am. Contract Bridge League (mem. pres. unit 220, accredited bridge dir., tchr., v.p. 1995—, Bronze Life Master), Hwy. Garden Club, Nat. Flute Assn. Methodist. Avocations: flute, painting, tennis, bridge, reading. Home: 410 Adams St Dumas AR 71639-2714

HUDSON, KAREN ANN SAMPSON, music educator; b. Greenville, Mich., Nov. 1, 1946; d. Elton J. Sampson and Freda Sampson Grunwald; m. James Gary Hudson, May 23, 1970; children: Alexander E., Annemarie M., Elaine K., Veronica L. BA, U. Mich., 1968. Piano tchr. Karen Hudson's Piano Studio, Reno, 1994—. Lay Carmelite Little Flower Lay Carmelites, Reno, l997—. Mem.: Nat. Music Tchrs. Assn., Autism Soc. Am. Democrat. Home: 2055 Severn Dr Reno NV 89503

HUDSON, KATHERINE RUTH MCCLAIN, elementary school educator; b. Dearborn, Mich., July 29, 1963; d. J.L. and Lorene (Nanney) McClain; m. Robert Wesley Hudson, Aug. 3, 1985; 1 child, Benjamin Robert. BS in Elem. Edn., Liberty U., 1985; MEd in Early Childhood Edn., Lynchburg Coll., 1994. Cert. Va., Nat. Bd. Profl. Tchg. Stds., 2000. Tchr. Amherst County Schs., Va., 1987—2002; tchr. Lynchburg City Schs., Va., 2002—. Mem. NEA, Va. Edn. Assn., Lynchburg Edn. Assn., Amherst Edn. Assn. (faculty rep. 1990), Kappa Delta Pi. Republican. Baptist. Avocations: sports, reading, cross-stitch, stock car racing. Home: 1301 Grove Rd Lynchburg VA 24502-2927

HUDSON, MILES, retired special education educator; b. Brewer, Maine, Aug. 22, 1940; s. Fredrick and Elsie (Bailey) H. BS, U. Maine, Farmington, 1963. Cert. spl. edn. tchr., Maine, Mass. Founder, program coord. spl. edn. program, Millinocket, Maine, 1963-68; founder spl. edn. class MDI H.S., Bar Harbor, Maine, 1968-70; unit leader spl. edn. Methuen (Mass.) Pub. Schs., 1970-74; vocat. spl. edn. tchr. Minuteman Vocational Tech. H.S., Lexington, Mass., 1974-80; spl. edn. tchr. Dr. Franklin Perkins Schs., Lancaster, Mass., 1980-83; head tchr. for autistic and psychotic children Devereaux Found., Rutland, Mass., 1985-86; vocat. instr. Bangor (Maine) Mental Health Inst., 1986-87; program dir. Capacito Learning Ctr., Ellsworth, Maine., 1986-87; spl. edn. tchr., founder summer program Town of Jonesport (Maine) Schs., 1987-90; ret., 1992. Mem. Countywide Regional Tchr. Support Com. Author: Survey of Special Education Classes in Maine, 1963. Home: 307 S Lubec Rd Lubec ME 04652-9627

HUDSON, SAMUEL CAMPBELL, JR., art educator, artist, sculptor, portraitist; b. Richmond, Va., Aug. 25; s. Samuel Campbell Sr. and Kizzie Morse (Barker) H.; m. Susan Holley Hudson (dec. 1966); children: Samuel Campbell III, Kimberly Ann; m. Sara Caroline Magers, Aug. 16, 1973. AA, Coll. William & Mary, 1963; BFA, Va. Commonwealth U., 1973; MFA, U. N.C., 1975. Art instr. U. N.C., Greensboro, 1973-74, Guilford Tech. C.C., Jamestown, N.C., 1974-76; asst. prof. art Nazareth Coll. Rochester, NY, 1978—83; prof. art, dean student affairs Studio Sch. Visual Rsch., Rochester, 1983-87; asst. prof. art, dir. O'Connor Gallery Rosary Coll., River Forest, Ill., 1988-98. Vis. artist Davidson C.C., Lexington, N.C., summer 1976; vis. prof. design U. Miss., University, 1976-77; dir. A.W. Mitchell & Co., Inc., Fredericksburg, Va., 1990-99; editl. adviser Collegiate Press, Alta Loma, Calif., 1991-93; cons. Greensboro Artists' League, 1985-87; art dir., founding ptnr. Capital Ideas, Inc., Richmond, Va., 1963-66; judge 14th Annual Keuka Lake Art Show, Hammondsport, N.Y., 1980, 1st Annual Poster Competition N.Y. Assn. Retarded Children, Rochester, 1980, Oak Park (Ill.) Art League Fall Festival '89 Exhibit; juror Annual Nazareth Coll. Art Student Competition and Exhbn., Rochester, N.Y., 1979-83; judge, juror Greensboro Artists' League's 13th Annual Nat. Painting, Drawing, and Sculpture Competition, 1982, Annual Rosary Coll. Fine Arts Club Competition and Exhbn., River Forest, Ill., 1991-93; cons. visual studies Cons. Assocs., Chgo., 1997—. One man shows include Ctrl. YWCA Art Gallery, Richmond, 1961, Richmond Profl. Inst., 1963, Weatherspoon Mus., Greensboro, N.C., 1975, Greensboro Coll., 1978, Little Gallery, Rochester, 1982, Studio Gallery Ctr. Creative Arts, Greenboro, 1986, O'Connor Gallery, River Forest, Ill., 1989, others; group exhbns. include Mariners Mus., Newport News, Va., 1967 (award), 68 (award), Va. Mus. Fine Arts, Richmond, 1967 (award), also travel exhbn., 1967-69, The 21st Nat. Art on Paper, 1984 (award 1985), The Marietta 11th Nat., 1977 (award 1978), Nat. On-Paper Show '82, 1982 (award 1982), Salmagundi Annual Summer Show, N.Y.C., 1982, 83, 84, 85,U. N.C.-Greensboro, 1986, Wehterholt Galleries, Washington, 1991, 92, 93, River Forest (Ill.) Pub. Lib. Gallery, 1993, others. Gallery asst. Civic Arts Coun. Kid Art, Oak Park, Ill., 1993; curator, judge Fra Angelico Art Found., River Forest, 1992; judge, juror Midwest Assn. Religious Talent, Milw., 1992. Grantee W.T.D. Pumphery Found., 1983-85. Mem. AAUP, Coll. Art Assn. Am., Nat. Trust for Hist. Preservation, Kappa Pi. Democrat. Avocations: in-line skating, weight-training, furniture design. Home: 149 W Park Dr Lombard IL 60148-3320

HUDSON, SUNCERRAY ANN, analyst, research grants manager; b. San Francisco, Jan. 20, 1960; d. Charles Hudson and Nan Katherine (Coleman) Wagoner. BA, U. San Francisco, 1982; student, S.E. C.C., San Francisco, 1988; student in Orgl. Mgmt., U. Phoenix, Calif., 2003—. Stock transfer clk. Bank Calif., San Francisco, 1983-85; prin. clk. U. Calif., San Francisco, 1985-87, adminstrv. asst. II, 1987-88, adminstrv. asst. III, 1988-95, adminstrv. analyst, 1995—; ind. dealer Nat. Safety Assocs., Inc., San Francisco, 1990-92. Art cons. Artistic Impressions, Inc., 1994—96; mem. Notary Pub. Commn., 1997—; shape rite distbr., 1997—99. Mem.: Nat. Coun. Negro Women, Acad. Bus. Officers' Group, Am. Soc. Notaries, Sharing the Wealth Social Club, Gamma Phi Delta. Avocations: donating to various orgns. and the homeless, rollerskating, reading. Office: U Calif Campus Box 0440 521 Parnassus Ave San Francisco CA 94122-2722

HUDSON, YVONNE MORTON, elementary education educator; b. Cin., July 25, 1943; d. Eugene Benjamin and Eura Selenora (Williams) Morton; m. McKinley Hudson, Aug. 27, 1966; children: Shawna, McKinley Jr. BS in Primary Edn., U. Cin., 1965; MEd, Boston U., Mons, Belgium, 1988. Cert. tchr., Calif.; advanced profl. cert., Md. Tchr. Cin. Bd. Edn., 1965-66, 67-68, 71-73, Anne Arundel County Pub. Schs., Annapolis, Md., 1968-69, 73-76, Dept. Def. Dependents Schs., Kaiserslautern, Fed. Republic Germany, 1980-83, San Francisco Unified Sch. Dist., 1989-94, Montgomery County Pub. Schs., Rockville, Md., 1994—. Mem. Sch. Adv. Bd., Kaiserslautern, 1981-83. Vice pres. PTO, Kaiserslautern, 1981-82, San Francisco, 1991, pres., Ft. McClellan, Ala., 1984-85; mem. Ft. McClellan Elem. Sch. Bd., 1984-85; troop leader Girl Scouts U.S.A., East Point, Ga., 1977-80, bd. dirs. North Atlantic coun., 1987-88. Recipient Patriotic Civilian Svc. award Dept. Army, 1988; named Parent of Yr. George Washington H.S., San Francisco, 1994. Mem. NEA, ASCD, AAUW, Internat. Reading Assn., Calif. Tchrs. Assn., United Educators San Francisco (rep. 1989-94, negotiating team 1989-94, ethnic leadership awareness com. 1989-94, exec. bd. dirs. 1992-94, tchr. ctr. policy bd. 1992), Montgomery County Edn. Assn. (bd. dirs., minority affairs com. 1998—, negotiating team 1999—), Nat. Coun. Negro Women, Presidio Officers Wives Club, Alpha Kappa Alpha. Avocations: reading, travel, shopping, collecting. Home: 13 Cabin Creek Ct Burtonsville MD 20866-1841 Office: Rock View Elem Sch 3901 Denfeld Ave Kensington MD 20895-1510

HUDZINSKI, LEONARD GERARD, social sciences educator, researcher; b. Aug. 14, 1946; BA in Psychology and Sociology, Findlay (Ohio) Coll., 1968; MSW, U. Mich., 1971; PhD, U. Pitts., 1975. Diplomate Clin. Social Work Examiners. Tchg. asst. dept. sociology Findlay Coll., 1966-68; psychology specialist Lyster Army Hosp., Ft. Rucker, Ala., 1969-70; psychiat. social worker Toledo (Ohio) Mental Health Ctr., 1972; instr. in applied social rsch. and social work Med. Coll. Ohio, 1974-77; head divsn. clin. social work Ochsner Med. Instns., New Orleans, 1977—2001; ret., 2001. Dir. Ochsner Ctr. for Elimination of Smoking; asst. clin. prof. psychiatry La. State U. Med. Ctr.; asst. clin. prof. Tulane Med. Ctr.; instr., social scis. dept., Tahoe Coll. South Lake Tahoe, Calif.; psychology and sociology faculty Lake Tahoe C.C., 2002-; program dir., adminstr. State of Ohio Epilepsy Deinstitutionalization Assistance Program, 1976-77. Contbr. articles to profl. jours.; mem. editorial bd. Headache Quar., 1989—. Bd. dirs. Biofeedback Certification Inst. Am., Wheat Ridge, Colo., 1995. With U.S. Army, 1968-70. Fellow Am. Assn. for Study of Headache; mem. Assn. for Advancement of Behavior Therapy, Assn. Applied Psychophysiology and Biofeedback, La. Assn. Applied Psychophysiology and Biofeedback (past pres.), Am. Assn. for Study of Headache, NASW, La. Assn. for Clin. Social Work Vendorship (bd. dirs., treas., pres.), ACSW, Am. Fedn. for Clin. Rsch. Home: P O Box 1182 Zephyr Cove NV 89448

HUEFNER, DIXIE SNOW, special education educator; b. Washington, Dec. 7, 1936; m. Robert Paul Huefner, July 30, 1960; children: Steven Frederick, Eric William; m. Robert Paul Huefner. BA in Polit. Sci., Wellesley Coll., 1958; MS in Spl. Edn., U. Utah, 1977, JD, 1986. Clin. instr. dept. spl. edn. U. Utah, 1978-86; jud. clk. to hon. Stephen H. Anderson U.S. Ct. Appeals (10th cir.), 1986-90; clin. asst. prof. dept. spl. edn. U. Utah, Salt Lake City, 1986-89, vis. asst. prof. dept. spl. edn., 1989-90, asst. prof. dept. spl. edn., 1990—94, assoc. prof., 1994—99, prof., 1999—. Presenter in field. Contbr. articles prof. jours.; author: (book) Getting Comfortable with Spl. Edn.Law /Christopher-Gordon Pub., 2000; co-author: Edn. Law and the Pub. Sch./ Christopher-Gordon Pub., 1998. Apptd. to Utah State Bd. Edn. Adv. Com. on the Handicapped. Mem. ABA, Coun. for Exceptional Children, Learning Disability Assn., Learning Disability Assn. Utah, Nat. Assn. for Retarded Citizens, Women Lawyers Utah, bd. mem. Utah parent ctr., Edn. Law Assoc.. Office: U Utah Dept Spl Edn 1705 E Campus Ctr Dr Rm 221 Salt Lake City UT 84112-9253

HUEG, WILLIAM FREDERICK, agronomy educator, dairy owner; b. N.Y.C., Jan. 12, 1924; s. William Frederick and Mary Lavinia (Lynch) H.; m. Alvina Louise Sauer, Feb. 5, 1949 (div. Mar. 1975); children: William III, Anne (dec. 1995), Thomas, John, Paul, Mark, Michael; m. Hella Lindemyer Mears, Aug. 12, 1978. BS, Cornell U., 1948; MS, Mich. State U., 1954, PhD, 1959; LLD (hon.), U. Minn., 1998. Asst. county agt. SUNY, Herkimer, 1948-50, instr. farm crops Alfred, 1950-55, Mich. State U., East Lansing, 1955-57; assoc. prof. agronomy U. Minn., St. Paul, 1957-62, asst. dir. agrl. expt. sta., 1962-66, dir. agrl. expt. sta., 1966-75, v.p. agr. for home econs., 1974-83, prof. emeritus agronomy and plant genetics, 1983—, hon. doctorate, 1998. Bd. dirs. NSF, Washington, 1976-82; pres., bd. dirs. Coun. Agrl. Sci. and Tech., Ames,. Iowa, 1977-84; owner, mgr. Bhella Holsteins, Hammond, Wis., 1984—; cons. Asian Devel. Bank, Manila, 1990—. Trustee United Bd. for Christian Higher Edn. in Asia, N.Y.C., 1991—, Nitrogen Fixing Tree Assn., Maui, Hawaii, 1992-95. Fellow AAAS, Crop Sci. Soc., Agronomy Soc. Baptist. Home: 1170 Dodd Rd Saint Paul MN 55118-1823

HUELLEMEIER, LORI ANN, art educator; b. Cin., May 8, 1962; d. Frank Shelby and Janet Mae Hodges; m. Kenneth Norbert Huellemeier, Aug. 1, 1999; children: Allison, Brandon, Ryan;1 child, Justin Leonard. BA in Art, Xavier U., 1984, MEd, 1996. Art tchr. North Norwood (Ohio) Elem. Sch., 1985—86, Fairfield (Ohio) Mid. Sch., 1986—, volleyball coach, 1986—91. Exhibitions include Mt. St. Joseph Coll., 1998, Cin. Pub. Libr., 1999, Cohen Gallery at Xavier U., 2002. Mem.: NEA, Fairfield Classroom Tchr. Assn., Ohio Edn Assn. Avocations: walking, drawing, artwork, volleyball. Office: Fairfield Mid Sch 1111 Nilles Rd Fairfield OH 45014

HUELSMANN, RICHARD THADDEUS, principal; b. Manchester, Conn., Feb. 14, 1944; s. Howard H. and Dorothy (Foukel) H.; m. Marianne Frances Jackson, Aug. 12, 1972; 1 child, Mark Richard. BS in Chemistry, U. Conn., 1966, MS in Chemistry, 1968, postgrad., 1973-78, St. Joseph Coll., West Hartford, Conn., 1973. Tchr. chemistry East Cath. H.S., Manchester, 1968-74; asst. prin. East Hampton (Conn.) H.S., 1974-77; prin. East Hampton Mid. Sch., 1977—. Bd. advisors Conn. Adolescent Ctr., New Haven, 1994-96. Recipient Principal of Yr., NASSP/MetLife State Principal of Yr., 2004. Mem. Conn. Assn. of Schs. (mid. level bd. control 1990-94, bd. dirs. 1994—), Conn. Assn. Middle Sch. Principals (chmn. 2000-03, Principal of Yr. 2003). Avocations: sailing, travel. Office: East Hampton Middle School 19 Childs Rd East Hampton CT 06424-1709

HUFF, C(LARENCE) RONALD, public policy and criminology educator; b. Covington, Ky., Nov. 10, 1945; s. Nathaniel Warren G. and Irene Opal (Mills) H.; m. Patricia Ann Plankenhorn, June 15, 1968; children: Tamara Lynn, Tiffany Dawn. BA, Capital U., 1968; MSW, U. Mich., 1970; PhD, Ohio State U., 1974. Social worker Franklin County Children's Svcs., Columbus, Ohio, 1968; social work intern Pontiac (Mich.) State Hosp. and Family Svc. Met. Detroit, 1969-70; dir. psychiat. social work Lima (Ohio) State Hosp., 1970-71; chief psychiat. social worker N.W. Cmty. Mental Health Ctr., Lima, 1971-72; grad. tchg. assoc. sociology Ohio State U., 1972-74; asst. prof. social ecology U. Calif., Irvine, 1974-76; asst. prof. sociology Purdue U., 1976-79; assoc. prof. pub. policy/mgmt. Ohio State U., Columbus, 1979-87, dir. Criminal Justice Rsch. Ctr., 1979-99, prof., 1987-99, prof. emeritus, 1999—, dir. Sch. Pub. Policy and Mgmt., 1994-99; dean Sch. Social Ecology U. Calif., Irvine, 1999—, prof. criminology, law and society, 1999—. Vis. prof. U. Hawaii, 1995; cons. Bur. Justice Stats., Nat. Inst. Justice, Nat. Inst. Corrections, Nat. Inst. Juvenile Justice and Delinquency Prevention, U.S. Senate Jud. Com., NSF, FBI, others; expert witness fed. and state cts. Author: Youth Violence: Prevention, Intervention, and Social Policy, 1999, Convicted But Innocent: Wrongful Conviction and Public Policy, 1996, (Outstanding Acad. Book award Choice Mag., 1996), The Gang Intervention Handbook, 1993, Gangs in America, 1990, 2d edit., 1996, 3rd edit., 2002, House Arrest and Correctional Policy: Doing Time at Home, 1988, The Mad, The Bad, and The Different: Essays in Honor of Simon Dinitz, 1981, Attorneys as Activists: Evaluating the American Bar Association's BASICS Program, 1979, Contemporary Corrections: Social Control and Conflict, 1977, Planning Correctional Reform, 1975, and others; mem. editl. bd. various jours.; contbr. articles to profl. jours., chpts. to books. Recipient Nat. Security award Mershon Found., 1980, prize New Eng. Sch. Law, 1981, Outstanding Tchg. award, 1985, Donald R. Cressey award Nat. Coun. on Crime and Delinquency, 1992, Paul Tappan award Western Soc. Criminology, 1993, Herbert Bloch award Am. Soc. Criminology, 1994; grantee ABA, 1974-77, Purdue U., 1978, Dept. Justice, 1978-79, 85-88, 91-95, Ohio Dept. Mental Health, 1982-83, 84-85, 85-87, Gov.'s Office Criminal Justice, 1985-88, 92-95, 98, Ohio Dept. Youth Svcs., 1989-90, Ohio State U./Ohio Bd. Regents, 1990-92. Fellow Western Soc. Criminology, Am. Soc. Criminology (exec. bd., pres.-elect 1999-2000, pres. 2000-01, Herbert Bloch award 1994); mem. Acad. Criminal Justice Scis., Nat. Coun. on Crime and Delinquency, Phi Kappa Phi, Phi Beta Delta. Office: U Calif Irvine Sch Social Ecology 300 Social Ecology I Irvine CA 92697-7050 E-mail: rhuff@uci.edu.

HUFF, JANET HOUSE, special education educator; b. Kansas City, Mo., Sept. 5, 1947; d. Arthur and Juanita House; m. William E. Huff, Dec. 20, 1975; children: Ryan, Anesi. BS in Edn., Emporia State U., 1970; MA in Edn., U. Phoenix, 1998, adminstr. license, 2001. Cert. Type A psychology, educationally handicapped and spl. tchr. I, Colo., Type D Elem./Middle. Tchr. spl. edn. Kansas City (Kans.) Unified Sch. Dist., 1970-73, S.W. Bd. Coop. Svcs., Cortez, Colo., 1973-74, Mesa County Valley Sch. Dist. 51, Grand Junction, Colo., 1974-86, Bakersfield (Calif.) City Schs., 1986-89, Fresno (Calif.) Unified Sch. Dist., 1989-90, Cherry Creek Sch. Dist. 5, Englewood, Colo., 1990-92, Jefferson County Sch. REI, 1992—. Lutheran. E-mail: jhuff@jeffco.k12.co.us.

HUFF, LULA LUNSFORD, controller, accounting educator; b. Columbus, Ga., July 5, 1949; d. Walter Theophilus and Sally Lunsford; m. Charles Efferidge Huff Jr., June 11, 1972; 1 child, Tamara Nicole. BA, Howard U., 1971; MBA, Atlanta U., 1973. CPA, Ga. Acct. Ernst and Young, Columbus, 1973-76; internal auditor First Consol. Gov., Columbus, 1976-84; instr., chair dept. acctg., dir. pers. mgmt. Troy State U., Phenix City, Ala., 1979-89; sr. fin./cost analyst Pratt and Whitney, Columbus, 1984-89, controller Southington, Conn., 1989-92, Columbus, 1992-95; contr. for Precision Components Internat. Pratt and Whitney Joint Venture, Columbus, 1995-96; tax commn. Muscogee County, Columbus, Ga., 1997—. Mem. fin. bd. Diocese of Savannah; mem. Liberty Theater Hist. Preservation Bd., Columbus Housing Authority Bd., Columbus Hist. Found. Bd., Columbus Literate Cmty. Program Inc. Bd., Columbus Beyond 2000, 1989-90; active Concharty coun. Girl Scouts, Inc., Women of Achievement, 1995; active Chattahoochee Valley Cmty. Found., Inc. Recipient Disting. Black Citizen award Sta. WOKS, 1978, Black Excellence award Nat. Assn. Negro Bus. and Profl. Women's Clubs, Inc., 1977, Outstanding Svc. award St. Benedict Cath. Ch., 1971-76, cert. of merit Congressman Jack Brinkley, 1976, Achievement award Links Inc., 1976, Outstanding Achievement and Svcs. award 1st African Bapt. Ch., 1975, Ga. Jaycees Outstanding Young Woman award, 1989, Leadership Columbus award C. of C., 1983-84, Women on the Move award Spencer Owlettes, 1992; named Outstanding Woman of Yr., Ledger Enquirer Newspaper, 1976, Profl. Woman of Yr., Iota Phi Lambda, 1977, Bus. Woman of Yr., 1979, Columbus Ga. Outstanding Young Woman, Jaycees, 1980, Columbus Young Woman, 1980. Mem. NAACP, Am. Mgmt. Assn., Ga. Soc. CPAs, Howard U. Alumnae Assn., Urban League, Push, Toastmasters Am., Links, Inc. (Achievement award 1976), Columbus C. of C., Delta Sigma Theta (auditor 1991). Roman Catholic. Avocation: swimming. Home: PO Box 1742 Columbus GA 31902-1742

HUFF, PATSY JO HERNANDEZ, elementary education educator; b. Prescott, Ariz., July 13, 1953; d. Pete L. and Rita M. Hernandez; m. John Stewart Huff, Nov. 18, 1978; 1 child, Sarah Elizabeth. AA, Yavapai Jr. Coll., 1973; BA in Elem. Edn., Ariz. State U., 1975; MA in Curriculum Edn., No. Ariz. U., 1982. Tchr. Prescott Pub. Schs., 1975-79, South Sioux City (Nebr.) Community Schs., 1979—. Named Tchr. of Week, McDonalds, 1989, # 1 Country Sch. Tchr., Country Mag., 1991. Mem. NEA, PTA (Founders Day award 1986), Loess Hills Audubon Soc. (edn. chmn. 1986). Democrat. Avocations: travel, antiques, gardening, reading. Home: 1927 Idylwild Way Prescott AZ 86305-7573 Office: Dakota City Elem Sch PO Box 455 Dakota City NE 68731-0455

HUFF, SHERRI LYNN, physical education educator; b. Owensboro, Ky., Sept. 29, 1963; d. John and Darleen Mae (Westphal) H. BS in Recreation, U. Ala., Birmingham, 1985; MA in Athletic Adminstrn., U. Ala., 1988, MA in Phys. Edn., 1990; EdS in Phys. Edn., U. Montevallo, 1994; ednl. specialist degree, Samford U., 1997, EdD in Edn. Adminstrn., 2001. Cert. Rank AA tchr. phys. edn. K-12, rank 1 ednl. adminstr. grades K-12, Ala. Pre-sch. tchr. Jewish Cmty. Ctr., Birmingham, Ala., 1985-88; phys. edn. tchr.'s aide, coach basketball Hewitt-Trussville Mid. Sch., Trussville, Ala., 1990-91; tchr. phys. edn. K-5 Washington Elem. Sch., Birmingham, 1991-92; basketball coach Washington Mid. Sch., Birmingham, 1991-92; volleyball coach Tarrant (Ala.) H.S., 1993-94; basketball coach Tarrant Mid. Sch., 1992-95; tchr. elem. phys. edn. K-4 Tarrant Elem. Sch., 1992-96; golf and basketball coach Tarrant H.S., 1995-96; mid. sch. volleyball ofcl., 1996; phys. edn. program specialist Birmingham City Schs., 1996—; girls basketball coach AAU, 1991, AAU, 1999—. Summer activities instr. U. Ala., Birmingham, 1988-95; com. mem. bldg. leadership team Tarrant Elem. Sch., 1994-96; com. mem. sch. accreditation Fultondale (Ala.) Elem. Sch.-So. Assn. of Colls. and Schs., 1994; Ala. State Textbook Com., 1997-98. Coord. Jump Rope for Heart program Am. Heart Assn., Birmingham, 1992-96; coord. Jingle Bell Run for Arthritis Found., Birmingham, 1994-96; vol. Spl. Olympics, Ala., 1997; apptd. State Textbook Com., Ala., 1997-98. Named Faculty Mem. of Nat. Blue Ribbon Sch., U.S. Dept. Edn., 1994; inducted into Apollo H.S. Athletic Hall of Fame, 1996; Mervyn Goldstein Meml. scholar U. Ala., 1985-86, Adminstrn. Samford U. scholar, 1995—. Mem. ASCD, NEA, AAHPERD, Nat. Fedn. Interscholastic Coaches Assn., Ala. State Assn. for Health, Phys. Edn., Recreation and Dance (Adminstr. of Yr. 2002, state bd. mem. dist. rep. 1993-95, v.p.-elect 1996-97, v.p. phys. edn. 1997-98, 99—, sec. 1998-99, v.p. U. Ala. Birmingham athletic alumni chap., 2001-02, com. mem. for Chem. Awareness Program, Birmingham, 2002-03), presenter phys. edn. workshop 1993, coord. fall and spring conf. store), Ala. H.S. Athletic Dirs. and Coaches Assn., Magic City Phys. Educators and Coaches Assn. (pres. 1992-93), Ala. State Assn. for Health, Phys. Edn., Recreation and Dance (sec. 1998—). Republican. Presbyterian. Avocations: golf, tennis, basketball, cycling. Home: 153 Ashford Ln Alabaster AL 35007-5160 Office: Rickwood Field Dept Ath Birmingham City Schs 1137 2nd Ave W Birmingham AL 35204-4502

HUFFMAN, CAROL KOSTER, retired elementary school educator; b. L.I., N.Y., Nov. 4, 1933; d. Harry C., Jr. and Mary M. (Wilchin) Koster; m. William Leslie Huffman. BS, Hofstra U., 1954, MS, 1967. Cert. elem., art, nursery and spl. edn. tchr. N.Y., advanced Irlen screener I and area coord. Dir. Child's World Sch., New Orleans; in-svc. instr. Half Hollow Hills Schs., Dix Hills, NY, resource, self-contained program, art and learning strategies tchr.; instr. in spl. edn. Hofstra U., Hempstead, NY; cons. curriculum, spl. edn. and reading; ret. Rschr. identification and ednl. accomodations students with visual disabilities affecting schoolwork. Editor: The Communicator, The Phoenix, Williamsburg Directory Sect. Former del. N.Y. State Retirement Sys.; former bd. dirs. Win-Gate Village Club, Orlando, Fla.; chair Neighborhood Beautification Grant Com., 2002—03. Recipient award, Orange County, Fla., 2001—02, 2002—03. Mem.: AFT, Half Hollow Hills Tchr. Assn., N.Y. State United Tchrs., Am. Assn. Those with Augsberger Syndrome, Kappa Delta Pi, Kappa Pi.

HUFFMAN, DONALD GERALD, special education educator; b. Woodman, Wis., Oct. 2, 1938; s. William Henry and Winifred Ruby (Coleman) H.; married; children: Jaki Ann, Sun Re, Wil Don. BS, Columbia County Tchrs. Coll., 1963, U. Wis., 1969, MS Guidance Counseling, 1978; Cert. Spl. Edn., U. Eau Claire, 1973. Cert. (life) tchr. spl. edn., elem. edn. adult basic edn., GED, EMR, TMR, ED/BD, Wis. Prin. Warrens (Wis.) Elem. Sch., 1963-64, Danbury (Wis.) Elem. Sch., 1964-65, Yahara Valley Elem. Sch., Edgerton, Wis., 1965-66, Barneveld (Wis.) Elem. Sch., 1966-69; dir. Edn. Assn. Retarded Citizens, Dubuque, Iowa, 1969-70; prin. DeSoto (Wis.) Elem. Sch., 1970-73; tchr. trainable mentally retarded Independence, Wis., 1973-74; tchr. EMR-ED/BD Iowa-Grant High Sch., Livingston, Wis., 1974-85; tchr. LD 29 Palms (Calif.) High Sch., 1985—. Wrestling coach Barneveld High Sch., 1966-69; tchr. ABE/GED Southwest Wis. Vocat. Tech. Coll., Fennimore, Wis., 1986-87; counselor Copper Mountain Coll., Joshua Tree, Calif., 1987-88; leader/tchr. You and Your World contest for good citizens, Middletown, Conn.; mentor tchr. Calif. Dept. Edn., 1990, Calif. New Tchrs. Project, 1991. Leader Boy Scouts Am., Warrens, 1963-64; lay person United Meth. Ch., Montfort, Wis., 1975-85. With USAF, 1957-61, Okinawa. Grantee San Bernardino County Solid Waste Mgmt. Dept., 1994; named Mr. Twentynine Palms, 1989; pub. recognition/commendation City Coun. of Twentynine Palms, 1993, 94. Mem. NEA, Coun. Execptional Children, Learning Disabilities Assn. Calif., Masons, Phi Delta Kappa. Avocations: helping students get jobs, fishing, speaking, family time, travel. Home: 72739 Two Mile Rd Twentynine Palms CA 92277-1535 Office: Morongo Unified Sch Dist 5717 Utah Trail Twentynine Palms CA 92277

HUFFMAN, DURWARD ROY, college system official, electrical engineer; b. Little Mountain, S.C., Jan. 22, 1939; s. Roy Otho and Mabel Amanda (Huffstettler) H.; m. Lillian Hope Farrell, Apr. 18, 1959; children: Donald Durward, Heatherlyn. BSEE, Heald Engring. Coll., 1963; MSEE, U. Colo., 1966; EdD in Higher Edn., U. Sarasota, 1980. Registered profl. engr., Pa. Asst. design engr. Westinghouse Elec. Corp., Sunnyvale, Calif., 1963-64; instr. elec. engring. U. Colo., Boulder, 1965-67; elec. engr. Corning (N.Y.) Glass Works, 1967-68; sr. process control engr. Corning Glass Works, Wellsboro, Pa., 1968; assoc. prof. elec.-electronic engring. tech. Luzerne County C.C., Wilkes-Barre, Pa., 1968-73, chmn. dept., 1971-73; faculty Midlands Tech. Coll., Columbia, S.C., 1973-75; assoc. dean Nashville State Tech. Inst., 1976-87, acting dean instrn., 1985-86; pres. No. Maine Tech. Coll., Presque Isle, 1987-2001; acad. officer Maine C.C. Sys., Augusta, 1994-2001, chief acad. officer, 2001—. Presenter in field; chair tech. accreditation commn. Accreditation Bd. Engring. and Tech., 1989-90. Editor-in-chief, Jour. Engring. Tech., 1990-92, pub. editor, 1987-89. Mem. steering com. Ctrl. Aroostook County (Maine) Job Opportunity Zone, 1988-91; bd. dirs. Leaders Encouraging Aroostook Devel., 1988-2001, sec., 1988-93; bd. dirs. Maine Rsch. and Productivity Coun., 1988-92; mem. pub. policy com. Maine Alzheimer's Assn., 2001—. Fellow Accreditation Bd. Engring. and Tech.; mem. IEEE (sr.), Am. Soc. Engring. Edn. (divsn. engring. tech. exec. bd. 1981-82, sec. 1982-84), Am. Tech. Edn. Assn., Am. Assn. C.C. (commn. on cmty. and workforce devel. 1995-97, com. on academic, student, cmty. devel. 1998-2001), Engring. Tech. Leadership Inst. (mem. exec. com. 1978-79, 86-87), New Eng. Assn. Schs. and Colls. (chairperson accreditation team 1990, 95, 97, 98, team mem. 1994-96), Rotary (chairperson com. on vocat. svc. 1988-89, dist. 7810 scholarships subcom. 1996-2000), Presque Isle Club, Eta Kappa Nu. Republican. Avocation: vol. work accreditation postsecondary ednl. instns. and programs. Office: Maine CC Sys 323 State St Augusta ME 04330-7131

HUFFMAN, JANICE KAY, middle school educator, curriculum coordinator; b. Mt. Pleasant, Mich., Nov. 5, 1941; d. Charles Emerald and Norma Ilene (Gilmore) Brien; m. Charles William Huffman, Jan. 15, 1966; children: Victoria Lynn, Mary Kathleen, Jasmine Rae. BA, North Ctrl. Coll., 1963; student, U. Fla., 1966-67; MA, Ctrl. Mich. U., 1982. Cert. elem. tchr., Mich., Ill., Fla. Elem. tchr. Comm. Cons. Sch. Dist. 15, Palatine, Ill., 1963-65, Midland (Mich.) Pub. Schs., 1965; 1-12 reading tchr. Alachua County Schs., Gainesville, Fla., 1966-67; 7-8 Title I Indian Culture tchr. Mt. Pleasant Pub. Schs., 1967-70, 7-8 reading tchr., 1967-72, 7-8 English, lang. arts tchr., 1972—2001, English/lang. arts coord., 1997—2001, K-12 curriculum coun. chmn., 1985-98. Mem. edn. com. Sag. Chip Tribe, Mt. Pleasant, 1968-73; strategic planner Mt. Pleasant Pub. Schs., 1994-96; adj. prof. tchr. edn. and profl. develop., Ctrl. Mich. U., 2003. Bd. dirs. Zion Luth. Nursery Sch., Mt. Pleasant, 1970-72; writing & pub. com. mem. Art Reach, Mt. Pleasant, 1989-94; edn. chmn. Countryside United Meth. Ch., 1975-2003; mentor Coun. Exceptional Children, 1985. Mem. AAUW, ASCD (assoc.), Phi Delta Kappa (v.p. program, 1999-2000, pres. 2001-03, Svc. award 1997), Delta Kappa Gamma (rsch. chair 198-85). Avocations: reading, music, travel, genealogy.

HUFFMAN, JOAN BREWER, history educator; b. Springfield, Ohio, Aug. 18, 1937; d. James Clarence and Berniece (Notter) Brewer; m. James Russell Huffman, Aug. 21, 1959; children: Jill Elizabeth, Jean Elaine. AB, Ohio U., 1959; MA, Ga. State U., 1968, PhD, 1980. Adj. prof. Wesleyan Coll., Macon, Ga., 1981-82; instr. history Macon State Coll., 1968-72, asst. prof., 1972-81, assoc. prof., 1981-86, prof., 1986-2000, prof. emerita, 2000—; owner The Printed Page, Macon, Ga., 1993-97, Picture Perfect, 1995—. Chmn. History adv. com. U. Sys. Ga., 1986—87. Contbr. articles to profl. jours. Mem., bd. dirs. Oklahatchee Pk., Perry, Ga., 1966-68, Macon State Coll. Found., 1985-90, Ga. Humanities Coun., Atlanta, 1983-87. Katharine C. Bleckley scholar English-Speaking Union, 1977; recipient Gov.'s award in the humanities, 1998. Mem. N.Am. Conf. on Brit. Studies, Am. Hist. Assn., Southern Hist. Assn. (membership com. 1988-89), Ga. Assn. Historians (pres. 1982-83), Phi Beta Kappa, Phi Alpha Theta (award 1978). Home: 135 Covington Pl Macon GA 31210-4445 E-mail: huffmanj@bellsouth.net.

HUFFMAN, KELLEY RAYE, reporter and columnist, former elementary educator; b. Smithville, Mo., Mar. 17, 1972; d. Loren Ray and Susan Eleanor (Newell) R. AA, Williams Bapt. Coll., 1992, BS in Elem. Edn., 1994. Cert. K-6 tchr., Tex. Home sch. tchr. Fgn. Mission Bd., Richmond, Va., 1994-95; tchr. kindergarten and ESL Ft. Worth Ind. Sch. Dist., 1996-98; reporter and columnist, editor Paragould (Ark.) Tribune, 1998—2003. Dir. coll. drama team Williams Bapt. Coll., Walnut Ridge, Ark., 1993. Tchr. Mission Friends Ch., Ft. Worth, 1997. Republican. Southern Baptist. Avocations: running, writing, reading, piano, kickboxing. Home: 2711 N 4 1/2 St Paragould AR 72450

HUFFMAN, KEVIN DALE, principal; b. Springfield, Mo., July 1, 1965; s. Raymond D. and Billie Jean (Bakewell) H.; m. Mary Elizabeth Mundt, Aug. 5, 1988. B in Music Edn., Evangel U., 1988; M in Ednl. Adminstrn., S.W. Mo. State U., 1992. Tchr. music Lakeland R-III Schs., Deepwater, Mo., 1988-89; grad. asst. S.W. Mo. State U., Springfield, 1991-92; tchr. music Everton (Mo.) R-III Schs., 1989-91, prin. grades 7 through 12, 1992-93, prin. grades kindergarten through 12, 1993-95; prin. grades kindergarten through 5 Springfield (Mo.) Sch. Dist., 1996—; music min. St. John's United Ch. of Christ, Springfield, 1991—. Active Springfield Regional Opera, 1988-89, Mid-Am. Singers, 1991-92; bd. dirs. North Springfield Betterment Assn., 1993—. Mem. Nat. Assn. Elem. Sch. Prins. (pub. rels. com.), Mo. Assn. Elem. Sch. Prins., Nat. Assn. Tchrs. of Singing (Outstanding Soloist 1988). Republican. Avocations: music, arts, drama. Home: 416 Hughes Rd Willard MO 65781-9548 Office: Springfield R-XII Sch Dist 940 N Jefferson Springfield MO 65802 E-mail: Khuffman@spsmail.org.

HUFFMAN, LOUISE TOLLE, middle school educator; b. Tallahassee, Fla., July 24, 1951; d. Donald James and Mary Alice (McNeill) Tolle; m. Terry Lee Huffman, July 17, 1976; children: Cody McNeill, Hunter Tolle. BSED in Spl. Edn./Elem. Edn., So. Ill. U., 1973; MSEd, No. Ill. U., 1979. Cert. elem. tchr., spl. edn. tchr. Ill. Title I reading tchr., Tonica, Ill., 1973-74; learning disabilities tchr. St. Charles, Ill., 1974-78; spl. edn. tchr. McWayne Elem. Sch., Batavia, Ill., 1978-80; tchr. grades 1, 3, 4, and 5 Steeple Run Elem. Sch., Naperville, Ill., 1980-98; tchr. Kennedy Jr. H.S., Naperville, 1998—. Com. to develop dual maj. in elem. edn. and sci. Benedictine U., Lisle, Ill., 1999—2000; curriculum developer Brookfield (Ill.) Zoo, 2001—02; facilitator of tchr. workshops Jurica Sci. Mus./ Benedictine U., Lisle, 1992—; facilitator sci. workshops Mus. Sci. and Industry, Chgo., 1991—96, Hamline U., St. Paul, 1990—93; Saturday Morning TV Sci. tchr. Dist. 203, Naperville, 1994; author Earth Rhythms Saturday Sch. program Benedictine U., 1996; tchr. summer sci. workshop Golden Apple Found., 1999—; mem. steering com. World Sch. Adventure Learning St. Thomas U., St. Paul, 1992—94; steering com. World Sch. Adventure Learning Hamline U., 1995, 2002. Co-author: Antarctica: A Living Classroom, 1991; contbg. author: Project Circles: The World School for Adventure Learning, 2002; contbr. articles to Cobblestone Mag., Good Apple Newspaper, Children's Digest; author of poetry. Bd. dirs. Cmty. United Meth. Ch. Sojourners Sunday Sch., Naperville, 1995-2000; confirmation class tchr. Cmty. United Meth. Ch., 1999-2001. Recipient award of Excellence, Ill. Sci. Tchrs. Assn., 1992, 1996, Golden Apple award, 2002, tchr. rsch. assistantship in Antarctica, NSF, 2001—03; grantee, Naperville Edn. Found., 1994, 2002, Jeanine Nicarico Lit. grant, 1999. Methodist. Office: Kennedy Junior High Sch 2929 Green Trails Dr Lisle IL 60532-6262 E-mail: lhuffman@ncusd203.org.

HUFFMAN, SANDRA JEAN, academic counselor, educator; b. El Dorado, Ark., Jan. 23, 1951; d. Roscoe N. and Sara Margaret (Thomas) Herring; m. Robert Terry Huffman, June 24, 1972 (div. 1984); children: Robby, Greg. BS in Edn., Henderson State Coll., 1972; MS in counseling, U. Ark., 1976; EdS in counseling and psych., Miss. Coll., 1996. Tchr. Prairie Grove Sch., Fayetteville, Ark., 1972-75; grad. asst. U. Ark., Fayetteville, 1975-76; guidance counselor St. Aloysius High Sch., Vicksburg, Miss., 1977-84; acad. counselor, psychology instr. Hinds C.C., Vicksburg, 1990—98, clin. dir. therapeutic group home for adolescent girls, 1998—2002; program dir. Child Abuse Prevention Ctr., 2002—. Pres. Mental Health Assn. Warren County, 1982-84; bd. dirs. Mental Health Assn. Miss., 1982-84. Avocations: reading, gardening.

HUFFMAN-HINE, RUTH CARSON, adult education administrator, educator; b. Spencer, Ind., Sept. 13, 1925; d. Joseph Charles Carson and Bess Ann Taylor; m. Joe Buren Hine; children: Paulette Walker, Larry K., Annette M. AA in Fine Arts, Ind. Cen. Coll., 1967; BS in Edn., Butler U., 1971; MS in Adult Edn., Ind. U., 1976; PhD in Ednl. Adminstrn., Greenwich U., 1995. Cert. elem. edn. Subs. tchr. Met. Sch. Dist. Wayne Twnshp., Indpls., 1956-60; tchr. of homebound Met. Sch. Dist. Decatur Twnshp., Indpls., 1964-66; adult edn. tchr. Met. Sch. Dist. Wayne Twnshp., Indpls., 1971-75, adminstr. adult edn., 1975—. Cons. Ind. Adoption System, Indpls., 1985—; regional rep. Ind. Assn. Adult Adminstrs., 1984—; program rep. Ind. Literacy Coordinators, Indpls., 1985—; speaker, mem. literacy research and evaluation com. Ind. Adult Literacy Coalition, Indpls., 1980-86. Author: Driving Regulations and Courtesies, It Happened at the Pond, 1997, We Build Walls, 1999; co-author Learning for Everyday Living, 1978, Table Approach to Education, 1984, Developing Educational Competencies for Individuals Determined to Excel, 6 vols., 1980 (ERIC System award 1980), (ERIC System award 1985), Collection, Evaluation, Dissemination of Special Research Projects, 1984, Automobile Driving Rules and Regulations, 1988. Vice com. person Rep. Orgn., Indpls., 1968-72; charter mem., sec. Project READ, LITERACY, 1988. Recipient Extra Mile award Met. Sch. Dist. Wayne Twp., 1990. Mem. Internat. Reading Assn. (Celebrate Literacy award 1984), Ind. Assn. for Adult & Continuing Edn. (treas. 1984—, pres. 1990-93, Outstanding Adult Educator 1979), Beta Phi Delta (pres. 1986—), Beta Phi, Delta Kappa Gamma (v.p. 1985-86, fellowship chmn. 1982-84), Phi Delta Kappa. Republican. Mem. Christian Ch. Avocations: reading, music, bicycling. Home: 138 Abner Creek Pkwy Danville IN 46123-9602 Office: Adult Basic Edn Ctr 5248 W Raymond St Indianapolis IN 46241-4700

HUG, CARL CASIMIR, JR., anesthesiology and pharmacology, educator; b. Canton, Ohio, Dec. 20, 1936; s. Carl Casimir and Aimee Cecelia (McArdle) H.; m. Marilyn Ann France, May 12, 1956; children: Patricia Ann DeStephano, Michael Stephen, Joan Marie Daniel, Mary Lynn Higgins, Lori Renee Mauldin. BS in Pharmacy summa cum laude, Duquesne U., 1958; PhD in Pharmacology, U. Mich., 1963, MD with distinction, 1967. Diplomate Am. Bd. Anesthesiology (bd. dirs. 1984-96, v.p. 1990-92, pres. 1992-93). From instr. to assoc. prof. pharmacology U. Mich., Ann Arbor, 1963-71; from assoc. prof. anesthesiology and pharmacology to emeritus prof. Emory U. Sch. Medicine, Atlanta, 1972—, dep. chmn. for rsch., 1987-95, dep. chmn. for acad. affairs, 1995—2001; faculty assoc. Emory U. Ctr. for Ethics, 2001—. Vis. rsch. prof. U. Leiden, The Netherlands, 1982. Author: Alfentanil: Pharmacology and Uses in Anesthesia, 1984; editor Pharmacokinetics of Anaesthesia, 1984; editor Anesthesiology, 1979-88. Chmn. St. Francis Sch. Bd., Ann Arbor, Mich., 1967—71; coach Little League, Ann Arbor, 1967—71; active Corpus Christi Cath. Ch., Stone Mountain, Ga., 1972—96, St. John Neumann Cath. Ch., Liburn, Ga., 1997—; bd. dirs. Found. for Anesthesiology Edn. and Rsch., 1993—2003, v.p., 1995—98, pres., 1998—2001. Named Tchr. of Yr. Emory U. Anesthesiology, 1989, hon. lectr. at multiple Univs. Fellow Royal Coll. Anaesthetists (Eng.) (hon.), Australian and New Zealand Coll. Anaesthetists (hon.); mem. Belgian Soc. Anesthesia and Reanimation (hon.), Am. Soc. Anesthesiologists (mem., chmn. various coms. 1976—, Rovenstine lectr. 1999). Office: Emory Univ Hosp Dept Anesthesiology 1364 Clifton Rd NE Atlanta GA 30322-1104 E-mail: carl_hug@emoryhealthcare.org.

HUGET, EUGENE FLOYD, dental educator, researcher; b. Flint, Mich., Sept. 20, 1931; s. Leonard John and Dorothy (Makey) H.; m. Barbara Claire Wisneiwski, June 22, 1957; children: Kirby Gene, Kristen Claire Huget Byrnes, Kathy Claire Huget Rather, Jason Gene. BS in Chemistry, Alma (Mich.) Coll., 1953; DDS, U. Mich., 1961; MS in Dental Materials, Georgetown U., 1967; MBA, Rensselaer Poly. Inst., 1983, MS in Mgmt., 1986. Enlisted man, radar and guided missile technician U.S. Army, Balt., 1953-55, commd. 1st lt., 1961, advanced through grades to col., 1978, gen. dentist, 1961-65; guest researcher Nat. Bur. Standards, Washington, 1965-68; rsch. dental officer U.S. Army Inst. Dental Rsch., Washington, 1968-74, chief div. dental materials, 1974-80; indsl. chemist Chevrolet Motor Co., Flint, Mich., 1955-57; dir. rsch. J.M. Ney Co., Bloomfield, Conn., 1980-87; prof dentistry U. Tenn., Memphis, 1987—, prof. emeritus restorative dentistry. Contbr. numerous monographs on dental biomaterials and articles to profl. jours., chpts. to 11 textbooks. Mem. policy coun. Shelby County Headstart Program, Memphis, 1989—. Chancellor's instrnl. devel. grantee U. Tenn., 1989, alumni rsch. grantee Coll. Dentistry, 1990, 93, 97, 98, 99. Mem. Internat. Assn. for Dental Rsch., Am. Assn. for Dental Rsch. (pres. Memphis chpt. 1990), Am. Assn. Dental Schs., Sigma Xi. Republican. Presbyterian. Avocations: gardening, writing, computer science. Home: 2539 Brachton Ave Memphis TN 38139-6409 Office: U Tenn Coll Dentistry 875 Union Ave Memphis TN 38103-3513 E-mail: efhuget@worldnet.att.net., ehuget@utmem.edu.

HUGGINS, CANNIE MAE COX HUNTER, retired elementary school educator; b. Belton, Tex., July 16, 1916; d. Jesse Daniel and Mary Alice (Hamilton) Cox; m. William Dudley Hunter, June 5, 1938 (div. 1967); children: Darline, Bob Roy; m. Bertrand Huggins, Aug. 4, 1979 (dec. July 19, 1980). BS, Mary Hardin Baylor Coll., 1940; MS, San Marcos Tchrs. Coll., 1942; postgrad., U. Tex., 1946-47, Tex. Tech. U., 1956-70, U. San Diego, 1975, St. Mary's U., 1976. Cert. educator, Tex. Tchr. pub. schs., Belton, 1935-38, Galveston, Tex., 1938-42; mem. staff testing dept. U. Ariz., 1942-43; reading cons. Phoenix Pub. Schs., 1943-45; tchr.-counselor pub. schs. Killeen, Tex., 1946-54; classroom tchr. Lubbock, Tex., 1954-74; tchr. first grade bilingual lang. devel. Posey Elem. Sch., Lubbock, Tex., 1974-96; pres. CM Corp. First aid chmn. ARC, Lubbock County, 1960-63, first aid instr., 1956—; area dir. March of Dimes, 1958-63; tchr. high sch. dept. First Bapt. Ch., Lubbock, 1960-82; state advisor U.S. Congl. Adv. Bd., 1985—; mem. Lubbock Hospice Vol. Program. Recipient Outstanding Svc. award ARC, 1966; Bronze award CONTACT Lubbock. Mem. Assn. Childhood Edn. Internat., NEA, Tex. Tchrs. Assn., Tex. Classroom Tchrs. Assn., Nat. PTA, Tex. Edn. Assn., Lubbock Educators Assn., Lubbock Classroom Tchrs. Assn., AAUW, Am. Bus. Women's Assn., South Plains Writers Guild, YWCA, Lubbock C. of C., Killeen C. of C., Univ. City Club (Lubbock). Baptist. Home: 4626 30th St Lubbock TX 79410-2423

HUGGINS, CHARLES EDWARD, obstetrician, gynecologist, educator; b. Hartsville, S.C., Nov. 16, 1944; s. Charles Witherspoon Huggins and Frances Sue (Fountain) Evans; m. Mary Ellen Esto, May 29, 1966; children: Chadwick Edward, Laura Ruth, Mary Elizabeth. BS, Wofford Coll., 1965; MD, Med. U. S.C., 1969. Diplomate Am. Bd. Ob-Gyn. Intern Strong Meml. Hosp., Rochester, 1969-70; resident in ob-gyn. Med. U. S.C. Hosp., Charleston, 1970-74; chief of ob-gyn. Roper Hosp., Charleston; chmn. ob-gyn. dept. Bon Secours St. Francis Hosp., Charleston, 1999—. Clin. assoc. prof. Med. U. S.C.; mem. exec. bd. Roper Hosp., Charleston,1992-95, perinatal adv. bd., Charleston, 1992-95. Leader Boy Scouts of Am., Mt. Pleasant, S.C., 1978-88; coach Hungry Neck Internat. Soccer, Mt. Pleasant, 1978-88. Lt. Cmdr. USN, 1974-76. Fellow ACOG, South Atlantic Assn. Ob-Gyn. (chair state com. 1995-98); mem. AMA, Am. Fertility Soc., NYAS, S.C. Med. Assn., Charleston County Med. Soc., Pi Kappa Phi (archon 1962—), Phi Rho Sigma. Presbyterian. Fax: (843) 577-4193.

HUGGINS, CHARLOTTE SUSAN HARRISON, secondary school educator, author, travel specialist; b. Rockford, Ill., May 13, 1933; d. Lyle Lux and Alta May (Bowers) Harrison; m. Rollin Charles Huggins Jr., Apr. 26, 1952; children: Cynthia Charlotte Peters, Shirley Ann Cooper, John Charles. Student, Knox Coll., 1951-52; AB magna cum laude, Harvard U., 1958; MA, Northwestern U., 1960, postgrad., 1971-73; cert. in conversation French, Berlitz Lang. Sch. Asst. editor Hollister Publs., Inc., Wilmette, Ill., 1959—65; tchr. advanced placement English New Trier H.S., Winnetka, Ill., 1965—, master tchr., 1979, leader tchr., 1988. With Task Force Commn. on Grading, 1973—74; Sabbatical project 1 yr. world travel History-Lit. Prospectus; cons. Asian Studies New Trier, 1987—88; mem. New Trier Supts. Commn. on Censorship, 1991; critic tchr. Northwestern U.; cons. McDougall-Littel's Young Writer's Manual, 1985—88; asst. sponsor Echoes, 1981—, Trevia, 1982, 83; sponsor New Trier News, 1988—; pres. Harrison Farms, Inc., Lovington, Ill., 1976—; spkr. North Suburban Geneal. Soc., 1990; presenter Asian lit. Ill. Humanities Coun., 1992, Nat. Scholastic Press Assn., No. Ill. Sch. Press Assn., 1992, 93, 94; instr., travel expert New Trier Adult Edn. Keys to the World's Last Mysteries, 1986—. Author: A Sequential Course in Composition Grades 9-12, 1979, A History of New Trier High School, 1982, Passage to Anaheim: An Historical Biography of Pioneer Families, 1984, Cambodia: A Place in Time, 1987; author: (video tapes) The Glory That was Greece, 1987; author: The World of Charles Dickens, 1987; editor: The Cornog Years, 2002. Women's bd. St. Leonard's House, Chgo., 1965—75; active Ctrl. Sch. PTA Bd., Wilmette, Ill., 1960—64; assocs. bd. Northwestern U. Settlement, Chgo., 1965—, pres., 1999—, fundraising com., 1997—, ctrl. bd. com., 2003—. Recipient Citizenship award, DAR, 1953, award, Phi Beta Kappa, 1957, Am. Legion, 1959, Cert. of Merit Graphic Arts Competition, Printing Industries of Am., 1983, 1st pl. award, Am. Scholastic Press Assn., 1990, Cert. of Merit, Am. Newspaper Pubs. Assn., 1990. Mem.: DAR (historian 1999—2000, regent 2000—02, parliamentarian 2002—), ASCD, MLA, NEA, IRTA, Ill. Journalism Edn. Assn. (sec. 1997—97, awards chmn., bd. dirs., Life Achievement award 2001), New Trier Edn. Assn. (sec. 1992, pres.-elect 1994, pres. 1995—96, parliamentarian 2003—), Ill. Assn. Tchrs. English, Ill. Edn. Assn., Nat. Scholastic Press Assn. (conv. del. 1991, spring conf. rep. 1991—92, 1992—93, 1993—94, presenter fall and spring conv. 1993—94, spring conf. rep. 1994—95, presenter fall and spring conv. 1994—95, 1994—95, spring conf. rep. 1995—96, presenter fall and spring conv. 1995—96, 1996—, newspaper judge, All-Am. Newspaper award 1990—91, Life Achievement award 2001), Nat. Coun. Tchrs. English, Harvard U. Alumni Assn. (admissions candidate interviewer), Radcliffe Coll. Alumnae Assn., Knox Coll. Alumni Assn., Terra Mus. Chgo. (charter), Chgo. Farmers, Mary Crane League, Women Comm., Inc., Nat. Huguenot Soc., Quill and Scroll (bd. dirs. 1992—93, George Gallup award 1990), Ill. Huguenot Soc., Columbia Scholastic Press Assn. (del. 1990, newspaper judge), Jr. Aux. U. Chgo. Cancer Rsch. Bd., Northwestern U. Alumni Assn., Art Inst. Chgo. (life), New Trier Ret. Tchrs. Assn. (newsletter editor), Lyric Opera (assoc.), Univ. Club Chgo., Mich. Shores Club, Women's Club Willmette, Pi Beta Phi (North Shore Chgo. alumnae bd., publicity chair). Home: 700 Greenwood Ave Wilmette IL 60091-1748 Office: 385 Winnetka Ave Winnetka IL 60093-4238

HUGGINS, MARY LOUISE WHITE, English educator, small business owner; b. Big Wells, Tex., Jan. 7, 1933; d. Edwin Horatio and Cora Edith (English) White; m. Chester Huelon Huggins, Sept. 23, 1961; children: Mary Catherine, Clarice Nell, Lloyd Jefferson, Henry Nuelon, Chester Horatio. BA in English and Spanish, Tarleton State U., Stephenville, Tex., 1979, MA in Teaching, 1981. Cert. secondary tchr., Tex. Sec., bookkeeper Hico (Tex.) Pub. Sch., 1969-76; instr. English, Tarleton State U., 1983—, dir. summer program, 1987—. Clk., bookkeeper Blair's Hardware, Hico, 1972-83; owner, operator Mary's Garden, Stephenville, 1987—. Pres. Erath County Women's Polit. Caucus, Stephenville; speaker to garden clubs, 1986—. Named Erath County Woman of Yr., Erath County Com., 1989. Mem. Conf. Coll. Tchrs. English, Assn. Tchrs. Tech. Writing, South Cen. Women's Studies Assn., Tarleton State U. Faculty Women's Forum (treas. 1988-89), AAUW (pres. Stephenville br. 1987), Am. Iris Soc., Johnson County Iris and Daylily Soc. (pres. 1987-88, 1st v.p. 1989-90). Avocations: writing, painting, gardening, home maintenance and remodeling. Home: 867 W Elm St Stephenville TX 76401-2415

HUGHES, EDWARD THOMAS, retired English educator, consultant; b. Elmira, N.Y., June 4, 1942; s. Henry Michael and Irene (Husar) H.; m. Judy Ann Lawrence, Sept. 20, 1969; children: Susan Jill, Anne-Marie. BA, SUNY, Albany, 1964, MA, 1968, MS, 1974. Cert. tchr. English, sch. adminstrn. and supervision, sch. dist. adminstrn. Tchr. English Horseheads (N.Y.) Ctrl. Schs., 1964-67, Shenendehowa Ctrl. Schs., Clifton Park, N.Y., 1967-99, chairperson English, 1973-99. Adj. prof. tchr. edn. SUNY, Albany, 1988-91; supr. student tchrs. Coll. St. Rose, 2000-; chairperson Profl. Performance Rev. Com. Shenendehowa Ctrl. Sch., Clifton Park, 1991-93, 96-99; participant field tests Nat. Bd. Profl. Teaching Stds., U. Pitts., Conn., 1993; cons. Project Lead The Way. Contbr. articles to Schenectady Sunday Gazette. Eucharistic minister St. Edward's Cath. Ch., Clifton Park, N.Y., 1990—, faith formation com., 1989-92; host chairperson Am. Field Svc.

Shenendehowa Pub. Libr., Clifton Park, 1980-85, bd. trustees, v.p., 1994-95. Named Outstanding Educator Cornell U., 1990, Educator of Excellence award N.Y. State English Coun., 1997. Mem. ASCD, Shenendehowa PTA (Life), English Educators Assn. (treas. capital dist.). Roman Catholic. Avocations: classical music, collecting figurines, reading.

HUGHES, EUGENE MORGAN, university president; b. Scottsbluff, Nebr., Apr. 3, 1934; s. Ruby Melvin and Hazel Marie (Griffith) H.; m. Margaret Ann Romeo; children: Deborah Kaye, Greg Eugene, Lisa Ann; stepchildren: Jeff, Mark, Christi. Diploma, Neb. Western Coll., 1954; BS in Math. magna cum laude, Chadron State Coll., 1956; MS in Math., Kans. State U., 1958; PhD in Math., George Peabody Coll. for Tchrs., Vanderbilt U., 1968; LHD (hon.), No. Ariz. U., 1997, Chadron State Coll., 2003. Grad. asst. dept. math. Kans. State U., Manhattan, 1956-57; instr. math. Nebr. State Tchrs. Coll. at Chadron, 1957-58; asst. prof. math., head dept. Chadron State Coll., 1958-66, assoc. prof., 1966-69, prof. math., 1969-70, dir. rsch., 1965-66, asst. to the pres., 1966-68, dean adminstrn., 1968-70; grad. asst. dept. math. George Peabody Coll. for Tchrs., Nashville, 1962-63, 64-65, asst. to undergrad. dean, 1964, asst. to pres., 1964-65; instr. Peabody Demonstration Sch., 1963-64; prof. math. No. Ariz. U., Flagstaff, 1970-93, prof. math. emeritus, 1993—, dean Coll. Arts and Scis., 1970-71, provost univ. arts and sci. edn., 1971-72, acad. v.p., 1972-79, pres., 1979-93, pres. emeritus, 1993—; pres. Wichita State U., 1993-98, pres. emeritus, 1998—; interim pres. Ea. Ky. U., 2001; prs. Mus. No. Ariz., 2002—03. Cons. Nebr. Dept. Edn., 1966-70; mem. adv. bd. United Bank Ariz., 1980-82; mem. nat. adv. bd. Ctr. for Study of Sport in Society, 1990; mem. adv. bd. Bank IV, 1993-97; bd. dirs. NationsBank N.A. (Midwest), mem. adv. bd., 1997-98, bd. dirs. First State Bank. Mem. staff bd. trustees Nebr. State Colls., Lincoln, 1969-70; co-dir. workshop tchr. edn. North Cen. Assn. U. Minn., 1968-70; officer fed. ednl. programs, Nebr., Ariz., 1966-93; mem. Ariz. Commn. Postsecondary Edn.; bd. fellows Am. Grad. Sch. Internat. Mgmt., 1980-93; mem. Gov.'s Com. Quality Edn., Chadron Housing Authority, 1968-70, Pres.' Commn. NCAA; mem. Ariz. State Bd. Edn., 1982-87, 90-93, pres., 1992-93; mem. Flagstaff Summer Festival, Ariz. Coun. Humanities and Pub. Policy, Mus. No. Ariz., Grand Canyon coun, Boy Scouts Am.; chair Ariz. Leadership Adv. Coun., 1990-93; mem. Ariz. Town Hall; commr. Western Interstate Commn. for Higher Edn., 1992-93; mem. Gov.'s Strategic Partnership for Econ. Devel., 1992; mem. Christopher Columbus Quincentenary Commn., 1990-91; sec., mem. Wichita/Sedgwick Partnership for Growth, 1993-97, Wichita/Sedgwick County Employment Tng. Bd., 1993-96; bd. dirs. Kids Voting Kans., 1997-98, Mus. North Ariz., 2002-03; trustee Assn. Western Univs. Inc., 1997-98. Ariz. Acad. NSF fellow, 1963, 64; recipient Chief Manuelito award Navajo Tribe, 1976, Disting. Svc. award Chadron State Coll., 1982, Flagstaff Citizen of Yr., 1988, Disting. Math. Grad. award Kans. State U., 1990, Cmty. Svc. award, 1994; named Hon. Chmn. black Bd. Dirs., 1989, Outstanding Citizen, Wichita Soc. of Profl. Engrs., 1998, Kans. Soc. Profl. Engrs., 1998. Mem. Am. Assn. State Colls.and Univs. (past chmn. & mem. com. on grad. sties 1979—, bd. dirs., mem. com. on accreditation, 1980—, treas.), Math. Assn. Am. (vis. lectr. secondary schs. Western Nebr. 1962), North Cen. Assn. Colls.nd Secondary Schs. (coord. 1968-72, cons./evaluator 1977—), Nat. Coun. Tchrs. of Math., Wichita Area C. of C., Flagstaff C. of C., Blue Key, Golden Key, Masons, Elks, Rotary (past pres., Paul Harris fellow 1975), Pi Mu Epsilon, Phi Delta Kappa, Kappa Mu Epsilon, Phi Kappa Phi.

HUGHES, FRANK LOUIS, high school band director; b. Lakewood, N.J., July 18, 1948; s. H. George and Dorothy (Pulcrano) H.; m. Denise Dipoalo, Dec. 6, 1975; children: Lara, Susanne, Frank Jr., Kelly. BA in Music Edn., Trenton State Coll., 1970, MA in Music, 1973. Cert. music tchr., supr., N.J. Asst. band dir. Lakewood High Sch., 1970-73; music tchr. Brick (N.J.) Schs., 1973-74; asst. band dir. Toms River (N.J.) High Sch. N., 1974-79, band dir., 1979—. Bugler Monmouth Park Race Track, Oceanport, N.J., 1973—; adj. instr. Ocean County Coll., Toms River, 1991—; coord. N.J. All-State Band, 1978-79, 84-85, solo chmn., 1980-90; chmn. curriculum revision in fine arts Toms River Schs., 1988-89. Composer Dedication Mass, various band works. Musical dir. Dover Twp. Mcpl. Band, Toms River, 1979—; coach Toms River Softball, 1991—; mem. Toms River Centennial Com., 1991-92. Named Band Dir. of Yr. Nat. Band Dirs. Hall of Fame, 1991. Mem. NEA, N.J. Music Edn. Assn. (all-state procedures 1980-90), Toms River Edn. Assn. (bldg. rep. 1989-90), Music Educators Nat. Conf., Elks, Am. Fedn. Musicians, Phi Mu Alpha. Republican. Roman Catholic. Avocations: golf, bowling, coaching tennis, collecting christmas records. Home: 1135 Lakewood Rd Toms River NJ 08753-4170 Office: Toms River High Sch N Old Freehold Rd Toms River NJ 08753

HUGHES, HARRISON G. horticulture educator; BS, Eastern Ill. U.; PhD, Purdue U. Prof., Dept. Horticulture Colo. State U., Fort Collins. Recipient Outstanding Extension Educator award. Office: Colo State U Dept Horticulture and Landscape Arch 210 Shepardson Bldg 1173 Campus Delivery Fort Collins CO 80523-1173 Office Fax: 970-491-7745. E-mail: hghughes@lamar.colostate.edu.*

HUGHES, JOHN HAROLD, surgeon, educator; b. New Rochelle, N.Y., Feb. 17, 1936; s. Harold Tegai and Ida (Erickson) H.; m. Janet Gail Williams, Mar. 7, 1964; children: Stephen A.T., Megan Elizabeth, John E.Q. BA, Yale U., 1957; MD, Cornell U., 1961. Diplomate Am. Bd. Surgery. Intern in surgery St. Luke's Hosp., N.Y.C., 1961-62, resident in surgery, 1962-66; chief of surgery Ft. Benjamin Harrison, Indpls., 1966-67; surgeon Hardin Meml. Hosp., Kenton, Ohio, 1968-74; asst. prof., dir. clinics Med. Coll. Ohio, Toledo, 1974-77; assoc. prof., dir. emergency svcs. U. Ariz., Tucson, 1977-81; surgeon, prof. surgery Naval Hosp. Long Beach, Calif., 1982-85; surgeon Naval Hosp. Oak Knoll, Oakland, Calif., 1990-91; med. dir. Casa Grande (Ariz.) Clinic, 1992-93; pvt. practice Casa Grande, Ariz., 1993—2000. Clin. instr. surgery Columbia U., N.Y.C., 1965-66; lectr. U. Ariz., Tucson, 1981—; clin. prof. surgery USUHS, Bethesda. 1990-96, adj. prof., 1996—; lectr. U. Ariz., 2002-03; cons. Paxis, 2002—. Contbr. over 65 articles to profl. jours.; editor emergency medicine jour. Hosp. Medicine, 1979—90; editorial reviewer jour. Mil. Medicine, 1987—; book reviewer jour. Profl. Safety, 1981—. Commr. health Hardin County, Ohio, 1969-74; pres. Hardin County Med. Soc., Kenton, Ohio, 1973-74. Capt. USNR, 1982—. Grantee Nat. Cancer Inst., 1976, NIMH, 1979. Fellow ACS; mem. AAAS, Assn. Mil. Surgeons, Soc. Med. Cons. to Armed Forces (assoc.), Pima County Med. Soc., Tucson Surg. Soc., Nanotech. Cluster of So. Ariz., Sigma Xi. Presbyterian. Home: 7712 E Oakwood Cir Tucson AZ 85750-2338

HUGHES, KAYLENE, historian, educator; b. Modesto, Calif., Aug. 4, 1952; BA, Miami-Dade (Fla.) Jr. Coll., 1972, Fla. Internat. U., 1976; MA, Fla. State U., 1977, PhD, 1985. Intern Fla. State Dept. Archives Records Mgmt., Tallahassee, 1977; Claims Control Supr. Sys. Devel. Corp., Tallahassee, 1978-81; editl. asst. Fla. Hotel and Motel Jour., Tallahassee, 1983-85; dir. edn., rsch. mgr. Fla. Hotel and Motel Assn., Tallahassee, 1985-87; historian U.S. Army Aviation & Missile Command, Redstone Arsenal, Ala., 1987—. Grad. asst. Fla. State U., Tallahassee, 1976-77, tchg. asst., 1981-83; adj. instr. history John C. Calhoun C.C., Huntsville, Ala., 1990—. Author: Florida's Lodging Industry: The First 75 Years, 1987, The Missile's Red Glare, 1992, Redstone Army Airfield: A Tradition of Aviation Support, 1992, Redstone Arsenal's Role in Operation Desert Shield/Desert Storm, 1992; contbr. articles to jours. and newspapers. Grantee Fla. State U., 1983. Mem. Phi Alpha Theta (sec. 1982-85), Phi Theta Kappa. Home: 342 Pawnee Trl SE Huntsville AL 35803-2280 E-mail: kaylene.hughes@redstone.army.mil.

HUGHES, KENNETH G. elementary school educator; b. Colorado Springs, Colo., Feb. 12, 1952; s. George V. and Martha (Stark) H. BS in Elem. Edn., U. Pitts., 1983; MEd in Edn. Leadership, U. Ctrl. Fla., 1993. Cert tchr., Fla., Pa., Ohio; cert. Level 1 adminstrv., Fla. Head tchr. Learning Tree, Inc., Pitts., 1983-85; tchr. 1st grade, 3d grade, 4th grade Dr. Phillips Elem. Sch., Orlando, Fla., 1985-89; tchr. 1st grade, 4th grade McCoy Elem. Sch., Orlando, 1989-91; tchr. curriculum resource Dr. Phillips Elem. Sch., Orlando, 1991-95; 1st grade tchr. Windsor Elem. Sch., Elyria, Ohio, 1998—. Adult edn. ESOL, Mid-Fla. Tech. Inst., Orlando, 1990-91. Recipient Innovative Classroom Practices award-Orange County, Walt Disney World, 1991,92. Mem. Phi Delta Kappa (exec. bd. Golden Crescent chpt. 2000—). Home: 401 Starling Ct Elyria OH 44035-9320

HUGHES, LAUREL ELLEN, psychologist, educator, writer; b. Seattle, Oct. 30, 1952; d. Morrell Spencer and Eleanore Claire (Strong) Chamberlain; m. William Henry Hughes Jr., Jan. 27, 1973; children: Frank, Ben, Bridie. BA in Psychology, Portland State U., 1980, MS in Psychology, 1986; D in Clin. Psychology, Pacific U., 1988. Lic. psychologist, Oreg. Counselor Beaverton (Oreg.) Free Meth. Ch., 1982-85; psychotherapist Psychol. Svc. Ctr., Portland, Oreg., 1986, Psychol. Svc. Ctr. West, Hillsboro, Oreg., 1987-89; pvt. practice Beaverton, 1990—. Adj. mem. faculty Portland C.C., 1990-91, U. Portland, 1992—, CU/Seattle, 1993-95; vis. asst. prof. U. Portland, 1991-92; psychol. cons. children's weight control group St. Vincent's Hosp., Portland, 1991. Author: How to Raise Good Children, 1988, How to Raise a Healty Achiever, 1991, Beginnings and Beyond, 1996; contbr. articles to profl. jours. Tchr. Sunday sch. Beaverton Free Meth. Ch., 1983-88; mother helper Walker Elem. Sch., Beaverton, 1988-90, 92-93; foster parent Washington County, Oreg., 1976-77, 79-80; vol. disaster mental health svcs. ARC, 1993—. Mem. APA, Oreg. Psychol. Assn. (bd. dirs. 1990-91, editor jour. 1990-91). Avocations: knitting, gardening, football, reading. Office: 4320 SW 110th Ave Beaverton OR 97005-3014

HUGHES, MARY ALICE, adult education educator; b. Natchitoches, La. d. J. Wesley and Mary Odeal (Ferguson) Stephens; children: Cary Wendell, Andrea Michelle. BA, Northwestern State U., 1960, MEd, 1982, postgrad., 1984; doctoral studies in developmental edn./instrnl. systems and tech., Grambling State U., 1990—. Cert. tchr., La. Tchr. Caddo Parish-Linwood Jr. High Sch., Shreveport, La., 1960-64, St. Tammany Parish-Salmen High Sch., Slidell, La., 1967-69, Rapides Parish-Adult Edn. Ctr., Alexandria, La., 1971—; coord., tchr. JTPA Acad. Remediation High Sch. Program, Alexandria, La., 1991-93; tchr. La. Bus. Coll., Alexandria, La., 1987-89; coord., tchr. St. Frances Cabrini Hosp.: Workplace Literacy Project, Alexandria, La., 1991—. Staff assoc. tchr. tng., assessment team mem. diagnostic/prescriptive evaluations, Youth Challange Program, 1993; coord. Mobile Automated Learning Lab, 1994; mentor adult edn. and insvc. grant Northwestern State U., 1991, cons. tng. tchrs. adult learners grant, 1993, evaluator Adult Learning Project grant program, 1993—; tutor in field; evaluator grant proposals Bur. Adult and Cmty. Edn., Baton Rouge, 1992-94. Participant support projects Battered Women's Program, Alexandria, 1989—, Shepard Ctr., Alexandria, 1989—, Food Bank, 1993—; rep. Gov.'s Forum on Literacy in the Workforce in Yr. 2000, Baton Rouge, 1991. Named Tchr. of Yr., La. Assn. Pub. Community and Adult Educators, 1987-88, named to Nat. Dean's List, 1991; recipient All Am. Scholar award U.S Achievement Acad., 1990. Mem. ASCD, La. Assn. Pub. Community and Adult Educators (state bd. dirs. 1981-88, state conv. coord. 1986), Assoc. Profl. Educators of La., Phi Delta Kappa, Kappa Kappa Iota. Methodist. Avocations: redesigning jewelry, playing piano, collecting carousels, nurturing houseplants. Home: PO Box 1382 Natchitoches LA 71458-1382 Office: 3441 Prescott Rd Alexandria LA 71301-3919

HUGHES, MICHAEL P. principal; BS in Social Studies/Secondary Edn., Kutztown State Coll., 1977; M in Secondary Edn., East Stroudsburg U., 1984; postgrad., Trenton State Coll., 1985, LaSalle U., 1997. Cert. social studies, tchr. of handicapped, adminstrv./prin., pupil pers. svcs., sch. adminstr. N.J., social studies, secondary prin., cert. of eligbility Pa. Prin. North Hunterdon H.S., 1998—; social studies tchr. Phillipsburg H.S., 1978—82, in-sch. suspension supr., 1980—83, tchr. of the handicapped, 1983—90, supr. spl. edn., 1987—90, acting adminstr. spl. svcs., 1989—90, dir. guidance svcs., 1990—91, ast. prin. for athletics and student activities, 1991—96, asst. prin. for curriculum, pers. and staff devel., 1996—98; prin. North Hunterdon H.S., 1998—. Mem.: NJSIAA (mem. exec. com., Hunterdon County rep. 2000—03, first v.p. 2002—03, pres. 2003—), Middle Atlantic States Assn. (validation team chair), Hunterdon County Adminstrs. Assn. (v.p. 2000—01), North Hunterdon - Voorhees Adminstrs. Assn., N.J. Prin. and Supr. Assn., Nat. Assn. Secondary Sch. Prins., North Hunterdon Rotary Club, Phi Delta Kappa (Lehigh Univ. chpt., v.p. programs Lehigh U. 1998—2000). Home: 4 Barberry Ln Easton PA 18045*

HUGHES, PATRICIA E. secondary education educator; b. Duluth, Minn., Jan. 11, 1940; d. Earl H. and Bernice Ione (Fuhrman) Dahlgren; m. Warren G. Hughes, June 1, 1958; children: Sherri, David, Michael. BS, Bemidji State U., 1967, MS, 1982. English tchr. Blackduck (Minn.) Pub. Sch., 1967-68; English tchr., German I, II mid. level Kelliher (Minn.) Sch., 1969—. Contbr. articles to profl. jours. Recipient Tchr. Achievement award Ashland Oil Co.; named to Minn. Honor Roll of Tchrs., 1993, Bemidji State U. Tchr. of Yr. Hall of Fame, 1998, Minn. Middle Level Educator of Yr., 2000. Mem. NEA, Nat. Coun. Tchrs. English, Minn. Coun. Tchrs. English, Minn. Edn. Assn., Minn. Coun. Tchrs. Fgn. Lang., Kelliher Edn. Assn. Home: 39085 Shiloh Dr NE Kelliher MN 56650-0059

HUGHES, ROBERT JOSEPH, vocational school educator; b. Phila., Nov. 17, 1944; s. Robert Joseph Sr. and Catherine Mary (Frederickson) H. BS, St. Joseph's U., 1968; MEd, Temple U., 1983, EdD, 1993. Cert. vocat. edn. tchr., Pa., tchr. data processing office tchs., Pa.; cert. elem. and secondary prin., Pa. Tchr. Sch. Dist. Phila., 1969-87, vocat. tchr., 1987—. Adj. tchr. Computers for Educators, St. Joseph's U., 1994—, adj. tchr. mgmt. info. sys. Charles Nash fellow Temple U., 1990, Samuel Caplan Meml. award, 1993, Epsilon Delta Epsilon award, 1993. Fellow Phi Delta Kappa (bd. dirs. 1991-92); mem. Am. Vocat. Assn., Pa. Vocat. Assn. (bd. dirs. Harrisburg chpt. 1989—), KC (4th degree color corp. 1980-85), Omicron Tau Theta (pres. Temple U. chpt. 1989-90, 94-95). Roman Catholic. Avocations: travel, dance, movies, sports, reading. Home: 1923 Fitzgerald St Philadelphia PA 19145-3612

HUGHES, THOMAS J.R. mechanical engineering educator, consultant; b. Bklyn., Aug. 3, 1943; s. Joseph Anthony and Mae (Bland) H.; m. Susan Elizabeth Weh, July 1, 1972; children: Emily Susan, Ian Thomas, Elizabeth Claire. B.M.E., Pratt Inst., Bklyn., 1965; M.M.E., Pratt Inst., 1967; MA in Math., PhD in Engrng. Sci., U. Calif.-Berkeley, 1974. Mech. design engr. Grumman Aerospace, Bethpage, N.Y., 1965-66; mgr. R & D Gen. Dynamics, Groton, Conn., 1967-69; lectr., asst. rsch. engr. U. Calif., Berkeley, 1975-76; assoc. prof. structural mechanics Calif. Inst. Tech., Pasadena, 1976-80; assoc. prof. mech. engring. Stanford U., Calif., 1980-82, prof., 1983—, chmn. divsn. applied mechanics, 1984-88, 94—, chmn. dept. mech. engring., 1988-89; founder, chmn. CENTRIC Engrng. Sys., Inc., 1990-99. Galileo vis. prof. Scuola Normale Superiore, Pisa, Italy, 1999; Eshbach vis. prof. Northwestern U., 2000; cons. in field. Author: A Short Course in Fluid Mechanics, 1976, Mathematical Foundations of Elasticity, 1983, The Finite Element Method: Linear Static and Dynamic Finite Element Analysis, 1987, Computational Inelasticity, 1998; editor: Nonlinear Finite Element Analysis of Plate and Shells, 1981, Computational Methods in Transient Analysis, 1983; editor Jour. of Computer Methods in Applied Mechanics and Engrng., 1980—; contbr. numerous articles to profl. jours. Recipient Computational Mechanics prize Japan Soc. Mech. Engrs., 1993. Fellow AAAS, ASME (Melville medal 1979, Worcester Reed Warner medal 1998), AIAA (assoc.), Am. Acad. Mechanics, U.S. Assn. Computational Mechanics (pres. 1990-92, von Neumann medal 1997), Nat. Acad. Engrng; mem. ASCE (Huber prize 1978), Internat. Assn. Computational Mechanics (pres. 1998-2002, Gauss-Newton medal), Sigma Xi, Phi Beta Kappa. Office: U Tex at Austin 1 University Sta C0200 201 E 24th St ACES 6 412 Austin TX 78712-0027

HUGHES, WILLIAM FRANCIS, JR., educational consultant; b. Altoona, Pa., Dec. 5, 1941; s. William Francis Hughes Sr. and Anna Martha (Burgoyne) Burgoon; m. Jocelyn Ursula Gonano, June 10, 1963 (div. Aug. 1978); children: William Joseph, Jennifer Allison; m. Kathleen Rose Chobody, Apr. 21, 1979. BS in Edn., Ind. U., Pa., 1963; postgrad., Yale U., 1967; MS in Teaching of Sci., Coll. William and Mary, 1970; cert. in multi-variant analysis, Ohio U., 1973. Tchr. physics Altoona Area Sch. Dist., 1963-70; from asst. dir. rsch. to dir. rsch. Pa. State Edn. Assn., Harrisburg, 1971-81, asst. exec. dir. rsch., 1989-96, asst. exec. dir. tech. support, 1981-88; pres. Keystone Rsch. Ctr., Harrisburg, 1996—. Recipient Excellence in Sch. Fin. Rsch. award State Edn. Rsch. Staff Assn., 1979. Mem. NEA (life), Am. Edn. Fin. Assn. (bd. dirs.), Nat. Tax Assn., Pa. State Edn. Assn. (life), Alliance for Sch. Aid Partnership (steering com. 1987-96), World Future Soc. Democrat. Presbyterian. Avocations: travel, investing in collectibles, music. Home and Office: 69 Fairway Dr Camp Hill PA 17011-2065

HUGO, NANCY, county official, alcohol and drug addiction professional; b. Cedar Rapids, Iowa, May 4, 1944; d. Roger S. and Phyllis Anita (Wenger) Conrad; m. Marshall G. Hugo (div.), Apr. 5, 1968; 1 child, Andrea. BS, Drake U., 1966; MS, Pepperdine U., 1987; adminstrn. credential, U. Calif., Irvine, 1989. Cert. adminstr., middle sch. educator, Calif. Tchr., asst. prin. Ocean View Sch. Dist., Huntington Beach, Calif., 1966-90; coord. alcohol and drug prevention edn., tobacco use prevention edn., sch. crisis response, program mgr. juvenile ct. schs. drug and alcohol programs Orange County Dept. Edn., Costa Mesa, Calif., 1990—, coord. phys. edn., 1991-93, coord. bus. edn. partnership, 1993-95. Author: No Butts...About Quitting Tobacco Use, A Tobacco Cessation Program, 1995; co-author: Snuff Out Teen Tobacco and Nix Spit, 1994. Mem. ASCD, NEA, Assn. Calif. Sch. Adminstrs., Calif. Edn. Assn., Calif. Assn. Health Phys. Edn. Recreation and Dance, Calif. Tchrs. Assn. Home: 93 Stanford Ct Irvine CA 92612-1671 Office: Orange County Dept Edn 200 Kalmus Dr Costa Mesa CA 92626-5922

HUHEEY, JAMES EDWARD, chemist, herpetologist and educator; b. Cin., Aug. 2, 1935; s. Edward O'Neill and Catherine (Smythe) H. BS, U. Cin., 1957; MS, U. Ill., 1959, PhD, 1961. Rsch. assoc. U. Mich., Ann Arbor, 1961; asst. prof. chemistry Worcester (Mass.) Poly. Inst., 1961-65; asst. prof. U. Md., College Park, 1965-68, assoc. prof., 1968-75, prof., 1975-98, U. Tenn., Knoxville, 1998—. Vis. prof. So. Ill. U., Carbondale, 1974-75, 89-90, UCLA, 1986, U. Tenn., Knoxville, 1998; pres., dir. Chem. Assocs. Md. Author: Inorganic Chemistry: Principles of Structure and Reactivity, 1972, 4th edit. 1993, (with Arthur Stupka) Amphibians and Reptiles of Great Smoky Mountains National Park, 1968, Diversity and Periodicity: An Inorganic Module, 1973, 78; contbr. articles to profl. jours. Recipient Young Chemists award D.C. chpt. Am. Inst. Chemists, 1971, Leo Schubert Teaching award, 1983; NSF grantee, 1965-67, 75-77, 78—; NSF fellow, 1959, duPont Teaching fellow, 1960; Sigma Xi grantee, 1963, Am. Philos. Soc. grantee, 1974. Fellow AAAS; mem. Am. Chem. Soc., Am. Soc. Ichthyologists and Herpetologists, Soc. Study Amphibians and Reptiles (dir.), Herpetologists League, Ecol. Soc. Am., Soc. Study Evolution. Home: Sourwood Mountain 215 Tucker Ln Lenoir City TN 37771-3405

HUIZER, EVELINE MARINA, special education educator; b. Schiedam, The Netherlands, May 26, 1966; came to U.S. 1977; d. Jan and Edith M. (Pacejka) H. AS, Vincennes (Ind.) U., 1987; BS, Ind. State U., 1989. Tchr. E.C.L.C. Daycare, Indpls., 1988; substitute tchr. Indpls. Pub. Schs., 1990, learning disabilities tchr., 1991—, tchr. inclusion/resource. Mem. Dutch Reformed Ch. Avocations: reading, horses, swimming, movies. Home: 2232 Braeburn East Dr Indianapolis IN 46219-2541 Office: Sch 15 2302 E Michigan St Indianapolis IN 46201-3198

HUJSAK, RUTH JOY, musician, educator; b. Buffalo, May 13, 1924; d. Frederic Cecil and Elfrieda (Fell) Detenbeck; m. Edward Josef Hujsak, June 27, 1953; children: Michael Kim, Jonathan Todd. MusB, U. Rochester, 1945. Cert. piano tchr. Instr. piano, organ, theory Marion (Va.) Coll., 1945-46; pianist Miss. State U. for Women, Columbus, 1946-47; pvt. music studio, concert work Kenmore, N.Y., 1947-53; lectr. harp U. Calif. San Diego, La Jolla, 1968-95; instr. harp San Diego State U., 1970-84; lectr. harp Point Loma Nazarene U., San Diego, 1977-95; instr. harp U. San Diego, 1980-84. Fellow Ctr. Mus. Experiment, U. Calif., San Diego, 1974; bd. dirs. Friends of Music, 1990—; propr. Mina-Helwig Co., 1976—; CEO Perigee West Co., 1989-95. Composer harp music, 1975—; contbr. articles to mags. Mem. music com. La Jolla Presbyn. Ch., 1980-92, also elder; past v.p. Cmty Music Sch. Buffalo. Recipient scholarship Schmitz Sch. Piano, 1948. Mem. Musicians Assn. San Diego, Chromatic Club Buffalo (life, pres. 1950), Mus. Merit Soc. San Diego (bd. dirs.), Am. Harp Soc. (chmn. religious music com., pres. San Diego chpt.), World Harp Congress, Sigma Alpha Iota (life). Republican. Avocations: reading, cooking, health foods. Home: 8732 Nottingham Pl La Jolla CA 92037-2128

HULCE, MARTIN RUSSELL, chemistry educator; b. Balt., Apr. 15, 1956; BS, Butler U., 1978; MA, Johns Hopkins U., 1980, PhD, 1983. Rsch. chemist E.I. du Pont de Nemours and Co., Wilmington, Del., 1983-85; asst. prof. U. Md. Balt. County, 1985-91; assoc. prof. Creighton U., Omaha, 1991—2002, prof., 2002—. Author: (book chpt.) Studies in Natural Products Chemistry, 1991, Comprehensive Organic Synthesis, 1991, Organic Reactions, vol. 38, 1990, Macmillan's Ency. of Chemistry; contbr. articles to profl. jours. Grantee Am. Cancer Soc., 1989-91, Petroleum Rsch. Fund, 1986-89, 92-94, Rsch. corp., 1993-95, NSF, 1993-96, 95-98; recipient RFK Meml. Student award for Tchg. Achievement, Creighton U. Mem. AAAS (pres., southwestern and mnt. divn., 2003), Am. Chem. Soc., Neb. Acad. Scis., mem. Nebr. Biomed. Rsch., Infrastructure Network Steering Com. Phi Kappa Phi, Sigma Xi, Omicron Delta Kappa. Achievements include research on chemistry of extended conjugated mixed hybridization state compounds, on ambiphilicity of allenyl enolates, and on tandem geminal dialkylation. Office: Creighton Univ Dept of Chem 2500 California Plz Omaha NE 68178-0001

HULL, CHARLES WILLIAM, retired special education educator; b. East St. Louis, Ill., Feb. 23, 1936; s. William Semple Hull and Jessie Marie (Brennan) Poole; m. Beverly Kay Julian, Aug. 19, 1967; 1 child, William Kenneth. BA in Econs., Cen. Meth. Coll., 1964; MEd, Olivet Nazarene Coll., 1974; AA (hon.), Joliet Jr. Coll., 1987. Tchr. elem. grades Taft Sch., Lockport, Ill., 1965-67; tchr. spl. edn. S.W. Cook County Coop. Assn. for Spl. Edn., Oak Forest, Ill., 1967-99; ret., 1999. Permanent exhibits include Tchr's Ret. Office Bldg., Springfield, Ill. Past bd. dirs., v.p., chmn. fund raising Easter Seals Will and Grundy Counties; dist. leader Am. Cancer Soc., 1984, residential campaign chmn., 1985; vol., mem. adv. bd. Big Bros.-Big Sisters Will County; Cub Scouts com. chmn. Boy Scouts Am., 1980-81, commr. Rainbow coun., bd. dirs. troop 6l; choir, past trustee Faith United Meth. Ch.; Will County walkathon chmn. March of Dimes, 1979; chmn. Canal Days events Will County Hist. Soc., 1987; mem. Nat. Trust for Hist. Preservation, Lockport Area Geneal. Hist. Soc.; bd. dirs. Joliet Project Pride, Will County Project Pride, 2000-03; life mem. Friends of Ill. and Mich. Canal. Cpl. USMC, 1955-58. Recipient Congl. Medal of Merit, 1985, Frederick Bartleson Meml. award Will County Hist. Soc., 1985, Citizen of Week award Sta. WBBM, Chgo., 1985, Leadership award Am. Cancer Soc., 1985, Outstanding Svc. award Big Bros.-Big Sisters Will County, letter of commendation Pres. of U.S., 1986, 89, Disting. Svc. award Joliet Jr. Coll., 1987, Citizen of Month award Southtown Economist, plaque KC; inducted into Joliet/Will County Hall of Pride, 2002. Mem. 1st Marine Divsn. Assn.,

Coalition for Citizens with Disabilities in Ill. (life), Will County Old-Timers Baseball Assn., Am. Legion, Masons (32 degree), Shriners (pres. Joliet club 1983, Shriner of Yr. 1989), KC, Medina Temple, Cumberland Scottish Rite Club, Lions (pres. Manhattan club 1984, chmn. youth and fgn. exch. dist. 1986-87, bd. dirs. Lockport chpt.), Will County Hist. Soc. (pres. 1989), Joliet Area Ret. Tchrs. Assn., Ill. Ret. Tchrs. Assn., Pleasant Hill Hist. Soc., Royal Order Scotland. Republican. Methodist. Home: PO Box 429 Pleasant Hill TN 38578

HULL, DAVID GEORGE, aerospace engineering educator, researcher; b. Oak Park, Ill., Mar. 27, 1937; s. John Lawrence Hull and Elizabeth Christine (Carstensen) Meyer; m. Meredith Lynn Kiesel, June 2, 1962 (div. July 1980); children: David, Andrew, Matthew; m. Vicki Jan Poole, June 30, 1983; children: Katherine, Emily. BS, Purdue U., 1959; MS, U. Wash., 1962; PhD, Rice U., 1967. Staff assoc. Boeing Sci. Research Labs., Seattle, 1959-64; research assoc. Rice U., Houston, 1964-66; asst. prof. U. Tex., Austin, 1966-71, assoc. prof., 1971-77, prof., 1977-85, M.J. Thompson Regents prof., 1985—. Cons. several aerospace cos. Assoc. editor 2 jours.; reviewer several engring. jours.; contbr. more than 55 articles to profl. jours. Recipient/co-recipient more than 50 grants and contracts; recipient award Best paper, AAS/AIAA Space Flt. Mechanics Conf., Albuquerque, 1995. Mem. AIAA (assoc. fellow, atmospheric flight mechanics tech. com. 1974-77, guidance and control tech. com. 1984-87), AAS (sr. mem.), Delta Tau Delta (treas. Purdue U. 1958-59). Office: U Tex ASE/EM C0600 Austin TX 78712-0235

HULL, DONNIE FAYE, special education director, educator; b. New Orleans, Apr. 15, 1945; d. Henry Frank and Laura (Mack) H. BA, So. U. A&M Coll., 1966, MEd, 1970; postgrad., La. State U., 1974, Southeastern La. U., 1974. Tchr. East Baton Rouge Sch. System, 1966-77, ednl. strategist, 1977-79, instructional specialist, 1979-81, supr. spl. edn., 1981-84, dir. spl. edn., 1984—. La. rep. to exchange program in Italy, 1991. Mem. exec. bd. March of Dimes, Baton Rouge, 1985—; pres. sr. choir Greater Phila. Bapt. Ch., Sunday sch. tchr., sponsor young adult choir; coord. spl. programs and events Young Women's Christian Auxiliary, sponsor community outreach ministry. Named one of Outstanding Educators, YWCA, 1981, Outstanding Leaders, Greater Phila. Bapt. Ch., 1984, Outstanding Vol. for La. Spl. Olympics, 1994; recipient Outstanding Tchr. award East Baton Rouge Parish Edn. Assn., 1973, Outstanding Leadership in Adminstrn. award 1990, Outstanding Adminstr. of Yr. award So. U., 1990. Mem. Nat. Assn. State Dirs. of Spl. Edn., Coun. for Exceptional Children, Found. for Exceptional Children, La. Assn. State Dirs. of Spl. Edn., La. Assn. Spl. Edn. Adminstrs., La. Sch. Suprs.' Assn., So. U. A&M Coll. Alumni Fedn. (life), La. Assn. Sch. Execs., Phi Delta Kappa (Disting. Svc. award 1990), Zeta Phi Beta (life, Mu Zeta chpt., asst. sec., chaplain, v.p., mem. exec. bd., pres. 1985-88, projects dir. so. region, regional life mem. dir., nat. dir. leadership devel., regional model chpt. coord., Pres. Svc. award 1988). Democrat. Baptist. Avocations: reading, shopping, travel, collecting angels. Home: PO Box 321 Zachary LA 70791-0321

HULL, ELIZABETH ANNE, retired English language educator; b. Upper Darby, Pa., Jan. 10, 1937; d. Frederick Bossart and Elizabeth (Schmik) H.; m. Dean Carlyle Beery, Feb. 5, 1955 (div. 1962); children: Catherine Doria Beery Pizarro, Barbara Phyllis Beery Wintczak; m. Frederik Pohl, July 1984. Student, Ill. State U., 1954-55; AA, Wilbur Wright Jr. Coll., Chgo., 1965; B in Philosophy, Northwestern U., 1968; MA, Loyola U., Chgo., 1970, PhD, 1975. Teaching asst. Loyola U., Chgo., 1968-71; prof. English, coord. honors program William Rainey Harper Coll., Palatine, Ill., 1971-2001; ret., 2001. Judge nat. writing competition Nat. Coun. Tchrs. of English, 1975-2002, John W. Campbell award, 1986—. Co-editor: (with F. Pohl) Tales from the Planet Earth; contbr. articles to profl. jours. Pres. Lexington Green Condominium Assn., Schaumburg, Ill., 1982-84; bd. dirs. Hunting Ridge Homeowner's Assn., Palatine, 1984-86; Dem. candidate for U.S. Ho. of Reps. for 8th Congl. Dist. Ill., 1996; bd. dirs. N.W. Cmty. Hosp. Aux., 2001-03; mem. steering com. Constituency on Vols. Ill. Hosp. Assn., 2001-03. Recipient Northwestern U. Alumni award for Merit, 1995, Thomas Clareson award Sci. Fictin Rsch. Assn., 1998, Excellence award Nat. Inst. for Staff and Orgnl. Devel., 1998. Mem. MLA, Midwest MLA, Popular Culture Assn., Sci. Fiction Rsch. Assn. (editor 1981-84, sec. 1987-88, pres. 1989-90), Ill. Coll. English Assn. (pres. 1975-77), World Sci. Fiction Assn. (N.Am. sec. 1978—, pres. Honors coun. Ill. region 1992-93), Palatine Area LWV (bd. dirs. 1991—, v.p. 1995-96, pres. 1998-2000), Am. Assn. for Women in C.C. (v.p. comm., bd. dirs. Harper Coll. chpt. 1993-96). Home: 855 Harvard Dr Palatine IL 60067-7026

HULL, GLYNDA, language educator; BA, Miss. U. for Women; PhD, U. Pitts. Co-editor (with Katherine Schultz): (book) School's Out! Bridging Out-of-School Literacies with Classroom Practice, 2002; author: Changing Work, Changing Workers: Critical Perspectives on Language, Literacy, and Skills, 1997; co-author (with J. Gee et al): The New Work Order: Behind the Language of the New Capitalism, 1996. Recipient Richard Braddock Meml. award for best article of yr. (2), Coll. Composition and Comm., award for best article reporting qualitative or quantitative rsch. related to tech. or sci. comm., Nat. Coun. Tchrs. English, 2001. Office: U Calif Berkeley Dept Edn 5629 Tolman Berkeley CA 94720-1670*

HULL, LOUISE KNOX, retired elementary educator, administrator; b. May 24, 1912; d. William E. and Ruby Joe (Bradshaw) Knox; m. Berrien J. Hull, Jan. 1, 1953. BS in Edn., S.W. Mo. State U., 1933; postgrad., U. Colo., 1939, Northwestern U., 1945; MA in Edn., NYU, 1951. Cert. elem. and secondary tchr., Mo. Elem. tchr. R12 Sch. Dist., Springfield, 1936-70, supr. tchr., 1956-70, mem. adv. com. to supt., 1955-57; ret., 1970. Chmn. Christian edn. com. Westminster Presbyn. Ch., 1953-66, trustee, 1983-86, chmn. bd. trustees, 1986, circle chmn., 1986-89, mem. women's adv. bd., 1987-89, rep. witness and fin. com., 1990, pres. Women of Ch., 1970-73, 90-92, pres. bd. trustees, 1983-86; life mem. Wilson Creek Found., Springfield, 1954-67; sec. greene County Hist. Soc., Springfield, 1960-96, also life mem.; mem. Springfield Little Theater Guild, 1970—, Hist. Preservation Soc., Springfield, 1980—; docent Mus. of Ozarks, Springfield, 1976-85; chmn. dist. III, John Calvin Presbytery, 1974-76, sec., 1977-80; vol. St. John's Regional Med. Ctr., 1970-78. Mem. Springfield Ret. Tchr. Assn. (life), Mo. Ret. Tchr. Assn. (life), Ozarks Genealogy Soc. (sec. 1985-87, pub. info. rep. 1987-89), DAR, Mo. Fedn. Women's Clubs (chmn. home life com. 1986-89), Springfield City Fedn. Women's Club (pres. 1990-92), Brige Dept. of Sorosis, 1995-2003; Audubon Dept. of Sorosis; Sorosis Club (pres. Springfield 1980-82, chmn. hobby dept. 1986-88, 94-96, chmn. fine arts dept. 1988-90, mem. perpetual endowment com. 1992-96, chmn. 1994, parliamentarian 1998-2000, chmn. Audubon dept. 2000-02, sec. bridge dept. 1995—), Ch. Women United, Alpha Delta Pi (treas. house corp. 1932-60), Alpha Delta Kappa (sec. 1965-67, corr. sec. Psi chpt. 1990-92).

HULL, MARGARET RUTH, artist, educator, consultant; b. Dallas, Mar. 27, 1921; d. William Haynes and Ora Carroll (Adams) Leatherwood; m. LeRos Ennis Hull, Mar. 29, 1941; children: LeRos Ennis, Jr., James Daniel. BA, So. Meth. U., Dallas, 1952; postgrad., So. Meth. U., 1960-61; MA, North Tex. State U., 1957; postgrad., R.I. Sch. Design, 1982. Art instr. W.W. Bushman Sch., Dallas Ind. Sch. Dist., 1952-57, Benjamin Franklin Jr. High Sch., Dallas, 1957-58, Hillcrest H.S., Dallas, 1958-61, dean, pupil personnel counselor, 1961-70; designer, coord. curriculum writing visual art cluster Skyline H.S., Dallas, 1970-76; developer curriculum writing/writing art cluster Booker T. Washington Arts Magnet H.S., Dallas, 1976-82, coord. visual arts careers cluster, 1976-82, artist, ednl. cons., 1982-96. Tchr. children's painting Dallas Mus. Fine Art, 1956-70; mus. reprodns. asst. Dallas Mus. Art, 1984-93. Group shows include Dallas Mus. Fine Arts, 1958, Arts Magnet Faculty Shows, 1978-82, Arts Magnet H.S., Dallas Art Edn. Assn. Show, 1981, D'Art Membership Show, Dallas, 1982-83; represented in pvt. collections. Trustee Dallas Mus. Art, 1978—84; vol. League Dallas Mus. Art, 1982—2002. Mem. Tex. Designer/Craftsmen, Craft Guild Dallas, Fiber Artists Dallas, Dallas Art Edn. Assn., Tex. Art Edn. Assn., Nat. Art Edn. Assn., Dallas Counselors Assn. (pres. 1968), Delta Delta Delta.

HULL, MARION HAYES, communications educator, researcher; b. Bronx, N.Y., Feb. 23, 1940; d. David Vernon and Jessie C. (Summerville) Hayes; m. Bernard Samuel Hull, Aug. 24, 1974; children: Karla Williams, Bernard S. II. BJ, L.I. U., 1961; MA in TV Writing, NYU, 1967; PhD in Polit. Sci., Am. U., 1996. Instr. Norfolk (Va.) State U., 1967-70; asst. prof. Shaw U., Raleigh, N.C., 1970-72; comm. specialist U.S. Dept. Justice, Washington, 1972-73; dir. telecom. programs Booker T. Washington Found., Washington, 1973-82; asst. prof. comm. Howard U., Washington, 1982—. Newscaster Sta. WAVY-TV, Portsmouth, Va., 1969-70; U.S. del. The World Adminstn. Radio Conf., (plan. com.) Washington, 1978-79; vis. scholar Rand Afrikaanse U., 1998. Author: (chpt.) Public-Cable Handbook, 1975-76; mem. editl. adv. bd. The Montgomery Times, 1990—; contbr. articles to profl. periodicals. Cmty. amb. City of Raleigh (N.C.), Sweden, 1971; exch. amb. Expt. Internat. Living, 1972—; com. Maryland Pub. Broadcasting Commn., 1998—; mem. The White House Conf. Minority Ownership, Washington, 1973; mem. cable comm. adv. com. Montgomery County (Md.) Govt., 1982-86, chmn. consumer adv. bd., 1989-95; chair clubs and orgns. United Negro Coll. Fund, Washington, 1989—; spkr. Montgomery County Pub. Schs., 1992—; bd. dirs., pres. Leadership Montgomery, 1996—. Recipient Excellence in Svc. award United Negro Coll. Fund, 1994, grad. Leadership Montgomery, 1995, Disting. Leadership award, Sprint and Nat. Assn. for cmty. leadership; Ford Found. grantee, 1968. Mem. Assn. Edn. Journalism and Mass Comm. (accreditation chair 1994—, vice chair commn. on status of minorities), Women's Inst. Freedom of the Press, Capital Press Club (pres., Leadership award 1977), Alpha Kappa Alpha (pres. local chpt. 1980-85, advisor to undergraduates 1990—, Leadership award 1984). Democrat. Baptist. Office: Howard U Sch Comm 525 Bryant St NW Washington DC 20059-0001

HULL, MARY FRANCES, elementary school educator; b. Valdosta, Ga., Jan. 30, 1955; d. Albert and Elizabeth (Fuller) Jennings; widowed; 1 child, Jimmy Karl III. BS in Elem. Edn., Midwestern State U., 1978; M Elem. Edn., Troy State U., 1987. Cert. elem. and lang. arts tchr., Ala. Title 1 chpt. 1 tchr. Robinson Springs Elem. Sch., Millbrook, Ala., 1978-81; elem. chpt. 1 tchr. Millbrook Mid. Sch., 1981-83, 4th grade lang. arts tchr., 1983—. Asst. brownie troop leader Girl Scouts U.S., Holtville, Ala., 1994. Mem. NEA, Ala. Edn. Assn., Elmore County Edn. Assn. Methodist. Avocation: reading. Home: PO Box 623 Millbrook AL 36054-0623

HULL, ROGER HAROLD, academic administrator; b. NYC, June 18, 1942; s. Max Harold and Magda Mary (Stern) H.; children: Roberto Franklin, Lincoln Macgregor. AB cum laude, Dartmouth Coll., 1964; LL.B., Yale U., 1967; LL.M., U. Va., 1972, SJD, 1974; LHD, Rockford Coll., 1988; LLD, Beloit Coll., 1992. Bar: N.Y. 1968. Assoc. firm White & Case, N.Y.C., 1967—71; spl. counsel to gov., Va., 1971—74; spl. asst. to chmn., dep. staff dir. Interagy. Task Force Law of Sea, NSC, 1974—76; v.p. devel. Syracuse U., 1976—79, v.p. devel. and planning, 1979—81; pres. Beloit (Wis.) Coll., 1981—90, Union Coll., Schenectady, 1990—; chancellor Union U., 1990—. Mem. U.S. del. Law of Sea Conf., 1974-76; adj. prof. Syracuse Univ. Law Sch., 1976-81; bd. visitors Coll. William and Mary, Williamsburg, Va., 1970-74; mem. pub. instns. task force Assn. Gov. Bds., 1975. Author: The Irish Triangle, 1976; co-author: Law and Vietnam, 1968. Co-founder, vice chair Schenectady 2000. Named Schenectady County Person of Yr., 1998, Patroon, 1999, Schnectady C. of C. Exec. of Yr., 2002 ; recipient Cmty. Leadership award, 1999. Mem. Am. Soc. Internat. Law, Univ. Club, Millbrook Golf and Tennis Club. Office: Union Coll Pres Office Schenectady NY 12308

HULL, WILLIAM EDWARD, theology educator; b. Birmingham, Ala., May 28, 1930; s. William Edward and Margaret (King) H.; m. Julia Wylodine Hester, July 26, 1952; children: David William, Susan Virginia. BA, Samford U., 1951; MDiv, So. Bapt. Theol. Sem., Louisville, 1954, PhD, 1960; postgrad., U. Gottingen, Germany, 1962-63, Harvard U., 1971. Ordained to ministry Bapt. Ch., 1950. Pastor Beulah Bapt. Ch., Wetumpka, Ala., 1950-51, Cedar Hill Bapt. Ch., Owenton, Ky., 1952-53, 1st Bapt. Ch., New Castle, Ky., 1953-58; from instr. to assoc. prof. So. Bapt. Theol. Sem., Louisville, 1954-67, prof., 1967-75, dean theology and provost, 1969-75; pastor 1st Bapt. Ch., Shreveport, La., 1975-87; provost Samford U., Birmingham, Ala., 1987-96, Univ. prof., 1987-2000, rsch. prof., 2000—. Author: Gospel of John, 1964, Broadman Bible Commentary, 1970, Beyond the Barriers, 1981, Love in Four Dimensions, 1982, The Christian Experience of Salvation, 1987, Southern Baptist Higher Education: Retrospect and Prospect, 2001, (with others): Professor in the Pulpit, 1963, The Truth That Makes Men Free, 1966, Salvation in Our Time, 1978, Set Apart for Service, 1980, Celebrating Christ's Presence Through the Spirit, 1981, The Twentieth Century Pulpit, Vol. II, 1981, Minister's Manual, 1983-87, 2000, 02, Biblical Preaching: An Expositor's Treasury, 1983, Preaching in Today's World, 1984, Heralds to a New Age, 1985, Getting Ready for Sunday: A Practical Guide for Worship Planning, 1989, Best Sermons 2, 1989, The University Through the Eyes of Faith, 1998, Southern Baptist Higher Education: Retrospect and Prospect, 2001; contbr. articles to profl. publs. Mem. Futureshape Shreveport (La.) Commn., 1985-87. Recipient Denominational Svc. award Samford U., 1974, Liberty Bell award Shreveport Bar Assn., 1984, Brotherhood and Humanitarian award NCCJ, 1987, Charles D. Johnson Outstanding Educator award Assn. So. Bapt. Colls. and Schs., 1999. Mem. Nat. Assn. Bapt. Profs. Religion (pres. 1967-68), Am. Acad. Religion, Soc. Biblical Lit., The Club (Birmingham), Vestavia Country Club (Birmingham), Rotary, Phi Kappa Phi, Phi Eta Sigma, Omicron Delta Kappa. Baptist. Home: 435 Vesclub Way Birmingham AL 35216-1357

HULLAH, ANN MARIE, elementary education educator; b. Buffalo, N.Y., Dec. 18, 1933; d. Paul and Ida (De Forest) Ronde; m. Eugene Henning, July 27, 1955 (dec. 1975); children: Anita Hasseler, Paul Henning, Karen Morris; m. Stanley Hullah, June 10, 1977; children: Stan Jr., Kris Kyle, Lynn Princl, Nocole Frances, Jacqueline, Les. BEd., Wis. State U., 1969; MST, U. Wis., Whitewater, 1981. Cert. elem. reading tchr., Wis. Tchr. Merrifield Sch., Milton, Wis., 1953-55, Crist Sch., Beloit, Wis., 1955-56, Turner Middle Sch., Beloit, 1970-91, reading specialist, 1981—; reading specialist, chpt. I Powers, Townview Schs., Beloit, 1991-95, ret., 1995. Team leader, reading curriculum writer Turner Middle Sch., Beloit, 1975—; lang. arts study group Turner Sch. Dist., Beloit, 1991-94. Organist Congregational Ch., Shopiere, Wis., 1960—. Recipient scholarshp Whitewater (Wis.) State Coll., 1951. Mem. ASCD, S. Kettle Moraine Reading Coun., Village and Valley Homemakers, Women of the Moose. Avocations: travel, music, golf, reading. Home: RR 1 Poplar Grove IL 61065-9801

HULSEY, RACHEL MARTINEZ, secondary school educator, columnist; b. Laredo, Tex., Jan. 30, 1950; d. Manuel Conrado and Julia (Solis) Martinez; children: John Travis, Marisa Andrea, Joseph Robert. BA, Our Lady of the Lake U., 1971; MA, U. Tex., 1977. Tchr. Harlandale Mid. Sch., San Antonio, 1971-77; reading supervisor Harlandale I.S.D., San Antonio, 1977-83; English tchr. Judson Ind. Sch. Tchr., San Antonio, 1983—; columnist SA Herald, 2002—. Writing trainer N.J. Writing Project in Tex., San Antonio, 1992—, reading trainer, 1995—, 6-Traits Trainer, 2001—, curriculum writer, 2001—; cons. in field. Mem. NEA, Tex. State Edn. Assn., San Antonio Romance Authors, Alamo Writers Assn. Roman Catholic. Avocations: writing, reading, collecting books, dancing, exercising.

HULTMAN, CAROL LINDA, middle school education educator; b. Janesville, Minn., Mar. 23, 1950; d. Henry Adolph and Margot (Kraft) Huelsnitz; m. John Kenneth Hultman, Aug. 3, 1974; children: Ann, Kristi, Lindsay. BS, U. Minn., 1972, MEd, 1984. Educator Ind. Sch. Dist. #624, White Bear Lake, Minn., 1972—. Coach Odyssey of the Mind. Recipient Golden Apple Achiever award Ashland (Ky.), Inc., 1996, 97; Tchr. Venture Fund grantee Edn. Ventures, Inc., 1992, 93. Fellow NEA. Nat. Sci. Tchrs. Assn., Minn. Edn. Assn.; mem. Gt. Explorations in Math. and Sci. (assoc.). Avocations: tennis, biking, skiing, coaching youth soccer, music. Office: Ctrl Middle Sch 4857 Bloom Ave Saint Paul MN 55110-2792

HULTMAN, CHARLES WILLIAM, economics educator; b. Oelwein, Iowa, Apr. 6, 1930; s. John William and Alma (Loeb) H.; m. Irene Oliver, June 7, 1957; children: Susan, Gregory. BA, Upper Iowa U., 1952; MA, Drake U., 1957; PhD, U. Iowa, 1960. Asst. prof. U. Ky., Lexington, 1960-64, prof. econs., 1967-98, chmn. dept., 1969-71, CSX prof. bus. and pub. policy, 1988-98, assoc. dir. Ctr. for Devel. Change, 1971-73, assoc. dean for rsch., 1976-85, prof. emeritus, 1998—; tchr. English, Luth. Ch., Pingxiang, China, summer 1999. Vis. assoc. prof. U. Calif., 1964-65, prof. of banking and fin. Univ. Coll., Dublin, Ireland, 1990; fall sememster Ford Found. prof. Fudan U., Shanghai, China, 1989. Author: International Finance, 1963, American Business and the Common Market, 1964, Problems of Economic Development, 1967, Ireland in the World Economy, 1969, (with M. Wasserman, R. Ware) International Economics, 1969, Comparison of Projected Unemployment Insurance Costs, 1973, The Environment of International Ban King, 1990; book rev. editor: Internat. Devel. Rev.; mem. editorial adv. bd. Sage Papers in Internat. Studies; assoc. editor internat. econs. Wall Street Rev. Books; acting editor: Jour. Growth and Change, 1979-86. Chmn. Ky. Coun.Econ. Advisors, 1976-85; mem. So. Growth Policies Bd., 1976-90. With U.S. Army, 1952-55. Fulbright lectr. Ireland, 1967-68 Mem. Eastern Econ. Assn. (exec. bd. 1980-84) Lutheran. Home: 3341 Crown Crest Rd Lexington KY 40517-2809

HUMBERD, DONNA SUE, retired social studies educator; b. Athens, Tenn., Apr. 7, 1949; d. Russell Hughes and Helen Jewell (Housley) H.; m. William P. Hemmings, Apr. 9, 1994; 1 stepchild, Julia Claire. BS, U. Tenn., 1971; MEd, Nicholls State U., 1980. Cert. secondary social studies tchr., adminstr. Tchr. McDonogh # 26 Jefferson Parish Schs., Gretna, La., 1971-76; tchr., dept. chair Worley Jr. H.S., Westwego, La., 1976-90; tchr. adult edn. Jefferson Parish Schs., Westwego, 1985-90; tchr., dept. chair J.Q. Adams Mid. Sch., Metairie, La., 1990-96; tchr. Riverdale H.S., Jefferson, La., 1997—2001, ret., 2001—. Mem. curriculum com. Sun King Exhbn., New Orleans, 1984; cons. Scott, Foresman and Co., 1985; reviewer Merrill Pub. Co., 1988, Instrnl. Design Assocs., Colo., 1988. Recipient Disting. Teaching award Advance Program for Young Scholars, Northwestern State U., 1994. Mem. Nat. Coun. for Social Studies. Avocations: gardening, baseball, cross-stitching, traveling, bird-watching.

HUMBYRD, SHIRLEY J. educational consultant, counselor, therapist; b. Allentown, Pa., July 28, 1951; d. Frederick H. and Julia (Davis) Kinsey; m. Danny E. Humbyrd, Jan. 26, 1974 (div. Jan. 1996); children: Casey Jo, Matthew, Chelsea, Zachary. BS, Huntington (Ind.) Coll., 1973; MA, U. Mich., 1977; MS, U. R.I., 1996. Cert. by Am. Counseling Assn., Am. Assn. Marriage and Family Therapy; lifetime guidance counselor. Vice-chairperson bd. mgmt. Kent County YMCA, 1993-95; guidance counselor WBCA, N. Kingstown, R.I., 1986-92, tchr., 1985-91; pres., founder Ednl. Interventions, E. Greenwich, R.I., 1992—; family therapist South Shore Mental Health Agy., 1995-97; guidance counselor Cranston (R.I.) pub. sch., 1997-98, Portsmouth (R.I.) pub. sch., 1998—. Mem. Jr. League, E. Greenwich, 1984-87; bd. dirs. Kent County YMCA, Warwick, R.I., 1985-95; children and youth dir. Bapt. Ch., N. Kingstown, 1986-92, dir. day campt, 1987-92; chairperson United Way Task Force on Teens, Warwick, R.I., 1990-91. Mem. Ortho Psychiat. Assn. (assoc.). Avocations: running, reading, rollerblading, bicycling. Home: 45 Hamilton Dr East Greenwich RI 02818-2108

HUME, HELEN DUNCAN, art educator; b. Kansas City, Kans., July 16, 1933; d. Edwin Wayne and Lula Evelyn (Johnson) Duncan; m. John Clyde Hume, Aug. 31, 1952; children: Susan Kay Hume Baker, David Duncan. Student, Kans. State U., 1951-52, U. Mo., St. Louis, 1970-71; BA, Webster U., 1973, MA, 1976. Cert. tchr. art, Mo. Instr. art, chair dept. Parkway West High Sch., St. Louis, 1973-79, 82—; tchr. art Sao Jose Internat. Sch., Sao Jose dos Campos, Brazil, 1979-82, Antwerp (Belgium) Internat. Sch., 1967-70, Florissant Valley C.C., St. Louis, 1992—97, Webster U., 1997—2002, Fontbonne U., 2002—. Author: Survival Kit for the Secondary Art Teacher, 1990, Art History and Appreciation Activities Kit, 1992, Am. Art Appreciation Activities Kit, 1996, The Art Teacher's Book of Lists, 2000, A Survival Kit for the Elementary/Middle School Art Teacher, 2001, The Art Lover's Almanac, 2003; contbr. articles to art jours. Mem. spl. com. edn. dept. St. Louis Art Mus., 1992, tchr. and youth programs adv. com., 1994—. Named Mo. Higher Art Educator of Yr., 2001. Mem. Nat. Art Edn. Assn., Greater St. Louis Art Suprs. (pres. 1989), St. Louis Artist's Guild (sec. 1989-92). Avocations: reading, golf, painting, theater, symphony.

HUME, SUSAN RACHEL, finance and economics educator; b. Englewood, N.J., Aug. 25, 1952; d. Philip and Anna Ann (Petrowski) Nachtigal; m. John Elliott Hume, Dec. 27, 1975; children: Philip John, Scot Elliott. BA, Douglass Coll., 1974; MBA, Rutgers U. Grad. Sch. Mgmt., 1976; PhD, CUNY, 2003. Bank analyst N.Y. Fed. Res. Bank, 1976-77, sr. credit analyst, 1977-79; sr. comml. loan officer 1st Pa. Bank, Phila., 1979-81; asst. v.p. Mfrs. Hanover Trust Co., N.Y.C., 1982-83, v.p., 1983-84, dept. head, hedge funding and asset liability mgmt., 1984-88; adj. assoc. prof. fin. and econs. Rider Coll., 1988-90; asst. adj. prof. Fairleigh Dickinson, Madison, N.J., 1991-93; adj. prof. dept. fin. and econs. Baruch Coll., N.Y.C., 1993—. Mem. Douglass Alumnae Endowment Fund Fin. Com., 1985—; pres. Douglass Coll. Class of 1974, 1990-; mem. internat. seminar interest rate risk mgmt. N.Y. Inst. Fin., N.Y.C., 1990-92. Mem. choir, Sunday Sch. tchr. Presbyn. Ch., Glendale; mem. investment com. Glendale Presbyn. Ch.; active Boy Scouts Am., PTO Cedar Hill and Ridge H.S.; former chairperson McGinn Elem. Sch. PTA Reading Program. Recipient Heller alumni award Rutgers U., 1976. Mem.: Beta Gamma Sigma.

HUMES, H(ARVEY) DAVID, nephrologist, educator; b. Honolulu, Nov. 20, 1947; s. William and Nancy Humes; m. Dolores Humes; 1 child, Michael David. BA, U. Calif., Berkeley, 1969; MD, U. Calif., San Francisco, 1973. Diplomate Am. Bd. Internal Medicine. Intern Moffit Hosp. and U. Calif. Hosps., San Francisco, 1973-74; resident U. Calif. Hosps., San Francisco, 1974-75; clin. fellow nephrology U. Pa. Hosp., Phila., 1975-76; rsch. fellow lab. kidney & electrolyte physiology Peter Bent Brigham Hosp., Boston, 1976-77; from instr. to asst. prof. medicine Peter Bent Brigham Hosp./Harvard Med. Sch., Boston, 1977-79; from asst. prof. to assoc. prof. internal medicine U. Mich., Ann Arbor, 1979-86, prof. internal medicine, 1986—, John G. Searle prof., chmn. internal medicine, 1996-2000; founder, gen. ptnr., mgr. EpiGenesis, LLC; founder, dir., chief sci. officer Nephros Therapeutics, Inc.; founder, pres. Innovative Biotherapies, Inc. Founder, pres. Innovative Biotherapies, Inc.; mem. sci. adv. bd. NephRx; cons. Sandoz Pharm., Bristol-Meyers-Squibb, Sterling-Winthrop, AmGen., Dow Chem.; dir., chief Nephrology Rsch. Labs., U. Mich., Ann Arbor, 1980-81; chief med. svc. VA Med. Ctr., Ann Arbor, 1983-96, chmn. internal medicine, 1996-2000. Editor: Current Opinion in Internal Medicine, 2001—; editor-in-chief: Kelley's Textbook of Internal Medicine, 1997—2001; mem. editl. bd. Am. Jour. Medicine, 1997—; mem. editl. bd.: Seminars in Nephrology, 1993—, Internat. Yearbook of Nephrology, 1989—; contbr. articles to profl. jours. Grantee Nat. Kidney Found., 1981-85, 87-88, PHS, 1987—, VA, 1982—. Am. Heart Assn., 1982-87, 94-95. Fellow: AAAS, ACP; mem.: Am. Soc. Artificial Internal Organs (trustee), Ctrl. Soc. Clin. Rsch. (past pres.), Nat. Kidney Found. Mich., Nat. Kidney Found. (Pres. award), Internat. Soc. Nephrology, Am. Fedn. Clin. Rsch., Am. Soc. Nephrology, Am. Heart Assn., Am. Soc. Clin. Investigation, Assn. Prof. Medicine, Am. Physiol. Soc., Phi Beta Kappa, Alpha Omega Alpha. Achievements include development of bioartificial kidney;

research in cellular basis of acute renal failure, biochemical basis of aminoglycoside-induced acute renal failure, cyclosporine nephrotoxicity, lipid alterations in ischemic acute renal failure, free-radical-induced mitochondrial injury, molecular basis of renal repair in acute renal failure, molecular basis of kidney tubulogenesis. Office: U Mich Med Sch Box 0644 7220 MSRB III 1150 W Medical Ctr Ann Arbor MI 48109

HUMITA, TIBERIUS TED, languages educator; b. Clui, Romania, Dec. 20, 1913; came to U.S., 1951, naturalized, 1956; s. Teodor and Teodosia (Abrudan) H.; m. Sophie Kisch, Sept. 20, 1954. Student U. Bucharest (Romania), 1937-39, U. Rome (Italy), 1946-50; BA, Wayne State U., 1958, MA in Polit. Sci., Tchrs. Coll., 1960, secondary teaching certificate, 1961. Sec., v.p. Romanian Polit. Refugee Welfare Com., Rome, Italy, 1948-50; worker, timekeeper, payroll clk. Chrysler Corp., Highland Park, Mich., 1951-60; tchr. fgn. langs. Detroit Pub. Schs., 1961-80. Corr., Romanian News America, Cleve., 1964—, Romanian cons. Greater Detroit Ethnic Group Project, 1968-75. Candidate, Mich. Constl. Conv., 1961; chmn. Romanian sect. nationalites div. Mich. Dem. Com., 1960—, v.p., 1965-66, treas., 1968-70. Contbg. mem. Iulia Maniu Found., N.Y., 1965—. Served to 1st lt. Romanian Army, 1939-40; polit. prisoner, Buchenwald, Germany, 1942-44. Recipient Service award Nationalites div. Mich. Dem. Com., 1967, M. Banciu award Romanian of Year, 1978, Aron Cotrus award, 1979, 1940 Moldova medal of Honor Romanian Am. Soc., 1993; Fonds European Secour Etud. Etranger, Switzerland scholar, 1949-50; Nat. Def. Edn. Act grantee N.Y. State U., 1963; Fed. grantee, P.R., 1966. Mem. Internat., Am. polit. sci. assns., Am. Fedn. Tchrs., Am. Acad. Polit. and Social Sci., Mich. Fgn. Lang. Assn., Anti-Defamation League. Editor Bull. Romanian Am. Nat. Com., Detroit, 1958-63; dir. sci. book exhibit Internat. Congress Dialectology. Louvain, Belgium, 1960. Home: 16424 Lincoln Ave Eastpointe MI 48021-3082

HUMMEL, MARILYN MAE, elementary education educator; b. Cleve., June 20, 1931; d. John Winfield and Meta E. (Timm) H. BS, Ohio U., 1953. Cert. elem. educator. Elem. tchr. Lakewood (Ohio) Bd. of Edn., 1953-83. Mem. Centennial Planning Com., Lakewood, Ohio 1989; vol. United Way, Lakewood Hosp. Jennings scholar, 1969-70; named Tchr. of the Yr., Franklin Sch., 1983. Mem.: Lakewood Hist. Soc., Kiwanis Club, Coll. Club West, Delta Kappa Gamma. Republican. Presbyterian.

HUMPHREY, CAMILLA MARIE, retired special education educator; b. Devils Lake, N.D., July 3, 1928; d. George O. and Annette Sophia (Monson) Loftness; m. Thomas Milton Humphrey, Dec. 26, 1950 (dec. Nov. 1992); children: Ana Oliva Johns, Marlena Marie Hensley. AA, Coll. Marin, 1948; student, U. Calif., Berkeley, 1948-49; BA in Edn., Pacific Luth. U., 1950; postgrad., U. Oreg., 1951-53, U. Nev., 1968. Cert. spl. edn. Oreg. Tchr. Albany (Oreg.) Elem. Sch., 1950-51; spl. edn. tchr. Children's Hosp. Sch., Eugene, Oreg., 1951-53, Eugene Jr. HS, 1953-54, Clark County Sch. Dist., Las Vegas, 1968-71; ret. Contbr. articles to profl. jours. Adv. world concerns children's issues, preservation natural beauty; bd. dirs. Adult Day Health Care, McKinleyville, 1994—95; nurse's aid Red Cross, Tripoli, Libya, 1958; fgn. rels. chmn. LWV, Carson City, Nev., 1963; mem. adv. bd. Salvation Army, Las Vegas, 1983—86; vol. English tchr. Luth. Mission, 1955—56; pres. Oil Wive's Club, Bogota, Colombia, 1956—57, Assistance League, Las Vegas, 1980—81; fin. sec. Gen. fedn. Women's Clubs, Las Vegas, 1983—84; vol. R.S.V.P., 1993—95, Thrift Store and Food Bank, McKinleyville, Calif., Patricks Point State Pk. Bookstore, Trinidad, Calif. Recipient 1st and 2d pl. photography award, Gen. Fedn. Women's Clubs, 1982, Nev. Short Story award, 1984, Vol. Svc. plaque, Help Ctr., Las Vegas, 1986, Silver Platter award, Evang. Luth. Ch. Am. Mission, Bogota, 1956. Mem.: DAV Aux., AAUW, Nat. Assitance League (at-large), Am. Polar Soc., Pacific Luth. U. Alumni Assn. Avocations: photography, reading, travel, art and sculpture, interior decorating. Home: 115 Maple Park Dr SE Olympia WA 98501-8701

HUMPHREY, DORIS DAVENPORT, publishing company executive, consultant, educator; b. Woodbury, Tenn., June 3, 1943; d. Luther and Gladys (Alexander) Davenport; m. John Sparkman Humphrey, Sept. 15, 1941 (dec.); children: Heather, Holly. BS, Middle Tenn. State U., 1965; MBE, Ga. State U., 1972, EdS, 1977, PhD, 1983; postgrad., Bryn Mawr Coll., 1989. Sec., coord. creative svcs., asst. to pres. Noble-Dury & Assocs., Nashville, 1965-69; asst. account exec. McCann-Erickson & Assocs., Atlanta, 1969-70; adj. and full-time instr. DeKalb C.C., 1970-79; coord. internship program Raymond Walters Coll., U. Cin., 1980-83, chmn. dept. office adminstrn., 1981-86; asst. dean bus. and office mgmt. Delaware County C.C., Media, Pa., 1987-90; pres. Career Solutions Tng. Group, Paoli, Pa., 1990. Lectr. in field; curriculum cons. Author: The Medical Office: A Reference Manual, 1997, Pediatric Associates, P.C., 2004, School to Work Series, 1994, 2001, Quick Skills Series, 2002; pub. Career Launcher, 1998, Reality, 1999, It's for Real, 2001, Hands on Academics, 2002, Data Entry for the Computer, 2004. Former trustee Harcum Coll., 1996—2002; elder Presbyn. Ch., 1999—2002; bd. dirs. Main Line C. of C. Mem. Nat. Bus. Edn. Assn., Am. Vocat. Assn., Friend Bus. Edn. State Pa., Delta Pi Epsilon. Presbyterian.

HUMPHREY, JOHN JULIUS, university program director, historian, writer; b. Booneville, Miss., Jan. 22, 1926; s. George Duke and Josephine (Robertson) H.; m. Mary Margaret Ryan, Jan. 19, 1949 (dec. June 1996); children: George Duke II, Laurie Ann. BS, Miss. State U., 1945; BA, U. Wyo., 1946, MA, 1964, postgrad., 1964-68, U. Ariz., 1969-71. Pres. J.J. Humphrey Co. Inc., Laramie, Wyo., 1947-68; lectr. History U. Ariz., Tucson, 1969-71, asst. dir. placement, 1969-70, dir. scholarships, awards, 1970-72, dir. office of scholarships and fin. aid, 1972-84, dir. scholarship devel., 1970-91; asst. to pres. western area Cumberland Coll., Williamsburg, Ky., 1991; v.p. bus. affairs Tucson Coll. Arts and Scis., 1992. Sec. Baird Found., Tucson, 1970—; bd. dirs. Bendalin Fund, Phoenix, 1976—, Cacioppo Found., Tucson, 1986—; cons. DeMund Found., St. Louis, 1970—; mem. Pres. Club U. Ariz. Found.; mem. Ariz. Assn. Fin. Aid Officers, 1970-91, pres., 1973-74; pres. Ariz. Coll. & Univ. Faculty Assn., 1972-73. Ivinson Meml. Hosp. Bd., Laramie, 1964-68. Recipient Spl. award U. Ariz. Black Student Govt., 1983, Black Alumni, 1990; study grantee U. Ariz., 1993—. Mem. Am. Indian Alumni Assn. (Spl. Appreciation for Svc. in Scholarships Native Ams. award 1982), Mormon History Assn., Masons (32 degree, Knight York Cross of Honor), Shriners. Methodist. Home: 5602 E Holmes Tucson AZ 85710

HUMPHREY, OWEN EVERETT, retired education administrator; b. Wautoma, Wis., Oct. 25, 1920; s. Marion A. and Flora A. (Helms) H.; m. Billye A. Cox, Apr. 6, 1946 (dec. Dec. 1974); children: Reba, Ivye. BS, U. Wis., Whitewater, 1947; MS, U. Ark., 1949; advanced cert., U. Ill., 1954. Life gen. supervisory cert. grades K-14. Elem. classroom tchr. Four Corners Sch., Plainfield, Wis., 1941-42; jr. high and sci. tchr. Jefferson Sch., Sheboygan, Wis., 1947-48; elem. classroom tchr. and prin. Holcomb, Mo., 1949-50, Lincoln Sch., Mattoon, Ill., 1950-55; supervising prin. various elem. schs., Peotone, Ill., 1955-57; elem. tchr. Nameoki Sch., Granite City, Ill., 1957-59; elem. prin. Maryville Sch., Granite City, 1959-67; curriculum coord. Sch. Dist. #9, Granite City, 1967-79; adminstrv. asst. Regional Supt. of Schs., Madison County, Ill., 1979-81, 85-87; ret., 1987. Leader parent study groups Ea. Ill. U., Mattoon, 1950-54; PTA field unit organizer Ill. Congress of Parents and Tchrs., Mattoon, 1952-54; coord. local dist. planning Sch. Dist. #9, Granite City, 1973-79; rep. Ill. State Curriculum Coun., Springfield, 1980-81. Co-author: The Greening of Gateway East, 1984; contbr. poetry to Nat. Libr. of Poetry anthologies; contbr. articles to profl. jours. Dir. chorus Area Coun. PTA, Mattoon, 1950-54, Granite City Area Coun. PTA, 1957-59; dir. Granite City Steel Mixed Chorus, 1958-60; actor Creative Arts Theatrical Soc., 1992--. Sgt. U.S. Army Infantry, 1942-45, ETO. Recipient Area Coun. PTA award Granite City, Ill., 1979. Mem. NEA (life), ASCD (life), Ill. ASCD (life, bd. dirs.), Internat. Poets Soc. (life), Creative Arts Theatrical Soc. (bd. govs.), Miners Inst. Found. (bd. dirs. 2002-03), Phi Delta Kappa (Gateway East chpt. sec., historian, v.p., pres., Svc. Key award 1984, George H. Reavis Assoc. award 1991). Avocation: composing music and lyrics. Home: 18 Wilson Park Dr Granite City IL 62040-3550

HUMPHREYS, DONALD WAYNE, environmental engineering educator; b. Iowa Falls, Iowa, Mar. 14, 1931; s. Wayne B. and Alta B. (Hyde) H.; m. Constance S. Severaid, June 12, 1954; children: Janet Krasner, Eric, Ann Sellers, Paul. BA, U. No. Iowa, Cedar Falls, 1953, MA, 1964; PhD, U. Iowa, Iowa City, 1972. Vis. prof. Ind. U., Bloomington, 1972-74; prof. sci. edn. Temple U., Phila., 1974-82, prof. environ. engring., 1982—2000, dir. undergrad. studies, 1996—, prof. emeritus, 2000—. Materials devel. NSF, Washington, 1990-92; environ. cons., Gilbertsville, 1974-95. Author: Aguide to Freshwater Protists and Metazoans, 1977. Dir., chair Berks/Mont Mcpl. Authority, Gilbertsville, 1978-88. With U.S. Army, 1953-55. NSF grantee, Washington, 1968-69; fellow Inst. Math. and Sci., Temple U., 1985-2000. Mem. APHA, Nat. Biology Tchrs. Assn. (dir. 1963—), Am. Soc. Engring. Edn. Office: Coll Engring Temple U 12th & Norris Sts Philadelphia PA 19122

HUMPHREYS, PAUL WILLIAM, philosophy educator, consultant; b. London, Jan. 17, 1950; came to U.S., 1971; s. William Edward and Florence C. (Didcock) H.; m. Diane Gail Snustad, July 14, 1984; children: Emily Victoria, Alexandra Elizabeth. BSc, U. Sussex, U.K., 1971; MA, MS, Stanford U., 1974, PhD, 1976. From asst. to assoc. prof. philosophy U. Va., Charlottesville, 1978-91, prof., 1991—, chmn., 1996-97, 99—; v.p. Assn. for Founds. Sci., 1995-99. Seminar dir. NEH, Va., 1991, 95; cons. EPA, CDC, BCG. Author: Chances of Explanation, 1989, Extending Ourselves, 2004; editor: Synthese, 1991—98, Foundations of Science, 1993—98, Oxford Studies in the Philosophy of Science, 1999—. Recipient Travel award Fulbright, 1971, Scholars award NSF, 1984. Mem. Am. Philos. Assn., Philosophy Sci. Assn. (mem. gov. bd. 1997-2000), Keswick Soc. (chmn. 2000—). Home: 323 Kent Rd Charlottesville VA 22903-2409 Office: U Va Dept Philosophy PO Box 400780 Charlottesville VA 22903-4780

HUMPHRIES, EDNA BEVAN, music educator, choir director; b. Cheyenne, Wyo., Sept. 21, 1922; d. Christopher Henry Droegemueller and Charlotte Adelheit Mueller; m. Elmer Wayne Bevan, Nov. 4, 1944 (div. Dec. 1988); children: David Wayne, Ronn Merrill, Paul Bevan (dec.), Philip Neal; m. John B. Humphries, Feb. 18, 1989. BS, U. Minn., 1943. Nat. and state cert. piano tchr. Freelance writer, Seattle, 1955—; piano tchr., 1955—; organist Luth. Ch., Seattle, 1950—80, choir dir., 1965—80; dir. bell choir John Knox Presbyn. Ch., Seattle, 1989—2002, Glendale Luth. Ch., Seattle, 1989—, Southminster Presbyn. Ch., Seattle, 2002—. Author: Christian Finger Plays and Games, 1955. Mem.: Wash. State Music Tchrs. Assn. (past treas., past pres. South King County chpt.). Avocation: square and folk dancing. Home: 830 SW Shoremont Ave Seattle WA 98166-3646

HUMPHRIES, FREDERICK S. university president; b. Apalachicola, Fla., Dec. 26, 1935; m. Antoinette Humphries; children: Frederick S., Robin Tanya, Laurence Anthony. BS magna cum laude, Fla. A&M U., 1957; PhD in Phys. Chemistry (fellow), U. Pitts., 1964. Pvt. tutor sci. and math., 1959-64; asst. prof. chemistry U. Minn., Mpls., 1966-67; asso. prof. chemistry Fla. A&M U., 1964-67, prof. chemistry, 1964-67, dir. 13 coll. curriculum program, 1967-68; dir. summer confs. Inst. for Services to Edn., 1968-74, dir. interdisciplinary program, 1973-74, dir. two-univs. grad. program in sci., 1973-74, v.p., 1970-74; pres. Tenn. State U., Nashville, 1974-85, Fla. A&M U., Tallahassee, 1985—. Cons. to various colls. and univs.; mem. bd. grad. advocates Meharry Med. Coll. 1976, co-chmn. Reston's Black Focus, 1973; bd. dirs. So. Growth, Nat. Merit Scholarship Corp. Bd.; bd. regents 5-Yr. Working Group for Agriculture, chmn. State Univ. System of Fla.; adv. coun. Panhandle Regional Ctr. Excellence in Math., Sci., Computers, Tech.-FAMU & U., West Fla.; Nat. Assn. Ednl. Opportunities sci. and tech. adv. com., vice chmn. bd. dirs.; mem. EIS adv. com. HBCUs. Contbr. articles on higher edn. to profl. publs. Chmn. Fairfax county Anti-Poverty Commn., 1972-74, White House Sci. and Tech. Adv. Com., on Edn. Blacks in Fla.; bd. dirs. YMCA, 1975—, Walmart Corp., Brinker Internat., Barnett Bank Tallahassee; bd. ann. minority bus. Youth Ednl. Svc. Embarkment; commn. Future of South, 1986, com. tech. and innovation commn.; steering com. Apalachicola Bay Area Resource Planning and Mgmt.; subcom. Fed. Student Fin. Assistance-Office for the Advancement of Pub. Black Colls., chmn. adv. com. Recipient Disting. Svc. to Advancement of Edn. for Black Americans award Inst. for Svcs. to Edn., Disting. Edn. and Adminstr.; Meritorious award Fla. A&M U., Human Rels. award Met. Human Rels. Commn., Nashville, 1978, Thurgood Marshall Ednl. Achievement award Johnson Publ. Co., 1990; named an Outstanding Alumnus of Pitts. U., 1986, Floridian of Yr., Orlando Sentinel, 1999. Mem. NIH (nat. adv. com. neurol. and communicative disorders and stroke coun.), AAUP, AAAS, NAACP, Am. Chem. Soc., Am. Assn. Higher Edn., Nat. Assn. State Univs. and Land-Grant Colls. (chmn.), Nat. Assn. Equal Opportunity Bd. Dirs. (chmn.), Assn. Minority Rsch. Univ., Alpha Kappa Mu (pres., award), Alpha Phi Alpha (Meritorious Svc. award). Office: Fla A&M U Office of President Tallahassee FL 32307

HUMPHRIES, JOAN ROPES, psychologist, educator; b. Bklyn., Oct. 17, 1928; d. Lawrence Gardner and Adele Lydia (Zimmermann) Ropes; m. Charles C. Humphries, Apr. 4, 1957; children: Peggy Ann, Charlene Adele. BA, U. Miami, 1950; MS, Fla. State U., 1955; PhD, La. State U., 1963; cert., W2RN Cable. Registered lobbyist State of Fla. Part-time instr. psychology dept. U. Miami, Coral Gables, Fla., 1964—66; prof. behavioral studies dept. Miami-Dade Coll., 1966—. Presenter, lectr. in field cruise ship Costa Romantica. Editl. staff, maj. author The Application of Scientific Behaviorism to Humanistic Phenomena, 1975, Rev. Edit., 1979, prodr. & host, Sigma Series video, cert.for TV Strategies in Global Modern Academia: Issues and Answers in Higher Education, 1993—94, Strategies in Global Modern Academia: Issues and Answers in Higher Education II, 1995; prodr.: (video series) Strategies in Global Modern Academia: Issues and Answers in Higher Education, III, 1996—97, Strategies in Global Modern Academia: Issues and Answers in Higher Education, IV, 2001—02, W2RN (cert.). Mem. Biofeedback Delegation, China, 1995; mem. Citizen Amb. Program Psychic Arts Delegation to Russia, 1997, Am. Mus. Natural History; life mem. Pastorius Home Assn., Inc., 2001; mem. Citizen Amb. Program Vizcayans Mus., Aldren Kindred of Am., Inc., Nat. Trust Hist. Preservation, The Charles F. Menninger Soc., People to People; mem. ladies aux. Fla. Soc. SAR; mem. Nat. Mus. Women in Arts; mem. women's history month com. Jr. Honor Women Recognition, women's leadership seminar. Recipient award in hon. of women recognition, Women's Hist. Month com. and Women's Leadership Seminar, 2003. Mem.: AAUP (Miami-Dade Coll. chpt., past v.p. Fl. conf. 1986—88, pres. 1986—, mem. exec. bd. Fl. conf. 1989—90, former v.p., sec.), AAAS, AAUW (life; former v.p. Tamiami br. 1983—88, Appreciation award 1977), APA (life), Dade-Monroe Psychol. Assn., Fla. Psychol. Assn., Biofeedback Soc. Fla. (pres. 1990—), Noetic Scis., N.Y. Acad. Scis. (life), Assn. Applied Psychophysiology and Biofeedback, Inst. Evaluation, Diagnosis and Treatment (past v.p. 1975—87, pres. 1987—, former bd. dirs.), Internat. Soc. for Study Subtle Energies and Energy Medicine (charter), Physicians for Social Responsibility, Am. Psychol. Soc. (charter), Biofeedback Soc. Am. (pres. 1989—), Am. Inst. Parliamentarians, Pilgrim John Howland Soc., Hist. Homeowners Coral Gables, Heredity Order Descs. of Colonial Govs., Regines in Miami, North Campus Spkrs. Bur. (Cmty. Lecture Series award), Internat. Platform Assn. (bd. govs. 1979—, Silver Bowl award 1993), Mexico Beach C. of C. (bus. 1991—95), Colonial Dames 17th Century, Soc. Mayflower Descs. (elder William Brewster colony), Cellar Club, Coral Gables Country Club (life), Jockey Club (life), Phi Lambda Pi, Phi Lambda (Founder's Plaque 1976, Appreciation award 1987). Democrat. Achievements include research in biofeedback and human consciousness. Home: 1311 Alhambra Cir Coral Gables FL 33134-3521 Office: Miami Dade Coll North Campus 11380 NW 27th Ave Miami FL 33167-3418

HUND, BARBARA MAURER, English educator and speech broadcasting educator; b. Wilkes-Barre, Pa., Dec. 11, 1930; d. Robert Henry and Nerline Maude (Smith) Maurer; m. Henry John Hund, June 10, 1961; children: Kirsten, John. BA in English and Edn., Hofstra U., 1952; cert. in devel. western civilization, U. Edinburgh, Scotland, 1952; cert. in English, art, lit. and music, U. London, 1955; MA in Speech and Broadcasting, U. Wis., 1957; cert. in conversational Chinese, Yale U., 1966; EdD in Higher Edn., Coll. William and Mary, 1987. Cert. elem. and secondary tchr., N.Y., Wis., N.J., Md., Va. Elem. tchr., Baldwin, N.Y., Madison, Wis., Montclair, N.J., 1952-58, Norfolk (Va.) Acad., 1972-76; tchr. TV, Washington County Sch. Sys., Hagerstown, Md., 1958-61; ednl. TV prodr. WMHT-TV Mohawk-Hudson Pub. Broadcasting, Schenectady, 1961-64; TV prodr. Chinese Broadcasting Co., Taipei, Taiwan, 1969-70; tchr. English, Taipei Am. Sch., 1969-70; prof. speech, English and broadcasting Tidewater C.C., Portsmouth, Va., 1976—, chmn. coll. internat. task force, 1995-96, chmn. distance edn. task force, 1995-99. Tchr. Beijing Broadcasting Inst., 1988-89, 1997; China coord. exch. agreement between Tidewater C.C. and Beijing Broadcasting Inst., 1989—; instr. Fulbright-Hays Study Seminar in Czech and Slovak Republics, summer 1993; instrnl. TV writer, prodr., broadcaster elem. math., sci. and enrichments lessons Washington County TV Project, 1958-61. Organizer, prodr., co-host comml. TV show Spotlight on Hampton Roads, Norfolk, 1986-87, Edn. chmn. Luth. Ch., 1973-85, lay reader, lector, communion asst., 1985—; mem. cmty. adv. bd. WHRO Pub. Broadcasting, Hampton Roads, Va., 1980-84; leader leadership edn. and devel.. for 12 Luth. chs., Hampton Roads area, 1981-83; speaker on China experiences to local civic group and local TV stas., 1989-91; participant 1st Sino-Am. Conf. on Women's Issues, China and Ednl. Exch., Beijing, summer 1990, spring 1997. Named Outstanding Tidewater C.C. Faculty Showcase Mem., Va. C.C. Assn., 1994; scholar Hofstra U., 1948-52. Mem. AAUW, Am. Women in Radio and TV (charter, v.p., treas. Commonwealth chpt. 1962-99). Avocations: travel, reading, tennis, other sports. E-mail: bhund@mindspring.com.

HUNDERT, EDWARD M. academic administrator; b. Woodbridge, N.J. m. Mary Hundert; 3 children. BS in Math. and History of Sci. and Medicine, summa cum laude, Yale U., 1978; MA in Philosophy, Politics and Econs., first class honors, Oxford U., 1980; MD, Harvard U., 1984. Diplomate Am. Bd. Neurology and Psychiatry. Med. intern Mount Auburn Hosp., Cambridge, Mass., 1984—85; resident in adult psychiatry, rsch. fellow, Labs. for Psychiatric Rsch. McLean Hosp., Belmont, Mass., 1985—88, chief resident, 1987—88; clin. fellow in psychiatry Harvard Med. Sch., Boston, 1984—88, instr. psychiatry, 1988—90, asst. prof. psychiatry, 1990—93, asst. prof. med. ethics, 1990—97, assoc. dean for student affairs, 1990—97, assoc. master, William B. Castle Soc., 1992—97, assoc. prof. psychiatry, 1994—97, faculty fellow, Harvard U. Mind/Brain/Behavior Initiative, 1996—99; prof. psychiatry U. Rochester Sch. Medicine and Dentistry, 1997—2002; prof. med. humanities U. Rochester (N.Y.) Sch. Medicine and Dentistry, 1997—2002, sr. assoc. dean for med. edn., 1997—2000, dean, 2000—02; pres. Case Western Res. U., Cleve., 2002—, prof. biomed. ethics, 2002—. Asst. psychiatrist McLean Hosp., Belmont, 1988—94, hosp. ethicist, 1988—97, assoc. psychiatrist, 1995—97; psychiatrist Strong Meml. Hosp., Rochester, NY, 1997—2002. Author: Philosophy, Psychiatry and Neuroscience: Three Approaches to the Mind, 1989, Lessons from an Optical Illusion: On Nature and Nurture, Knowledge and Values, 1995. Mem.: Phi Beta Kappa. Office: Case Western Res U Adelbert Hall 216 10900 Euclid Ave Cleveland OH 44106-7001

HUNDLEY, CAROL MARIE BECKQUIST, music educator; b. L.A., Oct. 19, 1936; d. Paul Albert and Virginia Mary (Noll) Beckquist; m. Norris Cecil Hundley, Jr., June 8, 1957; children: Wendy Michelle Hundley Harris, Jacqueline Marie Hundley Reid. Student, Mt. St. Mary's Coll., 1954-55; AA, Mt. San Antonio Coll., 1956; postgrad., Calif. State U., L.A., 1981-82, 85-86. Tchr. pvt. piano studio, Arcadia, Calif., 1955-58, Pacific Palisades, Calif., 1965-95; vocal coach Corpus Christi Sch., Pacific Palisades, Calif., 1980-95, dir. instrumental music, 1980-95. Vocal and instrumental accompanist Theater Palisades, Pacific Palisades, 1986-87, music arranger, 1970-95; accompanist in field. Author: (play) Bach to Broadway, 1986, The Spirit of America, 1987; arranger and choreographer in field. Piano recitals Tuesday Musicale Jrs., Pasadena, Calif., 1950-54; accompanist Arcadia (Calif.) Women's Club, 1953-54; choral music provider Optimist Club, Pacific Palisades, 1989-92. Recipient scholarship Tuesday Musical Srs., 1954, Mt. St. Mary's Coll., 1954. Mem.: Santa Barbara Symphony League. Democrat. Roman Catholic. Avocations: reading, walking, composition and improvisation, dancing, interior decorating. E-mail: hundley@history.ucla.edu.

HUNDLEY, NORRIS CECIL, JR., history educator; b. Houston, Oct. 26, 1935; s. Norris Cecil and Helen Marie (Mundine) H.; m. Carol Marie Beckquist, June 8, 1957; children: Wendy Michelle Hundley Harris, Jacqueline Marie Hundley Reid. AA, Mt. San Antonio Coll., 1956; AB, Whittier Coll., 1958; PhD (Univ. fellow), UCLA, 1963. Instr. U. Houston, 1963-64; asst. prof. Am. history UCLA, 1964-69, assoc. prof., 1969-73, prof., 1973-94, prof. emeritus, 1994—, chmn. exec. com. Inst. Am. Cultures, 1976-93, chmn. univ. program on Mex., 1981-94, acting dir. Latin Am. Ctr., 1989-90, dir. Latin Am. Ctr., 1990-94. Exec. com. U. Calif. Consortium on Mex. and the U.S., 1981-86; adv. com. Calif. water atlas project Calif. Office Planning and Research, 1977-79 Author: Dividing the Waters: A Century of Controversy Between the United States and Mexico, 1966, Water and the West: The Colorado River Compact and the Politics of Water in the American West, 1975, The Great Thirst: Californians and Water 1770s-1990s, 1992, Las aquas divididas: Un siglo de controversia entre México y Estados Unidos, 2000, The Great Thirst: Californians and Water-A History, 2001; co-author: The Calif. Water Atlas, 1979, California: History of a Remarkable State, 1982; editor: The American Indian, 1974, The Chicano, 1975, The Asian American, 1976; co-editor: The American West: Frontier and Region, 1969, Golden State Series, 1978-2002; mng. editor Pacific Hist. Rev., 1968-97; mem. editl. bd. Jour. San Diego History, 1970-79, Calif. Hist. Soc., 1980-89; contbr. articles to profl. jours. Bd. dirs. John and LaRee Caughey Found., 1983-2000, Henry J. Bruman Ednl. Found., 1983-2003, Forest History Soc., 1987-93. Recipient award of merit Calif. Hist. Soc., 1979; Am. Philos. Soc. grantee, 1964, 71, Ford Found. grantee, 1968-69, U. Calif. Water Resources Ctr. grantee, 1969-72, 91, 2000, Sourisseau Acad. grantee, 1972, NEH grantee, 1983-89, Hewlett Found. grantee, 1986-89, U. Calif. Regents faculty fellow in humanities, 1975, Guggenheim fellow, 1978-79, Hist. Soc. So. Calif. fellow, 1996—; Whitsett lectr., 2000. Mem. Am. Hist. Assn. (exec. coun. Pacific Coast br. 1968-97, v.p. 1993-94, pres. 1994-95), Western History Assn. (coun. 1985-88, 93-97, pres. 1994-95, Winther award 1973, 79), Orgn. Am. Historians. Office: UCLA Dept History Los Angeles CA 90095-1473 E-mail: hundley@history.ucla.edu.

HUNG, JENNY, development specialist; b. Taipei, Taiwan, Mar. 2, 1962; d. You Tsai and Yueh Chin (Yuan) H. BA, U. Calif., Riverside, 1983; MAS, Johns Hopkins U., 1987. Devel. specialist Modern Irrigation, Upland, Calif.; tech. writer City Nat. Bank, L.A. Researcher in field. Mem. Johns Hopkins U. Alumni Assn. Home: 1285 Clark St Upland CA 91784-1733

HUNG, MIEN-CHIE, cancer biologist; b. Taiwan, Sept. 4, 1950; BS in Chemistry, Nat. Taiwan U., 1973, MS in Biochemistry, 1977; MA, PhD, Brandeis U., 1983. Postdoctoral fellow Whitehead Inst. MIT, 1984-86; asst. prof. virology tumor biology dept. U. Tex. M.D. Anderson Cancer Ctr., Houston, 1986-91, assoc. prof., 1991-94, prof. virology, 1994—; dir. Breast

Cancer Basic Research Prog. and Hubert L. and Olive Stringer Endowed Prof., 1996—. Mem. spl. rev. com. for PO-1 Nat. Cancer Inst. L.A., 1990, grant rev. com. Israel Sci. Found., 1993-94, NIH Pathology B Study Sect., 1994—, nat. biochemistry study sect., 1994; mem. adv. bd. Inst. fur Klinische Chemie und Laboratoriumsmedizin-Zentrallaboratorium, Germany, 1993-94, Nat. Taiwan U. Hosp., 1992-94; cons. R Gene Therapeutics Inc., 1994-96, Devel. Ctr. for Biotechnology, Taipei, Taiwan, 1994; guest prof. Xiaman U., Peoples Republic of China, 1991-93, Shanghai Med. U., 1994-96. Mem. editl. bd. Oncology Reports, 1994—, Biomed. Jour., 1994-96; contbr. numerous articles to profl. jours. With Taiwanese Mil., 1973-75. Mem. Am. Assn. for Cancer Rsch., AAAS, Am. Soc. Microbiology, Metastasis Rsch. Sco., Soc. Chinese Bioscientists in Am. No., Am. Taiwanese Profs. Assn. Home: 5762 Birdwood Rd Houston TX 77096-2109 Office: U Tex MD Anderson Cancer Ctr BF 7-001 Box 79 Houston TX 77030

HUNG, PAUL PORWEN, biotechnologist, educator, consultant; b. Taipei, Taiwan, Sept. 30, 1933; s. Yao-Hsun and Shiu-Chin (Wu) H.; m. Nancy Kay Clark, May 4, 1956; children: Pauline E., Eileen K., Clark D. BS in Arts and Sci., Millikin U., 1956; PhD in Biochemistry, Purdue U., 1960; DSc (hon.), Millikin U., 1997. Head molecular virology and biology Abbott Labs., North Chicago, 1960-81; gen. mgr. Bethesda Rsch. Lab., Gaithersburg, Md., 1981-82; asst. v.p. Wyeth Ayerst Labs., Radnor, Pa., 1982-95, disting. rsch. fellow, 1993-95; adj. prof. Northwestern U. Med. Sch., Chgo., 1975-86; chmn. bd. RDNA Corp., Bryn Mawr, Pa., 1995—, Global Briotech Inc., Taiwan, 1998—. Mem. Nat. Vaccine Adv. Com., Washington, 1990-95; cons. Am. Inst. Biol. Sci., Washington, 1992, UN Indsl. Devel. Orgn., Vienna, Austria, 1981; vis. prof. Stanford U., 1969-1970. Author: (chpt.) Recombinant DNA, 1991, Hepatitis Vaccine, 1991; contbr. over 270 articles to profl. jours. Named Disting. Alumni of Yr., Purdue U., 1994, Alumnus of Yr., Millikin U., 2001; recipient Taiwanese Am. Found. Sci. and Tech. award, 2001. Mem. Am. Soc. Biochemistry and Molecular Biology, Am. Assn. Cancer Rsch., Internat. Assn. Biol. Standardization, Am. Inst. Chemists, Am. Soc. Microbiology, Am. Chem. Soc., AAAS, N.Y. Acad. Sci., Medalion Soc./Millikin U. Achievements include patents in field. Home: 506 Ramblewood Dr Bryn Mawr PA 19010-2041 Fax: 525-3595; Home Fax: 610-525-3595. E-mail: pphung@prodigy.net.

HUNGER, J(OHN) DAVID, business educator; b. May 17, 1941; s. Jackson Steele and Elizabeth (Carey) H.; m. Betty Johnson, Aug. 2, 1969; children: Karen, Susan, Laura, Merry. BA, Bowling Green (Ohio) State U., 1963; MBA, Ohio State U., 1966, PhD, 1973. Selling supr. Lazarus Dept. Store, Columbus, Ohio, 1965-66; brand asst. Procter and Gamble Co., Cin., 1968-69; asst. dir. grad. bus. programs Ohio State U., Columbus, 1970-72; instr. Baldwin-Wallace Coll., Berea, Ohio, 1972-73; prof. U. Va., Charlottesville, 1973-82; strategic mgmt. prof. Iowa State U. Coll. Bus., Ames, 1982—. Prof. bus. George Mason U., Fairfax, Va., 1986-87; past pres. bd. dirs. Iowa State U. Press; cons. to bus., fed. and state agys. Author (with T.L. Wheelen): Strategic Management and Business Policy, 1983, 8th rev. edit., 2002, An Assessment of Undergraduate Business Education in the U.S., 1980, Cases in Strategic Management, 1987, Essentials of Strategic Management, 1997, 3d edit., 2003; author: Concepts in Strategic Management and Business Policy, 2000, 2d edit., 2002; contbr. articles to profl. jours. Capt. Mil. Intelligence, U.S. Army, 1966-68. Decorated Bronze Star. Mem. Acad. Mgmt., N.Am. Case Rsch. Assn. (pres.), Soc. for Case Rsch. (past pres.), Strategic Mgmt. Soc., US Assn. for Small Bus. and Enterpreneurship (past v.p.). Office: Iowa State U Coll Bus 300 Carver Hall Ames IA 50011 E-mail: jdhunger@iastate.edu.

HUNGERFORD, DAVID SAMUEL, orthopedic surgeon, educator; b. Rochester, NY, May 4, 1938; s. Francis Samuel and Marjorie Ellen (Wilson) H.; m. Uta-Heide Jung, July 20, 1962; children: Marc Wilson, Kyle Sasha, Lars Daniel. BA, Colgate U., 1960; MD, U. Rochester, 1964. Diplomate Am. Bd. Orthopaedic Surgery. Asst. prof. orthopaedic surgery Johns Hopkins U., Balt., 1972-78; chief orthopaedic surgery VA Hosp., Balt., 1975-80, Good Samaritan Hosp., Balt., 1972—, chief div. arthritis surgery, 1979—2001; assoc. prof. orthopaedic surgery Johns Hopkins U. Sch. Medicine, Balt., 1978-86, prof. orthopaedic surgery, 1987—. Cons. Balt. City Hosp., 1972-85, Children's Hosp., 1972-80, East Balt. Med. Ctr., 1972-78; co-dir. Johns Hopkins U. Ctr. for Osteonecrosis Rsch. and Edn., 1995—; bd. dirs. Nat. Osteonecrosis Found. Author: Progress in Orthopaedics, 1977, Ischemia and Necroses of Bone, 1980, Total Knee Arthroplasty: A Comprehensive Approach, 1984, Total Hip Arthroplasty: A New Approach, 1984, Bone Circulation, 1984, Disorders of the Patello Femoral Joint, 1990, Videobook of Total Knee Arthroplasty, 1994; founding editor Jour. Arthroplasty, 1985-93. Elder Cen. Presbyn. Ch., Balt., 1974-83; dir. Crippled Children's United Rehab. Effort, 1997—, Christian Orthopaedic Ptrs., 1997—; chmn. bd. Med. Assistance Program Internat., 1998—. Maj. U.S. Army, 1969. Recipient George Hoyt Whipple award, 1965; named Disting. So. Orthopedist, So. Orthopedic Assn., 2002; Colgate U. scholar, 1956-59, GM scholar, 1956-59, U. Rochester scholar, 1959-61, Girdlestone Meml. scholar Oxford U., Eng., 1969-70; fellow USPHS, Paris, 1961-62, Carl Berg traveling fellow, 1973. Mem. Johns Hopkins Med. and Surg. Soc., Md. Orthopaedic Soc., Arthritis Found., Md. Soc. Rheumatic Diseases, Am. Rheumatism Assn., Orthopaedic Rsch. Soc., Hip Soc., Am. Assn. Orthopaedic Surgeons, Am. Assn. Hip Knee Surgeons, Soc. Internat. de Chirurgie Orthopedique et de Traumatologie, Knee Soc. (pres. 1994). Republican. Home: 10715 Pot Spring Rd Cockeysville Hunt Valley MD 21030-3019 Office: Good Samaritan Hosp Profl Office Bldg G-1 5601 Loch Raven Blvd Baltimore MD 21239-2991 also: Johns Hopkins U Sch Medicine Dept Orthopaedic Surgery Baltimore MD 21205 Business E-Mail: dhunger@jhmi.edu.

HUNGERFORD, JOHN CHARLES, mechanical engineer, educator; b. Detroit, Feb. 6, 1939; s. Joseph Vincent and Bertha Estelle (Warren) H.; m. Ruth Faye Wolkoff, Sept. 23, 1978; 1 child, Julia Michel. BSME, Ohio U., 1967, MS, 1968; PhD, Ohio State U., 1984. Diplomate Am. Coll. Forensic Examiners; cert. profl. ergonomist. Program analyst supr. Tenn. Dept. Mental Health, 1970-75; rsch. assoc. Ohio State U., 1975-79; assoc. prof. indsl. engring. U. Tenn., Knoxville, 1979—2002, prof. emeritus, 2002. Cons. to nuclear industry; former cons. mental health programs; accident reconstructionist, forensics cons. Office of Edn. tng. grantee, 1973. Transp. Rsch. fellow; Office of Edn. tng. grantee 1973; recipient Grad. Rsch. award Ohio State U., 1978-79. Mem. Am. Soc. Engring. Edn., Human Factors and Ergonomics Soc., Am. Soc. Safety Engrs., Md. Assn. Traffic Accident Investigation, Nat. Assn. of Profl. Accident Reconstrn. Specialists, Inst. Indsl. Engrs. (regional v.p. 1993-95), Ergonomics Soc. (registered), Soc. Automotive Engrs., Alpha Pi Mu. Home: 7120 Stagecoach Trl Knoxville TN 37909-1113 Office: U Tenn 309 E Stadium Hall Knoxville TN 37996-0700 E-mail: hungerfo@utk.edu.

HUNIA, EDWARD MARK, foundation executive; b. Sharon, Pa., Jan. 8, 1946; s. Edward and Estelle (Maleski) H.; m. Mary Sue Marburger, Sept. 25, 1976; children: Stephen, Adam. BSME, Carnegie Mellon U., 1967, MSME, 1968; MBA, U. Pitts., 1971. CFA. Sr. systems analyst Pitts. Plate Glass Industries, 1968-73; asst. to treas. Carnegie Mellon U., Pitts., 1973-76, dir. internal audit, 1976-78, asst. controller, dir. fin. systems, 1978-81, treas., 1981-90; v.p. for finance, treas. U. Pitts., 1990-92; sr. v.p., treas. The Kresge Found., Troy, Mich., 1992—. Mem. Assn. for Investment Mgmt. and Rsch., Fin. Analysts Soc. Detroit. Avocations: tennis, golf, running, books. Home: 4393 Barchester Dr Bloomfield Hills MI 48302-2116 Office: The Kresge Found PO Box 3151 Troy MI 48007-3151

HUNNICUTT, VICTORIA ANNE WILSON, education educator; b. Tyler, Tex., July 23, 1944; d. Leroy G. and N. Joseline (Bobo) Wilson; m. John Walter Hubble, July 29, 1967 (div. Oct. 1972); m. Buford D. Hunnicutt, Aug. 1, 1982. BA, Emory and Henry Coll., 1966; MEd, Mercer U., 1970; Ed Specialist, U. Ga., 1993; EdD, Ga. So. U., 1998. Tchr. Spanish/English Marion (Va.) Sr. H.S., 1966-67; tchr. Spanish Ballard Hudson Middle Sch., Macon, 1967-68; reading specialist Robins AFB Sch. System, Warner Robins, Ga., 1973-74, Spanish tchr., 1968-70, classroom tchr., 1970-86, computer/sci. specialist, 1986-90, prin. Robins Elem. Sch., 1991, curriculum coord., 1990-99; asst. prof. Early Childhood Ga. Coll. and State U., Macon, 1999—. Adj. prof. Tift Coll., Forsyth, Ga., 1985-88, Ft. Valley State Coll., 1993-99. Treas. Bibb County Dem. Women, Macon, Ga., 1986-88, membership chair 1989-93. Mem.: Nat. Coun. Tchrs. Math., NSTA, ASCD, Nat. Coun. Tchrs. English, Aerospace Edn. Found. (nat. bd. trustees 1998—, nat. sec. 2000—03, Tchr. of Yr. 1995, Jane Shirley McGee award 1990, Medal of Merit 1990, Exceptional Svc. award 1997, George C. Hardy award for excellence in aerospace edn. 1999, Pres.'s citation 2001), Air Force Assn. (treas. chpt. 296 1989—91, v.p. 1991—92, v.p. for aerospace edn. chpt. 296 1991—, v.p. for aerospace edn. Ga. State AFA 1992—97, v.p. chpt. 296 1993—94, regional v.p. for aerospace edn. 1997—, v.p. 1998—, v.p. for aerospace edn. Ga. State AFA 1998—), Ga. Assn. Tchr. Educators, Ga. Coun. Tchrs. of Math., Ocmulgee Audubon Soc. (edn. chair 1986—93), Nat. Audubon Soc., HOPE Coun. (pres. 1994—95), Internat. Reading Assn., Ga. Coun. of Internat. Reading Assn., Nat. Coun. Tchrs. of English, Bus. and Profl. Womens Club (Woman of Achievement local, regional, and state levels 1999), Phi Delta Kappa (chpt. sec. 2002—). Democrat. Methodist. Avocations: reading, gardening. Office: Ga Coll and State Univ 100 College Station Dr Macon GA 31206-5100 E-mail: vhunnicu@mail.gcsu.edu.

HUNSAKER, SCOTT LESLIE, gifted and talented education educator; b. Provo, Utah, Oct. 22, 1953; s. Melvin J and Ruth Lofthouse (Pulsipher) H.; m. Rebecca Naser, June 2, 1982; children: Adam Scott, Jacob Christian, Rachel Noelle. BA cum laude, Brigham Young U., 1977, MEd, 1982; PhD, U. Va., 1991. Classroom tchr. Alpine Sch. Dist., Orem, Utah, 1977-85, gifted coord. American Fork, Utah, 1986-87; rsch. asst. U. Va., Charlottesville, 1987-91; asst. prof. U. Ga., Athens, 1991-95, Utah State U., Logan, 1995-2000, assoc. prof., 2000—, chmn. ednl. policies curriculum subcom., 2002—. Presenter workshops and papers to internat., nat., state, and local confs. Co-author: Suggestions for Program Development in Gifted Education; contbr. articles to profl. jours. Mem. Mormon Tabernacle Choir. Named Coll. of Edn. Tchr. of Yr., Utah State U., 2002; Governor's fellow U. Va., 1989. Mem. Am. Edn. Rsch. Assn., Nat. Assn. Gifted Children (bd. dirs. 1992-98, edn. commn. 1999-2002, creativity div. chair 1989-90, John C. Gowan Grad. Student award 1989, Early Leader award 1991), Coun. Exceptional Children/The Assn. for Gifted, Utah Assn. for Gifted Children (3rd v.p. of publs. 1999-2001, pres. 2001-2003, past pres., 2003—). Mem. Lds Ch. Avocation: presidential trivia. Office: Dept Elem Edn Utah State Univ Logan UT 84322-2805 E-mail: scotthunsaker@usu.edu.

HUNSPERGER, ELIZABETH JANE, art and design consultant, educator; b. Phila., Aug. 30, 1938; d. Francis Charles and Elizabeth Julia Thorpe; m. Robert George Hunsperger, Sept. 13, 1958; 1 child, Lisa Marie. AA in Design, Santa Monica Coll., 1974; student, UCLA, 1975-76; BA in Art History, U. Del., 1978; postgrad., Rutgers U., 1978-81; MA in Edn., Del. State Coll., 1993; postgrad. in ednl. technology, U. Del. Designer Huntingdon Mills, Phila., 1960-63, Rothschild's, Ithaca, N.Y., 1963-65, Cornell U., Ithaca, 1965-67; freelance designer Malibu, Calif., 1967-76; art and design cons., lectr. Art & Sci. Assocs., Newark, Del., 1980—, Galena, Md., 2001—. Art tchr. Cath. Diocese of Wilmington, 1988-95, Kent County High Sch., Md., 2002-; art and spl. edn. tchr. Red Clay Consolidated Sch. Dist. A.I. duPont H.S., Greenville, Del., 1995-97, Shorehaven Sch., Chesapeake City, Md., 1997-99, A.I. duPont Inst., Wilmington, Del., 1999—; with Leech Sch., 1994; cons. Arts and Sci. Assocs., Ednl. and Design Svcs., Newark, Del., 1995—; coord. Delmarva Edn. Action Learning Project; educator Kent County (Md.) Pub. Schs., 2002. Exhbns. include Malibu Art Assn. Show, 1973-74, Newark Art Show, 1987-88. Founding mem. bd. dirs., v.p. Newark Housing Ministry, Inc., 1983-94, pres., 1989-91; mem. social concerns com. and drug and alcohol task force Del.; active Coun. Exceptional Children. Recipient Outstanding Svc. award YWCA, Santa Monica, Calif., 1972, award of recognition Missionhurst, 1982, Gov.'s Vol. of the Yr. award State of Del., 1990. Mem. Nat. Art Edn. Assn., Am. Craft Coun., Art Educators of Del. (bd. dirs., pres.), Debutante Assemlby Club (N.Y.C.). Episcopal. Home: 14040 S Mill Rd Galena MD 21635 E-mail: elizabeth_hunsperger@usa.net.

HUNT, COLLEEN A. educational consultant; b. Atlantic, Iowa, Feb. 24, 1950; d. Paul W. and Arvis A. (Saxton) McKeane; m. William D. Hunt, Apr. 11, 1981; children: Sarah N., Emily B. BS, N.W. Mo. State U., 1976; MS, Iowa State U., 1983. Coord., instr. Iowa Western C.C., Council Bluffs, 1978-89, asst. dir. vocat.-tech. edn., 1989-92, assoc. dean Sch. Applied Sci. and Tech., 1993-99; cons. Dept. Edn., 1999—. Exec. bd. State Coun. Vocat. Edn., Des Moines, 1988-95; mem. Council Bluffs Adv. Bd., 1989—. Mem. Assn. for Career and Tech. Edn. (region III rep.), Iowa Vocat. Assn. (pres. 1995), Iowa Bus. Edn. Assn. (area rep. 1986-92, Outstanding Postsecondary Bus. Educator 1988), S.W. Iowa Vocat. Assn. (pres. 1994), Phi Delta Kappa. Methodist. Avocations: reading, needlework, antiquing. Home: 12528 525th St Elliott IA 51532-4031

HUNT, EARL STEPHEN, federal agency administrator; b. Chattanooga, Nov. 28, 1948; s. Earl Gladstone, Jr. and Mary Anne (Kyker) Hunt; m. Edeltraut Gilgan, Sept. 6, 1986. BA with honors, Emory and Henry Coll., 1971; MA, Am. U., 1973; PhD, U. Va., 1979; MLS, CAS, Syracuse U., 2000. Instr. Fla. So. Coll., Lakeland, 1980-81; edn. cons. Nashville, N.Y.C., 1980-82; editor, cons. Washington, 1982-86; sr. rsch. analyst U.S. Dept. Edn., Washington, 1986—94, sr. internat. rels. specialist internat. affairs staff Office Undersecretary Edn., 2002—; planning dir. Nat. Libr. Edn., 1995—2002; mgr. U.S. Network Edn. Info., 1997—. Mem. drug prevention task force U.S. Dept. Edn., Washington, 1986—89; cons. U.S. Dept. Labor, Washington, 1990—, NSF, Washington, 1990—, U.S. Trade Rep., Washington, 1999—, U.S. Dept. Homeland Security, Washington, 2001—. Co-editor: (book) The Apocalyptic Premise: Nuclear Arms Debated, 1982; author: Drug Prevention Curricula, 1993, Mapping the World of Education: The Comparative Database System, 1994, Professional Workers as Learners, 1992, A Guide to the International Interpretation of U.S. Education Program Data, 1993; co-author: Classification of Instructional Programs, 1990, 2d edit., 2000; contbr. articles to profl. jours. Mem. Sangamore-Brooks Ln. Citizens' Assn., Bethesda, Md., 1990—. Grantee, USIA, 1982. Mem.: Acad. Polit. Sci., Am. Assn. Higher Edn., Nat. Contract Mgmt. Assn., Phi Delta Kappa, Blue Key, Phi Gamma Mu, Alpha Phi Omega (life). Methodist. Avocations: reading, travel, gardening, cooking. Home: 5209 Sangamore Rd Bethesda MD 20816-2324 Office: US Dept Edn Internat Affairs Staff OUS Rm 6W242 FB6 400 Maryland Ave SW Washington DC 20202 Fax: 202-401-2508. Business E-Mail: stephen.hunt@ed.gov.

HUNT, JANICE LYNN, adult education educator; b. Fairfield, Ill., Sept. 1, 1952; d. William Allen and Evelyn (Newby) Hunt. AA, Olney Ctrl. Coll., 1972; BA, So. Ill. U., 1974, MS in Edn., 1978; PhD, Southeastern U., 1982. Lic. optician, Fla. Computer panel operator So. Ill. U., Carbondale, 1975-79; dir. women's programs Kankakee (Ill.) C.C., 1980-81; counselor Family Shelter Svcs., Glen Ellyn, Ill., 1981-82; dir. partial hosp. program Green River Comp. Care Ctr., Henderson, Ky., 1982-84; exec. dir. Harbor House Shelter Svc., Kankakee, 1983-84; therapist Northside Mental Health Ctr., Tampa, Fla., 1985-89; owner-optician Internat. Optics, Tampa, 1990-93; instr. Baywinds, Tampa, 1993—. Mem. adv. bd. Tolentime Ctr. Grief Resolution, Olympia Fields, Ill., 1982, Ill. State Bd. Shelters, Springfield, 1983-84, St. Anthony's Hospice, Henderson, 1983, Henderson County Coun. on Human Svcs., 1983; spkr. U.S./China Joint Conf. on Women in Beijing, 1995. Children's support group leader MacDill AFB, Tampa, 1980-81; fundraiser YWCA, St. Petersburg, Fla., 1994, Tampa AIDS Network, 1996; spiritum assembly mem. Baha'i Faith, 1985-96. Recipient Vol. of Yr. award Constance Morris Family Crisis Ctr., 1982; Chgo. Refugee Found. grantee, 1984. Mem. NOW (newsletter editor 1995-96), AAUW, People for the Am. Way, U.S. Golf Assn. Pres. CEO, Feng Shui, USA, 1993. Avocations: golf, sailing, bicycling, photography, motorcycling. Home: 4201 Ohio Ave Tampa FL 33616-1203

HUNT, JOHN MORTIMER, JR., classical studies educator; b. Bryn Mawr, Pa., Sept. 21, 1943; s. John Mortimer and Ruth Pierson (Ott) H. AB, Lafayette Coll., 1965; MA, Bryn Mawr Coll., 1968, PhD, 1970. From asst. prof. to assoc. prof. classical studies Villanova (Pa.) U., 1970-91, prof., 1991—, chmn. dept. classical studies, 1993-99, dir. classical studies, 1999—. Instr. Latin Lafayette Coll., Easton, Pa., 1970; vis. assoc. prof. U. Calif., Santa Barbara, 1978—80. Mem. editl. bd. Classical Philology, 1976—2001; contbr. articles to profl. publs. Cornell U. fellow, 1965—66. Mem.: Delano Kindred, Roger Williams Family Assn., Colonial Soc. Pa., Soc. Colonial Wars in Pa., Soc. Mayflower Descs. Pa. (state historian 1999—2000, editor The Pa. Mayflower), Pa. Soc. S.R., Franklin Inn Club, Ancient and Honorable Artillery Co. Mass. Episcopalian. Avocations: genealogy, early American history, opera. Office: Villanova U Dept Classical and Modern Langs & Lits Villanova PA 19085-1699

HUNT, KEVIN DEAN, anthropologist, educator; b. Indpls., Mar. 16, 1957; s. David Guy and Norma Jean (Buck) H.; m. Marion Louise Gewartowski, Oct. 10, 1987; children: Daniel Walter, Marion Alison, David Lloyd. BA, U. Tenn., 1980; MA, U. Mich., 1982, PhD, 1989. Postdoctoral fellow Harvard U., Cambridge, Mass., 1989-91; asst. prof. anthropology Ind. U., Bloomington, 1991—96, assoc. prof., 1997—. Contbr. articles to profl. jours. NSF grantee, 1986, 91, 97, 99, 2002, Leakey Found. grantee, 1986. Mem. AAAS, Am. Soc. Primatologists, Am. Assn. Phys. Anthropologists, Sigma Xi. Achievements include research in function explanation of ape thorax shape; proposed a postural feeding hypothesis for origin of human bipedalism; interpretation of Australopithecus afarensis anatomy. Office: Indiana Univ SB 130 Bloomington IN 47405

HUNT, MARY ALICE, library science educator; b. Lima, Ohio, Apr. 14, 1928; d. Blair T. and Grace (Henry) H. BA, Fla. State U., Tallahassee, 1950, MA, 1953; PhD, Ind. U., Bloomington, 1973. Instr., librarian Fla. State U., Tallahassee, 1955-61, asst. prof., 1961-74, assoc. prof., 1974-82, prof., 1982-95, assoc. dean, 1986-95, prof. emerita, 1995—. Author: Transitions: An Informal History of a School Celebrating its 50th Anniversary, 1997; co-author: (book) Multimedia Indexes, Lists, etc., 1975; editor: (book) Multimedia Approach To Children's Literature, 1983, (periodical) FSU/SLIS Alumni Newsletter, 1966-95, Florida Libraries, 1961-67; assoc. editor: (book) Folders of Ideas for Library Excellence, 1991. Mem. ALA (councilor at large 1986-94, 96-2000), Southeastern Library Assn., Fla. Assn. Media in Edn., Delta Kappa Gamma, Pi Lambda Theta (life), Pi Kappa Phi, Beta Phi Mu. Avocations: gardening, reading, photography, pastel drawing and watercolor painting. Home: 1603 Kolopakin Nene Tallahassee FL 32301-4733

HUNT, MICHAEL O'LEARY, wood science and engineering educator; b. Louisville, Dec. 9, 1935; s. George Henry and Tressie (Truax) H.; children: Elizabeth H. Schwartz, Lynne T. Lattimer, Michael O. Jr. BS, U. Ky., 1957; M.Forestry, Duke U., 1958; PhD, N.C. State U., 1970. Product engr. Wood Products div. Singer Co., Pickens, S.C., 1959-60; asst. prof. wood sci. Purdue U., West Lafayette, Ind., 1960-70, assoc. prof., 1970-79, prof., 1979—, dir. Wood Rsch. Lab., 1979—2002. Contbr. articles over 80 articles to profl. jours. Chmn. campus preservation com. Wabash Valley Trust for Historic Preservation, Lafayette. Recipient Servaas Meml. award Hist. Landmarks Found. of Ind., 1994, H. Fannon award Lafayette Neighborhood Housing Svcs., 1998, Downie Meml. award Wabash Valley Trust, 2002. Mem. Forest Products Soc. (pres. 1990-91, Fred Gottschalk Meml. award 1984), Soc. of Wood Sci. and Tech., Rotary. Achievements include patent for lightweight, high-performance structural particleboard. Office: Purdue Univ Wood Rsch Lab West Lafayette IN 47907-2033

HUNT, PAMELA STAFFORD, retired secondary school educator; b. Altus, Okla. d. James P. Jr. and Edna Earle (Snyder) S.; m. W. Gaddis Hunt; children: Gregory Todd, Lari Anne. BS, Miss. State U., 1967, MEd, 1973. Cert. tchr., Miss. Tchr. Starkville (Miss.) Sch. Dist., 1972—99; ret., 1999—. Instr. Miss. State U., 1989-98; co-dir. Youth Leadership Conf., 1990-91; mem. com. Miss. Textbook State Rating Com., Jackson, 1992-93, Miss. Curriculum Revision Com., Jackson, 1990-92, 97-98; evaluator So. Accreditation for Colls. and Schs., Vicksburg, Miss., 1990-91; Miss. team leader Mid South Japan Schs. Project, 1992-93. Recipient Bettersworth award Miss. Edn. TV Authority, 1985, Nat. Disting. Tchr. award Nat. Coun. Geographic Edn., 1987; named Starkville (Miss.) Edn. Hall Fame, 1996. Mem. Miss. Coun. Social Studies (v.p. 1989-90, pres. 1990-91), Delta Kappa Gamma (corr. sec. 1992-95, 1st v.p. 2002-04), Phi Mu House Corp. (sec. 1993-95). Republican. Methodist. Avocations: travel, music, gardening. Home: 1106 E Lee Blvd Starkville MS 39759-9722

HUNT, RONALD DUNCAN, veterinarian, educator, pathologist; b. L.A., Oct. 9, 1935; s. Charles H. and Margaret (Duncan) H. BS, U. Calif.-Davis, 1957, D.V.M. with highest honors, 1959; student, UCLA, 1954-55. Research fellow pathology Harvard Med. Sch., 1963-64, research assoc. pathology, 1964-69, prin. assoc. pathology, 1969-72, assoc. prof. comparative pathology, 1972-77, prof. comparative pathology, 1977-99, prof. comparative pathology emeritus, 1999—. Dir. Animal Resources Center Harvard Med. Sch., 1979-89; dir. New Eng. Regional Primate Research Center, Southborough, Mass., 1976-98. Author: (with T.C. Jones) Veterinary Pathology, 1972, 5th edit., 1983, (with T.C. Jones and U. Mohr) Endocrine System, Respiratory System, Digestive System, Urinary System, Genital System; contbr. numerous articles on research on vet. pathology to profl. jours.; editorial bd.: Lab Animal Medicine, 1969—, Jour. Med. Primatology, 1977—, Internat. Life Scis. Inst, 1981—, Am. Jour. Vet. Research, 1978-80. Trustee Charles Louis Davis DVM Found., 1979—; exec. com. Tufts U. Sch. Vet. Medicine, 1979-82. Served with Vet. Corps U.S. Army, 1959-63. Mem. Am. Coll. Vet. Pathologists, AVMA, U.S. and Can. Acad. Pathology, Am. Soc. Exptl. Pathology, Am. Soc. Clin. Pathologists, Am. Assn. Lab. Animal Sci., Am. Soc. Primatology, Internat. Primatological Soc., Am. Assn. Accreditation of Lab. Animal Care (exec. com. 1989), Internat. Soc. Primatology.

HUNT, T(HOMAS) W(EBB), retired religion educator; b. Mammoth Spring, Ark., Sept. 28, 1929; s. Thomas Hubert and Ethel Clara (Webb) H.; m. M. Laverne Hill, July 22, 1951; children: Melana Claire Hunt Monroe. MusB, Ouachita Bapt. U., 1950; MusM, N. Tex. State U., 1957, PhD, 1967. Faculty Southwestern Bapt. Theol. Sem., Ft. Worth, 1963-87; life cons. for prayer Bapt. Sunday Sch. Bd., Nashville, 1987-94, ret., 1994. Lectr. in field; confs. on the five continents; mem. adv. coun. Life Action Ministries; mem. bd. ref. Union U., adv. coun. Life Action Ministries, bd. reference Union U. Author: The Doctrine of Prayer, 1985, Music in Missions, 1986, The Disciple's Prayer Life, 1988, Church Ministry Prayer Manual, 1994, The Mind of Christ, 1995, In God's Presence, 1995, From Heaven's View, 2002, The Life-Changing Power of Prayer, 2002; founder, author: course in music in missions. Bd. dirs. Life Action Ministries; Union Univ. Home: 3915 Cypress Hill Dr Spring TX 77388-5798

HUNT, VALERIE VIRGINIA, electrophysiologist, educator; b. Larwill, Ind., July 22, 1916; d. Homer Henry Hunt and Iva Velzora Ames. BS in Biology, Fla. State Coll., 1936; MA in Physiol. Psychology, Columbia U., 1941, EdD in Sci. Edn., 1946; DD, Phoenix Inst., San Diego, 1984. Sci. tchr. Anniston (Ala.) H.S., 1936-38; asst. anatomy nursing dept. Columbia U., N.Y.C., 1939-40; chmn. health edn. Boston YWCA, 1942-43; instr. Columbia U. Tchrs. Coll. and Coll. Physicians and Surgeons, N.Y.C.,

1943-46; asst. prof. U. Iowa, Iowa City, 1946-47; assoc. prof., dir. divsn. phys. therapy UCLA, 1947-64, prof. physiology, dir. electromyographic lab., 1964-80, prof. emeritus, 1980—; dir. BioEnergy Fields Lab. BioEnergy Fields Found., Malibu, Calif., 1980—; CEO Malibu Pub. Co., 1995—. Cons. Nat. Bd. YWCA, 1943-46, Nat. Early Childhood Edn., 1948-50, UCLA Sch. Engring. Prosthetics Inst., 1949-51, Calif. Dept. Edn., 1950-60, Chrysler Motor Co. Space Divsn. Rsch., 1952, NASA Space Biology, 1958, Grand Kamalani Wellness Ctr., Maui, Hawaii; field reader U.S. Dept. HEW, 1958-65; reviewer sci. textbooks McMillan Pub., Prentice-Hall, McGraw-Hill, W.B. Saunders & Co., 1959-67; cons. Fetzer Found. Energy Field Rsch., 1989, Heart Math Found., 1992. Author: Recreation for the Handicapped, 1955, Corrective Physical Education, 1967, Movement Education for Preschool, 1972, Guidelines for Movement Behavior: Curricula for Early Childhood Education, 1974, Infinite Mind: Science of the Human Vibrations of Consciousness, 1996, Mind Mastery Meditations, 1997, Naibhu, 1998; contbr. articles to profl. jours. Pres. United Cerebral Palsy, L.A., 1947-51; mem. adv. com. Harlan Shoemaker Clinic for Neurol. Disabilities, 1948-53; bd. dirs. Found. for Jr. Blind, 1949-52, Crippled Children Soc., 1953-58, YWCA, L.A., 1955-65; adv. com., Internat. Congress for Exceptional Children, 1964-72, Rory Found., L.A., 1998—; vestry bd. mem. St. Matthew Episcopal Ch., L.A., 1965-69. Rsch. grantee USPHS, 1957-61, Adelphi Found., 1960-63, Rolf Found., 1965-71; recipient Heritage award Calif. Dance Educator Assn., 1987, N.B. Rudman award Found. Exceptional Leadership, 1995; Dame Order of St. John of the Ams., 1996. Mem. NSF, N.Y. Acad. Scis., Pi Lambda Theta, Kappa Delta Pi. Achievements include patents pending for Aurameter. Avocations: travel, gardening, music, art, lecturing. Office: BioEnergy Fields Found PO Box 6653 Malibu CA 90264-6653 E-mail: vhunt@bioenergyfields.org.

HUNT, WAYNE PHILIP, psychologist, educator; b. Balt., Feb. 4, 1947; s. Henry Adus and Nancy Hanna Hunt; m. Janice Lee Staples; 1 child, Scott Waldo. BS, Mars Hill Coll., 1969; MS, Johns Hopkins U., 1974; EdD, George Washington U., 1982. Lic. psychologist; nat. cert. sch. psychologist. Cons. psychologist Cmty. Residential Facility for Youth, Balt., 1974; investigator Pre-Trial Release-Supreme Bench Baltimore City, 1973-76; intern psychologist Psychol. Svcs., Bd. Edn. Baltimore County, 1976; counseling psychologist Glass Mental Health Clinic, Balt., 1977-78; mental health counselor Health and Welfare Coun. Ctrl. Md., Balt., 1975-78; coord. counseling svcs. Counseling and Consultation Svcs., Balt., 1978-80; psychologist St. Francis Sch. Spl. Edn., Balt., 1978-83; cons. psychologist Chestnut Hill Devel. Ctr., Inc., 1982-84, bd. dirs., 1983-84; clin. psychologist Youth Diagnostic Ctr., State of Del., Wilmington, 1983-84; chief psychologist Md. Divsn. Correction Reception-Diagnostic and Classification Ctr., Balt., 1984—; psychologist Balt. Police Dept. Crisis Negotiation Team, 1989—. Psychologist Critical Incident Stress Debriefing Team, 1991—; dir. tng. Md. Dept. Pub. Safety and Correctional Svcs., Clin. Psychology Internship and Mental Health Svcs., 2000—; vis. assoc. staff Taylor Manor Hosp., 1989-2000; staff affiliate, clin. psychologist dept. psychiatry and behavioral scis. The Johns Hopkins Hosp., 1990—; asst. prof. dept. psychiatry and behavioral scis. Sch. Medicine Johns Hopkins U., 1992—, faculty assoc. Sch. Profl. Studies, 1993—. Lt. U.S. Army, 1969-72. Fellow Md. Psychol. Assn.; mem. APA, Md. Sch. Psychologists Assn., Am. Correctional Psychologists Assn., Johns Hopkins Club, Phi Delta Kappa. Home: 900 Old Barn Rd Parkton MD 21120-9421 Office: Psychology Dept 550 E Madison St Baltimore MD 21202-4239

HUNT-CLERICI, CAROL ELIZABETH, retired academic administrator, counselor; b. N.Y.C., Mar. 14, 1938; d. William Laubach and Mary Alice (Grace) Hunt; m. Francis Anthony Clerici, May 17, 1958; children: Francis Anthony Clerici Jr., David William Clerici, Paul Camilio Clerici. AB, Boston Coll., 1987, MA, 1990. Faculty pers. asst. academic v.p. office Boston Coll., Chestnut Hill, Mass., 1984-99; psychol. counselor Summerhill Ho., Norwood, Mass., 1989—2003; ret., 2003. Rep. staff adv. senate Boston Coll., Chestnut Hill, 1981—98, vice-chair, 1985—86, chair, 1986—88, Chestnut Hill, 1990—91; sec. Martin Luther King Jr. Com., 1989—98. Rep. Walpole (Mass.) Town Hall Meeting, 1977—82; vol. Friends of Wrentham; treas. CAMY 5K Run, DAVID 5K Walk Race. Mem.: APA (assoc.). Avocations: theater, reading, music, travel.

HUNTE, BERYL ELEANOR, mathematics educator, consultant; b. N.Y.C. BA, CUNY-Hunter Coll., 1947; MA, Columbia U., 1948; PhD, NYU, 1965. Instr. math. So. U., Baton Rouge, 1948-51; tchr. math. Bloomfield (N.J.) H.S., 1951-57; tchr. maths. Friends Sem., N.Y.C., 1957-62; asst. prof. maths. Rockland C.C., Suffern, N.Y., 1962-63; instr. maths., supr. tchr. trainees NYU, N.Y.C., 1964; chmn. dept. math. Borough of Manhattan C.C., N.Y.C., 1964-67, 70-73, prof. maths., 1970-95, prof. maths. emerita, 1996, acting dean students, 1985-87, acting dean acad. affairs, 1987-88; dean for spl. projects CUNY, 1988-89. Assoc. U. Seminar on Higher Edn., Columbia U., N.Y.C., 1989-95. Author: (with others) (textbook) Mathematics Through Statistics, 1973. NSF fellow, summer 1960, 1963-64, Chancellor's Faculty fellow CUNY, 1980. Mem. N.Y. Acad. Scis., Am. Math. Soc., CUNY Acad. for Humanities and Scis. (bd. dirs. 1991—, first v.p. 1994—), UN Assn. N.Y.C. (bd. dirs., sec. 1980-86). Avocations: opera, concerts, ballet, bridge.

HUNTER, ALYCE, school system administrator; b. Bayonne, N.J., Sept. 26, 1948; d. Theodore and Alyce (Matan) Psemeneki; m. Robert Howard Hunter, Dec. 19, 1970; children: Jay, Sean, Scott, Alyson, Jessica. AB, Douglass Coll., 1970; MEd, East Stroudsburg Univ., 1988; EdD, Lehigh Univ., 1996. Cert. tchr. English, elem. edn., supr., prin. Tchr. Dunellen (N.J.) High Sch., 1978-84, North Hunterdon Regional Sch. Dist., Annandale, N.J., 1986-89; instr. Hunterdon County Adult Edn., Flemington, N.J., 1989-90; tchr. Roxbury High Sch., Succsumna, N.J., 1990-91; dir., supr. Franklin Twp. Pub. Schs., Somerset, N.J., 1991-93; supr. West Windsor Plainsboro Mid. Sch., Plainsboro, N.J., 1993—. Adj. instr. Rariton Valley Community Coll., Somerville, N.J., 1989-90; presenterworkshops N.J. Coun. Tchrs. of English, 1993, Nat. Assn. Secondary Sch. Prins., Va., 1994, Coun. on English leadership, Ill., 1994, adv. bd., 1992— Contbr. articles to profl. jours. Mem. Middlesex (N.J.) Bd. Edn., 1977-80; trustee Fanny B. Abbot Meml. Scholarship Fund, 1988—. Grantee N.J. Coun. for Humanities, 1991, N.J. Title IV-C/State, 1980. Mem. ASCD, N.J. Prin. and Suprs. Assn. (adv. bd. mid. level 1991—), Mensa, Delta Kappa Gamma. Avocations: reading, walking. Office: West Windsor Plainsboro Mid Sch 55 Grovers Mill Rd Plainsboro NJ 08536-3105

HUNTER, BRINCA JO, education specialist; b. Athens, Ga., Feb. 24, 1940; d. Mattie Maude Patton; m. Levis Eugene Hunter, May 6, 1961 (dec. 1994); children: Daphne M. Inman, Jason L. BS in Spl. Edn., U. Akron, 1977, MS in Ednl. Supervision, 1992; PhD in Ministry, Shalom Sem., 1999. Instr. Medina (Ohio) County Bd. Mental Retardation and Devel. Disabilities, 1969-88, edn. specialist, 1988-99, ret., 1999; registrar Springs of Life Bible Coll. and Shalom Sem., 1999—. Mem. Medina City Citizens Adv. Com., 1978-84; bd. dirs. YWCA, Medina, 1978-84, Springs of Life Min.; fin. sec. 2d Bapt. Ch., Medina, 1978-82. Mem. ASCD, AAUW, Am. Assn. Mental Retardation, Profl. Assn. Retardation (gen. bd. dirs. 1996—, adult svcs. bd. 1995—, scholar 1982). Democrat. Avocations: crafts, reading. Home: 226 N Harmony St Medina OH 44256-1938

HUNTER, DAVID WILLIAM, physical education educator; b. Cleve., Dec. 18, 1957; s. James William and Ruth (Stroud) H. BA, Hiram Coll., 1979; MA, Ohio State U., 1981, PhD, 1988. Dir. recreation City of Obetz (Ohio), 1981-87; prof. Hampton (Va.) U., 1987-88, 89—, Old Dominion U., Norfolk, Va., 1988-89. Cons. Can. Football League Scouting Combine, 1994; health and fitness cons. Daycare mag., Atlanta; mem. adv. bd. Fitness and Aerobics Cert. Tng., Inc. Contbr. articles to profl. jours. Mem. AAHPERD, Va. Assn. Health, Phys. Edn. and Recreation, Am. Coll. Sports Medicine (S.E. chpt.), Nat. Strength and Conditional Assn. Avocations: photography, exercising, traveling, gardening. Home: 308 Vista Point Dr Hampton VA 23666-5342 Office: Hampton U Dept Phys Edn Norfolk VA 23668

HUNTER, BROTHER EAGAN (DONALD J. HUNTER), retired education educator; b. Cedar Rapids, Iowa, June 9, 1922; s. John William and Nellie (Connors) H. BA, U. Iowa, 1944; MEd, U. Tex., 1971. Tchr. Churchill Jr. H.S., Galesburg, Ill., 1944-45, Ctrl. Cath. H.S., South Bend, Ind., 1946-47, Msgr. Coyle H.S., Taunton, Mass., 1947-50; tchr., vice prin., dir. studies Notre Dame H.S., Sherman Oaks, Calif., 1950-61, prin., 1978-80; tchr., vice prin., dir. studies St. Francis H.S., Mountain View, Calif., 1961-64, prin., 1964-70, Notre Dame H.S., Biloxi, Miss., 1971-77; mem. staff St. Edward's U., Austin, 1977-78, prof. edn., 1980-2000. Pres. Archdiocese of L.A. English Com., 1951-53, Guidance Coun., 1955-60; cons. So. Assn. Colls. and Schs., 1974-77, State of Miss., Dept. Edn., 1974-77; reg. advisor Nat. Cath. Edn. Assn., Secondary Sch. Dept., 1974-77, reg. cons., 1977-80; del. Gov.'s Conf. on Edn., Miss., 1975; bd. trustees St. Edward's U., Austin, 1978-80; mem. liturgical commn. Diocese of Austin, 1980-88, coun. of religious, 1983, adminstrv. coun. mem., 1986-88; liaison rep. Intercollegiate Studies Inst., Inc., 1983-98, Tex. Elem. Prins. and Suprs. Assn., 1984-93; mem. sch. bd. St. Michael's Cath. Acad., Austin, 1984-85; mem. state selection com. U.S. Senate Youth Program, 1986; del. Study Mission to People's Rep. of China, 1987; liaison rep. Tex. Acad. Skills Project, 1988-89; del. Nat. Cath. Edn. Assn.'s Reg. Congress for Tex., Ark., Okla., N.Mex. from Diocese of Austin, 1991; mem. adv. com. Diocese of Austin, Tex., 2002—, com. cons. Contbr. numerous articles to profl. jours. Dir. Assocs. of Holy Cross in Prayer, 2000—. Recipient Disting. Profl. Svc. award Nat. Assn. Sec. Sch. Prins., 1978, Ednl. Leadership-Austin award St. Michael's Acad., 1992, Selective Service citations Pres. U.S., 1975. Home and Office: Saint Edward's Univ 3001 S Congress Ave Austin TX 78704-6425 E-mail: eagenh@admin.stedwards.edu.

HUNTER, JAIRY C., JR., academic administrator; b. Feb. 27, 1942; married; two children. Student, U. S.C., Lancaster, 1965-66; AA in Acctg. magna cum laude, Wingate (N.C.) Coll., 1967; BS cum laude, Appalachian State U., Boone, N.C., 1969, MA, 1970, MA in Bus. Adminstrn., 1971; PhD, Duke U., Durham, N.C., 1977. Pres. Charleston Southern U., Charleston, S.C., 1984—. Lectr. in field. Mem. Assn. S.C. Coll. & Univ. Pres's. (pres.), Assn. Colls. & Univs. South (pres.), Alpha Chi, Kappa Delta Pi. Office: Charleston So U Office of Pres PO Box 118087 Charleston SC 29423-8087 Home: 4272 Club Course Dr Charleston SC 29420-7506

HUNTER, JOHN ORR, college president; b. Newfane, N.Y., Mar. 17, 1933; s. Alexander and Jane (Robertson) H.; m. Lyla Beth Brown, Aug. 31, 1957; children: Elaine, John, Susan, Elizabeth. BA, U. Buffalo, 1959, MA, 1964; EdD, SUNY, Buffalo, 1968; postgrad., St. Bonaventure U., Harvard U., 1976. Prof. Niagara C.C., Sanborn, NY, 1963-69, dean, 1969-78; pres. Coll. Lake County, Grayslake, Ill., 1978-86, Alfred (N.Y.) State Coll., 1986-93; founding pres. Cambria County (Pa.) C.C., 1994—; pres. W.Va. No. C.C., 2000—. Spl. cons. FEPADE, El Salvador, 1988-94; mem. Afred Tech. Resources, Inc., 1990—; bd. dirs. Bank of Highland Park, Ill. Author: Values and the Future: Models of Community College Development, 1979; contbr. articles to jours. in field. Trustee Nioga Libr. System, 1973-78; mem. Abbott Scholarship Found., 1979-86, Lake County SBA Corp., 1980-86, Ill. Community Coll. Bd. Planning Adv. Coun., 1980-81, Lake County Econ. Devel. Commn., 1981-86, exec. coun. Steuben Area Boy Scouts Am., 1987-88; chmn. Wellsville adv. bd. Salvation Army, 1988—; bd. dirs. Hornell YMCA, 1989—. lst lt. arty. U.S. Army, 1954-57. Recipient award Lake County Freedom Found.; N.Y. Jaycees pub. speaking champion, 1964. Mem. U.S. Navy League (hon.), Ill. Coun. Pub. Community Coll. Presidents (curriculum com. chmn. 1981-82, econ. devel. com. chmn. 1983-84, sec., treas., 1984-85, chmn. elect 1985-86), Ill. Bd. Higher Edn. (spl. com. on undergrad. edn. reform 1985-86), Pres. Assn. of Colls. of Tech. Office: SUNY Coll Tech Alfred NY 14802 Home: Apt A6 98 Edgwood St Wheeling WV 26003-5739

HUNTER, LESLIE GENE, history educator; b. Meadville, Pa., Sept. 26, 1941; s. George Harper and Gladys Laverne (Bowland) H.; m. Cecilia Aros, Aug. 15, 1969; children: Louis, Raquel, Daniel, Joseph. BA in History, U. Ariz., 1964, MA in History, 1966, PhD in History, 1971. Asst. prof. Tex. A&M U., Kingsville, 1969-74, assoc. prof., 1974-81, prof., 1981—, Regents prof., 1998—, chmn. dept. history, 1986-90, 91-96. Mem. faculty exch. Kiev (Ukraine) Policy Inst., 1991. Editor: Historic Kingsville, Texas, 1994; author (computer software) Missions in Spanish Tex., 1987; editor Jour. South Tex., 1997—; rev. editor History Microcomputer Rev., 1987—; mem. editl. bd. Jour. South Tex., 1989—, Social Studies Texan, 1989—; contbr. articles to profl. jours. Chair hist. rev. bd. City of Kingsville, Tex., 1987—; amb. Inst. Texan Culture, 1994—. Mem. AAUP, Tex. Coun. Social Studies, Tex. Computer Edn. Assn., South Tex. Hist. Assn., S.W. Mission Rsch. Ctr., Phi Alpha Theta. Democrat. Episcopalian. Avocation: computer technology. Home: 811 W Alice Ave Kingsville TX 78363-4262 Office: Tex A&M U Dept History Kingsville TX 78363 E-mail: kflgh00@tamuk.edu.

HUNTER, LYNN, sales executive, writer, elementary school educator; b. Bronx, N.Y., Apr. 25, 1949; d. Harvey and Pearl (Weinstock) Handelsman; m. Casey Scott Hunter, Oct. 1, 1988. BA, Bklyn. Coll., 1970, MS, 1973; EdD, Nova Southeastern U., Ft. Lauderdale, Fla., 1995. Tchr. Bd. Edn. N.Y.C., Bklyn., 1970-80; prodr., writer WNYE-TV Bd. Edn., Bklyn., 1979-82; assoc. prodr. Broadway Prodns., N.Y.C., 1979-83; mktg. mgr. Account-A-Call, N.Y.C., 1980-85; spl. cons. Open Ct. Pub., Peru, Ill., 1985-89, ednl. rep., 1990-94, Ky. Ednl. TV, Lexington, 1988-92; regional mgr. Creative Publs., Mountainview, Calif., 1994—; distance learning coord. NYC Dept. Edn., 2001—. Judge Emmy awards children's TV, NATAS, N.Y.C., 1990—; mem. adv. bd. reading Open Ct. Pub., Peru, 1992—94; sales cons., pres. Edn. Media Enterprises, Jackson, NJ, 1992—; learning coord. N.Y.C. Bd. Edn.; ind. sales rep. variety textbook cos., N.Y. and N.J.; pub. rels. officer Brick Twp. Sch. Dist., 1998—2001. Author (children's book): Meet the Dooples, 1998, The Dooples and the Shapes, 2002; author, creator characters Dooples, prodr., writer pub. svc. announcements, WNYE-TV, 1989. Mem. ASCD, NATAS, NAFE, Nat. Coun. Tchrs. Maths., Am. Ednl. Rsch. Assn., Internat. Reading Assn., Assn. Math. Tchrs. N.J., N.J. Math. Coalition (adv. bd. 1992-94), N.Y. Assn. fo Edn. of Young Children. Home and Office: 51 Whitesville Rd Jackson NJ 08527-5116 also: 770 Anderson Ave Cliffside Park NJ 07010

HUNTER, MARIE HOPE, library media generalist; b. Troy, N.Y., Nov. 21, 1950; d. Roger Walter Joseph and Cecilia Yvonne (Daudelin) Miller; m. Robert Hutchinson Hunter, June 3, 1972 (div. Sept. 1978); 1 child, Teal Miller. BA, Johnson (Vt.) State Coll., 1972; MS in Edn., Ind. U., 1978. Elem. tchr. Lo Nisky Elem. Sch., U.S. V.I., 1972-74; libr. Lockhart Elem. Sch., U.S. V.I., 1974-77; evening libr. Johnson State Coll., 1978-79; libr. Ticonderoga (N.Y.) Mid. Sch., 1980-85; libr. media generalist Richmond Mid. Sch., Hanover, N.H., 1985—. Author: (student workbooks) The Topic Paper Workbook: A Guided Process, 1993, The Thesis Paper Workbook: A Guided Process, 1994. Trustee Lebanon (N.H.) Pub. Libr. Named Tchr. of Yr., Richmond Mid. Sch./U. Vt., 1992. Mem. Vt. Ednl. Media Assn., N.H. Edn. Media Assn. Avocations: travel, golf, racquetball, fishing. Office: Richmond Mid Sch 39 Lebanon St Hanover NH 03755-2147

HUNTER, MIRIAM EILEEN, artist, educator; b. Cin., June 6, 1929; d. James R. and Bertha (Oberlin) H. BS, Ball State U., 1951, MA in Art, 1957; EdD, Nova U., 1979. Tchr. art and English Madison-Marion Consol. Schs., 1951-52; tchr. art Wheaton Coll., Ill., 1952-84, chair art dept., 1969-70, 75-79; asst. prof. art Fine Arts Gallery, Chgo., then assoc. prof., 1971-84; dir. Sch. Edn. Calvin Simmons Coll., Lawrenceville, Ga., 1984—. Freelance art cons.; broker First Am. Nat. Securities Corp., 1982—; div. mgr. A.L. Williams Corp., Chgo. and Lilburn, Ga., 1982—; mgr. House of Frames, Frameland, Ltd. Edit. Galleries, 1985-99, night auditor Howard Johnson, Lithonia, Ga., Comfort Inn, Muncie Ind., 2002-03. Vol. Cook County Hosp., Chgo., 1955-58; mem. Wheaton Human Rels. Orgn., 1965-67. Recipient Ingersol award for painting, 1946, 47, 2nd place award DuPage Sesquicentennial, 1968, Outstanding Alumnus award Ball State U., 1975. Mem. Ill. Art Edn. Assn., Nat. Soc. Lit. and the Arts, Art Inst. Chgo., Delta Phi Delta, Sigma Tau Delta, Kappa Delta Pi. Home: 2800 N Timber Ln Muncie IN 47304-5430

HUNTER, PAMELA ANN, veterinarian, educator; b. Washington, Feb. 12, 1955; d. Melvin L. and Audrey Jean (Perry) Ailer. BS in Zoology, Howard U., 1976; BS in Animal Sci., Tuskegee U., 1980, DVM, 1981. Staff fellow NIH, Bethesda, Md., 1981-83; rsch. assoc. Fla. A&M U., Tallahassee, Fla., 1985-86, asst. prof., 1986-93, assoc. prof., 1993—; vet. med. officer Bur. Land Mgmt., Reno, Nev., 1993. Cons. FAMU, Tallahassee, 1986—. Vol. Sr. Citizen Coun., Tallahassee, St. Francis Wildlife Program, Thomasville, Ga., Nat. Zool. Soc., Washington. Mem. AVMA, Am. Assn. Women in Bus., Am. Soc. Animal Sci., Fla. Wildlife Assn., Magnolia Yoga Assn., Delta Sigma Theta, Friends Nat. Zoo. Avocations: horseback riding, reading, quilting, gardening, yoga. Office: Fla A&M U 306 S Perry-Paige Tallahassee FL 32301

HUNTER, TODD LEE, secondary school music educator; b. Phoenixville, Pa., July 7, 1954; s. Edward Gilmore and Mary Louise (Miller) H.; m. Deborah Ann Johnson, Oct. 9, 1976 (dec. Mar. 1996); 1 child, Lauren Elizabeth; m. Michele Suzanne DeLaunay, July 19, 1997; 1 child, Paul, Vanessa Victoria. B Music Edn., Mansfield U. of Pa., 1976; MusM in Edn., West Chester U. of Pa., 1983. Cert. music tchr., Pa. Instrumental and gen. music tchr. Minersville (Pa.) Area H.S., 1977-80; instrumental music tchr. Berwick (Pa.) Area Sr. H.S., 1980-87; music and instrumental music tchr. Ctrl. Bucks West H.S., Doylestown, Pa., 1987-88; music, instrumental music tchr., head dept. Dallas (Pa.) Sr. H.S., 1988—. Prin. trombone Bloomsburg (Pa.) U. and Cmty. Orch., 1976—, Schuylkill Symphony Orch., Pottsville, Pa., 1991-93; mem. trombone sect. Susquehanna Valley Chorale Orch., Selinsgrove, Pa., 1985-91; trombonist, vocalist, mem. aux. percussion sect. Daddy-O and the Sax Maniax, Scranton and Wilkes Barre, Pa., 1992—. Musician Gene Dempsey Orch., Scranton, 1980—, Penn Ctrl. Wind Band, Lewisburg, Pa., 1996—. Mem. NEA, Pa. Music Educators Assn., Music Educators Nat. Conf., Pa. State Edn. Assn., Phi Mu Alpha Sinfonia, Kappa Kappa Psi. Avocations: performing, arranging music, hunting, fishing, travel. Home: 382 Fowlersville Rd Bloomsburg PA 17815-6964 Office: Dallas Sr HS PO Box 2000 Dallas PA 18612-0720 E-mail: toddbone@ptdprolog.net.

HUNTER, WILLIAM ANDREW, education educator; b. North Little Rock, Ark., Sept. 6, 1913; s. William James Columbus and Jessie Dorothy (Berry) H.; m. Alma Rose Burgess, June 6, 1938. AA, Dunbar Jr. Coll., Little Rock, 1933; BS, Wilberforce (Ohio) U., 1936; MS, Iowa State U., 1948, PhD, 1952. Cert. tchr., Ark., Ala. Tchr. math. and sci. Dunbar H.S., Little Rock, 1936-42; asst. prof. edn. Tuskegee Inst., Ala., 1950-56, assoc. prof., 1956-63, prof. edn., 1964-73, dean sch. edn., 1957-73; dir. multicultural project Am. Assn. Colls. Tchr. Edn., Washington, 1973-74; dir. rsch. inst. Iowa State U., Ames, 1974-83, prof. edn. emeritus, 1983—. Chief acad. officer Tuskegee Inst.-Liberian Govt.-US AID to establish schs. in Liberia, West Africa, 1960-70; programs adv. bd. Ednl. Testing Svc., Princeton, N.J., 1973-77; adv. com. multicultural requirements Iowa State Dept. Edn., Des Moines, 1975-80; found. rep. CSRA/Phi Delta Kappa, Bloomington, Ind., 1984-86. Co-author: Educational Systems in Southeast Asia in Comparaison with Systems in U.S., 1979, Educational Computing: Needs Assessment, 1983; editor: Multicultural Education Through Competency Based Teacher Education, 1974. Mem. So. Poverty Law Ctr., Montgomery, Ala., 1984, Affirmative Action Com., Iowa State U., Ames, 1978-83; life mem. Tuskegee Civic Assn., 1950—; mem. Commn. on Christian Unity and Interreligious Affairs, 1988, chair, 1994—. With U.S. Army, 1942-46. Recipient Lagomarcino Laureate award for outstanding contbns. tchr. prep Iowa State U. Coll. Edn., 1981, Disting. Achievement award, 1973, Outstanding Svc. to Teaching Profession, Sch. Edn., Tuskegee Inst., 1972. Mem. Am. Assn. Colls. Tchr. Edn. (bd. dirs. 1966-73, pres. 1973-74, Pres.'s award 1974), NEA (life), Phi Delta Kappa, Kappa Delta Pi, Beta Kappa Chi, Kappa Alpha Psi. Methodist. Avocations: creative writing, gardening, oil painting, creative handiwork. Home: 2202 Country Club Ct Augusta GA 30904-3506

HUNTINGTON, CURTIS EDWARD, actuary; b. Worcester, Mass., July 30, 1942; s. Everett Curtis and Margaret (Schwenzfeger) H. BA, U. Mich., 1964, M.Actuarial Sci., 1965; JD, Suffolk U., 1976. With New Eng. Mut. Life Ins. Co., Boston, 1965-93, v.p., auditor, 1980-84, corp. actuary, 1984-93; prof. math., dir. actuarial program U. Mich., Ann Arbor, 1993—. Treas. Actuarial Edn. and Rsch. Fund, 1986-89, chmn., 1989-92, dir. 1985—, exec. dir., 1994—. Trustee The Actuarial Found., 1998—. Served with USPHS, 1965-67. Mem. Soc. Actuaries (gen. chmn. edn. and exam. com. 1985-87, bd. govs. 1986-89, v.p. 1989-91), Am. Acad. Actuaries (bd. dirs. 1997-2000), Am. Soc. Pension Actuaries (dir. 1996—), Am. Coll. Life Underwriters, Internat. Actuarial Assn. (sec., nat. corr. U.S.), New Zealand Soc. Actuaries. Office: U Mich Dept of Math 2864 East Hall Ann Arbor MI 48109-1109

HUNTINGTON, IRENE ELIZABETH, special education educator; b. Whitman AFB, Mo., Mar. 9, 1965; d. James Bartholomew Palacio and Martina Marlene (Vasquez) Brown, stepfather Gilbert Arthur Brown. BA, Oreg. State U., 1987; MS, Western Oreg. State Coll., 1989. Cert. tchr., Nev.; cert. reading specialist, 2003. Tchr. spl. edn. Kapa'a (Kauai, Hawaii) Elem. Sch., 1989-90, Kapa'a High Sch., 1990-91, Louisville (Colo.) Mid. Sch., 1991-96, Pau-Wa-Lu Mid Sch, Gardnerville, Nev., 1996-2000. Rural Cross cultural grantee for spl. edn. Western Oreg. State Coll., 1988-89. Mem. NEA, Alpha Omicron Pi. Avocations: travel, learning, outdoor activities, reading.

HUNTINGTON, MARY C. elementary school educator; b. West Hebron, N.Y., May 23, 1923; d. Fred and Agnes (Scott) Cary; m. David Huntington, July 17, 1949; children: Scot Lee, Debra Dee. BEd, Oneonta (N.Y.) State Coll., 1946; postgrad., Cornell U., 1952-53, U. Maine, 1963-64, Elmira (N.Y.) Coll., 1977-78. Cert. tchr., N.Y. Elem. tchr., Pine Bush, N.Y., 1946-51, Ithaca, N.Y., 1951-53, 1959-64; substitute tchr., 1976—. Mem. Alfred (N.Y.) Village Planning Bd., 1974-86; mem. grants com. Bethesda Found., 1985-91, sec. 1990-91, pub. rels. chair 1992; v.p. LWV, Maine, 1958-64; bd. dirs. Camp Fire Girls coun., Hornell, N.Y., 1976-84, Hornell Symphony; bd. dirs. Bethesda Hosp., 1975-85, Alfred State Coll. devel. bd., 1999; mem. So. Tier Health Mgmt. Bd., 1980-85; trustee Alfred Meth. Ch., 1993; com. mem. United Meth. Child Care Ctr., 1998; mem. edn. com. Bethesda Found., 1998; mem. Alfred State Coll. devel. bd., 1999. Mem. AAUW (v.p. 1988—), Woman's Golf Assn. (v.p. 1992—), Bethesda Found. (v.p. 1995, chairperson planning commn. 1995—), Habitat for Humanity (dir. 2000—). Republican. Avocations: physical fitness, bowling, traveling, reading, golf. Home: 5470 Jericho Hill Rd Alfred Station NY 14803-9743

HUNTINGTON, PENELOPE ANN, middle school educator; b. Houston, Apr. 21, 1942; d. William Chandler Cottingham and Bobbie Frances (Houlgrave) Goggan; m. Carlton W. Buesing, Aug. 1962 (div.); children: Bradley D., Kimberley D. Hill, Robert D. BS, Tex. Luth. Coll., 1963; MA, Tex. Tech U., 1974. Tchr. Lubbock (Tex.) Pub. Schs., 1964-69, chair social studies dept., 1966-67; tchr. Goose Creek Consol. Sch., Baytown, Tex., 1972-74, Norman (Okla.) Pub. Schs., 1980—; coord. Lamesa Campus of Howard Coll., Big Spring, Tex., 1975-77; core team leader, chair social studies dept. Longfellow Mid. Sch. Norman (Okla.) Pub. Schs., 1988-90.

Mem. Nat. Bill of Rights Workshop, Okla. Bar Assn., Tulsa County Bar Assn., 1992. Author curriculum in field. Ednl. rep. Okla. Mo. Synod Luth. Ch., Oklahoma City, 1985; edn. chmn. St. John's Luth. Ch., Moore, Okla., 1984. Recipient Tchr. medal Freedom Found., 1972, Finalist Okla. Supreme Ct. Tchr. of Yr., 1994, 95, 96, Okla. Supreme Ct. Tchr. of Yr., 1997; grantee Okla. Bar Assn., Oklahoma County Bar Assn., 1992, Pace V, 1994, Colonial Williamsburg, 1994, Pace VI, 1995, Pace VII, 1996, Pace VIII, 1997, James F. Ackerman Ctr. for Dem. Citizenship, Purdue U., 1995. Mem. Nat. Coun. Social Studies, Okla. Coun. Social Studies, Okla. Assn. Geog. Edn. (grantee 1989), PACE II (grantee 1989), PACE III (grantee 1992, mentor), PACE IV (grantee 1993, mentor), PACE V (mentor), PACE VI (mentor), PACE VII (mentor), Phi Delta Kappa. Democrat. Home: 1345 Dorchester Dr Norman OK 73069-7517 Office: Whittier Mid Sch 2000 W Brooks St Norman OK 73069-4297

HUNTLEY, DIANE E. dental hygiene educator; b. Concord, N.H., Oct. 1, 1946; d. George Williams and Esther A. (Gadwah) H. AS, Fones Sch. Dental Hygiene, Bridgeport, Conn., 1966; BA, U. Bridgeport, Conn., 1968; MA, SUNY, Buffalo, 1971; PhD, Kans. State U., 1985. Registered dental hygienist. Dental hygienist various gen. practice dentists, Conn., Colo., 1966-76; clin. instr. Fones Sch. Dental Hygiene, 1971-74; asst. prof. U. Colo. Dental Sch., Denver, 1974-76; asst. prof. dental hygiene Wichita (Kans.) State U., 1976-82, assoc. prof., 1982—. Vol. hygienist Good Samaritan Clinic, Wichita, 1989-90, 92—. Contbr. articles to profl. jours. Mem. dental adv. bd. United Meth. Urban Ministries, Wichita, 1990-92; mem. P.A.N.D.A. Coalition of Kans. Exec. Com., 1995—. Mem.: AAUP (Wichita State U. chpt. sec.treas. 1988—91), Am. Dental Hygienists Assn. (editl. dir. 1983—85, historian 1993—2001), Kans. Dental Hygienists assn. (del. 1989—93, treas. 1998—2000, parliamentarian 1998—2001, trustee 2000—03), Wichita Dental Hygienists Assn. (pres. 1982—83, treas. 1988—90, trustee 1990—91), Am. Dental Edn. Assn., Apha Eta, Phi Kappa Phi. Office: Wichita State U 1845 Fairmount St Wichita KS 67260-0144

HUNTSMAN, LEE, university provost, academic administrator; BSc in elec. engring., Stanford U., 1963; PhD in bioengineering, U. Pa., 1968. Dir, ctr. for bioengineering U. Wash., 1980—96, assoc. dean for sci. affairs, sch. of medicine, 1993—96, provost, v.p. acad. affairs, 1997—, interim pres., 2002—. Mem. Whitaker Found. Governing Com., 1994—98; chmn. Working Gorup on Rev. of Bioengineering and Tech. Instrumentation Develop. Rsch. for the Ctro for Sci. Rev of the NIH, 1998. Fellow: Am. Ins. of Med. and Biol. Engring., Am. Assn. for the Advancement of Sci. Office: Office of the Pres U of Wash 301 Gerberding Hall Box 351230 Seattle WA 98195

HUOT, RACHEL IRENE, biomedical educator, research scientist, physician; b. Manchester, N.H., Oct. 16, 1950; d. Omer Joseph and Irene Alice (Girard) Huot. BA in Biology cum laude, Rivier Coll., 1972; MS in Biology, Cath. U. Am., 1976, PhD in Biology, 1980; MD, La. State U. Health Sci. Ctr., Shreveport, 2000. Sr. technician Microbiol. Assocs., Bethesda, Md., 1974-77; chemist Uniformed Svcs. Univ. of Health Scis., Bethesda, 1977-79; biologist Nat. Cancer Inst., Bethesda, 1979-82; postdoctoral fellow S.W. Found. for Biomed. Rsch., San Antonio, 1982-85, asst. scientist, 1985-87, staff scientist, 1987-88; instr. U. Tex. Health Sci. Ctr., San Antonio, 1988-89; asst. prof., dir. basic urologic rsch. La. State U., New Orleans, 1990-96; resident in family practice Aultman Hosp., Canton, Ohio, 2001—02, U. Minn./Mayo Clinic, Waseca, 2002—. Judge sr. divsn. Alamo Regional Sci. Fair, San Antonio, 1989—90. Contbr. Vol. ARC, Christus Schumpert Hosp., Shreveport; patient educator vol. Martin Luther King Clinic, Shreveport, 1996—2000. Recipient Rsch. Svc. award, NIH, 1983—86, Searle Young Investigator award, 1994; grantee, NSF, 1972—74. Mem.: AMA, AAUW, LWV, AAAS, Minn. Acad. Family Practice, Am. Acad. Family Practice, Am. Soc. Experiment Biology, St. Vincent De Paul Soc., N.Y. Acad. Scis., Soc. In Vitro Biology, Fedn. Am. Scientists, Am. Soc. Cell Biology, Am. Assn. Cancer Rsch., Am. Soc. Microbiology, Sierra Club, Sigma Xi, Delta Epsilon Sigma, Iota Sigma Pi. Democrat. Roman Catholic. Avocation: Avocations: drawing, painting, roadracing, reading, Volksmarching. Home: 405 N 5th St Apt 416 Mankato MN 56001

HUQ, MANSUR U. KENNEDY, chemical engineer, materials scientist, educator, entrepreneur; b. Bangladesh, July 15, 1951; came to U.S., 1973; naturalized, 1986; s. A.T.M. Abdul Huq and Khondoker Saleha Khatun; m. Melinda Katherine Anne Fabiano; 1 child, Austin David. BS in Chem. Engring., Iowa State U., 1976, MS in Chem. Engring., 1981; PhD in Chem. and Materials Engring., U. Iowa, 1994. Process and product devel. and improvement engr. Iowa Limestone Co., Des Moines, 1977-83; coord., dir. R & D MixTrusion Engring., Ames, Iowa, 1983-84; rsch. engr. and sci., chem. and materials engring. dept. U. Iowa, Iowa City, 1984-86; pres., CEO Miracle Metals, Inc., Oakdale, Iowa, 1987—; pres., founder AgriCorp Bioproducts, Inc., Oakdale, Iowa. Presenter in field. Contbr. articles to profl. jours. Vol. Dem. Presdl. Elections, 1976—, Govt. of Bangladesh. Recipient Rsch. award Iowa Gov. High Tech. Coun., 1984-86. Mem. AIChE (Profl. Devel. Recognition cert. 1982), Metall. Soc. AIME, Inst. Briquetting & Agglomeration, Soc. Agrl. Engrs., Wire Assn. Internat. Achievements include three patents. Home: 2232 Oakleaf St Iowa City IA 52241-1365 Office: AgriCorp BioProducts Inc PO Box 156 Oakdale IA 52319-0156

HURD, ERIC RAY, rheumatologist, internist, educator; b. Columbus, Kans., July 5, 1936; s. Myron Alexander and Isobel (Moore) H.; m. Beverly Jean Button, June 14, 1962; children: Sherryl Lynn, Susan Rae, Brent Eric. BS, U. Tulsa, 1958; MD, U. Okla., 1962. Intern St. John's Hosp., Tulsa, 1962-63, resident in internal medicine, 1963-65; research fellow U. Tex., Dallas, 1965-67, instr. internal medicine, 1967-68, asst. prof., 1968-73, assoc. prof., 1973-80, prof., 1980—. Cons. rheumatologist, attending physician Parkland, VA Hosps.; dir. John Peter Smith Hosp. Arthritis Clinic, Ft. Worth; chief rheumatology VA Hosp., 1982—, mem. immunology research merit rev. bd.; assoc. Baylor Arthritis Ctr., 1981—; mem. med. and sci. com. North Tex. Arthritis Found., bd. med. dirs., 1988—, chmn. profl. edn. com.; traveling guest lectr. Tex. Med. Assn., Belgium and Fed. Republic Germany, 1990. Contbr. articles to profl. jours. Served to maj. U.S. Army, 1963-74. Recipient Clin. Scholar award Arthritis Found., 1975-77; named Outstanding Cons. Faculty Mem. John Peter Smith Hosp., 1983-84, Outstanding Part-time Clin. Prof. John Peter Smith Hosp., 1989-90. Mem. ACP, Am. Assn. Immunologists, Am. Fedn. Clin. Research, Am. Rheumatism Assn. (cooperating clinics com. 1968-74, Founding Fellow 1986), Tex. Rheumatism Assn. (sec.-treas. 1976-79, 2d v.p. 1979-80), Tex. Med. Soc., Dallas County Med. Soc., Phi Eta Sigma. Democrat. Methodist. Office: Arthritis Ctrs of Tex 712 N Washington Ave Ste 200 Dallas TX 75246-1632

HURLBUT, GERALDINE, retired elementary education educator; b. Lima, Ohio, Apr. 3, 1933; d. Maurice and Sadye (Keeley) Owens; m. Willis Hurlbut, Sept. 17, 1955 (dec.); children: Bill, Mary, John (dec.). BA, Barat Coll, Lake Forest, Ill., 1955. Cert. elem. tchr., Ill. Tchr. 5th grade Nelson Sch., East Maine Sch. Dist. 63, Niles, Ill., 1971-87, tchr. 2d grade, 1987—, ret., 2001. Past team leader 5th grade Nelson Sch.

HURLEY, ALFRED FRANCIS, historian, academic administrator emeritus, retired air force officer; b. Bklyn., Oct. 16, 1928; s. Patrick Francis and Margaret Teresa (Coakley) H.; m. Joanna Helen Leahy, Jan. 24, 1953; children: Alfred F., Thomas J., Mark P., Claire T., John K. BA summa cum laude, St. John's U., 1950; MA, Princeton U., 1958, PhD, 1961. Enlisted USAF, 1950, commd. lt., 1952, tng. officer, instr. navigator, 1952—56; from instr. to asst. prof. history USAF Acad., 1958—63, prof., head dept. history, 1966—80; navigator, exec. officer USAF Hdqrs., Germany, War Plans Staff, Joint Chiefs of Staff, 1963—66; bd. mem. Acad. Bd., 1977-80; advanced through grades to brig. gen. USAF, ret., 1980; v.p. adminstrv. affairs U. North Tex. (formerly North Tex. State U.), Denton, 1980-82, pres., 1982-2000, prof. history, 1981—; chancellor U. North Tex. Sys., 2000—02. Mem. adv. com. USAF hist. program sect. USAF, Washington, 1982-86, chmn., 1984-86; mem. bd. visitors Air U., 1993-97. Author: Billy Mitchell, Crusader for Air Power, 1964, (rev. edit.), 1975; contbg. author: Winged Shield, Winged Sword, History of the USAF, 1997; co-editor: Air Power and Warfare, 1979. Decorated Legion of Merit (2); Guggenheim fellow, 1971-72, Eisenhower Inst., Smithsonian fellow, 1976-77; recipient Pres.'s medal St. John's U., 1990. Mem.: Tex. Philos. Soc. (2d v.p. 2002—), Dallas Citizens Coun. (bd. dirs. 2000—02), North Tex. Commn. (bd. dirs. 1986—2000, chmn. 1995—97), Alliance for Higher Edn. of North Tex. (trustee 1983—89, chmn. coun. of pres. 1989—90), Tex. Coun. Pub. Univ. Pres. and Chancellors (chmn. 1987—89), Coalition Urban and Met. Univs. (co-chair 1993—2002, mem. exec. com. 2002—), Am. Hist. Assn. (chmn. NASA fellowship com. 1993—94), Am. Coun. Edn. (commn. leadership 1993—96), Am. Assn. State Colls. and Univs. (coun. state reps. 1989—92), Air Force Hist. Found. (trustee 1980—), Soc. for Mil. History (trustee 1973—78, 1981—85). Roman Catholic. Home: 828 Skylark Dr Denton TX 76205-8012 Office: U North Tex Dept History Denton TX 76203-0650

HURLEY, EILEEN BEVERLY, school system administrator; b. Hawley, Minn., July 29, 1937; d. Bernhard Olai and Ella Louise (Winjum) Renslow; m. Harlow William Hurley, Apr. 9, 1960; children: Lisa, Kent. BS, Moorhead State U., 1960; MS in Reading, Calif. State U., Fullerton, 1975; MA in Ednl. Adminstrn., Calif. Luth. Coll., 1983. Classroom tchr. Wadena (Minn.) Pub. Schs., 1956-58, Little Lake City Sch. Dist., Santa Fe Springs, Calif., 1958-60, Montebello (Calif.) Unified Sch. Dist., 1960-65, Whittier (Calif.) City Sch. Dist., 1974-79, reading specialist, 1979-83, sch. improvement specialist, 1983-85, instrnl. specialist, 1985-87, dir. categorical programs, 1987-93, dir. instrnl. svcs. and categorical programs, 1993—; clin. tchr. Reading Guidance Inst., Whittier, 1970-74. Treas., bd. dirs. Whittier Area Consortium, 1987—; mem. L.A. County Reading Recovery Consortium Adv. Bd., Downey, Calif., 1992— Mem. ASCD, Internat. Reading Assn., Calif. Assn. Gifted, Assn. Calif. Sch. Adminstrs., Whittier Area Adminstrv. Devel., Mill Sch.-Whittier PTA (hon. life), Delta Kappa Gamma (co-pres. 1992-94, pres. 1994—). Republican. Lutheran. Office: Whittier City Sch Dist 7211 Whittier Ave Whittier CA 90602-1123

HURLEY, PATRICIA ANN, college official; b. Williamsport, Pa., May 7, 1946; d. Daniel Joseph and Irene Gertrude (Doran) H BA, Nazareth Coll., 1968; MEd, Suffolk U., 1972; postgrad., Boston Coll., 1978—80; EdD, UCLA, 2003. Cert. adminstr., community coll. instr., student svcs., Calif. Asst. dir. fin. aid, placement Grahm Jr. Coll., Boston, 1969-71; dir. student employment, assoc. dir. fin. aid Boston Coll., Chestnut Hill, Mass., 1971-81; dir. fin. aid Computer Learning Ctr., San Francisco, 1981-86; dir. fin. aid and career programs Coll. of Marin, Kentfield, Calif., 1986-97; assoc. dean Glendale Com. Coll., 1998—. Mem. adv. bd. Sallie Mae Corp., 2003—. Fellow, UCLA and C.C. Leadership Commn. Mem. Calif. C.C. Student Fin. Aid Adminstrs. Assn. (past pres.),Calif. Student Fin. Aid Assn., N.E. Assn. Student Employment (hon. life, founding),Nat. Assn. Student Fin. Aid, The Coll. Bd., We. Regional Coun. Mem. Office: Glendale Com Coll 1500 N Verdugo Rd Glendale CA 91208-2809

HURLEY, WILLIAM JAMES, JR., English language educator; b. Chgo., Dec. 31, 1924; s. William James and Marian Josephine (Clark) H.; m. Jane Ellen Hezel, July 10, 1954; children: Ellen, Jane Ann, William III, Michael, Patrick, Matthew. AB in English, DePaul U., 1950, MA in Edn., 1952; MLS, Chgo. State U., 1982. Tchr. reading and English Chgo. Pub. Schs., 1950-61; instr. English Wright Jr. Coll., Chgo., 1950-54; lectr. edn. Loyola U., Chgo., 1960-63; instr. English Crane Jr. Coll., Chgo., 1963-65; asst. prof. English Chgo. State U., 1961-74, assoc. prof. curriculum and instrn., 1974—. Speaker, selected faculty Suwon U., South Korea, 1986; panelist World Forum, Atlanta, 1989, speaker, St. Paul, 1990; speaker Stow (Ohio) Pub. Libr., 1990, Purdue U., Calumet, 1995. Author 12 vols. Dan Frontier Reading Series, 1959-77; editor: Culturally Disadvantaged Children, 1966. With USAAF, 1943-45, lt. col. USAF, 74-76, brig. gen., Ill. ANG, ret. 1983. Ford Found. fellow, 1960; Mil. History fellow U.S. Mil. Acad. at West Point, 1992; recipient sabbaticl for study of dual track secondary schs., Germany, 1991, Jubilee medal of Liberty, Regional Coun. Lower Normandy, France, 1994, Medal of Jubilee of Liberty Regional Coun. of Lower Normandy for participation in the Battle of Normandy, 1944; named Conservation Farmer of Yr., U.S. Dept. Agr., Divsn. Soil Conservation for Van Buren County, Mich., 1993. Mem. ASCD, Nat. Geographic Soc., Smithsonian Assocs., NG Assn. of U.S., West Side Community Orgn., Air Force Assn., Quadrangle Club, Air War Coll. Alumni Assn. (life mem.), Eighth Air Force Hist. Soc., Octave Chanute Aerospace Mus. (life), Pi Gamma Mu. Roman Catholic. Avocations: numismatics, travel, flying light aircraft. Home: PO Box 1 Palos Heights IL 60463-0001 Office: Chgo State U 95th and King Dr Chicago IL 60628

HURST, LINDA WHITTINGTON, small business owner, educational administrator; b. Norfolk, Va., July 19, 1949; d. Leroy and Minnie Estella (Burgess) Whittington; m. Donald Grayson Hurst, Aug. 28, 1971; children: William Christopher, Donald Geoffrey. BS in Secondary Edn., Old Dominion U., 1971, MS in Edn., 1978; postgrad., East Tex. State U., 1982-89. Cert. tchr., Tex. Tchr. Tidewater Christian High Sch., Virginia Beach, Va., 1971-73, Victory Christian Sch., Norfolk, Va., 1976-78; substitute tchr. Dallas Ind. Sch. Dist., 1981-84, tchr., 1984-88; grad. asst. East Tex. State U., Commerce, 1988-89, adj. instr., 1989-91; owner, writer-editor Helping Hand Ednl. Svc. and Supplies, Garland, Tex., 1989—. Ednl. cons. H.O.P.E. for Tex., Austin, 1991—. Author, editor elem. curriculum The Classics, 1989-92, children's mag. Treasure Box, 1992. Sec. Parent Awareness League, Mesquite, Tex., 1990-91. Mem. Phi Delta Kappa. Avocations: music, art, gardening, cooking. Home and Office: PO Box 496316 Garland TX 75049-6316

HURST, MARY JANE, English language educator; b. Hamilton, Ohio, Sept. 21, 1952; d. Nimrod and Leckie Gaines; m. Daniel L. Hurst, June 5, 1974; 1 child, Katherine Jane. BA summa cum laude, Miami U., 1974; MA, U. Md., 1980, PhD, 1986. Tchr. Groveport (Ohio) H.S., 1974-77; tchg. asst. U. Md., College Park, 1978-79, master tchr., 1979-82; asst. prof. English, Tex. Tech U., Lubbock, 1986-92, assoc. prof., 1992-99, prof., 1999—, assoc. dean Coll. Arts and Scis., 2000—. Vis. scholar Stanford U., summer 1987; steering com. Nat. Cowboy Symposium, Lubbock, 1988-89. Author: The Voice of the Child in American Literature, 1990; tech. editor: HTLV-I and the Nervous System, 1989; book rev. editor S.W. Jour. Linguistics, 1995-98; contbr. articles to profl. jours. Active Lubbock Cultural Affairs Coun., 1986-92, Lubbock Symphony Guild, 1992—; vol. Meals on Wheel, Lubbock, 1986-97, Habitat for Humanity, Lubbock, 1986-97, Interfaith Hospitality Network, 1998—. Mem.: MLA, AAUP (regional v.p. 1990—94), AAUW (alt. fellowships panel in linguistics 1988—90), South Ctrl. MLA, Coll. Tchrs. English Tex., Linguistic Assn. S.W. (pres. 1996—97, exec. dir. 1998—2001), Linguistic Soc. Am., Phi Beta Kappa, Alpha Lambda Delta, Sigma Tau Delta, Phi Kappa Phi. Avocations: geneaology, travel, west highland white terriers. Office: Tex Tech U Dept English Lubbock TX 79409

HURT, DAVINA THERESA, educator; b. Yonkers, N.Y., May 11, 1972; d. David Wallace and Sadie Theresa (Jeffries) H. Grad. in vocal music, School of the Arts, 1990; BS, Hampton U., 1995, postgrad.; cert. bus. edn., Nazareth Coll., 1997, MS Ed., 2001. Student intern IBM, Rochester, 1991; factory worker ITT, Rochester, 1994; contractor Man Power, Rochester, 1992-95; acctg. First Federal S&L, Rochester, N.Y., 1995-97; substitute tchr. Rochester City Sch. Dist., 1998—99; computer tchr. Josh Lofton H.S., Shape Alternative H.S., 2000—01, Edison Tech. Occupational and Ednl. Ctr., 2001—02. Bd. dirs. Ctr. for Youth Svcs., 1988-90; life mem. Ch. of God and Saints of Christ. Mem. AAUW. Home: 22 Dejonge St Rochester NY 14621-4606

HURTIG, SHANE BRENT, multimedia and music industry writer, educator, consultant; b. Winnipeg, Man., Can., June 12, 1959; came to U.S., 1978; s. Jack Zane Hurtig and Beverly Nan Gershman Schlechter; m. Andrea M. Albi, Sept. 1, 1989. Student, Banff (Can.) Sch. Fine Arts, 1977; BA cum laude, Brandeis U., 1982. Tech. dir., disk jockey Sta. WBRS-FM, Waltham, Mass., 1979-82; dir. tech. sales Recording and Broadcast Supply, San Rafael, Calif., 1983-86; sr. editor GPI Books, Cupertino, Calif., 1987-89; editor in chief EQ, Cupertino, 1989-90. Rec. engr. Brandeis U., Waltham, 1978-82; instr. exploration program Wellesley (Mass.) Coll., 1982, Blue Bear Sch. Music, San Francisco, 1988; instr. Cogswell Coll., Cupertino, 1991—; sr. assoc. Montara Creative Group. Author: Multi-Track Recording for Musicians, 1988; editor: Synthesizers and Computers, 1987, Playing Synthesizers, 1988, What is Midi?, 1988, Basic Midi Applications, 1988, Advanced Midi Applications, 1988, Synthesizer Basics, 1988; editor, writer (bi-monthly newsletter) Home Recording, 1987-89; columnist (mag.) Keyboard Mag., 1988-93; performed for HRH Prince Charles, Winnipeg, 1976; performed numerous concerts 1973-82; contbg. editor New Media Mag., 1995—. Recipient First Place award classical guitar Manitoba Music Festival, 1976, 77, Eagle prize St. John's Ravenscourt, Winnipeg, 1977. Mem. Nat. Acad. Recording Arts and Scis., Audio Engring. Soc. Jewish. Avocations: canoeing, scuba diving, mountain trekking, travel.

HURWITZ, SAUNDRA HARRIET (SANDI HURWITZ), analyst, educator; b. Orange, N.J., May 19, 1937; d. Julius Meyer and Laura (Mann) H. BA, Calif. State U., 1958, MPA, 1972. Mgmt. specialist II City of L.A. Cmty. Devel. Dept., 1976-95; prin. devel. specialist County of L.A. Cmty. Devel. Commn., L.A., 1991-95; contract specialist L.A. Homeless Svcs. Authority, 1995-96; prof. Calif. State U., L.A., 1978—. Cons. SH & Assocs., 1997—. Chair Cmty. Devel. Commn., Monterey Park, Calif., 1985-94; bd. dirs. Plz. Cmty. Ctr., L.A., 1997—. Recipient Youth Achievement award Downtown Businessmen Assn., L.A., 1977, Outstanding Achievement Alumni appreciation Calif. State U. Alumni Assn., 1977. Mem. Am. Soc. Pub. Adminstrn. (bd. dirs.). Avocations: dancing, painting, gardening, cooking, crafts, needlework. Home and Office: 1940 College View Dr Monterey Park CA 91754-4438

HUSARIK, ERNEST ALFRED, educational administrator; b. Gary, Ind., July 2, 1941; m. Elizabeth Ann Bonnette; children: Jennifer, Amy. BA in History, Olivet Nazarene U., 1963; MS in Ednl. Adminstrn., No. Ill. U., 1966; PhD in Ednl. Adminstrn. and Curriculum Devel., Ohio State U., 1973. Supt. Ontario (Ohio) Pub. Schs., 1973—75, Euclid (Ohio) Pub. Schs., 1975—86, Westerville (Ohio) Pub. Schs., 1986—2000, Carmel Clay Sch. Corp., 2000—01; ednl. specialist MS Cons., Inc. Past pres. Sch. Study Coun. Ohio; gd. govs. Westerville Fund; mem. adv. and distbn. com. Martha Holden Jennings Found.; pres. Westerville chpt. Am. Heart Assn.; past chmn. Franklin County Ednl. Coun.; past mem. alumni adv. coun. Ohio State U.; bd. dirs. Carmel Symphony. Named Ohio Supr. of Yr., 1994; named one of top 100 Edn. Adminstrs. N.Am., Exec. Educator, 1993. Mem.: ASCD, Hamilton-Boone County Ednl. Svc. Ctr. (chmn.), Franklin County Area Supt.'s Assn. (exec. com.), Ind. Assn. Pub. Sch. Supts., Ohio Assn. Supervision and Curriculum Devel., Ohio State U. Edliners (pres.), Sci. amd Math. Achievement Required for Tomorrow, Ohio Math. and Sci. Coalition (exec. bd.), Buckeye Assn. Sch. Adminstrs. (bd. dirs., pres., Disting. Svc. award 2001), Am. Assn. Sch. Adminstrs., Olivet Nazarene U. Alumni Assn. (past mem. alumni bd. dirs.), Carmel C. of C., Westerville Area C. of C. (bd. dirs.), Rotary (pres. Westerville, Rotarian of Yr.), Sigma Tau Delta, Phi Delta Kappa (past chpt. pres.). Home: 1029 Wood Glen Rd Westerville OH 43081-3240 Office: 1029 Wood Glen Rd Westerville OH 43081-3240 E-mail: edwardH568@aol.com.

HUSBAND, ROBERT WAYNE, biology educator; b. Hesperia, Mich., May 21, 1931; s. Max Robert and Frieda Belle (Poe) H.; m. Patricia Sue Psalmonds, May 14, 1955; children: David O., Linda C., Suzanne M. BA, U. Mich., 1953; MA, Western Mich. U., 1960; PhD, Mich. State U., 1966. Commd. 1st lt. USAF, 1954, advanced through grades to maj., 1962, resigned, 1970; sci. tchr. Milwood Jr. High Sch., Kalamazoo, 1959-60; lab. instr. Mich. State U., E. Lansing, 1960-64; from asst. prof. to full prof. Adrian (Mich.) Coll., 1964—, chmn. dept. Biology, 1970-80, chmn. sci. div., 1974-76. Prof. emeritus, 1997; endocrinology rsch. asst. Upjohn Pharm. Co., Kalamazoo, 1959, 1960. Mem. editorial bd. Internat. Jour. Acarology, 1980—; contbr. articles to profl. jours. Bd. dirs. Assoc. Charities, Adrian, 1968-70, 1st Meth. Ch., Adrian, 1988-90; project dir. Civitan, 1970—. 1st lt. USAF, 1954-58; maj. Mich. Air N.G., 1962-70. Recipient rsch. award Gerber Baby Food Co., 1986, Lifelong Svc. award Internat. Jour. Acarology, 2001; named C.A.S.E. Prof. of Yr. Mich., 1987; Around the World Travel grantee Lilly Found., 1990; NSF Rsch. fellow, 1971-72, NIH fellow, 1963, Goldsmith European Study fellow, 1967, 82, 86. Mem. Am. Microscopical Soc. (treas. 1975-79), Acarological Soc. Am., Entomological Soc. Am., Mich. Entomological Soc. (pres. 1973-74), Mich. Acad. Sci. (sect. chmn. 1970, 1988, 1997), Sigma Xi. Achievements include description of 116 new species of mites from all continents except Antarctica; world authority on mite family Podapolipidae, many of which have potential in controlling agricultural pests. Home: 1035 Scottdale Dr Adrian MI 49221-3263

HUSHEK, JOSEPH CHARLES, chemistry educator; b. Milw., Feb. 1, 1954; s. Charles Joseph and Patricia Louise (Zimmerman) H.; m. Kathleen Louise McFall, July 22, 1983. BA, Occidental Coll., 1976; MA, Fresno Pacific U., 1991. Cert. tchr. Nat. Bd. Profl. Tchg. Stds. Sci. educator Selma (Calif.) Unified Sch. Dist., 1977—. Recipient yearbook dedication, 1988; fellow GIFT, GTE, 1991. Mem. NSTA, NEA, ASCD, Calif. Sci. Tchrs. Assn. Democrat. Roman Catholic. Avocations: golf, travel, scuba diving, snorkeling. Home: 1366 W Sample Ave Fresno CA 93711-2031 Office: Selma High 3125 Wright St Selma CA 93662-2499

HUSSAIN, SYED TASEER, biomedical educator, researcher; b. Lahore, Pakistan, Sept. 18, 1943; came to U.S., 1970; s. S. Fayyaz and Riaz (Fatima) H. BS, Punjab U., Pakistan, 1963, BS with honors, 1964, MS, 1965; PhD, U. Utrecht, The Netherlands, 1969. Instr. Howard U. Coll. Medicine, Washington, 1972-73, asst. prof., 1973-76, assoc. prof., 1977-85, prof. anatomy, 1985—; postdoc. fellow Am. Mus. Natural History, N.Y.C., 1970—72. Dir. gen. Pakistan Mus. of Natural History, Pakistan Sci. Found., Islamabad, 1985-87; grants reveiwer NSF, 1980—, NATO, 1987—, Nat. Geog. Soc., 1985—; frequent invited spkr. on evolutionary processes, biological changes, climate change and human health. Author, co-author over 50 publs. and several book chpts., contbr. articles to profl. jours. Grantee Smithsonian Instn., 1974-94, NSF, 1977—, Nat. Inst. Environ. Health Scis., 1994. Fellow Pakistan Acad. Geol. Scis.; mem. AAAS, Am. Assn. Anatomy, Soc. Vertebrate Paleontology. Achievements include research in evolution in locomotion and hearing mechanism in mammals; human health and forced climate change; influence of increased temperatures on diseases. Office: Howard Univ Coll Medicine 520 W St NW Washington DC 20001-2337

HUSTED, STEWART WINTHROP, dean, marketing educator, consultant; b. Roanoke, Va., Oct. 22, 1946; s. John Edwin and Kathryn Faye (Stewart) H.; m. Kathleen Lixey, June 22, 1974; children: Ryan Winthrop, Evan William. BS, Va. Poly. Inst. & State U., 1968; MEd, U. Ga., 1972; PhD, Mich. State U., 1977. Mgmt. trainee Macy's Dept. Stores, Atlanta, 1967; trainee Heironimus Dept. Stores, Roanoke, Va., 1967; mktg. edn. coord. and tchr. Towers HS, Decatur, Ga., 1972-75; vocat. counselor Lansing Comm. Coll., Mich., 1975-76; from asst. prof. to prof. bus. Ind.

State U., Terre Haute, 1977-89; Donaldson Brown disting. prof. bus. Lynchburg Coll., Va., 1989—2003, dean Sch. Bus., 1994—2002; Frederik Wachmeister prof., vis. chair Va. Mil. Inst., Va., 2002—03, John W. and Jane M. Roberts chair in free enterprise bus., 2003—. Reviewer McGraw-Hill, NYC, 1983-87, Southwestern Pub. Co., 1987, Dryden Press, 1993; liaison officer US Mil. Acad., 1987-95. Author: (with Sam Certo, Max Douglas) Business, 1st edit., 1984, 2d edit., 1987, 3rd edit., 1990, (with Ralph Mason, Pat Rath) Marketing Practices and Principles, 4th edit., 1986, 5th edit., 1995, (with others) Cooperative Occupational Education, 6th edit., 2003, (with Dale Varble and James Lowry) Principles of Modern Marketing, 1989, Marketing Fundamentals, 1993; contbr. articles to profl. jours., chpts. and cases to books. Rep. to curriculum consortium MarkEd, Ind. Dept. Pub. Instrn., 1978-85, also trustee; bd. dirs., treas. Big Bros./Big Sisters, 1977-80; bd. dirs., mem. exec. com. Lynchburg Bus. Devel. Ctr., 1999-2002. Served to lt. col. USAR, 1968-96, ret. 1996. Col. Va. Militia, 2002—. Named to Mktg. Edn. Hall of Fame, 1974; U.S. Office Edn. EPDA Nat. fellow, 1975-76. Mem. Am. Mktg. Assn. (pres. Blue Ridge chpt. 1991-92), Am. Soc. Tng. and Devel. (exec. com. sales and mktg. div. 1991), Mil. Order of World Wars, Delta Pi Epsilon, Beta Gamma Sigma, Epsilon Delta Epsilon (Research award 1978), Mu Alpha Mu, Phi Kappa Phi, Phi Eta Sigma. Methodist. Home: 2224 Surrey Pl Lynchburg VA 24503-3042

HUSZAGH, FREDRICK WICKETT, lawyer, educator, information management company executive; b. Evanston, Ill., July 20, 1937; s. Rudolph LeRoy and Dorothea (Wickett) H.; m. Sandra McRae, Apr. 4, 1959; children: Floyd McRae, Fredrick Wickett II, Theodore Wickett II. BA, Northwestern U., 1958; JD, U. Chgo., 1962, LLM, 1963, JSD, 1964. Bar: Ill. 1962, U.S. Dist. Ct. D.C. 1965, U.S. Supreme Ct. 1966. Market rschr. Leo Burnett Co., Chgo., 1958-59; internat. atty. COMSAT, Washington, 1964-67; assoc. Debevoise & Liberman, Washington, 1967-68; asst. prof. law Am. U., Washington, 1968-71; program dir. NSF, Washington, 1971-73; assoc. prof. U. Mont., Missoula, 1973-76, U. Wis., Madison, 1976-77; exec. dir. Dean Rusk Ctr., U. Ga., Athens, 1977-82; prof. U. Ga., 1982—. Chmn. TWH Corp., Athens, 1982—; chmn. Profession Mgmt. Techs., Inc., Athens, 1993-96; cons. TWH Scv. Corp.; cons. Pres. Johnson's Telcommunications Task Force, Washington, 1967-68; co-chmn. Nat. Gov.'s Internat. Trade Staff Commn., Washington, 1979- 81. Author: International Decision-Making Process, 1964, Comparative Facts on Canada, Mexico and U.S., 1979; editor Rusk Ctr. Briefings, 1981-82; contbr. articles to publs. Mem. Econ. Policy Coun., N.Y.C., 1981-89. NSF grantee, 1974-78. Republican. Presbyterian. Home: 151 E Clayton St Athens GA 30601-2702 Office: U Ga Law Sch Athens GA 30602 E-mail: huszagh@twhcorp.com.

HUTCHENS, EUGENE GARLINGTON, college administrator; b. Birmingham, Ala., Nov. 26, 1929; s. Wallace Luther and Reydonia (Corry) H.; m. Betty Frances Goode, Aug. 26, 1951; children: Dale Eugene, Wayne Goode, Dennis Wade. BA, Samford U., 1952; ThM, New Orleans Bapt. Theol. Sem., 1970; MS in Econs., U. Mo.-Columbia, 1972; D Arts in Theology, Emmanuel Sem., 1999. Ordained to ministry, 1952. Min. North Brewton (Ala.) Bapt. Ch., 1952-56, 1st Bapt. Ch., Ashland, Ala., 1956-63, Highlands Bapt. Ch., Huntsville, Ala., 1963-67; tchr. pub. schs. Huntsville, 1967-71; instr. econs. N.W. Ala. State Jr. Coll., 1972-77, acting pres., 1981, dir. Tuscumbia campus, 1977-89; adminstrv. asst. Shoals C.C., 1989-93, asst. to dean, 1993-95; pastor emeritus Weeden Heights Bapt. Ch., Florence, 1995; prof. Emmanuel Sem., 1995—. Owner radio stas., WKNI AM, Lexington, Ala., WFIX, Rogersville, Ala., 1991-96, mem. Ala. Bapt. State Exec. Bd., 1961-63; v.p. Ala. Bapt. State Pastors Conf., 1966, Ala. Bapt. Hist. Commn., 1992-2000. NSF grantee, 1971-72. Mem. NEA, Ala. Edn. Assn., Ala. Jr. and C.C. Assn. (exec. com. 1981-84), Phi Theta Kappa. Home: 801 E 2nd St Tuscumbia AL 35674-2206

HUTCHENS, JOAN REID, elementary school educator, reading specialist, consultant; b. Harrisonburg, Va., May 22, 1947; d. Paul Leslie and Mary (Holsinger) Reid; m. Harry Edward Hutchens, Dec. 27, 1969; children: Stacie Amelia, Kimberly Dawn. BS in Elem. Edn., James Madison U., 1969, MEd, 1994. Cert. tchr., Va.; lic. reading specialist, Va. Tchr. grades 1-7, reading specialist K-12 Rockingham County Pub. Schs., Harrisonburg, Va., 1969—. Cons., trainer W.R.I.T. &E. Project/Nat. Diffusion Network, Falls Church, Va. and Glassboro, N.J., 1988-91; writing workshops/assessment workshops Rockingham County Pub. Schs., 1991—, lang. arts curriculum com., 1985—, Blue Ridge Assessment Project Albemarle County Pub. Schs., Charlottesville, Va., 1993-94, Va. State Reading Assn. Presentation, 1995. Recipient grant Rockingham Pub. Sch. Bd., 1992, 93, Blue Ridge Assessment Participant award Va. State Dept. Edn., 1994. Mem. ASCD, Va. Reading Assn., Shenandoah Valley Reading Assn., Phi Beta Kappa. Mem. Brethren Ch. Avocations: boating, fishing, reading professionally, cooking, writing. Home: 14813 Runions Creek Rd Broadway VA 22815-9510 Office: John C Myers Elem Sch Rockingham County Pub Schs Raider Rd Broadway VA 22815

HUTCHEON, DUNCAN ELLIOT, physician, educator; b. Kindersley, Sask., Can., June 21, 1922; s. Robert Scott and Anne (McGibbon) H.; m. Jean-Marie Kirkby, June 7, 1946; children: Robert Gordon, Jean-Marie Daleo, Marcia Louise Gale, Megan M. Smith. MD, U. Toronto, 1945, BSc in Medicine, 1947; DPhil, Oxford U., 1950. Diplomate Am. Bd. Internal Medicine. Intern Toronto Gen. Hosp., 1945-46; asst. prof. to prof. pharmacology and medicine Univ. Medicine and Dentistry N.J. Med. Sch., Newark, 1957-91, prof. emeritus, hon., 1991—2003. Editor Jour. Clin. Pharmacology, 1978-85, editor emeritus, 1990—, editor and pub. Sci. edn., 2002-. Pres. CINé, Inc.; cons. urban edn.; pres. Inst. Sci. Edn. and Tech., 1999-2002; prod./dir. Percy Julian Symposia for Sci. Edn., 2003-. Nat. Research Council Can. fellow, 1948-50 Fellow ACP. Achievements include applying advances in infor.tech. for student presentations for the classroom, publ., and World Wide Web.

HUTCHEON, WALLACE SCHOONMAKER, history educator; b. N.Y.C., June 27, 1933; s. Wallace Schoonmaker and Dorothy Mae (Tate) H.; m. Margaret Marie Crossen, Sept. 29, 1963; children: Dorothy Lee, Hillary Ann. BS in Agrl. Econs., Pa. State U., 1954; MA in History, George Washington U., 1969, MPhil in History, 1971, PhD in History, 1975. Commd. ensign U.S. Naval Res., 1955, advanced through grades to comdr., 1970; comm. officer Fawtulant Naval Air Sta., Key West, Fla., 1955-59; edn. officer USS Kitty Hawk, 1962-64; air intelligence officer CVW-2, 1964-66, intelligence analyst DIA, 1966-70; released to inactive duty, 1970; ret., 1976; lectr. George Mason U., Fairfax, Va., 1970; instr. St. Marys Coll., Md., 1971; asst. prof. history No. Va. C.C., Annandale, 1971-75, assoc. prof., 1975-80, prof., 1980—, head dept., 1974—. Asst. chmn. divsn. social scis. and pub. svcs., 1979-; mgmt. tng. cons. Health Resources Adminstrn., HEW, Hyattsville, Md., 1978; cons. mil. evaluations program Am. Coun. Edn., Washington, 1980; cons. coll. hist. textbooks Houghton-Mifflin Co., Boston, Mass., 1992-; mem. adv. bd. Annual Editions, Dushkin Pub. Co.; pub. spkr. Mariners Mus., D.C. Historian Luncheon, others; cons. coll. history textbooks McGraw-Hill Co., 2003. Author: Robert Fulton: Pioneer of Undersea Warfare, 1981; contbr. to manuscripts collection U.S. Navy History Divsn. Mem. History of the City of Fairfax Roundtable, 1995-98; history day judge George Mason U., 1990-2002. Recipient Outstanding Contbns. to Edn. award, Alumni Fedn. No. Va. CC, 1993, 1995, 2003, Golden Apple award, Student Govt., 1999—2000. Mem. U.S. Naval Inst., Orgn. Am. Historian, No. Va. Assn. History (bd. dirs. 1994, v.p. 1994), U.S. Capitol Hist. Soc., Delta Chi. Democrat. Episcopalian. Avocations: swimming, reading, music, theatre. Home: 4425 Village Dr Fairfax VA 22030-5642 Office: No Va CC 8333 Little River Tpke Annandale VA 22003-3743 E-mail: whutcheon@nvcc.us.

HUTCHERSON, DONNA DEAN, retired music educator; b. Dallas, July 10, 1937; d. Lamar Shaffer and Lenora Fay (Newbern) Clark; m. George Henry Hutcherson, Jan. 31, 1959; children: Lamar, Michael, Mark Lee, Holly (dec.), Shela. B. Music Edn., Sam Houston State U., Huntsville, Tex., 1959; MA in Music, Stephen F. Austin State U., Nacogdoches, Tex., 1974; postgrad., Memphis State U., 1986-89. Cert. tchr. music K-12, Orff levels 1, 2, 3, Master. cert. computer literacy, Tex. Tchr. music 4th and 5th grades Carthage (Tex.) Ind. Sch. Dist., 1958-59; tchr. music grades 1-5 and H.S. choir Hallsville (Tex.) Ind. Sch. Dist., 1969-75, tchr. music K-4, 1975-78, tchr. music grades 3-4, 1978-86, tchr. music 4th grade, 1986-97; ret., 1997. Contbr. Jour. of Music Edn. Delegation to Vietnam Citizen Ambassador Program, 1993; chmn. Tex. Ann. Conf. United Meth. Ch. Commn. on Archives/History. Contbr. articles to profl. jours. Fellow United Meth. Musicians in Worship and Other Arts; mem. Music Educators Nat. Conf. (registered music educator), Tex. Music Educators Conf. (state Tri-M chmn. 1993-98), Tex. Music Educators Assn. (region IV chmn. 1975-93), Am. Orff Schulewerk Assn., Tri M Internat. Music Honor Soc. (local chpt. sponsor 1992—, hon. mem.). Methodist. Avocations: square dancing, sewing, travel, church work, summer mission trips. Home: 119 Mcpherson Rd Hallsville TX 75650-7707 E-mail: ddhutch@juno.com.

HUTCHINS, CYNTHIA BARNES, special education educator; b. Macon, Ga., Apr. 29, 1954; d. Robert O. and Emily Ann (Coody) Barnes; m. Joe Thrash Hutchins, June 15, 1975; children: Joey, Jason. BS in Edn., U. Ga., 1976, MEd, 1981; EdS, Brenau U., 1996. Cert. tchr., Ga.; cert. middle childhood generalist Nat. Bd. Profl. Tchg. Stds. Tchr. Bethlehem (Ga.) Elem. Sch., 1976-78, Winder (Ga.) Elem. Sch., 1983-85, Auburn (Ga.) Elem. Sch., 1985-92; tchr., staffing coord. Bramlett Elem. Sch., Auburn, 1992—. Mem. spl. edn. adv. com., mem. inclusion task force, mentor tchr., tchr. support specialist Barrow County, 1990—. Sunday sch. tchr. Midway Meth. Ch., Carl, Ga., 1975-80, 90-93; leader Boy Scouts Am., Barrow County, 1986-90; active PTO. Named Tchr. of Yr., Auburn Elem. Sch., 1986, Tchr. of Yr. Bramlett Elem., 1998, Barrow Co. Tchr. of Yr., 1998. Mem. ASCD, Coun. for Exceptional Children, Alpha Delta Kappa, Phi Delta Kappa. Avocations: crafts, reading, white water rafting, traveling. Home: 1165 Bankhead Hwy Winder GA 30680-3431

HUTCHINSON, ANN, management consultant; b. East Stroudsburg, Pa., May 15, 1950; d. David Ellis and Susie (Ingalls) Hutchinson; m. Paul Harrison McAllister, Jan. 2, 1986. BS in Vocat. Edn., Fla. Internat. U., 1985; MBA, Pepperdine U., 1990. Cert. advanced vocat. tchr. Fla., cmty. coll. educator Ariz., pub. mgr. Motorcycle technician, Ft. Lauderdale, Fla., 1973-78; machinist, 1978-79; instr., motorcycle tech. Sheridan Vocat. Tech. Sch., Hollywood, Fla., 1979-85; adminstr., tng. program Am. Honda Motorcycle Divsn., Torrance, Calif., 1985-86, curriculum developer motorcycles svc. tech., 1986-90, coll. program coord., 1990-94; ednl. devel. dir. Clinton Tech. Inst., Phoenix, 1994-96; dep. mgr. tng. unit Ariz. State Dept. Econ. Security, Phoenix, 1996-99, mgmt. cons. office of total quality, 1999-2001; instrnl. sys. specialist Bur. Land Mgmt. Nat. Tng. Ctr., 2001—. Adj. faculty Ariz. State U., 2001—; chmn. high tech. acad. steering com. Pasadena (Calif.) United Sch. Dist., 1991—94; ednl. cons. Ctr. for Occupation R & D Sch.-to-Work Awards, 1994—97; mem. cert. pub. mgr. program adv. bd. Ariz. State U., 1998—2001. Examiner Gov.'s Award for Excellence, 1997—99; mem. Ams. With Disabilities Act com. Ariz. Dept. Econ. Security, 1995—2001; mem. Desert Hill Improvement Assn., 1996—, bd. dirs., editor, 1998—99, v.p., 1999—2001, pres., 2001—; examiner Ariz. State Quality Awards, 1997—2002, mem. tech. integrity coun., 2003—. Recipient State of Ky. Col. award, 1990, Quality award examiner, Az. State, 1997—2002, Quality award tech. integrity coun., 2002—. Mem.: ASTD, Am. Vocat. Assn., Vocat. Indsl. Clubs Am. (co-chmn. motorcycle tech. com. 1988—90, 1994—95, automotive nat. tech. com. 1990—94, adv. Hollywood, Fla. 1979—85), Cert. Pub. Mgr. Assn., Am. Motorcycle Assn., Toastmasters Internat. (Zenger Miller cert. 1996—). Avocations: hiking, camping, st. motorcycle riding. Office: Bur Land Mgmt Nat Tng Ctr Office Total Quality 9828 N 31 Ave Phoenix AZ 85051 E-mail: behomes@attglobal.net.

HUTCHINSON, BARBARA WINTER, elementary school educator; b. Pitts., Dec. 20, 1952; d. Raymond Francis and Dorothy (Kunkel) Winter; m. Matthew Hutchinson, June 8, 1973; children: Matthew Martin, Jennifer Elizabeth. BA, Westminster Coll., 1974. Cert. tchr., Pa. Tchr. Shaler Area Sch. Dist., Glenshaw, Pa., 1975-84, North Allegheny Sch. Dist., Pitts., 1984—, staff devel. leader, 1991—. Mem. dist. adv. coun., profl. issues com. North Allegheny Sch. Dist., Pitts., 1993—, mem. instrnl. responsibility com., 1996-98, total quality in edn. process com., 1996-98, quality improvement team, 1996-97, strategic planning com., 1999—, total quality steering com., 1999-2000, negotiating team, 1999-2000, mem. profl. edn. com., 1998—; mem. mid. sch. day com., 2001—; presenter coop. learning workshops. Author: Primary Assistance, 1979, History of the Avonworth School District, 1990; co-author curriculum materials. Mem. Cmty. Presbyn. Ch. Ben Avon, Pa., 1976—; pres., program dir. Ben Avon Area Hist. Assn., 1988-2003; bd. dirs., sec., program chair Avon Club Found., 1990-93; mem. Ben Avon Centennial Com., 1990-93; co-leader local troop Girl Scouts U.S., 1991-92; bd. dirs. Sacred Heart Sch., Pitts., 1991-92. Recipient Found. Excellence award, 1996, Citation for Tchg. Excellence, Pa. Ho. of Reps., Outstanding Secondary Social Studies Program of Yr. award Pa. Coun. Social Studies Tchrs., 2002. Mem. Am. Fedn. Tchrs., North Allegheny Fedn. Tchrs. (mem. exec. coun. 1992-96, treas. 1996-98, secondary v.p. 1998-99, 1st v.p. 1999-2000, pres. 2000—), Pa. Fedn. Tchrs., Phi Delta Kappa. Avocations: sewing, wood refinishing, reading, writing, home decorating. Home: 205 Hillvue Dr Seven Fields PA 16046 Office: Marshall Middle Sch 5145 Wexford Run Rd Wexford PA 15090-7458 E-mail: bhutchinson@northallegheny.org.

HUTCHINSON, CHARLES EDGAR, engineering educator; b. Parkersburg, W.Va., Dec. 18, 1935; s. Charles Edgar and Elizabeth Hana (Eggleton) H.; m. Elva Anneta Butland, Aug. 20, 1960; children: Charles Edgar IV, John Mathew. BEE, Ill. Inst. Tech., 1957; MEE, Stanford U., 1961, PhD, 1963. Instr. USN ROTC, 1959-60; tchg. asst. Stanford (Calif.) U., 1960-63; lectr. UCLA, 1963-65; assoc. prof. U. Mass., Amherst, 1965-69, prof., 1969-84, acting assoc. dean acad. affairs, 1977, acting assoc. dean research affairs, 1977-78, head dept. electrical and computer engring., 1978-82; prof., dean Thayer Sch. Engring. Dartmouth Coll., Hanover, NH, 1984-94, 97-98, John H. Krehbiel Sr. prof. for emerging technologies, 1994—2003, emeritus, 2003—. Lectr. Sch. Medicine, Boston U., 1971-72; cons. The Analytic Scis. Corp., Reading, Mass., 1967-98, Molex, Inc., 1988—, Baxter Health, 1992-2003, Tally Sys., Inc., 1997—; bd. dirs. Markem Corp., Keene, N.H., Hypertherm, Inc., Hanover, N.H., Med. Media Sys., Inc., Lebanon, N.H., Dilion Tech., Inc., Newport News, Va., Microchips, Cambridge, Mass. Lt. USN, 1957-60. Mem. IEEE (chmn. edn. com. 1983-86, bd. govs. profl. group on aerospace and electronic sys. 1983-86, profl. groups on automatic control and on computers), Am. Soc. Engring. Edn. (chmn. computers in edn. divsn. 1975-77, New Eng. sect. 1965—), Assn. for Media-Based Edn. for Engrs. (vice chmn. 1983, bd. dirs. 1980-84), Sigma Xi, Eta Kappa Nu (nat. bd. dirs. 1966-69, chmn. nat. publicity com. 1968-73, faculty advisor 1966-68, 74-76), Tau Beta Pi (prof. 1967). Republican. Avocations: horse showing, horse breeding. Home: 89 Apple Blossom Ln Canaan NH 03741 Office: Dartmouth Coll Thayer Sch Engring Hanover NH 03755

HUTCHINSON, JOHN WOODSIDE, mechanical engineer, educator; b. Hartford, Conn., Apr. 10, 1939; s. John Woodside and Evelyn (Eastburn) Hutchinson; m. Lizzi Spanggaard; children: Leif, David, Robert. BS, Lehigh U., 1960; MS, Harvard U., 1961, PhD, 1963; DSc (hon.), Royal Inst. Tech., Stockholm, 1985, Tech. U. Denmark, Lyngby, 1992, Northwestern U., Evanston, 2002. Asst. prof. Harvard U., Cambridge, Mass., 1964-69, Gordon McKay prof. applied mechanics, 1969—. Contbr. articles to profl. jours. Fellow, Guggenheim Found., 1974. Fellow: ASME (Araprd L. Nadai award 1991, Timoshenko medal 2002); mem.: NAS, NAE, ASTM (Irwin medal 1982), AAAS. E-mail: hutchinson@husm.harvard.edu.

HUTCHISON, BRENDA LEE, elementary education educator; b. Campbellsville, Ky., Jan. 8, 1956; d. David Malcom and Rosa Allene (Carroll) Eastridge; m. Clarence Thomas Hutchison, May 30, 1980. BS, Campbellsville Coll., 1978; MEd, U. Louisville, 1983; postgrad., Bellarmine Coll., 1992—. Tchr. music Marion County Schs., Lebanon, Ky., 1978-79, Casey County Schs., Liberty, Ky., 1979-80, Bullitt County Schs., Shepherdsville, Ky., 1980-81; elem. tchr. St. Paul Sch., Louisville, 1985-93; music tchr. Bullitt County Schs., Shepherdsville, Ky., 1993—. Avocation: give music lessons.

HUTCHISON, JANE CAMPBELL, art history educator, researcher; b. Washington, July 20, 1932; d. James Paul and Leone Bailey (Warrick) H. BA fine arts, Western Maryland Coll., 1954; MA art history, Oberlin Coll., 1958; PhD art history, U. Wis., 1964. Tech. illustrator/ Dept. Model Basin U.S. Navy, Washington, 1954-56; rsch libr. Toledo Mus. of Art, 1957-59; teaching asst. U. Wis., Madison, 1959-60,61-63; vis. asst. prof. Temple U., Phila., summer 1968; from instr. to assoc. prof. U. Wis., Madison, 1964—, prof., 1975—, dept. chmn., 1977-80, 92-93. Expert witness U.S. Dist. Ct. (so. dist.) N.Y., 2000; cons. in field. Author: Master of the Housebook, 1972, Early German Artists, vol. 8, 1980, vol. 9, 1981, vol. 9 part 2, 1991, vol. 8 part 6, 1996, Albrecht Dürer: A Biography, 1990 (German edit., 1994), Albrecht Durer: A Guide to Research, 2000; mem. editl. bd. Studies in Iconography, 1997—, Source, 2003, Sixteenth Century Jour., 2003. Pres. Madison chpt. AAUP, 1979-81, Midwest Art History Soc., 1983-85, treas., 2001—; sec.-treas. Historians of Netherlandish Art, 1995-99; pres. St. Andrew's Soc. Madison, 1995—; mem. spl. com. on arts funding Wis. State Legis. Coun., 2000-01. Grad. fellow Oberlin Coll., 1955-57, fellow U. Wis., 1959-60, 61-63, Fulbright fellow Rijksuniversiteit Utrecht, Netherlands, 1960-61, rsch. grantee NEH, Germany, 1982, German Acad. Exch. Svc., Germany, summer 1989; Grant in aid Am. Coun. Learned Soc., Amsterdam, 1984; recipient Alumni award Western Md. Coll. Trustees, 1987. Mem. AAUP (pres. Madison chpt. 1979-81), Internat. Coun. Mus., Am. Assn. Mus., Medieval Acad. Am., Coll. Art Assn., Univ. Club U. Wis. (bd. dirs. 1976-80, pres. 1980), Wis. Assn. Scholars (v.p. Madison chpt. 1990-95), Midwest Art History Soc. (pres. 1983-85, treas. 2001--), Historians of Netherlandish Art (treas. 1995-99), Print Coun. Am., Wis. Acad. Scis., Arts and Letters, Minerva Soc. Home: 2261 Regent St Madison WI 53705-5321 Office: U Wis Dept Art History 800 University Ave Madison WI 53706-1414 E-mail: jchutchi@facstaff.wisc.edu.

HUTCHISON, WILLIAM ROBERT, history educator; b. San Francisco, May 21, 1930; s. Ralph Cooper and Harriet (Thompson) H.; m. Virginia Quay, Aug. 16, 1952; children: Joseph Cooper, Catherine Eaton, Margaret Sidney, Elizabeth Quay. BA, Hamilton Coll., 1951, DHL (hon.), 1991; BA (Fulbright scholar), Oxford U., 1953, MA, 1957; PhD, Yale U., 1956; MA (hon.), Harvard U., 1968. Instr. history Hunter Coll., 1956-58; assoc. prof. Am. studies Am. U., 1958-64, prof. history and Am. studies, 1964-68; Charles Warren prof. history of religion in Am. Harvard U., 1968—2000; master Winthrop House, 1974-79; USIA lectr. E. Asia & Pacific, August, 1983; Charles Warren rsch. prof. Harvard U., 2000—. Vis. asso. prof. history U. Wis., 1963-64 Author: The Transcendentalist Ministers: Church Reform in the New England Renaissance, 1959, The Modernist Impulse in American Protestantism, 1976, Errand to the World: American Protestant Thought and Foreign Missions, 1987; Religious Pluralism in America: The Contentious History of a Founding Ideal, 2003; editor: American Protestant Thought, the Liberal Era, 1968; co-editor and joint author: Missionary Ideologies in the Imperialist Era, 1982; editor and joint author: Between the Times: The Travail of the Protestant Establishment in America, 1900-1960, 1989; co-editor and joint author: Many are Chosen: Divine Election and Western Nationalism, 1994; contbr. articles to profl. jours. Recipient Brewer prize Am. Soc. Ch. History, 1957; Am. Religious Book award, 1976; Guggenheim fellow, 1960-61; fellow Charles Warren Ctr. for Studies in Am. History, Harvard, 1966-67; Fulbright Sr. Research scholar Free U., Berlin, 1976; Fulbright Disting. lectr. in Am. history India, summer 1981; Fulbright Western European Regional Research grantee, 1987; Fulbright Disting. lectr. in Am. hist. and rel., Indonesia, 1993; Olaus Petri lectr., Uppsala U. (Sw.), 1996. Mem. Am. Hist. Assn., Orgn. Am. Historians, Am. Studies Assn., Am. Soc. Ch. History (pres. 1981), Unitarian Universalist Hist. Soc., Mass. Hist. Soc., Phi Beta Kappa. Democrat. Mem. Soc. Of Friends. Home: 4 Ellery Square Cambridge MA 02138 Office: Widener N, Harvard Univ Cambridge MA 02138

HUTHLOFF, CHRISTA ROSE, library and information science educator; b. Aichelberg, Germany, Oct. 4, 1946; Grad., Libr. Sch., Hamburg, Germany, 1969. Head interlibr. loan Lower Saxonian State Libr., Hannover, Germany, 1969-76; lectr. Libr. Sch., Hannover, 1976-80; lectr. libr. & info. sci. Fach Hoch Sch, Hannover, 1980—. Author: GRIPS Fuer BRZN und DBI, 1991; co-author: Online - Bibliographieren in allgemeinbibliographiochen, 1985; editor: Informationsvermittling, 1988; contbr. articles to profl. jours. Mem. Berufsverband Information Bibliothek, Deutsche Gesellschaft für Informationswissenschaft und Informationspraxis. Office: Fach Hoch Sch Info und Komm Ricklinger Stadtweg 120 30459 Hannover Germany E-mail: Christa.huthloff@ik.fh-hannover.de.

HUTSON, BETTY SWITZER, art educator, artist; b. Brunswick, Mo., Aug. 14, 1930; d. Henry William and Pearl Evelyn (Sayler) Switzer; m. Don L. Hutson, Sept. 7, 1952; children: Eric, Sheila Hutson, Robin Hutson-Montoya, Heather Hutson Daye. BFA, Ctrl. Meth. Coll., 1952; postgrad., U. Mo., 1953-54, Kansas City Art Inst., 1958-60, Avila Coll., 1981; MA in Art Edn., U. Mo., Kansas City, 1986. Cert. tchr. grades K-12, Mo. Elem. art cons. Md. Pub. Schs., Rockville, 1954-58; art instr. Ruskin High Sch., Hickman Mills, Mo., 1958-60, East High Sch., Kansas City, Mo., 1961-62, N.E. Sr. High Sch., Kansas City, 1964-65; dir. edn. All Souls Unitarian Ch., Kansas City, 1975-77; art instr. Westport Jr. High Sch., Kansas City, 1977-87; art instr., cons. De LaSalle Edn. Ctr., Kansas City, 1987-88; art instr. Nelson Mus. Art, Kansas City, 1987-88; visual arts resource tchr. Kansas City Middle Sch. Arts, 1988—99; ret., 1999. Art instr. U. Md., College Park, summer, 1956; resource cons. U. Mo., Kansas City, 1984-86; arts ptnrs. devel. Kansas City Sch. Dist. Learning Exch., 1985-86; curriculum author, task force mem. Kansas City Middle Sch. the Arts, 1988-90, Paseo Acad. Fine & Performing Arts, Kansas City, 1988-90; supervising tchr. student and practicum tchrs. Rockhurst Coll., Kansas City, 1976-92, Avila Coll., Kansas City, 1976-92, U. Mo., Kansas City, 1976-92, 94, Truman U., 1996-97, Park U., 1997-98. Author: Sampling the Basics, 1985; one-woman shows include Unitarian Gallery, 1987, 2001, Lebanon Gallery, 1988, Tchrs. Credit Union Gallery, 1989-90, Le Fou Frog, 2002-03; exhibited in group shows at Unitarian Gallery, Kansas City, 1985, 87, 89, 91, 93, 95, 97, 99, 2001, Nelson Mus. Art, Kansas City, 1989, Fed. Res. Bank, Kansas City, 1990, Kaw Valley Gallery, Kansas City, 1990, Blue Springs (Mo.) Art Exhbn., 1990, 91, Heartland Art Festival, St. Joseph, Mo., 1990-93, Allied Arts Coun., St. Joseph, 1990-93, Bruce Watkins Cultural Ctr., Kansas City, 1993, 94, 95, Muse Gallery, Kansas City, 1995, Kansas City Artists Coalition, 2000, Ashby-Hodge Art Gallery, 2001, Cultures w/o Borders Exhbn., 2001, Open Studios, 2001, 02, others; illus. Children's History of AME Church, 1997. Den mother, art leader Boy Scouts of Am., Raytown, Mo., 1967-69, Girl Scouts of Am., Raytown, 1969-75; vol. AIDSWalk 1998, 99, 2000, 01, 02, 03, Habitat for Humanity, 1992, 93, 94, 96, 2002, soup kitchen Ward Chapel AME, World Federalists, Kansas City, 1989—, Scholastic Arts Regional Com.; vol., fundraiser Peaceworks, Kansas City, 1986—; vol., leader, officer PTA, Kansas City, 1965-76; Jr. Great Books, Picture Lady, Headstart, Planned Parenthood, Friends of the Zoo; trustee All Souls Unitarian-Universalist, 1976-79, 96-99; vol. usher various orgns.; bd. dirs. Unitarian Gallery, 1989—, curator Elizabeth

Layton exhibit, 1992. Recipient Disting. Svc. award All Souls Unitarian Ch., Kansas City, 1977, Outstanding Tchr. award Westport Jr. High Sch., Kansas City, 1987, Excellence in Tchtg. Art award, 1995. Mem. AAUW (v.p. 2002-04, art study chmn.), Nat. Art Edn. Assn., Art Edn. Connection (Svc. award 1991-92), Mo. Art Edn. Assn. (Outstanding Art Tchr. 1992), Friends of Art-Nelson Mus. Art, Demeters (pres. 1978-80, 90-91, v.p. 1965-68, 79, 89, co-pres. 2001-, Svc. award 1987), Kansas City Artists Coalition, Mo. Mid. Sch. Assn. Democrat. Unitarian Universalist. Avocations: travel, swimming, gardening, drawing, painting. Home: 7625 Baltimore Ave Kansas City MO 64114-1813

HUTSON, JACQUELYN COLLINS, pianist, educator; b. Gainesville, Ga., Sept. 5, 1938; d. Joseph Watson and Merta (Shuler) Collins; m. Billy Monroe Hutson, Jan. 1, 1959; children: Tamelyn Merta, Jonathan Monroe. AB, Young Harris Coll., 1957; BA in English, Tift coll., 1959; BA in Music, Mercer U., 1976. Tchr. pub. sch. Cobb County, Marietta, Ga., 1959-66; ind. piano tchr. Marietta, 1966—. Mem.: Cobb County Music Tchrs., Greater Marietta Music Tchrs. (v.p. chmn. solo festival 1997—99, pres. 2001—), Ga. Music Tchrs. Assn. (chmn. state conv. 1995, chmn. state piano auditions com. 1996—98), Ga. Music Educators Assn. (chmn. piano com.), Nat. Music Tchrs. Assn., Nat. Music Educators Assn. Republican. Baptist. Avocations: church choir, youth choir, accompanist. Home: 1827 Kimberly Dr SW Marietta GA 30008-4490

HUTTEN, ANGELA CLARE, special education educator; b. Rockford, Ill., Dec. 1, 1938; d. Elmer Edward and Alice Caroline (Bassetti) Englund; m. Francis Joseph Hutten, June 23, 1962; children: Caroline, Edward, Rosemary. BA in English, No. Ill. U., 1961, MS in English Edn., 1967. Cert. tchr. grades K-12 regular edn., learning disabilities, socially and emotionally disorders, lang. arts, Ill. English tchr. Ela-Vernon H.S., Lake Zurich, Ill., 1961-62, Waukegan (Ill.) Twp. H.S., 1962-65; spl. edn. tchr. Waukegan (Ill.) Unit Dist. 60, 1972—. Mem. curriculum coun. Waukegan (Ill.) Pub. Schs., 1980-84, site-based adv. com., 1991—. Bd. dirs., v.p. AAUW Nursery Sch., Waukegan, 1970-74; mem. Friends of the Waukegan (Ill.) Pub. Libr., 1975—, treas., 1984, v.p., 1990-92, pres., 1998-2002. Mem. AAUW (Waukegan br. treas. 1976-77, v.p. 2002--), Am. Fedn. Tchrs. (nat. trainer), Ill. Fedn. Tchrs., Lake County Fedn. Tchrs. (Waukegan coun. sec. 1982-2001, local site coord. Ednl. Rsch. and Dissemination Program 1989—, coord. profl. devel.), Delta Kappa Gamma (Beta Upsilon chpt. sec. 1985-86), Phi Delta Kappa (chpt. 1123 v.p. 1990-91, conv. del. 1994-95). Avocations: reading, education research, furniture refinishing, needle point. Home: 2912 Carriage Ln Waukegan IL 60085-3116 Office: Lake County Fedn Tchrs 248 Ambrogio Dr Gurnee IL 60031-3373

HUTTO, NORA MARGUERITE NELSON, education educator; b. Roswell, N.Mex., Jan. 16, 1952; d. Clarence Harvey and Roberta Ann (Caywood) Nelson; m. Rodney Dean Hutto, Aug. 16, 1975; children: Spurgeon Robert, Rodney Loran. BS in Home Econs. Edn., N.Mex. State U., 1972; MS, Tex. Tech. U., 1974, EdD, 1979, supt.'s profl. cert., 1990; mid-mgmt. cert., West Tex. State U., 1985. Cert. tchr., supt., mid-mgmt., Tex. Instr. Clarendon Jr. Coll., Pampa, Tex., 1982-84; prin. Allison (Tex.) Ind. Sch. Dist., 1985-86, supt., 1986-88; assoc. prof. edn. adminstrn. N.Mex. State U., Las Cruces, 1988-90; edn. program dir. Tex. Edn. Agy., Austin, 1990-91, field svc. agt. region III edn. svc. ctr. Victoria, 1991-93; assoc. prof. edn. adminstrn. U. Houston-Victoria, 1993—. Contbr. articles to profl. jours. Recipient Nat. Exemplary Project award U.S. Office Edn. Mem. ASCD, Nat. Secondary Prins. Assn., Phi Delta Kappa, Phi Kappa Phi, Pi Beta Phi. Avocations: tennis, writing, gardening, walking. Home: PO Box 4172 Victoria TX 77903-4172

HUTTON, JOHN EVANS, JR., surgery educator, retired military officer; b. N.Y.C., Sept. 9, 1931; s. John Evans and Antoinette (Abbott) H.; m. Barbara Seward Joyce, Apr. 15, 1961; children: John III, Wendy, James, Elizabeth. BA, Wesleyan U., 1953; MD, George Washington U., 1963. Diplomate: Am. Bd. Surgery, Am. Bd. Med. Examiners. Commd. 2d lt. USMC, 1953, advanced through grades to capt., 1962; discharged USMCR; commd. capt. U.S. Army, 1963, advanced through grades to brig. gen., 1989, intern, resident in gen. surgery Walter Reed Army Med. Ctr., 1963-68, fellow vascular surgery, 1969-70, asst. chief vascular surgery, 1970-71, mem. staff gen. surgery svcs., 1969-71, chief dept. surgery, 1981-84, White House physician, 1984-86, physician to the Pres., 1987-88, chief surgeon 91st Evacuation Hosp., Republic of Vietnam, 1968—69, chief vascular surgery, asst. chief gen. surgery Letterman Army Med. Ctr., 1971-74, chief gen. and vascular surgery, program dir., gen. surgery residency Letterman Army Med. Ctr., 1975-81; comdr. 47th Field Hosp., Honduras, 1984; commanding gen. Madigan Army Med. Ctr. U.S. Army, Tacoma, 1989-92; ret., 1992; prof. surgery, chief div. gen. surgery, dept. surg. Uniformed Svcs. U. Sch. Medicine, Bethesda, Md., 1992—, mem. faculty senate, 1996—99, mem. students promotion com., 1993-96, 2002—, mem. instl. rev. bd., 1993-96, mem. com. appointments, promotion and tenure, 1998-99, pres. elect faculty senate, 1997; pres. faculty senate Uniformed Svcs. U. Health Scis., Bethesda, 1998. Assoc. clin. prof. surgery U. Calif., San Francisco, 1978-81, mem. dean's adv. group, 1998-99; assoc. prof. surgery, vice chmn. dept. surgery Uniformed Svcs. U. Health Scis., Bethesda, 1981-84, prof. surgery, 1985—; clin. prof. surgery Tulane U. Sch. Medicine, 1988—, George Washington Sch. Medicine, Washington, 1985—. Contbr. articles, photographs to profl. publs., chpts. to books. Mem. men and boys choir Grace Cathedral, San Francisco, 1971-75. Decorated D.S.M., Bronze Star, Meritorious Svcs. medal with oak leaf cluster, Army Commendation Medal, Navy Commendation Medal, Joint Svc. Commendation Medal, Vietnam Svc. medal with four bronze svc. stars, Nat. DSM with two bronze svc. stars, Naval Occupation medal, WWII, Vietnam Honor medal 1st class, Vietnam Cross of Gallantry; recipient Barron Dominique Larrey award for excellence in surgery, Disting. Svc. medal, Uniformed Svcs. U. Sch. Medicine, 2000. Fellow: ACS; mem.: Soc. for Mil. Cons. to Armed Forces (councilor 1988—89, v.p. 2000, pres. 2001), Acad. Medicine Washington D.C., Chesapeake Vascular Soc., Soc. Mil. Vascular Surgery, Am. Assn. for Surgery of Trauma, Soc. Clin. Vascular Surgery, Am. Assn. for Vascular Surgery, Bay Surg. Soc. (hon.), U.S. Naval Acad. Sailing Squadron, St. Francis Yacht Club (membership com. 1978—81). Republican. Episcopalian. Avocations: music, photography, competitive sailing, coaching. Home: 1707 Priscilla Dr Silver Spring MD 20904-1610 Office: Uniformed Svcs U Health Scis Dept Surgery 4301 Jones Bridge Rd Bethesda MD 20814-4712

HUTTON, MARY J. guidance counselor; b. Kansas City, Mo., Nov. 21, 1951; d. Bill H. and Vera M. (Needels) Harmon; m. Douglas L. Hutton, June 1, 1974; children: Dylan M., Marissa S. Cert. in Elem. Edn., Northwest Mo. State U., 1973; M in Counseling, U. Iowa, 1985. Tchr. Mid-Buchanan Community Sch., St. Joseph, Mo., 1973-74; co-dir. Adolescent Ctr. FAMCO, Cedar Rapids, Iowa, 1974-76; employment specialist State of Iowa, Iowa City, 1976-80; employment mgr. Mercy Hosp., Iowa City, 1980-85; guidance counselor Linn Mar Community Sch., Cedar Rapids, 1985—. Mem. St. Paul's United Meth. Ch. Mem. NEA, Linn Mar Edn. Assn., Iowa Assn. for Counselors. Avocations: needle work, reading, children, tae kwon do (black belt). Home: 2366 Towne House Dr NE Cedar Rapids IA 52402-2228 Office: Bowman Woods 151 Boyson Rd NE Cedar Rapids IA 52402-1415

HUTTON, WINFIELD TRAVIS, management consultant, educator; b. LA, Aug. 17, 1935; s. Travis Calhoun and Frances (Gardemann) H. BS in Mgmt. summa cum laude, Ohio State U., 1956, MBA, 1957, PhD, 1959. Consumer economist Fed. Res. Bank Atlanta, 1959-62; prof. econs. Hunter Coll., CUNY, 1962-68; prof. European divsn. U. Md., 1968-79, 93-99; prof. Troy State U.-Europe, Germany, 1979-93. Cons. on mgmt., mktg. and econs. in Europe, 1968—. Author: (mgmt. computer simulations) City Finance, 1994, Simanage, 1998; author computer programs for rsch. stats.; contbr. articles to profl. jours. Lay reader St. Alban's Episcopal Ch., Kaiserslauten, Germany, 1981-88. Mem. AAUP, Am. Mktg. Assn. (manuscript reviewer 1983-94), Am. Econ. Assn., Beta Gamma Sigma. Avocations: opera, folk dancing, walking, cycling, travel. Address: 15138 Stone Ln N Apt B106 Shoreline WA 98133-6259 also: Goethestr 66 19053 Schwerin Germany

HUURMAN, WALTER WILLIAM, pediatric orthopaedic surgeon, educator; b. Rochester, N.Y., Mar. 16, 1936; s. Walter U. and Anna Mae (Lennon) H.; m. Lindsay Ann McGuiness, Dec. 16, 1967; children: Sean Patrick, Anne Lindsay. BS, U. Notre Dame, 1958; MD, Northwestern U., 1962. Diplomate Am. Bd. Orthopaedic Surgery. Intern Cook County Hosp., Chgo., 1962-63; flight surgeon USS Hornet, San Diego, 1964-66, NAS Miramar, San Diego, 1966-68; resident in orthopedic surgery Naval Regional Med. Ctr., Oakland, Calif., 1968-71; dir. pediatric orthopaedics USN, Oakland, Calif., 1973-77; prof. pediatrics and orthopaedics U. Nebr., Omaha, 1977—; dir. pediatric orthopedics U. Nebr./Children's Meml. Hosp., Omaha, 1977. Bd. dirs. Nat. Alumni, Northwestern U. Mem. editl. bd. Jour. Pediat. Orthopaedics, 1981-83, Jour. Bone and Joint Surgery, 1983-87, Pediatrics in Rev., 1995—; reviewer Clin. Orthopaedics and Related Rsch., 1985—, Jour. Am. Acad. Orthopaedic Surgeons, 1998—; contbr. articles to sci. and profl. jours. Pres., chmn. bd. dirs. Nebr. Arthritis Found., 1984. Capt. USN, 1963-77; res., 1980-95, ret. Fellow Am. Acad. Orthopaedic Surgery, Am. Acad. Pediatrics (chmn. orthopaedic sect. 1986-89), ACS; mem. AMA, Am. Orthopaedic Assn., Omaha Midwest Clin. Soc. (pres. 1994), Nebr. Orthopaedic Soc. (pres. 2000—), Pediat. Orthopaedic Soc. N.Am.(bd. dirs. 1994-2000), Acad. Orthoopaedic Soc., Northwestern U. Feinberg Sch. Medicine Alumni Assn. (pres.-elect 2003—). Roman Catholic. Office: U Nebr Med Ctr 600 S 42nd St Omaha NE 68198-1002

HUVOS, ANDREW, internist, cardiologist, educator; b. Budapest, Hungary, Apr. 23, 1930; came to U.S., 1950; s. Julian Gyula and Magdolna (Matyas) H.; m. Monique Chatriot, June 8, 1959; children: Christine, Anne, Philip. Student, Free U. Brussels, 1948-50, Harvard U., 1951; MD, Boston U., 1955. Diplomate Am. Bd. Internal Medicine, Am. Bd. Cardiovascular Disease. Resident in medicine Yale-New Haven Med. Ctr., 1955-59; fellow in cardiology Mass. Gen. Hosp., Boston, 1961-63; physician-in-charge cardiac catheterization lab. Univ. Hosp., Boston, 1963-70; chief cardiology Faulkner Hosp., Boston, 1970-74, chief medicine, 1974-95; lectr. medicine Harvard Med. Sch., Boston, 1974-86; lectr. medicine and physiology Boston U. Sch. Medicine, 1976—95; prof. medicine Tufts U. Sch. Medicine, Boston, 1985-97, prof. emeritus, 1997—. Dir. Tufts Assoc. Health Plan, 1979-81. Contbr. articles to med. jours., chpts. to books. Chmn. bd. trustees Ecole Bilingue, Inc., Arlington, Mass., 1970-74; trustee Boston Med. Libr., 1981-85. Capt. M.C., U.S. Army, 1959-61. Recipient Excellence in Teaching award Boston U. Sch. Medicine, 1974; USPHS grantee, 1977-83. Fellow: ACP, Mass. Med. Soc. (del., mem. com. on med. edn. 1981—95), Am. Heart Assn., Am. Coll. Chest Physicians (pres. New Eng. States chpt. 1981—83), Am. Coll. Cardiology; mem.: Roxbury Clin. Record Club, Dorchester Med. Club, Alpha Omega Alpha. Presbyterian. Avocations: opera, classical music. Office: Faulkner Hosp Boston MA 02130

HUXLEY, CAROLE FRANCES CORCORAN, educational adminstrator; b. Evanston, Ill., 1938; d. Harold Francis and Angela Mary (Dawson) Corcoran; m. Michael Remsen Huxley; children: Samuel, Ian. BA, Mount Holyoke Coll., S. Hadley, Mass., 1960; MAT, Harvard U., 1961. Tchr. Woodbury (Conn.) H.S., 1961-62; staff to sr. adminstr. AFS/Internat., N.Y.C., 1962-71; program officer, State Programs to Div. Dir. Nat. Endowment for Humanities, Washington, 1971-82; deputy commr. for Cultural Edn. N.Y. State Edn. Dept., Albany, 1982—. Bd. mem., vice chair N.Y. Coun. on Humanities, 1984—90; bd. mem. Commn. on Preservation and Access, Washington, 1987—97; reviewer Nat. Acad. Scis., 2000. Trustee, vice chair Mt. Holyoke Coll., South Hadley, Mass., 1982—87, 1988—, vice chair, 1994—99, 2003—; bd. mem. Albany Med. Ctr., 1984—90; bd. dirs. Rsch. Libr. Group, 1997—2003. Recipient Alumnae medal of honor, Mt. Holyoke Coll., 1990, Leadership award, Alliance for Arts Edn., N.Y., 1994, Disting. Svc. award, Rockefeller Inst. for Pub. Policy, 1999, Pres.'s award, Hudson Mohawk Assn., 2000, Libr. Advocacy award, N.Y. Libr. Assn., 2000. Home: 355 Loudon Rd Loudonville NY 12211-1701 Office: New York State Edn Dept Cultural Edn Ctr Rm 10a33 Albany NY 12230-0001 E-mail: chuxley@mail.nysed.gov.

HUYETT, DEBRA KATHLEEN, elementary education educator; b. Massillon, Ohio, Oct. 10, 1955; d. William Wilbur and Vivian Delores (Anderson) H. BA, Stetson U., 1978. Cert. elem. and early childhood edn. tchr., Fla. Dir. assistance and long distance operator Gen. Telephone, Myrtle Beach, S.C., summer 1974-76; desk clk. Bon Villa Motel, Myrtle Beach, summer 1976-79; tchr. Lake Orienta Elem. Sch., Altamonte Springs, Fla., 1978-88, Bear Lake Elem. Sch., Apopka, Fla., 1988-2000; outreach specialist Seminole County Sch. Bd., 2000-01; reading specialist Goldsboro Math., Sci. and Tech. Magnet Elem. Sch., 2001—. Curriculum rep. Lake Orienta Elem. Sch., 1980-88, v.p. PTA, 1984-85; mem. Sch. Adv. Bd., 1995-97. Campaign vol. City Coun. Rep., Massillon, 1973; counselor Orange County Jail Ministry, Orlando, Fla., 1988-91; cmty. counselor EurAuPair, 1996-98. Named to Most Admired Men and Women of the Yr., 1995. Mem. Fla. Reading Conv. (chairperson Orlando chpt. 1983-84, chairperson for transp. and tours 1985-86), Seminole Edn. Assn. (faculty rep. Sanford, Fla. chpt. 1980-81), Seminole County Reading Coun. (rep. for Goldsboro 2001—), Delta Kappa Gamma. Republican. Baptist. Avocations: travel, reading, beach. Home: 893 Little Bend Rd Altamonte Springs FL 32714-7514 E-mail: DKH551010@aol.com.

HWANG, HYEON-SHIK, orthodontist, educator, dean; b. Bonghwa, Korea (South), July 13, 1959; s. Eui-Sun Hwang and Ki-Nam Kim; m. Jung-Un Park, May 23, 1987; children: Ji-Sup, Joon-Sup. DDS, Yonsei U., Seoul, Republic of Korea, 1983, MSD, 1989, PhD, 1992. Cert. Dentist 1983. Instr. Yonsei U., 1990; prof. orthodontics Chonnam Nat. U., Gwangju, Republic of Korea, 1990—; chmn., dept. orthodontics Chonnam U. Hosp., Gwangju, Republic of Korea, 1994—; dir. Dental Sci. Rsch. Inst., Gwangju, Republic of Korea, 2000—; dean Coll. Dentistry Chonnam Nat. U., Gwangju, Republic of Korea, 2001—. Dir. Korean Adult Orthodontic Rsch. Inst., Seoul, 1993—, Korean Adult Occlusion Study Ctr., Seoul, 1996—; mem. coun. Chonnam U. Hosp., 2001—; vis. prof. U. Pa., Phila., 1993—94, U. Tenn., Memphis, 1995. Author: Adult Orthodontics, 1995, Lingual Orthodontics, 2000; editor: Clinical Orthodontics Year Book 99, 1999, Clinical Orthodontics Year Book 2001, 2001; contbr. chapters to books. Fellow: World Fedn. Orthodontists; mem.: Korean Assn. Orthodontists (mem. coun. 1996, Young Scientist Rsch. award 1996, Outstanding Rsch. award 2000, Outstanding Table Clinic award 2001), Internat. Assn. Dental Rsch., European Orthodontic Soc. (assoc.), Japan Orthodontic Soc., Am. Assn. Orthodontists. Home: 203-1002 Hyundai Apt Yongbong-Dong Pukgu Gwangju 500-070 Republic of Korea Office: Dept of Orthodontics Chonnam Univ Hospital, Hak-Dong Dong-Gu Gwangju 501-757 Republic of Korea Office Fax: +82 62 228 5403. Business E-Mail: hhwang@chonnam.ac.kr.

HWANG, SANTAI, electrical engineering educator; b. Tainun, Taiwan, July 14, 1958; came to U.S., 1985; s. Hotin and Yue Kue (Chen) H. BSME, Nat. Chung Hsing U., Taichung, Taiwan, 1980; MSEE, Youngstown State U., 1986; PhD in Engring. Sci., U. Toledo, 1991. Registered profl. engr. Ohio. Asst. engr. Yeu-Tyan Machinery Co., Taiwan, 1980-82; mechanization engr. Philip Elec., Ltd., Taiwan, 1983-84; maintenance engr. China Steel Corp., Taiwan, 1984-85; grad. asst. U. Toledo, 1987-91; asst. prof. Ind. U.-Purdue U., Ft. Wayne, Ind., 1991-96, assoc. prof., 1997—. Contbr. articles to Jour. Contorl and Measuring, Internat. Jour. Computer Controls, Internat. Jour. Computer Applications in Tech. Mem. IEEE (chmn. Ft. Wayne sect. 1994—, nat. chmn. 1994—), Indsl. Automation & Control Com. (nat. chmn. 1994—), Indsl. Applications Soc. (nat. chmn. 1994—), Am. Soc. Engrs. Edn., Engrs. Club Ft. Wayne. Office: Ind U-Purdue U Dept Elec Engring Tech 2101 E Coliseum Blvd Fort Wayne IN 46805-1445

HWANG, TE-LONG, neurologist, educator; b. Hualien, Taiwan, Republic of China, Nov. 4, 1943; came to U.S., 1976; s. Tien-Fu and Tien (Liu) Hwang; m. Ai-Yu Chau; children: Tang-Hau Jimmy, Tang-Chieh George. MD, Nat. Def. Med. Ctr., Taipei, Taiwan, 1970. Intern New Brunswick (N.J.) Affiliated Hosps., 1976-77; pathology resident North Shore Univ. Hosp., Manhasset, N.Y., 1977-79; neurology resident U. Tex. Med. Sch., Houston, 1979-82; neuro-oncology fellow U. Tex. M.D. Anderson Cancer Ctr., Houston, 1983-85; attending neurologist VA Hosp., Topeka, Kans., 1986-88, Columbia, S.C., 1988—. Assoc. prof. U. S.C. Sch. Medicine, Columbia, 1988-94, prof., 1994—, chief neurology, 2002-. Mem. Am. Acad. Neurology, Am. Stroke Assn., Nat. Stroke Assn., World Fedn. Neurology (neurosonology rsch. group), S.C. Neurol. Assn. Home: 7 Birchbark Ct Columbia SC 29229-9002 Office: 3555 Harden Street Ext Columbia SC 29203-6894 E-mail: tlh@gw.mp.sc.edu.

HYDE, FRANCES ELIZABETH, elementary school educator; b. Bklyn. d. Albert C. and Gertrude Zang; m. James Daniel Hyde, July 12, 1969; children: Donald, Catherine, Cynthia. AA, Nassau C.C., 1967; BS in Edn., SUNY, Oswego, 1969; MS in Edn., Russell Sage Coll., 1973. Cert. tchr., N.Y. 5th grade tchr. Green Meadow Sch. East Greenbush (N.Y.) Schs., 1969-70; substitute tchr. Wyantskill (N.Y.) Schs., 1972-73, Troy (N.Y.) City Schs., 1970-72, 75-77, 1st grade tchr. Sch. # 17, 1973, 5th grade tchr. Sch. # 2, 1977-91, 3d grade tchr. Sch. # 2, 1991-95, tchr. 4th grade, 1995— 96, tchr. 3d grade Sch. # 16, 1996—, math. mentor, 1999—. Scorer N.Y. State Edn. Dept., Albany, 1994—; reading tutor, Troy, 1992-93; scholastic news gr. 3 advisor, 2002—. Author: 5th Grade Social Studies Curriculum Guide, 1988. Troop com. mem. Boy Scouts Am., Troy, 1990-91; dir., chair grants Capitol Region Cmty. Found., Troy, 1984-93; mem. Troy Labor Coun., 1982—, trustee, 1991-94, treas. 1994—; v.p. Friends of Troy Pub. Libr., 1993—; mem. Hamilton Coll. Worldwide Admission Vol. Effort, 1994—. Recipient Cmty. Svc. award Troy Ednl. Pride Found., 1999. Mem. LWV (bd. dirs. 1990-92), N.Y. State United Tchrs. (del. conv. 1982—, sgt.-at-arms 1993), Troy Tchrs. Assn. (treas., past pres. 1989-91, exec. bd. rep.-at-large 1990—), Am. Fedn. Tchrs. (conf. del. 1986—), N.Y. State Reading Assn., Nat. Coun. Tchrs. English, Delta Kappa Gamma Soc. Internat. Roman Catholic. Avocations: travel, reading, water aerobics, church activities. Office: School Sixteen Walker and Collins Ave Troy NY 12180 E-mail: lighthousetroy@netscape.net.

HYDE, GERALDINE VEOLA, retired secondary school educator; b. Berkeley, Calif., Nov. 26, 1926; d. William Benjamin and Veola (Walker) H.; m. Paul Hyde Graves, Jr., Nov. 12, 1949 (div. Dec. 1960); children: Christine M. Graves Klykken, Catherine A. Graves Hackney, Geraldine J. Graves Hansen. BA in English, U. Wash., 1948; BA in Edn., Ea. Wash. U., 1960, MA in Edn., 1962. Cert. tchr. K-16, Wash.; life cert. specialist in secondary edn., Calif. English educator Sprague (Wash.) Consol. Schs., 1960-62, Bremerton (Wash.) Sch. Dist., 1962-63, Federal Way (Wash.) Sch. Dist., 1963-66; English, journalism and Polynesian humanities educator Hayward (Calif.) Unified Sch. Dist., 1966-86; ret., 1986. Charter mem. Hist. Hawaii Found., Honolulu, 1977-; founding mem. The Cousteau Soc., Inc., Norfolk, Va., 1973-; life mem. Hawaiian Hist. Soc., Honolulu, 1978-; mem. Molokai Mus. and Cultural Ctr., Kaunakakai, 1986-, Bishop Mus. Assn., Honolulu, 1973-, Mission House Mus., Honolulu, 1994, Bklyn. Hist. Assn., N.Y., 1994, Berkshire Family History Assn., Pittsfield, Mass., 1994-, Richville (N.Y.) Hist. Assn., 1994-, Swanton (Vt.) Hist. Soc., 1998-, N.Y. Geneal. and Biog. Soc., 1999-, New Eng. Hist. Genealogic Soc., 1998-, Gouverneur Hist. Assn., NY, 1998-, New Wing Luke Asian Mus., Seattle, 1994, Upham Family Soc., Inc., Melrose, Mass., 2001-, Calif. Ret. Tchrs Assoc. 2003. Mem. Libr. Congress Assocs. (charter), Nature Conservancy of Hawai'i, Smithsonian Inst. (contbg.), Nat. Geog. Soc., Nat. Trust Historic Preservation, Calif. Ret. Tchrs. Assn., Jr. League Spokane, U. Wash. Alumni Assn. (life), Ea. Wash. U. Alumni Assn. (life). Episcopalian. Avocations: historic and ecologic preservation, genealogy, shell collecting, needlework, crafts. Home: 5051 El Don Dr Apt 1301 Rocklin CA 95677-4470

HYDE, KENNETH EDWIN, chemistry educator; b. McKees Rocks, Pa., July 26, 1941; s. Kenneth Edwin Sr. and Helen (Czajkowski) H.; m. Elaine Wenderholm, Aug. 10, 1974 (div. Nov. 1987); 1 child, Valerie. BS, Carnegie-Mellon U., 1963; PhD, U. Md., 1969. Instr. U. Md., College Park, 1967-68; asst. prof. SUNY Coll., Oswego, 1968-71, assoc. prof., 1971-79, prof. chemistry, 1979-91, Disting. Teaching prof., 1991—, dept. chair, 2000—. Vis. scientist U. Frankfurt, Germany, 1976; software engr. GE, Syracuse, N.Y., 1981-85; vis. faculty rschr. Oak Ridge Nat. Lab., 1989-90, 96-97. Contbr. articles to profl. jours. Mem. Am. Chem. Soc. (chair Syracuse sect. 1982-83, award 1998). Avocations: biking, financial planning, hiking, running. Home: 4633 Aqua Dr Marcellus NY 13108-1003 Office: SUNY Dept Chemistry Oswego NY 13126

HYDER, BETTY JEAN, art educator; b. Elizabethton, Tenn., Oct. 19, 1940; d. Earl Bennick and Bonnie Thelma (Humphrey) Buck; m. Billy Joe Hyder, 1962 (div. 1990); 1 child, Billie Jean Hyder Wallace. BS, East Tenn. State U., 1962, MA, 1970, BA, 1971; postgrad. Tenn. Arts Acad., Belmont U., 1985-94. Visual art specialist grades K-5 Andrew Johnson Sch., Kingsport, Tenn., 1962—; visual art specialist Palmer Ctr. for Handicapped Students, Kingsport, 1976-80. Author: (art textbook) What's Cooking in Art?, 1987; works exhibited in one-woman show East Tenn. State U., 1979; interviewed and taught class for CNN Revolution in Edn., 1989; exhibited work at Renaissance Ctr., Kingsport, 1992, Arts and Crafts festival, Roan Mt., Tenn., 1990, Arts Acad. Capital Bldg., Nashville, 1991, Earth Day at Bays Mt., Kingsport, 1991-92; student art exhibited widely in Kingsport. Artist (booth art) Fun Fest, Kingsport, 1990; chairperson PTA cultural art com., Kingsport, 1989-94; chairperson Christian Fellowship for Singles, Kingsport, 1991-93; singer Christian Single Ensemble, Kingsport, 1991-94; presenter Tenn. Arts Acad., Nashville, 1993; host Pentel's Internat. Children's Exhibit from Japan, 1993; coord. Christine LaGuardia Phillips Cancer Ctr. exhibit, Kingsport, 1984-94; presenter East Tenn. Edn. Assn. art workshop, Knoxville, 1987, 90, 93; hospitality chair. Christian Fellowship for Singles; chair Kingsport Arts Assn., 1994; mem. Crackerjack Singers. Named Kingsport City Schs. Outstanding Educator of Yr., 1987. Mem. NEA, PTA, Tenn. Edn. Assn., Kingsport Edn. Assn. (publicity, pub. rels. chmn. 1962, chairperson edn. profl. stds. com. 1986-88), East Tenn. Art Edn. Assn., Nat. Art Edn. Assn., Delta Kappa Gamma (chairperson legis. com.), Madrigal Drama Players. Republican. Mem. Avoca Christian Ch. Avocations: floral design, water colors, ceramics, christian choir & ensemble. Office: Andrew Johnson Sch 1001 Ormond Dr Kingsport TN 37664-3235

HYMAN, ALBERT LEWIS, cardiologist, educator; b. New Orleans, Nov. 10, 1923; s. David and Mary (Newstadt) H.; m. Neil Steiner, Mar. 27, 1964; 1 son, Albert Arthur. BS, La. State U., 1943; MD, 1945; postgrad., U. Cin., U. Paris, U. London, Eng. Diplomate: Am. Bd. Internal Medicine. Intern Charity Hosp., 1945-46, resident, 1947-49, sr. vis. physician, 1959-63; resident Cin. Gen. Hosp., 1946-47; instr. medicine La. State U., 1950-56, asst. prof. medicine, 1956-57; asst. prof. Tulane U., 1957-59, assoc. prof., 1959-63, assoc. prof. surgery, 1963-70, prof. rsch. surgery in cardiology, 1970—, prof. clin. medicine Med. Sch., 1983—, adj. prof. pharmacology Med. Sch., 1974—, dir. Cardiac Catheterization Lab., 1957—, Mayerson meml. lectr. in physiology, 2000. Sr. vis. physician Touro Hosp., Touro Infirmary, Hotel Dieu; chief cardiology Sara Mayo Hosp.; cons. in cardiology USPHS, New Orleans Crippled Children's Hosp., St. Tammany Parish Hosp., Covington La. area VA, Hotel Dieu Hosp., Mercy Hosp., East Jefferson Gen. Hosp., St. Charles Gen. Hosp.; electrocardiographer Metairie Hosp., 1959-64, Sara Mayo Hosp., Touro Infirmary, St. Tammany Hosp.;

cons. cardiovascular disease New Orleans VA Hosp.; cons. cardiology Baton Rouge Gen. Hosp., U.S. Dept. Justice, Fed. Social Security Agy.; Barlow lectr. in medicine U. So. Calif., 1977; mem. internat. sci. com. IV Internat. Symposium on Pulmonary Circulation, Charles U., Prague; Mayerson meml. lectr. dept. physiology Tulane Med. Sch., 1999; Plenary lectr. gene therapy Internat. Congress Pulmonary Circulation, Prague, 1999; vis. prof. medicine SUNY, Stony Brook, 2001; vis. prof. pharmacology U. South Ala. Med. Sch., 2001; invited lectr. in field. Mem. editorial bd. Jour. Applied Physiology; contbr. over 250 articles to profl. jours. Recipient award for rsch. of the Hadassah, 1980, Vis. Scientist award Wellcome Found., Univ. Coll., London, 1991, Disting. Achievement award Am. Heart Assn., 1992, 93, Dickinson-Richards lectr., 1990, Albert Hyman award for excellence in cardiology Tulane U. Med. Sch., 1997, Disting. Achievement award in sci. and rsch. Orleand Parish Med. Soc., 2001; Tulane Med. Sch. Sect. on Cardiology fellow, 1997. Fellow ACP, Am. Coll. Chest Physicians, Am. Coll. Cardiology, Am. Fedn. Clin. Rsch.; mem. AAUP, Am. Heart Assn. (fellow coun. on circulation, fellow coun. on clin. cardiology, mem. coun. on cardiopulmonary medicine, regional rep. coun. clin. cardiology, chmn. sci. com. cardiopulmonary coun. 1981, chmn. cardiopulmonary coun., rsch. com. bd. dirs., editl. bd. mem. Circulation Rsch., edit. bd. mem. Am. Jour. Physiology, Heart Disease and Stroke, Jour. Applied Physiology, Dickinson Richards Meml. Lectr. 1986, 92, Disting. Sci. Achievement award 1990, 93), La. Heart Assn. (v.p. 1974, Albert L. Hyman Ann. Rsch. award, Wellcome Rsch. Found. Vis. Scientist award Univ. Coll. London 1992, Disting. Achievement award outstanding sci. contbns. to cardiopulmonary medicine), Am. Soc. Pharmacology and Exptl. Therapeutics, So. Soc. Clin. Investigation (chmn. membership com.), So. Med. Soc. (Seale-Harris award 1988), Am. Physiol. Soc., N.Am. Soc. Pacing and Electrophysiology, Orleans Surg. Soc. (hon.), New Orleans Surg. Soc. (hon.), N.Y. Acad. Scis., Nat. Am. Heart Assn. (vice-chmn. rsch. com.), Alpha Omega Alpha. Achievements include research in cardiopulmonary circulation. Home: 5467 Marcia Ave New Orleans LA 70124-1052 Office: 3601 Prytania St New Orleans LA 70115-3610

HYMAN, EDWARD JAY, forensic psychologist, cognitive and information scientist, consultant, educator, television news commentator; b. Roslyn, NY, Oct. 25, 1947; s. Herbert H. and Edith (Tannenbaum) H.; m. Deborah Anne McDonald, May 1, 1986; children: Cameron Scott, Devon Edward. AB, Columbia U., 1969; postgrad., Harvard U., 1969-70; PhD, U. Calif., Berkeley, 1975. Diplomate Am. Bd. Forensic Medicine, Am. Bd. Forensic Examiners, Am. Bd. Psychol. Specialties, lic. psychologist Calif. Editl. asst. Huntley-Brinkley Report NBC News, NYC, 1969; coord. Ctr. for Ednl. Change U. Calif., Berkeley, 1970-72, sr. fellow Ctr. for Social Rsch., 1972-74; intern Calif. Health Dept., Santa Cruz, Calif., 1974; lectr. U. Calif., Berkeley, 1975-76, asst. dean, 1976-77; chmn. bd. Assn. for Advanced Tng., LA, 1977-79; asst. prof. U. San Francisco, Calif., 1979-81; sci. dir. Ctr. for Social Rsch., Berkeley, Calif., 1981—; assoc. prof. psychiatry, psychology and law Ctr. Social Rsch., Berkeley, Calif., 1981-85; news commentator KRON-TV, 1981—88; prof. Ctr. Social Rsch., Berkeley, Calif., 1985-96, R. Nevitt Sanford prof. psychiatry, psychology & law, 1996—; news commentator NBC Network News, 1975—88, CBS Network News, 1988—, ABC Network News, 1990—. Cons. Union Am. Hebrew Congregations, 1967, Std. Oil Co., San Francisco, 1976—77, Exxon USA, 1976—77, Edison Electric Inst., Washington, 1977—80, NBC-TV, 1977—, Natural Resources Def. Coun., 1977—, Pacific Gas and Electric, 1986, PBS, 1997—, Frontline, 1997—, Weekend Today, 1997—; clin. dir. Inst. Labor & Mental Health, 1982—83. Co-author: Life Stress, 1983, Herbert Marcuse Festschrift, 1988; contbr. sci. papers and articles to profl. jour. Chair pub. rels. Tamalpais High Found., 2001—. Regents scholar U. Calif., 1974-75. Fellow: Calif. Inst. Forensic Scis.; mem.: APA, AAAS, AAUP, Am. Psychology-Law Soc., Am. Coll. Forensic Examiners, Soc. Psychol. Study Social Issues, Assn. Family and Conciliation Cts., Soc. Personality Assessment (conv. forensic issues chair), Am. Child Abuse Prevention Soc. (bd. dirs. 1975—, clin. dir. 1979—81, intern 1975—77), Internat. Congress Psychology (conv. com. 1980), Internat. Soc. Applied Psychology, Am. Coll. Forensic Psychology, Internat. Soc. Polit. Psychology (conv. com. 1987), Calif. Psychol. Assn., Am. Inst. Decision Scis., Alumni Club Columbia U. (No. Calif. bd. mem. 1995—, recruiting chair 1985—). Office: Ctr for Social Rsch 2029 Durant Ave Ste 301 Berkeley CA 94704 Office Fax: 415-388-5009.

HYMAN, HAROLD M. history educator, consultant; b. Bklyn., July 24, 1924; s. Abraham and Rebecca (Hermann) H.; m. Ferne Beverly Handelsman, Mar. 11, 1946; children: Lee Rosenthal, Ann Root, William Hyman. BA with honors, U. Calif. L.A., 1948; MA, Columbia U., 1950, PhD, 1952; LHD (hon.), Lincoln Coll., 1984. summer instr. Columbia U., 1953, U. Wash., 1960, Bklyn. Coll., 1962, U. Chgo., 1965; vis. asst. prof. UCLA, 1955-56; sr. Fulbright lectr. in Am. History and Law, grad. faculty polit. sci. U. Tokyo, 1973; faculty of law Keio U., 1973; adj. prof. legal history Bates Coll. Law U. Houston, 1977, of Am. legal history U. Tex. Law Sch., 1986; Meyer vis. disting. prof. legal history NYU Sch. Law, 1982-83; cons. and spkr. in field. Asst. prof. Earlham Coll., 1952-55; assoc. prof. Ariz. State U., 1956-57; prof. UCLA, 1957-63, U. Ill., 1963-68; William P. Hobby Prof. History Rice U., 1968-96, William P. Hobby prof. history emeritus, 1997—. Speaker in field. Author: Era of the Oath: Northern Loyalty Tests During the Civil War and Reconstruction (Albert J. Beveridge award Am. Hist. Assn. 1981), 1954, To Try Men's Souls: Loyalty Tests in American History (Sidney Hillman Found. prize 1960), 1981, Stanton: The Life and Times of Lincoln's Secretary of War, 1962, Soldiers and Spruce: Origins of the Loyal Legion of Loggers and Lumbermen: The Army's Labor Union of World War I, 1963, A More Perfect Union: The Impact of the Civil War and Reconstruction on the Constitution, 1973, Union and Confidence: The 1860s, 1976, (with William Wiecek) Equal Justice Under Law: Constitutional History, 1833-1880, 1982, paperback, 1983, Quiet Past and Stormy Present? War Powers in American History, 1986, American Singularity: The 1787 Northwest Ordinance, the 1862 Homestead-Morrill Acts, and the 1944 GI Bill, 1986, Oleander Odyssey: The Kempners of Galveston, 1870-1980, (Coral H. Tullis Meml. prize Tex. A&M U. Press 1990, T. R. Fehrenbach Book award Tex. Hist. Comsn. 1990, Ottis Lock Endowment award E. Tex. Hist. Assn. 1991), 1990, The Reconstruction Justice of Salmon P. Chase: In re Turner and Texas v. White, 1997, Character and Craftsmanship: A History of Houston's Vinson & Elkins Law Firm, 1917-1990s, 1998; editor (with Ferne B. Hyman) The Circuit Court Opinions of Salmon Portland Chase, 1972; contbr. numerous articles to profl. jours. Elected lay mem. Houston Bar Assn. Grievance Com., 1985-88; mem. numerous U. coms. The Constitution, Law, and Am. Life in the Nineteenth Century: A conf. named in his honor, Rice U. and NYU Sch. Law, 1989; named U.S. Presdl. appointee to permanent com. Oliver Wendell Holmes Trust, 1993-2001. Mem. Am. Hist. Assn. (numerous coms. and offices), Am. Soc. Legal History (pres . 1993-95), Orgn. Am. Historians (various coms. and offices), So. Hist. Assn. Avocation: fishing. Office: Rice University Dept History-MS 42 PO Box 1892 Houston TX 77251-1892

HYMAN, MARY BLOOM, science education programs coordinator; m. Sigmund M. Hyman, 1947 (dec.); children: Carol Hyman Piccinini, Nancy Louise. BA, Goucher Coll., 1971; MS, Johns Hopkins U., 1977. Asst. dir. Edn. Md. Sci. Ctr., Balt., 1976-81, dir. edn., 1981-90; coord. sci. edn. programs Loyola Coll., Balt., 1990—, coord. Inst. for Child Care Edn., 1992—. Trustee Goucher Coll., Franklin & Marchall Coll., Lancaster, Pa., 2003--; active Baltimore County Pub. Schs. Com. for Sch.-Based and Sch.-Linked Child Care; bd. dirs. Balt. Sch.-Age Child Care Alliance, Johns Hopkins U. Ctr. Talented Youth; mem. Gov.'s Task Force on Compensation of Child Care Providers, 1995-96. Recipient Disting. Women award Gov.'s Office, Annapolis, Md., 1981; Meritorious Svc. award Johns Hopkins U., 1983; Outstanding Svc. to Sci. Edn. award. Assn. Sci. Dept. Chairmen Balt. County Pub. Schs., 1989. Mem. Md. Assn. Sci. Tchrs. (bd. dirs.), Phi Beta Kappa, Phi Delta Kappa. Home: 10815 Longacre Ln Stevenson MD 21153-0665 E-mail: mhyman@loyola.edu.

HYMAN, MONTAGUE ALLAN, lawyer, educator; b. N.Y.C., Apr. 19, 1941; s. Allan Richard and Lilyan P. (Pollock) H.; m. susann Podell, Jan. 25, 1965; children: Jeffrie-Anne, Erik. BA, Syracuse U., 1962; JD, St. Johns U., 1965. Bar: N.Y. 1965, U.S. Dist. Ct. (so. and ea. dists.) N.Y. 1967, U.S. Ct. Appeals (2d cir.) 1982, U.S. Supreme Ct. 1973. Assoc. Warburton, Hyman, Deeley & Connolly, Mineola, NY, 1965-67; ptnr. Hyman & Deeley, 1967-69, Koeppel, Hyman, Sommer, Lesnick & Ross, 1969-72, Hyman & Hyman, P.C., Garden City, 1972-80, Costigan, Hyman, Hyman & Herman, P.C., Mineola, 1980-87, Certilman, Haft, Balin, Buckley, Adler & Hyman, 1988—, Certilman Balin Adler & Hyman, 1988—. Lectr. Hofstra U., Adelphi U., Columbia Appraisal Soc., Practicing Law Inst.; chmn. bd. Edn. and Assistance Corp. Contbr. articles to profl. jours. Bd. trustees North Shore L.I. Jewish Health System. Mem. Nassau County Bar Assn., N.Y. State Bar Assn., Inst. Property Taxation. Office: Certilman Balin Adler & Hyman LLP 90 Merrick Ave East Meadow NY 11554-1571 E-mail: ahyman@certilmanbalin.com.

HYMER, MARTHA NELL, elementary education educator; b. Magnolia, Ark., Apr. 2, 1956; d. Elton N. and Nell Merle (Hill) Amburn; m. Gerald Lee Hymer, Nov. 21, 1980; children: Angela Colleen, Melissa Nicole. BS in Edn., Lubbock Christian Coll., 1978. Tchr. R.L. Wright Elem. Sch., Sedgwick, Kans., 1979—99, Bloomingdale Pub. Sch., Mich., 2000—. Evaluator for Kans. literature, 1993; site based coun. mem. Unified Sch. Dist. 439, 1993, chairperson, 1996-97. Pres. Families with a Difference, Newton, Kans., 1985-87; sec. Cooper Parent Tchr. Orgn., 1991-97. Mem. Ch. of Christ. Avocations: family, cooking, sewing. Home: 862 N 30th St Galesburg MI 49053-8793

HYNES, JUDITH ANNE, secondary education educator; b. Brockton, Mass., June 18, 1961; d. William Henry and Alice Francis (Quitt) H. AS, N.H. Coll., 1981, BS, 1983; MEd, Bowling Green State U., 1984. Cert. vocat. edn. dir., comprehensive mktg. and bus. Instr. mktg. N.H. Coll., Manchester, 1985-89, Franklin Pierce Coll., Concord, N.H., 1985-90; mktg. tchr. Merrimack Valley High Sch., Penacook, N.H., 1987—, vocat. edn. coord., 1989—. Grad. scholar Bowling Green State U., 1983. Mem. N.H. Secondary Sch. Adminstrs., N.H. Mktg. Edn. Tchrs. Assn., N.H. Bus. Edn. Assn., N.H. Coun. Secondary Adminstrs. and Vocat. Educators (treas. 1993-94), Concord C. of C. (edn. adv. bd. 1991—). Avocations: coaching, softball, basketball. Office: Merrimack Valley High Sch 163 N Main St Penacook NH 03303-1106

HYNES, RICHARD OLDING, biology researcher, educator; b. Nairobi, Kenya, Africa, Nov. 29, 1944; s. Hugh Bernard Noel and Mary Elizabeth (Hinks) H.; m. Fleur Marshall, July 29, 1966; children: Hugh Jonathan, Colin Anthony. BA with honors, U. Cambridge, Eng., 1966, MA, 1970; PhD, MIT, 1971. Asst. prof. biology MIT, Cambridge, 1975-78, assoc. prof., 1978-83, prof. dept. biology, 1983—, assoc. head dept. biology, 1985-89, head, 1989-91, dir. Ctr. for Cancer Rsch., 1991-2001, Daniel K. Ludwig prof. cancer rsch., 1999—; investigator Howard Hughes Med. Inst., Chevy Chase, Md., 1988—. Author: Fibronectins, 1990; editor Tumor Cell Surfaces and Malignancy, 1979, Surfaces of Normal and Malignant Cells, 1979; contbr. articles to profl. jours. Guggenheim Found. fellow, 1982; recipient internat. award Gairdner Found., 1997. Fellow AAAS, Am. Acad. Arts and Scis., Royal Soc. London; mem. Inst. Medicine NAS,, Nat. Acad. Scis. Office: MIT Ctr Cancer Rsch EI7-227 77 Massachusetts Ave Cambridge MA 02139-4307 E-mail: rohynes@mit.edu.

HYTCHE, WILLIAM PERCY, university president; b. Porter, Okla., Nov. 28, 1927; s. Goldman and Bartha L. (Wallace) H.; m. Deloris Juanita Cole, Dec. 27, 1952; children— Pamelia Renee, Jaqueta Anita, William Percy Jr. BS, Langston U., 1950; MS, Okla. State U., 1958, EdD, 1967; LHD (hon.), Fisk U., 1995, Washington Coll., Md., 1995, U. Md., 1996; LLD (hon.), Tuskegee U., 1997. Tchr. math., Ponca City, Okla., 1952-60; asst. prof. math. Md. State Coll., Princess Anne, 1960-66, dean student affairs, 1968-70, Md. State Coll. (name changed to U. Md. Eastern Shore), 1970, assoc. prof. math., 1970-71; head dept. math. and computer sci., dir. Md. State Coll. (13 Coll. Curriculum Program), 1971-73, acting chmn. div. liberal studies, 1973-74, chmn. divsn. liberal studies, 1974-75, chancellor, pres., 1975-97, pres. emeritus, 1997—. Lectr. in field. Author: Step by Step to the Top: The Saga of a President of a Historically Black University, 1999; contbr. chpts. in books and articles to profl. jours. Mem. Somerset County Econ. Devel. Commn., Greater Salisbury Com., Joint Com. Agrl. R&D; mem. Pres.'s Bd. Advisors on Historically Black Colls. and Univs., 1988-92; adv. bd. Nat. Aquarium; bd. trustees Peninsula Regional Med. Ctr., 1978-94. NSF grantee, 1957-58, 60; recipient Thurgood Marshall Ednl. Achievement award Johnson Pub. Co., 1992; named to Hall of Fame, Okla. State U. Alumni Assn., 1993, George Washington Carver Pub. Svc. Hall of Fame Tuskegee U., 1994. Fellow Acad. Arts and Scis. (Okla. State U. 1978); mem. Nat. Assn. State Univs. and Land-Grant Colls. (exec. bd. 1988-91), Am. Coun. on Edn. (bd. dirs. 1988-90), Nat. Assn. Equal Opportunity Higher Edn. (bd. dirs. 1975-90), Phi Sigma, Phi Delta Kappa, Alpha Phi Alpha, Phi Kappa Phi. Methodist. Office: U Md Ea Shore Office President Emeritus Princess Anne MD 21853

IACONO, JAMES MICHAEL, research center administrator, nutrition educator; b. Chgo., Dec. 11, 1925; s. Joseph and Angelina (Cutaia) I.; children: Lynn, Joseph, Michael, Rosemary. BS, Loyola U., Chgo., 1950; MS, U. Ill., 1952, PhD, 1954. Chief Lipid Nutrition Lab. Nutrition Inst. Agrl. Rsch. Svc. USDA, Beltsville, Md., 1970-75, dep. asst. adminstrv. nat. program staff Washington, 1975-77, assoc. adminstr. office human nutrition, 1978-82, dir. Western Human Nutrition Rsch. Ctr. San Francisco, 1982-94. Adj. prof. nutrition Sch. Pub. Health UCLA, 1987—. Author over 100 rsch./tech. publs. and chpts. in books relating to nutrition and biochemistry and lipids. With U.S. Army, 1944-46. Recipient Rsch. Career Devel. award NIH, 1964-70. Fellow Am Heart Assn. (coun. on arteriosclerosis and thrombosis), Am. Inst. Chemists; mem. Am. Inst. Nutrition, Am. Soc. Clin. Nutrition, Am. Oil Chemists Soc. E-mail: JIacono25@aol.com.

IADIPAOLO, DONNA MARIE, educator, writer, director, artist, performer; b. Ventura, Calif., June 4, 1967; d. Rene and Sandra (Ciccarelli) I. BA in English and Edn. with honors, U. Mich., 1990; MA in Comms. and Theatre with honors, Ea. Mich. U., 1997. Cert. secondary English, math., social studies, journalism, and drama tchr., Mich. Freelance writer Metro Times, Ann Arbor, Mich., 1989-90, Village Voice, N.Y.C., summer 1990; mng. editor Ear Mag. of New Music, N.Y.C., 1991; editor Ins. and Tech. Mag., N.Y.C., 1991; tchr. High Scope Ednl. Found., Ypsilanti, Mich., 1993; tchr. Wylie E. Groves H.S. & Covington Mid. Sch. Birmingham (Mich.) Pub. Schs., 1993-95, h.s. and mid. sch. forensic coach, 1993-95; tchr. Dexter (Mich.) H.S., 1995-99. Tchr. adolescent summer sch. U. Mich.-Housing and Children Svcs., Ann Arbor, 1993; budget dir., mem. adv. bd. WCBN-FM Campus Radio Sta., 1993-94. Mem. Mich. Interscholastic Forensic Assn. (award 1994, 97, 98), Mich. Speech Coaches Assn., Mich. Interscholastic Press Assn., Nat. Assn. Student Activity Advisors, Nat. Coun. Tchrs. English, Edn. Theatre, Theatre Comm. Avocations: reading, music, nature, painting, theatre, creative writing.

IANNELLA, PENNY MARIE, learning disabilities educator, consultant; b. Dubuque, Iowa, Apr. 6, 1963; d. Thomas James and Elizabeth Ann (Schadle) Delaney. BA in Spl. Edn. and Elem. Edn. magna cum laude, Loras Coll., 1986; MA in Varying Exceptionalities, U. South Fla., 1994. Cert. elem. tchr., N.J., Fla., learning disabilities tchr., cons., N.J., tchr. of the handicapped, N.J., K-12 mentally handicapped tchr., Fla. Spl. edn. tchr. Brevard County Schs., Melbourne, Fla., 1986-89, Hernando County Schs., Brooksville, Fla., 1989-94; learning disabilities tchr., cons. Warren Hills Regional Sch. Dist., Washington, N.J., 1994-97; student success program tchr. South Orange & Maplewood (N.J.) Sch. Dist., 1997—. Cons., presenter, instr. Perfect Harmony, Inc., Fla. Dept. Edn., Fla. State U., Hernando County Schs., 1989—, part-time homebound instr., 1992-93; developer programs, presenter state and local workshops, 1993. Author: (arts and crafts program) Perfect Harmony, 1992; contbr. Reaching Out Manual, AAHPERD nat. and state jour.; contbr. brochures. Presenter tng. sessions for Perfect Harmony to numerous civic, parks and sch. orgns., 1990—; bd. dirs. Perfect Harmony Agy. of United Way of Hernando County, 1991-92; radio interviews on Perfect Harmony, 1992. Recipient Creative Concept award Fla. Assn. Health, Phys. Edn., Recreation and Dance, 1992, Best Practice award Fla. Vocat. Assn., Fla. Dept. Edn., 1993, 1st pl. in econs. Hernando County C. of C./Ptnrs. in Edn., 1991. Avocations: arts and crafts, tennis, bicycling, reading.

IANNUZZI, JOHN NICHOLAS, lawyer, author, educator; b. N.Y.C., May 31, 1935; s. Nicholas Peter and Grace Margaret (Russo) I.; m. Carmen Marina Barrios, Aug. 1979; children: Dana Alejandra, Christina Maria, Nicholas Peter II, Alessandro Luca; children from previous marriage: Andrea Marguerite, Maria Teresa. BS, Fordham U., 1956; JD, N.Y. Law Sch., 1962. Bar: N.Y., U.S. Dist. Ct. (so. and ea. dists.) N.Y. 1964, U.S. Dist. Ct. (no. and we. dists.) N.Y. 1965, U.S. Ct. Appeals (2d cir.) 1965, U.S. Supreme Ct. 1971, U.S. Dist. Ct. Conn. 1978, U.S. Tax Ct. 1978, U.S. Ct. Appeals (5th and 11th cirs.) 1982, U.S. Ct. Appeals (4th cir.) 1988, Wyo. 1994. Assoc. Law Offices of H.H. Lipsig, N.Y.C., 1962, Law Offices of Aaron J. Broder, N.Y.C., 1963; ptnr. Iannuzzi & Iannuzzi, N.Y.C., 1963—. Adj. prof. trial advocacy Fordham U. Law Sch. Author: (fiction) What's Happening, 1963, Part 35, 1970, Sicilian Defense, 1974, Courthouse, 1977, J.T., 1984, (non-fiction) Cross-Examination: The Mosaic Art, 1984, Trial Strategy and Psychology, 1992, Handbook of Cross-Examination, 1999, Handbook of Trial Strategy, 2000. Mem. ABA, N.Y. County Bar Assn., N.Y. Criminal Bar Assn., Columbian Lawyers Assn., Lipizzan Internat. Fedn. (v.p.). Roman Catholic. Home: 118 Via Settembre 9 Rome Italy Office: Iannuzzi & Iannuzzi 74 Trinity Place New York NY 10006 also: 775 Park Ave Huntington NY 11743-3976 also: 345 Franklin St San Francisco CA 94102-4427 also: 1592 Pine Ave W Montreal QC Canada also: 120 Adelaide St W Toronto ON Canada H3B 3G3 E-mail: jni@iannuzzi.net.

IAQUINTA, LEONARD PHILLIP, university official; b. Kenosha, Wis., Aug. 1, 1944; s. Anthony Sam and Mary Natalie (Gallo) I. BJ, Northwestern U., 1966; M in Journalism, Columbia U., 1967. Dir., coms. World Studies Data Bank Acad. for Ednl. Devel., N.Y.C., 1969-76; dir. field svcs. for alumni rels. Northwestern U., Evanston, Ill., 1977-81; dir. nat. alumni program Columbia U., N.Y.C., 1981-82; devel. officer, alumni dir. Bklyn. Coll. (CUNY), 1982-86; dir. devel. and alumni affairs Ind.-Purdue Univs., Ft. Wayne, 1986-95, Northeastern Ill. U., Chgo., 1995-2001; asst. dean, dir. devel. and alumni rels. Coll. Engring. and Applied Scis. U. Wis., Milw., 2001—03, devel. officer, 2003—. Spkr. various profl. confs. Assoc. editor: Notes on Negotiating, 1974; contbr. articles to profl. jours.; author various devel. manuals. Exec. dir. Kenosha United Way, 1976-77, mem. campaign cabinet, 2003; mem. fund adv. com. Greater Milw. Found., 2003. Recipient 4 nat. alumni programming and fundraising awards Council for Advancement and Support of Edn., 1981, 84, 88, 98; 15 Who Care awards, Vol. Connection of Switchboard of Ft. Wayne, 1990. Mem. Assn. Fundraising Profls., Coun. for Advancement and Support of Edn., East Wis. Planned Giving Coun., Rotary, Soc. Profl. Journalists. Mem. Congregational Ch. Avocations: gardening, reading, enjoying the arts, travel. Home: 9507 74th St Kenosha WI 53142-8194 Office: Univ Devel Office Hefter Conf Ctr 3271 N Lake Dr Milwaukee WI 53211-3125 E-mail: LPIaquinta@cs.com.

IBANEZ, MANUEL LUIS, university official, biological sciences educator; b. Worcester, Mass., Sept. 23, 1935; s. Ovidio Pedro and Esperanza Fe (Perez) I.; m. Jane Marie Bourquard, Oct. 16, 1970; children: Juana Lia Cristina, Vincent Ovidio, William Dayan, Marc Albert BS cum laude, Wilmington Coll., 1957; MS, Pa. State U., 1959, PhD, 1961. Asst. prof. Bucknell U., Lewisburg, Pa., 1961-62; postdoctoral fellow UCLA, 1962; sr. biochemist IICA de la OEA, Turrialba, Costa Rica, 1962-65; assoc. prof., chmn. dept. U. New Orleans, 1965-70, prof., 1977-90, assoc. dean grad. sch., 1978-82, assoc. vice chancellor acad. affairs, 1982-83, acting vice chancellor, 1983-85, vice chancellor acad. affairs, provost, 1985-89, prof. emeritus, 1990—; pres. Tex. A&M U., Kingsville, 1989-98, Disting. prof. biology, 1998—. Author: Basic Biology of Microorganisms, 1972; contbr. articles to profl. jours. Regent Smithsonian Inst., 1994—; mem. Alliance for Good Govt., New Orleans, 1980. NSF coop. fellow, 1958-61 Mem. Am. Assn. State Colls. and Univs., Kingsville C. of C. (pres. 1991), Rotary, KC, Sigma Xi Democrat. Roman Catholic. Avocations: chess, tennis, cycling, collections. Office: Tex A&M Univ-Kingsville Office Biol Scis Kingsville TX 78364-0101

IBEN, ICKO, JR., astrophysicist, educator; b. Champaign, Ill., June 27, 1931; s. Icko and Kathryn (Tomlin) I.; m. Miriam Genevieve Fett, Jan. 28, 1956; children: Christine, Timothy, Benjamin, Thomas. BA, Harvard U., 1953; MS, U. Ill., 1954, PhD, 1958. Asst. prof. physics Williams Coll., 1958-61; sr. rsch. fellow in physics Calif. Inst. Tech., Pasadena, 1961—64; assoc. prof. physics MIT, Cambridge, 1964-68, prof., 1968-72; prof. astronomy and physics, head dept. astronomy U. Ill., Champaign-Urbana, 1972-84, prof. astronomy and physics, 1972-89, disting. prof. astronomy and physics Urbana, 1989—99, disting. prof. emeritus, 2000; holder of Eberly family chair in astronomy Pa. State U., 1989-90. Vis. prof. astronomy Harvard U., 1966, 68, 70; vis. fellow Joint Inst. for Lab. Astrophysics U. Colo., 1971—72; vis. prof. astronomy and astrophysics U. Calif., Santa Cruz, 1972; vis. prof. physics and astronomy Inst. for Astronomy U. Hawaii, 1977; adv. panel astronomy sect. NSF, 1972—75; vis. com. Aura Observatories, 1979—82; vis. scientist astronomical coun. Union Soviet Socialist Rep. Acad. Sci., 1985; sr. vis. fellow Australian Nat. U., 1986; vis. prof. U. Bologna, Italy, 1986, Hokkaido U. Grad. Sch. Sci., 2001; sr. rsch. fellow U. Sussex, England, 1986; George Darwin lectr. Royal Astronomical Soc., London, 1984; McMillin lectr. Ohio State U., 1987; vis. eminent scholar U. Ctr. Ga., 1988; guest prof. Christian Albrechts U. Kiel, 1990; sr. fellow Nicolaus Copernicus Astron. Ctr., Warsaw, 2002. Contbr. articles to profl. jours. John Simon Guggenheim Meml. fellow, 1985-86; recipient Eddington medal Royal Astron. Soc., 1990. Fellow Japan Soc. for Promotion of Sci.; mem. Am. Astron. Soc. (councilor 1974-77, Henry Norris Russell lectr. 1989), U.S. Nat. Acad. of Scis., Internat. Astronom. Union. Home: 3910 Clubhouse Dr Champaign IL 61822-9280 Office: U Ill Dept of Astronomy 1002 W Green St Urbana IL 61801-3074

IBERS, JAMES ARTHUR, chemist, educator; b. Los Angeles, June 9, 1930; s. Max Charles and Esther (Imerman) I.; m. Joyce Audrey Henderson, June 10, 1951; children: Jill Tina, Arthur Alan. BS, Calif. Inst. Tech., 1951, PhD, 1954. NSF post-doctoral fellow, Melbourne, Australia, 1954-55; chemist Shell Devel. Co., 1955-61, Brookhaven Nat. Lab., 1961-64; mem. faculty Northwestern U., 1964—, prof. chemistry, 1964-85, Charles E. and Emma H. Morrison prof. chemistry, 1986—. Recipient Disting. alumni award Calif. Inst. Tech., 1997. Mem. NAS, Am. Acad. Arts and Sci., Am. Chem. Soc. (inorganic chemistry award 1979, Disting. Svc. in the Advancement of Inorganic Chemistry award 1992, Linus Pauling award 1994), Am. Crystallographic Assn. (Buerger award 2002). Home: 2657 Orrington Ave Evanston IL 60201-1760 Office: Northwestern U Dept Chemistry Evanston IL 60208-3113 E-mail: ibers@chem.northwestern.edu.

ICE, ORVA LEE, JR., history educator, retired; b. Elkhart, Ind., Mar. 10, 1920; s. Orva Lee Sr. and Frances Marian (Grimes) I.; m. Jean Ellen Ice, July 31, 1944. AB, U. Pitts., 1942; MA, U. Chgo., 1948; EdM, Wayne State U., 1959; PhD, Mich. State U., 1970. Cert. social worker, Mich. Export mgr.

J.C. Jensen Co., Chgo., 1949-52; counselor Gary (Ind.)-Lake County Schs.; tchr. East Detroit (Mich.) Pub. Schs.; registrar Macomb Community Coll., Warren, Mich., 1961-68, prof. history, 1971—, prof. spl. studies in Asia and Latin Am., 1984-98, ret., 1998. With U.S. Army, 1942-46. Fulbright fellow. Mem. ASCD, Latin Am. Studies Assn., Asian Studies Assn, Phi Delta Kappa. Home: 11926 15 Mile Rd Sterling Heights MI 48312-5108

ICHIISHI, TATSURO, economics and mathematics educator; b. Seoul, Dec. 16, 1943; came to U.S., 1970; s. Jitsuro and Tomiko Ichiishi; m. Barbara Ann Franklin, Sept. 7, 1973 BA in Econs., Keio U., Tokyo, 1966, MA in Econs., 1968; MA in Math., U. Calif., Berkeley, 1973, PhD in Econs., 1974. Rsch. assoc. Keio U., Tokyo, 1968-73; vis. rsch. fellow Cath. U. Louvain, Heverlee, Belgium, 1974-75; lectr., rsch. assoc. Northwestern U., Evanston, Ill., 1975-76; asst. prof. Carnegie-Mellon U., Pitts., 1976-80; assoc. prof. U. Iowa, Iowa City, 1980-83, prof., 1983-86, Ohio State U., Columbus, 1987—, Hitotsubashi U., Tokyo, 2001—02. Vis. prof. Bilkent U., Ankara, Turkey, 1997; guest prof. Keio U., Tokyo, 1999. Author: Game Theory for Economic Analysis, 1983, The Cooperative Nature of the Firm, 1993, Microeconomic Theory, 1997; editor (with Abraham Neyman and Yair Tauman): Game Theory and Applications, 1990; editor: (with Thomas Marschak) Markets, Games and Organizations: Essays in Honor of Roy Radner, 2002; series editor Math. Econs. and Game Theory, 2000—, assoc. editor Rev. Econ. Design, 1997—, mem. editl. bd. Internat. Jour. Game Theory, 1997—, Advances in Mathematical Economics, 1998—, Games and Economic Behavior, 1998—; contbr. articles. Recipient Nikkei-Tosho Bunka Sho award Nihon Keizai Shinbun and Japan Ctr. for Econ. Rsch., 1994; CORE fellow, 1974-75; NSF grantee, 1978-82, 82-85, 92-96. Mem.: Game Theory Soc. Office: Ohio State U Dept Econs 1945 N High St Columbus OH 43210-1172

IDE, JOHN EDWIN, physical education educator; b. Kingston, Pa., Aug. 11, 1946; s. John E. Sr. and Doris (McCarty) I.; m. Carole Fogg, May 25, 1968; children: Daniel, Barrett. BS in Health and Phys. Edn., East Stroudsburg U., 1968; MEd in Health and Phys. Edn., Trenton State Coll., 1972. Cert. tchr., N.J., Pa. Tchr. elem. phys. edn. Cherry Hill (N.J.) Sch. Dist., 1968-70; tchr. health and phys. edn. Klinger Jr. High Sch., Warminster, Pa., 1970-72, William Tennent Intermediate High Sch., Warminster, Pa., 1972-80, Davis Elem. Sch., Warminster, Pa., 1980-92, Klinger Mid. Sch., Southampton, Pa., 1992-93, Willow Dale/Leary Elem. Sch., 1993—. Co-owner, dir., coach, co-founder Southampton Gymnastic Club, Ivyland, Pa., 1974-97. Mem. NEA, AAHPERD, Pa. Edn. Assn., Centennial Edn. Assn., U.S. Gymnastic Fedn. Avocations: golf, skiing. Home: 1630 Franklynn Dr Furlong PA 18925-1441

IDOL, JAMES DANIEL, JR., chemist, educator, inventor, consultant; b. Harrisonville, Mo., Aug. 7, 1928; s. James Daniel and Gladys Rosita (Lile) I.; m. Marilyn Thorn Randall, 1977. AB, William Jewell Coll., 1949; MS, Purdue U., 1952, PhD, 1955, D.Sc. (hon.), 1980. With Standard Oil Co., Ohio, 1955-77, rsch. supr., 1965-68, rsch. mgr., 1968-77; mgr. venture rsch. Ashland Chem. Co., Columbus, Ohio, 1977-79, v.p., dir. corp. R & D, 1979—88; disting. prof. materials sci. and ceramics sch. engring. Rutgers U., New Brunswick, NJ, 1988—2002, dir. polymer sci. ctr. for advanced materials via immiscible polymer processing, 2002—. Adv. bd. NSF Presdl. Young Investigators Awards, Nat. Inst. Sci. and Tech., 1997—; cons. in field; lectr. chem. engring. dept. Northwestern U., 1978, Stanford U., 1982-83, U. Calif., Berkeley, 1986, Yale U., 1988 U. Chgo., 1998; lectr. Lawrence Berkeley Lab., 1985-86; v.p., program coord. 1st N.Am. Chem. Congress, 1975; program coord. 1st Pacific Rim Chem. Cong., 1979; indsl. rep. U.S. Coun. for Chem. Rsch., 1983—, governing bd., 1985—; panel on frontiers in fossil fuel energy rsch. NRC, 1986, com. on tracking toxic wastes, 1989-93, panel on polymers in the environ. Internat. Union of Pure and Applied Chemistry, 1996, com. on energy conservation in processing of indsl. materials; adv. bd. U. Tex., Tex. A&M, Ohio State U., Purdue U., Okla. State U., Ariz. State U., U. Mass., Case Western Reserve U., 1965-75; com. polymers recycling Internat. Union Pure and Applied Chem., 1993—; mem. U.S. Coun. Chem. Rsch., 1981-89, gov. bd. 1985-88. Chmn. editl. adv. bd.: Indsl. & Engring. Chemistry Jour., 1976—84, mem. editl. adv. bd.: Chem. and Engring. News, 1977—81, Am. Chem. Soc. Symposium Series, 1978—84, Advances in Chemistry Seris, 1979—84, Chem. Week Mag., 1980—82, Sci., 1986—91, Jour. Applied Polymer Sci., 1988—; contbr. chapters to books, articles to profl. jours., handbooks and encys. Active Cleve. Welfare Fedn. Recipient Modern Pioneer award NAM, 1965, Disting. Alumnus citation William Jewell Coll., 1971 Fellow AAAS, Am. Inst. Chemists (life; bd. dirs. 1981—, vice-chmn. 1986, chmn. 1987, Chem. Pioneer award 1968, Mems. and Fellows lectr. 1980); mem. Nat. Acad. Engring., Soc. Plastics Industry, Soc. Mfg. Engrs.-Composite Group, Am. Chem. Soc. (indsl. and engring. chemistry divsn., chmn. 1971, chem. innovator designation Chem. and Engring. News mag. 1971, adv. bd. Petroleum Rsch. Fund, 1974-76, Joseph P. Stewart Disting. Svc. award 1975, Creative Invention award 1975), Am. Mgmt. Assn. (R&D coun. 1985-88, Coun. award for Disting. Svc. pkg. coun. 1989-97, mfg. and tech. coun. 1997—), Dirs. of Indsl. Rsch., Am. Inst. Chem. Engrs., Licensing Execs. Soc., Soc. Plastics engrs., Indsl. Rsch. Inst. (rep., chmn. bd. editors 1983-86), Plastics Pioneers Assn., Soc. Chem. Industry (Perkin medal 1979), Ind. Acad. Sci., Catalysis Soc. (Ciapetti award/lectureship 1988), Cleve. Athletic Club, Cosmos Club (Washington), Worthington Hills Country Club, Masons, Shriners, Sigma Xi, Alpha Chi Sigma, Theta Chi Delta, Kappa Mu Epsilon, Alpha Phi Omega, Phi Gamma Delta. Mem. Christian Ch. (Disciples Of Christ). Achievements include invention of process for manufacture acrylonitrile (over 80 plants in 30 countries-this ammoxidation process was designated as Nat. Hist. Chem. Landmark 1996 by Am. Chem. Soc; patents in field. Office: Dept Ceramic & Materials Eng 607 Taylor Rd Rutgers Univ Piscataway NJ 08854-8065

IDOL, JOHN LANE, JR., English language educator, writer, editor; b. Deep Gap, N.C., Oct. 28, 1932; s. John Lane and Annie Lulu (Watson) I.; m. Marjorie Anne South, Nov. 24, 1955. BS, Appalachian State U., 1958; MA, U. Ark., 1961, PhD, 1964. English tchr. Blowing Rock (N.C.) Union Sch., 1958-59; English tchr., writer Clemson (S.C.) U., 1965-95. Dir. grad. studies in English Clemson U., 1969—74; table leader Ednl. Testing Svcs., Princeton, NJ, 1990—; vis. lectr. UNC, Chapel Hill, 2000. Author: Thomas Wolfe Companion, 1987; co-author: Hawthorne and the Visual Arts, 1991; editor: The Hound of Darnkess (Thomas Wolfe), 1986; co-editor: Mannerhouse (Thomas Wolfe), 1985, Nathaniel Hawthorne, The Contemporary Reviews, 1994, The Party at Jack's (Thomas Wolfe), 1995, Hawthorne and Women, 1999; contbr. articles and poems to lit. jours.; : Thomas Wolfe, 2001. Treas. Clemson Area Arts Coun. 1984-85; chmn. Adv. Com. on Accomodation Taxes, 1985-90; bd. mem. Friends of Orange County Libr., 2001—; pres. Friends of Clemson Community Libr., 1989-90; sec. Chapel Hill-Carrboro Cmty. Chorus, 1997-98; vol. tchr. Chapel Hill Sr. Citizens' Ctr. With U.S. Air Force, 1951-55. Recipient Award of Merit, AAUP, S.C. chpt., 1986; NDEA fellow U. Ark., 1959; named Alumni Disting. Prof., Clemson U., 1993. Mem. MLA, Nathaniel Hawthorne Soc. (pres. 1984-86, editor Nathaniel Hawthorne rev. 1983-92), Herman Melville Soc., Thomas Wolfe Soc. (pres. 1981-83), Southeastern Name Soc. (pres. 1988-90), Philol. Assn. of the Carolinas (pres. 1984, Honored Tchr. 1986), Soc. for Study of So. Lit. (v.p. 1992-94, pres. 1994-96), Mark Twain Circle, Phi Beta Kappa (Piedmont Area pres. 1981-83, 89-91), Phi Kappa Phi. Avocations: choral singing, softball, birding, photography, book collecting. Home: PO Box 413 Hillsborough NC 27278-0413

IDOS, ROSALINA VEJERANO, secondary school educator; b. Ligao, Philippines, Mar. 18, 1944; arrived in U.S., 1987; m. Salvador Salcedo Idos, Dec. 21, 1969; children: Nathaniel, Rey, Lady Lou. BSc in Edn., U. of the East, Philippines, 1965; MSc in Edn., Nat. U., 2000. Cert. single subject tchg. in English, social studies, Filipino Calif., 1989. Tchr. Mayon H.S., Ligao City, Philippines, 1965—67; master tchr. in charge of student tchrs. U. of the East, Manila, Philippines, 1967—69, prof., 1969—87; tchr. San Diego Unified Sch. Dist. Morse H.S., San Diego, 1988—. Workshop presenter in field; curriculum writer Project Inclusion San Diego City Schs., San Diego, 1993—95. Recipient Outstanding Tchr. award, U. Calif., 1995—96, Educator of the Decade award, Filipino-Am. Educators Assn. San Diego, 1999, Svc. award, Fgn. Lang. Coun. San Diego, 1999, Recognition award, Filipino-Am. Educators of Calif., 2000. Fellow: Calif. Fgn. Lang. Project; mem.: San Diego Internat. Lang. Network (leadership team), Filipino-Am. Parents Assn. (adv. 1993—), Kaisahan Club (adv. 1990—). Roman Catholic. Avocations: reading, writing. Home: 6333 Viewpoint Ct San Diego CA 92139 Office: Morse High School 6905 Skyline Drive San Diego CA 92114

IERARDI, ERIC JOSEPH, school system administrator; b. Bklyn., May 11, 1950; s. Joseph and Angelina (Vitale) I. BA, St. Francis Coll., 1973; MEd, Fordham U., 1987. Asst. dir. James A. Kelly Local Hist. Studies Inst., 1973; St. Francis Coll. tchr. St. Bartholomew's Sch., 1974-78; tchr. Our Lady of Grace Sch., Bklyn., 1978-86, St. Mary Star of Sea Sch., 1986-87, asst. on edn. to Bklyn. borough pres., 1979; dist. rep., mgr. Congressman Stephen J. Solarz, 1981-82; prin. St. Francis Xavier Sch., Vicksburg, Miss., 1987-89, St. Francis Paola Sch., Bklyn., 1989-91, St. Pius V, Jamaica, Queens, N.Y., 1991-96; adminstr. David A. Boody Intermediate Sch. 228, Bklyn. Instr. prof. Hinds C.C., Miss.; U.S. delegate Gruppo Savoia, 2000. Author: Gravesend: The Home of Coney Island, 1975, Gravesend: Brooklyn, Coney Island & Sheepshead Bay, 1996, Brooklyn in the 1920s, 1998; contbg. editor Bklyn. Mag., 1978-79. Past mem. Cmty. Planning Bd. 11, Bklyn.; past pres. Gravesend Dem. Club; commr. deeds City N.Y.; apptd. U.S. del. GRUPPO SAVOIA. Named Hon. Mayor, Gravesend, Eng., 1977, Knight Officier, Order of Merit of Savoy, 2002, Honored Guard, Royal Tombs at the Pantheon in Rome, 2003; recipient Calabrian of Yr. award Brutium Cultural Club, 1979; knighted, named to Order of Merit of Savoy, His Royal Highness Prince Victor Emmanuel IV of Savoy, 1999; promoted to Knight Officer (Ufficiale), Order of Merit of Savoy, 2002. Mem. Assn. Tchrs. Social Studies, Columbia Tchrs. Assn., Gravesend Hist. Soc. (pres.), Circolo Culturale Club, Univ. S. Fla. Club, Order Sons of Italy. Democrat. Roman Catholic. Home: PO Box 5 Upper Black Eddy PA 18972-0005 Office: IS 228 228 Avenue S Brooklyn NY 11223-2746

IFEDIORA, OKECHUKWU CHIGOZIE, nephrologist, educator; b. Onitsha, Nigeria, Mar. 1, 1955; came to U.S., 1986; s. Jeremiah Chukwudebe and Victoria Nonye (Menyua) I.; m. Efeti Osagie Udaze, Mar. 20, 1993; children: Amala Chukwu Tochukwu, Nwamaka Chidima. BSc with hons., U. Ife, Nigeria, 1978; MBChB, U. Ife, 1981. Diplomate Am. Bd. Internal Medicine, Am. Bd. Nephrology. Intern Gen. Hosp., Onitsha, 1981-82; med. officer Apex Med. Ctr., Igbo-Ukwu, Nigeria, 1982-86; resident Harlem Hosp., N.Y.C., 1987-90; fellow in nephrology Lankenau Hosp., Phila., 1990-92; cons. Nephrology Cons., Monroe, La., 1992-97; cons., v.p. Renal Assocs., Monroe, 1997—. Asst. clin. prof. La. State U., Conway Hosp., Monroe, 1994—. Contbr. articles to profl. jours. Fellow ACP; mem. AMA, Am. Soc. Nephrology, Internat. Soc. Nephrology, Ouachita Med. Soc., Nat. Kidney Found., Monroe C. of C., Monroe Atheletic Club. Avocations: tennis, photography, swimming, travelling. Home: 3102 Claiborne Cir Monroe LA 71201-2006

IGNATONIS, SANDRA CAROLE AUTRY, special education educator; b. Dixon Mills, Ala., June 6, 1942; d. Charles Franklin Autry; m. Algis Jerome Ignatonis, June 15, 1968; children: Audra Carole, David Jerome. BA, Samford U., 1964; cert. in Gifted Edn., Kennesaw State U., 1989. Cert. tchr., Ga. Tchr. Jefferson County Bd. Edn., Birmingham, Ala., 1964, Huntsville (Ala.) Bd. Edn., 1964-71, Epiphany Cath. Sch., Miami, Fla., 1981, Cobb County Bd. Edn., Marietta, Ga., 1982, Bartow County Bd. Edn., Cartersville, Ga., 1990-92, Sequoria Group, Inc., Roswell, Ga., 1996; with Atlanta real estate divsn. Regions Bank, Atlanta, 1997—. Mem. Sch. Self-Governance Com., Emerson, Ga., 1990-91, Soccer Adv. Bd., Marietta, 1985-89; judge, mem. Social Sci. Fair Competitions, Huntsville, 1964-71. Team mom Metro N. Youth Soccer Assn., Marietta, 1991-92; block parent Somerset Subdivision, Marietta, 1982-86, block capt., 1998-99; polit. chmn. Student Nat. Edn. Assn., Samford U., Birmingham, Ala., 1963-64; bd. dirs. Somerset Homeowners Assn., 1998-99. Recipient grant Samford U. Faculty, 1963. Mem. Ga. Supporters of Gifted, Profl. Assn. Ga. Educators. Republican. Roman Catholic. Avocations: tennis, bowling, gardening, needle work, reading. Office: Regions Bank 400 Embassy Row 6600 Peachtree Dunwoody Rd NE Atlanta GA 30328-1649

IHDE, MARY KATHERINE, retired mathematics educator; b. St. Louis, Jan. 19, 1942; d. Harold Orville and Katharine Marie Nanninga; m. Daniel Carlyle Ihde, Dec. 22, 1968; children: Steven Carlyle, Douglas Harold. BA in Math., Northwestern U., 1964; MS in Math. Edn., Stanford U., 1968. Cert. tchr., N.Y., Calif., Md. Tchr. math. Shawnee Mission (Kans.) H.S. Dist., 1964-67; math. specialist Columbia Grammar and Prep. Sch., N.Y.C., 1969-72; tchr. math. Georgetown Visitation Prep. Sch., Washington, 1981-84; lectr. math. Mt. Vernon Coll., Washington, 1984-85; tchr. math. Nat. Cathedral Sch. for Girls, Washington, 1985-93, chmn. dept., 1989-92; instr. math. Maryville U., St. Louis, 1994-95, Webster U., St. Louis, 1994-95; tchr. math., curriculum coord. Whitfield Sch., St. Louis, 1995-96; math. curriculum cons., 1996—2002; ret., 2002. Recipient 2nd place state level competition award Mathcounts, 1992, 4th place, 1993; fellow Shell Oil Corp., 1967-68. Mem. Nat. Coun. Tchrs. Math., Pi Lambda Theta. Address: 10805 Chicobush Dr NW Albuquerque NM 87114-5550

IHLANFELDT, WILLIAM, investment company executive, consultant; b. Belleville, Ill., Dec. 12, 1936; s. Raymond William and Olivia Anna (Boycourt) I.; m. D. Jeannine Huguelet, May 7, 1978; children: Troy, Kimberly, Holly. BS, Ill. Wesleyan U., 1959, LLD, 1980; MA, Northwestern U., 1963, PhD, 1970. Adminstr. Monticello Coll., Godfrey, Ill., 1959-60; tchr., coach Rich Twp. H.S., Park Forest, Olympia Fields, Ill., 1960-64; dir. fin. aid Northwestern U., Evanston, Ill., 1964-67, dean admission and fin. aid, 1973-78, v.p. instnl. rels., 1978-96; mng. dir. Hartline Investment Corp., Chgo., 1997—. Chmn. pub. policy Consortium Financing Higher Edn., Cambridge, Mass., 1979-83; chmn. Fedn. Ill. Ind. Colls. and Univs., Springfield, 1981-83; chmn. Fedn. Com. on State Funding, 1993-95; Student Loan Mktg. Assn., Washington, 1975-95, CyberMark, 1995-96, Constrn. Loan Assn., 1995-98; cons. in field. Author: Achieving Optimal Enrollments and Tuition Revenues, 1980; contbr. chpts. to books, articles to profl. publs. Founder, Northwestern U. Chgo. Action Project, Evanston, 1966; pres., CEO Northwestern U./Evanston Rsch. Park, 1986-96; co-founder Ill. Ind. Higher Edn. Loan Authority, Northbrook, 1981; founder Ill. Rsch. Park Authority, 1986. Wieboldt Found. grantee, 1966, 67, 68. Mem. Indian Hill Club (Winnetka, Ill.), Gainey Ranch Golf Club, Phi Delta Kappa. Avocations: tennis, golf, skiing. E-mail: williami@cox.net.

IHRIE, JOHN RICHARD, III, art educator; b. Washington; s. John R. Jr. and Mary Frances (Collins) I.; m. Mary Haddad, July 18, 1969. Student, Corcoran Sch. Art, 1935; LLB, Columbus U., 1942. Creator art tchg. srs. programs OASIS, Washington, 1994—, IONA, Washington, 1996—. Pastelist, watercolorist mediums used in painting series German Village, 1970's, Arlington House, Lee Mansion, 1970's, Nova Scotia P.E.I., 1987, Bicentennial for the TRS-Centennial Series on the Mall, Washington, DC 1973-76, Wash., DC Indsl. Sites, 1980's, England, Scotland, Ireland, 1991, Jerusalem and Palestine of 19th Century, 1991-96, Monet's Giverny, France, 1995, Le Baron, Beirot Roman Ruins, 1999. Mem. Corcoran Art Gallery Phillips, Smithsonian Instn. With USCG. Presbyterian. Avocation: singing irish songs. Home: Pastellery 3924 Livingston St NW Washington DC 20015-2922

IKENBERRY, STANLEY OLIVER, education educator, former university president; b. Lamar, Colo., Mar. 3, 1935; s. Oliver Samuel and Margaret (Moulton) Ikenberry; m. Judith Ellen Life, Aug. 24, 1958; children: David Lawrence, Steven Oliver, John Paul. BA, Shepherd Coll., 1956; MA, Mich. State U., 1957, PhD, 1960, LHD (hon.); LLD (hon.), Millikin U.; LHD (hon.), Millikin U., Ill. Coll., Rush U., W.Va. U., Towson State U., U. Nebr., Bridgewater (Va.) Coll., Bradley U., Shepherd Coll., Roosevelt U., Juniatta Coll., Pa., 2003, Northeastern U. Instr. office evaluation svc. Mich. State U., 1958—60, instr. instl. rsch. office, 1960—62; asst. to provost for instl. rsch., asst. prof. edn. W.Va. U., 1962—65, dean coll. human resources and edn., assoc. prof. edn., 1965—69; prof., assoc. dir. ctr. study higher edn. Pa. State U., 1969—71, sr. v.p., 1971—79; pres. U. Ill., Urbana, 1979—95, pres. emeritus, Regent prof., 1995—; pres. Am. Coun. on Edn., Washington, 1996—2001. Bd. dirs. Pfizer, Inc., N.Y.C., Aquila Inc., Kans. City; pres. bd. overseers Tchrs. Ins. and Annutiy Assn./Coll. Retirement Equities Fund. Named hon. alumnus, Pa. State U. Fellow: Am. Acad. Arts and Scis.; mem.: Assn. Am. Univs. (past chmn.), Tavern Club (Chgo.), Cosmos Club (Washington), Mid-Am. Club, Comml. Club Chgo. Office: U Ill 347 Education 1310 S 6th St Champaign IL 61820

ILCHMAN, ALICE STONE, foundation administrator, former college president, former government official; b. Cin., Apr. 18, 1935; d. Donald Crawford and Alice Kathryn (Biermann) Stone; m. Warren Frederick Ilchman, June 11, 1960; children: Frederick Andrew Crawford, Alice Sarah. BA, Mt. Holyoke Coll., 1957; MPA, Maxwell Sch. Citizenship, Syracuse U., 1958; PhD, London Sch. Econs., 1965; LHD, Mt. Holyoke Coll., 1982, Franklin and Marshall Coll., 1983. Asst. to pres., mem. faculty Berkshire C.C., 1961-64; lectr. Ctr. for South and S.E. Asia Studies U. Calif., Berkeley, 1965-73; prof. econs. and edn., dean Wellesley (Mass.) Coll., 1973-78; asst. sec. ednl. and cultural affairs Dept. State, 1978; assoc. dir. ednl. and cultural affairs Internat. Comm. Agy., 1978—81; advisor to sec. Smithsonian Instn., 1981; pres. Sarah Lawrence Coll., Bronxville, N.Y., 1981-98; chmn. bd. Rockefeller Found., N.Y.C., 1995—2000. Dir. Jeannette K. Watson Fellowships, 1999—; intern, asst. to Sen. John F. Kennedy, 1957; dir. Peace Corps Tng. Program for India, 1965-66; chmn. com. on women's employment NAS; sr. advisor Thomas Watson Found., 1999—; bd. dirs. NYNEX, Seligman Group of Investment Cos. Author: The New Men of Knowledge and the New States, 1968, (with W.F. Ilchman) Education and Employment in India, The Policy Nexus, 1976. Trustee Mt. Holyoke Coll., 1970-80, Mass. Found. for Humanities and Pub. Policy, 1974-77, East-West Ctr., Honolulu, 1978-81, Expt. in Internat. Living, The Markle Found., The Rockefeller Found., chmn. bd. dirs., acting pres., 1998; trustee The U. of Cape Town, South Africa, Corp. Adv. Bd., Hotchkiss Sch.; mem. Smithsonian Coun., Yonkers Emergency Fin. Control Bd., 1982-88, Am. Ditchley Found. Program Com., Internat. Rsch. and Exch. Bd., Com. for Econ. Devel., The Masters Sch., Save The Children, Chamber Music Soc. Lincoln Ctr.; bd. dirs. Pub. Broadcasting Corp., 2000—. Hon. fellow Wadham Coll., Oxford U. Mem. NOW Legal Def. Edn. Fund, Coun. Fgn. Rels., Century Assn. (N.Y.C.), Bronxville Field Club. Home: 18 Highland Cir Bronxville NY 10708-5908 Office: Jeannette K Watson Fellowships 31st Fl 810 Seventh Ave New York NY 10019 E-mail: ailchman@jkwatson.org.

ILES, LAWRENCE IRVINE, liberal arts educator, historian; b. Epsom, U.K., June 8, 1954; s. Irvine Edmund Douglas and Bridget Margaret (Dobson) I.; m. Betty Louise McLane. BA, U. Newcastle Upon Tyne, 1975; MA, U. London, 1978, U. Ill., 1982. Hon. vis. fellow Grad. Sch. Internat. Studies, Birmingham U., Edgbaston, U.K., 1987; adj. instr. Johnson County C.C., Overland Park, Kans., 1991-92; vis. tchr. Roedean Internat. Coll., Brighton, England, 1992-93; lectr. Oakland Coll., St. Albans, 1993; tutor Bartholomew's Coll., Brighton, 1992-93, 96; pvt. practice lectr., broadcaster polit. sci. and global perspectives Kirksville, Mo., 1996—. Vis. tchr. St. Mary's Coll., Brighton, 2002; presenter in field. Author: Modern History Course Planner, 1988; contbr. articles to profl. jours.; author 3 sects. The Routledge Ency. Contemporary Brit. Culture, 1999. State organizer Socialist Party USA, N.Y.C., 1994—; dep. chair (Hove Constituency) Brunswick and Goldsmid br. Labor Party U.K., 1996; U.S./Can. rep. Brit. Governing Labor Party Heritage Group. Mem.: MLA. Home: 503 S Stanford St Kirksville MO 63501-3878

ILES, ROGER DEAN, business educator; b. Detroit, June 11, 1950; s. Virgil Llewellyn and Mary Elizabeth (Lynn) I.; m. Gail Ann Swatzell, Jan. 10, 1971; 1 child, Gwendolyn Christine. AA, Regents Coll., 1990; BS magna cum laude, Crichton Coll., 1992; MBA, U. Memphis, 1997. Enlisted USN, 1969, advanced through grades to chief electronics technician, 1969-89; ret., 1989; switchman Mich. Bell Telephone Co., Dearborn, 1968-69; controller, alumni advisor Crichton Coll., Memphis, 1989-99. Mem. adj. faculty, mem. capital campaign steering com. Crichton Coll., Memphis, 1998—; mem. adj. faculty U. Memphis, 1998—; mem. online faculty U. Phoenix, 2003—; chmn., mgr. Shade Tree Engring., Inc., Munford, Tenn., 1992—. Mem. Gideons Internat. (area dir., pres. Tipton County South Camp). Republican. Baptist. Avocations: auto racing, target shooting. Home: 59 Jennifer Cv Brighton TN 38011-6056 Office: 2359 Beaver Rd Ste A Brighton TN 38011-6215 Fax: 901-837-0499. E-mail: etcsw@email.uophx.edu.

ILETT, FRANK, JR., trucking company executive, educator; b. Ontario, Oreg., June 21, 1940; s. Frank Kent and Lela Alice (Siver) I.; m. Donna L. Andlovec, Apr. 3, 1971; children: James Frank, Jordan Lee. BA, U. Wash., 1962; MBA, U. Chgo., 1969. CPA, Idaho, Ill., Wash. Acct. Ernst & Young, Boise, Cleve., Spokane, 1962-69, mgr. Boise, 1970-72, regional mgr. San Francisco, 1972-73; treas. Interstate Mack, Inc., Boise, 1973-81, pres., CEO, 1981-82; pres. Interstate NationLease, Inc., Boise, 1975-81, Contract Carriers, Inc., Boise, 1983-89, Ilett Transp. Co., Boise, 1985-90; chmn. Carriers/West, Inc., Salem, Oreg., 1986-89; CFO, White GMC Trucks, 1988-92; v.p., CFO, May Trucking Co., Payette, Idaho, 1992-94; acct., mng. ptnr. Frank Ilett, Jr., CPA, Boise, 1994—. Spl. lectr. Boise State U., 1964-67, 94—, St. Mary's Grad. Sch., Moraga, Calif., 1989-92 ; v.p. I.D.E.A.L., Inc., Nampa, Idaho, 1997-2002; cons. Calif. Hosp. Commn., 1973, Idaho Hosp. Assn., 1974; chmn. Mack Truck Western Region Distbr. Coun., 1979-82; nat. distbr. adv. com. Mack Trucks, Inc., 1980-82; dir. stds. enforcement Idaho State Bd. Accountancy, 1983-84; contr. Idaho Stampede, 2002—. Contbr. articles to profl. jours. Recipient Outstanding Prof. award KPMG, 2003; named Arthur Andersen Outstanding Acctg. Prof., 1996, 2001. Mem.: ACIPA, SAR, Gen. Soc. Mayflower Descs., Crane Creek Country Club, Shriners, Masons, Alpha Kappa Psi (Outstanding Bus. Prof. award 1997, named Disting. Faculty Mem., Coll. Bus. 2002). Episcopalian. Home: 1701 Harrison Blvd Boise ID 83702-1015 Office: 1910 University Dr Boise ID 83725 E-mail: frankilett@msn.com.

ILEY, MARTHA STRAWN, music educator; b. Marhsville, NC, June 1, 1925; d. Stephen Hasty and Lila Faircloth Strawn; m. Bryce Baxter Iley, Aug. 7, 1948; children: Deborah Iley Hodde, Sheila Iley McLean, Cheryl Iley Lindstrom, Stephanie Iley Salb. BA, East Carolina Tchrs. Coll., 1946; MA, Western Ky. State Coll., 1947; MusM, Winthrop Coll., 1973; EdM, U. NC, Charlotte, 1974; EdD, Nova U., 1979; M Theol. Studies, Gordon-Conwell Theol. Sem., 1998. Cert. Music Tchrs. Nat. Assn. Music tchr. Lincolnton City Sch., 1947—48, Alexander Graham Jr. HS, Charlotte, NC, 1948—52, Charlotte Country Day Sch., 1955—59; min. music Providence Bapt. Ch., Charlotte, 1954—57, Carmel Bapt. Ch., Charlotte, 1968—70, 1975—76; project dir. music edn. Ctrl. Piedmont C.C., Charlotte, 1974—83; founder, chmn. bd. dirs. Met. Music Ministries, Charlotte, 1984—. Editor: (newsletter) ARTY-FACTS, 1983. Bd. dirs., sec. Charlotte Cmty. Concert Assn., 1980—93; dir. recital series Shepherd Ctr., Charlotte, 1980—83; adjudicator piano and voice various orgns., NC, 1980—. Recipient Disting. Music Alumni award, East Carolina U., 2002. Mem.: Charlotte Piano Tchrs. Forum (bd. dirs., pres. 1979—81), Charlotte Clergy

Assn., NC Music Tchrs. Assn. (cert. chmn., v.p. 1981—83), Charlotte Music Club (bd. dirs.). Republican. Baptist. Avocations: writing, painting. Home: 10151 Robinson Church Rd Harrisburg NC 28075-6607 Office: Met Music Ministries Inc 1311 Paddock Cir Charlotte NC 28209-2443 Office Fax: 704-529-0256.

ILI, ESTHER KAILI, educational administrator; b. Honolulu, Nov. 2, 1945; d. Mitchell Kala and Flora Nakilau (Gonsalves) Kamana; m. Taugata To'oto'o Ili, July 29, 1970; children: Jan Kaleolani, Jeff Kamana, Brett Kahililani. BS, Ch. Coll. Hawaii, 1968; MEd, U. Hawaii, 1981. Cert. tchr., Hawaii, Am. Samoa; cert. adminstrn., Am. Samoa. Tchr. history Hawaii Radford High Sch., Honolulu, 1969-75; tchr. English, head dept. Samoana High Sch., Pago Pago, Am. Samoa, 1975-83; tchr. English ch. edn. system LDS Ch., Pesega, Upolu, Western Samoa, 1984-85; tchr. English, head dept. Tafuna High Sch., Pago Pago, 1986-89, vice prin., 1989-92; vice prin., bd. dirs. Nu'uuli Vocat. Tech. High Sch., Pago Pago, 1992-97, prin., 1997-99, consortia program dir., 1999—2003. Mem. English standing curriculum com. Am. Samoa Dept. Edn., 1995-99, mem. Tchr. of the Yr. com., 1994-99, 2001-2003, leadership team Dept. Edn., 2002-; team mem. Pacific Region Effective and Successful Schools; tech. com. Dept. of Edn., 1997-98. Tchr. LDS Ch., Pago Pago, 1975-99, advisor to young women; mem. PTA, Am. Samoa Territorial PTA; bd. dirs. C.D. 2000; active coop. dist. Pago Pago, Am. Samoa, 1996-99; counselor Young Women First, 2002; tchr. mia Maid, 2002-. Recipient nomination Internat. Citizen of Yr. for Hutt River, Australia, 1996; awarded hon. title Principality of Hutt River Province; named State Tchr. of Yr., Govt. Am. Samoa, 1982. Mem. Am. Samoa Edn. Assn., Dept. Hawaiian Home Lands, Brigham Young U.-Hawaii Alumni Assn., Ch. Coll. Hawaii Alumni Assn., Am. Vocat. Assn., Pvt. Industry Coun., Assn. Curriculum and Devel., Mālama O Mānoa, Young Adult Relief Soc. (tchr. 1994-96, chmn. state welfare com. 2000-2002), United Srs. Assn., Postal Commemorative Soc., Am. Samoa Career Guidance Assn. (adv. com. 1997-98), Assn. for Career and Tech. Edn., Phi Alpha Theta. Avocations: reading, sports. Home: PO Box 5094 Pago Pago AS 96799-5094 Office: Aiga Potopoto Resource Ctr D O E Pago Pago AS 96799 E-mail: estheri@doe.as.

ILLANES, ALEJANDRO MORA, physician, educator, researcher; b. Concepcion, Chile, May 10, 1928; s. Alejandro Benavides Illanes and Emelina Delord Mora; m. Javiera Araya, July 17, 1954 (dec. Jan. 1982); children: Alejandra, Javier; m. Eliana Giglio, July 8, 1983. B Math., U. Chile, Santiago, 1947, B Biology, 1948, lic. in medicine, 1955, MD, 1956; postgrad., Tulane U., 1961. Instr. Pharmacology Inst. U. Chile, 1956-61, asst. prof. Pharmacology Inst., 1961-68, prof., head exptl. medicine dept., 1969-73; subrogating prof. Bern (Switzerland) U. Physiol. Inst., 1974-75; vis. prof. pharmacology dept. Man. CHF, Winnipeg, Can., 1975-76; prof. pharmacology, chief physiol. scis. dept. Orient U., Bolivar, Venezuela, 1976-96. Fellow in pharmacology Harvard U. Sch. Medicine, 1962-63; mem. health com. Consejo Nacional de Investigacion, Santiago, 1970-73; founder, mem. Orient Ctr. Toxicology, Bolivar, 1978-81; med. rsch. cons. Ministry of Health, Govt. of Chile, 1970-73; pres., coord. med. scis. sect. Nat. Scis. Congress, 1972. Author, editor: Scorpion Venom Pharmacology, 1982; contbr. articles to profl. jours. Pres. Chilean Nat. Formulary Com., 1971-73; organizer, sec. Guayana sect. Venezuela Assn. for Advancement of Scis., Bolivar, 1984-90; organizer, editor bull. Sci., Tech. and Edn. of Guayana, Bolivar, 1984-90. Recipient Honor award Venezuelan Assn. for Advancement of Sci., 1994, U. Venezuela, 1996, Meritory Prof. award and diploma Nat. Univ. Sys., 1995, Meritory Rsch. award P.E.I.-UDO, Venezuela, 2000. Mem. Chilean Coll. Physicians, Internat. Soc. Heart Rsch., N.Y. Acad. Scis. Roman Catholic. Avocations: classic cars, writing, photography, collecting pens and watches.

ILTIS, HUGH HELLMUT, plant taxonomist-evolutionist, educator; b. Brno, Czechoslovakia, Apr. 7, 1925; came to U.S., 1939, naturalized, 1944; s. Hugo and Anne (Liebscher) I.; m. Grace Schaffel, Dec. 20, 1951 (div. Mar. 1958); children: Frank S., Michael George; m. Carolyn Merchant, Aug. 4, 1961 (div. June 1970); children: David Hugh, John Paul. BA, U. Tenn., 1948; MA, Washington U., St. Louis and Mo. Bot. Garden, 1950, PhD, 1952. Rsch. asst. Mo. Bot. Garden, 1948-52; asst. prof. botany U. Ark., 1952-55; asst. prof. U. Wis.-Madison, 1955-60, assoc. prof., 1960-67, prof., 1967-93, prof. emeritus, 1993—, curator herbarium, 1955-67, dir. univ. herbarium, 1967-93, dir. emeritus, 1993—. Vis. prof. U. Va., Biol. Sta., 1959; world-wide lectr. in field; expdns. to Costa Rica, 1949, 89, Peru, 1962-63, Mex., 1960, 71, 72, 77, 78, 79, 81, 82, 84, 87, 88, 90, 93, 94, 95, 96, Guatemala, 1976, Ecuador, 1977, St. Eustatius, P.R., 1989, USSR, 1975, 79, Nicaragua-Honduras, 1991, Venezuela, 1991, Hawaii, 1967; mem. adv. bd. Flora N.Am., 1970-73, Gov. Wis. Commn. State Forests, 1972-73; rsch. assoc. Mo. Bot. Gardens, Bot. Rsch. Inst. Tex.; co-instigator Reserva Biosfera Sierrra de Manantlán, Jalisco, Mex. Author: articles flora of Wis. and Mex., Capparaceae, biogeography, evolution of maize, human ecology, especially innate responses to, and needs for, nature, beauty, diversity and wild nature.; co-author: Flora de Manantlan, 1995, Atlas of the Wisconsin Prairie and Savana Flora, 2000, Checklist of the Vascular Plants of Wis., 2001; editor: Extinction or Preservation: What Biological Future for the South American Tropics?, 1978. With U.S. Army, 1944—46, ETO. Recipient Biologia award, U. Tenn., 1948, Feinstone Environ. award, SUNY, Syracuse, N.Y., 1990, Conservation award, Conservation Coun. Hawaii, 1990, Nat. Wildlife Fedn. Spl. Achievement award, 1992, Puga medal, U. de Guadalajara, Mex., 1994, Disting. Alumnus award, Missouri Bot. Gardens, 1999. Fellow AAAS, Linnean Soc. (London); mem. Am. Inst. Biol. Scis., Bot. Soc. Am. (Merit award 1996), Soc. Econ. Botany (Econ. Botanist of Yr. award 1998), Am. Soc. Plant Taxonomists (Asa Gray award 1994), Internat. Assn. Plant Taxonomy, Soc. Bot. Mex., Soc. Study Evolution, Ecol. Soc. Am., Wis. Acad. Arts, Sci. and Letters, Forum for Corr.-Internat. Ctr. Integrative Studies, Nature Conservancy (co-founder and trustee emeritus Wis. chpt., Nat. Oakleaf award 1963), Wilderness Soc., Sierra Club, Nat. Parks Assn., Citizens Natural Resources Assn. Wis., Natural Resource Def. Coun., Environ. Def. Fund, Friends of Earth, Zero Population Growth, Negative Population Growth, Soc. Conservation Biology (Disting. Achievement award 1994), Natural Areas Assn., Sigma Xi, Phi Kappa Phi. Achievements include co-discoverer Zea diploperennis, Z. nicaraguensi and lycopersicom chmielewskii (high sugar-content wild tomatoes). Home: 2784 Marshall Pky Madison WI 53713-1023 Office: U Wis Dept Botany 430 Lincoln Dr Madison WI 53706-1313 Fax: 608-262-7509. E-mail: tscochra@facstaff.wisc.edu.

IMBODEN, JOHN BASKERVILLE, psychiatry educator; b. Morrilton, Ark., Sept. 17, 1925; MD, Johns Hopkins U., Balt., 1950. Diplomate Am. Bd. Neurology and Psychiatry; lic. physician, Md. Intern Cin. Gen. Hosp., 1950-51; resident Johns Hopkin's Hosp., 1951-52, 54-56; pvt. practice psychiatry Balt., 1963—; chief dept. psychiatry Sinai Hosp. of Balt., 1969-90; assoc. prof. psychiatry Johns Hopkins U., Balt., 1963—. Co-author: Practical Psychiatry in Medicine; contbr. articles to profl. jours, chpts. to books. With U.S. Army, 1952-54. Fellow Am. Psychiat. Assn.; mem. Am. Psychoanalytic Assn. Office: 600 Wyndhurst Ave Baltimore MD 21210-2489 E-mail: houndz@erols.com.

IMHOFF, PAMELA M. marketing educator; b. Lone Pine, Calif., Jan. 12, 1955; d. Buel Franklin Avery and Barbara Ann (Cohen) Wallace; m. Dennis Wayne Wallace,Mar. 28, 1972 (dec. Feb. 1973); 1 child, Jennifer Michelle; m. John Allen Imhoff, July 15, 1989; 1 child, Joshua Avery. AS, Tulsa Jr. Coll., 1975; BS, N.E. Okla. State U., 1978; MS, Okla. State U., 1981. Mktg. tchr., coord. Charles C. Mason H.S., Tulsa, Okla., 1978-79, Meml. H.S., Tulsa, Okla., 1979-80, Union H.S., Tulsa, Okla., 1980-91; mktg. tchr., coord. mktg. edn. Tulsa Tech. Ctr., Okla., 1991—. Salesmanship instr. Tulsa Jr. Coll., Okla., 1980; sales rep. Advertising Everything, Tulsa, Okla., 1984-86. Contbr. articles to profl. jours.; presenter in field. Mem. Gracemont Bapt. Ch., 1973—, Sunday sch. tchr., 1973-78; vol. Nat. Govs. Assn. Conf., Okla., 1993; mem. Tulsa Fire Fighter's Women's Aux., 1989—; coord., sponsor Turkey Challenge for Tulsa Area Schs., 1991—; vol., fundraiser United Way, 1982-90, Muscular Dystrophy Assn., 1980-90, Salvation Army, 1980-90; sponsor Sr. Citizen Day Target Stores, 1980-90. Recipient Tchr. of Yr. award AVA, 1995. Mem. NEA, Am. Vocat. Assn. (nat. conf. 1989, 90, 92, 93, mem. resolutions com. 1993—, nat. policy leadership seminar 1993, 94, chmn. Am. Vocat. Assn. conf. mktg. edn. divsn. 1993, tchr. of yr. Am. Vocat. Assn. regional IV 1994, nat. tchr. of yr. 1995), Nat. Bus. Edn. Assn., Okla. Edn. Assn., Okla. Vocat. Assn. (strategic planning com. 1994, chmn., mem. awards com. 1992—, mem. polit. action com. 1989—, rep. regional and nat. confs., 1988—, mem. awards banquet planning com. 1993, mem. adv. com. and exec. com. 1988-92, mem. membership svcs. com. 1991-92. tchr. of yr. 1993), Okla. Mktg. Edn. Tchrs. (chmn. awards com. 1992—, chmn. consititution com. 1984-92, pres. 1990-91, 1991-92, pres.-elect 1989-90, sec., treas. 1988-89, reporter 1987-88, mktg. tchr. of yr. 1993), Mktg. Edn. Assn., DECA (sec. state activities and awards com. 1982-86, mem. state exec. coun. 1982, 84, 85, 87, 93, 94, adv. state officers 1982, 84, 85, 87, 93, 94, adv., presenter, participant state fall leadership devel. conf., CSU mini-conf., OSU DECAthalon 1978—, event mgr. nat. conf. 1986, 90, 93, series dir. nat. conf. 1993, adult asst. nat. conf. 1980-92, 94, adv. nat. and state winners 1978—), Tulsa Area Vo-Tech Assn. Classroom Tchrs. Avocations: aerobics, reading. Office: Tulsa Community Coll 909 S Boston Ave Tulsa OK 74119*

INAGAMI, TADASHI, biochemist, educator; b. Kobe, Japan, Feb. 20, 1931; m. Masako Araki, Nov. 12, 1961 BS, Kyoto U., Japan, 1953, D.Sc., 1963; MS, Yale U., 1955, PhD, 1958. Research staff Yale U., New Haven, 1958-59, research assoc., 1962-66; research staff Kyoto U., Japan, 1959-62; instr. biochemistry Nagoya City U., Japan, 1962; asst. prof. biochemistry Vanderbilt U., Nashville, 1966-69, assoc. prof., 1969-74, prof. biochemistry, 1975-91, dir. hypertension rsch. ctr., 1979-95, Stanford Moore prof. biochemistry, 1991—, prof. medicine, 1992—. Contbr. numerous articles to profl. jours. Fulbright fellow, 1954-55; recipient Roche Vis. Prof. award, 1980, Humboldt Found. award, 1981, Ciba award Am. Heart Assn., 1985, Spa award Belgium Nat. Funds Sci. Rsch., 1986, Sutherland prize Vanderbilt U., 1990, Okamoto Internat. award Japan Vascular Disease Rsch. Found., 1995, award for excellence in cardiovascular rsch. Bristol Meyers Squibb, 1996, award Japan Acad., 1996, Jokichi Takamine award Japan Cardiovascular Endocrine-Metabolism Soc., 1998. Fellow: High Blood Pressure Rsch. Coun.; mem.: Japan Soc. Cardiovascular Endocrinol. Metabolism, Japan Soc. Biochemistry, Japan Soc. Hypertension, Internat. Soc. Hypertension, Am. Soc. Hypertension, Soc. Neurosci., Am. Soc. Cell Biology, Japan Endocrine Soc. (hon.), Japan Soc. Agrl. Chemistry (hon.), Am. Heart Assn. (Rsch. Achievement award 1994), Am. Soc. Pharmacol. and Therapent, Am. Chem. Soc., Endocrine Soc., Am. Physiol. Soc., Am. Soc. Biol. Chemists and Molecular Biologists. Office: Vanderbilt U Sch Medicine Dept Biochemistry 23D Ave S And Pierce Ave Nashville TN 37232-0146 E-mail: tadashi.inagami@vanderbilt.edu.

INAMINE, SHARON OGAWA, elementary school administrator; b. Honolulu, Apr. 26, 1942; d. Joseph and Yaeko (Fujii) Ogawa; m. Wayne Seigi Inamine, July 9, 1966; children: Malcolm Scott and Marcus Stuart (twins). BEd in Elem. Edn., U. Hawaii, 1964, 5th yr. diploma, 1965, MEd in Edn. Adminstrn., 1987; MEd in Elem. Edn., Calif. State U., Long Beach, 1968. Cert. tchr., adminstr., Hawaii. Tchr. Palolo Sch. Dept. edn., Honolulu, 1965, Mckinley Elem. Sch., Long Beach, Calif., 1965-69, Kahala Elem. Sch. Hawaii Dept. of Edn., Honolulu, 1970-87; resource tchr. Honolulu Dist. Office, 1987-90; vice prin. intern Kapunahala Elem. Sch., Kaneohe, Hawaii, 1989-90; vice prin. Kauluwela Sch., Honolulu, 1990-93, Ahuimanu Elem Sch., Kaneohe, 1993—. Dir. summer sch. Aina Haina Sch., Honolulu, 1987, Kauluwela Sch., Honolulu, 1992, Enchanted Lake Summer Sch., 1994; bd. dirs. Hawaii Adv. Coun. for Gifted and Talented, Honolulu, 1986-89. Author: (handbook) Honolulu Dist. Middle Schs., 1988; editor: (manual) Honolulu Dist. Effective Teaching, 1990. Bd. dirs. Kaiser High Sch. Band Boosters, Honolulu, 1984-88, Niu Valley Intermediate Band Boosters, Honolulu, 1982-84; team mother Local soccer, basketball and baseball teams, 1976-85. Mem. ASCD, Hawaii Assn. Supervision and Curriculum Devel., Internat. Reading Assn., Hawaii Assn. Middle Schs. (conf. chmn.). Honolulu Dist. Vice Prins. Group, Hawaii Drug Abuse Resistance Edn. Officers Assn., Delta Kappa Gamma (chpt. sec.). Congregationalist. Avocations: jogging, reading, photography, cooking. Home: 1176 Kaluanui Rd Honolulu HI 96825-1350 Office: Ahuimanu Elem Sch 47-470 Hui Aeko Pl Kaneohe HI 96744-4599

INCE, LAUREL T. music educator; b. Gonzales, Tex. m. Joe C. Ince; children: Joe C. Ince, Jr.(dec.), Mark A., Susan I. Burns, William C. BMus, Trinity U., 1950. Piano tchr. Ince Piano Studio, Gonzales, 1950—. Performer various internat. workshops, Austria, Can., Switzerland, Scotland, France; south ctrl. coord. music Link Found., 1990—. Contbr. articles to profl. jours. Advisor City Coun., Gonzales; accompanist First Bapt. Ch., Gonzales; pres. Sesame Club, Gonzales. Recipient Tchr. of Yr. award, Austin Music Tchrs. Assn., 1995, Pillar of the Point award, Inspiration Point Fine Arts Colony. Mem.: Nat. Guild Piano Tchrs., Tex. Music Tchrs. Assn. (state pres., Tchr. of Yr. award 1995), Nat. Fedn. Music Clubs (life; chmn. FAMA 1991, recording sec., lectr., performer), Tex. Fedn. Music Clubs (state pres., founder jr. state festival 1975), Sigma Alpha Iota (life). Avocations: entertaining, travel. Home: 723 St Francis Str Gonzales TX 78629 Home Fax: 830-672-5808. Personal E-mail: ljince@gvec.net.

INCROPERA, FRANK PAUL, mechanical engineering educator; b. Lawrence, Mass., May 12, 1939; s. James Frank and Ann Laura (Leone) I.; m. Andrea Jeanne Eastman, Sept. 2, 1960; children: Terri Ann, Donna Renee, Shaunna Jeanne. BSME, MIT, 1961; MS, Stanford U., 1962, PhD, 1966. Jr. engr. Barry Controls Corp., Watertown, Mass., 1959; thermodynamics engr. Aerojet Gen. Corp., Azusa, Calif., 1961; heat transfer specialist Lockheed Missiles and Space Co., Sunnyvale, Calif., 1962-64; mem. faculty Purdue U., 1966-98, prof. mech. engring., 1973-98, head dept., 1989-98; dean of engring. U. Notre Dame, Ind., 1998—. Cons. in field. Author: Introduction to Molecular Structure and Thermodynamics, 1974, Fundamentals of Heat Transfer, 1985, 90, 96, 2001; Fundamentals of Heat and Mass Transfer, 1981, 85, 90, 96, 2001, Liquid Cooling of Electronic Devices by Single-Phase Convection, 1999; also articles. Recipient Solberg Teaching award Purdue U., 1973, 77, 86, Potter Teaching award, 1973, Von Humboldt sr. scientist award Fed. Republic Germany, 1988; named One of the 100 most frequently cited engrs. in the world Inst. for Sci. Info., 2000. Fellow ASME (Melville medal 1988, Heat Transfer Meml. award 1988, Worcester Reed Warner award 1995); mem. Am. Soc. Engring. Edn. (Ralph C. Roe award 1982, George Westinghouse award 1983), Nat. Acad. Engring. Achievements include invention of bloodless surg. scalpel. Office: U Notre Dame Coll Engring 257 Fitzpatrick Hall Notre Dame IN 46556 E-mail: fpi@nd.edu.

INDENBAUM, DOROTHY, musician, researcher; b. N.Y.C., Nov. 24; d. Abraham and Celia (Pine) Shapiro; m. Eli Indenbaum; children: Arthur, Esther. BA, Bklyn. Coll., 1942; MS, Queens Coll., 1962; PhD, NYU, 1993. Prof. Dalcroze Sch. Music, N.Y.C., 1957-93, chmn., 1995—; prof. Hunter Coll., N.Y.C., 1970-77. Assoc. dir. Aviva Players, N.Y.C., 1977—. Performed piano with chamber music ensembles. Chmn. Am. Jewish Congress, 1958-60, YIVO, 1980—, Bohemian Club, 1980—, 92nd St YMHA, 1985—. Mem. Am. Women Composers (bd. dirs. 1988-93), Internat. Alliance for Women in Music (bd. dirs. 1993—), Sonneck Soc., League for Yiddish, Musicians Club (bd. dirs. 1983—), Sigma Alpha Iota (program chmn.).

INFANTINO, NANCY STRONG, special education educator; b. Hartford, Conn., Mar. 21, 1947; d. Horace Stoddard and Lorraine Edith (Wilder) Strong; m. S. Joseph Infantino, Oct. 20, 1967 (div. May 1983); 1 child, Brian Christopher. BS in Elem. Edn., Ea. Conn. State U., 1977, MA in Human Rels., 1990; MS in Spl. Edn., So. Conn. State U., 1986. Cert. tchr., Conn. Tchr. spl. edn. Waterford Country Sch., Quaker Hill, Conn., 1980-85, Lisbon (Conn.) Cen. Sch., 1985-86, Groton (Conn.) Pub. Schs., 1986—; part-time lectr. spl. edn. Mohegan C.C., Norwich, Conn., 1987, 88. Teacher mentor Beginning Educator Support and Tng., Conn. State Dept. Edn., 1988—; rep. New England League Mid. Schs. Conf., Hyannis, Mass., 1987. Mentor Noank (Conn.) Bapt. Group Homes, 1991—; sponsor parent USCG Acad., New London, Conn., 1985-89; bd. dirs. Unitarian Universalist Ch. Norwich, 1988-90, 93—; mem. Sch. Improvement Team, Town of Groton, Southeastern Conn. Transition Team. Recipient Cert. of Accomplishment, Conn. State Dept. Edn., 1992. Mem. NEA, NOW, Conn. Edn. Assn. (rep. summer leadership conf. 1988), Coun. for Exceptional Children, Groton Edn. Assn., Amnesty Internat. Democrat. Avocations: gardening, classical music, reading, cooking. Home: 41 Beebe Rd Norwich CT 06360-1806 Office: Cutler Mid Sch 160 Fishtown Rd Mystic CT 06355-2012

ING, GRACE SACHIKO NAKAMURA, elementary education educator; b. Honolulu, Aug. 30, 1935; d. Masaichi and Hatsue (Akamine) Nakamura; m. Rudolph K. Y. Ing (div. 1979); children: Darcy, Tracy, Jon Randall. BS in Elem. Edn., U. Hawaii, 1957, cert. in 5th yr., 1958. Tchr. 6th grade Waimanalo (Hawaii) Elem. Sch., Dept. Edn., State Hawaii, 1958-60, tchr. 2d grade, 1960, tchr. remedial reading, 1961, coord. Chpt. I Reading program, 1963-69; HEP installation tchr. Windward Dist. Office, Kaneohe, Hawaii, 1969-73, tchr. lang. arts resource, 1973-74; team tchr. grades 4-6 Blanche Pope Elem. Sch., Waimanalo, 1974; tchr. first grade Ahuimanu Elem. Sch., Kaneohe, 1974, tchr. spl. projects incl. writing, gifted/talented, remedial, 1975—, chmn. NEA mastery in learning project Kaneone, 1985—. Mem. ASCD, NEA, AAUW, Internat. Reading Assn., Hawaii Assn. Supervision and Curriculum Devel., Hawaii State Tchrs. Assn. (bd. dirs. 1982-86, 88-90), Windward Hawaii State Tchrs. Assn. (pres.), Ahuimani Sch. Ohana, Ka Hu Helu Helu, HAwaii State Tchrs. Assn. (chpt. pres., bd. dirs., standing and spl. coms.), Nat. Sci. Tchrs. Assn. Democrat. Methodist. Avocations: reading, travel, collecting recipes, theater. Office: Ahuimanu Elem Sch 47-470 Hui Aeko Pl Kaneohe HI 96744-4599

INGE, MILTON THOMAS, American literature and culture educator, author; b. Newport News, Va., Mar. 18, 1936; s. Clyde Elmo and Bernice Lucille (Jackson) I.; m. Betty Jean Meredith, 1958 (div. 1977); 1 child, Scott Thomas; m. Tonette Long Bond, 1982 (div. 1991); 1 stepchild, Michael Gordon Bond; m. Donaria Romeiro Carvalho, 1998. BA, Randolph-Macon Coll., 1959; MA, Vanderbilt U., 1960, PhD, 1964. Instr. English Vanderbilt U., 1962-64; asst. prof. Am. thought and lang. Mich. State U., 1964-68, assoc. prof., 1968-69; assoc. prof. English Va. Commonwealth U., Richmond, 1969-73, prof., 1973-80, chmn. dept. English, 1974-80; prof., chmn. dept. English, Clemson U., S.C., 1980-84; resident scholar in Am. studies USIA, Washington, 1982-84; Blackwell prof. English and humanities Randolph-Macon Coll., Ashland, Va., 1984—. Reader English Composition Test Coll. Entrance Exam Bd., 1967, 69, 77, 80; Va. Cultural Laureate, 92; dir. USIA Summer Inst. in Am. Studies, 1993—95; liberal studies disting. scholar-in-residence U. Louisville, 2003. Author: Donald Davidson: Essay and Bibliography, 1965, (with T.D. Young) Donald Davidson, 1971, The American Comic Book, 1985, Comics in the Classroom, 1989, Great American Comics: 100 Years of Cartoon Art, 1990, Comics as Culture, 1990, Faulkner, Sut, and Other Southerners, 1992, Perspectives on American Culture: Essays on Humor, Literature, and the Popular Arts, 1994, Anything Can Happen in a Comic Strip: Centennial Reflections on an American Art Form, 1995; editor: (books) Sut Lovingood's Yarns, 1966, 2d edit. 1987, High Times and Hard Times, 1967, Agrarianism in American Literature, 1969, A.B. Longstreet, 1969, Faulkner: A Rose for Emily, 1970, Wm. Byrd of Westover, 1970, Studies in Light in August, 1971, Frontier Humorists: Critical Views, 1975, Ellen Glasgow: Centennial Essays, 1976,(with J. Bryer and M. Duke) Black American Writers: Bibliographic Essays, 2 vols., 1978, Handbook of American Popular Culture, Vol. I, 1978, Vol. II, 1980, Vol. III, 1981, 3 vols. rev. and expanded edits., 1989, Concise Histories of American Popular Culture, 1982, (with E.E. MacDonald) James Branch Cabell: Centennial Essays, 1983, (with J. Bryer and M. Duke) American Women Writers: Bibliographical Essays, 1983, Huck Finn Among the Critics: A Centennial Selection, 1984, rev. edit., 1985, Truman Capote: Conversations, 1987, Naming the Rose: Essays on Umberto Eco's "The Name of the Rose", 1988, Handbook of American Popular Literature, 1988, A Nineteenth Century American Reader, 1988, The Comics, 1991, (with Sergei Chakovsky) Russian Eyes on American Literature, 1992, Dark Laughter: The Satiric Art of Oliver W. Harrington, 1993, Why I Left America and Other Essays of Oliver W. Harrington, 1993, William Faulkner: The Contemporary Reviews, 1994, (with James E. Caron) Sut Lovingood's Nat'ral Born Yarnspinner: Essays on George Washington Harris, 1996, Mark Twain's A Connecticut Yankee in King Arthur's Court, 1997, The Achievement of William Faulkner: A Centennial Tribute, 1998; Conversations with William Faulkner, 1999, "Co. Aytch," or a Side Show of the Big Show and Other Sketches by Samuel R. Watkins, 1999, Charles M. Schulz: Conversations, 2000, (with Ed Piacentino) The Humor of the Old South, 2001, (with Dennis Hall) Greenwood Guide to American Popular Culture, 4 vols., 2002; editor jours. Resources for American Literary Study, 1971-79, American Humor: An Interdisciplinary Newsletter, 1974-79; gen. editor Greenwood Press Bio-Bibliographies and Reference Guides in Popular Culture, Cambridge U. Press Am. Critical Archives, U. Press Miss. Studies in Popular Culture; book reviewer: Nashville Tenneseean, Richmond Times-Dispatch. Bd. dirs. Friends of Richmond Pub. Libary; bd. dirs. San Francisco Acad. Comic Art, James Br. Cabell Libr. Assocs., Va. Commonwealth U., Edgar Allen Poe Mus. Recipient Bd. Govs. award Am. Cultural Assn., 1999; fellow So. Fellowship Fund, 1959-62, Newberry Libr., 1987, Va. Found. Humanities, 1987, 93; grantee Fulbright-Hays, 1967-68, 71, 79, 88, 94, Mich. State U., 1965, 66, 68, Am. Philos. Soc., 1970, Clemson U., 1981, NEH, 1986, 91, 92; recipient Disting. Alumnus award Randolph-Macon Coll., 1995. Mem. MLA (hon. life, del. assembly 1976-78, 2001-03, chmn. elections com. 1980), South Atlantic MLA (program com. 1982-85, chmn. 1986, v.p. 1987, pres. 1988-89), Am. Studies Assn., Popular Culture Assn., Am. Humor Studies Assn. (pres. 1978, 88, Charlie award 1996), Soc. Study So. Lit. (exec. coun. 1971-73, 78-80, 86-88), Melville Soc., Ellen Glasgow Soc. (exec. coun. 1974-84, pres. 1987-88), Mus. Cartoon Art (nominating com. Hall of Fame 1975-95), European Assn. Am. Studies, So. Studies Forum (founder, exec. coun. 1988—), Popular Culture Assn. in South (v.p. 1987-88, pres. 1988-89), Mark Twain Cir. (chmn. nominating com. 1987-88), Mark Twain Cir. Am. (hon.), Cosmos Club, Phi Beta Kappa, Omicron Delta Kappa, Pi Delta Epsilon, Lambda Chi Alpha. Home: PO Box 129 Ashland VA 23005-0129 E-mail: tinge@rmc.edu.

INGELS, JACK EDWARD, horticulture educator; b. Indpls., Mar. 28, 1942; s. Carl Eugene and Mary Louise (Fultz) I. BS, Purdue U., 1964; MS, Rutgers U., 1966; postgrad., Ball State U., 1968-70. Rsch. asst. Rutgers U., New Brunswick, N.J., 1964-66; prof. SUNY, Cobleskill, 1966-89, disting. teaching prof., 1990—. Hort. cons. J.C. Penney Corp., N.Y.C., 1966-69; landscape designer, 1966—; hort. and/or landscape cons. numerous small cos., 1970—; pres. J. Ingels Assocs., 1991—. Author: Landscaping: Principles and Practices, 6th edit., 2003, Ornamental Horticulture: Science, Operations, and Management, 3d edit., 2000. Chmn. Cobleskill Restoration and Devel., Inc., 1991—, bd. dirs., 1988—; pres. Timothy Murphy Gourmet Soc., 1989—; mem. Schoharie County Coun. on Arts, Cobleskill, Albany Inst. of History and Art; bd. dirs. Cobleskill Partnership, 1996—. Named one of top ten landscape educators in Am., Landscape Mgmt. mag., 1995. Mem. Associated Landscape Contractors Am., Northeastern N.Y. Nursery Assn., Genesee-Finger Lakes Nursery Assn., Univ. Club (Albany, N.Y.), Moose, Elks. Avocations: gourmet cooking, landscape garden history, travel. Home: 139 Jay St Cobleskill NY 12043 Office: SUNY Horticulture Dept Cobleskill NY 12043

INGERSOLL, ANDREW PERRY, planetary science educator; b. Chgo., Jan. 2, 1940; s. Jeremiah Crary and Minneola (Perry) I.; m. Sarah Morin, Aug. 27, 1961; children: Jeremiah, Ruth Ingersoll Wood, Marion Ingersoll Quinones, Minneola, George. BA, Amherst Coll., 1960; PhD, Harvard U., 1965. Rsch. fellow Harvard U., Cambridge, Mass., 1965-66; asst. prof. planetary sci. Calif. Inst. Tech., Pasadena, 1966-71, assoc. prof., 1971-76, prof., 1976—2003, Earle C. Anthony prof. planetary sci., 2003—. Mem. staff summer study program Woods Hole (Mass.) Oceanographic Inst., 1965, 70-73, 76, 80, 92; prin. investigator Pioneer Saturn Infrared Radiometer Team, NASA; mem. Voyager Imaging Team, NASA, Cassini Imaging Team; interdisciplinary scientist, Mars Global Surveyor Project, Galileo Project, NASA. Bd. trustees Poly. Sch., Pasadena. Fellow AAAS, Am. Geophys. Union, Am. Acad. Arts and Scis.; mem. Am. Astron. Soc. (vice-chmn. div. planetary sci. 1988-89, chmn. 1989-90). Office: Calif Inst Tech Dept Planetary Sci 150 21 Pasadena CA 91125-0001

INGERSOLL, GARY MICHAEL, educational psychologist; b. Utica, N.Y., Mar. 20, 1944; s. Robert James and Elnora (Bracken) I.; m. Helen Westbrook O'Connell, Nov. 26, 1966; children: Kristin Jean, Robert O'Connell Ingersoll, John O'Connell Ingersoll. BS, SUNY, Oswego, 1966; PhD, Pa. State U., 1970. Asst. prof. Sch. Edn. Ind. U., Bloomington, 1970-73, assoc. prof., 1973-86, prof. edn1. psychology, 1986—, dir. edn. core, Diabetes Rsch. and Tng. Ctr. Indpls., 1988-92, assoc. dean for rsch. and devel. Bloomington, 1990-92, exec. assoc. dean, 1992—97. Part-time prof. pediat. Ind. U. Sch. Medicine, Indpls., 1989—; cons. Madison (Ind.) State Hosp., 1976-90, Warsaw (Ind.) Cmty. Schs., 1987-89, Denver Pub. Schs., 1985-88, Mayer Corp., Dayton, Ohio, 1981-88, Ind. Profl. Stds. Bd., 1996-2001, NCATE Bd. Examiners, 1998—. Author: Adolescents, 2d edit., 1989; contbg. author: Child/Adolescent Psychology and Social Development, 1991; co-author: (monograph) Adolescent Behaviour and Development, 1988, Performance-Based Teacher Licensure. Bd. dirs. Ind. Am. Diabetes Assn., 1988-91, Am. Assn. Diabetes Educators, 1991—; ctrl. coun. Am. Diabetes Assn., 1991-92. Recipient Showcase award for Evaluation, Ind. Gov.'s Conf. on Mental Health, 1985; named Hon. Alumnus, Sch. of Dentistry, Ind. U. Mem. Am. Edn. Rsch. Assn., Soc. For Rsch. in Child Devel., Soc. for Adolescent Medicine, Sigma Xi. Roman Catholic. Avocations: reading, bridge, swimming. Home: 2542 S Spicewood Ln Bloomington IN 47401-4343 Office: Ind U 201 S Rose Ave Bloomington IN 47408-1006

INGERSOLL, MARGARET LEE, personnel professional; b. Columbus, Ga., Aug. 2, 1950; d. Thad and Charlie (Josey) Lee; m. Rudolph Ingersoll; children: Brandi, Brandon. BS cum laude, Mercer U., 1972; MEd, Ga. State U., 1975, EdS, 1983, postgrad., 1983-86. Cert. tchr., Ga. Tchr. biology Muscogee County Sch. Dist., Columbus, 1972-74; tchr. hearing impaired pvt. sch. and Muscogee County Sch. Dist., Columbus, 1974-86; prin. 30th Ave Elem. Sch., Columbus, 1986-91, River Rd. Elem. Sch., Columbus, 1991-98, ctrl. officer pers. coord., 1998—. Named to Outstanding Young Women of Am., 1983. Mem. ASCD, Nat. Assn. Elem. Prins., Ga. Assn. Elem. Prins. (Sch. Bell award 1990, Outstanding 4-H Prin. 1997), Muscogee Elem. Prins. Assn. (sec. 1988-90, pres.-elect 1994-95, pres. 1995-96), Ga. Assn. Ednl. Leaders, Soc. of Human Resource Mgmt., Jack and Jill of Am., Inc., Leadership Columbus Alumni. Baptist. Avocations: singing, reading, swimming, gardening. Office: Muscogee County Sch Dist 1200 Bradley Dr Columbus GA 31906-2806 E-mail: mingersoll@mcsd.ga.net.

INGERSOLL, MARYANN E. PATTERSON, health educator, holistic nurse; b. Durham, NC, Aug. 22, 1951; d. Hubert Clifton Jr. and Elizabeth R. (Fox) Patterson; m. Dennis Scott Ingersoll, Dec. 20, 1975; children: Christopher Scott, Elizabeth Patterson. BSN, U. N.C., 1973; MN in Parent and Child Health Nursing, La. State U., 1985; secondary vocat. health occupation cert., U. Houston, 1994. RN, N.C. Staff RN intermediate neonatal care nursing Tex. Children's/St. Luke's Hosp., Houston, 1975-76; pediat. staff nurse Meml. Pediat., Houston, 1976-79; clin. staff nurse Inwood Pediat., Houston, 1979-80; instr. med. terminology Phillips Jr. Coll., New Orleans, 1981-83; founder, dir. Parents Plus Parenting Ctr., New Orleans, 1985-86; substitute tchr., RN Humble (Tex.) Ind. Sch. Dist., 1986-90; nursing instr. No. Harris C.C., Humble, 1990-91; health occupations edn. instr. New Caney (Tex.) Ind. Sch. Dist., 1991-99; ret., 1999. Adv. bd. mem. tech. prep. program No. Harris C.C., Humble, 1992—, adv. bd. mem. ADN program, 1995-96; bd. mem. New Horizons, New Caney, Tex., 1994-95; adv. bd. mem. respiratory care program No. Harris C.C./Kingwood Coll., 1995-96. Tchr., mem. PTSA-New Caney H.S., 1992—97; mem. KW Athletic Boosters, Kingwood, 1992—97, Parents of Cheerleaders Club; fundraiser, dir. Thesbians Kingwood H.S. Dept. Drama, 1995—96; mem., vol. docent Houston Fine Arts Mus.; mem., vol. Tex. Children's Hosp., Houston, Dorrell Martin Dance Fusion, KUHF-NPR, Houston. Mem. Sigma Theta Tau, Alpha Delta Pi (scholarship award 1972). Avocations: travel, reading, yoga, sailing. Home: 1111 Hermann Dr 6-C Houston TX 77004 E-mail: mpi082251@aol.com.

INGHAM, NORMAN WILLIAM, Russian literature educator, genealogist; b. Holyoke, Mass., Dec. 31, 1934; s. Earl Morris and Gladys May (Rust) I. AB, Middlebury Coll. in German and Russian cum laude, 1957; postgrad. Slavic philology, Free U. Berlin, 1957-58; MA in Russian lang. and lit., U. Mich., 1959; postgrad. in Russian lang. and lit., Leningrad (USSR) State U., 1961-62; PhD in Slavic langs. and lit., Harvard U., 1963. Cert. genealogist. Postdoctoral researcher Czechoslovak Acad. Scis., Prague, Czechoslovakia, 1963-64; asst. prof. dept Slavic langs. and lits. Ind. U., Bloomington, 1964-65; asst. prof. Harvard U., Cambridge, Mass., 1965-70, lectr., 1970-71; assoc. prof. U. Chgo., 1971-82, prof., 1982—, chmn. dept., 1977-83, dir. Eastern Europe and USSR lang. and area ctr., 1978-91. Mem. Am. Com. Slavists, 1977-83; mem. com. Slavic and Ea. European studies U. Chgo., 1979-91, chmn., 1982-91, also other coms.; dir. Ctr. for East European and Russian/Eurasian Studies, 1991-96; rep. internat. Rsch. and Exch. Bd.; cert. genealogist, 1994—. Author: E.T.A. Hoffman's Reception in Russia, 1974; editor: Church and Culture in Old Russia, 1991; co-editor: (with Joachim T. Baer) Mnemozina: Studia litteraria russica in honorem Vsevolod Setchkarev; mem. editorial bd. Slavic and East European Jour., 1978-87, adv. bd., 1987-89; assoc. editor Byzantine Studies, 1973-81; contbg. editor The Am. Genealogist, 1995—; contbr. and translator articles and book revs. Fulbright fellow, 1957-58, vis. fellow Dumbarton Oaks Ctr. for Byzantine Studies, 1972-73. Mem. Am. Assn. Advancement Slavic Studies (rep. coun. on mem. instns. 1985-96, area rep. nat. adv. com. for Ea. European lang. programs 1985-96), Am. Assn. Tchrs. Slavic and East European Langs., Early Slavic Studies Assn. (v.p. 1993-95, pres. 1995-97), Chgo. Consortium for Slavic and East European Studies (v.p. 1982-84, 98, pres. 1984-86, 98-2000, exec. coun. 1992-94), Phi Beta Kappa. Office: U Chgo Slavic Dept 1130 E 59th St Chicago IL 60637-1539 E-mail: ningham@uchicago.edu.

INGIS, GAIL, interior designer, educator, writer, photographer, artist; b. Nov. 1, 1935; d. Bernard and Claire Gerber; m. Thomas H. Claus; children: Linda, Richard, Paul. Student, CUNY, 1953; grad. in interior architecture-design, N.Y. Sch. Interior Design, 1973, BFA, 1980; postgrad., Pratt Inst., N.J. Ins. Tech., Parsons Sch. Design. Prin. Ingis Design Assocs., Woodcliff Lake, N.J., Fairfield, Conn., 1970—. Adj. prof. U. Bridgeport, Conn., 2001—, U. New Haven, 2002—. Exhibitions include Agora Gallery SOHO, N.Y.C. Troop leader U.S. Girl Scouts, N.Y.C. and Woodcliff Lake, 1964—69; bd. trustees The Lockwood Mathews Mansion Mus., Norwalk, Conn. Recipient Watercolor Painting award, Wall St. Gallery, 1997, Cooper Lighting award, 23d Ann. Nat. Lighting Competition, 1999. Mem.: AIA (profl. affiliate), Westport Arts Ctr., Wilton Arts Coun., Rowayton Art Assn., Milford Arts Coun., Lyme Art Assn., New Haven Arts League, Shoreline Alliance for Arts, Guilford Art League, Madison Art Soc., Interior Design Educators Coun., Illuminating Engring. Soc. N.Am., Am. Soc. Interior Designers (admissions com. N.J. chpt. 1978, edn. chmn. 1978—86, co-chmn. pro-licensing com. 1984—86, bd. dirs. 1985—97, com. legis. for interior designers 1988—90, edn. chmn. 1994—95, bd. dirs. Conn. chpt. 1996—97, editor newsletter 1996—2002, Svc. award 1978, 1982—87), U.S. Profl. Tennis Assn. (cert. instr.), Westport Arts League. Home and Office: 200 Old Black Rock Tpke Fairfield CT 06825-

INGLE, JAMES CHESNEY, JR., geology educator; b. Los Angeles, Nov. 6, 1935; s. James Chesney and Florence Adelaide (Geldart) I.; m. Fredricka Ann Bornholdt, June 14, 1958; 1 child, Douglas James BS in Geology, U. So. Calif., 1959, MS in Geology, 1962, PhD in Geology, 1966. Registered geologist, Calif. Research assoc. Univ. So. Calif., 1961-65; vis. scholar Tohoku U., Sendai, Japan, 1966-67; asst., assoc. to full prof. Stanford U., Calif., 1968—, W.M. Keck prof. earth scis., 1984—, chmn. dept. geology, 1982-86. Co-chief scientist Leg 31 Deep Sea Drilling Project, 1973, co-chief scientist Leg 128 Ocean Drilling Program, 1989; geologist U.S. Geol. Survey W.A.E, 1978-81 Author: Movement of Beach Sand, 1966; contbr. articles to profl. jours. Recipient W.A. Tarr award Sigma Gamma Epsilon, 1958; named Disting. lectr. Am. Assn. Petroleum Geologists, 1986-87, Joint Oceanographic Institutions, 1991; A.I. Leverson award Am. Assn. Petroleum Geologists, 1988. Fellow Geol. Soc. Am., Calif. Acad. Scis.; mem. Cushman Found. (bd. dirs. 1984-91), Soc. Profl. Paleontologists and Mineralogists (Pacific sect. 1958—, pres. 1993-94), Am. Geophys. Union. E-mail: ingle@pangea.stanford.edu.

INGLE, KAY SUE, elementary education educator; b. Portland, Ind., July 14, 1941; d. William Ivan and Lucille Jean (Haviland) Wood; m. Robert Lee Ingle, Aug. 31, 1962; children: Allen Wood, Daniel Robert. BA, Ball State U., 1963, MA, 1966. Profl. cert. tchr. kindergarten to 8th grade, Ohio, life cert. tchr. kindergarten to 6th grade, Ind., Iowa. Elem. tchr. Elkhart (Ind.) Schs., 1963-65, Southwest Allen County Schs., Fort Wayne, Ind., 1965-67; elem. supr. Fort Wayne (Ind.) State Hosp. and Tng. Ctr., 1967-68; reading tchr. Keokuk (Iowa) City Schs., 1972-74; elem. tchr. Sylvania (Ohio) City Schs., 1976—. SEc. Sylvania (Ohio) Communiity Action Team, 1986-87; mem. Red Ribbon Campaign, Slyvania, 1988, 90, 90, 91, 92, 93. Recipient Grant for Reading, Acad. Excellence Found., Sylvania, 1992. Avocations: aerobics, phys. fitness, travel. Home: 8515 Augusta Ln Holland OH 43528-8393 Office: Whiteford Elem 4708 Whiteford Rd Toledo OH 43623-2763

INGLE, MARTI ANNETTE, protective services official, educator; b. Waynesville, N.C., Apr. 3, 1972; d. William Carroll Ingle, Shirley Grooms Ingle. Student, East Coast Bible Coll., 1987—89; EMT-paramedic cert., Haywood C.C., Clyde, NC, 1993, tech. rescue and fire fighting, 1996; degree culinary arts and scis., Alaska Vocat. Tech. Coll., Seward, AK, 2000—01. Cert. emergency rescue technician 1996; tech. rescue instr., swiftwater rescue technician II 1997, haz mat ops. 1994, sr. fire investigations 1999, emergency boat ops. 1999, personal watercraft rescue 1999, PALS 1991, ACLS 1992, advanced trauma life support 1991, pediat. emergencies for prehospital providers 2001, tchr. Alaska, 2001. EMT-paramedic Haywood County Emergency Med. Svcs., Waynesville, NC, 1991—2002; EMS/tech. rescue instr. Haywood C.C., Clyde, NC, 1994—2002; EMS evaluator State of N.C., Raleigh, 1994—2002; EMS/tech. rescue instr. Blue Ridge C.C., Hendersonville, NC, 1995—2002, Tri-County C.C., Murphy, NC, 1996—2002, Southwestern C.C., Sylva, NC, 1998—2002; EMS/fire/rescue instr. Alaska Vocat. Tech. Coll., Seward, Alaska, 2001—. Mem.: N.C. Assn. Paramedics, N.C. EMS and Rescue Assn., N.C. Assn. Fire Svc. Instrs., Haywood County Rescue Squad (life; 1st lt. and sgt. 1994—99). Avocations: travel, white-water rafting, cooking, reading, mountain biking. Home: 151 Children St Waynesville NC 28786 Office: 215 N Main St Waynesville NC 28786 Personal E-mail: rafty981@yahoo.com.

INGLETT, BETTY LEE, retired director; b. Augusta, Ga., Oct. 6, 1930; d. Wilfred Lee and Elizabeth Arelia (Crouch) Inglett. BS in Edn., Ga. State Coll. Women, 1953; MA in Libr., Media and Edn. Adminstrn., Ga. So. U., 1980; EdD in Edn. Adminstrn., Nova U., 1988. Tchr. James L. Fleming Elem. Sch., Augusta, 1953-63, Murphey Jr. HS, Augusta, 1963-64, Sego Jr. HS, Augusta, 1964-68, Glenn Hills HS, Augusta, 1968-75; media specialist Nat. Hills Elem. Sch., Augusta, 1975-80; prin. Lake Forest Elem. Sch., Augusta, 1980-84, Joseph R. Lamar Elem. Sch., Augusta, 1984-86; dir. ednl. media services Richmond County Bd. Edn., Augusta, 1986-92; ret., 1992. Owner, operator Betty Inglett Enterprises, Augusta. Contbr. articles to profl. jours. Mem. coun. PTA, 1985; del. Dem. State Conv., 1982; bd. dirs. Am. Heart Fund, 1975—80, Am. Cancer Fund, 1986—. Named Adminstr. of the Yr., 1988—89. Mem.: NEA, AAUW (v.p. 1957—59), Ctrl. Savannah River Area Libr. Assn., Profl. Leadership Assn., Ga. Assn. Curriculum Instrnl. Supr., Ga. Assn. Instrnl. Tech., Ga. Libr. Assn., Ga. Libr. Media Dept., Ga. Assn. Ednl. Leaders, Ga. Assn. Edn., Richmond County Edn. Assn. (sec., v.p. 1961—63, Adminstr. of the Yr. 1989—90), Phi Delta Kappa, Phi Delta Pi, Alpha Delta Kappa. Episcopalian.

INGOLD, CATHERINE WHITE, academic administrator; b. Columbia, S.C., Mar. 15, 1949; d. Hiram Hutchison and Annelle (Stover) White; m. Wesley Thomas Ingold, June 13, 1970; 1 child, Thomas Bradford Hutchison. Student, U. Paris-Sorbonne, 1969; BS in French with honors, Hollins Coll., 1970; MA in Romance Langs., U. Va., 1972, PhD in French, 1979; DHum honoris causa, Francis Marion U., Florence, S.C., 1992. Assoc. prof. romance langs. Gallaudet U., Washington, 1973-88, dir. hons. program, 1980-85, dean arts and scis., 1985-86, provost, v.p. acad. affairs, 1986-88; pres. Am. U. of Paris, 1988-92, Curry Coll., Milton, Mass., 1992-96. Dep. dir. Nat. Fgn. Lang. Ctr. Johns Hopkins U., 1996—2000, U. Md., 2000—. Recipient Prix Morot-Sir de Langue et Littérature françaises (Hollins). Mem. MLA, Nat. Collegiate Honors Coun., Lychnos Soc. (U.Va.), Phi Beta Kappa. Episcopalian. Home: 2015 N Brandywine St Arlington VA 22207-2200 Office: Nat Fgn Lang Ctr 1029 Vermont Ave NW Washington DC 20005-3517 E-mail: cwingold@nflc.org.

INGOLFSSON-FASSBIND, URSULA G. music educator; b. Zurich, Switzerland, Dec. 22, 1943; arrived in U.S., 1980; d. Franz Bernardin Fassbind and Gertrud M. Schmucki; m. Ketill Ingolfsson; children: Katla Soffia, Judith, Mirjam, Bera Bjorg. Nat. tchrs. diploma, Conservatory Zurich, 1965, soloist diploma, 1968; postgrad., U. Ariz., 1969—70. Tchg. asst. Conservatory Zurich, 1966—68; with Reykjavik (Iceland) Music Coll., 1970—79, Settlement Music Sch., Phila., 1987—2000; founder, dir., tchr., performer Leopold Mozart Acad. and Franz Fassbind Found., Phila., 2001—. Founder, dir. The Leopold Mozart Chamber Music Concerts, 2002—. Grantee Excellency in Tchg. grant, Wilmington (Del.) Piano Co., 2003. Mem.: Am. Composers Guild, Music Tchr. Nat. Assn. Democrat. Avocations: painting, gardening. Home and Office: Leopold Mozart Acad 4833 Pulaski Ave Philadelphia PA 19144

INGRAM, ARTONYON S. psychology educator; b. Fremont, N.C., Dec. 2, 1962; s. Gliffie and Doris Ingram. BS, BS, Atlantic Christian Coll., 1985; cert. in drugs and alcohol abuse, AA, Pierce Coll., Steilacoom, Wash., 1993; MEd, City U., Bellevue, Wash., 1995; cert. parent educator, Clover Pk. Tech. Coll., 1995. Cert. in drug and alcohol abuse, 1993. Teaching parent Onslow Mental Health Ctr., Jacksonville, N.C., 1987-89; social svcs. asst. Rainer Vista Health Care, Puyallup, Wash., 1990-91, Lakewood Health Care, Tacoma, Wash., 1990-91; group life counselor Jessie Dyslin Boys Ranch, Tacoma, Wash., 1991-92; case mgr. Puget Sound Ctr., Tacoma, Wash., 1991; counselor intern Dotters Counseling Ctr., Puyallup, Wash., 1992-93, Cross Rd. Treatment Ctr., Tacoma, 1993; instr. Clover Pk. Tech. Coll., Tacoma, 1993—. Counselor First Bapt. Ch., Jacksonville, N.C. With USNG, 1981-88. Army Nat. Guard scholar, 1978-81, L.N. Forbes scholar, Boeing Engring. scholar, 1993. Mem. Nat. Assn. Alcoholism and Drug Abuse Counselors, Chem. Dependency Profls. Home: 4302 S Center St Apt H101 Tacoma WA 98409-8620 Office: Tacoma Washington Clover Pk Tech Coll Psych Tacoma WA 98498

INGRAM, GLADYS ALMENAS, secondary school educator; b. Caguas, P.R., Dec. 4, 1937; d. Arcadio and Francisca Almenas; m. Wayne L. Ingram, Aug. 25, 1960; children: Wayne Karl, Paul Andrew, Gladys Irene. BBA cum laude, U. P.R., 1962; MEd summa cum laude, Winthrop U., 1986; EdS, U. Madrid, 1990. Tchr. Latta (S.C.) High Sch., 1982-90, Wilson High Sch., Florence, S.C., 1990-91, Hartsville (S.C.) High Sch., 1992—. Tchr. Lang. Teaching, Columbia, 1991-93; del. S.C. Curriculum Congress, 1992; adv. bd. So. Conf. Lang. Teaching. Mem. Am. Assn. Tchrs Spanish and Portuguese, Phi Kappa Phi. Avocations: travel, reading, bird watching. Office: Hartsville High Sch 701 Lewellyn Dr Hartsville SC 29550-5235

INGRAM, GLORIA BATIE, science educator; b. Centre, Ala., Sept. 23; d. Jones and Dorothy Batie; children: Nathan Ingram, Alicia Ingram. BS, Mich. State U., 1973; MA in Tchg., Wayne State U., 1982. Cert. tchr., Mich. Dietetic foods instr. Wayne County C.C., Detroit, 1976; food inspector Mich. Dept. Agr., Lansing, 1974-76; consumer affairs coord. Chatham Supermarket, Warren, Mich., 1977-79; math. tchr., adolescence skills tchr. Detroit Pub. Schs., 1980-85, mid. sch. sci. tchr., 1985—2000, ret., 2000, prof. devel. facilitator, 1997-2000; cohort leader Wayne State U., 2000—. Pres., co-founder African Am. Assn. Ind. Sch. Parents, Southfield, Mich., 1990-94; mem. AME Ch. Recipient Recognition cert. Nat. Bd. Profl. Tchg. Stds., 1993-94; grantee Detroit Pub. Schs. Mem. Delta Sigma Theta (Epsilon Epsilon chpt.). E-mail: g.ingram@wayne.edu.

INGRAM, JOHNNYE HUGHES, artist, educator; b. Silverton, Tex., Apr. 28, 1904; d. James Monroe and Maude Ethel (McCann) Hughes; m. Abner Clay Ingram, July 17, 1922 (dec.); 1 child, Clark Hughes Ingram. Grad. high sch., Winnfield, La., 1922. Tchr. ceramics, china painting, Smackover, Ark., 1936-45; art lectr. various schs. and orgns., Ark., 1940-80; art tchr. Singer Sewing Machine Studio, El Dorado, Ark., 1976-83, South Ark. U., El Dorado, 1982-83, South Ark. Art Ctr., El Dorado, 1984; art lectr. Ark. Oil & Brine Mus., Smackover, 1991—. Art tchr., Smackover, 1970-88; art lectr. Springhill (La.) Art League, 1986; judge Ouachita County Fair, Camden, Ark., 1985-87, Columbia County Fair, Magnolia, Ark., 1980, Union County Fair, El Dorado, 1960-69; mem. bd. visual arts South Ark. Art Ctr. Active gray lady svc. ARC, Smackover, 1960-69, Easter Seals, Smackover, 1955; bd. dirs. Tuberculosis Bd. Union County, El Dorado, 1935, Union County Human Svcs., 1985-90, Ret. Sr. Vol. Program, 1982; active Maple Ave. Bapt. Ch. Mem. South Ark. Art Ctr. (bd. dirs. 1985-91), United Daus. Confederacy. Avocations: collecting rare antique lace, lapidary, reading, art. Home: 600 E 12th St Smackover AR 71762-2125

INGRAM, JUDITH ELIZABETH, writer, counselor, educator; b. Alameda, Calif., May 6, 1951; d. William Ralph and Elizabeth (Lelis) Madler; m. Frank David Ingram, Sept. 4, 1971; 1 child, Melanie Anne. AA, Chabot Coll., Hayward, Calif., 1972; BS in Biology summa cum laude, Calif. State U., Hayward, 1978; MA in Counseling, St. Mary's Coll. of Calif., Moraga, 1996. Tech. writer Tech. Writing Svcs., Dublin, Calif., 1990-93; counselor trainee Valley Christian Counseling, Dublin, 1995-96, counselor, dir. devel., 1996-97. Mem.: ACA, Writer's Internat. Network/Writer's Inter-Age Network, Soc. Tech. Comm., Assn. for Spiritual, Ethical and Religious Values in Counseling, Am. Assn. Christian Counselors, We. Assn. Counselor Edn. and Supervision (bd. officer, newsletter editor). Presbyterian. Avocations: writing, desktop publishing and computer graphic designing, reading psychology, philosophy and women's issues. Home: 8724 Augusta Ct Dublin CA 94568-1063 E-mail: jingramtws@aol.com.

INGRAM, RICHARD THOMAS, educational association executive; b. McKeesport, Pa., Sept. 29, 1941; s. Henry Stephen and Jean Catherine (Lis) I.; m. Mollie Mangan Brown, Apr. 6, 1968; children: Kirsten Collins, David Thomas. BS, Indiana U. Pa., 1963; MEd, U. Pitts., 1964; EdD, U. Md., 1969. High sch. tchr. Monroeville (Pa.) Sch. Dist., 1963-64; dir. psychometric svcs. U. Md., College Park, 1965-69; adj. instr. U. So. Calif., 1976, U. Va., 1971-79; program assoc. Assn. Governing Bds. of Univs. and Colls., Washington, 1971-74, exec. dir., 1974-78, exec. v.p., 1978-92, pres., 1992—. Dir. United Educators Ins. Risk Retention Group, Inc., Washington, 1988-99, Am. Coun. on Edn., 1995-96; adv. commr. Edn. Commn. of States, Denver, 1985-95; trustee Dickinson Coll., Pa., 1995-2002. Editor, author: Governing Public Colleges and Universities, 1993, Governing Independent Colleges and Universities, 1993. Trustee U. Charleston, W.Va., 1980—89, Connelly Sch. Holy Child, Potomac, Md., 1987—93, Dickinson Coll., Pa., 1996—2002. Capt. U.S. Army, 1969—71, Vietnam. Recipient Disting. Alumni award Ind. U. Pa., 1992, Outstanding Alumnus Citation, Pa. Coll. Alumni Assn., 1994, Coll. Edn. Alumni Assn. award U. Md., 1996. Mem. Am. Assn. Higher Edn., Cosmos Club, Phi Delta Kappa. Democrat. Avocations: skiing, camping, fly fishing. Home: 12017 Gregerscroft Rd Potomac MD 20854-2148 Office: Assn Governing Bds Univ and Colls 1 Dupont Cir NW Ste 400 Washington DC 20036-1136

INGRAM, ROBERT JOHN, business education educator; b. Batavia, N.Y., Oct. 5, 1926; s. George F. and Florence (Bousser) I.; m. Joan Elizabeth Geisler, Apr. 19, 1952; children: Charles, Kathleen, Paula. BS in Acctg., U. Buffalo, 1950; MBA, U. Detroit, 1955. Bus. planner Chrysler Corp., Highland Park, Mich., 1954-70; adminstr. CPA Orgns., Detroit, Southfield, Mich., 1970-77; instr. bus. Detroit Coll. Bus., Warren, Mich., 1976—, St. Mary's Coll., Orchard Lake, Mich., 1990-91; supr. acctg. Volkswagen Am., Warren, 1978-80; mgr. gen. acctg. auto div. United Techs., Dearborn, Mich., 1980-82; regional mgr. Primerica Fin. Svcs., Warren, 1982—; program chmn. grad. program Fla. Inst. Tech., Selfridge N.G. Base, Mich., 1988-90; instr. bus. Union Inst. Cin., Wayne, Mich., 1990—; divsn. chair for bus. St Mary's Coll, Orchard Lake, Mich., 1992—; asst. prof. St. Mary's Coll., Orchard Lake, Mich., 1993—. Lectr. bus. seminars Madonna Coll., Livonia, Mich., 1980-88; adj. instr. Northwood U., 1992—. Mem. Rep. Nat. Com., 1991; charter mem. Citizens Against Govt. Waste, Washington, 1991; active state legis. campaigns, Warren, 1987-90. Mem. Alpa Kappa Psi. Republican. Roman Catholic. Avocations: counseling, consulting, sports. Home: 31242 Bretz Dr Warren MI 48093-1672 Office: St Marys Coll Indian Trail Orchard Lake MI 48324

INGRAM, SANDY GOGGANS, elementary school educator; b. Dallas, Aug. 10, 1958; d. Wilfert Leon and Jere (Cleveland) Goggans; m. Sam C. Ingram, Dec. 17, 1988; 1 child, Christopher. AAS, Brookhaven Coll., Dallas, 1986; BS magna cum laude, Tex. Woman's U., 1988. Cert. elem. tchr., ESL tchr., Tex. Tchr. ESL, Dallas Ind. Sch. Dist., 1988—. Historian Obadiah Knight Sch. PTA, Dallas, 1989-90, edn. com. chairperson 1992-93, membership chairperson, 1993—. Nina Scott Hulsey scholar, 1987-88. Mem. NEA, Tex. State Tchrs. Assn., Classroom of Tchrs. Dallas, Nat. Hist. Soc., Smithsonian Assocs., Phi Lambda Theta. Republican. Methodist. Avocations: children, reading, ceramics, pets, camping. Office: Obadiah Knight Elem Sch 2615 Anson Rd Dallas TX 75235-3702

INLOW, D(AVID) RONALD, university administrator, food service consultant, consumerism lecturer; b. Cheyenne, Wyo., Mar. 18, 1943; s. Gail Maurice and Joanne Francis (Currie) I.; m. Beverly Jean Walden, June 20, 1964; children— Deborah Sue, Robert John, Jennifer Lynn. B.A., No. Ill. U., 1965, M.S., 1972. Food service mgr. No. Ill. U., DeKalb, 1965-72; dir. food service Valparaiso U., Ind., 1972-78; dir. food service U. Richmond, Va., 1978-80, dir. aux. services, 1980— ; evaluator profl. standards Nat. Assn. Coll. and Univ. Food Services, East Lansing, Mich., 1984— ; cons. to various colls. and health bds., 1983—. Speaker on the citizens with disabilities in the work force, 1985-93; announcer nat. synchronized swimming competition Olympics Sports Festival, summer 1987; bd. govs. food mgrs. profl. cert. program. U. Richmond. Sec. Community Involvement Citizens Adv. Group to sch. system, Richmond, 1983— ; elder Gayton Kirk Presbyn. Ch., Richmond, 1984— ; originator Sanitation Certification Program Richmond, Va., Valparaiso, Ind., 1981, Meals on Wheels Program, Valparaiso, 1973. Recipient Disting. Service award Nat. Inst. for Food Service Industry, 1977. Adminstr./Staff award U. Richmond Student Govt., 1979, Meritorious Svc. award Pres.'s Com. on Employment of Handicapped, 1986, Silver Plate award Internat. Foodservice Mfrs. Assn., 1990, Ivy award Restaurant & Institutions Mag., 1992. Mem. Nat. Assn. Coll. and Univ. Food Services (regional pres. 1976-78, nat. pres. 1987-88), Nat. Restaurant Assn., Am. Personnel and Guidance Assn., Va. Coll. Book Store Assn., Internat. Food Service Exec. Assn., Nat. Inst. for Food Service Industry (cert.), DeKalb Jaycees (pres. 1970-71). Club: Octopi Synchronized Swimming (pres. 1981-83) (Richmond). Lodge: Rotary (bd. dirs. 1975-77). Avocations: coaching Little League baseball, administration of synchronized swimming activities at regional level. Home: 11402 Creekside Dr Richmond VA 23233-4610 Office: U Richmond Commons Bldg 3d Fl Richmond VA 23173

INMAN, ANA M. JIMENEZ, secondary education educator; b. Rio Piedras, P.R., Jan. 5, 1962; d. Antonio Jiménez del Toro and Ana E. Colon Fontan. BA, U. P.R., 1985, postgrad. Cert. secondary Spanish tchr., P.R., profl. edn. cert. continuing tchr. English 4-12, Spanish K-12, Wash., DSHS Med. and Social Svcs. interpreter/translator in Spanish, Wash., notary public, Wash.; cert. cmty. first aid and safety instr. ARC. Tutor La Mansion, Rio Piedras; tchr. Colegio Mater Salvatoris, Cupey, P.R., Colegio Nuestra Senora de Altagracia, Rio Piedras, Colegio San Jose, Rio Piedras; Am. Sch., Bayamón, P.R.; Escuela Superior Católica de Bayamón; clk. I-II, interpreter Seafirst Bank-Trust Vault, Seattle; office mgr., adminstrv. asst. El Centro de la Raza, Seattle; adminstrv. team leader, mgr. Las Brisas housing program Consejo Counseling and Referral Svc., Seattle, vocat. rehab. program mgr.; instr. Spanish Rites Of Passage Experience program Ctrl. Area Motivation Program. Pvt. tutor in Spanish and all subject matters; acad.-vocat. counselor/tchr. Sea Mar, Seattle. Vol., cert. instr. ARC. Mem. ASCD, Nat. Notary Assn., Wash. State Ct. Interpreters & Translators Soc., Phi Delta Kappa. Avocations: music, reading, literature, painting, crafts. Home: 895 Wildwood Blvd SW Issaquah WA 98027

INMAN, DANIEL JOHN, mechanical engineer, educator; b. Shawano, Wis., May 10, 1947; s. Glen and Wilma (Sidebotham) I.; m. Catherine Little, Sept. 18, 1982; children: Jennifer W., Angela W., Daniel J. BS, Grand Valley State, Allendale, Mich., 1970; MAT, Mich. State U., 1975, PhD, 1980. Instr. physics Grand Rapids (Mich.) Ednl. Park, 1970-76; tech. staff Bell Labs., Whippany, N.J., 1978; rsch. asst. Mich. State U., East Lansing, 1976-79, 79-80, instr., 1978-79; prof. SUNY, Buffalo, 1980; chmn. U. Buffalo, 1989-92; Samuel Herrick prof. engring., sci., mechanics Va. Tech., 1992-97, dir. Ctr. for Intelligent Material Sys. and Structures, 1997—, Goodson prof. mech. engring. Dir. Mech. Sys. Lab., Buffalo, 1984; adj. prof. Brown U., Providence, 1986; cons. Kistler Instrument Corp., Amherst, N.Y., 1985-90, Kodak, 1990-93; bd. visitors Army Rsch. Office, 1995-97; cons. United Techs. Rsch. Ctr., 1995—, Los Alamos Nat. Labs., 2000—. Author: Vibration: Control Stability and Measurement, 1988, 90, Eng Vibration, 1994, 96, 2d edit., 2000, Statics, 1998, Dynamics, 1998; assoc. editor SEM Jour. of Theoretical and Exptl. Modal Analysis, 1986, Mechanics of Structures and Machines, Jour. Intelligent Material Sys. and Structures, 1992—, Jour. Smart Materials and Structures, 1993—2000; editor Jour. Intelligent Material Sys. and Structures, Shock and Vibration, Shock and Vibration Digest. Presdl. Young Investigator NSF, 1984-89. Fellow ASME (chair Buffalo sect. 1986-87, assoc. editor Vibration, Acoustics, Stress and Reliability in Design, 1984-89, Jour. Applied Mechanics, tech. editor Jour. Vibration and Acoustics 1990-2000, Disting. Lectr. 1995—; Adaptive Structure award 2000), AIAA, Am. Acad. Mechs. Internat. Inst. for Acoustics and Vibration. Home: 3545 Deer Run Rd Blacksburg VA 24060-9091 Office: Va Tech Inst Dept Mech Engring Blacksburg VA 24061-0261

INNESS, SHERRIE ANNE, English language educator; b. Palo Alto, Calif., Mar. 16, 1965; d. Lowell Edwin Inness and Ruth Caroline Ebelke. BA, Wellesley Coll., 1986; MA, U. Calif., San Diego, 1991, PhD, 1993. Prof. English Miami U., Hamilton, Ohio, 1993—2003. Author: The Lesbian Menace, 1997, Intimate Communities, 1995, Tough Girls: Women Warriors and Wonder Women in Popular Culture, 1999; editor: (anthology) Nancy Drew and Company, 1997, Delinquents and Debutantes, 1998, Millennium Girls, 1998; co-editor: (anthology) Breaking Boundaries, 1997, Kitchen Culture in America, 2000, Running for Their Lives: Pozole, Pilaf, and Pad Thai: American Women and Ethnic Food, 2001. Office: Miami U 1601 Peck Blvd Hamilton OH 45011-3399

INOS, RITA HOCOG, school system administrator; MA in Sch. Adminstrn. and Supervision, San Jose State U., 1983; EdD in Ednl. Planning, Policy and Adminstrn, USC, 1993. Commr. No. Mariana Islands Pub. Sch. System, Saipan, 2002—. Office: No Mariana Islands Pub Sch System 3rd Fl Retirement Fund Bldg Capitol Hill Saipan MP 96950*

INSALACO-DE NIGRIS, ANNA MARIA THERESA, middle school educator; b. N.Y.C., Oct. 18, 1947; d. Salvatore and Rosaria (Colletti) Insalaco; m. Michael Peter De Nigris, July 12, 1969; children: Jenniffer Ann, Tamara Alicia. BA in English and Langs., CCNY, 1969; MA in English Linguistics, George Mason U., 1988; postgrad., U. Va. Cert. endorsement in Adminstrn. and Supervision U. Va., 2002, English secondary tchr. Va. Tchr. Spanish and core subjects St. John's, Rubidoux, Calif., 1969-70; ESL specialist Sunset Hills Elem. Sch., San Diego, 1980; tchr. Sunrise Acres Elem. Sch., Las Vegas, Nev., 1984-85; tchr. 1st grade Talent House Pvt. Elem. Sch., Fairfax, Va., 1987-88; tchr. ESL Hammond Jr. High Sch., Alexandria, Va., 1988-90, Washington Irving Intermediate Sch., Springfield, Va., 1990-91; tchr. ESL 6th grade Ellen Glassgow Mid. Sch., Alexandria, 1991-92; tchr. ESL and English 7th grade Cooper Mid. Sch., McLean, Va., 1992-93; tchr. ESL Poe Mid. Sch., Annandale, Va., 1993-94; tchr. ESL and social studies Longfellow Mid. Sch., Falls Church, Va., 1994-95; tchr. ESL Herndon (Va.) Mid. Sch., 1995—; summer sch. asst. prin. Longfellow Mid. Sch., 2002. Tchr. adult ESL George Mason H.S., Falls Church, Va., 1988—89; chmn. for multicultural forum Coun. for Applied R&D George Mason U., 1990—94; mem. steering com., faculty adv. com. Herndon Mid. Sch., 1995—, program sponsor Reach for Tomorrow; coach for Krasnow Inst. George Mason U., 2000—; mem. sch. adoption com. Va. Dept. Transp., 1991, human rels. com., 1990—96, ESL Portfolio Assessment com., 1993—98; sch.-based mem. for minority achievement in prin.'s cabinet F.C. Hammond Jr. H.S., Alexandria, 1989—90; mem. Continuing Edn. Bd. Fairfax County, 1998—; co-chair WATESOL Secondary Interest Group, 1998—99, chair, 1999—2001; presenter in field. Vol. Family Svcs., Wright Patterson AFB, Ohio, 1971-72, ARC, Ohio and S.C., 1971-73; leader Girl Scouts U.S., 1980-87; Fairfax Edn. Assn. scholarship sponsor. Mem. Va. Edn. Assn. (del. 1990—), Nat. Assn. Bilingual Edn., ESL Multi-Cultural Conv. (presenter, facilitator 1989, socio-polit. concerns immigrant rights advocate 1995—), Tchrs. ESL, Washington Tchrs. ESL, Calif. Tchrs. ESL, Va. Assn. Tchrs. English, Fairfax Edn. Assn. (sch. rep., del. Va. Edn. Assn. and NEA), Italian-Am. Caucus (v.p. 1997-2000, pres. 2000—). Roman Catholic. Avocations: writing, reading, politics, helping others. Home: 8814 Hayload Ct Springfield VA 22153-1213 E-mail: denigris@erols.com., annamaria.denigris@fcps.edu.

INSELMAN, LAURA SUE, pediatrician, educator; b. Bklyn., Nov. 2, 1944; d. Alexander M. and Rae (Bloom) Inselman. BA, Barnard Coll., 1966; MD, Med. Coll. Pa., 1970. Diplomate Am. Bd. Pediatrics, Am. Bd. Pediatric Pulmonology. Intern and resident St. Lukes Hosp. Ctr., N.Y.C., 1970-73; fellow in pediatric pulmonary disease Babies Hosp., N.Y.C., 1973-76; chief pediatric pulmonary divsn. Interfaith Med. Ctr., Bklyn., 1976-81, Newington Con. Children's Hosp., 1987-92; pulmonologist, med. dir. dept. respiratory care duPont Hosp. for Children, Wilmington, Del., 1992-99, med. dir. pulmonary function lab., 1992—. Asst. prof. pediatrics Cornell U. Med. Coll., N.Y.C., 1981-86; asst. clin. prof. pediatrics, Yale U. Sch. Medicine, New Haven, 1987-92; asst. prof. pediatrics, U. Conn. Health Ctr., Farmington, 1987-92; assoc. prof. pediatrics, Jefferson Med. Coll. Thomas Jefferson U. Hosp., Phila., 1992—; mem. staff Good Samaritan Hosp., West Islip, N.Y., 1982-87. Bd. dirs. Am. Lung Assn. Nassau-Suffolk, East Meadow, N.Y., 1983-86, Del., 1992—. Fellow Am. Acad. Pediatrics, Am. Coll. Chest Physicians; mem. Am. Thoracic Soc., Am. Fedn. Med. Rsch., N.Y. Acad. Medicine, Harvey Soc., Soc. Pediatric Rsch. Office: DuPont Hospital for Children 1600 Rockland Rd Wilmington DE 19803-3607 E-mail: linselm@nemours.org.

INSLER, STANLEY, philologist, educator; b. N.Y.C., June 23, 1937; AB, Columbia Coll., 1957; postgrad., U. Tubingen, 1960-62; PhD, Yale U., 1963. Mem. faculty Grad. Sch., Yale U., 1963—, now prof. Sanskrit and comparative philology. Cons. NEH Contbr. numerous articles on ancient langs. and lits. of India and Iran to profl. publs; translator Songs of Zarathustra. Recipient fellowships Ford Found., fellowships Woodrow Wilson Found., fellowships Yale U. Mem.: Societe Asiatique, Assn. Française des Sanskritists, Royal Asiatic Soc. Gt. Brit. and Ireland, Philological Soc., Cambridge, Eng., Deutsche Morgenlandische Gesellschaft, Am. Oriental Soc. (pres., fin. dir.), Am. Acad. Arts and Scis. Office: Yale U Dept Linguistics Box 208236 New Haven CT 06520-8236 E-mail: insler-stanley@yale.edu.

IOFFE, GRIGORY, geography educator, researcher; b. Moscow, Oct. 21, 1951; s. Victor and Raisa I.; m. Yelena Kulagina, May 12, 1979; children: Mikhail, Nataliya. MA in Geography, Moscow State U., 1974; PhD in Geography, USSR Acad. Scis., 1980. Rsch. assoc. Inst. Rural Constrn. & Physical Planning, Moscow, 1974-80, Inst. Geography, USSR Acad. Scis., Moscow, 1980-88, dept. chair, 1988-89; asst. prof. geography Radford (Va.) U., 1990-94, assoc. prof. geography, 1994-00, full prof. geography, 2000—. Cons. com. on population NAS, Washington, 1994. Author: Agriculture in Non-Chernozem Zone, 1990; co-author: Continuity and Change in Rural Russia, 1997; co-editor: Population Under Duress: Geodemography of Post-Soviet Russia, 1999; ; co-author: The Environs of Russian Cities, 2000; mem. editl. bd. Columbia Gazeteer of the World, N.Y.C., 1998, Eurasian Geography and Economics, 2002—. Recipient Nat. Coun. for Soviet and East European Rsch., Washington 1995, 97, 99, NSF, 2002. Mem.: Am. Assn. Advancement Slavic Studies, Assn. Am. Geographers.

IORIO, JOHN EMIL, retired education educator; b. Bklyn., Dec. 20, 1932; s. Frederick and Helen (Grandillo) I.; m. Helen Capobianco, Dec. 20, 1958; children: Frederick Joseph, John Richard. BS in Polit Sci., Manhattan Coll., 1954; MS in Elem. Edn., Bklyn. Coll., 1967; profl. diploma Adminstrn./Supervision, Fordham U., 1984. Cert. elem. tchr., adminstr., prin. supt. N.Y.S., N.Y.C. Elem. tchr. N.Y.C., 1965-72; adminstrv. asst. P.S. 214K, Dist. 19, N.Y.C., 1972-74, asst. prin., 1974-75; adminstr. Office of Fed. and State Reimbursable Programs, N.Y.C., 1975-76; asst. prin. Ps. 153Q, Dist. 24, N.Y.C., 1976; asst. prin., head of sch. PS 128Q Dist. 24, Queens, N.Y., 1976-79, prin., 1979-87; community supt. Dist. 24, Queens, 1987-90. Adj. prof. Fordham U., 1991; presenter at many ednl. confs. and workshops. 1983-90. Contbr. articles to profl. jours. Recipient Builder of Brotherhood award, Nat. Conf. Christians and Jews, 1981, Arts in Edn. Programs award, Young Audiences of N.Y., 1989, Project Innovation Spl. Merit award, Education mag., 1990, others; named Educator of Yr. Assn. Tchrs. of N.Y., 1988; grantee Nat. Endowment for Humanities, 1981. Home: 155-57 Bridgeton St Howard Beach NY 11414-2809

IOVIENO-SUNAR, MARY SUSAN, secondary education educator; b. Worcester, Mass., May 21, 1951; m. Erdogan Sunar, Oct. 8, 1988. BA, Newton Coll. of Sacred Heart, 1973; MFA, Boston U., 1978; postgrad., U. Conn., 1975, Brockton Art Mus. Sch., 1983-88. Jr. H.S. art instr. Town of Winthrop Pub. Schs., 1974; art instr. West Jr. H.S., Town of Walpole Pub. Schs., 1975-81; art instr. Qualters Mid. Sch. Town of Mansfield (Mass.) Pub. Schs., 1981-83, visual arts instr., dept. chair Mansfield H.S., 1983—, dir. visual and performing arts, 1985—. Adult edn. life drawing instr. Walpole Pub. Schs., 1983-85; guest lectr. Mass. Coll. Art, U. Mass., Dartmouth U.; reader AP Studio Art Portfolios, Princeton, N.J., 2003; presenter workshops in field. One woman shows include Boston City Hall, 1973, Cushing-Martin Libr., Stonehill Coll., Easton, Mass., 1985, Attleboro (Mass.) Mus., 1987, Mid. Ea. Tech. U., 1998; exhibited in group shows at Walpole Arts Coun., 1975-81, Brockton (Mass.) Art Mus., 1984—, Ames Estate, Borderlands State Park, Easton, Mass., 1984; prin. works include welded assemblage II at Digital Corp., Shrewbury, Mass.; represented in permanent collection at New Moon Festival, Attleboro, Mass., Shrewsbury Pub. Libr., Starr Hair Stylists, Boston, also numerous pvt. collections; contbr. articles to profl. jours.; contbg. editor Mass. Dept. Edn. Arts Curriculum Frameworks, 1994-96; contbr. Discovery Art History, 3d edit. Recipient Outstanding Arts Educator award State of Mass., 1988, Mass. Alliance Arts Edn. award, Outstanding Bus.-Edn. Collaboration Mass. award, 1990; Mass. State Arts Lottery Fund grantee, 1984. Mem. Southeastern Mass. Arts Collaborative (chair bd. dirs. 1989—, founding mem., steering com. curriculum writer 1986—), Mass. Dirs. Art Edn. (v.p. 1996-97, pres. 1997—). Home: 10 Ray Rd Wrentham MA 02093-1818 Office: Mansfield Pub Schs care MHS 250 East St Mansfield MA 02048-2526

IRELAND, ROBERT ABNER, JR., education consultant; b. Winterville, Miss., Nov. 13, 1918; s. Robert A. Sr. and Clara Lee (Johnson) I.; children: Robert A. III (dec.), Daniel G., Merry L., Kathleen, Joseph K., John E., Christopher M. BA, U. Va., 1941; MS, Columbia U., 1947; MA, Pepperdine U., 1974. Cert. counselor, Calif., career counselor. Commd. 2nd lt. U.S. Army, 1941, advanced through grades to lt. col., 1961, ret., 1972, edn. svcs. officer, counselor ednl.-vocat., 1976-80; cons. edn. U.S. Navy, L.A., 1981-93; ind. cons. career devel. L.A., 1988-93. Mem. AACD, APA, Academic and Profl. Soc. in Counseling, Am. Ednl. Rsch. Assn., Nat. Coun. on Measurement in Edn., Nat. Soc. for the Study of Edn., Mil. Testing Assn., Phi Delta Kappa, Chi Sigma Iota, Kappa Delta Pi. Office: Apt 302 537 S Wilton Pl Los Angeles CA 90020-4922

IRISH, ROBERT MICHAEL, principal; b. Newburgh, N.Y., Oct. 22, 1953; s. Thomas Edward and Doris Evelyn (Stahl) I.; m. Eileen Mary Claffey, Sept. 22, 1990. AA, Orange C.C., Middletown, N.Y., 1974; BA, SUNY, New Paltz, 1976, MS, 1983, cert. advanced study, 1991. Cert. tchr., supr., adminstr., N.Y. Reading tchr., social studies tchr. Monticello (N.Y.) Sch. Dist., 1978-91; prin. summer sch., athletic dir., asst. prin. Wallkill (N.Y.) Sch. Dist., 1991-92; asst. prin. Valley Cen. High Sch., Montgomery, N.Y., 1992—. Bd. dirs. Sarah Wells Girl Scout Coun., Middletown, N.Y., 1988. Mem. NASSP, Nat. Mid. Sch. Assn., Nat. Coun. Social Studies, Mid-Hudson Coun. Social Studies, Sch. Adminstrs. Assn. N.Y., N.Y. State Coun. Social Studies, N.Y. State Basketball Coaches Assn. Democrat. Roman Catholic. Home: 108 Lakeside Rd Newburgh NY 12550-5716

IRIYE, AKIRA, historian, educator; b. Tokyo, Oct. 20, 1934; s. Keishiro and Naoko (Tsukamoto) I.; m. Mitsuko Maeda, May 14, 1960; children: Keiko, Masumi. BA, Haverford Coll., 1957; PhD, Harvard U., 1961. Instr. in history Harvard U., Cambridge, Mass., 1961-64, lectr. in history, 1964-66; asst. prof. history U. Calif., Santa Cruz, 1966-68; assoc. prof. U. Rochester, 1968-69, U. Chgo., 1969-71, prof., 1971-89, disting. service prof., 1983-89, chmn. dept. history, 1979-85; prof. history Harvard U., 1989—91, Charles Warren prof. history, 1991—, chmn. dept. history, 2002—. Vis. prof. Ecole des Hautes Etudes en Sciences Sociales, Paris, 1986-87, London Sch. Econs., 1992. Author: books, including After Imperialism, 1965, Across the Pacific, 1967, Pacific Estrangement, 1972, The Cold War in Asia, 1974, Power and Culture, 1981, The Origins of the Second World War in Asia and the Pacific, 1987, China and Japan, 1992, The Globalizing of America, 1993, Cultural Internationalism and World Order, 1997, Japan and the Wider World, 1997, Global Community, 2002; editor: The Chinese and the Japanese, 1980, other books. John Simon Guggenheim fellow, 1974-75 Mem. Am. Hist. Assn. (pres. 1988), Am. Acad. Arts and Scis., Orgn. Am. Historians, Soc. Historians Am. Fgn. Relations (pres. 1978) Office: Harvard U Dept History Cambridge MA 02138

IRIZARRY, ESTELLE DIANE, foreign language educator, writer, editor; b. Paterson, N.J., Nov. 13, 1937; d. Morris Jerome and Ceil Pearl (Schwartz) Roses; m. Manuel Antonio, Dec. 14, 1963; children: Michael Carl, Steven Edward, Nelson Paul. BA, Montclair State U., 1959; MA, Rutgers U., 1963; PhD in Philosophy, The George Washington U., 1970. Tchr. Glen Rock (N.J.) H.S., 1958-60, Ramapo (N.J.) Regional H.S., 1960-63; instr. U. P.R., Rio Piedras, 1963-66, Howard U., Washington, 1966-68, George Washington U., Washington, 1968-70; prof. Georgetown U., Washington, 1970—. Editor Spanish sect. Humanities Computing Yearbook, Oxford, U.K., 1988, Hispania, 1993-2000. Author: Escritores-pintores españoles, 1990, Estudios Sobre Rafael Dieste, 1992, Informática y Literatura, 1997. Recipient Tomas Barros Essay prize, La Coruna, Spain, 1990, Spanish Cross of the Civil Order of Alphonse the Sage, 1998; grantee Quincentennial grant, P.R. Com. for the Quincentenary, 1989. Mem. Am. Assn. Tchrs. Spanish and Portuguese, N.Am. Acad. of the Spanish Lang., Royal Spanish Acad. (corr.), Sigma Delta Pi. Avocations: writing, painting, literary computing. Home: 1600 N Oak St Apt 1615 Arlington VA 22209-2758

IRVIN, HELEN ARLENE, vocational education educator; b. Glenford, Ohio, May 30, 1932; d. Frank Harold and Frankie Louise (Rath) Bowser; m. Charles A. Irvin, Dec. 23, 1956; children: Elizabeth C. Weidig, Bonnie Louise O'Neil, Robert Dean Irvin. BS in Home Econ., Ohio State U., 1955; MS, Ohio U., 1985. Cert. home economist, pre-kindergarten and vocat. edn. tchr., Ohio. Home econ. tchr. Keene Ohio Sch., 1955-57, Maysville Sch., South Zanesville, Ohio, 1957-59; LPN program tchr. Muskingum Area Vocat. Sch., Zanesville, Ohio, 1970-74; family life dir. Mid-East Ohio Vocat. Sch. Dist., Zanesville, 1974-92. Project dir. children's trust fund project Muskingum County, Guernsey and Perry Counties, 1986-92. Author: (with others) Ohio Family Life Curriculum Guide. Mem. AAUW (Zanesville chpt.), Am. Home Econ. Assn., Ohio Home Econ. Assn., Ohio Vocat. Assn., Ohio State Home Econ. Alumni Assn. (key alumni 1979-87), Nat. Assn. Edn. Young Children, Ohio Assn. Edn. Young Children, Zane Trace Assn. for Edn. Young Children, Phi Upsilon Omicron Gamma Alumni Assn, Omicron Nu. Republican. Protestant. Avocations: reading, family activities, traveling, sewing. Home: 1255 Pfeifer Dr Zanesville OH 43701-1353

IRVINE, ROSE LORETTA ABERNETHY, retired communications educator, consultant; b. Kingston, N.Y., Nov. 14, 1924; d. William Francis and Julia A.; m. Robert Tate Irvine Jr., Dec. 18, 1965 (dec. June 1968). BA, Coll. St. Rose, 1945; MA, Columbia U., 1946; PhD, Northwestern U., 1964. Tchr. English, Kingston H.S., 1946-47; tchr. English and speech Croton-Harmon H.S., Croton-on-Hudson, NY, 1947-49; instr. speech SUNY, New Paltz, 1949-53, asst. prof. New Paltz, 1953-57, assoc. prof., 1957-64, prof. speech communication, 1964-85, prof. emeritus, 1985—. Guest prof. Yon Sei U., Seoul, 1970; U.S. del. U.S. Bi-Nat. Conf., Manila, 1976; adv. bd. Rondout Nat. Bank Norstar (now Fleet Bank), 1973-85; U. Chancellor's adv. bd. SUNY Senate, Albany, 1974-80; guest prof. Celtic lore Princess Grace Libr., Monaco, 1987; mem. faculty sr. rsch. partnership program SUNY, Albany, 1999—; cons., rschr., writer, 1985—; presenter in field. Contbr. articles to Speech Tchr., Ednl. Forum, Readers Theatre, others; writer, performer hist. scripts. Active Nat. Jr. League, Kingston, 1958-90; dir. Puppet Theater for Srs., N.Y., 1982-83; bd. trustees Friends of the Senate House State Hist. Site, Kingston, 1996-99, pres. 1999; bd. Ulster County adv. coun. to Office for Aging, 1998—, v.p., 2000—, pres. 2001—; mem. Gov. Pataki's Adv. Coun. Aging Svcs., 2000—; allocations com. United Way, Ulster County, 1998-2000; mem. Cornell Coop. Extension Program Com., 2003--. Honor Tuition scholar Coll. St. Rose, Albany, N.Y., 1941; named Outstanding Educator of Am., 1971. Mem. AAUW (liaison SUNY New Paltz 1966-85), Speech Comm. Assn. (mem. legis assembly 1967-68, emeritus), N.Y. State Speech Assn. (emeritus), Zeta Phi Eta, Delta Kappa Gamma, Kappa Delta Pi, Pi Lambda Theta. Roman Catholic. Avocations: historic preservation, historic research "John Vanderlyn Holters from Paris", golf, swimming, travel, local history. Home: 105 Lounsbury Pl Kingston NY 12401-5231 Office: SUNY Communications Dept New Paltz NY 12561

IRVING, BRENDA A. secondary education educator; b. St. Louis, May 11, 1947; d. Fred V. and Corzetta (Jones) I. BS, Lincoln U., 1969; EMR cert., Harris-Stowe U., 1972; MA, N.E. Mo. State U., 1978; student, Paris Am. Acad., 1978. Cert. home economics, Mo. Tchr. St. Louis (Mo.) Pub. Schs., 1969—. Sec. adv. bd. DePaul's Hosp., St. Louis, 1971-73. Camp dir. Girl Scout Coun. Greater St. Louis, 1970-86, bd. mem., 1975-79; asst. dir. St. Louis (Mo.) Progressive Christian Edn., 1976-79, Mo. Progressive Christian Edn., St. Louis, Kansas City, 1987—; dir. Mo. Progressive Missionary Baptist Conv., Congress of Christian Edn., 1993; sec. 27th Ward Polit. Orgn., St. Louis, 1984; mem. Congress Christian Edn.; tchr. Midwest Region Congress Christian Edn. Progressive Nat. Bapt. Conv. Inc., Washington, 1991—. Recipient Thanks badge Girl Scout Coun. St. Louis, 1972, Make-A-Difference award Continental Socs. Inc., 1996, 20 Yr. Svc. award Greater Mt. Carmel Bapt. Ch., St. Louis, 1987; Mo. Home Econs. Assn. exec. bd. scholar, 1994. Mem. Am. Home Econs. Assn., Mo. Home Econs. Assn. (bd. dirs. 1986-89, scholarship com. 1992—, chmn. 1994—, sec. dist. B 1993—), Mo. Home Econs. Tchrs. Assn., St. Louis Tchrs. Home Econs. Assn. (pres. 1987-89), Mo. Vocat. Assn., Mo. Assn. Family and Consumer Scis. (dist. B pres. 1996-97), Lincoln U. Alumni Assn., Delta Sigma Theta (parliament 1968-69), Phi Delta Kappa. Baptist. Avocations: traveling, reading, photography, camping, history. Home: 4919 Lotus Ave Saint Louis MO 63113-1704

IRVING, THOMAS BALLANTINE, retired Spanish language educator, consultant; b. Preston, Ont., Can., July 20, 1914; s. William John and Jessie Christina (MacIntyre) I.; m. Amanda Antillón, Aug. 17, 1950 (div. 1955); children: Diana, Lillian, Nicholas; m. Evelyn Esther Uhrhan, June 30, 1961. BA, Toronto U., 1937; Maîtrise ès Lettres, Montreal U., 1938; PhD, Princeton U., 1940. Instr. Spanish U. Calif., Berkeley, 1940-42, Carleton U., Ottawa, Can., 1942-44; dir. Colegio Nueva Granada, Bogotá, Colombia, 1944-45; asst. prof. Wells Coll., Aurora, N.Y., 1945-46; catedrático U. de San Carlos, Guatemala, 1946-48; from assoc. prof. to prof. U. Minn., Mpls., 1948-65; prof. North Ctrl. Coll., Naperville, Ill., 1965-67, U. Guelph, Ont., Can., 1967-69, U. Tenn., Knoxville, 1969-80, ret., 1980. Dir. summer sch. U. San Carlos, Guatemala City, 1946-48; trustee, dean Am. Islamic Coll., Chgo., 1981-86; vis. prof. U. Americas, Puebla, Mex., 1984. Author: Darío y la patria, 1958, Falcon of Spain, 1954, Islam Resurgent, 1979, Kalilah and Dimnah, 1980, The Maya's Own Words, 1986, The Qur'an: First American Version, 1985, Selections from the Noble Reading, 1968, rev. edit., 1980. Lt. Royal Can. Naval Svc., 1942-44. Fulbright fellow, Iraq, 1956-57; recipient Star Imtiaz, Govt. Pakistan, 1983. Mem. Lions Club. Moslem. Avocations: transculturation, islamic world, central america. Home: 3721 Mercier Dr Pascagoula MS 39581-2351

IRWIN, ANNA MAE, English language educator; b. Petrolia, Kans., Aug. 19; d. Clarence Newton and Elsie Mildred (Stump) Williams; m. Everett Irwin, Sept. 1, 1938; children: Stanley, Pamela, Steven. BS, Northeastern

State U., Tahlequah, Okla., 1940; postgrad., Denver U. and Colo. U., 1960-80. Bookkeeper, typist Fed. Bur. Pub. Rds., Denver, 1942-45; tchr. Denver Pub. Schs., 1945-46; typist State Dept. Employment, Denver, 1958-60; tchr. Aurora (Colo.) Pub. Schs., 1960-84; tutor ESL for refugees State Dept. Edn., Denver, 1988-91. Mem. adv. bd., bd. dirs. Unity Ch., Denver, 1986—; mem. and pres. aux. Goodwill Industries, Denver, 1996—, 2d v.p., 1st v.p. 1992-96, pres. 1993-96; state del., county del., congl. del., precinct com. woman Rep. Party, Denver, 1970-84. Recipient Mary Venable Svc. award for vol. work Goodwill Industries, 1996. Mem. Book Review Club (v.p., program chmn. 1990-93), Cherry Creek Womens Club. Avocations: bridge, travel, book review, ceramics.

IRWIN, DEBORAH JO, secondary education educator, flutist; b. Ellensburg, Wash., Aug. 3, 1952; m. Brent Willard Irwin, June 15, 1974; children: Tony, Nick. BA in Music Edn., Cen. Wash. U., 1974, MA in Music, 1978. Tchr. Federal Way (Wash.) Schs., 1974-75, Auburn (Wash.) Schs., 1975—; prin. flutist Tacoma Concert Band, 1982—, Renton (Wash.) Pks. Band, 1978-82; tchr. The Flute Studio, Federal Way, 1983-84; piccolo player, flutist Fed. Way Philharm., 1997—. Mem., historian Fireside Concert Series, Auburn, 1983-84. Mem. mus. groups Windsong, Scirrocco. Mem. NEA, Seattle Musicians Union, Seattle Flute Soc. Home: 12110 SE 312th St Apt C201 Auburn WA 98092-3325

IRWIN, JOHN THOMAS, humanities educator, educator; b. Houston, Apr. 24, 1940; s. William Henry and Marguerite Harriet (Hunsaker) I.; m. Laura Elizabeth Scott, Sept. 23, 1978 (div. 1991); m. Meme Amosso, May 29, 1993. BA, U. St. Thomas, 1962; MA, Rice U., PhD, 1970. Supr. public affairs library NASA Manned Spacecraft Center, Houston, 1966-7; asst. prof. English, Johns Hopkins U., 1970-74, prof. writing seminars, 1977—, Decker prof. in humanities, 1984—, chmn., 1977-96; editor Ga. Rev., U. Ga., 1974-77. Author: Doubling and Incest/Repetition and Revenge, 1975, expanded edit., 1995, The Heisenberg Variations, 1976, American Hieroglyphics, 1980, The Mystery to a Solution, 1994, Just Let Me Say This About That, 1998; editor: Johns Hopkins Press Fiction and Poetry series, 1978—; mem. editl. bd. Poe Studies, Ariz. Quar.; contbr. articles to profl. jours. Served with USNR, 1963-66. Recipient John Gardner medal Rice U., 1970, Christian Gauss prize, 1994, Scaglione prize for comparative lit., 1994; Danforth fellow, 1962, Guggenheim fellow, 1991. Mem.: Tudor and Stuart Club, F. Scott Fitzgerald Soc., Faulkner Soc., Poe Studies Assn. (v.p. 1995—97), Assn. Lit. Scholars and Critics. Home: 5313 Springlake Way Baltimore MD 21212-3413 Office: Johns Hopkins U Writing Seminars Gilman 135 Baltimore MD 21218

IRWIN, MARGARET LYNN, secondary education educator; b. Port Arthur, Tex., Jan. 10, 1962; d. Charles Weldon and Marjory (Barton) I. BA, U. Tex., 1984; MA, U. Tex., San Antonio, 1992; postgrad., St. Mary's U., 1985-86. Cert. tchr., Tex. Social studies tchr. Taft H.S., San Antonio, 1986—. Adj. instr. history Palo Alto C.C., San Antonio, 1993—; advanced placement test grader College Bd., San Antonio, 1995; state secondary social studies com. Tex. Edn. Agy., Austin, 1994, evaluator grant application com., 1995. Advocate ATPE, 1989, 93, 95; mem. bond proposal com. Northside Ind. Sch. Dist., San Antonio, 1992. Recipient Leon Jaworski award for law related edn. Young Lawyers' Assn., 1993. Mem. AAUW, Assn. Tex. Profl. Educators (regional pres. 1991-93, dir. 1994-96), U. Tex. Ex-Students Assn., Phi Delta Kappa. Republican. Methodist. Avocations: pub. speaking, travel, reading, writing hist. fiction. Office: Taft HS 11600 W Fm 471 San Antonio TX 78253-4802

IRWIN, MICHELLE KATHLEEN, artist, educator; b. Boston, July 23, 1950; BA in Edn., So. Conn. State U., 1972; MA in Tech. Edn., W.Va. U., 1987; postgrad., Internat. Sch., London, Eng., 1973. Cert. tchr., Calif. Tchr. trainer Nat. Tchr. Tng. Coll., Maseru, Lesotho, Africa, 1975-77, crafts technician mohair spinning project, 1977-79; office mgr. Bus. Internat., San Francisco, 1980-83; muralist Marine World/Africa U.S.A., Vallejo, Calif., 1984; bd. dirs., adv. bd. mem. Precita Eyes Mural Arts Ctr., San Francisco, 1984—2002; artist, cons. Learning Through Edn. in the Arts Project, San Francisco, 1989—96, Dr. Charles R. Drew Sch., San Francisco, 1990—95; tech. resource isntr. Dr. G.W. Carver Sch., San Francisco, 2002—. Instr. computers New Coll. of Calif., San Francisco, 1994-96; cons. San Francisco Unified Schs., 1989—. Author, artist: Resources in Technology, Vols. I and II, 1983; muralist Food for the People, 1988. Vol. S.H.A.R.E. Self-Help Food Distbn., San Francisco, 1988-92. Mem. NEA, Am. Fedn. Tchrs., Calif. Fedn. Tchrs. Home and Office: 1222 Palou Ave San Francisco CA 94124-3333

IRWIN, MILDRED LORINE WARRICK, library consultant, civic worker; b. Kellerton, Iowa, June 21, 1917; d. Webie Arthur and Bonnie Lorine (Hyatt) DeVries; m. Carl Wesley Warrick, Feb. 11, 1937 (dec. June 1983); children: Carl Dwayne, Arthur Will; m. John B. Irwin, Feb. 1, 1994 (dec. Apr. 10, 1997). BS in Edn., Drake U., 1959; M of Librarianship, Kans. State Tchrs. Coll., 1970. Cert. tchr., libr., Iowa. Elem. tchr. Monroe Ctr. Rural Sch., Kellerton, Iowa, 1935-37, Denham Rural Sch., Grand River, Iowa, 1945-48, Grand River Ind. Sch., 1948-52, Woodmansee Rural Sch., Decatur, Iowa, 1952-55, Centennial Rural Sch., Decatur, 1955-56; elem. tchr., acting libr. Cen. Decatur Sch., Leon, Iowa, 1956-7l, media libr. jr. and sr. high sch., 1971-79; libr. Northminster Presbyn. Ch., Tucson, 1984-93, advisor, 1994—. Media resource instr. Graceland Coll., Lamoni, Iowa, 1971-72; lit. dir. S.W. Iowa Assn. Classroom Tchrs., 1965-69; instr. workshop Tucson Mall, Ariz., 2002, 03. Editor (media packet) Mini History and Quilt Blocks, 1976, Grandma Lori's Nourishing Nuggets for Body and Soul, 1985, As I Recall (Loren Drake), 1989, Foland Family Supplement III, 1983; author: (with Quentin Oiler) Van Der Vlugt Family Record, 1976; compiler, editor Abigail Specials, 1991, Abigail Assemblage, 1996; compiler Tribute to Ferm Mills 1911-1992, 1992; co-editor: (with Dorothy Heitlinger) Milestones and Touchstones, 1993, Musings From the Heart, 1999; compiler Musical Ministry, 2002; contbr. articles to publs. Leader Grand River 4-H Club for Girls, 1954-58; sec. South Ctrl. Iowa Quarter Horse Assn., Chariton, 1967-68; chmn. Decatur County Dems., 1981-83, del., 1970-83; pianist Salvation Army Amphi League of Mercy Rhythm Noters, 1984-90; pianist, dir. Joymakers, 1990—; Sunday Sch. tchr. Decatur United Meth. Ch., 1945-54, 80-83, lay speaker, 1981-83, dir. vacation Bible sch., 1982, 83. Named Classroom Tchr. of Iowa Classrom Tchrs. Assn., 1962, Woman of Yr., Leon Bus. and Profl. Women, 1978, Northminster Presbyn. Ch. Women, 1990; named to Internat. Profl. and Bus. Women Hall of Fame for outstanding achievements in field of edn. and libr. sci., 1995; English and reading grantee Nat. Dept. Edn., 1966. Mem. NEA (life), AAUW (chmn. Tucson creative writing/cultural interests 1986-87, 89-93, historian, 1994—, Honoree award for ednl. found. programs Tucson br., Svc. award 1991), Internat. Reading Assn. (pres. Clarke-Ringgold-Decatur chpts. 1967-68), Cen. Cmty. Tchrs. Assn. (pres. 1961-62), Pima County Ret. Tchrs. Assn. (pres. 1989-90), Decatur County Assn. (pres. 1961-63), Decatur County Ret. Tchrs. Assn. (historian 1980-83), Iowa Edn. Assn. (life), Presbyn. Women (hon. life 1990—), Luth. Ch. Libr. Assn. (historian Tucson area chpt. 1991-92, v.p. 1993-94, pres. 1994-95), Delta Kappa Gamma (pres. Iowa Beta XI chpt. 1974-76, sec. 1984-85, historian Ariz. Alpha Gamma chpt. 1986-89). Democrat. Presbyterian. Avocations: walking, computing, horseback riding, reading, writing. Home: 2879 E Presidio Rd Tucson AZ 85716-1539

IRWIN, SARA, retired secondary school educator; b. Texarkana, Ark., Aug. 21, 1936; d. Carlin Lanier and Dilla Belle (Russell) Rodgers; m. Wayne Irwin, Dec. 23, 1956; children: Sheila Irwin Waits, Lisa Irwin Thomas. BSE, Henderson Coll., 1957; MSE, George Peabody Coll., 1963. Cert. secondary tchr., Ark. Bus. edn. tchr. Cutter Morning Star High Sch., Hot Springs, Ark., 1957-62; bus. edn. tchr. Springdale (Ark.) Jr. High Sch., 1962-63, High Sch. Rehab. Ctr., Hot Springs, Ark., 1963-67, Lakeside High Sch., Hot Springs, 1967—97, ret., 1997. Sec.-treas. Irwin Engring. Co., Inc., Hot Springs, 1963—; exec. sec. Home Ins. Co., Dallas, 1957. Sunday sch. tchr. First Bapt. Ch., Hot Springs, 1968-73. Mem. Ark. Vocat. Edn. Assn., Ark. Bus. Edn. Assn., Nat. Vocat. Edn. Assn., Garland County Ret. Tchrs. Assn., Ark. Ret. Tchrs. Assn., Delta Pi Epsilon. Democrat. Baptist. Avocations: sewing, walking, step aerobics, quilting, cross stitch. Home: 198 Carol St Hot Springs National Park AR 71901-9777

ISA, SALIMAN ALHAJI, electrical engineering educator; b. Okene, Kogi, Nigeria, Aug. 13, 1955; came to U.S., 1983; s. Isa Onusagba and Mariyamoh (Anawureyi) I. MSEE, Syracuse U., 1984, PhD, 1989. Elec. engr. Radio Oyo (NYSC), Ibadan, Nigeria, 1979-80, Aladja Steel Plant, Warri, Nigeria, 1980-82; grad. tchg. asst. Syracuse (N.Y.) U., 1985-89; assoc. prof. S.C. State U., Orangeburg, 1989—. Contbr. articles to profl. jours. Bd. dirs. Rev. Ravanel Scholarship Fund, Charleston, S.C., 1990—; pres. Nigerian Student Union, Syracuse U., 1986-89. Mem. IEEE, Material Rsch. Soc., Am. Vacuum Soc., Phi Beta Delta Honor Soc. Office: SC State Univ PO Box 7355 300 College St NE Orangeburg SC 29117-0001

ISAAC, WALTER LON, psychology educator; b. Seattle, May 31, 1956; s. Walter and Dorothy Jane (Emerson) I.; m. Susan Victoria Wells. BS, U. Ga., 1978; MA, U. Ky., 1983; postgrad., U. Ga., 1988-89; PhD, U. Ky., 1989. Advanced EMT Athens Gen. Hosp., 1977-79; teaching asst., rsch. asst. U. Ky., Lexington, 1979-87, instr. gifted student program, 1985, 87; instr. evening classes U. Ga., Athens, 1988, temp. asst. prof., 1989; asst. prof. psychology, mem. grad. faculty East Tenn. State U., Johnson City, 1989-98; assoc. prof. psychology Ga. Coll. and State U., Milledgeville, 1998—, tenure, 2002. Councilor for Coun. on Undergrad. Rsch, 1999—; reviewer McGraw-Hill Pub. Co., Cambridge, Mass., 1990—. Contbg. author: Aging and Recovery of Function, 1984; contbr. articles to profl. jours. Bd. dirs. Upper East Tenn. Sci. Fair, Inc., 1992-98; advisor to honor socs. Gamma Beta Phi, 1994-97, Psi Chi, 1999—. Mem. Am. Psychol. Soc., Southeastern Psychol. Assn., Soc. for Neurosci., Coun. on Undergrad. Rsch. (coun. 1999), Sigma Xi (grantee 1987). Avocations: stained glass, photography, canoeing. Home: 286 Old Plantation Trail Milledgeville GA 31061

ISAAC NASH, EVA MAE, educator; b. Natchitoches Parish, La., July 24, 1936; d. Earfus Will Nash and Dollie Mae (Edward) Johnson; m. Will Isaac Jr., July 1, 1961 (dec. May 1970). BA, San Francisco State U., 1974, MS in Edn., MS in Counseling, San Francisco State U., 1979; PhD, Walden U., 1985; diploma (hon.), St. Labre Indian Sch., 1990. Nurse's aide Protestant Episcopal Home, San Francisco, 1957-61; desk clk. Fort Ord (Calif.) Post Exchange, 1961-63; practical nurse Monterey (Calif.) Hosp., 1963-64; tchr. San Francisco Unified Schs., 1974; counselor, instr. City Coll. San Francisco, 1978-79; tchr. Oakland (Calif.) Unified Sch. Dist., 1974—. Pres. sch. adv. coun., Oakland, 1977-78, faculty adv. coun., 1992-93; advt. writer City Coll., San Francisco, 1978; instr. vocat. skill tng., Garfield Sch., Oakland, 1980-81; pub. speaker various ednl. insts. and chs., Oakland, San Francisco, 1982—; lectr. San Jose State U., 1993; creator Language Arts-Step By Step program E. Morris Cox Elem. Sch., Oakland, 1995, 96; author, presenter material in field. Author video tape Hunger: An Assassin in the Classroom, 1993-94. Recipient Community Svc. award Black Caucus of Calif. Assn. Counseling and Devel., 1988, Cert. of Recognition, 1990; named Citizen of the Day, Sta. KABL, 1988. Mem. ASCD, Internat. Reading Assn., Nat. Assn. Female Execs., Am. Personnel and Guidance Assn., Calif. Personnel and Guidance Assn., Internat. Platform Assn. (Hall Fame 1989, Profl. Speaking cert. 1993), Phi Delta Kappa. Democrat. Avocations: travel, hiking, tennis, music, dancing. Office: Oakland Unified Sch Dist 1025 2nd Ave Oakland CA 94606-2296

ISAACS, ANDREA, editor, publisher, dancer, choreographer, former educator; b. Chgo., July 16, 1952; d. William H. and Sally (Shapiro) I. BFA, U. Ill., 1975; MA, U. Iowa, 1985. Cert. secondary tchr. Founder, artistic dir., pres. Moving Images Dance Co., Chgo. and Troy, N.Y., 1976-94; artist-in-residence Ill. Arts Council, Chgo., 1978-86; dance dir. Emma Willard Sch., Troy, 1986-94; founder, tchr. phys. intelligence U.S., Italy, France, Eng., Can.; founder Phys. Intelligence, Inc. Presenter Internat. Enneagram Assn. Confs., Balt., 1997, Denver, 1998, Toronto, 1999, San Francisco, 2000. Choreographer Village, 1985, Travelers, 1986, Dancing with a Foot in Two Worlds, 1988, Sacred Dream, 1989, Raven, 1990, Borrowed Ledges, Cocoon and Trinity, 1992, Avalon, 1992, Awakening, 1992, No Slack for You, 1993, Walking to the Falls, 1993, Northern Lights, 1993, Red Sea, 1994, Don't Worry Be Happy, 1994; editor: Enneagram Monthly, 1994—; pub. Enneagram Monthly, 1994—, founder EnneaMotion; author: Buddhist Six Realms of Being and the Enneagram, 1995, Movement as a Bridge Between Thought and Feeling, 1995, Using EnneaMotion to Explore the Nine Types, 1995, Experiencing the Types through EnneaMotion, 1995, Enneagram Demographic and the MBTI, 1996, Setting the Record Straight, 1996, EnneaMotion, 1997, Out of the Abyss: A Creative Journey of Self-Discovery, 1997, Frogs, Neuron Pathways and EnneaMotion, 1998, EnneaMotion-Transformation Through Movement, 1999, Beyond Type: Transformation Through Movement, 1999, EnneaMotion: The Somatic Enneagram, 2000, Conversation with Sandra Maitri, 2001, Physical Intelligence and Will, 2003. Ill. Arts Coun. fellow, 1980; Ill. Arts Coun. grantee, 1978-86; recipient N.Y. State Arts Decentralization awards, 1988, 89, 90, 92, 93. Mem. Dance Alliance (chmn. 1987—), Chgo. Dance Arts Coalition. Avocations: bookbinding, horses, biking, swimming, poetry. Home and Office: 117 Sweetmilk Creek Rd Troy NY 12180-9105 E-mail: andreais@earthlink.net .

ISAACS, HAROLD, history educator; b. Newark, Dec. 19, 1936; s. Albert Lewis and Bertha (Wohl) I.; m. Doris Carol Mack, Apr. 25, 1974. BS in History, U. Ala., University, 1958, MA in History, 1960, PhD in History, 1968. Grad. tchg. fellow in history U. Ala., University, 1959-62; instr. in history Memphis State U., 1962-65; asst. prof. history Ga. Southwestern State U., Americus, 1965-70, assoc. prof. history, 1970-79, prof. history, 1979—. Bd. dirs. World Communities Theater, bd. advs. Ency. Developing World; scholar cons. Jimmy Carter Residency Program. Author: Jimmy Carter's Peanut Brigade, 1977; founder, editor Jour. of Third World Studies, 1984—. Advisor Young Dems., Ga. Southwestern State U., 1965-80, chmn. faculty capital campaign, 2003; founder, coord. Third World in Perspective Program Seminar Series, 1981—; coord. Black Leaders Lecture Series, 1981. Recipient Tchr. of Yr. award Alpha Phi Alpha, 1982, Outstanding Svc. award Americus Early Bird Civitan Club, 1983, Outstanding Historian and Humanitarian award SABU, 1994, Presdl. Citation for Disting. Svc., 1995, Outstanding Svc. to African Am. and Third World Studies SABU 1996-97, 1997, All-Africa award African Studies and Rsch. Forum, 2001. Mem. Assn. Third World Studies, Inc. (founder, pres., exec. dir., 1983-91, treas. 1983-97, proceedings editor 2002—, Presdl. award 1992, Harold Isaacs award). Democrat. Jewish. Home: 180 Lakeshore Dr Americus GA 31719-8233 Office: Ga Southwestern State U Dept History & Polit Sci 800 Wheatley St Americus GA 31709

ISAACS, KATHLEEN TAYLOR, secondary education educator; b. Madison, Wis., Dec. 20, 1940; d. Robert and Fannie (Turnbull) Taylor; m. Arnold R. Isaacs, Nov. 22, 1962; children: Jennifer, Katherine, Robert. BA, Wellesley Coll., 1962; MLS, U. Md., 1980; MS, Johns Hopkins U., 1994. 5th grade tchr. Hong Kong Internat. Sch., 1973-74, libr., high sch., 1974-78; 5th grade tchr. Park Sch. Lower Sch., Brooklandville, Md., 1980-82; humanities and math. tchr. Park Sch. Mid. Sch., Brooklandville, 1982-90, chair dept. humanities, 1987-90; English tchr. N.W. U., Xi'an, China, 1990-91; young adult specialist Enoch Pratt Free Libr., Balt., 1991-93; chair English dept. Yeshiva of Greater Washington, Silver Spring, Md., 1993-94; coord. 6th grade and new tchrs. Edmund Burke Sch., Washington, 1994—. Mem. adv. com. on gifted and talented edn., Balt. County, Towson, Md., 1987-90. Contbr. articles and book reviews to profl. publs. Singer, mem. coun. Balt. Choral Arts Soc., 1978—; singer, sect. leader Choir of Cathedral of Mary Our Queen, Balt., 1987-93; mem. Newbery Roundtable, Balt. County Libr., Towson, 1988, 89, 91. Dalsheimer grantee, 1981, 83, 85, 88; Am. Memory fellow, 1999. Mem. ASCD, ALA (Newbery com. 1997, Margaret Edwards com. 2000, Sibert com. 2001, Batchelder com. 2002, Great Web Sites com. 1998-2003, BBYA 2003-2004), Nat. Coun. Tchrs. English (lit. based on lang. arts instrn. com. 1987-91), Wellesley Coll. Alumnae Assn. (class sec. 1992-97). Home: 1788 Chesapeake Pl Pasadena MD 21122-5803 Office: Edmund Burke Sch 2955 Upton St NW Washington DC 20008-1107

ISAACS, KENNETH S(IDNEY), psychoanalyst, educator; b. Mpls., Apr. 7, 1920; s. Mark William and Sophia (Rai) I.; m. Ruth Elizabeth Johnson, Feb. 21, 1951 (dec. 1967); m. Adele Rella Bodroghy, May 17, 1969; children: Jonathan, James; stepchildren: John, Curtis, Peter and Edward Meissner. BA, U. Minn., 1944; PhD, U. Chgo., 1956; postgrad., Inst. Psychoanalysis, 1957-63. Intern Worcester State Hosp., Mass., 1947-48; trainee VA Mental Hygiene Clinic, Chgo., 1948-50; chief psychologist outpatient clinic system Ill. Dept. Pub. Welfare, 1949-56; research assoc., assoc. prof. U. Ill. Med. Sch., Chgo., 1956-63; practice psychoanalysis Evanston, Ill., 1960—. Supr. psychiat. residency program Evanston Hosp., Northwestern U., 1972-81, Northwestern Meml. Hosp.; pres. Chgo. Ctr. Psychoanalytic Psychology, 1984-87; cons. to schs., hosps., clinics, pvt. practitioners and industry; sr. cons. Beta Consulting Ltd.; pres. Kenisa Drilling Co., 1982-93, Kenisa Securities Co., 1982-93, Kenisa Oil Co., 1982-95. Author: Again with Feeling, 1989, Uses of Emotion, 1998, (syndicated newspaper column) A Psychologist's Notebook; contbr. articles to profl. publs. Served with AUS, 1943-45, ETO. Mem.: Chgo. Psychoanalytic Soc., Am. Bd. Profl. Psychology (bd. trustees 1994—2001), Am. Bd. Psychoanalysis (chair bd. dirs.), APA (bd. dirs. divsn. pschoanalysis), AAAS, Sigma Xi. E-mail: isaacs@storm.cncoffice.com.

ISABELL, GENE PAUL, SR., school district administrator; b. Call, Tex., Sept. 21, 1946; s. William Franklin and Billie Jean (Roebuck) I.; m. Rosa Kathleen Sory, July 13, 1968; children: Paula Kathleen, Gene Paul Jr. BS, Lamar U., 1969; MEd, Prairie View A&M U., 1975. Cert. counselor, prin., supt., Tex. Tchr., coach Beaumont (Tex.) Ind. Sch. Dist., 1969-75; head coach Warren (Tex.) Ind. Sch. Dist., 1976-78, elem. prin., 1978-81; jr. high prin. Woodville (Tex.) Ind. Sch. Dist., 1981-85; high sch. prin. Hardin-Jeffersin Ind. Sch. Dist., Sourlake, Tex., 1985-91, asst. supt., 1991-92; supt. Cen. Heights Ind. Sch. Dist., Nacogdoches, Tex., 1992—. Bd. dirs. Lions Club, Sour Lake, Tex., 1985-91, Boy Scouts Am., Woodville, Tex,. 1981-85. Mem. ASCD, Tex. Assn. Sch. Adminstrs., Tex. Assn. Secondary Sch. Prins. (bd. dirs. 1987-90, Prin. of Yr. 1989-90, region 5, Outstanding Prin. award 1989-90), Sabine-Neches Adminstrn. and Sch. Bd. Mems. Assn., Nacodoches County C. of C. (bd. dirs., chmn. edn. com.), Region VII Supts. Study Group, Phi Delta Kappa. Office: RR 13 Box 2390 Nacogdoches TX 75965-9840

ISACSON, OLE, neuroscientist, educator; b. Kristianstad, Skåne, Sweden, May 27, 1959; came to U.S., 1989; s. Dan S. and Gunnie Isacson. Student, Atlantic Coll., Wales, 1976-78; Degree in Biochemistry, U. Coll. Kalmar, Sweden, 1979; DrMedSci, U. Lund, Sweden, 1987. Rsch. asst., lectr. U. Lund, 1981—87; rsch. fellow U. Cambridge, England, 1987—89; asst. prof. Harvard U., Boston, 1989—92; assoc. prof. Harvard U., Mass. Gen. Hosp., Cambridge, 1992—; prof. neurosci. and neurology Harvard Med. Sch., 2002—. Dir. NRL, McLean Hosp Labs., Belmont, Mass., 1989—; cons. Biotech., Boston, 1992—; dir. Ctr. for Neuroregeneration Rsch., McLean Hosp. Harvard Med. Sch., Belmont, 1999—. Author: Neural Grafting, 1987, Cell Transplantation, 1994; contbr. articles to Nature, Sci., Procs. NAS. Adv. presenter Parkinson's disease rsch. U.S. Senate Spl. Com. on Aging and U.S. Ho. of Reps. Subcom. on Health and Environment, 1995, U.S. Senate Appropriations Com., 2002, others. Recipient Lindahl award Royal Swedish Acad. Scis., 1987; Fernström Found. scholar, 1987; NIH grantee, 1991, 92, 95, 97, 99, 2000, 2001, Internat. Soc. Transplantation medal, 2000, B. Sanberg Meml. Brain Rsch. awardee, 2002. Fellow Am. Soc. Neural Transplantation (coun. 1994-96, pres.-elect 1997, pres. 1998); mem. AAAS, Soc. Neurosci., Am. Acad. Neurology, World Fedn. Neurology, Mus. Fine Arts. Achievements include research in new methods for treatments of nerve cell loss in neurodegenerative diseases. E-mail: isacson@hms.harvard.edu.

ISAYEV, AVRAAM ISAYEVICH, polymer engineer, educator; b. Privolnoe, Azerbaijan, Russia, Oct. 17, 1942; s. Isai S. and Basia Isayev; m. Lubov M. Dadasheva, July 26, 1969; 1 child, Daniela. MSChemE, Azerbaijan Inst. Oil & Chem., Baku, 1964; PhD in Polymer Engring., USSR Acad. Scis., Moscow, 1970; MS in Applied Maths., Inst. Electronic Machine Bldg., Moscow, 1975. Rsch. assoc. State Rsch. Inst. Nitrogen Industries, Severodonetsk, Russia, 1965—66; predoctoral Inst. of Petrochem. Synthesis Russia Acad. Sci., Moscow, 1967—69, rsch. assoc., 1970—76; sr. rsch. fellow Israel Inst. Tech., Haifa, 1977—78; sr. rsch. assoc. Cornell U., Ithaca, NY, 1979—83; assoc. prof. Inst. Polymer Engring., U. Akron, Ohio, 1983—87, prof., 1987—2001, dir. mold tech., 1987—, disting. prof., 2001—. Guest prof. U. Aachen, Germany, 1986, U. Linz, Austria, 1993, Kyoto Inst. Technology, Japan, 1996, Inst. Polymer Rsch., Dresden, Germany, 1997, U. Sao Carlos, Brazil, 1997; expert on plastics processing technologies, Malaysia, 1995. Editor: Injectioon Compression Molding Fund, 1987, Modelling of Polymer Processing, 1991, Liquid Crystalline Polymer Systems Technological Advances, 1996; contbr. articles Internat. Ency. of Composites, Ency. of Polymer Sci. and Engring., Ency. of Matter, Sci. and Tech. and others. Expert witness U.S. Ho. of Reps., Washington, 1988; expert U.S. Army Rsch. Office, 1991; rev. panel NSF, Washington, 1991, 94, 2000-01. NASA fellow, 1985; recipient Laureate of Young Scientists USSR Acad. Scis., 1970, Cert. of Appreciation, U. Akron Bd. Trustees, 1988, 93, Outstanding Rschr. award U. Akron Alumni Assn., 1996, Silver medal The Inst. Materials, London, 1997, Vinogradov prize G. V. Vinogradov Soc. Rheology, Moscow, 2000, Omnova Solutions Signature Univ. award, Akron, 2000; named Disting. Corp. Inventor, Am. Soc. Patent Holders, 1995. Mem. Am. Chem. Soc. (Melvin Mooney Disting. Tech. award rubber divsn. 1999), N.Y. Acad. Scis., Soc. Plastics Engrs. (Cert. of Recognition 1994), Polymer Processing Soc. (treas. 1989-91), Soc. Rheology. Jewish. Achievements include 22 patents for Self-Reinforced Composites, Devulcanization of Rubbers and Decrosslinking of Crosslinked Plastics, in-situ copolymerization in polymer blends, multi-layer conductive and nonconductive polymers; fundamental research in polymer and composite processing. Office: U Akron Inst Polymer Engring 260 S Forge St Akron OH 44325-0301 E-mail: aisayev@uakron.edu.

ISBELL, DAVID BRADFORD, lawyer, educator; b. New Haven, Feb. 18, 1929; s. Percy Ernest and Dorothy Mae (Crabb) I.; m. Florence Bachrach, July 21, 1971; children: Christopher Pascal, Virginia Anne, Nicholas Bradford. BA, Yale U., 1949, LLB, 1956. Bar: Conn., 1956, D.C. 1957. Assoc. Covington & Burling, Washington, 1957-59, 61-65, ptnr., 1965-98, sr. counsel, 1998—; asst. staff dir. U.S. Commn. on Civil Rights, Washington, 1959-61. Lectr. Sch. Law U. Va., 1962—, Georgetown U. Law Ctr., 1996—. Bd. dirs. ACLU, 1965-92; chmn. exec. bd. Vets. Consortium Pro Bono Program, 1992—. 2nd lt. U.S. Army, 1951-53. Mem.: ABA (mem. ho. dels. 1986—96, chmn. com. on ethics & profl. responsibility 1991—94), D.C. Bar (gov. 1978—82, pres. 1983—84), Cosmos Club. Home: 3709 Bradley Ln Bethesda MD 20815-4256 Office: Covington & Burling 1201 Pennsylvania Ave NW Washington DC 20004 E-mail: disbell@cov.com.

ISBERNER, BRAD JOSEPH, health and safety educator, coach; b. New Ulm, Minn., Jan. 26, 1953; s. Edgar R. and Carol (Groebner) I.; m. Sandra Kay Schultz, Aug. 10, 1975; children: Joshua, Jacob, Zachary. AA in Gen. Edn., Worthington (Minn.) C.C., 1974; BS in Phys. and Health Edn. cum laude, St. Cloud (Minn.) State U., 1977, MS, 1979; PhD, LaSalle U., Mandeville, La., 1999. Phys. and health edn. specialist, adapted phys. edn.

Kimball (Minn.) Elem. Sch., 1977-88; tchr. traffic safety and cons. Cathedral H.S., St. Cloud, 1978—; asst. prof. health and safety, asst. coach men's basketball St. Cloud State U., 1986-95, assoc. prof. health and safety, asst. coach men's basketball, 1995—, driver edn. tchr., licensure program coord., 1995—. Health edn. cons. St. Cloud Sch. Dist. 742, 1993-94, Nay Ah Shing Native Am. Sch., Onamia, Minn., 1993-94; tchr. driver edn. Buffalo (Minn.) H.S., summers 1978-79; presenter in field; advisor, cons. AIDE program Minn. pub. and pvt. secondary schs.; asst. to state coord. Minn. Student Safety Program. Contbr. articles to profl. publs. and newsletters. Brainard scholar St. Cloud State U., 1976. Mem. AAHPERD, NEA, Minn. Edn. Assn., Am. Driver and Traffic Safety Edn. Assn., Minn. Driver and Traffic Safety Edn. Assn., Inter Faculty Orgn., Nat. Safety Coun., MADD, Am. Diabetes Assn., Am. Heart Assn., Minn. H.S. Coaches Assn., Fellowship Christian Athletes, Nat. Colls. Athletic Assn., Nat. Assn. Basketball Coaches, Parochial Athletic Assn. St. Cloud, St. Cloud Youth Basketball Assn., St. Cloud Youth Soccer Assn. Republican. Roman Catholic. Office: St Cloud State U AHH 247 720 4th Ave S Saint Cloud MN 56301-4498 E-mail: BJIsberner@stcloudstate.edu.

ISBISTER, JENEFIR DIANE WILKINSON, microbiologist, researcher, educator, consultant; b. Rahway, N.J., June 4, 1936; d. Edwin Guy and Alvira Marie (Andrews) Wilkinson; m. James David Isbister, July 23, 1960; children: Wendy Jill Isbister Kalavritinos, Kirstin Ann Isbister Hammond. BS, Newberry (S.C.) Coll., 1957; MS in Med. Tech., Jefferson Med. Sch., Phila., 1958; PhD in Microbiology, U. Md., 1977. Med. technologist Princeton (N.J.) Hosp., 1958-60; instr. med. tech. sch. George Washington U., Washington, 1960-62, rsch. asst., 1976-77; rsch. microbiologist Environ. Biospherics, Inc., Rockville, 1978-80; group leader environ. microbiology dept. Atlantic Rsch. Corp., Alexandria, Va., 1980-89; pvt. practice cons. microbiologist Potomac, Md., 1989—; sr. tech. advisor ARCTECH, Inc., Chantilly, Va., 1989-92. Adj. prof. George Mason U., 1988-92, rsch. prof., 1992—; cons. Orkand Corp., Silver Spring, Md., 1979-80, U.S. DOE, Pitts., 1988-89, Advancis Pharm., Gaithersburg, Md., 2001—. Contbr. to book, articles to profl. jours. Sci. fair judge Montgomery and Fairfax County Schs., Md. and Va., 1975—; bd. dirs. Bedford (Pa.) Springs Music Festival, 1984-89. Va.-Carolina Chem. Corp. scholar, 1953; recipient Congl. High Tech. award Congl. Caucus for Sci. and Tech., 1985. Mem. ASTM (vice chair 1983-92, 99-2002), Am. Soc. for Microbiology, Am. Soc. for Clin. Pathologists, Cosmos Club, Phi Kappa Phi, Phi Sigma, Chi Beta Phi. Episcopalian. Avocations: reading, music, tennis, restoring old houses and furniture. Home: 9521 Accord Dr Rockville MD 20854-4302 Office: George Mason U Rm 303E Prince William II 10900 University Blvd Manassas VA 20110 E-mail: jisbiste@osf1.gmu.edu.

ISELIN, JOHN JAY, foundation president; b. Greenville, S.C., Dec. 8, 1933; s. William Jay and Fannie Harrington (Humphreys) I.; m. Josephine Lea Barnes, Sept. 8, 1956; children: William Jay II, Benjamin Barnes, Josephine Lea, Fannie I. Minot, Alison Jay Russell. AB, Harvard U., 1956, PhD, 1965; BA, Corpus Christi Coll., U. Cambridge, Eng., 1958, MA, 1963; hon. degree, Adelphi U., L.I. U., Lander Coll. Rsch. fellow Brookings Inst., Washington, 1960-61; sr. writer Congl. Quar., Washington, 1961; corr.-editor Newsweek mag., 1962-65, sr. editor nat. affairs, 1965-69; v.p., pub. Harper & Row Publs. Inc., N.Y.C., 1969-71; pres., trustee Ednl. Broadcasting Corp., Channel 13, sta. WNET, N.Y.C., 1971-87; pres. The Cooper Union for the Advancement of Sci. and Art, N.Y.C., 1988-2000; pres. and dir. Marconi Internat. Fellowship Found., 2000—. Adj. prof. Columbia U., 2000—. Mem. bd. overseers Harvard U., 1970-76; mem. Acad. Polit. Sci., mem. Nat. Geog. Soc., Josiah Macy Jr. Found., Ventures in Edn.; Waterford Inst.; mem. Cathedral of St. John the Divine, N.Y. State Archives Inst. Recipient Disting. Citizen award trustees SUNY. Mem. Coun. on Fgn. Rels., Century Club, Harvard Club of N.Y.C. Office: Marconi Foundation 500 Mudd Hall Columbia Univ New York NY 10027 Home: Apt C606 200 E 66th St New York NY 10021-9185 E-mail: jji9@columbia.edu.

ISELY, HENRY PHILIP, association executive, integrative engineer, writer, educator; b. Montezuma, Kans., Oct. 16, 1915; s. James Walter and Jessie M. (Owen) I; m. Margaret Ann Sheesley, June 12, 1948 (dec. 1997); children: Zephyr, LaRock, Lark, Robin, Kemper, Heather Capri; m. Jelica Kungulovska, 2001. Student, South Oreg. Jr. Coll., Ashland, 1934-35, Antioch Coll., Yellow Springs, Ohio, 1935-37. Organizer Action for World Fedn., 1946-50, N.Am. Coun. for People's World Conv., 1954-58, World Com. for World Constl. Conv., 1958, sec. gen., 1959-66, World Constn. and Parliment Assn., Lakewood, Colo., 1966—; organizer worldwide prep. confs. World Constnl. Convention, 1963, 66, 67, 1st session People's World Parliament and World Constl. Conv., Switzerland, 1968; editor assn, jour. Across Frontiers, 1959—; co-organizer Emergency Coun. World Trustees, 1971, World Constituent Assembly, Innsbruck, Austria, 1977, Colombo, Sri Lanka, 1978-79, Troia, Portugal, 1991; organizer Provisional World Parliament 1st session, Brighton, Eng., 1982, 2nd Session, New Delhi, India, 1985, 3d Session, Miami Beach, Fla., 1987; mem. parliament, 1982—. Sec. Working Commn. to Draft World Constn., 1971-77, pres. World Svc. Trust, 1972-78; co-founder Builder Found., Vitamin Cottages, 1955—, (chmn. bd. dir s., 1985—), pres. Earth Rescue Corps., 1984-90, sec.-treas. Grad. Sch. World Problems, 1984-99, pres., 1999—, cabinet mem. Provisional World Govt., 1987—, pres. World Govt. Funding Corp., 1986—, Emergency Earth Rescue Adminstrn., 1995—, co-organizer Global Ratification and Elections Network, 1991— (sec. 1992—), prin. organizer 4th session Provisional World Parliament, Barcelona, Spain, 1996, 5th session, Malta, 2000, organizer first More Oxygen for the World conf., San Antonio, 1998; prof. world problems Grad. Sch. World Problems, 1990—; organizer Com. Five Global Expositions, 2001—. Author: The People Must Write the Peace, 1950, A Call to All Peoples and All National Governments of the Earth, 1961, Outline for the Debate and Drafting of a World Constitution, 1967, Strategy for Reclaiming Earth for Humanity, 1969, Call to a World Constituent Assembly, 1974, Proposal for Immediate Action by an Emergency Council of World Trustees, 1971, Call to A Provisional World Parliament, 1981, People Who Want Peace Must Take Charge of World Affairs, 1982, Plan for Emergency Earth Rescue Administration, 1985, Plan for Earth Finance Credit Corporation, 1987, Climate Crisis, 1989, Technological Breakthroughs for A Global Energy Network, 1991, Bill of Particulars: Why the U.N. Must Be Replaced, 1994, Manifesto for the Inauguration of World Government, 1994, Call to the Fourth Session of the Provisional World Parliament, 1995, Fifth Session, 1997, Critique of the Report of the Commission on Global Governance, 1995, Using Crtedit Careds and Electronic Accountin to Initiate New Global Accounting, Credit and Finance System, 1996, Double Jeopardy and the Phytoplankton Project, 1997, The Fallacy of Treating Labor as a Commodity, 2000, The Immediate Economic Benefits of World Government, 2000, The First Fifteen Global Ministries of World Government, 2002; co-author, editor: A Constitution for the Federation of Earth, 1974, rev. edit., 1991, also author several other world legis. measures adopted at Provisional World Parliament, 1968-96; co-author: Plan for Collaboration in World Constituent Assembly, 1991, Creator treatment for screen drama History Hangs by a Thread, 1993; designer: prefab modular panel sys. constrn., master plan Guacamaya project, Costa Rica; planner five world fairs, five sessions World Parliament, 2000. Candidate for U.S. Congress, 1958. Recipient hon. rsch. doctorate in edn., 1989, Honor award Internat Assn. Educators for World Peace, 1975, Ghandi medal, 1977, Honor award Internat Soc. Universalism, 1993. Mem. ACLU, Am. Acad. Polit. Sci., Fellowship of Reconciliation, World Union, World Federalist Assn., World Future Soc., Earth Island Inst., Populatin Reference Bur., Earth Action, People's Congress, Life Ext. Found., Interfaith Alliance, Internat. Assn. for Hydrogen Energy, Friends of Earth, Wilderness Soc., Solar Energy Soc., Sierra Club, Amnesty Internat., World Resources Inst., Human Rights Watch, Nat. Nutritional Foods Assn., Environ. Def. Fund, Greenpeace, Ctr. for Study of Democratic Instns., War Resistors League, Audubon Soc., Worldwatch Inst., Internat. Assn. Constl. Law, Earth Regeneration Soc., Zero Population Growth, Cancr Control Soc., Mt. Vernon Country Club, Lakewood Country Club. Socialist. Home: Lookout Mountain 241 Zephyr Ave Golden CO 80401-9589 Office: 8800 W 14th Ave Lakewood CO 80215-4817 Fax: 303-237-7685, 303-526-7933. E-mail: wcparliament@uswest.net.

ISEMINGER, GARY HUDSON, philosophy educator; b. Middleboro, Mass., Mar. 3, 1937; s. Boyd Austin and Harriet Herring (Hudson); m. Andrea Louise Grove, Dec. 18, 1965; children: Andrew, Ellen. BA, Wesleyan U., 1958; MA, Yale U., 1960, PhD, 1961. Instr. philosophy Yale U., 1961-62, Carleton Coll., Northfield, Minn., 1962-63, asst. prof., 1963-68, assoc. prof., 1968-73, prof., 1973-94, William H. Laird prof. philosophy and liberal arts, 1994—2002, Stephen R. Lewis, Jr. prof. philosophy and liberal learning, 2002—. Vis. fellow Kings Coll., London, 1966, U. Lancaster, 1991; chair student-faculty adminstrn. com. Carleton Coll., 1970-71, dept. philosophy, 1972-75, 86-89, 98—, ednl. policy com., 1973-74, English dept. rev. com., 1973-74, com. Lucas Lectrs. in Arts, 1977-81, presdl. inauguration, 1987, edn. dept. rev. task force, 1988, Am. studies program rev. com., 1992, mem. tenure and devel. rev. com., 1985-87, Coll. Coun., 1987, Coll. Marshall, 2001—; acad. vis. London Sch. Econs., 1971; vis. prof. philosophy U. Minn., 1979, Mayo Med. Sch., 1986, 87, U. Lancaster, 1994, Trinity Coll. Dublin, 2000, Lingnan U., Hong Kong, 2003; Belgum meml. lectr. St. Olaf Coll., 1997; panelist divsn. fellowships NEH, 1980, 91; commentator Minn. Pub. Radio, 1981; dir. London arts program Associated Colls. Midwest, 1982; cons. Harvard U. Press, Univ. Calif. Press, Prentice-Hall, Cornell U. Press, Holt, Rinehart and Winston, Vanderbilt U. Press, Jour. Aesthetics and Art Criticism, Dialogue, Notre Dame Jour. Formal Logic, Jour. of Philosophy and Phenomenological Rsch., Inquiry; external reviewer, evaluator various philosophy depts.; presenter in field. Author: An Introduction to Deductive Logic, 1968, Logic and Philosophy: Selected Readings, 1968, 2d edit., 1980, Knowledge and Argument, 1984, Intention and Interpretation, 1992; mem. editl. bd. Am. Philos. Quar., 1989-92, Jour. of Aesthetics and Art Criticism, 1993—; contbr. articles, revs. to profl. jours. Mem. Minn. Humanities Commn., 1984-90, chair 1988-89 Grantee NSF Coun. Philos. Studies, 1968, Bush Found., 1983, Sloan Found. 1984, Faculty Devel. Endowment, 1989, 94, 2000, NEH, 1990, 91; recipient summer stipend NEH, 1971, 78, Disting. Alumnus award Wesleyan U., 1993; Woodrow Wilson fellow, 1958, fellow Univ. Coll., London, 1975, 78, Inst. Adv. Studies in the Humanities, U. Edinburgh, 1985; vis. scholar Cambridge U., 1996, York U., 2002. Mem. AAUP (pres. Carleton chpt. 1967-68), Am. Philos. Assn. (program com. western divsn. 1982, task force on the philosophy major 1989-90, program com. ctrl. divsn. 1991, chmn. com. on tchg. philosophy 1993-96, com. to award Matchette prize in philosophy 1993-95, bd. officers 1993-96), Am. Soc. Aesthetics (trustee 1996-99), Minn. Philos. Soc. (pres. 1978-79), Phi Beta Kappa (pres. Carleton chpt. 1968-69). Avocations: classical percussion, jazz vibraphone, choral singing. Office: Carleton College One North College St Northfield MN 55057-4002 E-mail: giseming@carleton.edu.

ISENBARGER, ROSALIE ADAMS, retired secondary school educator; b. Bristol, Ind., June 12, 1934; d. G.W. and Ruth G. (Gregory) Adams; m. John Philip Raney, July 18, 1955 (div. July 1959); 1 child, Rosalie Kay Whited; m. Jerry Ross Isenbarger, Nov. 22, 1975; stepchildren: Tim S., Gary A., James L., also Russell K. Yoder (grandson). BS, Purdue U., 1956; MA in Tchg., Ind. U., 1962. Cert. secondary sch. tchr., Ind. English tchr. Middlebury (Ind.) Jr. H.S., 1957-58, West Side Mid. Sch., Elkhart, Ind., 1958-60, 61-92, chair English dept., 1962-82, 89-92; chair jr. H.S. English dept. Elkhart Cmty. Schs., 1967-87. Rep. Elkhart Cmty. Schs. in Japan; active numerous coms. in Elkhart Schs., including curriculum and advanced tng. approval coms., sponsored yearbook, newspaper, dance clubs, equestrian club, others; mem West Side Mid. Sch. Prin.'s Cabinet, Ind. Retired Tchrs. Assn. steering coms. Author: Youth Serving Organizations in Elkhart, Indiana, 1962. Chmn. bd. dirs. Christian Sci. Ch., Elkhart, 1994-95; chmn. usher com., mem. lectr. com. Christian Sci. Ch., Hudson, Fla., 1996—; mgr. Teen Turntable radio program for teens; V.p. Rice Sch. PTA, 1967-68; mem. Middlebury Schs. Bargaining Com.; sec. Elkhart Tchrs.' Assn.; past pres., v.p., numerous coms. AAUW; Brownie troop leader Girl Scouts U.S.; Y-teen leader YWCA; ednl. chmn. City of Elkhart Bicentennial Commn., 1976; mem. steering com. transition from jr. high to mid. sch., Elkhart, com. establishing gifted and talented Program. Elkhart Cmty. Schs. Tchrs.' Assn. scholar, 1952, Finnell Sys. Inc. scholar Purdue U., 1952-56; named to Outstanding Young Women of Am., 1967. Mem. NEA (life), Ind. Coun. Tchrs. English, Ind. Ret. Tchrs.' Assn., Delta Kappa Gamma (world fellowship chmn. 1996—, past pres., v.p., sec., numerous coms., parliamentarian, charter mem., Runner-Up Tchr. of Yr. City of Elkhart, Ind. 1968, State of Ind. 1970), Sigma Delta Pi (conductress, hostess). Avocations: music, travel, reading, learning ventriloquism. Home: 20901 Tanger Rd Land O Lakes FL 34639

ISENBERG, SHELLY SCONYERS, elementary education educator; b. Augusta, Ga., July 21, 1951; d. James Anthony and Beulah (Wise) Sconyers; children: Kimberly Nicole, Sean Bradley; m. Paul David Isenberg, May 25, 1979. AA, Seminde Community Coll., 1971; BA, Univ. Cen. Fla., 1973; MS, Nova Univ., 1992. Cert. elem. tchr., Fla. 3rd grade tchr. Lake Mary (Fla.) Elem. Seminole Co., 1973-79; 1st grade tchr. Hollywood Hills (Fla.) Elem Broward Co., 1979-81; ass. mgr. Toys R Us, Plantation, Fla., 1981-82; 3rd grade tchr. Nova Blanche Forman Elem. Broward Co., Davie, Fla., 1983-86; 5th grade tchr. Griffin Elem., Davie, Fla., 1986-89; 3rd grade tchr. Hawkes Bluff Elem. Broward Co., Davie, Fla., 1989-94; asst. prin. Riverglade Elem. Sch., Parkland, Fla., 1994—. Cons. Hardcourt, Brace, Jovanorich, Ft. Lauderdale, 1985-86. Asst. troop leader Girl Scouts, Davie., 1991-93. Recipient grant Hawkes Bluff Elem., 1991, 90. Mem. Fla. Assn. Supervision & Curriculum Devel. Republican. Methodist. Avocations: reading, biking, swimming. Home: 13940 Monticello St Davie FL 33325-1262 Office: Riverglades Elem Sch 7400 Parkside Dr Parkland FL 33067-1642

ISETT, DEBORAH MICHELE GUNTHER, elementary education educator; b. Allentown, Pa., Nov. 26, 1949; d. William Harrison and Virginia (Quigley) Gunther; m. James Douglas Isett, Aug. 10, 1973; children: David Joseph, Chadley James. BS in Elem. Edn., Kutztown U., 1972, MEd, 1975, postgrad., 1992—, Pa. State U., 1992—, Millersville U., East Stroudsburg U., U. Alaska, Pa. State U., Kutztown U. Educator Boyertown (Pa.) Area Sch. Dist., 1972—; elem. edn. educator Kutztown U. Mem. math. guide com. Boyertown Area Sch. Dist., 1992-93, mem. math. curriculum writing, 1997—, mentor for new tchrs.; mem. instrnl. support team (WIST), Washington Elem. Sch., Barto, Pa., 1989-96. Com. mem. Boy Scouts Am., 1973-76; com. chmn. Colebrookdale Twp. Anniversary, 1991; coun. v.p. Huff's Luth. Ch., Barto, 1987, coun. mem., 1984-87. Mem. NEA, Pa. State Edn. Assn., Boyertown Edn. Assn. (mem.-at-large 1982), Berks Talkline. Lutheran. Avocations: travel, reading, fitness walking, swimming, basket weaving. Home: 290 N Funk Rd Boyertown PA 19512-8616 Office: Washington Elem Sch 1406 Route 100 Barto PA 19504-8704

ISHIKAWA-FULLMER, JANET SATOMI, psychologist, educator; b. Hilo, Hawaii, Oct. 17, 1925; d. Shinichi and Onao (Kurisu) Saito; m. Calvin Y. Ishikawa, Aug. 15, 1950; 1 child, James A.; m. Daniel W. Fullmer, June 11, 1980. B of Edn., U. Hawaii, 1950, MEd, 1967, MEd, 1969, PhD, 1976. Diplomate Am. Acad. Pain Mgmt. Prof. Honolulu Bus. Coll., 1953-59; prof., counselor Kapiolani Community Coll., Honolulu, 1959-73; prof., dir. counseling Honolulu Community Coll., 1973-74, dean of students, 1974-77; psychologist, pres., treas. Human Resources Devel. Ctr., Inc., Honolulu, 1977—. Cons. United Specialties Co., Tokyo, 1979, Grambling (La.) State U., 1980, 81, Filipino Immigrants in Kalihi, Honolulu, 1979-84, Legis. Ref. Bur., Honolulu, 1984-85, Honolulu Police Dept., 1985; co-founder Waianae (Hawaii) Child and Family Ctr., 1979-92. Co-author: Family Therapy Dictionary, 1991, Manabu: The Diagnosis and Treatment of a Japanese Boy with a Visual Anomaly, 1991; contbr. articles to profl. jours. Commr. Bd. Psychology, Honolulu, 1979-85; co-founder Kilohana United Meth. Ch. and Family Ctr., 1993—. Mem. APA, ACA, Hawaii Psychol. Assn., Pi Lambda Theta (sec. 1967-68, v.p. 1968-69, pres. 1969-70, 96-98), Delta Kappa Gamma (sec., v.p. scholarship 1975, Outstanding Educator award 1975, Thomas Jefferson award 1993, Francis E. Clark award 1993). Avocations: jogging, tennis, dancing. Home: 154 Maono Pl Honolulu HI 96821-2529 Office: Human Resources Devel Ctr 1750 Kalakaua Ave Apt 809 Honolulu HI 96826-3725

ISHIMARU, AKIRA, electrical engineering educator; b. Fukuoka, Japan, Mar. 16, 1928; came to U.S., 1952; s. Shigezo and Yumi I.; m. Yuko Kaneda, Nov. 21, 1956; children: John, Jane, James, Joyce. BSEE, U. Tokyo, 1951; PhD, U. Wash., 1958. Registered profl. engr., Wash. Engr. Electro-Tech. Lab, Tokyo, 1951-52; tech. staff Bell Telephone Lab, Holmdel, N.J., 1956; asst. prof. U. Wash., Seattle, 1958-61, assoc. prof., 1961-65, prof. elec. engring., 1965-98, prof. emeritus, 1998—. Vis. assoc. prof. U. Calif., Berkeley, 1963-64; cons. Jet Propulsion Lab., Pasadena, Calif., 1964—, The Boeing Co., Seattle, 1984—. Author: Wave Propagation & Scattering in Random Media, 1978, Electromagnetic Wave Propagation, Radiation and Scattering, 1991; editor: Radio Science, 1982; founding editor Waves in Random Media, U.K., 1990. Recipient Faculty Achievement award Burlington Resources, 1990; Boeing Martin professorship, 1993. Fellow IEEE (editl. bd., Region VI Achievement award 1968, Centennial medal 1984, Antennas and Propagation Disting. Achievement award 1995, Heinrich Hertz medal 1999), IEEE Geosci. and Remote Sensing (Disting. Achievement award 1998, Third Millennium medal 2000), Acoustical Soc. Am., Optical Soc. Am. (assoc. editor jour. 1983), Inst. Physics U.K. (chartered physicist); mem. NAE, Internat. Union Radio Sci. (chmn. commn. B, John Howard Dellinger Gold medal 1999). Home: 2913 165th Pl NE Bellevue WA 98008-2137 Office: U Wash Dept Elec Engring PO Box 352500 Seattle WA 98195-2500 E-mail: ishimaru@ee.washington.edu.

ISOM, VIRGINIA ANNETTE VEAZEY, retired nursing educator; b. Tallapoosa County, Ala, Nov. 19, 1936; d. Jimmy L. and Bessie (Pearson) Veazey; m. William G. Isom, May 1959; children: William Gary, Marleah, James Leland. BSN, Tuskegee Inst., 1959; MSN, Syracuse U., 1974; PhD, Howard U., 1997. Cert. in nursing adminstrn. Am. Nurses' Credentialing Ctr.; cert. med.-surg. nursing. Asst. prof. med. surg. nursing Howard U. Coll. Nursing, Washington, 1975-86; edn. and tng. quality assurance coord. Howard U., Washington, 1986-87; patient care coord. Howard U. Hosp., Washington, 1987-88, coord. for spl. projects, 1988-90; prof. nursing Prince George's C.C., Largo, Md., 1992—2003; ret., 2003. Contbr. articles to profl. jour. Mem. ANA (cert. clin. specialist med. surg. nursing), Nat. League Nursing, Acad. Med. Surg. Nurses, Md. Nurses' Assn. Home: 534 Round Table Dr Fort Washington MD 20744-5638 E-mail: visom97@aol.com.

ISRAEL, JEROLD HARVEY, law educator; b. Cleveland, Ohio, June 14, 1934; s. Harry and Florence S. (Schoenfeld) I.; m. Tanya M. Boyarsky, Sept. 28, 1959; children— Lewis, Laurie, Daniel BBA, Western Res. U., 1956; LLB, Yale U., 1959. Bar: Ohio 1959, Mich. 1967. Law clk. to Justice Potter Stewart U.S. Supreme Ct., Washington, 1959-61; asst. prof. Law Sch. U. Mich., Ann Arbor, 1961-64, assoc. prof., 1964-67, prof., 1967-96, Alene and Allan F. Smith prof., 1983-96, prof. emeritus, 1996—; Ed Rood Eminent Scholar in trial advocacy and procedure U. Fla. Coll. Law, Gainesville, 1993—. Exec. sec. Mich. Law Revision Commn., 1972-92; co-reporter Uniform Rules of Criminal Procedure, Nat. Conf. Commrs. Uniform State Laws; Alene and Allen F. Smith prof. emeritus U. Mich., Ann Arbor, 1996—. Co-author: Criminal Procedure Treatise, 1999, Criminal Procedure Hornbook, 2000, Modern Criminal Procedure, 2002, Criminal Procedure and the Constitution, 2002, White Collar Crime, 1996. Office: U Fla Law Sch Gainesville FL 32611-2038

ISSEROFF, HADAR, molecular parasitologist; BS in Biology, Bklyn. Coll., 1960; MS, Purdue U., 1963, PhD, 1966. Postdoctoral fellow Rice U., Houston, 1965-68; asst. prof. SUNY, Buffalo, 1968-72, assoc. prof., 1973-78, prof., 1978—. Vis. assoc. prof. Sackler Sch. Medicine, Tel-Aviv, 1975; vis. scientist Dept. Molecular & Cell Biology, Roswell Park Meml. Inst., Buffalo, 1983, vis. prof., scientist, 1990—; vis. scientist NIAID-NIH, 1997; cons. U.S. Dept. Agr. Reviewer Jour. Parasitology, John Wiley & Sons; contbr. articles to profl. jours., chpts. to books. NIH postdoctoral fellow, Dept. HEW-NIH, 1966-68; NIH grantee, 1972-75, 76-79, 81-83; recipient Pres. Award for Scholarship and Creativity SUNY, 1987. Fellow AAAS; mem. Am. Physiol. Soc., Am. Soc. Parasitologists, Am. Soc. Zoologists. Jewish. Achievements include discovery that proline released by liver fluke, Fasciola, causes bile duct cells to multiply and enlarge bile duct, and that proline regulates development of bile duct and causes anemia and weight loss. Office: SUNY 1300 Elmwood Ave Buffalo NY 14222-1004

ITAYA, STEPHEN KENJI, neuroanatomist, educator; b. Cleve., Jan. 11, 1947; m. Patricia Williams, Mar. 24, 1973; children: Catherine, Michael. BA, Washington U., St. Louis, 1968; PhD, U. Tenn. Ctr. Health Sci., 1974. Postdoctoral fellow U. Tenn. Ctr. for Health Sci., Memphis, 1974-76, U. Iowa, Iowa City, 1976-78, asst. prof., 1978-84, U. Ill., Chgo., 1984-87; assoc. prof. U. South Ala., Mobile, 1987-99, prof., 1999—, chair biomed. sci., 1993—. Contbr. articles to profl. publs. Mem. Soc. for Neurosci. Office: U South Ala Dept Biomed Sci Ucom6000 Mobile AL 36688-0001 E-mail: sitaya@usouthal.edu.

ITZKOWITZ, NORMAN, history educator; b. N.Y.C., May 6, 1931; s. Jack and Gussie (Schmier) I.; m. Leonore Krauss, June 13, 1954; children: Jay Noah, Karen Lisa. BA magna cum laude, CCNY, 1953; MA, Princeton U., 1956, PhD, 1959. Instr. depts. history and Oriental studies Princeton U., 1958-61, asst. prof. Oriental studies, 1961-66, assoc. prof. Near Eastern studies, 1966-73, prof., 1973—, master Wilson Coll., 1975-89. Vis. prof. CCNY, summer 1959, Tchrs. Coll., Columbia U., 1964, N.Y. U., 1969, 72, 74, Hebrew U., Jerusalem, 1970, U. B.C., summer 1971 Author: (with V. Volkan and A. Dod) Richard Nixon: A Psychobiography, 1997, Ottoman Empire and Islamic Tradition, 1980, (with V. Volkan) The Immortal Atatürk, 1984 Ford Found. fellow, 1954-59; HEW, SSRC, Littauer Found. fellow, 1970, 74 Mem. Am. Hist. Assn., Am. Oriental Soc. Jewish. Office: Princeton U 108 Jones Dr Princeton NJ 08540

IVANOV, LYUBEN DIMITROV, naval architecture researcher, educator; b. Varna, Bulgaria, Apr. 14, 1941; came to U.S., 1991; s. Dimitar Dimov and Petra Christova (Grozdeva) I.; m. Svetlana Zekova, Aug. 14, 1965 (div. July 1977); children: Ognyan, Iskra; m. Irina Radeva, Aug. 18, 1977; stepchildren: Ivelin, Michaela. Diploma for Naval Architecture, Higher Naval Sch., Varna, Bulgaria, 1964; PhD, Leningrad Shipbuilding Inst., USSR, 1970. Chartered engr., U.K. Designer Inst. for Shipbuilding, Varna, 1964-66; asst. Tech. Univ., Varna, 1966, reader, head of dept., 1970-74, vice-dean for rsch., 1975-76, vice-dean for continuing edn., 1985-86, dean of faculty of shipbuilding, 1987-89, reader on ship structures, 1989-91; sr. engr. Am. Bur. Shipping, N.Y.C., 1991—. Vis. researcher Univ. Newcastle upon Tyne, U.K., 1974-75; dep. dirs. Inst. for Shipbuilding, Varna, 1986-87, mng. dir. 1987-89; v.p. Bulgarian Shipbuilding Corp., Varna, 1987-88. Mem. editorial bd. Marine Structures Jour., 1988-93. Founder, sec. Union of Bulgarian Scientists in Shipbuilding, Varna, 1982. Recipient badge of Honor, Presidium of the Union of Bulgarian Scientists, Sofia, 1984. Mem. Royal Instn. Naval Architects/U.K. (mem. internat. standing com. practical design of ships and mobile units symposium 1987-93), Soc. Naval Architects and Marine Engrs. Achievements include research in application of probabilistic methods in ship structures design and analysis. Home: 12 Brentwood Oaks Ct The Woodlands TX 77381-2525 Office: Am Bur Shipping ABS Plaza 16855 Northchase Dr Houston TX 77060-6006 Fax: 281-877-5820. E-mail: livanov@eagle.org.

IVERSEN, DAVID STEWART, librarian; b. Ames, Iowa, Sept. 5, 1963; s. James Delano and Margery Lynne (Peters) Iversen. BA in English, Dana Coll., 1986; MA in Libr. Sci., U. Iowa, 1987; MA in Scandinavian Studies, U. Wis., 1990. Multisvc. libr. Concordia Coll., Moorhead, Minn., 1990-91; libr. catalogue serials Rider U., Lawrenceville, N.J., 1991-95; head of cataloging Cowles Libr., Drake U., Des Moines, 1995-96; cataloging libr. Olson Libr., Minot (N.D.) State U., 1996—. Translator: (book chpt.) 1986: A Danish-American Family Saga, 1986, (short story) Old Hans Nielsen's Last Christmas, 1987; compiler (bibliography) Danish Utopias in America, 1988; reviewer: (by Niels Peter Stilling and Anne Lisbeth Olsen) A New Life: Danish Emigration to North America as Described by the Emigrants Themselves in Letters, 1842-1946, 1997; translations of article and short stories by Carl Hansen from Danish to English. Travel grantee U. Wis., 1989. Mem. ALA, Danish Am. Heritage Soc., Danish Immigrant Mus., Red River Danes, Alpha Mu Gamma. Lutheran. Avocations: reading, singing, theater. Office: Minot State U Gordon B Olson Libr 500 University Ave W Minot ND 58707-0002 E-mail: iversen@minotstateu.edu.

IVERSON, ROBERT LOUIS, JR., internist, physician; b. Borden, Ind., Sept. 3, 1944; s. Robert L. and Agnes Maxine (Knight) I.; m. Elsa Maschmeyer, Sept. 3, 1967 (div. 1982); children: Nathan, Kirsten; m. Deborah A. Budd, June 16, 1984 (dec. May 1996); children: Richard, Colin; m. Amy M. Neidert, May 9, 1998. Student, Wabash Coll., 1962-64; BA, Ind. U., 1970, MD, 1974, Intern, 1974-75. Diplomate Am. Bd. Internal Med., diplomate in critical care medicine, Am. Bd. Internal Med. Intern Ind. U., Indpls., 1974-75; resident (internal med.) Methodist Hosp., Indpls, 1975-77; co-dir. critical care, mem. tchg. staff dept. medicine Meth. Hosp., Indpls., 1977-84; fellow in critical care med. U. So. Calif. Shock Rsch. Unit, Ctr. for Critically Ill, L.A., 1977; vis. lectr. U. So. Calif., L.A., 1977; co-dir. critical care, teaching staff, Dept. of Med. Methodist Hosp., Indpls, 1977-84; asst. prof. medicine Wayne State U., Detroit, 1984-96, assoc. prof. clin. medicine, 1996-2000; dir. med. affairs Hutzel Hosp., Detroit, 1996-97, vice chief med. staff, 1995-97, dir. ICU, 1986-2000, chief critical care medicine, 1988-2000; chief critical care svcs. Vassar Bros. Hosp., Poughkeepsie, NY, 2000—02. Mem. bd. Rudgate Neighborhood Assocs., Bloomfield Hills, Mich. 1996-98; mem. physician leadership coun. Detroit Med. Ctr., 1996-2000; participant Ind. Malpractice Rev. Panels, 1981-85; chief med. officer Oakland County (Mich.) Sheriff's Dept., 1997-2000, tactical med. officer Spl. Response Team (SWAT), 1997-2000. Author: (with others) Respiratory Care of the Neurosurgical Patient, 1983, Septic Shock in Critical Care Clinics, 1988; established adminstrv. core curriculum for intensivists Critical Care Clinics, 1993; contbr. abstracts and articles to profl. jours. Med. advisor to Ind. Coun. Emergency Response Teams, 1980-85, mem. Ind. Symphonic Choir, 1970-84, trustee, 1983-84; hon. dep. sheriff Marion County Sheriff's Dept., 1982-84; bd. dirs. City of Bloomfield Hills, Mich., Rudgate Neighborhood Assn., 1996-98. With U.S. Army, 1964-67, Vietnam. Fellow ACP, Am. Coll. Chest Physicians; mem. AMA, Soc. Critical Care Medicine, Am. Coll. Physician Execs., Wayne County Med. Soc. (elected del. 1990-91), Phi Beta Kappa. Avocations: music, shortwave radio communications, sailing, astronomy, astrophotography. Home: 5421 Ashley Pkwy Sarasota FL 34241

IVEY, CHRISTYNE GLORIA, private school administrator; b. Ridgeland, S.C. d. Katie (Beaton) Smith; m. Jim L. Ivey; children: Christopher, Jason. BS in Elem. Edn., Coppin State Coll., 1963; MS in Early Childhood Edn., Towson State U., 1974. Cert. advanced profl., Md. Tchr., supr. Balt. City Pub. Schs., 1965-78; owner, adminstr. Ivey League Learning Ctr., Balt., 1978—. Commr. early learning years Md. State Dept. Edn., 1990-92; co-chair salaries task force Md. Com. for Children, 1990—, bd. dirs.; panelist child care issues WBAL-TV. Co-author: Shortchanging Our Children, 1992. Sec. Harambee Presbytn., Balt., 1992—. Recipient awards Mayor's Office of Children and Youth, City Child Care Assn. and Dept. Social Svcs.-Child Care Divsn.; cover feature The Child Care Information Exchange, Nov., 1992. Mem. Nat. Assn. for Colored People (life), Nat. Bus. League, Nat. Child Care Assn., Nat. Assn. for the Edn. Young Children, Md. Assn. for the Edn. Young Children, Md. Child Care Assn. (bd. dirs. 1982—), Md. Com. for Children (pub. policy com. 1985—), Ctrl. Md. Assn. for the Edn. Young Children (bd. dirs. 1982-85), Balt. Bus. League (1st v.p., bd. dirs. 1985—), Balt. Child Care Assn. (pres. 1992—), Delta Sigma Theta. Avocations: singing, cooking, travel, reading. Home: 2608 Beethoven Ave Baltimore MD 21207-6752 Office: Ivey League Learning Ctr 1010 E 43rd St Baltimore MD 21212-4916

IVIE, EVAN LEON, computer science educator; b. May 15, 1931; s. Horace Leon and Ruth (Ashby) Ivie; m. Betty Jo Beck, Mar. 29, 1957; children: Dynette, Mark, Joseph, Robert, Ann, Rebecca, John, James, Mette, Emily, Peter. BS, BES, Brigham Young U., 1956; MS, Stanford U., 1957; PhD, MIT, 1966. Instr. MIT, Cambridge, 1960—66; mem. tech. staff Bell Labs., Murray Hill, NJ, 1966—79; prof. computer sci. Brigham Young U., Provo, Utah, 1979—; pres. Ivie Computer Corp., Provo, 1979—; dir. Joseph Smith Acad., Nauvoo, Ill., 2003—. Expert witness on computers for 12 lawsuits, 1983—; instr., dir. Joseph Smith Acad., Ill., 2002—. Leader Boy Scouts Am., 1954—83; mem. Warren Sch. Bd., NJ, 1975—78; developer Pioneer Ancestral Past, Utah Sesquicentennial, 1997. 1st lt. USAF, 1957—60. Recipient Fulbright scholarship, Kiev Poly. Inst., Ukraine, 1992—93; fellow, Stanford U., 1956—57. Mem.: IEEE (sr.), Assn. Computing Machinery. Republican. Mem. Lds Ch. Achievements include invention of Data Base Computers, 1972; Programmer's Workbench, 1975; Electronic Yellow pages, 1978; Reader's Workbench, 1984. Home: 1131 Dover Dr Provo UT 84604-5255 Office: Brigham Young U Provo UT 84602 also: 145 Wells St Rm 30 Nauvoo IL 62354 E-mail: evan@cs.byu.edu., evan@ivies.org.

IVORY, GOLDIE LEE, retired social worker, educator; b. Apr. 19, 1926; d. Percey Carr and Edna M. (Scott) Carr Williams; m. Sam Ivory, Aug. 7, 1947; children: Kenneth L., Kevin D. BS, Ind. U., 1949; MA, U. Notre Dame, 1956; MSW, Ind. U.-Purdue U., Indpls., 1977. Registered cert. clin. social worker, Ind. Juvenile probation officer St. Joseph County Juvenile Probation Dept., South Bend, Ind., 1949-56, intake supr., 1956-59; chief probation officer South Bend City Ct., 1959; psychiat. social worker Beatty Meml. Hosp., Westville, Ind., 1960; instr. sociology Ind. U., South Bend, 1960-67; relocation rep. Urban Redevel. Commn., South Bend, 1960-62; social worker Elkhart (Ind.) Cmty. Schs., 1962-66, supr. social svcs., 1966-69, dir. human rels., 1970-87; mem. faculty Goshen (Ind.) Coll., 1971—, asst. prof. social work, 1981-91, assoc. prof. social work emerita, 1993—. Pvt. practice social work Ivory Caring Corner, 1981-87; family therapist Family Learning Ctr., South Bend, 1987-94, clinician emerita, 1994—; workshop cons. human social svcs.; instr. sociology and social work St. Mary's Coll., 1967-69, dir. Upward Bound program, 1970; guest lectr. dept. sociology U. Swaziland, South Africa, 1983. Author articles in field. Recipient Human Svc. award Acad. Human Svcs., 1974-75, Merit award Indpls. Pub. Schs. Dept. Social Work, 1977, Designation BCD award Am. Bd. Examiners in Clin. Soc., 1985, plaque for cmty. svcs. Mayor of Elkhart, 1981, Black Achiever award in edn. Ind. Black Expo, 1983; state chpt. Delta Kappa Gamma scholar, 1969-70. Mem. NASW, AAUW, Nat. Black Child Devel. Inst., Nat. Assn. Black Social Workers, Acad. Cert. Social Workers, The Links, Delta Kappa Gamma, Delta Sigma Theta, Alpha Delta Mu. Mem. Church of God in Christ. Home: 1309 Bissell St South Bend IN 46617-2108

IWANSKI, MARY, parochial school educator; b. Sacramento, Feb. 12, 1947; d. John Joseph Iwanski and Philomena Astorino Iwanski Glassy. BS, Benedictine U., Lisle, 1969; MS, U. Wis., Milw., 1973; postgrad., Corcordia U., River Forest, Ill., 1992-93, U. Calif., 1980-82, 91. Cert. high sch. tchr., Ill.; joined Inst. Blessed Virgin Mary, 1964. Tchr. high sch. physics and math. Loretto Cath. Ctrl. High Sch., Sault Sainte Marie, Mich., 1969-71; tchr. high sch. algebra and phys. sci. Sault Area Pub. High Sch., Sault Sainte Marie, 1971; tchr. high sch. geometry and physics St. Francis High Sch., Wheaton, Ill., 1971-72; tchr. math., physics, physical sci. Unity Cath. High Sch., Chgo., 1972-76; jr. high sch. tchr. math. and sci., cons. Our Lady of the Assumption, Carmichael, Calif., 1976-82; 8th grade tchr. math. and sci. St. John of the Cross Sch., Western Springs, Ill., 1982-88; high sch. math. tchr. Mother McAuley Liberal Arts High Sch., Chgo., 1989—. Sci. cons. St. John of the Cross Sch., 1982-88, math. coach/cons., 1983-88; mem. faculty/staff coun. Mother McAuley Liberal Arts H.S., Chgo., 1990-93, Math Macs team coach, 1994—; sci. fair, sci. cons. Our Lady Assumption Sch., 1976-82. Recipient Photography award Joliet (Ill.) Park Dist., 1977; Heart of the Sch. award, 1995-96. Mem. Assn. Women Math., Nat. Coun. Tchrs. Math., Nat. Cath. Ednl. Assn., Sigma Pi Sigma. Avocations: music (accordion playing), photography, hiking, reading. Office: Mother McAuley Libl Arts HS 3737 W 99th St Chicago IL 60655-3133

IWERKS, CAROL JOY, minister; b. Webster, S.D., Oct. 30, 1935; d. John William and Petra Amanda (Dahl) Grebner; m. E. Donald Iwerks, Apr. 4, 1960; children: Edie J., Bryce J., Elyce J. BS in Home Econs., S.D. State U., 1957. Tchr. Millbank (S.D.) High Sch., 1957-60; nursery sch. tchr. YWCA, Aberdeen, S.D., 1975-78; edn. dir. First United Meth. Ch., Aberdeen, 1978—; interim pastor Ch. of All Nations, Aberdeen, 1987-90. Cons. in field. Bd. dirs. United Way, Aberdeen, 1986-90, Aberdeen Child Care Ctr., 1980—. Recipient Svc. to Mankind award Sertoma, 1989. Mem. Christian Educators Fellowship, Lab. Workers Network, AAUW (pres. 1970-71), Zonta (pres. 1988-89), Toastmasters. Republican. United Methodist. Office: First United Meth Ch 502 S Lincoln St Aberdeen SD 57401-4321

IYECHAD, THEODORE MELENGOES, youth program director; b. Koror, Republic of Palau, Dec. 16, 1953; s. Iyechad and Kerengerong (Ibluuk) I.; 1 child, Metelleklang Kevin. BS in Rhetoric and Comm., U. Oreg., 1978; MEd in Adult Edn., Colo. State U., 1982. 4-H and youth ext. agt. Coll. Agr. and Life Scis. U. Guam, Mangilao, 1979—, resident instrn. coord. Coll. Agr. and Life Scis., 1984-86. Chmn. Charter Day com. U. Guam, 1989-90; coach Triton Men's Varsity Softball Team, 1986-87; resident instrn. sect. summer work conf. divsn. agr. Nat. Assn. State and Land Grant Colls., Honolulu and Hilo, 1985 condr. workshops in field. Author: Guam's One-on-One 4-H Baseball, 1982, Public Speaking You and Me, 1989, 4-H Gardening Program, 1990; co-author: 4-H Leader's Handbook, 1992, What is 4-H, 1993; contbr. articles to profl. jours. Mem. Cen. Planning Com. for Sr. Citizen Month, 1989-91; mem. Substance Abuse Task Force-Mental Health, 1989-91; vol. Holiday Hotline, 1989. Mem. Assn. for Internat. Agrl. and Ext. Edn., Nat. Rural Edn. Assn., Assn. Leadership Educators, Nat. Safety Coun., Nat. Geography Soc., Assn. for Gerontology in Higher Edn., Epsilon Sigma Phi (Tau Alpha chpt.). Avocations: fishing, photography, various sports. Office: U Guam Coll Agr & Life Scis 4-H & Youth U Guam Station Mangilao GU 96923

IZAWA, CHIZUKO, psychologist, researcher; b. Tokushima, Japan; came to U.S., 1961; m. Robert G. Hayden, July 15, 1973; 1 child, Althea J.E.K. Izawa-Hayden. BA in Psychology, U. Tokyo, 1960; MA in Psychology, Stanford U., 1962, PhD in Psychology, 1965. Asst. prof. psychology San Diego State U., Calif., 1965-67; postdoctoral fellow Inst. Human Learning U. Calif., Berkeley, 1967-68; asst. prof. psychology SUNY, Buffalo, 1968-72; assoc. prof. psychology Tulane U., 1972-80, prof. psychology, 1980—. Cons., question constructor Am. Assn. State Psychology Bds.; examiner, interviewer selection com. JET program Consulate Gen. Japan, 1983—; invited vis. fgn. scientist U. Tsukuba, Japan, 2001; co-organizer, chair 4th Tsukuba Internat. Conf. on Memory, 2003-; visiting scholar, Univ. Tsukuba, 2001. Author: Current Issues in Cognitive Processes, 1989, Cognitive Psychology Applied, 1993, On Human Memory, 1999; reviewer numerous jours. including Am. Psychologist, Am. Jour. Psychology, Jour. Exptl. Psychology: Gen. Jour. Exptl. Psychology: Learning, Memory, and Cognition, Memory & Cognition, Jour. Math. Psychology, Jour. Appl. Psychology, Japanese Jour. Psychonomic Sci., Cognitive Psychology, others; cons. reviewer NSF, NIMH, Oxford U. Press, Cambridge U. Press, Stanford U. Press, Harcourt, Sage, others; review panelist Directorate Sci. Edn., Div. Sci. Manpower Improvement, NSF; contbr. numerous articles to profl. jours.; presenter in field. NIMH grantee; Flowerree Found. grantee; Japanese Edn. Rsch. Publ. grantee; Japanese Edn. Min. grantee; Aron Found. grantee; Japanese Monbusho, educ. ministry grantee. Fellow APA, WPA, Am. Psychol. Soc. (charter), WPA; mem. AAUP, Asian Am. Psychol. Assn., Japanese Psychol. Assn., Southeastern Psychol. Assn. (co-chair annual meeting local arrangements subcom. 1972-73, co-chair commn. for status women student rsch. awards 1975-78, chair com. on equality profl. opportunity rsch. awards 1978-80, various program coms. 1975-90, program com. learning, memory, cognition 1995—, chair com. equality profl. opportunity minority interest group 1996-98, exec. com. mem.-at-large 1998-2001, chair spl. grad. rsch. awards 1998-2000), Regional Psychol. Assn., Psychonomic Soc., Psychometric Soc., Soc. Math. Psychology, Soc. Cross-Cultural Psychology, Soc. Cross-Cultural Rsch., Internat. Coun. Psychologists (co-chair annual meeting local arrangements 1973-74), Southeastern Workers in Memory (chmn. 1974-75), Japan Prize World-Wide Nomination Com., Sigma Xi. Office: 411 Pine St New Orleans LA 70118-3715

IZZI, JOHN, educator, author; b. Providence, Dec. 31, 1931; s. Joseph and Elizabeth (Kinney) I.; m. Barbara Ann Freethy, Dec. 18, 1954; children: Kathleen, Donna, James; m. Patricia Margaret Crowley, Aug. 27, 1979; children: John, Matthew, Jessica. BA, Providence Coll., 1953; MEd, R.I. Coll., 1965; postgrad. (NSF grantee), U. Vt., 1959, 60, 63, Seton Hall U., 1961, Yale U., 1966; doctoral candidate (NSF grantee), Boston U., 1968—70. Tchr. LaSalle Acad., Providence, 1955-58, Warren (R.I.) H.S., 1958-60, Warwick (R.I.) Vets. H.S., 1960-62, Pilgrim H.S., Warwick, 1962—66, 1999—2001, head math. dept., 1968-72, 1968—72, Seekonk (Mass.) H.S., 1966-67; state supr. math. Mass. Dept. Edn., 1967-68; head math. dept. Toll Gate HS, Warwick, 1972—88, 2001—02; coord. secondary sch. R.I. Hosp., 1988-89; tchr. math. and sci. Westport (Mass.) H.S., 1989-91, math. adviser, biology/sci. tchr.; adj. faculty Bristol C.C., Mass., 1992-94. Pres. Smallstate Co., Warwick, 1975—; prin. Warwick Adult Edn., 1987-88; ext. lectr. U. R.I., 1976—; math. coach Toll Gate Acad. Decathlon State Champions, 1985, New Eng. Math. League Divsn. Champions, 1989-90; dir. Prep. Inst., Warwick, Math. Edn. Svc., Providence, 1965-66, Toll Gate Metrication Project, Warwick, 1972-73; creator 1st federally funded sch. metrication project in U.S., 1972, Izzi Metric Slide Chart, 1974, Izzi Decimal Notation, 1974; dir. Smallstate Math. Inst., Warwick, 1989-90, Smallstate Scholarship Svc., Warwick, 1991-93; pres. Smallstate Pub., 1994-96; advisor Am. Security Coun., 1973-79; pres. P & J Izzi Assocs., Warwick, 1997-99; metrication cons. Nat. Coun. Tchrs. Math., 1973—, computer software reviewer, textbook reviewer, 1981-88; adj. faculty C.C. R.I., 1981-85, Bristol C.C., Mass., 1992-94; metrication cons. State Depts. Edn., New England, Pa. and NY, 1977-80. Textbook reviewer AAAS, 1968-74; book reviewer Phi Delta Kappan, 1974-76; author: Metrication, American Style, 1974, Looking at the Metric System, 1977, Adult Metric Guide, 1977, Basic Metric Competency Test, 1977, My Irish, Voices of America, 1991; editl. adviser New Eng. Math. Jour., 1982-85; contbr. articles to various publs. Mem. Mass. Gov.'s Hwy. Safety Act Com., 1967-68. With U.S. Army, 1953-55. Recipient Disting. Achievement award Ednl. Press Assn. Am., 1974; named Best Math. Tchr. in Am., Ky. Ednl. TV, 1990. Mem. ASCD, NEA, Am. Fedn. Tchrs., Nat. Coun. Tchrs. Math., Am. Assn. Sch. Adminstrs. Metric Assn., Assn. Tchrs. Math. in New Eng., New Eng. Regional Metric Assn. (edn. commr. 1976-80), Mass. Dept. Edn. Assn. (v.p. 1967-68). Home: 243 Greenwood Ave Warwick RI 02886-2015 E-mail: johnizzi@aol.com.

IZZO, HERBERT JOHN, language and linguistics educator, researcher; b. Saginaw, Mich., July 17, 1928; s. Joseph Anthony and Eleanor Bertha (Karau) I.; m. Barbara Suzanne McLaughlin, Sept. 22, 1958 (div); children: Victoria Sue Gutierrez, Alexander John, Sylvia Rachel Hunter, Daniel Stanley; m. Olga Frances Koutna, Dec. 30, 1989. BA in Spanish, U. Mich., 1950, MA in Spanish and Italian, 1951, BS in Chemistry, 1953, PhD in Linguistics, 1965. Chargé de cours Huê (Vietnam) U., 1958-59; instr. Spanish U. Ariz., Tucson, 1960-61; instr. Spanish and linguistics Stanford (Calif.) U., 1961-64; asst. prof. Spanish San Jose (Calif.) State U., 1964-68; from assoc. to prof. linguistics U. Calgary, Alberta, Can., 1968-88, prof. emeritus, 1988—. Vis. asst. prof. fgn. langs. Mansfield (Pa.) State Coll., 1957; vis. prof. Romance linguistics U. Mich., Ann Arbor, 1977-78, 93-94; vis. prof. linguistics U. Bucharest, Romania, 1975-76; vis. prof. Italian, Stanford U., 1990-91; vis. scholar U. Mich., 1997—; adv. bd. Quaderni d'Italianistica, Can., 1979—. Author: Tuscan and Etruscan, 1972; editor: The Sixth LACUS Forum, 1980, Italic and Romance, 1985; editor for linguistics Am. Jour. Italian Studies, 1988-2002; translator Lost Papers of Ludwig von Mises, 1998-2001, Italian Dialect Studies of Carl L. Fernow, 2003. Bd. dirs. Fathers Alberta, Calgary, 1986-87. Grad. fellow U. N.Mex., 1953, Award for Advanced Study, Am. Coun. Learned Socs., 1963, Fulbright-Hays award U.S. Dept. State, 1966, 75. Mem. Am. Assn. Italian Studies, Linguistic Assn. Can. and U.S. (conf. organizer 1978), N.Am. Assn. for History of Lang. Scis. (v.p. 1977-80), Am. Assn. Tchrs. Italian (life), Linguistic Soc. Am. (life), Am. Classical League, Am. Assn. Tchrs. of Spanish and Portuguese (life), Can. Soc. Italian Studies (nominating com. 1977-78, adv. bd. 1974-80), Internat. Soc. Phonetic Scis., Nat. Assn. Scholars, Phi Beta Kappa, Phi Kappa Phi. Avocations: music, history, running. Home: 2515 Deake Ave Ann Arbor MI 48108-1330 E-mail: hizzo@umich.edu.

JABARA, FRANCIS DWIGHT, merchant banker, educator, entrepreneur; b. Cambridge, Kans., Oct. 13, 1924; s. Farris George and Helen (Hourany) J.; m. Geri Ablah, Dec. 30, 1956; children: Leesa, Lori, Harvey F.G. BS, Okla. State U., 1948; MBA, Northwestern U., 1949. CPA, Ill. Faculty Wichita (Kans.) State U., 1949-89, assoc. prof. acctg., 1954-59, prof., 1959-89, head dept., 1962-64, dean Coll. Bus. Adminstrn., 1964-71, Wichita Soc. Accts. Disting. prof. bus., 1971-89, founder, dir. Ctr. for Entrepreneurship, 1977-89; pres. Jabara Ventures Group, 1989—; chmn. Jabara Family Found. Bd. dirs. Commerce Bank of Wichita, Sheplers, Inc.; chmn. bd. dirs. Kans. Coliseum Corp.; chmn. Kans. delegation to White House Conf., 1986. Mem. Gov. Kans. Adv. Bd. to Bd. Accountancy, 1962-86; founder Venture Kids. Recipient George Washington medal of Honor, Freedoms Found., Leavy award, Pres.'s medal Wichita State U., 2002, Faculty Lifetime Achievement award Coll. Bus. Adminstrn., Wichita State U., 2001, Fin. Svcs. Advocate of Yr. award U.S. SBA, 2003; named to Hall of Fame Okla. State U.; named laureate Wichita Bus. Hall of Fame, 1997; Jabara Hall, Wichita State U., dedicated 1997. Mem. AICPA, Kans. Soc. CPAs, Wichita C. of C., Rotary, Alpha Kappa Psi, Beta Alpha Psi, Phi Kappa Phi, Alpha Tau Omega. Republican. Mem. Greek Orthodox Ch. Home: 35 Hampton Rd Wichita KS 67207-1054

JABLE, JOHN THOMAS, physical education educator; b. Trenton, N.J., Dec. 21, 1940; s. John Thomas and Stella Helen (Cezus) J.; m. Mary Christine Anderson, June 14, 1969 (dec. Oct. 1978); 1 child, Joy; m. Betsy Jane Glantz, May 1, 1982. BS, U. Dayton, 1962; MEd in Phys. Edn., Pa. State U., 1965, MA in History, 1973, PhD in Phys. Edn., 1974. Swimming instr., lifeguard Dayton Boys Club, 1962; instr. Pa. State U., McKeesport, 1965-70, asst. prof., 1973-75; assoc. prof., chair dept. exercise and movement sci. William Paterson U., Wayne, NJ, 1975-81, 96-01, prof., 1981—. Chmn. Ctr. Rsch. Coll. Sci. and Health, 2002-; mem. adv. coun. Passaic County (N.J.) Title VII Nutrition Project, Paterson, 1977-81. Contbr. articles to profl. jours. Chmn. bd. Lake Neepaulin Cmty. Club Assn., Wantage, N.J., 1991, sec., 1992-95; pres. Friends of Lake Neepaulin, Inc., 1997—. 1st lt. inf. U.S. Army, 1962-64. State of N.J. higher edn. act Title I grantee, 1978-79; NEH summer grantee, 1989. Fellow Am. Acad. Kineseology and Phys. Edn.; mem. AAHPERD (fellow rsch. consortium 1984, chair coun. on aging and adult devel. 1986-87, chair history acad. 1995-96), N.Am. Soc. for Sport History (pres. 1983-85), Orgn. Am. Historians, Internat. Soc. for History of Phys. Edn. and Sport. Office: William Paterson Dept Exercise/Movement Sci Wayne NJ 07470 E-mail: jablet@wpunj.edu., jable26t@webtv.net.

JACKIW, ROMAN, physicist, educator; b. Lublinec, Poland, Nov. 8, 1939; came to U.S., 1949; s. Nicholas and Zenobia (Kostyk) J.; m. So-Young Pi, Sept. 4, 1981; children: Simone Ahlborn, Nicholas, Stefan Pi. BA, Swarthmore Coll., 1961; PhD, Cornell U., 1966; Doctorate (hon.), U. Uppsala, Sweden, 2000, U. Torino, Italy, 2000, Bogolyubov Inst., Kiev, Ukraine, 2003. Jr. fellow Harvard Soc. of Fellows, Cambridge, Mass., 1966-69; from asst. prof. to Jerrold Zacharias prof. physics MIT, Cambridge, 1969—. Vis. prof. Rockefeller U., N.Y.C., 1977-78, U. Calif., L.A., Santa Barbara, 1980, Columbia U., N.Y.C., 1989-90. Contbr. over 150 articles to profl. jours. Alfred P. Sloan fellow Sloan Found., 1969-71, J.S. Guggenheim fellow Guggenheim Found., 1977-78; recipient Dannie Heineman prize in math. physics Am. Phys. Soc., 1995, Dirac medal and prize Internat. Ctr. for Theoretical Physics, Trieste, Italy, 1998. Fellow Am. Acad. of Arts and Scis., Am. Phys. Soc.; mem. NAS, Nat. Acad. Scis. Ukraine (fgn. mem.). Achievements include research on fundamental processes in nature. Office: MIT 6-320 77 Massachusetts Ave Cambridge MA 02139-4307 E-mail: jackiw@lns.mit.edu.

JACKMAN, HARRY EMEKONA, III, special education educator; b. Honolulu, Sept. 7, 1961; s. Harry E. II and Toby (Kearns) J.; m. Sandra Diaz Guerrero, Oct. 10, 1984 (div. Oct. 1990). BA, Incarnate Word Coll., San Antonio, 1990. Tchr. fine arts and devel. phys. edn. St. Pius X Sch., San Antonio, 1985-86; tchr. gifted and talented edn. Christ The King Sch., San Antonio, 1989-90; tchr. spl. edn. Harlandale Ind. Sch. Dist., San Antonio, 1991—. Fundraiser Royal Sovereign Inperial Ct. Alamo Empire, 1990—. Mem. ASCD, Tex. Tchrs. Assn. (polit. action team 1991—, sec. region VII 1994-95), Harlandale Tchrs. Assn. (bd. dirs. 1991), Asian-Pacific Islander Caucus. Democrat. Eastern Orthodox Catholic. Home: 3127 Stoney Orch San Antonio TX 78247-3991

JACKO, JEAN ANNE, nurse, educator; b. Columbus, Ohio, June 27, 1963; d. John Anthony and Norma Mary (Competti) Gurklis. BSN summa cum laude, Ohio State U., 1985, MS, 1986, PhD in Nursing, 1992. Staff nurse Doctors Hosp. North, Columbus, Ohio, 1985-86, Riverside Meth. Hosp., Columbus, 1986-87, Ohio State U. Hosps., Columbus, 1988-92; grad. teaching assoc. Ohio State U. Coll. Nursing, Columbus, 1987-90, grad. fellow, 1990-92; assoc. prof. nursing Capital U. Sch. Nursing, Columbus, 1992—. Manuscript review panel Nephrology Nursing Jour.; contbr. articles to profl. jours. Bremer scholar, 1987-90; recipient various grants. Mem.: ANA, Am. Nephrology Nurses Assn., Midwest Nursing Rsch. Soc., Ohio Nurses Assn., Golden Key, Phi Eta Si, Alpha Lambda Delta, Phi Kappa Phi, Sigma Theta Tau. Home: 2840 N Star Rd Columbus OH 43221-2959 Business E-Mail: jjacko@capital.edu.

JACKSON, ALETHEA WHITE, secondary educator; b. Hilton Head Island, S.C., June 12, 1944; d. Johnny LaSalle and Matilda (Williams) White; m. David Jackson, June 6, 1970; children: David Christopher, Lauren Alethea. BS, Savannah State Coll., 1967; MS in Edn., CCNY, 1972. Cert. permanent tchr., N.Y., N.J. Tchr. Jr. Acad., Bklyn., 1967-68, Bd. Edn., Bklyn., 1972, Madison Twp. Pub. Schs., Matawan, N.J., 1968-73; tchr.

headstart program St. Alban's Congl. Ch., Jamaica, N.Y., 1968-69; tchr. Elmont (N.Y.) Pub. Schs., 1973—. Mem. sch. discipline com. Clara H. Carlson Sch. Vol. pack 48 Cub Scouts Am., Uniondale, N.Y., 1983-87. Mem. N.Y. State Tchrs. Retirement Sys., Elemont Tchrs. Assn., Clara Carlson Tchrs. Assn., Telstar. Baptist. Avocations: reading, sewing, gardening, shopping, dancing. Home: 108 Lincoln Rd Hempstead NY 11550-5216

JACKSON, BARBARA TALBERT, education educator; b. Washington, Dec. 25, 1937; d. Wilbert Allen and Barbara Lee (Duckett) Talbert; m. Charles H. Jackson, Apr. 1, 1961; 1 child, Charles H. Jr. BS, D.C. Tchrs. Coll., 1959; MA, Antioch Coll., Yellow Springs, Ohio, 1971; PhD, Union Inst., 1982. Tchr. D.C. Pub. Schs., 1959-67, prin., 1972-77, asst. to asst. supt., 1977-82, asst. supt., 1982-87, exec. asst., 1987-90, vice supt., 1990-91, exec. dir., 1991—95; local advisor follow through U.S. Office Edn., Washington, 1967-71; dir. edn. Antioch Coll., 1971-72; asst. prof. Bowie State U., 1999—. Chair, bd. dirs. Nannie Helen Burroughs Sch., Washington, 2001—; mem. adv. bd. nat. hist. stds. UCLA, 1992—. Contbr. articles to profl. publs. Bd. dirs. Stoddart Nursing Home, Washington, 1990—. Ford Found. internat. studies fellow, 1967; recipient Disting. Pub. Svc. proclamation Mayor of Washington, 1993, Profl. Leadership proclamation Mayor of Ponce, P.R., 1993. Mem. ASCD (nat. pres. 1993-94, adv. bd. urban edn. initiative 1993—), Nat. Alliance of Black Sch. Educators, The Society (sec. 2003), Coalition of 100 Black Women, Phi Delta Kappa, Delta Kappa Gamma, Sigma Gamma Rho (Leadership award 1993). Democrat. Baptist. Avocations: interior decorating, reading, gardening, travel. Home: 1461 Leegate Rd NW Washington DC 20012-1211 Office: DC Pub Schs 415 12th St NW Washington DC 20004-1905

JACKSON, BETTY EILEEN, music and elementary school educator; b. Denver, Oct. 9, 1925; d. James Bowen and Fannie (Shelton) J. MusB, U. Colo., 1948, MusM, 1949, MusB in Edn., 1963; postgrad., Ind. U., 1952-55, Hochschule fur Musik, Munich, 1955-56. Cert. educator Colo., Calif. Tchr., accompanist, tchr. H.L. Davis Vocal Studios, Denver, 1949-52; tchg. assoc. Ind. U., Bloomington, 1952-53, U. Colo., Boulder, 1961-63, vis. lectr., summers 1963-69; tchr. Fontana (Calif.) Unified Sch. Dist., 1963—2002; pvt. studio, 1966—. Lectr. in music Calif. State U., San Bernardino, 1967-76; performer, accompanist, music dir. numerous musical cos. including performer, music dir. Fontana Mummers, 1980—, Riverside Cmty. Players, Calif., 1984—; performer Rialto Cmty. Theatre, Calif., 1983—; head visual and performing arts com. Cypress Elem. Sch., 1988-92. Performances include numerous operas, musical comedies and oratorios, Cen. City Opera, Denver Grand Opera, Univ. Colo., Ind. Univ. Opera Theater (leading mezzo), 3 tours of Fed. Rep. Germany, 1956-58; oratorio soloist in Ind., Ky., Colo., and Calif., West End Opera (lead roles), Riverside Opera (lead roles). Judge Inland Theatre League, Riverside, 1983-92; mem. San Bernardino Cultural Task Force, 1981-83; bd. dirs. Riverside-San Bernardino Counties Met. Auditions, 1988—; mem. adv. bd. Riverside Concert Opera, 1990-95. Fulbright grantee, Munich, 1955-56; named outstanding performer Inland Theatre League, 1982-84; recipient Outstanding Reading Tchr. award, 1990, Tchr. of Yr. nominations, 1990, 91, hon. svc. award, 1992. Mem. AAUW (bd. dirs., cultural chair 1983-86), NEA, Nat. Assn. Tchrs. Singing (exec. bd. 1985-89), Internat. Reading Assn., Music Educators Nat. Conf., Calif. Tchrs. Assn., Calif. Elem. Educators Assn., Fontana Tchrs. Assn., Music Tchrs. Assn., Arrowhead Reading Coun., San Bernardino Valley Concert Assn. (bd. dirs. 1977-83), Internat. Platform Assn., Nat. Assn. Preservation and Perpetuation of Storytelling, Order Eastern Star, Kappa Kappa Iota (v.p. 1982-83), Sigma Alpha Iota (life), Chi Omega. Avocations: community theater and opera, travel, collecting hummels and plates. Home: PO Box 885 Rialto CA 92377-0885

JACKSON, CHERYL K. English educator; b. Shreveport, La., Feb. 19, 1945; d. Elmer Nelse and Virginia Mae (DeVore) Kellerman; m. Donald T. Jackson, Aug. 7, 1971; 1 child, Brian Christopher. BA in English, Westminster Coll., New Wilmington, Pa., 1967; MEd in Sec. Edn./English, Pa. State U., 1976. Cert. tchr. sec. English, reading, Pa. Tchr. English Gateway Sr. H.S., Monroeville, Pa., 1967-71, I.C. Norcom H.S., Portsmouth, Va., 1972-73; adj. instr. English Tidewater C.C.-Portsmouth Campus, Portsmouth, 1981-92; instr. Tidewater C.C. Portsmouth Campus, 1992-95, asst. prof., 1995—; dir. Ethelyn Hardesty Morgan scholarship Tidewater C.C.-Portsmouth Campus, Portsmouth, 1996—. Seminar instr. effective bus. comm., stress mgmt., others. Co-author: New Handbook of Basic Writing Skills, 2002. Lector Ch. of the Resurrection, Portsmouth, 1980-88. Frick scholar for tchrs. The Frick Found., Pitts., 1970. Avocations: reading, travel. Office: Tidewater Cmty Coll 7000 College Dr Portsmouth VA 23703-6158

JACKSON, CYNTHIA LYNN, academic dean; b. N.Y.C., July 7, 1950; d. William Simon and Mary Henrietta (Saunders) J. BA, Spelman Coll., 1972; MA, Atlanta U., 1975; PhD, Ohio State U., 1982. Cert. K-8 tchr., Ga., K-12 tchr., sch. adminstr., Fla. Classroom tchr. DeKalb County Pub. Schs., Decatur, Ga., 1973-78; rsch. assoc., trainer Ohio State U., Columbus, 1978-82; head outreach and rsch. N.C. Sch. Sci. and Math., Durham, N.C., 1982-84; supr. instnl. analysis Duval County Pub. Schs., Jacksonville, Fla., 1984-87; dir. practicum rsch. Nova U., Ft. Lauderdale, Fla., 1987-89; pvt. practice ednl. cons., 1981—; dir. PhD program Barry U., Miami, Fla., 1991-92; asst. dean grad. sch., gra. sch. faculty mem. Union Inst., Cin., 1993—. Evaluator Fla. Dept. Edn., Tallahassee, 1990-91; cons. Miami-Dale C.C., 1990, N.C. A&T State U., Greensboro, 1990, U. N.C., Greensboro, 1989. Contbr. articles to profl. publs., chpts. to books. Chair edn. bd. Ascension Presbyn. Ch., Ft. Lauderdale, 1989-93; chair bd. dirs. Fla. Micro Bus., Ft. Lauderdale, 1992. Named to Women of Achievement Durham YWCA, 1984;' recipient Bd. Trustees Resolution for Svc. award N.C. Sch. Sci. and Math., 1984. Mem. Am. Ednl. Rsch. Assn., Phi Delta Kappa, Pi Lambda Theta (rsch. grantee 1992). Office: Union Inst 440 E Mcmillan St Cincinnati OH 45206-1925

JACKSON, CYNTHIA MARIE, elementary school educator; b. Phila., Dec. 18, 1941; d. Clarence and Dorothy (Booker) Cook; m. Howard C. Jackson, Nov. 14, 1964 (div. May 1983); 1 child, Michelle Yvette. BS in Edn., Cheyney (Pa.) U., 1964. Cert. tchr. elem. edn., Pa. Elem. tchr. Phila. Sch. Dist., 1964-67, Chester-Upland Sch. Dist., Chester, Pa., 1967—. Mem. ASCD, Nat. Coun. Tchrs. English. Democrat. Baptist. Avocations: classical music, opera, museums, shopping. Office: Smedley Middle School 1701 Upland St Chester PA 19013-5734 Home: 1246 E Sydney St Philadelphia PA 19150-2812

JACKSON, DAVID LEE, industrial education educator; b. Seminole, Okla., Sept. 4, 1952; s. Lemuel James Jr. and Bernice Hellen (Hurst) J.; m. Pamela June Haley, Feb. 2, 1974; children: Dalton Lee, Travis Wayne. Student, U. Cent. Okla., 1992--. Cert. tchr. Okla. Apprentice H and H Builders, Oklahoma City, Okla., 1970-73, Harrison Electric, Oklahoma City, 1973-74; electrician Univ. Hosp., Oklahoma City, 1974-89; supr. bldg. Okla. Med. Ctr., 1989-91; instr. electricity, indsl. tech. Moore Norman (Okla.) VoTech Ctr., 1991--. Electrical contractor, mechcanical journeyman, Noore Norman Votech, 1991--. Panel mem. Okla. State Electrical Inspectors, Norman, 1992; bd. dirs. Tecumseh Youth Program, Okal., 1979, 80, 81, 82. Recipient Star award Moore Norman Votech. Mem. Vocat. Indsl. Clubs Am. (advisor), Nat. Vocat. Honor Soc. (advisor). Democrat. Baptist. Avocations: skiing, hunting, fishing, golf, traveling. Office: Moore Norman Vocat-Tech Ctr 4701 12th Ave NW Norman OK 73069-8308

JACKSON, DAVID ROBERT, school system administrator; b. Long Beach, Calif., Jan. 15, 1945; s. Harlan Leroy and Helen Louise (Worthen) J.; m. Stacey Ann Bryan, Nov. 13, 1971; children: David, Daniel, Chad, Lcren, Darcy. Student, Fullerton Coll., 1963-64, Brigham Young U., 1965-67, Santa Ana Coll., 1977, Orange Coast Coll., 1977-78. Mgr. trainee Carl Karcher Enterprizes, Fullerton, Calif., 1964; asst. mgr. Household Fin. Co., Santa Ana., Calif., 1964-65; mgr. Chateau Apres Lodge, Park City, Utah, 1965-69; pres. Aero Wash Co., Santa Ana., Calif., 1970-79; pres., exec. dir. Fairmont Schs. Inc., Anaheim, Calif., 1979—. Former leader Boy Scouts Am.; bishop LDS Ch., Corona, 1990-96; chmn. Orange County 2000, Calif., 1991-93, also bd. dirs. Mem. Nat. Ind. Pvt. Sch. Assn. (bd. dirs. 1981—, founding mem., pres. 1993-98), Calif. Assn. Nationally Recognized Schs. (founder, pres. 1992-93), Orange County Pvt. Sch. Assn. (pres. 1990-93, founder). Republican. Avocations: snow skiing, geneology, private pilot. Office: Fairmont Sch 1575 W Marble St Anaheim CA 92802

JACKSON, DIANE WEST, special education educator, consultant; b. Boston, May 28, 1953; d. Karl Henry Jr. and Dorothy (Nielsen) West; m. Mark Jackson, Dec. 20, 1975; children: Jennifer Lynn, Nicholas Benjamin. BS, Framingham State Coll., 1975; MS, U. Maine, 1993, postgrad., 2000. Tchr. Leland Hall, Norfolk, Mass., 1975; spl. edn. tchr. Kingston (Mass.) Elem. Sch., 1975-79, Southport (Ind.) Mid. Sch., 1979-82; tchg. asst. U. Maine, Orono, 1994-99; spl. edn. cons. Bangor, Maine, 1996—; clin. instr. U. Maine, 1999—. Mem. adv. bd. United Techs. Ctr., Bangor, 1996-00; presenter in field. Vol. advocate for spl. edn., Maine pub. schs., 1994—. Mem. Learning Disabilities Assn. (exec. bd. dirs. 1996—), Coun. for Exceptional Children, Nat. Ctr. for Learning Disabilities, Maine parent Fedn., Assn. for Higher Edn. and Disability, Nat. Assn. for Devel. Edn., Phi Kappa Phi, Phi Delta Kappa. Home: 381 Howard St Bangor ME 04401-4151

JACKSON, EDWIN ATLEE, physicist, educator; b. Lyons, N.Y., Apr. 18, 1931; s. Frederick Wolcott and Helen Jean (Carroll) J.; m. Cynthia Ann Gregg; children: Eric Hugh, Mark Wolcott. BS in Physics, Syracuse U., 1953, MS in Physics, 1955, PhD in Physics, 1958. Asst. lectr. Brandeis U., Waltham, Mass., 1957-58; postdoctoral Airforce Cambridge Rsch. Ctr., Bedford, Mass., 1958-59; rsch. staff Princeton (N.J.) U., 1959-61; asst. prof. U. Ill., Urbana, 1961-64, assoc. prof., 1964-77, physics prof., 1977—. Dir. ctr. for complex systems rsch. Beckman Inst. U. Ill., Urbana, 1989—; vis. faculty FOM-Inst. Voor Plasma Fysica, Jutphaas, The Netherlands, 1967-68; vis. staff Los Alamos (N.Mex.) Sci. Lab., 1971; vis. prof. Chalmers U., Göteberg, Sweden, 1984; JIFT prof. Nagoya (Japan) U., 1984; core rschr. Santa Fe Inst., 1992—. Author: Equilibrium Statistical Mechanics, 1968, Perspectives of Nonlinear Dynamics, vol. 1, 1989, vol. 2, 1990, Exploring Nature's Dynamics, 2001; contbr. more than 80 articles to profl. jours. Fellow Am. Phys. Soc. Office: U Ill Dept Physics 1110 W Green St Dept Physics Urbana IL 61801

JACKSON, ERNESTINE HILL, elementary education educator; b. Gray, Ga., Oct. 24, 1939; d. William Thomas and Thelma (Lamar) Hill; m. Robert E. Blakeney, Jr., June 9, 1962 (div. Mar. 1971); 1 child, Alda Marcia; m. Albert Jackson, 1980. BS, Ft. Valley (Ga.) State Coll., 1961, postgrad., 1971, Ind. U., 1962-65, U. Calif., Santa Barbara, 1971. Cert. K-12 tchr., Ga. Tchr. Burke County Bd. Edn., Waynesboro, Ga., 1961-63, Atlanta Pub. Schs., 1965-69; libr. cataloguer U. Calif., 1970-71; tutor Atlanta Urban League, 1971-72; tchr. Atlanta Pub. Schs., 1973-80; tchr.'s aid Scott North Sch., O'Fallon, Ill., 1981; ednl. specialist Atlanta Urban League, 1983-83; tchr. early childhood edn. Atlanta Pub. Schs., 1965-69, 73-80, 83—. Recipient trophy Ragsdale Elem. Sch., Atlanta, 1974, plaque, 1975, 77, 78, C-Flag Pen, Pres. of U.S., 1989. Mem. Am. Fedn. Tchrs. (bldg. rep. 1983—), Am. Bus. Women's Assn. (chpt. formation chmn. 1990, sec., bull. chmn., Friendship Star award 1989, cert. 1990, Stars in Her Crown award 1990, pres. Atlanta Peach chpt. 1992, Inner Circle award 1993). Democrat. Home: 81 Oak Dr SW Atlanta GA 30354-2643 Office: Atlanta Pub Schs 399 Macedonia Rd SE Atlanta GA 30354-2854

JACKSON, GUIDA MYRL, writer, magazine editor, book editor, publisher; b. Clarendon, Tex., Aug. 30; d. James Hurley and Ina (Benson) Miller; m. Prentice Lamar Jackson (div. Jan. 1986); children: Jeffrey Allen, William Andrew, James Tucker, Annabeth Broomall Davis; m. William Hervey Laufer, Feb. 14, 1986. BA, Tex. Tech U.; MA, Calif. State U., Dominguez Hills, 1986; PhD, Greenwich U., Hilo, Hawaii, 1990. Tchr. secondary sch. English, Houston Ind. Sch. Dist., 1951-53, Ft. Worth Ind. Sch. Dist., 1953-54; pvt. tchr. music, freelance writer, Houston, 1956-71; editor newsletter Tex. Soc. Anesthesiologists, Austin, 1972-80; editor-in-chief Tex. Country mag., Houston, 1976-78; mng. editor Touchstone, lit. mag., Houston, 1976—. Contbg. editor Houston Town and Country mag., 1975—76; book editor Arte Publico, 1987—88; editor, pub. Panther Creek Press, 1999—; lectr. English U. Houston, 1986—95; instr. Montgomery Coll., 1996—; freelance writer, Houston, The Woodlands, Tex., 1978—. Author: (novels) Passing Through, 1979, A Common Valor, 1980, (play) The Lamentable Affair of the Vicar's Wife, 1989, (biog. reference) Women Who Ruled, 1990 (best reference lists award Libr. Jour. and Sch. Libr. Jour. 1990), (nonfiction) Virginia Diaspora, 1992, Virginia Diaspora CD-ROM, 2001, (lit. reference) Encyclopedia of Traditional Epic, 1994 (best reference list award ALA), (lit. reference) Traditional Epics: A Literary Companion, 1995, Encyclopedia of Literary Epics, 1996, (play) Showdown at Nosegay Cottage, 1997, (play) The Man From Tegucigalpa, 1998, (reference) Women Rulers Throughout the Ages, 1999, (play) Julia is Peculiar; editor: (anthologies) Heart to Hearth, 1989, African Women Write, 1990, Fall From Innocence, Memoirs of the Great Depression, 1998, (nonfiction) Legacy of the Texas Plains, 1994, Through the Cumberland Gap, 1995. Mem.: Houston Writers Consortium, Writers' Forum, Montgomery Lit. Arts Coun., Dramatists Guild, Woodland Writers Guild, Houston Writers Guild, PEN Ctr. West, Women in Comm. Avocations: music, gardening, poetry. Office: Panther Creek Press PO Box 130233 Spring TX 77373-0233 E-mail: panthercreek3@hotmail.com.

JACKSON, HERB, artist, educator; b. Raleigh, NC, Aug. 16, 1945; s. Walter H. and Virginia (Rogers) Jackson; m. Laura Dudley Grosch, June 9, 1967; children: Leif, Ulysses. BA, Davidson Coll., 1967; postgrad., Philips Universität; M.F.A., U. N.C., 1970. William H. Williamson Prof. Art Davidson Coll., NC, 1969—, chmn. dept. art, 1977-94; dir. Art Gallery, 1974-95; mem. artist adv. bd. Mint Mus. Art, Charlotte, NC, 1979-85. Bd. adv. Light Factory, Charlotte, 1990—, NC Dance Theater, NC, 1998. One-man shows include: Mint Mus. Art, Charlotte, 1973, U. Nev., Reno, 1973, Rahr Mus., Manitowoc, Wis., 1973, Jane Haslem Gallery, Washington, 1974, Nielsen Gallery, Boston, 1974, Impressions Gallery, Boston, 1975, 81, Hahn Gallery, Phila., 1976, Dryden Gallery, Charlotte, 1976, Van Straaten Gallery, Chgo., 1977, Frances Aronson Gallery, Atlanta, 1978, NC Mus. Art, Raleigh, 1979, Rowe Gallery, U. NC, Charlotte, 1979, Southeastern Center for Contemporary Art, Winston-Salem, NC, 1981, Phyllis Weil Gallery, NYC, 1981, 83, 85, 87, 88, 90, Princeton Gallery Fine Art, 1982, 83, Oxford Gallery (Eng.), 1982, DBR Gallery, Cleve., 1983, 84, Mint Mus. Art, Charlotte, NC, 1983, Springfield Mus. Art (Mo.), 1983, Asheville Mus. Art (NC), 1983, Nat. Acad. Scis., Washington, 1983, Cheekwood Art Ctr., Nashville, 1983, Reading Art Mus. (Pa.), 1984, Gulbenkian Found., Lisbon, Portugal, 1984, Huntsville Mus. Art (Ala.), 1984, Jerald Melberg Gallery, Charlotte, NC, 1984, 85, 87, 88, 90, 92, 93, 94, 96, 97, 98, 99, Fay Gold Gallery, Atlanta, 1986, 88, 92, Cumberland Gallery, Nashville, 1987, 96, Judy Youens Gallery, Houston, 1988, Peden Gallery, Raleigh, NC, 1988, 92, 93, Asheville (NC) Mus. Art, 1988, Allene Lapides Gallery, Santa Fe, 1989-90, Maurine Littleton Gallery, Washington, 1990, Hickory (NC) Mus. Art, 1993, St. Johns Mus. Art, Wilmington, NC, 1993, Bi-Nat. Cultural Ctr., Arequipa, Peru, 1994, parchman Stremmel Gallery, San Antonio, Tex., 1995-2001, Somerhill Gallery, Chapel Hill, NC, 1995, 98, Christa Faut Gallery, Cornelius, NC, 1996, 97, 99, 2000, 02, 03, La. Tech. U., Ruston, 1999, Lmar Dodd Art Ctr., La Grange, Ga., 1999, Greenville (NC) Mus. Art, 2000, Les Yeux du Monde, Charlottesville, Va., 2001, GSI Fine Art, Cleve., 2001, Fayetteville (NC) Mus. Art, 2002; numerous group shows, 1962—, latest being Internat. Print Biennale, Bradford, Eng., 1979, Mint Mus., Charlotte, 1979, 81, Southeastern Center Contemporary Art, Winston-Salem, 1979, Internat. São Paulo (Brazil) Bienal, 1979, Spring Mills Ann. Competition, Lancaster, SC, 1980, Weatherspoon Gallery, Greensboro, NC, 1980, Impressions Gallery, Boston, 1980, Associated Am. Artists, Phila., 1980, Am. Acad. and Inst. Arts and Letters, NYC, 1981, 1987, Bklyn. Mus. Art, 1981, World's Fair, Knoxville, Tenn., 1982, Davos, Switzerland, 1983, Palazzo Venezia, Rome, 1984, Miss. Mus. Art, 1984, U. Denver, 1984, Albuequerque Mus. Art, 1985, Fla. State U., 1985, St. John's Mus. Art, Wilmington, NC, 1986, U. Tex., San Antonio, 1987, Contemporary Arts Ctr. New Orlean, 1988, Kunstsammlungen der Veste Coburg, Fed. Republic Germany, 1988, Lorenzelli Fine Art, Milan, 1989, Exhbn. Hall of Union of Moscow Artists, Moscow, 1989, Samuel P. Harn Mus., Gainesville, Fla., 1990, New Orleans Mus. Art, 1995, Shanxia Govt. Art Gallery, Xian, China, 1996, Morris Mus. Art, Augusta, Ga., 1997, Mus. Del Vidrio, Monterey, Mex., 1999, Vanessa Suchar Fine Arts, London, Eng., 2000, Thomas McCormick Gallery, Chgo., 2002; represented in permanent collections: Balt. Mus. Art, Phila. Mus. Art, Victoria and Albert Mus., London, Whitney Mus. Art, NYC, Mpls. Inst. Arts, Nat. Acad. Sci., Washington, Indpls. Mus. Art, Bklyn. Mus., USIA, Japan, U. Wis., Sheboygan, Yale U., New Haven, Mus. Fine Arts, Boston, NY Public Library, Library of Congress, Washington, Mint Mus., Charlotte, So. Ill. U., Edwardsville, Kalamazoo Inst. Arts, Mus. Fine Arts, Springfield, Mass., Utah Mus., Salt Lake City, U. Nebr., Lincoln, U. Calif., Riverside, Minn. Mus. Art, St. Paul, Brit. Mus., London, others. Fellow Southeastern Ctr. for Contemporary Art Southeastern Seven, 1981, N.C. Visual Arts, 1984, Nat. Endowment for Arts and So. Arts Fedn., 1986; recipient N.C. award, 1999, Hunter-Hamilton Love of Tchg. award, 2003. Mem. Coll. Art Assn., So. Graphics Council, Charlotte Artists Coalition (dir. 1980-81), Mecklenberg-Charlotte Arts and Sci. Council (dir. 1977-79), Southeastern Coll. Art Conf. Home: PO Box 10 Davidson NC 28036-0010 Office: PO Box 7117 Davidson NC 28035-7117 Fax: 704 894-2691. E-mail: hejackson@davidson.edu.

JACKSON, JACQUELYN C. federal agency administrator; BA, Howard U.; M in edn., Doctorate in edn., George Washington U. Dir. student achievement sch. accountability programs US Dept. Edn., Wash., 2002—; staff US Dept. Edn., Off. Spec. Edn. and Rehab. Svcs., Wash.; tchr., adminstr. Pub. Schs., DC; adj. prof. George Washington U., Wash.; tchr. Trinity Coll., U. DC, Wash., DC. Office: US Dep Edn Student Achievement Sch Accountability 400 Maryland Ave FOB-6 Rm 3W230 Washington DC 20202*

JACKSON, JAMES SIDNEY, psychology educator; b. Detroit, July 30, 1944; s. Pete James and Johnnie Mae (Wilson) J. BS, Mich. State U., 1966; MA, U. Toledo, 1970; PhD, Wayne State U., 1972. Probation counselor Lucas County Juvenile Ct., Toledo, Ohio, 1967-68; tchg. and rsch. asst. Wayne State U., Detroit, 1968-71; from asst. prof. to prof. psychology U. Mich., Ann Arbor, 1971—, faculty assoc. Rsch. Ctr. Group Dynamics, 1971—, dir. Rsch. Ctr. Group Dynamics, 1996—, rsch. scientist, 1986—, faculty assoc. Inst. Gerontology, 1976—, faculty assoc. Ctr. Afro-Am. and African Studies, 1982—, dir. Ctr. Afro-Am. and African Studies, 1998—, assoc. dean Rackham Sch. Grad. Studies, 1987-92, prof. pub. health, 1990—, dir. program for rsch. on Black Ams., 1976—, Daniel Katz Disting. Univ. prof. psychology, 1995—, Daniel Katz Collegiate prof., 1994-95; Hill Disting. vis. prof. U. Minn., 1995. Chair sociol. psychology tng. program U. Mich., 1980-86, 93-96; cons. Emergency Sch. Aid Project, 1973-74, Commn. on Equal Opportunity in Psychology, 1970, Project to Provide Psychol. Svcs. to Head Start Programs, 1973-74, European Econ. Commn. Project on Racism, Xenophobia and Immigration, 1989—; mem. com. on aging and com. on status of Black Ams., panel on race, ethnicity and health in later life, Nat. Acad. of Scis., NAS; mem. com. on African Am. Population Year 2000 and 2010 U.S. Census Bur.; mem. nat. adv. com. Boston Mus. Sci., 1998—; mem. Nat. Adv. Coun. on Aging, NIH, 1996-99; mem. bd. sci. counselors, Nat. Inst. Aging; invited rschr. École des Hautes Etudes en Scis. Sociales, Paris, 1992—; disting. lectr. gerontology UCLA, 1992; mem. steering com. Nat. Acad. Aging Soc., 1995—. Author: The Black American Elderly: Research on Physical and Psychosocial Health, 1988, African American Elderly, 2d edit., 1997, (with Gurin P., Hatchett S.) Hope and Independence: Blacks Response to Electoral and Party Politics, 1989, Life in Black America, 1991, (with Chatters L., Taylor R.) Aging in Black America, 1993, (with H. Neighbors) Mental Health in Black America, 1996, (with R. Taylor and L. Clatters) Family Life in Black America, 1997; editor: New Directions: African Americans in a Diversifying Nation, 2000; editl. cons. Jour. Behavioral and Social Scientists; editl. bd. Jour. Gerontology, Applied Social Psychology Ann., Psychol. Bull., Jour. Social Issues; cons. editor Psychology and Aging; contbr. articles to profl. jours. Bd. dirs. Pub. Commn. on Mental Health, Ronald McDonald House, Ann Arbor, 1993—; bd. trustees Greenhills Sch., Ann Arbor, 1997-2003, v.p., 2002-03. Recipient Disting. Faculty Svc. award U. Mich., 1976, Harold R. Johnson Diversity Svc. award U. Mich., 2000; Urban Studies fellow Wayne State U., 1969-70; NSF fellow, 1969; Sr. Postdoctoral fellow Groupe d'Études et de Recherches sur la Science, École des Hautes Études en Sciences Sociales, 1986-87; Sr. Ford Found. Minority Postdoctoral fellow, 1986-87; Fogarty Sr. Internat. fellow, 1993-94; Robert W. Kleemeier award for rsch., Gerontol. Soc. Am. Fellow APA (divs. 9-20, policy and planning bd., fin. com. 1984-86, award for early contbns. 1983, Tenth Anniversary Peace and Social Justice award Soc. for the Study of Peace, Conflict and Violence, Peace Psychology divsn. 2000, com. on internat. relations, 1999-02, cahir 2001-02, Disting. Career Contbns. ro Rsch. award Divsn. 45, 2001), Am. Psychol. Soc., Gerontol. Soc. Am. (task force on minority issues in gerontology, chmn. 1988-92, ann. sci. conv. program com.); mem. AAAS (chair-elect sect. social, econ. and polit. scis.), Assn. Advancement of Psychology (trustee 1973-89, chmn. 1978-80), Inst. of Medicine, Nat. Acad. of Scis., Black Students Psychol. Assn. (nat. chmn. 1970-71), Assn. Black Psychologists (nat. chmn. 1972-73), Soc. Psychol. Study of Social Issues, World Future Soc., Assn. Behavioral and Social Scientists, Gerontol. Soc. Am. (chair behavioral and social scis. sect. 1997-98), Internat. Platform Assn., NIMH (nat. mental health coun. 1989-93, panel on equal access com. on instl. cooperation 1989-92), Psi Chi, Alpha Phi Alpha. Home: 340 Orchard Hills Dr Ann Arbor MI 48104-1832 Office: U Mich 5110 Inst Social Rsch 426 Thompson St Ann Arbor MI 48104-2321

JACKSON, JANIS LYNN, biology educator; b. Houston, May 9, 1952; d. Harrell James and Patricia Ann (Vernon) Odom; m. James Arthur Jackson, May 18, 1974; 1 child, Megan Michelle. AA, San Jacinto Coll., 1972; BS, East Tex. State U., 1974, MS, 1976. Biology instr. McLennan C.C., Waco, Tex., 1975—. Mem. chmn. instrn. subcom. McLennan C.C., Waco, 1980-81, chmn. faculty coun. rep., 1981-82, compensation com., 1990, co-chmn. instl. self study, 1990-91, profl. devel. com., 1992-93, mem. Tartan Scholars design com., 1995; judge paper presentations North Tex. Biol. Assn., Commerce, 1983, Tex. Acad. Sci., Nacodoches, 1990; vol. Assn. Locally Involved Vols. in Edn., Inc., Waco, 1979; rep. Gt. Tchrs. Workshop, Waco, 1989. Co-author: Basic Biological Concepts, 1983, rev. edit., 1984, 90, 95. Co-leader Camp Fire, Inc., Waco, 1993—; mem. Parents Assn.-St. Louis, Waco, 1991—. Recipient Nat. Inst. Staff and Orgn. Devel. Excellence award Internat. Conf. on Tchg. Excellence, 1991, 94. Mem. Tex. Jr. Coll. Tchrs. Assn., Instns. Master Plan Task Force (steering com. 1989). Republican. Presbyterian. Avocations: raising, training and showing hunter/jumpers, gardening, raising and showing poultry. Home: 307 Rogers Hill Spur Waco TX 76705-5733 Office: McLennan C C 1400 College Dr Waco TX 76708-1402

JACKSON, JO ANNE, speech pathologist; b. Lincoln, Nebr., Jan. 17, 1951; d. George B. and Evelyn Moore (Shirley) Scott; m. Joe Ellis Jackson, Dec. 18; children; Ty Joe, Clay Scott, Kyle Thomas, Jay Jordan. BA, N.Mex. State U., 1973, MA, 1992. Speech lang. pathologist Capitan (N.Mex.) Schs., 1987-88, High Plains Regional Ctr. Coop., Springer, N.Mex., 1988-95; speech/lang. pathologist The Children's Workshop,

Raton, N.Mex., 1989—; speech lang. pathologist Clayton Mcpl. Schs., 1995—2002; provider speech/lang. svcs. Texline (Tex.) Ind. Sch. Dist., 1995—2001; speech/lang. pathologist Maxwell Schs., 2001—, Cimarron Mcpl. Schs., 2002—. Mem. Am. Speech Lang. Hearing Assn. (cert.), N.Mex. Speech Lang. Hearing Assn. Avocations: baking, roping.

JACKSON, JOHN HOWARD, lawyer, educator; b. Kansas City, Mo., Apr. 6, 1932; s. Howard Clifford and Lucile (Deischer) J.; m. Joan Leland, Dec. 16, 1962; children: Jeannette, Lee Ann, Michelle. AB, Princeton U., 1954; JD, U. Mich., 1959. Bar: Wis. 1959, Mo. 1959, Calif. 1964, Mich. 1970. Pvt. practice law, Milw., 1959-61; assoc. prof., prof. law U. Calif., 1961-66; prof. law U. Mich., 1966-97; univ. prof. law Georgetown U., Washington, 1998—, dir. Inst. of Internat. Econ. Law. On leave gen. counsel U.S. Office Spl. Trade Rep., 1973-74, acting deputy spl. rep. for trade, 1974; vis. prof. U. Brussels, 1975-76; vis. fellow Inst. for Internat. Econs., Washington, 1983; Hessel E. Yntema prof. law U. Mich., 1983-97, assoc. v.p. acad. affairs, 1988-89; disting. vis. prof. law Georgetown Law Ctr., Washington, 1986-87, 93; Ford Found. cons. legal edn., vis. prof. U. Delhi, India, 1968-69; Hersch Lauterpacht Meml. lectr. Cambridge (Eng.) U., 2002. Author: World Trade and the Law of GATT, 1969, Contract Law in Modern Society, 1973, 2d edit., 1980, Legal Problems of International Economic Relations, 1977, 4th edit. (with William Davey and Alan Sykes), 2002; (with Jean-Victor Louis and Mitsuo Matsushita) Implementing the Tokyo Round, 1984; (with Edwin Vermulst) Anti-Dumping Law & Practice: Comparative Study, 1989; The World Trading System, 1989, 2d edit., 1997, Restructuring the GATT System, 1990; (with Alan Sykes) Implementing the Urugauy Round, 1997, World Trade Organization, 1998, The Jurisprudence of GATT and the WTO, 2000; editor-in-chief Jour. Internat. Econ. Law; bd. editors: Am. Jour. Internat. Law, Jour. Law and Policy in Internat. Bus., others; contbr. articles to profl. jours. With M.I. U.S. Army, 1954-56. Recipient Wolfgang Friedman Memorial award Columbia U., 1992; Rockefeller Found. fellow for study European community law Brussels, 1975-76 Mem. ABA, Am. Soc. Internat. Law (v.p. 1990-92), Am. Law Inst., Council Fgn. Relations, Phi Beta Kappa, Order of Coif. Office: Georgetown U Law Ctr 600 New Jersey Ave NW Washington DC 20001-2022

JACKSON, JOHN CHARLES, retired secondary education educator, writer; b. Columbus, Ohio, Mar. 12, 1939; s. John Franklin and Mari Jane (Lusch) J.; m. Carol Nancy Tiggelbeck, June 24, 1990. Tchr. social studies Buckeye Local Sch., West Mansfield, Ohio, 1961-62, Grandview Heights (Ohio) City Schs., 1962-91; ret., 1991. Cooperating tchr. Project Bus. program Jr. Achievement, Grandview, 1984-91. Recipient Career Tchr. award Ohio State U. Coll. Edn. Alumni Soc., 1995; Martha Holden Jennings Found. scholar, 1968-69. Mem. Ohio Ret. Tchrs. Assn. (life.), Franklin County Ret. Tchrs. Assn. (life), Ohio State U. Alumni Assn. (life), Am. Mensa Ltd. Republican. Methodist. Avocations: reading, tennis, college football. Home: 5741 Aspendale Dr Columbus OH 43235-7506

JACKSON, JUANITA WALLACE, educational consultant; b. Cin., Mar. 7, 1931; d. William J. and Viola D. (Shively) Wallace; m. John Arter Jackson, Apr. 21, 1967; children: Karon Gibson-Mueller, Blaine Gibson. BS, U. Cin., 1955; MEd, Miami U., Oxford, Ohio, 1963. Cert. elem. tchr., Md., elem. prin., Mass., tchr., shpr., adminstr., Ohio. Sr. supr. Mass. State Dept. Edn.; dir. kindergarten edn. Wilmington (Mass.) Pub. Schs.; coord. reading Cin. Pub. Schs.; exec. dir. Schoharie County Child Devel. Coun., Cobleskill, N.Y.; dir. bus. maintenance orgn. SUNY Rsch. Found., Albany. Cons. in field. Contbr. articles, book revs. to profl. publs. Chmn. N.Y. State Legis. Forum. Recipient cert. of achievement Schenectady County Reps., Schenectady County Community Coll., 1985, Tribute to Women award Albany YWCA, declaration of Mayor Whalen Juanita Wallace Jackson Day, Albany, July 10, 1990. Mem. AAUW (mem. edn. found., past pres. Schenectady br.), Woman's Club McLean (pres. 1994), LINKS Inc. (pres.), Delta Kappa Gamma (past pres. Alpha Kappa chpt.). Home: 1417 Trap Rd Vienna VA 22182-1642

JACKSON, JUDITH ANN, elementary education educator; Reading tchr. Gulfview Elem., Hancock County, Miss., 1993—. Office: Hancock County Sch. Dist. 17304 Highway 603 Kiln MS 39556-8210

JACKSON, LAMBERT BLUNT, academic administrator; b. Wilmington, Del., July 27, 1940; s. Wendell Ford and Margaret (Blunt) J.; m. Doris Vidal Jackson; children: L. Blunt, Margaret Julia Chantal, Etienne Vidal. BA, U. Del., 1964, MA in Am. Studies, 1965, PhD in History of Am. Civilization, 1976. Master The Marvelwood Sch., Cornwall, Conn., 1965-67; tchg. asst. dept. English U. Del., 1970-72, instr. dept. history, 1973-76, interim dir. Am. Studies Program, 1974; rsch. assoc. acad. founds. dept. Rutgers U., Camden, N.J., 1976-77, 78-79, acting dir., 1977-78, 80-81, adj. faculty dept. English, 1980-88, asst. dir. acad. founds. dept., 1984-87, acting dir., 1987, dir. Edn. Opportunity Fund Program, from 1988, assoc. dept. urban studies, from 1989, mem. grad. English faculty, from 1995. Mgmt. cons. Hispanic Health and Mental Health Assn. of So. N.J., Inc., 1981; supr. student tchr. English Rutgers-Camden Dept. Edn., 1983-85; project dir. City of Camden Youth Commn., 1986; devel. cons. Casa PRAC, Vineland, N.J., 1987; workshop leader Episcopal Diocese of N.J., 1989; cons. Hispanic Family Ctr., Camden, 1988. Author: They Serve: A History of And Salute to Service Clubs in Delaware, 1976, The American Poet, The Prairie Poet. Mem. Urban Coun. of Camden City Episcopal Parishes, 1983—; mem., v.p. Hispanic Task Force of Camden County, 1985-94; mem. Bishop's Hunger Task Force Episcopal Diocese of N.J., 1985, chair, 1986; del. rep. from diocese of N.J. to Nat. Impact Conf., Washington, 1986; mem. bd. trustees William Alexander Procter Found., 1986-92; warden, mem. vestry, clk. Grace Episcopal Ch., Haddonfield, N.J., 1986-90; commn. on ministry Diocese of N.J., Trenton, 1988—, anti-racism commn., 1997—, Hispanic commn., 1997—; trustee, treas. Shepherd's Gate, 1989—; curriculum com. Camden Bd. Edn., 1997-2000; officer Freinds of the Camden Libr., 1998—; pres. N.J. Minority Edn. Devel. Program. Grantee N.J. Dept. Higher Edn., 1979-80, 1990—, Pew Charitable Trust, 1987-90, Divsn. of Women, State of N.J., 1988-89, HUD, 1992-94, NSF, 1994-97, Bell Atlantic, 1997-98; recipient Andelot fellowship, 1964-65, 68-69, Univ. fellowship, 1968-69, 69-70, Tchg. assistantship, 1970-71, 71-72, Disting. Svc. award Rutgers Adminstrv. Assembly, 1990. Episcopalian. Avocations: collector of Am. and Chinese antiques, hist. restoration, garden design. Home: Haddonfield, NJ. Deceased.

JACKSON, LOLA HIRDLER, art educator; b. Faribault, Minn., Mar. 2, 1942; d. Earl Arthur and Marian Barbara (Pavek) Hirdler; children: Carilyn, Cherilyn, Marc. BS in Art Edn., Mankato State U., 1972, MA, 1975. Cert. tchr. Instr. art YWCA, Mankato, 1968-70; art instr. Mankato Area Vocat. Tech. Inst., 1971-72; pres., tchr., art dir. Jackson Studios, Mankato, 1969-78; art tchr. New Richland (Minn.) High Sch., Mankato (Minn.) State U., 1973-74; pres. Lola Ltd. Lt'ee Art Distbn., N.C., 1976—; tchr. art Lincoln Sch. Math. and Sci. Tech., Greensboro, N.C., 1988-90, chmn. dept., 1988, 89-90; tchr., chmn. art dept. Shallotte Mid. Sch., 1990—; instr. art Brunswick C.C., Supply, N.C., 1990-92; co-owner, pres. Jackson Carpenter Galleries, Ltd., Little River, S.C., 1997-99. Staff artist The Reporter, 1970-73; pres., bd. dirs. Fine Arts Inc., Gallery 500, Mankato, 1972-75. Bd. mem. Mankato Area Found., 1976-83. Recipient award Busch Found. Minn. Arts Coun., Nat. Endowment Arts, 1974. Mem. Profl. Pictures Framers Assn., N.C. Assn. of Edn. Republican. Roman Catholic. Avocations: stamp collecting, botany, birdwatching, biking, ballroom dancing.

JACKSON, MARY JANE MCHALE FLICKINGER, principal; b. Cleve., Feb. 23, 1938; d. Thomas William Flickinger and Margaret Julia (Lydon) Flickinger Nichols; m. Robert Lowell Jackson, June 27, 1959; children: Julia Anna Jackson Somers, Patricia Lauck, Margaret Jacqueline Jackson Tyler. BS in Speech, St. Louis U., 1959; postgrad., U. Copenhagen, 1961-62; MS in Spl. Edn., Southern Ill. U., 1965; EdD, George Washington U., 1977. Cert. tcht. Md. 1972. Tchr. Ritenour Sch. Dist., Overland, Mo., 1959-60; tutor Spl. Sch. Dist. Handicapped, St. Louis, 1960-61; tchr. Rugaards Franske Skole, Copenhagen, Denmark, 1961-62; substitute tchr., primary tchr. St. Louis and Ladue, Mo., 1962-65; tchr. L.A. City Schs., 1966-67, Woodlin Elem. Sch., Silver Spring, Md., 1967-68; various teaching positions, 1968-71, 73-81; asst. prin. Ritchie Park Elem. Sch., Rockville, Md., 1971-73, various supr. positions, 1974-79; asst. prin. Stephen Knolls Sch., Kensington, Md., 1981-88, prin., 1988-97; adj. prof., supr. spl. edn. student tchrs. Trinity Coll., 1997—. V.p. Concerned Citizens Exceptional Edn., Washington, 1968-70; surrogate parent Assn. Retarded Citizens, Washington. Bd. dirs. Archdiocesan of Washington, 1986-91; pres. Bd. Edn., Washington, 1990-91; bd. dirs. United Cerebral Palsy, Montgomery County, 1992—; presenter Young Adult Insts. Internat. Conf., 1994. Recipient Lisa Kane award, 1964; Fulbright scholar, Russia, 2002. Mem. Wash. Hearing Soc. (bd. dirs. 1969-81), Coun. Exceptional Children (exec. bd., pres. Montgomery county chpt. 1992-93, polit. action coord. for Md. fedn. 1993, exec. com. divsn. of internat. spl. edn. and svcs. 1993), Alexander Graham Bell Assn. (pub. rels. com. 1979—), Rotary (pres. Wheaton-Kensington club 2000-2001), AAUW (bd. v.p. for programs 2003—). Roman Catholic. Home: 9900 Georgia Ave Apt T-11 Silver Spring MD 20902-5241 E-mail: jacksonjb@aol.com.

JACKSON, MILES MERRILL, retired university dean; b. Richmond, Va., Apr. 28, 1929; s. Miles Merrill and Thelma Eugertha (Manning) J.; m. Bernice Olivia Roane, Jan. 7, 1954; children: Miles Merrill III, Marsha, Muriel, Melia. BA in English, Va. Union U., 1955; MS, Drexel U., 1956; postgrad., Ind. U., 1961, 64; PhD, Syracuse U., 1974. Br. libr. Free Libr., 1955-58; acting libr. C.P. Huntington Meml. Libr., Hampton (Va.) U., 1958-59, libr., 1959-62, asst. prof. libr. sci., 1958-62; territorial libr. Am. Samoa, 1962-64; chief libr. Trevor Arnett Libr., Atlanta U., 1964-69; also lectr. Sch. Libr. Sci.; assoc. prof. State U. N.Y., Geneseo, 1969-75; prof. U. Hawaii, 1975—, dean, 1983-95, chmn. interdisciplinary program in communication and info. scis., 1985-89; cons. in field, 1995—. Fulbright lectr. U. Tehran, Iran, 1968-69; libr., cons. Fiji, Samoa, Papua New Guinea, Micronesia, USIA India, 1993, Pakistan, 1985, Nat. Libr. Edn., 1996, Govt. Am. Samoa, 1997, Hawaii Pub. Libr. Found., 1986-2000; chmn. bd. Hawaii Lit., Inc., 1985-88; commr. Hawaii Libr. Commn., 1996-97. Editor: A Bibliography of Materials on Negro History and Culture for Young People, 1968, Comparative and International Librarianship, 1971, International Handbook of Contemporary Developments in Librarianship, 1981, Pacific Island Studies: Review of the Literature, 1986, Linkages Over Space and Time, 1993, And They Came: A Brief History of Blacks in Hawaii, 2001; mem. editl. bd. Internat. Jour. Info. Mgmt., Internat. Libr. Rev., 1982-87; founder, editor Pacific Info. and Libr. Svcs. Newsletter; contbr. articles to profl. jours.; book reviewer. Bd. dirs. Cen. YMCA, 1986-94, Hawaii Gov.'s Coun. on Literacy, 1986-96, Hawaii ACLU, 1990-94, office holder in Dem. party of Hawaii, 1992—. With USNR, 1946-48. Recipient Outstanding Alumnus award Va. Union U., 1987; Rsch. grantee Am. Philos. Soc., 1966; Coun. on Libr. Resources fellow, 1970, vis. fellow Republic of China, 1986; Harold Lancour fgn. travel awardee Beta Phi Mu, 1976 Mem. ALA (chmn. Internat. Rels. Roundtable 1988-89), Assn. for Libr. and Info. Sci. Edn. (pres. 1989-90), Coll. Lang. Assn. (hon. mention poetry 1954, 2d prize award short story 1955) Democrat.

JACKSON, PATRICIA MARIE, retired elementary education educator; b. Kansas City, Kans., July 9, 1937; d. William Taylor and Oma Belle (Bixler) Carter; m. James L. Jackson, Aug. 26, 1960; children: Jon Carter, Juli Gayle. BS in Edn., Abilene Christian U., 1959; MS in Edn., East Tex. U., 1972; postgrad., Tenn. State U., 1990. Music tchr., Abilene, Tex., 1960-61; tchr. Club Hill Elem., Garland, Tex., 1975-78; kindergarten tchr. McGavock, Cole Sch., Nashville, 1978-84; chpt. 1 tchr. Tom Joy Metro Sch., Nashville, 1984-86; kindergarten tchr. Glendale Mid. Sch., Nashville, 1986—91, ret., 2001. Adj. prof. David Lipscomb U., 1993—, music tchr. Tusculum Elem. Sch., 1999-2001. Recipient Career Ladder III award State of Tenn., 1986—. Mem. NEA, Tenn. Edn. Assn., Metro Nashville Edn. Assn. (Tchr. of Yr. 1992). Home: 3800 Belmont Blvd Nashville TN 37215-3006

JACKSON, RANDALL W. geography educator; b. Richland, Wash., Mar. 12, 1954; s. Max Eliot and Wilma Marie (Miller) J.; m. Leslie Marie Pennell, Aug. 11, 1979; children: Adam Douglas, Timothy Clay. BS, U. Utah, 1976; MS, U. Ill., 1980, PhD, 1983. Asst. prof. No. Ill. U., DeKalb, 1983-86; assoc prof. dept. geography Ohio State U., Columbus, 1986—2001; cons., pres. Bus. & Econ. Geographics, Columbus, 1988—2001; prof. geology, geography West Va. U., 2002—. Assoc. dir. rsch. computing Ohio State U., 1990-92, adj. prof., 2002—; adj. prof. econs. U. Pitts., 2003—. Contbr. articles to profl. jours.; editl. bd. Profl. Geographer, Geographical Analysis, Australasian Jour. Regional Studies, Jour. Regl. Sci. Mem. Regional Sci. Assn. Internat. (editor nat. newsletter 1997—, editor website 2000), Am. Assn. Geographers (bd. dirs. indsl. geog. splty. group 1989-90, bd. dirs. math models and quant. meth. splty. group 1998—), Internat. Input-Output Assn. Home: 199 Hickory Ridge Rd High View WV 26808 Office: Regional Rsch Inst 511 N High St Morgantown WV 26506

JACKSON, REBECCA M. elementary education educator, English as a second language educator; b. Franklin, Tenn., Oct. 29, 1962; d. Ralph Newton and Dewey Fay Miller. AA, Western Tex. Coll., Snyder, 1984; BS cum laude, All-Am. Tex. Tech U., 1987. Cert. tchr., tex. Tchr. Klondike Ind. Sch. Dist., Ackerly, Tex., 1988—89, Highland Bapt. Sch., Lubbock, Tex., 1991—92, Union Ind. Sch. Dist., Brownfield, Tex., 1993—96, Coahoma (Tex.) Ind. Sch. Dist., 1997—98, Grandfalls (Tex.)-Royalty Ind. Sch. Dist., 1998—99; ESL instr. Odessa (Tex.) Coll., 1998—99; ESL instr., ESL coord. Dalby Correctional Facility, Post, Tex., 1999—2003, Northeast Elem. Sch., Tex., 2003—. Recipient Outstanding Achievement award Adult Basic Edn. Program. Mem. Tex. Classroom Tchrs. Assn., Delta Psi Kappa (v.p.), Golden Key, Phi Epsilon Kappa (Outstanding scholar 1986-87). Baptist. Home: 1203 R Miller Rd Fluvanna TX 79517-3027

JACKSON, RICHARD PERRY, secondary school educator; b. Chgo., Sept. 7, 1950; s. Charles and Genevieve Jackson. BA, Midland Coll., 1974; MA, Chgo. State U., 1999. Basketball and track coach Emerson Sch. Dist. 152, 1974—79; phys. edn. instr. Harvey Sch. Dist. 152, 1974—97; varisty football and basketball coach Thornton High Sch., 1979—83; site supr. and program dir. Holmes Elem. Sch., 1993—95; pks. dept. chairperson of phys. edn. Sch. Dist 147, 2000—; adminstrv. asst. Rosa L. Park, 2001—, chair dept. phys. edn. Mem.: Tri County Official Assn., South Suburban Officals Assoc., Ctrl. Officals Assoc., Met. Officals Assoc., Am. Fed. Police, Fraternal Order of Police. Avocations: stepping, swimming, jogging, sports, music. Office: Rosa Parks Mid Sch 14700 Robey Ave Harvey IL 60426-1526

JACKSON, ROBERT LORING, science and mathematics educator, academic administrator; b. Mitchell, S.D., June 8, 1926; s. Olin DeBuhr and Edna Anna (Hanson) J.; divorced; children: Charles Olin, Catherine Lynne, Cynthia Helen. BS, Hamline U., 1950; MA, U. Minn., 1959, PhD, 1965. Tchr. math. and sci. pub. schs., Heron Lake, Minn., 1950-52; tchr. math. Lakewood (Colo.) Sr. H.S., 1952-53, Nouassuer Air Force Sch., Casablanca, Morocco, 1953-54, Baumholder (Germany) Elem. Sch., 1954-55, U. Minn. Univ. Lab. Sch., Mpls., 1955—60; asst. prof. Sci. and Math. U. Minn., Mpls., 1965-66, assoc. prof., 1966-70, prof., 1970-94, emeritus prof., 1994—, head sci. and math. edn., 1980-84, assoc. chmn., dir. undergrad. studies, curriculum-instrn., 1984-88, assoc. chmn., 1989-92. Vis. prof. Hamline U., St. Paul, 1958, Mont. State U., Bozeman, 1981, Bethel Coll., St. Paul, 1981, No. Mich. U., Marquette, 1983-84; cons. math. Minn. Dept. Edn., St. Paul, 1960-62. Co-author: (book/man series) Laboratory Mathematics, 1975-76. Bd. dirs. Oratorio Soc. Minn.; bd. dirs. Minn. Chorale, Mpls., 1973-88, pres., 1978-80. With U.S. Army, 1944-46. Decorated Purple Heart; recipient 1st Alumni award U. Minn., 1988, Disting. Tchg. award Coll. Edn., 1984. Mem. Nat. Coun. Tchrs. Math. Methodist. Home: 810 Purple Sage Ter Henderson NV 89015-5692

JACKSON, ROSA M. educator; b. Columbia, S.C., Dec. 8, 1943; d. Alvin Jr. and Rosa Lee (Reese) Oree; m. Olin D. Jackson, June 14, 1969; children: Zandra Lalita, Delin Jawaski. BA, Benedict Coll., 1966; MEd, S.C. State U., Orangeburg, 1981. Cert. tchr. Tchr. 1st grade Richmond County Bd. Edn., Augusta, Ga.; tchr. 2nd grade McDuffie County Bd. Edn., Thomson, Ga.; tchr. 5th grade Lancaster County Bd. Edn., Kershaw; tchr. 2nd grade Richmond County Bd. Edn., Augusta, Ga. Mem. Richmond County Schs. Leadership Team. Sci. tchr. in residence. Mem. GAE, RCAE, NEA, Nat. Sci. Tchrs Assn., Ga. Sci. Tchrs. Assn., GA Staff Devel. Coun., Assn. for Multicultural Sci. Edn. Home: 3003 Bramble Wood Trl Augusta GA 30909-4105

JACKSON, RUTH NAOMI, primary school music educator; b. Buffalo, Dec. 8, 1940; d. Frank Earl and Violet Arietta (Walker) Stevick; m. Ernest George Jackson, June 25, 1966 (div. Feb. 1980). AA, Pensacola Jr. Coll., 1975; BA, U. West Fla., 1977, MA, 1982. Music tchr. Dixon Primary Sch., Pace, Fla., 1977—, acting asst. to prin., 1994-99, mem. sch. adv. coun., 1994-95. Choral coord. Santa Rosa Sch. Bd., Milton, Fla., 1990—; mem. choir Northridge Ch.; mem. sch. improvement team Dixon Elem. Sch., Pace, 1991-93. Sec.-treas. Pace Civic Assn., Inc., 1992—; mem. Choral Soc. of Pensacola, 1991—; mem. Chamber Singers Choral Soc. Pensacola, 1996-98; mem. sch. adv. coun. S.S. Dixon Primary Sch., 1997-99. Named S.S. Dixon Elem. Tchr. of Yr., 1985; Mini-grantee Jr. League of Pensacola, 1984-85, Santa Rosa Sch. Bd., 1993. Mem. NEA, Fla. Tchg. Profession, Santa Rose Profl. Educators, Music Educators Nat. Conf., Fla. Elem. Music Edn. Assn., Am. Orff-Schulwerk Assn., Delta Kappa Gamma (pres. chpt. 1997-2000). Republican. Avocations: travel, reading, gardening, sewing, crafts. Home: 4372 W Avenida De Golf Pace FL 32571-3060 Office: Dixon Primary Sch 4585 SS Dixon St Pace FL 32571 E-mail: ruthnjackson@mchsi.com., jacksonrn@mail.santaroas.k12.fl.us.

JACKSON, SHARON BROOME, elementary educator; b. Sarasota, Fla., Sept. 3, 1952; d. Stanley Frank and Aileen Rita (Murphy) Broome; m. Thomas Harold Jackson Jr., Nov. 22, 1975; children: Thomas Harold III, Stanley David. Student, Ga. So. Coll., 1970-71; BS in Edn., U. Ga., 1973, MS in Edn., 1976; postgrad., West Ga. Coll., 1976. Cert. tchr. Kindergarten-8th grades, Ga., supervising tchr. child abuse edn., drug/alcohol awareness tchr. Tchr. 7th and 8th grades Winder-Barrow Mid. Sch., Winder, Ga., 1973-75; tchr. 5th and 6th grades Dunson Elem. Sch., LaGrange, Ga., 1975-80; tchr. 4th grade Oconee County Schs., Watkinsville, Ga., 1980-97, tchr. 3d grade, 1997—2003, tchr. early intervention program, 2003—. Presenter, tchr. tng. Ga. Assn. Marine Sci. Educators, 1990; presenter tchr. stress mgmt. workshop, Watkinsville, 1990. Vol. local shelter for the homeless, local soup kitchen; mem. 1st United Meth. Ch., pres. United Meth. Women's Circle. Named Oconee County Tchr. of Yr., 1989-90; one of 20 tchrs. statewide chosen to participate in Marine Sci. Edn. program, 1989. Mem. Profl. Assn. Ga. Educators, Ga. Sci. Tchrs. Assn., Nat. Coun. Tchrs. Math. Avocation: reading historical fiction. Home: 1021 N Rossiter Ter Watkinsville GA 30677-5124 Office: Oconee County Elem Sch Hog Mountain Rd Watkinsville GA 30677

JACKSON, SHEILA BERNICE, principal; b. N.Y.C. d. Samuel Alex and Louise (Rodgers) J. Bachelors in Elem. Edn., Morgan State U., 1970; Masters in Reading, CCNY, 1975; Diploma in Edn. Adminsrtn. and Supr., Fordham U., 1980. Cert. bldg. adminstr. N.Y. Tchr. PS 161 Manhattan CSD 5, N.Y.C., 1970-75, PS 269 Bklyn. CSD 22, 1983-75, adminstrv. asst., 1983-84; prin. PS 30 Queens CSD 28, Jamaica, N.Y., 1991--. Adj. prof. Coll. New Rochell, N.Y., 1989--. Named Educator of Yr. Cath. Tchrs. Assn., 1988. Mem. N.Y. Assn. Black Educators, Alpha Kappa Alpha (pres. 1986). Office: PS 30 Queens 12610 Bedell St Jamaica NY 11434-3199

JACKSON, SHELIA LUCYLE, physical education educator, consultant; b. Newport, Ark., Sept. 28, 1960; d. Charles Wayne Jackson nd Marette McCauley Stiritz. BSE, So. Ark. U., 1981; MEd, U. Ark., 1984; PhD, Tex. Woman's U., 1988. Tchr. phys. edn. and health Crossett (Ark.) H.S., 1982-83; adapted phys. edn. asst. Richardson Ctr., Fayetteville, Ark., 1983-84; instr. NCAA Youth Sports program U. Ark., Fayetteville, 1984-85; biomechs. lab. asst. Tex. Woman's U., Denton, 1986; adapted phys. edn. cons. Duncanville (Tex.) Sch. Dist., 1987; asst. prof., dir. tennis U. Puget Sound, Tacoma, 1987-90; asst. prof. kinesiology U. N.C., Charlotte, 1990-95, U. Ctrl. Ark., Conway, 1995-98; assoc. prof. phys. edn. Ark. Tech. U., Russellville, 1998—. Coord. elem. conf. U. Ctr. Ark., 1997; cons. Charlotte Observer. Contbr. chpt. to book, articles to profl. jours. Vl. tchr. First Presbyn. Aftersch. Program, Conway, 1995; volleyball marathon team mgr. Easter Seals, Charlotte, 1992-93; event coord. Charlotte Mecklenburg Sr. Games, 1992, Valleyfeast, Russellville, 2003; bd. dirs. So. Assn. for Women in Physical Activity, Sport, and Health, 2003 Recipient Young Alumni award So. Ark. U., 1999; rsch. and tchg. grantee PEAK Performance Techs., 1997, U. Ctrl. Ark., 1996. Mem. AAHPERD (presider 1993), Ark. Alliance for Health, Phys. Edn., Recreation and Dance (bd. dirs. 1998—), Profl. Disc Golf Assn. (chmn. women's com. 1997-98, Women's Disc Golf Rookie of Yr. award 1995, Women's Disc Golf Master World Champion award 1997), Internat. Soc. Biomechanics in Sports, Internat. Fedn. Adapted Phys. Activity, USTA. Christian. Avocations: tennis, volleyball, cycling, backpacking, badminton. Office: Ark Tech U Dept Phys Edn Russellville AR 72801 Home: 278 Carothers Ln Russellville AR 72802-8227

JACKSON, STANLEY EDWARD, retired special education educator; b. Washington, Sept. 3, 1918; s. Eugene Edward and Inez Christine (Booth) Jackson. BS, Miner Tchrs. Coll., Washington, 1939; MA, Columbia U., 1947, profl. diploma, 1948, EdD, 1958; postgrad., Johns Hopkins U., Peabody Inst. Elem. tchr. DC Pub. Schs., 1940-58, elem. sch. prin., 1958-66, dir. spl. edn., 1966-72; gov.-at-large Coun. Exceptional Children, Reston, Va., 1971-72, asst. exec. dir., membership, 1972-82; ret., 1982. Lectr. Cath. U., Washington, 1965—66, asst. prof. edn., 1967; instr. DC Tchrs. Coll., 1971—72, initiator Tchr. Aide Program Spl. Edn. Classes, 1968; founder Juvenile Decency Corps Uplift House, 1964; co-planner Mamie D. Lee Sch. Mentally Retarded, 1968. Author: School Organization for the Mentally Retarded, 1973, Educational Strategies and Services for Exceptional Children, 1976. Pres. Area K Bd. Commrs. Youth Coun., Washington, 1959—65; founder UPLIFT Cmty. House, Washington, 1963, pres. Chpt. 49, 1962—64, 1st pres. Fedn. 524, 1965—66; bd. dirs. Found. Exceptional Children, 1978. With U.S. Army, 1941—45, WWII. Decorated 4 Battles Stars; named Stanley E. Jackson Scholarship in his honor, Peabody Pres., Johns Hopkins U., 1988. Found. for Exceptional Children, 1980, Philanthropic Honor Roll, George Washington U., 1949—2001; recipient Yes I Care award, Found. for Exceptional Children, 1992, Plaque for Outstanding Svc., Commr. Coun., Washington, 1963, Outstanding Ret. Tchr. award, Jr. Citizens Corps, 1979, Stanley E. Jackson Spl. Edn. award established in his honor, Bd. Edn. D.C. Pub. Schs., 1973, Cert. of Appreciation, Nat. Fedn. Blind, 2001. Mem.: NAACP, AAUP, NEA, Dept. Elem. Sch. Prins., Coun. Exceptional Children, DC Congress Parents and Tchrs., Johns Hopkins Assoc. Program, Urban League, AMVETS, Phi Delta Kappa, Kappa Delta Pi. Avocations: music, numismatics, writing, philanthropy. Home: Apt 703 One E University Pky Baltimore MD 21218

JACKSON, THOMAS HUMPHREY, academic administrator, lawyer; b. Kalamazoo, June 20, 1950; s. William Humphrey and Louise Longstreth (Cone) Jackson; m. Bonnie Eileen Gelb; children: Richard, Steven. BA, Williams Coll., 1972; JD, Yale U., 1975. Bar: N.Y. 1976, Calif. 1979. Law clk. to judge U.S. Dist. Ct. N.Y., 1975—76; law clk. to justice U.S. Supreme

Ct., Washington, 1976—77; asst. prof., assoc. prof. to prof. Stanford U. Law Sch., Calif., 1977—86; prof. Harvard U. Law Sch., Cambridge, Mass., 1986—88; dean Sch. Law, U. Va., Charlottesville, 1988—91, v.p., provost, 1991—93; pres. U. Rochester, NY, 1994—. Assoc. Heller, Ehrman, White & McAliffe, San Francisco, 1979—81, spl. counsel, 1981—86. Co-author: Secured Transactions, 1982, Secured Transactions, 3d edit., 2000, Bankruptcy, 1985, Bankruptcy, 3d edit., 2000; author: Logic and Limits of Bankruptcy Law, 1986; mem. editl. bd.: The Found. Press, Inc. Trustee George Eastman House. Office: University of Rochester 240 Wallis Hall Rochester NY 14627-0011

JACKSON, THOMAS MICAJAH, former state legislator, lawyer; b. Radford, Va., May 22, 1957; m. Cynthia Paylette Jones; children: Thomas M. III, Jenna Katharine. BA, Hampden-Sydney Coll., 1979; JD, Coll. William & Mary, 1982. Mem. Va. State Legis., 1988—2002, mem. edn. com., mem. appropriations com., mem. agrl. com., mem. militia & police com.; county atty. Carol County, Va., 1983, 1987; atty. Thomas M. Jackson, Jr. and Assoc., Hillsville; mem. Va. State Bd. of Edn., 2002—, pres., 2003—. Democrat. Methodist. Office: Thomas M Jackson Jr and Assoc 227 N Main St PO Box 130 Hillsville VA 24343

JACKSON, VIVIAN MICHELE, church administrator, consultant; b. Yonkers, N.Y., Feb. 17, 1953; d. Evelyn Green Alexander-Booker; m. Harry R. Jackson, Jr., Dec. 25, 1976; children: Joni Michele, Elizabeth Rountree. BA in Edn., Wittenberg U., 1975; MA in Edn., Northeastern U., 1980; MA in Theology, Logos Bible Coll., Fla., 1986. Tchr. Cleve. Pub. Schs., 1975-77, Cin. Pub. Schs., 1977-78, Boston Pub. Schs., 1978-79; grad. asst. Northeastern U., Boston, 1979-80; pres. Word of Life Broadcast, Christian Hope Ctr., Corning, N.Y., 1981-84, assoc. pastor, 1981-88; founder, dir. Hope Christian Acad., Corning, 1987-88, College Park, Md., 1989-96; prof. Hope Bible Coll., College Park, 1994—2002; cons. Hope Christian Ch., College Park, 1988—, dir. children's ministry, 1989-92, assoc. pastor, 1994—. COO, 1996—; mgr. svcs. Christian Hope Ministries, 2002—. Cons. Hope Christian Ch., 1988—. Named one of Outstanding Young Women of Am., 1981, 1984. Avocations: swimming, reading, women's issues, public speaking, missions.

JACKSON-HOLMES, FLORA MARIE, lawyer, educator; b. Miami, Fla., June 1, 1957; d. Andrew and Elizabeth (Oliver) Jackson; m. Myron William Holmes, Apr. 16, 1988. BS, Fla. Meml. Coll., 1978; JD, Howard U., 1982. Bar: Fla. 1984, U.S. Dist. Ct. (so. dist. Fla.). Staff atty. James E. Scott Cmty. Assn., Miami, 1985-87, sr. atty., 1987-89; pvt. practice Miami, 1990—. Code enforcement hearing officer Dade County; adj. prof. law, Fla. Meml. Coll., Miami, 1989—; legal advisor Delta Sigma Theta Alumnae of Dade County, 1997. Recipient Pro Bono award Domestic Violence Legal Aid of Greater Miami, 1996, Cert. Appreciation Charles R. Drew Elem. Sch., 1997, Miami Golden Glades Optimists, 1996. Mem. Nat. Black Lawyers (treas. 1986-87), Fla. Bar Assn. (women lawyer's divsn.), NBAWLD (sec. 1996), Delta Sigma Theta. Democrat. Baptist. Avocations: reading, working with youth, travel. Home: 15728 NW 7th Ave Miami FL 33169-6255 Office: 10735 NW 7th Ave Miami FL 33168-2103

JACOB, BRUCE ROBERT, law educator; b. Chgo., Mar. 26, 1935; s. Edward Carl and Elsie Berthe (Hartmann) J.; m. Ann Wear, Sept. 8, 1962; children: Bruce Ledley, Lee Ann, Brian Edward. BA, Fla. State U., 1957; JD, Stetson U., 1959; LLM, Northwestern U., 1965; SJD, Harvard U., 1980; LLM in Taxation, U. Fla., 1995. Bar: Fla. 1959, Ill. 1965, Mass. 1970, Ohio 1972. Asst. atty. gen. State of Fla., 1960-62; assoc. Holland, Bevis & Smith, Bartow, Fla., 1962-64; asst. to assoc. prof. Emory U. Sch. Law, 1965-69; rsch. assoc. Ctr. for Criminal Justice, Harvard Law Sch., 1969-70; staff atty. Cmty. Legal Assistance Office, Cambridge, Mass., 1970-71; assoc. prof. Coll. Law, Ohio State U., 1971-73, prof., dir. clin. programs, 1973-78; dean, prof. Mercer U. Law Sch., Macon, Ga., 1978-81; v.p., dean, prof. Stetson U. Coll. Law, St. Petersburg, Fla., 1981-94, dean emeritus and prof., 1994—. Contbr. articles to profl. jours. Mem. Fla. Bar, Sigma Chi. Democrat. Home: 1946 Coffee Pot Blvd NE Saint Petersburg FL 33704-4632 Office: Stetson U Coll Law 1401 61st St S Saint Petersburg FL 33707-3246 E-mail: jacob@law.stetson.edu.

JACOB, DEIRDRE ANN BRADBURY, manufacturing executive, business educator, consultant; b. Providence, Mar. 7, 1952; d. John Joseph and Marion Damon (Shute) Bradbury; m. Thomas Keenan, Nov. 15, 1975 (div. Dec. 1980); 1 child: Victoria Irene; m. Robert A. Jacob, June 22, 1996; 1 child, Meggin Rosemary. BA in Govt. and Law, Lafayette Coll., 1973. Supr. Procter & Gamble Mfg. Co., S.I., N.Y., 1973-76, mgr. warehouse dept., 1976-79, mgr. shortening and oils, 1979-81, fin. mgr. food plant, 1981-82, mgr. personnel, 1982-86, mgr. total quality and pub. affairs, 1986-91; ptnr. Avraham Y. Goldratt Inst., New Haven, Conn., 1991—. Cons. Procter & Gamble, S.I., 1987—89, Cin., 1989—91. Trustee Lafayette Coll., 1985-90. Mem. Lafayette Coll. Alumni Assn. (pres. 1992-94, Clifton P. Mayfield award), Maroon Club (Easton, Pa., pres. 1987-89). Roman Catholic. Avocation: singing. Office: Avraham Y Goldratt Inst 442 Orange St New Haven CT 06511-6201

JACOB, ELIZABETH ANN, elementary education educator; b. Highland Park, Mich., May 14, 1950; d. Theodore George and Helen Mae (Kressbach) J. BS, Ea. Mich. U., 1972; MA, Cen. Mich. U., 1976. Master gardener, 1999—. Tchr. Tawas City (Mich.) Elem. Sch., 1972—. Dir. region II MCTM, 1995; co-chair NCA 1995-2001. Sunday sch. tchr. Zion Luth. Ch., Tawas City, 1976-89, mem. bd. edn., 1990, 2000-02, mem. bd. fin., 1995-96; instr. water safety Oscoda-Iosco County chpt. ARC, 1979-90; treas. Animal Humanitarians Iosco, 1995-2003. Office: Tawas City Elem Sch 825 2nd St Tawas City MI 48763-9191

JACOB, PAUL BERNARD, JR., electrical engineering educator; b. Columbus, Miss., June 9, 1922; s. Paul Bernard and Sarah Dorsey (Jamison) J.; m. Mildred Evelyn Hammack, Aug. 20, 1946; children: William Boswell, Paul Bernard, III. BS in Elec. Engring., Miss. State U., 1944; MS, Northwestern U., 1948. Registered profl. engr., Miss. Engr., Tenn. Eastman Corp., Oak Ridge, 1944-46; mem. faculty Miss. State U., 1946-88, prof. elec. engring., 1956-88, prof. emeritus, 1988—, assoc. head dept., 1962-88, Paul B. Jacob high voltage lab. and endowed prof. chair elec. and computer engring. dept. Cons. in field; mem. steering com. Internat. Symposium on High Voltage Engring., 1987—. Author articles on high voltage engring. Recipient Alumnus of Yr. award Miss. State U., 1987, UOP Tech. award Instrument Soc. Am., 1988 Mem. IEEE (life), Power Engring. Soc. (chmn. com., Com. Disting. Svc. award), Am. Soc. Engring. Edn., Sigma Xi, Tau Beta Pi, Eta Kappa Nu (dir. 1962-63, nat. v.p. 1982-83, nat pres. 1983-84), Phi Kappa Phi, Sigma Alpha Epsilon (bd. dirs. 1961-69, nat. pres. 1969-71, Disting. Svc. award 1975, Highest Effort award for profl. accomplishments 1986, Merit Key award, Order of the True Gentleman 1994), Omicron Delta Kappa. Clubs: Rotary (past pres. Starkville, Miss.). Baptist. Home and Office: 102 Kenswick Ct Starkville MS 39759-9493 E-mail: pbj@ece.msstate.edu.

JACOB, ROBERT JOSEPH KASSEL, computer scientist, educator; b. Nov. 11, 1950; s. Ezekiel Joseph and Ethel Charlotte (Behr) Jacob; m. Kathryn Ann Allamong, June 9, 1973; children: Charlotte Allamong, Anne Elizabeth. BA, Johns Hopkins U., 1973, MSE, 1974, PhD, 1976. Tchg. asst., rsch. asst. Johns Hopkins U., Balt., 1972—76; computer scientist Naval Rsch. Lab., Washington, 1977—94; assoc. prof., lectr. George Washington U., Washington, 1978—94; assoc. prof. Tufts U., Medford, Mass., 1994—. Vis. prof. media lab. MIT, Cambridge, Mass., 2000—01. Assoc. editor: ACM Trans on Computer-Human Interaction, 1992—; contbr. chpts. to books, articles to profl. publs. Fellow, Johns Hopkins U., 1973—75. Mem.: IEEE, Human Factors Soc., Assn. Computing Machinery (vice chmn. Spl. Interest Group Computer-Human Interaction 2001—, recognition of svc. award 1999). Jewish. Avocations: sailing, piano, designing electronic organs. Home: 30 Valleyfield St Lexington MA 02421-7908 Office: Tufts U Dept Computer Sci Medford MA 02155

JACOB, STANLEY WALLACE, surgeon, educator; b. Phila., 1924; s. Abraham and Belle (Shulman) J.; m. Marilyn Peters; 1 son, Stephen; m. Beverly Swarts; children: Jeffrey, Darren, Robert; m. Gail Brandis; 1 dau., Elyse. MD cum laude, Ohio State U., 1948. Diplomate: Am. Bd. Surgery. Intern Beth Israel Hosp., Boston, 1948-49, resident surgery, 1949-52, 54-56; chief resident surg. service Harvard Med. Sch., 1956-57, instr., 1958-59; asso. vis. surgeon Boston City Hosp., 1958-59; Kemper Found. research scholar A.C.S., 1957-60; asst. prof. surgery U. Oreg. Med. Sch., Portland, 1959-66, asso. prof., 1966—; Gerlinger prof. surgery Oreg. Health Scis. U., 1981—. Author: Structure and Function in Man, 5th edit, 1982, Laboratory Guide for Structure and Function in Man, 1982, Dimethyl Sulfoxide Basic Concepts, 1971, Biological Actions of DMSO, 1975, Elements of Anatomy and Physiology, 1989; contbr. to: Ency. Brit. Served to capt. M.C. AUS, 1952-54; col. Res. ret. Recipient Gov.'s award Outstanding N.W. Scientist, 1965; 1st pl. German Sci. award, 1960; Markle scholar med. scis., 1960 Mem. Phi Beta Kappa, Sigma Xi, Alpha Omega Alpha. Achievements include co-discovery of therapeutic usefulness of dimethyl sulfoxide and MSM. Home: 1055 SW Westwood Ct Portland OR 97201-2708 Office: Oreg Health Scis U Dept Surgery 3181 SW Sam Jackson Park Rd Portland OR 97201-3011 E-mail: jacobs@ohsu.edu.

JACOBE, CAROL ANN, secondary school educator; b. Mt. Vernon, NY, May 12, 1950; d. John Benjamin and Rose Jean (Spinelli) Troini; m. Ivan William Jacobe (div. 1983). B.Music Edn., Syracuse U., 1972; M.Music Edn., Syracuse U., 1973. Mid. sch. choral and gen. music tchr. Soule Rd. Mid. Sch., Liverpool, NY, 1972—81; music, chorus and voice tchr. C.W. Baker H.S., Baldwinsville, NY, 1981—. Composer: (choral) Sing of Live and Peace Alleluia, 1980. Founder, dir. Silk & Satin Vocal Jazz Ensemble, 1981—. Named Tchr. of the Yr., C.W. Baker H.S., 1994, Outstanding Music Educator, Syracuse U., 1985; recipient Pride of Workmanship award, Rotary, 1994, gold ratings throughout the U.S. and Can. in competitions. Mem.: Onondaga County Music Educators Assn., N.Y. State Sch. Music Assn. (asst. chairperson 1981—82, chairperson 1982—85, all-state vocal jazz judge 1982—, asst. chmn. 2002—), Internat. Assn. of Jazz Educators, Am. Choral Dirs. Assn. Avocations: rollerblading, skiing.

JACOBS, ALAN MARTIN, physicist, educator; b. N.Y.C., Nov. 14, 1932; s. Samuel J. and Amelia M. (Ziegler) J.; m. Evelyn Lee Banner, Aug. 7, 1955 (dec. Jan. 1977); children: Frederick Ethen, Heidi Joelle; m. Sharon Lynn Auerbach, Oct. 14, 1978; children: Aaron Michael, Seth Joseph. B.Engring. Physics (John McMullen scholar, LeVerne Noyes scholar, Clevite scholar), Cornell U., Ithaca, N.Y., 1955; postgrad., Oak Ridge Sch. Reactor Tech., 1955-56; MS, in Physics, Pa. State U., 1958, PhD, 1963. Research asso. nuclear reactor facility Pa. State U., 1956-63, mem. faculty, 1963—, prof. nuclear engring., 1968-80; prof. U. Fla., Gainesville, 1980—, chmn. dept. nuclear engring. scis., 1980-82; chief scientist Future Tech, Inc., Gainesville, 1986-87. Cons. to industry. Co-author: Basic Principles of Nuclear Science and Reactors, 1960; patentee dynamic radiography, control of radiation beams by vibrating media, multichannel radiograph, digital x-ray imaging system NSF sci. faculty fellow, 1960-61; recipient Glenn Murphy award for nuclear sci. edn. ASEE, 1994. Mem.: Tau Beta Pi, Sigma Xi, Pi Mu Epsilon. Home: 3718 SW 80th Dr Gainesville FL 32608-3662 Office: Dept Nuclear & Radiol Engring U Fla Gainesville FL 32611-8300 E-mail: jacobs@ufl.edu.

JACOBS, ARTHUR DIETRICH, educator, researcher, health services executive; b. Bklyn., Feb. 4, 1933; s. Lambert Dietrich and Paula Sophia (Knissel) Jacobs; m. Viva Jane Sims, Mar. 24, 1952; children: Archie(dec.), David L., Dwayne C., Dianna K. Hatfield. BBA, Ariz. State U., 1962, MBA, 1966. Enlisted USAF, 1951, commd. 2d lt., 1962, advanced through grades to maj., 1972, ret., 1973; indsl. engr. Motorola, Phoenix, 1973-74; mgmt. cons. State of Ariz., 1974-76, Productivity Internat., Tempe, Ariz., 1976-79; faculty assoc. Coll. Bus. Adminstrn. Ariz. State U., Tempe, 1977-94, sr. lectr., 1995, ret., 1996. Productivity advisor Scottsdale Meml. Health Svcs. Co., Ariz., 1979—84; rschr. U.S. Internment of European-Am. Aliens and Citizens of European Ancestry during World War II. Author: (book) The Prison Called Hohenasperg: An American Boy Betrayed by His Government During World War II, 1999; editor, pub.: Freedom of Information Times; co-editor: The World War Two Experience - The Interment of German-Americans, Documents, vol. IV (now in spl. collections of USAF Acad.); contbr. Bd. dirs. United Way of Tempe, 1979—85. Recipient Meritorious Svc. award, Coll. Ozarks, Mo., 2000. Mem.: Ops. Rsch. Soc. Am., Inst. Indsl. Engrs. (pres.ctrl. Ariz. chpt. 1984—85), Am. Soc. Quality Control, Ariz. State U. Alumni Assn. (bd. dirs. 1973—79), Optimist (life), Delta Sigma Pi, Beta Gamma Sigma, Sigma Iota Epsilon. Achievements include research in the special collections of the United States Air Force Academy. E-mail: adjacobs@foitimes.com.

JACOBS, DOROTHY PATRICIA, elementary education educator; b. Detroit, July 13, 1940; d. Alexander Mackery and Lillian (Bondarchuk) Lovchuk; m. Richard Chester Jacobs, Jan. 7, 1978. BA, Mich. State U., 1962; EdM, Oregon State U., 1975. Cert. tchr., Tex., Calif. Elem. sch. tchr. Fremont (Calif.) Unified Sch. Dist., 1962-65, Corona Unified Sch. Dist., Norco, Calif., 1965-66, Riverside (Calif.) Unified Sch. Dist., 1966-69; reading tchr. Fremont (Calif.) Unified Sch. Dist., 1969-71; lang., learning disabilities tchr. Pasadena (Tex.) Ind. Sch. Dist., 1975-77, spl. edu. resource tchr., 1977-81, reading specialist, 1981-90, peer facilitator, 1991-95. Mem., program chmn. Assn. for Children with Learning Disabilities, Pasadena, 1976-80; mem. Greater Houston Area Reading Coun., Houston, 1988-90. Mem. NEA, Tex. State Tchrs. Assn., Pasadena Educators Assn. (v.p. 1991-93, editor newsletter 1992-95), Tex. State Reading Assn., Internat. Reading Assn., Am. Volksport Assn., Sierra Club. Avocations: choir singing, piano playing for ch., hiking, travel. Home: 9487 N Twinkling Shadows Way Tucson AZ 85743-5492

JACOBS, GRACE GAINES, retired gerontologist, adult education educator; b. Mpls., Aug. 29, 1919; d. Abe S. and Ruth (Justman) Gaines; m. Michael M. Jacobs, Mar. 30, 1943; children: Laurence Bruce, Yana Arlene, Robert Marc. AA, Santa Monica City Coll., 1969; BA in Anthropology, Calif. State U., Northridge, 1971, MA in Ednl. Psychology, 1973. Owner, editor, pub. Publicraft Assocs., Detroit, 1948-50; instr. adult edn. L.A. City Schs., 1974-80. Writer: (handbook) Teaching Older Adults, 1978. Nat. program chair Gray Panthers, Phila. and Washington, 1982-84, mem. nat steering com., 1978-86; host Speaking of Seniors radio program KPFK-Pacifica, L.A., 1976-85; mem. Consumer Action Bd., San Francisco, 1988-93; mem. Pacific Bell Intelligent Network Task Force, San Francisco, 1984-87; mem. housing adv. com. City of Santa Cruz, Calif., 1984-90; obtained funding and site for startup SeniorNet Computer Ctr., Santa Cruz, 1989. Mem. Am. Soc. Aging, AAUW, LWV (chair 2 yr. study on nat health Santa Cruz, Calif., 1993-95), Geneal. Soc., Lifelong Learners Univ. Santa Cruz (pres. 1993-94). Democrat. Avocations: writing, family history.

JACOBS, HYDE SPENCER, soil chemistry educator; b. Declo, Idaho, May 15, 1926; s. Rex Haynes and Clare Julia (McHale) J.; m. Gareldene Marchant, Aug. 4, 1950; children: Stanalee, Ruth, Julia Jacobs Spresser, Merrie Jacobs Houser, Marcia. MS, U. Idaho, 1954; PhD, Mich. State U., 1957. Cert. profl. agronomist; cert. profl. soil scientist. Prof. soils Kans. State U., Manhattan, 1967-95, asst. dir. ext., 1981-86, asst. to dean of agr., 1986-95, dir. Evapotranspiration Lab., 1964-80; dir. Kans. Water Resources Rsch. Inst., Manhattan, 1964-74, 88-95. Liaison rep. Gt. Plains Agrl. Coun., Ft. Collins, Colo., 1987-92; sec. Kans. Food and Agrl. Coun., Manhattan, 1984-92; legis. liaison Agrl. Expt. Sta., Manhattan, 1986-93, Coop. Ext. Svc., 1986-93. Contbr. articles to profl. jours. Fellow Am. Soc. Agronomy, Soil Sci. Soc. Am., Soil and Water Conservation Soc.; mem. Kans. Crop Improvement Assn. (hon. mem.). Mem. Lds Ch.

JACOBS, JEFFREY LEE, lawyer, education network company executive; b. Boston, Jan. 20, 1951; s. Philip and Millicent T. (Katz) J.; m. Deborah R. Rath, June 7, 1981; children: Alison, Hannah. BA, U. Pa., 1973; MPA, U. So. Calif., 1979; JD, Pace U., 1985. Bar: Conn. 1985, N.Y. 1988. Asst. to comptroller gen. U.S. Gen. Acctg. Office, Washington, 1976-80; sr. rsch. assoc. Nat. Acad. Pub. Adminstrn., Washington, 1980-83; dir. of seminars Prentice Hall, Clifton, N.J., 1985-87; pres. Profl. Edn. Network, Inc., Westport, Conn., 1987—. Lectr. Ga. Tax Inst., Ohio Fed. Tax Inst.; adj. prof. Quinnipiac Coll., Univ. New Haven; cons. SmartPros Ltd. Co-author: GAO: Government Accountability, 1979; producer, writer TV series The CPA Report, 1988-91; producer, writer radio series Legal Practice Alert, 1990—. Trustee Westport Pub. Libr. Mem. ABA (taxation sect.), Acad. Legal Studies in Bus. Home: 16 Janson Dr Westport CT 06880-2568 Office: SmartPros Ltd 12 Skyline Dr Hawthorne NY 10532-2133 E-mail: jeffjacobs@aol.com.

JACOBS, JOSEPH BARRY, otolaryngologist, educator; b. Newark, 1948; MD, Albert Einstein Coll. Medicine, 1974. Diplomate Am. Bd. Otolaryngology. Intern Montefiore Hosp. Med. Ctr., Bronx, N.Y., 1974-75; resident in otolaryngology Bellevue Hosp. Ctr.-NYU Hosp., N.Y.C., 1975-78; fellow in plastic surgery UCLA, 1978-79; prof. otolaryngology NYU Sch. Medicine, N.Y.C., 1996—, vice chmn. dept. otolaryngology, 1999—. Dir. rhinology dept. otolaryngology, NYU Hosp., N.Y.C., 1991—; pvt. practice, N.Y.C. Fellow ACS, Am. Rhinologic Soc. (v.p., pres. elect), Am. Triologic Soc.; mem. Am. Acad. Facial Plastic & Reconstructive Surgery, Am. Acad. Otolaryngology Head & Neck Surgery, Am.Coll. Otolaryngology. Office: NYU Dept Otolaryngology 530 1st Ave New York NY 10016-6402

JACOBS, KENNETH A. composer, educator; b. Sept. 13, 1948; s. Harvey C. Jacobs; children: Jennifer, Michael, David, Sarah. BA, N.Mex. State U., 1969, MusM, 1970; DMA, U. Tex., 1975. Prof. N.Mex. Western U., 1971, U. Tenn., 1974—. Composer: (orch.) Caravans, Symphony #1, Symphony #2-Gypsy Nights, Symphony #3, Symphony #4-Wonderland's Gifts, Concerto for violin and orch., flute concerto-Angels Speak No Words, clarinet concerto-Imaginings on the Wind; (wind ensemble) Again Wild Spring; (soprano and string trio) Midsummer Vocalise; (string quartet) Canopy of Dreams; (computer synthesized tape) Saffron, Elena, Woman on the Dunes, Little Birds, Second Touch, The Sun Gatherer; (ballet) Magic of the Rainbow Man, Secret World, Spirit Dances; (piano) Windows to Three, Treasures of a Captured Sun, Tracing Infinity, Ring of Gold, Portraits; (woodwinds) Bookends, While Children Sleep; (brass quintet) Ambassadors of Fortune; (choir and keyboard) Letters of Love, Five Biblical Songs, In His Hand; (voice and percussion) The Pine Planters; (trumpet) Through the Hourglass; (horn) Night Covers All, Rivulet, Snowman; (tuba) Mountain Mischief; (viola) Drifter's Heart; (oboe) Sand Castles; (flute) Legends, Jenny's Delight, Indian Summer; (clarinet) Fragments Torn From the Heart; (string bass) Anxious Arrivals; (alto sax) The Wind at the Top of the Hill; (bassoon) Twilight Voices; (songs) Bow to Your Partner, And You Hold Me, Gestures in the Face of Time, others; (multimedia with photography) Private Obsessions, Savanna Afternoon; (multimedia with synchronized artwork projections) Passage to Honor House, Draw Down the Dark Moon, Celestial Illusions, A Model, Winter Strategy, Walk in Many Lands, Scenes from the Earth; guest artist numerous orgns.; commns. Balt. Sch. Arts, DeReggi Interarts Ensemble, U. Tenn. Orch., U. Tenn. Bicentennial, Tenn. Music Tchrs. Assn.; contbr. articles to jours. U. Tenn. grantee; recipient Disting. Composer award Tenn. Music Tchrs. Assn., 1988, 95, Bergen Festival, 1996, S.A.I./Cath. U. award, 1998, Brown U. Choral prize, 1982, Tex. Music Edn. Assn. award, 1974, CCNY award, 1985, Internat. New Music Composers Competition, 1988, Tenn. Composer Competition award, 1988, others. Mem. Broadcast Music Inc., Coll. Music Soc., Soc. of Composers, Southeastern Composers League, Phi Kappa Phi, Pi Kappa Lambda. Home: 1229 Westbury Rd Knoxville TN 37922-8010

JACOBS, LINDA ROTROFF, elementary school educator; b. Peebles, Ohio, June 10, 1942; d. Joseph Harold Rotroff and Mary Lucille (Peterson) Rotroff Nixon; m. Donald Eugene Jacobs, Nov. 29, 1968; 1 child, Donald Brett. BS in Edn., Ohio State U., 1963; MA in Edn., U. Cin., 1968; postgrad., U. Cin., Miami U., Xavier U., 1968—, Coll. Mt. St. Joseph, 1968—. Cert. tchr., Ohio. Tchr. K-8 Forest Hills Bd. Edn., Cin., 1963-74, 77—; tchr. kindergarten Chillicothe (Ohio) Bd. Edn., 1974-77; tchr. reading adult edn. Cin., 1975; tchr. kindergarten Mercer Elem. Forest Hills, Cin., 1977—, tchr. pupil enrichment program, 1997—. Cooperating tchr. student tchrs. Ohio U., U. Cin., No. Ky. U., 1965—; tchr. summer sch. 4th-7th grades math./lang. arts, Cin., 1964-68, kindergarten and 1st grade Forest Hills, Cin., 1978-82; tchr. rep. Head Start, Chillicothe, 1975-77; kindergarten coord. Forest Hills and Hamilton County, Cin., 1965-70, 83-85; mem. supt.'s coun. Forest Hills, Cin., 1979, 82, 88; tchr. rep. PTA, Cin., 1967, 73, 82, 89; facilitator Forest Hills Summer Sch., 1993-96, 97-99; master tchr./advisor entry tchrs. Forest Hills, 1993—; career mentor Ashford-McCarthy Resources, Inc., 1993-94; coord. early entrance screening Hamilton County, 1994, 95, faculty mem. Intervention Based Multifactored Evaluation Com., 1994, 95, mem. Collaboration Team for Inclusion of Spl. Children, 1994, 95; mem. responsive classroom team, 1996-97; mem. steering com. accelerated schs., 1997-98, mem. diversity cadre Accelerated Schs., Great Aspirations pilot program Mercer Elem. Sch., mem. profl. devel. cadre, 1999-2000. Author: Getting Ready for Kindergarten, 1978, Parenting Tips, 1982, Intervention Assistance Team Handbook, 1992 Cons. Women Helping Women, Cin., 1989. Recipient Ohio State U. Scarlet and Gray award, 1995; named Hamilton County Tchr. of Yr., 1965, Educator of Yr., Anderson Hills C. of C., 2000. Mem. NEA, Nat. PTA (rep.) Tchrs. Applying Whole Lang., Ohio Edn. Assn. (del. 1965), Southwestern Ohio Edn. Assn., Forest Hills Educators Assn. (sec. 1964-68, Martha Holden Jennings scholar 1976-77), DAR, Ohio State U. Alumni Club of Clermont County (sec. 1995—), Anderson Hills Hist. Soc., Forest Hills Ret. Staff Assn., Hamilton County Ret. Tchrs. Assn., Police Officers Hall of Fame (hon.), Clermont County Herb Soc., Alpha Kappa Delta (sec. 1975—). Mem. Ch. of Christ. Avocations: interior decorating, writing stories/poems, music, landscaping, reading.

JACOBS, MARILYN ARLENE POTOKER, gifted education educator, consultant, author; b. N.Y.C., Oct. 22, 1940; m. David Jacobs, Dec. 10, 1960. BA in Psychology, Hunter Coll. CUNY, 1961, MS in Edn., 1963; cert. in gifted edn., U. South Fla., 1977. Cert. elem. edn., gifted and early childhood edn., Fla. Tchr. Yonkers (N.Y.) Pub. Schs., 1961-63; dir., tchr. Creative Corners Pre-Sch., Pomona, N.Y., 1971-74; tchr. of gifted, tchr. trainer Pinellas County Schs., Clearwater, Fla., 1975—. Pvt. practice computer edn. cons., 1987—; freelance grant writer, 1976—, freelance curriculum writer, 1993—. Contbr. articles to profl. jours. Recipient numerous county, state and nat. Econs. Edn. Curriculum awards, 1982—. Mem. NEA, ASCD, Coun. for Exceptional Children (Educator of the Yr. 1985), Assn. for Gifted, Fla. Assn. Computer Educators, Phi Delta Kappa, Phi Beta Kappa, Kappa Delta Pi, Psi Chi. Office: Eisenhower Elem Sch 2800 Drew St Clearwater FL 33759-3010

JACOBS, MERLE EMMOR, zoology educator, researcher; b. Nov. 30, 1918; s. Paul Anthony and Trello Elizabeth (Risch) J.; m. Elizabeth Beyeler, June 6, 1959. BA, Goshen Coll., 1948; PhD, Ind. U., 1953. Assoc. prof. Duke U., Durham, N.C., 1953-57; prof. Bethany (W.Va.) Coll., 1957-61, Ea. Mennonite Coll., Harrisonburg, Va., 1961-64; rsch. prof. Goshen (Ind.) Coll., 1964-86. Contbr. articles to profl. jours. Recipient Eigenmann award Ind. U., 1950. Office: Goshen Coll 1700 S Main St Goshen IN 46526-4724 Home: 344 Northeast St Smithville OH 44677-9725

JACOBS, PETER ALAN, artist, educator; b. N.Y.C., Jan. 31, 1939; s. Peter A. and Elsie Katherine (Hirchi) J.; m. Nanci Gardner, Apr. 1, 1961; children: Christopher P.D., Cathi Kottenstette. BS, SUNY, New Paltz, 1960, MS, 1962; EdD, Vanderbilt U., 1965. Assoc. prof. art SUNY, New Paltz, 1961-62; prof. art and dept. chair U. Wis., Whitewater, 1965-70, No. Ariz. U., Flagstaff, 1970-74, Ctrl. Mich. U., Mt. Pleasant, 1975-76, Colo. State U., Ft. Collins, 1976-86, prof. art, 1988—; vis. prof. and dept. head U. Wyo., Laramie, 1987-88. Founder, 1st pres. Nat. Coun. Art Adminstrs., 1972; pres. The Douglas Soc., Native Arts Dept.; pres. Denver Art Mus., 1994-95, bd. dirs., 1993—; mem. Semester at Sea faculty U. Pitts., 1998; vis. prof. Guangxi Normal U., Guilin, China; mediation officer Colo. State U. Over 65 one-artist exhbns. in 14 states including Nicolaysen Art Mus., Casper, Wyo., 1991, Wyo. State Mus., Cheyenne, 1991, Julliet Denious Gallery, Carnegie Ctr. for Arts, Dodge City, Kans., 1990, Banares Hindu U., Varanasi, India, Gallery Bog, Boulder, Colo., Scottsdale (Ariz.) Fine Arts Ctr., Port Huron (Mich.) Mus. of Art, Ohio State U., Columbus, Northwestern U., Evanston, Ill.; exhbns. in Italy, India, Poland, Germany, Can., Bulgaria; numerous juried exhbns. Bd. dirs. Nightwalker Enterprises, Ft. Collins, Colo., 1985—, One-West Contemporary Art Ctr., Ft. Collins, 1979-86, Artists' Adv. Com., 1994-95, No. Colo. Intertribal Pow-wow Assn. Fulbright scholar, India, 1981-82. Mem. Coll. Art Assn., Native Am. Art Study Assn., Artist Adv. Coun. One-West Contemporary Art Ctr. Lutheran. Avocation: canoeing. Office: Colo State U Dept Art Fort Collins CO 80523-0001

JACOBS, RUTH ANN, program director; b. Toledo, Apr. 5, 1954; d. Ralph Clare and Toshi (Murakami) J.; m. Nathan Douglas Jacobs. Student, U. Toledo, 1980-81; A. in Electronic Engring. Tech., Stautzenberger Coll., 1986; student, Owens Tech. Coll., 1990, Heidelberg Coll., 1991. Cert. netware instr., netware engr. Ranch hand H.H. Green Ranch, Houston, 1973; tropical fish breeder Silent World, Gretna, La., 1974-75; machine operator Lindsay Design Assocs., Toledo, 1975; mem. sales Colony Generator, Toledo, 1976; control clk. Union 76 Oil Co., Millbury, Ohio, 1976-85; fabrication T.L. Industries, Toledo, 1986; biomed. engring. temp Med. Coll. Ohio, Toledo, 1986-87, computer technician, 1994—; program coord. Stautzenberger Coll., Toledo, 1987—; computer technician Med. Coll. Ohio, Toledo, 1994—. Vol. zookeeper Toledo Zoo, 1986-88. Mem. Mensa, Internat. Soc. Cert. Electronic Technicians (cert., journeyman in computers 1990). Avocations: tropical plants, tropical fish, rockhounding, silver smithing, weight lifting. Home: 760 Bronx Dr Toledo OH 43609-1724 Office: Stautzenberger Coll 5355 Southwyck Blvd Toledo OH 43614-1581

JACOBS, THOMAS PRICE, internal medicine educator; b. N.Y.C., June 13, 1942; s. Thomas Price and Anne Snowden (Brennan) J.; m. Janice Marie Carmody, Feb. 24, 1968; children: Kevin, Michael, Timothy, Jennifer, Brian. AB, Amherst Coll., 1964; MD, Johns Hopkins U., 1968. Diplomate in internal medicine and endocrinology Am. Bd. Internal Medicine. Resident in medicine Presbyn. Hosp., N.Y.C., 1968-70, 72-73; fellow in endocrinology U. Wash., Seattle, 1973-75; asst. prof. clin. medicine Columbia U., N.Y.C., 1975-81, assoc. prof., 1981-93, prof., 1993—. Examiner Physician for Human Rights. Contbr. articles to med. jours. Pres. Tenafly (N.J.) Jr. Soccer League, 1989-2003; trustee Am. U. Beirut, 1996—. Maj. M.C., U.S. Army, 1970-72, Vietnam. Fellow ACP; mem. Am. Soc. for Bone and Mineral Rsch., Endocrine Soc., Pituitary Soc., Phi Beta Kappa, Sigma Xi, pres. Tennis Club, N.J., Soccer League, 1989-2003. Home: 66 Magnolia Ave Tenafly NJ 07670-2121 Office: Columbia-Presbyn Med Ctr 161 Fort Washington Ave New York NY 10032-3713

JACOBS-CIRANNI, MARY LAURALEE, elementary education educator; b. Ft. Meade, Md., July 1, 1962; d. Ronald Matthew and Leona Rosemary (Gagnon) J. BA in Edn. and German, Coll. of St. Catherine, St. Paul, 1984. Cert. elem. edn. tchr., Md. Tchr. 2d grade Holy Cross Elem. Sch., Garrett Park, Md., 1984-86, dir. after care program, 1985-90, tchr. kindergarten, 1986-90; tchr. kindergarten thru 2d grade Buechel Elem. Sch., Kennfus, Fed. Republic of Germany, 1990-93. Dir. summer camp Holy Cross Elem., summer 1985, 86, 87, 88, 89. Roman Catholic. Avocations: reading, travel, skiing. Address: 102 Indian Rock Cir # 1 Minot Afb ND 58704-1101

JACOBSEN, CHARLENE MARIE, middle school music educator, band director; b. Chgo., Nov. 21, 1942; d. Edmund S. and Florence D. (Krause) Berchert; m. Lloyd H. Jacobsen, July 11, 1970 (dec. May, 1992); 1 child, Gretchen M. BS in Music Edn., Ea. Ill. U., 1964; MS in Music Edn., U. Ill., 1968; postgrad., Vander Cook Coll. of Music, Chgo., 1988-92. cert. tchr. music. elem., secondary, jr. coll., Ill. Tchr. Dixon (Ill.) Pub. Schs., 1964-66, River Trails Pub. Sch., Mt. Prospect, Ill., 1966-73, 1980—, Immanuel Sch., Des Plaines, Ill., 1976-77. Parish music dir. Immanuel Luth. Ch., Des Plaines, 1986-88; founding mem. Fine Arts Network, Arlington Heights, Ill., 1989-92. chair person, 1992-93. Mem. NEA, Ill. Edn. Assn., River Trails Edn. Assn. (pres. 1969-71, chair person 1969-73, negotiating team 1989-92), Music Educators Nat. Conf. (registered music educator), Ill. Music Educators Assn., Alumni Assn. Ea. Ill U., U. Ill. Avocations: sewing, knitting, gardening. Home: 802 E Jennifer Ct Arlington Heights IL 60004-4000 Office: River Trails Middle Sch 1000 N Wolf Rd Mount Prospect IL 60056-1551

JACOBSEN, EGILL LARS, dentist, educator; b. Copenhagen, Dec. 20, 1940; came to U.S., 1969; s. Haukur and Inge Liss (Kristensen) J.; m. Ruth C. Jacobsen, Aug. 2, 1974; children: Mikael Lars, Anna Liss. BS in Bus., Comml. Coll., Reykjavik, Iceland, 1961; DDS, U. Iceland, Reykjavik, 1967; postgrad., U. Pa., 1972. Lic. dentist, Iceland, Ill. Pvt. practice dentistry, Iceland, 1967-69; pvt. practice endodontics, 1973-80; teaching fellow dept. endodontics U. Pa., Phila., 1969-70; asst. prof. dept. endodontics Health Sci. Ctr., U. Conn., Hartford, 1972-73; assoc. prof. endodontics U. Iceland, Reykjavik, 1973-80, U. Ill., Chgo., 1980-97. Part-time practice endodontics, Ill., 1983—. Contbr. articles to profl. jours. Fulbright scholar, 1969-72, NATO scholar, 1971-72, Icelandic Rsch. Found. scholar, 1971-72. Mem. Icelandic Dental Assn., Am. Assn. Endodontists, Midwest Soc. Electron Microscopists, Edgar Coolidge Endodontic Study Club.

JACOBSON, ALBERT HERMAN, JR., industrial and systems engineer, educator; b. St. Paul, Minn., Oct. 27, 1917; s. Albert Herman and Gertrude Jacobson; m. Elaine Swanson, June 1960; children: Keith, Paul. BS Indsl. Engring./Adminstrn. cum laude, Yale U., 1939; SM Bus. and Engring. Mgmt., MIT, 1952; MS in Applied Physics, U. Rochester, 1954; PhD in Indsl. and Mgmt. Engring., Stanford U., 1976. Registered profl. engr., Calif. Pers. asst. Yale U., New Haven, Conn., 1939-40; indsl. engr. in electronics Radio Corp. of Am., Camden, N.J., 1940-43; prodn. officer USN BuORD, 1943-44; RINSMAT USN Colonial Radio Corp. (Sylvania), Buffalo, 1944-45; INSORD USN Eastman Kodak Co., Rochester, N.Y., 1945-46; chief engr., dir. quality control Naval Ordnance Office, Rochester, N.Y., 1946-57; staff engr. Space Satellite Program Eastman Kodak Co., Rochester, 1957-59; assoc. dean Coll. Engring. and Architecture Pa. State U., University Park, Pa., 1959-61; v.p., gen. mgr. to pres. Knapic Electro-Physics Inc., Palo Alto, Calif., 1961-62; prof. of indsl. and systems engring. Coll. of Engring. San Jose State U., 1962—, co-founder, coord. Cybernetic Systems grad. program, 1968-88. Cons. in field, Lockheed, Motorola, Santa Fe R.R., 20th Century Fox, Alcan-Aluminium Corp., Banner Container, Sci. Mgmt. Corp., No. Telecom, Siliconix, others. Author: Military and Civilian Personnel in Naval Administration, 1952, Railroad Consolidations and Transportation Policy, 1975; editor: Design and Engineering of Production Systems, 1984; contbr. articles to profl. jours. Mem., chmn. Pers. Commn. City of Mountain View, Calif., 1968-78; troop chmn., scoutmaster, mem. Stanford Area Coun. Boy Scouts of Am., Palo Alto, 1970-83; chmn. Campus Luth. Coun. San Jose State U., 1981-86; mem. Santa Clara Valley Luth. Parish Coun., 1991—; pres. N.Y. State Young Adults Coun. YMCA, 1954-55. Lt. comdr. USNR. Recipient commendation USN, 1946; Alfred P. Sloan fellow Program Exec. Devel. MIT, 1951-52, NSF fellow, Stanford U., 1965-66; recipient Scouters Key and Award of Merit Stanford Coun. Boy Scouts Am., 1976. Mem. Am. Soc. Engring. Edn., Inst. Indsl. Engrs., Am. Prodn. and Inventory Control Soc. (bd. dirs. 1975—), Masons, Sigma Xi, Tau Beta Pi. Lutheran. Avocations: orchestra and choir, swimming, tennis, skiing, photography. Home: 1864 Limetree Ln Mountain View CA 94040-4019 Office: San Jose State U Coll Engring 1 Washington Sq San Jose CA 95192-0001

JACOBSON, HOWARD NEWMAN, obstetrics and gynecology educator, researcher; b. St. Paul, Aug. 13, 1923; s. Irvin Oliver and Nora Henrietta (Olson) J.; m. Barbara Jane Dinger, Aug. 20,1961. BSc in Medicine, Northwestern U., Chgo., 1947, BM, 1950, MD, 1951. Intern Presbyn. Hosp., Chgo., 1950-51, resident in ob-gyn, 1951-52; fellow, rsch. fellow in obstetrics, mem. family clinic Harvard Sch. Pub. Health, Boston, 1952-55; resident Boston Lying-In Hosp. and Free Hosp. for Women, Brookline, Mass., 1955-58; obstetrician, physiologist Lab. Neuroanat. Scis., Nat. Inst. Nervous Disease and Blindness, NIH, Bethesda, Md., 1958-60; instr., asst. prof. Harvard Med. Sch., Boston, 1960-65; assoc. prof. U. Calif., San Francisco, Berkeley, 1965-69; dir. Macy program Med. Sch. Harvard U., 1969-74; prof. dept. cmty. medicine Coll. Medicine and Dentistry NJ, Piscataway, NJ, 1974-78; dir. Inst. Nutrition, clin. prof. U. NC, Chapel Hill, 1978-88; rsch. prof. Coll. Pub. Health U. So. Fla., 1988—2003; prof. dept. ob-gyn U. South Fla. Med. Sch., Tampa, 1990-96, facilitator spl. programs Health Sci. Ctr., 1996—2003. Cons. Children's Bur., HEW, Washington, 1964-73, GAO, Washington, 1974-83, AMA, 1980-82, 88—; mem. food and nutrition bd. NRC/NAS, Washington, 1971-74; prof. dept. biology and Sch. Home Econs., U. N.C., Greensboro, 1978-88, Ellen Swallow Richards lectr., 1978; cons. pregnancy and nutrition study U. Minn., Mpls., 1979—; adj. prof. dept. food, nutrition and instn. mgmt. East Carolina U. Sch. Home Econs., Greenville, 1981-88; mem. nutrition grad. faculty N.C. State U., Raleigh, 1979-88. Contbr. over 130 articles and abstracts to FMA Today, Jour. Nurse-Midwifery, Clin. Nutrition, Contemporary Internal Medicine, Food and Nutrition News, Nutrition Today, New Eng. Jour. Medicine, chpt. to books. Panel vice chmn. White House Conf. on Food, Nutrition and Health, Washington, 1969; chmn. Quality of Life Conf., Mass. Med. Soc., Boston, 1972; mem. hunger com. Episcopal Ch. S.W. Fla., 1990-94; mem. Fla. Health Start Initiative working Group, 1991—. Lt. (j.g.) USNR, 1943-46, PTO. Recipient Agnes Higgins award March of Dimes and APHA, 1987; recipient Career Devel. award NIH, 1963-65. Fellow Am. Coll. Ob-Gyn (assoc.); mem. Am. Soc. Clin. Nutrition, Am. Physiol. Soc., Mass. Med. Soc. (chmn. commn. 1972-74), Fla. Pub. Health Assn. (chmn. sect. 1990-91), Am. Dietetic Assn. (hon.). Democrat. Achievements include co-develop. of guides for clin. nutrition studies, portable ultrasound for body composition; co-determination of nature of cardiovasc. changes at birth; co-intro. of computer assisted methodology in nutrition; co-initiation of modern nutrition standards for healthy pregnancy. Office: U South Fla Coll Pub Health 13201 Bruce B Downs Blvd Tampa FL 33612-3805

JACOBSON, KAREN, retired elementary school educator; b. N.Y.C. d. Lawrence and Doris (Case) J. BA in Elem. Edn., SUNY, Potsdam, 1966; MS in Elem. Edn., SUNY, Cortland, 1975; AAS in Advt. Design and Prodn., Mohawk Valley C.C., 1997. Cert. tchr., N.Y. Kindergarten tchr. Mohawk (N.Y.) Sch., summers 1966-72; primary grades tchr. Oriskany (N.Y.) Ctrl. Sch., 1966—; curator Oriskany Mus., 1998—. Mem. Oriskany PTA; bd. trustees Oriskany Pub. Libr., 1995-2000; mem. Battle of Oriskany Hist. Soc., Friends of Oriskany Battlefield. Mem. Oriskany Tchrs. Assn., N.Y. State United Tchrs. Avocations: church, golf, watercolor painting. Home: Box 152 109 Ridge Rd Oriskany NY 13424-4723 E-mail: kjake152@aol.com.

JACOBSON, NORMAN MARON, computer science educator; b. Hollywood, Calif., May 30, 1954; s. Eugene and Sylvia J. BA in Math., U. Calif., Irvine, 1976; BS in Info. & Computer Sci., U. Calif., 1976. Cert. tchr., Calif. V.p. Custom Software, Inc., Mission Viejo, Calif., 1979-85; programmer Office of Housing and Transp. U. Calif., Irvine, 1974-85, sr. program analyst Pub. Policy Rsch. Orgn., 1975-84, programmer Office of Vice Chancellor, 1977-78; articulation officer Sch. Info. and Computer Sci. U. Calif., Irvine, 1985—98, 2002—; asst. chair undergrad. affairs dept. info. and computer sci. Am. Indian Summer Sci. Inst., U. Calif., Irvine, 1994—98. Instr. summer sessions Sch. Info. and Computer Sci., U. Calif., 1979—, software cons. Visual Resource Collection, Irvine, 1986—; writer, host ednl. TV series The New Literacy, 1984; expert witness in computer-related cases, 1984—. Author: Structured Programming Using Think Pascal on the MacIntosh, 1992. Mem. Assn. Computing Machinery. Avocations: hammer dulcimer, philately. E-mail: jacobson@uci.edu.

JACOBSON, PHILLIP LEE, architect, educator; b. Santa Monica, Calif., Aug. 27, 1928; s. Allen Wilhelm and Greta Percy (Rohde) J.; m. Effie Laurel Galbraith, Nov. 6, 1954; children: Rolf Wilhelm, Christina Lee, Erik Mackenzie. B. Archtl. Engring. with honors, Wash. State U., 1952; postgrad. (Fulbright scholar), U. Liverpool, Eng., 1952-53; M.Arch., Finnish Inst. Tech., Helsinki, 1969. Field supr. Gerald C. Field Architect, 1950; designer, draftsman John Maloney Architect, 1951, 53-55; designer, project mgr. Young, Richardson, Carleton & Detlie Architects, 1955-56; designer, project architect John Carl Warnecke Architect, San Francisco, 1956-58; ptnr., design dir. TRA, Seattle, 1958-92; prof. architecture and urban design and planning Coll. Architecture and Urban Planning, U. Wash., Seattle, 1962—2000. Author: Housing and Industrialization in Finland, 1969, The Evolving Architectural Design Process, 1969; contbr. articles to profl. jours.; major archtl. works include Aerospace Research Lab., U. Wash., Seattle, 1969, McCarty Residence Hall, 1960, Highway Adminstrn. Bldg., Olympia, Wash., 1970, Sea-Tac Internat. Airport, 1972, Issaquah (Wash.) High Sch., 1962, State Office Bldg. 2, Olympia, 1976, Sealaska Corporate Hdqrs. Bldg., Juneau, Alaska, 1977, Group Health Hosp., Seattle, 1973, Metro Shelter Program, Seattle, 1977, N.W. Trek Wildlife Preserve, 1976, Rocky Reach/Rock Island Recreation Plan, 1974, master plan mouth of Columbia River, 1976, U. Wash. Biol. Sci. Bldg., 1981, Wegner Hall, Wash. State U., 1982, Wash. Conv. Ctr., 1988, King County Aquatics Ctr., 1990, Albuquerque Airport, 1989, U. Wash. Health Scis. H Wing, 1993. Mem. Seattle Planning and Redevel. Council, 1959-69, v.p., 1966-67; mem. Seattle Landmark Preservation Bd., 1976-81; trustee Pilchuck Sch., 1982-2001, Northwest Trek Found., 1987-94, AIA/Seattle Archtl. Found., 1986-92. With U.S. Army, 1946-47. Fulbright-Hays Sr. Rsch. fellow Finland, 1968-69; named to Order of White Rose Govt. of Finland, 1985; recipient Silver plaque Finnish Soc. Architects, 1992; recipient numerous design awards. Fellow AIA (pres. Wash. state Council 1965, dir. Seattle chpt. 1970-73, sr. council 1970—, Seattle chpt. medal 1994); mem. Am. Inst. Cert. Planners, Phi Kappa Phi, Tau Beta Pi, Tau Sigma Delta, Scarab, Sigma Tau (outstanding alumnus 1967). Home: PO Box 45368 Seattle WA 98145-0368 Office: U Wash PO Box 355720 Seattle WA 98195-5720

JACOBSON, SHELDON HOWARD, engineering educator; b. Montreal, Sept. 9, 1960; BSc, McGill U., 1981, MSc, 1983; PhD, Cornell U., 1988. Asst. prof. Case Western Res. U., Cleve., 1988—93; assoc. prof. Va. Tech. U., Blacksburg, 1993—99, U. Ill., Urbana, Ill., 1999—2002, prof., 2002—, assoc. Ctr. for Advanced Study, 2002—03. Mem. sci. adv. bd. BioPop Inc., Charlotte, NC, 2000—02. Recipient Best Application award, Inst. Indsl. Engring. Ops. Rsch. Divsn., 1998, Aviation Security Rsch. award, Aviation Security Internat., 2002; Willett Faculty scholar, U. Ill., 2002—, Guggenheim fellow, 2003. Office: University of Illinois 1206 West Green Street (MC-244) Urbana IL 61801

JACOBSON, VERA LEE, theater educator; b. San Francisco, Jan. 14, 1952; d. Leo David and Doris Bush (Mulford) Jacobson; m. Paul Vasiliy Kopeikin, Nov. 27, 1975 (div. Feb. 1990); 1 child, Katie Elizabeth Kopeikin; m. Leonard Flores, Jr., Dec. 29, 1993 (div. Feb. 1999). BA in Theatre Arts, Calif. State U., Hayward, 1992; M in Arts Edn., San Francisco State U., 1998. Cert. tchr. English/drama Calif. Realtor Trotter Realty, Burlingame, Calif., 1977-79; tchr. Visitacion Valley Sch., San Francisco, 1994-96; tchr. drama, media, coord. arts Potrero Hill Mid. Sch. of the Arts, San Francisco, 1996-98; tchr. drama, media edn. Carlmont HS, Belmont, Calif., 1998—, chair dept. Bus. Tech. Acad., 2001—. Mem. leadership team Visitacion Valley Sch., 1995—96; judge Shakespeare Festival Calif. State U., Hayward, 1994—95. Dir.: (musical) The Wiz, 1995, Little Shop of Horrors, 1996, 2000, Around the World, 1998, Murder for Rent, 1998, Kiss Me Kate, 1999, Harvey, 1999; actor: Internat. Greek Theatre Festival, 2001, Edinburgh (Scotland) Fringe Festival, 2002. Mem.: Calif. Arts Project (tchr.), Nat. Urban Alliance, Women in Arts, Epilepsy Soc. Am., Calif. Ednl. Theatre Assn. (bd. dirs., New Tchr. of the Yr. 1998), Autism Soc. Am., Performing Arts Libr. Mus., San Francisco Mus. Modern Art. Democrat. Episcopalian. Avocations: running, performing, sailing, painting, travel. Office: Carlmont H S 1400 Alameda de las Pulgas Belmont CA 94002 E-mail: vjacobso@sel.org.

JACOBUS, SARA WILSON, special education educator; b. Lynn, Mass., Sept. 19, 1943; d. William Broyles and Evelyn French (Scott) Wilson; m. Paul Bailey Francis, Mar. 18, 1964 (div. Feb. 1980); children: Gregory Scott Francis, William Paul Francis. BS in Zoology, Memphis State U., 1965; MEd in Spl. Edn., Ga. State U., 1976; EdS in Adminstrn. and Supervision, U. Tenn., 1989. Cert. career ladder III Tenn. Med. rsch. technician med. unit U. Tenn., Memphis, 1965-66; gen. sci. tchr. Rochester (N.Y.) City Schs., 1967-68; tchr. Montessori Dean Meml. Learning Ctr., Dallas, 1972-74; tchr. spl. edn. DeKalb County Schs., Atlanta, 1977-83, Maryville (Tenn.) City Schs., 1984-96, systemwide homebound tchr., assessment specialist, 1996—, coord. homebound svcs., 2000—, coord. gifted svcs., 2003—. Counselor, co-leader Adventure Camp for At Risk Youth, Maryville City Schs., 1993, 94. Co-author: (book) Learning Disabilities Handbook, 1980. Edn. dir. Girls Club Blount County, Maryville, 1984; apptd. mem. Maryville Hist. Zoning Commn., 1998—; vice chair Maryvill Hist. Zoning Commn., 2003—; apptd. mem. Maryville Downtown Rev. Bd., 1999—. Mem.: Coun. Exceptional Children, Phi Delta Kappa, Phi Kappa Phi. Home: 1815 E Westwood Dr Maryville TN 37803-6357

JACOBY, THOMAS S. cultural organization administrator; b. Konigsberg, Fed. Republic Germany, May 13, 1935; came to U.S., 1939; s. Berthold and Anni (Pfingst) J.; m. Adrienne Zacansky, Apr. 14, 1962; children: Michael, Melissa. BS in Edn., West Chester U., 1958; EdM, Temple U., 1961. Cert. health, phys. edn. tchr. Tchr. Sch. Dist. of Phila., 1958-69, dept. head, athletic dir., 1969-71, supr. health and phys. edn., 1971-90, curriculum coord. phys. edn. and athletics, 1990-93, adminstrv. asst. to regional supt., 1993-95, adminstrv. asst. student svcs., 1995-97, dir. svcs. to students with disabilities, 1997-99; ednl. cons., 1999-2000; exec. dir. Phila. Reads, 2000—. Adj. asst. prof. Temple U., Phila., 1976—; cons. Tech. Adv. Svc. for Attys., Blue Bell, Pa., 1977—; bd. dirs. Lake Owego Camp for Boys, Greeley, Pa. Author: (pamphlets) Physical Education for the Bicentennial, 1976, Street Games of Philadelphia, 1985; contbg. editor: Unique Games and Sports Around the World, 2001. Pres. Phila. Coun. B'nai B'rith, Phila., 1985, Jewish Cmty. Rels. Coun., 1998-2000, co-chmn. edn. com. Jewish Coun. on Pub. Affairs, 2001—. Mem. AAHPERD (2003 conv. mgr., Honor award 2002), Pa. State Assn. Health, Phys. Edn., Recreation and Dance (pres. 1980, conv. mgr. 1975, 79, exhibits mgr. Ea. Dist. 1988-92, pres. elect Ea. Dist. 1993, pres. Ea. Dist. 1994, Profl. Honor awards 1973, 90, Elmer B. Cottrell award 1984), ASTM, ASCD, Am. Assn. Sch. Adminstrs., Am. Camping Assn., Phi Delta Kappa. E-mail: T.Jacoby@verizon.net.

JACOFF, RACHEL, Italian language and literature educator; b. N.Y.C., Apr. 5, 1938; d. Richard and Natalie (Wiener) J. BA, Cornell U., 1959; MA, Harvard U., 1960, MPhil, 1963; PhD, Yale U., 1977. Acting asst. prof. U. Va., Charlottesville, 1974-78; asst. prof. Italian, Wellesley (Mass.) U., 1978-83, assoc. prof., 1983-85, prof., 1985—, Carlson prof. comparative lit., 2001—. Vis. prof. Cornell U., Ithaca, N.Y., 1984; vis. prof. Stanford (Calif.) U., 1989, dir. NEH Stanford Dante Inst., 1988. Co-author: Inferno II: Lectura Dantis Americana, 1989; editor: (essays) Dante: The Poetics of Conversion, 1986 (hon. mention Marraro prize 1987), The Poetry of Allusion, 1991, The Cambridge Companion to Dante, 1993, The Poets' Dante, 2001. Fellow NEH, 1981-82, 91-92, Bunting Inst., 1981, Villa I Tatti, 1982, Stanford Humanities Ctr., 1986-87, Rockefeller Found. Bellagio, 1993, 99, Bogliasco Found., 1999. Mem. MLA, Dante Soc. Am. (coun. 1989-92), Medieval Acad. (asst. editor Speculum 1986-99), Save Venice Charter. Office: Wellesley Coll Dept Italian 106 Central St Wellesley MA 02481-8268

JACOX, ADA KATHRYN, nurse, educator; b. Centreville, Mich. d. Leo H. and Lilian (Gilbert) Jacox. BS in Nursing Edn., Columbia U., 1959; MS in Child Psychiat. Nursing, Wayne State U., 1965; PhD in Sociology, Case Western Res. U., 1969. RN. Dir. nursing Children's Hosp.-Northville State Hosp., Mich., 1961—63; assoc. prof., then prof. Coll. Nursing Univ. Iowa, Iowa City, 1969—76; prof., assoc. dean Sch. Nursing U. Colo., Denver, 1976—80; prof., dir. rsch. ctr. sch. nursing U. Md., Balt., 1980—90, dir. ctr. for health policy rsch., 1988—90; prof. sch. nursing, Independence Found. chair health policy Johns Hopkins U., Balt., 1990—95; prof., assoc. dean for rsch. Coll. Nursing Wayne State, Detroit, 1996. Co-chmn. panels to develop clin. guidelines for pain mgmt. U.S. Agy. for Health Care Policy and Rsch., 1990—94; chair AIDS study sect. NIH, 1990—92. Co-author: Organizing for Independent Nursing Practice, 1977 (named Book of Yr., Am. Jour. Nursing), A Process Measure for Primary Care: The Nurse Practitioner Rating Form, 1981 (named Book of Yr., Am. Jour. Nursing); editor: Pain: A Sourcebook for Nurses, 1977 (named Book of Yr., Am. Jour. Nursing). Recipient Disting. Achievement in Nursing Rsch. and Scholarship, Alumni Assn., Columbia U. Tchrs. Coll., 1975, Disting. award for spl. achievement, Nat. Coalition for Cancer Survivorship, 1994, Cameo award for rsch. excellence, Sigma Theta Tau, 1996, Rozella Schlotfeldt Leadership award, MAIN, 1997; fellow Carver fellow, U. Iowa, 1972. Fellow: Am. Acad. Nursing; mem.: Wayne State U. Alumni Assn. (Disting. Alumni award 1994), Inst. of Medicine, NAS (com. on nat. needs for biomed. and rsch. pers. 1984—87), Am. Acad. Nursing, Am. Health Quality Assn. (bd. dirs. 1998—2001), Am. Pain Soc. (chair clin. practice guidelines com. 1995—2000, bd. dirs. 1999—2001), Am. Nurses Found. (pres. 1982—85), AMA (mem. health policy agenda work group 1983—86), ANA (dir. 1978—82, 1st v.p. 1982—84). Office: Wayne State U Coll Nursing 5557 Cass Ave Detroit MI 48202-3615

JAEGER, MARC JULIUS, physiology educator, researcher; b. Berne, Switzerland, Apr. 4, 1929; came to U.S., 1970; s. Francis K. and Jeanne (Perrin) J.; m. Frances Dick, Dec. 1960 (div. 1972); children: Dominic, Olivia; m. Ina Claire Burlingham-Forbes, June 23, 1973. BA, Gymnasium, Berne, 1948; MD, U. Berne, 1954. Diplomate Swiss Bd. Pulmonary Diseases. Resident, fellow U. Hosp. of Berne, 1954-63; asst. prof. U. Fribourg, Switzerland, 1963-69; assoc. prof. U. Fla. Coll. Medicine, Gainesville, 1970-76, prof. physiology, 1976—2000, prof. emeritus, 2000—. Contbr. over 50 articles to profl. jours., including papers on the separation of gases and isotopes such as U235 and deuterium. Democrat. Achievements include 6 patents for a Method of Separating Solutes and Gases, for a method to Transport Large Amounts of Heat without Coolant and on ventilation of spaces, filled with granules, which have only one opening; research in mechanics of breathing, deep sea diving, air pollution and its effects on the lungs, smoking and its effects on the lungs. Home: 5915 SW 36th Way Gainesville FL 32608-5150 Office: U Fla Coll Medicine Gainesville FL 32610 E-mail: mjaeger@phys.med.ufl.edu.

JAFFE, ARTHUR MICHAEL, physicist, mathematician, educator; b. N.Y.C., Dec. 22, 1937; s. Henry and Clarisse Jaffe; m. Nora Frances Crow, July 24, 1971; 1 child, Margaret Collins; m. Sarah Robbins Warren, Sept. 12, 1992. AB, Princeton U., 1959; BA, Cambridge U., 1961; PhD, Princeton U., 1966; MA, Harvard U., 1970. Acting asst. prof. math. Stanford U., 1966-67; asst. prof. physics Harvard U., Cambridge, Mass., 1967-69, assoc. prof., 1969-70, prof. physics, 1970-77, prof. math. physics, 1977-85, Landon T. Clay prof. math. and theoretical sci., 1985—, chmn. dept. math., 1987-90. Rsch. fellow Princeton U., 1965—66, vis. prof. math. physics, 1971; rsch. fellow Stanford Linear Accelerator Ctr., 1966—67; mem. Inst. for Advanced Study, 1967; vis. prof. Eidgenössische Technische Hochschule, Zurich, 1968, Rockefeller U., 1977, U. Rome, 1993, Boston U., 2001; Porter lectr. Rice U., 1982; Hahn lectr. Yale U., 1985; Hendrik lectr. Math. Assn. Am., 1985; mem. pres.'s com. Nat. Medal of Sci., 1997—2002, acting chair, 2001—02; mem. sci. bd. Santa Fe Inst., 1998—; founding mem. and pres. Clay Math. Inst., 1998—2002; bd. dirs. Internat. Math. Olympiad 2001, 1998—, Inst. Schs. of the Future, 2001—. Author: Vortices and Monopoles, 1980, Quantum Physics, 1981, 87, Quantum Field Theory and Statistical Mechanics, Expositions, 1985, Constructive Quantum Field Theory, 1985; assoc. editor Jour. Math. Physics, 1970-72; mem. editl. coun. Annals of Physics, 1975-77, asst. editor, 1977-2002; editor Communications Math. Physics, 1976-2000, chief editor, 1979-2000; mem. adv. bd. Letters in Math. Physics, 1975—; editor Progress in Physics, 1979-86, Selecta Mathematica Sovetica, 1980—, Revs. in Mathematical Physics, 1990; contbr. articles to profl. jours. Alfred P. Sloan Found. fellow, 1968-70; Guggenheim Found. fellow, 1977-78, 92; award Math. and Phys. Scis., N.Y. Acad. Sci., 1979; Dannie Heineman prize for Math. Physics, 1980; NSF fellow, 1961-64; NAS Air Force Office Sci. Rsch. fellow, 1965-67. Fellow AAAS (chair math. section, 2001), Am. Phys. Soc., Am. Acad. Arts and Scis.; mem. U.S. Nat. Acad. Scis., Am. Math. Soc. (exec. com. of coun. 1991-95, pres. 1997-98), Internat. Assn. Math. Physics (pres. 1991-96), Coun. of Scientific Soc. Pres. (chmn. 2000), Joint Policy Bd. for Math. (chair 1998). Home: 27 Lancaster St Cambridge MA 02140-2837 E-mail: jaffe@math.harvard.edu.

JAFFE, GWEN DANER, museum educator; b. NYC, July 8, 1937; d. Izzy and Selma (Hess) Daner; m. Anthony R. Jaffe; children: Thomas, Elizabeth. BA in Art History, Skidmore Coll., 1957; cert. in elem. tchg., Hofstra U., 1960; postgrad., N.Y. Sch. Interior Design, 1964, Columbia U., 1973. Spl. edn. tchr. Payne Whitney Hosp., 1958-65, Bd. Coop. Ednl. Svcs., Westchester, N.Y., 1958-65; designer Jaffe-Halperin Design Firm, N.Y.C., 1965-86; tour guide Walker Art Ctr., Mpls., 1987-89; tchr. Art Express Sch. mus. program Carnegie Mus. of Art, Pitts., 1989—; mem. staff Peace Arts Exch. program Pitts. Children's Mus., 1992-93; interior designer pvt. practice, 1998—. Designer briefcases and handbags Gwynne Collection, 1993-95. Mem. Fiber Arts Guild. Home: 1056 Lyndhurst Dr Pittsburgh PA 15206

JAFFE, LOUISE, English language educator, creative writer; b. Bronx, NY, May 17, 1936; d. Joseph and Anna (Movitz) Neuwirth; m. Steven Jaffe, Aug. 26, 1962 (div. 1975); 1 child, Aaron Lawrence; m. Leo Gerber, 1993. BA, Queens Coll., 1956; MA, Hunter Coll., 1959; PhD, U. Nebr., 1965; MFA, Bklyn. Coll., 1991. From instr. to prof. English Kingsborough C.C., Bklyn., 1965-95, prof. emerita, 1995—. Author: Hyacinths and Biscuits, 1985, Wisdom Revisited, 1987, Light Breaks, 1995, The Great Horned Owl's Proclamation and Other Hoots, 1997; author numerous poems and fiction stories; mem. editl. bd. Cmty. Review CUNY, 1984—. Recipient First prize N.Y. Poetry Forum, 1980, First prize, First honorable mention Shelley Soc. N.Y., 1983-84, others. Mem.: Am. Mensa. Democrat. Jewish. Avocations: creative writing, scrabble, crossword puzzles., people watching, poetry. Home: 2411 E 3rd St Brooklyn NY 11223-5357 Office: Kingsborough Cmty Coll Oriental Blvd Brooklyn NY 11235-4906 E-mail: athena9x@aol.com.

JAFFE-BLACKNEY, SANDRA MICHELLE, special education educator; b. El Paso, Tex., Oct. 6, 1966; d. Stanley Harris and Rhoda (Rosenfield) J.; m. David Charles Blackney, June 26, 1998. BS in Edn., U. Tex., 1990. Lic. cosmetologist, 1985; cert. generic spl. edn. K-12, regular edn. K-8, ESL instr., mediator for cts. With domestics dept. K-Mart, El Paso, 1980-85; work study Regis Coll., El Paso, 1985-87; vol. Austin (Tex.) Ind. Sch. Dist., 1988-90, student tchr., substitute tchr., 1990; tchr. spl. edn. Garland (Tex.) Schs., 1990—, 3d grade ESL tchr., 1995-97, Title I reading specialist, ESL instr., LPAC chair, SCE scribe, 1997-98, ESL tchr. pre-kindergarden, kindergarden, 3d grade, 1998; hair stylist/asst. mgr. Great Clips for Hair, 2001—02. Substitute tchr. Dallas Ind. Sch. Dist., 1990-91; tchr. spl. edn., mentally retarded/learning disabilities/emotionally disabled, Dallas, 1991-94; tchr., tutor Exemplary Ctr. for Reading Instrn., Dallas, 1991-94; instr. ESL for adults; tchr. Jumpstart 3-4 yr.-olds speaking only Spanish, summer 1999; tchr. technologist 1999-2000; balanced literacy instr. Dallas Reading Plan-Dallas Pub. Schs., 1999-2000; tchr. Title I ESL, 1999-2000; mem. Fannie C. Harris Elem. Campus Instrnl. Leadership Team; LPAC chair, PK-3/ESL; adminstr. Woodcoak-Munoz Lang. Survey, 1997—; others. Tchr., trainer, vol. Spl. Olympics, 1993-94; vol. CHAMPS-Children Have and Model Positive Peer Skills, 1994, El Paso Pub. Schs., 1981-82. Recipient Student medals Spl. Olympics, 1993, award Dallas Reading Plan-Dallas Pub. Schs., 1999-2000. Mem. NEA, Vocat. Indsl. Clubs Am., Tex. Edn. Assn., Texas Exes (life), Classroom Tchrs. Dallas, Coun. for Exceptional Children, Tex. State Tchrs. Assn. Democrat. Jewish. Avocations: swimming, walking, bike riding, raising poodles, water polo. Home: 2021 Via Corona Carrollton TX 75006-4614 Office: 6929 Town North Dr Dallas TX 75231-8117

JAFFREY, IRA, oncologist, educator; b. N.Y.C., July 28, 1939; s. Mack and Elaine (Schneider) J.; m. Jane Sharon Friedman, Dec. 26, 1964 (div. Mar. 1979); children: Jonathan David, Marc Jason; m. Sandra Read, June 17, 1979; 1 child, Marc Read. AB, Columbia Coll., N.Y.C., 1960; MD, SUNY, Bklyn., 1965. Intern Jewish Hosp., Bklyn., 1965-66; chief resident Elmhurst Gen. Hosp., N.Y.C., 1970; asst. resident Mt. Sinai Hosp., N.Y.C., 1968-69, resident, 1969-70, chief resident, 1970, ednl. fellow dept. hematology, 1970-71, asst. clin. prof. dept. medicine divsn. neoplastic disease, 1980—99; pres. Palisades Oncology Assocs. P.C., Pomona, 1972—; asst. clin. prof. dept. medicine U. Colo. Health Scis., Denver, 2000—. Lt. USNR, 1961-65. Oak Ridge (Tenn.) Inst. fellow, 1965. Fellow ACP, Am. Cancer Soc. (pres. Rockland City unit 1973-74), Rockland City Med. Soc. (v.p. 1992, pres. 1993-94), Mt. Sopris County Med. Soc. (pres. 2002-03). Office: Western SLOPE Oncology Assoc P C PO Box 1148 Basalt CO 81621-1148 Office Fax: 970-384-2276.

JAGACINSKI, CAROLYN MARY, psychology educator; b. Orange, N.J., Apr. 12, 1949; d. Theodore Edward and Eleanor Constance (Thys) Jagacinski; m. Richard Justus Schweickert, Dec. 27, 1980; children: Patrick, Kenneth. AB with honors in psychology, Bucknell U., 1971; MA in Psychology, U. Mich., 1975, PhD in Psychology and Edn., 1978. Rsch. assoc. U. Mich., Ann Arbor, 1978-79, Purdue U., West Lafayette, Ind., 1979-80, vis. asst. prof., 1980-83, rsch. psychologist, 1983-86, vis. lectr., 1986-88, asst. dean, 1988-89, asst. prof. psychology, 1988-94, assoc. prof., 1994—. Contbr. articles to profl. jours. U. Mich. predoctoral fellow, 1977-78, dissertation grantee, 1977-78; Exxon Edn. Found. grantee, 1983-84. Mem. APA, Midwestern Psychol. Assn., Soc. for Judgment and Decision Making, Am. Ednl. Rsch. Assn., Psychonomic Soc., Sigma Xi, Psi Chi. Avocations: tennis, reading. Office: Purdue Univ Dept Psychol Scis West Lafayette IN 47907

JAGASICH, PAUL ANTHONY, language educator, translator; b. Budapest, Hungary, Mar. 30, 1934; came to U.S., 1965, naturalized 1971; s. Peter Kalman and Etelka (Tar) J.; m. Ea Jane Nagy, oct. 15, 1960; children: Diana, Yvonne. MA, U. N.C., 1970, 71, PhD, 1973; MA, Middlebury Coll., 1983. Med. librarian Med. U., Budapest, 1958-61; major domo, sec. Motel Assn., Budapest, 1961-64; tchr. French and Russian, St. Bernard's Sch., Gladstone, N.J., 1966-68; grad. tchg. asst. U. N.C., Chapel Hill, 1968-73; chmn. prof. fgn. langs. Hampden-Sydney Coll., Va., 1973—. Language educator, translator; b. Budapest, Hungary, Mar. 30, 1934; came to U.S., 1965, naturalized, 1971; s. Peter Kalman and Etelka (Tar) J.; m. Ea Jane Nagy, Oct. 15, 1960; children— Diana, Yvonne. M.A., U. N.C., 1970, 71, Ph.D., 1973; M.A., Middlebury Coll., 1983. Med. librarian Med. U., Budapest, 1958-61; major domo, sec. Motel Assn., Budapest, 1961-64; tchr. French and Russian, St. Bernard's Sch., Gladstone, N.J., 1966-68; grad. teaching asst. U. N.C., Chapel Hill, 1968-73; chmn. prof. fgn. langs. Hampden-Sydney Coll., Va., 1973—. Translator: The Casting of Bells, 1983 (Metthauer award 1985); Mozart in Prague, 1985; Eight Days, 1985, Halley's Comet, 1987, My Cobwebbed Appletree, 1990, Dressed in Light, 1990, Short Love Song About Ctirad and Sarka, 1991, Song About Viktorka, 1991, Maminka, 1991, To Be a Poet, 1992, Starving Artist So Sees the World, 1992, Bozena Nemcova's Fan, 1992, Honeymoon Ride, 1992, The Nightingale Sings Out of Tune, 1992, Over the Waves of TSF, 1992, Only Love, 1994; author Dictionary of Oriental Lexical Elements in Hungarian, 1985, (essay) Heinar Kipphardt, 1986, (essay) All the Beauty of the World, 1991; also short stories and poems, Two Faces of the English Channel, 1991, A Course in Russian Conversation through Videotapes, 1993. Recipient O'Clee Jub. trophy; Named to Internat. Swimming Hall of Fame, 1991; Men. Am. Assn. Tchrs. German, Am. Translators Assn., Am. Literary Translators Assn., Am. Assn. Tchrs. Slavic and East European Langs., Phi Sigma Iota. Republican. Roman Catholic. Translator: The Casting of Bells, 1983 (Metthauer award 1985), Mozart in Prague, 1985, Fight Days, 1985, Halley's Comet, 1987, My Cobwebbed Appletree, 1990, Dressed in Light, 1990, Short Love Song About Ctirad and Sarka, 1991, Song about Viktorka, 1991, Maminka, 1991, To Be a Poet, 1992, Starving Artist So Sees the World, 1992, Bozena Nemcova's Fan, 1992, Honeymoon Ride, 1992, The Nightingale Sings Out of Tune, 1992, Over the Waves of TSF, 1992, Only Love, 1994; author Dictionary of Oriental Lexical Elements in Hungarian, 1985 (essay) Heinar Kipphardt, 1986 (essay) All the Beauty of the World, 1991; also short stories and poems, Two Faces of the English Channel, 1991, A Course in Russian Conversation through Videotapes, 1994. Recipient O'Clee Jub. trophy; named to Internat Swimmin Hall of Fame, 1991. Mem. Am. Assn. Tchrs. German, Am. Translators Assn., Am. Literacy Translators Assn., Am. Assn. Tchrs. Slavic and Eart European Langs., Phi Sigma Iota. Republican. Roman Catholic. Home: PO Box 81 Hmpden Sydney VA 23943-0081 Office: Hampden-Sydney Coll College Rd Hampden Sydney VA 23943

JAGGERS, VELMA MARY LEE, foundation administrator, educator; b. McAlester, Okla., Dec. 12, 1919; d. John Jaggers; m. O. Lee Jaggers, June, 1957; 1 child, Robin. Student, U. of World Ch., 1965; MA, Nat. Eccles U., London, 1970; PhD, DLitt. Ordained to ministry. Pres. Arch Elder's Commn. Internat., Inc., L.A., Miss Velma's Found., Inc., L.A.; univ. tchr. L.A. Contbr. articles to profl. publs. Recipient citation Pres. of U.S., V.P. of U.S., various govs., mayors, fgn. potentates. Address: 119 N Lake St Los Angeles CA 90026-5320

JAGO, DEIDRE ELLEN BERGUSON, kinesiology educator, tennis and volleyball coach; b. Blossburg, Pa., May 26, 1948; d. Walter Bernard and Iris Lorraine (Strong) Berguson; m. John William Jago, May 29, 1971; children: Jocelyn Anne, William Thomas. BS in Health and Phys. Edn. cum laude, East Stroudsburg (Pa.) U., 1970, MEd in Phys. Edn., 1972. Cert. instr. Profl. Tennis Registry. Tchr. T.A. Edison High Sch., Elmira Heights, N.Y., 1970-71; grad. asst. East Stroudsburg U., 1971-72; from instr. health and phys. edn. to asst. prof. Pa. State U., Hazleton, 1972—92, asst. prof. kinesiology, 1992—, asst. dir. academic affairs, 2003—. Participant People to People Citizen Amb. Women in Sport Del. to Russia and Belarus, 1993; coach women's volleyball team, U. Pa., 1992—, men's tennis team, 1992—, co-ed tennis team, 2001—; sec. faculty senate, Pa. State U., 2001-02, u. faculty senate, 1979-91, 96—. Instr. trainer water safety Hazleton chpt. ARC, 1976—; mem. Hazleton Area Sch. Bd., 1987-95, v.p., 1989, pres., 1990; mem. consistory Christ Ch., United Ch. of Christ, 1986-88, 98-2000, 2003—, sec., 1986-87, pres. 1999, treas., 2001—; Pa. Interscholastic Athletic Assn. Volleyball and Swimming Ofcl., 1993—; bd. mgrs. Hazleton Area Pub. Libr., 1987-89, 94, trustee, 1987-89, 95. Recipient vol. svc. award Hazleton chpt. ARC, 1990; mem. PEARL award for edn. YWCA, 1994. Mem. AAHPERD, AAUW (Risk Challenge award Pa. divsn. 1989, named gift to Marilyn Kreidler Gardner Endowment Hazleton br. 1989). Home: 20 Lissa Ln Sugarloaf PA 18249-9701 Office: Pa State U Highacres Hazleton PA 18201 E-mail: dej1@psu.edu.

JAGTIANI, JULAPA A. economist, educator; b. Bangkok, Dec. 28, 1957; came to the U.S., 1980; d. Sathien and Apa (Arunin) Rungakasiri; m. Anil R. Jagtiani, Dec. 31, 1990. BBA in Acctg., Thammasat U., Bangkok, 1979; MBA in Fin., NYU, 1982, MPhil, 1986, PhD in Fin. and Internat. Fin., 1989. Instr. in internat. fin. NYU, 1989; asst. prof. fin. U. Calgary, Canada, 1989—90, Syracuse (N.Y.) U., 1990—94; assoc. prof. fin. Baruch Coll., CUNY, N.Y.C., 1994—97; sr. economist Fed. Res. Bank Chgo., 1998—2001, Fed. Res. Bank Kansas City, Mo., 2001—. Contbr. articles to profl. jours. Supporter United Way, Kansas City, 2001—. Rockefeller Found. fellow, 1980-85; Alberta Energy Co. grantee, 1990. Mem. Am. Fin. Assn., Am. Econ. Assn., Fin. Mgmt. Assn., So. Fin. Assn. Avocations: piano, yoga, spiritual activities, photography. Office: Fed Res Bank Kansas City 925 Grand Blvd Kansas City MO 64198 Home: 1000 Westover Rd Kansas City MO 64113-1124 Fax: 816-523-3597. E-mail: julapa.jagtiani@kc.frb.org.

JAHNKE, JESSICA JO, university administrator, dean; b. Appleton, Wis., Nov. 4, 1949; d. Howard Tod Jahnke and Evelyn Marie Appleton Blunck. BS in Secondary English Edn., Silver Lake Coll., Manitowoc, Wis., 1971; MA in Humanities/English, Roosevelt U., Chgo., 1975; PhD in Edn., Ohio State U., 1981. Tchr. Hauser Jr. High Sch., Riverside, Ill., 1971-73; instr. Coll. Edn. Ohio State U., Columbus, 1981-82, dir. accreditation and state evaluation Coll. Edn., 1981-84, coord. program devel./adminstrn. Office Acad. Affairs, 1984-85; asst. prof. edn., exec. asst. to pres. U. Maine, Farmington, 1985-88, assoc. prof. edn., 1988-90, chair dept. elem., secondary and early childhood edn., 1988-90; dean Ctr. for Tchr. Edn. Shawnee State U., Portsmouth, Ohio, 1990—. Presenter in field. Contbr. articles to profl. jours. Mem. ASCD, Am. Ednl. Rsch. Assn., Am. Assn. Colls. Tchr. Edn. (instl. rep.). Address: PO Box 704 Fletcher NC 28732-0704

JAHNKE, SUSAN ALICE, primary education educator; b. Hartford, Conn., Jan. 24, 1950; d. Walter Henry and Alice Ruth (Strecker) J. BS in Early Childhood Edn., So. Conn. State U., 1974, MS in Early Childhood Edn., 1977; Kindermusik cert., Westminster Choir Coll., 1989; postgrad., Sacred Heart U., 1992—. First grade tchr. John F. Kennedy Sch., Milford, Conn., 1974—. Mem. Right to Read Task Force, 1980; del. Gov.'s Leadership Symposium on Career Edn., 1980; mem. com. Rev. Bd. Edn. Goals, 1981; adv. Nat. Jr. Honor Soc., 1982; faculty rep. ARC, 1982-86. Editor: Milford Edn. Assn. Communique, 1983-85; writer, dir. Submarine Band, 1978; co-editor (newsletter) Burning the Midnight Oil, 1985. Mem. Stratford (Conn.) Oratorio Choir, 1989, 91. Named Tchr. of Yr., Milford (Conn.) Jaycees, 1984-85. Mem. NEA, Internat. Reading Assn., Milford Edn. Assn., Conn. Edn. Assn., Tchrs. Advocating Whole Lang., Kappa Delta Epsilon (past pres. Phi chpt. and Beta Theta chpt.). Republican. Lutheran. Avocations: piano, voice, interior decorating, gardening, theatre. Home: 125 Warner Hill Rd Stratford CT 06614-1424 Office: John F Kennedy Sch West Ave Milford CT 06460

JAIN, MOHINDER (MONA JAIN), daycare administrator, educator; b. India, Oct. 8, 1936; came to U.S., 1964; d. Beant Singh and Bhagwati Kohli Sethi; m. Kailash M. Jain, Oct. 20, 1957; 1 child, Anila. BSc, BEdn., Delhi U., 1956 1961; MS, Fla. State U., 1971; EdS, Nova U., Ft. Lauderdale, Fla., 1981; PhD, U. South Fla., 1984; MD, Spartan Health Scis. U., 1987. Cert. tchr. Fla. Tchr. Delhi Pub. Schs., New Delhi, India, 1961-64, educator, adminstr., 1966-70; educator, Fulbright scholar Sch. Bd. of Sarasota, Fla., 1964-66; educator Sch. Bd. Manatee County, Bradenton, 1970-82; practicum advisor Nova U., Ft. Lauderdale, Fla., 1988-90; health dir. Manatee County Head Start, Bradenton, Fla., 1990—. Adj. prof. health, edn., Nova U., Ft. Lauderdale, Fla., 1987-90, Bethune-Cookman Coll., Daytona Beach, Fla., 1990—. Author: (science text) Inquiry into Science, 1968, (lab. manual) Investigations into the World of Living Things, 1970. Past chmn. Manatee Commn. on Status of Women, Bradenton, 1987—; mem. exec. com. Fla. Commn. on Status of Women, Tallahassee, 1991—; bd. dirs. UN Assn., Bradenton-Sarasota, 1987—; mem. exec. com. Manatee Human Rels. Commn., Bradenton, 1991—. Fulbright scholar U.S. Ednl. Found., Washington, 1964-66, Internat. scholar Delta Kappa Gamma, Tex., 1981-84, U. South Fla. Named scholar, Tampa, 1982—. Mem. AAUW (past pres. Bradenton, Edn. Leadership award 1978, 91), APHA, Am. Med. Women's Assn., Pres. Coun. U. South Fla., Fla. Sci. Tchrs. Assn., Fla. Assn. Profl. Health Educators, Planned Approach to Community Health, Community Health Edn. Coun., Kiwanis Internat., Phi Delta Kappa, Phi Kappa Phi. Democrat. Sikhism. Avocations: travel, reading, svc. and action projects. Home: 10309 Braden Run Bradenton FL 34202-1744 Office: Manatee County Head Start 1707 15th St E Bradenton FL 34208-3423

JAIN, SURINDER MOHAN, electronics engineering educator; b. Patiala, Punjab, India, Sept. 19, 1945; came to U.S., 1983; s. Chhajju Ram and Kamla Jain; m. Harmit Kaur, June 9, 1974; children: Sumit, Preeti. MSc in Physics, Punjabi U., Patiala, 1967, post MS diploma, 1972. Rsch. assoc. Punjabi U., 1967-71, asst. prof., 1972-74, 75-83; vis. prof. Eindhoven (The Netherlands) Tech. U., 1974-75; asst. prof. Sinclair C.C., Dayton, Ohio, 1983-88, prof., head elec. engring., 1985—, tng. coord., 1985—. Nat. electronics program evaluator Am. Coun. on Edn., Washington, 1989—; writer spl. programs GE, Ohio Bell Co., Dayton Power and Light Co.; developer tng. ctr. Pace, Inc., Laurel, Md., Textronix; co-dir. USAID, UDLP grant for India, Sinclair Coll., 1992-97; established Ctr. for Excellence at CVE, Madras, India, 1994. Author lab. manual, Analog Electronics, 1983. Social sec. Physics Assn., Punjabi U., 1974-83; career expert Explorer program Boy Scouts Am., Dayton, 1988-95. Hewlett-Packard grantee, 1988, Ohio Learning Network grantee, 2001. Mem. IEEE, Am. Soc. Engring. Edn., Tau Alpha Pi (hon.). Jianist. Achievements include development of special computer aided programs for corporate retraining of employees. Home: 1102 Kenworhty Pl Centerville OH 45458-3661 Office: Sinclair CC 444 W 3rd St Dayton OH 45402-1421

JAITE, GAIL ANN, music educator; b. Painesville, Ohio, Mar. 11, 1953; d. Gail Clarence King and Barbara Mary Safick; m. Charles E. Jaite, Jr., Mar. 22, 2003. BA, Hiram Coll., 1975. Music tchr. Jordak Elem. Sch., Middlefield, Ohio, 1975—; prin., owner Tall Pines Dog Tng., 2002—. Instr. dog agility Kenston Cmty. Edn., Auburn, Ohio, 2000—; dir. tri-sch. honors band Cardinal Schs., Middlefield, 1984—. Active in cmty. theatre; soloist Geauga County hunger task force. Mem.: Music Educators Nat. Conf., Northeastern Ohio Edn. Assn. (leader workshops), Ohio Music Edn. Assn., LELRC Dog Club, Northeastern Ohio Dog Club (pres.), Buckeye Retriever Club, Delta Kappa Gamma. Home: 13769 Old State Rd Middlefield OH 44062

JAJI, LAZARUS MUSEKIWA, educational administrator, leadership educator, consultant, researcher; b. Makumbe Mission Hospital, Zimbabwe, July 29, 1939; s. Tafa Shereni and Victoria Chenzira (Mungure) J.; m. Gail Louise Hoover, Dec. 20, 1975; children: Tsitsi Ella, Tafirenyika Christopher. BS, Morningside Coll., 1974; MEd, U. Zimbabwe, 1983; PhD, U. Ill., 1987. Youth conf. president United Meth. Ch., Zimbabwe, 1964-68; sch. choir and ch. choir dir. United Meth. Schs., Zimbabwe, 1964-77; tchr. math., dept. head Murewa (Zimbabwe) H.S., 1976-77, Harare (Zimbabwe) H.S., 1978-83; chmn. ednl. adminstrn. dept. U. Zimbabwe, 1989-93, 1989, 91, 92, chmn. team tchrs. to Germany, 1993; vis. prof. ednl. leadership Ohio U., Athens, 1993—, chair electronic roundtable rsch. African Devel., 1994—. Contractor/facilitator workshops Internat. Inst. Ednl. Planning, Paris, 1990, 91; chmn. edn. and devel. workshop U. Zimbabwe and Graz, Austria, Harare, 1989; mem. United Meth. Bd. Edn. Conf., Zimbabwe, 1993-94. Author: Grade Four Math Revision Book, 1984 (chpt.) Education in the New Zimbabwe, 1988; editor Tchrs. Bull. jour., 1989-93; contbr. articles to profl. jours. Recipient scholarships United Meth. Ch., Govt. of Zimbabwe and United Meth. Bd. Missions, 1956-62, 71, Zimman-USAID PhD Study grant U. Ill., 1984-87. Mem. Am. Edn. Rsch. Assn., Zimbabwe Edn. Rsch. Assn., Zimbabwe Math. Tchrs. Assn. (exec. mem 1980-83), Comparative Internat. Edn. Soc., N.Am. Fishing Club, Phi Delta Kappan. Zanu-PF. Avocations: church choir singing, fishing, soccer, walking, working in garden.

JAJICH, JAMES GARY, elementary and middle school educator; b. Highland Park, Mich., July 21, 1947; s. Milosav and Olga (Protasevich) J.; m. Margaret Helen Bolton, May 8, 1971; children: Dmitri, Audrey. BA, Mich. State U., 1969; MEd, No. Mich. U., 1976, EdS, 1989. Tchr., chmn. dept. history St. John's Sch. of Alta., Stony Plain, Can., 1973-74; elem. tchr. Marquette (Mich.) Area Schs., 1977-82, 86—; asst. prof. U.S. Army ROTC No. Mich. U., Marquette, 1982-86. Dir. pers. and cmty. activities Camp Grayling (Mich.) Tng. Site, 1992—, comdr. 117th Quartermaster Bn., Kingsford, Mich., 1990-92, exec. officer, 1987-90; instr. Mich. Mil. Acad., Augusta, 1981-90; chief tng. divsn. Mich. Army Nat. Guard Hqrs., Lansing, 1995—; dir. Intelligence Tng. (G-2) Hdqtrs. Mich. Army Nat. Guard dir. region E Total Army Sch. Sys., 1995; middle sch. track coach, apptd. to state com. to devel. Mich.'s Elem. Tchg. Proficiency Exam., 1990-91. Active Marquette Interfaith Forum, 1985—, Racial Harmony Task Force, Marquette, 1990—; bd. dirs. Marquette Women's Ctr., 1995—; mem. pub. rels. com. Habitat for Humanity, Marquette, 1991—; jr. warden St. Paul's Episc. Ch., Marquette, 1993-96. Col. N.G. Mem. ASCD, Phi Delta Kappa, Phi Alpha Theta. Democrat. Avocations: running, reading, canoeing, restoring and riding vintage bmw motorcycle. Home: 328 W Park St Marquette MI 49855-3329

JAMAR, JOHN WOODBRIDGE, technology education educator, consultant; b. Duluth, Minn., Oct. 23, 1929; s. Warren St. John and Lydia (Woodbridge) J.; m. Frances Lucile Edlund, Sept. 7, 1957; children: Judith Anne Jamar Jones, John Philip. BSME, Mich. Technol. U., Hougton, Mich., 1952. Cert. in aircraft structural design. Asst. mgr. mining machinery div. Lake Shore, Inc., Iron Mountain, Mich., 1956-61; v.p., co-owner Jasper Engring. & Equipment Co., Hibbing, Minn., 1961-69; projects engr. and pers., benefits mgr. Champion, Inc., Iron Mountain, 1978-83; asst. prof., lectr. Sch. Tech. Mich. Technol. U., Hougton, 1984-95; ret., 1995. Asst. v.p. Cable Constructors, Inc., Iron Mountain, 1989—; engring. mgmt. cons. MTU Tech. Transfer, Houghton, 1985—. Textbook manuscript reviewer. Served to 1st lt. USAF, 1952-56, Europe. Mem. ASME, Kiwanis (pres. 1989-90, Gov.'s Trophy 1989-90, pres. Golden K 1998-2000), Tau Beta Pi (life). Presbyterian. Avocations: hunting, fishing, camping, travel. Office: Cable Constructors Inc 105 Kent St Iron Mountain MI 49801-1507 E-mail: john.senior@cciinc.us.

JAMAR, STEVEN DWIGHT, law educator; b. Ishpeming, Mich., May 11, 1953; s. Dwight W. and Lorraine (Persgard) J.; m. Shelley June Von Hagen-Jamar, May 19, 1979; children: Alexander S., Eric D. BA, Carleton Coll., 1975; JD cum laude, Hamline U., 1979; LLM with distinction, Georgetown U., 1994. Bar: Minn. 1979, D.C. 1993, U.S. Supreme Ct. 1985. Jud. clk. Minn. Supreme Ct., St. Paul, 1979-80; pvt. practice law Minn.,

1980—89; prof. law U. Balt., 1989-90; prof. Sch. Law, Howard U., Washington, 1991—, dir. legal rsch. and writing program, 1990—2002; assoc. dir. Inst. Intellectual Property and Social Justice, 2003—. Cons. on Environ. Legal Info. Sys. project NASA, 1998-2002; cons. on Global Legal Info. Network to Law Libr. of Congress, 1999—. Co-author: Essential Lawyering Skills: Interviewing, Counseling, Negotiation, and Persuasive Fact Analysis, 1999; contbr. articles to profl. jours. Rsch. fellow Law Libr. Congress, 2000-01. Mem. ABA, ACLU, Legal Writing Inst. (pres. 1997-98), Am. Soc. Internat. Law, Amnesty Internat., Assn. Legal Writing Dirs., Sierra Club. Avocations: canoe camping, soccer, go, photography, guitar. Office: Howard U Sch Law 2900 Van Ness St NW Washington DC 20008-1106

JAMES, BARBARA FRANCES, school nurse, special education educator; b. Elizabeth, N.J., June 29, 1941; d. Edward Joseph and Frances Veronica (Szypula) Turkiewicz; 1 child, John Wayne James. Certificate in group tchg., Kean Coll., 1981; diploma, Elizabeth Gen. Sch. Nursing, 1962; BS magna cum laude, Jersey City State Coll., 1994. Cert. tchr. health edn., cert. sch. nurse, cert. infant specialist, cert. family svc. provider trainer, N.J.; RN, N.J. Oper. room nurse Alexian Bros. Hosp., Elizabeth, 1962-63; obstetrical nurse Rahway (N.J.) Hosp., 1964-65; pvt. duty nurse Alexian Bros., St. Elizabeth and Elizabeth Gen. Hosps., 1964-65; office nurse Stephan S. Halabis, MD, Linden, N.J., 1965-71; tchr. developmentally disabled Assn. for Retarded Citizens, Winfield, N.J., 1971-76; early intervention tchr., home trainer The Arc of Union County/Kohler Child Devel. Ctr., Winfield, 1976—; sch. nurse Kohler Child Dev. Ctr., Winfield, N.J., 1976—. Guest lectr. developmental disabilities Kean Coll., Middlesex County Coll., Rutgers U., Jersey City State Coll., Fla. Atlantic U., Union Coll., 1980-92; mem. pres. com. on mental retardation U.S. Dept. Health and Human Svcs., N.J. State Nurses Assn., Elizabeth Pub. Schs. One-woman shows include Elizabeth Gen. Med. Ctr., Woodbridge, N.J., 1984; exhibited in group shows at N.J. State Mus., Trenton, 1959, Elizabeth Gen. Med. Ctr., 1960-62, Found. Arts and Scis., Long Beach Island, 1981, Kean Coll., Union, N.J., 1981, Woodbridge (N.J.) Mall, 1981; author, illustrator (booklet) Recognizing Childhood Illness, 1973. Mem. legis. com. Union County Protection Coun., Elizabeth, 1975; mem. supervisory com. Winfield Fed. Credit Union, 1977; active Dem. com. Twp. of Winfield, 1978, mem. drug alliance coun., 1990; active local, county and state health fairs. Recipient Health Fair Pub. Svc. award State of N.J., Rutgers U., 1986; Garwood (N.J.) Women's Club scholar, 1959; named Teacher of the Year ARC of Union County, 1981. Mem. Coun. for Exceptional Children, League for Ednl. Advancement of Nurses. Avocation: fine arts painting. Home: 66B Wavecrest Ave Winfield Park NJ 07036-6633 Office: Arc Kohler Sch 1137 Globe Ave Mountainside NJ 07092

JAMES, CHARLES CLINTON, science education educator, consultant; b. Washington, Nov. 11, 1957; s. Charles Clinton and Harriet Fae (Bempkins) J.; m. Mary Beth Cline; children: Clinton Carty, Mariah Fae. MS in Geology, George Mason U., 1984, EdM, 1986. Chair sci. dept., dir. summer programs St. Patricks Episcopal Sch., Washington, 1982-93; dir. Carnegie Acad. Sci. Edn., Carnegie Instn. Washington, 1993—; edn. and pub. outreach NASA Astrobiology Inst., 1994—. Author: Exploring Together, 1994, Design Connections, 1995. Dir. First Light, Washington, 1989—. Recipient Presdl. Sci. Tchg. award Nat. Sci. Tchrs. Assn., 1991, 94. Episcopalian. Avocations: photography, scuba diving. Office: Carnegie Inst Washington 1530 P St NW Washington DC 20005-1933

JAMES, CHARLES FRANKLIN, JR., engineering educator, educator; b. Des Arc, Mo., July 16, 1931; s. Charles Franklin and Beulah Frances (Kyte) J.; m. Mollie Keeler, May 18, 1974; children: Thomas Elisha, Matthew Jeremiah. BS, Purdue U., 1958, MS, 1960, PhD, 1963. Registered profl. engr., Wis. Sr. indsl. engr. McDonnel Aircraft Co., 1963; asst. prof. U. R.I., 1963-66, prof., chmn. dept. indsl. engring., 1967-82, co-founder, mem Robotics Rsch. Ctr., 1980-83; C. Paul Stocker prof. engring. Ohio U., Athens, 1982-83; dean Coll. Engring. and Applied Sci., U. Wis.-Milw., 1984-95; v.p. academics Milw. Sch. of Engring., 1995-2000; ret., 2000. Cons. Asian Productivity Orgn.; arbitrator Fed. Mediation and Conciliation Service, Am. Arbitration Assn.; bd. dirs. Badger Meter Co., Milw. Contbr. articles to profl. jours. With USAF, 1951-55. Recipient Silver medal Tech. U. Budapest, Hungary, 1989. Mem. NSPE, ASME, Wis. Soc. Profl. Engrs. (pres. Milw. chpt. 1993-94, Outstanding Profl. Engr. in Edn. 1993, statewide treas. 1994-96), Inst. Indsl. Engrs., Am. Soc. Engring. Edn., Soc. Mfg. Engrs., Am. Foundrymen's Soc., Engrs. and Scis. of Milw. (bd. dirs. 1988-95, v.p. 1991-93, pres.-elect 1993-94, pres. 1994-95).

JAMES, DOROTHY LOUISE KING, special education educator; b. Columbus, Miss., Jan. 1, 1952; d. T.B. and Dorothy (Lee) King; m. Willie Earl James, July 7, 1979, children: Ebun, Shantana, Leah, Trinita, Caleb. BS magna cum laude, Harris Stowe Coll., 1979; M in Spl. Edn., U. Mo., 1988; EdD in Guidance Counseling, Lael Coll. and Grad. Sch., 1998. Itinerant resource instr. Northwest High Sch., St. Louis, 1978-80; instr. learning disabilities Cleveland High Sch., St. Louis, 1980-84, Clinton Mid. Sch., St. Louis, 1984-91; resource tchr., unit leader A-team for alternative edn. Stevens Mid. Sch., St. Louis, 1992—2002; resource tchr. Vashon H.S., 2003—. Team leader, resource tchr., The New Vashon HS, 2003—; "A" team unit leader alternative edn. Stevens Mid. Sch. 1988-2000, Drug Free Schs. and Communities Program, 1993; counselor King-James Enterprises, St. Louis, 1988—; team leader, resource tchr., founder Student Response Team, St. Louis, 1988—. Editor (speech) Internat. Yr. of the Child, 1979 (Bravo award Youth Adv. Comsn. St. Louis County Youth Programs), Clinton Middle School Student Handbook, 1989, team leader Drug Free Schools Community Program. Youth adv. mem. Conflict Mediation, 1992-96; mem. support coun. Stevens Mid. Sch., 1992-96; active New Ebenezer Bapt. Ch. Recipient Excellence in Drug Prevention award U.S. Dept. Edn., 1994, cert. of commendatio, 1994; granteee Power X, The Positive Peer Coalition; winner KPLR-TV Promoting Pers. and Comty Health, 1997. Mem. Coun. for Exceptional Children, Alpha Kappa Alpha. Avocations: reading, walking, stamp collecting, cooking. Home and Office: 2431 Strawberry Fields Ct Florissant MO 63033-1765

JAMES, HELEN FOSTER, education director; b. San Diego, Sept. 3, 1951; d. Seth Charles and Naomi Charlene; m. Robert Paul James, May 25, 1987. BA, San Diego State U., 1973, MEd, 1980; DEd, No. Ariz. U., 1990. Cert. adminstrv. svcs., libr. svcs., C.C. credential, elem. credential. Elem. tchr. Jamul (Calif.) Sch. Dist., 1978-82; media specialist San Diego (Calif.) County Office Edn., 1982-89; coord. libr. media svcs. Santee (Calif.) Sch. Dist., 1989-96, San Diego State U., 1996—. Publs. adv. bd. Ednl Horizons, Bloomington, Ind., 1988-92; adv. bd. mem. Sch. Book Fairs, St. Petersburg, Fla., 1993-95; com. mem. Calif. Young Reader Medal Com., Calif., 1994-98; mem. Carnegie Com., 2001-02. Author: Across the Generations, 1997, Day Adventures, 2003. Adv. cons. San Diego (Calif.) Children's Mus., 1982-94; bd. mem. Carlsbad (Calif.) Children's Mus., 1994-96. Fellow Calif. State U. L.A., 1986. Mem. Internat. Reading Assn., Calif. Tchrs. English, Soc. Children's Book Writer's and Illustrators, Greater San Diego Reading Assn. (pres. 1985-86, bd. mem., award of excellence 1993), Pi Lambda Theta (com. mem., Anna Tracey Meml. award 1993). Avocations: hiking, camping, backpacking. Home and Office: 3818 Riviera Dr Apt 1 San Diego CA 92109-6307

JAMES, HERMAN DELANO, former college administrator; b. St. Thomas, V.I., Feb. 25, 1943; s. Henry and Frances (Smith) J.; m. Marie Nannie Gray, Feb. 25, 1964; children— Renee, Sybil, Sidney BS, Tuskegee Inst., 1965; MA, St. John's U., N.Y.C., 1967; PhD, U. Pitts., 1972; LLD (hon.), Tuskagee U., 1996. Asst. prof. U. Mass., Boston, 1973-78, assoc. provost, 1975-77, asst. chancellor, 1977-78; vice provost Calif. State U.-Northridge, 1978-82; v.p. Rowan Coll. N.J., 1982-84; pres. Rowan U., Glassboro, 1984-98, pres. emeritus, disting. prof., 1998—. Bd. dirs. Mid. States Assn., S. Jersey Industries. Contbr. articles to profl. jours. Bd. dirs. Gloucester County (N.J.) United Way; mem. transition team for gov.-elect James Florio, N.J. NIH fellow, 1968-71; recipient Outstanding Achiever award Boston YMCA, 1977, Outstanding Contbr. award Nat. Ctr. for Deafness, 1982, Civic award Cherry Hill Minority Civic Assn., N.J., 1985; Tosney award, Amer. Assn. of Univ. Admin., 1994. Mem. Am. Assn. Higher Edn., Am. Sociol. Assn., N.J. C. of C. (bd. dirs.). Avocation: basketball. Office: Rowan U 201 Mullica Hill Rd Glassboro NJ 08028-1702*

JAMES, MARIE MOODY, clergywoman, musician, vocal music educator; b. Chgo., Jan. 23, 1928; d. Frank and Mary (Portis) Moody; m. Johnnie James, May 25, 1968. B Music Edn., Chgo. Music Coll., 1949; postgrad., U. Ill., Champaign-Urbana, 1952, 72, Moody Bible Inst., Chgo., 1963-64; MusM, Roosevelt U., 1969, MA, 1976; DD, Internat. Bible Inst. and Sem., Plymouth, Fla., 1985; postgrad., Trinity Evang. Div. Sch., Deerfield, Ill., 1995; DRE, Logos Grad. Sch., 1995. Key punch operator Dept. Treasury, Chgo., 1950-52; tchr. Posen-Robbins Bd. Edn., Robbins, Ill., 1952-59; tchr. vocal music Englewood High Sch., Chgo., 1964-84; music counselor Head Start, Chgo., 1965-66. Exec. dir. House of Love DayCare, 1983, 88, Mary P. Moody Christian Acad., 1989, supt., 1989; dir. Handbell Choir for Srs. Maple Park United Meth. Ch., 1988-92; bd. dirs. Van Moody Sch. Music, Chgo. Composer, arranger choral music: Hide Me, 1963, Christmas Time, 1980, Come With Us, Our God Will Do Thee Good, 1986, The Indiana House, 1987, Behold, I Will Do a New Thing, 1989, Mary P. Moody Christian Academy School Song 1989, Glory and Honor, 1992. Organist Allen Temple A.M.E. Ch., 1941-45; asst. organist Choppin A.M.E. Ch., 1945-49; organist-dir. Progressive Ch. of God in Christ, Maywood, Ill., 1950-60; missionary Child Evangelism Fellowship, Chgo., 1955-63; unit leader YWCA, New Buffalo, Mich., 1956-58; min. of music God's House of All Nations, Chgo., 1960-80; pastor God's House of Love, Prayer and Deliverance, Robbins, 1982—; chmn. Frank and Mary Moody Scholarship Com., 1984—; dir. music Christian Women's Ourtreach Ministry, 1984-88; mem. Robbins Community Coun., 1987-88; camp counselor Abraham Lincoln Ctr., 1951-53. Coppin A.M.E. Ch. scholar, 1946; recipient Humanitarian award God's House of Love, Prayer and Deliverance, 1992, Disting. Leadership award God First Ministries, 2002. Mem. Music Educators Nat. Conf., Good News Club (tchr. 1987-90, Robbins, Ill.). Home: 8154 S Indiana Ave Chicago IL 60619-4712

JAMES, MARK OLOV, education educator; b. Jamestown, N.D., Oct. 10, 1954; s. Robert Louis and Joan Dee (Lillie) James; m. Choon Huay Chua, June 30, 1978; children: Robert, Mark, Jeremy, Daniel, Tiffany. BA, Brigham Young U., Laie, Hawaii, 1979; MA, Brigham Young U., 1981; PhD, U. Hawaii, 1996. From English instr. to assoc. prof. Brigham Young U. Hawaii Campus, Laie, 1981-92; dir. study program Tchrs. English to Speakers Other Lang., Laie, 1992—. Author: (book) Beyond Words, 1989. Pres. fgn. lang. instrn. com. Laie Elem. Sch., 1991—95, assoc. dean lang. and linguistics, 1997—. U.S. Dept. Edn. fellow, 1990—91. Mem.: TESOL (editor 1992—, TESL reporter), Internat. Assn. World Englishes (charter). Mem. Lds Ch. Office: Brigham Young Univ PO Box 1834 Laie HI 96762 E-mail: jamesm@byuh.edu.

JAMES, NANCY IRENE, elementary education educator; b. Stigler, Okla., Dec. 1, 1933; d. Charles Alfred and Lamina (Alverson) Dilday; m. Leroy Murrow James, May 3, 1953; children: Bill, Mike, Nancy. AA, Carl Albert State Coll., 1975; BS in Edn., Northeastern State U., 1978, MEd, 1983. Cert. elem. edn., spl. endorsement in kindergarten and social studies. Tutor for Indian students Poteau (Okla.) Pub. Schs., spring 1978; kindergarten tchr. Panama (Okla.) Pub. Schs., 1978—. Sec. Panama Classroom Tchrs. Assn., 1986-87; sec.-treas. Leflore County Okla. Edn. Assn., 1986-91; del. Okla. Edn. Assn., Oklahoma City, NEA, Okla., 1986-91. Mem. Internat. Reading Assn., Okla. Reading Coun., Leflore County Reading Coun. (hon. coun. chmn. 1986-96, pres. 1989), Alpha Delta Kappa (chaplain Delta chpt. 1984, pres. 1986, rec. sec. 1994-96, dist. 3 chairperson 1986-88, state chaplain 1989, state rec. sec. 1992-94, sgt.-at-arms 1994-96) Democrat. Baptist. Avocations: reading, sewing, gardening, traveling.

JAMES, SHERMAN ATHONIA, social epidemiologist, educator; b. Hartsville, S.C., Oct. 25, 1943; s. Jerome and Helen Genese (Bachus) J.; m. Vera Lucia Moura; children: Sherman Alexander, Scott Anthony. AB, Talladega Coll., 1964; PhD, Washington U., 1973. Prof. epidemiology U. N.C., Chapel Hill, 1973-89, U. Mich., Ann Arbor, 1989—, assoc. dean acad. affairs Sch. Pub. Health. Cons. NIMH, NIH, Bethesda, Md., 1979-83, Nat. Heart, Lung and Blood Inst., 1985—, Nat. Inst. Environ. Health Sci., 1990—; cons. NAS, Washington, 1994—. Contbr. articles to profl. jours. Capt. USAF, 1964-69. Fellow Soc. of Fellows, U. Mich., 1993—. Fellow Am. Heart Assn., Acad. Behavioral Medicine Rsch., Soc. Behavioral Medicine, Am. Coll. Epidemiology; mem. Am. Men and Women of Sci. Inst. Medicine. Avocations: travel, photography, tennis, nature walks. Office: Univ Mich 109 Observatory St Ann Arbor MI 48109-2029

JAMES, SUSANNE MARIE, biology educator; b. Sacramento, Oct. 5, 1951; d. Donald Frederick James and Carma (Covey) Thomas; children: Larissa Celeste Anderson, Hilary Renee Anderson. BA in Sociology, Calif. State Coll., 1974; MA in Biology, U. Calif., Riverside, 1979, PhD in Botany, 1983. Postdoctoral rsch. scientist Savannah River Ecology Lab., Aiken, S.C., 1987-90; open space adminstr. City of Thousand Oaks (Calif.), 1984-86; county planner County of Ventura, Ventura, Calif., 1983-84; rsch. scientist U.S. Forest Svc., Riverside, Calif., with fire mgmt. San Bernandino, Calif., 1974-83; lect. Berry Coll., Rome, Ga., 1990-93, asst. prof., 1993-94; lectr. We. Wash. U., Bellingham, 1995—99, dir. deg. programs and summer session, 1998—. Author: Prescribed Fire, 1984; contbr. articles to profl. jours. Civil rights cons. Inst. for Land and Resource Mgmt., San Bernardino. Mem. Bot. Soc. Am., Ecol. Soc. Am., Soc. Wetland Scientists, Internat. Assn. Wildland Fire, Sigma Xi.

JAMES, TANYS GENE, biology educator, consultant; b. Freeport, Ill., Feb. 25, 1945; d. E.W. and Phyllis Aline (Race) Strawn; m. William H. Ostermeyer, Sept. 13, 1969 (dec. May 1972); m. Cecil Dow James, Aug. 10, 1974; children: Matthew, Phyllis K. BA, North Ctrl. Coll., 1968; MS, No. Ill. U., 1969; AAS in Nursing, Elgin (Ill.) C.C., 1974; MEd, Tex. A&M U., 1991. Cert. tchr., Tex.; cert. adminstrn., prin., Tex.; RN, Tex. Homebound tchr. Cmty. Sch. D # 300, Dundee, Ill., 1971-72; LVN Dr. E.S. Hernandez, Elgin, Ill., 1972-74; CCU RN Dallas Meth. Hosp., 1974-75; geriat. RN cons. Beverly Enterprises, Graham, Tex., 1976-85; nursing instr. Vernon (Tex.) Regional Jr. Coll., 1992—; sci. and psychology instr. Ranger (Tex.) Coll., 1977—; sci. dept. chmn. Graham H.S., 1983—. Contbr. articles to profl. jours. including Sci. Tch., NCC Sci. Tchr. Pres. Heart of Tex. Girl Scouts USA, Brownwood, 1992—. G.I.F.T. fellow G.T.E. Corp., 1989-90; Tandy Tech. scholar, 1991-92. Mem. NSTA, NEA, Tex. Assn. Biology Tchrs., Nat. Assn. Biology Tchrs., Graham Tchrs. Assn. (pres. 1987-89), Sci. Tchrs. Assn. Tex. (region IX dir. 1989—), Phi Delta Kappa, Delta Kappa Gamma (area XVI coord. 1997—, pres. 1990-92, Chpt. Achievement award 1996). Republican. Episcopalian. Avocations: needlework, reading, piano performance, golfing, walking. Home: 1625 S Rodgers Dr Graham TX 76450-5012 Office: Graham HS/Ranger Coll 1000 Brazos St Graham TX 76450-3944

JAMES, THOMAS NAUM, cardiologist, educator; b. Amory, Miss., Oct. 24, 1925; s. Naum and Kata J.; m. Gleaves Elizabeth Tynes, June 22, 1948; children: Thomas Mark, Terrence Fenner, Peter Naum. BS, Tulane U., 1946, MD, 1949. Diplomate Am. Bd. Internal Medicine (mem. bd. govs. 1982-88), Bd. Cardiovasc. Diseases (bd. dirs. 1972-78). Intern Henry Ford Hosp., Detroit, 1949-50, resident in internal medicine and cardiology, 1950-53, staff, 1959-68; instr. medicine Tulane U., New Orleans, 1955-58, asst. prof., 1959; prof. medicine U. Ala. Med. Ctr., Birmingham, 1968-87, prof. pathology, 1968-73, assoc. prof. physiology and biophysics, 1969-73, dir. Cardiovasc. Rsch. and Tng. Ctr., 1970-77, chmn. dept. medicine, dir. divsn. cardiovasc. disease, 1973-81, Mary Gertrude Waters prof. cardiology, 1976-87, Disting. prof., 1981-87; prof. medicine, prof. pathology U. Tex. Med. Br., Galveston, 1987—, pres., 1987-97, dir. WHO Cardiovasc. Ctr., 1988-98, Thomas N. and Gleaves T. James disting. chair cardiol. scis., 1997—. U. Tex. Med. Br., Galveston, 1997—; physician-in-chief U. Ala. Hosps., 1973-81; mem. adv. coun. Nat. Heart Lung and Blood Inst., 1975-79; pres. 10th World Congress Cardiology, 1986; mem. cardiology del. invited by Chinese Med. Assn. to China, 1978; Campbell orator Queens U., Belfast, No. Ireland, 1982; Mikamo lectr. Japan Circulation Soc., 1982; Sir Thomas Lewis lectr. Brit. Cardiac Soc., 1983, Einthoven lectr. U. Leiden, The Netherlands, 1993, Bailey K. Ashford lectr. U. P.R., 1995; hon. lectr. U. Padua, 1998. Author: Anatomy of the Coronary Arteries, 1961, The Etiology of Myocardial Infarction, 1963; Mem. editl. bd. Circulation, 1966-83, Am. Jour. Cardiology, 1968-82, Am. Heart Jour, 1976-79; contbr. articles to profl. jours. Capt. M.C. U.S. Army, 1953-55. Recipient Sesquicentennial Medal of Honor Paul Tulane Coll. Tulane U., 1997, 50-year Lifetime Achievement award Tulane Med. Alumni Assn., 1999, James B. Herrick award, Am. Heart Assn., 1999. Fellow ACP (gov. Ala. 1975-79, master 1983)); mem. AMA, Am. Clin. and Climatological Assn. (v.p. 1992-93, councillor 1992-93), Assn. Am. Physicians, Am. Soc. Clin. Investigation, Assn. Univ. Cardiologists (pres. 1978-79), Am. Heart Assn. (pres. 1979-80, Herrick award Coun. on Clin. Cardiology 1999), Am. Coll. Cardiology (v.p. 1970-71, trustee 1970-71, 76-81, First Disting. Scientist award 1982, chmn. publs. com. 1994-97), Am. Soc. Pharmacology and Exptl. Therapeutics, Soc. Exptl. Biology of Medicine, Am. Coll. Chest Physicians, Ctrl. Soc. Clin. Rsch., Internat. Soc. and Fedn. Cardiology (pres. 1983-84), WHO (expert adv. panel on cardiovascular diseases 1988-97), So. Soc. Clin. Investigation, Am. Fedn. Clin. Rsch., Ala. Acad. Honor. Philos. Soc. Tex., Phi Beta Kappa, Sigma Xi, Omicron Delta Kappa, Alpha Omega Alpha, Alpha Tau Omega, Phi Chi. Clubs: Cosmos, Mountain Brook, Galveston Artillery. Presbyterian. Office: U Tex Med Br 301 University Blvd Galveston TX 77555-0175

JAMES, VIRGINIA SCOTT, elementary school educator; b. Mobile, Ala., Feb. 5, 1955; d. Timothy Varian and Sarah (Watts) Scott; m. Jeffery Thomas Heathcock, June 7, 1980 (widowed, July 1988); m. Colvin Jerome James, Mar. 22, 1991. BS, Mobile Coll., 1978; grad. in pub. speaking, Dale Carnegie Sch., 1978. Cert. tchr. grades kindergarten through 8, Ala. Tchr. grades 1 and 2 Cypress Shores Christian Sch., Mobile, 1983-84; tchr. grade 2 Irvington Christian Sch., Mobile, 1984-85; early intervention tchr. reading and math. grades 1 through 8 Riggins Elem. Sch., Birmingham, Ala., 1985—, title one 3d grade tchr., 1995—. Sponsor various 3rd through 5th grade Just Say No Clubs, Riggins Elem. Sch., 1986—; choir Warrior United Meth. Ch. Mem. Ala. Edn. Assn., Birmingham Edn. Assn., Birmingham Area Reading Coun., Ala. Classroom Tchrs. (social dir. Birmingham chpt. 1991-92). Methodist. Avocations: hiking, horseback riding, reading, collecting dolls while traveling. Home: 3680 Goblers Knob Rd Warrior AL 35180-3154

JAMES, VIRGINIA STOWELL, retired elementary, secondary education educator; d. Austin Leavitt and Doris Carolyn Stowell; m. William Hall James, June 24, 1950; 1 child, Hillery. BA, Middlebury Coll., 1947; MA, Yale U., 1955; PhD, U. Conn., 1988. Cert. tchr.. cert. art tchr. Elem. tchr. Bd. Edn., Westport, Conn., 1950-58; art tchr. grades 6-9 Wallingford (Conn.) Bd. Edn., tchr. gifted/talented grades 4-5, kindergarten, 1958-91; ret., 1991. Contbr. articles to profl. jours. Mem. NEA, AAUW, DAR, Soc. of Children's Book Writers and Illustrators, Nat. Assn. for Gifted Children, Conn. Assn. for the Gifted, Conn. Edn. Assn., Nat. Mus. Women in Arts, Phi Delta Kappa, Pi Lambda Theta, Delta Kappa Gamma. Address: PO Box 234 Northford CT 06472-0234

JAMESON, GARY, art educator; b. Aurora, Ill., Jan. 18, 1950; BFA, U. Ill., 1972; MA, No. Ill. U., 1975, MFA, 1976; student, Skowhegan (Maine) Sch., 1972. Profl. artist, 1972—; art tchr. The Calverton Sch., Huntingtown, Md., 1989—, chmn. arts dept., 1993—. Adj. faculty Coll. So. Md., La Plata, Md., 1989—; artist/restoration artist Carlson-Jameson, Inc., North Beach, Md., 1979—. Councilman Town of North Beach, 1982-90, 94-98, mem. Hist. Dist. Commn., 1987—; mem. Ann-Marie Sculpture Garden com., Calvert County, Md., 1993—. Office: The Calverton Sch 300 Calverton School Rd Huntingtown MD 20639-9499 E-mail: gjameson@calvertonschool.org.

JAMESON, SANFORD CHANDLER, education educator; b. Toronto, Ohio, Feb. 12, 1932; s. Sanford Frank and Dorothy Lee (Robinson) J.; m. Joan Sheridan, June 29, 1963; children: Jennifer Joan, Julie Jo. BS, Miami U., Oxford, Ohio, 1954; MA, Case Western Res. U., 1960. Asst. dir. admission Case Western Res. U., Cleve., 1957-60; assoc. dir. admissions Carleton Coll., Northfield, Minn., 1960-63; asst. regional dir. Coll. Entrance Exam. Bd., Evanston, Ill., 1963-66, asst. dir. internat. edn. Ctrl. Office N.Y.C., 1966-69, assoc. for internat. edn., 1969-71, dir. internat. edn. Washington, 1971-94, dir. emeritus, 1994—. Chmn. Nat. Coun. Evaluation Fgn. Ednl. Credentials, 1974-78, active, 1964-94; chmn. Alliance for Internat. Ednl. Exch., 1986-88, active, 1980-94; mem. Internat. Sch. Svc., 1974-81, 83-90, 2001—, chmn., 1988-90, Author, editor workshop reports in field. Lt. USNR, 1954-57. Recipient cert. of appreciation, U.S. Dept. State, 1992. Mem. SAR, Nat. Assn. Coll. Admission Counselors, NAFSA: Assn. Internat. Educators (life, mem., bd. dirs., chmn. admissin sect., pres. 1976-77), Am. Assn. Collegiate Registrars and Admission Officers (chmn. nat. liaison com. fgn. student admissions 1972-74, sec., 1974-87, cert. of appreciation 1995), Soc. Mayflower Descs., Md. Mayflower Soc. (bd. dirs. 1997—, Soc. of Cincinnati (docent Anderson House), Masons (32d degree), Shriners, Sigma Alpha Epsilon. Presbyterian (elder). Home and Office: 4948 Sentinel Dr Bethesda MD 20816-1239

JAMIESON, STUART WILLIAM, surgeon, educator; b. Bulawayo, Rhodesia, July 30, 1947; came to U.S., 1977; MB, BS, U. London, 1971. Intern St. Mary's Hosp., London, 1971; resident St. Mary's Hosp., Northwick Park Hosp., Brompton Hosp., London, 1972-77; asst. prof. Stanford U., Calif., 1980-83, assoc. prof., 1983-86; prof., head cardiac surgery U. Minn., Mpls., 1986-89, U. Calif., San Diego, 1989—. Dir. Minn. Heart and Lung Inst., Mpls., 1986-89; pres. Calif. Heart and Lung Inst., San Diego, 1991-95. Co-author: Heart and Heart-Lung Transplantation, 1989; editor: Heart Surgery, 1987; contbr. over 600 papers to med. jours. Recipient Brit. Heart Found. Fellowship award, 1978, Irvine H. Page award Am. Heart Found., 1979, Silver medal Danish Surg. Soc., 1986. Fellow ACS, Royal Coll. Surgeons, Royal Soc. Medicine, Am. Coll. Chest Physicians, Am. Coll. Cardiology; mem. Royal Coll. Physicians (licentiate), Internat. Soc. for Heart Transplantation (pres. 1986-88), Calif. Heart and Lung Inst. (pres. 1991—), Internat. Soc. Cardiothoracic Surgery (pres. 2003-.). Office: U Calif Divsn Cardiothoracic Surgery 200 W Arbor Dr San Diego CA 92103-8892

JAMISON, MARY RUFFIN, special education educator; b. Sussex, Va., Jan. 27, 1953; d. James Andrew and Otelia (Diggs) R.; m. O'Berry Kelly Houpe, Jan. 12, 1973 (dec. June 1977); 1 child, Kelly Alonda; m. David Lee Jamison, Nov. 15, 1980; 1 child, LaKeesha Daveene. BS, Va. State U., 1980; student, Va. Commonwealth U., 1983-86; MS, Va. State U., 1992. Cert. tchr., Va. Spl. edn. tchr. Southside Va. Tng. Ctr., Petersburg, 1980-89, Petersburg Pub. Schs., 1989—. Treas. Area 16 Spl. Olympics, Petersburg, 1985-88; mem. exec. bd. PTA. Mem. Coun. for Exceptional Children, Kappa Delta Pi (Iota Epsilon chpt.). Baptist. Avocations: writing poetry, traveling, bowling, reading, piano. Home: 2909 Tinsberry Dr Colonial Heights VA 23834-5121

JAN, COLLEEN ROSE, secondary school educator; b. Toledo, Ohio, Sept. 1, 1953; d. Robert James and Irene Dolores (Bartnikowski) Kegerreis;

children: Brett Robert Jan, Shawna Michele Jan. AA, Monroe County C.C., Mich., 1973; BS, U. Toledo, 1975, JD, 1978, MEd, 1992, postgrad., 1992-98. Cert. in secondary edn., Mich. Sec. Family Planning, Monroe, 1971-73; paralegal Bedford Legal Bldg., Temperance, Mich., 1973-80; tchr. Bedford Pub. Schs., Lambertville, Mich., 1989—, lang. arts chair, 1996, social studies chair, 1996—. Mem. negotiating team Bedford Pub. Schs., 1997—; mem. NCA Outcomes Visitation Team, Birney Middle Sch., Southfield, Mich., 1993—; mem. dist. assessment and profl. devel. com., 1995-96. Creater video: Winning at the MEAP, 1991. Expository com. co-chair Sch. Improvement/Bedford, Temperance, 1991—, steering com., 1992—; social studies core curriculum mem. Intermediate Sch. Dist., Monroe, 1993-94, Bedford Pub. Schs., 1994—; co-chair NCA steering com., 1994—; co-advisor Students United Against Drugs, Temperance, 1990-96; designer The Cmty. Svc. Alternative, Temperance, 1993-94; facilitator Lion's Club Quest Program, Temperance, 1989-91; campaign mgr. Sch. Bd. Mem., 1987-88; 3d v.p. PTA, Lambertville, Mich., 1998-99; pres. PTSA Bedford Jr. H.S., 1998-99. Mem. AAUW, Nat. Coun. for the Social Studies, Bedford Edn. Assn. (pres. 2000—), Phi Delta Kappa, Phi Kappa Phi. Avocations: travel, reading, woodworking, cards. Office: Bedford Jr High Sch 8405 Jackman Rd Temperance MI 48182-9498

JANAVARAS, BASIL JOHN, business educator, consultant; b. Corinth, Corinth, Greece, Nov. 1, 1943; came to U.S., 1962; s. John Basil and Loukia Demetra (Tzakona) J.; m. Linda Mae Larson, Aug. 19, 1972; children: Loukia Linda, John Basil (dec.). BA, Minot State U., 1967; MS, U. N.D., 1969; EdD, No. Ill. U., 1974. Bus. instr. Mankato (Minn.) State U., 1969-72, asst. prof., 1974-76, assoc. prof., 1977-80, prof., 1980—; dir. Internat. Bus. Inst., Mankato, 1986-89, chairperson, dir., 1986-91; pres., CEO Ianavaras & Assocs. Internat., Inc., 1990—; dir. internat. bus. studies U. St. Thomas, St. Paul, 1992—. Pres. Odyssey Gift Shops, Mankato, 1978-94; dir. Internat. Bus. Exec. Program, St. Paul, 1988—, Minn. State U. Sys., Vienna, Austria, 1990-92. Author: Student Guide to International Business, 1988, Student Resource Manual, 1992, Global Marketing Management System, 1998; contbr. articles to profl. jours. Grantee Mankato State U., 1988-89, U.S. Dept. Edn., 1988-90, So. Minn. Initiative Fund, 1988-90. Mem. Acad. Internat. Bus., Minn. World Trade Week (bd. dirs. 1983—, pres. 1989), Minn. Dist. Export Coun., Minn. World Trade Assn. Home: 27 Capri Dr Mankato MN 56001-4119 Office: Minn State U Mankato 150 Morris Hall Mankato MN 56001-6044 E-mail: basil.janavaras@mnsu.edu.

JANCUK, KATHLEEN FRANCES, educational administrator; b. Balt., Apr. 1, 1950; d. Joseph Frank and Dorothy Jane (Lowry) J. BA in Elem. Edn., Notre Dame Coll., Balt., 1974; MEd in Reading, Towson State U., 1985. MEd in Adminstrn., Loyola Coll., Balt., 1992. Cert. tchr., reading specialist, adminstr. and supr., Md. Substitute tchr. St. Wenceslaus, Balt., 1970-72; tchr. 5th grade St. Boniface, Phila., 1972-77, Cath. C.C., Balt., 1977-82, reading specialist K-5, 1982-88; reading specialist K-8 St. Mary's Elem. Sch., Annapolis, Md., 1988-91; prin. St. Clare Sch., Balt., 1991-97, St. John Neumann Sch., Cumberland, Md., 1997—2002; dir. elem. sch. Bishop Walsh Sch., Cumberland, 2002—. Non-voting mem. St. Clare Sch. Bd., Balt., 1991-97, St. John Neumann Sch. Bd., 1997-2002; mem. Sch. Sisters of Notre Dame, 1991—; mem. area pastoral coun., 1993-97. Recipient Recognition of Svc. award Archdiocese of Balt., 1993. Mem. ASCD. Elem. Sch. Prins. Assn. (exec. bd. dirs. 1994-97), Nat. Cath. Ednl. Assn., Internat. Reading Assn., Mid. States Assn. Sch. Evaluation Teams. Democrat. Roman Catholic. Avocations: collecting clowns, puppetry, swimming, singing, playing guitar and piano. Office: Bishop Walsh School 700 Bishop Walsh Rd Cumberland MD 21502

JANDRIS, THOMAS PAUL, program director; b. Chgo., Sept. 6, 1948; s. Raymond R. and Marie J. (McLean) J.; m. Theresa M. Bellert, Aug. 14, 1992; children: Brody, Ryan. BS in Edn., Ea. Ill. U., 1970; MEd, Wayne State U., 1974; PhD, U. Minn., 1978. Cert. secondary tchr., gen. adminstrn.; lic. consulting psychologist. With Nat. Security Agy., Berlin, 1971-74; asst. prof. U. Minn., Mpls., 1974-76; asst. prin. Downers Grove (Ill.) North H.S., 1976-79; prin. Springfield (Ill.) H.S., 1979-80, Barrington (Ill.) H.S., 1980-83; mng. ptnr. Mainstream Access Inc., N.Y.C., 1983-88; owner, mng. ptnr. Enterchange, Inc., Westchester, Ill., 1988-92; prin. H.S. Dist. 209, Hillside, Ill., 1992-94; dir. secondary edn. Unit Sch. Dist. 131, Aurora, Ill., 1994—. Conf. speaker Internat. ASCD, Arlington, Va.; bd. dirs. Drucker Found., N.Y.C., Rainbows for All Children, Schaumburg, Ill. Author: RIFed, 1979, Silent Echos, 1990. Chmn. bd. dirs. Fellowship of Christian Athletes, Chgo., 1976-82; mem. Lions Club, Barrington, 1980-86. Served with U.S. Army, 1971-74. Recipient U.S. Presdl. Spirit of Honor medal, U.S. Army, 1971; mem. U.S. Olympic team U.S. Team Handball Fedn., 1972-76. Mem. ASCD, AASA, Nat. Assn. Secondary Sch. Prins., Ill. Prin. Assn. Avocations: triathlon competition, marathon running, golf.

JANE, JAY-LIN, food science educator; b. Taipei, Taiwan, Mar. 10, 1951; came to U.S., 1975; d. Tung Hsiang and Chih Fei Cheng. BS, Nat. Chung-Hsing U., Taichung, Taiwan, 1973; MS, Tex. Woman's U., 1978; PhD, Iowa State U., 1984. Rsch. assoc. Kans. State U., Manhattan, 1984-87; prof. food sci. Iowa State U., Ames, 1987—. Assoc. editor Cereal Chemistry, 1988-92; mem. editl. bd. Jour. Polymer and Environ., Bioimacromolecules, Carbohydrate Polymers; contbr. chpt. to book, articles to profl. jours. Corn Refiners Assn. fellow, 1992, 93; DuPont Co. ednl. aid grantee, 1994, 97, 98; recipient award for utilization rsch. Am. Soybean Assn., 1995. Mem. Am. Chem. Soc. (exec. com. 1994-98, Best Paper award 1991), Am. Assn. Cereal Chemists (Gedds lectr. N.W. sect. 1997, divsn. chair 1996-97), Bio-Environ. Degradation Polymer Soc. (treas. 1994-96), Sigma Xi (pres.-elect 2003). Achievements include patent on methods of making granular cold-water soluble starch; 7 patents on biodegradable plastics; invention of methods of making small-particle starch; understanding of granular structure of starch.

JANEWAY, RICHARD, university official; b. LA, Feb. 12, 1933; s. VanZandt and Grace Eleanor (Bell) J.; m. Katherine Esmond Pillsbury, Dec. 23, 1955; children: Susan Kent, David VanZandt, Elizabeth Anne. AB, Colgate U., 1954; MD, U. Pa., 1958. Diplomate Am. Bd. Psychiatry and Neurology. Intern Hosp. U. Pa., 1958—59; resident N.C. Baptist Hosp., Winston-Salem, 1963—66; mem. faculty Bowman Gray Sch. Medicine (now Wake Forest U. Sch. Medicine), Winston-Salem, 1966—; prof. neurology Wake Forest U., Winston-Salem, 1971—2003, prof. medicine and mgmt., 1997—2003, prof. emeritus, 2003—, dir. Cerebral Vascular Rsch. Ctr., Bowman Gray Sch. Medicine, 1969—71; dean Bowman Gray Sch. Medicine Wake Forest U., Winston-Salem, 1971—85, exec. dean, 1985—94, v.p. health affairs, 1983—90, exec. v.p. health affairs, 1990—97. Exec. com. So. Nat. Bank, Winston-Salem, N.C., 1982-92; exec. com. BB&T Corp., chmn. exec. com. 2001-03; nat. adv. coun. regional med. programs HEW. 1974-77; mem.-at-large Nat. Bd. Med. Examiners, 1979-87; mem. N.C. Joint Conf. Com. on Med. Care, Inc., 1983-2003; mem. N.C. Inst. Medicine. Active Winston-Salem Forsyth County Bd. Edn., 1970-73; bd. dirs. Nat. Assn. for Biomed. Rsch., 1993-96; Ams. for Med. Progress, Inc., 1993-97, Winston-Salem Found., 1994-2002, chmn., 1997, 98; trustee Colgate U., 1988-95, Winston-Salem State U., 1991-95. Capt. USAF, 1959—63. USPHS fellow, 1956; Markle scholar, 1968-73 Fellow: ACP, Am. Heart Assn (coun. on stroke), Am. Acad. Neurology; mem.: AMA, Soc. Med. Adminstrs., Greater Winston-Salem C. of C. (bd. dirs. 1985—89, 1991—95, chmn 1992), Inst. Medicine of NAS, Am. Clin. and Climatol. Assn., Assn. Am. Med. Colls. (exec. coun. 1977—86, mem. accreditation coun. on grad med. edn. 1981—85, chmn. coun. of deans 1982—83, exec. com. 1982—86, chmn. 1984—85), Am. Neurol. Assn., Rotary (dir. 1977—80, v.p. 1981—82, pres. 1982—83), Alpha Omega Alpha, Sigma Xi, Phi Beta Kappa. E-mail: rjaneway@triad.rr.com.

JANIGA, MARY ANN, art educator, artist; b. Lackawanna, N.Y., June 14, 1950; d. Jacob and Julia (Zatlukal) Mazurchuk; m. William B. Janiga, Nov. 23, 1972; children: Nicholas, Matthew. BS, State U. Coll., Buffalo, 1972, MS, 1974, cert. advanced study, 1995. Cert. in sch. adminstrn. and supervision. Tchr. art Buffalo Pub. Schs., 1972—. Art facilitator Olmsted Sch., Buffalo, 1985—; supervising tchr. State Univ. Coll., Buffalo; liaison Albright-Knox Art Gallery, 1994—; art presenter fed. pre-kindergarten program, 1998; wrote art curriculum Buffalo Pub. Sch., 2002. Carnegie Hall, N.Y.C., 2002; co-ordinated with Fisher-Price Designers, Buffalo Pub. Sch. Art Program, 2003. Exhibited in group shows at Cheektowaga (N.Y.) Art Guild, 1979, Erie County Parks Art Festival, 1979, Lockport Art Festival, 1980, Allentown Art Exhibit, Kennan Ctr. Recipient various awards for art; grantee Buffalo Tchr. Ctr., 1986-90, Olmstead Home Sch. Assn., 1991-97, Allentown Village Soc., 1994; grantee Fisher Price, 2003. Mem. NEA, PAT (life), Olmsted Home Sch. Assn., SUNY-Buffalo Alumni Assn., Buffalo Tchrs. Fedn., Buffalo Fine Arts Acad., Buffalo Soc. Natural Scis., Zool. Soc. of Buffalo, Lancaster H.S. Home Sch. Assn. (rec. sec. 1998-99, co-pres. 1999-01). Avocations: reading, concerts, theater, art exhibits. Office: Olmsted Sch 64 874 Amherst St Buffalo NY 14216-3502

JANIS, ELINOR RAIDEN, artist, educator; b. N.Y.C., Dec. 8, 1934; d. Edward and Lea Raiden; m. Leon Janis, July 14, 1957 (div. Jan. 5, 1970); children: Madeline, Richard, Cheryl. BA in Elem. Edn., UCLA, 1957; MFA, Instituto Allende, San Miguel De Allende, Mex., 1975. Instr. elem. schs., 1957—66, Woman's Workshop, Granada Hills, Calif., 1971—73; painting instr. Instituto Allende, 1974, 1976—77, Santa Monica (Calif.) Pks. and Recreation, 1977; instr. L.A. City Schs., 1978—86; profl. artist, 1986—. One-woman shows include Galeria Conde, San Miguel de Allende, Mex., 1974, Beyond Baroque Gallery, Venice, Calif., 1977, Canyon Cafe, Glendale, Calif., 2000—01, exhibited in group shows at Barnsdall Pk., L.A., 1972, Emerson Gallery, 1972, Brentwood (Calif.) Art Ctr., 1973, Geleria Pintora de Jovenes, Mexico City, 1974, McCaffery Galleries, L.A., 1973, Ryder Gallery, 1973, Galeria Pintora de Jovenes, Mexico City, 1974, Powerhouse Gallery, Montreal, Can., 1975, Woman's Bldg., L.A., 1975, Woman's Ctr., Ridgefield, Con.., 1975, Assn. Humanist Artists, San Francisco, 1975, Museo de Arte Contemporaneo, San Miguel de Allende, 1977, others. Mem. Amnesty Internat., L.A., 1995—2001, NOW, 1985—2001, Handgun Control, 1990—2001. Recipient scholarship, Instituto Allende, 1974, 2d prize, Burbank Creative Arts Ctr. Show, 2001. Mem.: Valley Artists Guild, L.A. County Mus. Art. Democrat. Jewish. Avocations: pottery, stone carving, etching. Office: Elinor Janis Studio 14417 Chase St # 298 Panorama City CA 91402

JANKOVIC, JOSEPH, neurologist, educator, scientist; b. Teplice, Czechoslovakia, Mar. 1, 1948; came to U.S., 1965; m. Cathy Sue Inselberg, May 26, 1973; children: Jason, Daniel, Zachary. MD, U. Ariz., 1973. Diplomate Am. Bd. Neurology. Med. intern Baylor Coll. Medicine, Houston, 1973-74, asst. prof. neurology, 1977-84, assoc. prof., 1984-88, prof., 1988—; resident in neurology Columbia U., N.Y.C., 1974-76, chief resident in neurology, 1976-77. Dir. Parkinson's Disease Ctr. and Movement Disorder Clinic, Houston, 1977—; sr. attending physician Meth. Hosp., Houston, 1988—. Author over 500 articles and book chpts. in field; editor/co-editor 16 med. books; mem. editorial bd. jours. Movement Disorders, Clin. Neuropharmacology, Neurology Jour., Jour. Neurology Psychiatry. Chmn. sci. adv. bd. Blepharospasm Rsch. Found.; mem. adv. bd. Dystonia Med. Rsch. Found., Internat. Tremor Found., Tourette's Syndrome Med. Adv. Bd. Grantee disease rsch. founds., pharmaceutical cos., NIH Fellow Am. Acad. Neurology; mem. AMA, Am. Neurol. Assn., Soc. for Neurosci., Movement Disorders Soc. (pres.-elect 1991-94, pres. 1994-96). Avocations: tennis, family activities, music. Office: Baylor Coll Medicine 6550 Fannin St Ste 1801 Houston TX 77030-2744

JANKOWSKA, MARIA ANNA, librarian, educator; b. Jarocin, Poland, Aug. 12, 1952; d. Tadeusz and Aleksandra (Ruszkowska) Nocun; m. Piotr L. Jankowski, Jan. 14, 1978; children: Pawel Pat, Marta Maja. MA, Sch. Econs., Poznan, Poland, 1975, PhD, 1983; M Libr. Info. Sci., U. Calif., Berkeley, 1989. Rsch. and tchg. asst. Sch. Econs., Poznan, 1976-83, asst. prof., 1983-85; catalog libr., asst. prof. U. Idaho, Moscow, 1989-94, network resources libr., assoc. prof., 1995—, prof., 2001—. Author: Electronic Guide to Polish Research and University Libraries, 1996, Idaho Geospatial Data Center, 1998; founding editor Green Libr. Jour., 1991-94; gen. editor Electronic Green Jour., 1994—. Recipient Movers and Shakers award Libr. Jour., 2002; guest scholar Smithsonian Inst., Woodrow Wilson Internat. Ctr., Washington, 1985; fellow U Calif., Berkeley Sch. Libr. and Info. Studies, 1989; grantee Rsch. Coun. Grant, U. Idaho, 1990, 95, 2001, Internat. Rsch. and Exchs. Bd., Washington, 1995, 96. Mem. ALA (chair task force on environ. 1993-95, 98—), Idaho Libr. Assn., Beta Phi Mu. Office: U Idaho Libr Rayburn St Moscow ID 83844-0001 Fax: (208) 885-6817. E-mail: majanko@uidaho.edu.

JANOVY, KAREN ANNE ONETH, art museum educator, curator; b. El Reno, Okla., Aug. 1, 1940; d. Glenn T. and Evelyn Winola (Lucas) Oneth; m. John Janovy Jr., Aug. 7, 1961; children: Cynthia Anne, Jenifer Lynn, John III. BFA, U. Okla., 1961; MA, U. Nebr., 1993. Project asst. Sheldon Meml. Art Gallery, U. Nebr., Lincoln, 1984-87, edn. coord., 1987-94, catalogue co-editor, 1991—; lectr. mus. studies grad. program U. Nebr., Lincoln, 1993—, curator edn., 1995—. Co-editor The American Painting Collection of the Sheldon Memorial Art Gallery, 1988. Bd. dirs. Lincoln Arts Coun., 1985-91; bd. dirs.-at-large Lincoln Found., 1980's; pres. Jr. League of Lincoln, 1982-83; exec. dir. Lincoln Community Concert Assn., 1973-82. Mem. Nat. Art Edn. Assn., Nebr. Art Tchrs. Assn.(Art Educator of Yr., 1992, 95, 99), Am. Assn. Mus. Vols., Am. Assn. Mus., Nebr. Mus. Assn. (membership co-chair 1990—), Mountain Plains Mus. Assn. Home: 421 Sycamore Dr Lincoln NE 68510-4352 Office: Sheldon Meml Art Gallery 12th And R St Lincoln NE 68588-0300

JANOWITZ, GERALD SAUL, geophysicist, educator; b. N.Y.C., Apr. 5, 1943; s. Leo and Yetta (Caress) J.; m. Barbara Susan Kantrowitz, Mar. 23, 1968; 1 child, David. BS, Poly. Inst. Bklyn., 1963; MS, Johns Hopkins U., 1965, PhD, 1967. Asst. prof. Case Western Res. U., Cleve., 1968-75; assoc. prof. N.C. State U., Raleigh, 1975-80, prof., 1980—. Contbr. over 60 articles to profl. jours. Mem. Am. Geophys. Union, Sigma Xi. Office: NC State U PO Box 8208 Raleigh NC 27695-8208 Home: 208 Hogan Farm Rd Apex NC 27523-5441

JANSZ, BARBARA RAYMOND, elementary education educator; b. Naperville, Ill., May 29, 1947; d. Robert James and Mae Edith (Roche) Raymond; m. Thomas Wayne Kavanagh Jansz, Apr. 11, 1970. Student, Miss. State Coll. for Women, 1965-67; BA in Elem. Edn., No. Ill. U., 1969, MS in Elem. Edn., 1970. Tchr. 3d, 4th, 5th, 6th grades Dist. # 131, East Aurora, Ill., 1969-89; tchr. 3rd, 4th, 5th, 6th grades, 1969-89; tchr. 4th grade, curriculum resource specialist, 1989-92; instrnl. coord., 1989-92; tchr. 1st grade, 1992-95; tchr. 2nd grade, 1995—. Participant math. project Problem Solving Critical Thinking; coord. Scholastic On-Line Network, N.Y.C., 1992—; scholastic cons. Elec. Book Project, N.Y.C., 1991—; tchr. advisor Scholastic's Literacy Pl., 1993; early lit. in-svc. facilitator Rigby Co., Cary, Ill., 1990—; with North Cen. Regional Edn. Lab., Oak Brook, Ill., 1992—. Treas. East Aurora (Ill.) Coun. IFT, 1982-84; bldg. rep. Naperville (Ill.) Edn. Assn., 1991; sec. Naperville Saddle Club, 1993—. Named Young Educator of Yr., Aurora (Ill.) Jaycees, 1980, Disting. Educator Ill. State Bd. Edn., Springfield, 1981, Kane County Educator of Yr., 1983. Mem. Ill. Coun. Tchrs. Math., Nat. Coun. Tchrs. Math., Ill. Reading Coun., Internat. Reading Assn., Nat. Coun. Tchrs. English, Nat. Assn. Edn. Young Children. Republican. Roman Catholic. Avocations: horseback riding, trail riding, quilting. Home: 106 N Morley Rd Elizabeth IL 61028 Office: Dist # 203 Naperville Schs Webster and Hillside Naperville IL 60540

JANTOLAK, LAURA JEAN, elementary school educator; b. Apr. 4, 1946; BA in Edn., U. Ariz., 1968; MA in Tchg., Nat. U., 2003. Tchr. 5th grade Centralia Sch. Dist., Buena Pk., Calif., 1968-75, tchr. 6th grade, 1975—, tchr. 5th & 6th grades, 1990-91, 98-99; ednl. cons. TeachSoft, 1994—, TeachSoft.com, 1997—, gifted and talented edn. coach (GATE), 2002—. Home: 1616 S Euclid St Spc 58 Anaheim CA 92802-2437

JANTZEN, J(OHN) MARC, retired education educator; b. Hillsboro, Kans., July 30, 1908; s. John D. and Louise (Janzen) J.; m. Ruth Patton, June 9, 1935; children: John Marc, Myron Patton, Karen Louise. AB, Bethel Coll., Newton, Kans., 1934; A.M., U. Kans., 1937, PhD, 1940. Elementary sch. tchr., Marion County, Kans., 1927-30, Hillsboro, Kan., 1930-31; high sch. tchr., 1934-36; instr. sch. edn. U. Kans., 1936-40; asst. prof. Sch. Edn., U. of Pacific, Stockton, Calif., 1940-42, assoc. prof., 1942-44, prof., 1944-78, prof. emeritus, 1978—, also dean sch. edn., 1944-74, emeritus, 1974—, dir. summer sessions, 1940-72. Condr. overseas seminars; mem., chmn. commn. equal opportunities in edn. Calif. Dept. Edn., 1959-69; mem., chmn. Commn. Tchr. Edn. Calif. Tchrs. Assn., 1956-62; mem. Nat. Coun. for Accreditation Tchr. Edn., 1969-72. Bd. dirs. Ednl. Travel Inst., 1965-89. Recipient hon. svd. award Calif. Congress Parents and Tchrs., 1982, McCaffrey disting. Svc. award in recognition of leadership in higher edn., cmty. relationships and internat. svc. San Joaquin Delta Coll., 1996. Mem. NEA, Am. Edn. Rsch. Assn., Calif. Edn. Rsch. Assn. (past pres. 1954-55), Calif. Coun. for Edn. Tchrs., Calif. Assn. of Colls. for Tchr. Edn. (sec., treas. 1975-85), Rotary (Outstanding Rotarian of Yr. award North Stockton 1990, Paul Harris fellow 1980), Stockton Coun. PTA Found., Phi Delta Kappa. Methodist. Home: Folsom, Calif. Died Aug. 26, 2001; Stockton, Calif..

JARABA, MARTHA E. (BETTY JARABA), secondary school educator; b. San Pedro Sula, Honduras, Feb. 27, 1952; d. G.E. and Francisca L. (Reynaud) Donaldson; children: Janine Ilene, Jimmy. BA in French, Spanish, La. State U., 1972; M in Ednl. Supervision, Northwestern U., 1998. Cert. tchr. French, Spanish, ESL. Foundation dir. El Paso (Tex.) Ind. Sch. Dist., 1993—. Examiner for Ednl. Testing Svc.; mentor New Tchrs. Assistance Program; presenter in field. Published author. Panelist in edn. Tex. Commn. on the Arts; pres. City of El Paso Arts Resource Dept.; bd. dirs. The Opera Co.; mem. standing com. on arts, culture, and recreation for the U.S. Conf. of Mayors. Named Tchr. of Yr., Tex. Tchr. Task Force. Mem. NEA, TESOL, Tex. TESOL, Assn. Fundraising Profls., Tex. State Tchrs. Assn., El Paso Tchrs. Assn. Home: 6629 Camino Fuente Dr El Paso TX 79912-2407 Office Fax: 915-521-4727.

JARCHO, JUDITH LYNN, artist, art educator; b. Mpls., Mar. 24, 1944; d. Paul and Lillian (Garetz) Brazman; m. Michael Jarcho, Nov. 24, 1968; children: Jason M., Johanna Molly. BFA, Mpls. Coll. Art & Design, 1968; tchg. credential elem. and art edn., Coll. St. Rose, Albany, N.Y., 1975. Grades K-6 art tchr. Albany Sch. Dist., 1971-74; art tchr. Portrait Soc., La Jolla, Calif., 1996, San Digeto Art Assn., Del Mar, Calif., 1996, El Cajon (Calif.) Art Assn., 1997. Juror Del Mar Art Fair/Art Exhbn., 1995, El Cajon Art Assn. Annual Exhbn., 1996, San Diego Art Inst., 1998. Works exhibited San Diego Mus. Art, 1994, Rose-Hulman Inst. Tech., Terre Haute, Ind., 1994, Nat. Arts Club, N.Y.C., 1994, Poudre Valley Artist League, Denver, 1995, Tijuana (Mexico) Cultural Ctr., 1995, Hampton Classic, Bridgehampton, N.Y., 1995, Perry House Galleries, Old Town Alexandria, Va., 1995, Linda Joslin Gallery, La Jolla, Calif., 1995, Mpls. Found., 1996, Robert Mondavi Food & Wine Ctr., Orange County, Calif., 1996, The Parrish Art Mus., South Hampton, N.Y., 1996, San Diego Mus. Art, 1995-99, Univ. Club, San Diego, 1998. Philantropist Helen Woodward Animal Ctr., Rancho Santa Fe, Calif., 1996-98; past pres. San Diego Mus. of Art Artist Guild. Named Entrepreneur of Yr., Vishe Corp., San Diego, 1998, Best Canine Artist, Manhattan Guest mag., 2001, Overall Gold award ann. report competition League Am. Comm. Profls., 2001. E-mail: jjarcho@msn.com.

JARCZYNSKI, ELAINE CHILDS, nurse educator; b. Rockledge, Fla., Aug. 14, 1957; d. Joseph Francis Jarczynski and Patricia Ann Sturrock. Grad. in nursing, Brevard C.C., 1977; BSN, U. Ctrl. Fla., 1985, postgrad., 2003—04. RN Fla., cert. wound care nurse, legal nurse cons. Clin. therapy specialist HILL-ROM Co., Batesville, Ind., 1987—. Lectr., educator on wound mgmt. and issues related to immobility. Author: (with Oscar Alvarez) Pressure Ulcers: Physical, Supportive and Local Aspects of Management, 1991; co-author: Fourth National Pressure Ulcer Survey, 1997, also sci. posters. Mem. AACN, Am. Assn. Geriatric Nursing, Wound Healing Soc. (assoc.), Wound, Ostomy and Continence Nurses Soc., Sigma Theta Tau. Avocations: walking, biking.

JARMA, DONNA MARIE, secondary education educator; b. Portsmouth, Va., Aug. 31, 1949; d. Harry A. Sr. and Dreau M. (Schaedel) J. AA, Temple (Tex.) Jr. Coll., 1969; BA, U. Mary-Hardin Baylor, 1971; MA, Tex. Woman's U., 1990, PhD, 2003. Tchr. English and Spanish Troy H.S., 1971—77, Howe H.S., 1977—2002. Mem. campus improvement com., Howe Ind. Sch. Dist., 1995-96, mem. curriculum com., 1993; instr. English Grayson County Coll.; instr. Tex A&M U., Commerce, Tex. Contbr. articles to The Leaflet and Inland, English in Tex. Lector and Cath. Christian Doctrine, St. Mary's Cath. Ch., Sherman, Tex., 1988—. Named Tchr. of the Yr., Region 10, Tex. Edn. Assn., 1999, Tchr. of Yr. Wal-Mart, 2000. Mem. NCTE (presenter 1999), Tex. Coun. Tchrs. English (presenter 1994-2003, English and Lang. Arts Educator of Yr. 1998-99), Tex. Gifted/Talented (presenter, Austin, 1993-97). Roman Catholic. Avocations: writing, music, book collecting, bicycling, computers. Home: 2300 W Taylor St Sherman TX 75092-2765 E-mail: djarm@texoma.net.

JARMAN, MARK FOSTER, English language educator; b. Mt. Sterling, Ky., June 5, 1952; s. Donald Ray and Bo Dee (Foster) J.; m. Amy Lynn Kane, Dec. 28, 1974; children: Claire Marie, Zoe Anne. BA, U. Calif., Santa Cruz, 1974; MFA, U. Iowa, 1976. Instr. Ind. State U., Evansville, 1976-78; vis. lectr. U. Calif., Irvine, 1979-80; asst. prof. English Murray (Ky.) State U., 1980-83, Vanderbilt U., Nashville, 1983-86, assoc. prof. English, 1986-92, prof. English, 1992—. Mem. Associated Writing Programs, Norfolk, Va., 1980—, Poets' Prize Com., N.Y.C., 1988-2002. Author: Iris, 1992, The Black Riviera, 1990, 2d edit., 1995, Far and Away, 1985, The Rote Walker, 1981, North Sea, 1978, 2d edit., 1989, The Reaper Essays, 1996, Questions for Ecclesiastes, 1997, Unholy Sonnets, 2000, The Secret of Poetry, 2001, Body and Soul: Essays on Poetry, 2002; editor: Rebel Angels: 25 Poets of the New Formalism, 1996. Winner Poets' prize, 1991, Lenore Marshall Poetry prize, Acad. of Am. Poets and The Nation Mag.,1998; John Simon Guggenheim Meml. Found. poetry fellow, 1991-92, Robert Frost fellow, Bread Loaf Writer's Conf., 1985: NEA grantee, 1977, 83, 92; recipient Joseph Henry Jackson award SF Found., 1974. Mem. Nat. Book Critics Cir. Mem. Christian Ch. Office: Vanderbilt U Dept English Nashville TN 37235

JARNIGAN-GRAY, ANGELA RENEE, elementary school educator; b. Savannah, Ga., Mar. 14, 1956; d. Walter Edwin and Marie Antoinette (Hardrick) Jarnigan; m. Kevin Darnell Gray, Dec. 26, 1997; children: Albert Clayton Smith II, Alisha Colette McKinnis. Student, S.C. State U., Orangeburg, 1974-77; BS, Armstrong State Coll., Savannah, 1989. Cert. tchr. elem. edn., Ga. Tchr. Young World, Greensboro, N.C., 1979-81, Parent and Child Day Care, Savannah, 1982-83; switchboard operator Hyatt Regency-Savannah, 1982, 83; para-profl. Chatham-Savannah Bd. Edn., 1984-88; tchr. 1st grade Windsor Forest Elem. Sch., Savannah, 1989—. Camp tchr. Meml. Day Sch., Savannah, 1987; mentor Savannah-Chatham County Bd. Edn., 1994—. Mem. NEA, Ga. Assn. Educators, Chatham Assn. Educators. Roman Catholic. Avocations: sewing, computers. Home: 1705 Vassar St Savannah GA 31405-3862

JAROS, DEAN, university official; b. Racine, Wis., Aug. 23, 1938; s. Joseph and Emma (Kotas) J. BA, Lawrence Coll., Appleton, Wis., 1960; MA, Vanderbilt U., 1962, PhD, 1966. Asst. prof. polit. sci. Wayne State U., Detroit, 1963-66; from asst. prof. to prof. polit. sci. U. Ky., 1966-78, assoc. dean Grad. Sch., 1978-80; dean Grad. Sch. No. Ill. U., DeKalb, 1980-84, Colo. State U., Ft. Collins, 1984-91, assoc. provost, 1991—; dir. Soc. Sr. Scholars. Author: Socialization to Politics, 1973, Political Behavior: Choices and Perspectives, 1974, Heroes Without Legacy, 1993, also articles.; Mem. editorial bds. profl. jours. Mem. Exptl. Aircraft Assn. Office: Colo State U Grad Sch Fort Collins CO 80523-0001

JARRARD, JAMES PAUL, school program administrator; b. Flint, Mich., July 5, 1951; s. Donald and Virginia Bernadine J. BA with honors, Mich. State U., 1975; MS in Edn., U. So. Calif., University Park, 1982; postgrad., Boston U. Tchr. lang. arts and reading Agrl. Migrant Sch., Immokalee, Fla., 1976-78; tchr. lang. art. and social studies Flint Community Schs., 1978-81; tchr. computer sci., and lang. arts Makiminato Schs. Dept. Def. Schs., Naha, Okinawa, Japan, 1981-84, tchr. computer sci. Mannheim (Fed. Republic Germany) High Sch., 1984-86, tchr. computer sci. Munich High Sch., 1986, dist. computer coord. Germany Region, 1986-89, sch. info. mgr. Atlantic Region London, 1989-92, mgr. sch. info. sys. devel. Arlington, Va., 1992-94; knowledge mgmt. officer Peace Corps, 2000—02; nat. def. coord. Nat. Assess Edn. Progress, 2002—. Edn. tech. rschr. and developer Dept. Def. Edn. Activity, 1994-96. career tech. coord., 1996-97, coord. electronic comm., 1997-99, chief internat strategist. 1999-2001; chief knowledge officer Peace Corps, 2001—. Mem. ASCD, Overseas Edn. Assn. (NEA). Home: 6917 Lodestone Ct Alexandria VA 22306-1216

JARRARD, LEONARD EVERETT, psychologist, educator; b. Waco, Tex., Oct. 23, 1930; s. Thomas Ivan and Levis Everett (Lasswell) J.; m. Janet Grier Shoop, Aug. 16, 1958; children: Alice Grier, David Frazier, Hugh Everett. BA, Baylor U., Waco, 1955; MS, Carnegie Inst. Tech., Pitts., 1957, PhD, 1959. Asst. to asso. prof. psychology Washington and Lee U., 1959-66; assoc. prof. to prof. psychology Carnegie-Mellon U., 1966-71; Robert L. Telford prof. psychology Washington and Lee U., Lexington, Va., 1971-2001, prof. emeritus, 2001—. Vis. lectr., prof. exptl. psychology U. Oxford, Eng., 1975-76; interim assoc. prof. anatomy U. Fla., 1965-66; acad. visitor Inst. Psychiatry, U. London, 1988-89. Editor: Cognitive Processes of Nonhuman Primates, 1971; cons. editor: Jour. Comparative and Physiol. Psychology, 1970-75, Behavioral Neurosci. Psychology, 1995-2001. Served with USAF, 1952-54. Fellow AAAS, APA, APS; mem. Soc. for Neurosci., Psychonomics Soc., Va. Acad. Sci. So. Soc. Philosophy and Psychology, Phi Beta Kappa, Omicron Delta Kappa, Sigma Xi. Home: RR 5 Box 1067 Lexington VA 24450-9805 Office: Washington and Lee U Dept Psychology Lexington VA 24450

JARRELL, IRIS BONDS, elementary school educator, business executive; b. Winston-Salem, N.C., May 25, 1942; d. Ira and Annie Gertrude (Vandiver) Bonds; m. Tommy Dorsey Martin, Feb. 13, 1965; 1 child, Carlos Miguel; m. 2d, Clyde Rickey Jarrell, June 25, 1983; stepchildren: Tamara, Cris, Kimberly. Student, U. N.C., Greensboro, 1960-61, 68-69, student, 1974-75, Salem Coll., 1976; BS in Edn., Winston-Salem State U., 1983; M in Elem. Edn., Gardner-Webb Coll., 1992. Cert. tchr., N.C. Tchr. Rutledge Coll., Winston-Salem, 1982-84; owner, mgr. Rainbow's End Consignment Shop, Winston-Salem, 1983-85; tchr. elem. edn. Winston-Salem/Forsyth County Sch. Svcs., 1985-96; dir. Knollwood Bapt. Pre-Sch., 1996-97; tchr. gifted/talented students Winston-Salem/Forsyth County Schs., 1998; tchr. Clemmons Elem. Sch., 1998—. Contbr. poetry to mags. Mem. Assn. of Couples for Marriage Enrichment, Winston-Salem, 1985-86; mem. Winston-Salem Symphony Chorale; mem. Planned Parenthood. Mem. NOW, Internat. Reading Assn., N.C. Assn. Adult Edn., Forsyth Assn. Classroom Tchrs., World Wildlife Fund, Greenpeace, KlanWatch. Democrat. Baptist. Avocations: singing, writing, sewing, gardening, reading. Home: 101 Cheswyck Ln Winston Salem NC 27104-2905 E-mail: ijarrell@bellsouth.net.

JARRELL, ROSEANN, elementary school educator; b. New Orleans, Dec. 12, 1949; d. Emmit Marvin and Betty Joan (Russo) J. BS, Our Lady of Holy Cross, Algiers, La., 1973; MEd, U. New Orleans, 1976, postgrad., 1982. Cert. tchr. elem., early childhood edn., reading specialist. Tchr. 1st grade River Oaks Acad., Belle Chasse, La., 1973-82; tchr. kindergarten Allemands Elem. Sch., Des Allemands, La., 1982—, Dial R coord., 1990—. Early childhood cons.; lectr. in field; cons. Therapeutic Foster Care, Algiers, 1988—. Cons. Interested Citizens of New Orleans, 1988—; parent/tchr. Disability Coun., New Orleans, 1992—; therapeutic foster care parent/cons. Gulf Coast Tchr., 1988—; mem. St. Michael Guild. Mem. ASCD, St. Charles Reading Coun., Agenda for Children, La. Assn. for Edn. Young Children. Roman Catholic. Avocations: reading, working with handicapped children, beaded ornaments. Home: 126 Downing Ct Belle Chasse LA 70037-2358 Office: Allemands Elem Sch 1471 Wpa Rd Des Allemands LA 70030-3027

JARRETT, CRAIG ALLEN, elementary school educator; b. Lewisburg, Pa., Oct. 17, 1953; s. Richard Leon and Marian Edna (Klingler) J.; m. Nanette Marie Graziano, Nov. 15, 1980; children: Jason Andrew, Justin Daniel, Jonathan Nathaniel. BS, Millersville (Pa.) U., 1974; MEd, Pa. State U., 1979. Tchr. tech. edn. Milton (Pa.) Mid. Sch., 1975—. Advisor Tech. Student Assn., Milton, 1988—, bd. dirs. Region 7, 1990—. Scoutmaster Boy Scouts Am., New Columbia, Pa., 1994—; Little League coach West Milton/Newky League, New Columbia, 1993—97. Recipient Silver Beaver award, Boy Scouts Am., 2001, Wood badge, 1985, Vigil-Order of Arrow, 1985; Edcore grantee, 1993—98. Mem. NEA, Pa. State Edn. Assn., Tech. Edn. Assn. Pa. (Supr. of Yr. 1994), NRA (life), Boy Scouts Am. (life., Eagle Scout). Republican. Lutheran. Avocations: woodcarving, hunting, camping, smallbore silhouette shooting. Home: 299 Graylyn Crest Dr New Columbia PA 17856-9729 Office: Milton Mid Sch 700 Mahoning St Milton PA 17847-2231 E-mail: cjarrett@evenlink.com., caj01@milton.k12.pa.us.

JARRETT, GRACIE MAE, middle school guidance counselor; b. Kansas City, Kans., Feb. 8, 1944; d. Hosea George Washington and Sylvia Ann (McCluney) Canady; m. Gennie Jarrett, Jr., July 11, 1987; children: Tony Jarrett, André D. Oden, Dale Marie Jarrett. AA, Coffeyville (Kans.) JUCO, 1964; BS, Kans. State Coll., 1968; MS, Troy (Ala.) State U., 1975. Cert. tchr.; cert. guidance counselor. Nurse aide, cashier Kansas City U. Med. Ctr., 1962-67; phys. edn. tchr. Kansas City Mo. Dist., 1968-73; sch. social worker Okaloosa County Schs., Ft. Walton Beach, Fla., 1973-76; spl. agt. tng. FBI, Quantico, Va., 1976; substitute tchr. Berryessa Sch. Dist., San Jose, Calif., 1976; personal lines underwriter Reliance Ins. Co., Shawnee Mission, Kans., 1977-81; vocat. edn. counselor Operation P.U.S.H., Kansas City, Mo., 1981; casemanager Kansas Youth Trust, Kansas City, Kans., 1982-83; guidance counselor Sch. Dist. #204, Bonner Springs, Kans., 1983—. Trainer, spkr. U. Mo., Kansas City, 1989—; trainer Adult Illiteracy Program, Kansas City, 1993-94; del. Minority Leadership Tng., Bonner Spring, 1995. Co-sponsor, chaperone Spl. Olympics of Fla., Fort Walton Beach, 1973-75; vol. Community Action Program, Kansas City, 1978-82, Hotline, Kansas City, 1978-80; mem. Kansas Polit. Action, Bonner Springs, 1994—; nominating com. Senator Al Ramirez, Bonner Springs, 1991-93. Scholarship Delta Sigma Theta, 1964; named Kappa Sweetheart Kappa Alpha Psi. Mem. NEA, ACA, NAACP (bd. dirs. 1977-98), ASCD, AARP, Kans. Nat. Edn. Assn. (HCR commr. chair 1994-95, pres. 1990, constn./bylanws com. 1999—, mem. com. 1992-94, black caucus 1994—, bd. dirs. 1997—, Wyandotte United Uniserv bd. 1994—), Bonner Springs Edn. Assn. (pres., rep., del. 1982—, co-head negotiator 1996), Delta Kappa Gamma. Baptist. Avocations: swimming, sewing, reading, public speaking, writing poetry. Home: 1746 S 98th St Kansas City KS 66111-3528 Office: Robert E Clark Middle Sch 420 N Bluegrass St Bonner Springs KS 66012-1608

JARRETT, POLLY HAWKINS, secondary education educator, retired; b. Columbia, S.C., May 6, 1929; d. William Harold and Ann Beatrice (Carson) Hawkins; m. Nov. 21, 1953 (dec. Aug. 1984); children: William Guy Jr., Henry Carson. Student, Montreat Coll., 1947-49; BS in Secondary Edn., Longwood Coll., 1951. Tchr. 7th grade McDowell County Schs., Marion, N.C., 1951-52; tchr. 8th grade Marion City Schs., 1952-53, Burke County Schs., Morganton, N.C., 1954-56; tchr. 7th grade Wake County Schs., Raleigh, N.C., 1956-58, Durham (N.C.) County Schs., 1958-59; tchr. 7th and 8th grade Raleigh City and Wake County Schs., Raleigh, 1959-79; tchr. social studies Wake County Pub. Schs., Raleigh, 1979-90, ret., 1990. Adv. bd. State Employees Credit Union, Raleigh, 1988-92, 94-00. Mem. United Daus. of the Confederacy (chpt. pres. 1978-81, 91-96, divsn. historian 1981-83, dist. VI dir. 1983-85, divsn. chaplain 1986-90, divsn. parliamentarian 1994-96, chmn. bd. trustees 1990-91), Delta Kappa Gamma (chpt. pres. 1988-90, regional dir. 1990-92, state 2d v.p. 1997-99, chmn. N.C. divsn. State Conv. 2001, mem. S.E. regional steering com. 2003), Kappa Delta Pi, Pi Delta Epsilon, Pi Gamma Mu. Democrat. Methodist. Avocations: travel, growing roses, reading, pets. Home: 3405 White Oak Rd Raleigh NC 27609-7620

JARRETT, TWILA MARIE, special education educator; b. Devils Lake, N.D., Dec. 10, 1954; d. William O. and Della C. (Marchand) Folendorf; m. Greg A. Jarrett, Aug. 4, 1979 (dec. Jan. 1988); children: Sara, Elizabeth. BS in Edn., Minn. State U., Moorhead, 1977; postgrad., Minn. State U., Minot State Coll., N.D. State U., U. N.D.; MS in Counseling and Guidance, No. State U., 1995. Spl. edn. tchr.-TMH Brainerd (Minn.) State Hosp., 1977-79; adult edn. tchr. Pride Industries, Bismarck, N.D., 1979-81; spl. edn. tchr.-EMH Bismarck High Sch., 1981-88, vocat. resource educator, 1989—. Advisor student coun., 1983—. Vol. Big Brother/Big Sister Program, Brainerd, 1977-79; tchr. religious edn., Brainerd and Bismarck, 1977—; vol. Mental Health Assn., Bismarck, 1983-84; mem. adv. bd. Office of Separate, Divorced and Widowed, Bismarck, 1990—. Mem. ASCD, Am. Vocat. Assn., N.D. Assn. Vocat. Edn. of Spl. Needs Pers., Begnining Experience of Western N.D. (facilitator, v.p. 1991—, pres.). Avocations: walking, reading, gardening, volleyball, piano. Home: 1220 Michigan Ave Bismarck ND 58504-5939 Office: Bismarck High Sch 800 N 8th St Bismarck ND 58501-3997

JARUSSI, PATRICIA LILLIAN, elementary education educator; b. Lower Burrell, Pa., Apr. 18, 1956; d. Donald G. and Cladinora (Iarussi) J. BS in Elem. Edn., Edinboro State Coll., 1978; M in Elem. Edn., Marshall U., 1998. Cert. tchr., W.Va. Tchr. Madison (W.Va.) Elem. Sch., 1978—94, Danville Elem., 1994—97, Brookview Elem., Foster, W.Va., 1997—2003. Workshops, inservices coord. Active County Take A Kid To Dinner, Madison, Grandparent Involvement Program and Parent Vols., Madison; mem. Danville Lion Club. Mem. NEA, W.Va. Edn. Assn., Madison-Danville Jaycees (coms.), Lions (pres. 2002-03), Alpha Delta Kappa. Avocations: teaching aerobics, cross-stitch, arts and crafts, dance, outdoor sports. Home: PO Box 319 Madison WV 25130-0319

JARVIS, GILBERT ANDREW, humanities educator, writer; b. Chelsea, Mass., Feb. 13, 1941; s. Vernon Owen and Angeline M. (Burkard) J.; m. Carol Jean Ganter, Jan. 26, 1963; children: Vicki Lynn, Mark Christopher. BA, St. Norbert Coll., De Pere, Wis., 1963; MA, Purdue U., 1965, PhD, 1970. Prof. Ohio State U., Columbus, 1970-95, chmn. humanities edn., 1980-83, assoc. chmn. dept. ednl. theory and practice, 1983-87, chmn. dept. ednl. studies, 1987-95, dir. ESL programs, 1994-2000, chmn. prof. emeritus, 1995—. Cons. Internat. Edn. Program, U.S. Dept. Edn., Washington, 1977-84, many schs., agys. and pub. cos. Author: Et Vous?, 1983, 86, 89; Invitation, 1979, 2d edit., 1984, 3d edit., 1988, 4th edit., 1993, Y tu?, 1986, 2d edit., 1988, Connaitre et se connaitre, 3d edit., 1986, Invitation Essentials, 1991, 2d edit., 1995, Invitation au monde francophone, 2000; editor: The Challenge for Excellence, 1984; mem. editl. bd. Modern Lang. Jour., 1979-86; adv. bd. Can. Modern lang. Rev., 1982—. Mem. Am. Coun. Tchg. Fgn. Langs. (editor Rev. Fgn. Lang. Edn. 1974, 75, 76, 77), Phi Delta Kappa. Avocations: travel, photography. Home: 8337 Evangeline Dr Columbus OH 43235-1136

JARVIS, ROBERT MARK, law educator; b. NYC, Oct. 17, 1959; s. Rubin and Ute (Hacklander) J.; m. Judith Anne Mellman, Mar. 3, 1989. BA, Northwestern U., 1980; JD, U. Pa., 1983; LLM, NYU, 1986. Bar: N.Y. 1984, Fla. 1990. Assoc. Haight Gardner Poor & Havens, N.Y.C., 1983-85, Baker & McKenzie, N.Y.C., 1985-87; asst. prof. law ctr. Nova Southeastern U., Ft. Lauderdale, Fla., 1987-90, assoc. prof., 1990-92, prof., 1992—. Chmn. bd. dirs. Miami Maritime Arbitration Bd., 1993-94; vice chmn. bd. dirs. Miami Internat. Arbitration and Mediation Inst., 1993-94; mem. adv. bd. Carolina Acad. Press, 1996—, Sports Law Reporter, 2000—, hospitalitylawyer.com, 2000—. Co-author: AIDS: Cases and Materials, 1989, 3d edit, 2002, AIDS Law in a Nutshell, 1991, 2d edit., 1996, Notary Law and Practice: Cases and Materials, 1997, Travel Law: Cases and Materials, 1998, Sports Law: Cases and Materials, 1999, Art and Museum Law: Cases and Materials, 2002, Gaming Law: Cases and Materials, 2003; author: Careers in Admiralty and Maritime Law, 1993, An Admiralty Law Anthology, 1995; editor: Maritime Arbitration, 1999, Law of Cruise Ships, 2000; co-editor: Prime Time Law: Fictional Television as Legal Narrative, 1998, Bush v. Gore: The Fight for Florida's Vote, 2001, Amicus Humoriae: An Anthology of Legal Humor, 2003; mem. editl. bd. Washington Lawyer, 1988-94, Jour. Maritime Law and Commerce, 1990-92, 2001—, assoc. editor, 1993-95, editor, 1996-2000, Maritime Law Reporter, 1991-99, Hospitality Law, 1999-2001; adv. bd. Transnat. Lawyer, 1991—, World Arbitration and Mediation Report, 1990—, U. San Francisco Maritime Law Jour., 1992-95, 2002—; contbg. editor Preview U.S. Supreme Ct. Cases, 1990-95, 99-2002. Mem.: ABA (vice chmn. admiralty law com. young lawyers divsn. 1992—93, chair 1993—94), Phi Delta Phi (province pres. 1989—91, coun. 1991—93), Assn. Am. Law Schs. (chmn.-elect maritime law sect. 1991—93, chmn. 1993—94), Maritime Law Assn. U.S., Fla. Bar Assn. (admiralty law com. 1988—95, vice chmn. 1991—92, chmn. 1992—93, exec. coun. internat. law sect. 1992—96), Acacia, Northwestern U. Club South Fla. (v.p. 1992—93, pres. 1993—95), Phi Beta Kappa. Democrat. Jewish. Avocations: theatre, running. Office: Nova Southeastern U Law Ctr 3305 College Ave Fort Lauderdale FL 33314-7721 Business E-Mail: jarvisb@nsu.law.nova.edu.

JARVIS, SARA LYNN, elementary education educator; b. Indpls., May 2, 1948; d. Richard Lee and Betty Morris (Stockton) Jones; children: Patrick William, Kelley Lynn; m. Steven Kent Jarvis, Oct. 14, 1989. BS, Ball State U., 1971, MA in Edn., 1976. Cert. elem. tchr., Ind. Elem. sch. tchr. Muncie (Ind.) Cmty. Schs., 1978—. Bd. dirs. Wapehani Girl Scout Coun., Muncie, 1989-95; sponsor, founder Washington Carver Earth Keepers, Muncie, 1990—, Mother/Daughter Connection, Muncie, 1996-99; chmn. Young Author's Conf.-Muncie Area Reading Coun., 1983-84, All County Artfest-Delaware County Girl Scout Coun., 1994-97; mem. com. Action for Women and Girls, Muncie, 1997—. Recipient Golden Broom award Muncie Clean and Beautiful, 1993, PResdl. Excellence in Math and Sci. Tchg. award, 2002; sci. grantee Harvard U., 1994, Purdue U., 1997, Vivian Conley Cmty. Svc. award, 1998. Mem. AAUW (Eleanor Roosevelt Tchr. fellow 1996), NSTA, Nat. Assn. Sci. Tchrs. (Ind. Presdl. award for excellence in sci. and math tchg. 1998, 99, 2001, 02), Environ. Edn. Assn. Ind., Hoosier Assn. of Sci. Tchrs., Inc., Muncie Tchrs. Assn., Muncie Area Reading Coun. (treas. 1979, 80), Pi Lambda Theta (pres., v.p.). Presbyterian. Office: Washington Carver Elem Sch 1000 E Washington St Muncie IN 47305-2046

JARVIS, TERESA LYNN, art educator, artist; b. Huntington, W.Va., May 10, 1956; d. Thomas Richard and Lovetta (Qualls) McComas; m. Roger Dale Jarvis, July 28, 1992; children; Richard Allen, Sarah Elizabeth. BA, Marshall U., 1979, MA, 1988. Cert. art and elem. tchr., W.Va. Tchr. St. Joseph Grade Sch., Huntington, 1979-88, Crum (W.Va.) Elem. and Mid. Schs., 1988—. Editl. cartoonist (newspaper) The Martin County-Tug Valley Mountain Citizen, 1991. Mem. ASCD, Nat. Art Educators Assn., Internat. Reading Assn., Am. Fedn. Tchrs., W.Va. Edn. Assn., Wayne County Reading Coun., Delta Kappa Gamma (Sigma chpt.). Democrat. Baptist. Avocations: drawing, painting, reading, walking, country line dancing. Home: PO Box 483 Kermit WV 25674-0483

JARZAVEK, JOHN BRIAN, English and art history educator; b. Middletown, Conn., Sept. 18, 1941; s. John Celestin and Stephanie Teresa (Kaminski) J. Carte de assiduité, Sorbonne, Paris, 1961; BA, Wesleyan U., Conn., 1963; MA, Yale U., 1965. English dept. tchr. Rivers Sch., Weston, Mass., 1965—98, art history tchr., 1968—, chmn. English dept., 1970-84. Reader advanced placement art history exam., Ednl. Testing Svc., Princeton, 1987—, reader English achievement, 1986-91. Fulbright fellow Bristol U., England, 1963, Woodrow Wilson fellow Wilson Found., 1964. Mem. Phi Beta Kappa. Democrat. Roman Catholic. Avocation: vocal classical record collecting. Office: Rivers Sch 333 Winter St Weston MA 02493-1071 E-mail: j.jarravek@rivers.org.

JASIEWICZ, RONALD CLARENCE, anesthesiologist, educator; b. Suffern, N.Y., June 8, 1964; s. Clarence William and Adele Helen (Rucki) J. AAS in Sci. and Math., SUNY, Rockland, 1984; BS in Life Sci., N.Y. Inst. Tech., 1987; DO, N.Y. Coll. Osteo. Medicine, 1992; AAS in Emergency Med. Tech., SUNY, Rockland, 1993. Diplomate Am. Bd. Anesthesiology, Am. Osteo. Bd. Anesthesiology, Nat. Bd. Osteo. Med. Examiners. Unit asst. Good Samaritan Hosp., Suffern, 1980-87; paramedic Empress Ambulance Svc., Yonkers, N.Y., 1985-86, Nyack (N.Y.) E.M.S., 1986-87; intern in medicine and surgery Wilson Meml. Regional Med. Ctr., Johnson City, N.Y., 1992-93; asst. clin. instr. Stony Brook (N.Y.) Med. Sch., 1993-96; resident in anesthesiology Univ. Med. Ctr., 1993-96; fellow pediatric anesthesiology Children's Hosp. of Buffalo, 1996-97; clin. instr. Buffalo Med. Sch., 1996-97; pediatric anesthesiologist U. Med. Ctr. Stony Brook, N.Y., 1997—; asst. prof. anesthesiology SUNY Sch. Medicine, Stony Brook, 1997—. Mem. admission com. SUNY Stony Brook Med. Sch., 1998-2001, mem. cirriculum com., 2001-. Bd. mgrs., treas. Stonington at Port Jefferson-Condominium II, 1998—2001; bd. dirs. Stonington at Port Jefferson HOA, 1998—2001. Med. corps. USNR, 1998—. Am. Osteo. Coll. Anesthesiologists, Am. Osteo. Assn., Sigma Omicron. Roman Catholic. Avocations: downhill skiing, travel, kayaking, physical fitness, the arts. Office: U Med Ctr at Stony Brook Dept Pediatric Anes Stony Brook NY 11794-0001

JAVARAS, BARBARA KARIOTIS, special education educator; b. Chgo., Oct. 3, 1946; d. Theodore and Bessie (Janopoulos) Kariotis; children: John Nicholas, Christine Nicole; m. Paul Basil Javaras, June 24, 1983. Assoc. in Liberal Arts, Wright Jr. Coll., Chgo., 1972; BS, Chgo. State U., 1974; MA, Northeastern Ill. U., 1979. Cert. tchr., prin., adminstr. and supr. of spl. edn., spl. edn. tchr., pre-vocat. coord., Ill. Educator New Horizon Ctr. for Handicapped, Chgo., 1975; rehab. supr. Leyden Devel. Ctr., Franklin, Ill., 1977-78; ednl. facilitator Chgo. Regional Project Chpt. 1, 1978-90; ednl. specialist Chgo. Pub. Schs., 1990—. Info. specialist Juvenile Ctr. Cir. Ct. Cook County, 1997—, ct.-apptd. spl. advocate; advocate for grandparents rights in Ill.; treas. Learning Games Libr. Assn., Oak Park, Ill., 1985—, coord., 1983-86, assisted with catalog, 1986; presenter programs in field. Dem. election judge, Elmwood Park, Ill., 1976; troop leader Elmwood Park area Boy Scouts Am., 1975-77; bd. dirs. Plato Greek Sch., Chgo., 1986-89; adv. bd. West Suburban Spl. Recreation Assn., Elmwood Park, 1986-87. Mem. Coun. Exceptional Children, Greek Womens Univ. Club (pres. 1995, 96, 97, 99), Hellenic Profl. Soc., Phi Delta Kappa. Avocations: knitting, sewing, dance, professional clowning for children with disabilities. Home: 7223 Oak Ave River Forest IL 60305-1935 Office: Chgo Pub Schs Info Office Juvenile Ctr Cir Ct Cook Co 1100 S Hamilton Ave Fl 2D Chicago IL 60612-4207

JAVITCH, DANIEL GILBERT, comparatist, educator; b. Cannes, France, June 13, 1941; m. Leila Laughlin, 1968; children: Arielle, Daphne. AB, Princeton U., 1963; BA, Cambridge U., 1965, MA, 1970; PhD, Harvard U., 1971. Asst. prof. Columbia U., N.Y.C., 1970-78; from assoc. prof. to prof. NYU, 1978—. Dir. New Directions Publ. Corp., N.Y.C., 1972—, Ctr. for Rsch. in Mid. Ages and Renaissance, NYU, 1994-95, chmn. dept. comparative lit., 1997-98; resident Am. Acad. Rome, 1995, fellow 1989-90; resident Bellagio Study Ctr., 2000. Author: Poetry and Courtliness in Renaissance England, 1978, Proclaiming a Classic, the Canonization of Orlando Furioso, 1991; editor: Norton Critical Edition of Castiglione's Courtier, 2002. Guggenheim fellow, 1995-96. Mem. Renaissance Soc. Am. (exec. bd. 1993—), Am. Comparative Lit. Assn., Modern Lang. Assn. (com. mem. Comparative Studies in Renaissance Lit. 2000—). Home: 110 Riverside Dr New York NY 10024-3715 Office: NYU Dept Comparative Lit 19 University Pl New York NY 10003-4556

JAX, CHRISTINE, educational administrator, education educator; b. Detroit, Jan. 2, 1959; d. Donald P. and Merilyn E. (Baker) J.; m. Len F. Biernat, Apr. 1, 1989; children: Shelley, Marie, Ellen, Laura. BA in Child Psychology, U. Minn., 1991; MA in Pub. Adminstrn., Hamline U., 1994; PhD in Ednl. Policy and Adminstrn., U. Minn., 1998. Owner Christine's Child Care, Mpls., 1985-88; dir. Kinder Care Lng. Ctr., Shoreview, Mn., 1988-90, Working for Children, Mpls., 1989-92, Mayflower Nursery Sch., Mpls., 1991-92; exec. dir., founder Learning Ctr. for Homeless Families, Mpls., 1992-96; prof. edn. St. Mary's U., Minn., 1998-99. Commr. edn. State Minn., 1999—, mem. Gov.'s cabinet, 1999—; bd. dirs. Child Care Resource Ctr., Mpls., 1991-95, Minn. Coalition for the Homeless, 1992-95; mem. exec. rels. coun. Gillette Children's Hosp., Mpls.. 1994—. Author: Your Book: Ethics for Children, 1994; contbr. articles to law jours. Campaign mgr. various candidates, Mpls., 1989-96; mem. Early Edn. Com. Mpls. Schs., 1990-92, appointed mem. Mayor's Sch. Readiness Group, Mpls., 1991; resource person LWV's Valuing Children, 1993. Recipient Leadership in Child Care award Greater Mpls. Day Care Assn., 1989, Bush Leadership fellowship, Bush Found., St. Paul, 1996. Mem. AAUW, LWV, Citizens League, Pi Lambda Theta. Democrat. Avocations: scuba diving, golf, skiing, fgn. travel. Home: 2246 Lincoln St NE Minneapolis MN 55418-3824

JAY, BARBARA, educational consultant; b. Detroit, Dec. 9, 1942; d. William Priestman and Mary Elizabeth (Connor) Thorpe; m. John Elden Jay, Aug. 1, 1964; children: Michael, Robert. BS, Wayne State U., 1964, MA in Edn., 1978. Cert. spl. edn. K-12. Pres. Learning Power, Inc., Rye, N.Y., 1985—. Cons. computer based ednl. enrichment and remediation. Mem. Pi Lambda Theta. Home: Forest Ave Rye NY 10580 Office: Learn Power Inc 13 3rd St Rye NY 10580-2934

JAY, KARLA, English language educator, women's studies educator; b. Bklyn., Feb. 22, 1947; d. Abraham N. and Rhoda (Ginsberg) Berlin; life ptnr. Karen F. Kerner. AB, Barnard Coll., 1968; MPhil in Comparative Lit., NYU, 1978, PhD, 1984. Assoc. adj. prof. Pace U., N.Y.C., 1974-83, asst. prof., 1983-87, assoc. prof., 1987-90, prof., 1990—, dir. women's studies, 1995—2000, 2002—03; Disting. prof. of English, 2000. Reader CLEP English Exams., Princeton Ednl. Testing Svc., 1982; program com. Internat. Interdisciplinary Congress on Women, Hunter Coll., 1990; outside grant evaluator CUNY, 1990-91; co-chair seminar on homosexualities Columbia U., 1992-94, assoc. seminar for invited faculty, 1991-98; chair panel on politics of translation Out/Write Conf., 1992; speaker Gay Studies Conf., Yale U., 1989, Coll. Art Assn., 1986, Harvard U., 1987; panelist Am. Studies Assn., 1987; lectr. West Chester (Pa.) U., 1991, Fla. Atlantic U., Boca Raton, Fla., 1991, Pa. State U., State College, Pa., 1992, Russell Sage Jr. Coll., Albany, N.Y., 1992, Harvard U., Cambridge, Mass., 1994, Fla. State U., Tallahassee, 1995, UCLA, U. So. Calif., L.A., 1996, W.Va. U., Morgantown, 1996, U. Nev., Las. Vegas, 1996, U. Ky., Lexington, 1996,

Rice U., Houston, Tex., 1998, U. Oreg., Eugene, 1999, Western Wash. U., Bellingham, 1999, U. Wash., Seattle, 1999. Author: (with Allen Young) The Gay Report, 1979; author: The Amazon and the Page: Natalie Clifford Barney and Renée Vivien, 1988, Tales of the Lavender Menace: A Memoir of Liberation, 1999; co-editor: (with Young) After You're Out: Personal Experiences of Lesbians and Gay Men, 1975, Out of the Closets: Voice of Gay Liberation, 1972, 20th Anniversary edit., 1992; (with Joanne Glasgow) Lesbian Texts and Contexts: Radical Revisions, 1990; editor: Lesbian Erotics, 1995, Dyke Life: From Growing Up to Growing Old-A Celebration of The Lesbian Experience, 1995; assoc. editor: Concerns, 1992-99; bd. adv. Ms. Mag., 1992—; mem. editl. bd. Jour. Lesbian Studies, 1995-99, Lesbian Review of Books, 1994-2001, One Inst. U. So. Calif., 1996—; contbr. articles to profl. jours. Bd. dir. Ctr. for Lesbian and Gay Studies CUNY, N.Y.C., 1988-89; bd. dir. Barbara Deming Meml. Fund, 1979-86, pres. 1979-85. Recipient Best Journalist award Stonewall Awards Found., 1983, Best Lesbian Studies Book, 1995, medal of honor Vet. Feminists of Am., 1997; Travel grantee NEH, 1984, 89, Getty Found., 1985, Lambda Literary Award, Lambda Literary Found., 1996, recipient Kenan award Excellence in Teaching, 2000; named Grand Marshal Heritage of Pride Parade, N.Y.C., 2002 Mem. MLA (del. 1988-90, exec. com. divsn. gay langs. and lit. 1988-92, co-chair lesbian and gay caucus 1993-95, Michael Lynch Svc. award 1995), Nat. Womens Studies Assn. Avocations: cycling, travel.

JAYJOCK, MICHAEL ANTHONY, environmental engineer, educator; b. Kingston, Pa., Apr. 17, 1946; s. Michael Charles and Florence Marjorie (Gill) Jayjock; m. Kay Louise Kemmerer, Sept. 12, 1970; children: Emily Anne, Eric Michael. BS, Pa. State U., 1968; MS, Drexel U., 1981, PhD, 1984. Engr. Rohm & Haas Co., Bristol, Pa., 1969-82, product safety engr. Phila., 1984-90, mgr. risk assessment, 1990—, tech. fellow, mgr. risk assessment Rsch. Lab. Spring House, Pa., 1990—. Rsch. asst. Drexel U., Phila., 1982—83, adj. prof., 1991—; mem. tech. rev. panel EPA, 1986—90. Contbr. articles to profl. jours. Mem.: NAS (EPA sci. adv. bd. 1999—, Best Com. Exposure Assessment 1985—87), Am. Chemistry Coun. (chmn. task group exposure assessment 1987—2002), Soc. Risk Analysis (pres.-elect Phila. chpt.), Brit. Occupl. Hygiene Soc., Am. Indsl. Hygiene Assn. (exposure assessment strategies 1989—). Avocations: golf, personal computers. Office: Rohm & Haas Co Rsch Labs 727 Norristown Rd Spring House PA 19477-0904 E-mail: mjayjock@ronmhaas.com.

JAYNES, CHERIE LOU, early childhood education educator; b. Sioux City, Iowa, Aug. 2, 1942; d. Ronald Ray and Helen Adrian (Pounds) Diller; m. Jerome B. Jaynes, Oct. 14, 1960 (div. July 1992); children: Rick, Randy, Melissa. Child Ctr. cert., Riverside (Calif.) C. C., 1990-92. Cert. early childhood edn. tchr., Calif. Tchr.'s asst. Anna M. Glazier Sch., Norwalk, Calif., 1975-81; home day care provider Norwalk, 1981-83; owner, operator JJ's Donuts, Moreno Valley, Calif., 1984-89; tchr., para-profl. Primary Intervention Program, Moreno Valley, 1989—; tchr. presch. lab. Coll. Lab. Sch. Riverside C. C., 1990-91; tchr. La Petite Acad., Moreno Valley, 1992—. Sunday sch. supt. United Meth. Ch., Moreno Valley, 1985-89; Sunday sch. tchr. United Meth., Bellflower, Calif., 1983-84, Calvary Chapel of Moreno Valley, 1989—. Home: 2603 Alegre Ave Hemet CA 92545-1118

JEAN, ROGER V. mathematician, educator; b. Montreal, Que., Can., Oct. 20, 1940; s. Paul-Emile and Irène (Mongeau) Jean Bachelors degree, U. Montreal, 1968, Masters degree, 1970; Doctorate, U. Paris, 1977, Doctorate d'Etat, 1984. Demonstrator IBM, Que., 1967; prof. Colls. Montreal, 1967-70; prof. math., biomathematician U. Que., Rimouski, 1970—. Academician Acad. Creative Endeavors, Russia; critical reviewer Am. Math. Soc., 1987—; lectr. in field. Author: Mesure et Integration, 1975, rev. edit., 1989—, Phytomathematique, 1978—, Morphogenesis (Patterns), 1984—, Phyllotaxis, 1994; editor: Approche Mathematique de la Biologie, 1989; editor-in-chief Jour. Biol. Systems, Singapore, 1991—, Series on Biol. Systems; editorial bd. Symmetry: Culture and Science, 1989—, Symmetry in Plants, 1998; contbr. over 100 articles to scholarly jours. Recipient Cert. award Systems Rsch. Found., 1987, Nicholas Rashevsky award, 1991, Herman Weyl prize Acad. Creative Endeavors, 1992; hon. grantee Gov. of Que., 1969; grantee Can. Coun., 1974, 75, 77. Address: 560 Chemin des Bains St Irénée Canada G0T 1V0

JEANNE, ROBERT LAWRENCE, entomologist, educator; b. NYC, Jan. 14, 1942; s. Armand Lucien and Ruth (Stuber) Jeanne; m. Louise Grenville Bluhm, Sept. 18, 1976; children: Thomas Lucien, James McClure. BS in Biology, Denison U., 1964; postgrad., Justus-Liebig U., Giessen, Fed. Republic Germany, 1964-65; MA, Harvard U., 1968, PhD in Biology, 1971. Instr. biology U. Va., Charlottesville, 1970-71; asst. prof. biology Boston U., 1971-76; asst. prof. entomology U. Wis., Madison, 1976-79, assoc. prof., 1979-83, prof., 1983—. Rschr.: numerous publs. on social insects. Fellow Rotary Found., 1964—65, Guggenheim Meml., 1986—87; grantee NSF, 1972—. Mem.: Wis. Acad. Scis., Arts and Letters, Animal Behavior Soc., Internat. Union Study Social Insects (chmn. protempore, sec.-treas. 1979—80, pres. western hemisphere sect. 1981, assoc. editor insectes Sociaux 1986—2002), Assn. Tropical Biology, Phi Beta Kappa, Sigma Xi. Achievements include numerous discoveries relating to nest construction, nest architecture, commmunication, defense, caste polymorphism, polyethism, social organization, and life histories in social wasps. Office: U Wis Dept Entomology 1630 Linden Dr Madison WI 53706-1520 E-mail: jeanne@entomology.wisc.edu.

JEBSEN, HARRY ALFRED ARTHUR, JR., history educator; b. Chgo., Apr. 8, 1943; s. Harry Alfred Arthur Jebsen; m. Elaine Claire Melchert, Sept. 5, 1964; children— Timothy Paul, Christopher Warren. B.A., Wartburg Coll., 1965; M.A., U. Cin., 1966, Ph.D., 1971. Prof. history Texas Tech U., Lubbock, 1969-81, dir. urban studies, 1972-81, assoc. dean arts and scis., 1980-81; dean Coll. of Arts and Scis., Capital U., Columbus, Ohio, 1981-88, provost, 1988-95, prof. history, 1995—. Author: History of Dallas, Texas Park System, 1971. Contbr. articles to profl. jours. Bd. dirs. Luth. Council for Community Action, Lubbock, 1970-78, U. Ministries of Lubbock, 1971-81, Luth. Social Services of Central Ohio, Columbus, 1984-92. Recipient Fish and Loaves award Luth. Council for Community Action, Lubbock, 1977; NDEA fellow, Cin., 1966-69. Mem. Am. Assn. Higher Edn., N.Am. Soc. Sport Historians. Democrat. Avocations: golf, reading. Home: 1397 Goldsmith Dr Westerville OH 43081-4526 Office: Capital U 2199 E Main St Columbus OH 43209-2394 E-mail: hjebsen@capital.edu.

JEFFERIES, WILLIAM MCKENDREE, internist, educator; b. Richmond, Va., Oct. 1, 1915; s. Richard Henry and Mary Adeline (Harris) J.; m. Jeanne Telfair Mercer, Dec. 28, 1946 (dec. Dec., 1991); children: Richard Mercer, Scott McKendree, Colin Tucker, Leslie McLaurin. BA summa cum laude, Hampden Sydney Coll., 1935; MD, U. Va., 1940. Diplomate Am. Bd. Internal Medicine. Instr. in Math., Physics, Chemistry McGuires Univ. Sch., Richmond, Va., 1936; resident Mass. Gen. Hosp., Boston, 1940-42; flight surgeon San Antonio Aviation Cadet Ctr., 1942; post surgeon India China Div. Air Transport Command, 1943-45, divsn. med. inspector, 1945; rsch. fellow Am. Cancer Soc. Com. on Growth NRC Harvard Med. Sch., Boston, 1946-49; from instr. to asst. prof. medicine Case Western Reserve Med. Sch., Cleve., 1949-92; clin. prof. medicine U. Va. Sch. of Medicine, Charlottesville, 1993—. Mem. internship com. Univ. Hosps., Cleve., 1955-65; bd. dirs. Brush Found., 1966-67; mem. com. for human investigation Luth. Med. Ctr., Cleve., 1977-92; chmn. diabetes adv. com. Euclid Gen. Hosp., Cleve., 1979-82. Author: (med. books) Safe Uses of Cortisone, 1981, Safe Uses of Cortisol, 1996; contbr. articles to profl. jours., chpts. to books. Com. mem. Boy Scouts Am., Shaker Heights, Ohio, 1957-68; past chmn. coun. of deacons, bd. of ministry and fellowship Plymouth Ch. of Shaker Heights. Lt. col. med. corps U.S. Army (attached to air force) India Burma Theatre. Fellow ACP; mem. AAAS, SAR, AMA, N.Y. Acad. Scis., Albemarle County Med. Soc., Am. Thyroid Assn. (Van Meter award 1949), Clin. Immunology Soc., Endocrine Soc., Am. Fertility Soc., Am. Fedn. for Clin. Rsch., Ctrl. Soc. for Clin. Rsch., Friends of Nat. Libr. of Medicine, Am. Legion, Cheshire Cheese Club, Raven Soc., Phi Beta Kappa, Omicron Delta Kappa, Alpha Omega Alpha, Kappa Alpha, Phi Beta Pi. Avocations: golf, fly fishing, skiing.

JEFFERIS, BERNICE K. education educator; b. Cleve., Oct. 5, 1931; BS in Edn., Cleve. State U., 1970, M of Edn., 1975. Cert. elem. tchr. Tchr. Cleveland Heights, University Heights (Ohio) Bd. Edn. Vis. prof. Miami U. Mythology Inst.; mem. Cleve. Heights-Univ. Heights Bd. Edn. Mem. Cleveland Heights-University Heights Bd. Edn., 2002—, 2002—. Fellow Aeneid Inst. Miami U., Oxford, Ohio; Martha Holden Jennings scholar. Mem. Greater Cleve. Tchr. Ctr. Adv. Coun. (chmn. bd.), Tchr. Resource Ctr., Cleve. Mus. Art, Elem. Tchrs. Classics (pres.), Phi Delta Kappa. Presbyn.

JEFFERS, BARBARA CLARK, learning clinic administrator; b. Washington, Jan. 9, 1938; d. E. Kent and Catherine Reagan (Groseclose) Clark; m. John Herrick Jeffers, June 22, 1957; children: David Kent, Jennifer Lee. BA, U. South Fla., 1969, MA, 1971. Tchr. Hillsborough Pub. Sch., Tampa, Fla., 1969—70, U. South Fla., Tampa, 1970—71; clinician Tampa Reading Clinic, 1971—83; owner, dir. Brevard Learning Clinic, Melbourne, 1983—97. Apptd. by Gov. Martinez South Brevard Water Authority Bd., 1990—97; bd. dirs. COPE Brevard Prevent!. Bd. dirs., pers. Bayshore Presbyn. Apts., Tampa, 1977—83, Sharahome. Mem.: Leadership Brevard (alumni rep. 1989—), Internat. Dyslexia Assn., Orton Dyslexia Soc. (legis. rep. 1984—, bd. dirs. 1984—), Internat. Reading Assn., Assn. Children Learning Disabilities (pres. 1984—86), AAUW (local) (v.p. 1984—), Melbourne C. of C., Soroptimist Internat. (pres. 1986—88), Delta Kappa Gamma (grantee 1984, leader workshops). Republican. Avocations: sailing, needlecrafts, antiques, quilts. Office: Brevard Learning Clinic 1900 S Harbor City Blvd Melbourne FL 32901-4749

JEFFERSON, KATHLEEN HENDERSON, retired secondary education educator; b. Pine Bluff, Ark., Sept. 20, 1928; d. Horace and Fannie Henderson; children: Ellen, Regina. BS in Chemistry, U. Ark., 1951; MEd in Maths. Edn., Tuskegee (Ala.) Inst., 1973. Cert. tchr., D.C., Ark. Tchr. Ark. Pub. Schs., Pine Bluff, 1952-78, U. Ark., Monticello, 1978-79, D.C. Pub. Schs., Washington, 1979—; chairperson maths. dept., tchr. Dunbar Sr. High Sch., Washington, 1982-96; ret., 1996. Adj. prof. U. D.C., 1997—. Mem. LWV, Pine Bluff, 1973-77, St. Francis De Sales Ch., Washington; vol. mathematics tutor, St. Francis De Sales Sch., 2000—. NSF fellow, 1960, Internat. Paper Co. fellow, 1970-73. Mem. ASCD, D.C. Coun. Tchrs. of Maths., D.C. Tchrs. Union Local, Delta Sigma Theta. Roman Catholic. Avocations: reading, swimming, chess.

JEFFERSON, KURT WAYNE, political science educator; b. Macomb, Ill., Jan. 17, 1966; s. Robert Wayne and Sally Ann (Wallace) J.; m. Lori Jeanene Merriman, Aug. 8, 1992; children: Kelly Lynn, Megan Leigh, Nicole Layne. BA in Polit. Sci. magna cum laude, Western Ill. U., 1988; MA in Polit. Sci., U. Mo., 1989, PhD in Polit. Sci., 1993. Grad. tchg. asst. dept. polit. sci. U. Mo., Columbia, 1988-91, instr. dept. polit. sci., 1992; instr. dept. social and cultural studies Stephens Coll., Columbia, 1992-93; asst. prof. polit. sci. dept. polit. sci. Westminster Coll., Fulton, Mo., 1993-99, assoc. prof. polit. sci. dept. polit. sci., 1999—, chair dept. polit sci., 1999-2000, 2002—. Vis. asst. prof. dept. polit. sci. U. Mo., Columbia, summer, 1993; dir. Churchill Acad., Westminster Coll., Fulton, 1996—99, coord. leadership studies, 1997—; cons. U. Mo. Rsch. Bd., U. Mo. Sys., St. Louis, 1996; editl. adv. bd. Collegiate Press, Alta Loma, Calif., 1997—98. Contbr. articles to profl. jours.; author: Christianity's Impact on World Politics: Not by Might, nor by Power, 2002. Soccer coach Columbia Soccer League, 1993—94, 2001—02; prayer coord. Men Without Fear men's ministry, Columbia, 2002—; bd. dirs. Christian Chapel Assembly of God, Columbia, 2003—. Mem.: Brit. Politics Group, Am. Polit. Sci. Assn. Avocations: bible reading, sports, banjo playing, reading. Home: 3701 Triple Crown Dr Columbia MO 65202-4849 Office: Westminster Coll 501 Westminster Ave Fulton MO 65251-1129 Fax: 573-592-5191. E-mail: jefferk@jaynet.wcmo.edu.

JEFFRESS, CHARLES H. retired art educator; b. San Francisco, May 21, 1920; s. Charles Howard and Mary O. Jeffress; m. Jane Jeffress, June 6, 1944; children: Jane H., Charles H. III, George W., John D. BA, La. Coll., 1971; MA, Stephen F. Austin State U., Nacogdoches, Tex., 1972, MFA, 1976. Cert. pilot, instr. Prof. La. Coll., Pineville, La., 1973, prof. art emeritus, 1985—. Instr., pilot Basic Flying Sch., Shaw AFB; instr. instrument Shaw AFB. Exhibitions include over 20 galleries, Represented in permanent collections. Nat. Guard, 1937—39, lt. col. USAF, 1940—80, China, 2nd. Lt. pilot Nat. Guard, 1943, 1st. Lt. pilot Nat. Guard, 1944, capt. Nat. Guard, 1946 reserves USAF, 1946, maj. reserves USAF, 1955, lt. col. reserves USAF, 1964. Recipient pair of Chinese airforce wings. Mem.: China-Burma-India Hump Pilots Assn., Daedalians. Republican. Methodist. Avocations: golf, fishing. Home: 1713 Simmons St Alexandria LA 71301

JEKEL, JAMES FRANKLIN, physician, public health educator; b. St. Louis, Oct. 14, 1934; s. Oscar Henry and Frances Sarah (Newell) J.; m. Janice Marilyn Clark, Aug. 30, 1958; children: Clifford R., Mark R., Linda F., Timothy W. AB, Wesleyan U., 1956; MD, Washington U., St. Louis, 1960; MPH, Yale U., 1965. House officer Hartford (Conn.) Hosp., 1960-62; epidemiologist Ctrs. for Disease Control, Atlanta, 1962-67; asst. prof. pub. health Yale U. Sch. Medicine, New Haven, 1967-71, assoc. prof., 1971-80, prof., 1980-97, prof. emeritus, 1997—, C.E.A. Winslow prof. pub. health, 1982-97, dir. residency program in gen. preventive medicine, 1975-93; asst. dir. Robert Wood Johnson Scholar Program Robert Wood Johnson Clin. Scholar Program, New Haven, 1976-95; dir. sect. preventive medicine and cmty. health Griffin Hosp., Derby, Conn., 1996—. Pres. Bd. Health Quinnipiack Valley Health Dist., Hamden, Conn., 1986-91. Lt. comdr. USPHS, 1962-67. Fulbright Faculty fellow The Bahamas, 1985-86; recipient various rsch. grants, 1968—. Fellow Am. Coll. Preventive Medicine, Am. Sci. Affiliation; mem. Am. Pub. Health Assn., Christian Med./Dental Soc. Presbyterian. Office: Griffin Hosp 130 Division St Derby CT 06418

JELINEK, FREDERICK, electrical engineer, educator; b. Prague, Czechoslovakia, Apr. 18, 1932; arrived in U.S., 1949, naturalized, 1955; s. William and Trudy (Kocmanek) J.; m. Milena Tobolova, Feb. 4, 1961; children— Hannah, William. BS, MIT, 1956, MS, 1958, PhD, 1962; DS Math. and Physics (hon.), Charles U., Prague, 2001. Instr. MIT, Cambridge, 1959-62; lectr. Harvard U., Cambridge, 1962; asst. prof. Cornell U., Sch. Elec. Engring., Ithaca, N.Y., 1962-66, assoc. prof., 1966-72, prof., 1972-74; vis. scientist MIT, Lincoln Lab., 1964, 65, IBM, 1968-69; sr. mgr. continuous speech recognition IBM, T.J. Watson Research Center, Yorktown Heights, N.Y., 1972-93; prof., dir. Ctr. Lang. and Speech Processing Whiting Sch. Engring. Johns Hopkins U., Balt., 1993—. Author: Probabilistic Information Theory, 1968, Statistical Methods for Speech Recognition, 1998; contbr. articles to profl. jours. Chmn. Liberal Party, Ithaca, N.Y., 1970-72, mem. state exec. com., 1971-73. Recipient Outstanding Achievement in the Field of Speech Comm. European Speech Comm. Assn., 2000; named One of top 100 innovators in speech recognition by Tech. Mag., 1981. Fellow IEEE (life; pres. Info. Theory Group 1977, bd. govs. 1970-79, 81-86, Info. Theory Group best paper award 1971, Soc. award Signal Processing Soc. 1998, Golden Jubilee Paper award Info. Theory Soc. 1998, Third Millennium medal 2000, Computer, Speech and Lang. paper award 2002). Office: Johns Hopkins U Ctr Lang and Speech Processing Barton Hall 3400 N Charles St Baltimore MD 21218 E-mail: jelinek@jhu.edu.

JELINEK, VERA, university director; b. Kosice, Czechoslovakia, Dec. 16, 1935; came to U.S., 1947; d. Joseph and Margit (Lefkovits) Schnitzer; m. Josef E. Jelinek, June 19, 1960; children: David, Paul. BA in History, CUNY, 1956; MA, Johns Hopkins U., 1958; PhD in Modern European History, NYU, 1977; diploma, Sch. Advanced Internat. Study, Bologna, Italy. Translator Rockefeller Bros. Fund, N.Y.C., 1958-59; exec. dir. U.S. Youth Coun., N.Y.C., 1959-63; dir. internat. programs, social and natural scis. NYU, N.Y.C., 1985—, dir. Lillian Vernon Ctr. for Internat. Affairs, 2000—, dir. The Energy Forum, 2000—. Mem. adv. com. N.Y.C.-Budapest Sister City Program, 1991-94; prin. dir. pilot tng. program for new UN diplomats NYU, 1996-97. Author audio cassette: Before You Go-Italy, 1985. Mem. edn. com. Mus. Am. Folk Art, N.Y.C.; edn. co-chair The Am. Antiques Show, 2002—03. Recipient fellowship Ford Found., 1960, grant NYU Curriculum Challenge Fund, 1989, 90, 99, Phillip E. Frandson award Nat. Univ. Continuing Edn. Assn., 1991. Mem. Am. Folk Art Soc., Carnegie Coun. on Ethics and Internat. Affairs, Women's Fgn. Policy Group, Phi Beta Kappa. Democrat. Avocations: tennis, jogging, folk art, cooking, travel. Office: Lillian Vernon Ctr Internat Affairs 58 W 10th St New York NY 10011

JELLISON, KATHERINE KAY, historian, educator; b. Garden City, Kans., Jan. 5, 1960; d. Billy Dean and Margaret Ruth (Brown) Jellison; m. David John Winkelmann, Aug. 10, 1985. BA, Ft. Hays (Kans.) State U., 1982; MA, U. Nebr., 1984; PhD, U. Iowa, 1991. Asst. prof. Memphis State U., 1991-93, Ohio U., Athens, 1993-96, assoc. prof. history, 1996—. Author: Entitled to Power: Farm Women and Technology, 1913-1963, 1993. Named Outstanding Young Alumni Ft. Hays State U., 1994; recipient Excellence in Feminist Pedagogy award Ohio U., 1994; Smithsonian Instn. fellow, 1989. Mem. NOW, Am. Hist. Assn., Orgn. Am. Historians, Berkshire Conf. on History of Women, Social Sci. History Assn., Ohio Acad. History. Democrat. Methodist. Avocations: hiking, watching old movies. Office: Ohio University Dept History Bentley Annex Athens OH 45701 E-mail: jellison@ohio.edu.

JELSMA, ELIZABETH BARBARA, music educator; b. Newark, N.J., Aug. 24, 1934; d. Joseph Augsdorfer and Clara Stiehl; m. Lawrence Franklin Jelsma, June 15, 1967 (div. Sept. 30, 1976); children: Deborah Lynn, Lawrence Frank, Elizabeth Louise, Mark Andrew. Degree in Music Edn., Northwestern U., 1959, MusM, 1961. Tchr. 1st grade Jenner Sch., Chgo.; tchr. music grades K-8, Yavapai Sch., Scottsdale, Ariz.; pvt. piano tchr. N.J., Ill. and Ariz. Judge piano Ariz. State U., Tempe, Ariz., 1962—63; accompanist Bach Madrigal Soc., Phoenix, 1964—66. Recipient various awards for solo performances. Republican. Roman Catholic. Avocations: reading, travel, swimming.

JEMIELITY, THOMAS JOHN, language educator; b. Cleve., Dec. 17, 1933; s. Joseph Henry and Margaret Anne (Wielgus) Jemielity; m. Barbara Gray, Aug. 7, 1965; children: David Christopher, Samuel Andrew, Sarah Margaret. MA, John Carroll U., Cleve., 1958; PhD, Cornell U., 1965. Lectr. English Carleton U., Ottawa, Canada, 1962-63; instr. U. Notre Dame, Ind., 1963-65, asst. prof. English, 1965-70, assoc. prof., 1970-90, prof., 1990—2003, prof. emeritus, 2003—. Vis. lectr. Lancaster (Eng.) U. Author: (book) Satire and the Hebrew Prophets, 1992; contbr. articles to profl. jours. Summer fellow, Ind. Com. Humanities, 1988. Mem.: Johnson Soc. Ctrl. Region (pres. 1985), Johnson Soc. London, Johnson Soc. (Lichfield, Eng.), Jane Austen Soc. N.Am., Am. Soc. 18th Century Studies. Home: 20408 Kern Rd South Bend IN 46614-5046 Office: U Notre Dame Dept English Notre Dame IN 46556

JEN, FRANK CHIFENG, finance and management educator; b. Shanghai, May 15, 1931; came to U.S., 1957; s. Seybold E. and Susan (Lin) J.; m. Daisy Chi, Aug. 26, 1962; children: Amy K., Wendy K., Edward K. BS, N. Central Coll., 1959; MBA, U. Wis., 1960, PhD, 1963. Asst. prof. finance SUNY, Buffalo, 1964-66, assoc. prof., 1966-68, prof., 1968-97, chmn. dept. fin., 1967-70, Mfrs. & Traders Trust Co.'s prof. banking/fin. to emeritus, 1972-97, 97—, Univ. rsch. scholar, 2002—, chmn. dept. fin., 1967-70, chmn. dept. operating analysis, 1970-77, dir. bank mgmt. inst. and advanced comml. lending program, 1977-97, co-dir., dir. China MBA program, 1984-91, univ. rsch. scholar, 2002—. Vis. prof. Dalian (China) U. Tech., 1980—; Am. dir. Consulting and Rsch. Ctr. Nat. Mgmt. Ctr., Dalian U. Tech., 1995—. Contbr. articles to profl. jours. Mem. Am. Fin. Assn., Am. Econ. Assn., Soc. Econ. and Fin. Mgmt. in China (pres. 1985-88), Pi Gamma Mu, Beta Gamma Sigma. Home: 287 Forestview Dr Buffalo NY 14221-1439 Office: SUNY Buffalo Sch Mgmt Jacobs Ctr Amherst NY 14260-0001 E-mail: frankjen@buffalo.edu.

JENKINS, ALICE MARIE, secondary school educator; b. Adair, Iowa, June 7, 1922; d. Charles Erwin Hall and Elizabeth Catherine Clarke Hall; m. Doyce Gwendon Pitts, June 27, 1943 (dec. Mar. 27, 1977); 1 child, Beverly Lou; m. Richard Jenkins, June 24, 1978. BA, Drake U., 1963. Tchr. rural and county schs., 1940—54, Linden (Iowa) Pub. Sch., 1954—55, Woodward (Iowa) State, 1955—60, 1971—93, Boone (Iowa) Pub. Sch., 1960—71, Woodward Cmty., 1993—. Mem.: VFW, Am. Legion Aux. (past pres.), Alpha Delta Kappa (past pres.). Democrat. Methodist. Avocations: cooking, reading, music. Office: Woodward-Granger HS 306 W 3rd St Woodward IA 50276-1033

JENKINS, BEVERLY ANN, education specialist; b. Mt. Pleasant, Tex., Apr. 30, 1956; d. Morris and Bertha (Craddock) Hurndon; m. Raymond Paul Jenkins, Sept. 11, 1982 (div.); children: Kelvin Martel Brookins, Britany Rae. BS, East Tex. State U., 1977. Tchr. Longview (Tex.) Ind. Sch. Dist., 1979-86, Mt. Pleasant (Tex.) Ind. Sch. Dist., 1986-92; edn. specialist Region VIII Edn. Svc. Ctr., Mt. Pleasant, 1992—. Mem. Assn. Tex. Profl. Educators, Tex. Social Studies Suprs. Assn., Titus County Progressive Women (sec. 1988-94), Lady Majaji (pres., sec. 1987-94), Delta Kappa Gamma. Baptist. Avocation: reading. Home: 1102 W Pecan St Mount Pleasant TX 75455-5508 Office: Region VIII Edn Svc Ctr 2230 N Edwards Ave Mount Pleasant TX 75455-2036

JENKINS, BONNIE BUCH, elementary education educator; b. West Point, Va., Apr. 25, 1949; m. Garland E. Jenkins. children: Eric Lee, Elliot Garland. AS, Ferrum Jr. Coll., 1969; BS, Va. Commonwealth U., 1977. Cert. tchr. Va. Tchr. West Point Elem. Sch., Va., 1977—. Sunday sch. tchr., vestry mem., altar guild mem., St. John's Episcopal Ch., West Point, 1949—. Mem. Assoc. for Supervision & Curr. Dev., Va. Edn. Assn., Nat. Edn. Assn., Richmond Area Reading Council, West Point Edn. Assn. Home: 3470 Southern Ave West Point VA 23181-9355

JENKINS, BRENDA GWENETTA, early childhood and special education specialist; b. Durham, N.C., Aug. 11, 1949; d. Brinton Alfred and Ophelia Arden (Eaton) Jenkins. BS, Howard U., 1971, MEd, 1972; postgrad., Trinity Coll., Am. U., U. D.C., Marymount Coll., 1976—. Cert. tchr., Washington; cert. Advanced Grad. Studies Spl. Edn., aerobics instr., Nat. Dance Exercise Instr.'s Tng. Assn. Cheerleading coach Howard U., Washington, 1971-86; aerobics instr. D.C. Pub. Schs., Washington, 1982-97, tchr.; v.p. Nerdlihc Corp., Washington, 1985—; co-owner Fantasia Early Learning Acad., Washington, 1985-98; ptnr. Jenkins, Trapp-Dukes and Yates Partnership., Washington, 1984; instr. aerobics Washington Dept. Recreation, Washington, 1988-93; instr. You Fit, Inc. Nat. Children's Ctr. Washington, 1991-93, Anthony Bowen YMCA, Washington, 1992-93; instr. health, nutrition support Rockville, Md., 1992; instr., coach Maryvale PomPom/cheerleaders, Montgomery County, Md., 1992-94, asst. chmn. tchr. collabrative program, 1992-94, co-chair program com. tchr. collaborative, 1995-96; fitness instr. Oxedine Performing Arts Acad., Prince George's County, 1995-96; Goals 2000 English, lang. arts, history writer D.C. Pub. Schs., 1995-96. Aerobic instr. handicapped Coun. Exceptional

Children, Washington, 1982, recreation svcs., City of Rockville, 1986—; developer My Spl. Friend program, 1984, BJ's Thinking Cap, 1991, Learning Creations, 1994, Girlfriends; bldg. rep. Washington Tchrs. Union AFT, AFL-CIO, 1987-89, 91-94, 1996, asst. bldg. rep., 1990-91, 94-95, bldg. rep. 1997—; supr. foster grandparent program Sharpe Health Sch., 1988—; trainer AIDS in Workplace, 1990, Early Childhood Substance Abuse Project Tng., 1992-93, Substance Abuse Prevention Edn., 1995, Metro Foster Grandparent Program, Washington, 1992-93; mem. preschool adv. bd. D.C. Pub. Schs., 1992-93, coordinating curriculum coun., 1994-96; master tchr. Coop. Tchr. Corp., 1993; curriculum writer, 1993; v.p. spl. edn. Washington Tchrs. Union Local 6, 1994--; stds. specialist, 1997—; presenter in field; del. 75th convention Am. Fed. Tchrs., 1998; mem. adv. bd. Supt.'s Tchr. Affairs, 1999; mem. Spl. Edn. State Adv. Panel, Washington, 1998-2000, D.C. Parent Tng. and Info. Ctr., ARC, Inc. Adv. Panel; exec. bd. dirs. Assembly of Petworth, 1998--; D.C. Pub. Schs. recruiter Nat. Alliance Black Sch. Educators, Nashville, 1999, resident mentor tchr., 1999--; mem. Disting. Educators Roundtable, 1998; presenter creative dance workshops Washington Srs. Wellness Ctr., 2003. Singer: 2000 Voices Lincoln Meml., 2000. Active D.C. Spl. Edn. State Adv., 1998, presenter AFT Civil, Human, Women's Rights Conf., 1998; Internat. Space Camp, Huntsville, Ala., 1998. Recipient Outstanding Svc. award Kappa Delta Pi, 1978, 79, 81, 82, 84, citation Washington Tchr. Union, 1985, State winner Elem. Level Nat. Citizenship Edn. Tchr.'s award Ladies Aux. VFW, Washington, 2002-03.; named DC Tchr. of Yr. Coun. Chief State Sch. Officers, 1998; grantee spl. edn. DC Pub. Sch. state office, 1993, Citibank, 1994; named to Hall of Fame Bison Found. Inc., Howard U., 1995; recipient Washington Post grants in the arts, 1999-2000, 2000-01, 01-02, Masonic Scottish Rite Educator excellence award, 2001, recipient Elem. Level Nat. Citizenship Edn. Tchr. award VFW, 2002-2003. Mem.: ASCD, Am. Fedn. Tchrs. (presiding officer WTU Spl. Educator and Svc. Provider Forums 1998—, tchr. speaker on Capitol Hill 1999, 2000, sch. to careers tchr. extern 2001, tchr. speaker on Capitol Hill 2001, DCPS new tchr. orientation trainer 2001, new tchr. coord. 2001—, DCPS new tchr. orientation trainer 2002, 2003, mem. 2000 voices at Lincoln Meml., Washington, D.C., Nat. State Tchrs. of Yr.), Coun. Exceptional Children, Howard Alumni Cheerleaders Assn. (co-founder 1977, pres. 1990—94, v.p. 1998—, Outstanding Recognition award 1984, Recognition award named Brenda G. Jenkins Outstanding Cheerleader award 1987), D.C. Parents and Friends of Children with Special Needs (mem. critical ptnrs. group/supts. task force 2003, bd. dirs.), Kappa Delta Pi (convocation presenter, Balt. 1999, exec. com. Theta Alpha chpt.). Democrat. Avocations: alumni cheerleading, fashion design, cooking, dancing, poetry writing.

JENKINS, CLARA BARNES, psychology educator; b. Franklinton, N.C., 1943; d. Walter and Steffa (Griffin) Barnes; m. Hugh Jenkins, Dec. 24, 1949 (div. Feb. 1955). BS, Winston-Salem State U., 1939; MA, N.C. Ctrl. U., 1947; EdD, U. Pitts., 1964; postgrad., NYU, 1947—48, U. N.C., 1963, N.C. Agrl. and Tech. State U., 1971. Cert. notary pub. N.C. Tchr. pub. schs., Wendell, NC, 1939—43, Wise, NC, 1943—45; mem. faculty Fayetteville State U., 1945—53, Rust Coll., Holly Spring, Miss., 1953—58; asst. prof. Shaw U., 1958—64; prof. edn. and psychology St. Paul's Coll., Lawrenceville, Va., 1964—91. Vis. prof. edn. Friendship Jr. Coll., Rock Hill, SC, 1947, N.C. Agrl. and Tech. State U., 1966—83. Former mem. bd. dirs. Winston-Salem State U.; bd. dirs. annual giving fund U. Pitts. Named United Negro Coll. Fund Faculty fellow, 1963—64; grantee, Am. Bapt. Conv., 1963—64. Mem.: APA, AAAS, AAUW, NEA, AAUP, So. Poverty Law Ctr., Leadership Coun., Soc. Profls. Edn., Philosophy Edn. Soc., Jean Piaget Soc., Soc. Rsch. in Child Devel., Acad. Polit. Sci., Am. Soc. Notaries, Am. Assn. Higher Edn., Doctoral Assn. Educators, History Edn. Soc., Assn. Tchr. Educators, Internat. Platform Assn., Am. Acad. Polit. and Social Sci., Va. Edn. Assn., Am. Hist. Assn., Nat. Soc. for Study Edn., Kappa Delta Pi, Phi Delta Kappa, Zeta Phi Beta, Phi Eta Kappa. Episcopalian. Died Apr. 2, 1999.

JENKINS, DANIEL EDWARDS, JR., retired physician, educator; b. Omaha, July 19, 1916; s. Daniel Edwards and Anne (Finley) J.; m. Dora Solis, Aug. 1, 1942; children: Daniel Edwards III, Mark Schering, Tessa Ann. Student, Hampden-Sydney Coll., 1934; BA, U. Tex., 1936, MD, 1940. Intern, then resident U. Mich. Hosp., 1940-44; asst. prof. medicine, chief med. tuberculosis unit U. Mich. Med. Sch., 1946-47; asst. prof. medicine Baylor Coll. Medicine, 1947-55, prof. internal medicine, 1956-2001, chief sect. pulmonary diseases, 1947-74, chief sect. environ. medicine, 1974-91; part-time pvt. practice, 1947-91; pvt. practice Respiratory Cons. of Houston, 1991-96; chief pulmonary disease service Harris County Hosp. Dist., 1947-74; ret., 2001. Cons. VA, 1949-75 Contbr. articles to profl. jours. Med. bd. dirs. Harris County Hosp. Dist., 1967-90. Recipient So. Conf. award So. Tb Conf., 1967 Fellow A.C.P., Am. Coll. Chest Physicians (pres. So. chpt., 1958); mem. AMA, Am. Thoracic Soc. (pres., 1958-59), Am. Fedn. Clin. Research, Am. Clin. and Climatol. Assn., Am. Lung Assn. (dir., 1958-75, pres., 1967-68, Hall of Fame, 1980), Tex. Tb and Respiratory Disease Assn. (dir., 1949-82, pres., 1966-67, hon. dir., 1982—), Alpha Omega Alpha, Alpha Kappa Kappa, Sigma Alpha Epsilon. Home: 3550 Sun Valley Dr Houston TX 77025-4146 Fax: 713-668-0028.

JENKINS, GEORGANN KLAUS, librarian; b. Oct. 9, 1950; d. Francis William and Mary Ida (Steingraber) Klaus; m. Robert M. Jenkins, Jr., Aug. 24, 1974; children: Andrew Klaus, Jeffrey Robert. BS in Edn., Edinboro (Pa.) U., 1972; MLS, U. Pitts., 1977, postgrad. suprs. program, 1986. Cert. sch. libr. Pa. Libr. grades 5-8 Pitts. Pub. Schs., 1972-74; libr. grades K-8, dist. audio-visual coord. Baldwin-Whitehall Sch., Pitts., 1974-87; asst. dir., children's libr. Whitehall Pub. Libr., Pitts., 1987-88; head libr. grades K-6 Whitehall Elem. Sch. Baldwin-Whitehall Sch. Dist., 1988-97; head libr. Harrison Mid. Sch., Pitts., 1997—. Instrnl. materials reviewer Allegheny intermediate unit, Wilkinsburg, Pa.; review coord. Librs. Book Review Program, Allegheny County, Pa., 1991—; rec. sec. Pitts. Newspaper Unions Unity Coun. Women's Orgn., 1992-99; guest lectr. Sch. Sociology, U. Pitts., 1982. Contbr. book revs. to profl. jours. Mem. ALA, Pa. Edn. Assn., Am. Assn. Sch. Librs., Coun. Sch. Librs. (S.W. Pitts. chpt.), Pa. Sch. Librs. Assn., Beta Phi Mu. Democrat. Home: 520 Clair Dr Pittsburgh PA 15241-2013 Office: J E Harrison Middle Sch 129 Windvale Dr Pittsburgh PA 15236-1854

JENKINS, JACQUELINE ANN MOORE, secondary education educator; b. N.Y.C., Dec. 8, 1948; d. Samuel and Minnie Mae (Patterson) Canion; widowed; children; Britt, Kiirsten, Sheva, Jaeron, LeAnise. AS in Edn., Atlanta Jr. Coll., 1978; BS in Elem. Edn. cum laude, Ga. State U., 1980, MEd, 1984, MEd in Adminstrn. and Supervision, 1991. Cert. tchr. and adminstr., Ga. Tchr. elem. Atlanta Bd. of Edn., 1980-83, tchr. mid. grade, 1983—. Tchr. Word In Action Ministries, Atlanta, 1988—, prin., summer, 1992. Author plays. Organizer Youth Challengers, N.Y.C., 1969; recereation leader Fulton County Parks and Recreation, Atlanta, 1978; organizer, dir. Inman's Heritage Ensemble, Atlanta, 1990. Apple Corps grantee, 1988; named Tchr, of the Yr. Atlanta Pub. Schs. Systemwide and Middle Grades, 1991-92. Mem. Nat. Coun. Social Studies, Atlanta Coun. Social Studies, Kappa Delta Epsilon. Pentecostal. Avocations: writing songs and plays, volleyball, singing, board games, playing piano.

JENKINS, JAMES BOSWELL, secondary educator; b. Jefferson City, Mo., July 7, 1952; s. Ray Boswell and Nora Elizabeth (Claybrook) J.; m. Diana Jean Jenkins, Aug. 18, 1974; children: Matthew Lee, Megan Elizabeth. BS in Edn., Ctrl. Mo. State U., 1974, MS in Edn., 1977. Cert. life tchr., Mo. Sci. tchr., dept. chair St. James (Mo.) R-I Schs., 1974—. Adj. grad. faculty S.W. Bapt. U., Bolivar, Mo., 1994; adj. faculty Mo. Bapt. Univ., St. Louis, adj. chemistry faculty East Ctrl. Coll., Union, Mo., 2003—; goals 2000 pre-svc. sci. S.W. Mo. State U., Springfield, 1997; participant 4 Howard Hughes Med. Inst. programs, other workshops. Computer cons. James Meml. Libr., 1990—; scholarship chair St. James Kiwanis Club, 1986—. Named Outstanding Chemistry Tchr. South Ctrl. Mo. ACS, 1996, Sci. Tchr. of Yr. U. Mo.-Rolla Sigma Xi, 1986, Midwest Regional Outstanding H.S. Chemistry Tchr., ACS, 1997. Mem. Sci. Tchrs. of Mo. (bd. dirs. 1992-99, awards dir. 1992-99), Nat. Sci. Tchrs. Assn. (awards and recognition com.). Avocations: design and construction stained glass windows, stamp collecting. Home: 507 Saint Francis Cir Saint James MO 65559-1519 Office: John F Hodge High Sch 101 E Scioto St Saint James MO 65559-1717

JENKINS, JIMMY RAYMOND, university president; b. Selma, N.C., Mar. 18, 1943; s. Alma (Street) Jenkins; m. Faleese Moore-Jenkins; children: Lisa, Ginger, Jimmy R. BS, Elizabeth City State U., 1965; MS, Purdue U., PhD in Sci. Edn., 1972. Asst. acad. dean Elizabeth City State U., 1972-73, assoc. prof., 1973-75, vice chancellor, 1977-83, chancellor, 1983-97; pres. Edward Waters Coll., Jacksonville, Fla., 1997—. Mem. N.C. Bd. Sci. Tech., N.C. State Adv. Team Examiners Coll. Licensing, N.C. Humanities Com. Author: The Mini Patt Approach to Individualized Instruction, 1973, The Ultimate Evidence of Scholarship: The Meaning of a Good Education, 1979, Competency Based Approach Stresses Individualization, 1981 Mem. Am. Assn. Higher Edn., Nat. Sci. Tchr. Assn., Am. Biology Tchrs. Assn., Nat. Alliance Black Sch. Educators, Assn. Supervision and Curriculum Devel., Nat. Caucus Black Aged Mem. Christian Ch. (Disciples Of Christ). Office: Edward Waters Coll Office of Pres 1658 Kings Rd Jacksonville FL 32209-6167*

JENKINS, JOHN SMITH, retired academic dean, lawyer; b. Pittston, Pa., Dec. 11, 1932; s. Walter Hershel and Mildred (Lewis) J.; m. Marilyn Lewis, Aug. 23, 1958; 1 child, John Smith Jr. BA, Lafayette Coll., Easton, Pa., 1954; JD with honors, George Washington U., 1961; MA, Am. U., 1967. Bar: Va. 1961, U.S. Ct. Appeals for the Armed Forces, 1964, U.S. Supreme Ct. 1982. Commd. ensign U.S. Navy, 1955, advanced through grades to rear admiral, 1978; stationed at naval communications sta. Pearl Harbor, Hawaii, 1955—56; duty on U.S.S. Rochester, 1956-57; with Bur. Naval Personnel, 1957-62; with Hdqrs. 1st Naval Dist. Boston, 1962-64; staff Office Navy JAG, 1964-65; staff Office Legis. Affairs, 1969-71; staff Office of Asst. Sec., 1971-73; spl. counsel to sec. Office of Sec., 1973-76; asst. civil law JAG, 1976-78; dep. JAG, 1978-80; JAG, 1980-82; asst. dean Nat. Law Ctr. George Washington U., Washington, 1982-86, assoc. dean, 1986-2000, sr. assoc. dean, 2000—01, sr. assoc. dean emeritus, 2001. Decorated D.S.M. Legion of Merit. Fellow Am. Bar Found.; mem. ABA (ho. of dels., chair standing com. on lawyers in the armed forces 1991-94, standing com. on delivery of legal svcs. 1997-2001, standing com. on legal assistance for mil. pers. 2001-), FBA, Judge Advs. Assn., Army and Navy Club (gov. 1988-98), George Washington U. Club. Episcopalian. Home: 5809 Helmsdale Ln Alexandria VA 22315-4138 E-mail: jsjmlj@aol.com.

JENKINS, MARGIE KLINE, secondary school educator; b. Beaufort, S.C., Aug. 11, 1943; d. Eddie and Frances (Jones) Kline; m. Manuel Edward Jenkins. BA, Benedict Coll., 1965; postgrad. studies, Bridgewater State Coll., 1970, '73, U. S.C., Clemson U. Tchr. Jasper County Sch., Ridgeland, S.C., 1965-67, Beaufort (S.C.) County Schs., 1967—. Mem. team total quality mgmt. Beaufort County Sch. Dist.; co-developer Project Accelerate. Mgr. poll Beaufort County Election Commn., 1984—, dep. registrar Beaufort Voter's Registration Commn., 1984—; Dem. precint pres., Burton, S.C., 1988; mem. Dem. exec. com., Burton, 1990—. Named Outstanding Contbr., Beaufort County Pub. Edn. Found. Mem. NEA, S.C. Edn. Assn. (bd. dirs.), Beaufort County Edn. Assn. (pres.), Nat. Coun. Social Studies, S.C. Coun. Social Studies, Nat. Middle Sch. Assn. Baptist. Avocations: reading, shopping, traveling. Home: RR 3 Box 36-e Beaufort SC 29906-9803

JENKINS, MARIE PRESCOTT, art and music educator; m. D. Paul Jenkins, 1961; children: Kristi, Donald, Audrey, Justin, Jon. Secretarial cert., Armstrong Bus. Coll., 1959. Cert. art specialist. Pvt. vocal tchr., Grace, Idaho, 1962-2000; pvt. piano tchr., 1970-99; pvt. art/workshop tchr. Intermountain Area, Idaho, 1980-2000; art tchr., specialist K-12 Soda Springs (Idaho) Pub. Sch. Dist. 150, 1992-93; owner Jenkins Arts and Solfelt Music. Profl. fine artist in mediums of watercolor, oil, acrylic, Utah and Idaho and travelling shows (solo gallery shows); music dir. Broadway musical prodns. 3 murals for Guys and Dolls, for Caribou County Theatre Guild; developed art dept. Caribou County Fair Bd., 1968; adjudicator County Fair Art Competitions. Polit. cartoonist, 1969-70; illustrator children's books, 1990-91. Sudden Opportunity grantee Idaho Arts Coun. Mem. Idaho Watercolor Soc., Utah Watercolor Soc. Avocations: sewing, playing banjo, gardening, cross country skiing, composing inspirational music, directing and producing church and community concerts and variety shows. E-mail: artsmusicm@yahoo.com.

JENKINS, PEGGY JEAN, nurse educator; b. Amsterdam, N.Y., Apr. 16, 1958; d. Charles Wendell and Leah Inazetta (Hunter) Olendorf; m. Paul Llewellyn Jenkins, July 30, 1988 (div.); children: Paul Llewellyn, Stephen Charles, Ryan James. BSN, Keuka Coll., 1980; MSN, Russell Sage Coll., 1984; postgrad., SUNY, Albany, 1987—. CCRN. ICU staff nurse Ellis Hosp., Schenectady, N.Y., 1980-91; tchg. asst. Russell Sage Coll., Troy, N.Y., 1982-84; clin. preceptor Albany (N.Y.) Med. Ctr. Hosp., summer 1983; ICU staff nurse Bassett Hosp., Cooperstown, N.Y., summer 1993—; instr. Jr. Coll. Albany, N.Y., 1984-85; assoc. prof. Hartwick Coll., Oneonta, N.Y., 1985—. Critical care presentations, Hartwick Coll., Oneonta, 1987, 89; curriculum cons.Bassett Hosp., Cooperstown, N.Y., 1989-90; expert witness, Binghamton, 1989—; manuscript reviewer multiple pub. cos., 1992—; presenter in field. CPR instr. Am. Heart Assn., Cooperstown, 1994. Mem. N.Y. State Nurses Assn. (pres. dist. 15 1994-98, chmn. functional unit nurse educators), Rebekahs, Sigma Theta Tau. Presbyterian. Avocations: hiking, embroidery, reading, tennis, traveling.

JENKINS, SANDRA MARIE, physical education educator, coach; b. Chgo., Jan. 27, 1948; d. James Clarence and Betty Louise (Windom) J.; m. Melvin Johnson, Feb. 1, 2003; children: La'Sandra Bi'Arbra, Oronde' Jeremiah Christopher. AA, Kennedy King Jr. Coll., Chgo., 1970; BS, George Williams Coll., Downers Grove, Ill., 1972; MS, U. Ill., 1977; MA, Roosevelt U., 1980. Tchr. health edn., driver edn. Chgo. Bd. Edn., 1972—; coach boys and girls track CVS High Sch., Chgo., 1974-91; women's track coach Chgo. State U., 1991—2000, girls volleyball coach, 2000—. Coach freshman and sophomore track and field Calumet Career Prep. Acad., 2001—. Mem. Nat. Alliance Black Sch. Educators, Am. Alliance Health, Phys. Edn., Recreation and Dance, Ill. Assn. Health, Phys. Edn., Recreation and Dance (membership chmn. 1990—). Avocations: walking, jogging, bible reading, exercising. Home: 10508 S Wentworth Ave Chicago IL 60628-2540 Office: 8131 S May St Chicago IL 60620-3007

JENKINS, WILLIAM KENNETH, electrical engineering educator; b. Pitts., Apr. 12, 1947; s. William Kenneth and Edna Mae (Treusch) J.; m. Suzann Heinricher, Aug. 22, 1970 BSEE, Lehigh U., 1969; MSEE, Purdue U., 1971, PhD, 1974. Grad. instr., teaching asst. Purdue U., West Lafayette, Ind., 1969-74; research sci. assoc. Lockheed Corp., Palo Alto, Calif., 1974-77, cons., 1983—; asst. prof. elec. engring. U. Ill., Urbana, 1977-80, assoc. prof., 1980-83, prof., 1983-99, dir. coordinated sci. lab., 1986-99; prof., head elec. engring. Pa. State U., University Park, 1999—. Hon. vis. prof. U. York, U.K., 1995-96; vis. prof. Naval Postgrad. Sch., Monterey, Calif., 1996; cons. Ill. State Water Survey, Urbana, 1978, Siliconix, Inc., Santa Clara, Calif., 1979-81, Bell Labs., North Andover, Mass., 1984, AT&T Bell Labs, Lockheed Missiles and Space Co. Fellow IEEE (Millenium medal 2000); mem. IEEE Circuits and Systems Soc. (pres. 1985, editor reprint vol. 1986, Disting. Svc. award 1990), Signal Processing Soc. Avocations: tennis, swimming, sports cars, music. Home: 1517 Ridge Master Dr State College PA 16803-3164 Office: 129 EE East Bldg University Park PA 16802

JENKINS-SMITH, EFFIE SHARON, educational administrator; b. Queens, N.Y., Aug. 12, 1955; d. Winfred Joseph and Elizabeth (Harrell) Jenkins; m. Clyde T. Smith, Jan. 24, 1986; 1 child, Kyle T. Smith. BS, Morgan State U., Balt., 1977; M in Ednl. Adminstrn., U. So. Miss., Hattiesburg, 1984. Cert. paralegal. Tchr. Pleasantville (N.J.) Bd. Edn., 1977-86, supr., 1986-88, dir. alternative/cmty. edn., 1988—, Affirmative Action officer, 1994—. Mem. Child Fedn., Pleasantville, 1994—. Sec. Mcpl. Alliance, Pleasantville, 1993—. Sgt. Air N.G., 1979—. Fellow IDEA, 1995; recipient Commendation award Air N.G., 1992, Outstanding Educator award N.J. Alliance Black Sch. Educators, Newark, 1994. Mem. N.J. Prins./Suprs. Assn., Assn. for Lifelong Learning, Nat. Alliance Black Sch. Educators, Nat. Comty. Edn. Assn. Methodist. Avocations: travel, crafts, reading. Office: Alternative/Comty Edn 350 S Franklin Ave Pleasantville NJ 08232-3051 Home: 8042 English Creek Ave Egg Harbor Township NJ 08234-7272

JENKS-DAVIES, KATHRYN RYBURN, retired daycare provider and owner, civic worker; b. Lynchburg, Va., Oct. 9, 1916; d. Charles Arthur and Jessie Katherine (Moorman) Ryburn; m. Thomas Edgar Jenks Jr., Sept. 9, 1941 (dec. June 1975); children: Thomas Edgar III, Jessika, Timothy; m. Robert E. Davies, Dec. 27, 1986 (dec. Mar. 1996). BS, State Tchr. Coll., 1938; postgrad., Mary Washington Coll., 1947-48, U. Va., 1957-58, William and Mary Coll., 1967-68, Va. Commonwealth U., 1969-70. Elem. tchr. various schs., Grundy, Va., 1939-41; phys. therapist U.S. Army, Ft. Bragg, N.C., 1942, operator motor pool Ft. Still, Okla., 1943-44, occupational therapist Augusta, Ga., 1944-45; instr. phys. edn. King George (Va.) High Sch., 1947-48, Stafford (Va.) High Sch., 1949-50, substitute tchr., 1950-53; owner, dir. Kay's Kindergarten, Fredericksburg, Va., 1959-83; ret., 1983. Featured in Fredericksburg Times mag., The Free Lance-Star and Richmond Newspapers. Counselor Girl Scouts U.S.A., Grundy, Va., 1939-41; life mem. Kenmore Assn., 1949—; mem. Hist. Fredericksburg Found., Inc., 1953—, vol. Garden Week and Christams Open House; mem. Mental Health Bd., 1978-84; founder Ford Franklin Found., 1968-78; mem. Fredericksburg Clean Cmty. Commn., 1987—; rep. United Way, Fredericksburg; instr. art ceramics Cmty. Ctr. Fredericksburg, 1950-80; bd. dirs. Miss Fredericksburg Fair Pageant, 1965-88; participant cmty. parades; coord. Fredericksburg Agrl. Fair 18th Century Craft People and Artisans, 1988-93, also others; bd. dirs. Antique Farm Implements, Gas and Steam Engines, 1989-93, Fredericksburg Fair, 1994-96; active State Fair of Va., 1981-95, Am. Heritage Showcase Endl. Reenactment Pioneer Farmstead, 1981-96. Recipient Virginia Ellison Vol. Svc. award Fredericksburg Clean Community Commn., 1976-87, Recognition of Svc. award, 1983-84, 1st, 2nd. and 3rd pl. trophies cmty. parades, awards radio Stas. WFLS and WFVA, 1949-89; honored by Kiwanians for travelogue for fund raiser, 1995—, vol. award, 1997. Mem. AAUW (advt. chmn. travelogue 1971-89, Donor Honoree award 1983, 98, bd. dirs. 1971-79), Lioness Club (bd. dir. 1968-87, Lioness Tamer 1984—, bd. dirs. 1996-97, Tongue Wagger 1985, 96—), Soroptimist Internat. Fredericksburg (life mem., sec. 1971-73, pres. 1973-75, bd. dirs. 1971-78, co-chmn. Soroptimist Travelogue 1991-93, First Class Pub. Recognition Trophy 1986, Women Helping Women award 1982, named 1 of 5 who have made a difference in cmty. 1994), Order of Eastern Star (hostess 1995, 96, 97, 98), Nat. League of Fredericksburg (bd. dir., Svc. Recognition Trophies 1963, 69, 80), Izaac Walton League (bd. dir. Dog Mart parade 1965-72). Republican. Episcopalian. Avocations: ceramics, drama, dancing, travel, golf. Home: 8 Blair Rd Fredericksburg VA 22405-3025

JENNERICH, EDWARD JOHN, university official and dean; b. Bklyn., Oct. 22, 1945; s. William James and Anna Johanna (Whicker) J.; m. Elaine Zaremba, May 27, 1972; children— Ethan Edward, Emily Elaine BA, Trenton State Coll., 1967; MSL.S., Drexel U., 1970; PhD, U. Pitts., 1974. Cert. tchr., learning resources specialist. Tchr. U.S. history Rahway High Sch., N.J., 1967-70; librarian Westinghouse High Sch., Pitts. Pub. Sch., 1970-74; adminstrv. intern U. Pitts, 1973; chmn. dept. library sci. Baylor U., Waco, Tex., 1974-83; dean Sch. Library Sci. So. Conn. State U., New Haven, 1983-84; v.p. acad. affairs Va. Intermont Coll., Bristol, 1984-87; grad. dean Seattle U., 1987-89; assoc. provost for acad. adminstrn., dean Grad. Sch., 1989-97; pres. Knowledge N.W. Inc., 1997—. Mem. rev. panel Fulbright Adminstrv. Exch., 1983-86. Co-author: University Administration in Great Britain, 1983, The Reference Interview as a Creative Art, 1987, 2d edit., 1997; contbr. articles to profl. jours. Bd. dirs. Waco Girls Club, Tex., 1977-83 Mem. ALA (office for libr. pers. resources 1980-82), Am. Assn. Univ. Adminstrs. (bd. dirs. 1980-82, 83-86, 89-93, 94—, v.p. 1996—, exec. com. 1982-87, chmn. overseas liaison com. 1982-87, Eileen Tosney Adminstrv. Excellence award 1985), Assn. for Coll. and Rsch. Librs. (exec. bd. dirs. 1984-88), Phi Delta Kappa. Republican. Episcopalian. Avocations: collecting and painting military miniatures, reading, travel, outdoor sports, sailing. Home: 6935 NE 164th St Kenmore WA 98028-4282

JENNETT, JOSEPH CHARLES, retired academic administrator, engineering educator; b. Dallas, June 11, 1940; s. James C. and Rita (Gavin) Buchanan; m. Linda Ellis, Aug. 2, 1963; children: Erin, Brian. BS in Civil Engring., So. Meth. U., 1963, MS in Civil Engring., 1966; PhD, U. N.Mex., 1969. Registered profl. engr. Mo., N.Y., S.C., Tex. Field engr. Pitometer Assocs., U.S., Can., 1964-65, 69; instr. civil engring. U. N.Mex., Albuquerque, 1965-66; asst. prof. civil engring. U. Mo., Rolla, 1969-73, assoc. prof. civil engring., 1973-75; assoc. prof., chmn. civil engring. Syracuse (N.Y.) U., 1975-78, prof., chmn. civil engring., 1978-81; prof. environ. systems engring. Clemson (S.C.) U., 1981—, dean engring., 1981—96, provost, v.p. acad. affairs, 1991—96; pres. Tex. A&M U., Laredo, Tex., 1996—2001, pres. emeritus, 2001—. Adj. prof. civil engring. Syracuse U., 1981-87; constr. engr. Dept. of Water Resources, State of Calif., 1963-64, Projects in N. Sydney, New Waterford, Halifax, Can., 1969; cons. Pitometer Assocs., Pa., Ga., Mich., Ky., 1964-65, Calspan Corp., Litton Industries, Schwitzer Corp., Dow Chem., Union Carbide, Martin Marietta, 1969, 85—. Co-author: Lead in the Environment, Geochemistry and the Environment; contbr. articles to profl. jours. Vol. troop 235 Boy Scouts Am., Clemson; adviser Water and Wastewater Treatment Authorities, Natal, Brazil, Wesley Found.; patron Greenville (S.C.) Theatre on the Green. Named Outstanding Young Engr. of Yr. Mo. Soc. Profl. Engrs., 1974. Fellow ASCE; mem. NAS, NSPE, Am. Soc. Engring. Edn. (bd. dirs. 1986-89), Am. Acad. Environ. Engrs. (bd. dirs. 1988-91), S.C. Soc. Profl. Engrs. (pres. Piedmont chpt. 1987-88, Outstanding Engr. of Yr. Piedmont chpt. 1990, S.C. Engr. of Yr. 1990), U. N.M. Outstanding Coll. Engring. Alumni, Water Pollution Control Fedn., Nat. Rsch. Coun. Commn. (life scis. com.), Order of Engr. (bd. dirs. 1988-91). Episcopalian. Avocations: photography, travel, camping, fishing, reading, skiing. Home: PO Box 2761 Wimberley TX 78676*

JENNINGS, ALFRED HIGSON, JR., music educator, actor, singer; b. Danbury, Conn., Dec. 24, 1959; s. Alfred Higson and Linda (Keating) J. BS, U. Conn., 1982, MMus, 1984. Cert. profl. educator, Conn. Teaching asst., choral dept. U. Conn., Storrs, 1982-84; tchr. music Danbury Pub. Schs., 1985—; ptnr. Jennings Oil Co., 1999—. Asst. condr. Concert Choir/Chamber Singers, U. Conn., 1982-84, asst. dir. Annual Elizabethan Christmas Dinner Concert, 1983; musical dir. for theatrical prodns. Danbury High Sch., 1985-88; baritone soloist St. Matthew Episcopal Ch. Choir, Wilton, Conn., 1986—. Vocal dir. plays The Sound of Music, 1986, Camelot, 1988, Annie, 1990, others; actor in plays Godspell, 1985, South Pacific, 1987, Oklahoma!, 1988, You're a Good Man, Charlie Brown, 1988, Into the Woods, 1991, Assassins, 1992, Sweeney Todd, 2001, others; actor, in opera Amahl and the Night Visitors, 1998, 2000. Named Tchr. of Yr., South St. Elem. Sch., 1990, 97, Roberts Ave. Elem. Sch., 1997; recipient Project Redesign grant Danbury Pub. Schs., 1991-92, Exemplary Program award, Conn. Assn. Schs., 1997. Mem. NEA, Musicals at Richter, Inc. (sec. 1987-88, v.p. 1988-89, program editor 1991-94), Orff-Schulwerk Assn., Conn. Edn. Assn., Music Educators Nat. Conf., Conn. Music Educators

Assn. Avocations: singing, conducting, theatre. Home: 8 Cipolla Ln Brookfield CT 06804-1511 Office: Danbury Pub Schs 63 Beaver Brook Rd Danbury CT 06810-6211 E-mail: ahj@aol.com.

JENNINGS, GARY HAROLD, college administrator; b. Coos Bay, Oreg., May 10, 1941; s. Harold D. Jennings (dec.) and Georgia E. (Davenport) Perez; m. Susan B. Boreman, Mar. 26, 1988; children: Eliza, Jennifer, Daniel, Michael, David. BBS, Nat. U., 1983, MS in Edn., 1985. Enlisted USN, 1959, advanced through grades to lt., ret., 1979; dean, contract mgr. San Diego C.C. Dist., Orlando, Fla., 1980—. Contbr. articles to profl. jours. Pres. Stop Turning Out Prisoners, Seminole County, Fla., 1993-94; chmn. edn. com. Seminole County Rep. Exec. Com., Fla., 1993-94; mem. Gov.'s Com. on Edn. in Fla., 1993-94. Mem. ASCD. Mem. Lds Ch. Home: 644 Wilbur Ct Gurnee IL 60031-3132

JENNINGS, NANCY ANN, retired elementary education educator; b. Bristow, Okla., July 11, 1932; d. John Linard and Charlie Estelle (Hooper) Stucker; m. Jerald Leon Jennings, June 4, 1951; children: Jan, Catherine Jennings Hackman, Elizabeth. BS, U. Okla., 1956; MS, Washburn U., Topeka, Kans., 1974. Cert. elem. tchr., Kans. Tchr. Whitson Grade Sch. Dist. 501, Topeka, 1970-75, Delia Grade Sch Dist. 321, St. Marys, Kans., 1978-79, Silver Lake (Kans.) Grade Sch. Dist. 372, 1979-85, ret., 1985. Mem. Kans. Hist. Soc. Mem. NEA (life), AAUW (bd. dirs.), DAR (regent Topeka chpt. 1989-91, sec.-treas. N.E. dist. Kans. 1992-95, chmn. pres.-gen.'s project state com. 1992-95, co-chair Kans. DAR geneal. records), Topeka Area Ret. Tchrs. Assn. (v.p. 1992-93), Internat. Reading Assn. (sec. 1983-84), Topeka Aux. Kans. Engring. Soc. (pres. 1987-88), Woman's Club (2d v.p. 1989-91), PEO Kans. (corr. sec. 1993—, guard 1994—, pres. 1995-97), Alpha Delta Kappa (pres. 1989-91), Kappa Delta Pi, Alpha Phi (2d v.p. 1989-90). Presbyterian. Avocations: genealogy, reading, sewing, gardening, bridge. Home: 11340 NW 13th St Topeka KS 66615-9620

JENNINGS, PAUL CHRISTIAN, civil engineering educator, academic administrator; b. Brigham City, Utah, May 21, 1936; s. Robert Webb and Elva S. (Simonsen) J.; m. Millicent Marie Bachman, Aug. 28, 1981; m. Barbara Elaine Morgan, Sept. 3, 1960 (div. 1981); children: Kathryn Diane, Margaret Ann. BSCE, Colo. State U., 1958; MSCE, Calif. Inst. Tech., 1960, PhD, 1963. Prof. civil engring., applied mechanics Calif. Inst. Tech., Pasadena, 1966—2002, chmn. divsn. engring., 1985-89, v.p., provost, 1989-95, acting v.p. for bus. and fin., 1995, 98-99, prof. emeritus, 2002—. Mem. faculty bd. Calif. Tech. Inst., 1974-76, steering com., 1974-76, chmn. nominating com., 1975, grad. studies com., 1978-80; cons. in field. Author: (with others) Earthquake Design Criteria. Contbr. numerous articles to profl. jours. 1st lt. USAF, 1963-66. Recipient Honor Alumnus award Colo. State U., 1992, Achievement in Academia award Coll. Engring., 1992; Erskine fellow U. Canterbury, New Zealand, 1970, 85. Fellow AAAS, New Zealand Soc. Earthquake Engring.; mem. ASCE (Walter Huber award 1973, Newmark medal 1992), Seismol. Soc. Am. (pres. 1980), Earthquake Engring. Rsch. Inst. (pres. 1981-83), Athenaeum Club. Avocations: fly fishing, hiking. Home: 640 S Grand Ave Pasadena CA 91105-2423 Office: Calif Inst Tech Mail Code 104-44 Pasadena CA 91125-0001 E-mail: pcjenn@caltech.edu.

JENRETTE, THOMAS SHEPARD, JR., music educator, choral director; b. Roanoke, Va., Feb. 1, 1946; s. Thomas Shepard and Virginia Catherine (Harris) J. BA, U. N.C., 1968, MusM, 1970; D of Mus. Arts, U. Mich., 1976. Choral dir. Cummings High Sch., Burlington, N.C., 1969-72; dir. cultural arts Burlington (N.C.) City Schs., 1972-73; dir. choral activities S.W. State U., Marshall, Minn., 1976-79, East Tenn. State U., Johnson City, 1979—. Dir. music First Christian Ch., Johnson City, 1981-84, Covenant Presbyn. Ch., Johnson City, 1991—; dir. East Tenn. State U. Chorale European Tour, 1985, 98, 2001; guest condr. choral festival N.C. High Sch., Raleigh, 1987, 2002, Govs. Sch. for Arts, Murfreesboro, Tenn., 1987, Nat. Seminar of Intercollegiate Men's Choruses, Inc., 1992; guest condr. N.C. All-State Male Choir, 1997, All-East Tenn. H.S. Male Choir, 1998, Tenn. All-State H.S. Male Choir, 2001, S.C. All-State Male Choir, 2002, Ga. All-State H.S. male choir, 2003, Nat. Condrs. Conf., U. So. Miss., 2000; so. divsn. repertoire and stds. chair for male choirs Am. Choral Dirs. Assn., 1999—. Grantee East Tenn. State U., 1988, 90, 96, 99. Mem. Am. Choral Dirs. Assn. (life, conductor 1986, 88, 94, 2000, so. divsn. convs., 89, 99 nat. conv., so. divsn. repertoire and stds. chair for male choirs 1999—), Tenn. Music Educators Assn. (conductor state convs. 1990, 91, 94, 2000, dir. White House, Christmas 1989, 2001, Canticum Novum Festival, Caracas, Venezuela, 1996), Internat. Fedn. Choral Music, Nat. Assn. Tchrs. Singing, The Coll. Music Soc. (life), Music Educators Nat. Conf. (condr. so. divsn. conv. 1997), Phi Mu Alpha (hon.), Omicron Delta Kappa, Pi Kappa Lambda. Home: 2734 E Oakland Ave Apt C-25 Johnson City TN 37601-1887 E-mail: jenrette@etsu.edu.

JENSEN, ANNA BERNICE, retired special education educator and nurse; b. Wilkinsburg, Pa., Oct. 1, 1914; d. August Anderson and Anna Lovisa Jönsson; m. William F. Jensen, July 26, 1941 (dec. Oct. 1990); children: William Maehr (dec.), Robert Russell, Richard Bryan. RN, Bellevue Sch. Nursing, 1936; BA, Trenton State Coll., 1969, MA, 1972, supervisory cert., 1979. Charge nurse surgery Gouverneer Hosp., N.Y.C., 1936-39; indsl. nurse Todd Shipyard, Bklyn., 1939-41; substitute tchr. Hillsborough (N.J.) Sch. Sys., 1965-71; tchr. McNamara Sch. Presbyn. Ch., Flemington, N.J., 1972-73; title I tchr. Somerville (N.J.) Sch. Sys., 1973-75. Dir. Hillsborough Leisure Time Learning Ctr., Jointure Adult Edn. Bd., Brook Hillsboro, others, 1979-83; tchr. creative writing Hunterdon Adult Edn., Flemington, 1976-79; dir. vols. Somerset County Chaplaincy to the Elderly, 1985-89; vol. Somerset Med. Ctr., 1981-92. Editor: (booklet) We Walk In Their Footsteps, 1976, 2d edit., 1977; rschr.: (book) Ladies At the Crossroads, 1978; contbr.: (books) Poems—Elder Hostel U. of Iowa, 1986, 87, 88, Memoirs—Elder Hostel U. of Iowa, 1991, 94. Coord. lit. program Older Wiser Program, Somerset County Libr., Bridgewater, N.J., 1986—, tchr. creative writing and memoirs, 1995—, mem. planning com., 1985—; mem. adv. com. RSVP Somerset County Office of Aging, Bridgewater, 1993-96; coord., founder Sixty Plussers, Good Shepherd Ch., Somerville, 1990—; statistician Women's Rsch. Ctr., Somerville, 1985—. Recipient award Adult Comty. Edn.—N.J., 1981. Mem. NEA, Am. Assn. Ret. Persons, Bellevue Alumnae Assn., Princeton Y. Lutheran. Avocations: writing poetry, needlework, volunteering, reading, speaking and reading swedish.

JENSEN, ARTHUR ROBERT, psychology educator; b. San Diego, Aug. 24, 1923; s. Arthur Alfred and Linda (Schachtmayer) J.; m. Barbara Jane DeLarme, May 6, 1960; 1 child, Roberta Ann. BA, U. Calif., Berkeley, 1945; PhD, Columbia U., 1956. Asst. med. psychology U. Md., 1955-56; research fellowInst. Psychiatry U. London, 1956-58; prof. ednl. psychology U. Calif., Berkeley, 1958-94; prof. emeritus, 1994—. Author: Genetics and Education, 1972, Educability and Group Differences, 1973, Educational Differences, 1973, Bias in Mental Testing, 1979, Straight Talk about Mental Tests, 1981, The g Factor, 1998; contbr. to profl. jours., books. Guggenheim fellow, 1964-65, fellow Ctr. Advanced Study Behavioral Scis., 1966-67 Fellow AAAS, Am. Psychol. Assn., The Glaton Inst., Am. Psychol. Soc.; mem. Psychonomic Soc., Am. Soc. Human Genetics, Soc. for Social Biology, Behavior Genetics Assn., Psychometric Soc., Sigma Xi. Office: U Calif Sch Edn Berkeley CA 94720-0001

JENSEN, BAIBA, principal; Prin. Hawkins Elem. Sch., Brighton, Mich. Recipient Elem. Sch. Recognition awards U.S. Dept. Edn., 1989-90. Office: Hawkins Elem Sch 8900 Lee Rd Brighton MI 48116-2000

JENSEN, DAVID GRAM, marketing professional, consultant, sales trainer; b. New Britain, Conn., Jan. 24, 1955; s. Robert and Vera (Ericksen) J. BS, Cen. Conn. State U., 1977; MS, U. Wis., 1979. Assoc. dir. phys. dept. New Britain (Conn.) YMCA, 1975-77; grad. asst. LaCrosse (Wis.) Exercise Program, 1978-79; staff rsch. assoc. U. Calif., San Diego, 1979-81, coord. rsch. cardiology, 1981-83; med. application cons. Med. Data Systems, San Diego, 1983-84; med. sales specialist Siemens Med. Systems, Mission Viejo, Calif., 1984-90; chief adminstrv. officer UCLA, 1990-95; pres. Scientific Selling Systems, L.A., 1993—. Cons. Western Imaging, Denver, 1991—. Contbr. articles to profl. jours. Mem. Nat. Speakers Assn., Inst. for Mgmt. Cons. Avocations: pub. speaking, exercise, motivational books and tapes. Home and Office: 3518 Barry Ave Los Angeles CA 90066-2802

JENSEN, HARLAN ELLSWORTH, veterinarian, educator; b. St. Ansgar, Iowa, Oct. 6, 1915; s. Bert and Mattie (Hansen) J.; m. Naomi Louise Geiger, June 7, 1941; children: Kendra Lee Jensen Belfi, Doris Eileen Jensen Futoma, Richard Harlan. DVM, Iowa State U., 1941; PhD, U. Mo., 1971. Diplomate: Charter diplomate Am. Coll. Vet. Ophthalmologists (v.p. 1970-72, pres. 1972-73). Vet. practice, Galesburg, Ill., 1941-46; small animal internship New Brunswick, N.J., 1946-47; small animal practice Cleve., 1947-58, San Diego, 1958-62, Houston, 1962-67; mem. faculty U. Mo., Columbia, 1967-80, chief ophthalmology, 1967-80, prof. emeritus Vet. Sch., 1980—, assoc. prof. ophthalmology Med. Sch., 1972-80. Cons. in vet. ophthalmology to pharm. firms; guest lectr., prof. ophthalmology Vet. Sch. U. Utrecht, The Netherlands, 1973; tchr., lectr. various vet. meetings; condr. seminar World Congress Small Animal Medicine and Surgery, 1973, 77. Author: Stereoscopic Atlas of Clinical Ophthalmology of Domestic Animals, 1971, Stereoscopic Atlas of Ophthalmic Surgery of Domestic Animals, 1974; co-author: Stereoscopic Atlas of Soft Tissue Surgery of Small Animals, 1973, Clinical Dermatology of Small Animals, 1974; contbr. articles to profl. jours. Recipient Gaines award AVMA, 1973 Mem. Am. Vet. Radiology Soc. (pres. 1956-57), Am. Vet. Ophthalmology Soc. (pres. 1960-62), Farm House Frat., Rotary (pres. Pacific Beach, Calif. 1960-62, pres. Columbia 1977-78), Sigma Xi, Phi Kappa Phi, Phi Zeta, Gamma Sigma Delta. Mem. Bible Ch. Achievements include invention of instrument for ear trimming in dogs, 1949, breathing apparatus, 1953; designer sound proof animal hosps.; developer 3-D study program for vet. ophthalmology, 1969. Home: 1600 Texas St Apt 301 Fort Worth TX 76102-3481

JENSEN, JOSEPH (NORMAN), priest, educator; b. Mannheim, Ill., Nov. 22, 1924; s. Harry and Annette (Gerbing) J. BA, Cath. U. Am., 1951, STD, 1971; lic. in Sacred Theology, Collegio San Anselmo, Rome, 1955; S.S.L., Pontifical Bibl. Inst., Rome, 1968. Joined Benedictine Order, Roman Cath. Ch., 1948, ordained priest, 1954. Assoc. prof. Cath. U. Am., Washington, 1961—; prior St. Anselm's Abbey, Washington, 1981-85. Author: The Use of Tora by Isaiah, 1977, God's Word to Israel, 1982, Isaiah 1-39, 1984; mng. editor Old Testament Abstracts, 1977—. 2d lt. USAAF, 1943-45. Mem. Cath. Bibl. Assn. (exec. sec. 1970—), Soc. Bibl. Lit., Joint Com. Cath. Learned Socs. (sec. 1977-82, del. 1974-98), Coun. on Study of Religion (treas. Waterloo, Can. chpt. 1970-77, del. 1970—, sec. 1985-92, v.p. 1992—). Home: St Anselm's Abbey 4501 S Dakota Ave NE Washington DC 20017-2753 Office: Cath Bibl Assn 314 Caldwell Hall Cath U Am Washington DC 20064

JENSEN, RICHARD JORG, biology educator; b. Sandusky, Ohio, Jan. 17, 1947; s. Aksel Carl and Margaret (Wolfe) J.; m. Faye Robertson, May 30, 1970. BS, Austin Peay State U., 1970, MS, 1972; PhD, Miami U., 1975. Asst. prof. Wright State U., 1975-79; prof. St. Mary's Coll., 1979—. Guest prof. U. Notre Dame, Ind., 1981—, dir. Greene-Nieuwland Herbarium, 1988—; sr. rsch. fellow Ctr. for Field Biology, Austin Peay State U., 1986-88; vis. scholar dept. botany Miami U., 1987; panelist systematic biology program NSF, 1983-87. Assoc. editor Am. Midland Naturalist, 1988—; mem. exec. com. Am. Midland Naturalist, 1989—; mem. editl. bd. Plant Systematics and Evolution, 1990-96; assoc. editor Systematic Botany, 1996-2000. Recipient Award for outstanding tchg. Wright State U., 1978, Maria Pieta award for outstanding tchg. St. Mary's Coll., 1997; named to Austin Peay State U. Acad. Hall of Fame, 1998; NSF grantee, 1973, 79, 85, 87, 95, Rsch. Corp. grantee, 1984, Eli Lilly grantee, 1990. Fellow: Ind. Acad. Sci. (co-chair program com. 1988, fellow com., biol. survey com., publ. com., grantee 1983, 1991); mem.: Internat. Oak Soc. (bd. dirs. 1997—, webmaster 2000—, membership chair 1997—), Soc. Systematic Biology, Internat. Assn. Plant Taxonomy, Bot. Soc. Am., Am. Soc. Plant Taxonomists (rsch. com. 1987—90, chmn. 1989—90, treas. 1991—96, coun. mem. at large 2000—, honors and awards com. 2000—, chair 2001, Disting. Svc. award 1996), Sigma Xi (grantee 1974). Democrat. Avocations: reading, computing, genealogy research. Home: 2044 Carrbridge Ct South Bend IN 46614-3514 Office: St Mary's Coll Dept Biology Notre Dame IN 46556 also: Greene-Nieuwland Herbarium Univ of Notre Dame Dept Biology Notre Dame IN 46556 E-mail: rjensen@saintmarys.edu., sparky0408@msn.com.

JENSEN, ROBERT TRAVIS, physician, educator, researcher; b. Minot, N.D., Mar. 19, 1926; s. John and Katherine N. (Arnold) J.; m. Rosemary Elizabeth McEachern; children: Janet, Katherine, Tova Marie. Student, Concordia Coll.; BA, Denison U., 1946; MD, U. Minn., 1949; Diploma in Tropical Medicine and Hygiene, London Sch. Hygiene and Tropical Medicine, 1958; MPH, Johns Hopkins U., 1967. Diplomate Am. Bd. Internal Medicine, Am. Bd. Preventive Medicine. Commd. capt., physician officer Med. Corps U.S. Army, Japan, Korea, 1950-51, advanced through grades to col., 1967, ret., 1976, physician officer Med. Corps., 1950-51, physician officer Brooke Army Hosp., Walter Reed Inst. Rsch., 1952-55, physician officer Ft. Meade Hosp., 1955-57, chief dept. pub. health Acad. Health Sci., 1971-76; missionary physician Luth. Ch., Tanzania, 1957-66; chief dept. health, edn. and welfare U.S. Civil Adminstrn., Okinawa, Ryuku Isls., 1969-71; supt. state chest hosps. Dept. Health State of Tex., San Antonio, 1977-82; assoc. prof. dept. family practice Health Scis. Ctr. U. Tex., San Antonio, 1983-97, ret., 1997; pvt. practice in internal medicine, 1997-98; ret., 1998. Lectr., cons. in field. Contbr. articles to med. jours. Decorated Silver Star, Bronze Star, Legion of Merit cluster. Fellow Am. Coll. Physicians, Am. Coll. Preventive Medicine; mem. Am. Soc. Tropical Medicine and Hygiene. Republican. Presbyterian. E-mail: drrtj@aol.com.

JENSEN, WALTER EDWARD, lawyer, educator; b. Chgo., Oct. 20, 1937. AB, U. Colo., 1959; JD, Ind. U., 1962, MBA, 1964; PhD (Univ. fellow), Duke U., 1972. Bar: Ind. 1962, Ill. 1962, D.C. 1963, U.S. Tax Ct. 1982, U.S. Supreme Ct. 1967. Prof. bus. law U. Colo., Boulder, 1958-62; assoc. prof. Colo. State U., 1964-66, U. Conn., Storrs, 1966-67, Ill. State U., 1970-72; prof. bus. adminstrn. Va. Poly. Inst. and State U., beginning 1972, prof. fin., ins. and law, 1972-; with Inst. Advanced Legal Studies, U. London, 1983-84; prof. U.S. Air Force Grad. Mgmt. Program, Europe, 1977-78, 83-85; Duke U. legal rsch. awardee, rschr., Guyana, Trinidad and Tobago, 1967; vis. lectr. pub. internat. law U. Istanbul, 1988, Roberts Coll. U. Bosporous, Istanbul, Uludag U., Turkey, 1988; rschr. U. London Inst. Advanced Legal Studies, London Sch. Econs. and Inst. Commonwealth Studies, 1969, 71-74, 76; Ford Found. Rsch. fellow Ind. U., 1963-64; faculty rsch. fellow in econs. U. Tex., 1968; Bell Telephone fellow in econs. regulated pub. utilities U. Chgo., 1965. Recipient Dissertation Travel award Duke U. Grad. sch., 1968; Ind. U. fellow, 1963, 74, scholar, 1963-64. Mem. D.C. Bar Assn., Ill. Bar Assn., Ind. bar Assn., ABA, Am. Polit. sci. Assn., Am. Soc. Internat. Law, Am. Judicature Soc., Am. Bus. Law Assn., Alpha Kappa Psi, Phi Alpha Delta, Pi Gamma Mu, Pi Kappa Alpha, Beta Gamma Sigma. Contbr. articles to profl. publs.; staff editor Am. Bus Law Jour., 1973— ; vice chmn. assoc. editor for adminstrv. law sect. young lawyers Barrister (Law Notes), 1975-83; book rev. and manuscript editor Justice System Jour: A Mgmt. Rev., 1975— ; staff editor Bus. Law Rev., 1975— . Home: 3358 Glade Creek Blvd 5 Roanoke VA 24012 Office: Va Poly Inst and State U Blacksburg VA 24060

JENSEN, WILLIAM AUGUST, plant biology educator; b. Chgo., Aug. 22, 1927; s. William McKinley and Gertrude Rose (Hild) J.; m. Joan nancy Sell, June 20, 1947 (div. Dec. 28, 1987); children: Scott William, Christina Catherine; m. Beverly Joyce Bailey, Dec. 31, 1987. PhB, U. Chgo., 1948, MS, 1950, PhD, 1953. Postdoctoral fellow Calif. Inst. Tech., Pasadena, 1953-55, U. Brussels, 1955-56; asst. prof. U. Va., Charlottesville, 1956-57, U. Calif., Berkeley, 1957-60, assoc. prof., 1960-63, prof., 1963-84, Ohio State U., Columbus, 1984—. Chair dept. botany U. Calif., Berkeley, 1980-82, chair dept. instrn. in biology, 1982-89, from asst. dean to assoc. dean Coll. of Letters and Sci., 1962-65; dean Coll. of Biol. Scis., Ohio State U., Columbus, 1984-89. Author: Botanical Histochemistry, 1962, Botany: An Ecological Approach, 1972, 84, Biology, 1979; contbr. 110 rsch. articles to profl. jours. With U.S. Army, 1946-47. Recipient Ohaus/Nat. Sci. Tchr. award, 1976, Tchg. award U. Calif., Berkeley, 1960, Outstanding Tchg. award Ohio State U. Alumni Assn., 1992, Outstanding Tchg. award Ohio State U. Coll. Letters and Sci., 1997. Fellow AAAS; mem. Bot. Soc. Am. (program officer 1962-67, v.p. 1975, pres. 1978, N.Y. Botanic Garden award for rsch. in botany 1964, Merit award 1982). Achievements include development of audio-tutorial slide-tape modules and multi-image lectures in botanical and biological topics; research in the ultrastructure of fertilization in flowering plants, in the structure of pollen, pollen tubes, the embryo sac, and the early embryo in a variety of plants, in cell development in root tips and plant embryos. Home: 396 Pebble Creek Dr Dublin OH 43017-1369 Office: Ohio State U Dept Plant Biology 1735 Neil Ave Columbus OH 43210-1220

JENSH, RONALD PAUL, anatomist, educator; b. NYC, June 14, 1938; s. Werner G. and Dorothy (Hensle) J.; m. Ruth Eleanor Dobson, Aug. 18, 1962; children: Victoria Lynn, Elizabeth Whitney BA, Bucknell U., 1960, MA, 1962; PhD, Jefferson Med. Coll., 1966. Instr. in anatomy Thomas Jefferson U., Phila., 1966—68, asst. in radiology, 1966—68, asst. prof. radiology and anatomy, 1968—74, assoc. prof. radiology, 1968—92, assoc. prof. anatomy, 1968—74, prof. anatomy, 1982—94, vice chmn., 1984—94, prof. pathology, anatomy and cell biology, 1994—, assoc. prof. pediatrics, 1992—, chmn. curriculum com., 1987—93, head anatomy div. Coll. Allied Health Scis., 1975—88, co-dir. pre-doctoral tng. program, 1971—79, course coord. histology, 1988—. Staff Op. Concern Inc., Cherry Hill, N.J., 1970-72; cons. reproductive biology Bio-Search Inc., Argus Rsch. Lab. Inc., Ortho Rsch. Found. Contbr. articles to sci. jours. Task force com. on comm. S. Jersey Methodist Conf., 1974-80; chmn. Learning Resources Ctr., Haddonfield United Meth. Ch., NJ, 1976-79. Recipient Christian R. and Mary F. Lindback Found. Disting. Teaching award, 1978, Disting. Alumnus award, 1985, Faculty Achievement award Burlington Northern Found., 1989, Jefferson Med. Coll. Portrait, 1994, Award for Disting. Alumnus in a Chosen Profession, Bucknell U., 1997. Mem. AAAS, Am. Soc. Zoologists, N.Y. Acad. Scis., Teratology Soc. (treas. 1989-92), Behavioral Teratology Soc. (pres. 1985-86), Am. Assn. Anatomists, Soc. Am. Mus. Natural History, Inst. Social Ethics and Life Scis., Jefferson Med. Coll. Alumni Assn. (hon. life), Phi Beta Kappa, Sigma Xi, Psi Chi, Phi Sigma. Home: 230 E Park Ave Haddonfield NJ 08033-1835 Office: 562 Jefferson Alumni Hall 1020 Locust St Philadelphia PA 19107-6799 E-mail: ronald.jensh@jefferson.edu.

JENSON, PAULINE ALVINO, retired speech and hearing educator; b. Orange, N.J. m. Bernard A. Jenson; 1 child, Mark J. BS, Trenton State Coll., 1948; MA, Columbia U., 1950, PhD, 1969. Tchr. English and history Bordentown (N.J.) H.S., 1948-49; tchr. Lexington Sch. for Deaf, N.Y.C., 1950-51, with rsch. dept., 1969-70; tchr. N.J. Sch. for Deaf, West Trenton, 1951-56, 58-61, St. Mary's Sch. for Deaf, Buffalo, 1956-58; speech pathologist Hunterdon Med. Ctr., Flemington, N.J., 1959-60, dir. speech and hearing, 1960-62; asst. prof. Trenton (N.J.) State Coll., 1962-65; instr., lectr. Teacher's Coll., Columbia U., N.Y.C., 1966-69; prof. dept. speech pathology and audiology Trenton (N.J.) State Coll., 1970-95; Yrbk Dedica, 1978; prof. dept. lang. and comm. sci. Coll. N.J. (formerly Trenton State Coll.), 1995-98, chmn. dept., 1991-94, prof. emerita, 1998. Cons. Universal Films & Visual Arts, N.Y.C., 1968-70, State Agys. and Schs. for Handicapped, N.J., N.Y., 1976-98; evaluator Coun. on Edn. of Deaf, Washington, 1979-83. Author: (with others) Speech for the Deaf Child, 1971; inventor cueing system for deaf speakers, 1976; editor: (info. booklets) Topics, Princeton, N.J., 1980-86 Help line vol. N.J. Assn. for Children with Hearing Impairments, Princeton, 1973-95; co-author, cons. Senate Bills on Deafness, Trenton, 1979-98; commr. Legislative Commn. to Study Svcs. for Hearing Impaired Children, Trenton, 1988-90. Post Master's scholar U.S. Office Edn., Tchrs. Coll., Columbia U., 1965-66; grantee N.J. Dept. Edn., 1973, N.J. Dept. Human Svcs., 1992-96. Mem. N.J. Assn. for Children with Hearing Impairment (founder, exec. dir. 1973-95, Pauline Jenson award at The Coll. of N.J. named in her honor, 1996), N.J. Speech, Lang. and Hearing Assn. (life, Disting. Svc. award 1985, disting. clin. svc. award 1998), Am. Speech, Lang. and Hearing Assn. (cert., life). Avocation: bibliophic. Office: PO Box 1336 Princeton NJ 08542-1336

JENTSCH, LYNDA JEANNE, language educator; b. Harlingen, Tex., Nov. 9, 1953; d. Theodore Werner Jentsch and Elinor Jean Elwert; m. Bart Grooms, Aug. 4, 1979; children: Walker Elwert, Owen Michael. BA, Kutztown State Coll., 1975; MA, Vanderbilt U., 1979, PhD, 1983. Tchg. asst., sr. tchg. fellow Vanderbilt U., Nashville, 1978—79; instr. Jefferson C.C., Louisville, 1979—81; from instr. to asst. prof. Spanish U. Ala., Birmingham, 1982—92; from asst. prof. to assoc. prof. Spanish Samford U., Birmingham, 1992—. Author: Exile and the Process of Individuation, 1986. Mem.: Am. Lit. Translators Assn., Ala. Assn. Fgn. Lang. Tchrs., Am. Assn. Tchrs. Spanish & Portugese.

JENTZ, GAYLORD ADAIR, law educator; b. Beloit, Wis., Aug. 7, 1931; s. Merlyn Adair and Delva (Mullen) Jentz; m. JoAnn Mary Hornung, Aug. 6, 1955; children: Katherine Ann, Gary Adair, Loretta Ann, Rory Adair. BA, U. Wis., 1953, JD, 1957, MBA, 1958. Bar: Wis. 1957. Pvt. practice law, Madison, 1957-58; from asst. prof. to assoc. prof. bus. law U. Okla., 1958-65; assoc. prof. U. Tex., Austin, 1965-68, prof., 1968-98, Herbert D. Kelleher prof. bus. law, 1982-98, prof. emeritus, 1998—, chmn. gen. bus. dept., 1968-74, 80-86. From vis. instr. to vis. prof. U. Wis. Law Sch., Wis., 1957—65. Author (with others): Texas Uniform Commercial Code, 1967; author: rev. edit., 1975; author: (with others) Business Law Text and Cases, 1968, Business Law Text, 1978, Legal Environment of Business, 1989, Texas Family Law, 7th edit., 1992, Business Law Today-Alternate Essentials Edition, 4th edit., 1997, Fundamentals of Business Law, 5th edit., 2002, West's Business Law: Text and Cases, 9th edit., 2004, West's Business Law: Alternate Edition, 9th edit., 2004, Law for E-Commerce, 2002, West's Business Law-Case Study Approach, 2003, Business Law Today-Interactive Text, 6th edit., 2003; dep. editor: Social Sci. Quar., 1966—82, mem. editl. bd.:, 1982—94, editor-in-chief: Am. Bus. Law Jour., 1969—74, adv. editor:, 1974—. With U.S. Army, 1953—55. Named to CBA Hall of Fame, 1999; recipient Outstanding Tchr. award, U. Tex. Coll. Bus., 1967, Jack G. Taylor Tchg. Excellence award, 1971, 1989, Joe D. Beasley Grad. Tchg. Excellence award, 1978, CBA Found. Adv. Coun. award, 1979, Grad. Bus. Coun. Outstanding Grad. Bus. Prof. award, 1980, James C. Scorboro Meml. award for outstanding leadership in banking edn., Colo. Grad. Sch. Banking, 1983, Utmost Outstanding Prof. award, 1989, CBA award for excellence in edn., 1994, Banking Leadership award, Western States Sch. Banking, 1995, Civitatis award, U. Tex., 1997. Mem.: So. Bus. Law Assn. (pres. 1967), Wis. Bar Assn., Tex. Assn. Coll. Tchrs. (pres. Austin chpt. 1967—68, mem. exec. com. 1979—80, state pres. 1971—72), Acad. Legal Studies Bus. (pres. 1971—72, mem. exec. com. 1989—94), Am. Arbitration Assn. (nat. panel 1966—96), Southwestern Fedn. Adminstrv. Disciples (v.p. 1979—80, pres. 1980—81), Phi Kappa Phi (pres. 1983—84), Omicron Delta Kappa. Home: 4106 N Hills Dr Austin TX 78731-2826 Office: U Tex MSIS Dept McCombs Sch Bus CBA 5 202 1 University S Austin TX 78712

JERGENS, MARIBETH JOIE, school counselor; b. Cleve., May 3, 1945; d. Raymond Wenceslaus and Elsie Koryta J.; children: Annemarie Gurchik, Keith Robert Gurchik. Student, St. Joseph Acad., Cleve., 1959—63, U. Vienna, Austria, 1965; BS in Elem. Edn., Coll. Mt. St. Joseph on-the-Ohio, 1967; MEd in Ednl. Counseling, Cleve. State U., 1984; cert. in Ednl. Adminstrn., Akron U., 1988; postgrad. in edn. and clin. psychology, Kent State U., 1989—. Cert. elem., spl. edn. and adult edn. tchr., counselor. Coord. info. svcs. Halle Bros., Cleve., 1961—67; tchr. North Olmstead (Ohio) City Schs., 1967-75; tchr. adult basic edn. Polaris Vocat. Sch., Berea, Ohio, 1977-78; tchr. adult edn., ESL Lakewood (Ohio) City Schs., 1978-79; tchr. 2d grade St. Rose Sch., Lakewood, 1979-80; tchr. learning disabled students, tutor Cleve. Pub. Schs. Watterson-Lake Elem. Sch., 1980-85; tutor handicapped Cleve. Christian Home, 1982-84; elem. sch. counselor, tchr. learning disabilites Cleve. Pub. Schs., A.B. Hart Mid. Sch., 1995-97; tchr. human devel. and learning Kent (Ohio) State U., 1997-98; sch. psychologist asst. PSI Assocs., Inc., 1998-99; tchr. Wade Park Sch. Cleve. Mcpl. Sch. Dist., 1999-2000; pvt. practice Rocky River Psychol. Svcs., Ohio, 1999—2003; intervention specialist Dike Montessori Magnet Sch., 2000-01. Counselor West Side Cmty. Mental Health Ctr., Cleve., 1983-84; sales mgr. Field Enterprises Inc., Cleve., 1975-77; fund raising spkr., vol. Cerebral Palsy Camp Rosemary Home for Children United Torch, Cleve., 1961-65; coordinated vol. svcs. area colls. Allen Halfway Ho., Cin., 1965-67; rschr. interventions children with guns and violence in Am. schs., 1998-99; elem. counselor Cleve. Pub. Schs. Adams-Rhodes Cluster, 1985-94; spkr. in field. Contbr. articles to newspapers. Vol. Fairview Gen. Hosp., Cleve., 1959-63, Cerebral Palsy Camp, 1959-63, Allen Halfway House for Children, Cin., 1963-67; co-founder Westshore Separated, Div. and Remarried Caths., Cleve., 1975-85; chair North Olmsted Jr. Women's Club; parish coun. St. Brendan Ch., North Olmstead, 1975-87, founder cath. separated and div. ministry, 1976-85, counselor; mem. com. Cleve. Symphony, Cleve. Art Mus.; summer civil rights activist to implement Fed. Ct. Order Desegregation, Ctrl. H.S., Little Rock, 1957, New Orleans, 1958, Mobile, Ala., 1959; active Am. Aeobics and Fitness Assn., Audobon Soc., Cleve. Natural History Mus., Cleve. Mus. Art, Dem. Party, Edgewater Yacht Club (NCSS), English-Speaking Union, Holden Arboretum, St. Malachi Cath. Ch., Cath. Ch. Spl. Commn. on Priests Sexual Abuse, 2002-03; mem. rev. bd. Cleve. Cath. Diocese, 2003--. Recipient Speaker's United Torch award United Way, Cleve., 1st Pl. prize in clothing design Stretch & Sew, 1975, 1st Pl. prize in needlepoint Framemakers Art, 1983, 1st Pl. in three interstate art contests, musical recording, singing with the Cleve. Symphony Orch., NCSS regatta. Mem. Am. Assn. Counseling and Devel., AAUW, Am. Assn. Marriage and Family Therapists, Am. Psychol. Assn., Assn. for Curriculum and Supervision, Am. Sch. Counselor Assn., N.E. Ohio Counselors Assn., Ohio Counselors Assn., Ohio Assn. Counseling and Devel., Coun. for Exceptional Children, Am. Sch. Counselor Assn., ASCD, Gestalt Inst., Audubon Soc., Cleve. Psychol. Assn., Cleve. Mus. Art, Cleve. Natural History Mus., Cleve. Tchrs. Union, Gestalt Inst., Am. Aerobics and Fitness Assn., Edgewater Yacht Club, English Speaking Union, Holden Arboretum, Pi Lambda Theta. Democrat. Avocations: aerobics, art, cycling, dancing, gardening. Home: 727 Tollis Pkwy Broadview Heights OH 44147

JERGER, EDWARD WILLIAM, mechanical engineer, university dean; b. Milw., Mar. 13, 1922; s. Nickolaus and Ann (Huber) J.; m. Dorothy Marie Post, Aug. 2, 1944 (dec. 1981); children: Betty Ann Murphy, Barbara Lee Smyth; m. Elizabeth Cordiner Sweitzer, Mar. 27, 1982. BS in Mech. Engring, Marquette U., 1946; MS, U. Wis., 1948; PhD, Iowa State U., 1951. Registered profl. engr., Iowa, Ind. Process engr. Wis. Malting Co., Manitowoc, 1946-47; asst. prof. mech. engring. Iowa State U., 1948-55; asso. prof. mech. engring. U. Notre Dame, 1955-61, prof., head mech. engring., 1961-68, asso. dean, 1968-82, prof. mech. engring., 1982-97, prof. emeritus, 1989—. Cons. U. Madre De Maestra Santiago, Dominican Republic, 1965-71 Bd. dirs. Beaufort County Schoolbook Found. Served with USAAF, 1943-46. Mem. ASME, Am. Soc. Engring. Edn., Nat. Soc. Profl. Engrs., Internat. Assn. Housing Sci. (dir.), Nat. Fire Protection Assn., Internat. Assn. Arson Investigators, Sigma Xi, Phi Kappa Phi, Pi Tau Sigma (nat. v.p. 1969-74, pres. 1974-78), Tau Beta Pi. Home: 4 Coburn Ct Okatie SC 29909-4560 Office: Univ Notre Dame Coll Engring Notre Dame IN 46556-5637 E-mail: profjerger@aol.com.

JERMIASON, JOHN LYNN, elementary school educator, farmer, rancher; b. Rochester, Minn, Jan. 9, 1958; s. Orlyn and Evelyn S. Jermiason; m. Ann M. Gebhardt, June 30, 1990. BA in Music, Psychology, St. Olaf Coll., 1981; AS in Agr., N.D. State U., 1982; BS in Edn., Minot State U., 1990. Sales rep. Century 21 Real Estate, Minot, ND, 1989; ind. farmer, rancher Minot, 1982—. Substitute elem. tchr. Minot Pub. Sch., 1993—. Prin. violist Minot Symphony Orch., 1983—, bd. dir., 1996—; mem. ch. coun. Augustana Luth. Ch., Minot, 1989-91; mem. No. Lights String Quartet. Mem.: Elks, Kappa Delta Pi, Phi Mu Alpha. Avocation: church choir. Home and Office: PO Box 452 Minot ND 58702-0452

JERMINI, ELLEN, educational administrator, philosopher; b. Krefeld, Germany, Aug. 25, 1939; came to U.S., 1986. d. Maximilian and Mathilde (Wachtberger) Wilms; m. Helios Jermini, 1961 (div. June 1989); children: Mariella Arnoldi, Diego Jermini. PhB, U. Healing, 1984, M in Healing Sci., 1985, PhD, 1986; PhB, U. Philosophy, 1992. Sec., Germany, Switzerland, 1962; pub. translator, 1984—; seminar organizer, 1983—; dir. U. Philosophy/European Found., 1986—; pres., also chmn. bd. dirs. U. Healing, Campo, Calif., 1986-99, 99—; pres. U. Philosophy, Campo, 1986—; abbot Absolute Monastery, Campo, 1986-99; chmn. bd. Regent. Editor: (newsletter in Italian) Absolute, (newsletter in German) Absolute. Spkr. various univs. and orgns. in Calif. and N.Y., 1989-99, St. Petersburg, Moscow, 1991, Africa, 1994, Egypt, 1995, various seminars and workshops, Ghana, Nigeria, Can., Bahamas, Europe, New Zealand, Australia, The Philippines, China. Mem. Toastmasters Internat. (Able Toastmaster, chmn. bd., mktg. dir.). Avocations: writing, skiing, swimming, playing tennis, flying. Home and Office: U Healing 1101 Far Valley Rd Campo CA 91906-3213

JERNIGAN, SHARON REYNOLDS, school system administrator, educator; b. Dallas, Apr. 29, 1947; d. Robert Lee and Angie (Monk) Reynolds; m. Ross V. Jernigan, Mar. 14, 1985. BA, Dallas Bapt. U., 1971; MEd, Stephen F. Austin State U., 1976; EdD, U. of North Tex., 1986. Cert. elem. tchr., supr., Tex; cert. tchr. grades P-8, leadership, Ga. Tchr. Grand Prairie (Tex.) Ind. Sch. Dist., 1971-72, Duncanville (Tex.) Ind. Sch. Dist., 1972-75, Cedar Hill (Tex.) Ind. Sch. Dist., 1975-78, Garland (Tex.) Ind. Sch. Dist., 1978-85; spl. instrnl. assistance, tchr. Cobb County Pub. Schs., Marietta, Ga., 1985—. Mem. ASCD, NEA, Ga. Assn. Educators, Cobb County Assn. Educators, Nat. Assn. Elem. Sch. Prins., Ga. Assn. Elem. and Secondary Prins., Internat. Reading Assn., Phi Delta Kappa.

JERNSTROM, JOAN, retired secondary school educator; b. South Bend, Ind., July 15, 1934; d. James Nevins and Anne Hermena Jakel; m. Donald Leon Jernstrom Sr., Oct. 17, 1959; children: Donald Leon II, Jan R. Jernstrom Broeders. BA in Bus. Econs., U. South Fla., 1977; MEd, St. Leo Coll., 1982. Cert. electronics technician. Farmer, Zephryhills, Fla.; electronics technician Honeywell, St. Petersburg, Fla.; enlisted USN, 1978-87; tchr. Raymond B. Stewart Mid. Sch., Zephyrhills, Fla.; ret., 2003—. Speaker computer presentation USF workshop leadership conf.; active sch. programs. With USAF, 1952-57; active mem. U.S. Coast Guard Aux. Mem. FFA (hon.), Nat. Women in the Mil. (charter), Am. Vocat. Assn., Fla. Vocat. Assn., Fla. Assn. Computers Am., Pasco County Vocat. Assn., Delta Kappa Gamma (treas.), Am. Legion (past adjutant, past judge advocate Post 118, svc. officer), Air Force Assn. Home: 5534 Darlene St Weeki Wachee FL 34607-1517

JEROME, JAMES JOHN, secondary education educator; b. Milw., Nov. 19, 1962; s. Ronald Francis and Lauralee Ann (McCoy) J.; m. Deborah Jean Rader, Apr. 23, 1994. BS, U. Wis., Milw., 1987; MS, U. Wis., Whitewater, 2001. Cert secondary edn., biology and life sci., chemistry and gen. sci. Sci. tchr. Kern H.S. Dist., Bakersfield, Calif., 1989-91; sci. tchr., chair sci. dept. Waterford (Wis.) Union H.S., 1991—. Mem. NEA, Nat. Assn. Biology Tchrs., Wis. Soc. Sci. Tchrs., So. Lakes Edn. Assn. Roman Catholic. Avocations: reading, fishing, outdoors activities. Home: 534 Small Farm Rd Mukwonago WI 53149-1463 Office: Waterford Union HS 100 Field Dr Waterford WI 53185 E-mail: jjerome@waterforduhs.k12.us.

JERRY, ROBERT HOWARD, retired education educator; b. Brazil, Ind., July 25, 1923; s. Floyd W. and Zetta (Hoffman) J.; m. Marjorie O. Collings, July 23, 1950; children: Robert Howard II, E. Claire. BS, Ind. State U., 1949, MS, 1951; Ed.D., Ind. U., 1963; postgrad., Colo. U., 1951. Tchr. elem. sch., Fowler, Ind., 1949-50; high sch. Delphi, Ind., 1951-57; prin. Covington (Ind.) High Sch., 1957-60; supt. Worthington (Ind.) Schs., 1961-63; mem. faculty Ind. State U., Terre Haute, 1963-85, prof. edn., 1974-85, rep. of Sch. of Grad. Studies, 1986-98; ret. Dep. state supt. public instrn., Ind., 1967-69; active North Central Assn. Colls. and Schs. Co-author: Legal Rights and Responsibilities of Indiana Teachers. Served with USNR, 1943-46. Mem. Ind. Ret. Sch. Adminstrs., Kiwanis, Exch. Club (pres. 1973174), Blue Key, Theta Alpha Phi, Pi Gamma Mu, Phi Delta Kappa, Phi Delta Theta. Home: 2908 Crawford St Terre Haute IN 47803-2848

JERRYTONE, SAMUEL JOSEPH, financial broker; b. Pittston, Pa., Mar. 21, 1947; s. Sebastian and Susan Teresa (Chiampi) J.; children: Sandra, Cheryl, Samuel, Sebastian. Assoc. in Bus., Scranton (Pa.) Lackawanna Jr. Coll., 1966. Mgr. House of Jerrytone Beauty Salon, West Pittston, Pa., 1967-68; regional sales dir. United Republic Life Ins., Harrisburg, Pa., 1970-76; night instr. Wilkes-Barre (Pa.) Vo-Tech High Sch., 1976-78; spl. sales agt. Franklin Life Ins. Co., Wilkes-Barre, 1978-80; instr. Jerrytone Beauty Sch., Pittston, Pa., 1968-69, supr., 1969-95, pres., CEO, 1975, Jerrytone Tng. Ctrs., Pittston, 1989, Las Vegas, 1989; fin. broker Exec. Bus. Mgmt. and Property Svcs., 2001—. Prof. sch. evaluator Nat. Accrediting Com. Arts and Scis., 1974-95; mem. adv. craft com. Wiles-Barre Vo-Tech H.S., 1988. Mem. com. Rep. Presdl. Task Force, Washington, 1984, mem. parish coun. Guardian Angel Cathedral, Las Vegas, 1997. Mem. Pa. Hairdressers Assn., Nat. Accrediting Com. Cosmetology, Am. Coun. Cosmetology Educators, Masons (3d degree award 1983, 32d degree award Lodge Coun. chpt. consistory 1984), Shriners (Irem temple). Roman Catholic. Avocations: reading, golf, bowling, music, video filming. E-mail: s.jerrytone@att.net.

JERVIS, JANE LISE, college official, science historian; b. Newark, N.J., June 14, 1938; d. Ernest Robert and Helen Jenny (Roland) J.; m. Kenneth Albert Pruett, June 20, 1959 (div. 1974); children: Holly Jane Pruett, Cynthia Lorraine Pruett; m. Norman Joseph Chonacky, Dec. 26, 1981; children: Philip Joseph Chonacky, Joseph Norman Chonacky. AB, Radcliffe Coll., 1959; MA, Yale U., 1974, MPhil, 1975, PhD in History of Sci., 1978. Freelance sci. editor and writer, 1962-72; lectr. in history Rensselaer Poly. Inst., 1977-78; dean Davenport Coll., lectr. in history of sci. Yale U., 1978-82; dean students., assoc. prof. history Hamilton Coll., 1982-87; dean coll., lectr. in history Bowdoin Coll., 1988-92; pres. Evergreen State Coll., Olympia, Wash., 1992-2000. Cons. in field. Author: Cometary Theory in 15th Century Europe; contbr. articles to profl. jours.; book reviewer; presenter in field. Trustee Maine Hist. Assn., 1991-92, Stonehill Coll., 1996-02, Providence St. Peter's Hosp., 1997-2000; chair Maine selection com. Rhodes Scholarship Trust, 1990-92, chair N.W. selection com., 1992-93; commr. N.W. Assn. Schs. and Colls. Commn. on Colls., 1994-99. E-mail: jjervis99@comcast.net.

JERVIS, KATHE, educational consultant, researcher; b. Denver, May 3, 1942; d. William and Bettye (Prinz) Weil; m. Robert Jervis, June 19, 1967; children: Alexa, Lisa. BA in History, U. Colo., 1963; M in European History, NYU, 1966; M in Human Devel., Pacific Oaks, 1978. Cert. tchr. N.Y., Calif. Tchr. Dalton Sch., N.Y.C., 1966-67, Shady Hill, Cambridge, Mass., 1967-72, Ctr. Early Edn., L.A., 1974-78, L.A. Unified Sch. Dist., 1978-80, N.Y.C. Pub. Schs., 1980-90; staff assoc., N.Y. coord. Urban Sites Writing Network Inst. for Literacy Studies, Lehman Coll., Bronx, NY, 1991-93; sr. rsch. assoc. Nat. Ctr. Restructuring Edn., Schs. & Tchg. Tchrs. Coll., Columbia U., N.Y.C., 1993—99; coord. Columbia Urban Educators, 2001—. Bd. dirs. Nat. Network Progressive Educators. Author: (book) Eyes on the Child: Three Portfolio Stories, 1996; founding editor: book Pathways: A Forum for Progressive Educators, 1983—93; editor: Education for Democracy, 1988, Progressive Education for the 1990s, 1991; contbr. articles to profl. jours. Grantee, Nat. Coun. Tchrs. English, 1989—90, Dept. Edn., 1996—99. Mem.: N.D. Study Group Evaluation, Am. Edn. Rsch. Assn. Democrat. Home: 1170 5th Ave New York NY 10029-6527 Office: Columbia U MC 3347 420 W 118 St 13th Fl New York NY 10029 E-mail: kj29@columbia.edu.

JESBERG, ROBERT OTTIS, JR., educational consultant, science educator; b. Springfield, Ill., Nov. 17, 1947; s. Robert O. Sr. and Catharine I. (Patton) J.; m. Ruth Marie Andreas, Aug. 21, 1971; children: Kate Debra, Amy Lyn. BA in Biology, Susquehanna U., 1969; MEd, Temple U., 1971, secondary prin. cert., 1974. Cert. secondary biology and gen. sci. tchr., secondary sch. prin. Sci. tchr. Centennial Schs., Warminster, Pa., 1969—, asst. prin., 1979, 85, 88; sci. cons. K'NEX Industries, Inc., Hatfield, Pa., 1994—; sci. coord. Centennial Schs., Warminster, Pa., 1996-98; mem. adv. com. Gov.'s Sci. Inst. Carnegie Mellon U., 1999—; cons. edn. K'nex Edn., Hatfield. Site dir., instr. Lawrence Hall of Sci., NSF Summer Insts., U. Calif., Berkeley, 1990-92; sci. cons. Singapore Am. Schs., 1993; dir. adult edn. Centennial Schs., Warminster, Pa., 1984-97, staff devel. trainer, 1985—; instr. Pa. Commonwealth Excellence in Sci. Tchg. Alliance, Franklin Inst. Mus., Phila., 1996—. Author: (with others) K'NEX Racer Energy Educator Guide, 1996, K'NEX Bridges Educator Guide, 1996. Elder Lenape Valley Presbyn. Ch., New Britain, Pa., 1988—. Recipient Outstanding Sci. Supr. in Pa. Pa. Sci. Suprs. Assn., 1989; named Outstanding Educator in Bucks County, Pa. Bucks County ASCD, 1987, Outstanding Contbn. and Svc. to Bucks County ASCD, 1987. Mem. Nat. Sci. Tchrs. Assn., Pa. Math/Sci. Eisenhower Consortium (chairperson 1997-98, 2003-), Bucks County Sci. Tchrs. Assn. (pres. 1992-99). Republican. Home: 116 Blue Jay Rd Chalfont PA 18914-3104 Office: K'Nex Edn 2990 Bergey Rd Hatfield PA 19440-0700

JESCHKE, THOMAS, gifted education educator; Dir. spl. edn. Des Moines Pub. Schs., 1975-93, exec. dir. student and family svcs., 1993—. Recipient Coun. of Admin. of Spec. Edn. Outstanding Admin. award, 1994. Office: Des Moines ISD Adminstrv Office 1801 16th St Des Moines IA 50314-1902

JESINSKY, SUSAN GAIL, special education educator; b. Las Cruces, N.Mex., Mar. 3, 1947; d. Joseph Hartful and Georgia Miram (Cothern) Arnold; m. Dennis Randolph Jesinsky, July 15, 1967; 1 child, Amber Elizabeth. BS in Secondary Edn., N.Mex. State U., Las Cruces, 1969, MA in Edn. Specialities, 1982. Cert. spl. edn. tchr., instrnl. leader, ednl. diagnostician, N.Mex. Social worker N.Mex. Dept. Human Svcs., Dona Ana County, 1969-71, social work supr., 1971-76; social worker III Children in Need of Supervision, N.Mex. Dept. Human Svcs., Dona Ana County, 1976-77; special edn. tchr. Gadsden Independent Schs., Anthony, N.Mex., 1980-82, edn. diagnostician, 1982-85, special edn. tchr.-behavior disorders, 1985-97; edu. diagnostician Ysleta Ind. Sch. Dist., El Paso, Tex., 1997—. Mem. Coun. for Exceptional Children, Phi Delta Kappa. Democrat. Baptist. Avocation: horses. Home: PO Box 353 Santa Teresa NM 88008-0353 Office: Ysleta Ind Sch Dist Spl Edn Dept 9600 Sims Dr El Paso TX 79925-7200

JESSE, SANDRA ELIZABETH, special education educator; b. Green Bay, Wis., Nov. 22, 1960; d. Albert Henry and Janice Elizabeth (Schroeder) J. BA in Edn., Ariz. State U., 1983; MA, No. Ariz. U., 1990. Cert. spl. edn. tchr., adminstr. Special edn. educator Peoria (Ariz.) Unifed Sch. Dist. # 11, 1983—98. Religious edn. tchr. St. Helens Ch., Glendale, Ariz., 1989—2000, mem. religious edn. bd., 1994—. Mem. NEA, Am. Fedn. Tchrs., Learning Disabilities Assn. Roman Catholic. Avocations: music, swimming, spectator sports, gardening, music. Office: Sky View Sch 8624 W Sweetwater Ave Peoria AZ 85381-8101

JESSEP, JANE (NORDLI), elementary education educator; b. Bridgeport, Conn., Oct. 30, 1947; d. William and Elizabeth (Glenn) Nordli; m. John Jessep, Dec. 16, 1978 (div. 1985); 1 child by previous marriage, Tara Walsh. BS, Skidmore Coll., 1969; M Voice, Manhattan Sch. Music, 1977; postgrad., Lincoln Ctr. Inst., 1992-96. Cert. tchr., Conn. Tchr. music Title I Schs., Omaha, 1970-71, Hillspoint Sch., Westport, Conn., 1971-72, Coleytown Jr. HS, 1977-82, Hart Sch., Stamford, 1984-85, Hurlbutt Elem. Sch., Weston, 1985—. Soloist New Haven Opera, 1974-77, Delphi Opera, Conn., 1980-84, Danbury Symphony and Danbury Orch., 1996, 97; chorister Am. Guild Musical Artists, 1976-83; chorus mem. Met. Opera, NYC, 1980-83, NYC Ballet, 1980-86; tchr. music history Adult Edn. Program, Westport, 1984-87. Vol. AIDS hospice Bread and Roses. Recipient Celebration of Excellence award Dept. Edn. Recognition Program, 1995. Mem. NEA, LWV, Amnesty Internat., People for the Am. Way, NYC Ballet Guild, Met. Opera Guild, Conn. Edn. Assn., Weston Tchr. Assn., Music Educators Nat. Conf. (cert. music educator), New Eng. Assn. Schs. and Colls. (steering com. 1990-92). Democrat. Avocations: singing, piano, tennis, bicycling, writing. Home: 12 Northfield Dr Westport CT 06880-1516

JESSIMAN, MARILYNN R. library media specialist; b. Buffalo, Aug. 22, 1946; d. Allan E. and Eleanor (Dougherty) Roy; m. Eric W. Jessiman, Oct. 4, 1969; children: Elizabeth Anne, Brian Eric. BA, SUNY, Buffalo, 1968, MLS, 1971. Tchr. Skaneateles (N.Y.) Central Schs., 1969-70; libr. media specialist, dept. chmn. Niagara Falls (N.Y.) City Schs., 1970—. Workshop leader on children's lit. and curriculum devel.; mem. dist. ednl. tech. implementation com. Co-author: Rainbows and Realities. Numerous dist. grants. Mem. N.Y. Libr. Assn. Sch. Libr. Media Sect., Soc. Sch. Librs. Internat. (past pres., speaker), Sch. Librs. Assn. Western N.Y. Office: 607 Walnut Ave Niagara Falls NY 14301-1729

JESSUP, JOE LEE, business educator, management consultant; b. Cordele, Ga., June 23, 1913; s. Horace Andrew and Elizabeth (Wilson) J.; m. Janet Amis, Apr. 16, 1989. BS, U. Ala., 1936; MBA, Harvard U., 1941; LLD (hon.), Chung-Ang U., Seoul, Korea, 1964. Sales rep. Proctor & Gamble, 1937-40; liaison officer bur. pub. rels. U.S. War Dept., 1941; spl. asst. and exec. asst. Far Ea. div. and office exports Bd. Econ. Warfare, 1942-43; exec. officer to chief of staff Svcs. of Supply-Europian Theatre, 1943-44; exec. officer, office deptl. adminstrn. Dept. State, 1946; exec. sec. adminstr.'s adv. coun. War Assets Adminstrn., 1946-48; v.p. sales Airken, Capitol & Service Co., 1948-52; assoc. prof. bus. adminstrn. George Washington U., 1952, prof., 1952-77, prof. emeritus, 1977—, asst. dean Sch. Govt., 1951-60; pres. Jessup and Co., Ft. Lauderdale, Fla., 1957—2002. Bd. dirs. Giant Food, Inc., Washington, mem. audit com., 1971—75; bd. dirs. Hunter Assn. Labs., Fairfax, Va., mem. exec. com., 1966—69, exec. v.p., 1967, coord. Air Force Regources Mgmt. program, 1951—57; del. in edn. 10th Internat. Mgmt. Conf., Sao Paulo, Brazil, 1954, 11th Internat. Mgmt. Conf., Paris, 1957, 12th Internat. Mgmt. Conf., Sydney and Melbourne, Australia, 1960, 13th Internat. Mgmt. Conf., Rotterdam, The Netherlands, 1966, 14th Internat. Mgmt. Conf., Tokyo, 1969, 15th Internat. Mgmt. Conf., Munich, 1972; mem. Md. Econ. Devel. Adv. Commn., 1973—75. Mem. Civil Svc. Commn., Arlington County, Va., 1973—75; trustee Tng. Within Industry Found., Summit, NJ, 1954—58; mem. bd. overseers Lynn U., Boca Raton, Fla., 1991—2002; mem. adv. bd. Youth Automotive Tng. Ctr., Hollywood, Fla., 1993—; trustee Philharm. Orch., Fla., 1986—91; mem. nat. adv. coun. Ctr. Study of Presidency, 1974—99; mem. Atlanta regional panel selection of White House fellow, 1990—95, mem. Miami regional panel. Decorated Bronze Star; recipient cert. of appreciation Sec. of Air Force, 1957 Mem.: Royal Palm Yacht and Country Club, Univ. Club (Washington), Harvard Club (N.Y.C.). Home: 133 Coconut Palm Rd Boca Raton FL 33432-7975

JESSUP, SALLY ANN, adult educator, educational consultant; b. Owosso, Mich., Sept. 20, 1949; d. William Ivan and Arlene Effie (Jessop) Jessup. BA in Theatre, U. Mich., Flint, 1980; secondary teaching cert., U. Mich., Ann Arbor, 1991; reading endorsement K-12, U. Mich., 1991; social sci. endorsement, U. Mich., Flint, 1997. Adult edn. instr. Owosso Pub. Schs., 1990-96; lang. arts cons. Waverly Pub. Schs., Lansing, Mich., 1991-93, reading support, 1992-93; lang. arts cons. Atherton Pub. Schs., Burton, Mich., 1993-94; Chpt. I/Title I reading support Perry (Mich.) Pub. Schs., 1994-96; lang. arts at-risk specialist New Buffalo (Mich.) Schs., 1996—2000; edn. cons. Co-Nect, Inc., 2000—. Mem. State Content Literacy Com., Lansing, 1991—; lang. expert North Ctrl. Outcomes Accreditation, Lowell, Mich., 1992-97. Author ednl. materials. Recipient Selah Performing Arts award U. Mich., Flint, 1989; Continuing Edn. for Women grantee, 1988, scholar, 1989. Mem. ASCD, Mich. Reading Assn., Kappa Delta Phi. Presbyterian. Avocations: writing, reading, walking, swimming, sketching. Home: 7995 S M 52 Owosso MI 48867-9249 Office: New Buffalo H S New Buffalo MI 48872

JEWELL, H. RICHARD, English language educator; b. Monmouth, Ill., Jan. 21, 1949; s. Louis C. and Helen I. (Stevens) J. BA in Philosophy, Monmouth Coll., 1970; MA in Theology, San Francisco Theol. Seminary, 1972, MDiv, 1973; MA in English, St. Cloud State U., 1985. Freelance writer, Little Falls, Minn., 1977-85; instr. dept. English St. Cloud (Minn.) State U., 1985-90, North Hennepin C.C., Brooklyn Park, Minn., 1989-93, Anoka (Minn.) Ramsey C.C., 1993-96; edn. specialist in composition dept. English U. Minn., Mpls., 1996—2001; instr. dept. English Inver Hills C.C., Inver Grove Heights, Minn., 2001—. Mem. MLA, The Loft Writers' Orgn., Nat. Coun. Tchrs. of English, Midwest MLA, Minn. Coun. Tchrs. of English. Democrat. Congregationalist. Avocations: web authoring, academic writing, camping, reading, travel. Home: 410 Groveland Ave Apt 401 Minneapolis MN 55403-3208

JEYNES, MARY KAY, college dean; b. Miami, Fla., Oct. 31, 1941; d. Nasrallah and Martha (Jabaly) Demetry; m. Paul Jeynes, Sept. 30, 1978. BS, Fla. State U., 1963. Program dir. Orange County YMCA, Orlando, Fla., 1964-69, Ea. Queens YMCA, Belrose, N.Y., 1970-73; regional coord. N.Y. State Park and Recreation Commn., N.Y.C., 1974-77; dir. health, fitness and recreation YWCA of N.Y.C., 1978-79; dean continuing edn. and adult programs Marymount Manhattan Coll., N.Y.C., 1980—. Mem.: East Manhattan (N.Y.) C. of C. (pres. 1996—97, chmn. bd. dirs. 1998—2002). Office: Marymount Manhattan Coll 221 E 71st St New York NY 10021-4532

JIAN, HAORAN, microbiology educator; b. Kowloon, China, Dec. 26, 1911; s. Yintang and Yue-E (Mai) J.; m. Xingyuan Liu, June 6, 1936; children: Tanwei, Chanwei, Shenwei, Shùnwei. BS, Sun Yat-Sen U., 1934, MS, 1937, PhD, U. Wis., 1948. Chemist Guangdong Agrl. Bur., Yuebei, China, 1938-43; assoc. prof., prof. Sun Yat-Sen U., Guangdong, 1944-49; prof. environ. sci. Ctrl. South Hygenics Coll., Wuhan, China, 1951-55; prof. microbiology Chinese Acad. Scis., 1956-76, prof. virology, 1976—; prof.

Guangdong Inst. Microbiology, 1986—. Developed the concept and implementation of bioremediation to environ. pollutants. Mem. Guangzhou Soc. Genetic Engring. (chmn.), Am. Soc. Microbiology, N.Y. Acad. Sci., Chinese Acad. Microbiology, Sigma Xi. Home: 504 26 81 Ctrl Xianlie Rd 510070 Guangzhou China Office: Guangdong Inst Microbiology 100 Ctrl Xianlie Rd 510070 Guangzhou China

JIMENEZ, JACQUELYN, elementary education educator; b. Gary, Ind., Mar. 1, 1953; d. Frank Vasquez and Carmen (Martinez) J. BA in Elem. Edn., Purdue U., 1978, MS in Edn., 1982. Cert. tchr., Ind. Tchr. Indiana Harbor Cath. Elem. Sch., East Chicago, Ind., 1978-85, Sacred Heart Elem. Sch., Whiting, Ind., 1985-88; tchr. English as 2d lang. School City of East Chicago, 1988-89; tchr. Washington Elem. Sch., East Chicago, 1988—. Student tchr. supr. Purdue U., Hammond, Ind., 1990-91; chmn. proficiency-based accreditation com., Washington Elem. Sch., 1991-92; cons. curriculum revision School City of East Chicago, 1992—. Mem. Am. Fedn. Tchrs. Roman Catholic. Avocations: creative writing, guitar.

JIMENEZ, PRAXEDSIS, middle school educator; b. Orange Grove, Tex., June 13, 1947; s. Jose and Maria (Garza) J.; m. Raquel S. Jimenez, Aug. 27, 1977; 1 child, Rebecca Jo. BEd, Tex. A&I, 1974; LLB, Del Mar Coll., Corpus Christi, Tex., 1989. Lic. tchr., Tex. Tchr. Mathis (Tex.) Ind. Sch. Dist. Mem. ins. bd. Mathis Ind. Sch. Dist. Mem. Orange Grove Sch. Bd., 1992—. Mem. ATPE Tchrs. Assn., Orange Grove Lions (past zone chmn., past sec., pres. 1989-93), W.O.W., Coastal Bend Peace Officers. Roman Catholic. Avocations: camping, hunting. Office: Mathis Intermediate 516 E Saint Marys St Mathis TX 78368-2698

JIMENO, CHERI ANNETTE, dean; b. Hamilton, Mont., Mar. 10, 1950; d. Max Charita and Gladys Montana (Buhl) J.; children: Shawna Sutherland, Shayne Sutherland. BS in Bus., U. Mont., 1972; MS in Bus., Mont. State U., 1985, PhD in Edn. and Bus. Info. Systems, 2000. Prodn. typist Hoerner Waldorf Corp., Missoula, Mont., 1972-73; adminstrv. asst. U. Mont., Missoula, 1973-74; instr. bus. and govt. Dixon (Mont.) High Sch., 1974-75; instr. bus. Warm Springs (Mont.) State Hosp., 1976-83; instr. vocat. bus. Mountain View Girl's Schs., Helena, Mont., 1984-85; assoc. prof. bus. U. Mont., 1985—, MIS tng. officer, 1986-88, div. chmn., 1988-90; lectr. Fulbright Coll. of the Bahamas, Nassau, 1990-91. Contbr. grant proposals and articles to profl. jours. Recipient Merit award Western Mont. Coll., 1987, 92. Mem. Nat. Bus. Edn. Assn., Internat. Soc. Bus. Educators, Mont. Bus. Edn. Assn. (pres. elect 1989-90), Mont. Data Processing Soc., Dillon Lioness Club (pres. 1987-88), Profl. Ski Inst. Am. Democrat. Avocations: skiing, golf, travel, reading. Office: U Mont 710 S Atlantic St Dillon MT 59725-3511

JIMMAR, D'ANN, elementary education educator, fashion merchandiser; b. Leighton, Ala., Dec. 10, 1942; d. Harry D. Qualls and Lillian Jimmar. BS in Elem. Edn., Ala. A&M U., 1965, MS in Urban Studies, 1973; PhD in Higher Edn., Iowa State U., 1986. Elem. tchr. Limestone County Bd. Edn., Athens, Ala., 1966-68, Huntsville City Bd. Edn., Ala., 1968-71; instr. dept. cmty. planning and urban studies Ala. A&M U., Huntsville, Ala., 1973-78; rsch. asst. dept. sociology and anthropology Iowa State U., Ames, Iowa, 1978-79, rsch. aide, 1980-81, 82-83; ednl. aide, substitute tchr. Ames Cmty. Sch. Dist., Iowa, 1983-86; coord. practicums Nova U., Ft. Lauderdale, Fla., 1986-87; tchr. Downtown Adult Edn. Ctr., Ft. Lauderdale, Fla., 1987-88, Apollo Mid. Sch., Hollywood, Fla., 1988-89, Greenview Elem. Sch., Columbia, SC, 1989-91; dir. rsch. edn. NuWAE Ent., Houston, 1991-92; cosmetic cons., counter mgr. Elizabeth Arden Foley's/May Co., 1992-99; resource cons. RCI, Inc., Tex. So. U., 1999-2000; ed. cons. Houston, 2000—. Sec.-treas. Ames Tenant Landlord Svcs., 1982-83, bd. dirs. 1982-, 83, 84-85, chmn., 1984-85. Recipient svc. award Local Govt. Study Commn., Huntsville, 1972, Ms. Alumni award Ala. A&M U., 1978. Mem. ASCD, Ala. A&M U. Alumni Assn. (chaplain 1977-78), Phi Delta Kappa, Delta Sigma Theta. Home: 8001 W Tidwell Rd Apt 416 Houston TX 77040-5536

JINKERSON, MAXINE LOUISE, gifted education educator; b. Gary, Ind., Aug. 10, 1936; d. Elias Daniel and Vessey Jane (Ralph) Spry; m. Donald Howard Wintermute, Aug. 11, 1956 (div. May 1980); children: Donine Marie Wintermute Schwartz, Mark Weston, Charles Martin, Bradford Earl; m. Marvin Wayne Jinkerson, July 12, 1985. Student, N.W. Mo. State U., 1954-56, U. Mo., 1964; BA in Edn., Harris Tchrs. Coll., 1971; MA in Edn., S.E. Mo. State U., 1983. Cert. elem., social studies and gifted edn. tchr., Mo. 2d grade tchr. Auxvasse (Mo.) Consol. Sch., 1956-59; organist Cedar Hill (Mo.) Presbyn. Ch., 1960-63, St. Andrews United Meth. Ch., De Soto, Mo., 1977—; 5th grade Hillsboro (Mo.) R-3 Schs., 1971-83, gifted edn. tchr., 1983-98. Coord. Jefferson County Conf. for Gifted Children and Their Parents, Jefferson Coll., Hillsboro, 1988-98. Mem. Mo. State Tchrs. Assn. (pres. Hillsboro Cmty. Tchrs. Assn./Mo. State Tchrs. Assn. 1995-96), Gifted Assn. Mo. (S.E. Mo. dist. dir. 1986-89), Nat. assn. for Gifted Children, PEO Sisterhood (chaplain 1979-80, corr. sec. 1986, rec. sec. 1999, pres. 2000-03), Jefferson County Sq. Dance Club (treas. 1987-89). Avocations: organ, piano, travel, genealogy, dulcimer.

JINRIGHT, NOAH FRANKLIN, vocational school educator, security executive; b. Banks, Alabama, Dec. 5, 1936; s. William Carroll and Ila Marie (Garrett) J.; m. Sarah Ann (Graham) Nickolson, Nov. 21, 1959 (div. Sept. 1974); children: Charlene M., Lisa A., Michael D.; m. Frances Lenora (Gaskins), June 11, 1978; children: Diana Carol, Jonathan Franklin. Cert. archtl. and mech. drafting, Columbus Tech., GA., 1971, CNC, 1983, cert. plate and pipe welder, 1984. Lic. ins. agt., Ga; cert. security officer. Operator scale Bibb Textiles, Columbus, Ga., 1954-56; operator press and share Columbus Iron Works, Columbus, Ga., 1957-58; ins. agt. Interstate Life, Columbus, Ga., 1958-61; operated winder, starter, generator Joe Hooten, Inc., Columbus, Ga., 1960; fireman City of Columbus, Columbus, Ga., 1960-66; ins. agt. Murray Meadows Ins. Agy., Columbus, Ga., 1960—67; advt. rep. Jinright Enterprises, Columbus, Ga., 1966; ins. agt. Security Life of Ga., Columbus, Ga., 1966; operator share and press Pascoe Steel, Columbus, Ga., 1966-67; machinist Goldens' Foundry and Machine Works, Columbus, Ga., 1967; carpenter, roofer Muscogee County Sch. Dist., Columbus, Ga., 1968-72; pattern maker Pekor Iron Works, Columbus, Ga., 1972-78; instr. metals tech. Spencer H.S., Columbus, Ga., 1978-91, Carver H.S., Columbus, Ga., 1991-94; security officer Sizemore Security Internat., 1994-95, 97-99; instr. metals tech. Kendrick H.S., Columbus, Ga., 1994-99; ret., 1999; security officer Sizemore Security Internat., 1999-2001, The Wackenhut Corp. Security Internat., 2001—03, Securitas Security Svc., USA, Inc., 2003—. Past mfg. rep. printing and advtg. specialties; cons. Voc. Tng. and Rsch. Inst., Seoul, Korea, 1989-90; instr., ptnr. with M. Davis; fire protection supr. 9311th A.F.Rescuer Squadron Columbus, Ga., (Tech. Sgt.). Contbg. articles to local newspapers. Sponsor Spencer H.S. AWS Club, 1979-81; exec. trainer Precision Metalforming Assn., 1996-99; past trustee Epworth United Meth. Ch., ch. usher; mem. Columbus Confederate Drill Team; adv. bd. Am. Biog. Inst., 1999—. Tech. sgt. USAFR, 1963-65. Mem. NEA, Internat. Soc. Welding Educators (1st symposium program adv. bd. mem.), Am. Foundry Soc., Am. Welding Soc. (adv. bd.), Vocat. Indsl. Clubs Am. (advisor, cert. of appreciation region VIII 1996), Trade and Indsl. Educators Ga. (mem. West Ga. Sch. to work-evaluation team 1994-99), Muscogee Edn. Assn., Ga. Assn. Educators, Ga. Vocat. Assn., Am. Vocat. Assn., Precision Metalforming Assn., Am. Foundrymen's Soc., Ga. Teacher's Union, So. Assn. Colls. and Schs., Ga. Assn. Educators, Methodist. Avocations: fishing, hunting, camping, model building, photography. Home: PO Box 63 Columbus GA 31902-0063 Office: 2040 Lee Rd 427 Phenix City AL 36867 Fax: 334-297-7545.

JISCHKE, MARTIN C. academic administrator; b. Chgo., Aug. 7, 1941; m. Patricia Fowler; children: Charles, Marian. BS in Physics with honors, Ill. Inst. Tech., 1963; MS in Aeronautics and Astronautics, MIT, 1964, PhD in Aeronautics and Astronautics, 1968. Engr. Rand Corp., Santa Monica, Calif., 1965; research engr. Battelle N.W. Lab., Richland, Washington, 1970; research fellow Donald W. Douglas Lab., Richland, 1971, Nat. Aeronautics and Space Adminstrn., Moffett Field, Calif., 1973; from asst. prof. to prof. aerospace, mech. and nuclear engring. U. Okla., 1968-75, prof., dir. Sch. Aerospace, Mech. and Nuclear Engring., 1977-81, interim pres., 1985, dean Coll. Engring., 1981-86, mem. various coms., 1985; White House fellow, spl. asst. to sec. of transp. U.S. Dept. Transp., Washington, 1975-76; chancellor U. Mo., Rolla, 1986-91; pres. Iowa State U., Ames, 1991-2000, Purdue U., 2000—. Bd. dirs. Kerr McGee Corp., Wabash Nat. Corp., Mo. Alliance for Sci., 1987-91, The Keystone Found., 1984-90, Mo. Corp. for Sci. and Tech., vice-chmn., 1990-91; participant Japanese Econ. Found. Vis. Leaders Program, 1983; mem. Gov.'s Coun. on Sci. and Tech. State of Okla., 1983-84, Gordon Rsch. Conf. on Geophysics; mem. planning com. for 80's Okla. State Regents for Higher Edn.; mem. organizing com. 14th Midwestern Mechanics Conf.; mem. adv. com. for engring. sci. NSF Engring. Directorate, 1985-88; mem. com. on statewide postsecondary telecomm. policy Mo. Coordinating Bd. for Higher Edn., 1987-91; chmn. Congrl. Aero. Adv. Com., 1987-89; sci. adviser to Gov. of Mo., 1990-91; mem. Am. Coun. on Edn. Com. on Math. and Sci., 1990-91. Contbr. articles and reports to profl. publs. Civilian aide Sec. of Army, State of Mo. East, 1987-91; bd. dirs. Bankers Trust, 1995—, Iowa Spl. Olympics, Am. Coun. on Edn., 1996—, Nat. Merit Scholarship Corp., 1997—; mem. Kellogg Commn. on the Future of State and Land-Grant U., 1995—; founding pres. Global Consortium of Higher Edn. and Rsch. for Agr., 1999. Recipient Ralph Teetor award Soc. Automotive Engrs., 1971, Brandon H. Griffith award U. Okla., U. Okla. Regents award for superior teaching, 1975, IIT Prof. Achievement award, 1992, Delta Tau Delta Achievement award, 1992, Engrs. Club St. Louis Achievement award, 1991, Dept. Army Outstanding Civilian Svc. medal, 1991; NASA fellow, 1966; NSF fellow, 1965; AEC/NORCUS summer faculty fellow, 1970-71, NASA/ASEE fellow, 1973. Fellow AAAS, AIAA (assoc., sec.-treas. Okla. chpt., vice chmn., chmn.); mem. ASME, AAUP (v.p., pres. Okla. chpt.), NSPE, Am. Phys. Soc., Am. Soc. Engring. Edn. (Centennial Medallion 1993), Nat. Assn. State Univs. and Land Grant Colls. (bd. dirs., chair 1997-98), Assn. Big Twelve Univs. (pres. 1994-96), Mo. Soc. Profl. Engrs., Rotary, Phi Beta Kappa, Tau Beta Pi, Sigma Xi, Pi Tau Sigma, Sigma Gamma Tau, Sigma Pi Sigma, Phi Eta Sigma. Home: 500 McCormick Rd West Lafayette IN 47906 Office: Purdue U Office of the Pres West Lafayette IN 47906

JIVIDEN, LORETTA ANN HARPER, secondary school educator; b. Charleston, W.Va., Jan. 30, 1939; d. Murry Deane and Marie Frances (Allison) Harper; m. Gay Melton Jividen, Jan. 30, 1959; children: Jon David, Ann Marie. BA in Sociology, N.C. State U., 1970, MEd in Curriculum and Instrn., 1979. Tchr. Our Lady of Lourdes, Raleigh, N.C., 1970-72, Wake County Pub. Sch. System, Raleigh, 1972-87, supr. Academically Gifted Program, 1987-90, tchr., 1990-92, math., computer specialist, 1992—. Mem. steering com. NCNet Day 96; bd. dirs. Durant Rd. Elem. Sch. Found., Inc. Co-author: The EXCEL Program grant for Wake County Pub. Sch. System; past editor Special Edit., Parent Edit., Wake County Pub. Schs. Special Programs newsletters; adviser The Poacher's Payback. Mem. state employees' credit union adv. com. for the biennium, 1996-98; bd. dirs. ExplorNet, N.C. Mem. NEA, Coun. for Exceptional Children, N.C. Assn. for the Gifted (pres. elect 1988-90, pres. 1991-93), N.C. Assn. Sch. Adminstrs., Parents for Advancement of Gifted Edn. (past v.p., past bd. dirs.), Nat. Assn. Gifted Children, Nat. Coun. Tchrs. Math., N.C. Assn. for the Gifted and Talented (Tchr. of Yr. award 1984), Profl. Educators N.C., Delta Kappa Gamma Soc. Internat. (past pres., past coordinating coun. pres.). Avocations: piano, reading, computer programming, painting, sewing. Home: 12501 Shallowford Dr Raleigh NC 27614-9664 Office: Durant Rd Elem Sch 9901 Durant Rd Raleigh NC 27614-9369

JOEHL, RAYMOND JOSEPH, surgeon, educator; b. Alton, Ill., July 20, 1948; m. Julia Nelle Garrels, Aug. 28, 1970; children: Jacob, Samuel, Hillarie, Sarah, Claudia, Hannah. BA, U. Pa., 1970; MD, St. Louis U., 1974. Diplomate Am. Bd. Surgery. Resident in surgery Pa. State U., Hershey, 1974-79, rsch. fellow, 1979-80, from asst. to assoc. prof. surgery, 1980-85; from assoc. prof. to prof. surgery Northwestern U., Chgo., 1985-91, James R. Hines prof. surgery, 1993—2003; prof. surgery Loyola U., Maywood, Ill., 2003—. Chief divsn. gen. surgery and dir. residency in surgery, 1995-2000, attending surgeon Northwestern Meml. Hosp., VA Chgo. Health Care Sys.-Lakeside divsn., 1985-2003, Hershey Med. Ctr., 1980-85, Loyola U. Med. Ctr., Maywood, 2003—; chief surg. svc., VA Chgo.-Lakeside, 1987-95, 2001-03, Hines VA Hosp., Ill., 2003—. Fellow ACS, Am. Surg. Assn.; mem. Soc. Univ. Surgeons, Soc. for Surgery Alimentary Tract, Alpha Omega Alpha. Episcopalian. Avocations: children, advocate for disabled especially blind, teaching. Office: Loyola U Med Ctr Dept Surgery 2160 S 1st Ave Maywood IL 60153 Business E-Mail: raymond.joehl@med.va.gov.

JOEL, RICHARD MARC, academic administrator, law educator, dean; b. NYC, Sept. 9, 1950; s. Avery Joel and Annette (Bloom) Ashwal; m. Esther Duora Ribner, Nov. 11, 1973; children: Penina, Avery, Arielle, Noam. BA, NYU, 1972, JD, 1975. Bar: N.Y. 1976, U.S. Dist. Ct. (ea. dist.) N.Y. 1976. Asst. dist. atty. Borough of Bronx, N.Y., 1975-78; dir. alumni affairs Yeshiva U., N.Y.C., 1978-80, asst. dean Cardozo Sch. Law, 1980-82, assoc. dean Cardozo Sch. Law, 1982—, adj. prof. law, 1985—, pres., 2002—. Sec. Hebrew Acad. Long Beach, N.Y., 1983—; bd. dirs. Jewish Community Council Oceanside, N.Y., 1977-81, Young Israel Oceanside, 1986—. Root-Tilden scholar NYU, 1972-75. Mem. ABA. Democrat. Jewish. Avocations: music, youth work. Home: 712 Hermleigh Rd Silver Spring MD 20902-1601 Office: Yeshiva U Cardozo Sch Law 55 5th Ave New York NY 10003-4301

JOHANNSEN, CHRIS JAKOB, agronomist, educator, administrator; b. Randolph, Nebr., July 24, 1937; s. Jakob J. and Marie J. (Lorenzsen) J.; m. Joanne B. Rockwell, Aug. 16, 1959; children: Eric C., Peter J. BS, U. Nebr., Lincoln, 1959, MS, 1961; PhD, Purdue U., 1969. Program leader lab. for applications of remote sensing Purdue U., 1966-69, from asst. prof. to assoc. prof. agronomy, 1969-77, dir. ag data network, 1985-87, dir. lab. for applications of remote sensing, 1985—; prof. U. Mo., Columbia, 1977-84, dir. geogrpahic resources ctr., 1981-84; dir. Ag Data Network, Purdue U., 1985-87, Lab. for Applications of Remote Sensing, 1985—; prof. Purdue U. W. Lafayette, Ind., 1985—; dir. Nat. Resources Rsch. Inst., 1987-93, Environ. Scis. and Engring. Inst./Purdue U., West Lafayette, 1994-96. Vis. prof. U. Calif., Davis, 1980—81; cons. Lockheed Electronics, Houston, 1975—76, NOAA, Columbia, Mo., 1978—80, FAO UN, Nairobi, Kenya, 1983, 87, Rome, 87, U.S. Agy. Internat. Devel., Ea. Africa, 1983, USDA-Soil Conservation Svc., Washington, 1984—85, IBM, 1991, Ball Aerospace Corp., 1995, Space Imaging Inc., 1996—, Aventis CropSci. Inc., 1998—, RapidEye Corp., 2001—; pres. Ecologistics Ltd., 1996—2002, assoc., 2002—; vis. chief scientist Space Imaging Inc., 1996—97; adj. prof. Katholieke U. Leuven (Belgium). Pres. coun. St. Andrew's Luth. Ch., Columbia, 1975-77; asst. scoutmaster Boy Scouts Am., Gt. Rivers coun., Columbia, 1979-84, West Lafayette, 1985-91; pres. Purdue Luth. Ministry, 1989-95; apptd. mem. West Lafayette Redevel. Authority, 2001-2004. Recipient Tech. Innovation Rsch. award NASA, 1979, Disting. Svc. award Mo. Assn. Soil and Water Conservation Dists., 1982, Agr. Alumni Merit award U. Nebr., 1995. Fellow: Ind. Acad. Scis., Soil and Water Conservation Soc. (pres. 1982—83), Am. Soc. Agronomy, Soil Sci. Soc. Am., Am. Soc. Photogrammetry and Remote Sensing (Outstanding Svc. award 1992); mem.: Geosci. and Remote Sensing Soc. of IEEE, Internat. Union Soil Sci., World Assn. Soil and Water, Rotary (Lafayette chpt. bd. dirs. 1995—98), Epsilon Sigma Phi (Internat. award 2000). Home: 209 Cedar Hollow Ct West Lafayette IN 47906-1671 Office: Purdue Univ LARS/AGRY 500 Central Dr West Lafayette IN 47907-2022 E-mail: johan@purdue.edu.

JOHANSEN, EIVIND HERBERT, special education services executive, former army officer; b. Charleston, S.C., Mar. 7, 1927; s. Andrew and Ruth Lee (Thames) J.; m. Dolores E. Klockmann, June 9, 1950; children: Chris Allen, Jane Elizabeth. BS, Tex. A&M U., 1950; MS, George Washington U., 1968; postgrad., Harvard U., 1955, Army Command and Gen. Staff Coll., 1963, Naval War Coll., 1968, Advanced Mgmt. Program, U. Pitts., 1971. Quartermaster officer U.S. Army, 1950-79, advanced through grades to lt. gen., 1977; strategic planner Office Joint Chiefs of Staff, 1968-69, group comdr., 1969-70; army dir. distbn., 1970-72; army dir. materiel, 1972-75; comdg. gen. Army Aviation Systems Command, St. Louis, 1975-77; army dep. chief staff for logistics Washington, 1977-79; ret., 1979; pres., CEO Nat. Industries for Severely Handicapped, Inc., 1979-92. Mem. exec. council, chmn. mgmt. improvement com. Fed. Exec. Bd., St. Louis, 1975-77; bd. advs. Am. Def. Preparedness Assn., St. Louis, 1975-77, tech. and mgmt. adv. bd., Washington, 1977-79; chmn. Army Logistics Policy Council, 1977-79; bd. advs. Army Logistic Mgmt. Coll., 1978-79, Army Mgmt. Engring. Coll., 1978-79 Contbr. articles to profl. jours. Mem. President's Com. for Purchase from Blind and Other Severely Handicapped, Washington, 1973-74, chmn., 1975; mem. President's Com. on Employment of Handicapped; bd. dirs., chmn. ind. ops. com. Mo. Goodwill Industries, 1975-77; chmn. youth program Jr. Achievement, St. Louis, 1975-77; sponsor Air Explorer Post, Boy Scouts Am., 1975-77; bd. dirs. Q.M. Found., 1979-88, 92-93. Decorated DSM, Legion of Merit with two oak leaf clusters, Bronze Star, numerous others; recipient Tex. A&M Disting. Alumnus award, 1985, Hall of Honor award Tex. A&M, 1997, Disting. Svc. award Nat. Industries for Severely Handicapped, 1992, Disting. Career award Nat. Assn. Rehab. Facilities, 1992; named to Quartermaster Hall of Fame, U.S. Army, 1992. Mem. Assn. U.S. Army (bd. advisors St. Louis 1975-77), Am. Helicopter Soc., Army Aviation Assn. Am., Ret. Officers Assn., Nat. Rehab. Assn., Tex. A&M Alumni Assn. Washington (exec. bd. 1974, 78-79, pres. 1975, bd. dirs. 1993-95), George Washington U. Alumni Assn., U. Pitts. Alumni Assn., Harvard U. Alumni Assn., Toastmasters. Home: 3084 Darby Rd Keswick VA 22947-2720

JOHN, HUGO HERMAN, natural resources educator; b. Natoma, Kans., Feb. 13, 1929; s. Lorenz Louis and Clara Marie (Doehrmann) J.; m. Prudence Patricia Shuck, Sept. 9, 1950; children: Patrick, Peter, Sarah. BS, U. Minn., 1959, MS, 1961, PhD, 1964. From asst. prof. to assoc. prof. Coll. Forestry U. Minn., St. Paul, 1964-69, prof., 1969-72; prof. Coll. Forestry, Wildlife and Range Scis., assoc. dean U. Idaho, Moscow, 1972-74; dean, prof. Sch. Natural Resources U. Vt., Burlington, 1974-83; dean Coll. Agriculture and Natural Resources, dir. Agrl. Expt. Sta. and Coop. Extension U. Conn., Storrs, 1983-87, prof. natural resources, 1987-94, prof. emeritus, 1994—. Forestry expert UN Food and Agr. Orgn., Puerto Cabezas, Nicaragua, 1965-66, Nat. Univ. Medellin, Colombia, 1969-71; cons. Taconic Found., N.Y.C., Internat. Paper Co., N.Y.C., 1981-84; sr. cons. UN Devel. Programme, Humane Soc. of U.S., 1993—; devel./planning cons. Internat. Exec. Svcs. Corps., Zimbabwe, 1996, Ukraine, 1998. Contbr. articles to profl. jours. Mem., treas. bd. dirs. Smokey House Project, Danby, Vt., 1976—; bd. dirs. Merek Forest Found., Rupert, Vt., 1980-83, Ea. States Expn., West Springfield, Mass, 1989—, mem. Conn. trustees, 1984—, chmn., 1989-94. With U.S. Army, 1950-52. Mem. Soc. Am. Foresters (chmn. accreditation com. 1981-84), Am. Forestry Assn. Avocations: gardening, woodworking. Home: Box 732 501 4th Ave SE Mapleton MN 56065-9782

JOHN, LEWIS GEORGE, political science educator; b. Waco, Tex., Nov. 25, 1936; s. Lewis Hervin and Margaret Reese J.; m. Annette Louise Church, June 3, 1961; children: Andrew Lewis, Christopher Donald. BA, Washington & Lee U., 1958; M in Pub. Affairs, Princeton U., 1961; PhD, Syracuse U., 1973. Asst. dean students, dir. fin. aid and placement Washington & Lee U., Lexington, Va., 1963-66, assoc. dean students, 1968-69, dean students, prof. politics and adminstrn., 1969-90, prof. politics and adminstrn., 1969—. Leader workshops and seminars, various colls., 1981-85; presenter symposia and confs. Contbr. articles to profl. jours. and chpts. to books. Chmn. Lexington Sch. Bd. 1979-80; pre-law adviser NCAA Faculty Athletics, 1993-2001, rep., 1998-2001 Served to 1st lt. US Army, 1961-63. Woodrow Wilson fellow Princeton U., 1959-60; Fulbright scholar U. Edinburgh, 1958-59. Mem. ASPA, Nat. Assn. Student Personnel Adminstrs. (bd. dirs. 1977-79, 87-89, region III exec. bd. 1980-85, chmn. career devel. and profl. standards div. 1987-89, Disting. Svc. award 1982), Va. Assn. Student Personnel Adminstrs. (pres. 1975, Outstanding Profl. award 1983), Am. Polit. Sci. Assn., Phi Beta Kappa, Beta Gamma Sigma, Omicron Delta Kappa (faculty sec. Washington and Lee chpt. 1987-90, 98-2001, faculty advisor 1990-98), Omicron Delta Epsilon, Pi Sigma Alpha. Democrat. Presbyterian. Avocation: sports. Home: 8 Edmondson Ave Lexington VA 24450-1904 Office: Washington & Lee U Williams Sch 101B Lexington VA 24450 E-mail: johnl@wlu.edu.

JOHN, MARTHA TYLER, dean, education educator; b. Saranac Lake, N.Y., Apr. 22, 1930; d. Albert Carlos and Helen Escha (Moss) Tyler; m. Floyd I. John, Aug. 8th, 1952; children: Floyd A., Bruce, David. A.B., Eastern Nazarene Coll., 1951; M.S., Purdue U., 1958; Ed.D., Stanford U., 1966; Asst. prof., assoc. prof. Boston U., 1967-74; assoc. prof. Bowie State Coll., Bowie, Md., 1974-77; research assoc. U. Dar-es-Salaam, Tanzania, 1978—; prof., chmn. div. edn. and psychology, phys. edn. Mid-Am. Nazarene Coll., Olathe, Kans., 1977-85; dean Sch. Edn. and Human Services, Marymount U., Arlington, Va., 1986—; Fulbright prof. U. Botswana, 1979; prof., head Ednl. Found., U. Swaziland, 1983-84; dean Marymount U., Arlington, Va., 1985—; chmn. Swaziland Ednl. Research Assn., 1984; cons. curriculum Nat. Curriculum Ctr., Swaziland, 1983-84, Lesotho (Africa) project Aurora Assocs. (for USAID), 1987-88; vol. instr. Powhatan Nursing Ctr., Arlington, 1986—; judge children's writing Catholic Daughters of Charity, Arlington, 1987—; com. mem. Arlington Agy. on Aging, 1987—; active Youth Diversion Group, 1982-84. Mem. Internat. Coun. in Edn. for Teaching, 1984—, Internat. Reading Assn., Nat. Council for Social Studies, Kans. Assn. for Aging in Higher Edn., Swaziland Ednl. Rsch. Assn (charter chairperson 1983), Assn. Advancement Policy, rsch., and Devel. in Third World, 1987—, Assn. Supervision and Curriculum Devel. Internat. Assn. Cross Cultural Psychology, Pi Lambda Theta, Kappa Delta Pi, Phi Delta Kappa. Author: A Guide for Elementary Social Studies Teacher, 1972, 78; Using Media in the Elementary Classroom, 1979; Teaching and Learning: Philosophical, Psychological and Curricular Applications, 1975; Practice in Research and Study Skills, 1980; The Research Project, 1981; Teaching and Loving the Elderly, 1983; Geragogy: A Theory for Teaching the Elderly, 1986, Story Writing in a Nursing Home: A Patchwork of Memories, 1991; author (with others) Academic Role Models for Females in the Third World, 1991; editor Swaziland Inst. Edn. Research Bull., 1984; editorial cons. Internat. Jour. Psychology, 1991; contbr. articles to profl. jours. Avocations: reading, fishing, knitting, travel. Office: Marymount U 2807 N Glebe Rd Arlington VA 22207-4299

JOHNS, BEVERLEY ANNE HOLDEN, special education administrator; b. New Albany, Ind., Nov. 6, 1946; d. James Edward and Martha Edna (Scharf) Holden; m. Lonnie J. Johns, July 28, 1973. BS, Catherine Spalding Coll., 1968; MS, So. Ill. U., 1970; postgrad., Western Ill. U., 1973-74, 79-80, postgrad., 82, U. Ill., 1984-85. Cert. adminstr., tchr. Ill. Demonstration tchr. So. Ill. U., Carbondale, 1970-72; instr. MacMurray Coll., Jacksonville, Ill., 1977—79, 1990—93, 2002—03; intern Ill. State Bd. Edn., Springfield, 1981; program supr. Four Rivers Spl. Edn. Dist., Jacksonville, 1972—2003; learning and behavior cons., 2003—. Chair Ill. Spl. Edn.; conf. coord. Ill. Alliance, Champaign, 1982-94; lectr., cons. in field. Author: Report on Behavior Analysis in Education, 1972; author: (with V. Carr) Techniques for Managing Verbally and Physically Aggressive Students, 2002; author: (with V. Carr and C. Hoots) Reduction of School Violence: Alternatives to Suspension, 1997; author: (with B. Johns, E. Crowley & E. Guetzloe) Effective Curriculum for Students with Behavioral

Disorders, 2002; author: (with J. Keenan) Techniques for Managing a Safe School, 1997; editor: Position Papers of Ill. Council for Exceptional Children, 1981; contbr. articles to profl. jours. Bd. dirs. Jacksonville Area Assn. Retarded Citizens, v.p., 1993-94, sec. 1996-99; govt. rels. chair Internat. Coun. Exceptional Children, 1984-87; fed. liason Ill. Adminstrs. Spl. Edn., 1985-86. So. Ill. U. fellow, 1968; resolution honoring Beverly H. Johns Internat. Coun. for Exceptional Children Conv., 1982; recipient Recognition cert. Ill. Atty. Gen., 1985, Outstanding Leadership award Internat. Coun. Exceptional Children, 2000; named Jacksonville Woman of Yr., Bus. and Profl. Women, 1988, Unsung Hero Jacksonville Jour.-courier, 1993. Mem. ASCD, Assn. Retarded Citizens (com. 1982-85), Ill. Coun. for Children with Behavioral Disorders (founder, past pres., pres. Ill. divsn. for learning disabilities 1991-92, Presdl. award 1985), Ill. Alliance for Exceptional Children (v.p. 1982-94), Learning Disabilities Assn. (bd. dirs., pres. 2000-03), Ill. Coun. Exceptional Children (past pres., chair govt. rels. com. 1982-95, 97-98, governing bd. 1984-95, Presdl. award 1983, Lifetime Achievement award 1989, First Lady 1993), Internat. Coun. for Children with Behavioral Disorders (pres. 1997), West Cen. Assn. for Citizens with Learning Disabilities (founder, com. chair 1997), Internat. Pioneer Press (editor CEC pioneer divsn., pres. internat. pioneers divsn.), Internat. Divsn. Learning Disabilities (exec. bd.), Delta Kappa Gamma (chpt. pres. 1988-90, state exec. bd. 1991—), Phi Delta Kappa. Roman Catholic. Avocation: world travel. Home: PO Box 340 Jacksonville IL 62651-0340 E-mail: bevjohns@juno.com.

JOHNS, CHRISTINE MICHELE, elementary school principal; b. Spangler, Pa., Nov. 11, 1965; d. George Warren and Walterine Johns. BS, U. Pitts., 1988; MS, Johns Hopkins U., Balt., 1992. Early childhood tchr. Salvation Army, Pitts., 1985-87; summer counselor YWCA, Pitts., summers 1987-88; tchr. sci. and math. Prince George's (Md.) County Pub. Schs., 1988-91, magnet sch. coord., 1991-92, instructional specialist, 1992-94; prin. Fort Foote Elem. Sch., Ft. Washington, Md., 1994—. Tchr. trainer Lego Dacta Ednl. Sys., Enfield, Conn., 1988-92; tchr. adult edn. Prince Georges County Pub. Schs., 1993-94; sci. trek steering com. Prince George's C.C., 1988-92. Recipient Outstanding Adminstr.'s award Prince George's C. of C., 1996; grantee Nat. Found. for Improvement of Edn., 9191, 92, Mid-Atlantic Japan in the Schs., U. Md., 1989, Gov.'s Acad. for Math. and Sci., Md. Dept. Edn., 1992, Harvard U., 1996. Mem. ASCD, Md. Assn. Supervision and Curriculum Devel. Avocations: softball, volleyball, skiing. Office: Prince Georges Co Pub Sch Fort Foote Elementary Sch 8300 Oxon Hill Rd Fort Washington MD 20744-4719

JOHNS, DIANA, secondary education educator; BS, Mich. State U.; MS, U. Mich. Jr. high school tchr. Crestwood Dist. Schools, Dearborn Heights, Mich., sr. high sch. tchr., sci. dept. chair. Outstanding Earth-Sci. Tchr. award, 1992, Tchr. of the Year award Crestwood Sch. Dist., Scholarship award Crestwood High Sch. Chpt. NHS. Mem. Nat. Assn. Geology Tchrs., Mich. Earth Sci. Tchrs. Assn. Office: Crestwood Sr High Sch 1501 N Beech Daly Rd Dearborn Heights MI 48127-3403

JOHNS, DOLORES YUILLE, educational administrator; b. Altavista, Va., Sept. 27, 1934; d. William Everett and Helen Ruth (Dabney) Yuille; m. William Lawrence Johns Jr., Apr. 19, 1957; children: Deborah, Linda, Lawrence, Anthony. BS in Bus. Edn., Va. State U., 1955; MS in Mktg. Edn., Va. Commonwealth U., 1970; EdD, Va. Tech. U., 1981. Lic. profl. counselor, Va.; cert. tchr., Va. Tchr. bus. edn. Botecourt County Pub. Schs., Fincastle, Va., 1955-65; tchr. mktg. edn. Roanoke (Va.) City Pub. Schs., 1965-69, supr., guidance counselor, 1982-84, dir. fed. programs, 1985—; dir. spl. svcs. Va. Western C.C., Roanoke, 1970-75, assoc. prof., 1980-82; asst. prof. edn. Va. Tech. U., Blacksburg, 1975-79. Cons., presenter U.S. Dept. Edn., 1989, 92, Va. State Bd. Edn., 1987-88, Internat. Reading Assn., 1988, 90, 93; cons. Va. Dept. Fed. Programs, Richmond, 1988, 90, 91. Mem. Roanoke City Libr. Bd., 1981-83; dir. ednl. svcs. High St. Ch., Roanoke, 1985—, chair Community Ctr. com., 1985—; mem. health svcs. bd. Catawba (Va.) Hosp., 1988-91; bd. dirs. YWCA, Roanoke, 1989. Ednl. profl. devel. fellow Va. Dept. Edn.; named amont Top 100 C.C. Women in Nation Found. for Improvement Secondary Edn., Am. Assn. Jr. and Community Colls., 1982; recipient Outstanding Svc. award High St. Ch., Roanoke, 1986. Mem. Nat Assn. Fed. Educators, Internat. Reading Assn., Va. Reading Assn., Va. Assn. Fed. Educators, Phi Delta Kappa, Alpha Kappa Alpha, Omnia Bona (pres. 1975-77, Svc. award 1980). Baptist. Avocations: reading, bowling. Office: Roanoke City Schs 40 Douglas Ave NW Roanoke VA 24012-4611

JOHNS, JAYNE HOWELL, elementary education educator, administrator, achievement specialist; b. Roanoke, Va., Dec. 15, 1939; d. Vernard Clinton and Sally Gertrude (Taylor) Terry; m. Adolphus J. Howell, Feb. 27, 1967 (div.); 1 child, Adrion J. Howell. BA, Va. State U., 1962; MA, George Mason U., 1977. Cert. in adminstrn./supervision, Md. Tchr. Carver Sch., Salem, Va., 1962, Capitol Heights (Md.) Elem., 1966-69; tchr., adminstr. James Ryder Randall Elem., Clinton, Md., 1973-92. Leadership chairperson Prince George's Tchrs. Union, Upper Marlboro, Md., 1978. Active Coalition 100 Women, Montgomery County, Md., 1985—. Mem. Alpha Kappa Alpha. Democrat. Baptist. Avocations: real estate, travel, theatre, reading, mentoring. Home: 12017 Deka Rd Clinton MD 20735-1128 Office: James Ryder Randall Elem Sch 5410 Kirby Rd Clinton MD 20735-1421

JOHNS, KAREN KAY, elementary education educator; b. Tecumseh, Nebr., Sept. 8, 1953; d. Victor John and Esta Katherine (Schweppe) Dierking; m. James Lee Johns, Apr. 1, 1972; children: Laura Xiao, Shawnee Phung. BEd., Peru (Nebr.) State Coll., 1975; MEd, U. Nebr., 1989. Cert. in elem. edn., endorsement in early childhood, curriculum and instrn., Nebr. Elem. tchr. Sch. Dist. #58, Syracuse, Nebr., 1975-76, 78-79, Sch. Dist. #19, Tecumseh, Nebr., 1979-87; libr. elem. art Johnson-Brock Schs., 1987-88, elem. tchr., 1988—. Mem. Dwight D. Eisenhower Adv. Coun., Auburn, Nebr., 1992-2000; presenter, cons. Activities Integrating Math and Sci., Fresno, Calif., 1991-96. Compiler, editor: Johns Family History, 1986, Petersen Family History, 1985. Active Zion Lutheran Ch., 1974—; mem. Johnson County Chamber, Tecumseh, 1986-2000; pres., sec. Women Involved in Farm Econs., 1980-2000; mem. Nat. Farmer's Orgn., 1972-82. Named Outstanding Young Woman, Jaycee Women, Johnson, 1985; recipient Honorable Mention for Tchr. in Space, NASA, Nebr., 1985. Mem. Johnson-Brock Edn. Assn. (sec., negotiating sec.), Johnson County Edn. Assn. (pres., sec.), Internat. Reading Assn. (sec. 1989-91, pres. 1981-82, 91-93), Phi Delta Kappa, Delta Kappa Gamma. Republican. Lutheran. Avocations: reading, photography, sewing, crafts, gardening. Home: RR 3 Box 148 Tecumseh NE 68450-9561

JOHNS, RICHARD JAMES, physician, educator; b. Pendleton, Oreg., Aug. 19, 1925; s. James Shanard and Pearl (McKenna) Johns; m. Carol Greacen Johnson; children: Richard Clark, Robert Shanard, James Ashmore. BS, U. Oreg., 1947; MD, Johns Hopkins U., 1948. Diplomate Am. Bd. Internal Medicine. Intern Johns Hopkins Hosp., Balt., 1948—49, asst. resident, 1951—53, fellow in medicine, 1953—55, resident, 1955—56, instr., 1955—57, physician, 1956—, asst. prof., 1957—61, assoc. prof., 1961—66, asst. dean admissions, 1962—66, prof. medicine, 1966—, dir. subdept. biomed. engring., 1966—70, mem. adv. bd., prin. profl. staff Applied Physics Lab., 1967—, prof., dir. dept. biomed. engring., 1970—91, disting. svc. prof., 1991—. Bd. dirs. Sparton Corp. Bd. visitors Sch. Engring., Duke U., 1986—; chmn. adv. com. Divsnl. Health Scis. and Tech., Harvard-MIT, 1987—92; mem. com. sci., engring. and pub. policy NAS, 1988—90; mem. sci. adv. com. GM, 1991—97; sec., vice chmn., chmn. med. bd. Myasthenia Gravis Found.; trustee Am. Bd. Clin. Engring., pres., 1976—83; bd. dirs. Whitaker Found., 1991—94. Capt. M.C. U.S. Army, 1949—51. Fellow: Royal Soc. Medicine, Am. Inst. for Biol. and Med. Engring. (founding), AAAS, ACP; mem.: Inst. Medicine-NAS (coun. 1987—90), IEEE (pres. group on engring. in medicine and biology 1970—72), Biomed. Engring. Soc. (bd. dirs. 1972—75, pres. 1978—79), Assn. Am. Physicians, Am. Soc. Clin. Investigation, Am. Clin. and Climatol. Assn. (v.p. 1977—78, sec.-treas. 1979—85, pres. 1986—87), Sparton Corp. (dir. 2002—), Annapolis Yacht Club, Caduceus Club, Elkridge Club, Johns Hopkins Club (v.p. 1969—70), Peripatetic Club, Interurban Clin. Club (pres. 1980—81), Johns Hopkins Med. Soc. (pres. 1968—69), Tau Beta Pi, Nu Sigma Nu, Phi Kappa Psi, Alpha Omega Alpha, Sigma Xi. Home: 203 E Highfield Rd Baltimore MD 21218-1105 Office: Johns Hopkins U Sch Med 1830 E Monument St Ste 501 Baltimore MD 21287 E-mail: rjohns@jhmi.edu.

JOHNSEN, BARBARA PARRISH, writer, educator; b. Fort Madison, Iowa, Feb. 21, 1933; d. Lloyd Lynn and Genevieve Agnes (Peter) P.; m. James Cotten Johnsen (dec.); 1 child, Holly Ann. BA, Fla. So. Coll., 1959; MEd, Boston U., 1964. Cert. tchr., Calif. Account exec. Ledger Pub. Co., Lakeland, Fla., 1954-62; tchr., counselor Long Beach (Calif.) Unified Sch. Dist., 1965-74; owner Ednl. Counseling and Cons., Cazenovia, N.Y., 1990-2000. Mem. Madison County Coun. on Alcohol and Substance Abuse, 1986-92. Chair Madison County Cmty. Svcs. Bd., 1987-95; v.p. LWV N.Y. State, Albany, 1993-97. Avocations: writing, poetry, travel.

JOHNSEY-ROBERTSON, ANITA COLLEEN, special education educator; b. Birmingham, Ala., June 14, 1966; d. Judith Colleen (Bradberry) Steger. BS in Spl. Edn./Mental Retardation, Livingston (Ala.) U., 1988, MEd in Spl. Edn./Mental Retardation, 1990; EdS in Spl. Edn./Mental Retardation, U. Ala., 1994; EdD, U. So. Miss., 1997—2000. Lic. tchr. spl. edn, area mental retardation. Tchr. multihandicapped Linden (Ala.) Elem. Sch., 1988-90; tchr. mentally retarded Jefferson County Schs., Hillview Elem. Sch., Birmingham, Ala., 1990-94, Jefferson County Schs., Pittman Mid. Sch., Birmingham, Ala., 1994-98, Jefferson County Schs., Lipscomb Elem., 1999—2000, Oak Grove H.S., 2000—. Del. Citizens Ambassador Program, 1995. Mem. Coun. Exceptional Children (presenter Ala. conf. 1996, 2000, nat. conf. 1996), Ala. Edn. Assn., Phi Delta Kappa. Avocations: reading, special olympics. Home: 1510 Lilly Ln Bessemer AL 35023-4377

JOHNSON, ADDIE COLLINS, secondary education educator, former dietitian; b. Evansville, Ind., Feb. 28; d. Stewart and Willa (Shamell) Collins; m. John Q. Johnson, Sept. 6, 1958 (dec. Aug. 1991); 1 child, Parker. BS, Howard U., 1956; MEd, Framingham State Coll., Mass., 1967. Registered dietitian, Mass. Dietitian Boston Lying-In Hosp., 1957-61; dietitian Diet Heart Study, Harvard U. Sch. Pub. Health, Boston, 1962-63; tchr. Foxboro (Mass.) Pub. Sch., 1968-2000; dietitian Sch. Medicine Boston U., 1975-77, Westinghouse Health Systems, Boston; faculty Dept. Nursing Boston State Coll., 1979-82; real estate sales assoc. Century 21, Sharon, Mass., 2001—. Nutrition cons. Head Start program Westinghouse Sch., Boston, 1979-82; instr. dept. nursing U. Mass., 1981-89, Bridgewater (Mass.) State Coll., 1982-97; mem. state adv. coun. Dept. Edn Bur. Nutrition Edn., 1981-83; participant NSF Project Seed, 1992; chmn. edn. com., bd. dirs. Consumer Credit Counseling Svcs. of Mass., Inc., 1996-99. Bd. dirs. Norfolk-Bristol County Home Health Assn., Walpole, Mass., 1975-78; presenter Nat. Social Studies Assn., Boston, 1984-85; instr./trainer health svcs. edn. ARC, 1987-90. Nominated for Mass. Tchr. of Yr., 1999. Mem.: AAUW, NAACP (life), Consumer Credit Counseling Svc. (bd. chair edn. com. 1998—99), Mass. State Dept. Edn. (adv. bd. 1995—98), Soc. Nutrition Edn., Mass. Tchrs. Assn. (higher edn. com. 1984—87), Ea. Mass. Home Econs. Assn. (bd. dirs. 1978), Am. Home Econs. Assn., Am. Dietitic Assn., Delta Kappa Gamma (journalist Iota chpt. 1986—88, membership com. 1988—92, v.p. 1994, pres. Iota chpt. 1996—98, state world fellowship chairperson, Internat. Area Achievement award 2001). Avocations: travel, bicycling. Home: 92 Morse St Sharon MA 02067-2719

JOHNSON, ALEX CLAUDIUS, English language educator; b. Freetown, Sierra Leone, Aug. 14, 1943; came to U.S., 1991; s. Eunice Angela (Thorpe) Johnson; m. Daphne Marvel Taylor; children: Marvin(dec.), Joyemi. BA in English Lang. and Lit. with honors, U. Durham, Eng., 1968; MA in English and Am. Lit., U. Kent, Canterbury, Eng., 1971; MPhil in Linguistics, U. Leeds, Eng., 1974; PhD in English, U. Ibadan, Nigeria, 1982. Tchr. various h.s., Freetown, Sierra Leone, 1968-69, 71-72; sr. lectr., lectr. English dept. Fourah Bay Coll., Sierra Leone, 1974-88, sr. lectr., acting head classics/philosophy dept., 1987-88, assoc. prof., head English dept., 1988-91; vis. prof. English lang. and Creole studies U. Bayreuth, Germany, 1982-84; vis. prof. S.C. State U., Orangeburg, 1991-92, prof., 1992. Acting vice prin. Fourah Bay Coll., summer 1989, 90, dean faculty of arts, 1989-91; cons. UNESCO, 1985-89; external assessor U. Cape Coast, Ghana, 1988. Contbr. articles to internat. profl. jours., papers to internat. confs. and symposia. Chief examiner West Africa Examinations Coun., Accra, Ghana, 1978-91, Inst. Edn., U. Sierra Leone, 1980-91; chair Nat. Primary Curriculum Revision Com., 1981. Mem. SAMLA, South Ea. Renaissance Conf., Coll. Lang. Assn., African Lit. Assn., West African Linguistic Soc. (sec., organizer 13th West African Langs. Congress, Freetown, 1978), West African MLA (exec. com. 1981-82). Episcopalian. Home: 767 Windmill Way Orangeburg SC 29118-2838 E-mail: johnsonac@scsu.edu.

JOHNSON, ALICE JEAN SHUMATE, elementary education educator; b. Tipple, W.Va., Jan. 7, 1947; d. Wanus Eli Shumate and Lorene Virginia Phillips Shumate Collier; m. Jack Woodrow Johnson, Oct. 6, 1973; children: Karen Paige, Joel Wesley. BS, Concord Coll., Athens, W.Va., 1969. Cert. tchr. grades 4-8. Tchr. 4th grade Raleigh County Pub. Schs., Beckley, W.Va., 1969; tchr. 5th grade Hampton (Va.) City Pub. Schs., 1969-70; tchr. 7th grade Petersburg (Va.) Pub. Schs., 1970-72, tchr. 5th grade, 1972-74, 87-92, tchr. 6th grade, 1992—. Staff devel. trainer Petersburg City Pub. Schs., 1988—, mem. math. grading criteria task force, 1991; cooperating tchr. Va. State U., Ettrick, 1992; participant various symposia; cons. Va. Dept. Edn., 1993-94, state planning process for funding under Improving Am.'s Schs. Act, 1995. Leader Cub Scouts Robert E. Lee Coun. Boy Scouts Am., 1991-92, cubmaster, 1992-94, staff day camp Cub Scouts, 1992; mem. officer Hopewell (Va.) High Sch. Band Boosters, 1987-92. Mem. ASCD, NEA, Va. Edn. Assn., Petersburg Edn. Assn., Nat. Coun. Tchrs. Math., Va. Theatre Assn., Va. Middle Sch. Assn. Office: Petersburg City Pub Schs 141 E Wythe St Petersburg VA 23803-4535

JOHNSON, ANDREW W. secondary education educator; b. Abington, Pa., May 5, 1975; s. Ralph Walton and Catherine H. Johnson; m. Heather Marie Arnold, June 27, 1998. BS in Math., Ursinus Coll., Collegeville, Pa., 1997; MA in Math., Villanova U., 2001. Instrnl. II cert. for secondary schs., Pa. Teller, info. cons. Harleysville (Pa.) Nat. Bank, 1994-98; tchr. math. Souderton (Pa.) Area Sch. Dist., 1997—. WWW home-page designer Ursinus Coll., 1994-96; mentor Indian Valley Mid. Sch., Harleysville, 1999—; educator academically talented students Carnegie Mellon U.; C-Mites Instr., 2002—. Mem. Phi Beta Kappa. Republican. Mennonite. Avocations: singing in choirs, listening to mahler's music. Office: Indian Valley Mid Sch 130 Maple Ave Harleysville PA 19438-1796

JOHNSON, ARTHUR V., II, secondary education educator; BA in Math. and History, Tufts U., 1967; postgrad., Lowell U., 1968-74, MEd in Cirriculum and Adminstrn., 1977; postgrad., Northeastern U., 1977-79, U. N.H., 1984-88, Boston U., 1990-91. Tchr. jr. high sch., Nashua, N.H., 1967-69; tchr. sr. high sch., 1969—. Dir. digital computer bus program, 1984; dir., instr. Critical Skills Insts., 1985—; instr. geometry Inst. at Groton Sch., 1990, 91; instr. geometry seminar U. N.H., 1991; instr. geometry and patterns seminar Nat. Coun. Math., 1993—; mem. F.I.P.S.E. Program, U. N.H., 1986-88, NSF Inst. U. N.H., 1986-88, Tsongas Ctr., U. Lowell, 1990. Author Math That Matters, 1991, Mathematics History for the Classroom, 1992; contbr. articles to profl. jours.; host videotape series MATH: The Basics, Ky. Ednl. TV, 1990. Family ch. counselor, 1980—; instr. Kid's Kollege, 1984-90; instr., avdisor Challenge Program, River Coll., 1986-91. Recipient N.H. award Taxpayer Edn. Program, 1990, Presdl. Excellence in Teaching award, 1992; named N.H. Tchr. of Yr., 1992. Mem. Nat. Coun. Tchrs. Math. (chmn. joint articulation com. with Math. Assn. Am. 1985-87, chair publs. Boston regional conf. 1988, chair publicity Nasha regional conf. 1991), Pi Lambda Theta (hon.). Home: 7 Steadman St Hudson NH 03051 Office: Nashua Sr High Sch 36 Riverside Dr Nashua NH 03062-1312

JOHNSON, BADRI NAHVI, sociology educator, real estate business owner; b. Tehran, Iran, Dec. 1, 1934; came to U.S., 1957; d. Ali Akbar and Monir Khazraii Nahvi; m. Floyd Milton Johnson, July 2, 1960; children: Rebecca, Nancy, Robert. BS, U. Minn., 1967, MA, 1969, PhD, 2001. Stenographer Curtis 1000, Inc., St. Paul, 1958-62; lab. instr. U. Minn., Mpls., 1966-69, teaching asst., 1969-72; chief exec. officer Real Estate Investment and Mgmt. Enterprise, St. Paul, 1969—; prof. emeritus sociology Anoka-Ramsey C.C., Coon Rapids, Minn., 1973—2003. Pub. speaker, bd. dirs., sponsor pub. radio KFAI, Mpls., 1989-93; established an endowed scholarship for women Anoka Ramsey C.C., 1991. Radio talk show host KCW, Brookline Parks, Minn., 1993. Organizer Iranian earthquake disaster relief, 1990; bd. dirs. dist. 7 Cmty. Coun., 1996-98. Recipient Earthquake Relief Orgn. citation Iranian Royal Household, 1968, Islamic Republic of Iran citation for organizing earthquake disaster relief, 1990. Mem.: NEA, Sociologists of Minn., Minn. Edn. Assn., Women's Leadership Forum, Nat. Social Scis. Assn., U. Minn. Alumni Assn. Avocations: world travel, classical and historical novels, exotic food, gardening. Home: 1726 Iowa Ave E Saint Paul MN 55106-1334 Office: Anoka-Ramsey Cmty Coll 11200 Mississippi Blvd NW Minneapolis MN 55433-3470 E-mail: john1800@tc.umn.edu.

JOHNSON, BARBARA ANN, health services educator; b. Rochester, N.Y., July 3, 1953; d. Ray Clifford and Helen Frances (Lindgren) J.; m. William A. Perison, Feb. 28, 1986 (dec. 1998); 1 child, Alyssa Ann. BSEd, Worcester State COll., 1975; MA, U. Mass., 1977; PhD, U. Fla., 1982. Lic. speech-lang. pathologist, Tex., La., N.Y., Calif. Speech therapist Killingly Pub. Schs., Danielson, Conn., 1975-76; grad. tchg. asst. dept. comm. disorders U. Mass., Amherst, 1976-77; level II trainee VA Med. Ctr., Gainesville, Fla., 1977-78; grad. tchg. asst. Eng. Lang. Inst. U. Fla., Gainesville, 1978-79, grad. tchg. asst. speech dept., 1980-81; pvt. practice speech-lang. pathologist North Ctrl. Fla., 1980-81; asst. prof. speech sci., pathology and audiology dept. St. Cloud (Minn.) State U., 1983-84; dir. speech-lang. pathologist South County Speech-Hearing-Learning Ctr., Gilroy, Calif., 1984-85; vis. asst. prof. speech dept. Nat. Inst. for Deaf Rochester (N.Y.) Inst. Tech., 1985-90; asst. prof. speech dept. La. Tech. U., Ruston, 1990-92; assoc. prof., chair/dir. dept. comm. disorders U. Tex.-Pan Am., Edinburg, 1992-96, interim dean, assoc. prof. Coll. Health Scis. & Human Svcs., 1996-98, prof., chair dept. comm. disorders, 1998-99; prof., chair dept. speech pathology and audiology Ithaca (N.Y.) Coll., 2000—. Presenter, mentor in field. Author: Language Disorders in Children: An Introductory Clinical Perspective, 1996; contbr. articles to profl. publs. Grantee Crippled Children's Soc. Santa Clara County, 1985, U.S. Dept. Edn., 1993, 94, U. Tex.-Pan Am., 1994, Pro-Tec Equipment, 1995, Health Career Opportunity Program, 19965. Mem. Am. Speech-Lang.-Hearing Assn. (cert. clin. competence, Svc. Recognition award 1993, mem. profl. svcs. bd. 1991-93, multi-site com. 1991-93), Tex. Speech-Lang.-Hearing Assn., Coll. Health Deans, Tex. Soc. Allied Health Professions, Coun. Grad. Programs in Comm. Scis. and Disorders, Coun. Suprs. in Speech-Lang. Pathology and Audiology (pres. 1997), Kappa Delta Pi. E-mail: bjohnson@ithaca.edu.

JOHNSON, BARBARA ELAINE SPEARS, retired education educator; b. Chgo., May 24, 1932; d. William Everett and Sadie Mae (Fennoy) Spears; m. John Gilbert Johnson, July 29, 1967 (dec. Jan. 1985); children: Steven W., Jeri-Lynn Johnson Jackson. AB, U. Chgo., 1952; EdB, Chgo. Tchrs. Coll., 1954; EdM, Loyola U., Chgo., 1967; EdS, U. Ill., Chgo., 1982; MSEd in counseling, Chgo. State U., 1986. Tchr. Chgo. Pub. Schs., 1954-64, counselor, 1964-70; evening tchr. Chgo. Pub. High Schs., 1964-66; dir. resource skills City Colls. of Chgo., 1970-84, dir. audio visual, 1985-86, coordinator academic support ctr., 1986-87, prof. acad. support, 1988-93; prof. emeritus City Colls. of Chgo., 1993—. Faculty coun. City Colls. of Chgo., v.p. 1989-90, pres. 1990-91. Coordinator food ministry Cosmopolitan Community Ch., Chgo., 1983-90. Recipient Dedication to Youth award McCosh Sch. Council, 1985, citations of recognition Ill. Community Coll. Bd., 1982, 84. Fellow Ill. Com. Black Concerns in Higher Edn. (plaque 1984); mem. AARP (exec. bd. mem. 1997—, v.p. 2000), Ill. C.C. Faculty Assn. (life, exec. bd. 1979—, pres. 1981-82, plaque 1982), Ill. Assn. Personalized Learning Programs (exec. bd., treas. 1975-85, Outstanding Contbn. award 1985), U. Ill. Mothers Assn. (chair 1977-81), Ill. C.C. Annuitants Assn. (exec. bd. dirs. 1993—, pres. 1995-97), Sr. Friends, Alpha Kappa Alpha (50 yr. mem. award 2002). Home: 8610 S Vernon Ave Chicago IL 60619-6015

JOHNSON, BETH MICHAEL, school administrator; b. New Orleans, Dec. 7, 1938; d. Carney Leon and Amy Juanita (Monju) J. BA, St. Mary's Dominican, 1963; MEd, U. New Orleans, 1978. Cert. elem. tchr., prin., sch. supt., supr. student teaching, parish supr. of instruction, La. Tchr. Holy Rosary, New Orleans, 1959-68, Cath. High, New Roads, La., 1968-69; prin. St. Ignatius, Grand Coteau, La., 1969-71; asst. prin. Lourdes Community, New Orleans, 1972-74, prin., 1974-77; asst. prin., guidance counselor Our Lady of Prompt Succor, Westwego, La., 1977-78; prin. Our Lady of Perpetual Help, Belle Chasse, La., 1978-85; asst. prin. Archbishop Chapelle H.S., Metairie, La., 1985-89, prin., 1989-97, pres., 1997—. Author: (workbook) A Study Guide of Europe, 1983. Recipient Exemplary Sch. award U.S. Dept. Edn., 1986, 91. Mem. ASCD, Nat. Cath. Edn. Assn. Secondary Prin. Assn. (exec. bd. 1991—, pres. 1993—), Nat. Assn. Secondary Sch. Prins. (pres. 1993), Elem. Prins. Assn. (exec. bd. 1974-80, pres. 1976-80). Democrat. Roman Catholic. Avocation: travel. Office: Archbishop Chapelle High Sch 8800 Veterans Memorial Blvd Metairie LA 70003-5235

JOHNSON, BETTY LOU, secondary education educator; b. Stockwell, Ind., Apr. 4, 1927; d. Paul Stanley Jones and Ethel Leona (Royer) J.; m. Kenneth Odell Johnson, Aug. 5, 1950; children: Cynthia Jo (Mrs. James P. Greaton), Gregory Alan. BS in Home Econs., Purdue U., 1948; postgrad., Northwood Inst. Culinary Arts, 1981, 83. Cert. home economist. Tchr. LaCrosse (Ind.) Jr.-Sr. High Sch., 1948-49, Wendell L. Willkie High Sch., Elwood, Ind., 1949-51, Thomas Carr Howe High Sch., Indpls., 1951-57; substitute tchr. Gt. Oaks Joint Vocat. Sch. Dist., Cin. Mem. AAUW, Am. Home Econs. Assn. (life), Ohio Home Econs. Assn. (life), John Purdue Club, Purdue Pres.'s Coun., Purdue U. Alumni Assn. (life), Gamma Sigma Delta. Home: Cincinnati, Ohio. Deceased.

JOHNSON, BONNIE SUE, piano educator; b. Macon, Ga., Aug. 17, 1958; d. Herbert Franklin and Betty Jean (Gattis) Green; m. Michael Marwood Johnson, July 10, 1982; children: Pamela Elaine, Phillip Michael. B of Music Edn., Wesleyan Coll., 1980. Ch. pianist Lynmore Meth. Ch., Macon, 1985-86, Cross Keys Bapt. Ch., Macon, 1986-87, Park Meml. Meth. Ch., Macon, 1987-97, Bass United Meth. Ch., Macon, 1997-98; tchr.'s aide Northminister Presbyn. Pre-Sch., 2001—. Composer (tape) Unspoken Melodies, 1996, S & S Cafeteria comml., 1996, (song) Macon's Cherry Blossom, 1996. Accompanist grand chorus 1st Bapt. Ch., 1997—; ch. pianist Tattnall Sq. Presbyn. Ch., 1999—. Fellow Macon Music Tchrs. Assn. (v.p. membership 1996-98, v.p. publicity. 1999); mem. Music Tchrs. Nat. Assn., Morning Music Club. Avocations: walking, swimming, reading. Home: 4731 Leo Pl Macon GA 31210-3001

JOHNSON, BRIAN KEITH, electrical engineering educator; b. Madison, Wis., Mar. 11, 1965; s. Alton Cornelius and Virginia Rae (Korener) Johnson; m. Elizabeth M. Williams, Jan. 3, 1998; children: Erica Pearl,

Mark Macrae. BS, U. Wis., 1987, MS, 1989, PhD, 1992. Registered profl. engr., Wis., Idaho. Teaching asst. U. Wis., Madison, 1988, rsch. asst., 1988-92; engr. Lawrence Livermore Nat. Labs., Livermore, Calif., 1989; asst. prof. U. Idaho, Moscow, 1992-97, assoc. prof., 1997—. Instr. Coll. Engring. Tchg. Asst. Tng., U. Wis., Madison, 1988, Engring. profl. devel., 1992-98; co-advisor Iron Cross Leadership Soc., Madison, 1988-92, U. Idaho IEEE Student Chpt., 1995—; dir. Western Virtual Engring., 1996-99. Lodge chief Order of the Arrow, Boy Scouts Am., 1982-84, dir. Brownsea Double 2Course, Madison, 1987, advisor, 1990-92. Recipient Vigil Hon. Membership, Order of the Arrow, Boy Scouts Am., 1988, Leadership award, Exploring Boy Scouts Am., 1986, Outstanding Young Faculty award U. Idaho Coll. Engring., 1995. Mem. IEEE (chair working group on utility applications of supercondrs. 1999—, sec. IEEE working group on modeling and simulation of distributed resources, 2001—, mem. AdCom intelligent transp. systems coun., ITS coun.), Am. Soc. Engring. Edn., Internat. Coun. on Large Electric Sys. Lutheran. Avocations: cross country skiing, bicycling, backpacking. Office: U Idaho Dept Elec Engring Moscow ID 83844-0001

JOHNSON, CARLA RAE, sculptor, art educator; b. East Chicago, Ind., Mar. 9, 1947; d. Carl Einor and Ruth Elizabeth (Steele) J. BS, Ball State U., 1969; MA, U. Iowa, 1974, MFA, 1975. Lectr. SUNY, Plattsburgh, 1975-76, Miss. State U., Starkville, 1977-80; adj. lectr. contemporary sculpture Westchester art workshop Westchester C.C., White Plains, NY, 1985—93; adj. lectr. ceramics/sculpture Kingsborough C.C., Bklyn., 1986—93; assoc. prof. art, chair art dept. Marymount Coll. of Fordham U., Tarrytown, NY, 1993—2003; asst. prof. art Westchester C. C., Valhala, NY, 2003—. Rep. Ceres Gallery, N.Y.C., Maxwell Fine Arts, Peekskill, NY. Sculpture installation, Gray Matters, 1990, Elizabeth Found. Arts, N.Y.C., 2002. Design commn. Westchester Arts Coun., White Plains, NY, 2003. Pollock-Krasner fellow Pollock-Krasner Found., N.Y.C., 1990. Mem. Internat. Sculpture Ctr., Women's Caucus for Art, Soho 20 Artists (pres. 1988-89, chmn. bd. 1989-90, vice chair 1990-91).

JOHNSON, CAROL J. principal; Prin. Meadow Lake Elem. Sch., Birmingham, Mich. Recipient DOW Elem. Sch. Recognition award, 1990-91. Office: Meadow Lake Elem Sch 7100 Lindemere Bloomfield Hills MI 48301

JOHNSON, CAROLYN LOUISE, elementary education educator; b. Chgo., Dec. 20, 1952; d. John Henry and Essie Beatrice (McDonald) Crawford; m. Henry Johnson Jr., July 17, 1971; children: Henry Johnson II, Christopher L., Chaun L. BA, Northeastern Ill. U., Chgo., 1976, MA, 1986. Tchr. Chgo. Pub. Schs., 1976-77; elem. thcr. Archdiocese of Chgo., 1977—. Mem. ASCD, Nat. Sci. Tchrs. Assn., Black United Front Ednl. Div. (dir. tutoring program 1986), Westside Confedn. of Tchrs. Democrat. Pentecostal. Avocations: singing, reading, boating, baseball, tennis.

JOHNSON, CHARLES N. elementary education educator; Tchr., vice prin. Morgan (Utah) Middle Sch.; prin. Clinton (Utah) Elem., 1997-99, Burton Elem., Kaysville, Utah, 1999—. Recipient Tchr. Excellence award Internat. Tech. Edn. Assn., 1992. Office: Burton Elem 827 E 200 S Kaysville UT 84037-2299

JOHNSON, CHRISTINE, educational administrator; b. Antelope Wells, N.Mex., Feb. 6, 1953; d. Charles and Rosa (Vera) J.; m. Ronald D. Sherbon, June 30, 1978 (div. Aug. 1984); m. Carlyle F. Griffin, July 7, 1989. BS in Secondary Edn., N.Mex. State U., 1975; MA in Edn. Adminstrn., Colo. U., 1977, PhD in Edn. Adminstrn., 1984. Tchr. Thomas Jefferson H.S., Denver, 1975-80; spl. asst. Ctrl. Adminstrn., Denver, 1980-81; asst. prin. Abraham Lincoln H.S., Denver, 1981-83, prin., 1986-91, Horace Mann Mid. Sch., Denver, 1984-85; rsch. fellow Colo. Dept. Edn., Denver, 1985-86; exec. dir. K-12 edn. Littleton (Colo.) Pub. Schs., 1991-93; urban policy dir. Edn. Commn. of States, Denver, 1993—. Chair com. Nat. Assessment for Edn. Progress, Washington, 1990-94; mem. governing bd. Cross City Campaign, Chgo., 1993—, Prins. Ctr., 1988-90; mem. adv. bd. Nat. Sch. Based Health, Washington, 1993—. Contbr. articles to profl. publs. Chair State Higher Edn. Bd., Denver, 1994—; v.p. Prevention Ctr., Denver, 1992; mem., chair com. Colo. Achievement Commn., Denver, 1993; mem., chair prins. adv. bd. Colo. Gen. Assembly, Denver, 1991-93. Kellogg Found. fellow, 1993, Danforth fellow, 1987. Mem. ASCD, Colo. Commn. on Higher Edn. (chair 1991—), Am. Assn. Sch. Adminstrs., Denver C. of C. (mem. Leadership Denver 1990, award 1990), Phi Delta Kappa. Avocations: jogging, skiing, hiking.

JOHNSON, CLIFTON HERMAN, historian, archivist, former research center director; b. Griffin, Ga., Sept. 13, 1921; s. John and Pearl (Parrish) Johnson; m. Rosemary Brunst, Aug. 2, 1960; children: Charles, Robert, Virginia. Student, U. Conn., 1943—44; BA, U. N.C., 1948, PhD, 1959; MA, U. Chgo., 1949; postgrad., U. Wis., 1951. Tutor LeMoyne Coll., Memphis, 1950—53, asst. prof., 1953—56, prof., 1960—61, 1963—66; asst. prof. East Carolina Coll., 1958—59; asst. libr. and archivist Fisk U., 1961—63; exec. dir. Amistad Rsch. Ctr., New Orleans, 1966—92, emeritus, 1992. Author (with Carroll Barber): The American Negro: A Selected and Annotated Bibliography for High Schools and Junior Colleges, 1968; author: A Legacy of La Amistad: Some Twentieth Century Black Leaders, 1989, Abolitionism in the Antislavery Movement, 1997; editor: God Struck Me Dead: Religious Conversions and Experiences and Autobiographies of Ex-Slaves, 1969. Exec. bd. dirs. All Congregations Together, 1997—; bd. dirs. La. World Expn., 1980—82, Lillie Carroll Jackson Mus., 1978—89, Countee Cullen Found., 1981—87, Friends of Archives La., 1978—90, La. Folklife Commn., 1982—85, Ctr. for Black Music Rsch., 1986—, New Orleans Urban League, 1994—; cons. DreamWorks Prodns., 1997. With AUS, 1940—45. NEH fellow, 1994. Mem.: Nat. Assn. Human Rights Workers, Orgn. Am. Historians, Assn. for Study Negro Life and History, Soc. Am. Archivists, So. Hist. Assn. E-mail: clifton@peak.org.

JOHNSON, CONSTANCE ANN TRILLICH, web site designer; b. Chgc., Apr. 16, 1949; d. Lee and Ruth (Goodhue) Trillich; m. Robert Dale Neal, Dec. 25, 1972 (div. 1988); 1 child, Adam Danforth; m. Lewis W. Johnson Jr., Feb. 14, 1990. BA in French, U. Tenn., 1971; cert., Sorbonne, Paris, 1970; MLn, Emory U., 1979; JD, Mercer Law Sch., 1982; PhD magna cum laude, Internat. Sem., 1995. Bar: Ga. 1982. Reservationist AAA, Tampa, 1971-72; libr. tech. asst. I Mercer U., Macon, Ga., 1973-74, libr. tech. asst. II, 1974-78; tchg. asst. Mercer Law Sch., Macon, 1981; asst. prof. Mercer Med. Sch., Macon, 1980-82; pvt. practice Macon, 1982-86; min. Ch. Tzaddi, 1986-89; writer/rschr.ADC Project 1988-89; min. Alliance of Divine Love, 1988—; co-owner Cmtys. OnLine, Winter Park, Fla., 1990—, Christians on the Net, Winter Park, Fla., 1995—; of counsel Read Found., Evansville, Ind., 1989. Mgr. Lifestream Assocs., 1989; freelance editor Page Design Co., 1989; assoc. AA Computer Care, Winter Park, 1989; founder House of the Lord, 1989—; rsch. asst. Ctr. Constnl. Studies, Macon, 1983; instr. bus. Wesleyan Coll., Macon, 1982; web designer Christians on the Net, 1995—; curator Angel Art Gallery, 1995—; internet editor, Discovery Newspaper, Orlando, Fla., 1998—; assoc. prof., libr., Internat. Sem., Plymouth, Fla., 1991; founder Ruth G. Trillich Meml Sch., Flywheeler Park, Ft Meade, Fla. Author: Treasures From Heaven, 1995; editor (periodical) Ray of Sunshine, 1989. Bd. dirs. Unity Ch., Middle, Ga., 1987, sec., 1987; bd. dirs. Macon Coun. World Affairs, 1981-82, Light of Creative Awareness, Northville, Mich., 1989; mem. Friends Emory Librs., Atlanta, 1980-87, Friends Eckerd Coll. Libr., St. Petersburg, Fla., 1980-87. Mem. ABA, AAUW, Am. Soc. Law and Medicine, Am. Judicature Soc., DAR (DuVall chpt.), Mercer U. Women's Club (treas. 1974, pres. 1986, bd. dirs. 1987), Fla. Flywheelers Antique Engine Club (edn. chairperson 2001—), Friends of the Libr., Mid. Ga. Gem and Mineral Soc., Macon Mus. Arts and Scis., La Leche League (sec. 1985), Phi Alpha Delta. Republican. Office: Communities OnLine 1416 Pelican Bay Trl Winter Park FL 32792-6131 E-mail: drjphd@yahoo.com.

JOHNSON, CURTIS, alumni affairs administrator, enrollment management administrator; b. Aberdeen, Miss., Dec. 11, 1961; s. William White and Emma Johnson; 1 child, Latoya H. Braylock. BS in Psychology, Jackson State U., 1985, MEd in Guidance/Counseling, 1994. Bldg. supr. Miss. State Hosp., Whitfield, 1983-84; asst. counselor Jackson (Miss.) State U., 1984-86, counselor/recruiter, 1986-93, interim dir. alumni affairs, 1993-94, dir. alumni affairs, 1994—. Mem. Devel. Found., Jackson State U., 1993—, scholarship chmn. Jackson-Hinds chpt., 1992—. Sponsor Jackson Police Dept., 1994. Recipient Outstanding Achievement award Omega Psi Phi, 1994; named one of Outstanding Young Men of Am., 1988. Mem. Coun. for Nat. Alumni Assn. (com. chair 1994), Jackson State U. Alumni Assn. (exec. dir. 1993—), Inter-Alumni Coun., Fgn. Student Adv. Coun., Sports Hall of Fame Com., T.C. Almore Lodge # 242 (sec. 1994), Order of Ea. Star (Worthy Patron 1992-94). Avocations: reading, softball, basketball, biking, volleyball. Office: Jackson State Univ PO Box 17820 Jackson MS 39217

JOHNSON, DAVID CHESTER, university chancellor, sociology educator; b. Jan. 21, 1933; s. Chester Laven and Olga Henriett (Resnick) J.; m. Jean Ann Lunnis, Sept. 10, 1955 (dec. 1996); children: Stephen, Andrew, Jennifer. BA, Gustavus Adolphus Coll., 1954; MA, U. Iowa, 1956, PhD, 1959; LLD, Luther Coll., 1993. Instr. to prof. sociology Luther Coll., Decorah, Iowa, 1957-69; dean arts and scis. East Stroudsburg (Pa.) U., 1969-76; v.p. acad. affairs St. Cloud (Minn.) State U., 1976-83; dean Gustavus Adolphus Coll., St. Peter, Minn., 1983-90; chancellor U. Minn., Morris, 1990-98; cons. to Scandinavian univs., 1999—. Leader of numerous hiking groups to Norwegian mountains. Mem. bd. Friends of Libr., U. Minn. Librs., 2003—. NSF sci. faculty fellow Inst. Social Rsch., Oslo, 1965-66, adminstrv. fellow Am. Coun. Edn., Luther Coll., 1968-69, Summer Leadership fellow Bush Found., Inst. Edn. Mgmt., Harvard U., 1981; Kennedy Swedish Fund grantee, 1976. Mem. Elder Learning Inst. U. Minn. (pres), U. Minn. Retirees Assn. (pres.), Am. Swedish Assn. Democrat. Lutheran. Home: 1235 Yale Pl Apt 1705 Minneapolis MN 55403-1948

JOHNSON, DEBORAH CROSLAND WRIGHT, mathematics educator; b. Winston-Salem, N.C., July 17, 1951; d. Clayton Edward and Elizabeth Elliott (Bradley) Crosland; married; children: Jacqueline, Stephanie. BS in Math. Edn. magna cum laude, Appalachian State U., 1973; MEd in Math., U. N.C., Greensboro, 1976, cert., 1984. Cert. tchr., N.C., academically gifted; nat. bd. cert. adolescent/young adulthood math. Tchr. math. Mt. Tabor H.S., Winston-Salem, 1973-76, McDowell H.S., Marion, N.C., 1976-78, Ctrl. Cabarrus H.S., Concord, N.C., 1978-81, Walter M. Williams H.S., Burlington, N.C., 1981—. Mem. sch. improvement team Walter M. Williams H.S., 1989-92. Active First Presbyn. Ch., Burlington, 1988—. Mem. NEA, N.C. Assn. Educators, Nat. Coun. Tchrs. Math., N.C. Coun. Tchrs. Math., N.C. Assn. Gifted and Talented, Alpha Delta Kappa (hon. tchrs. sorority). Democrat.

JOHNSON, DELORES, special education educator; b. Balt., Aug. 30, 1948; d. Jay Vee and Mary Bert (Lawrence) Alderman; m. Franklin Blaney Johnson (div.); children: Francine Bonita Johnson, Kimberly Nikole Johnson Goitia. BS, Coppin State Coll., Balt., 1986, M in Spl. Edn., 1998. Cert. in respite care tng. Tchr. aide Balt. City Pub. Schs., 1974-86, spl. edn. tchr., 1986—. Cons. Latchkey/Alternative Learning Program, Balt., 1994, Adventures In Travel, Balt., 1999—. Mem. bd. edn. Pennsylvania Ave. African Meth. Episcopal Zion Ch., 1992-97. Methodist. Avocations: sewing, travel.

JOHNSON, DENNIS D. elementary school principal; Prin. Pine Tree Elem. Sch., Kent, Wash., 1986—. Recipient Elem. Sch. Recognition award U.S. Dept. Edn., 1989-90. Office: Pine Tree Elem Sch 27825 118th Ave SE Kent WA 98031-8778

JOHNSON, DORIS ANN, educational administrator; b. Marinette, Wis., Dec. 4, 1950; d. Jerome Louis and Jean Fern (Henry) La Plant; m. Daniel Lee Leonard, June 10, 1972 (div. June 1987); children: Jeremiah Daniel, Erica Leigh, Wesley Cyril; m. Paul Robert Johnson, Oct. 21, 1989; stepchildren: Kindra Michelle, Tanya Mari. Student, U. Wis., Oshkosh, 1969-70; BA in Edn., U. Wis., Eau Claire, 1973; MS in Edn., U. Wis., Whitewater, 1975; postgrad., Oreg. State U., 1988. Reading specialist Brookfield (Wis.) Cen. High Sch., 1975-79; lead instr. N.E. Wis. Tech. Coll., Marinette, 1979-87; dir. adult basic edn. Umpqua C.C., Roseburg, Oreg., 1987-95, dir. developmental edn., 1995—2003, dir. grants, 2003—. Founding bd. dirs. Project Literacy, Umpqua Region, Roseburg, 1989-98; mem. adv. bd. Umpqua Cmty. Action Network, Roseburg, 1987-94; mem. State Dirs. of Adult Edn., Oreg., 1987-2002, vice chair, 1992-93, chair, 1993-94; dir. Title III grant, 2002; mem. Adminstrn. Assn., Roseburg, 1989—, chair, 1993-94, 94-95; bd. dirs. Greater Douglas United Way, 1994-2000; adv. bd. Oreg. Literacy Line, 1994-96. Co-author literacy module Communication Skills, 1988; author ednl. curriculum. Founding mem., bd. dirs. St. Joseph Maternity Home, Roseburg, 1987-90; mem. Literacy Theater, Roseburg, 1988-95; mem. Project Leadership, Roseburg, 1988-89; mem. adv. bd. Oreg. Literacy Line, 1994-96; mem. Roseburg Valley Rep. Women, 1994-96. State legalizatoin assistance grantee Fed. Govt., 1988-93, homeless literacy grantee Fed. Govt., 1990-91, family literacy grantee Fed. Govt., 1991-93, intergenerational literacy grantee State of Oreg., 1991, literacy expansion grantee Fed. Govt., 1992-95, literacy outreach grantee Fed. Govt., 1992-2002, staff devel. spl. projects grantee Fed. Govt., 1992-93, Title III grantee Fed. Gov., 2002—. Fellow TESOL, Inst. Inst. Leadership Devel., Am. Assn. Adult and Continuing Edn., Oreg. Assn. Disabled Students, Oreg. Developmental Edn. Studies, Oreg. Assn. for Children with Learning Disabilities, Western Coll. Reading and Learning Assn., Am. Assn. Women in Coll. and Jr. Coll., Roseburg Valley Rep. Women, Altrusa Internat. Club of Roseburg (chair literacy com. 1993-97), Rep. Women. Republican. Lutheran. Avocations: peer counseling, reading, hiking, cooking, running support groups. Home: 761 Garden Grove Dr Roseburg OR 97470-9670 Office: Umpqua CC PO Box 967 Roseburg OR 97470-0226 E-mail: doris.johnson@umpqua.edu.

JOHNSON, DOROTHY CURFMAN, elementary education educator; b. Smithsburg, Md., Nov. 21, 1930; d. Paul Frank and Rhoda Pearl (Witmer) Curfman; m. Robert Nelson Johnson, Jan. 24, 1953 (div. Dec. 1965); children: Gregory Nelson, Eric Paul. Student, Gettysburg Coll., 1948-50, Waynesboro Bus. Coll., 1950, Broward C.C., Ft. Lauderdale, Fla., 1967; BS in Edn., Fla. Atlantic U., 1969, postgrad., 1975-76. Cert. tchr., Fla. Sec. to prodn. mgr. Westinghouse Elec. Corp., Sunbury, Pa., 1951-53; sec. to v.p., sales Metal Carbides Corp., Youngstown, Ohio, 1966; tchr. Sch. Bd. of Broward County, Ft. Lauderdale, Ohio, 1969-93, curriculum specialist, 1993-96. Masters in Edn. Prog., 1973-74, team coord. Sanders Park Elem., Pompano Beach, Fla., 1985-96; mem. North Area Adv. Bd., Pompano Beach, 1990-96; sec. Sanders Park PTA, Pompano Beach, 1994-96. Sec.-treas. Georgen Arms Bd. of Dirs., Pompano Beach, 1997—; dir. Georgen Arms Condo, Inc., Pompano Beach, 1974—; active Jr. League, Youngstown. Recipient Master Tchr. award State of Fla., 1981-82. Mem. Alpha Xi Delta. Lutheran. Home: 280 S Cypress Rd Apt 5 Pompano Beach FL 33060-7038

JOHNSON, DOROTHY SUTHERLAND, school guidance counselor; b. Phila., Sept. 28, 1951; d. Robert Archibald and Lillian Mae (Armstrong) Sutherland; m. Maurice Hugo Johnson, Feb. 26, 1985. BS in Edn., Temple U., 1972; MA, Villanova U., 1976; postgrad., Pa. State U., 1995. Cert. elementary tchr and guidance counselor, elem. prin. Pa. Tchr. Sch. Dist. of Phila., 1972-85; guidance counselor Sch. dist. of Phila., 1985-91, Colonial Sch. Dist., New Castle, Del., 1991-2000; asst. prin. Red Clay Consolidated Sch. Dist., Wilmington, Del., 2000—. Recipient Ruth W. Hayre Community Svc. award Sch. Dist. of Phila., 1988, SuperStars! in Edn., Del. State C. of C., 1995. Mem. ASCD, Pa. Sch. Counselors Assn. (exec. bd. 1987-89), Phi Delta Kappa. Avocations: needlework, gourmet cooking, collecting fine wine. Home: 119 Ridgewood Dr Landenberg PA 19350-9101 Office: Castle Hills Elem Sch Moores Ln New Castle DE 19720

JOHNSON, DUANE P. retired academic administrator, consultant; b. Wadena, Minn., Mar. 19, 1937; s. Julian C. and Lillian M. (Petri) J.; m. Mary E., Oct. 22, 1960; children: Michael D., Gregory P. BS, Iowa State U., 1959; MEd, Colo. State U., 1970. County extension agt. 4-H Oreg. State U., Gresham, 1959-70, ext. specialist 4-H and youth devel. Corvallis, 1970-80, state leader 4-H, 1980-94, prof. adult edn., ext. specialist program devel., 1994-2000; ednl. cons., 2000—; prof. emeritus Oreg. State U., 2001—. Cons. Nat. 4H Japanese Exch. Program, 2000—. Contbr. numerous articles to profl. jours. Recipient Am. Spirit award USAF Recruiting Svc., 1991. Mem. Nat. Assn. Ext. 4-H Agts. (Disting. Svc. award 1979), Assn. Vol. Adminstrn., ASCD, Oreg. State U. Ext. Assn., Epsilon Sigma Phi (we. regional v.p. 2003—, Disting. Svc. award 1995). E-mail: johnsodu@onid.orst.edu.

JOHNSON, EDITH CURTICE, art education administrator; b. Auburn, N.Y., May 21, 1932; d. Charles Wellman and Michaleine Neilsen (Hansen) Witherell; m. Claude Lee Curtice, Dec. 7, 1958 (dec. Jan. 1968); children: Christian Lee, Alison Ann, Brian Wellman; m. Homer Martin Johnson, Apr. 7, 1972 (div. Jan. 1992). BS in Elem. Edn., SUNY, Potsdam, 1954; MS in Art Edn., Ind. U., 1970, EdD in Art Edn., 1976; MA in Counseling, Calif. State U., Fresno, 1984. Cert. tchr., C.C. tchr., supr., instr., counselor, Calif. 2d grade tchr. South Orange (N.J.)/Maplewood Schs., 1954-55; instrumental music tchr. Wrangell (Alaska) Inst., 1955-57; 2d grade music tchr. Yokota (Japan) AFB, 1957-58; visual arts tchr., libr. Tulsa Pub. Schs., 1958-59; 4th grade tchr. North Little Rock (Ark.) Schs., 1961-62; 5th grade tchr. Kirkwood (Mo.) Sch. Dist., 1963; visual arts specialist Clayton (Mo.) Sch. Dist., 1964-69; evaluation specialist CEMREL, Inc. Edn. Lab., St. Louis, 1972-73; supr. art K-12 University City (Mo.) Sch. Dist., 1973-74; profl. assoc. Homer Johnson Assocs., Monterey, Calif., 1977-78; instr. art edn. and phys. edn. Calif. State U., Fresno, 1980-82, 84, 85; curriculum writer art edn. Migrant Edn. PASS Program, Calif. County, Calif., 1985, 91; dir. edn. Fresno Met. Mus., 1986-88; media arts cons. Fresno County Office Edn., Fresno, 1989-90; adminstrv. dir. Calif. Consortium Visual Arts Edn., Fresno, 1988—. Lectr. in art edn. Pacific Cultural Found., Taiwan, 1980; mem. edn. com. Fresno Art Mus., 1988-94, Fresno Met. Mus., 1993-94; visual arts cons. Improving Visual Arts Edn., Washington, 1988-91; dir. summer Insts. in Discipline Based Art Edn., Ctrl. Calif. Hawaii, 1994. Author aesthetics cards Not Just A Bunch of Grapes, 1990. Bd. dirs. Pacific Grove (Calif.) Art Ctr., 1974-77, Fresno (Calif.)-Madera Counties ARC, 1990-94. Recipient numerous awards from Calif. Art Edn. Assn., including Douc Langur award, 1981, Outstanding Mus. Educator, 1988, Ruth Jansen award, 1989, award of merit, 1990, 94, also Outstanding Svc. award Nat. Art Assn., 1994. Mem. Nat. Art Edn. Assn. (v.p. Pacific region 1991-93, contbr. column to Nat. Art Edn. News 1992-94), Calif. Art Edn. Assn. (bd. dirs. 1983-91, pres. 1987-89, contbr. column to newsletter 1987-89), Calif. Alliance for Arts Edn., Phi Delta Kappa. Avocations: music, piano, opera, ice skating, art, travel. Home: 3035 E Buckingham Way Fresno CA 93726-4229 Office: Calif Consortium Visual Arts 1111 Van Ness Ave Fresno CA 93721-2002

JOHNSON, EDWARD ELEMUEL, psychologist, educator; b. Jamaica, B.W.I., July 25, 1926; came to U.S., 1941, naturalized, 1948; s. Edward and Mary Elizabeth (Blake) J.; m. Beverley Jean Morris, Jan. 26, 1955; children— Edward Elemuel, Lawrence Palmer, Robin Jeannine, Nathan Jerome, Cyril Ulric. BS, Howard U., 1947, MS, 1948; PhD, U. Colo., 1952. Assoc. prof. psychology Grambling Coll., La., 1954-55; prof. So. U., Baton Rouge, 1955-60, prof., head dept. psychology, 1960-69, assoc. dean univ., 1969-72, dir. Regional Head Start Evaluation and Research Ctr.; clin. prof. La. State U. Med. Sch., New Orleans, 1969-72; dir. United Bd. for Coll. Devel., 1972-74; dir. 13 coll. curriculum program So. U., Baton Rouge; clin. prof. psychiatry Emory U. Med. Sch., Atlanta, 1973-74; prof. psychiatry Robert Wood Johnson Med. Sch., Piscataway, N.J., 1974—; pres. Limited Liability Corp. in Forensic Psychology, 2002—. Cons. collaborative child devel. project; cons. State Indsl. Sch. Scotlandville, La., 1973-74, VA Hosp., Lyons, N.J., 1987; mem. Med. Rev. Panel, State of N.J., 1976—, chmn., 1993; vocat. cons. HEW; mem. mental health adv. group Westinghouse Health Systems, 1978-82; region II mental health coordinator Head Start Program, 1978—; mem. gen. research support rev. com. NIH, 1980—; mem. acad. council Thomas A. Edison Coll. of N.J., 1978-83; mem. adv. bd. Office Pub. Guardian, State of N.J., 1988—; chmn. minority and cultural concerns com. div. Mental Health and Hosps. of State of N.J., 1989—; psychol. evaluator Middlesex County Superior Ct., 1996—; cons. forensic psychology. Contbr. articles to profl. jours. Bd. dirs. Crossroads Theatre Co., New Brunswick, N.J. Served to 1st lt. AUS, 1951-53. Fellow AAAS; mem. Am. Psychol. Assn. (com. on adv. svcs. for edn. and tng. 1968-69, task group on faculty devel. for minority and non-minority faculty to implement culturally relevant curriculum 1992), N.Y. Acad. Scis. (life), Masons, Sigma Xi, Sigma Pi Phi, Alpha Phi Alpha, Beta Beta Beta, Pi Gamma Mu, Psi Chi. Home: PO Box 597 East Brunswick NJ 08816-0597

JOHNSON, ELEANOR MAE, education educator; b. St. Paul, Mar. 22, 1925; d. Emil H. and Leona W. (Warner) Busse; m. Edward Charles Johnson, May 13, 1950; 1 child, Mary Jo Johnson Tuckwell. BS, U. Wis., Stout, 1946, MS, 1959, edn. specialist, 1981. Cert. home economist, tchr., Wis. Instr. home econs. various pub. schs., Wis., 1946-48, 56-64; home economist U. Wis. Extension, various locations, 1948-51, 52-56; tchr. educator U. Wis.-Stout, Menomonie, 1965-87; ret., 1987. Summer session guest prof. U. Man., Winnipeg, Can., 1970, 71, S.D. State U., Brookings, 1978; dir. Native Am. curriculum for home econs. Fed. Vocat. Project, U. Wis.-Stout, 1978-80; cons. vocat. evaluation team U. Wis.-Stout, 1982-90; presenter at profl. confs.; team mem. interdisciplinary consumer edn. teaching materials Joint Coun. Econ. Edn., 1980-82. Editor teaching materials for Native Ams., 1978-80. Sr. statesman Wis. Coalition on Aging, 1990-2003; adv., vol. Office of Aging, 1992-2003. Mem. Am. Home Econs. Assn. (del. nat. and internat. confs., Inner City fellow 1970), Life mem. with - Am. Vocat. Assn., Wis. Edn. Assn., U. Wis.-Stout Alumni, Assn. Tchr. Educators and Am. Assn. Ret. Persons. Avocations: national and international travel, collecting historical canning jars, stamps, antique dolls, genealogy. Home: 623 Elm Ave Barron WI 54812-1712

JOHNSON, ELIZABETH ERICSON, retired educator; b. Rockford, Ill., Oct. 5, 1927; d. Gunnar Lawrence and Victoria Amelia (Carlson) Ericson; m. Barent Olaf Johnson, June 2, 1951; children: Ann E. Arellano, Susan M. Taber. BA, U. Ill., 1949; MSEd, No. Ill. U., 1969. Tchr. Sch. Dist. 205, Rockford, Ill., 1949-53, 65-92. Mem. Ct. Appointed Spl. Advocate, Rockford, 1992—. Mem. AAUW, LWV (bd. dirs. 1994-96, local bd.), Ill. Ret. Tchrs. Assn., Winnebago Ret. Tchrs. Assn. (various bds.), Phi Delta Kappa emeritus. Avocations: music, viola, musician, violist. Home: 1902 Valencia Dr Rockford IL 61108-6818 E-mail: evebridge@aol.com.

JOHNSON, FLORA GILCHRIST, school principal; b. Jamestown, Va., Oct. 20; d. Floyd and Vessie Alma (Haskett) Gilchrist; m. richard Johnson, Dec. 15, 1956; children: Kevin R., Kirk R. BS, Va. State U., 1955; MEd, Johns Hopkins U., 1970; postgrad., Loyola Coll., Towson State U., Morgan State U., U. Md. Cert. advanced profl. adminstr. and supr. Ednl. specialist, asst. prin., tchr. Balt. City Pub. Schs., prin., Mary E Rodman Elem. Sch., Balt. Trustee Trinity Presbyn. Ch., dir. children's choir. Mem. ASCD, Md. Assn. Elem. Sch. Adminstrs., Pub. Schs. Adminstrs. and Suprs. Assn, Nat.

Assn. Negro Bus. and Profl. Women (pres. Balt. chpt., Top Ladies of Distinction), Nat. Coun. Negro Women, League of Women Voters, Garrison Blvd. United Neighbors Assn. (exec. bd.), Phi Delta Kappa, Phi Delta Gamma, Delta Sigma Theta. Office: Mary E Rodman Elem Sch 3510 W Mulberry St Baltimore MD 21229-3040

JOHNSON, GARY ROBERT, political scientist; b. Shenandoah, Iowa, June 30, 1949; s. Glen Robert and Norma Jean (Otte) J.; m. Margaret Delaina Maddox, Aug. 30, 1975; children: Samuel Maddox, Katherine Elizabeth. BA, Augustana Coll., Rock Island, Ill., 1972; MA, U. Cin., 1975, PhD, 1979. Teaching asst., rsch. asst. U. Cin., 1972-78; rsch. cons. Frost & Jacobs, Attys.at Law, Cin., 1976; instr., then asst. prof. polit. sci. Lake Superior State U., Sault Ste. Marie, Mich., 1978-84, assoc. prof. polit. sci., 1984-90, head dept. social scis., 1981-89, prof. polit. sci., 1990—. Vis. lectr. Drake U., Des Moines, 1986-87; manuscript referee various jours., pubs., 1986—; mem. faculty workgroup on undergrad. instrnl. quality Gov.'s Commn. on Future of Higher Edn. in Mich., 1984. Bibliography co-editor Politics and the Life Scis. jour., 1986-91, editor, 1991-2001; contbr. articles, book revs. to profl. jours., edited books. Grantee State of Mich., 1987. Mem. Am. Polit. Sci. Assn. (panel discussant, chair 1989—, sect. program chair 1990-91), Assn. Politics and Life Sci. (exec. dir. 1996-2001, conf. chair 1998, 99, 2000), Internat. Soc. Human Ethology, Human Behavior and Evolution Soc. Avocations: genealogy, old books, racquetball. Home: 924 Johnston St Sault Sainte Marie MI 49783-3324 Office: Lake Superior State U 650 W Easterday Ave Dept Polit Sault Sainte Marie MI 49783-1643 E-mail: gjohnson@lssu.edu.

JOHNSON, HENRY L. superintendent of education; b. Tuscaloosa, Ala. married; 3 children. BS in Biology, Livingston Coll., Salisbury, N.C., 1968; MA in Tchg., U. N.C., Chapel Hill., 1975; DEd in Sch. Adminstrn., N.C. State U., 1990. Tchr. Wake County Pub. Schs., 1969—75, prin. elem. sch., 1975—78, middle sch. dir., 1979—81; asst. supt. for curriculum and instrn. Johnston County Schs., 1986—92; assoc. state supt. instruction and accountability svcs. N.C. Dept Edn., 1997—2002; supt. of edn. Miss. State Dept. Edn., 2002—. Named to Livingston Coll. Hall of Fame, 2002; recipient N.C. Disting. Alumnus award, N.C. State U., 1994, Presidl. citation, Livingstone Coll., 1999. Office: State Dept Edn PO Box 771 359 N West St Jackson MS 39205 Office Fax: 601-359-3242.

JOHNSON, HERBERT ALAN, history and law educator, lawyer, chaplain; b. Jersey City, Jan. 10, 1934; s. Harry Oliver and Magdalena Gertrude (Diemer) J.; m. Barbara Arlene (Balcerak), Sept. 24, 1955 (dec. Nov. 1980); children: Amanda Blair, Vanessa Paige.; m. Jane (McCue), June 4, 1983. AB, Columbia U., 1955, MA, 1961, PhD (Schiff fellow), 1965; LLB, N.Y. Law Sch., 1960; postgrad., Luth. Theol. So. Sem., 1981-84. Bar: N.Y. 1960; U.S. Supreme Ct. 1965; D.C. 1967; S.C. 1983; ordained vocat. deacon, 1991. Jr. clk. First Nat. City Bank of N.Y., N.Y.C., 1955; adminstrv. asst. Chase Manhattan Bank, N.Y.C., 1957—60; practiced in N.Y.C., 1960—67; rsch. asst. Papers of John Jay, Columbia U., 1961—63; lectr. Hunter Coll., N.Y.C., 1964—65, asst. prof. history, 1965—67; assoc. sem. on history of legal polit. thought Papers of John Jay, Columbia U., 1966—77; assoc. editor Papers of John Marshall, Inst. Early Am. History and Culture, Williamsburg, Va., 1967—70; assoc. sem. on early Am. history Columbia U., 1967—77; co editor Papers of John Marshall, Inst. Early Am. History and Culture, 1970—71, editor, 1971—77; prof. law and history U. S. C., Columbia, 1977—90, Ernest F. Hollings prof. constl. law, 1991—2002, disting. prof. law emeritus, 2002—. Lectr. Coll. William and Mary Williamsburg, 1967-77; Bostick vis. rsch. prof. So. studies program U. S. C., 1976, 77; mem. com. rsch., publ. Heritage '76 Com. Am. Revolution Bicentennial Commn., 1972-73; mem. bd. adjustments, appeals, Williamsburg, 1970-77; trustee Fund for Preservation of John Marshall House, 1972-74; Fund Coop. Editl. Rsch. Am. Antiquarian Soc., 1972-76; mem. profl. adv. bd. Angel Homehealth & Hospice, 2002-. Author: The Law Merchant and Negotiable Instruments in Colonial New York, 1664-1730, 1963; John Jay, 1745-1829, 1970; Imported Eighteenth Century Law Treatises in Am. Libraries 1700-1799, 1978; Essays on New York Colonial Legal History, 1981; History of Criminal Justice, 1988, 3d edit., 2002; John Jay: Colonial Lawyer, 1989; The Chief Justiceship of John Marshall, 1997; Wingless Eagle: U.S. Army Aviation Through World War I, 2001; co-author: Historical Courthouses of New York State-18th and 19th Century Halls of Justice Across the Empire State, 1977; Foundations of Power, John Marshall, 1801-15, vol. 2, History of the Supreme Court of the U.S., 1981; editor: The Papers of John Marshall, Vol. 1, 1974, Vol. II, 1977, South Carolina Legal History, 1980; Am. Legal and Constitutional History: Cases and Materials, 1994, 2d edit., 2000; gen. editor Chief Justiceships of the U.S. Supreme Court Series, 1989—; contbg. articles to profl. jour. Chaplain assoc. Bapt. Med. Ctr., Columbia, 1983-2002; hospice legal svc. vol., 1986-2000; chaplain Angel Hospice, Franklin, N.C., 2002-; mem. ethics com. S.C. Episcopal Home, Still Hopes, 1989-99; 1st lt. USAF, 1955-57; ret. col., Res. Recipient: William P. Lyons Masters' Essay Award Loyola U., 1962; Paul S. Kerr History prize N.Y. State Hist. Assn., 1970; U. S. C. Edn. Found. Rsch. Award profl. sch., 2000; Am. Council Learned Soc. Fellow, 1974-75; Inst. Humane Studies Fellow, 1981, 85; vis. fellow Centre for Comparative Constl. Studies, U. Melbourne Law Faculty, 1992; vis. rsch. scholar U. Toronto Law Faculty, 1995; vis. prof. Univ. of Birmingham, (Eng.), 1998. Mem. Am. Hist. Assn. (Littleton-Griswold com. 1976-81, interim com. Bicentennial era 1976-77), Selden Soc. (state corr. for S.C. 1988-2002), Stair Soc., Air Force Assn., Am. Law Inst., Assn. Am. Law Sch. (chmn. legal history sect. 1979), Am. Soc. Legal History (pres. 1974-75, del. Am. Coun. Learned Soc. 1977-80, bd. dirs. 1999-2001), U. South Caroliniana Soc., Res. Officers Assn., Assn. Profl. Chaplains, Nat. Eagle Scout Assn. Episcopalian. Home: 245 Laurel Falls Rd Franklin NC 28734-9527 E-mail: janeherb@dnet.net.

JOHNSON, HERMAN, secondary education educator; b. Chgo., Feb. 25, 1940; s. William and Beatrice (Beamon) J.; m. Elaine Glenn, Dec. 10, 1960; children: Pamela, Herman II, Joseph, Tessa, Verna, Ivan. BS in Edn., Chgo. State U., 1971; MA, Northeastern Ill., 1974; MEd, DePaul U., 1982. Cert. tchr. elem. 3-8, secondary 9-12, Ill. Data files clk. VA, Chgo., 1962-63; clk., carrier U.S. Post Office, Chgo., 1963-69; tchr. Chgo. Bd. Edn., 1972-95, ret., 1995. Bd. dirs. Chgo. Tchr. Ctr., 1980-85, Ill. State Tchr. Ctr., Springfield, 1982-83. Bd. dirs. Friends of Oak Park Libr., 1975; commr. Community Rels. Commn., Oak Park, 1976, N.E. Ill. Planning Commn., Chgo., 1977. With USAF, 1959-62, Korea. Recipient Outstanding Svc. award, Ill. State Bd. Edn., Springfield, 1983, Meritorious Svc. award, Chgo. Police Dept. Mem. Am. Fedn. Tchrs. (del.), Ill. Fedn. Tchrs. (del.), Chgo. Tchrs. Union (del., dist. supt. 1972—), Nat. Coun. Social Studies, Am. Legion, Alpha Phi Alpha, Phi Beta Kappa. Home: 325 Rowan Ct Naperville IL 60540-7822

JOHNSON, JAMES JOSEPH SCOFIELD, lawyer, judge, educator, author; b. Washington, Apr. 28, 1956; s. Richard Carl and Harriette (Benson) J.; m. Sherry Bekki Hall; children: Andrew Joel Schaeffer Johnson. AA with high honors, Montgomery Coll., Germantown, Md., 1980; BA with honors, Wake Forest U., 1982; JD, U. N.C., 1984; ThD with highest honors, Emmanuel Coll. Christian Studies, 1996, DASc with highest honors, 2000; PhD with highest honors, Cambridge Grad. Sch., Springdale, Ark., 1996, MSc, M of Liberal Arts, 1999. Bar: Tex. 1985, U.S. Dist. Ct. (no. dist.) Tex. 1986, U.S. Dist. Ct. (ea. dist.) Tex. 1987, U.S. Ct. Appeals (5th cir.) 1989, U.S. Dist. Ct. (we. and so. dists.) Tex. 1990, U.S. Supreme Ct. 2000; bd. cert. bus. bankruptcy law Tex. Bd. Legal Specialization, 1990, 95, 2000, Am. Bankruptcy Bd. Cert., 1992; cert. water quality monitor Tex. Natural Resource Conservation Commn., 1994-1997. Assoc. various orgns., Dallas, 1985—; pvt. practice law Dallas, 1993—. Adj. prof., master faculty LeTourneau U., Dallas, 1991—, Dallas Christian Coll., 1995—; lectr. History, Geography, Ecology, Culture, Norwegian Cruise Lines, 1998—; Bibl. langs. instr. Cross Timbers Inst., 2001—. Author: Introduction to Environmental Studies, 1995, 98, Doxological Zoology and Zoogeography, 1998, How Texas is Addressing Administrative Law Issues in School Law Contexts, 2003; sr. editl. staff N.C. Jour. Internat. Law and Comml. Regulation, 1983-84; conf. issue editor Harvard Jour. Law & Pub. Policy, 1984; contbr. articles to profl. jours. Protestant chaplain Boy Scouts Am., Goshen, Va., 1976; libr. vol. N.W. Bible Ch., Dallas, 1991-2000; cmty. program dir. Southwestern Legal Founds. Conf. on Internat. and Am. Law, 1991-92; scripture chmn. Gideons Internat., North Dallas, Tex., 1993-94. Recipient award for excellence in biblical studies and biblical langs. Am. Bible Soc., 1982. Mem. Near East Archaeology Soc., Sangre de Cristo Mountain Coun., Icelandic Geneal. Soc., Creation Rsch. Soc., Evangel. Theol. Soc., Norwegian Soc. Tex., Icelandic Soc. of Dallas, Sons of Norway (historian). Republican. Avocations: reading, writing, birding, traveling, hiking. Office: PO Box 2952 Dallas TX 75221-2952

JOHNSON, JAMES TERENCE, lawyer, educator, minister; b. Springfield, Mo., Oct. 25, 1942; s. Clifford Lester and Margaret Jeanne (Wallace) Johnson; m. Martha Susan Mitchell, May 2, 1964; children: Jennifer Jeanne, Emily Jill. BA, Okla. Christian Coll., 1964; JD, So. Meth. U., 1967; LLD (hon.), Pepperdine U., 1980. Min., Okla., Tex., 1961—; staff counsel, asst. prof. Okla. Christian Coll., Oklahoma City, 1968-72; pvt. practice Oklahoma City, 1969—; v.p. Okla. Christian U., 1972-73, exec. v.p., 1973-74, pres., 1974-95, chancellor, 1995—2000. Co-founder Enterprise Sq., 1982, Cascade Coll., 1993. Named to Okla. Higher Edn. Hall of Fame, 2000. Mem.: Okla. Bar Assn., Phi Delta Theta.

JOHNSON, JAMIESON DREGALLO, women's athletics director; b. June 24, 1951; d. Frank and Phyllis Arlene (Griffiths) Dregallo; m. Stephen B. Johnson; children: Lindsay Benedict, Christopher Sheldon. BA with honors, Lindenwood Coll., St. Charles, Mo., 1973; M Sport Sci., U.S. Sports Acad., Mobile, Ala., 1987. Cert. life K-12 health and phys. edn. tchr., Mo. Tchr. phys. edn. Berkeley Sch. Dist., St. Louis, 1973-77; asst. to headmaster for girls activities Casady Sch., Oklahoma City, 1977-81; dir. women's sports Tex. Mil. Acad., San Antonio, 1981-82; varsity coach, dormitory head Berkshire Sch., Sheffield, Mass., 1982-86; dir. fitness Danbury Health Racquetball Club, Bethel, Conn., 1987-88; dir. women's athletics Greens Farms (Conn.) Acad., 1988—. Personal trainer, Greens Farms, 1987— Named Outstanding Coll. Athlete Am., 1973. Mem. Am. Coll. Sports Medicine (cert. health & fitness instr.), Am. Coun. Exercise, Fairchester Athletic Assn. (sec., treas. 1992-97, pres. 1997—). Episcopalian. Avocations: tennis, (mem. USTA tennis team/radnked #5 in New Eng. in 1994), collecting antiques, squash. Office: Greens Farms Acad 35 Beachside Ave Greens Farms CT 06436 Home: PO Box 847 Middlebury CT 06762-0847

JOHNSON, JEANNETTE SELBY, vocational education educator; b. Warren, Ohio, July 20, 1950; d. William Edward and Agnes (Newell) Selby; m. Dan Frederick Johnson, Mar. 16, 1974; children: Shelley, Robyn, Kimberly. BS in Home Econs., Ohio State U., 1972, MA in Edn., 1974; AAS, Hocking Coll. Cert. tchr., Ohio; RN, Ohio. Student pers. asst. Ohio State U., Columbus, 1972-74; home economist Children's Hosp., Columbus, 1976-80; instr. Sch. Home Econs. Ohio U., Athens, 1987-89, vis. prof. Sch. Theater, 1989; substitute tchr. Athens City Schs., 1989; adult instr. family life edn. Tri-County Vocat. Sch., Nelsonville, Ohio, 1989-92, adult instr. displaced homemakers, 1993-94; tchr. home econs. Trimble Mid. Sch., Glouster, Ohio, 1992-93; adult instr. On My Own Tri-County Vocat. Sch., Nelsonville, Ohio, 1994—; cmty. health nurse coord. childhood immunization and post partem program Ohio U. Coll. Osteopathic Medicine, Athens, 1997—. Dir. day camp Girl Scouts U.S., Athens, 1990-91; instr. aerobics YWCA, Columbus, 1978-80; mem. Ohio Studen Aid Commn. S.E. adv. com., 1995. Leader 4-H Clubs Am., Columbus, 1978-79; v.p. Dennison Pl. Community Orgn., Columbus, 1978-84; co-chair Residents for Community Revitalization, Columbus, 1983; tchr. Sunday sch. 1st Presbyn. Ch., Athens, 1989-94. Recipient award of recognition Pres.'s Com. on Employment of Handicapped, 1972, Outstanding Leader award Girl Scouts U.S., 1990. Mem. Ohio State U. Alumni Assn. Avocations: reading, camping, piano, bicycling, sewing. Home: 10 Marietta Ave Athens OH 45701-1815

JOHNSON, JEROME LINNÉ, cardiologist, educator; b. Rockford, Ill., June 19, 1929; s. Thomas Arthur and Myrtle Elizabeth (Swanson) J.; m. Molly Ann Rideout, June 27, 1953; children: Susan R. Johnson, William Rideout. BA, U. Chgo., 1951; BS, Northwestern U., 1952, MD, 1955. Diplomate Nat. Bd. Med. Examiners. Intern U. Chgo. Clinics, 1955-56; resident Northwestern U., Chgo., 1958-61; chief resident Chgo. Wesley Meml. Hosp., 1960-61; mem., v.p. Hauch Med. Clinic, Pomona, Calif., 1961-88; pvt. practice cardiology and internal medicine Pomona, 1988—. Clin. assoc. prof. medicine, U. So. Calif., L.A., 1961—; mem. staff Pomona Valley Hosp. Med. Ctr., chmn. coronary care com. 1967-77; mem. staff L.A. County Hosp. Citizen ambassador, People to People; mem. Town Hall of Calif., L.A. World Affairs Coun. Lt. USNR, 1956-58; bd. dirs. Claremont chpt. ARC, 1993-2000; bd. dirs., health com. Mt. San Antonio Gardens Retirement Home, 1993-2000. Fellow Am. Coll. Cardiology, Am. Geriatrics Soc., Royal Soc. Health; mem. Galileo Soc., Am. Heart Assn. (bd. dirs. L.A. County div. 1967-84, San Gabriel div. 1963-89), Am. Soc. Internal Medicine, Inland Soc. Internal Medicine, Pomona Host Lions. Avocations: photography, swimming, bicycling, medical and surgical antiques, travel. Home: 648 Delaware Dr Claremont CA 91711-3457

JOHNSON, JERRY DOUGLAS, biology educator; b. Salina, Kans., Sept. 1, 1947; s. Maynard Eugene and Norma Maude (Moss) J.; m. Kathryn Ann Johnson, May 12, 1973; children: George Walker, Brett Arthur. BS in Zoology, Fort Hays State U., 1972; MS in Biology, U. Tex., El Paso, 1975; PhD in Wildlife Sci., Tex. A&M U., 1984. Teaching asst. biology dept. U. Tex., El Paso, 1973—75; instr. biology El Paso C.C., 1975—2000, Piper prof., 1989—90; prof. biol. scis. U. Tex., El Paso, 2000—; dir. Indio Mountains Rsch. Station, 2000—. Councilor bd. scientists Chihuahuan Desert Rsch. Inst., Alpine, Tex., 1991—. Co-author: Middle American Herpetology, 1988; editor: Meso Am. Herpetology, 2001; contbr. articles to profl. jours. Bd. dirs. Meml. Park Improvement Assn., 1987—, El Paso Coun. for Internat. Visitors, 1988—, v.p., 1996, Parks and Recreation Bd., El Paso, 1991-94. Recipient El Paso Natural Gas Faculty Achievement award, 1995—96, Nat. Inst. Staff and Orgnl. Devel. Tchg. Excellence award, 1995—96, EPCC Honors Program Outstanding Honors Faculty award, 1998—99; grantee, Sigma Xi, 1974, Theodore Roosevelt Found. Am. Mus. Natural History, 1979, Exline Corp., 1980, NSF, 1992—95, 2001—, NIH, 1992—2000, Tex. Pks. and Wildlife Dept., 1998—2000. Mem. NSF, Nat. Ctr. for Acad. Achievement, Nat. Inst. Gen. Med. Sci., Soc. for Study of Amphibians and Reptiles (elector 1980, assoc. editor Geog. Distbn. Herpetol. Rev. 1993—), Southwestern Assn. Naturalists (assoc. editor 1977-85, bd. govs. 1985-89), Tex. Herpetol. Soc. (v.p., pres. 1995-96), El Paso Herpetol. Soc. (pres. 1993-95), Herpetologists League, others. Home: 3147 Wheeling Ave El Paso TX 79930-4321 Office: U Tex Dept Biol Scis El Paso TX 79968-0001 E-mail: jjohnson@utep.edu.

JOHNSON, JOHN PATRICK, neurosurgeon, educator; b. Great Falls, Mont., Apr. 16, 1956; s. Alexander Charles and Jane (Koepper) J.; m. Nancy Tripp, Oct. 11, 1993; 1 child, Alexander Charles. BS, The Citadel, 1978; MD, Oreg. Health Scis. U., 1981, MD, 1986. Intern in surgery UCLA Med. Ctr., 1986-87, resident in neurosurgery, 1987-92; fellow Nat. Hosp. Neurology and Neurosurgery, Queen Square, Eng., 1991, Spine fellow dept. neurosurgery, 1992; staff neurosurgeon Harbor/UCLA Med. Ctr., Torrance, Calif., 1992—, Wadsworth VA Med. Ctr., L.A., 1992—; chief adminstrv. and clin. affairs divsn. neurosurgery Olive View/UCLA Med. Ctr., Sylmar, Calif., 1993-97; co-dir. UCLA Comprehensive Spine Ctr., L.A., 1994—; dir. UCLA Spinal Neurosurgery Fellowship Program, L.A., 1995—; co-dir. UCLA Ctr. Autonomic Disorders, L.A., 1996—. Asst. prof. divsn. neurosurgery UCLA Sch. Medicine, L.A., 1993—; tech. cons. Depuy-Motech, Wabash, Ind., 1996. Contbr. articles to profl. jours. Rsch. grantee UCLA Acad. Senate Grant, L.A., 1994-95, 95-96, Radionics, Inc., Burlington, Mass., 1996—; rsch. fellow N.Am. Spine Soc., 1994-95. Mem. AMA, ACS, Am. Assn. Neurol. Surgeons, N.Am. Spine Soc., Congress Neurol. Surgeons, Calif. Assn. Neurol. Surgeons. Avocations: skiing, hunting, fishing, family ranch business, traveling.

JOHNSON, JUDITH ANN, special education educator; b. Peoria, Ill., Aug. 14, 1939; d. Fred Joseph and Bernadine Mary (Bucklar) Hadank; m. Herbert Brooks Johnson, June 10, 1961; children: Nancy Sharon, Linda, Susan, Julie, Ann, Kathleen. BA, Marycrest (Iowa) Coll., 1960; M in Spl. Edn., Ill. State U., 1988. Tchr. 4th grade Kellar Grade Sch., Peoria, 1960-61; tchr. 3d grade McKinley Sch. Dist. 150, Peoria, 1961-63; homebound tutor Dist. 150, Peoria, 1977-85; tchr. 1st grade Bo Peep Nursery Sch., Peoria, 1985-87; tchr. Brimfield (Ill.) Grade SCh., 1987-90, Dunlap (Ill.) Grade Sch., 1990—99; supr. student tchrs. U. Wisconsin, Whitewater, 1999—. Cons. Regional Supt. of Schs., Peoria, 1984-86; tchr., dir. Bo Peep Nursery Sch., Peoria, 1980-85; chairperson primary com. St. Vincent de Paul Sch., Peoria, 1985-87. Mem. Christian Environment Com., Peoria, 1988—, 90-99; Sunday sch. tchr. St. Vincent de Paul Sch., Peoria, 1972-79, coord. picture lady program, 1972-75; bd. dirs. parent club Bergan High Sch., Peoria, 1983-85. Mem. Coun. Excptional Children (chmn. membership com. 1988-89, pres. 1989-90, past pres. 1990-92), Kappa Delta Pi, Phi Delta Kappa. Roman Catholic. Avocations: sailing, swimming, biking, sewing.

JOHNSON, JUDY DIANNE, elementary education educator; b. Houston, Oct. 1, 1947; d. Thomas Hunter and Roxie Pauline (Swink) Mitchell; m. Dennis Carlton Johnson, June 4, 1971; children: Juli Lyn, Jill Nicole. BS, U. Houston, 1969; MEd, Stephen F. Austin U., 1981. Cert. supr., tchr., Tex. Elem. tchr. Humble (Tex.) Independent Sch. Dist., 1969-92, Katy Ind. Sch. Dist., Tex., 1992—. Mem. Assn. Tex. Profl. Educators, Katy Profl. Educators, Coun. for Advancement of Math. Teaching, Asns. for Supervision and Curriculum Devel., Tex. Coun. Tchrs. Math. Baptist. Avocation: reading. Office: Bear Creek Elem Sch 4815 Hickory Downs Dr Houston TX 77084-3654

JOHNSON, KAREN, legislation and congressional affairs secretary; BA comm., Appalachian State Univ., NC. Asst. Conv. Mgr. for Pub. Liaison Rep. Nat. Conv., 2000; instr. of Polit. comm. and Pub. Rels. Internat. Rep. Inst.; asst. sec. of edn. for legis. and congl. affairs U.S. Dept. Edn., Washington, 2003—; v.p. of Soc. Mark. and Pub. Affairs Porter Novelli. Fellow: Univ. of Pa. Annenberg Sch. for Comm. She also traveled to China and Hong Kong to serve as a delegate for the Am. Coun. of Young Polit. Leaders. Office: Dept of Ed 400 Maryland Ave SW Rm 7E307 Washington DC 20202*

JOHNSON, KAREN ELAINE, secondary school educator, tax specialist; b. San Diego, Calif., Feb. 7, 1957; d. Alan Jerome and Clarex Irene Johnson. AA, Mesa Coll., San Diego, 1978; BA, San Diego State U., 1981; MA, Calif. State U, San Bernardino, 1985; MS, Nat. U., Vista, Calif., 1993. Cert. Ryan Single Subject Teaching Credential 1981, Reading Specialist Credential 1985, Administrative Services Credential 1992. Tchr. William S. Hart Union HS Dist., Newhall, Calif., 1982; tchr. San Jacinto (Calif.) Unified Sch. Dist., 1982—85, Grossmont Union HS Dist., La Mesa, Calif., 1985—86, Oceanside Unified Sch. Dist., Oceanside, Calif., 1986—; tax preparer H & R Block, Encinitas, Calif., 1996—2001. Member Oceanside Unified Sch. Dist. Strategic Plan Com., 1996—; dept. chair-8th Grade Language Arts/Social Studies Oceanside Unified Sch. Dist., 1989—99. Mem.: AAUW (bd. dirs Carlsbad, Calif. 1992—2001, legal advocacy v.p. 2000—, bd. dirs Carlsbad, Calif. 2002—, named Gift Honoree 1993, 1996, 1999), Delta Kappa Gamma (recording sec. Carlsbad chpt. 1993—95, 1997—99, corr. sec. 2000—). Avocations: crocheting, knitting, music, reading. Home: 2651 Regent Rd Carlsbad CA 92008-6413 Office: Oceanside Unified Sch Dist 2111 Mission Ave Oceanside CA 92054 Personal E-mail: bigbodaciousbabe@yahoo.com.

JOHNSON, KATHY VIRGINIA LOCKHART, art educator; b. Aberdeen, Miss., May 5, 1951; d. Clovis Clinton and Marium Kathleen (Bowen) Lockhart; m. Gary Wayne Johnson, Aug. 5, 1973; 1 child, Daniel Clinton. BFA, Miss. U. Women, 1973; postgrad., U. Ala., 1973—92. Cert. tchr. Ala. Inventory clk. Johnson Showroom, Columbus, Miss., 1970—73; student tchr. Amory Mid. Sch., Amory, 1973; tchr. art Huntsville Art League, Huntsville, 1974, 1983—84, Evangel Sch., 1974—75, 1st Christian Early Childhood, 1984—88, Huntsville Mus. Art, 1990, Huntsville City Schs., 1989—. One-woman shows include, 1974, Tchr. Show Youth Art Month, 1994, Ann. NASA Picnic, 1998. Mem.: Huntsville Edn. Assn., Ala. Edn. Assn., Nat. Art Edn. Assn., Alpha Delta Kappa (bd. dirs. 1999—, pres. 1996—, sec. 1999—2002). Mem. Christian Ch. (Disciples Of Christ). Avocations: painting, gardening, football. Home: 122 Regent Ctr Madison AL 35758

JOHNSON, KEVIN RAYMOND, law educator; b. Culver City, Calif., June 29, 1958; s. Kenneth R. Johnson and Angela J. (Gallardo) McEachron; m. Virginia Salazar, Oct. 17, 1987; children: Teresa, Tomás, Elena. AB in Econs. with great distinction, U. Calif., 1980; JD magna cum laude, Harvard U., 1983. Bar: Calif. 1985, U.S. Dist. Ct. (no., ea. and so. dists.) Calif. 1985, U.S. Ct. Appeals (9th cir.) 1985, U.S. Supreme Ct. 1991. From rsch. asst. to Charles Haar prof. Harvard U., Cambridge, Mass., 1982-83, instr. legal writing, 1982; law clk. to Hon. Stephen Reinhardt, U.S. Ct. Appeals (9th cir.), L.A., 1983-84; atty. Heller Ehrman White & McAuliffe, San Francisco, 1984-89; acting prof. law U. Calif., Davis, 1989-92, prof., 1992—, prof. Chicano studies, 2000—, assoc. dean acad. affairs, 1998—, dir. Chicano studies program, 2000—01. Instr. civil procedure, complex litig., immigration law, refugee law, acting dir. clin. legal edn., 1992; instr. Latinos and Latines and the law, 2001; instr. critical race theory, 03; mem. legal del., El Salvador, 1987. Author: (book) How Did You Get To Be Mexican? A White/Brown Man's Search for Identity, 1999, Race, Civil Rights, and the Law: A Multiracial Approach, 2001, Mixed Race America and the Law: A Reader, 2002; editor: Harvard Law Rev., 1981—83; contbr. articles to profl. jours. Bd. dirs. Legal Svcs. No. Calif., 1996—, mem. exec. com., 1997—, v.p., 2001—03, pres., 2003—; bd. dirs. Yolo County ACLU, 1990—93, chmn. legal com., 1991—93; magistrate merit selection panel U.S. Dist. Ct. (ea. dist.) Calif.; vol. Legal Svcs. Program, San Francisco, Sacramento; mem. Lawyers Com. Civil Rights San Francisco Bay Area, 1991—; various pro bono activities. Recipient commendation, Calif. State Bar, 1985—90, Chancellor's Cmty. and Diversity award, 2001. Mem.: ABA (mem. coordinators com. immigration 1998—), Calif. Bar Assn. (mem. standing com. legal svcs. for poor 1992—94, mem. gov. com. continuing edn. bar 1993—98, mem. minority affairs com., mem. law sch. admission coun. 1999—2001), U. Calif. Alumni Assn. (class sec. Class of 1980), Phi Beta Kappa. Democrat. Roman Catholic. Office: U Calif Sch Law King Hall Davis CA 95617

JOHNSON, KIRSTEN DENISE, elementary education educator; b. L.A., Sept. 21, 1968; d. Daniel Webster Johnson and Marinella Venesia (Ishem) Johnson Miller; 1 child, Khari Malik Manning-Johnson. BBA in Ins., Howard U., 1990; student, Southwestern Sch. Law, L.A., 1991-92, Calif. State U., Dominguez Hills, 1994-97. Asst. Ctr. for Ins. Edn. Howard U., Washington, 1988-89; intern Cigna Ins. Co., L.A., 1989; agt. asst. McLaughlin Co., Washington, 1989-90; legal sec. Harris & Baird, L.A., 1990-92; legal asst. Hamrick & Garrotto, L.A., 1992-94; tchr. 5th grade L.A. Unified Sch. Dist., 1993—; intern Travelers Cos., 1987—. Free-lance writer Calif. Mus. Sci., L.A., 1994—; workshop presenter in field. Participant UCLA/CSP Sci. Project; tutor Delinquent Teenage Group Home Residents, 1998—. Nat. Dean;s List, 1987, 88, All Am. scholar, 1989, John

Schumacher scholar, 1991, Martin Luther King Jr. scholar, 1996. Mem. NEA (RA del.), UTLA (mem. ho. of reps.), CTA, Internat. Soc. Poets. Democrat. Avocations: reading, traveling, movies, weight lifting.

JOHNSON, LAVERNE ST. CLAIR, retired elementary school educator; b. Danville, Va. d. Emanuel Linwood and Lula St. Clair (Yarbrough) White; m. Cornell A. Johnson, Apr. 10, 1955 (div. Apr. 1982); children: Cassandra St. Clair, LeBrahne Cornell. Student, Howard U., 1950-55, Allen U., 1955; BA, Queens Coll., 1977, MA, 1986. Cert. and lic. in reading edn., common br., N.Y. Asst. tchr. 1st Hebrew Day Nursery, Bklyn., 1967-75; tchr. United Youth Action Day Care, Bklyn., 1977-80, Charles R. Drew Day Care Ctr., Queens Village, N.Y., 1980-83, N.Y.C. Bd. Edn., Bklyn., 1983-95; ret., 1995. Composer childrens' music; author: (childrens' poems) Fall Time Fall Time, 1974. Mem. Com. to Eliminate Media Offensive to African People, St. Albans, N.Y., 1988—, Dem. Club, St. Albans, Bklyn. Philharmonic Chorus, St. Albans Congl. Ch. choir, Howard U. Choir, Carr-Hill Singers, Cambria Heights Civic Assn., other choral groups. Mem. United Fedn. Tchrs. Howard U. Alumni Club (sec. L.I. chpt. 1970-79), Lioness (v.p. Cambria Heights, N.Y. 1980-82, cert. of appreciation 1980-89). Avocations: musical composition, poetry, aerobics, church activities, community groups.

JOHNSON, LESLIE DIANE HORVATH, artist, graphic designer, small business owner, educator; b. Trenton, N.J., Sept. 10, 1951; d. Lester Walter and M. Lee (Green) Horvath; m. Douglas James Johnson, Sep. 1, 1973. BA in Art Edn., Ohio State U., 1973. Graphic artist, tchr. various orgns., 1973-84; owner Southwind Studios, Forest, Va., 1981—2001, Art Bus. Acad., Raleigh, NC, 2002—. Lectr. Liberty U., Forest Pub. Schs., Lynchburg Pub. Schs., Heritage Bapt. Ch., Lynchburg Art Club, En Plein Air Art and Discovery, others. One woman shows include The Framery, Lynchburg, Va., 1987, Lychburg Art Club, 1990, Lynchburg Area Art Show, 1991, Gallery 3, Roanoke, Va., 1989, 92, McClendon Fine Art, Washington, 1993, Sakias, Lynchburg, 1996, Warm Springs (Va.) Gallery, 1997, Art on a Mission, Roanoke, 2001, The Little Gallery, Moneta, Va., 1995, 2000, 03; group shows include Lynchburg Area Art Show, 1985, 89, Gallery 3, Roanoke, 1992-94, Maymont Found., Richmond, Va., 1994, Art Alliance of Fla., 2002, The Little Gallery, Moneta, 1987-2002; Illus.: If I Had Long, Long Hair, 1986 (award 1987); artist pastel and acrylic paintings, 1985—. Recipient George Innes Jr. Meml. award for best pastel The Salmagundi Club, N.Y.C., 1991. Mem. Nat. Assn. Fine Artists, Pastel Soc. of Am., Nat. Acad. Profl. Plein Air Painters, Nat. Acrylic Painters Assn. (U.K.), Plein Air Fla. Home and Office: 404 Kellyridge Dr Apex NC 27502-9639

JOHNSON, LONNIE, special education educator; b. Atoka, Okla., Feb. 28, 1934; s. Della (Wright) J.; m. Grace Malone, Dec. 26, 1962; children: Donna Renee, Lonnie Jr. BA in Polit. Sci., Northeastern U., Tahlequah, Okla., 1965; D Religion, Jackson Sem., North Little Roc, Ark., 1970; MA in Teaching, Oklahoma City U., 1983; LittD (hon.), Immaculate Conception Sem., Troy, N.Y., 1971. Cert. spl. edn. and polit. sci. tchr., Okla.; ordained to ministry A.M.E. Ch., 1958. Commr. City of Sapulpa, Okla., 1958-60; social worker Dept. Pub. Welfare, Tulsa, 1960-62; tchr. Kansas City (Mo.) Pub. Schs., 1962-65; counselor, dir. Neighborhood Youth Corp., Lawton, Okla., 1965-70; pres. Shorter Coll., North Little Rock, 1970-72; officer-in-charge USDA, Oklahoma City, 1972-78; pastor Allen Chapel A.M.E. Ch., Oklahoma City, 1978-81; tchr. spl. edn. Capital Hill High Sch., Oklahoma City, 1981—. Cons. Govt. of Lesotho, Maseru, 1980—, A.M.E. Ch. in Haiti, 1981—. Founder World Hunger Orgn., 1978; cons. Walters for Gov., Oklahoma City, 1990. With USAF, 1955-56. Mem. Coun. for Exceptional Children, Am. Fedn. Tchrs., Alpha Phi Alpha (life). Democrat. Avocation: gardening. Home: 6209 SE 57th St Oklahoma City OK 73135-5401

JOHNSON, LUCILLE MERLE BROWN, elementary school principal; b. Brown's Town, St. Ann, Jamaica, Nov. 5, 1936; came to U.S., 1970; d. Ezekiel and Christina (Hawthorne) Brown; m. Carl Wesley Johnson, Oct. 26, 1958 (div. 1974); children: Carl Anthony, Michael Ian. BE, Bethlehem Coll., 1957; MEd, Nat. Coll. Edn., 1976, cert. advanced study, 1980; EdD, Clayton U., 1990. Cert. elem. tchr., Ill. Div. head St. Ann Schs., Jamaica, 1968-69; reading facilitator Sch. Dist. #64, North Chicago, Ill., 1973-76, coordinator tchr. inservice, 1976-80, prin., 1980—; supr. Dist. 187 Yeager Elem. Sch., North Chicago, 1980-92; prin. Dist. 187 Neal Sch., North Chicago, 1992. Mem. North Chicago I-SEARCH; sec. Lake County Community Service League, Waukegan/North Chicago, Ill., 1985-88; trustee North Chicago Pub. Library; bd. mem. Big Brother/Big Sister of Lake County, North Chicago Ctr. of Cultural Art; dir. I Have a Dream Program, High Sch. Students, Lake Forest, 1993. Mem. Nat. Assn. Elem. Sch. Princs., Nat. Alliance Black Sch. Educators, Lake County Alliance Black Sch. Educators (sec.). Avocations: bowling, dancing, travel, reading. Office: Neal Elem Sch Argonne And Lewis Ave North Chicago IL 60064

JOHNSON, MARIAN ILENE, education educator; b. Hawarden, Iowa, Oct. 3, 1929; d. Henry Richard and Wilhelmina Anna (Schmidt) Stoltenberg; m. Paul Irving Jones, June 14, 1958 (dec. Feb. 1985); m. William Andrew Johnson, Oct. 3, 1991. BA, U. La Verne, 1959; MA, Claremont Grad. Sch., 1962; PhD, Ariz. State U., 1971. Cert. tchr., Iowa, Calif. Elem. tchr. Cherokee (Iowa) Sch. Dist., 1949-52, Sioux City (Iowa) Sch. Dist., 1952-56, Ontario (Calif.) Pub. Schs., 1956-61, Reed Union Sch. Dist., Belvedere-Tiburon, Calif., 1962-65, Columbia (Calif.) Union Sch. Dist., 1965-68; prof. edn. Calif. State U., Chico, 1972-91. Avocation: travel. Home: 26437 S Lakewood Dr Sun Lakes AZ 85248-7246

JOHNSON, MARJORIE R. special education educator; b. Boston, Jan. 3, 1929; d. Irving Benjamin and Florence Emma (Alling) Akerson; m. Richard Johnson, May 19, 1951; children: William Benjamin, Gerald Dennis, Peter Charles. BS in Occupational Therapy, Columbia U., N.Y.C., 1951. Cert. tchr. spl. edn., primary edn. and occupational therapy, Pa. Occupational therapist ABC Children's Clinic, Reading, Pa., 1951-52; clerk Kaiser Metal Co., Bristol, Pa., 1952-54; spl. edn. tchr. Chester Co. Intermediate Unit, Coatesville, Pa., 1964-91; ret., 1991. Union v.p. CCIU branch PSEA, 1964, pres. 1965. Active in establishing group homes ARC, Chester County, 1973. Mem. Soc. Pa. Archaeology (sec. 1984-86, v.p. 1996-99). Avocations: archaeology, thread arts. Home: 40 Forrest Rd Honey Brook PA 19344-1731

JOHNSON, MARK PAUL, obstetrics and gynecology educator, geneticist; b. Fargo, N.D., Sept. 28, 1953; s. Milton Leslie Johnson and Jean Nora (Edhlund) McNeil; m. Christine Marie Jerpbak, May 5, 1984; children: Jennifer, Erik, Rolf. BA in Biology magna cum laude, Concordia Coll., Moorhead, Minn., 1976; MS in Med. Genetics, U. Minn., 1980, MD, 1984. Diplomate Am. Bd. Ob-Gyn., Am. Bd. Med. Genetics. Grad. rsch. fellow dept. lab. medicine and pathology U. Minn. Med. Ctr., Mpls., 1979-80; resident in ob-gyn. U. Mich. Med. Ctr., Ann Arbor, 1984-88; fellow in med. genetics, clin. instr. ob-gyn. Wayne State U. Sch. Medicine, Detroit, 1988-90, clin. instr. dept. molecular biology and genetics, 1988-90, asst. prof. ob-gyn., molecular medicine-genetics, pathology, 1990-96, assoc. prof. ob-gyn., molecular medicine-genetics, pathology, 1997-98, assoc. dir. div. reproductive genetics, 1990-98, assoc. dir. Ctr. for Fetal Diagnosis and Therapy, 1990-98, assoc. dir. grad. program in genetic counseling, 1996-98; assoc. prof. ob-gyn. and surgery U. Pa., Phila., 1998—; dir. obstetrics svcs., divsn. fetal surgery Children's Hosp., Phila., 1998—. Vis. asst. prof. ob-gyn. Med. Coll. Ohio, Toledo, 1991-93; numerous presentations, condr. workshops in field. Editor: (with others) Maternal Genetic Disease, 1995, Invasive Outpatient Procedures in Reproductive Medicine, 1996; mem. editl. bd. Fetal Diagnosis and Therapy, 1991—; contbr. numerous articles, abstracts and revs. to med. jours., chpts. to books. Recipient Bronze Beeper award Galens Med. Soc., 1987, 1st place award for outstanding rsch. paper Wayne State U.-Hutzel Hosp., 1990, Faculty Achievement award Alpha Omega Alpha, 1998; grantee March of Dimes Birth Defects Found., 1991, Nat. Inst. Child Health and Human Devel., 1994-97. Fellow ACOG (1st place award for outstanding rsch. paper 1990), Am. Coll. Med. Genetics (founding); mem. AMA, Am. Soc. Human Genetics, Internat. Fetal Medicine and Surgery Soc. (pres. 1997), Soc. Maternal-Fetal Medicine, Ctrl. Assn. Obstetricians and Gynecologists, Mich. Med. Soc. (med. ethics com. 1995), Wayne County Med. Soc. (med. ethics com. 1993-98), Sigma Xi, Alpha Omega Alpha. Avocations: sailing, fly fishing, classic cars. Office: Pediatric Gen and Thoracic Surgery Childrens Hosp of Phila 34th and Civic Ctr Blvd Philadelphia PA 19104

JOHNSON, MARKES ERIC, geology educator; b. Cedar Rapids, Iowa, Dec. 30, 1948; s. Clifford O. and Agnes M. (Carey) J.; m. Martha J. Riley, Aug. 12, 1972 (div.); m. Gudveig Baarli, Mar. 16, 1984; 1 child, Erlend M. BA, U. Iowa, 1971; PhD, U. Chgo., 1977. Asst. prof. Williams Coll., Williamstown, Mass., 1977-84, assoc. prof., 1984-89, prof. dept. geosci., 1989—, chmn. dept., 1996—2000. Chmn. Subcommn. on Silurian Stratigraphy, 1992-2000. Author: Discovering the Geology of Baja California-Six Hikes on the Southern Gulf Coast, 2002; editor, author: (rsch. vol. 318) Geological Society of America Special Papers, 1997, (rsch. vol. 491) N.Y. State Mus., 1998. Achievements include development of global sea-level curve for Silurian Period; studies on the rocky-shore ecosystem through geologic time. Home: 758 N Hoosac Rd Williamstown MA 01267-2323 Office: Williams Coll Dept Geoscis 947 Main St Williamstown MA 01267-2606

JOHNSON, MARLYS MARLENE, elementary school educator; b. Omak, Wash., Mar. 13, 1946; d. Beverly Wayne and Mary Etta (Greene) McGrath; m. Gary Vaughn Johnson, Aug. 13, 1967 (div. June 3, 2001); children: Chad, Shane, Aubrey. BS in Edn., Wash. State U., 1967, MEd, 1991. Cert. profl. educator Wash., tchr. Va. Substitute tchr. Pullman (Wash.) Sch. Dist., 1970—80, home hosp. tutor, 1973—77, tchr. 2d grade, 1980—2001; tchr. 5th grade Alexandria (Va.) City Pub. Schs., 2001—02, tchr. 1st grade, 2002—03, tchr. 3d grade, 2003—. Pres. Profl. Edn. Adv. Bd. Office Supt. Pub. Instrn. and Wash. State U., Olympia and Pullman, 2000; tchr. leader Curriculum Instrn. Leadership Coun., Pullman, 1996—2001; presenter in field. Contbr. articles to profl. jours. Host family chair Wash. State Jr. Miss, Pullman, 1998—2001; awards chairperson Pullman Swim Club; mother advisor Rainbow for Girls; mem. scholarship com. 4-H. Recipient Christa McAuliffe Excellence in Edn. award, State of Wash./OSPI, 1990; grantee Contextual Tchg. grantee, U.S. Dept. Edn., 1999—2001, Rsch. Tech. grantee, RMC Rsch. Corp., Pullman, 1999—2000. Mem.: Wash. Edn. Assn. (rep. assembly del.), Pullman Edn. Assn. (exec. sec.), Phi Kappa Phi. Methodist. Home: 1501 N Highview Ln #110 Alexandria VA 22311

JOHNSON, MARY ANN, vocational school owner; b. Chgo., June 26, 1956; d. Truly and Pearlie Mae (Bell) J.; children: Pamela Ann, Russell Alan Jr. AA, Joliet (Ill.) Jr. Coll., 1990; student mgmt. info. systems, Governor State U. Student intern Argonne (Ill.) Nat. Lab., 1972-79; owner, pres. Tech. Soft Svcs., Chgo., 1991—. Lectr., condr. seminars on running small bus. Author: Running a Small Business, 1996. Avocations: self-defense, computer and software edn. Office: Tech Soft Svcs 160 E Illinois St Ste 603 Chicago IL 60611-3859

JOHNSON, MARY BETTINA BLACK, physical education educator, athletic trainer; b. Salt Lake City, Mar. 2, 1952; d. Wayne Lythgoe and Bettina Loewen (Rothrock) Black; m. Carl Lowell Johnson, July 26, 1974; children: Robert Wayne Rā, Wyatt Lowell Giuseppi, Dylan Parnell Giovanni. BS, U. Utah, 1974, MS, 1984, PhD, 1990. Cert. tchr., Utah. Phys. edn. tchr. Mt. Jordan Jr. High Sch., Sandy, Utah, 1974-78, Alta High Sch., Sandy, Utah, 1978-84; adj. faculty U. Utah, Salt Lake City, 1986-89; assoc. athletic trainer U.S. Olympic Com., Colorado Springs, Colo., 1986; athletic trainer Salt Lake Sports Medicine, 1987-89; grad. asst. athletic trainer U. Utah Athletics, Salt Lake City, 1985-89; asst. prof. athletic tng./pre-phys. therapy San Diego State U., 1989-93; assoc. prof., dir. athletic tng. dept. human performance Met. State Coll. Denver, from 1993. Presenter in field. Mem. editl. bd. Jour. Athletic Tng.; contbr. articles to profl. jours. Named one of Outstanding Young Women of Am., 1979; Affirmative Action grantee, Rsch. scholar and Creative Arts grantee San Diego State Univ. Mem. AAHPERD, Nat. Athletic Trainers Assn. (cert., grad. student scholarship 1984, membership rsch. grant 1991), Far West Athletic Trainers Assn., Rocky Mountain Athletic Trainers Assn., Colo. Athletic Trainers Assn., Calif. Athletic Trainers Assn., Utah Athletic Trainers Assn. Democrat. Home: Golden, Colo. Died Dec. 29, 2001.

JOHNSON, MARY ELIZABETH, music educator, pianist; b. Tyler, Tex., Mar. 29, 1933; d. Robert Edward and Mamie Oberia (Walters) Spaulding; m. George Devereaux Johnson, Mar. 31, 1955; children: Bradford D., Robin Elizabeth. BFA, So. Methodist U., 1955; pvt. study with Bomar Cramer, Dallas, 1964-69. Music tchr. Dallas Country Day Sch., 1955; tchr. Dayton (Ohio) pub. schs., 1956-57; pvt. tchr. piano Dallas, 1962—; profl. accompanist, 1965—; duo-pianist, 1965—; sponsor-tchr. creative and performing arts program Dallas Ind. Sch. Dist., 1981-82, 83, 84. Sponsor Jr. Melodie and Jr. Harmonie. Mem. Northwest Bible Ch. Dallas, 3-score com. N.W. Bible Ch. Named to Hall of Fame, Am. Coll. Musicians, 1981. Mem. Nat. Guild Piano Tchrs. (cert., named to honor roll 1971), Tex. Fedn. Music Clubs (historian 1974-76, state chmn. music svc. in the community 1971-73, dist. jr. counselor 1971-78, dist. chmn. music svc. in the community 1971-78; rec. sec. 5th dist. 1975-76, 1st v.p. 1977-78, jr. festival chmn. 1977-80, dist chmn. Jr. Gold Cup awards 1980, 84, 85, 86, 87, 88, asst. chmn. North Dallas div. 5th dist. jr. festival 1981-82), Music Tchrs. Nat. Assn., Jr. Pianists Guild of Dallas (chmn. jr. recitals 1983, chmn. sr. recitals 1984, treas. 2003-2004), Tex. Music Tchrs. Assn., Dallas Music Tchrs. Assn., Music Study Club Dallas (chmn. piano program 1981-82), Music Study Club, Dallas Fedn. Music Clubs (del. 1969-78, 1st v.p. 1977), Daus. Republic Tex. (1st v.p. Bonham chpt. 1975-76), Alpha Delta Pi, Melodie Club (pres. 1969-71, 2d v.p. 1977—, choral accompanist, counselor jr. club, historian, press sec. 1981-82, 1st v.p. 2003-2004), Kalista Club (yearbook chmn. 1983-2000, v.p. 1984-85, pres. 1986-87), Park Cities Club, Tower Club, Kermis Club, Rondo-Carrousel Club, Trippers Club, Steinway Hall's Partners in Performance, Northwest Bible Ch., Mu Phi Epsilon (patron). Home: 3848 Cedarbrush Dr Dallas TX 75229-2701

JOHNSON, MARY ELIZABETH, retired elementary education educator; b. St. Louis, Sept. 17, 1943; d. Richard William Blayney and Alice Bonjean (Taylor) Blayney Needham; m. Clyde Robert Johnson, Aug. 31, 1963; children: Brian (dec. 1991), Elizabeth Johnson Meyer, David. BS cum laude, U. Ill., 1966; MA, Maryville U., 1990; postgrad., So. Ill. U., 1990. Cert. elem. tchr., Ill., Mo. Tchr. Hazelwood Sch. Dist., Florissant, Mo., 1971-93, positive intervention tchr., 1989-91. Author play: Say No to Drugs, 1991. Author: Secret Study Skills for Third Graders, 1990. Mem. Hazelwood Schs. Music Boosters, 1980-88; mem. coms. Townsend PTA, Florissant, 1976—; contbr. Schlarship Run-Walk, 1982—; mem. Children's United Rsch. Effort in Cancer, 1986—; vol. Spl. Love, Inc., camp for children with cancer, 1986—; active The Children's Inn, Bethesda, Md., 1990—, Bailey Scholarship Fund, U. Ill., 1994—; mem. scholarship com. Clark County Sch. Dist., Las Vegas, Nev., 2001-03. Fred S. Bailey scholar, 1962-66, Edmund J. James scholar, 1964-65; named Townsend Tchr. of Yr., 1989-90. Mem. NEA, Internat. Platform Assn., Kappa Delta Pi, Alpha Lambda Delta, Phi Kappa Phi. Baptist. Avocations: travel, reading, crafts, writing, music. Home: 2016 Bay Tree Sun City Las Vegas NV 89134-5235

JOHNSON, MARY KATHERINE (KATIE JOHNSON), elementary education educator; b. Prescott, Wis., June 12, 1945; d. Walter Frank and Mary Jane (Larson) Johnson; m. William F. Hilton, June 23, 1968 (div. 1985); children: Bradley Eric, Karin Louise. BA, Mich. State U., 1967, MA, 1970; postgrad., U. Calif., Berkeley, 1970—. Cert. elem. tchr., Calif. Tchr. East Lansing (Mich.) Pub. Schs., 1967-68, Hall's Crossroads Sch., Aberdeen, Md., 1968-69, Oakland (Calif.) Pub. Schs., 1970-82; tchr., cons. Bay Area Writing Project, Berkeley, 1978—, Bay Area Math. Project, Berkeley, 1994—, Bay Area Calif. Arts Project, Berkeley, 1997—; cons. Child Devel. Project, San Ramon, Calif., 1985; tchr. Berkeley Unified Sch. Dist., 1986—, support provider, beginning tchr. support and assessment program, 2000—; coord. pub. programs, math. edn. program Lawrence Hall of Sci., U. Calif., Berkeley, 1996-98; curriculum developer, writer U. Calif. Bot. Gardens, 2001—. Mem. MATHTEQ U. Calif., Berkeley, 1987-90; mem. com. of credentials Commn. for Tchr. Preparation and Licensing, Sacramento, 1974-76; spkr. Asilomar Math. Conf., 1991—, mem. program com., 1995-2000; spkr. Calif. chpt. Assn. for Persons with Severe Handicaps Conf., 1992, 94, 97, 98, 2000, bd. dirs., 1997—; spkr. Assn. for Persons with Severe Handicaps Internat. Conf., 1993, 2001, Supported Life Conf., 1992; rep. No. Regional Spl. Edn. Local Plan Area Com., Region III Full Inclusion Task Force for State of Calif., 1994-98; participant Calif. Rsch. Inst., 1992; mem. adv. task force on tchr. preparation in mainstreaming Calif. Commn. on Tchr. Credentialling, 1996; adv. bd. Profl. Internship Program., U. Calif., Berkeley; tchr. leader Profl. Insvc. for New and Experienced Tchrs., 1997—; pres. AC3ME-Alameda/Contra Costa County Math Educators, 2000—; mem., tchr.-leader Profl. Instrn. for New and Established Tchrs., 1998-2002. Contbg. author: Portfolio Assessment in Mathematics, 1990, Teacher Handbook on Homework, C.M.C. Communicator, 1993. Coord. children's coun. Epworth Meth. Ch., Berkeley, 1985-88, 96-98, Youth Coun., 1993-95; cert. lay spkr. Bay View dist. Calif.-Nev. United Meth. Ch., Berkeley, 1989—, trustee, 1994-96, 98-2002; pres. bd. trustees Maya's Music Therapy Fund, 1994—; mentor tchr. Berkeley Unified Sch. Dist., 1996, 99; mem. adv. bd. Calif. Urban Partnership program U. Calif., Berkeley, 1999—. Recipient Outstanding Alumni K-12 Tchr. award Mich. State U. Coll. Edn. Alumni Assn., 2002; named Math. Tchr. of Yr. Alameda/Contra Costa Counties Math. Educators, 1996; Berkeley Pub. Edn. Found. grantee, 1988, 89, 90, 92, 94, 95, 98, 2000-03, In Dulce Jullibo Inc. grantee, 1989, 90, 92, 94, 95, 99, 2003, BAMP grantee, 1995, Calif. Math. Coun. grantee, 1995; fellow Bay Area Math. Project, 1994, Oakland-Bay Area Writing Project, 1977, Bay Area Writing Project, 1978, 98, Bay Area Calif. Arts Project, 1997. Mem. Nat. Coun. Tchrs. English, Nat. Coun. Tchrs. Math., Calif. English Coun., Calif. Math. Coun., P.E.O., Profl. Instr. for New and Established Teacher; bd. dirs. CA Chpt. Assn. Persons with Severe Handicaps, 1997—, Alameda-Contra Costa County Math. Educators (pres. 2000—). Democrat. Avocations: singing, jogging, swimming, gourmet cooking, sewing. Home: 1016 Keeler Ave Berkeley CA 94708-1404 Office: Oxford Sch 1130 Oxford St Berkeley CA 94707-2624

JOHNSON, MARY LOU, lay worker, educator; b. Moline, Ill., July 15, 1923; d. Percy and Hope (Aulgur) Sipes; m. Blaine Eugene Johnson, May 30, 1941 (dec.); children: Vivian Johnson Sweedy Maday, Michael D. (dec.), Amelia Johnson Harms Thomas, James Michael (dec.). Grad. high sch., Moline. From chmn. Christian edn. to dir. 1st Christian Ch., Moline, 1971—88, dir. Christian edn., 1988—93, ret., 1993, chmn. Christian edn., 2001—03. Sunday sch. tchr. 1st Christian Ch., Moline, 1958-84; cluster del. Christian Chs. Ill. and Wisc., Moline, 1988-89. Author: (poem) What Is A Mother?, 1965. Officer various positions PTA, Moline, 1972-75, hon. life mem. State of Ill., 1972; leader, dist. chair Girl Scouts U.S., Moline, 1955-65; chmn. skywatcher USAF Ground Observer Corps, Moline, 1955-57; vol. telethon coord. Muscular Dystrophy Assn., Moline, 1971-94; del. lt. gov.'s Commn. on Aging, Springfield, Ill., 1990; historian 1st Christian Ch., Moline, 1996—, libr., 2000—; vol. C.A.R.E. Ministry, 1999—, Ring for Care, 1999-2002, Western Ill. Area Agy. on Aging, 1998-2003. Recipient Appreciation award Muscular Dystrophy Assn., 1964-94. Republican. Home: 2014 9th St Moline IL 61265-4779 E-mail: grmalou624@aol.com.

JOHNSON, MARY LYNN, chemistry educator, consultant; b. Pampa, Tex., Mar. 12, 1938; d. E. Ray and L. Hortense (Allison) Miller; m. James Jefferson Johnson, Jr., Aug. 17, 1957; children: Melinda Ann, James Jefferson III. Student, West Tex. State U., 1955-57; BS in Scis., U. Tex., El Paso, 1958; MS, N.Mex. State U., 1961; PhD, Pa. State U., 1970. Air pollution chemist El Paso City-County Health Dept., Tex., 1959-60, 61-63, Tex. State Health Dept., El Paso, 1963-64; air pollution spl. fellow USPHS, HEW, Univ. Pk., N.Mex., 1960-61, 1964-68; asst. prof. chemistry U. Tex.-Arlington, 1968-75; chemistry instr. Hockaday Sch., Dallas, 1975-86, Brookhaven Coll., Dallas, 1979-87, 91-93, Highland Pk. Ind. Sch. Dist., 1986-95; retired, 1995; air pollution spl. fellow USPHS, HEW, Univ. Pk., Pa., 1964—68. Indsl. cons. combustion and air pollution problems, 1965-75. Contbr. articles to profl. jour. Mem. People to People Citizen Ambs., Fellow Am. Inst. Chemists; mem. Am. Chem. Soc., Internat. Union Pure and Applied Chemistry, Combustion Inst., Alpha Chi, Iota Sigma Pi. Democrat. Congregationalist. Avocations: reading, antiques, piano. Home: 3004 Croydon St Denton TX 76209-1300

JOHNSON, MARYANN ELAINE, educational administrator; b. Franklin Twp., Pa., Nov. 1, 1943; d. Mary I. Sollick; married. BS in Elementary Edn., Mansfield State U., Pa., 1964; MS in Elementary Edn., U. Alaska, College, 1973; EdD, Wash. State U., Pullman, 1981. Tchr. Nayatt Sch., Barrington, R.I., 1964-66, North Sch., North Chicago, Ill., 1966-67, Kodiak (Alaska) On-Base Sch., 1967-71, Eastmont Sch. Dist., 1971-74, reading coord., 1974-77, adminstrv. asst., 1977-82; asst. supt. Sec. Parent Advisory Com., 1982-93, South Kitsap Sch. Dist., Port Orchard, Wash., 1993-95, Clarkston Sch. Dist., Wash., 1995-97; chair Wash. State Discover Card Scholarship, 1993-97; pvt. cons. Reach for the Future, Inc., 1997—, Learning Workshop, 1999—. Active Ctrl. Wash. Hosp. Bd., 1991-93, Ctrl. Wash. Hosp. Found. Bd., 1992-93. Named Eastmont Tchr. of the Year, 1973-74. Mem. Assn. Supervision and Curriculum Devel. (review coun. 1993-99), Wash. State Assn. Supervision and Curriculum Devel. (bd. dirs. 1986-89, pres. elect 1989-90, pres. 1990-91, Educator of Yr. 1981), NEA, Wash. Assn. Sch. Adminstrs. (bd. dirs., chmn. curriculum and instrn. Job-Alike, profl. devel. com., Project Leadership, pres. elect 1986-87, pres. 1987-88, leadership award, 1986, award of merit 1992, Exec. Educator 100 1988, 93, chmn. WASA 21st century scholarship com. 1988-96, leadership acad. 1993), Am. Assn. Sch. Adminstrs. (resolutions com. 1988-89, com. for advancement of sch. adminstrs. 1989-92), East Wenatchee C. of C. (bd. dirs. 1990-93, chair edn. com. 1990-91), Delta Kappa Gamma (pres. 1982-83), Phi Delta Kappa, Phi Kappa Phi. E-mail: mjohnson@i70west.com.

JOHNSON, MILDRED SNOWDEN, retired nursing educator; b. Elgin, Tex., Nov. 15, 1915; d. Milton Foy and Pearl Mae (DeLoach) Snowden; children: Roy B. Johnson, Betty Carol Johnson. BSN, U. Tex., Galveston, 1965; MSN, U. Tex., Austin, 1972. Cert. clin. nurse spl. adult psychol./mental health. Psychiatric nurse tech. State Hosp., Austin, 1959-63; head nurse Holy Cross Hosp., Austin, 1967, St. David's Hosp., Austin, 1968-69; acting dir. Ctrl. Tex. Coll., Kileen, Tex., 1969-70; asst. prof. nursing U. Tex., Galveston, 1970-93; ret., 1993. Mem. ANA, Nat. League Nursing, Tex. Nurses Assn., Tex. League Nursing, Sigma Theta Tau Internat. Home: 2116 Fordham Ln Austin TX 78723-1332

JOHNSON, MONICA LYNN, elementary education educator; b. Dubuque, Iowa, Mar. 8, 1962; d. Hugo and Arlene Isabel Fritz; children: Justus, Kyle. BS, No. Ill. U., 1985. Cert. Gare ceramics tchr., 1995. Elem. art educator Saratoga Elem. Sch., Morris, Ill., 1987-92, 94—, Immaculate Conception Sch., Morris, Ill., 1991-92, Troy Shorewood-Dist. 30C, Joliet, Ill., 1992-94. Muralist Saratoga Sch., Morris, 1990, 95, Immaculate Conception Sch., Morris, 1991, 92, Mary Crest Sch., Joliet, 1991, Troy Shorewood Sch., Joliet, 1993; owner Monicom, Personalized Children's Books, Morris. Mem. Nat. Art Edn. Assn., Ill. Art Edn. Assn. (cert. Duncan ceramics tchr. 1994). Avocation: multimedia painting.

JOHNSON, NANCY ANN, education educator; b. Worcester, Mass., May 12, 1932; d. Arthur Eugene and Anna Evelyn (Erickson) J. BA, Clark U., 1955, MA in Edn., 1957; EdD, Boston U., 1977. Tchr. pub. schs., Auburn, Mass., 1956-63, reading supr. Groton, Mass., 1963-68; asst. prof. edn. Worcester State Coll., 1968-78, assoc. prof., 1978, prof., 1982, chair dept. edn., 1982-84, 91, coord. student teaching, 1980-83; adv. bd., local sch. Mem. pastoral com. Peoples Ch., Worcester, 1973-80, Christian edn. com., 1978-91, sec., 1990-94, ch. libr. extension, 1992-93, adult edn. coord.; mem. exec. bd. Friends of Worcester Pub. Libr., 1980—, sec., 1981-82; coord. book sale vols.; corporator Worcester YWCA; mem. state lit. coun.; bd. dirs. Brittan Sq. Neighborhood Coun.; docent Worcester Hist. Mus., 1995—; sec. Clark Alumnae Coun., 1961-66; grant writer tree project City of Worcester-Brittan Sq. Neighborhood Coun.; docent Preservation Worcester, 1999, mem. endangered prop. com.; bd. dirs., lectr. Friends of Hope Cemetery; chair scholarship com. Worcester Women's Club. Mem. AAUW, Mass. Assn. Tchr. Educators (pres. 1987-88), Delta Kappa Gamma (sec. Tay chpt. 1974-76, 1st v.p. chpt. 1976, pres. 1990-92), Pi Lambda Theta (pres Alpha Gamma chpt. 1979-81, mem. exec. bd. chpt. 1975-79), Phi Delta Kappa (Educator of Yr. 1993, advisor ctrl. chpt. chair rsch. ctrl. Mass. chpt. found. rep., scholarship chair), Kappa Delta Pi (co-counselor), Worcester Womens Club (scholarship chair), Boston U. Womens Club (pres.), Boston U. Alumni Club Worcester County (pres. 1992-94, nominating chair, scholarship chair). Friends of Hope Cemetery Program Chr. Office: 486 Chandler St Worcester MA 01602-2832

JOHNSON, NEAL FREDERICK, psychological scientist, educator; b. Willmar, Minn., May 1, 1934; s. Malcolm Ruben and Helen Laura Johnson; m. Kathleen A. Crimmins, Sept. 9, 1960 (dec. Jan. 2000); children: Neal, Margaret (dec. Sept. 1999), Elizabeth, Michael. BA, U. Minn., 1956, PhD, 1961. Prof. psychology Ohio State U., Columbus, 1961—. Vis. prof. U. Calif., Berkeley, 1965, 74, 75, 77, 78, 83. Contbr. articles to profl. jours.; assoc. editor Jour. Memory and Lang., 1984-88; consulting editor Jour. Verbal Learning and Verbal Behavior, 1965-84, Memory & Cognition, 1972-82, Jour. Exptl. Psychology: Human Perception and Performance, 1978-82, Jour. Exptl. Psychology: Learning, Memory and Cognition, 1982-89, Jour. Memory and Lang., 1988-94, Gen. Psychology Rev., 1996—. Mem. com. Troop 312 Boy Scouts Am., Columbus, 1974-81. Rsch. scholar Tozer Found., Stillwater, Minn., 1959; grantee U.S. Office Edn., NIH, NSF. Fellow APA (pres. Soc. Gen. Psychology 1995, pres. divsn. exptl. psychology 1996), AAAS (governing coun. 1998-2000, chair psychology sect. 2002—); mem. Psychonomic Soc. (pres. 1997), Coun. Sci. Soc. Presidents, Midwestern Psychol. Assn. (pres. 1987). Presbyterian. Avocations: downhill skiing, fencing. Home: 5478 Rockwood Rd Columbus OH 43229-4324 Office: Dept Psychology Ohio State U Columbus OH 43210 E-mail: johnson.64@osu.edu.

JOHNSON, OLIN CHESTER, education educator; b. Phila., Sept. 19, 1941; s. Benjamin F. and Eva M. Johnson; m. Vernetta Dudley, Nov. 22, 1964; children: Quanda, Olin Jr. BS, Cheyney State Coll., 1965; MEd, Temple U., 1969; MS, U. Pa., 1972. Cert. elem. edn., social studies, elem. prin., secondary prin., supt., Pa. Tchr. Phila. Sch. Dist., 1965-68, supr., 1968-72, dir., coord. urban career ednl. ctr., 1973-75, prin., 1976—, William Bryant Sch., 1977-80, Charles R. Drew Sch., 1981—. Mem. secondary sch. com. U. Pa., Phila.; adj. asst. prof. Drexel U., Phila., 1989—, mem. ednl. adv. com. Chmn. Cmty. Concern 13, Inc., 1970—, B.F. Johnson Scholarship Fund, 1971—; vice-chmn. Phila. M.H. Multi-Purpose Learning Ctr., 1975-85; bd. dirs. Open Door Bapt. Ch.; exec. adminstr. B.F. Johnson Found., 1989—. Recipient award Nat. Tchr. Corp., 1970, Four Chaplains Cmty. Svc. award, 1971, 73, Phila. Prin. Merit award Phila. Sch. Dist. #1, 1978, OIC commendation, 1973, Pa. Dept. Edn. Planning and Testing citation, 1987, Prin. Outstanding Leadership C.R. Drew award, 1987, Strawbridge Civic award, 2001; Ford Found. fellow U. Pa., 1971-74. Mem. Am. Assn. Sch. Adminstrs., Pa. Congress Sch. Adminstrs., Phi Delta Kappa, Kappa Alpha Psi.

JOHNSON, PATRICIA HARDY, early childhood specialist pre-school provider; b. Washington, Sept. 14, 1933; d. Dennis and Ira Bell (McGarrah) Hardy. BS, Miners Tchrs. Coll., Washington, D.C., 1955; MA, NYU, 1962; EdD, U.S. Internat. U., San Diego, 1989. Cert. tchr. elem. physically handicapped, mentally handicapped, learning handicapped, supervision, sch. psychologist, adminstrn. Resource specialist L.A. Unified Sch. Dist., 1981-84; asst. prin. L.A. Child Guidance Clin., 1984-86, prin., 1986-89; owner, pres. Raintree Inn, Inc., L.A., 1985—. Author: Raintree Inn Incorporated's Complete Child Care Center's Curriculum Guide, 0-27 Months; contbr. articles to profl. jours. Mem. usher bd. and hospitality com. Eternal Promise Bapt. Ch., L.A. Spl. Edn. grantee State of Calif.; numerous fellowships received from Univs. Mem. NAFE, Am. Assn. Ret. Persons, NYU Alumni, UCLA Alumni, Beta Pi Sigma, Gamma Theta Upsilon. Democrat. Avocations: homemaking, gourmet cooking, traveling. Home: 6611 Rugby Ave Apt A Huntington Park CA 90255-4094 Office: 6611 Rugby Ave Apt A Huntington Park CA 90255-4094

JOHNSON, PAUL CHRISTIAN, physiologist, educator; b. Ironwood, Mich., Feb. 3, 1928; s. George Herman and Sophia (Kliemola) J.; m. Genevieve Ruth Shanklin, Sept. 3, 1955; children: Ciri, Philip, Christopher. AA, Gogebic Jr. Coll., 1948; BS in Physics, U. Mich., 1951, MA in Physiology, 1953, PhD, 1955; MD (hon.), U. Limburg, The Netherlands, 1986. Instr. dept. physiology U. Mich., Ann Arbor, 1955-56, Case Western Res. U., Cleve., 1956-58; asst. prof. Ind. U., Bloomington, 1958-61, assoc. prof., 1961-67; prof. physiology U. Ariz, Tucson, 1967-94, head dept., 1967-87; adj. prof. bioengring. U. Calif. San Diego, La Jolla, 1994—. Mem. study sect. on physiology NIH, 1968-72. Mem. editl. bd. Am. Jour. Physiology, 1964-70, co-editor, 1976-78; mem. editl. bd. Jour. Applied Physiology, 1964-70, Circulation Rsch., 1971-76, 81-86; contbr. articles to profl. jours. NIH Spl. postdoctoral fellow, 1965-66; rsch. grantee NIH, 1960—. Mem. Am. Physiol. Soc. (chmn. circulation group 1973-74, mem. coun. 1978-82, Wiggers award lectr. 1981, chmn. publs. com. 1985-89), Microcirculatory Soc. (pres. 1967-68, Landis award lectr. 1976), Basic Sci. Coun., Am. Heart Assn. (exec. com. 1973-75, 82-85, rsch. grantee 1960-72). Democrat. Home: 2411 El Amigo Rd Del Mar CA 92014-3118 Office: U Calif San Diego Dept Bioengring La Jolla CA 92093-0412

JOHNSON, PAULA BOUCHARD, preschool administrator, educator, consultant; b. St. Albans, Vt., Dec. 9, 1954; d. Leo Paul and Irene Mary (Goldsbury) B.; m. John Howard Johnson, July 1, 1978; children: Mathieu, Meredith, Marc. BA in French and Drama, Marymount Coll., Tarrytown, N.Y., 1977; cert., Cath. Inst., Paris, 1975; EdM in Bilingual Edn., Boston U., 1981. Cert. 7-12 French tchr., N.Y.; cert. profl. std. 7-12 French tchr., K-12 bilingual and bicultural tchr., prin. lic. grades K-12, Vt.; cert. ESL tchr. Bilingual specialist Enosburg (Vt.) Elem. Sch., 1977-78; adminstrv. asst. Bilingual Resource and Tng. Ctr., Boston, 1979-80; dir. Title VII Elem. & Secondary Edn. Act bilingual program Franklin N.E. Supervisory Union, Richford, Vt., 1980-82; tchr. French, Enosburg Falls (Vt.) H.S., 1983-84; instr. French, C.C. of Vt., St. Albans, 1985-92; co-owner, tr. Kinderhaüs Pre-Sch., St. Albans, 1990-95; French tchr. Bellows Free Acad., St. Albans, Vt., 1999—. Mem. adj. faculty Johnson State Coll., 1981-82; French cons. Berkshire (Vt.) Elem. Sch., 1984-86; coord. A Bilingual Curriculum Guide for the Classroom, Tchr. Vols. I, II and III, 1982; fgn. lang. cons. Milton Sch. Dist.; Vt. ESL instr. Berkshire (Vt.) Elem. Sch. Mem. St. Albans City Elem. Sch. Bd., 1988—, vice chmn., 1994-95, chair, 1995-96; justice of peace Bd. Civil Authority, St. Albans, 1994—; vice-chair Franklin County Rep. Com., 1997—. Mem. ASCD, Vt. Fgn. Lang. Assn. (bd. dirs. 1991-93), Vt. Assn. for Edn. Young Children. Avocations: tennis, genealogy, running. Home: 54 High St Saint Albans VT 05478-1651

JOHNSON, PHILIP CALVIN, school administrator; b. Washington, Aug. 14, 1963; s. Paul Calvin and Clara Madelyn (Campbell) J.; m. Haeryeon Kim, Aug. 10, 1985; children: Kristopher Juhun, Samuel Kirk. BA, Washington Bible Coll., 1985; MS, Pensacola Christian Coll., 1994; postgrad., Andrew Jackson U. Tchr. Old Nat. Christian Acad., College Park, Ga., 1985-88; tchr., supr. Mt. Zion Christian Acad., Jonesboro, Ga., 1988-94, adminstr., 1994—. Republican. Baptist. Avocations: piano, song writing, running. Office: Mt Zion Christian Acad 7102 Mount Zion Blvd Jonesboro GA 30236-2518

JOHNSON, RAYMONDA THEODORA GREENE, humanities educator; b. Chgo., Jan. 12, 1939; d. Theodore T. and Eileen (Atherley) Greene; m. Hulon Johnson, June 27, 1964; children: David Atherley, Theodore Cassell, Alexander Ward. BA in English, DePaul U., 1960; MA in English, Loyola U., Chgo., 1965. Cert. high sch. English tchr., Ill. Tchr. high sch. English, Chgo. Pub. Schs., 1960-65; instr. English, Harold Washington Coll. (formerly Loop Coll.), City Coll., Chgo., 1965-66, asst. prof., 1966-91, assoc. prof., 1991-96, faculty advisor coll. newspaper, 1989-92, 96-98, pres. faculty coun., 1990-92, mem. faculty coun., 1990-94, chairperson English and Speech Dept., 1992—, coord. coll. assessment plan com., 1995-99, prof., 1996—. Mem. Brit. Partnership Articulation team, 1997—. Middle sch. v.p. parents coun. Latin Sch., Chgo., 1974-76, trustee, 1987-93; mem. adv. bd. high jump program Latin Sch. Chgo., 1989-98; cubmaster, leader cub scouts Boys Scouts Am., Chgo., 1974-81; mem. black creativity adv. com. Mus. Sci. and Industry, Chgo., 1984-96; mem. steering com. St. Thomas the Apostle Anti-Racism Ethnic Sensitivity, 1999—; chmn. St. Thomas the Apostle Parish Diversity Dinners, 1999—. Recipient svc. award religious edn. program St. Thomas the Apostle Ch., Chgo., 1984. Mem. Twigs Mothers Club (pres. 1982-84), Alpha Kappa Alpha. Democrat. Roman Catholic. Avocations: reading, sewing, modern dance, theater, music. Home: 6747 S Bennett Ave Chicago IL 60649-1031 Office: Harold Washington Coll 30 E Lake St Rm 602A Chicago IL 60601-2403 E-mail: rajohnson@ccc.edu.

JOHNSON, REX RAY, automotive education educator; b. Buckhannon, W. Va., June 27, 1949; s. Virgil Melvin and Vesta Matilda (Carpenter) J.; m. Beverly Ann Ashcraft, Aug. 18, 1973. BA in Edn., Fairmont State Coll., 1972. Welder T & T Machine Co., Morgantown, W.Va., 1971; tchr. Norwood (Ohio) City Schs., 1972; technician Cecil Jackson Equipment, Oakland, Md., 1973-76; assoc. prof. automotive tech. Allegany C.C., Cumberland, Md., 1976—. Dir. Automotive Tech. and Transp., Cumberland, 1984—. Recipient Miriam D. Sanner award for Outstanding Teaching, 1989-90, 2001-02. Mem. Nat. Assn. Coll. Automotive Tchrs., Inc. (charter), Md. Tchrs. Assn., I-Car Assn. (chair 1989-90). Avocation: drag racing. Office: Allegany Community Coll Willowbrook Rd Cumberland MD 21502

JOHNSON, RICHARD AUGUST, English language educator; b. Washington, Apr. 18, 1937; s. Cecil August and Esther Marie (Nelson) J.; m. Michaela Ann Memelsdorff, Aug. 20, 1960; children— Nicholas, Patrick, Hong, Loeun. BA, Swarthmore Coll., 1959; PhD, Cornell U., 1965. Instr. English U. Va., Charlottesville, 1963-65; asst. prof. Mt. Holyoke Coll., South Hadley, Mass., 1965-71, assoc. prof., 1971-74, prof., chmn. dept., 1974-80, 1988-91, prof. Alumnae Found., 1980-86, Lucia, Ruth and Elizabeth MacGregor prof. English, 1986—. Vis. prof. Amherst Coll., 1979, 84-88. Author: Man's Place: An Essay on Auden, 1973; co-author: Common Ground: Personal Writing and Public Discourse, 1992, Finding Common Ground, 1996; contbr. articles to profl. jours. Mem. MLA, AAUP, Phi Beta Kappa Democrat. Episcopalian. Office: Mount Holyoke Coll Dept English 50 College St South Hadley MA 01075-1423 E-mail: rjohnson@mtholyoke.edu.

JOHNSON, ROBERT GLENN, geology and geophysics educator; b. Iowa, Dec. 12, 1922; m. Elizabeth Louise Gulliver, July 17, 1949. BS, Case Western Res. U., 1947; PhD, Iowa State U., 1952. Project engr. Bendix Aviation Inc., Red Bank, N.J., 1952-55; scientist Honeywell Inc., Mpls., 1955-74, staff scientist, 1974-90; adj. prof. dept. geology and geophysics U. Minn., Mpls., 1990—. Contbr. articles to profl. publs. Achievements include 23 patents on control technology sensors; pioneering research in silicon microstructure sensor technology; contributions to understanding of glacial climate change. Office: U Minn Dept Geology-Geophys 310 Pillsbury Dr SE Minneapolis MN 55455-0219 E-mail: johns088@johns088.email.umn.edu.

JOHNSON, ROBERT LEE, JR., physician, educator, researcher; b. Dallas, Apr. 28, 1926; s. Robert L. and Doris (Miller) J.; m. Aileen Johnson, 1952; children: Stephen Lee, Robert Edward. BS, So. Meth. U., 1947; MD, Northwestern U., 1951. Intern Cook County Hosp., Chgo., 1951-52; resident in internal medicine Parkland Meml. Hosp., Phila., 1952-55; fellow nat. foun. infantile paralysis and clin. instr. U. Tex. Southwestern Med. Ctr., Dallas, 1955-56; fellow dept. physiol. and pharmacology Grad. Sch. Medicine U. Pa., Phila., 1956-57; asst. prof. U. Tex. Southwestern Med. Ctr., Dallas, 1959-65, assoc. prof., 1965-69, prof. medicine, 1969—; John Butler Meml. lectr. U. Wash., Seattle, 2001. Vis. staff Parkland Meml. Hosp., Dallas, 1957—, Zale Lipshy U. Hosp., Dallas, 1989—, St. Paul Hosp., Dallas, 2000-; cons. chest diseases VA Hosp., Dallas, 1966—; dir. sarcoidosis clinic Parkland Meml. Hosp., 1983—; mem. parent rev. com. Nat. Heart, Lung, and Blood Inst. for Spl. Ctrs. of Rsch. proposals, 1983-85; mem. Nat. Heart, Lung, and Blood Rsch. Rev. Com., 1985-89; mem. respiratory and applied physiology study sect. NIH, 1991-94. Mem. editl. bd.: Jour. Clin. Investigation, 1972—77, Jour. Applied Physiology, 1980—82, Circulation, 1996—, guest referee editor: Jour. Applied Physiology, —, Am. Jour. Physiology, —, Chest, —, Circulation, —, Circulation Rsch., —, Am. Jour. Med. Sci., —, Am. Jour. Respiration and Circulation Medicine, —, Jour. Clin. Investigation, —, Early Human Devel., —, Kidney Internat., —. With Naval ROTC, 1945-46; with USNR, 1944-46; maj. USAR, 1962. Mem. Am. Heart Assn. (cardiopulmonary coun. exec. com. mem. 1990-92, nominating com. cardiopulmonary coun. 1989-93, chmn. 1990-92), Am. Thoracic Soc. (planning com. mem. 1987-90, com. proficiency standards 1985-94, Scientific Accomplishment award 1996), Am. Coll. Chest Physicians, Am. Fedn. Clin. Rsch., Am. Physiol. Soc., Am. Soc. Clin. Investigation, Assn. Am. Physicians, Cen. Soc. Clin. Rsch., So. Soc. Clin. Rsch., Soc. Sigma Xi. Office: UT Southwestern Med Ctr 5323 Harry Hines Blvd Stop 9034 Dallas TX 75390-9034

JOHNSON, ROBERT OLIVER, JR., school system administrator; b. Galesburg, Ill., Mar. 10, 1940; s. Robert Oliver and Veda Margaret J.; B.S., Western Ill. U., 1963, M.S., 1968, Ed.S., 1972; Ed.D., Western Colo. U., 1975; m. Patricia Ann O'Field, Apr. 7, 1979; children— Ray, Greg, William. Tchr., adminstr. Ill. schs., 1963— ; prin. Knoxville (Ill.) Jr. High Sch., 1973-87, curriculum coordinator, 1970—, asst. supt., 1983— ; regional supt. Knox County Schs., 1995—. mentor Ill. Adminstrv. Acad., Springfield, 1989—; alderman Knoxville City Council. Bd. dirs. Carl Sandburg Jr. Coll. Found; treas. Knox County Rep. Party, 1990-92; co-chmn. Knox County United Way, Galesburg, 1991-92; mayor Knoxville City, 1993—; active Knox County Multi-Handicapped Bd., Galesburg, 1987-92; found. mem. Leadership Galesburg. Mem. Am. Lung Assn., Ill. Jr. High Sch. Assn. (pres.), Assn. Ill. Middle Schs., Ill. Assn. Reg. Supts., Phi Delta Kappa (pres.-elect Galesburg chpt., advisor), Masons, Lions (pres. Galesburg evening lions), Eastern Star (second v.p. 1993). Lutheran. Avocations: reading, power walking, travel. Home: PO Box 19 208 W North St Knoxville IL 61448-1044 Office: 700 Mill St Knoxville IL 61448-1522

JOHNSON, RUTH ALLEN, elementary school educator; b. Saltillo, Miss., Dec. 11, 1941; d. William Henry and Ruby R. (Harwood) Nichols; m. Charles Lee Johnson, Nov. 10, 1962; children: Stephen Lee, William Allen. BS, Miss. State U., 1963; MEd, U. Miss., 1975, EdS, 1978. Cert. elem. tchr., Miss. Elem. tchr. Lee County Schs., Tupelo, Miss., 1962-69, Columbus (Miss.) Pub. Schs., 1969-71, Tupelo City Schs., 1971-94; instr. adult basic edn. Itawomba C.C., 1994—. Chairperson 5th Grade Reading Curriculum, Tupelo, 1980-94; cons. Cooperative Learning in Elem. Classroom, Portfolio Assessment, Miss. Writing/Thinking Inst. Named Profl. Educator of Yr. Columbus City Schs., 1969-71, one of 2000 Notable Am. Women. Mem. AAUW, Miss. Profl. Educators, ASCD, Delta Kappa Gamma (pres. 1987-89), Phi Delta Kappa (sec. 1978-79). Baptist. Home: 1222 Oakview Dr Tupelo MS 38804-1604

JOHNSON, RUTH CRUMLEY, economics educator; b. Bristol, Tenn., Feb. 13, 1936; d. Glenn Fine and Marian Grace (Thomas) Crumley; m. Robert William Johnson, June 10, 1971 (dec. May 1995); m. Edwin Douglas Smiley, Aug. 2, 1998. BS, U. Tenn., 1970, MS, 1971, PhD, 1981. Grad. rsch. asst. U. Tenn., Knoxville, 1978-79; rsch. assoc. Oak Ridge (Tenn.) Nat. Lab., 1979-80, Oak Ridge Associated Univs., 1980-82; pres., co-founder Econ. Sys. Analysis, Inc., Oak Ridge, 1983-85; economist Sci. & Tech., Inc., Oak Ridge, 1986-88; mem. adj. faculty Pellissippi State Tech. C.C., Knoxville, 1988—. Mem. People to People Internat. del. of economists to USSR, 1989. Contbr. articles to profl. jours. Chairperson Anderson County Youth Workers Coun., Oak Ridge, 1977; bd. dirs. Anderson County Health Coun., Oak Ridge, 1975-77, Anderson County Cmty. Action Commn., Clinton, Tenn., 1972-74; chairperson bd. dirs. United Ch., Oak Ridge, 1997. Mem. AAUW, Am. Econ. Assn., Phi Kappa Phi, Gamma Sigma Delta, Omicron Nu. Avocations: gardening, hiking, travel, genealogy. Home: 105 Adelphi Rd Oak Ridge TN 37830-7807

JOHNSON, RUTH FLOYD, educational consultant; b. Plateau, Ala., Apr. 19, 1935; d. Nathan Daniel and Ora Anna (Ellis) Floyd; children: Anthony, Walter, Camille, Quinitta, Annette. Student, Tuskegee Inst., 1951-53; BS in History, Bowie (Md.) State U., 1970; MEd in Counseling, U. Md., 1977; PhD in Human Svcs. Adminstrn., Univ. for Humanistic Studies, San Diego, 1982. Cert. tchr., counselor. Radio personality Sta. WMOZ, 1953-56; owner, dir. Azalea Sch. Dance, 1954-56; numerous posts for fed. govt., 1957-69; tchr., adminstr. Pub. Schs. of Prince George's County, Md., 1970-78; tchr.-counselor Dunbar S.T.A.Y. Sch., Washington, 1974-75; instr. child and youth study divsn. U. Md., 1977-78; CEO Diametron Corp., 1979-81; tchr. L.A. Unified Sch. Dist., 1980-82, Pasadena (Calif.) Unified Sch. Dist., 1982-83, Rialto (Calif.) Unified Sch. Dist., 1984—; profl. devel. coord. Calif. State Polytech. U., 1995—. Author: Remediating Mass Poverty: Development of a Model Program, 1982, Pep Squad handbook, 1991, (with others: Government/Contemporary Issues: A Curriculum Guide, 1976. Active PTAs; mem. organizing com. Peppermill Village Civic Assn., 1966; vol. Boy Scouts Am., 1968-72, Sr. Citizens of Prince George's County, 1974-76; bd. dirs.Mill Point Improvement Assn., 1975-78, Combined Communities in Action, 1976-78; mem. Prince George's County Hosp. Commn., 1978; mem. Altadena Town Coun., 1983; founder Rialto Freedom and Cultural Soc., 1988; mem. Calif. 36th Dist. Bicentennial Adv. Com., 1989; mem. exec. com. Rialto Police/Community Rels. Team, 1993. Recipient Outstanding Svc. to Children and Yourh award Md. Congress PTA, 1969, Services to Boy Scouts Am. award, 1969, Svcs. to Sr. Citizens award, 1975, Community Svc. award Rialto Freedom and Cultural Soc., 1993, others. Mem. NEA, NAACP, Nat. Assn. Univ. Women, Nat. Coun. Negro Women, Zeta Phi Beta, Gamma Phi Delta. Avocations: world travel, theatre, tennis, spectator sports, outdoor activities. Home: PO Box 1946 Rialto CA 92377-1946 Fax: 909-820-6001.

JOHNSON, SAMUEL FREDERICK, English and literature educator emeritus; b. Pitts., July 22, 1918; s. Samuel Frederick and Estella Helen (Kitsch) J. BA, Haverford Coll., 1940; MA, Harvard U., 1941, PhD, 1948; postgrad., Ind. U., 1943, The Sorbonne, 1945-46. Instr. Harvard U., Cambridge, Mass., 1948-49; asst. prof. NYU, N.Y.C., 1949-54; from asst. prof. to prof. English and comparative renaissance lits. Columbia U., N.Y.C., 1954-84, prof. emeritus, 1984—. Vis. prof. Washington U., St. Louis, 1963; mem. supervising com. English Inst., N.Y.C., 1957-59. Editor: Julius Caesar, 1960, rev. edit., 1969; author: Early Elizabethan Tragedies of the Inns of Court, 1987; festschrift: Shakespeare and Dramatic Tradition, 1989. With U.S. Army, 1942-46. Guggenheim fellow, 1954; Huntington Libr. grantee, 1972. Mem. MLA (asst. sec., editor 1951-52), Renaissance Soc. Am. (assoc. editor 1967-84), Shakespeare Assn. Am. (assoc. editor 1956-57, mem. edit. bd. Shakespearean Internat. Yearbook 1996-99), Phi Beta Kappa. Democrat. Avocations: chamber music, opera. Home and Office: 285 Riverside Dr Apt 7C New York NY 10025-5227

JOHNSON, SANDRA LYNN TERRY, education consultant; b. Mesa, Ariz., Apr. 14, 1942; d. Kenneth Cade and Merlyn Grace (Mattes) Terry; m. Olin Neal Johnson, June 2, 1961; children: Diane Lynn Johnson McLean, Keith Terry Johnson. BS, Tex. Tech U., 1967; MA, U. Tex., 1983, PhD, 1994. Cert. secondary, elem., kindergarten, and gifted edn. tchr., Tex. Tchr. various pvt. schs., Austin, Tex., 1969-84, Austin Ind. Sch. Dist., 1974-76; dir. University Avenue Early Learning Ctr., Austin, 1976-84; cons. Johnson Cons., Austin, 1984-91, edn l. cons., 1998—; cons. region XIII, Edn. Svc. Ctr., Austin, 1991-98; adj. faculty U. Tex., Austin, 1998. Trainer AP Environ. Sci. for Coll. Bds., 1996-98. Editor: Hands Across Texas, 1991, Fulfilling a Dream, 1997, And There Was Light, 1998, Foundation for the Future, 2000; contbg. author mongraph: Perspectives in Gifted Education: Young Gifted Children, Rickes Center for Gifted Children, U. Denver; contbr. articles to profl. jours., mags., newspapers and profl. newsletters; featured in PBS video The Equitable Classroom. Sunday sch. tchr. University Avenue Ch. of Christ, Austin, 1975-83; master tchr. Nat. Tchr. Tng. Inst. for PBS, 1993-96. Scholar Nat. Honor Soc., 1960, Hardin Simmons U., 1960; Advanced Micro Devices grantee, 1997, Eisenhower grantee, 1997. Mem. Nat. Sci. Tchrs. Assn., Nat. Assn. for Rsch. in Sci. Tchg., Nat. Assn. for Gifted Children, Austin Assn. for Edn. Young Children (v.p. 1971-73, pres. 1973-74, chmn. Week of Young Child 1974-75, newsletter editor 1975-76, historian 1983-86, conf. chmn. 1971-72), Tex. State Tchrs. Assn., Phi Kappa Phi, Kappa Delta Pi. Democrat. Avocations: swimming, reading, painting, hiking, camping, yoga. Office: Johnson Cons Svcs 604 E Covington Dr Austin TX 78753-2712 E-mail: dr_s_johnson@hotmail.com.

JOHNSON, SHARI, early childhood educator; b. Phila., Apr. 5, 1955; d. Solomon and Evelyn (Spector) Haas; m. Andrew Johnson, Aug. 6, 1989; children: Jessica Ariel, Benjamin Paul. BS, Pa. State U., 1975; MEd, Chestnut Hill Coll., Phila., 1985; postgrad., U. of the Arts, Phila., 1993-94, C.C. of Phila., 1993-94. Cert. in early childhood edn., elem. edn., Pa. Tchr. Phila. Housing Authority, 1977-82; sr. career tchr. pre-kindergarten Head Start Sch. Dist. Phila., 1982—. Bd. dirs. Multiple Opportunities for Many Youths. Mem. Nat. Assn. for Edn. of Young Children, Assn. for Childhood Edn. Internat., World Orgn. for Early Childhood (France). Avocations: dancing, sewing, swimming, basket weaving. Office: Sch Dist Phila Cook-Wissahickon Sch 201 E Salignac St Philadelphia PA 19128

JOHNSON, SHERILYN RAE, music educator; b. Atlanta, Sept. 15; d. W. Lewis and Bernice C. Johnson. BMus, Furman U., 1975; MEd in Early Childhood Edn., Ga. State U., 1980, MMus, 1982; EdS in Early Childhood Edn., Mercer U., 1995; postgrad., Nova Southeastern U. Cert. tchr. early childhood edn. and music, T-6. Music specialist K-7 DeKalb County Bd. Edn., Decatur, Ga., 1975—, Avondale Elem., 1975-88, Glen Haven Elem., 1980-88, Brockett Elem., 1988—. Chairperson county honor chorus DeKalb County Bd. Edn., 1987-89. Editor/author musical plays, 1975—. Vol., pres.-elect Ga. Shakespeare Festival Soc., Atlanta, 1987-93; vol. asst. dir. Atlanta Dogwood Festival Queen's Pageant, 1975-90; bd. dirs. Miss DeKalb County Scholarship Pageant, Atlanta, 1993—. Named to Outstanding Young Women of Am., 1985. Republican. Lutheran. Home: 887 Jami Ct Lawrenceville GA 30045-7412 Office: Brockett Sch 1855 Brockett Rd Tucker GA 30084-6433

JOHNSON, SYLVIA S. retired secondary school educator; b. Jefferson City, Tenn., Sept. 20, 1937; d. David and Agnes Marie (Ingram) Barnett; m. Charles Johnson Jr., Aug. 28, 1960; 1 child, Sylvia Charlene. BS in Home Econs, Berea Coll.; MS in Family Life, Wayne State U. Tchr. Pershing High Sch., Detroit, 1967-74, 1980-96; counselor Murray Wright Day Care, Detroit, 1974-80; ret., 1996. Vol. tchr. ARC, Detroit, 1980—; sec. Can-Do Block Club, Detroit, 1987—; mem. pres.'s coun. Berea Coll., 1987—. Democrat. Methodist. Avocations: tennis, basketball. Home: 19335 Greydale Ave Detroit MI 48219-1889

JOHNSON, SYLVIA SUE, university administrator, educator; b. Abiline, Tex., Aug. 10, 1940; d. SE Boyd and Margaret MacGillivray (Withington) Smith; m. William Ruel Johnson; children: Margaret Ruth, Laura Jane, Catherine Withington. BA, U. Calif., Riverside, 1962; postgrad., U. Hawaii, 1963. Elem. edn. credential, 1962. Chmn. bd. regents U. Calif., 2000—. Mem. bd. regents U. Calif.; mem. steering com. Citizens Univ. Com., chmn., 1978-79; bd. dirs., charter mem. U. Calif.-Riverside Found., chmn. nominating com., 1983—; pres., bd. dirs. Friends of the Mission Inn, 1969-72, 73-76, Mission Inn Found., 1977—, Calif. Bapt. Coll. Citizens Com., 1980—; bd. dirs. Riverside Comty. Hosp., 1980—, Riverside Jr. League, 1976-77, Nat. Charity League, 1984-85; mem. chancellors blue ribbon com., devel. com. Calif. Mus. Photography; state bd. dirs. C. of C., 2003. Named Woman of Yr., State of Calif. Legislature, 1989, 91, Citizen of Yr., C. of C., 1989; recipient Golden Key award Soroptomist Internat., 2000, Chancellor's medal U. Calif. Riverside, 2002; recipient Silver Raincross medal, Jr. League Riverside, 1993. Mem. U. Calif.-Riverside Alumni Assn. (bd. dirs. 1966-68, v.p. 1968-70), Calif. C. of C. (bd. dirs. 2003—).

JOHNSON, TESLA FRANCIS, data processing executive, educator; b. Altoona, Fla., Sept. 2, 1934; s. Tesla Farris and Ruby Mae (Shockley) J.; m. Eleanor Mary Riggs, Oct. 17, 1975. BSEE, U. S.C., 1958; MS in Ops. Rsch., Fla. Inst. Tech., 1968; PhD in Adminstrv. Mgmt., Walden U., Mpls., 1989. Machinist apprentice Seaboard Airline Ry., 1952-54; asst. computer engr. So. Ry. System, Washington, 1958-61; sr. sci. programmer NCR, Dayton, Ohio, 1961-66; staff programmer IBM, East Fishkill, N.Y., 1966-72; mgr. Jay Turner Co., Grace, Idaho, 1973-74; programmer, analyst Ccybernetics & Systems, Inc., Jacksonville, Fla., 1974-77; systems analyst lst Nat. Bank Md., Balt., 1977-78; sr. systems analyst GM, Detroit, 1978-80; tech. analyst Sunbank Data Corp., Orlando, Fla., 1980-81; mgr. data adminstrn. dept. Martin Marietta Corp., Orlando, 1981-92; dir. technology Computer Bus. Assocs., 1993-96; program mgr. GTE Through Computer Horizons, 1997-2000; ret., 2000—. Adj. prof. bus. adminstrn. Valencia C.C., Orlando, 1989-94, Orlando Coll., 1990-92, Fla. Inst. Tech., Melbourne; mentor grad. sch. of computer resource mgmt. Webster U., 1993-94. Recipient cert. of appreciation NASA, 1969, Excalibur award. Mem. Tau Beta Pi, Sigma Phi Epsilon. Republican. Baptist. Avocations: stamp collecting, playing the organ. Home: 36649 Sundance Dr Grand Island FL 32735 E-mail: teslafjohnson@hotmail.com.

JOHNSON, THOMAS G., JR., lawyer; b. Norfolk, Va., Apr. 4, 1942; BA, U. Va., 1964, LLB, 1969. Bar: Va. 1969. Atty. Willcox & Savage P.C., Norfolk, Va.; chmn. Wilcox & Savage P.C., Norfolk, Va. Mem. Va. State Bd. Edn., 2003—; bd. dir. Va. Found. Ind. Colls. Bd. editors: Va. Law Rev., 1967-69. Mem. Norfolk (Va.) Sch. Bd., 1976—90, chmn., 1981—90; bd. dir. Southside Boys and Girls Clubs. Mem. Raven Soc., Order of Coif, Phi Beta Kappa, Norfolk Sch. Bd., 1976-90, chmn., 1981-90. Democrat. Office: Willcox & Savage PC One Commercial Plz Ste 1800 Norfolk VA 23510*

JOHNSON, THOMAS STEPHEN, banker; b. Racine, Wis., Nov. 19, 1940; s. H. Norman and Jane Agnes (McAvoy) Johnson; m. Margaret Ann Werner, Apr. 18, 1970; children: Thomas Philip, Scott Michael(dec.), Margaret Ann. AB in Econs., Trinity Coll., 1962; MBA, Harvard U., 1964. Instr. Grad. Bus. Sch. Ateneo de Manila U., Philippines, 1964-66; spl. asst. to contr. U.S. Dept. Def., Washington, 1966-69; with Chem. Bank, N.Y.C., 1969-89, pres., dir., 1983-89, Mfrs. Hanover Trust Co., N.Y.C., 1989-91; chmn., CEO GreenPoint Fin. Corp., GreenPoint Bank, N.Y.C., 1993—. Bd. dirs. Alleghany Corp., R.R. Donnelley & Sons, Inc., The Phoenix Cos., Inc., Lower Manhattan Devel. Corp. Trustee, past chmn. Trinity Coll.; chmn., bd. trustees U.S. Japan Found.; chmn. bd. dirs. Inst. Internat. Edn.; bd. dirs. Cancer Rsch. Inst., Channel 13-WNET, United Way N.Y.C. Mem.: Coun. Fgn. Rels., Harvard Club N.Y.C., Links N.Y.C., River Club N.Y.C., Palm Beach Polo and Country Club, Montclair Golf Club. Roman Catholic. Office: GreenPoint Fin Corp 90 Park Ave Fl 4 New York NY 10016-1301

JOHNSON, VALERIE ANNE, elementary education educator; b. Plainfield, N.J., May 29, 1942; d. Keith W. and Vivian M. (Craig) Hall; children: Monica Lei, Michael Keith. BA in English, Bloomfield (N.J.) Coll. & Sem., 1964; cert., Kean Coll., 1965, Trenton State U., 1966; MLitt, Drew U., 1980. Cert. elem. and secondary English tchr., prin., supr., asst. supt., N.J. Tchr. 4th grade Mansfield Elem. Sch., Port Murray, N.J., 1964-65; tchr. 6th grade Washington Elem. Sch., Plainfield, N.J., 1965-72, tchr. kindergarten-1st grade, 1972-90, computer resource tchr., 1988—, tchr. 2d grade, 1990-93; tchr. 5th grade Woodland Elem. Sch., Plainfield, 1993—. Therapist, ednl. program dir. Newark Counseling Ctr., 1987-89. Drew U. scholar, 1978. Mem. ASCD, N.J. Assn. for Ednl. Tech., N.J. Northeast Coalition of Ednl. Leaders Inc. Episcopalian. Avocations: video productions, bowling. Home: 1744 Mountain Ave Scotch Plains NJ 07076-1060

JOHNSON, WILLARD RAYMOND, political science educator, consultant; b. St. Louis, Nov. 22, 1935; s. Willard and Dorothy (Stovall) J.; m. Vivian Robinson, Dec. 15, 1957; children: Caryn L., Kimberly E. BA, UCLA, 1957; MA, Johns Hopkins U., 1961; PhD, Harvard U., 1965. Asst. prof. polit. sci. MIT, Cambridge, Mass., 1964-69, assoc. prof., 1969-73, prof. polit. sci., 1973-96, prof. emeritus, 1996—. Vis. assoc. prof. Harvard U. Sch. Bus., Cambridge, 1969; exec. dir. Circle Inc., Roxbury, Mass., 1968-70; adj. prof. Fletcher Sch., Medford, Mass., 1971-82; cons. U.S. Nat. Commn. for Minority Enterprise, Washington, 1969; bd. dirs. Interfaith Housing Corp., Boston, 1970; chmn. bd. Circle Inc. subs. Greater Roxbury Devel. Corp., 1970; mem. U.S. Commn. for UNESCO, Washington, 1960-66 Author: The Cameroon Federation, 1970, (with Vivian R. Johnson) West African Governments and Volunteer Development Organizations, 1990; contbr. articles to Daedalus, 1973-82; New Eng. dir. Jour. African Civilizations, 1979-82, Jour. Modern African Studies, 1983, Negro History Bull., 2001; mem. editl. bd. Africa Today, 1975-2001. Bd. dirs. TransAfrica and TransAfrica Forum, Washington, 1978-95, chmn., 1984-86, pres. Boston chpt., 1980-84, 89-90; chmn. Africa Policy Task Force, McGovern for Pres. campaign, 1972; sr. adv. bd. Boston Pan-African Forum, Inc., 1997—; pres. Kans. Inst. African Am. and Native Am. Family History, 1997—. Recipient M.L. King Jr. award MIT Pres.'s Office, 1982—, YMCA Black Achiever's award, 1988; fellow and grantee Ford Found.; grantee Social Sci. Research Council, 1975, Rockefeller Found., 1977; Fulbright grantee, 1987; resident fellow Rockefeller Study Ctr., Bellagio, Italy, Sept. 1987; Fulbright scholar Indonesia, summer 1991. Mem. Coun. Fgn. Rels., Assn. Concerned African Scholars (bd. dirs. 1977—, nat. co-chmn. 1984-89), African Studies Assn., Nat. Conf. of Black Polit. Scientists. Democrat. Baptist. Office: MIT Dept Polit Sci 30 Wadsworth St Cambridge MA 02142-1320

JOHNSON, YVONNE AMALIA, elementary education educator, science consultant; b. DeKalb, Ill., July 1, 1930; d. Albert O. and Virginia O. (Nelson) J. BS in Edn., No. Ill. State Tchrs. Coll., 1951; MS in Edn., No. Ill. U., 1960. Tchr. Love Rural Sch., DeKalb, 1951-53, West Elem. Sch., Sycamore, Ill., 1953—2002; coord. Media Ctr. West Sch. Ill. honors sci. tchr., ISU, 1985-87. Contbr. articles to profl. publs. Bd. dirs. Sycamore Pub. Libr., 1974-98, pres. bd. dirs., 1984-98, chmn. maj. fund drive for addition to libr., 1994-98; founder Dekalb County Excellence in Edn. award, 1999. Named DeKalb County Conservation Tchr., 1971, Gov.'s Master Tchr., State of Ill., 1984, Outstanding Agrl. Tchr. in the Classroom Dekalb County Farm Bur., 1993; grantee NSF, 1961, 62, 85, 86, 87, NASA, 1988; Sci. Lit. grantee State of Ill., 1992-94. Mem. NEA, NSTA (cert. in elem. sci.), Ill. Sci. Tchrs. Assn., Ill. Edn. Assn., Sycamore Edn. Assn., Coun. for Elem. Sci. Internat. Office: West Elem Sch 240 Fair St Sycamore IL 60178-1641

JOHNSON-BROCK, LETHER SHEREE, secondary education educator; b. Bamberg, S.C., Mar. 6, 1953; m. Michael Steven Brock, July 3, 1991. BS, Claflin Coll., 1975; MAT, Howard U., 1977; MA, U. D.C., 1986. Tchr. D.C. Pub. Schs., Washington, 1975—, Tchr. Corps., 1975-76, Taft Jr. High Sch., 1976-79, Francis Jr. High Sch., 1979-92, Anacostia Sr. High Sch., 1992—; tchr. adult edn. Prince Georges County Pub. Schs., Hyattsville, Md., 1992-93; tchr. Ballou Sr. H.S., Washington, 1993—. Facilitator Backus Sci./Math. Ctr., Washington, 1987-92; internat. faculty mem. Challenger Ctr., Alexandria, Va., 1992—. Recipient Tchr.'s award Cafritz Found., 1989, Growth Initiatives for Tchrs. award GTE Found., 1991; Earthwatch fellow, 1987, Dept. of Def., 1985, NASA/Nat. Sci. Tchrs. Assn., 1991; named Outstanding Sci. Tchr. United Black Fund, 1993. Mem. Nat. Sci. Tchrs. Assn., D.C. Sci. Educators Assn. (v.p. 1991-93), D.C. Network Minority Women in Sci. (membership chair 1983), Claflin Coll. Alumni Assn. (treas. 1983—). Methodist. Avocations: traveling, hiking, cooking, reading, exploring. Office: Ballou Sr HS 3401 4th St SE Washington DC 20032-5499

JOHNSON-CHAMP, DEBRA SUE, lawyer, educator, writer, artist; b. Emporia, Kans., Nov. 8, 1955; d. Bert John and S. Christine (Brigman) Johnson; m. Michael W. Champ, Nov. 23, 1979; children: Natalie, John. BA, U. Denver, 1977; JD, Pepperdine U., 1980; postgrad., U. So. Calif., 1983-84. Bar: Calif. 1981. Pvt. practice, Long Beach, Calif., 1981-82, L.A., 1981-87, Woodland Hills, Calif., 1993-99; of counsel Greenbaum & Champ, 1999—. Legal reference librarian, instr. Southwestern U. Sch. Law, L.A., 1982-88; adj. prof. law, 1987-88; atty. Contos & Bunch, Woodland Hills, 1988-93; free lance writer/artist; owner The Purple Iguana, 1997—; of counsel Greenbaum & Champ LLP, 1999—. Editor-in chief: Southern Calif. Assn. Law Libraries Newsletter, 1984-85; mem. law rev. Pepperdine U., 1978-80; contbr. articles to profl. jours. Trustee United Meth. Ch., Tujunga, Calif., 1986-88. West Pub. Co. scholar, 1983; recipient H. Wayne Gillis Moot Ct. award, 1980, Vincent S. Dalsimer Best Brief award 1979. Mem. ABA, So. Calif. Assn. Law Libr., Am. Assn. Law Libr., Calif. Bar Assn., Southwestern Affiliates, Friends of the Libr. L.A. Democrat. Home and Office: 5740 Valerie Ave Woodland Hills CA 91367-3967 E-mail: legaldebi2@prodigy.net.

JOHNSON-COLE, LUELLA EMILY, educator; b. Modesto, Calif., Jan. 10, 1945; d. Lloyd E. and Lue Elizabeth (Alcorn) Swanson; m. Larry T. Cole, June 28, 2003; children: Katherine Gandy, Scott Johnson. AA in English, Modesto Jr. Coll., 1964; BA in English, U. Calif., 1966; MA in Spl. Edn., Calif. State U., 1977. Tchr. Hart-Ransom Elem. Sch., Modesto, Calif., 1966-67, Patterson (Calif.) Unified Sch. Dist., 1967-69, Kings Canyon Unified Sch. Dist., Reedley, Calif., 1969-70; dir., tchr. Patterson Coop. Presch., 1973-74; resource specialist Turlock (Calif.) Elem. Sch. Dist., 1977-79; resource specialist, coord. Oakdale (Calif.) Elem. Sch. Dist., 1979-80, tchr. spl. edn., 1980-81; resource specialist, tchr. Stanislaus Union Elem. Sch. Dist., Modesto, 1981, adminstr. summer sch., 1990. Mem. Christian edn. commn. Ch. of the Brethren, Modesto, 1989-91, mem. worship and spiritual life commns., 1993-97, mem. witness commn. 1999—. Mem. NEA, Calif. Tchrs. Assn. (negotiating team 1984-86, chpt. sec. 1982, chpt. v.p. 1988-89), Delta Kappa Gamma (chpt. treas. 1994-98, chpt. sec. 1992-94). Democrat. Avocations: reading, gardening, needlecraft, home improvement. Home: 3544 Traveler Ct Modesto CA 95355-3663 Office: Prescott Sr Elem Sch 2243 W Rumble Rd Modesto CA 95350 E-mail: luellaj@worldnet.att.net., luellacole@hotmail.com.

JOHNSON-COUSIN, DANIELLE, French literature and cultural studies educator; b. Geneva; d. Edouard Henri and Suzanne Louise Cousin; m. Harry Morton Johnson, Jan. 25, 1970; 1 child, Eliza Suzanne Johnson. Cert. de Maturité cum laude, Coll. of Geneva, 1962; BA, U. Alaska, 1966; MA, Purdue U., 1968; PhD, U. Ill., 1977; postgrad., Oxford U., 1968, Northwestern U., Evanston, Ill., 1968-69, Maximilian U., Munich, 1970, Mellon Regional Seminar Lit. Crit., Vanderbilt U., 1987. Vis. lectr. U. Ill., Urbana-Champaign, 1976-77; asst. prof. French Amherst Coll., 1979-82; asst. prof. French, Andrew W. Mellon fellow Vanderbilt U., Nashville, 1982-88, dir. Vanderbilt-in-France program Aix-en-Pce, 1984-85; assoc. prof. French Fla. Internat. U., 1988—2002. Cons. Social Scis. and Humanities Rsch. Coun. of Can., Ottawa, 1994—. Contbr. articles to profl. jours. Named U. Mass. Oxford scholar, 1968; fellow, U. Ill., 1971—73, Inst. Advanced Studies in Humanities, U. Edinburgh, Scotland, 1979, numerous others. Mem. Nat. Assn. Scholars, Am. Assn. Tchrs. French (emeritus), Am. Soc. 18th-Century Studies, Assn. Lit. Scholars and Critics, Soc. des Professeurs Francais et Francophones en Am., Assn. J.J. Rousseau (Neuchatel), Soc. Vaudoise d'Histoire & d'Archéologie (Lausanne), Internat. Soc. for Study of European Ideas, Internat. Parliament of Writers (Strasbourg), Internat. Dir. of 18th Century Studies, Oxford, Oglala Lakota Coll. Alumni (hon.), Pi Delta Phi (hon.). Home: 9805 SW 115th Ct Miami FL 33176-2582

JOHNSON-LAIRD, PHILIP NICHOLAS, psychologist; b. Rothwell, Eng., Oct. 12, 1936; s. Frederick Ryberg and Dorothy (Blackett) J.-L.; m. Maureen Mary Sullivan, Aug. 1, 1959; children: Ben, Dorothy. BA with honors, Univ. Coll., London, 1964; PhD, Univ. Coll., 1967; Doctorate (hon.), U. Gothenburg, Sweden, 1983, Padua (Italy) U., 1997, Trinity Coll., Dublin, Ireland, 2000, Nat. U. Distance Edn., Madrid, Spain, 2000, U. Ghent, Belgium, 2002. Asst. lectr., then lectr. psychology Univ. Coll., London, 1966-73; vis. mem. Inst. for Advanced Study, Princeton, N.J., 1971-72; reader, prof., chair exptl. psychology Sussex U., Brighton, Eng., 1973-82; spl. appointment, asst. dir. Med. Rsch. Coun. Applied Psychology Unit, Cambridge, Eng., 1982-89; prof., Stuart prof. psychology Princeton U., 1989—. Vis. prof. cognitive sci. Stanford (Calif.) U., 1980, vis. prof. psychology, 1985; vis. prof. Trieste (Italy) U., 1990, Univ. Coll., 1992, NYU, 1996, Padua, 2000. Author: Mental Models, 1983, The Computer and the Mind, 1988, (with Ruth Byrne) Deduction, 1991, 7 others; contbr. over 200 articles to profl. jours. Mem. Campaign for Disarmament, London, 1959-82. Recipient Medaglia D'Onore, U. Florence, Italy, 1989. Fellow: Royal Soc. U.K., Brit. Acad.; mem.: Soc. Exptl. Psychologists, Brit. Psychol. Soc. (Spearman medal 1974, Pres.'s award 1985), Am. Psychol. Soc. Avocations: modern jazz piano, arguing. Office: Princeton U Dept Psychology Princeton NJ 08544-0001 E-mail: phil@princeton.edu.

JOHNSON-LEESON, CHARLEEN ANN, former elementary school educator, insurance agent, insurance consultant, regional executive assistant; b. Battle Creek, Mich., June 10, 1949; d. Kenneth Andrews Leeson and Ila Mae (Weed/Lesson) McCutcheon; m. Lynn Boyd Johnson, Aug. 8, 1970; children: Eric Andrew, Andrea Johnson McGrath. BA, Spring Arbor Coll., 1971; MS, Reading Specialist, Western Ill. U., 1990. Cert. elem. and secondary tchr., Mich., elem. tchr., Ill., reading K-9, Ill. Tchr. Hanover (Mich.) Horton Schs., 1972-73, Virden (Ill.) Elem. Sch., 1984-90; ins. agt. State Farm Ins., Virden, Ill., 1991-95, cons. Springfield, Ill., 1995-97, regional exec. asst. Bloomington, Ill., 1997-99, agt. Myrtle Beach, S.C., 1999—. Collegiate and jr. high sch. cheerleading advisor in field; course leader Agt. Schs. 1, 2, and 3. Music dir., pianist Zion Luth. Ch., Farmersville, Ill., 1979-88, organist, pianist Olive St. Friends, Battle Creek, 1961-67. Recipient Honor the Educator award World Book, 1988, 89, Soaring Eagle award Millionair/Amb. Club, 1991-98, Amb. Club, 2001-02; Wilson Stone scholar, 1990, Mich. State scholar, 1967. Mem. AUA, Internat. Reading Assn., S.C. Assn. Life Underwriters, Nat. Assn. Ins. and FIn. Advisors, Alpha Upsilon Alpha. Avocations: music (piano and organ), writing. Home: 9621 Chestnut RIdge Dr Myrtle Beach SC 29572 Office: 119 Waccamaw Med Park Conway SC 29526-8902 Office Fax: 843-347-9326. E-mail: charleen.johnson.cyxd@statefarm.com.

JOHNSON-MILLER, CHARLEEN V. teacher coordinator; b. Cleve., Ohio, Jan. 17, 1948; d. Leroy and Alice Vivian Carter; m. Sammy Richard Miller, Dec. 24, 1980; 1 child, Patrice. BS in Edn., Ctrl. State U., 1970; MS in Edn., Cleve. State U., 1979; postgrad., Clevel. State U., 1985, John Carroll U., 1983. Permanent tchg. cert. Ohio, 1985. Cleve. Tchrs. Union rep. Cleve. Pub. Schs., 1982—86, cons. tchr., mentor, 1988—93, guidance/drug liaison, 1992—95; lead tchr. Cleve. Mcpl. Schs., 1995—99, grade level chairperson, 1996—2000, safety patrol dir., 1998—, Helping One Student to Succeed/tutor vol. coord., 1999—. Cons. tchr., facilitator human devel. Kent (Ohio) State U., 1983—90; program developer, curriculum planner guidance program Cleve. Pub. Schs., 1985—91, dist. prof. developer, 1993—99. Mem. Present Day Bapt. Ch. Scholar Martha Holden Jenning scholar, Martha Holden Jennings Found., Cleve., 1990. Mem.: Cabinettes, Scrabblers (past pres., v.p., sec.), Alpha Kappa Alpha, Phi Delta Kappa, Inc. (life). Avocations: tennis, bowling, aerobics, kickboxing, line dancing.

JOHNSTON, CALVIN GEORGE, secondary education educator; b. Lincoln, Nebr., Apr. 5, 1942; s. Stewart Arthur and Elizabeth Louise (Hogle) J.; m. Frances Delana Aldrich, Aug. 14, 1966 (div. 1992); children: Price Johnston, Rob Sontag, Deborah Sontag, Emily Johnston; m. Joann Balhorn, March 20, 1993. BS, U. Nebr., 1963, MEd, 1969. Cert. tchr. Colo. Tchr. sci. and social studies Byron Pub. Schs., Nebr., 1963-64; tchr. sci. Montrose County Region I J Pub. Schs., Colo., 1964-66; tchr. sci. and social studies Columbus City Schs., Nebr., 1966-68; tchr. sci. Albuquerque Pub. Schs., N.Mex., 1968-69; tchr. sci. and social studies Wheat Ridge Jr. High, Colo., 1969-74; tchr. social studies Bear Creek High Sch., Lakewood, Colo., 1974—. Advisory education com. Denver Post Newspaper, 1990—, Chapter II Colo. State Dept. Edn., 1993—. Vol. probation counselor Jefferson County Ct., Littleton, 1969-74; com. mem. Close Up Community Svc. Project for Colo., 1992; candidate U.S. Congress, Colo. 5th Congl. Dist., 1990. Mem. Colo. Coun. Social Studies (chair. 1992—), Nat. Edn. Assn., Colo. Edn. Assn., Jefferson County Edn. Assn., Nat. Coun. for Social Studies. Democrat. Methodist. Avocations: photography, travel, hiking, bicycling. Home: 8160 Storm King Peak Littleton CO 80127-4023 Office: Bear Creek High Sch 3490 S Kipling St Denver CO 80227-4309

JOHNSTON, CAROLYN S. elementary education educator, reading specialist; AA, Marymount U.; BA, George Washington U.; MEd, Salisbury State U.; EdD, U. Md. Cert. elem. tchr. grades 1-6, reading specialist grades K-12, elem. and middle sch. prin. and supr., Md. Career edn. coord. Delmana Adv. Coun., Salisbury, Md.; Chpt. 1 reading and math. coord. Wicomico County Bd. Edn., Salisbury. Mem. Teaching Effectiveness Network, coord.; editorial adv. bd. Scholastic, Inc., N.Y.C. Contbr. articles to profl. jours. Mem. Wicomico County Arts Coun. Mem. NEA, Md. State Tchrs. Assn., Internat. Reading Assn., Ea. Shore Reading Coun., Wicomico County Tchrs. Assn., Habitat for Humanity. Home: 922 Colony Dr Salisbury MD 21804-8758

JOHNSTON, JAMES H. elementary school educator; b. Hartford, Conn., June 10, 1947; s. James H. and Phyllis M. (Mortensen) J.; m. Barbara A. Swallow, Aug. 22, 1975; children: Karin E., Margaret A. BA, U. Conn., 1969; MS in Elem. Edn., Ctrl. Conn. State U., 1973, cert. in reading, 1990. Cert. K-8 tchr., K-12 lang. arts cons., Conn. Tchr. Bloomfield (Conn.) Bd. Edn., 1969-95; lang. arts specialist Tolland (Conn.) Bd. Edn., 1995—2002. Dir. Impact II, N.Y.C., 1993-95; adj. prof. reading Ctrl. Conn. State U. Contbr. column to Jour. Mid. Sch. Reading, also articles to profl. jours. Chair subcom. Town Govt., South Windsor, 1994; pres. Timothy Edwards, PTO, South Windsor, 1991-95; chair outreach bd. Wapping Cmty. Ch., South Windsor, 1994—, pres. couples club, 1994-95. Grantee New Eng. Reading Assn., 1989, Cigna Corp., 1992. Mem. Nat. Coun. Tchrs. English (bd. dirs. Jr. High/Mid. Sch. sect. 1994—, chair 1999-2001), Conn. Tchrs. English (bd. dirs. 1993—), Conn. Reading Assn. (bd. dirs. 1990-92), Internat. Reading Assn., Nat. Mid. Sch. Assn., Conn. Coun. English (bd. dirs. 1993), Celebrations of Excellence (bd. dirs. 1991-95). Mem. United Ch. of Christ. Avocations: reading, computers. Office: Ctrl Conn State U Reading Dept 1615 Stanley St New Britain CT 06050 E-mail: jimjceleb@aol.com.

JOHNSTON, JOYCE ASHMORE, secondary education educator; b. San Antonio, May 31, 1955; d. James Edward and Bonnie Aleen (Duncan) Ashmore; m. Jack Russell Hinds, Sr., June 4, 1976 (div. 1985); 1 child, Jack Russell Jr.; m. Bobb Johnston, Aug. 6, 1986; 1 child Bonnie Carole. BS, Northeastern State U., 1978, MEd, 1989. Cert. tchr., reading specialist, Okla. Freelance artist, Tahlequah, Okla., 1973-80; photojournalist Cherokee County Chronicle, Tahlequah, Okla., 1973-78; tchr. Woodall (Okla.) Pub. Sch., 1978-79; instr. ACT Talking Leaves Job Corps Ctr. NSU, Tahlequah, 1979-80; artist Arts of Tulsa; asst. dir. computer programing Bryan Inst., Tulsa, 1981-82; freelance artist McAlester, Okla., 1982-83; photojournalist, typesetter Latimer County News Tribune, Wilburton, Okla., 1982-88; tchr. Wilburton Pub. Schs., 1988—; coach cheerleaders Wilburton High Sch., 1992—. Mem. evaluation team North Ctrl. Assn. Colls. and Schs., Okla., 1991, 92; dir. Little Digger Cheer Camp, Wilburton, 1992; mem. Okla. learner outcomes, reading com. Okla. Dept. Edn. Contbr. articles to newspapers; author, designer Salute to Working Women, 1992. Charter mem. PTA, Wilburton, 1988; coord. pub. rels. Latimer County Outdoor Recreation Park, Wilburton, 1991-93; dir. Learn to Swim, Wilburton, 1991, 92, Fall Soccer Program, Wilburton, 1991, 92. Mem. AAUW (v.p. programs 1991-93, pres. 1993-95), Bus. and Profl. Women U.S.A. (corr. sec. 1991-92), Nat. Reading Assn., Okla. Reading Assn., Okla. Edn. Assn., Wilburton Edn. Assn., Okla. Secondary Schs. Activity Assn., Cherokee Nation Okla., Nat. Cheerleader Assn., Order Ea. Star (star point 1990-91), Beta Sigma Phi. Republican. Baptist. Avocations: photography, freelance writing, typesetting, serigraphy. Home: 720 Nickell Ln Wilburton OK 74578-9565 Office: Wilburton High Sch 1201 W Blair Ave Wilburton OK 74578-2009

JOHNSTON, MARY ELLEN, retired nursing educator; b. Roswell, N.Mex., June 4, 1951; d. E. Bernard and Jane (Shugart) J. BSN, Baylor U., 1973; MSN, Oral Roberts U., 1982. Staff nurse crit. care dept. Tucson Med. Ctr., 1973-74; charge nurse med. unit St. Mary's Hosp., Roswell, 1975; instr. nursing Ea. N.Mex. U., Roswell, 1975-2000; ret., 2000. Mem. ANA (cert. med.-surg. nurse), N.Mex. Nurses Assn. (past pres. dist. V), Baylor U. Nurses Alumni Assn., Philanthropic and Ednl. Orgn. (N.Mex. state officer), Daus. of Am. Colonists, Altrusa Club Roswell, DAR, Sigma Theta Tau. Republican. Methodist. Home: 2715 N Kentucky Ave Apt 16 Roswell NM 88201-5868

JOHNSTON, MICHAEL (WILLIAM JOHNSTON), political science educator, university administrator; b. Omaha, Nebr., Nov. 1, 1949; s. William M. and Margaret Mary (Ryan) J.; m. Bette Bennett, 1976; children: Michael Joseph, Patrick Brendan Ryan. BA in Polit. Sci summa cum laude, Macalester Coll., St. Paul, 1971; MPhil in Polit. Sci., Yale U., 1974, PhD in Polit. Sci., 1977. Teaching fellow, acting instr. Yale U., 1972-76; instr. U. Pitts., 1976-77, asst. prof., 1977-82, assoc. prof., 1982-86; from assoc. prof. to prof. Colgate U., Hamilton, NY, 1986—2003, Charles A. Dana prof. polit. sci., 2003—. Chmn. Colgate U. Rsch. Coun.; vis. lectr. politics, vis. fellow Ctr. Urban and Regional Rsch. U. Glasgow, Scotland, 1983—84; vis. fellow dept. politics and Inst. Rsch. in Social Scis. U. York, England, 1991; vis. fellow St. Aidan's Coll., 1997; vis. fellow dept. politics U. Durham, England, 1997; rsch. assoc. Cogen, Holt and Assocs., New Haven, 1974—75; Pitts. on-site coord. cmty. devel. block grants evaluation ABT Assocs., Cambridge, Mass., 1979—80; leader US Info. Agy. Seminar on corruption and democracy, Mongolia, 1999; participant anti-corruption confs.; participant, working group chair Ditchley (Eng.) Conf., 1998; coord. rsch. on case studies Internat. Political Bribery, Italy, 2000; bd. dirs., coun. governance Transparency Internat. USA; co-organizer program on governance and democratization 2nd Conv. European Assn. Advancement Social Scis., Cyprus, 1997, U.S. AID Ptnrs.' Conf., Washington, 2000; spkr. in field; cons. in field; presenter in field. Author: Political Corruption and Public Policy in America, 1982, Fraud, Waste and Abuse in Government, 1986, Political Corruption: A Handbook, 1989; co-editor: Political Corruption, 2002; contbr. articles to profl. jours. NSF fellow, 1972-76; grantee U. Pitts., 1983, Nuffield Found., 1984, Fulbright/British Coun. Higher Edn., 1984, Colgate U. Rsch. Coun. Maj. Grants com., 1987, New Liberal Arts program Colgate U./Sloan Found., 1988, 90, Leverhulme Trust/Social and Cmty. Planning Rsch., 1998, NEH fellow 2002-03. Mem. Internat. Polit. Sci. Assn., Internat. Studies Assn., Am. Polit. Sci. Assn., Beta Kappa, Pi Sigma Alpha. Democrat. Roman Catholic. Avocations: computing, baseball, trains. Home: 41 W Main St Earlville NY 13332-1900 Office: Colgate U Dept Polit Sci 13 Oak Dr Hamilton NY 13346-1383 Fax: 315-228-7883. E-mail: mjohnston@mail.colgate.edu.

JOHNSTON, NORMAN JOHN, retired architecture educator; b. Seattle, Dec. 3, 1918; s. Jay and Helen May (Shultis) J.; m. Lois Jane Hastings, Nov. 22, 1969. BA, U. Wash.-Seattle, 1942; B.Arch., U. Oreg., 1949; M. in Urban Planning, U. Pa.-Phila., 1959, PhD, 1964. Registered architect, Wash. City planner Seattle City Planning Commn., 1951-55; asst. prof. arch. U. Oreg.-Eugene, 1956-58; assoc. prof. architecture and urban planning U. Wash.-Seattle, 1960-64, prof., 1964-85, prof. emeritus, 1985—, assoc. dean, 1964-76, 79-84, chmn. dept. architecture, 1984-85. Mem. nat. exams. com. Nat. Coun. Archtl. Registration Bds., Washington, 1970-81, 88-99; vis. prof. Tokyo Inst. Tech., 1991, 98; Fulbright prof. Istanbul Tech. U., 1968-69; mem. Wash. State Archtl. Registration Bd., 1989-2000, chmn., 1988-89. Author: Cities in the Round, 1983, Washington's Audacious State Capitol and its Builders, 1988 (Gov.'s Book award 1984, 89), The College of Architecture and Urban Planning, 75 Years at the University of Washington: A Personal View, 1991, The Fountain and the Mountain - The University of Washington Campus, 1895-1995, 1995-2003, National Guide Series: The University of Washington, 2001; editor: NCARB Architectural Registration Handbook, 1980; contbr. articles to profl. jours. Mem. King County Policy Devel. Commn., Seattle, 1970-76; mem. Capitol campus design adv. com. State of Wash., Olympia, 1982-2000, chmn., 1980-88, 96; trustee Mus. History and Industry, 1997-2000. Recipient Wash. Disting. Citizen award, 1987, Barney award AIA Coll. of Fellows, 2003. Fellow AIA (pres. Seattle chpt. 1981, AIA medal Seattle chpt. 1991, Wash. Coun. medal 1997); mem. Phi Beta Kappa, Sigma Chi, Tau Sigma Delta. Presbyterian. Home: 900 University St Apt Au Seattle WA 98101-1778 Office: U Wash C Architecture & Urban Planning PO Box 355726 Seattle WA 98195-5726 E-mail: njjo@u.washington.edu.

JOHNSTONE, CRAIG S. elementary education educator; Tchr. Page (Ariz.) Mid. Sch., 1992-94. Recipient Tchr. Excellence award Internat. Tech. Edn. Assn., Ariz., 1992. Home: 7811 East Lindon St Tucson AZ 85715*

JOHNSTONE, D. BRUCE, university administrator; b. Mpls., Jan. 13, 1941; s. D. Bruce and Florence Morton (Elliott) J.; m. Gail Eberhardt, July 30, 1965; children: Duncan Bruce, Cameron. BA, Harvard U., 1963, M.A.T., 1964; PhD, U. Minn., 1969; D (hon.), Towson St U., 1995, D'Youville Coll., 1995, Calif. State U., San Diego, 1997. Tchr. econs. and history, Westport, Conn., 1964-65; asst. dir. U. Minn. Center for Econ. Edn., 1966-69; adminstrv. asst. to Sen. Walter F. Mondale, 1969-71; project specialist Ford Found., 1971-72; exec. asst. to pres. U. Pa., 1972-77, assoc. prof. edn., 1976-79, v.p. for adminstrn., 1977-79; pres. State U. Coll. at Buffalo, 1979-88; chancellor SUNY Sys. Office SUNY, Albany, 1988-94, prof. Buffalo, 1994—. Author: New Patterns for College Lending, 1973, Sharing the Costs of Higher Education, 1986; co-editor: The Funding of Higher Education: International Perspectives, 1993, In Defense of American Higher Education, 2001; contbr. articles to profl. jours. Bd. dirs. Buffalo Arts Commn.; bd. trustees D'Youville Coll. Democrat. Episcopalian.

JOHNSTONE, JOYCE VISINTINE, education educator; b. Columbus, Ohio, Nov. 12, 1943; d. James Joseph and Virginia (Vogel) Visintine; m. James S. Luckett, Nov. 27, 1965 (dec. May 1969); children: Anne, Robert; m. William E. Kuhn, Sept. 1, 1995. BA, Cath. U. Am., 1965; MA, Butler U., 1974; PhD, Ind. U., 1994. Tchr. Columbus Pub. Schs., 1965-68, Hawaii Pub. Schs., Wahiawa, 1968-69, Montgomery County (Md.), Wheaton, 1969-70; chair edn. dept. Marian Coll., Indpls., 1975-98; Ryan dir. ednl. Outreach U. Notre Dame, South Bend, 1998—, fellow Inst. for Ednl Initiative, 1998—. Dir. Ind. Cath. Prins. Inst., 1989-94. Cath. Prins. Inst. grantee Lilly Endowment, Indpls., 1990, Project Enhance grantee Ind. Bell, Indpls., 1991, 95; Parent Partnership grant Danforth Found., 1995-97. Mem. ASCD, Assn. Tchr. Educators (pres. 1990-91, Turkey Run Outstanding Educator 1990), Ind. Assn. Colls. for Tchr. Edn. (pres., 1990-92, Outstanding Svc. award 1995). Roman Catholic. Office: Inst Ednl Initiative Univ Notre Dame Notre Dame IN 46556

JOHNSTONE, SALLY MAC, educational association administrator, psychology educator; b. Macon, Ga., Dec. 8, 1949; d. Ralph E. and Maxine A. J.; m. Stephen R. Tilson, 1977; 1 child, Emma. BS, Va. Poly. Inst., 1974, MS, 1976; PhD, U. N.C., 1982. Lectr. European div. U. Md., Heidelberg, Germany, 1982-84, instr. psychology College Park, 1984-89, asst. dean, 1984-86, dir. Ctr. for Instructional Telecom., 1986-89; dir. Western Coop. for Ednl. Telecom., Boulder, Colo., 1989—. Cons. Northwest Legis. Leadership Forum, Seattle, 1990, Pacific Northwest Econ. Region, Whistler, B.C., 1991, Calif. State U. System, 1993; invited panelist U.S. Dept. Edn., Washington, 1990, 97, Aspen Inst., Washington, 1990, Pacific Northwest Econ. Region, 1991-92; presenter Pacific Rim Pub. U. Pres. Conf. Asia Found., Bangkok, Thailand, 1990, Workshops Pacific Telecom Coun., Honolulu, 1991, 99; spkr. edn. commn. states' Legislator's Workshop, Cin., 1992; meeting Nat. Assn. State Univs. & Land Grant Colls. Distance Edn. & Telecomm. Working Group; witness U.S. Senate Subcom. Edn., Humanities and Arts, Washington, 1991; study advisor Corp. Pub. Broadcasting, 1993; spkr. So. Assn. Schs. and Colls., 1997, Nat. Assn. State Univs. and Land Grant Colls., 1997; advisor Western Govs. U., 1996-98. Author: Lessons on Accommodations for Colleges and Rural High Schools Linking Electronically, 1996; co-author: (with Witherspoon and Wasem) Rural TeleHealth: Telemedicine, Distance Education and Informatics, 1993; co-editor: (with Markwood) New Pathways to a Degree: Technology Opens the College, 1994; editl. bd. Tech. Svc., Internat. Jour. Edn. Telecom. Judge sci. fair U. Hills Elem. Sch., Md., 1986-89; mem. adv. com. Boulder Valley Sch. Bd., 1999; bd. trustees U.S. Open Univ.; adv. com. Nat. Info. Ctr. Hispanic Edn., 1999, Consortium Advancement Pvt. Higher Edn., 1998—; com. co-chair Nat. Postsecondary Edn. Coop., 1998—. Grantee Annenberg/CPB Project, 1988, 91-96, Fund for Improvement of Postsecondary Edn., 1993, 96, Dept. Commerce Nat. Telecomms. and Info. Adminstrn., 1994, U.S. Dept. Edn., 1991, 99, Western Assn. Schs. and Colls., 1997; recipient Disting. Rsch. award Nat. U. Continuing Edn. Assn., 1989. Mem. Am. Psychology Assn., Am. Assn. Higher Edn. (bd. mem. 1998). Avocations: hiking, cross-country skiing, photography. Office: Western Coop Ednl Telecoms 1540 30th St Boulder CO 80303-1012

JOHNSTONE, STOWELL, former state agency administrator; Grad., U. Idaho, 1953, MA in Edn./Adminstrn., 1960. Tchr. Moscow (Idaho) High Sch., 1956-58; tchr., dir. driver edn. Moscow Sch. Dist. # 28, 1957-66; acting prin. Moscow Mid. Sch., 1958-59; prin. Moscow Jr. High, 1959-61; dir. secondary curriculum Moscow Sch. Dist., 1961-62, adminstrv. asst. to supt. schs., 1962-64; prin. Moscow High Sch., 1964-67, West Anchorage (Alaska) High Sch., 1967-70; dir. audio-visual svcs., libr. processing and TV prodn. Anchorage Sch. Dist., 1970-71, dir. secondary edn., 1971-78, asst. dep. supt. secondary sch. mgmt., 1978-81, asst. dep. supt. ednl. planning, 1981-82; chair Alaska Bd. Edn., Juneau, 1994-98; pres. Stowell and Assoc., 1982—. Instr. U. Idaho, 1958-60; part time supr. maintenance pers. Moscow Sch. Dist., 1963-67; part time instr. U. Alaska, Anchorage, 1956-85, Anchorage C.C.; trustee Alaska Coun. Econ. Edn., 1977-85. Active exec. com. Jr. Achievement of Alaska, 1966-85; chmn. Alaska Pub. Broadcasting Commn., 1969-83; bd. dirs. Alaskan of Yr. Com., 1979-82; v.p., mem. Alaska Repertory Theatre Statewide Bd., 1979-85; v.p. Alaska March of Dimes Bd., 1988-89. With USAF, 1953-56, col. Res. ret. Recipient Outstanding Young Men of America award, Disting. Svc. award, Moscow, 1966, Gov.'s award for Outstanding Svc. to Alaska, 1979, Disting. Svc. award Alaska Assn. Secondary Sch. Prins., 1980, Exec. of Yr. award City of Anchorage, 1980. Mem. Northwest Assn. Schs. and Colls. (chmn. Alaska com. 1973-78, pres. commn. schs. 1978-82, sec. 1983—, pres. 1991-94), Northwest Assn. of Schs. and Colls.

JOINER, THOMAS, psychology educator; Bright-Burton prof. psychology Fla. State U., Tallahassee, 2000—, dir. univ. psychology clinic. Recipient Young Investigator award, Nat. Alliance Rsch. on Schizophrenia and Affective Disorders, 1994, David Shakow Early Career award for disting. scientific contbn., Divsn. Clin. Psychology APA, 1997, Disting. Scientific award for early career contbn. to psychology, APA, 1999, Edwin S. Schneidman award for scientific contbns. to suicide rsch., Am. Assn. Suicidology, 2001; fellow, John Simon Guggenheim Meml. Found., 2003. Office: Fla State U Dept Psychology 315 Psychology Bldg Tallahassee FL 32306-1270*

JOINES, KEITH P. See PERRYMAN-JOINES, KEITH

JOKLIK, WOLFGANG KARL, biochemist, virologist, educator; b. Vienna, Nov. 16, 1926; s. Karl F. and Helene (Giessl) J.; m. Judith Vivien Nicholas, Apr. 9, 1955 (dec. Apr. 1975); children: Richard G., Vivien H.; m. Patricia Hunter Downey, Apr. 23, 1977. B.Sc. with 1st class honors, U. Sydney, Australia, 1948, M.Sc., 1949; D.Phil. (Australian Nat. U. scholar), U. Oxford, Eng., 1952. Australian Nat. U. research fellow, Copenhagen, Denmark, 1953, Canberra, Australia, 1954-56; fellow, 1957-62; assoc. prof. cell biology Albert Einstein Coll. Medicine, Bronx, N.Y., 1962-65, prof. cell biology, 1965-68, Siegfried Ullmann prof. biochem. virology, 1966-68; prof., chmn. dept. microbiology and immunology Duke U. Med. Ctr., Durham, N.C., 1968-92, James B. Duke Disting. prof. microbiology and immunology, 1972-92, James B. Duke prof. microbiology, 1992-96, James B. Duke prof. emeritus, 1996—. Sr. author: Zinsser Microbiology, 15th, 16th, 17th, 18th, 19th, 20th edits.; editor-in-chief Virology, 1975-93, Microbiological Rev., 1991-95; contbr. articles to profl. jours. Recipient Sr. U.S. award Alexander Humboldt Found., 1985, ICN Internat. prize for virology, 1991. Mem. NAS, Inst. Medicine of NAS, Am. Soc. Virology (pres. 1982-83), Am. Soc. Microbiology, Am. Soc. Biol. Chemists. Address: Duke U Med Ctr Dept Molecular Genetics and Microbiology PO Box 3020 Durham NC 27710-0001 E-mail: joklikb@aol.com.

JOLLES, MITCHELL IRA, engineering consultant; b. Bronx, N.Y., Feb. 10, 1953; BS in Aerospace Engring., MS in Applied Mechanics, Poly. Inst. Bklyn., 1973; PhD in Engring. Mechanics, Va. Poly. Inst., 1976. Instr. engring. sci. and mechanics Va. Poly. Inst., Blacksburg, 1973-76; asst. prof. aerospace and mech. engring. U. Notre Dame, Ind., 1976-79; assoc. prof. mech. and aerospace engring. U. Mo., Columbia, 1979-82; head of fracture mechanics sect. Naval Rsch. Lab., Washington, 1982-88; chmn. mech. engring. Widener U., Chester, Pa., 1988-91, prof. mech. engring., 1988-97; sr. sys. developer Towers Perrin, Phila., 1997-2000; sr. tech. cons. Hewlett-Packard, Phila., 2000—. Dir. Wallingford (Pa.)-Swarthmore Sch. Dist., 1991-95. Contbr. articles to profl. jours. and procs. Recipient Jimmie Hamilton award Am. Soc. Naval Engrs., 1989, Alan Berman Rsch. Publ. award Naval Rsch. Lab., 1989, Ralph R. Teetor award Soc. Automotive Engrs., 1979, Dow Outstanding Young Faculty award Am. Soc. Engring. Educators, 1979. Mem. Sigma Xi, Tau Beta Pi, Phi Kappa Phi. E-mail: mjolles@home.com.

JOLLEY, BETTY CORNETTE, history educator; b. Taylors Valley, Va., Apr. 3, 1927; d. Benjamin Harrison and Joyce Joanne (Stamper) Cornette; m. Harley Edison Jolley, Dec. 24, 1949; children: Benjamin Joseph, Stuart Lynn. BS, Appalachian State U., 1949, MA, 1955; postgrad., U. N.C., Chapel Hill, U. London. Tchr. Haynes Sch., Winston Salem, N.C., 1949-50, Newton Elem. Sch., Asheville, N.C., 1950-52, Nathans Creek (N.C.) Sch., 1952-53; asst. librarian Mars Hill (N.C.) Coll., 1953-55, prof. history, 1955--. Cons. various N.C. public schs., 1970--; supr. social studies tchrs., Mars Hill Coll., 1970--; prof. tchr. Continuing Edn. Program, Mars Hill Coll., 1970--; workshop leader, 1986; mem. Southern Assn. Accreditation Com., 1987, social studies tchr., edn. coord., Tchr. Evaluation Com., N.C. Edn. Assn.; chair Appalachian Consortium Regional coop. and Devel. Com., 1990--; advisor local coll. chpt. Phi Alpha Theta, 1982--. Co-author: (video) North Carolina: A Goodly Land and a Hardy People, 1985; contbr., advisor (workbook) Appalachian Studies. Precinct chmn. Madison County (N.C.) Constitutional Bicentennial Com., 1987-91, Dem. precinct chair, Mars Hill, 1986-89; judge Optimist Club, Buncombe County, N.C., 1984-89, N.C. Western dist. judge dist. oratorical/CCHI finals, 1993; speaker various N.C. churches, 1989—. Piedmont U. study/travel grantee, London, Paris, 1966, faculty devel. grantee, 1991, NEH grantee, 1967, N.C. Humanities Media grantee, 1969, Nat. Humanities travel/study grantee, China, 1989; recipient Disting. Service and Mentor award Mars Hill Coll., 1985. Mem. Western N.C. Historical Assn., Hist. Preservation Orgn., Delta Kappa Gamma (pres. Alpha Phi chpt.). Baptist. Avocations: reading, travel, cooking, rockhounding, writing poems.

JOLLEY, WELDON BOSEN, surgery educator, research executive; b. Gunnison, Utah, Sept. 8, 1926; s. Edward Mckinley Jolley and Rosella (Elvira) Bosen; m. Dorathy Timms, Dec. 21, 1954 (dec. Jan. 1983); children: Elizabeth Price, Kathleen Cope, Phillip Jolley; m. JoLane Laycock, Aug. 20, 1983; children: Jessica, Brian. BA, Brigham Young U., 1952; PhD, U. So. Calif., 1959; postdoctoral, UCLA, 1960. Prof. surgery, physiology and biophysics Loma Linda (Calif.) U., 1969—, assoc. dir. surg. research lab., 1969—; dir. surg. research VA Hosp., Loma Linda, 1979-85; pres. Nucleic Acid Research Inst., Costa Mesa, Calif., 1985—95. Bd. dirs. SPI Pharms., Inc.; sr. v.p., bd. dirs. ICN Pharms., Inc.; sci. adv. Viratek, Inc. Contbr. tech. articles to publs. Named McPherson Soc. Clin. Prof. of Yr., 1982. Home: 3825 E Woodbine Rd Orange CA 92867-8008

JOLLIN, PAULA, special education educator; b. Worcester, mass., Apr. 16, 1943; d. Robert Alfred and Norma (Goulet) Jollin; children: Jeffrey David, Michelle Suzanne. BS, Syracuse U., 1965, MS, 1968; cert. in learning disabilities, Montclair State Coll., 1979. Cert. tchr., N.J., N.Y., Md. Tchr. East Syracuse (N.Y.)-Minoa Bd. Edn., Montgomery County Bd. Edn., Bethesda, Md.; reading specialist South Orange (N.J.)-Maplewood Bd. Edn.; learning disabilities specialist Hackensack (N.J.) Med. Ctr. Inst. Child Devel.; tchr., cons. learning disabilities Elmwood Park (N.J.) Bd. Edn., 1984—. Adj. reading specialist Montclair State Coll., Upper Montclair, N.J.; ind. cons. learning disabilities diagnosis, remediation, Glen Ridge, N.J., 1979—; presenter at profl. confs.; presenter workshops. Speaker on learning disabilities to civic orgns. Mem. NEA, AAUW, N.J. Edn. Assn., Elmwood Park Edn. Assn., Coun. Exceptional Children, N.J. Spl. Educators Assn., Phi Delta Kappa. Home: 1034 Ash Dr Mahwah NJ 07430-2349 Office: Elmwood Park Bd Edn 475 Boulevard Elmwood Park NJ 07407-2029

JOLLY, DANIEL EHS, dental educator; b. St. Louis, Aug. 25, 1952; s. Melvin Joseph and Betty Ehs (Koehler) Jolly; m. Paula Kay Haas, 1972 (div.); 1 child, Farrell. BA in Biology and Chemistry, U. Mo., Kansas City, 1974, DDS, 1977. Resident in hosp. dentistry VA Med. Ctr., Leavenworth, Kans., 1977-78; pvt. practice Newcastle, Wyo., 1978-79; asst. prof. U. Mo., Kansas City, 1979-87; chief restorative dentistry Truman Med. Ctr., Kansas City, 1979-87; dir. dental oncology Trinity Luth. Hosp., 1982-87; assoc. prof., dir. gen. practice residency program Ohio State U., Columbus, 1987—, prof., dir. gen. practice residency program, 1993—. Dir. Honduras Clinic Project, 1992—; bd. dirs. Rinehart Found. U. Mo. Dental Sch., Kansas City, 1985—87; cons. Lee's Summit (Mo.) Care Ctr., 1984—87, Longview Nursing Ctr., Grandview, 1986—87; sec. Combined Hosp. Dental Staff, Columbus, 1989—90, v.p., 1990—91, pres., 1991—92. Author: (manual) Hospital Dental Hygiene, 1984, Hospital Dentistry, 1985, OSU Manual Hospital Dentistry, 1989—, (booklet) Nursing Home Dentistry, 1986, Dental Oncology, 1986. Mem. profl. adv. coun. Easter Seal Soc., 1986—92, sec. bd. dirs. Easter Seal Rehab. Ctr., 1990—93, mem. regional coun. Kansas City, 1985—87; pres. Health Profls. Serving Humanity. With U.S. Naval Sea Cadet Corps, 1998—99. Recipient Alumni Achievement award in dentistry, U. Mo., Kansas City, 1995. Fellow: Pierre Fauchard Acad., Am. Coll. Dentistry, Acad. Dentistry Handicapped (pres. 1992), Am. Assn. Hosp. Dentists (regional v.p. 1993—, sec., pres.-elect 2002—03, pres. 2003—), Am. Soc. Dentistry Children, Acad. Gen. Dentistry, Am. Soc. Geriatric Dentistry, Acad. Dentistry Internat.; mem.: ADA, Ohio Dental Assn. (Humanitarian award 1998), Internat. Soc. Oral Oncology, S.W. Oncology Group, Fedn. Spl Care Orgns. Dentistry (chmn. 1992—93), Greater Kansas City Dental Soc., Internat. Assn. Dentistry handicapped (pres. 1994—96, past pres. 1996—98, editor 1998—), Magna Charta Barons Club. Avocations: photography, skiing, scuba diving, swimming, horses. Home: 1601 W Fifth Ave # 118 Columbus OH 43212-2310 Office: Ohio State U Coll Dentistry PO Box 182357 305 W 12th Ave Columbus OH 43218-2357 E-mail: jolly.4@osu.edu.

JOLLY, MICHAEL JOHN, college administrator; b. Oct. 24, 1960; s. John T. and Lois E. (Sumpter) J. BS, Adams State Coll., 1984, MA, 1985. Dir. housing and residence life Adams State Coll., Alamosa, Colo., 1986—2001; dir. univ. housing Idaho State U., Pocatello, Idaho, 2001—. Student counselor Adams State Coll., 1986—2001, lab. instr., 1986—2001. Mem.: Assn. Coll. and U. Housing Officers, Assn. Student Judicial Affairs, Assn. Intermountain Housing Officers (treas. 2000—), West Region Nat. Assn. Coll. Auxiliary (bd. dirs. 1999—2001, nominations com. 2002), Nat. Assn. Coll. Auxiliary (profl. devel. com. 2002—, svcs. awards com. 2000—01), Am. Coll. Pers. Assn., Elks, Phi Delta Kappa. Office: Idaho State University Housing Campus Box 8083 Pocatello ID 83209 E-mail: jollmich@isu.edu.

JOLLY, WILLIAM THOMAS, foreign language educator; b. Helena, Ark., Apr. 8, 1929; s. Sidney Eugene and Eva (Jones) J. BA, Southwestern at Memphis, 1952; MA, U. Miss., 1958; PhD, Tulane U., 1968. Assoc. ancient langs., chmn. dept. Millsaps Coll., Jackson, Miss., 1959-65; assoc. prof. Greek and Latin Rhodes Coll., Memphis, 1965-75, prof., 1975-94, chmn. dept. fgn. langs., 1975-79, prof. emeritus, 1994—. With USN, 1953-55. Recipient Clarence Day award Day Found., 1991. Mem. Am. Philol. Assn/, Linquistic Soc. Am., Archaeol. Inst. Am., Classical Assn. Mid. West & South, Tenn. Classical Assn., Tenn. Philol. Assn., Am. Classical Legue. Democrat. Methodist. Home: 697 University St Memphis TN 38107-5138 Office: Rhodes Coll 2000 N Parkway Memphis TN 38112-1690

JONAKAIT, GENE MILLER, developmental neurobiologist, neuroimmunologist, educator; b. Evanston, Ill., May 15, 1946; d. William Cleveland and Mary Gene (Herren) Knopf; m. Randolph N. Jonakait, Mar. 21, 1970; 1 child, Amelia. AB, Wellesley (Mass.) Coll., 1968; MA, U. Chgo., 1969; PhD, Cornell U. Med. Coll., 1978. Postdoctoral fellow Cornell U. Med. Coll., N.Y.C., 1978-81, asst. prof., 1981-85, Rutgers U., Newark, 1985-90, assoc. prof., 1990-94, prof., 1994—2001, chmn. dept. biol. scis., 1994—96, 2000—01, assoc. dean, 1996-98; dean Coll. Sci. and Liberal Arts NJ Inst. Tech., 2001—, disting. prof., 2003—. Chmn. conf. com. N.Y. Acad. Scis., N.Y.C., 1991-92; chmn. summer conf. neuroimmunology Fedn. Am. Socs. Exptl. Biology, Bethesda, Md., 1994, 96; co-chmn. Gordon Conf. in Glial-Neuronal Interactions, 2003. Assoc. editor Jour. Neurosci.; contbr. articles to profl. jours. including Neuron, Jour. Neurosci., Exptl. Neurology, Jour. Neurosci. Rsch., Jour. Neuroimmunology, Trends in Neurosci., Devel. Biology, Adv. Pharmacol., others. Recipient award for Excellence in Rsch., Rutgers U. Bd. Trustees, 1990; Wellesley scholar, 1968; grantee NIH, 1982-84, 86-89, 93-96, BRSG, 1986-90, Rutgers U. Busch grantee, 1990—, grantee Johnson & Johnson, 1987-89, NIMH, 1990-93, Office Naval Rsch., 1990-93, NSF, 1993—, Merck Rsch. Labs., 1994-95. Fellow AAAS; mem. Soc. Neurosci. Achievements include research in regulation of cholinergic differentiation, neuropeptide regulation of microglial function. Office: NJ Inst Tech 504 Cullimore Newark NJ 07102-

JONAS, HARRY S. medical education consultant; b. Kirksville, Mo., Dec. 3, 1926; s. Harry S. and Sarah (Laird) J.; m. Connie Kirby, Aug. 6, 1949; children— Harry S., III, William Reed, Sarah Elizabeth. BA, Washington U., St. Louis, 1949, MD, 1952. Intern St. Luke's Hosp., St. Louis, 1952-53; resident Barnes Hosp., St. Louis, 1952-56; practiced medicine specializing in ob-gyn., Independence, Mo., 1956-74; prof. ob-gyn, chmn. dept. ob-gyn Truman Med. Center; asst. dean U. Mo-Kansas City Sch. Medicine, 1975-78, dean, 1978-87, med. edn. cons., 2000—, spl. cons. to the dean; asst. v.p. med. edn. AMA, Chgo., 1987-2000. Mem. Independence City Council, 1964-68; mem. Jackson County (Mo.) Legislature, 1973-74. Mem. ACOG (pres. 1986-87), Ctrl. Assn. Obstetricians and Gynecologists, Assn. Profs. Gynecology and Obstetrics, Assn. Am. Med. Colls., A.C.S., AMA, Mo. Med. Assn., Jackson County Med. Soc., Kansas City Gynecol. Soc., Chgo. Gynecol. Soc. Home: 207 NW Spruce St Lees Summit MO 64064-1430 Office: U Mo-Kansas City Sch Medicine 2411 Holmes St Kansas City MO 64108-2741

JONAS, SARAN, neurologist, educator; b. N.Y.C., June 24, 1931; s. Myron and Margaret (Wurmfeld) J.; m. Ruth Haber, Sept. 16, 1956; children: Elizabeth Ann, Frederick Jonathan. BS, Yale U., 1952; MD, Columbia U., 1956. Diplomate Am. Bd. Psychiatry and Neurology, Am. Bd. Internal Medicine. Intern Bellevue Hosp., N.Y.C., 1956-57, resident and fellow in medicine and neurology, 1957-62; practice medicine specializing in neurology N.Y.C., 1964—; from clin. instr. to assoc. prof. clin. neurology NYU Sch. Medicine, 1964-77, prof. clin. neurology, 1977—, acting chmn. dept. neurology, 1987-91. Assoc. dir. neurology NYU Hosp., 1970-87, dir., 1987-91, dir. electroencephalography, 1969-94; acting dir. neurology Bellevue Hosp., N.Y.C., 1987-91, assoc. dir., 1991—, dir. electroencephalography, 1994—. Served with USN, 1962-64. N.Y. State fellow in rheumatic diseases, 1962-64 Mem. Am. Acad. Neurology, Assn. for Rsch. in Nervous and Mental Diseases, Am. Heart Assn. (Stroke Coun., Epidemiology Coun.), Am. Epilepsy Soc. Office: 530 1st Ave New York NY 10016-6402

JONASSAINT, JEAN, French and Francophone literatures educator; MA in Lit. Studies, U. Que., Montreal, 1981; PhD in French Studies, U. Montreal, 1990. Sr. lectr. U. Que., Montreal, 1979-96; cultural adviser City of Montreal, 1988-95; asst. prof. French and francophone lit. Duke U., Durham, N.C. Literary commentator News Paper, Le Devoir, Montreal, 1991-92. Author: La Déchirure du texte et autres brèches, 1984, Le Pouvoir des mots, les maux du pouvoir. Des romaniers haïtiens de l'exil, 1986, Des romans de tradition haïtienne. Sur un récit tragique, 2002; editor, guest editor De l'autre littérature québécoise Autoportraits, supplement Lettres Québécoises, 1992; editor, pub. Dérives, 1975-87; mem. assoc. editors bd. Nepantla: Views from South; mem. reading and evaluation com. Jour. Études Francophones; contbr. articles to profl. jours. Rsch. grantee Can. Coun. for the Arts Explorations, 1981, Can. Coun. for the Arts, 1986, Sec. State Can./Multiculturalism, 1994-95, Trent Found., Duke U., 2000; PhD fellow Fonds Formation Chercheur et Action Concertée, 1983-85. Mem.

MLA, Conseil Internat. d'etudes Francophones, Am. Comparative Lit. Assn., Assn. des éditeurs de périodiques culturels québécois (pres. 1979-80). Office: Duke Univ Romance Studies Box 90257 Durham NC 27708-0257 Office Fax: 919-684-4029. E-mail: /jonj1996/@duke.edu.

JONES, ALICE SAMUELS, elementary education educator, reading specialist; b. Fayetteville, N.C., Mar. 20, 1931; d. Jerry Meyer and Maggie Lee (Graham) Samuels; m. Thomas Roosevelt Jones, Jr., Oct. 29, 1954; children: Michelle S. Jones, Thomas R. III. BS in Elem. Edn., Hampton (Va.) U., 1952; MEd in Reading, Boston U., 1958. Elem. tchr. Carver Elem. Sch., Richmond, Va., 1952-56, Charles Houston Elem. Sch., Alexandria, Va., 1956-58, Greenleaf Elem. Sch., Washington, 1958-60, Blow Elem. Sch., Washington, 1961-65; reading specialist Reading Clinic, Eaton Sch., Washington, 1965-67, Langdon, Plummer, Bacchus, Janney Elem. Sch., Washington, 1967-71, Green Elem. Sch., Washington, 1971-93. Writer: Competency Based Curriculum Guide K-12, 1982-93; editor Silver Tongues, 1985-86, Green Sch. News, 1990-93; assoc. editor Ten Talks, 1988-89. Named Tchr. of Yr. Edn. Inst., Washington, 1975; recipient Competency Based Curriculum Exemplary award D.C. Pub. Schs., 1979, Plaque D.C. Reading Coun. Internat. Reading Coun., Washington, 1990, Grant, D.C. Pub. Schs., 1985. Mem. ASCD, NAACP, Am. Assn. Retired Persons, African Am. Women's Assn., Internat. Reading Assn., Internat. Comm. In Reading (pres. 1992-93), D.C. Columbia Reading Coun. (rec. sec. 1992-93), Silver Tongues Club (pres.), Pi Lambda Theta (pres. 1984-85, plaque 1984). Democrat. Mem. Plymouth Congregation. Avocations: swimming, reading, gardening, traveling. Home: 824 Kennedy St NE Washington DC 20011-2731

JONES, ALMA ARLENE, elementary education educator; b. Atlanta, Nov. 7, 1932; d. Lloyd Emanuel and Gussie Marguerite (Hogan) Field; m. David Max Holder, June 19, 1954 (dec.); children: David Marcus, Samuel Wade, Lloyd Michael; m. Earl Clayborne Jones II, July 17, 1981. AS, Tyler Jr. Coll., 1956; BS in Elem. Edn., U. Houston, 1968; MEd in Reading, Stephen F. Austin U., 1975. Cert. profl. reading specialist, Tex. 2d grade tchr. Webster (Tex.) Elem. Sch., 1968-69; 3d grade tchr. Dickinson (Tex.) Elem. Sch., 1969-72; 5th grade tchr. Westwood Elem. Sch., Palestine, Tex., 1972-77; 3d and 4th grade tchr. Goliad Elem. Sch., San Angelo, Tex., 1977-79; 5th, 6th-8th grade reading specialist Creekwood and Kingwood Mid. Sch., Humble, Tex., 1979-82; 1st grade tchr. Jasper (Tenn.) Elem. Sch., 1982-85; 6th grade tchr. Patton Elem. Sch., Chattanooga, 1985-86; third grade tchr. Lookout Mountain (Tenn.) Sch., 1986—. Mem. staff Career Ladder III, Tenn. State Schs., 1985—; chmn. sch. improvement coun. Lookout Mountain Schs., 1993-95; faculty rep. Image/Hamilton County Schs., Lookout Mountain, 1993-94. Exhibited paintings at local cmty. fairs. Mem. choir First Bapt. Ch., 1986. Named to Tenn. Gov.'s Acad. for Tchrs. of Writing, 1993. Mem. Order of Ea. Star (chaplain 1995), 100th Bomb Group-8th Air Force. Republican. Avocations: reading, travel, crafts, writing short stories. Office: Lookout Mountain Sch 321 N Bragg Ave Lookout Mountain TN 37350-1299

JONES, ALPHA BELLE, physical education educator; b. Charleston, S.C., Sept. 24, 1956; d. Lewis Earle and Dolores (Page) J. BS in Edn., U. Ga., 1978; MEd, Furman U., 1986. Cert. health and phys. edn. tchr., S.C. Tchr. elem. phys. edn. Sch. Dist. Greenville (S.C.) County, 1978—; coach basketball, track, tennis Wade Hampton High Sch., Greenville, 1979-86, coach softball, 1990—. Asst. to athletic dir. aiding girl's sports Wade Hampton High Sch., Greenville, 1990—; mem. recreation com. Edwards Rd. Bapt. Ch., Greenville. Mem. AAHPERD, S.C. AAHPERD, S.C. Athletic Coaches Assn., Palmetto State Tchrs. Assn. Avocations: playing sports, needlepoint, traveling, choir, saxophone.

JONES, ANITA KATHERINE, computer scientist, educator; b. Ft. Worth, Mar. 10, 1942; d. Park Joel and Helene Louise (Voigt) J.; m. William A. Wulf, July 1, 1977; children: Karin, Ellen. AB in Math., Rice U., 1964; MA in English, U. Tex., 1966; PhD in Computer Sci., Carnegie Mellon U., 1973, PhD in Sci. and Tech. (hon.), 2000. Programmer IBM, Boston, Washington, 1966-69; assoc. prof. computer sci. Carnegie-Mellon U., Pitts., 1973-81; founder, v.p. Tartan Labs. Inc., Pitts., 1981-87; free-lance cons. Pitts., 1987-88; prof., head computer sci. dept. U. Va., Charlottesville, 1988-93, prof., 1997—, univ. prof., 1998—, Lawrence A. Quarles prof. engring. and applied sci., 1999; dir. def. rsch. and engring. Dept. Def., Washington, 1993-97. Mem. Def. Sci. Bd., Dept. Def., 1985-93, 98—; mem. sci. adv. bd. USAF, 1980-85; governing bd. Nat. Sci. Found.; vice-chair governing bd. NSF, 1998-2000; bd. dirs. Sci. Applications Internat. Corp., InQTel; trustee Mitre Corp., 1989-93, chair Va. Rsch. and Technology Adv. Commn., 1999-2002, Commonwealth of Va. Advs. Commn.; mem. corp. Charles Stark Draper Labs., 1999—. Editor: Perspectives on Computer Science, 1977, Foundations of Secure Computation, 1971. Recipient Air Force Meritorious Civilian Svc. award, 1985, Medal for Disting. Pub. Svc. Dept. of Def., 1996, Disting. Svc. award Computing Rsch. Assn., 1997. Fellow IEEE, AAAS, Assn. Computing Machinery (editor-in-chief Transactions on Computer Sys. 1983-91), Am. Acad. Arts and Scis.; mem. Nat. Acad. Engring., Sci. Found. of Ireland (bd. dirs. 2000-2003), Sigma Xi. Avocation: gardening. E-mail: jones@virginia.edu.

JONES, ARNEITHA R. middle school educator; b. Westmoreland, Va., July 31, 1961; d. James L. and Etta H. (Hughes) Reed; m. Owaiian Maurice, Aug. 13, 1983; children: Shadei Ebony, Owaiian W., Jamal M. BS cum laude, Va. State U., 1983, MS cum laude, 1993. Tchr., Knoxville, Tenn., 1983-86, King George (Va.) Middle Sch., 1986—. Chmn. spl. edn. dept. King George Middle Sch., 1990-91. Mem. Dem. Party. Mem. Va. State U. Alumni Assn. (treas.). Democrat.

JONES, ARTHUR EDWIN, JR., library administrator, English and American literature educator; b. Orange, N.J., Mar. 20, 1918; s. Arthur Edwin and Lucy Mabel (Alpaugh) J.; m. Rachel Evelyn Mumbulo, Apr. 24, 1943; 1 child, Carol Rae Jones Jacobus BA, U. Rochester, 1939; MA, Syracuse U., 1941, PhD in English, 1950; MLS, Rutgers U., 1964. Instr. English Syracuse U., N.Y., 1946-49, Drew U., Madison, N.J., 1949-52, asst. prof., 1952-55, assoc. prof., 1955-60, prof. English and Am. lit., 1960-86, dir. libraries, 1956-85, prof., libr. emeritus, 1986—. Evaluator Middle States Assn. Colls., Phila., 1955-85. Author: Darwinism and American Realism, 1951; contbr. articles to profl. jours.; book reviewer Library Jour., 1956-75, Choice, 1969— Trustee Madison Pub. Library, N.J., 1958-79, pres., 1976-79. Served to 1st lt. U.S. Army, 1941-46 Named to U. Rochester Athletic Hall of Fame, 1997; Lilly Endowment scholar Am. Theol. Libr. Assn., 1963-64 Mem. MLA, Nat. Coun. Tchr. of Eng., ALA (councillor 1970-71), Am. Theol. Libr. Assn. (pres. 1967-68), AAUP, Lions Club, Habitat for Humanity. Democrat. Home: 400 Avinger Ln Apt 409 Davidson NC 28036-9718

JONES, BARBARA ANN, elementary education educator; b. Rockville Centre, N.Y., Nov. 2, 1946; d. Robert C. and Doris M. (Felten) J. BS in Edn., St. John's U., 1968; MA, Hofstra U., 1971; MS, Coll. New Rochelle, 1996. Tchr. Our Lady of Peace Sch., Lynbrook, N.Y., 1968-86, Uniondale (N.Y.) Pub. Schs., 1986—; pers. trainer A & S, Hempstead, 1985-87. Leader 4-H Club, Franklin Square, N.Y., 1973-84, corr. sec. leaders coun.; active PTA. Roman Catholic. Avocations: crafts, needlework, stamp collecting. Office: Uniondale Pub Schs Smith St Sch 780 Smith St Uniondale NY 11553-3399

JONES, BARBARA CHRISTINE, linguist, creative arts designer, educator; came to U.S., 1964, naturalized, 1971; d. Martin and Margarete (Roth-Rommel) Schulz von Hammer-Parstein; m. Robert Dickey, 1967 (div. 1980); m. Raymond Lee Jones, 1981. Student, U. Munich, 1961, Philomatique de Bordeaux, France, 1962; BA in German, French, and Speech, Calif. State U., Chico, 1969, MA in Comparative Internat. Edn., 1974. Cert. secondary tchr., C.C. instr., Calif. Fgn. lang. tchr. Gridley Union H.S., Calif., 1970-80, home econs., decorative arts instr., cons., 1970-80, English study skills instr., 1974-80, ESL coord., instr. Punjabi, Mex. Ams., 1970-72, curriculum com. chmn., 1970-80; program devel. adv. Program Devel. Ctr. Supt. Schs., Butte County, Oroville, Calif., 1975-77; opportunity tchr. Esperanza H.S., Gridley, Calif., 1980-81, Liberty H.S., Lodi, Calif., 1981-82, resource specialist coord., 1981-82; Title I coord. Bear Creek Ranch Sch., Lodi, Calif., 1981-82, instr., counselor, 1982-83; sub. tchr. Elk Grove (Calif.) Unified, 1982-84. Freelance decorative arts and textiles designer, 1982-95; internat. heritage and foods adv. AAUW, Chico, Calif, 1973-75; lectr. German, Schreiner Coll., Kerrville, Tex., 1993; workshop dir. Creative Arts Ctr., Chico, 1972-73; workshop dir., adv. Bus. Profl. Women's Club of Gridley, 1972-74; mem. Cowboy Artists Mus., Kerrville, 1996-99; v.p. Golden State Mobile Home League, Sacramento, 1980-82; mem. publicity Habitat for Humanity, Kerrville br., 1992-94. Weavings-wall hangings (1st pl. 10 categories, Silver Dollar Fair, Chico, Calif., 1970). Vol. Ariz. Superior Ct., Foster Care Review Bd., 2003. Mem.: AAUW (publicity dir. cultural activities Kerrville br. 1991—92), Am. Assn. German Tchrs., German Texan Heritage Soc., Turtle Creek Social Cir. (pioneer 1992—99), USAR Non-Commd. Officer's Assn. (ednl. adv. 1984—86), Am. Cancer Soc. (publicity 1992—95), Kerrville Garden Club (publicity 1993—97), United European Am. Club, Kappa Delta Pi. Avocations: textile design, swimming, travel, real estate, mosaics. Home: 3350 Pasadena Ave Kingman AZ 86401-5046

JONES, BONNIE DAMSCHRODER, government agency administrator; b. Cocoa, Fla., Dec. 20, 1945; d. Eugene Edward and Lu Jeanette (Hufford) Damschroder; m. Robert Kirk Jones, June 8, 1968; children: Kelly Anne, Jennifer Graham. BS in Edn., Capital U., Columbus, Ohio, 1967; MS in Edn., George Mason U., 1976; transition specialist cert., U. Hawaii, 1988; EdD, Columbia U., 2000. Tchr. mental retardation Waterford (Conn.) Pub. Schs., 1967-68; tchr. mentally retarded Escambia County Schs., Pensacola, Fla., 1968-70; tchr. learning disabilities Fairfax County Schs., Fairfax, Va., 1975-78; curriculum specialist Newport News (Va.) Pub. Schs., 1978-80; program coord. Peninsula Area Coop. Ednl. Svcs. Day Treatment Regional Sch., Newport News, 1980-81; dist. transition coord. Hawaii Dept. Edn., Honolulu, 1984-88; program specialist Kans. Dept. Edn., Topeka, 1988-90; rsch. asst. Columbia U. Tchrs. Coll., N.Y.C., 1991-92; tchr. learning disabilities Fairfax County Pub. Schs., Fairfax, Va., 1992-94, tchr., dept. chairperson, 1994-96; program specialist U.S. Dept. Edn. Office of Spl. Edn. Programs, 1997—2002, edn. rsch. analyst, 2002—. Adj. faculty Grad. Sch. Edn., George Mason U., Fairfax, 1976, Fairfax, 1997—, Baruch Coll., 1992, Grad. Sch. Edn., Johns Hopkins U., Columbia, Md., 2002—; supervising tchr. Hampton (Va.) Inst., 1981, U. Hawaii, Honolulu, 1998, George Mason U., 1996; mem. exceptional needs standards com. Nat. Bd. for Profl. Tchg. Standards, 1994—98; nat. adv. com. on assessment of exceptional needs standards, 1998—. Co-author: Identifying Handicapping Conditions, 1978, Career Awareness for Students with Handicaps, 1986, Implementing Transition Goals, 1992, 2d edit., 1999, Student Led IEPs, 2000; mem. editl. bd. Career Devel. for Exceptional Individuals, 2000—. Mem. Jr. League, Portland, Maine, Honolulu, Topeka, and No. Va., 1983—; pres. USCG Officers' Wives Club, Portland, 1983, bd. dirs. Newport News, 1978-79, Honolulu, 1984-88, N.Y.C., 1991; co-chmn. carnival booth Punahou Sch., Honolulu, 1987, 88; treas. Red Hill Sch. PTA, Honolulu, 1985-87; bd. dirs. Internat. Divsn. Career Devel., 1989-94, treas., 1992-94; pres. Kans. Divsn. Career Devel., 1989-90. Recipient cert. of appreciation USCG, Boston, 1983, community svc. award, N.Y.C., 1991; Vocat. Educator of Yr. award Hawaii Vocat. Edn. Assn., 1987, Outstanding Contbn. to Transition award Kans. Div. on Career Devel., 1990, Outstanding Alumni award George Mason U. Grad. Sch. Edn., 1998. Mem. ASCD, Am. Ednl. Rsch. Assn., Coun. for Exceptional Children (subcom. on knowledge and skills profl. standards com. 1990-94, rsch. com. tchr. edn. divsn. 2000—), Phi Delta Kappa. Home: 7726 Silver Sage Ct Springfield VA 22153-2126 E-mail: bonnie.jones@ed.gov.

JONES, BONNIE JILL, elementary education educator; b. Canton, Ohio, Apr. 10, 1948; d. Billie George and Marjorie Ruth (Brandt) Kessler; m. Thomas Earl Jones, Aug. 20, 1966 (dec. 1977); 1 child, Jill Marie (dec. May 2001). BS in Elem. Edn., Malone Coll., 1986; M in Edn., Ashland U., 1996. Cert. tchr., Ohio. 2d grade tchr. Perry Local Sch., Massillon, Ohio, 1986-87, 3d-4th grade tchr., 1987-88, 3d grade tchr., 1988-89, 89-90, 4th grade tchr., 1990-91, 1st grade tchr., 1991-97, 2d grade tchr., 1997—2001, ret., 2001—. Lang. arts rep. Perry Local Schs. Deaconness Emmanuel Christian Ch., Massillon, 1992-94, sec. ch. gen. bd., 1992, choir mem., 1972—, Sunday sch. tchr.; mem. Calvary Chapel. Named Tchr. of Yr. East Ohio Gas Co., 1988-89; grantee Honeywell Corp., 1993-94. Mem. Kappa Delta Phi (chmn. ways and means 1991-92, rec. sec. 2000-04), Delta Tau. Avocations: singing, reading, walking, cooking. Home: 5935 Bosford St SW Navarre OH 44662-8408 Office: Genoa Elem Sch 519 Genoa Ave SW Massillon OH 44646-3772

JONES, BRENDA GAIL, school district administrator; b. Winnipeg, Man., Can., Nov. 5, 1949; d. Glen Allen and Joyce Catherine (Peckham) McGregor. BA, San Francisco State U., 1972; MA, U. San Francisco, 1983. Cert. tchr., sch. adminstr., Calif. Tchr. Lakeport (Calif.) Unified Sch. Dist., 1973-82, asst. prin., 1982-88, dir. ednl. svcs. and spl. projects, 1988-2000; dir. pupil personnel svcs. Redwood City (Calif.) Sch. Dist., 2000—. Instr. English Mendocino Coll., Ukiah, Calif., 1977-82. Mem. Assn. Calif. Sch. Adminstrs. (past pres. 1987, Lake County charter), Order Ea. Star (past matron Clear Lake chpt. 1995, dep. grand matron 1999). Democrat. Episcopalian. Avocations: health, fitness, walking, reading, gardening. Home: 1315 20th St Lakeport CA 95453-3051 Office: Redwood City sch Dist 750 Bradford St Redwood City CA 94063

JONES, BRIAN W. federal official; BSBA in Fin., Georgetown U.; JD, UCLA. Atty. Sheppard, Mullin, Richter & Hampton, San Francisco; pres. Ctr. New Black Leadership, Washington; counsel U.S. Sen. Jud. Com., Washington, 1999; dep. legal affairs sec. to Calif. Gov. Pete Wilson, 1999; atty. Curiale Dellaverson Hirschfield Kelly & Kraemer, LLP, San Francisco; gen. counsel Dept. Edn., Washington, 2001—. Contbr. (on air polit. and news analysis) MSNBC-TV. Office: Dept Edn Gen Counsel 400 Maryland Ave SW Washington DC 20202-2110*

JONES, CHARLOTT ANN, museum director, art educator, retired; b. Jonesboro, Ark., May 27, 1927; d. Arthur Philip and Mary Lillian (Falk) J. BA, St. Scholastica Coll., Duluth, Minn., 1962; MS in Edn., N. Tex. State U., 1970; PhD, Pa. State U., 1978. Tchr. St. Andrews Sch., Little Rock, 1947-51, Holy Souls Sch., Little Rock, 1951-55, Sacred Heart Sch., Muenster, Tex., 1955-56; prin. Holy Souls Sch., 1956-61, Sacred Heart High Sch., 1962-69; instr. art Ark. State U., Jonesboro, 1972-84, assoc. prof., 1974-90, mus., 1983—; mus. dir. Ark. State U. Mus., Jonesboro, 1983—2002; ret., 2002. Cons., writer art standard com. State of Ark., 1984; curator Ark. Women Artists Exhibit, Nat. Mus. Women in Arts, 1990-92. Contbr. articles to profl. jours. Grantee Inst. Mus. Svcs., Washington, 1986, 1995-97, Ark. Endowment Humanities, 1986, 88, 89, Ark. Historic Resources/Mus. Svcs., 1994. Mem. am. Assn. Mus., Nat. Art Edn. Assn. (Outstanding 18-state Region educator 1983), Ark. Mus. Assn. (pres. 1994-95, Outstanding Ark. Art Educator award 1983), Delta Kappa Gamma Internat. (arts com. chmn. 1982—), Phi Kappa Phi (pres. 1993-94). Democrat. Avocations: watercolor painting, canoeing.

JONES, CHARLOTTE, principal; b. Elk City, Okla., Dec. 21, 1949; d. S.G. and Mary Kathryn (Hartman) McLaury; m. Ray Loyd Jones, Apr. 3, 1969; children: Kathryn Denise, Ryan MacRay, Joshua Kyle. BS in Edn., U. Okla., 1976; MEd, Southwestern Okla. State U., 1991. Cert. tchr. math., counseling, social studies, lang. arts. Prin. Madison Elem. Sch., Norman, Okla. Mem.: ASCD, Nat. Assn. Elem. Sch. Prins., Okla. Assn. Elem. Sch. Prins., Rotary, Phi Delta Kappa. Home: 4409 Oxford Way Norman OK 73072-3160 E-mail: cjones@norman.K12.OK.us.

JONES, CHRISTOPHER PRESTIGE, classicist, historian; b. Kent, U.K., 1940; s. William Prestige and Irene May (McCreddie) J. BA, Oxford U., 1962; PhD Classical Philology, Harvard U., 1965. From lectr. to prof. U. Toronto, Can., 1965-92, chair dept. classics, 1986-90; prof. classics and history Harvard U., Cambridge, 1992-97, George Martin Lane prof. classics and history, 1997—. Vis. lectr. Harvard U., 1968; assoc. prof. Ecole Normale Supérieure de Jeunes Filles, Paris, 1979, Ecole Normale Supérieure, Paris, 1992; acting vice dean Faculty Arts and Scis., U. Toronto, 1985-86. Author: Philostratus: Life of Apollonius of Tyana, 1971, Plutarch and Rome, 1971, The Roman World of Dio Chrysostom, 1978, Culture and Society in Lucian, 1986, Kinship Diplomacy in the Ancient World, 1999; co-editor: Le Martyre de Pionios, prêtre de Smyrne, 1994; contbr. numerous articles to profl. jours. Fellow Royal Soc. Can., Am. Numismatic Soc.; mem. Am. Philol. Assn. (chair subcom. epigraphical bibliog. 1981-89, subcom. cartography 1986-90), Am. Acad. Arts and Scis., German Archeol. Inst. (corr. mem. 1992—), Am. Philos. Soc. Home: 130 Mount Auburn St Apt 107 Cambridge MA 02138-5757 Office: Harvard U Boylston Hall Cambridge MA 02138 E-mail: cjones@fas.harvard.edu.

JONES, CLAIRE BURTCHAELL, artist, teacher, writer; b. Oakland, Calif. d. Clarence Samuel and Florence Mallett (Hinchman) Burtchaell; m. E.C. Jones; children: Holland Mallett, Lela Claire, S. Evan. AB, Stanford U.; postgrad., Laguna Beach Sch. Art, 1972-73, San Diego Art Acad., 1980-82. Freelance art tchr., Park Ridge, Ill., 1967; tchr. Jade Fon Group, Pacific Grove, Calif., 1972-73, Merced Coll., Sierra Mountains, Calif., 1973; freelance pvt. workshop, painting for commns. and galleries Calif., 1973—. Bd. reviewers Dorland Mountain Arts Colony, 1990—. Author: First The Blade (ann. collection), 1939, Arrows in the Air, 1947-51, Utah Sings, 1953; editor: Watercolor West Newsletter, 1978-83; contbr. articles to profl. jours. Bd. reviewers Dorland Mountain Arts Colony, Temecula, Calif., 1985—. Recipient numerous awards for artwork. Mem. Nat. Mus. Women in the Arts (founding mem.), Assn. Western Artists (bd. dirs. 1970-71), Watercolor West (bd. dirs. 1978-81, 86—, membership chmn. 1988-96), Stanford Alumni Assn., Literati West (founder, sec.-treas. 1994—).

JONES, CLYDE ADAM, art educator, artist; b. Cobleskill, N.Y., Nov. 10, 1924; s. Lester L. and Myra (Karker) Jones. BFA, Syracuse U., 1948, MA, 1954; EdD, Pa. State U., 1961. Tchr. art North H.S., Binghamton, NY, 1948—49, 1950—56; instr. ceramics Jr. League of Binghamton, 1950—53; guest instr. ceramics Rehab. Guild, Saranac Lake, NY, 1951—54; asst. prof. art edn. Edinboro (Pa.) State Coll., 1956—58; instr., summer creative arts workshop Cornell U., Ithaca, NY, 1958; asst. prof. child devel. U. Conn., Storrs, 1961—66, asst. dean Sch. Home Econs. and Family Studies, 1976—79, assoc. prof. huyman devel. and family rels., 1966—85, prof. emeritus, 1985—; trustee Syracuse U. Libr. Assocs., 1970. Cons. Head Start program, Conn., 1965—66. One-man shows include Rehab. Guild, Saranac Lake, Windham Hosp., Willimantic, Conn., Art Bldg., Pa. State U., Student Union, U. Conn., exhibited in group shows at Roberson Meml., Binghamton, N.Y., Erie (Pa.) Art Mus., Munson-Williams-Proctor Inst., Utica, N.Y., Mus. Fine Arts, Syracuse, Norwich (Conn.) Art Mus., Schoharie County Arts Coun., Albany Inst. History and Art, Essex (Conn.) Art Assn., Rochester (N.Y.) Meml. Art Gallery, illustrations for history vols. of Sch. of Home Econs. and Family Studies and Sch., U. Conn. Mem. Gov.'s Commn. on Status of Women, Conn., 1965—67; governing bd. Nat. Assn. Creative Children and Adults, 1986—; bd. dirs. Greater Mansfield Arts Coun., 1986—, adv. bd., 1989—; dir., bd. dirs. Cobleskill Hist. Soc. Served U.S. Army, 1943—45. Recipient Hon. mention, Ceramic Nat. Exhbn., 1954. Mem.: Conn. Home Econs. Assn. (del., dir. 1978—82, newsletter editor 1984—, named Home Economist of Yr. 1992), Assn. for Childhood Edn. Internat., Internat. Soc. Edn. thru Art, Nat. Art Edn. Assn. (rsch. trainee 1965), Nat. Soc. Study of Edn., Soc. Rsch. in Child Devel., Nat. Assn. Edn. of Young Children, Hartford Assn. Edn. of Young Children (pres. 1967—69), New Eng. Assn. Edn. of Young Children (editor newsletter 1963—65, publs. com. 1980—, fin. com. 1999—), Conn. Assn. Edn. of Young Children (v.p. 1970—72), Phi Delta Kappa. Home: 52 Storrs Heights Rd Storrs Mansfield CT 06268-2322 Office: U Conn Sch Family Studies Storrs Mansfield CT 06269-0001

JONES, CONNIE JEANNE, primary school educator; b. Dayton, Ohio, July 23, 1950; d. Roger Glen and Anna Marie (Klein) Dils; m. David William Jones, July 4, 1987; children: Carrie Beth Grugin, Nicholas Scott Grugin. BS in Elem. Edn., Ea. Ky. U., 1972, MA in Elem. Edn., 1976, rank I elem. prin. and supr. of instrn., 1990. Tchr. 5th grade Croftshire Elem. Sch., Kettering, Ohio, 1972; primary tchr. Collins Lane Elem., Frankfort, Ky., 1972—, gifted and talented tchr., extended sch. supr., 1994-95. Tchr. rep. Interagy. Task Force on Family Resource and Youth Svc. Ctrs., Frankfort, 1991—, Site Base Decision Making Coun., Frankfort, 1992—, Adv. Coun., Frankfort, 1992-93. Bldg. chairperson United Way, Frankfort, 1989-90, Cystic Fibrosis, Frankfort, 1990-91; mem. Triangle Circle, First United Meth. Ch., Frankfort, 1986—. Named Outstanding Young Educator of Yr. Frankfort Jaycees, 1979; recipient Outstanding Tchr. award Franklin County Schs. by Ky. State U., 1978. Mem. ASCD, Ky. Edn. Assn., Franklin County Edn. Assn. (bldg. rep. 1989, 90, 91, 94-95, publicity chairperson 1990, 91). Avocations: arts and crafts, golf, travel. Home: 100 Thistle Rd Frankfort KY 40601-4463 Office: Collins Lane Elem Sch 1 Cougar Ln Frankfort KY 40601

JONES, DAVID ALWYN, geneticist, botany educator; b. Colliers Wood, Surrey, Eng., June 23, 1934; came to U.S., 1989; s. Trefor and Marion Edna Jones; m. Hazel Cordelia Lewis, Aug. 29, 1959; children: Catherine Susan, Edmund Meredith, Hugh Francis. BA, MA in Natural Scis., U. Cambridge, Eng., 1957; DPhil in Genetics, U. Oxford, Eng., 1963. Chartered biologist, UK. Lectr. genetics U. Birmingham, Eng., 1961-73; prof. genetics U. Hull, Eng., 1973-89, head dept. plant biology and genetics, 1983-88; prof. botany U. Fla., Gainesville, 1989—2003, chmn. dept. botany, 1989—98. Chmn. membership com. Inst. of Biology, London, 1982-87. Co-author: Variation and Adaptation in Plant Species, 1971, Analysis of Populations, 1976, What is Genetics?, 1976, Zmiennosc i przystosowanie roslin, 1977; contbr. over 100 articles to profl. jours. Fellow Linnean Soc., Inst. Biology; mem. AAAS, Am. Soc. Naturalists, Bot. Soc. Am., Internat. Soc. Chem. Ecology (coun. 1983-84, 89-91, keynote spkr. ann. meeting 1984, pres. elect 1986-87, pres. 1987-88, past pres. 1988-89, co-editor Jour. Chem. Ecology 1994-2000, Outstanding Svc. award 2001), Brit. Assn. Advancement of Sci. (chmn. coord. com. for cytology and genetics 1974-87), Genetical Soc. Gt. Britain (convenor ann. meetings profs. of genetics 1983-88), Ecol. Genetics Group, Population Genetics Group, Soc. for Study of Evolution, Gamma Sigma Delta, Sigma Xi (pres. U. Fla. chpt. 2000-01). Achievements include research in practical population biology especially in ecological genetics and chemical ecology of cyanogenic plants. Home: 7201 SW 97th Ln Gainesville FL 32608-6378 Office: U Fla Dept Botany 220 Bartram Hall Gainesville FL 32611-8526

JONES, DIONNE JUANITA, health scientist administrator, educator, researcher, consultant; b. Georgetown, Guyana, Sept. 14, 1945; came to U.S., 1970; d. Henry Hamilton and Beryl Marjorie (Williams) J.; children—Marcus Anthony, Dustin Troy, Dayton Lance. B.S. Howard U., 1974, M.S.W., 1976, PhD, 1987. Lectr., Putney Coll., London, 1968-70; instr. Walter Reed Med. Ctr., Washington, 1971-73; research assoc. Mental Health Ctr., Washington, 1976-78; publ. specialist Inst. Urban Affairs, Washington, 1978-79; research cons. M.Battle Assocs. and L.S.C., Washington, 1979-81; coordinator edn. and tng. Howard U. Hosp., Washington, 1982-84, sr. research assoc., Nat. Urban League, 1986-93, adj. prof., Howard U., 1988-90; sr. rsch. scientist Pacific Inst. Rsch. Evaluation,

Bethesda, 1993-98; adj. assoc. prof. U. Md., Adelphi, 1996—; health science adminstr. Nat. Inst. Drug Abuse, NIH, Bethesda, 1998—. Co-author: Higher Education and High Risk Students: Future Trends, 1990; author (with others) Mental Health: A Challenge to the Black Community, 1978; editor: Teenage Pregnancy: Developing Strategies for Change in the 21st Century, 1989, Prescriptions and Policies: The Social Well-being of African Americans in the 1990s, 1990; assoc. editor Black Caucus Jour., 1977-79, The Urban League Rev., 1986-88; editor Urban Research Rev., 1977-79, The Urban League Rev., 1988—; contbr. articles to profl. jours. Mem. adv. bd. dirs. St. Gabriel's Ch., Washington, 1977-78, tchr. Sunday Sch., 1977-79; mem. Ladies Guild, Trinity Episcopal Ch., Washington; speaker area high schs., Washington, 1978-79; mem. parents adv. com. YMCA, Washington, 1989-98. Mem. APA, Am. Ednl. Rsch. Assn., Am. Evaluation Assn. (editl. bd.), Ea. Evaluation Rsch. Assn. (exec. bd.), Assn. Social and Behavioral Scientists (mem. editl. bd., exec. com.), Phi Beta Kappa. Democrat. Home: 705 Hillsboro Dr Silver Spring MD 20902-3218 Office: Nat Inst Drug Abuse NIH 6001 Exec Blvd Bethesda MD 20892

JONES, DOROTHY JEFFERSON, elementary education educator; b. Washington, Jan. 13, 1948; d. Lawson Sayles and R. Irene (Valentine) Jefferson; m. John Christopher Jones, June 28, 1975. B in Elem. Edn., Va. Union U., 1969; MA, Trinity Coll., 1972; M Specialist, George Washington U., 1990. Cert. elem. tchr., D.C. Tchr. D.C. Pub. Schs., Washington, 1969—, dir. ednl. before and after program, 1986—. Fellow Inst. Ednl. Leadership; mem. Nat. Coun. Tchrs. Math., Internat. Reading Assn., Phi Delta Kappa (sec. 1988). Baptist. Avocations: reading, sports. Home: 9658 Boyett Ct Fairfax VA 22032-2829 Office: 1050 21st St NW Washington DC 20036-4904

JONES, ELAINE HANCOCK, humanities educator; b. Niagara Falls, N.Y., Feb. 17, 1946; d. Roy Elmer and June Edna (Clark) Hancock; m. Ralph Jones III, Oct. 9, 1971 (div. June 1981). AAS in Comml. Design, U. Buffalo, 1962; BFA, SUNY, Buffalo, 1971, MFA in Painting, 1975; postgrad., Fla. State U., 1993—. Med. illustrator Roswell Park Meml. Inst., Buffalo, 1967-70; designer, animator Acad. McLarty Film Prodns., Buffalo, 1970-73; publs. designer Buffalo/Erie County Hist. Soc., 1974-78; dir. publs. Daemen Coll., Amherst, N.Y., 1978-80; owner, art dir. Plop Art Prodns., Melbourne, Fla., 1981-86; instr. humanities Brevard C.C., Melbourne, 1986—; prof. humanities Brevard campus Rollins Coll., Melbourne, 1995—. One-woman shows include SUNY, Buffalo, 1974, Upton Gallery, N.Y., 1975, Gallery Wilde, Buffalo, 1978; exhibited in group shows at Fredonia Coll., N.Y., 1975, Upton Gallery, 1975, Brevard Art Mus., Melbourne, Fla., 1987. Mem. docent program Art Mus./Sci. Ctr., Melbourne, 1983-84, mem. edn. com., 1995—; officer Platinum Coast chpt. Sweet Adelines Internat., 1984-90. Nat. Merit scholar, 1971-75; recipient cert. of merit Curtis Paper Co., 1977; N.Y. State Coun. on Arts grantee, 1975. Republican. Home: 2240 Sea Ave Indialantic FL 32903-2524 Office: Brevard CC Liberal Arts Dept 3865 N Wickham Rd Melbourne FL 32935-2310

JONES, EMMA JEAN, principal; b. Monroe, La., Mar. 15, 1937; d. Percy and Lottie (Lewis) Gordon; m. Nathan Jones, Jr., July 31, 1960 (dec. Apr. 1989); children: Nathan Jones III, Natalie Renae Jones. BA, So. U., 1959; MEd, Northeast La. U., 1969, postgrad., 1979, 90. Cert. tchr., La. Tchr. 5th, 6th grades Monroe (La.) City Sch. Bd., 1959-73, supr. on site, 1973-75, dir. emergency sch. Aid Act Project, 1975-79; grad. ast. Northeast La. U., Monroe, 1979-80, reading lab. chpt. I, 1979-80, prin. Martin Luther King, Jr. Elem. Sch., 1981-89, 90—, grad. asst., 1989-90. Mem. steering com. Expect the Best, Monroe, 1981—; mem. selection com. La. State Prin. of Yr., 1993. Mem. Ouachita League of Women Voters, Monroe, past pres., 1990. Named Prin. of Year, Monroe City Schools, 1992. Mem. Nat. Assn. U. Women, La. Reading Assn. (adv. bd. dirs. 1983), La. Assn. Prins., La. Assn. Sch. Execs., State Selection Com. for Prin. of Yr., Phi Delta Kappa (com. 1990), Kappa Delta Pi, Alpha Kappa Alpha (past tamiouchous, 1st v.p. Somoans civic and social club, chmn. logistics regional conf. 1993). Democrat. Baptist. Avocations: reading, aerobic exercise, writing, shopping, traveling. Home: 1202 Crescent Dr Monroe LA 71202-3010

JONES, ERVIN, physician, educator; b. Emerson, Ark., May 10, 1943; s. William McKinley and Charity L. Jones; m. Elaine A. Jones, June 19, 1982; 1 child, Mark Rojette. BS, U. Ark., 1966; PhD, U. Ill., 1971; MD, U. Calif., Irvine, 1977. Diplomate Am. Bd. Reproductive Medicine. Fellow in pathology U. Claif., Irvine, 1976, resident in ob-gyn., 1977-81; rsch. assoc. Yale U. Sch. Medicine, New Haven, 1982-83, instr., 1983-85, asst. prof., 1985-90, assoc. prof., 1991-99, prof., 1999—. Cons. NIH/Alcohol, Drug Abuse and Mental Health Adminstrn. USPHS, 1995—; dir. assisted reprodn. dept. ob-gyn. Yale U. Med. Sch., New Haven. Contbr. articles to profl. jours. Advisor assisted reprodn. Conn. State Legislature, Hartford, 1999—. Mellon fellow, 1982-83, NIH fellow, 1971-73, 1991. Fellow: ACOG; mem.: AAUP, Soc. for Gynecol. Investigation, Soc. Assisted Reproductive Tech., Nat. Med. Assn., Assn. Profs. Gynecology (Excellence in Tchg. award 1992), Am. Soc. Reproductive Medicine. Avocation: outdoor activities. Office: Yale U Sch Medicine 333 Cedar St New Haven CT 06510-3289

JONES, EVELYN GLORIA, medical technologist, educator; b. Roanoke, Va., Aug. 13, 1940; d. William Darnell and Elizabeth (Harris) Powell; m. Theodore Joseph Jones, Aug. 21, 1965. BS in Biology, Tenn. State U., 1973; cert. in med. tech., Vanderbilt U., 1974; MEd in Adminstrn. and Supervision, Tenn. State U., 1993. Cert. clin. lab. scientist Nat. Cert. Agy. Med. Lab Pers. Med. technologist Metro Gen. Hosp., Nashville, 1974-78, Vanderbilt Med. Ctr., Nashville, 1978-97; microbiologist Tenn. Dept. Health Lab. Svcs., Nashville, 1997—. Tech. cons. Vanderbilt Point of Care Program, 1993-96; lectr. St. Thomas Program Med. Tech., Nashville, 1991-94, Tenn. State U./Meharry Med. Tech. Program, Nashville, 1991—; instr. tchg. faculty Pub. Health Lab. Svcs., State Tenn., Nashville. Nashville bd. dirs. Tenn. Valley Region ARC Blood Svcs., 1996-2002; asst. sec. Hendersville area chpt. The Links, Inc., 1997-2002; docent Frist Mus.; info. guide Fisk U. Mem.: AAAS, So. Assn. Clin. Microbiology, Am. Soc. Clin. Pathologist (assoc.; cert. med. technologist), Alpha Kappa Alpha, Phi Delta Kappa. Roman Catholic. Home: 1003 Cross Bow Dr Hendersonville TN 37075-9403 Office: Tenn Dept Health Lab Svcs Dept Microbiology Nashville TN 37202 E-mail: EvelynJones@mail.state.tn.us.

JONES, FELICIA M. director; b. N.Y.C., June 20, 1961; d. Michael W. Toreno, Myrna L. Toreno. BS, Butler U., 1984; MS in Edn., Old Dominion U., 1997, student. Registered diagnostic med. sonographer, vascular technologist, diagnostic cardiac sonographer Am. Registry Diagnostic Med. Sonographers. Instr. Hillsborough C.C., Tampa, Fla., 1988—90; sect. leader sonography Mary Washington Hosp., Fredericksburg, Va., 1990—92; program dir. Tidewater C.C., Virginia Beach, Va., 1992—; chief sonographer Preferred Diagnostic Svcs., Inc., Largo, Fla., 1985—88. Coord. distance learning Tidewater C.C., Virginia Beach, 1998—2000; site visitor Joint Rev. Com. on Edn. in Diagnostic Med. Sonography, Bedford, 2000—. Contbr. book Ultrasonography: An Introduction to Normal Structure and Function, 1995, book Ultrasound Scanning: Principles and Protocols, 1999. Grantee, Va. C.C. Sys. Profl. Devel. Com., 1997, Tidewater C.C., 1998. Mem.: N.C. Ultrasound Soc., Am. Inst. Ultrasound in Medicine, Soc. Diagnostic Med. Sonographers. Office: Tidewater CC 1700 College Crescent Virginia Beach VA 23453 Home Fax: 757.427.1338; Office Fax: 757.427.1338. Business E-Mail: fjones@tcc.edu.

JONES, FERDINAND TAYLOR, JR., psychologist, educator; b. N.Y.C., May 15, 1932; s. Ferdinand Taylor and Esther (Haggie) J.; m. Antonina Laub, Sept. 26, 1953 (div. Mar. 1967); children: Joanne Esther, Terrie Lynn; m. Myra Jean Rogers, Nov. 25, 1967. AB, Drew U., 1953; PhD, U. Vienna, Austria, 1959. Staff psychologist Riverside Hosp., Bronx, N.Y., 1959-62; chief psychologist Westchester County Community Mental Hosp. Bd., White Plains, N.Y., 1962-67; tng. cons. Lincoln Hosp. Mental Health Services, Bronx, 1967-69; tchr. psychology Sarah Lawrence Coll., Bronxville, N.Y., 1968-72; prof. psychology Brown U., Providence, 1972-97, prof. emeritus, 1997, dir. psychol. svcs., 1972-1992; clin. lectr. Emeritus in Psychiatry and Human Behavior, 2002. Scholar-in-residence The Schomburg Ctr. for Rsch. in Black Culture, 1987; cons. St. Peter's Head Start, Yonkers, N.Y., 1967-71, Bronx State Hosp., 1969-72; vis. prof. U. Dar es Salaam, Tanzania, 1993, Oberlin Coll., 1997, 98, U. Cape Town, 1999, Sarah Lawrence Coll., 2001. Co-editor: The Triumph of the Soul: Cultural and Psychological Aspects of African American Music. Bd. dirs. Am. Orthopsychiat. Assn., 1984-87. Served with AUS, 1953-56. Mem. APA, Am. Orthopsychiat. Assn. (pres. 1989-90), Ea. Psychol. Assn., Westchester County Psychol. Assn. (past pres.), Assn. Black Psychologists, Soc. Psychol. Study Social Issues, Internat. Assn. for Jazz Edn. Achievements include developing (with Myron W. Harris) small group method for reduction of distance and dissonance in interracial communication. Home: 182 Sessions St Providence RI 02906 Office: Brown U 79 Waterman St Providence RI 02912-9079 E-mail: ferdinand_jones@brown.edu.

JONES, FLORENCE M. music educator; b. West Columbia, Tex., Apr. 11, 1939; d. Isaiah and Lu Ethel (Baldridge) McNeil; m. Waldo D. Jones, May 29, 1965; children: Ricky, Wanda, Erna. BS, Prairie View A&M U., 1961, MEd, 1968; postgrad., Rice U., 1988, U. Houston, 1980. Cert. tchr. elem. edn., math. Tchr. English and typing Lincoln High Sch., Port Arthur, Tex., 1961-62; tchr. grades three and four Houston Ind. Sch. Dist., 1963-90, tchr. gifted and talented, 1990-94; tchr. piano Windsor Village Liberal Arts Acad., Houston, 1994—. Dist. tchr. trainer Houston Ind. Sch. Dist., 1985-90; shared decision mem. Sch. decision Making Team, 1993-94; coord. gifted/talented program, Petersen Elem. Sch., Houston, 1990-94; participant piano Recital Hartzog Studio, 1985-88; film previewer Houston Media Ctr. Curriculum writer Modules to Improve Science Teaching, 1985; author sci. pop-up book, 1980, gifted/talented program, 1994; contbr. poems to lit. jours. Youth camp counselor numerous non-denominational ch. camps, U.S., 1961-89; active restoration of Statue of Liberty, Ellis Island Found., N.Y.C., 1983-85; lay minister Ch. of God, 1961-94; charter founder The Am. Family History Immigration Ctr., Ellis Island, N.Y.C. Recipient Letter of Recognition for Outstanding Progress in Edn., Pres. Bill Clinton, 1994, Congresswoman Sheilia Jackson Lee, Tex. Gov. George Bush, State Rep. Harold V. Sutton Jr., Houston Mayor Bob Lanier, Tex. Gov. Ann Richards; Gold Cup/Highest Music award Hartzog Music Studio, 1987, Diamond Key award Nat. Women of Achievement, 1995, Editors Choice award Nat. Library Poetry, 1995, cert. recognition Quaker Oats Co. and NCNW Inc., 1999, Youth Advisors trophy and New Millennium Leader plaque Nat. Women Achievement, 2001, others; inductee The Internat. Poetry Hall of Fame. Mem. NEA, Houston Assn. Childhood Edn. (v.p. 1985-88), Assn. for Childhood Edn. (bd. dirs. 1979-91), Houston Zool. Soc., World Wildlife Fund, Nat. Storytelling Assn., Tejas Storytelling Assn. (life), Soc. Children's Book Writers and Illustrators, Nat. Audubon Soc., Am. Mus. Natural History, Tex. Ret. Tchrs. Assn. (life), Internat. Soc. Poets (disting. life mem.), others. Democrat. Avocations: writing, reading, storytelling, collecting sea shells, arts and crafts. Home: 3310 Dalmatian Dr Houston TX 77045-6520

JONES, FLORESTA D. English educator; b. Hopewell, Va., Dec. 24, 1950; d. William A. Sr. and Florine (Brown) Jones. BA, Berry Coll., 1972; MA, Mich. State U., 1975; doctoral student, Rutgers, The State U. Assoc. dir. ednl. opportunity program, instr. Georgian Court Coll., Lakewood, N.J.; co-dir. Learning Through Writing Project Brookdale C.C., Lincroft, N.J., prof. English. Adj. faculty in modern langs. and history depts.; faculty coord. for Diversity across Curriculum; faculty participant N.J. Project on Inclusive Scholarship, Curriculum, and Tchg.; Nat. Site coord. Brookdale Am. Assn. Colls. and Univs. Contbr. articles to profl. jours. FICE matching-funds grantee, 1986-88. Mem. AAUW, Nat. Coun. Tchrs. English, N.J. Edn. Assn., N.J. TESOL (bilingual edn.). Home: 64 Jefferson Dr Spotswood NJ 08884-1240 Office: Brookdale CC Newman Spring Rd Lincroft NJ 07738

JONES, GARTH NELSON, business and public administration educator; b. Salt Lake City, Feb. 25, 1925; s. Harry H. and Sophronia Dubois (Nelson) J.; m. Verda Marie Clegg, Sept. 29, 1950; children: Edward Hood, Garth Kevin, Drew Luke. BS, Utah State U., 1947; MS, U. Utah, 1948, PhD, 1954. Mem. faculty Brigham Young U., Provo, Utah, 1953-56; with AID, Indonesia, 1957-61, 1967-69; mem. faculty U. So. Calif., 1961-67; sr. scholar East-West Center, Hawaii, 1969-70; mem. faculty Colo. State U., 1970-72; with UN, N.Y.C., 1972-73; mem. faculty U. Alaska, Anchorage, 1973—, founding dean Coll. Bus. and Pub. Policy, 1974—79. Vice chmn. Alaska Coun. Edn.; cons. to govt. and industry World Bank, UN Population Program, Ford Found. Rural Devel., U.S. Dept. State; mem. citizen's adv. bd. Bur. Land Mgmt., 1989-96; bd. dirs. Alaska World Affairs Coun.; mem. faculty U. Gadjah Madjah, Indonesia, U. Punjab, Pakistan, Nat. Chengci U., Taiwan; mem. adv. coun. Coll. Bus. and Pub. Policy, U. Alaska. Mem. bd. editors profl. jours.; contbr. articles to profl. jours. Chmn. Anchorage Mayor's Ad Hoc Govtl. Rev. Commn., 1978, Anchorage Urban Obs.; Anchorage Mayor-elect's transition team, 1987. Fulbright-Hayes scholar, Taiwan, 1981-82; named Disting. Alumnus Old Main Soc. Utah State U., 1996. Mem. Lds Ch. Office: U Alaska 3221 Providence Dr Anchorage AK 99508-4614

JONES, GRAHAM ALFRED, mathematics educator; b. Brisbane, Queensland, Australia, Oct. 29, 1937; came to U.S., 1991; s. Charles Henry and Doris Beatrice (Powell) J.; m. Marion Rose Rudge, Dec. 15, 1962; children: Timothy Charles, Cameron Philip. BSc, U. Queensland, 1960, BEd with 1st honors, 1964; MA, San Diego State U., 1968; PhD, Ind. U., 1974. Tchr. Cavendish Rd. High Sch., Brisbane, 1961-66; Fulbright Exch. tchr. John Francis Poly., L.A., 1966-67; head dept. math. Kelvin Grove Tchrs. Coll., Brisbane, 1968-71, Kelvin Grove Coll. Advanced Edn., Brisbane, 1974-76, dean of sci., 1976-82; campus prin. Brisbane Coll. Advanced Edn., Carseldine campus, Brisbane, 1982-85; pro-vice chancellor, prof., dir. Gold Coast (Australia) Univ. Coll., Griffith U., 1985-91; prof. math. Ill. State U., Normal, 1991—. Mem. Bd. Tchr. Edn., Brisbane, 1982-86; chair Math. Adv. Com. of Queensland, Brisbane, 1968-71, 74-76. Author monographs, reports and rsch. articles. NSF scholar, 1967-68. Fellow Australian Inst. Mgmt., Australian Coll. Edn.; mem. Math. Edn. Rsch. Group of Australasia (life, founding pres. 1980-84), Am. Ednl. Rsch. Assn., Nat. Coun. Tchrs. Math. (reviewer for jours. 1991—). Presbyterian. Avocations: surfing, wind-surfing, theatre, tennis, cryptic crosswords. Home: Unit 62 Belle Maison 129 Surf Parade Broadbeach QLD 4218 Australia Office: Ill State U Dept Math Stevenson Bldg Normal IL 61790-0001

JONES, JANICE COX, elementary school educator, writer; b. Jackson, Miss., Nov. 4, 1937; d. Eugene Debs and Thelma Corelli (Beard) Cox; m. June 20, 1959 (div. June 1985); children: Allison Jones Griffiths, Tamara Jones McKee. BS with highest distinction, Miss. Coll., 1959; MEd magna cum laude, U. Miami, 1968. Cert. elem. edn. Tchr. Jackson Pub. Sch., 1959-60, Arlington (Tex.) Pub. Schs., 1960-63, Houston Pub. Schs., 1963-64, Miami-Dade County Pub. Schs., 1967-1980, 1988—97; pres. Palm Tree Prodns., Ltd., 1980-88. Tchr. English ESOL Say Sch., Tokyo, 1985; tutor, child welfare worker CBS, Twentieth Century Fox, N.Y.C., Miami, 1981-; pvt. tutor, owner Think, Ink!, Miami, 1983-; piano tchr. MDCPS Cmty. Sch., Miami, 1991-; participant Miss. Gov.'s Edn./Econ. Task Force, 1990-91; workshop presenter Children's Cultural Coalition & Arts for Learning; speaker/poet in field; usher Coconut Grove Playhouse, Actor's Playhouse, Gablestage, Biltmore. Author several books of poetry, Geography Fun Facts: A Trip Across the U.S.A. in Poetry, Numbered & Named: A Preventive for Math Anxiety in Children and Adults. Dist. exec. adv. com. to sch. bd. for gifted edn. Miami-Dade County Pub. Schs., 1987-91; adv. bd. Metro-Dade Rapid Transit, 1974-77; parent sponsor Olympics of the Mind Team, 1984; parent sponsor Queen's Ct., Jr. Orange Bowl, Coral Gables, Fla., 1983; vol. pianist, organist, music dir. Village Green Baptist Mission, Miami, 1973; vol. Habitat for Humanity, 1991-. Recipient nat. poetry award, Byline Mag., 2002, ann. conf. scholarship, World Future Soc.; grantee, NEA, 1973. Mem. Am. Fedn. Tchrs., Dade Heritage Trust (edn. com., writer), Miami Writer's Club, Fla. Freelance Writers Assn., Nat. Writers Assn. South Fla. chapt. (bd., exec. sec. 1997-, nat. writing contest chair, 1998-2001), United Tchrs. Dade (bldg. steward 1976-78), Tropical Audubon Soc., Coun. for Internat. Visitors, Internat. Platform Assn. (red carpet com.), Soc. Children's Book Writers and Illustrators, Miami Arts Exch., Nature Conservancy, Sierra Club. Avocations: Broadway plays and musicals, museums, fishing, photography, travel, accordion, accordion. Home: 6301 SW 93rd Ct Miami FL 33173-2317

JONES, JEAN CORREY, organization administrator; b. Denver, Jan. 12, 1942; d. Robert Magnie and Elizabeth Marie (Harpel) Evans; m. Stewart Hoyt Jones, Aug. 3, 1963; children: Andrew and Correy. BS in History, Social Studies and Secondary Edn., Northwestern U., 1963. Cert. non-profit mgr. History tchr. Glenbrook South H.S., Glenview, Ill., 1963-65; advocacy rsch. dir. Episc. Diocese of Denver, 1977-80; pub. affairs adminstr. United Bank of Denver, 1980-82; pres., CEO Mile Hi coun. Girl Scouts U.S., Denver, 1982—. Substitute tchr. Denver Pub. Schs., 1965-80. Active Minoru Yasui Cmty. Vol. Award com., 1979-201, Women's Forum of Colo., 1989-2002, Leadership Denver (Member of Yr., 1988), 1988—; pres. Jr. League, Denver, 1979-80, Rotary, Denver, 1995—, pres., 1995-96, commr., chair Colo. Civil Rights commn., Denver, 1987-96, vice chair Health One, Denver, 1996; bd. dirs. Hist. Denver, Inc., 1994—, Samaritan Inst., Denver, 1999; chair, trustee Colo. Trust, 2002; pres. Women's Forum of Colo. Inc., 1999—; trustee Rotary Found., Am. Humane Assoc., 2002—, Colo. Health Inst., 2003—; v.p. Univ. Club, 2002—. Named Profl. Woman of Achievement Colo. Women's Leadership Coalition and Colo. Easter Seal Soc., 1995, Martin Luther King Social Responsibility award. Mem. Denver Metro C. of C., Univ. Club. Republican. Episcopalian. Avocations: swimming, tennis, reading. Office: Girl Scouts Mile High Coun PO Box 9407 Denver CO 80209-0407

JONES, JEANNE PITTS, pre-school administrator; b. Richmond, Va., Oct. 19, 1938; d. Howard Taliaferro and Anne Elizabeth (Warburton) Pitts; m. Jack Hunter Jones, Nov. 17, 1962; children: Jack Hunter, Jr., Judith Anne, James Howard, Jon Martain. BA, Marshall U., 1961, postgrad., 1962, Presbyn. Sch. Christian Edn., Richmond, 1974, 94, Va. Commonwealth U., 1987-88, MEd in Early Childhood Edn., 2000. Cert. tchr. Va. Tchr. Richmond Pub. Schs., 1961-65; founder Bon View Sch. Early Childhood Edn., Richmond, 1971, tchr., 1971-91, dir., 1971—. Validator Nat. Assn. for Edn. of Young Children, 1993—, mentor, 1994-98; acad. affairs chmn. Good Shepherd Episcopal Sch. Bd., Richmond, 1985-88; mentor Ecumenical Child Care Network Nat. Coun. Chs., Washington, 1990-92. Chmn. room parents Crestwood Sch. PTA Bd., Richmond, 1974-80; publicity chmn. Va. Swimming, Richmond, 1978-88, children's coord. Bon Air United Meth. Ch., Richmond, 1985-93, v.p. Bon Air United Meth. Women, 1991-94; dir. Camp Friendship, Bon Air UMC, Richmond, 1992—; Va. Children's Action Network, Va. Conf. of United Meth. Ch., rep., 1993-95; Va. Conf. United Meth. Ch., weekday com. 1992-94. Recipient Spl. Mission recognition Bon Air United Meth. Women, Richmond, 1987. Mem.: Success by Six Mentor, Va. Assn. for Early Childhood Edn. (bd. dirs. 2002—, mentor "Success by Six" 2002), Chesterfield Coalition Early Childhood Educators (bd. dirs. 1993—97), Presch. Assn. Ch. Ednl. Dirs. (pres. 1993—95), Richmond Early Childhood Assn. (mem.-at-large 1994—96, rec. sec. 1996—98, 1998—2000, v.p. membership 2000—02, pres.-elect 2001—02, pres. 2002—, Early Childhood Adv. of the Yr. 2002). Republican. Avocations: aerobics, reading. Home: 9103 Whitaker Cir Richmond VA 23235-4053 Office: Bon View Sch Early Childhood Edn 1645 Buford Rd Richmond VA 23235-4274

JONES, JOEL MACKEY, academic administrator; b. Millersburg, Ohio, Aug. 11, 1937; s. Theodore R.a nd Edna Mae (Mackey) Jones; children: Carolyn Mae, Jocelyn Corinne. BA, Yale U., 1960; MA, Miami U., Oxford, Ohio, 1962; PhD, U. N.Mex., 1966. Dir. Am. studies U. Md., Balt., 1966-69; chmn. Am. studies U. N.Mex., Albuquerque, 1969-73, asst. v.p. acad. affairs, 1973-77, dean faculties, assoc. provost, prof. Am. studies, 1977-85, v.p. adminstrn., 1985-88; pres. Ft. Lewis Coll., Durango, Colo., 1988-99, pres. emeritus, 1999—; interim supr. of schs. Durango Pub. Schs., 1999; interim pres. Salisbury State U., 1999—2000. Bd. dirs. 1st Nat. Bank. Contbr. numerous essays, articles and chpts. to books. Founder Rio Grande Nature Preserve Soc., Albuquerque, 1974—; bd. dirs., mem. exec. com. United Way, Albuquerque, 1980-83; na. bd. cons. NEH, 1978—; bd. dirs. Mercy Hosp., 1990-94; mem. ACE Commn. on Leadership. Farwell scholar Yale U., New Haven, 1960; sr. fellow NEH, 1972; adminstrv. fellow Am. Coun. Edn., Washington, 1972-73. Mem. Am. Studies Assn., Am. Assn. Higher Edn., Am. Assn. State Colls. and Univs. (chair com. on cultural diversity, Colo. state rep. 1994—).*

JONES, JOHN ANDERSON, JR., retired school system administrator; b. New Orleans, June 15, 1940; s. John Anderson and Irene Wells (Bennett) J.; divorced; children: Cheryl Lynn Jones Williams, Cyril Ivan Jones. BS in Social Studies, So. U., 1962, MA in African-Am. Studies, 1972; postgrad., La. State U., 1971, U. New Orleans, 1975, Tulane U., 1975, Harvard U., 1989. Cert. tchr., prin., supr., adminstr., supt., La. Rsch. asst. La. Dept. Edn., Baton Rouge, 1976-77; tchr. New Orleans Pub. Schs., 1962-75, supr. social studies, 1977-84, supr. instrs., 1984-85, spl. asst. prin., 1985-86, assoc. dir., 1990-98, dir. govtl. liaison, 1992-98; ret., 1998; acting dir. dept. adult and continuing edn. New Orleans Pub. Schs. Cons., presenter in field; teaching asst. Tulane U., New Orleans, 1976-77, Xavier U., New Orleans, 1989, So. U., New Orleans, 1990, U. New Orleans, 1992; rschr. Consortium for Internat. Studies for West Africa, New Orleans, 1981; chmn. bd. dirs. New Orleans Home Mortgage Authority, 1989-95; book reviewer in field. Co-author: Educating Black Male Youth: A Moral and Civic Imperative, 1988; also contbr. to profl. publs. Res. dep. civil sheriff Res. Dep. Civil Sheriffs Assn., New Orleans, 1984; mem. Commn. on Excellence in Inner City Schs., La. Legislature, Baton Rouge, 1990; chmn. bd. New Orleans Home Mortgage Authority, 1989-95; mem. La. Gov.'s Edn. Transition Team, 1991; mem. pub. rels. com. United Way; mem. New Orleans Human Rels. Commn., 1998—, chmn., 1999-2003; trustee New Orleans chpt. PUSH/Excel; bd. dirs. New Orleans Coun. on Aging, 2000—, Econ. Devel. Unit New Orleans, 2002—; mem. adv. bd. New Orleans East Econ. Devel. Found., 2001—. 1st lt. U.S. Army, 1963-65. Named Tchr. of Yr., Fortier H.S., 1974, 75; recipient cert. of appreciation ABA, 1981, young lawyers sect. La. Bar Assn., 1989, trophy Cox Cable and New Orleans Pub. Schs., 1991; also others; scholar Tulane U., 1976-77; fellow Close Up Found., 1979, 80, 82, 83, 86-90; grantee Harvard U., 1989. Mem. Nat. Coun. for Social Studies (plaque 1980), La. Coun. for Social Studies (plaque 1984), Nat. Social Studies Suprs. Assn., La. Coun. on Econ. Edn. (trustee 1984—, plaque 1990), Profl. Pers. Assn. (organizing, co-chmn.), Phi Delta Kappa, Pi Gamma Mu, Omega Psi Phi (reporter 1989-90). Democrat. Baptist. Avocations: billiards, travel, chess, sports. Home: 7001 Cove Dr New Orleans LA 70126-3032

JONES, JULIA PEARL, retired elementary school educator; b. Kesler, W.Va., Nov. 22, 1942; d. Wallace Leon and Wilda Thelma (Doss) Frazier; m. James Victor Jones, Jr., Nov. 26, 1961; children: Julie Lorraine Lynch, Jamie Lynn Dunston Smith. BS in Elem. Edn. cum laude, Memphis State U., 1979; MEd cum laude, U. Va., 1986; MLS summa cum laude, James Madison U., 1998. Cert. elem./mid. sch. prin., supr., K-7th grade tchr., art tchr. Tchr. 4th grade Spotsylvania County (Va.) Schs., 1979-91, reading resource specialist, 1991-96, sch. libr., 1996—2002. Mem. ASCD, Nat. Tchrs. Assn., Va. Edn. Assn., Spotsylvania Edn. Assn., Nat. Congress of Parents and Tchrs., Internat. Reading Assn., Va. Reading Assn. Rappahannock Reading Coun. (past pres., Reading Tchr. of Yr. 1993-94), Va. Edn./Media Assn., Christian Bus. and Profl. Women, Internat. Platform Assn., Order Ea. Star, Kappa Delta Pi, Phi Delta Kappa. Methodist. Avocation: art. Home: 1563 Fiarmont Ave Morgantown WV 26501

JONES, KATHRYN ANNE, academic administrator; b. Stillwater, Okla., Jan. 25, 1948; d. Alexander Nova and Dorothy Margaret (Lotka) Wilson; m. Ralph Lee Jones, Aug. 13, 1983; 1 child, Layne Lee. AA, No. Okla. Coll., 1968; BS in Edn., Northwestern Okla. State U., 1969, MEd, 1973; EdD, Okla. State U., 1989. Debate, drama coach U.S.D. #300, Coldwater, Kans., 1969-75, Unified Sch. Dist. #484, Fredonia, Kans., 1975-78; computer analyst Conoco Oil Co., Ponca City, Okla., 1978-79; dir. theatre No. Okla. Coll., Tonkawa, 1979-84, dir. sch. and alumni rels., 1984-90; dir. Enid (Okla.) Higher Edn. Program, 1990—. Bd. dirs., chair St. Mary's Hosp., Pegasys, 1995 Author: Northern Dormitories, 1988 (Paragon award 1989). Pres. Leadership Greater Enid, (class I 1991-92, alumni 1992—); active mem. Leadership Okla. (class VI 1992-93), Okla Acad. State Goal, 1993—. Bd. dirs. Ponca Playhouse, Ponca City, 1975-78, Fredonia's Art Coun., 1975-78; v.p., bd. mem. S.E. Kans. Area Study of Aging, Independence, 1976-78, Fredonia Child Care Ctr., 1976-78. Mem. Nat. Coun. Mktg. and Pub. Rels. (Okla. dir. 1989), Okla. Assn. Community and Jr. Colls. (v.p. commn. 1987-88, del. 1988-89), Am. Bus. Clubs, Enid Lions Club, Enid Am. Too Ambucs. Democrat. Methodist. Avocations: reading, attending theatre, flower gardening. Office: Enid Higher Edn Program 2929 E Randolph Ave Enid OK 73701-4667

JONES, KELSEY A. law educator, law administrator; b. Holly Springs, Miss., July 15, 1933; m. Virginia Bethel Ford; children— Kelsey Jr., Cheryl Darline Jones Campbell, Eric Andre, Claude Anthony. B.A. in English summa cum laude, AB magna cum laude, Miss. Indsl. Coll., 1955, D.D., 1969; Garrett Theol. Sem. M.Div., Northwestern U., 1959; postgrad. U. Mich. Med. Ctr., 1960; cert. clin. pastoral care and counseling, Wesley Med. Ctr., Wichita, Kans., 1967. Staff counselor State Prison So. Mich., Jackson, 1959-62; chmn. Kans. Bd. Probation and Parole, 1965-70; vis. lectr. in Black history, Fed City Coll. (Univ. DC Mt. Vernon Campus), 1973-75, INTER/MET, dir. Bace & Liason consult, 1973-77; prof. social scis. Univ. DC (Van Ness Campus), Washington, 1972-77, chmn. dept. social/behavioral scis., 1977-78, prof. criminal justice, 1978-79, assoc. for prof., 1978-82, chmn., 1979-91, prof., 1982-94, spl. asst. to pres. for environ. health, occupl. safety and instl. security, 1984-86, justice prof. emeritus, 2003-; Public spkr. and lectr.; resident facilitator, The Think Tank at Emeritus Manor, Takoma Park, MD; developer of published curriculum at pre-coll., undergraduate and graduate levels; participated in dispute resolutions; conducted workshops & seminars on juvenile violence and fashioned paradigms for adolescent aggression; chaired depts. in three distinct disciplines; author and published many papers and articles; generated scores of intellectual properties, including documents prepared for publ., An Environmental Approach to Environmental Health, Occupational Safety and Institutional Security, Dynamics and Diversity, Exploring Implications for Accountability in Crime, Drug, Public, and Social Policy and Education in the Inductive Mode, A Collection of Constructs on the Philosophy of Alternative Modes in Education, are in consistent demand; post career-Cultural Ethicist, Soc. Behaviorist and Policy Analyst; Bd. dirs. D.C. Corrections Found., Bros Inc.; dean Leadership Educ. of 3rd Episcopal Dist.; trustee Washington Internat. Coll.; sec. NY/WA ann. conf. Vis. Chapel Meth. Pop Cook County Jail, 1956-58, KS/MO ann.conf., 1962-70; del. Gen. Conf. of Christ Meth. Episcopal Ch., 1966, Centennial Session Gen Conf., 1970. Apptd. Staff receptionist, Diag Ctr. MI Correct Commn., 1961; mem. Acad. of Criminal Justice Scis., North Atlantic Conf. of Criminal Justice Educators, Inst. for Criminal Justice Ethics, Nat. Criminal Justice Assn., Northeastern Assn. of Criminal Justice Educators, Am. Soc. for Indsl. Security, Nat. Assn. Chief of Police, Am. Soc. Pub. Adminstrn., ASHE (Am. Assn for Higher Edn.), Phi Alpha Mu Lamda Chpt., DC, Alpha Phi Alpha; chmn. State Bd. of Probation and Parole, 1967; First pres. Wichita Urban League, LEAP com for Desegration of pub. Sch. in Wichita. Recepient: Presdl. citation Nat. Assn. for Equal Opportunities in Higher Edn., 1979, Alumnus of the Year, Disting. Service award Howard U. without Walls, Washington, 1980, Disting. Service award, Lorton Student Govt. Assn. (Lorton Prison Project), Univ. DC, 1980.; Awarded cert. for workshop on Crime Prevention for Coll. And Univ., Campus Crime Prevention Programs, 1985. Office: Justice Prof Emeritus Resident Facilitator Think Tank at Emeritus Manor Takoma Park PO Box 60379-0379 Washington DC 20039-0379

JONES, KENNETH D. secondary education educator, coach; b. May 23; s. James C. and Lucille M. Jones. BS in Edn. in Math. Edn., U. Ill., 1982; MA in Ednl. Adminstrn., Ea. Ill. U., 1993. Tchr. math. Casey (Ill.)-Westfield Schs., 1989-91, Edinburg (Ill.) Sch. Dist., 1983-89, 91—. Scholar FMC Corp., 1980. Mem. NEA, Nat. Coun. Tchrs. Math., Ill. Edn. Assn., Ill. H.S. Assn. (ofcl.), Edinburg Athletic Club. Avocation: youth sports. Office: Edinburg Sch Dist 100 E Martin St Edinburg IL 62531-9713

JONES, KENNETH DON, secondary education educator; b. Washington, Sept. 4, 1947; s. Oscar Don and Edna Adele (Chambers) J.; children: Lisa Salonge, Sean Kenneth. BS in Biology, Knoxville Coll., 1971; MS in Linguistics, Fed. City Coll., Washington, 1974; MA in Adminstrn. and Supervision, U. D.C., 1985; EdD, Va. Poly. Inst., 1992. Cert. secondary tchr., D.C. Tchr. sci. Eliot Jr. High Sch., Washington, 1971; tchr. sci., coach Kramer Jr. High Sch., Washington, 1971-85; prin. Spingarn Sch. to Aid Youth, Washington, 1985—. Owner Jones' Tax Svc., Temple Hill, Md., 1980—; monitor Assocs. for Renewal in Edn., Washington, 1989; asst. adj. prof. U. D.C., Washington, 1988—. Mem. ASCD, NEA, NASSP, Am. Edn. Rrsch. Assn., Entrepreneur of Am., D.C. Coaches Assn., D.C. Tchrs. Sci. Assn., Prophecy Homeowner's Assn. Baptist. Avocations: reading, sports, speaking, jogging, writing. Home: 10053 Edgewater Ter Fort Washington MD 20744-5766

JONES, KEVIN SCOTT, materials science educator; b. Gainesville, Fla., Feb. 20, 1958; s. William Maurice and Elizabeth Rose (Nordwall) J.; m. Debra Lillene Dauphin, July 1, 1983; children: Britta Elyse, Ryan Scott, Sean Michael. BS in Materials Sci. & Engrng. honors, U. Fla., 1980; MS in Materials Sci. & Engrng., U. Calif., Berkeley, 1985, PhD in Materials Sci. & Engrng., 1987. Lab. asst. dept. materials sci. and engrng. U. Fla., Gainesville, 1975-80; tech. process engr. E.I. DuPont and Co., Parkersburg, W.Va., 1980-82; cons. TRW, Inc., L.A., 1985, 86; teaching/rsch. asst. dept. materials sci. & mineral engrng. U. Calif., Berkeley, 1982-87, postdoctoral researcher dept materials sci./mineral engrng, 1987; asst. prof. dept. materials sci. and engrng. U. Fla., Gainesville, 1987-92, assoc. prof. dept. materials sci. and engrng., 1992-96, prof., 1996—, chmn. dept. material sci. and engrng., 2002—. Chmn., co-organizer of 1992 Internat. Ion Implantation Tech. Meeting, elected. gen. sec. tech. com.; co-organizer symposium nat. meeting 176th Electrochem. Soc., 1989, meeting chmn., 2000; tech. presenter in field. Editor: Ion Implantation for Elemental and Compound Semiconductors, 1990; contbr. numerous refereed publs. to profl. jours., books; reviewer Material Rsch. Soc., Jour. Electrochem. Soc., Jour. Vacuum Sci. and Tech., Ion Implantation Tech. Conf., Applied Physics Letters. Named Viola P. Tarrent scholar U. Fla., 1978-79; recipient NSF Presdl. Young Investigators award, 1990. Mem. Materials Rsch. Soc. (meeting chmn. 2001), Am. Soc. Metals, The Metall. Soc., Electrochem. Soc., U. Fla. Ultimate Frisbee Club (faculty advisor), Alpha Sigma Mu, Tau Beta Pi. Democrat. Avocations: ultimate frisbee, running, gardening. Home: 13814 SW 72nd Ter Archer FL 32618-5806 Office: U Fla Dept Materials Sci & Engring 533 Engring Bldg Gainesville FL 32611-2066

JONES, LACINDA, assistant principal; b. Baton Rouge, Mar. 1, 1962; d. Carl Lester and Joan (Alford) J. BS, La. State U., 1984; MEd in Guidance/Counseling, Southeastern La. U., 1990; postgrad., Southern U., Baton Rouge, 1990-92. Cert. tchr., elem. sch. prin., adminstr., supr., guidance counselor, resource devel., leadership, supervision of student tchrs. Tchr. grades 1-4 Livingston Parish (La.) Sch. Bd., 1985-89; tchr. grade 5 East Baton Rouge Sch. Bd., 1989-90, guidance counselor, 1990-95, adminstrv. intern, 1993-94, asst. prin., 1995—. Lectr. in field; condr. workshops for tchrs./adminstrs., and parents; asst. in implementing Reading Recovery program for at-risk students; assisted other sch. dists. in implementing their guidance programs, diversity trainer; helped implemented La. Bd. Elem. and Secondary Edn./La. Quality Ednl. Support Fund Grant, 1993-94. Featured on WFMF Radio Pub. Affairs program; featured in articles in Baton Rouge Advocate, Ctrl. News newspapers, other pubs.; pub. handbook: Parent-Student Handbook, 1993. Tutor underprivileged children, Baton Rouge, 1986-90; libr. vol. Goodwood Libr., Baton Rouge, 1990; Sunday sch. tchr. Deerford United Meth. Ch., Baton Rouge, 1980-84; vol. fundraiser Acad. Distinction, Baton Rouge, 1990-94; vol. Vols. in P ub. Schs. (VIP), Baton Rouge, 1993. Grantee Exxon Chem. Edn. Involvement Fund, 1996, South Ctrl. Bell, La., 1989, Nat. 4-H Found., 1991, Acad. Distinction Fund, Baton Rouge, 1991, 93. Mem. ASCD, La. Assn. Prins., Am. Sch. Counselor Assn. (membership chair 1990), La. Sch. Counselor Assn. (elem. v.p. 1993-94), East Baton Rouge Counselor Assn. (elem. v.p. 1992-93), Assoc. Prof. Educators (La. membership rep. 1992), East Baton Rouge Counselor Assn. (pres.-elect 1995—), Prins. and Asst. Prins. Adv. Coun. to Supt., Coun. of Asst. Prins. for Instrn., Coun. of Asst. Prins. of Adminstrn., Delta Kappa Gamma (historian 1994), Phi Delta Kappa. Democrat. Avocations: aerobics, exercise, reading, water sports. Office: Northeast Elem Sch PO Box C Pride LA 70770 Home: 1450 Lake Pointe Ave Zachary LA 70791-7305

JONES, LARRY DEE, principal; b. Princeton, Ill., Dec. 12, 1947; s. Herbert E. and Florence (Adams) J.; m. Judy Ann Reddick, Aug. 8, 1970; children: Marti, Jonna, Shauna, Adam. BS in Edn. with high honors, Ill. State U., 1973, MS in Edn., 1982. Tchr. Woodrow Wilson Grade Sch., Peoria, Ill., 1974, 77-86, Longfellow Grade Sch., Peoria, 1974-77; asst. prin. Sterling Mid. Sch., Peoria, 1986, Trewyn Mid. Sch., Peoria, 1986-88; prin. Glen Oak Primary Sch., Peoria, 1988-94, Briar Glen Sch., Wheaton, Ill., 1994—. Multi-age cons. Mid Illini ESC # 12, Creve Coeur, Ill., 1990—, Peoria Dist. # 150, 1990—, spl. edn. task forc, 1992, early childhood adv. bd., 1992; presenter numerous confs. Mem. ASCD, Internat. Reading Assn., Nat. Assn. Elem. Sch. Prins., Nat. Coun. Tchrs. Math., Ill. Adminstrs. Acad., Peoria Assn. Sch. Adminstrs. (pres. 1993—), Phi Delta Kappa. Home: 104 Balmoral Ct Washington IL 61571-9502 Office: Briar Glen Sch 1800 Briarcliffe Blvd Wheaton IL 60187-8499

JONES, LEE BENNETT, chemist, educator, university official; b. Memphis, Mar. 14, 1938; s. Harold S. and Martha B. J.; m. Vera Kramar, Feb. 8, 1964; children: David B., Michael B. BA magna cum laude, Wabash Coll, 1960; PhD, M.I.T., 1964; DSC (hon.), Wabash Coll., 1992. Faculty U. Ariz., Tucson, 1964-85, prof. chemistry, 1972-85, asst. head dept. chemistry, 1971-73, head dept., 1973-77, dean Grad. Coll., 1977-79, provost Grad. Studies and Health Scis., 1979-82, v.p. rsch., 1982-85; prof. chemistry, exec. v.p., provost U. Nebr., Lincoln, 1985—2002, exec. v.p., provost emeritus, 2002—. Chmn. bd. dirs. Coun. Grad. Schs., 1986; mem. Grad. Records Exam. Bd., 1986-91; mem. Midwest Higher Edn. Commn., 1995—. Mem. editl. bd. Jour. Chem. Edn, 1975-79; contbr. numreous articles to sci. jours. Mem. Nebr. R&D Authority, 1985—, Midwest Higher Edn. Commn.; vice chmn. Nebr. Ednl. Telecomm. Commn., 1987-88, 91-92. NSF fellow, 1961-63, 64— Mem. AAAS, AAUP, Am. Chem. Soc., Chem. Soc. (London), N.Y. Acad. Scis., Phi Beta Kappa. Home: 1611 Kingston Rd Lincoln NE 68506-1526 Office: U Nebr 106 Varner Hall 3835 Holdrege St Lincoln NE 68503-1435

JONES, LESLIE SUSAN, special education educator; b. Denver, Jan. 11, 1958; d. Arthur Henry and Marilyn Clark (Wycoff) J.; m. Larry Jay Westrum, Aug. 11, 1984 (div. Aug. 10, 1992). BA in Biol. Scis., Univ. No. Colo., 1981, MA in Severe Needs Affective, 1990. Jr. high sci. instr. Holyoke (Colo.) RE-1 Sch. Dist., 1982-84; patient edn. instr. Boulder (Colo.) Psychiatric Inst., 1985-88; instr., severe needs jr. high SIED Poudre R-1 Sch. Dist., Ft. Collins, Colo., 1988-89; instr., severe needs SIED San Antonio Ind. Sch. Dist., 1990; resource instr. East Yuma County Sch. Dist., Wray, Colo., 1991; elem. SIED instr. Poudre R-1 Sch. Dist., 1991—. Guest speaker Sci. Edn. Dept. Univ. No. Colo., Greeley, 1987; team mem. Adolescent Health Adv. Coun., Ft. Collins, Colo., 1988, Outcomes Based Accreditation Com., Wray, 1991; presenter Connections Workshop, Ft. Collins, 1993; adminstrv. asst., Irish Elem., Ft. Collins, 1993; mem. Mid. Sch. Rsch. Team, Irish Elem., Ft. Collins, 1993. Author: Steppin' To Success, 1990. Precinct co-capt. Larimer County Dem. Party, 1988; coach Spl. Olympics, Wray, 1991. Mem. NEA, Coun. for Exceptional Children, Kappa Delta Pi. Mem. Soc. Of Friends. Home: 563 S 9th St Berthoud CO 80513-1400 Office: Irish Elem Sch 515 Irish Dr Fort Collins CO 80521-1524

JONES, LILLIAN BARNES, elementary school principal; b. Balt., Nov. 20; d. Lawrence B. and Emily L. (Johnson) B.; m. Barton Williams, Feb. 16, 1957 (div. 1970); 1 child, Michael David; m. Adolph Jones, Oct. 28, 1973. BS, Morgan State U., 1970; MEd, Johns Hopkins U., 1980; cert. of advanced studies, Loyola U., Balt., 1986. Tchr. Balt. City Pub. Schs., 1973-80, demonstration tchr., 1980, reading specialist, 1980-84, support tchr., 1984-86, master tchr., 1986-89, asst. prin., 1989-93, prin., 1993—. Advisor to partnership U.S. Army Recruitment, 1993-94. Named Tchr. of Yr., Mayor Balt., Gov. Md., 1989; recipient Citizen citation, Mayor Balt., 1992. Mem. Internat. Reading Assn., Pub. Sch. Adminstrs. Mem. African Meth. Ch.

JONES, LINDA JACKSON, professional educator; b. Huntington, N.Y., Apr. 16, 1952; d. Henry Thomas and Susan (Keels) Jackson; m. Lawrence Jones, Aug. 12, 1973; children: Malcolm, Lia, David. BA in Elem. Edn., Howard U., 1974; MEd, Bowie State Coll., 1988; PhD in Edn. Policy/Planning/Adminstrn., U. Md., 1993. Cert. in elem. edn., mid. and elem. adminstrn. and supervision; cert. prin., supt. Tchr. St. Mary's County Bd. Edn., Leonardtown, Md., 1974—75; tchr., adminstr., resource specialist Prince George's County Pub. Schs., Upper Marlboro, Md., 1975—2000; prin. Montgomery County Pub. Schs., Md., 2000—. Adj. faculty Bowie (Md.) State U.; mentor prin. Johns Hopkins U., U. Md. Tchr. Sunday sch. Largo Cmty. Ch. Recipient United Way Gold award Leadership, 1981, 82, 85, 86, Kettering Elem. Outstanding Educator award, 1991, P.G.C.P.S. Outstanding Educator Countywide award, 1995. Mem. ASCD, Md. Assn. Supervision, Curriculum Devel. (network facilitator), United Tchg. Profession, Nat. Alliance Black Sch. Educators, Kappa Delta Pi, Alpha Kappa Alpha.

JONES, LINDA KAREN, speech, language pathologist; b. Lindsay, Okla., July 5, 1949; d. Howard Curtis and Berniece (Farrow) Swindell; m. Wayne Arbey, Aug. 29, 1968 (div. Oct. 1973); children: Misty, Brian; m. David Ray Jones, Nov. 6, 1980; children: Robbie, Noah. BS, Okla. State U., 1984, MA, 1987. Lic. speech/lang. pathologist, Okla. Speech/lang. pathologist Winfield (Kans.) State Hosp. and Tng. Ctr., 1987-88, Pauls Valley (Okla.) State Sch., 1988-90, Developmental Disabilities Svcs. Divsn., Pauls Valley, 1990-92, J.D. McCarty Ctr. for Children with Developmental Disability, Norman, Okla., 1992—. Cons. Dept. Human Svcs., Pauls Valley, 1992—, Saber Mgmt., Ardmore, 1994—. Vol. Spl. Olympics, Stillwater, Okla., 1986-88, Health Fair, Stillwater, 1985-88. Mem. Am. Speech/Lang./Hearing Assn. (cert., award 1994), Okla. Soc. for Augmentative and Alternative Comm., Golden Key, Phi Kappa Phi. Avocations: antiques, camping, snow skiing. Office: JD McCarty Ctr Children DD 1125 E Alameda St Norman OK 73071-5254

JONES, LINDA W. federal agency administrator; B in bus. admin., U. DC, 1973; M in pub. admin., U. Maryland, 1976. Dir. fund for improvement of Edn. US Dept. Edn., Innovation and Improvement, Wash., 2002—; contracting off. rep. for tech asst. contracts Eisenhower Nat. Clearinghouse for Math. and Sci. Edn.; mgr. Eisenhower Profl. Devel. Fed. Activities Program; adminstr. Nat. Bd. for Profl. Tng. Standards, Eisenhower Regional Consortia for Math. and Sci. Edn. and Civic Edn., Javits Gifted and Talented Students Edn. Program. Office: US Dept Edn Innovation and Improvement 555 NJ Ave NW IES Rm 502D Capitol Pl Washington DC 20202*

JONES, LLEWELLYN WILLIAMS, special education educator; b. Wilson, N.C., Sept. 9, 1951; d. Henry Ely and Mattie Belle (Davenport) Williams; m. Stephen Thomas Jones, Jan. 23, 1970; children: Stephen Jr., Benjamin Wade, Philip Lee. BS cum laude, Atlantic Christian Coll., 1973; MA, Calif. State U., Northridge, 1983. Lic. tchr., prin., supr., curriculum instrn. specialist. Presch. tchr. Ea. N.C. Sch. for the Deaf, Wilson, N.C., 1973-76, 84—, multi-handicapped tchr., 1976-81, tchr., coordinator multi-handicapped program, 1981-84, tchr. presch., 1984-90, supervising tchr., asst. prin., 1990—, dir. student support svcs., 1990—93, deafblind children's specialist, resource tchr., 1993—. Mem. State Task Force, N.C., 1985—, presenter, 1987—. Bd. dirs. Wilson County Spl. Olympics, 1981-85, Wilson County Residential Services, 1986—. Calif. State U. fellow, 1983. Mem. AAUW, Council Am. Instrs. of Deaf, N.C. Assn. Interpreters, N.C. Registry of Interpreters for Deaf. Republican. Baptist. Avocations: reading, camping, tennis. Office: Ea NC Sch for the Deaf Hwy 301 Wilson NC 27893-5517

JONES, LUCIA JEAN, physical education educator; b. Racine, Wis., Apr. 24, 1942; d. Lawrence E. and Laura (Westphall) J. BS, U. Ariz., 1964; MS, Ariz. State U., 1967. Cert. tchr., Ariz. Tchr., chair women's phys. edn., coach Leysin (Switzerland) Am. Sch., 1964-65; prof., coach U. Ariz., Tucson, 1965-66; chair, coach phys. edn. dept. Hohokam Elem. Sch., Scottsdale, Ariz., 1967-68; instr. phys. edn., coach Alhambra High Sch., Phoenix, 1968-83; instr. phys. edn., health Trevor Browne High Sch., Phoenix, 1983-89; instr. physical edn. Alhambra High Sch., Phoenix, 1989-91, physical edn., health dept. chair, 1992-95. Delegate citizen amb. to Russia and Belarus, Temple Univ., 1993; program head golf profl. Ogontz White Mountain Resort, Lisbon, N.H., 1962-65; instr. Swiss Ski Sch., Leysin, 1964-65; tennis teaching profl. Top Seed Tennis Club, Phoenix, 1974-78; bd. dirs. Phoenix Dist. Tennis Assn., 1974-82; dir. European Study Tours, 1981-83; tennis coach Phoenix Coll., 1983-86; Jr. Wightman Cup coach Phoenix Dist. Tennis Assn., 1979-80. Contbr. articles to profl. publs.; author curriculum materials. Tchr. golf Scottsdale YWCA, 1967-71; bd. dirs. Ariz. Interscholastic Assn., Phoenix, 1968-92; cons. Phoenix Rackets Profl. Tennis Team, 1973-76; cons., bd. dirs. Phoenix Dist. Tennis Assn., 1973-92. Recipient Championship Recognition award Phoenix Union H.S. Sys., 1979-81, AIA Svc. award, 1993; named Wonder Woman Coach Tennis West Publications, 1979, Phoenix Metro Coach of Yr. softball Metro Phoenix Coaches Assn., 1981. Mem. NEA, AAHPERD, Ariz. AAHPERD (Secondary Phys. Edn. Tchr. of Yr. 1990), Phoenix Futures Forum, U.S. Tennis Assn. Umpires Coun., Ariz. Edn. Assn., Ariz. Interscholastic Assn. (Earl McCullar award 1979), Delta Psi Kappa. Republican. Avocations: travel, music, theater, golf, tennis. Home: 7108 N 15th Dr Phoenix AZ 85021-8506 Office: Alhambra High Sch 3839 W Camelback Rd Phoenix AZ 85019-2598

JONES, LYLE VINCENT, psychologist, educator; b. Grandview, Wash., Mar. 11, 1924; s. Vincent F. and Matilda M. (Abraham) Jones; m. Patricia Edison Powers, Dec. 17, 1949 (div. 1979); children: Christopher V., Susan E., Tad W. Student, Reed Coll., 1942—43; BS, U. Wash., 1947, MS, 1948; PhD, Stanford U., 1950. Nat. Research fellow, 1950—51; asst. prof. psychology U. Chgo., 1951—57; vis. assoc. prof. U. Tex., 1956—57; assoc. prof. U. N.C., 1957—60, prof., 1960—69, Alumni disting. prof., 1969—92, rsch. prof., 1992—, dir. L.L. Thurstone Psychometric Lab., 1957—74, 1979—92, vice chancellor, dean Grad. Sch., 1969—79. Pres. Assn. Grad. Schs., 1976—77; cons. in field. Author: Studies in Aphasia: An Approach to Testing, 1961, The Measurement and Prediction of Judgment and Choice, 1968, An Assessment of Research-Doctorate Programs in the United States, 5 vols., 1982, Indicators of Precollege Education in Science and Mathematics, 1985; Psychometrika, 1956—61, mem. editl. com. for psychology Mc-Graw-Hill, 1965—77; contbr. articles to profl. jours. Mng. trustee J. McKeen Cattell Fund, 1974—. With Air Corps U.S. Army, 1943—46. Recipient Thomas Jefferson award, U. N.C., 1979; fellow, Ctr. Advanced Study in Behavioral Scis., 1964—64; grantee, NIH, 1957—63, NSF, 1960—63, 1971—74, 1982—84, 1993—97, NIMH, 1963—74, 1979—87. Fellow: AAAS, APA (pres. divsn. 1963—64), Am. Statis. Assn., Am. Psychol. Soc., Am. Acad. Arts and Scis.; mem.: Psychometric Soc. (pres. 1962—63), Inst. Medicine, Nat. Coun. Measurement Edn., Am. Ednl. Rsch. Assn. Home: 6578 US Highway 15 501 N Pittsboro NC 27312-7793 Office: U NC CB 3270 Davie Hl Chapel Hill NC 27599-0001 E-mail: lvjones@email.unc.edu.

JONES, MARGUERITE JACKSON, English language educator; b. Greenwood, Miss., Aug. 12, 1949; d. James and Mary G. (Reedy) Jackson; m. Algee Jones, Apr. 4, 1971; 1 child, Stephanie Nerissa. BS, Miss. Valley State U., 1969; MEd, Miss. State U., 1974; EdS, Ark. State U., 1983; postgrad. U. Ark., 1982. Tchr. English Henderson High Sch., Starkville, Miss., 1969-70, creative writing Miami (Fla.) Coral Park, 1970-71, English, head dept. Marion (Ark.) Sr. High Sch., 1971-78, East Ark. Community Coll., Forrest City, 1978-79; migrant edn. supr. Marion (Ark.) Sch. Dist., 1979-83; mem. faculty Draughons Coll., Memphis, 1978-83; assoc. prof. State Tech., 1984—; cons. writing projects; condr. workshops for ednl., bus., civic groups. Bd. dirs. Bountiful Blessings Christian Acad., Memphis; dir. Leadership Tng. Inst. for 4th Eccles. Jurisdiction, Tenn.; Christian edn. dir. Temple Deliverance-The Cathedral Bountiful Blessings, Memphis. Mem. ASCD, Nat. Coun. Tchrs. English, Ark. Assn. Profl. Educators, Memphis Assn. Young Children, Tenn. Assn. Young Children, Nat. Assn. Young Children, Phi Delta Kappa. Home: 1239 Meadowlark Ln Memphis TN 38116-7801 Office: State Tech Inst 5983 Macon Cv Memphis TN 38134-7642

JONES, MARK LOGAN, educational association executive, educator; b. Provo, Utah, Dec. 16, 1950; s. Edward Evans and Doris (Logan) J.; m. Catherine A. Bailey. BS, Ea. Mont. Coll., 1975; postgrad. in labor rels., Cornell U.; postgrad., SUNY, Buffalo. Narcotics detective Yellowstone County Sheriff's Dept., Billings, Mont., 1972-74; math tchr. Billings (Mont.) Pub. Schs., 1975-87; rep. Nat. Edn. Assn. of N.Y., Buffalo, Jamestown, 1987-91, Nat. Edn. Assn. Alaska, Anchorage, 1991—. Mem. Alaska Tchr. Licensure Task Force, Tchr. Edn. Adv. Coun., Adv. Com. on Tchr. Stds., Alaska Partnership Tchr. Enhancement; bd. mem. Alaska staff Devel. Network; mem. various coms. Alaska Dept. Edn. Photographs featured in 1991 N.Y. Art Rev. and Am. Artist. Committeeman Yellowstone Dem. Party, Billings, 1984-87; exec. com. Dem. Cen. Com., Billings, 1985-87; bd. dirs. Billings Community Ctr., 1975-87; concert chmn. Billings Community Concert Assn., 1980-87; bd. dirs. Chautauqua County Arts Coun.; bd. dirs. Big Brothers and Big Sisters Anchorage. With U.S. Army, 1970-72. Recipient Distinguished Svc. award, Billings Edn. Assn., 1985, Mont. Edn. Assn., 1987. Mem. ACLU, Billings Edn. Assn. (bd. dirs. 1980-82, negotiator 1981-87, pres. 1982-87), Mont. Edn. Assn. (bd. dirs. 1982-87), Ea. Mont. Coll. Tchr. Edn. Project, Accreditation Reviewer Team Mont. Office Pub. Edn., Big Sky Orchard, Masonic, Scottish Rite. Avocations: bonsai, photography, reading, classical and jazz music, hunting, fishing. Home: PO Box 102904 Anchorage AK 99510-2904 Office: Nat Edn Assn Alaska 1840 S Bragaw St Ste 103 Anchorage AK 99508-3463

JONES, MARLENE ANN, retired education supervisor; b. Bluffton, Ohio, Nov. 22, 1936; d. Waldo J. and Blanche M. (Criblez) Wilkins; m. Marvin O. Jones, July 3, 1965; children: John O., Dianne M. BS, Bowling Green State U., 1958, EdS, 1978; MA, Ohio State U., 1962. Cert. family and consumer scis. Vocat. home econs. tchr. 7-12 Liberty Ctr. (Ohio) Bd. Edn., 1958-61; asst. state supr. Ohio Dept. Edn., Columbus, 1962-65; chair home econs. techs. Owens C.C. (formerly Penta Tech. Coll.), Toledo, 1965-71; supr. Penta County Vocat. Sch., Perrysburg, Ohio, 1965—2001. Pres. United Meth. Women, Colton, Ohio, 1967—. Named 1 of 10 Outstanding Women in Toledo Jaycees, 1971-72; recipient Disting. Centennial Svc. award Ohio Agrl. and Home Econs. Rsch. and Devel. Ctr., 1982, Home Econs. Grad. fellowship award Am. Vocat. Assn., 1990; named Alum of Yr. Coll. of Edn., Bowling Green State U., 1990. Mem. ASCD, Am. Ohio Vocat. Assn., Am. Family and Consumer Svcs. Assn. (past state pres.), Ohio Vocat. Family and Consumer Svcs. Suprs. Assn. (treas.), N.W. Ohio FHA/HERO Alumni Assn. (sec.), Phi Delta Kappa, Phi Upsilon Omicron (past pres. Alumni chpt. 1965—). Methodist. Home: 5-212 US Hwy 24 Liberty Center OH 43532 E-mail: marvin.marlenejones@gateway.net.

JONES, MARLENE WISEMAN, elementary education educator, reading specialist; b. Zanesville, Ohio, Oct. 8, 1939; d. Mark Andrew Wiseman and Elizabeth Wiseman (Wilkins) Doughty; m. Herbert Pearce Jones, Sept. 2, 1961. BS in Edn., Muskingum Coll., New Concord, Ohio, 1962; MEd, Ohio U., Zanesville, 1984. Elem. tchr. Zanesville City Schs., 1962-65, reading specialist, 1967-97, ret., 1997. Reading instr. Ohio U., Zanesville, 1984, Muskingum Area Tech. Coll., Zanesville, 1991-94; part time with Finley Fine Jewelry Co./Lazarus Dept. Store, 1999. Co-author book Diagnosis for Reading, 1975; creator Games for Reading, 1973. Mem. jr. assembly Bethesda Hosp., 1998-2002; treas. Salvation Army, 1999-2001; 1st v.p. Y-City Women's Club, 1999-2000, pres., 2000-01; pres. Brock Welding Golf League (pres. 2000-01). Recipient Outstanding Elem. Tchr. award, 1973. Mem. Salvation Army Womem's Aux., Y-City Women's Club, Zanesville Women's Club, Swarovski, Ohio Ret. Tchrs. Assn., Muskingum County Ret. Tchrs. Assn. (legis. chmn. 2000—), Zanesville Art Ctr., Order Ea. Star. Democrat. Lutheran. Avocations: golf, reading, crafts, painting, gardening. Home: 2219 Hazel Ave Zanesville OH 43701-2022

JONES, MYRA KENDALL, elementary school educator; b. Thomaston, Ga., June 1, 1947; children: Julius Jones II, Sharlene Deann Jones. AA, Palm Beach C.C., Lake Worth, Fla., 1970; BS, Fla. Atlantic U., Boca Raton, 1973. Cert. tchr. elem., Montessori. Assembly operator ITT, West Palm Beach, Fla., 1969-70; Headstart Ctr. dir. Cmty. Action Coun., Lake Worth, 1970-73; head tchr. day care Palm Beach C.C., Lake Worth, 1973-75; tchr. 2d grade Palm Beach County Pub. Schs., Delray Beach, 1975-76, tchr. 1st and 3d grades, 1979-84, tchr. 1st grade and Chpt. I, 1985—; recruiter/counselor Urban League, West Palm Beach, Fla., 1976-79; code enforcement officer City of Boynton Beach, Fla., 1984-85. Part-time ins. agt. Mass. Indemnity, West Palm, Fla., 1982-86. Pres. Concerned Citizens, Boynton Beach, 1982-83; counselor Yes/To Me Club, Drug Prevention Program for Youths; bd. dirs. Urban League, West Palm Beach, 1981-83; alt. mem. Civil Svc. Bd., Boynton Beach; hon. mem. Met. Ministerial Alliance, Boynton Beach, 1993. Recipient Tchr. of Yr. award Alpha Phi Alpha, 1992. Mem. NAACP, Urban League. Democrat. Baptist. Avocations: golf, reading. Home: 311 NW 4th Ave Boynton Beach FL 33435-4060 Office: Plumosa Elementary School 1712 NE 2nd Ave Delray Beach FL 33444-4198

JONES, PATRICIA LOUISE, elementary counselor; b. Moorhead, Minn., Aug. 20, 1942; d. Harry Wilfred and Myrtle Louise Rosenfeldt; m. Edward L. Marks (div.); m. Curtis C. Jones, July 16, 1973; children: Michon, Andrea, Nathan, Kirsten, Leah. BS, Moorhead State U., 1965; MS, Mankato State U., 1990. Cert. K-12 sch. counselor, Minn. Tchr. Anoka (Minn.) Hennepin Schs., 1966-68; pvt. practice Youth Ctr., Truman, Minn., 1969-72; bookkeeper Fairmont (Minn.) Glass & Sign, 1973, Truman Farmers Elevator, 1973-87; libr. Martin County Libr., Truman, 1988-89; sch. counselor St. James (Minn.) Schs., 1989—. Coord. Internat. Fun Fest, St. James, 1992, 96; originator, advisor Armstrong After Sch. Hispanic Club, St. James, 1991-2001. Coord. Truman Days Parade, 1991, 92, 94-2000; mem. adv. bd. Watonwan County Big Buddy Program, 1993—; mem. Watonwan County Corrections Adv. Bd., 1998-2002; foster parent, 1999. Mem. ACA, Am. Sch. Counselors Assn., Minn. Sch. Counselors Assn. (bd. dirs. 1997-99), S.W. Minn. Counselors Assn. (Elem. Counselor of Yr. 1993, pres. 1997-99). Avocations: genealogy, walking, photography. Office: Saint James Sch Dist 500 8th Ave S Saint James MN 56081 E-mail: pjones@stjames.k12.mn.us.

JONES, PIRKLE, photographer, educator; b. Shreveport, La., Jan. 2, 1914; s. Alfred Charles and Wilie (Tilton) J.; m. Ruth-Marion Baruch, Jan. 15, 1949 (dec. Oct. 1997). Grad., Calif. Sch. Fine Arts, 1949; PhD in Fine Arts (hon.), San Francisco Art Inst, 2003. Profl. free-lance photographer, 1949—; asst. to Ansel Adams, 1949—53; faculty Calif. Sch. Fine Arts, 1953-58, San Francisco Art Inst., 1971-97. Tchr. Ansel Adams Workshops, Yosemite.; Mem. Archtl. Adv. Com., Mill Valley, Calif., 1963-67 Exhibited in leading art mus.; photographic archive established Spl. Collections Libr., U. Calif., Santa Cruz; author: Portfolio One, 1955, (with Dorothea Lange) Death of a Valley, 1960, Portfolio Two, 1968; (with Ruth-Marion Baruch) Black Panthers, 1968, 2d edit., 2002, The Vanguard, A Photographic Essay on the Black Panthers, 1970; author: Berryessa Valley, The Last Year, 1995, Pirkle Jones California Photographs, 2001. Nat. Endowment for Arts photography fellow, 1977; recipient award of honor for exceptional achievement in field of photography Arts Commn. of City and County of San Francisco, 1983 Home: 663 Lovell Ave Mill Valley CA 94941-1086 E-mail: pirkle@earthlink.net.

JONES, RAYMOND MOYLAN, strategy and public policy educator; b. Phila., Dec. 28, 1942; s. Raymond and Elizabeth (Shaw) J.; m. Barbara Ann Donaghue, May 22, 1965; children: Andrea Marie, Audra Marie. BS, U.S. Mil. Acad., 1964; MBA, Harvard U., 1971; JD, U. Tex., 1973; PhD, U. Md., 1993. Bar: Tex. 1973, U.S. Supreme Ct. 1993. Commd. 2d lt. U.S. Army, 1964, advanced through grades to capt., 1966, ret., 1969; legal asst. to chmn. Occidental Petroleum Corp., L.A., 1973-75; pres. Oxy Metal Industries Internat., Geneva, 1975-77, Occidental Resource Recovery Corp., Irvine, Calif., 1978-81; v.p. Hooker Chem. Corp., Houston, 1977-78; pvt. practice cons. Austin and Irvine, 1981-86; lectr. Calif. State U., Long Beach, 1986, U. Md., College Park, 1986-90, Loyola Coll., Balt., 1990—. Cons. to multinational and domestic orgns. Author: Strategic Management in a Hostile Environment: Lessons from the Tobacco Industry, 1998; contbr. articles, book rev. to profl. publs. Mem. Friends of Austin Symphony Orch.; mem. Ludwig Von Mises Inst., Burlingame, Calif., 1987—. Intercoll. Studies Inst., Bryn Mawr, Pa., 1987—; mgmt. con. ARC, Balt., 1988—. Grantee U. Md. 1987, Loyola Coll. 1993. Mem. Am. Econ. Assn., Acad. Internat. Bus., Strategic Mgmt. Soc., Acad. Mgmt., State Bar Tex., Harvard Club. Roman Catholic. Home: 305 Kernewy Baltimore MD 21212-4714 Office: Loyola Coll Sellinger Sch Bus Mgmt Baltimore MD 21210-2699 E-mail: rjones@loyola.edu.

JONES, RICHARD JEFFERY, internist, educator; b. Cleve., Apr. 6, 1918; s. Edward Safford and Frances Christine (Jeffery) J.; m. Helen Hart, Oct. 5, 1946; children: Christopher, Ruth, Jeffery, Catherine. AB, Oberlin Coll., 1938; MA, SUNY, Buffalo, 1942, MD, 1943. Diplomate Am. Bd. Internal Medicine. Intern U. Chgo. Hosps., 1944, resident in internal medicine, 1947-49; assoc. prof. medicine U. Chgo., 1958-76; assoc. prof. clin. medicine Northwestern U., Chgo., 1976-92, pvt. practice specializing in cardiology, 1976—92. Vis. assoc. prof. Rockefeller U., 1965. Author: Chemistry and Therapy of Chronic Cardiovascular Disease, 1961; mem. editl. bd. Nutrition Revs., 1964-72. Lt. USNR, 1944-46, PTO. Recipient Presdl. letter of commendation Pres. of U.S., 1946. Fellow Am. Heart Assn.; mem. AMA (dir. sci. activities 1976-83, coun. sec. 1976-83), Ctrl. Soc. Clin. Rsch., Soc. Exptl. Biol. and Medicine (editl. bd. 1964-74). Unitarian Universalist. Home: 5550 South Shore Drive Ste 1014 Chicago IL 60637-5058 E-mail: rjones@ais.net.

JONES, RICHARD LAMAR, entomology educator; b. Charleston, Miss., May 31, 1939; s. Raymond Lee and Tyna Louise (Holland) J.; m. Anne Marchman, June 6, 1964; children: Katherine Mathis, Margaret Holland; m. Joan Marie Wood, Nov. 29, 1997. BS, Miss. State U., 1963, MS, 1965; PhD, U. Calif., Riverside, 1968. Rsch. entomologist Agrl. Rsch. Svc., USDA, Tifton, Ga., 1968-77; assoc. prof. entomology U. Minn., St. Paul, 1977-84, prof., head dept., 1984-91, dean Coll. Agr., 1991-95; dean of rsch., dir. Fla. Agrl. Expt. Sta. U. Fla., Gainesville, Fla., 1995—. Editor, author: Semiochemicals, 1974; also over 70 articles. With USN, 1958-60. Scholar NIH, 1965-68, Fulbright scholar, Leiden, The Netherlands, 1980. Mem. AAAS, Entomol. Soc. Am. (fin. com. 1989-96), Am. Chem. Soc. Avocations: golf, fishing. Office: U Fla PO Box 110200 Gainesville FL 32611-0200

JONES, ROBERT CLAIR, middle school educator; b. Norfolk, Va., Apr. 9, 1949; s. Leon Herbert and Barbara Dean (Jones) J.; m. Geri Lee Siebels, Feb. 13, 1977; children: Adam, Matthew, Aaron, Lee. BS, Old Dominion U., 1971, MS, 1981. Tchr. Virginia Beach (Va.) Jr. High Sch., 1971-73, Kempsville Jr. High Sch., Virginia Beach, 1973—. Adj. faculty Old Dominion U., Norfolk, Va., 1990—; co-chmn. faculty coun. Kempsville Mid. Sch., 1992-93, curriculum coord., grade level chair, 1993—; program devel. com. for mid. schs., Virginia Beach City Schs., 1990-91, chmn. social studies curriculum adv. com., 1990-91, instr. staff devel., 1989-91; speaker in field. Contbr. articles to profl. jours.; featured in Oasis mag. Baseball coach Pony Colt League, Virginia Beach, 1991-92; vol. Make A Wish Found., Virginia Beach, 1990-92. Named Tchr. of Yr., Va. Coun. Social Studies, 1987—. Mem. ASCD, NEA, Nat. Coun. Social Studies, Va. Edn. Assn., Va. Coun. Social Studies, Virginia Beach Edn. Assn. Avocations: profl. musician, collecting records, Beatles memorobilia. Home: 812 Yearling Ct Virginia Beach VA 23464-3214 Office: Kenpsville Mid Sch 260 Churchill Dr Virginia Beach VA 23456

JONES, ROBERT LYLE, emergency medical services leader, financial planner, educator; b. Washington, Feb. 14, 1959; s. Herman Aven and Dorothy Edith J.; m. Cynthia Celia Bogdanowicz, May 15, 1996. B in Gen. Sci., U. Kans., 1982; MA in Adult and Continuing Edn., U. Mo., 1990. Registered paramedic, Kans.; cert. emergency med. svcs. instr./coord.; chartered mut. funds counselor; accredited investor SEC. Paramedic team leader Johnson County (Kans.) Med. Action, 1983-89, dist. supr., 1989-92, edn. supr., 1992—2002, bn. chief, 2002—; chmn., CEO Bercalso Investments, 2001—; pres., chief investment officer NorthTail Real Estate Co., 2002—. BCLS instr., 1979-87, affiliate faculty, 1987—, ACLS instr., 1985-88, prehosp. trauma life support instr., 1986—, affiliate faculty, 1988—, PALS instr., 1993—; PEPP instr./coord., 2003—. Served to Capt. USAR, 1979-94. Mem.: Fin. Planning Assn., Assn. Profls. in Infection Control and Epidemiology. Avocations: bicycling, backpacking, running. Office: Johnson County Med Action 111 S Cherry St Ste 300 Olathe KS 66061-3421

JONES, ROBERT THADDUES, principal; b. Manhattan, N.Y., Jan. 11, 1938; s. Monte Jones and Adelle (Brown) Ousmane; m. Geneva Alafair Thomas, Nov. 24, 1957; 1 child, Terry David. BA, Claflin Coll., Orangeburg, S.C., 1961; postgrad., S.C. State U., 1962-67, U. S.C., 1967-68; MEd, LaVerne (Calif.) U., 1977. Cert. guidance, elem. and secondary supr., elem. and secondary prin., art. Art tchr., guidance counselor Bryson H.S., Fountain Inn, S.C., 1960-69; 1st and 5th grade tchr. Hayne Elem. Sch., Greenville, S.C., 1969-70; art tchr., biracial coord. Northwood Mid. Sch., Taylors, S.C., 1970-71; guidance counselor Berea Mid. Sch., Greenville, S.C., 1971-79, asst. prin., 1982-83, Woodmont H.S., Piedmont, S.C., 1979-82, N.W. Mid. Sch., Travelers Rest, S.C., 1983-84; prin. Cone Elem. Sch., Greenville, 1984-88, Alexander Elem. Sch., Greenville, 1988—2000; ret. Greenville County Schs., 2000. Asst. formulator model for S.C. schs. Guidance By Objectives, 1977. Vice chmn. Freetown Crime Watch Com., Greenville, 1986—; chmn. Parker Sewer & Fire Subdist., Greenville, (elected 1988 & 1999-), vice-chmn. commn., 1998; precinct pres. Tanglewood Dem. Precinct, Greenville, 1990; vice chmn. Greenville County Planning Commn., 1994; sec.-treas. N.W. Area Coun. Chamber, Greenville, 1994 (plaque 1994); v.p. for membership Blue Ridge Coun. Boy Scouts Am., Greenville, 1992; mem. Greenville Marchers Against Drugs, 1993-94 (plaque 1993). Recipient Silver Beaver award Boy Scouts Am., Greenville, 1988; named Ben E. Craig Outstanding Educator First Union Bank, Greenville, 1991, N.W. Area Bus. Edn. Partnership Prin. of Yr., Greenville, 1993. Mem. Palmetto State Law Enforcement Officers Assn. (sec. 1979-94, Plaque 1988), SC Law Enforcement Officers Assn., Masons, United Teaching Profession (retired 2001). Methodist. Avocations: photography, tennis computer technology. Home: 202 Hollywood Dr Greenville SC 29611-7320 Office: Parker Sewer & Fire Subdistrict 117 Smythe St Greenville SC 29611

JONES, ROGER CLYDE, retired electrical engineering educator; b. Lake Andes, S.D., Aug. 17, 1919; s. Robert Clyde and Martha (Albertson) J.; m. Katherine M. Tucker, June 7, 1952; children: Linda Lee, Vonnie Lynette. BS, U. Nebr., 1949; MS, U. Md., 1953; PhD U. Md., 1963. With U.S. Naval Research Lab., Washington, 1949-57; staff sr. engr. to chief engr. Melpar, Inc., Falls Church, Va., 1957-58, cons. project engr., 1958-59, sect. head physics, 1959-64, chief scientist for physics, 1964; prof. dept. elec. engring. U. Ariz., Tucson, 1964-89, dir. quantum electronics lab., 1968-88, adj. prof. radiology, 1978-86, adj. prof. radiation-oncology, 1986-88, prof. of radiation-oncology, 1988-89, prof. emeritus, 1989—; guest prof. of exptl. oncology Inst. Cancer Research, Aarhus, Denmark, 1982-83; tech. dir. H.S.C. and A., El Paso, 1989-96. Patentee in field. Served with AUS, 1942-45. Fellow AAAS; mem. IEEE, NSPE, Am. Phys. Soc., Optical Soc. Am., Internat. Soc. Optical Engring., Bioelectromagnetics Soc., NSPE, Am. Congress on Surveying and Mapping, N.Mex. Acad. Sci., N.Y. Acad. Sci., Eta Kappa Nu, Pi Mu Epsilon. Home: 5809 E 3rd St Tucson AZ 85711-1519

JONES, ROGER WALTON, English language educator, writer; b. Morristown, N.J., Nov. 22, 1953; s. Chastine Walton and Gloria (Gamble) J.; m. Sue Chang, Aug. 3, 2003. BA in eng., Kenyon Coll., 1976; MA in eng., Southern Ill. U., 1979; PhD in eng., Tex. A&M U., 1989. Teaching asst. Southern Ill. U., Carbondale, 1978-79; adj. prof. Kean Coll., Newark, N.J., 1980; instr. Lamar U., Beaumont, Tex., 1981-83; teaching asst. Tex A&M U., College Station, 1984-89, lecturer, 1990; asst. prof. Howard Payne U., Brownwood, Tex., 1990-91; dir. acad. honors Ranger (Tex.) Coll., 1991—, head dept. humanities and social & behavioral scis., 1998—. Author: Larry McMurtry and the Victorian Novel, 1994; contbr. articles to profl. jours. Contbr., mem. Dem. Nat. Com., Washington. Recipient Merit Incentive award Lamar U., 1983. Mem. Modern Lang. Assn., S. Cen. Modern. Lang. Assn. Democrat. Episcopalian. Avocations: reading, writing, oil painting, swimming. Office: Ranger Coll College Cir Ranger TX 76470 E-mail: rjones@ranger.cc.tx.us.

JONES, ROSEMARY, college official; b. Washington, Pa., Aug. 15, 1951; d. Roy F. and Grace Vivian (Beton) J. BA in Sociology, Ohio State U., 1974, MA in Pub. Adminstrn., 1977. Mgmt. analyst office planning studies Ohio State U., Columbus, 1974-76; staff assoc., edn. rev. com. Ohio Gen. Assembly, Columbus, 1977-78; from adminstr. to asst. dir. info. systems and rsch. Ohio Bd. Regents, Columbus, 1978-90; from project dir. instl. rsch. to dir. rsch. planning Lakeland C.C., Mentor, Ohio, 1990-93; dist. dir. instl. planning evaluation Cuyahoga C.C., Cleve., 1994—. NPECSS planning com. Dept. Edn., 1994-96, NPEC student outcomes data working group, 1996, NCES coop. sys. fellows program, 1996; com. on revising info. sys. for higher edn. Ohio Bd. Regents, Columbus, 1994-96, subsidy consultation com., 1996, 2002, cons., 1990-91, com. on resource analysis revision, 1994-96, 2002, vice-chair higher edn. info. adv. com., 1996-98, chair, 1999-2001, chair subcom. on data access and reporting, 1998-99; mem. Ohio Awards for Excellence Coun., 1999-2001; com. on performance Ohio Bd. Regents, 2000-2002. Consumer adv. bd. United Health Plan, Columbus, 1978-82, chair, 1980-82; vol. Ronald McDonald House, Columbus, 1989, operating bd. mem., 1989; bd. dirs. Netcare Found., Columbus, 1988; state and regional conf. chair ASPA, Columbus, 1981, 83-84; steering com. Ctrl. Ohio Salute to Pub. Employees, Columbus, 1983; mem. strategic planning com. Mentor Pub. Libr., 1998-2001. Recipient Pres.'s award of achievement Cuyahoga C.C., 2000. Mem. Assn. Instl. Rsch., Ohio Conf. for Coll. and Univ. Planning (two-yr. campus coun. rep. 1997-99), Ohio Assn. Instl. Rsch. (two-yr. campus coun. rep. 1994-96), Cleve. Planning Forum, Soc. for Coll. and Univ. Planning, Cleve. Commn. on Higher Edn. Strategic Planning Com. (temp. chair 1991), Ohio Assn. C.C.s (performance measurement study team 1999-2001), Oxford U. Roundtable. Office: Cuyahoga CC 700 Carnegie Ave Cleveland OH 44115-2833

JONES, SARAH DOWNING, visual arts educator; b. S.I., N.Y., Jan. 11, 1960; d. Burton Hathaway and Jean (Reinbrecht) J. BS in Art Edn., East Carolina U., 1983. Art tchr. Williston Middle Sch., Wilmington, N.C., 1983-92, New Hanover High Sch., Wilmington, N.C., 1992—. Lead specialist for visual arts New Hanover County, Wilmington, 1991-92. Named Human Rels. Tchr. of Yr., Williston Middle Sch., 1986; recipient Prin.'s award for Arts Edn., 1986-92, Prin.'s award for Mentorship, 1989, Prin.'s award for So. Assn. Chairperson, 1991. Mem. NEA, N.C. Art Edn. Assn. (art awards chair 1989-91, presenter of workshops 1991-92, mid. sch., jr. high divsn. chair 1991-93), Arts Coun. of the Lower Cape Fear, N.C. Alliance for Art Edn., St. Johns Mus. of Art, New Hanover County Human Rels. Com. Democrat. Avocations: painting, drawing, portraits. Office: New Hanover High Sch 1307 Market St Wilmington NC 28401-4399

JONES, SARAH LUCILLE, supervisor, consultant; b. Pinewood, S.C., Aug. 12, 1947; d. Aaron Mack and Sarah Jane Green; m. Flynn Raymond Jones, June 5, 1976; 1 child, Flynn Raymond Jones Jr. BS, S.C. State U., 1970; MS, Drexel U., 1974; Cert. in Supervision and Adminstrn., Georgian Ct. Coll., 1993. Cert. tchr. N.J., N.Y., Pa., Ind., S.C. Head tchr. Head Start, Phila., 1970—76; tchr. Rochester (N.Y.) City Schs., 1977—79; dir. ACEOC Head Start, Ft. Wayne, Ind., 1979—82; tchr. Freehold Regional H.S., Englishtown, NJ, 1982—2000; edn. specialist Brookdale C.C., Lincroft, NJ, 1989—95; dept. supr. Manalapan (N.J.) H.S., 2000—. Nutrition cons. MCEOC Head Start, New Brunswick, NJ, 1985—; state trainer AHEA/NJHEA, NJ, 1987—88; daycare cons. Espic Diocese, Keyport, NJ, 1987—88; mem. numerous curriculum coms., faculty rep., faculty advisor Freehold Regional H.S. Dist. Mem.: N.J. Assn. Family and Cons. Sci. (treas. 1992—93, corr. sec. 1993—94), Mon-Ocean Assn. Family and Cons. Sci. (pres. 1989—90, councilor 1994—, v.p. program 1999—2002). Avocations: reading, gardening. Office: Freehold Regional HS Dist 11 Pine St Englishtown NJ 07726

JONES, SUEJETTE ALBRITTON, basic skills educator; b. Kinston, N.C., Mar. 27, 1923; d. Clyde A. and Carrie (Jackson) Albritton; m. William Edward Jones, Mar. 15, 1946 (dec.); 1 dau., Jocelyn Suejette. B.S. in Pub. Sch. Music, Va. State U., 1943; postgrad. U. Pa. Sch. Music, 1945, Winston-Salem State U., 1950-51, A&T State U., 1959-61, Shaw U., 1952, East Carolina U., 1970. Tchr. music, Greenville, N.C., 1943-45; clk. typist Navy Dept., Washington, 1945; interviewer N.C. Employment Security Commn., Kinston, 1946-47; tchr., choral dir. Bethel (N.C.) Union Sch., 1950-52; tchr. C.M. Eppes Sch., 1952-54, S. Greenville Sch., 1954-69, Eastern Elem. Sch., 1969-80; chorus accompanist, tchr. Wahl Coates Lab. Sch., East Carolina U., Greenville, 1980-85, ret., 1985; exec. dir. Partnership for Progress After Sch. Tutorial, 1992-93; instr. basic skills Pitt C.C., Greenville, 1993—. Former mem. Greenville Choral Soc., Tarboro Jubilee Singers. Mem. NEA, Opportunities Industrialization Ctrs. (bd. dirs. 1992-93), N.C. Assn. Educators, So. Assn. Colls. and Schs. (vis. com. 1983-85), Delta Kappa Gamma, Alpha Kappa Alpha. Mem. Ch. of Christ. Lodge: Daus. of Isis. Composer: O Isis Dear, 1956.

JONES, SUSAN MATTHEWS, elementary educator educator; b. Pueblo, Colo., Nov. 2, 1945; d. Zolton and Cecilia (Barnhoft) Orosz. BS in Edn., Ark. State U., 1968. Cert. elem. tchr., Ark., Okla., art tchr., Ark., Okla., Mo. 1st grade tchr. Cherokee Elem. Sch., Hardy, Ark., 1969-70, Madill (Okla.) Elem. Sch., 1979-86, T. G. Smith Elem. Sch., Springdale, Ark., 1986—; high sch. art tchr. Warren County R-III Sch., Warrenton, Mo., 1970-74; jr. high art tchr. Moore (Okla.) West Ju. High Sch., 1974-75. Presenter workshops in math and reading. Creator, pub. memory aid books and posters, 1984—. Recipient Presdl. award for Excellence in Math. Tchg., 1996; State recognition exemplary grantee Ark. Dept. Edn., 1988-89, Christa McAuliffe fellowship program grantee, 1990-91. Mem. NEA, ASCD, Ark. Edn. Assn., Ark. Reading Coun. Home: 1623 Terry Dr Fayetteville AR 72703-4133 E-mail: susan@memoryaids.com.

JONES, SUSAN MCGOWAN, gifted and talented educator; b. Alameda, Calif., May 12, 1959; d. Thomas and Gladys Mae (Prutzman) McG.; m. Warren Howard Jones, Oct. 31, 1980 (div.); children: Kelly Hardcastle, Reilly James. AS in Edn., No. Va. Community Coll., 1988; BA in Russian Area Studies, George Mason U., 1991; MEd, Marymount U., 1994; EdD candidate, Coll. William & Mary, 2003—. Cert. nat. bd. cert. tchr. Va. State Lic. Data processor Tracor, Inc., Virginia Beach, Va., 1982-83; computer operator Hughes, Bendix, Holmes and Narver, Virginia Beach, 1983-84; data analyst Tracor, Inc., Virginia Beach, 1984; systems analyst Advanced Tech., Inc., Virginia Beach, 1984-85, computer programmer Reston, Va., 1986-87; tech. writer Swiger Group, Reston, 1987; tchr. 3rd grade Loudoun County Day Sch., Leesburg, Va., 1991-93; tchr. 4th and 5th grade Loudoun County Pub. Schs., 1994—2000, Va. Beach City Pub. Sch., 2001—. Master tchr. Nat. Tech. Tchr. Inst., WNVT, Fairfax, 1998-99; cand. Nat. Bd. for Profl. Teaching Certification, 1999; translation cons. Systems Ctr., Inc., Reston, 1990—. Mem. ASCD, World Affairs Coun., Golden Key, Phi Theta Kappa, Alpha Chi. E-mail: smjones59@aol.com.

JONES, THOMAS WILLIAM, secondary education educator, consultant; b. Charleroi, Pa., Mar. 13, 1952; s. Frank Jr. and Margaret (Powk) J.; m. Daryl Vernau, Mar. 13, 1975; children: Joshua Thomas, Gwynenn Taylor. BS in Edn., California (Pa.) U., 1974, MS in Earth Sci., 1982, MEd, 1990; postgrad., Indiana U. of Pa., 1996—. Tchr. elem. sch. Rockwood (Pa.) Sch. Dist., 1974-82, tchr. secondary sch., 1982—, acting adminstr., 1989-90. Assoc. dir. Bus./Edn. Partnerships, U. Pitts. at Johnstown, 1992—; owner DEC Cons. Svcs., Pa., Highland Computers, Pa.; environ. cons. Allegheny Mountain Rsch., Berlin, 1986-88; instr. Appalachia Intermediate Unit 08, Ebensburg, Pa., 1987-89; edn. cons. ERB Cons., Berlin, 1990—; owner DEC Cons. and Webmaster Svcs. Author curriculum materials, ednl. materials. Officer Rotary Internat., Meyersdale, Pa., 1984-87; organizer Casselman Watershed Assn., Rockwood, 1988, Cen. Pa. Sci. Alliance, Ebensburg, 1989; county organizer, Skywarn vol. NOAA-Nat. Weather Svc., Pitts., 1989—; vol. Pa. Dept. Conservation and Natural Resources, 1998. Recipient Equipment award Spectroscopy Soc. Pitts., 1991, Participant award U.S. Dept. Energy (STRIVE), 1992. Mem. ASCD (internat. network for sci., facilitator 1992-94), NSTA, Nat. Assn. Ptnrs. in Edn., Mid-Atlantic Consortium for Math. and Sci. Edn. (steering com. 1994-95, co-chair 1995-96, chair Pa. Eisenhower state team), Alliance for Tchg. of Sci. (chmn., pres. 1989—, network facilitator 1992-94, PSTA convestion publicity chmn. 1991, tech. chair, internet developer), Nat. Parks Conservancy, Gamma Theta Upsilon, Phi Kappa Theta. Republican. Avocations: martial arts, woodworking. Home: 700 Diamond St Berlin PA 15530-1519 Office: Univ Pitts Johnstown 110 Biddle Hall Johnstown PA 15904

JONES, TINA CHARLENE, music educator, genealogy and law researcher; b. Washington, May 27, 1961; d. Charles Timothy Jones and Tiney Ruth (Marion) Haynie; James H. Haynie (stepfather). Cert. paralegal, George Washington U., Washington, 1986. Music educator Creative Music Melodies Co., Silver Spring, Md., 1984—. Freelance geneal. and legal rschr., Silver Spring, 1986. Contbr. articles on geneal. rsch. to The Afro-American Newspaper, 1994-95. Recipient grants Delta Sigma Theta, 1979, Nat. Christian Choir, 1986. Mem. Am. Coll. Musicians, Nat. Piano Found., Music Educators Nat. Conf., Internat. Ctr. Rsch. in Music Edn. Avocations: singing, travel, reading. Home: 13810 Carter House Way Silver Spring MD 20904-4854 Office: 13810 Carter House Way Silver Spring MD 20904-4854 E-mail: jones61@bellatlantic.net.

JONES, TRINA WOOD, special education educator; b. Murfreesboro, N.C. d. James Elton I and Sarah Virginia (Bishop) Wood; 1 child, Ashleigh Erin. BA in Early Childhood Edn., N.C. Cen. U., 1977, MEd in Mental Retardation, 1978. Educator Granville County Pub. Schs., Stovall, N.C., 1978-81, Norfolk (Va.) Pub. Schs., 1981-84, Chgo. Pub. Schs., 1984—. Mem. Coun. for Exceptional Children. Avocations: coin and stamp collecting, writing, reading, travel. Home: 5230 S Cornell Ave Chicago IL 60615-4200 Office: Jackie Robinson Elem Sch 4225 S Lake Park Ave Chicago IL 60653-3064 E-mail: twj195@aol.com.

JONES, ULYSSES SIMPSON, JR., agronomy and soils educator, consultant; b. Portsmouth, Va., Feb. 14, 1918; s. Ulysses Simpson and Annie Virginia (Fraser) J.; m. Ann Gayle Plummer, June 7, 1941; 1 child, Josephine Jones Allen. BS, 1939, Va. Poly. Inst. & State U., 1939; MS, Purdue U., 1942; PhD, U. Wis., 1947. Assoc. prof. Miss. State U., Starkville, 1947-53; chief agronomist OLIN Corp., Little Rock, 1953-60; prof. and head dept. agronomy and soils Clemson (S.C.) U., 1960-83, prof. emeritus soils, 1983—2002; dir. Rural Devel. Inst. Cuttington U., Liberia, 1983-85; vis. Fulbright prof. U. Zimbabwe, Harare, 1986-88; cons. W. E. Gilbert and Assocs., Greenville, 1988-91; Fulbright prof. Estonian Agr. U. Tartu, 1992. Dir. Coun. on Fertilizer Application, Washington, 1965-71; mem. adv. bd. Nat. Soybean Improvement Coun., Ames, Iowa, 1965-71; vis. Fulbright prof. Coun. Internat. Exch. of Scholars, Izmir, Turkey, 1975; vis. scientist Internat. Rice Rsch. Inst. NSF, 1980; vis. prof. U. Philippines, 1981; cons. UN Devel. Program, N.Y.C., 1982. Author: Fertilizers and Soil Fertility, 1982; (with others) Atmospheric Sulfur Deposition, 1980, Sulfur in Agriculture, 1986, Detecting Mineral Nutrient Deficiencies, 1989; contbr. over 50 articles to scholarly jours. including Soil Sci., Agronomy Jour. Bd. dirs., v.p. Rotary Internat., Clemson, 1965. Col. U.S. Army, 1939-78, World War II and Korea. Fellow Am. Soc. Agronomy, Soil Sci. Soc. Am. Republican. Episcopalian. Achievements include research on use of radioactive elements in soil and fertilizer, on Wetland rice nutrient deficiencies, on influence of pH on growth and nutrient composition of maize in flowing nutrient solutions, and on 4 soil test extractants for Zimbabwe soils. Home: Clemson, SC. Died Sept. 11, 2002.

JONES, VIRGINIA ALLEN, secondary education educator, site director; b. Manson, N.C., Sept. 25; d. Jarvis and Magnolia (Hargrove) Allen; m. Douglas Lee Jones, Sr., Aug. 16; children: Moneefa, Malaika, Douglas Jr., Marvin, Jarvis. BS in English, A & T State U., 1969; MS in English, Converse Coll., 1973. Lang. arts tchr. Spartanburg (S.C.) H.S., 1971-78, 79-81, 1988-92, Boiling Springs Jr. H.S., Spartanburg, 1982-88; cities in schs., tchr., site dir. Whitlock Jr. H.S., Spartanburg, 1993-95; tchr./site dir. cities in schs. Carver Jr. H.S., Spartanburg, 1995—. BSAP writing com. State Dept. of Edn., Columbia, S.C., 1985—; writing cons. Thornwell Sch., Clinton, S.C., 1992-94. Mem. Assn. Supervision and Curriculum Devel., Palmetto State Tchrs Assn., Internat. Alliance for Invitational Edn., Women of Color Literary Guild, Alpha Kappa Alpha (philacter 1995). Avocations: reading, writing, working with youth groups, traveling. Office: Carver Jr HS 449 S Church St Spartanburg SC 29306-5211

JONES, WILBERT, school principal; b. Jersey City, Dec. 16, 1947; s. Robert W. and Peacola (Cooper) J.; m. Screll Page Hudson, Aug. 14, 1971; children: Wilbert Robert, Charla Screll. BA, Benedict Coll., 1969; MA, Montclair State Coll., 1973. Elem. tchr. Jersey City Sch. Dist., 1969-73, elem. guidance counselor, 1973-75, high sch. guidance counselor, 1975-79, sch. prin., 1979-80, asst. supt. schs., 1980-81, sch. prin., 1981—. Bd. dirs. Hudson County Sickle Anemia Soc., Jersey City. Bd. of deacon First Bapt. Ch., South Orange, N.J. Recipient Donald Hampton Meml. Bd., 1979, Outstanding Young Man of Am. award, 1979, 80. Mem. NEA, Jersey City Adminstr. and Supr. Assn., Jersey City Men's Prin. Assn. Home: 5606 Flintlock Ln Columbus OH 43213-2627

JONES, WILLIAM DENVER, physicist, educator; b. Jenkinjones, W.Va., Apr. 14, 1935; s. William Clyde and Verda Lucille (Shrewsbury) J.; m. Melba R. Mayberry, Sept. 13, 1958 (div. 1982); children: Mark Allen, Lisa Gayle. MS in Physics, Vanderbilt U., 1962, PhD, 1963. Rsch. assoc. Oak Ridge (Tenn.) Nat. Lab., 1963-70; prof. physics U. South Fla., Tampa, 1970—. Cons. Solar Kit of Fla., Tampa, 1975-80, Naval Rsch. Lab, 1985-87. Author: Linear Theories and Methods of Electrostatic Waves in Plasmas, 1985; contbr. articles to Basic Rsch. In Plasma Physics, 1964—. Grantee Atomic Energy Commn., 1970-78, Dept. of Energy, 1973-76, USAF, 1972-74, Tampa Electric Co., 1971-73. Fellow Am. Phys. Soc.; mem. Union Concerned Scientists, Public Citizen, NOW, Sigma Xi. Republican. Office: U South Fla 4202 E Fowler Ave Tampa FL 33620-8000

JONES, WILLIAM ERNEST, chemistry educator; b. Sackville, N.B., Can. s. Frederick W. and Jennie E. (Tuttle) J.; m. Norma Florence McKinney Reid, Aug. 9, 1958; children: Mary Ellen E., Jennifer A.J., Sarah A.L., K. Martha M. B.Sc., Mt. Allison U., 1958, M.Sc., 1959; PhD, McGill U., 1963. Asst. prof. Dalhousie U., Halifax, 1962—68, assoc. prof., 1968—73, prof. chemistry, 1973—91, chmn. dept. chemistry, 1974—83, chmn. univ. senate, 1983—89, Saint Mary's U., Halifax, 1989—91, prof. chemistry, dean faculty sci., 2001—; prof. chemistry, v.p. acad. affairs U. Windsor, 1991—98, prof. chemistry, 1991—2001; adj. prof. chemistry St. Mary's U., 2001—, acting dean faculty grad. studies and rsch. Contbr. articles to profl. jours. Fellow Chem. Inst. Can. Home: 17 Shaw Crescent Halifax NS Canada B3P 1V2 Office: St Mary's U Office Faculty Grad Studies & Rsch Halifax NS Canada B3H 3C3 E-mail: wjones@stmarys.ca.

JONES, WILLIAM REX, law educator; b. Murphysboro, Ill., Oct. 20, 1922; s. Claude E. and Ivy P. (McCormick) J.; m. Miriam R. Lamy, Mar. 27, 1944; m. Gerri L. Haun, June 30, 1972; children: Michael Kimber, Jeanne Keats, Patricia Combs, Sally Horowitz, Kevin. BS, U. Louisville, 1950; JD, U. Ky., 1968; LLM, U. Mich., 1970. Bar: Ky. 1969, Ind. 1971, U.S. Supreme Ct. 1976. Exec. v.p. Paul Miller Ford, Inc., Lexington, Ky., 1951-64; pres. Bill's Seat Cover Ctr., Inc., Lexington, Ky., 1952-65, Bill Jones Real Estate, Inc., Lexington, Ky., 1965-70; asst. prof. law Ind. U., Indpls., 1970-73, assoc. prof., 1973-75, prof., 1975-80; dean Salmon P. Chase Coll. Law. No. Ky. U., Highland Heights, 1980-85, prof., 1980-93, prof. emeritus, 1993—. Vis. prof. Shepard Broad Law Ctr., Nova Southeastern U., Ft. Lauderdale, Fla., 1994-95; mem. Ky. Pub. Advocacy Commn., 1982-93, 97-2000, chmn., 1986-93; chmn. existing structures appeal bd., City of Newport, Ky., 2002—. Author: Kentucky Criminal Trial Practice, 3d edit., 2001, Kentucky Criminal Trial Practice Forms, 3d edit., 2000. 1st sgt. U.S. Army, 1940-44. Cook fellow U. Mich., 1969-70, W.G. Hart fellow Queen Mary Coll. U. London, 1985. Mem. Order of Coif. E-mail: jonesw@nku.edu., wrexjones@zoomtown.com.

JONES, WINONA NIGELS, retired library media specialist; b. Feb. 24, 1928; d. Eugene Arthur and Bertha Lillian (Dixon) Nigels; m. Charles Albert Jones, Nov. 26, 1994; children: Charles Eugene, Sharon Ann Jones Allworth, Caroline Winona Jones Pandorf. AA, St. Petersburg Jr. Coll., 1965; BS, U. So. Fla., 1967, MS, 1968; advanced MS, Fla. State U., 1980. Libr. media specialist Dunedine (Fla.) Comprehensive H.S., 1967-76; libr. media specialist, chmn. dept. Fitzgerald Mid. Sch., Largo, Fla., 1976-87; dir. media svcs. East Lake H.S., Tarpon Springs, Fla., 1987-93; ret., 1993. Dir., vol. North Pinellas Hist. Mus.; active Palm Harbor Hist. Soc., Pinellas County Hist. Soc.; del. White Ho. Conf. Libr. and Info. Svcs. Named Educator Yr. Pinellas County Sch. Bd. and Suncoast C. of C., 1983, 88, Palm Harbor Woman Yr. Palm Harbor Jr. Women's club, 1989, Palm Harbor Citizen Yr., Palm Harbor C. of C., 2002. Mem. ALA (coun. 1988-92), NEA, AAUW, ASCD, Assn. Ednl. Comm. and Tech. (divsn. sch. media specialist, coms.), Am. Assn. Sch. Librs. (com., pres.-elect 1989, pres. 1990-91, mem. exec. bd. 1991-92), Southeastern Libr. Assn., Fla. Libr. Assn., Fla. Assn. Media Edn. (pres.), U. So. Fla. Alumni Assn., Fla. State Libr. Sci. Alumni Assn., U. So. Fla. Libr. Sci. Alumni Assn. (pres. 1991-92, 92-93), Phi Theta Kappa, Phi Rho Pi, Beta Phi Mu, Kappa Delta Pi, Delta Kappa Gamma (parliamentarian 1989-90, legis. chmn. 1990, sec. 1994-96), Inner Wheel Club, Pilot Club, Civic Club, Order Ea. Star (Palm Harbor, past worthy matron). Democrat. Home: 911 Manning Rd Palm Harbor FL 34683-6344

JONES-BLAND, VALERIE QUINETTA BREWER, secondary education educator; b. Little Rock, Dec. 29, 1953; d. Curtis and Maggie Helene (Taylor) Brewer; m. Keith Fredrick Jones, Apr. 18, 1984 (div. Aug. 1987); 1 child, Jeremy Michael; m. Melvin Bland, Jr., Feb. 6, 1993. BA, Spelman Coll., 1975; MA, U. Iowa, 1976. Cert. spl. edn. and computer edn. tchr., Ill. Pre-sch. tchr. Holy Cross Cath. Sch., Chgo., 1976-77; tchr. elem. spl. edn. LeMoyne Pub. Sch., Chgo., 1977-78; elem. tchr. Parkside Pub. Sch., Chgo., 1978-82, tchr. kindergarten, 1982-89, tchr. computers, coord. computer lab., 1989—, sec. local sch. coun., 1992—. Contbr. articles to mags. Literacy vol. South Ctrl. Cmty. Ctr., Chgo., 1989-94; mentor, vol. Greer Pregnant Teen Home, Chgo., 1994-95; bd. dirs., sec. 3100 Condo Assn., Chgo., 1986-91. Named Outstanding Tchr. of Yr. award Parkside Sch. Chgo. Pub. Sch., 1989, Outstanding Tchr. Svc. award Parkside Sch. PTA, 1990; Spelman Coll. Alumnae of Yr., United Negro Coll. Fund, 1994. Mem. Chgo. Tchrs. Union (coord. restructuring 1991-95, Quest award 1993), Nat. Alumnae Assn. Spelman Coll. (pres. Chgo. chpt. 1992-94), Alpha Kappa Alpha (grad. advisor 1989-94, Soror of Yr. award 1990, Grad. Advisor of Yr. award ctrl. region 1993). Democrat. Lutheran. Avocations: drama, dance, skating, administration, travel. Home: 9824 S Beverly Ave Chicago IL 60643-1377

JONES-GREGORY, PATRICIA, secondary art educator; b. La Grange, Ga., Apr. 15, 1944; d. Eddie Burrel Jones (dec.), Samuel Lee (stepfather) and Mildred Jones (Johnson) Turrentine; m. Bernard Gregory, Oct. 12, 1985. BFA in Art Edn., Pratt Inst., 1966; MS in Photography, Ill. Inst. Tech., 1970; postgrad. in African Studies and Rsch., Howard U., 1970-74; EdD in Ednl. Adminstrn. and Supervision, Seton Hall U., 1994. Cert. prin./supr., supr., ednl. adminstrn. and supervision, art tchr. grades K-12. Art tchr. Westfield (N.J.) Sch. Dist., 1966-68; art instr. Howard U., Washington, 1970-71; art tchr. Newark (N.J.) Sch. Dist., 1974-79, Irvington (N.J.) Sch. Dist., 1979-80, South Orange (N.J.)-Maplewood (N.J.) Sch. Dist., 1980-81, Montclair (N.J.) Sch. Dist., 1981-82; art instr., docent Newark (N.J.) Mus., 1982-84; art tchr. Weequahic H.S., Newark, 1983-98. Mem. com. textbook evaluation curriculum svcs. Bd. Edn., Newark, 1983—; art dir. Ergo-Weequahic H.S., Newark, 1984-93, founder, advisor Kuumba Art Club, 1989-94, PB Graphics Design, liasion, City Without Walls Art Reach mentor program, 1997-98. Author: Many Moods of the Afro-American Woman, 1971, Multicultural Arts Exhibition Catalog, 1992, Pathways to Empowerment, 1997; editor, pub. The Harvester, 1979-83, The Beauty of Holiness, 1997, The Clarion: The Voices That Lead to Righteousness, 1999-2000, Friendship With the World, 2000, Metamorphosis of the Christian, 2001, Intermezzo in l'Italia. Rschr. Goldman and Kennedy The New York Urban Athlete, Simon and Schuster, N.Y., 1983; vol. tchr., counselor local ch. Grace B. Monroe grantee Pratt Inst., Bklyn., 1964; Grad. scholar Ill. Inst. Tech., Chgo., 1968-70; Rsch. fellow Howard U., Washington, 1972-73; recipient Cert. of Recognition, Gov.'s Tchr. Recognition Program, N.J., 1993. Mem. ASCD, Nat. Assn. for Multicultural Edn., Nat. Assn. Art Educators, Newark Mus., Newark Art Coun., Studio Mus. in Harlem, Kappa Delta Pi. Avocations: art, travel, discussion, reading, writing. Home: 78 Woodland Ave East Orange NJ 07017-2006

JONES-JOHNSON, GLORIA, sociologist, educator, consultant; b. Donaldsonville, Ga., Feb. 4, 1956; d. Willie James Jones and Annie Lois (Backey) Facen; m. Willie Roy Johnson, Aug. 14, 1982; children: Kyle Jamary Johnson, Nia Kiara Johnson. BA, Talladega Coll., 1978; MA, Bowling Green State U., 1980; PhD, U. Mich., 1986. Teaching asst. Bowling Green (Ohio) State U., 1978-80; rsch. asst. U. Mich., Ann Arbor, 1980-84, teaching asst., 1984-85; lectr. Wayne State U., Detroit, 1986; asst. prof. Iowa State U., Ames, 1986-92, assoc. prof., 1992-2000, prof., 2000—, administrv. intern, 1997-98. Cons. United Rubber Workers, Des Moines, 1988—, TVA, Nashville, 1987—; vis. scholar U. Ga., Athens, 1996—. Grant reviewer NSF, 1988—, U.S. Dept. Edn., 1991—; editl. bd. The Sociol. Quar. and the Nat. Jour. of Sociology; contbr. articles to Jour. Social Psychology, Jour. Applied Social Psychology, Am. Sociologist, and others. Mem. Am. Sociological Assn., Midwest Sociological Soc. (state dir. Iowa 1991—), Assn. Black Sociologists, Rural Sociological Soc. (assoc. editor 1990—), Indsl. Rels. Rsch. Assn., Alpha Chi, Sigma Xi. Democrat. Roman Catholic. E-mail: GJJ@iastate.edu.

JONES-KOCH, FRANCENA, school counselor, educator; b. Bunnell, Fla., Dec. 3, 1948; d. Roosevelt Jones and Naomi Stafford; m. William H. Koch, July 1976 (div. Aug. 1980); 1 child, Ahmad Yussef Shaw. BS, Fla. Meml. Coll., 1972; M in Elem. Edn., Nova Southeastern U., 1984, specialist degree, 1994. Intermediate tchr. Miami (Fla.) Dade County Pub. Schs., 1973—88, guidance counselor, 1988—. Adj. prof. Fla. Meml. Coll., Miami, 1984—87; juvenile GED instr. Women's Detention Ctr., Miami, 1994—96; planner summer 2000 Inmate to Inmate Tutoring Program Dept. Corrections, Miami, 2000; mem. region 5 steering com. Dade County Pub. Schs., Miami, mem. dist.'s student svcs. adv. coun., 2002—; amb. United Way-Dade County Pub. Schs., Miami; pres. Dade Counseling Assn., Miami, 2002—; dir. comms. Herstory Inc., 1975—2000. Vol. United Way Dade County, Miami, 1999—. Mem.: Am. Sch. Counselor Assn., AAUW (Miami br. chair Gwen Cherry awards 2000—, designer 21st Century Women's Wisdom Project 2001, prodr. 21st Century Women's Wisdom Project 2001), Fla. Counseling Assn., United Tchrs. Dade County, United Way of Dade County, Zeta Phi Beta Sorority, Inc. (pres. Beta Zeta chpt. 1997—99). Avocations: reading, community service, creative writing, travel, visiting book stores. Home: 10850 SW 164th St Miami FL 33157

JONES Y DIEZ ARGUELLES, GASTON ROBERTO, language educator, educator; b. Cardenas, Cuba, Dec. 6, 1910; came to U.S., 1963, naturalized, 1971; s. Guillermo Rafael Jones and Maria de Los Angeels Diez Arguelles; m. Dolores Carricarte, May 19, 1950. BLetters and Scis., Matanzas Inst. Cuba, 1928; DrLaw, U. Havana, 1937. Practice law, Havana, 1937-60; mcpl. judge, 1938-40; cons. atty. Cuban Treasury Dept., 1943-60; instr. dept. fgn. langs Sacred Heart Coll., Cullman, Ala., 1965-70, St. Bernard Coll., Cullman, 1967-70; asst. prof. U. Ala., Birmingham, 1971-81. Author: Eternidad, 1996, Y Para Que Vinieron? Y Otros Cuentos, 1997, Blanca Eternidad (El inmortal Qje Queria Morir); contbr. articles to profl. jours. Mem. Nat. Bicentennial Com. for Celebration of Nat. Fgn. Lang. Discovery Week, 1975-83. Mem. Am. Assn. Tchrs. Spanish and Portuguese (past pres. Ala. chpt., chmn. so. and mountain states regional pub. rels. com. 1975-77, chmn. nat. pub. rels. and publicity com. 1977-81), Ala. Assn. Fgn. Lang. Tchrs. (past dir., chmn. com. fo advancement fgn. langs. in Ala. 1973-81), Birmingham-Coban Ala.-Guatemala Ptnrs. of Ams. (v.p. 1971-81), Sociedad Nacional Hispanica, Cuban Bar Assn. in Exile, Miami Rowing Club (Outstanding Contbn. award 1985), Coral Gables Country Club, Cuban Rotary in Exile, Sigma Delta Pi, Omicron Delta Kappa. Roman Catholic. Achievements include successfully promoting national campaign to make Americans aware of need for foreign languages in U.S. Home: 1311 SW 102nd Ct Miami FL 33174-2700

JONKOUSKI, JILL ELLEN, materials scientist, ceramic engineer, educator; b. Chgo. d. Joseph and Ruth Jonkouski. BS in Ceramic Engring., MS in Ceramic Engring., U. Ill. Former rschr. Battelle Meml. Inst., Columbus, Ohio; former ceramic engr. Austenal Dental, Inc., Chgo.; former rsch. scientist BIRL Indsl. Rsch. Lab. Northwestern U., Evanston, Ill.; ceramics mfg. engr., program mgr. rsch. and engring., energy efficiency and renewable energy program Office of Programs and Project Mgmt. divsn. U.S. Dept. Energy, Argonne, Ill., 1991—. Past adj. faculty Triton Coll., River Grove, Ill.; presenter Nat. Thermal Spray Conf., 1991, 92, Pacific Coast regional meeting Am. Ceramic Soc., 1994, Coal-Fired Sys. 94, 1994, Ceramic Industry Mfg. Conf. & Exposition, 1995; chair Internat. Gas Turbine Inst., ASME Turbo Expo, 2002, 2003, chair Ann. Conf. on Composites, Materials and Structures, 1997-2003; presenter 17th Ann. Midwest Cogeneration Assn. Mem. Am. Ceramic Soc. (spkr., tech. presenter 1983, 84, 95, 96, chair Chgo.-Milw. sect. 1993-94), U.S. Figure Skating Assn., U. Ill. Alumni Assn. Avocations: ice skating, hiking, flying, tennis. Office: US Dept Energy Office Programs and Project Mgmt 9800 S Cass Ave Argonne IL 60439-4899 E-mail: jill.jonkouski@ch.doe.gov.

JONSEN, RICHARD WILIAM, retired educational administrator; b. San Francisco, Mar. 29, 1934; s. Albert Rupert and Helen Catherine (Sweigert) J.; m. Ann Margaret Parsons, Nov. 20, 1955; children: Marie Wood, Eric, Gregory, Stephen, Matthew. BA, U. Santa Clara, 1955; MA, San Jose (Calif.) State U., 1970; PhD, Stanford U., 1973. Pub.'s rep. Hearst Advt. Service, San Francisco, 1955-58; alumni dir. U. Santa Clara, Calif., 1958-70; dir. admissions, asst. dean. Sch. Edn., asst. prof. Syracuse (N.Y.) U., 1972-76; project dir. Edn. Commn. States, Denver, 1976-77, Western Interstate Commn. Higher Edn., Boulder, Colo., 1977-79, dep. dir., 1979-90, exec. dir., 1990-99; ret., 1999; instr. ESL Front Range Cmty. Coll., Colo., 1999—. Vis. prof. U. Tamaulipas, Mex., 1996-97; cons. Consortium for N.Am. Higher Edn. Collaboration; bd. regents U. Santa Clara, 2002—. Author: State Policy and Independent Higher Education, 1975, Small Liberal Arts Colleges, 1978, Lifelong Learning: State Policies, 1978, The Environmental context for Postsecondary Education, 1986; editor: Higher Education Policies in the Information Age, 1987. Roman Catholic. Home: 363 Troon Ct Louisville CO 80027-9592 E-mail: dickjonsen@att.net.

JONSSON, BJARNI, mathematician, educator; b. Draghals, Iceland, Feb. 15, 1920; came to U.S., 1941, naturalized, 1963; s. Jon and Steinunn (Bjarnadottir) Petursson; m. Amy Sprague, Dec. 16, 1950 (div. 1967); children: Eric M., Meryl S.; m. Harriet Parkes, Jan. 17, 1970; child, M. Kristin. BA, U. Calif. at Berkeley, 1943, PhD, 1946. Faculty Brown U., 1946-56, asst. prof., 1948-56; vis. prof. U. Iceland, 1954-55; vis. asso. prof. U. Calif. at, Berkeley, 1955-56; vis. prof., research mathematician U. Calif., Berkeley, 1962-63; faculty U. Minn., 1956-66, assoc. prof., 1956-59, prof., 1959-66; disting. prof. Vanderbilt U., Nashville, 1966-93, disting. prof. emeritus, 1993—. Mem. AAUP, Am. Math. Soc. Achievements include research, publs. in lattice theory, universal algebra, founds. of algebra, group theory. Office: Vanderbilt U Dept Math 2305 W End Ave Nashville TN 37203-1700 Address: 5810 Vine Ridge Dr Nashville TN 37205-1326 E-mail: jonsson@vanderbilt.edu.

JOPLIN, CLAUDIA PHILLIPS, state education administrator; b. Montclair, N.J., Feb. 14; d. George M. and R.W. P.; m. B. Charles Joplin; 1 child, Vincent E. BS, Glassboro State Coll., 1972; MEd, Howard U., 1974. Cert. tchr., Tex., N.J.; cert. guidance counselor, Tex.; cert. migrant edn. tchr., N.J. Adj. prof. English Trenton (N.J.) State Coll., 1977-79; ednl. specialist, cons. Ft. Dix U.S. Army Sch., Pemberton, N.J., 1979-80; migrant counselor, tchr. Burlington (N.J.) Sch. Dist., 1980-85; tchr. Sheldon Sch. Dist., Houston, 1985-86; guidance counselor Houston Ind. Sch. Dist., 1986-89; coord. elem. guidance Tex. Dept. Edn., Austin, 1989—. Presenter workshops locally and nationally; presenter at profl. confs. Mem. Nat. Alliance Black Educators, Jack and Jill of Am., Lions Internat., Austin Chpt. Links, Alpha Kappa Alpha. Avocations: creative writing, public speaking. Home: 7205 Meadowood Dr Austin TX 78723-1617

JORAJURIA, ELSIE JEAN, elementary education educator; b. Flagstaff, Ariz., June 28, 1946; d. Frank Y. and Elsie (Barreres) Auza; m. Ramon Jorajuria, June 23, 1973; children: Tonya, Nina. BS in Edn., No. Ariz. U., 1971, MA in Elem. Edn., 1975. Cert. elem. edn., Ariz. First grade tchr. Kinsey Sch., Flagstaff, Ariz., 1971-73; third grade tchr. Mohawk Valley Sch., Roll, Ariz., 1973-77, migrant edn. coord., 1980-83, second lang. English Kindergarten tchr., 1983-84, first grade tchr., 1984—; tchr. ESL Ariz. Wester Coll., Yuma, Ariz., 1987. Cheerleader sponsor, Roll, Ariz., 1984-99; vol. 4-H, Roll, 1986-97, project leader, 1990-97, cmty. leader, 1994-97, sponsor Student Coun., Roll, 1994-95, 2000; 4-H supt., 1998-99; pres. Mohawk Valley Sch. Assn., 2003-04. Named Tchr. Yr., Mohawk Valley Sch., 1987-88, 88-89, 95-96. Mem.: NEA, Bus. Profl. Women (pres. 2003—04, Woman Yr. 1994), Ariz. Wool Growers Assn., Mohawk Valley Tchrs. Assn. (pres. 1992—99, v.p. 2000—01), Ariz. Edn. Assn. Democrat. Roman Catholic. Home: PO Box 485 40154 Colorado Ave Tacna AZ 85352 Office: Mohawk Valley Sch PO Box 67 Roll AZ 85347

JORDAHL, KATHLEEN PATRICIA (KATE JORDAHL), photographer, educator; b. Summit, N.J., Aug. 23, 1959; d. Martin Patrick and Marie Pauline (Quinn) O'Grady; m. Geir Arild Jordahl, Sept. 24, 1983. BA in Art & Art History magna cum laude with distinction, U. Del., 1980; MFA in Photography, Ohio U., 1982. Lifetime credential in art and design, Calif. Teaching assoc. Sch. Art Ohio U., Athens, 1980-82; adminstrv. asst. A.D. Coleman, S.I., N.Y., 1981; placement asst. career planning & placement U. Calif., Berkeley, 1983; instr. Coll. for Kids, Hayward, Calif., 1987-88; supr. student/alumni employment office Chabot Coll., Hayward, 1983-87, tchr. photography, 1987-97; assoc. prof. photography and digital imaging Foothill Coll., Los Altos Hills, Calif., 1997—. Workshop coord. Friends of Photography, San Francisco, 1990; instr., workshop leader, coord. Photo-Cen. Photography Programs, Hayward, 1983—; mem., co-coord., publ. evaluation accreditation com. Chabot Coll., Hayward, 1984, instrnl. skills workshop facilitator, 1994, speaker opening day, 1986, coord. ann. classified staff devel. workshop, 1985; workshop leader Ansel Adams Gallery, Yosemite, Calif., 1991, 92, artist-in-residence Yosemite Nat. Park Mus., 1993; ind. curator numerous exhbns., 1984—; coord., curator Ann. Women's Photo Workshop & Exhbn., 1993—; spkr. Let Me Learn, Rowen U., N.J., 2000. Exhibited in group shows Parts Gallery, Minn., 1992, The Alameda Arts Commn. Gallery, Oakland, 1992, Panoramic Invitational, Tampere, Finland, 1992, Photo Forum, Pitts., 1992, Photo Metro Gallery, San Francisco, 1993, Ansel Adams Gallery, Yosemite, 1994, Yosemite Mus., 1994, 96, Vision Gallery, San Francisco, 1994, 95, San Francisco Mus. Modern Art Rental Gallery, 1994, Photographer's Gallery, Palo Alto, 1997, Hayward Art Coun. Members Show, 1997, Hayward City Hall Gallaria, 1998, Ansel Adams Gallery, Mona Lake, 1999, Yogenji Temple, Tokyo, 1999, Himawarmosato Gallery, Yokahama, Japan, 1999, Mumm Winery, 2000, Euphrat Mus., Cupertino, Calif., 2001; represented in permanent collections Muse Gallery, Phila., 1982, Ohio U. Libr. Rare Books Collection, Athens, 1982, Yosemite Mus., 1994, Bibliotheque Nationale de France, Paris, 1996; contbr. photos and articles to photography mags. and publs. Recipient Innovative New Program award Calif. Parks and Recreation Soc., 1990; Sons of Norway scholar U. Oslo, summer 1996. Mem. Internat. Assn. Panoramic Photographers, Soc. Photographic Edn., Friends of Photography, Phi Beta Kappa. Democrat. Avocations: travel, bicycling, reading. Office: PO Box 3998 Hayward CA 94540-3998 E-mail: kate@jordahlphoto.com.

JORDAN, BERNICE BELL, retired elementary school educator; b. Calvert, Tex. d. Ocie Wade and Nannie B. (Westbrook) Bell; m. William B. Jordan, Sept. 28, 1956; children: Beverly, Terrence, Keith. Student, Prairie View A&M, Tex. Western Coll.; BA, San Jose State Coll., 1959, MA, 1985. Cert. elem. edn., fine arts, multi-cultural tchr., specially designed acad. instrn. English. Writer curriculum guide, fine arts Alum Rock Union Elem. Sch. Dist., San Jose, Calif., elem. tchr., 1959—99; writer sch. plan Goss Elem.; ret., 1999. Mem. adv. com., tchr.-cons. writing project San Jose U., 1992—. Mem.: NEA, ASCD, Calif. Ret. Tchrs. Assn., Santa Clara County Reading Coun., Calif. Elem. Edn. Assn., Calif. Reading Assn., Calif. Tchrs. Assn., Alum Rock Edn. Assn., Nat. Coun. Negro Women, Delta Kappa Gamma, Alpha Delta Kappa. Home: 3282 Fronda Dr San Jose CA 95148-2015

JORDAN, BETTY SUE, retired special education educator; b. Lafayette, Tenn., Sept. 4, 1920; d. Aubrey Lee and Geneva (Freeman) West; m. Bill Jordan, Oct. 22, 1950; 1 child, L. Nicha. Student, David Lipscomb Coll., 1939-41; BS, U. Tenn., 1943; registered dietitian, Duke U. Hosp., 1945; MEd, Clemson U., 1973. Dietitian U. Ala., Tuscaloosa, 1945-46, Duke U., Durham, N.C., 1946-48, Stetson U., DeLand, Fla., 1948-50, Furman U., Greenville, S.C., 1950-52; elem. tchr. Greenville County Schs., S.C., 1952-66, tchr. orthopedically handicapped, 1966-85. With Shriners Hosp. for Crippled Children Sch. Pres. Robert Morris S.S. class U. Meth. Ch., 1992, pres. Susanna Wesley S.S. Class, 2003—. Named Outstanding Judge, Carolina Dist. Rose Soc., 2001. Mem. NEA, Assn. Childhood Edn. (treas. 1980-85), United Daus. Confederacy (pres. Greenville chpt. 1978-99), Greenville Woman's Club (exec. bd. 1991-94), Lake Forest Garden Club (pres. 1970-71, 77-79, 80-81, historian 1981-87, 1st v.p. 1991-92, Woman of Yr. awards 1991, 91, Rachel McKaughan Horticulture award 1992, 94, 95, Lois Russel Arrangement award 1993-95), Greater Greenville Rose Soc. (pres. 1983-84, bronze medal 1996), Am. Rose Soc. (accredited rose judge 1986, rose arrangement judge, cons., Rosarian, Outstanding Judge Carolina dist. 2003), Clarice Wilson Garden Club (pres. 1987-89, Woman of Yr. 1991, 2003, Award for Arrangements, Bette Jackson award 1997, Canal Ins. award 1999, Lena Whatley Wallace award 1999, Clarice Townsend Wilson award), Greenville Garden Club (recipient Past Pres.'s Silver Punch Bowl 1998-99, Hall of Fame cert. 2000, Mary Griffith Stevens award, Horticulture Achievement award 2003, Cert. Appreciation, others), Delta Kappa Gamma (pres. Tau chpt. 1976-78, state chmn. comm. 1979-81, state chmn. rsch. 1983-85, leadership/mgmt. seminar Austin, Tex. 1989), Kappa Kappa Iota (state pres. 1972-73, conclave pres. 1983-85). Avocations: collecting antiques, growing roses, flower arranging. Home: 21 Lisa Dr Greenville SC 29615-1350

JORDAN, DAVID CRICHTON, ambassador, educator; b. Chgo., Apr. 30, 1935; s. Edwin Pratt and Marjorie (Crichton) J.; m. Anabella Guzman, Dec. 14, 1964; children— Stephen, Victoria, Anne AB, Harvard U., 1957; LLB, U. Va., 1960; PhD, U. Pa., 1964. Asst. prof. Pa. State U., State College, 1964-65; asst. prof. U. Va., Charlottesville, 1965-68, assoc. prof., 1968-72, prof., 1972—; ambassador to Peru U.S. Dept. State, Lima, 1984-86. Author: (with others) Nationalism in Latin America, 1966, World Politics in Our Times, 1969, Revolutionary Cuba and the End of The Cold War, 1993; contbr. articles to profl. jours. Office: U Va Dept Govt and Fgn Affairs University Station Charlottesville VA 22906

JORDAN, IRVING KING, university president; Pres. Gallaudet U., Washington, 1988—. Office: Gallaudet U Office of President 800 Florida Ave NE Washington DC 20002-3660 E-mail: president@gallaudet.edu.

JORDAN, JOHN LESTER (GAUDEAMUS), artist; b. Houston, Dec. 21, 1944; s. Jesse Peavy and Catherine Myrtle J.; m. Irena Veronika (sep.); 1 child, Najel Solomon. Student, U. Houston, 1963-65, St. Thomas U., 1974. Artist Hurlock Real Estate Co., Houston, 1963-65; salesman-designer Dennis Sleep Shop, Houston, 1967-71; dir. Jerusalem Jewels, Denver, 1979-84, 1985; art rep. Whitney-Morse Art Group, Saugerties, N.Y., 1988-90; tchr. Onteora Sch. Dist., Woodstock, N.Y., 1988-91; dir. Gaudeamus-Jordan, Woodstock, 1985—; prodr. Panaramblecam Prodns., Woodstock, 1990—. Host, prodr.: (tv show) Ramble On, 1990—; exec. prodr.: Woodstock Winter Video Festival, 1994, Pete Seeger on Solar, 1997; sculptor; prodr. TV video Peter Max in Woodstock, 1994; prodr. (video) The Sand Painters of Tashi Lhunpo, 2002, The Dharma Bums in Woodstock, 2002-03; prodr. Goddess Festival Woodstock TV, 2003. Master of ceremonies Hiroshima to Now, Catskill Alliance, Woodstock, 1990; asst. organizer for Catskill Alliance for Peace, Woodstock, 1990; chmn. Earth Day, Hiroshima Day Show, 1993; organizer Woodstock UFO Network, 1998. With USAF, 1965-67. Mem. Woodstock Guild, Woodstock Artists Assn. Avocations: tv hosting and producing, recycling resource research. Home: PO Box 932 Woodstock NY 12498-0932 Office: Gaudeamus-Jordan 205Wittenberg Rd Bearsville NY also: Hillhouse Studios 205 Wittenberg Rd Bearsville NY

JORDAN, JOSEPH TANDY, mathematics educator; b. Conway, Ark., Mar. 12, 1939; s. Edwin Dwight and Anna Marie (Hiegel) J.; m. Mary Carroll Brown, Aug. 10, 1967; children: Joseph T. Jr., James Richmond. BS in Physics, St. Edward's U., Austin, Tex., 1961; MEd in Adminstrn. and Supervision, Va. Commonwealth U., 1971. Math. and sci. tchr. Holy Cross H.S., New Orleans, 1961-62; math. tchr., coach St. Joseph's H.S., Conway, 1962-64, Little Rock (Ark.) Cath. H.S., 1964-68; assoc. prof. math. John Tyler C.C., Chester, Va., 1968—. Mem. Greater Richmond Coun. Tchrs. Math., Va. Coun. Tchrs. Math., Va. C.C. Assn. Democrat. Roman Catholic. Avocations: aerobics, weight lifting, reading. Home: 11515 Rolling Brook Rd Chester VA 23831-2032 E-mail: JJordan@jt.cc.edu.

JORDAN, JUDITH VICTORIA, clinical psychologist, educator; b. Milw., July 28, 1943; d. Claus and Charlotte (Backus) J.; m. William M. Redpath, Aug. 11, 1973. AB, Brown U., 1965; MA, Harvard U., 1968, PhD, 1973; DHL (hon.) (hon.), New Eng. Coll., 2001. Diplomate Am. Bd. Profl. Psychology. Psychologist Human Relations Service, Wellesley, Mass., 1971-73; assoc. psychologist McLean Hosp., Belmont, Mass., 1978-93, psychologist, 1993—, dir. women's studies program, 1988—, dir. tng. in psychology, 1991, dir. Women's Treatment Network, 1992—. Vis. scholar Stone Ctr. Wellesley Coll., 1985—; asst. prof. psychiatry Harvard Med. Sch., 1988—; co-dir. Jean Baker Miller Tng. Inst., Wellesley Coll. 1998; adv. bd Fox TV Network, Women First healthcare., 1998; disting. prof. Menninger Clinic, 1999. Author: Empathy and Self Boundries, 1984, Women's Growth in Connection, 1991, (with others) The Self in Relation, 1986; editor, author: Relational Self in Women; editor: Women's Growth in Diversity, 1997. Recipient Outstanding Contbn. award, Feminist Therapy Inst., 2002. Fellow Am. Psychol. Assn.; mem. Mass. Psychol. Assn. (bd. dirs. 1983-85, Career Achievement award for outstanding contbns. to advancement of psychology as a sci. and a profession), Phi Beta Kappa. Office: McLean Hosp 114 Waltham St Lexington MA 02421-5415

JORDAN, JULIA CRAWFORD, secondary education educator; b. Memphis, Oct. 17, 1934; d. Elijah Cornelius and Zeffa Louise (Simms) Crawford; divorced; 1 child, Cheryl Lynn. BA, Harris Stowe State Coll., 1967; MA, Wash. U., St. Louis, 1973. Cert. tchr., Mo. Tchr., dept. head social studies dept. St. Louis (Mo.) Bd. Edn. Chmn. No. Ctrl. Vis. Com. Rosary H.S., St. Louis, 1977; mem. tchr. work group on acad. stds. Dept. of Elem. and Secondary Edn., State of Mo., 1993—, Regional Commerce and Growth Assn. Mem. Persona Players, rec. sec., pres. 1985-89; vol. Brean Homeless Ctr., St. Louis, 1990—. Recipient Cert. Exemplary Citizen Participation Citizen Edn. Clearing House, Letter of Appreciation Nat. Kidney Found., 1984-93. Mem. ASCD, Top Ladies of Distinction, Nat. Coun. of Negro Women (life), Annie Malone Children's Home, Democrat. Baptist. Avocations: reading, needle crafts, traveling. Home: 8406 January Ave Saint Louis MO 63134-1414 Office: Vashon HS St Louis Bd Edn 3035 Cass Ave Saint Louis MO 63106-1604

JORDAN, KARLA SALGE, early childhood education educator; b. Berlin, July 4, 1943; came to U.S. 1965; d. Hubert Ernst Richard and Irmgard Klara Salge; m. William Jackson Jordan, May 28, 1963 (div. 1980); 1 child, Michael Bond. BA, Berlin Tchrs. Coll., 1964, Meth. Coll., Fayetteville, N.C., 1974; MA, Fayetteville State U., 1986. Cert. tchr., N.C., ednl. supr., 1995, cert. early childhood generalist Nat. Bd. Edn., 2000. Tchr. Eastover Elem. Sch., Fayetteville, 1974-75, Montclair Elem. Sch., Fayetteville, 1975—. Workshop presenter Cumberland County Sch., Fayetteville, spring 1983, 92-95; mem. bldg. leadership team Montclair Elem. Sch., 1992-93, chair, 1994-95, grade chair, 1980-90, 99-2001, 2002-03, sch. improvement team chair, 1995-98, 2001-03. Treas. Montclair PTA, 1987-88, sec., 1988-90, pres. 1985, 86; youth choir dir. Eureka Bapt. Ch., Fayetteville, 1990—, min. of music, 1995—; mem., bible study leader for German fellowship Walstone Bapt. Ch., Fayetteville, German fellowship coord., 1999—. Fayetteville Jr. League mini grantee, 1991; named Tchr. of the Yr. Montclair Elem. Sch., 1987-88; recipient Fayetteville Tchr. of the Week Jr. League and the Huntington Learning Ctr., 1997. Mem. ASCD, Cross Creek Reading Coun. (rec. sec. 1990), Fayetteville Assn. for Edn. of Young Children, N.C. Assn. of Edn. (bldg. rep. 1981-83), Pi Lambda Theta. Republican. Baptist. Avocations: sewing, crafts, gardening, travel, reading. Home: 845 Mary Jordan Ln Fayetteville NC 28311-7075 Office: Montclair Elem Sch 555 Glensford Dr Fayetteville NC 28314-2326 E-mail: karlasjs@msn.com., karlajordan@ccs.k12.nc.us.

JORDAN, LINDA SUSAN DARNELL, elementary school educator; b. Greenville, Tex., Sept. 5, 1955; d. Charles Albert and Dorothy Nell (Everheart) Darnell; m. Mark Alan Jordan, Sept. 1, 1979; children: Sarah Tison, Michael Albert. BE, East Tex. State U., 1977. Cert. elem. edn. tchr. 1-8, secondary edn. tchr. 9-12. County ext. agt. Tex. A & M U., Wise County, Tex., 1977-81; tchr. Decatur (Tex.) Ind. Sch. Dist., 1981-87, 91—. Tech. planning com. Decatur Ind. Sch. Dist., 1991-95, mem. campus improvement com., 1992-94, 98-99. Sun. sch. educator First United Meth. Ch., Decatur, 1992-96, acolyte coord., 1990-91, 95-96, Sun. sch. coord., 1989-90; mem. Decatur Jr. Woman's Club, 1977-79. Recipient Apple of the Month award Twin Lakes Hosp., 1992. Mem. Tex. Classroom Tchrs. Orgn. Avocations: quilting, cake decorating, phys. fitness activities, reading, smocking. Home: 173 PR 4231 Decatur TX 76234-9802 Office: Decatur Elem Sch 1300 Deer Park Rd Decatur TX 76234-4403

JORDAN, MARK D. school administrator; b. Chgo., Oct. 22, 1953; s. Herbert and Lavina Eliza (Holgate) J.; m. Verna Zemorra Harris, Aug. 1, 1981; 1 child, Jeremy Ajani. BA in Edn., Chgo. State U., 1976; MEd, Nat. Louis U., 1993. Cert. tchr., Ill. Tchr. Chgo. Pub. Schs., 1976—; asst. prin. Gompers Fine Arts Sch., Chgo., 1989—. Bd. dirs. Suzuki Music Acad. Chgo., 1978-87; adviser leadership conf. Ill. State Bd. Edn., Springfield, 1990—; child expert panelist McDonalds Corp., Chgo., 1990; facilitator Nat. Bd. Profl. Teaching Standards, Chgo., 1991; oresebter address Presdl. Commn. on Music Edn., Chgo. and Washington, 1990. Organist Greater Instnl. Meth. Ch., Chgo., 1983—; accompanist Chgo. All-City Youth Chorus, 1984—. Named Disting. Educator Ill. State Bd. Edn.-Milken Family Found., 1989, Maremont Dedicated Tchr. Chgo. Region PTA, 1989; recipient Nat. Excellence in Edn. award Burger King/Nat. Assn. Secondary Sch. Prins., 1990, Cert. Appreciation Ednl. Svc. Region Cook County, Ill., 1993, Mayoral Proclamation of Ednl. Excellence from Hon. Mayor Richard M. Daley, Chgo., 1993, Thanks to Tchrs. award Sta WBBM-TV, Bennigan's Corp., Chgo. State U., 1993; grantee Chgo. Found. Edn., 1991. Mem. Assn. Supervision and Curriculum Instrn., Music Educators Nat. Conf., Ill. Music Educators Assn., Am. Choral Dirs. Assn., Ill. Alliance Arts Edn., Nat. Dropout Prevention Assn. Avocations: reading, travel. Home: 8156 S Rhodes Ave Chicago IL 60619-5024 Office: Gompers Fine Arts Sch 12302 S State St Chicago IL 60628-6811

JORDAN, MARY LEE, retired elementary education educator; b. Cin., Oct. 22, 1931; m. T. Paul Jordan, July 29, 1975 (dec. 1988); children: Aaron, Marc, Carrie. BS in Edn., U. Cin., 1965, AA, 1984. First grade tchr., St. Louis County, Mo., 1963-65; first grade, kindergarten tchr. Cin., 1965-80; sec. personnel dept. Longview State Hosp., 1983; word processor Nat. Inst. Occupational Safety & Health, 1984; bookkeeper L. Levine & Co., Inc., 1985-88. Bd. dirs., membership chmn., newsletter co-producer Cin. Alliance for the Mentally Ill, 1983-86; park ranger U.S. Nat. Park Svc., Cin., 1993-96. Author: History of Camp Dennison, Ohio, 1956. Pres. Cin. chpt. Zero Population Growth, 1976. Mem. AAUW (v.p. Cin. br. 1994-96, bd. dirs. 1970-71), LWV (pres. N.C. br. 1994-96, program coord. 1970-71), Am. Horse Show Assn., Ohioana Libr. Assn., DAR (vice-regent, mus. trustee Mariemont, Ohio chpt. 1988-89, regent 1990-91). Avocations: equestrian events, community video producer. Home: 27 Sherry Rd Cincinnati OH 45215-4225

JORDAN, PATRICIA JAMES, secondary education educator; Math. tchr. Roslyn (N.Y.) High Sch. Named N.Y. State Tchr. of Yr., 1993, Outstanding Tchr. Math. Disney Am. Tchr. Awards. Office: Roslyn High Sch Round Hill Rd Roslyn Heights NY 11577

JORDAN, PAUL HOWARD, JR., surgeon, educator; b. Bigelow, Ark., Nov. 22, 1919; s. Paul Howard and Marie Theresa (Lewis) J.; m. Lois Regnell, Apr. 6, 1944; children: Kristine Jordan Henyey, Craig T., Patricia Jordan Johnson. BS, U. Chgo., 1941, MD, 1944; MS, U. Ill., 1950. Intern St. Luke's Hosp., Chgo., 1944-46; resident in surgery U. Ill., Chgo., 1948-50, Hines VA Hosp., 1950-53; from instr. to clin. prof. surgery UCLA Med. Sch., 1953-58; asso. prof. U. Fla. Med. Sch., Gainesville, 1959-64; prof. surgery Baylor Coll. Medicine, Houston, 1964—; chief surgery VA Hosp., Houston, 1964-83, chief staff, 1969. Mem. sr. attending staff Methodist Hosp., Houston; cons. staff St. Luke's Episcopal Hosp., Houston. Author articles on gastroenterologic surgery, chpts. in books. Served to capt. M.C. AUS, 1946-48. SpI. NIH fellow Karolinska Inst., Stockholm, 1958-59; recipient Acrel medal Swedish Surg. Soc., 1974, Disting. Alumni Service award U. Chgo.; corr. fellow Brazilian Surg. Soc., 1976; named Disting. Houston Surgeon, 1989. Mem. ACS (chpt. councilor 1978-81), Soc. Surgery Alimentary Tract (past recorder, pres. 1983-84), Assn. VA Surgeons (past pres., Disting. Service award 1979), Am. Surg. Assn. (v.p.,1999), Soc. Internat. Chururgie, Soc. Univ. Surgeons, Am. Physiol. Soc., Am. Gastroenterol. Assn., Am. Soc. Gastrointestinal Endoscopy, Soc. Exptl. Biology and Medicine, Western Surg. Assn., So. Surg. Assn. (v.p., 2000), Tex. Surg. Soc., Harris County Med. Soc., Houston Surg. Soc. (past pres.), Houston Gastroenterol. Soc. (past pres.), U. Chgo. Med. Alumni Assn. (Disting. Sci. Service award 1984). Methodist. Office: Baylor Coll Medicine One Baylor Plaza Houston TX 77030

JORDAN, RAMONA PIERCE, home economics educator, art education educator, elementary education educator; b. Orlando, Fla., Jan. 24, 1954; d. Arthur Lloyd and Mildred (Duke) Pierce; m. William Winford Jordan, 1986. BS in Home Econs., U. Montevallo, 1974, cert. elem. edn., art, 1977; recert. in reading, Auburn U., 1984. Tchr. reading Elmore County Bd. Edn., Millbrook, Ala., 1977-78; learning disabilities tchr. Minor High Sch., Birmingham, Ala., 1978-79; tchr. reading Wetumpka (Ala.) Elem. Sch., 1982-90; tchr. home econs. Elmore County High Sch., Eclectic, Ala., 1990—. County contact Elmore County Home Econ. Assn., Eclectic, 1992—; judge Eclectic Beautiful Contest, 1992—; cookoff judge Elmore County Cattlemen Assn., 1991-92. Mem. Ala. Vocat. Assn., Nat. Vocat. Assn., Eastern Elmore County Assn. of Retarded Citizens (bd. dirs. 1992—), Alpha Delta Kappa (historian 1991-93). Baptist. Avocations: traveling, sewing, cooking, gardening, crafts. Home: 1105 Morrison Rd Equality AL 36026-2630

JORDAN, THERESA JOAN, psychologist, educator; b. Irvington, N.J., Sept. 17, 1949; d. Ernest Anthony and Helen Joan (Debski) Balazs; 1 child, Theresa-Helena. BA, NYU, 1971, MA, 1972, PhD, 1979. Lic. psychologist, N.Y., N.J.; diplomate Am. Bd. Forensic Medicine, Am. Bd. Forensic Examiners, Am. Bd. Forensic Psychologists. Grad. fellow Nat. Inst. Occupational Safety and Health, N.Y.C., 1971-74; rsch. asst., rsch. coord. Project City Sci. NYU, 1974-79, assoc. dir. for rsch. Ctr. for Devel. Studies, 1979-82; asst. prof. medicine N.J. Med. Sch., Newark, 1982-92; assoc. prof. applied psychology NYU, 1992—. Dir. Ctr. for Med. Info. N.J. Med. Sch., Newark, 1989—; cons. Ctrs. for Disease Control, Atlanta, 1990; spkr. Am. Lung Assn., N.Y., 1990-96, Am. Thoracic Soc., N.Y., 1998-99; spkr. Asia-Pacific Congress on Lung Diseases, Bangkok, Thailand, Bali, Indonesia. Author: Overcoming the Fear of Riding, 1996, Understanding Medical Information, 1999; contbr. articles to profl. jours. Mem. U.S. Icelandic Demonstration Team. Mem. APA, Assn. for the Advancement Ednl. Rsch. (pres.-elect 1998—), Soc. for Med. Decision-Making, Eastern Ednl. Rsch. Assn. (2d v.p. 1985-87), Mem. Internat. Union Against Tuberculosis & Lung Disease. Avocation: rider and trainer of icelandic horses. Office: NYU Dept Applied Psychology 239 Greene St New York NY 10003-6674

JORDAN, THOMAS HILLMAN, geophysicist, educator; b. Coco Solo, C.Z., Republic of Panama, Oct. 8, 1948; s. Clarence Eugene and Beulah J.; m. Margaret Jordan; 1 child, Alexandra Elyse. BS, Calif. Inst. Tech., 1969, MS in Geophysics, 1970, PhD in Geophysics and Applied Math., 1972. Asst. prof. Princeton (N.J.) U., 1972-75, Scripps Instn. of Oceanography, U. Calif. San Diego, La Jolla, 1975-77, assoc. prof., 1977-82, prof., 1982-84, MIT, Cambridge, 1984-85, U. So. Calif., L.A., 2000—. Contbr. over 140 articles to profl. jours. Fellow AAAS, Am. Geophys. Union (James B. Macelwane award 1983, George P. Woolard award 1998); mem. NAS, Am. Philosophical Soc. Office: Dept Earth Scis U So Calif Los Angeles CA 90089-0740 E-mail: tjordan@usc.edu.

JORGENSEN, DANIEL FRED, academic executive; b. May 3, 1947; m. Susan Jorgensen, June 20, 1969; children: Kari, Becky. BA in Journalism, S.D. State U., 1969, MS in Journalism, 1974; postgrad., Colo. State U.; grad. with honors, U.S. Army's Def. Info. Sch., 1970. Writer news and sports Sioux Falls (S.D.) Argus-Leader, 1969-70; asst. editor news and sports, part-time instr. S.D. State U. Comm. Office, 1972-74; from publ. editor to asst. dir. Colo. State U., 1974-78; editor news and sports Hot Springs (S.D.) Star, 1978-81; exec. dir. Black Hills (S.D.) Girl Scout Coun., 1981-83; dir. devel. and pub. rels. St. Martin's Acad., Rapid City, S.D., 1983-84; dir. news svc. St. Olaf Coll., Northfield, Minn., 1984-88, dir. pub. rels., 1988-97; v.p. comm. Scholarship Am., 1997-2000; dir. pub. rels. Augsburg Coll., 2000—. Author and co-author six books; contbr. numerous articles to mags. and jours. Chair bd. Northfield Hosp., 1990-2001, United Way, 1989-91, chair 1990-91; chair bd. Northfield Rotary, 1987-92, v.p., 1990-91, pres. 1991-92; officer various other cmty. orgns.; mem. coms. Northfield Sch.; governing bd. Minn. Hosp. Assoc., 1998—2003. 1st lt. U.S. Army, 1970-72. Named to first class Leadership Rapid City, 1982-83; honored for community svc. City of Northfield, 1992; recipient Rice County Vol. award, 1992. Mem. Coun. for the Advancement and Support of Edn. (nat. coms. mem. 1991—), Nat. Assn. Sci. Writers, Nat. Edn. Writers Assn., Kappa Tau Alpha, Sigma Delta Chi. Avocations: sports, youth activities, writing, community theatre. Home: 505 Wilson Ct Northfield MN 55057-1374 Office: Augsburg Coll 2211 Riverside Ave Minneapolis MN 55454 E-mail: jorgensd@augsburg.edu.

JORGENSEN, GERALD THOMAS, psychologist, educator, lawyer; b. Mason City, Iowa, Jan. 15, 1947; s. Harry Grover and Mary Jo (Kollasch) J.; m. Mary Ann Reiter, Aug. 30, 1969; children: Amy Lynn, Sarah Kay, Jill Kathryn. BA, Loras Coll., Dubuque, 1969; MS, Colo. State U., Ft. Collins, 1970, PhD, 1973; Juris Canonici Licentiae, Cath. U. Am., 1998. Lic. psychologist, Iowa; lic. canonist Cath. Ch.; cert. health svc. provider Nat. Register, Iowa; ordained to ministry Roman Cath. Ch. as deacon, 1979. Psychology intern Counseling Ctr., Colo. State U., Ft. Collins, 1971-72, VA Hosp., Palo Alto, Calif., 1972-73; psychologist Loras Coll., Clarke Coll., Dubuque, 1973-76; asst. prof. psychology Loras Coll., 1976-80, assoc. prof., 1981-93, dir. Ctr. for Counseling and Student Devel., 1977-86, assoc. dean of students, 1985-86, dean of students, v.p. for student devel., 1986-93; cons. and supervising psychologist Gannon Ctr. for Cmty. Mental Health, 1977—. Assoc. med. staff Mercy Med. Ctr., 1989—, mem. credentials com., 1992—; asst. dir. for formation Office of Permanent Diaconate, Archdiocese of Dubuque, 1979-93, dir., 1993-96, auditor, 1993-98; cons. psychologist Met. Tribunal, 1993—, judge, 1998—; mem. Iowa Bd. Psychology Examiners, Des Moines, chairperson, 1984-90, coord. continuing edn., 1983; sec.-gen. First Internat. Congress on Licensure, Certification and Credentialing of Psychologists, New Orleans, 1995. Contbr. articles to profl. jours. Treas. Dubuque County Assn. Mental Health Inc., 1975-82, v.p., 2002—. NDEA fellow, 1969-72. Fellow Assn. State and Provincial Psychology Bds. (exec. com. 1986-89, pres. 1989-92, Morton Berger award 1996); mem. Am. Coll. Pers. Assn. (chmn. com. VII 1980-82), Am. Assn. Counseling Devel., Am. Psychol. Assn., Iowa Psychol. Assn. (treas. 1976-80, mem. exec. coun. 1980-83, highest honors 1990), Nat. Assn. Diaconate Dirs. (sec. 1983-85, treas. 1985-90, award 1991), Canon Law Soc. Am. (sec. 2002—), Iowa Student Pers. Assn., Fedn. Assns. Reg. Bds. (v.p. 1993-94, 96-97, pres. 1994-96), Delta Epsilon Sigma, Phi Kappa Phi, Sigma Tau Phi. Democrat. Roman Catholic. Office: Archdiocesan Ctr 1229 Mount Loretta Ave Dubuque IA 52003-7826 Home: 480 Woodland Ridge Dubuque IA 52003-6723 E-mail: dbqcmtaud@arch.pvt.k12.ia.us.

JORGENSEN, JUDITH ANN, psychiatrist, educator; b. Parris Island, S.C. d. George Emil and Margaret Georgia Jorgensen; m. Ronald Francis Crown, July 11, 1970 (dec. Oct. 1996). BA, Stanford U., 1963; MD, U. Calif., 1968. Intern Meml. Hosp., Long Beach, Calif., 1969-70; resident County Mental Health Svcs., San Diego, 1970-73; staff psychiatrist Children and Adolescent Svcs., San Diego, 1973-78; practice medicine specializing in psychiatry La Jolla, Calif., 1973—. Staff psychiatrist County Mental Health Services of San Diego, 1973-78, San Diego State U. Health Services, 1985-87; psychiat. cons. San Diego City Coll., 1973-78, 85-86; asst. prof. dept. psychiatry U. Calif., 1978-91, assoc. prof. dept. psychiatry, 1991-96; chmn. med. quality rev. com. Dist. XIV, State of Calif., 1982-83. Fellow: Am. Psychiat. Assn.; mem.: Sex Therapy and Edn., Soc. Sci. Study of Sex, San Diego Soc. Adolescent Psychiatry (pres. 1981—82), Am. Soc. Adolescent Psychiatry, San Diego Psychiat. Soc. (chmn. membership com. 1976—78, v.p. 1978—80, fed. legis. rep. 1985—87, fellowship com. 1989—), Rowing Club. Office: 470 Nautilus St Ste 211 La Jolla CA 92037-5981 Fax: (858) 551-0964.

JOSBENO, LARRY JOSEPH, physics educator; b. Elmira, N.Y., Oct. 21, 1938; s. Samuel Joseph and Katherine Lorena (Jessup) J.; m. Cecile Ann Quatrano, Sept. 15, 1962; children: Deborah Ann, John Lawrence. BS in Math., St. Bonaventure U., 1962; MS in Chemistry, U. N.H., 1970. Cert. tchr., N.Y. Tchr. Horseheads (N.Y.) High Sch., 1965-89; prof. Corning (N.Y.) C.C., 1989—; faculty assn. chair, 1995. Vis. scientist Cornell U., Ithaca, N.Y., 1986-87; adj. prof. Elmira Coll.; cons. State Edn. Dept., Albany, N.Y., 1987, Math Matrix, Ithaca, 1987—. Author: ARCO Physics Review Book, 1983; contbr. articles to profl. jours. Mem. bd. govs. Notre Dame H.S., Elmira, 1977-82; trustee Steele Meml. Lab., Elmira, 1985-94, pres., 1993; obs. presenter Elmira Corning Astron. Soc., Corning, 1968—; trustee So. Tier Libr. Sys., 1995-2000. Capt. arty. U.S. Army, 1963-65. Recipient N.Y. State Chancellor's award, 1995, Excellence in Tchg. award Bd. Trustees, 1998. Fellow Sci. Tchrs. Assn. N.Y. (pres. 1989-90); mem. Math. Assn. Am., Am. Phys. Soc. (N.Y. state sect./treas. 2001—), Am. Chem. Soc., Am. Physics Tchr. Assn. (N.Y. state sect., bd. dirs. 1996-2000, pres. 2002—, N.Y. State svc. award 2000), So. Tier Libr. Assn. (trustee 1995), Alpha Sigma Lambda (Tchr. of Yr. 1985). Democrat. Roman Catholic. Home: 539 W Franklin St Horseheads NY 14845-2356 E-mail: josbenlj@corning-cc.edu.

JOSEPH, GERI MACK (GERALDINE JOSEPH), former ambassador, educator, journalist; b. St. Paul, June 19, 1923; BS, U. Minn., 1946; LLD, Bates Coll., 1982; DHL (hon.), Macalester Coll., 1997; LLD, Carleton Coll., 1998; DHL (hon.). Staff writer Mpls. Tribune, 1946-53, contbg. editor, 1972-78; amb. to The Netherlands, Am. Embassy, The Hague, 1978-81; sr. fellow internat. programs U. Minn. Hubert H. Humphrey Inst. Pub. Affairs, Mpls., 1984-94, chmn. adv. bd., 1997—; dir. Mondale Policy Forum, 1990-94. Bd. dirs. Nat. Dem. Inst. for Internat. Affairs, George A. Hormel Co.; mem. U.S. President's Commn. on Mental Health, Minn. Supreme Ct. Commn. on Mentally Disabled and the Cts., mem. Coun. on Fgn. Rels., 1985—; mem. com. on Mid. East, Brookings Instn., 1987. Vice chmn. Gov.'s Commn. on Taxation, 1983-84; trustee Carleton Coll., 1975-94; mem. Democratic Nat. Com., 1960-72, vice chmn., 1968-72; pres. Nat. Mental Health Assn., 1970-72, co-chairperson Minn. Women's Campaign Fund, 1982-84; co-chmn. Atty. Gen.'s Com. on Child Abuse within the Family, 1986. Democrat. E-mail: gerimj@cs.com.

JOSEPH, JENEEN KAY, elementary education educator; b. Delta, Colo., Feb. 13, 1950; d. Edward Sheldon and Nellie (Pagotto) Smith; m. John Edwin Joseph, June 19, 1971; children: Jennifer, Judy. AS, Mesa Coll., 1970; BS with highest distinction, Colo. State U., 1972, MEd, 1976; M in Elem. Edn., U. St. Thomas, 1992. Cert. elem. and vocat. tchr., Tex., Colo. Instr. home econs. Jefferson County Pub. Schs., Lakewood, Colo., 1972-81; instr. early childhood Oaks Acad., Spring, Tex., 1985-91; instr. kindergarten Conroe (Tex.) Ind. Sch. Dist., 1991-92, tchr. 1st grade, 1992—. Instr. adult edn. Arapaho C.C., Denver, 1983-84; curriculum writer, instr. Emily Griffith Opportunity Sch., Denver, 1983-84. Mem. Nat. Coun. Tchrs. English, Nat. Coun. Tchrs. Math., Nat. Coun. for Social Studies, Nat. Assn. for Edn. Young Children, Nat. Sci. Tchrs. Assn., Internat. Reading Assn., Assn. Childhood Edn. Internat., Internat. Inst. Literacy Learning, Tex. Assn. Improvement of Reading, Coun. for Exceptional Children, Phi Kappa Phi, Kappa Delta Phi. Home: 17726 Treeloch Ln Spring TX 77379-7858

JOSEPH, LYNNE CATHIE, art educator; b. Manchester, N.H., Aug. 14, 1965; d. George and Jane Helen (Nita) J. BA, Notre Dame Coll., 1987; MEd, Lesley Coll., 1995. Cert. tchr., prin., technologist, N.H. Art tchr. Manchester Schs., 1987-88, East Derry (N.H.) Meml. Schs., 1989-93, Hood Middle Sch., Derry, 1993-94, West Running Brook Mid. Sch., Derry, 1995-2000, Timberlane Regional Mid. Sch., Plaistow, N.H., 2000—. Asst. dir., spl. events dir. Camp Mataponi, Naples, Maine, 1989-94, dir. Camp Runels, Pelham, N.H, 1995; site coord., mem. adv. bd. Scholastic Art Awards, Boston, 1985-93, 2000-02. Mem.: Nat. Assn. Elem. Sch. Prins. Avocations: art, sports, music. Home: 50 Harrington Ave Manchester NH 03103-6561

JOSEPH, RICHARD SAUL, cardiologist, educator; b. N.Y.C., Mar. 27, 1937; s. Charles Irving and Lillian (Horowitz) J.; m. Frances B. Rappaport, Jan. 27, 1963; children: Lauryl, James, Alisa, Jennifer. BA magna cum laude, Hofstra Coll., 1958; MD, Albert Einstein U., 1962. Intern U. Utah Affiliated Hosp., Salt Lake City, 1962-63; resident in chest medicine Bronx (N.Y.) Mcpl. Hosp., 1963-64; resident in internal medicine Mt. Sinai Hosp., N.Y.C., 1966-68; fellow in cardiology Nassau County Med. Ctr., East Meadow, N.Y., 1968-69; pvt. practice cardiology Huntington (N.Y.) Hosp., 1969—, chief cardiology, 1981-90, attending cardiology, 1973—; asst. prof. clin. medicine (cardiology) SUNY, Stony Brook, 1973—. Cons. in cardiology Kings Park (N.Y.) Hosp., 1971—; electro cardiographer Huntington Hosp., 1971—, co-dir. cardiac stress lab., 1975—; dir. Huntington Cardiac Rehab., 1977-94; adj. attending cardiologist St. Francis Hosp., Roslyn, N.Y., 1993-2000. Contbr. articles to profl. jours. Speaker med. adv. bd. Suffolk County Heart Assn., Blue Point, N.Y., 1971-73; speaker med. dir. Huntington (N.Y.) YMCA, 1973-77. Lt. USN, 1964-66. Recipient Pres. prize Hofstra Coll., Uniondale, N.Y., 1954; named Valedictorian Hofstra Coll., Uniondale, N.Y., 1958. Fellow Am. Coll. Cardiology; mem. Alpha Omega Alpha. Jewish. Avocations: jogging, classical and popular piano. Office: 205 E Main St Huntington NY 11743-2923

JOSEY, E(LONNIE) J(UNIUS), librarian, educator, former state administrator; b. Norfolk, Va., Jan. 20, 1924; s. Willie and Frances (Bailey) J.; m. Dorothy Johnson, Sept. 11, 1954 (div. Dec. 1961); 1 dau., Elaine Jacqueline. AB, Howard U., 1949; MA, Columbia U., 1950; MLS, SUNY, Albany, 1953; LHD, Shaw U., 1973; DPS, U. Wis., Milw., 1987; HHD, N.C. Cen. U., 1989; LittD, Clark Atlanta U., 1995; LHD (hon.), Clarion Univ. of Pa., 2001. Desk asst. Columbia U. Libraries, 1950-52; libr. tech. asst. central br. N.Y. Pub. Libr., N.Y.C., 1952; libr. I Free Libr., Phila., 1953-54; instr. social scis. Savannah State Coll., 1954-55, libr., assoc. prof., 1959-66; libr., asst. prof. Del. State Coll., 1955-59; assoc. divsn. libr. devel. N.Y. State Edn. Dept., Albany, 1966-68; chief Bur. Acad. and Rsch. Libraries, 1968-76, Bur. Specialist Libr. Svcs., 1976-86; prof. U. Pitts. Sch. Libr. and Info. Scis., 1986-95, prof. emeritus, 1995—. Mem. bd. advisors Children's Book Rev. Service, Bklyn., 1972— Editor, contbg. author: The Black Librarian in America, 1970, What Black Librarians Are Saying, 1972, New Dimensions for Academic Library Service, 1975; co-compiler, co-editor: Handbook of Black Librarianship, 1977; co-editor: A Century of Service: Librarianship in the United States and Canada, 1976, Opportunities for Minorities in Librarianship, 1977, The Information Society: Issues and Answers, 1978, Libraries in the Political Process, 1980, Ethnic Collections in Libraries, 1983, Libraries, Coalitions, And the Public Good, 1987, Politics and the Support of Libraries, 1990, Festchaift E.J. Josey: an Activist Librarian, 1992, The Black Librarian in America Revisited, 1994, Handbook of Black Librarianship, 2001; mem. editl. bd. Dictionary of Am. Library History, 1974— ; mem. editl. adv. bd. ALA Yearbook, 1975-83; spl. advisor: World Ency. Black People, 1974-80; contbr. numerous articles to profl. jours. Mem. Albany Interracial Coun., 1972—86; state youth advisor Ga. Conf., 1962—66, 1st v.p., 1981—82, pres., 1982—86, life mem., 1971—, chmn. program, 1972—76, trustee; mem. tech. task force Econ. Opportunity Authority of Savannah, 1964—66; mem. adv. coun. Sch. Libr. Sci. N.C. Ctrl. U.; mem. adv. coun. Sch. Libr. and Info. Sci. SUNY, Albany, Sch. Libr. and Info. Sci. Queen's Coll. CUNY; mem. exec. bd. Savannah (Ga.) br. NAACP, 1960—66; mem. exec. bd. Albany br. Ga. Conf., 1970—72; mem. exec. bd. Albany Opportunity Authority; bd. dirs. Freedom to Read Found., 1987—91. With AUS, 1943—46. Recipient cert. of Appreciation Savannah br. NAACP, 1963, NAACP award Savannah State Coll. chpt., 1964, Merit award for work on econ. opportunity task force Savannah Chatham County, 1966, award for disting. service to librarianship Savannah State Coll. Library, 1967, Jour. Library History award, 1970, N.Y. Black Librarians Inc. award, 1979, N.J. Black Librarians Network award, 1984, Joseph W. Lippincott award, 1980, Disting. Alumnus of Yr. award SUNY Albany Sch. Library and Info. Sci. and Policy, 1981, 89, Disting. Service award Library Assn. of CUNY, 1982, Martin Luther King Jr. award for disting. community leadership SUNY, Albany, 1984, award for contbns. to librarianship D.C. Assn. Sch. Librarians, 1984, award Kenyan Library Assn., 1984, Disting. Service award Afro-Caribbean Library Assn., Eng., 1984; ALA Hon. Mem. Award, 2002. Mem.: ACLU, AAUP, ALA (hon.; founder, chmn. Black Caucus 1970—71, mem. coun. 1970—, mem. exec. bd. 1979—86, v.p./pres.-elect 1983—84, pres. 1984—85, John Cotton Dana award 1962, 1964, Black Caucus award 1979, ALA Equality award 1991, Black Caucus Demco award for disting. svc. to librarianship 1994, Wash. office award 1996—, Humphrey/OCLC/Forest Press award for contbns. to internat. librarianship 1998), Am. Soc. Info. Scis., Internat. Platform Assn., N.Y. Libr. Assn. (Disting. Svc. award 1985), Am. Acad. Polit. and Social Sci., Assn. Study Afro-Am. Life and History, Pa. Libr. Assn. (Disting. Svc. award 1996), N.Y. Libr. Club, Kappa Phi Kappa, Alpha Phi Omega. Democrat. Home: 5 Bayard Rd Unit 505 Pittsburgh PA 15213-1905 Office: U Pitts Sch Info Scis Bldg Pittsburgh PA 15260 E-mail: ejjosey@mail.sis.pitt.edu.

JOSLIN, LINDA JOY HARBER, elementary education educator; b. Abilene, Tex., Dec. 16, 1946; d. William E. and Frances Rowena (Robinson) Harber; m. Fred Leon Joslin, May 29, 1970; 1 child, Jeremy Lee. BS in Elem. Edn., Sul Ross State U., 1968; cert. educable emotionally mentally handicapped, Hardin Simmons U., 1972, MS in Reading, 1983. Cert. tchr., Tex. 2d and 4th grade tchr. Lamesa (Tex.) Ind. Schs., 1968-72; educable emotionally mentally handicapped tchr. Tri-County Edn. Co-op, Anson, Tex., 1972-73, Taylor/Calahan County Edn. Co-op, Merkel, Tex., 1973-75; 3d grade tchr., jr. high educable emotionally mentally handicapped Snyder (Tex.) Ind. Schs., 1975-77; 11-12 yr. olds educable emotionally mentally handicapped tchr. Midland (Tex.) Ind. Schs., 1977-78; 1st grade tchr. Deltac-7 Pub. Schs., Deering, Mo., 1978-95; tchr. grade 1 Malden Pub. Sch., 1995—; ret., 1999. Mem. profl. devel. com. County and Sch. Dist. Delta C-7 and Pemiscot County, 1992—, tchr. Caruthersville Summer Sch. Acad., 1994-95 (del. 1993-95), presenter Mo. State Tchrs. Convention Workshop, Kansas City, 1994. Contbr. articles in profl. jours. Summer food program monitor Pemiscot Health Ctr., Hayti, Mo., 1990-93; workshop facilitator for Early Literacy. Mem. Mo. State Tchrs. Assn. (del. 1993-94), Delta C-7 Classroom Tchrs. Assn. (pres., v.p., recording sec. 1978—), Beta Sigma Phi (Girl of Yr. 1980-82), Delta Kappa Gamma. Baptist. Avocations: reading, travel, volleyball, meeting interesting people, learning new things. Home: 1003 Collins Ave Caruthersville MO 63830-1741

JOSLYN, CATHERINE RUTH, art educator, artist; b. Cleve., May 18, 1950; d. Richard Owen and Mary Ellen (See) Joslyn. BA, Colby Coll., 1972; MFA, Ind. U., 1977. Owner Woven Images, Kansas City, 1973-77; vis. artist Kansas City Art Inst., 1978-79; asst. prof. Clarion (Pa.) U., 1979-85; dir. Clarion Festival of Arts, 1984-86; founding dir. univ. honors program Clarion (Pa.) U., 1986-88. Commonwealth speaker Pa. Humanities Coun., Phila., 1991; internat. lectr. and exhibitor. Contbr. articles to Grove's Dictionary Art and profl. jours.; works included in juried and solo exhibits, pvt. and corp. collections nat. and internat., 1973—. Grantee Pa. Coun. on the Arts, 1985; J. William Fulbright Sr. scholar, Peru, 2002. Mem. Surface Design Assn. (bd. dirs 1982-87, 91). Avocations: gardening, reading, music, dance, sailing, yoga. Office: Clarion U Dept Art Clarion PA 16214

JOSS, PAUL CHRISTOPHER, astrophysicist, atmospheric physicist, educator; b. Bklyn., May 7, 1945; s. Everett Henry and Magda Anna (Hohorst) J.; m. Marjorie Jean Axton, Jan. 24, 1970 (div.); 1 child, Susan Elizabeth; m. Karen Elizabeth Murray, July 3, 1992 (div.); 1 child, Matthew Albert Henry. BA, Cornell U., 1966, PhD, 1971. Mem. Inst. for Advanced Study, Princeton, N.J., 1971-73; asst. prof. MIT, Cambridge, 1973-78, assoc. prof., 1978-83, prof., 1983—, mem. Ctr. for Theoretical Physics, 1973—, mem. Ctr. for Space Rsch., 1973—, assoc. head astrophysics divsn., 1983-88. Vis. scientist Weizmann Inst. Sci., Rehovot, Israel, 1974—75, 1978, Inst. Astronomy, Cambridge, England, 1977, 93; vis. staff mem. Los Alamos (N.Mex.) Sci. Lab., 1979—80, cons., 1980—92, Visidyne Inc., Burlington, Mass., 1979—82, 1992—93, spl. asst. to pres., 1993—2000, sr. scientist, 2000—; mem. adv. com. Inst. Geophysics and Planetary Physics Los Alamos Nat. Lab., 1987—92; mem. High Energy Astrophysics Mgmt. Ops. Working Group NASA, 1988—91; mem. Astronomy and Space Physics Sci. Coun. Univs. Space Rsch. Assn., 1988—92; mem. Inst. for Theoretical Physics U. Calif., Santa Barbara, 1991; pres. Joss Consulting Assocs., 1992—. Contbr. 140 articles to profl. jours.; editor 140 articles to profl. jours. Woodrow Wilson Found. fellow, 1966; NSF fellow, 1970; Alfred P. Sloan Found. fellow, 1976. Mem. Am. Astron. Soc. (Helen B. Warner Prize 1980, exec. com. High Energy Astrophysics div. 1983-85), Am. Phys. Soc., Internat. Astron. Union, Phi Beta Kappa. Avocations: classical music, chess. Office: MIT Dept Of Physics Rm 37-607 Cambridge MA 02139 E-mail: joss@space.mit.edu.

JOSSEM, EDMUND LEONARD, physics educator; b. Camden, N.J., May 19, 1919; BS, CCNY, 1938; MS, Cornell U., 1940—42, PhD in physics, 1950. Asst prof. Cornell U., 1946—50, assoc. prof., 1950—52, chmn Dept. Physics, 1967—80; prof. physics Ohio State U., 1964—89, prof. emeritus, 1989—. Exec. sec. Cmty. Coll. Physics, 1963—65, chmn., 1966—71, mem. commn. on coll. physics; mem. Nat. Adv. Coun. Edn. Profl. Devel., 1967—70; bd. dirs. Mich.-Ohio Edn. Lab., 1967—69; hon. bd. Internat. Conf. X-ray and Atomic Inner Shell Physics, 1981—82; mem. sci. staff Advanced Divsn. Lost Alamos, 1942—47; mem. com. tchg. sci. Internat. Coun. Sci. Unions; cons. World Bank-Chinese U. Devel. Project, China; hon. prof. physics Beijing (China) Normal U. Fellow: AAAS; mem.: Am. Assn. Physics Tchrs. (v.p. 1971—72, pres. 1973—74, chmn. com. tchr. preparation 2002—, Phillips award 1985, Oersted award 1994), Am. Physics Soc., Sigma Xi. Home: 174 W 18th Ave Columbus OH 43210-1106*

JOURNEAY, GLEN EUGENE, physician, educator; b. Orange, Tex., June 14, 1925; s. Fred Young and Gertrude (Martin) J.; m. Betty Cooper, Sept. 4, 1948; children: Carol Journeay-Kaler, David, Stephen, Nancy Journeay Jackson, Janet Journeay Slack. BA, Rice U., 1945, BS in Chem. Engring., 1947; PhD, U. Tex, 1951; MD, U. Tex, Galveston, 1960. Diplomate Am. Bd. Family Physicians. Chemist Monsanto Chem. Co., Texas City, Tex., 1951-56; lectr. St. Mary's Sch. Nursing, Galveston, 1957-61; physician Beeler Manske Clinic, Texas City, 1961-63; lectr. U. Tex., Austin, 1964—2000; physician pvt. practice, Austin, 1963-92. Contbr. articles to profl. jours. Mem. Tex. Air Control Bd. Resources Panel, Austin, 1989-93, Imported Fire Ant Adv. Bd., Austin, 1988-92; bd. dir. Austin Trade and Tech. Sch., 1982-85, Galveston County Heart Assn., 1961-63, Capital Area Coun. Boy Scouts Am., 1966-69, scoutmaster, 1964-70. Lt. (j.g.) USN, 1943-45. Recipient Silver Beaver award Boy Scouts Am., 1968. Fellow Am. Inst. Chemists, AMA; mem. Tex. Med. Assn. (editorial com., ho. of dels.), Am. Acad. Family Physicians, Tex. Acad. Family Physicians (pres. 1983-84), Am. Chem. Soc., Sigma Xi, Alpha Omega Alpha, Phi Lambda Upsilon. Avocations: painting, photography, hunting, sailing, camping.

JOY, CARLA MARIE, history educator; b. Denver, Sept. 5, 1945; d. Carl P. and Theresa M. (Lotito) J. AB cum laude, Loretto Heights Coll., 1967; MA, U. Denver, 1969, postgrad., 1984-87. Instr. history Cmty. Coll., Denver; prof. history Red Rocks C.C., Lakewood, Colo., 1970—. Cons. for innovative ednl. programs; reviewer fed. grants, 1983-89; mem. adv. panel Colo. Endowment for Humanities, 1985-89. Contbr. articles to profl. publs. Instr. vocat. edn. Mile High United Way, Jefferson County, 1975; participant Jefferson County Sch. Sys. R-1 Dist., 1983-88; active Red Rocks C.C. Spkrs. Bur., 1972-89, strategic planning com., 1992-97; chair history discipline Colo. Gen. Edn. Core Transfer Consortium, 1986-96, faculty transfer curriculum coun., 1997—; mem. Colo. C.C. curriculum com., 1999—; mem. history, geography, civics stds. and geography frameworks adv. com. Colo. Dept. Edn., 1995-96; steering com. Ctr. Tchg. Excellence, 1991-92, 96-97; with North Ctrl. Self-Study Process, 1972-73, 80-81, 86-88, 96-98; with K-16 Linkages Colo. Commn. for Higher Edn., 1997-98; mem. evaluation team for Colo. Awards, edn. and civic achievement for Widefield Sch. Dist. #3, 1989; mem. Red Rocks C.C.-Clear Creek Sch. Sys. Articulation Team, 1990-91; mem. Statue of Liberty-Ellis Island Found. Inc., 1987—. Ford Found. fellow, 1969; recipient Cert. of Appreciation Kiwanis Club, 1981, Telecomm. Coop. for Colo.'s Cmty. Colls., 1990-92, Master Tchr. award U. Tex.-Austin, 1982. Mem. NEA, Am. Hist. Assn., Am. Assn. Higher Edn., Nat. Coun. Social Studies, Nat. Geog. Soc., Omohundro Inst. Early Am. History and Culture, Colo. Edn. Assn., Colo. Coun. Social Studies, World Hist. Assn., Orgn. Am. Historians, The Colo. Hist. Soc., Colo. Geog. Alliance, Soc. Hist. Edn., Phi Alpha Theta. Home: 1849 S Lee St Apt D Lakewood CO 80232-6252 Office: Red Rocks C C 13300 W 6th Ave Lakewood CO 80228-1213

JOYCE, ANN IANNUZZO, art educator; b. Scranton, Pa., May 23, 1953; d. Albert Joseph and Lucy (Giumento) Iannuzzo; m. Patrick Francis Joyce, July 23, 1977; children: Ryan Patrick, Shawn Patrick. BFA, Maryland Inst., Balt., 1975; MS, U. Scranton, 1988; postgrad., Pa. State U., 1990—. Mech. artist Internat. Corr. Schs., Scranton, Pa., 1975-77; layout artist Lynn Orgn., Wilkes-Barre, Pa., 1977-78; prodn. coord. Jewelcor Merchandising, Wilkes-Barre, 1978-82; adj. lectr. Kings Coll., Wilkes-Barre, 1981-89; art dir. WVIA-TV Pub. Broadcasting, Pittston, Pa., 1985-86; publs. dir. U. Scranton, 1986-89; asst. prof. King's Coll., Wilkes-Barre, 1989—. Exec. bd. v.p. Northeastern Pa. Writing Coun., Wilkes-Barre, 1993—; edn. co-chair Northeast Pa. Ad Club, 1994-96. Contbg. author: Handbook of Classroom Assessment: Learning, Achievement, and Adjustment, 1996; group show Everhart Mus., Scranton, Pa., 1997. Cub Scout leader Boy Scouts Am., Moosic, Pa., 1992-95. Mem. ASCD, Nat. Art Edn. Assn., Am. Inst. Graphic Arts (Phila. chpt.), Calligraphers Guild, Artists for Art, Pa. Art Edn. Assn., Nat. Assn. Desktop Pubs., Seminar for Rsch. in Art Edn., Caucus for Social Theory in Art Edn. Democrat. Roman Catholic. Avocations: mixed media art, writing, vegetarian cooking. Home: 148 Joyce Dr Moosic PA 18507-2113 Office: King's Coll 133 N River St Wilkes Barre PA 18711-0851 Address: 148 Joyce Dr Moosic PA 18507-2113

JOYCE, CAROL BERTANI, social studies educator; b. NYC, Apr. 9, 1943; d. Joseph and Ethel Marie (Bracchi) Bertani; m. William Leonard Joyce, Aug. 13, 1967; children: Susan A., Michael J. BA, Coll. New Rochelle, 1964; MA, St. John's U., 1966; postgrad., U. Mich., 1970-71. Cert. tchr., NJ, NY, Mass., Mich.; cert. supr., NJ, Nat. Bd. Cert. Tchr. Tchr. Christ the King HS, Mid. Village, NY, 1966-67, Willow Run HS, Ypsilanti, Mich., 1967-68, Notre Dame Acad., Worcester, Mass., 1974-81, Salesian HS, New Rochelle, NY, 1981-82, Ursuline Sch., New Rochelle, NY, 1982-88, Burlington Twp. Sch., NJ, 1988-89; edn. planner Dept. Edn., Trenton, NJ, 1989-91; tchr. Princeton Regional Sch., NJ, 1991—. Participant Tri-States Global Workshop, Boylston, Mass., 1980, NEH summer seminar fellowship U. Mass., Dartmouth, North Dartmouth, 1993, Tchrs. Inst. in History, Princeton U., 1994, 97, Seminar in African-Am. Studies for Secondary Sch. Tchrs. Princeton U., 1995-96, Nat. Consortium for Tchg. about Asia seminars, 2002-03, NBPTS Renewal Team, 2003; tchr., counselor European tour Am. Leadership Study Group, 1987; master tchr. DeWitt-Wallace World History Tchrs. Summer Inst., Woodrow Wilson Nat. Scholarship Found., Princeton, 1992. Tchr. religious edn. various parishes in Mass., N.Y., 1974-83; chair edn. com. LWV, Pelham, N.Y., 1983-84; vol. Profl. Roster, Princeton, 1989, Profl. Svc. Group, New Brunswick, N.J., 1991; panelist N.J. Bar Found. High Sch. Curriculum Panel on Law-Related Edn., 1993-96. Grantee Women's Ctr. U. Mich., 1970-71. Mem. Nat. Coun. for Social Studies (participant social studies coun. meeting N.E. regional conf. 1981), Nat. Coun. for History Edn. Avocations: travel, crafts. Office: Princeton High Sch 151 Moore St Princeton NJ 08540-3399 Home: 42 Grande Blvd Princeton Junction NJ 08550-2429

JOYCE, EDWARD ROWEN, retired chemical engineer, educator; b. St. Augustine, Fla., Oct. 20, 1927; s. Edward Rowen and Annie Margaret (Cobb) J.; m. Leland Livingston White, Sept. 11, 1954; children: Leland Ann, Julia, Edward Rowen III, Theo, Adele. BS in Chem. Engring., U. Miss., 1950; M of Engring., U. Fla., 1969; MBA, U. North Fla., 1975. Registered profl. engr., Fla. Petroleum engr. Texaco, Harvey, La., 1953-55; project engr. Freeport Sulphur Co., New Orleans, 1955-59; chem. engr. SCM Corp., Jacksonville, Fla., 1959-81; profl. engr. Jacksonville Electric Authority, 1981-93, ret., 1993. Adj. prof. U. North Fla., Jacksonville, 1977—, Jacksonville U., 1989—; newspaper columnist Fla. Times Union, Jacksonville, 1970-87. Co-author: Sulfate Turpentine Recovery, 1971; author booklet; patentee in field. Sci. fair judge Duval County Sch. System, Jacksonville, 1960-92; co-chmn. adv. com. U. North Fla., 1981-85; merit badge advisor Boy Scouts Am., Jacksonville, 1960—; advisor Jr. Achievement, Jacksonville, 1963; vestryman, lay Eucharistic minister, sr. warden local Episcopal ch. Comdr. USN, 1950-53, Korea. Fellow Fla. Engring. Soc. (pres. Jacksonville chpt. 1983); mem. AICE (pres. Peninsular Fla. chpt. 1963-64), Phi Kappa Phi, Alpha Pi Mu, Gamma Sigma Epsilon. Democrat. Avocations: stamp collecting, coin collecting, water sports, camping. Home: 5552 Riverton Rd Jacksonville FL 32277-1361

JOYCE, JOHN JOSEPH, English language educator; b. Buffalo, Aug. 1, 1930; s. Leo A. and Margaret Louise (Edgar) J.; m. Carole J. King, Aug. 22, 1970; children: Stephen Leo, Patrick John. BA, Canisius Coll., 1952, MA, 1960; PhD, SUNY, Binghamton, 1977. Ins. agt., Buffalo, 1954-59; tchr. Lackawanna (N.Y.) Sr. High Sch., 1959-65; lectr. SUNY, Buffalo, 1964-65; prof. Nazareth Coll. Rochester, N.Y., 1965-99, prof. emeritus, 1999—. Chmn. English dept. Nazareth Coll., Rochester, 1980-87, coll. marshall, 1995—. Reader textbook publs. and jours.; contbr. articles to profl. jours. and ref. texts. Trustee Rochester Regional Libr. Coun. Sgt. major U.S. Army Infantry, 1952-54, Korea. Recipient Disting. Tchg. award Nazareth Coll. Alumni, 1990, numerous rsch. grants. Mem. MLA, Coll. English Assn. (exec. dir. 1984-94, Disting. Svc. award 1991), N.Y. Coll. English Assn. (newsletter editor 1978-84, bd. dirs., v.p. 1979—), Assn. Lit. Scholars and Critics, English Coalition (organizing com. 1985-87). Roman Catholic. Avocations: golf, gym work-out, music, architecture, painting. Office: Nazareth Coll Rochester English Dept Rochester NY 14618

JOYCE, JOSEPH PATRICK, economist, educator; b. Bklyn., Nov. 16, 1951; s. Joseph P. Joyce Sr. and Mary Ellen Connolly; m. Catherine Clark. BSFS, Georgetown U., 1973; MA, Boston U., 1976, PhD, 1984. Lectr. dept. econs. Wellesley (Mass.) Coll., 1981-83, asst. prof., 1983-89, assoc. prof., 1989—96; prof. Wellesley Coll., 1996—. Vis. scholar Internat. Affairs, Harvard U., Cambridge, Mass., 1987-90, Fed. Res. Bank Boston, 2000-01; intern Fed. Res. Bd., Washington, 1980, IMF, Washington, 1980; guest scholar Brookings Instn., Washington, 1993-94. Contbr. articles to profl. jours. Mem. Am. Econs. Assn. Democrat. Roman Catholic. E-mail: jjoyce@wellesley.edu.

JOYCE, MARY ANN, principal; b. Bklyn., May 29, 1935; d. Alfred and Antoinette (Polito) Lo Sasso; m. Michael J. Joyce, Jr., Mar. 2, 1957 (dec. 1982); children: Michael, Debra Grammer, Patricia Sommers. BA in Elem. Edn., Social Scis., Mount St. Mary Coll., 1972; MS in Elem. Edn., Reading, SUNY, New Paltz, 1975, CAS in Ednl. Adminstrn., 1983. Cert. tchr. N-6, N.Y., reading tchr., K-12, N.Y., sch. dist. administr., N.Y., sch. administr./supr., N.Y. Tchr. grades 3 and 4 Temple Hill Sch., Newburgh, N.Y., 1972-74, tchr. reading, 1974-83, tchr. gifted and talented, 1976-83, asst. prin., 1983-85; prin. Horizons-on-the-Hudson Magnet Sch., Newburgh, 1985-98; exec. dir. curriculum and instrn. Newburgh Enlarged City Schs., 1998—. Tchr. summer sch. Newburgh (N.Y.) Free Acad., 1976-81; adj. prof. SUNY, New Paltz, 1989-91; nat. review panelist Blue Ribbon Sch. Competition, 1991, 92, FIRST family-sch. partnership program, 1992; speaker numerous confs., seminars. Recipient Elem. Sch. Recognition award U.S. Dept. Edn., 1989-90, 93-94, Excellence in Adminstrn. award Mid-Hudson Sch. Study Coun., 1993, award for Outstanding Leadership, Achievements and Contributions Toward Making the Edn. of our Nation's Youth a Safe and Productive Experience, 1991. Mem. ASCD, Am. Assn. Female Execs., Nat. Assn. Elem. Sch. Prins. (Excellence in Edn. award 1990, 94), State Adminstrs. Assn. N.Y. State (Elem. Schs. Excellence award 1990, 94), Newburgh Suprs. and Adminstrs. Assn., United Univ. Profs., Delta Kappa Gamma. Avocations: reading, sewing, needlework. Office: Newburgh Enlarged City Schs 124 Grand St Newburgh NY 12550-4615

JOYCE, MICHAEL DANIEL, personal resource management therapist and consultant, neurolearning therapist; b. St. Cloud, Minn., June 8, 1948; s. Francis Daniel and Bernadette (Ferkinhoff) J.; m. Patricia Mary Boom, July 7, 1969. BA in Psychology and Sociology, St. Cloud State U., 1973, postgrad., 1977, Moorhead State U., 1993, Atwood Inst., 1993, Biofeedback Tng. and Treatment Ctr., 1994. Cert. behavior analyst, rsch. analyst, Minn., master practitioner of neuro-linguistic programming, Colo.; cert. hypnotherapist, neurolearning therapist; cert. in hemisphere specific auditory stimulation; cert. to practice hemisphere specific auditory stimulation; cert. in biofeedback; cert in EEG neurofeedback. Resident mgr. Dan J. Brutger, Inc., St. Cloud, 1969-71; rsch. analyst Faribault (Minn.) State Hosp., 1974-75, behavior analyst, 1975-76; therapist/behavior analyst Ctrl. Minn. Mental Health Ctr., St. Cloud, 1977-78; emotional/behavior disabled facilitator, chpt. 1 tutor Perham (Minn.) Dent Schs., 1978-92, dir. neurofeedback svcs. Tech. cons. Inclusive Edn. Tech. Assistance Team, Region IV, State of Minn., Perham, 1991-93, Personal Resource Strategies, Vergas, Minn., 1994-99; dir. neurotechnology svcs. A Chance To Grow, Mpls., 1999—; trainer and mentor Minn. Learning Resource Ctr., Mpls., 1999—. Co-author: Life-Threatening Behavior: Analysis and Intervention, 1982, Audio-Visual Entrainment Program as a Treatment for Behavior Disorders in a School Setting—Journal of Neurotherapy, 2001. Coord. Youth Assn. for Retarded Citizens, St. Cloud, 1977-78; respite care provider Ctrl. Minn. Mental Health Ctr., St. Cloud and Perham, 1977-78, 79-86; vol. Perham Schs., 1978—, Spl. Olympics - Winter Games, Duluth, Minn., 1980, 81. Named Mem. of Yr. Minn. Sch. Employees Assn., 1989. Mem. Neuro-Linguistic Programming (cert. master level), Internat. Med. and Dental Hypnotherapy Assn. (cert. neurolearning therapist). Avocations: organic gardening and orcharding, tree farming, basketball, computers, psychotechnology hardware and software. Home: 1749 Roselawn Ave W Saint Paul MN 55113-5757 E-mail: mdmjoyce@hotmail.com., mjoyce@mail.actg.org.

JOYCE, PHYLLIS NORMA, educational administrator; b. Bronx, N.Y., June 8, 1955; d. Philip Emmanuel and Dolores (Pizzolanella) Malizio; m. Thomas Patrick Joyce, June 11, 1983; 1 child, Diana. BA, CUNY, 1978; MA, Nova U., 1995. Tchr. St. Raymond's Sch., Bronx, 1980-83; tchr., head English dept. St. Anne Sch., Las Vegas, Nev., 1983-94, prin., 1994—, coord. jr. high Sch., 1988-94. Spl. Olympics vol. KC, Las Vegas, 1983-90; vol. Sons of Erin, Las Vegas, 1990—; pastoral coun. St. Anne Parish, 1996—. Democrat. Roman Catholic. Avocations: tennis, working out, family recreational activities. Office: St Anne Sch 1813 S Maryland Pky Las Vegas NV 89104-3104

JOYCE, STEVEN JAMES, German and comparative studies educator; b. Green Bay, Wis., Dec. 13, 1950; s. Emmett and Dolores (Remmel) J.; m. Mary Delphine Tomino; children: Alexander, Genevieve, Brendan. BA cum laude, St. Norbert Coll., De Pere, Wis., 1973; postgrad., Lawrence U., Appleton, Wis., 1973-74; MA in Comparative Lit., Purdue U., 1982; PhD in Comparative Lit., U. N.C., 1988. Assoc. prof. German, English, comparative studies Ohio State U., Mansfield, 1988—. Author: Transformations and Texts: G.B. Shaw's Buoyant Billions, 1992. Recipient Disting. Teaching award Ohio State U., Mansfield, 1988, 2000; Fulbright grantee, Bonn, West Germany, 1987; Fulbright Rsch. fellow, Vienna, Austria, 1983-84, 92. Mem. MLA, Fulbright Alumni Assn., Am. Assn. Tchrs. German, Phi Beta Delta. Home: 60 Stewart Ave S Mansfield OH 44906-3207 Office: Ohio State Univ 1680 University Dr 317 Ovalwood Mansfield OH 44906 E-mail: joyce.3@osu.edu.

JOYCE, VICKI MARIE, special education educator; b. Chgo., Sept. 8, 1936; d. Walter and Victoria Juckins; m. Robert Daniel Joyce, Aug., 1956 (div. 1974); children: Jennifer Brining, David. BA, Calif. State U., L.A., 1962; MA, Calif. State U., San Bernardino, 1992. Home econs. tchr. L.A. City Sch. Dist., 1962-65; real estate broker Homes Unltd., Orange County, Calif., 1970-82; tchr. Riverside and San Bernardino County (Calif.) Sch. Dists., 1982-95; resource specialist San Bernardino Unified Sch. Dist., 1995—. Author: A Theoretical Meta-Analysis and Review of Kinesis For Special Education Teachers and Resource Specialists, 1993. Named Outstanding Tchr. Orton Dyslexia Soc., 1993. Mem. Calif. Tchrs. Assn., San Bernardino Tchrs. Assn., Nat. Tchrs. Assn., Nat. Assn. Resource Specialists. Avocations: reading, writing, painting, theater, grandchildren. Home: 3958 Park View Ter Riverside CA 92501-2360

JOYCE, WILLIAM LEONARD, librarian; b. Rockville Centre, N.Y., Mar. 29, 1942; s. John Francis and Mabel Clare (Leonard) J.; m. Carol Gail Bertani, Aug. 13, 1967; children: Susan, Michael. BA, Providence Coll., 1964; MA, St. John's U., 1966; PhD, U. Mich., 1974. Manuscripts libr. William L. Clements Libr. U. Mich., Ann Arbor, 1968-72; curator manuscripts Am. Antiquarian Soc., Worcester, Mass., 1972-81, edn. officer, 1977-81; asst. dir. for rare books and manuscripts N.Y. Pub. Libr., N.Y.C., 1981-86; assoc. univ. libr. for rare books and spl. collections Princeton U., 1986-2000; Dorothy Foehr Huck chair for spl. collections Pa. State U., 2000—. Numerous cons. assignments including assessment and reporting project Nat. Hist. Publs. and Records Commn., Washington, 1982; lectr. Clark U., 1975-77; adj. faculty Sch. Library Service, Columbia U., N.Y.C., 1984-92; vis. prof. Grad. Sch. Libr. & Info. Sci. UCLA, 1994. Author: Editors and Ethnicity: A History of the Irish-American Press, 1848-1883, 1976; co-author: Documenting America: Assessing the Condition of Historical Records in the States, 1984; booklet Evaluation of Archival Institutions, 1982; co-editor: Printing and Society in Early America, 1983; editor: Catalog of Manuscripts Collections of the American Antiquarian Society, 4 vols., 1979; contbr. articles, revs. to profl. jours. Bd. dirs. Conservation Ctr. for Art and Hist. Artifacts, 1992-2000, chmn., 1995-98; mem. J.F.K. Assassination Records Rev. Bd., 1994-98; mem. adv. bd. Cannery Row Mus. Found., 1998-2000; mem. adv. com. Ctr. for Jewish History, 2000—, chmn., 2001—. Fellow Soc. Am. Archivists (coun. mem. 1981-85, pres. 1986-87); mem. Am. Hist. Assn. (mem. profl. div. com. 1979-81), Bibliog. Soc. Am. (chmn. fellowship com. 1982-85), Orgn. Am. Historians, Am. Antiquarian Soc., ALA (rare books and manuscripts sect., publs. com. 1985-88, chmn. 1987-88, mem. ARL spl. collections task force 2000-), Grolier Club (coun. 1990-93), Internat. Coun. on Archives (com. on lit. and art, 1993-97), Princeton Club (N.Y.C.). Office: Pa State Librs 110 Paterno Library University Park PA 16802-1808 E-mail: wlj2@psulias.psu.edu.

JOYNER, NINA WOMBLE, elementary education educator; b. Richmond, Va., Aug. 10, 1950; d. Lewis Earl and Marie (Price) Womble; 1 child, Jason Lewis. AA in Edn., Paul D. Camp C.C., 1976; BS in Elem. Edn., Old Dominion U., 1978. Cert. tchr., Va. Tchr. Franklin (Va.) City Pub. Schs., 1978—, adult edn. tchr., 1988—, tutorial tchr. Va. Literacy Test, 1992—. Avocations: horseback riding, kite making, boating, swimming.

JOYNER, WEYLAND THOMAS, physicist, educator, business consultant; b. Suffolk, Va., Aug. 9, 1929; s. Weyland T. and Thelma (Neal) J.; m. Marianne Steele, Dec. 3, 1955; children: Anne, Weyland, Leigh. BS, Hampden-Sydney Coll., 1951; MA, Duke U., 1952, PhD, 1955. Teaching fellow Duke U., Durham, N.C., 1954, rsch. assoc., 1958; physicist Dept. Def., Washington, 1954-57; rsch. physicist U. Md., 1955-57; asst. prof. physics Hampden-Sydney Coll., 1957-59, assoc. prof., 1959-63, prof., 1963—, physics chmn., 1968-82, 85-87, Elliott prof., 1995-98; rsch. assoc. Ames Lab. AEC, 1964-65; vis. prof. Pomona Coll., 1965; staff Commn. on Coll. Physics, Ann Arbor, Mich., 1966-67; vis. fellow Dartmouth Coll., 1981. Mem. Panel on Preparation Physics Tchrs., 1967-68; nuclear physics cons. Oak Ridge Inst. Nuclear Studies, 1960-67; NASA-Lewis faculty fellow, 1982-84; pres. Piedmont Farms, Inc., 1958-75, Windsor Supply Corp., 1966-82, Three Rivers Farms, Inc., 1971-74, Windsor Seed & Livestock Co., 1969-83; ednl. cons. numerous colls. and univs., 1965-75; mgmt. cons., 1966—. Contbr. articles profl. jours. Bd. dirs. Prince Edward Acad., 1971-92, exec. com., 1975-92; trustee Prince Edward Sch. Electoral Bd., 1979-80. NASA prin. investigator, 1985-87. Fellow AAAS; mem. Am. Phys. Soc., Am. Assn. Physics Tchrs., IEEE, Va. Acad. Sci. (past mem. council, sect. pres.), Am. Inst. Physics (regional counselor, past dir. Coll. Program), Phi Beta Kappa, Sigma Xi, Lambda Chi Alpha. Presbyn. (trustee). Home: Venable Pl Hampden Sydney VA 23943 Office: Hampden Sydney Coll Gilmer Sci Ctr Hampden Sydney VA 23943

JOYNES, AMELIA C. art educator; b. Bridgeport, Conn. m. Thomas J. Joynes; two children. BA, Hiram Coll., 1967; MEd, Cleve. State U., 1984. Art educator Mentor (Ohio) Sch. Dist., 1967-68, Orange Sch. Dist., Pepper Pike, Ohio, 1968-70, Kenston Sch. Dist., Chagrin Falls, Ohio, 1978—2001; adj. faculty mem. Cleve. State U., 1987—, lectr. edn. dept., 1987—; lectr. Case Western Res. U., 2002—. Mem. adv. bd. State of Ohio Dept. Edn.; mem. tchr. resource adv. bd. Cleve. Museum of Art; arts presenter Ohio Alliance for Art, 1998—. Textbook reviewer Harper Collins Pub. Co., 1990, 94; contbr. articles to profl. jours. Named Reg. Outstanding Art Educator Northeast Ohio, 1999. Mem. Nat. Art Edn. Assn., Nat. Mid. Sch. Assn., Ohio Art Edn. Assn. (state sec. 1984-85, elem. divsn. chmn. 1985-88), Ohio Alliance. Avocations: reading, theater, travel.

JREISAT, JAMIL ELIAS, public administration and political science educator, consultant; b. Apr. 9, 1935; came to U.S., 1960; s. Elias E. and Hanieh J. (Khory) J.; m. Andrea Brunais, July 9, 1977; children: Mark Ramsey, Leila Martine. BA, Am. U., Washington, 1962; MPA, U. Pitts., 1963, PhD, 1968. Sr. ofcl. Govt. Jordan, 1957-60; lectr. pub. adminstrn. and polit. sci. U. South Fla., Tampa, 1968—, chmn. dept. polit. sci., 1976-80. Vis. prof. U. Jordan, 1983, U. Riyad (Saudi Arabia), 1981-82; cons. UN Devel. Program, Internat. Mgmt. Devel. Inst.-U. Pitts., Arab Orgn. Adminstrv. Devel., others. Author: Administration and Development in the Arab World, 1986, Managing Public Organizations, 1992, Politics Without Process, 1997, and others; contbr. articles to profl. jours. and chpts. to books; mem. editl. bd. Internat. Jour. Pub. Adminstrn. Mem. ASPA, Am. Polit. Sci. Assn., Arab-Am. Univ. Grads. (bd. dirs., pres. 1991-93), Middle East Club. Home: 6713 Maybole Pl Tampa FL 33617-3831 Office: U South Fla Pub Adminstrn Program Tampa FL 33620

JUBERG, RICHARD KENT, mathematician, educator; b. Cooperstown, N.D., May 14, 1929; s. Palmer and Hattie Noreen (Nelson) J.; m. Janet Elisabeth Witchell, Mar. 17, 1956 (div.); children: Alison K., Kevin A., Hilary N., Ian C.T.; m. Sandra Jean Vakerics, July 8, 1989. BS, U. Minn., 1952, PhD, 1958. Asst. prof. U. Minn., Mpls., 1958-65; sci. faculty fellow Univerista di Pisa, Italy, 1965-66; assoc. prof. U. Calif., Irvine, 1966-72, U. Sussex, Eng., 1972-73; prof. U. Calif., Irvine, 1974-91, prof. emeritus, 1991—. Vis. prof. U. Goteborg, Sweden, 1981; mem. Courant Inst. Math. Scis., NYU, 1957-58. Contbr. articles to profl. jours. With USN, 1946-48, Guam. NSF Faculty fellow, Univ. Pisa, Italy, 1965-66. Mem. Am. Math. Soc., Tau Beta Pi. Democrat. Avocation: bird watching.

JUBINSKA, PATRICIA ANN, ballet instructor, choreographer, artist, artist; b. Norfolk, Va. d. Joseph John and Lucy (Babey) Topping; children: Vanessa Meredith, Courtney Hilary. Student, Md. State Ballet Sch., Sch. Am. Ballet, N.Y.C.; BA, R.I. Coll.; MA, Wesleyan U.; PhD, Union Inst., 1999. Mem. N.Y.C. Ballet; freelance artist Chamber Ballet of L.A., San Antonio Ballet, Md. State Ballet; artistic dir. Blackstone Valley Ballet, Harrisville, R.I., 1983-84, Am. Ballet, Pascoag, R.I., 1984-92; asst. artistic dir. Odessa Ukrainian Dancers, Woonsocket, R.I., 1991-92; freelance guest artist, 1992—; mem. Mandrivka Dancers of Boston, 1993—; mem. faculty Fine Arts West Warwick Sch., 1995—; mem. faculty Roger Williams U., 2000—. Avocation: equestrian. Home: 110 Gold Mine Rd Chepachet RI 02814

JUCHNICKI, JANE ELLEN, secondary education educator; b. Greenfield, Mass., Jan. 18, 1949; d. Francis W. and Helen (Helstowski) J. BS in Secondary History Edn., U. Vt., 1970; MS in Colonial U.S. History, Ctrl. Conn. State U., 1976; MA in Archeology, U. Conn., 1979. Tchr. social studies, history Gideon Wells Jr. High Sch., Glastonbury, Conn., 1970-72, Glastonbury Adult Edn., 1976-86, Glastonbury High Sch., 1972—. Mem. Pub. Archeology Survey Team, Storrs, Conn., 1978-79, Secondary Social Studies Curriculum Devel. Com., 1989—. Author: (booklet) Career/Resume Prep Unemployment, 1979. Active Fulbright Assn., Washington, 1990—; vol. Smithsonian Excavation, Tell Jemmeh, Israel, 1976. Fellow U.S. Dept. Edn., Egypt, 1987; Fulbright-Hayes Found. tchr. exch., London, 1987-89, tchr. rsch. fellow U. London, 1992. Mem. NEA, Conn. Edn. Assn., Glastonbury Edn. Assn. Democrat. Avocations: archeology, sailing, skiing, golf. Office: Glastonbury HS 330 Hubbard St Glastonbury CT 06033-3047

JUDAH, FRANK MARVIN, retired school system administrator; b. Guymon, Okla., Sept. 13, 1941; s. Frank Morris and Margaret (Vaughan) J.; m. Rita Kay Paschal, Oct. 28, 1966; children: Frances Margaret (dec.), Frank Martin. BA, Tex. Tech. U., 1965; MA, Tex. A&M U., 1975, PhD, 1980. Cert. tchr., ednl. adminstr., Tex. Tchr. Reagan County Ind. Sch. Dist., Big Lake, Tex., 1967-73; adminstrv. asst. City of Sweetwater, Tex., 1974-76; dir. purchasing Killeen (Tex.) Ind. Sch. Dist., 1977-81; asst. supt. for adminstrn. Seguin (Tex.) Ind. Sch. Dist., 1981-85; asst. supt. for bus. DeSoto (Tex.) Ind. Sch. Dist., 1985-97; ret., 1997. Civil svc. commr. City of DeSoto, 1988-93; trustee DeSoto Ind. Sch. Dist., 2000-2003, bd. sec., 2003. Mem. Tex. Assn. Sch. Bus. Ofcls. (vice-chmn. cert. com. 1984-97), Assn. Sch. Bus. Ofcls. Internat., Rotary (pres., sec. DeSoto club 1986-89), Masons (treas. DeSoto lodge 1409 1987-90, 98-99). Avocations: numismatics, gardening, physical fitness, recreational reading. Home: PO Box 90 Moody TX 76557-0090 E-mail: texpony@ev1.net.

JUDD, BRIAN RAYMOND, physicist, educator; b. Chelmsford, Eng., Feb. 13, 1931; s. Harry and Edith (Saltmarsh) J. BA, Brasenose Coll., Oxford U., 1952, MA, D.Phil., Brasenose Coll., Oxford U., 1955. Fellow Magdalen Coll., Oxford U., 1955-62; instr. U. Chgo., 1957-58; assoc. prof. U. Paris, 1962-64; staff mem. Lawrence Radiation Lab., Berkeley, Calif., 1964-66; prof. physics Johns Hopkins U., Balt., 1966-96, chmn. dept. 1979-84, Gerhard H. Dieke prof., 1992-96, prof. emeritus, 1997-98, Gerhard H. Dieke prof. emeritus, 1998—. Vis. Erskine fellow U. Canterbury, Christchurch, New Zealand, 1968; vis. fellow Australian Nat. U., Canberra, 1975; hon. fellow Brasenose Coll., Oxford U., 1983—. Author: Operator Techniques in Atomic Spectroscopy, 1963, reprinted, 1998, Second Quantization and Atomic Spectroscopy, 1967, (with J.P. Elliott) Topics in Atomic and Nuclear Theory, 1970, Angular Momentum Theory For Diatomic Molecules, 1975. Recipient Spedding award for rare-earth rsch. Rhone-Poulenc, Inc., 1988. Fellow Am. Phys. Soc. Office: Johns Hopkins U Dept Physics and Astronomy Baltimore MD 21218

JUDD, GARY, university administrator; b. Czechoslovakia, Sept. 24, 1942; came to U.S., 1946, naturalized, 1951; s. Joe and Arlene (Zipser) J.; m. Rosalind Sandra Dixter, July 26, 1964; children: Robin, Jennifer, Jason. B.Mat.E., Rensselaer Poly. Inst., 1963, PhD in Phys. Metallurgy, 1967. Mem. faculty Lally Sch. Mgmt. and dept. materials sci. and engring. Rensselaer Poly. Inst., Troy, NY, 1967—, assoc. prof., 1972-76, prof., 1976—, acting dept. chmn., 1974-75, vice provost plans and resources, 1975-78, dean grad. sch. and vice provost for acad. affairs, 1979-93, acting provost, 1982-83, 85, dean of faculty, 1993—??. Cons. Oak Ridge Nat. Labs., McGraw-Hill Ency. Sci. and Tech., Watervliet Arsenal, N.Y. State Edn. Dept., N.J. State Edn. Dept.; mem. Doctoral Coun. N.Y. State, 1982-97. Contbr. articles to profl. jours. Mem. bd. of edn. Hebrew Acad. of Capital Dist., 1974-79, 81-83; trustee Rensselaer at Hartford, 1996-98. Fellow ASM Internat.; mem. ASEE, Acad. of Mgmt., Microbeam Analysis Soc., Sigma Xi, Tau Beta Pi, Alpha Sigma Mu, Phi Lambda Upsilon. Jewish. Home: 3 Harding St Albany NY 12208-1601 Office: Rensselaer Poly Inst 110 8th St Troy NY 12180-3522

JUDD, WILLIAM ROBERT, engineering geologist, educator; b. Denver, Aug. 16, 1917; s. Samuel and Lillian (Israelske) J.; m. Rachel Elizabeth Douglas, Apr. 18, 1942; children: Stephanie (Mrs. Chris Wadley), Judith (Mrs. John Soden), Dayna (Mrs. Erick Grandmason), Pamela, Connie. AB, U. Colo., 1941, postgrad., 1941-50. Registered profl. engr., Colo., engring. geologist, Oreg. Engring. geologist Colo. Water Conservation Bd., 1941-42; supervisory engring. geologist Denver & Rio Grande Western R.R., Colo. and Utah, 1942-44; head geology sect. No. 1, acting dist. geologist-Alaska U.S. Bur. Reclamation, Office of Chief Engr., Denver, 1945-60; head basing tech. group RAND Corp., Santa Monica, Calif., 1960—66; prof. rock mechanics Purdue U., Lafayette, Ind., 1966-87, head geotech. engring., 1976-86; tech. dir. Purdue U. Underground Excavation and Rock Properties Info. Center, 1972-79, prof. emeritus civil engring., 1988—. Geotech. cons., U.S., Mexico, Cuba, Honduras, Greece, 1950— ; geoscience editor Am. Elsevier Pub. Co., 1967-71; chmn. panel on ocean scis. Com. on Instl. Cooperation, 1971-85; founder and chmn. Nat. Acad. Sci. U.S. Nat. Com. on Rock Mechanics, 1963-69, co-chmn. panel on rsch. requirements, 1977-81, chmn. panel on awards, 1972-82; mem. U.S. Army Adv. Bd. on Mountain and Arctic Warfare, 1956-62, USAF Sci. Adv. Bd. Geophysics Panel Study Group, 1964-67; com. on safety dams NRC, 1977-78, 82-83; Nat. dir. Nat. Ski Patrol System, Inc., 1956-62; Alex du Toit Meml. lectr., S.Africa and Rhodesia, 1967; owner Rayanbill Galleries, 1986—. Author: (with E.F. Taylor) Ski Patrol Manual, 1956, (with D. Krynine) Principles of Engineering Geology and Geotechnics, 1957, Sitzmarks or Safety, 1960; editor: Rock Mechanics Research, 1966, State of Stress in the Earth's Crust, 1964; co-editor: Physical Properties of Rocks and Minerals, 1981; editor-in-chief: Engring. Geology, 1972-92, hon. editor, 1996—. Recipient Spl. Rsch. award NRC, 1982; named to Colo. Ski Hall of Fame, 1983; named hon. life mem. Nat. Ski Patrol System, Inc., 1988. Fellow ASCE, Geol. Soc. Am. (Disting. Practice award engring. geology divsn. 1989), South African Inst. Mining and Metallurgy; mem. Assn. Engring. Geologists (hon.), Internat. Assn. Engring. Geologists (Hans Cloos medal 1994), Ind. Soc. Engring. Geology (life), Ind. Acad. Scis., U.S. Com. on Large Dams (exec. coun. 1977-83, com. on earthquakes 1976-90), U.S. Ski Assn. (hon. life), U.S. Recreational Ski Assn. (hon. life). Home and Office: 1051 Cumberland Ave West Lafayette IN 47906

JUDY, JANICE M. nurse, educator; b. North Platte, Nebr., Aug. 26, 1950; d. J. Garnet and Rosemary (Welsh) Walters; m. Leland S. Judy, Dec. 29, 1972; children: Allison, Brian, Kyle. Diploma, West Nebr. Sch. Nursing, 1972; BSN, Marshall U., 1981; MSN, U. Wyo., 1992. Staff nurse Perkins County Hosp., 1972, Berlin Army Hosp., 1973-75; charge nurse ICU-CCU Cabell Huntington (W.Va.) Hosp., 1975-80; staff nurse ICU-CCU Regional West Med. Ctr., Scottsbluff, 1980—81; instr. lic. practical nursing program West Nebr. Community Coll., Scottsbluff, 1980-84; instr. West Nebr. Sch. Nursing, Scottsbluff, 1984-88; instr. nursing Western divsn. U. Nebr., Scottsbluff, 1988—. Mem. ANA, Nebr. Nurses Assn. (dist. treas., membership chmn.), Sigma Theta Tau. Home: 1010 13th St Gering NE 69341-3254

JUEL, TWILA EILEEN, elementary education educator; b. Audubon, Iowa, Feb. 8, 1948; d. Niels Christian and Norma Eileen (Wahlert) J. BE, Dana Coll., Blair, Nebr., 1970; MEd, U. Nebr. Omaha, 1975. Cert. tchr., Nebr. Tchr. Millard Pub. Schs., Omaha, 1970—2003; ret., 2003. Mem. NEA, Nebr. Edn. Assn., Millard Edn. Assn., Phi Delta Kappa. Democratic. Lutheran. Home: 16146 Arbor Ct Omaha NE 68130-1736

JUETTNER, DIANA D'AMICO, lawyer, educator; b. N.Y.C., Jan. 21, 1940; d. Paris T.R. and Dina Adele (Antonucci) D'Amico; m. Paul J. Juettner, June 29, 1963; children: John, Laura. BA, Hunter Coll., 1961; postgrad., Am. U., 1963; JD cum laude, Touro Coll., 1983. Bar: N.Y. 1984, U.S. Dist. Ct. (so. dist.) N.Y. 1984, U.S. Supreme Ct. 1987. Office mgr. Westchester County Dem. Com., White Plains, NY, 1976-79; dist. mgr. for Westchester County U.S. Bur. Census, N.Y.C., 1979-80; pvt. practice Ardsley, NY, 1984—; prof. law, program dir. for legal studies Mercy Coll., Dobbs Ferry, NY, 1985—, co-chair social and behavioral scis. divsn., 2002—, asst. chair dept. law, criminal justice-safety adminstrn., 1994-98, pres. faculty senate, 1996—98, 2000—02. Arbitrator small claims matters White Plains City Ct., 1985-89. Co-author: (booklet) Your Day in Court, How to File a Small Claims Suit in Westchester County, 1976; assoc. editor N.Y. State Probation Officers Assn. Jour., 1990-92; editor-in-chief Jour. Northeast Acad. Legal Studies in Bus., 1996-98; contbr. articles to profl. jours. Councilwoman Town of Greenburgh, N.Y., 1992—; vice chair law com. Westchester County Dem. Com., White Plains, 1987-91; corr. sec. Greenburgh Dem. Town Com., Hartsdale, N.Y., 1986-91; mem. Westchester County Citizens Consumer Adv. Coun., White Plains, 1975-91, chair, 1991; chair Ardsley (N.Y.) Consumer Adv. Commn., 1974-79. Mem. Am. Assn. for Paralegal Edn. (model syllabus task force 1992-95, chair legis. com. 1995-97), N.Y. State Bar Assn. (elder law sect. com. on pub. agy. liaison and legis. 1992-95), Westchester County Bar Assn. (chair paralegal subcom. 1990—, chair bicentennial U.S. Constitution com. 1987-91), Westchester Women's Bar Assn. (v.p. 1989-91, dir. 1994-96, co-chair tech. com. 1996-2000), Women's Bar Assn. State N.Y. (chair profl. ethics com. 1997-98). Avocations: sailing, walking. Office: Mercy Coll 555 Broadway Dobbs Ferry NY 10522-1134 Business E-Mail: djuettner@mercy.edu.

JUGENHEIMER, DONALD WAYNE, advertising and communications educator, university administrator; b. Manhattan, Kans., Sept. 22, 1943; s. Robert William and Mabel Clara (Hobert) J.; m. Bonnie Jeanne Scamehorn, Aug. 30, 1970 (dec. 1983); 1 child, Beth Carrie; m. Kaleen B. Brown, July 25, 1987. BS in Advt., U. Ill.-Urbana, 1965, MS in Advt., 1968, PhD in Communications, 1972. Advt. copywriter Fillman & Assocs, Champaign, Ill., 1963-64, 66; media buyer Leo Burnett Co., Chgo., 1965-66; asst., assoc. prof. U. Kans., Lawrence, 1971-80, prof. journalism, dir. grad. studies and rsch., 1980-85; Manship prof. journalism La. State U., Baton Rouge, 1985-87; prof., chmn. dept. communications and speech Fairleigh Dickinson U., Teaneck, N.J., 1987-89, 92-95, dean coll. liberal arts, 1989-92; chair dept. English, lang. and philosphy, 1995; prof. Sch. Journalism So. Ill. U., Carbondale, 1995—. Dir. Sch. Journalism So. Ill. U., Carbondale, 1995-2002; adj. faculty Turku (Finland) Sch. Econs., 1999—; adv. cons. U.S. Army, Fort Sheridan, Ill., Pentagon, Washington, 1981-90, Am. Airlines, 1989-91, IBM Corp., 1989—, U.S. Dept. Def.; cons. editor Grid Publ., Columbus, Ohio, 1974-84; grad. and rsch. dir. U. Kans., 1978-84, adv. chmn., 1974-78; adj. prof. Turku (Finland) Sch. Econs. and Bus. Adminstrn., 1998—. Author: Advertising Media Sourcebook and Workbook, 1975, 3d edit., 1989, 4th edit. 1996, Strategic Advertising Decisions, 1976, Basic Advertising, 1979, 2d edit., 1991, Advertising Media, 1980, Problems and Practices in Advertising Research, 1982, Advertising Media: Strategy and Tactics, 1992, Advertising Media Planning: A Brand Management Approach, 2003; bd. editors Jour. Advt., 1985-89, Jour. Interactive Advt., 2000—, Jour. Current Issues and Rsch. in Advt., 1990—. Advvertising Needs Planning: A Broad Management Approach, 2003. Subscription mgr. Jour. of Advt., 1971-74, bus. mgr., 1974-79; chmn. U. Div. United Fund, Lawrence, 1971-72; pres. Sch.-Cmty. Rels. Coun., Lawrence, 1974-75. Recipient Hope Tchg. award U. Kans, 1977, 78, Kellogg Nat. fellow W.K. Kellogg Found., 1984-88; named Outstanding Young Men in Am. Nat. Jaycees, 1978. Mem. AAUP, Am. Acad. Advt. (pres. 1984-86), Assn. For Edn. in Journalism (head advt. divsn. 1977-78), Kappa Tau Alpha, Alpha Delta Sigma. Presbyterian. Avocations: skiing; sailing; writing; travel; reading. Home: 110 Tecumseh Dr Carbondale IL 62901-7113 Office: So Ill U Sch Journalism Carbondale IL 62901-6601

JUHLIN, DORIS ARLENE, French language educator; b. Atlanta, Dec. 1, 1942; d. Lawrence Alfred and Doris (South) J. BA, Greenville (Ill.) Coll., 1964; MA, Baldwin-Wallace Coll., 1979. Cert. elem. and secondary French and reading tchr., Ohio. Tchr. French Cleve. Bd. Edn., 1965—. Chmn. bldg. activities Cleve. Pub. Schs., 1983-93, writer French curriculum, 1980, Acad. Challenge, Cleve., 1995; workshop presenter Ohio Modern Lang. Tchrs. Assn., Columbus, Ohio, 1978; fgn. lang. cons. WV12-TV (PBS), Cleveland, Ohio, 198 0; contbr. CP's Fgn. Lang. Exploratory Program, 1995-96. Cons. and tchr.: Exploring Languages video series, Cleve. Pub. Schs., 1994-95. Dir. jump for heart sch. program Am. Heart Assn., 1986-90; v.p. Womens Ministries Internat.; speaker, editor ann. program resource books Free Meth. Ch., Indpls., 1985-95; sec. Free Meth. Ohio Conf. Bd. Camping Dirs., Mansfield, Ohio, 1990-94; organist, Sunday Sch. tchr. Free Meth. Ch., Westlake, Ohio, 1964—; vol. Nat. Welsh Home for Aged, Rocky River, Ohio, 1970—; mem. task force Edn. 2000, 1992-93. Jennings scholar Martha Holden Jennings Found., 1980. Mem. Ohio Fgn. Lang. Assn., Cleve. Tchrs. Union, Nat. Audubon Soc., MENSA (gifted child coord. 1985-94, columnist Graffiti 1986-94. Democrat. Avocations: reading, walking, piano. Home: 3745 W 213th St Cleveland OH 44126-1216 Office: Wilbur Wright Mid Sch 11005 Parkhurst Dr Cleveland OH 44111-3601

JULIAN, ROSE RICH, music educator, director; b. Asheboro, N.C., Sept. 9, 1937; d. Herbert C. and Esther Dennis Rich; m. Cecil Perry Julian, May 30, 1959 (div. Apr. 1977); children: Alan Perry, Keri Dawn Julian Sorensen, Derrick Kyle. AA in Voice, Mars Hill Coll., 1957; BS in Music, East Carolina U., 1959; postgrad., U N.C., 1971—79, Western Carolina U., 1995. Cert. music tchr. N.C. Dir. music USAF Chapel Choir, 1960—71; tchr. Rowan/Salisbury (N.C.) Schs., 1972—79, 1988—; dir. music Thyatira Pres Ch., Salisbury, 1982—88, Coburn U. N.C., Salisbury, 1991—97. Conductor Salisbury Choral Soc., 1993; pianist 1st Bapt. Ch., Salisbury, 1999—; judge Protestant Chapels of Europe, Frankfurt, Germany, 1970. Mem.: AOSA, NAE, Nat. Assn. Tchrs. Singing, Music Educators Assn., Piano Guild. Baptist. Home: 36 Old Farm Rd Salisbury NC 28147

JULIEN, CATHERINE, history educator; BA in Anthropology, U. Calif., Berkeley, 1971, MA in Anthropology, 1975, PhD in Philosophy, 1978. Dir. mus. programs Courthouse Mus., Merced, Calif.; lectr. and internat. study tour leader Smithsonian's Am. Mus. Natural History and Calif. Alumni Assn.; instr. Calif. State U., U. Bonn (Germany), U. Calif., Berkeley; assoc. prof. history We. Mich. U., Kalamazoo, 1996—. Author: Reading Inca History (Erminie Wheeler-Voegelin prize, 2000, Katherine Singer Kovacs prize MLA). Fellow, John Simon Guggenheim Meml. Found., 2003. Office: We Mich U Office Univ Rels 1903 W Michigan Ave Kalamazoo MI 49008-5433*

JUNG, BETTY CHIN, epidemiologist, research analyst, educator, medical/surgical nurse; b. Bklyn., Nov. 28, 1948; d. Han You and Bo Ngan (Moy) C.; m. Lee Jung, Oct. 1, 1972; children: Daniel, Stephanie. AA, King's Coll., 1968; BS, Columbia U., 1971; MPH, So. Conn. State U., 1993. RN, Conn., Miss., N.Y.; cert. health edn. specialist. Adminstrv. asst. Columbia U., N.Y.C., 1968-69; practical nurse Babies Hosp., N.Y.C., 1969-70, charge nurse, 1974-76; staff nurse Columbia-Presbyn. Hosp., N.Y.C., 1971-73; sch. nurse Nassau County Sch. System, Long Island, N.Y., 1984-85; grad. asst. So. Conn. State U., New Haven, 1991-92; coop. edn. intern Conn. Dept. Health Svcs., Hartford, 1991-92; intern North Ctrl. Dist. Health Dept., Enfield, Conn., 1992; epidemiologist Conn. Dept. Pub. Health, Hartford, Conn., 1992-98, health program assoc., 1998-2001, cardiovascular health epidemiologist, 2003—; staff nurse Quinnipiac Coll. Student Health Svcs., 1998; mem. multicultural adv. coun. Conn. Dept. Children and Families, assoc. rsch. analyst, 2001—03. Health promotion cons. dept. pub. health So. Conn. State U., New Haven, 1991, mem. adv. coun. dept. pub. health, 1999—, lectr., adj. faculty, 1998—, tchg. asst., 1992, curriculum developer, 92, vol. rsch. analyst, 93, founder grad. alumni mentor program, 1993—94, mem. adv. coun., 1997—, webmaster E-comm. web site, 2000—, univ. asst. webmaster, 2001—; instr. Albertus Magnus Coll., 1995—96; computer cons., course dir. contg. edn. program dept. pub. health So. Conn. State U., 1998—; health columnist Baldwin Newcomers Club, NY, 1977—78; coord. Dept. Pub. Health and Svcs./Conn. EPI Info. Network, Hartford, 1994—2001; mem. Nat. Lead Info. Ctr. Spkrs. Bur., 1997—98; vol. scientist Sci.-By-Mail, 1997—98; mem. Nat. Safety Coun. Environ. Health Ctr. Spkrs. Referral Bur., 1998—2001; apptd. mem. Conn. Dept. Pub. Health's Affirmative Action Employee Adv. Com., 1998—2001; mem. permanent commn. Status of Women, 1996—, chair news subcom., editor affirmative action newsletter, 2001; apptd. mem. multicultural adv. coun. Conn. Dept. Children and Families, 2002—03; cons. medicine policy Anthem, 2003; supercourse lectr. U. Pitts., 1999—; pilot reviewer CDC Pub. Health Tng. Network, 2002—. Mem. editl. bd.: Data Quality, 1994—98, mem. manuscript rev. bd.: Jour. Clin. Outcomes Mgmt., 1995—, Pub. Health Reports, 1997—98, Women's Health in Primary Care, 1998—; contbg. editor: Episource, A Guide to Resources in Epidemiology, 1998—99; editor/web pub.: SCSU Pub. Health E-News Bull., 2000—01, Public Health E-news, 2001—, Public Health Jobs Electronic Newsletter, 2000—, pilot reviewer: Ctr. for Disease Control, 2003—; contbr. articles to profl. jours. Vol. nurse health educator, coord. Chinatown's First Ann. Health Fair, 1971-72; treas. Tenant Assn., Bronx, N.Y., 1976-77; pre-confirmation tchr. Bethlehem Luth. Ch., Baldwin, N.Y., 1981-85. Recipient cardiovascular health grant, CDC, 2003—; grantee, USPHS, 1992—98, Fed. HUD, 1995—98, U.S. Preventive Health and Health Svcs., 1998, block grant, Maternal Child Health, 1998—2001; scholar Merit, Kings Coll., 1968, Columbia U., 1968—69, Women's Florist Assn., 1968, Bessie Lee Gambrill scholar, So. Alumni Assn., 1992. Fellow: Soc. for Pub. Health Edn.; mem.: Pub. Health Expertise Network of Mentors (program dir. 2002—), Internat. Assn. Webmasters and Designers, Boston Mus. Sci., Nat. Acad. Sci. (mentor career planning ctr. beginning scientists & engrs. 1997—98), Columbia U. Sch. Nursing Alumni Assn. (survey cons. 1994—95), Conn. Women in Healthcare Mgmt., Inc., So. Conn. State U. Alumni Assn. (founder pub. health chpt. 1994, interim pres, then pres. 1994—98, founder, coord. pub. health alumni mentor program 1994—2002, chair coms. 1994—, numerous other positions 1994—, editor MPH Alumni Record 1995—, founder, dir., coord. pub. health alumni spkrs. bur. 1997—, founder, program dir. pub. health expertise network of mentors 2002—, Alumni Appreciation award 1998), Internat. Assn. IT Trainers (assoc.), Conn. Pub. Health Assn., Nat. Lead Info. Ctr. Spkrs. Bur., Conn. State and Territorial Epidemiologists (alternate cons. 1996—, co-leader Healthy People 2010 1999—2001, lead diabetes 2002—, lead cardiovasc. disease 2002—), Am. Statis. Assn. (OSPA media experts list 1997—), Am. Med. Writers Assn., APHA (health care reform activist network, peer assistance the model stds. project). Avocations: reading, writing, research, web development and design, bicycling. Home: 25 Driftwood Ln Guilford CT 06437-1929 Office: Conn Dept Pub Health 410 Capitol Ave Hartford CT 06106

JUNG, DAVID JOSEPH, law educator; b. St. Louis, Aug. 19, 1953; s. Joseph Henry and Leona Louise Jung; m. Jennifer Beryl Hammett, Oct. 15, 1951; children: David O'Grady Hammett, Brennan Joseph Hammett. BA, Harvard U., 1975; JD, U Calif., Berkeley, 1980. Lectr. in law U. Calif., Berkeley, 1980-82, from asst prof. to assoc. prof. Hastings Coll. Law San Francisco, 1982-88, prof., 1988—. Vis. prof. U. Hamburg, Germany, 1992, U. Iowa, Iowa City, 1993—; dir. Pub. Law Rsch. Inst., 1994—. Co-author: Remedies: Public and Private, 2d edit., 1996; contbr. articles to profl. jours. Bd. dirs. San Francisco Neighborhood Legal Aid, 1983, North of Market Child Car Ctr., 1984-86; sec. El Cerrito Youth Baseball, 1997-99, pres., 1999-2000. Recipient U.S. Law Week award U.S. Law Week, 1980, 1066 Found. award 1066 Found., 1986. Mem. Am. Assn. Law Schs. (remedies section, exec. com. 1991-92). Office: U Calif Hastings Coll Law 200 Mcallister St San Francisco CA 94102-4707

JUNGE, CHERYL MARIE, elementary education educator; b. Great Falls, Mont., Mar. 25, 1961; d. Raymond Lawrence and Elizabeth Gertrude Seerup; m. William Gordon Junge, Aug. 16, 1986; children: Rebecca Ann, Katherine Elizabeth, Bryan Christopher. BS in Elem. & Spl. Edn. with honors, Ea. Mont. Coll., 1986. Cert. tchr., Wyo., Mont. Tchr. Great Falls (Mont) Pub. Schs., 19861-91, Natrona County Schs., Casper, Wyo, 1991-92, tchr., work study coord., 1992—. Cosn. Mont. Sch. for Deaf and Blind, Great Falls, 1990. Recipient Cert. of Appreciation Indian Edn. Program, 1989, Spl. Educator's award Spl. Edn. Adv. Bd., 1993. Mem. ASCD, Wyo. Assn. for Persons in Supported Employment, Nat. Assn. Vocat. Edn. Spl. Needs Pers., Coun. for Exceptional Children (Profl. Recognition Spl. Educator 2000), Phi Detla Kappa. Republican. Roman Catholic. Avocations: dancing, sewing, crafts. Home: 1150 Donegal St Casper WY 82609-3217 Office: Natrona County Schs Kelly Walsh HS 3500 E 12th St Casper WY 82609-1827 E-mail: cheryl_junge@ncsd.k12.wy.us.

JURASEK, JOHN PAUL, mathematics educator, counselor; b. Flushing, NY, June 23, 1959; s. John Steven and Eleanor Rita Jurasek; m. Gale Marie Abrahamsen, May 22, 1993; 1 child, John IV. BS, Fairleigh Dickinson U., 1982; BA, SUNY, New Paltz, 1991; MS, Iona Coll., 1995. Cert. pub. sch. math. tchr., N.Y., N.J. Acct. Sony Corp., Park Ridge, N.J., 1982-85; learning ctr. coord. Rockland C.C., Suffern, NY, 1985-91; math. instr. Collegiate Sch., Passaic, N.J., 1991-92, Ridgefield Park (N.J.) Schs., 1992—99, Cresskill (NJ) Schs., 2000—. Map chair NY/NJ Trail Conf. Contbr. articles to profl. jours. Mem. Town Dem. Com., Piermont, N.Y., 1980. Recipient Above and Beyond award RAMAQUOIS, Pomona, 1990, Counselor of Yr. award 1990. Mem. Internat. Soc. Technology in Edn., Math. Assn. Am., Nat. Coun. Tchrs. Math., N.J. Edn. Assn., Northvale Rifle and Pistol Club, Am. Mensa, Brit. Mensa, Appalachian Mountain Club. Democrat. Roman Catholic. Avocations: model rocketry, target shooting, computer programming, hiking. Home: 193 Howard Ave Orangeburg NY 10962-2314 Office: Cresskill Schs 1 Lincoln Dr Cresskill NJ 07626 E-mail: jurasek@optonline.net.

JURDAK, MURAD EID, mathematics educator; b. Marj'ayoun, Lebanon, June 8, 1943; s. Eid Hannoush and Nahia Farha J.; m. Muna Mitri Shami Jurdak, Sept. 13, 1970; children: Hania, Raja. BS in Math., Am. U. Beirut, 1966, MS in Math., 1968; PhD in Math. Edn., U. Wis., 1973. Asst. tchr., tng. specialist UNRWA/UNESCO Inst. Edn., Beirut, 1968-71; asst. prof. Am. U. Beirut, 1973-79, assoc. prof., 1979-85, prof., 1986—. Dept. chmn., ctr. dir., div. dir., Am. U. Beirut, 1979-82, 83-86, 86—; cons. UNESCO, World Bank, govts. Middle East. Author chpts. to books, sci. papers; contbr. articles to profl. jours.; editor math. textbook series. Mem. Internat. Group for Psychol. of Math Edn., ASCD. Avocations: swimming, walking, music, cinema, reading. Office: Am Univ Beirut PO Box 236 Beirut Lebanon

JUREWICZ, JOHN THOMAS, university dean, engineer; b. Wilkes-Barre, Pa., Mar. 16, 1945; s. Benjamin Urevitch and Sophia (Blotski) J.; m. Kathleen C. Vander Heyden, June 10, 1978; 1 child, Joseph; stepchildren: Stephen Unmuth, Elizabeth Unmuth. BA in Math., King's Coll., 1968; BS in Aero, Engring., Pa. State U., 1968; MS in Mech. Engring., Wash. State U., 1973, PhD in Engring. Sci., 1976. Rsch. engr. Pratt & Whitney Aircraft, E. Hartford, Conn., W. Palm Beach, Fla., 1968-70; tchr. Bishop Hoban H.S., Wilkes-Barre, Pa., 1970-71; asst. prof. Inst. Paper Chemistry, Appleton, Wis., 1976-78, W. Va. U., Morgantown, 1978-79, from asst. prof. to prof., 1981-86, assoc. dean of engring., 1986-91, interim dean of engring., 1991-92; rsch. engr. Kimberly Clark Corp., Neenah, Wis., 1979-81; dean of grad. studies and rsch. Fla. Atlantic U., Boca Raton, Fla., 1993—, acting dean of engring., 1996—. Dir. W. Va. Space Grant Consortium, Morgantown, 1989-91; bd. dirs. W. Va. Rsch. Corp., 1989-92, Fla. Atlantic Univ. Rsch. and Devel. Authority, Boca Raton, 1994-97; pres. Fla. Atlantic Rsch. Corp., Boca Raton, 1993-97. Editor (4 books) Gas-Solid Flows, 1986-91; assoc. editor ASME Jour. of Fluids Engring., 1984-86; contbr. articles to 10 profl. jours. Home: 2712 NW 27th Ter Boca Raton FL 33434-6001 Office: Fla Atlantic U 777 Glades Rd Boca Raton FL 33431-6424

JURGEVICH, NANCY J. retail executive, educator; b. Stoystown, Pa., July 20, 1940; d. Peter and Ruth Leone (Kimmel) J. BBA, George Washington U., Washington, 1973; MGT, U.S. Army Command & Gen. Staff Coll., Ft. Leavenworth, Kans., 1976; MS, U. Utah, 1977; postgrad., Cath. U., Washington, D.C., 1981. Enlisted U.S. Army, 1958, advanced through grades to lt. col., 1984; ret., 1984; adj. prof. Embry Riddle Aero. U., Daytona Beach, Fla., Brevard Community Coll., Cocoa Beach, Fla.; mgr. PO Depot, Inc., Palm Bay, Fla. Author: Development of Business Plan, Psychological Effects of Erosion of Military Benefits, Leadership Principals in the Bible. Decorated Legion of Merit, Bronze Star; recipient Western Union award for Increase in Sales. Home: PO Box 100077 Palm Bay FL 32910-0077

JURICIC, DAVOR, mechanical engineering educator; b. Split, Croatia, Aug. 2, 1928; came to U.S., 1968; s. Mate and Slavka (Franceschi) J.; m. Milesa L. Harris, Mar. 10, 1984; 1 child, Ivanna Albertin. Dipl.Ing., U. Belgrade, Yugoslavia, 1952, DSc, 1964. Stress analyst Icarus Aircraft Industries, Zemun, Yugoslavia, 1953-58; rsch. engr. Inst. Aeronautics, Belgrade, 1958-63; asst. prof. U. Belgrade, 1963-65, assoc. prof., 1965-68, S.D. State U., Brookings, 1968-73, prof., 1973-75; vis. prof. Stanford (Calif.) U., 1975-78; prof. mech. engring. U. Tex., Austin, 1978-98, prof. emeritus, 1998—. Contbr. numerous articles to profl. jours. Rsch. grantee various agencies, 1962—. Mem. ASME, Am. Soc. Engring. Edn. (Chester F. Carlson award 1993), Sigma Xi. Achievements include research in suspension system for railway vehicles (patent). E-mail: juricic@mail.utexas.edu.

JURKAT, MARTIN PETER, mathematician, statistician, management educator; b. Berlin, July 23, 1935; came to U.S., 1946, naturalized, 1951; s. Ernest Herman and Dorothy (Bergas) J.; m. Mayme Porter, May 31, 1958; children: Martin Alexander, Susanna, Maria. BA in Math. and Stats. with honors, Swarthmore (Pa.) Coll., 1957; MA, U. N.C., 1961; PhD, Stevens Inst. Tech., Hoboken, N.J., 1972. Programmer Burroughs Corp. Research Lab., Paoli, Pa., 1960-61; sr. program analyst ITT Corp., Paramus, N.J., 1961-64; dir. Center Mcpl. Studies and Services Stevens Inst. Tech., 1975-77, chief transp. analysis div. Davidson Lab., 1964-75, Alexander Crombie Humphreys prof. mgmt. sci., 1979—2001. Cons. Tank-Automotive Devel. Command, U.S. Army, 1975-88, AT&T, 1995-2001, Lucent, 1996-2001; dir. Cause project NSF, 1978-81. Co-author: The NATO Reference Mobility Model, 1980; author studies, reports on mobility, transp., human factors, math. edn. Mem. Assn. Computing Machinery. Democrat. Mem. Soc. Of Friends. Home and Office: 2822 Don Quixote Santa Fe NM 87505 E-mail: mpeterj@comcast.net.

JURKIEWICZ, MARGARET JOY GOMMEL, secondary education educator; b. Indpls., Sept. 5, 1920; d. Dewey Ezra and Joy Agnes (Edie) Gommel; m. Walter Stephen Jurkiewicz, Jan. 1, 1942; children: Mary Margaret, Dewey John, Walter Stephen Jr., Hugh Louis. BS, Ind. U., 1941; postgrad., U. Minn., 1942-43, Butler U., 1950-51, U. Cin., 1958-60, Ind. U., 1971-72, Ball State U., 1974-75. Cert. secondary tchr., Ind., Ohio. Tchr. home econ. Plymouth HS, Ind., 1941-42, Indpls. Pub. Sch., Ind., 1949-57, Mt. Confort-Hancock Co. Sch., Mt. Comfort, Ind., 1957-58, Cin. Pub. sch., 1958-61; tchr. 6th grade Plymouth Sch. corp., Ind., 1961-63; tchr. home econ. and art Argos Cmty. Sch., Ind., 1963-67; tchr. home econ. Penn-Harris-Madison Sch., Mishawaka, Ind., 1967-83; tchr. chpt. I South Bend Sch. Corp., Ind., 1983-85; vol. tchr. art various sch., Ind., 1985—, various sch., Mich., 1985—96, various sch., Ill., 1985-96. Author newsletter and booklet Polish Cultural Soc., 1979—. Bd. dir. Area Agy. on Aging Coun., Plymouth, Ind., 1987-94, Garden Cts. Sr. Housing, Plymouth, 1989—; mem. legis. com. Five County Area Agy. on Aging, 1994—; vol. tchr. sch., libr., children's mus. and sr. ctr., 1985—. Mem.: AARP (editor newsletter Marshall County chpt. 1993—), AAUW (pres., chair various coms.), Plymouth Pub. Libr. Friends (pres., chair various coms.), Marshall County Ret. Tchr. (pres. 1993—95), Ind. Assn. Family and Consumer Sci., Am. Assn. Family and Consumer Sci., PEO, Tippecanoe Audubon Soc., Ind. Polish Cultural Soc. (v.p., chair various coms.). Methodist. Avocations: gardening, camping, travel, football games, sewing. Home: 11570 9th A Rd Plymouth IN 46563-9581 E-mail: mjjurkiewicz@yahoo.com.

JUSTESON, JOHN S. anthropologist, educator; PhD, Stanford U., 1978, MS in Computer Sci., 1988. Prof. anthropology SUNY, Albany, 1990—. Contbr. articles to profl. jours. Fellow, John Simon Guggenheim Meml. Found., 2003. Office: SUNY Dept Anthropology Rm 237 1400 Washington Ave Albany NY 12222*

JUSTIZ, MANUEL JON, education educator, researcher; b. Havana, Cuba, Dec. 26, 1948; came to U.S., 1961; s. Manuel L. and Elena (Odriasola) Justiz. BA, Emporia State U., 1970, MS, 1972; PhD, So. Ill. U., 1976; HHD (hon.), St. Leo's Coll., 1983; LLD, Tex. Southmost Coll., 1983; LittD. (hon.), Emporia State U., 1985. Assoc. dir. Latin Am. programs in edn. U. N.Mex., Albuquerque, 1978-79, dir. Latin Am. programs, 1979-82; dir. Nat. Inst. Edn. U.S. Dept. Edn., Washington, 1982-85, spl. cons. to sec. of edn., 1985; prof. edn. U. S.C., Columbia, 1985—, chaired prof. edn., 1986—; dean Coll. of Edn. U. Tex., Austin, 1990—. Mem. governing bd. Office of Econ. and Devel., Ctr. for Ednl. Rsch. in Improvement, Paris, 1984-85; A.M. Aikin Regents chair Edn. Leadership, 1990—, Lee Hage Jamail Regents chair in edn., 1997—. Mem. editorial adv. bd. Educational Record, Am. Coun. Edn., 1985-97. Bd. dirs. All Faiths Receiving Home, Albuquerque, 1980-82, Albuquerque Opera, 1981-82, Albuquerque Libr., 1982, Am. Coun. of End., 1992-93, mem. Commn. on Innovation Calif. Cmty. Coll., 1992-95, mem. exec. com. Edn. Commn. of the States, Denver, 1990-95, commn. rep. State of Tex Edn. Commn. of States, Denver. Avocations: bicycling, running, swimming. Office: SZB 210 Austin TX 78712 Home: 1 University Station D5000 Austin TX 78712-4525

JUSTUS, CAROL FAITH, linguistics educator; b. Lodi, Ohio, Mar. 21, 1940; d. Ernest and Esther Mary (Cockrell) J.; m. Rahim Raman; div. 1976. BA in French, King Coll., 1960; MA in Linguistics, U. Minn., 1966; PhD in Linguistics, U. Tex., 1973. Assoc. prof., asst. prof., linguistics coord. SUNY, Oswego, 1973-77; asst. prof. U. Calif., Berkeley, 1977-82; rsch. assoc. U. Tex., Austin, 1982-84; tech. staff Microelectronics & Computer Tech. Corp., Austin, 1984-88; rsch. fellow U. Tex., 1988-89; assoc. prof. San Jose (Calif.) State U., 1989-94, linguistics coord., 1989-93; sr. rsch. fellow U. Tex., 1994—; adj. assoc. prof. Ctr. for Mid. Eastern Studies and Classics, 1995—. Rev. editor Diachronica, 1988—91; editor: Gen. Linguistics, 1999—; mem. editl. bd. Jour. Indo-European Studies, North-Western European Language Evolution: Odense, NOWELE; contbr. articles to profl. jours. and encys. NEH grantee, 1976. Mem.: MLA (divsn. chair 1979, 1981, 1984, 1987, del. 1991—93), Am. Oriental Soc., Linguistic Soc. Am. (Inst. dir. 1976). Avocations: swimming, walking. Home: 306 W 35th St Austin TX 78705-1412 E-mail: cjustus@mail.utexas.edu.

JUSZCZAK, NICHOLAS MAURO, psychology educator; b. Chorely, Lancashire, Eng., May 19, 1955; came to U.S. 1956; s. Adam and Augusta (Lugnan); 1 child, Amanda; m. Margie Nina Malkin, Oct. 9, 1988; children: Kimberly, Melissa, Nina, Nicole. BA cum laude, Baruch Coll., N.Y.C., 1980; MS, Hunter Coll., N.Y.C., 1984. Rschr. psychophysiology lab Baruch Coll., N.Y.C., 1980-88, instr. psychology, 1984—. Cons. statistics BOE/CUNY Student Mentor Program, 1987-91; creator, pres. world wide web Homeroom Dot Net, 1997—. Contbr. articles to profl. jours. Cons. Office of Instructional Tech., N.Y. State Bd. Edn., 1999—. Mem. N.Y. Acad. Sci. Home: 26 Spiral Ln Levittown NY 11756 E-mail: nmj@homeroom.net.

JUVET, RICHARD SPALDING, JR., chemistry educator; b. L.A., Aug. 8, 1930; s. Richard Spalding and Marion Elizabeth (Dalton) J.; m. Martha Joy Myers, Jan. 29, 1955 (div. Nov. 1978); children: Victoria, David, Stephen, Richard P.; m. Evelyn Raeburn Elthon, July 1, 1984. BS, UCLA, 1952, PhD, 1955. Research chemist Dupont, 1955; instr. U. Ill., 1955-57, asst. prof., 1957-61, assoc. prof., 1961-70; prof. analytical chemistry Ariz. State U., Tempe, 1970-95, prof. emeritus, 1995—. Vis. prof. UCLA, 1960, U. Cambridge, Eng., 1964-65, Nat. Taiwan U., 1968, Ecole Polytechnique, France, 1976-77, U. Vienna, Austria, 1989-90; air pollution chemistry and physics adv. com. EPA, HEW, 1969-72; adv. panel on advanced chem. alarm tech., devel. and engring. directorate, def. sys. divsn. Edgewood Arsenal, 1975; adv. panel on postdoctoral associateships NAS-NRC, 1991-94; mem. George C. Marshall Inst., 1998—. Author: Gas-Liquid Chromatography, Theory and Practice, 1962, Russian edit., 1966; editl. advisor Jour. Chromatographic Sci., 1969-85, Jour. Gas Chromatography, 1963-68, Analytica Chimica Acta, 1972-74, Analytical Chemistry, 1974-77; biennial reviewer for gas chromatography lit. Analytical Chemistry, 1962-76. Deacon Presbyn. Ch., 1960—, ruling elder, 1972—, commr. Grand Canyon Presbytery, 1974-76; moderator, communion com. Valley Presbyn. Ch., Scottsdale, Ariz., 1999-2001. NSF sr. postdoctoral fellow, 1964-65; recipient Sci. Exch. Agreement award to Czechoslovakia, Hungary, Romania and Yugoslavia, 1977. Fellow Am. Inst. Chemists; mem. AAAS, Am. Chem. Soc. (nat. chmn. divsn. analytical chemistry 1972-73, nat. sec.-treas. 1969-71, divsn. com. on chem. edn., subcom. on grad. edn. 1988—, councilor 1978-89, coun. com. analytical reagents 1985-95, co-author Reagent Chemicals, 7th edit. 1986, 8th edit. 1993, 9th edit. 2000, chmn. U. Ill. sect. 1968-69, sec. 1962-63, directorate divsn. officers' caucus 1987-90), Internat. Union Pure and Applied Chemistry, Internat. Platform Assn., Am. Radio Relay League (Amateur-Extra lic.), Sigma Xi, Phi Lambda Upsilon, Alpha Chi Sigma (faculty adv. U. Ill. 1958-64, Ariz. State U. 1975-95, profl. rep.-at-large 1989-94, chmn. expansion com. 1990-92, nat. v.p. grand collegiate alchemist 1994-96, trustee ednl. found. 1994—). Achievements include rsch. on gas and liquid chromatography, instrumental analysis, computer interfacing, plasma desorption mass spectroscopy. Home: 4821 E Calle Tuberia Phoenix AZ 85018-2932 Office: Ariz State U Dept Chem and Biochem Tempe AZ 85287-1604 E-mail: rsjuvet@juno.com.

KAAS, JON H. psychology educator; BA, Northland Coll., 1959; PhD, Duke U., 1965. With Vanderbilt U., 1973—, now Centennial prof. psychology. Office: Vanderbilt U Dept of Psychology 301 Wilson Hl Nashville TN 37240-0001

KABACINSKI, STANLEY JOSEPH, health and physical education educator, consultant, speaker; b. Duryea, Pa., May 23, 1949; s. Bernard Merlyn and Anna (Polaski) K.; m. Mary Claire Finnerty, June 26, 1971; children: Ryan Michael, Michael Joseph. BS in Health, Phys. Edn. and Dance, East Stroudsburg State Coll., 1971, MEd in Health, Phys. Edn. and Dance, 1975; postgrad., Millersville U., 1981. Tchr., coach basketball, softball, soccer, volleyball Washington (N.J.) Boro Elem., 1971-78; asst. football coach, head coach offense, scouting coord. East Stroudsburg (Pa.) State Coll., 1971-78, cooperating tchr. for student tchrs., 1974-78; asst. prof. Millersville (Pa.) U., 1978—, offensive coord., adminstrv. asst., recruiting coord., strength coach, 1978-88, coord., minor in athletic coaching, 1989—, grad. program coord. MEd in sport mgmt., 1999—, chair health and phys. edn. dept., 1999—. Chair dept. health and phys. edn.; cons. Sch. Dist. of Lancaster, 1991—, Clarion (Pa.) U., 1991—, Gov's. Coun. on Phys. Fitness and Sports, Harrisburg, Pa., 1991—, East Stroudsburg U., 1994—, Mansfield U., 1998—; rschr. U.S. Mil. Acad. Performance Enhancement Ctr., West Point, N.Y., 1989, Am. Coaching Effectiveness Program and Coaching Minor Nat. Survey, Millersville, 1989; motivational cons., 1991—; ASEP instr. coaching principles, sport 1st aid, sport psychology; clinician various tng. programs and spkr. in field; also TV appearances. Dir., asst. activities in field Warren County Elem., Washington, N.J., Willow St. (Pa.) Elem., Ch. of Apostles Pre-Sch., Rohrerstown, Pa., Hans Herr Elem., Lampeter, Pa., Willow St. Family Festival, Fulton Elem. Sch., Lancaster, Pa.; head coach, cons. Willow St. Youth Baseball, 1987-91; cons. Willow St. PTO, 1983-87; coord. Elks Hoop Shoot, Washington, N.J., 1971-78. Mem. AAHPERD, Am. Football Coaches Assn., Pa. State Assn. Health, Phys. Edn., Recreation and Dance, Assn. Pa. State Coll. and Univ. Profs., Pa. Scholastic Football Coaches Assn., N.J. State Football Coaches Assn., Lancaster County Quarterback Club, Phi Epsilon Kappa. Avocations: coaching, baseball and football card collecting, model railroading, landscaping. Office: Millersville U Pucillo Gymnasium Millersville PA 17551

KABIS, REBECCA SLOOP, elementary education educator; b. Salisbury, N.C., Oct. 28, 1949; d. Carl Eugene and Joy (Smith) Sloop; m. Richard Alan Kabis, Mar. 18, 1978. AB in Elem. Edn. and Social Studies, Pfeiffer Coll., 1970; postgrad., U. So. Calif., 1970; MA in Elem. Edn. and Reading, U. South Ala., 1974. Cert. tchr., N.C. Elem. tchr. Bethel Luth. Sch., Van Nuys, Calif., 1971-72, South Elem. Sch., Pascagoula, Miss., 1972-73, Kreole Elem. Sch., Moss Point, Miss., 1973-74, St. Martin East Elem. Sch., Ocean Springs, Miss., 1975-82, A.B. Combs Elem. Sch., Raleigh, N.C., 1984—. Del. Edn. Day, Wake County Schs., Raleigh; del. Elem. Leadership Math., Raleigh; participant Quail Roost Conf., Raleigh, 1987; prodr., dir. musicals A.B. Combs Elem. Sch., 1989, 92, student tchr. supr. Author original raps and various ednl. songs and stories. Former dir. children's choir Christus Victor Luth. Ch., Ocean Springs, Miss.; assisting min. Holy Trinity Luth. Ch., Raleigh, 1984-91; coach Dutchman Downs Swim Team, Raleigh. Recipient merit pay tchr. award Wake County Schs., 1987-92. Mem. Internat. Reading Assn. (publicity chmn. Wake County chpt. 1989-90), N.C. Coun. Tchrs. Math., N.C. Assn. Educators, Epsilon Sigma Alpha. Republican. Avocations: scuba diving, piano, trumpet, bridge, tennis. Home: 5228 Leiden Ln Raleigh NC 27606-9553 Office: AB Combs Elem Sch 2001 Lorimer Rd Raleigh NC 27606-2661

KAC, VICTOR G. mathematician, educator; b. Buguruslan, USSR, Dec. 19, 1943; came to U.S., 1977; s. Gersh and Clara (Landman) K.; m. Elena Bourdenko; children: Luba, Marianne. Diploma, Moscow State U., 1965, cand. of sci., 1968. Asst. Moscow Inst. Electronic Machine Bldg., 1968-71; sr. tchr. MIEM, Moscow, 1971-76; assoc. prof. MIT, Cambridge, Mass., 1977-81, prof., 1981—. Author two books on infinite-dimensional Lie algebras, a book on vertex algebra and a book on quantum calculus; contbr. numerous articles to profl. jours. Recipient Medal Coll. de France, 1981, Wigner medal Group Theory Found., 1994; Guggenheim fellow, 1985, Sloan fellow, 1981. Mem. Am. Math. Soc., Moscow Math. Soc. (hon.). Achievements include structure and representation theory of infinite-dimensional groups and algebras that arise in mathematics and physics. Home: 273 Mason Ter Brookline MA 02446 Office: MIT Math Dept 77 Massachusetts Ave Cambridge MA 02139-4307

KACHUR, BETTY RAE, elementary education educator; b. Lorain, Ohio, June 12, 1930; d. John and Elizabeth (Stanko) Kachur. BS in Edn., Kent State U., 1963; MEd, U. Ariz., 1971. Cert. tchr., in reading. Tchr. Lorain City Schs., 1961-94. Bd. dirs. Habitat for Humanity Lorain County, 1997—2001, Lorain Pub. Libr., Ohio Friends LIbrs.; treas. Lorain Downtown Ministerial Assn.; profl. storyteller Northeastern Ohio Western Res. Assn. for Preservation and Perpetuation of Storytellers. Mem.: AAUW (social com., scholarship com. 1999), Daniel T. Gardner Reading Assn. (pres. 1978—79, treas. 1988—94), Internat. Reading Assn. (by-laws com. Ohio Coun.). Mem. United Ch. Of Christ. Avocations: reading, writing, quilting, travel.

KACZOREK, SHARON CAPS, parochial school educator; b. Poteau, Okla., July 22, 1947; d. James William and Grace (Schroetter) Caps; m. Thaddeusz Kaczorek, Dec. 28, 1973; children: Andrew David, Marie Susan. BS, Kans. U., 1969; MS, Vanderbilt U., 1970. Tchr. Ritenour Consol. Sch. Dist., St. Louis, 1970-74, Tullahoma (Tenn.) City Schs., 1974-77, 88-89, St. Paul the Apostle Sch., Tullahoma, 1990—. Home: 217 Lake Circle Dr Tullahoma TN 37388-3330 Office: 306 W Grizzard Tullahoma TN 37388

KADEN, LEWIS B. law educator, lawyer; b. 1942; AB, Harvard U., 1963, LLB, 1967. Bar: N.Y. 1970, N.J. 1974. Harvard scholar Emmanuel Coll., Cambridge U., 1963-64; law clk. U.S. Ct. Appeals, 1967; legis. asst. Senator Robert F. Kennedy, 1968; ptnr. Battle, Fowler, Stokes & Kheel, 1969-73; chief counsel to gov. State of N.J., 1974-76; assoc. prof. Columbia U., 1976-79, prof., 1979-84, adj. prof., 1984—, dir. Ctr. for Law and Econ. Studies, 1979-83; ptnr. Davis, Polk & Wardwell, N.Y.C., 1984—. Bd. dirs. Bethlehem Steel Corp.; chmn. U.S. Govt. Overseas Presence Adv. Panel, 1999. Chmn. N.Y. State Indsl. Coop. Coun., 1986-92. Office: Davis Polk & Wardwell 450 Lexington Ave Fl 31 New York NY 10017-3982 E-mail: kaden@dpw.com.

KADISH, KATHERINE, artist, art educator; BFA, Carnegie Mellon U., 1961; MA, U. Chgo., 1966. Co-dir. art gallery Harpur Coll. SUNY, Binghamton, 1963-66; curator, slide and print collection dept. art and art history, SUNY Binghamton, 1963-66, vis., adj. asst. prof. dept. art and art history, 1974-82; master tchr. N.Y. State Summer Sch. Visual Arts, 1979-82; asst. prof. art Broome C.C., Binghamton, 1982-84; vis. lectr. art dept. Ohio State U., Columbus, 1985-86; artist-in-residence Montpelier Cultural Arts Ctr., Laurel, Md., 1986; adj. assoc. prof. dept. art and art history Wright State U., Dayton, Ohio, 1987-88; vis. asst. prof. dept. art Wittenberg U., Springfield, Ohio, 1989-90, vis. assoc. prof., Wright State U., 1992; vis. artist Arrowmont Sch. Arts and Crafts, Gatlinburg, Tenn., 1992—, Cleve. Inst. Art, 1994. Solo exhbns. include Denison U., Granville, Ohio, 1975, Hobart Coll., Geneva, N.Y., 1977, Arnot Art Mus., Elmira, N.Y., 1978, SUNY Buffalo, 1980, Va. Ctr. Creative Arts, Sweet Briar, 1981, Univ. Art Gallery SUNY Binghamton, 1981, SUNY Plattsburgh, 1981, Atlantic Gallery, N.Y.C., 1983, Wheaton Coll. Watson Gallery, Norton, Mass., 1984, NW La. U., Natchitoches, 1985, Leigh Gallery, London, 1985, 87, Springfield (Ohio) Art Mus., 1986, Malton Gallery, Cin., 1986, 88, Montpelier Cultural Arts Ctr., Laurel, Md., 1986, Nanjing (People's Republic of China) Arts Coll., 1987, Clemson (S.C.) U. Gallery, 1992, Roberta Kuhn Gallery, Columbus, Ohio, 1992, Yvonne Rapp Gallery, Louisville, 1992, Marta Hewett Gallery, Cin., 1994, Dayton (Ohio) Art Inst., 1994, Gallery East and West, Chgo., 1995, Interchurch Ctr. Gallery, N.Y.C., 1995Zella Gallery, London, 1996, Va. Mus.Fine Arts, Richmond, 1999, Univ. Va., Charlottesville, 1999, Purdue U., West Lafayette, Ind., 2002, Washington State U., Pullman, 2003, others; group exhbns. include Libr. Congress, Washington, 1973, Galerie de l'Esprit, Montreal, Que., Can., 1975, Evans Gallery, Toronto, Ont., Can., 1975, Pleiades Gallery, N.Y.C., 1976, Okla. Art Ctr., Okla. City, 1976, Empire State Plz., Albany, 1977, SUNY, Albany, 1981, N.Y. State Mus., Albany, 1981, Nat. Mus. Am. Art, Washington, D.C., traveling exhbn. to 13 states, 1981, U. N.D., Grand Forks, 1983, Whitney Mus. Am. Art/Downtown, N.Y.C., 1983, Quinton Green Fine Arts, London, 1984, Hopkins Gallery Ohio State U., Columbus, 1986, Cadogan Contemporary Gallery, London, 1990, Ohio Arts Invitational, Tokyo, 1991, Oxford (Eng.) Gallery, 1993, Anita Shapolsky Gallery, N.Y.C., 1995, Nat. Mus. Women in Arts, Washington, 1996, Boston Print Makers N. Am. Print Biennial, 1999, Bowling Green U., 2001, Fine Arts Bldg Gallery, Chgo., 2002, Korea Internat. Contemporary Print Exhbn., Seoul, 2003, many others; represented in public and corp. collections Broome C.C., Binghamton, N.Y., Charter Oaks Bank, Columbus, 1st Federal of Boston, Cin., Fries and Fries Corp., Cin., GTE Corp., Indpls., Herbert F. Johnson Mus. Cornell U., Ithaca, N.Y., Marine Midland Bank, Binghamton, Merrill Lynch, Metel Corp., Cin., N.Y. State Coun. Arts, N.Y.C., Va. Ctr. Creative Arts, Brit. Mus., London, Victorial & Albert Mus., London, N.Y.C. Pub. Libr., Nat Mus. Women in Arts, Washington, others. Recipient six awards, Ohio Arts Coun., 1st Annual Artist-in- Residency award Montpelie Cultural Arts Ctr., 1986, Creative Artists Pub. Svc. Program grantee N.Y. State Coun. on Arts, 1973, Travel grantee Unied Bd. Christian Higher Edn. in Asia, 1986; Residency fellow Yaddo, 1977, 78, 80, Tyrone Guthrie Ctr. for Arts, Ireland, 1988, Va. Ctr. Creative Arts, 1978-82, 87, 89, 95, 98, 2002, Vt. Studio Colony, 1990, Ludwig Vogelstein Found., 1990. Home: 1062 State Route 343 Yellow Springs OH 45387-9799 also: 222 W 14th St # 13A New York NY 10011-7200 E-mail: kkadish123@aol.com.

KADISON, RICHARD VINCENT, mathematician, educator; b. N.Y.C., July 25, 1925; married, 1956; 1 child. MS, U. Chgo., 1947, PhD, 1950; hon. doctorate, U. d'Aix-Marseille, 1986, U. Copenhagen, 1987. NRC fellow math. Inst. Advanced Study, 1950-52; from asst. prof. to prof. Columbia U., 1952-64; Kuemmerle prof. math. U. Pa., 1964—. Fulbright rsch. grantee, Denmark, 1954-55; Sloan fellow, 1958-62; Guggenheim fellow, 1969-70. Mem. NAS (chmn. math. sect. 2003—), Am. Math. Soc. (Steele prize for lifetime achievement 1999), Royal Danish Acad. Sci. and Letters (fgn. mem.), Norwegian Acad. Sci. and Letters (fgn. mem.), Sigma Xi. Office: U Pa Dept Math Philadelphia PA 19104-6395

KAFKA, BARBARA POSES, writer; b. N.Y.C., Aug. 6, 1933; d. Jack and Lillian (Shapiro) Poses; m. Ernest Kafka, June 19, 1959; children: Nicole, Michael. AB cum laude, Radcliffe Coll., 1954. Cons. in field. Author: American Food California Wine, 1981, 94, (Tastemaker award), Microwave Gourmet, 1987 (N.Y. Times Best Seller), Food for Friends, 1987, 93, Microwave Gourmet Healthstyle Cookbook, 1989, (Tastemaker award), Party Food, 1992, Roasting A Simple Art, 1995 (Julia Child Cookbook award), Soup, A Way of Life, 1998; compiler, editor pro bono: The James Beard Celebration Cookbook, 1990; editor: The Four Seasons, 1980, The Cook's Catalogue, (mags.) Cooking, The Pleasures of Cooking; contbg. editor Vogue, 1981-89, Gourmet, 1988-96; contbg. columnist N.Y. Times, 1987—; contbr. articles to profl. jours. Mem. Internat. Assn. Culinary Profls., Am. Inst. Wine and Food, Culinary Historians Boston, James Beard. Home and Office: 23 E 92nd St New York NY 10128-0607

KAGAN, CONSTANCE HENDERSON, philosopher, educator, consultant; b. Houston, Sept. 16, 1940; d. Bessie Earle (Henderson) Davis; m. Morris Kagan, May 27, 1967. BA, Baylor U., 1962; MSSW, U. Tex. Austin, 1966; PhD, U. Okla., 1979. Dir. Acacia Pk. Ctr. for Continuing Edn., Great Falls, Va., 1996—. Congl. fellow, 1981-82. Mem. Am. Philos. Assn. Office: PO Box 1290 Great Falls VA 22066-1290 Business E-Mail: ckagan@continuingedu.org.

KAGAN, ELENA, law educator; b. 1960; BA summa cum laude, Princeton, 1981; MPhil, Worchester Coll., Oxford, 1983; JD magna cum laude, Harvard Law School, 1986. Law clk. US Ct. of Appeals for Judge Abner Mikva of the US Supreme Ct. for the DC Circuit, 1986—87, US Ct. of Appeals for Justice Thurgood Marshall of the US Supreme Ct., 1987—88; assoc. Williams & Connolly, Wash., DC, 1989—91; faculty mem. Univ. of Chgo. Law Sch., Chgo., 1991—99; nominated to serve as judge US Supreme Ct. of Appeals, Wash., DC, 1999; asst. prof. Univ. of Chgo. Law Sch., 1991, prof. of law tenure, 1995; assoc. counsel to the Pres. White House, Wash., DC, 1995—96, dep. asst. to the Pres. for Domestic Policy, 1997—99, dep. dir. of the Domestic Policy Coun., 1997—99; vis. prof. Harvard Law Sch., Cambridge, Mass., 1999, prof., 2001—, dean, 2003—, Charles Hamilton Houston prof. of law, 2003—. Author: (article) Harvard Law Rev. Article, "Pres. Admin.", 2001 (honored as the year's top scholarly article by the Am. Bar Assoc. Section on Admin. Law and Reg. Pract., 2001). Kagan has also written on a range of First Amendment issues, including the role of governmental motive in different facets of First Amendment doctrine, and the interplay of libel law and the First Amendment. Mem.: Harvard Law Sch. faculty appt. comm., Harvard Law Sch. Locational options comm. (chair 2001—02). Kagan is a prof. of law at Harvard fLaw Sch. where she teaches admin. law, constitutional law, and civil procedure. Her recent sholarship focuses primarily on the role of the Pres. of the US in formulating and influencing fed. admin. and regulatory law. Office: Harvard Law Sch Griswold 200 1563 Mass Ave Cambridge MA 02138*

KAGAN, GLORIA JEAN, secondary education educator; b. Kansas City, Mo., Oct. 6, 1946; d. Charles A. and Betty Lou (Mour) Glass; m. Stuart Michael Kagan, Aug. 1, 1971; children: Jennifer Anne, Abigail Elizabeth. BA, U. Mo., 1968; MEd, U. Ariz., 1970. Cert. secondary edn. tchr. Tchr. Ctr. Sch. Dist., Kansas City, Mo., 1970-73, N. Chgo. Sch. Dist., 1974-75, Hyman Brand Hebrew Acad., Overland Park, Kans., 1988—. Mem. edn. com. Hyman Brand Hebrew Acad., 1993—. Author poetry. Mem. B'Nai Brith Women, Kansas City, 197—, Hadassah, Kansas City, 1971—, LWV, Kansas City, 1976—. Nominated for Outstanding Tchr. of the Yr., Kansas City C. of C., 1991, High Sch. Tchr. Recognition award U. Kans., 1994. Mem. Nat. Coun. Tchrs. of English. Avocations: reading, writing, travel. Home: 12005 Overbrook Rd Leawood KS 66209-1149 Office: Hyman Brand Hebrew Acad 5801 W 115th St Overland Park KS 66211-1824

KAGAN, JEROME, psychologist, educator; b. Newark, Feb. 25, 1929; s. Joseph and Myrtle (Liebermann) K. BS, Rutgers U., 1950; PhD, Yale, 1954. Instr. psychology Ohio State U., 1954-55; research assoc. Fels Research Inst., Yellow Springs, Ohio, 1957-59, chmn. dept. psychology, 1959-64; assoc. prof. psychology Antioch Coll., 1959-64; rsch. prof. psychology Harvard U., 1964-2000, dir. Mind Brain Behavior Initiative, 1996-2000, rsch. prof., 2000—. Adv. com. Nat. Inst. Child Health and Devel. Author (with G.S. Lesser): Contemporary Issues in Thematic Apperceptive Methods, 1961; author: (with Moss) Birth to Maturity, 1962; author: (with Mussen, Conger and Huston) Child Development and Personality, 7th edit., 1990; author: (with Segal) Psychology, 7th edit., 1991; author: (with Janis, Mahl and Holt) Personality, 1969, Understanding Children, 1971, Change and Continuity in Infancy, 1971; author: (with Kearsley and Zelazo) Infancy, 1978; author: (with Brim) Constancy and Change, 1980, The Second Year, 1981, The Nature of the Child, 1984; author: Unstable Ideas, 1989, Galen's Prophecy, 1994, Three Seductive Ideas, 1998, Surprise, Uncertainty and Mental Structures, 2002. Served with AUS, 1955-57. Recipient Lucius Cross medal Yale U., 1981; Phi Beta Kappa scholar, 1988-89. Fellow AAAS, APA (Disting. Sci. Contbn. award 1987, G. Stanley Hall award 1995), Am. Acad. Arts and Scis., Soc. Rsch. Child Devel. (Disting. Sci. Contbn. award 1989); mem. NAS, Inst. Medicine, Ea. Psychol. Assn. Home: 210 Clifton St Belmont MA 02478-2605 Office: Harvard U Dept Psychology William James Hall 33 Kirkland Hl Cambridge MA 02138 E-mail: jk@wjh.harvard.edu.

KAHALAS, HARVEY, business educator; b. Boston, Dec. 3, 1941; s. James and Betty (Bonfeld) K.; m. Dianne Barbara Levine, Sept. 2, 1963; children: Wendy Elizabeth, Stacy Michele. BS, Boston U., 1965; MBA, U. Mich., 1966; PhD, U. Mass., 1971. Data processing coord. Ford Motor Co., Wayne, Mich., 1963-66; lectr. Salem (Mass.) State Coll., 1966-68; asst. prof. bus. Worcester (Mass.) Poly. Inst., 1970-72; asst. prof. Va. Poly. Inst. and State U., Blacksburg, 1972-75, assoc. prof., 1975-77, SUNY, Albany, 1977-79, assoc. dean, 1979-81, prof., 1979-89, dean, 1981-87; pres. HKE Inc., 1987-97; prof. U. Mass., Lowell, 1989-94, dean, 1989-94, exec. dir. Ctr. Indsl. Competitiveness, 1990-94, Commonwealth disting. prof., 1994-97; dir. Ctr. for Bus. Rsch. and Competitiveness, U. Mass., Dartmouth, 1994-97; prof., dean Wayne State U., 1997—, exec. dir. Inst. for Orgn. and Indsl. Competitiveness, 2001—. Program dir. Aspen Inst., 1994—97; exec. dir. Inst. Orgnl. and Indsl. Competitiveness Wayne State U., 2001—; bd. dirs. Lumigen Inc., Southfield, Mich.; cons. Aspen Inst./Fund for Corp. Initiatives, N.Y.C., 1980—94, GE, Schenectady, NY, 1981—85, GM, Tarrytown, NY, 1987—89. Contbr. articles to profl. jours. Bd. dirs. Nat. Found. Ileitis and Colitis, Albany, NY, 1982—89, Fund for Corp. Initiatives, N.Y.C., 1980—, Blue Cross Northeastern N.Y., Albany, 1983—89, Capital Dist. Bus. Rev., Albany, 1984—, Greater Detroit Area Health Coun., 1998—2001, Greater Detroit Conv. and Visitors Bur., 2001—. Named Disting. Alumni, U. Mass., 1982, Disting. Lectr. USIA, 1985, Am. Participant USIA, 1989; Fulbright scholar, 1987, 88, Aspen Inst. scholar, 1997. Mem. Fulbright Assn. (life), Acad. Mgmt. (treas. 1971-73, mem. exec. com.), Human Resource Planning Soc. (hon.), Human Resource Systems Profls. (hon.), Pers. Accreditation Inst. (life), Beta Gamma Sigma, Sigma Iota Epsilon, Delta Tau Kappa. Office: Wayne State Univ Sch Bus Adm 226 Prentis Bld 5201 Cass Ave Detroit MI 48202-3930

KAHAN, WILLIAM M. mathematics educator, consultant; b. Toronto, Ont., Can., June 5, 1933; s. Myer and Gertrude (Rosenthal) K.; m. Sheila K. Strauss, Sept. 5, 1954; children: Ari J., Simon H. BA in Math., U. Toronto, 1954, MA in Math., 1956, PhD in Math., 1958; DEng (hon.), Chalmers Tech. U., Sweden, 1993; PhD (hon.), U. Waterloo, Can., 1998. Lectr. U. Toronto, Can., 1954-58, from asst. prof. to prof., 1960-68; postdoctoral rsch. student math. lab. Cambridge (Eng.) U., 1958-60. Vis. prof. Stanford (Calif.) U., 1966; cons. IBM, N.Y.C. and Austin, Tex., 1967—1984, calculator div. Hewlett-Packard, Cupertino, Calif. and Corvallis, Oreg., 1974-80, Intel, Santa Clara, Calif., 1977—1990; cons. Co-inventor Intel 8087, 1980; contbr. articles to profl. jours. Fellow: ACM (1st G.E. Forsythe Meml. award 1972, A.M. Turing prize 1990); mem.: Am. Acad. Arts. and Sci., IEEE Computer Soc. (E. Piore award 2000), Soc. Indsl. and Applied Math. (John von Neumann lectr. 1997). Jewish. Avocation: repairing household appliances and cars. Office: U Calif Dept Elec Engring Comp Sci 1776 Berkeley CA 94720-1776

KAHANA, EVA FROST, sociology educator; b. Budapest, Hungary, Mar. 21, 1941; came to U.S., 1957; d. Jacob and Sari Frost; m. Boaz Kahana, Apr. 15, 1962; children: Jeffrey, Michael. BA, Stern Coll., Yeshiva U., 1962; MA, CCNY, CUNY, 1965; PhD, U. Chgo., 1968; HLD (hon.), Yeshiva U., 1991. Nat. Inst. on Aging predoctoral fellow U. Chgo. Com. on Human Devel., 1963-66; postdoctoral fellow Midwest Council Social Research, 1968; with dept. sociology Washington U., St. Louis, 1967-71, successively research asst., research assoc., asst. prof.; with dept. sociology Wayne State U., Detroit, 1971-84, from assoc. prof. to prof., dir. Elderly Care Research Ctr., 1971-84; prof. Case Western Res. U., Cleve., 1984—, Armington Prof., 1989-90, chmn. dept. sociology, 1985—, dir. Elderly Care Research Ctr., 1984—, Pierce and Elizabeth Robson prof. humanities, 1990—. Cons. Nat. Inst. on Aging, Washington, 1976-80, NIMH, Washington, 1971-75. Author: (with E. Midlarsky) Altruism in Later Life, 1994; editor: (with others) Family Caregiving Across the Lifespan, 1994; mem. editl. bd. Gerontologist, 1975-79, Psychology of Aging, 1984-90, Jour. Gerontology, 1990-94, Applied Behavioral Sci. Rev., 1992—; contbr. articles to profl. jours., chpts. to books (recipient Pub.'s prize 1969). Bd. dirs. com. on aging Jewish Community Fedn., Cleve.; vol. cons. Alzheimer's Disease and Related Disorders Assn., Cleve. NIMH Career Devel. grantee, 1974-79, Nat. Inst. Aging Merit award grantee, 1989—; Mary E. Switzer Disting. fellow Nat. Inst. Rehab., 1992-93; recipient Arnold Heller award excellence in geriatrics and gerontology Menorah Park Ctr. for Aged, 1992, Diekhoff awrd for disting. grad. tchg., 2002; named Disting. Geontological Rschr. in Ohio, 1993. Fellow Gerontol. Soc. Am. (chair behavioral social sci. com. 1984-85, chair 2000—, Disting. Mentorship award 1987, Polisher award 1997); mem. Am. Sociol. Assn. (coun. sect. on aging 1985-87, Disting. Scholar award sect. on aging and life course 1997, chair sect. on aging and life course, 2000-2001), Am. Psychol. Assn., Soc. for Traumatic Stress, Wayne State U. Acad. Scholars (life), Sigma Xi. Avocations: reading, antiques, travel.

KAHN, BERND, radiochemist, educator; b. Pforzheim, Baden, Germany, Aug. 16, 1928; came to U.S., 1938; s. Eric Herman and Alice Dora (Meyer) K.; m. Gail Pressman, Aug. 6, 1961; children: Jennifer, Elizabeth. BSChemE, N.J. Inst. Tech., 1950; MS in Physics, Vanderbilt U., 1952; PhD in Chemistry, MIT, 1960. Commd. officer USPHS, 1954, advanced through grades to capt., 1970, health physicist, radiochemist, Oak Ridge (Tenn.) Nat. Lab., 1951-54, engr. various facilities, 1954-74, ret., 1974; prof. nuc. engring. and health physics Ga. Inst. Tech., Atlanta, 1974-96, prof. emeritus, 1996—, dir. Environ. Resources Ctr., 1974—. Co-editor: Management of Low-Level Radioactive Waste, 1979; co-inventor recovery of magnesium salts from sea water. Mem. Nat. Coun. Radiation Protection and Measurments (hon.), Am. Chem. Soc., Am. Phys. Soc., Health Physics Soc. Achievements include research specialization: radiochemistry and environmental radioactivity. Office: Ga Inst Tech Nuclear Engring Health Physics Atlanta GA 30332-0335 E-mail: bernd.kahn@me.gatech.edu.

KAHN, DAVID MILLER, lawyer, educator; b. Port Chester, N.Y., Apr. 21, 1925; m. Barbara Heller, May 9, 1952; children: William, James, Caroline. BA, U. Ky., 1947; LLB cum laude, N.Y. Law Sch., 1950. Bar: N.Y. 1951, U.S. Dist. Ct. (ea. and so. dists.) N.Y. 1953, U.S. Supreme Ct. 1958. Sole practice, White Plains, N.Y., 1951-60; ptnr. Kahn & Rubin, White Plains, 1960-66, Kahn & Goldman, White Plains, 1967-80; sr. ptnr. Kahn & Landau, White Plains, Palm Beach, Fla., 1980-88, Kahn and Kahn, Fla., N.Y., 1988-95, Kahn, Kahn & Scutieri Esq., Palm Beach Gardens, 1995—. Lectr. N.Y. Law Sch., 1982—; spl. counsel Village Port Chester, N.Y., 1960-63; commr. of appraisal Westchester County Supreme Ct., 1973-77; counsel Chemplex Industries, Inc., BIS Communications Corp., Bilbar Realty Co. Chmn. Westchester County Citizens for Eisenhower, 1950-52; pres. Westchester County Young Reps. Clubs, 1958-60; founder, chmn. bd. dirs. Port Chester-Rye Town Vol. Ambulance Corps, 1968-77; pres. Driftwood Corp., Amagansett, L.I., N.Y., 1984-91. Served with Counter Intelligence Corps USAF, 1942-46. Recipient John Marshall Harlan fellow N.Y. Law Sch., 1990-93, lifetime achievement award Westchester County Bar Assn, 2001. Fellow Am. Acad. Matrimonial Lawyers (bd. govs. N.Y. chpt. 1976-79); mem. ABA, N.Y. State Bar Assn., Westchester County Bar Assn., White Plains Bar Assn., N.Y. Law Sch. Alumni Assn. (bd. dirs. 1970-80), Elmwood C.C. (legal counsel), Eastpointe Country Club. Home and Office: 6419 Eastpointe Pines St Palm Beach Gardens FL 33418 also: 175 Main St White Plains NY 10601-3105

KAHN, MARK LEO, arbitrator, educator; b. N.Y.C., Dec. 16, 1921; s. Augustus and Manya (Fertig) K.; m. Ruth Elizabeth Wecker, Dec. 21, 1947 (div. Jan. 1972); children: Ann Mariam, Peter David, James Allan, Jean Sarah; m. Elaine Johnson Morris, Feb. 12, 1988. BA, Columbia U., 1942; MA, Harvard U., 1948, PhD in Econs., 1950. Asst. economist U.S. OSS, Washington, 1942-43; tchg. fellow Harvard U., 1947-49; dir. case analysis U.S. WSB, Region 6-B Mich., 1952-53; mem. faculty Wayne State U., Detroit, 1949-85, prof. econs., 1960-85, prof. emeritus, 1985—, dept. chmn., 1961-68, dir. indsl. rels. M.A. program, 1978-85. Arbitrator union-mgmt. disputes. Co-author: Collective Bargaining and Technological Change in American Transportation, 1971; mem. editl. bd. Employee Responsibilities and Rights Jour., 1988-96; contbr. articles to profl. jours. Bd. govs. Jewish Welfare Fedn. Detroit, 1976-82; bd. dirs. Jewish Home for Aged, Detroit, 1978-93, Lyric Chamber Ensemble, Southfield, Mich., 1995-97, Detroit Empowerment Zone Devel. Corp., 1996-99. Pvt. to Capt. AUS, 1943-46. Decorated Bronze Star; recipient Disting. Svc. award U.S. Nat. Mediation Bd., 1987, Am. Arbitration Assn., 1992. Mem. AAUP (past chpt. pres.), Nat. Acad. Arbitrators (bd. govs. 1960-62, v.p. 1976-78, chmn. membership com. 1979-82, pres. 1983-84, chmn. nominating com. 1995-96), Indsl. Rels. Rsch. Assn. (pres. Detroit chpt. 1956, exec. sec. 1979-89, nat. exec. bd. 1985-88), Soc. Profls. in Dispute Resolution (v.p. 1982-83, pres. 1986-87). Home and Office: 15151 Ford Rd Apt 321 Dearborn MI 48126-5027 E-mail: mleokahn@aol.com.

KAHN, NORMAN, pharmacology and dentistry educator; b. N.Y.C., Dec. 28, 1932; s. Louis Meyer and Dorothy (Simon) Kohn; m. Dale Krasnow, Mar. 30, 1958 AB, Columbia U., 1954, D.D.S., 1958, PhD, 1964. Lic. dentist, N.Y. State. Dental intern Montefiore Hosp., Bronx, N.Y., 1958-59; instr. Coll. Physicians and Surgeons, Columbia U., N.Y.C., 1962-65, asst. prof., 1965-72, assoc. prof., 1972-80, prof. pharmacology, 1980-99, prof. dentistry, 1980-92, Edwin S. Robinson prof. dentistry, 1992-99; assoc. dean acad. affairs Sch. Dental and Oral Surgery, Columbia U., 1989-94, acting dean, 1994-95; attending dentist Presbyn. Hosp., N.Y.C., 1985-99, Robinson prof. dentistry & pharm. emeritus, spl. lectr., 1999—, cons. dentist, 1999—. Vis. assoc. prof. UCLA, 1978; chair instl. rev. bd. Columbia-Presbyn. Med. Ctr., N.Y.C., 1981-91; cons. pharmcologist Harlem Hosp., N.Y.C., 1966-80; vis. scientist U. Pisa, Italy, 1965-66. Contbr. chpts. to books, articles to profl. jours. NIH grantee, 1969-75, Nat. Fund Med. Edn. grantee, 1973; recipient Outstanding Contbn. to Teaching award Columbia U. Coll. Physicians and Surgeons, 1980, Physicians & surgeons Disting. Svc. award in Pre-Clinical Yrs., 2001; hon. research fellow Univ. Coll., London, 1986. Mem. Am. Physiol. Soc., ADA, Am. Assn. Dental Schs., Confrerie des Chevaliers du Tastevin, Alpha Omega Alpha, Omicron Kappa Upsilon Jewish. Avocation: oenology. Office: Columbia U 630 W 168th St New York NY 10032-3795

KAHN, SIGMUND BENHAM, retired internist and dean; b. Phila., May 18, 1933; s. Maxwell Louis and Clara (Parris) K.; m. Joanne Pokras, June 11, 1955; children: Marc L., Elissa Kahn Petrosky, Hillary Kahn Roth, Lauren B. Westlake. BA, U. Pa., 1954, MD, 1958. Diplomate Am. Bd. Internal Medicine; cert. hematology and med. oncology. Rotating intern Albert Einstein Med. Ctr., Phila., 1958-59; resident in internal medicine Hosp. of U. Pa., Phila., 1959-61, fellow in hematology, 1961-62, USPHS rsch. fellow dept. hematology, 1962-63; assoc. in hematology medicine Hahnemann U. Hosp., Phila., 1963-66, asst., assoc., then prof. medicine, 1966-99; prof. dept. neoplastic disease Hahnemann Univ. Hosp., Phila., 1978-99, dir. edn., vice chmn. dept., 1978-94; assoc. dean Hahnemann U., Phila., 1986-94; prof. emeritus, 1999—2002; prof. dept. medicine divsn. hematology/ med. oncology Med. Coll. Pa./Hahnemann U., Phila., 1992-94, assoc. dean edn., 1992-94, prof. emeritus, 1999—2002, Drexel U. Coll. of Med., 2002—. Cons., chmn. dean's com. Wilkes-Barre (Pa.) VA Hosp., 1987-92. Mem. editl. bd. Jour. Cancer Edn., 1985-95, Am. Jour. Clin. Oncology; contbr. articles to profl. jours. Instl. rep. Boy Scouts Am., 1970-75; pres. Temple Beth Sholom, Cherry Hill, N.J., 1977-80; mem. med. bd. Lupus Found., Delaware Valley, 1977-79. Mem. AMA, ACP, Phila. County Med. Soc., Phila. Hematology Soc., Pa. Med. Soc., Am. Fedn. Clin. Rsch., Am. Hematology Soc., Am. Assn. Cancer Rsch., Am. Soc. Clin. Oncology, Am. Assn. Cancer Edn., Am. Cancer Soc. (chmn. patient svc. com. Phila. divsn. 1981-83, chmn. med. subcom. profl. edn. com. 1979-81, fin. com. 1981), Phi beta Kappa, Alpha Omega Alpha. Jewish. Home: 2307 Sagemore Dr Marlton NJ 08053-4315

KAHN, SY MYRON, humanities educator, poet; b. N.Y.C., Sept. 15, 1924; s. Max Kahn, Sophie (Wagner) Kahn; m. Marion Belefant, June 15, 1947 (div. Oct. 1, 1962); 1 child, David Matthew; m. Nancy Dennis, Apr. 20, 1963 (div. Apr. 20, 1979); m. Janet Aline Baker, Nov. 25, 2000. BA, U. Pa., 1948; MA, U. Conn., 1951; PhD, U. Wis., 1957. Prof. English and drama U. of Pacific, Stockton, Calif., 1963—86. Exec. dir. Fallon House Theatre, Columbia, Calif., 1970—84; vis. prof. Am. Studies U. Wales, Swansea, 1987, Swansea, 97; vis. prof. theatre Justus Liebig U., Giessen, Germany, 1987; prof. Am. Lit. Fulbright Commn., Salonika, Greece, 1957—58, Warsaw, 1966—67, Vienna, 1970—71, Porto, Portugal, 1985—86. Author: Between Tedium and Terror, 1993; author: (poetry) Our Separate Darkness, 1963, Triptych, 1964, A Later Sun, 1966, Fight is With Phantoms, 1966, Another Time, 1968, Facing Mirrors, 1980; editor: Interculture, 1975, Devour the Fire, 1984. Cpl. U.S. Army, 1943—45, PTO. Recipient Gardner Writing award, 1955, 1956, Borestone Poetry award, 1964, Promethean Lamp prize, 1966, Grand Prize Poetry, 1985, Angel of the Arts award, Port Townsend, 2003. Mem.: Modern Lang. Assn., Key City Players (v.p. 2000—, pres. 2002—03). Home: 1212 Holcomb St Port Townsend WA 98368

KAHNE, STEPHEN JAMES, systems engineer, educator, academic administrator, engineering executive; b. N.Y.C., Apr. 5, 1937; s. Arnold W. and Janet (Weatherlow) Kahne; m. Irena Nowacka, Dec. 11, 1970; children: Christopher, Kasia. BEE, Cornell U., 1960; MS, U. Ill., 1961, PhD, 1963. Asst. prof. elec. engring. U. Minn., Mpls., 1966-69, assoc. prof., 1969-76; dir. Hybrid Computer Lab., 1968-76; founder, dir., cons. InterDesign Inc., Mpls., 1968-76; prof. dept. sys. engring. Case Western Res. U., Cleve., 1976-83, chmn. dept., 1976-80; dir. divsn. elec., computer and sys. engring. NSF, Washington, 1980-82; prof. Poly Inst. N.Y., 1983-85, dean engring., 1983-84; pres. Oreg. Grad. Ctr., Beaverton, 1985-86, prof. dept. applied physics and elec. engring., 1985-89; chief engr. civil systems divsn. MITRE Corp., McLean, Va., 1989-90, chief scientist Washington Group, 1990-91, cons. engr. Ctr. for Advanced Aviation Sys. Devel., 1991-94; exec. dir., CEO Triangle Coalition for Sci. and Tech. Edn., 1994; chancellor, v.p. Embry-Riddle Aeronautical U., Prescott, Ariz., 1995-97, prof. engring., 1995—. Cons. in field; exchange scientist NAS, 1968, 75. Editor: IEEE Transactions on Automatic Control, 1975-79; hon. editor: Internat. Fedn. of Automatic Control, 1975-81, dep. chmn. mng. bd. publs., 1976-87, chmn., 1999—, v.p., 1987-90, pres.-elect, 1990-93, pres., 1993-96, advisor, 1999—; assoc. editor: Automatica, dep. chmn. editl. bd., 1976-82; mem. editl. bd. IEEE Spectrum, 1979-82; contbr. articles to sci. jours. Active Mpls. Citizens League, 1968-75; regent L.I. Coll. Hosp., Bklyn., 1984-85; trustee Yavapi Regional Med. Ctr., 1999—; chmn. Beaverton Sister Cities Found., 1986-89. Served with USAF, 1963-66. Recipient Amicus Poloniae award POLAND Mag., 1975, John A. Curtis award Am. Soc. Engring. Edn., Outstanding Svc. award Internat. Fedn. Automatic Control, 1990; Case Centennial scholar, 1980 Fellow: AAAS, IEEE (life; pres. Control Sys. Soc. 1981, bd. dirs. 1982—86, v.p. tech. activities 1984—85, Centennial medal 1984, Disting Mem. award 1983, Richard Emberson award 1991, Disting. Lectr. 1998—2000); mem.: Air Traffic Control Assn., Am. Soc. Engring. Edn., Eta Kappa Nu. Office: Embry Riddle Aero U 3700 Willow Creek Rd Prescott AZ 86301-3721 E-mail: s.kahne@ieee.org.

KAHRMANN, ROBERT GEORGE, educational administrator; b. New Brunswick, N.J., Dec. 12, 1940; s. Robert George and Susan Rose (Budish) K.; m. Linda Irene Bradshaw, Aug. 22, 1993; children: Kellie, Jeffrey, Jeannette. BS, Monmouth U., West Long Branch, N.J., 1963; MA in Edn., Seton Hall U., 1964; EdD, NYU, 1970. Tchr. social studies Middletown Twp. (N.J.) H.S., 1964—66; asst. dir. Jersey City State Coll., 1968—71; dir. continuing edn. Somerset County Coll., Somerville, NJ, 1971—77, Seton Hall U., South Orange, NJ, 1977—78, 1978—84; mgr. continuing engring. edn. IEEE, Piscataway, NJ, 1984—95; dean Pa. Inst. of Tech., Media, 1995—98; v.p. acad. affairs Berkeley Coll., West Paterson, NJ, 1998—99; assoc. dean enrollment svcs. Hudson County C.C., Jersey City, 1999—2001; dir. enrollment svcs. Middlesex C.C., Edison, NJ, 2001—02; ret., 2002. Adj. prof. Seton Hall U., 1977-83; cons. N.J. Funeral Dirs. Assn., 1978-84, Westmoreland County (Pa.) C.C., 1975, N.Y.C. Fire Lts. Assn., 1974-75. Editor: Fire Problems in Modern Building, 1971; contbr. articles to profl. jours. Pres., treas. H.S. Band Parents, North Brunswick, N.J., 1985-93; chmn. Charter Study Commn., North Brunswick, 1981-82; chmn. and mem. Parks and Recreation Com., North Brunswick, 1984-92, Devel. Com., 1977-83. Recipient TAB Pioneer award IEEE Computer Soc., 1988, Edn. award N.J. Ind. Ins. Agts., 1982, Founder's Day award NYU, 1971. Mem.: Am. Philat. Soc., Internat. TV Assn., Phi Delta Kappa. Avocations: travel, stamp collecting, model trains. Personal E-mail: bobkahrmann@aol.com.

KAHWAJI, GEORGE ANTOINE, computer and mathematics educator; b. Beirut, Oct. 27, 1959; came to U.S., 1979; s. Antoine Youssef and Jamile Toufic Kahwaji; m. Charlotte Lynn Cunningham, Aug. 27, 1985 (div. Nov. 1995); children: Jessica Noel, Anthony George Edwin. BSMe, W. Va. Inst. Tech., 1983; MSME, U. Akron, 1988; postgrad., U. Mo., Kansas City, 1989—. Grad. asst. U. Akron, Ohio, 1983-84; cons. Aviation Cos., various locations U.S., 1984-87; lectr. Cen. Mo. State U., Warrensburg, 1985-87, instr., 1989-94; grad. asst. CRINC Rsch. Ctr., Lawrence, Kans., 1988-89. Pres. Flight-Ware, Ltd., Lee's Summit, Mo., 1992—; cons. Aircraft Systems, Miami, 1991-94; food costing analyst/software Sonic Restaurants, USA. Author, creator: (software) Aviation Systems, 1992; author, creator restaurant mgmt. system, point of sale system to fast food industry. Mem. Math. Assn. Am. (best paper presentation 1992), Am. Math. Soc., Kappa Mu Epsilon. Roman Catholic. Office: Flight-Ware Ltd 1111 SE Broadway Dr Lees Summit MO 64081-4602

KAILATH, THOMAS, electrical engineer, educator; b. Poona, India, June 7, 1935; arrived in U.S., 1957, naturalized, 1976; s. Mamman and Kunjamma (George) K.; m. Sarah Jacob, June 11, 1962; children: Ann, Paul, Priya, Ryan. BE, U. Poona, 1956; SM, MIT, 1959, ScD, 1961; Dr. Tek (hon.), Linkoping U., Sweden, 1990; Doctorate (hon.), U. Carlos III, Madrid, 1999; D honoris causa, Strathclyde U., Scotland, 1992, U. Bordeaux, France, 2003. Comm. rschr. Jet Propulsion Labs., Pasadena, Calif., 1961-62; faculty Stanford (Calif.) U., 1963—, prof. elec. engring., 1968—, Hitachi Am. prof. engring., 1988—2001, Hitachi Am. prof. emeritus, 2001—; dir. Info. Systems Lab., 1971-81, assoc. chmn. dept., 1981-87. Vis. prof., cons. univs., industry, govt. Author: Linear Systems, 1980, Least-Squares Estimation, 2d edit, 1981, Linear Estimation, 2000; mem. editl. bd. various jours.; contbr. articles to profl. jours. Recipient Edn. award Am. Control Coun., 1986, Tech. Achievement and Soc. awards Signal Processing Soc. IEEE, 1989, 91, Donald G. Fink Prize award, 1996, Shannon award, 2000; Sr. Vinton Hayes fellow MIT, 1992, Guggenheim fellow, 1970, Churchill fellow, 1977, Michael fellow Weizmann Inst., Israel, 1984, Royal Soc. guest rsch. fellow, 1989; Alexander Humboldt fellow, 2003. Fellow: IEEE (Edn. medal 1995), Am. Acad. Arts and Scis., Inst. Math. Stats.; mem.: NAS, Royal Spanish Acad. Engring., Third World Acad. Scis., Soc. Indsl. and Applied Math., Am. Math. Soc., Nat. Acad. Engring., Indian Nat. Acad. Engring., Sigma Xi. Home: 1024 Cathcart Way Palo Alto CA 94305-1047 Office: Stanford U Dept Elec Engring Stanford CA 94305-9510 E-mail: kailath@stanford.edu.

KAIN, PHILIP JOSEPH, philosophy educator; b. San Francisco, May 21, 1943; s. Joseph Frank and Laura (Fino) K.; m. Helen Yuko Nakamura, Apr. 2, 1967; children: Joseph Naoki, Benjamin Tadashi. BA in Philosophy, St. Mary's Coll., 1966; PhD in Philosophy, U. Calif., San Diego, 1974. Asst. prof. U. Calif., Santa Cruz, 1974-82; lectr. Stanford (Calif.) U., 1982-86; prof. Santa Clara (Calif.) U., 1988—. Author: Schiller, Hegel, and Marx, 1982, Marx' Method, Episemology, and Humanism, 1986, Marx and Ethics, 1988, Marx and Modern Political Theory, 1993. Mem. Am. Philos. Assn., Hegel Soc. Am. Office: Santa Clara U Dept Philosophy Santa Clara CA 95053-0310 E-mail: pkain@scu.edu.

KAINZ, HOWARD PAUL, philosophy educator; b. Inglewood, Calif., June 9, 1933; s. Howard Paul and Cecelia Gertrude (Gallas) K.; m. Cathryn Louise Drozdik, Feb. 28, 1970; children: Alexander, Monica, Erika. BA, Loyola Marymount Coll., L.A., 1957; MA, St. Louis U., 1964; PhD, Duquesne U., 1968. Asst. prof. philosophy Duquesne U., Pitts., 1966-67, Marquette U., Milw., 1968-74, assoc. prof., 1974-80, prof., 1980—2002, prof. emeritus, 2003—. Author: Hegel's Phenomenology, Part I, 1976, Hegel's Phenomenology, Part II, 1983, Democracy East and West, 1984, Paradox, Dialectic and System, 1988 (Choice Disting. Scholarly Book award), Ethics in Context, 1988, Democracy and the Kingdom of God, 1993, An Introduction to Hegel, 1995, G.W.F. Hegel: The Philosophical System, 1996, Politically Incorrect Dialogues, 1998, Natural Law: a Reevaluation, 2004; translator: Hegel's Phenomenology Selections, 1994; editor: Philosophical Perspectives on Peace, 1987. Mem. Internationale Hegel Gesellschaft, Hegel Soc. Am., Am. Philos. Assn. Roman Catholic. Avocations: piano, racquetball. Office: Marquette U Dept Philosophy Milwaukee WI 53233 E-mail: kainzh@mu.edu.

KAISER, EDWIN MICHAEL, chemistry educator; b. Youngstown, Ohio, Oct. 15, 1938; s. Edwin Carl and Mary Lavern (Harris) K.; m. Judith Ann Boyer, Nov. 7, 1959; children: Kim Suzette, Kay Lynnette, Karla Annette, Kevin Michael, Kurt Eric, Karenda Jeannette (dec.). BS, Youngstown State U., 1960; PhD, Purdue U., 1964; postgrad., Duke U., 1966. Asst. prof. U. Mo., Columbia, 1966-70, assoc. prof., 1970-75, prof., 1975—2002, dir. hons. coll., 1984-91, assoc. chair chemistry, 1994-96, curators disting. tchg. prof. chemistry, 1995—2002, prof. emeritus, 2002—. Vis. prof. U. East Anglia, Norwich, U.K., 1991, U. Western Cape, Cape Town, South Africa, 1992, 97, 2002; cons. in field. Contbr. articles to profl. jours. Mem. planning and zoning commn. City of Columbia, 1978-79, mem. city coun., 1985-89; various offices United Ch. of Christ, Columbia, 1966—. Mem. Am. Chem. Soc., Sigma Xi. Avocations: reading, family, travel. Home: 202 Old 63 N Columbia MO 65201-6364 Office: U Mo 123 Chemistry Columbia MO 65211-0001

KAISER, HANS ELMAR, pathology educator, researcher; b. Prague, Czech Republic, Feb. 16, 1928; arrived in U.S., 1961. s. Rudolf and Charlotte (Thiel) K.; m. Charlotte (Moehring), Oct. 12, 1960. ScD, U. Tuebingen, Fed. Republic of Germany, 1958. Rsch. prof. U. Md., Balt., 1988; hon., sci. dir. Internat. Inst. Anticancer Rsch., Attiki, Greece. Hon. cons. Bulgarian Med. Acad., Sofia; vis. prof. Martin Luther U., Halle-Wittenberg, Fed. Republic of Germany, U. Vienna, Austria; pres. Internat. Soc. for Study of Comparative Oncology, German Soc. Comparative Oncology, Inc. Author: Das Abnorme in der Evolution, 1970; Morphology of Sirenia, 1972; Species Specific Potential of Invertebrates, 1980; editor, author: Nepolasms, Comparative, Pathology of Growth. . ., 1981; Cancer Growth and Progression, 10 vols., 1989; others; mem. editorial bd. Anticancer Rsch., in Vivo. Mem.: Physikalisch Medizinische Societaet Erlangen (corr.), Turkish Kanseroloji ve Ekoloji Dernegi (hon.). Home: 433 Southwest Dr Silver Spring MD 20901-4420

KAISER, MARK JOHN, research scientist, science educator; b. Ft. Thomas, Ky, June 22, 1965; Degree in agr. engring., Purdue U., 1985, degree in indsl. engring., 1988, degree in indsl. engring., 1991. Rsch. asst. Purdue U., West Lafayette, Ind., 1985-91, instr., 1988-91, rsch. fellow, 1990-91; instr. Ind. Vocat. Tech. Coll., Lafayette, Ind., 1990-91; asst. prof. indsl. engring. Auburn U., Ala., 1991-94; vis. asst. prof. Am. U. Armenia, Yerevan, 1995, vis. assoc. prof. earthquake and indsl. engring., 1996; asst. prof. indsl. and mfg. engring. Wichita State U., Kans., 1996—, grad. coord. dept. indsl. and mfg. engring., 1997—2001; assoc. prof. La. State U., 2001—. Assoc. prof., Ctr. Energy Studies, La. State U., 2001-. Contbr. articles to profl. jour. Achievements include the initiation of the fields of geometric metrology and constructive convex geometry, developed meta-modeling analysis of fiscal regimes; national expert on LIHEAP and WAP allocation mechanisms. Office: Center for Energy Studies, LSU Energy Coast & Environ Bldg Nicholson Extension Dr Baton Rouge LA 70803-0301

KAISER, MARTHA WINNIFRED, elementary school educator; b. Boston, Sept. 9, 1948; d. William Burrows and Jane Phillips (Thompson) Mercaldi; m. Christopher Barina Kaiser, June 27, 1970; children: Justin, Matthew, Patrick. AB in Edn., Smith Coll., 1970; MA in Reading, Western Mich. U., 1989, postgrad., 1992-93. Cert. reading and Reading Recovery tchr., Mich. 6th grade tchr. Centerville Sch., Beverly, Mass., 1970-71; 3d and 4th grade tchr. George Watsons' Boys Coll., Edinburgh, Scotland, 1971-74; presch. tchr. Presbyn. Coop., Holland, Mich., 1977-78; 2d grade tchr. Zeeland (Mich.) Pub. Schs., 1988-91, 1st grade tchr., 1991-92, Reading Recovery tchr., 1992—. Classroom tchr. mini-grantee State of Mich., 1989. Mem. NEA, Mich. Edn. Assn., Zeeland Edn. Assn., Internat. Reading Assn., Mich. Reading Assn., Reading Recovery Coun. of NAm. Office: Zeeland Pub Schs Roosevelt Sch 175 W Roosevelt Ave Zeeland MI 49464-1127

KAISER, MICHAEL BRUCE, elementary education educator; b. New Albany, Ind., Mar. 6, 1949; s. Bobby Bruce and Maxine Delores (Roberts) K.; m. Patricia Gibson, Aug. 15, 1970; children: Lesa, Kevin, Todd. BS in Elem. Edn., Ind. U., Jeffersonville, 1971; MS in Elem. Edn., Ind. U., New Albany, 1977, MS, 1989. Reading tutor S. Ellen Jones Sch., New Albany, 1968-69; summer sch. aide Hazelwood Jr. High, New Albany, 1969-70; elem. tchr. Pine View Elem. Sch., New Albany, 1971—; gifted and talented coord. Project AHEAD, Ind. U. Southeast, New Albany, 1987—. Tchr. creativity fellow Lilly Found., Ind., 1988 Recipient Profl. Best Leadership award Learning Mag., Oldsmobile Corp., Mich. State U., 1990, State Tchr. of Yr. award, Ind., Coun. of Chief State School Offices, 1992, Burger King Nat. Edn. award, 1992, Presdl. Svc. award, 1998; inducted into Nat. Tchrs. Hall of Fame, 1995; Christa McAuliffe fellow, 1994. Mem. NEA, Ind. State Tchrs. Assn., New Albany-Floyd County Edn. Assn. Avocations: bubbleology, volleyball, camping. Office: Pine View Sch 2524 Corydon Pike New Albany IN 47150-6126

KAISER, WALTER, English language educator; b. Bellevue, Ohio, May 31, 1931; AB magna cum laude, Harvard Coll., 1954; PhD, Harvard U., 1960. Allston Burr sr. tutor Eliot House Harvard U., 1957-58, from instr. to assoc. prof. English, comparative lit., 1960-62, prof. English, comparative lit., 1969—, chmn. dept., 1969-75, 82-85. Mem. coms. degrees in history and lit. Harvard U., 1960—, Faculty coun., 1971-74, libr. com., 1971-74; dep. dir. Villa I Tatti, Florence, 1971-86, dir. 1988-2002. Author: Praisers of Folly: Erasmus, Rabelais, Shakespeare, 1964, Essays of Montaigne, 1964; co-author Program in Literature and the Arts for the Core Curriculum, 1977; transl.: (with intro.) Three Secret Poems, (George Seferis), 1969, Alexis (Marguerite Yourcenar), 1984, Two Lives and a Dream (Marguerite Yourcenar), That Mighty Sculptor, Time (Marguerite Yourcenar), 1992; edit. bd. Studies in English Lit., 1977-88; editor-in-chief I Tatti Studies: Essays in the Renaissance, 1988-2002; editor (with M. Mallon) On Artists and Art Historians: Selected Book Reviews of John Pope Hennessy, 1994; contbr. numerous articles, reviews, poems to profl. jours. Chair ad hoc vis. com. to Addison Gallery Am. Art, 1978; trustee Michael Rockefeller Meml. Fellowship, 1965-68, 69-70, Rockefeller Family Fund, 1973-79, Mus. Fine Arts, Boston, 1978-88, Bogliasco Found., 2001—; bd. dirs. Philip H. Rosenbach Found., 1974-78. Fulbright fellow U. Paris, 1954-55; Tower fellow Ecole Normale Supérieure Paris, 1955-56; fellow to Rome Am. Coun. Learned Socs., 1964-65; Walter Channing Cabot fellow Fac. Arts. and Scis., 1977-78. Mem. PEN, Boston Athenaeum, Am. Comparative Lit. Assn., Renaissance Soc. Am., Signet Soc. (assoc.), Modern Greek Studies Assn., Shakespeare Assn. Am., Coun. Fgn. Rels., Knickerbocker Club, Somerset Club, Harvard Club, Old Salopian, Boston Libr. Soc., Century Assn., Phi Beta Kappa. Home and Office: 25 Sutton Pl S Apt 20M New York NY 10022 E-mail: walter_kaiser@harvard.edu.

KAISER-BOTSAI, SHARON KAY, early childhood educator; b. Waterloo, Iowa, Aug. 9, 1941; d. Peter A. Ley and Lorraine (Worthington) Burton; m. Hugh W. Kaiser, Aug. 28, 1968 (div. 1981); 1 child, Kiana; m. Elmer E. Botsai, Dec. 5, 1981; children: Kiana, Don, Kurt. BSBA, U. Ariz., 1963; MEd, U. Hawaii, Honolulu, 1970; postgrad., U. Hawaii, 1972-88. Cert. elem. edn. tchr., Hawaii. Sec. Donald M. Drake, San Francisco, 1964-66; tchr. St. Mark's Kindergarten, Honolulu, 1966-73; head tchr. Cen. Union Preschool, Honolulu, 1967-77; tchr. Waiokeola Preschool, Honolulu, 1974-76, 77-88; tchr. staff instruction Honolulu Dist. Dept. of Edn., 1989-90; tchr. students of ltd. English proficiency Kaahumanu Sch., Honolulu, 1990-94; tchr. kindergarten Palolo Sch., Honolulu, 1991-97, Waialae Chartered Sch., 1997—2003. Pvt. instr. in Hawaiian dance, 1977-79; workshop leader marine sea crafts Sea Grant Inst. for Marine Educators, 1977, HAEYC Conf., 1979, 82, 84, 85, 86, chair workshops in music and creative drama, 1977, drama workshop, 1994, Drama Nat. Conf. workshop leader, 1982, multiple intelligences workshop leader, 1998; speaker Celebration of Life Sta. KHON-TV, 1979; workshop leader MECAP Conf., 1985; mem. com. Improvement Symphony Performance for Preschoolers, 1977; art advisor, coord. Sunday sch. program Waiokeola Ch., 1973, speaker creative communication, 1984; validator accreditation program Nat. Acad. for Edn. of Young Children, 1986—; asst. to co-chair conf. Hawaii Assn. for Edn. Young Children, 1987-88; Hawaii State Tchrs. Assn. rep. Palolo Sch., 1993; lectr. in field. Author: Creative Dramatics, 1990; co-author: Preschool Activities, 1990. Actress Presido Playhouse, San Francisco, 1962, Little Theatre, Honolulu Zoo, 1976; instr. spl. edn. students Kaneohe YWCA, 1967; troop co-leader Girl Scouts U.S.A., 1981-84; bd. dirs. Zoo Hui, 1984-86; trustee, stewardship chmn. Waiokeola Ch., 1986-88. Mem. Hawaii Assn. for Edn. of Young Children (First recipient Phyllis Loveless Excellence in Teaching award 1979), Delta Delta Delta. Lutheran. Avocations: tennis, water and snow skiing, creative drama, traveling, scuba diving. Home: 321 Wailupe Cir Honolulu HI 96821-1524

KAISERSHOT, EDWARD JOSEPH, elementary education educator, coach; b. Dickinson, N.D., Dec. 24, 1956; s. Edward A. and Margaret M. (Ridl) K.; children: Derrik E., David J. BS in Elem. Edn. and Physical Edn., Dickinson State U., 1979; certificate of edn. computing, Calif State Univ., San Bernardino, 1992. Elem. tchr., track-baksetball coach, asst. football coach New England (N.D.) Pub. Sch., 1979-80; equipment operator, western region chemist Dowell div. Dow Chem. Co., Dickinson, 1980-83; tchr., track and basketball coach Tioga (N.D.) Pub. Schs., 1983-86; elem. tchr. phys. edn., basketball coach El Camino Real Acad. WBT/SIL, Bogota, Colombia, 1986-88; elem. tchr. phys. edn. Del Rosa Christian Sch., San Bernardino, Calif., 1988-89; tchr. kindergarten San Bernarndino City Unified Sch. Dist., 1989—. Asst. track coach Dickinson State Univ., 1983—; tech. liaison for sch. site San Bernardino City Unified Sch. Dist. 1992—, sch. site sci. fair coord., 1991—; bd. dirs. Computer Using Educators, San Bernardino and Riverside Counties, Calif., 1995—. Camp counselor Child Evangelism Fellowship, N.D., 1984-85, bd. dirs. So. Calif., 1995—; judge Inland Empire Sci. and Engring. Fair, San Bernardino, 1994; bd. dirs., trustee Temple Bapt. Sch., Redlands, Calif., 1995—; leader Children's Bible Club, N.D., Bogota, 1983-88, Calif., 1990—; trustee 1st Bapt. Ch. Tioga, 1984-86; vol. Tioga Community Nursing Home and Hosp., 1983-86; coach N. D. Spl. Olympics; vol. San Bernardino Spl. Olympics, 1995—. Avocations: bible study, chess, basketball, fishing, relaxing. Office: San Bernardino City Unified Schs 777 N F St San Bernardino CA 92410-3017

KAISH, LUISE CLAYBORN, sculptor, former educator; b. Atlanta, Sept. 8, 1925; d. Harry and Elsa (Brown) Meyers; m. Morton Kaish, Aug. 15, 1948; 1 child, Melissa. BFA magna cum laude, Syracuse U., 1946, MFA, 1951; student, Escuela de Pintura y Escultura, Escuela de las Artes del Libro, Taller Grafico, Mexico, 1946-47. Artist-in-residence Dartmouth Coll., 1974; prof. sculpture and painting, 1980-93, chmn. div. painting and sculpture Columbia U., 1980-86, prof. emerita, 1993; vis. artist U. Wash., Seattle, Battelle seminars and study program, Seattle, 1979; artist-in-residence U. Haifa, Israel, 1985. One-man shows Meml. Art Gallery, Rochester, N.Y., 1954, Sculpture Ctr., N.Y.C., 1955, 58, Staempfli Gallery, N.Y.C., 1968, 81, 84, 87, 88, Minn. Mus. Art, St. Paul, 1969, Jewish Mus., N.Y.C., 1973, U. Ark., 1990, The Century Assn., 1998; exhibited (with Morton Kaish), Rochester Meml. Art Gallery, 1958, USIS, Rome, 1973, Dartmouth Coll., 1974, Oxford Gallery, Rochester, 1988; represented in permanent collections Whitney Mus. Am. Art, N.Y.C., Met. Mus. Art, N.Y.C., Jewish Mus., N.Y.C., Export Khleb, Moscow, Minn. Mus. Art, Gen. Mills Corp., Minn., Rochester Meml. Art Gallery, Smithsonian Instn., Nat. Mus. Am. Art, Washington, also numerous pvt. collections, commns., Syracuse U., Temple B'rith Kodesh, Rochester, Temple Israel, Westport, Conn., Holy Trinity Mission Sem., Silver Springs, Md., Temple Beth Shalom, Wilmington, Del., Beth-El Synagogue Ctr., New Rochelle, N.Y., Temple B'nai Abraham, Essex City, N.J., Continental Grain Co., N.Y. Trustee Am. Acad. in Rome, 1973-81, mem. exec. com., 1975-81, trustee emerita, 1994; trustee St. Gaudens Found., 1978-90, mem. exec. com., 1980-90. Recipient awards Everson Mus., Syracuse, 1947, awards Rochester Meml. Art Gallery, 1951, awards Ball State U., 1963, awards Ch. World Service, 1960, awards Council for Arts in Westchester, 1974, Emily

Lowe award, 1956, Audubon Artists gold medal, 1963, Honor award AIA, 1975, Arents Pioneer medal, Syracuse U., 1989; Louis Comfort Tiffany grantee, 1951; Guggenheim fellow, 1959; Rome prize fellow Am. Acad. in Rome, 1970-72 Mem. Nat. Acad. Design, The Century Assn., Eta Pi Upsilon. Home and Office: 610 W End Ave # 9-a New York NY 10024-1605

KAJI, AKIRA, microbiology scientist, educator; b. Tokyo, Jan. 13, 1930; came to U.S., 1954; s. Kiichi and Chiyo (Hanai) K.; m. Hideko Katayama, Aug. 22, 1958; children: Kenneth, Eugene, Naomi, Amy. BS, Tokyo U., 1953; PhD, Johns Hopkins U., 1958; MS (hon.), U. Pa., 1973. Rsch. fellow Johns Hopkins Hosp., Balt., 1958-59; guest investigator Rockefeller U., N.Y.C., 1959; rsch. assoc. microbiology Vanderbilt Med. Sch., Nashville, 1959-62; vis. scientist Oak Ridge (Tenn.) Nat. Lab., 1962-63; assoc. U. Pa. Med. Sch., Phila., 1963-64, asst. prof. microbiology, 1964-67, assoc. prof., 1967-72, prof., 1972—. Permanent mem. bd. sci. councilors Nat. Eye Inst., Bethesda, Md., 1987-92; prof., chair Tokyo U. Faculty Pharm. Scis., 1972-73; vis. prof. Kyoto U. Virus Rsch. Inst., 1985. Contbr. over 200 articles to profl. jours. Recipient Fulbright-Smith-Mundt award, 1954, Helen Hay Whitney award, 1964-69, John Simmon Guggenheim award, 1972-73, Fogarty Internat. Sr. award, 1985-86 Mem. Am. Soc. Biol. Chemistry and Molecular Biology, Am. Soc. Cell Biology, Am. Soc. Microbiology, Am. Soc. Chemistry. Avocations: ice dancing, swimming. Office: U Pa Sch Medicine Dept Microbiology Johnson Pavilion Philadelphia PA 19104

KAJI, HIDEKO, pharmacology educator; b. Tokyo, Jan. 1, 1932; came to U.S., 1954; d. Sakae and Tsuneko (Matsuda) Katayama; m. Akira Kaji, Aug. 23, 1958; children: Kenneth, Eugene, Naomi, Amy. BS, Tokyo U. Pharm. Scis., 1954; MS, U. Nebr., 1956; PhD, Purdue U., 1958. Vis. scientist Oak Ridge (Tenn.) Nat. Lab., 1962-63; assoc. U. Pa., Phila., 1963-64; rsch. assoc. The Inst. Cancer Rsch., Phila., 1965-66, asst. mem., 1966-76; vis. mem. Max Planck Inst. Molek. Gen., Berlin, 1972-73, Nat. Inst. Med. Rsch., London, 1973; assoc. prof. Jefferson Med. Coll., Phila., 1976-82; vis. prof. Wistar Inst., Phila., 1984-85; prof. biochemistry and molecular pharmacology Jefferson Med. Coll., Phila., 1983—. Cons. Nippon Paint Co., Ltd., Tokyo, 1990—, Coatesville (Pa.) VA Hosp., 1982-84. Contbr. articles to profl. jours. Fellow NIH (bd. dirs. 1986-89); mem. Am. Soc. Biochemistry and Molecular Biology, Am. Soc. Pharmacol. and Exptl. Therapeutics, Am. Soc. Microbiology, Sigma Xi. Home: 334 Fillmore St Jenkintown PA 19046-4328 Office: Jefferson Med Coll 1020 Locust St Philadelphia PA 19107-6731 Business E-Mail: hideko.kaji@jefferson.edu.

KALAI, EHUD, decision sciences educator, researcher in economics and decision sciences; b. Tel Aviv, Dec. 7, 1942; came to U.S., 1963; s. Meir and Elisheva (Rabinovitch) K.; m. Marilyn Lott, Aug. 24, 1967; children: Kerren, Adam. AB with distinction, U. Calif. at Berkeley, 1967; MS, Cornell U., 1971, PhD in Applied Math., 1972. Asst. prof. dept. statistics Tel Aviv U., 1972-75; vis. asst. prof. decision scis. J.L. Kellogg Grad. Sch. Mgmt. Northwestern U., Evanston, Ill., 1975-76, assoc. prof. decision scis., 1976-78, prof. managerial econs. and decision scis., 1978-82, The Charles E. Morrison Chair prof. decision scis., 1982-2001, prof. math., 1990—, IBM rsch. chair managerial econs., 1980-81, J.L. Kellogg rsch. chair in decision theory, 1981-82, chmn. meds. dept., 1983-85; dir. Ctr. for Strategic Decision-Making Kellogg Sch. Mgmt., Northwestern U., 1995—. Oskar Morgenstern rsch. prof. game theory NYU, 1991; expert testimony in ct. cases, 1982—; cons. Israeli Def. Forces, 1974-75, 1st Nat. Bank Chgo., 1987, Arthur Anderson, 1990, Kaiser Permanente, 1995, Nath Sonnenschein and Rosenthal, 1999, Baxter Healthcare Corp., 1999—; James J. O'Conner Distinguished Prof. of Decision and Game Scis., 2001—. Founder, editor Games and Econ. Behavior Jour., 1988—; editl. bd. Math. Social Scis., 1980-90, Jour. Econ. Theory, 1980-88, Internat. Jour. Game Theory, 1984—; contbr. numerous articles on game theory and econs. to profl. jours. Sgt. Israeli Def. Forces, 1960-63. NSF grantee, 1979—; Sherman Fairchild Disting. scholar, Calif. Inst. Tech., 1994-95. Fellow Econometrics Soc.; mem. Am. Math. Soc., Pub. Choice Soc., Game Theory Soc. (founder, exec. v.p 1998—), Beta Gamma Sigma. Home: 1110 N Lake Shore Dr Apt 23S Chicago IL 60611-1023 Office: Kellogg Grad Sch of Mgmt Northwestern Univ Evanston IL 60208-0001 E-mail: kalai@kellogg.northwestern.edu.

KALAMAROS, ANASTASIA ANN, educational psychology educator; b. South Bend, Ind., May 2, 1963; d. Edward Nicholas and Marilyn Jane (Foster) K. BA in Psychology, Hanover Coll., 1985; MA in Ednl. Psychology, U. Denver, 1986, PhD in Sch. Psychology, 1991. Cert. sch. psychologist, Colo. Spl. edn. intern, mini course tchr. Cherry Creek Schs., Englewood, Colo., 1985-86; grad. rsch. asst. U. Denver, 1986-88; psychologist Douglas County Sch. Dist., Castle Rock, Colo., 1988-92; chairperson Douglas County dist. crisis team Douglas County Schs., Castle Rock, Colo., 1989-92; asst. rsch. prof. U. Colo., Denver, 1992—. Residential counselor Rocky Mountain Talent Search, Denver, summer, 1985-86, residential dir., summer, 1986-88; presenter in field. Mem. APA (mem. com. for children, families and youth 1992-93), ASCD, Nat. Assn. Sch. Psychologist, Colo. Soc. Sch. Psychologist (chairperson legis. com. 1992—). Presbyterian. Avocations: skiing, travel, volley ball, music. Home: 7540 S Homesteader Dr Morrison CO 80465-2839 Office: U Colo Sch Edn Campus Box 106 PO Box 173364 Denver CO 80217-3364

KALAPOS, FELICIA ZERA, elementary school educator, writer; b. Bridgeport, Conn., July 5, 1953; d. Aloyzy John and Florence (Dobieski) Zera; m. George Julius Kalapos, Jr., May 26, 1974; children: Jennifer, Jessica, Jaclyn, Jeffrey. BS Elem. Edn. cum laude, So. Conn. State U., 1974; MS Elem. Edn., U. Bridgeport, 1976. Cert. profl. educator Conn. State Bd. Edn. Grade 6 tchr. Fairfield (Conn.) Bd. Edn., 1974—77, gifted tchr., 1979—81, grade 5 tchr., 1988—90, chpt. I math tutor, tchr., 1991—92, math resource tchr., 1993—, gifted math tchr., 2000—; homebound pvt. corp. tutor Fairfield and Stratford (Conn.) Bd. Edn., 1981—88. Ednl. cons. Environ. Mgmt. Con., Shelton, Conn., 1990; guest lectr. ESOL class Fairfield (Conn.) U., 2000; guest lectr. U. R.I., Kingston, 2000; spkr. in field. Author: (novels) Love on a Shoestring, 2000. Active PTA, 1974—. Mem.: Nat. Edn. Assn., Conn. Edn. Assn., Fairfield Edn. Assn., Nat. Coun. Tchrs. Math. Republican. Roman Catholic. Avocations: collecting old books, cooking, writing. Home: 502 Allyndale Dr Stratford CT 06614-4308 Office: Fairfield Bd Edn Stratfield Sch 1407 Melville Ave Fairfield CT 06825

KALAYJIAN, ANIE, psychotherapist, nurse, educator, consultant; b. Aleppa, Syria; came to U.S., 1971; d. Kevork and Zabelle (Mardikian) Kalayjian; m. Shahé Navasart Sanentz, Dec. 16, 1984 (div. 1999). BS, L.I. U., 1979; MEd, Columbia U., 1981, EdD, 1985, profl. nursing tng. course, 1984; cert. photography, Pratt Inst., 1979; DSc (hon.), L.I. U., 2001. RN, N.Y., N.J., Conn.; cert. psychiat. mental health specialist; Dutch diplomate in logotherapy; advanced cert. in Eye Movement Desensitization and Reprocessing, advanced cert. in disaster mgmt. ARC; bd. cert. expert in traumatic stress; cert. expert in crisis mgmt. Psychiat. nurse Met. Hosp., N.Y.C., 1979-84; staff psychiat. mental health nurse Project Renewal, N.Y.C., 1978-2000; instr. Hunter Coll., N.Y.C., 1980-82; prof. Bloomfield Coll., N.J., 1984-85; lectr. Jersey City Coll., N.J., 1985; prof. Seton Hall U., South Orange, N.J., 1985-87; assoc. prof. grad. program St. Joseph Coll., 1987-91; prof. John Jay Coll. Criminal Justice, 1991-92, Fairleigh Dickinson U., 1991—92; vis. prof. Pace U., N.Y.C., 1994-95. Adj. prof. Coll. Mt. St. Vincent, Riverdale, NY, 1995—97, Fordham U., 1998—, Coll. New Rochelle, 1998—99; disting. lectr. Columbia U., N.Y.C., 1995; spkr. in field; keynote spkr. Mid Am. Logotherapy Inst., 1995, Coll. Mt. St. Vincent, 1995, Hollins Coll., Va., 1995, UN; NGO exec. com. vice-chair, 2000—; chair DPI/NGO annual conf.; lectr., Argentina, Toronto, Ireland, U.N., 2003. Author: Disaster and Mass Trauma: Global Perspectives on Post Disaster Mental Health Management, 1995; contbr. articles to profl. jours., chapters to books; reviewer: Readings: A Journal of Reviews and Commentary in Mental Health, 1990—; TV appearances ABC, CNN, NY1, Tokyo TV, —, radio appearances WSOU, WFUV, WBAI, Voice of America, —. Active com. for presdl. task force on nursing curriculum Soc. for Traumatic Stress Studies; co-founder, East coast coord. Mental Health Outreach to Earthquake Survivors in Armenia; program dir. Mental Health Outreach to Earthquake Survivors in Turkey, 1999; dir. Julia Richman-Pace U.-N.Y. State Bd. Edn.-Visiting Nurse Svc.-Partnership program, 1991-92; UN rep. World Fedn. for Mental Health, mem. mental health/human rights com., 1996—. Recipient Clark Found. scholarship award, 1985, Outstanding Rsch. award Columbia U., 1993, ABSA Outstanding Achievement award APA, 1995; rsch. grantee Pace U., 1992; Endowed Nursing Edn. Columbia U., scholar, 1984; Armenian Relief Soc. scholar, 1976-77, Armenian Students Assn. Am. scholar, 1976-78, Columbia U. Tchrs. Coll. Outstanding Rsch. award, 1993. Fellow Am. Orthopsychiat. Assn., N.Y. State Nursing Assn. (planning com. nursing edn.), APA (outstanding achievement award 1995); mem. Coun. on Continuing Edn., Psychiat. and Mental Health Nursing, Am. Psychol. Soc., Am. Psychiat. Nurses Assn., Am. Acad. Experts in Traumatic Stress, Internat. Coun. Psychologists, Internat. Trauma Counselors, Inst. for Psychodynamics and Origins of Mind, Armenian Students Assn. (treas. 1980-81, pres. 1981-83, scholarship chairperson 1983-85, v.p. ctrl. exec. com. 1987-88, pres. 1988-89, nat. pres. 1988-90), Armenian Info. Profls. (corr. sec. 1992—), Armenian-Am. Soc. for Studies on Stress and Genocide (founder, pres. 1988—), N.Y. RN's Assn. (chair edn. com. 1989-99), World Fedn. for Mental Health (UN rep. 1994—, treas., sec., UN com. on human rights 1994—, chair human rights com. 1996—), Univ. for Peace (corr. sec. UN com.), Internat. Soc. Traumatic Stress Studies (v.p. N.Y. chpt. 1993-95, pres. 1995—), Global Soc. for Nursing and Health (pres., co-founder), N.Y. Counties RN Assn. (Jane Delano Disting. Svc. award 1994), Kappa Delta Pi (advisor 1989-90), Sigma Theta Tau. Avocations: aerobics, photography, acting, hiking. Office: 130 W 79th St New York NY 10024-6477 E-mail: kalayjiana@aol.com.

KALBFLEISCH, JOHN MCDOWELL, cardiologist, educator; b. Lawton, Okla., Nov. 15, 1930; s. George and Etta Lillian (McDowell) K.; m. Jolie Harper, Dec. 30, 1961. AS, Cameron A&M U., Lawton, 1950; BS, U. Okla., 1952, MD, 1957. Diplomate Am. Bd. Internal Medicine, Am. Bd. Cardiovascular Disease. Intern U. Va. Hosp., 1957-58; resident and fellow U. Okla. Med. Ctr., 1958-62, instr. medicine, 1964-66, asst. prof., 1966-69, assoc. clin. prof., 1970-78, clin. prof. Tulsa br., 1978—; pvt. practice Tulsa, 1969—; founder, chmn. bd., CEO Cardiology of Tulsa, Inc., 1969—; dir. cardiovascular svcs. St. Francis Hosp., Tulsa, 1975—. Physician adv. bd. City of Tulsa, 1978-81; bd. dirs. St. Francis Hosp., exec. com., 1987-97, 2001—; exec. v.p., chief med. officer St. Francis Health Sys., 1998-99; treas. Tulsa Med. Edn. Found., 1988-89, v.p., 1990-92, pres., 1992-94; med. dir., chmn. bd. Warren Clinics, 1990-97; mem. Okla. Ctr. for Advancement of Sci. and Tech., 1989-95; mem. adv. com. Ctr. for Lasser Devel. and Applications, Okla. State U. Contbr. articles to profl. jours. With USPHS, 1962-64. Recipient Lifelong Svc. award, Tulsa Med. Edn. Found./U. Okla. Coll. Medicine, 2002. Fellow ACP (gov.-elect Okla. 1990-91, gov. 1991-95, Okla. Laureate award 1995), Am. Coll. Cardiology (gov. Okla. 1978-81); mem. AMA, AAAS, Tulsa County Med. Soc., Okla. State Med. Assn., Am. Heart Assn. (Fellow coun. on clin. cardiology), tchg. scholar 1967-69), Okla. Soc. Internal Medicine v.p., pres.-elect 1983-84, pres. 1985-86), Am. Soc. Internal Medicine, Am. Fedn. Clin. Rsch., Am. Inst. Nutrition, U. Okla. Med. Alumni Assn. (Physician of Yr. in Pvt. Practice 1999), Delta Upsilon. Republican. Presbyterian. Office: 6151 S Yale Ave Ste 400 Tulsa OK 74136-1933

KALER, ERIC WILLIAM, chemical engineer, educator; b. Burlington, Vt., Sept. 23, 1956; s. Ronald Maurice and Mary Elizabeth (Kindred) K.; m. Karen Fults, Dec. 30, 1979. BS, Calif. Inst. Tech., 1978; PhD, U. Minn., 1982. Asst. prof. chem. engring. U. Wash., Seattle, 1982-87, assoc. prof., 1987-89; assoc. prof. chem. engring. U. Del., Newark, 1989-91, prof., 1991-98, chair dept. chem. engring., 1996-2000, Elizabeth Inez Kelley prof., 1998—, dean Coll. Engring., 2000—. Vis. prof. U. Graz, Austria; cons. Shell Devel. Co., 1983-90, BP Am., 1987-88, DuPont, 1988—, numerous other cos. Conbr. numerous articles to profl. jours. Elder Andrew Riverside Presbyn. Ch., Mpls., 1980-82, Northminster Presbyn. Ch., Seattle, 1984-88. Named Presdl. Young Investigator, NSF, Washington, 1984; recipient Curtis W. McGraw Rsch. award Am. Soc. Engring. Edn., 1995; Presdl. scholar Dept. Edn., Washington, 1978. Fellow AAAS; mem. AIChE (Chilton award 2002), Am. Chem. Soc. (award in Colloid or Surface Chemistry 1998, DE Sect. award 1998). Lodges: Masons. Republican. Home: 11 Bridlebrook Ln Newark DE 19711-2003 Office: U of Del Dept Chem Engring Newark DE 19716 E-mail: Kaler@che.udel.edu.

KALIN, D(OROTHY) JEAN, artist, educator; b. Kansas City, Mo., Feb. 11, 1932; d. William Warner and Esther Dorothy (Peterson) Johnson; m. John Baptist Kalin, Jr., Jan. 5, 1952; children: Jean Loraine, Debra Ann, Diana Yvonne. AA, St. Joseph (Mo.) Jr. Coll., 1951. Artist Hallmark Cards, Inc., Kansas City, Mo., 1952-53, 73-93; freelance artist Kansas City, 1953-72; owner Portraits of Life, Kansas City, 1986—, art tchr., 1988—. Illustrator article for Directory of Am. Portrait Artists, 1985; featured in Rockport Pubs. Best of Watercolor 2 and Painting Light and Shadow, 1997, Am. Artist Mag., 1998, 2000, Splash 5, 1998, Best of Collected Watercolor, 2002, Midwest Art, 2003, The Artists' Mag., 2003. Kansas City Art Inst. scholar, 1951-52. Mem. Nat. Oil and Acrylic Painters Soc. (signature mem.), Nat. Acrylic Painters Assn. (signature mem.), Kans. Watercolor Soc. (signature mem.), Women Artists of the West (signature mem.), Am. Watercolor Soc. (assoc.), Nat. Watercolor Soc. (assoc.), Midwest Watercolor Soc. (assoc.), Nat. Mus. Women in the Arts (charter mem.), Mo. Watercolor Soc. (signature mem., bd. dirs. 1999—), Western Colo. Watercolor Soc. (signature mem.), Internat. Platform Assn. Avocations: gardening, traveling. Address: 20650 State Rt 371 Platte City MO 64079-9344

KALIN, KARIN BEA, retired secondary school educator, consultant; b. N.Y.C., June 22, 1943; d. Lawrence Leon and Celia (Siskind) Elkind; children: Laura, Howard. BS, SUNY, Oswego, 1965; MS, CUNY, 1967. Cert. social studies tchr., N.Y. Tchr. Benjamin Franklin H.S., N.Y.C., 1965-66, Grover Cleveland H.S., Ridgewood, N.Y., 1967-73, Aviation H.S., L.I. City, N.Y., 1979-99, sex equity coord., 1982-90, local equal opportunity coord., 1983-91, sch. recruiter, 1985-91; ret., 1999. Curriculum developer OEO N.Y.C. Bd. Edn., fall, 1985; global studies curriculum writing, 1997—98; panelist Aerospace Edn. Workshop for Elem. Tchrs., Career Exploration Seminar, Aerospace Edn. Conf., 1990; placement counselor East Meadow (N.Y.) Sch. Dist., 1989—; cons. Coll. Aerospace, NY, 1986, Profl. and Clerical Employees of Internat. Ladies Garment Workers Union, N.Y.C., 1989; with L.I. Coun. for Equal Edn. and Employment, 1990; placement counselor N.Y.C. H.S., 2000—; with N.Y.C. H.S. Transfer Ctr., 2000. Mem. Women on the Job, Port Washington, NY, 1986—91, L.I. Coun. Equal Edn. and Employment, 1990—, Coalition to Advocate for Women of Color in Edn.; vol. Goodwill Games, 1998, Empire State Games, 1999, Hamlet Cup, 1999—, Friends of the Arts, 1999—, L.I. Fair at Old Bethpage Restoration, 1999, L.I. Studies Inst., 2000, Divsn. 1 NCAA Women's Swimming & Diving Championship, 2001, Big East NCAA Women's Swimming & Diving Championship, 2001, 2002; mem. com. Nassau Dem. Com., Westbury, NY, 1988—. William Robertson Coe fellow, 1992; grantee Columbia U., 1967, 69, N.Y.C. Bd. Edn., 1983, Nat. Coun. for Humanities, 1985, Project Voice/Move, 1984-85; named to Nat. Women's Hall of Fame. Mem.: AFL-CIO, LWV, NAFE, AAUW (roundtable on gender equity in classroom 1992, co-chair social justice 2000—, Nassau County chair Sister to Sister 2001), NOW (chair conciousness raising com. 1982, chair women and employment com. 1987—90, chair social justice), Nat. Women's Hall of Fame, Nat. Women's History Mus., Assn. Tchrs. of Social Studies, United Fedn. Tchrs., Nat. Women's Hall of Fame, Nat. Women's Polit. Caucus (chair polit. action com. 1990—96, bd. dirs.), N.Y. State Alliance for Women and Girls in Tech., Bachelor and Bachelorettes for Square Dancing (pres. L.I. chpt. 1994—96, founder). Jewish. Avocations: swimming, reading, visiting museums, square dancing, round dancing, bridge. Home: 700 Barkley Ave East Meadow NY 11554-4501 E-mail: karin622@att.net.

KALIN, ROBERT, retired mathematics educator; b. Everett, Mass., Dec. 11, 1921; s. Benjamin and Celia (Kraff) K.; m. Shirley Sharney, Oct. 22, 1944; children: Susan Leslie, John Benjamin; m. 2d Madelyn Pildish, Aug. 17, 1962; 1 child, Richard Dean. Student, Northeastern U., 1940-43; BS, U. Chgo., 1947; MAT, Harvard U., 1948; PhD, Fla. State U., 1961. Tchr. math. Holten H.S., Danvers, Mass., 1948-49, Beaumont H.S., Hadley Tech. Sch., Soldan-Blewitt H.S., St. Louis, 1949-52; ednl. statistician Naval Air Tech. Tng. Ctr., Norman, Okla., 1952-53; test specialist, assoc. in research Ednl. Testing Svc., Princeton, N.J., 1953-55; exec. asst. Commn. on Math. of Coll. Entrance Exam. Bd., 1955-56; instr. dept. math. edn. Fla. State U., Tallahassee, 1956-61, asst. prof., 1961-63, assoc. prof., 1963-65, prof., 1965-90, prof. emeritus, 1990, assoc. dept. head, 1968-73, program chmn., 1975-78. Co-author: Elementary Mathematics, Patterns and Structure, 11 vols., 1966, (with George Green) Modern Mathematics for the Elementary School Teacher, 1966, (with E.D. Nichols) Analytic Geometry, 1973, Holt School Mathematics, 9 vols., 1974, rev. 1978, Holt Mathematics, 9 vols., 1981, rev., 1985, (with M.K. Corbitt) Prentice Hall Geometry, 1990, rev. edit., 1993. Mem., treas. Brownsville-Haywood County Libr. Bd., 1991-95, chmn., 1995-97; bd. dirs. Friends of Tenn. Librs., 1995-2002, sec., 1996-97, pres.-elect, 1997-99, pres., 1999-2000, past pres., 2000-02; pres. Temple Adas Israel, 1992-94, treas., 1994-2000; bd. dirs. Jewish Hist. Soc. of Memphis and the Mid-South, 1998-2001, sec., 2000-01. Mem. Math. Assn. Am. (sec.-treas. Fla. sect. 1985-91, Svc. award Fla. sect. 1991), Fla. Coun. Tchrs. Math. (pres. 1960-61), Fla. Assn. Math. Educators (pres. 1984-86), Nat. Coun. Tchrs. Math. (chmn. external affairs com. 1972-73), Nat. High Sch. and Jr. Coll. Math. Clubs (gov. 1972-75, pres. 1978-80). Home: 7 Stoneleigh Pl Brownsville TN 38012-2463 E-mail: r_kalin@bellsouth.net.

KALIPOLITES, JUNE ELEANOR TURNER, rehabilitation professional; b. Grasmere, NH; d. Louis O. and Edith Mae (Allen) Turner; m. Nicholas G. Kalipolites, Feb. 12, 1955; children: George, Stephanie, Athena. AA secretarial sci., Hesser Coll., Manchester, NH, 1977; B of Gen. Studies, U. NH, 1980; MS in Rehab. Adminstrn. and Svc., So. Ill. U., Carbondale, 1982; EdD in Ednl. Adminstrn., Vanderbilt U., 1992. Cert. rehab. counselor. Office mgr. Harris Upham and Co., Inc., Manchester; mgr. Amoskeag Bank & Trust Co.; rehab. counselor Div. Vocat. Rehab., Nashua, NH; rehab. cons. NH Divsn. Vocat. Rehab., Concord, NH, 1986-94, tng. coord., 1993-94; rehab. cons. spl. svc. NH Divsn. Adult Learning and Rehab., Concord, 1995-2000; pvt. practice Manchester, 1999—. Author: Profile of Women in Rehabilitation Administration: A Common Theme, 1992, Projects with Industry: A Unique Concept for Providing Rehab. Svc. to Persons with Severe Disabilities, 1982. LaVerne Noyes scholar. Mem. ACA, ASTD, AAUW, Am. Rehab. Counseling Assn., Nat. Rehab. Assn. (bd. dir. 1977-81, 82-2000, nat. bd. dir. 1994-97), Nat. Rehab. Counseling Assn. (bd. dir. 1986-87), Nat. Rehab. Adminstrn. Assn. (nat. bd. dir. 1983-87, 92-94), NE Rehab. Counseling Assn. (pres. 1986-87, bd. dir. 1986-88), NE Rehab. Assn. (pres. 1999, bd. dir. 1999—), NH Rehab. Assn. (bd. dir. 1977-80, treas. 1978-79, 89-92, sec. 1977-78, 1982-2000), Rho Sigma Chi, Chi Sigma Iota. Democrat. Greek Orthodox. Avocations: swimming, travel, research, genealogy.

KALISCH, KATHRYN MARY, elementary education educator; b. N.Y.C., June 05; d. Henry Arthur and Lenore (Morey) K. BA, Marymount Manhattan Coll., 1974; MEd, William Paterson Coll. N.J., 1988; postgrad., Oxford U., 1995. Cert. tchr., supr. N.J. Instr. basic skills Hasbrouck Hts. (N.J.) Bd. Edn., 1977-92, instr. gifted & talented, 1983-89, 4th grade tchr., 1992—. Presenter grad. studies symposium, Jersey City State Coll., 1992. Counselor Hasbrouck Hts. Youth Guidance Coun., 1976-81; bd. dir. Hasbrouck Hts. Free Pub. Libr., 1990-91. Mem. NEA, ASCD (bd. dirs. northeast region 1990—), N.J. Edn. Assn., N.J. Assn. Supervision and Curriculum Devel. (gen. chairperson northeast reg. conf. 1992, exec. bd. mem. 1990—), Bergen County Edn. Assn., Hasbrouk Hts. Edn. Assn., People to People Internat. (vis. Viet Nam Reading Del. of Citizen's Ambassador Program) 1995). Roman Catholic. Avocation: travel. Home: 240 Prospect Ave Apt 380 Hackensack NJ 07601-2595

KALLENDORF, CRAIG WILLIAM, English, speech and classical languages educator; b. Cin., June 23, 1954; s. Earl Roy and Hazel Greene (Griffith) K.; m. Hilaire Richey, Oct. 16, 1993. BA, Valparaiso U., 1975; MA, U. N.C., 1977, PhD, 1982. Asst. prof. dept. English Tex. A&M U., College Station, 1982-88, assoc. prof. English and classics, 1988-93, prof. English, classics and speech, 1993—, interim head modern and classical langs., 2001—. Cons. NEH, Washington, 1987—. Author: Bibliography of Latin Influences..., 1982, Petrarch: Selected Letters, 1987, In Praise of Aeneas, 1989, Epistle of St. Paul to the Romans, 1991, A Bibliography of Venetian Editions of Virgil, 1470-1599, 1991, Vergil: The Classical Heritage, 1993, A Bibliography of Renaissance Italian Translations of Virgil, 1994, Aldine Press Books, 1998, Virgil and The Myth of Venice, 1999, Landmark Essays on Rhetoric and Literature, 1999, Humanist Educational Treatises, 2002; editor Jour. Allegorica, 1989-2000, Rhetorica, 1993-96, Neo-Latin News, 1992—; contbr. articles to prof. jours. Grantee Tex. A&M U., 1983—, South Ctrl. MLA, 1984, NEH, 1985, 90-92, Delmas Found., 1987, 92, ACLS, 1992, Humanities Rsch. Ctr., U. Tex., 1994., U. Utah Humanities Ctr., 2000-01. Lutheran. Office: Tex A&M U Dept English College Station TX 77843-4227 E-mail: kalendrf@tamu.edu.

KALMAN-COBURN, ELAINE PRISCILLA, elementary school educator; b. Washington, Aug. 16, 1958; d. Benjamin and Doris (Spector) K.; m. Jeff Coburn, Apr. 8, 1989; children: Nathan, Tyler. BS, Towson State U., 1980; MS in Reading Edn., Johns Hopkins U., 1987. Tchr. Swansfield Elem. Sch. Howard County Pub. Schs., Columbia, Md., 1981-84; tchr. Bushy Park Elem. Sch. Fairfax County Pub. Schs., Glenwood, Md., 1984-87; tchr. Mt. Vernon High Sch., 1988—92, Hybla Valley Elem. Sch., 1992—. Mem. NEA, Va. State Reading Assn., Howard County Edn. Assn., Am. Fedn. Tchrs., Md. State Tchrs. Assn., Va. Edn. Assn.

KALMUS, ELLIN, art historian, educator; b. N.Y.C. d. Victor and Mata (Heineman) Roudin; m. Murray L. Silberstein, Oct. 6, 1949 (dec. 1968); children: James, Barbara Silberstein Keezell, John; m. Allan H. Kalmus, May 16, 1969 (dec. 1997). BA cum laude, Vassar Coll., 1946. Asst. dept. publs. and exhbns., asst. tchr. Mus. Modern Art, N.Y.C., 1946-50; lectr. Riverdale Country Sch., N.Y.C., 1970-90, Dalton, Trinity, Columbia Grammar, Birch Wathen Schs., N.Y.C., 1971-83, Fifth Ave. Presbyn. Ch., St. James Episcopal Ch., N.Y.C., 1982-83. Vis. com. photograph and slide libr. Met. Mus. Art, N.Y.C., 1978—; tchg. staff Ethical Culture Sch. for Adult Edn., New Sch. for Social Rsch., 1980-81; lectr. in field. Trustee, head edn. com. Riverdale Country Sch., N.Y.C., 1978-84. Pierpont Morgan Libr. fellow, 1986, Frick Collection fellow, 1992. Mem. Cosmopolitan Club, Sunningdale Club (Scarsdale, N.Y.), Phi Beta Kappa. Home: 125 E 72d St New York NY 10021-4250

KALONJI, GRETCHEN, engineering educator; Degree in Engring., MIT, 1980, PhD, 1982. Asst. to assoc. prof. MIT, 1982—90; prof. dept. materials sci. & engring. U. Wash., 1990—. Dir. Engring. Coalition Schs. Excellence Edn. and Leadership U. Wash; lectr. Symposium Japanese Soc. Engring. Edn. Tokyo; with Tech. Edn. Resource Ctr.; vis. scholar Max Planck Inst., Stutgart, U. Paris. Recipient Young Investigator award 1984, George Westinghouse award ASEE, 1994. Fellow: AAAS. Office: U Wash Box 352120 Seattle WA 98195-2120 Office Fax: 206-543-3100.*

KALTSOS, ANGELO JOHN, electronics executive, educator, photographer; b. Boston, Aug. 19, 1930; s. John Angelo and Rita Thomas (Goudas) K.; m. Verna Kay Wilson, June 30, 1952 (dec. Jan. 1973); children: Pamela, Elaine, Gregory, Stephanie, Lenora, Demetra, Dana. Student, Mass. Radio and TV Sch., Boston, 1955-57, Harvard Coll. Extension, 1964, Boston State Coll., 1965-67, U. N.M., 1976, Fitchburg State Coll., 1977. Clk. U.S. Postal Svc., Boston, 1954-57; electronic rsch. technician Crosley div. Avco, Cin., 1957; electronic rsch. production technician Raytheon Mfg. Co., Waltham, Mass., 1957-63; educator Cambridge (Mass.) Sch. Dept., 1961-81; ind. ethnology rsch. N.Mex., 1969—; mgr. Pampas, Inc., Boston, 1987-90. Bd. dirs. Expansion Dance Co., Boston; cons. 5 P.I.E., Albuquerque, 1976—, Indian Tribal Group, N.Mex.; lectr. S.W. Indian Culture in Boston, Cambridge area, 1990—; pres., treas. Spartan Enterprises, Inc., 1965-69. Author: Southwest Indian, 1986; one-man shows include Christmas Tree Gallery, Manteo, N.C., 1977, 4th St. Photo Gallery, N.Y.C., 1980, Cambride Rindge and Latin Sch., Mass., 1981, Jay's, Cambridge, Mass., 1983, Here Today Gallery, Boston, 1984, Andover (Maine) Town Hall, 1984, 86, Piedmont Art Assn., Martinsville, Va., 1985-86, Cambalache Gallery, Boston, 1986-87, The 4th St. Gallery, N.Y.C., 1990, Andover (Maine) Pub. Libr., 1997-98; contbg. journalist in field. Chmn. No Thank Q Hydro Quebec, Andover, Maine, 1988-91, coord., Dryden, Maine, 1991-2001; regional and media coord. N.E. Alliance to Protect James Bay, 1990-91, exec. bd., adv. bd., treas., 1991-2001, project dir., 1995-2001; project dir., treas. Hydro Electric Watch, 2001—; senate faculty Cambridge Sch. Dept., 1980-81; sec. New Eng. Model Car Assn. of Raceways, 1966-69; educator Cambridge Adult Ctr., 1990-97, Paulist Ctr., Boston, 1991-92; judge Andover amateur photo contest, 1996-99, coord., judge, 2001-. Recipient Robert Sweeney award Rindge Alumni Assn., 1996. Mem. Appalachian Mountain Club (life). Greek Orthodox. Avocations: ethnography, entomology, cooking, gardening, hiking. Home: PO Box 33 Andover ME 04216-0033

KALUDIS, GEORGE, management consultant, book company executive, educator; b. Balt., Oct. 7, 1938; s. Steven George and Theresa (Topal) K.; m. Eugenia Leone Mihalakis, July 21, 1962; children: Stephen George, Michele Maria, William Michael, Kirk Jamie. BA, U. Md., 1960, MEd, 1965; PhD, Fla. State U., 1968. Asst. dean student life U. Md., 1960-65; resident instr. U. S. Fla., 1965-66; dir. div. planning and evaluation State Univ. Sys. Fla., 1966-70; vice chancellor ops. and fin. planning, assoc. prof. mgmt. Vanderbilt U., 1970-76, adj. assoc. prof. mgmt., 1976-78; exec. v.p. Ingram Book Co., 1976-78; chmn., pres. Kaludis Consulting, Washington, 1978—. Mem. tech. coun. Nat. Ctr. Higher Edn. Mgmt. Sys., 1970—72, bd. dirs., 1972—76, chmn. bd., 1975—76; pres., bd. dirs. Frat. Advisors Group, Inc., Tallahassee, 1968—70; mem. com. chmn. Nat. Com. on Financing Postsecondary Edn., 1972—74. Editor: Strategies for Budgeting, new Directions in Higher Education, 1973; mem. editl. bd.: On the Horizon, 1996—2001, contbg. author: Mission Management a New Synthesis, vol. 1, Dollars, Distance and Online Education. Bd. dirs. NCCJ, Nashville, St. Photios Nat. Shrine, 1986-87; 1st v.p. Family and Children's Svcs., Inc., 1978-80; chmn. Spl. Com. on Cable TV, Nashville, 1982-95; mem. parish coun. Holy Trinity Greek Orthodox Ch., 1971-94, pres., 1972-78, 81-83, 92-94, Stewardship Commn., Greek Orthodox Archdiocese, 1993-95, archdiocesan coun., 1994-98, 2000—, co-chmn. com. on strategic and long range planning, 1994-97, diocese coun., N.J., 1999—, v.p.; parish coun. St. George Greek Orthodox Ch., Bethesda, 1998, sec., chair stewardship com., 2000, pres.; del. World Clergy-Laity Congress, Greek Orthodox Ch., Istanbul, 2000, mem. Leadership 100, 2001; mem. Nat. Capital campaign com. Fla. State U., 2001; bd. trustees Internat. Orthodox Christian Charities, 2003—. With U.S. Army, 1962-64. Recipient Medal of St. Paul award Greek Orthodox Archdiocese, 1992, Disting. Alumnus award U. Md. Coll. Edn., 1995, Order of St. Andrew of Ecumenical Patriarch, 2003—. Mem. Am. Assn. Higher Edn., Assn. Instnl. Rsch., Nat. Assn. Coll. and Univ. Bus. Officers, Fin. Execs. Inst. (pres. Nashville chpt. 1975), Nashville Area C. of C. (gov.), Am. Hellenic Ednl. Progressive Assn., U. Md. alumni ctr. cabinet, U. Md. arena seating planning com., Omicron Delta Kappa, Pi Sigma Alpha, Sigma Phi Epsilon (chmn. commn. on univ. rels. 1992-93). Office: Ste 440 1919 M St NW Washington DC 20036

KALUZA, SHERYLE SIEGFRIED, music educator, singer, songwriter; b. Mpls., Jan. 4, 1950; d. Ervin Vern and Dorothy Lorraine Siegfried; m. Charles Leo Kaluza, Apr. 14, 1972; children: Karl Nicholas, Ruth Alayne. BA, Augsburg Coll., Mpls., 1972. Cert. tchr., Mo. Tchr. vocal music Memphis (Mo.) Sch. Dist., 1972, Immaculate Mary Cath. Sch., Kirksville, Mo., 1973-76; asst. choir dir. St. Edmund's Cath. Ch., Warren, Mich., 1977-81; choir dir. Ch. of Redemption, Bartlett, Tenn., 1981-84, Emmanuel Presbyn. Ch., West Linn, Oreg., 1984-85, Ch. of Resurrection, West Linn, 1987-94, music coord., 1993-95; instr. voice Marylhurst (Oreg.) Coll., 1994-96, Heartsong Studio, West Linn, 1985—; voice cons. Eastmoreland Ear, Nose and Throat Clinic, Portland, Oreg. Instr. Liturgical Arts Resource Ctr., 1989; participant Nat. Assn. Tchrs. Singing, Superior, Wis., 1987; participant vocal master class Linfield Coll., McMinnville, Oreg., 1989, 90, Nat. Pastoral Musicians Composers Forum, St. Paul, 1992. Composer: (song cycle) The Lark Songs, 1991; singer, arranger rec. Real Lullabies, 1989. Ch. cantor Ch. of Resurrection, 1985—, also mem. choir; pres. Portland Aux. Osteo. Physicians and Surgeons Oreg., 1986-87; asst. dir. Ah! Chantez, Marylhurst, 1988-89. Mem. Music Tchrs. Nat. Assn. (soloist for song cycle Summer Fragments composer competition 1992), Oreg. Music Tchrs. Assn. Avocations: watercolor, glass painting, decorating, walking, fishing. Office: Eastmoreland Ear Nose & Throat Clinic 2816 SE Steele St Portland OR 97202-4525

KALYANARAM, GURUMURTHY, engineering educator, consultant; b. India, Sept. 28, 1956; came to U.S., 1981; s. P.R. Gurumuthy and Bhavani Kalyanaram. B of Engring., U. Madras, 1978; MBA, U. Tex., 1983; PhD, MIT, 1989. Asst. prof. U. Tex., Dallas, 1990—; pres. GK Assocs., Dallas, 1991—. Cons. Am. Airlines, Dallas, 1990, Russia and Slovenia, 1991—, Rockwell Internat., 1993. Contbr. articles to profl. jours. Cons. presdl. campaigns of senators Joseph Biden and Paul Simon, 1987, 88. Mem. MIT Alumni Club, Inst. of Mgmt. Scis., Am. Mktg. Assn., Mensa. Avocations: political biography, poetry, politics, public policy. Office: 5353 Keller Springs Rd Ste 1523 Dallas TX 75248

KAM, THOMAS KWOCK YUNG, accountant educator; b. Honolulu, Nov. 12, 1955; s. William Kwock Yung and Mae S. M. (Yee) K.; m. Sally Ben Huai, July 9, 1983; children: Tiffany L. M., Stephen C. M. BBA, U. Hawaii, 1975, MBA, 1978, postgrad., 1993—. CPA, Hawaii; CMA. Intern Coopers & Lybrand, Honolulu, 1975-76; instr. Beckers CPA Rev. Course, Honolulu, 1982-83; statis. asst. Hawaiian Elec. Co., Inc., Honolulu, 1976-78, assoc. budget analyst, 1978-86; adult edn. tchr. Farrington Cmty. Sch., Honolulu, 1978-84, McKinley Cmty. Sch., Honolulu, 1978-86; lectr. West Oahu Coll., Honolulu, 1986; asst. prof. acctg. and fin. Hawaii Pacific U., Honolulu, 1984—. Mem. Neighborhood Bd. (Liliha-Kapalama), 1980-83; treas., fin. com. chmn. Neighborhood Bd. (Pearl City), 1985-88, vice chair health, edn. and welfare com. 1985, chmn., 1988-93, chmn. devel., planning and zoning com. 93-97; auditor Kams' Soc., 1984-89, 3d v.p., 1990-91, 2d v.p., 1992-93, 1st v.p., 1994-95, pres., 1996-97, bd. dirs. 1998—; mem. loan com. Native Hawaiian Revolving Loan Fund, 1989-91; co-facilitator Pearl City Highlands Elem. Sch. SCBM Coun., 1992-93, 95-96; dir. Pearl City Highlands Elem. Sch., Kokua Hui, 1992-93, treas., 1993-97, pres. 1998-2001; chmn. Leeward Dist. Sch. Adv. Coun., 1995-97. Named Co-Adult Edn. Tchr. of Yr., Hawaii Adult Edn. Assn., 1988. Mem. AICPA, Hawaii Adult Edn. Assn. (dir. 1978-79, treas. 1979-81, pres. 1981-83), Hawaii Bus. Educators Assn., Inst. Mgmt. Accts., Hui Luna Club (dir. 1978, 85, auditor 1979, treas. 1980, 81), Friends of the Libr. of Hawaii, Toastmasters (Kam 720 Club treas. 1981-82, Disting. Toastmaster 1985, Dist. 49 audit com. chmn. 1981-82, treas. 1982-84, speechcraft chmn. 1984-85). Office: Hawaii Pacific Univ 1188 Fort Street Mall Ste 252 Honolulu HI 96813-2713 E-mail: tkam@hpu.edu.

KAM, VERNON TAM SIU, accounting educator; b. Honolulu, Sept. 2, 1933; s. Henry K.F. and Maizie Y.C. (Ching) K.; m. Alice T. Takizawa, Aug. 15, 1965; children: Carolyn, Garret. BA, U. Hawaii, 1955; MBA, U. Calif., Berkeley, 1959, PhD, 1968. CPA, Ill. Auditor L.A. County, 1959-60; asst. prof. U. Ill., Chgo., 1965-69; prof. Calif. State U., Hayward, 1969-87, chair dept., 1987—. Author: Accounting Theory, 1986, 2d edit., 1990, Consolidation of Financial Statements, 1981, 2d edit., 1991, 3d edit., 1996; co-author: Financial Accounting, 1995, 97, Financial Statements: Composition and Analysis, 1999; contbr. articles to profl. jours. 1st lt. U.S. Army, 1955-57, Korea. Mem. AICPA, Am. Acctg. Assn. Office: Calif State U Dept Acctg Hayward CA 94542

KAMANAROFF, CHARLENE, elementary education educator; b. Gary, Ind., Oct. 18, 1948; d. Charles and Sue (Petrovich) Markovich; m. Mike P. Kamanaroff, July 24, 1971; 1 child, Christie Michelle. BS in Elem. Edn., Ball State U., 1970; MS in Elem. Edn., Purdue U., 1974. Elem. tchr. Merrillville (Ind.) Community Schs. Corp., 1970—, developer lang. arts curriculum, 1981—2001. Mem. Delta Kappa Gamma (v.p. 1980-82, pres. 1990-92), Pi Beta Phi (pres. Southlake Alumnae club 1973-75, 86-88, 96—). Roman Catholic. Avocations: reading, downhill and cross country skiing. Home: 7728 Delaware Pl Merrillville IN 46410-5635 Office: Homer Iddings Sch 7249 Van Buren St Merrillville IN 46410-3857

KAMISAR, YALE, lawyer, educator; b. N.Y.C., Aug. 29, 1929; s. Samuel and Mollie (Levine) K.; m. Esther Englander, Sept. 7, 1953 (div. Oct. 1973); children: David Graham, Gordon, Jonathan; m. Christine Keller, May 10, 1974 (dec. 1997); m. Joan Russell, Feb. 28, 1999. AB, NYU, 1950; LLB, Columbia U., 1954; LLD, CUNY, 1978. Bar: D.C. 1955. Rsch. assoc. Am. Law Inst., N.Y.C., 1953; assoc. Covington & Burling, Washington, 1955-57; assoc. prof., then prof. law U. Minn., Mpls., 1957-64; prof. law U. Mich., Ann Arbor, 1965-92, Clarence Darrow disting. univ. prof., 1992—. Vis. prof. law Harvard U., 1964-65, San Diego U., 2000-02; disting. vis. prof. law Coll. William and Mary, 1988; cons. Nat. Adv. Commn. Civil Disorders, 1967-68, Nat. Commn. Causes and Prevention Violence, 1968-69; mem. adv. com. model code pre-arraignment procedure Am. Law Inst., 1965-75. Reporter-draftsman: Uniform Rules of Criminal Procedure, 1971-73; author: (with J.H. Choper, S. Shiffrin and R.H. Fallon), Constitutional Law: Cases, Comments and Questions, 9th edit., 2001; (with W. LaFave, J. Israel and N. King) Modern Criminal Procedure: Cases and Commentaries, 10th edit., 2002, Criminal Procedure and the Constitution: Leading Cases and Introductory Text, 2002; (with F. Inbau and T. Arnold) Criminal Justice in Our Time, 1965; (with J. Grano and J. Haddad) Sum and Substance of Criminal Procedure, 1977, Police Interrogation and Confessions: Essays in Law and Policy, 1980; contbr. articles to profl. jours. Served to 1st lt. AUS, 1951-52. Recipient Am. Bar Found. Rsch. award, 1996. Home: 2910 Daleview Dr Ann Arbor MI 48105-9684 Office: U Mich Law Sch 625 S State St Ann Arbor MI 48109-1215

KAMM, JACQUELINE ANN, elementary reading specialist; b. Santa Monica, Calif., Aug. 22, 1958; d. Philip Schuyler Jr. and Juanita (Jones) K. BA in History, U. Calif., L.A., 1980; MS in Edn., Curriculum and Instrn., U. So. Calif., 1987, postgrad., 1989—. Cert. instr. multiple subjects, reading specialist, Calif. Tchr. 1st grade Bonner Sch., L.A., 1981-82, Curtis Sch., L.A., 1982-88; reading specialist Culver City (Calif.) Unified Sch. Dist., 1988—, mentor tchr., 1995—. Adj. prof. Grad. Sch. Edn. and Psychology, Pepperdine U., Culver City, 1994-96; tchr. cons. writing project U. So. Calif., 1996—. Dir. St. Matthew's Summer Day Camp, Pacific Palisades, Calif., 1989-94; mem. Strategic Planning Task Force I, Curriculum, Culver City, 1989—; active Jr. Charity League. Culver City Edn. Found. grantee, 1990, 92, 93, 94, 95, 96. Mem. ASCD, Internat. Reading Assn., Santa Monica Bay Area Reading Assn. (pres.), Coronets of Nat. Charity League, Grad. Sch. Edn. Alumni Assn. (charter), Phi Kappa Phi, Phi Delta Kappa. Home: 500 Lombard Ave Pacific Palisades CA 90272-4347 Office: La Ballona Sch 10915 Washington Blvd Culver City CA 90232-4045

KAMM, ROGER DALE, biomedical engineer, educator; b. Ashland, Wis., Oct. 10, 1950; s. Rudolph Wilhelm and Betty Jane (White) K.; m. Judith Mary Brown, Sept. 1, 1974; 1 child, Peter Martin. BS, Northwestern U., 1972; SM, MIT, 1973, PhD, 1977. Lectr. MIT, Cambridge, 1977-78, asst. prof., 1978-81, assoc. prof., 1981-87, prof. mech. engring. and bioengring., 1987—, assoc. dir. Ctr. for Biomed. Engring., 1995—. Vice chmn. U.S. Nat. Com. on Biomech., 2003—. Contbr. more than 130 articles to profl. jours. Fellow Am. Inst. Med. and Biol. Engring. (founding); mem. ASME (chmn. summer bioengring. conf.), Am. Physiol. Soc., Biomed. Engring. Soc. (sr., chmn. awards com. 1989-91, bd. dirs. 1994-97), World Coun. on Biomechanics (sec./treas., vice-chmn. 2002—). Home: 31 Newton Rd Weston MA 02493-1021 Office: MIT 77 Massachusetts Ave Rm NE47-321 Cambridge MA 02139-4307

KAMMASH, TERRY, nuclear engineering educator; b. Sult, Jordan, Jan. 27, 1927; came to U.S., 1946; m. Sophie C. Kammash, Dec. 31, 1956; 1 child, Dean. BS, Pa. State U., 1952, MS, 1954; PhD, U. Mich., 1958. Instr. engring. mechs. Pa. State U., University Park, 1952-54, U. Mich., Ann Arbor, 1954-58, from asst. prof. to assoc. prof. nuclear engring., 1958-67, prof. nuclear engring., 1967—. Physicist Lawrence Livermore Lab., Livermore, Calif., 1961-62; rsch. scientist Los Alamos (N.Mex.) Nat. Lab., summer 1958; cons. Battelle N.W. Labs., Richland, Wash., 1975-78, Argonne (Ill.) Nat. Lab., 1972-77. Author: Fusion Reactor Physics, 1975; editor/author: Fusion Energy in Space Propulsion, 1995. Fellow AIAA (assoc., nuclear propulsion com. 1993)), Am. Nuclear Soc. (fusion tech. com. 1979), Arthur Holly Compton award 1977, Outstanding Achievement award 1977), Am. Phys. Soc. (plasma physics com. 1977). Office: U Mich Dept Nuclear Engring and Radiol Scis Ann Arbor MI 48109

KAMMEN, CAROL KOYEN, historian, educator; b. Plainfield, N.J., Nov. 14, 1937; d. Elmer Albert and Helen Edith (Kingberry) Koyen; m. Michael Kammen, Feb. 26, 1961; children: Daniel Merson, Douglas Anton. BA, George Washington U., Washington, 1959. Tchr. Am. history Ithaca (N.Y.) H.S., 1971-73; lectr. history Tompkins Cortland C.C., Dryden, N.Y., 1973-84, Cornell U., Ithaca, 1983-85, lectr., 1986-92, sr. lectr., 1992—. Cons. Nat. Humanities Faculty, Atlanta, 1981—; project dir. Nat. Youth Grant Ithaca H.S., 1972—74; dir. Tompkins County Arts Coun., Ithaca, 1984; cons., historian Empire State Partnership on Arts in Edn. Program, Hangar Theater, 1991—2001; appt. historian Tompkins County, Ithaca, 2000—; lectr. and cons. various hist. socs.; local history adv. bd. N.Y. Commr. Edn., 2002—. Author: Simeon DeWitt Proprietor of Ithaca, 1969; author: What They Wrote, 1978, Lives Passed, 1984, Peopling of Tompkins County, 1986 (RCHA award of Merit 1987), On Doing Local History, 1986, repub., 1996 (Merit award 1987), rev. edit., 2003, Plain as a Pipestem, 1989; editor: One Day in Ithaca, 1989 (Spl. award 1989), The Finger Lakes of New York, 1996, Pursuit of Local History, 1997, Cornell University: Glorious to View, 2003; author plays, including: Central New York (video script) 1978, Between the Lines, 1985, Testimony for Black Voices, 1986, Counting Wheat Street, 1986, Jazz a la Mode, 1987, A Chamber Entertainment with Clowns, 1988, Flight to Ithaca, 1995, Womens' Proper Place, 1997, Peaches and Bird, 1998, Ain't I a Man, Too?, 1998, Escape to the North, 1999, Juneteenth: The Ithaca Connection, 2000, The Day the Women Met, 2000; columnist The Ithaca Jour., 1978—; ednl. writer History News, 1995—; contbg. editor Ency. of New York; editor: The Local History Ency., 2000; contbr. articles to profl. jours. Local history adv. coun. NY State Commr., 2002—. Recipient award of excellence Tompkins County Trust Co., Ithaca, 1995. Mem. Am. Assn. State and Local History (editl. writer History News 1995—), Assn. Pub. Historians N.Y. State. Democrat. Home: 16 Sun Path Ithaca NY 14850-9781 Office: Cornell U Dept History 433 McGraw Hall Ithaca NY 14853 E-mail: ckk6@cornell.edu.

KAMMERAAD, STEPHANIE D. special education educator; b. Dearborn, Mich., Dec. 21, 1977; d. Allen Thomas and Catherine Jane Wenner. BA in Psychology/Spl. Edn., Grand Valley State U., 2001. V.p., sec. Cooperfly Books, Inc. Mem.: Mich. Reading Assn., Autism Soc. Mich. Home: 538 Eleanor NE Grand Rapids MI 49505 E-mail: stephanie@tomatocollection.com.

KAMMERZELL, SUSAN JANE, elementary school educator, music educator; b. Greeley, Colo., Mar. 4, 1953; d. Carl Warren and Charlotte Josephine Strandberg; m. Arnold Henry Kammerzell, Sept. 11, 1976; 1 child, Jeffrey Scott. BA in Elem. Edn., U. No. Colo., 1975. Elem. tchr. grade 1 Ft. Morgan (Colo.) Sch. Dist., 1975—76; presch. dir., tchr. Wiggins (Colo.) Presch., 1987—89; elem. tchr. grade 1 Wiggins Sch. Dist., 1989—91, elem. tchr. kindergarten, 1991—96, elem. tchr. gen. music, 1996—. Sunday sch. tchr. grades 4 and 5 Wiggins Cmty. Ch., 1996—. Mem.: Nat. Assn. for Music Edn. Republican. Mem. United Church Of Christ. Avocations: travel, reading, music. Home: 5446 Road O Wiggins CO 80654 Office: Wiggins Sch Dist RE-50J Wiggins Elem 320 Chapman Wiggins CO 80654

KAMP, CYNTHIA LEA, elementary education educator; b. Johnstown, Pa., June 29, 1956; d. Charles Jr. and Helen Lois (Paff) Lane; m. Robert Thomas Kamp, June 9, 1979; children: Jason, Meghan, Jordan. BFA, Miami U., Oxford, Ohio, 1978, MA, 1984. Cert. fine arts tchr., Ohio. Tchr. art Mt. Healthy City Schs., Cin. Mem. ASCD, Ohio Arts Edn. Assn., Ohio Edn. Assn. Home: 25 Brompton Ln Cincinnati OH 45218-1314 Office: Greener Elem Sch 2400 Adams Rd Cincinnati OH 45231

KAMPE, CAROLYN JEAN, elementary art and special education educator; b. Chicago Heights, Ill., July 8, 1943; d. Fred H. and Harriet (Bobrowski) K. Student, Mt. St. Clare Jr. Coll., Clinton, Iowa, 1966-68; BA in Art, St. Ambrose U., 1970; MA in Cultural Studies, Gov. State U., 1974; EdD in Art Edn., Ill. State U., 1990. Cert. art tchr.; cert. spl. edn.; cert. K-12 specialist. Art supr., coord., and elem. art tchr. Dist. 170, Chicago Heights, 1970-87; grad. asst. art dept. Ill. State U., Normal, 1987-90; spl. edn. tchr. Hugh Jr. H.S., Matteson, Ill., 1990-91, Burr Oak, Calumet Park, Ill., 1991-92; homebound tchr. Dist. 162, Matteson, 1991-98; art edn. for spl. edn. Dist. 170, Chicago Heights, 1992—; art tchr. Field Sch. Dist. 152, Harvey, Ill., 1994, Vogt Visual Art Ctr., Tinley Park, Ill., 1996—2003; spl. edn. tchr. Hufford Jr. H.S., Joliet, Ill., 1996-98; with South Suburban Spl. Edn. Recreation Assn., Frankfort, Ill., 2000—02; spl. edn. tchr. Homewood-Flossmoor Park Dist., 2002. Vis. faculty and adaptive art specialist St. Norbert Coll., DePere, Wis., 1990-92; active in Put Your Heart Illinois Youth Art Month, 1985-86 and 1993-94, spl. edn. "Earth Day" Art Exhbn. (200 works on display); homebound tchr. Dist. 162 and 227, 1991-98; bd. dirs. Very Spl. Arts, Ill. State U., Normal, 1992-96. Group exhbns. include Chicago Heights Libr., Chicago Heights Mcpl. Bldg., 1993-94, Wash. Jr. H.S., Chicago Heights, 1994; contbr. articles to profl. jours. Bd. dirs. Very Spl. Arts Ill., Ill. State U., Normal, 1992-94; Ill. Coalition for Disabilities, Normal, 1985-86; pres. Self Help for Hard of Hearing, Ill., 1984-86; mem. White House Exhbn. Com., Chgo., 1992-93; vol. Chgo. Pub. Libr., 1993; mem. Put Your Heart in Month, Ill. Youth Art Month, 1985-86; art judge Girl Scout Art Contest, 1982, Chicago Heights Jaycees, 1982-83. Named One of 5 Best and Brightest Outstanding Disabled Coll. Grads., Mainstream Mag. and Am. Bus. Women's Assn., 1990, to Hall of Fame for Outstanding Achievement, Mt. St. Clare Coll., 1996, to Hall of Fame for Fine Art, Marian Cath. H.S. Alumni Assn., 1997; recipient Kohl Internat. Tchg. award 1993. Mem. Nat. Assn. Art Edn., Ill. Art Edn. Assn. (Best Art Tchr. award 1984), South Surburban Spl. Recreation Assn. Roman Catholic. Achievements include: first deaf female doctoral graduate from Ill. State Univ.

KAMPFE, NANCY LEE, communications educator; b. Lemmon, S.D., May 6, 1946; d. Kenneth and Joyce Rose (Bartell) Preszler; m. Gregory Stephen Kampfe, Aug. 15, 1970; children: Leanne, Janice, Carole, Amy. BA in English, U. S.D., 1968; MA in English, S.D. State U., 1970. Cert. secondary tchr., S.D. Halftime freshman composition S.D. State U., Brookings, 1968-70; tchr. speech and English Sioux Valley Sch., Volga, S.D., 1970-72; tchr. White River (S.D.) Sch. Dist., 1977-78; tchr. English Crazy Horse Sch., Wanblee, S.D., 1985-90; tchr. English, speech and journalism Bennett County Schs., Martin, S.D., 1990—. Yearbook adv., photographer Bennett County H.S., 1990-2002; com. co-chair lang. arts. curriculum revision com., 1991-93; com. chair reading curriculum revision com., 1992-94. Organist St. Paul's Evang. Luth. Ch., White River, S.D.; mem. SD Lang. Arts Stds. Revision Com., 2002-03. Mem. Nat. Coun. Tchr. of Eng., NEA, S.D. Edn. Assn., Bennett County Edn. Assn., S.D. Coun. Tchrs. of Eng. (v.p. 1999-01, pres. 2001-03), Nat. Writing Project (pub. chair Y2K Regional NCTE-NWP Conf. 2000), Dakota Writing Project (presenter regional workshops 2000, 02, 03). Avocations: piano, reading, cooking, writing poetry. Home: PO Box 536 Martin SD 57551-0536 Office: Bennett County H S PO Box 580 Martin SD 57551-0580

KAMPITS, EVA, accrediting association administrator, educator; b. Budapest, Hungary, Feb. 22, 1946; came to U.S., 1951; d. Ernest Michael and Ilona (Gondi) K.; m. Dan Catalin Stefanescu, Aug. 4, 1979; children: Andreea N., Cristina F. Cert., U. Innsbruck, Austria, 1963; BA, Harvard U., 1968; MA, Boston Coll., 1971, PhD, 1977. Instr. freshman seminars MIT, Cambridge, 1973—80, freshman advisor, 1975-80, sophomore advisor, 1976-80, adminstrv. officer Artificial Intelligence Lab., 1967-78, asst. to dir. Lab. for Computer Sci., 1987-88, rsch. affiliate Media Lab., 1987-88; acad. dean Pine Manor Coll., Chestnut Hill, Mass., 1980-94, dir. sponsored programs, grad. sch. dean, 1994; dir. sch. and coll. rels. New Eng. Assn. Schs. and Colls., Inc., Bedford, Mass., 1994—2003, Ctr. Ednl. Improvement, 2003. Mem. NEARnet, 1989-94, Gov.'s Ednl. Tech. Adv. Coun., 1990-93; mem. steering com. Mass. Telecomputing Coalition, 1991-95, New Eng. Network Acad. Alliances in Fgn. Langs. and Lits., 1995-98, Eisenhower Regional Alliance for Math. and Sci. Reform, 1996-98; trustee Boston Archtl. Ctr., 1996-2000, overseer, 2000—; cons. Regional Ednl. Lab. of Northeast and Islands, Brown U., 1997—; mem. editl. adv. bd. Dominion Press, Eng., 1998—; rsch. assoc. Nat. Ctr. for Cmty. Innovation, Montpelier, Vt., 1999—; adv. bd. Dorcas Place, 2000; bd. dirs. Nat. Staff Devel. Coun., 2000; cons. Ministry of Edn., China, 2001—; advisor PBS Access to Coll. documentary, 2003—. Founding mem. bd. editors NER-Comp Jour. Founding mem. bd. visitors Brimmer and May Sch., Chestnut Hill, Mass., 1992-97. Republican. Roman Catholic. Avocations: natural history, marine studies, arts, travel, tennis. Office: New Eng Assn Schs & Colls Inc 209 Burlington Rd Bedford MA 01730-1422

KANDEL, WILLIAM LLOYD, lawyer, mediator, arbitrator, educator, writer; b. NYC, Apr. 25, 1939; s. Morton H. and Lottie S. (Smith) K.; m. Joyce Roland, Jan. 27, 1974; 1 child, Aron Daniel (Ari). AB cum laude, Dartmouth Coll., 1961; JD, Yale U., 1964; LLM in Labor Law, NYU, 1967. Bar: N.Y. 1965, U.S. Dist. Ct. (ea. dist.) N.Y. 1978, U.S. Dist. Ct. (so. dist) N.Y. 1980, U.S. Dist. Ct. (no. dist.) N.Y. 1988, U.S. Ct. Appeals (2d cir.) 1982, U.S. Ct. Appeals (3d cir.) 1997, U.S. Ct. Appeals (5th cir.) 2000. Assoc. Lorenz, Finn & Giardino, N.Y.C., 1964-66; labor atty. NAM, N.Y.C., 1966-68; with Singer Co., N.Y.C., 1968-79, asst. v.p. pers. dept., 1973-76, mng. counsel pers. office of gen. counsel, 1976-79; assoc. Skadden, Arps, Slate, Meagher & Flom, N.Y.C., 1979-85; ptnr. Finley, Kumble, Wagner, Heine, Underberg, Manley, Myerson & Casey, N.Y.C., 1985-87, Myerson & Kuhn, N.Y.C., 1987-89, McDermott Will & Emery, 1989-97, Orrick, Herrington & Sutcliffe, 1997-2000; full-time mediator and arbitrator, 2000—; mediator U.S. Dist. Ct. (so. and ea. dists.), Supreme Ct. N.Y., 2001—; pvt. mediator and arbitrator, 2000—. Adj. prof. employment law Fordham U., 1983-86; lectr. Practising Law Inst.'s Ann. Inst. on

Employment Law, 1980—, co-chair, 1995, chair, 1996-2002; vol. mediator U.S. EEO Commn., 2000—; spl. master Appellate Divsn. of Supreme Ct., N.Y., 2002—; panelist comml. and employment, Am. Arbitration Assn., 2002—; arbitrator Nat. Assn. Securities Dealers, 2002—. Contbg. editor: Employee Rels. Law Jour., 1975—; contbr. over 100 articles to profl. jours. V.p., bd. dirs. Assn. for Integration Mgmt., 1979-85; bd. dirs. N.Y. chpt. Am. Jewish Com., 1980-82; mem. human resources com. N.Y. YMCA, 1994—. Recipient award of Merit, Nat. Urban Coalition, 1979. Mem.: Am. Arbitration Assn. (comml. and employment panels 2001—), Bar Assn. of City of N.Y., University Club. Democrat. Jewish. Home and Office: Mediator/Arbitrator 880 Fifth Ave New York NY 10021 E-mail: wlkandel@hotmail.com.

KANDRAC, JO ANN MARIE, school administrator; b. Warren, Ohio, May 5, 1943; d. Clyde Joseph and Micheline (Vescera) Battista; m. Thomas Michael Kandrac, Sept. 25, 1965; children: Michael, Richard, David. B Music in Edn., Youngstown U., 1965, MS in Edn., 1983. Cert. tchr., administrator, Ohio. Tchr. St. Mary Sch., Warren, 1965-66, Blessed Sacrament Sch., Warren, 1967-68, 70-86, Plew Elem. Sch., Niceville, Fla., 1968-70; prin. Saints Mary and Joseph Sch., Newton Falls, Ohio, 1986-91, Blessed Sacrament Sch., Warren, 1991-97, St. Thomas Aquinas Sch., St. Cloud, Fla., 1997—2000; founding prin. City of Kissimmee (Fla.) Charter Sch., 2000—. Area chair United Way, Warren, 1986-97. Tchr. of Yr. award Diocese of Youngstown, 1981. Mem. Trumbull Assn. Reading Coun., Rotary, Delta Kappa Gamma. Roman Catholic. Avocations: travel, reading, cross-stitch, knitting, ceramics. Office: City of Kissimmee Charter Sch 2850 Bill Beck Blvd Kissimmee FL 34744

KANE, CHERYL MARIE, education program developer; b. Great Barrington, Mass., Dec. 26, 1947; d. Alexander and Mildred (Tatsapaugh) Shmulsky. BA, U. Mass., 1969; MA, U. Colo., 1979; PhD, Fla. State U., 1988. Project dir. Colo. State Dept. Edn., Denver, 1977-79; rsch. assoc. Nat. Inst. Edn., Washington, 1979-81; pvt. practice cons. Washington, 1981-88; assoc. exec. dir. Nat. Found. for the Improvement of Edn., Washington, 1988-92; dir. rsch. Nat. Edn. Commn. on Time and Learning, Washington, 1992-94; dir. strategy New Am. Schs. Devel. Corp., Arlington, Va., 1994-99; sr. assoc. office ednl. rsch./improvement U.S. Dept. Edn., 1999-2000, exec. dir. nat. commn. on H.S. sr. yr., 2000—01, sr. rsch. assoc., 2001—. Cons. U.S. Dept. Edn., Washington, World Bank, Washington, Acad. for Edn. Devel., Washington, 1981—88. Author: Prisoners of Time: What We Know and What We Need to Know, 1994; contbr. chpts. in books. Sec. Logan Circle Cmty. Assn., Washington, 1993. Mem.: Am. Edn. Rsch. Assn., Phi Delta Kappa. Avocations: sailing, gardening, photography, travel. Home: 1325 13th St NW Apt 6 Washington DC 20005-4453 Office: Rm 4W307 400 Maryland Ave SW Washington DC 20202

KANE, EDWARD JOSEPH, elementary and secondary school educator; b. Somers Point, N.J., Sept. 26, 1951; s. Joseph James and Ruth Marina (Ramirez) K.; m. Joan L. Davis, Feb. 11, 1978; children: Jonathan E., Daniel J., Rebecca A. BA, LaSalle Coll., Phila., 1978; MEd, Widener U., Chester, Pa., 1988. Cert. tchr. Rsch. technician Franklin Inst. Rsch., Phila., 1971-74; auditor Holiday Inn Midtown, Phila., 1975-76; corr. officer Pa. Dept. Justice, Graterford, Pa., 1976-78; tchr. St. Gabriel's Hall, Phoenixville, Pa., 1978-79, Harriton High Sch., Rosemont, Pa., 1979, William Penn Sch. Dist., Yeadon, Pa., 1979-89; tchr. English and Spanish Faith Mennonite High Sch., Kinzers, Pa., 1989-97; tchr. math. Manheim Twp. Middle Sch., Lancaster, Pa., 1997—2001; tchr. project Landis Valley, 2001—. Mem. Nat. Sci. Tchrs. Assn., Internat. Reading Assn., Nat. Coun. Tchrs. Math., Nat. Middle Sch. Assn., Hist. Soc. Pa., Phila. Libr. Co., Lancaster Mennonite Hist. Soc., Appalachian Trail Conf., Nat. Coun. Tchrs. English. Amish-Mennonite. Avocations: astronomy, walking, bicycling, writing. Home: 167 Maple St Gordonville PA 17529-9546 Office: Manheim Twp Mid Sch School Rd Lancaster PA 17601-5134 E-mail: ejkane@redrose.net., ed_kane@mail.mtwp.K12.pa.us.

KANE, JAMES PATRICK, superintendent, educator; b. Staten Island, N.Y., Apr. 4, 1933; s. Frank J. and Della A. (Harte) K.; m. Maureen D. Kane, Aug. 13, 1955; children: Deirdre, Donna. BS in edn., Fordham U., 1954; MA, Columbia U., 1962, profl. diploma, 1964; PhD in Edn., Fairleigh Dickinson U., 1974. Diplomate in sch. adminstrn. Eng. tchr. Peekskill (N.Y.) MA, 1958-66, dean of students, 1958-66; headmaster Nyack Prep. Sch., Southampton, N.Y., 1966-75; supr. of schs. Hamburg (N.J.) Pub. Schs., 1975—; lectr. William Paterson U. Adj. faculty post Ramapo Coll., Mahwah, N.J., 1983—; adj. prof. William Paterson U., Wayne, N.J., 1998—; spkr. Americana Lectrs., Newton, N.J., 1999; author school plays, Hamburg Drama Soc., 1981—. Contbr. articles to profl. jours. Trustee Franklin Mineral Mus., Franklin, N.J., 1985—; trustee Green Chimneys Sch., Brewster, N.Y., 1962-66; active Hamburg Drug Alliance Coun., 1985—. Capt. USMC, 1954-58. Recipient Reinhardt Excellence in Edn. award SCSAA, 1989, Cummings Disting. Svc. award SCEA, 1993, Fordham U. Alumni Achievement award, 1995, Excellence in Arts award SC Arts Coun., 1991, Disting. Svc. award NJASA; named Man of Yr. Hamburg, N.J., 1985, N.J. Gov.'s Award in Arts, 1997. Mem. N.J. Assn. Sch. Adminstrs. Disting. Svc. award), Am. Legion, N.J. Congress of Parents & Tchrs. (life), Roundtable Assn., Phi Delta Kappa. Avocation: summer cruising. Home: 38 Elmwood Ter Wayne NJ 07470-4334 Office: Hamburg Pub Sch Dist Linwood Ave Hamburg NJ 07419

KANE, KAREN ANN, speech language pathologist; b. Lakewood, Ohio, Apr. 29, 1966; d. John Joseph and Roberta Clare (Quigley) Kelley; m. Christopher Joseph Kane, June 24, 1989; children: Christopher Joseph Jr., Megan Clare. BS, Marquette U., Milw., 1988; MA, Cleve. State U., 1996. Cert. clin. competence speech-lang pathology. Speech lang. pathologist PSI Affiliates, Twinsburg, Ohio, 1992-94, Lakewood (Ohio) Bd. Edn., 1994-95, Fairview Park (Ohio) Bd. Edn., 1995-96; pvt. practice speech and lang. pathology, 1996-99; speech and lang. pathologist The Achievement Ctrs. for Children, Cleve., 1998-2000, Berea City Sch. Dist., 1999—. Mem. Am. Speech and Hearing Assn., Ohio Speech and Hearing Assn., Nat. Stutterers Assn., WestSide Irish Am. Club. Roman Catholic. Avocations: sports enthusiast, spending time with my children. Home: 1366 Hall Ave Lakewood OH 44107-2326

KANE, LOANA, foreign language educator; b. Sarzana, Liguria, Italy, Dec. 15, 1940; d. Leonardo and Maria (Colombini) Fumagalli; m. William D. Kane, July 10, 1964; children: David C., Jonathan A. BA, U. Messina, Italy, 1967; MA, Tufts U., 1971; PhD, U. Messina, 1985. Cert. china painter; qualified lang. specialist Italian/Sicilian FBI, 1987; Italian lang. proficiency tester CIA Lang. Sch., 1985; qualified courtroom interpreter U.S. Fed. Cts., 1996. Teaching asst. Tufts U., Medford, Mass., 1969-72; instr. French Fairfax County (Va.) Pub. Schs., 1980-81; instr. ESL Am. Embassy, Caracas, Venezuela, 1981-82; instr. Italian C.I.A. Lang. Sch., Arlington, Va., 1985-86; lectr. French George Mason U., Fairfax, Va., 1986-88, coord. Italian studies, 1988-90; asst. prof. Latin and Romance lang. Gallaudet U., Washington, 1990-95; Romance langs. prof. U.S. Dept. Agr. Grad. Sch., Washington, 1995—; Italian lang. proficiency examiner John Hopkins U., Washington, 1995—; Spanish lang. interpreter Fairfax County Dist. Ct. for Juvenile and Domestic Rels., Fairfax, Va., 1996—. Dir. Italian cultural activities Tufts U., 1969-72; guest spkr. Italian Cultural Soc., Washington, 1989, Order Sons of Italy in Am. Heritage Lodge, 1990, Greater Washington Area Tchrs. Fgn. Langs. Conf., 1994; keynote spkr. Italian Festival, Alexandria, Va., 1993; organizer confs. in field including Pride in Our Heritage, Sons of Italy Heritage Lodge, Fairfax, Va., 1989, The Panare Indians, Am. Embassy, Caracas, Venezuela, 1983, others. Author: Everyday Italian, 3 vols., 1988, Signs of Italy, 1992; co-author: Theodor Billroth, 1994; co-author Inaugural Conf. Soc. Sicilian Surgeons, 1989, 90, 91; china painting exhbns., 1982, 84, 86, 90; co-host (cable TV show) Our Place, Fairfax, Va., 1992-93; translator monograph Italian Gestures and Am. Sign Langs. TV program Communicating Today, Fairfax County Cable TV, 1995. Sec. exec. bd. Am. Nursery Sch., Bonn, Germany, 1976-77; pres. Am. Embassy Women Assn., Caracas, Venezuela, 1982-83. Faculty Devel. Fund. Study grantee Gallaudet U., 1991, Italian Govt. study grantee, 1990; recipient Disting. Mem. award Order Sons of Italy, 1989, Gold Medal award C. of C. Italy, 1991. Mem. MLA, AAUP, China Painters Assn., Tufts U. Alumni Assn., Tufts Washington Alliance, Order Sons of Italy in Am., Italian Cultural Soc. Washington, Am. Assn. Tchrs. Italian (pres. Washington chpt.). Roman Catholic. Avocations: china painting, oil painting.

KANE, MARY KAY, dean, law educator; b. Detroit, Nov. 14, 1946; d. John Francis and Frances (Roberts) K.; m. Ronan Eugene Degnan, Feb. 3, 1987 (dec. Oct. 1987). BA cum laude, U. Mich., 1968, JD cum laude, 1971. Bar: Mich. 1971, N.Y., Calif. Rsch. assoc., co-dir. NSF project on privacy, confidentiality and social sci. rsch. data sch. law U. Mich., 1971-72, Harvard U., 1972-74; asst. prof. law SUNY, Buffalo, 1974-77; mem. faculty Hastings Coll. Law U. Calif., San Francisco, 1977—, prof. law, 1979—, assoc. acad. dean, 1981-83, acting acad. dean, 1987-88, acad. dean., 1990-93, dean, 1993—; chancellor U. Calif., San Francisco, 2001—. Vis. prof. law U. Mich., 1981, U. Utah, 1983, U. Calif., Berkeley, 1983-84, sch. law U. Tex., 1989; cons. Mead Data Control, Inc., 1971, 74, Inst. on Consumer Justice, U. Mich. Sch. Law, 1972, U.S. Privacy Protection Study Commn., 1975-76; lectr. pretrial mgmt. devices U.S. magistrates for 6th and 11th cirs. Fed. Jud. Ctr., 1983; Siebenthaler lectr. Samuel P. Chase Coll. Law, U. North Ky., 1987; reporter ad hoc com. on asbestos litigation U.S. Jud. Conf., 1990-91, mem. standing com. on practice and procedure, 2001—; mem. 9th Cir. Adv. Com. on Rules Practice and Internal Oper. Procedures, 1993-96; spkr. in field. Author: Civil Procedure in a Nutshell, 1979, 5th edit., 2003, Sum and Substance on Remedies, 1981; co-author: (with C. Wright and A. Miller) Pocket Supplements to Federal Practice and Procedure, 1975—, Federal Practice and Procedure, vols. vol. 7, 3d edit., 2001, 10, 10A and 10B, 3d edit., 1998, vols. 7-7C, 2d edit., 1986, vols. 6-6A, 2d edit., 1990, vols. 11-11A, 2d edit., 1995, (with J. Friedenthal and A. Miller) Hornbook on Civil Procedure, 3d edit., 1999, (with C. Wright) Hornbook on the Law of Federal Courts, 2002, Federal Practice Deskbook, 2002; mem. law sch. divsn. West. Adv. Editl. Bd., 1986—; contbr. articles to profl. jours. Mem. standing com. on rules of practice and procedure U.S. Jud. Conf., 2000—. Mem. ABA (mem. bar admissions com. 1995-2000), Assn. Am. Law Schs. (com. on prelegal edn. statement 1982, chair sect. remedies 1982, panelist sect. on prelegal edn. 1983, exec. com. sect. on civil procedure 1983, 86, panelist sect. on tchg. methods 1984, spkr. new tchrs. conf. 1986, 89, 90, chair sect. on civil procedure 1987, spkr. sects. civil procedure and conflicts 1987, 91, chair planning com. for 1988 Tchg. Conf. in Civil Procedure 1987-88, nominating com. 1988, profl. devel. com. 1988-91, planning com. for workshop in conflicts 1988, planning com. for 1990 Conf. on Clin. Legal Edn. 1989, chair profl. devel. com. 1989-91, exec. com. 1991-93, 2000-02, pres.-elect 2000, pres. 2001), Am. Law Inst. (co-reporter complex litigation project 1988-93, coun. 1998—), ABA/Assn. Am. Law Schs. Commn. on Financing Legal Edn., State Bar Mich. Home: 8 Admiral Dr Ste 421 Emeryville CA 94608-1567 Office: U Calif Hastings Coll Law 200 Mcallister St San Francisco CA 94102-4707

KANE, MICHAEL BARRY, social science research executive; b. Taunton, Mass., July 2, 1944; s. Julius J. and Dorothy M. (Moscoff) K.; children: Jared E., Stacy E., Matthew D. BA in Polit. Sci., NYU, 1966; MA in Ednl. Adminstrn., Columbia U., 1968, MEd in Ednl. Adminstrn., 1970, EdD in Ednl. Adminstrn., 1974. Tchr. Roosevelt Sch., Stamford, Conn., 1966-67; asst. to dir. New Lincoln Sch., N.Y.C., 1969; spl. asst. to dep. commr. for devel. U.S. Office of Edn., Washington, 1970-71; headmaster Downtown Community sch., N.Y.C., 1971-73; coord. program for situational analysis and program for ednl. leadership Columbia U. Tchrs. Coll., N.Y.C., 1970-73; group mgr., project dir. Abt Assocs., Inc., Cambridge, Mass., 1973-79; asst. dir., assoc. dir. Nat. Inst. Edn., U.S. Dept. Edn., Washington, 1979-82; pres. MCK Assocs., Inc., Tallahassee, Fla., and Annapolis, Md., 1982-87; prin. Pelavin Assocs., Inc., Washington, 1988-94; v.p. Am. Inst. for Rsch., Washington, 1995—, sr. v.p., dir. program on individual and orgnl. performance, 1998—. Chmn. Profl. Tchr. Career Devel. Coun., Fla.; vis. scholar Fla. State U.'s Ctr. for Needs Assessmtn and Planning; pres. Citizen's Coun. Edn., Fla.; chmn. Fla. Bus. and Edn. Coalition; lectr. numerous workshops. Author, co-author or editor: Minorities in Textbooks: A Study of Their Treatment in Social Studies Texts, Improving Schools: Using What We Know, Changing the Odds: Factors Increasing Access to College, Implementing Performance Assessments: Promises, Problems, and Challenges, Principles and Practices of Performance Assessment; contbr. articles to profl. jours. Avocations: boating, photography, scuba diving. Home: 1307 35th St NW Washington DC 20007

KANE, PATRICK J. high school principal; b. Cleve., June 14, 1955; s. Eugene F. and Elizabeth A. Kane; m. Heidi C. Kane, Oct. 9, 1982; children: Erin E., Jacqueline A. BS in Edn., Kent State U., 1977; MS in Athletic Adminstrn., Seattle Pacific U., 1989, cert. adminstrn., 2000. Cert. elem. tchr., Wash. Spl. edn. instr. Mentor (Ohio) Sch. Dist., 1977-78, Browning (Mont.) Sch. Dist., 1978-79; elem. tchr. Cut Bank (Mont.) Sch. Dist., 1979-81; mem. collections staff Ford Motor Credit, Portland, Oreg., 1981-84; tchr. Port Angeles (Wash.) Schs., 1984—; track coach Port Angeles H.S., 1984-93, soccer coach, 1993—2000. Intern Sport for Understanding, Washington, summer 1989, West Seattle YMCA, summer 1988. Pres. Port Angeles Jr. Soccer, 1986-91, North Olympic Soccer Referees, 1986-92; tournament dir. Jr./Sr. Babe Ruth, Port Angeles, 1990-92. Mem. Nat. Soccer Coaches Assn. Am. Avocations: hiking, weight lifting, reading. Home: 350 Viewcrest St Port Angeles WA 98362-6979 Office: Port Angeles HS 304 E Park Ave Port Angeles WA 98362-6934

KANE, RUTH ANNE, principal, educator; b. Beaumont, Tex., Jan. 20, 1948; d. Lewis Barclay "Red" III and Lois Virginia (Metzke) Herring; m. Gabriel Christopher Kane, Apr. 27, 1974 (div. Sept. 24, 1980); children: David Kane, Elijah Kane. BS, U. Tex. at Austin, 1981; MEd, 1982, PhD, 1991. Cert. secondary English, Spanish, spl. edn., adminstrn. Tchr. Adventure Bound Sch., Charlottesville, Va., 1978-79, Austin State Sch., Tex., 1979-80, Clear Lake H.S., Houston, 1982-84, McCallum H.S., Austin, Tex., 1984-88; adminstrv. intern Fulmore Middle Sch., Austin, Tex., 1988; tchr. Travis H.S., Austin, Tex., 1988-89; asst. prin. Martin Jr. H.S., Austin, Tex., 1989-90, Reagan H.S., Austin, Tex., 1990-93; prin. Lanier H.S., Austin, Tex., 1993—. Cons. Ednl. Svc. Ctr. Region XIII, Austin, Tex., 1989—; instr. ExCet Reviews, Austin, 1991—; test adminstr. Nat. Evaluation Sys., Mass., 1991-93; adj. prof. S.W. Tex. State U., 1997—. Co-author: Futurism in Education, 1988, Special Education ExCet Review Guide, 1993. Vol. AIDS Svcs. of Austin, Tex., 1993-94; mem. City of Austin Joint Truancy Task Force, Austin, 1993—, Leadership Austin, Tex., 1994-95. Career Advancement scholarship Bus. and Profl. Woman's Assn., 1980, Am. Bus. Women's Assn. scholarship Austin-Lake Travis chpt., Austin, Tex., 1980, 81, Jesse H. Jones scholarship Kappa Delta Pi Internat., 1990, Univ. fellowship U. Tex. at Austin, 1981; recipient Peacemaker award Dispute Resolution Ctr., 1997, Heroin Edn. award Readers Digest Am., 1997. Mem. ASCD, Austin Assn. Secondary Sch. Adminstrn., Nat. Assn. Secondary Sch. Prin./ Tex/ Assn. Secondary Sch. Prin., Phi Delta Kappa, Delta Kappa Gamma. Avocations: theatre, music, reading. Office: Lanier H S 1201 Payton Gin Rd Austin TX 78758-6616 Home: 320 Maple Dr Hitchcock TX 77563-3042

KANE, STEPHANIE C. social anthropologist, educator; b. N.Y.C., Jan. 24, 1951; d. Bernard David and Gerry Kane. BA in Biology, Cornell U., 1972; MA in Zoology, U. Tex., 1981, PhD in Social Anthropology, 1986. Tchg. asst. Biology and Physiology Labs, Dept. Zoology, U. Tex., Austin, 1981, Dept. Anthropology, U. Tex., Austin, 1985-86; resident faculty Sch. for Field Studies, Virgin Islands, 1987; adj. asst. prof. Dept. Anthropology, Ind. U., 1992—; asst. prof. Dept. Criminal Justice, Ind. U., 1992-99, assoc. prof., 1999—. Author: The Phantom Gringo Boat, 1994, AIDS Alibis: Sex, Drugs and Crime in the Americas, 1998; co-editor: Crime's Power: Anthropologists & the Study of Crime, 2003; contbr. to profl. papers and jours. Recipient rsch. grant Inst. Latin Am. Studies U. Tex., Austin, 1979-80, 84-85, Fulbright rsch. grant Coun. for Internat. Exch. of Scholars, 1989-90, rsch. grant Rural Ctr. for Study and Promotion of HIV/STD Prevention, Ind., 1995, rsch. grant Wenner-Gren Found. for Anthropol. Rsch., 1995-96, 99-2000, rsch. and travel grantee INd. U., 2001, 02; scholarship U. Tex., Austin, 1979-83; Lang. and Area Studies fellowship Inst. Latin Am. Studies, U. Tex., Austin, 1982-83, Tng. fellowship Orgn. Am. States, 1984-85, Rockefeller Humanities fellowship rsch. grant SUNY, Buffalo, 1991-92, Coll. Arts and Scis. Summer Faculty fellowship Ind. U., Bloomington, 1994. Mem. NOW, Am. Anthropol. Assn. (mem. task force on AIDS, 1991-93), Am. Soc. Criminology, Law and Soc. Assn., Amnesty Internat. Avocations: art, gardening, travel. Office: U Ind Dept Criminal Justice and Gender Studies 302 Sycamore Hall Bloomington IN 47405

KANE, STEVEN MICHAEL, psychotherapist, educator; b. Boston, July 25, 1947; s. Harry and Annette (Oranburg) K. AB, Boston U., 1971; MA, U. N.C., 1973; PhD, Princeton U., 1979. Staff psychotherapist Mass. Treatment Ctr., Bridgewater, Mass., 1985-86; staff psychologist Bridgewater State Hosp., 1986-89; pvt. practice psychotherapy Providence, R.I., 1990—; psychologist R.I. Sex Offender Treatment Program, 1995-2000. Dir. sr. empowerment program Westminster Sr. Ctr., Providence, 1998-2003; vis. asst. prof. U. N.C., 1978-79, Conn. Coll., New London, 1982-83; asst. prof. Gen. Motors Inst., Flint, Mich., 1981-82; rsch. scientist Brown U. Child Study Ctr., 1984-85; instr. Brown U. Learning Cmty., 1998—; dir. clin. edn. Interfaith Counseling Ctr., Providence, 1988-2002; part-time faculty RISD, Providence, 1989-99, U. R.I., Providence, 1992—; spl. lectr. Providence Coll., 1990-94; cons. and spkr. in field. Reviewer Internat. Assn. of Jazz Record Collectors Jour.; contbr. articles to profl. jours. Bd. dir. The Music Sch., Providence, 1993-95; founder, dir. Life-Enrichment Ctr. New Eng., Providence, 2002-. Recipient Outstanding Faculty award U. R.I./Providence Ctr., 1997; Nat. Def. Edn. Act Title IV fellow Fed. Govt.-U. N.C., 1971-73, Postdoctoral Social Sci. Rsch. fellow NIMH, 1979-81; Rsch. grantee NSF, 1975-76; RI Dept. Elderly Affairs minority health promotion grantee, 1998-2003. Fellow Am. Anthropol. Assn.; mem. Soc. for Psychol. Anthropology, Soc. for the Anthropology of Consciousness, Am. Assn. of Pastoral Counselors, Broadway Renaissance (pres. 2001--), Psi Chi. Avocations: jazz pianist, writer on jazz, jazz educator. Home and Office: 451 Broadway Providence RI 02909-1625

KANE, THOMAS JAY, III, orthopaedic surgeon, educator; b. Merced, Calif., Sept. 2, 1951; s. Thomas J. Jr. and Kathryn (Hassler) K.; m. Marie Rose Van Emmerik, Oct. 10, 1987; children: Thomas Keola, Travis Reid, Samantha Marie. BA in History, U. Santa Clara, 1973; MD, U. Calif., Davis, 1977. Diplomate Am. Bd. Orthopaedic Surgery. Intern U. Calif. Davis Sacramento Med. Ctr., 1977-78, resident in surgery, 1978-81; resident in orthopaedic surgery U. Hawaii, 1987-91; fellowship adult joint reconstruction Rancho Los Amigos Med. Ctr., 1991-92; ptnr. Orthop. Assocs. of Hawaii, Inc., Honolulu, 1992—; asst. prof. surgery U. Hawaii, Honolulu, 1993—, chief divsn. implant surgery, 1993—. Contbr. articles to profl. jours. Mem. AMA, Am. Assn. Hip and Knee Surgeons, Hawaii Med. Assn., Hawaii Orthop. Assn. (v.p. 2003—), Am. Acad. Orthop. Surgery, Western Orthopedic Assn., Alpha Omega Alpha, Phi Kappa Phi. Avocations: tennis, golf, skiing, music, surfing. Office: Orthopaedic Svcs Co LLP 1380 Lusitana St Ste 608 Honolulu HI 96813-2442

KANE, THOMAS REIF, engineering educator; b. Vienna, Mar. 23, 1924; came to U.S., 1938, naturalized, 1943; Ernest Kanitz and Gertrude (Reif) K.; m. Ann Elizabeth Andrews, June 4, 1951; children: Linda Ann, Jeffrey Thomas. BS, Columbia U., 1950, MS, 1952, PhD, 1953; D Tech. Scis. (hon.), Tech. U. Vienna, Austria, 1990. Asst. prof., assoc. prof. U. Pa., Phila., 1953-61; prof. Sch. Engring. Stanford U., Calif., 1961-93, prof. emeritus, 1993—. Cons. NASA, Harley-Davidson Motor Co., AMF, Lockheed Missiles and Space Co., Vertol Aircraft Corp., Martin Marietta Co., Kellet Aircraft Co. Author: (vol. 1) Analytical Elements of Mechanics, 1959, (vol. 2), 1961, Dynamics, 1972, Spacecraft Dynamics, 1983; Dynamics: Theory and Applications, 1985; contbr. over 150 articles to profl. jours. Served with U.S. Army, 1943-45, PTO. Recipient Alexander von Humboldt prize, 1988. Fellow Am. Astron. Soc. (Dirk Brouwer award 1983); mem. ASME (hon.), Sigma Xi, Tau Beta Pi. Office: Stanford University Dept Mechanical Engring Stanford CA 94305

KANEKO, SYLVIA YELTON, clinical social worker, educator; b. Marion, N.C., Mar. 31, 1935; d. Harvey Rayburn and Annie Laurie (Phillips) Yelton; m. Shozo Kaneko, 1960 (div. 1963). BA, U. N.C., 1959; MSW, U. Hawaii, 1964; PhD, Smith Coll., 1971. Lic. clin. social worker, Mass.; bd. cert. diplomate Am. Bd. Examiners Clin. Social Work. Editl. asst. TV Guide mag., Hollywood, Calif., 1957-59; psychiat. social worker Ceders-Sinai Med. Ctr., L.A., 1965-69; pvt. practice Brookline and Newton, Mass., 1971—; asst. prof. treatment methods Smith Coll., Northampton, Mass., 1971-72; dir. social work Valleyhead Psychiat. Hosp., Carlisle, Mass., 1972-75; assoc. prof., chair casework Boston U., 1978-86; assoc. prof. dept. social work U. N.H., Durham, 1995-96; faculty mentor doctoral program Human Svcs. Walden U., 1998—. Adj. asst. prof. treatment methods and rsch. Smith Coll., Northampton, 1973-88; participant Brit.-Am. Conf. on Psychodynamic Social Work, 1979, faculty mentor doctoral program Human Svcs., Walden U., 1998—; Schwartz rounds facilitator New Eng. Sinai Hosp., 2001—. Contbr. articles to profl. jours. Internat. Women's Yr. grantee Internat. Mktg. Inst., 1979. Fellow Am. Orthopsychiat. Assn.; mem. NASW (chair com. 1978-82, bd. dirs. 1988-90), Mass. Acad. Clin. Social Workers (legis. and ednl. com. 1972-83, 86-89). Unitarian Universalist. Avocations: theatre, dance, art, music, writing, traveling. Office: Acorn Psychotherapy Assocs 1400 Center St Ste 105 Newton Centre MA 02459-1754 E-mail: sykjp@aol.com., skaneko@waldenu.edu.

KANE-VANNI, PATRICIA RUTH, lawyer, paleontology educator; b. Phila, Pa, Jan. 12, 1954; d. Joseph James and Ruth Marina (Ramirez) Kane; m. Francis William Vanni, Feb. 14, 1981; 1 child, Christian Michael. AB, Chestnut Hill Coll., 1975; JD, Temple U., 1985; postgrad., U. Pa. Bar: Pa. 1985, US Ct. Appeals (3d cir.) 1988. Freelance art illustrator, Phila., 1972-80; secondary edn. instr. Archdiocese of Phila., Pa., 1980-83; contract analyst CIGNA Corp., Phila., 1983-84; jud. aide Phila. Ct. of Common Pleas, Pa., 1984; assoc. atty. Anderson and Dougherty, Wayne, Pa., 1985-86; atty. cons. Bell Tele. Co. of Pa., Pa., 1986-87; sr. assoc. corp. counsel Independence Blue Cross, Phila., 1987-96; pvt. practice law, 1996-97; dinosaur educator Acad. Natural Scis., Phila., 1997—. Atty. cons., 1996-2003; counsel Reliance Ins. Co., Phila., 1998-2000, contract atty., 2000-2003; counsel Westmont Law Assoc., 2002; atty. Westmont Assoc., Haddonfield, NJ, 2002; legal counsel, Ho. Authority, Phila., Pa., 2003-; cons. Coll. Consortium on Drug and Alcohol Abuse, Chester, Pa., 1986-89; paleo-sci. educator Pa. Acad. Natural Sci., 1997—; paleontology field expdns. include Mont., 1999. 2000, Isle of Wight, Eng., 1999, Bahariya Oasis, Egypt, 2000; spkr. in field. Contbr. articles and illustrations to profl. mag.; performer: Phila. Revels. Judge Del. Valley Sci. Fairs, Phila., 1986, 87, 98, 99; Dem. committeewomen, Lower Merion, Pa., 1983-87; ch. cantor, soloist, mem. choir Roman Cath. Ch.; bd. dir. Phila. Assn. Ch. Musicians. Recipient Legion of Honor award Chapel of the Four Chaplins, 1983. Mem. ABA, Pa. Bar Assn., Phila. Bar Assn. (Theatre Wing), Phila. Assn. Def. Counsel, Phila. Vol. Lawyers for Arts (bd. dir.), Nat. Health Lawyers Assn. (spkr. 1994 ann. conv.), Hispanic Bar Assn., Soc. Vertebrate Paleontology, Pa. Acad. Nat. Sci. (vol.), Delaware Valley Paleontol. Soc. (v.p. 1998—). Democrat. Avocations: choral and solo vocal music, portrait painting and illustrating, paleontology. Home: 119 Bryn Mawr Ave Bala Cynwyd PA 19004-3012 E-mail: pkv1@erols.com., Paleopatti@hotmail.com.

KANFER, RUTH, psychologist, educator; b. St. Louis, Feb. 1, 1955; d. Frederick H. and Ruby Kanfer. BA, Miami U., Oxford, Ohio, 1976; MA, PhD, Ariz. State U., 1981. Med. psychology intern health scis. ctr. U. Oreg., Portland, 1980-81; NIMH postdoctoral fellow U. Ill., Champaign, 1981-83, vis. asst. prof. psychology, 1983-84; asst. prof. psychology U. Minn., Mpls., 1984-89; office naval rsch. summer faculty rsch. fellow USN Personnel Rsch. and Devel., San Diego, 1987; vis. scholar Stanford U., Palo Alto, Calif., 1988; assoc. prof. psychology U. Minn., Mpls., 1989-93, prof., 1993-97; prof. psychology Ga. Inst. Tech., 1998—. Editl. bd. Jour. Applied Psychology, 1990—2001, Human Perf, 1997—, Orgnl. Behavior and Human Decision Processes, 1989-98, Applied Psychology: An Internat. Rev., 1991—, Basic and Applied Social Psychology, 1994-97, Contemporary Psychology, 1992-97; co-editor: Abilities Motivation and Methodology: The Minnesota Symposium on Learning and Individual Differences, 1989, Emotions in the Workplace, 2002; contbr. articles to profl. jours. Fellow NIMH, 1976; recipient Disting. Scientific award for early career contribution to psychology APA, 1989. Fellow APA, APS, SIOP, Am. Psychol. Soc.; mem. Acad. Mgmt. Assn. (Outstanding Publ. in Orgnl. Behavior award 1989, chair org. Divsn. Program 1998, Divsn. chair 2000), Internat. Assn. Applied Psychology, Psychonomic Soc., Midwestern Psychol. Assn., Sigma Xi. Office: Ga Inst Tech/Psychology Mc 0170 274 5th St Atlanta GA 30332-0001 E-mail: rk64@prism.gatech.edu.

KANNADY, PAM, secondary school educator; b. Tulsa, May 10, 1964; d. B.F. and Barbara J. (Dedmon) K. BA in Edn. summa cum laude, Northeastern State U., Tahlequah, Okla., 1986, MEd., 1989. Cert. tchr. Tchr. English Owasso (Okla.) H.S., 1987—2002; English instr. Tulsa C.C., 2002—. Mem. Okla. Coun. Tchrs. English, Alpha Chi.

KANNE, ELIZABETH ANN ARNOLD, retired secondary school educator; b. Atlanta, Sept. 16, 1945; d. Robert Earl and Elizabeth Ann (Jetton) A.; m. Robert Edward Lee, Jr., Aug. 20, 1967 (div. Oct. 1977); children: Robert Edward III, Edward Andrew; m. William Rudolph Kanne, Jr., June 4, 1979; 1 child, William Edward. BA, Furman U., 1967; MA, U. S.C., 1978, MEd, 1996. Cert. elem., early childhood, mid. sch. tchr., sch. adminstrn. S.C. 1st grade tchr. Aiken (S.C.) County Schs., 1967-70, 4th and 5th grade tchr., 1978-90, guidance counselor, 1990-92, 6th grade math. tchr., 1992-97, prin. mid.-sch., 1997—99, prin. elem. sch., 1999—2001; ret., 2001. Mem. S.C. Curriculum Congess, Columbia, 1991-94, Dist. Screening Team, Aiken, 1991—, Sch. Improvement Coun., Aiken, 1992-97. S.C. Ednl. Improvement Act grantee State Dept. Edn., 1991-92, 93-94. Mem. NEA, S.C. Edn. Assn., S.C. Mid. Sch. Assn., Aiken County Edn. Assn. Avocation: playing piano. Office: Kennedy Mid Sch 274 E Pine Log Rd Aiken SC 29803-6158

KANNER, RICHARD ELLIOT, physician, educator; b. Bklyn., Oct. 1, 1935; s. William W. and Elsie Alice (Karpf) K. AB, U. Mich., 1958; MD, SUNY, Bklyn., 1962. Diplomate Am. Bd. Internal Medicine, sub-bd. pulmonary disease. Intern then resident in internal medicine U. Utah Hosps., Salt Lake City, 1962-65; fellow pulmonary medicine Columbia Presbyn. Med. Ctr., N.Y.C., 1965-66, U. Utah Med. Ctr., 1968-70; from instr. to prof. medicine U. Utah Sch. Medicine, Salt Lake City, 1970-91, instr. medicine, 1970-71, asst. prof. medicine, 1971-77, assoc. prof. medicine, 1977-91, prof. medicine, 1991—. Vis. assoc. prof. medicine Harvard Med. Sch., Boston, 1980-81. Mem. air quality bd. Dept. Environ. Quality, State of Utah, 1988-97, chmn., 1995-97. Served to lt. comdr. USNR, 1966-68, Vietnam. Fellow ACP, Am. Coll. Chest Physicians (chmn. coun. of govs. 1991), mem. Am. Thoracic Soc. Office: U Utah Sch Medicine 701 Wintrobe Bldg 26 North 1900 East Salt Lake City UT 84132-4701 E-mail: kanner@med.utah.edu.

KANO, HISAO, director; b. Tokyo, Dec. 13, 1938; s. Hisaichi and Kikue Kano; m. Kazuko Kunieda, Apr. 21, 1968; children: Tetsuo, Ayuko. BA Bus. & Commerce, Keio U., 1962. Staff Sumitomo Elec. Industries, Ltd., Tokyo, 1962—71, sr. cons., 1971—75, mgr. Hokuriku Office, 1975—80, mgr. fiber optics sales, 1980—84; dep. gen. mgr. corp. planning Nuclear Fuel Indistries, Ltd., 1984—87, exec. asst. gen. mgr. corp. planning & adminstrn., 1987—98; dir. Kano Inst., Fujisawa, 2001—. Author, translator: Counseling Programs for Employees in the Workplace, 1997. Pres. The Ishizaka Sem., Tokyo, 1961—62. Grantee Fulbright grantee, Japan-U.S. Ednl. Comm., Tokyo, 1992. Mem.: APA, Acad. Human Resource Devel., Japanese Assn. Counseling Sci., Internat. Coach Fedn. Home: 3-9-M-108 Tsujido Higashi Kaigan Fujisawa-shi 251-0045 Japan

KANOFSKY, JACOB DANIEL, psychiatrist, educator; b. Phila., Apr. 16, 1948; s. Philip and Mollie (Edelstein) K. BA in Physics, Temple U., 1965-69; MD, Thomas Jefferson Med. Coll., Phila., 1974; MPH in Epidemiology, Johns Hopkins U., 1978. Diplomate Am. Bd. Psychiatry and Neurology. Intern Met. Hosp., N.Y.C., 1974-75; resident in psychiatry St. Luke's-Roosevelt Hosp. Ctr., Columbia U., N.Y.C., 1978-80, fellow in psychiat. epidemiology, 1980-82; asst. editor-in-chief Med. Tribune, N.Y.C., 1984-85; ward chief rsch. unit Bronx (N.Y.) Psychiat. Ctr., 1986, assoc. clin. dir., 1986-87, acting clin. dir., 1987, pres. med. staff orgn., 1987-89; assoc. dir. schizophrenia rsch. Albert Einstein Coll. Med./Bronx Psychiat. Ctr., 1989-90, sr. rsch. psychiatrist, 1989—, asst. prof. psychiatry, 1986—; asst. prof. epidemiology and social medicine Albert Einstein Coll. Med., 1993—. Lectr. in psychiatry Columbia U., N.Y.C., 1980—; attending psychiatrist St. Luke's-Roosevelt Hosp. Ctr., 1980—; contbg. editor Med. Tribune, 1986—; nutrition cons. Office of Alternative Medicine, NIH, 1992, Time Life Books, 1994—. Consulting editor Jour. of the Am. Coll. of Nutrition, 1990—; contbr. over 50 articles to profl. jours. Fellow Am. Coll. Nutrition; mem. Am. Psychiat. Assn. Jewish. Avocations: swimming, hiking, piano. Office: Bronx Psychiat Ctr 1500 Waters Pl Bronx NY 10461-2723

KANTOR, MEL LEWIS, dental educator, researcher; b. N.Y.C., 1956; s. Irving and Sarah Kantor. BA in Chemistry and Math., CUNY, 1977; DDS, U. N.C., 1981; MPH, U. Medicine and Dentistry N.J., Rutgers U., 1999. Diplomate Am. Bd. Oral and Maxillofacial Radiology. Resident Hennepin County Med. Ctr., Mpls., 1981-82, U. Conn. Health Ctr., Farmington, 1982-84; asst. prof. U. N.C. Sch. Dentistry, Chapel Hill, 1984-88, U. Conn. Sch. of Dental Medicine, Farmington, 1988-92; assoc. prof. N.J. Dental Sch., U. Medicine and Dentistry N.J., Newark, 1993—2003; prof. N.J. Dental Sch. Um. Medicine and Dentistry, Newark, 2003—; clin. assoc. prof. N.J. Med. Sch. U. Medicine and Dentistry N.J., Newark, 1993-2000; health svcs. rsch. fellow Robert Wood Johnson Med. Sch., 1997-99. Cons. dental selection criteria panel FDA, 1985-87; test constructor Nat. Bd. Dental Exams., 1989-93, 96-99, 2002--; bd. dirs. Acad. Radiology Rsch., 2000—, Am. Bd. Oral and Maxillofacial Radiology, 2001—. Assoc. editor Jour. Dental Edn., 1986-2001, Radiology, 2003—; mem. editl. bd. Dentomaxillofacial Radiology, 1997—, Oral Surgery. Oral Pathology, Oral Medicine, Oral Radiology and Endodntics, 2003—; contbr. articles to Jour. Chem. Physics, Jour. ADA, Jour. Dental Rsch., Oral Surgery, Oral Medicine and Oral Pathology, Jour. Dental Edn., Dentomaxillofacial Radiology. Mem. Internat. Assn. Dental Rsch. (founding mem. diagnostic sys. group, group program chmn. 1993-97), Am. Acad. Oral and Maxillofacial Radiology (chair consitution and bylaws com., rsch. and tech. com.), Am. Assn. Dental Schs., Internat. Assn. Dentomaxillofacial Radiology, Radiol. Soc. N.Am., Soc. for Med. Decision Making, Soc. for Health Svcs. Rsch. in Radiology, Phi Beta Kappa, Sigma Xi, Omicron Kappa Upsilon. Office: UMDNJ-NJ Dental Sch 110 Bergen St Rm D860 Newark NJ 07101-1709

KANYUK, JOYCE STERN, secondary art educator; b. Irvington, N.J., June 29, 1951; d. Paul Stern and Jean Hannah (Oberdofer) Dubin; m. Peter Kanyuk, June 10, 1973; 1 child, Paul. BFA in Art Edn., Syracuse (N.Y.) U., 1973; MA, Coll. of New Rochelle, 1977. Art tchr. Felix Festa Mid. Sch., West Nyack, 1973—. Exhibited in group shows at Orangeburg Town Hall, 1991, Nanuet Libr., 1992, 93, 94, 95, 97, Suffern Libr., 1992, 93, Allendale Borough Hall, 1992, N.E. Watercolor Soc., 1991, 94, 97, Audubon Artists Ann. Exhbn., 1994-97, Cmty. Arts Assn. Tri-State Open Juried Show, 1990, 91, 92, 96, South Nyack Fine Arts Festival, 1989-95, Ringwood Manor Assn. of the Arts Open Juried Show, 1990, 92, 1992 Morris County ARt Assn. Tri-State Juried Exhbn., Mari Galleries Nat. Fine Arts Exhbn., 1992, 93, 94, Exhibit of Mixed Media, Nabisco Gallery, 1993. Recipient Best of Show award Milburn-Short Hills Art Fair, 1994, Second Pl. award Mari Galleries, 1994, Honorable Mention Morris Count Art Assn., 1992, South Shore Watercolor Artists award East Islip Arts Coun., 1994, 95. Mem. Arts Coun. of Rockland, Cmty. Arts Assn. (membership chmn.), Ringwood Manor Art Assn., Audubon Artists, North East Watercolor Soc., N.Y. State Art Tchrs. Assn., Piermont Fine Arts Gallery. Avocations: figure skating, bicycling, cross country skiing. Home: 29 John St New City NY 10956-3650 Office: Felix Festa Mid Sch 30 Parrot Rd West Nyack NY 10994-1028

KAO, YASUKO WATANABE, retired library administrator; b. Tokyo, Mar. 30, 1930; came to U.S., 1957; d. Kichiji and Sato (Tanaka) Watanabe; m. Shih-Kung Kao, Apr. 1, 1959; children: John Sterling, Stephanie Margaret. BA, Tsuda Coll., 1950; BA in Lit., Waseda U., 1955; MSLS, U. So. Calif., 1960. Instr., Takinogawa High Sch., Tokyo, 1950-57; catalog librarian U. Utah Library, 1960-67, Marriott Library, 1975-77, head catalog div., 1978-90; dir. libr. Teikyo Loretto Heights U., 1991-95. Contbr. articles to profl. jours. Vol., Utah Chinese Am. Community Sch., 1974-80, Asian Assn. Utah, 1981-90. Waseda U. fellow, 1958-59. Mem. ALA, Asian Pacific Librs. Assn., Assn. Coll. and Rsch. Librs., Beta Phi Mu. Home: 2625 Yuba Ave El Cerrito CA 94530-1443

KAPEL, DAVID EDWARD, retired academic administrator, education educator; b. Wilmington, Del., July 11, 1932; s. Edward M. and Adele (M.) K.; m. Marilyn Brown, Aug. 27, 1955; children: Michael, Larry, Amy. BS in Edn., Temple U., 1955, MEd, 1957, EdD, 1964. Cert. tchr. of history, math., adminstr./prin., Pa. Tchr. of history, math. Phila. Sayre Jr. High Sch. Dist., 1955-57; tchr. of math. Elkins Park Jr. High, Cheltenham, Pa., 1957-59; tchr. of history, math. Cen. High Sch., Phila., 1959-64; prof. edn. Glassboro (N.J.) State Coll., 1964-69, Temple U., Phila., 1969-76; assoc. dean U. Nebr., Omaha, 1976-80, U. Louisville, 1980-86; dean U. New Orleans, 1985-88, Rowan U., Glassboro, NJ, 1988-98, prof. edn., 1998—2002; ret., 2002. Cons. various sch. dists. and colls. nationwide. Co-author: Metric Measure Simpl. 1974, Am. Educator's Encyclopedia, 1982 (ALA award 1982), 2d edit., 1991; contbr. articles to profl. jours. Staff sgt. USAF, 1951-52. Post-doctoral rsch. fellow U.S. Office Edn., Pitts.-AIR, 1966-67. Mem. ASCD, Am. Ednl. Rsch. Assn., Assn. Tchr. Educators (diplomate, dist. tchr. educator 1990—, honored as one of 70 Leaders in Edn. 1990), Am. Assn. Polit. and Social Sci. Democrat. Jewish. Avocations: reading, walking, fishing. Home: 217 Uxbridge Dr Cherry Hill NJ 08034-3731 E-mail: dmkapel@aol.com.

KAPETANAKOS, CHRISTOS ANASTASIOS, science administrator, physics educator; b. Xirokabi, Lakonia, Greece, Jan. 2, 1936; s. Anastasios and Alexandra (Doukas) K.; m. Ioanna Plafoutzi, June 23, 1962 (div. 1993); children: Anastasios, Yula. Diploma, Nat. U. Greece, Athens, 1960; M in Nuclear Engring., MIT, 1964; PhD, U. Md., 1970. Rschr. U. Tex., Austin, 1970-71; br. head, sect. head, rschr. Naval Rsch. Lab., Washington, 1971-92; acting dir. Inst. Plasma Physics, U. Crete, Iraklion, Crete, Greece, 1993-95; prof. of physics U. Crete, Iraklion, 1993-96; pres. Leading Egde Tech. Corp., Washington, 1995—. Cons. Fuel and Mineral Resources, Reston, Va., Icarus Rsch. Inc. Bethesa MD., Naval Rsch. Lab., Washington, SFA. Inc., Largo, Md., FERMI Nat. Accelerator Lab. Patentee in field; contbr. over 110 articles and more than 50 tech. reports to profl. publs. 2d lt. Artillery, 1960-62, Greece. Grantee Dept. Def., Washington, Dept. Energy, Washington, Office of Naval Rsch. Def. Advanced Project Agy., Washington, ELINOIL, Athens, Naval System Command, Fermi Lab. Fellow Am. Phys. Soc., Washington Soc. Scis. Home: 4431 Macarthur Blvd NW Washington DC 20007-2564 E-mail: let-kapetanakos@starpower.net.

KAPITAN, MARY L. retired nursing administrator, educator; b. Lawrence, Mass., July 9, 1920; d. Vincent and Concetta (Tomaselli) Zazzo; m. John A. Kapitan, Sept. 6, 1947. Diploma, Somerville (Mass.) Hosp., 1944; BS in Nursing Edn., DePaul U., Chgo., 1960, MS in Nursing Adminstrn., 1962. RN; lic. health facility adminstr., Ind. Occupational health nurse E. I. duPont de Nemours & Co., Lincolnwood, Ill., Senco Corp., Newtown, Ohio; asst. prof. psychiat. and med. nursing No. Ky. U., Highland Heights; nursing coord. VA Hosp., Butler, Pa.; instr. psychiat. nursing Ohio Valley Community Hosp., McKees Rocks, Pa.; dir. nursing svc. Presbyn. Home, Evanston, Ill., Edgewater Hosp., Chgo., Franklin Blvd Hosp., Chgo. 1st lt. U.S. Army Nurse Corps, 1944-47. Mem. ANA, Am. Assn. Occupational Health Nurses, Am. Coll. Health Facility Adminstrs., Ohio Nurses Assn., Ill. Nurses Assn., Ind. Nurses Assn., Mass. Nurses Assn., Southwestern Ohio Assn. Occupational Health Nurses (chmn. legislation and edn. com.), Women in Mil. Svc. for Am., Women's Meml. Found.

KAPLAN, ALAN LESLIE, gynecology educator, oncologist; b. Atlanta, Sept. 10, 1930; divorced; children: John, Robert. AB, Washington and Lee U., 1951; MD, Columbia U., 1955. Diplomate Am. Bd. Ob-Gyn. Intern Jackson Meml. Hosp., Miami, Fla., 1955-56; resident in ob-gyn Columbia-Presbyn. Med. Ctr., N.Y.C., 1956-59, 61-63; prof. dept. ob-gyn, dir. divsn. gynecologic oncology Baylor Coll. Medicine, Houston, 1963—. Med. dir. gynecologic oncology program Meth. Hosp., Houston, 1989—. Capt. M.C., U.S. Army, 1959-61. Mem. ACS, AMA, Am. Coll. Obstetricians and Gynecologists, Am. Cancer Soc., Am. Soc. Clin. Oncology, Soc. Gynecol. Oncology, Houston Gynecol. and Obstet. Soc. Office: Baylor Coll Medicine 6550 Fannin St Ste 801 Houston TX 77030-2738 E-mail: akaplan@bcm.tmc.edu.

KAPLAN, BETSY HESS, school board member; b. Bridgeton, N.J., Aug. 12, 1926; d. Alfred N. and Betsy (Bolton) Hess; m. Robert Leon Kaplan, June 11, 1953; children: Bruce Alfred, James Edward, Joan Ann. AB, Wesleyan Coll., 1947; BFA, Wesleyan Conservatory, 1948. Cert. tchr., Fla. Tchr. 4th grade Miami (Fla.)-Dade County Pub. Schs., 1950-53; edn. and cultural arts adv., 1961—88; instr. Miami Dade Cmty. Coll., 1979-81; admintrv. asst. to Ethel K. Beckham Miami-Dade County Sch. Bd., 1980-82, mem. sch. bd., 1988—, chair, 1993-95. Chair fed. rels. network Fla. Sch. Bds., Tallahassee, 1996-98; bd. dirs. New World Sch. of Arts, Miami; mem. Performing Arts Ctr. Trust, Miami, 1993—, student mentor. Mem. Emily's List, Washington, 1990—, Women's Emergency Network, Miami, 1990—, Women's Polit. Caucus, 1988—; cultural amb. Heart of the City cultural series Miami-Dade Park and Recreation Dept., 2002. Named Woman Worth Knowing, Miami Beach Commn. on Status of Women, 1994, Woman of Yr., King of Clubs, 2000; recipient Alumnae Disting. Achievement award, Wesleyan Coll., 1987, French Acad. Palms award, French Min. of Edn. of Youth and Sports, 1991, Co. of Women, Pioneer award, Miami-Dade County Pks. Dept., 1997, Ruth Wolkowsky Greenfield award, Am. Jewish Congress, 1993, Woman of Impact award, Cmty. Coalition for Women's History, 1995, Red Cross Spectrum award, Women in Edn., 1997, Trailblazer award, Women's Com. of 100, 1993, Lifetime Svc. to Music Edn. in Fla. and U.S., Fla. Music Educators Assn., 2000, Branches of Learning award, Women's Divsn. Greater Miami State of Israel Bonds Orgn., 2001. Mem.: AAUW (Phoenix award 1999), LWV, Alliance for Aging (mem. adv. bd. 1996—), Fla. Sch. Bds. Assn. (bd. dirs. 1990—99, Pres.'s award 2001), Phi Kappa Phi, Delta Kappa Gamma, Phi Delta Kappa. Democrat. Jewish. Avocations: studying art history, reading and interpreting poetry, studying and practicing French language, cooking. Home: 6790 SW 122d Dr Miami FL 33156-5459 Office: Miami Dade County Sch Bd 1450 NE 2d Ave Ste 700 Miami FL 33132 E-mail: bakaplan60@aol.com., bkaplan@sbab.dade.k-12.fl.us.

KAPLAN, ERICA LYNN, typing and word processing service company executive, pianist, educator; b. Aug. 6, 1955; d. George William and Raylia (Eagle) Kaplan; m. James Laurence Kellermann, Feb. 26, 1982. B in Mus., Manhattan Sch. Music, N.Y.C., 1976, M in Mus., 1979. Pres. Erica Kaplan Typing/Word Processing/Music Svcs., N.Y.C., 1980—; from accompanist to tchr. Stuyvesant Adult Ctr., N.Y.C., 1988—97, tchr. performance singing, 1997—. Accompanist Literally Alive/Victory Theatrical, 2000—, mus. dir., 2001—. Transl., annotator with additional mus. examples: L'Anacrouse dans la Musique Moderne, 1978; composer: (songs) Four by Feiffer, 1978, Hey Boys, 1984, Unborn Child, 1988, Neighbor, 1991, Watch the Closing Doors, 2001; arranger Postcards from the Apple, 1993, Isn't It Romantic, 1996. Mem. Common Cause, Washington, 1983—, SANE/FREEZE, 1988—. Mem.: Am. Fedn. Musicians, Mensa. Democrat. Jewish. E-mail: ELKK@aol.com.

KAPLAN, FRADA M. retired principal, special education educator; b. Bklyn., Sept. 3, 1940; d. Irving Kaplan and Naomi (Berger) Benezra; children: Irvin, Adley, Heidi Gartenstein; m. Lawrence R. Haley, Aug. 19, 1990. BA, Bklyn. Coll., 1978, cert., 1981; MS, Adelphi U., 1979; EdD, Columbia U., 1992. Tchr. vacation playgrounds N.Y.C. Bd. of Edn., Bklyn., 1968-71, tchr., coord. Bur. for Visually Handicapped, 1971-76, spl. asst. div. spl. edn., 1976-81; asst. prin. N.Y.C. Bd. Edn. 811K, Bklyn., 1981-88, prin., 1988-96, supr. prin.; adjunct prof. L.I. U., 1995-98. Mem. Midwood Civic Action Coun., Bklyn., 1970-96; chairperson Bklyn. Borough Pres.'s Adv. Com. on People with Disabilities, 1987-95; pres. N.Y.C. Adminstrv. Women in Edn. Recipient Educator of Yr. award Doctorate Assn. N.Y. Educators, 1993. Mem. Coun. for Exceptional Children, Assn. for Persons with Severe Disabilities, Assn. for the Help of Retarded Citizens, Assn. for Children with Retarded Mental Devel., N.Y. State Assn. Tchrs. for the Handicapped, N.Y. Acad. Pub. Edn., Kappa Delta Pi. Avocations: mastiff dogs, knitting, spinning fiber. Home: 26 Thorpe Rd Lyman NH 03585-3315

KAPLAN, HAROLD, humanities educator, author; b. Chgo., Jan. 3, 1916; m. Isabelle M. Ollier, July 29, 1962; three children. BA, U. Chgo., 1937, MA, 1938; postgrad., 1938-40. Instr. Rutgers U., New Brunswick, N.J., 1946-49; faculty dept. lit. Bennington (Vt.) Coll., 1949-72; prof. dept. English Northwestern U., Evanston, Ill., 1972—, chmn. Program in Am. Culture, 1973-75, acting chmn. dept. English, 1980-81. Fulbright-Hays lectr. U. Bari, Italy, 1956-57, U. Poitiers, France, 1960, U. Clermont-Ferrand, France, 1961, U. Aix-Marseille, France, 1967-68; vis. prof. Hebrew U., Jerusalem, 1981-82; acad. cons. Jan Krukowski Assocs., N.Y.C.; chmn. Fulbright Adv. Com. Am. Lit. Author: The Passive Voice: An Approach to Modern Fiction, 1966, Democratic Humanism and American Literature, 1972, Power and Order: Henry Adams and the Naturalist Tradition in American Fiction, 1981, Conscience and Memory: Meditations in a Museum of the Holocaust, 1994; contbr. articles and lit. criticism on Am. Lit. to scholarly publs., books revs. to lit. jours. Served to capt. USAAF, 1942-46. Ford Found. research grantee, 1970; Nat. Endowment Humanities grantee, summer, 1977; Rockefeller Found. fellow, 1981-82

KAPLAN, JEAN GAITHER (NORMA KAPLAN), reading specialist, retired educator; b. Cumberland, Md., Dec. 14, 1927; d. Frank Preston and Elizabeth (Mcneil) Gaither; m. Robert Lewis Kaplan, Dec. 4, 1959; 1 child, Benjamin Leigh. AB in Edn., Madison Coll., Harrisonburg, Va., 1950; MA in Edn., U. Va., 1956; postgrad., U. Va., William and Mary, 1958-61; reading specialist degree, U. Va., 1976. Tchr. Frederick County Sch. System, Winchester, Va., 1950-51, Washington County Sch. System, Hagerstown, Md., 1951-55, Charlottesville (Va.) Sch. System, 1955-60, York County (Va.) Sch. System, 1962, Newport News Sch. System, Denbigh, Va., 1963, Internat. Sch. Bangkok, 1965-67; tutor Reston Reading Ctr., Fairfax County, Va., 1972-74; tutor homebound, substitute tchr. Fairfax County Sch. Systems, 1974-78; pvt. practice pvt. tutor McLean/Middleburg, Va., 1978-89. Pres. Tutorial Svcs., Inc., McLean, 1985-87; sec. The Rumson Corp., Middleburg, 1981—. Mem. No. Va. Conservation Coun., Fairfax County, 1976-81; bd. dirs. Nat. Environ. Leadership Coun.; active Piedmont Environ. Coun. Mem. AAUW, LWV, Bangkok Am. Wives Assn., Tuesday Afternoon Club (pres. 1974-75, treas. 1995-96), Ayr Hill Garden Club, Soc. John Gaither Descs. Inc., Bluestone Soc., Kappa Delta Pi, Alpha Sigma Tau. Avocations: reading, theater, concerts, travel. Home and Office: PO Box 1943 Middleburg VA 20118-1943 E-mail: JK9600K@juno.com.

KAPLOW, LOUIS, law educator; b. Chgo., June 17, 1956; s. Mortimer and Irene (Horwich) K.; m. Jody Ellen Forchheimer, July 11, 1982; children: Irene Miriam, Leah Rayna. BA, Northwestern U., 1977; AM, JD, Harvard U., 1981, PhD, 1987. Bar: Mass. 1983. Prof. law Harvard U., Cambridge, Mass., 1982—, assoc. dean for rsch. and spl. programs, 1989-91. Co-author: Antitrust Analysis, 1997, Fairness Versus Welfare, 2002; contbr. articles to profl. jours.; mem. editl. bd. Jour. of Law, Econs. and Orgn., 1989—, Nat. Tax Jour., 1995—, Legal Theory, 1995—, Jour. Pub. Econs., 2001—. Faculty rsch. assoc. Nat. Bur. Economic Rsch., Cambridge, Mass., 1985—. Mem. AAAS, Am. Acad. Arts and Scis., Am. Econ. Assn., Nat. Tax Assn., Am. Law and Econs. Assn. Jewish. Office: Harvard U 1575 Mass Ave Rm 322 Cambridge MA 02138-2801

KAPLOWITZ, LISA GLAUSER, physician, educator; b. Phila., Apr. 18, 1951; d. Felix E. and Charlotte (Gordy) Glauser; m. Paul Bernard Kaplowitz, Dec. 28, 1970; children: Joshua Michael, Daniel Steven. BS, U. Mich., 1970; MD, U. Ill., Chgo., 1975; MS in Health Adminstrn., Va. Commonwealth U., 2002. Diplomate Am. Bd. Internal Medicine; Am. Bd. Infectious Diseases. Resident U. N.C., Chapel Hill, 1976—78, post grad. fellow, 1978—80, instr. dept. medicine, 1980—82; asst. prof., dept. medicine Med. Coll. Va., Richmond, 1982—89, assoc. prof., 1989—; dir. HIV/AIDS Ctr., Va. Commonwealth U., Richmond, 1993—2002, asst. v.p. fed. health policy; med. dir. ambulatory care Va. Commonwealth U. Health Sys., Richmond, 2000—02; dep. commr. for emergency preparedness and response Va. Dept. Health, Richmond, 2002—. Bd. dirs. AIDS Action Coun., Washington, 1995-96; mem., 1999-2000 class Exec. Leadership in Acad. Medicine Program for Women, MCP Hahnemann U. Contbg. (book chpt.) Conn's Current Therapy, 1985, 2d rev. edit., 1988, 3d edit., 1998; Principles of Critical Care Medicine, 1992. Mem. adv. bd. Va. League for Planned Parenthood, Richmond, 1993—, Richmond AIDS Ministry, 1988-92; Leadership Metro Richmond, 1992-93; grad. Exec. Leadership in Acad. Med. for Women, MCP-Hahnemann U., 2000. Named Woman of Yr. Va. Commonwealth U., 1995; mem. Va. Women's Hall of Fame; Coun. on Status of Women, 1992; health policy fellow, Inst. Medicine, 1996-97; fellow, Office of Senator Jay Rockefeller, 1997. Fellow ACP, Infectious Disease Soc. Am.; mem. APHA; Am. Soc. Microbiology. Avocation: piano. Office: Dept Commr Va Dept Health 1500 E Main St Richmond VA 23219 E-mail: lkaplowitz@vdh.state.va.us.

KAPPNER, AUGUSTA SOUZA, academic administrator; b. Bronx, June 25, 1944; d. Augusto and Monica Thomasina (Fraser) Souza; m. Thomas Kappner, Aug. 14, 1965; children: Tania, Diana. AB, Barnard Coll., 1966; MSW, Hunter Coll., N.Y.C., 1968; DSW, Columbia U., 1984. Cert. social worker, N.Y. Lectr., community affairs specialist Dept. Urban Affairs, Grad. Div., Hunter Coll., 1968-70; adj. instr., field supr. N.Y.C. C.C., 1970-71; instr., coord. urban leadership unit Columbia U. Sch. Social Wk., 1970-72; asst. prof., dir. admissions and student svcs. SUNY, Stony Brook, 1973-74; assoc. prof., chmn. human svcs. divsn. LaGuardia C.C., 1974-78, prof., dean continuing edn., 1978-84; dean acad. affairs Adult & Continuing Edn., CUNY, 1984, dean acad. affairs, instructional rsch., adult learning, 1984-86; pres. Borough of Manhattan C.C./CUNY, 1986-92; asst. sec. of vocat. and adult edn. Dept. of Edn., Washington, 1993-95; pres. Bank Street Coll., N.Y.C., 1995—. Cons. in field; lectr. in field; mem. adv. bd. Fund for the Improvement of Post Secondary Edn., U.S. Dept. of Edn, Adult Literacy Media Alliance; mem. adv. panel Nat. Ctr. for Innovation in Governing Am.

Edn., Nat. Writing Project; mem. N.Y.C. Bd. Edn. Adv. Bd. for Universal Pre-Kindergarten; former mem. Commn. for Nation of Lifelong Learners; commr., Commn. Higher Edn., Middle States Assn. Trustees Marymount Manhattan Coll.; mem. N.Y. State Edn. Commr.'s Task Force for the Edn. of Children and Youth at Risk, N.Y. State Gov.'s Coun. on Literacy, N.Y.C. Bd. Edn. Chancellor's U./Schs. Collaborative steering com.; appointed by Mayor of City of N.Y. to Joint Commn. on Integrity in Pub. Schs.; bd. dirs. N.Y. Urban Coalition; mem. N.Y.C. Coun. on Econ. Edn. Whitney M. Young Jr. fellow, 1982, USPHS awardee, 1981, Ford Found. fellow, 1973, Silverman Fund awardee, 1968, NIMH fellow, 1967, others; recipient Harlem Sch. Arts Humanitarian award, 1990, Am. Assn. Women in Community and Jr. Colls. Presdl. award, 1989, Asian Ams. for Equality Community Svc. award, 1989, Columbia U. Medal of Excellence, 1988, Barnard Coll. medal of distinction, 1988, Found. for Child Devel. Centennial award, 1999, Morris T. Keeton award Coun. for Adult and Exptl. Learning, others. Mem. Am. Coun. on Edn.

KAPPOS, STEVEN WAYNE, secondary social studies educator; b. Des Moines, Apr. 15, 1957; s. Theodore Kappos and Gretchen Mae (Vlassis) Aldrich; m. Stephanie Crawford, Aug. 2, 1980; children: Ashley Lynne, Molly Anne. BS in Edn., Drake U., 1979. Profl. teaching cert. Tchr. h.s. social studies Marshalltown (Iowa) Comty. Schs., 1979-80, Interstate 35 Comty. Schs., Truro, Iowa, 1980-81, Forest City (Iowa) Cmty. Schs., 1981—. Mem. ASCD, Forest City Edn. Assn. (pres. 1989-90, 93-94, 2003—, negotiations chair 1997-2000). Home: 110 Indian Ave Forest City IA 50436-2321 Office: 206 W School St Forest City IA 50436-1439 E-mail: skappos@forestcity.k12.ia.us.

KAPRAL, FRANK ALBERT, medical microbiology and immunology educator; b. Phila., Mar. 12, 1928; s. John and Erna Louise (Melching) K.; m. Marina Garay, Nov. 22, 1951; children: Frederick, Gloria, Robert; m. Esther McKenzie, May 10, 2003. BS, U. of the Scis. in Phila., 1952; Ph.D, U. Pa., 1956. With U. Pa., Phila., 1952-66, assoc. in microbiology, 1958-66; assoc. microbiologist Phila Gen. Hosp., 1962-64, chief microbiology research, 1964-66, chief microbiology, 1965-66; asst. chief microbiol. research VA Hosp., Phila, 1962-66; assoc. prof. med. microbiology Ohio State U., Columbus, 1966-69, prof. med. virology, immunology and med. genetics, 1969—95, prof. emeritus dept. molecular virology, immunology and med. genetics, 1995—. Cons. Ctr. Disease Control, Atlanta, 1980, Proctor and Gamble Co., 1981-87. Contbr. articles to profl. jours. Active Ctrl. Ohio Diabetes Assn., 1992-93. With AUS, 1946-47. Grantee, Ctrl. Ohio Diabetes Assn., 1992—93; Rsch. grant, NIH, 1959—95. Fellow Am. Acad. Microbiology, Infectious Diseases Soc. Am.; mem. AAAS, Am. Soc. for Microbiology, Am. Assn. for Immunologists, Sigma Xi. Democrat. Roman Catholic. Achievements include patents for implant chamber. Home: 873 Clubview Blvd S Columbus OH 43235-1771 Office: 2166B Graves Hall Columbus OH 43223-3226

KAPTEYN, HENRY CORNELIUS, physics and engineering educator; b. Oak Lawn, Ill., Jan. 21, 1963; m. Margaret Mary Murnane, 1988. BS, Harvey Mudd Coll., 1982; MA, Princeton U., 1984; PhD, U. Calif., Berkeley, 1989. Postdoctoral rschr. U. Calif., 1989-90; asst. prof. physics Wash. State U., Pullman, 1990-95, assoc. prof., 1995, U. Mich., Ann Arbor, 1996-99; prof. JILA, U. Colo., Boulder, 1999—. Contbr. articles to profl. jours. Regents fellow U. Calif., 1985, Sloan rsch. fellow, 1995. Fellow Optical Soc. Am. (Adolph Lomb medal 1993), Am. Phys. Soc.; mem. IEEE, Soc. Photo-Optical Instrumentation Engrs. (scholar 1988). Office: JILA Univ Colo Boulder CO 80309-0440 E-mail: kapteyn@jila.colorado.edu.

KAPUSINSKI, ALBERT THOMAS, economist, educator; b. Greenport, N.Y., Oct. 16, 1937; s. Casimir Thomas and Anne Mary (Olbrys) K.; m. Margaret Catherine Eichler, Sept. 3, 1963 (dec. March, 1982); children: Albert J., George T., Frank P.; m. Theresa Tafuri, Dec. 27, 1987. BBA, St. Johns U., N.Y.C., 1961, MBA, 1966; PhD, NYU, 1981. Economist Lionel D. Edie & Co., 1962-64; mem. faculty Caldwell (N.J.) U., 1964-2000, from assoc. prof. to prof. econs., 1969-2000, chmn. bus. dept., 1970-79, prof. emeritus, 2000; owner Kapusinski Prodns. Mem. Faculty Senate, 1969-75; assoc. sr. economist Hans Klunder Assocs., Hanover, N.H., 1966-69, ENVICO, Windsor, Vt., 1969-73; owner, operator Albert T. Kapusinski & Assoc., 1966—; econ. cons. to various industries in N.Y. and Vt.; mem. faculty Adirondack Coll., 1966, NYU, 1970-71, Merrill-Lynch Tng. Ctr. for Brokers, N.Y.C., 1973-74. Author: The Economy of Greene County, New York, 1972; contbr. articles to profl. jours. Chmn. Pro-Life del. World Population Conf. Forum, Bucharest, Rumania, 1974; bd. advisors U.S. Coalition for Life, Export, Penn., Ednl. Opportunities Fund, 1973-75. Served with USAR, USNG, 1953-61. Recipient K.L. Kiernan award; Gen. Electric Faculty fellow U. Chgo., 1970, Found. for Econ. Edn. fellow, 1971. Mem. Am. Econ. Assn., AAUP, Assn. Social Econs., Inst. Social Rels. Newark (adv. bd. 1972-74), Univ. Devel. Inst. (pres. 1967-68), Omicron Delta Epsilon. Office: Eichler Dr PO Box 80 Huletts Landing NY 12841 E-mail: drcapp@aol.com.

KARABATSOS, ELIZABETH ANN, career counseling services executive; b. Geneva, Nebr., Oct. 25, 1932; d. Karl Christian and Margaret Maurine (Emrich) Brinkman; m. Kimon Tom Karabatsos, Apr. 21, 1957 (div. Feb. 1981); children: Tom Kimon, Maurine Elizabeth, Karl Kimon. BS, U. Nebr., 1954; postgrad., Ariz. State U., 1980; Cert. contemporary exec. devel., George Washington U., 1985; M Orgnl. Mgmt., U. Phoenix, 1994; cert. tchg., Scottsdale (Ariz.) C.C., 1999. Myers Briggs Type Indicator Qualified Profl. Provider. Instr. bus. Fairbury (Nebr.) H.S., 1954—55; staff asst. U.S. Congress, Washington, 1955—60; with Karabatsos & Co. Pub. Rels., Washington, 1960—73; conf. asst. to asst. adminstr. and dep. adminstr. Gen. Services Adminstrn., Washington, 1973—76; dir. corr. Office Pres.-Elect, Washington, 1980; assoc. dir. adminstrv. svcs. Pres. Pers.-White House, Washington, 1981; dept. asst.to Sec. and Dep. Sec. Def., Washington, 1981—86, asst. to, 1987—89; dir. govt. and civic affairs McDonnell Douglas Helicopter Co., Mesa, Ariz., 1989—90, gen. mgr. gen. svcs., 1990—92, co. ombudsman, community rels. exec., 1992—95; exec. asst. to dir. adminstrn. State of Ariz., 1995—96; prin., owner Karabatsos & Assocs., bus. consulting and mediation svcs., Scottsdale, 1995—. Bur. chief Office Prevention and Health Promotion Ariz. Dept. Health Svcs., 1997-98. Mem. Nat. Mus. Women in Art, Washington; bd. dirs. U.S. C. of C. Com. on Labor & Tng.; mem. Gov.'s Sci. and Tech. Com.; mem. Ariz. Com. Employer Support the Guard and Res., 1991; active Gov. Com. for Ariz. Clean and Beautiful, World Affairs Coun. Ariz. Mem.: ASTD, AAUW, Ariz. Dispute Resolution Assn. (bd. dirs.), Assn. Conflict Resolution, Am. Arbitration Assn., Women in Def., U. Nebr. Cather Group, Internat. Friends Transformative Art, Order Ea. Star, Pi Beta Phi, Pi Omega Pi. Episcopalian. Home and Office: 4446 E Camelback Rd # 110 Phoenix AZ 85018 Fax: (602) 954-0225. E-mail: ebkarabats@aol.com.

KARAN, BRADLEE, lawyer, educator; b. Greensburg, Pa., Aug. 26, 1938; s. Nicholas and Anna (Bonovich) K.; m. Audette Rheta Cushman, May 5, 1961; children: Nicholas, Bradlee B., Jeffrey, Gregory. BA summa cum laude, Pa. State U., 1960; MA, U. Minn., 1965, PhD, 1967; JD, U. Akron, 1981. Bar: Ohio 1981, Minn. 1982, U.S. Dist. Ct. Minn. 1982. Assoc. prof. polit. sci. Mich. State U., East Lansing, 1965-69; prof. polit. sci. Coll. of Wooster, Ohio, 1969-81; assoc. Stuurmans & Kelly P.A., Mpls., 1982-83; ptnr. Stuurmans & Karan P.A., Mpls., 1983-94; pvt. practice Mpls., 1994—. Nat. Def. Edn. Act fellow. Mem. Minn. Bar Assn., Hennepin County Bar Assn. Democrat. Home: 11000 National St NE Blaine MN 55449-7020 Office: 2420 Centre Village 431 S 7th St Minneapolis MN 55415-1821

KARAN, HIROKO ITO, organic chemistry educator; b. Osaka City, Japan, Jan. 7, 1942; arrived in US, 1965; d. Seito and Haruko Ito; m. Jeffrey David Karan, Dec. 28, 1972; 1 child, Elizabeth Mika. MS, Wilkes Coll., Wilkes-Barre, Pa., 1967; PhD, Brown U., 1972. Rsch. asst. Hoshi Coll. Pharmacy, Tokyo, 1964-65; rsch. assoc. Fels Rsch. Inst., Temple U., Phila., 1971-72; rsch. scientist NYU, N.Y.C., 1972-73, 76-77; vis. instr. Hoshi Coll. Pharmacy, Tokyo, 1973-74; asst. prof. organic chemistry Medgar Evers Coll. CUNY, Bklyn., 1977-85, assoc. prof. Medgar Evers Coll., 1985-90, prof. Medgar Evers Coll., 1990—; asst. dean Medgar Evers Coll., 1993-98, dean, 1998—. Contbr. articles to profl. jours. Recipient svc. award Medgar Evers Coll., 1984, 90; grantee NIH, 1979—. Mem. Am. Chem. Soc. (chmn., bd. dirs. Bklyn. subsect. 1982-88, chmn. metrowomen chemists com. 1989, bd. dirs. N.Y. sect. 1985, 89-90, sec. 1989-90, Outstanding Svc. award 1993), Sigma Xi. Office: CUNY Medgar Evers Coll 1150 Carroll St Brooklyn NY 11225-2201 E-mail: hiroko@mec.cuny.edu.

KARANT-NUNN, SUSAN CATHERINE, history educator; b. Evanston, Ill. d. Max and Catherine (Cass) Karant; m. Frederick M. Nunn. BA, Cornell Coll., Mt. Vernon, Iowa, 1963; MA, Ind. U., 1967, PhD, 1971. Asst. prof. Portland (Oreg.) State U., 1970-76, assoc. prof., 1976-83, prof., 1983—. Author: Luther's Pastors, 1979, Zwickau in Transition, 1987; co-editor: Germania Illustrata, 1992; contbr. articles to profl. jours. Recipient Kathryn McHale fellowship Ind. AAUW, 1968, grad. fellowship Ind. U., 1969, Travel grant to German Dem. Republic Am. Coun. Learned Socs., 1975, Exchange fellowships Internat. Res. and Exchanges Bd. to German Dem. Republic, 1977, 86, Travel grant to Germany Am. Philosophical Soc., 1979. Mem. Soc. for Reformation Rsch. (coun. mem. 1992—), Sixteenth Century Studies Conf. (pres. 1991-92). Office: Portland State Univ PO Box 751 Portland OR 97207-0751

KARBER, JOHNNIE FAYE, elementary education educator; b. Enid, Okla., June 24, 1949; d. William Harvard Sr. and Marilyn Faye (Morehead) Benton; m. Jerry Lynn Karber, June 7, 1969; children: Jason Kelly, Jennifer Lyn, Julee Dawn. BS, Okla. Panhandle State U., 1972; postgrad., Wichita State U. and West, Tex. State U. Tchr., kindergarten and music Goodland (Kans.) Unified Sch. Dist.; tchr., music Perryton (Tex.) Ind. Sch. Dist. Active church and community orgns. Mem. Tex. Music Educators Assn., ATPE, Kodaly Educators of Tex. Avocation: pianist.

KARDAS, SIGMUND JOSEPH, JR., secondary education educator; b. Phila., Jan. 14, 1940; s. Sigmund Joseph Sr. and Mary Olga (Sambor) K. BSc in Geology, Villanova U., 1962; postgrad., U. Madrid, 1971. Lic. tchr. N.J., Mass. Prof. sci. English U. Madrid, 1964-65; tchr. sci. Am. Sch. Madrid, 1966-69; chmn. dept. sci. Am. Sch. of Las Palmas, Spain, 1969-71; prof. sci. English, phys. anthropology and palaeontology U. La Laguna, Spain, 1971-78; tchr. sci. Mid. Twp. High Sch., Mays Landing, N.J., 1980-81, Trenton (N.J.) Pub. Schs., 1982—97. Bd. dirs. Lab. Investigaciones Sobre Biorritmos Humanos, Tenerife, Spain; editorial assoc. Metron Publs., Princeton, 1982-84; vis. scientist Senckenberg Inst., Wilhelmshaven, Fed. Republic Germany, 1964. Contbr. articles to profl. jours. Grantee NATO Paleoclimate Conf., 1963, Internat. Biorhythm Rsch. Assn., 1977, NSF Geology Inst., 1985; named Hon. Rsch. Assoc. Japanese Biorhythm Lab., Tokyo, 1976. Mem. Fedn. Study of Environ. Factors (adv. bd. 1989—), Nat. Speleolog. Soc., Internat. Soc. Biometerology, Real Sociedad Espanola de Historia Natural, Nat. Sci. Tchrs. Assn. Achievements include description of new subspecies of Pleistocene walrus; correlation of solar activity cycle MHz radiation to human behavior; first use of x-rays to study internal structure of stalactites; used polymer resin to make molds of underground nests of parasitic wasps; research in solar cycle-Earth relationships, especially climate and human behavior. Office: Lab Investigations SBH Huerta Bicho 27 38350 Tacoronte Spain

KARDON, PETER FRANKLIN, foundation administrator; b. N.Y.C., May 5, 1949; s. Leonard and Annette (Rappaport) K. AB, Dartmouth Coll., 1970; MA, U. Chgo., 1975, PhD, 1984. Asst. to exec. dir. MLA of Am., N.Y.C., 1980-84; acad. affairs assoc. Office of Chancellor, NYU, N.Y.C., 1984-86, dir. acad. projects, 1986-88; dir. planning John Simon Guggenheim Meml. Found., N.Y.C., 1988-98, dir. L.Am. program, 1991-2001, dir. info., 1998-2001, v.p., 2001—. Adj. prof. medieval and Renaissance studies NYU, N.Y.C., 1986—. Bd. dirs. TeenAIDS PeerCorps, Inc., 2002—. Reynolds scholar Dartmouth Coll., 1970-71; Fulbright-Hayes fellow, 1973-74, Georges Lurcy fellow, 1976-77, Whiting fellow U. Chgo., 1978-79; NYU Golden Dozen Disting. Tchg. award, 1996. Office: JS Guggenheim Meml Found 90 Park Ave New York NY 10016-1301 E-mail: pk@gf.org.

KARELIS, CHARLES HOWARD (BUDDY KARELIS), former academic administrator, humanities educator; b. Denver, July 7, 1945; s. Lloyd Howard and Annabelle (Weinberg) Karelis; m. Judith Theodora Johanna Johnston, June 10, 1972 (div. 1991); children: Alexander O., Oliver L. BA, Williams Coll., 1966; PhD, Oxford (Eng.) U., 1972; LHD, Phillips U., Okla., 1990; HHD, Marietta Coll., 1993. Assoc. producer WGBH-FM, WGBH-TV, Boston, 1967—68; lectr. in philosophy Williams Coll., Williamstown, Mass., 1972—73, asst. prof., 1973—79, assoc. prof., 1979—85, prof., 1985—99; spl. asst. to sec. Dept. Edn., Washington, 1985, dir. Fund for Improvement of Postsecondary edn., 1985—99; pres. Colgate U., Hamilton, 1999—2001; vis. prof. philosophy George Washington U., Washington, 2001—. Vis. assoc. prof. philosophy Wesleyan U., Middleton, Conn., 1980—81; bd. dirs. (sec.) Charter Schools Develop. Corp.; mem. of governing bd. U.S. Dept. of Agrl. Contbr. articles to profl. jours. Mem.: Phi Beta Kappa. Office: George Washington U Dept Philosophy 801 22nd St NW Washington DC 20052 also: 1090 Vermont Ave NW Ste 800 Washington DC 20005*

KARESH, JANICE LEHRER, special education consultant; b. N.Y.C., May 22, 1924; d. Maxwell and lillian (Cohen) Lehrer; m. Irwin Karesh, June 15, 1947 (dec. 1959); children: Sara, Hyman, Ann, Charles. BS in Pre-Medicine, Rutgers U., 1945; MA in Psychol. Counseling, NYU, 1946. Tchr. algebra Chicora H.S., Charleston, S.C., 1946-47; tchr. math. Charleston H.S., 1963; tchr. gifted Addleston Hebrew Acad., Charleston, 1963-64; tchr. physics, biology Rivers H.S., Charleston, 1964-65; cons. spl. edn. S.C Dept. Mental Retardation, Charleston, 1966-69; dir. spl. svcs. Beaufort (S.C.) Sch. Dist., 1969-89; ind. cons. spl. edn. Charleston, 1989—. Vol. advocate guardian at litem, Family Ct., S.C., 1990—; mem. exec. com. Charleston Democratic Party, 1994—. Mem. LWV (past bd. dirs.), Nat. Coun. Jewish Women (pres. 1951, past bd. dirs.), Coun. for Exceptional Children, Poetry Soc. of S.C., Douglass Alumnae Assn. (v.p. 1995—). Democrat. Jewish. Avocations: needlepoint, writing poetry and essays, child advocacy issues. Home: 150 Wappoo Creek Dr Apt 9 Charleston SC 29412-2140 E-mail: j.karesh@bellsouth.net.

KARETZKY, STEPHEN, library director, educator, researcher; b. Bklyn., Aug. 29, 1946; s. Harry and Lillian Dorothy (Abrams) K.; m. Deborah Ann Shaw, Apr. 12, 1970 (div. July 1972); Joanne Louise Ballestrasse, Mar. 17, 1985. BA, CUNY, Flushing, 1967; MLS, Columbia U., 1969, DLS, 1978; MA, Calif. State U., Dominguez Hills, 1991. Libr. Bklyn. Pub. Libr., 1969-70; asst. prof. SUNY, Buffalo, 1974-76, Geneseo, 1977-78; assoc. prof. U. Haifa, Israel, 1978-81, San Jose (Calif.) State U., 1982-85; researcher, editor Shapolsky/Steimatzky Pub., N.Y.C., 1981-82; sr. editor Shapolsky Pubs., N.Y.C., 1985-86; libr. dir. Felician Coll., Lodi, N.J., 1986—. Author: Reading Research and Librarianship: A History and Analysis, 1982 (2d place award for Best Book of Yr. Am. Soc. Info. Sci 1983), The "Cannons" of Journalism, 1984; editor: The Media's War Against Israel, 1985, The Media's Coverage of the Arab-Israeli Conflict, 1989, Not Seeing Red: American Librarianship and the Soviet Union, 2002; bd. advisors Directory of American Scholars, 1999-2001; contbr. articles to profl. jours. Exec. dir. Ams. for a Safe Israel, N.Y.C., 1985-86. Mem.: Author's Guild, Orgn. Am. Historians, Am. Hist. Assn., Am. Soc. Info. Sci. and Tech. Jewish. Avocation: book collecting. Office: Felician Coll Libr 262 S Main St Lodi NJ 07644-2117

KARIN, SIDNEY, computer science and engineering educator; b. Balt., July 8, 1943; BSME, CCNY, 1966; MS in Nuclear Engring., U. Mich., 1967, PhD in Nuclear Engring., 1973. Registered profl. engr., Mich. Computer programmer, nuc. engr. ESZ Assocs., Inc., Ann Arbor, Mich., 1968-72; sr. engr., sect. leader Gen. Atomics (formerly GA Techs., Inc.), San Diego, 1973-75, mgr. fusion divsn. Computer Ctr., 1975-82, dir. info. sys. divsn., 1982-85; dir. San Diego Supercomputer Ctr., 1985-2001, Nat. Partnership for Advanced Computational Infrastructure, 1997-98. Bd. dirs. Corp. for Ednl. Network Initiatives in Calif.; prof. computer sci. and engring., 1986—; chair Fed. Networking Adv. Com., 1991-97; mem. adv. com. CISE Directorate, NSF. Contbr. articles to profl. jours. NDEA fellow, AEC fellow. Fellow AAAS, Assn. for Computing Machinery; mem. IEEE Computer Soc., Computing Rsch. Assn. (bd. dirs. 1998—). Avocations: flying, technical rock climbing, motorcycle riding, alpine skiing, reading. Home: 748 Avocado Ct Del Mar CA 92014-3911 Office: U Calif San Diego Supercomputer Ctr 9500 Gilman Dr La Jolla CA 92093-5003 E-mail: skarin@ucsd.edu.

KARKHECK, JOHN PETER, physics educator, researcher; b. N.Y.C., Apr. 26, 1945; s. John Henry and Dorothy Cecilia (Riebling) K.; m. Kathleen Mary Shiels, Nov. 8, 1969; children: Lorraine, Michelle, Eric. BS, LeMoyne Coll., 1966; MA, SUNY, Buffalo, 1972; PhD, SUNY, Stony Brook, 1978. Various positions Grumman Corp., Bethpage, N.Y., 1964-68; grad. asst. SUNY, Buffalo, 1968-70; tchr. secondary schs. Mattituck (N.Y.) Sch. Dist., 1970-71, Shelter Island (N.Y.) Sch. Dist., 1971-73; grad. asst. SUNY, Stony Brook, 1973-78, postdoctoral fellow, 1978-79, rsch. assoc., 1979-81; asst. prof. physics GMI Engring. and Mgmt. Inst., Flint, Mich., 1981-84, assoc. prof., 1984, prof., dir. physics, 1988-89, head. dept. sci. and math., 1989-93; prof., chmn. dept. physics Marquette U., Milw., 1993—2003, dir. physics for medicine program, 2003—. Physics assoc. Brookhaven Nat. Lab., Upton, N.Y., 1975-79, cons., 1979-85, STS, Hauppauge, N.Y., 1983, BID Ctr., Flint, 1985-90; acad. assoc. Mich. State U., 1988, 90, vis. scholar, 1989, vis. scientist, 1991; reviewer Addison-Wesley Pub., 1990, 93; regional dir. Mich. Sci. Olympiad, 1991-92, 92-93; co-dir. NATO Advanced Study Inst., 1998, editor, 1999-2000. Contbr. numerous articles to profl. jours. Den leader Cub Scouts Am., Flint, 1987-91; leader Boy Scouts Am., 1991-98; bd. dirs. Flint Area Sci. Fair, 1991-93; mem. sci. curriculum adv. com. Milw. Acad. Sci., 2000-; judge local sci. fairs. Dept. Energy rsch. grantee, 1977-79, NATO travel grantee, 1983-86, 89, NATO ASI grantee, 1998. Mem. Am. Phys. Soc., AAAS, AAPT, Sigma Xi (v.p. Marquette U. chpt. 1998-99, pres., 1999-2000). Roman Catholic. Avocations: swimming, reading, bicycling, travel, learning german. Home: 6592 N Bethmaur Ln Glendale WI 53209-3320 Office: Marquette Univ Dept Physics PO Box 1881 Milwaukee WI 53201-1881 E-mail: John.Karkheck@marquette.edu.

KARL, GABRIEL, physics educator; b. Cluj, Romania, Apr. 30, 1937; came to Can., 1960; s. Alexander and Frida (Izsak) K.; m. Dorothy Rose Searle, Apr. 10, 1965; 1 child, Alexandra PhD, U. Toronto, Ont., Can., 1964. Research assoc. Oxford U., Eng., 1966-69; prof. physics U. Guelph, Ont., Can., 1969—. Contbr. articles to profl. jours. German-Canadian Research Prize (Deutsch-Kanadischer Forschungspreis). Fellow Royal Soc. Can.; mem. Am. Phys. Soc., Can. Assn. Physicists (CAP medal 1991). Office: U Guelph Macnaughton Bldg 50 Stone Rd E Guelph ON Canada N1G 2W1 E-mail: gk@physics.uoguelph.ca.

KARL, HELEN WEIST, pediatric anesthesia and pain management educator, researcher; b. NYC, Oct. 28, 1948; d. Edward C. and Louise (Stursberg) Weist; m. Stephen R. Karl, June 1, 1974 (div. 1990); children: Katherine L., Thomas R., John W. BA in Philosophy, Smith Coll., 1970; MD, U. Va., 1976. Diplomate Am. Bd. Anesthesiology, Nat. Bd. Med. Examiners. Intern Hartford (Conn.) Hosp., 1976-77, resident in anesthesia, 1977-79; fellow pediat. anesthesiology Children's Hosp. of Phila., 1979-81; staff anesthesiologist St. Christopher's Hosp. for Children, Phila., 1981; asst. prof. anesthesiology and pediatrics Pa. State U., Hershey, 1981-90; asst. prof. anesthesiology U. Washington, 1990-97, assoc. prof. anesthesiology, 1997—; Parker B. Francis fellow in pulmonary rsch. Pa. State U., Hershey, 1986-88; dir. pain mgmt. Children's Hosp., Seattle, 1994-99. Adj. assoc. prof. dental pub. health scis., U. Wash., 1997-2000. Contbr. articles to profl. jours. Mem.: AAUW, Wash. Soc. Anesthesiologists, Am. Med. Women's Assn., Am. Soc. Anesthesiologists. Avocations: swimming, trumpet. Office: Children's Hosp & Med Ctr 4800 Sand Point Way NE Seattle WA 98105-3901 E-mail: helen.karl@seattlechildrens.org.

KARLIN, BERNARD RICHARD, retired educational administrator; b. Chgo., Apr. 4, 1927; s. Louis and Sara (Banen) K.; m. Betty Ann Baehrend, June 17, 1950 (dec. Mar. 1988); children: Kristine, Kathleen, Larry Kimberly. BS, DePaul U., 1950, MEd, 1961. Cert. Type 75 administr., Ill. With Otis Playground Chgo. Pub. Schs., 1951, tchr. elem. sch., 1951-63, cons. spl. edn., 1973-75; tchr. spl. edn. Montefiore Spl. Sch., Chgo., 1963-68, prin., 1982-93; ret., 1993; administr. Chgo. Parental Sch., 1968-73; prin. Key Sch., Chgo., 1975-82; mem. adv. bd. local sch. coun. Chgo. Pub. Schs., 1993—. Instr. adj. faculty Northea. Ill. U., Chgo., 1968-75, Harper Coll., Palatine, Ill., 1975-93, Coll. Lake County, Grayslake, Ill., 1979—; adv. bd. Uniform Code of Discipline, Chgo., 1986-90, Dist. 4 Supt.'s Com., Chgo., 1990-93, Corp. Schs. Am., 1990-91, Gen. Supt.'s Roundtable, Chgo., 1990-91, Chgo. Bd. Edn. tchrs. Union, 1992-93. Active Key Sch. PTA, Chgo., 1975-82, Montefiore PTA, Chgo., 1982-90, Montefiore Local Sch. Coun., Chgo., 1990-93. With USNR, 1945-46. Named Educator of Yr. Phi Delta Kappa, 1980-86; recipient Whitman award Ednl. Excellence Whitman Corp., 1988, Spl. Ednl. Leadership award Ind. U., 1991, Exec. Educator 100 award, 1990, U. Ill. Med. Sch. Leadership award, 1993. Mem. DePaul Alumni Assn. Avocations: sports, gardening, movies, music, photography. Home: 4800 N Ozark Ave Norridge IL 60706-3310

KARLIN, SAMUEL, mathematics educator, researcher; b. Yonova, Poland, June 8, 1924; s. Morris Karlin; m. Elsie Karlin (div.); children: Kenneth, Manuel, Anna. BS in Math., Ill. Inst. Tech., 1944; PhD in Math., Princeton U., 1947; DSc (hon.), Technion-Israel Inst. Tech., Haifa, 1985. Instr. math. Calif. Inst. Tech., Pasadena, 1948—49, asst. prof., 1949—52, assoc. prof., 1952—55, prof., 1955—56; vis. asst. prof. Princeton U., 1950—51; prof. Stanford U., Calif., 1956—. Wald lectr., 1957; Andrew D. White prof.-at-large Cornell U., 1975—81; Wilks lectr. Princeton U., 1977; pres. Inst. Math. Stats., 1978—79; Commonwealth lectr. U. Mass., 1980; 1st Mahalanobis meml. lectr. Indian Statis. Inst., 1983; prin. invited spkr. XII Internat. Biometrics Meeting, Japan; prin. lectr. Que. Math. Soc., 1984; adv. dean math. dept. Weizmann Inst. Sci., Israel, 1970—77; Britton lectr. McMaster U., Hamilton, Ont., Canada, 1990; Cockerham lectr. N.C. State U., 1996. Author: Mathematical Methods and Theory in Games, Programming, Economics, Vol. I: Matrix Games, Programming and Mathematical Economics, 1959, Mathematical Methods and Theory in Games, Programming, Economics, Vol. II: The Theory of Infinite Games, 1959, A First Course in Stochastic Processes, 1966, Total Positivity Vol. I, 1968; author: (with K. Arrow and H. Scarf) Studies in the Mathematical Theory of Inventory and Production, 1958; author: (with W.J. Studden) Tchebycheff Systems: With Applications in Analysis and Statistics, 1966; author: (with H.Taylor) A First Course in Stochastic Processes, 2d edit., 1975; author: A Second Course in Stochastic Processes, 1980, An Introduction to Stochastic Modeling, 1984; author: (with C. Michelli, A. Pinkus, I.I. Schoenberg) Studies in Spline Functions and Approximation Theory, 1976. Recipient Lester R. Ford award, Am. Math. Monthly, 1973, Robert Grimmett Chair Math., Stanford U., 1978, The John Von Neumann Theory prize, 1987, award, U.S. Nat. Medal Sci., 1989, The Karlin prize in Math. Biology named in honor, Stanford U. Dept. Biol. Scis., 1992; fellow Proctor, 1945, Bateman Rsch., 1947—48, Guggenheim Found., 1959—60, NSF, 1960—61. Fellow: AAAS, Inst. Math. Statis., Internat. Statis. Inst.; mem.: NAS (award in applied math. 1973), Am. Philos. Soc., Human Genome

Orgn., Am. Naturalist Soc., London Math. Soc. (hon.), Genetics Soc. Am., Am. Soc. Human Genetics, Am. Acad. Arts and Scis., Am. Math. Soc. Office: Stanford U Bldg 380 Stanford CA 94305-2125 E-mail: karlin@math.stanford.edu.

KARLINS, M(ARTIN) WILLIAM, composer, educator; b. NYC, Feb. 25, 1932; s. Theodore and Gertrude Bertha (Leifer) K.; m. Mickey Cutler, Apr. 6, 1952; children: Wayne, Laura. MusB, MusM, Manhattan Sch. Music, 1961; PhD in Composition, U. Iowa, Iowa City, 1965; studied with, Frederick Piket, Vittorio Giannini, Stefan Wolpe, Philip Bezanson, Richard Hervig. Asst. prof. music Western Ill. U., 1965-67; assoc. prof. theory and composition Northwestern U. Sch. Music, Evanston, Ill., 1967-73, prof., 1973—, dir., co-dir. Contemporary Music Ensemble, 1967—, apptd. Harry N./Ruth F. Wyatt prof. music theory/composition, 1998—2002, prof. emeritus, 2003—. Vis. guest composer Ariz. State U., 1978, Ill. Wesleyan U., 1978; guest composer Nazareth Coll., Rochester, NY, 1978, Bowling Green State U., 1982, 89, Navy Band, Washington, 1988, Nat. Conf. for Condrs., Chgo., Ball State U., Bloomington, Composer's Symposium U. N.Mex., Albuquerque, 1991, Alta. (Can.) Coll. Conservatory Music, 1991, Sigma Alpha Iota Internat. Am. Music Awards Competition, 1993; featured guest composer We. Ill. U., Macomb, 1994; articipant Coll. Band Dirs. Nat. Assn. Nat. Conf., Northwestern U., 1987; coord. composers workshops Internat. World Congress Saxophones, London; lectr., composer-in-residence World Saxophone Congress, Bordeaux, France, 1974, Nat. Saxophone Tng. Course, Duras, France, 6th Stage de Saxophone, Duras, France, 1991; panelist Nat. Conf. Am. Symphony Orch. League; lectr., guest composer Franz Liszt Acad. Music, Budapest, Franz Liszt Musical Coll., Győr, Hungary, 1995; vis. composer U. Fla., Gainesville, 2003; composer, coord. Stefan Wolpe Festival, Northwestern U., 2001; guest composer Budapest Spring Festival, 1999, U. Louisville, Ky., 2003; honored composer, Sofia, Bulgaria, 1997; honored composer and lectr. 3rd Music Rsch. Seminar, Escola de Música e Artes Cênicas da Universidade Federal de Goiás, Goiânia, Brazil, 2003; guest lectr., composer Vienna, Austria, 1999, Bowdoin Coll., Maine, 1999. Composer: Concert Music 1 through 5, Lamentations-In Memoriam, Elegy for Orchestra, Reflux (concerto for double bass and wind ensemble), Symphony No. 1, Concerto Grosso I and II, Academic Festival Fanfare for wind ensemble, Woodwind Quintet I and II, Saxophone Quartet I and II, Night Light Quartet No. 3 for Saxophones, 3 Plano Sonatas, Outgrowths-Variations for Piano, Suite of Preludes for piano, Humble Harvest for piano, Catena I (clarinet and chamber orch.), Catena II (soprano saxophone and brass quintet), Catena III (concerto for horn and orch.), Birthday Music I (flute, bass clarinet/clarinet and double bass) and II (flute and double bass), Under and Over (flute and double bass), Variations on Obiter Dictum (cello, piano and percussion), Music for Cello Alone I and II, Music for Oboe, Bass Clarinet and Piano, Music for Tenor Saxophone and Piano, Music for Alto Saxophone and Piano, Music for English Horn and Piano, Four Inventions and a Fugue for Bassoon, Piano and Female Voice, Infinity for Oboe d'amore, clarinet, viola and female voice, Song for Soprano with Alto Flute, Cello, Three Songs for Soprano, Flute and Piano, Chameleon for Harpsichord, Drei Kleine Cembalostücke (harpsichord), Celebration for Flute, Oboe and Harpsichord, Kindred Spirits for mandolin, guitar and harp, Quintet for Alto Saxophone and String Quartet, Impromptu for Saxophone and Organ, Nostalgie for 12 Saxophones Ensemble, Introduction and Passacaglia for 2 Saxophones and Piano, Just A Line From Chameleon, for 2 clarinets, Fantasia for tenor saxophone and percussion, Saxtuper for Saxophone, Tuba, and Percussion, Seasons for solo saxophonist, Concerto for Alto Saxophone and Orch., String Quartet with soprano in the last movement, Chidlren's Bedtime Songs for mixed chorus, Three Love Songs for male chorus, Three Poems for mixed chorus, Looking Out My Window for Treble Chorus and viola; (bass clarinet solo) Improvisations on Lines Where Beauty Lingers; recs. include Music for Tenor Saxophone and Piano, Music for Alto Saxophone and Piano, Variations on Obiter Dictum for cello, piano and percussion, Introduction and Passsacaglia for 2 saxophones and piano, Solo Piece with Passacaglia for clarinet, Sonata No. 2, Sonata No. 3 for piano and Outgrowth Variations for Piano, Saxophone Quartets Nos. 1 and 2, Chameleon for harpischord, Drei Kleine Cembalostücke (harpsichord), Quintet for alto saxophone and string quartet, Nostalgie for 12 saxophone ensemble, Impromptu for alto saxophone and organ, Reflux (concerto for amplified double bass and winds), Quartet for Strings with soprano in the last movement, Song for Soprano, with alto flute and cello, Four Inventions and a Fugue for bassoon, piano, and soprano, Kindred Spirits for mandolin, guitar and harp, Concerto Grosso # 1 for 9 instruments, Catena II for soprano saxophone and brass quintet; CDs include Klecka Plays Broege and Karlins, Salvatore Spina Piano Music By Karlins, Lombardo and Stout, Nostalgie, A Retrospective of Saxophone Music by M. William Karlins, Works by M. William Karlins, Howard Sandroff, Charles Tomlinson Griffes, Carl Ruggles, Chicago Saxophone Quartet, Joseph Wytko Saxophones-Wytko Saxophone Quartet, Midwest Composers-Music for Winds, America's Millennium Tribute to Adolphe Sax, Vol II, Lifting the Veil, Mixed Company, Héliosaxo, Shaking the Pumpkin, Conicality. Grantee MacDowell Colony, Nat. Endowment for Arts, 1979, 85, Meet the Composer, 1980, 84-85, 90, 95, Ill. Arts Coun., 1985, 87, 90, 96, 98, 2003. Mem. Am. Music Ctr., Broadcast Music, Inc., Am. Woman Composers (trustee Chgo. chpt.), Pi Kappa Lambda, Sigma Alpha Iota (nat. arts. assoc.). Office: Northwestern U Sch Music Evanston IL 60208-1200 E-mail: m-karlins@northwestern.edu.

KARLSRUD, GARY MICHAEL, administrator, consultant; b. Gary, Ind., Oct. 31, 1946; s. Gilbert and Jessica Mae (Rutherford) K.; m. Patricia Lynn Matheus, Apr. 12, 1975; 1 child, Kim Mee. AAS in Dental Technology, Milw. Area Tech. Coll., 1971; BS in Sociology, SUNY, Albany, 1977; MA in Health Care Edn., Ctrl. Mich. U., 1978; EdD in Ednl. Leadership, U. Sarasota, 1994; PhD, Greenwich U., 1996. Trainee dental technician Kramer Dental Studio, Mpls., 1968-69; dental technician Baasch Dental Lab., Deerfield, Ill., 1972; gen. mgr. Glaze Dental Lab., Waukesha, Wis., 1972-73; v.p. Sanford Dental Lab., Milw., 1973-79; lab. pres., group v.p. Nat. Dentex Corp., Boston, 1979-84; pres., owner Mesa Dental Ceramics, Louisville, Colo., 1984-87; dir. dental lab. svcs. U. Conn. Sch. Dental Medicine, Farmington, 1987—; pres. Dental Tech. Svcs., 1995—. Adj. faculty Greenwich U., 1996—; mem. adv. bd. Allied Dental Programs-Tunxis C.C., Farmington, 1990—; presenter in field; examiner cert. dental technician program, 1996—. Author: Inservice Training in the Dental Lab, 1978. Mem. John Patterson Sch. PTO, Newington, Conn., 1994. With USN, 1969-72. Mem. Am. Assn. Dental Schs., Am. Soc. Allied Health Profls., Conn. Dental Lab. Assn. (acting pres., edn. chair 1990—), High I.Q. Soc., Mensa, Tau Theta Epsilon, Pi Lambda Theta. Lutheran. Avocations: jogging, tennis, hiking, camping, golf. Home: 24 Stuart St Newington CT 06111-3741 Office: U Conn Sch Dental Medicine 263 Farmington Ave Farmington CT 06032-1956

KARNI, EDI, economics educator; b. Tel Aviv, Mar. 20, 1944; s. Eliezer and Sara (Vitis) K.; m. Barbara Shapiro, Mar. 16, 1980; children: Anat, Anna. BA in Econs., Hebrew U., 1965, MA in Econs., 1970, U. Chgo., 1970, PhD in Econs., 1971. Asst. prof. Ohio State U., Columbus, 1971-72; fellow Inst. for Advanced Studies/Hebrew U., Jerusalem, Israel, 1976-77; vis. prof. U. Chgo., 1977-79; assoc. prof. Tel Aviv U., 1972-81; prof. econs. Johns Hopkins U., Balt., 1981—. Disting. vis. prof. Vanderbilt U., 1987. Author: Decision Making Under Uncertainty, 1985; contbr. articles to profl. jours. Fellow: Econometric Soc.; mem.: Am. Econ. Assn. Jewish. Home: 6208 Sareva Dr Baltimore MD 21209-3530 Office: Johns Hopkins U Dept Econs Baltimore MD 21218

KARNOFSKY, MOLLYNE, artist, poet; b. New Orleans, July 19, 1932; d. Samuel and Lena (Gaethe) Finegold; m. Dave E. Winston, Sept. 17, 1952 (div. Sept. 1975); children: Craig T. Winston, Janelle R. Winston Lewis. BBS in Bus. Adminstrn., Tulane U., New Orleans, 1966; student in Art Studio Courses, Tulane, Newcomb Coll., New Orleans, 1966-70; MAT in Painting and Teaching, Tulane U., New Orleans, 1972. Lic. teaching La., 1972, N.Y.C. Bd. Edn., 1986. Dir., owner La. Lic. Art Sch., New Orleans, 1972-77; art tchr., art workshops N.Y.C., 1977—. Mem. univ. course and policy study com. Tulane U., 1952; panelist Artists Talk on Art, N.Y.C., 1993, 94; guide to internat. artists, Mid. Am. Arts Alliance, N.Y.C., 1994. One-woman shows include Vincent Mann Gallery, New Orleans, 1974, Spirit of New Orleans, 1976, Viridian Gallery, N.Y.C., 1977, 79, Spring St. Performance Painting for Artists' Day, N.Y.C., 1977, PS1 Inst. Art and Urban Resources, Long Island City, N.Y., 1978, Contemporary Art Ctr., New Orleans, 1978, Galerie Forum, Stockholm, 1980, Satellite gallery Bronx Mus. Art, N.Y., 1980, Galerie Leger, Malmö, Sweden, 1980, Ave. B Gallery, 1985, Asphalt Green Cmty. Ctr., N.Y.C., 1988, N.Y. Pub. Libr., 1988, Leonard Stern Bldg. NYU, 1994, Galerie Lafitte, New Orleans, La., 2001, (Site Specific: Found Spaces and Other Places) Eclectic Properties, 1979, Rudolph Bass Power Tool Co., N.Y.C., 1982, Galeriex, Istanbul, Turkey, 2003; exhibited in group shows at Judson Poets Theater, N.Y.C., 1977, World Trade Ctr., N.Y.C., 1979, Ear Inn, N.Y.C., 1979, Artists' Day Art Parade, 1979, 83, Bklyn., Atlantic Ave. Galleries, Bklyn., 1979, Bklyn. Arts Cultural Assn., 1981, Emily Harvey Gallery, N.Y.C., 1983, WPA Gallery, Washington, 1983, Jack Tilton Gallery, N.Y.C., 1983, Jon Leon Gallery, N.Y.C., 1984, Franklin Furnace, N.Y.C., 1984, Minor Injury Gallery, Williamsburg, Bklyn., 1989, World Congress Arts and Medicine, N.Y.C., 1992, Tribeca 148, N.Y.C., 1993, 94, Printmaking Workshop, N.Y.C., 1997, Chuck Levitan Gallery, N.Y.C., 1998, Broome St. Gallery, N.Y.C., 2000, Lyman-Eyer Gallery, Newton, Mass., 2001, 2002, Gallery X, N.Y.C., 2002, Lyman Eyer Gallery, Provincetown, Mass., 2001-02, Ch. of All Sts., 2002, Extreme Exteriors, 2002, Lyman Eyer Gallery, Newton and Provincetown, Mass., 2001-02, Ch. of All Souls, N.Y.C., 2002; permanent collections include Cigna, Insurance Co. of N.Am., Mollyne Karnofsky Papers, NYU Library, Anthology Film Archives, N.Y.C., 1996, Chuck Levitan Gallery, N.Y.C, 1998; subject of art Coll. Art Assn., N.Y.C., 1980; documentary video of art exhbn. Vesteras Mus., Sweden, 1981; documentary video of art ehbn. and interview Fuji Network, Japan, 1981; contbr. articles to profl. jours. Pres. Tulane Commerce Women's Club, New Orleans, 1951; publicity dir. Chevra Thilim Sisterhood, New Orleans, 1960-63; com. mem. Coun. of Jewish Women, New Orleans, 1965-70; tour dir. Spring Fiesta Assn., New Orleans, 1965. Grantee for performance poetry, Poets and Writers, N.Y.C., 1982, 92, 98; named Artist in Residence Avenue B. Gallery, N.Y.C., 1985, honorarium, spl. project, Coal Bin PSI Inst. for Arts and Urban Resources, Queens, N.Y., 1978, Contemporary Art Ctr., New Orleans, 1978. Mem. Tulane Alumni Assn. (bd. dirs. 1970-71, editor bus. review 1971), Artists Equity, Mcpl. Art Soc. Avocations: writing, music, urban archaeology. E-mail: MKarnArt@aol.com.

KARNOK, KEITH J. agronomist, educator; b. Cleve., Mar. 20, 1950; s. Albert A. and Emily Karnok; m. Melinda Susan Webb, Jan. 23, 1971; children: Kristen, Kara, Keith, Kortney. BS in Agronomy, U. Ariz., 1973, MS, 1974; PhD, Tex. A&M U., 1977. Asst. prof. Ohio State U., Columbus, Ohio, 1977-82, U. Ga., Athens, Ga., 1983-87, assoc. prof., 1987-93, prof., 1993—. Author: Principles of Turfgrass Management, 1993, Turfgrass Science and Culture Lab Manual, 1978. Mem. adv. bd. recreation County of Oconee, Ga., 1990—; mem. booster club Oconee County High Sch., 1994—. Recipient So. Region Excellence in Tchg. award, USDA. Fellow AAAS, Nat. Assn. Colls. and Tchrs. of Agr. (Regional Outstanding Tchr. award 1995), Am. Soc. Agronomy (Agronomy Resident Edn. award 1994), Crop Sci. Soc. Am. (Nat. Tchg. award, Fred V. Grau Turfgrass Sci. award 1998), Golf Course Supts. Assn. Am., Sports Turf Mgrs. Assn., Profl. Lawn Care Assn. Am. Avocations: coaching youth sports, magic. Home: 1101 Hillcrest Dr Watkinsville GA 30677-2351 Office: U Ga Dept Crop and Soil Scis Miller Plant Scis Bldg Athens GA 30602*

KAROL, VICTORIA DIANE, educational administrator; b. Bremerhaven, Germany, Sept. 22, 1956; d. Arthur Lee and Esther Marie Stephens; m. Eugene Karol; 1 child: Theodore L. BS in Elem. Edn. magna cum laude, Towson State U., 1978; M Adminstrn. and Supervision, Bowie State U., 1992; EdD in Ednl. Leadership, Nova Southeastern U., Fla., 1996. Cert. tchr., Md. Tchr. Calvert County Pub. Schs., Prince Frederick, Md., 1978-89, asst. dir. staff devel. and art and dance Title IV, Tchr. Ctr., student tchrs., media svcs., 1989—. Cons. coop. learning strategies, adult learners, team-building strategies tech., dimensions of learning, supervision, sch. to work, internet, multicultural edn., 1990—; adv. com. Bowie (Md.) State U., 1990-91. Bd. dirs. St. Mary's Elem. Sch., sec., 1990—; mem. adv. coun. on Multicultural Edn. Md. State Dept. of Edn. Mem. Calvert Assn. Suprs. and Adminstrs. (pres.), Calvert County Pub. Sch. Ctrl. Office Social Com. (chairperson), So. Md. Tri-County Staff Devel. Consortium. Roman Catholic. Avocations: dance, sports, baton twirling, gardening. Office: Calvert County Pub Schs 1305 Dares Beach Rd Prince Frederick MD 20678-4208

KARON, BERTRAM PAUL, psychologist, educator; b. Taunton, Mass., Apr. 29, 1930; s. Harold Banny and Celia (Silverman) K.; m. Mary Kathryn Mossop, Oct. 17, 1957; 1 son, Jonathan Alexander. AB, Harvard U., 1952; MA, Princeton U., 1954, PhD (USPHS fellow), 1957; grad. Social Sci. Research Council Inst. Maths. for Social Scientists, Dartmouth, summer 1953. Diplomate in clin. psychology and psychoanalysis Am. Bd. Profl. Psychology. Rsch. fellow psychometrics Ednl. Testing Svc. and Princeton, 1952-55; intern in direct analysis John N. Rosen, M.D., Gardenville, Pa., 1955-56; sr. clin. psychologist Annandale (N.J.) Reformatory, 1958; psychologist, dir. rsch. Akron (Ohio) Psychol. Cons. Ctr., 1958-59; rsch. psychologist Phila. Psychiat. Hosp., 1959, USPHS fellow, 1959-61; practice clin. psychology Phila., 1961-62; asst. prof. psychology Mich. State U., 1962-63, assoc. prof., 1963-68, prof., 1968—. Vis. lectr. Calif. Sch. Profl. Psychology, L.A., 1972; vis. scholar Wright Inst., L.A., 1979; rsch. cons. U.S. Naval Hosp., Phila., 1962, U. Pa., 1962; lectr. psychiatry Ypsilanti (Mich.) State Hosp., 1964-65; cons. VA Hosp., Allen Park, Mich., 1966-75, Ann Arbor, Mich., 1971-72 Author: The Negro Personality: A Rigorous Investigation of the Effects of Culture, 1958, rev. edit., Black Scars, 1975, (with others) Psychotherapy of Schizophrenia: The Treatment of Choice, 1981; contbg. author: Projective Techniques in Personality Assessment, 1968, Techniques for Behavior Change, 1971, The Schizophrenic Syndrome: An Annual Review, 1971, The Construction of Madness, 1976, Assessment with Projective Techniques: A Concise Introduction, 1981, Comprehensive Textbook of Psychotherapy, 1994, Dynamic Therapies for Psychiatric Disorders (Axis I), 1995; editor: Affects, Imagery, and Consciousness (Silvan S. Tomkins), vols. 1 and 2, 1962, 63; contbr. articles to profl. jours. Recipient Fowler award for disting. grad. tchg. APA Grad. Students, 1990; named disting. psychoanalyst Soc. for Psychoanalytic Tng., N.Y., 1988; NIMH grantee, 1966-71 Fellow APA (divsn. psychotherapy, clin. psychology, divsn. psychoanalysis, pres. 1990-91); mem. Soc. Psychotherapy Rsch., Am. Statis. Assn., Psychologists Interested in Study Psychoanalysis (pres. 1987-89), Mich. Psychoanalytic Coun. (pres. 1993-95). Home: 420 Wayland Ave East Lansing MI 48823 Office: 108 Psychology Rsch East Lansing MI 48824-1117

KARP, STEFANIE, special education educator; b. Phila., June 30, 1966; d. Steven Francis and Rosemarie (Martino) Whelan; m. Murray David Karp, July 21, 1990. BA in Psychology cum laude, Rutgers U., 1988, MEd, 1998, MEd +30, 1999. Cert. tchr. handicapped K-8, N.J. Tchr. perceptually impaired in grades 4-6 Manalapan-Englishtown (N.J.) Pub. Schs., 1988—, tchr. advocate disaffected program, 1990, advocate in mentoring program, 1992-93, piloted math. textbook com., 1993-94, home instrn./tutor, 1988—. Cooperating tchr. coll. students; trainer/asst. Tournament of Champions, Monmouth County, 1991—; curriculum writer sci., math., reading, lang. arts, mem. book rev. com., evaluator for various subjects. Named Tchr. of Yr. for Lafayette Mills Sch. Bd. Edn., 1993. Mem. Coun. Exceptional Children, Persons Associated with Spl. Svcs. Mem., Pupil Assistance Com., Kappa Delta Pi. Avocations: family, reading, running, music, sports, miami dolphins. Home: 24 Mccue Rd Morganville NJ 07751-1615

KARPLUS, MARTIN, chemistry educator; b. Vienna, Mar. 15, 1930; came to U.S., 1938; s. Hans and Isabella (Goldstern) K.; m. Marci Anne Hazard. BA, Harvard U., 1950; PhD, Calif. Inst. Tech., 1953; DSc (hon.), U. Sherbrooke, Que., Can., 1998; MA (hon.), Oxford U., 1999. NSF fellow Oxford (Eng.) U., 1953-55; asst. prof. chemistry U. Ill., 1957-60, assoc. prof., 1960; prof. Columbia U., N.Y.C., 1960-66, Harvard U., Cambridge, Mass., 1966—, Theodore William Richards prof. chemistry, 1979-99, Theodore William Richards rsch. prof., 1999—. Prof. U. Paris VII, 1974-75, Coll. de France, Paris, 1980; prof. associè U. Paris-Sud, 1980-81, U. Louis Pasteur, Strasbourg, France, spring 1992, 94-95, prof. conventionné, 1995—; Eastman prof. Oxford U., 1999-2000. Author: (with R.N. Porter) Atoms and Molecules: An Introduction for Students of Physical Chemistry, 1970, (with C.L. Brooks III and B.M. Pettitt) Proteins: A Theoretical Perspective of Dynamics, Structure and Thermodynamics, 1988; also articles. Recipient Fresenius award Phi Lambda Epsilon, 1965, Harrison Howe award Am. Chem. Soc., 1967, Outstanding Contbn. award Internat. Soc. Quantum Biology, 1979, Disting. Alumni award Calif. Inst. Tech., 1986, Irving Langmuir award Am. Phys. Soc., 1987, Theoretical Chemistry award Am. Chem. Soc., 1993, Joseph O. Hirschfelder prize in theoretical chemistry U. Wis. Theoretical Chemistry Inst., 1995, Computers in Chem. and Pharm. Rsch. award Am. Chem. Soc., 2001, Anfinsen award portein Soc., 2001; nat. lectr. Biophys. Soc., 1991; Westinghouse scholar, 1947. Mem. NAS, Am. Acad. Arts and Scis., Internat. Acad. Quantum Molecular Sci., Netherlands Acad. Art and Scis. (fgn.), Royal Soc. U.K. (fgn.). Office: Harvard U Dept Chemistry 12 Oxford St Cambridge MA 02138-2902

KARR, JAMES RICHARD, ecologist, educator, research director; b. Shelby, Ohio, Dec. 26, 1943; s. Rodney Joll and Marjorie Ladonna (Copeland) K.; m. Kathleen Ann Reynolds, Mar. 23, 1963 (div. Nov. 1982); children: Elizabeth Ann, Eric Leigh; m. Helen Marie Herbst Serrano, Dec. 22, 1984. BS, Iowa State U., 1965; MS, U. Ill., 1967, PhD, 1970. Fellow in biology Princeton (N.J.) U., 1970-71, Smithsonian Tropical Rsch. Inst., Balboa, Panama, 1971-72, dep. dir., 1984-87, acting dir., 1987-88; asst. prof. biology Purdue U., Lafayette, Ind., 1972-75; assoc. prof. U. Ill., Urbana, 1975-80, prof., 1980-84; Harold H. Bailey prof. biology Va. Poly. Inst. and State U., Blacksburg, 1988-91; prof. zoology, fisheries, environ. health, civil engring. and pub. affairs U. Wash., Seattle, 1991—, dir. Inst. Environ. Studies, 1991-95. Cons. on water resources EPA, 1978—, OAS, Washington, 1980, South Fla. Water Mgmt. Dist., West Palm Beach, 1989—; cons., gen. counsel Fla. Dept. Environ. Protection, 2002-03. Grantee EPA, 1972-85, 93-2000, U.S. Forest Svc., 1980-81, 90-91, U.S. Fish and Wildlife Svc., 1979-82, NSF, 1982-84, 1997-2000, TVA, 1990-93, Dept. Energy, 1995-2002. Fellow AAAS, Am. Ornithologists Union. Achievements include development of Index of Biotic Integrity, now used in North and South America, Asia, Australia, and Europe to assess directly the quality of water resources. Office: U Wash PO Box 355020 Seattle WA 98195-5020

KARRAKER, DAVID FRANKLIN, secondary educator, reading consultant; b. Knoxville, Tenn., June 5, 1942; s. David Franklin and Sarah (Cleveland) K.; m. Laraine Belanich, June 29, 1968; children: Katherine Elizabeth, Audrie Laraine. BS, Mid. Tenn. State U., 1965; cert., U. Hawaii, 1969, Western Conn. State U., 1980; MS in Secondary Edn., U. Bridgeport, 1973. Vol., tchr. St. John's Episcopal Mission, Peace Corps, Liberia, 1965-67; tchr. Rhodes Elem. Sch., Phila., 1967-68, Waianae (Hawaii) Intermediate Sch., 1968-70; tchr. social studies and reading, soccer-volleyball coach Cen. Mid. Sch., Greenwich, Conn., 1970—, team leader, 1988-91. Contbr. articles to profl. publs. Mem. choir Bethel (Conn.) Congl. Ch., 1982—, youth min., 1989—, trustee, 1989—; coord. Dorothy Day Hospitality House, soup kitchen and shelter, Danbury, Conn., 1982—. Recipient Celebration of Excellence award State of Conn., 1989. Mem. NEA, ASCD, Conn. Edn. Assn. (del. 1991), Greenwich Edn. Assn. (bldg. rep., bd. dirs. 1988—), Nat. Coun. for Social Studies, Returned Peac Corps Vols. Assn. (rep. for lobbying com. 1990-92). Democrat. Avocations: gardening, rebuilding old houses, singing in quartet, hiking, camping. Home: 67 Putnam Park Rd Bethel CT 06801-2908 Office: Cen Mid Sch 9 Indian Rock Ln Greenwich CT 06830-4004

KARSEN, SONJA PETRA, retired American-Hispanic literature educator; b. Berlin, Apr. 11, 1919; came to U.S., 1938, naturalized, 1945; d. Fritz and Erna (Heidermann) K. Titulo de Bachiller, 1937; BA, Carleton Coll., 1939; MA (scholar in French), Bryn Mawr Coll., 1941; PhD, Columbia U., 1950. Instr. Spanish Lake Erie Coll., Painesville, Ohio, 1943-45; instr. modern langs. U. P.R., 1945-46; instr. Spanish Syracuse U., 1947-50, Bklyn. Coll., 1950-51; asst. to dep. dir. gen. UNESCO, 1951-52, Latin Am. Desk, tech. assistance dept., 1952-53, mem. tech. assistance mission Costa Rica, 1954; asst. prof. Spanish Sweet Briar Coll., Va., 1955-57; assoc. prof., chmn. dept. Romance langs. Skidmore Coll., Saratoga Springs, N.Y., 1957-61, chmn. dept. modern langs. and lits., 1961-79, prof. Spanish, 1961-87, prof. emerita, 1987; cons. Hudson-Mohawk Assn. Colls. and Univs., 1990. Faculty rsch. lectr. Skidmore Coll., 1963; mem. adv. and nominating com. Books Abroad, 1965-67; Fulbright lectr. Free U. Berlin, 1968; lectr. U. Gesamthochschule, Paderborn, Germany, 1995, 99. Author: Guillermo Valencia, Colombian Poet, 1951, Educational Development in Costa Rica with UNESCO's Technical Assistance, 1951-54, 1954, Jaime Torres Bodet: A Poet in a Changing World, 1963, Selected Poems of Jaime Torres Bodet, 1964, Versos y prosas de Jaime Torres Bodet, 1966, Jaime Torres Bodet, 1971, Ensayos de Literatura E Historia Iberoamericana/Essays on Iberoamerican Literature and History, 1988, Papers on Foreign Languages, Literature and Culture, 1982-87, 88, Bericht Über Den Vater: Fritz Karsen 1885-1951, 1993; translator: The Role of the Americas in History (Leopoldo Zea), 1992; editor Lang. Assn. Bull., 1980-83; mem. editl. adv. bd. Modern Lang. Studies, 1977-93; contbr. articles to profl. jours. Decorated Chevalier dans l'Ordre des Palmes Académiques, 1964; recipient Leadership award N.Y. State Assn. Fgn. Lang. Tchrs., 1973, 76, 78, Nat. Disting. Leadership award, 1979, Disting. Service award, 1983, 86, Capital Dist. Fgn. Language Disting. Service award, 1987; recipient Spanish Heritage award, 1981, Alumni Achievement award Carleton Coll., 1982; exchange student auspices Inst. Internat. Ednl. at Carleton Coll., 1938-39; Buenos Aires Conv. grantee for research in Colombia, 1946-47; faculty research grantee Skidmore Coll., summer 1959, 61, 63, 64, 67, 69, 70, 73, ad hoc faculty grantee, 71, 78, 85. Mem. Am. Assn. Tchrs. Spanish and Portuguese (emeritus), Nat. Assn. Self-Instructional Lang. Programs (v.p. 1981-82,pres. 1982-83), AAUW (life), AAUP (life), MLA (del. assembly 1976-78, Mildenberger medal selection com 1984-86), El Ateneo Doctor Jaime Torres Bodet (founding mem.), Nat. Geog. Soc., Asociación Internacional de Hispanistas, UN Assn. U.S.A., Am. Soc. French Acad. Palms, Fulbright Alumni, Phi Sigma Iota, Sigma Delta Pi. Home: 1755 York Ave Apt 37A New York NY 10128-6875

KARST, NANCY JOAN SHOBE, dental hygiene educator; b. Great Bend, Kans., Mar. 8, 1942; d. Philip D. and Effie L. (Jackson) Shobe; m. Larry K. Karst, 1960; 1 child, Laurie K. Olson. AA, Mo. So. State Coll., 1980, AS, 1987; BS, Pitts. State U., 1982, MS, 1992. Cert. dental asst. Dental asst. various dentists, 1960-75; instr. Mo. So. State Coll., Joplin, 1975-86, asst. prof., 1986-99. Presenter various seminars on dental hygiene; oral hygiene cons. Early Head Start, Joplin, Mo. Author slide tape series; author: Dental Anatomy: A Self Instructional Program, 10th edit., 1997, Head and Neck Histology and Anatomy, 2000. Sunday sch. tchr. St. Paul's United Meth. Ch., Joplin, 1980-90. Mem. Am. Assn. Dental Schs., Mo. Dental Hygiene Assn. (past bd. dirs.), Am. Dental Asst. Assn. (life). Avocations: horseback riding, bell choir. E-mail: lnKarst@joplin.com.

KASBERGER-MAHONEY, ELVERA A. educational administrator; b. Oak Park, Ill., July 2, 1952; d. Lawrence and Aura Louise (Rutledge) Petrongelli; m. Daniel Mahoney, July 14, 1988. BA, Northeastern Ill. U., 1974, MA, 1978; grad., Calif. Sch. Leadership Acad., 1990. Tchr. Social Emotionally Disturbed Children Warren Twp. High Sch., Gurnee, Ill.; dean of students Adlai Stevenson High Sch., Prairie View, Ill.; asst. prin. Hesperia (Calif.) Unified Sch. Dist.; prin., supt. schs. San Bernardino County, 1988-90; asst. prin. Elsinore High Sch., Lake Elsinore, Calif., 1990-95, Temescal Canyon H.S., Elsinore, 1995-96; asst. prin. of student svcs. Jurupa Valley H.S., Jurupa Unified Sch. Dist., Mira Loma, Calif., 1996—. Chpt. I grantee; Job Tng. Partnership grantee. Mem. ASCD, Assn. Calif. Sch. Adminstrs., Coun. for Exceptional Children.

KASCH, JULIA ANN, social sciences educator; b. Shreveport, La., Sept. 30, 1933; d. Jasper M. and Vida Alvina (Jenison) Johnson; m. Milton Edward Kasch, Aug. 4, 1956 (dec. July 3, 1991); children: Robert Edward, Lawrence Steven. BS in Edn., U. Ala., Tuscaloosa, 1954; MA in History, S.W. Tex. State U., 1960. Tchr. San Marcos (Tex.) Bapt. Acad., 1954-58, Ector County Ind. Sch. Dist., Odessa, Tex., 1958-60, Cuero (Tex.) Jr. High Sch., 1964-66; instr. Frank Phillips Coll., Borger, Tex., 1966—. Pres. Women of Rotary, Borger, 1988-89; v.p. Altrusa Internat., Borger, 1989-91; vol. St. Anthony's Hospice, Amarillo, Tex., 1985-86; mem. Jenison Hist. Assn., Frank Phillips Coll. Devel. Corp., Hutchinson County Hist. Commn., Hutchinson County Mus., bd. dirs.; elder 1st Presbyn. Ch., Borger. Mem. DAR, Tex. Jr. Coll. Tchrs. Assn., Tex. State Tchrs. Assn., Magna Charta Dames and Barons, Magic Plains Art Coun., Rotary Internat., Colonial Dames XVII Century, Daus. of Am. Colonists, Am. Cancer Soc. (bd. dirs.), Olivia's Angels, Plainsmen Ptnrs., Kappa Delta Pi (hon.), Delta Kappa Gamma. Avocations: collecting antique butter molds, genealogy, reading, needlework. Home: 102 Rigdon St Borger TX 79007-6518

KASHDIN, GLADYS SHAFRAN, painter, educator; b. Dec. 15, 1921; d. Edward M. and Miriam P. Shafran; m. Manville E. Kashdin, Oct. 11, 1942 (dec.). BA magna cum laude, U. Miami, 1960; MA, Fla. State U., 1962, PhD, 1965. Photographer, N.Y.C. and Fla., 1938-60; tchr. art Fla. and Ga., 1956-63; from asst. prof. humanities to assoc. prof. to prof. U. South Fla., Tampa, 1965-87, prof. emerita, 1987—. Lectr., adv. bd. Hillsborough County Mus., 1975—84. Exhibitions include 68 one-woman shows, 55 group exhbns., The Everglades, 1972—75, Aspects of the River, 1975—80, Processes of Time, 1981—91, Retrospective, 1941—96, Tampa Mus. Art, 1996, Appleton Mus. Art, Ocala, 1999, 2001—02, Mus. Sci. and Industry, Tampa, 2003, Represented in permanent collections, Taiwan, China, Columbus Mus. Arts, LeMoyne Art Found., Tampa Internat. Airport, Tampa Mus. Art, Appleton Mus. Art, Ocala, Mus. Sci. and Industry, Tampa, Miss. Mus. Art, Jackson, Jan Kaminis Platt Libr., Tampa. Mem. U.S. Fla. Status of Women Com., 1971-76, chmn., 1975-76; mem. nat. bd., Mus. Sci. and Industry, Tampa, 2003—. Recipient Women Helping Women in Art award Soroptimist Internat., 1979, Citizens Hon. award Hillsborough Bd. County Commrs., 1984, Mortar Bd. award for tchg. excellence, 1986, Recognition award for lifetime achievement in arts and scis. So. Acad. Letters, Arts and Scis., 2002. Mem. AAUW (1st v.p. Tampa br. 1971-72), Phi Kappa Phi (chpt.-pres. 1981-83, artist/scholar award 1987). Home: 441 Biltmore Ave Temple Terrace FL 33617-7207

KASHEF, ALI EBRAHIM, industrial technology educator; b. Tehran, June 28, 1957; came to U.S., 1976, naturalized, 1986. s. Iraj Ebrahimi and Kokab (Amini) K.; m. Farah L. Kashef, July 17, 1990; children: Omeed Ebrahimi, Raud Ebrahimi. BS, Lincoln U., Jefferson City, Mo., 1980; MS in Indsl. Mgmt., Ctrl. Mo. State U., Warrensburg, 1981; PhD in Vocat. Edn. Studies, So. Ill. U., 1990. Nuc. power plant engr. Sys. Coordination Inc., Fulton, Mo., 1981—84; instr. Ea. Ill. U., Charleston, 1984—85; program dir. W.Va. State Coll., Institute, 1985—88; asst. prof. Montclair State U., Upper Montclair, NJ, 1988—92; asst. prof. dept. indsl. tech. U. No. Iowa, Cedar Falls, 1992—96, assoc. prof. dept. indsl. tech., 1996—2001, prof., 2001—, coop. edn. coord., 2001—, tech. mgmt. coord., 2003—. Acad. specialist Montclair State Coll., 1990-91; cons. Charleston (W.Va.) Job Corps Ctr., 1987-88. Contbr. articles to nat. and internat. profl. jours. UN devel. program grantee, 1994. UN Devel. Programme grantee, 1994. Avocations: soccer, volleyball, travel. Office: U No Iowa Dept Indsl Tech Cedar Falls IA 50614-0001 E-mail: kashef@uni.edu.

KASIK, MARIBETH MONTGOMERY, special education educator, educator; b. Chgo., Feb. 10, 1952; d. Leland Thomas and Esther Marie (McCambridge) Montgomery; 1 child, Jamie Montgomery. BS, So. Ill. U., 1973; MEd, U. Ill., 1978; PhD, So. Ill. U., 1983. Cert. elem. and spl. edn. tchr., Ill. Teaching asst. instr., grad. asst. So. Ill. U., Carbondale, 1982-83; vis. asst. prof. U. Wis., Stout, Menomonie, 1983-84; prof., coord. special edn. Govs. State U., University Park, Ill., 1984—. Vis. asst. prof. U. Wis., Menomonie, 1982-84; cons. chair higher edn. adv. com. Ill. Bd. Edn.; faculty adv. com. Ill. Bd. Higher Edn., 1992—; writer of State Vision for Tchr. Pers. Devel. in Ill. Author: Psychosocial Aspects of Learning Disabilities; contbr. articles to profl. jours. Commr. 204th Gen. Assembly, Presbyn. Ch. USA; ruling elder Morgan Pk (Ill.) Presbyn. Ch., 1978-93. Mem. NASP, Am. Ednl. Rsch. Assn., Coun. for Exceptional Children (tchr. edn. divsn.), Univ. Profls. of Ill. (chpt. pres.), Phi Delta Kappa. Home: 1727 W 103rd St Chicago IL 60643-2820

KASIPATHI, CHINTA, geologist, educator, consultant, researcher; b. Rajahmundry, India, Oct. 17, 1955; s. Chinta Veerabhadra Rao and Chinta M. Viyyuri Manikyamba; m. Chinta Hemalatha, May 9, 1979; children: Anand Chinta, Pramod Chinta. BS, Andhra U., Visakhapatnam, India, 1973, MS, 1976, PhD, 1981. Rsch. assoc. Andhra U., 1981-84, officer, 1984, lectr., 1984-86, reader, 1986-94, prof., 1994—, dir. rsch., 1984—. Rschr., Andhra U., 1976—, tchr., 1980—, cons., 1981—, pres., 1983—; expert India Bur. Mines, 1995—. Contbr. articles to profl. jours. Gemologist, Visakhapatnam, 1992—; geoscientist, Visakhapatnam, 1976—; vol. Helpless Pub., Andhra Pradesh, 1973—. Recipient Young Scientist award Wadia Inst. Himalian Geology, Dept. Sci. and Tech., India, 1985. Fellow Indian Sci. Congress (life), Internat. Geol. Congress, Indian Nuc. Soc., Assn. Environ. Geochemistry, Indian Soc. Applied Geochemistry; mem. Instn. Geoscientists India (life), Soc. Geoscientists and Allied Techs. (life). Avocations: tourism, scientific pursuits, music, games, tv. Home: P8 Andhra Univ Quarters Sivajipalem Visakhapatnam 530017 India Office: Andhra Univ Dept Geology 530 003 Visakhapatnam India E-mail: kasigeolau@rediff.com., kasigeolau@yahoo.com.

KASKINEN, BARBARA KAY, author, composer, songwriter, musician, music educator; d. Norman Ferdinand and Martha Agnes (Harju) Kaskinen. AA, Broward C.C., Coconut Creek, Fla., 1978; BA with honors, Fla. Atlantic U., 1981, MA, 1995; postgrad., U. Miami, 2000—. Instr. adult piano Atlantic H.S., Delray Beach, Fla., 1981-82; organist, combo dir. Affirmation Luth. Ch., Boca Raton, Fla., 1981-86; studio musician, composer/arranger Electric Rize Prodns., Margate, Fla., 1982-94; ind. instr. piano, electronic keyboard and guitar. Margate, 1979-91. Co-founder Oasis Coffee House, Boca Raton, Fla., 1990—92; co-owner Electric Rize Publ, 1991; mem adj faculty Fla Atlantic Univ, 1995—; asst dir TOPS Piano Camp, 1994—96; mem. adj. faculty Broward C.C., Coconut Creek, 1996—. Musician (bass, keyboard player): Electric Rize Band, 1982—91; composer: Hansen House, 1987—88; author: Adult Electronic Keyboard Course Book I, 1988, Adult Electronic Keyboard Course Books II and III, 1989. Mem.: ASCAP, Nat. Piano Found., Music Guild Boca Raton, Broward County Music Tchr's Asn (treas), Fla State Music Tchr's Asn, Nat Guild Piano Tchrs, Fla Atlantic Univ Alumni Asn. Home: 6601 NW 22nd St Pompano Beach FL 33063-2117 Address: 6601 NW 22 St Margate FL 33063 E-mail: neniksa@aol.com.

KASPAR, LORI JAYNE, elementary school educator; b. Sioux City, Iowa, Jan. 19, 1957; d. George S. and Bertha M. (Gunderson) Kaspar; m. David M. Bennett, June 2, 1981; 1 child, Anna Kathleen. BA in Edn., Nat. Coll. Edn., 1978; MA in Edn., Tex. Woman's U., 1991; postgrad., U. North Tex., 1995—99, Tex. Wesleyan U., 2001—. Cert. tchr., Tex. 7th grade tchr. East Main Schs., Des Plaines, Ill., 1978-79; 6th-8th grade tchr. Grand Prairie (Tex.) Schs., 1979-81, Rocksprings (Tex.) Schs., 1982-84; coord. cmty. edn. Ctrl. Tex. Coll., Killeen, 1984-87; K-5, 8th grade tchr. White Settlement Schs., Ft. Worth, 1987-94; 4th-6th grade tchr. Hurst-Euless-Bedford (Tex.) Schs., 1994—. Cons. in field. Author: Plug In The sun, 1991, Think Plus Science, 1992, Aviation Explorations, 1994. Recipient Letter of the Month award Ft. Worth Star Telegram, 1988, 91. Mem. ASCD, Nat. Assn. for Gifted Children, Assn. Tex. Profl. Educators, Tex. Assn. for Gifted and Talented, Moot Ct. Honor Soc. Lutheran. Office: Harrison Lane Elem Sch 1000 Harrison Ln Hurst TX 76053-5002

KASPAR, VICTORIA ANN, school administrator; d. Rudolph Hans and Rose Marie Boysen; m. Ronald Michael Kaspar, 1948; children: Ron Jr., John, Jim. BS in Secondary Edn., U. Nebr., Omaha, 1974, MS in Secondary Adminstrn., 1995; EdD, U. Nebr., 2003. Tchr. English Bellevue (Nebr.) Pub. Schs., 1974-75; dir. daycare pvt. practice, Omaha, 1978-88; tchr. English Millard South H.S., Omaha, 1988-98, chair dept. English, 1995-98, asst. prin., 1998—. Author of poems. Mem. Friends of Omaha Pub. Libr. Mem. LWV, Internat. Soc. for Tech. in Edn., Nat. Coun. Sch. Adminstrs., Nat. Assn. Secondary Sch. Prins., Nebr. Assn. Secondary Sch. Adminstrn. (Region II), Nat. Coun. Staff Devel., Alpha Xi Delta, Phi Delta Kappa. Avocations: reading, gardening, writing.

KASPERBAUER, ISABEL GILES, art educator; b. Huancayo, Peru, Jan. 26, 1940; came to the U.S., 1960; d. Andres Humberto and Sofia Catalina (Saez) Giles; m. Michael John Kasperbauer, June 3, 1962; children: Maria Isabel, John Michael, Paul Andrew, Sandra Anne. BS, Iowa State U., 1962; BA, U. Ky., 1980. Cert. tchr., Ky. Art and Spanish tchr. Newman Ctr. U. Ky., Lexington, 1975-77; art tchr. Living Arts and Sci. Ctr., Lexington, 1980-82; after sch. art tchr. So. Elem. Sch., Lexington, 1980-82; art and Spanish tchr. Lexington Sch., 1982-85, art tchr., 1985-96. Del. Internat. Woman's Yr. Conf., Houston, 1977; co-chair dept. fine arts Lexington Sch., 1993-96. V.p. Lexington Assn. for Parent Edn., 1967; treas. Lexington Talent Edn. Assn., 1971; co-pres. PTA James Lane Allen Sch., Lexington, 1978. Recipient Martha V. Shipman award Kappa Delta Pi, 1980. Mem. Ky. Art Edn. Assn. (sec. 1981-82, Art Educator of Yr. 1993), Am. Art Edn. Assn. Avocations: world travel, videography, painting.

KASPIN, SUSAN JANE, child care specialist; b. Bklyn., May 28, 1950; d. Stanley Engel and Thelma Rosenblum; m. Jeffrey Marc Kaspin, Apr. 17, 1977; children: Jodi-Anne, Stacey, Melanie. BA, Bklyn. Coll., 1972. Cert. tchr. N.J. Adminstrv. asst. Stone & Webster Mgmt. Cons., N.Y.C., 1972-74, Am. Electric Power Co. (formerly in N.Y.C.), Columbus, Ohio, 1974-78; program dir. Office for Youth/Sch. Age Child Care Twp. of East Brunswick, NJ, 1989—98; mgr. Sch. Age Child Care/Alliance, 1999—. Staff liaison East Brunswick Alliance for the Prevention of Alcoholism and Drug Abuse, 1990—. Mem. twp. ad-hoc com., N.J. tpk. expansion, East Brunswick, 1985-90; mem. adv. bd. Local Law Enforcement Block Grant Program. Mem. N.J. Sch. Age Child Care Coalition, Nat. Sch. Age Care Alliance, Assn. for Children of N.J. (John Alexander Outstanding Project award 1992), Middlesex County Mcpl. Alliance Network.

KASSOUF, ESTHER KAY, education educator; b. Kinston, NC, Apr. 19, 1950; d. William Gid and Josephine (Smith) Holland; m. John Michael Kassouf Jr., May 8, 1976. AS, Mt. Olive (N.C.) Jr. Coll., 1970; BS, Atlantic Christian Coll., 1972; MEd, U. Nev., 1990. Tchr. 6th grade Kinston City Pub. Schs., 1972-76; tchr. 5th, 7th, 8th grades Clark County Sch. Dist., Las Vegas, Nev., 1976—; project facilitator Presvc. Tchrs. Avocations: reading, shopping, crafts. Office: Clark County Sch Dist 3950 S Pecos McLeod Las Vegas NV 89121-4396

KASTEN, KARL ALBERT, painter, printmaker, educator; b. San Francisco, Mar. 5, 1916; s. Ferdin and Barbara Anna Kasten; m. Georgette Gautier, Mar. 29, 1958; children: Ross, Lee, Beatrix, Joellen, Cho-An. MA, U. Calif., 1939; postgrad., U. Iowa, 1949; student, Hans Hofmann Sch. Fine Arts, 1951. Instr. Calif. Sch. Fine Arts, 1941, U. Mich., 1946-47; asst. prof. art San Francisco State U., 1947-50; prof. U. Calif., Berkeley, 1950-83. Bibliography appears in Etching (Edmondson), 1973, Collage and Assemblage (Meilach and Ten Hoor), 1973, Modern Woodcut Techniques (Kuroski), 1977, California Style (McClelland and Last), 1985, Art in the San Francisco Bay Area (Albright), 1985, Breaking Type: The Art of Karl Kasten (Landauer), 1999, The Stamp of Impulse, Abstract Expressionist Prints (David Acton), 2001; group shows include San Francisco Mus. Art, 1939, Chgo. Art Inst., 1946, Whitney Mus., 1952, Sao Paolo Internat. Biennials, 1955, 61, Achenbach Found., 1976, World Print III Traveling Exhbn., 1980-83, Gallery Sho, Tokyo, 1994, Inst. Franco-Americain, Rennes, 1995, Calif. Heritage Gallery, 1999, Robert Green Fine Arts Gallery, 2002; patentee etching press. Capt. U.S. Army, 1942-46. Decorated 4 battle stars; fellow Creative Arts Inst., 1964, 71, Tamarind Lithography Artist Fellowship, 1968, Regents Humanities, 1977. Mem. Berkeley Art Ctr. Assn. (bd. dirs. 1987-92), Calif. Soc. Printmakers (Disting. Artist award 1997), Univ. Faculty Club, Univ. Arts Club. Home: 1884 San Lorenzo Ave Berkeley CA 94707-1841 Office: Univ Calif Berkeley Art Dept Berkeley CA 94707

KASTENBERG, WILLIAM EDWARD, engineering educator, science educator; b. N.Y.C., June 25, 1939; s. Murray and Lillian Kastenberg; m. Berna R. Miller, Aug. 18, 1963; children: Andrew, Joshua, Lillian; m. Gloria Hauser, May 3, 1992. BS, UCLA, 1962, MS, 1963; PhD, U. Calif., Berkeley, 1966. Asst. prof. Sch. Engring. and Applied Sci. UCLA, 1966-71, assoc. prof., 1971-75, assoc. dean Sch. Engring. and Applied Sci., 1981-85, chmn. mech. aerospace and nuc. engring., 1985-88, prof. mech., aerospace and nuc. engring. dept., 1975-94; sr. fellow U.S. NRC, Washington, 1979-80; prof. nuc. engring. dept. U. Calif., Berkeley, 1995—, chmn. nuc. engring. dept., 1995-2000, Chancellor's prof., 1996—99, Daniel Tellep disting. prof. engring., 1999—. Guest scientist Karlsruhe (Fed. Republic Germany) Nuc. Rsch., 1972—73; mem. Nat. Rsch. Com. Reactor Safety, 1985—86; chmn. peer rev. com. U.S. NRC, Washington, 1987—88; mem. adv. com. nuc. facility safety Dept. of Energy, 1988—92; mem. adv. com. Diablo Canyon Nuc. Power Plant, 1999—2000; dir. risk and sys. analysis control toxics program UCLA, 1989—95, chmn. Ctr. Clean Tech., 1992—94; project dir. Ctr. Nuc. and Toxic Waste Mgmt. U. Calif., Berkley, 1995—2000. Contbr. articles to profl. jours. Recipient Disting. Tchg. award, Am. Soc. Engring. Edn., 1973. Fellow: AAAS, Am. Nuc. Soc. (chmn. nuc. safety 1984—85, Arthur Holly Compton award); mem.: NAE. Office: Univ Calif Nuclear Engring Dept 4155 Etcheverry Hall Berkeley CA 94720-1731

KASTENS, BEVERLY ANN, special and elementary education educator; b. Wichita, Kans., June 22, 1941; d. Ray Francis and Ava Marie (Lambert) Poole; children: Kelly, Cyndi; m. Gary Michael Kastens, Apr. 22, 1978. BA in Elem. Edn. magna cum laude, Wichita State U., 1973; MS in Edn., Kans. State U., 1980. Cert. tchr., Kans. Math. lab. instr. Goddard (Kans.) Sch. Dist., Unified Sch. Dist. #265, 1973-74, reading lab. instr., 1975-76, 8th grade remedial reading tchr., 1976, 6th grade tchr., 1977-78, 5th grade tchr., 1979-91, tchr. gifted grades K-9, 1992—. Faculty advisor Intermediate Learning Ctr., Goddard, 1979, 81, 83, gifted screening com., 1980-83, dept. head, 1984-91; curriculum com. Unified Sch. Dist. #265, Goddard, 1987-88. Author: (teaching curriculum) Christmas Traditions, 1979, (poetry) Memoirs of Grandma, 1979, Memoirs of Student, 1982. Facilitator Wichita (Kans.) Park Bd., 1988-89; cast Voices of Ctrl. Community, Wichita, 1990—, Majesty of Christmas-Easter, Wichita, 1990—. Named Master Tchr., Intermediate Learning Ctr., Goddard, 1985, 87, 89; recipient grant in literature Kans. State Dept. Edn., Topeka, 1987. Mem. Nat. Assn. for Gifted Children, Nat. Rsch. Ctr. on the Gifted and Talented, Kans. Nat. Edn. Assn. (negotiator 1973-91, faculty rep.-negotiation team NEA, Goddard 1985-88). Republican. Mem. Church of God. Avocations: traveling, photography, music, walking, reading, arts and crafts. Home: 547 Pamela St Wichita KS 67212-3733 Office: Clark Davidson Sch 333 S Walnut St Goddard KS 67052-7004

KASTNER, MARC AARON, physics educator; b. Toronto, Ont., Can., Nov. 20, 1945; came to U.S., 1952; s. Jacob and Ida Pearl (Shidlowsky) K.; m. Marcia Jill Paul, Aug. 27, 1967; 2 children. BS in Chemistry, U. Chgo., 1967, MS, 1969, PhD in Physics, 1972. Rsch. fellow Harvard U., Cambridge, Mass., 1972-73; asst. prof. physics MIT, Cambridge, 1973-77, assoc. prof., 1977-83, prof., 1983-89, Donner prof. of physics, 1989—. Dir. Consortium for Superconducting Electronics, 1989-91, Ctr. for Materials Sci. and Engring, 1993-98; head MIT Dept. Physics, 1998—. Recipient David Adler Lectureship award Am. Physical Society, 1995 Fellow AAAS, Am. Phys. Soc. (councillor at large 1991-94, Oliver E. Buckley prize 2000). Achievements include discovery of single electron effects in nanostructures and research in electronic, optical and magnetic properties of condensed matter, including semiconductors and high temperature superconductors.

KATEB, GEORGE ANTHONY, political science educator; b. Bklyn., Feb. 27, 1931; s. Anthony Francis and Victoria Anna (Mesnooh) K. AB, Columbia U., 1952, A.M., 1953, PhD, 1960; D.H.L. (hon.), Amherst, 1989. Mem. faculty Amherst Coll., 1957, prof., 1967-87, Kenan prof. polit. sci., 1974-78, Joseph B. Eastman prof. polit. sci., 1980-87; prof. politics Princeton U., 1987—, William Nelson Cromwell prof. politics, 1999—2002, William Nelson Cromwell prof. politics emeritus, 2002—. Vis. lectr. Mt. Holyoke Coll., 1958, Yale U., 1973, Harvard U., 1986. Author: Utopia and Its Enemies, 2d edit., 1972, Political Theory: Its Nature and Uses, 1968, Utopia, 1971, Hannah Arendt: Politics, Conscience, Evil, 1984, The Inner Ocean: Individualism and Democratic Culture, 1992 (Spitz prize Conf. for Study Polit. Thought 1994), Emerson and Self-Reliance, 1994; co-editor: (with David Bromwich) John Stuart Mill, On Liberty; mem. editl. bd. Mass. Rev., 1961-70, Polit. Theory, 1972—, Am. Polit. Sci. Rev., 1976-81, Jour. History Ideas, 1976—, Jour. Utopian Studies, 1977-80, Raritan, 1980-2002; cons. editor: Polit. Theory, 1983-2000. Univ. fellow Columbia U., 1953-54; fellow Soc. Fellows, Harvard U., 1954-57; Guggenheim fellow, 1971-72 Mem. AAUP, Am. Acad. Arts and Scis., New Eng. Polit. Sci. Assn. (exec. com. 1965-66, pres. 1978-79), Am. Soc. Polit. and Legal Philosophy (v.p. 1972-74), Conf. for Study of Polit. Thought, ACLU, Phi Beta Kappa. Office: Princeton U Dept Politics Princeton NJ 08544-0001

KATES, MORRIS, biochemist, educator; b. Galati, Romania, Sept. 30, 1923; arrived in Can., 1924, naturalized, 1944; s. Samuel and Toby (Cohen) K.; m. Pirkko Helena Sofia Makinen, June 14, 1957; children: Anna-Lisa, Marja Helena, Ilona Sylvia. Student, Parkdale Coll., 1936-41; BA, U. Toronto, Ont., Can., 1945, MA, 1946, PhD, 1948. Research asst. Banting Inst., U. Toronto, 1948-49; postdoctoral fellow Nat. Research Council Can., Ottawa, Ont., 1949-51, research officer bioscis. div., 1951-68; prof. chemistry U. Ottawa, 1968-69, prof. biochemistry, 1969-89, prof. emeritus, 1989—, vice-dean research Faculty Sci. and Engring., 1978-82, staff research lectr., 1981, chmn. dept. biochemistry, 1982-85. Author: Techniques of Lipidology, 1972, 2d edit., 1986; co-editor: Metabolic Inhibitors vols. II and IV, 1972, 73, Biomembranes vol. 12, 1984, Handbook of Lipid Rsch., vol. 6, 1990, Biochemistry of Archaea (Archaebacteria), 1993; co-editor: Can. Jour. Biochemistry, 1974-84; contbr. numerous articles on lipid rsch. to profl. jours. Fellow Chem. Inst. Can., Royal Soc. Can.; mem. Can. Biochem. Soc. (pres. 1987-88), Am. Chem. Soc., Am. Soc. Biol. Chemists, Biochem. Soc. (London, Morton lectr. 1995), Am. Oil Chemists Soc. (Supelco rsch. award 1984), Ottawa Biol. and Biochem. Soc. (Sci. prize 1977, pres. 1974-75). Achievements include rsch. on lipid biochemistry. Home: 1723 Rhodes Crescent Ottawa ON Canada K1H 5T1 Office: U Ottawa Dept Biochemistry 40 Marie Curie Ottawa ON Canada KIN 6N5 E-mail: mkates@science.uottawa.ca.

KATZ, ALAN MARTIN, secondary education educator; b. Bronx, N.Y., Apr. 14, 1945; s. Joseph and Alice (Laster) K.; m. Gale Idette Dubin, July 4, 1971; children: Lawrence, Elyse. BA, U. Bridgeport, 1966; MS, Fla. State U., 1968. Cert. tchr., N.Y. Tchr. sci. Commack (N.Y.) Pub. Schs., 1968—. Ednl. asst. Maldemar Med. Rsch. Found., Woodbury, N.Y., 1971-72, rsch. asst., 1973; instr. marine biology Bd. Coop. Ednl. Svcs. Inst. for Gifted and Talented, Dix Hills, N.Y., 1974-88; adj. instr. Suffolk County C.C., 1981-84; program dir. Babylon (N.Y.) Consortium for Marine Studies, 1987-90, Commack Summer Marine Sci. Program, 1990—; chairperson sci. dept. Commack H.S., 1995. Co-author: Marine Science Curriculum for High School, 1989. Recipient Outstanding Tchr. award Tandy Corp., 1991-92, cert. of honor N.Y. Sci. Talent Search, 1992, cert. of honor Westinghouse Sci. Talent Search, 1991, 92. Mem. N.Y. State Sci. Tchrs. Assn., Suffolk County Sci. Tchrs. Assn., Pine Barrens Soc. Avocations: scuba diving, golf, sailing.

KATZ, ALAN ROY, public health educator; b. Pitts., Aug. 21, 1954; s. Leon B. and Bernice Sonia (Glass) K.; m. Donna Marie Crandall, Jan. 19, 1986; 1 child, Sarah Elizabeth. BA, U. Calif., San Diego, 1976; MD, U. Calif., Irvine, 1980; MPH, U. Hawaii, 1987; postgrad., U. So. Calif., 1980-81, U. Hawaii, 1982-83. Staff physician emergency medicine L.A. County U. So. Calif. Med. Ctr., 1981-82; staff physician, med. dir. Waikiki Health Ctr., Honolulu, 1983-87; dir. AIDS/STD prevention program Hawaii State Dept. of Health, Honolulu, 1987-88; asst. prof. dept. pub. health scis. U. Hawaii, Honolulu, 1988-94, assoc. prof., 1994—. Dir. preventive medicine residency program U. Hawaii, Honolulu, 1994-99; com. mem. Chlamydia control workgroup USPHS, 1985-87, sci. adv. bd. Hawaii AIDS Clin. Trials Rsch. Program; staff physician, lab. dir. Diamond Head STD Clinic, Hawaii State Dept. Health, 1998—. Contbr. articles to profl. jours. Leptospirosis ad hoc com. Hawaii State Dept. Health, Honolulu, 1988—; mem. com. human subjects U. Hawaii, 1989—. USPHS Chlamydia Prevalence Survey grantee, Hawaii, 1986, Tuberculosis Survey grantee U. Hawaii, 1991; recipient presdl. citation for meritorious teaching, U. Hawaii, 1989, Regents medal excellence in teaching, 1992. Fellow Am. Coll. Preventive Medicine; mem. Am. Pub. Health Assn., Soc. Epidemiologic Rsch., Delta Omega. Office: U Hawaii Medicine Dept Pub Health Sci 1960 E West Rd Honolulu HI 96822-2319 E-mail: katz@hawaii.edu.

KATZ, ANNE HARRIS, biologist, educator, writer, aviator; b. Long Branch, N.J; BS, Ursinus Coll., Collegeville, Pa., 1966; MS, U. Mass., 1974, PhD, 1976. Cert. pvt. pilot. Tchr. biology Middletown (N.J.) Twp. High Sch., 1966-69; instr. biology Holyoke (Mass.) Community Coll., 1969; teaching and research assoc. U. Mass., 1969-76; asst. prof. biology Fordham U., N.Y.C., 1977-83; assoc. prof. biology, asst. dean Coll. St. Elizabeth, Convent Station, N.J., 1983-86; assoc. dean Coll. Natural Scis. and Math. Ind. U. Pa., 1987-91, interim dean Coll. Natural Scis. and Math., 1988-89; dean of the coll., prof. biology Lycoming Coll., Williamsport, Pa., 1991-93. Cert. pvt. pilot; cert. ecologist. Founder, editor, pub. Aviation Mus. & Event News, 1993; contbr. abstracts and articles to profl. jours. Vis. scholar Drew U., Madison, N.J., 1984-87; grantee Ctr. Field Rsch., Watertown, Mass., 1981-82, Geraldine R. Dodge Found., Morristown, N.J., 1981-83, N.J. DEP, 1983, Pa. Dept. Edn., 1989, GTE, 1990, CDC, 1991. Mem. AAAS, Ecol. Soc. Am., Aircraft Owners and Pilots Assn., Ninety Nines (aerospace edn.), Civil Air Patrol (aerospace edn. officer, pub. affairs officer), Soc. Study Reprodn., Am. Inst. Biol. Scis., N.Y. Acad. Sci., N.J. Acad. Sci., Pa. Acad. Sci., Ecol. Soc. Am. Avocations: hiking, traveling, writing, flying small airplanes.

KATZ, BARBARA S. special education educator; b. Springfield, Mass., July 22, 1933; d. Harry and Pearl (Black) Stein; m. Charles Murry Katz,

July 14, 1957; children: Helen Lee, Robert Alan. BS, Am. Internat. Coll., Springfield, 1956, MA in Ednl. Psychology in Learning Disabilities, 1979. Cert. in elem. edn., moderate spl. needs, Mass. Elem. tchr. Springfield Pub. Schs., 1956-60; Jr. Great Books discussion leader, 1968-69; Gillingham remedial tchr. Pub. Schs., Longmeadow, Mass., 1975-78, spl. edn. tchr. Chicopee, Mass., 1978-98, reader, 1998—. Reader Pioneer Valley Collaborative, East Longmeadow, Mass., 1998—. Pres. Kodimoh Synagogue Women's Group, Springfield, 1972-74; troop leader Girl Scouts U.S., Longmeadow, 1967-70. Horace Mann grantee, 1988. Mem. NEA, Mass. Tchrs. Assn. Avocations: painting, reading, walking, swimming. Home: 407 Bliss Rd Longmeadow MA 01106-1538

KATZ, JANE, swimming educator; b. Sharon, Pa., Apr. 16, 1943; d. Leon and Dorthea (Oberkewitz) Katz BS in Edn., CCNY, 1963; MA, NYU, 1966; MEd, Columbia Tchrs. Coll., 1972, EdD, 1978. Faculty Bronx C.C., CUNY, 1964—, prof. phys. edn., 1972—. Mem. U.S. Round-the-World Synchronized Swim Team, 1964; synchronized swimming solo tour of Eng., 1969; founding co-organizer, coach 1st Internat. Israeli Youth Festival Games, 1970; mem. winning U.S. Maccabiah Swim Team, 1957; vice-chair U.S. Masters All-Am. Swim Team, 1974—; mem. Nat. Masters All-Am. Swim Team, 1974—, synchronized swimming solo champion, 1975; spkr. judge in field. Author: Swimming for Total Fitness, A Progressive Aerobic Program, 1981, rev. ed. 1993, Swimming Through Your Pregnancy, 1983, W.E.T. Workouts: Water Exercises and Techniques to Help You and Tone Up Aerobically, 1985, Fitness Works: Blueprint for Lifelong Fitness, 1988, Swim 30 Laps in 30 Days, 1991, The Workstation Workout, 1994, Aquatic Handbook for Lifetime Fitness, 1996; author: (video) The New W.E.T. Workout, 1994, The All-American Aquatic Handbook: Your Passport to Lifetime Fitness, 1996, The W.E.T. Workout, 1996; contbr. Encyclopedia Britannica Med. and Health Ann., 1997, Swim Basics Video, 2001, Synchro Video, 2003, Aqua Fit Book, 2003; papers in field. Trainee Fed. Adminstrn. Aging, 1971-72; mem. Internat. Hall of Fame, Ft. Lauderdale. Named Healthy Am. Fitness Leader U.S. Jaycees and the Pres's. Coun. on Phys. Fitness, 1987, Outstanding Masters Synchronized Swimming, 1987; recipient CCNY Towsend Harris Acad. medal, 1989, Outstanding Lifetime Leadership award Fedn. Internat. Nat. Amateur, 1999, cert. of merit Fedn. Internat. de Natation Amateur (FINA), Sydney, Australia, 2000, Lifetime Contbrn. to Swimming award Internat. Olympic Com., 2000. Mem.: AAHPER, Internat. Aquatics (Hall of Fame Paragon award), U.S. Com. Sports for Israel (co-chmn. women's swimming com. 1970—, dir.), Internat. Swimming Hall of Fame (bd. of dir. 2002—). Address: 400 2nd Ave Apt 23B New York NY 10010-4052 E-mail: jkatz@jjay.cuny.edu.

KATZ, LEON, theatre and drama educator; b. Bronx, N.Y., July 10, 1919; s. Bernard and Rachel (Koslow) K.; children: Elia, Fredric. BSS., CCNY, 1940; MA, Columbia U., 1946, PhD, 1962. Instr. Cornell U., 1946-47, Hunter Coll., N.Y.C., 1947-49; asst. prof. Vassar Coll., 1949-58; lectr. Columbia, 1958-60; assoc. prof. Manhattanville Coll., Purchase, N.Y., 1960-64; vis. assoc. prof. Stanford, 1964-65; prof. San Francisco State Coll., 1965-68; Andrew Mellon vis. prof. Carnegie-Mellon U., Pitts., 1968-69, prof. drama dept., 1969-77; prof. dept. speech and theater arts U. Pitts., 1977-81; prof. Yale U., 1981-89, prof. emeritus, 1989—. Resident dramaturg Mark Taper Forum, L.A., 1990-92; vis. prof. Theater and Film Dept. UCLA, 1991—2003. Drama critic, sta. WQED-TV, San Francisco, 1966-68; film critic syndicated on radio, 1970-72; playwright TV writer; Author: plays Three Cuckolds, 1958, Dracula: Sabbat, 1972, Making of Americans, 1973, Astapovo, 1982, Odyssey, 1986, The Greek Myths, 1987, Midnight Plays, 1992, GBS in Love, 1995, Dear Bosie, 1996, Pinocchio, 1996, Beds, 2000, Classical Monologues from Aeschylus to Bernard Shaw, 4 vols., 2003—; TV dramas Confrontation, 1969; Necessity, 1972; co-editor: QED and Other Early Writings by Gertrude Stein, 1970. Co-dir. N.Y. Writers Workshop; curator Am. Theatre Collection. Served to capt. USAAF, 1942-46. Nat. Endowment for Humanities Research grantee, 1972-73; Ford Found. fellow, 1952-53. Mem. AAUP, AFTRA, Actors Equity, Authors Guild, Dramatists Guild. Jewish. Home: 6212 Lubao Ave Woodland Hills CA 91367-3823

KATZ, STANLEY NIDER, law history educator; b. Chgo., Apr. 23, 1934; s. William Stephen and Florence (Nider) K.; m. Adria Holmes, Jan. 16, 1960; children: Derek Holmes, Marion Holmes. AB, Harvard U., 1955, MA, 1959, PhD, 1961; LLD (hon.), Stockton State Coll., 1981; DHL (hon.), U. Puget Sound, 1994, C.W. Post/L.I. U., 1997, Sacred Heart U., 1997; LLD, Ohio State U., 1998, U. Hartford, 1998; DHL (hon.), Roosevelt U., 2003, Ursinus Coll., 2003; DLA (hon.), Dickinson Coll., 2003. Asst. prof. history Harvard U., 1961-65, U. Wis., Madison, 1965-71; prof. legal history Law Sch. U. Chgo., 1971-78; Class of 1921 Bicentennial prof. history Am. law and liberty Princeton U., 1978-86, sr. fellow Woodrow Wilson Sch., 1986-97, lectr. with rank of prof. Woodrow Wilson Sch., 1997—; pres. Am. Council Learned Socs., N.Y.C., 1986-97; dir. Ctr. for Arts and Cultural Policy Rsch./Woodrow Wilson Sch., 1998—. Vis. prof. law U. Pa., 1978-86; mem. Oliver Wendell Holmes Devise, Washington, 1976-84; bd. govs. Inst. European Studies, Chgo., 1976—; chmn. Coun. on Internat. Exchange Scholars, Washington, 1981-85; adj. prof. Cardozo Law Sch., 1999-2000. Author: Newcastle's New York, 1968; editor: The Case and Tryal of John Peter Zenger, 1963, rev. edit., 1972, Oliver Wendell Holmes Devise History of U.S. Supreme Court, 1984—, Colonial America, 1971, 76, 83, 92, 2000, American History: Promise and Progress, 1983, Constitutionalism and Democracy, 1993, The Life of Learning, 1994, Philanthropy in the World's Traditions, 1998, Mobilizing for Peace, 2002. Active N.J. Com. for Humanities, 1978—84, 1996—; trustee So. Meth. U., 1988—2000, Nat. Cultural Alliance, 1990—97, chmn., 1997—98; trustee Rsch. Librs. Group, 1991—93, 1997—99, Brit.-Am. Arts Assn., 1991—, Newberry Libr., Chgo., ind. sector, 1989—92, Toynbee Prize Found., 1994—97, pres., 1995—97, Nat. Faculty, 1995—2001, Fulbright Internat. Ctr., 1995—, Copyright Clearance Ctr., 1997—, civic edn. project, 1997—; bd. dirs. Social Sci. Rsch. Coun., N.Y.C., 2002—; v.p. Friends of the Law Libr., Libr. of Congress, 1991—, Surpeme Ct. N.J., disciplinary oversight com., 1994—2000, N.J. Ethics Commn., 1991—94, com. model rules of profl. conduct, 1982—83, com. sale of law practices, 1983—84, 1989. Fellow Am. Soc. Legal History (pres. 1978-81); mem. AAAS, Papers of the Founding Fathers (chair 1985—), Inst. Early Am. History and Culture (coun. 1974-76, 90-93, 97-98), Am. Hist. Assn. (v.p. rsch. 1997-2000), Orgn. Am. Historians (exec. com. 1976-79, pres. elect 1986-87, pres. 1987-88), Am. Antiquarian Soc., Mass. Hist. Soc., Am. Philos. Soc., Soc. Am. Historians, Coun. Fgn. Rels., Phi Beta Kappa. Clubs: Princeton (N.Y.C.). Democrat. Jewish. Office: Princeton U Woodrow Wilson Sch Princeton NJ 08544-0001 E-mail: snkatz@princeton.edu.

KATZMAN, ROBERT, medical educator, neurologist; b. Denver, Nov. 29, 1925; s. Maurice and Leah K. (Schnitt) K.; m. Nancy Bernstein, Sept. 2, 1947; children: David Jonathan, Daniel Mark. BS, U. Chgo., 1949, MS, 1951; MD cum laude, Harvard U., 1953. Diplomate Am. Bd. Psychiatry and Neurology. Intern Boston City Hosp., 1953-54; chief resident Neurol. Inst. Columbia Presbyn. Hosp., N.Y.C., 1956-57; faculty mem. Albert Einstein Coll. Medicine, N.Y.C., 1957-84, prof., chmn. neurology dept., 1964-84, dir. Resnick Gerontology Ctr., 1979-84; chmn. dept. neuroscis. U. Calif., San Diego, 1984-90, Florence Riford prof. neuroscis. and rsch. in Alzheimer's disease, 1984-94, rsch. prof. neuroscis., 1994—2002, prof. emeritus neurosci., 2003—. Mem. clin. rsch. adv. com. Nat. Found. March of Dimes, 1975-76; mem. adv. coun. Nat. Inst. on Aging, 1982-85; chmn. med. and sci. bd. Alzheimer Disease and Related Disorders Assn., Chgo., 1979-85; mem. adv. panel on Alzheimer's disease HHS, 1987-93. Co-author: Brain Electrolytes and Fluid Metabolism, 1973, Neurology of Aging, 1983, Alzheimer Disease: The Changing View, 2000; co-editor: Basic Neurochemistry, 1972-81, Principles of Geriatric Neurology, 1992, Alzheimer Disease, 1994, Alzheimers Disease, 2d edit., 1999; mem. editl. bd. Clin. Neuroscience Rsch. Jour., ARNMD, 2001--. With USN, 1944-46, PTO. Recipient Humanitarian Award Alzheimer's Disease and Related Disorders Assn., 1985, Disting. Svc. award, 1989, Allied Achievement in Aging award Allied Signal Corp., 1985, Henderson Meml. award Am. Geriatric Soc., 1986, 7th Ann. Chgo. Rita Hayworth Gala award recipient, Alzheimer's Assn., 1994, Crystal Tower award Alzheimer's Assn., 1998. Fellow Am. Acad. Neurology (S. Weir Mitchell award 1960, George W. Jacoby award 1989, co-recipient Potamkin prize for Alzheimer's disease rsch. 1992); mem. Assn. for Rsch. in Nervous and Mental Disorders (pres. 1977), Am. Physiol. Soc., Inst. Medicine NAS, Am. Neurol. Assn. (pres. 1985-86), Internat. Soc. for Alzheimer's Disease Rsch. (pres. 1996—), Alpha Omega Alpha. Office: U Calif San Diego Sch Medicine 9500 Gilman Dr Dept 0949 La Jolla CA 92093-0949 E-mail: rkatzman@ucsd.edu.

KAUFER, CONNIE TENORIO, retired reading specialist; b. Saipan, No. Mariana Islands, June 12, 1945; d. Lino Pangelinan and Magdalena Faosto (Arriola) Tenorio; m. Leonard James Kaufer, Jan. 20, 1974; 1 child, Lucile Tenorio. AA in Elem. Edn., Chaffey Coll., 1968; BS in Lang. Arts, Calif. State Poly. U., 1971; MA in Edn., San Jose State U., 1983. Cert. tchr., Calif., Mariana Islands. Elem. tchr. Marianas Dept. Edn., Chalan Kanoa, Saipan, Mariana Islands, 1964-66, 74-76, 80-84, elem. and h.s. tchr., 1970-71, elem. sch. supr. Lower Base, Saipan, 1971-74, elem. sch. prin. Tanapag Village, Saipan, 1979-80; comprehensive lang. arts skills project dir. Pub. Sch. Sys., Lower Base, Saipan, 1984-87, reading specialist, 1984-94, trainer Marianas instrument for obs. of tchr. activities, 1986—94, trainer onward to excellence, 1988—94; ret., 1994. Part-time instr. U. Guam Ext., No. Marianas Coll., Saipan, 1993—; sec. Diocesan Bd. Edn. Saipan, 1985-90; trainer pacific region pacific effective schs. Pacific Region Edn. Lab., Honolulu and Saipan, 1991-93; presenter in field. Mem. Mariana Islands rep. Trust Ter. Curriculum Coun., Saipan, 1970-72; coord. cross cultural Peace Corps, Saipan, 1973, coord. Chamorro lang., 1975; pres. Chalan Kanoa Sch. Saipan Tchrs. Assn., 1981-83. Scholar Marianas Edn. Found., 1966-70, Bilingual Edn. scholar Trust Ter. Dept. Edn., 1975. Mem. ASCD, AAUW, Internat. Reading Assn. (Saipan chpt. pres. 1975-76), Pacific Islands Bilingual/Bicultural Assn., Phi Delta Kappa. Roman Catholic. Avocations: raising orchids, cooking, baking. Home: PO Box 7611 Saipan MP 96950

KAUFFMAN, GEORGE BERNARD, chemistry educator; b. Phila., Sept. 4, 1930; s. Philip Joseph and Laura (Fisher) K.; m. Ingeborg Salomon, June 5, 1952 (div. Dec. 1969); children: Ruth Deborah (Mrs. Martin H. Bryskier), Judith Miriam (Mrs. Mario L. Reposo); m. Laurie Marks Papazian, Dec. 21, 1969; stepchildren: Stanley Robert Papazian, Teresa Lynn Papazian Baron, Mary Ellen Papazian. BA with honors, U. Pa., 1951; PhD, U. Fla., 1956. Grad. asst. U. Fla., 1951-55; rsch. participant Oak Ridge Nat. Lab., 1955; instr. U. Tex., Austin, 1955-56; rsch. chemist Humble Oil & Refining Co., Baytown, Tex., 1956, GE, Cin., 1957, 59; asst. prof. chemistry Calif. State U., Fresno, 1956-61, assoc. prof., 1961-66, prof., 1966—. Guest lectr. coop. lecture tours Am. Chem. Soc., 1971; vis. scholar U. Calif., Berkeley, 1976, U. Puget Sound, 1978; dir. undergrad. rsch. participation program NSF, 1972. Author: Alfred Werner— Founder of Coordination Chemistry, 1966, Classics in Coordination Chemistry, Part I, 1968, Part II, 1976, Part III, 1978, Werner Centennial, 1967, Teaching the History of Chemistry, 1971, Coordination Chemistry: Its History through the Time of Werner, 1977, Inorganic Coordination Compounds, 1981, The Central Science: Essays on the Uses of Chemistry, 1984, Frederick Soddy (1877-1956): Early Pioneer in Radiochemistry, 1986, Aleksandr Porfirevich Borodin: A Chemist's Biography, 1988, Coordination Chemistry: A Century of Progress, 1994, Classics in Coordination Chemistry, 1995, Metal and Nonmetal Biguanide Complexes, 1999; contbr. articles to profl. jours.; contbg. editor: Jour. Coll. Sci. Tchg., 1973—, The Hexagon, 1980—, Polyhedron, 1983-85, Industrial Chemist, 1985-88, Jour. Chem. Edn., 1987—, Today's Chemist, 1989-91, The Chemical Intelligencer, 1994-2000, Today's Chemist at Work, 1995—, Chemical Heritage, 1996—, The Chemical Educator, 1998—, Chem. 13 News, 1998—; guest editor: Coodination Chemistry Centennial Symposium (C3S) issue, Polyhedron, 1994; editor tape lecture series: Am. Chem. Soc, 1975-81. Named Outstanding Prof., Calif. State U. and Colls. Sys., 1973; recipient Exceptional Merit Svc. award, 1984, Meritorious Performance and Profl. Promise award, 1986-87, 88-89, Coll. Chemistry Tchr. Excellence award Mfg. Chemists Assn., 1976, Chugaev medal, 1976, Kurnakov medal, 1990, Chernyaev medal, 1991, USSR Acad. Sci., George C. Pimentel award in chem. edn. Am. Chem. Soc., 1993, Dexter award in history of chemistry, 1978, Marc-Auguste Pictet medal Soc. Physique et d'Histoire Naturelle de Genève, 1992, Pres.'s medal of Distinction, Calif. State U., Fresno, 1994, Rsch. award at an Undergraduate Instn., Am. Chem. Soc., 2000, Laudatory Decree Inst. History of Sci. and Tech. Russian Acad. Sci., 2000; Rsch. Corp. grantee, 1956-57, 57-59, 59-61, Am. Chem. Soc. Petroleum Rsch. Fund grantee, 1963-64, 69-70, NSF grantee, 1960-61, 63-64, 67-69, 76-77, NEH grantee, 1982-83; John Simon Guggenheim Meml. Found. fellow, 1972-73, grantee, 1975; Strindberg fellow Swedish Inst., Stockholm, 1983. Fellow: AAAS; mem.: Mensa, Am. Chem. Soc. (chmn. divsn. history of chemistry 1969, mem. exec. com. 1970, councilor 1976—78, George C. Pimentel award in chem. edn. 1993, Helen M. Free Pub. Outreach award 2002), Soc. History Alchemy and Chemistry, History of Sci. Soc., Assn. Univ. Pa. Chemists, AAUP, Gamma Sigma Epsilon, Alpha Chi Sigma, Phi Kappa Phi, Phi Lambda Upsilon, Sigma Xi. Home: 1609 E Quincy Ave Fresno CA 93720-2309 Office: Calif State U Dept Chemistry Fresno CA 93740-8034 E-mail: georgek@csufresno.edu.

KAUFFMAN, KAETHE COVENTON, art educator, artist, author; b. Washington, Aug. 12, 1948; d. Richard G. and Kathleen B. (Coventon) K.; m. James William Hite, Oct. 23, 1983; children: James Haydn, Kauffman Hite. BA, U. Wash., 1970, U. Nev., 1975; MFA, U. Calif., Irvine, 1978; PhD, Union Inst. Cin., 1989. Art dept. faculty U. Nev., Las Vegas, Mount St. Mary's Coll., L.A.; chmn. art dept. Sierra Nevada Coll., Incline Village, 1989-91, assoc. prof., 1991-2001, Chaminade U., Honolulu, 2001—, adj. faculty, 2001—. Faculty dept. art U. Calif., Irvine; bd. dirs. Buddhist Studies Ctr. Press. Author: Sex and the Avant-Garde: A Gender Revolution in the Visual Arts 1830-1993, Female Forms of Originality and the New, Women Artists in the Avant-Garde, How Art Professors Teach Avant-Garde Values, Women Artists Deconstruct the Male Avant-Garde, A Modern Renaissance of the Arts; columnist: Lake Tahoe World newspapers; art exhibited at Utrecht, Holland, 1977, Inst. Modern Art, Brisbane, Australia, 1978, George Patton Gallery U. Melbourne, Australia, 1979, Newport Harbor Art Mus., Calif., 1980, Fiberworks Gallery, Berkeley, Calif., 1981, Galerie Triangle, Washington, 1982, Nev. Mus., Reno, 1983, Schoharie Nat., Cobleskill, N.Y., 1984, Pinnacle Gallery, N.Y., 1986, Space Gallery, Las Vegas, Nev., 1988, Manville Gallery, U. Nev., Reno, 1989, Galerie Art-Jeunesse, Montreal, Que., 1990, Kleinert Gallery, N.Y., 1991, West Gallery, Claremont Grad. Sch., 1992, Sierra Nev. Coll. Art Gallery, Lake Tahoe, Nev., 1995, Exhbn. Hall U. Prague, Czech Republic, CERES Gallery, N.Y., Women's UN Conf., Beijing, Nat. Mus. Women in Arts, Washington, Gallery of the Pali, Honolulu, Czech Mus. Fine Arts, Prague; represented in permanent collections Women's Studio Workshop, N.Y.C., Calif. Mus. Photography, L.A., Fluor Corp., L.A., Harris Found., Las Vegas, Nev., Computer Scis. Corp., L.A., Sheraton Plaza Inn, L.A., Glendale Fed. Bank, L.A.; mem. editl. bd. Collegiate Press. Juror 3d biennial Nev. Craft Show. Recipient Max H. Block award for Humanism, Juror's award Am. Pen Women Bienniale, Dr. Wu and Elsie Ject-Key meml. award for photography Nat. Assn. Women Artists, N.Y.; Laguna Beach Festival of the Arts fellow; TOSCO Corp. grantee; Artists grantee Sierra Arts Found. Mem. Nat. Mus. Women in Arts, Women's Caucus for Art, Nat. Assn. for Women Artists (medal of honor for works on paper, Elizabeth Morse Genius Found. award), Ceres Gallery, Am. Pen Women (3 awards for non-fiction writing nat. competition), Arts and Letters, Natl. Assn. for Women Artists.

KAUFFMAN, TERRY, broadcast and creative arts communication educator, artist; b. San Francisco, Aug. 24, 1951; d. Raymond Roger and Patricia Virginia Kauffman. BA in Journalism with hons., U. Calif., Berkeley, 1974; MA in Comm. summa cum laude, U. Tex., 1980; PhD in Psychology, Comm., and Creative Expression with distinction, Union Inst., 1996. With Alta. Ednl. TV, 1976; sr. writer, prodr. and dir. Ampex Corp., Calif., 1980; writer, news prodr., reporter, anchor ABC, Tex., 1974-75; mem. faculty dept. radio, TV and motion pictures U. N.C., Chapel Hill, 1985; mem. faculty dept. comm. N.C. State U., Raleigh, 1986—2001; founder, artist Cozy Cards, Cards by Terry, 2000—. Adj. prof. music, theatre and comm. dept. Meredith Coll., Raleigh, 1990—; adv. bd., chmn. publicity Raleigh Conservatory Music; v.p. Wake Visual Arts Assn. and Gallery; tchr. art Meredith Coll., 1995—; founder, owner Creative Spaces; founder Cards by Terry Kauffman, 2003; expressive art therapist at psychit. hosps. and pvt., 1994—. Author: I'm Clueless, Confessions of a College Teacher, The Script as Blueprint, 1994, 8 vol. set poetry including Psalms of Teresa, Secret Place, Just Visiting, others; author numerous poems; composer, prodr., dir. When the Wind Blows, The Rainbow, The Seasons of Change, PBS, Women Today, Profiles in Leadership, Little Miss Puppet Talks to the Angels, I'm One Person or Another, One; commd. and exhibited in solo shows (1st place painting), San Francisco, Raleigh; artist for documentary series, rschr., writer, Alta., Can., 1976; prodr., dir., writer, composer I'm One Person...Or The Other, Thanksgiving (PBS), 1980—; writer, prodr. Consumer Hotline, PBS, Customs Operations at the Border; main character, vocalist, composer Little Miss Puppet Talks to the Angels; pub. music book: Songs by Terry Kauffman. Singer/composer for chs. and retirement homes; past bd. dirs. Tex. Consumer Assn., Wake visual Arts. Named Outstanding Lectr. of Yr., Coll. of Humanities and Social Scis., N.C. State U., 1996; recipient Emmy nomination for documentary Otters from Oiled Waters, 1991, more than 15 1st place nat. awards in TV, including writing, producing, directing, music composition, acting, art and photography, vrious art and music shows. Mem. APA, NATAS, Internat. TV Assn. (judge nat. contests), Nat. Broadcasting Soc. (8 1st place nat. awards 1973—, named Outstanding Mem., 1993-94, Profl. Mem. of Yr. 1994), Internat. Expressive Art Therapists Assn., Calif. Scholastic Fedn. (life), Calif. Scholastic Assn., Berkeley Honor Soc., Am. Psychol. Assn., Phi Kappa Phi. Home: 407 Furches St Raleigh NC 27607-4017

KAUFMAN, ALAN STEPHEN, psychologist, educator; b. NYC, Apr. 21, 1944; s. Max and Blanche (Levine) K.; m. Nadeen Laurie Bengels, Dec. 20, 1964; children: Jennie Lynn, David Scott, James Corey. BA, U. Pa., 1965; MA, Columbia U., 1967, PhD, 1970. Assoc. prof. psychology U. Ga., Athens, 1974-79, U. Ill., Chgo., 1979-80; prof. psychology Nat. Coll. Edn., Evanston, Ill., 1980-82, Calif. Sch. Profl. Psychology, San Diego, 1982-84; rsch. prof. U. Ala., Tuscaloosa, 1984-95; sr. rsch. scientist Psychol. Assessment Resources, Inc., Odessa, Fla., 1995-97; clin. prof. psychology Yale U. Sch. Medicine, New Haven, 1997—. Author: Intelligent Testing with the WISC R, 1979, Assessing Adolescent and Adult Intelligence, 1990, Intelligent Testing with the WISC-III, 1994, (with Nadeen Kaufman) Clinical Evaluation of Young Children, 1977, Specific Learning Disabiities in Children and Adolescents, 2001; (with E. Lichtenberger) Essentials of WAIS-III Assessment, 1999, Assessing Adolscent and Adult Intelligence, 2d edit., 2002; writer tests (with Nadeen Kaufman) including K-ABC and others; co-editor: Research in the Schools; mem. editl. bd. Sch. Psychology Quar., Archives Clin. Neuropsychology, Psychology in Schs., Jour. Psychoednl. Assessment, Ednl. and Psychol. Measurement; patentee psychol. testing device. Recipient Outstanding Rsch. award Ariz. Assn. Sch. Psychologists, 1980, Award for Excellence, Mensa Edn. and Rsch. Found., 1989. Fellow APA (Sr. Scientist award divsn. 16, 1997), Am. Psychol. Soc.; mem. Nat. Assn. Sch. Psychologists, Nat. Coun. Measurement in Edn., Coun. for Exceptional Children, Am. Ednl. Rsch. Assn., Mid-South Ednl. Rsch. Assn. (Outstanding Rsch. award 1988, 93), Phi Beta Kappa, Sigma Xi. Avocation: researching baseball. Home: 8721 Sherwood Forest Ct Escondido CA 92026 Office: Yale Child Study Ctr PO Box 207900 New Haven CT 06520-7900 E-mail: alanadeen@att.net.

KAUFMAN, ANDREW LEE, law educator; b. Newark, Feb. 1, 1931; s. Samuel and Sylvia (Meltzer) K.; m. Linda P. Sonnenschein, June 14, 1959; children: Anne, David, Elizabeth, Daniel. AB, Harvard U., 1951, LL.B., 1954. Bar: D.C. 1954, Mass. 1979, U.S. Supreme Ct. 1961. Assoc. Bilder, Bilder & Kaufman, Newark, 1954-55; law clk. to Justice Felix Frankfurter U.S Supreme Ct., 1955-57; ptnr. Kaufman, Kaufman & Kaufman, Newark, 1957-65; lectr. in law Harvard U., Cambridge, Mass., 1965-66, prof., 1966-81, Charles Stebbins Fairchild prof. law, 1981—, assoc. dean, 1986-89. Author: (with others) Commercial Law, 1971, 82, Problems in Professional Responsibility, 1976, 84, 89, 2002, Cardozo, 1998. Treas. Shady Hill Sch., 1969-76; treas. Hillel Found. Cambridge, Inc., 1977-86. Mem. Mass. Bar Assn. (chmn. com. profl. ethics 1982—). Office: Harvard U Law Sch Cambridge MA 02138 E-mail: kaufman@law.harvard.edu.

KAUFMAN, HAROLD RICHARD, mechanical engineer and physics educator; b. Audubon, Iowa, Nov. 24, 1926; s. Walter Richard and Hazel (Steere) K.; m. Elinor Mae Wheat, June 25, 1948; children: Brian, Karin, Bruce, Cynthia. Student, Evanston Community Coll., 1947-49; BSM.E., Northwestern U., 1951; PhD, Colo. State U., 1971. Researcher in aerospace propulsion NACA, Cleve., 1951-58; mgr. space propulsion research NASA, Cleve., 1958-74; prof. physics and mech. engrng. Colo. State U., Ft. Collins, 1974-84, prof. emeritus, 1984—, chmn. dept. physics, 1979-84; pres. Kaufman & Robinson, Inc., Ft. Collins, 1984—; v.p. R&D Commonwealth Sci. Corp., Alexandria, Va., 1984-96. Pioneer in field of electron bombardment ion thruster, 1960; cons. ion source design and applications. Contbr. over 140 publs. and 30 patents in field. Served with USNR, 1944-46. Recipient NASA medal for exceptional sci. achievement, 1971. Fellow Am. Vacuum Soc. (Albert Nerken award 1991), AIAA (assoc. fellow, James H. Wyld Propulsion award 1969); mem. Tau Beta Pi, Pi Tau Sigma. Office: Kaufman & Robinson Inc 1306 Blue Spruce Dr Ste 2A Fort Collins CO 80524-2067

KAUFMAN, HENRY, financial services executive; b. Wenings, Germany, Oct. 20, 1927; came to U.S., 1937; s. Gustav and Hilda (Rosenthal) K.; m. Elaine Reinheimer, Sept. 15, 1957; children: Glenn, Craig, Daniel. BA, NYU, 1948, PhD, 1958; MS, Columbia U., 1949; LLD (hon.), NYU, 1982; LHD, Yeshiva U., 1986. Asst. chief economist research dept. Fed. Res. Bank N.Y., 1957-61; with Salomon Bros., Inc., N.Y.C., 1962-88, gen. partner, 1967-88, mem. exec. com., 1972-88, mng. dir., 1981-88, also chief economist, charge bond market research, industry and stock research and bond portfolio analysis research and corp. bond research depts., also vice-chmn.; founder Henry Kaufman & Co., N.Y.C., 1988—. Pres. Money Marketeers, N.Y. U., 1964-65 Bd. dirs. Fed. Home Loan Mortgage Corp. Trustee Whitney Mus. of Am. Art; pres. Animal Med. Ctr.; bd. govs. Tel-Aviv U.; chmn. bd. overseers Stern Sch. of Bus. NYU; chmn. Inst. Internat. Edn. Mem. Am. Econ. Assn., Am. Fin. Assn., Conf. Bus. Economists, Econ. Club N.Y.C. (dir.), UN Assn. (bd. dirs., co-chmn. econ. policy council), Council Fgn. Relations. Office: Henry Kaufman & Co 65 E 55th St New York NY 10022-3219

KAUFMAN, JANICE HORNER, foreign language educator, women's and gender studies educator; b. Mattoon, Ill., Apr. 30, 1949; d. Daniel Ogden and Julia Betty (McDermid) Horner; m. Richard Boucher Kaufman, June 24, 1972 (div. Mar. 27, 2002); children: Julia Ogden, Richard Pearse. AB, Duke U., 1971; MA in Liberal Studies, Hollins Coll., 1979; postgrad., NYU, 1986; PhD in French, U. Va., Charlottesville, 1997. Tchr. in French Roanoke (Va.) City Pub. Schs., 1971-72, North Cross Sch., Roanoke, Va., 1974-82; instr. French Va. Poly. Inst. and State U., Blacksburg, 1984-86, 88, 90, 94, 98, asst. dir. fgn. lang. camps, 1984-85, administrv. dir., 1986; French, English interpreter, translator Coll. Architecture and Urban Studies, Blacksburg, 1988; instr. ESL U. Cmty. Internat. Coun., Cranwell Internat.

Ctr., Blacksburg, 1987-89; instr. French Hollins Coll., Roanoke, Va., 1989-90, Radford (Va.) U., 1989-90; grad. tchg. asst. U. Va., Charlottesville, 1992; adj. assoc. prof. French No. Va. C.C., Woodbridge and Alexandria, 1997-99; asst. prof. French and women's and gender studies SUNY-Oneonta, 2000—. Student counselor Am. Inst. Fgn. Study, Greenwich, Conn., 1977; session leader Russell County Pub. Schs., Lebanon, Va., 1985, Va. Assn. Ind. Schs., Richmond, 1986; asst. tchr. Am. Coun. for Internat. Studies "Toujours en France," 1995; faculty cons. advanced placement exam in French, Ednl. Testing Svc., Trenton State Coll., 1991-95, 97-98; adj. prof. French, George Mason U., Fairfax, Va., 1999-2000; acad. dir. study abroad in Strasbourg, France, George Mason U. Ctr. for Global Edn., summer 2000; presenter in field. Contbr. articles to profl. jours. Mem. MLA, Am. Assn. Tchrs. French, African Lit. Assn., Women in French, Pi Delta Phi, Phi Sigma Iota. Avocations: reading, travel, hiking. E-mail: kaufmajh@oneonta.edu.

KAUFMAN, MARY SUSAN, elementary education educator; b. Ellwood City, Pa., Sept. 8, 1946; d. Richard Francis and Harriet Augusta (Stillwagon) Oswald; m. Lawrence William Kaufman, Nov. 21, 1970; children: Steven, Kristina, Amy. BS in Elem. Edn., Clarion State U., 1968; Master Equivalency, Slippery Rock U., 1992. Cert. elem. edn. Reading tchr. Aliquippa (Pa.) Area Sch. Dist., 1968; tchr. grades 1 and 2 Blackhawk Sch. Dist., Beaver Falls, Pa., 1969-79; tchr. grades 4 and 6 Pittsburgh Diocese, Beaver Falls, 1985-87; tchr. grade 6 Beaver (Pa.) Area Sch. Dist., 1987—. Mem. steering com. Regional Math Sci. Collaborative, Pitts., 1994—. Rschr., author: Twentieth Century History of Beaver County, 1989. Mem., past pres. New Brighton (Pa.) Area PTA, 1980-85; trustee, rec. sec. Beaver County Hist. and Landmarks Found., Beaver, 1987-91. Recipient Scholarship award West Mayfield PTA, Beaver Falls, 1974, Beaver County Times Cmty. Svc. award Beaver County Times, Beaver, 1985; named Environ. Educator of Yr., Beaver County Conservation Dist., 1996. Mem. Pa. Sci. Tchrs. Assn. Democrat. Roman Catholic. Avocations: oil painting, reading, sewing, travel, biking. Home: 1058 6th St Beaver PA 15009-1824 Office: Beaver Area Sch Dist College Square Sch 375 College Ave Beaver PA 15009-2238 E-mail: kaufman@basd.k12.pa.us.

KAUFMAN, SUSAN NANETTE BLAND, secondary school educator; b. Medicine Lodge, Kans., Nov. 23, 1961; d. Marvin Lee and Leora Jean (Ruggles) Bland; m. Alan Keith Kaufman, Aug. 4, 1984; children: Kristen Leigh, Kelli Bryn. BA, Bethany Coll., 1983; MS, Kans. State U., 1984. Cert. K-12 gifted elem. tchr., 7-12 English, 7-12 art, k-12 phys. edn., Tex. Gifted edn. tchr. Valley Ctr. (Kans.) Pub. Schs., 1984-88; elem. tchr. Maize (Kans.) Unified Sch. Dist. # 266, 1988—95; jr. high tchr. HEBISD, 1995—97; art tchr., coach Trinity HS, Euliss, Tex., 1997—. Mem. Crown of Life Luth. Ch. Mem. Tex. Nat. Edn. Assn. (resolution com. 1984-92, student NEA pres. 1983-84), Tex. Art Educators Assn., Tex. Girls Coaching Assn., Am. Volleyball Coaches Assn. Avocations: reading, drawing, crafts, athletics. Home: 3809 Horizon Dr Bedford TX 76021-2630 Office: Trinity HS 500 N INdsl Blvd Euless TX 76039

KAUFMAN, WILLIAM MORRIS, engineer consultant; b. Pitts., Dec. 31, 1931; s. Nathan and Sarah M. (Paper) K.; m. Iris F. Picovsky, June 21, 1953; children: Nathan E., Marjorie L., Emily M. BSEE, Carnegie Inst. Tech., 1953, MSEE, PhD in EE, Carnegie Inst. Tech. Registered profl. engr. Supr. Westinghouse Electric Corp., Pitts., 1955-62; dir. rsch. Gen. Instrument Corp., Newark, 1962-65; cons. engr. GE, Valley Forge, Pa., 1965-66; mgr. med. engr. dept. Hittman Assocs. Inc., Columbia, Md., 1966-71; v.p. engring. ENSCO, Springfield, Va., 1971-83; v.p. Ocean Data Systems Inc., Rockville, Md., 1984-85; v.p. applied rsch., dir. Carnegie Mellon Rsch. Inst. Carnegie Mellon U., Pitts., 1985-97, mem. tech. transfer bd., 1989-94, mem. employee retirement and welfare benefit plan com., 1988-97. Chmn. tech. adv. group Fostin Capital, Pitts., 1986-95; mem. adv. bd. Pitts. Seed Fund, 1986-97; bd. dirs. Mellon Pitt Carnegie Corp., Maglev, Inc., Tech. Devel. and Edn. Corp. Patentee in field. Mem. adv coun. on regional devel. U. Pitts., 1986; bd. dirs. Ben Franklin Tech. Ctr. of Western Pa., 1988-97, treas., 1997; cons. tech. acquisition. Fellow IEEE (life); mem. Sigma Xi, Tau Beta Pi, Eta Kappa Nu. Home and Office: 38 Sheridan Rd Swampscott MA 01907-2045 E-mail: billkaufman@cmu.edu.

KAUTZMAN, JEAN L. PFLIGER, nurse educator; b. Hazen, N.D., Oct. 4, 1942; d. Lawrence Raymond and Louise A.M. (Hagerott) Pfliger; m. Raymond L. Kautzman, Aug. 1, 1969 (dec.); children: Jerry, Linda, Timothy, Terry, Marty, Tracy(dec.). Diploma, Bismarck Hosp. Sch. Nursing, 1963; BSN, Mary Coll., 1969; MSN, S.D. State U., 1984; postgrad., U. N.D., N.D. State U.; MSU, U. Mary. RN, N.D. Head nurse pediatrics Bismarck (N.D.) Hosp.; faculty mem. Bismarck Hosp./Medcenter One; acting dir. sch. nursing Medcenter One Coll. Nursing, Bismarck, home healthcare nurse, assoc. prof., dir. alumni affairs. Editor: The Alumni Connection. Dist. dir. Center Pub. Sch. Recipient Medcenter One Coll. Nursing Svc. award, You're Number One Medenter One award, Inez G. Hinsvark Founder's award; grantee, Helene Fuld Health Trust, Oliver County Ambulance Assn. Mem.: ANA (cert. nursing adminstr.), N.D. Nurses Assn. (former dir. at large, DNA 6 v.p., v.p. chairperson, bylaws and resolutions com., Hon. Recognition award, Dist. #6 Hall of Fame award), Lewis and Clark Dist. Nurses Assn., N.D. Childhood Immunization Program, N.D. Bd. Nursing (mem. entry into practice com.), Bismarck Hosp./Medcenter One Nursing Alumni Assn. (1st v.p.), Bismarck C. of C. (higher edn.com.), Epsilon Sigma Kappa Rho (counselor), Kappa Upsilon (bylaws chairperson). Home: 2130 41st Ave SW Center ND 58530-9767

KAVADAS-PAPPAS, IPHIGENIA KATHERINE, preschool administrator, educator, consultant; b. Manchester, N.H., Oct. 24, 1958; d. Demetrios Stefanos and Rodothea (Palaiologou) K.; m. Constantine George Pappas, July 29, 1979; children: George Demetrios, Rodothea Constance. BA magna cum laude, U. Detroit, 1980; MAT summa cum laude, Oakland U., 1985. Cert. tchr., Mich. Pre-sch. tchr. Assumption Nursery Sch., St. Clair Shores, Mich., 1977-80, interim dir., 1984, bd. dirs., 1980—; Sunday sch. tchr. Assumption Greek Orthodox Ch., St. Clair Shores, 1985—; chairperson pre-sch. curriculum com. Greek Orthodox Archdiocese Dept. Religious Edn., Brookline, Mass., 1987—. Cons. Assumption Nursery Sch., 1985—; validator preschs. program for cert. Co-author: Pre-school Curriculum Manual for Greek Orthodox Archdiocese, 1990, Pre-School Curriculum for National Use, 1991. Mem. Assumption Greek Orthodox Ch. Philoptochos Soc., 1978-87; trustee Assumption Nursery Sch., 1979—, Sunday sch. presch. tchr., 1985—; spl. events coord. Assumption Sunday Sch., 1999—; vol. svcs. Bemis Elem. Sch., Boulan Park Mid. Sch., 1991-96; mem. Nat. Ctr. for the Early Childhood Work Force; vol. Troy H.S., 1996—, Rainbow Connection Orgn. Recipient Vol. Svc. award Angus Elem. Sch., 1989. Mem. AAUW, Nat. Assn. for the Edn. Young Children (validator presch. programs for accreditation), Nat. Multiple Sclerosis (adv. bd. 2000). Office: Assumption Greek Orthodox 21800 Marter Rd Saint Clair Shores MI 48080-2464

KAVANAGH, JOHN JOSEPH, medical educator; b. Phila., Aug. 7, 1947; s. John and Christine Kavanagh; m. Teresa Ann Brown. BA, Sch. Internat. Svc., Washington, 1969; MD, Jefferson Med. Coll., 1975. Clin. asst. prof. U. Nebr., Omaha, 1980-81; instr., asst. internist M.D. Anderson Cancer Ctr., Houston, 1981-82, asst. prof., chief sect. gynecologic med. oncology, 1983-85, assoc. gynecologist, 1987—, assoc. prof., chief sect. gynecologic med. oncology, 1987—; assoc. prof. H. Lee Moffitt Cancer Ctr., Tampa, Fla., 1985-87; assoc. prof. ob-gyn. and reproductive scis. U. Tex. Health Sci. Ctr., Houston, 1991—, prof. dept. clin. investigation, 1996—. Cons. S.W. Oncology Group, San Antonio, 1994—; mem. faculty European Sch. Oncology. With USAR, 1969-71. Grantee ASTA Medica, Inc., Hackensack, N.J., 1994, Hoffman-LaRoche, Nutley, N.J., 1994. Fellow ACP, European Soc. Gynecol. Oncology (assoc.); mem. Internat. Gynecologic Cancer soc. (chmn. membership com., exec. com.), So. Oncology Assn. (pres. 1991-92), So. Med. Assn. (Presdl. com. on endowments 1993—), Tex. Soc. Med. Oncology (founding). Avocations: fishing, boating, reading. Office: M D Anderson Cancer Ctr 1515 Holcombe Blvd # 39 Houston TX 77030-4009

KAVANAGH, RALPH WILLIAM, physics educator; b. Seattle, July 15, 1924; s. Ralph W. and Esther (Weken) K.; m. Joyce Eberhart, July 31, 1948; children: Kathleen, Janet, Stephanie, Linda, William Leonard. BA, Reed Coll., 1950; MA, U. Oreg., 1952; PhD, Calif. Inst. Tech., 1956. Mem. faculty Calif. Inst. Tech., Pasadena, 1956—, assoc. prof. physics, 1965-70, prof., 1970—2000, prof. emeritus, 2000—; rsch. assoc. Centre de Recherches Nucleaires, U. Strasbourg, France, 1967-68; rsch. assoc. Sch. Physics U. Melbourne, Australia, 1983. Contbr. articles to profl. jours. Served with USNR, 1942-46. Fellow Am. Phys. Soc. Home: 450 Bonita Ave Pasadena CA 91107-5064

KAWCZYNSKI, DIANE MARIE, elementary and middle school educator, composer; b. Milw., Jan. 22, 1959; d. Adalbert Lawrence and Joan (Zernia) K. BMus, Lawrence U., 1981; MMus, U. Wis., 1985. Cert. music tchr. Va., adminstrn. and supervision pre-K-12 Va. Suzuki violin instr., string methods instr. Brandon (Manitoba, Can.) Univ. Sch. Music, 1982-83; violin/viola instr., univ. prep program U. Wis. Sch. of Music, Madison, 1983-85; elem. and middle sch. string instr. Albuquerque Pub. Schs., 1985-86; middle sch. string and chorus instr. Ft. Morgan (Colo.) Pub. Schs., 1986-87; elem. string instr., middle sch. orchestra instr. Norfolk Pub. Schs., 1987—. Mem. NEA, Am. String Tchr. Assn., Music Educators Nat. Conf. Avocations: knitting, walking, crafts. Home: 860 Gaslight Ln Virginia Beach VA 23462-1232 E-mail: dkawczynksi@blairms.nps.k12.va.us.

KAWMY, SUSAN YOST, educational consultant; b. Bklyn., Feb. 14, 1950; d. John Gantt and June Ardith (Goodman) Yost; m. Karim Fred Kawmy, Aug. 17, 1974; children: Jumana Maria, Rashad Fouad, Marya Melissa, Elie Wadiah. BS, Colo. State U., 1972; MEd, U. Ariz., 1973. Resource tchr. Edn. Svc. Unit, Hastings, Nebr., 1973-74, 85-87, Scottsdale (Ariz.) Pub. Schs., 1974-76; resource tchr., cons. Universal Am. Sch., Kuwait, 1977-78, Am. Sch. Kuwait, 1979, Al Bayan Sch., Kuwait, 1979-82; pvt. practice Susan Kawmy Lang. and Learning Specialist, Kuwait, 1976-84; resource tchr., diagnostician Hastings Pub. Schs., 1986-87, 90-91; spl. edn. cons. Kawmy and Assocs., Kuwait, 1987-89; outreach project dir. Kuwait Spl. Edn. Soc., 1989—; pvt. practice Cairo, 1991—, Dubai, Kuwait, 1992, Jeddah, Saudi Arabia, 1992-93, Riyadh, Saudi Arabia, 1993—. Cons. Al Bayan Sch., Ctr. for Evaluation and Teaching; founder, mem. sch. bd. Khalifeh Sch.; designer mainstream support team Kuwait Pvt. Schs.; spl. cons. New Spl. Needs Sch., Kuwait, Spl. Edn. Libr. for Women, Jeddah. Mem. Mental Health Specialists Support Group. Mem. Kuwait Spl. Edn. Soc., YWCA Internat. Club. Republican. Episcopalian. Avocations: horseback riding, swimming, reading, gardening. Home: Joumaiah Bottling Co PO Box 210 Riyadh Saudi Arabia also: c/o Dr J G Yost RR 4 Box 4 Hastings NE 68901-9804

KAY, CYRIL MAX, biochemist, educator; b. Calgary, Alta., Can., Oct. 3, 1931; s. Louis and Fanny (Pearlmutter) K.; m. Faye Bloomenthal, Dec. 30, 1953; children: Lewis Edward, Lisa Franci. B.Sc. in Biochemistry with honors (J.W. McConnell Meml. scholar), McGill U., 1952; PhD in Biochemistry (Life Ins. Med. Research Fund fellow), Harvard U., 1956; postgrad., Cambridge (Eng.) U., 1956-57. Phys. biochemist Eli Lilly & Co., Indpls., 1957-58; asst. prof. biochemistry U. Alta., Edmonton, 1958-61, assoc. prof., 1961-67, prof., 1967—, co-dir. Med. Rsch. Coun. Group on Protein Structure and Function, 1974-95, mem. protein engring. network Centre of Excellence, 1990—, chmn. internat. rsch. adv. com. to protein engring. network Centre of Excellence, 2000—; v.p. rsch. Alta. Cancer Bd., 1999—. Med. Rsch. Coun. vis. scientist in biophysics Weizmann Inst., Israel, 1969-70, summer vis. prof. biophysics, 1975, summer vis. prof. chem. physics, 1977, 80; mem. biochemistry grants com. Med. Research Council, 1970-73; mem. Med. Rsch. Coun. Can., 1982-88; Can. rep. Pan Am. Assn. Biochem. Socs., 1971-76; mem. exec. planning com. XI Internat. Congress Biochemistry, Toronto, Ont., Can., 1979; mem. med. adv. bd. Gairdner Found. for Internat. awards in Med. Sci., 1980-89; chmn. Internat. Scientific adv. com. on protein engring., 2000—. Contbr. numerous articles to profl. publs.; asso. editor Can. Jour. Biochemistry, 1968-82; editor-in-chief Pan Am. Assn. Biochem. Socs. Revista, 1971-76. Decorated Order of Can.; recipient Ayerst award in biochemistry Can. Biochem. Soc., 1970, Disting. Scientist award U. Alta. Med. Sch., 1988. Fellow N.Y. Acad. Scis., Royal Soc. Can.; mem. Order of Can., Can. Biochem. Soc. (coun. 1971—, v.p. 1976-77, pres. 1978-79). Home: 9408-143d St Edmonton AB Canada T5R 0P7 Office: U Alta Dept Biochemistry Med Scis Bldg Edmonton AB Canada T6G 2H7 E-mail: ckay@gpu.srv.ualberta.ca.

KAY, DOUGLAS HAROLD, optometrist, educator; b. Oakland, Calif., Oct. 7, 1949; s. Marvin Jack and Lois Natalie (Bernstein) K. AB, U. Calif., 1971, BS in Optometry, 1973, OD, 1975. Registered optometrist. Optometrist Calif. Assoc. Woodland Clin. Med. Group, Davis, 1975-78; cons. Calif. Vision Svc. Plan, Sacramento, 1977-82; pvt. practice optometry, Davis, 1978—; indsl. vision cons. Hunt-Wesson Foods, 1980—99. Asst. clin. prof. Sch. Optometry, U. Calif., Berkeley, 1983-93; chmn. supervisory com. Calif. Optometric Credit Union; pres. Calif. Vision Project, 1996-98; expert witness Calif. State Bd. Optometry, 1995—; clin. examiner Nat. Bd. Examiners in Optometry, 1995—; qualified med. evaluator Calif. Indsl. Med. Cou. Dept. Indsl. Rels., 1994—. Bd. dirs. Valley Artist Prodns., Libr. Assocs., U. Calif., Davis, Salvation Army, Davis., Econ. Devel. Coun. Davis, 1985-87; mem. Davis Comic Opera Co.; chmn. south Davis Traffic Study Com., 1984, Davis 2000 Study Com., 1985; trustee Sutter Cmty. Health Found., 1998—. Mem. Am. Optometric Assn. (chmn. polit. action com. Calif., nat. keyperson coord. 1995-96, mem. coun. contact lens sect. 1997—), Calif. Optometric Assn. (trustee 1993-96, chair polit. action com. 1996-98), Sacramento Valley Optometric Soc. (pres. 1985-86, Young Optometrist of Yr. 1981, Optometrist of Yr. 1997), Vision Conservation Inst., C. of C. (dir. membership Davis Area (sec. 1981-93), Rotary asst. sec. 1993-2003). Office: 1111 Kennedy Pl Ste 6 Davis CA 95616-1266

KAY, HERMA HILL, education educator; b. Orangeburg, S.C., Aug. 18, 1934; d. Charles Esdorn and Herma Lee (Crawford) Hill. BA, So. Meth. U., 1956; JD, U. Chgo., 1959. Bar: Calif. 1960, U.S. Supreme Ct. 1978. Law clk. to Hon. Roger Traynor Calif. Supreme Ct., 1959-60; from asst. prof. to assoc. prof. law U. Calif., Berkeley, 1960-62, prof., 1963, dir. family law project, 1964-67, Jennings prof., 1987-96, dean, 1992-2000, Armstrong prof., 1996—; co-reporter uniform marriage and div. act Nat. Conf. Commrs. on Uniform State Laws, 1968-70. Vis. prof. U. Manchester, England, 1972, Harvard U., 1976; mem. Gov.'s Commn. Family, 1966. Author (with Martha S. West): (book) Text Cases and Materials on Sex-Based Discrimination, 5th edit., 2002; author: (with D. Currie and L. Kramer) Conflict of Laws: Cases, Comments, Questions, 6th edit., 2001; contbr. articles to profl. jours. Trustee Russell Sage Found., NY, 1972—87, chmn. bd. trustees, 1980—84; trustee, bd. dirs. Equal Rights Advs., Calif., 1987—88, chmn., 1976—83; pres., bd. dirs. Rosenberg Found., Calif., 1987—88, bd. dirs., 1978—. Recipient Rsch. award, Am. Bar Found., 1990, Margaret Brent award, ABA Commn. Women in Profession, 1992, Marshall-Wythe medal, 1995; fellow, Ctr. Advanced Study Behavioral Sci., Palo Alto, Calif., 1963. Mem.: ABA (sect. legal edn. and admissions to bar coun. 1992—99, sec. 1999—2001), Order of Coif (nat. pres. 1983—85), Am. Philos. Soc., Am. Acad. Arts and Scis., Assn. Am. Law Schs. (exec. com. 1986—87, pres.-elect 1988, pres. 1989, past pres. 1990), Am. Law Inst. (mem. coun. 1985—), Calif. Women Lawyers (bd. govs. 1975—77), Bar U.S. Supreme Ct., Calif. Bar Assn. Democrat. Office: U Calif Law Sch Boalt Hall Berkeley CA 94720-7200 E-mail: kayh@law.berkeley.edu.

KAY, JAMES FRANKLIN, religion educator; b. Kansas City, Mo., May 18, 1948; s. Bob Burton and Mary Lenore (Branstetter) K. BA, Pasadena (Calif.) Coll., 1969; MDiv, Harvard U., 1972; MPhil, Union Seminary, N.Y.C., 1984, PhD, 1991. Pastor No. Lakes Parish, Beltrami County, Minn., 1974-78; campus minister United Ministries, Bemidji, Minn., 1977-79; cons. PHEWA, N.Y.C., 1980-82; instr. Princeton Theol. Seminary, NJ, 1988-91, asst. prof., 1991-95, assoc. prof., 1995-97, Joe R. Engle assoc. prof., 1997-2001, Joe R. Engle prof., 2001—, chair dept. practical theology, 2001—; dir. Joe R. Eagle Inst. Preaching, 2002—. Warrack lectr. St. Andrews U., Scotland, 1997. Author: Christus Praesens, 1994, Seasons of Grace, 1994; editor: Women, Gender, and Christian Community, 1997; book rev. editor The Princeton Sem. Bull., 1991-94. editor, 1994-2000. Vice-pres. Bemidji Home Loan Improvement, 1978. Mem. Am. Acad. Religion, Acad. Homiletics, Duodecim Theol. Soc., Karl Barth Soc. of N.A., New Haven Theol. Discussion Group, Phi Delta Lambda. Office: Princeton Theol Seminary PO Box 821 Princeton NJ 08542-0803 E-mail: james.kay@ptsem.edu., drjfkay@aol.com.

KAYE, GAIL LESLIE, healthcare consultant, educator; b. Upland, Pa., Aug. 6, 1955; d. Ronald E. and Doris T. (Welfley) K. BS, W.Va. Welseyan Coll., 1977; MS, Ohio State U., 1982, PhD, 1989. Lic. profl. clin. counselor; registered dietitian. Asst. dir. food svc., chief clin. dietitian Albert Einstein Med. Ctr., Phila., 1983; asst. prof. Ind. State U., Terre Haute, 1983-85; nutrition cons. Ohio State U. Hosp. Clinics, Columbus, 1986-88, grad. rsch. asst., 1986-89; legis. rep. Ohio Assocs. Counseling and Devel., Columbus, 1988-89; rsch. cons. State Dept. Edn., Columbus, 1988-89; lectr. counselor edn. Ohio State U., Columbus, 1989-93; program devel. and clin. rschr. Ross Labs., Columbus, 1990-94; pres. Kaye Consultation Svcs., Inc., 1994—. Mem. faculty dept. human nutrition Ohio State U., 1998—, dir. MS/DI program in diebetics. Inventor in field; contbr. articles to profl. jours. Recipient Pres. award Ohio Mental Health Counselors Assn., 1990. Mem. Am. Dietetics Assn., Ohio Dietetics Assn. Avocations: swimming, piano, reading, hiking, painting, theatre. Home and Office: 365 Helmbright Dr Gahanna OH 43230-3290

KAYE, JANET MIRIAM, psychologist, educator; b. New Haven, Mar. 2, 1937; d. Al and Rose (Marcus) Sovitsky; m. Donald Kaye, June 26, 1955; children: Kenneth, Karen, Kendra, Keith. BS, NYU, 1958, MA, 1960; PhD, Med. Coll. of Pa., 1980. Clin. instr. Med. Coll. Pa., Phila., 1980-82, asst. prof., 1982-86, assoc. prof., 1986-94, Med. Coll. Pa. Hahnemann Sch. Medicine, Phila., 1994-96, prof., 1996—2002; prof. coll. medicine Drexel U., Phila., 2002—. Contbr. articles to profl. jours. Mem. APA, Am. Assn. Cancer Edn., Am. Soc. Clin. Hypnosis, Soc. Health and Human Values, Gerontol. Soc. Am., Am. Soc. Psychiat. Oncology, Coll. Physicians Pa., Internat. Soc. Exptl. Hypnosis. Avocations: jogging, working out, swimming, reading.

KAYE, ROBERT, pediatrics educator; b. NYC, July 17, 1917; s. Harry and Anna (Brisk) K.; m. Ellen Eskin, Nov. 16, 1960; children: Elizabeth, Margaret, Hillary, Sanford, Anthony. BA, Johns Hopkins U., 1939, MD, 1943. Intern Johns Hopkins Hosp., Balt., 1943, resident, 1944-45; instr. pediatrics Johns Hopkins Med. Sch., Balt., 1945; assoc. physiology Harvard Sch. Pub. Health, 1946-48; prof. pediatrics U. Pa., 1964-73, 86-88; prof., chmn. pediatrics Hahnemann Med. Coll. and Hosp., Phila., 1973-86; chmn. dept. pediatrics Med. Coll. Pa., Phila., 1988-92, prof., 1992-95; prof. emeritus Med. Coll. Pa., U. Pa., Hahnemann Med Coll., Phila. Contbr. articles to profl. jours. With U.S. Army, 1942—46. Nat. Found. Infantile Paralysis fellow, 1946-48. Mem. AAAS, Am. Pediatric Soc., Soc. Pediatric Rsch., Am. Diabetes Assn., Brodhead Forest and Stream Assn., Bala Golf Club. Jewish. Home: 200 Locust St Apt 22bc Philadelphia PA 19106-3914

KAYE JOHNSON, SUSAN, educational consultant; b. N.Y.C., Jan. 23, 1932; d. Albert and Goldie (Feldman) Sroge; m. Carroll F. Johnson, Jan. 16, 1990; children from previous marriage: Richard M. Kaye, Gillian Kaye Karran. BA in History, Bklyn. Coll., 1953, MS in Counseling, 1958; MEd in Adminstrn., Columbia U., 1976, EdD in Adminstrn., 1978. Cert. adminstr., supr. N.Y., N.J., guidance counselor, history tchr., N.Y. Tchr. 3d grade Ollie Perry Storm Sch., San Antonio, 1954-55; tchr. social studies Jr. High Sch. 214, Bklyn., 1955-57; guidance counselor Jr. High Schs. 214 and 10, Bklyn., 1957-59; evaluation asst., coord. career devel. Great Neck (N.Y.) Pub. Sch., 1966-71, dir. chpt. I, 1971-79; dir. pupil svcs. Bellmore-Merrick High Sch. Dist., Long Island, N.Y., 1979-83; asst. supt. schs. Longwood Sch. Dist., Middle Island, N.Y., 1983-89; supt. schs. Florham Park (N.J.) Pub. Schs., 1989-92; ednl. cons. Longboat Key, Fla., 1992—; adminstr. Sarasota (Fla.) Safe Place and Rape Crisis Ctr., 1996-97. Chair women's caucus Am. Assn. Sch. Adminstrs., 1980-82; cons. superintendency searches, Casper Wym., St. Loius, Mo., Riverdell, N.J., Monctair, N.J., Manatee City, Fla. Co-author: An Analysis of Problems in a School District, 1980, Managing Schools in Hard Times, 1981. Assoc. trustee Dowling Coll., Long Island, 1983-87; trustee Women Svcs. Divsn., Brookhaven, N.Y., 1986, Brookhaven Twp. Youth Bd., 1987, Adult Sch., Florham Park, 1989-92; adv. commn. on the status of women Sarasota County, Sarasota, Fla. Mem. AAUW, NOW, Archael. Inst. Am., Phi Delta Kappa. Avocations: archaeology, tennis. Home and Office: 2077 Gulf Of Mexico Dr Longboat Key FL 34228-3202

KAYWELL, JOAN, education educator; b. West Palm Beach, Fla., Mar. 1, 1956; d. Bernard E. and Grace H. Kaywell; 1 child, Stephen Matthew. BA in Edn., U. Fla., 1979, MEd, 1980, PhD, 1987. Prof. U. South Fla. Coll. Edn., Tampa, 1988—, interim chair secondary edn. Award winning tchr. and presenter in field. Author: Adolescent Literature as a Complement to the Classics (4 vols. 1993, 95, 97, 2000), Adolescents At Risk: A Guide to Fiction & Nonfiction for Young Adults, Parents and Professionals, 1993; series editor Using Literature to Help Troubled Teenagers Cope, 6-book series, 1999, 2000, 2001. Mem.: ASCD, Assembly on Lit. for Adolescents (past pres.), Fla. Coun. Tchrs. English (past pres., Honor award 2000), Eastern Ednl. Rsch. Assn., Am. Ednl. Rsch. Assn., Nat. Coun. Tchrs. English, Tau Beta Sigma, Phi Delta Kappa. Avocations: cooking, boating, writing, reading. Office: U South Fla Coll Edn 162 Tampa FL 33620-5650

KAZHDAN, DAVID, mathematician, educator; b. Moscow, June 20, 1946; came to U.S., 1975; s. Alexander and Rimma (Ivanskaya) K.; m. Helena Slobodkina, Mar. 22, 1968; children: Eli, Dina, Misha, Daniel. MA, Moscow State U., 1967, PhD, 1969; BA (hon), Harvard U., 1977. Researcher Moscow State U., 1969-75, vis. prof., 1975-77; prof. Harvard U., Cambridge, Mass., 1977—. MacArthur fellow. Mem. NAS. Office: Harvard U 1 Oxford St Cambridge MA 02138-2901

KAZIMI, MUJID SULIMAN, nuclear engineer, educator; b. Jerusalem, Nov. 20, 1947; came to U.S., 1969; s. Suliman Ishak Kazimi and Fikrat Nuseibeh; m. Nazik D. Denny, Sept. 1, 1973. B. Engring., Alexandria U., Arab Republic of Egypt, 1969; MS, MIT, 1971, PhD, 1973. Sr. engr. Westinghouse Electric Corp., Madison, Pa., 1973-74; assoc. scientist Brookhaven Nat. Lab., Upton, N.Y., 1974-76; asst. prof. MIT, Cambridge, 1976-79, assoc. prof., 1979-86, prof., 1986—, head dept. nuclear engring., 1989-97. Tokyo Elec. Power Co. (TEPCO) chair for nuc. engring. at MIT, 2000—; dir. Ctr. Advanced Nuc. Energy Systems, 2000—; chmn. high-level waste tank safety adv. panel U.S. Dept. Energy, Washington, 1990-95, chmn. new prodn. reactor severe accident group, 1990-91. Co-author: (with Neil Todreas) Nuclear Systems: Volume I: Thermal Hydraulic Fundamentals, 1990, Nuclear Systems: Volume II: Elements of Thermal Hydraulic Design, 1990; editor: Perspectives on Technological Development in the Arab World, 1978. Pres. Assn. Arab-Am. Univ. Grads., Belmont, Mass., 1980, 87. Fellow Am. Nuclear Soc. (bd. dirs. N.E. chpt. 1978, 80, exec. com. thermal hydraulics divsn. 1988-90); mem. ASME, AAAS, AIChE (chmn. nuclear heat transfer com. 1980-83), Am. Soc. for Engring. Edn. (exec. com. nuclear engring. divsn. 1995-97). Office: MIT Dept Nuc Engring 77 Massachusetts Ave Rm 24-215 Cambridge MA 02139-4307 E-mail: kazimi@mit.edu.

KAZMAREK, LINDA ADAMS, secondary education educator; b. Crisfield, Md., Jan. 18, 1945; d. Gordon I. Sr. and Annie Ruby (Sommers) Adams; m. Stephen Kazmarek, Jr., Aug. 2, 1981. B of Music Edn., Peabody Conservatory of Music, 1967; postgrad., Morgan U., Towson U. Cert. advanced profl. tchr., K-12, Md.; nat. cert. tchr. Mayron Cole piano method. Organist, choir dir. Halethorpe United Meth. Ch., Balt., min. music, 1978-92, 93-99; organist, choir dir. Olive Branch United Meth. Ch., 1973-77, 1978-83, 93—; piano tchr. Modal Cities Program, Balt., Balt. Community Schs; tchr. vocal music Balt. City Schs., 1967-99; min. music Halethorpe Meth. Ch., 1978-92, 93-99, St. John's Episcopal Parish Day Sch., 1999-2001; music specialist. Piano accompanist Witness Sing, 2000, Christian Choir, 2000-01; pianist Chestnut Ridge Bapt. Ch., 2001; pianist and performer Joppa Gospel Tabernacle, 2002-; pvt. tchr. piano and organ, concert artist. Composer, arranger: A Family of Care (award, 1991, Praise Song, 1992, Thy Way, Lord, 1993, Peace and Rest, 1994, Sing Praise to Jesus, 1994, Trilogy for piano solo, 1994, Shine Your Light, 1994, Resurrection, 1995, 1-800-Heaven, 1995, God Has A Plan for You, 1995, Christmas Joy, 1998, His Name is Jesus, 1998, Only Love, 1999, Be Still and Listen, 1999, Awesome Love, 2001, The Gifts of the Vine, 2002, (piano arrangements) The First Noel, Angels We Have Heard on High, O Come All Ye Faithful, All Through the Night/Lullaby, I Heard the Bells on Christmas Day/Silent Night Christmas Medley, I Saw Three Ships; rec. Christmas CD His Name is Jesus, 2000, Gifts of the Vine, 2002; guest performer S.W. Emergency Svcs., 1999, Joppa Gospel Tabernacle; CD Praise, Peace and Promise, 2002; rec. America the Beautiful/America, Jesus Loves Me, The Promise, Blessings, His Eye Is on the Sparrow, I Bowed on My Knees and Cried Holy, Praising My Saviour, 2002. Concert perfomer for Halethorpe Meth. Ch., 1994, Meth. Bd. Child Care, 1989, Balt. S.W. Emergency Svcs., 1991; guest performer Balt. City Tchrs. Appreciation Banquet, 1991, S.W.E.S. 18th Yr. Celebration, 1999; concert artist and performer, 2001—. Recipient vol. award for music enrichment summer program, 1973, award for voluntarism Fund. for Ednl. Excellence, 1985; Fund for Ednl. Excellence grantee, 1988. Mem. NEA, Md. State Tchrs. Assn., Balt. City Tchrs. Assn., Md. Music Educators Assn. (award for 30 yrs. of svc. in music and music edn. 1997), Music Educators Nat. Conf., Md. State Music Tchrs. Assn., Nat. Music Tchrs. Assn., Gospel Music Assn., Peabody Alumni Assn. E-mail: Kazmarekl@comcast.net.

KAZRAGYS, LINDA KAYAN BUBLIS, elementary school educator; b. East Chicago, Ind., Nov. 26, 1946; d. Bert Charles and Irma Aldonna (Matuck) Bublis; m. Vitas Joseph Kazragys, June 22, 1968; children: Amanda, Julianna, Adam. BSE, Ball State U., 1968; MSE, Purdue U., 1984. Elem. tchr. East Chicago Pub. Schs., 1968-70, 73-78; dir. nursery sch. St. John the Bapt. Sch., Whiting, Ind., 1978-83, elem. tchr. Dicoese of Gary, 1983—, mem. home and sch. com., chair lang. arts and sci. dept. On-site rev. team performance based accreditation INd. Dept. Edn. Dir. adult edn. Girl Scouts Calumet Council, Highland, Ind., 1982-84. Recipient St. Anne's award Girl Scouts of Calumet Council, Gary, Ind., 1972, Thanks Badge, Highland, Ind., 1978. Mem. Nat. Cath. Educators Assn. Democrat. Avocations: traveling, outdoor activities, reading, art, music. Home: 2028 Lake Ave Whiting IN 46394-1832 Office: St John the Bapt Sch 1844 Lincoln Ave Whiting IN 46394-1532

KEA, JONATHAN GUY, instrumental music educator; b. Honolulu, June 2, 1960; s. Gilbert Halemano and Goldie Lee Gum (Chun) K. BMus, cert. teaching, Coe Coll., Cedar Rapids, Iowa, 1982. Band dir. James Campbell High Sch., Ewa Beach, Hawaii, 1982—. Asst. condr. Honolulu Cmty. Band, 1988-94; dir. Honolulu Cmty. Jazz Band, 1993—. Mem. NEA, Oahu Band Dirs. Assn., Hawaii Music Educators Assn., Music Educators Nat. Conf., Phi Mu Alpha. Office: James Campbell High Sch 91-980 North Rd Ewa Beach HI 96706-2746

KEAN, THOMAS H. academic administrator, former governor; b. N.Y.C., Apr. 21, 1935; m. Deborah Bye; children: Thomas, Reed, Alexandra. AB, Princeton; MA, Columbia. Tchr. history and govt.; mem. N.J. Assembly, 1967-77, speaker, 1972, minority leader, 1974; acting gov., 1973; gov., 1981-89; pres. Drew U., Madison, N.J., 1990—. Bd. dirs. Beneficial Corp., Carnegie Corp. of N.Y., Robert Wood Johnson Found. Bd. dirs. World Wildlife Fund/Conservation Found. Address: Drew U Ofc of Pres 36 Madison Ave Madison NJ 07940-1434*

KEANE, JOHN PATRICK, retired secondary education educator; b. N.Y.C., Nov. 28, 1931; s. John and Mary (Walsh) K.; m. Lucille Ann Dunn, Apr. 3, 1976. BA in English, Iona Coll., 1954; JD, Fordham U., 1963, MS in Edn., 1965; EdM, Columbia U., 1973; MA in English, CUNY, 1984. Cert. secondary tchr. (English), adminstr., N.Y.C., N.Y. State. Tchr. area jr. h.s., N.Y.C., 1962-65; tchr. h.s. English N.Y.C. Bd. Edn., Bklyn., 1965-93; dean of boys W.H. Taft H.S., Bronx, 1969-72; reading, writing coord. John F. Kennedy H.S., Bronx, 1985-91; tchr. English advanced placement John F. Kennedy H.S., Manhattan Coll., Bronx, 1991-93, retired, 1993. Editor, compiler: (manual) Handbook for Teachers of Reading and Writing, 1987, Writing Sampler (student's work), 1989-91 biannual. Founder Hamilton Heights Dems., 1965-69; candidate N.Y. State Assembly, 1965; Dem. candidate 1st Selectman, North Stonington, 1997; past mem. North Stonington, Conn. Bd. Edn; justice of peace North Stonington; chmn. North Stonington Dem. Town Com.; music min. St. Mary's Ch., Groton. MA thesis placed on permanent display as model, Lehman Coll., CUNY, Bronx, 1984. Mem. NEA (del. local 2), Am. Fedn. Tchrs. (del. local 2), United Fedn. Tchrs. (del N.Y. State, chpt. leader, unity com.), N.Y. State United Tchrs., Delta Kappa Pi, Phi Delta Kappa. Roman Catholic. Avocations: poetry, drama, environmentalist. Home: 6 Wyassup Lake Rd North Stonington CT 06359-1124

KEANE HERNANDEZ, NOREEN B(ERNADETTE), elementary education educator; b. Louisburg, Mayo, Ireland, Feb. 10, 1947; came to U.S., 1972. d. Austin and Bridget Theresa (O'Malley) Keane; m. Pablo Arturo Hernandez, June 17, 1972; children: Tara Marie Hernandez, Sean Paul Hernandez. BA, Univ. Coll., Dublin, Ireland, 1972, BS, 1976; MA, U. Tex., San Antonio, 1988. Cert. tchr., reading specialist, supr., Tex. Tchr. elem. edn. Little Flower Cath. Sch., San Antonio, 1983-84, Buena Vista Elem. Sch., San Antonio, 1984-86, Lackland Elem. Sch., San Antonio, 1986—. Mem. ASCD, Internat. Reading Assn., Nat. Coun. Social Studies, Nat. Coun. Tchrs. English, Lackland Tchrs. Assn. (sec. 1988-89, 92-93, historian 1989-90). Republican. Roman Catholic. Avocations: traveling, music, poetry, reading, arts and crafts.

KEANINI, RUSSELL GUY, mechanical engineering educator, researcher; b. Denver, June 29, 1959; s. Russell Eldridge and Patricia Ann (Regan) K.; m. Tracy Jo. BS, Colo. Sch. of Mines, Golden, 1983; MS, U. Colo., Denver, 1987; PhD, U. Calif., Berkeley, 1992. Bldg. specialist Nicor Exploration, Golden, 1984-85; structural designer Commerce City Supply, 1985-86; grad. rsch. asst. U. of Colo., Denver, 1985-87, U. of Calif., Berkeley, Calif., 1987-92; asst. prof. U. N.C., Charlotte, 1992-98, assoc. prof., 1998—. Contbr. articles to profl. jours. Recipient Engring. Found. Rsch. Initiation award Engring. Found. and ASME, 1993-94, Alcoa Found. award, 1995, Jr. Faculty Enhancement award Oak Ridge Assoc. Univs., 1995; Colo. Sch. Mines scholar, 1982-83; NASA grad. rsch. fellow, 1988-89. Mem. AIAA, ASME, Am. Phys. Soc. Office: U NC Charlotte Dept Mech Engring Charlotte NC 28223 Home: 16014 Woodcote Drive Huntersville NC 28078 E-mail: rkeanini@uncc.edu.

KEARFOTT, KIMBERLEE JANE, nuclear engineer, health physicist, educator; b. Oakland, Calif., Jan. 30, 1956; d. William Edward and Edith (Chamberlin) K. BSc, St. Mary's U., Halifax, N.S., Can., 1975; ME in Nuclear Engring., U. Va., 1977; ScD, MIT, 1980. Coop. engr. Babcock & Wilcox Co., Lynchburg, Va., 1975-77; rsch. asst. Mass. Gen. Hosp., Boston, 1980; asst. prof. Cornell U. Med. Sch., N.Y.C., 1980-84; rsch. assoc. Sloan-Kettering Cancer Ctr., N.Y.C., 1980-84; from asst. to assoc. prof. Ariz. State U., Tempe, 1984-89; assoc. prof. Ga. Inst. Tech., Atlanta, 1989-93; assoc. prof. Med. Sch. Emory U., Atlanta, 1990-93; prof. U. Mich., Ann Arbor, 1993—, dir. faculty devel. Coll. Engring., 1994-97. Contbr. articles to Jour. Health Physics, Jour. of Nuc. Medicine, Jour. Computer Assisted Tomography, Jour. Med. Physics. Mem. IEEE, AAUW, Am. Nuc. Soc. (bd. dirs. 1996-01, Women's Achievement award 1995), Soc. Nuc. Medicine (Tetalman award 1991), Assn. Women in Sci., Soc. Women Engrs., Health Physics Soc. (bd. dirs. 1992-95, Anderson award 1992), Order of Engr. Office: U Mich Dept Nuclear Engring and Radiol Sci Ann Arbor MI 48109-2104

KEARNEY, ANNA ROSE, history educator; b. Mount Pleasant, Pa., Mar. 1, 1940; d. John Joseph and Marguerite Costello (Gettings) K. BA, St. Mary's Coll., Notre Dame, Ind., 1962; MA, U. Notre Dame, 1967, PhD, 1975; MLS, Ind. U., 1983; JD, U. Louisville, 2002. Cert. tchr., Pa. Tchr. Hempfield Area Schs., Greensburg, Pa., 1962-66, Mishawaka (Ind.) Sch. Dist., 1967-68; teaching asst. U. Notre Dame, 1968-70, libr. clk., 1974-76, libr. assoc., 1976-86; divsn. chair gen. edn. Ind. Vo-Tech. Coll., South Bend, 1970-72; asst. to univ. libr. U. Louisville, 1986-89; prof. Am. history Jefferson C.C./Ky. Tech. and C.C., Louisville, 1989—. Faculty cons. Ednl. Testing Svc., San Antonio, 1993, 96, 2000, 01. Contbr. articles to profl. jours. Judge Nat. History Day, Louisville and Indpls., 1990-94; exec. on loan United Way of St. Joseph County, South Bend, 1982; food coord. Ethnic Festival, South Bend, 1974; lector Our Lady of Lourdes Ch., Louisville, 1987—. Grantee U. Louisville, 1987, U. Notre Dame, 1988, Ky. Libr. Assn., 1988, NEH, 1990-92, 95. Mem. Assn. of Coll. and Rsch. Librs. (exec. com. for 5th nat. conf. 1987-89), Orgn. Am. Historians, So. Hist. Assn., Cath. Hist. Assn., Ky. Assn. Tchrs. History, Nat. Coun. of Women's Studies Assn., St. Mary's Coll. South Bend Alumnae Assn. (pres. 1984-85), Phi Alpha Theta. Democrat. Roman Catholic. Avocations: knitting, sewing, reading, computers. Home: 3316 Cawein Way Louisville KY 40220-1908 Office: Jefferson Cmty Coll/KCTCS 109 E Broadway Louisville KY 40202-2005

KEARNEY, BONNIE HELEN, elementary education educator; b. Greenwood, Miss., Feb. 17, 1947; d. John Whitfield and Beryl Alice (Brewerton) K. BA in Edn., U. Miss., 1969, MS in Early Edn., 1970. Cert. early childhood tchr., elementary tchr., English Speakers of Other Langs., Fla. Tchr.kindergarten Mirror Lake Elem., Plantation, Fla., 1970-71, 72—, tchr. 1st grade, 1971-72, tchr. phys. edn., 1974-75. Tchr. kindergarten summer sch. Lauderdale Paul Turner Elem., Lauderhill, Fla., 1981. Campaign worker mayoral election, Plantation, Fla., 1971-72; mem. com. St. Patrick's Day parade, Fort Lauderdale, Fla., 1988—. Recipient Superior Science Class Project Broward County (Fla.) Sci. Fair, 1987-92, Excellent in County, 1989, Best in Show, 1991. Mem. NEA. Democrat. Presbyterian. Avocations: swimming, boating, seasonal decorating, cooking. Office: Mirror Lake Elementary 1200 NW 72nd Ave Fort Lauderdale FL 33313-6095

KEARNEY, LINDA LEE, secondary education educator; b. Pitts., Sept. 6, 1947; d. Richard Joseph Bracco and Vada Ilene (Conner) Bracco Learn; m. Charles Ray Kearney, June 12, 1971; children: Robert Charles, Richard Leslie, Debra June. BS in Edn., Clarion (Pa.) State U., 1969; MEd Equivalency, Pa. State U., 1975. Tchr. English 11th and 12th grade DuBois (Pa.) Area Sch. Dist., 1969—2002, secondary lead tchr., 1994; lead tchr., mem. profl. devel. and gifted adv. coms., 1991-94; ptnr. Human Tng. Cons., 2001—. Co-founder, adviser Kids Saving Kids Club, DuBois Area Jr. H.S., 1988—; advisor sr. h.s. yearbook, 1996-2000; coord. Sch. Excellence Program 2000, 1997-98, peer mediation coord., 1996-2002, grad. project com., 1999—, sr. h.s. co-coord. peer mediation program 2000-02. Chair edn. com., Sunday sch. supr. Moorhead Meth. Sch., Brockway, Pa., 1988-90; neighborhood dir. Brockway Girl Scouts, 1993—, coord. Rising Star Girl Scout Area Tng.; coord., mem. coun. splty. and coun. trainer Keystone Tall Tree, Brockway, 1990—; mem. Brockway Recreation Bd., 1996—; dir. Brockway Sch., 1999—; mem. Brockway Recreation Bd., 1999-2001; regional cabinet mem. PSBA, 2000-02. Recipient Cross and Flame award Moorhead United Meth. Ch., 1996; mini-grantee or grantee Pa. Acad. for Execllence in Tchg. and Intermediate Unit 6, 1992; Pa. Rivers Writing Project fellow, 1990. Mem. Nat. Coun. Tchrs. English, DuBois Area Edn. Assn. (1st v.p.), Delta Kappa Gamma, Alpha Sigma Alpha (chpt. pres. 1967-68). Avocations: reading, camping, gardening, writing, crafts. Home: RR 2 Box 415A Brockway PA 15824-9453 Office: 400 Orient Ave Du Bois PA 15801-2436

KEARNEY, PATRICIA ANN, university administrator; b. Wilkes-Barre, Pa., May 15, 1943; d. William F. and Helen L. (Hartz) K. BA, Mich. State U., 1965; MSEd, Ind. U., 1966. Head resident advisor Western Ill. U., Macomb, 1966-68; asst. v.p. SUNY, Buffalo, 1968-70; asst. dean student life Lock Haven (Pa.) State Coll., 1970-72; dir. residential life U. Calif., Davis, 1974-83, bus. mgr., 1983-85, dir. housing and food services, 1985-95, exec. dir. housing and fin. aid, 1996—. Speaker nat. and state convs. Contbr. articles to profl. jours. Mem. Am. Coll. Personnel Assn. (pres.), Assn. Coll. and U. Housing Officers Internat., Sierra Club. Avocations: tennis, cross country skiing, hiking, cooking. Home: 4155 Tallman Ln Winters CA 95694-9660 Office: U Calif 127 Student Housing Davis CA 95616

KEARNEY-NUNNERY, ROSE, nursing administrator, educator, consultant; b. Glen Falls, NY, July 8, 1951; d. James J. and Helen F. (Oprandy) K.; m. Jimmie E. Nunnery. BS(hon.), Keuka Coll., 1973; M of nursing, U. Fla., 1976, PhD, 1987. Asst. prof. La. State U. Med. Ctr., New Orleans, 1976-87; project coord., indigent health care U. Fla., Gainesville, 1984-85; asst. prof. U. of South Fla., Tampa, Fla., 1987-88; dir. nursing programs State Univ. of N.Y., New Paltz, NY, 1988-94; project dir. MS in gerontol. nursing advanced nursing edn. grant U.S. Health Resources and Svc. Adminstrn. Div. Nursing, 1992-94; head nursing dept. Tech. Coll. of the Low Country, Beaufort, SC, 1995-97, v.p. acad. affairs, 1997—. Author: Advancing Your Profession Concepts for Profl. Nursing, 1997, Advancing Your Profession: Concepts for Profl. Nursing, 2001. Bd. dirs. Beaufort Co. First Steps, 2000-01; Ulster County unit Am. Cancer Soc., 1991-94; nursing edn. com., 1990-92; bd. dir. Mid-Hudson Consortium for Advancement Edn. for Health Profl., 1988-94; nursing edn. com., 1988-92; scholarship com., 1989-93; com. chmn., 1990-93, treas., 1992-94; prof. devel. program SUNY, Albany, 1989-92; adv. coun. Ulster CC, 1989-94; adv. regional planning group for early intervention svc. United Cerebral Palsy Ulster County Inc., Children's Rehab. Ctr., 1989-91; mem. Ulster County adv. com. Office for Aging, 1991-94; state del. S.C. Conf. on Aging, 1995; bd. dir. Beaufort County Coun. on Aging, 1995; cmty. adv. bd. Hilton Head Med. Ctr. and Clinics, 1996-2000; mem. SC Bd. Nursing, 2000—, pres. 2000-03; accreditation evaluator So. Assn. Coll. and Sch. Commn. on Coll. Mem. ANA, S.C. Nurses Assn. (editl. bd. 1994-99, chair 1996-99); Nat. Coun. of State Bd. of Nursing (mem. practice, regulation, and edn. com. 2001—); Sigma Theta Tau. Roman Catholic. Home: 80 Peninsula Dr Hilton Head Island SC 29926-1119

KEARNS, ELLEN HOPE, health sciences educator; b. N.Y.C., Apr. 25, 1942; AA, Lasell Jr. Coll., Auberndale, Mass., 1961; BS with honors, N.Y. Inst. Tech., 1976; MS with honors, SUNY, Stony Brook, 1987. Med. technologist New Eng. Deaconess Hosp., Brookline, Mass., 1962-64; rsch. asst. pathology lab. Cancer Rsch. Inst., Brookline, Mass., 1964-66; lab. supr. North Shore Univ. Hosp. Cornell Med. Ctr., Manhasset, N.Y., 1973-84; asst. prof. med. tech. SUNY, Stony Brook, N.Y., 1984-90; prof. health sci., coord. MS in Clin. Sci. program Calif. State U., Dominguez Hills, Calif., 1990—. Clin. adj. faculty L.I. U., Greenvale, N.Y., 1979-84, N.Y. Inst. Tech., Old Westbury, 1979-84; judge Health Occupations Students of Am., Nat. Competitive Events; dir. CSUDH Study and Cultural program, Eng., 1991, dir. Internat. Health Seminar, Australia, 1989; co-dir. study and cultural program U. Uppsala Karolinska Inst., Sweden, U. Oslo, Norway, 1988; presenter in field. Contbr. articles to profl. jours. Cmty. leader Campaign to Prevent Handgun Violence Against Kids, 1996—; mentor Calif. Acad. Math and Scis., 1990-95; univ. rep. Long Beach (Calif.) Pub. Safety Summit, 1995-96; mem. nat. com. World Food Day, 1991-94; vol. Long Beach Civic Light Opera, 1994-95; mem. vol. Long Beach Symphony Guild, 1994—; mem. docent Long Beach Mus. Art, 1996—; mem. L.A. World Affairs Coun., 1996-97. Recipient numerous grants. Fellow Royal Soc. Arts; mem. AAUW, Am. Soc. Sch. Allied Health Professions, Am. Soc. Clin. Pathologists (state adv., specialist in hematology, regional assoc. mem. award 1998), Calif. Assn. Med. Lab. Tech., Am. Assn. for World Health, N.Am. Consortium Nursing and Allied Health (bd. dirs.), Coalition for Allied Health Leadership, Alpha Eta (pres. chpt. 1996—, bd. dirs. 1991—). Office: Calif State U Divsn Health Scis Sch of Health 1000 E Victoria St Carson CA 90747-0001 E-mail: ehope@soh.csudh.edu.

KEARNS, TERRANCE BROPHY, English language educator; b. Staten Island, N.Y., July 15, 1946; s. Francis and Geraldine Mae (Brophy) Kearns; m. Jean Theresa Watts, Feb. 23, 1968; children: Sean Brophy Kearns, Gwendolyn Elizabeth Kearns. BA cum laude, Holy Cross Coll., 1968; PhD, Ind. U., 1978. Teaching asst. Ind. U., Bloomington, 1969-74; instr. U. Cen. Ark., Conway, 1974-78, asst. prof., 1978-83, assoc. prof., 1983-89, prof. English, chair English dept., 1990-98. Campus rep. Mellon Fellowships in the Humanities, U. Cen. Ark., Conway, 1982-90. Assoc. editor SLANT: A Jour. of Poetry, 1986-90; contbr. articles to profl. jours.; cons. (coll. textbooks) About Language, 1988, Discovering Language, 1991. Dist. commr. Boy Scouts Am., Conway, 1983, dist. com., 1984-89, mem. troop 71 com., 1990-91, dist. com., 1992—. Fenwick scholar Holy Cross Coll., 1967; Woodrow Wilson fellow Woodrow Wilson Found., Ind. U., 1968; recipient Dist. Award of Merit, Boy Scouts Am., Little Rock, 1989, Silver Beaver award, 2002. Mem. Assn. Lit. Scholars and Critics, Ark. Philol. Assn. (assoc. editor 1979-90), Mo. Philos. Assn. Office: U Cen Ark Dept English Conway AR 72035-0001

KEATING, THOMAS PATRICK, health care administrator, educator; b. Cleve., Jan. 5, 1949; s. Thomas Wilbur and Margaret (Gahllagher) K.; m. Carolyn Elizabeth Kraft, Sept. 4, 1976; children: Jerrod Patrick, Kerri Ann, Zane, Kriste, Marite. BS in Bus., Cleve. State U., 1971; MS in Bus., U. Toledo, 1973. Cert. health care exec. Asst. dir. facilities U. Kans. Med. Ctr., Kansas City, 1977-80; dir. mgmt. svcs. Charleston (S.C.) County Park and Recreation Commn., 1980-84; adminstr. Children's Health Sys., Med. U. of S.C., Charleston, 1984-2001, instr., 1987-2001, preceptor adminstrv. residency, master health svcs. adminstrn., 1990-93; asst. supt. Bibb County Schs., 2001—. Adj. instr. Cen. Mich. U., Mt. Pleasant, 1979—, Rockhurst Coll., Kansas City, 1979-80, Kansas City (Kans.) Cmty. Jr. Coll., 1978-80, Fayetteville (N.C.) Tech. Inst., 1974-75; accredited cons. SBA, Charleston, 1980-91; adj. prof. Webster U., St. Louis, 1981-2000, faculty U. Ala., New Coll., 1974; nursing home cons. Charleston County Mental Retardation Bd., Charleston, 1987-88. Contbr. articles to profl. jours. Vol. Driftwood Health Care Ctr., Charleston, 1981-83. Capt. U.S. Army, 1973-77, lt. col. USAR ret. Fellow Am. Coll. Health Care Execs., Am. Acad. Med. Adminstrs.; mem. Toastmasters (adminstrv. v.p. 1985-86), Sigma Phi Epsilon (com. chmn. 1970-71), Alpha Kappa Psi (com. chmn. 1972-73), KC. Roman Catholic. Home: 110 Trophy Ct Macon GA 31211-6042

KEATON, MOLLIE M. elementary school educator; d. Lorenzo and Katie Mae (Thomas) K. BS, Kent State U., 1976; MA, Atlanta U., 1980, EdD, 1985. Counselor, asst. prin. DeKalb County Bd. Edn., Decatur, Ga.; rsch. asst. Atlanta U.; tchr. Canton (Ohio) Bd. Edn. Mem. Assn. for Supervision and Curriculum Devel., Phi Delta Kappa. Home: 4076 Chapel Mill Bnd Decatur GA 30034-5335

KEATON, WILLIAM THOMAS, academic administrator, pastor; b. England, Ark., Aug. 29, 1921; m. Theresa Simpson, July 29, 1946; children: Sherrye Ann, William II, Bernard, Denise, Edwin, Karen, Renwick, Zelda, Aloysius. AA, Ark. Bapt. Coll., 1940-42; BA, U. Ark., 1948; MA, Columbia U., 1951. Supt. Howard County Sch. Dist. #38, Mineral Springs, Ark., 1951-56, East Side Sch. Dist., Menifee, Ark., 1956-61; prin. Quachita County High Sch., Bearden, Ark., 1961-68, Peake High Sch., Arkadelphia, Ark., 1968-70; coord. state programs Ark. Dept. Edn., Little Rock, 1970-85; pres. Ark. Baptist Coll., Little Rock, 1985—. Vis. prof. Ala. State U., 1972; researcher Office of Edn., Washington, 1973; state insvc. coord. Region VI-AR, staff devel. specialist, Little Rock, 1970-85; staff assoc. adult edn. U. Tex., Austin, 1967-70, Lafayette, La., 1972; pastor Greater Mt. Zion Bapt. Ch., Ashdown, Ark., 1951-72, Greater Pleasant Hill Bapt. Ch., Arkadelphia, Ark., 1972-79, Canaan Missionary Bapt. Ch., Little Rock, 1979—; mem. pres. adv. bd. dirs. Historically Black Colls. and U., 1989. Mem. NCCJ, NEA (life), NAACP (life), Ark. Edn. Assn., Ark. Adult Edn. Assn. (pres. 1969-70), Union Dist. Assn. (dean 1980—), Nat. Assn. Pub. Continuing Edn., Nat. Assn. Equal Opportunity Higher Edn. (sec. 1988-93, bd. dirs. 1989), Masons, Alpha Phi Alpha, Phi Delta Kappa. Democrat. Baptist. Office: Ark Bapt Coll 1600 Bishop St Little Rock AR 72202-6067

KEATS, DONALD HOWARD, composer, educator; b. N.Y.C., May 27, 1929; s. Bernard and Lillian K.; m. Eleanor Steinholz, Dec. 13, 1953; children: Jeremy, Jennifer, Jeffrey, Jocelyn. MusB, Yale U., 1949; MA, Columbia U., 1951; PhD, U. Minn., 1962; student, Staatliche Hochschule fur Musik, Hamburg, Germany, 1954-56. Teaching fellow Yale U. Sch. Music, New Haven, Conn., 1948-49; instr. music theory U.S. Naval Sch. Music, Washington, 1953-54; post music dir. Ft. Dix, N.J., 1956-57; faculty Antioch Coll., Yellow Springs, Ohio, 1957-76, prof., 1967-76, chmn. music dept., 1967-71; vis. prof. music U. Wash. Sch. Music, 1969-70, Lamont Sch. Music, U. Denver, 1975-76; composer-in-residence Colo. Music Festival, 1980, Arcosanti, 1986; vis. composer Aspen Music Festival, 1987; prof. music, composer-in-residence Lamont Sch. Music, U. Denver, 1975-99, Phipps Prof. in the humanities, 1982-85, prof. emeritus, 1999—. Concerts devoted solely to his music often with his participation as pianist, London, 1973, Tel Aviv, 1973, Jerusalem, 1973, N.Y.C., 1975, Denver, 1984, 91; Composer: Sonata for Clarinet and Piano, 1948, String Trio, 1948, Divertimento for Winds and Strings, 1949, The Naming of Cats, 1951, The Hollow Men, 1951, String Quartet 1, 1952, Concert Piece for Orchestra, 1952, Variations for Piano, 1955, First Symphony, 1957, Piano Sonata, 1960, An Elegiac Symphony, 1962, Anyone Lived in a Pretty How Town, 1965, String Quartet 2, 1965; ballet New Work, 1966; Polarities for Violin and Piano, 1968-70, A Love Triptych, 1970, Dialogue for Piano, and Winds, 1973, Diptych for Cello and Piano, 1975, Upon the Intimation of Love's Mortality, 1975, Branchings for Orch., 1976, Four Puerto Rican Love Songs: Tierras del Alma for soprano, flute and guitar, 1978, Musica Instrumentalis for chamber group, 1980, Concerto for Piano and Orch., 1990, Revisitations for Violin, Cello and Piano, 1992, Elegy for chamber orch., 1995, Fanfare for Brass, 1996, String Quartet No. 3, 2001. Served with U.S. Army, 1952-54. Recipient ASCAP awards, 1964— ; awards from Ford, Danforth and Lilly founds., Nat. Endowment for Arts; winner Rockefeller Found. Symphonic Competitions, 1965, 66; Guggenheim fellow Europe, 1964-65, 72-73; Nat. Endowment for Arts grantee, fellow, 1975; Fulbright Scholar, 1954-56. Mem. ASCAP, Am. Music Ctr., Phi Beta Kappa. Home: 12854 Buckhorn Rd Littleton CO 80127 E-mail: dkeats@du.edu.

KEAULANA, JERALD KIMO ALAMA, secondary education educator; b. Honolulu, May 10, 1955; s. David Kau'inohea and Geraldine Harriet Maile (Sousa) Alama. AA, Honolulu C.C., 1984; BEd, U. Hawaii, 1986, profl. diploma, 1987, MEd, 1992. Cert. tchr., Hawaii. Tchr. social studies Moloka'i (Hawaii) High and Intermediate Sch., 1986-87, Washington Intermediate Sch., Honolulu, 1987-89, Kalani High Sch., Honolulu, 1989-

92, chair dept. social studies, 1992—. Lectr. Kapi'olani C.C., Honolulu, 1990—; student tchr. trainer, U. Hawaii, 1988—; mem. leadership team Consortium for Teaching the Pacific and Asia in the Schs., Honolulu, 1989-92; developer curriculum Hawaii Dept. Edn., 1991—. Editor: Puke Mele: Vol. 1, 1988. Mem. ASCD, Nat. Coun. Social Studies, Nat. Geographic Soc., Ahahui Ka'iulani. Avocations: hawaiian language translation, hawaiian music and dance documentation. Office: Kalani High Sch 4680 Kalanianaole Hwy Honolulu HI 96821-1299

KEAY, CHARLES LLOYD, elementary school educator; b. Cleve., Dec. 12, 1959; s. Richard Thomas and Betty Eleanor (Dixon) K. BS, Kent (Ohio) State U., 1984; postgrad., U. West L.A., 1984-86; MS, Nat. U., San Diego, 1990. Tchr. L.A. Unified Sch. Dist., 1985-90, Euclid (Ohio) Pub. Schs., 1990—. Exch. tchr. Nahara-Machi, Japan, 1998-99. With U.S. Army, 1978-82. Mem. ASCD, NEA, Ohio Edn. Assn., Soka GAkki Internat. (culture dept.), Euclid Tchrs. Assn., United Tchrs. L.A. (co-chmn. local chpt.). Home: 23651 Glenbrook Blvd Euclid OH 44117-1960 also: 2-1 Aza Kanetsukido Ohaza-Kitada Naraha-Machi Fukushima-ken 979-06 Japan E-mail: ckeay@aol.com.

KECK, DAVID MICHAEL, school administrator; b. Toledo, Nov. 17, 1947; s. Marvin Wendell and Eleanor Lucille (Elwing) K.; children: Christian David, Stephen Patrick. Student, U. Toledo, 1967; BS in Edn., Ohio U., 1969, MEd, 1971; postgrad., Ohio State U., 1981—. Cert. tchr., prin., Ohio. Tchr. social studies Athens High Sch., The Plains, Ohio, 1969-73, Westerville (Ohio) South High Sch., 1973-86, Dublin (Ohio) High Sch., 1986-92, adminstrv. asst., 1992—, summer sch. adminstr., 1987-95. Pres. Ohio Capital Conf. Acad. League, 1995-96; pres. Ctrl. Ohio H.S. Soccer league, Columbus, 1975-77; vrsity soccer coach Westerville South H.S., 1974-85, Watterson H.S., 1985-86, Dublin H.S., 1986-88. Editor: Crew Chief, 1991; contbr. articles to profl. jours. Chmn. high sch. youth edn. com. Columbus Coun. World Affairs, 1990-91; issues adviser, staff mem. Linda Reidelbach for U.S. Congress, Columbus, 1992. Recipient Citizen Achievement award Westerville Parks and Recreation Dept., 1979; named Coach of Yr. Ohio Capital Conf., Franklin County, 1982. Mem. ASCD, Nat. Coun. Social Studies, John Dewey Soc., Ohio Assn. Secondary Sch. Adminstrs., Theodore Roosevelt Assn., Licking County Soccer Ofcls. Assn., Ohio U. Coll. Edn. Soc. Alumni and Friends (bd. dirs.), Ohio Scholastic Soccer Coaches Assn. (pres. 1982-85), Ohio Geneal. Soc. (v.p. 1988-89, trustee 1988-92), Maumee Valley Hist. Soc., Phi Delta Kappa. Republican. Lutheran. Avocations: genealogy, softball, reading, travel. Home: 203 S Westgate Ave Columbus OH 43204-1980 Office: Dublin Scioto High Sch 4000 Hard Rd Dublin OH 43016-8358

KECK, LOIS T. anthropology educator; b. Bklyn., Jan. 19, 1947; d. Joseph Francis and Madeline Teresa (Donnelly) K.; m. Thomas Gregory Raslear, Aug. 7, 1971. BA in Anthropology, CUNY, 1969, MA in Anthropology, 1974; PhD in Anthropology, SUNY, Binghamton, 1986; MPH in Internat. Health, Johns Hopkins U., 1992; cert. health edn. specialist, Nat. Commn. for Health Edn., 1994. Reader in anthropology and archaeology undergrad. program Queens Coll., CUNY, 1968-70, rsch. asst. Archaeology Lab., 1968-69, field instr. archaeology Summer Field Sch., 1969; tchg. asst. dept. anthropology Brown Univ., Providence, 1969-70; assoc. prof. dept. anthropology George Washington U., Washington, grad. advisor for students in women and disability; chief rsch. scientist Nat. Coun. on Disability, Washington. Cons. D.C. Women's Coun. on AIDS, 1989-95; mem. study group for peer rev. panel on grants Nat. Inst. on Disability Rsch. and Rehab.-Dept. Edn.; mem. Montgomery County (Md.) Com. on Ethnic and Minority Affairs; adj. asst. prof. CUNY-Kingsborough C.C., fall 1974; vis. asst. prof. Howard U., Washington, fall 1988; guest lectr. U. Md., fall 1988, Am. U., 1994; adj. prof. U. Md.-Univ. Coll.; sr. rsch. assoc. LTG Assocs., Inc., Turlock, Calif., 1993-94. N.Y. State Regents Nursing scholar, 1964, N.Y. State Regents scholar, 1964; Mary Switzer fellow Nat. Inst. for Disability Rsch. and Rehab., 1995-96. Fellow Am. Anthropol. Assn. (commn. on disability, advisor for students with disabilities); mem. AAAS, APHA, Am. Ethnol. Assn., Soc. for Applied Anthropology, Ctr. for Women's Policy Studies, Soc. for Med. Anthropology, Washington Evaluators Assn., Washington Assn. Profl. Anthropologists (pres. 1996-97, sec. 1993-96, 1999—), Anthropol. Soc. Washington, Washington Assn. Profl. Anthropologists (sec. 1999—), Nat. Assn. Practicing Anthropologists, Md. Pub. Health Assn., N.Y. Acad. Scis., Middle East Inst. Home: 1408 Woodman Ave Silver Spring MD 20902-3905 Office: Nat Coun on Disability 1331 F St NW Ste 1050 Washington DC 20004-1138

KECK, VICKI LYNN, special education educator; b. Lancaster, Ohio, Mar. 22, 1961; d. Robert Harvey and Trudy Gay (Fishbaugh) K.; 1 child, Alexandra Joy. BS in Edn., Bowling Green (Ohio) State U., 1983; MEd, Ohio U., 1991. Cert. tchr. of learning disabled, gifted/talented, Ohio, elem. edn. and learning behavior, disorders. Learning disabilities tchr. South Dade Sr. High Sch., Dade County Sch. System, Homestead, Fla., 1983-85; learning disabilities tutor Pickerington (Ohio) High Sch., 1985-86; learning disabilities tchr. Groveport (Ohio)-Madison Mid. Sch. South, 1986—, tchr. regular 6th grade gifted/talented, 1995—. Cheerleading advisor Groveport-Madison Mid. Sch. South, 1986-90, student coun. advisor, 1986—; flag corps advisor South Dade Sr. High Sch., 1984-85; workshop speaker student coun. Ohio Assn. Elem. Sch. Adminstrs., Columbus, 1988-92, 98, spkr. Contextual Tchg. and Learning Conf. for Bowling Green State Univ., 1999. Facilitator: (book of student poetry) American Association of Poetry, 1992, 94, 96, 97, 98. Vol. Faith Mission, Long St., Columbus, 1989-92. Named one of All-Ohio Student Coun. Advisors, Ohio Assn. Student Couns., 1989, 1st in State of Ohio, Project Citizen, 7th in the nation, 1998, Ashland Gold Apple Tchr. Awd., 1996. Mem. NEA, Ohio Edn. Assn., Assn. Supervision and Curriculum Devel., Am. Assn. Poetry. Avocations: stained glass, reading, student sports and activities, travel. Office: Groveport-Madison Mid Sch S 4400 Glendenning Dr Groveport OH 43125-9292

KEE, HOWARD CLARK, religion educator; b. Beverly, N.J., July 28, 1920; s. Walter Leslie and Regina (Corcoran) K.; m. Janet Burrell, Dec. 15, 1951; children: Howard Clark III, Christopher Andrew, Sarah Leslie. AB, Bryan (Tenn.) Coll., 1940; Th.M., Dallas Theol. Sem., 1944; postgrad., Am. Sch. Oriental Research, Jerusalem, 1949-50; PhD (Two Bros. fellow), Yale, 1951. Instr. religion and classics U. Pa., 1951-53; from asst. prof. to prof. N.T. Drew U., 1953-68; Rufus Jones prof. history of religion, chmn. dept. history of religion Bryn Mawr (Pa.) Coll., 1968-77; William Goodwin Aurelio prof. Biblical studies Boston U., 1977-89, chmn. grad. div. religious studies, 1977-86; sr. rsch. fellow U. Pa., 1987—. Vis. prof. religion Princeton U., 1954-55, Brown U., 1985; vis. lectr. U. of Durham, 1987, Claremont Sch. of Theology, 1991; Rsch. scholar, Miss. state U., 1992, vis. scholar, Princeton Theological Seminary, 1993; mem. archaeol. teams at Roman Jericho, 1950, Shechem, 1957, Mt. Gerizim, 1966, Pella, Jordan, 1967, Ashdod, Israel, 1968; chmn. Coun. on Grad. Studies in Religion; cons. for transls. Am. Bible Soc., 1989—. Author: Understanding the New Testament, 1957, 4th edit., 1983, 5th edit., 1992, Making Ethical Decisions, 1958, The Renewal of Hope, 1959, Jesus and God's New People, 1959, Jesus in History, 1970, 3d edit., 1995, The Origins of Christianity: Sources and Documents, 1973, The Community of the New Age, 1977, Christianity: An Historical Approach, 1979, Christian Origins in Sociological Perspective, 1980, Miracle in the Early Christian World, 1983, The New Testament in Context: Sources and Documents, 1984, Medicine, Miracle and Magic in New Testament Times, 1986, Knowing the Truth: A Sociological Approach to New Testament Interpretation, 1989, What Can We Know About Jesus?, 1990, Good News to the Ends of the Earth: The Theology of Acts, 1990, Christianity: A Social and Cultural History, 1991, 2d edit., 1998, Who Are the People of God? Early Christian Models of Community, 1995, To Every Nation Under Heaven: The Acts of the Apostles, 1997; editor: Biblical Perspectives on Current Issues, 1976-83, Understanding Jesus Today, 1985—; editor Cambridge UP Annotated Study Bible, 1993, Cambridge Annotated Study Apocrypha, 1994, Cambridge Companion to the Bible, 1997, Removing Anti-Judaism From the New Testament, 1996, Removing Anti-Judaism From the Pulpit, 1998, The Evollution of the Synagogue, 1999; librettist: New Land, New Covenant (Howard Hanson), 1976; contbr.: Interpreter's Dictionary of the Bible, 1962, supplement, 1976, Harper's Bible Dictionary, Dictionary of Bible and Religion, The Books of the Bible, Anchor Bible Dictionary. Bd. mgrs. Am. Bible Soc., 1956-89, chmn. transls. com., 1985-89; chmn. transls. com. United Bible Socs., 1985-89; bd. dirs. Mohawk Trail Concerts, Inc., Charlemont, Mass.; mem. adv. bd. Yale U. Inst. Sacred Music; exec. bd. Liberty Mus. Am. Assn. Theol. Schs. fellow Germany, 1960; Guggenheim fellow Israel, 1966-67; Nat. Endowment Humanities grantee Eng., 1984 Mem. Soc. Values in Higher Edn., Phila. Seminar on Christian Origins, Am. Acad. Religion, Soc. Bibl. Lit., Bibl. Theologians, Studiorum Novi Testamenti Societas, New Haven Theol. Discussion Group, Assn. for Sociology of Religion (pres.), Am. Interfaith Inst. (pres.). Presbyterian. Home: 3300 Darby Rd Haverford PA 19041-1061

KEE, SHIRLEY ANN, retired elementary education educator; b. Ewing, Mo., Dec. 21, 1935; d. Marion L. and Ida (Pauline) Becktell; m. Byron Eugene Kee, Aug. 18, 1956; children: Daniel G., Kristin S. Student, Western Ill. U., 1954-59, Ball State U., 1969-70; BA, Trinity Christian Coll., 1975; MEd, U. Ill., 1982. Tchr. 1st grade La Harpe (Ill.) Grade Sch., 1958-60, South Holland (Ill.) Sch Dist. 151, 1960-66, 68, 1971; tchr., adminstr. St. Andrews Nursery Sch., Homewood, Ill., 1972-73; tchr. 1st, 2d grades North Palos Dist. 117, Hickory Hills, Ill., 1975-84, Mansfield (Ohio) City Schs., 1984—96; founder vol. reading program Prospect Sch., Mansfield, 1997—. Pres. Parent Edn. Groups, Palos Park, Ill., 1974-81. Mem. AAUW, Alpha Kappa (historian, sec., pres.-elect, pres.). Presbyterian. Avocations: golf, bridge, cross stitch, crafts. Home: 770 Courtwright Blvd Mansfield OH 44907-2220

KEEBLER, LOIS MARIE, elementary school educator; b. Jasper, Ala., Nov. 24, 1955; d. Roosevelt T. and Marie (Smiley) K. Student, Cen. State U., Wilberforce, Ohio; cert., North Ala. Regional Hosps., 1981. Cert. tchr., Ala. Tchr. Mamani Vallied Children Devel. Ctr., Dayton, Ohio. Vol. pub. schs. Democrat. Baptist. Avocation: bowling.

KEEFE, DEBORAH LYNN, cardiologist, educator; b. Oklahoma City, Nov. 23, 1950; d. Stanley William and Gloria Jean (Kelsoe) Denton; m. Richard Alan Keefe, May 14, 1971; children: Jennifer, Colin, Corwin. BA, Rice U., 1973; MD, N.Y. Med. Coll., 1976; MPH, Columbia U., 1990. Diplomate Am. Bd. Internal Medicine, Am. Bd. Cardiovascular Disease, Am. Bd. Critical Care, Am. Bd. Clin. Pharmacology. Intern and resident St. Vincent's Hosp., N.Y.C., 1976-79; fellow in cardiology Stanford (Calif.) Univ. Hosp., 1979-81; dir. CCU Bronx (N.Y.) Mcpl. Hosp., 1981-87; assoc. dir. Am. Cyanamid, Pearl River, N.Y., 1987-88; assoc. mem. Sloan-Kettering Meml. Hosp., N.Y.C., 1988-94, mem., 1994—2001; dir. clin. devel. Berlex Labs., 2001—. Asst. prof. medicine Albert Einstein Coll. Medicine, Bronx, 1981-87; assoc. prof. medicine Cornell U., N.Y.C., 1988-95, prof. medicine, 1995—; regent Am. Coll. Clin. Pharmacology, 1985-89, 92-96, treas., 1992-94. Assoc. editor Jour. Clin. Pharmacology, 1985-94, editor, 1994—; contbr. articles to Clin. Pharm. Therapeutics, Jour. Cardiovascular Pharmacology, Am. Jour. Cardiology, Seminars in Oncology. Fellow Am. Coll. Cardiology, Am. Coll. Chest Physicians, Am. Coll. Critical Care Medicine, Am. Coll. Clin. Pharmacology (hon. regent). Office: Berlex Labs PO Box 1000 Montville NJ 07045-1000 E-mail: dkclinpharm@aol.com., Deborah_Keefe@Berlex.com.

KEEFFE, EMMET BRITTON, medical educator; b. San Francisco, Apr. 12, 1942; s. Emmet Britton and Corinne M. (Walsh) K.; m. Melenie M. Laskey, June 18, 1966; children: Emmet III, Brian, Meghan. BS, U. San Francisco, 1964, secondary teaching credential, 1965; MD, Creighton U., 1969. Intern Oreg. Health Sci. U., Portland, 1969-70, resident, 1970-73, fellow gastroenterology, 1973-74, asst. prof. medicine, 1979-83, assoc. prof. medicine, 1983-89, prof. med., 1989-92; fellow gastroenterology U. Calif., San Francisco, 1977-79, clin. prof. medicine, 1992—95; chief divsn. gastroenterology, hepatology Calif. Pacific Med. Ctr., San Francisco, 1992—95, med. dir. liver transplant program, 1992—95; prof. medicine, chief of hepatology, co-dir. liver transplant program Stanford Univ. Med. Ctr., 1995—. Author: Flexible Sigmoidoscopy, 1985, Handbookof Liver Disease, 1998, Atlas of Gastrointestinal Endoscopy, 1998; editor: Liver Update, 1991—94; mem. editl. bd. Hepatology, 1993—, assoc. editor Liver Transplantation and Surgery, 1995—2000, Digestive and Nutrition, 1999—, Reviews in Gastroenterological Disorders, 2000—, sec. editor Current Opion in Organ Transplatation, 2000—; contbr. chapters to books, articles to profl. jours. Lt. comdr. USN, 1974-77. Fellow ACP, Am. Coll. Gastroenterology; mem. AMA, Am. Liver Found. (bd. dirs. 1991-95), Am. Gastroenterologic Assn. (v.p. 2002-03, pres.-elect 2003—), Am. Assn. Study Liver Diseases, Am. Soc. Gastrointestinal Endoscopy (sec. 1991-94, pres.-elect 1994-95, pres. 1995-96), Am. Soc. Transplantation, Am. Fedn. Clin. Rsch., North Pacific Soc. Internal Medicine, Internat. Liver Transplantation Soc., Internat. Assn. for Study of Liver, Western Gut Club (pres. 1991). Home: 22 Weatherly Dr Mill Valley CA 94941-3272 Office: Stanford University Med Ctr 750 Welch Rd Ste 210 Palo Alto CA 94304-1509

KEEGAN, LISA GRAHAM, state agency administrator; m. John Keegan; 5 children. BS in Linguistics, Stanford U.; MS in Comm. Disorders, Ariz. State U., 1983. Mem. Ariz. Ho. of Reps., 1991-95, chair edn. com., joint legis. budget com., 1993-94; state supt. of pub. instrn. Dept. of Edn., State of Ariz., Phoenix, 1994—2001; CEO Edn. Leaders Coun., Washington, 2001—. Office: 1225 19th St NW Ste 400 Washington DC 20036*

KEEHN, JEFFREY JAMES, mathematics educator; b. Gary, Ind., Oct. 7, 1965; s. James Wilfred and Sandra Kaye (Spence) K.; m. Janet Louise Porubyanski, Aug. 5, 1989; children: Valerie, Mark. BS in Math., Purdue U., 1987. Math. tchr. Calumet H.S., Gary, Ind., 1988—. Home: 6368 Mulberry Ave Portage IN 46368-3818 Office: Calumet HS 3900 Calhoun St Gary IN 46408-1753

KEELE, KERRY LEANNE, elementary school educator, counselor; b. Salem, Ill., July 19, 1962; d. Kenneth Lee and Wanda Faye (Maxey) K. BS in Elem. Edn. magna cum laude, Carson Newman Coll., 1985; MS in Ednl. Guidance and Counseling, Ea. Ill. U., 1993. Cert. tchr. K-9, Ill., guidance and counseling for sch. svc. pers., Ill. Receptionist, assembler H&R Block, Salem, 1976-82; children's choir worker First Bapt. Ch., Jefferson City, Tenn., 1985; substitute tchr. Bond County Sch. Dist., Greenville, Ill., 1985-86; tchr. aide Greenville (Ill.) Elem. Sch., 1986-87; lifeguard Kingsbury Park Dist., Greenville, 1986-87; asst. mgr., swim lessons dir., instr., lifeguard City of Salem Parks and Recreation, 1981-94; elem. tchr. Wash. Sch. Vandalia (Ill.) Cmty. Schs., 1987—, asst. dir./choreographer of musicals, 1987—; mem./counselor student assistance program N000, 1993—, student assistance program team leader, 1995—; student tchr. supr. Wash. Sch. Vandalia (Ill.) Cmty. Schs., 1992-93. Marching band flag & rifle coach Wash. Sch. Vandalia (Ill.) Comty. Schs., 1987—; presenter Ill. Counselor Assn., 1994; mem. Ill. Task Force for Developmental Counseling, 1994—. Aquatics instr. Marion County chpt. ARC, Salem, 1992—. Mem. Am. Counseling Assn., Ill. Sch. Counselors Assn., Ill. Reading Coun., Alpha Delta Kappa, Delta Omicron. Republican. Baptist. Avocations: performing vocal and instrumental music, basketweaving, swimming, bowling. Home: 4334 Tonti Rd Salem IL 62881-4714 Office: Wash Sch 301 S 8th St Vandalia IL 62471-2713

KEELER, THEODORE EDWIN, economics educator; b. Enid, Okla., Mar. 25, 1945; s. Clinton Clarence and Lorene Adda Keeler; m. Marjorie Ann Nathanson, Aug. 29, 1982; 1 child, Daniel C. BA, Reed Coll., 1967; S.M., MIT, 1969, PhD, 1971. Asst. prof. econs. U. Calif.-Berkeley, 1971-77, assoc. prof., 1977-83, prof., 1983—. Key faculty Robert Wood Johnson Postdoctoral Fellows Program, 1993-2001. Author: Railroads, Freight, and Public Policy, 1983; co-author: Regulating The Automobile, 1986; also articles; editor: Research in Transportation Economics, vol. I, 1983, vol. II, 1985 Grantee NSF, 1973-75, 80-82, dept. transp. program, 1988-90, 93-94, NIH, 1990-91, Nat. Inst. on Aging, 1995-96; prin. investigator Sloan Found., 1975-80, Robert Wood Johnson Found., 1996-99; sr. fellow, vis. scholar Brookings Instn., Washington, 1980-82; co-prin. investigator Tobacco Tax Project Calif. Tobacco-Related Disease Fund, 1990-94, 99-2000 Mem. Am. Econs. Assn. Democrat. Office: U Calif Dept Econs Berkeley CA 94720-3880

KEELING, RITA D. elementary educator; b. Richmond, Va., Mar. 31, 1955; BS, Longwood Coll., 1977, M, 1980. Tchr. Halifax County Sch. System, Hanover County Sch. System. Chmn. talented and gifted screening program Mem. of Fine Screening for the Talented and Gifted Program for Halifax County; reading placement tester. Mem. Phi Delta Kappa. Home: PO Box 38 Keysville VA 23947-0038

KEEN, MARIA ELIZABETH, retired educator; b. Chgo., Aug. 19, 1918; d. Harold Fremont and Mary Eileen Honore (Dillon) K. AB, U. Chgo., 1941; postgrad., U. Wyo., summer 1943; MA, U. Ill., 1949; postgrad., U. Mich., 1957. Tchr. high sch., Wyo., 1942-43, 1943-44; tchr. Am. Coll. for Women, Istanbul, Turkey, 1944-47; mem. faculty U. Ill., Urbana, 1947-88, prof. emerita, 1988—. Mem. Champaign Community Devel. Com. Mem. AAUW, AAUP (past treas.), AAAS, LWV, Animal Protection Inst., Defenders of Wildlife, Am. Inst. Biol. Scis., Nat. Coun. Tchr. Educators, U. Ill. Athletic Assn. (sec., bd. dirs.), Ont. Geneal. Soc., Orton Dyslexia Soc., Art Inst. Chgo., Women's Philharm. (charter), Women in Arts (charter), Women's Humane Soc., Illini Union (faculty staff social com.), Nat. Humane Soc., Phi Kappa Epsilon (hon.). Baptist. Home: 608 S Edwin St Champaign IL 61821-3834

KEEN, RACHEL, psychology educator; b. Burkesville, Ky., Oct. 5, 1937; d. James Em and Regina Elizabeth (Simpson) Keen; m. Charles E. Clifton, Aug. 20, 1965 (div. 2002); children: Ramona, Catherine. BA, Berea (Ky.) Coll., 1959; MA, U. Minn., 1960, PhD, 1963. Fellow U. Wis., Madison, 1963-65; rsch. assoc. U. Iowa, Iowa City, 1966-68; from asst. prof. to assoc. prof. U. Mass., Amherst, 1968-76, prof., 1976—. Vis. prof. Stanford U., Palo Alto, Calif., 1975-76, U. Sussex, Brighton, Eng., 1981-82, U. Cambridge, Eng., 1989-90; mem. rsch. rev. com. NIMH, 1983-87; mem. human devel. study sect. NIH, 1990-94. NIMH fellow U. Minn., 1961-63; grantee NIMH, NIH, NSF, 1968—; named Disting. Alumna Berea Coll., 1994. Fellow APA, AAAS, Acoustical Soc. Am.; mem. Soc. Rsch. Child Devel. (sec. 1979-85, assoc. editor jour. 1977-79, editor Monographs 1993-99), Fedn. Behavioral, Psychol. and Cognitive Sc is. (sec. 1987-90), Soc. Psychophysiol. Rsch. (bd. dirs. 1975-78, assoc. editor jour. 1972-75), Internat. Soc. Infant Studies (pres. 1998-00). Democrat. Congregationalist. Avocations: playing piano, reading. Office: U Mass Dept Psychology Amherst MA 01003

KEENA, DOLORES MAY, retired elementary education educator; b. Delta, Colo., Aug. 1, 1935; d. Cleve Shannon and Myrtle May (Cross) Buckmaster; m. Earl E. Keena, Aug. 21, 1960; children: James, Dennis, Melody, Carol. BA in Elem. Edn., Pasadena (Calif.) Coll., 1961. Cert. elem. tchr. Telephone operator Mountain States Bell Telephone, Delta, 1953-58; tchr. Garvey Sch. Dist., South San Gabriel, Calif., 1962-64, Thermalito Sch. Dist., Oroville, Calif., 1968-96. Sec. Poplar Ave. Sch. Site Coun., Oroville, 1990-96. Mem. Arbor Day Found., 1990; mem. Rep. Nat. Com., Washington, 1989. Pres. scholar Pasadena Coll., 1958, PTA scholar, 1959. Mem. Thermalito Tchrs. Assn. (former sec. 1968—), Calif. Tchrs. Assn. Avocations: stamp collecting, gardening, reading. Home: 2160 D St Oroville CA 95966-6672

KEENAGHAN, PATRICIA ANNE, principal, educator; b. N.Y.C., Jan. 24, 1951; d. Michael W. and Mary Elizabeth (Cronin) Smith; m. Daniel J. Keenaghan, Aug. 16, 1975; children: Daniel J. Jr., Michael, Brian, Claire. BA, CUNY, Jamaica, 1972; MS, CUNY, Flushing, 1975. Tchr. 8th grade math. Incarnation Sch., Queens Village, N.Y., 1972-77; 7th and 8th grade tchr. St. Michael's Sch., Bklyn., 1977-78; tchr. 10th grade social sci. Moore Cath. High Sch., Staten Island, N.Y., 1979; tchr. math. and sci. Our Lady of Mercy Sch., Park Ridge, N.J., 1988-98; prin. St. Catharine Internat. Sch./Acad. of Our Lady, Glen Rock, NJ, 1998—. Confraternity of Christian Doctrine tchr. Sacred Heart, S.I., N.Y., 1981-85, Blessed Sacrament, S.I., 1985-87, Our Lady Mother of the Christ, Woodcliff Lake, N.J., 1987-2001. Host Project Children, 1992-98. Home: 24 Highview Ave Woodcliff Lake NJ 07677-8016 Office: Acad of Our Lady 180 Rodney St Glen Rock NJ 07452

KEENAN, EDWARD LOUIS, history educator; b. Buffalo, May 13, 1935; s. Edward Louis and Emma (Boudiette) K.; m. Joan Glasser, Nov. 25, 1961 (div. Oct. 1986); children: Edward, Christopher, Nicholas, Matthew (dec.); m. Judith Kapp Davison, Jan. 4, 1987. AB, Harvard U., 1957, MA, 1962, PhD, 1966; postgrad., Leningrad State U., 1959-61. From tchg. fellow to prof. Harvard U., Cambridge, Mass., 1962—91, Mellon prof. humanities, 1991—98; dir. Dumbarton Oaks Rsch. Libr. and Collections, Washington, 1998—. Lectr. Slavic Workshop, Ind. U., 1962-64; dir. Ctr. for Mid. Ea. Studies, 1981-83, 86-87, 93, 95. Author: The Kurbskii-Groznyi Apocrypha, 1972, Joseph Dobrovsky and the Origins of the Igor Tale, 2003; contbr. articles to profl. jours. Bd. govs. Reza Shah Kabir U., 1975—. Guggenheim fellow, 1970 Mem. Am. Assn. for Advancement Slavic Studies (pres. 1994). Democrat. Office: Dumbarton Oaks 1703 32nd St NW Washington DC 20007

KEENAN, JOHN PAUL, leadership and management educator, consultant, psychologist; b. Boston, Mar. 18, 1944; s. John W. and Claire (Gallagher) K.; m. Kathleen Lennon, Aug. 7, 1976; children: Christopher, Sean Patrick. BA, U. Santa Clara, 1967; MA, San Jose State U., 1969; PhD, U.S. Internat. U., San Diego, 1978. Instr. Chapman Coll., Orange, Calif., 1971-79; asst. prof. mgmt. Coll. of St. Rose, Albany, N.Y., 1979-83; dean C.C. Low County, Beaufort, S.C., 1983-86; assoc. prof. mgmt., dir. leadership devel. programs Mgmt. Inst., U. Wis. Sch. Bus., Madison, 1986-98; exec. dir. leadership programs ACCEL-Medaille Coll., Amherst, NY, 2001—02. Acting dean Sch. of Leadership and Human Devel., exec. dir. Leadership programs ACCEL-Medaille Coll., Amherst, NY; pres., CEO John Keenan & Assocs., Orchard Park, NY, 1986—; exec. v.p. Coun. on Employee Responsibilities and Rights, Norfolk, Va., 1993—98; spkr. in field; presenter in field; pres./CEO John P. Keenan & Assocs., Internat.; pres. Internat. U. Leadership and Global Edn., 2003—. Co-author: Whistleblowing: Managing Dissent in the Work Place, 1985, Whistleblowing Research, 1985, Foundations of Leadership: New Manager Leadership Guide, 1997, Foundations of Leadership: Facilitator's Guide, 1997, Fastart: An Indepth Seminar for New Managers, 1998, Organizational Behavior, 1998, Managing Human Resources, 1999, Strategic Planning, Leadership Development, Decision Making and Problem Solvine and Conflict Resolution, 2003; editor-in-chief Employee Responsibilities & Rights Jour., 1999—; contbr. over 120 articles to profl. jours. Mem. APA, ASTD, Acad. Mgmt., Decision Scis. Inst., Inst. Mgmt. Scis., Soc. for Indsl. and Orgnl. Psychology, Assn. on Employment Practices and Principles (pres.1998—, program chmn. 1993, 97, 2000), Assn. Employment Practices and Prins. Avocations: swimming, hiking, all sports. Home: 2 Hillsboro Dr Orchard Park NY 14127-3411 E-mail: jkeenan945@aol.com.

KEENAN, RETHA ELLEN VORNHOLT, retired nursing educator; b. Solon, Iowa, Aug. 15, 1934; d. Charles Elias and Helen Maurine (Konicek) Vornholt; m. David James Iverson, June 17, 1956; children: Scott, Craig; m. Roy Vincent Keenan, Jan. 5, 1980. BSN, State U. Iowa, 1955; MSN, Calif. State U., Long Beach, 1978. Cert. nurse practitioner adult and mental health. Pub. health nurse City of Long Beach, 1970-73, 94-96, cons., 1998, 99, 2000, coord. continuing edn., 1999, 2000. Pub. health nurse Hosp. Home Care, Torrance, Calif., 1973-75; patient care coord. Hillhaven, L.A., 1975-76; mental health cons. InterCity Home Health, L.A., 1978-79; instr. C.C. Dist., L.A., 1979-87; instr. nursing El Camino Coll., Torrance, 1981-86; instr. nursing Chapman Coll., Orange, Calif., 1982, Mt. St. Mary's Coll., 1986-87; cons., pvt. practice, Rancho Palos Verdes, Calif., 1987-89, 98, 99. Contbg. author: American Journal of Nursing Question and Answer Book for Nursing Boards Review, 1984, Nursing Care Planning Guides for Psychiatric and Mental Health Care, 1987-88, Nursing Care Planning Guides for Children, 1987, Nursing Care Planning Guides for Adults, 1988, Nursing Care Planning Guides for Critically Ill Adults, 1988. Mem. Assistance Leauge of Temecula Valley, Calif. NIMH grantee, 1977-78. Mem. Sigma Theta Tau, Phi Kappa Phi, Delta Zeta. Republican. Lutheran. Avocations: traveling, writing, reading. Home: PO Box 205 Temecula CA 92593-0205

KEENE, JOHN CLARK, lawyer, educator; b. Phila., Aug. 17, 1931; s. Floyd Elwood and Marthe (Bussiere) K.; m. Ana Maria Delgado, July 21, 1973; children: Lisa Keene Kerns, John, Suzanna Tonra, Katharine, Peter; stepchildren: Carlos, René, Mario, Raúl, Silvio Navarro, Carmen Peláez. BA, Yale U., 1953; JD, Harvard U., 1959; M in City Planning, U. Pa., 1966. Bar: Pa. 1960. Assoc. Pepper, Hamilton & Scheetz, Phila., 1959-64; prof. city and regional planning U. Pa., Phila., 1968—, chmn., 1989-93, univ. ombudsman, 1978-84, chmn. faculty senate, 1998-99; ptnr. Coughlin, Keene & Assocs., Phila., 1981—2000, Keene and Assoc., Phila., 2001—; chair doctoral program in city and regional planning U. Pa., 2002—. Vis. prof. U. Paris X, 1991. Author: (with Robert E. Coughlin) The Protection of Farmland, 1981, Growth Without Chaos, 1987, (with others) Untaxing Open Space, 1976, (with Samuel Hamill) Growth Mgmt. in NJ, 1989, (with Robert Coughlin and Joanne Denworth) Guiding Growth: Managing Urban Growth in Pa., 1991, 93, (with Julia Freedgood) Saving Am. Farmland: What Works, 1997. Trustee ex officio Phila. Mus. Art, 1978-80; mem. sci. and tech. adv. com. Chesapeake Bay Program. Lt. USN, 1953-56. Fulbright fellow Tunisia, 1985. Mem. Am. Inst. Cert. Planners, Phila. Club, Merion Cricket Club. Home: 1527 Montgomery Ave Bryn Mawr PA 19010-1659 Office: U Pa 127 Meyerson Hall Philadelphia PA 19104 E-mail: keenej@pobox.upenn.edu.

KEESLING, JAMES EDGAR, mathematics educator; b. Indpls., June 26, 1942; s. Fred Edgar and Martha Belle (Grimes) K.; m. Marian Ellen Calley, Jan. 26, 1963; children: James Jr., Marian Esther, Timothy Carl, Ruth Emily. BS in Indsl. Engring., U. Miami, 1964, MS in Math., 1966, PhD in Math., 1968. Asst. prof. math. U. Fla., Gainesville, 1967-71, assoc. prof. math., 1971-75, prof. math., 1975—; pres. pro-tempore Coll. of Liberal Arts and Scis., U. Fla., 1989-90. Vis. faculty U. Ga., 1976-77, U. Utah, 1991-92; vis. lectr. Soc. Indsl. and Applied Math., 1992—; lectr. numerous nat. and internat. conf. in math., 1969—. Contbr. articles to math. jours.; mng. editor Topology and its Applications. Elder, ch. chmn. Creekside Community Ch. (Evangelical Free Ch. of Am.), Gainesville, 1987-90, 94-97, 2001-2003. Recipient Tchg. award U. Fla., 1994, 98. Mem. Am. Math. Soc., Math. Assn. Am., Soc. Indsl. and Applied Math., Tau Beta Pi, Phi Kappa Phi. Home: 710 NE 6th St Gainesville FL 32601-5566 Office: U Fla Dept Math Gainesville FL 32611-8105 E-mail: jek@math.ufl.edu.

KEETER, LYNN CARPENTER, English educator; b. Charlotte, N.C. d. John Franklin and Georgiana (LaVender) Carpenter; children: John Blair, Eric William. BA in English, Gardner-Webb U., 1980, MA in Edn., 1985, MA in English, 1994; devel. educator specialist, Ariz. State U.; postgrad., The Union Inst., Cin. Instr. Taylor Finishing, Charlotte, 1970-74, Gardner-Webb U., Boiling Springs, N.C., 1980-86, prof. English, 1988—; tchr. self-devel. classes for underprivileged women Robeson County Schs., Lumberton, N.C., 1986-88. Founder, dir. personal devel. program for women; freelance writer for vintage clothing jours.; storyteller Appalachian folklore. Co-author: Fundamentals of Reading and Writing, 1997; writer children's stories. Mem. Internat. Reading Assn. (award 1997), A.C.E.I., pres. local chpt. N.C.R.A., N.C.Reading Assn. (pres. local coun. 1998—), Woman's Club Internat. (v.p., pres., Outstanding Woman 1980), Woman's Prayer Assn. (pres.), Coll. English Assn. (editor newsletter 1993—), Beta Sigma Phi (pres., v.p., sec., Woman of Yr. award 1991, 92, Alpha Omega award 1992), Sigma Tau Delta, Phi Delta Kappa. Avocations: antiques, interior decorating, dancing.

KEFALIDES, NICHOLAS ALEXANDER, physician, educator; b. Alexandroupolis, Greece, Jan. 17, 1927; came to U.S., 1947, naturalized; s. Athanasios and Alexandra (Aematidou) K.; m. Eugenia Georgia Kutsunis, Nov. 24, 1949; children: Alexandra Jane (dec.), Patricia Ann, Paul Thomas. BA, Augustana Coll., Rock Island, Ill., 1951; BS, U. Ill., Chgo., 1953, MS in Biochemistry, MD, U. Ill., Chgo., 1956, PhD in Biochemistry, 1965; MS (hon.), U. Pa., 1971; doctorate (hon.), U. Reims, France, 1987. Resident in internal medicine U. Ill. Coll. Medicine, Chgo., 1960-62, NIH fellow in infectious disease, 1962-64, asst. prof. medicine, 1964-65, U. Chgo., 1965-69, assoc. prof. medicine, 1969-70; assoc. prof. medicine and biochemistry U. Pa., Phila., 1970-74, prof. medicine, 1974—, prof. biochemistry and biophysics, 1975—; assoc. dean rsch. U. Pa. Sch. Medicine, 1994-95. Vis. prof. Oxford (England) U., 1977—78, 1984—85; mem., chmn. pathobiochemistry study sect. NIH, 1982—86; dir. project on burns NIH, USPHS, Lima, Peru, 1957—60, Connective Tissue Rsch. Inst., Phila., 1977—2002; chmn. Instn. Rev. Bd. U. Pa., 1995—98, exec. chmn., 1998—; initiator, chair Gordon Rsch. Confs. on Basement Membranes, 1982. Contbr. chpts. to books, articles to profl. jours. Served as surgeon USPHS, 1957-60. Recipient Borden Rsch. Found. award, 1956, award for pioneering rsch. on connective tissue Collagen Gordon Confs. and Collagen Corp., 1997; Guggenheim fellow, 1977. Fellow AAAS; mem. Am. Assn. Pathologists, Am. Soc. Clin. Investigation, Am. Soc. Biochemistry and Molecular Biology, Am. Soc. Cell Biology. Achievements include discovery of Collagen type IV in basement membranes and its role in suppressing tumor cell growth. Office: U Pa Univ City Sci Ctr 3701 Market St Rm 468 Philadelphia PA 19104-5502

KEFELI, VALENTIN ILICH, biologist, botanist, educator, researcher; b. Moscow, July 12, 1937; s. Ilia Josef Kefeli and Alisa Michailovna Kefeli-Tongur; m. Galina Michailovna Mzen, Jan. 9, 1932; 1 child, Maria Valentinovna. Student, Agrl. Acad., Moscow, 1954-59; cand. of sci., Inst. Plant Physiology, Moscow, 1965, DSc, 1971. Asst. Inst. Phytopathology, Moscow region, 1959-61; sci. jr. Inst. Plant Physiology, Moscow, 1961-69, sci. sr., 1969-88, head lab., prof. biology, 1988—; dir. Inst. of Soil Sci. and Photosynthesis, Moscow region, 1988—. Vis. then assoc. prof. biology Slippery Rock U., Pa., 1995—; advisor wetland project & master programs Coll. Health & Human Svcs., 1998—. Author: Natural Growth Inhibitors, 1978, 2002; editor: Development of Acetabularia, 1979. V.p. Presidium of Pushchino Biol. Ctr., Moscow region, 1989. Recipient prize Russian Chek Acad., Moscow, 1979. Mem. Plant Physiol. Soc. (pres. 1993—), N.Y. Acad. Sci. Home: 329 N Main St Slippery Rock PA 16057-1019

KEGGEREIS, NORMA JEAN, music educator, composer, arranger, arranger, vocalist, keyboard artist; b. July 20, 1942; d. Marvin Ray and Rhonda Ruth (Mayo) Taylor; m. Everett Paul Keggerels; children: David Gene Mitchell, Merle Wayne Mitchell, Vikki Lynn Keggereis Chaffin, Jana Lynn. Cert. in piano pedagogy, Mus. Arts Conservatory, Amarillo, Tex., 1972. Cert. vocat. music evangelist. Pvt. educator piano, organ, Dallas, 1969—83; accompanist Weekly Gospel TV Program, Dallas, 1968-71; co-owner, dir. schs. Dallas, 1977—2002. Tchr. adult theory classess. Composer: This is the Way, 1971, One Day at a Time, 1973, My Best Friend, 1974, I Don't Mind...So It Don't Matter, 1975, others. Evangelistic pianist, organist Prof. Ch., Dallas, 1952—; ch. organist Orchard Hills Bapt. Ch., Garland, Tex., 1967-79, Lochwood Bapt. Ch., Dallas, 1980-81, Northlake Bapt. Ch., Garland, Tex., 1985-91, Criswell Coll., Dallas, 1988-95; music counselor, instl. rep. Dist. Cir. 10 coun. Boy Scouts Am., 1973-77; mem. North Am. Mission Bd. Nat. So. Bapt. Evangelist Assn., Tex. Bapt. Evangelist Assn. Mem. Nat. Dunning Piano Tchrs., Assn. Nat. Coll. Musicians (honor roll tchr.), Nat. Guild Piano Tchrs., Organ and Piano Tchrs. Assn., Tex. Fedn. Music Clubs, Dallas Dunning Piano Tchrs. (pres. 1973-78). Home and Office: 1650 E Quail Run Rd Rockwall TX 75087-7211

KEGLEY, CHARLES WILLIAM, JR., political science educator, author; b. Evanston, Ill., Mar. 5, 1944; s. Charles William and Elizabeth Euphemia (Meck) K.; m. Ann Curry Taylor, Apr. 1, 1966 (div.); 1 child, Mrs. Suzanne, Mitchell Douglas; m. Pamela Ann Holcomb, July 2, 1975 (div.); m. Debra Annette Jump, July 6, 2002.. BA, Am. U., 1966; PhD, Syracuse U., 1971. Asst. prof. Sch. Fgn. Svc., Georgetown U., 1971-72, prof., chmn. dept. govt. and internat. studies, 1981-85; dir. Byrnes Internat. Ctr. U. SC, 1986—88, holder Pearce chmn. internat. rels., 1985—. Vis. prof. U. Tex., 1976; Moses Back Peace prof., Rutgers U., New Brunswick, N.J., 1989. Author: A General Empirical Typology of Foreign Policy Behavior, 1973; co-author, co-editor (with William Coplin): A Multi-Method Introduction to International Politics: Observation, Explanation and Prescription, 1971, Analyzing International Relations: A Multi-Method Introduction, 1975; co-author: (with Eugene R. Wittkopf) American Foreign Policy: Pattern and Process, 1979, 6th edit., 2003, World Politics: Trend and Transformation, 1981, 9th edit., 2003; (with Gregory A. Raymond) When Trust Breaks Down: Alliance Norms and World Politics, 1990, A Multipolar Peace? Great-Power Politics in the 21st Century, 1994, How Nations Make Peace, 1999, From War to Peace: Fateful Decisions in International Politics, 2002, Exorcising the Ghost of Westphalia: Building World Order in the New Millennium, 2002; co-editor: (with Robert W. Gregg) After Vietnam: The Future of American Foreign Policy, 1971; (with Gregory A. Raymond, Robert M. Rood, Richard A. Skinner) International Events and the Comparative Analysis of Foreign Policy, 1975; (with Patrick J. McGowan) Challenges to America: U.S. Foreign Policy in the 1980's, 1979, Threats, Weapons, and Foreign Policy, 1980, The Political Economy of Foreign Policy, 1981, Foreign Policy: USA/USSR, 1983; (with Eugene R. Wittkopf) Perspectives on American Foreign Policy, 1983, The Global Agenda: Issues and Perspectives, 1984, 6th edit., 2001 (with Patrick McGowan) Foreign Policy and the Modern World System, 1983; (with Eugene R. Wittkopf) The Nuclear Reader: Strategy, Weapoons, War, 1985, 2d edit., 1989; (with Charles F. Hermann and James N. Rosenau) New Directions in the Study of Foreign Policy, 1987, (with Eugene R. Wittkopf) The Domestic Sources of American Foreign Policy, 1988, (with Kenneth Schwab) After the Cold War: Questioning the Morality of Nuclear Deterrence, 1991, (with Eugene R. Wittkopf) The Future of American Foreign Policy, 1992; editor: The Long Postwar Peace: Contending Explanations and Projections, 1990, International Terrorism: Characteristics, Causes, Controls, 1990, Controversies in International Relations Theory: Realism and the Neoliberal Challenge, 1995, The New Global Terrorism, 2003; contbr. chpts. to books, articles to profl. jours. Trustee Carnegie Coun. Ethics and Internat. Affairs, 1992-98, 2000—. Recipient Disting. Alumni award Am. U., 1984; R.M. Davis scholar, 1962-66; Maxwell fellow, 1968-69, 70-71; N.Y. State Regents fellow, 1969-70; Fulbright sr. scholar, 1978, Russell rsch. awardee in humanities and social scis., 1982. Mem. Am. Polit. Sci. Assn., Am. Soc. Internat. Law, Am. Soc. Advancement Sci., Internat. Polit. Sci. Assn., Internat. Studies Assn. (assoc. dir. 1980-84, pres. 1993-94), Midwest Polit. Sci. Assn., Peace Sci. Soc., Peace Rsch. Soc., So. Polit. Sci. Assn., Pi Sigma Alpha, Omicron Delta Kappa, Delta Tau Kappa, Alpha Tau Omega. Home: 35 Veranda Ln Blythewood SC 29016-7602 Office: U SC Dept Polit Sci Columbia SC 29208-0001

KEHLER, ABBEJEAN, economist, educator; b. Balt., June 12, 1952; d. Richard Jay and Mary Elizabeth (Lenhardt) K. BS in Edn., U. N.D., 1975, MEd, 1977. Instr. dept. econs. Wichita State U., 1977-8; instr., asst. dir. Ctr. Econ. Edn. Ball State U., Muncie, Ind., 1978-80; instr. dept. econs. Ind. U., Bloomington, 1980-81; field dir. Fla. Coun. Econ. Edn., Tampa, 1981-86; assoc. dir. Cen. Ohio Ctr. Econ. Edn. Ohio State U., Columbus, 1986-93, dir. Cen. Ohio Ctr. Econ. Edn., 1993—; pres. Ohio Coun. Econ. Edn., Columbus, 1991—. Mem. social studies adv. com. Ohio Dept. Edn., Columbus, 1992-94. Editor profl. newsletters. Recipient Univ. Teaching award Joint Coun. Econ. Edn., 1989. Mem. Nat. Assn. Econ. Educators (long-range planning com. 1990-93, 94—, Moore Svc. award 1995), Columbus Assn. Bus. Economists, Nat. Coun. Social Studies, Phi Delta Kappa, Omicron Delta Epsilon. Avocations: desk-top publishing, travel. Office: Ohio State U CETE Bldg 1900 Kenny Rd Columbus OH 43210-1016

KEIGHER, SHARON, physical education educator; b. West Orange, N.J., Sept. 7, 1965; d. James Joseph and Marilyn Lois (Morahan) K. BA, Seton Hall U., 1987; MA in Edn., Columbia U., 1999. Writer, developer Enhanced Comms., Inc., New Providence, N.J., 1987-88; pub. rels. dir. Adtech Advt., Passaic, N.J., 1988-90; unit dir. Boys' & Girls' Clubs Newark, 1988-92; aquatic dir., curriculum designer Asphalt Green, N.Y.C., 1992-94; faculty Trinity Sch., N.Y.C., 1994—. Mem. Eagle Rock Civic Assn., West Orange, N.J., 1993— Mem. ARC (instr.), Afterschool Program Dirs. Network, Am. Swim Coaches Assn., Nat. Swimming Pool Operators Assn., Garden State Soccer Assn., Assn. Athletics in Ind. Schs. (coach 1994—), Assn. Tchrs. in Ind. Schs. (bd. dirs.), Nat. Interscholastic Swim Coaches Assn., Sportsfriends Women's Soccer Club, Kappa Delta Pi. Avocations: swimming, writing, reading, hiking, kayaking, sailing. Home: 10 Moore Ter West Orange NJ 07052-5014 Office: Trinity Sch 139 W 91st St New York NY 10024-1399

KEILLER, JAMES BRUCE, college dean, clergyman; b. Racine, Wis., Nov. 21, 1938; s. James Allen and Grace (Modder) K.; m. Darsel Lee Bundy, Feb. 8, 1959; 1 dau., Susanne Elizabeth. Diploma, Beulah Heights Bible Coll., 1957; BA, William Carter Coll., 1963, EdD (hon.), 1973; LLB, Blackstone Sch. Law, 1964; MA, Evang. Theol. Sem., 1965, BD, 1966, ThD, 1968; MA in Ednl. Adminstrn., Atlanta U., 1977; degree, Nat. Tax Tng. Sch., Monsey, N.Y., 1986; postgrad., Atlanta Law Sch., Harvard U., 2001—03; Eds, Georgia State U., 1987; DD, Heritage Bible Coll., 2001. Ordained to ministry Internat. Pentecostal Assemblies, 1957. Pastor Maranatha Temple, Boston, 1957-58, Midland (Mich.) Full Gospel Ch., 1958-64; v.p. acad. dean Beulah Heights Bible Coll., Atlanta, 1964—, trustee, 1964-92; nat. dir. youth and Sunday sch. dept. Internat. Pentecostal Assemblies, 1958-64, dir. world missions, 1964-76; missionary editor Bridegroom's Messenger, 1964—; dir. global missions Internat. Pentecostal Ch. of Christ, 1976—, mem. exec. com., 1976—; mem. exec. bd. Mt. Paran Christian Sch., 1980-91. Named Alumnus of Yr. William Carter Coll., 1965. Fellow: Coll. of Preceptors; mem.: Soc. for Bibl. Lit., Am. Acad. Religion, Little Mountain Village Condo Assn. (bd. dirs. 1994—), Intercollegiate Studies Inst., Nat. Fedn. for Decency (bd. dirs.), Evang. Theol. Soc., Am. Bd. Master Educators (cert.), Am. Inst. Parliamentarians, Ind. Order Foresters, So. Accrediting Assn. Bible Colls. (exec. sec. 1970—93), Kiwanis (lt. gov. Ga. dist. 1986—87, chmn. human values state com. Ga. dist. 1989—90). Republican. E-mail: bhbc@beulah.org. Fax: (404)-627-0702. Home: 21A Little Mountain Vlg Ellenwood GA 30294-3150 Office: Beulah Heights Bible Coll 892 Berne St SE Atlanta GA 30316-1873

KEIM, DONALD BRUCE, finance educator; b. Bethlehem, Pa., Feb. 7, 1953; s. Elwood Benjamin and Doris Mae (Wanamaker) K.; m. Susan Langshaw, July 10, 1976; children: Sarah Elizabeth, Julia Diane. BSBA, Bucknell U., 1975; MBA, U. Chgo., 1980, PhD, 1983; MS (hon.), U. Pa., 1988. Rsch. assoc. Fed. Deposit Ins. Corp., Washington, 1978; lectr. Loyola U. of Chgo., 1981-82; asst. prof., fin. U. Pa., Phila., 1982-88, assoc. prof. fin., 1988-94, prof. fin., 1994—98, John B. Neff prof. fin., 1998—. Vis. prof. INSEAD, Fontainebleau, France, 1994, 96-98; vis. scholar Dimensional Fund Advisors, Santa Monica, Calif., 1990, 1995-96; mem. acad. adv. bd. Brandywine Asset Mgmt., Wilmington, Del., 1993-2000. Assoc. editor Jour. of Fin. and Quant. Analysis, 1993-2001; co-editor European Fin. Rev., 1998—; contbr. articles to profl. jours. Rsch. grantee Inst. for Quantitative Rsch., 1984, 92, 99; recipient Graham and Dodd award Fin. Analysts Fedn., 1987, 99, N.Y. Stock Exch. award, 1996. Mem. Am. Fin. Assn., Western Fin. Assn. (program com. 1992-96, 2000-2003), European Fin. Assn. (program com. 1996-2003). Avocations: music, photography, golf, gardening. Office: Univ Pa The Wharton Sch 2300 Steinberg Hall Philadelphia PA 19104

KEISER, CATHERINE ANN, band director; b. Neenah, Wis., Apr. 8, 1958; d. Clinton L. and Dolores Clark; m. John T. Ludgate, Dec. 22, 1979 (div. June 1989); children: Kelly Lynn, Jennifer Ann; m. Richard L. Keiser, July 15, 1995; stepchildren: Ryan, Jennifer, Lindsey. BFA in Music Edn., U. S.Dak., 1980. Gen. music tchr. St. James Elem., Omaha, 1980—81; band & vocal dir. Roncalli H.S., Omaha, 1981—82; music dir. Father Flanagan's Boys Town, Boys Town, Nebr., 1983—2002; asst. dir. bands Millard North High Sch., Omaha, 2002—. Scholar, Arrow Stage Line, 1992. Mem.: Boys Town Education Assn., Nebr. Education Assn., Nebr. State Bandmaster Assn. (treas. 1986—96, Jack R. Snider Young Band Dir. award 1990), Music Educators Nat. Conf., Nebr. Music Educator Assn., Phi Beta Mu (treas. 1999—). Republican. Avocations: tennis, skiing, motorcycle touring with husband. Home: 13955 Arbor Circle Omaha NE 68144 Office: Millard North High Sch 1610 S 144th St Omaha NE 68144 E-mail: ckeiser@hotmail.com.

KEISER, MARY ANN MYERS, special education educator; b. Phila., Feb. 13, 1932; d. Edgar Miller and Mary (Bickley) Myers; m. John F. Keiser, Jr., Dec. 25, 1963 (wid. Sept. 1977); children: Jill, Kimberly, Beth (tiwns), Mary Ann, Meg (twins). BA, Dickinson Coll., 1954; MS, Temple U., 1957; MEd, Pa. State U., 1979. Tchr. sci. Media (Pa.) H.S., 1954-56; elem. tchr. Phoenixville (Pa.) Sch. Dist., 1956-57, Springfield (Pa.) Sch. Dist., 1957-64, Neshaminey Sch. Dist., Langhorne, Pa., 1964-65; reading tchr., cons. Main Line Day Sch., Haverford, Pa., 1971-79; spl. edn. tchr. West Chester (Pa.) Sch. Dist., 1979-97. Vol. R.S.V.P. and West Chester Sch. Dist. Ford Found. grantee Temple U., Phila., 1954-57. Mem. NEA, Pa. Edn. Assn. (life), Chester County Hist. Soc., PSEA-R, DAR (sr. state pres. Pa.), Children Am. Revolution (past sr. state pres. Pa.). Methodist. Avocations: doll collector, tutor for care children, travel, reading. Home: 423 Gateswood Dr West Chester PA 19380-6324

KEITH, CAROLYN AUSTIN, secondary school counselor; b. Mobile, Ala., July 15, 1949; d. Lloyd James Jr. and Aletia Delores (Taylor) Austin; m. Carlos Lamar Keith Sr., Aug. 14, 1971; children: Carlos Lamar Jr., Carolyn Bernadette Austin Keith. BA in English and History, Mercer U., 1971; Cert. in Gifted Edn., Valdosta State Coll., 1979, MEd in Counseling, 1982, postgrad., 1987, Nova Southeastern U., 1997—. Tchr. English Crisp County High Sch., Cordele, Ga., 1971-77; tchr. gifted Tift County Jr. High Sch., Tifton, Ga., 1977-81, Dooly County Sch. System, Vienna, Ga., 1981-82; counselor Worth County High Sch., Sylvester, Ga., 1982-86, Monroe Comprehensive High Sch., Albany, Ga., 1986-91, Dougherty County Alternative Sch., Albany, 1991-98, Dougherty County Mid. Sch., Albany, 1998—. Cons. Ga. State U., Atlanta, 1986-89, Dept. Family and Children Svcs., Albany, 1993, 94; presenter Nat. Dropout Prevention Fall conf., 1997. Mem. West Point Parent's Club, U.S. Mil. Acad., 1992-96, Dougherty County Commn. on Children/Youth, Albany, 1991—; mem. adv. bd. Southwest Ga. Prevention Resource Ctr., Teen Plus Clinic, 1998, S.W. Ga. Area Health Edn. Ctr., 1996—; mem. Nat. Family Life Inst., U. N.C., Charlotte, 1997; presenter Nat. Dropout Prevention Fall Conf., 1997. Named Vol. of Yr., Dougherty County Coun. on Child Abuse, 1993, Student Assistance Program Counselor of Yr. for State of Ga., 1994. Mem. Am. Counseling Assn., Ga. Sch. Counselors Assn. (sec. 2d dist. 1985-91, Counselor of Yr. 1993), Am. Sch. Counselors Assn., Nat. Bd. Cert. Counselors (cert. family life instr.), Ga. Lic. Profl. Counselors, South Ga. Regional Assn. Lic. Profl. Counselors, Delta Sigma Theta. Democrat. Roman Catholic. Avocations: reading, classical music. Office: PO Box 50261 Albany GA 31703-0261

KEITH, JENNIE, anthropology educator and administrator, writer; b. Carmel, Calif., Nov. 15, 1942; d. Paul K. and Romayne Louise (Fuller) Hill; m. Marc Howard Ross, Aug. 25, 1968 (div. 1978); 1 child, Aaron Elliot Keith Ross; m. Roy Gerald Fitzgerald, June 21, 1980; 1 child, Kate Romayne Keith-Fitzgerald. BA, Pomona Coll., 1964; MA, Northwestern U., 1966, PhD, 1968; Dr.Letters (hon.), Pomona Coll., 2002. NIMH fellow, Paris, 1968-70; asst. prof. anthropology Swarthmore Coll., 1970-76, assoc. prof., 1976-82, prof., 1982—, Centennial prof. anthropology, 1990—, chmn. sociology and anthropology, 1987-92, provost, 1992-2001; exec. dir. Eugene M. Lang Ctr. for Civic and Social Responsibility, 2002—. Mem. rsch. edn. rev. com. NIMH, Washington, 1979-82; co-dir. workshop on age and anthropology Nat. Inst. Aging, Washington, 1980-81, task group leader nat. rsch. plan on aging, 1981; mem. human devel. rev. bd. NIH, 1985-89; mem. adv. coun. Brookdale Found., 1990-93. Author: Old People, New Lives, 1977, 2d paperback edit., 1982 (Am. Jour. Nursing Book of Yr. 1978), Old People as People, 1982; co-author: The Aging Experience, 1994 (Richard Kalish award Gerontol. Soc. Am. 1994); co-editor: New Methods for Old-Age Research, 1980, 2d edit., 1986, Age in Anthropological Theory, 1984; mem. editorial bd. Gerontologist, 1981-89, Jour. Gerontology, 1987-91, Jour. Aging Studies, 1989-98; assoc. editor Rsch. on Aging, 1981-88. Bd. dirs. Cmty. Svcs., Folsom, Pa., 1980-82, Inst. Outdoor Awareness, Swarthmore, 1980—; bd. dirs. Kendal-Crosslands, 1987-92, chmn., 1989-92, Kendal Corp., 1992-95. Conf. grantee Nat. Inst. Aging, 1980, rsch. grantee, 1982-90. Fellow Am. Anthrop. Assn., Gerontol. Soc. Am. (exec. bd. behavioral and social scis. sect. 1985-87, program chmn. 1989, chair 1989-90, publs. com. 1993-95); mem. Assn. Anthropology and Gerontology (founder, sec. 1980-81). Office: Swarthmore Coll Lang Ctr for Civic and Social Responsibi Swarthmore PA 19081 E-mail: jkeith1@swarthmore.edu.

KEITH, KENT MARSTELLER, academic administrator, educator, writer, lawyer; b. N.Y.C., May 22, 1948; s. Bruce Edgar and Evelyn E. (Johnston) K.; m. Elizabeth Misao Carlson, Aug. 22, 1976. BA in Govt., Harvard U., 1970; BA in Politics and Philosophy, Oxford (Eng.) U., 1972, MA, 1977; JD, U. Hawaii, 1977; EdD, U. So. Calif., 1996. Bar: Hawaii 1977, D.C. 1979. Assoc. Cades, Schutte, Fleming & Wright, Honolulu, 1977-79; coord. Hawaii Dept. Planning and Econ. Devel., Honolulu, 1979-81, dep. dir., 1981-83, dir., 1983-86; energy resources coord. State of Hawaii, Honolulu, 1983-86, chmn. State Policy Coun., 1983-86; chmn. Aloha Tower Devel. Corp., 1983-86; project mgr. Mililani Tech. Park Castle and Cooke Properties, Inc., 1986-89, v.p. pub. rels. and bus. devel., 1988-89; pres. Chaminade U., Honolulu, 1989-95; v.p. devel. and comm. YMCA Honolulu, 1998—2001, sr. v.p., 2001—. Author: Jobs for Hawaii's People: Fundamental Issues in Economic Development, 1985, The Paradoxical Commandments: Finding Personal Meaning in a Crazy World, 2001, Anyway: The Paradoxical Commandments, 2002; contbr. articles on ocean law to law jours. Trustee Hawaii Loa Coll., 1986—89, vice chmn., 1987—89; bd. dirs. St. Louis Sch., 1990—95, Hanahauoli Sch., 1990—98, Cath. Charities, 1997—2003; chmn. Manoa Neighborhood Bd., 1989—91; mem. platform com. Hawaii Dem. Conv., 1982, 1984, 1986; pres. Manoa Valley Ch., Honolulu, 1976—78; mem. Diocesan Bd. Edn., 1990—95, chmn., 1990—93. Rhodes scholar, 1970; named one of 10 Outstanding Young Men of Am., U.S. Jaycees, 1984; recipient Disting. Alumni award U. Hawaii, 1993. Mem. Am. Assn. Rhodes Scholars, Internat. House of Japan,

Nature Conservancy, Pla. Club, Pacific Club, Harvard Club Hawaii (Honolulu, bd. dirs. 1974-78, sec. 1974-76), Rotary (Honolulu Sunrise). Home: 2626 Hillside Ave Honolulu HI 96822-1716 E-mail: kentkeith@hotmail.com.

KEITH, MARY AGNES, food scientist, educator; b. Bellefonte, Pa., Apr. 12, 1947; d. Robert Bruce and Rose Alma (Gillespie) K. BS in Secondary Edn. and Chemistry, Pa. State U., 1969, MS in Food Sci., 1979, PhD, 1983; cert., Swahili Lang. Inst., 1989. Home econs. vol. U.S. Peace Corps-Paraguay, Washington, 1970-75; internat. job counselor Internat. Agriculture Programs Pa. State U., University Park, 1976-82; asst. prof., extension specialist Ill. Cooperative Extension U. Ill., Urbana, 1983-88; nutritionist, missionary Maryknoll (N.Y.) Lay Mission Program, 1989-91; pvt. practice Urbana, 1991-92; dir. house ops., adminstr., trainer summer mission program St. Augustine's Cath. Ctr., U. Fla., Gainesville, 0192—1994; pub. health nutritionist WIC, Tampa, 1994—2000; ext. agt., dietitian U. Fla., 2001—. Faculty liaison Internat. Colloquium, Urbana, 1983—87; spkrs. bur. Office Internat. Affairs, Champaign, Ill., 1985—88. Co-author: Food Safety for Dietitians, 1991. Translator Champaign-Urbana Com. on Sanctuary, 1984-88. Mem. Inst. Food Technols. (del. 1987-88, chair lecture com. 1987-88, Pitts. sect. fellow 1979, Foremost-McKesson fellow 1980), Assn. Women in Internat. Devel., Am. Home Econs. Assn., Internat. Assn. Milk, Food and Environ. Sanitarians. Democrat. Roman Catholic. Avocations: painting, birdwatching, handicrafts. Home: 2106 E Annie St Tampa FL 33612-8326

KEITH, PENNY SUE, mayor, educator; b. Louisville, Sept. 15, 1949; d. John G. Jr. and Edna Lee (Butler) K. AS, U. Ky., 1974; BS, U. Louisville, 1978, MEd in Spl. Edn., 1982, MEd in Curriculum Studies, 1984. Cert. tchr., Ky. Adv. tchr. St. Stephan Martyr Sch., Louisville, 1978-80; tchr. learning disabled students South Oldham Mid. Sch., Crestwood, Ky., 1980-87; dir., prodr. WSOM News, 1988—; pub. rels. liason South Oldham Mid. Sch., 1987-90; mayor City of Parkway Village, Ky., 1990—. Prodr./dir. WSOM News, South Oldham Middle Sch., 1988—, WSOH News, South Oldham High Sch., 1994—. Editor: Through the Eyes of 6th Graders, 1978, Interview with Famous People in the Louisville Times, 1987, An Interview with Diane Sawyer, Louisville Mag.. Nov. 1992. Commr. City of Parkway Village, Louisville, 1982-85, 88-89; treas., 1986; mem. Regional Airport Authority, Louisville, 1992-93; mem. Community Adv. Com., Louisville, 1992. Mem. NEA, Ky. Mcpl. League, Ky. Cols., Oldham County Edn. Assn., Atwood Sr. Citizens (pres. 1985-90). Democrat. Methodist. Home: 850 Melford Ave Louisville KY 40217-2006 Office: South Oldham Mid Sch 6403 W Highway 146 Crestwood KY 40014-9792

KEITH, TIMOTHY ZOOK, psychology educator; b. Providence, R.I., May 7, 1952; s. Charles Herbert and Julia Mercer (Zook) K.; m. Mary Anne Forbes, Aug. 16, 1975 (dec. Mar. 1989); children: Davis Henry, Scott Forbes, William Howe; m. Patricia Josephine Berg, Sept. 15, 1990. BA, U. N.C., 1974; MA, East Carolina U., 1978; PhD, Duke U., 1982. Licensed psychologist, N.C. Lead psychologist Montgomery County Schs., Troy, N.C., 1978-80; sch. psychologist Durham (N.C.) City Schs., 1981-82; asst. prof. U. Iowa, Iowa City, 1982-85, assoc. prof., 1985-87, Va. Poly. Inst. and State U., Blacksburg, Va., 1987-91, prof., 1991-93, Alfred (N.Y.) U., 1993-97, Powell prof. of psychology and schooling, 1997—2001; prof. of ednl. psychology U Tex., 2001—. Rsch. cons. Iowa Dept. Corrections, 1985-86, Iowa Dept. Edn., Des Moines, 1983-87; nat. adv. com. mem. Buros Inst. Mental Measurements, 1992—95. Contbr. articles to profl. jours.; author: (videotape) Sch. Psychologist's Applications of Computers in Edn., 1984; mem. editl. bd. Sch. Psychology Rev., 1985-, assoc. editor, 1987-90, Jour. Sch. Psychology, 1987-99, Jour. Psychoednl. Assessment, 1994—; assoc. editor Sch. Psychology Quarterly, 1996-2000. Recipient award, N.C. Sch. Psychology Assn., 1981, Disting. Rsch. award, N.C. Assn. Rsch. in Edn., 1981, 1993, Ea. Ednl. Rsch. Assn., 1993, Rsch. Excellence award, Iowa Ednl. Rsch. and Evaluation Assn., 1985, Women's Rsch. award, Iowa Psychol. Assn., 1987, Presdl. award, Iowa Sch. Psychologists Assn., 1987, Outstanding Article award, Sch. Psychology Quar., 1993, Jour. Sch. Psychology, 1999, Articles of Yr. award, Sch. Psychology Rev., 1999, Rsch. Excellence award, Mensa Internat., 2001; fellow sr. rsch. fellow, Office Ednl. Rsch. and Improvement, U.S. Dept. Edn., 1998—2001, Measurement/Learning/Cons., LLC, 2000, Riverside Pub., 2001, Woodcock-Muñoz Found., 2003; grantee, Iowa Measurement Rsch. Found., 1984—85, U. Iowa, 1983—84, 1985—86, Va. Dept. Edn., 1991—93, sr. rsch. fellow, Office Ednl. Rsch. and Improvement, U.S. Dept. Edn., 1987—88. Fellow APA (mem. membership com. sch. psychology divsn. 1985, program co-chmn. 1993-95, Lightner Witmer award 1988); mem. NASP, Am. Ednl. Rsch. Assn., Am. Psychol. Soc., Sigma Xi. Episcopalian. Home: PO Box 160427 Austin TX 78716 Office: Dept of Ednl Psychology U Tex SZB 504 Austin TX 78712 E-mail: tim.keith@mail.utexas.edu.

KELDERMAN VAN POLEN, CAROLE ANN, special education educator; b. Oskaloosa, Iowa, June 7, 1950; d. Robert Elmer Kelderman and Evelyn Ruth (Van Ommen) Cunningham; m. Jerry Lee Van Polen, Aug. 10, 1989; children: Amy Catherine, Angela Jo, Jason Lee. BA in Psychology and Sociology, Ctrl. U. of Iowa, 1972; MA in Spl. Edn., N.E. Mo. State U., 1991. Cert. tchr., Iowa, Wash., Ariz. Spl. edn. tchr. Oskaloosa Jr. and Sr. High Schs., 1979-83; adminstr. Mahaska Diamond Shelter, Oskaloosa, 1983-85; substitute tchr. Cartwright Sch. Dist., Phoenix, 1985-87; spl. edn. tchr. K-12 multicategorical resource rm. Firemont (Iowa) Sch., 1987-89; spl. edn. tchr. K-6 mutlicategorical program Eddyville (Iowa) Sch., 1989—. Adj. prof. psychology Buena Vista Coll., Ottumwa, Iowa, 1991—; adv. bd. Mahaska Diamond Shelter, Oskaloosa, 1980-82, bd. dirs., 1983-85; cons. phase III North Ctrl. Regional Ednl. Lab. Mayor Kirkville, Iowa; vol. campaign State Rep. Candidate, 1984; fund raiser Mahaska Diamond Shelter, Oskaloosa, 1983-85. Mem. NEA, Iowa State Edn. Assn., Nat. Assn. for Learning Disabilities, Iowa Assn. for Learning Disabilities, Coun. for Exceptional Children, LWV, Dem. Women. Methodist. Avocations: wine and beer making, antique collecting, twig furniture building. Home: RR 1 Box 73 B Eddyville IA 52553-9801

KELEMEN, CHARLES F. computer science educator; b. Mt. Vernon, N.Y., Jan. 7, 1943; s. Frank K. and Eleanor E. (Scott) K.; m. Sylvia J. Brown, July 26, 1975; children— Rebecca, Colin, Elizabeth. BA, Valparaiso U., 1964; MA, Pa. State U., 1966, PhD, 1969. Asst. then assoc. prof. Ithaca Coll., N.Y., 1969-80; prof. LeMoyne Coll., Syracuse, N.Y., 1980-84, Swarthmore Coll., Pa., 1984—, chmn. divsn. natural scis. and engring., 2000—03, Edward Hicks Magill prof. math. and natural scis., 2002—. Cons. in field; chair computer sci. dept. Swarthmore Coll., 1984-99, 2001—; vis. assoc. prof. Cornell U., Ithaca, N.Y., 1978, summers 1979-81. Co-author: (with others) Fundamentals of Computing II Abstraction Data Structures, and Large Software Systems, 1995, Fundamentals of Computing II C++ Laboratory Manual, 1995. Grantee NSF, 1977-81 Mem. Assn. Computing Machinery, IEEE, Computer Soc., Math. Assn. Am. Office: Swarthmore Coll Dept Computer Sci Swarthmore PA 19081 E-mail: ckeleme1@swarthmore.edu.

KELEMEN, JOHN, neurologist, educator; b. Nyíregyháza, Hungary, Apr. 28, 1948; s. Ignac and Anna (Hartman) K. BA, SUNY, Binghamton, 1970; MD, Georgetown U., 1974. Cert. Am. Bd. Psychiatry and Neurology-Neurology, Am. Bd. Electrodiagnostic Medicine. Med. intern Nassau County Med. Ctr., East Meadow, N.Y., 1974-75, neurology resident, 1975-78, staff neurologist, 1980-85, dir. MDA clinic, 1980-85, chief neuromuscular program, 1981-85; neuromuscular fellow Tufts U.-New Eng. Med. Ctr., Boston, 1978-80; pntr. Island Neurol. P.C., Plainview, N.Y., 1985—; clin. asst. prof. neurology NYU Sch. of Medicine, 1996—. Clin. asst. prof. neurology Cornell U. Med. Coll., N.Y.C., 1986-95; tchg. residents and med. students Stony Brook U., Cornell U., NYU, Manhasset, East Meadow, 1980—; lectr. in field. Contbr. chpts. to books and articles to profl. jours. Rsch. grantee Muscular Dystrophy Assn., Boston, 1979, Nassau Heart Assn., East Meadow, 1984. Fellow Am. Acad. Neurology. Avocations: tennis, sailing, skiing, computers, cinema. Office: Island Neurol PC 824 Old Country Rd Plainview NY 11803-4935

KELLAM, BECKY, business educator, consultant; b. Austin, Tex., Sept. 7, 1938; d. Carruth Brisco and Madge Lee (Swindell) K.; m. June 20, 1958 (div. 1979); m. Thomas G. Dougherty, June 21, 1987. BA, Calif. State U., Hayward, 1973; postgrad., U. San Diego, 1978-79, U. So. Calif., L.A., 1979; MBA, Nat. U., 1982. Legal sec. Neil Strain, San Mateo, Calif., 1967-69, Hrusoff & Graham, Attys., La Mesa, Calif., 1975-77; owner, mgr. DataText, San Diego, 1976-80; paralegal Miller, Boyko and Bell, San Diego, 1976-77; legal adminstr. Gade & Hayne, Attys., San Diego, 1977-79, Thacher & Hurst, P.C., San Diego, 1979-80; mgmt. cons. Profl. Bus. Svcs., San Diego, 1980-84; instr. Kings River Community Coll., Reedley, Calif., 1984-97, pres. senate, 1992-94; instr. Madera (Calif.) C.C., 1997—, bus. dept. chair, 1998—. State rep. Calif. Acad. Senate, Sacramento, 1984-87; cons. post secondary edn. Calif. State Dept. of Edn., Sacramento, 1985-88; computer cons. Bus. Solutions, Fresno, Calif., 1988—. Coord. Faculty Assn. of Community Colls., Sacramento, 1985—; bd. dirs. Women's Polit. Inst., L.A., 1982-84, Children Svcs. Network, Fresno, 1990—. Named Outstanding Leader of the Yr., Las Mujeres of Calif., 1982. Mem. Am. Assn. Women of Cmty. and Jr. Colls., Nat. Fedn. Bus. and Profl. Women, Fresno Bus. and Profl. Women (pres. 1989-90, Fresno County Woman of the Yr. 1990), Office Automation Soc. Internat. (editl. bd. dirs. 1989—), Delta Kappa Gamma, Alpha Psi (pres. 1992-94). Presbyterian. Avocations: travel, antique collector, gardening, quilting. Office: Clovis Community Coll 390 W Fir Clovis CA 93612-8321

KELLAR, MARIE TERESE, special education educator; b. St. Louis, Oct. 11, 1934; d, Paul and Frances Marie (O'Hallaron) Robyn; m. John Cullen Hagerty, Jan. 17, 1959 (dec. 1972); children: John Cullen Jr., Anne Rose; m. John W. Kellar, Dec. 26, 1974 (dec.); children: Stephen, Joyce, Robert, Barbara, Michael, Richard. BS in Elem. Edn., Maryville Coll., St. Louis, 1956; MAT, Webster U., 1975; postgrad., Fontbonne Coll., Clayton, Mo., 1981. Cert. elem. edn., social studies, English, learning disabilities, emotionally disturbed, behavior disordered. 1st grade tchr. Kratz Sch., St. Louis County, 1956-63; homebound tchr. Sch. Dist. Webster Groves, Mo., 1964-67, Spl. Sch. Dist. St. Louis County, 1965-67; tchr. Webster U., 1974-75, Miriam Sch., Webster Groves, 1980—84; adminstr., 1984-89; pvt. practice, 1989—. Learning cons. St. Ambrose Sch., 1989—; presenter and spkr. in field. Contbr. articles to profl. jours. Active St. Gerard Majella Ch.; vol. March of Dimes, ARC, Am. Cancer Soc. Mem. Coun. for Exceptional Children, Mo. Assn. for Children with Learning Disabilities (Tchr. of Yr. 1984), Nat. Cath. Edn. Assn. (Disting. Tchr. award 2002), Adults With Learning Disabilities, Delta Epsilon Sigma, Pi Lambda Theta Roman Catholic. Avocations: drawing, painting, reading.

KELLAR, WILLIAM HENRY, university official, history educator; b. Cleve., Feb. 11, 1952; s. William Leo and Mary Jane (Sachrison) K. BA in History Edn., U. Houston, 1983, MA in History, 1990, PhD in History, 1994. Cert. secondary tchr., Tex. History tchr. Houston Ind. Sch. Dist., 1984-93, curriculum writer, 1990-93; adj. instr. history Houston C.C., 1992-98, Kingwood (Tex.) Coll., 1995-97, U. Houston, 1997—, dir. scholars' cmty., 1997—2003, exec. dir., 2003—; pub. historian W.H. Kellar Cons., LLC, Houston, 1995—. Cons. Mus. Fine Arts, Houston, 1989, Rice U., Houston, 1990. Author: Piping Technology and Products, 1998, Make Haste Slowly, 1999; co-author: Service Corporation International, 1999, Kelsey-Seybold Clin., 1999. Fellow NEH, 1985, Petroleum Inst. for Edn., 1986; grantee Houston Bus. Com. Ednl. Excellence, 1986, 88, 89. Mem. Am. Hist. Assn. (life), Am. Assn. Higher Edn., Assn. for Study of Afro-Am. Life and History (life), Houston Coun. for Social Studies (bd. dirs. 1985-94), So. Hist. Assn. (life), Tex. State Hist. Assn. (life, Commendation 1989). Avocations: theater, symphony, sports, travel, writing. Office: U Houston Scholars Cmty Houston TX 77204-0001 E-mail: Wkellar@uh.edu.

KELLER, BARBARA LYNN, special education educator, reading teacher; b. Great Falls, Mont., July 18, 1941; d. Edward Jerome and Alvina Elizabeth (Kampsnider) Daly; m. Ray B. Keller, Dec. 28, 1961; 1 child, Forest Ry. Student, Ea. Mont. Coll., 1967-69; BA, U. Mont., 1976; MEd, Mont. State U., 1996. Tchr. grades 1-4 Pub. Schs. Birch Creek Hutterite Colony, Dupuyer, Mont., 1962-63; tchr. grade 2 Pub. Sch. Blackfeet Indian Reservation, Heart Butte, Mont., 1963-64; tchr. reading remediation Pub. Sch., Fort Benton, Mont., 1967-68; tchr. emotionally disturbed Manzanita Ranch Residential Sch., Hyompom, Calif., 1968-69; tchr. reading remediation Pub. Schs., Bigfork, Mont., 1975-78; tchr. ESL Flathead C.C., Kalispell, Mont., 1978-82; pvt. practice tchr. reading, ESL, emotionally disturbed Bigfork, 1982-85; tchr. spl. edn. Pub. Schs. Blackfeet Indian Reservation, Browning, Mont., 1985-94; tchr. study skills and reading, coord. Parents' Ctr. Browning (Mont.) H.S., 1994-99, sch. wide team leader, dir. reading lab., 1997-99, Parents' Ctr. coord.; pres. Reading Essentials Inc., from 1999, from 1999. Pres. Eagle's View Publs., Bigfork, 1989—; author-in-residence Am. Edn. Inst., 1994—; cons. adult edn. Author: Reading Pals—A Handbook for Volunteers, 1990, Reading Pals—A Teacher's Manual, 1990, The Parents' Guide—Studying Made Easy, 1991, Gifts of Love and Literacy—A Parent's Guide to Raising Children Who Love to Read, 1993, Read With Your Child—Make a Difference, 1994; (ednl. program) Studying Made Easy—The Complete Program, 1992, The Students' Guide—Studying Made Easy, 1996, Teachers Manual Studying Made Easy, 1996, Read to Your Child, Make a Difference, 1997. Reading cons. Personal Vol. Svc., Bigfork, 1970—, Browning, Mont., 1985-99. Recipient Author of Yr. award Am. Edn. Inst., 1993. Mem. ASCD, Internat. Reading Assn., Am. Fedn. Tchrs., Literacy Vols. Am., Mont. Counseling Assn., Learning Disabilities Assn., SPAN (Small Publs. Assn. No. Am.). Avocations: cross country skiing, traveling, reading. Home: Bigfork, Mont. Died July 12, 2002.

KELLER, CHARLES DALE, secondary school educator; b. Forrest City, Ark., Feb. 5, 1946; s. Hugh Alvin Keller, Sr. and Mary Evelyn (Moore) Starr; m. Brenda Sue Adams, Aug. 7, 1950; 1 child, Megan. BSE, Ark. State Coll., 1966; MSE, Ark. State U., 1970; postgrad., Ark. State U., U. Nev. Grad. asst. Ark. State U., Jonesboro, 1966-67; tchr. Jonesboro H.S., 1967-68, South Pemiscot H. S., Steele, Mo., 1968-69, Beatty (Nev.) H.S., 1969-72; internat. tchg. fellow Echuca H.S., Victoria, Australia, 1972-74; ednl. devel. and tng. officer Royal Melbourne Inst. of Tech., Australia, 1975-76; tchr. Eagle Valley Jr. High, Carson City, Nev., 1990-93, Carson H.S., 1993-95, dean of students, 1995-99, asst. prin. alt. edn. divsn., 1999—. Pres. Seminar and Counseling Svcs., Carson City, 1988-90; dir. Citizen Outreach, Carson City, chmn. joint svcs. coun. Chmn. Joint Svc. Coun., Carson City, 1988-90; elder First Presbyn. Ch., Carson City, 1990-93; adv. bd. Carson City Children's Mus., Carson City, 1990-95; mem. Nev. Day Com., 1988-93. Recipient Internat. Tchg. Fellowship, Victoria Dept. Edn., Australia, 1972-73. Mem. Australian Coll. Edn., Ormsby County Edn. Assn., Kiwanis (Kiwanian of Yr. 1988-89, 91-92, Disting. Lt. Gov., Calif./Nev., Hawaii, 1991-92, life mem.). Office: 225 E Park St Carson City NV 89706-3017 E-mail: cdkeller@aol.com, ckeller@carson.k-12nv.us.

KELLER, DENNIS JAMES, management educator; b. July 6, 1941; s. Ralph and Dorothy (Barckman) K.; m. Constance Bassett Templeton, May 28, 1966; children: Jeffrey Breckenridge, David McDaniel, John Templeton. AB, Princeton U., 1963; MBA, U. Chgo., 1968. Account exec. Motorola Comm., Chgo., 1964-67; v.p. fin. Bell & Howell Comm., Waltham, Mass., 1968-70; v.p. mktg. Bell & Howell Schs., Chgo., 1970-73; pres. Keller Grad. Sch. Mgmt., Chgo., 1973-81, chmn., CEO, 1981—2002, chmn., co-CEO, 2002—. Chmn. bd., CEO DeVry Inc., 1987-2002, chmn., co-CEO, 2002—; cons., evaluator North Central Assn., Chgo., 1979-84; bd. dirs. Templeton Kenly & Co., Broadview, Ill., Nicor Inc. Trustee Glenwood (Ill.) Sch. for Boys, 1980-2002, Chgo. Zool. Soc., Brookfield, Ill., 1979-, Princeton (N.J.) U., 1994-98, 2000-, Lake Forest Acad.-Ferry Hall, Ill., 1980-87, George M. Pullman Found., Chgo., 1987-2002; bd. trustees U. Chgo., 1998-; bd. dirs. Great Books Found., Chgo., 1986-98; chmn. U. Chgo. Grad. Sch. Bus. Coun., 1994-2002, Princeton U. Sch. Engring. and Applied Scis. Leadership Coun., 1992-; commr. North Cen. Assn.-Commn. on Instns. of Higher Edn., 1985-88. Nat. Merit scholar, 1959-63; U. Chgo. Grad. Sch. Bus. fellow, 1967-68. Mem. Hinsdale Golf Club, Econ. Club, Comml. Club Chgo., Chgo. Club, Nantucket Golf Club, Sankaty Head Golf Club. Republican. Mem. United Ch. of Christ. Office: DeVry Inc 1 Tower Ln Ste 1000 Oakbrook Terrace IL 60181

KELLER, EDWARD LOWELL, electrical engineer, educator; b. Rapid City, S.D., Mar. 6, 1939; s. Earl Lowell and E. Blanche (Oldfield) K.; m. Carole Lynne Craig, Sept. 1, 1963; children: Edward Lowell, Craig, Morgan. BS, U.S. Naval Acad., 1961; PhD, Johns Hopkins U., 1971. Mem. faculty U. Calif., Berkeley, 1971—, assoc. prof. elec. engring., 1977-79, prof., 1979-94, prof. emeritus, 1994—; assoc. dir. Smith Kettlewell Eye Rsch. Inst., San Francisco, 1998—; chmn. bioengring. program U. Calif., Berkeley and San Francisco, 1989; chmn. engring. sci. program Coll. of Engring. U. C., Berkeley, 1991-94. Contbr. articles to sci. jours. Served with USN, 1961-65. Sr. Von Humboldt fellow, 1977-78 Fellow IEEE; mem. AAAS, Assn. for Rsch. in Vision and Ophthalmology, Soc. for Neurosci., Internat. Neural Network Soc. Achievements include rsch. on oculomotor system and math. modelling of nervous system. Office: Smith-Kettlewell Eye Rsch Inst 2318 Fillmore St San Francisco CA 94115-1813 E-mail: elk@ski.org.

KELLER, GEORGE CHARLES, higher education consultant, writer; b. N.J., Mar. 14, 1928; s. Charles and Elizabeth K.; m. Gail Faithfull, 1960 (div. 1973); children: Bayard, Elizabeth; m. Jane Eblen, 1975. AB, Columbia U., 1951, MPhil, 1954. Academic dir. Gt. Books Found., Chgo., 1954-56; instr. polit. sci. Columbia U., N.Y.C., 1957-59, asst. dean, 1959-61, editor, 1962-70; asst. to chancellor SUNY, Albany, 1970-78; asst. to pres. U. Md., College Park, 1979-82; sr. v.p. Barton-Gillett Co., Balt., 1983-88; sr. fellow Grad. Sch. Edn. U. Pa., Phila., 1988-94. Author: Academic Strategy, 1983; co-author: Post-Land Grant University, 1981, The Best of Planning, 1997; editor: Planning for Higher Education, 1990-97; contbr. numerous articles, revs. to ednl. publs. With USN, 1946-48. Recipient Sibley award, Coun. for Advancement and Support of Edn., 1963, 64, 65, U.S. Steel Found. award, 1965; named Best U.S. Edn. Writer, Atlantic mag., 1968; James Fisher Award from CASE,2003. Mem. Assn. Study Higher Edn., Soc. Coll. and Univ. Planning (Founders award 1988). Office: 4900 Wetheredsville Rd Baltimore MD 21207-6625

KELLER, JAMI ANN, special education educator; b. Hastings, Nebr., Jan. 4, 1961; d. Donald Lee and Gail Angela (England) Stilley; m. Mark Lee Keller, June 19, 1982; children: William England, Robert John Thomas, Alexander James Stilley, Clare Jana Lee, Elyse Markie Ann, Jack Marcus Gust. BS with distinction, U. Nebr., 1984. Tchr. spl. edn. Grand Island (Nebr.) Pub. Schs., 1985-92, Papillon (Nebr.)/La Vista Pub. Schs., 1992-93. PTA scholar Nebr. PTA, 1983, Beach-Byer scholar, 1983. Mem. NEA, Nebr. Edn. Assn., Pi Lambda Theta, Mu Epsilon Nu.

KELLER, JANICE GAIL, principal; b. Providence, R.I., Jan. 30, 1950; d. Harry A. and Naomi (Dressler) K. BA, U. R.I., 1972, MA, 1975. Cert. elem. tchr., critic tchr., elem. prin., R.I. Tchr. 6th grade East Providence (R.I.) Schs., 1972-90; prin. James R.D. Oldham Sch., East Providence, 1990—, Meadowcrest Sch., Riverside, R.I., 1992—. Bd. dirs. local PTA. Recipient grant Commr. Edn., St. Bd. Regents; named East Providence Tchr. of the Yr., 1988-89, East Bay Women's Club Outstanding Educator of the Yr., 1989. Mem. NEA, ASCD, Nat. Assn. Elem. Sch. Prins., Nat. Coun. Tchrs. of English, Nat. Sci. Tchrs. Assn., Nat. Coun. Tchrs. Math., Internat. Reading Assn., Assn. Childhood Edn. Internat.

KELLER, JOSEPH BISHOP, mathematician, educator; b. Paterson, N.J., July 31, 1923; s. Isaac and Sally (Bishop) Keller; m. Evelyn Fox, Aug. 29, 1963 (div. Nov. 17, 1976); children: Jeffrey M., Sarah N. BA, NYU, 1943, MS, 1946, PhD, 1948. Prof. math. Courant Inst. Math. Scis., NYU, 1948—79; chmn. dept. math. Univ. Coll. Arts and Scis. and Grad. Sch. Engring. and Sci., 1967—73; prof. math. and mech. engring. Stanford U., 1979—93, prof. emeritus, 1993—. Hon. prof. math. scis. Cambridge U., 1990—; rsch. assoc. Woods Hole Oceanographic Instn., 1965—; Gibbs lectr. Am. Math. Soc., 1977; von Neumann lectr. Soc. Indsl. and Applied Math., 1983; Rouse Ball lectr. U. Cambridge, Eng., 1993. Contbr. articles to profl. jours. Recipient von Karman prize, Soc. Indsl. and Applied Math., 1979, Eringen medal, Soc. Engring. Scis., 1981, Timoshenko medal, ASME, 1984, U.S. Nat. medal of Sci., 1988, NAS award in Applied Math. and Numerical Analysis, 1995, Frederic Esser Nemmers prize in math., Northwestern U., Evanston, Ill., 1996, Wolf prize, Israel, 1997. Mem.: NAS, Soc. Indsl. and Applied Math., Am. Phys. Soc., Am. Math. Soc., Am. Acad. Arts and Scis., Royal Soc. (fgn.). Home: 820 Sonoma Ter Stanford CA 94305-1072 Office: Stanford U Dept Math Stanford CA 94305-2125

KELLER, JULIE ELIZABETH, elementary and learning disabilities educator; b. Portsmouth, Ohio, Jan. 29, 1960; d. Charles Curtis and Mary Margaret (Greer) Caulley; m. Paul Jeffrey Keller, Nov. 4, 1978; children: Jennifer, Joshua. Student, Shawnee State U., 1987-88, Ohio U., 1987-88; BS in Edn., U. Rio Grande (Ohio), 1989-90; MEd summa cum laude, Ohio U., 1995. Cert. elem. tchr., learning disabilites tchr., Ohio. Priv. music tchr., Minford, Ohio, 1979-86; sch. bus driver Minford Local Sch. Dist., 1985-89; vol. tchr. aide Minford Primary Shc., 1988-89; in-sch. suspension monitor Green Local Sch. Dist., Franklin Furnace, Ohio, 1990-91; learning disabilites tchr., asst. basketball coach Wheelersburg (Ohio) Elem. Sch., 1991—; adult basic edn. instr. Northwest Local Sch. Dist., Minford Ctr., 1991-92; priv. home tutor Wheelersburg Schs., 1991-92. Com. person U. Rio Grande Grad. Program, 1990-91, bd. of review mem., 1992—; cons. appendix to bd. policy Emergency Procedure Plan, 1990. Author: (booklet) Athletic, Activity Handbook, 1991 (bd. recognition award 1991); designer In-Sch. Suspension Program, 1990 (bd. recognition award 1991). Program dir. Music Recital and Review, Minford, 1983-86, Daily Vacation Bible Sch. Fairview Bapt. Ch., Minford, 1984-86; activity asst. Silver Spurs 4-H Club, Minford, 1989-91; pianist Fairview Missionary Bapt. Ch., 1973-94; asst. musician, choir mem. Wheelersburg Baptist Ch., 1994—. Recipient Ohio Student Choice award, Rio Grande, 1989. Mem. NEA (1st v.p. 1995-96), Wheelersburg Edn. Assn. (spl. areas rep. liaison com. 1992-94, exec. com. 1992—, negotiating com. 1994—, pres. 1996—), Wheelersburg 200 Club, Wheelersburg PTO. Republican. Baptist. Avocations: horseback riding, hiking, playing piano, travel, sports. Home: 687 Gleim Rd Wheelersburg OH 45694-8322 Office: Wheelersburg Elem Sch 1731 Dogwood Ridge Rd Wheelersburg OH 45694-9474

KELLER, KENNETH HARRISON, engineering educator, science policy analyst; b. N.Y.C., Oct. 19, 1934; s. Benjamin and Pearl (Pastor) K.; m. Dorothy Robinson, June 2, 1957 (div.); children: Andrew Robinson, Paul Victor; m. Bonita F. Sindelir, June 19, 1981; children: Jesse Daniel, Alexandra Amelie. AB, Columbia U., 1956, BS, 1957; MS in Engring., Johns Hopkins U., 1963, PhD, 1964. Asst. prof. dept. chem. engring. U. Minn., Mpls., 1964-68, assoc. prof., 1968-71, prof., 1971—, prof. Hubert H. Humphrey Inst. Pub. Affairs, 1996—, Charles M. Denny Jr. prof., assoc. dean Grad. Sch., 1973-74, 99—, acting dean Grad. Sch., 1974-75, head dept. chem. engring. and materials sci., 1978-80, v.p. acad. affairs, 1980-85, pres., 1985-88; Philip D. Reed sr. fellow for sci. and tech. Coun. on Fgn. Rels., 1990-96, sr. v.p., 1993-95. Cons. in field; mem. cardiology adv. com. NIH, 1982-86; mem. sci. and tech. adv. panel to dir. CIA, 1995-99; mem. commn. on phys. scis., math. and applications NRC, 1996-2000; bd. dirs.

LASPAU: Acad. and Profl. Programs for the Ams., 1996—; trustee Sci. Mus. Minn., 1997—; chmn. Med. Technology Leadership Forum, 1998—. Mem. adv. com. program for Soviet emigré scholars, 1974-82; bd. govs. Argonne Nat. Lab., 1982-85; bd. dirs. Walker Art Ctr., 1982-88, Charles Babbage Found., 1991-99. Served from ensign to lt. USNR, 1957-61. NIH Spl. fellow, 1972-73; vis. fellow Woodrow Wilson Sch. of Pub. and Internat. Affairs, Princeton U., 1988-90. Founding fellow Am. Inst. for Med. and Biol. Engring.; fellow AAAS; mem. Am. Soc. Artificial Internal Organs (pres. 1980-81), AIChE (Food and Bioengring. award 1980), Am. Coun. for Emigrés in the Professions (dir. 1972-80), Nat. Acad. Engring., Mpls. C. of C. (bd. dirs. 1985-88), Coun. Fgn. Rels., Phi Beta Kappa, Sigma Xi (nat. lectr. 1978-80). Office: Hubert H Humphrey Inst U Minn 301 19th Ave S Ste 300 Minneapolis MN 55455-0411

KELLER, MICHAEL JAY, research director; b. Bklyn., May 25, 1946; s. Leonard and Vivian (Slamm) K. BS in Journalism, Ohio U., 1968; MA in Polit. Sci., Miami U., 1973. Dir. student life rsch. Miami U., Oxford, Ohio, 1976-82; rsch. specialist Md. Higher Edn. Commn., Annapolis, 1982-91, assoc. dir. policy analysis and rsch., 1991-93, dir. policy analysis and rsch., 1993—. Co-author: (textbook) Understanding Political Science, 1977; contbr. articles to profl. jours. Bd. dirs. Peace Action, Washington, 1989—; chpt. coord. Anne Arundel Peace Action, Annapolis, 1985—; chmn. Annapolis Human Rels. Commn., 1996—; bd. dirs. Anne Arundel Conflict Resolution Ctr., 1993-96. With U.S. Army, 1969-72. Cooperative Systems fellow Nat. Ctr. Edn. Statis., Washington, 1993, Adminstrv. fellow Miami U., 1982. Mem. Assn. Instl. Rsch. (Md. exec. com. 1990-93). Democrat. Avocations: peace activism, political campaign management, stamp collecting. Office: Md Higher Edn Commn 839 Bestgate Rd Ste 400 Annapolis MD 21401-3013 E-mail: mkeller@mhec.state.md.us., mjkeller@worldnet.att.net.

KELLER, MICHELLE R. science educator, secondary education educator; b. Rolla, N.D., Aug. 15, 1951; d. Raymond Charles Halone and Yvonne M. (Klier) Edwards; m. Fred F. Keller, June 30, 1973; 1 child, Brent F. BS in Foods and Nutrition, N.D. State U., 1973; cert. sci. edn., Minot State U., 1977; MEd in Secondary Sci. Edn., N.Dak. State U., 2001. Instr. sci. Bisbee (N.D.)-Egeland H.S., 1975—. Judge Seiko Youth Challenge, 1993, 94; mem. N.Dak. State Sci. Stds. com., N.Dak. Stds. Awareness facilitator. Access Excellence fellow Genentech/NSF, 1994; recipient Presdl. award for excellence in sci. tchg., 1993, Edn.'s Unsung Hero award 1998; named Hon. Mention Tchr., Radio Shack/Tandy scholars program, 1998, 99. Mem. Am. Assn. Physics Tchrs. (pres. N.D. sect. 2001—), Nat. Sci. Tchrs. Assn., N.D. Sci. Tchrs. Assn., N.D. Orienteering Alliance, Nat. Edn. Assn., N.D. Edn. Assn. Democrat. Roman Catholic. Avocations: walking, reading, gardening. Home: PO Box 265 201 3rd Ave W Bisbee ND 58317-0265 Office: Bisbee-Egeland H S P O Box 217 204 3rd Ave W Bisbee ND 58317 E-mail: mkeller@alum.ndsu.nodak.edu.

KELLER, NANCY CAMILLE, secondary educator; b. Charleston, W.Va., Aug. 17, 1954; d. William Henry and Helen Irene (Anglin) K. BA summa cum laude, Morris Harvey Coll., 1976; MA, W.Va. Coll. Grad. Studies, 1982. Tchr. French and English, Kanawha County Schs., Charleston, W.Va. Mem. AAUW, Dtrs. Am. Colonists, United Dtrs. Confederacy, Colonial Dames 17th Century, Nat. Coun. Tchrs. English, Am. Assn. Tchrs. French, DAR, Alpha Lamba Delta, Sigma Tau Delta, Phi Delta Phi, Kappa Delta Pi. Home: HC 36 Box 54 Blount WV 25025-9702

KELLER, THOMAS FRANKLIN, business administration educator; b. Greenwood, S.C., Sept. 22, 1931; s. Cleaveland Alonzo and Helen (Seago) K.; m. Margaret Neel Query, June 15, 1956; children: Thomas Crafton (dec.), Neel McKay, John Caldwell. AB, Duke U., 1953; MBA, U. Mich., 1957, PhD, 1960; HHD (hon.), Clemson U., 1987. CPA, N.C. Mem. faculty Fuqua Sch. Bus. Duke U., Durham, N.C., 1959—, assoc. prof., 1962-67, prof., 1967-74, R.J. Reynolds prof., 1974—, chmn. dept. mgmt. scis., 1974-96, vice provost, 1971-72, dean Fuqua Sch. Bus., 1974-96; dean Fuqua Sch. Bus. Europe, Frankfurt, 1999-2001. Mem. editorial bd. Duke U. Press, 1970-87; vis. assoc. prof. Carnegie Mellon U., 1966-67, U. Wash., Seattle, 1963-64; cons. to govt. and industry; Fulbright-Hays lectr., Australia, 1975; bd. dirs. Hatteras Income Securities Inc., Charlotte, N.C., Nations Funds Inc., Charlotte, Wendy's Internat., Dublin, Ohio, DIMON Inc., Danville, Va., Biogen, Cambridge, Mass. Author: Accounting for Corporate Income Taxes, 1961, Intermediate Accounting, 1963, 68, 74, Advanced Accounting, 1966, Financial Accounting Theory vol. 1, 1964, 73, 84, vol. 2, 1969, Earnings or Cash Flows: An Experiment on Functional Fixation and the Valuation of the Firm, 1979; editor: monographs Financial Information Needs of Security Analysts, 1977, The Impact of Accounting Research on Practice and Disclosure, 1978; contbr. articles to profl. jours. Elder Presbyn. Ch.; trustee Stillman Coll., Tuscaloosa, Ala.; dir. N.C. Zool. Soc., Rsch. Triangle Regional Partnership, Research Triangle Park, N.C. With AUS, 1953-55. Recipient Outstanding Educator award, N.C. Assn. CPA's, 1997, Univ. medal, Duke Univ., 2001; fellow Haskins and Sells Found., U. Mich., 1959, Ford Found., Duke U., 1960, 1961. Mem. AICPA, Am. Acctg. Assn. (v.p. 1967-68, editor jour. 1972-75), N.C. Assn. CPAs, Fin. Execs. Inst., University Club, Phi Beta Kappa, Phi Kappa Sigma, Beta Gamma Sigma, Alpha Kappa Psi. Avocations: hiking, fishing, reading, sailing. Office: Duke U Fuqua Sch Bus Durham NC 27708-0120 E-mail: tfk1@mail.duke.edu.

KELLER, TONI L. elementary education educator; b. Cin., Sept. 19, 1945; d. Umberto Giacomo and Dora (Casagrande) Colussi; m. Thomas L. Keller, Aug. 21, 1971; children: Sara, Karen, Ann. BA, Thomas More Coll., Ft. Mitchell, Ky., 1971; MA in Edn., Coll. Mount St. Joseph, Cin., 1985. Cert. reading specialist. Elem. tchr. Detroit Parochial Schs., 1966-68, Sycamore Cmty. Sch., Cin., 1969-77, Our Lady of Visition Sch., Cin., 1983-85, St. Teresa of Avila Sch., Cin., 1986—; adjunct instr. Coll. Mount St. Joseph, Cin., 1990-98. Edn. adv. bd. Coll. Mount St. Joseph, Cin., 1992—; sci. adv. com. St. Teresa of Avila Sch., Cin., 1994—; curriculum devel. Sci., Archdiocese of Cin., 1993-94; lectr. No. Ky. U., Highland Heights, 1998—. Mem. Nat. Cath. Edn. Assn., Ohio Cath. Edn. Assn., St. Teresa Parent Tchr. Group, Internat. Reading Assn., St. Teresa Edn. Commn., Nat. Sci. Tchrs. Assn., Internat. Reading Assn. (Ohio coun.), Ky. Reading Assn.

KELLER-AUGSBACH, LINDA JEAN, elementary school educator; b. Glendale, W.Va., June 7, 1951; d. Ernest Nelson and Pearl (Henry) Keller. AA, Minn. Bible Coll., 1971; postgrad., Ky. Christian Coll., 1973-74; BS, Malone Coll., 1975. Cert. elem. tchr., Fla., Ohio. 1st-8th grade tutor CETA program Minerva (Ohio) Local Schs., 1976-77; 1-2d grade tchr. Christian Schs. Cin., 1977-78; substitute tchr. Canton (Ohio) City Schs., 1978-82, Pasco County Schs., New Port Richey, Fla., 1982-83, chpt. I 6th grade tchr. Dade City, Fla., 1983-87, 4th grade tchr. New Port Richey, Fla., 1987-88, 6th grade tchr., 1988-91, 4th grade tchr., 1991—96, 4th, 5th grade tchr., 1996—99, Mittye P. Locke Elem. Sch., Elfers, Fla., 2000—. Attendee Gov. Bush Ann. Educators Leadership Summit, 2002. Mem. Concerned Women for Am. Republican. Avocations: creative teaching materials, crafts, sewing, reading, writing. Home: 3644 Pensdale Dr New Port Richey FL 34652-6244

KELLERMAN, JAMES S. educational association administrator; b. Johnstown, Pa., Mar. 14, 1934; s. James B. and Annie S. K.; m. Patricia G., Feb. 14, 1981; children: Gwendolyn, Bradley, Ashley. BS, Fla. State U., 1958, MS, 1961; EdD, Nova U., 1975. Tchr. Pinellas County (Fla.) Schs., 1958-65; asst. registrar St. Petersburg (Fla.) Jr. Coll., 1965-67; dir. admissions Valencia Community Coll., Orlando, Fla., 1967-69, dean student svcs., 1969-74, provost West campus, 1974-76; exec. dir., CEO Fla. Assn. Community Colls., Tallahassee, 1977-81, Calif. Community Coll. Assn., Sacramento, 1982-85; vice chancellor North Orange County Community Coll., Fullerton, Calif., 1985-86, chancellor, 1986-89; exec. dir., CEO Mo. Community Coll. Assn., Jefferson City, 1989—. Pres. H/K Assocs., Inc., Jefferson City, 1989—. Contbr. articles to profl. jours. With U.S. Army, 1952-54. Recipient Outstanding Leadership award Minority CEOs, Calif., 1989, Alumni Achievement award Nova U., 1986, Disting. Leadership award, Fla. State U., 1981. Fellow Missourians for Higher Edn., Nat. Coun. of State Assoc. Execs., Nat. Ctr. for Rsch. in Vocat. Edn. (policy forum on vocat. edn.), Nat. Coun. on Resource Devel. Address: Missouri Community College 200 E Mccarty St # 100 Jefferson City MO 65101-3113

KELLER-MATHERS, SUSAN, elementary educator, adult education educator; b. Buffalo, May 3, 1962; d. Charles Joseph and Mildred (Ackermann) Keller; m. Gordon Mathers, Aug. 20, 1988; children: Christopher, Rebecca. BS in Elem. Edn., SUNY, Buffalo, 1984, MS in Creativity and Innovation, 1990. Tchr. New Orleans Pub. Schs., 1984-87; lectr. Ctr. for Studies in Creativity, SUNY, 1988-90; asst. prof. SUNY, Learning Lab., 1990-91; tchr. Buffalo Pub. Schs., 1991—2002; lectr. creative studies Ctr. Studies Creativity, Buffalo State Coll., 2002—. Adj. asst. prof. Ctr. Studies Creativity, 1992-2002 Recipient Creative Studies Alumni Achievement award. Mem. NAGC (past chair creativity divsn.), Phi Delta Kappa (exec. bd., past pres.). Home: 874 Lafayette Ave Buffalo NY 14209-1202 Office: Buffalo State Coll Chase Hall 239 Internat Ctr Studies Creativity 1300 Elmwood Ave Buffalo NY 14222 E-mail: kellersm@buffalostate.edu.

KELLEY, ALBERT JOSEPH, global management strategy consultant; b. Boston, July 27, 1924; s. Albert Joseph and Josephine Christine (Sullivan) K.; m. Virginia Marie Riley, June 7, 1945 (dec. Aug. 1988); children: Mark, Shaun, David. BS, U.S. Naval Acad., 1945; BSEE, MIT, 1948, ScD, 1956; postgrad., U. Minn., 1954, Carnegie-Mellon U., 1974. Commd. ensign USN, 1945, advanced through grades to comdr., 1961, carrier pilot, 1950-51, exptl. test pilot Naval Air Test Ctr., 1951-53, program engr. F-4 aircraft Bur. Aeros., 1956-58, program mgr. Eagle missile program Bur. Weapons, 1958-60; mgr. Agena program NASA, 1960-61, dir. electronics and control advanced rsch. and technology, 1961-64, dep. dir. Electronics Research Ctr., 1964-67; dean sch. mgmt. Boston Coll., 1967-77; pres. Arthur D. Little Program Systems Mgmt. Co., Cambridge, Mass., 1977-85, chmn., 1985-88; sr. group v.p. Arthur D. Little Inc., Cambridge, Mass., 1985-88; sr. v.p. strategic planning United Tech. Corp., Hartford, Conn., 1988-90; dep. undersec. of def. internat. programs U.S. Dept. Def., Pentagon, Washington, 1990-93; fellow Kennedy Sch. Harvard U., Cambridge, Mass., 1993-94; rsch. group leader MIT, Cambridge, 1994-96, rsch. affiliate, 1994—2000; ret. Chmn. Bd. Econ. Advisors, Commonwealth of Mass., 1970-74; chmn. bd. dirs. Arthur D. Little Valuation Inc., 1985-86; corp. mem. C.S. Draper Lab. Corp., Cambridge, 1975-90; cons. The White House; mem. NRC Space Applications Bd., 1976-82. Author: Venture Capital, 1977, New Dimensions of Project Management, 1982; contbr. articles to profl. jours. Trustee Milton (Mass.) Acad., 1975-83; bd. dirs. Mass. Bus. Devel. Corp., Boston, 1969-78, Am. Assembly Collegiate Schs. Bus., 1970-76, State Street Co., State Street Bank and Trust, 1975-93, Mass. Tech. Devel. Corp., Boston, 1979-82, other mfg. cos. Recipient exceptional svc. medal NASA, 1967, outstanding svc. medal U.S. Sec. Def., 1993. Fellow IEEE, AIAA (assoc.); mem. Internat. Acad. Astronautics, Armed Forces Comms. and Electronics Assn. (v.p. 1962-65), Algonquin Club, Army Navy Country Club, Milton-Hoosic Club, Sigma Xi, Tau Beta Pi, Eta Kappa Nu, Sigma Gamma Tau. Avocations: golf, hiking, travel. Home: 522 Ocean St PO Box 2519 Ocean Bluff MA 02065-2519

KELLEY, ALOYSIUS PAUL, university administrator, priest; b. Carlisle, Pa., Oct. 4, 1929; s. Aloysius Paul and Teresa (Barron) K. AB, St. Louis U., 1955, MA, PhL, St. Louis U., 1956; STL, U. Innsbruck, Austria, 1963; PhD, U. Pa., 1968; LLD (hon.), Sacred Heart U., 1985. Joined S.J., 1949; ordained priest Roman Catholic Ch., 1962; chmn. dept. classics Georgetown U., 1969-71, asst. acad. v.p., 1971-72, acting acad. v.p., 1972-74, exec. v.p. for acad. affairs and provost, 1974-79; pres. Fairfield (Conn.) U., 1979—. Trustee Georgetown Prep. Sch., 1969-72, Loyola Coll., Balt., 1971-75, Scranton U., 1974-80, Bridgeport Area C. of C., 1979-82, St. Joseph's U., Phila., 1980-86, Georgetown U., 1982-88, 89-95, Conn. Grand Opera, 1980-82, John Carroll U., 1987-93, LeMoyne Coll., 1993-99, The Gesu Sch., 1993-97, St. Joseph's Prep. Sch., 1997—2002, St. Peter's Coll., 1998—, Nat. Assn. Ind. Colls. and Univs., 1997-2000; mem. D.C. Commn. Postsecondary Edn., 1974-79; vice chmn. Conn. Conf. Ind. Colls., 1980-81, chmn., 1981-83; pres. New Eng. Colls. Fund, 1993-95. Fulbright-Hayes fellow, 1971 Mem. Am. Philol. Assn., Am. Assn. Univ. Adminstrs., Am. Assn. Higher Edn., Patterson Club, Newcomen Soc. Democrat. Home and Office: Fairfield U Office of the Pres 1073 N Benson Rd Fairfield CT 06824-5195

KELLEY, BARBARA BANNIN, physical education educator; b. Far Rockaway, N.Y., Feb. 29, 1952; d. Robert Joseph and Regina (Auspitzer) Bannin; m. Edward L. Kelley, Feb. 14, 1976; children: Ryan Patrick, Timothy Bannin. BS, Longwood Coll., 1974; MEd, U. Maine, 1976. Cert. tchr., Maine. Phys. edn. tchr. Mecklenburg County Schs., South Hill, Va., 1974-75, Bangor (Maine) Sch. Dept., 1975—. Mem. Nat. Bd. Profl. Teaching Standards, Washington, 1992—. Named Coach of Yr., Maine High Sch. Coaches Assn., 1981, Tchr. of Yr., Maine Assn. Health, Phys. Edn., Recreation and Dance. Mem. NEA (bd. dirs. 1991—), Maine Tchrs. Assn. (bd. dirs. 1986—), Bangor Edn. Assn. (chief negotiator 1985-92). Democrat. Avocation: tennis. Home: 60 Washington St Brewer ME 04412-1851 Office: Vine St Sch Bangor ME 04401

KELLEY, DAVID BRIAN, community college dean, educator, consultant; b. Somerville, Mass., June 30, 1951; s. John Dennis and Mary Agnes Kelley; m. Jane Aria, Oct. 13, 1974; children: Kathleen, MaryElizabeth. BS, Salem State Coll., 1974; MS, Simmons Coll., 1976; EdD, Boston U., 1985. Libr. Fitchburg (Mass.) State Coll., 1977-79; dean No. Essex C.C., Haverhill, Mass., 1979—; exec. dir. Mass. Colls. Online, 2002—. Ednl. tech. cons. numerous cos. and colls., 1977—; bd. dirs. Tchg. Academic Survival Skills. Author: Analysis of Training and Human Resource Development Programs, 1985. Chair various statewide ednl. policy groups. Recipient Edn. Policy fellowship Inst. Ednl. Leadership, 1984-85. Mem.: Assn. Ednl. Comms. and Tech. Avocations: sailing, skiing, travel, reading. Home: 65 Cochrane St Melrose MA 02176-1504 Office: No Essex CC Elliott Way Haverhill MA 01830-2399 E-mail: dkelley@mca.mass.edu.

KELLEY, EARL W., JR., managed care administrator; b. Bellefonte, Pa., Jan. 10, 1953; s. Earl W and Lois Janet (Rishel) K. Law Enforcemen and Corrections/Bus. Adminstrn. and Mgmt., Pa. State U., 1973; PhD in Criminology. Pres., owner Kelley & Assocs., Lemont, Pa., 1974-91; exec. v.p., CEO Emergency Svcs. Edn and Tng., Inc., State Coll., Pa., 1987-91; pres., co-owner Kelley, Krise & Assocs., Lemont, Pa., 1991-93; exec. dir. Keystone Community Svcs., Inc., Bellefonte, Pa., 1993—. Bd. dir. SPE Federal Credit Union, State Coll., Pa. Developed courses Indsl. Health and Safety and Employee Assistance Programs, 1980-82, Total Quality Mgmt., 1986—. Vol. Alpha Vol. Fire Co., State College, 1981-89; mem. exec. com. Alpha Cmty. Ambulance Svc., State College, 1984-90; instr. Motorcycle Safety Found., State College, 1988-94; bd. govs. Healthsouth Nittany Valley Rehab. Hosp., Pleasent Gap, Pa., 1993—. Mem. Free & Accepted Masons Lodge #700, Williamsport Consistory, Pa. State Alumni Assn., Ctrl. Pa. AIDS Coalition. Avocations: motocycles, photography, carpentry. Home: PO Box 53 Lemont PA 16851-0053 Office: Keystone Cmty Svcs Inc 111 E High St Bellefonte PA 16823-3001

KELLEY, HENRY PAUL, university administrator, psychology educator; b. Cleburne, Tex., July 4, 1928; s. Henry Rowell and Jane Frances (Wynn) K.; m. Lucerle DeCourcy Scott, Aug. 18, 1949; children: Roger Wynn, Scott Franklin, Gordon Henry. BA in Pure Math., U. Tex., 1949, MA in Ednl. Psychology, 1951; AM, PhD in Psychology, Princeton U., 1954. Cert. and lic. psychologist, Tex. Psychometric fellow Ednl. Testing Svc., Princeton, N.J., 1951-54; pers. mgmt. and evaluation psychologist pers. and tng. rsch. ctr. USAF, San Antonio, 1954; aviation exptl. psychologist U.S. Naval Sch. Aviation Medicine, Pensacola, Fla., 1955-57; coord. measurement svcs., testing and counseling ctr., from asst. to assoc. prof. ednl. psychology U. Tex. Austin, 1958-64, lectr., 1964-67, dir. measurement and evaluation ctr., prof. ednl. psychology, 1967—99, prof. emeritus ednl. psychology, 1999—; regional dir. southwestern office Coll. Entrance Exam. Bd., Austin, 1964-67. Regional coord. Project TALENT, Austin, 1959-61; mem. southwestern regional adv. com. Coll. Entrance Exam. Bd., Austin, 1968-73, vice-chmn. com. rsch. and devel., N.Y.C., 1970-73, chmn., 1973-76, mem. adv. panel econ. implications recognizing prior learning, 1979-80; vis. faculty mem. ann. inst. coll. entrance, acad. placement and student fin. assistance Coll. Entrance Exam. Bd. and U. N.C., Chapel Hill, 1975-94; tech. reviewer, panel mem. rsch. projects br., bur. edn. handicapped, office edn. HEW, Washington, 1977; asst. hearing officer minimum competency study Nat. Inst. Edn., 1980-81; mem. gen. faculty U. Tex. Austin, 1960-64, 67-99, sec., 1981-87, mem. faculty senate, 1972-74, 81-95, sec., 1975-79, adminstrv. adviser ednl. policy com., 1968-99; reviewer comprehensive program fund improvement secondary edn. U.S. Dept. Edn., 1983; mem. rsch. adv. panel, manpower and pers. divsn. Air Force Human Resources Lab., Brooks AFB, San Antonio, 1984-86; mem. com. testing, coordinating bd. Tex. Coll. and Univ. Sys., Austin, 1985-86, mem. adv. com. basic skills testing, coordinating bd., 1987; mem. basic skills test rev. panel Tex. Edn. Agy., Austin, 1987; mem. Tex. acad. skills coun. Tex. Higher Edn. Coord. Bd., 1987-93, chmn. adv. com. tests and measurements Tex. acad. skills coun., 1987-93; mem. planning com. Ann. Tex. Testing Conf., 1987-94; cons., spkr. in field. Author: (with Bruce Walker) Self-Audit of CLEP Policies and Procedures: A Guide to Policy Decisions for Colleges and Universities, 1981; contbr. articles to profl. jours. and publs. Lt. USNR. Recipient Edward S. Noyes award Coll. Bd., 1976, Advanced Placement Spl. Recognition award, 1985; recipient numerous grants in field. Fellow APA, Am. Psychol. Soc.; mem. Am. Assn. Applied and Preventive Psychology, Am. Ednl. Rsch. Assn., Nat. Coun. Measurement Edn., Nat. Soc. Study Edn., Am. Assn. Higher Edn., Am. Evaluation Assn., Measurement Svcs. Assn., Nat. Coll. Testing Assn., Psychometric Soc., Phi Beta Kappa, Phi Delta Kappa, Phi Eta Sigma, Phi Kappa Phi, Sigma Xi. Methodist. Avocations: reading, bridge. Home: 2522 Jarratt Ave Austin TX 78703-2433 Office: U Tex Austin Ednl Psychology Dept 1 Univ Station D5800 Austin TX 78712-0383

KELLEY, JANE HOLDEN, archaeology educator; b. Abilene, Tex., Aug. 31, 1928; came to Can., 1968; d. Wiliam Curry and Ira Olive (Price) Holden; m. David Humiston Kelley, June 11, 1958; children: Rebecca Ann, Thomas Michael, Dennis W.C., Nancy Megan. BA, Tex. Tech U., 1949; MA, U. Tex., 1951; PhD, Harvard U., 1966. Instr. Tex. Tech U., Lubbock, 1957-63; assoc. curator Nebr. State Mus., Lincoln, 1964-68; assoc. prof. U. Calgary, Alta., Can., 1968-76, prof., 1976-93, emeritus, 1993—, assoc. to v.p. rsch., 1995—97. Dir. Calgary Inst. Humanities, 1992—99. Author: The Tall Candle, 1971, Yaqui Women, 1978, (with Marsha Hanen) Archaeology and The Methodology of Science, 1988, Cihuatan, El Salvador: A Preliminary Study in Intra-Site Variability, 1988. Home: 2432 Sovereign Crescent Calgary AB Canada T3C 2M2 Office: Dept Archeology U Calgary Calgary AB Canada T2N 1N4

KELLEY, JOHN H. school system administrator; b. Seneca, S.C., July 4, 1946; s. John H. and Earlene (Godwin) K. BA, Ctrl. Wesleyan Coll., 1968; MEd, Clemson U., 1973. Tchr. Pendleton (S.C.) High Sch., 1968-89, Walhalla (S.C.) Mid. Sch., 1969-72, 82-84, counselor, 1972-74, asst. prin., 1974-82; coord. gifted and talented Oconee Sch. Dist., Walhalla, 1984-86, dir. elem. edn., 1986-89, asst. supt. elem. edn., 1990—. Bd. dirs. College St. Bapt. Ch., 1975—, chmn. bd. 1981, 85, 88, sec. bd. 1977, mem. sanctuary choir, 1972—; mem adv. coun. dept. elem. edn Clemson U., 1989-90, adv. coun. coll. elem. and secondary edn., 1990-91). Recipient E. Bruce Anderson Meml. award 1977. Mem. NEA, Am. Assn. Sch. Adminstrs., S.C. Edn. Assn., S.C. ASCD, S.C. Assn. Sch. Adminstrs., S.C. Dept. Edn. (selection com. 1989-90, 90-91, reading recovery adv. com. 1989—), Oconee County Edn. Assn., Jaycees (Walhalla club internal v.p. 1972), Rotary (pres. 1990, Rotarian of Yr. 1991), Phi Delta Kappa (historian 1985, v.p. 1987). Baptist. Home: PO Box 81 312 S Lovingood Ave Walhalla SC 29691-1523 Office: Oconee Sch Dist PO Box 649 101 E North Broad St Walhalla SC 29691-1907

KELLEY, LUCILLE MARIE KINDELY, dean, psychosocial nurse; m. Robert Kelley; children: Ryan Patrick, Megan Maura. Diploma, St. Vincent Hosp., Bridgeport, 1965; BSN, U. Conn., 1969; MNursing, U. Wash., 1973, PhD, 1990. Assoc. prof., RNB program dir. Seattle Pacific U., 1985-99, dean Sch. Health Sci., 1998—. Sr. cons. healthcare The Effectiveness Inst., Redmond, Wash., 1984-99. Pres. Nat. Coun. Cmty. Mental Health Ctrs., 1983-84. Recipient Disting. Svc. award Eastside Mental Health, 1987, Tchg. award Burlington No., 1993. Mem. Sigma Theta Tau. Office: Seattle Pacific U Sch Health Sci Marston Hall 3307 3rd Ave W Seattle WA 98119-1940

KELLEY, MARIE ELAINE, retired director; b. St. Johns, Mich., Feb. 6, 1941; d. Berl Louis and Doris Louise (Tait) Foerch; m. Edgar Allen Kelley, Aug. 10, 1963; 1 child, Wesley Lynn. BA, Ctrl. Mich. U., 1963; MA, Mich. State U., 1965, PhD, 1973; EdS, U. Nebr., Lincoln, 1976. Tchr. Ovid Elsie (Mich.) Area Schs., 1963—67, Colon (Mich.) Cmty. Schs., 1967—68, Lincoln (Nebr.) Pub. Schs., 1970—78; asst. prin. instrn. Lincoln East-Jr. Sr. High Sch., 1978—85; prin. Caledonia (Mich.) Jr. HS, 1985—89, tchr., 1989—90; curriculum dir. Fennville (Mich.) Pub. Schs., 1990—95; ret. Vis. prof. U. Nebr., Lincoln, 1976—77, Lincoln, 1980—81, Western Mich. U., Kalamazoo, 1988—96; founder, bd. dirs. Discovery Elem. Sch., a Pub. Sch. Acad., Fennville, Mich., 1996—; originator, 1st dir. Lincoln Writing Lab., 1975—78. Contbr. articles to profl. jours. Mem.: Assn. for Supervision and Curriculum Devel., Alpha Lambda Delta, Phi Delta Kappa, Mortar Bd. Home: PO Box 586 Fennville MI 49408-0586 E-mail: mkelley@accn.org.

KELLEY, MIKE, artist; b. Detroit, 1954; Performances include L.A.C.E., L.A., 1978, 81, 83, La Jolla (Calif.) Mus. Contemporary Art, 1978, Found. Art Resources, L.A., 1979, 80, Calif. Inst. Arts, Valencia, 1980, Hallwalls, Buffalo, 1981, Mus. Contemporary Art, L.A., 1984, L.A. Mcpl. Art Gallery Theatre, 1985, Sta. KPFK, L.A., 1986, Artists Space, N.Y.C., 1986; one-person exhbns. include Mizuno Gallery, L.A., 1981, Felsen Gallery, L.A., 1983, Rosamund Felsen Gallery, L.A., 1984, 85, 87, 89, 90, Galerie Peter Pakesch, Vienna, 1989, 91, Galerie Ghislaine Hussenot, 1990, Hirshorn Mus., Washington, 1991, Galeria Juana de Aizpuru, Madrid, 1991, Jablonka Galerie, Cologne, Germany, 1991, Basel Kunsthalle, Basel, Swizerland, 1992, Inst. Contemporary Art, London, 1992, capcMusee, Bordeaux, France, 1992, Whitney Mus. Am. Art, N.Y.C., 1993;group exhbns. include Annina Nosei Gallery, N.Y., 1980, Mizuno Gallery, 1981, Rosamund Felson Gallery, 1983, 84, Newport Harbor Art Mus., Newport Beach, Calif., 1983, 84, 91, Mus. Contemporary Art, 1988, 89, 91, 92, Weatherspoon Art Gallery, Greensboro, N.C., 1983, Art Gallery New South Wales, Sydney, Australia, 1984, Whitney Mus. Am. Art, 1985, 87, 88, 89, 91, 92, 93, Milw. Art Mus., 1985, 90, 92, Concord Gallery, N.Y., 1985, L.A. Inst. Contemporary Art, 1985, Corcoran Gallery Art, Washington, 1986, L.A. County Mus. Art, 1987, 88, Mus. Modern Art, Tokyo, 1987, Mus. Fine Arts, Boston, 1988, 90, Inst. Contemporary Art, Boston, 1988, Kunsthalle Dusseldorf, 1988, Kunstsammlung Nordrheim-Westfalen, 1988, Kunstverein fur die Rheinlande und Westfalen, 1988, La Biennale di Venezia, Venice, 1988, Stadmuseum Graz, Austria, 1988, Pat Hearn Gallery, N.Y., 1989, La Foret Art Mus. Tokyo, 1989, Rooseum Malmo, Sweden, 1989, Daniel Weinberg Gallery, L.A., 1989, 90, Suzanne Hilberry Gallery, Birmingham, Mich., 1989, Robbin Lockett Gallery, Chgo., 1989, Galerie Schurr, Stuttgart, 1989, Galerie Gisela Capitain, Koln, Germany, 1990,

Interim Art, London, 1990, Jay Gorney Modern Art, N.Y., 1990, Loughelton Gallery, N.Y., 1990, Galerie Ghislaine Hussenot, Paris, 1990, 93, Villa Arson, Nice, France, 1990, Seibu Contemporary Art Gallery, Tokyo, 1990, Simon Watson Gallery, N.Y., 1990, John Good Gallery, N.Y., 1990, Fahey/Klein Gallery, L.A., 1990, Grazer Kunstverein, Graz, Austria, 1990, Stux Gallery, N.Y., 1990, Mincher/Wilcox Gallery, San Francisco, 1991, Fundacion Caja de Pensiones, Madrid, 1991, ALdrich Mus. Contemporary Art, Ridgefield, Conn., 1991, L.A. Mcpl. Art Gallery, 1991, Sezon Mus. Art, Tokyo, 1991, Tsukashin Hall, Osaka, Japan, 1991, Meyers/Bloom Gallery, L.A., 1991, Martin-Gropius-Bau, Berlin, 1991, 93, Carnegie Mus. Art, Pitts., 1991, Newport Harbor Art Mus., 1991, Galerie Max Hetzler, Cologne, 1992, 93, Anders Tornberg Gallery, Lund, Sweden, 1992, Hayward Gallery, London, 1992, Mus. Modern Art, N.Y.C., 1992, Musee d'Art Contemporarin, Pully/Lausanne, Swizerland, 1992, Castello di Rivoli, Turin, Italy, Deste Found., Athens, Greece, 1992, Deichtorhallen, Hamburg, Germany, 1992, Israel Mus., Jerusalem, 1992, Mus. Ludwig, Cologne, 1992, Museo d'Arte Sezione Contemporanea, Trent, Italy, 1992, Schurmann Sammlung, Ludwig Forum fur Internationale Kunst, Aachen, Germany, 1992, Galerie Nationale Du Jeu de Paume, Paris, 1992, Spazio Opos, Milan, 1992, Galerie Krinzinger, Vienna, 1992, Royal Acad. Art, London, 1993, Galerie Jennifer Flay, Paris, 1993, Kunstlerhaus Bethanien, Berlin, 1993; permanent collections include Whitney Mus. Am. Art, Mus. Modern Art, N.Y.C., Mus. Fine Arts, Boston, capc Musee, Bordeaux, L.A. County Mus. Art, Mus. Contemporary Art, L.A., Mus. Boymans van Beuningen, Rotterdam, Mus. van Hedendaadse Kunst, Ghent, Belgium. Office: Metro Pictures 519 W 24th St New York NY 10011-1104

KELLEY, PATRICIA COLLEEN, education educator, researcher; b. Winchester, Mass., Oct. 14, 1953; d. Joseph Sayward Kelley and Florence Patricia Dougherty; children: Brian, Brandon, Daniel. BA cum laude, U. N.H., 1978; MBA, Boston U., 1985, DBA with honors, 1988. Asst. to pers. dir. Huntington Gen. Hosp., Boston, 1975-76; asst. adminstrv. mgr. Coopers and Lybrand, Boston, 1976-78; adminstrv. mgr. Allyn & Bacon, Inc., Boston, 1978-80; teaching asst. Sch. of Mgmt. Boston U., 1981-83, writing coord. Sch. of Mgmt., 1985-88; asst. prof. Sch. of Bus. U. Wash., Seattle, 1988-90, Western Wash. U., Bellingham, 1990-95; adj. prof. bus. U. Wash., Bothell, Wash., 1995-99, sr. lectr., 1999—. Cons. various projects relative to ethical decision making and bus.-polit. interaction. Contbr. articles to profl. jours. Coach Lake Hill Soccer Club, King County, Wash., 1989-92; rm. mother Bellevue Schs., 1988-92, 98—, Sacred Heart Sch., Bellevue, 1994—; instr. Sacred Heart Ch., Bellevue, 1988-92; treas. Boy Scouts Am., Bellevue, 1989-91; merit badge counselor Boy Scouts of Am., 1994—. Mass. Bd. Higher Edn. scholar, 1972-75, Boston U. scholar, 1985-87. Mem. Acad. of Mgmt. (social issues in mgmt. divsn. 1988—, fin. com. SIM divsn. 1993—, chairperson, 1990-93, sec. editor 1992-95).

KELLEY, PATRICIA HAGELIN, geology educator; b. Cleve., Dec. 8, 1953; d. Daniel Warn and Virginia Louise (Morgan) Hagelin; m. Jonathan Robert Kelley, June 18, 1977; children: Timothy Daniel, Katherine Louise. BA, Coll. of Wooster, 1975; AM, Harvard U., 1977, PhD, 1979. Instr. New Eng. Coll., Henniker, N.H., 1979; asst. prof. U. Miss., University, 1979-85, assoc. prof., 1985-89, acting assoc. vice chancellor acad. affairs, 1988, prof., 1989-92, assoc. dean, 1989-90; program dir. NSF, Washington, 1990-92; prof., chmn. dept. geology U. N.D., Grand Forks, 1992-97; prof. U. NC, Wilmington, 1997—, chmn. dept. earth scis., 2003—. Contbr. articles to profl. jours. Deacon Bethel Presbyn. Ch., Olive Branch, Miss., 1985-90. Rsch. grantee NSF, 1986-89, 90-99, 2000-03; NSF fellow, 1976-79. Fellow Geol. Soc. Am.; mem. AASS, Paleontol. Soc. (coun. 1984-85, 95-96, 98—, chair S.E. sect. 1984-85, chair N.C. sect. 1995-96, pres.-elect 1998-2000, pres. 2000-2002, past pres. 2002—), Assn. Women Geosci. (Outstanding Educator award 2003), (Paleontol. Rsch. Inst. (trustee 2003-), Soc. Econ. Paleontologists and Mineralogists, Sigma Xi, Phi Beta Kappa. Presbyterian. Avocations: family, ch. work, writing, music, travel. Office: Dept Earth Scis Univ NC Wilmington NC 28403 E-mail: kelleyp@uncw.edu.

KELLEY, SHARON LEE, physical education educator; b. Utica, N.Y., Dec. 4, 1941; d. Lee G. and Vera M. (Byrns) K. BA, State Univ. Coll. at Cortland, N.Y., 1963; MA, U. Iowa, 1969. Phys. edn. tchr. and coach Pine Plains (N.Y.) Ctrl. Sch., 1963-66; grad. asst. U. Iowa, Iowa City, 1966-68, tchr. phys. edn., 1968-69; phys. edn. tchr. Luther Coll., Decorah, Iowa, 1969-70, Glens Falls (N.Y.) Elem. and Jr. H.S., 1970-71, Fowler Elem. Sch., Gouverneur, N.Y., 1971—. Author and presenter in field. Recipient Outstanding Leadership in Swimming and Aquatics award ARC, 1965, others; grantee in field. Mem. AAHPERD (life), N.Y. State Assn. for Health, Phys. Edn. and Recreation, Gouverneur Tchrs. Assn./United Tchrs., Girls and Women's Sports. Avocations: writing poetry, observing nature, swimming, kayaking and canoeing, mountain climbing. Home: 3 Bolton Rd New Hartford NY 13413-2511

KELLEY, WILLIAM NIMMONS, physician, educator, science administrator, dean; b. Atlanta, June 23, 1939; s. Oscar Lee and Willa Nimmons (Allen) Kelley; m. Lois Faville, Aug. 1, 1959; children: Margaret Paige, Virginia Lynn, Lori Ann, William Mark. MD, Emory U., 1963; MA (hon.), U. Pa., 1989. Diplomate Am. Bd. Internal Medicine (chmn. 1985-1986). Intern in medicine Parkland Meml. Hosp., Dallas, 1963—64, resident, 1964—65; sr. resident medicine Mass. Gen. Hosp., Boston, 1967—68; clin. asso., sect. on human biochem. genetics NIH, 1965—67; teaching fellow medicine Harvard U. Med. Sch., 1967—68; asst. prof. to prof. medicine, asst. prof. to asso. prof. biochemistry, chief div. rheumatic and genetic diseases Duke U. Sch. Medicine, 1968—75; Macy faculty scholar Oxford U., 1974—75; prof., chmn. dept. internal medicine, prof. dept. biol. chemistry U. Mich. Med. Sch., Ann Arbor, 1975—89; Robert G. Dunlop prof. medicine, biochemistry and biophysics U. Pa., Phila., 1989—2000, dean Sch. Medicine, 1989—2000; CEO U. Pa. Med. Ctr. and Health System, Phila., 1989—2000; prof., 2000—. Human gene therapy subcom. NIH, 1986—92, recombinant DNA com., 1988—92, dirs. adv. com., 1992—95; bd. dirs. Merck & Co., Beckman Coulter, Inc., Advanced Biosurfaces, GenVec, Inc. Author (with J.B. Wyngaarden): Gout and Hyperuricemia, 1976; author: (with I.M. Weiner) Uric Acid, 1979; author: (with Harris, Ruddy and Sledge) Textbook of Rheumatology, 1981, 5th edit., 1997, Arthritis Surgery, 1994; author: (with M. Osterweiss and E.R. Rubin) Emerging Policies for Bio-Medical Research (Health Policy Annual III), 1993; editor-in-chief: Textbook of Internal Medicine, 1989, Textbook of Internal Medicine, 3rd edit., 1997, Essentials of Internal Medicine, 1994; contbr. articles to profl. jours. Trustee Emory U., 1992—, Emory U., Woodruff Health Scis. Ctr. Recipient C.V. Mosby award, 1963, John D. Lane award, USPHS, 1969, Rsch. Career Devel. award, 1972—75, Geigy Internat. prize rheumatology, 1969, Heinz Karger Meml. Found. prize, 1973, Disting. Med. Achievement award, Emory U., 1985, John Phillips Meml. award and medal, ACP, 1990, Nat. Med. Rsch. award, Nat. Health Coun., 1993, Robert H. Williams award, Assn. Profs. of Medicine, 1995, David E. Rogers award, Assn. Am. Med. Coll., 1999, Emory medal, 2000; scholar, Mead Johnson, 1967, Josiah Macy Found., 1974—75; Clin. scholar, Am. Rheumatism Assn., 1969—72. Master: ACP; fellow: AAAS, Am. Coll. Rheumatology, Am. Philos. Soc., Am. Acad. Arts and Scis.; mem.: Assn. Profs. Medicine (sec.-treas. 1987—89), Am. Soc. Internal Medicine, Am. Soc. Human Genetics, Ctrl. Rheumatism Soc. (pres. 1978—79), Australian Rheumatism Assn. (hon.), Royal Coll. Physicians Ireland (hon.), Am. Coll. Rheumatology (editl. bd. 1972—77, pres. 1986—87, Gold Medal award 1997), Assn. Am. Physicians (sec.-treas. 1987—89), Am. Fedn. Med. Rsch. (pres. 1979—81), Am. Soc. Biochemistry and Molecular Biology (editl. bd. 1976—81), Am. Soc. Clin. Investigation (editl. bd. 1974—79, pres. 1983—84), Inst. Medicine of NAS (chmn. sect. 4 1988—90, chmn. membership com. 1990—94, coun. mem., exec. com. 1996—2001), Ctrl. Soc. for Clin. Rsch. (pres. 1986—87), Alpha Omega Alpha, Sigma Xi. Home: 768 Woodleave Rd Bryn Mawr PA 19010-1709 Office: Univ of Pa Health Sys 757 Biomed Rsch Bldg II/III Philadelphia PA 19104 E-mail: kelleyw@hotmail.com.

KELLEY-BROCKEL, KATHLEEN FRANCES, principal; b. Phila., Apr. 4, 1948; d. James J. and Frances M. (Stiegler) Kelley; m. Thomas E. Hoats, Aug. 8, 1970 (div. Jan. 1989); children: Christina, Melissa, Michael; m. Robert L. Brockel Sr., Sept. 28, 1991; children: Robert, Scott, Arlene, Curt. BS, Coll. Misericordia, 1970; MS, Marywood Coll., 1983; student, Lehigh U., 1993. Cert. prin., Pa. Tchr. grade 4 Allentown (Pa.) Sch. Dist., 1970; tchr. grades 3, 4 and 5 St. Paul's Sch., Allentown, 1979-87; prin. Christ the King Sch., Whitehall, Pa., 1987-93; asst. prin. So. Lehigh Mid. Sch., Center Valley, Pa., 1993—. Mem. ASCD, Pa. ASCD, Nat. Assn. Secondary Sch. Prins. Roman Catholic. Office: So Lehigh Mid Sch 3715 Preston Ln Center Valley PA 18034-9453

KELLISON, DONNA LOUISE GEORGE, accountant, educator; b. Hugoton, Kans., Oct. 16, 1950; d. Donald Richard and Zepha Louise (Lowry) George. BA in Elem. Edn. with honors, Anderson (Ind.) U., 1972; MS in Elem. Edn., Ind. U., 1981. CPA, Ind.; lic. tchr., Ind.; lic. in ins., Ind.; cert. gen. securities rep.; cert. investment advisor. Tchr. elem. Maconaquah Sch. Corp., Bunker Hill, Ind., 1972-73; office mgr. Eskew & Gresham, CPA's, Louisville, Ky., 1973-78; para-profl. Blue & Co., Indpls., 1979-83, tax compliance specialist, 1983-84, tax sr., 1984-86, tax supr., 1986-87, tax mgr., 1987-90, tax prin., 1990-92, tax sr. mgr., 1992-94, tax dir., 1995—; pres. Blue Benefits Cons., Inc., 1998—, Olympic Fin. Svcs. LLC, 1999—. Vol. Children's Clinic, Indpls., 1985-92; chairperson Most Wanted campaign Am. Cancer Soc., 1995; bd. dirs. Indpls. Estate Planning Coun., 1995—, sec., 1995-96, vice-chair, 1998, chair 1998-99. Mem. AICPA, Ind. CPA Soc. (tax inst. com. 1989-93, govt. rels. com. 1994-95), Ind. Tax Inst. (chair 1993). Presbyterian. Home: 382 Pintail Ct Carmel IN 46032-9125 Office: 12800 N Meridian St Ste 400 Carmel IN 46032

KELLNER, ROBERT DEAN, college official; b. Worthington, Minn, Mar. 7, 1956; s. Carl Deane and Mary Ann (Bingham) K. BS, U. S.C., 1978, MEd, 1980; MPA, Valdosta State Coll., 1991. Dir. Columbia Hall U. SC, Columbia, SC, 1979-80; dir. Marguerite Hall St. Louis U., 1980-81; dir. housing U. Southern Colo., Pueblo, 1981-83; dir. housing and residence life Valdosta State Univ., Ga., 1983-98, instr., 1994—, asst. dean students, 1998-99, dir. aux. svc., 1999—. Mem. Episcopal Diocese Commn. in Higher Edn., Ga., 1986-87; vol. coach YMCA, Valdosta, 1989-90. Mem. Nat. Assn. Coll. Aux. Svc., Assn. Coll. and Univ. Housing Officers (chmn. legis. issues com. 1990-93), Southeastern Assn. Housing Officers (state rep. 1987-88), Am. Coll. Pers. Assn., Nat. Assn. Student Pers. Adminstrs., Ga. Assn. Housing Officers (co-founder), Valdosta/Lowndes C. of C. (census com. 1998-2001, chmn. 2000-01, govt. affairs com. 2001—, metro. com. chair 2001-03), Rotary Internat. (sgt. at arms 2000-01, pres.-elect 2002-03, pres. 2003—), Theta Xi (advisor 1984-89), Habitat for Humanity, Jimmy Carter Work Projucet, Libr. chair, 2003. Avocations: volleyball, softball. Office: Valdosta State Univ Aux Svcs Office Valdosta GA 31698-0001 E-mail: rkellner@valdosta.edu.

KELLOGG, FREDERIC RICHARD, religious studies educator; b. San Angelo, Tex., Dec. 16, 1939; s. John Franklin III and Naomi Lucille (Cory) K.; m. Jeannette Villeret Boykin, June 1, 1963; children: Christopher, Mark. BS summa cum laude, La. Tech. U., 1962; ThM with honors, So. Meth. U., 1965; postgrad., U. Goettingen, 1965-66; PhD, Yale U., 1972. Ordained to ministry Meth. Ch., 1969. Asst. prof. religion Emory & Henry Coll., Emory, Va., 1969-75, assoc. prof., 1975-83, Floyd Bunyan Shelton prof., 1984—, acting dean faculty, 1993-94. Mem. Am. Acad. Religion, Soc. Biblical Lit., Mid. East Studies Assn. Democrat. Home: PO Box 24 Emory VA 24327-0024 Office: Emory & Henry Coll Dept Religion PO Box 947 Emory VA 24327

KELLOGG, HERBERT HUMPHREY, metallurgist, educator; b. N.Y.C., Feb. 24, 1920; s. Herbert H. and Gladys (Falding) K.; m. Jeanette Halstead, July 20, 1940; children—Thomas Bartlett, Jane Falding, David Humphrey, Elizabeth Ann. BS, Columbia, 1941, MS, 1943. Asst. prof. mineral preparation Pa. State U., State Coll., 1942-46; faculty Columbia U., N.Y.C., 1946—, Stanley-Thompson prof. chem. metallurgy, 1968-90, prof. emeritus, 1990—. Chmn. titanium adv. com. Office Def. Mblzn., 1954-58 Research; contbr. numerous articles to publs. Recipient Best Paper award extractive metals div. Am. Inst. Mining., Metall. and Petroleum Engrs.; James Douglas Gold medal Am. Inst. Mining, Metall. and Petroleum Engrs., 1973 Fellow AIME (chmn. extractive metallurgy div. 1958), Metall. Soc., Instn. Mining and Metallurgy (London); mem. NAE, Sigma Xi, Tau Beta Pi. Home: Closter Rd Palisades NY 10964

KELLOGG, ROBERT LELAND, English language educator; b. Ionia County, Mich., Sept. 2, 1928; s. Charles Edwin and Lucille Jeanette (Reasoner) K.; m. Joan Alice Montgomery, Apr. 4, 1951; children: Elizabeth Joan, Jonathan Montgomery, Stephen Robert. BA, U. Md., 1950; MA, Harvard U., 1952, PhD, 1958. Mem. faculty U. Va., 1957-99, prof. English, 1967-99, chmn. dept., 1974-78, dean Coll. Arts and Scis., 1978-85, prof. emeritus, 1999—; prin. Monroe Hill Coll., 1985-88. Vis. prof. U. Iceland, 1999—2001. Author: (with Robert Scholes) The Nature of Narrative, 1966, A Concordance to Eddic Poetry, 1988; translator of works from Icelandic; contbr. to profl. jours. Served with USAR, 1954-56. Am.-Scandinavian Found. fellow, 1956-57; Guggenheim fellow, 1968-69 Mem. Medieval Acad. Am., Modern Lang. Assn., South Atlantic Modern Lang. Assn. (pres. 1974-75), Raven Soc., Phi Beta Kappa (pres. local chpt. 1981) Clubs: Colonnade. Democrat. Home: 261 E Jefferson St Charlottesville VA 22902-5175 Office: U Va Bryan Hall Charlottesville VA 22904-4121 E-mail: rlk@virginia.edu.

KELLOGG FAIN, KAREN, retired history and geography educator; b. Pueblo, Colo., Oct. 10, 1940; d. Howard Davis and Mary Lucille (Cole) Kellogg; m. Sept. 1, 1961; divorced; 1 child, Kristopher. Student, U. Ariz., 1958-61; BA, U. So. Colo., 1967; MA, U. No. Colo., 1977; postgrad., U. Denver, 1968, 72-93, Colo. State U., 1975, 91, Chadron State Coll., 1975, U. No. Ill., 1977, 83, Ft. Hayes State Coll., 1979, U. Colo., 1979, 86-87, 92, Ind. U., 1988. Cert. secondary tchr. Colo. Tchr. history and geography Denver Pub. Schs., 1967-96; tchr. West H.S., Denver, 1992-96. Area adminstr., tchr. coord. Close Up program, Washington, 1982-84; reviewer, cons. for book Geography, Our Changing World, 1990. Vol., chmn. young profls. Inst. Internat. Edn. and World Affairs Coun., Denver, 1980—; mem. state selection com. U.S. Senate and Japan Scholarship Com., Denver, 1981-89, Youth for Understanding, Denver; mem. Denver Art Mus., 1970—; vol. Denver Mus. Natural History, 1989—, Am. Cancer Soc. "Jail and Bail", 1996, "Climb the Mountain", 1996, Denver Conv. Bur., 1997; bd. overseas Dept. Def. Dependents Sch., Guantanamo Bay, Cuba, 1990-91; screening panelist Tchr. to Japan Program Rocky Mtn. Regional Fulbright Meml. Fund, 1997; vol. tour guide Colo. State Capitol, 1997-2001. Fulbright scholar Chadron State Coll., Pakistan, 1975; Geog. Soc. grantee U. Colo., 1986; recipient award for Project Prince, Colo. U./Denver Pub. Schs./Denver Police Dept., 1992. Mem.: AAUW, Colo. Coun. on Internat. Orgns. (mem. bd. 1999—), Colo. Geographic Alliance (steering com. 1986), Rocky Mountain Regional World History Assn. (steering com. 1984—87), Am. Forum for Global Edn., Fulbright Assn. (bd. dirs. and regional liaison Colo. chpt. 2001—), World History Assn., Nat. Coun. Social Studies (del. 1984), Colo. Coun. Social Studies (sec. 1984—86), Denver Bot. Gardens, Kappa Kappa Iota, Gamma Phi Beta. Episcopalian. Avocations: traveling, hosting international visitors, swimming, reading. Home: 12643 E Bates Cir Aurora CO 80014-3315 E-mail: karenfain@hotmail.com.

KELLOGG-SMITH, PETER, sculptor; b. N.Y.C., Apr. 21, 1920; s. Jewell and Margaret (Shearer) Kellogg-Smith; children by guardianship: Peter von Pein, Lee von Pein Schreitz, Ruth Bueneman, Cynthia Taylor Dax; grad. Putney Sch., Vt., 1939; studied yacht design with Franz Plunder, 1940-43; AB, St. John's Coll., Annapolis, Md., 1943; MA in Philos. Edn., Putney-Antioch Grad. Sch. Tchr. Edn., 1962; postgrad. U. Md., 1968. Tchr. Ojai (Calif.) Valley Sch., 1944-47; founding dir.-tchr. Happy Valley Sch., Ojai, 1948; yacht designer, broker, Chestertown, Md. 1949-57; asst. head, tchr. Gunston Sch., Centerville, Md., 1950-57; tchr. Grapho-English, Abana, Turkey, 1956; founding dir., tchr. Key Sch., Annapolis, Md., 1958-62; founding dir., hands-on tchr. oceanography Bay Country Sch., Arnold, Md., 1963-72; tchr. stone carving Acad. Arts, Easton, Md., 1972-76. Prin. works include marble carving under Etienne Desmet, Carrara, Italy, 1972, under Kenneth Davis, Carrara, 1974, drawing and modeling with Reuben Kramer, modeling and bronze casting with Arthur Benson, 1975-79; patentee new type engine and marine hardward. Bd. dirs. Fairhaven "free" sch.; ind. counselor students and parents on ednl. problems. Westinghouse Sci. fellow MIT, 1952; recipient Best in Show award Chestertown Arts League Show, numerous awards for sculpture. Avocations: traveling, playing music, sailing. Address: 202 Divinity Ln Arnold MD 21012-1301

KELLY, ANN TERESE, elementary education educator; b. St. Louis, Jan. 29, 1954; d. Robert Victor and Mary Magdalen (Debrecht) K. BS in Elem. Edn., U. Mo., St. Louis, 1977, student, 1978—79, U. Mo., 1986—88, Webster U., St. Louis, 1990, U. Mo., Columbia, 1990—92, SUNY, Brockport, 1994, U. Mo., 1995, SUNY, Brockport, 1997, Webster U., 1999, SUNY, Brockport, 2000. Tchr. 4th grade St. Paul (Mo.) Sch., 1974-75, Assumption Sch., O'Fallon, Mo., 1977-79; tchr. grades 6 to 8 St. Raphael, St. Louis, 1979-86; tchr. grade 7 Our Lady of Sorrows, St. Louis, 1986-88, tchr. grade 5, 1988—. Tchr. trainer Sci. Olympiad, St. Louis, 1987—; presenter weather workshops, 1991—; trainer Gr. 5 Developmental Approaches in Sci. and Health, 1993, Archdiocese of St. Louis, 1994—; Am. Meteorol. Soc./Nat. Oceanic and Atmospheric Adminstrn. workshop presenter Maury Project oceanographic studies, 1994—, local team leader, 2000—. Recipient Alumni of the Heart award Our Lady of Sorrows Sch., 1996, Shining Star award St. Louis (Mo.) Sci. Ctr., 2002. Mem. Nat. Sci. Tchrs. Assn., Sci. Tchrs. Mo., Cath. Educators Network. Roman Catholic. Avocations: singing, dancing, walking, photography. Home: 10126C Puttington Dr Saint Louis MO 63123-5258 Office: Our Lady of Sorrows 5831 S Kingshighway Blvd Saint Louis MO 63109-3571

KELLY, DOROTHY HELEN, pediatrician, educator; b. Fitchburg, Mass., July 29, 1944; BS in Nursing magna cum laude, Fitchburg State Co., 1966; BS with distinction, Wayne State U., 1968, MD with distinction, 1972. Diplomate Am. Bd. Pediatrics, Pediatric Pulmonology. Intern Children's Svc. Mass. Gen. Hosp., Boston, 1972-73, resident in pediatrics, 1973-75, fellow in pediatrics pulmonary medicine, 1976-79, co-dir. pediat. pulmonary lab., 1976—83, assoc. dir. pediatric pulmonary unit, 1983—95; teaching fellow Harvard Med. Sch., Boston, 1973-75, clin. fellow, 1972-75, instr. in pediatrics, 1975-81, asst. prof. pediatrics, 1981-89, assoc. prof. pediatrics, 1989-95, U. Tex., Galveston, 1995-97, Houston, 1995—; assoc. dir. S.W. SIDS Rsch. Inst. Meml. Herman S.W. Hosp., Houston, 1995—. Cons. Bur. Community Health Svcs., NEW, 1979-80, FDA, 1986, 88-92, ECRI, 1987-88, also others; chmn. apnea adv. com. Nat. Sudden Infant Death Syndrome Found., 1979-81; mem. com. anesthesiology and respiratory devices panel Ctr. for Devices and Radiol. Health, FDA, 1990-94; chmn. physicians' com. Nat. Assn. Apnea Profls., 1990-91, also others; reviewer numerous jours. in field. Contbr. numerous articles to profl. jours. Recipient Woman of Vision award Nat. Soc. for Prevention of Blindness, Mass. Affiliate, 1981, First Disting. Alumni award Fitchburg State Coll., 1984, grants in field. Mem. Am. Med. Woman's Assn., Am. Acad. Pediatrics (task force on prolonged apnea 1978), Am. Thoracic Soc., Soc. Pediatric Rsch., Internat. Pediatric Soc., Assn. for Psychophysiol. Study Sleep, Soc. for Pediatric Rsch., Tex. Thoracic Soc., Tex. Med. Assn., Tex. Pediatric Soc., Am. Autonomic Soc. Office: SW SIDS Rsch Inst Meml Hermann SW Hosp Houston TX 77030 E-mail: swsids@ev1.ent.

KELLY, EAMON MICHAEL, university president emeritus; b. N.Y.C., Apr. 25, 1936; s. Michael Joseph and Kathleen Elizabeth (O'Farrell) K.; m. Margaret Whalen, June 22, 1963; children: Martin (dec.), Paul, Andrew, Peter. BS, Fordham U., 1958; MS, Columbia U., 1960, PhD, 1965. Officer in charge Office of Social Devel., Ford Found., N.Y.C., 1969—74; officer in charge program related investments Ford Found., 1974—79; exec. v.p. Tulane U., New Orleans, 1979—81, pres., 1981—98, prof. Payson Ctr. Internat. Devel. and Tech. Transfer, 1998—. Dir. policy formulation div. Econ. Devel. Adminstrn., Dept. Commerce, Washington, 1968; spl. asst. to adminstr. SBA, Washington, 1968-69; spl. cons. to sec. Dept. Labor, 1977; bd. dirs. So. Edn. Found., La. Land and Exploration Co., Nat. Captioning Inst., Assn. Gov. Bds. Colls. and Univ., Econ. Devel. Commn. State of La.; mem. Nat. Sci. Bd., Nat. Security Edn. Bd., Humphrey Fellows Nat. Adv. Bd., Bus. Higher Edn. Forum, com. econ. devel. Gabelli Enterprises Inc., exec. com. Assn. Am. Univs.; pres. Commission NCAA, Found. for Biomed. Rsch., Nat. Sci. Bd., 1996; former chair Presidential Adv. Bd.; chair Nat. Sci. Bd. Pres. city coun., councilman-at-large City of Englewood, N.J., 1974-77; bd. advocates Planned Parenthood of La. Mem. AAUP, La. Conf. Univs. and Colls., La. Assn. Ind. Colls. and Univs., Bus. Coun. New Orleans, City Club, Inc., Met. Area Com., New Orleans Ednl. Telecom. Consortium. Democrat. Roman Catholic. Office: Tulane U Payson Ctr Bldg 7 Rm 300 6823 Saint Charles Ave New Orleans LA 70118-5698*

KELLY, EILEEN PATRICIA, management educator; b. Steubenville, Ohio, Oct. 24, 1955; d. Edward Joseph and Mary Bernice (Cassidy) K. BS, Coll. Steubenville, 1978; MA, U. Cin., 1979, PhD, 1982. LPA, Ohio; sr. profl. in human resources. Lectr. U. Cin., 1981-82; asst. prof. bus. Creighton U., Omaha, 1982-87, chmn. mgmt., mktg. and sys. dept., 1986-88, assoc. prof., 1987-88, coordinator project Minerva, 1987-88; assoc. prof. La. State U., Shreveport, 1988-93, chmn. dept. mgmt. and mktg., 1988-93; assoc. prof. Ithaca (N.Y.) Coll., 1993-99, prof., 1999—, chmn. mgmt. dept., 1993-95. Contbr. articles to profl. jours. and acad. presentations. Mem. Acad. Mgmt., Acad. Legal Studies in Bus., Soc. Human Resource Mgmt., Soc. for Bus. Ethics, Beta Gamma Sigma (faculty adviser 1985-88, 92-93). Roman Catholic. Avocations: genealogical research, antique collecting, travel. Office: Ithaca Coll Sch Bus Ithaca NY 14850

KELLY, JAMES ARTHUR, JR., educator; b. St. Louis, Oct. 5, 1934; s. James A. and Fern (Oesterle) K.; m. Marjorie Weist Kelly, June 1956 (div. 1972); children: Susan Elizabeth, Robert James, David Charles, John Duncan; m. Mariam C. Noland, June 13, 1981. BA, Shimer Coll., 1954; MA, U. Chgo., 1956; PhD, Stanford U., 1966. From asst. prof. to assoc. prof. Tchrs. Coll. Columbia U., New York, 1966-74; exec. assoc. Nat. Urban Coalition, Washington, 1968-69; program officer Ford Found., New York, 1970-81; pres. Spring Hill Ctr., Wayzata, Minn., 1981-85, Ctr. for Creative Studies, Detroit, 1985-87, Nat. Bd. for Profl. Teaching Standards, Detroit, 1987—. Bd. dirs. Inst. for Ednl. Leadership, Washington; cons. Carnegie Corp. N.Y., 1983, 86, Cleve. Found., 1987. Chmn. U.S.-Australia Edn. Policy Project, Detroit, 1987—; mem. Detroit Com. Fgn. Rels., 1987—; trustee Met. Opera in Upper Midwest, Mpls., 1983-85, Mich. Opera Theater, Detroit, 1988; commr. Edn. Commn. States, Denver, 1975-77; bd. dirs. Blake Schs., Mpls., 1983-85. Recipient Finis Engleman award Am. Assn. Sch. Adminstrs., 1966. Mem. Am. Ednl. Rsch. Assn. (chmn. program com. 1968-70), Detroit Club, Mpls. Club. Home: 203 Cloverly Rd Grosse Pointe MI 48236-3316 Office: Nat Bd Profl Teaching Standards 333 W Fort St Bsmt 2070 Detroit MI 48226-3134

KELLY, JANICE HELEN, elementary school educator; b. Akron, Ohio, Nov. 28, 1951; d. Joe Ralph and Barbara Ann (Goins) Long; m. W. Gary Kelly, May 10, 1973; children: Benjamin, Chad. BS in Elem. Edn., Akron

U., 1984; M in Edn., Kent (Ohio) State U., 1994. Cert. elem. tchr., Ohio; nat. bd. cert. Mid. Child. Gen., 1999. Tchr. Suffield United C.C. Coop., Suffield, Ohio, 1984-86, Mogadore (Ohio) Local Schs., 1986—. Cadre mem. Summit County Tech. Acad., Cuyahoga Falls, Ohio, 1994; classroom tchr. SBC Ameritech, Kent State, Ohio, 2000, 2002. Mem., tchr. Randolph (Ohio) United Meth. Ch., 1973—. Recipient Outstanding Educator award Somers Elem. PTA, Mogadore, 1989, Crystal Apple award Plain Dealer, 2003; Eisenhower grantee Kent State U., 1990-92, Tech., Industry, Environ. Edn. grantee Gen Corp, 1993. Mem. ASCD, Ohio Edn. Assn., Mogadore Edn. Assn. (sec. 1990-92, v.p. 1995—, co-pres. 2001-03), Sci. Edn. Coun. Ohio. Avocations: doll-making/collecting, computer technology, golf, swimming. Home: 534 Hartville Rd Atwater OH 44201-9785 Office: Somers Elementary School 3600 Herbert St Mogadore OH 44260-1199

KELLY, JUDITH JOHANNA COVA, elementary language arts consultant; b. Detroit, Jan. 27, 1947; d. Vasile and Margaret Ilene (Gehrke) Cova; m. Daniel Ward Golds, Mar. 19, 1966 (div.); 1 child, Jeffrey Alan; m. Michael Thomas Kelly, Jan. 3, 1981. BS, Wayne State U., 1972; MA in Reading, Ea. Mich. U., 1977. From pre-sch. tchr. to chpt. I reading tchr. Monroe (Mich.) Pub. Schs., 1972-91, elem. lang. arts cons., 1991—. Co-facilitator Mich. English Lang. Arts Framework project Monroe Pub. Schs., 1994-96; presenter at numerous confs. Coord. African-Am. Read-In, Monroe, 1994-2000. Honoree, Soroptimist of Monroe County, 2003; Fellow Ea. Mich. Writing Project, 1993, 94. Mem. Internat. Reading Assn., Nat. Coun. Tchrs. English, Whole Lang. Umbrella (conf. co-chair 1995, sec./treas. 1999-01), Mich. Coun. Tchrs. English, Mich. Reading Assn., Ctr. for the Expansion of Lang. and Thinking. Avocations: reading, walking, travel, swimming. Office: Monroe Pub Schs 908 E 2nd St Monroe MI 48161-1950 E-mail: kelly@monroe.k12.mi.us.

KELLY, KATHLEEN S(UE), communications educator; b. Duluth, Minn., Aug. 6, 1943; d. Russell J. and Idun N. Mehrman; m. George F. Kelly, Apr. 29, 1961; children: Jodie A., Jennifer L. AA, Moorpark (Calif.) Coll., 1971; BS in Journalism, U. Md., College Park, 1973, MA in Pub. Rels., 1979, PhD in Pub. Communication, 1989. Accredited pub. rels.; cert. fundraising exec. Dir. pub. info. Bowie (Md.) State U., 1974-77; asst. to dean, instr. Coll. Journalism U. Md., College Park, 1977-79, assoc. dir. devel., 1979-82; v.p. Mt. Vernon Coll., Washington, 1982-83; dir. devel. U. Md., College Park, 1983-85, assoc. dean, lectr. Coll. Journalism, 1985-88, asst. dean Coll. Bus. and Mgmt., 1988-90; prof. U. La., Lafayette, 1991—2003; prof., chair dept. pub. rels. U. Fla., Gainesville, 2003—. Cons. NASA, NIH, Mt. St. Marys Coll., 1986—; lectr. CASE, Pub. Rels. Soc. Am., 1987—. Author: Fund Raising and Public Relations: A Critical Analysis, 1991, Building Fund-Raising Theory, 1994, Effective Fund-Raising Management, 1998. Named PRIDE Book award winner Speech Comm. Assn., 1991, article award winner 1994, John Grenzebach award winner for rsch. on philanthropy CASE and Am. Assn. Fund-Raising Coun., 1991, 98, PRIG award winner for outstanding dissertation Internat. Comm. Assn., 1990, winner 1995 Pathfinder award Inst. for Pub. Rels. Rsch. and Edn., Staley/Robeson/Ryan/St. Lawarence prize for rsch. on fund raising and philanthropy Nat. Soc. Fundraising Execs., 1998, Jackson, Jackson & Wagner Behavioral Sci. prize, Pub. Relations Soc. Am. Found., 1999. Fellow Pub. Rels. Soc. Am. (chmn. ednl. and cultural orgn. sect. 1989, pres. Md. chpt. 1986-87, Pres.' Cup 1981, nat. bd. dirs. 1994-96, Jackson Jackson and Wagner Behavioral Sci. prize 1999); mem. Nat. Soc. Fund Raising Execs. (mem. rsch. coun.), Coun. Advancement and Support of Edn. (women's forum 1983), Phi Kappa Phi. Democrat. Avocations: travel, reading. Home: 1922 NW 4th Ave Gainesville FL 32603 Office: U Fla Dept Pub Rels PO Box 118400 Gainesville FL 32611-8400

KELLY, LUCIE STIRM YOUNG, nursing educator; b. Stuttgart, Germany, May 2, 1925; came to U.S., 1929; d. Hugo Karl and Emilie Rosa (Engel) Stirm; m. J. Austin Young, Aug. 30, 1946 (div. Feb. 1971); m. Thomas Martin Kelly, 1972 (dec. 2003); 1 child by previous marriage, Gay Aleta (Mrs. Donald Meyer). BS, U. Pitts., 1947, MLitt, 1951, PhD (HEW fellow), 1965; D in Nursing Edn. (hon.), U. R.I., 1977; LHD (hon.), Georgetown U., 1983; DSc (hon.), Widener U., 1984, U. Mass., 1989; D of Pub. Svc. (hon.), Am. U., 1985; DHL (hon.), SUNY, 1996. Instr. nursing McKeesport (Pa.) Hosp., 1953-57, asst. adminstr. nursing, 1966-69; asst. prof. nursing U. Pitts., 1957-64, asst. dean, 1965; prof., chmn. nursing dept. Calif. State U., Los Angeles, 1969-72; co-project dir. curriculum research Nat. League for Nursing, 1973-74; project dir. patient edn., office consumer health edn., also adj. asso. prof. community medicine Coll. Medicine and Dentistry N.J.-Rutgers Med. Sch., 1974-75; prof. pub. health and nursing Sch. Pub. Health and Sch. Nursing Columbia U., N.Y.C., 1975-90, prof. emeritus Sch Pub. Health, Sch. Nursing, 1990—, assoc. dean acad. affairs Sch. Pub. Health, 1988-90, hon. prof. nursing edn. Tchrs. Coll., 1977-93, acting head div. health adminstrn. Sch. Pub. Health, 1980-81, 86-88; on leave as exec. dir. Mid-Atlantic Regional Nursing Assn., 1981-82. Cons. U. Nev., Las Vegas, 1970-72, Ball State U., Ind., 1971, Long Beach (Calif.) Naval Hosp., 1971-72, Travis AFB, Calif., 1972, Brentwood VA Hosp., L.A., 1971-72, Ctrl. Nursing Office VA, Washington, 1971-94, N.J. Dept. Higher Edn., 1974-78, John Wiley Pub., 1974-76, Sch. Nursing Am. U. Beirut; mem. spl. med. adv. group VA Dept. Medicine and Surgery, Washington, 1980-84; cons. nursing com. AMA, 1971-74, Citizen's Com. for Children, N.Y.C.; v.p. Pa. Health Coun., 1968-69; mem. adv. com. physicians assts. Calif. Bd. Med. Examiners, adv. com. Cancer Soc. L.A., 1970-72, com. nursing VA, Washington, 1971-74, chair 1975-90, regional med. programs, Pa., 1967-69, Calif. 1970-72; mem. spl. adv. com. on med. licensure and profl. conduct N.Y. State Assembly, 1977-79, mem. nat. adv. com. Encore (nat. YWCA post-mastectomy group rehab. project), 1977-83; assoc. mem. N.Y. Acad. Medicine, 1988-90; mem. ethics com. Palisades Med. Ctr., 1993—, bd. govs., 1995—, mem. profl. and quality rev. com., 1995—, chair, 1998—, exec. com., 1998-99; 2d vice chair N.Y. Presbyn. Healthcare Sys., Palisades Med. Ctr., 1999-2003, 1st vice chair 2003—; lectr., cons., guest Beijing Med. Coll., China, 1982, Aga Khan U., Pakistan, 1990; bd. visitors U. Pitts. Sch. Nursing, 1986-93; mem. editl. adv. bd. Am. Jour. Pub. Health, 1992, chair, 1993-97; nat. and internat. lectr. in field; chair adv. com. grad. program in pub. health U. Medicine and Dentistry of N.J., 1995-2000. Author: (textbooks) Dimensions of Profl. Nursing, 8th edit., 1999, The Nursing Experience: Trends, Challenges, Transitions, 4th edit., 2001; contbg. editor: (jour.) Jour. Nursing Adminstrn., 1975—82; columnist: jour. Nursing Outlook, editor-in-chief, 1982—91; mem. bd. advisors (jour.) Nurses Almanac, 1978, Nurse Manager's Handbook, 1979, Nursing Administration Handbook, 1992; editor (editl. bd.): (jour.) Am. Health, 1981—91; editl. bd. (jour.) Nursing and Health Care, 1991—95, Internat. Nursing Index, 1997—2001. Bd. dirs. ARC, Los Angeles, 1971-72; bd. dirs. Vis. Nurse Service N.Y., 1980-2001, mem. exec. com., chmn. human resources, 1989-2001; bd. dirs. Concern for Dying, 1983-89; trustee Calif. State Coll. L.A. Found., 1971-72, U. Pitts., 1984-90, mem. exec. com. 1988-90; chair bd. visitors U. Pitts. Sch. Pub. Health, 1988-90; bd. visitors U. Miami Sch. Nursing, 1986—; mem. health services com. Children's Aid Soc., N.Y., 1978-84; v.p. Am. Nurses Found., 1980-82; mem. nat. adv. council on nurse tng. HRA, 1981-85; mem. nurses leadership coun. Chlorine Chemistry Coun., 1999—; hon. bd. dirs. NOVA Found., 1998—, Health Professions Panel, Am. Legacy Found., 2000—. Named Outstanding Alumna U. Pitts. Sch. Nursing, 1966, Pa. Nurse of Yr., 1967, Roll of Honor N.J. State Nurses Assn., 1990; named to Tchrs. Coll. Columbia U. Nursing Edn. Alumni Hall of Fame, 1999; recipient Disting. Alumna award U. Pitts. Sch. Edn., 1981, Shaw medal Boston Coll., 1985, Bicentennial Medallion of Distinction, U. Pitts., 1987, R. Louise McManus Medallion for Disting. Svc. to Nursing, Tchrs. Coll. Columbia U., 1987, Dean's Disting. Svc. award Columbia Sch. Pub. Health, 1995, Second Century award in health care, Columbia U. Sch. Nursing, 1996. Fellow Am. Acad. Nursing (named Living Legend 2001); mem. ANA (dir. 1978-82, Hon. Recognition award 1992), APHA (Ruth Freeman Pub. Health Nursing award 1993), Pa. Nurses Assn. (pres. 1966-69), Nat. League Nursing (bd. govs. 1991-95), Nurses Ednl. Funds Bd., U . Pitts. Sch. Nursing Alumni (pres. 1959), Vis. Nurse Assn. Ctrl. Jersey (bd. dirs. 1999-2001, mem. bd. trustees), Am. Hosp. Assn. (com. chmn. 1967-68), Assn. Grad. Faculty Cmty. Health/Pub. Health Nursing (v.p. 1980-81), Sigma Theta Tau (sr. editor Image 1978-81, pres.-elect 1981-83, pres. 1983-85, nat. campaign chair Ctr. for Nursing Scholarship 1987-89, chair devel. com. 1989-95, spl. advisor 1995-97, planned giving task force 1998-2001, Mentor award 1985, 93, 97, Spirit of Philanthropy award 1997), Pi Lambda Theta, Alpha Tau Delta (Cert. of Merit 1968). Achievements include collection of papers in Mugar Library, Boston U. Home: 6040 Boulevard E Apt 11G West New York NJ 07093-3827

KELLY, MAE BAKER, secondary education educator; b. Goose Creek, Tex., Jan. 5, 1938; d. Rex John and Eva Mae (Copeland) Baker; m. Theodore Chilton Kelly (dec.), Dec. 22, 1962; 1 child, Theodore Chilton Kelly II. BS in Home Econ., Southwest Tex. U., 1960. Cert. Sec. Tchr., Vocat. Edn. for Handicapped. Vocat. home econ. Kenedy (Tex.) I.S.D., 1960-62, Poth (Tex.) I.S.D., 1962-66, Hull-Dasietta I.S.D., Dasietta, Tex., 1967-68; lang. arts Dilley (Tex.) I.S.D., 1969-71; vocat. home econ. coop. Cotulla (Tex.) I.S.D., 1972-74; food svc. vocat. edn. for handicapped Harlandale I.S.D., San Antonio, 1974-89, teen age parenting, 1990—. Mem. Am. Vocat. Assn., Tex., 1960-92, Vocat. Home Econ. Tchrs. Assn., Tex., 1963-92; advisor Young Homemakers Tex., 1966, 68, 70-74. Co-author: Vocational Orientation for VEH Students, 1981. Mem., instr. Girl Scouts Am., La Porte, Tex., 1946-56; den mother Boy Scouts Am., Cotulla, Tex., 1972-74; 1st chmn. Nueces County Fair, Cotulla, Tex., 1973-74; clarinet player Beethoven Concert Band, San Antonio, Tex., 1986-92. Recipient Outstanding Tchr., Trinity Campus award, Harlandale Alternative Ctr., 1984, 85. Mem. Order Rainbow Girls, Order of Eastern Star, Harp and Shamrock Soc. Tex., Daughters of the King, Harp and Shamrock Irish Singers. Republican. Episcopalian. Avocations: music, story telling, genealogy, irish cooking, teen advocate. Office: Teen Age Parent Program 1406 Fitch St San Antonio TX 78211-1406

KELLY, MARY JOAN, librarian; b. Baton Rouge, Nov. 25, 1947; d. Theodore McKowen Sr. and Patricia Marilyn (Faul) Wilkes; m. Karl Joseph Nix; 1 child, Patricia Lynn Woodworth. BS, La. State U., 1970, MEd, 1973, EdD, 1980. Cert. English and social studies tchr., city/parish materials and/or media ctr. dir., sch. libr., La. Instr. conversation class La. State U., Baton Rouge, 1979-80; writer, prodr. The Video Co., Baton Rouge, 1983-90; freelance writer, pre and post video prodn., storyteller DBA-The BookDoctor, Baton Rouge; tchr. East Baton Rouge Parish Sch. Bd., ret., 1991; prin. St. Isidore Mid. Sch., 1991-95; libr. Holy Family Sch., Port Allen, La., 1995—2001, East Baton Rouge Parish Sch. Bd., 2001—. Presenter in field. Contbr. numerous articles to profl. jours.; sponsor yearbook and lit. mags.; storyteller and spkr. Mem. Non-Pub. Sch. Commn., La. Bd. Elem. and Secondary Edn., 1992-97; mem. adminstrn. commn. St. Aloysius Cath. Ch., 1989—, mem. comms. com., 1987—, chmn., 1989—. Mem. NEA, ASCD, La. Assn. Educators (mem. com. 1978-91), East Baton Rouge Parish Assn. Educators (v.p.), La. Assn. Classroom Tchrs. (mem. com. 1972-81), East Baton Rouge Parish Assn. Classroom Tchrs. (pres.), Assn. Ednl. Comm. and Tech., La. Assn. Ednl. Comm. and Tech., Internat. Platform Assn., La. Libr. Assn., Capital Area Reading Coun., Cath. Diocese of Baton Rouge Librs. Assn. (sec. 1996-97, pres. 99-01), East Baton Rouge Parish Librs. Assn., Gamma Beta Phi, Pi Lambda Pi, Phi Delta Kappa. Home: 2005 Lee Dr Baton Rouge LA 70808-3932 Office: Park Forest Elem 10717 Elain St Baton Rouge LA 70814 Business E-Mail: mkelly@ebrpsb.k12.la.us. E-mail: marykelly14@prodigy.net.

KELLY, MARY SUSAN, psychologist, educator; b. N.Y.C., July 15, 1954; d. James J. and Veronica (Jacob) Kelly; m. James Houlihan, July 18, 1992. BA, Boston Coll., 1976; MA, Columbia U., 1980, PhD, 1987. Tchr. Kennedy Meml. Hosp., Brighton, Mass., 1976—79; adj. asst. prof. Teachers Coll., Columbia U., N.Y.C., 1987—93; assoc. prof. Western Conn. State U., Danbury, 1993—94; assoc. prof. clin. pediatrics Albert Einstein Coll. of Medicine, Bronx, 1994—. Dir. Fisher Landau Ctr. for Treatment of Learning Disabilities, Albert Einstein Coll. Medicine. Contbr. articles to profl. jours., including Jour. Sch. Psychology, Brain & Cognition, Jour. Learning Disabilities, Jour. Am. Bd. Family Practice, Contemporary Pediats. Grantee: U.S. Dept. Edn., 1987-89, Fisher-Landau Found., N.Y.C., 1987-91, Bd. Edn. Yonkers, N.Y., 1991-93, LD Access Found., 2001-03. Mem. APA, Am. Psychol. Soc. (charter), Am. Ednl. Rsch. Assn., Internat. Reading Assn., Internat. Dyslexia Assn. Office: Fisher Landau Ctr for Treatment of Learning Disabilities Albert Einstein Coll Med 1165 Morris Park Ave Bronx NY 10461-1915 E-mail: mskelly@aecom.yu.edu.

KELLY, MICHAEL JOSEPH, academic administrator, consultant; b. NYC, July 2, 1931; s. Hugh and Mary Agnes (Harrison) K.; m. Helen Janet Nee, Oct. 4, 1969; children: Joan T., Jean M. BA, Marist Coll., 1955; BEE, Cath. U., 1960, MEE, 1961; DEng, U. Detroit, 1968. Tchr. U. Detroit, 3 yrs., dir. Computer Ctr.; tchr., adminstr. Marist Coll., 4 yrs.; assoc. prof. electrical and mech. engring., dir. engring. case program Stanford U.; mgr. CAD, litho sys. IBM, East Fishkill, NY, 1969-79, mgr. Mfg. Tech. Ctr. Boca Raton, Fla., 1979-84, dir. Quality Inst., 1984, mgr. quality improvement and profl. devel. programs systems tech. divsn., 1986-87; dir. computer integrated mfg. and tech. transfer NJ Inst. Tech., NJ, 1987-89; dir. def. mfg. office Def. Advanced Rsch. Projects Agy., 1989-91; exec. dir. Nat. Adv. Com. on Semiconductors, 1989-91; dir. Mfg. Rsch. Ctr. Ga. Inst. Tech., Ga., 1991-96, prof. technology mgmt., 1995-96; Northrop-Grumman endowed chair mfg. and design Calif. State U., LA, 1996-99; ind. mgmt. and ednl. cons., 1999—. Home: 31 Lieper St Huntington Station NY 11746

KELLY, PATRICIA ALINE, physical education educator, coach; b. Indian Town Gap, Pa., Nov. 6, 1952; d. James Grant and Mary Maria (Weber) K. BS in Health and Phys. Edn., Slippery Rock State U., 1974; MEd in Phys. Edn., East Carolina U., 1981. Cert. health and phys. edn. tchr., Pa., phys. edn. tchr., Tex. Tchr., coach Ind. (Pa.) Area Sch. Dist., 1974-80; grad. asst. East Carolina U., Greenville, N.C., 1980-81; instr., asst. basketball coach Lamar U., Beaumont, Tex., 1981-83; tchr., coach Monsignor Kelly High Sch., Beaumont, Tex., 1983-84, Lumberton (Tex.) Ind. Sch. Dist., 1984—. Named Coach of Yr., Tri-County Ofcls. Assn., 1977-78, 78-79, Ctrl. Western Girls Basketball Conf., 1977-78, 78-79, Coach West All-Stars, Pa. Interscholastic Athletic Assn., 1979 Mem. NEA, Am. Alliance Health, Phys. Edn., Recreation and Dance, Tex. State Tchrs. Assn., Tex. Assn. Health, Phys. Edn., Recreation and Dance, Delta Psi Kappa.

KELLY, SEAN DORRANCE, philosophy educator; BS with honors, MS in Cognitive and Linguistic Scis., Brown U., 1989; PhD in Philosophy, U. Calif., 1992. Tchg. asst. philosophy U. Calif., Berkeley, 1989—97, Ralph K. Church departmental fellow in philosophy, 1997—98, instr. philosophy, 1996; lectr. philosophy Stanford U., Calif., 1998—99; asst. prof. philosophy Princeton (N.J.) U., 1999—. Jonathan Edwards Bicentennial preceptor, 2002—, Old Dominion faculty fellow, 2000—01, chair Old Dominion Faculty Fellows, 2001—02. Vis. scholar U. Calif., Berkeley, 2000; lectr. in field. Author: The Relevance of Phenomenology to the Philosophy of Language and Mind, 2000; contbr. articles. Campbell's Coll. Scholarship, Brown U., 1985—89, Fellowship in Complex Sys., Santa Fe Inst. and Los Alamos Labs., 1989, Howison fellowship in philosophy, U. Calif., 1995—96, fellow, NEH Summer Inst. on Consciousness and Intentionality, 2002, James S. McDonnell sr. fellowship in philosophy and neuroscis., 2000—, fellow, John Simon Guggenheim Meml. Found., 2003—, vice-chancellor's rsch. grant in the humanities, U. Calif., 1995, Humanities Grad. Rsch. grant (2), 1996. Mem.: Am. Philosoph. Assn. Office: Princeton U Dept Philosophy 1879 Hall Princeton NJ 08544-1006*

KELM, BONNIE G. art museum director, educator; b. Bklyn., Mar. 29, 1947; d. Julius and Anita (Baron) Steiman; m. William G. Malis; 1 child, Michael Darren. BS in Art Edn., Buffalo State U., 1968; MA in Art History, Bowling Green (Ohio) State U., 1975; PhD in Arts Adminstrn., Ohio State U., 1987. Art tchr. Toledo Pub. Schs., 1968—71; ednl. cons. Columbus (Ohio) Mus. Art, 1976—81; prof. art Franklin U., Columbus, 1976—88; legis. coord. Ohio Ho. of Reps., Columbus, 1977; pres. bd. trustees Columbus Inst. for Contemporary Art, 1977—81; tech. asst. cons. Ohio Arts Coun., Columbus, 1984—88; dir. Bunte Gallery Franklin U., Columbus, 1978—88; dir. art mus. Miami U., Oxford, Ohio, 1988—96, assoc. prof., 1988—96; dir. Muscarelle Mus. of Art Coll. William and Mary, Williamsburg, Va., 1996—2002, assoc. prof. art and art history, 1996—2002; dir. Univ. Art Mus. U. Calif., Santa Barbara, 2002—. Adj. prof. dept. art history U. Art Mus. U. Calif., Santa Barbara; grant panelist Ohio Arts Coun., Columbus, 1985-87, 91-95; art book reviewer William C. Brown Pub., Madison, Wis., 1985-92; mem. acquisitions adv. bd. Martin Luther King Ctr., Columbus, 1987-88; field reviewer Inst. Mus. Svcs., Washington, 1990—; chairperson grant panel Art in Pub. Places, 1992-95; trustee Ohio Mus. Assn., 1993-96; state apptd. mem. adv. com. Ohio Percent for Art, 1994-96; bd. dirs. U.S. Nat. Com. Internat. Coun. Museums, 1998—; bd. dirs., southeast rep. Assn. Univ. & Coll. Mus. Galleries, 1998—. Author, editor (mus. catalogues) Connections, 1985, Into the Mainstream: Contemporary Folk Art, 1991, Testimony of Images: PreColumbian Art, 1992, Collecting by Design: The Allen Collection, 1994, Photographs by Barbara Hershey: A Retrospective, 1995, Georgia O'Keeffe in Williamsburg, 2001; contbr. chpt. to book Modernism Gender & Culture, 1997, articles to profl. jours. Founding mem., mem. adv. coun. Columbus Cultural Arts Ctr., 1977-81; coord., curator Cultural Exch. Program, Honolulu-Columbus, 1980; mem. acad. women achievers YWCA, 1991—; guest spkr. 1991 Scholastic Arts Award, Cin., 1991; keynote spkr. Ohio Mus. Assn., ann. meeting, 1992; spkr. Internat. Coun. Mus. Triennial Conf., Quebec City, 1992, Internat. Coun. Mus. Triennial Congress, Barcelona, Spain, 2001, session chair; session chair Midwest Mus. Assn. ann. meeting, St. Louis, 1993; session chair Am. Assn. Mus. ann. meeting, Balt., 2000; presenter East-West Ctr. Internat. Conf., Honolulu, 2000. Recipient Marantz Disting. Scholar award Ohio State U., 1995, Gelpe award YWCA, 1987, Cultural Advancement of City of Columbus award, The Columbus Dispatch, 1984, Disting. Svc. award, Columbus Art League, 1984, Critic's Choice award Found. for Cmty. of Artists, N.Y., 1981; Fulbright scholar USIA, 1988 (The Netherlands); NEH fellow East-West Ctr., Honolulu, 1991. Mem. Am. Assn. Mus. (advocacy task force, surveyor mus. assessment program 1996—, nat. program com. 2001), Assn. of Coll. and Univ. Mus. and Galleries, Western Mus. Assn., Assn., Fulbright Assn., Coll. Arts Assn. (session chair, spkr. ann. meeting 2003), Internat. Coun. Mus., Calif. Assn. Mus. Office: Univ Art Mus U Calif Santa Barbara 1626 Arts Bldg Santa Barbara CA 93106 E-mail: bgkelm@uam.ucsb.edu.

KELSCH, JOAN MARY, elementary education educator; b. Allentown, Pa., Jan. 19, 1953; d. Paul Thomas and Dorothy Mildred (Grim) Reichart; m. William Joseph Kelsch, July 27, 1974; children: Daniel, Dorothy. BS, West Chester (Pa.) State Coll., 1974. Cert. tchr., Pa. Elem. tchr. St. Francis Acad., Bally, Pa., 1974-79, 86—, substitute tchr., 1979-82, establisher, tchr. kindergarten, 1982-86, coord. reading, 1976-79, coord. religion, 1986—; head tchr. St. Francis Academy, Bally, Pa., 2000—; mentor tchr. St. Francis Acad., Bally, Pa., 1986-87; coord. Rainbows Peer Support Program, 1993-95. Mem., chairperson Mid. States Evaluation Coms., 1986-87, 98-99; playground supr. Bally Recreation Com., summer 1990, pool mgr., summer 1991; trained mem. IST, 1995; instr. homebound, 1999. Mem. Internat. Reading Assn., Home and Sch. Assn. (faculty rep.), Tri-County Reading Assn., Keystone State Reading Assn., Allentown Diocese Assn. Lay Tchrs. Avocations: reading, sewing, travel, collecting, crafts. Home: 331 Main St Bally PA 19503 Office: Saint Francis Acad 7th And Pine Sts Bally PA 19503

KELSEY, CLYDE EASTMAN, JR., philosophy and psychology educator; b. Wadena, Minn., Mar. 30, 1924; s. Clyde Eastman and Lorraine (Lamb) Bagley) K.; m. Betty Jean Williams, Apr. 1, 1949 (dec.); children: Becky Kelsey Marcin, Nancy Kelsey Eargle; m. Jamie Lee Reagan, 1987. BA, U. Tex., El Paso, 1948; MA, U. Tulsa, 1951; PhD, U. Denver, 1960; hon. degree, U. de Oriente, Venezuela, 1969. Dir. counseling bur. U. Tex., El Paso, 1951-61, prof., head dept. philosophy, psychology, 1961-62, vice chmn. dept. philosophy and psychology, 1951-61; dean students, dir. Inter-Am. Inst., 1962-66; program adv. Venezuela, Ford Found., 1966-69; vice chancellor public affairs U. Denver, 1969-72; v.p. devel. and univ. relations Tex. Tech U., Lubbock, 1972-81, prof. edn., 1981-88, prof. emeritus, 1988—; sr. rsch. fellow Nat. Center Higher Edn. Mgmt., 1983-87. Lectr. 4th Army U.S., 1961-65; cons. U.S. Dept. State, Peace Corps, 1961-66; mem. adv. bd. Kans. Wesleyan Coll., 1960-71; vis. scientist NSF, 1962-66; v.p. Colo. Ptnrs. of Alliance, 1971-73; examiner, cons. Tex. State Bd. of Examiners of Psychologists, 1992-98; cons. Agy. for Internat. Devel., Coll. Bd., Civil Svc. Commn., World Bank to India, Saudi Arabia, Turkey, Republic of Mauritius, InterAm. Bank to Guyana, S.A. Contbr. articles to profl. jours. Bd. dirs. El Paso Mental Health Assn., 1951-58, pres. 1953-55; bd. dirs. El Paso Sch. Retarded Children, 1952-57, pres., 1953-55; bd. dirs. Lubbock Goodwill Industries, 1972-85, v.p., 1973-77, pres., 1978-80; bd. dirs. St. Mary's Hosp. Found., 1986-2000, chmn., 1994-96. With USNR, 1942-45. Decorated Order San Carlos Republic Colombia, 1964; recipient Disting. Alumni Service award U. Denver, 1972; Fulbright scholar Colombia, 1960-61 Fellow Tex. Acad. Sci.; mem. APA, Tex. Psychol. Assn., Phi Beta Delta. Home: 13413 North Shore Dr Montgomery TX 77356

KELTY, PAUL DAVID, physician, educator; b. Louisville, Oct. 2, 1947; s. William Theadore and Mary Frances (Hinton) K. BEE, U. Louisville, 1970, MD, 1978; MS, Ohio State U., 1971. Mem. tech. staff Bell Labs., Whippany, N.J., 1970-72; design engr. Gen. Electric Co., Louisville, 1972-74; intern St. Mary's Med. Ctr., Evansville, Ind., 1978-79, resident in ob-gyn., 1979-82; practice medicine, specializing in ob-gyn. Corydon, Ind., 1982—. Clin. instr. Dept. Ob-Gyn U. Louisville (Ky.) Sch. Medicine, 1987—. Mem. AMA, Am. Soc. Reproductive Medicine, Am. Inst. Ultrasound in Medicine, N.Y. Acad. Scis., Sigma Xi, Phi Kappa Phi, Tau Beta Pi, Sigma Tau, Sigma Pi Sigma, Eta Kappa Nu, Gamma Beta Phi, Omicron Delta Kappa. Roman Catholic. Home and Office: 2000 Edsel Ln NW Corydon IN 47112

KEMNA, RITA MARIE, primary/elementary school educator; b. St. Louis, Dec. 31, 1946; d. Arthur Henry Jr. and Nellie Mae (Fitzgerald) K. BA, U. Mo., St. Louis, 1969, MEd, 1976. Cert. tchr. elem., early childhood, remedial reading and spl. edn., Mo. Tchr. spl. edn./learning disabilities Mo. Schs., 1969—; tchr. spl. edn.-learning disabled St. Louis Schs., 1983-87, tchr. kindergarten, 1987—. Adj. prof. Maryville U., St. Louis, 1990-93; supervising tchr. Harris-Stowe Coll., St. Louis, 1991, U. Mo., St. Louis, 1992; Mo. del. Fine Arts Seminar, Taiwan, 1980; del. Ednl. Seminar, Russia and China, 1983; presenter, panel mem. profl. confs. and workshops. Mem. Gov.'s Com., Jefferson City, Mo., 1979; judge Monsanto/Post Dispatch Sci. Fair, St. Louis, 1983-93; mem. steering and curriculum coms. for development of magnet sch., St. Louis, 1988-89; hon. mem. St. Louis Spina Bifida Assn., 1982—. Named Bd. Mem. of Yr., St. Louis Spina Bifida Assn., 1985. Mem. ASCD, Assn. for Childhood Edn. (v.p. 1977-79, 87-93, pres. 1979-81, mem. exec. bd. 1973-77), Sherlock Holmes Soc., Alpha Delta Kappa (v.p. 1988-90, pres. 1990-92, mem. exec. bd. 1986). Office: Wilkinson Early Childhd Ctr 7212 Arsenal St Saint Louis MO 63143-3404

KEMP, ARTHUR DEREK, psychology educator; b. Raeford, N.C., May 24, 1959; s. Arthur Brooks and Annie (Johnson) K.; m. Gina Bell, June 30, 1984; children: Austin Danté, Anson DuBois, Arrington Demetrius. BA in Psychology magne cum laude, N.C. A&T State U., 1980; MA in Psychology, So. Ill. U., 1982, PhD in Psychology, 1989. Intern in counseling psychology Tex. Tech. U. Counseling Ctr., Lubbock, 1987-88; postdoctoral summer fellow in clinical neuropsychology VA Med. Ctr., Leavenworth, Kans., 1989; therapist South Kansas City (Mo.) Mental Health Ctr., 1989; counseling psychologist Counseling Ctr. Cen. Mo. State U., Warrensburg, 1988-90, asst. prof. dept. psychology, 1990-92, 94-95, assoc. prof. dept. psychology, 1995—; postdoctoral fellow in clin. neuropsych. behavioral medicine St. Louis U. Health Sci. Ctr., 1992-94; adj. asst. prof. dept. psychology St. Louis U., 1993-94. Cons. Chem. Decontamination Tng. Ctr., Ft. McClellan, Ala., 1987, Tex. Rehab. Commn. Tex. Tech. U., 1988, Cen. Mo. State U. dept. inst. rsch., 1989, Northwest Mo. State U., 1991, Ctrl. Methodist Coll., 1992. Contbr. articles to profl. jours. Mem. APA, Nat. Acad. Neuropsychology, Alpha Phi Alpha, Phi Kappa Phi, Psi Chi, Alpha Chi, Alpha Phi Omega, Alpha Kappa Mu (Excellence in Tchg. award), Phi Delta Kappa. Democrat. Avocations: gospel organ music, reading, sports, bible study, pastor. Home: 910 Coventry Ct Warrensburg MO 64093-9634 Office: Central Mo State U Dept Psych Warrensburg MO 64093 also: Enlightened World Christian Ctr PO Box 634 708 N College Ave Warrensburg MO 64093-1220 Fax: (660) 429-2441. E-mail: drkemp@sprintmail.com.

KEMP, PATRICIA MARY, reading educator; b. Milw., Dec. 8, 1944; d. William F. and Charlotte R. (Spangenberg) Marten; m. Croydon Leigh Kemp, Sept. 14, 1968 (div. Aug. 1994). B, Mich. State U., 1967; M, Cardinal Stritch Coll., 1977. Tchr. 5th grade Greendale (Wis.) Sch. Dist., 1967-68, tchr. 2d grade, 1969-93, tchr. reading K-6, 1993-2000, tchr. reading k-2, 2000—. Roman Catholic. Avocations: golf, stitchery, reading, swimming, walking. Home: 1960 Lone Oak Cir E Brookfield WI 53045-5036

KEMP, SUZANNE LEPPART, elementary education educator, clubwoman; b. N.Y.C., Dec. 28, 1929; d. John Culver and Eleanor (Buxton) Leppart; m. Ralph Clinton Kemp, Apr. 4, 1953; children— Valerie Gale, Sandra Lynn, John Maynard, Renee Alison. Grad. Ogontz Jr. Coll., 1949; B.S., U. Md., 1952. Elem. sch. tchr. Mem. Nat. Soc. Women Descs. of Ancient and Hon. Arty. Co., Nat. Soc. Daus. of Founders and Patriots of Am. (corr. sec.), Nat. Soc. Sons and Daus. of Pilgrims, Nat. Soc. U.S. Daus. of 1812 (chpt. organizing Md. state pres. 1977-79, chpt. v.p. 1979—), Nat. Soc. New Eng. Women (colony pres. 1978-80, Nat. Soc. Colonial Dames XVII Century (state chmn. heraldry and coats of arms 1977-79), Nat. Soc. D.A.R. (chpt. regent 1970-73, chpt. v.p., Md. soc. chmn. transp. 1976-79), Md. State Officers Club, Md. Hist. Soc., Friends of Animals, Defenders of Animal Rights Inc., U. Md. Alumni, English Speaking Union, Star Spangled Banner Flag House Assn., Potter-Balt. Clayworks, Balt. Mus. Art, Walters Art Gallery, Dames of the Court of Honor, Kappa Delta Alumni. Clubs: Baltimore Country; Lago Mar (Ft. Lauderdale, Fla.); Roland Park Women's; Woodbrook-Murray Hill Garden Club, Federation Garden Clubs. Editor; The Spinning Wheel, 1973-76. Home: 7 Ruxton Green Ct Baltimore MD 21204-3548

KEMPER, ROBERT VAN, anthropologist, educator, minister; b. San Diego, Nov. 21, 1945; s. Ivan L. and Roberta (King) K.; m. Sandra L. Kraft, Sept. 9, 1967; 1 child, John Kraft. BA, U. Calif., Riverside, 1966; MA, U. Calif., Berkeley, 1969, PhD, 1971; MDiv, So. Meth. U., 1999. Ordained to ministry Presbyn. Ch., 1999. Postdoctoral fellow U. Calif., Berkeley, 1971-72; asst. prof. So. Meth. U., Dallas, 1972-77, assoc. prof., 1977-83, prof., 1983—, chmn., 1992-94. Visiting rsch. scholar U. Iberoamericana, Mexico City, 1970, 79-80, Ctr. U.S.-Mex. Studies, LaJolla, Calif., 1983, U. Nat. Autónoma Mex., Mexico City, 1990-91, El Colegio de Michoacán, Zamora, Mex., 1991; sec. Inst. Study of Earth and Man, Dallas, 1989-92; Coun. Preservation Anthrop. Records; founding chair Commn. Anthropology Tourism, Internat. Union Anthrop. and Ethnol. Scis., 1993-96. Author: Migration and Adaptation, 1977; co-author: History of Anthropology, 1977; co-editor: Anthropologists in Cities, 1974, Migration Across Frontiers, 1979, (series) Contemporary Urban Studies, 1990—, Chronicling Cultures, 2002; editor Socio Cultural Anthropology, Am. Anthropologist, 1985-90, Human Orgn., 1995-98; mem. editl. bd. Ency. World Cultures, 1990-96, Ency. Urban Cultures, 1999—2002. Elder North Pk. Presbyn. Ch., Dallas, 1987-89, 95-97; parish assoc. Trinity Presbyn. Ch., 1999-2002; mem. Mcpl. Libr. Adv. Bd., Dallas, 1975-79; bd. dir. Oasis Housing Corp., 2000—, Presbyn. Assn. Cmty. Transformation, 2003—. Fulbright fellow, 1979-80, 91-92, Wenner-Gren fellow, 1974-76, 79-83, Woodrow Wilson fellow, 1966-67. Fellow AAAS, Am. Anthrop. Assn. (bd. dirs. 1990-92), Soc. Applied Anthropology (chmn. Malinowski award com. 1979-80, bd. dirs. 1995-98); mem. Latin Am. Studies Assn. (co-chmn. XI Internat. Congress 1983), Soc. Urban Anthropology (pres. 1988-90), Soc. Latin Am. Anthropology (pres. 1981-82), Phi Beta Kappa (pres. chpt. 1987-88). Home: 10617 Cromwell Dr Dallas TX 75229-5110 Office: So Meth Univ Dept Anthropology 3225 Daniel Ave Dallas TX 75205-1437

KENDA, JUANITA ECHEVERRIA, artist, educator; b. Tarentum, Pa., Nov. 12, 1922; d. Carlos Porfirio and Jane Amelia (Gummert) Echeverria; m. William Kenda, Aug. 18, 1945; children: Linda Jane, Carlos Paul, William Porfirio. Student, Stephens Coll., 1940-41, Art Students' League, N.Y.C., 1941-42; BFA, Temple U. and Tyler Art Sch., 1945; student, U. Hawaii, 1969-72. Instr. Phila. Mus. Art, 1940-45, Punahou Sch., Honolulu, 1948-49; dir. art edn. Hawaii Dept. Edn., Honolulu, 1952-60; head, creative art sect. Honolulu Acad. Arts, Honolulu, 1958-63; community relations officer, Eastwest Ctr. U. Hawaii, Honolulu, 1967-70; instr. in watercolors Honolulu Acad. Arts, from 1983. Pres. Nat. Soc. Arts and Letters, Downtown Gallery, Honolulu, 1969-76, Am. Women's Club, Asuncion, Paraguay, 1981-83; trustee Tennant Found., Honolulu, 1984—. One woman exhbns. include Duncan Gallery, N.Y., Da Vinci Gallery, Phila., Downtown Gallery, Honolulu, Pali Art Gallery, Honolulu, 1991, King Hooper Mansion, 1995; represented in collections of pres. of Mex., State of Hawaii, many others; invited guest artist Art of Hawaii, 1993. Bd. dirs. Hawaii Art Coun., Honolulu, 1984-90; hon. Mex. Consul Hawaii, 1969-77; mem. Allentown Art Mus., Peabody Mus., Honolulu Acad. Arts. Mem. Hawaii Artist's League (pres. 1984-87), Hawaii Water Color Soc., Am. Assn. Mus., Nat. Penn Women, Internat. Coun. Mus., Am. Fedn. Women's Club, PEO, Oahu Country Club, Plaza Club, 21st Century Club (founder, chmn. 1987), Nat. Soc. Arts & Letters, Am. Assn. Univ. Women, Water Color Art Soc. Houston, Mus. of Fine Arts. Republican. Episcopalian. Home: Houston, Tex. Died Sept. 26, 2000.

KENDALL, LAUREL ANN, geotechnical engineer; b. Detroit, Dec. 4, 1956; d. James McNair and Dorothy Mildred (Frost) K. BSE in Environ. Sci., U. Mich., 1979, MSCE, 1983. Registered profl. engr., Mich., Ill., Ohio. With Bechtel Assocs. P.C., 1979-84; project mgr. NTH Cons., 1984-90; gen. mgr. solid waste ops. Wayne Disposal, Inc. (purchased by Allied Waste Industries), 1990-97, dist. landfill gen. mgr., 1997-99, dist. environ. mgr., 1999-2000; dir. landfill ops. The Environtl. Quality Co., 2000—01; mgr. geoenviron. svcs. The Mannik & Smith Group, Inc., 2002—. Instr. Lawrence Inst. Tech., Southfield, Mich., 1985-91, Wayne State U., 1991—. Mem. ASCE (past pres. Mich. sect.), Mich. Soc. Profl. Engrs. (past pres. Oakland chpt.), Engrng. Soc. Detroit (landfill design conf. organizing com. 1995—). Congregationalist. Avocations: gardening, jogging, mountain biking, cross-country skiing. Office: Mannik & Smith Group 15300 Rotunda Dr Dearborn MI 48120

KENDLER, HOWARD H(ARVARD), psychologist, educator; b. NYC, June 9, 1919; s. Harry H. and Sylvia (Rosenberg) K.; m. Tracy Seedman, Sept. 20, 1941 (dec. July 2001); children: Joel Harlan, Kenneth Seedman. AB, Bklyn. Coll., 1940; MA, U. Iowa, 1941, PhD, 1943. Instr. U. Iowa, 1943; research psychologist OSRD, 1944; asst. prof. U. Colo., 1946-48; assoc. prof. NYU, 1948-51, prof., 1951-63; chmn. dept. Univ. Coll., 1951-61; prof. U. Calif., Santa Barbara, 1963-89, prof. emeritus, 1989—, chmn. dept. psychology, 1965-66. Project dir. Office Naval Rsch., 1950-68; prin. investigator NSF, 1953-65, USAAF, 1951-53; mem. adv. panel psychobiology NSF, 1960-62; tng. com. Nat. Inst. Child Health and Human Devel., 1963-66; cons. Dept. Def., Smithsonian Instn., 1959-60, Human Resources Rsch. Office, George Washington U., 1960; vis. prof. U. Calif., Berkeley, 1960-61, Hebrew U., Jerusalem, 1974-75, Tel Aviv U., 1990; chief clin. psychologist Walter Reed Gen. Hosp., 1945-46. Author: Basic Psychology, 1963, 3d edit., 1974, Basic Psychology: Brief Version, 1977, Psychology: A Science in Conflict, 1981, Historical Foundations of Modern Psychology, 1987, Amoral Thoughts About Morality: The Intersection of Science, Psychology, and Ethics, 2000; co-author: Basic Psychology: Brief Edition, 1970; co-editor: Essays in Neobehaviorism: A Memorial Volume to Kenneth W. Spence; assoc. editor: Jour. Exptl. Psychology, 1963-65; contbr. to profl. jours., chpts. to books. Served as 1st lt. AUS. Fellow Center for Advanced Studies in Behaviorial Scis., Stanford, Calif., 1969-70; NSF grantee, 1954-76 Mem. Am. Psychol. Assn. (pres. div. exptl. psychology 1964-65, pres. div. gen. psychology 1967-68), Western Psychol. Assn. (pres. 1970-71), Soc. Exptl. Psychologists (exec. com. 1971-73), Psychonomic Soc. (governing bd. 1963-69, chmn. 1968-69), Sigma Xi. Home and Office: 300 Hot Springs Rd Santa Barbara CA 93108 E-mail: kendler@psych.ucsb.edu.

KENDRICK, RICHARD LOFTON, university administrator, consultant; b. Washington, Nov. 19, 1944; s. Hilary Herbert and Blanche (Lofton) K.; m. Anne Ritchie, Mar. 5, 1966; children: Shawn Elizabeth, Christopher Robert. BS in Bus. and Mktg., Va. Poly. Inst., 1971; postgrad., U. Ky., 1978-80. Adminstr. U.S. Army Security Agy., Washington, 1965-69; with credit, sales and adminstrv. depts. U.S. Plywood-Champion Internat., Pa., N.C. and Va., 1971-77; purchasing dir. James Madison U., Harrisonburg, Va., 1977-78, fin. officer, 1978-85; cons. Systems and Computer Tech. Corp., Malvern, Pa., 1986; dir. fin. svcs. Hillsborough C.C. System, Tampa, Fla., 1986-87; agt. Mass Mut. Life Ins., Harrisonburg, 1987-88; asst. vice chancellor/treas. U. Ark., Fayetteville, 1988-92; dir. fin. svcs. Clinch Valley Coll. U. Va., Wise, 1992-97; cons. Computer Mgmt. and Devel. Systems, Harrisonburg, 1997-98; CFO RMC, Inc., Harrisonburg, 1998; fin. mgr. Massanetta Springs, Harrisonburg, 1998-99; dir. fin. and adminstrn. U. South Fla. Sarasota/New Coll., 1999—2002; v.p. bus. Luth. Theol. So. Sem., Columbia, SC, 2002—. Affirmative action, equal opportunity officer treas., CVC Found., affirmative action-equal opportunity officer; credit cons. to plywood and lumber industry; cons. to higher edn. Leader, treas. Boy Scouts Am., Harrisonburg, 1977-86; mem. Ashbury United Meth. Ch., 1975-77, Trinity United Meth. Ch., 1992-97. Served with Security Agy., U.S. Army, 1965-69. Recipient New Idea award U.S. Plywood-Champion Internat., 1972; named Profl. Pub. Buyer Nat. Inst. Govt. Purchasers, 1977. Mem. Am. Mktg. Assn., Nat. Assn. Accts., Nat. Assn. Coll. and Univ. Bus. Officers, Fin. Officers of State Colls. and Univs., So. Assn. Coll. and Univ. Bus. Officers, Internat. Platform Assn., Ark. Assn. of Univ. and Coll. Bus. Officers, Nat. Assn. Cash Mgrs., Exchange (Harrisonburg), Kiwanis. Avocations: home building, designing world war ii dioramas. Home: 1431 Bluewater Rd Harrisonburg VA 22801-8646 Office: Luth Theol So Sem 4201 N Maine St Columbia SC 29203-5898 E-mail: rkendrick@ltss.edu.

KENEN, PETER BAIN, economist, educator; b. Cleve., Nov. 30, 1932; s. Isaiah Leo and Beatrice (Bain) K.; m. Regina Horowitz, Aug. 21, 1955; children: Joanne Lisa, Marc David, Stephanie Hope, Judith Rebecca. AB, Columbia U., 1954; MA, Harvard U., 1956, PhD, 1958. Mem. faculty Columbia U., 1957-71, prof. econs., 1964-71, chmn. dept., 1967-69, provost univ., 1969-70; prof. econs. and internat. fin. Princeton (N.J.) U., 1971—, dir. internat. fin. sect., 1971-99; Ford rsch. prof. U. Calif., Berkeley, 1979-80. Rschr. on internat. monetary theory and policy; cons. Coun. Econ. Advisors, 1961, U.S. Treasury, 1962-68, 77-80, 95-98, Bur. Budget, 1964-68, IMF, 1990, 92. Author: British Monetary Policy and the Balance of Payments (1951-1957), 1960, Giant Among Nations, 1960; author: (with A.G. Hart and A. Entine) Money, Debt and Economic Activity, 4th edit., 1969; author: (with R. Lubitz) International Economics, 3d edit., 1971; author: A Model of the U.S. Balance of Payments, 1978; author: (with P.R. Allen) Asset Markets, Exchange Rates and Economic Integration, 1980; author: Essays in International Economics, 1980, Managing Exchange Rates, 1988, Exchange Rates and Policy Coordination, 1989, Exchange Rates and the Monetary System, 1994, Economic and Monetary Union in Europe, 1995, International Economy, 4th edit., 2000, The International Financial Architecture: What's New? What's Missing?, 2001; editor: International Trade and Finance, Frontiers for Research, 1975; editor: (with others) The International Monetary System Under Flexible Exchange Rates, 1982; editor: (with R.W. Jones) Handbook of International Economics, 1984; editor: Managing the World Economy, 1994, Understanding Interdependence, 1995; editor: (with A.K. Swoboda) Reforming the International Monetary and Financial System, 2000; contbr. articles to profl. jours. Recipient David A. Wells prize Harvard U., 1958-59, Univ. medal Columbia U., 1977; Ctr. Advanced Study Behavioral Scis. fellow, 1971-72, John Simon Guggenheim Found. fellow, 1975-76, Res. Bank Australia fellow, 1983-84, Royal Inst. Internat. Affairs fellow, 1987-88, German Marshall Fund fellow, 1987-88, Houblon-Norman fellow Bank of Eng., 1991-92, fellow Res. Bank New Zealand, 2002. Mem. Am. Econ. Assn., Coun. Fgn. Rels., Royal Econ. Soc., Group of Thirty. Home: 176 Western Way Princeton NJ 08540-7208 Office: Princeton U Dept of Econs Fisher Hall Princeton NJ 08544-1021

KENKEL, JAMES LAWRENCE, economics educator; b. Cin., Mar. 25, 1944; s. Lawrence J. and Mildred (Schmidt) K.; children: Julie, Tim. BA, Xavier U., Cin., 1966; MA, Purdue U., 1968, PhD, 1969. Prof. econs. U. Pitts., 1969—; cons. Fed. Home Loan Bank Bd, Washington, 1971-72, Jones & Laughlin Steel, Pitts., U.S. Steel, Pitts., Sony Corp., Nat. Steel, EPA, Mellon Bank, Westinghouse. Author: Risk in Mortgage Lending, 1973, Linear Dynamic Economic Models, 1974; Statistics for Management, 1996. Mem. Am. Econ. Assn., Am. Statis. Assn., Econometric Soc. Avocations: tennis, skiing, baseball. Home: 807 Academy Pl Pittsburgh PA 15243-2000 Office: U Pitts Forbes Quad Pittsburgh PA 15260

KENNAN, KENT WHEELER, composer, educator; b. Milw., Apr. 18, 1913; s. Kossuth Kent and Sara Louise (Wheeler) K. Student, U. Mich., 1930-32; B.Mus. in Composition and Theory, Eastman Sch. of Music U. Rochester, 1934, M.Mus. in Composition, 1936; student, Royal Acad. of Santa Cecilia, Rome, 1938. Mem. faculty Kent (Ohio) State U., 1939-40; tchr. composition, orchestration, counterpoint and theory U. Tex., Austin, 1940-42, 45-46, 49-83, prof. emeritus; tchr. theory Ohio State U., 1947-49; tchr. composition, orchestration Eastman Sch. of Music, summers 1954, 56. Composer music performed under Toscanini, Ormandy, Hanson, Stokowski, others, by N.Y. Philharm. Symphony, Phila. Orch., Chgo., Houston, Detroit, San Antonio, Boston Symphonies, others; composer: Night Soliloquy, other orch. works, 5 Preludes for Piano, Retrospectives (12 pieces for piano), Sonata for Trumpet and Piano, also vocal, choral and chamber music; author: Counterpoint, 4th edit., 1999; (with D. Grantham) Technique of Orchestration, 6th edit., 2002. Served with USAAF, 1942-46. Recipient Prix de Rome in Music, 1936 Mem.: ASCAP, Pi Kappa Lambda, Phi Mu Alpha, Delta Tau Delta. Address: 1034 Liberty Park Dr Apt 248 Austin TX 78746-6852 E-mail: kwhe@earthlink.net.

KENNARD, EMILY MARIE, secondary school art educator, watercolor artist; b. Cleve., Oct. 23, 1947; d. Stephen George and Cora Charlotte (Barto) Duke; children: Erin Marie, Coreen Marie. BA, Notre Dame Coll., South Euclid, Ohio, 1969; postgrad., Cleve. State U., 1980-83, Kent State U., 1983, Cleve. Inst. Art, 1987, U. Akron, 1988-92; MA in Curriculum and Instrn., Ashland U., 1997. Cert. secondary tchr., cert. tchr. visual art grades kindergarten through 12, Ohio. Tchr. art Nazareth Acad., Parma, Ohio, 1969-72; asst. office mgr. Cosmo Plastics Co., Cleve., 1973-74; tchr. art Cleve. Pub. Schs., 1974-75, Padua Franciscan High Sch., Parma, 1979-83, St. Joseph High Sch., Cleve., 1983-88; tchr., chairperson dept. art Elyria (Ohio) Cath. High Sch., 1988—; freelance artist Brooklyn Heights, Ohio. Mem. adv. bd. Lorain (Ohio) County Scholastic Art Assn., 1988—. Exhibited watercolor Notre Dame Coll., 1986 (Best of Show); one-person show Morse Graphic Arts, Parma, 1984; group exhbn. Lorain County Bd. Edn., Elyria, 1988—. Com. chairperson Brooklyn Heights Svc. Orgn., 1983-89; active Cleve. Mus. Art. Recipient Citation for Excellence, Nat. Scholastic Art Assn., N.Y.C., 1990-91. Mem. Nat. Art Educators Assn., Ohio Art Edn. Assn., Cath. High Sch. and Acad. Lay Tchrs. Assn. (rep. 1988—), Ohio Cath. Edn. Assn. (mem. art com., chairperson conv. 1991), Ohio Watercolor Soc. Avocations: Tae Kwon Do, huntstyle riding, golf, bowling, piano. Office: Elyria Cath High Sch 725 Gulf Rd Elyria OH 44035-3648

KENNARD, MARGARET ANNE, middle school educator; b. Dayton, Ohio, Nov. 28, 1944; d. Dwight Clinton and Martha Ellen (Risser) K. BA, Asbury Coll., Wilmore, Ky., 1967; MA, Eastern Mich. U., 1972; EdD, Western Mich. U., 1983; postgrad., Wayne State U., 1984-85. Cert. tchr., Mich. Tchr. L'Anse Creuse Schs., Harrison Twp., Mich., 1967—. Adj. prof. Oakland U., Rochester, Mich., 1989, Embry Riddle Aeronautical U., Daytona Beach, Fla., 1997; twp. trustee Harrison Twp., Mich., 1984-92; participant Tchr. in Space program NASA, Washington, 1985-86; chair visitation team Mich. Accreditation Program, Lansing, 1990-95; accreditation facilitator North Ctrl. Accreditation Assn., Ann Arbor, Mich., 1986-90. Author: (poetry) On Turning Fifty, 1995. Mem. State of Mich. Hazardous Waste Commn., 1992-96; sec., mem. Zoning Bd. Appeals, Harrison Twp., 1983-88; sec., trustee Econ. Devel. Corp.; vice-chmn. Harrison Twp., 1982-92; mem. Selective Svc. Bd., Mt. Clemens, Mich., 1993-96; mem. bd. advisors Lake St. Clair Task Force, 1996, Harrison Twp. Hist. Commn., 1992-96; vol. Detroit Inst. Arts, Gt. Lakes Maritime Inst. Recipient Famous Women of Macomb County, Girl Scouts, 1995. Mem. Kiwanis Internat. (pres. 1998—). Avocations: scuba diving, flying, skiing, writing, world travel. Home: 34720 E Lake Dr Harrison Township MI 48045-3327 Office: L'Anse Creuse Schs 38000 Reimold Harrison Township MI 48045-5501

KENNEDAY, ELIZABETH, fine arts educator; b. Orange, Calif., Dec. 7, 1950; m. John Kenneth Corathers II. BA, Calif. State U., Long Beach, 1972, MA, 1980; MFA, The Claremont Grad. U., 1988; PhD, Claremont Grad. U. Lectr. art edn., photography Calif. State U., Long Beach, 2000—. Works in collections of Lydia Pierce, Nathan Pettengill, Thomas Peckenpaugh, Alaska State Mus., Fairbanks, Calif. State U. Spl. Collections, Long Beach. Exhibited in solo and group shows at Angels Gate Cultural Ctr., House of Photographic Art, Goldwyn Hollywood Gallery; rsch. publs. Local Landscapes/Global Issues, 2002, Landscape Into Place, 2003, Beauty, the Subline and Ecological Disaster, The Salton Sea, 2003 Claremont Grad. U. rsch. grantee, 1987, Visual Arts Ctr. of Alaska grantee, 1984, Fulbright grantee, 2003-04. Mem. InSEA, NAEA, CAEA, WIPI, Angels Gate Cultural Ctr. Artist. Roman Catholic. Office: Calif State Univ Art Dept 1250 Bellflower Blvd Long Beach CA 90840

KENNEDY, B(YRL) J(AMES), medicine and oncology educator; b. Plainview, Minn., June 24, 1921; s. Arthur Sylvester and Anna Margaret (Fassbender) K.; m. Margaret Bradford Hood, Oct. 21, 1950; children: Sharon Lynn, James Bradford, Scott Douglas, Grant Preston. BA, BS, U. Minn., 1943, MB, 1945, MD, 1946; MS in Exptl. Medicine, McGill U., Montreal, Que., Can., 1951. Diplomate Am. Bd. Internal Medicine, Am. Bd. Med. Oncology. Intern in medicine Mass. Gen. Hosp., Boston, 1945-46, resident in medicine, 1946, 51-52; fellow in medicine Harvard Med. Sch.-Mass. Gen. Hosp., 1947-49; rsch. fellow in medicine McGill U. Med. Sch., 1949-50; fellow in medicine Cornell U. Med. Sch., N.Y.C., 1950-51; asst. prof. medicine U. Minn. Med. Sch., Mpls., 1952-57, assoc. prof., 1957-67, prof., 1967-91, Masonic prof. oncology, 1970-91, prof. emeritus, 1991—, Regents prof. medicine, 1988-91, Regents prof. emeritus, 1991—, B.J. Kennedy chair in clin. med. oncology, 2000. Contbr. articles to profl. jours. Past chmn. bd. Presbyn. Homes of Minn., St. Paul, bd. dirs., 1964-93. Recipient Nat. Divsn. award Am. Cancer Soc., 1975, Recognition award Assn. Comty. Cancer Ctrs., 1985, Spl. Recognition award Am. Soc. Internal Medicine, 1989, Charles Bolles Bolles-Roger award Hennepin Med. Soc., 1996; B.J. Kennedy Lectureship in Oncology named in his honor Minn. Med. Found., 1990, B.J. Kennedy Oncology Scholarship named in his honor Minn. Med. Found., 1998, B.J. Kennedy Chair in Med. Oncology named in his honor Minn. Med. Found., 1999. Fellow ACP (master 1996, Laureate award Minn. 1992); mem. AMA (Sci. Achievement award 1992), Am. Cancer Soc. (Disting. Svc. award 1991, Medal of Honor-Clin. Rsch. award 1996), Am. Soc. Clin. Oncology (pres. 1987-88), Am. Assn. Cancer Rsch., Am. Assn. Cancer Edn. (pres. 1982-83, Margaret Hay Edwards Achievement medal 1990), Minn. Med. Alumni (Harold S. Diehl award 1999), Town and Country Club (St. Paul). Avocation: photography. Home: 1949 E River Pky Minneapolis MN 55414-3675 Office: U Minn Med Sch and Hosp MMC 286 Mayo 420 Delaware St SE Minneapolis MN 55455-0374 E-mail: kenne018@tc.umn.edu.

KENNEDY, CYNTHIA LYNN THIAN, secondary educator; b. Biloxi, Miss., Oct. 6, 1948; d. Steve Julius and Mary (Zorich) T.; m. Michael Randall Kennedy, Oct. 19, 1991. BS, Delta State U., Cleveland, Miss., 1970; MS, U. So. Miss., 1976. Elem. tchr. Biloxi Sch. System, 1970-71, Harrison County Pvt. Sch. Found., Biloxi, 1971-74; therapeutic dietitian Jefferson County Hosp., Pine Bluff, Ark., 1975-77; adminstrv. dietitian Chalmette (La.) Gen. Hosp., 1977-78; tchr. biology Jackson County Schs., Biloxi and Vancleave, 1978—. Instr. William Carey Coll. on Gulf Coast, Gulfport, Miss., 1989-91; safety chmn. Regional Sci. Fair, Biloxi, 1989-91, Tchr. Cath. Christian doctrine program Diocese of Biloxi, 1988-89, 91-92. Recipient Apple award Vancleave High Sch., 1991; President's acad. scholar Delta State U., 1966, home mgmt. fellow U. So. Miss., 1976. Mem. NSTA (del. 1990), Nat. Assn. Educators, Miss. Assn. Educators, Am. Dietetic Assn. Home: 2014 Rue Ulysse Biloxi MS 39531-2432 Office: Vancleave High Sch 12424 Highway 57 Ocean Springs MS 39565-8608

KENNEDY, DALLAS CLARENCE, II, physicist, educator, writer; b. Washington, Nov. 1, 1962; s. Edwin Dallas and Dora (Funari) K. BS, U. Md., 1984; MS, Stanford U., 1986, PhD, 1989. Asst. engr. Nat. Security Agy., Fort G.G. Meade, Md., 1983-84; grad. tchg. and rsch. asst. Stanford U., Calif., 1984-89; postdoctoral fellow U. Pa., Phila., 1989-91; rsch. assoc. Fermi Nat. Accelerator Ctr., Batavia, Ill., 1991-93; asst. prof. U. Fla., Gainesville, 1993-00. Sr. tech. writer The MathWorks; contbr. articles to profl. jour, Am. Red Cross, Hyattsville, 1976-1984 Advisor First Amendment Coalition, Gainesville, 1994-96. Mem. Am. Phys. Soc. (particles and fields and astrophysics divsn.), George C. Marshall Inst. Sci. and Pub. Policy, U. Fla. Hillel Found. (faculty advisor 1994-2000), Sigma Pi Sigma, Phi Beta Kappa. Office: The Mathworks Inc 3 Apple Hill Dr Natick MA 01760 E-mail: helioplex@earthlink.net.

KENNEDY, DANE KEITH, history educator; b. Bonne Terre, Mo., May 30, 1951; s. William Joseph Kennedy and Helen Marie Mueller; m. Martha Hoeprich, June 16, 1974; 1 child, Aline Elizabeth. BA, U. Calif., Berkeley, 1973, MA, 1975, PhD, 1981. Asst. prof. U. Nebr., Lincoln, 1981—87, assoc. prof., 1987—94, prof., 1994—2000, chair dept. history, 1997—2000; Elmer L. Kayser prof. George Washington U., Washington, 2000—. Vis. fellow Davis Humanities Ctr. U .Calif., Davis, 1989—90. Author: Islands of White, 1987, The Magic Mountains, 1996, Britain and Empire, 1880-1945, 2002. Bd. dirs. German Hist. Inst., Washington, 2000—; chair internat. com. Am. Hist. Assn., Washington, 2000—. Crossing Borders grantee, Ford Found., 1997—2002, Indo-Am. fellow, Coun. for Internat. Exch. of Scholars, 1991, Guggenheim fellow, 2003—. Fellow: Royal Hist. Soc. Home: 9741 Water Oak Dr Fairfax VA 22031 Office: George Washington U Dept History Washington DC 20052 Office Fax: 202-994-6231.

KENNEDY, DANIEL, mathematics educator; b. Rochester, N.Y., July 19, 1946; s. Daniel Gerald and Nancy Helen (Colgan) K. AB in Math., Coll.

Holy Cross, Worcester, Mass., 1968; MS in Math., U. N.C., 1971, PhD in Math., 1973. Camp dir. Camp Pathfinder, Algonquin Park, Ont., Can., 1976-91, program dir., 1976-95; dormitory parent/advisor The Baylor Sch., Chattanooga, 1980—, Cartter Lupton disting. prof., 1981—, chmn. math., 1976-94. Mem. Advanced Placement Calculus Test Devel. Com. The Coll. Bd., N.Y.C., 1986-94, chair, 1990-94, math. scis. adv. bd. mem., 1991-95; exam leader Advanced Placement Calculus Ednl. Testing Svc., Princeton, N.J., 1994-97; advanced placement cons. Coll. Bd., Atlanta, 1980-2003. Recipient Presdl. award for Excellence in Sci. and Math. Tchg. NSF Presdl. Awards Com., 1995; Tandy tech. scholar Tandy Corp., 1992, Siemens Advanced Placement scholar, 1998. Mem. Math. Assn. Am., Nat. Coun. Tchrs. Math. (program chmn. regional meeting 1990, referee and reviewer 1982—), Tenn. Math. Tchrs. Assn. (v.p. 1987-89), Chattanooga Area Math. Tchrs. Assn. (v.p. 1979-81, pres. 1983-89, editor 1981-86). Democrat. Roman Catholic. Avocations: cooking, cryptic crosswords, 45 rpm record collecting, art. Home and Office: Baylor Sch PO Box 1337 Chattanooga TN 37401-1337 E-mail: dkennedy@chattanooga.net.

KENNEDY, DAVID MICHAEL, historian, educator; b. Seattle, July 22, 1941; s. Albert John and Mary Ellen (Caufield) Kennedy; m. Judith Ann Osborne, Mar. 14, 1970; children: Ben Caufield, Elizabeth Margaret, Thomas Osborne. BA, Stanford U., 1963; MA, Yale U., 1964, PhD, 1968; MA, Oxford U., 1995; D (hon.), LaTrobe U., 2001. From asst. prof. history to prof. Stanford U., Calif., 1967—80, prof., 1980—, chmn. program in internat. relations, 1977—80, assoc. dean Sch. Humanities and Scis., 1981—85, William Robertson Coe prof. history and Am. studies, 1987—93, Donald J. McLachlan prof. history, 1993—, chair, history dept., 1990—94. Vis. prof. U. Florence, Florence, Italy, 1976—77; lectr. Internat. Comms. Agy., 1976—77, Ireland, 1980; vis. prof. Am. history Oxford U., 1995—96, Tanner lectr., 2003. Author: Birth Control in America: The Career of Margaret Sanger, 1970, Over Here: The First World War and American Society, 1980; author: (with Thomas A. Bailey and Lizabeth Cohen) The American Pageant: A History of the Republic, 12th edit., 2002; co-editor: Power and Responsibility: Case Studies in American Leadership, 1986; author: Freedom from Fear: The American People in Depression and War, 1929-1945, 1999; mem. adv. bd. (TV program) The American Experience, Sta. WGBH, 1986—. Mem. planning group Am. Issues Forum, 1974—75; bd. dirs. CORO Found., 1981—87, Environ. Traveling Companions, 1986—, Stanford U. Bookstore, 1994—, The Pulitzer Prizes, 2002—. Recipient Bancroft prize, 1971, John Gilmary Shea prize, 1970, Richard W. Lyman award, Stanford U. Alumni Assn., 1989, Pulitzer prize, 2000, Frances Parkman prize, 2000, Ambs. Book prize, 2000, Calif. Book award, 2000; fellow, Am. Coun. Learned Socs., 1971—72, John Simon Guggenheim Meml. Found., 1975—76, Ctr. for Advanced Study in Behavioral Scis., 1986—87, Stanford Humanities Ctr., 1989—90. Fellow: Am. Philos. Soc., Am. Acad. arts and Scis.; mem.: Soc. Am. Historians, Orgn. Am. Historians, Am. Hist. Assn. Democrat. Roman Catholic. Office: Stanford U Dept History Stanford CA 94305 E-mail: dmk@stanford.edu.

KENNEDY, DONALD, editor, environmental scientist, educator; b. NYC, Aug. 18, 1931; s. William Dorsey and Barbara (Bean) Kennedy; children: Laura Page, Julia Halestepchildren: Cameron Rachel, Jamie Christopher. AB, Harvard U., 1952, AM, 1954, PhD, 1956; DSc (hon.), Columbia U., Williams Coll., U. Mich., U. Ariz., U. Rochester, Reed Coll., Whitman Coll., Coll. William & Mary. Mem. faculty Stanford (Calif.) U., 1960-77, prof. biol. scis., 1965-77, chmn. dept., 1965-72, sr. cons. sci. and tech. policy Exec. Office of Pres., 1976, commr. FDA, 1977-79, provost, 1979-80, pres., 1980-92, prof. emeritus, Bing prof. environ. sci., 1992—. Bd. overseers Harvard U., 1970—76; bd. dirs. Health Effects Inst., Nat. Commn. Pub. Svc., Carnegie Commn. Sci., Tech. and Govt. Author: Academic Duty, 1997; mem. editl. bd. Jour. Neurophysiology, 1969—75, Sci., 1973—77; editor-in-chief: Sci., 2000—; contbr. articles to profl. jours. Bd. dirs. Carnegie Endowment Internat. Peace. Fellow: AAAS, Am. Acad. Arts and Scis.; mem.: NAS, Am. Philos. Soc. Office: Stanford U Inst for Internat Studies Encina Hall 401 Stanford CA 94305-6055 Business E-Mail: kennedyd@stanford.edu.

KENNEDY, ELLEN WOODMAN, elementary and home economics educator; b. Laconia, N.H., June 23, 1950; d. Arthur Stone and Rosemary (Jackson) Woodman; m. Thomas Daniel Kennedy, July 27, 1974 (dec. Aug. 1988); children: Susan Elaine, Margaret Ann. Student, Westbrook Coll., 1968-69; BEd, Keene State Coll., 1973; MS in Elem. Edn., So. Conn. State U., 1982, postgrad. in Nutrition Edn., 1991—. Cert. tchr., N.H. Tchr. home econs. Ctrl. H.S., Manchester, N.H., 1974-75, High and Mid. Schs., West Haven, Conn., 1975-83; adult edn. tchr. Derry (N.H.) Adult Edn., 1974, 92; devel. 1st grade instr. North Sch., Londonderry, N.H., 1996—. Spl. svcs. tchr. grade 1-6, spl. edn. tutor, North Sch., Londonderry. Author: New England Saturday Night Suppers, 1988. Republican. Congregationalist. Avocations: all hand embroidery, camping, doll collecting, geneaology. Home and Office: 452 Mammoth Rd Londonderry NH 03053-2370

KENNEDY, EUGENE CULLEN, psychology educator, writer; b. Syracuse, N.Y., Aug. 28, 1928; s. James Donald and Gertrude Veronica (Cullen) K.; m. Sara Connor Charles, Sept. 3, 1977. AB, Maryknoll Coll., 1950; STB, Maryknoll Sem., 1953, MRE, 1954; MA, Cath. U. Am., 1958, PhD, 1962; LHD (hon.), Barat Coll., 1990. Instr. psychology Maryknoll Sem., Clarks Summit, Pa., 1955-56, Cath. U., Washington, 1959-60; prof. psychology Maryknoll Coll., Glen Ellyn, Ill., 1960-69, Loyola U., Chgo., 1969-95, prof. emeritus, 1995—. Cons. Menninger Found., 1965-67; mem. profl. adv. bd. Chgo. Dept. Mental Health; bd. dirs., cons. King Kullen Grocery Co., 1985—, mem. exec. com., 1994—; ptnr. Associated Growth Investors, 1992—; bd. dirs. Crown Mktg. Group, Inc. Author 40 books, including Himself! The Life and Times of Richard J. Daley, 1978 (Carl Sandburg award 1978), Father's Day, 1981 (Soc. of Midland Authors fiction award 1981, Friends of Lit. award 1981, Carl Sandburg award 1981), Queen Bee, 1982, The Now and Future Church, 1984, (with Sara Charles) Defendant, 1985, Tomorrow's Catholics, Yesterday's Church, 1988, Fixes, 1989, Cardinal Bernardin, 1989, (with Sara Charles) On Becoming a Counselor, 1990, (with Sara Charles) Authority, 1996, This Man Bernadin, 1996, My Brother Joseph, 1997, The Unhealed Wound, 2001, Thou Art That, 2001, Meditations at the Center of the World, 2002, Cardinal Bernardin's Stations of the Cross, 2003; author TV play: I Would Be Called John, PBS, 1987; also articles, book revs.; columnist Religion News Svc., 1991-92, 97—, Chgo. Tribune, 1992-93. Trustee U. Dayton, 1977—86. Recipient Thomas More medal, 1972, 78, Wilbur award Religious Pub. Relations Council. Fellow Am. Psychol. Assn. (div. pres. 1975-76); mem. Authors Guild. Democrat. Roman Catholic. Home: 1300 N Lake Shore Dr Chicago IL 60610-2169

KENNEDY, FREDERICK MORGAN, retired secondary school educator; b. Oklahoma City, May 5, 1943; s. Fredrick Theodor and Ruthy Marie Kennedy; m. Claudette Alberta Carter, Aug. 14, 1966; children: Kimberly Michelle, Cheryl Ann. BS, Langston U., 1965; MA, Kent State U., 1979. Cert. tchr., Ohio; ordained local elder African Meth. Episcopal Ch.; lic. life health ins., Securities. Tchr. math., occupational work adjustment Cleve. City Schs., 1965-96. Curriculum writing com. Cleve. City Schs., 1987, 89, 92. Treas. Quinn Chapel AME Ch., Cleve., 1985-97, 2001—, ch. adminstr., 1989-97, 2002—. Mem. Ohio Vocat. Assn. (life), Indsl. Arts Club (membership com. 1992), Occupational Work Adjustment (instrs. div.), Langston U. Nat. Alumni Assn. (life, pres. Cleve. chpt.), Phi Beta Sigma (life). Democrat. Home: 17201 Dynes Ave Cleveland OH 44128-3320 E-mail: fckck@core.com.

KENNEDY, JACK, secondary education journalism educator; b. Iowa City, Iowa, July 12, 1950; s. John William and Barbara Fern (Guffey) K.; m. Kathleen Ann Gowey, Sept. 25, 1971; children: Lesley Kathleen, Sara Ann, Philip John. BA in English, U. Iowa, 1976, MA in Edn., 1981. Tchr., journalism adviser Regina High Sch., Iowa City, 1976-80, City H.S., Iowa City, 1980-99, vice prin., 1999—2001; tchr. Heritage H.S., Littleton, Colo., 2002—. Journalism adv. Heritage H.S., 2002—. With USAF, 1971-74. Nat. HS Journalism Teacher of the Yr., Dow Jones Newspaper Fund, 1993. Mem.: NEA, Journalism Edn. Assn. Democrat. Avocations: reading, singing, coaching youth sports. Office: Hertiage High Sch 1401 W Geddes Ave Littleton CO 80120 Home: 2268 W Ashwood Ln Highlands Ranch CO 80129

KENNEDY, JAMES WILLIAM, JR., (SARGE KENNEDY), special education administrator, consultant; b. Santa Rosa, Calif., Oct. 6, 1940; s. James William and Kay Jean (Eaton) Kennedy; m. Lorene Adele Dunaway, May 12, 1962 (div. Sept. 1971); children: Sean, Erin, Mark; m. Patricia Carter Critchlow, Nov. 5, 1988; stepchildren: Jennifer, Dayna, Joy; m. Carolyn Judith Nighsonger, Mar. 30, 1972 (div. Dec. 1979). BA, San Francisco State U., 1964, MA, 1970. Tchr., prin., coord. spl. edn., dir. Spl. Edn. Local Plan Area Napa County (Calif.) Schs., 1968-83; spl. edn. compliance cons. overseas dependent schs. Mediterranean region Dept. Def., 1983-84; adminstr. Spl. Edn. Local Plan Area and dir. spl. programs Tehama County Dept. Edn., Red Bluff, Calif., 1985-99, asst. supt. student programs/ Spl. Edn. Local Plan Area Ops., 1999—. Editor: (profl. jour.) Calif. Fed. Coun. Exceptional Children Jour., 1971—77, 1981—83. Mem. Wilson Riles Spl. Edn. Task Force, Calif., 1981—82, Spl. Edn. Fiscal Task Force, Calif., 1987—89. Named Outstanding Spl. Edn. Adminstr. Calif., Spl. Edn. Adminstrs. in County Offices of Edn. in Calif., Spl. Edn. Local Plan Area Adminstrs.. Calif., and Calif. Fedn. Coun. Exceptional Children, 1998. Mem.: Spl. Edn. Adminstrs. in County Offices of Edn. in Calif., Spl. Edn. Local Plan Area Adminstrs. Assn. Calif. (co-chair fin. com. 1993—), Coun. for Adminstrs. Spl. Edn., Calif. Fedn. Coun. Exceptional Children (treas. 1992—), Internat. Coun. for Exceptional Children (sgt. at arms 1980—95), Profl. Football rschers. Assn., San Francisco State Alumni Assn. Democrat. Avocations: sports history, pop music history, Spanish and Portuguese cultures. Office: Tehama County Dept Edn PO Box 689 Red Bluff CA 96080-0689 E-mail: skennedy@tcde.tehama.k12.ca.us.

KENNEDY, JOSEPH PAUL, JR., retired elementary school educator; b. Bakersfield, Calif., Jan. 27, 1951; s. Joseph Paul Kennedy and Joellyn Mary (Brite) Kennedy Hardin. BA in English, Calif. State U., Fresno, 1974. Substitute tchr. Kern County Schs., Bakersfield, 1976-78; weighmaster Superior Farms, Bakersfield, 1977; price marker Brock's Dept. Store, Bakersfield, 1988; reader for the blind CSB Found., Bakersfield, 1979; camera salesman Ardan's, Bakersfield, 1979; tchr. Greenfield Union Sch. Dist., Bakersfield, 1981-99; ret., 1999. Children's book evaluator Greenfield Schs., 1984, mem. CTIIP com., 1987; mem. mentor selection com. W.A. Kendrick Sch., Bakersfield, 1989, 92, 95, mem. 4th grade leadership team, 1991—. Contbr. poems to profl. publs. Active Am. Found. AIDS Rsch., P-Flag, Gorilla Found., Challenger Ctr., KCET, ARC, Planned Parenthood, Am. Inst. for Cancer Rsch., Am. Lung Assn., Nat. Heart Found., Am. Diabetes Assn., JFK Libr. Found., African Wildlife Found., Irish-Am. Partnership, Grand Canyon Trust, USMC Toys for Tots, others. Recipient Outstanding Tchr. award Greater Bakersfield C. of C., 1989; grantee Bakersfield Jr. League, 1992. Mem. Greenfield Educators Assn. (pres. 1990-91, membership chair 1992-95), World Wildlife Fund, Greenpeace, Nature Conservancy, Earthwatch, Wilderness Soc., Nat. Geog. Soc., Sierra Club, Medecins sans Frontieres, Habitat for Humanity Internat., Fox Theater Found., Calif. State Parks Found., Names Project Fund, Native Am. Rights Found., Nat. Parks Found., Project Angel Food, Project Open Hand, Smithsonian Inst., Simon Wiesenthal Ctr. Avocations: gardening, fitness, travel, music, reading. Home: 2809 N Inyo St Bakersfield CA 93305-1820

KENNEDY, KAY FRANCES, physical education educator, social studies educator; b. Springfield, Ill., July 7, 1946; d. Carl M. and A. Mildred (Wells) K. BS in Edn., Ill. State U., 1969; MA, U. No. Colo., 1971; postgrad., U. So. Fla. Tchr. phys. edn. Chenoa (Ill.) H.S., 1968-70; tchr. phys. edn., coach Calif. State U., Chico, 1972-73; tchr. phys. edn. Solano (Calif.) C.C., 1973-74; coach phys. edn. Glenroy H.S., Melbourne, Victoria, Australia, 1974-76; tchr. phys. edn. and history Pinellas Schs., Clearwater, Fla., 1977—. Swimming instr. ARC, Clearwater, 1964—. Mem. AAHPERD, Am. Assn. Coll. Women, Phi Delta Kappa. Avocations: reading, golf, computers, boating. Home: 3412 Briarwood Ln Safety Harbor FL 34695-4604 Office: Safety Harbor Mid Sch 1257th St N Safety Harbor FL 34695-3538

KENNEDY, KEN, computer science educator; b. Washington, Aug. 12, 1945; s. Kenneth Wade and Audrey Ruth K. BA in Math. summa cum laude, Rice U., 1967; MS in Math., NYU, 1969, PhD in Computer Sci., 1971. Asst. prof. dept. math. scis. Rice U., Houston, 1971-76, assoc. prof., 1976-80, prof., 1980-84, Noah Harding prof. dept. computer sci., 1985-97, chmn. computer sci. program com., 1982-85, chmn. dept. computer sci., 1984-88, 90-92, dir. Computer and Info. Tech. Inst., 1986-92, dir. Ctr. for Rsch. on Parallel Computation, 1989—. Vis. prof. computer sci. dept. Stanford U., 1985-86; v.p. R.M. Thrall & Assocs., Inc., 1974-81, pres., 1981-93; mem. programming langs. and implementation sub-area panel computer sci. and engring. rsch. Div. Computer Rsch. NSF, 1975-77, mem. adv. com. for computer rsch., 1984-88, chmn., 1985-87, adv. commn. computer and info. sci. and engring., 1995—; vis. scientist Space Shuttle Program Lead Office NASA, 1975, Dept. Computer Sci. IBM Thomas J. Watson Rsch. Ctr., Yorktown Heights, N.Y., 1978-79, cons., 1979—, Lawrence Livermore Nat. Lab., 1985—; vis. staff mem. computer div. Los Alamos Sci. Lab., 1977—; mem. exec. com. CSNET, 1984-86, computer sci. and telecom. bd., NRC, 1992-94, mem. commn. phys. scis., math. and applications, 1995-97; co-chair adv. com. high performance computin gand comm. Indo. Tech. and Next Generation Internet, 1997—; presenter numerous prof. meetings; dir. numerous masters theses, PhD dissertations. Mem. editorial bd. Jour. Parallel and Distributed Computing, 1988—, Concurrency: Practice and Experience, ACM Transactions on Software Enging. and Methodology, 1989—; sect. editor langs. and programming Jour. Supercomputing, 1986-93; contbr. numerous chpts. to books, articles to profl. jours. Bd. dirs. Houston Soc. Performing Arts, 1986—, v.p. artistic adv., 1987—. Grantee NSF, 1973—, IBM, 1979-94, DARPA, 1987—, W.M. Keck Found., 1990-92, Office of Gov. State of Tex., 1990-95, Office Naval Rsch., 1993-96, NASA, 1993-96; Woodrow Wilson Nat. fellow, 1967-68; NSF grad. fellow, 1968-71; recipient NYU Founders Day award for Acad. Achievement, 1972. Fellow IEEE (W. Wallace McDowell award 1995), AAAS, ACM (program com. SIGPLAN nat. conf. 1982, 84, chmn. program com. principles of programming langs. confs. 1983, software sys. award com. 1983-85, chmn. 1984, chmn. program com. Supercomputing 1992); mem. Soc. Indsl. and Applied Math., Nat. Acad. Engring., Phi Beta Kappa, Sigma Xi. Home: 2238 Southgate Blvd Houston TX 77030-1121 Office: Rice U Computer Info Tech Inst 6100 Main St Houston TX 77005-1892

KENNEDY, LAWRENCE ALLAN, mechanical engineering educator; b. Detroit, May 31, 1937; s. Clifford Earl and Emma Josephine (Muller) K.; m. Valaree J. Lockhart, Aug. 3, 1958; children: Joanne E., Julie A., Janet A., Raymond L., Jill M., Brian G. BS, U. Detroit, 1960; MS, Northwestern U., 1962, PhD, 1964. Registered profl. engr., N.Y. Chmn. dept., prof. mech. and aero. engring. SUNY-Buffalo, 1964-83; chmn. dept. mech. engring., prof. Ohio State U., Columbus, 1983-93, Ralph W. Kurtz disting. prof., 1992-95; dean coll. engring. U. Ill., Chgo., 1995—, prof. mech. engring. and chem. engring., 1995—, Standley Kaplan prof., 2002—. Vis. assoc. prof. mech. and aero. engring. U. Calif.-San Diego, 1968-69, VonKarman Inst., Rhode-St. Genese, Belgium, 1971-72; Goebel vis. prof. mech. and aero. engring. U. Mich., Ann Arbor, 1980-81; vis. prof. mech. & aerospace engring. Princeton U., 1993-94; cons. Cornell Aero. Lab., Buffalo, 1968-72, Tech. Adv. Service, Fort Washington, Pa., 1969—, Ashland Chem. Corp., Dublin, Ohio, 1983-90, Mech. Enging. Sci. and Application, Buffalo, 1972-83, Columbia Gas, 1987-92; vis. faculty fellow mech. and aerospace engring. Princeton U., 1994. Contbr. numerous articles on engring. to profl. jours.; editor: Progress in Astronautics and Aeros., Vol. 58, 1978, Exptl. Thermal and Fluid Scis., 1987-95; editor in chief Jour. Thermal & Fluid Scis., 1997—; assoc. editor Applied Mechanics Revs., 1985-88, Jour. Propulsion & Power, 1992-98. Recipient Ralph R. Teetor award 1984, AT&T Found. award, 1987, Ralph Coats Roe award, 1993; NATO fellow, 1971-72, NSF fellow, 1968-69, W.P. Murphy fellow, 1960-63; Agard lectr., 1971-72. Fellow AIAA, ASME, AAAS, Am. Phys. Soc.; mem. Combustion Inst., Am. Soc. Engring. Edn., Soc. Automotive Engrs. Roman Catholic. Avocations: skiing, squash, hiking, music. Home: 24306 Turnberry Ct Naperville IL 60564-8127 Office: Coll Engring M/C 159 851 S Morgan St Chicago IL 60607-7042

KENNEDY, LINDA LOUISE, secondary education educator; b. Albany, N.Y., Oct. 6, 1952; d. Robert Joseph and Ruth Irene (Bopp) Havens; m. Brian Francis Kennedy, Aug. 19, 1989 (div.). BS, SUNY, Albany, 1974, MS, 1982. Cert. secondary edn. tchr., N.Y. Tchr. math. Vincentian Inst., Albany, 1974-77, Job Corps, Glenmont, N.Y., 1977-78, Cath. Cen. High Sch., Troy, N.Y., 1978-84, Rensselaer (N.Y.) Mid. High Sch., 1984—. Adj. tchr. Hudson Valley C.C. Mem. Assn. Math. Tchrs. N.Y. State, Nat. Coun. Tchrs. Math., Am. Fedn. Tchrs., N.Y. State United Tchrs. (bldg. rep.), Rensselaer Tchrs. Assn. (sec. 1982-84). Roman Catholic. Avocations: reading, ceramics, tennis, walking. Home: 24 Marsdale Ct Selkirk NY 12158-9772 Office: Rensselaer Mid High Sch 555 Broadway Rensselaer NY 12144-2608

KENNEDY, LINDA MARIE, elementary school educator, curriculum director; b. Mason City, Iowa, Mar. 20, 1942; d. Clement George and Marie Louise (DeWeerdt) Weiss; m. Michael Kelly Kennedy, Aug. 14, 1965; 1 child, Cara. BA, Coll. St. Theresa, Winona, Minn., 1964; MA in Reading and Lang. Arts, U. No. Iowa, 1992; Degree in Adminstrn., Iowa State U., 2001. Adminstrv. licensee, Iowa State U., 2000. Tchr. 1st grade Creekside Elem. Sch., Bloomington, Minn., 1964-65, Hoover Elem. Sch., Iowa City, 1966-68, New Hampton (Iowa) Elem. Sch., 1968-70; pre-sch. instr., organizer Winne the Pooh Pre-Sch., New Hampton, 1970; 2d grade tchr. New Hampton Elem. Sch., 1978—94; dir. curriculum New Hampton Comty. Sch. Dist., 1994—. Instr. Headstart profram McKinley Sch., Mason City, summer 1964, Robert Lucas Sch., Iowa City, summer 1966, 67. Organizer Friends of Children's Library, 1973-80; sec. Physicians Recruitment com., New Hampton, 1970—. Mem. Dem. Women's Club (pres. 1973-75), New Hampton Edn. Assn. (pres. 1984-86, govt. affairs chmn., 1986-88, v.p. 1986-88), N.E. Iowa Lang. Arts Council, N.E. Iowa Reading Council, Iowa Council Tchrs. English, Sch. Adminstrs. Iowa, New Hampton Golf and Country Club (pres. 1988-89). Democrat. Roman Catholic. Avocations: golf, reading, writing. Office: New Hampton Elem Sch 206 W Main St New Hampton IA 50659-2037

KENNEDY, MARIAN ELIZABETH, secondary school educator; b. Goldsboro, N.C., Feb. 28, 1962; d. Louie Coltrain Kennedy. AS, Mount Olive Coll., 1982; BMus, Campbell U., 1984; M in Music, East Carolina U., 1987. Cert. tchr. N.C. Music tchr. E.B. Frink Mid. Sch. and N. Lenoir HS, LaGrange, NC, 1985, Belvoir/Pactolus Elem., Greenville, NC, 1987—88; music and drama tchr. N. Lenoir HS, LaGrange, NC, 1988—. Dir. sch. musicals N. Lenoir HS, LaGrange, NC, 1988—2001, cheerleading coach, 1988—2000. Actor: (plays and musicals) Steel Magnolias, Guys and Dolls, and others, 1999. Vol. ch. choir dir. LaGrange First Free Will Bapt., LaGrange, NC, 1985—. Mem.: N.C. Educators Assn., N.C. Music Educators Assn., Delta Kappa Gamma. Democrat. Baptist. Avocations: singing, musicals, church activities. Home: 311 Forest Dr La Grange NC 28551 Office: N Lenoir HS 2400 Institute Rd La Grange NC 28551 Office Fax: 252-527-8672. Personal E-mail: mekennedy@hotmail.com. Business E-Mail: mekennedy@hotmail.com.

KENNEDY, MARK ALAN, secondary school educator; b. Oklahoma City, Okla., July 20, 1951; s. Millford Gordon and Lyn (Cheaney) Kennedy. BA with honors, Calif. State U., 1978; postgrad., Western Sem., 1978-79, Fuller Sem., 1980-83; MEd, U. LaVerne, 1997. Cert. tchr., Calif. Sales mgr. Kennedy Investments, Ontario, Calif., 1980-83; regional v.p. A.L. Williams, Rancho Cucamonga, Calif., 1983-89; loan officer Funder's Mortgage Corp., Covina, Calif., 1989-90; math., social sci. tchr., lang. devel. specialist Ontario-Montclair Sch. Dist., 1990-96, San Bernardino County Cmty. Sch., 1996—, lead tchr., 1998—2000, acting prin., 1998-99. Tchg. asst. Western Sem., Portland, Oreg., 1978-79; instr. Cmty. Inst., 1979; adj. prof. tchr. edn. Chapman U., 2001—; soccer coach DeAnza Mid. Sch., Ontario, 1990-93, core team leader, coop tchr., 1992-95, student coun. advisor, 1992-93, bilingual adv. coun., 1992-96, dist. lang. arts/social sci. trainer, 1993-94; advisor U. Calif. Riverside Honors Students' Inner City Literacy Program, 1993-95; mentor tchr. Ontario-Montclair Sch. Dist., 1994-95; cons. Inst. in Local Self Govt., Sacramento, 1994-96, Assn. Calif. Sh. Adminstrs., 1994-2002; learning styles cons., 1994—; mem. sch. attendance rev. bd., 1996-99. Author: Lessons from the Hawk, 2001, Dance of the Dolphin, 2003; contbr. some 20 articles to profl. jours. With USN, 1971-75. Named Tchr. of Yr., Inland Coun. for Social Studies, 2000, San Bernardino County Alternative Educators, 2003. Mem. ASCD, Assn. Calif. Sch. Adminstrs., Calif. Tchrs. Assn. (mem. joint program quality rev. bd.), Nat. Dropout Prevention Network, Phi Alpha Theta (mem. chair 1976-78). Episcopalian. Avocations: German and Latin philosophy and literature, exegesis of koine Greek, conversational Spanish, Shaolin Kempo, Kung Fu San Soo. Office: West End Cmty 1135 W 4th St Ontario CA 91762-1796

KENNEDY, MARY PATT, principal; b. Chgo., July 8, 1946; d. William and Margaret (Ahearn) Atkins; m. John R. Kennedy, Jan. 18, 1969; children: Jason, Jonathan, Justin. BA in Edn., Dominican Coll., Racine, Wis., 1968; MEd in Spl. Edn., Stetson U., Deland, Fla., 1980; EdS in Ednl. Leadership, Nova U., Ft. Lauderdale, Fla., 1989; EdD in Ednl. Leadership, U. Ctrl. Fla., 1994. Tchr. Norridge Pub. Sch., Rosemont, Ill., 1968-69, Hendricks Day Sch., Jacksonville, Fla., 1973-74, Sheffield Elem. Sch., Jacksonville, 1974-76, Samsula (Fla.) Elem. Sch., 1977-78, Edgewater (Fla.) Pub. Sch., 1978-84, New Smyrna Beach (Fla.) H.S., 1984-86, New Smyrna Beach Middle Sch., 1986-89; asst. prin. Ormond Jr. H.S., Ormond Beach, Fla., 1989—; prin. Indian River Elem. Sch., Edgewater, Fla., 1990—. Adv. bd. News & Observer Newspaper, New Smyrna Beach. Mem. referral bd. United Way, Daytona Beach, Fla.; chairperson S.E. Volusia Visions, New Smyrna Beach, 1993—. Recipient award Qualitative/Quantitative Dissertation Internat. Edn. Planning Coun., 1995. Fellow Inst. for Devel. Edn. Activities; mem. AAUW, Am. Assn. Sch. Adminstrs., Fla. Assn. Sch. Adminstrs., Phi Delta Kappa. Home: 3055 Lucas Ln Edgewater FL 32132-2806

KENNEDY, MELBA FAULKNER, secondary education educator; b. Jackson, Miss., July 10, 1962; d. Huey Paul and Martha Bell (Mace) Faulkner; m. Gerald Nolan Kennedy, June 25, 1983; 1 child, Justin Gerard. BS in Bus. Edn., So. U., 1985, MEd, 1988. Tchr. Scotlandville Magnet High Sch., Baton Rouge, 1985—, coach, 1987-92. Mem. La. Assn. Bus. Edn., So. Bus. Edn. Assn., Nat. Bus. Edn. Assn., Gamma Sigma Sigma. Democrat. Roman Catholic. Office: Scotlandville Magnet High Sch 9870 Scotland Ave Baton Rouge LA 70807-3999

KENNEDY, PAUL MICHAEL, history educator; b. Wallsend, U.K., June 17, 1945; came to U.S., 1983; s. John Patrick and Margaret (Hennessy) K.; m. Catherine Urwin, Sept. 2, 1967 (dec. June 1998); children: James, John, Matthew; m. Cynthia Farrar, Aug. 18, 2001. BA, Newcastle (Eng.) U., 1966; PhD, Oxford (Eng.) U., 1970; MA, Yale U., 1983; hon. doctorate, U. Ohio, 1989, U. New Haven, 1989, U. Newcastle, 1991, L.I. U., 1993, Union Coll., 1994, Alfred U., 1994, U. East Anglia, 1994, Conn. Coll., Quinnipiac Coll., 1999, U. Leuven, 2001. Lectr. history U. East Anglia, U.K., 1970-74, reader, 1974-82, prof., 1982-83; Dilworth prof. history Yale U., New Haven, 1983—; dir. Internat. Security Studies, 1990—. DeVane lectr.,

1992-93; Lewis lectr. Princeton U., 1990; Ford's lectr. Oxford U., 1984; Gabriel Silver lectr. Columbia U., 1988; Brodie lectr. UCLA, 1993; 1st ann. Nobel Peace lectr., Oslo, 1992; Bruno Keisky lectr., Vienna, 1994; Roskill Meml. lectr., Cambridge, 1997; rsch. asst. Sr. Basil Liddell Hart, 1966-70; vis. fellow Ins. for Advanced Study, Princeton, N.J., 1978-79; co-dir. of Secretariat to report on UN in Its Second-Half Century, 1993-96. Author, editor 13 books including Preparing for the Twenty-First Century, The Rise and Fall of Great Powers, Strategy and Diplomacy, The War Plans of the Great Powers. Recipient Wolfson prize Wolfson Found., U.K., 1989, Acqui Storia prize, Italy, 1990; fellow Alexander von Humboldt Found., 1968, 72; named Comdr. of the British Empire, 2000. Fellow Royal Hist. Soc., Am. Acad. Arts and Scis., Am. Philos. Soc., Brit. Acad.; mem. Assn. Am. Historians. Roman Catholic. Home: 409 Humphrey St New Haven CT 06511-3710 Office: Yale U Internat Security Studies 31 Hillhouse Ave New Haven CT 06511-3704

KENNEDY, PRISCILLA ANN, elementary school educator; b. Chattanooga, July 23, 1941; d. Jesse Spurgeon and Agnes Adaline (Barnes) Deal; m. Steven Ray Kennedy, Aug. 16, 1964 (div. Apr. 1982); children: Cherie Michelle, Amy Heather, Matthew Steven. BA, Bob Jones U., Greenville, S.C., 1964; MA in Humanities (Theatre Arts), U. Houston, Clear Lake, 1983. Cert. elem. tchr. Tchr. grades 1 and 3 N.E. Houston Ind. Sch. Dist., 1964-67; tchr. grades 2-4 Houston Ind. Sch. Dist., 1967-69, 71-72; Chpt. I reading tchr. Pearland (Tex.) Ind. Schs., 1980-95, tchr. 2nd grade, 1995-98, tchr. drama PK-4, 1998—. Mary Kay Beauty cons., 1980-99. Mem. Young Reps. of Houston, 1968. Mem. Internat. Reading Assn., Tex. Reading Assn., Bay Area Reading Coun. (sec., v.p., pres., past pres. 1980-99), Kappa Delta Pi (Houston Alumni chpt. treas. 1994, v.p. 1995, pres. 1996, past pres. 1997). Republican. Soc. Friends. Avocations: theatre, gardening, infant swimming. Home: 213 Palm Aire Dr Friendswood TX 77546-5640

KENNEDY, ROBERT SPAYDE, electrical engineering educator; b. Augusta, Kans., Dec. 9, 1933; s. Kirk Randel and Marene Lucile (Spayde) K.; m. Eleanor Emma Stagliola, June 27, 1981; children: Carole Lesley, Nancy Allison, Nina Margret. BSEE, U. Kans., 1955; MSEE, MIT, 1957, DSc in EE, 1963. Instr. engring. MIT, Cambridge, 1958-63, asst. prof., 1963-67, assoc. prof., 1967-74, prof., 1974-94; prof. emeritus, 1994—. Dir. MIT Communication Forum, 1986-88; housemaster MacGregor House, MIT, 1985-91; pres. Eastport Healthcare, Inc. Author: Fading Dispersive Communication Channels, 1968; contbr. numerous articles to jours. in field. Pres., chief pilot Quoddy Air. Fellow IEEE (pres. info. theory group 1976-77). Avocations: flight instructor, pilot. Home: 3 Green St Eastport ME 04631-1315 Office: PO Box 311 Eastport ME 04631-0311 E-mail: alias@ptc-me.net.

KENNEDY, ROGER GEORGE, museum director, park service executive; b. St. Paul, Aug. 3, 1926; s. Walter J. and Elisabeth (Dean) K.; m. Frances Hefren, Aug. 23, 1958; 1 dau., Ruth. Grad., St. Paul Acad., 1944; BA, Yale, 1949; LL.B., U. Minn., 1952. Bar: Minn. 1952, D.C. 1953. Atty. Justice Dept., 1953; corr. NBC, 1954-57; dir. Dallas Council World Affairs, 1958; spl. asst. to sec. Dept. Labor, 1959; successively asst. v.p., v.p., chmn. exec. com., dir. Northwestern Nat. Bank St. Paul, 1959-69; v.p. finance, exec. dir. Univ. Found., Minn., 1969-70; v.p. financial affairs Ford Found., N.Y.C., 1970-78, v.p. arts, 1978-79; dir. Nat. Mus. Am. History Smithsonian Instn., Washington, 1979-92, dir. emeritus, 1993—; dir. Nat. Park Svc., Washington, 1993-97. Spl. asst. to sec. HEW, 1957, cons. to sec., 1969 Author: Minnesota Houses, 1967, Men on a Moving Frontier, 1969, American Churches, 1982, Architecture, Men, Women and Money, 1985, Orders from France, 1989, Greek Revival America, 1989; editl. dir.: Smithsonian Guide to Historic America, 12 vols., 1989-90, Rediscovering America, 1990, Mission 1993, Hidden Cities, 1993, Burr, Jefferson, and Hamilton, 1999, Mr. Jefferson's Last Cause, 2003; appearances on NBC radio and TV Today, also others, 1954-57; contbr. articles to mags. and profl. jours. Served with USNR, 1944-46. Address: 1008 Massachusetts Ave Apt 702 Cambridge MA 02138

KENNEDY, SAMUEL VAN DYKE, III, journalist, educator; b. Auburn, NY, July 18, 1936; s. Samuel V., Jr. and Marion Huse (Blanchard) Kennedy; m. Bourke Larkin, Oct. 10, 1969 (div. 1994); children: Mary Morgan, Larkin Ellen, Lesley Chandler. BA, Cornell U., 1959; MA, Syracuse U., 1976, PhD, 1993. Reporter/editor Citizen-Advertiser, Auburn, 1960-75; asst. prof. Syracuse U., 1976-80, assoc. prof., 1980-2001. Cons. in field, Syracuse, 1985—. Author: (book) Samuel Hopkins Adams and the Business of Writing, 1999. Bd. dirs. Auburn Players Cmty. Theater, 1961—; trustee Osborne Meml. Assn., Auburn, 1973—. Mem.: Orgn. Am. Historians, Am. Journalism Historians Assn., Assn. Edn. Journalism & Mass Comm. Avocation: community theater. Home: 3692 Ensenore Rd Moravia NY 13118 E-mail: samkennedy@baldcom.net.

KENNEDY, SUSAN ORPHA, education consultant, sports official, physical education educator; b. Torrington, Conn., June 1, 1951; d. Sidney Robinson Jr. and Dorothy Rose (Deering) K. BS in Phys. Edn., Ithaca Coll., 1973; MS in Phys. Edn., U. Oreg., 1978; PhD in Phys. Edn., Tex. Woman's U., 1991. Cert. K-2 tchr., N.Y. Tchr., coach Regional Dist. #1, Housatonic Valley Regional H.S., Falls Village, Conn., 1973-76; grad. teaching fellow U. Oreg., Eugene, 1976-78; substitute tchr., girls basketball coach Lake County Sch. Dist. #7, Lakeview, Oreg., 1978-80; instr., coach, athletic trainer Chadron (Nebr.) State Coll., 1980-84; rsch. asst. Tex. Woman's U., Denton, 1984-86, 88-89. Adj. faculty, U. North Tex., Denton, 1988-90. Author: (video) Prevention and Care of Athletic Injuries: Taping Techniques, 1984; coord.: (puppet show) Kids on the Block, Tex. Woman's U., 1985-86.; contbr. articles to profl. jours. Basketball ofcl.; ofcl. U.S. Field Hockey Assn., U.S. Women's Lacrosse Assn.; bd. dirs., sec. Conn. Field Hockey Ofcls., 1995—; vol. Conn. Vols. Svcs. for Visually and Physically Handicapped, rec. sec., 1999—; mem. Inland Wetlands Commn., Litchfield, Conn., chair, 1999—. Recipient Outstanding Official, Conn. Field Hockey Coaches Assn., 2001, Vol. of Yr., Nutmeg State Games, 2000, Ofcl. of Yr., 2000; scholar Acad. All-Am., 1987, All-Am., U.S. Achievement Acad., 1989, 1991. Mem. AAHPERD, Nat. Athlete Trainers Assn., Am. Coll. Sports Medicine, Nat. Assn. Sport Ofcls., Conn. Interscholastic Athletic Conf. Avocations: sea kayaking, cycling, weight training, backpacking, sailing, officiating. Home and Office: PO Box 1426 266 Norfolk Rd Litchfield CT 06759-2517

KENNEDY, WILLIAM BRUCE, theatre educator, writer; b. Pitts., Oct. 9, 1957; s. Charles Milton Kennedy III and Helen Edna Buck. BA, Grove City Coll., 1979; MA, U. Pitts., 1981; PhD, Kent State U., 1987. Dir. theatre John Carroll U., Cleve., 1985-88, Waynesburg (Pa.) Coll., 1988-90, Ark. Coll., Batesville, 1990-91; instr. theatre Clarion (Pa.) U., 1991-92; dir. theatre Capital U., Columbus, Ohio, 1993—. Author: (plays) Brother Love, 1978, Emeritus, 1986, Cabaret Confidential, 1997, Oedipus Tex, 1998, What You Will, 1999, If I Knew, 1999, Fierce Beauty: The Story of Medea, 999. Clown various groups, Columbus, 1995-97; spkr. Rotary, 1998; tchr. Brookwood Ch., Columbus, 1998. Mem. Assn. Theatre Higher Edn., Christians in Theatre Arts, World Clown Orgn. Presbyterian. Avocations: magic, music, walking, puppet construciton.

KENNELLY, SISTER KAREN MARGARET, retired academic administrator, church administrator, nun; b. Graceville, Minn., Aug. 4, 1933; d. Walter John Kennelly and Clara Stella Eastman. BA, Coll. St. Catherine, St. Paul, 1956; MA, Cath. U. Am., 1958; PhD, U. Calif., Berkeley, 1962. Joined Sisters of St. Joseph of Carondelet, Roman Cath. Ch., 1954. Prof. history Coll. St. Catherine, 1962-71, acad. dean, 1971-79; exec. dir. Nat. Fedn. Carondelet Colls., 1979-82; province dir. Sisters of St. Joseph of Carondelet, St. Paul, 1982-88; pres. Mt. St. Mary's Coll., L.A., 1989-2000, pres. emerita, 2000—; congl. dir. Sisters of St. Joseph of Carondelet, St. Louis, 2002—. Cons. N. Ctrl. Accreditation Assn., Chgo., 1974—84, Ohio Bd. Regents, Columbus, 1983—89; trustee colls., hosps., Minn., Mo., Wis., Calif., 1972—; chmn. Sisters St. Joseph Coll. Consortium, 1979—82. Editor, co-author: Am. Cath. Women, 1989; author (with others): Women of Minnesota, 1977; author: Women Religious and the Intellectual Life: The North American Achievement, 1996; co-editor: Gender Identities in American Catholicism, 2001; : Cath. Coll. Women in Am., 2002. Bd. dirs. Am. Coun. on Edn., 1997—99, Nat. Assn. Ind. Colls. and Univs., 1997—2000, Assn. Cath. Colls. and Univs., 1996—2000, Western Region Nat. Holocaust Mus., 1997—2000. Fellow Fulbright, 1964. Mem.: Western Assn. Schs. and Colls. (sr. commn. 1997—2000), Assn. Cath. Colls. and Univs. (exec. bd. 1996—2000), Am. Coun. Edn. (bd. dirs. 1997—99), Nat. Assn. Ind. Colls. and Univs. (bd. dirs. 1997—99), Am. Assn. Rsch. Historians Medieval Spain, Medieval Acad., Am. Cath. Hist. Assn. Avocations: skiing, cuisine. Office: Congl Ctr 2311 Lindbergh Blvd Saint Louis MO 63131 E-mail: kkennelly33@hotmail.com.

KENNEVAN, WALTER JAMES, computer science educator; b. N.Y.C., Aug. 29, 1912; s. David A. and Ellen Kathleen (Grogan) K.; m. Marguerite Roberta Stevens, Oct. 12, 1940; children: JoEllen Kennevan Berlin, Steven David. BS in Commerce, Columbus U. Am., 1938; MS in Commerce, Cath. U. Am., 1940, M Fiscal Adminstrn., 1943. Mgmt. supr. Nat. Capital Housing Authority, Washington, 1942-48; asst. comptroller Bur. Ordnance U.S. Dept. Navy, Washington, 1948-57; dir. computer systems Office of Navy Comptroller Washington, 1957-69; prof. info. sci. Am. U., Washington, 1969-77, prof. emeritus, 1977—. Cons. NIH, Washington, 1964-65, U.S. Dept. State, Washington, 1964-65, U.S. Civil Svc. Commn., Washington, 1964-65. Author: Management and Computer Systems, 1973; contbr. articles to numerous publs. Mem. Cen. Suffrage Com. D.C., 1946-47, Vets. of the Battle of the Bulge. Staff sgt. U.S. Army, 1943-46, ETO. Mem. Am. Legion, Soc. Info. Mgmt. (nat. sec. 1975), Acad. Mgmt., Assn. Systems Mgmt., Ancient Order of Hibernians, Kenwood Country Club. Democrat. Roman Catholic. Avocation: golf. Home: 3356 S Lambert St Eugene OR 97405

KENNEY, ESTELLE KOVAL, artist; b. Chgo., Feb. 15, 1928; d. Hyman English and Florence (Browman) Koval; B.F.A., Art Inst. Chgo., 1976, M.F.A., 1978; postgrad. Yale U., 1980; m. Herbert Kenney, Feb. 6, 1948; children— Carla, Robert. Art therapist Grove Sch., Lake Forest, Ill., 1973-78, New Trier High Sch. and Central High Sch., Winnetka, Ill., 1978-79, Mosely Sch., Chgo., 1979, Cove Sch., Evanston, Ill., 1979-82; dir. art therapy concentration, instr. painting and drawing Loyola U., Chgo., 1981— ; pres., art dir. Nuts on Clark Inc., Chgo.; one woman shows: Evanston (Ill.) Library, 1971, Zaks Gallery, Chgo., 1977, 79, 82, Renaissance Soc.-Bergman Gallery, U. Chgo., 1980; group shows include: Ill. State Mus., 1975, Women Artists, Here and Now, 1976, Chgo. Connections travelling exhbn., 1976-77, Nat. Women's Caucus for Art, 1977, Nancy Lurie Gallery, 1978, Marycrest Coll. Gallery, Davenport, Iowa, 1982, Chgo. Internat. Art Expo, 1981, 82, 83, Notre Dame U. Gallery, South Bend, Ind., 1982; represented in permanent collections: Ill. State Mus., Springfield, Union League Club of Chgo. Mem. Am. Art Therapy Assn., Ill. Art Therapy Assn. (pres. 1979—), Coll. Art Assn. Home: 3830 N Clark St Chicago IL 60613-2812 Office: Loyola University of Chicago Dept Fine Arts 6525 N She Ridan Rd Chicago IL 60626 E-mail: estellekenneynutsonclark@nutsonclark.com.

KENNEY, JOSEPH EDMUND, special education educator; b. Ware, Mass., May 5, 1951; s. George Thomas and Joan F. (Keating), K.; m. Linda Siiri Perkins, Oct. 13, 1978. AA, Mt. Wachussett C.C., Gardner, Mass., 1971; BS, Fitchburg State Coll., 1974, MEd, 1993. Cert. tchr. secondary social sci, moderate spl. needs. Night counselor Brandon Sch., Petersham, Mass., 1970-74; tchr. spl. edn. Mahar Regional Sch., Orange, Mass., 1974—. Coach Mahar Regional football, Orange, 1981—, tennis, 1988. Coach Little League Baseball, Petersham, 1975-82; asst. chmn. Dem. Town Com., Petersham, 1984; mem. Senators Boosters Club, Orange, Mass., 1985—. Petersham Cemetry Commn., 1991—. Recipient Alumni Recognition award Fitchburg State Coll., 1993; nominated for Mass. Tchr. of Yr. award, Walt Disney award, Miller award. Mem. NEA, Mass. Tchrs. Assn., Nat. Geograpic Soc., Coun. Exceptional Children, Lions Club Internat. Roman Catholic. Avocations: stamp collecting, golf, yard work, reading. Home: PO Box 202 Petersham MA 01366-0202

KENNON, PAMELA CANERDAY, secondary school educator; b. Opelika, Ala., Nov. 9, 1961; d. Thomas Donald and Norma (Fowler) Canerday; m. John Carlton Kennon, Jr., Jan. 12, 1985; children: Kate, Carly, Jake, Sam. Student, Chipola Jr. Coll., Marianna, Fla., 1980-81; BS in Edn. cum laude, U. Ga., 1984; MEd, Brenau U., 1994. Phys. edn. tchr. Greensboro (Ga.) Primary Sch., 1984-85; tchr. 2d grade Jefferson (Ga.) Elem. Sch., 1985-93; tchr. 4th grade Oconee County Intermediate Sch., Watkinsville, Ga., 1993—. Softball coach Jefferson (Ga.) High Sch., 1988-92, Oconee County High Sch., 1993—, head softball coach; pvt. tutor. Named Tchr. of Yr., Tchr. of Month Jefferson Elem. Sch., 1988, 90, N.E. Ga. Softball Coach of Yr., 1997. Mem. Golden Key Hon. Soc. Baptist. Avocations: softball, walking, traveling. Home: 1640 S Barnett Shoals Rd Watkinsville GA 30677-2215

KENNY, SHIRLEY STRUM, academic administrator; b. Tyler, Tex., Aug. 28, 1934; d. Marcus Leon and Florence (Golenternek) Strum; m. Robert Wayne Kenny, July 22, 1956; children: David Jack, Joel Strum, Daniel Clark, Jonathan Matthew, Sarah Elizabeth. BA, BJ, U. Tex., 1955; MA, U. Minn., 1957; PhD, U. Chgo., 1964; LHD (hon.), U. Rochester, 1988, Chonnam U., 1996, Donguk U., 2000. Chair English dept. U. Md., College Park, 1973-79, provost Arts and Humanities, 1979-85; pres. CUNY Queens Coll., Flushing, 1985-94, SUNY, Stony Brook, 1994—; chair Brookhaven Sci. Assocs. Mem. regional adv. bd. Chase Manhattan Corp. Author: The Conscious Lovers, 1968, The Plays of Richard Steele, 1971, The Performers and Their Plays, 1982, The Works of George Farquhar, 2 vols., 1988, British Theatre and the Other Arts, 1984; contbr. articles to profl. jours. Bd. dirs. Goodwill Greater N.Y., L.I. Assn. Named Outstanding Woman, U. Md., 1983, Outstanding Alumnus, U. Tex. Coll. Comm., 1989, Disting. Alumna, U. Tex., 1999; recipient Disting. Alumnus award, U. Chgo. Club Washington, 1980, Svc. and Leadership award, N.Y. Urban League, 1988. Mem.: Boyer Comm. Educating Undergrads (chair), Assn. Am. Colls. and Univs. (bd. dirs. 1988—96). Office: SUNY 310 Adminstrn Bldg Stony Brook NY 11790-0701

KENOFER, DORIS DILLON See DILLON, DORIS

KENT, ALLEN, library and information sciences educator; b. N.Y.C., Oct. 24, 1921; s. Samuel and Anna (Begun) K.; m. Rosalind Kossoff, Jan. 24, 1943; children: Merryl Frances Kent Samuels, Emily Beth Kent Yeager, Jacqueline Diane Kent Maryak, Carolyn May Kent Hall. BS in Chemistry, CCNY, 1942. Sci. editor Intersci. Pubs., 1946-51; research assoc. Ctr. Internat. Studies, MIT, 1951-53; prin. documentation engr. Battelle Meml. Inst., Columbus, Ohio, 1953-55; asso. dir. Ctr. for Documentation and Communication Research; prof. library sci. Western Res. U., Cleve., 1955-63; dir. office communications programs, chmn. interdisciplinary doctoral program info. sci., prof. info. sci., edn. and computer sci. U. Pitts., 1963-76; Univ. Disting. Service prof. library and info. sci. and assoc. dean U. Pitts. Sch. Library and Info. Sci., 1976-91, interim dean, 1985-86, prof. emeritus, 1992. Mem. mgmt. info. com. Health and Welfare Assn. Allegheny County, Pa., 1972-80; dir. Marcel Dekker, Inc., N.Y., 1978-93. Author (with others): Machine Literature Searching, 1956; author: (with J.W. Perry) Documentation and Information Retrieval, 1957; author: Tools for Machine Literature Searching, 1958, Centralized Information Services, 1958, Mechanized Information Retrieval, 1962, 2d edit., 1966, also fgn. transls. Specialized Information Centers, 1965, Information Analysis and Retrieval, 1971, Resource Sharing in Libraries, 1977, On-Line Revolution in Libraries, 1978, Structure and Governance of Library Networks, 1979, Use of Library Materials, 1979, Information Technology, 1982; editor, co-editor numerous books in field, exec. editor Ency. Libr. and Info. Sci., 1968—2003, Ency. Computer Sci. and Tech., 1972—2002, Ency. Microcomputers, 1984—2001, Ency. of Telecomm., 1988—98. Chmn. bd. Interuniv. Comms. Coun. Inc., 1971-74. Served with USAAF, 1942-46. Recipient Info. Tech. Merit award Eastman Kodak Co., 1968 Fellow AAAS; mem. ALA, Assn. Computing Machinery, Am. Soc. Info. Sci. (award of merit 1977, award for Best Info. Sci. Book of Yr. 1980, Pioneer in Info. Sci. 1987), Acad. Sr. Profls. Eckerd Coll. Home: 5108 Brittany Dr S Apt 601 Saint Petersburg FL 33715-1525

KENT, CATHARINE HAZEN, elementary education educator; b. Memphis, Nov. 15, 1950; d. Charles Edward and Emily (Novak) Hazen; m. William Clarence Kent Jr., Oct. 21, 1973; children: Wendy, David. BSE, Memphis State U., 1972. Cert. tchr., Tenn. Tchr. 6th grade math. Shelby County Schs., Memphis, 1972—; chmn. dept. math. Collierville Mid. Sch., Collierville, 1989—. Chmn. Mathaton for St. Jude Children's Hosp., 1989—; workshop presenter. Coord. Angel Tree Project; Sunshine chmn. Recipient awards, grant. Mem. NEA, Tenn. Edn. Assn., Shelby County Edn. Assn., Nat. Coun. Tchrs. Math., Kappa Delta Pi. Republican. Roman Catholic. Avocation: photography. Home: 1372 Harbert Ave Memphis TN 38104-4803 Office: Collierville Mid Sch 146 College St Collierville TN 38017-2625

KENT, JACK THURSTON, retired mathematics educator; b. Sardis, Tenn., Sept. 26, 1908; s. John Franklin and Daisy Josephine (Craven) K.; m. Pauline Elizabeth Oates, May 27, 1936; children: Christine Elizabeth Johnson Ellis, David Harbet. AB, Lambuth Coll., 1930, MA, U. Ark., 1931; postgrad., Ohio State U., 1931-33, Yerkes Obs., U. Chgo., Williams Bay, Wis., 1949-52. Prof. of math. Lambuth Coll., Jackson, Tenn., 1930; grad. asst. U. Ark., Fayetteville, 1930-31, Ohio State U., Columbus, 1931-33; prof., head math. dept. Ft. Smith (Ark.) Jr. Coll., 1933-35, Ark. Tech. Coll., Russellville, 1935-36; from instr. to assoc. prof. Tex. A&M U., College Station, 1936-74; retired, 1974. Vis. lectr. Tex. Acad. Sci./NSF, 1957-65; area dir. Am. Meteor Soc., Ark., Mo., Tex., 1930-45, Moon Watch Program, Bryan, Tex., 1957-61. Author: Unified Mathematics for High Schools; editor: Binary Stars; contbr. sci. papers in astronomy to profl. publs. Chmn. March of Dimes, Bryan, 1953; mem. Equalization Bd., College Station, 1951; scoutmaster to coun. Boy Scouts Am., Russellville, Ark., 1936, Bryan, 1952-65. Ford Found. grantee, 1949-52. Democrat. Methodist.

KENT, ROBERT B. artist, educator; b. Cleve., June 23, 1924; m. Celeste Zalk, Dec. 18, 1948; children: William, Kenneth, Brian. BA, Western Res. U., 1950, MA, 1951; postgrad, Columbia U., 1952-53; EdD, U. Calif., Berkeley, 1968. Cert. expressive therapist. Art instr. El Paso (Tex.) City Schs., 1953-54, Stockton (Calif.) Unified Schs., 1954-56, Tamalpais High Sch., Mill Valley, Calif., 1956-67; assoc. prof. U. Ga., Athens, 1967-93, emeritus, 1993—. Lectr. Denmark, Sweden and Israel. Mem. editorial bd. Ill. State U. Publ.; contbr. articles to profl. jours. Mem. Am. Art Therapy Assn., Nat. Expressive Therapy Assn., World Assn. for Prevention Drug and Alcohol Abuse (internat. bd. govs.). Home: 332 Stonybrook Cir Athens GA 30605-6029

KENYON, DAPHNE ANNE, economics educator; b. Augusta, Ga., Aug. 14, 1952; d. Lawrence Austin and Shirley (Knaus) Kenyon; m. Peter George Kachavos, Oct. 22, 1988. BA, Mich. State U., 1974; MA in Econs., U. Mich., 1976, PhD in Econs., 1980. Asst. prof. Dartmouth Coll., Hanover, N.H., 1979-83; sr. analyst U.S. Adv. Commn. on Intergovt. Relations, Washington, 1983-85; fin. economist U.S. Treasury Dept., Washington, 1985-87; sr. research assoc. Urban Inst., Washington, 1987-88; Lincoln fellow Lincoln Inst. of Land Policy, Cambridge, Mass., 1988-89; asst. prof. econs. Simmons Coll., Boston, 1989-90, assoc. prof. econs., 1991-98, chair dept. econs., 1996-99, prof. econs., 1998-2000; pres. The Josiah Bartlett Ctr. for Pub. Policy, 1999—2002; prin. D.A. Kenyon & Assocs., 2002—. Cons. U.S. IRS Adv. Panel, Washington, 1987-99; appt. to Mass. Dept. of Revenue Adv. Group, 1991; bd. dirs. New Eng. Econ. Project, v.p., 1997-98, pres., 1999. Assoc. editor Urban Studies, 1988-93, mem. U.S. editl. adv. com., 1993—; co-editor: Coping with Mandates, 1990, Competition Among States and Local Governments, 1991; N.H. corr. State Tax Notes, 1990-93; mem. editl. bd. Mass. Benchmarks, 1997-99; columnist: State Tax Notes, 2003—; contbr. articles to profl. jours. Active NH Gov.'s Revenue Adv. Com., Concord, 1982, 98, N.H. State Consensus Revenue Estimating Panel, 2000-03, Windham NH Sch. bd., 2000-03, vice chmn. 2002-03. Fellow Grad. fellow, NSF, 1974. Mem. Am. Econ. Assn. (com. on the status of women in econs. profession 1995-98), Nat. Tax Assn. (bd. dirs. 1996-99, chair intergovernmental fiscal rels. com. 1996-98, program chair 1999), Nat. Tax Jour. (referee Ea. Econ. Jour.). Episcopalian.

KENYON, ELINOR ANN, retired social worker; b. Otto, Tex., July 8, 1936; d. William Karl and Anna Malinda (Achelpohl) Hannusch; m. Curtis E. Kenyon; children: John Kyle, Joel Leonard. L.A., St. John's Coll., 1956; BA, Valparaiso U., 1958; MSW, U. Kans., 1961. Adoption worker/dir. Kansas City Area Office Luth. Social Svc., 1958-71; area rep. Luth. Immigration and Refugee Svc., Met. Luth. Ministry, Kansas City, Mo., 1979-83; domestic adoption worker Family and Children Svcs. of Kansas City, 1983-85; pvt. practice social worker Kansas City, 1985-87; coord. refugee family stress edn. program Cmty. Svc. Ctr., Kansas City, Kans., 1987-88; sch. social worker Turner Unified Sch. Dist., Kansas City, Kans., 1988—2001; ret., 2001. Co-author: Resources for Refugee Resettlement, 1981. Mem. NASW, Kans. NEA, Coun. Exceptional Children, Kans. Assn. Sch. Social Workers, Valparaiso U. Guild. Lutheran.

KENYON, JUDITH, primary school educator; b. Barre, Vt., Feb. 21, 1939; d. Fletcher Thomas and Dorothy (Davidson) K. BS, Johnson State Coll., 1963; postgrad, U. Vt., 1985. Cert. tchr. Vt. Tchr. Milton (Vt.) Elem. Sch., 1963-65, 67-68, Ext. Vol., Chgo., 1965-66; tchr., extension vol. Salida, Colo., 1966-67; tchr. South Burlington (Vt.) Sch. System, 1968—. Sponsor Children Internat., 1985—. Mem. NEA, Nat. Coun. Tchrs. Math., New Eng. Reading Assn., Vt. Educators Assn., South Burlington Educators Assn., Citizens for Responsible Growth, Nature Conservancy, Delta Kappa Gamma. Roman Catholic. Avocations: reading, collectables, music, travel, aerobics. Home: 53 Northview Ct Williston VT 05495-9530 Office: Orchard Elem Sch 2 Baldwin Ave South Burlington VT 05403-7316

KEOHANE, NANNERL OVERHOLSER, university president, political scientist; b. Blytheville, Ark., Sept. 18, 1940; d. James Arthur and Grace (McSpadden) Overholser; m. Patrick Henry III, Sept. 16, 1962 (div. May 1969); 1 child, Stephan Henry; m. Robert Owen Keohane, Dec. 18, 1970; children: Sarah, Jonathan, Nathaniel. BA, Wellesley Coll., 1961, Oxford U., Eng., 1963; PhD, Yale U., 1967. Faculty Swarthmore Coll., Pa., 1967—73, Stanford U., Calif., 1973—81, fellow Ctr. for Advanced Study in the Behavioral Scis., 1978—79, 1987—88; pres., prof. polit. sci. Wellesley (Mass.) Coll., 1981—93, Duke U., Durham, NC, 1993—. Bd. dirs. IBM. Author: Philosophy and the State in France: The Renaissance to the Enlightenment, 1980; co-editor: Feminist Theory: A Critique of Ideology, 1982. Trustee Colonial Williamsburg Found., 1988—2001, Nat. Humanities Ctr., 1993—, Doris Duke Charitable Found., 1996—. Named to National Women's Hall of Fame, 1995; fellow Dissertation fellow, AAUW; scholar Marshall scholar, 1961—63. Fellow: Am. Philos. Soc., Am. Acad. Arts and Scis.; mem.: Coun. on Fgn. Rels., Watauga Club, Saturday Club, Phi Beta Kappa. Democrat. Episcopalian. Office: Duke Univ Box 90001 207 Allen Bldg Durham NC 27708-0001

KEPPLER, DONALD JOHN, secondary education educator; b. Seattle, Dec. 20, 1937; s. Donald Robert and Ruth Esther (Carlson) K.; m. Elizabeth Ann Bartleson, Dec. 23, 1966; 1 child, Kirk Donald. BA in Edn., Pacific Luth. U., 1961; MS in Teaching, U. Puget Sound, 1968. Cert. tchr., Wash. Tchr. phys. sci., gen. math., algebra, geometry Gault Jr. High, 1961-71; tchr. geology, biology, oceanography and forestry Lincoln High Sch., Tacoma, Wash., 1971-92, chmn. indsl. arts dept., 1971-92; owner Olympic Sprinklers, 1973—. Hunter edn. instr. Wash. Dept. Wildlife, 1983-87. Ski instr. Ski Profls., Inc., 1969; coach Gault Jr. h.S., 1961-71; jr. varsity baseball coach Lincoln H.S., 1971-73, asst. football coach, asst. track coach, 1974-79; advisor Future Farmers Am., 1980-92; pres. Tacoma N.W. Camp of the Gideons, Internat. Recipient Cert. Appreciation award City of Tacoma, 1990, Outstanding Dedication and Svc. award Pierce County Coop., 1984-85 Mem. Nat. Edn. Assn, Wash. Sci. Tchrs. Assn. (rec. sec.), Wash. Edn. Assn., Wash. Vocat. Assn. (Outstanding Vocat. Tech. Project, 1992), Wash. Vocat. Agrl. Tchrs. Assn., Tacoma Assn. Classroom Tchrs. Avocations: photography, skiing, hunting, woodworking, fishing, flytying. Home: PO Box 607 Sisters OR 97759-0607

KERATA, JOSEPH J. secondary education educator; b. Cleve., Jan. 20, 1949; s. Joseph John and Lillian (Potocky) K.; m. Lynne E. Armington, July 20, 1990. BS in Edn., Ohio State U., 1971; MEd, Cleve. State U., 1978; postgrad., Ohio Wesleyan U., Princeton U. Tchr. sci. grades 7-8 Spellacy Jr. High Sch., Cleve., 1972-73; tchr. BSCS and gen. biology grades 10-12 Willoughby South High Sch., 1973-79; tchr. earth sci., physics, biology grades 10-12 Colegio Roosevelt, Lima, Peru, 1979-80; tchr. English adult edn. Academia Secretaria Y Typografia, Lima, 1980; tchr. gen. sci. grades 7-9 Eastlake Jr. High Sch., Willowick, Ohio, 1980-83; tchr. AP and honors biology Eastlake North High Sch., Willowick, 1983—, chair dept. sci., 1984—. Mem. North Ctrl. Evaluation Team, 1978, cirriculum devel. and revision com., 1978, 85; judge sci. fairs several sch. dists., 1977—. Recipient Krecker Outstanding Sci. Dept. award, 1976, Outstanding Educator award Edinboro U., 1984, Sci. Tchr. of Yr. award Lubrizol Corp., 1991, Gov.'s Ednl. Leadership award, 1992, Ohio Tchr. of Yr. award, 1993; Martha Holden Jennings scholar, 1990; Woodrow Wilson Nat. fellow, 1992. Mem. NEA, Nat. Sci. Tchrs. Assn., Nat. Assn. Biology Tchrs., Ohio Edn. Assn., Ohio Acad. Sci., Willoughby-Eastlake Tchrs. Assn. (grievance chmn. 1981—), Cleve. Regional Assn. Biologists (original). Office: Eastlake North High Sch 34041 Stevens Blvd Eastlake OH 44095-2905

KERBER, LINDA KAUFMAN, historian, educator; b. N.Y.C., Jan. 23, 1940; d. Harry Hagman and Dorothy (Haber) Kaufman; m. Richard Kerber, June 5, 1960; children: Ross Jeremy, Justin Seth. AB cum laude, Barnard Coll., 1960; MA, NYU, 1961; PhD, Columbia U., 1968; DHL, Grinnell Coll., 1992. Instr., asst. prof. history Stern Coll., Yeshiva U., N.Y.C., 1963-68; asst. prof. history San Jose State Coll., (Calif.), 1969-70; vis. asst. prof. history Stanford U., (Calif.), 1970-71; asst. prof. history U. Iowa, Iowa City, 1971-75, prof., 1975-85, May Brodbeck prof., 1985—. Vis. prof. U. Chgo., 1991-92. Author: Federalists in Dissent: Imagery and Ideology in Jeffersonian America, 1970, paperback edit., 1980, 97, Women of the Republic: Intellect and Ideology in Revolutionary America, 1980, paperback edit., 1986, Toward an Intellectual History of Women, 1997, No Constitutional Right to Be Ladies: Women and the Obligations of Citizenship, 1998, paperback edit., 1999 (Littleton-Griswold prize in legal history Am. Hist. Assn., Joan Kelley prize in womens history Am. Hist. Assn.); co-editor: Women's America: Refocusing the Past, 1982, 5th edit., 2000, U.S. History As Women's History, 1995; mem. editl. bd. Signs: Jour. Women in Culture and Society, Jour. Women's History; contbr. articles and book revs. to profl. jours. Fellow Danforth Found., NEH, 1976, 83-84, 94, Am. Coun. Learned Socs., 1975, Nat. Humanities Ctr., 1990-91, Guggenheim Found., 1990-91, Radcliffe Inst. for Advanced Study, 2003. Mem. Orgn. Am. Historians (pres. 1996-97), Am. Hist. Assn., Am. Studies Assn. (pres. 1988), Am. Soc. for Legal History, Berkshire Conf. Women Historians, Soc. Am. Historians, Japan U.S. Friendship Commn., PEN/Am. Ctr., Am. Acad. Arts and Scis. Jewish. Office: U Iowa Dept History Iowa City IA 52242

KERBIN, DIANE LEITHISER, history educator; b. Havre de Grace, Md., Oct. 20, 1941; d. William Austin and Mildred (Tweed) Leithiser; m. William Howard Kerbin, June 8, 1963; children: Laura, William. BA, Western Md. Coll., Westminster, 1963; MEd, Salisbury (Md.) State U., 1984. Cert. Secondary History, Social Studies, Md. Tchr. Worcester County Bd. Edn., Newark, Md., 1963-65; exec. sec. Pocomoke City (Md.) C. of C. and Bus. Assn., Md., 1979-81; adult lit. program coord. Worcester County Libr., Snow Hill, Md., 1982-83; counselor Worcester County Health Dept., Snow Hill, Md., 1983-84; tchr. Worcester County Bd. Edn., Newark, Md., 1984—. Mem. sch. Improvement Team, Pocomoke, Md., 1991-92, Sch. Improvement Adv. Com., 1990-91, 92—. Past mem. Jr. Woman's Club, Pocomoke City, Md., 1970-75, Worcester County (Md.) Garden Club, 1970-80; vol. tutor Citizens Involved with Today's Youth, Pocomoke City, Md., 1992—. Named Pocomoke Mid. Tchr. of Yr., 1993-94. Mem. Nat. Coun. for Social Studies, Orgn. of Am. Hist., Alpha Delta Kappa. Democrat. Episcopalian. Avocations: church work, painting, calligraphy. Office: Pocomoke Mid Sch 800 8th St Pocomoke City MD 21851-1599

KERES, KAREN LYNNE, English language educator; b. Evanston, Ill., Oct. 22, 1945; d. Frank and Bette (Pascoe) K.; m. Walter Wilson Berg. BA, St. Marys Coll., 1967; postgrad., U. Notre Dame, 1967-68; MA, U. Iowa, 1969. Assoc. prof. English, humanities and fine arts William Rainey Harper Coll., Palatine, Ill., 1969-95, prof., 1995—, Palomar Coll., San Marcos, Calif., 1990-93. Cons. in field. Mem. MLA, Ill. Assn. Tchrs. English, Am. Fedn. Tchrs., Nature Conservancy, Mensa. Home: 222 Fairfield Dr Island Lake IL 60042-9622 Office: William Rainey Harper Coll Dept Liberal Arts Palatine IL 60067

KERIKAS, SHARON MAREL, special education educator; b. South Bend, Ind., Jan. 14, 1943; d. Edward John and Mary Agnes (Babinski) Nawrocki; m. Emanuel John Kerikas, July 11, 1970. BS, Ball State U., Muncie, Ind., 1963; MA, Northwestern U., 1964. Cert. in elem. edn., secondary edn., spl. edn. Educator Gallaudet U., Washington, 1964-65; tchr. Utah Sch. for the Deaf, Salt Lake City, 1965—2002, mentor tchr., 1990—; ednl. svcs. coord. Judge Meml. Cath. H.S., Salt Lake City, 2002—. Named Tchr. of Yr., Utah Sch. for the Deaf, 1991; recipient Jon S. Huntsman award, Huntsman Chem. Internat. Corp., 2002. Mem. Utah Edn. Assn., Internat. Reading Assn., Alexander Graham Bell Assn. Avocations: sewing, hand work, walking, gardening. Home: 1428 Ambassador Way E Salt Lake City UT 84108-2859 Office: Judge Meml Cath HS 650 S 1100 East Salt Lake City UT 84102

KERKEL, LYNN, retired middle school educator; b. Baton Rouge, Nov. 14, 1942; d. Peter Phillip and Rosa Emaline (Dunnam) K.; m. James O. Skidmore, Dec. 23, 1972 (div. Jan. 6, 1978). AA, Mt. San Antonio Jr. Coll., 1962; BE, Kent State U., 1965, MEd in Reading, 1973. Cert. elem. educator, reading specialist, Ariz., Mich. Elem. educator Willoughby (Ohio) Eastlake Bd. Edn., 1965-84, mid. sch. educator, 1984-98. Inservice instr. Willoughby-Eastlake Bd. Edn. Recipient Jennings grant Martha Holden Jennings Found., 1992; Named to South High Sch. Hall of Fame Willoughby-Eastlake Bd. Edn., 1989; Jennings grantee Martha Holden Jennings Found., 1992, scholar, 1978-79. Mem. NEA (rep. 1979—), AAUW, Willoughby Eastlake Tchr. Assn. (past pres. 1981-86, grievance co-chair 1965—), Galilee Shrine #41 Order of the White Shrine of Jerusalem, Am. Profl. Partnership for Lithuanian Edn., Ohio Edn. Assn. (rep. 1970—), Northeastern Ohio Edn. Assn., Internat. Reading Assn., Delta Kappa Gamma Soc. Internat. Democrat. Methodist. Avocations: cross country skiing, walking, aerobic dancing, sewing, painting. Home: 5457 Millwood Ln Apt D Willoughby OH 44094-3284

KERKOC, RUTH ANN, Spanish educator; b. New Orleans, Aug. 24, 1930; d. Ernest Edward and Alta Mai (Jacobs) Clark; m. Anto Kerkoc, Sept. 3, 1966; 1 child, Kristina Maria. BA, Wellesley (Mass.) Coll., 1951; MA, Yale U., 1959, U. Calif., Berkeley, 1966. Cert. tchr., Calif. Adminstrv. asst. U.S. Govt., Washington, 1951-55; 2nd grade tchr. Karl C. Parrish Sch., Barranquilla, Colombia, 1955-57; Spanish and German tchr. Yorktown H.S., Arlington, Va., 1959-64; teaching assst. German U. Calif., Berkeley, 1964-66; tchr. Spanish Piedmont, Calif., 1966-67; tchr. German DeAnza Coll.q, Cupertino, Calif., 1968; tchr. Spanish part time West Valley Coll., Campbell, Calif., 1968-69; tchr. social studies Young Mothers Program, San Jose, 1969-84; tchr. Spanish Leland H.S., San Jose, 1984—. Mem. pacesetter Soanish Coll. Bd., N.Y.C., 1994—; nat. com. ednl. Testing Svc., Princeton, N.J., 1997—; trainer pacesetter Spanish Coll. Bd., 1995—. Named Fullbright Teaching Asst., Aachen, Germany, 1957-58. Mem. AAUW, Am. Coun. Teaching Fgn. langs., Calif. lang. Assn., Fgn. lang. Assn. Santa Clara County. Democrat. Episcopalian. Avocations: reading, travel, walking. Home: 6198 Cecala Dr San Jose CA 95120-2709 Office: Leland High School San Jose CA 95120

KERMODE, JOHN COTTERILL, pharmacology educator, researcher; b. Changi, Singapore, June 10, 1949; arrived in U.S. 1983; s. Alfred Cotterill and Rose Price (Roberts) K.; m. Jaehwa Choi, June 27, 2000. BA with honors, Cambridge (Eng.) U., 1970, MA, 1974; PhD, London U., 1983. Rsch. scientist U. Coll. Hosp. Med. Sch., London, 1970-74; rsch. biochemist U. Coll. Hosp., London, 1975-83; postdoctoral fellow U. Conn. Health Ctr., Farmington, Conn., 1983-87; postdoctoral assoc. U. Vt., Burlington, 1987-90; rsch. chemist McGuire VA Med. Ctr., Richmond, Va., 1990-93; rsch. asst. prof. Med. Coll. Va., Richmond, 1990-93; asst. prof., dept. pharmacology and toxicology U. Miss. Med. Ctr., Jackson, Miss., 1993-98, assoc. prof., 1998—. Mem. editl. bd. Jour. Receptor & Signal Transduction Rsch., 1991-2002; contbr. articles to profl. jours. Recipient Earnest G. Spivey Meml. Rschr. award, 1994; Cambridge (Eng.) U. scholar, 1967, Basic Sci. All Star Prof. award Carl G. Evers, M.D., Soc., 2000, 2001, 2002, 2003; Am. Heart Assn. grantee, Va., 1991, Miss., 1994, 97, Southeast, 1999, 2003, Nat. Heart Found. grantee, 1997, 98, Am. Lung Assn. grantee, 1997. Mem. Internat. Soc. Thrombosis and Haemostasis, Am. Soc. Pharmacology & Exptl. Therapeutics (councilor divsn. Cardiovasc. Pharmacology 2002—). Avocations: photography, travel, tennis, contract bridge, downhill skiing. Home: 57 Redbud Ln Madison MS 39110-9260 Office: U Miss Med Ctr 2500 N State St Jackson MS 39216-4500

KERN, JEAN GLOTZBACH, elementary education educator, gifted education educator; b. Fargo, N.D., Mar. 31, 1944; d. Clifford William and Edna Baker (Sullivan) Glotzbach; m. Peter Kern III, Oct. 11, 1974; 1 child, Adam Baker. BGS, Kent State U., 1973; student, SUNY, Buffalo, 1989; MEd., U. So. Fla., 1994. Cert. early childhood, elem. sch., gifted K-12, creative studies, Fla. Elem. educator Fruitville Elem. Sch., Sarasota, Fla., 1977-79, Sch. Bd. Sarasota County, Sarasota, Fla., 1977—, Ashton Elem. Sch., Sarasota, Fla., 1979-85; elem. educator gifted students Pine View Sch., Osprey, Fla., 1985-95, Bay Haven Sch. of Basics Plus, 1995; tchr. trainer Peace Corps, Cape Verde, 1996—. Directing tchr. in internship program U. So. Fla., 1985—; chair elem. dept. Sarasota County Sch. Bd., 1992-93; teaching intern Dr. Donald Treffinger's Ctr. for Creative Learning, 1991, coord. Treffinger creativity project, 1992—; tchr. ESE model demonstration; spkr in field. Selby Found. grantee, 1989; Dept. Edn. grantee, 1985-86. Mem. Internat. Reading Assn. (sch. site contact person 1984—), Fla. Assn. for Gifted, Tchrs. Applying Whole Lang., Delta Kappa Gamma. Avocations: travel, reading, dieting, watching sunsets, creating. Home: 1846 W Leewynn Dr Sarasota FL 34240-9664 Office: care Peace Corp CP 109 Corpo da Paz Assomada Santa Catarina Cape Verde

KERN, RONALD PAUL, computer company executive, academic dean, curriculum consultant; b. Chickasha, Okla., Sept. 2, 1947; s. John Edward Kern and Winona Briscoe Evans; m. Stephanie Perry, May 30, 1970; children: Stephanie Rachel, Jayson Paul. BS, U. Ctrl. Okla., 1970; MA, U. Tex., San Antonio, 1977; PhD, U. North Tex., 1990. Dept. chair, tchr. Permian H.S., Odessa, Tex., 1981-84; prof. Odessa (Tex.) Coll., 1984-85, dean, curriculum dir., 1990-97; curriculum dir. Maypearl (Tex.) Ind. Sch. Dist., 1985-88; coord. Collin County C.C., Plano, Tex., 1988-90; v.p. acad. affairs We. Okla. State Coll., 1997-99; dir. Tex. Tech Univ.-Acad. 2000, Plano, 1999—2002; prin., owner Xstream Computers, 2002—. Cons. Tex. colls. and univs., 1988—; master tchr. Nat. Inst. for Staff and Orgnl. Devel., Austin, Tex., 1991. Contbr. articles to profl. jours. Mem. Tex. Assn. Instructional Adminstrs., Tex. Assn. Tech. Educators, Tex. Tech. Soc., Am. Indian Sci. and Engring. Soc., Odessa Optimist Club (bd. dirs. 1991-93). Office: 3301 Preston Rd Ste 6 Frisco TX 75034 E-mail: ron@xstreamcomputers.com.

KERNER, HOWARD ALEX, English and communications educator, writer, literary manager; b. N.Y.C., Jan. 1, 1951; BA, SUNY, Albany, 1971, MA, 1972; postgrad., U. Va., 1972-73. Tchr. Clifton-Fine High Sch., Star Lake, N.Y., 1973-80; prof. English and speech Empire State Coll., Watertown, N.Y., 1979-87, Syracuse (N.Y.) U., 1985-87, Jefferson C.C., Watertown, N.Y., 1979-89, Polk C.C., Winter Haven, Fla., 1989—. Literary mgr. Syracuse Stage, 1986—; arts editor Sta. WWNY-TV, Watertown, 1985-88; weekly columnist The Watertown Daily Times, 1985-89; monthly columnist Syracuse New Times, 1986-89. Contbr. over 350 articles to publs.; actor, dir. 60 dramatic and musical theatre prodns. Mem. S.E. Conf. on English in Two Yr. Coll., Nat. Coun. Tchrs. English, Fla. Coll. English Assn., Outer Critics Circle. Office: Polk CC Div Arts Letters and SS 999 Avenue H NE Winter Haven FL 33881-4256

KERNSTOCK, ELWYN NICHOLAS, political science educator, author; b. Bronx, N.Y., Dec. 24, 1917; s. Charles Henry and Irene (Paollilo) K.; m. Peggy Giles, Dec. 20, 1947; children: Stephan Giles, Nicholas Charles, Christopher John, Wendy Kernstock Robinson. BS in Edn., Ctrl. Conn. State Coll., 1963, MS, 1965; PhD, U. Conn., 1972. Commd. 2d lt. U.S. Army, 1943, advanced through grades to maj., 1962, ret., 1962; instr., chmn. social studies various secondary schs., Conn., 1962-70; faculty St. Michael's Coll., Winooski, Vt., 1971-88, prof. emeritus, 1988—; prof. Acad. Sr. Profls. U. West Fla., 2000—. Pres. New Britain Edn. Assn., 1964; del. Conn. Dem. Conv., 1970, Vt. Dem. Conv., 1972, 1974, 1976, 1980, 1984, 1992, 1994; adv. to chmn. Vt. Dem. Com., 1974—76; Dem. candidate for Congress Vt., 1978; Fla. state legis., 2000; elected committeeman Santa Rosa County, Fla., 1996, Esambia County, Fla., 2001; Dem. candidate for state legis. Fla., 2000; pres. New Britain Unitarian Universalist Soc., 1962. Co-recipient 9th Ann. Freedom of Choice award Pro Choice Vt., 1994. Mem. Am. Polit. Sci. Assn., New Eng. Polit. Sci. Assn., Americans United for Separation Ch. and State (mem. adv. bd. 1987-93, 98—, 99-, pres. N.W. Fla. chpt.), Ret. Officers Assn. Home: 10100 Hillview Rd # 2105 Pensacola FL 32514-5436 E-mail: ekernstock@yahoo.com.

KERN-YSTAD, CAROL RAE, special education educator; b. Ladysmith, Wis., Dec. 20, 1957; d. Clarence Everett and Mary Anita (Kroll) K.; m. Randy Ystad, May 9, 1996; 1 child, Sayre; stepchildren: Brent, Tyler, Jared. AS in Gen. Studies, U. Wis., 1978; MS in Spl. Edn., U. Wis., Eau Claire, 1991; BA, Cardinal Stritch Coll., 1980. Clerical aide U. Wis., Rice Lake, 1976-78; nurses' aide Northland Care Ctr., Rice Lake, 1978, 82, 83; clerical aide Cardinal Stritch Coll., Milw., 1978-80; 1st and 2d grade tchr. St. Mary's Sch., Greenwood, Wis., 1980-84; evening recreation coord. Adult Devel. Svc., Greenwood, 1984-85; tchr. aide for cognitively delayed Sch. Dist. Greenwood, 1985-86, long-term substitute tchr., 1986-87, exceptional edn. needs tchr., chpt. I presch. tchr., 1990—; exceptional edn. needs tchr. Sch. Dist. Loyal, Wis., 1987-90. Grad. asst. dept. spl. edn. U. Wis., Eau Claire, 1989, 90; evaluator spl. edn. component Head Start, Greenwood, 1991, 92, 93, 94; mem., leader wellness com. Sch. Dist. Greenwood, 1993-94. Emergency med. tech. Greenwood Area Ambulance, 1994-96; leader Greenwood Girl Scouts, 1986-87; religious educator St. Mary's Parish, Greenwood, 1982-84, 86-87, Holy Family Parish, Willard, Wis., 1984-85, 94-95. Mem. Jaycees, Delta Epsilon Sigma, Kappa Gamma Pi, Phi Kappa Phi. Roman Catholic. Avocations: fishing, hiking, child care, elderly care. Home: N10637 Madison Ave Greenwood WI 54437-8339 Office: Sch Dist Greenwood 708 E Division St Greenwood WI 54437-9330

KERPER, MEIKE, family violence, sex abuse and addiction educator, consultant; b. Powell, Wyo., Aug. 13, 1929; d. Wesley George and Hazel (Bowman) K.; m. R.R. Milodragovich, Dec. 25, 1963 (div. 1973); children: Dan, John, Teren, Tina, Stana. BS, U. Mont., 1973; MS, U. Ariz., 1975; postgrad., Ariz. State U., 1976-78, Columbia Pacific U., 1990—. Lic. marriage and family therapist, Oreg.; cert. domestic violence counselor, alcoholism and drug abuse counselor, mental health profl. and investigator. Family therapist Cottonwood Hill, Arvada, Colo., 1981; family program developer Turquoise Lodge, Albuquerque, 1982; co-developer abusers program Albuquerque Shelter Domestic Violence, 1984; family therapist Citizens Coun. Alcoholism and Drug Abuse, Albuquerque, 1984-86; pvt. practice cons., trainer family violence and treatment Albuquerque, 1987—. Developer sex offender program Union County, Oreg. Co-author: Court Diversion Program, 1985; author Family Treatment, 1982. Lobbyist CCOPE, Santa Fe, 1983-86; bd. dirs. Union County Task Force on Domestic Violence, 1989-91; developer Choices program treatment of sex offenders and victims union, Wallowa and Baker Counties, Oreg. Recipient commendation Albuquerque Shelter Domestic Violence, 1984. Mem. Assn. for the Treatment Sexual Abusers (Ea. Oreg. rep.), Nat. Assn. Marriage and Family Therapists, PEO Club, Delta Delta Delta. Republican. Episcopalian. Avocations: art history, reading, indian culture, swimming, public speaking. Home: 61002 Love Rd Cove OR 97824-8211

KERR, BARBARA PROSSER, research scientist, educator; b. Asheville, N.C., Dec. 28, 1925; d. George Holcomb and Gertrude Berenice (Parker) Prosser; m. William Albert Kerr, June 18, 1950 (div. May 1959); 1 child, Diana. BA, U. Chgo., 1951; MSW, Ariz. State U., 1971. Cert. clin. social worker, psychiatry and mental health nursing. Exec. sec. Union Theol. Sem., N.Y.C., 1961-67; case worker Dept. Pub. Welfare, Wilmington, Del., 1967-69; psychiatric nurse St. Luke's Hosp. and Med. Ctr., Phoenix, 1969-70; emergency rm. social worker Maricopa Med. Ctr., Phoenix, 1971-82; dir. Kerr-Cole Sustainable Living Ctr., Taylor, Ariz., 1983—. Adv. Solar Cookers Internat., Sacramento, 1993—. Author: The Expanding World of Solar Box Cookers, 1991; inventor Solar Box Cooker, 1976, Solar Wall Oven, 1986. Home: PO Box 576 Taylor AZ 85939 E-mail: kerrcole@skyboot.com.

KERR, CLARK, academic administrator emeritus; b. Stony Creek, Pa., May 17, 1911; s. Samuel William and Caroline (Clark) K.; m. Catherine Spaulding, Dec. 25, 1934; children: Clark E., Alexander W., Caroline M. BA, Swarthmore Coll., 1932, LLD, 1952; MA, Stanford U., 1933; postgrad., London Sch. Econs., 1936, 39; PhD, U. Calif., 1939; LLD, Harvard U., 1958, Princeton U., 1959, others. Traveling fellow Am. Friends Svc. Com., 1935-36; instr. econs. Antioch Coll., 1936-37; tchg. fellow U. Calif., 1937-38; Newton Booth fellow, 1938-39; acting asst. prof. labor econs. Stanford, 1939-40; asst., later assoc. prof. U. Wash., 1940-45; assoc. prof., prof., prof. emeritus, dir. Inst. Indsl. Rels., U. Calif., Berkeley, 1945-52, chancellor, 1952-58, pres., 1958-67, pres. emeritus, 1974—. Chmn. Carnegie Commn. on Higher Edn., 1967-73, Carnegie Coun. Policy Studies in Higher Edn., 1974-79; vice chmn. divsns. War Labor Bd., 1943-45; nat. arbitrator Armour Co. and United Packing House Workers, 1945-52; impartial chmn. Waterfront Employers, Pacific Coast and Internat. Longshoremen's and Warehousemen's Union, 1946-47; pub. mem. Nat. WSB, 1950-51; various arbitrations in pub. utilities, newspaper, aircraft, canning, oil, local transport and other industries, 1942— ; mem. adv. panel Soc. Sci. Rsch., NSF, 1953-57; chmn. Armour Automation Com., 1959-79; chmn. bd. arbitrators U.S. Postal Svc. and Nat. Assn. Letter Carriers (AFL-CIO) and Am. Postal Workers Union (AFL-CIO), 1984 Author: (with E. Wight Bakke) Unions, Management and the Public, rev. edit., 1960, 67, (with Dunlop, Harbison, Myers) Industrialism and Industrial Man, rev. edit., 1964, 73, The Uses of the University, rev. edit., 1972, 82, 95, 2001, Labor and Management in Industrial Society, 1964, Marshall, Marx and Modern Times, 1969, Labor Markets and Wage Determination: The Balkanization of Labor Markets and Other Essays, 1977, Education and National Development: Reflections from an American Perspective during a Period of Global Reassessment, 1979, The Future of Industrial Societies, 1983, (with Marian L. Gade) The Many Lives of Academic Presidents, 1986; editor: (with Paul D. Staudohar) Industrial Relations in a New Age, 1986, Economics of Labor in Industrial Society, 1986, (with Dunlop, Lester, Reynolds; editor Bruce E. Kaufman) How Labor Markets Work: Reflections on Theory and Practice, 1988, (with Marian L. Gade) The Guardians: Boards of Trustees of American Colleges and Universities, 1989, The Great Transformation in Higher Education, 1960-80, 1991, Troubled Times for American Higher Education: The 1990s and Beyond, 1994, Higher Education Cannot Escape History: Issues for the Twenty-First Century, 1994, (with Paul D. Staudohar) Labor Economics and Industrial Relations: Markets and Institutions, 1994, The Gold and the Blue, Vol. 1: Academic Triumphs, 2001. Vol. II Pol. Turmoil, 2003. Trustee Rockefeller Found., 1960-76; mem. bd. mgrs. Swarthmore Coll., 1969-80, life mem., 1981. Recipient Harold W. McGraw Jr. prize in Edn., 1990; named Hon. fellow London Sch. Econs. Mem. Am. Econ. Assn., Royal Econ. Assn., Am. Acad. Arts and Scis., Indsl. Rels. Rsch. Assn., Nat. Acad. Arbitrators, Phi Beta Kappa, Kappa Sigma. Mem. Soc. Of Friends. Home: 8300 Buckingham Dr El Cerrito CA 94530-2530 Office: U Calif Inst Indsl Rels 2521 Channing Way # 5555 Berkeley CA 94720-5556

KERR, GARY ENRICO, lawyer, educator; b. Kewanee, Ill., Feb. 8, 1948; s. Roy Harrison and Marietta (Dani) K.; m. Eileen Elizabeth Straeter, Aug. 18, 1978; 1 child, Victoria Elizabeth. BA, No. Ill. U., 1970; JD, Northwestern U., Chgo., 1973. Bar: Ill. 1974, U.S. Dist. Ct. (cen. dist.) Ill. 1982, U.S. Ct. Appeals (7th cir.) 1983, U.S. Supreme Ct. 1983. Adminstrv. asst. Office Supt. Pub. Instrn. State Ill., Chgo., Springfield, 1971-74; asst. legal advisor Ill. State Bd. Edn., Springfield, 1974-78; spl. counsel Ill. State Comptroller, Springfield, 1978-79; pvt. practice Springfield, 1979—. Adj. faculty Sangamon State U. (now Ill. State U.), Springfield, Ill., 1994; pres., dir. counsel Kerr Products, Inc., Kewanee, Ill., 1980—; instr. paralegal program Robert Morris Coll., Springfield, 1992. Atty. South County Democrats, Sangamon County, Ill.; founder, mgr., Springfield (Ill.) Area Youth Jazz Band. Fellow Ednl. Policy program Inst. Ednl. Leadership, George Washington U., 1976-77. Mem. Ill. State Bar Assn. (chmn. sch. law sect. coun. 1983-84), Sangamon County Bar Assn., Automotive Parts and Accessories Assn. (mem. govtl. affairs and internat. trade com. 1997). Avocations: snow skiing, tennis, fishing. Office: Gary Kerr Ltd 1020 S 7th St Springfield IL 62703-2417 E-mail: kerrltd@aol.com.

KERR, MARGARET ANN, elementary education educator; b. Ashland, Ohio, Jan. 8, 1951; d. Wallace Amander and Beulah Elizabeth (Westerfeld) Canfield; m. Roger William Kerr Jr., June 12, 1970; children: Robert, Thomas. BS in Edn., Ashland U., 1973; MA in Edn., LaVerne Coll., 1975. Cert. elem. tchr., reading specialist, nat. bd. cert. tchr. Tchr. Ruggles-Troy Sch., Ohio, 1973-76, Nankin (Ohio) Sch., 1977-79, Mapleton Sch. Dist., 1981-82; kindergarten tchr. Mapleton Sch., 1982-92; tchr. chpt. 1 extended day kindergarten Mapleton Schs., 1992-94, reading recovery tchr., 1994—2001, tchr. 1st grade, 2001—. Organizer, tchr. pre-sch., 1981; coord. for active parenting Mapleton Schs., 1992-94. Treas. PTA; co-chmn, Mapleton New Bldg. Campaign; mem. Nankin Fedn. Ch., Mapleton Acad. Booster, Mapleton Sports Booster. Mem. NEA, Ohio Edn. Assn., Mapleton Edn. Assn. Avocations: reading, walking, computers, working with young people. Home: 705 State Route 302 Ashland OH 44805-9529 E-mail: mkerr@bright.net.

KERREBROCK, JACK LEO, aeronautics and astronautics engineering educator; b. Los Angeles, Feb. 6, 1928; s. Oscar A. and Florence (Hoy) K.; m. Bernice Veverka, Apr. 11, 1953; children: Christopher, Nancy, Peter. Student, U. Oreg., 1946-47; BS, Oreg. State Coll., 1950; MS, Yale, 1951; PhD, Calif. Inst. Tech., 1956. Aero. research scientist Lewis Lab., NASA, Cleve., 1951-53; research fellow Calif. Inst. Tech., 1955-56; engring. leader Oak Ridge Nat. Lab., 1956-58; sr. research fellow Calif. Inst. Tech., 1958-60; mem. faculty M.I.T., 1960-2001, Richard C. Maclaurin prof. aeros. and astronautics, 1975-96, dir. Gas Turbine and Plasma Dynamics Lab., 1969-78, head div. energy conversion and propulsion, 1970-81, head dept. aeros. and astronautics, 1978-81, 83-85, assoc. dean engring., 1985-89, acting dean, 1989; assoc. adminstr. Office Aeros. and Space Tech., NASA, Washington, 1981-83. Mem. Air Force Sci. Adv. Bd., 1972-88; mem. NASA Rsch. and Tech. Adv. Com., 1975-77; mem. Aeronautics and Space Engring. Bd. NRC, 1976-81, 92-95; mem. aero adv. com. NASA, 1978-81, Nat. Commn. on Space, 1984-86; mem. Air Force Studies Bd. NRC, 1990-92, com. on Earth-Orbit Propulsion, 1991-92; mem. adv. com. Space Sta. NASA, 1987-92; chm. com. Space Sta. NRC, 1992-95; trustee Inst. for Def. Analysis, 1984-2000, Aerospace Corp., 1986-88; bd. dirs. Orbital Scis. Corp., Aerodyne Rsch. Inc. Recipient Gas Turbine Power award ASME, 1971, John Leland Atwood award ASEE and AIAA, 1992; Fairchild Disting. scholar Calif. Inst. Tech., 1990. Fellow AIAA (hon.); mem. Nat. Acad. Engring., Am. Acad. Arts and Scis. Home: 108 Tower Rd Lincoln MA 01773-4403

KERRIGAN, JOHN E. academic administrator; Chancellor emeritus U. Wis., Oshkosh; interim pres. Loras Coll., Dubuque, Iowa, 2002—. Office: Loras College PO Box 178 Dubuque IA 52004-0178*

KERR-NOWLAN, DONNA COURTNEY, pre-school administrator; b. Wellsboro, Pa., Sept. 25, 1940; d. Sylvan LaRue and Mildred Fowler Kerr; children from previous marriage: Craig Kerr Nowlan, Brent Fowler Nowlan. Cert., Jean Summers Bus. Sch., N.Y., 1956; student, Corning C.C., Mansfield (Pa.) State Tchrs. Coll., 1960. Owner, bridal cons. Bridal Bower, 1960—63; owner Victorian Fingerlakes Tour Guides, 1963—72; dir., owner Building Block Nursery & Pre-K, Elmira, NY, 1969—. Coord. Civil War prison camp Chemung County C. of C., Elmira, 2000—; pres. Hist. Near Westside Bd. Dirs. and Assn., 1985—89; mem. planning commn. City of Elmira; mem. Chemung County Planning Bd.; dir. Found. for Ctrl. Diocese Episcopal Ch., Syracuse, NY, 1981. Named Woman of Achievement, Chemung County Coun. of Women, 1993; named to Legion of Honor, Chaplin of Four Chaplins, Valley Forge, Pa., 1994; recipient Cmty. Svc. award, Hist. Near Westside Neighborhood Assn., 1982, cert. of appreciation, Elmira Coll., 1985, 1994, Robert Goostrey award, Chemung County C. of C., 1990. Mem.: Twin Tier Jazz Soc. (bd. dirs. 1989—, pres. 2000—), Hal Roach Soc. (bd. dirs. 1987—), Soroptimist Internat. (pres. Elmira chpt. 1989—99, Outstanding Cmty. Svc. award 1994, Outstanding Club Mem. 1995, Outstanding Cmty. Vol. 1996, Outstanding Vol. Svc. award 1986). Republican. Episcopalian. Avocations: walking, gourmet cooking, reading, painting. Home: 715 Winsor Ave Elmira NY 14905 Office: Building Block Pvt Nursery Sch 308 College Ave Elmira NY 14901 E-mail: dnowlan@stny.rr.com.

KERSCHNER, LEE R(ONALD), academic administrator, political science educator; b. May 31, 1931; m. Helga Koller, June 22, 1958; children: David, Gabriel, Riza. BA in Polit. Sci. (Univ. fellow), Rutgers U., 1953; MA in Internat. Relations (Univ. fellow), Johns Hopkins U., 1958; PhD in Polit. Sci. (Univ. fellow), Georgetown U., 1964. From instr. to prof. polit. sci. Calif. State U., Fullerton, 1961-69, prof., 1988—; state univ. dean Calif. State Univs. and Colls. Hdqrs., Long Beach, 1969-71, asst. exec. vice chancellor, 1971-76, vice chancellor for adminstrv. affairs, 1976-77, vice chancellor acad. affairs, 1987-92; exec. dir. Colo. Commn. on Higher Edn., Denver, 1977-83, Nat. Assn. Trade and Tech. Schs., 1983-85, Calif. Commn. on Master Plan for Higher Edn., 1985-87; interim pres. Calif. State U., Stanislaus, 1992-94, spl. asst. to the chancellor, 1994-97; exec. vice chancellor Minn. State Colls. and Univs., St. Paul, 1996-97; vice chancellor emeritus Calif. State U., 1997—. Mem. Calif. Student Aid Commn., 1993-96; cons. in field. Mem. exec. com. Am. Jewish Com., Denver, 1978-83; internat. bd. dirs. Amigos de las Americas, 1982-88 (chmn. 1985-87). Served with USAF, 1954-58; col. Res., ret. Home: PO Box 748 Weimar CA 95736-0748

KERYCZYNSKYJ, LEO IHOR, county official, educator, lawyer; b. Chgo., Aug. 8, 1948; s. William and Eva (Chicz) K.; m. Alexandra Irene Okruch, July 19, 1980; 1 child, Christina Alexandra. BA, BS, DePaul U., 1970, MS in Pub. Svc., 1975; JD, No. Ill. U., 1979; postgrad., U. Ill., Chgo., 1980-82. Bar: Ill. 1981, U.S. Dist. Ct. (no. dist.) Ill. 1981, U.S. Ct. Appeals (7th cir.) 1981, U.S. Tax Ct. 1981, U.S. Ct. Claims 1982, U.S. Ct. Mil. Appeals 1982, U.S. Ct. Appeals (fed. cir.) 1983, U.S. Supreme Ct. 1984. Condemnation awards officer Cook County Treas.'s Office, Chgo., 1972-75, adminstrv. asst., 1975-77, dep. treas., 1977-87, chief legal counsel, 1987-96, dir. fin. svcs., 1988-96; pvt. practice, 1996-98; adv. Office of Profl. Stds. Chgo. Police Dept., 1998—. Adj. prof. DePaul U., Chgo., 1979-95; elected chmn. bd. dirs., 1st Security Fed. Savs. Bank Chgo., 1992-93. Capt. Ukrainian Am. Dem. Orgn., Chgo., 1971. Recipient Outstanding Alumni award Phi Kappa Theta, 1971. Mem. ABA, Ill. State Bar Assn., Ill. Trial Law Assn., Ukrainian Am. Bar Assn., Chgo. Bar Assn., Ill. Assn. County Ofcls., Internat. Assn. Clerks, Recorders, Election Ofcls. and Treas., Shore Line Interurban Hist. Soc. (bd. dirs., legal counsel 1987-2001, pres. and chmn., 1993-98), Theta Delta Phi. Ukrainian Catholic. Home: 2324 W Iowa St Apt 3R Chicago IL 60622-4720 Office: Office Profl Stds 10 W 35th St Chicago IL 60616

KESLER, JAY LEWIS, academic administrator; b. Barnes, Wis., Sept. 15, 1935; s. Elsie M. Campbell Kesler; m. H. Jane Smith; children: Laura, Bruce, Terri. Student, Ball State U., 1953-54; BA, Taylor U., 1958, LHD (hon.), 1982; Dr. Divinity (hon.), Barrington Coll., 1977; DD (hon.), Asbury Theol. Sem., 1984, Anderson U., 1999; HHD (hon.), Huntington Coll., 1983; LHD, John Brown U., 1987; LLD (honoris causa), Gordon Coll., 1992; DD (hon.), Union U., 2000, Trinity Internat. U., 2001; LHD (honoris causa), So. Wesleyan U., 2002. Dir. Marion (Ind.) Youth for Christ, 1955-58, crusade staff evangelist, 1959-60, dir. Ill.-Ind. region, 1960-62, dir. coll. recruitment, 1962-63, v.p. personnel, 1963-68, v.p. field coordination, 1968-73, pres., 1973-85, also bd. dirs.; pres. Taylor U., Upland, Ind., 1985-2000, chancellor, 2000—03, pres. emeritus, 2003—; tchg. pastor Upland Cmty. Ch., 2002—. Bd. dirs. Star Fin. Group, Christianity Today, Brotherhood Mut. Ins. Co., Nat. Ass. Evangs., Youth for Christ Internat., Youth for Christ U.S.A.; mem. bd. reference Christian Camps Inc.; mem. Council for Christian Colls. and Univs., bd. mem., 2001; chmn. United Christian Coll. Fund; mem. adv. bd. Christian Bible Soc.; co-pastor 1st Bapt. Ch., Geneva, 1972—85; mem. faculty Billy Graham Schs. Evangelism; lectr. Staley Disting. Christian Sch. Lecture Program; past gov.'s appointee Ind. Commn. on Youth. Spkr. on Family Forum (daily radio show and radio program), 1973-98; mem. adv. com. Campus Life mag.; author: Let's Succeed With Our Teenagers, 1973, I Never Promised You a Disneyland, 1975, The Strong Weak People, 1976, Outside Disneyland, 1977, I Want a Home with No Problems, 1977, Growing Places, 1978, Too Big to Spank, 1978, Breakthrough, 1981, Parents & Teenagers, 1984 (Gold Medallion award), Family Forum, 1984, Making Life Make Sense, 1986, Parents and Children, 1986, Being Holy, Being Human, 1988, Ten Mistakes Parents Make With Teenagers (And How to Avoid Them), 1988, Is Your Marriage Really Worth Fighting For?, 1989, Energizing Your Teenagers' Faith, 1990, Raising Responsible Kids, 1991, Grandparenting: The Agony and the Ecstasy, 1993, Challenges for the College Bound, 1994, Emotionally Healthy Teenagers, 1998; contbr. articles to profl. jours. Bd. advisors Prison Fellowship Internat., Christian Camps Inc., Christian Educators Assn. Internat., Evangelicals for Social Action, Love and Action, Venture Middle East, Internat. Com. of Reference for New Life 2000. Named sr. fellow, Coun. Christian Coll., 2000, Sagamore of the Wabash, 2000; recipient Angel award, Religion in Media, 1985, Outstanding Youth Leadership award, Religious Heritage Am., 1989. Office: Taylor U Office Pres 236 W Reade Ave Upland IN 46989-1002

KESLER, KENNETH ALLEN, thoracic surgeon, educator; b. Indpls., Apr. 12, 1953; s. Jack Allen and Jacqueline Rita (Schaeffer) K. AB in Math., Ind. U., 1975; MD, Ind. U., Indpls., 1979. Bd. cert. Am. Bd. Surgery, Am. Bd. Thoracic Surgery. Gen. surgery resident Ind. U., Indpls., 1979-85; thoracic surgery resident St. Louis (Mo.) U., 1985-87; asst. prof. surgery thoracic surgery divsn. Ind. U. Sch. Medicine, Indpls., 1987-93, assoc. prof. surgery thoracic surgery divsn., 1993—; surg. dir. thoracic oncology program Ind. U., Indpls., 1993—2000; prof. surgery thoracic surgery divsn. Ind. U. Sch. Medicine, Indpls., 2000—. Thoracic surgery subcom. Ea. Coop. Oncology Group, 1992—. Contbr. chpts. to books and articles to profl. jours. Recipient Liebig Found. award for original rsch. Soc. Vascular Surgeons, 1985. Fellow ACS; mem. Am. Assn. Thoracic Surgeons, Soc. Thoracic Surgeons, Soc. Surg. Oncology, Gen. Thoracic Surg. Club, U.S. Triathlon Med. Assn., Sigma Xi. Avocations: triathlon, golf. Office: Ind U Dept Surgery Thoracic Divsn 545 Barnhill Dr # 212 Indianapolis IN 46202-5112

KESSEL, JOHN HOWARD, political scientist, educator; b. Dayton, Ohio, Oct. 13, 1928; s. Arthur V. and Helen (Hopkins) K.; m. Margaret Sarah Wagner, Aug. 22, 1954; children— Robert Arthur, Thomas John. Student, Purdue U., 1946-48; BA, Ohio State U., 1950; PhD, Columbia U., 1958. Instr. Amherst and Mt. Holyoke colls., 1957-58; instr., asst. prof. Amherst Coll., 1958-61; asst. prof. U. Wash., 1961-65; Arthur E. Braun prof. polit. sci. Allegheny Coll., Meadville, Pa., 1965-70; prof. polit. sci. Ohio State U., Columbus, 1970-94, prof. emeritus, 1994—. Vis. prof. U. Calif., San Diego, 1977, U. Wash., 1980, Am. U., 1980. Author: The Goldwater Coalition: Republican Strategies in 1964, 1968, The Domestic Presidency, 1975, Presidential Campaign Politics: Coalition Strategies and Citizen Response, 1980, 4th edit., 1992, Presidential Parties, 1984, Presidents, the Presidency, and the Political Environment, 2001; co-editor: Micropolitics-Individual and Group Level Concepts, 1970, Theory Building and Data Analysis in the Social Sciences, 1984, Researching the Presidency: Vital Questions, New Approaches, 1993; editor Am. Jour. Polit. Sci, 1974-76; contbr. articles to profl. jours. Mem. exec. council Inter-Univ. Consortium for Polit. Research, 1964-65, 67-68; Exec. dir. Nixon-Lodge Vols. Mass., 1960; dir. arts, scis. div. Republican Nat. Com., 1963-64. Served with USN, 1950-53. Guest scholar, Brookings Inst., 1972, vis. scholar, Am. Enterprise Inst., 1980—82. Mem. Am. Polit. Sci. Assn. (exec. council 1969-71), Midwest Polit. Sci. Assn. (pres. 1978-79) Home: 516 E Schreyer Pl Columbus OH 43214-2273 E-mail: kessel.1@osu.edu.

KESSLER, BETTY DEAN, academic administrator; b. Oak Ridge, Tenn., July 30, 1945; d. Joseph Brown and Louise Elizabeth (Kinder) K. BA in Elem. Edn., Marshall U., 1967, MA in Elem. Edn., 1973. Cert. reading specialist, adminstr. Elem. tchr. Walled Lake (Mich.) Schs., 1967-70, Newark/New Castle County Schs., 1970-78; reading resource tchr. Christina Schs., Newark, 1978-2000; adj. instr. Grad. Sch. Wilmington (Del.) Coll., 1993—; supr. Coll. of Edn. U. Del., 2000—. Reading instr. U. Del., Newark, summer 1981, 82; cons. Harper and Row Co., N.Y.C., summer 1973; rep. People to People, Internat. Russian-Am. Reading Coun., 1991; speaker in field; state performance com. testing benchmark (grade 3), outstanding papers, 1998. Contbr. (video) HOSTS-tutor/mentoring program, 1990. Vol. Com. to Re-elect State Treas. Del., Wilmington, 1992-94; trustee Ebenezer United Meth. Ch., Newark, 1988-90; bd. dirs. Multiple Schlerosis Read-a-thons, 1988-94; vol., co-coord. Del. Hospice Camp New Hope, Festival Trees for Youth Activities, 1996—. Recipient Del. Tchr. Ctr. Svc. award, 1988, Super Stars in Edn. award Del. C. of C., 1990. Mem. NEA, Del. Edn. Assn., Newark Edn. Assn., Delta Kappa Gamma (state pres. 1991-93), Phi Delta Kappa. Methodist. Avocations: reading mystery novels, tennis, bridge, travel, raising miniature schnauzers. Home: 4 Parliament Ct Newark DE 19711-6954

KESSLER, EDWIN, meteorology educator, consultant; b. Bklyn., Dec. 2, 1928; s. Edwin and Marie Rosa (Weil) K.; m. Lottie Catherine Menger; children: Austin Rainier, Thomas Russell. AB, Columbia Coll., 1950; MS in Meteorology, MIT, 1952, ScD in Meteorology, 1957. Chief synoptic meteorology sect. Weather Radar br. Air Force Cambridge Rsch. Lab., Bedford, Mass., 1954-61; sr. rsch. scientist Travelers Rsch. Ctr., Hartford, Conn., 1961-62, dir. atmospheric physics div., 1962-64; dir. Nat. Severe Storms Lab., Norman, Okla., 1964-86; adj. prof. U. Okla., 1964—. Vis. prof. MIT, 1975-76, McGill U., Can., 1980; bd. dirs. LINK, Norman, N.Am. Transp. Inst., Norman Area Land Conservancy, Inc., Norman chpt. LWV. Editor: Thunderstorms, A Social Scientific and Technological Documentary, 3 vols., 1982, 2d edits., 1983-88, paperback edits., vol. 1, 1988, vol. 2, 1992; contbr. over 250 reports, and about 100 peer-reviewed articles to profl. jours. State chair Common Cause, Okla., 1993-99, vice chair, 1999-. With U.S. Army, 1946-47. Recipient award for outstanding authorship NOAA, 1971 Fellow AAAS, Am. Meteorol. Soc. (nat. councilor 1966-69, past mem. coms. on hurricanes, atmospheric electricity, agr. and forestry, cloud and precipitation physics, severe local storms, past chmn. com. on weather radar, cert. cons. meteorologist, Cleveland Abbe award for disting. svc. 1988); mem. AIAA (sr. mem.), LWV, Royal Meteorol. Soc. (fgn.), Am. Geophys. Union, Sigma Xi. Achievements include research in agriculture and energy; manager of 350 acres of pasture, streams and wilderness in central Oklahoma. Office: U Okla 100 E Boyd St Rm 684 Norman OK 73019-1028 Fax: 405-360-3246. E-mail: kess3@swbell.net.

KESSLER, HERBERT LEON, art historian, educator, university administrator; b. Chgo., July 20, 1941; s. Ben and Bertha K.; m. Johanna Zacharias, Apr. 24, 1976; 1 dau., Morisa. AB, U. Chgo., 1961; MFA, Princeton U., 1963, PhD, 1965. Asst. prof. U. Chgo., 1965-68; assoc. prof., 1968-73; prof., 1973-76; chmn. dept. art, univ. dir. fine arts, 1973-76; prof. Johns Hopkins U., Balt., 1976—, chair dept. art, 1976-89, 95-98. Guest prof. Bibliotheca Hertziana, Rome, 1996-97, dean Sch. Arts and Scis., 1998-99; vis. prof. Harvard U., 2000, Ecole des Hautes Etudes, 2000. Author: French and Flemish Illuminated Manuscripts, 1969, The Illustrated Bibles from Tours, 1977, The Cotton Genesis, 1986, The Dura Synagogue Frescoes and Christian Art, 1990, Studies in Pictorial Narrative, 1994, The Poetry and Paintings in the First Bible of Charles the Bald, 1997, The Holy Face and the paradox of Representation, 1998, Rome 1300: On the Path of the Pilgrim, 2000, Spiritual Seeing: Picturing God's Invisibility in the Middle Ages, 2000. Old St. Peter's and Ch. Decoration in medieval Italy, 2002. Sr. fellow Dumbarton Oaks, Washington, 1980-86; Woodrow Wilson fellow; Inst. Advanced Study fellow; Am. Council Learned Socs. fellow; Am. Philos. Soc. fellow; Guggenheim fellow; fellow Am. Acad. in Rome Fellow Medieval Acad. Am., Am. Acad. Arts and Scis.; mem. Coll. Art Assn., Phi Beta Kappa. Home: 3601 Greenway Apt 809 Baltimore MD 21218 Office: Johns Hopkins U Baltimore MD 21218 E-mail: hlk@jhu.edu.

KESSLER, JOAN MIRIAM, retired special education educator, learning consultant; b. N.Y.C., July 22, 1933; d. David and Bess (Nagin) Keiles; m. Frederick M. Kessler, May 2, 1954; children: Fran Yungher, Andrew, Rachel Park. BS in Edn., CCNY, 1954; MS in Edn., Rutgers U., 1969. Cert. learning disabilities tchr.-cons., reading specialist, N.J. Elem. tchr. N.Y.C. Schs., 1954-56; learning disabilities tchr.-cons. Bridgewater-Raritan (N.J.) Schs., 1966-94; ret., 1994. Author: Guidebook for High School Personnel: The Match Book, 1990, The College Match Book-A Guidebook for Students with Learning Disabilities, for High School Personnel, Parents and Students, 1994; co-author: (transition to coll. for the learning disabled student) Building Bridges, 1991. Bd. dirs. Coop. Nursery Sch., Bound Brook, N.J., 1966-80, Temple Sholom-Hebrew High Sch. Bridgewater, 1973-75, Solomon Schecter Day Sch., Bridgewater, 1984-86. Mem. N.J. Assn. Learning Cons. Avocations: reading, travel, tennis, golf.

KESSLER, MARK ALLEN, political scientist, educator; b. McKeesport, Pa., Jan. 3, 1955; s. Robert and Rae (Alpern) K.; m. Stephanie Weko, Aug. 14, 1983. BA, U. Pitts., 1977; MA, Pa. State U., 1979, PhD, 1985. Prof. politi. sci. Bates Coll., Lewiston, Maine, 1983—, chair polit. sci., 1993-97, chair divsn. social sci., 2000—. Author: Legal Services for the Poor, 1987; co-author: The Play of Power, 1996; contbr. articles to profl. jours. NSF grantee, 1981. Mem.: Law and Soc. Assn., Am. Judicature Soc., Am. Polit. Sci. Assn. Democrat. Jewish. Home: 241 5th St Providence RI 02906-3763 Office: Bates Coll 174 Pettingill St Lewiston ME 04240-5324 E-mail: mkessler@bates.edu.

KESTENBAUM, LAWRENCE, political science educator; b. Chgo., Sept. 13, 1955; s. Justin Louis and Maryhelen (Dietrich) K.; m. M. Janice Gutfreund, Nov. 17, 1990. BA in Econs., Mich. State U., 1979; JD, Wayne State U., 1982; postgrad., Cornell U., 1988-90. Bar: Mich. Atty., cons., East Lansing, Mich., 1983-88, Ithaca, N.Y., 1988-90, Ann Arbor, Mich., 1990—; commrs. Ingham County, Mason, Mich., 1983-88; program assoc. Mich. Citizen's Lobby, Lansing, 1983-85; computer lab. dir. Sch. Criminal Justice, Mich. State U., East Lansing, 1992-95, acad. specialist polit. sci. dept., 1995-98; sr. specialist health and retirement study Inst. for Social Rsch., U. Mich., 1998—; creator, owner Polit. Graveyard web site, 1996—. Adj. faculty Ea. Mich. U., Ypsilanti, 1991-2000. Contbg. author: At the Campus Gate, 1976; contbr. articles to profl. jours. Mem. planning commn. City of E. Lansing, 1977-79; replacement del. Dem. Nat. Mid-term Conv., 1978; county commr. Ingham County, Mason, Mich., 1983-88; mem. hist. dist. commn., City of Ann Arbor, 1992-98, chair hist. dist. commn., 1997-98; bd. dirs. Mich. State U. Student Housing Corp., East Lansing, 1978-79, Ann Arbor Hist. Found., 1992-2000, Arbornet, Inc., Ann Arbor, 1993-95; mem. univ. planning com., Wayne State U., Detroit, 1980-82; vice-chmn. Ann Arbor Dem. Party, 1994-98; candidate Mich. Ho. of Reps., 1998; county commr. Washtenaw County, Ann Arbor, Mich, 2000-2002. Recipient Arthur F. Lederle scholarship Wayne State U. Law Sch., Detroit, 1979. Mem. State Bar of Mich., Nat. Trust for Historic Preservation, Pittsfield Union Grange. Democrat. Jewish. Avocations: folk dancing, cemeteries, science fiction, local history, given names. Home: 1726 W Stadium Blvd Ann Arbor MI 48103-5225 Office: U Mich 3132 Inst Social Rsch 426 Thompson St Ann Arbor MI 48104-2321 Personal E-mail: polygon@potifos.com.

KESTER, DALE EMMERT, pomologist, educator; b. Audubon, Iowa, July 28, 1922; s. Raymond and Fannie (Ditzenberger) K.; m. Daphne Dougherty; children: William Raymond, Nancy Inman. BS in Horticulture, Iowa State Coll., 1947; MS in Horticulture, U. Calif., Davis, 1949, PhD in Plant Physiology, 1951. Rsch. asst. dept pomology U. Calif., Davis, Calif., 1947-51, lectr., jr. pomologist, 1951-53, asst. prof., asst. pomologist, 1953-60, assoc. prof., assoc. pomologist, 1960-69, prof., pomologist, 1969-91, prof. emeritus, 1991—. Vis. scholar dept. genetics U. Wis., Madison, 1962-63, Volcanic Rsch. Inst., Bet Dagan, Israel, 1975. Co-author: Plant Propagation: Principles and Practices, 1959, 7th revised edit., 2002; contbr. numerous articles to profl. and popular publ. 1st lt. USAF, 1943-45, ETO. Fellow Am. Soc. Hort. Sci. (Stark award 1980); mem. Internat. Plant Propagators Soc. (sec. 1961, 1st v.p. 1996, pres. 1997), Alpha Zeta, Gamma Sigma Delta, Phi Beta Kappa, Pi Alpha Xi. Republican. Presbyterian. Achievements include introduction of 7 almond cultivars and 3 almond rootstocks. Home: 1515 Shasta Dr Apt 2327 Davis CA 95616-6684 Office: U Calif Dept Pomology Davis CA 95616

KESTNER, CHERYL LYNN, elementary school educator; b. Mendota, Ill., Dec. 1, 1951; d. Giles Culver and Mary Margaret (Nelson) Culver; m. Kenneth Kestner, Aug. 18, 1973; children: Theresa, Kristine. BS, Western Ill. U., 1973, M of Sci. Edn., 1997. Tchr. Sch. Dist. 15, Beardstown, Ill., 1973-78, Sch. Dist. #3, Camp Point, Ill., 1978-81, 90—, St. James Luth. Ch., Quincy, Ill., 1982-90. Bd. dirs. PTO, Camp Point, 1992-93. Mem. Nat./Ill. Sci. Tchrs. Lutheran. Avocations: reading, quilting.

KETCHAM, MADALINE SUE, elementary school educator; b. Neosho, Mo., Mar. 25, 1956; d. Robert Irl and Marjorie Faye (Daugherty) Carnes; m. Richard Glenn Ketcham, Feb. 20, 1987; 1 child, Kellen Brett. Cert. elem. tchr., Mo. Remedial lang. and math. tchr. Purdy Sch. Dist., Mo., 1978-80, 6th grade tchr., 1980-82, 5th and 6th grade math. tchr., 1982-83, 6th grade math. tchr., 1983—94; elem. tchr. So. Elem. Sch., Neosho, Mo., 1994—. Bible sch. tchr. High St. Christian Ch., Neosho. Mem. Internat. Reading Assn. (treas. S.W. dist. 1990—), Mo. Coun. Tchr. of Math., Internat. Reading Assn., Purdy Cmty. Tchr. Assn. (treas. 1981, pres. 1983), Mo. State Tchr. Assn, Neosho Cmty. Tchr. Assn., Delta Kappa Gamma; Spcl. Olympics. Avocations: bowling, reading, children. Office: South Elem Sch 911 Wornall Rd Neosho MO 64850 Home: 317 N Jefferson St Neosho MO 64850-1558

KETCHAM, WARREN ANDREW, psychologist, educator; b. Manistee, Mich., June 28, 1909; s. Perry Warren and Anna Ella (Ulrich) K.; m. Edna May Wearne, Nov. 23, 1962 (dec. Mar. 1991). BM, U. Mich., 1932, MA, 1947, PhD, 1951. Lic. psychologist Mich., Tex. Tchr. Reed City (Mich.) Pub. Schs., 1934-36, Melvindale (Mich.) Pub. Schs., 1936-38; supr. Dearborn (Mich.) Pub. Schs., 1938-43; sch. psychologist Ferndale (Mich.) Pub. Schs., 1950-53; prof., sch. psychologist U. Mich., Ann Arbor, 1953-77, prof. emeritus, 1978—; pvt. practice clin., indsl., orgnl. psychology Mich. and Tex., 1964—. Cons. Am. Sch., Guatemala City, Guatemala, 1958-80. Sgt. U.S. Army, 1943-45, PTO. Fulbright scholar Leeds U., 1959, Hinsdale scholar U. Mich., 1951. Fellow Am. Psychol. Assn.; mem. Am. Soc. Clin. Hypnotists, Mich. Soc. Clin. Psychologists, Mich. Psychol. Assn., Nat. Registered Health Svc. Providers in Psychology. Home and Office: 608 E Lake Rd Harbor Springs MI 49740-1220

KETEFIAN, SHAKÉ, nursing educator; b. Beirut, Dec. 29, 1939; d. Krikor and Zaghganoush (Soghomonian) K. BSN, Am. U. Beirut, 1963; MEd, Columbia U., 1968, EdD, 1972. From asst. prof. nursing to prof. NYU Sch. Edn., Health, Nursing and Arts Professions, N.Y.C., 1972-84; dir. continuing edn. in nursing NYU, N.Y.C.; with U. Mich., 1984—; prof., assoc. dean for grad. studies, dir. doctoral and postdoctoral studies, dir. internat. affairs U. Mich. Sch. Nursing, Ann Arbor, acting dean, 1991-92. Contbr. articles to profl. jours. Fellow AAUW, Am. Acad. Nursing (governing coun.); mem. ANA, Am. Orgn. Nurse Execs., Midwest Nursing Rsch. Soc. (chair sci. integrity task force 1994-96, 2001-03), Mich. Nurses Assn., Assn. for Moral Edn., Internat. Network for Doctoral Edn. in Nursing (co-founder, chmn.), Sigma Theta Tau. Office: U Mich Sch Nursing 400 N Ingalls Ann Arbor MI 48109

KETRON, CARRIE SUE, secondary school educator; b. Clifton, Tex. d. Randolph Allen and Mary (Waggoner) Ogden; m. N.M. Ketron, Aug. 4, 1984; children: John, Robert. B of Applied Arts and Scis., U. North Tex., 1990, MEd, 1993. Tchr. Duncanville (Tex.) High Sch., 1982--. Named Tchr. of Yr., Tex. Vocat. Tech. Assn., 1990, Outstanding Nat. Career & Tech. Tchr. of Yr., 1997. Mem. Golden Key Honor Soc., Am. Vocat. Assn., Cosmetology Instructors' of Pub. Schs. (parliamentarian 1989-90), Vocat. Indsl. Clubs Am. (advisor 1986-93), Iota Lambda Sigma Sigma (pres. 1995-96), Phi Theta Kappa, Alpha Chi. Baptist.

KETT, JOSEPH FRANCIS, historian, educator; b. N.Y.C., Mar. 11, 1938; s. Joseph Francis and Anne (Barry) K.; m. Eleanor Hess, June 26, 1965; children: Jennifer, John. BA magna cum laude, Coll. Holy Cross, 1959; MA, Harvard U., 1960, PhD, 1964. Instr. in history Harvard U., Cambridge,

Mass., 1964-65; asst. prof. U. Va., Charlottesville, 1966-69, assoc. prof., 1970-76, prof., 1976—, chmn. dept. history, 1985-90. Author: The Formation of the American Medical Profession, 1780-1860: The role of Institutions, 1968, Rites of Passage: Adolescence in America, 1790—, 1977, The Pursuit of Knowledge Under Difficulties, 1994; co-author: The Enduring Vision, 1989, (with E. Donald Hirsch and James Trefil) Dictionary of Cultural Literacy, 1988, 2d edit., 1993, 3d edit. 2002; contbg. author: Cultural Literacy: What Every American Needs to Know (Hirsch), 1986; also articles. Fellow Charles Warren Ctr. Harvard U., 1969-70. Office: U Va Dept History Randall Hall Charlottesville VA 22903-3284

KETTERLING, DEBRA M. secondary school educator; b. Lamoure, North Dakota, July 21, 1951; d. Harold E. and Hilda L. Weixel; m. Lynn Ketterling, Dec. 28, 1968; children: Darin, Dustin. EdM, U. Mary VCSU, Bismarck, N.D., 1974. Tchr., Killdeer, ND, Veblen, SD, White, SD, Richardton, ND, Bismarck, ND. Mem. coll. adv. bd. U. Mary Masters, Bismarck, ND, 1998; tchr., adv. bd. Century H.S., Bismarck, ND, 1989—. Home: 2905 Vancouver Ln Bismarck ND 58503 Office: Century HS 1000 Century Ave E Bismarck ND 58503

KETTERLING, MELISSA CARY, elementary school educator; b. Mandan, North Dakota, Dec. 4, 1967; d. Allan Edgar and Cary Elizabeth (Fetch) U. AA, Bismarck Coll., Bismark, ND.; BS, U. Mary, Bismarck, ND. Nautilus instr. Mandan Cmty. Ctr., Mandan, ND, 1987-90; substitute tchr. Bismarck and Mandan Sch., ND, 1990-93; tchr. Immanuel Christian Elem. Sch., Mandan, ND, 1993—2002; stay at home mother with a set of twins and another baby on the way. Fellow NEA, mem. N.D. Edn. Assn. Avocations: boating, volleyball, softball, camping, sports. Home: 656 16th St NW Mercer ND 58559-9322

KETTLE, SALLY ANNE, consulting company executive, educator; b. Omaha, Feb. 2, 1938; d. H. Eugene and Elaine Josephine (Winston) Smiley; m. William Frederick Kettle, July 20, 1968 (div. 1973); children: Christopher, Winston. BEd, U. Nebr., 1960, postgrad. Cert. tchr., S.C., Nebr. Tchr. Dist. 66 Pub. Schs., Omaha, 1966-72; owner, mgr. The Rick Rack, Ltd., Lakewood, Colo., 1974-75; coord. merchandising communications 3M, St. Paul, 1978-80, sr. coord. internat. corp. comm., 1981-83; corp. dir. communications Intran Corp., St. Paul, 1984; pres. Sally Kettle & Co., Bloomington, Minn., 1985-95, Apple Valley, Minn., 1994—. Mem. cmty. faculty Met. State U., Mpls., 1983-90, 97—, St. Olaf Coll., Northfield, Minn., 1992-94, asst. prof. econs., 2000-01; mem. adj. faculty U. Minn. Sch. Journalism and Mass Comm., Mpls., St. Thomas U., 1994-95, Northwestern Coll., 1998-2000. TV hostess City of Bloomington Cable TV, 1984-86. Co-founder Women's Resource Ctr., bd. dirs., mem. adv. bd., 1978-88; chair 13th Precinct, Bloomington, 1978-83; bd. dirs. 41st Sen. Dist., Bloomington, 1982-83; cable TV commr. Bloomington City Coun., 1984-85; pub. rels. com. U.S. Olympic Festival, 1989-90; bd. dirs. Minn. Prayer Breakfast Bd., 1984—; mem. Better Bus. Bur.; founder Ad Rev. Coun.; v.p. Christian Mgmt. Assn., Minn.; internat. com. bd. Carlson Grad. Sch. Mgmt., U. Minn.; mem. state ctrl. com. and platform commn. DFL, 1988-90; bd. dirs. Fellowship of Christian Athletes, 1988-89; pub. rels. com., vice chair bd. comms. '96 Billy Graham Minn. Crusade, 1996; bd. commrs. Shoreland Zoning Commn. Dakota County, Minn., 1996—, vice chair, 1998—. Named one of Outstanding Young Women of Am., 1965. Mem. Am. Advt. Fedn. (conf. com. 1985-87, pub. svc. com. 1986-88), Pub. Rels. Soc. Am., Advt. Fedn. Minn. (bd. dirs. 1982-86), Minn. Women's Econ. Roundtable, Internat. Platform Assn., Nat. Grad. Women's Honor Soc., Minn. Press Club (co-chair newsmaker com., bd. dirs. 1989-92), Phi Delta Gamma, Kappa Alpha Theta. Avocations: reading, sewing, entertaining, volunteering. Home: 13390 Gunflint Path Apple Valley MN 55124-7376

KETTLEWELL, GAIL BIERY, academic administrator; b. Dresden, Ohio, Apr. 5, 1939; d. Graydon Adams and Mildred K. (Cox) Biery; m. Charles G. Kettlewell, Sept. 9, 1960; children: Christian, Abigail, Nathaniel. BA, Muskingum Coll., 1961; MA, Old Dominion U., 1973; EdD, Va. Poly. Inst. and State U., Blacksburg, Va., 1985. Librarian Knox County Library, Mt. Vernon, Ohio, 1961-62; tchr. Fairfax County Pub. Schs., Alexandria, Va., 1968-70, Portsmouth (Va.) Pub. Schs., 1962-68, 70-72; assoc. prof. Tidewater C.C., Portsmouth, 1974-83; vice chancellor So. Ark. U. Tech., Camden, 1984-90; provost No. Va. C.C., Manassas, 1990—2002; dir. D.A. program George Mason U., 2002—. Chmn. Internat. Applied Arts and Scis. Inst., 1999—2001. Author: Guide for Peer Tutors, 1981; co-author: (with Alice Hedrick) An Approach to Language, 1978, (with Betty J. Perkinson) Reading/Thinking/Writing, 1983, 2d edit., 1989, 3d edit., 1994; mem. editl. bd. Workforce, 1994. Bd. dirs. Ark. Literacy Coun., Little Rock, 1988, Prince William County cht. ARC, 1991-94, 96-01, Prince William Litter Control Coun., 1991, Manassas Mus. Assocs., 1991-94, Manassas Ctr. for Arts, 1994-99, Prince William/I66 Partnership, 1994-2002, Prince William/Manassas Conv. and Visitors Bur., 2001; pres. Prince William Habitat for Humanity, 2001—; mem. Ark. Tech. Com., Little Rock, 1989-90, Am. Coun. Edn. Commn. on Women, 1994-97, Manassas Tourism Coun., 1994-96, Manassas Bus. Coun., 1994-96; coord., organizer Ouachita-Calhoun Literacy Coun., Camden, Ark., 1987-89; active Cmty. Theatre, 1983—. Fellow Western Carolina U., 1976, Old Dominion U., 1967; recipient Community Svc. award, Portsmouth, Va. Mem. AAUW, ASTD, NAFE, Am. Coun. Edn. (com. on women 1994-97), Va. Assn. Female Execs., Manassas Bus. Coun., DAR, North Ctrl. Assn. Schs. and Colls. (rev. com. 1987—), Ark. Assn. for Devel. Edn. (pres. 1988-89), Children Am. Revolution (orgn. sr. pres. 1989-90), Fedn. Civic Clubs (v.p. 1980, pres. 1981—), Prince William/Greater Manassas C. of C. (bd. dirs. 1994-2002), Rotary (bd. dirs. 1992-94), Delta Kappa Gamma (internat. fellowship 1982, v.p. 1980-81, pres. 1988-89, 1st v.p. 1992-93), Phi Theta Kappa (hon.), Phi Delta Kappa. Episcopalian. Office: George Mason U Coll of Arts and Scis Fairfax VA 22030-4444 Home: 13456 Victory Gallop Ln Gainesville VA 20155 E-mail: gkettlew@gmu.edu.

KETTS, SHARON DAVIS, elementary education educator; b. Bklyn., Oct. 23, 1946; d. Claude D. and Selma R. (Gottlieb) Davis; m. Jeffrey Lee Ketts, Nov. 12, 1966; children: Jeffrey Lee Jr., Kevin Patrick. AA, Santa Fe C.C., Gainesville, Fla., 1981; BA Edn., U. Fla., 1986, MEd, 1991. Cert. elem. edn., reading edn. Music dir. K-8 St. Patrick's Sch., Gainesville, 1981-84; 1st grade tchr. Archer (Fla.) Cmty. Sch., 1986-89, 4th grade tchr., 1989-92; 3rd grade tchr. Prairie View Elem. Sch., Gainesville, 1992—. Reviewer, cons. Tchrs. Cert. Exam. Bd., Gainesville, 1991, 92; cons. textbook adoption Sch. Bd. of Alachua County, Gainesville, 1990; cons. portfolio assessment U. Fla. Office Instrnl. Resources, Gainesville, 1993-94; coord. Prairie View Elem. Sch./U. Fla. Profls. Devel. Sch. Project, 1995-97. State conv. del. Dem. Party Davis County, Layton, Utah, 1978. Creative teaching grantee Sch. Bd. Alachua County, Gainesville, 1993. Mem. Internat. Reading Assn., Nat. Coun. Tchrs. English, Fla. Reading Assn. (dist. dir. VI 1992—), Alachua County Reading Coun. (pres. 1992-96, v.p., treas. 1988-92), North Fla. Classical Guitar Soc. (pres. 1989—), North Ctrl. Fla. Tchrs. Applying Whole Lang. Avocation: classical guitar. Home: 7710 SW 51st Pl Gainesville FL 32608-4431

KEULEGAN, EMMA PAULINE, special education educator; b. Washington, Jan. 21, 1930; d. Garbis H. and Nellie Virginia (Moore) K. BA, Dumbarton Coll. of Holy Cross, 1954. Cert. tchr. elem. and spl. edn. Tchr. St. Dominic's Elem. Sch., Washington, 1954-56, Sacred Heart Acad., Washington, 1956-59, Our Lady of Victory, Washington, 1959-63, St. Francis Acad., Vicksburg, Miss., 1963-78, Culkin Acad., Vicksburg, 1978-91, substitute tchr. spl. edn., 1991—. Treas. PTA, Vicksburg, 1980; pres. Vicksburg Genealogical Soc., 1999. Mem.: DAR (chpt. regent 1967—69, sec. 1994, chpt. chaplain 1996, chpt. libr. 2002, chpt. membership chmn.), Daus. of United Confederacy (chpt. chaplain), Soc. Descs. of Knights of Most Noble Order of the Garter, Sovereign Colonial Soc. Am. Royal Descent, Soc. Magna Charta Dames and Barons (state chaplain 2001), Daus. of the War of 1812 (state chaplain 1998, hon. state pres. 2002, state pres. 2002—, hon. state pres. 2003), Daus. Am. Colonists (chaplain 1985—89, state pres. 1992—94, hon. state pres. 1994—), Colonial Dames 17th Century (state v.p. 1987—89, state pres. 1989, hon. state pres. 1991—), Internat. Reading Assn. (pres. Warren County chpt.), Vicksburg Geneal. Soc. (pres. 2003). Republican. Roman Catholic. Avocations: stamp and coin collecting, needlework, reading. Home: 215 Buena Vista Dr Vicksburg MS 39180-5612 Office: Cedars Elem School 235 Cedars School Circle Vicksburg MS 39180-2571

KEVORKIAN, JIRAIR, applied mathematics, aeronautics and astronautics educator; b. Jerusalem, May 14, 1933; came to U.S., 1952; s. Leon and Araxie (Kalemkerian) K.; m. Seta Tabourian, Mar. 8, 1980. BS, Ga. Inst. Tech., 1955, MS, 1956; PhD, Calif. Inst. Tech., 1961. Aerodynamicist Convair, Ft. Worth, 1956-57, Calif. Inst. Tech., Pasadena, 1961-64; asst. prof. U. Wash., Seattle, 1964-66, assoc. prof., 1966-71, prof. applied math., aeros. and astronautics, 1971—2002, prof. emeritus, 2002—, acting chmn. applied math., 1986-87, 88-90. Vis. prof. U. Paris, 1971-72; Fulbright-Hayes vis. lectr., 1975-76. Author: Partial Differential Equations, 1990; co-author: Perturbation Methods in Applied Mathematics, 1981, Multiple Scale and Singular Perturbation Methods, 1996. Home: 3730 W Commodore Way Seattle WA 98199-1104 Office: U Wash Dept Applied Math PO Box 352420 Seattle WA 98195-2420

KEY, HELEN ELAINE, accountant, educator, consulting company executive; b. Cleve., Jan. 16, 1946; d. Maud and Helen (Key) Vance. BS, W.Va. State Coll., 1968; MEd, Cleve. State U., 1977, PhD, 2003. Prin. Cleve. Bd. Edn., 1968—. Instr. Cuyahoga Community Coll., Cleve., part-time, 1969—, Dyke Coll., Cleve., part-time, 1979-85; pres. H.E. Key & Assos., Cleve., 1983—; treas. BK4W Inc., Cleve., 1981; sec. Progressive Pioneers, Inc. Mem. AAUW, NAACP, NEA, Am. Assn. Notary Pubs., Women Bus. Owners Assn., Cleve. Area Bus. Tchrs., Toastmistress Club (sec. 1978), Pi Lambda Theta, Alpha Kappa Alpha. Democrat. Baptist. Home: 564 Wilkes Ln Cleveland OH 44143-2622 E-mail: hekey-clev@worldnet.att.net.

KEY, OTTA BISCHOF, retired educator; b. Englewood, Colo., May 19, 1907; d. Herbert and Lulu Bonita (Kitterman) Bischof; m. Elra Richard Key, Aug. 21, 1938 (dec. June 1993); children: Paul, Kathryn. BFA, Kans. U., 1933; MA, Ctrl. Mich. U., 1967. Cert. Christian educator. Tchr., Luray, Kans., 1923; elem. tchr., 1924-26; tchr. jr. h.s. Russell, Kans., 1926-29; tchr. art Meml. H.S., Lawrence, Kans., 1934-38; instr. art edn. Maryville (Mo.) U., 1937-38, Saginaw (Mich.) Valley Coll., 1957-70; ednl. asst. Meml. Presbyn. Ch., Midland, Mich., 1958-73; ednl. asst. religion dept. Millikin U., Decatur, Ill., 1976-84. Student adviser Meml. H.S., Lawrence, 1934-38, dir. art exhibits, 1934-38; tchr. synod schs. Presbyn. Ch., 1955-58; mem. edn. City Ch. Coun., Decatur, Ill., 1978-84. Author: Teaching Volunteers Teachers, 1984. Cooperator Decatur Ch. coun., 1976-84, Ch. Women United, Decautur, 1974-93; supporter Am. United, Washington, 1970-97, Presbyn. Ch., 1973-93. Scholarships established McCormick Presbyn. Sem., Louisville Presbyn. Sem.; recipient award Presbyn. Ch., 1958-93. Mem. Assn. of Presbyn. Ch. Educators, Assn. of Great Lakes Ch. Educators. Democrat. Ecumenical. Avocations: reading current events, ecumenical activities, visual arts, family education. Home: 2025 E Lincoln St # 1221 Bloomington IL 61701-5995

KEY, RITA KAY, secondary education educator; b. Galax, Va., Sept. 21, 1951; d. John Howard and Dora V. (Spicer) K. AS, Wytheville (Va.) C.C., 1977; BS, Radford U., 1979; MEd, Va. Poly. Inst. and State U., 1986. Cert. tchr., Va. Instrl. aide Galax High Sch., 1980-84, tchr., 1985—, sci. dept. chair. Mem. adv. bd. Southwest Va. Gov.'s Sch., Pulaski, 1992—. Named Tchr. of Yr., Wal-Mart, 2000, Va. Region VII Tchr. of Yr., 2001. Mem. Va. Assn. Sci. Tchrs., Va. Instrs. of Physics, Southwest Va. Assn. Sci. Tchrs., Alpha Delta Kappa. Methodist. Avocations: flying, biking, sewing, cooking, reading. Home: PO Box 291 Galax VA 24333-0291 Office: Galax High Sch Maroon Tide Dr Galax VA 24333 E-mail: rkey1115@yahoo.com.

KEYE, WILLIAM RICHARD, JR., physician, educator; b. Mineola, NY, Oct. 31, 1943; s. William Richard and Jane Elizabeth (Snell) Keye; m. Suzanne Marie Edstrom, Aug. 13, 1965; children: Deborah Sue, Jeffrey Scott. BA, U. Minn., 1965, BS, MD, U. Minn., 1969. Diplomate Am. Bd. Ob-Gyn., Am. Bd. Reproductive Endocrinology. Intern U. Minn., Mpls., 1969—70, resident, 1970—72, U. Mich., 1972—73, U. Calif., San Francisco, 1973—77; physician Caylor-Nickel Clinic, Bluffton, Ind., 1977—78; asst. prof. U. Utah, Salt Lake City, 1979—84, assoc. prof., 1984—90; dir. divsn. reproductive endocrinology and infertility William Beaumont Hosp., Royal Oak, Mich., 1990—; clin. assoc. porf. U. Mich., 1992—. Editor: Laser Surgery in Obstetrics and Gynecology, 1984, 2d edit., 1990, PMS, 1988, Infertility: Diagnosis and Treatment, 1995; contbr. articles to profl. jour. Med. advisor Resolve of Utah, Salt Lake City, 1979—90. Maj. USAF, 1974—76. Fellow: ACOG, Am. Soc. Reproductive Medicine (bd. dirs. 1994—97, 1999—2003, pres. 2001—03); mem.: Soc. Reproductive Surgeons, Gynecol. Laser Soc., Soc. Reproductive Endocrinology (treas. 1990—91, sec. 1991—92, v.p. 1992—93, pres. 1993—94). Office: William Beaumont Fertility Ctr 3535 W 13 Mile Rd Royal Oak MI 48073-6710

KEYES, DAVID ELLIOT, scientific computing educator, researcher; b. Bklyn., Dec. 4, 1956; s. Elliot Fuller and Edna (Corsini) K.; married; 2 children. BSME, Princeton U., 1978; MS in Applied Math., Harvard U., 1979, PhD in Applied Math., 1984. Rsch. assoc. dept. computer sci. Yale U., New Haven, 1984-85, asst. prof. dept. mech. engring., 1986-90, assoc. prof. dept. mech. engring., 1990-94; assoc. prof. dept. computer sci. Old Dominion U., 1993—99, teletechnet broadcast instr., 1996—2003, Richard F. Barry chair prof. math. and stats., 1999—2003, chmn. dept. math. and stats., 1999—2001, dir. Ctr. for Computational Sci., 2001—03; dir. Program in High Performance Computing and Comm., Va. Inst. for Computer Applications and Sci. Engring., NASA, Langley Rsch. Ctr., 1994—2000; acting dir. Inst. Sci. Computer Rsch. Lawrence Livermore Nat. Lab., 1999—; Fu Found. prof. applied math., dept. applied physics and applied math. Columbia U., N.Y.C., 2003—. Vis. scientist Inst. Computer Applications in Sci. and Engring., Hampton, Va., 1990, sr. rsch. assoc., 1993-2002. Editor: Domain Decomposition Methods in Partial Differential Equations, 1991, Domain-based Parallelism and Problem Decomposition Methods, 1995, Domain Decomposition Methods in Scientific and Engineering Computing, 1995, 98, 02, 03, Parallel Numerical Algorithms, 1996, Parallel Computational Fluid Dynamics, 2000; mem. editl. bd. Internat. Jour. for Supercomputer Applications, 1994—, Lecture Notes in Computational Sci. and Engring., 1996—, Soc. for Indsl. and Applied Math. Jour. Sci. Comput., 1999-2000; contbr. articles to profl. jours. Named Presdl. Young Investigator, NSF, Washington, 1989, Gordon Bell prize winner IEEE Supercomputing '99, Portland, 1999. Mem. ASME, AIAA (coun. mem. 1991-93, chair 1992-93), IEEE Computer Soc., Soc. Indsl. and Applied Math. (sec. 1991-93, vis. lectr. 1992—, coun. 1999—), Assn. for Computing Machinery, The Combustion Inst., Tau Beta Pi, Sigma Xi, Phi Beta Kappa. E-mail: David.Keyes@columbia.edu.

KEYES, GORDON LINCOLN, history educator; b. Kearney, Ont., Can., Mar. 5, 1920; s. Arthur Beverley and Edna (File) K.; m. Mary Ferguson, June 9, 1945; children: Katherine Mary Keyes Ewing, John Thomas David. BA, U. Toronto (Ont.), 1941, MA, 1942; PhD, Princeton U., 1944. Lectr. in Greek McMaster U., Hamilton, Ont., 1941-42; asst. prof. Birmingham-So. Coll., Ala., 1945-47; faculty Victoria Coll., U. Toronto, 1947—, prof. Greek and Roman history, 1963-83, Nelles prof. ancient history, 1967-83, prof. emeritus, 1983—, also chmn. combined depts. classics, 1967-69, chmn. dept. classics, 1971-75; prin. Victoria Coll., 1976-81. Author: Christian Faith and the Interpretation of History: A Study of St. Augustine's Philosophy of History, 1966. Can. Council sr. research fellow, 1959-60 Mem. Soc. Promotion Roman Studies, Am. Philol. Assn., Classical Assn. Can. Home: 204 #7255 South Ridge Ave Prince George BC V2N 4Z3 Canada

KEYES, JOAN ROSS RAFTER, education educator, author; b. Bklyn., Aug. 12, 1924; d. Joseph W. and Hermia (Ross) Rafter; m. William Ambrose, Apr. 26, 1947 (dec.); children: William, Peter, Dion, Kenzie. BA, Adelphi U., Garden City, N.Y., 1945; MS, Long Island U., Greenvale, N.Y., 1973. Prodn. asst. CBS Radio, N.Y., 1943-44; cub news reporter Bklyn. Daily Eagle, 1945-46; advt. copywriter Gimbel's Dept. Store, N.Y., 1946-47; adj. prof. L.I. U., Greenvale, N.Y., 1984—; tchr. Port Wash. Pub. Schs., N.Y., 1970-94. Lectr., cons. pub. sch. dists. nationwide, 1978—; workshop leader Tchrs. English to Speakers Other Langs. convs., 1981—. Author: Beats, Conversations in Rhythm, 1983, (video program) Now You're Talking, 1987, (computer program) Quick Talk, 1990, Oxford Picture Dictionary for Kids Program, 1998; contbr. articles to ednl. mags. Lectr., catechist Our Lady of Fatima Ch., Port Washington, 1987—; vol. Earthwatch, Mallorca, 1988. Australia/New Zealand ednl. grantee Port Washington Pub. Schs., 1992. Mem. Tchrs. of English to Speakers of Other Languages, Am. Fedn. of Tchrs., N.Y. State United Tchrs., Port Wash. Tchrs. Assn. Republican. Roman Catholic. Avocations: music, painting, travel, tennis, golf. E-mail: joanrosskeyes@aol.com.

KEYS, MARTHA MCDOUGLE, educational administrator; b. Erie, Pa., May 20, 1938; d. Marshall and Helen (Siegel) McD. BA in English, Grove City Coll.; MEd in Counseling, U. Rochester, N.Y.; EdD, Calif. Coast U. Field supr. Calif. Sch. Profl. Psychology, 1969-75, Sonoma (Calif.) State U., 1969-75, U. Santa Clara, Calif., 1969-75; counselor, instr. Stanford (Calif.) U., 1969-75; counselor The Door, N.Y., 1975-76; lang. arts coord. Learning Skills Ctr., Coll. of New Rochelle (N.Y.), 1980-87; assoc. dir. Coun. for Internat. Understanding of Myrin Inst., 1987-89; exec. dir. Moorhead Kennedy Inst., N.Y.C., 1990-96. V.p.Moorhead Kennedy Assocs.; exec. prodr. 360 Degree Prodns., Inc.; pres. Something In Common, Inc., 1996—. Author simulations (with Moorhead Kennedy) Hostage Crisis, 1987, Death of a Dissident, 1989, Sacrilege in Talbotsville, 1990, Fire in the Forest, 1990, Hinomaru, 1992, Metalfabriken, 1993, Grocery Store, 1993, Toxic International, 1993, Atomic, 1994; (films) Cultural Baggage, 1995, Read My Lips, 1996, Sign of the Times, 1998. Home: 15915 84th Dr Jamaica NY 11432-2528

KEYSER, DANIEL, atmospheric scientist, educator; b. Phila., Dec. 21, 1953; s. Gerson and Evelyn (Mokren) K.; m. Wendy Joy Leichter, Oct. 31, 1982; 1 child, Michael Gerson. BS with highest distinction, Pa. State U., 1975, MS, 1977, PhD, 1981. Rsch. meteorologist Naval Postgrad. Sch., Monterey, Calif., 1977-78, Rsch. and Data Systems, Inc., Lanham, Md., 1981-82, NASA/Goddard Space Flight Ctr., Greenbelt, Md., 1982-87; assoc. prof. U. Albany, SUNY, 1987-92, prof., 1992—. Earth and atmospheric scis. evaluation panel for associateship programs NRC, Washington, 1995—2001. Contbr. chpts. to books, articles to profl. jours.; editor Monthly Weather Rev., 1991-93, assoc. editor, 1986-90, 94-97. Recipient Disting. Authorship award NOAA/Environ. Rsch. Labs., 1987. Mem.: Am. Meteorol. Soc. (chair com. on mesoscale processes 1987—90, Clarence Leroy Meisinger award 1989, Editor's award 1989), Royal Meteorol. Soc., Sigma Xi. Office: U Albany SUNY Dept Earth/Atmospheric Scis 1400 Washington Ave Albany NY 12222-0100

KEYT, DAVID, philosophy and classics educator; b. Indianapolis, Feb. 22, 1930; s. Herbert Coe and Hazel Marguerite (Sissman) K.; m. Christine Harwood (Mullikin) June 25, 1975; children by previous marriage: Sarah, Aaron. AB, Kenyon Coll., 1951; MA, Cornell U., 1953, PhD, 1955. AB Kenyon Coll., 1951; instr. dept. philosophy U. Wash., Seattle, 1957-60, asst. prof., 1960-64, assoc. prof., 1964-69, acting chmn. dept. philosophy, 1967-68, 70, 86, prof., 1969—, chmn. dept. philosophy, 1971-78, adj. prof. classics, 1977-79, winter and spring of, 94. Vis. asst. prof. dept. philosophy UCLA, 1962-63; vis. assoc. prof. Cornell U., 1968-69; vis. prof. U. Hong Kong, autumn 1987, Princeton U., autumn 1988, U. Calif., Irvine, autumn 1990; vis. scholar Social Philosophy and Policy Ctr., Bowling Green State U.,autumn, 2001. Co-editor: (with Fred D. Miller Jr.) A Companion to Aristotle's Politics, 1991; Author: Aristotle Politics, Books V, VI, 1999; contbr. articles in field to profl. jour. Served with U.S. Army, 1955-57. Inst. for Rsch. in the Humanities fellow U. Wis., 1966-67; Ctr. for Hellenic Studies fellow, 1974-75; mem. Inst. for Advanced Study, 1983-84. Mem., Am. Philos. Assn., Soc. Ancient Greek Philosophy. Home: 12032 36th Ave NE Seattle WA 98125-5637 Office: U Wash Box 353350 Dept Philosophy Seattle WA 98195-3350 E-mail: keyt@u.washington.edu.

KHABEER, BERYL JEAN, poet, playwright, educator; b. Cleve., Jan. 7, 1952; d. Berry James and Doris Lamerle Thompson. BA, Brandeis U., 1976; MPh, Cleve. State U., 1992. Cert. tchr., Ohio. Tchr., tutor Cleve. Bd. Edn., 1985-88; tchg. asst. Cleve. State U., 1989-92; philosophy instr. Cuyahoga C.C., Cleve., 1993-94; substitute tchr. East Cleveland (Ohio) Bd. Edn., 1994, 97—. Bd. dirs. New Day Press. Author: (poems) The Eighth Level of Awareness; contbr. poems to lit. publs.; author: He Calls My By the Thunder, 1998, (plays) The Way They Play House, 1970, The Souls of Men, 1970. Civil Rights scholar, 1973; recipient Playwright award ACLU, 1970, Outstanding Achievement in Poetry award Nat. Libr. Poetry, 1994. Home: Apt 4 3040 S Moreland Blvd Cleveland OH 44120-2756

KHACHATOURIANS, GEORGE (GHARADAGHI), microbiologist, educator; b. Nov. 21, 1940; s. Sumbat and Mariam (Ghazarian) Khachatourians; m. Lorraine M. McGarth, Oct. 14, 1974; 1 child, Ariane K. BA, Calif. State U., San Francisco, 1966, MA, 1969; PhD, U. B.C., Vancouver, Can., 1971. Postdoctoral fellow Biol. Div. Oak Ridge (Tenn.) Nat. Lab., 1971-73; rsch. assoc. U. Mass. Med. Sch., Worcester, 1973-74; from asst. prof. to assoc. prof. microbiology dept. U. Sask., Saskatoon, Canada, 1974—80, prof., 1980-81, prof. applied microbiology and food sci., 1981—, coord. ag-biotech. human resources tng. and rsch., 1998—, head dept., 2001—, dir. agrl. biotechnology initiative. Mem. task force biotechnology Govt. of Can., Ottawa, Ont., 1980—81; mem. oper. grants panel Can. Agr., 1981—84; mem. biomedical grants panel Sask. Health Rsch., 1988—91; pres. Khachatourians Enterprises Inc.; vis. prof. U. B.C., Vancouver, 1992; advisor Food Biotechnology Commn. Network, Ottawa, 1996—98, Biotechnology Human Resources Coun. Task Force, Ottawa, 1997—99; bd. dirs. Nutraceuticals Network Sask. Sci. Adv., Cell Cultivation Pilot Plant Facility, PhilomBios Inc., Biolin Rsch. Inc., Dumas Enterprises Inc., Mycogen Corp.; founding dir. BioInsecticide Rsch. Labs., Ctr. Molecular Agr. Applied Biotechnology. Co-editor: (book series) Food Biotechnology-Microorganisms, 1995, Applied Mycology and Biotechnology, 2001—; assoc. editor: Can. Jour. Microbiology and Food Biotech.; assoc. editor Agr. and Food Prodn., vol. 1, 2001; assoc. editor: Applied Mycology and Biotech., The Biotechnology Revolution in Global Agriculture, 2001; assoc. editor Agr. and Food Prodn., vol. 1, 2002; sr. editor: Transgenic Plants and Crops, 2002, sr.editor: Fungal Genomics, 2003; contbr. ency. chpts. Bd. dirs. Can. Coll. Microbiologists, Biotechnology Human Resources Coun. Can., Coll. Univ. Program Task Force. Recipient Golden Wheel award, Rotary Internat., 1996; grantee, Nat. Sci. Engring. Rsch. Coun., Ottawa, 1974—92, 2001—, Sask. Agr. Rsch. Found., 1981—85, NRC, 1977—78, Agrl. Devel. Found., Regina, 1985—, Agri-Food Innovation Fund, 1998—. Mem.: AAAS, Sask. Adv. Technol. Assn. (bd. dirs.), Am. Assn. Integrative Studies, Soc. Invertabrate Pathology, Am. Entomol. Soc., Can. Soc. Microbiology, Am. Soc. Microbiology, Am. Chem. Soc. Achievements include patents for aneucleated live E. coli vaccines. Home: 1125 13th St E Saskatoon SK Canada S7H 0C1 Office: U Sask Applied Micro-Food Sci Dept Saskatoon SK Canada S7N 5A8 Fax: 306-966-8898. E-mail: khachatouria@sask.usask.ca.

KHACHIAN, ELISA ARPENIA, artist, educator; b. Worcester, Mass., May 6, 1935; d. Mihran and Hrag (Sohigian) Tufenkjian; m. Richard Khachian, June 16, 1957; children: Carol Garinther, Nancy Quinn, Gary, Sue Hendricks. BS, R.I. Sch. Design, 1957. Art tchr. elem. schs., Concord, Mass., 1958-59; art vol. tchr. Fairfield (Conn.) Sch. Sys., 1972-79; art instr. Darien (Conn.) Arts Coun., 1990-94. Pvt. tchr. and cons., Fairfield, 1989—. Represented in permanent collections Nat. Assn. Women Artists, Zimmerli Mus., Rutgers U., New Haven Paint & Clay Club; group shows include Inheritance Project, Beacon St. Gallery, Chgo., 2002, NAWA Millenium Collection, UN, N.Y., 2002, Silvermine Guild Galleries, 2002; contbr. articles to profl. mags. Vol. Fairfield Sch. Sys., 1972-87. Recipient Charlie Fischer Prize Brush, Palette Club, 1988, Best drawing/painting award Discovery Mus. Barnum Festival, Best Featured Artist, Conn. Women Artists, 2000, Conn. Watercolor Soc. award, 2000; Conn. Commn. for Arts grantee, 2002. Mem.: Conn. Watercolor Soc. (award 1989, 1994, Woman Artist of Yr. 1996, award 2000, 2001, numerous other awards), Silvermine Arts Ctr. (bd. dirs. 1995), Art. Pl. Gallery (sec. 1990—95), Conn. Women Artists (award 2000, 2001, numerous other awards), Am. Assn. Women Artists (numerous awards), Internat. Arts Soc. (assoc. mem., Hon. Menetion 1998), New Haven Paint and Clay Club (merit award 2001). Avocations: grandchildren, gardening, writing, travel, walking, teaching. Home and Office: 213 Hollydale Rd Fairfield CT 06430-2231

KHALIMSKY, EFIM, mathematics and computer science educator; b. Odessa, USSR, June 23, 1938; came to U.S., 1978; s. David Khalimsky and Olga Weizman; m. Elena Merems, May 19, 1962; 1 child, Olga. MS in Math. with honors, Pedagogical Inst., Odessa, 1960; PhD in Math., Pedagogical Inst., Moscow, 1969. Tchr. high sch., Odessa, 1960-66; assoc. prof. Pedagogical Inst., Magnitogorsk, USSR, 1969-72; sr. research scientist Research and Prodn. Inst. for Food Industry, Odessa, 1972-73, Econs. Inst. Acad. Sciences, Odessa, 1973-77; asst. prof. Manhattan Coll., Riverdale, N.Y., 1980-85; assoc. prof. CUNY, 1979-80, Coll. of Staten Island (N.Y.), 1985-89; prof. Cen. State U., Wilberforce, Ohio, 1989—. Author: Ordered Topological Spaces, 1977, (with others) The Planning of Economic and Ecological Research at Sea Basins, 1976, (with others) Economical and Ecological Management of Water Resources, 1976, (with others) Methodological Foundations on Developing MIS System for Water Resources, 1976; area editor Jour. Applied Math. and Simulation, 1987—; contbr. numerous articles to profl. jours. Named Best Scientist USSR Acad. Sciences, 1986. Mem. IEEE, Am. Math. Soc., Assn. Computing Machinery, Soc. Indsl. and Applied Math., Ops. Research Soc. Am. Home: 1260 Brentwood Dr Dayton OH 45406-5713

KHAN, M. WASI, academic administrator; PhD in Edn. Adminstrn., Ind. U. Chancellor East-West U., Chgo. Office: East-West U 816 S Michigan Ave Chicago IL 60605-2185*

KHANZHINA, HELEN P. English educator, translator; b. Perm, Russia, Aug. 28, 1954; came to U.S., 1995; d. Pavel L. and Dina B. Wexler; m. Yevgenii A. Khanzhin, Dec. 4, 1975 (div. Jan. 1984); 1 child, Dmitri. MA in English Lit., U. Perm, 1976; PhD in World Lit., U. St. Petersburg, 1985; assoc. prof. diploma, USSR State Com. Nat. Edn., Moscow, 1991. Asst. then assoc. prof. dept. world lit. U. Perm, 1976-95; lectr. dept. English div. continuing edn. U. Va., Charlottesville, 1996-98. Interpreter Lang. Learning Enterprises, Washington, 1996—; libr. joint state govt. commn. gen. assembly Commonwealth Pa., Harrisburg, 1998—; lectr. divsn. comm., arts and social sciences Harrisburg C.C., 1998—; lectr. Sch. of Humanities Pa. State U., Harrisburg, 1999—2000. Author: The Making of the National Tradition in American Romantic Poetry and William Cullen Bryant's Creative Work, 1987, Genre, Mode and Style in American Romantic Poetry, 1998; editor: Problems of Method and Poetics in World Literature of the Nineteenth and Twentieth Centuries, 1995, 97; contbr. articles to profl. jours. Vis. scholar grantee USIA, 1993-94, Brit. Coun. Beatrice Ward Found., 1990. Mem. MLA, Am. Assn. Tchrs. Slavic and E. European Langs., Pa. Libr. Assn., Spl. Librs. Assn. Avocations: classical music, jazz, ballet, painting, sculpture. Office: Joint State Govt Commn 108 Fin Bldg Harrisburg PA 17120 E-mail: ykhanzhina@legis.state.pa.us.

KHEIRME, SHARON LYNN, elementary education educator; b. Washington, Oct. 27, 1951; d. Bobbie Herbert and Irene Roslyn Belcher; children: John R. Jenkins, Michele L. Sessoms. BS Elem. Edn. cum laude, Carson-Newman Coll., 1973; Masters equivalent/music endorsement, Cen. Wash. U., 1982. Cert. elem. tchr. 1-6, mid. sch., tchr. music K-6. Tchr. kindergarten and music Green Acres Kindergarten, Louisville, 1974-75; elem. grade Grant County Sch. Dist., Corinth, Ky., 1976-78; long-term elem. substitute tchr. Bracken County Sch. Dist., Brooksville, Ky., 1978-79; long-term substitute bilingual-Spanish tchr. Moses Lake (Wash.) Sch. Dist., 1980-81, long-term substitute elem. tchr., 1981-84; elem. tchr. Wicomico County Sch. Dist., Salisbury, Md., 1984-88, tchr. elem. sch. music, 1988—. Music dir. of choirs and congregations/pianist, Ky., Tenn., Wash. and Md., 1971-88; tchr. pvt. piano lessons various communities; tchr. Vacation Bible Sch., Tenn., Wash., Ky. and Md., 1971-88; presenter 1st U.S./Russia Joint Conf. on Edn., Moscow. Organizer/author: Vocabulary and Science Activities (curriculum to accompany textbook), 1982; author: (elem. holiday musical program) Symbols of Holidays, 1995, To Russia with Music, 1997; author/organizer music curriculum, 1994, lessons on multicultural music activities and traditions, 1988—, others; presenter at univ. confs., 2002; singer New Cmty. Singers, 2001-. Mem. Delmar (Md.) elem. Sch. PTA, 1990-; singer Salisbury Choral Soc., 1985-95; adult choir dir. Oak Ridge Bapt. Ch., Salisbury, 1994-95. Del. to 1st U.S./Russia Joint Conf. on Edn., Citizen Ambassador Program, Moscow, 1994. Mem. NEA, Md. State Tchrs. Assn., Wicomico County Edn. Assn., People-to-People Internat., Md. State Music Tchrs. Assn., Music Educators Nat. Conf., Md. Music Educators Assn., Delta Omicron. Avocations: collecting music in various mediums, sewing, cooking, movies, travel. Office: Delmar Elem Sch 811 S 2nd St Delmar MD 21875-1782 E-mail: sennis@wcboe.org.

KHOSLA, VED MITTER, oral and maxillofacial surgeon, educator; b. Nairobi, Kenya, Jan. 13, 1926; s. Jagdish Rai and Tara V. K.; m. Santosh Ved Chabra, Oct. 11, 1952; children: Ashok M., Siddarth M. Student, U. Cambridge, 1945; L.D.S., Edinburgh Dental Hosp. and Sch., 1950, Coll. Dental Surgeons, Sask., Can., 1962. Prof. emeritus, dir. postdoctoral studies in oral surgery Sch. Dentistry U. Calif., San Francisco, 1968—; chief oral surgery San Francisco Gen. Hosp. Lectr. oral surgery U. of Pacific, VA Hosp.; vis. cons. Fresno County Hosp. Dental Clinic.; Mem. planning com., exec. med. com. San Francisco Gen. Hosp. Contbr. articles to profl. jours. Examiner in photography and gardening Boy Scouts Am., 1971-73, Guatemala Clinic, 1972. Granted personal coat of arms by H.M. Queen Elizabeth II, 1959 Fellow Royal Coll. Surgeons (Edinburgh), Internat. Assn. Oral Surgeons, Internat. Coll. Applied Nutrition, Internat. Coll. Dentists, Royal Soc. Health, AAAS, Am. Coll. Dentists; mem. Brit. Assn. Oral Surgeons, Am. Soc. Oral Surgeons, Am. Dental Soc. Anesthesiology, Am. Acad. Dental Radiology, Omicron Kappa Upsilon. Clubs: Masons. Home: 1525 Lakeview Dr Hillsborough CA 94010-7330 Office: U Calif Sch Dentistry Oral Surgery Div 3D Parnassus Ave San Francisco CA 94117-4342

KHOURI, FRED JOHN, political science educator; b. Cranford, N.J., Aug. 15, 1916; s. Peter and Mary (Rizk) K.; m. Catherine McLean, June 24, 1964. Student, Union Jr. Coll., Roselle, N.J., 1934-36; BA, Columbia U., 1938, MA, 1939, PhD, 1953. Instr. Brownsville Jr. Coll. and High Sch., Tex., 1939-40; instr. polit. sci. U. Tenn., 1946-47, U. Conn., 1947-50; asst. prof. Villanova U., Pa., 1951-61, prof., 1964-86, prof. emeritus, from 1986. Vis. prof. Am. U. of Beirut, Lebanon, 1961-64; mem. Brookings Instn. Middle East Study Group, 1975-76; sr. fellow Middle East Ctr U. Pa., 1978-79, 80-81; lectr. in field Author: The Arab States and the UN, 1954, The Arab Israeli Dilemma, 1968, 2d edit., 1976, 3d edit., 1985; assoc. editor: Jour. South Asian and Middle Eastern Studies; contbr. to books and profl. jours. Served with U.S. Army, 1941-45. Decorated Order of Cedars Lebanon Fellow Middle East Studies Assn.; mem. Middle East Inst., Am. Polit. Sci. Assn., Am. Soc. Internat. Law, Am. Coun. for Study Islamic Socs., UN Assn. of U.S.A., World Affairs Coun., Phi Kappa Phi. Democrat. Roman Catholic. Home: Wynnewood, Pa. Died Jan. 28, 2001.

KHOURY, BERNARD V. educational administrator; Asst. dean Grad. Studies and Rsch. U. Md.; assoc. exec. sec. Assn. Am. U.; exec. dir. Grad. Record Examinations Program Ednl. Testing Svc.; assoc. v.p. Academic Affairs U. Md. Sys., assoc. vice chancellor Policy and Planning; exec. officer Am. Assn. Physics Tchrs., 1990—. Office: Am Assn Physics Tchrs One Physics Ellipse College Park MD 20740-3845*

KHOURY, PHILIP S. academic administrator; b. Washington, D.C., Oct. 15, 1949; s. Shukry E. and Angela Mansur (Jurdak) K.; m. Mary Christina Wilson, Aug. 28, 1980. BA with hons., Trinity Coll., 1971; PhD, Harvard U., 1980. Asst. prof. MIT, Cambridge, Mass., 1981-84; assoc. prof. Mass. Inst. Tech., Cambridge, Mass., 1984-90, prof., 1990—, assoc. dean Sch. Humanities, Arts, and Social Sci., 1987-90, acting dean, 1990-91, dean, 1991—, Kenan Sahin dean, 2002—, 2002—. Mem. editl. bd. Jour. Interdisciplinary History, 1987—, Hist. Abstracts, 1990—, The Beirut Rev., 1991-93. Author: Urban Notables and Arab Nationalism, 1983, Syria and the French Mandate, 1987; co-editor Tribes and State Formation in the Middle East, 1990, The Modern Middle East: A Reader, 1993, 2nd ed. 2003, Recovering Beirut: Urban Design and Post-war Reconstruction, 1993. Trustee Am. U. Beirut, 1997—, Toynbee Prize Found., 1998—, World Peace Found., 1999—, Trinity Coll., 2000—; dir. Harvard Coop. Soc., 1998—. Fellow Am. Acad. of Arts Scis., 2002-. Thomas J. Watson fellow Watson Found., 1971-72; Fulbright scholar, 1976-77; Post-Doctoral Social Sci. Rsch. Coun., 1983-84; Mellon fellow Aspen Inst., 1984-85; Class of 1922 Career Devel. Professorship, MIT, 1984-86. Mem. AAAS, Am. Hist. Assn. (George Louis Beer Prize 1987), Middle East Studies Assn. (pres. 1998, dir. 1990-92, 97-2000), Brit. Soc. for Middle East Studies; Pi Gamma Mu. Avocation: tennis. Office: MIT Office Dean Sch Hum/Arts/Social Scis 77 Massachusetts Ave Cambridge MA 02139-4307 E-mail: khoury@mit.edu.

KHOUZAM, HANI RAOUL, psychiatrist, physician, educator; b. Heliopolis, Egypt, June 5, 1950; came to U.S., 1980; s. Raoul Aniss Khouzam and Jeannette (Guindi) Roufael; m. Lynda Margaret Dickerson, Nov. 20, 1982; children: Andrea Adahlia, Andrew Amaris, Adam Yurie Alexander. MB BCh, Faculty Medicine Cairo, Egypt, 1977; MPH, Tulane U., 1981. Diplomate Am. Bd. Psychiatry and Neurology with spl. certification in Geriatric Psychiatry; cert. ednl. commn. fgn. med. grads. Med. house officer Cairo U. Teaching Hosps., 1978-79; psychiatrist Shaalan M.D., Inc., Cairo, 1979-80; rsch. scholar Okla. Med. Rsch. Found., Oklahoma City, 1982-83; resident in psychiatry U. Okla. Health Scis. Ctr., Oklahoma City, 1983-87; staff psychiatrist Okla. County Crisis Intervention Ctr., Oklahoma City, 1987-90; med. dir., inpatient psychiatry unit VA Med. Ctr., Oklahoma City, 1990-92, dir. consultation liaison psychiatry Manchester, NH, 1992—95; asst. prof. psychiatry dept. psychiatry and behavioral scis. Coll. Medicine U. Okla., Oklahoma City, 1990—92; staff psychiatrist VA Med. Ctr., N.H., 1992-2000, VA Ctrl. Calif. Health Care Sys., Fresno, Calif., 2000—, med, dir. chem. dependency treatment program, 2000—. Adj. asst. prof. psychiatry Dartmouth Med. Sch., Lebanon, NH, 1992—95, adj. assoc. prof. psychiatry, 1995—2000; clin. instr. in medicine Harvard Med. Sch., Boston, 1994—; assoc. clin. prof. psychiatry U. Calif. San Francisco Med. Edn. Program, Fresno, 2001—. Author: Emergency Psychiatric Interventions, 1988; contbr. to profl. jours. Hubert H. Humphrey fellow in pub. health, USIA, New Orleans, 1980-81. Fellow Egyptian Sci. Soc., Am. Psychiatric Assn.; mem. Egyptian Med. Assn., N.H. Psychiatric Soc. Coptic Catholic Christian. Avocations: reading, writing, bible study, music, stamp collecting. Home: 7377 N Carruth Ave Fresno CA 93711-0513 Office: VA Ctrl Calif Health Care Sys Dept Psychiatry 2615 E Clinton Ave Fresno CA 93703

KHOZEIMEH, ISSA, electrical engineer, educator; b. Tehran, Iran, Dec. 25, 1939; came to U.S., 1959; s. Ismail and Zohreh (Alam) K.; m. Nahid Khozeimeh; children: Lili, Nini. BSEE, George Washington U., Washington, 1966; MSEE, 1973, D in Engring., 1984, DSc in Engring. Mgmt., 1993. Registered profl. engr. Jr. engr. Potomac Electric Power Co., Washington, 1967-68; substation engr., 1968-73; design standrads engr., 1973-79; sr. engr. substation design, 1979-80; dept. head, chief elec. engr. David Volkert and Assocs., Bethesda, Md., 1980-88; mgr. Util. Svcs. Metro. Washington Airports Auth. Dulles Internat. Airport, 1988—; prof. engring. and mgmt. U. Md., Balt., 1998—; prof. mgmt. U. Balt., 1999—. Pres. Internat. Mktg. and Consulting Corp., Washington, 1980-82; v.p. Horizon Internat., Washington, 1982-88; pres. Forum Internat. Glen Echo, Md., 1988—; prof. U. Md., Balt., 1998—, U. Balt., 1999—. Author: An Automated Maintenance Management System for International Airports, 1993; contbr. articles to profl. jours. Recipient Sch. of Engring Svcs. award, 1976, Gen. Alumni Assn. Svc. award, 1971, George Washington U., 1976, Engr. Coun. Cert. of Appreciation, 1984, 85, Disting. Svc. award 1986, Disting. Alumni Svc. award George Washington U. Alumni Assn., 1998, Tech. Forum Leadership award, 1999, Outstanding Profl Efforts award Met. Washington Airport Authority, 2000. Mem.: NSPE, IEEE (sr.), Washington Soc. Engrs., Md. Soc. Prof. Engrs. (pres. 1995—96, 2002—, Disting. Sr. Engr. award 1997), Instrument Soc. Am. Republican. Moslem. Avocations: water skiing, snow skiing, hiking, reading, publishing, lecturing, travel. Home: PO Box 557 Glen Echo MD 20812-0557 Office: Metro Washington Airports Authority Dulles Internat Airport PO Box 17045 Washington DC 20041-7045 E-mail: khozeimeh@hotmail.com., issa.khozeimeh@mwaa.com.

KHURI, FADLO RAJA, oncologist, educator; b. Boston, Sept. 13, 1963; s. Raja Najib and Soumaya Makdisi Khuri; m. Lamya Raja Tannous, June 15, 1991; children: Raja, Layla, Rayya. Student, Am. U. of Beirut, 1982; BS, Yale U., 1985; MD, Columbia U., 1989. Cert. bd. cert. diplomate. Intern in internal medicine Boston City Hosp., Boston U., 1989—90; resident Boston City Hosp., 1990—92; fellow in hematology and med. oncology Tufts-New Eng. Med. Ctr., Boston, 1992—95; instr. medicine U. Tex. M.D. Anderson Cancer Ctr., Houston, 1995—96, asst. prof., 1996—2001, assoc. prof., 2001—02; assoc. dir. clin. and translational rsch. Winship Cancer Inst., Emory U., Atlanta, 2002—; Blomeyer prof. hematology, oncology, medicine, pharmacology and otolarngology. 1st author: clin. investigation Nature Medicine, 2000, Journal of the National Cancer Institute, 1997, Journal of Clinical Oncology, 2000. Recipient Career Devel. award, Am. Cancer Soc., 1996; scholar R.G. Haddad scholar, 1985—89; funding, NIH/Dept. of Def., 1996—. Mem.: Radiation Therapy Oncology Group (chmn. chemoprevention com. 1998—2002), Am. Soc. for Clin. Oncology, Am. Assn. for Cancer Rsch. Office: Emory U Winship Cancer Inst Hematology and Oncology Ste B4100 1365 Clifton Rd Atlanta GA 30322 Office Fax: 404-778-5016. E-mail: fadlo_khuri@emoryhealthcare.org.

KIBRICK, ANNE, retired nursing educator and university dean; b. Palmer, Mass., June 1, 1919; d. Martin and Christine (Grigas) Karlon; m. Sidney Kibrick, June 16, 1949; children: Joan, John. RN, Worcester (Mass.) Hahnemann Hosp., 1941; BS, Boston U., 1945; MA, Columbia Tchrs. Coll., 1948; EdD, Harvard U., 1958; LHD (hon.), St. Joseph's Coll., Windham, Maine, 1973. Asst. edn. dir. Cushing VA Hosp., Framingham, Mass., 1948—49; asst. prof. nursing Simmons Coll., Boston, 1949—55; dir. grad. div. Boston U. Sch. Nursing, 1958—63, dean, 1963—68, prof., 1968—70; chmn. dept. nursing Boston Coll. Grad. Sch. Arts and Sci., 1970—74; founding chmn. Sch. Nursing Boston State Coll., 1974—82; founding dean Sch. Nursing U. Mass., Boston, 1974—88, prof., 1988—93, prof. emeritus, 1993—. Mem. editl. bd. Mass. Jour. Cmty. Health. Mem. Brookline Town Meeting, 1995—2000; mem. nat. adv. bd. Hadassah Nurses Coun., 1996—; bd. dirs. Brookline Mental Health Assn., Met. chpt. ARC, Children's Ctr. Brookline and Greater Boston, Inc., 1984—89, Boston Health Care for Homeless, 1988—90, Landy-Kaplan Nurses Coun., 1992—, treas., 1994—96. Named to, Nursing Edn. Alumni Assn. Tchr.'s Coll., Columbia U. Hall of Fame, 1999. Fellow: Am. Acad. Nursing; mem.: Inst. of Medicine of NAS, Mass. Blueprint 2000, Mass. Orgn. Elder Ams. (bd. dirs. 1988—2000), Mass. Med. Soc. (postgrad. med. inst. 1983—96, bd. dirs. 1983—96, exec. com. 1989—96), Nat. Acads. of Practice, Mass. Nurses Found. (v.p. 1983—86), AIDS Internat. Info. Found. (founding mem. 1985), Mass. Nurses Assn. (dir. 1982—86, charter inductee to Hall of Fame 2000), Nat. Mass. League Nursing (pres. 1971—73), ANA, Pi Lambda Theta, Sigma Theta Tau. Home: # 312 130 Seminary Ave Auburndale MA 02466

KICKISH, MARGARET ELIZABETH, elementary school educator; b. Atlantic City, N.J., Nov. 30, 1949; d. James Bernard and Margaret Elizabeth (Egan) Parlett; m. Robert Anthony Kickish, June 30, 1973; children: Eileen, Kathleen, Robert Jr. BS, Franciscan U., 1971; MEd, Coll. N.J., 1977. Cert. elem. tchr., learning disabilities tchr. cons. Tchr. Our Lady Star of the Sea Sch., Atlantic City, 1971-75, Weymouth Twp. Elem. Sch., Dorothy, NJ, 1975-89; curriculum coord. Port Republic (N.J.) Sch., 1990-91; tchr. Brigantine (N.J.) Bd. Edn., 1991-94, supr. curriculum and instrn., 1995—. Cognetics coach St. Joseph Sch., Somers Point, NJ, 1989—. Treas. PTA, Somers Point, 1987—89, pres., 1989—90; asst. coach Somers Point Softball Assn., 1991—; rec. sec. Parents Orgn. Mainland Regional HS, 2001—; mem. choir St. Joseph Ch., Somers Point, 1985—. Mem.: ASCD, NEA, AAUW, Assn. Learning Cons., Coun. Exceptional Children, Prins. and Suprs. Assn., N.J. Edn. Assn., S. Jersey Irish Cultural Soc., Seashore Mother of Twins Club, Phi Delta Kappa, Delta Zeta, Kappa Delta Pi. Democrat. Roman Catholic. Avocations: swimming, bicycling, reading, travel, crafts. Home: 526 9th St Somers Point NJ 08244-1458 Office: Brigantine Bd of Edn 301 E Evans Blvd Brigantine NJ 08203-3424 E-mail: mskick@aol.com.

KIDD, JAMES MARION, III, allergist, immunologist, naturalist, educator; b. Baton Rouge, Dec. 15, 1950; s. James Marion Jr. and Germaine Elizabeth (Hunt) K.; children: Mackenzie Elizabeth, Katherine Anne. MD, La. State U., 1976. Diplomate Am. Bd. Internal Medicine, Am. Bd. Allergy and Immunology; lic. physician, La., Fla., Wis. Resident physician La. State U. Sch. Medicine, New Orleans, 1977—79; rsch. fellow Med. Coll. Wis., Milw., 1980-82; pvt. practice in allergy and immunology Allergy, Asthma, and Immunology Clinic, Baton Rouge, 1982—; clin. asst., prof. medicine La. Sch. Medicine, New Orleans, 1982—; clin. asst., prof. community medicine and pub. health Tulane U. Sch. Medicine, New Orleans, 1992—2003. Dir. Baton Rouge Pollen Counting Sta., Nat. Allergy Bur. Fellow Am. Coll. Physicians, Am. Acad. Pediat., Am. Acad. Allergy and Immunology, Royal Soc. of Medicine (U.K.), La. Allergy Soc. (pres. 1989-90, exec. sec.-treas. 1992-96), Baton Rouge Allergy Soc. (pres. 1990-95), Rotary (Paul Harris fellow). Office: James M Kidd III MD 8017 Picardy Ave Baton Rouge LA 70809-3538 Fax: 225-768-7642. E-mail: drjmkidd3@aol.com.

KIDDA, MICHAEL LAMONT, JR., psychologist, educator; b. Jackson, Miss., May 24, 1945; s. Michael Lamont and Annie Laurie (McKeithen) K.; m. Ellen Gordon, Aug. 23, 1977; children: Patrick Gordon, John McKeithen. BA in English, Centenary Coll., Shreveport, La., 1969; MDiv, U. South, Sewanee, Tenn., 1972; MS in Social Psychology, U. Ga., 1984, PhD in Social Psychology, 1987. Youth cons. Cathedral of St. Philip, Atlanta, 1974-76; counselor All Saints' Sch., Vicksburg, Miss., 1977-79; coord. of assessment J.C. Smith U., Charlotte, N.C., 1989-94, assoc. prof. psychology, 1985—, dept. head, 1987—89, 1999—2002. Coord. Grad. Student Conf./Personality and Social Psychology, Athens, 1981; bd. trustees N.E. Ga. Area Cmty. Resource Coun., Athens, 1980—83, v.p., 1982, tech. adminstrn., 84; data analysis cons., Athens, 1980—83; corp. sec. Kidda Enterprises, 1999—, Carolina Cupboard, 2002—; pres. Higher Edn. Evaluation and Devel., 2002—; presenter in field. Contbr. articles to profl. jours. and to On-line and CD-Rom data bases; author newsletter ETS Higher Edn. Assessment, 1993. Com. mem. cub scouts pack 19 Boy Scouts Am., Huntersville, NC, 1994—97; com. mem. Lions Club, Huntersville, 1997—99, Davidson, 1999—2002, membership com., 2000—01, Hickory Grove, 2003—; mem. adv. bd. Washington Heights Project Nat. Children's Def. Fund, Charlotte, 1994; chair evaluation com. Fighting Back Against Drugs, Charlotte, 1992—94; bd. dirs. Lions Svcs. for the Blind, Charlotte, 1999—, pers. com., 2002—. Recipient Nat. Retention Excellence award Noel-Levitz Ctrs., Cross of Nails award St. Michael's Cathedral, Coventry, Eng., cert. of appreciation Washington Hts. Youth Svcs. Acad., 1997; Retention and Performance grantee Pew Charitable Trusts, 1994, Equipment grantee AT&T Found., 1991, grantee APA, 1996, United Negro Coll. Fund, 1996; Inst. Non-Traditional Ministries rsch. fellow, 1994-99. Mem. Am. Statis. Assn., Soc. Southeastern Social Psychologists, Lions, Sigma Xi (site coord. celebration of undergrad. rsch. 1999), Sigma Tau Delta, Psi Chi (chpt. adviser 2001—). Achievements include empirical demonstration of superiority of college-level inquiry curriculum over remediation in post-secondary education; research on effects of social control on prosocial behavior; research of causal attribution on evaluation of people with disabilities; research on effects of accepting non-reciprocal aid; devel. of relationship mapping as a curriculum assessment tool. Office: Johnson C Smith Univ 100 Beatties Ford Rd Charlotte NC 28216-5398 E-mail: mkidda@jcsu.edu.

KIDWELL, GEORGIA BRENNER, elementary education educator; b. Madison, Wis., Aug. 20, 1932; d. Clarence E. and Loraine R. (Brenner) Tipton; m. John C. Kidwell, Aug. 10, 1954; children: Jeffrey, Susan. BS in Edn., U. Kans., 1953; MA in Edn., Tex. Woman's U., 1989; student, Beloit Coll., 1949-51. Cert. tchr., Tex. Elem. tchr. Kansas City (Mo.) Sch. Dist., 1953-54, Lawrence (Kans.) Sch. Dist., 1954-56; substitute tchr. Hurst-Euless Bedford Ind. Sch. Dist., Bedford, Tex., 1969-76, 80-85, elem. tchr., 1985—2002; ret., 2002. Pres. LWV Tarrant County, Ft. Worth, 1979-80; voters svc. dir. LWV Tex., Ft. Worth, 1980-84; mem. Circle T coun. Girl Scouts U.S.; leadership Ft. Worth United Way. Recipient Appreciation award for svc. Circle T. Girl Scouts U.S.A., Ft. Worth, 1978, Thanks Badge, Girl Scouts U.S.A., 1993. Mem. AAUW (pres. Hurst br. 1969-71), Pi Lambda Theta (treas. 1988—), Delta Kappa Gamma, Kappa Alpha Theta. Democrat. Episcopalian. Avocations: music, reading, handwork, sewing. Home: 308 Brookview Dr Hurst TX 76054-3506

KIEBALA, SUSAN MARIE, accounting and management educator; b. Bay City, Mich., Aug. 22, 1952; d. Edwin Edward and Ruth May (Jarvela) Bukowski; children: Jems, Adam, Kara. BS, Ferris State Coll., 1973; MBA, Western Mich. U., 1977. Acct. Consumers Power Co., Jackson, Mich., 1973-76, Eaton Corp., Marshall, Mich., 1976-78; instr. acctg. Kellogg Community Coll., Battle Creek, Mich., 1978-89; asst. prof. Olivet (Mich.) Coll., 1989—, chair Dept. Bus. Adminstrn. and Econs., 1992—; dir. Olivet (Mich.) Coll. Evening Program, 1992-94. Adj. instr. Davenport Coll., Kalamazoo, 1989-90. Coord. Youth Soccer League, Marshall, 1986—; sec./treas. Marshall Soccer Boosters, 1987-88; chmn. Marshall Citizens for Quality Schs., 1988; treas. Com. for Quality Schs., 1989; co-chmn. Fin. Com. Millage, 1989; neighborhood capt. Am. Cancer Soc., 1987—; treas. St. Joseph's Guild of St. Mary's Ch., Marshall, 1989-91. Recipient Gold Apple award Marshall Pub. Schs., 1988. Mem. Am. Acctg. Assn., Inst. Mgmt. Acct. Avocations: reading, golf, racquetball. Home: 527 Sherman Dr Marshall MI 49068-9661 Office: Olivet Coll 407F Mott Olivet MI 49076

KIEFER, JACQUELINE LORRAINE, special education educator, consultant; b. Dayton, Ohio, Nov. 6, 1947; d. Elmer Louis Kiefer and Lorraine (Siefert) K. BS in Educ., U. of Dayton, 1969; MED in Curr and Super., Wright STate U., 1978; MED, Wright State U., 1987. Sp. edn. tchr. Milton

Union Village Sch., West Milton, Ohio, 1969-88; spl. edn. cons. Medina (Ohio) County Bd. Edn., 1988—. Supr. part-time Amateur Trap Shooting Assn., Vandalia, Ohio, 1969-93. Author: Packets of Activities - Kids N Summer, math Box of Activities, Math Box. Chairperson Disaster Services, Am. Nat. Red Cross, Dayton, Ohio, Fund raiser, Cancer Soc., Heart Assn., Dayton; mem. Women in Ednl. Leadership; vol. Miami Valley Hosp., Ohio Pub. Images, Miami Valley Spl. Edn. Regional Resource Ct. Recipient Disting. Service award, Spl. Olympics, Ohio, Cert. of Merit, Milton Union Sch., Council of Exceptional Children. Mem. Ohio Assn. Supr., N.E. Ohio Suprs. Assn., Coun. Exceptional Children, Assn. Curriculum Supervision, Lizotte Reading Coun., Assn. Curiculum Devel., Dayton Ski Club, Kappa Delta Pi, Phi Delta Kappa. Avocations: skiing, tennis, crafts, reading, travel. Home: 10 W Sherry Dr Trotwood OH 45426-3522

KIEFFER, CONNIE WELCH, academic administrator; b. Portland, Oreg., July 31, 1944; d. Lorenz Carl and Lillian A. (Grassel) Plog; m. David B. Welch, Dec. 30, 1966 (div. Dec. 1974); 1 child, Jason Michael Welch; m. Edward L. Kieffer, Aug. 5, 1978. BS, Oreg. State U., 1967; MA, NYU, 1974; EdD, Nat.-Louis U., 1996. Home econs. faculty New Trier H.S., Winnetka, Ill., 1968-72; mem. interior design faculty Marymount Coll., Tarrytown, N.Y., 1972-73; mem. home econs. faculty Highland Park (Ill.) H.S., 1974-83, chair dept. applied arts, 1983-86, chair fine and applied arts, 1986—2001; chair dept. applied arts Deerfield (Ill.) H.S., 1983-86, summer sch. prin., 1984-87; asst. prof. secondary edn. Nat. Louis U., Wheeling, Ill., 2001—. Bd. dirs. Ctr. for New Deal Studies, Roosevelt U., Chgo. Contbr. articles to profl. jours.; co-author (with Arnie Barbknecht): Peer Coaching: The Learning Team Approach, 2001; author (website): Learning Through Historic Art and Architecture, 2003. Bd. dirs. Jubilate Children's Choir, Winnetka, 1994—, Highland Pk. Hist. Soc., 2002—; elder 1st Presbyn. Ch., Deerfield, 1997—; founding mem. Nat. New Deal Preservation Assn., treas., exec. dir. Midwest chpt.; active Nat. Louis U. Alumni Bd. Dirs. Mem. ASCD, Am. Edn. Rsch. Assn., Nat. Coun. for the Social Studies, Nat. Art Edn. Assn., Nat. Staff Devel. Coun., Delta Kappa Gamma. Avocation: architectural history. Home: 1204 Dartmouth Ln Deerfield IL 60015-4130 Office: Nat Louis U Wheeling 1000 Capitol Dr Wheeling IL 60090 E-mail: ckieffer@nl.edu.

KIEHLBAUCH, SHERYL LYNN, elementary education educator; b. Las Vegas, Apr. 6, 1950; d. William Bert and Grace (Homan) Berk; m. John Howard Kiehlbauch, Aug. 19, 1972; children: John Karl, Jason Kyle. BS, U. Nev., Las Vegas, 1972; MEd, U. Nev., 1980. Cert. tchr. K-8, reading K-12, reading improvement tchr., computer coord., literacy specialist, adminstr. Data processing specialist First Nat. Bank of Nev., Las Vegas; elem. tchr. Clark County Sch. dist., Las Vegas. Named Elem. Computer Using Tchr. of the Yr., Nev., 1989, Excellence in Edn. Program participant; recipient Presdl. Excellence in Elem. Sci. Edn. State award Nev., 1991. Mem. PTA, Computer Using Educators So. Nev. (pres.), Southern. Nev. Sci. Tchrs. Assn., Nev. Math. Coun., Nev. State Sci. Tchrs. Assn. (pres. 1994, dist. dir., 1998—), Delta Kappa Gamma (v.p.), Phi Delta Kappa (pres.), others.

KIELBORN, TERRIE LEIGH, secondary education educator; b. Miami, Fla., Sept. 25, 1955; d. Gerald and Dolores Eloise (Adams) Carter; m. Gerald Albert Kielborn, Mar. 31, 1979; children: Carl Gerald, Katie Leigh, Sarah Beth. BA in Edn., Fla. Atlantic U., 1977; MA with honors, U. South Fla., 1986; PhD in Sci. Edn., Fla. State U. Cert. mid. sch. tchr., Ga. 8th grade sci. tchr. S. Paulding (Ga.) Mid. Sch. Presenter in field. Co-editor SERVE Monograph: Meaningful Science: Teachers Doing Inquiry and Teaching Science, 1999, SERVE Monograph: Georgia Goes Global: Monitoring the Global Environment through Authentic Science, 2002; rschr., writer Ga. AG in the Classroom newsletter; textbook reviewer; contbr. articles to profl. jours. Chair bd. dirs. environ. edn. com. Marion County Audubon Soc., 1991, pres., 1992-93; mem. mid. sch. sci. curriculum com. Marion County, 1994-98, chair sch. adv. coun. 1993-95. Named Tchr. of Yr., 1979, 92, 94; Phi Theta Kappa scholar, 1975, Minigrants, 1990-99, Profl. Enhancement Program grantee, 1989-96, PTO grantee, Dreams grantee, 1995, Tech. grantee, 1993-95, Marion County Soil and Conservation grantee, Fla. Growers and Nurseryman grantee, Dow Chem. grantee, 1998-99, Fla. Sci. Inst. grantee, 1999, P-16 Collaboration grantee, 2000, SERVE grantee, 2001, DCSS PET grantee, 2001; recipient NEWEST award, 1991, Sci. Grasp award Upjohn, 1992, Golden Apple award Marion County, 1992, Fla. Explorer's! Workshop award, 1995-98, Tchr. and Rschr. Update Experience (TRUE) Program award, 1997, Fla. Through a Global Lens award, Tchr. Quest Program award, 1998, Fla. Mid. Sch. Sci. Tchr. of Yr., 1997, Target Tchr. Scholarship award, 1999, Pyramid Rsch. award, 2001, awardee Environ. Health Partnership Workshop for Tchrs., 2001; nominated for presdl. award for excellence in sci., 1991, 94, 95, 96, 97, 98; Ag in the Classroom Best Idea award, 1996, Delta Exn. Outstanding Science Activity award, 1993, others; field rsch. on exotic grass of a state park, 1996. Mem. NSTA (presenter nat. conf. 1992, 95, 96, 2000, 02, S.E. regional conf. 1993, local leader 1994), Nat. Assn. Rsch. in Sci. Tchg. (nat. conf. presenter 1996, 97), Nat. Assn. Earth Sci. Tchrs., Assn. Edn. Tchg. Scis., Fla. Assn. Earth Sci. Tchrs., Fla. Coun. Tchrs. Math. (regional bd. dirs. 1992-94, presenter state conf. 1992, 93), Fla. Assn. Sci. Tchrs. (presenter state conf. 1996, 97, 98, regional dir. Region III 1995-99), Ga. Sci. Tchrs. Assn. (coll. rep., bd. dirs. 2001—, chair publicity com.), League Environ. Educators Fla., Marion Edn. Assn.-Fla. Tchrs. Profession (rep. 1986-87), Fla. Native Plant Soc. (co-v.p. Big Scrub 1992), Nat. Mid. Level Sci. Tchrs. Assn., Carroll County Assn. Gifted Children (bd. rep. 2000-02), Tchrs. Involved in Maths. Edn., Alpha Delta Kappa (sgt.-at-arms 1990-91, v.p. 1992-94), Phi Delta Kappa (rsch. rep. 1997-99, pres. W. Ga. chpt. 2001-02), Phi Lambda Theta. Office: State Univ West Ga Middle Sch Secondary Sci Carrollton GA 30118-0001

KIERNAN, DEIRDRE, secondary education educator; b. Middletown, N.Y., Nov. 15, 1946; d. Charles James and Kathleen Patricia (O'Carolan) Klingman; m. Paul Kiernan, Sept. 21, 1968 (div. 1984); children: Siobhan, Caitlin, Moira. AA, Orange County C.C., 1980; BS in Edn., SUNY, New Paltz, 1984, postgrad, 1984—. Tchr. English John S. Burke High Sch., Goshen, N.Y., 1984-89; lead tchr. English Orange-Ulster BOCES, Goshen, 1989—. Office: Orange-Ulster BOCES Gibson Rd Goshen NY 10924

KIESLER, CHARLES ADOLPHUS, psychologist, academic administrator; b. St. Louis, Aug. 14, 1934; m. Teru Morton, Feb. 28, 1987; 1 child, Hugo; children from previous marriage: Tina, Thomas, Eric, Kevin. BA, Mich. State U., 1958, MA, 1960; PhD (NIMH fellow), Stanford U., 1963; D (hon.), Lucian Blaga U., Romania, 1995. Asst. prof. psychology Ohio State U., Columbus, 1963-64, Yale U., New Haven, 1964-66, assoc. prof., 1966-70; prof., chmn. psychology U. Kans., Lawrence, 1970-75; exec. officer Am. Psychol. Assn., Washington, 1975-79; Walter Van Dyke Bingham prof. psychology Carnegie Mellon U., Pitts., 1979-85, head psychology, 1980-83, acting dean, 1981-82, dean Coll. Humanities and Social Scis., 1983-85; provost Vanderbilt U., 1985-92; chancellor U. Mo., Columbia, 1992-96, Weil Disting. prof. health svcs. mgmt., 1996-98; prof., sr. advisor San Diego State U., 1998-99. Pres., CEO, Virtual Univ. Internat., 1996-97. Author: (with B.E. Collins and N. Miller) Attitude Change: A Critical Analysis of Theoretical Approaches, 1969, (with S.B. Kiesler) Conformity, 1969, The Psychology of Commitment: Experiments Linking Behavior to Belief, 1971, (with N. Cummings and G. VandenBos) Psychology and National Health Insurance: A Sourcebook, 1979, (with A.E. Sibulkin) Mental Hospitalization: Myths and Facts About a National Crisis, 1987, (with C. Simpkins) The Unnoticed Majority: Psychiatric inpatient care in general hospitals, 1993. Served with Security Service USAF, 1952-56. Recipient Disting. Alumnus award Mich. State U., 1987, Gunnar Myrdal award for Evaluation Practice Am. Evaluation Assn., 1989. Fellow AAAS, APA (Distng. Contbr. to Rsch. in Pub. Policy award 1989), Am. Psychol. Soc. (founding past pres. 1988-90); mem. AAUP, Inst. of Medicine of Nat. Acad. Scis., Sigma Xi, Psi Chi, Phi Kappa Phi. Home and Office: 3427 Mount Laurence Dr San Diego CA 92117-5649 E-mail: ckiesler@san.rr.com.

KIESLICH, ANITA FRANCES, school system administrator; b. St. Albans, Vt., July 8, 1941; d. George E. and Doris E. (Rogers) Hilliker; m. Karl V. Kieslich, May 16, 1964; children: Karin, Karl John, Kathleen, Kevin. BEd, Johnson State Coll., 1964; MA, Wayne State U., 1974; specialist degree in reading, U. S.C., 1985. Cert. tchr., adminstr., counselor S.C. Tchr. Vt. Pub. Schs., Burlington, 1964, Georgia, 1967-68; sub. tchr. DOD Schs., Germany, 1965-67, Colo. Pub. Schs., Denver, 1968-72; tchr. reading DOD Schs., Turkey, 1972-75; guidance counselor, tchr. reading Millwood Elem. Sch., Sumter, S.C., 1975-89; asst. prin. Lemira Elem. Sch., Sumter, 1989-94; coord. parenting & extended day programs Sch. Dist. #17, Sumter, 1994-95, dir. early head start and parenting, 1995—; adj. instr. U. S.C., Sumter, 1990-91, Carolina Cent. Coll., Sumter, 1992—. Presenter S.C. Palmetto's Tchrs. Assn., Charleston, 1992; grant reader DOE Washington, 1992; cons. on grants Sumter Dist. 17 Sch., 1992—; Parent As Tchr. educator, 1994; Motheread facilator, 1995. Author: Teaching Reading Through Bulletin Boards, 1989; host for daily T.V. show. Adv. bd. Boys and Girls Club, Sumter, 1989-94; chmn. edn. Bicentennial Women's Club, Sumter, 1987-90; tchr. St. Jude's Cath. Ch., Sumter, 1988-95; adv. bd. RSVP, Sumter, 1991—. Mem. S.C. Assn. Sch. Administrs., S.C. Assn. Elem. and Mid. Sch. Prins. (S.C. Disting. Asst. Principal of Yr. 1993), S.C. Assn. for Elem. Prins., Pee Dee Reading Assn., S.C. Assn. for Counseling and Devel., S.C. Network for Women Adminstrs. in Edn., S.C. Assn. for the Edn. of Young Children, Nat. Head Start Assn., S.C. Assn. for School Age Care (comm. chmn.), Leadership Inst. for Child Care, Nat. Assn. for Early Young Child, Phi Delta Kappa, Kappa Delta Epsilon (charter pres. 1962), Delta Kappa Gamma. Avocations: reading, crafts, drawing. Home: 22 Conyers St Sumter SC 29150-3202

KIGER, ROBERT WILLIAM, botanist, science historian, educator; b. Washington, Oct. 4, 1940; s. William Joseph and Marian (Calvert) K.; m. Suellen Montgomery, June 11, 1968; children: David M., James R. AA with honors, Montgomery Jr. Coll., 1964; BA in Spanish with Social Scis. minor, Tulane U., 1966; MA in History, U. Md., 1971, PhD in Botany, 1972. Tchr. Poolesville Elem. Sch., Md., 1966-67; grad. teaching asst. dept. history U. Md., College Park, 1968-69, grad. teaching asst. dept. botany, 1969-70, grad. rsch. asst. dept. botany, 1969-70; assoc. editor, rsch. botanist Flora N.Am. Program dept. botany Smithsonian Inst., Washington, 1972-73; asst. dir., sr. rsch. scientist Hunt Inst. Bot. Documentation, Carnegie Mellon U., 1974-77, dir., prin. rsch. scientist, 1977—; rsch. assoc. sect. botany Carnegie Mus. Natural History, Pitts., 1978—. Adj. scientist Pitts. Poison Ctr., Children's Hosp., 1990—; adj. prof. biol. scis. dept. biol. scis. Carnegie Mellon U., 1984-99, history of sci. dept. history, 1979—, disting. svc. prof. botany dept. biol. scis., 1999—; mem. internat. com. Internat. Congress Systematic and Evolutionary Biology, 1980-90, asst. treas., 1980-90, sec.-gen., 1990-96; mem. adv. com., editorial com. Flora of N.Am. Project, 1983—; cons. Chgo. Botanic Garden, Glencoe, Ill., 1980-83, 87-88, 89, Carnegie Mus. Natural History, Pitts., 1984, European Sci. Found., Stasbourg, France, 1987, Commn. Preservation and Access, Wye, Md., 1991, FBI, Martinsburg, W.Va., 1997. Editor: Memoirs of the Torrey Botanical Club, 1975-88, Huntia, 1978-92, bibliographic editor (all vols.) and taxonomic editor (various families), Flora of North America, 1987—; exec. editor Hunt Inst. publs., 1977—; contbr. articles to profl. jours. Chmn. Lawrence Meml. Award Com., 1979—; steering group Com. Organize a Flora of N.Am. Project, 1982-83; sec. for N.Am. Commn. Taxonomic Database Plant Sci. IUBS, 1986-89, working parties for devel. various standards, 1986—, program com., 1987-90, global plant species info. group, 1990—; mem. adv. com. computer databasing Mo. Botanical Garden, St. Louis, 1988-89, Rocky Mountain Flora Project, 1993—; botanical info. adv. workshop BIOSIS, Washington, 1990; chmn. judges for botany Internat. Sci. and Engring. Fair, Pitts., 1989. With USMC, 1960-61, USMCR, 1960-66. Grantee NSF, 1971-73, 78-80, 90; recipient Full Merit scholarship Montgomery Jr. Coll., 1963-64, Partial Merit scholarship Tulane U., 1964-66, NSF Grad. traineeship U. Md., 1970, Carroll E. Cox award U. Md., 1972-73. Fellow Linnean Soc. London; mem. AAAS, Botanical Soc. Am. (sec./treas. hist. sect. 1979-92, chmn. archives and history com. 1985-86), Am. Assn. Botanical Gardens and Arboreta, Am. Inst. Biol. Scis., Am. Soc. Plant Taxonomists, Internat. Assn. Plant Taxonomy, Internat. Soc. for History and Philosophy Sci., Assn. Tropical Biology, Coun. Botanical and Horticultural Librs., History Sci. Soc., Soc. Econ. Botany, Soc. Study Evolution, Soc. Systematic Biology, Torrey Botanical Club (assoc. editor 1975—), New Eng. Botanical Club. Avocations: music, model aviation, bicycling, motorcycling, photography. Home: 1183 Bucknell Dr Monroeville PA 15146-4319 Office: Carnegie Mellon U Hunt Inst Bot Documentation 5000 Forbes Ave Pittsburgh PA 15213-3890 E-mail: rkiger@andrew.cmu.edu.

KIHM, KENNETH DAVID (KEN KIHM), mechanical engineering educator; b. Seoul, Korea, Jan. 27, 1957; came to U.S., 1981; s. Hong-Chul and Yang-Ja (Park) K.; m. Jennie Cha, Sept. 18, 1988; children: Grace, Christina. BS, Seoul Nat. U., 1979, MS, 1981; PhD, Stanford U., 1987. Registered profl. engr., Tex. Postdoctoral fellow mech. engring. Stanford U., Palo Alto, Calif., 1987; rsch. scientist mech. engring. Carnegie-Mellon U., Pitts., 1987-88; asst. prof. mech. engring. Tex. A&M U., College Station, 1989-94, assoc. prof. mech. engring., 1994—2001, prof. mech. engring., 2001—. Dir. Microscale Fluidics and Heat Transfer Lab. U. Tex. A&M, College Station. Recipient Select Young Faculty Fellow award Tex. Engring. Experiment Sta., 1990. Fellow: ASME; mem.: AIAA, Inst. Liquid Atomization and Spray Systems, Sigma Xi. Achievements include development and applications of advanced visualization techniques for microscale heat and mass transport problems. Office: Tex A&M U Mech Engring Dept College Station TX 77843-3123

KILABUK, PETER, education and human resources minister; b. Pangnirtung, Nunavut, Sept. 27, 1960; m. Rosie Kilabuk; children: Wayne (dec.), Lynn, Jenna, Joseph. Commercial fisherman Self Employed; tour guideand outfitter Self Employed; elected to first legislative assembly Province of Nunavut, Canada, 1999—; named minister of edn. Nunavut Legislative Assembly, Iqualuit, Canada, 1999—, named minister of human resources. Other ministries of Peter Kilauk include min. cmty. govt. and transp., culture, lang., elders and youth, min. responsibke for status of women coun. Mem. Northern Rangers; chmn. Panignirtung Fisheries; patrol officer Parks Canada, Renewable Resources; mgr. Hunters and Trappers Ora, Pangnirtung; bd. dirs. Housing Assn. Local Hamlet; coroner Local Hamlet. Avocations: hockey, volleyball. Office: Box 1200 Iqualuit NU X0A 0H0 Canada Office Fax: 867-975-5090.

KILBOURN, WILLIAM DOUGLAS, JR., law educator; b. Colorado Springs, Colo., Dec. 9, 1924; s. William Douglas and Clara Howe (Lee) K.; m. Barbara Ruth Neff, Sept. 16, 1950; children: Jonathan VI, Katharine Ann. BA, Yale U., 1949; postgrad., Columbia U., 1949-50, LLB, 1953. Bar: Mass. 1962, Oreg. 1953, Minn. 1974. Acct. Arthur Andersen & Co., 1949-50; assoc. Davies, Biggs, Strayer, Stoel & Boley, Portland, Oreg., 1953-56; asst. prof. law U. Mont., 1956-57; assoc. prof. law U. Mo., 1957-59; prof. law, founding dir. grad. tax program Boston U., 1959-71; prof. law U. Minn., 1971-98, prof. emeritus, 1998—. Dir. U. Mont. Tax Inst., 1956; of counsel Palmer & Dodge, Boston, 1964-75, Oppenheimer, Wolff & Donnelly, St. Paul and Mpls., 1980-94; mem. exec. com. Fed. Tax Inst. New Eng., 1966-72; mem. adv. com. Western New Eng. Coll. Tax Inst; vis. prof. law Duke U., 1974-75, U. Tex., 1977, Washington U., St. Louis, 1977; past ednl. advisor Tax Execs. Inst.; lectr. in 31 states, Mex., The Caribbean, D.C.; expert witness in field. Editor: Estate Planning and Income Taxation, 1957; contbr. articles to profl. jours. Dist. dir. United Fund, Belmont, Mass., chair fair practices com. Recipient numerous tchg. awards; Kent scholar, Stone scholar Columbia U. Law Sch. Mem. ABA (tax sect., corp. stockholder rels. com. 1962-76, chair subcom. inc. 1968-73), Boston Bar Assn. (chair tax sect. 1967-70), Boston Tax Forum, Boston Tax Coun. Avocations: tennis, botany, landscape gardening. Home: 2681 E Lake Of The Isles Pkwy Minneapolis MN 55408-1051

KILBOURNE, DIANE CUSTEAU, special education educator; b. Glen Ridge, N.J., Feb. 25, 1946; d. Emile Michel and Helen Mildred (Lombard) Custeau; m. Lincoln F. Kilbourne, June 29, 1968 (div. Feb. 1984); children: Charles Evans III, Elizabeth Brooke. BA, Wells Coll., 1968; MA, Duquesne U., 1972. Cert. tchr., Fla. Sec. GE, Schenectedy, N.Y., 1968-69; instr. Duquesne U., Pitts., 1970-72; client svcs. rep. Merrill Lynch, Pierce, Fenner & Smith, Inc., Schenectady, 1984-86; investment broker A.G. Edwards & Sons, Inc., Schenectady, 1986-89; instr. SUNY, Cobleskill, 1990; tchr. U.S. history Taylor County Mid. Sch., Perry, Fla., 1990—. Bd. dirs. Alcoholism Coun. and Clinic, Schenectady, 1979-82. Named Outstanding Young Women of Am., 1978. Mem. NEA, FTP. Republican. Avocations: tennis, mountain climbing, gardening.

KILBURN, KAYE HATCH, medical educator; b. Logan, Utah, Sept. 20, 1931; d. H. Parley and Winona (Hatch) K.; m. Gerrie Griffin, June 7, 1954; children: Ann Louise, Scott Kaye, Jean Marie. BS, U. Utah, 1951, MD, 1954. Diplomate Am. Bd. Internal Medicine, Am. Bd. Preventive Medicine. Asst. prof. Med. Sch. Washington U., St. Louis, 1960-62; assoc. prof., chief of medicine Durham (N.C.) VA Hosp., 1962-69; prof., dir. environ. medicine Duke Med. Ctr., Durham, 1969-73; prof. medicine and environ. medicine U. Mo., Columbia, 1973-77; prof. medicine and cmty. medicine CUNY Mt. Sinai Med. Sch., 1977-80; Ralph Edgington prof. medicine U. So. Calif. Sch. Medicine, L.A., 1980—. Pres. Neurotest Inc., 1988—; pres. Workers Disease Detection Svc. Inc., 1986-95. Author: Chemical Brain Injury, 1998, Endangered Brains, 2003; editor-in-chief Archives of Environ. Health, 1986—; editor Jour. Applied Physiology, 1970-80, Environ. Rsch., 1975—, Am. Jour. Indsl. Medicine, 1980—; contbr. more than 250 articles to profl. jours. Capt. M.C., U.S. Army, 1958-60. Avocations: travel, oil painting, swimming, hunting. Home: 3250 Mesaloa Ln Pasadena CA 91107-1129 Office: 1000 S Fremont St Bldg 7/401 Alhambra CA 91803 E-mail: kilburn@usc.edu.

KILCULLEN, MAUREEN, librarian, educator; b. Canton, Ohio, Oct. 29, 1954; d. Thomas Vincent and Betty Jane (Rawley) Kilcullen. BA in History, Kent State U., 1981, MLS, 1984. Libr. reference/audiovisual Barberton Pub. Libr., Barberton, Ohio, 1985—90; assoc. prof., reference libr. Stark Campus Kent State U., Canton, Ohio, 1990—. Contbr. chapters to books, articles to profl. jours. Vol. Dublin Irish Festival, Dublin, Ohio, 1995—. Recipient Regional Campus Vice Provost award Outstanding Service, Kent State U. Regional Campuses, 1997. Mem.: ALA, Acad. Libr. Assn. Ohio, Assn. Coll. and Rsch. Librs. Democrat. Roman Catholic. Avocations: reading, gardening, genealogy, photography. Office: Kent State Univ Stark Campus 6000 Frank Ave Canton OH 44720 Office Fax: 330-494-6212. Personal E-mail: mkilcullen@stark.kent.edu. Business E-Mail: mkilcullen@stark.kent.edu.

KILDE, SANDRA JEAN, nurse anesthetist, educator, consultant; b. Eau Claire, Wis., June 25, 1938; d. Harry Milan and Beverly June (Johnson) K. Diploma, Luther Hosp. Sch. Nursing, Eau Claire, 1959; grad. anesthesia course, Mpls. Sch. Anesthesia, 1967; BA, Met. State U., St. Paul, 1976; MA, U. St. Thomas, 1981; EdD, Nova Southeastern U., 1987. RN, Wis., Minn. Oper. rm. nurse Luther Hosp., Eau Claire, 1959-61, head nurse oper. rm., 1961-63; supr. oper. rm. Midway Hosp., St. Paul, 1963-66; staff anesthetist North Meml. Med. Ctr., Robbinsdale, Minn., 1967-68, St. Joseph's Hosp., St. Paul, 1992-99, R.C. Shefland Anesthesia, Ltd., Bemidji, Minn., 2003—. Program dir. Mpls. Sch. Anesthesia, St. Louis Park, Minn., 1968-96; adj. assoc. prof. St. Mary's U., Winona, Minn., 1982-96, adj. prof., 1996—, program dir. Masters Degree Program, 1984-96, staff anesthetist, R.C. Shefland Anesthesia, Ltd., 2003-; nurse anesthesia cons., 1996—; ednl. cons. accreditation visitor Coun. on Accreditation of Nurse Anesthesia Ednl. Programs, Park Ridge, Ill., 1983-92, 99—, elected to coun., 1992-99, vice chmn., 1994-97, chmn., 1997-99; corp. mem. Aitkin Cmty. Hosp., Inc. dba Riverwood HealthCare Ctr., 2000—, also bd. dirs.; presenter in field. Choir dir. Grace Luth. Ch., McGregor, Minn., 1988—, mem. ch. coun., 1992—97, 1998—2001, pres. ch. coun., 1992—97. Recipient Good Neighbor award Sta. WCCO, Mpls., 1980, Disting. Alumni Achievement award Nova Southeastern U., 1993, Lifetime Achievement for Excellence in Edn. award Mpls. Sch. Anesthesia Class of 1999, 1999, Cert. of Appreciation Aitkin County Bd. Commrs. and Aitkin County Health and Human Svc. Adv. Com., 2001. Mem. Am. Assn. Nurse Anesthetists (pres. 1981-82, pres. and bd. dirs. Edn. and Rsch. Found., 1981-83, cert. profl. excellence 1976, Program Dir. of Yr. award 1992), Minn. Assn. Nurse Anesthetists (pres. 1975-76). Lutheran. Avocations: gardening, fishing, photography, choir directing, playing guitar and piano. Home and Office: PO Box 80 Palisade MN 56469-0080

KILE, KENDA JONES, educational consultant; b. Milford, Del., May 11, 1949; d. Kendal Taylor and Louisa Jane (Bennett) Jones; m. Vernon Richard Kile, Aug. 22, 1986 (div. June 1988); stepchildren: Daphne Lynne, Richard Edward. BS in Child Devel., U. Del., 1971, MEd in Elem. Reading, 1976, postgrad., 1998. Cert. reading supr., reading cons., reading specialist, learning disabilities specialist, tchr. kindergarden/nursery, special edn. tchr., Del. Kindergarten tchr. Colonial Sch. Dist., New Castle, Del., 1972-73, spl. edn. tchr., 1973-78, 1991, reading resource tchr., 1978-80, 1980-91, chpt. I coord., 1980—, elem. tchr., 1991-94, dist. lang. arts com., 1993-94, futures com., 1992-93; v.p. ednl. divsn. Get Real, Inc., L.A., 1994—. Spkr. Ea. Regional Reading Conf., Wilmington, Del., 1990; facilitator, participant Assn. Computers in Edn./Computer Using Educators Leadership Inst. Ednl. Tech., Lewes, Del., 1990. Mem. Immanuel-on-the-Green Ch., New Castle, 1972—; vol. Army Hosp., Ft. Lee, Va., 1971-72; mem. Officer's Wives Chorus, Ft. Lee, 1971-72. Grantee Dept. Edn., 1989-91; fellow Divsn. Social Svcs., 1970. Mem. Internat. Reading Assn., Internat. Soc. Tech. in Edn., Coun. Exceptional Children, Nat. Assn. Tchrs. English, Reading Coun. No. Del., Diamond State Reading Assn., Del. State Assn. for Computers in Edn. (bd. dirs. 1989—). Democrat. Episcopalian. Avocations: needlework, reading, walking, metaphysics, water sports. Home and Office: 709 West St Laurel DE 19956-1927

KILE, MARCIA ANN, education consultant; b. York, Pa., Mar. 2, 1947; d. Earl Henry and Catherine Edith (Ernst) Bose; m. Bruce Walter Kile, Aut. 9, 1969; 1 child, Hayley Ayne. AA, York Jr. Coll., 1967; BS, Millersville U., 1969. Cert. tchr. Pa. Tchr. Shippensburg U. Migrant Child Devel. Program, 1979-85; program cons. migrant edn., ESL coord. Lincoln Intermediate Unit #12, Gettysburg, Pa., 1986—. Mem. adv. bd. Gettysburg Adolescent Parenting Program, 1992; mem. Rep. William Goodling's Edn. adv. bd., Pa., 1993. Testifier U.S. Ho. of Reps. Edn. Com., Washington, 1993. Mem.: ASCD, Nat. Assn. Bilingual Edn., Tchrs. English to Spkrs. Other Langs. Avocations: historical restoration, herb gardening. Home: 960 Flohrs Church Rd Biglerville PA 17307-9559 Office: Lincoln Intermediate Unit 12 Migrant and ESL Program 57 North 5th St Gettysburg PA 17325-1870 E-mail: mkile@blazenet.net.

KILGOUR, FREDERICK GRIDLEY, librarian, educator; b. Springfield, Mass., Jan. 6, 1914; s. Edward Francis and Lillian Bess (Piper) K.; m. Eleanor Margaret Beach, Sept. 3, 1940; children: Martha, Alison, Meredith. AB, Harvard U., 1935; student, Columbia Sch. Library Service, summers 1939-41; LLD (hon.), Marietta Coll., 1980, Coll. of Wooster, 1981; DHL (hon.), Ohio State U., 1980, Denison U., 1983, U. Mo., Kansas City, 1989. Staff Harvard Coll. Library, 1935-42, OSS, 1942-45; dep. dir. office of intelligence collection and dissemination U.S. Dept. State, 1946-48; librarian Yale Med. Library, 1948-65; asso. librarian for research and devel. Yale U. Library, 1965-67; mng. editor Yale Jour. Biology and Medicine, 1949-65; lectr. in history of sci. Yale U., 1950-59, lectr. history of tech., 1961-67; fellow Davenport Coll., 1950-67; pres., exec. dir. Online Computer Library Ctr., OCLC, Inc., 1967-80, vice chmn. bd. trustees Online Computer Library Ctr., 1981-83; founder trustee Online Computer Libr. Ctr., 1984—; Disting. rsch. prof. U. N.C., Chapel Hill, 1990—. Author: Library of the Medical Institution of Yale College and Its Catalogue of 1865, 1960, The Library and Information Science CumIndex, 1975, The Evolution of the Book, 1998; co-author: Engineering in History, 1956, 90; author: Collected Papers, 2 vols., 1984; editor: Book of Bodily Exercises, 1960, Jour. Library Automation, 1968-71; contbr. articles to profl. jours. Served as lt. (j.g.) USNR, 1943-45, overseas duty. Decorated Legion of Merit; recipient Margaret Mann citation in cataloging and classification, 1974, Melvil Dewey medal, 1978; Acad./Research Librarian of Year, 1979; Library Info. Tech. award, 1979, numerous others Mem. ALA, Am. Soc. Info. Sci. (Merit award 1979), Cosmos Club. Home: 207 Carolina Meadows Villa Chapel Hill NC 27517-8500 Office: Sch Info & Libr Sci U NC 100 Manning Hall CBH3360 Chapel Hill NC 37599-3360 E-mail: kilgour@ils.unc.edu.

KILLEBREW, ELLEN JANE (MRS. EDWARD S. GRAVES), cardiologist, educator; b. Tiffin, Ohio, Oct. 8, 1937; d. Joseph Arthur and Stephanie (Beriont) K.; m. Edward S. Graves, Sept. 12, 1970. BS in Biology, Bucknell U., 1959; MD, N.J. Coll. Medicine, 1965. Diplomate in cardiovasc. disease Am. Bd. Internal Medicine. Intern U. Colo., 1965-66, resident, 1966-68; cardiology fellow Pacific Med. Ctr., San Francisco, 1968-70; dir. coronary care Permanent Med. Group, Richmond, Calif., 1970-83; asst. prof. U. Calif. Med. Ctr., San Francisco, 1970-83, assoc. prof., 1983-93; clin. prof. medicine U. Calif., San Francisco, 1992—, mem. admissions panel, 1998—. Admissions panel joint med. program U. Calif. San Francisco/U. Calif. Berkeley, 1998—; expert med. reviewer Calif. Med. Br., 1999; expert med. reviewer Bd. of Med. Examiners Calif., 1999—. Contbr. chpt. to book. Recipient Physician's Recognition award continuing med. edn., Lowell Beal award excellence in tchg., Permante Med. Group/House Staff Assn., 1992; Robert C. Kirkwood Meml. scholar in cardiology, 1970. Fellow ACP, Am. Coll. Cardiology; mem. Fedn. Clin. Rsch., Am. Heart Assn. (rsch. chmn. Contra Costa chpt. 1975—, v.p. 1980, pres. chpt. 1981-82, chmn. CPR com. Alameda chpt. 1984, pres. Oakland Piedmont br. 1995—, bd. dirs. western affiliate). Home: 30 Redding Ct Belvedere Tiburon CA 94920-1318 Office: 280 W Macarthur Blvd Oakland CA 94611-5642 also: 901 Nevin Ave Richmond CA 94801-3143 E-mail: Ellen.Killebrew@k.p.org.

KILLIAN, GREG, mental health services professional; b. Louisville, 1952; m. Marcia Killian; children: Justin, Mark. Grad., Gardner-Webb U., 1974; MSW, U. S.C., 1977. Dir. child, adolescent and family svcs. Waccoma Ctr. for Mental Health, 1993—. Pres. S.C. State Bd. Edn., 2003—. Avocations: archery, surfing, leading Scouts, coaching youth sports teams, teaching water safety. Address: 701 45th Ave North Myrtle Beach SC 29577*

KILLIAN, WILLIAM CLARENCE, elementary education educator; b. Altoona, Pa., Aug. 7, 1950; s. William Kenneth and Rosalia J. (Kuhn) K.; m. Kathy Jane Ruggles, July 23, 1977. Assoc. in Bus. Adminstrn., Altoona Sch. Commerce, 1972; BS in Elem. Edn., Pa. State U., 1976; Masters in Edn., St. Francis Coll., 1980. Cert. tchr., prin., Pa., Ohio. Tchr. Altoona Area Sch. Dist., 1976—; dept. head Fisher's Dept. Store, Altoona, 1977—. Mem. Phi Delta Kappa. Home: 610 6th Ave Altoona PA 16602-2622

KILLINGSWORTH, ELIZABETH ANN, educational consultant; b. Longview, Tex., May 7, 1950; d. Carl and Martha Katherine (Brown) Rogers; m. Pascal Leroy Killingsworth, Nov. 24, 1972; 1 child, Pascal Leroy Killingsworth, Jr. AS, Kilgare Jr. Coll., 1970; BSin Edn., Stephen F. Austin U., 1971, MEd, 1980. Cert. speech pathologist all levels, cert. tchr. learning disabled, emotionally disturbed, mentally retarded, multi handicapped. Speech therapist Henderson (Tex.) Ind. Sch. Dist., 1971-74, Longview (Tex.) Ind. Sch. Dist., 1974-75; tchr. multi-handicapped Jacksonville (Tex.) Ind. Sch. Dist., 1975-83; tchr. mentally retarded, speech therapist Tyler (Tex.) Ind. Sch. Dist., 1983-85; tchr. mentally retarded, multi-handicapped Beaumont (Tex.) Ind. Sch. Dist., 1985-87; tchr. mentally retarded, learning disabled Brazosport (Tex.) Ind. Sch. Dist., 1987-90, cons. instructional materials support, 1990—2001; pvt. practice, 2001—. Leader Girl Scouts Am., Brazosport Area, 1990-98; scoutmaster, scout leader, Boy Scouts Am., 1990-2001, adv. explorer post, 1991-2001, cub master, Cub Scout leader, 1989-2001. Mem. Tex. State Tchrs. Assn., Nat. Edn.Assn., Brazosport Ednl. Assn., Delta Kappa Gamma. Methodist. Avocations: sailing, reading, unusual crafts. Home: 7 Ken Cir Little Rock AR 72207-5116 E-mail: packann@swbell.net., ann@asep.net.

KILLINGSWORTH, MAXINE ARMATHA, special education educator; b. Ft. Worth, Apr. 29, 1935; d. Marshall Raphael and Jewel Catherine (Robertson) Reliford; m. Prince B. Oliver Jr., June 16, 1963 (div.); m. Lee Killingsworth Jr., Sept. 4, 1975; 1 child, Saladin Charles. BS, Bethune-Cookman Coll., 1957; teaching cert., N. Tex. State U., 1957; MEd, Prairie View U., 1960; postgrad., Tex. Christian U., 1971-75. Cert. elem. tchr., spl. ednl. tchr., Tex., Wis. Classroom tchr. Ft. Worth Ind. Sch. Dist., 1958-63, 64-90, 1997—, Milw. Pub. Schs., 1964. Pvt. piano tchr., Ft. Worth, 1966-76. Organist, pianist, min. of music Mt. Hermon Missionary Bapt. Ch., Ft. Worth, 1986—, dir. of music, 1985—, dir. Bapt. tng. union, 1976—; chmn. Black Arts Festival, 1961; campaign sec. John Hill for Gov., Ft. Worth. Ft. Worth Ind. Sch. Dist. grantee, 1986; recipient Music Ministry Svc. award Mt. Zion Bapt. Ch., 1980, Svc. award Mt. Hermon Bapt. Ch., 1986, Campfire Girls, Inc., 1960. Mem. Ft. Worth Classroom Tchr. Assn. (Tchr. of Yr. 1961, faculty rep. 1958-62), NEA, Tex. State Tchr. Assn., Coun. for Exceptional Children, Bethune-Cookman Alumni Assn., Delta Sigma Theta (pres. Ft. Worth alumnae chpt. 1961-65, Leadership award 1984). Democrat. Avocations: organ, piano, music, sewing, travel, cooking. Home: 2612 Glen Gardens Ave Fort Worth TX 76119-2721

KILLMASTER, JOHN HENRY, III, artist, educator; b. Dec. 2, 1934; s. John H. and Ora Mae (Backus) K.; m. Rosemary Olsen, 1996; children: John Henry IV. BA cum laude, Hope Coll., Holland, Mich., 1968; MFA, Cranbrook Acad. Art, Bloomfield Hills, Mich., 1969. Artist, designer Ambrose Assocs., 1953-56, LaDriere Inc., Detroit, 1957-62; asst. prof. art Ferris State Coll., Big Rapids, Mich., 1966-67, 69-70; prof. art emeritus Boise State U., 1970—. Important works include: exterior mural Boise Gallery of Art, 1974, sculpture City of Portland, 1977, lobby mural Morrison Knudsen Corp., Boise, 1982, wall sculpture Idaho First Nat. Bank, 1980, wall relief mural Morrison Performing Arts Ctr., 1984; exhibitions include Denver Art Mus., 1980, Nat. Mus. Am. Art Smithsonian Instn., 1979, 83, San Francisco Mus. Modern Art, 1984, Laval Art Mus., Montreal, 1986, Barcelona (Spain) Art Gallery, 1988, Color and Image, N.Y.C., 1989. Recipient Gov.'s award for excellence in the arts State of Idaho, 1978; Western States Art Found. grantee, 1975. Mem.: N.W. Designers and Craftsmen, Internat. Enamelist Soc. (Lifetime Achievement award 2001). Home: 23919 Tyler Ln Middleton ID 83644-5658

KILMANN, RALPH HERMAN, business educator; b. N.Y.C., Oct. 5, 1946; s. Martin Herbert and Lilli (Leob) Kilmann; children: Catherine Mary, Christopher Martin, Arlette Martin. BS, Carnegie Mellon U., 1970; MS, Carnegie-Mellon U., 1970; PhD, UCLA, 1972. Instr. U. Pitts. Katz Grad. Sch. Bus., 1972, asst. prof., 1972-75, assoc. prof., 1975-79, prof., 1979—, George H. Love prof. orgn. and mgmt., 1991—2001, coord. orgnl. studies group, 1981-84, 86-89, dir. program in corp. culture, 1983—; pres. Organizational Design Cons., Pitts., 1975—; vis. scholar Calif. State U. Long Beach Coll. Bus. Adminstrn., 2002—03. Author: Social Systems Design: Normative Theory and the MAPS Design Technology, 1977, Beyond the Quick Fix: Managing Five Tracks to Organizational Success, 1984, Managing Beyond the Quick Fix: A Completely Integrated Program for Creating and Maintaining Organizational Success, 1989, Escaping the Quick Fix Trap: How to Make Organizational Improvements That Really Last, 1989, Workbook for Implementing the Five Tracks: Vols. I and II, 1991, Logistics Manual for Implementing the Five Tracks: Planning and Organizing Workshop Sessions, 1992, Workbook for Continuous Improvement: Holographic Quality Management, 1993, Quantum Organizations: A New Paradigm for Achieving Organizational Success and Personal Meaning, 2001 ; co-author: Methodological Approaches to Social Science: Integrating Divergent Concepts and Theories, 1978, Corporate Tragedies: Product Tampering, Sabotage and Other Catastrophes, 1984, The Management of Organization Design: Vols. I and II, 1976, Producing Useful Knowledge for Organizations, 1983, Gaining Control of the Corporate Culture, 1985, Corporate Transformation: Revitalizing Organizations for a Competitive World, 1988, Making Organizations Competitive: Enhancing Networks and Relationships Across Traditional Boundaries, 1991, Managing Ego Energy: The Transformation of Personal Meaning into Organizational Success, 1994; mem. editorial bd. Jour. Mgmt., 1983-86, Acad. Mgmt. Exec., 1987-90, Jour. Organizational Change Mgmt., 1988—; developed Kilmann Insight Test, Learning Climate Questionnaire, Thomas-Kilmann Conflict-Mode Instrument in Ednl. Testing Svc., MAPS Design Tech. for Social Systems Design, Kilmann-Saxton Culture-Gap Survey, Kilmann's Organizational Belief Survey; contbr. chpts. to books, articles to profl. jours. Mem. Eastern Acad. Mgmt. (treas. 1975-76, dir. 1983-86), Am. Psychol. Assn., Inst. Mgmt. Scis. (1st prize Nat. Coll. Planning competition 1976), Beta Gamma Sigma, Sigma Xi.

KILMARTIN, CHRISTOPHER THOMAS, psychology educator; b. Altoona, Pa., Jan. 19, 1955; s. James Edward and Josephine (Lily) K. BS, Frostburg (Md.) State U., 1976, MS, 1978, Va. Commonwealth U., 1986, PhD, 1988. Unit coord. Regional Inst. for Children and Adolescents, Rockville, Md., 1980-83; asst. prof. of psychology Albright Coll., Reading, Pa., 1987-88, Mary Washington Coll., Fredericksburg, Va., 1988—. Mem. Am. Psychol. Assn., Va. Psychol. Assn., Pi Kappa Phi. Avocation: professional stand-up comedian. Office: Mary Washington Coll Dept Psychology Fredericksburg VA 22401

KILMER, JOSEPH CHARLES, secondary school educator; b. Omaha, Nov. 21, 1942; s. Randall Delmore and Helen June (Barber) K.; m. Marietta Josée van Eek, Dec. 21, 1963; children: Jason Robert, Ryan Patrick, Derek Christian. BS, U. Wash., 1965, MA, 1970. Cert. secondary tchr., Wash. Tchr. Sch. Dist. # 121, Port Angeles, Wash., 1965-95; ret., 1995; coach various sports Sch. Dist. #121, Port Angeles, 1966-78; computer lab./rsch. ctr. supr. Chrysalis Sch. for Ind. Study, Woodinville, Wash., 1996-97. Cons. tchr., classroom instr. Chrysalis Sch. for Ind. Study, 1997—; bldg. rep. Port Angeles Edn. Assn., 1966-68, 88-90, treas., 1968-69; tchr. assistance program mentor Olympic Endl. Svc. Dist., 1992-93; curriculum and instrn. cons. with Sch. Dist. # 121, 1995-96; enrichment class instr. for N.W. Svcs. Pvt. Industry Coun., summers, 1992-96. Active Port Angeles Children's Theatre, 1982-85, Port Angeles Cmty. Players, 1987-95; mem. exec. bd. Port Angeles YMCA, 1968-71, v.p. bd., 1969, pres. bd., 1970; cubmaster Port Angeles coun. Boy Scouts Am., 1979-84, exec. coun. Mt. Olympus dist., 1979-84; coach YBA youth soccer and basketball, 1979-86; precinct com. person Dem. Com., 1988-96, King County Dem. Party, 1997-2002; pres. Clallam County Dem. Club, 1993-96; mem. Friends of the Fine Arts Ctr., Friends of the Libr.; vol. Arboretum Found., 1997—. Mem. nat. com. Princeton Parents Assn., 1993-95. Recipient Cubmaster of Yr. award Boy Scouts Am., 1982, Mt. Olympus Dist. Extra Mile award, 1982, Profl. Excellence award Northwest Svcs./Pvt. Industry Coun., 1993. Mem. NEA, Port Angeles Edn. Assn., Wash. Edn. Assn. (500-Hour Service award 1969), Phi Delta Kappa. Avocations: travel, reading, gardening.

KILPATRICK, GEORGIA LEE, nurse educator; b. Utica, N.Y., Feb. 4, 1938; d. Eugene James Crave and Helen Elizabeth Jones; m. Geoffrey A. Kilpatrick (div. 1974); children: Kevin, Karen Kilpatrick La Plante, Michael. R.N. diploma, Marcy (N.Y.) Psychiat. Ctr., 1958; student, Marist Coll., 1972-73; BA, Syracuse U., 1978; postgrad., Colgate U., 1978-79. Educator nursing Hudson River Psychiat. Ctr., Poughkeepsie, N.Y.; dir. nursing svcs. Masonic Home of Cen. N.Y., Utica; health care administr., home care Quality Care, Inc., Rockville Center, N.Y.; nurse educator Hutchings Psychiat. Ctr., Syracuse. Chmn. profl. growth and devel. com. nursing. Recipient scholarship Colgate U., Bus. and Profl. Women's Orgn. Mem. Bus. and Profl. Women's Orgn. (Woman of the Month).

KILPATRICK, JEAN ANN, elementary education educator; b. Clinton, Iowa, July 25, 1957; d. James Irwin and Barbara Elizabeth (Gillespie) K. BS in Edn., Western Ill. U., 1979. Cert. elem. tchr., Ill. Tchr. Galesburg (Ill.) City Unified Sch. Dist. 205, 1979—. Deacon 1st United Presbyn. Ch., Galesburg, 1989-91; mem. state steering com. Ill. Network Accelerated Schs., 1990-92; lay leader Chrysalis, Galesburg, 1992; supt. Bethel Bapt. Asst. Sunday Sch., 1993. Recipient Thomas B. Herring Cmty. Svc. award Galesburg C. of C., 1991, Ill. State Bd. Edn. Award of Excellence, 1991. Mem. Galesburg Community Chorus (pres. 1990-92), Altrusa Club (Galesburg). Republican. Baptist. Avocations: sports, concerts, movies, reading. Office: 1480 W Main St Galesburg IL 61401-3318

KILSON, MARION, college dean; b. New Haven, May 8, 1936; d. J.G. and Emily L. (Greene) Dusser de Barenne; m. Martin L. Kilson, Aug. 8, 1959; children: Jennifer Kilson-Page, Peter, Hannah Kilson Kuchtic. BA, Radcliffe Coll., 1958; MA, Stanford U., 1959; PhD, Harvard U., 1967. Instr., asst. prof. U. Mass., Boston, 1966-68; fellow Radcliffe Inst., 1968-70; assoc. prof. Simmons Coll., Boston, 1969-73; prof. sociology Newton (Mass.) Coll., 1973-75; dir. rsch., and dir. Bunting Inst., Cambridge, Mass., 1975-80; dean Emmanuel Coll., Boston, 1980-86; rsch. fellow Harvard Div. Sch., Cambridge, 1986; assoc. editor Simon & Schuster, Newton, Mass., 1987-89; dean Arts and Scis. and Grad Sch., Salem (Mass.) State Coll., 1989—2001; ret., 2001. Mem. adv. bd. Bunting Inst., 1992-98; chair New Eng. Bapt. Hosp. Sch. Nursing, Boston, 1992-97. Author: Kpele LaLa, 1971, African Urban Kinsmen, 1974, Royal Antelope & Spider, 1976, Mother of the Japan Mission, 1991, Claiming Place, 2001. Bd. dirs. AAUW Edn. Found., 1993-99, program v.p., 1996-99. Fellow Am. Anthropologist, Anthropology Assn.; grantee NIMH, 1965—66, NEH, 1968, 1972, 1974. Fellow Am. Anthropol. Assn.; mem. AAUW (Mary Lyon award 1994, pres. Mass. chpt. 2000—), Mass. Women in Pub. Higher Edn. (pres. 1995-96). Home: 4 Eliot Rd Lexington MA 02421-5610 E-mail: marionkilson@worldnet.att.net.

KIM, CHONG LIM, political science educator; b. Seoul, Korea, July 17, 1937; came to U.S., 1962; s. Soo Myung and Chung Hwa (Moon) K.; m. Eun Hwa Park, Aug. 21, 1963; children: Bohm S., Lahn S., Lynn S. BA, Seoul Nat. U., 1960; MA, U. Oreg., 1964, PhD, 1968. Instr. U. Oreg., Eugene, 1965-67; asst. prof. U. Iowa, Iowa City, 1968-70, assoc. prof., 1970-75, prof., 1975—. Author: Legislative Connection, 1984, Legislative Process in Korea, 1981, Patterns of Recruitment, 1974; editor: Legislative Systems, 1975, Political Participation in Korea, 1980; contbr. numerous articles to profl. jours. Mem. Am. Polit. Sci. Assn., Midwest Polit. Sci. Assn. Avocations: reading, travel. Office: U Iowa Dept Polit Sci Iowa City IA 52242 E-mail: chong-kim@uiowa.edu.

KIM, DAVID SANG CHUL, publisher, evangelist, retired seminary president; b. Seoul, Republic of Korea, Nov. 9, 1915; arrived in U.S., 1959; m. Eui Hong Kang, Jan. 6, 1942; children: Sook Hee, Sung Soo, Hyun Soo, Young Soo, Joon Soo. BA in English Lit., Chosen Christian Coll., Seoul, 1939; postgrad., U. Wales, 1954-55, Western Conservative Bapt. Sem., 1959-61, U. Oreg., 1962-63, MA, 1965; post grad., Pacific Sch. Religion, Berkeley, Calif., 1965-66; PhD, Pacific Columbia U., 1988. Staff Chosen Rubber Industry Assn., Seoul, 1939-45; fin asst. US Mil. Govt., Kunsan City, Republic of Korea, 1945-48; govt. ofcl. Ministry of Fin., Ministry of Social Affairs and Health, Ministry of Fgn. Affairs Govt. of Republic of Korea, Seoul, 1948-59; charter mem. Unification Ch., Seoul, 1954—, 1st missionary to Eng., 1954-55, missionary, evangelist, 1959-70; counseling supr. Clearfield Job Corps Ctr., Utah, 1966-70; founder, pres., owner The Cornerstone Press (now Rose of Sharon Press), 1978-85; charter mem., trustee World Relief Friendship Found., Inc. (now Internat. Relief Friendship Found., Inc.), 1974—; pres. Internat. One World Crusade Inc., 1975—. Founder, United Faith, Inc., Portland, Oreg., 1970—, Global Edn. R & D Fund, Inc., 1981-96; pres. Unification Theol. Sem., 1974-94; charter mem., trustee Nat. Coun. Ch. and Social Action, 1976-96; adv. fin. supporter Global Congress of World Religions, Inc., 1978-96; charter mem. Internat. Religious Found., Inc., 1982—; v.p. Unification Thought Inst., 1989-97; founder, pres. Marriage and Family Inst. Am., 1994—; chmn. inauguration The Family Fedn. for Unification and World Peace, The Netherlands, 1996—; pres. emeritus Unification Theol. Sem., 2000—. Author: Individual Preparation for His Coming Kingdom: Interpretation of the Principle, 1964, Victory Over Communism and the Role of Religion, 1972; exec. editor: (book series) Day of Hope in Review, Part 1-1972-1974, 1974, Part 2-1974-1975, 1975; exec. prodr.: (radio) The Unification Hour, 1975—2001; editor: (book series) Part 3-1976-1981, 1981; exec. prodr.: (radio) True Love Journey, 1993—2001; contbr. articles to profl. jour. Recipient Byzantine Golden medal Am. Inst. Patristic Byzantine Studies, Inc., 1992, Spl. Award for disting. Svc. Unification Ch., Internat., 1996. Address: PO Box 1755 South Rd Sta Poughkeepsie NY 12601-0755

KIM, DOJIN, science educator; b. Daejon, S. Korea, June 14, 1956; s. Heung-Kyu and Hee-Soon (Yu) K.; m. Kyung-Hee Cho, Mar. 27, 1983; children: Ji-Hyun, Kook-Han. BS, Seoul Nat. U., 1979; MS, Korea Advanced Inst. Sci. and, Tech., Seoul, 1981; PhD, U. So. Calif., L.A., 1989. Rschr. Korea Inst. of Electronics Technology, Gumi, Korea, 1981-83; sr. rschr. Electronics and Telecomms. Rsch. Inst., Daejon, Korea, 1984-91, prin. rschr., 1992; prof. Chung-Nam Nat U., Daejon, Republic of Korea, 1992—. Dir. Electronics and Telecomms. Rsch. Inst., Daejon, 1991—; councilor Korea Materials Rsch. Soc., Seoul, 1994—, Korea Vacuum Soc., Seoul, 1991—. Author rsch. papers in field. Rsch. grantee Korea Govt., 1993-95, Electronics and Telecom. Rsch. Inst., 1993—. Mem. N.Y. Acad. Scis., Am. Assn. Advanced Sci. Roman Catholic. Office: Chung-Nam Nat Univ 220 Gung-Dong Yuseong-Gu Taejon Republic of Korea E-mail: dojin@cnu.ac.kr.

KIM, HYUN WANG, mechanical engineering educator; b. Chulsangun, Korea, Feb. 23, 1945; came to US, 1973; s. Chong M. and Sookrim K.; m. Heasoon Karen, Nov. 13, 1971; 1 child, Anthony. BS Seoul Nat. U., Korea, 1968; MS, U. Mich., 1975; PhD, U. Toledo, 1980. Registered profl. engr. Ohio. Naval architect Korea Inst. of Sci., Seoul, 1971-73; rsch. asst. U. Mich., Ann Arbor, 1975-77; vis. asst. prof. Rochester Inst. Tech., NY, 1980-83; asst. prof. Youngstown State U., Ohio, 1983-88, assoc. prof., 1988-95, prof., 1995—, chair dept. mech. & indsl. engring., 1996—; dir. Hydraulics Res. & Ed. Ctr., 2002. Cons. Heat and Fluid Engring., Youngstown, 1986—, RMI, Youngstown, 1987, Keystone Rolls, Wheatland, Pa., 1994, Glowe-Smith Industry, Warren, Ohio, 1995. Contbr. articles to Internat. Jour. Heat and Mass Transfer, Jour. of Thermophysics and Heat Transfer, Jour of Math. and Computer Modeling. Mission specialist UN Maritime Orgn., NYC, 1982; pres. Korean Assn. Youngstown, Ohio, 1988-89; chmn. bd. trustees Korean Ch. of Youngstown, 1993-95. Lt. j.g. Korean Navy, 1968-71. Named Outstanding Engr., Korean Naval Shipyard, Chinhae, Korea, 1971. Mem. ASME, (ASEE)Am. Soc. for Engring. Edn., SAE, Phi Kappa Phi, Sigma Xi, Pi Tau Sigma. United Methodist. Achievements include design of high speed hydrofoil craft and rsch. in fluid power and control for Korean Navy. Office: Younstown State Univ Mech Engring Dept Youngstown OH 44555-0001

KIM, IL-WOON, accounting educator; b. Seoul, Korea, Sept. 30, 1949; s. Joon-Hwang Kim and Sook-Il Park; m. Jinwon Lee, Mar. 11, 1978; children: Andrew, Daniel, David. BBA, Yonsei U., Seoul, 1976; MBA, Ariz. State U., 1980; PhD, U. Nebr., 1985. Mem. sr. acctg. staff Doosan Corp., Seoul, 1975-78; asst. prof. acctg. U. Akron, Ohio, 1986-90, assoc. prof. acctg., 1990—. Adv. bd. Young Jin Trading Co., Cleve., 1992—. Author: Advanced Manufacturing Technology, 1989, Making Effective Investment Decisions, 1990, An Investor's Guide to the Korean Capital Market, 1992; editorial bd. So. Ohio Bus. Rev., 1988—; contbr. articles to acctg. and fin. jours. Mem. Nat. Assn. Accts. (bd. dirs. Akron chpt. 1986-90, Mem. of Yr. 1988-89, 89-90, cert. of merit 1990), Inst. Mgmt. Accts. (officer Akron chpt. 1991-92), Am. Acctg. Assn., So. Fin. Assn., Decision Scis. Inst. Office: U Akron Sch Accountancy Akron OH 44325-0001

KIM, JAEGWON, philosophy educator; b. Taegu, Korea, Sept. 12, 1934; came to U.S., 1955, naturalized, 1966; m. Sylvia Hughes, June 18, 1961; 1 child, Justin Lee. AB, Dartmouth Coll., 1958; PhD, Princeton U., 1962. Instr. philosophy Swarthmore Coll., 1961-63; asst. prof. philosophy Brown U., 1963-67, vis. prof., 1975, William Perry Faunce prof. philosophy, 1987—; chair dept. Borwn U., 1990-99; assoc. prof. philosophy U. Mich., 1967-70, prof., 1971-87, chmn. dept., 1979-87, Roy Wood Sellars prof. philosophy, 1986-87. Assoc. prof. Cornell U., 1970-71; prof. Johns Hopkins U., 1977-78; vis. prof. Stanford U., 1967; Fulbright lectr., Republic of Korea, 1984, Seoul Nat. U., 2000; vis. McMahon-Hank prof. U. Notre Dame, 1999, 2001—. Author: Supervenience and Mind, 1993, Philosophy of Mind, 1996, Mind in a Physical World, 1998; editor: (with Alvin I. Goldman) Values and Morals, 1978, (with A. Beckermann and H. Flohr) Emergence or Reduction?, 1992; (with E. Sosa) A Companion to Metaphysics, 1995, Metaphysics: An Anthology, 1999, Epistemology: An Anthology, 2000, Supervenience, 2002; co-editor: Nous; contbr. numerous articles to profl. publs. Fellow Am. Coun. Learned Soc., 1980-81, NEH, 1985; NSF grantee, 1977-79. Mem. Am. Philos. Assn. (chmn. com. on status and future of profession 1976-81, mem. bd. officers 1976-81, 88-90, v.p. ctrl. divsn. 1987-88, pres. 1988-89), Philosophy of Sci. Assn. (mem. governing bd. 1979-81), Am. Acad. Arts and Scis., Coun. Philos. Studies. Office: Brown U Dept Philosophy Providence RI 02912-0001

KIM, JAI SOO, physics educator; b. Taegu, Korea, Nov. 1, 1925; came to U.S., 1958, naturalized, 1963; s. Wan Sup and Chanam (Whang) K.; m. Hai Kyou Kim, Nov. 2, 1952; children: Kami, Tomi, Kihyun, Himi. BSc in Physics, Seoul Nat. U., Korea, 1949; MS in Physics, U. Sask., Can., 1957, PhD, 1958. Asst. prof. physics Clarkson U., Potsdam, N.Y., 1958-59, U. Idaho, Moscow, 1959-62, assoc. prof., 1962-65, prof., 1965-67; prof. atmospheric sci. and physics SUNY, Albany, 1967-95, chmn. dept. atmospheric sci., 1969-76; emeritus prof., 1995—; rep. Univ. Corp. for Atmospheric Research SUNY, Albany, 1970-76, cons. Korean Studies Program Stony Brook, 1983-85. Vis. prof. Advanced Inst. Sci. and Tech., Seoul, Korea, 1983; cons. U.S. Army Research Office, 1978-79, Battelle Meml. Inst., 1978-81, Environ. One Corp., 1978-84, N.Y. State Environ. Conservation Dept., 1976-82, Norlite Corp., 1982-84, Korean Antarctic Program, 1988—. Contbr. articles to profl. jours. Mem. Am. Inst. Physics, Am. Geophys. Union, Sigma Xi. Home: 22 Westover Rd Slingerlands NY 12159-3646 Office: 1400 Washington Ave Albany NY 12222-0100 E-mail: kim9664@msn.com.

KIM, JEONGBIN JOHN, mechanical engineering educator; b. Seoul, Korea, Oct. 20, 1947; came to U.S., 1972; s. Wanson Kim and Ilyun Wu; m. Mee-Joo Julie Kim, June 18, 1977; 1 child, June M. BS, Seoul Nat. U., 1970; MS, Brown U., 1974; PhD, Stanford (Calif.) U., 1978. Nat. rsch. coun. fellow NASA Ames Rsch. Ctr., Moffett Field, Calif., 1978-80; asst. prof. Stanford U., 1980-82; rsch. scientist NASA Ames Rsch. Ctr., Moffett

Field, 1982-87, sect. head., 1987-93, branch chief, 1992-93; prof. U. Calif., L.A., 1993—. Fellow Am. Phys. Soc. Democrat. Presbyterian. Office: U Calif Dept Mech/Aerospace Engring 420 Westwood Plz Los Angeles CA 90095-1597

KIM, KE CHUNG, entomology, systematics, and biodiversity educator, researcher; b. Seoul, Mar. 7, 1934; came to U.S., 1957, naturalized, 1973; s. Yong Shik Kim and Yong Im Cho, m. Young Hee Kim, Apr. 11, 1964; children: Stuart, Sally. BS, Seoul Nat. U., Korea, 1956; MA, U. Mont., 1959; PhD, U. Minn., 1964. Rsch. assoc. U. Minn., St. Paul, 1964-68; asst. prof. entomology Pa. State U., University Park, 1968-72, assoc. prof., 1972-79, prof., 1979—, dir. Ctr. for BioDiversity Rsch., 1988—. Fulbright lectr., rschr., Korea, 1975-76; vis. prof. Seoul Nat. U., 1993-94; Gast prof. Heidelberg U., 1976; chmn. Internat. Adv Coun. for Biosystematic Svcs. in Entomology, 1985-92; pres. Pa. Biol. Survey, 1996-97. Author, editor: Coevolution of Parasitic Arthropods and Mammals, 1985, Sucking Lice of North America, 1986, Black Flies, 1987, Evolution of Insect Pests, 1993, Biodiversity and Landscapes: A Paradox of Humanity, 1994, Biodiversity Korea 2000: A Strategy to Save, Study and Sustainably Use Korea's Biotic Resources, 1994, Biodiversity, Our Living World: Your LIfe Depends On It!, 2001. Mem. coun. Trinity Luth. Ch., State College, Pa., 1983-86; bd. dirs. Temporary Housing, Inc., State College, 1988-93. Fulbright sr. scholar, 1993-94. Mem. Entomol. Soc. Am. (chmn. Sect. A 1985-86), Entomol. Soc. Pa., Entomol. Soc. Washington, Soc. Systematic Biologists, Soc. Conservation Biology, Assn. Systematics Collections (chmn. coun. on applied systematics and society 1985-87), Korea Acad. Sci. and Tech. (life), Sigma Xi (chpt. pres. 1992-95). Avocations: photography, nature conservation, walking, music. Office: Pa State U Dept Entomology 501 ASI Bldg University Park PA 16802 also: Pa State U Ctr for BioDiversity Rsch Land and Water Bldg University Park PA 16802 E-mail: kck@psu.edu.

KIM, KI HOON, economist, educator; b. Taegu City, South Korea, Jan. 23, 1933; came to the U.S., 1957; s. Yoon Sung and Ha Hyang (Kwon) K.; m. Soo Wha Chai, June 6, 1964; children: Albert Sung-Chan, Noel Mi-Hye. BA, Seoul Nat. U., 1956; MRE, N.Y. Theol. Sem., 1960; MA, Clark U., 1962; PhD, U. Conn., 1968. Bank clk. Bank of Korea, Seoul, 1956-57; grad. asst. U. Conn., Storrs, 1963-67; asst. prof. Cen. Conn. State U., New Britain, 1967-72, assoc. prof., 1972-81, prof., 1981—. Mem. exec. com. World Univ. Svc., Geneva, 1959-60; cons. Stanley Works, New Britain, 1987-88; dir. Korean studies Cen. Conn. State U., 1989-90, dir. Inst. for Asian and Am. Studies, 1990—; fellow Yale U., 1982-83; columnist The Korea Ctrl. Daily/N.Y., 1991-92. Contbr. articles to profl. jours. Spl. advisor to mayor, New Britain, 1982-89, water commr., 1984-90, 94—; chmn. New Britain-Atsugi Sister City Com., 1989—, bd. dirs., 1990—; founding mem. Greater Hartford Korean Sch., 1985-87. With Korean Air Force, 1956-57. Devel. fellow Inst. Internat. Edn., 1965-67; recipient Spl. award Conn. World Trade Assn., 1987, Cert. Appreciation SBA, 1987, Plaque Appreciation Han Nam U., 1988, Alumni Assn., 1985, 86, 88, 93,, official commendation City of Atsugi, Japan, 1995; named Ki Hoon Kim scholarship fund Ctrl. Conn. State U., 1993; scholarship fund named in his honor Ctrl. Conn. State U., 1993. Mem. Am. Econ. Assn., AAUP, Korean-Am. U. Profs. Assn. (regional conf. dir. East 1990—), Korean-Am. Econ. Assn., Korean-Am. Soc. Conn. (bd. dirs. 1987-90), Greater Hartford C. of C., Omicron Delta Epsilon. Congregationalist. Avocation: travel. Home: 497 Commonwealth Ave New Britain CT 06053-2407 Office: Cen Conn State U 1615 Stanley St New Britain CT 06053-2439

KIM, SONJA CHUNG, elementary education educator; b. Seoul, Sept. 23, 1941; came to U.S., 1967; d. Sung Kwon and BoSoon (Chun) Chung; m. Man Jae Kim, Mar. 24, 1964; children: Richard S., Lesley S. BA, Seoul Nat. U., 1964; MA, Ohio State U., 1969; postgrad., Mich. State U., 1970-71, Western Mich. U., 1973-74. Cert. tchr., Mich., Korea. Tchr. Kalamazoo Korean Sch., 1987-90, prin., 1993-94; tchr., educator White Pigeon (Mich.) Community Schs., 1971—. Pres. Kports & Co., Portage, Mich., 1985—. Mem. NEA, Mich. Edn. Assn., Mich. Music Edn. Assn., Seoul Nat. U. Alumni Assn. (pres. 1989—). Avocations: travel, reading. Home: PO Box 1423 Portage MI 49081-1423

KIM, THOMAS KUNHYUK, college administrator; b. Shanghai, Peoples Republic of China, Feb. 18, 1929; came to U.S., 1948, naturalized, 1960; s. Hong Suh and Chong (Kim) K.; m. Martha Alice Zoellers, June 4, 1958; children— Lawrence Thomas, Catherine Ann. BA, Berea Coll., 1952; MBA, Ind. U., 1954; PhD, Tulane U., 1961; L.H.D., Southwestern U., 1973; LHD, Berea Coll., 1993. Asst. prof. econs. U. Akron, O., 1961-62; asso. prof. Baker U., Baldwin, Kans., 1962-65; prof. Tex. Tech. U., Lubbock, 1965-70; pres. McMurry U., Abilene, Tex., 1970-93, chancellor, 1993-94; disting. prof. econ Hardin & Simmons U., 1994—. Author: Introductory Mathematics for Economic Analysis, 1971. Mem. Phi Kappa Phi, Omicron Delta Epsilon. Methodist (del. gen. conf. 1972). Office: 1 City Ctr 241 Pine St Ste 8ld Abilene TX 79601-5935

KIM, YOON BERM, immunologist, educator; b. Pyongnam, Korea, Apr. 25, 1929; came to U.S., 1959, naturalized, 1975; s. Sang Sun and Yang Rang (Lee) K.; m. Soon Cha Kim, Feb. 23, 1959; children: John, Jean, Paul. MD, Seoul Nat. U., 1958; PhD, U. Minn., 1965. Intern Univ. Hosp. Seoul Nat. U., 1958-59; asst. prof. microbiology U. Minn., Mpls., 1965-70, assoc. prof., 1970-73; mem., head lab. ontogeny of immune system Sloan Kettering Inst. Cancer Research, Rye, N.Y., 1973-83; prof. immunology Cornell U. Grad. Sch. Med. Scis., N.Y.C., 1973-83, chmn. immunology unit, 1980-82; prof. microbiology, immunology and medicine, chmn. dept. micorbiology and immunology Finch U. Health Scis., Chgo. Med. Sch., 1983—, acting dean Sch. Grad. and Postdoctoral Studies, 1994-95. Mem. Lobund adv. bd. U. Notre Dame, 1977-88. Contbr. numerous articles on immunology to profl. jours. Recipient rsch. career devel. award USPHS, 1968-73, Morris Parker Meritorius Rsch. award U. Health Scis., Chgo. Med. Sch., 1984, Ham Choon Disinction in Med. Rsch. Grand prize Seoul Nat. U. Coll. Medicine Alumni Assn., 2003. Fellow Am. Acad. Microbiology; mem. AAAS, Korean Acad. Sci. and Tech., Assn. Gnotobiotics (pres.), Internat. Assn. for Gnotobiology (founding), Am. Assn. Immunologists, Am. Soc. Microbiology, Am. Assn. Pathologists, Korean-Am. Med. Assn., N.Y. Acad. Scis., Soc. for Leucocyte Biology, Internat. Soc. Devel. Comparative Immunology, Harvey Soc., Internat. Soc. Interferon and Cytokine Rsch., Korean Acad. Sci. and Tech., Chgo. Assn. Immunologists (pres.), Assn. Med. Sch. Microbiology and Immunology Chairs, Internat. Endotoxin Soc. (charter), Soc. Natural Immunity (charter), Sigma Xi, Alpha Omega Alpha. Achievements include discovery of the unique germfree dolostrum-deprived immunologically "virgin" piglet model used to investigate ontogenic development and regulation of the immune system including T/B lymphocytes, natural killer/killer cells, and macrophages; research on ontogeny and regulation of immune system, immunochemistry and biology of bacterial toxins, host-parasite relationships and gnotobiology. Home: 313 Weatherford Ct Lake Bluff IL 60044-1905 Office: Finch U Health Scis Chgo Med Sch 3333 Green Bay Rd North Chicago IL 60064-3037 E-mail: kimy@finchcms.edu.

KIM, YOUNG JEH, political science educator; b. Seoul, Republic of Korea, Jan. 24, 1939; s. Chul Soo and Soon Rae Kim; m. Ock Joo Han, Dec. 22, 1968; children— Michelle, Peter, Charlie. B.A., Kon-Kuk U., Seoul, 1962; M.A., U. Cin., 1968; Ph.D., U. Tenn., 1977. Asst. prof. polit. sci. Alcorn State U., Lorman, Miss., 1968-74, 77-81, assoc. prof., 1981-87, prof., 1987—; teaching asst. U. Tenn.-Knoxville, 1974-77. Author: Korea's Future and East Asian Politics, 1977; Roads for Korea's Future Unification, 1980; (with others) Korean Reunification, 1984; The Political Unification of Korea in the 1990's: Key to World Peace, 1989, Unification Theory of Korean Peninsula: Theory and Practice (Korean), 1990. Guest editor Asian Profile, Dec. 1983; mem. internat. editorial adv. com. Asian Research Service, Hong Kong, 1985; contbr. articles to profl. jours. Grantee U.S. Dept. Edn., 1985, Lilly Found., 1985. Fellow Internat. Ctr. for Asian Studies; mem. Am. Polit. Sci. Assn., So. Polit. Sci. Assn., Miss. Polit. Sci. Assn., Assn. for Asian Studies. Baptist. Avocations: Golf; skiing. Home: 497 E California Blvd Apt 323 Pasadena CA 91106-3791 Office: Alcorn State U Lorman MS 39096

KIM, ZAEZEUNG, allergist, immunologist, educator; b. Hamhung, Korea, Feb. 21, 1929; came to U.S., 1967; s. Suh and Suyeo (Hahn) K.; m. Youngju Kim, June 2, 1961; children: Keungsuk, Maria. Student, Hamhung Med. Coll., Korea, 1946-50; MD, Seoul U., Korea, 1960; PhD in Immunology, U. Cologne, Fed. Republic of Germany, 1968. Diplomate Am. Bd. Allergy and Immunology. Intern Seoul Nat. U. Hosp., 1960-61, resident in medicine, 1961-63, Heidelberg U. Hosp., Fed. Republic of Germany, 1963-64; research fellow Max-Planck Inst., Cologne, 1965-67; fellow in hematology U. Tex., Houston, 1967-68; resident in allergy and immunology Temple U. Hosp., Phila., 1968-69; fellow in medicine Ohio State U., Columbus, 1969-71; instr. medicine Med. Coll. Wis., Milw., 1972-75, asst. prof., 1975-78, assoc. clin. prof., 1978—; practice medicine specializing in allergy and immunology Racine, Wis. Contbr. articles to profl. jours. Fellow Am. Acad. Allergy and Immunology, Am. Coll. Allergists; mem. AMA. Home: 461 W Sunnyview Dr Apt 13 Oak Creek WI 53154-3893 Office: 461 W Sunnyview Dr Apt 13 Oak Creek WI 53154-3893

KIMBALL, ANNE SPOFFORD, French language educator; b. Bangor, Maine, July 2, 1937; d. Spofford Harris and Marian Stevens Kimball. BA, Mt. Holyoke Coll., 1959; MA in Tchg., Harvard U., 1960; MA, Middlebury Sch. French, Paris, 1961; PhD, U. wis., 1969. Asst. U. de Lille, France, 1960-61; instr., then asst. prof. Mt. Holyoke Coll., South Hadley, Mass., 1963-74, assoc. dean studies, 1974-75; acad. dean., assoc. prof. French Randolph-Macon Woman's Coll., Lynchburg, Va., 1975-82, assoc. prof., then prof. French, 1982-99, Dana prof. French, 1999-2000, prof. emeritus, 1999. Author: Max Jacob: Lettres a Marcel Jouhandeau, 1979, 31 Jours en France, 1984, Max Jacob: Lettres a Nino Frank, 1989, Max Jacob: Lettres a Pierre Minet, 1990, Max Jacob Jean Cocteau Correspondance, 2000, Marcel Jouhandeen: Letters a Max Jacob, 2002. Pres., v.p., program chair, bd. dirs. Alliance Française, Lynchburg, 1976—. Recipient award Fulbright Found., 1960-61, 61-62, 83-84, Young Humanist award NEH, 1981-82, award Am. Coun. on Learned Socs., 1988-89, Am. Philos. Soc., 1988-89, 97-98; Danforth fellow 1965-66, 66-67. Mem. MLA, FLAVA, Am. Assn. Tchrs. French, Soc. des Amis de Max Jacob, Soc. des Amis de Jean Cocteau, Soc. des Amis de Jean Paulhan. Democrat. Unitarian Universalist. Avocations: bell ringing, duplicate bridge, hiking, kayaking, travel. Home: HC 77 262 B Shore Rd Hancock ME 04640 E-mail: askimball7@aol.com.

KIMBALL, MARY HOLT, retired secondary school educator; b. Janesville, Wis., Oct. 2, 1934; d. Earle Frank and Mildred (Beahm) Holt; m. Robert Parker Kimball, June 30, 1962; children: Emily Beth, Laura Ann, Peter Markham. BA in French, Beloit (Wis.) Coll. Cert. tchr. in English-as-second-lang. French/history tchr. Piedmont High Sch., Piedmont, Calif., 1958-60; French tchr. Garfield Jr. High, Madison, Wis., 1960—62; English/social studies tchr. La Vista Jr. High, Hayward, Calif., 1962—64; French tchr. Burlingame Intermediate, Burlingame, Calif., 1964-66; tchr. English-as-second-lang. Klein Forest High Sch., Houston, 1982—94. Author: The Heritage of North Harris County, 1977; editor: SCRAPS, a collection of notes, mementos, and photos left by Mildred Beahm Holt (1903-20002). Mem. AAUW, NEA, Tex. State Tchrs. Assn., Tex. Tchrs. Speakers Other Langs., Phi Beta Kappa. Republican. Presbyterian.

KIMBLE, BETTYE D. retired educational administrator; b. Tulsa, June 21, 1936; d. J.C. and Ethel (Brown) K.; children: Jay Charles, Cheleste Kimble Botts. BME, Tulsa U., 1959; MS, Peperdine U., 1980; postgrad., Mo. U.; HHD (hon.), London Inst. Applied Rsch., 1992. Tchr., choral dir. Sapulpa (Okla.) Sch. Dist., 1959-61; dir., music edn. Hamlin (Kans.) Sch. Dist., 1961-62; tchr., vocal music edn. Kansas City (Mo.) Bd. Edn., 1962-67; vocal dir. Centennial High Sch., Compton, Calif., 1967—; supr. visual and performing arts dept. Compton Unified Sch. Dist., 1991-94, ret., 1994; part-time tchr. Inglewood Unified Sch. Dist., New Rds. Pvt. Sch. Lectr. in field. Author: Music Book of Songs, 1978. Dir. music So. Calif. AME Missionary Choir, 5th Dist. AME Choir, L.A. Ecumenical Choir, Kimble Cmty. Choir. Named Tchr. of Yr., 1982; recipient Outstanding Ednl. Contributions in Music Edn. award. Mem. NEA, CTA, Nat. Assn. Negro Musicians, Phi Delta Kappa. Home and Office: Bedekay Music Pub 8013 Crenshaw Blvd Inglewood CA 90305-1217

KIMBLER, DELBERT LEE, JR., industrial engineering educator; b. Whitman, W.Va., Sept. 8, 1945; s. Delbert and Jewell (Browning) K.; m. Elisabeth Moore Davidson, May 18, 1967. BS Engring. with distinction, U. South Fla., 1976; PhD in Indsl. Engring. and Ops. Rsch., Va. Poly. Inst. and State U., 1980. Registered profl. engr., S.C. Asst. prof. dept. indsl. and mgmt. systems engring. U. South Fla., Tampa, 1980-84, assoc. prof. dept. IMSE, 1984-86; assoc. prof. dept. indsl. engring. Clemson (S.C.) U., 1986-90, head dept. indsl. engring., 1989-90, prof. dept. indsl. engring., 1990—, chair dept. indsl. engring., 1995—2000. Acad. adviser Systems Modeling Corp., State College, Pa., 1983-86; cons. engr. CIBA Vision Corp., Ga., 1992-93; coun. mem. Coll. Industry Coun. for Material Handling Edn., Charlotte, N.C., 1984-87; program evaluator Accreditation Bd. for Engring. and Tech., 1997—. Author: TQM-Based Project Planning, 1996; editor: (procs.) 19th Annual Simulation Symposium, 1986, (std.) ANSI Z94.17 in Industrial Engineering Terminology, 1990, (newsletter) Comms. of SIM-IIE, 1989-90; sr. editor Jour. Mfg. Sys., 1991-2001; area editor Computers in Ind. Engring. 2002—. Mem., chmn. Zoning Bd. Ajustment, Clemson, 1989-92; unit commr. Boy Scouts Am., Clemson, 1990-92; mem. Planning Commn., Clemson, 1994-2000. With U.S. Army, 1966-70. Grantee 19 different sponsors, 1980-2003; named Engring. Educator of Yr., S.C. Soc. Profl. Engrs., Piedmont chpt. 1992. Fellow Inst. Indsl. Engrs. (sr., pres. SIM 1988-90, Mfg. System award 1988); mem. NSPE, Am. Soc. for Engring. Edn., Sigma Xi, Tau Beta Pi, Alpha Pi Mu. Democrat. Achievements include research in quality and the I.E. function in research and development. Office: Clemson U 110 Freeman Hl Clemson SC 29634-0001

KIMBRELL, EDWARD MICHAEL, university administrator, journalism educator, talk show host; b. Oak Park, Ill., May 3, 1939; s. Lloyd Lee and Marguerite (Graves) K.; children: Amy, Dow. BS in Journalism, Northwestern U., Evanston, Ill., 1961, MS in Journalism, 1967; PhD, U. Mo., 1972. Founding chmn. dept. mass comm. Mid. Tenn. State U., Murfreesboro, 1971-89, dean Coll. of Mass Comm., 1989-93, spl. gifts officer Devel. Office, prof. journalism, 1993-95, spl. asst. to v.p. for mktg. communications, 1995—. Trustee Mid. Tenn. State U. Found., 1985-91; cons. IBM, 1993, Peabody Coll., Access Group, 1992, Chaz Taylor Pub. Rels., Nashville, 1989—, Leadership Nashville, 1988—, Tenn. Forestry Assn., Nashville, 1988—, Christensen and Assocs. Advt., Murfreesboro, 1984; expert witness Baker, Worthington, Croscle Stansberry & Woolf, Attys. at Law, 1982; bd. dirs. George Polk awards L.I. Univ.; speaker in field. Editor: The Hyping of America, 1988; reviewer Mass Media Law, 1988; editor Freedom of Info. periodical, 1970-72; host Metro Jour. with Ed Kimbrell, 1989—; mem. editl. bd. Journalism Abstracts, 1981-92, Intermediary, 1977. Mem. adv. coun. Tenn. Commn. on Film, Music and Entertainment, 1987-89, 89-91; mem. Rutherford County Bicentennial Commn., 1987-89; mem. exec. bd. Rutherford County Heart Assn., 1986, Murfreesboro-Rutherford County Arts Coun., 1986. 2d lt. U.S. Army, 1961-63, 1st lt. USAR, 1967-69. Named Educator of Yr., Tenn. Speech Comm. Assn., 1992. Mem. NATAS (nat. trustee 1989-93, Nashville chpt. trustee 1986-93, pres. 1989-90, pub. rels. coun. 1993—, edn. com. 1992—, 4 Emmys, Telly award 1995), Tenn. Press Assn. (ednl. outreach com. 1992—). Democrat. Methodist. Avocations: writing, politics. Office: Mid Tenn State Univ Vp Devel Ofc Murfreesboro TN 37132-0001

KIMBRELL, GRADY NED, writer, educator, retired school system administrator; b. Tallant, Okla., Apr. 6, 1933; s. Virgil Leroy Kimbrell and La Veria Dee Underwood; m. Marilyn Louise King, May 30, 1953 (div.); m. Mary Ellen Cunningham, Apr. 11, 1973; children: Mark Leroy, Lisa Christine, Joni Lynne. BA, Southwestern Coll., Winfield, Kans., 1956; MA, Colo. State Coll., 1958. Cert. tchr. (life), Calif., Colo.; cert. adminstr., Calif. Bus. tchr. Peabody (Kans.) High Sch., 1956-58, Santa Barbara (Calif.) High Sch., 1958-65, coordinator work edn., 1965-75, dir. research and evaluation, 1975-88. Author: Introduction to Business and Office Careers, 1974, The World of Work Career Interest Survey, 1986; co-author: Succeeding in the World of Work, 1970, 7th rev. edit., 2003, Entering the World of Work, 1974, 3rd rev. edit., 1988, The Savvy Consumer, 1984, Personal and Family Economics, 1996, Marketing Essentials, 1991, 2nd edit., 1997, 3d edit., 2003, Office Skills, 1998, 3d edit., 2003, Advancing in the World of Work, 1992, Exploring Business and Computer Careers, 1998, Employment Skills for Office Careers, 1998. With U.S. Army, 1953-55. Mem. NEA, Calif. Assn. Work Experience Educators, Nat. Work Experience Edn. Assn., Calif. Tchrs. Assn., Coop. Work Experience Assn. Republican. Avocations: breeding and racing quarter horses, photography. E-mail: gradykim@cox.net.

KIMES, SHERYL ELAINE, business educator; b. St. Louis, Apr. 14, 1954; d. John Alfred and Alpha Louise (Johnson) K. AB, U. Mo., l975; MA in Pub. Adminstrn., U. Va., 1977; MBA, N.Mex. State U., 1983; PhD, U. Tex., 1987. Energy coord. St. Louis County, St. Louis, 1978-79; energy analyst Londe-Parker-Michels, St. Louis, 1979-82; teaching asst. N.Mex. State U., Las Cruces, 1982-83; project mgr. Technol. Innovation Ctr., Las Cruces, 1983-84; asst. instr. bus. U. Tex., Austin, 1984-85, rsch. asst., l985-86; asst. prof. bus. N.Mex. State U., Las Cruces, l986-88, Cornell U., Ithaca, N.Y., 1988-93, assoc. prof., 1993-2000, prof., 2000—. U. Tex. fellow, 1984-86. Mem. Decision Sci. Inst., Inst. Mgmt. Sci., Ops. Mgmt. Assn. Avocations: swimming, bridge, wine, puzzles. Office: Cornell U 335 Statler Hall Ithaca NY 14853-6902

KINCADE, DORIS HELSING, apparel marketing educator; b. Roanoke, Va., Nov. 15, 1951; d. Carl Edward and Katherine Elizabeth (May) Helsing; m. William James Kincade, June 10, 1972. BS, East Carolina U., 1973, MS in Home Econs., 1974; PhD, U. N.C., Greensboro, 1988. Lectr. Peace Coll., Raleigh, N.C., 1974-78, dept. coord., 1978-86; market analyst HKH Partners, Research Triangle Park, NC, 1982—2000; asst. statistician Cone Mills Corp., Greensboro, N.C., 1987-88; lectr. U. N.C., Greensboro, 1988-89; asst. prof. Auburn U., Ala., 1989-92, Va. Poly. Inst. and State U., Blacksburg, Va., 1992-96, assoc. prof., 1996—; chmn. outreach commn. Clothing and Textiles Area Leader, 2001—03. Cons. Triangle L & C, Rsch. Triangle Pk., 1986-93, S.E. Region Ala. Apparel Mfrs., 1990-92; mem. New Century Coun., 1993-95; rsch. reviewer Internat. Textile and Apparel Assn.; rsch. reviewer Am. Collegiate Retailing Assn., Flexible Automation and Intelligent Mfg., Atlantic Mktg. Assn.; guest lectr. East Carolina U., 1983. Contbr. articles to profl. jours. Grantee Rayon/Acetate Coun. N.Y., 1989, Russell Corp., 1990, Vanity Fair Corp., 1992, J.C. Penney Retail Rsch., 1992, Vol. Inter-Industry Coun. Stds., 1993, Va. Tech. Found., 1995, Human Resources Collaboration, 1996, Reach Out, 1998; fellow Textile Clothing Tech. Corp., Nat. Apparel Rsch. Ctr. Mem. Am. Collegiate Retailing Assn., Internat. Textile and Apparel Assn. (reviewer, assoc. editor, pub. Clothing and Textile Rsch. Jour., conf. planner 2003—), Phi Kappa Phi, Phi Upsilon Omicron, Kappa Omicron Nu. Avocations: apparel design & production, hiking, boating. Office: 109 Wallace Hall Va Poly Inst and State U Blacksburg VA 24061-0410

KINCAID, CAROLYN WADE, special education educator; b. Cynthiana, Ky., Aug. 22, 1948; d. Joseph Daniel and Norma Vivian Martin; m. Wilburn R. Kincaid, June 5, 1966; children: Wil, Jennie, Richard. BA in Sociology and History, Ea. Ky. U., 1985, MA in Spl. Edn., 1991. Cert. secondary tchr., tchr. of exceptional children. Rank I spl. edn. tchr. Pulaski County Bd. Edn., Somerset, Ky., 1987—. Info. giver Spl. Olympics, Somerset, 1987-94. Mem. NEA, Ky. Edn. Assn., Pulaski County Edn. Assn., Kappa Delta Pi. Avocations: reading, crafts, boating, water skiing, dancing. Home: 210 Linwood Dr Somerset KY 42501-1121

KINCANON, GARY LEE, elementary school educator; b. Muleshoe, Tex., Sept. 2, 1952; s. O.B. and Dorothy Lee (Thompson) K. AA, S. Plains Coll., 1973; BS in Edn., Tex. Tech U., 1975, MEd, 1978. Cert. elem. tchr., Tex. High sch. tchr. Lubbock (Tex.) Ind. Sch. Dist., 1976-77; presch. tchr. Oakwood Child Devel. Ctr., Lubbock, 1977-78, Forrest Heights Child Devel. Ctr., 1978-79; elem. tchr. Lamesa (Tex.) Ind. Sch. Dist., 1979-81, Ralls (Tex.) Ind. Sch. Dist., 1981-88, Lubbock (Tex.) Ind. Sch. Dist., 1988-92; ednl. diagnostician Plainview (Tex.) Ind. Sch. Dist., 1992—. Mem. Tex. Assn. for Improvement of Reading, Assn. Tex. Profl. Educators (pres. Ralls local unit 1986-87), Tex. Ednl. Diagnosticians Assn. (treas. Caprock region 17 1995-97). Democrat. Baptist. Avocations: singing, writing.

KINCH, JANET CAROLYN BROZIC, English and German language and literature educator, academic administrator; b. Cleve., Mar. 6, 1954; d. H. Joseph Brozic and Eleanor Ruth Peters; m. Timothy Lee Kinch, July 30, 1983. AB in English, Kenyon Coll., 1976; postgrad., U. Salzburg, Austria, 1976-79, 80-81; MA in English, Bowling Green State U., 1981, MA in German, 1982, PhD in English, 1986. Counselor Am. Inst. Fgn. Study, Salzburg, Austria, 1975, 76, acting dean Vienna, 1977; Fulbright tchg. asst. Austrian Fulbright Commn., St. Johann im Pongau, Pongau, Austria, 1977-79; tchg. fellow Bowling Green (Ohio) State U., 1981-86, instr. English, 1986-87, asst. prof., 1987-88; from asst. to assoc. prof. Edinboro U. of Pa., 1988—, dir. univ. honors program, 1998—2001, exec. dir. Pa.-Canadian Studies Consortium, 2000—. Founder, coord. HIV/AIDS awareness and edn. Edinboro U. of Pa., 1993—; rep., charter mem. The Pa. Canadian Studies Consortium, 1993—, dir. 2000—; advisor English and Humanities Club, 1993—, Alpha Chi Nat. Honor Soc., Pa. Zeta Chpt., 1998—; founder, advisor Sigma Tau Delta Internat. English Honors Soc., Alpha Eta Chi Chpt., 1999—; conf. coord. the Chuck Palahniak Internat. Acad. Conf., U. Pa., 2001, 03. Author: Mark Twain's German Critical Reception, 1989; contbr.: Mark Twain Encyclopedia, 1993. Mem. Erie (Pa.) AIDS Network, 1993—; mem. Univ. Senate, sec., 1995-98, mem. exec. com., 1995—2000. Univ. fellow Bowling Green State U., 1984-85. Mem. Mark Twain Cir., Can. Studies Consortium of Pa. (exec. dir., exec. mem., steering com. 1997—), Sigma Tau Delta, Phi Sigma Iota, Alpha Sigma Lambda. Avocations: community service, travel, indoor and outdoor gardening, interior design, collecting Pacific Northwest native art. Office: Edinboro U of Pa 114 Centennial Hall Edinboro PA 16444-0001

KINDER, KAREN DEANN, art educator; b. Webster, SD, Dec. 8, 1950; d. Sidney Orville and Elsie Jean (Patton) Jacobson; m. Keith Lee Kinder, Aug. 2, 1980; children: Kevin Jacob, Kimberly Ann. BS in Edn. summa cum laude, No. State U., Aberdeen, S.D., 1973. Cert. tchr. art K-12. Elem. art tchr. Sioux Falls (S.D.) Ind. Sch. Dist., 1973—83; art tchr. Madison (S.D.) Jr. H.S., 1991, Brookings (S.D.) Pub. Schs., 1991—. Participant Tech. for Tchg. and Learning Acad., 1998. One-woman shows include Old Firehouse Gallery, Madison, 1990, 95, S.D. State U., Brookings, 1991, No. State U., Aberdeen, 1991, Oscar Howe Art Ctr., Mitchell, S.D., 1991, Dakota State U., Madison, 1991, Mt. Marty Coll., Yankton, S.D., 1998; exhibited in group shows at LaGrange (Ga.) Nat. XU, 1990 (Jurors Merit award), Old Courthouse Mus., Sioux Falls, 1991, Six-State Competitive, McCook, Nebr., 1992 (Patron award), Mitchell Juried Art Show, 1992 (2d pl. award), Holiday Biennial, Spirit Lake, Iowa, 1992 (Merit award), Nobles County Art in the Courtyard, Worthington, Minn., 1994 (Best of Show), Oscar Howe Art Ctr., Mitchell, 1995 (Pick of the Crop award), Granary Rural Cultural Ctr., Groton, S.D., 1998 (Best of Show); invitational exhbn.: Washington Pavilion of Arts and Sci., Visual Arts Ctr., Sioux Falls, 2002.

Vol. Spl. Olympics, Sioux Falls, 1977-82. Mem.: Nat. Art Edn. Assn., Alpha Delta Kappa. Baptist. Avocations: singing in choir, drawing, painting. Home: 205 Santee Pass Brookings SD 57006-3722 Office: Hillcrest Elem Sch 304 15th Ave Brookings SD 57006-2363

KINDRICK, ROBERT LEROY, academic administrator, dean, English educator; b. Kansas City, Mo., Aug. 17, 1942; s. Robert William and Waneta LeVeta (Lobdell) K.; m. Carolyn Jean Reed, Aug. 20 1965. BA, Park Coll., 1964; MA, U. Mo., Kansas City, 1967; PhD, U. Tex., 1971. Instr. Ctrl. Mo. State U., Warrenburg, 1967-69, asst. prof. to assoc. prof., 1969-78, prof., 1978-80, head dept. English, 1975-80; dean Coll. Arts and Scis.; prof. English Western Ill. U., Macomb, 1980-84; v.p. acad. affairs, prof. English Emporia State U., Kans., 1984-87; provost, v.p. acad. affairs, prof. English Eastern Ill. U., Charleston, 1987-91; provost, v.p. acad. affairs, dean grad. studies, dean grad. sch., prof. English, U. Mont., 1991-2000; v.p. for acad. affairs and rsch. Wichita State U. Author: Robert Henryson, 1979, A New Classical Rhetoric, 1980, Henryson and the Medieval Arts of Rhetoric, 1993, William Matthews on Caxton and Malory, 1997, The Poems of Robert Henryson, 1997; editor: Teaching the Middle Ages, 1981—, (jour.) Studies in Medieval and Renaissance Teaching, 1975-80; co-editor: The Malory Debate, 2000; contbr. articles to profl. jours. Chmn. bd. dirs. Mo. Com. for Humanities, 1979-80, Ill. Humanities Coun., 1991; pres. Park Coll. Young Dems., 1963; v.p. Mo. Young Dems., Jefferson City, 1964; campus coord. United Way, Macomb, Ill., 1983; mem. study com. Emporia Arts Coun., 1985-88; mem. NFL Edn. Adv. Ed., 1995—. U. Tex. fellow, 1965-66; Am. Coun. Learned Socs. travel grantee, 1975; Nat. Endowment for Humanities summer fellow, 1977; Medieval Acad. Am. grantee, 1976; Mo. Com. Humanities grantee, 1975-84; Assn. Scottish Lit. Studies grantee, 1979. Mem. Mo. Assn. Depts. English (pres. 1978-80), Mo. Philol. Assn. (founding pres. 1975-77), Medieval Assn. Midwest (councillor 1977—, ex officio bd. 1980—, v.p. 1987-88, exec. sec. 1988—), Ill. Medieval Assn. (founding exec. sec. 1983-93), Mid-Am. Medieval Assn., Rocky Mtn. MLA, Assn. Scottish Lt. Studies, Early English Text. Soc., Societe Rencesvals, Medieval Acad. N.Am. (exec. sec. com. on ctrs. and regional assns.), Internat. Arthurian Soc., Sigma Tau Delta, Phi Kappa Phi, Rotary (editor Warrensburg club). Home: PO Box 20110 Wichita KS 67208-1110 Office: Wichita State U 109 Morrison Hall Wichita KS 67208 E-mail: Robert.Kindrick@Wichita.edu.

KINDT, JOHN WARREN, lawyer, educator, consultant; b. Oak Park, Ill., May 24, 1950; s. Warren Frederick and Lois Jeannette (Woelffer) K.; m. Anne Marie Johnson, Apr. 17, 1982; children: John Warren Jr., James Roy Frederick. AB, Coll. William and Mary, 1972; JD, U. Ga., 1976, MBA, 1977; LLM, U. Va., 1978, SJD, 1981. Bar: D.C. 1976, Ga. 1976, Va. 1977. Advisor to gov. State of Va., Richmond, 1971-72; asst. to Congressman M. Caldwell Butler, U.S. Ho. of Reps., Washington, 1972-73; staff cons. White House, Washington, 1976-77; asst. prof. U. Ill., Champaign, 1978-81, assoc. prof., 1981-85, prof., 1985—. Cons. 3d UN Conf. on Law of Sea; lectr. exec. MBA program U. Ill. Author: Marine Pollution and the Law of the Sea, 4 vols., 1981, 2 vols., 1988, 92, Economic Impacts of Legalized Gambling, 1994; contbr. articles to profl. jours. Caucus chmn., del. White House Conf. on Youth, 1970; co-chmn. Va. Gov.'s Adv. Coun. on Youth, 1971; mem. Athens (Ga.) Legal Aid Soc., 1975-76. Rotary fellow, 1979-80; Smithsonian ABA/ELI scholar, 1981; sr. fellow London Sch. Econs., 1985-86. Mem. Am. Soc. Internat. Law, D.C. Bar Assn., Va. Bar Assn., Ga. Bar Assn. Home: 801 Brookside Ln Mahomet IL 61853-9545 Office: U Ill 350 Commerce W Champaign IL 61820

KINEE-KROHN, PATRICIA, special education educator; b. Phila. d. William J. and Lillian L. (Long) K.; m. Eugene J. Krohn, July 21, 1995. BS, Westchester State Coll., 1982; AB, Immaculata Coll., 1988; MEd, St. Joseph's U., 1992. Cert. spl. edn. tchr., elem. edn. tchr., reading specialist. Spl. edn. tchr. Holly Hills Elem., Mt. Holly, N.J., 1982-84; elem. edn. tchr. St. James Elem. Sch., Falls Church, Va., 1987-88, Most Blessed Sacrament, Phila., 1988-90; spl. edn. tchr Kingsway Learning Ctr., Haddonfield, N.J., 1991-97; spl. day class instr. learning handicapped Vannoy Elem. Sch., Castro Valley, Calif., 1997-98; program specialist Kingsway Learning Ctr., Haddonfield, N.J., 1998—. Instr. Immaculata (Pa.) Coll., 1994-97, 98—, Chestnut Hill Coll., 1996-97; in-svc. devel. Gesu Sch., Phila., 1994-97, reading cons., 1992-97; tutor Progressive Edn. Svcs., Sewel, N.J., 1993-95. Vol. Trinity Hospice, Runnemede, N.J., 1993-97; CCD instr. Annunciation Cath. Ch., Bellmawr, N.J., 1994-95. Mem. Internat. Reading Assn., So. Jersey Reading Assn., Alpha Zeta (v.p. 1993-95). Avocations: cross stitching, bowling, reading. Home: PO Box 1183 Haddonfield NJ 08033-0716 Office: Kingsway Learning Ctr 144 Kings Hwy W Haddonfield NJ 08033-2190

KING, ADELE COCKSHOOT, French language educator; b. Omaha, July 28, 1932; d. Ralph Waldo and Thera Cecil (Brown) Cockshoot; m. Bruce Alvin King, Dec. 28, 1955; 1 child, Nicole Michelle. BA, U. Iowa, 1954; MA, U. Leeds, England, 1960; Doctorate in French Lit., U. Paris, 1970. Lectr. in French U. Ibadan, Nigeria, 1963-65, U. Lagos, Nigeria, 1967-70; reader in French Ahmadu Bello U., Zaria, Nigeria, 1973-76; prof. French Ball State U., Muncie, Ind., 1986—2003, chmn. dept. fgn. langs., 1991-94. Vis. assoc. prof. U. Mo., Columbia, 1976-77, mem. editl. bd. rsch. in African Lit., 2003—. Author: (critical studies) Camus, 1964, 3d edit., 1968, Proust, 1968, Paul Nizan: écrivain, 1976, The Writings of Camara Laye, 1980, French Women Novelists: Defining a Female Style, 1989, Rereading Camara Laye, 2003; (study guides) L'Enfant Noir, L'Etranger, Farewell to Arms, The Power and the Glory, Ghosts, 1980-82; editor: Camus's L'Etranger Fifty Years On, 1992, From Africa: New Francophone Stories, 2003; co-editor Modern Dramatists, 1982—, Women Writers, 1987—; contbr. articles to profl. jours. Summer Rsch. grantee Ball State U., 1987, 90, 95, 2001; postdoctoral fellow AAUW, 1977-78. Mem. MLA, Assn. Drs. of Univs. of France (v.p. 1991-01), Am. Comparative Lit. Assn., Soc. des Etudes Camusiennes, Am. Assn. Tchrs. French, Women in French (sec. 1988-92, v.p. 1996-98, editor Women in French Studies 1996-2000). Avocation: dancing. Office: Ball State Univ Dept Modern Langs Muncie IN 47306-0001 Address: 145 Quai de Valmy 75010 Paris France

KING, ALGIN BRADDY, retired marketing educator; b. Latta, S.C., Jan. 19, 1927; s. Dewey Algin and Elizabeth (Braddy) K.; m. Barbara I. Kelley, Nov. 29, 1997: children: Drucilla Ratcliff, Martha Louise. BA in Retailing and Polit Sci. cum laude, U. S.C., 1947; MS, NYU, 1953; PhD, Ohio State U., 1966. Exec. trainee Sears, Roebuck & Co., 1948-48; instr. retailing U. S.C., 1948-51; chief econ. analysis br. dist. OPS, 1951-53; exec. dir. Columbia (S.C.) Mchts. Assn., 1953-54; asst. prof. Tex. A&M U., 1954-55; mem. faculty Coll. William and Mary, 1955-72, prof. bus. adminstrn., 1959-72, dir. Bur. Bus. Research, 1959-63, assoc. dean Sch. Bus. Adminstrn., 1968-72; prof., dean Ctrl. Conn. State U. Sch. Bus., Avon, 1972-73; prof., head dept. bus. and econs. James Madison U., 1973-74; prof., dean Western Carolina U. Sch. Bus., Cullowhee, N.C., 1974-76; prof. mktg. and mgmt. Christopher Newport U., Newport News, Va., 1976-87, dean Sch. Bus. Adminstrn. and Econs., 1977-87; prof. mgmt. and mktg. Towson (Md.) State U. Sch. Bus. and Econs., 1987-96; ret., 2003—. Pres. Bus. and Adminstrv. Cons. Ltd. (mgmt. and mktg. cons.); teaching asst. Ohio State U., 1963-64; professorial lectr. George Washington U.; mgmt. cons. CSC, U.S. Army. Author: (with others) Hampton Waterfront Economic Study, 1967, The Source Book of Economics, 1973, Management Perceptions, 1976, International Marketing by Dabringer & Muellach Instrn. Manual, 1991; contbr. chpts. to books and articles to profl. jours. Mem. finance resource group Conn. Council Higher Edn., 1972-73; mem. U.S. Senatorial Bus. Adv. Bd. W.T. Grant Retailing scholar, 1947. Mem. Am. Mktg. Assn., Acad. Mgmt., Am. Inst. Decision Scis., Phi Beta Kappa. Episcopalian. E-mail: aking@towson.edu.

KING, ALMA JEAN, former health and physical education educator; b. Hamilton, Ohio, Feb. 28, 1939; d. William Lawrence and Esther Mary (Smith) K. BS in Edn., Miami U., Oxford, Ohio, 1961; MEd, Bowling Green State U., 1963; postgrad., Fla. Atlantic U., 1969, '92, Nova U., Ft. Lauderdale, Fla., 1979. Cert. elem. and secondry tchr., Ohio, all levels incl. coll., Fla. Tchr. health, physical edn. Rogers Middle Sch., Broward County Bd. Pub. Instrn., 1963-64; assoc. prof. health, phys edn., recreation, dance Broward C.C., Fort Lauderdale, Fla., 1964-94; ret., 1994. Dir. Intramurals and Extramurals Boward C.C., Fort Lauderdale, Fla., 1964-67, chair person Women's Affairs, 1978, health and safety com., 1975, faculty evaluation com. 1980-85, mem. faculty ins. benefits com. 1993-94. Sponsor Broward County Fire Fighters, Police; active mem. Police Benevolent Assn.; Historical Soc. Grantee Broward C.C. Staff Devel. Fund, 1988. Mem. AAHPERD, NEA, Fla. Edn. Assn., Fla. Assn for Health, Physical Edn., Recreation and Dance, Am. Assn. for Advancement of Health Edn., United Faculty of Fla., Fla. Assn. of C.C., Order of the Eastern Star (past Worthy Matron), Order of Shrine. Avocations: concerts, theater, art, historic museums, recreational activities. Home: 4310 Buchanan St Hollywood FL 33021-5917

KING, AMANDA ARNETTE, elementary school educator; b. Conway, S.C., Feb. 6, 1951; d. James Hilton and Maisie (Dunn) Arnette; m. Roachel Dent King III, Dec. 31, 1972; children: Roachel Dent IV, Amanda Catherine. AB, Coker Coll., 1973; MEd of Early Childhood Edn., U. S.C., 1997. Tchr. Darlington (S.C.) County Sch. Dist., 1972-75, 78-81, James F. Byrnes Acad., Florence, S.C., 1981-88, Darlington County Sch. Dist., 1988—. Part-time adult edn. instr. Rosenwald/St. David's Elem. Sch., SC, 1992—. Mem. Society Hill (S.C.) Rescue Squad, Woodmen of World, Palmetto Project; bd. dirs., vice chmn. Darlington County Libr. Sys.; bd. dirs. Mental Health Assn. Darlington County, First Steps Bd., Darlington County, Darlington County Dept. Disabilities and Spl. Needs; dir. 5th-6th grade Sunday Sch. Recipient Golden Apple award, 1993-94, Tchr. of the Yr. award James F. Byrnes Acad., 1988, Rosenwald/St. David's Elem. Sch., 1990, 93, 97; named Star Tchr. Time Warner Cable, 1998, S.C. Part-Time Adult Edn. Tchr. of Yr., 2001. Mem. Nat. Coun. Tchrs. English, S.C. Coun. Tchrs. Math., Internat. Reading Assn., Palmetto State Tchrs. Assn. (mem. com., pres. Darlington County Sch. Dist.), Coker Coll. Alumni Assn. (2d v.p. 1988—, Outstanding Alumni com. 1989-90, 93—), Pilot Club (Hartsville, S.C.). Baptist. Home: PO Box 58 Society Hill SC 29593-0058

KING, AMY CATHRYNE PATTERSON, retired, mathematics educator, researcher; b. Douglas, Wyo., Dec. 30, 1928; d. John Francis and Mabel Eloise (Wear) Patterson; m. Don R. King, Aug. 8, 1949 (dec. 1985). BS, U. Mo., 1949; MA, U. Wichita, 1960; PhD, U. Ky., 1970. Tchr. Goddard (Kans.) Pub. Schs., 1956-58, U. Wichita, 1960-62; asst. instr. U. Kans., Lawrence, 1962-65; instr. Washburn U., Topeka, 1966-67; teaching asst. U. Ky., Lexington, 1967-70; prof. math. Ea. Ky. U., Richmond, 1970-98; Found. prof. emeritus, 1998—. Presenter in field. Author: instr.'s manual for College Algebra, 1981; (with Cecil B. Read) Pathways to Probability, 1963; contbr. (with others) articles to profl. jours. Departmental rep. for United Way, 1983; pres. Cokesbury Sunday Sch., Centenary United Meth. Ch., 1995-96, tchr. 3-yr.-olds. Recipient Award in Teaching, Ea. Ky. U., Richmond, 1982, Ea. Ky. U. Found. Professorship, 1993. Mem. Am. Math. Soc., Math. Assn. Am. (mem. various coms., 1st award for Disting. Coll. or Univ. Teaching 1992), Nat. Coun. Tchrs. Math., Assn. for Women of Math., Ky. Coun. Tchrs. Math. (Maths. Edn. Svc. and Achievement award 1998), Women in Math. Edn., Ky. Acad. Computer Users' Group, AAUP (treas. local chpt. 1984-86), Pi Mu. Epsilon, Kappa Mu Epsilon, Pi Lambda Theta, Sigma Delta Pi, Delta Kappa Gamma (pres. Omicron chpt., 1994-96), Sigma Xi. Phi Kappa Phi. Methodist. Office: Ea Ky Univ Wallace Bldg # 114 Richmond KY 40475-3102

KING, ANN D. educational consultant; b. Pottsville, Pa., Oct. 31, 1947; d. Robert Donald Francis and Marion Clare (Nevils) Devers; children: Christopher J., Michael T., Colleen C., John R. BS in Elem. Edn., Gwynedd Mercy Coll., Gwynedd Valley, Pa., 1969; MEd in Psychology of Reading, Temple U., 1972. Cert. tchr. elem. edn., spl. edn., early childhood, reading. Tchr. Penn Delco Sch. Dist., Aston, Pa., 1969-73, learning disabled resource tchr., 1973-74, reading specialist, 1974-76; presch. curriculum coord. St. James Parent Coop, Langhorne, Pa., 1986-91; ednl. cons. Langhorne, 1989—. Covey facilitator Bucks County I.U., Doylestown, Pa., 1993—; Title I program evaluator Pa. Dept. Edn., Harrisburg, 1976-78; presch. program dir. Coatesville YWCA, 1976-78. Bd. dirs. Neshaminy Sch. Disti Langhorne, 1989-63, Neshaminy Ednl. Found., Langhorne, 1993-97. Mem. ASCD, Pa. Assn. Supervision and Curriculum Devel., Internat. Reading Assn., Keystone State Reading Assn., N.J. Reading Assn., Nat. Coun. Tchrs. Math, Nat. Soc. for Performance and Instr., Pa. Coun. of Tchrs. of Math, Assoc. of Math Tchrs. of N.J. Democrat. Home: 371 Barnsbury Rd Langhorne PA 19047-8105

KING, CAROLYN MARIE, mathematics educator; b. Carlisle, Pa., May 11, 1943; d. Charles C. and Ethel M. (Woods) Carothers; m. James E. King, June 6, 1964; children: J. Edward, Scott D. BS magna cum laude, Elizabethtown Coll., 1965; postgrad., Millersville U., 1966-68. Tchr. math. Middletown (Pa.) High Sch., 1965-71, substitute tchr., 1978-84; tchr. math. Derry Twp. Sch. Dist., Hershey, Pa., 1984—. Author: This is St. Peter: A History of St. Peter Lutheran Church, 1993; editor Scroll, 1985—. Mem. NEA, Nat. Coun. Tchrs. Math., Pa. State Edn. Assn., Pa. Coun. Math. Tchrs., Hershey Edn. Assn. Republican. Lutheran. Avocation: crafts. Home: 409 Spring Run Dr Mechanicsburg PA 17055-5574 Office: Derry Twp Sch Dist PO Box 898 Hershey PA 17033-0898 E-mail: cking@hershey.k12.pa.us.

KING, CARY JUDSON, III, chemical engineer, educator, university official; b. Ft. Monmouth, N.J., Sept. 27, 1934; s. Cary Judson and Mary Margaret (Forbes) K., Jr.; m. Jeanne Antoinette Yorke, June 22, 1957; children: Mary Elizabeth, Cary Judson IV, Catherine Jeanne. B. Engring., Yale, 1956; S.M., Mass. Inst. Tech., 1958, Sc.D., 1960. Asst. prof. chem. engring. MIT, Cambridge, 1959-63; dir. Bayway Sta. Sch. Chem. Engring. Practice, Linden, N.J., 1959-61; asst. prof. chem. engring. U. Calif., Berkeley, 1963-66, assoc. prof., 1966-69, prof., 1969—, vice chmn. dept. chem. engring., 1967-72, chmn., 1972-81, dean Coll. Chemistry, 1981-87, provost profl. schs. and colls., 1987-94; vice provost for rsch. U. Calif. Sys., Oakland, 1994-96, interim provost, sr. v.p. acad. affairs, 1995-96, provost, sr. v.p. acad. affairs, 1996—. Cons. Procter & Gamble Co., 1969-87; bd. dirs. Coun. for Chem. Rsch., chmn., 1989, Am. U. of Armenia Corp., chmn., 1995—, Calif. Assn. for Rsch. in Astronomy, 2001—. Author: Separation Processes, 1971, 80, Freeze Drying of Foods, 1971; contbr. numerous articles to profl. jours.; patentee in field. Active Boy Scouts Am., 1947-86; pres. Kensington Community Council, 1972-73, dir., 1970-73. Recipient Malcolm E. Pruitt award Coun. for Chem. Rsch., 1990. Mem. AIChE (Inst. lectr. 1973, Food, Pharm. and Bioengring Divsn. award 1975, William H. Walker award 1976, Warren K. Lewis award 1990, bd. dirs. 1987-89, Clarence G. Gerhold award 1992); mem. AAAS, Nat. Acad. Engring., Am. Soc. Engring. Edn. (George Westinghouse award 1978), Am. Chem. Soc. (Separations Sci. and Tech. award 1997). Home: 7 Kensington Ct Kensington CA 94707-1009 Office: U Calif Office of Pres 1111 Franklin St Fl 12 Oakland CA 94607-5201

KING, CHARLES MARK, dentist, educator; b. Ft. Benning, Ga., Mar. 15, 1952; s. Charles Ray and Marilyn Anita (Alexander) K.; children: Kelley Michelle, Kevin Marcus, Mark Alexander. BS, U. Ala., 1973, MS, 1977, DMD, 1981; JD, Birmingham Sch. Law, 1997. Lab technician Med. Lab. Assn., Birmingham, Ala., 1973-74; rsch. asst. dept. surgery Univ. Hosp., Birmingham, 1974-76, dept. anesthesiology, 1976-78; gen. practice dentistry Birmingham, 1981—. Clin. instr. U. Ala. Sch. Dentistry, Birmingham, 1982-89; mem. bd. advisors Dist. Dental Assts. Soc., 1984-90. Contbr. articles to profl. jours. Mem. Am. Legion Boys State; active Boy Scouts Am. Lt. col. USAR. Named Best Clin. Instr., Student Body U. Ala. Sch. Dentistry 1985. Mem.: Assn. Mil. Surgeons U.S., Am. Legion, Masons, Scottish Rite, Shriners, Delta Sigma Delta. Republican. Baptist. Avocations: archery, martial arts, hunting, water sports, flying. Office: PO Box 94805 Birmingham AL 35220-4805

KING, CLYDE RICHARD, journalism educator, writer; b. Gorman, Tex., Jan. 14, 1924; s. Clyde Stewart and Mary Alice (Neill) K. AS, John Tarleton State Coll., 1943; BA, U. Okla., 1948, MA, 1949; PhD, Baylor U., 1962. Dir. news svc., instr. journalism Mary Hardin-Baylor Coll., Belton, Tex., 1950; asst. prof. English Tarleton State Coll., Stephenville, Tex., 1951; dir. news svc., instr. journalism East Tex. State Coll., Commerce, 1952-56; asst. prof., assoc. prof. U. Tex., Austin, 1956-62, prof. journalism, 1965—; mem. faculty adv. com. U. Tex. Press, 1977—; freelance writer, 1948—. Author: Ghost Towns of Texas, 1953, Wagons East, 1965, Mañana With Memories, 1964, Watchmen of the Walls, 1967, Susanna Dickinson, Messenger of the Alamo, 1976, A Birthday in Texas, 1980, The Lady Cannoneer, 1981; editor: Letters From Fort Sill, 1886-1887, 1971, Victorian Lady on the Texas Frontier, 1971, Brit. edit., 1972, Fred Gipson: Before Old Yeller, 1980, A Pinch of Pride, 1993, Step by Step, 1997, The Pride of Stephenville: A History of the Stephenville Lions Club, 1998, Golden Days of Purple and White: The John Tarleton College Story, 1998, James Clinton Neill: The Shadow Commander of the Alamo, 2002, The Dick Smith Library: Into the Second Century, 2003. Mem. Winedale Adv. Com., 1969-72; pres. bd. Stephenville Hist. House Mus., 1976-79, 83-98; bd. dirs. Stephenville Area Little Theatre, 1987-90; mem. adminstrv. bd. Stephenville 1st Meth. Ch., 1986-87; bd. dirs., Friends of the Dick Smith Libr., 2001—. With AUS, 1943-45, ETO. Rsch. grantee U. Tex., 1960, Rsch. grantee U.S. Ednl. Found. in India, 1980. Mem. Tex. Hist. Assn., West Tex. Hist. Assn., Cross Timbers Fine Arts Assn., Masons, KT (master 1988-89, dist. dep. grand master 1990), Stephenville Lions Club, Sigma Phi Epsilon, Sigma Delta Chi (life). Methodist. Home: 830 Alexander Rd Stephenville TX 76401-5125

KING, D. KENT, education commissioner; b. Preston, Mo., 1943; m. Sandy King; 3 children. BA, Ctrl. Mo. State U., 1964; MA, Drury Coll., Springfield, 1967; PhD in Ednl. Adminstrn., Okla. State U., 1972. From tchr. to prin. Houston Sch. Dist., Tex. County, Mo., 1964—70; supt. Licking Sch. Dist., Mo., 1971—77, Rolla Sch. Dist., Mo., 1977—96; dir. Mo. Sch. Improvement Program, 1996—99; dep. commr. Mo. Dept. Edn., Jefferson City, Mo., 1999—2000, commr., 2000—. Office: Mo Dept Elem and Sec Edn 205 Jefferson St 6th Fl Jefferson City MO 65102 Office Fax: 573-751-1179.

KING, EILEEN ELIZABETH, secondary education educator; b. Two Rivers, Wis., June 10, 1950; d. Milton James and Loyola Ann (Ellerman) Barry; m. Ervin R. King Jr., Sept. 22, 1973; children: Barry, Andy, Betsy. BA in Biology and Life Scis., Cardinal Stritch Coll., 1975. Cert. biology and life scis. tchr. Tchr. biology Ozaukee High Sch., Fredonia, Wis., 1974-75; tchr. sci. St. Peter Alcantara Sch., Port Washington, Wis., 1975-78; substitute tchr. Port Washington High Sch., 1978-92, tchr. biol., 1992—. Avocations: horses, camping, fishing, home remodeling. Home: 3234 Highway W Port Washington WI 53074-9650 Office: Port Washington High Sch 427 W Jackson St Port Washington WI 53074-1899

KING, GEORGEANN CAMARDA, elementary education educator; b. N.Y.C., Aug. 5, 1966; d. Leonard Thomas and Theresa (Gentile) Camarda; m. Robert Michael King, Oct. 16, 1994. BA, Rutgers U., 1988, MEd, 1990. Tchrs. asst. Bridgewater (N.J.) - Raritan Sch. dist., 1991; tchr. 3d grade Mountain Lakes (N.J.) Bd. Edn., 1991-99; tchr. 5th grade Mountain Lakes (N.J.), 1999—; tchr. art Morris Plains (N.J.) Country Day Sch., 1994, 95. Tutor Cmty. Families, Mountain Lakes, 1992-99. Avocations: painting, reading, cooking, travel, writing. Office: Wildwood Elem Sch Glen and Kenilworth Rds Mountain Lakes NJ 07046

KING, GUNDAR JULIAN, retired university dean; b. Riga, Latvia, Apr. 19, 1926; came to U.S., 1950, naturalized, 1954; s. Attis K. and Austra (Dale) Kenins: m. Valda K. Andersons, Sept. 18, 1954; children: John T., Marita A. Student, J.W. Goethe U., Frankfurt, Germany, 1946-48; BBA, U. Oreg., 1956; MBA, Stanford U., 1958, PhD, 1964; DSc (hon.), Riga Tech. U., 1991; D Habil. Oecon., Latvian Sci. Coun., 1992. Asst. field supr. Internat. Refugee Orgn., Frankfurt, 1948-50; br. office mfr. Williams Form Engring. Corp., Portland, Oreg., 1952-54; project mgr. Market Rsch. Assocs., Palo Alto, Calif., 1958-60; asst. prof., assoc. prof. Pacific Luth. U., 1960-66, prof., 1966—, dean Sch. Bus. Adminstrn., 1970-90. Vis. prof. mgmt. U.S. Naval Postgrad. Sch., 1971-72, San Francisco State U., 1980, 1987-88; internat. econ. mem. Latvian Acad. Scis., 1990—; regent Estonian Bus. Sch., 1991-99; vis. prof. Riga Tech. U., 1993-97; dir. Baltic Studies fund, 1995—. Author: Economic Policies in Occupied Latvia, 1965, additional books on business, last four in Latvian, 1999—2002; contbr. articles to profl. publs. Mem. Gov.'s Com. Wash. State Govt., 1965-88; mem. study group on pricing U.S. Commn. Govt. Procurement, 1971-72; pres. N.W. Univs. Bus. Adminstrn. Conf., 1965-66. With AUS, 1950-52. Spidola prize Latvian Culture Found., 1999; Fulbright-Hayes scholar, Thailand, 1988, Fulbright scholar, Latvia, 1993-94. Mem. AAUP (past chpt. pres.), Am. Mktg. Assn. (past chpt. pres.), Assn. Advancement Baltic Studies (pres. 1970), Western Assn. Collegiate Schs. Bus. (pres. 1971), Latvian Acad. Scis., Alpha Kappa Psi, Beta Gamma Sigma. Home: PO Box 44401 Tacoma WA 98444-0401 Office: Pacific Lutheran U Tacoma WA 98447-0003 E-mail: Kingga@plu.edu.

KING, HUESTON CLARK, retired otolaryngologist, educator; b. Bklyn., Feb. 3, 1929; s. William Clark and Alice Packard (Hueston) K.; m. Wilma Marguerite Grove, June 13, 1953; children: Brian G., Melinda K. AB in Biology, Princeton U., 1950; MD, Columbia U., 1954. Diplomate Am. Bd. Otolaryngology; lic. physician, Fla.; cert. Nat. Bd. Med. Examiners. Intern Jackson Meml. Hosp., U. Miami (Fla.) Sch. Medicine, 1954-55; resident in otolaryngology Walter Reed Army Med. Ctr., Washington, 1956-58; staff Coral Gables (Fla.) Hosp., 1962-82, Bapt. Hosp., 1962-82, Mercy Hosp., 1962-82, South Miami Hosp., Fla., 1962-82, Cedars of Lebanon Hosp., 1962-82, Jackson Meml. Hosp., 1962-82; with Venice (Fla.) Hosp., 1983-94. From clin. faculty to assoc. prof. dept. otolaryngology U. Miami Med. Sch., 1962-82; clin. prof. dept. otolaryngology U. Tex. Southwestern Med. Ctr., Dallas, U. Fla.; lectr. in field. Author: (textbook) An Otolaryngologist's Guide to Allergy, 1991; sr. author: (textbook) A Practical Guide to Management of Nasal and Sinus Disorders, 1993, Allergy in ENT Practice: A Basic Guide, 1998; editor: Otolaryngologic Allergy, 1981; editor Allergy Digest, food allergy sect. Current Sci., allergy sect. Current Opinion, 1999-01; contbr. chpts. to books, articles to profl. jours. Bd. dirs. Woodmere at Jacaranda, Venice, 1997-99; committeeman Venice Found., 1995-97. Fellow ACS (emeritus), Am. Acad. Facial Plastic and Reconstructive Surgery (emeritus), Am. Acad. Otolaryngic Allergy (past pres. 1979-80, dir. med. edn. 1983-88), Am. Coll. Allergy, Asthma and Immunology; mem. Fla. Med. Assn., Sarasota County Med. Assn., Venice Yacht Club. E-mail: drhking@juno.com.

KING, IMOGENE M. retired nursing educator; b. West Point, Iowa, Jan. 30, 1923; Diploma, St. John's Hosp., 1945; BSN, St. Louis U., 1948, MSN, 1957; EdD, Columbia U., 1961; PhD (hon.), So. Ill. U., 1980, Loyola U., Chgo., 1998. Instr. med.-surg. nursing, asst. DON St. John's Hosp., St. Louis, 1947-58; from asst. prof. nursing to assoc. prof. Loyola U, Chgo., 1961-66, prof., dir. grad. program in nursing, 1972-80; prof. U. South Fla., Tampa, 1980-90, dir. rsch., 1982-85, prof. emeritus, 1990—. Asst. chief rsch. grants br. div. nursing HEW, Washington, 1966-68; prof., dean sch. nursing Ohio State U., Columbus, 1968-72; mem. def. adv. com. on women in svcs. Dept. Def., 1972-75; adj. prof. U. Miami Sch. Nursing, 1986-89;

cons. VA Hosp., health care agencies. Author: Toward a Theory for Nursing, 1971, transl. to Japanese, 1975, A Theory for Nursing: Systems, Concepts, Process, 1981, transl. to Japanese, 1983, transl. to Spanish, 1985, Curriculum and Instruction in Nursing, 1986; mem. editl. bd. Theria: The Journal of Nursing Theorica, Malmo, Sweden; contbr. articles to profl. jours., chpts. to books. Alderman, chmn. fin. com. Ward 2, Wood Dale, Ill., 1975-79; bd. dirs. operation PAR Inc., Pinellas County, Fla., 1990-92. Recipient Founders award St. Louis U., 1969, Recognition of Contbns. to Nursing Edn. award Columbia U. Tchrs. Coll., 1983, Disting. Scholar award U. So. Fla., 1988-89, Award for Outstanding Cmty. Svc. U. Tampa, 1997, Imogene King Rsch. award U. Tampa, 1997, Fla. Gov.'s medal for contbn. to nursing and health care, 1997, Dirs. award Fla. League Nursing, 1997. Fellow Am. Acad. Nursing (hon.); mem. ANA (Jessie M. Scott award 1996, conv. lectr. 1996), Ill. Nurses Assn. (highest recognition award 1975, award 19th dist. 1975), Fla. Nurses Assn. (life, dir. region 2 1981-83, 2d v.p. 1983-85, bd. dirs. 1997-2001, Nurse of Yr. 1984, Nursing Rsch. award 1985), Dist. IV Fla. Nurses Assn. (del. to Fla. Nurses Assn. 1981-96, pres.-elect 1982-83, del. to ANA conv. 1982-2003, pres. 1983-84, Advancing the Nursing Profl. award), Fla. Nurses Found. (sec. 1986-88, pres. 1988-91), Sigma Theta Tau (counselor Delta Beta chpt. 1981-83, pres.-elect 1986-87, pres. 1987-89, disting. lectr. 1990-91, co-chmn. biennial conv. 1991, nominating com. 1993-95, Founders award for excellence in nursing edn. 1989, life, Virginia Henderson fellow 1993) Sigma Theta Tau, Phi Kappa Phi (scholar award 1988).

KING, INGRID PAYTON, special education educator; b. Norfolk, Va., Dec. 13, 1959; d. Arthur Jordan Sr. and Beatric Virginia (Osborne) Payton; m. Robert Lee King Jr., July 9, 1988; 1 child, Robert Lee III. BS in Mental Retardation, Norfolk State U., 1983, MS in Severely Profoundly Handicapped, 1986. Tchr. learning disabilities resource Chesapeake (Va.) Pub. Schs., 1984-91, tchr. self-contained learning disabilities, 1991—, chmn. Dept. Spl. Edn., 1997—. Chair child study team Chesapeake Pub. Schs., 1992—, sec., 1986-88. Mem. NEA (bldg. rep. 1990-94, Tchr. of Yr. award 1997), Va. Edn. Assn., Chesapeake Reading Assn., Chesapeake Edn. Assn.. Baptist. Avocations: reading, bowling, travel. Office: Chesapeake Pub Schs Southwestern Elem Sch 4410 Airline Blvd Chesapeake VA 23321-2802

KING, IVAN ROBERT, astronomy educator; b. Far Rockaway, N.Y., June 25, 1927; s. Myram and Anne (Franzblau) K.; m. Alice Greene, Nov. 21, 1952 (div. 1982); children: David, Lucy, Adam, Jane; m. Judith Schultz, Apr. 20, 2002. AB, Hamilton Coll., 1946; AM, Harvard U., 1947, PhD, 1952; Laurea Honoris Causa (hon.), U. Padua (Italy), 2002. Instr. astronomy Harvard U., 1951—52; mathematician Perkin-Elmer Corp., Norwalk, Conn., 1951—52; methods analyst U.S. Dept. Def., Washington, 1954—56; with U. Ill., 1956—64; assoc. prof. astronomy U. Calif., Berkeley, 1964—66, prof., 1966—93, chmn. astronomy dept., 1967—70, prof. emeritus, 1993—; rsch. prof. U. Wash., Seattle, 2002—. Mem. faint object camera team Hubble Space Telescope. Contbr. numerous articles to sci. jours. Served with USNR, 1952-54. Fellow AAAS (chmn. astronomy sect. 1974), NAS, Am. Acad. Arts & Scis., Am. Astron. Soc. (councillor 1963-66, chmn. div. dynamical astronomy 1972-73, pres. 1978-80), Internat. Astron. Union. Achievements include rsch. study of stellar systems. Office: U Wash Dept Astronomy Seattle WA 98195-1580

KING, JANE CUDLIP COBLENTZ, volunteer educator; b. Iron Mountain, Mich., May 4, 1922; d. William Stacey and Mary Elva (Martin) Cudlip; m. George Samuel Coblentz, June 8, 1942 (dec. June 1989); children: Bruce Harper, Keith George, Nancy Allison Coblentz Patch; m. James E. King, August 23, 1991 (dec. Jan. 1994). BA, Mills Coll., 1942. Mem. Sch. Resource and Career Guidance Vols., Inc., Atherton, Calif., 1965-69, pres., CEO, 1969—. Part-time exec. asst. to dean of admissions Mills Coll., 1994-99. Proofreader, contbr. Mills Coll. Quarterly mag. Life gov. Royal Children's Hosp., Melbourne, Australia, 1963—; pres. United Menlo Park (Calif.) Homeowner's Assn., 1994—; nat. pres. Mills Coll. Alumnae Assn., 1969-73, bd. trustees, 1975-83; bd. govs. Mills Coll. Alumnae Assn., 1966-73, 75-83, 98-2000, v.p., 2001—. Named Vol. of Yr., Sequoia Union H.S. Dist., 1988, Disting. Woman Mid-Peninsula (forerunner San Mateo County Women's Hall of Fame), 1975; recipient Golden Acorn award for Outstanding Cmty. Svc., Menlo Park C. of C., 1991. Mem. AAUW (Menlo-Atherton br. pres. 1994-96, v.p. programs 1996-97, editor Directory and Acorn, 1994—), Atherlons, Palo Alto (Calif.) Area Mills Coll. Club (pres. 1986), Phi Beta Kappa. Episcopalian. Avocations: reading, gardening.

KING, JANET CARLSON, nutrition educator, researcher; b. Red Oak, Iowa, Oct. 3, 1941; d. Paul Emil and Norma Carolina (Anderson) Carlson; m. Charles Talmadge King, Dec. 25, 1967; children: Matthew, Samuel. BS, Iowa State U., 1963; PhD, U. Calif., Berkeley, 1972. Dietitian Fitzsimmons Gen. Hosp., Denver, 1964-67; NIH postdoctoral fellow dept. nutrition sci. U. Calif., Berkeley, 1972-73, asst. prof. nutrition dept. nutrition sci., 1973-78, assoc. prof. nutrition dept. nutrition sci., 1978-83, prof. nutrition dept. nutrition sci., 1983—, chair dept. nutrition sci., 1988-94; dir. USDA Western Human Nutrition Rsch.Ctr., Davis, Calif., 1995—2002; sr. scientist Children's Hosp. Oakland Rsch. Inst., 2003—; prof. internal medicine U. Calif., Davis, 2003—. Frances E. Fischer Meml. nutrition lectr. Am. Dietetic Assn. Found., 1985, Lotte Arnrich Nutrition lectr. Iowa State U., 1985; Massee lectr. N.D., 1991, Lydia J. Roberts lectr. U. Chgo., 1995, Virginia A. Beal lectr. U. Mass., 1998; vis. prof. U. Calif., Davis, 1998—. Contbr. articles to Jour. Am. Diet. Assn., Am. Jour. Clin. Nutrition, Jour. Nutrition, Nutrition Rsch., Obstetrics and Gynecology, Brit. Jour. Obstetrics and Gynaecology. Recipient Lederle Labs. award in human nutrition Am. Inst. Nutrition, 1989, Internat. award in human nutrition, 1996. Mem. AAAS, Nat. Acad. Scis. Inst. Medicine, Am. Dietetic Assn., Am. Inst. Nutrition, Am. Soc. Clin. Nutrition. Office: Childrens Hosp Oakland Rsch Inst 5700 MKL Jr Way Oakland CA 94609 E-mail: jking@chori.org.

KING, JOHN ETHELBERT, JR., academic administrator; b. Oklahoma City, r, July 29, 1913; s. John Ethelbert and Iosa (Koontz) K.; m. Glennie Beanland, Dec. 25, 1936; children: Wynetka Ann King Reynolds, Rebecca Ferriss King Stevens. BA, N. Tex. U., 1932; MS, U. Ark., 1937; PhD, Cornell U., 1941; LLD (hon.), Coll. of Ozarks, 1965; LHD (hon.), No. Mich. U., 1966, U. S.C., 1989. Latin tchr., coach Frisco (Tex.) Pub. High Sch., 1933-35; missionary to Native Ams. Presbyn. Ch. U.S.A., Okla., Ariz., 1938-43; asst. prof. N.Y. State Coll. Agr., Cornell U., Ithaca, 1945-47; acad. dean, provost, prof. U. Minn., Duluth, 1947-53; pres., prof. Emporia (Kans.) U., 1953-66; prof., pres. U. Wyo., Laramie, 1966-67; prof., chmn. dept. So. Ill. U., Carbondale, 1967-83; Disting. vis. prof., interim dean U. S.C., Columbia, 1984-90. Ednl. adviser Civilian Conservation Corps, U.S. Forest Svc., Ozone, Ark., 1935-37; mentor Assn. Governing Bds. Univs. and Coll., Washington, 1977-90. Editor: Work and the College Student, 1967, Money, Marbles and Chalk, 1978. Life trustee U. Ozarks, Clarksville, Ark., 1965—. Officer USN, 1943-45, PTO. Recipient Disting. Alumnus award N. Tex. U., Denton, 1965, U. Ark., Fayetteville, 1983. Mem. NEA (life), Am. Assn. Colls. Tchr. Edn. (pres. 1966-67), Rotary, Blue Key, Omicron Delta Kappa, Lambda Chi Alpha, Sphinx Club, Phi Delta Kappa. Avocations: native Am. studies, western U.S. history. E-mail: texasglennie@aol.com.

KING, JOSEPH, JR., government administrator, educator, consultant; b. Charleston, W.Va., June 8, 1950; s. Joseph and Jessie Ree (May) K.; m. Linda Streeter, Sept. 4, 1986. BA, Ohio State U., 1972; MS, Xavier U., 1975; EdD, U. Cin., 1982; diploma, U.S. Army War Coll., 1999. Investigator U.S. EEOC, Cin., 1976-79, tng. officer Washington, 1979-82; EEO advisor U.S. Army, Washington, 1982-84, EEO officer Giessen, Germany, 1984-86, Nurenburg, Germany, 1986-89, dir. EEO St. Louis, 1989-99. Dir. The King Group, St. Louis, 1989—, command exec. officer, 1999—; prof. Boston U., 1984-89, Webster U., 1989—; expert witness U.S. Fed. Dist. Ct., 1996; cons. in field. Author: Discretionary Equality, 1982. Unit commr. Boy Scouts Am., St. Louis, 1990; congrl. intern. Congrl. Black Caucus, Washington, 1980. Sgt. USAF, 1979-82. Mem.: ASTD, Soc. for Profls. in Dispute Resolution, Soc. Human Resource Mgmt., Am. Mgmt. Assn., World Future Soc. Independent. Avocations: jogging, fitness, martial arts. Home: 4520 Chouteau Ave Saint Louis MO 63110-1518 Office: USAR Personnel Command 1 Reserve Way Saint Louis MO 63132-5299

KING, KATHLEEN PALOMBO, adult education educator, consultant; b. Providence, June 8, 1958; d. Joseph Christopher and Catherine Ann (Walsh) Palombo; m. James Perry King, Jr., Sept. 3, 1983 (div. 1996); children: James Joseph, William Everett. BA in Biochemistry, Brown U., 1981; MA in Missions, Columbia (S.C.) Internat. U., 1983; MEd in Adult Edn., Widener U., 1994, EdD in Higher Edn., 1997. Oper. room technician Kent County Meml. Hosp., Warwick, R.I., 1978; rsch. asst. in biochemistry Brown U., Providence, 1979; rehab. counselor Talbot House, Providence, 1981; owner, cons., educator KP King Computer Svcs., N.J., 1991-98; mem. faculty Pa. Inst. Tech., Media, Pa., 1991-97, coord. continuing edn., 1995; asst. prof. grad. sch. edn. Lincoln Ctr. Fordham U., N.Y.C., 1997-2001, assoc. prof., 2001—03, prof., 2003—, dir. Regional Ednl. Tech. Ctr., 2003—; dir., prin. investigator Fund for the Improvement of Postsecondary Edn. Learning Anytime Anyway Partnerships, 2000—. Adv. bd. Glencoe Publs., 1994-2001, WNET TV, N.Y.C.; reviewer Jour. Women and Minorities in Sci. and Engring., 1994-98; spkr. at tech. and edn. confs.; organizing advisor Pa. Inst. Tech. Soc. of Women Engrs.; adj. faculty Holy Family Coll. Grad. Sch., Phila., 1996-97, Widener U., Chester, Pa., 1997; presenter in field. Author: A Guide to Perspective Transformation and Learning Activities, 1998, Keeping Pace with Technology: Educational Technology that Transforms, Vol. 1, 2002, Vol. 2, 2003; co-author: (with Lawler) Planning for Effective Faculty Development, 2000; editor Conf. Procs., 1998-2000; tech. editor Jour. Afro-L.Am. Studies and Lit., 1993-97; mem. editl. bd. New Horizons in Adult Edn., 1998—, PAACE Jour. Lifelong Learning, 2001--; mem. rev. bd. Adult Basic Edn., Jour., 1999—; founding editor: Perspectives Jour., 2001-; contbr. articles to profl. jours., reference and text books. Tchr. religious edn., 1985-90. Recipient Adminstr. of Yr., Fordham chpt. Phi Delta Kappa, 2002, Creative Use of Tech. award, Assn. Continuing Higher Edn., 2003. Mem. AAUW, Internat. Soc. for Tech. in Edn., Am. Assn. for Adult Continuing Edn., Commn. Profs. of Adult Edn. (sec.-treas. 2001-02), Am. Assn. Adult and Continuing Edn., N.Y. Assn. Continuing Cmty. Edn. (bd. dirs. 1999-2001, v.p. 2001-03, pres.-elect 2003—), Pa. Assn. Adult Continuing Edn., Am. Ednl. Rsch. Assn., Internat. Conf. of Univ. Adult Edn., Phi Kappa Phi, Kappa Delta Pi. Avocations: computers, biking. Office: Fordham U Lincoln Ctr 113 W 60th St Rm 1102 New York NY 10023-7484 E-mail: kpking@fordham.edu.

KING, KAY WANDER, academic administrator, design educator, fashion designer, consultant; b. Houston, Oct. 16, 1937; d. Aretas Robert and Verna Elizabeth (Klann) Wander; m. George Ronald King, Feb. 21, 1960; 1 child, Collin Wander. BA, U. North Tex., 1959; M of Liberal Arts, Houston Bapt. U., 1991. Fashion designer Kabro Houston, Inc., 1959-66, Joe Frank, Inc., Houston, 1966-68; fashion dir. Foley's, Houston, 1968-70; prin. Kay King Designer/Cons., Houston, 1970—; chair fashion dept. Houston C.C., 1981-97, chair fashion and interior design dept., 1997—2003; cultural exch. prof. fashion design Jinan, China, 2000; interim dean workforce devel. Houston C.C., 2000—01, chmn. Dept. Applied Arts, 2003—. Mem. adv. bd. Spring (Tex.) Ind. Sch. Dist. Tech. Edn., 1990—; bd. dirs. Make it Yourself with Wool, Tex., nat. judge, Tex., 1997—2001; Tex. Workforce Edn. Course Manual Facilitator, 1997—2001; site evaluator Tex. Coord. Bd. for Higher Edn., 1994, 99, 2000. Designer Mrs. Am., 1966, Houston Oilers Cheerleaders, 1968-92, Astroworld and The Astrodome, 1968-69, Brian Boru Opera, 1991, Design Industries Found. Fighting AIDS, 1994-96, Houston Comets/Houston Rockets, 1997. Chair Gulf Coast area United Cerebral Palsy Telethon, 1981; chair Whiteley Endowment Scholarship Awards, Houston, 1990-93, Sickle Cell Found., Houston, 1995-2000; adminstr. Bedichek Faculty Devel. Grants, 1995-96; pres. Spring Br. Ind. Sch. Dist. Coun., PTAs, Houston, 1987-88; bd. dirs. Houston C.C. Found., 1988-93, Mus. Fine Arts Costume Inst., Houston, 1991—, acquisitions com., 1993—. Named Woman to Watch, Houston Woman mag., 1991, Woman of Excellence, Fedn. Houston Profl. Women, 1992; recipient Freedoms Found. at Valley Forge Nat. award, 2001, Exemplary Program awards for fashion design and fashion merchandising, Tex. Higher Edn. Coord. Bd., 2001, Yellow Rose of Tex., Gov. Tex., 1982, Nat. Inst. for Staff and Orgnl. Devel. Tchg. Excellence award, U. Tex., 1993, Award of Excellence, Houston C.C. Faculty Assn. Coun., 1995, Fin. Advisors' Excellence in Cmty. Leadership award, Am. Express, 1996, Innovation award, Houston C.C., 1996, Chancellor's Medallion award, 1996, Tony Chee Tchg. Excellence award, 1996, Bedichek Outstanding Cmty. Svc. award, 1997, Athena award, Sickle Cell Assn., 1997, Fine Arts Fashion award, Mus. Fine Arts Houston, 1999, Fashion Forum award, Foley's Dept. Store and Fashion Group Internat., 2000, Women's Archives honoree, U. of Houston, 1998—99; grantee Bedichek Faculty Devel. grantee, 1986, 1989, 1990, 1993, 1994. Mem. Nat. PTA (life, hon., coun. pres. 1987-88), Costume Soc. Am. (awards chair 1992-93, exec. bd. dirs., sec. 1993-99, v.p. 2000—), Tex. Jr. Coll. Tchrs. Assn. (sect. chair 1990-92), Fashion Group Internat. (bd. dirs. 1969—, cultural exch. chair 1965-71, regional dir. 1969-70, program dir., chair career conf. 1994, retail chair 1995, Keynote address 1997), Houston C.C. Women Adminstrs. Assn. (bd. dirs. 1993-95, v.p. 1994-95, Star award 1989, Keynote address 1996), Houston Fashion Designers Assn. (charter, publicity chair 1989-93, v.p. bd. dirs. 1993-97), Tex. Sheep and Goat Raisers Assn. (Achievement award 2003), Fedn. Houston Profl. Women (bd. dirs., program dir. 1993, adminstrv. sec. 1994, pres.-elect 1995, pres. 1996, past pres. 1997, travel chair 1998—, charter mem. Classy Clown Corps 1994-2000), Zeta Tau Alpha (charity showhouse chair 1985, Nat. Cert. of Merit 1986). Avocations: opera, ballet, travel, graphic computer design, professional football. Office: Houston CC System 1300 Holman St # 325A Houston TX 77004-3834

KING, KENNETH PAUL, science educator; b. Omaha, Oct. 28, 1960; s. Richard Carlyle King and Karen (Cushman) Cheyney; m. Tina Anne, July 6, 1990; children: Marshall, Harrison. BS, Iowa State U., 1986; MS in Edn., No. Ill. U., 1990, EdD, 1998. Cert. secondary edn., Iowa, adminstrv., Ill. Writer, editor Quaransan Group, Northbrook, Ill., 1991; tchr. physics Sch. Dist. #46, Elgin, Ill., 1986-95; grad. asst. No. Ill. U., DeKalb, 1995-98, instr. sci. tchg. methods, 1996-98, assoc. prof. tchg. and learning, 1998—. Mem. editl. bd. Contemporary Issues in Tech. and Edn., Electronic Jour. Sci. Edn., Assn. History and Computing; mem. publs. bd. Sch. Sci. and Math. Camp dir. Boys Scouts Am., St. Charles, Ill., 1992, 96, sect. dir. nat. camping sch., Naperville, Ill., 1983-92, 96, 2001, 03. Recipient U. Chgo. Teaching Commendation award, 1993. Mem. ASCD, Nat. Assn. Rsch. Sci. Tchg., Ill. Assn. for Supervision and Curriculum Devel., Assn. for the Edn. of Tchrs. of Sci., Sch. Sci. and Math. Achievements include development of telecommunications applications for elementary education, development of technology applications to develop science process skills. Home: 128 Delcy Dr Dekalb IL 60115-1902 Office: No Ill U Gabel Hall Dekalb IL 60115 E-mail: kking1@niu.edu.

KING, K(IMBERLY) N(ELSON), computer science educator; b. Apr. 28, 1953; s. Paul Ellsworth and Marcelia Jeannette King; m. Cynthia Ann Stormes, Sept. 5, 1981 (div. Nov. 1991); m. Susan Ann Cole, Aug. 9, 1996. BS with highest honors, Case Western Res. U., 1975; MS, Yale U., 1976; PhD, U. Calif., Berkeley, 1980. Asst. prof. info. and computer sci. Ga. Inst. Tech., Atlanta, 1980-86, rsch. scientist, 1986-87; assoc. prof. computer sci. Ga. State U., Atlanta, 1987—. Cons. Norfolk So. Rwy., 1991. Author: Modula-2: A Complete Guide, 1988, C Programming: A Modern Approach, 1996, Java Programming: From The Beginning, 2000; columnist Jour. Pascal, Ada, and Modula-2, 1989-90; contbr. articles to profl. jours. Vol. Ga. Radio Reading Svc., Atlanta, 1989—. Grad. fellow NSF, 1975-78; NSF grantee, 1981-84. Mem. AAUP, IEEE Computer Soc., Assn. for Computing Machinery (chmn. program com. 36th annual southeast conf. 1998), Tau Beta Pi. Office: Ga State U Computer Sci Atlanta GA 30303 E-mail: knking@gsu.edu.

KING, LAWRENCE PHILIP, lawyer, educator; b. Schenectady, N.Y., Jan. 16, 1929; s. Louis D. and Sonia K.; children— David J. Kaufman, Deborah J. King. BSS., CCNY, 1950; LL.B., NYU, 1953; LL.M., U. Mich., 1957. Bar: N.Y. 1954, U.S. Supreme Ct. 1963. Atty. Paramount Pictures Corp., N.Y.C., 1955-56; asst. prof. law Wayne State U., 1957-59; asst. prof. NYU, 1959-61, assoc. prof., 1961-63, prof., 1963—, Charles Seligson prof. law, 1979—, assoc. dean Sch. Law, 1973-77; of counsel Wachtell, Lipton, Rosen & Katz, N.Y.C. Cons. Commn. to Study Bankruptcy Law U.S., 1970-73, advisor nat. bankruptcy rev. com., 1996-97; assoc. reporter adv. com. on bankruptcy rules U.S. Jud. Conf., 1968-76, reporter, 1979-83, mem. adv. com. on bankruptcy rules, 1983-92; vis. faculty law Hebrew U., Jerusalem, 1971, 87, 94, Haifa U., 1994, 96, 97, 98, 99, Tel Aviv U., 1987, 94, Temple U. Sch. Law, U. Calif. Law Sch., Berkeley; lectr. Bar Ilan U., U. Stockholm, U. Innsbruck, Fed. Ct. Author: (with R. Duesenberg) Sales and Bulk Transfers Under the U.C.C., 1966, supplement, 1999, (with M. Cook) Creditors Rights, Debtor's Protection and Bankruptcy, Cases and Materials, 1985, 2d edit., 1989, 3d edit., 1997; contbr. articles, book revs. to legal jours.; edtor-in-chief: Collier on Bankruptcy, 1964, 15th edit. rev., 1979—; co-editor-in-chief: Collier Bankruptcy Practice Guide, 1981—. Trustee Village of Saltaire (N.Y.), 1980-84, mayor, 1984-86, acting justice, 1988—. Recipient NYU Law Alumni Achievement award, 1976, NYU Law Alumni 25-Yr. Faculty Svc. award, 1984, legal teaching award, 1993, award Bankruptcy Lawyers divsn. UJA-Fedn., 1984, Man of Yr. award Comml. Law League Am., 1969, Disting. Svc. award Am. Coll. Bankruptcy, 1997, Excellence in Edn. award Nat. Conf. Bamkruptcy Judges, 2000. Mem. ABA, N.Y. State Bar Assn., Assn. of Bar of City of N.Y., Nat. Bankruptcy Conf., Am. Law Inst. Home: New York, NY. Died Apr. 1, 2001.

KING, MARGARET ANN, communications educator; b. Marion, Ind., Feb. 27, 1936; d. Paul Milton and Janet Mary (Broderick) Burke; m. Charles Claude King, Aug. 25, 1956; children: C. Kevin, Elizabeth Ann, Paul S., Margaret C. Student, Ohio Dominican, 1953-56, U. Kans., 1980-81; BA in Communication, Purdue U., 1986, MA in Pub. Communication, 1990. Regional rep. Indpls. Juv. Justice Task Force, 1984-85; vis. instr. dept. communication Purdue U., West Lafayette, Ind., 1992-96; v.p. King Mktg. Cons., Inc., 1996—2002; adj. lectr. U. Cin., 2002—. Bd. dirs. Vis. Nurse Home Health Svcs.; adj. instr. U. Cin., 2002—. Contbr. chpt. to book. Grad. mem. Leadership Lafayette, 1983. Purdue U. fellow, 1986-87. Mem. AAUW, Ctrl. States Comm. Assn. (conf. presenter 1989), Golden Key, Phi Kappa Phi. Republican. Roman Catholic. Avocations: poetry writing, vocal and piano music. Home: 7938 Wild Orchard Ln Cincinnati OH 45242-4309

KING, MARGARET LEAH, history educator; b. N.Y.C., Oct. 16, 1947; d. Reno C. and Marie (Ackerman) King; m. Robert E. Kessler, Nov. 12, 1976; children: David King Kessler, Jeremy King Kessler. BA, Sarah Lawrence Coll., 1967; MA, Stanford U., 1968, PhD, 1972. Asst. prof. dept. history Calif. State Coll., Fullerton, 1969-70; asst. prof. Bklyn. Coll., CUNY, 1972-76, assoc. prof., 1976-86; prof. Bklyn. Coll. and Grad. Ctr., CUNY, 1987—, Claire and Leonard Tow disting. prof., 2000-02. Disting. guest prof. Centre for Reformation and Renaissance Studies, U. Toronto, 1995. Author: (textbook) Western Civilization: A Social and Cultural History, 2d edit., 2002; Venetian Humanism in an Age of Patrician Dominance, 1986, Women of the Renaissance, 1991, The Death of the Child Valerio Marcello, 1994; contbr. articles to profl. jours.; mem. editorial bds. Recipient Howard R. Marraro prize, Am. Cath. Hist. Assn., 1986, Tow award for distinction in scholarship, Bklyn. Coll., 1994—95; fellow, Danforth Found., 1967—72, Woodrow Wilson Found., 1967—68, Am. Coun. Learned Socs., 1977—78, NEH, 1986—87, Leonard and Claire Tow Disting. fellow, 2000—; grantee, Am. Coun. Learned Socs., 1976, Gladys Krieble Delmas Found., 1977—78, 1980—81, 1990, Am. Philos. Soc., 1979, 1990, NEH, 1984. Mem. Am. Hist. Assn. (Howard and Helen Mararro prize 1996), Hist. Soc., Renaissance Soc. Am. (exec. dir. 1988-95, editor Renaissance Quar. 1984-88, 97-2002). Home: 324 Beverly Rd Little Neck NY 11363-1125 Office: CUNY Bklyn Coll Dept History 2900 Bedford Ave Brooklyn NY 11210-2814 E-mail: mking@nyc.rr.com.

KING, MARY ANN, secondary education educator; b. Jacksonville, N.C., June 22, 1961; d. Hiram and Dorothy N. (Roberts) K. AS in Horticulture, Abraham Baldwin Agrl. Coll., Tifton, Ga., 1982; AS in Edn., South Ga. Coll., 1984; BS in Edn., Ga. So. Coll., 1986. Lic. social sci. tchr., Ga. Tchr. social sci. Ware County High Sch., Waycross, Ga., 1986-94; tchr. social studies Alpha Ctr., Waycross, Ga., 1994-98, Ware County H.S., Waycross, Ga., 1998—. Named Outstanding Educator Waycross (Ga.) Jaycees, 1988-89, Tchr. of Yr., 1995. Mem. Nat. Coun. Social Studies, Ga. Assn. Educators, Delta Kappa Gamma. Baptist. Avocations: walking, gardening, exercising, reading. Home: 6560 Hidoma Ln Millwood GA 31552-9793

KING, MAXWELL CLARK, former academic administrator; b. Ft. Pierce, Fla., Jan. 1, 1928; s. Hiram and Ida (Chandler) K.; m. Doris Warren, Jan. 29, 1953; children: Maxwell Clark II, Pamela King Jones, Carol, Russell E., Dori King Knodel. BS, Auburn (Ala.) U., 1950; MS in Edn., U. Fla., 1954, EdD, 1956; postgrad., U. Tex., 1958-59. Tchr. St. Lucie County High Sch., Ft. Pierce, 1950-51; prin. Dan McCarty High Sch., Ft. Pierce, 1956-60; pres. Indian River Community Coll., Ft. Pierce, 1960-68, Brevard Community Coll., Cocoa, Fla., 1968-99; ret. Cons. overseas liaison com. Am. Coun. on Edn., India, 1978; chmn. C.C.'s for Internat. Devel., Cocoa, 1976—. Fla. Gov.'s Summer Colls. Coun., Tallahassee, 1988-90; mem. exec. com. S. Regional Edn. Bd., Atlanta, 1987-91; bd. dirs. Am. Bank South, Merritt Island, Fla., First Nat. Bank of Merritt Island, Am. Bank, First United Bank, Cmty. Bank of South. Contbr. articles to profl. jours. Bd. dirs. United Way Brevard County, Cocoa, 1969—, Eugene Wuesthoff Meml. Hosp., Rockledge, Fla., 1970—; chmn. bd. dirs. Wuesthoff Health Svcs., Rockledge, 1986—. 1st lt. U.S. Army, 1951-53. Recipient Norm Keller Disting. Svc. award Melbourne Jaycees, 1986, Patrick Henry medal Mil. Order World Wars, 1986, Thomas J. Peters Nat. Leadership award U. Tex., 1989, DeBus award Nat. Space Club, 1997; Eileen Tosney Outstanding Am. Community-Univ. Adminstr., Am. Assn. Univ. Adminstrs., 1989; named laureate Brevard Bus. Leadership Hall of Fame, Jr. Achievement, Cocoa, 1988; Fulbright scholar, India, 1979-81, Republic of China, 1987. Mem. Cmty. Coll. Internat. Devel. (founder, chmn. 1976-98), Assn. Community Coll. Trustees (Nation's Outstanding Community Coll. Pres. award 1976), Am. Assn. Community and Jr. Colls. (bd. dirs. 1978-81), Fla. Assn. Colls. and Univs. (pres. 1971-72), Fla. Assn. Community Colls. (pres. 1965-66), Nat. Pres. Acad. (chmn. 1975-76), Cocoa Beach Area C. of C. (bd. dirs. 1988-91), Kappa Delta Pi, Phi Delta Kappa. Avocations: golf, reading. E-mail: Kingm@worldnet.att.net.

KING, NANCY, communications educator; b. Blytheville, Ark., May 10, 1945; d. Willie Lee and Janie (Jones) Garrett; m. Perry King, June 17, 1967; children: Perry Jr., Tiffany, Christopher. BA in Speech Communication, Calif. State U., L.A., 1974, MA in Speech Communication, 1981; MA in Psychology, Chapman U., 1998. Asst. supr. Pacific Telegraph & Telephone, 1968-70; computer operator West Coast Community Exch. Fenton & Lavine, L.A., 1970-71, So Gas Co., L.A., 1972-81, communication cons., 1982—; devel. lang. specialist Charles Drew Headstart Program, L.A.; prof. speech dept. Marymount Coll., Rancho Palos Verdes, Calif., 1986—. Speechwriter various regional ofcls.; instr. Calif. State U., L.A., 1979-86; mem. Calif. Libr. Svcs. Bd., 1984-94, pres., 1988-89, 90-91; mem. Calif. Libr. Networking Task Force, 1985-2000, Calif. Librs. Adv. Bd., 1984-94, Orange County Friends of Libr. Found., 1988-94, Calif. Alliance for Literacy Task Force, 1988, 92; faculty coord. Webster U., 1996—; intern counselor Am. Inst. Family Counselors, 1997, Human Options Counseling Ctr., 2000. Contbr. articles to profl. jours. Co-chmn. black coun. Orange County Hist. and Cultural Found., pres. bd., 1992; campaign mgr. Fran Williams for Santa Ana City Coun. Mem. NEA, Nat. Speech Communication Assn., Western Speech Communication Assn., Am. Fedn. Tchrs., AAUW, L.A. Southcentral Planning Coun. (bd. dirs.). Republican. Roman Catholic. Office: Marymount Coll 30800 Palos Verdes Dr E Palos Verdes Peninsula CA 90274 E-mail: nking@marymountpv.edu.

KING, ORA STERLING, education educator, consultant; b. Delta, Ala., Oct. 15, 1931; d. William and Mary (Fielder) Sterling; m. Lonnie C. King, Jr., June 12, 1993; 1 child, Sherri Anderson Manear. BA, Spelman Coll., 1954; MA, Atlanta U., 1969; PhD, U. Md., 1982. Cert. tchr., Ga. With Atlanta Pub. Schs., 1954-72, headstart prin., summer 1969, instructional coord., 1969-72; adj. prof. Fed. City Coll., Washington, 1973-75, chairperson dept. reading, 1975-78; master tchr. reading clinic U. Md., College Park, summer 1979, reading clinic adminstr., summer 1980; asst. prof. U. D.C., Washington, 1978-81; dean edn. Coppin State Coll., Balt., 1988-91, dean edn. and grad. studies, 1990-91, prof. edn., coord. MA in Tchg. Program, 1991—99, dir. MEd in Curriculum and Instrn. program, 1999—2001. Author: Reading & Study Skills, 1984, 2d edit., 1988; contbr. articles to profl. jours. Mem. NAACP; mem. various orgns. Recipient Disting. Alumni Citation, NAFEO, 1988. Mem. Nat. Alumnae Assn., Spelman Coll. (pres. 1986-88, life mem.), Coll. Reading Assn. (membership chair 1978-80, exec. sec. 1996-99), Internat. Reading Assn., Am. Assn. Colls. for Tchr. Edn., Assn. for Supervision and Curriculum Devel., Alpha Kappa Alpha. Democrat. Baptist. Avocations: reading, bridge, dancing. Home: 9537 Kilimanjaro Rd Columbia MD 21045-3942

KING, PAUL IRVIN, aerospace engineering educator; b. Balt., Apr. 20, 1944; s. James Irvin and Mary Josephine (Sclafani) K. Cert. in mech. engring., Johns Hopkins U., 1967; BSME, Ariz. State U., 1971; MS in Astronautics, Air Froce Inst. of Tech., 1972; PhD, Oxford U., 1986. Design engr. Black & Decker Mfg. co., Towson, Md., 1963-68; aircraft mechanic USAF Mil. Airlift Command, Fairfield, Calif., 1968-69; aerospace engr. USAF Logistics Command, Sacramento, Calif., 1973-78; instr. aeronautics USAF Acad., Colorado Springs, Colo., 1978-87; asst. prof. aerospace engring. USAF Inst. of Tech., Dayton, 1987-90, assoc. prof. aerospace engring., 1991—; assoc. prof. mech. engring. Cleve. State U. Cons. Wright Patterson Aeropropulsion Lab., Dayton, 1987—. Contbr. articles to profl. jours. Senator Faculty senate, 1992-95; chmn. Acad. Stds. Com., Air Force Inst. of Tech., 1993-95. Recipient Phoenix Blue Print award Phoenix Soc. of Mech. Engrs., 1970. Mem. AIAA, ASME, Sigma Xi, Tau Beta Pi, Sigma Gamma Tau. Achievements include research in the field of aerodynamics mixing in the compressor component found in jet engines. Home: 726 Wilfred Ave Dayton OH 45410-2733 Office: Air Force Inst of Techn 2950 P St Wright Pat OH 45433-7765

KING, R. PETER, science educator, academic center director; b. Springs, Transvaal, South Africa, Mar. 12, 1938; came to U.S., 1990; s. Frank H. and Rose M. (Seeley) K.; m. July 29, 1961; children: Jeremy P., Andrew J., Janet M. BSc, U. Witwatersrand, Johannesburg, 1958, MSc, 1962; PhD, U. Manchester, Eng., 1963. Lectr. U. Witwatersrand, 1963-65, U. Natal, Durban, South Africa, 1965-73, U. Manchester, 1973-74; prof. U. Witwatersrand, 1974-90, U. Utah, Salt Lake City, 1990—. Dir. comm. ctr. U. Utah, 1990-96; mem. Prime Minister's Sci. Adv. Coun., South Africa, 1979. Author: Modeling and Simulation of Mineral Processing Systems, 2001, Introduction to Practical Fluid Flow, 2002; editor: Principles of Flotation, 1982; editor Internat. Jour. Mineral Processing; contbr. articles to profl. jours. Fellow South African Inst. Mining and Metallurgy (pres. 1983-84); mem. Nat. Acad. Engring., Soc. Mining, Metallurgy and Exploration, Soc. Indsl. and Applied Math. Home: 2055 E 1300 S Salt Lake City UT 84108-2241 Office: U Utah 135 S 1460 E Rm 412 Salt Lake City UT 84112-0114

KING, RICHARD AULD, education educator; b. Utica, NY, Oct. 13, 1947; s. Harold F. and Rye (Auld) K.; m. Janet Van Ingen, Dec. 19, 1970; children: Richard II, Laura W., Sarah H. BA in Math. Edn., SUNY, Oswego, 1969, MS, 1972; PhD ed. adminstrn., SUNY, Buffalo, 1976. Math. tchr. Liverpool HS, NY, 1969-72; co-dir. SUNY Tchg. Ctr., Buffalo, 1973-76; asst. prof. SUNY, Fredonia, 1976-77; assoc. prof. U. N.Mex., Albuquerque, 1977-84, U. N.C., Chapel Hill, 1984-89; chmn. ednl. adminstrn. program U. NC, Chapel Hill, 1986-88; prof. U. No. Colo., Greeley, 1989—, interim assoc. v.p. for rsch. and grad studies, 1998-99, dir. divsn. ednl. leadership and policy studies, 2000—; vis. prof. Univ. of Lincoln, England, 1999—. Co-author: School Finance: Achieving High Standards with Equity and Efficiency 1991, 3d rev. edit., 2003; contbr. chpt. to books, articles to profl. jour. Rsch. grantee Ednl. Testing Svc., Princeton, NJ, 1982, Spencer Found., 1986-87, 96. Mem. Am. Edn. Fin. Assn., Am. Ednl. Rsch. Assn., No. Rocky Mt. Ednl. Rsch. Assn., Phi Delta Kappa. Home: 7420 Vardon Way Fort Collins CO 80528-8866 Office: U No Colo 418 McKee Hall Box 103 Greeley CO 80639-0001 E-mail: richard.king@unco.edu.

KING, RICHARD WAYNE, principal; b. Pitts., Mar. 27, 1952; s. Ralph Lewis and Pauline (Pyle) K.; m. Cheryl Louise Brea, June 22, 1974; children: Ashley, Adam, Allyson. BA in Psychology, Mt. Union Coll., 1974; MEd in Spl. Edn., U. Pitts., 1976, PhD in Ednl. Adminstrn., 1989. Cert. tchr., prin., Pa. Tchr. multiple-handicapped students Allegheny Intermediate Unit, Pitts., 1976-88, tchr. life skills support class, 1989-93; prin. Barrett Elem. Sch. Steel Valley Sch. Dist., Munhall, Pa., 1993—, chair Title I com., 1993—. Assoc. dir. summer program for exceptional children Camp Shining Arrow, Penn Hills, Pa., 1979-86, dir. adult program, 1980-84; chair Ea. Area Pub. Rels. Com., Pitts.,1 981-82, Ea. Area Vocat. Edn. Com., Pitts., 1987; insvc. trainer Allegheny Intermediate Unit, Pitts., 1988; sci. edn. amb. Carnegie Sci. Ctr., Pitts.; co-chair Steel Valley Strategic Planning Tech. Com., 1994; mem. site leadership com. Barrett Elem. Sch., 1993—. Dir. edn. 1st United Meth. Ch., East McKeesport, Pa., 1989—; cub den leader North Versailles area Boy Scouts Am., 1990—; bd. dirs. Family Ctr. for Child Devel.; mem. Steel Valley Elem. Adv. Coun., Steel Valley Adminstrv. Cabinet, 1993—, Steel Valley Communications Curriculum Com., 1994—. Mem. NEA, ASCD, Pa. State Edn. Assn. Avocation: home remodeling. Home: 412 3rd St North Versailles PA 15137-1220 Office: Barrett Elem Sch 221 E 12th Ave Homestead PA 15120-1690

KING, RONOLD WYETH PERCIVAL, physics educator; b. Williamstown, Mass., Sept. 19, 1905; s. James Percival and Edith Marianne Beate (Seyerlen) K.; m. Justine Merrell, June 22, 1937 (dec. Aug. 1990); 1 son, Christopher Merrell; m. Mary M. Govoni, June 1, 1991. AB, U. Rochester, 1927, S.M., 1929; PhD, U. Wis., 1932; student, U. Munich, Germany, 1928-29, Cornell U., 1929-30. Asst. in physics U. Rochester, 1927-28; Am.-German exchange student, 1929-30; White fellow in physics Cornell U., 1929-30; U. fellow in elec. engring. U. Wis., 1930-32, research asst., 1932-34; instr. physics Lafayette Coll., 1934-36, asst. prof., 1936-37; Guggenheim fellow Berlin, Germany, 1937-38; with Harvard U., 1938—, successively instr., asst. prof., assoc. prof., 1938-46, prof. applied physics, 1946-72, prof. emeritus, 1972—. Cons. electromagnetics and antennas, 1972— Author: Electromagnetic Engineering, Vol. 1, 1945, 2d edit, Fundamental Electromagnetic Theory, 1963, Transmission Lines, Antennas and Wave Guides, (with A.H. Wing and H.R. Mimmo), 1945, 2d edit., 1965, Transmission-Line Theory, 1955, 2d edit., 1965, Theory of Linear Antennas, 1956, (with T.T. Wu) Scattering and Diffraction of Waves, 1959, (with R.B. Mack and S.S. Sandler) Arrays of Cylindrical Dipoles, 1968, (with C.W. Harrison, Jr.) Antennas and Waves: A Modern Approach, 1969, Tables of Antenna Characteristics, 1971, (with G.S. Smith et al) Antennas in Matter, 1981 (with S. Prasad) Fundamental Electromagnetic Theory and Applications, 1986, (with M. Owens and T.T. Wu) Lateral Electromagnetic Waves Theory and Applications to Communications, Geophysical Exploration and Remote Sensing, 1992 (with G. Fikioris and R.B. Mack) Cylindrical Depole Arrays, 2002; also articles in field. Guggenheim fellow Europe, 1937, 58, IBM scholar Northeastern U., 1985; recipient Disting. Service citation U. Wis., 1973, Pender award U. Pa., 1986. Fellow IEEE (Centennial medal 1984, Grad. Edn. award 1997, Disting. Educator award 2001), AAAS, Am. Acad. Arts and Scis., Am. Phys. Soc.; mem. IEEE Antennas and Propagation Soc. (Disting. Achievement award 1991, Chento Tai Disting. Educator award 2001), AAUP, Internat. Sci. Radio Union, Bavarian Acad. Sci. (contbg. mem.), Phi Beta Kappa, Sigma Xi. Home: 92 Hillcrest Pky Winchester MA 01890-1440 Office: Gordon McKay Lab 9 Oxford St Cambridge MA 02138-2901

KING, SHARON A. elementary school educator; b. Owensboro, Ky., May 17, 1947; d. Charles Franklin and Catherine (Brown) Whitaker; m. Ronald Holton King, Oct. 8, 1966; children: Christopher, Tom, Cindy. BA, No. Ky. U., 1989, MEd, 1992. Cert. tchr. K-6, Ky.; cert. RANK I adminstrn. Head cashier/bookkeeper Liberty Loan Co., Cin., 1965-66; tchr. grade 4 Dayton (Ky.) Ind. Schs., 1990-92, 93—; tchr. grades 2-3 Bracken County Schs., Brooksville, Ky., 1992-93; tchr. grade 5-6 Lincoln Elem. Sch., Dayton. Supr. intern program Ky. Intern Program/Lincoln Elem. Sch., Dayton, 1994—; assoc. Region 4 Svc. Ctr., 1996. Mem. ASCD, AAUW, NEA, Ky. Edn. Assn., Dayton Edn. Assn., Ky. Assn. Supervision and Curriculum Devel., Kappa Delta Pi (historian), Phi Delta Kappa. Republican. Home: RR 1 Box 319 Brooksville KY 41004-9756

KING, SHERYL JAYNE, secondary education educator, counselor; b. East Grand Rapids, Mich., Oct. 29, 1945; d. Thomas Benton III and Bettyann Louise (Mains) K. BS in Family Living, Sociology, Secondary Edn., Cen. Mich. U., 1968, M in Counseling, 1971. Educator Newaygo (Mich.) Pub. Schs., 1968-72; interior decorator Sue King Interiors, Grand Rapids, Mich., 1972-73; dir. girl's unit Dillon Family and Youth Svcs., Tulsa, 1973-74; mgr. Fellowhip Press, Grand Rapids, Minn., 1974-76; educator, counselor Itasca Community Coll., Grand Rapids, 1977-81, Dist. 318, Grand Rapids, 1977—, dept. head, 1977-81, 85-87. Bd. dirs., chairperson program com. Marriage and Family Devel. Ctr., Grand Rapids, 1985-89. Treas. Cove Whole Foods Coop., 1978-80; chmn. bd. Christian Community Sch., 1977-78; jr. high softball coach, 1983-86; mem. issues com. No. Minn. Citizens League, Grand Rapids, 1984—, Blandin Found. Study, 1985-86; chair Itasca County Women's Consortium, Grand Rapids, 1983-87, Women's Day Conf., Grand Rapids, 1983-87; bd. dir. audio tech. Fellowship of Believers, Grand Rapids, 1974-87, 90-98, deaconess, 1974—; bd. dir. audio tech Camp Dominion, Cass Lake, Minn., 1976-80; mem. fitness com., chmn. aquatic com., YMCA, Grand Rapids, 1974-87. Recipient 6 Outstanding Svc. awards Fellowship of Believers, 1974-79. Mem. Alpha Delta Kappa. Republican. Avocations: photography, tennis, sailing, softball, travel, writing. Home: 1914 Mckinney Lake Rd Grand Rapids MN 55744-4330

KING, STEPHEN EMMETT, educational administrator; b. Hopkinsville, Ky., June 1, 1942; s. Emmett Southall and Ruth Virginia (Burchfield) K.; m. Linda Johnston, Nov. 11, 1967. MusB, West Ky. U., 1964; MS, Radford U., 1975; EdD, Va. Poly. Inst. and State U., 1991. Dir. bands Coeburn (Va.) H.S., 1964-68, William Byrd H.S., Vinton, Va., 1968-86; supr. fine arts Roanoke County Schs., Roanoke, Va., 1986-97; vis. asst. prof. music edn. Va. Poly. Inst. and State U., Blacksburg, 1997—. Contbr. articles to profl. jours. Active Roanoke Symphony Soc. Bd., 1994-2000—, chair edn. com. 1997-2000—; legis. com Art Coun. Blue Ridge, 1998-2002. Mem. Music Educators Nat. Conf., Va. Edn. Assn., Va. Band and Orch. Dirs. Assn. (sec. 1984-86, pres.-elect 1986-88, pres. 1988-90, Philip Fuller Svc. award 2000), Am. Sch. Band Dirs. Assn. (state chmn. 1986-88), Va. Alliance for Arts Edn. (bd. dirs. 1991-96, sec. 1993-96), Va. Music Edn. Assn. (exec. bd. dirs., pres.-elect 1990-92, pres. 1992-94, v.p. 1994-96, chair editl. bd. 1996-98), Phi Delta Kappa, Phi Beta Mu, Phi Mu Alpha Sinfonia. Home: 5250 Keffer Rd Catawba VA 24070-2122 Office: Va Poly Inst and State U Dept Musc 241 Squires (0240) Blacksburg VA 24061 E-mail: sking@infionline.net.

KING, TANYA, counseling administrator, public school educator; b. Detroit, Apr. 28, 1954; d. Arthur Neal and Bonney (Shapiro) K.; s. Herman, widowed; 1 child, Samantha. BA in Edn., U. Mich., 1978; postgrad., U. Hawaii, 1989-90. Tchr. Hawaii Sch. Sys., Kona, 1986-87, Waianae, 1987-90, Commonwealth of the No. Mariana Islands Pub. Sch. Sys., Saipan, Hawaii, 1990-92, Rota, Hawaii, 1992—. Performance stds. task force Commonwealth of the No.Mariana Islands Pub. Sch. Sys., 1994, OTE task force, 1990-92, coun. steering comm., 2003, Nat. Honor Soc. adv., 2000—, v.p. of the Women's affairs office, accreditation team West. Assoc. Sch. and Coll. Author: Students of the Pacific Cooperative Algebra Lab, 1992 (award). Treas. PTA, Rota, 1992—; active WTA Parents' Networking, Rota, 1992, Mayors Task Force. Recipent numerous Fed. Grants, 1992, 1994 Mem. ASCD. Avocations: writing, illustrating children's books. Home: PO Box 523 Rota MP 96951-0523 Office: Pub Sch Sys PO Box 1370 Saipan MP 96950-1370

KING, THOMAS CREIGHTON, thoracic surgeon, educator; b. Salt Lake City, Apr. 10, 1928; s. Creighton G. and Alice (Edwards) K.; m. Joan Peters, Aug. 23, 1952; children— John Creighton, Elizabeth, Thomas David, Patrick Edward. BS, U. Utah, 1952, MD, 1954; MA in Ednl. Psychology, U. Mo., Kansas City, 1963. Diplomate: Am. Bd. Surgery, Am. Bd. Thoracic Surgery; cert. in critical care. Intern Columbia-Presbyn. Hosp., N.Y.C., 1954-55; resident U. Utah Hosps., 1955-59; asst. prof. surgery U. Kans., 1960-64; asso. chief staff, dir. research labs. Kansas City Vets. Hosp., 1962-64; asso. prof. surgery U. Ill., 1964-66, Asso. prof. ednl. psychology, 1964-66, chief of tng. Center for Study Med. Edn., 1964-66; attending surgeon U. Ill. Research and Edn. Hosp., 1964-66; asso. attending surgeon Cook County Hosp., Chgo., 1964-66; asso. prof. surgery, asso. dean Coll. Medicine, U. Utah, Salt Lake City, 1966-68; acad. v.p. U. Utah, 1968-69, provost, 1969-73, prof. surgery, 1969-73, v.p. health affairs, 1970-73; staff surgeon U. Utah Med. Center, 1966-73; chief thoracic surgery VA Hosp., Salt Lake City, 1968-73; prof. surgery Columbia Coll. Physicians and surgeons, N.Y.C., 1973—, Ferrer prof. surgery, 1983—; attending surgeon Presbyn. Hosp., N.Y.C., 1973—. Cons. med. edn. WHO; mem. Utah Bd. Health, 1967-73 Contbr. articles to profl. jours. Mem. ACS, Soc. U. Surgeons, Assn. Am. Med. Colls., Am. Assn. Thoracic Surgery, Am. Surg. Assn., Soc. for Critical Care Medicine, Soc. Internat. de Chirurgie. Home: 35 Claremont Ave # 6S New York NY 10027-6802

KING, THOMAS M. theology educator, priest; b. Pitts. s. William Martin and Catherine (Mulvihil) K. BA, U. Pitts., 1951; MA, Fordham U., 1959; Doctorat es Sci. Religeuse, U. Strasbourg, 1968. Joined Jesuits, 1951, ordained priest Roman Cath. Ch., 1964. Prof. Theology Georgetown U., Washington, 1968—. Author: Sartre and the Sacred, 1974, Teilhard's Mysticism of Knowing, 1981, Teilhard de Chardin, 1988, Enchantments, 1989, Merton: Mystic at the Center of America, 1992; editor: Teilhard and the Unity of Knowledge, 1983, Letters of Teilhard and Lucile Swan, 1993, Jung's Four and Some Philosophers, 1999. Co-founder, bd. dirs. Cosmos & Creation, Loyola Coll., Balt., 1982—, Univ. Faculty for Life, Washington, 1989—. Roman Catholic. Home: Jesuit Community Georgetown U Washington DC 20057-0001 Office: Georgetown U Dept Theology Washington DC 20057-0001

KING, VERNA ST. CLAIR, retired school counselor; b. Berwick, La.; d. John Westley and Florence Ellen (Calvin) St. C.; A.B., Wiley Coll., 1937; M.A., San Diego State U., 1977; m. Alonzo Le Roy King, Aug. 27, 1939 (dec.); children— Alonzo Le Roy, Joyce Laraine, Verna Lee Eugenia King Bickerstaff, St. Clair A., Reginald Calvin (dec.). Tchr., Morgan City, La., 1939-40; tchr. San Diego Unified Sch. Dist., 1955-67, parent counselor, 1967-78, counselor grades 1-9, 1978-86; cons. Tucson Sch. Dist., 1977—, dir. compensatory edn., 1983—. Mem. Calif. Democratic State Central Com., 1950—, Dem. County Central Com., 1972—, del. nat. conv., 1976, 84, mem. exec. bd. Dem. State Central Com., 1982—; mem. San Diego County Sander Adv. Commn., 1982; hon. life mem. PTA; bd. dirs. YWCA, 1983—, v.p., 1987-88; chair Dem. County Ctrl. fundraising, 1992—; del. Dem. Nat. Com., 1992. Recipient Key to City, Mayor C. Dail, 1955, cert. United Negro Coll. Fund dr., 1980, Urban League Pvt. Sector award, 1982, 4th Ann. Conf. on Issues in Ethnicity and Mental Health Participants award, 1982 ; named Woman of Dedication, Salvation Army, 1985, Citizen of Yr., City Club and Jaycees, 1985, Woman of Achievement, Pres.' Council, 1983, Henry Auerbach award San Diego Dem. Party Ctrl. Com., 1997; numerous other honors. Mem. NEA (women's council 1980-82), AAUW, Calif. Tchrs. Assn. (state council 1979—, area dir. 1985—), San Diego Tchrs. Assn. (dir. 1958, 64, sec. 1964-67), Nat. Council Negro Women, San Diego County Council Dem. Women (pres. 1986-88), Compensatory Edn. Assn. (area dir. 1982-87), Pres. Women, Inc., Alpha Kappa Alpha (pres. 1978-80), Delta Kappa Gamma. Methodist. Clubs: Women's Inc., Order Eastern Star. Home: 5721 Churchward St San Diego CA 92114-4011

KING, WILLARD FAHRENKAMP (MRS. EDMUND LUDWIG KING), Spanish language educator; b. Roswell, N.Mex., July 13, 1924; d. W.F. and Willard (Pickerill) Fahrenkamp; m. Edmund Ludwig King, Jan. 29, 1951. Student, Tex. Christian U., 1940-41; BA, U. Tex., 1943, MA, 1946; PhD, Brown U., 1957. Instr. Spanish U. Tex., 1946-47, 49-50; instr. Spanish Brown U., 1950-51, Bryn Mawr (Pa.) Coll., 1958-60, asst. prof., 1960-64, assoc. prof., 1964-70, prof. Spanish, 1970—, Dorothy Nepper Marshall prof. Hispanic studies, 1976—, chmn. dept. Spanish, 1964-89, dir. Hispanic studies program, 1971-92. Corporator Internat. Inst. in Spain, resident dir., 1991-93. Author: Prosa novelística y academias literarias en el siglo XVII, 1963, Juan Ruiz de Alarcón, letrado y dramaturgo, 1989; also articles; editor, translator: Lope de Vega, El Caballero de Olmedo, 1972; translator: Amèrico Castro, The Spaniards, 1971; editor, commentator Agustín Moreto, El desdén, con el desdén, 1996. Guggenheim fellow, 1965-66 Mem. MLA, Renaissance Soc. Am., Phi Beta Kappa. Home: 171 Western Way Princeton NJ 08540-7207 Office: Thomas Libr Bryn Mawr Coll Bryn Mawr PA 19010

KINGDON, JOHN WELLS, political science educator; b. Wisconsin Rapids, Wis., Oct. 28, 1940; s. Robert Wells and Catherine (McCune) K.; m. Kirsten Berg, June 16, 1965; children: James, Tor. BA, Oberlin Coll., 1962; MA, U. Wis., 1963, PhD, 1965. Asst. prof. polit. sci. U. Mich., Ann Arbor, 1965-70, assoc. prof., 1970-75, prof., 1975-98, prof. emeritus, 1998—, chmn. dept. polit. sci., 1982-87. Author: Candidates for Office, 1968, Congressmen's Voting Decisions, 1973, 3d rev. edit., 1989, Agendas, Alternatives and Public Policies, 1984, 2d edit., 1995, America the Unusual, 1998. NSF grantee, 1978-82, Soc. Sci. Research Council grantee, 1969-70; Guggenheim fellow, 1979-80, Ctr. for Advanced Study in Behaviorial Scis. fellow, 1987-88. Fellow Am. Acad. Arts and Scis.; mem. Midwest Polit. Sci. Assn. (pres. 1987-88). Office: U Mich Dept Polit Sci Ann Arbor MI 48109

KINGDON, MARY ONEIDA GRACE, retired elementary education educator; b. Canton, Ohio, Aug. 11, 1934; d. Virgil Ezra and Donnie Mabel (Rowe) Sell; m. Harold Ivor Edwin Kingdon, Feb. 22, 1957; children: Sheryl Lynn, Harold Ivor Edwin Jr., Jill Renée, James Todd Ezra. BA in History and Social Sci., Houghton Coll., 1956; postgrad., U. Ky., 1963-67, SUNY, Geneseo, 1969-71; MS in Edn., Alfred U., 1983. Cert. permanent N-6 elem. tchr., reading tchr., N.Y. Tchr. English, Cherry Street City Sch., Canton, 1956-57; tchr. English Mercer County Pub. Sch., Harrodsburg, Ky., 1963-64, Cardinal Valley Fayette County Sch., Lexington, Ky., 1965-67; intermediate tchr. Friendship (N.Y.) Cen. Sch., 1967-97; ret., 1997. Primary tchr. Bearss Acad., Jackson, Miss., 1983-84. Mem. N.Y. State Tchrs. Retirement Assn. (Allegany and Cattaraugus counties del. 1985-94), N.Y. State Union Tchrs., Friendship Ctrl. Sch. Tchrs. Assn. (sec. 1970-72, pres. 1982-83, 92-93). Republican. Mem. Wesleyan Ch. Avocations: travel, cross-stitching, flower gardening. Home: 9810 Fancher Hts Houghton NY 14744-8711

KING-GARNER, MIRIA, elementary education educator; b. Gadsden, Ala., May 29, 1949; d. Carl Jr. and Joyce Elrod (Gore) King; m. James Rickey Garner, June 2, 1968; 1 child, Micah. BS in Edn., Auburn U., 1972; MA, U. Ala., 1975, AA, 1981; Master's Endorsement in Adminstrn., 1995. Tchr. 6th-8th grades Etowah County Bd. Edn., Gadsden; asst. prin. Sardis H.S. Named Etowah County System Elem. Tchr. of Yr., 1988-89; inducted in Tchr. Hall of Fame (elem.) 1989. Mem. NEA, Ala. Edn. Assn., Etowah Edn. Assn., Delta Kappa Gamma.

KINGSBURY, REX ALAN, elementary education educator, administrator; b. Rockford, Ill., Feb. 22, 1957; s. Floyd Wolcott and Lois Muriel (Dahlgren) K.; m. Sandra Lynn Ferguson, Aug. 15, 1981; children: Michael, Jennifer. AA, Rock Valley Coll., 1977; BS in Elem. Edn., Bemidji State U., 1979; MS in Edn., No. Ill. U., 1986; cert. in adminstrn., Tri-Coll., 1987. Cert. tchr., sch. prin., Minn. Elem. tchr. Rockford Pub. Schs., 1979-85, Perham (Minn.) Pub. Schs., 1985-86, 90—, elem. sch. prin., 1986-90. Mem. new bldg. facility com. Perham Schs., 1988-90, numerous curriculum and policy coms. Recipient Outstanding Tchr. Achievement award Ashland Oil Co., 1993; named Bemidji State U. Educator's Hall of Fame, 1995; selected mem. Minn. Dept. Edn. Reading Best Practice Team, 1995. Mem. NEA, Minn. Edn. Assn., Nat. Elem. Sch. Prins. Assn., Minn. Elem. Sch. Prins. Assn., Perham Parent-Tchr. Orgn., Perham Rotary, Perham C. of C. Lutheran. Avocations: creative writing, reading. Office: Heart of the Lakes Elem Sch 810 2nd Ave SW Perham MN 56573-1600 Home: 38234 N Little Mcdonald Dr Frazee MN 56544-8930

KINLAW, HILDA HESTER, primary education educator; b. Elizabethtown, N.C., June 21, 1938; d. Joseph Woodrow and Mildred Lucille (Butler) Hester; m. William Robert Kinlaw, Aug. 2, 1957; children: Richard William, Gary Lynn, Lisa Faye. Grad. in cosmetology, Fayetteville Beauty Acad., 1957; BS, Pembroke (N.C.) State U., 1976, K-12 reading cert., MEd, 1979. Cosmetologist, Dublin, N.C., 1957-59, 60-76; sec. Edwards Store, Charleston, S.C., 1959-60; K-6 tchr. reading Bladen County Schs., Elizabethtown, 1960-76, tchr., 1983-90, 91—. Adv. bd. Bladen County Nursing Homes, 1990-93, Bladen County Hosp., 1990—; fund chmn. Dublin (N.C.) Area Heart Fund, 1985; area chmn. bike-a-thon St. Jude Hosp. Recipient NCAE human rels. commn. dist. 13 award Bladen County, 1983. Mem. ASCD, N.C. Assn. Educators, Homemakers Club. Avocations: reading, travel, crafts, exercise. Home: PO Box 237 Dublin NC 28332-0237 Office: PO Box 27347 Raleigh NC 27611-7347

KINNAIRD, MARY ANN, physical education educator; b. Queens, N.Y., July 10, 1952; d. John Arlington and Edith (Martin) K. BS in Phys. Edn. and Psychology, Russell Sage Coll., 1974; MS in Edn. Psychology, Albany State U., 1977. Cert. tchr., N.Y. Instr. phys. edn. Albany (N.Y.) High Sch., 1974-86, Philip Schuller Elem. Sch., Albany, 1986-93, Montessori Magnet Sch., Albany, 1993—. Bd. dirs. Albany Fund Edn., 1997—. Mem. N.Y. United Tchrs. (del. 1990—), Albany Pub. Sch. Tchrs. Assn. (polit. action com. 1990—, mem. com. tchrs. and adminstrs. 1990-93, mem. shared decision making team 1993—). Avocations: skiing, weight training. Home: PO Box 191 Altamont NY 12009-0191

KINNAIRD, SUSAN MARIE, special education educator; b. Grosse Pointe, Mich., May 3, 1954; d. William Burl and Ida Mae (Diehl) Cunningham; m. Henry Wayne Kinnaird Jr., Nov. 30, 1985. BA in Edn., Wayne State U., 1978; MA in Ednl. Adminstrn., U. Houston at Clear Lake, 1990. Cert. elem. tchr., spl. edn. tchr., spl. edn. supr., instrnl. supr., ESL tchr., Tex. Parent trainer Dept. Mental Health, Warren, Mich., 1977-78; spl. edn. tchr. Houston Ind. Sch. Dist., 1978-95, spl. edn. coord., 1995—. Asst.

coach Spl. Olympics, Houston, 1982, 84, 88-91; bell choir mem. Cen. Presbyn. Ch., Houston, 1979—. Grantee Houston Bus. Com. for Ednl. Excellence 1991, 92. Mem. Coun. for Exceptional Children (chpt. 100 newsletter editor 1990-92, sec. 1992-93, pres.-elect 1993-94, pres. 1994-95). Roman Catholic. Avocations: sewing, handcrafts, music, reading, travel. Home: 4111 Mona Lee Ln Houston TX 77080-1768 Office: Houston Ind Sch Dist Office of Spl Edn 3830 Richmond Houston TX 77027-

KINNEL, MARY LOU, college recruitment executive; b. Dawson, Ga., Sept. 3, 1945; d. James Kinnel and Flora M. (Bunts) Burdine; m. James Riley Lewis, 1964 (div.); children: Anthony, Reginald, Vickie; m. George Wayne Harris; 1 child, Kevin. Student, Gibbs Jr. Coll., St. Petersburg, Fla., 1963-64; BS, Ft. Valley (Ga.) State Coll., 1980, postgrad., 1987—. Tchr. home econs. Monroe County Middle Sch., Forsyth, Ga., 1980-82, Cen. High Sch., Macon, Ga., 1985-86, Wilkinson County Jr. High Sch., Irwinton, Ga., 1987; recruitment cons. Ft. Valley State Coll., 1986, recruitment specialist, 1987—. Tchr. arts and crafts, Camp John Hope, Marshallville, Ga., 1980-82. Mem. Ga. Vocat. Assn., Am. Vocat. Assn., NAFE, Assn. Supervision and Curriculum Devel., DAV Aux., Delta Kappa Rho. Democrat. Baptist. Avocations: arts, crafts, sewing, cooking.

KINNEY, ARTHUR FREDERICK, literary history educator, writer, editor; b. Cortland, N.Y., Sept. 5, 1933; s. Arthur F. and Gladys (Mudge) K. BA magna cum laude, Syracuse U., 1955; MS, Columbia U., 1956; PhD, U. Mich., 1963. Instr. Yale U., New Haven, Conn., 1963-66; asst. prof. U. Mass., Amherst, 1966-69, assoc. prof., 1969-73, prof., 1973-85, Copeland Prof., 1985—. Adj. prof. Clark U., 1973—, NYU, 1990—; dir. Mass. Ctr. for Renaissance Studies, Amherst; spkr. in field. Author: Faulkner's Narrative Poetics, 1978, Resources of Being: Flannery O'Connor's Library, 1984, Humanist Poetics, 1986, John Skelton: Priest as Poet, 1987, Continental Humanist Poetics, 1989, Dorothy Parker Revisited, 1997, Renaissance Drama, 1999, 2nd edit., 2001, Cambridge Companion to English Literature 1500-1600, 2000, Blackwell Companion to Renaissance Drama, 2001, Lies Like Truth: Shakespeare, Macbeth and the Cultural Moment, 2001, New Essays on Hamlet, 2001, Shakespeare by Stages, 2003; editor: Rogues, Vagabonds, and Sturdy Beggars, 1973, 2nd edit., 1990, Elizabethan Backgrounds, 1974, revised edit., 1990, Renaissance Historicism, 1987, English Literary Renaissance jour., (book series) Twayne English Authors Series-Renaissance, Massachusetts Studies in Early Modern Culture; mem. editl. bd. several jours.:, editl. cons. in field:. With AUS, 1956-58. Recipient Disting. Tchg. award U. Mass., 1990, Chancellor's medal, 1985, Univ. Rsch. fellowship, 1976; named Fulbright fellow, Christ Ch., Oxford U., 1977-78, Sr. Huntington Libr. fellow, 1973-74, 78, 83, Sr. NEH fellow, 1973-74, 87-88, Sr. Folger Shakespeare Libr. fellow, 1974, 90, 92. Mem. MLA (pres. coun. of editors of learned jours. 1971-73, 81-83), Shakespeare Assn. Am. (trustee 1995—), Renaissance Soc. Am. (coun. mem.), Renaissance English Text Soc. (pres. 1985—), Sixteenth-Century Studies Conf. Assn, Internat. Sidney Soc. (pres.). Avocations: published photographer, jazz. Home: 25 Hunters Hill Cir Amherst MA 01002-3116 Office: English Dept U Mass Amherst Amherst MA 01003 also: Ctr Renaissance Studies PO Box 2300 Amherst MA 01004-2300

KINNEY, BEVERLY JEAN, English language educator; b. Yakima, Wash., Apr. 17, 1926; d. Vesper Lewis and Ethel Annetta (Silvers) Cox; m. Lyle B. Kinney, Aug. 21, 1948. BA, Ctrl. Wash. U., 1948; MA in Reading, U. Mo., 1968; cert. in edn. adminstrn., Western Wash. U., 1976. Mem. dist. reading team Port Angeles (Wash.) Pub. Schs., 1969-75, prin. Franklin Elem. Sch., 1975-89, supr. student tchrs., 1968-90; instr. Peninsula Coll., Port Angeles, 1992; prin. Queets-Clearwater Sch. Dist. Ednl. Svcs. Dist., Bremerton, Wash., 1993-94; supr. student tchrs. Olympic Peninsula Ednl. Svcs. Dist., Bremerton, Wash., 2000—. Fellow Fla. Inst. Tech., Melbourne, 1983, Inst. for Devel. Ednl. Activities, Claremont, Calif., 1978-88; tchr. NEA Tchg. Corps, Sierra Leone, summers, 1965, 67; tchr. English, Shijiazhuang (China) Hebei Tchrs. Coll., 1990-91, 92-93, 94. Active YMCA, Port Angeles, 1956-61, Girl Scouts of U.S., Port Angeles, Women in Politics, Beijing, Shanghai, People to People, George Washington U. Recipient Friendship award People's Republic of China, 1994, Disting. Alumni award Coll. Edn. and Profl. Studies, Ctrl. Wash. U. Alumni Assn., 1997. Mem. AAUW, LWV, Delta Kappa Gamma, Soroptimists. Democrat. Methodist. Avocations: outdoors, gardening, hiking, walking, reading. Home and Office: 253 Cedar Park Dr Port Angeles WA 98362-8430

KINNEY, DICK JOSEPH, private school educator, coach; b. Sheldon, Iowa, Jan. 29, 1957; s. James Paul and Maybelle Emma (Bohlke) K. BA magna cum laude, Buena Vista Coll., Storm Lake, Iowa, 1979; MA magna cum laude, U. No. Iowa, Cedar Falls, 1983. Cert. tchr., Iowa, Colo., EMT. Tchr., coach Alden (Iowa) H.S., 1979-81; tchr.'s asst. U. No. Iowa, 1981-83; coach, tchr., advisor Orme Sch., Mayer, Ariz., 1983-87; tchr., coach, advisor Graland Country Day Sch., Denver, 1987—, head sci. dept., 2003—. Camp counselor Camp Deerhorn, Rhinelander, Wis., 1980-2003; emergency med. technician, Denver, 1994. Mem. Fellowship of Christian Athletes. Roman Catholic. Avocations: reading, running, sports, travel. Home: 1811 S Quebec Way Apt 45 Denver CO 80231-2670 Office: Graland Sch 30 Birch St Denver CO 80220-5634

KINNEY, DOROTHY JEAN, retired elementary school educator; b. Bklyn., Mar. 25, 1935; d. Joseph Salvatore and Ida (DiCamillo) Longo; m. Robert Frank Masessa, Apr. 3, 1954 (dec. May 1984); children: Robert C., Joseph M., Jeffrey T.; m. Lester Frederick Kinney, Mar. 22, 1986. BA, William Paterson Coll., 1974, MA, 1981. Elem. sch. tchr. West Milford (N.J.) Bd. Edn., 1974-95; ret., 1995. Remedial reading tutor St. Paul's Parochial Sch., Haledon, N.J., 1974. Scout leader Boy Scouts Am., West Milford, N.J., 1964-74; mem. com. Queen of Peace Ch., West Milford, 1960-84. Mem. NEA, N.J. Edn. Assn., West Milford Edn. Assn. Republican. Roman Catholic. Home: 15 Hickory Way Mount Arlington NJ 07856-1367 also: Apshawa Sch 7867 Gardner Dr Naples FL 34109-0608

KINNEY, JEANNE KAWELOLANI, English studies educator, writer; b. Bayville, N.Y., Nov. 22, 1964; d. Robert Warren Stewart and Genevieve Lehuanani (Okilauea) Kinney. BA, Linfield Coll., 1986; MFA, Bowling Green State U., 1988. Tchr. Hawaii Bus. Coll., Honolulu, 1993-95; ESL tchr. GEOs Lang. Corp., Osaka and Kobe, Japan, 1996-97; English tchr. St. Joseph's H.S., Hilo, Hawaii, 2000. Poet-in-the-schs. Dept. Edn., Honolulu, fall 1994; sub. English tchr. St. Andrew's Priory, Honolulu, 1993; adj. English tchr. Chaminade U., Honolulu, spring 1993, 94; basic skills instr. Kamehameha Schs., Honolulu, 1991-92; English tchr., speech coach Punahou Sch., Honolulu, 1989-91. Contbr. to profl. publs. including Hawaii Rev., Kaimana, Ascent, Seattle Rev., Bamboo Ridge Press. Precinct ops. cood. Office Lt. Gov., Hawaii Elections Divsn., 1991-93, precinct worker trainer, 1989-91; v.p. Hawaii Lit. Arts Coun., Honolulu, 1990; pub. rels. officer Hawaii Speech League, Honolulu, 1991. Avocations: dance, swimming, writing, travel, foreign languages. Home: 10 Ululani St # 10 Hilo HI 96720-2979

KINNEY, MARY MAY, secondary education educator; b. Lebanon, Mo., Apr. 11, 1954; d. Oscar Junior and Rilda May (Moss) Kelso; m. Richard L. Kinney, Oct. 11, 1986; children: Jesse Ryan, Kyle Thomas. BS in Social Sci. Edn. and English, S.W. Bapt. Coll., Bolivar, Mo., 1977. Cert. social sci. and English tchr. 7-12, Mo. Tchr. English and history Macks Creek (Mo.) Sch., 1977—. Mem. Nat. Coun. Social Studies, Mo. Coun. Social Studies, Mo. State Tchrs. Assn., Macks Creek Cmty. Tchrs. Assn., PTO. Republican. Mem. Assembly of God Ch. Avocations: reading, crossword puzzles, walking. Office: Macks Creek Sch 245 State Rd N Macks Creek MO 65786-0038 E-mail: mkinney@mail.mcreek.k12.mo.us.

KINNEY, PATRICIA MAY, elementary art educator; b. Princeton, N.J., July 30, 1951; d. David Duffield and Vera Frances (Webb) Wood; m. W. Grant Kinney, July 21, 1973; children: Laura E. Kinney, John D. Kinney. BS, SUNY, New Paltz, 1973; grad. Sch. Theology, U. of the South, 1996. Cert. N.Y. Art tchr. Moravia (N.Y.) Ctrl. Sch., 1973—, gifted/talented tchr., 1986—, gifted/talented coord., 1991—. Gifted/talented adv. bd. BOCES, Auburn, N.Y.; coach, judge, sch. coord. Odyssey of the Mind, 1986—; rep. for faculty Compact for Edn., Moravia, 1993; leader People to People Student Amb. program, 2003. Artist ceramic wall, commissioned mural, 1991. Pres. Episcopal Ch. Women, St. Matthew's Episcopal Ch., Moravia, 1988-93, warden, 1998-2000, mem. vestry, 1997— ; mem., lt., sec. Four Town First Aid, Moravia, 1974-79. Mem. N.Y. State Art Tchrs., N.Y. State United Tchrs. (bldg. rep. 1989-98, sec. 2002—), N.Y. State Acad. for Tchg. and Learning (charter), Delta Kappa Gamma. Episcopalian. Avocations: downhill skiing, reading, travel, crafts. Office: Moravia Ctrl Sch 24 S Main St Moravia NY 13118-2310

KINNEY, THOMAS JOHN, academic administrator; b. Dansville, NY, Jan. 31, 1946; s. John Vernon and Elinor (Fox) K.; m. Linda G. Gates, Dec. 12, 1970; children: Matthew, Andrew. BA, Syracuse U., 1968; MSW in Mgmt., U. Albany, 1974; postgrad. in edn., Nova U., 1995—. Case worker Livingston County Social Svc., Geneseo, N.Y., 1969-72; tng. specialist N.Y. State Dept. Social Svcs., Albany, 1974-76; dir. continuing edn. U. Albany SUNY, Albany, 1976-82, dir. profl. devel., 1983—; prof., co-founder Russian-Am. Ctr. Adult/Continuing Edn. Inst. Pedagogics Russian Acad. of Edn., Moscow, 1992—; chief learning officer, v.p. edn. and devel. Premier Inc., Oak Brook, Ill., 1999—2001; CEO, Kinney and Assocs., 1999—; mem. faculty U. Phoenix, 2000—, Keller Grad. Sch. Bus., 2001—. Adv. com. Am. Coll. Testing Program, Iowa City, Iowa, 1993—; bd. dirs. Synquest Technologies, Raleigh, N.C. Editor: Jour. of SW Continuing Edn., 1981—; series editor: (10 books) A Resource Guide Series for Human Service Professionals, 1985-90, A Resource Guide for Managers and Supervisors in Human Services, 1990—; contbr. articles to profl. jours. Mem. N.Y. State assembly task force on Employee Assistance Programs, Albany, 1988—; bd. dirs. Ctr. for Dispute Resolution, Albany, 1989—. Named to Adult and Continuing Edn. Hall of Fame. Fellow State Acad. for Pub. Adminstrn.; mem. Nat. U. Continuing Edn. Assn. (divsn. chair 1984—), Am. Assn. Adult and Continuing Edn. (treas. 1990-95, bd. dirs., pres. 1998-2000, Outstanding Svc. medallion 1994), Assn. Continuing Higher Edn., Work in Am. Inst., Am. Assn. Higher Edn. Avocation: wood carving. Home and Office: PO Box 770536 Ocala FL 34477

KINNEY, YVONNE MARIE, primary grades educator; b. Saginaw, Mich., Apr. 3, 1944; d. Harold William and Leola Rose (Beardsley) Johnson; m. Gerald Warren Kinney, Aug. 5, 1967; children: Meghan Marie, Andrew Gerald. BA in Elem. Edn., Mich. State U., 1965; MA in Elem. Edn., Ctrl. Mich. U., 1977. Cert. tchr., Mich. 1st grade tchr. Longfellow Sch., Saginaw, Mich., 1965—. Mem. NEA, Mich. Edn. Assn., Saginaw Edn. Assn. Methodist. Avocations: doll collecting, gardening, reading, church activities. Home: 5564 Adrian St Saginaw MI 48603-3659 Office: Longfellow Sch 1314 Brown St Saginaw MI 48601-2603

KINNINGHAM, ALAN GOODRUM, music educator, composer/arranger; b. Huntingdon, Tenn., Apr. 18, 1956; s. Troy Edward and Evelyn Clara (Goodrum) K.; m. Jennifer Lynn Bennett, May 30, 1977; children: William Andrew, Thomas Bennett. BS in Music Edn., U. Tenn., Martin, 1977; MusM in Music Composition, Tex. A&M Commerce, 1978; DMA in Music Composition, U. Memphis, 1990. Cert. tchr., Tenn. Dir. bands Martin (Tenn.)-Westview High Sch., 1978-85, Covington (Tenn.) High Sch., 1985-87; tchg. asst. band dept. U. Memphis, 1987-89; assoc. dir. bands Munford (Tenn.) High Sch., 1990, Haywood County High Sch., Brownsville, Tenn., 1990-97; dir. music Covington (Tenn.) Crestview Mid. Sch., 1997-2000, Covington H.S., 2000—. Nat. adv. bd. U.S. Achievement Acad., 1985; founder Kinningham Music Svcs., Covington, 1978—. Composer: Freedom's Cries: 1989, 1990, String Quartet #1, 1988, Sonaire #2, 1992, Echoes Past of Future Dreams, 1993, Prospect Variations, 2001, Nettleton Variants, 2002, Overlord, 2003, Sing To Me A Painting, 2003. Music dir. Brighton (Tenn.) Ch. of Christ, 1989-95, treas., 1989-95; deacon Covington (Tenn.) Ch. Christ, 1999—2003, elder, 2003—. Recipient Rafferty award for young composers Evanston (Ill.) Twp. High Sch., 1984, Key to City of Martin, 1985, Haimsohn Composition award U. Memphis, 1988, All-Am. Scholar award U.S. Achievement Acad., 1990. Mem. NEA, Music Educators Nat. Conf., Soc. of Composers, Inc., Am. Soc. Composers and Publishers, Southeastern Composers League, Phi Delta Kappa, Phi Kappa Phi. Avocations: photography, camping. Home: 1834 Kimbrough Dr Covington TN 38019-3612 Office: Covington HS 803 S College Covington TN 38019 E-mail: akinningha@aol.com.

KINNISON, WILLIAM ANDREW, retired university president; b. Springfield, Ohio, Feb. 10, 1932; s. Errett Lowell and Audrey Muriel (Smith) K.; m. Lenore Belle Morris, June 11, 1960; children— William Errett, Linda Elise, Amy Elisabeth. AB, Wittenberg U., 1954, BS in Edn., 1955; MA, U. Wis., 1963; PhD (1st Flesher fellow), Ohio State U., 1967; postgrad., Harvard U. Inst. Ednl. Mgmt., 1970; LL.D., Calif. Luth. Coll., 1983; Th.D., John Carroll U., 1983; LLD, Lenoir-Rhyne Coll., 1987; LHD, Capital U., 1995. Asst. dean admissions Wittenberg U., Springfield, 1958-65, asst. to pres., 1967-70, v.p. for univ. affairs, 1970-73, v.p. adminstrn., 1973, pres., 1974-95, pres. emeritus, 1995—; pres., CEO Heritage Ctr. of Clark County, 1997—2002. Author: Samuel Shellabarger: Lawyer, Jurist, Legislator, 1969, Building Sullivant's Pyramid: An Administrative History of the Ohio State University, 1970, Concise History of Wittenberg University, 1976, An American Seminary, 1980, Springfield and Clark County: an Illustrated History, 1985, also articles. Asst. to dir. Sch. Edn. Ohio State U., Columbus, 1965-67; past chmn. Assn. Ind. Colls. and Univs. Ohio; trustee Ohio Found. Ind. Colls., 1974-95, chair bd. trustees, 1995; chmn. standing com. Luth. World Ministries, 1976-82; mem. exec. coun. Luth. Ch. in Am., 1978-86; mem., chmn. Commn. for a New Luth. Ch., 1982-86; bd. dirs. Am. Assn. Colls., 1982-84. With U.S. Army, 1956-58. Mem. Clark County Hist. Soc. (trustee 1963—), Orgn. Am. Historians, Blue Key, Phi Beta Kappa, Phi Delta Kappa, Kappa Phi Kappa, Pi Sigma Alpha, Tau Kappa Alpha, Delta Sigma Phi, Omicron Delta Kappa. Clubs: Cosmos, Rotary. Home: 1820 Timberline Dr Springfield OH 45504-1236

KINSEY, JAMES LLOYD, chemist, educator; b. Paris, Tex., Oct. 15, 1934; s. Lloyd King and Elaine Mills K.; m. Berma McDowell, July 28, 1962; children: Victoria, Samuel, Adam. BA, Rice U., 1956, PhD, 1959; NSF fellow, U. Uppsala, Sweden, 1959-60; postdoctoral fellow, U. Calif., Berkeley, 1960-62. Asst. prof. dept. chemistry M.I.T., 1962-67, asso. prof., 1967-74, prof., 1974-88, chmn. dept., 1977-82; D.R. Bullard-Welch Found. prof. sci. Rice U., Houston, 1988—; dean natural scis., 1988-98; interim provost Rice U., Houston, 1993-94. Cons. Los Alamos Nat. Labs., external rev. com. chemistry and laser sci. divsn., 1983—89; Miller rsch. fellow, 1960—62; mem. NAS-NRC Bd. Chem. Scis., 1980—83, co-chmn., 1981—83; mem. steering com. U.S. Army Basic Sci. Rsch.-NRC, 1981—86; mem. oversight rev. com. chemistry divsn. NSF, 1989; mem. vis. com. for divsn. chemistry and chem. engring. Calif. Inst. Tech., 1999—; mem. com. of chemistry facilities and infrastructure U. Calif.-Berkeley, 1992—93; mem. corp. vis. com. for dept. chemistry MIT, 1994—; vis. com. for chemistry Stanford U., 1993—96; mem. external rev. com. for chemistry U. Pa., 2000; mem. adv. com. on rsch. projects State of Tex. Higher Edn. Coordinating Bd., 2000—02; mem. adv. bd. for engring. and scis. Internat. U. Bremen, Germany, 2000—. Assoc. editor Jour. Chem. Physics, 1981-84; mem. editorial adv. bd. Jour. Phys. Chemistry, 1984-88, Ann. Rev. Phys. Chemistry, 1985-89; mem. adv. editorial bd. Chem. Physics Letters, 1992-97; mem. Coun. of Am. Acad. of Arts and Scis., 1997-2001; contbr. articles to profl. jours. Recipient E.O. Lawrence award U.S. Dept. Energy, 1987; Alfred P. Sloan fellow, 1964-68, Guggenheim fellow, 1969-70. Fellow AAAS, Am. Phys. Soc. (exec. com. divsn. chem. physics 1985-88, Earle K. Plyler prize 1995), Am. Acad. Arts and Scis.; mem. NAS, Am. Chem. Soc. (chmn. divsn. phys. chemistry 1985, Nobel Laureate Signature award for grad. edn. 1990), Sigma Xi. Office: Rice U MS-600 PO Box 1892 Houston TX 77251-1892 E-mail: jlkinsey@rice.edu.

KINSINGER, JACK BURL, chemist, educator; b. Akron, Ohio, June 23, 1925; s. William Franklin and Idelle (Althaus) K.; m. Addie Jean Parker, Sept. 2, 1946 (div. 1987); children: Paul Craig, Amy Jo; m. Gladys Styles Johnston, 1997. BA, Hiram Coll., 1948; MS, Cornell U., 1951; PhD, U. Pa., 1958. Group leader rsch. Rohm & Haas Co., Phila., 1951-56; from asst. prof. to prof. chemistry Mich. State U., East Lansing, 1957-82, assoc. chmn. dept. chemistry, 1965-69, chmn. dept., 1969-75, asst. v.p. rsch. and devel., 1977, assoc. provost, 1977-82; prof. chemistry Ariz. State U., Tempe, 1982-87, v.p. acad. affairs, 1982-87; pres., CEO, Chgo. Osteo. Health Systems and Midwestern U., 1987-96; ret. Cons. Union Carbide Co., 1958-80, vice chmn. div. polymer chemistry, 1966-68, chmn., 1969; dir. chemistry div. NSF, 1975-77; trustee Kirksville Osteo. Med. Coll., 1984-87, Ariz. State U. Res. Park; exec. com. Fed. Independent Ill. Colls. and Univs., 1993-95. Editor computer symposium Jour. Polymer Sci., 1968. 2nd lt. USAAF, 1943-45. Recipient Disting. Alumnus award Hiram Coll., 1984. Fellow AAAS; mem. Am. Chem. Soc., Coun. Chem. Rsch. (vice chair exec. com. 1980-81). Home: 24548 N 121st Pl Scottsdale AZ 85255 E-mail: jbkgsj623@msn.com.

KINSOLVING, SYLVIA CROCKETT, musician, educator; b. Berkeley, Calif., Sept. 30, 1931; d. Harold Waldo and Louise (Effinger) Crockett; m. Charles Lester Kinsolving, Dec. 18, 1953; children: Laura Louise, Thomas Philip, Kathleen Susan. AA in Voice, Piano magna cum laude, No. Va. Community Coll., 1983; BA, U. Calif., Berkeley, 1953. Solo vocalist various chs., Va., 1982—; pvt. tchr. piano, 1983—. Singer, soloist Unity Ch., Oakton, Va., 1980—, St. Andrew's Anglican Ch., Alexandria, Va., 1985—; active numerous local musical prodns., 1959—. Tour leader Vienna Newcomers, 1980. Mem. PEO, U. Calif. Alumni Club, Fairfax West Music Fellowship (sec. 1990—), Phi Theta Kappa, Pi Beta Phi. Democrat. Episcopalian. Avocations: walking, swimming, music, reading. Home: 1517 Beulah Rd Vienna VA 22182-1417

KINTNER, PHILIP L. history educator; b. Canton, Ohio, Jan. 23, 1926; s. William Wagner and Effie (Erwin) K.; m. Anne Genung, Dec. 27, 1951; children: Karen, Judith, Jennifer. BA, Wooster Coll., 1950; MA, Yale U., 1952, PhD, 1958. Instr. Trinity Coll., Hartford, Conn., 1954-56, Reed Coll., Portland, Oreg., 1957-58, Trinity Coll., 1958-59, asst. prof., 1959-64; vis. assoc. prof. U. Iowa, Iowa City, 1964-65; assoc. prof. Grinnell (Iowa) Coll., 1964-69; coll. entrance bd. exam commissioner European History, Princeton, N.J., 1968-70; chief reader advanced placement European history, 1969-72; ACM prof. Florence (Italy) Program, 1989-90; prof. Grinnell Coll., 1970-96, Rosenthal prof. humanities, 1976-96; prof. emeritus, 1996—. With U.S. Army, 1944-46. Recipient numerous travel/study grants for rsch. in Germany. Mem. Sixteenth Century Studies Conf. Avocations: woodworking, gardening, cooking, mineral hunting. Home: 716 Broad St Grinnell IA 50112-2226 Office: Grinnell Coll PO Box 805 Grinnell IA 50112-0805 E-mail: kintner@grinnell.edu.

KINZELL, LA MOYNE B. school health services administrator, educator; b. Melstone, Mont., May 4, 1930; d. William Edward and Iro Millicent (Keeton) Berger; m. Les Kieth Kinzell, Sept. 18, 1954; children: Yvette Li Goins, Anitra Elise Chew, Antony Mikhail Kinzell. BS, Mont. State U., 1954; MA, Calif. State U., Northridge, 1982. RN Calif. Instr. surg. nursing Mont. Deaconess Hosp., Great Falls, 1954-55; instr. nursing arts St. Patrick's Hosp., Missoula, Mont., 1957-59; instr. sci. Palmdale (Calif.) Sch. Dist., 1966-86, dir. health svcs., 1986-2000. Adv. bd. facilitator Palmdale Healthy Start, 1992-2000; com. mem. Am. Cancer Soc., 1986—, United Way, 1991—; bd. dirs. A.V. Ptnrs. in Health, 2000—. Mem. Citizen Amb. Sch. Nursing Del. to Europe, 1994; treas. campaign sch. bd. mem., Palmdale, 1989, 93, 97; bd. dirs. A.V. Symphony Orch. and Master Choral, 2000—, A.V. Light Found., 2001-. Recipient Tchr. of Yr. award Palmdale, 1985-86, Los Angeles County Sheriffs Dept. award, 1985, Nat. Every Child by Two, Immunization Ptnrs. award, 1995; grantee Drug, Alcohol and Tobacco Edn., 1987, Healthy Start Planning, 1994, 95, Healthy Start Operational award, 1996, 98. Mem. Am. Heart Assn. (bd. dirs. 1997-2001), Am. Lung Assn. (chair edn. 1988-94), Calif. Sch. Nurse Orgn. (sec. 1992-95), Health Careers Acad. (adv. com. 1995—), Phi Kappa Phi, Alpha Tau Delta, Sigma Theta Tau, Delta Kappa Gamma (area IX chair legislature 1993-95, area IX dir. 1995-97, area IX sec. 2001—03, mem. Chi state expansion com. 1997-99, leadership com. 1999-2001, chair leadership com. 2001-03, profl. affairs com., 2003—). Democrat. Episcopalian. Avocations: traveling, gardening, geology, marine biology, swimming. Home: 38817 2nd St E Palmdale CA 93550-3201 E-mail: l.kinzell@worldnet.att.net.

KINZEY, OUIDA BLACKERBY, retired mathematics educator, photographer, photojournalist; b. Leeds, Ala., Feb. 6, 1922; d. George W. and Kate (Spruiell) Blackerby; m. William Thomas Kinzey, Feb. 6, 1943. AB, Birmingham So. Coll., 1942, EdM, 1959; advanced profl. diploma, U. Ala., 1964. Tchr. math. Phillips High Sch., Birmingham, Ala., 1942-44, Humes High Sch., Memphis, 1944-45; mem. math. dept. Woodlawn High Sch., Birmingham, 1945-69, chmn. math dept., 1965-69; assoc. prof. math. Birmingham So. Coll., 1969-84, prof. emeritus, 1984—, dir. vis. profs. program, 1971-75, mem. alumni leadership bd., Gala adv. bd.; vis. math. prof. Samford U., 1989, 90, 91, 92, 93; cons., lectr., speaker and workshop dir. throughout S.E. region. Author: (audio-visual text) Creative Teaching Mathematically, 1973, (video) The World of Mathematics, 1990, (video) A Mathematical Adventure, 1991; author, photographer: (photographic essays) Back Roads of Alabama, Alabama's Covered Bridges, Coal Mining in Alabama, A Place to Worship, The Art of Awareness, Highlights of St. Clair County, A Tour of Blount County; photographs exhibited one man shows including Birmingham So. Coll., 1984, Samford U., 1985, Med. Ctr. East, 1986, Univ. Hosp., 1989, U. Ala., Birmingham, 1989, Birmingham Mus. of Art, 1989, Baptist Med. Ctr., Princeton, 1991, 92, Art Gallery Birmingham Pub. Libr., 1991, Mervyn Sterne Libr., 1991, 93, 94, 95, Jefferson County Ct. House Gallery, 1992, 93, Vincent's Gallery, 1992, St. Vincents Hosp., 1992, Children's Hands On Mus., Tuscaloosa, Ala., 1992, 93, 94, Ala. State Coun. on the Arts, Montgomery, Ala., 1993, Gadsden Cultural Ctr., Gadsden, Ala., 1994, Corp. Hdqs. Atrium, Ala. Power Co., 1995, Art Gallery, Brookwood Med. Ctr., 1995, Vestavia Ctrl., 1996, 97, Hoover Libr., 1996; Permanent Exhibition: Marguerite Jones Harbert Bldg., Birmingham Southern Coll., Ala. Grantee NSF, 1959, 61, 64, 71, Kellogg Found., 1978, Mellon Found., 1980, 81, 84, Title III, 1982; recipient Grand Nat. award NEA/Kodak, 1984, Bruno-Found. award Birmingham Mus. Art, 1999, Cert. of Lifetime Personal Achievement Birmingham So. Coll., 1990, Disting. Alumni award Birmingham-So. Coll. Nat. Alumni Assn., 1992, Scholarship named in her honor, 1984; named an Outstanding Educator of Am., 1972. Mem. AAUW, Ala. Assn. Coll. Tchrs. Math., Ala. Acad. Sci., United Daus. Confederacy, Nat. Coun. Tchrs. Math., Math. Assn. Am., Am. Math Soc. (joint policy bd. math. pub. info. resources com.), Ala. Edn. Assn., Ala. Poetry Soc. Ala. Writers' Conclave, Nat. League Am. PEN Women, Patrons Art Coun. East, Nat. League Arts and Letters, Phi Beta Kappa, Kappa Delta Pi, Delta Kappa Gamma, Kappa Delta Epsilon, Kappa Mu Epsilon, Theta Sigma Lambda, Delta Phi Alpha, Alpha Lambda Delta. Speech Arts Club (pres., v.p., sec., treas.). Republican. Methodist. Avocations: photography, collecting rocks, Indian artifacts and antiques. Home: 3103 Altaloma Cv Birmingham AL 35216-4207

KIPFERL, CHRISTIANA A. special education educator; b. Elmira, N.Y., June 6, 1953; d. Martin Joseph and RosaLea (VanMarter) Burke; m. H. LaVerne Kipferl, Aug. 9, 1986; stepchildren: Kevin, Keith, Kayla, Kerry,

Kory, Kelly. AA, Corning C.C., 1973; BS, Mansfield State Coll., 1975, MEd, 1993. Sr. exec. sec., travel coord. Imaging & Sensing Technology Corp., Horseheads, N.Y., 1988-95; resource rm. tchr. Elmira (N.Y.) City Sch. Dist., 1995-96; affective educator Steuben-Allegany BOCES, Bath, N.Y., 1996-97; learning support resource rm. tchr. North Tioga Sch. Dist., Westfield (Pa.) Area Elem. Sch., 1997—. Sunday sch. tchr. Jackson Summit (Pa.) Bapt. Ch.; mem. Corning C.C. Alumni Chorus. Mem. Coun. Exceptional Children. Republican. Baptist. Avocations: fishing, music, camping, working with children, reading. Home: RR 1 Box 32K Millerton PA 16936-9712

KIPNIS, DAVID MORRIS, physician, educator; b. Balt., May 23, 1927; s. Rubin and Anna (Mizen) Kipnis; m. Paula Jane Levin, Aug. 16, 1953; children: Lynne, Laura, Robert. AB, Johns Hopkins U., 1945, MA, 1949; MD, U. Md., 1951. Intern Johns Hopkins Hosp., 1951—52; resident Duke Hosp., Durham, NC, 1952—54, U. Md. Hosp., 1954—55; asst. prof. medicine Washington U. Sch. Medicine, St. Louis, 1958—63, assoc. prof., 1963—65, prof., 1965—, Busch prof., chmn. dept. medicine, 1973—92; disting. prof. medicine Washington U. Sch. of Medicine, St. Louis, 1992—; asst. physician Barnes Hosp., assoc. physician, 1963—72, physician-in-chief, 1973—93, disting. univ. prof., 1993—. Chmn. endocrine study sect. NIH, 1963—64, diabetes tng. program com., 1970—; chmn. Nat. Diabetes Adv. Bd. Editor: Diabetes, 1973; mem. editl. bd.: Am. Jour. Medicine, 1973, Am. Jour. Med. Scis.; contbr. articles to profl. jours. Served with U.S. Army, 1945—46. Named Banting lectr., Brit. Diabetes Assn., 1972; scholar Markle scholar in med. scis., 1957—62. Mem.: NAS (coun. mem. 1997—2000), Nat. Acad. Scis., Inst. Medicine, Am. Acad. Arts and Scis., Am. Soc. Biol. Chemists, Endocrine Soc. (Oppenheimer award 1965), Am. Diabetes Assn. (Lilly award 1965, Banting medal 1977, Best medal 1981), Am. Fedn. Clin. Rsch., Assn. Am. Physicians (Kober medal 1994), Am. Soc. Clin. Investigation. Home: 7200 Wydown Blvd Saint Louis MO 63105-3023 Office: Barnes Hosp Dept Medicine PO Box 8212 660 S Euclid Ave Saint Louis MO 63110-1010

KIPP, BEVERLY J. elementary and secondary education educator; b. Cambridge, N.Y., Apr. 28, 1948; d. LeRoy John Sr. and Joan Marie (Kinney) Hunt; m. David Kenneth Kipp Sr., May 27, 1966; children: Tonya, Trista, David Jr., Tobias. AA, Clinton C.C., 1990; BS, SUNY, Plattsburgh, 1992. Cert. elem. tchr., N.Y. Tchr. elem. grades and secondary social studies. Presdl. scholar, 1990-91. Mem. Phi Theta Kappa (pres. 1989-90, Leadership award 1990), Alpha Sigma Lambda. Avocations: writing, sewing, needle work, camping. Home: 4757 Route 9N Corinth NY 12822-2414

KIRBY, DAVID, literature educator; m. Barbara Hamby; children: Will, Ian. PhD, Johns Hopkins U. Robert O. Lawton Disting. Prof. English Fla. State U., Tallahassee; W. Guy McKenzie prof. English Emerson Coll., 1989—. Author: (poems) Saving the Young Men of Vienna, 1987, Writing Poetry, 1989, Mark Strand and the Poet's Place in Contemporary Culture, 1990, Herman Melville, 1993, (poems) Big Leg Music, My Twentieth Century, 1999; contbr. essays and poems to jours. Recipient Coll. Tchg. award, 1990, Univ. Tchg. award, 1992, Univ. Tchg. Incentive award, 1994; fellow, John Simon Guggenheim Meml. Found., 2003. Mem.: Nat. Book Critics Circle. Office: Fla State U 421 Williams Bldg Tallahassee FL 32306-1580*

KIRBY, DEBORAH LOUANNA, nursing administrator; b. Lake City, Fla., Nov. 8, 1954; d. Woodrow Wilson and Vera Sue Lee (Kerce) Edenfield; married, 1971 (div. 1986); children: Jeanne, Alan; m. Joel Edwin Kirby, Oct. 14, 1989; children: Chad, Michelle. ASN, Lake City Comty. Coll., 1988. RN, Fla. CNA Dept. Corrections-Reception and Med. Ctr., Lake Butler, Fla., 1980-85, correctional med. technician, 1985-88; RN North Fla. Reception Ctr., Lake Butler, 1988-90, nursing program specialist-nursing edn., 1990—. Nurse preceptor North Fla. Reception Ctr. Hosp., Lake Butler, 1989—, Am. Heart Assn. contact, 1989—, mem. forms com., 1991—, nursing quality rev. com., 1992—. Mem. Fla. Nurses Assn., Union County Riding Club. Baptist. Avocations: family, horseback riding, sports, sewing, reading.

KIRBY, JAMIE MCGUIRE, gifted and talented educator; b. St. Louis, June 23, 1952; d. William F. and Florence J. (Bell) McG.; m. Edgar W. Kirby III, June 22, 1974; children: Anna Kimmins, Edgar Wilson IV. BA in Psychology/Early Childhood Edn., Queens Coll., Charlotte, N.C., 1974; MEd in Learning Disabilities, East Carolina U., 1985. Psychol. asst. Mecklenburg County Schs., Charlotte, 1974-75, learning disabilities tchr., 1975-76, Pitt County Schs., Greenville, N.C., 1985—. Active St. Timothy's Episcopal Ch., Greenville. Mem. NEA, N.C. Edn. Assn., Coun. for Exceptional Children (membership chmn. local chpt. 1989-90), Internat. Reading Assn., N.C. Coun. of Tchrs. of Math., N.C. Assn. Gifted and Talented, Delta Kappa Gamma. Avocations: snow skiing, water sports, reading. Office: Sadie Saulter Sch Fleming St Greenville NC 27834

KIRCHER, JOHN JOSEPH, law educator; b. Milw., July 26, 1938; s. Joseph John and Martha Marie (Jach) K.; m. Marcia Susan Adamkiewicz, Aug. 26, 1961; children: Joseph John, Mary Kathryn. BA, Marquette U., 1960, JD, 1963. Bar: Wis. 1963, U.S. Dist. Ct. (ea. dist.) Wis. 1963, U.S. Ct. Appeals (7th cir.) 1992. Sole practice, Port Washington, Wis., 1963-66; with Def. Research Inst., Milw., 1966-80, research dir., 1972-80; with Marquette U., 1970—, prof. law, 1980—, assoc. dean acad. affairs, 1992-93. Chmn. Wis. Jud. Council, 1981-83. Author: (with J.D. Ghiardi) Punitive Damages: Law and Practice, 1981, 2d edit (with C.M. Wiseman), 2000; editor Federation of Defense and Corporate Counsel Quarterly; mem. editorial bd. Def. Law Jour.; contbr. articles to profl. jours. Recipient Teaching Excellence award Marquette U., 1986, Disting. Service award Def. Research Inst., 1980, Marquette Law Rev. Editors' award, 1988. Mem. ABA (Robert B. McKay Professor award 1993), Am. Law Inst., Wis. Bar Assn., Wis. Supreme Ct. Bd. of Bar Examiners (vice chair 1989-91, chair 1992), Am. Judicature Soc., Nat. Sports Law Inst. (adv. com. 1989—), Assn. Internationale de Droit des Assurances, Scribes. Roman Catholic. Office: PO Box 1881 Milwaukee WI 53201-1881

KIRCHHOFF, LOUIS VAUGHN, biomedical researcher, educator, internist; b. Elmhurst, Ill., Nov. 3, 1943; s. Walter and Emily (Seibel) K.; m. Karen E. McClelland, Mar. 31, 1973 (div.); children: Alicia R., Aaron V. AB, Harvard U., 1966; BA, U. Calif., San Diego, 1972; MD, MPH, Yale U., 1977. Diplomate Am. Bd. Internal Medicine. Resident in internal medicine U. Mich., Ann Arbor, 1977-80; fellow in geog. medicine U. Va., Charlottesville, 1980-81; med. staff fellow NIAID, NIH, Bethesda, Md., 1981-85; asst. prof. U. Iowa, Iowa City, 1985-90, assoc. prof., 1990-97, prof., 1997—; pres. Goldfinch Diagnostics Inc., 1998—. Cons. Dept. State, Washington, 1993. Contbr. articles to profl. jours. including New Eng. Jour. Medicine, Annals of Internal Medicine, Jour. Infectious Diseases, Jour. Biol. Chemistry, Molecular & Biochem. Parasitology, Transfusion, Am. Jour. Tropical Medicine and Hygiene, Transactions Royal Soc. Tropical Medicine and Hygiene, among others. Grantee Am. Heart Assn., 1990, Am. Found. for AIDS Rsch., 1996, NIH SBIR Program, 1998; recipient Scholars award Syntex Inc., 1986; Nat. Bd. Found. scholar, 1998. Democrat. Home: 204 Lexington Ave Iowa City IA 52246-2413 Office: U Iowa 4-403 BSB Iowa City IA 52242 E-mail: louis-kirchhoff@uiowa.edu.

KIRCHNER, MARY KATHERINE, singer, music educator; b. Omaha, Apr. 22, 1937; d. Ferdinand Anthony and Loretta Agnes (Brady) Dascher; m. John Edmund Kirchner, Jr., June 20, 1959; children: J. Kevin, Mark A., Patrick D., Edmund J., Thomas J. BA, Loretto Heights Coll., 1959. Pvt. voice tchr., Edina, Minn., 1982—. Voice tchr. Performing Arts Ctr., Edina, 1982—95; adj. faculty voice tchr. Edina H.S., 1982—99; pres. Thursday Musical, Mpls., 1992—94. Sec. Senate Dist. 42 Rep. Party, 1983-85. Mem. Nat. Assn. Tchrs. Singing, Minn. Music Tchrs. Assn. (cert., adminstr. non-keyboard programs 1987-89), Mu Phi Epsilon (pres. 1988-90, dist. dir. 1995-98). Roman Catholic. Avocations: reading, walking. Home: 7470 Cahill Rd Edina MN 55439

KIRK, AIDA MONTEQUIN, secondary education Spanish and home economics educator; b. Arecibo, P.R., Oct. 20, 1952; d. Arturo and Aida (del Rosario) Montequin; m. Robert Lynn Kirk, Mar. 30, 1985. BA Edn. in Home Econs. magna cum laude, U. P.R., 1974; MS in Home Econs., Ohio State U., 1977. 7th grade home econs. tchr. Palm Beach County Sch. Bd., West Palm Beach, Fla., 1978-84; Spanish and home econs. tchr. Indian River County Sch. Dist., Vero Beach, Fla., 1984—. Mem. sch. improvement team, electives dept. chairperson Sebastian (Fla.) River Mid. Sch. Mem. Fla. Fgn. Lang. Assn., Treasure Coast ESOL Assn. Roman Catholic. Avocations: crafts, birds, travel, reading, sewing. Office: Sebastian River Mid Sch 9400 State Road 512 Sebastian FL 32958-6402

KIRK, CHERYL LINDA, elementary education educator; b. Jersey City, June 21, 1952; d. Louis William and Ada Mae (Scobie) Freese; m. George William Kirk, Nov. 22, 1980. BA in Elem., Early Childhood Edn., Wittenberg U., 1974; MEd in Reading Supervision, Kent State U., 1978. Cert. tchr. elem., reading specialist, elem. and secondary, (life) Ohio. Tchr. Kirtland (Ohio) Elem. Sch., 1974-81; substitute tchr. Trumbull County Bd. Edn., 1981-84; tchr. grade 2 Southington (Ohio) Local Elem. Sch., 1982-83, tchr. grade 4, 1984—. Leader collaboration team Southington Elem. Sch., 1992-93; co-author Martha Holden Jennings Grant application, Southington, 1988; mentor tchr. Trumbull County Bd. Edn., Warren, Ohio, 1991. Active missions com. Ch., Southington, Ohio, 1989-92. Scholar Martha Holden Jennings, 1991. Mem. Internat. Coun. of Reading, Ohio Coun. of Reading (lit. com.), Trumbull Area Reading Coun. (treas. 1993—, bd. dirs. 1991-93). Avocations: sewing, crafts, camping. Home: 4598 State Route 305 Southington OH 44470-9721 Office: Southington Local Schs 4432 State Route 305 Southington OH 44470-9721

KIRK, DEBORAH DIANNE, private school educator, curriculum developer; b. Lawrenceburg, Tenn., May 24, 1953; d. L.E. and Dovie (Tankersley) Garner; m. Jerry Ray Kirk, Aug. 17, 1974; children: Shelley MeRae, Allan Trevor. AA, Martin Coll., Pulaski, Tenn., 1972; 2BA in Bus. Edn., Harding U., 1974; elem. cert., Mid. Tenn. State U., 1976; MA in Supervision and Curriculum Devel., Trevecca Coll., Nashville, 1986. Secondary tchr. Lawrence County Bd. Edn., Lawrenceburg, 1975-78, elem. tchr., 1978-80; instr. bus. edn. and JTPA Columbia (Tenn.) State C.C., 1987-88; elem. tchr. Columbia Acad., 1989-91, K-9 tchr. computers, 1991-92, tchr. computers and bus. edn., 1992—, designer computer curriculum, 1990—. Bd. dirs. Columbia Acad. PTO, 1992, adv. com., 1993. Named Outstanding Ednl. Vol., New Prospect Elem. Sch., Lawrenceburg, 1986; recipient Outstanding Teaching award Columbia State C.C., 1987, Tchr. of Week award Nashville Tennessean, 1990. Mem. ASCD. Mem. Ch. of Christ. Avocations: writing poetry, travel, assistant coaching in youth league sports. Home: 1004 Claremont Dr Columbia TN 38401-6207 Office: Columbia Acad 1101 W 7th St Columbia TN 38401-3098

KIRK, DONALD JAMES, accountant, consultant; b. Cleve., Nov. 28, 1932; s. John James and Helen Anna (Pilskaln) K.; children: J. Alexander, Bruce D.; m. Mary (Mimi) Colgage Bullock, Jan. 31, 1998. BA, Yale U., 1959; MBA, NYU, 1961; LLD (hon.), Lycoming Coll., 1979. Acct. Price Waterhouse & Co., N.Y.C., London and Washington, 1959-73, ptnr., 1967-73; from mem. to chmn. Fin. Acctg. Stds. Bd., Stamford, Conn., 1973-86; prof. acctg. Columbia U. Grad. Sch. Bus., N.Y.C., 1987-94, exec.-in-residence, 1995-2000; cons., corp. dir. Trustee Fidelity Group Mut. Funds, 1987—; dir. Gen. Re Corp., 1987-98, Valuation Rsch. Corp., 1993-95; pub. gov. Nat. Assn. Securities Dealers, Inc., 1996-2002, Am. Stock Exch., 2001—. Officer, bd. dirs. Urban League of Southwestern Fairfield County, Conn., 1971-77; mem. Greenwich (Conn.) Rep. Town Mtg., 1971-77, Greenwich Bd. of Estimate and Taxation, 1977-89; bd. dirs. Nat. Arts Stabilization Fund, 1983-2002, chmn., 1995-2000, bd. overseers NYU Schs. Bus., 1985-89; bd. trustees The Greenwich Hosp. Assn., 1989—, chmn., 1996-2000, Greenwich Found. for Comty. Gifts, 1991-93; bd. dirs. Yale-New Haven Health Sys., 1998—. Recipient Alumni Achievement award NYU Grad. Sch. Bus. Adminstrn., 1980; named to Acctg. Hall of Fame Ohio State U., 1996. Mem. AICPA (governing coun. 1987-90, pub. oversight bd. of SEC practice sect. 1995-2002, vice-chmn. 1999-2002, Gold medal for disting. svc. 1986), Am. Acctg. Assn., Fin. Execs. Inst. (bd. dirs. N.Y.C. 1990-94), Yale Alumni Assn. Greenwich (bd. dirs. 1988-91), Stanwich Club (past pres.), Yale Club N.Y.C. E-mail: djkirk@optonline.net.

KIRK, JAMES ALLEN, mechanical engineering educator; b. Cleve., Nov. 3, 1944; s. Charles J. and Helen T. (Tulas) K.; m. Cynthia L. Ambler, Feb. 6, 1976; 1 child, Heather E. BSEE, Ohio U., 1967; MSME, MIT, 1969, PhD, 1972. Registered prof. engr., Md., Ohio. Rsch. engr. Ford Motor Co., Dearborn, Mich., 1966-67; rsch. assoc. MIT, Cambridge, Mass., 1968-72; asst. prof. mech. engring. U. Md., College Park, 1972-77, assoc. prof. mech. engring., 1977-86, prof. mech. engring., 1986-98, prof. emeritus mech. engring., 1998—; pres. Flywheel Sys., Inc., 1997-2000. Pres. FARE, Inc., College Park, Md. 1988—; owner Kirk Cons. Co., College Park, Md., 1977-88. Author: Scientific Automobile Accident Reconstruction, 1992, Vehicle Dynamics and Tire Forces, 1993, Forensic Engineering, 1993; contbr. articles to profl. jours. Mem. ASME, ASM Internat., Am. Soc. Engring. Edn. (Dow Outstanding Young Faculty award 1977), Soc. Automotive Engring. (Ralph Teetor award 1975), Nat. Assn. Profl. Accident Reconstrn. Specialists, Soc. Mfg. Engrs. Achievements include designed magnetically suspended flywheel for NASA and emergency stopping system for U.S. capitol-house subway system. Home: 7210 Windsor Ln Hyattsville MD 20782-1045 Office: Far Inc 7210 Windsor Ln Hyattsville MD 20782-1045 E-mail: jkirk@eng.umd.edu.

KIRK, JILL, educational association administrator; BA, U. Oreg. Corp. dir. human resources/orgnl. devel. Tektonix, Inc., group human resources mgr.; dir. cmty. affairs Tektronix, Inc., 1994; exec. dir. Tektronix Found., 1991; founder The Kirk Group LLC, 1999—; ptnr. Lindberg/Kirk/Millar, 2000—. Mem. bd. dirs., exec. bd., govt. affairs com. Am. Electronics Assn.; bd. dirs. Associated Oreg. Industries; chair deputies com. Oreg. Bus. Coun., vice chair edn. com., mem. higher edn. task force, mem. pub. fin. com. Mem. Oreg. State Bd. Edn., 1996—, chairperson, 2001—, mem. exec. com., mem. joint bds. working group, mem. econ. devel. joint bds. working group; trustee Portland Art Mus., 1998—2001, 2001—; mem. adv. com. Portland Ctr. for the Performing Arts; bd. dirs. Portland Youth Philharm.; mem. strategic planning com. United Way Columbia-Willamette; active Oreg. Profl. Devel. Coun.; bd. chair Lintner Ctr. for Advanced Edn.; active Govs. Task Force on Higher Edn., Govs. Task Force on Quality Edn.; bd. dirs. Japanese Gardent Soc., 2001—, STARS, Portland Edn. Network, N.W. Bus. for Culture and the Arts, Nat. Alliance Bus. Western Region. Mem.: Portland C. of C. (bd. dirs.). Office: Oreg Dept Edn 255 Capitol St NE Salem OR 97310-0203*

KIRK, ROBLEY GORDON, mechanical engineering educator; b. Coeburn, Va., Feb. 14, 1944; s. Robley Neal and Leona Margie (Robinette) K.; m. Janie Louise Isaacs, June 26, 1965; children: Timothy Alan, Andrea Denise. BSME, U. Va., 1967, MSME, 1969, PhD in Mech. Engring., 1972. Registered profl. engr., Va. Instr. U. Va., Charlottesville, Va., 1970-71, research engr., 1971-72; sr. engr. Pratt & Whitney Aircraft, East Hartford, Conn., 1972-75; devel. engring. Ingersoll-Rand Turbo Div., Phillipsburg, N.J., 1975-78, supr., rotor dynamics, 1978-85; assoc. prof. Va. Poly. Inst. and State U., Blacksburg, 1985-91, prof., 1991—. Cons. Dresser-Rand, Olean, N.Y., 1987-96, Ingersoll-Dresser Pump Co., Phillipsburg, N.J., 1989-96, No. Rsch., Woburn, Mass., 1994-95. Patentee in field. Leader, Webelos, Boy Scouts Am., Blacksburg, Va., 1986. Named Young Engr. of Yr., NSPE, 1979, Equipment grantee, 1987; Walter Hudson award, ASLE, 1978. Mem. ASME, Soc. Tribology and Lubrication Engrs., Am. Soc. Lubrication Engrs., Sigma Xi, Tau Beta Pi. Republican. Avocations: coin collecting, woodworking. E-mail: gokirk@vt.edu.

KIRK, VICTOR CLARK, special education educator; b. Monroe, La., Aug. 13, 1949; s. Rogers and Alberta (Williams) K.; children: Melanie R., Victor C. II. BS, So. U., Baton Rouge, La., 1971, MEd, 1979, postgrad., 1990. Cert. spl. edn. tchr., La. Sr. counselor Community Advancement, Inc., Baton Rouge, 1971-72; various adminstrv. positions La. Dept. Health and Human Resources, Baton Rouge, 1972-78; mgmt. analyst Office of the Gov. of La., Baton Rouge, 1978; dir. planning and instl. rsch. Grambling (La.) State U., 1979; planning analyst La. Dept. Health and Human Resources, Baton Rouge, 1980-84, dir. One Ch./One Family Adoption program, 1984-86, reimbursement planning analyst, 1986-87; pres. Victor C. Kirk Inc., Mgmt. Cons., Baton Rouge, 1983—. Adj. prof. So. U., 1992—. V.p. Sister Cities, Baton Roube, 1990-92; bd. dirs. Mayor/Pres. Coun. Internat. Rels., 1990-92; v.p. La. Assn. for Sickle Cell Anemia, New Orleans, 1976. State of La. grantee, 1990-92; Loyola U. Inst. Politics fellow, 1975. Mem. La. Assn. Devel. Edn., Kappa Delta Phi (v.p. 1991). Democrat. Baptist. Home: PO Box 3933 Baton Rouge LA 70821-3933 Office: PO Box 3933 Baton Rouge LA 70821-3933

KIRK-DUGGAN, MICHAEL ALLAN, retired law, economics and computer sciences educator; b. Stevens Point, Wis., Dec. 15, 1931; s. Frank E. and Dorothy Ada (Darrow) Duggan; married July 1956 (div. Jan. 1981); children: Michelle, Cheryl, Michael, Christopher, Robert, Siobhan, Mary; m. Cheryl Ann Kirk, Jan. 1, 1983. BS in Math., Coll. Holy Cross, 1953; postgrad., U. Minn., 1953—56; JD, LLB, Boston Coll., 1956; M in Patent Law, Georgetown U., 1959. Bar: Mass. 1956, U.S. Supreme Ct. 1961; qualified trial/def. counsel Gen. Cts. Martial, 1965; cert. cmty. based conflict resolution, 1994. Sr. engr. Sylvania Programming Lab., Needham, Mass., 1960—61; trial atty. antitrust divsn. U.S. Dept. Justice, 1961—67; asst. prof. econs. Whittemore Sch., U. N.H., Durham, 1967—69; comdr. U.S. Naval Intelligence Res., 1956—78; adminstrv. judge Atomic Safety and Licensing Bd. Panel, Washington, 1972—89; prof. bus. law and computer scis. U. Tex., Austin, 1969—93, prof. emeritus, 1993—. Apptd. adv. procurator Tribunal, Diocese of Raleigh, 1995-97; editor-in-chief Computing Revs., N.Y.C., 1969-74. Author: Antitrust & U.S. Supreme Court, 1829-1984, 1984, Computer Utility, 1972, Law and the Computer, 1973, Paul Robeson Movies and Discography, 1998, Amazon Reviews; editor: Legal Developments, J. Marketing, 1967-93, Legal Comments; contbr. numerous articles to profl. jours. Head Profs. for Johnson, Durham, 1968; eucharistic min., lector, lay pres. St. Columba Cath. Ch., Oakland, Calif., 1997—; del. Tex. Dem. Com., Austin, 1972; IRS Vol. Income Tax Assistance, 1993-97. Mem. Mensa, Friend of Bill W. Democrat. Avocations: computer guru/hacker, semi-pro photographer, choral. Home: 4872 Reno Ln Richmond CA 94803-3850 E-mail: kirkdugg@attbi.com.

KIRKLAND, NANCY CHILDS, secondary education educator, consultant; b. Ideal, Ga., July 20, 1937; d. Millard Geddings and Bessie Vioda (Forbes) C.; m. Allard Corley French, Jr., Apr. 22, 1961 (div. Dec. 7, 1978); children: Vianne Elizabeth French Ouzts, Nancy Alysia French Joyce; m. Clarence Nathaniel Kirkland, Jr., Dec. 12, 1987. AB in Speech and Religious Edn., LaGrange Coll., 1959; MS, Troy State U., 1977; EdD in Child and Youth Studies, Nova U., 1993. Cert. tchr. English, Religion; cert. instr. Profl. Refinements in Developing Effectiveness, Tchr. Effectiveness and Classroom Handling. Dir. Christian edn. First Meth. Ch., Thomson, Ga., 1959-61; tchr. English Flanagan (Ill.) Jr.-Sr. H.S., 1962-63; tchr. English and social studies Woodland Jr. H.S., Streater, Ill., 1963-64; tchr. 5th grade Sheridan Elem. Sch., Bloominton, Ill., 1964-65; tchr. English Samson (Ala.) H.S., 1965, Choctawhatchee H.S., Fort Walton Beach, Fla., 1966-68, Marianna (Fla.) H.S., 1972-77; dir. devel. reading lab. Chiefland (Fla.) H.S., 1979-82; tchr. English Buchholz H.S., Gainesville, 1982—. Co-founder, cons. KPS Leadership Specialists, Jonesboro, Ga., 1993—; chairperson Buchholz facilitis com., Gainesville, Fla., 1993—; instr. English Santa Fe C. C., Gainesville, Fla., 1982-87, 96; asst. chairperson Buchholz English Dept., Gainesville, Fla., 1989-92. Contbr. articles to profl. jours. Sec., co-chmn., mem. Buchholz sch. adv. coun., Gainesville, 1994-95; tchr., dir., tchr. trainer Sunday sch., vacation sch., Fla.; actress, dir. Little Theaters, ch. groups, Ill., Ga., Ala.; coord. Gainesville Sister Cities Youth Correspondence Program, 1991-93. Mem. AAUW, ASCD, Alachua Multicultural Coun. (grantee 1992), Nat. Coun. Tchrs. English, Fla. Coun. Tchrs. English, Alachua Coun. Tchrs. English (v.p. 1991-92, pres. 1992-93), Gainesville C. of C. Methodist. Avocations: crafts, sewing, fishing, traveling. Home: 1728 NW 8th St Gainesville FL 32606-5570 Office: Buchholz H S 5510 NW 27th Ave Gainesville FL 32606-6405

KIRKPATRICK, ANNE MARY, elementary education educator; b. Ridgway, Pa., Nov. 3, 1952; d. Anthony Joseph and Antoinette (Guaglianone) Marrone; m. John Berkley Kirkpatrick, July 15, 1978 (dec. 1981); 1 child, Beth Anne. BS in Mental Retardation, Clarion U., 1973, MS in Spl. Edn., 1976. Cert. tchr., spl. edn. tchr., Pa. Tchr. spl. edn. Intermediate Unit # 9 Seneca Highlands Sch., St. Marys, Pa., 1974-79; coord., tchr. early intervention pre-sch. Elk County Soc. Spl. Svcs., St. Marys, 1985-90; tchr. elem. sch. Johnsonburg (Pa.) Area Sch. Dist., 1991—. Mem. troop com. Johnsonburg area Girl Scouts U.S., 1985-92; pres. Elk County Children and Youth Svc., Ridgway, Pa., 1989-92; mem. Ridgway Community Nurse Svc., 1989-92, Elk County Coun. on Arts, Ridgway, 1989-92; Rep. precinct chair, Johnsonburg, 1991-92. Mem. NEA, Coun. Exceptional Childre, Pa. Edn. Assn., Kappa Delta Pi. Home: 185 East Ave Johnsonburg PA 15845-1015

KIRKPATRICK, DONALD ROBERT, secondary school educator; b. Ft. Belvoir, Va., Aug. 15, 1956; s. Robert Wilbur and Marsha Beatrice (Watson) K. BS, James Madison U., 1979; postgrad., U. Kans., 1979-81; MEd, U. S.C., 1994. Aid dept. paleobiology Nat. Mus. Natural History, Washington, 1979; rsch. asst. U. Kans., Lawrence, 1979-81; sci. tchr. 8th grade Johnakin Mid. Sch., Marion, SC, 1989—2003; sci. tchr. grades 9-12 Marion HS, 2003—. Rsch. assoc. Horry County Mus., Conway, 1990—; fossil collector/donor Nat. Mus. Natural History, 1979—; presenter in field; instr. part-time Coastal Carolina U., Conway, S.C., 1992—, Francis Marion U., Florence, S.C., 1998—. Lt. USNR, 1981-89. Mem. NEA, ASCD, Nat. Assn. Geosci. Tchrs., Nat. Sci. Tchrs. Assn., Nat. Assn. Biology Tchrs., SC Sci. Coun., SC Acad. Sci., Astronomical Soc. Pacific, Paleontological Rsch. Inst., Soc. Vertebrate Paleontology, Nat. Ctr. Sci. Edn., Assn. for Curriculum Devel. Episcopalian. Avocations: collecting fossils, walking, reading, swimming. Home: 1321 Snider St Conway SC 29526-3120 Office: Marion High Sch 1205 S Main St Marion SC 29571 Business E-Mail: dkirkpatrick@marion1.k12.sc.us. E-mail: drki@sccoast.net.

KIRKPATRICK, DOROTHY LOUISE, retired education educator, program coordinator; b. Winnsboro, SC, Aug. 23, 1937; d. Joseph Leslie and Mamie Annie (Kinard) K. BS, Winthrop Coll., 1959; MS, U. Tenn., 1962; EdD, U. Ky., 1975. Head lifeguard, swim coach Winnsboro Mills Pool, 1955-61; tchr. Thomas Jefferson Jr. H.S., Miami, Fla., 1959-61; recreation therapist Ea. Tenn. Psychiat. Hosp., Knoxville, 1961-62; prof., coord. secondary edn., dir. women's phys. edn. Ea. Ky. U., Richmond, 1962-97, prof. emeritus, 1997—. Cons. Ea. Ky. U. Consortium Area 1, Manchester, 1992, Consortium Area 2, Richmond, 1992, Consortium Area 3, Somerset, 1992, 94; intern cert. evaluator Ky. Dept. Edn., 22 county area, 1985-95; faculty Commonwealth Inst. for Tchrs., U. Ky., Commonwealth Inst. for Tchrs., Ea. Ky. U. Contbr. articles to profl. jours. Olympic devel. com. Nat. Inst. Girl's and Women's Sports, Lansing, Mich., 1966; deacon 1st Presbyn. Ch., Richmond, 1981-85, elder, 1987-90, clk. of session, 1990, trustee, 1992-98, chair bldg. com. 1994-97; pres. Isabell Bennett Philanthropic

Corp., 1992—; chair bd., pres., v.p. Deacon Hills Homeowners Assn. Recipient Hellams award Winthrop Coll., 1959, Regents award Ea. Ky. U., 1964, cert. of appreciation ARC, 1974, Disting. Phys. Edn. Alumnus award Winthrop U., 2001. Mem. AAHPERD, ASCD, So. AAHPERD, Ky. AHPERD (conv. mgr. 1968, v.p. 1973, 90, pres. 1990-91, Past President's award 1991, Disting. Svc. award 1992), Assn. Tchr. Educators, So. Assn. Phys. Edn. for Coll. Women (conv. mgr. 1985), Ky. Assn. Tchr. Educators (conv. mgr. 1970), Citizens for Sport Equity, Phi Kappa Phi (hon.), Phi Delta Kappa (hon.). Democrat. Presbyterian. Avocations: gardening, swimming, bird watching, crafts.

KIRKPATRICK, HOLLY JEAN, elementary education educator, special education educator; b. Santa Cruz, S.Am., Mar. 21, 1953; d. John Meridith and Alice Louise (Mitchell) K. BA, Earlham Coll., 1975; MA, U. Evansville, 1979. Cert. tchr., Ind. Tchr. Richmond (Ind.) Community Schs., 1975-76; substitute tchr. Indpls. Pub. Schs., 1976-77, North Gibson Schs., Princeton, Ind., 1977-79; tchr. Kokomo (Ind.) Ctr. Schs., 1979—. Bd. dirs. Kokomo unit Am. Heart Assn., 1990—; mem. communications coun. United Way, Kokomo, 1990—; mem. Mayor's Substance Abuse Adv. Coun., Kokomo, 1990—, Howard County Child Abuse Coun., Kokomo, 1990—. Named Master Tchr. for Ind. Migrant Edn. Coun., 1986, Outstanding Young Hoosier, Kokomo Jaycees, 1986, 92. Mem. NEA, ASCD, Internat. Reading Assn. (Honor Coun. 1992), Ind. State Reading Assn. (Honor Coun. 1992), Kokomo Area Reading Coun. (v.p. 1990-91, pres. 1991-92, Honor Coun. 1990-92), Ind. State Tchrs. Assn., Kokomo Tchrs. Assn. (pres. 1987—), Phi Delta Kappa, Delta Kappa Gamma. Methodist. Avocations: reading, cross-stitch, sewing. Home: 1206 Gleneagles Dr Kokomo IN 46902-3184 Office: Roosevelt Sch 2200 N Washington St Kokomo IN 46901-5840

KIRKPATRICK, JEANE DUANE JORDAN, political scientist, government official; b. Duncan, Okla. d. Welcher F. and Leona (Kile) Jordan; m. Evron M. Kirkpatrick; children: Douglas Jordan, John Evron, Stuart Alan. AA, Stephens Coll.; AB, Barnard Coll.; MA, PhD, Columbia U.; postgrad. (French govt. fellow), Inst. Polit. Sci., U. Paris; LHD (hon.), Georgetown U., U. Pitts., U. Charleston, Hebrew U., Colo. Sch. Mines, St. John's U., Universidad Francisco Marroquin, Guatemala, Coll. of William and Mary, U. Mich., Syracuse U.; hon. degree, Loyola U., U. Rochester, Chgo. Asst. prof. polit. sci. Trinity Coll., 1962-67; assoc. prof. polit. sci. Georgetown U., Washington, 1967-73, prof., 1973—, Leavey prof., 1978—2002, prof. emeritus, 2002—; sr. fellow Am. Enterprise Inst. for Pub. Policy Rsch., 1977—; mem. cabinet U.S. permanent rep. to UN, 1981-85; mem. Def. Policy Rev. Bd. (DPB), 1985-93; chair Commn. on Fail Safe and Risk Reduction (FARR), 1990-92; mem. Pres.'s Fgn. Intelligence and Adv. Bd. (PFIAD), 1985-89; head U.S. Delegation to Human Rights Commn., 2003. Author: Elections USA, 1956, Perspectives, 1962, The Strategy of Deception, 1963, Mass Behavior in Battle and Captivity, 1968, Leader and Vanguard in Mass Society; The Peronist Movement in Argentina, 1971, Political Woman, 1974, The New Presidential Elite, 1976, Dismantling the Parties: Reflections on Party Reform and Party Decomposition, 1978, The Reagan Phenomenon, 1983, Dictatorships and Double Standards, 1982, Legitimacy and Force (2 vols.), 1988, The Withering Away of the Totalitarian State, 1990; syndicated columnist, 1985-97; contbr. articles to profl. jours.; editor, contbr. various pubs. Trustee Helen Dwight Reid Ednl. Found., 1972—, pres., 1990—. Recipient Disting. Alumna award Stephens Coll., 1978, B'nai B'rith Humanitarian award, 1982, Award of the Commonwealth Fund, 1983, Gold medal VFW, 1984, French Prix Politique, 1984, Dept. Def. Disting. Pub. Svc. medal, 1985, Bronze Palm, 1992, Disting. Svc. medal Mayor of N.Y.C., 1985, Presdl. Medal of Freedom, 1985, Jamestown Freedom award, 1990, Centennial medal Nat. Soc. DAR, 1991, Disting. Svc. award USO, 1994, Laureate of the Lincoln Acad. of Ill., Medallion of Lincoln, 1996, Jerusalem 2000 award, 1996, Casey medal of hon., 1998, Tomas Garrigue Masaryk Order, 1998, Chauncey Rose award Rose-Hulman Inst. Tech., 1999, Hungarian Presdl. Gold medal, 1999, Living Legends medal Libr. Congress, 2000, Grand Officier du Wissam Al Alaoui medal King of Morocco, 2000; Kirkpatrick professorship of internat. affairs chair established in her honor Harvard U., 1999; Coun. on Fgn. Rels. established Jeane Kirkpatric chair in nat. security, 2002. Mem. Internat. Polit. Sci. Assn. (exec. coun.), Am. Polit. Sci. Assn. (Hubert Humphrey award 1988), So. Polit. Sci. Assn. Office: Am Enterprise Inst 1150 17th St NW Washington DC 20036-4603 E-mail: jkirkpatrick@aei.org.

KIRKSEY, KENN M. nursing educator; b. Ft. Worth, Jan. 31, 1954; s. Woodville Cicero and Ila Kay (Weehunt) K. BSN, Tex. Woman's U., 1978, PhD in Nursing, 1993; MSN, U. Tex., Arlington, 1981. RN, Tex.; CEN; cert. clin. nurse specialist, Tex.; cert. specialist ANCC. Instr. Lamar U., Beaumont, Tex., 1983-86; asst. prof. nursing U. Tex. Med. Br., Galveston, 1986-88, U. Tex. Health Sci. Ctr., San Antonio, 1988-96; assoc. prof. Tex. A&M U., Corpus Christi, 1996—. Bd. dirs. Cmty. Care for AIDS, Inc., Galveston, 1986-88. Contbr. articles to profl. publs., chpts. to books; contbg. editor jour. Critical Care Nurse, 1994—; reviewer for jours. in field; mem. editl. bd. AACN, Clin. Issues: Advanced Practice in Acute and Critical Care. Bd. dirs., vice chair The Passage AIDS Hospice, Corpus Christi. NIH/NINR RO1 grantee, 1994—. Mem. AACN, Tex. Nurses Assn. (Dist. 6 v.p. 1987-88; Dist. 17 bd. dirs. 1997—), Sigma Theta Tau (pres.-elect 1994-95, pres. 1995-96, bd. dirs. 1994-96; region 3 chairperson multimedia awards 1996—). Office: Tex A&M U Sch Nursing and Health Scis 6300 Ocean Dr Corpus Christi TX 78412-5503

KIRKWOOD, NANCY LYNNE, elementary education educator; b. Phila., June 6, 1961; d. Donald Francis and Joan Isabelle (Miller) Sleesman; m. James Mace, Oct. 4, 1986; 1 child, Colin James. BS of Edn., Millersville State Coll., 1983. Tchr., pre-kindergarten, asst. dir. Kinder-Care Learning Ctr., Camp Hill, Pa., 1983-85; remedial tchr. Upper Dauphin Area Schs., Elizabethville, Pa., 1985-86; tchr. York (Pa.) City Schs., 1986-87, Kindergarten-Kinder Care, Newark, Del., 1987-88, Millersburg (Pa.) Area Sch. Dist., 1988—. Pharmacy technician Rite Aid Corp. Camp Hill, Pa., 1988—; pvt. tutor, Millersburg, 1989—; color guard advisor Millersburg Area H.S. Band, 1988—, Upper Dauphin Area H.S. Band, Elizabethville, 1992-93; treas. Ednl. Horizons Inc. Active N.Y. Skyliners Drum and Bugle Corp, 1991—, Reading Buccaneers Aluni. Mem. Nat. Coun. Curriculum and Devel., Nat. Coun. for Social Studies, Pa. State Edn. Assn. (bldg. rep. 1992-93), Pa. State Edn. Assn., Millersburg Area Edn. Assn. Republican. Lutheran. Avocations: traveling, reading, cooking, music, theater. Home: 394 Rising Sun Ln Millersburg PA 17061-1456

KIRMSE, SISTER ANNE-MARIE ROSE, nun, educator, researcher; b. Bklyn., Sept. 23, 1941; d. Frank Joseph Sr. and Anna (Keck) K. BA in English cum laude, St. Francis Coll., 1972; MA in Theology with honors, Providence Coll., 1975; PhD in Theology, Fordham U., 1989. Joined Sisters of St. Dominic, Roman Cath. Ch., 1960; cert. elem. tchr., N.Y. Tchr. elem. sch. Diocese Bklyn., 1962-73; instr. adult edn. Diocese Rockville Centre, N.Y., 1974—; dir. religious edn. St. Anthony Padua Parish, East Northport, N.Y., 1975-83; dir. spiritual programs Diocese of Rockville Centre, 1979—. Demonstration tchr. Paulist Press, N.Y.C., 1968-70; cons. Elem. Sch. Catechetical Assocs., Bklyn., 1971-73; mem. adj. faculty grad. program Sem. Immaculate Conception, Huntington, N.Y., 1979-80; adj. instr. Molloy Coll., Rockville Centre, 1985, St. Joseph's Coll., Patchogue, N.Y., 1990-91; adj. asst. prof. Ignatius Coll., Bronx, N.Y., 1996-98; adj. assoc. prof. Fordham Coll. Liberal Studies, 1998—; asst. to Card. Avery Dulles, Fordham U., Bronx, 1988—, rsch. assoc. Laurence J. McGinley chair in religion and society, 1989-2003. Recipient Kerygma award Diocese of Rockville Centre, 1980; Dominican scholar Providence Coll., 1973, Presdl. scholar Fordham U., 1988; McGinley fellow Fordham U., 1988. Mem. Cath. Theol. Soc. Am., Coll. Theology Soc., Amnesty Internat., Kiwanis (pres. Fordham U. 1997-2000, Tablet of Honor 2000, KY dist. chmn. Internat. Understanding/Student Exch., 2001-03, lt. gov. Bronx-Westchester South divsn. 2003—, KPTC fellow 2001). Democrat. Roman Catholic. Avocations: swimming, needlework, cooking, traveling, reading. Office: Fordham U Faber Hall 255 Bronx NY 10458 E-mail: kirmse@fordham.edu.

KIRPES, ANNE IRENE, elementary education educator; b. Dubuque, Iowa, Oct. 6, 1966; d. Raymond Louis and Norma Jean Margaret (Kern) K. BA, U. No. Iowa, 1989; EdM, Harvard U., 1997. Lic. elem. edn. Tchr. 1st grade Western Ave Sch., Sch. Dist. 161, Flossmoor, Ill., 1989-93, Serena Hills Sch., Sch. Dist. 161, Chicago Heights, Ill., 1993-96; tchr. 3d grade Wheelock Lab. Keene (N.H.) State Coll., 1997-98; reading/lang. arts test devel. specialist Riverside Pub. Co., Itasca, Ill., 1998—2002; reading test devel. dir. Data Recognition Corp., Maple Grove, Minn., 2002—. Exch. team mem. Rotary Group, Paris, 1995. Recipient Silver Congl. award U.S.A., 1988, Gold Congl. award, 1991, Young Alumni award U. No. Iowa Alumni Assn., Cedar Falls, 1994. Mem. ASCD, Nat. Coun. Tchrs. English, Whole Lang. Umbrella, Internat. Reading Assn., Kappa Delta Pi (internat. nominations com. 1988-90), Phi Delta Kappa, Alpha Upsilon Alpha, Omicron Delta Kappa. Avocations: reading, travel, puzzles, butterfly memorabilia, board games. Home: 9461 Jewel Ln North Maple Grove MN 55311

KIRSCH, MARY ANNE GWEN, elementary education educator; b. Chgo., July 9, 1951; d. Steven R. and Helen S. (Krawczyk) Wilczynski; m. Robert Romano (div.); 1 child, Jeff Romano; m. Ronald T. Kirsch, July 21, 1973; 1 child, Justin. BA with high honors, Elmhurst Coll., 1991; MEd, Nat. Louis U., 1995. Cert. elem. tchr., Ill. Tchr. St. Isidore Sch., Bloomingdale, Ill., 1991-92, Elmwood Sch. Dist. #401, Elmwood Park, Ill., 1992—, gifted coord., 2002. Mem. West Suburban Reading Coun., Illinois Assoc. for Gifted Chilren (IAGC), Phi Kappa Phi.

KIRSCH, ROSLYN RUTH, art educator, painter, printmaker; b. N.Y.C., Dec. 30, 1928; d. Harry Morris and Lillian (Zemachson) Friedenberg; m. Louis Kirsch, Dec. 26, 1948; children: Libby Ann, Andrew Lawrence. Student, Queens Coll., 1946-48; BA, Hunter Coll., 1950. Art dir. Ladies' Ready-to-Wear Buying Office, N.Y.C., 1948-50; profl. artist, self employed, 1965—; art educator Armory Art Ctr., West Palm Beach, Fla., 1987—, Boca Raton Mus. Art Sch., Boca Raton, Fla., 1990—. One-person shows include J&W Gallery, New Hope, Pa., Capitol Gallery, Tallahassee, Fla., S&W Gallery, New Hope, Pa., Peter Drew Galleries, Fla., Ken Elias, Habitat Gallery, West Palm Beach, Fla., Joel Kessler Gallery, Fla., Indigo Gallery, Fla., Palm Beach Internat. Airport; exhibited in group shows Ann. Hortt Exhbn., Mus. of Art, Ft. Lauderdale, 1994 (award), Nat. Assn. Women Artists, West Palm Beach, 1995 (award), Mus. Art (invitational exhibit), Ft. Lauderdale, 1998, Boca Raton Mus. Art, Fla., 1999; represented in permanent collections including Mus. Art., Ft. Lauderdale, Boca Raton Mus. Art. Recipient Honorable Mention award Mus. Art, Ft. Lauderdale, 1994, others. Mem. Nat. Assn. Women Artists, Boca Raton Mus. Artists Guild, others. Avocations: golf, fundraising. E-mail: kirschfineart@yahoo.com.

KIRSCHNER, RUTH BRIN, elementary education educator; b. Mpls., Mar. 12, 1924; d. Sigman and Leah (Chazankin) Brin; m. Norman Bernard Kirschner, June 19, 1949; children: Sally Jo Kirschner Minsberg, William Arthur. BS cum laude, U. Minn., 1946. Primary tchr. Robert Fulton Sch., Mpls., 1946-52; elem. tchr. St. Louis Park (Minn.) Schs., 1962—. Tchr. religious sch. Adath Jeshurun Synagogue, Mpls., 1946-83, Bnai Emet Synagoguue, St. Louis Park, 1989—; primary tchr. Latch Key, Mpls., 1986-88; nursery sch. tchr. Westwood Luth. Ch., St. Louis Park, 1989—; customer svc. rep. Am. Automobile Assn., St. Louis Park, 1985—. Sec. 4th Dist. Dem. Com., St. Louis Park, 1986-90; state del. St. Louis Park Dem. Com., 1986, 88, 90; mem. Cmty. Rels. coun. St. Louis Park, 1986-88; mem. St. Louis Park Charter Commn., 1997—; pres. Friends of St. Louis Park Libr., 1987-88, sec., 1990—; pres. St. Louis Park Friends, 1991-92, 93-94; del. to 44th Dist. Dem. Farmer Labor Exec. Bd.; alt. to 5th Dist. Dem. Farmer Labor ctrl. com., del. to conv., 1998; apptd. mem. charter commn. St. Louis Park, 1993—; mem. Visions, 1994; bd. dirs. Suburban Alliance, 1994. Mem. AAUW (sec.-treas. 1970-72, parliamentarian 1974-76), Lioness (pres. Lyn-Lake 1995—, v.p. 1993-95), Alpha Delta Kappa (state scholarship chmn. 1988-90, sec. Gamma chpt. 1990—, Gamma pres. 2003—). Jewish. Avocations: reading, music, embroidery, telling stories, travel. Home: 3135 Colorado Ave S Minneapolis MN 55416-2050

KIRST, MICHAEL WEILE, education educator, researcher; b. Westreading, Pa., Aug. 1, 1939; s. Russell and Marian (Weile) K.; m. Wdndy Burdsall, Sept. 6, 1975; children: Michael, Anne. AB summa cum laude, Dartmouth Coll., 1961; MPA, Harvard U., 1963, PhD, 1964. Budget examiner U.S. Bur. Budgets, Office of Edn., Washington, 1964-64; assoc. dir. President's comsn. on White House fellows Nat. Adv. Coun. on Edn. Disadvantaged Children, Washington, 1966; dir. program planning and evaluation Bur. Elem. and Secondary Edn., U.S. Office Edn., Washington, 1967; staff dir. U.S. Senate Subcommittee Manpower, Employment and Poverty, Washington, 1968-69; with Ca. State Bd. Edn., Sacramento, 1975-77, pres., 1977-81; prof. edn. Stanford (Calif.) U., 1969—. Prin. investigator Policy Analysis for Calif. Edn., Berkeley, 1984—, Ctr. Policy Rsch. in Edn., Rutgers U., Stanford U., Mich. State U., 1984—, Reform Up Close, 1988-92; chmn. bd. comparative studies in edn. U.S. Nat. Acad. Scis., 1994—. Author: Government Without Passing Laws, 1969, (with Frederick Wirt) The Political Web of American Schools, 1972, (with Joel Berke) Federal Aid to Education: Who Governs, Who Benefits, 1972, State School Finance Alternatives, 1975, (with others) Contemporary Issues in Education: perspectives from Australia and U.S.A., 1983, (with others) Who Controls Our Schools: American Values in Conflict, 1984, (with Frederick Wirt) Schools in Conflict: Political Turbulence in American Education, 1982, 3d edit., 1992, Political Dynamic of American Education, 2001, Betraying the College Dream, 2003; editor: The Politics of Education at the Local, State, and Federal Levels, 1970, State, School and Politics, 1972; author numerous monographs; contbr. numerous articles to profl. jours., newspapers and mags. Pres. Calif. State Bd. Edn., Sacramento, 1977-80. Mem. NAS (chmn. bd. international comparative studies in edn.), Nat. Acad. Edn., Am. Edn. Rsch. Assn. (v.p.), Internat. Acad. Edn., Phi Beta Kappa. Office: Stanford U Sch Edn MC 3096 Stanford CA 94305

KIRSTEIN, JANIS ADRIAN, art educator; b. Louisville, July 7, 1955; d. John Audelbert and Myrl Oleen (Baxter) K.; m. John Brooke Rigor, Apr. 4, 1955. Student, Ind. U.; BA, U. Louisville, 1977; MFA, U. Mass., 1981. Cert. tchr., Ky. Art instr. Ind. U., Bloomington, 1984, U. Louisville, 1983-89, 2000; fine arts instr. Oldham County H.S., Louisville, 1986-88, Western Hills H.S., Frankfort, Ky., 1988—, Gov.'s Scholars Program, Louisville, 1994-97. One-person shows John Harriman Gallery, 2002, Peruvian Brit. Cultural Ctr., Peru, 2002, Bellarmine Coll., Louisville, 1994, Zephyr Gallery, Louisville, 2000-02, British Consulate Gallery, Lima, Peru, 2003; group shows include Digital Art Exhbn., Ky. State U. (Purchase award), Cin. Art Consortium, 1993, SC Mus. Art, 1993, Assemblage/Collage Invitational Exhbn., Seoul Inst. Arts, 1988. Fellow Ky. Arts Coun., 1983-2001, Ky. Found. for Women, 1989. Mem. AAUW (Eleanor Roosevelt award for Civic Svc. 1989, chair Edn. Found. Louisville chpt. 1989), Nat. Art Edn. Assn., Ky. Edn. Assn. Democrat. Home: 2001 Spring Dr Apt 11 Louisville KY 40205-1551 Office: Western Hills HS 100 Doctors Dr Frankfort KY 40601-4102 E-mail: jkirstei@franklin.k12.ky.us.

KIRTLEY, JANE ELIZABETH, law educator; b. Indpls., Nov. 7, 1953; d. William Raymond and Faye Marie (Price) K.; m. Stephen Jon Cribari, May 8, 1985. BS in Journalism, Northwestern U., 1975, MS in Journalism, 1976; JD, Vanderbilt U., 1979. Bar: N.Y. 1980, D.C. 1982, Va. 1995, U.S. Dist. Ct. (we. dist.) N.Y. 1980, U.S. Dist. Ct. D.C. 1982, U.S. Ct. Claims 1982, U.S. Ct. Appeals (4th cir.) 1982, U.S. Ct. Appeals (D.C. cir.) 1985, U.S. Ct. Appeals (10th cir.) 1996, U.S. Ct. Appeals (5th cir.) 1997, U.S. Ct. Appeals (6th cir.) 1998, U.S. Ct. Appeals (6th and 11th cir.) 1998, U.S. Supreme Ct. 1985. Assoc. Nixon, Hargrave, Devans & Doyle, Rochester, N.Y., 1979-81, Washington, 1981-84; exec. dir. Reporters Com. for Freedom of Press, Arlington, Va., 1985-99; Silha prof. media ethics & law U. Minn. Sch. Journalism & Mass Comm., Mpls., 1999—; dir. Silha Ctr. for Study of Media Ethics and Law, Mpls., 2000—; mem. affiliated faculty U. Minn. Law Sch., 2001—. Mem. adj. faculty Am. U. Sch. Comm., 1988-98; mem. affiliated law faculty U. Minn., 2001—. Exec. articles editor Vanderbilt U. Jour. Transnat. Law, 1978-79; editor: The News Media and the Law, 1985—, The First Amendment Handbook, 1987, 4th edit., 1995, Agents of Discovery, 1991, 93, 95, Pressing Issues, 1998-99; columnist NEPA Bull., 1988-99, Virginia's Press, 1991-99, Am. Journalism Rev., 1995—, W.Va.'s Press, 1997-99, Tenn. Press, 1997-99; mem. editl. bd. Comm. Law and Policy. Bd. dirs. Sigma Delta Chi Found., Indpls. Mem. ABA, N.Y. State Bar Assn., D.C. Bar Assn., Va. State Bar Assn., Sigma Delta Chi. Home: 3645 46th Ave S Minneapolis MN 55406-2937 Office: 111 Murphy Hall 206 Church St SE Minneapolis MN 55455-0488 E-mail: kirtl001@tc.umn.edu.

KIRWAN, WILLIAM ENGLISH, II, mathematics educator, university official, academic administrator; b. Louisville, Apr. 14, 1938; s. Albert Dennis Kirwan and Elizabeth (Heil) Kirwan; m. Patricia Ann Harper, Aug. 27, 1960; children: William English III, Ann Elizabeth. BA, U. Ky., 1960; MS (NDEA fellow 1960-63), Rutgers U., 1962, PhD, 1964. Instr. Rutgers U., 1963—64; mem. faculty U. Md., College Park, 1964, prof. math., 1972, chmn. dept., 1977—81, vice chancellor for acad. affairs, 1981—86, provost, 1986—88, acting pres., 1988—89, pres., 1989—98, Ohio State U., Columbus, 1998—2002; chancellor Univ. of Maryland, 2002—. Vis. lectr. London U., 1966—67; program dir. NSF, 1975—76. Contbr. articles to profl. jours. MS 2000 Com. for NRC; mem. adv. bd. Montgomery County (Md.), 1975—79; bd. dirs. Nat. Assn. State Univs. and Land Grant Colls., 1995—, Greater Washington YMCA, 1994—; World Trade Ctr. Inst., 1990—. Decorated officer Order King Leopold II (Belgium); named Disting. Alumnus, U. Ky., 1989. Mem.: NCAA (pres. commn. 1995—), Coun. for the Internat. Exch. of Scholars, Math. Assn. Am., Am. Assn. Colls. and Univs. (bd. dirs. 1993—, 1994—), Am. Math. Soc. (coun. 1980—82, editor Proc. 1977—82). Office: University System of Maryland Chancellor's Office 3300 Metzerott Rd, Suite 2C Adelphi MD 20783

KISER, KENNETH M(AYNARD), chemical engineering educator; b. Detroit, Nov. 28, 1929; s. Kenneth Chapman and Emma (Kutkuhn) K.; m. Florence Mary Sclafani, June 26, 1954; children: David, Thomas, James, John, Melissa. BS in Chem. Engring., Lawrence Tech. U., 1951; MS in Chem. Engring., U. Cin., 1952; D.Engring., Johns Hopkins U., 1956. Registered profl. engr., N.Y. Chem. engr. Gen. Electric Co., Schenectady, N.Y., 1956-64; asst. prof. chem. engring. SUNY-Buffalo, 1964-65, assoc. prof., 1965-80, prof., 1980—, acting chair chem. engring. dept., 1977, 78, assoc. dean engring., 1978-95, chair chem. engring. dept., 1995-97, prof. emeritus, 1997—; adj. prof. Rensselaer Poly. Inst., Troy, N.Y., 1962-64; chem. engring. cons., 1965—. Contbr. articles to profl. jours., 1957—. Patentee in field. Recipient Chancellor's award SUNY-Buffalo, 1974; grantee NSF, Heart Assn., others, 1965-80. Mem. Am. Inst. Chem. Engrs., Am. Soc. Engring. Edn., Alpha Chi Sigma, Sigma Xi, Tau Beta Pi (Tchr. award 1973). E-mail: ken_kiser@hotmail.com.

KISER, STEPHEN, artist, educator; b. Koloa, Hawaii, Feb. 4, 1944; s. Mary A. Kiser; m. Kathleen A. Cahill, Jan. 14, 1973; children: Lisa, Kari. Cert., Brooks Inst. Photography, 1965; BA, San Jose State U., 1976, MA, 1978. Freelance photojournalist, 1964-66, 72-74; photographer Pace Publs., L.A. and N.Y.C., 1966-68; exec. and artistic dir. Tidewater Young Performers, Norfolk, Va., 1968-69; owner Steve Kiser Prodns., Orange, Calif., 1970-72; coord. dir. Ctr. for Creative Arts and Scis., San Francisco, 1976-78; owner Steve Kiser Studios, Palo Alto, Calif., 1995—; assoc. prof. Foothill Coll., Los Altos Hills, Calif., 1974—2000; prof. City Coll. San Francisco, 1995—. Trustee, v.p. Am. Indian Contemporary Arts, San Francisco, 1988—. Exhibiting artist with numerous one man and group shows, 1970—. Event coord. Calif. Winter Spl. Olympics, Momouth, Calif., 1975-80; v.p. Hands Across the Water, U.S./Indonesia, 1984-93; advisor Leadership Mid-Peninsula, 1995. With USN, 1968-69. Fellow Rotary, Brazil, 1970; Arts fellow for Contemporary Native Am. Artist, Ednl. Found. Am., 1996. Mem. Am. Soc. Media. Photographers, Internat. Sculpture Assn., Soc. for Photog. Edn., Coll. Art Assn., Hale Naua III. Avocation: exploring new places and concepts. Home: 3302 Vernon Ter Palo Alto CA 94303-4203 Office: 4000 Middlefield Rd # 3 Palo Alto CA 94303-4739 E-mail: Steve@SteveKiser.com.

KISH, ELISSA ANNE, educational administrator, consultant; b. Bklyn., Sept. 29, 1934; d. Robert Joseph and Yolanda Filomina (Romano) Lucadamo; m. Joseph Laurence Kish Jr., Oct. 16, 1955; children: Grace Edna Kish, Joseph Robert, Frances Caroline Kish Burrell. BA, CUNY, 1956; EdM, Rutgers U., 1965. Elem. tchr. N.Y. City Pub. Schs., Bklyn., 1956-57, U.S. Army Dependent Schs., Hanau, West Germany, 1958, Piscataway (N.J.) Pub. Schs., 1961-62, New Brunswick (N.J.) Pub. Schs., 1965, 71-76; vice prin. Hopatcong (N.J.) Pub. Schs., 1977-78; asst. supt. Dunellen (N.J.) Pub. Schs., 1978-80; supr. K-12 instrn. Elmwood Park (N.J.) Pub. Schs., 1980-90; interim high sch. adminstr. Dunellen Pub. Schs., 1991-92; adminstr. ctrl. office Elmwood Park Pub. Schs., 1992-96. Cons. Newark Pub. Schs., 1976-77; evaluator Middle States Assn., Navesink, N.J., 1988; cons. State U. N.Y., Garden City, 1992, Mt. Vernon Pub. Schs., N.Y., 1992; mem. fine arts & humanities coun. Town of Wareham, Mass., 1996—. Author: Nutrition Program For Schools, 1979; contbng. author: Curriculum & Values: An Inquiry, 1976. Mem. strategic planning team Town of Elmwood Park, 1993-95; officer, mem. Westfield Coll. Women's Club, Westfield, N.J., 1969-92; founder, 1st pres. Vocational Adv. Coun., Elmwood Park, 1980-90; trustee Christopher Montessori Acad., Westfield, 1968-72. Recipient numerous grants for rsch. and curriculum devel., 1979—. Mem. ASCD, NEA, Elmwood Park Prins. and Suprs. Assn. (pres. 1989-90), Elmwood Park Adminstrs. Assn. (pres. 1986-89), Nat. Geographic Soc., Smithsonian Assocs., Kappa Delta Pi, Alpha Epsilon Phi. Avocations: theatre, opera. Home and Office: 635 4th Ave Lindenwold NJ 08021

KISHMAN, RACHEL TRESSLER, elementary education educator; b. Warsaw, Ind., Jan. 9, 1948; d. Joseph Ward and Agnes (Fay) Tressler; m. Harvey Byron Kishman, Jan. 13, 1989; children: Sheryl Lynn Sayre, Tamara Sayre Gee. BS in Elem. Edn., Grace Coll., 1969; postgrad. in gifted edn., Bowling Green State U., 1981, cert. in kindergarten teaching, 1990; postgrad. in gifted curriculum, Ashland U., 1994. Cert. tchr., Ohio. Tchr. Atkinson Elem. Sch., Fremont, Ohio, 1972-74; tchr. talented/gifted program Ottawa County Bd. Edn., Oak Harbor, Ohio, 1980-82; tchr. Townsend Elem. Sch., Vickery, Ohio, 1987-91, tchr. 6th grade ind. study program, 1990-92; tchr. Bogart Elem. Sch., Castalia, Ohio, 1991—. Tchr. 2d grade Ann. Studies and Coop. Learning Program, 1993; organizer Ann. Parent Thank You Dinner, 1993—; participant Ann. Grandparent Program, 1994—; core team mem. Multiple Intelligences Network, 1995—; mem. tech. com., 1995—. Contbg. author curriculum and enrichment materials for gifted program, integrated lang. arts program. Grantee Ohio Dept. Edn., 1991-94, Wal-Mart, 1992-93, STEP grantee Ohio Gifted Edn., 1993-95. Mem. NEA, Ohio Edn. Assn., Margaretta Tchrs. Assn. (bldg. rep. 1992-93), Bogart Tchrs. Assn. (sunshine rep. 1991-95). Avocations: fishing, cooking, piano, boating, computer. Home: 1921 N Nan St Marblehead OH 43440-9799 Office: Bogart Elem Sch 5906 Bogart Rd W Castalia OH 44824-9714

KITCH, EDMUND WELLS, lawyer, educator, private investor; b. Wichita, Kans, Nov. 3, 1939; s. Paul R. and Josephine (Pridmore) K.; m. Joanne Steiner, 1966 (div. 1976); 1 child, Sarah; m. Alison Lauter, Jan. 29, 1978 (div. 2000); children: Andrew, Whitney; m. Gail Lettwich Apr. 26,

2003. BA, Yale U., 1961; JD, U. Chgo., 1964. Bar: Kans. 1964, Ill. 1966, U.S. Supreme Ct. 1973, Va. 1986. Asst. prof. law Ind. U., 1964-65; mem. faculty U. Chgo., 1965-82, prof., 1971-82; prof., mem. Ctr. Advanced Studies U. Va., Charlottesville, 1982-85, Joseph M. Hartfield prof., 1985—2003, Sullivan and Cromwell rsch. prof., 1996-99, Mary and Daniel Loughran prof., 2003—, E. James Kelly Jr. Class of 1965 rsch. prof., 2003—. Vis. prof. Bklyn. Law Sch., 1995, Northwestern U., 1996, Georgetown U., 2002, U. Nebr., 2002; spl. asst. solicitor gen. U.S. Dept. Justice, 1973-74; exec. dir. Adv. Com. on Procedural Reform CAB, 1975-76; reporter Com. on Pattern Jury Instruction, Ill. Supreme Ct., 1966-69; mem. com. on pub.-pvt. sector rels. in vaccine innovation Inst. of Medicine, NAS, 1982-85, mem. com. on evaluation polio vaccine, 1987-88. Author: (with Harvey Perlman) Intellectual Property, 5th edit., 1997; Regulation, Federalism and Interstate Commerce, 1981. Contbr. articles to profl. jour. Mem. Va. Bar Assn., Am. Law Inst., Order of Coif, Phi Beta Kappa. Office: U Va Sch Law 580 Massie Rd Charlottesville VA 22903-1738

KITCHELL, KENNETH FRANCIS, JR., classical studies educator; b. Brockton, Mass., Oct. 24, 1947; s. Kenneth Francis, Sr. and Ellen Mary (LaRose) K.; m. Theresa Jean Barre, June 27, 1970; 1 child, Elizabeth Anne. BA in Classics (magna cum laude), Coll. of the Holy Cross, 1969; MA in Classics, Loyola U., 1972, PhD in Classics, 1977; postgrad., Am. Sch. Classical Studies, Athens, Greece, 1972-73. Latin tchr. Quigley High Sch., Chgo., 1974-76; instr. classics La. State U., Baton Rouge, 1976-78, asst. prof., 1978-84, assoc. prof. classics, 1984-94, prof., head of classics dept., 1994—98; prof. classics U. Mass., Amherst, 1998—, head grad. program in classics, 2000—03. Cons. and presenter in field. Author: (with H. Dundee) A Trilogy on the Herpetology of Linnaeus's Systema Naturae, 1994; co-author: Albertus Magnus De Animalibus: A Medieval Summa Zoologica, two vols., 1999; contbr. numerous articles to profl. jours. Grantee NEH, La. Endowment for Humanities, La. State U., U. Mass.; Hetty Goldman fellow Am. Soc. Classical Studies, 1972-73, Gertrude Smith prof. Am. Sch. Classical Studies, 1989. Mem. Am. Philol. Assn. (Excellence in Teaching in the Classics award 1983, v.p. edn. divsn. 1998-2002, bd. dirs. 1998-2002), Archaeol. Assn. Am., Am. Classical League (pres. 2002—), Assn. Ancient Historians, Classical Assn. Middle West and South (pres. 1990-91, v.p. com. for promotion of Latin 1978-82, region III rep. 1982-85, chair 1985-88, Ovatio 1994), Classical Assn. of New Eng. Avocations: stamp collecting, blues music, murder mysteries, short wave listening, barber shop quartet singing. Home: 471 State St Belchertown MA 01007-9476

KITHIER, KAREL, pathologist, educator; b. Prague, Czechoslovakia, Dec. 6, 1930; came to U.S. 1968, naturalized, 1978; s. Karel and Marie (Bohackova) K.; m. Viktorie Svecova, May 6, 1961; 1 child, Karel. MD, Charles U., Prague, 1962, PhD, 1967. Rsch. scientist Rsch. Inst. for Child Devel., Prague, 1967-68, Child Rsch. Ctr. of Mich., Detroit, 1968-71, Mich. Cancer Found., Detroit, 1972-74; asst. prof. pathology Wayne State U Sch. Medicine, Detroit, 1974-78, assoc. prof. pathology, 1978-95; chief, clin. immunology Detroit Receiving Hosp. and Univ. Health Ctr., Detroit, 1978-89, assoc. head clin. chemistry, 1978-89, med. dir. spl. chemistry, 1989-96; staff pathologist VA Med. Ctr., Allen Park, Mich., 1976—2001. Contbr. articles to profl. jours. Fellow Nat. Acad. Clin. Biochemistry; mem. Am. Assn. Cancer Research, Am. Assn. Immunologists, Am. Assn. Clin. Chemists, Internat. Soc. Oncodevelopmental Biology and Medicine. Avocation: fishing. E-mail: K.Kithier@wayne.edu. Office: Wayne State U Sch Medicine 540 E Canfield St Detroit MI 48201-1928

KITNER, JON DAVID, art educator; b. El Paso, Tex., Oct. 26, 1946; s. Harold C. and Joyce M. (LaPaz) K.; m. Debra S. Johnsen, June 12, 1976; 1 child, Jason R. BFA, Kent State U., 1969, MA, 1971. Instr. Stark Campus, Kent State U., Canton, Ohio, 1970-73, Broward Community Coll., Ft. Lauderdale, Fla., 1973-76; instr. Miami (Fla.)-Dade Cmty. Coll., 1973-76; assoc. prof. fin art Miami (Fla.)-Dade Community Coll., 1976-91, prof., 1991—, chmn. dept., 1988—94, mem. honors faculty, 1981-86, dir. art gallery, 1985-86. Ofcl. evaluator Fla. Internat. U., Fla. Endowment for Humanities, Miami, 1987; arts program coord. Visual Arts Honors Conservatory, 2002—. One-man shows include Meeting Point Gallery, Miami, 1981, Green Gallery, Miami, 1984, Wakefield Galleries, Yorkshire, Eng., 1989; exhibited in group shows Mus. Art, Ft. Lauderdale, Fla., 1984 (award of Merit), Barbara Scott Gallery, 1993; monthly columnist Miami-Herald, 1988-89. Recipient U.S. Disting. Tchr. award U.S. Dept. Edn., 1986, Outstanding Faculty award Miami-Dade C.C., 1988, Nat. Tchg. Excellence award U. Tex. Nat. Inst. for Staff Devel., 1989, Arthur Hertz Endowed Tchg. Chair for Fine Arts and Humanities, 1994-97, Nat. Inst. for Staff and Orgnl. Devel. award for ednl. excellence 2d superior leadership U. Tex., 1995, Miami-Dade County Arts Educator of Yr. award Children's Cultural Coalition, 1999, Simon Bolivar Endowed Tchg. chair, 2000-03, award Nat. Inst. for Staff and Devel., 2001; Fulbright scholar, 1988-89. Mem.: Miami Art Mus., Fulbright Alumni Assn. Office: Miami-Dade CC North Campus Dept Art & Philosophy 11380 NW 27th Ave Miami FL 33167-3418 E-mail: jkitner@mdcc.edu.

KITTELL, ANDREW JOHN, educational administrator; b. St. Albans, Vt., Apr. 2, 1957; s. Everett Clifford and Sheila D. Kittell; m. Patricia Anne McNally, Dec. 27, 1989. BS in Edn., Springfield (Mass.) Coll., 1980; MS, Johns Hopkins U., 1993. V.p., ednl. coord. Equitable Life, N.Y.C., 1980-86; tchr. social studies Kettering Mid. Sch., Upper Marlboro, Md., 1989-92; asst. dir. admissions The Am. Sch. in Switzerland (Eng. campus), Thorpe, Surrey, Eng., 1992-95; dir. admissions, dean of admissions Am. Cmty. Schs. Eng. Ltd., London, 1995—. Tchr., cons. Md. Geog. Alliance, Balt., 1990-92. Mem. Rep. Presdl. Task Force, Washington, 1992; adv. Mo. Pub. Interest Rsch. Group, St. Louis, 1985. With USN, 1986-89. Fellow Nat. Geog. Soc., Taft Inst. Govt.; mem. ASCD, NEA, Nat. Coun. for Social Studies, Environ. Law Found., Johns Hopkins Club, Phi Alpha Delta, Psi Chi. Roman Catholic. Avocations: marathons, video and still photography, travel to far east and africa. Home: 7 Wildwood Grove London NW3 7HU England Office: Am Cmty Schs Eng Ltd Woodlee London Rd (A30) Egham TW20 OHS England

KITTERMAN, JOAN FRANCES, education educator; b. Muncie, Ind., July 27, 1951; d. Thomas Harvey and Ruth (Jackson) K. BS in Elem. Edn. magna cum laude, Ball State U., 1973, MA in Elem. Edn., 1976, EdD in Spl. Edn., 1984. Cert. gen. elem. edn., reading; cert. tchr. learning disabled/neurologically impaired, Ind. Tchr. phys. edn. and music Morrison Christian Schs., Taiwan, 1973-74, tchr. 4th grade, 1974-75; title I reading tchr. Blackford County Schs., Hartford City, Ind., 1976-77, Liberty-Perry Community Schs., Selma, Ind., 1977-81; doctoral fellow Ball State U., Muncie, Ind., 1981-83; asst. prof. English as a fgn. lang. Seoul (Korea) Theol. Sem., 1984-86; asst. prof. spl. edn. and reading Ohio No. U., Ada, 1986-88; asst. prof. grad. studies Georgetown (Ky.) Coll., 1988-90, interim dean grad. studies, 1990-91, dean grad. edn., 1991-93; assoc. prof. edn. Ind. Wesleyan U., Marion, 1993-94, Taylor U., Upland, Ind., 1994-96, chair edn. dept., 1996-2000, prof. edn., dir. tchr. edn., 1997-2000, prof. edn., 2000—. Workshop presenter in field. Mem.: TESOL, Internat. Reading Assn., Coun. for Exceptional Children, Phi Delta Kappa. Avocations: reading, cross-stitching. Office: Taylor U 236 W Reade Ave Upland IN 46989-1002 E-mail: jnkitterm@tayloru.edu.

KITTOCK, CLAUDIA JEAN, education educator; b. Rochester, Minn., May 3, 1952; d. Garth William and Betty Louise (Kline) Evarts; m. Richard Carl Kittock, Dec. 23, 1978; children: Tyler Richard, Ryne Jackson. AA, Rochester (Minn.) Community Coll., 1972; BA, Gustavus Adolphus Coll., 1974; MA, U. Minn., 1977, PhD, 1986. Cert. elem. and secondary tchr., Minn. Vocal dir. Byron (Minn.) H.S., 1974-76, Rockford (Minn.) High Sch., 1977-81; behavior specialist St. Francis (Minn.) High Sch., 1981-85; edn. instr. Gustavus Adolphus Coll., St. Peter, Minn., 1985-86; behavior specialist Forest View Elem. Sch., Forest Lake, Minn., 1986-87; prof. psychology Cambridge (Minn.) Community Coll., 1987—, chair psychology dept. Adj. prof. edn. St. Mary's U., Minn., 1991—; cons. in field. Mem. Educators of the Emotionally Disturbed, Minn. Psychol. Assn., AAUW. Avocations: skiing, swimming, biking. Office: Cambridge Community Coll Highway 95 NW # 70 Cambridge MN 55008-9164

KITTROSS, JOHN MICHAEL, retired communications educator; b. NYC, Apr. 25, 1929; s. John H. and Lucile S. (Vossen) K.; m. Sally Sprague, Dec. 27, 1951; children— David M., Julia Ann. AB, Antioch Coll., 1951; MS, Boston U., 1952; PhD, U. Ill., 1960. Various positions broadcasting, summer stock, motion picture prodn., 1946-52; rsch. asst. U. Ill. Inst. Comm. Rsch., Urbana, 1955-59; from instr. to assoc. prof. dept. telecomm. U. So. Calif., Calif., 1959-68; prof. comm. Temple U., 1968-85, asst. dean Sch. Comm. and Theater, 1971-73, assoc. dean, 1973-80; dean Emerson Coll., Boston, 1985, provost, v.p. acad. affairs, 1985-87, prof. dept. mass comm., 1987-93. Vis. prof., dir. Temple U. Sch. Comms. and Theater London Programme, 1994; mng. dir. K.E.G. Assocs., 1995—. Author: Television Frequency Allocation Policy in the United States, 1979; co-author: Stay Tuned: A Concise History of American Broadcasting, 1978, 3d edit., 2002, Controversies in Media Ethics, 1996, 2nd edit., 1999; editor: Free and Fair: Courtroom Access and the Fairness Doctrine, 1970, Jour. Broadcasting, 1960-72, Documents in American Telecommunications Policy, 1977, Administration of American Telecommunications Policy, 1981; editor: Media Ethics, 1989—; compiler: Bibliography of Theses and Dissertations in Broadcasting, 1920-73, 1978; contbg. editor: Comm. Booknotes Quar., 1997—; contbr. articles to profl. jours. Trustee Upper Moreland Free Pub. Library, 1976-82. Served with AUS, 1952-54. Mem. AAUP, Broadcast Edn. Assn. (Disting. Broadcast Edn. award 1990), Assn. Edn. in Journalism and Mass Comm., Radio-TV News Dirs. Assn., Soc. Profl. Journalists, ACLU. Unitarian (trustee ch. 1966-68). Home: 164 High St Acton MA 01720-4218

KJAR, NANCY, elementary school educator; b. Hot Springs, SD, Apr. 17, 1947; d. Kenneth Winton and Marjorie Loraine Krutsch; m. Donald Robert Kjar, June 13, 1970; children: Steven Todd, Scott Ryan. BS in Edn., Chadron State U., 1969. Cert. tchr., Minn. 5th grade tchr. Sidney (Nebr.) Pub. Schs., 1969-70; 3d grade tchr. Eden Valley (Minn.) Watkins Pub. Sch., 1970-73, 4th grade tchr., 1986—2002. Mem. ch. choir Meth. Ch. Recipient Leadership in Ednl. Excellence award, Resource Tng. and Solutions (formerly Ctrl. Minn. Svc. Coop.), 2002. Mem.: Minn. Edn. Assn. Republican. Avocations: reading, music, walking, travel, needlecrafts. Office: Eden Valley-Watkins Pub Sch PO Box 100 Eden Valley MN 55329-0100

KJELSTRUP, CHERYL ANN, librarian; b. Madison, Wis., Sept. 23, 1947; d. Robert A. and Katherine E. (Benish) Heiman; m. Glen W. Wildenberg, Apr. 6, 1968 (div. June 1984); 1 child, William G. Wildenberg; m. Rod R. Kjelstrup, Jan. 3, 1987; children: Christopher M., Andrew J. BA in Social Scis., Kans. State U., 1970; student, U. Wis., Oshkosh, 1983; M of Libr. and Info. Sci., U. Wis., Milw., 1997. Cert. K-12 libr. and computer instr., Wis. Libr. aide Two Rivers (Wis.) Pub. Schs., 1976-88; libr. Wrightstown (Wis.) Cmty. Schs., 1988-90; libr., computer coord. Brillion (Wis.) Schs., 1990—. Bd. dirs. Cmty. Concerts Assn., Manitowoc, Wis., 1980-88, Manitowoc-Calumet County Libr., 2001—; long-rang planning com. Brillion Pub. Libr., 1993-94. Delta Kappa Gamma Sigma scholar, 1994-95. Mem. Wis. Ednl. Media Assn. (mem. info. literacy com. 1992-93), Brillion Fedn. Tchrs. (pres. local 1994-96, 98-2000), Delta Kappa Gamma (pres. 1992-94). Avocations: competitive pistol shooting, deer hunting, needlework, sewing. E-mail: kjelstrup@lakefield.net' ckjelstr@brillion.k12.wi.us. Home: 14415 Jambo Creek Rd Mishicot WI 54228-9734 Office: Brillion Pub Schs 315 S Main St Brillion WI 54110-1294

KLANCHER, JON PAUL, English language educator; b. San Francisco, Sept. 22, 1949; s. John A. and Patricia M. (McMahan) K.; m. (div.); 1 child, Emily; m. Nancy Arnold Belcher, July 21, 1990; children: Sophia, Maya. BA, Pitzer Coll., 1972; MA, UCLA, 1975, PhD, 1981. Mellon postdoctoral instr. Calif. Inst. Tech., Pasadena, 1984-86; asst. prof. English Boston U., 1986-90, assoc. prof. English, 1990—, Carnegie Mellon U., Pitts. Vis. lectr. lit. UCLA, 1981-84. Author: The Making of English Reading Audiences, 1987; contbr. articles to profl. jours. NEH fellow, 1989-90, John Simon Guggenheim Found. fellow, 1990-91. Mem. MLA, Wordsworth Coleridge Assn. (pres. 1992-93), Soc. for Critical Exch. Office: Carnegie Mellon Univ Dept English 259 Baker Dr Pittsburgh PA 15237-3602

KLAPPER, MOLLY, lawyer, educator; b. Berlin; came to U.S., 1950; d. Elias and Ciporah (Weber) Teicher; m. Jacob Klapper; children: Rachelle Hannah, Robert David. BA, CUNY, MA, 1964; PhD, NYU, 1974; JD, Rutgers U., 1987. Bar: N.J. 1987, U.S. Dist. Ct. N.J. 1987, N.Y. 1989, U.S. Dist. Ct. (so. and ea. dists.) N.Y. 1989, D.C. 1989, U.S. Supreme Ct. 1991, U.S. Ct. Appeals (2d cir.) 1992; cert. arbitrata, Better Bus. Bur., 2000, cert. arbitrator (NASD) Nat. Assn. of Security Dealers, 2003. Prof. English Bronx C.C., CUNY, 1974-84; law intern U.S. Dist. Ct. N.J., Newark, 1987; law sec. to presiding judge appellate div. N.J. Supreme Ct., Springfield, 1987-88; assoc. Wilson, Elser, Moskowitz, Edelman and Dicker, N.Y.C., 1988-96; adminstrv. law judge Dept. Finance, N.Y.C., 1997—; adj. prof. law Touro Law Ctr., Huntington, N.Y., 2001—. Small claims ct. arbitrator, 1994—; mediator N.Y. State Supreme Ct., comml. divsn., 2000—; jud. nominee State Supreme Ct., 2d dist., 1999; mediator Nat. Assn. Sec. Dirs., 2002—. Author: The German Literary Influence on Byron, 1974, 2d edit., 1975, The German Literary Influence on Shelley, 1975; contbr. to profl. publs. NEH fellow, 1978; grantee Am. Philos. Soc., 1976. Mem. Assn. Bar of City of N.Y., Adminstr. Law Com., 2003. Avocations: bicycling, skiing, roller skating, walking, hiking. Office: 720 Ft Washington Ave New York NY 10040-3708

KLARFELD, JONATHAN MICHAEL, journalism educator; b. Springfield, Mass., Dec. 11, 1937; m. Patricia Holland, Sept. 7, 1974; children: Victoria, Alexander. AB, Colgate U., 1960. Reporter, editor Holyoke (Mass.) Transcript-Telegram, 1962-65, UPI, Springfield, Boston, 1965-66, Boston Globe, 1966-68; press sec. Boston Parks/Redevel. Auth., 1968-70; reporter, writer Boston Record-Am., 1970-72; mgr. pub. info. Mass. Blue Cross, 1972-74; assoc. professor journalism Boston U., 1975—, dir. print journalism, 1979-96, dir. print and online journalism program, 1996—. Editl. cons. Lawyers Weekly Pubs., Boston, Lansing, Mich., Richmond, Va., Providence, 1983-92; press analyst Oxbow Corp., West Palm Beach, Fla., 1984-96; news media critic/columnist Boston Herald, 1994, 95; cons. in libel and invasion of privacy cases. Contbr. articles to numerous newspapers, periodicals. Mem. New Eng. Gilbert and Sullivan Soc., Sorcerers Rugby Club (pres. 1974-80), Newton Squash and Tennis Club (bd. govs. 1999-2003), Delta Kappa Epsilon. Unitarian Universalist. Avocations: squash, tennis, Gilbert and Sullivan. Office: Boston U Sch Journalism Boston MA 02215 E-mail: jklar@bu.edu.

KLARIK, BELA WILLIAM JAMES CLARK, retired school system administrator; b. Masontown, Pa., Aug. 7, 1931; s. Louis Klarik and Margaret Irma (Soltesz) Clark; children from previous marriage: Frank, Roxana, Steven, Louis M. AB in Edn. cum laude, Fairmont State Coll., 1957; postgrad., Antioch Coll., 1960, U. Md., 1965—75, W.Va. U., 1958—59; MEd, U. Ga., 1961. Cert. ednl. supr. and adminstr., math. sci. and phys. edn. tchr. Ohio, Md. Profl. baseball player minor leagues Bklyn. Dodgers, 1953-55; tchr. math., coach Madison (Ohio) Meml. HS, 1957-60; tchr. math. and sci. Euclid (Ohio) City Schs., 1961-62; head dept. math. Richard Montgomery High Sch., Montgomery County Pub. Schs., Rockville, Md., 1962-65; Nat. Assn. Secondary Sch. Prins. adminstrv. intern John F. Kennedy HS, Silver Spring, Md., 1965-66; vice-prin. Col. E. Brooke Lee Jr. HS, Silver Spring, 1966-67; supr. math. Montgomery County Pub. Schs., Rockville, 1967-75, dir. dept. acad. skills, 1975-91; ret., 1991. Staff sgt. U.S. Army, 1949—52. NSF Summer Inst. fellow, Antioch Coll., 1960, NSF Acad. Yr. Inst. fellow, U. Ga., 1960—61, NSF fellow, W.Va. U., 1963, U. Ga. fellow, 1961. Mem.: ASCD, Inst. for Ednl. Leadership, Burnt Store Isles (Fla.) Assn., Montgomery County Ret. Tchrs. Assn., Md. Ret. Tchrs. Assn., Burnt Store Isles Boat Club, Am. Legion. Democrat. Roman Catholic. Avocations: travel, boating, sports, gourmet cuisines and wines. Home: 5006 Ovideo St Punta Gorda FL 33950-8000 E-mail: ldsleigh@comcast.net.

KLASKO, HERBERT RONALD, lawyer, law educator, writer; b. Phila., Nov. 26, 1949; s. Leon Louis and Estelle Lorraine (Baratz) K.; m. Marjorie Ann Becker, Aug. 27, 1977; children: Brett Andrew, Kelli Lynn. BA, Lehigh U., 1971; JD, U. Pa., 1974. Bar: Pa. 1974, U.S. Dist. Ct. (ea. dist.) Pa. 1974, U.S. Ct. Appeals (3d cir.) 1981. Assoc. Fox, Rothschild, O'Brien & Frankel, Phila., 1974-75; ptnr., chmn. immigration dept. Abrahams & Loewenstein, Phila., 1975-88, Dechert, Price & Rhoads, Phila., 1988—. Instr., mem. adv. bd. Inst. for Paralegal Tng., Phila., 1974-81; instr. Temple Law Sch. Grad. Legal Studies, Phila., 1984; adj. prof. Villanova U. Law Sch., Pa., 1985-90. Co-author: (with Matthew Bender and Hope Frye) Employer's Immigration Compliance Guide, 1985; bd. editors: Immigration Law and Procedure Reporter. Exec. committeeman, bd. dirs. Jewish Community Rels. Coun., Phila., 1977—; chmn. exec. com., com. on unprosecuted Nazi war criminals Nat. Jewish Community Rels. Adv. Coun., N.Y.C., 1983-90; v.p. Hebrew Immigrant Aid Soc., Phila., 1977—; pres. Coun. of Tenants Assn., Southeastern Pa., 1980-81. Recipient Legion of Honor award Chapel of Four Chaplains, 1977. Mem. ABA (coordinating com. on immigration), Phila. Bar Assn., Am. Immigration Lawyers Assn. (chmn. Phila. chpt. 1980-82, bd. govs. 1980—, nat. sec. 1984-85, 2d v.p. 1985-86, 1st v.p. 1986-87, pres.-elect 1987-88, pres. 1988-89, exec. com. 1984-90, 96-99, gen. counsel, 1996-99, Founders award 1999), Am. Immigration Law Found. (bd. dirs. 1987-90). Avocations: politics, sports, traveling, organizations. Office: Dechert Price & Rhoads 4000 Bell Atlantic Tower 1717 Arch St Lbby 3 Philadelphia PA 19103-2713 E-mail: ronald.klasko@dechert.com.

KLASS, SHEILA SOLOMON, English language educator, writer; b. N.Y.C., Nov. 6, 1927; d. Abraham Louis and Regina (Glatter) Solomon; m. Morton Klass, May 2, 1953; children: Perri, David, Judy. BA, Bklyn. Coll., 1949; MA, State U. Iowa, 1951, MFA, 1953. English tchr. Julia Ward Howe Jr. H.S., N.Y.C., 1951-57; prof. English, Borough of Manhattan C.C./CUNY, N.Y.C., 1965-2000; prof. writer N.Y.C., 1950—. Author: (young adult novels) Nobody Knows Me in Miami, 1981, To See My Mother Dance, 1981, Alive and Starting Over, 1983, The Bennington Stitch, 1985, Page Four, 1986, Credit-Card Carole, 1987, Kool Ada, 1991, Rhino, 1993, Next Stop: Nowhere, 1995, A Shooting Star, 1996, Little Women Next Door, 2000; (adult novels) Come Back on Monday, 1960, Bahadur Means Hero, 1969, A Perpetual Surprise, 1981, In a Cold Open Field, 1997; (juvenile) The Uncivil War, 1997; (memoir) Everyone in This House Makes Babies, 1964. Mem. Author in the Schs. Vol. Program, N.Y.C., 1990—. Mem. PEN. Jewish. Avocation: travel. Home: 900 W 190th St Apt 2O New York NY 10040-3653

KLASSEK, CHRISTINE PAULETTE, behavioral scientist; b. Chgo., Dec. 28, 1947; d. Walter and Pauline (Bogolin) Strom; m. Alexander George Klassek, June 14, 1969; 1 child, Margaret Mary. BA in Applied Behavioral Sci., Nat. Louis U., 1989, cert. in leadership, 1993. Asst. juvenile libr. Bolingbrook (Ill.) Fountaindale Libr., 1974-79; behavior modification counselor, dir. vol. svcs. J.P. Kennedy Sch. for Exceptional Children, Palos Park, Ill., 1982-86; tchr. spl. edn. Little Friends Orgn., Downers Grove, Ill., 1986-89; program dir. Carmelite Carefree Village, Darien, Ill., 1989—, adminstrv. liaison, 1997—. Bd. mem. Benedictine Univ. Adv. Bd. for Sr. Programs and Issues, 1996; dep. registrar for Carefree Village, Dupage County, 1998—; notary public, 1999—; panelist Long Term Care Forum by Congresswoman Judy Biggert and Ill. Dept. of Aging, 2000. Treas. Young Democrats Will County, 1972; chmn., pres. bd. dirs. Dem. Women's Com. DuPage Twp., Ill., 1973-76; leader Campfire Girls Assn.; mem. adv. coun. case mgmt. Little Friends Assn., 1988; cert. pastoral min. care St. Charles Borromeo Pastoral Ctr.; vol. Pub. Action to Deliver Svc., Helping Hands Rehab. Ctr., Ray Graham; active Cath. Coun. Women; bd. dirs., mem. human rels. com. J.P. Kennedy Sch. Exceptional Children. Recipient Cert. of Appreciation, Am. Cancer Soc., 1991, Achievement award Life Svcs. Network Ill., 1995, DuPage County Consortium Intergenerational Task Force, 1996, 2000 Nat. award for sr. program devel. Sr. Network, Inc. Mem. LWV, Assn. Sr. Svc. Providers, Ill. Activity Profl. Assn., Suburban Activity Therapists Assn., Notary Public Assn. Am., Jaycees. Roman Catholic. Avocations: arts and crafts, reading, walking, classical music, writing poetry, needle point. Home: 240 Davis Ln Bolingbrook IL 60440-2369 Office: Carmelite Carefree Village 8419 Bailey Rd Darien IL 60561-5361

KLATT, MELVIN JOHN, library consultant; s. John Edward and Marie Barbara K.; m. Shirley Ann Ryan, Aug. 31, 1957; children: Mary, John, Peter. BS in History and Econ., U. Wis., 1956; MA in Libr. Sci., U. Denver, 1958; postgrad., Ind. U., 1969-72. Circulation asst. Wis. State Hist. Soc., Madison, 1955; head br. librs. Milw. Pub. Libr., 1958-62; head acquisitions dept. U. Ill., Chgo., 1962-65; head tech. svcs. U. Denver, 1965-67, dir. librs., 1967-69; asst. dean Dominican U. Grad. Sch. Libr. Sch., River Forest, Ill., 1972-74; head Libr. Elmhurst (Ill.) Coll., 1974-94; prof. emeritus Elmhurst Coll., 1997. Chair Suburbia and the Am. Dream Conf., Elmhurst, 1977; cons. St. Xaviers Coll., Chgo., 1982. Author-contbr.: Dictionary of Wisconsin Biography, 1960; book compiler Directory of Human Resources, 1979; co-editor Colo. Acad. Librs., 1968. Chmn. S.W. Denver Human Rels., Denver, 1968-69, v.p. polit. action com., 1968-70; judge, visual arts com. Ill Arts Coun., Chgo., 1979-81. With U.S. Army, 1951-53, Korea. City of Milw. scholar, 1957, Ill. Acad. Libr. of the Yr. award Ill. Assn. Coll. and Rsch. Librs., 1994; recipient Mel George award LIBRAS, 1996; NDEA fellow, 1969, 70, 71. Mem. ALA, LIBRAS Consortium (pres. 1979-81, Libr. of Yr. Ill. consortium 1994), AAUP (exec. com. 1964-65), North Ctrl. Accreditation Assn. (chair resources com. 1979), Ill. Libr. Assn., Pvt. Acad. Librs. Ill. (pres. 1979-81), Chgo. Libr. Club (v.p. 1979-80, pres. elect 1983-85), Beta Phi Mu, Omicron Delta Kappa.

KLAUCK, JUDITH LYNN, middle school educator; b. East St. Louis, Ill., July 26, 1945; d. James L. and Lydia L. (Arnold) K. BS in Home Econs. Edn., So. Ill. U., 1969, MS in Home Econs. Edn., 1978; cert. in guidance, So. Ill. U., Edwardsville, 1989. Cert. tchr., Ill. Home econs. tchr. Althoff Cath. H.S., Belleville, Ill., 1969-89, guidance counselor, 1989-98; family and consumer sci. tchr. North Jr. H.S., Collinsville, Ill., 1998—. Mem. Am. Assn. Family and Consumer Scis. (past pres., treas. Dist. 5 chpt. 1969—), Delta Kappa Gamma Soc. Internat. (chpt. pres. 2000-).

KLAUSNER, SAMUEL ZUNDEL, sociologist, educator; b. Bklyn., Dec. 19, 1923; s. Edward Solomon and Bertha (Adler) K.; m. Bracha Turgeman, Oct. 26, 1948 (div. 1960); children: Rina Ellen Klausner Spence, Jonathan David; m. Madeleine Suringar, Feb. 20, 1964 (div. 1982); children: Daphne Klausner Genyk, Tamar; m. Roberta Sands, Nov. 26, 1992. BS, NYU, 1947; MA, Columbia U., 1951, EdD, 1952, PhD, 1963. Cert. psychologist, N.Y., D.C. Lectr. edn. CCNY, 1951-52, 55-57; lectr. sociology Columbia U., 1957-63; instr. psychology Hebrew U., Jerusalem, 1952-53; lectr. religion and psychiatry Union Theol. Sem., 1961-63; assoc. prof. sociology U. Pa., Phila., 1967-70, prof., 1970-96; dir. Ctr. for Rsch. on the Acts of Man, 1971-88, chmn. grad. group in sociology, 1984-86; prof. emeritus U. Pa., Phila., 1996—. Clin. psychologist Govt. Mental Hosp., Jerusalem, 1954-55; program dir. Bur. Applied Social Rsch., Columbia U., 1956-61; sr. rsch. assoc. Bur. Social Sci. Rsch., Washington, 1964-67; exec. sec. Soc. for

Study of Religion, 1964-70; cons. U.S. Dept. Commerce, 1968-69, U.S. Naval Chaplains Sch., 1973-81, Nat. Libr. Medicine, 1969, NRC, 1967-81, others; vis. prof. Al Mansoura U., Egypt, 1983, Muhammad V. Univ., Morocco, 1986. Author: Psychiatry and Religion, 1964, The Quest for Self-Control, 1965, The Study of Total Societies, 1967, Why Man Takes Chances, 1968, Society and Its Physical Environment, 1970, On Man in His Environment, 1971, Eskimo Capitalists, 1981; author, editor: The Nationalization of the Social Sciences, 1986; also articles. With USAAC, 1943-45; with Israel Air Force, 1947-48. Ford Found. area rsch. fellow, 1952-53; Fulbright scholar, 1983. Mem. APA, AAAS, Am. Sociol. Assn., Assn. Sociol. Study of Jewry (pres. 1980), Soc. Sci. Study of Religion (v.p. 1974), Am. Vets. Israel (pres. 1951, 98-2000, newsletter editor 1998—). Jewish. Home: 7055 Greenhill Rd Philadelphia PA 19151-2322 Office: Univ Pa Dept Sociology Philadelphia PA 19104 E-mail: sklausner@ucwphilly.rr.com.

KLAVANO, ANN MARIE, school librarian; b. Pullman, Wash., Oct. 8, 1956; d. Paul Arthur and Martha Emma Klavano. M in Libr. and Info. Studies, U. Tex., 1986; BA, Washington State University, Pullman WA, 1976. Reference libr. Mercy Coll. Librs., Dobbs Ferry, NY, 1986—97; reference libr. external scvs. Buena Vista U., Storm Lake, Iowa, 1997—. Chair social concerns ministry St. Mark Luth. Ch., Storm Lake, 2000—01; bd. dirs. Midnight Run, Dobbs Ferry, 1994—97. Lutheran. Office: Buena Vista U Libr 610 W 4th St Storm Lake IA 50588

KLAYMAN, ELLIOT IRWIN, adult education educator; b. Cin., May 20, 1945; s. Samuel Norton and Lillian (Appel) K.; m. Joyce Beth Reichman, Aug. 18, 1974; children: Seth Nathaniel, Rhena Cheryl. BBA, U. Cin., 1966, JD, 1969; LLM, Harvard U., 1970. Bar: Ohio 1969, U.S. Dist. Ct. (so. dist.) Ohio 1971. Ptnr. Brown, Dennison & Klayman, Cin., 1970-78; asst. prof. bus. law Ohio State U., Columbus, 1978-84, assoc. prof., 1984—. Author: Legal Environment of Business, 6th edit. 2003, Real Estate Law, 5th edit 2003, Irwin's Business Law, 1994; editor Midwest Bus. Law Jour., 1982-85, Am. Bus. Law Jour., 1984-87, Real Estate Law Jour., 1992—, The Messianic Outreach, 1985—, Kesher, 1999—; editor-in-chief Jour. Legal Studies Edn., 1994-95; contbr. articles to profl. jours. Recipient Merit plaque Ohio State U. Real Estate Inst., 1979, Am. Soc. Appraisers, 1981. Mem. Acad. Legal Studies in Bus., Union Messianic Jewish Congregations (pres. 1986-90), Beta Gamma Sigma, Phi Alpha Delta, Phi Alpha Kappa. Home: 5984 Hilltop Trail Dr New Albany OH 43054 Office: Ohio State Univ Fisher Hall 2100 Neil Ave Rm 844 Columbus OH 43210-1144 E-mail: klayman.1@osu.edu.

KLECK, ROBERT ELDON, psychology educator; b. Archbold, Ohio, Aug. 3, 1937; AB in Philosophy, Denison U., 1959; PhD in Social Psychology, Stanford (Calif.) U., 1963. Postdoctoral fellow Stanford U., 1963-64; asst. prof. Williams Coll., Williamstown, Mass., 1964-66; asst. to assoc. prof. Dartmouth Coll., Hanover, N.H., 1966-75, prof. psychology, 1975—, John Sloan Dickey Third Century Prof. of Social Scis., 1985-90, chmn. dept. psychology, 1993-99. Vis. rsch. prof. Boy's Town Ctr. Study of Youth Devel., Stanford U., 1974-75; cons. VA Stroke Project, 1983-86, Disadvantaged Children in N.H., 1974, Bur. Devel. Disabilities, Concord, N.H., 1975-80, Crotchet Mountain Rehab. Ctr., 1973, Abilities, Inc., Albertson, N.Y., 1979-81, Can. Rsch. Coun., NSF, USPHS; faculty sponsore USPHS Post-doctoral fellowship, 1977-78. Cons. editor Jour. Personality and Social Psychology, 1974-78, assoc. editor 1971-72; mem. editorial bd. Jour. Nonverbal Behavior, 1990-93; mem. editorial adv. bd. Action for Children's TV, 1975-79; editorial cons.various jours.; contbr. articles to profl. jours. Danforth fellow, 1959-63; Gen. Motors scholar, 1955-59. Mem. Am. Psychol. Soc., Internat. Soc. Rsch. on Emotion, Soc. Experimental Social Psychology, New Eng. Psychol. Assn., Soc. Kent and Danfoth Fellows, Sigma Xi, Phi Beta kappa. Home: 6207 Moore Hall Hanover NH 03755-3578 Office: Dartmouth Coll Dept Of Psychology Hanover NH 03755 E-mail: r.kleck@dartmouth.edu.

KLEE, VICTOR LA RUE, mathematician, educator; b. San Francisco, Sept. 18, 1925; s. Victor La Rue and Mildred (Muller) K.; BA, Pomona Coll., 1945, DSc (hon.), 1965; PhD, U. Va., 1949; Dr. honoris causa, U. Liège, Belgium, 1984, U. Trier, Germany, 1995. Asst. prof. U. Va., 1949-53; NRC fellow Inst. for Advanced Study, 1951-52; asst. prof. U. Wash., Seattle, 1953-54, assoc. prof., 1954-57, prof. math., 1957-97, adj. prof. computer sci., 1974—98, prof. applied math., 1976-84; prof. emeritus, 1998—. Vis. asso. prof. UCLA, 1955-56; vis. prof. U. Colo., 1971, U. Victoria, 1975, U. Western Australia, 1979; cons. IBM Watson Research Center, 1972; cons. to industry; mem. Math. Scis. Research Inst., 1985-86; sr. fellow Inst. for Math. and its Applications, 1987. Co-author: Combinatorial Geometry in the Plane, 1963, Old and New Unsolved Problems in Plane Geometry and Number Theory, 1991, Convex Polytopes, 2003; contbr. more than 200 articles to profl. jours. Recipient Rsch. prize U. Va., 1952, Vollum award for disting. accomplishment in sci. and tech. Reed Coll., 1982, David Prescott Burrows Outstanding Disting. Achievement award Pomona Coll., 1988, Max Planck rsch. prize, 1992; NSF sr. postdoctoral fellow, Sloan Found. fellow U. Copenhagen, 1958-60, fellow Ctr. Advanced Study in Behavioral Scis., 1975-76, Guggenheim fellow, Humboldt award U. Erlangen-Nürnberg, 1980-81, Fulbright fellow U. Trier, 1992. Fellow AAAS (chmn. sect. A 1975), Am. Acad. Arts and Scis.; mem. Am. Math. Soc. (assoc. sec. 1955-58, mem. exec. com. 1969-70), Math. Assn. Am. (pres. 1971-73, L.R. Ford award 1972, Disting. Svc. award 1977, C.B. Allendoerfer award 1980, 99), Soc. Indsl. and Applied Math. (mem. coun. 1966-68), Internat. Linear Algegra Soc., Phi Beta Kappa, Sigma Xi (nat. lectr. 1969). Home: 13706 39th Ave NE Seattle WA 98125-3810 Office: U Wash Dept Math PO Box 354350 Seattle WA 98195-4350 E-mail: klee@math.washington.edu.

KLEEMAN, DIANE ELIZABETH, music educator; b. Flint, Mich., Dec. 5, 1950; d. Donald James and Grace Elizabeth (Pettengill) Vought; m. Robert Kleeman Jr., July 7, 1973 (div. May 1995); children: Robert III, Erin, Andrew. AA, Mott C.C., Flint, Mich., 1971; BA, Marian Coll., Indpls., 1975; M Music Edn., Butler U., 1984. Cert. music edn. tchr. Music tchr. grades 1-8 St. Luke's Sch., Indpls., 1980-82; organist N.E. United Ch. of Christ, Indpls., 1985-90; music tchr. K-5 Acton Elem., Indpls., 1983—; pvt. piano tchr. Indpls., 1966—. Organist N.E. United Ch. of Christ, Indpls., 1988-90, Bethany Moravian Ch., 1995—; handbell dir. Zion United Ch. of Christ, Indpls., 1982-89; chairperson Indpls. (Ind.) South Jr. Festival. Vol. Indpls. (Ind.) Guardian Children's Home, 1995—. Mem. Orgn. Am. Kodaly Educators, Am. Orff-Schulwerk, Indpls. Piano Tchrs., Indpls. Group Piano Tchrs. Methodist. Avocations: reading, antiques, walking. Home: 2535 Wayward Wind Dr Indianapolis IN 46239-9444 Office: Acton Elem 8010 Acton Rd Indianapolis IN 46259-1547

KLEEMAN, NANCY GRAY ERVIN, retired special education educator; b. Boston, Feb. 19, 1946; d. John Wesley and Harriet Elizabeth (Teuchert) Ervin; m. Brian Carlton Kleeman, June 27, 1969. BA, Calif. State U., Northridge, 1969; MS, Calif. State U., Long Beach, 1976, cert. resource specialist, 1982. Cert. spl. edn., learning disabilities and resource specialist tchr., Calif. Tchr. spl. edn., resource specialist Downey (Calif.) Unified Sch. Dist., 1972-86; tchr. spl. day class Irvine (Calif.) Sch. Dist., 1986-2001. Tutor in field; spkr. Commn. for Handicapped, L.A., 1975; advisor Com. to Downey Unified Sch. Dist., 1976-82; owner ISIS Design Publs. Author: Rhyme Your Times, 1990; author numerous greeting cards. Vol. sec. UN, L.A., 1980—83; vol. coord., art dir., educator Sierra Vista Mid. Sch., Irvine, 1986—88; liaison Tustin (Calif.) Manor Convalescent Home and Regents Point Retirement Home, Irvine, 1988—2000; fundraiser Ronald McDonald House, Orange, Calif.; vol. Sr. Cheer Project, 1986—2001, Vets. Cheer Project, 1996—2001, Make-A-Wish Found., Children in Crisis, Alexander Cohen Hospice, Modesto, Calif.; vol. horticulture program Sierra Vista Mid. Sch., 1999—2001; mem. Nat. Youth Svc., Washington. Recipient award Concerned Students Orgn., Downey, 1984; named Tchr. Yr. Sierra Vista Middle Sch., 1988. Mem.: Nat. Hist. Soc., Save Our Strays, Yankee Golden Retriever Rescue, Dogs for the Blind. Avocations: restoring antique carousel horses, canoeing, numerology, stained glass design, sculpting.

KLEIJNEN, JACK P. simulation and information systems educator; b. Maastricht, Limburg, The Netherlands, Nov. 22, 1940; s. Michael and Maria (Maesen) Kleijnen; m. Wilma A. Smulders, Dec. 10, 1966; children: Mara W., Jakko M. BS, Cath. U. Tilburg, The Netherlands, 1961; MS, Cath. U. Tilburg, 1964, PhD, 1971. Rsch. assoc. Econ. Inst. Tilburg, 1964—65, Cath. U. Tilburg, 1965—80, prof. simulation and info. systems, 1980—. Vis. scholar UCLA, 1967—68; vis. scholar (summers) Duke U., Durham, NC, 1968, 69; vis. prof. IBM, San Jose, Calif., 1974, Ind. U., Bloomington (summer), 1979; vis. scholar (summer) IBM, Yorktown, NY, 1981, Pritsker & Assocs., West Lafayette, Ind., 1984. Author: Statistical Techniques in Simulation, 1974 (hon. mention Lanchester prize Ops. Rsch. Soc. Am., 1975, transl. into Russian), also other books and numerous articles. Grantee, IBM, San Jose, 1974, Netherlands Nat. Sci. Found., 1974, Balzola, Madrid, 1975, Brit. Coun., 1970. Mem.: Netherlands Soc. for Informatics, Netherlands Soc. for Stats., Soc. for Computer Simulation, Ops. Rsch. Soc. Am., Inst. Mgmt. Sci., also others. Home: Schout Crillaerstraat 25 5037 MS Tilburg Netherlands Office: Tilburg U 2 Warandelaan 5000 LE Tilburg Netherlands E-mail: kleijnen@uvt.nl.

KLEIN, BENJAMIN GARRETT, mathematics educator, consultant; b. Durham, N.C., Jan. 24, 1942; s. James Raymond and Lenetta Mae (Garrett) K.; m. Rosemary Therese McAndrew, June 19, 1971; children: David Garrett, Peter Raymond. BA, U. Rochester, 1963; MA, Yale U., 1965, PhD, 1968. Lectr., asst. prof. NYU, N.Y.C., 1967-71; asst. prof. to prof. math. Davidson Coll., N.C., 1971—, vice chmn. faculty, 1985-88, appt. Dana prof. math., 1990-93, appt. Dolan prof. math., 1993—, chair dept. math., 1994-98, mem. advanced placement calculus devel. com., 1999—2003. Cons. N.C. Dept. Pub. Instrn., Raleigh, 1981-85, 90—. Mem. editl. bd. The Coll. Math. Jour. Elder Davidson Coll. Presbyterian Ch., 1981-83, 87-89, 94-96. Recipient Thomas Jefferson award, 1990; named N.C. Prof. of Yr. Coun. for Advancement and Support of Edn., 1991. Mem.: N.C. Assn. Advanced Placement Math. Tchrs., N.C. Coun. Tchrs. Math., Nat. Coun. Tchrs. Math., Math. Assn. Am. (chair S.E. sect. 1993—95), Am. Math. Soc. Democrat. Office: Davidson Coll PO Box 6937 Davidson NC 28035-6937 Business E-Mail: beklein@davidson.edu.

KLEIN, ELAINE CHARLOTTE, school system administrator; b. Herreid, S.D., June 14, 1939; d. Herman F. and Minnie (Weigum) Klein; 1 child, Erika Katherine. BA, U. Puget Sound, 1961; MA, U. Wash., 1964; cert. in adminstrn., Seattle U., 1976; postgrad., Western Wash. U., 1986. Cert. secondary sch. adminstr. Wash., K-12 tchr. Wash. Tchr. Edmonds Sch. Dist., Lynnwood, Wash., 1961-77; asst. prin. Meadowdale Jr. HS, Lynnwood, Wash., 1977-80, Mountlake Terrace (Wash.) HS, 1981-93, prin., 1993-97; exec. dir. cmty. svcs. Frederick (Md.) County Pub. Schs., 1997—. Adj. faculty Heritage Inst., Antioch U., Seattle Pacific U., Western Wash. U.; instr. Mt. St. Mary's Coll., Emmitsburg, Md.; cons. Am. Coll. Testing Passport Portfolio, Iowa City, 1995—97; presenter in field. Co-author: (book) ACT Manual for Administrators, 1997; grant writer:. Pres. Pacific N.W. region Internat. Tng. Comm., Alaska, 1993—94. Named Wash. State Prin. of the Yr., 1997, Adminstr. of the Yr., Md. Assn. Edn. Office Pers., 1999, Friend of Edn., M. St. Mary's Coll., 1999, Outstanding Contbr., Hood Coll., 2002; recipient award for Excellence in Edn., Wash. State Legislature, 1997. Mem.: ASCD, Nat. Assn. Secondary Sch. Prins. and Affiliates, Am. Assn. Sch. Adminstrs., Rotary (Mountlake Terrace pres. 1996—97). Methodist. Avocations: public speaking, reading, travel, advocating for public schools. Office: Frederick County Pub Schs 115 E Church St Frederick MD 21701-5403 E-mail: elaine.klein@fcps.org.

KLEIN, ELAYNE MARGERY, retired elementary education educator; b. L.I., N.Y., Apr. 25, 1947; d. Jack and Anne (Fialkow) K. BS, L.I. U., 1969, MS, 1972. Cert. elem. tchr., cert. in guidance edn., N.Y. Student tchr. 2nd, then 4th grades Robbins Lane Elem. Sch., Syosset, N.Y., 1968-69; tchr. 5th grade West Islip (N.Y.) Pub. Schs., 1969—2002. Co-organizer/supr. 5th and 6th grade drama club West Islip Pub. Schs., 1972. Mem. Am. Fedn. Tchrs., N.Y. State United Tchrs., N.Y. State Congress Parents and Tchrs. (hon. life), Iota Alpha Pi. Avocations: reading, opera, ballet, travel, collecting antiques.

KLEIN, GEORGIA ANN, retired secondary school educator; b. Harrisonville, Mo., July 28, 1942; d. Armour Alfred and Anna May (Voltmer) Sprague. BS in Edn., Emporia (Kans.) State U., 1964; MS in Edn., U. Kans., 1976. Home missionary Wesley Community Ctr., St. Joseph, Mo., 1964-66; social studies tchr. Colony (Kans.) Sch. Dist., 1966-68, Kansas City (Kans.) Sch. Dist., 1968-78; coord., tchr. homebound/hosp. prog. Shawnee Mission (Kans.) Schs., 1978—97, ret., 1997. Tchr. continuing edn. Johnson County Community Coll., Shawnee Mission; founder A+ Tours. Mem. Coun. for Exceptional Children. Mem. NEA, U. Kans. Alumni Assn., Phi Delta Kappa (sec. 1985-86), Delta Kappa Gamma (pres. 1986-88, chmn. state leadership devel., state v.p. 1993-95, state pres. 1995-97, chmn. internat. scholarship com. 2003—). Democrat. Presbyterian. Avocation: travel. Home: 4724 Mullen Rd Shawnee KS 66216-1161

KLEIN, HOWARD BRUCE, lawyer, law educator; b. Pitts., Pa, Feb. 28, 1950; s. Elmer and Natalie (Rosenzweig) K.; m. Lonnie Jean Wilets, Dec. 12, 1977; children: Zachary B., Eli H. Student, Northwestern U., 1968-69; BA, U. Wis., 1972; JD, Georgetown U., 1976. Bar: Wis. 1976, Pa. 1981, U.S. Ct. Appeals D.C., 1978, U.S. Dist. Ct. Pa. 1981, U.S. Ct. Appeals (3rd cir.) 1982, U.S. Supreme Ct. 1983. Law clk. to justice Robert Hansen Wis. Supreme Ct., Madison, 1976-77; asst. atty. gen. dept. justice State of Wis., 1977-80; chief criminal divsn. U.S. Atty.'s Office, Phila., 1980-87; ptnr. Blank, Rome & McCauley, Phila., 1987-96, chmn. litigation dept., 1991-94; prin. Law Offices of Howard Bruce Klein, Phila., 1996—; dir. in house tng. Am. Law Inst.-ABA, 1996—. Regional, nat. instr. Nat. Inst. Trial Advocacy, Phila. and Boulder, Colo., 1987-98; adj. prof. evidence and trial advocacy Temple U. Law Sch., 1984—; instr. Atty. Gen. Advocacy Inst., Washington, 1983-87; lectr. pub. corruption and trial advocacy; cons. Pa. Valley Neighborhood Assn., 1984—. Contbr. to profl. jours. Advisor Phila. Police Dept. Reform Commn., 1986—; campaign issues dir. Pa. Atty. Gen. campaign, Phila., 1988, 92; bd. dirs. Citizens Crime Commn. Delaware Valley, Phila. Mem. Fed. Bar Assn. (chmn. criminal law com.), Phila. Bar Assn., Wis. Bar Assn., D.C. Bar Assn., U.S. Attys. Alumni Assn. (co-founder, exec. bd.), Vesper Club (Phila.). Democrat. Jewish. Avocations: golf, basketball, hiking. Office: 1700 Market St Ste 2632 Philadelphia PA 19103-3903 E-mail: howbrklein@aol.com.

KLEIN, JEROME OSIAS, pediatrician, educator; b. N.Y.C., Feb. 10, 1931; s. Max N. and Elizabeth (Schlanger) K.; m. Linda Sue Breskin,June 19, 1955; children: Andrea, Bennett, Adam. AB, Union Coll., 1952; MD, Yale U., 1956. Diplomate Am. Bd. Pediatrics. Intern U. Minn. Hosps., Mpls., 1956-67; residnt in pediatrics Boston City Hosp., 1959-61, assoc. dir. pediatrics, 1967-72, dir. pediatric infectious diseases, 1973-96; vice chmn. acad. affairs dept. pediats. Boston Med. Ctr., 1996—; assoc. prof. pediatrics Harvard U. Med. Sch., Boston, 1967-74; prof. Boston U. Sch. Medicine, 1974; lectr. Harvard U. Med. Sch., Boston, 1974—. Cons. dept. pediats. Mass. Gen. Hosp., 1970-74; cons. adv. com. on vaccines and biologics, FDA, 1983-85. Author/editor: (with J.S. Remington) Infectious Diseases of the Fetus and Newborn Infant, 1976, 5th edit., 2001; author: (with C.D. Bluestone) Otitis Media in Infants and Children, 1987, 3d edit., 2001; editor: Report of the Committee on Infectious Diseases, Am. Acad. Pediats., 19th edit.; assoc. editor Revs. of Infectious Diseases, 1978-89, Pediat. Infectious Diseases Jour., 1982-92; contbr. numerous articles on rsch. in infectious diseases of children to profl. jours. Asst. surgeon, USPHS, 1957-59. Recipient Disting. Physician award Pediat. Infectious Diseases Soc., 1995, Maxwell Finlany award for sci. achievement Nat. Found. for Infectious Diseases, 2002; Peabody fellow Harvard U., 1963-64; grantee Nat. Inst. Allergy and Infectious Diseases. Mem. Am. Acad. Pediats. (com. on infectious diseases 1974-82), Infectious Diseases Soc. Am. (councellor 1980-83, treas. 1987-92, Bristol award 1995), Phi Beta Kappa, Alpha Omega Alpha. Office: Boston Medical Center Maxwell Finland Lab Infectious Diseases Boston MA 02118

KLEIN, LAWRENCE ROBERT, economist, educator; b. Omaha, Sept. 14, 1920; s. Leo Byron and Blanche (Monheit) Klein; m. Sonia Adelson, Feb. 15, 1947; children: Hannah, Rebecca, Rachel, Jonathan. BA, U. Calif.-Berkeley, 1942; PhD, MIT, 1944; MA, Lincoln Coll., Oxford U., 1957; LLD (hon.), U. Mich., 1977, Dickinson Coll., 1981; ScD (hon.), Widener Coll., 1977, Elizabethtown Coll., 1981, Ball State U., 1982, Technion, 1981, U. Nebr., 1983; D (hon.), U. Vienna, 1977; EdD, Villanova U., 1978; D (hon.), Bonn U., 1974, Free U. Brussels, 1979, U. Paris, 1979, U. Madrid, 1980; DSc, Nat. Central Univ. Taiwan, 1985; DHC, So. Helsinki Sch. Econs., 1986; Dr. Humane Letters, Bard Coll., 1986, Bilkent U., 1989, St. Norbert Coll., 1989; DHC, Univ. Lodz, 1990; D. Litt, Univ. Glasgow, 1991; DSc, Rutgers Univ., 1992; PhD (hon.), Bar Ilan U., 1994; D. honors (hon.), Carleton Univ., 1997; DHC, U. Piraeus, 1999, Acad. Economic Studies, Romania, 1999, U Toronto, 2002, Konan U., Japan, 2002, Keio U., 2002. Faculty U. Chgo., 1944—47; research assoc. Nat. Bur. Econ. Research, 1948—50; faculty U. Mich., 1949—54; research assoc. Survey Research Center, 1949—54, Oxford Inst. Stats., 1954—58; faculty U. Pa., Phila., 1958—, prof., 1958—, Univ. prof., 1964—, Benjamin Franklin prof., 1968—, prof. emeritus; vis. prof. Osaka U., Japan, 1960, U. Colo., 1962, CUNY, 1962-63, 82, Hebrew U., 1964, Princeton U., 1966, Stanford U., 1968, U. Copenhagen, 1974; Ford vis. prof. U. Calif. at Berkeley, 1968, Inst. for Advanced Studies, Vienna, 1970, 74; hon. prof. Shanghai Jiao Tong Univ., 1984; honorary prof. Nankai Univ., 1993, Shanghai Acad. Soc. Sci., 1994; dir. W.P. Carey & Co., 1984—; adv. State Information Ctr., Beijing, 1992—; hon. chmn. Pa. Inst. for Econ. Rsch. Adv. Bd., 2002—. Cons. Can. Govt., 1947, UNCTAD, 1966, 75, 77, 80, McMillan Co., 1965—74, E.I. du Pont de Nemours, 1966—68, State of N.Y., 1969, AT&T, 1969, Fed. Res. Bd., 1973, UNIDO, 1973—75, Congl. Budget Office, 1977—, Coun. Econ. Advisers, 1977—80; chmn. bd. trustees Wharton Econometric Forecasting Assocs., Inc., 1969—80, chmn. profl. bd., 1980—; trustee Maurice Falk Inst. for Econ. Rsch., Israel, 1969—75; adv. coun. Inst. Advanced Studies, Vienna, 1977—; chmn. econ. adv. com. Gov. of Pa., 1976—78; mem. com. on prices Fed. Res. Bd., 1968—70; prin. investigator econometric model project Brookings Instn., 1963—72, Project LINK, 1968—; sr. adviser Brookings Panel on Econ. Activity, 1970—; mem. adv. com. Inst. Internat. Econs., 1983; hon. mem. Chinese Bd. Soc. Scis., 1997, Romanian Acad., 1999—; coord. Jimmy Carter's Econ. Task Force, 1976; mem. adv. bd. Strategic Studies Ctr., Stanford Rsch. Inst., 1974—76; corr. fellow Brit. Acad., 1991—. Author: The Keynesian Revolution, 1947, Textbook of Econometrics, 1953, An Econometric Model of the United States, 1929-1952, 1955, Wharton Econometric Forecasting Model, 1967, Essay on the Theory of Economic Prediction, 1968, An Introduction to Econometric Forecasting and Forecasting Models, 1980; author, editor: Brookings Quar. Econometric Model of U.S., Ecometric Model Performance, 1976, Lectures in Econmetrics, 1983; editor: Internat. Econ. Rev., 1959—65; assoc. editor:, mem. editl. bd.: Empirical Econs., 1976—. Recipient William F. Butler award, N.Y. Assn. Bus. Economists, 1975, Golden Slipper Club award, 1977, Pres.'s medal, U. Pa., 1980, Alfred Nobel Meml. prize in econs., 1980. Fellow: Nat. Assn. Bus. Economists, Am. Acad. Arts and Scis., Econometric Soc. (past pres.), Brit. Acad. (corr.); mem.: NAS, Russian Acad. Sci. (fgn.), Ea. Econ. Assn. (pres. 1974—76), Am. Econ. Assn. (exec. com. 1966—68, pres. 1977, John Bates Clark medalist 1959), Social Sci. Rsch. Coun. (fellow 1945—46, 1947—48, com. econ. stability, dir. 1971—76), Am. Philos. Soc. Office: U Pa Mc Neil Bldg Rm 335 3718 Locust Walk Philadelphia PA 19104-6209 Address: WP Carey 50 Rockefeller Plaza New York NY 10020

KLEIN, LAWRENCE ALLEN, accounting educator; b. Harrisburg, Pa., Jan. 14, 1946; s. Samuel Edward and Ella Violet (Loeb) K. AB, Franklin and Marshall Coll., 1969; MBA, Pa. State U., 1974, PHD, 1978. Adminstrv. asst. dept. acctg. and mgmt. info. sys. Pa. State U., State College, 1975-76; asst. prof. acctg. U. Houston, 1978-79, U. Wyo., Laramie, 1982-84; asst. prof. bus. adminstrn. Franklin and Marshall Coll., Lancaster, Pa., 1979-82; assoc. prof. accountancy Bentley Coll., Waltham, Mass., 1984—. Vis. prof. econ. and mgmt. Vesalius Coll., Brussels, 1996; presenter in field. Author study guides for books in field; co-editor conf. procs., 1976. Program/conf. coord. N.E. Am. Acctg. Assn., State College, 1976; small bus. coun. Laramie Area C. of C., 1973-74. With USAF, 1969-70. Grantee Am. Acctg. Assn., Hasking & Sells Found. Mem. AAUP, NRA (life), AARP, Nat. Retired Tchrs. Assn., Inst. Mgmt. Accts. (I. Wayne Keller award, Ray E. Longnecker award 1980, Cert. Merit Manuscript award), Am. Acctg. Assn. (Sectional Best Paper award 1987), Inst. Internal Auditors, Decision Scis. Internat. (chmn. acctg. track N.E. sect. 1992), Mass. Soc. CPAs (acad. assoc.), Fin. Execs. Internat., Am. Legion (life), Am. Inst. Physics, U.S. Golf Assn., U.S. Tennis Assn. (life), Elks (permanent benefactor), Marine Meml. Club (perpetual benefactor), Jewish War Vets. (life), Beta Gamma Sigma, Beta Alpha Psi, Omicron Delta Kappa. Republican. Jewish. Avocations: tennis, golf, reading, swimming. Home: 521 Katahdin Dr Lexington MA 02421-6452 E-mail: lklein@bentley.edu.

KLEIN, MARY ANN, special education educator; b. Ridgewood, N.J., Jan. 31, 1956; d. Julius R. and Nancy M. Pascuzzo; m. Thomas F. Klein, July 16, 1983. B in Elem. Edn. & Spl. Edn., Adelphi U., Garden City, N.Y., 1978; M in Spl. Edn. & Reading, Adelphi Univ., Garden City, N.Y., 1980. Cert. in spl. edn. Learning disabilities specialist Merrick UFSD, Merrick, NY, 1978—. Swimming instr. disabled children and adults Village of Garden City, 1974—79; pvt. piano instr., NY, 1978—82; clinician & diagnostician Adelphi U. Reading Clinic, Garden City, 1980—84; ednl. cons. BOCES of Nassau County, Merrick, NY, 1993—94, SETRC of Nassau County, Westbury, NY, 1995—96; founder peer tutoring program Birch Sch., Merrick, NY; spl. edn. rep. Birch Child Study Team, Merrick, NY. Co-author: (curriculum guide) Foundations for Learning, 1991; author: (resource guide) Strategies to Assist Learning Disabled Children in the Classroom Setting, 1995. Mem. Merrick PTA, 1978—, tchr. liaison, 1994—97; mem. Merrick SEPTA, 1983—, Com. on Spl. Edn., 1983—, Nassau Reading Coun., 1996—; co-founder Students Against Destructive Decision-Making, Birch Sch., Merrick, NY; apptd. Crisis Mgmt. Team, Birch Sch. Mem.: State Congress of Parents & Tchrs. (hon.), Coun. for Exceptional Children, Kappa Delta Pi. Avocations: piano, travel.

KLEIN, MICHAEL LAWRENCE, research chemist, educator; b. London, Mar. 13, 1940; s. Julius and Bessie (Bloomberg) K.; m. Brenda May Woodman, June 3, 1962; children— Paula Denise, Rachel Anne B.Sc., Bristol U., Eng., 1961; PhD, Bristol U., 1964. Research fellow CIBA-GEIGEY, Genoa, Italy, 1964-65; research fellow Imperial Chem. Industries (UK), Bristol, Eng., 1965-67; research assoc. Rutgers U., New Brunswick, N.J., 1967-68; research officer NRC of Can., Ottawa, Ont., 1968-87; prof. chemistry U. Pa., Phila., 1987—91, William Smith prof. chemistry, 1991—93, Hepburn prof. phys. scis., 1993—, dir. Lab. for Rsch. on the Structure of Matter. Part-time prof. chemistry Mc Master U., Hamilton, Ont., 1977-89; mem. internat. relations com. Natural Scis. and Engring. Research Council, Ottawa, 1982-84, mem. NSERC chem. panel, 1985-86, NSF panels, 1993—, NIH panels, 1996, 97, 99; mem. FDA Panel, 1999; vis. prof., Paris, Lyon, France, Kyoto, Japan, Amsterdam, Canberra, Australia, Florence, Italy; fellow commoner Trinity Coll., Cambridge, Eng., 1985-86; dir. NSF Materials Rsch. Lab., 1993-96, NSF MRSEC, 1996—; Miller prof. U. Calif., Berkeley, 1997, Linnett prof. U. Cambridge, 1998; fellow Sydney-Sussex Coll., Cambridge, U.K., 1998. Editor: Rare Gas Solids, Vol. I, 1976, Vol. II, 1977, Inert Gases, 1984; mem. editl. bd. Chem. Physics,

1986—, Physics Reports, 1986—, Jour. Phys. Chemistry, 1990-95, Molecular Physics, 1992-99, Computational Materials Sci., 1992—, Jour. Chem. Soc. Farady Trans., 1993-98, Jour. Phys. Condensed Matter, 1994-97, Phys. Chemistry Chem. Physics, 1999—; contbr. numerous articles to profl. jours. IBM World Trade fellow, 1970, Guggenheim fellow, 1989, Humboldt fellow, 1995; grantee Natural Scis. and Engring. Rsch. Coun., 1979-89, NSF, 1988—, NIH, 1988—. Fellow Royal Soc. Can., Chem. Inst. Can., Am. Phys. Soc. (Rahman prize 1999), Am. Acad. Arts and Scis.; mem. Am. Chem. Soc. (Phila. Sect. award 1998), Royal Soc. Chemistry (U.K.). Home: 133 W Atlantic Blvd Ocean City NJ 08226-4603 Office: Univ Pa 141 CHEM/6323 3451 Walnut St Philadelphia PA 19104*

KLEIN, MILES VINCENT, physics educator; b. Cleve., Mar. 9, 1933; s. Max Ralph and Isabelle (Benjamin) K.; m. Barbara Judith Pincus, Sept. 2, 1956; children: Cynthia Klein-Banai, Gail. BS, Northwestern U., 1954; PhD, Cornell U., 1961. NSF postdoctoral fellow Max Planck Inst., Stuttgart, Germany, 1961; prof. U. Ill., Urbana, 1962—. Co-author: Optics, 1986; contbr. articles to profl. jours. A.P. Sloan Found. fellow, 1963. Fellow AAAS, Am. Phys. Soc. (Frank Isakson prize 1990), Am. Acad. Arts and Scis.; mem. IEEE (Sr.), Nat. Acad. Scis. Office: Materials Rsch Lab 104 S Goodwin Ave Urbana IL 61801-2902

KLEIN, MORTON, industrial engineer, educator; b. N.Y.C., Aug. 9, 1925; s. Norbert and Lottie (Wigdor) K.; m. Gloria Ritterband, July 31, 1949; children: Lisa, Melanie. BSM.E., Duke U., 1946; MS, Columbia U., 1952, D.Engring. Sci., 1957. Engr. Picatinny Arsenal, Dover, N.J., 1950-54; instr. Sch. Engring and Applied Sci., Columbia U., N.Y.C., 1956, asst. prof., 1957-61, asso. prof., 1961-69, prof. indsl. engring, ops. rsch., 1969—, chmn. dept. indsl. engring. and ops. research, 1982-85, 94-95. Cons. to industry, govt. Author: (with Cyrus Derman) Probability and Statistical Inference for Engineers, 1959; editor: Managment Science, 1960-77; rsch. and publs. on prodn. planning, scheduling early cancer detection examinations, network flows and statis. quality control. Served with USN, 1943-46. Mem. Am. Inst. Indls. Engrs., Pi Tau Sigma, Alpha Pi Mu, Omega Rho. Home: Haworth, NJ. Died Apr. 26, 2001.

KLEIN, SCOTT RICHARD, acting and directing educator; b. Aberdeen, South Dakota, June 2, 1959; s. Richard Lewis and Jalois Mae (Janish) K. BA, Gustavus Adolphus Coll., 1981; MFA, Mankato State U., 1983. Actor, tchr. Ark. Arts Ctr., Little Rock, 1983-84; assoc. dir. Permian Playhouse, Odessa, Tex., 1984-89; instr. acting and directing, coach Cameron Univ., Lawton, Okla., 1989-92, asst. prof., 1992-95, chmn., 1994—, assoc. prof., 1997—. Directed plays including Echoes, 1983; Vanities, 1985; A.B.C., 1986; Wiley and the Hairy Man, 1988; Night of January 16th, 1988; The Foreigner, 1989; The Barber of Seville, 1991; The Lion in Winter, 1992; Seascape, 1993; Betty the Yeti, 1995; Night Sky, 2002 (ACTF OK I Respondent's Chioce Award); appeared in plays The Glass Menagerie, 1989; Anything Goes, 1989; A Funny Thing Happened, 1989; Charley's Aunt, 1986; The Crucible, 1991; Christopher Columbus: The Gypsy's Fortune, 1992; Guys and Dolls, 2000; comml. for Kent Kwik, 1987 (Addy Award). Rep., United Way, Lawton, Okla., 1989-2000. Recipient Excellence in Direction Award, ACTF region V north, 1983; Best Dir. Award, Kaleidoscope Co., 1988; Alpha Psi Omega, 1990; Outstanding Rsch. Performance, C.U. Sch. Fine Arts, 1994; OK I Excellence in Direction Award ACTF, 2001; named Vol. of Yr. Arts for All S.W. Okla. Opera Guild, 1997; Vol. of Yr. S.W. Theatre Assn., 2000; Lawton Arts and Humanities Educator in the Arts, 2002. Mem. Tex. Non-Profit Theatres (cons. 1984—, adjudicator 1995, 97-99); Assn. Theatre in Higher Edn., S.W. Theatre Assn. (v.p. promotions 1997-2000, webmaster 2000—); Okla. Cmty. Theatre Assn., S.W. Okla. Opera Guild, 1994— (pres. 1995-96); Arts for All, Inc. (bd. dir. 1996-99); Lawton Cmty. Theatre (bd. dir. 1995-); Phi Kappa Phi. Avocations: music, dancing, books, videotapes. Home: 717 N W 36th St Lawton OK 73505-5123 Office: Cameron Univ 2800 W Gore Blvd Lawton OK 73505-6377 E-mail: scottk@cameron.edu.

KLEIN, WILLIAM WADE, religious educator; b. Weehawken, N.J., Feb. 11, 1946; s. William Carl and Eleanor (Kinkel) K.; m. Phyllis Gail Merritt, June 29, 1968; children: Alison, Sarah. BS, Wheaton (Ill.) Coll., 1967; MDiv, Denver Seminary, 1970; PhD, U. Aberdeen, Scotland, 1978. Ordained pastor Bapt. Ch., 1974. Assoc. pastor Calvary Bapt. Ch., Los Gatos, Calif., 1970—74; instr. Columbia (S.C.) Internat. U., 1977—78; prof. Denver Sem., 1978—, assoc. dean, 1994—2001. Author: The New Chosen People, 1990, Ephesians: An Annotated Bibliography, 1996; author, editor: Introduction to Biblical Interpretation, 1993, 2d edit., 2003; contbr. articles and book revs. to profl. jours. Named one of Outstanding Young Men Am., 1978; King William scholar U. Aberdeen, 1976. Fellow Inst. for Bibl. Rsch., Tyndale Fellowship for Bibl. Rsch.; mem. Soc. Bibl. Lit., Evang. Theol. Soc. Democrat. Office: Denver Seminary PO Box 100000 Denver CO 80250-0100

KLEINER, DIANA ELIZABETH EDELMAN, art history educator, administrator; b. N.Y.C., Sept. 18, 1947; d. Morton Henry and Hilda Rachel (Wyner) Edelman; m. Fred S. Kleiner, Dec. 22, 1972; 1 child, Alexander Mark. BA magna cum laude, Smith Coll., 1969; MA, MPhil, Columbia U., 1970, 74, PhD, 1976; MA (hon.), Yale U., 1989. Lectr., asst. prof. U. Va., Charlottesville, 1975-76, 76-78; vis. asst. prof. U. Mass., Boston, 1979; Mellon faculty fellow Harvard U., Cambridge, Mass., 1979-80; asst. prof. Yale U., New Haven, 1980-82, assoc. prof., 1982-89; fellow Whitney Humanities Ctr., Yale U., New Haven, 1984-87; master Pierson Coll., Yale U., New Haven, 1986-87; dir. grad. studies dept. history of art Yale U., New Haven, 1988-90; prof. history of art and classics Yale U., New Haven, 1989-95, dir. grad. studies dept. classics, 1991-94, chair dept. classics, 1994-95, Dunham prof. classics and history of art, 1995—, dep. provost for the arts, 1995—2003; liaison for faculty programs AllLearn, 2000—. Adv. bd. Archaeol. News, Tallahassee, 1980—, Am. Jour. Archaeology, Boston, 1985-98; mem., chair program for ann. meetings com. Archaeol. Inst. Am., Boston, 1988-93. Author: Roman Group Portraiture, 1977, The Monument of Philopappos in Athens, 1983, Roman Imperial Funerary Altars with Portraits, 1987, Roman Sculpture, 1992, paperback edit., 1994; editor: I, Clavdia: Women in Ancient Rome, 1996, I Clavdia II: Women in Roman Art and Society, 2000, (electronic course for AllLearn) eClavdia: Women in Ancient Rome, 2001—. Bd. dirs. Westville Cmty. Nursery Sch., New Haven, 1989-90, The Foote Sch., New Haven, 1994-2000; regional rep. Deerfield (Mass.) Acad., 2001—, mem. parent's com., 2002—. Grantee: Am. Coun. Learned Socs., 1979, NEH, 1980, 95, Am. Philos. Soc. 1982, The John Paul Getty Trust, 1992. Mem. Archaeol. Inst. Am., Am. Philol. Assn., Coll. Art Assn. Home: 102 Rimmon Rd Woodbridge CT 06525-1941 E-mail: diana.kleiner@yale.edu.

KLEINFELD, ELIZABETH ANNE, English literature educator; b. Hempstead, NY, June 18, 1969; d. Robert J. and Therese (O'Regan) K.; m. Travitt Lee Hamilton, Mar. 16, 1992. BS in History, Bradley U., 1992; MS in English, Ill. State U., 1994. Editor-in-chief Broadside Literary Jour., Peoria, Ill., 1988—91; instr. of English Ill. State U., Normal, 1993-94, Red Rocks C.C., Lakewood, Colo., 1995—; resident instr. English C.C. of Aurora, Colo., 1996—2000. Editor-in-chief Inscape Lit. Mag., 1997—2000. Mem.: MLA, Nat. Coun. Tchrs. English. Office: Red Rocks CC 13300 W 6th Ave Lakewood CO 80228 Home: 411 Pearl St Denver CO 80203-3807

KLEINSMITH, LEWIS JOEL, cell biologist, educator; b. Detroit, Apr. 13, 1942; s. Ralph Louis and Sylvia (Raphael) K.; m. Cynthia Weinstein, June 14, 1964; children: Alyssa Jan, Francesca Lynn. BS, U. Mich., 1964; PhD, Rockefeller U., 1968. Asst. prof. dept. zoology U. Mich., Ann Arbor, 1968-71, assoc. prof., 1971-74, prof. biology, 1975—, Arthur F. Thurnau prof., 1988. Vis. prof. biochemistry U. Fla. Med. Sch., Gainesville, 1974-75 Author: The World of the Cell, 5th edit., 2003, Principles of Cell and Molecular Biology, 2d edit., 1995; editor: Chromosomal Proteins and Their Role in the Regulation of Gene Expression, 1975; contbr. chpts. to books, articles to profl. jours.; developer of ednl. computer software. Recipient Henry Russel award, 1971; Distinguished Service award U. Mich., 1971; Higher Edn. Software award EDUCOM, 1988; Guggenheim fellow, 1974-75 Fellow AAAS; mem. Am. Soc. Biol. Chemists, Am. Soc. for Cell Biology, Am. Inst. Biol. Scientists, Phi Beta Kappa, Sigma Xi. Home: 2642 Essex Rd Ann Arbor MI 48104-6554

KLEJMENT, ANNE, historian, educator; b. Rochester, N.Y., Apr. 27, 1950; d. A. Henry and Alice Klejment. BA cum laude, Nazareth Coll., 1972; MA, SUNY, Binghamton, 1974, PhD, 1981. Instr. history Vassar Coll., 1978-79; adminstr. Historians-in-Residence Cornell U., Ithaca, N.Y., 1979-81; vis. asst. prof. history SUNY, Plattsburgh, 1981—83, dir. women's studies program, 1982-83; asst. prof. hist. U. of St. Thomas, St. Paul, 1983-88, assoc. prof., 1988—97, prof., 1997—. Muriel Ford lectr. Briar Cliff Coll., 1986. Author: The Berrigans: A Bibliography, 1979, Dorothy Day and The Catholic Worker: A Bibliography and Index, 1986; co-editor: American Catholic Pacifism, 1996; contbr. articles to profl. jours. and anthologies. SUNY Found. fellow, 1976-77; NEH Travel to Collections grantee, 1991; recipient Burlington No. Award for Scholarship, 1986, Pax Christi USA Book award, 1997. Mem. Am. Cath. Hist. Assn. (exec. bd. 1992-94), Peace History Soc., Orgn. Am. Historians. Office: U St Thomas Dept History Mail # 4188 Saint Paul MN 55105

KLEMPERER, WILLIAM, chemistry educator; b. N.Y.C., Oct. 6, 1927; s. Paul and Margit (Freund) K.; m. Elizabeth Cole, Jan. 12, 1949; children: Joyce Hillary, Paul, Wendy Judith AB, Harvard U., 1950; PhD, U. Calif., Berkeley, 1954; DSc, U. Chgo., 1996. Instr. chemistry Harvard U., Cambridge, Mass., 1954-57, asst. prof., 1957-61, assoc. prof., 1961-65, prof., 1965—. Asst. dir. NSF, Washington, 1979-81; vis. scientist Bell Telephone Lab., 1963-83; Evans lectr. Ohio State U., 1981, Pratt lectr. U. Va., 1984, Rollefson lectr. U. Calif., 1985, Oesper lectr. U. Cin., 1987, Kolthoff lectr. U. Minn., 1987, Mary E. Kapp lectr. Va. Commonwealth U., 1987, Linus Pauling Disting. lectr. Oreg. State U., 1988, Harry Emmett Gunning lectr. U. Alta., Can., 1988, Fritz London Meml. lectr. Duke U., 1989, Hinshelwood lectr. Oxford U., Eng., 1989, Neckers lectr. So. Ill. U., 1990; George C. Pimentel meml. lectr. U. Calif., Berkeley, 1992, vis. Miller prof., 1998; Joe L. Franklin meml. lectr. Rice U., 1994, E.K.C. Lee Fellowship lectr. U. Calif., Irvine, 1994; Richard C. Lord lectr. MIT, Cambridge, Mass., 1997; Bernstein lectr. UCLA, 1997. Served with A.C., USN, 1944-46 Recipient Wetherill medal Franklin Inst., 1978, Disting. Svc. medal NSF, 1981, Bomem Michelson award Coblentz Soc., 1990, Faraday Medal and Lectureship Royal Soc. Chemistry, 1995; named hon. citizen City of Toulouse, France, 2000. Fellow Am. Phys. Soc. (Earle Plyler prize 1983); mem. NAS, Am. Acad. Arts and Scis., Am. Chem. Soc. (Irving Langmuir award 1980, Peter Debye award in phys. chemistry 1994, E. Bright Wilson award in spectroscopy 2001, Remsen award Md. sect. 1992), Achievements include research in molecular structure, energy transfer and intermolecular forces using experimental spectroscopic methods; modelling molecule formation and detection in the interstellar medium. Home: 53 Shattuck Rd Watertown MA 02472-1310 Office: Harvard U Dept Chemistry and Chem Biology 12 Oxford St Cambridge MA 02138-2902 E-mail: klemperer@chemistry.harvard.edu.

KLENK, JACK, federal agency administrator; Graduated, U. Pitts.; diploma in edn., Makerere U. Coll., Uganda; MDiv, Harvard Divinity Sch. Acting dir. non-pub. edn. US Dept. Edn., Wash., 2001—; served White House Off. Policy Devel., Wash.; dir. issues analysis staff US Dept. Edn., Planning and Evaluation Svc.; tchr. Uganda. Office: US Dept Edn Non-Pub Edn 400 Maryland Ave SW FOB-6 Rm 4W306 Washington DC 20202

KLENK, TERRY ALLEN, theater educator; b. Cleve., Mar. 24, 1956; s. Kenneth John and Janet (Chisholm) K. BA, Miami U., Oxford, Ohio, 1978; MA, Kent State U., 1986; MFA, U. Fla., Gainesville, 1989. Asst. curator Western Res. Hist. Soc., Cleve., 1979-84; tchg. asst. dept. theater Kent (Ohio) State U., 1985-86, U. Fla., Gainesville, 1986-89; instr. Hippodrome State Theater, Gainesville, 1988-89; vis. lectr. dept. theater U. Fla., Gainesville, 1989; instr. Santa Fe Cmty. Coll., Gainesville, 1990-96; assoc. prof. Santa Fee C.C., Gainesville, 1996—. Dir.: (theater prodns.) Working, 1993, Queen of Hearts, 1993, Kennedy's Children, 1994, The Quilt, A Celebration, 1995, The Boys Next Door, 1996, Boy's Life, 1997, A Sense of Place, 2000, Bleacher Bums, 2002, Onionheads, 2003; dir., founder music theater group Swing Shift, 1993—. Mem. Actor's Equity Assn., South Eastern Theater Conf., Assn. of Theater in Higher Edn., Phi Kappa Phi. Democrat. Avocation: collecting antiques. Home: 7014 NW 52nd Ter Gainesville FL 32653-7008 Office: Dept Theater Santa Fe Cmty Coll 3000 NW 83rd St Gainesville FL 32606-6210

KLEPER, MICHAEL LAURENCE, graphic arts educator; b. New Haven, Apr. 23, 1947; s. Sidney Hillard and Rosaline Claire (Oliver) K.; m. Gwenyth E. Sykes, Nov. 5, 1972; children: Jodi Lisa, Scott Jeremy. AS, Rochester Inst. Tech., 1966, BS, 1969, MS, 1972. Ednl. specialist Rochester (N.Y.) Inst. Tech., 1969-71, asst. prof. graphic arts, 1972-77, assoc. prof., 1978-84, prof., 1984—, Paul and Louise Miller disting. prof., 2000—. Faculty assoc. RIT Printing Industry Ctr. Alfred P. Sloan Found. Author: The Illustrated Dictionary of Typographic Composition, 1984, The Illustrated Handbook of Desktop Publishing and Typesetting, 1987, 2d edit., 1990, The Handbook of Digital Publishing, 2001; editor: Personal Composition Report, 1979—, Today's Press and Publishing Technology, 1993—, The Kleper Report on Digital Publishing, 1996—; contbr. articles to profl. jours. Recipient Disting. Svc. award Nat. Composition Assn., 1984, Gitner Family prize 2002; Fulbright scholar 2001. Mem. House Printing Craftsmen, Phi Kappa Phi (pres. 1995—), Gamma Epsilon Tau. Office: Rochester Inst Tech 9 Lomb Memorial Dr Rochester NY 14623-5603 E-mail: mkleper@printerport.com., mlkpp4@rit.edu.

KLEPPER, ROBERT RUSH, science educator; b. Sculthorpe AFB, Norfolk, Wales, Nov. 8, 1957; came to U.S., 1958; s. Norman Eugene and Rosalind Violet (Rush) K.; m. Laurene Kay Wycoff, June 25, 1991; children: April Kaylynn, Candace Rose. AS, Iowa Lakes C.C., Estherville, Iowa, 1987; BS, Buena Vista Coll., Storm Lake, Iowa, 1990; MS, Iowa State U., 1992; PhD, Columbia Pacific U., San Rafael, Calif., 1994. Mgr. Milford (Iowa) Nursery, 1985-89; rsch. assoc. Iowa State U., Ames, 1989-90; adj. prof. Iowa Ctrl. C.C., Storm Lake, 1992—; dir. R&D TransAgra Internat., Storm Lake, 1990-97; prof. biology and chemistry Iowa Lakes C.C., Estherville, 1997—. Ind. cons., Linn Grove, Iowa, 1991—; sci. advisor Mus. Sci., Boston, 1994—; sci. day advisor Buena Vista U., Storm Lake, 1990—, adj. prof., 1996—; adj. prof. Iowa Lakes C.C., Spencer, 1994—, prof., Emmetsburg, 1997—; prof. Estherville, 1998—. Mem. Plant Growth Regulator Soc. Am., Am. Soc. Plant Physiologists, Coun. Agrl. Sci. and Tech., Am. Soc. Agronomy. Avocations: playing guitar, riding bike, hiking, reading. Home: 105 S 3d St Box 86 Terril IA 51364 Office: Iowa Lakes Cmty Coll 300 S 18th St Estherville IA 51334-2721 E-mail: rklepper@ilcc.cc.ia.us.

KLEPPNER, DANIEL, physicist, educator; b. N.Y.C., Dec. 16, 1932; s. Otto and Beatrice (Taub) K.; m. Beatrice Spencer; children: Paul, Sofie, Andrew. BS, Williams Coll., 1953; BA, Cambridge (Eng.) U., 1955; PhD, Harvard U., 1959. Asst. prof. physics Harvard U., Cambridge, Mass., 1962-66; assoc. prof. MIT, Cambridge, 1966-73, prof., 1974—, Lester Wolfe prof. physics, 1986—, assoc. dir. Rsch. Lab. of Electronics, 1987—. Author: Introduction to Mechanics, 1973, Quick Calculus, 1986. Recipient Oersted medal, AAPT, 1996. Fellow Am. Phys. Soc. (Davisson-Germer prize 1986, Julius Edgar Lilienfeld prize 1991), AAAS, Optical Soc. Am. (William F. Meggars award 1991), Am. Acad. Arts and Scis.; mem. NAS, Am. Assn. Physics Tchrs. (Oersted medal). Office: MIT Dept Physics 77 Mass Ave Rm 26237 Cambridge MA 02139-4307

KLEVEN, BRUCE ALAN, academic administrator; b. Rice Lake, Wis., Nov. 20, 1951; s. Gordon and Louise (Cameron) K.; m. Merrily Faith Thornton, Aug. 4, 1979; children: Joseph Cameron, Kyli Amanda. BS, U. Wis., Menomonie, 1973; MEd, U. Alaska, 1983, EdS, 1987. Cert. tchr., adminstr., Alaska; cert. adminstr., N.Y., Wis. Tchr. St. Paul Pub. Schs., St. Paul, 1974-76; tchr., coord. Yukon-Koyukuk Sch. Dist., Nenana, Alaska, 1976-80, dir. various programs, 1984-90; prin. Huslia (Alaska) Elem. and Secondary Sch., 1980-84; supt. Kake (Alaska) City Sch. Dist., 1990-92; dean adminstrn. and fin. Arctic Sivunmun Ilisagvik Coll., Barrow, Alaska, 1992-94; prin. Alaskan Ednl. Cons. Svc.; dist. adminstr. Sch. Dist. of Solon Springs, Wis., 1995—. Apptd. to Alaska Job Tng. Coun., 1993-96; apptd. bd. dirs. Arctic Devel. Coun.; apptd. Solon Springs Devel. Coun., 1995—; budget rev. com., policy rev. com., econ. devel. com., compensation bd., North Slope Borough, Alaska, 1993-94. Pres. 4 Mile Rd. Community Coun., Nenana, 1988-91, Valley Borough Support Committee, Nenana, 1989-91; mem. Valley Family Health Svc. Bd., Nenana, 1989-91. Avocations: hunting, fishing, flying. Office: Sch Dist Solon Springs 8993 E Baldwin Ave Solon Springs WI 54873-8144

KLIMEK, JOSEPH JOHN, physician, educator; b. Wilkes-Barre, Pa., Sept. 14, 1946; s. Joseph John and Frances Carol (Pavloski) K.; m. Jane Marie Stout, June 26, 1971 (div.); 1 child, Adam. AB cum laude, Princeton U., 1968; MD, Pa. State U., 1972. Diplomate Am. Bd. Internal Medicine, Am. Bd. Infectious Diseases. Intern, resident in internal medicine Hartford (Conn.) U., then fellow in infectious disease, 1972-76, chief epidemiology, 1976-87, dir. subsplty. medicine, 1985-87, assoc. dir. medicine, 1987-90, assoc. dir. dept. medicine and chmn. AIDS program, 1987-90, dir. dept. medicine, 1990—, chmn. AIDS task force, 1985-90, assoc. chmn. dept. medicine, 1995—; asst. prof. medicine U. Conn., Farmington, 1977-84, assoc. prof., 1984-90, prof., 1990—; assoc. chmn. dept. medicine U: Conn. Sch. Medicine, 1995—. Conn. mem. numerous faculties pharm. industry. Sr. assoc. editor Am. Jour. Infection Control, 1980-95; med. editor Asepsis, The Infection Control Forum; also mem. numerous editl. bds. in field; contbr. articles to med. jours. Recipient Disting. Alumnus award, 1978, ARC award, 1986. Fellow ACP, Infectious Disease Soc. Am.; mem. APHA, AAAS, Am. Profls. in Infection Control, Am. Soc. Microbiology, Am. Fedn. Clin. Rsch., Soc. Hosp. Epidemiologists Am., Am. Venereal Disease Assn., Am. Med. Writers Assn. Achievements include integrated internal medicine residency of Hartford Hospital with University of Connecticut School of Medicine; developed hospital community linkage network for AIDS care in Greater Hartford; introduced primary care medicine practice model to all ambulatory services; expanded care to indigent with two bilingual satellite practices; developed hospital cardiac services product line; initiated formal hospitalist program for care of inpatients. Home: 31 Main St Farmington CT 06032-2229 Office: Hartford Hosp 80 Seymour St Hartford CT 06115-2701 E-mail: jklimek@harthosp.org.

KLINE, BONITA ANN, middle school guidance counselor, educator; b. Charleroi, Pa., Sept. 25, 1952; d. Milton Paul Kobaly and Ann Marie (Gohosky) George; m. Dennis Charles Kline, Aug. 8, 1981. BS in Elem. Edn., U. Pitts., 1973; MEd, Calif. (Pa.) U., 1986; postgrad., U. Pitts., 1986—. Cert. elem. tchr., Pa., elem. guidance counselor, Pa., elem. prin., Pa., secondary guidance counselor, Pa., asst. supt., Pa. Juvenile probation officer Westmoreland County Court System, Greensburg, Pa., 1974; elem. tchr. Belle Vernon (Pa.) Area Sch. Dist., 1975—. Mem. Ea. Pa. Profl. Womens Group, Tri-State Area Sch. Study Coun., PTO. Democrat. Roman Catholic. Avocations: reading, fishing, traveling, swimming, gardening. Home: 1415 Willowbrook Rd Belle Vernon PA 15012-4329 Office: Belle Vernon Area Sch Dist 250 Crest Ave Belle Vernon PA 15012-4200

KLINE, CAROLE JUNE, special education educator; b. Youngstown, Ohio, June 16, 1947; d. Stephen and Mary (Kuzniak) Yourst; m. Ronald Edward Kline, Aug. 3, 1968 (dec. Dec. 2000); children: Christopher John, Melinda Marie. BS in Elem. Edn., Kent State U., 1968, MEd in Spl. Edn., 1970; postgrad., L.I. U., 1987. Cert. tchr. spl. edn., elem. and nursery sch., N.Y. Libr. I reference rm. Kent (Ohio) State U., 1968; intermediate EMR tchr. Niles (Ohio) City Schs., 1969-75; tchr. elem. spl. edn. Fulton (N.Y.) City Schs., 1984-88; subs. tchr. Baldwinsville (N.Y.) Ctrl. Schs., 1982-84, resource tchr. jr. h.s., 1984, resource and spl. edn. tchr. jr. h.s., 1988—. Homebound instr. Baldwinsville Ctrl. Schs., 1988—, inclusion com., 1998-99; adv. bd. OCM BOCES Career Exploration Program, 1997-98. Bd. dirs. Seneca Gardens Homeowners Assn., Baldwinsville, 1998—, Baldwinsville Cmty. Band, 1988—, Baldwinsville Cmty. Connection, 1995-97, steering com., 1996. Mem. NEA, Nat. Edn. Assn. N.Y. (del. 1993, 94, 95, 96), Baldwinsville Tchr.'s Assn. (exec. com. 1990-97, bldg. rep. 1988-97), Coun. for Exceptional Children (rsch. divsn. 1990-97), Coun. for Children With Behavioral Disorders (divsn. for learning disabilities 1990-97), Kent State Alumni Assn. Democrat. Roman Catholic. Avocations: floral and landscape design, needlework. Home: 1607 S Ivy Trl Baldwinsville NY 13027-9047 Office: Durgee Jr High Sch E Oneida St Baldwinsville NY 13027

KLINE, DAVID ADAM, lawyer, educator, writer; b. Keota, Okla., Sept. 27, 1923; s. David Adam and Lucy Leila (Wood) K.; m. Ruthela Deal, Aug. 25, 1947; children: Steven, Timothy, Ruthanna. JD, Okla. U., 1950. Bar: Okla. 1949. Law clk., spl. master U.S. Dist. Ct. Okla., 1952-61; 1st asst. U.S. atty. We. Dist. Okla., 1961-69; judge We. Dist. Okla. U.S. Bankruptcy Ct., Oklahoma City, 1969-82; sr. shareholder Kline Kline Elliott Castleberry & Bryant, P.C., Oklahoma City, 1983—. Pres. Nat. Conf. Bankruptcy Judges 1977-78; mem. arbitration panel program U.S. Dist. Ct. (we. dist.) Okla., 1985— mem. faculty Fed. Jud. Ctr., Washington, Nat. Seminar Bankruptcy Judges, 1971-86; adj. prof. law Oklahoma City U., 1980-84; cons. Norton Bankruptcy Law and Practice, 1986, Callaghan & Co.; bd. dirs. Consumer Credit Counseling Svc. Ctr., Okla., 1973-2001, chmn., 1992. Author: A Little Book (A New Thing in the Earth), 1993, A Little Book II (The Blood of the Lion), 1995, A Little Book III (The Revelation), 1997, A Little Book IV (A Still Small Voice), 1998, A Little Book V (Law and Liberty), 2003; digest editor Am. Bankruptcy Law jour., 1974—77; contbr. Cowans Bankruptcy Law and Practice, 1983, Cowans Bankruptcy Law and Practice 2d edit., 1986; co-author: Briefcase, 1988—2000. Fellow Am. Coll. Bankruptcy. Office: Kline Kline Elliott Castleberry & Bryant PC Kline Law Bldg 720 NE 63rd St Oklahoma City OK 73105-6405 E-mail: dkline@klinefirm.org.

KLINE, HARRIET DENNIS, psychologist, school psychologist; b. Sheridan, Wyo., Oct. 4, 1943; d. Thomas Gordon and Anna Townsend (Pyle) Dennis; m. Alan Herbert Kline, June 15, 1964 (div. Dec. 1976); children: Rebecca, David, Benjamin. BA, NYU, 1969; MS, SUNY, Potsdam, 1977; PhD, Temple U., 1988; cert. in sch. psychology, Bryn Mawr Coll., 1986; postgrad., Family Inst. Philadelphia, 1992-95. Lic. psychologist, Pa.; cert. tchr., N.Y., N.J., Pa. Reading tchr. Lake Placid (N.Y.) Sch. Dist., 1974-81; tchg. assoc. Temple U., Phila., 1981-84; dir. Ednl. Records Bur., Phila., 1985-90, Main Line Ednl. Svc., Rosemont, Pa., 1990—; sch. psychologist Chester (Pa.) Uplands Sch. Dist., 1990-91, 98—, Gladwyne (Pa.) Montessori Sch., 1991-94, Upper Moreland Sch. Dist., Willow Grove, Pa., 1994-95. Vis. lectr. Rutgers U., Immaculata Coll. Contbr. articles to profl. jours. Founder Hunterdon Recycling Ctr., Flemington, N.J., 1969-71; founding mem. Literacy Vols., Saranac Lake, N.Y., 1979-81. Mem. APA, NASP, Pa. Psychol. Assn., Orton Soc., Temple U. Sch. Edn. Alumni Assn. (bd. dirs. 1988—). Office: Main Line Ednl Svcs 1062 W Lancaster Ave Bryn Mawr PA 19010-2612 E-mail: hdkline_phd@nni.com.

KLINE, HOWARD JAY, cardiologist, educator; b. White Plains, NY, Nov. 5, 1932; s. Raymond Kline and Rose Plane; divorced; children: Michael, Ethan; m. Ellen Sawamura, June 13, 1987; 1 child, Christopher. BS, Dickinson Coll., 1954; MD, N.Y. Med. Coll., 1958. Intern San Francisco Gen. Hosp., 1958—59; resident Mt. Sinai Hosp., N.Y.C., 1959—61; sr. resident U. Calif. Med. Ctr., San Francisco, 1961—62; cardiology fellow Mt. Sinai Hosp., N.Y.C., 1962—64; dir. cardiology tng. program St. Mary's Hosp., San Francisco, 1970—90, Calif. Pacific Med. Ctr., San Francisco, 1992—. Clin. prof. medicine and cardiology U. Calif. Med. Ctr., San Francisco, 1984—; vis. prof. Nihon U., Tokyo, 1986; dir. cardiology Valley Forge Gen. Hosp. Cardiology editor Hosp. Practice, Cardiology, 1992—; contbr. articles to profl. jours. Lt. col. U.S. Med. Corps, 1967-69. Fellow ACP, Am. Heart Assn., Am. Coll. Cardiology, Am. Coll. Chest Physicians; mem. Burkes Tennis Club, U. San Francisco Masters Swim Team. Avocations: painting, reading, running, skiing, tennis. Office: 2100 Webster St Ste 516 San Francisco CA 94115-2382

KLINE, SUSAN ANDERSON, medical school official and dean, internist; b. Dallas, June 4, 1937; d. Kenneth Kirby and Frances Annette (Demorest) Anderson; m. Edward Mahon Kline, Dec. 26, 1964 (dec. July 1990). BA, Ohio U., 1959; MD, Northwestern U., 1963. Diplomate Am. Bd. Internal Medicine, Nat. Bd. Med. Examiners (bd. dirs. 1977-81). Asst. physician NY Hosp., 1967—68, physician-to-outpatients, 1968—69, electrocardiographer, 1968—70, asst. attending physician, 1969—76, physician-in-charge cardiopulmonary lab., 1970—71, dir. adult cardiac catheterizaion lab., 1970—71, dir. adult cardiac catheterization lab., 1971—79, assoc. attending physician, 1976—85, emeritus attending physician, 1985—, emeritus dir. adult cardiac catheterization lab., 1985—; assoc. dean student affairs Cornell U. Med. Coll., N.Y.C., 1974—78; assoc. dean admissions and student affairs Cornell Med. Sch., Ithaca, NY, 1978—80; mgr. occupl. med. programs GE Co., 1980—84; sr. assoc. dean student affairs N.Y. Med. Coll., Valhalla, 1984—94, interim dean, v.p. med. affairs, 1994—96, exec. vice dean acad. affairs, vice provost univ. student affairs, 1996—. Chmn. unmatched student com. Nat. Residency Matching Program, 1998—2000; mem. test com. Ednl. Commn. on Fgn. Med. Grads., Phila., 1985—92; mem. U.S. med. licensing exam test accommodations com. Nat. Bd. Med. Examiners, Phila., 1992—; bd. dirs. Nat. Resident Matching Program, 1996—, bd. dirs., mem. exec. com., 2003—; mem. Liaison Com. on Med. Edn., 1998—, chair ad hoc subcom. rev. accreditation stds., 2000—01, exec. com., 2002—; policy com. Liaiaon Com. on Med. Edn/, 2003—; chmn. adv. com. Electronic Residency Application Svc., 1996—2001. Bd. visitors Coll. Arts, Ohio U., Athens, 1981—91; bd. dirs. Burke Rehab. Hosp., White Plains, 1997—. Recipient Leaders of the Future award, Nat. Coun. Women, N.Y.C., 1978, Cert. of Appreciation, Ohio U., 1978. Fellow: ACP, Am. Soc. Internal Medicine, Am. Coll. Cardiology; mem.: Phi Kappa Phi, Am. Assn. Med. Colls. (chmn. 1989—93, chmn. N.E. group on student affairs, mem. sr. mgmt. adv. com. 2001—), N.Y. Cardiologists Soc., Am. Heart Assn. (fellow coun. on clin. cardiology), Cruising Club Am., Alpha Omega Alpha, Phi Beta Kappa. Avocation: sailing. Home: 561 Pequot Ave Southport CT 06490-1366 Office: New York Medical College Sunshine Cottage Valhalla NY 10595 E-mail: kline@nymc.edu.

KLINE, SYBIL ROSE, researcher; b. San Francisco; d. Samuel Henry and Louise (Holdforth) K. BA, Humboldt U., 1972, MA in Psychology, 1975; PhD, U. Calif., Santa Cruz, 1996. Lic. ednl. psychologist; Cert. sch. psychologist, bilingual cert. Sch. psychologist Monterey (Calif.) Peninsula Unified Sch. Dist., 1980-81, Oak Grove Unified Sch. Dist., San Jose, Calif., 1981-82, Santa Cruz (Calif.) County Office of Edn., 1982-83, Santa Cruz City Schs., 1983-96; cons. psychologist San Jose Unified Sch. Dist., 1992; practitioner, researcher, connection coord. U. Calif. Santa Cruz Ctr. for Rsch. on Cultural Diversity, 1992-96, Santa Cruz (Calif.) City Schs., 1982-96. Rschr. prin. investigator Alternative Assessment Project, CREDE, UCSC, US Dept. Edn.; lecturer edn. dept., UCSC, 1998-01 Author: PASS+S Dynamic Assessment, 1995, One-Minute Attention Test, 1995; co-author: (manual) Guidelines for the Linguistically and Culturally Different Exceptional Student, 1987. Regents fellow U. Calif., Santa Cruz, 1990; grantee Dept. Edn.; Fellow Office Bilingual Edn. and Minority Lang. Affairs, 1993-96. Mem. APA, Nat. Assn. Sch. Psychologists, Am. Edn. Rsch. Assn., Soc. Rsch. in Child Devel., Coun. Exceptional Children (divsn. culturally/linguistically diverse learners), Calif. Assn. Sch. Psychologists (multicultural com., Psychologist of Yr. 1986). Office: Univ Calif CREDE Santa Cruz CA 95064 E-mail: sybil@cats.ucsc.edu.

KLING, PHRADIE (PHRADIE KLING GOLD), small business owner, educator; b. NYC, July 2, 1933; d. Samuel A. and Mary Leah (Cohen) K.; m. Lee M. Gold, Sept. 5, 1955 (div. 1976); children: Judith Eileen, Laura Susan, Stephen Samuel, James David. BA, Cornell U., 1955; MA in Human Genetics, Sarah Lawrence Coll., 1971. Genetic counselor assoc. Coll. Medicine and Dentistry N.J., Newark, 1970-73; assoc. genetic counselor Sarah Lawrence Coll., Bronxville, N.Y., 1970-73; genetic counselor N.Y. Fertility Rsch. Found., N.Y.C., 1971-73; staff assoc., genetic counselor depts. pediatrics, ob-gyn and neurology Columbia U. Coll. Physicians and Surgeons, N.Y.C., 1973-78; asst. in genetics St. Luke's Hosp. Ctr., N.Y.C., 1977-79; health program assoc. Conn. Dept. Health Svcs., Hartford, 1978-84; edn. cons. Conn. Traumatic Brain Injury Assn., Rocky Hill, 1984-85; office mgr. Anderson Turf Irrigation Inc., Plainville, Conn., 1986-92; owner, mgr. KlingWorks, contract adminstrn., Avon, Conn., 1992—. Speaker, instr. on health and health ethics issues, Conn., N.Y., N.J., 1971-85; dir. confs. on genetics and traumatic brain injury, 1980-85; project dir. ednl. field testing Biol. Scis. Curriculum Study, 1981-83; scientist AAAS Sci.-by-Mail, 1991-2000. Active Farmington River Watershed Assn., Simsbury, Conn., 1988—; docent Sci. Mus. Conn., West Hartford, 1989-90. Recipient citation for dedicated svc. Conn. Safety Belt Coalition, 1985. Mem. Am. Human Genetics Soc., Bus. and Profl. Microcomputer Users Group (bd. dirs.), Conn. Assn. for Jungian Psychology (bd. dirs.), Am. Mensa (chpt. coord. gifted children 1985—), Cornell Club Greater Hartford. Home and Office: 33 Hunter Rd Avon CT 06001-3618

KLINGE, CAROLYN MURIEL, biochemist, educator; b. Utica, N.Y., May 20, 1957; d. Victor Stephen and Edith Muriel (Jones) K. BA in Biology magna cum laude, Keuka Coll., 1979; MS in Genetics, Pa. State U., 1981, PhD in Pharmacology, 1984. Postdoctoral fellow U. Rochester (N.Y.) Sch. Medicine, 1984-89, rsch. asst. prof. biochemistry, 1989-96; asst. prof. biochemistry U. Louisville Sch. Medicine, 1996—2001, assoc. prof., 2001—. Contbr. articles to Jour. Biol. Chemistry, Cancer Rsch., Jour. Steroid Biochemistry, Molecular Endocrinology. Recipient New Investigator award Nichols Inst., 1990. Mem. AAAS, Am. Assn. Cancer Rsch., N.Y. Acad. Scis., Endocrine Soc. Democrat. Presbyterian. Achievements include rsch. in mechanisms regulating normal versus neoplastic mamary cell growth, regulation of estrogen receptor interaction with specific DNA sequences, estrogen reponsive elements, in vitro, molecular basis of estrogen versus antiestrogen action. Office: U Louisville Sch Medicine Dept Biochemistry Louisville KY 40292-0001

KLINGER, THOMAS SCOTT, biology educator; b. Kalamazoo, May 4, 1955; s. Theodore Courtney Klinger and Marilyn Yvonne (Wright) Fuller; m. Signe Dolloff, July 25, 1987; children: Austin, Pepin. MA, U. South Fla., 1979, PhD, 1984. Teaching asst. U. South Fla., Tampa, 1976-83, adj. lectr., 1983-84; adj. prof. Saint Leo (Fla.) Coll., 1984-85; asst. prof. Bloomsburg (Pa.) U., 1985-90, assoc. prof., 1990-96, prof., 1996—. Curriculum cons. Sarasota (Fla.) County Schs., 1984; instr. Pasco-Hernando Community Coll., New Port Richey, 1984; v.p. academics Marine Sci. Consortium, Wallops Island, Va., 1988—, dir., 1986—. Mem. editl. bd. Am. Zoologist, 1998—; contbr. over 60 articles to scholarly and profl. jours. Grantee Pa. State System of Higher Edn., 1987-96, Bloomsburg U., 1988-96, U. Queensland, 1996, NSF, 1998. Mem. AAAS, Am. Soc. Integrative and Comparative Biology, Am. Soc. Zoologists, Commonwealth of Pa. Univ. Biologists (v.p. 1988-89), Assn. of Pa. State Coll. and Univ. Faculties, Sigma Xi (Grant-in-Aid Rsch. 1982). Achievements include research in the characterization of the digestive enzymology of sea urchins, quantification of nutritional energetics and behavior ecology of sea urchins and sea cucumbers. Office: Bloomsburg U Biology Dept 400 E 2nd St Bloomsburg PA 17815-1399

KLINGER, WAYNE JULIUS, secondary education educator; b. Chgo., Dec. 2, 1934; s. Walter Otto and Katherine Veronica (Murtha) K.; m. Dona Larene Sandkuhl, Sept. 26, 1967 (div. 1980); m. Ellen Jane Lawseth, July 7, 1991 (div. Mar. 1996); children: Susan Jackson-Woods, David; m. Annie Fumie Kuriki, June 19, 1999. BA, Villanova U., 1957; MS, Cath. U. Am., 1963. Cert. tchr., Ill., Mich., Calif., Oreg., Minn. Tchr. Order St. Augustine, Rockford, Ill., 1961-62, Detroit, 1962-63, tchr., dir. studies Chgo., 1963-66, tchr., activity dir. Holland, Mich., 1966-67; tchr. Palo Alto (Calif.) Unified Sch. Dist., 1967-72, Salem (Oreg.) Pub. Schs., 1972-77, Stockton (Calif.) Unified Sch. Dist., 1986—. NSF inst. participant Ill. Inst. Tech., 1963-64, Harvard Project Physics, Santa Clara, Calif., 1969, geology practicum We. Wash. State U., 1971, laser inst. San Jose State U., 1990; participant Woodrow Wilson Found. Physics Inst., U. Calif.-Santa Cruz, 1988, 89, 92-93, Physics Tchrs. Resource Agts., 1994-95; pres. Sch. Site Coun., 1991-92; participant numerous workshops. Founder, dir. Cardboard Boat Regatta, Stockton, 1988—. Mem. NEA, Nat. Sci. Tchrs. Assn., Am. Assn. Physics Tchrs., Calif. Sci. Tchrs. Assn., Valley Assn. Sci. Tchrs., Stockton Tchrs. Assn., Tech. Fellowship Team. Democrat. Roman Catholic. Avocations: skiing, camping. Home: 1927 Gerber Dr Stockton CA 95209-4514 Office: Edison H S 1425 S Center St Stockton CA 95206-2016

KLINGERMAN, KAREN NINA, elementary school educator, teacher consultant, course coordinator; b. Rahway, N.J., Sept. 12, 1952; d. Nelson Randolph and Alma Margaret (Magnani) Terry; m. William Robert Klingerman, May 25, 1975; children: Bryan William, Brad Nelson. BS in Secondary Edn., Bloomsburg (Pa.) U., 1974; MEd, Trenton State Coll., 1977; Elem. Edn. Cert., Holy Family Coll., Phila., 1992. Cert. secondary edn. educator, elem. edn. educator, Pa. Tchr. Bensalem (Pa.) Sch. Dist., 1974—; tchr. cons., course coord., asst. dir. for new fellows Pa. Writing Project West Chester (Pa.) U., 1988—; instrnl. facilitator to improve students' writing Bensalem Twp. Sch. Dist., 2002—, tchr. on spl. assignment, 2002—. Assoc. dir. New Fellows Pa. Writing Project, 2003. Contbr. articles to Pa. Writing Project Newsletter. Mem. James A. Michener Art Museum, Doylestown, 2001-. Grantee Just for the Kids Edn. Found., 2001; recipient Bucks County IU # 22 grant, 1986, Award for Innovative Teaching, Pa. State Educators Assn., 1988. Fellow Pa. Writing Project; mem. NEA, Pa. State Edn. Assn. Avocations: colonial crafts, antiques, sports spectator, summers at N.J. shore. Home: 49 Sharon Dr Richboro PA 18954-1049 Office: Bensalem Sch Dist 3000 Donallen Dr Bensalem PA 19020-1829

KLINGMAN, JOHN PHILIP, architect, educator; b. Phila., July 31, 1947; s. John Philip and Ethel Iva (Serfas) K. BSCE, Tufts U., 1969; postgrad., Stanford U., 1969-70; MArch, U. Oreg., 1983. Registered architect, La. Constrn. coord., project mgr. Payette Assocs., Inc., Boston, 1972-81; mem. design team Fairchild Biochemistry Bldg. Harvard U., 1977—78; project architect LaBouisse & Waggonner Inc. Architects, New Orleans, 1986-89; cons. architect Waggonner & Ball, Inc. Architects, New Orleans, 1990-96; design, planning and preservation U.S. Customhouse, New Orleans, 1996—. Asst. prof. Sch. Architecture Tulane U., New Orleans, 1983-90, assoc. prof., 1990-96, prof., 1996—, assoc. dean, 1991-93; mem. archtl. rev. com. Historic Dists. Landmarks Commn., 1995—. Author: New New Orleans Architecture, New Orleans Mag., 1997-2002; co-editor: Talk About Architecture: A Century of Architectural Education at Tulane, 1993. Recipient GSA Honor award for customhouse projects, 1996. Avocation: wood sculpture. Home: 1309 Harmony St New Orleans LA 70115-3424 Office: Tulane U Sch Architecture New Orleans LA 70118

KLINMAN, JUDITH POLLOCK, biochemist, educator; b. Phila., Apr. 17, 1941; d. Edward and Sylvia Pollock; m. Norman R. Klinman, July 3, 1963 (div. 1978); children: Andrew, Douglas. BA, U. Pa., 1962, PhD, 1966; PhD (hon.), U. Uppsala, Sweden, 2000. Postdoctoral fellow Weizmann Inst. Sci., Rehovoth, Israel, 1966—67; postdoctoral assoc. Inst. Cancer Rsch., Phila., 1968—70, rsch. assoc., 1970—72, asst. mem., 1972—77, assoc. mem., 1977—78; asst. prof. biophysics U. Pa., Phila., 1974—78; assoc. prof. chemistry U. Calif., Berkeley, 1978—82, prof., 1982—, prof. molecular and cell biology, 1993—, chair dept., 2000—03. Mem. ad hoc biochemistry and phys. biochemistry study sects. NIH, 1977—84, phys. biochemistry study sect., 1984—88. Mem. editl. bd.: Jour. Biol. Chemistry, 1979—84, Biofactors, 1991—98, European Jour. Biochemistry, 1991—95, Biochemistry, 1993—, Ann. Rev. Biochemistry, 1996—2000; contbr. Fellow, NSF, 1964, NIH, 1964—66, Guggenheim, 1988—89. Mem.: NAS, Am. Philos. Soc., Am. Soc. Biochemistry and Molecular Biology (membership com. 1984—86, pub. affairs com. 1987—94, program com. 1995, pres.-elect 1997, pres. 1998, past pres. 1999), Am. Acad. Arts and Scis., Am. Chmn. Soc. (exec. coun. biol. divsn. 1982—85, chmn. nominating com. 1987—88, program chair 1991—92, Repligen award 1994), Sigma Xi. Office: U Calif Dept Chemistry Berkeley CA 94720-0001

KLIR, GEORGE JIRI, systems science educator; b. Prague, Czechoslovakia, Apr. 22, 1932; arrived in U.S., 1966, naturalized, 1972; s. Jan and Emilie (Přitasilová) K.; m. Milena Řeholová, Jan. 26, 1962; children: Jane, John. MSEE, Czech Tech. U., Prague, 1957; PhD, Czechoslovak Acad. Scis., Prague, 1964; D (hon.), Prague U. Econs., Prague, 1994, Tech. U. in Brno, Moravia, 1997, Czech Tech. U., Prague, 1998. Rsch. fellow Inst. Computer Research, Prague, 1960-64; lectr. U. Baghdad, Iraq, 1964-66, UCLA, 1966-68; assoc. prof. Fairleigh Dickinson U., 1968-69, Sch. Advanced Tech., SUNY, Binghamton, 1969-72, prof. systems sci., 1972—, disting. prof. T.J. Watson Sch., 1984—, chmn. dept. systems sci., 1977-94. Dir. Internat. Conf. Applied Gen. Systems Rsch., 1977, Ctr. for Intelligent Systems, T.J. Watson Sch., 1995-2000. Author: Cybernetic Modelling, 1967, An Approach to General Systems Theory, 1969, Methodology of Switching Circuits, 1972, Architecture of Systems Problem Solving, 1985, 2d edit., 2003, Fuzzy Sets, Uncertainty, and Information, 1988, Facets of Systems Science, 1991, 2d edit., 2001, Fuzzy Measure Theory, 1992, Fuzzy Sets and Fuzzy Logic, 1995, Uncertainty-Based Information, 1998, Fuzzy Sets, 2000; author, co-author or editor other books; editor-in-chief: Book Series on Basic and Applied General Systems Research, 1978-82, Book Series on Frontiers in System Science: Implications for the Social Sciences, 1978-84, International Jour. Gen. Systems, 1974—, IFSR Book Series on Systems Science and Engineering, 1984—; mem. editl. bds. other profl. jours.; contbr. numerous articles to profl. jours. Recipient award for outstanding contbns., Austrian Soc. Cybernetics, 1976, award, Netherland Soc. Sys. Rsch., 1976, Bernard Bolzano gold medal in math. scis., Czech Acad. Scis., 1994, Lotfi A. Zadeh Best Paper award, 1994, Disting. Leadership award, ISSS, 1994, award for highest achievement in scholarship, Simon Bolivar U. in Caracas, 1997, Arnold Kaufmann's Gold Medal prize for excellence in uncertainty rsch., 2000, award, Internat. Conf. on Computing Anticipatory Sys., 2001, CASYS award for outstanding work on anticipatory and intelligent sys.; fellow rsch., IBM, 1969, Netherlands Inst. Advanced Studies, 1975—76, 1982—83, Japan Soc. for Promotion of Sci., 1980. Fellow IEEE (life), Internat. Fuzzy Systems Assn(pres. 1993-95); mem. AAAS, Internat. Soc. Sys. Scis. (mng. dir., v.p. 1978-80, pres. 1980-81, disting. leadership award 1994), Internat. Fedn. Sys. Rsch. (pres. 1980-84), N.Am. Fuzzy Info. Processing Soc. (pres. 1988-91). Home: 401 Manchester Rd Vestal NY 13850-3606 Office: SUNY/Dept Sys Sci/Indsl Eng Thomas J Watson Sch Engring and Applied Sci Binghamton NY 13902-6000 E-mail: gklir@binghamton.edu.

KLITZMAN, BRUCE, physiologist, plastic surgery educator, researcher; b. Dayton, Ohio, Nov. 4, 1951; m. Hardee Burt Brown; children: Rachel Hardee, Page Hardee. BS in Biomed. Engring. cum laude, Duke U., 1974; PhD, U. Va., 1979. Rsch. assoc. physiology U. Ariz. Coll. Medicine, Tucson, 1979-81; asst. prof. physiology, biophysics La. State U. Sch. Medicine, Shreveport, 1981-85; assoc. prof., 1985; sr. dir. Kenan plastic surgery rsch. labs., asst. rsch. prof. surgery and biomed. engring., assoc. prof. cell biology and biochem. engring. Duke U. Med. Ctr., Durham, NC, 1985—. Adj. prof. biomed. engring. La. Tech. U., Ruston, 1982-86; session chmn. Third, Fourth and Fifth World Congresses for Microcirculation, 1984, 87, 91; speaker, lectr. various symposia and seminars. Contbr. articles to profl. jours., chpts. to books; assoc. editor Jour. Reconstructive Microsurgery; editl. bd. Cell Transplantation, Am. Jour. Physiology, Jour. Reconstructive Microsurgery, Microvascular Rsch., Microcirculation. Recipient Instl. Nat. Rsch. Svc. award NIH, 1974-81, Machiko-Kuno Med. Student Rsch. award, U. N.C. at Chapel Hill, 1992, first prize investigator category, Plastic Surgery Ednl. Found., 1988; fellow U. Va., 1979, NATO, 1980; grantee Am. Heart Assn., 1982-85, NIH, 1985—. Mem. Am. Physiol. Soc., Am. Heart Assn. (circulation coun. 1984, grantee 1982-85, rsch. com. La. chpt. 1985), Am. Soc. Reconstructive Microsurgery (chmn. sci. session), Microcirculatory Soc. (sec. 1993-97, program com. 1983-84, mem. com. 1984-87, pres. 1998-99), Soc. Biomaterials, Plastic Surgery Rsch. Coun. (sci. adv. bd. 1998), European Soc. Microcirculation (travel award 1980), Internat. Soc. Oxygen Transport to Tissue, Controlled Release Soc.. Home: 3015 Wade Rd Durham NC 27705-5630 Office: Duke U Med Ctr Plastic Surgery Rsch Lab PO Box 3906 Durham NC 27710-0001 E-mail: Klitz@duke.edu.

KLOC, EMILY ALVINA, retired elementary school principal; b. Chgo., Apr. 8, 1933; d. Francis Joseph and Emily Mary (Gucwa) K. BMus, Mundelein Coll., Chgo., 1954; MEd, Loyola U., Chgo., 1960. Grade 2 tchr. Our Lady Help of Christians, Chgo., 1954-58; grades 5, 6, 7, 8 tchr. St. Mary of the Angels, Chgo., 1958-87, prin., 1987-95; ret., 1995. Mem. Near N.W. Orgn., Chgo., 1988—. Summer grantee U. Ill. NDEA Inst., Chgo., 1968; recipient Excellence in Mgmt. award Office Cath. Edn., Chgo., 1991, Tchr. Achievement award St. Mary of Angels Sch., Big Shoulders Fund, Chgo., 1992. Mem. ASCD, Nat. Cath. Educators Assn., Archdiocesan Prins. Assn. (chmn. coun. III-5A 1991-95). Roman Catholic. Avocations: reading, walking, classical music record collecting. Home: 1721 N Wood St Chicago IL 60622-1357 Office: St Mary of the Angels 1810 N Hermitage Ave Chicago IL 60622-1101

KLOMPMAKER, JAY EDWARD, business administration educator; b. Harvey, Ill., Feb. 15, 1941; s. Edward and Helen Joanne (Triemstra) K.; m. Mary Ann Hatfield, Sept. 7, 1963; children: Elizabeth Ann, Susan Mary, Caroline Jayne. BS in Metall. Engring., Ill Inst. Tech., 1963; MBA, U. Chgo., 1967; PhD, U. Mich., 1973. Sales engr. Midwestern divsn. Wyman-Gordon Co., Harvey, 1963-68; sales engr. Dynatech Corp., Cambridge, Mass., 1968-69; rsch. asst. grad. sch. bus. adminstrn. U. Mich., 1969-72; lectr. in bus. adminstrn. U. N.C., Chapel Hill, 1972-73, asst. prof. bus. adminstrn., 1973-78, assoc. prof. bus. adminstrn., 1978-83, prof. bus. adminstrn., 1983—, assoc. dean for devel. and corp. rels., 1984-86, dir. Ctr. for Internat. Mktg., 1986-89, dir. exec. program, 1989-90. Mem. undergraduate policy com. U. N.C., 1974-76, agenda com., 1974-76, continuing edn. com., 1976-77, steering com. student activities ctr. bldg. fund campaign, 1980, MBA admissions com., 1980-83, MBA Moregead selection com., 1980-90, MBA exec.-in-residence com., 1981-91, univ. licensing adv. com. 1982—, MBA program com., 1983-86, computer policy com., 1984-86, exec. com., 1984-86, univ. self study task group I., 1984-85, dean's adv. com., 1988-91, chancellor's adv. com. for greek affairs, 1991—, Kenan-Flagler Bus. Sch. adv. bd., 1991—, exec. edn. adv. com., 1992—, past mem. evaluation com. bus. program King's Coll.; gen. coll. advisor, 1973-77; dir. Young Execs. Inst., 1977-83, Exec. Program, 1990; faculty adv. Clef Hangers, 1979—, Undergraduate Honor Ct., 1979—, Kappa Delta, 1989—; faculty sponsor Interdisciplinary Studies Program, 1979—; exec. com. Sports Mgmt. Inst., 1989—; exec. dir. Bus. Found. N.C. Inc., 1984-86; chmn. acad. affairs State Employees Combined Campaign, 1988, 91; bd. dirs. Harriet and Henderson Yarns, Inc., Scott, Madden and Assocs., L. P. Thebault Co.; faculty assoc. Gemini Consulting, Cambridge, Mass., Scott, Madden and Assocs., Raleigh, N.C., Hamilton Cons., Cambridge, Loch Consulting, Atlanta. Author: (with David L. Kurtz and H. Robert Dodge) Professional Selling, 5th edit., 1988, Instructor's Manual to Accompany Professional Selling, 5th edit., 1988; mem. editorial bd. Mktg. Mgmt. Review; ad hoc reviewer Jour. Mktg. Rsch., Jour. Ops. Mgmt., Indsl. Mktg. Mgmt.; joint editori spl. issue Jour. Ops. Mgmt., 1991; contbr. articles, reports and reivews to profl. jours. Ruling elder Univ. Presbyn. Ch., 1967-83; area coord. acad. affairs divsn. United Fund Chapel Hill-Carrboro, 1979; mgr. campus fin. campaign Bill Cobey for Lt. Gov., 1980; bd. dirs., exec. and finance coms. YMCA, 1983. Mem. Am. Mktg. Assn. (judge doctoral dissertation competition 1981, 82, chmn. ad hoc conf. com. triangle chpt. 1982, reviewer paper competition 1982), Inst. for Rsch. in Social Sci., Chapel Hill Country Club (bd. dirs. 1983-85), Phi Eta Sigma, Tau Beta Phi, Honor I. Republican. Avocations: golf, music, travel. Home: 705 Pinehurst Dr Chapel Hill NC 27517-6530 Office: U NC Kenan-Flagler Sch Bus PO Box 3490 Chapel Hill NC 27515-3490

KLOPPER, STEPHANIE RUDOLPH, secondary education educator; b. Long Beach, Calif., Nov. 14, 1950; d. Dewey and E. Julie (Tunnell) Rudolph; m. Harold G. Klopper, June 15, 1986; children: Danny, Courtney. BA, UCLA, 1972; student, Calif. State U., Long Beach, 1973; MA in Edn., U. Phoenix, 1989. Cert. tchr. secondary social studies and drama, jr. coll. history, cinema, humanities and comm., Calif., Ariz. Tchr. L.A. Unified Schs., 1973-86; tchr., desegregation specialist Phoenix Union H.S. Dist., 1986—; instr. Rio Salado C.C. Maricopa C.C. Dist., Maricopa County, Ariz., 1992—; chair social studies dept. Central H.S., Phoenix, 1998—. Mem. sch. site coun. B.T. Washington Elem. Sch., Mesa, Ariz., 1994-2002; mem. site coun. Rhodes Jr. H.S., 2002—; mem. Ariz. State Task Force on Social Studies Curriculum, 2003—; spkr. at confs. Precinct committeeperson Dem. party, Mesa, 1994-98. Mem. ASCD, Classroom Tchrs. Assn. (mem. coun. of reps. 1992-94), Nat. coun. Social Studies, Ariz. Coun. Social Studies, Phi Delta Kappa. Home: 2528 W Madero Ave Mesa AZ 85202-6904

KLOSINSKI, DEANNA DUPREE, medical educator, consultant; b. Goshen, Ind., Dec. 28, 1941; d. George C. and Gertrude (Todd) Dupree; m. William L. Collins, Jan. 2000; children from previous marriage: Elizabeth, John, Robert, Lara. BS, Ind. State U., 1964; MS, Purdue U., 1972; PhD, Wayne State U., 1990. Cert. med. technologist. Lab. specialist Home Hosp., Lafayette, Ind., 1968-74; program dir. Ind. Vocat. Tech. Coll., Lafayette, 1968-75; clin. asst. prof. Oakland U., Rochester, Mich., 1985-97; med. technologist South Bend (Ind.) Med. Found., 1959-68; cons. Delta Initiatives, Bloomfield Hills, Mich., 1999—. Program dir., asst. adminstr. William Beaumont Hosp., Royal Oak, Mich., 1979—96, chair adv. com. Schs. Allied Health, 1990—92, 1996; adj. assoc. prof. Mich. State U., East Lansing, 1991—96, 2000—; asst. prof. Sch. Medicine Wayne State U., Detroit, 1996—98, adj. asst. prof. Coll. Pharmacy and Allied Health, 1999—2000; cons., dir. benchmarking svcs. Chi Lab. Sys., Ann Arbor, Mich., 1998; adj. online instr. Baker Coll., Owosso, Mich., 2001—; cons. in field. Co-author: (videotape) Routine Venipunture, 1989, (book) Molecular Biology and Pathology, 1993, Clinical Laboratory Science Education and Management, 1997; author: (videotape) Blood Collection: The Difficult Draw, 1992; contbg. editor: (book) Outline Review of Clinical Laboratory Science, 2001. Website chair Women's Com. for Hospice Care, 2003—; mem. pastoral coun. St. Hugo Cath. Ch., Bloomfield Hills, 1991—94. Named Outstanding Bus. Person, Mich. Coun. Vocat., 1992, Mich. Clin. Lab. Scientist, 1993; recipient Donna M. Duberg Mentorship award, Mich., 1997; Rsch. grantee, William Beaumont Hosp., 1989—90. Mem.: Wayne

State U. Alumni Assn. (leadership devel. com. 2001—03, dir., v.p. comm. 2003—, cmty. rels. com. 2001—03), Mich. Soc. Clin. Lab. Sci. (treas. 1984—86, 1988—92, pres. 1995—96, past pres. 1996—97, ann. meeting gen. chair 1996—97), Internat. Fedn. Clin. Chemistry (edn. and mgmt. divsn. com. programs and courses 1996—98), Assn. Women in Sci., Am. Soc. Clin. Lab. Sci. (mem. edn. sci. assembly, co-chairperson clin. lab. edn. conf. 1991, bd. dirs. edn. and rsch. fund 1996—98), Am. Assn. Clin. Chemistry (mem. mgmt. edn. group 1995—98, mgmt. scis. divsn. com. 1997, faculty, mgmt. course com. 1997), Am. Soc. Clin. Pathologists (chmn. tech. sample 1984—93, editor Profl. Perspectives 1993—94, mem. editl. bd. Lab. Medicine 1993—96, Technologist of the Yr. 1994, diplomate in lab. mgmt.), Sigma Xi (sec. Oakland U. chpt. 1994—96), Delta Gamma Regional (4), Delta Gamma Alumnae (treas. 1978—81, v.p. 1991—93, pres. 1993—95, Region IV housing dir. 2003—, women's com. for hospice care, website chair 2003—), Alpha Mu Tau (scholar 1985, 1987, 1990). Office: Delta Initiatives 715 Brockmoor Ln Bloomfield Hills MI 48304-1416 E-mail: ddkdeltai@aol.com.

KLOSKOWSKI, VINCENT JOHN, JR., educational consultant, writer, educator; b. Sept. 30, 1934; s. Vincent and Mary Kloskowski; m. Gerri K.; 1 child, Vincent John III. B.S. with honors, Seton Hall U., N.J., 1960, M.A., 1971; postgrad. Newark State Coll., 1960-62, Trenton (N.J.) State Coll., 1961-64; M.Ed. (Asian Found. scholar), Rutgers U., 1964; Ph.D., Philathea Coll., Western Ont., 1971; postdoctorate Harvard U., 1975, Appalachian State U., 1975; Ed.D. in Ednl. Adminstrn., Nova S.E. U., Fla., 1976. Substitute tchr. South River (N.J.) High Sch., 1958-60; tchr. Madison Twp. (N.J.) Pub. Schs., 1960-64; co-adj. mem. staff Rutgers U., 1961-64; remedial specialist North Brunswick (N.J.) Public Schs., 1964-65; vice prin. Jamesburg (N.J.) High Sch., 1965-66; asst. supt., child study coord., curriculum coord., fed. coord. urban funding Pub. Schs. Jamesburg, 1966-77, prin. elem., jr. high sch. and spl. edn. bldg., 1966-77; ednl. specialist N.J. Dept. Edn., 1977-91; cons. to para-profls. Mercer County Community Coll., Trenton, 1972; pvt. practice ednl. counseling, 1973—; speaker ann. conf. on incoming students Seton Hall U., Jamesburg Pub. Schs. In-Service Program, Middlesex County Child Study Team, PTA Jamesburg Pub. Schs., 1970, 72, Middlesex County Curriculum Council, East Brunswick Vocat. Sch., Holy Innocence Soc., Avenel, N.J., St. Catherines PTA, Clayton, N.J.; panelist child study devel. Madison Twp. Pub. Schs.; participant Internat. Reading Assn., Somerville, N.J., 42d Summer Sch. Conf. Sch. Adminstrn., Harvard U., Scott Foresman New Programs in Reading, Freehold, N.J., Ann. Reading Inst., Rutgers U., McGraw-Hill-Sullivan Reading Program, Hightstown, N.J., use of para-profls. in pub. schs. N.J. State Dept.-Middlesex County Community Coll., Edison; cons. Setting Up Pvt. Spl. Edn. Facility, South Brunswick, Ednl. Cons. Service N.J., 1971—, reading techniques for para-profl. Mercer County Community Coll., Trenton, 1971; merit badge counselor Boy Scouts Am.; mem. alumni resource bank counsel, mem. staff and adv. bd. transition program Rutgers U. Coll. Kettering Found. fellow. Mem. MENSA, Acad. Fellows (speaker nat. confs.), Am. Assn. Sch. Adminstrs., N.J. Assn. Sch. Prins., NEA (life), N.J., Middlesex County, Jamesburg edn. assns., Nat. Ednl. Assn. Sch. Prins., N.J. Classroom Tchrs. Assn., N.J. Assn. Retarded Children, Internat., N.J. reading assns., Middlesex County Audio-Visual Assn., Am. Soc. Notaries, Phi Delta Kappa, Alpha Epsilon Mu, Kappa Delta Pi. Author: Didacticism-Montessori and the Special Child, 1969; Amish School System and Special Education; asst. editor Seton Hall U. Newspaper and Coll. Yearbook, 1959-60; book reviewer Narod Polski, nat. Polish-Am. newspaper, 1976— . Home and Office: Hart Brook Farm PO Box 194 Hampshire Rd Brownfield ME 04010-0194

KLOTZ, LEORA NYLEE, retired music educator, vocalist; b. Canton, Ohio, Oct. 17, 1928; d. Clarence Karl and Nellie (Jacoby) Dretke; m. Kenneth Gordon Klotz, June 29, 1963. BMus and B.Pub. Sch. Music, Mount Union Coll., Alliance, Ohio, 1950; MA, Western Res. U., Cleve., 1954. Cert. vocal music tchr. Ohio. Elem. music supr. Canton City Schs., Ohio, 1950—60, h.s. vocal dir., 1955—60; elem. music tchr. Louisville City Schs., Ohio, 1960—71, h.s. vocal dir., 1960—81; adult choir dir. Perry Christian Ch., Canton, 1959—87; ret., 1987; mem. young artists competition com. Canton Symphony Orch. Bd., 1981—89; dir. Trirosis choir. Soprano soloist The Messiah Canton Symphony Orch., 1954—55; soprano soloist First Christian Ch., 1946—65, North Canton Cmty. Christian Ch., numerous vocal (solo) appearances N.E. Ohio. Composer choral octavos. Soprano soloist Rep. Civic Celebration, Canton, Ohio, 1950—60. Recipient Outstanding Young Ohio Composer, Ohioana Libr. Assn., 1959. Mem.: Mount Union Women, Canton Symphony League, Am. Guild Organists, ASCAP, Ohio Ret. Tchrs. Assn., Am. Choral Dirs. Assn. (life), Stark County Ret. Tchrs. Assn. (life), MacDowell Chorale (hon.), Canton Woman's Club, MacDowell Music Club (hon.), Order Ea. Star, PEO Sisterhood, Mu Phi Epsilon, Delta Kappa Gamma. Republican. Avocations: collecting Hummel figurines, reading, cooking. Home: 5036 Parkhaven Ave NE Canton OH 44705

KLOTZ, LOUIS HERMAN, structural engineer, educator, consultant; b. Elizabeth, N.J., May 21, 1928; s. Herman Martin and Edna Theresa (Kloepfer) K.; m. Virginia Helen Roll, Apr. 3, 1966 (dec. Oct. 1995); Emily Louise, Jennifer-Claire Virginia. BSCE, Pa. State U., 1951; MCE, N.Y.U., 1956; PhD, Rutgers U., 1967. Registered profl. engr., N.J., N.H. Structural engr. various firms, N.Y., N.J. metro area, N.Y., N.J., 1951-65; asst. prof. civil engring. U. N.H., Durham, 1965-69, assoc. prof. civil engring., 1969-86, chmn. dept. civil engring., 1971-74; spl. projects dir. ASCE, N.Y.C., 1986-87; cons. Klotz Assocs., Inc., New Castle, N.H., 1987-88; project mgr. Universal Engring. Corp., Boston, 1988-91; exec. dir. New Eng. States Earthquake Consortium, 1991-94; pres. Klotz Consultants Group, Inc., New Castle, N.H., 1994—; reservist FEMA, 1999—2002. Cons., evaluator Office of Energy Related Inventions, Gaithersburg, Md., 1978—; mem. energy policy adv. group N.H. Ho. of Reps., Concord, 1979-82; founding mem. N.H. Legis. Acad. Sci. & Tech., Concord, 1980-83. Editor: Energy Sources, The Promises and Problems, 1980; author: Users Manual Small Hydroelectric Financial/Economic Analysis, 1983; (monograph) Water Power, Its Promises and Problems; contbr. articles to Procs. of 1st Internat. Conf. on Computing in Civil Engring., Hydro Rev. Advisor Environ. Protection div. N.H. State Atty. Gen.'s Office, Concord, 1972-76; mem. New Castle (N.H.) Budget Com., 1977-79; tech. reviewer N.E. Appropriate Tech. Small Grants program Dept. Energy, Boston, 1979-80; bd. dirs. Family Svcs. Assn. Portsmouth, 1995-98, Seacoast Hospice, 1996-98. Ford Found. fellow, 1962-65, Ford Found. grant, 1968, Systems Design fellow, NASA, Assn. for Engring. Edn., Houston, 1975; named Gen. Acctg. Office Faculty Fellow, U.S. Gen. Acctg. Office, Washington, 1975-76. Mem. AAAS, ASCE (com. on coordination outside ASCE 1978-86), Am. Assn. Engring. Edn., N.Y. Acad. Scis. Republican. Episcopalian. Home: 90 Mainmast Cir New Castle NH 03854 Office: Klotz Consultants Group Inc PO Box 204 New Castle NH 03854-0204 E-mail: lhk@comcast.net.

KLUCKING, GAIL MARIE, education educator; b. Trenton, NJ, Feb. 17, 1958; d. Laurence Patrick and Christina Thelma Minnick; m. Tony Vaughn Klucking, June 5, 1987; 1 child, Sara. BA, Mo. Bapt. Coll., 1984; MPA, Troy State U., 1991; MPhil, U. Oxford, England, 1993; PhD, Auburn U., 1999. Instr. English Kubaski H.S., Okinawa, Japan, 1987-89; founding dir., com. mem. Taylor Rd. Kindergarten, Montgomery, Ala., 1988-98. Adj. instr. Auburn U., Montgomery, 1993—; field rep. European Region Troy State U., Upper Heyford, England, 1990-91; adv. 21st century adminstr. evaluatin program task force State of Ala., Dept. Edn., Taylor Rd. Edn. Adhoc Com., Montgomery. Sunday sch. tchr. O'Fallon (Ill.) Bapt. Ch., 1980-85, Taylor Rd. Bapt. Ch., 1994-2002; coach Spl. Olympics, Seattle, 1987; pres. Student Govt. Assn., Mo. Bapt. Coll., 1984. With USAF, 1985-87. Mem.: Am. Soc. Pub. Adminstrn., Phi Kappa Phi, Phi Sigma Alpha. Republican. Avocations: fitness training, reading.

KLUGE, CHERYLE DARLENE JOBE, secondary education educator; b. Atlanta; d. Lonnie Dewitt and Gracie Beatrice (Shelton) Jobe. BS, Calif. State Poly. Coll.; MEd, U. Houston. Cert. secondary English and Spanish tchr. Tchr. Ascension Parish Sch. Dist., Donaldsonville, La., Spring Br. Ind. Sch. Dist., Houston, Cypress-Fairbanks Ind. Sch. Dist., Houston. Tchr. Chinese Culture Ctr., Houston. Mem. Nat. Assn. for Gifted Children, Tex. Assn. Gifted and Talented, Golden Key Nat. Honor Soc. Avocations: gardening, reading, painting, autography.

KLUGE, LEN H. director, actor, theater educator; b. Lakeview, Mich., Oct. 28, 1945; s. Leonard H. and Edna Alvena (Paris) Kluge; m. Heather Lenartson, 2002. Diploma, Am. Acad. Dramatic Arts, 1967; student, Actors Studio, N.Y.C., 1968-69; BFA, Cen. Mich. U., 1977, MA in Counseling, 1978. Actor various mediums, N.Y., Calif., 1967-75; therapist Ionia County Mental Health Dept., Mich., 1978-79; exec. dir. Nat. Coun. on Alcoholism, Lansing, Mich., 1979-81; artistic dir. Spotlight Theatre, Grand Ledge, Mich., 1982—; prof. theater Spring Arbor Coll., 1993-95. Dir. The Actors Workshop and Ensemble Acting Co., Lansing, 1986—. Appeared in: (soap opera) Another World, 1968-69, (off-Broadway play) Man with the Flower in His Mouth, 1969, (film) Rennaisance Man, 1994, spl. performance as Clarence Darrow for Do the Right Thing program, Punta Gorda, Fla., 1996, 97, 98; performed for Boarshead Pub. Theatre, 1997-2001. Mem. Ctr. for the Arts, Lansing; bd. dirs. Child Abuse Prevention Svcs., 1993—; spl. Recipient Obie award, 1969, Thespie X award Lansing State Jour., 1982, 84, 86-90, 2001, Decade of Excellence award for body of work, 1993, Barney award Okemos Barn Theatre, Lansing, 1984, Riverwalk Theater, 91, 95, 96, 99, Star X award Spotlight Theatre, 1984-97. Lutheran. Avocations: baseball, writing, teaching, lecturing, travel, cigars. Home: 1937 Byrnes Rd Lansing MI 48906-3402 E-mail: wilieloman@aol.com.

KLUGE, STEVE, secondary education educator; Sci. tchr. Foxlane High Sch., Bedford, N.Y., 1987—. Project coord. Morgenthau Nature Conservancy. Developed AP course in physical geology. Recipient Outstanding Earth Sci. Tchr. award, 1992. Office: Fox Lane High Sch PO Box 390 Rte 172 Bedford NY 10506

KLUKA, DARLENE ANN, human performance educator, researcher; b. Berwyn, Ill., Oct. 6, 1950; d. Aloysius Louis and Lillian (Malkovsky) K. BA, Ill. State U., 1972, MA, 1976; PhD, Tex. Woman's U., 1985. Educator, coach Fenton High Sch., Bensenville, Ill., 1972-73, New Trier East High Sch., Winnetka, Ill., 1973-80; coach Bradley Univ., Peoria, Ill., 1980-82; grad. teaching asst. Tex. Woman's Univ., Denton, 1982-85; prof. Newberry (S.C.) Coll., 1985-86; prof., rschr., dir. Human Performance Ctr., Grambling (La.) State U., 1986-90; asst. prof. human studies and sport adminstrn. U. Ala., Birmingham, 1990-94, rschr., dir. Motor Behavior and Sports Vision Lab, 1990-94; dir. grad. program U. Ctrl. Okla., Edmond, 1994-97; prof., coord. kinesiology and sport studies Grambling (La.) State U., 1997—. Head of del. Internat. Olympic Acad., Olympia Greece, 1990; dep. del. U.S. Olympic Com., 1996-2000; adv. bd. Women's Sports Found., 1992—; U.S.A. Volleyball Sports Medicine and Performance Commn., 1994—; bd. dirs. U.S.A. Volleyball, v.p. rels. and human resources, 1996-2000. Author: Visual Skill Enhancement for Sport Exercises, 1989, Volleyball Drills, 1990, Volleyball, 4th edit., 2000, Motor Behavior: From Learning to Performance, 1999; founding co-editor Internat. Jour. Sports Vision, 1991-97; founding editor Internat. Jour. Volleyball Rsch., 1997—, mem. editl. bd., Coaching Volleyball Jour., 1988—. ICHPERSD dir. Girls and Women in Sport Commn., 1993—2001; mem. La. Gov.'s Coun. on Phys. Fitness and Sports, 2003—. Recipient Rsch. award So. Assn. Phys. Edn. Coll. Women, 1994, 96, USA Volleyball Leader award, 1998, Joseph Andera Rsch. award Internat. Acad. of SportsVision, 1999, Disting. Svc. award AAALF Internat. Rels. Coun., 1999, Disting. Achievements award Ill. State U. Alumni Assn., 1997; LAHPERD scholar, 1999-2000, Honor award 2002, So. Dist. Honor award 2003. Mem. AAHPERD (rsch. fellow, bd. govs. 1993-96, So. dist. scholar 2001. So. Dist. Honor award 2003), AAUP (Disting. scholar award 1997), Nat. Assn. for Girls and Women in Sport (bd. dirs., exec. com. 1989-92, 93-96, pres. 1990-91, Honor award 1996), Internat. Coun. for Sport Sci. and Phys. Edn. (exec. bd. 1997-02, treas. 2002—, editl. bd. 1998—), Internat. Acad. Sports Vision (adv. bd. 1989-98, v.p. 1993-01), Am. Volleyball Coaches Assn. (mem. editl. bd. Coaching Volleyball Jour., 1988-, bd. dirs. 2003—, chmn. edn. and publs. com. 2003—, Disting. Scholar in Sport award 1995, Excellence in Edn. award 1999, Kluka/Love Young Rsch. Award named in her honor 2001), Women's Sports Found. (internat. coun. 1993—, edn. & rsch. coun. 1995—, Pres.'s award 1996, Darlene A. Kluka rsch. award named in her honor 2001), Internat. Assn. Phys. Edn. and Sports for Girls and Women, Girls and Women in Sport (bd. cons. 2000—). Roman Catholic. Avocations: jogging, photography, collecting olympic games memorabilia, bicycling.

KLUMP, JANE F. HARRAD, elementary school educator; b. Little Falls, N.Y., Nov. 26, 1947; d. Cecil Charles and Florence Louise (Pierce) Harrad; m. James Reuben Smith, July 16, 1983 (dec. May 1998); m. Ronald A. Klump, June 29, 2002. AA, Dutchess C.C., Poughkeepsie, N.Y., 1967; BS, Oneonta State Coll., 1970. Cert. tchr. (permanent or life) nursery-6, 7-9 English, N.Y. 6th grade tchr. Dolgeville (N.Y.) Ctrl. Sch., 1970—. Cims math. coord. Dolgeville Ctrl. Sch., 1984—. Chmn. trustees Hoyer Hill Cemetery (historic landmark), 1983—. Mem. DAR (regent 1977-83, 1999-, registrar Henderson chpt. 1987-2000). Republican. Methodist. Avocations: antiques, stamp collecting, gardening. Home: PO Box 7 5922 Park Rd Van Hornesville NY 13475-0007 Office: Dolgeville Ctrl Sch Slawson St Extension Dolgeville NY 13329

KLUTH, HARRIET ANN HAMLET, elementary education educator; b. Cameron, Mo., Sept. 29, 1956; d. Albert Thomas Sr. and Evelyn Marie (Swords) Hamlet; m. Robert William Kluth, June 10, 1989. BS in Elem. Edn., Mo. Western State Coll., 1979; MS in Elem. Edn., Southwest Mo. State U., 1988, EdS, 1993. Cert. tchr., Mo. Elem. tchr., sixth grade Hamilton (Mo.) R-2, 1979-84, Neosho (Mo.) R-5, 1984-91, gifted edn. grades 6-8, 1991—; instr. in English Crowder Jr. Coll., Neosho, Mo., 1993—. Mem. Gifted Assn. Mo., NEA, Mo. Mid. Sch. Assn., ASCD, Nat. Assn. Supr. Secondary Sch. Prins., Delta Kappa Gamma. Roman Catholic. Avocations: aerobics, reading. Home: 514 W Hickory St Neosho MO 64850-1727 Office: Neosho R-5 Sch Dist 511 S Neosho Blvd Neosho MO 64850-2049

KLUTH, IRMA LEE, music educator; b. Chgo., July 18, 1942; d. Irwin Charles and Thelen L. Gerke; m. Gerald Buchner, Aug. 16, 1980 (dec. May 1985); m. John Robert Kluth, Aug. 26, 1995; children: Corinda S. Sherman, Paul Henry Sherman; m. Ralph Sherman (div. Sept. 1978). BA, Roosevelt U., 1964, M in Music Edcn., 1965. Music tchr. Rhodes Sch., River Grove, Ill., 1964—66, Richards Vocat. Sch., Chgo., 1966—67, Longfellow Middle Sch., LaCrosse, Wis., 1968—70, Virogua, Wis., 1971—89; piano tchr. LaCrosse, 1970—; music tchr. Coulee Region Christian Sch., West Salem, Wis., 1995—97. Singer, mem. worship team Evangelical Free Ch., La-Crosse. Recipient Nat. Roller Skate Dance Championship Gold Medal award, State of Wis., 1961. Mem.: LaCrosse Area Music Tchrs. Assn. (sec. 1994, treas. 1997, pres. 2001). Evangelical. Avocations: downhill skiing, horses, camping, gardening, travel. Home and Studio: N135 Christiansen Rd Coon Valley WI 54623

KMETZ, DONALD R. retired academic administrator; Dean Sch. Medicine U. Louisville, 1981-98; ret.; v.p. health affairs U. Louisville, 1992-98; ret. Office: U Louisville Sch Medicine Health Scis Ctr 323 E Chestnut St Louisville KY 40202-1823

KNABENSHUE, CATHERINE SUE, special education educator; b. South Bend, Ind., Oct. 19, 1953; d. Joseph Francis and Marjorie Ann (Steenbergen) Goepfrich; m. Kerry Lee Knabenshue, Oct. 4, 1975; children: Tara, Christopher, Rebecca. BS, Ind. U., 1976, MS, 1983. Tchr. Holy Family Sch., South Bend, 1977-79; preschool tchr. Sunshine Corner Nursery Sch., South Bend, 1982-84; tchr. Holy Cross, South Bend, 1984-86; first grade tchr. St. Mary of the Assumption, South Bend, 1986-87; jr. high tchr. St. Bavo, Mishawaka, Ind., 1987-89; second grade tchr. St. Matthew, South Bend, 1987-94, resource tchr. spl. svcs. and pub. rels., 1994—. Mem. Super Tchrs. Educating Pupils for Success (STEPS), 1996—; computer curriculum Ft. Wayne/South Bend Diocese, 1991-94, math curriculum selection com., 1997-98; pub. rels. dir. St. Matthew Sch., 1993—, math. textbook com., 1997-98; presenter in field, mem. various textbook coms.; team leader Intervention Team, St. Matthew, 1993—; mem. com. to develop sch. year, 1992-93. Vol. Right to Life, South Bend; CCD instr. Holy Family, 1977-79, St. Matthew, 1975-78. Recipient Cert. of Completion Profl. Edn. Resources, 1994. Mem. CHADD, Nat. Assn. Catholic. Sch. Tchrs. Roman Catholic. Avocations: ceramics, cooking, cross-stitch.

KNAPP, CHARLES BOYNTON, economist, educator, university president; b. Ames, Iowa, Aug. 13, 1946; s. Albert B. and Anne Marie (Taff) K.; m. Lynne Vickers, Aug. 25, 1967; 1 dau., Amanda. BS, Iowa State U., 1968; MA, PhD, U. Wis., 1972. Asst. prof. econs., research assoc. Ctr. for Study of Human Resources, U. Tex., Austin, 1972-76; spl. asst. to Sec. of Labor Dept. Labor, Washington, 1977-79, dep. asst. sec. labor, 1979-81; assoc. prof. pub. policy George Washington U., 1981-82; assoc. prof. econs. Tulane U., New Orleans, 1982-87, sr. v.p., 1982-85, exec. v.p., 1985-87; pres., prof. econs. U. Ga., Athens, 1987-97; pres. Aspen Inst., 1997-99; ptnr. Heidrick & Struggles Internat., Inc., Atlanta, 2000—. Bd. dirs. AFLAC Inc. Contbr. articles to profl. jours. Office: Heidrick & Struggles Internat Inc 303 Peachtree St NE Ste 3100 Atlanta GA 30308-3200

KNAPP, CHARLES LINCOLN, law educator; b. Zanesville, Ohio, Oct. 22, 1935; s. James Lincoln and Laura Alma (Richardson) K.; m. Beverley Earle Trott, Aug. 23, 1958 (dec. 1995); children: Jennifer Lynn, Liza Beth. BA, Denison U., 1956; JD, NYU, 1960. Bar: N.Y. 1961. Assoc. Paul, Weiss, Rifkind, Wharton & Garrison, N.Y.C., 1960-64; asst. prof. law NYU Law Sch., N.Y.C., 1964-67, assoc. prof., 1967-70, prof. law, 1970-88, Max E. Greenberg prof. contract law, 1988-98, Max E. Greenberg prof. emeritus contract law, 1998—, assoc. dean, 1977-82. Vis. prof. law U. Ariz. Law Sch., Tucson, 1973, Harvard U. Law Sch., Cambridge, Mass., 1974—75, Bklyn. Law Sch., 2003, Hastings Coll. Law, San Francisco, 1996—97, disting. prof. law, 1998—2000, Joseph W. Cotchett Disting. prof. law, 2000—. Author: Problems in Contract Law, 1976, (with N. Crystal and H. Prince) 5th edit., 2003; editor-in-chief: Commercial Damages, 1986. Mem. Am. Law Inst., Order Coif, Phi Beta Kappa. Office: Hastings Coll Law 200 McAllister St San Francisco CA 94102-4707 E-mail: knappch@uchastings.edu.

KNAPP, JANIS ANN, elementary school educator; b. Coffeyville, Kans., Nov. 15, 1949; d. Harry Clarence and Dorothy (Lehr) Herman; m. Stephen Foxall Knapp, Feb. 12, 1972; children: Marysa Monica, Stephen Weslee, Alexandria Annastasia, Janna Jacqualan. BE, U. Kans., 1971; MEd, Pittsburg State U., 1983, EdS, 1986. Cert. elem. tchr., Fla. Tchr. Overland Park (Kans.) Elem. Sch., 1971-72, Alamo Heights (Tex.) Jr. High Sch., 1972-73, Hoover Elem. Sch., Bartlesville, Okla., 1974, 79-80, Limestone Elem. Sch., Bartlesville, 1975-76, Whittier Elem. Sch., Coffeyville, 1980-83, Edgewood Elem. Sch., Coffeyville, 1983-85, J.C. Mitchell Community Sch., Boca Raton, Fla., 1985-88; math. specialist Palm Beach County Schs., Riviera Beach, Fla., 1988-90; tchr. Meadow Park Elem. Sch., Palm Beach, Fla., 1990-91, Conniston Mid. Sch., Palm Beach, 1991-93, Pine Grove Elem. Sch., Delray Beach, Fla., 1993-99, Calusa Elem. Sch., Boca Raton, Fla., 1999—. Vol. high sch. debate judge, Delray Beach, Fla., 1990; Heart Fund vol., Ft. Lauderdale, 1985-91; assoc. mem. Rep. Club, Boca Raton, 1990—. Mem. AAUW, Fla. Palm Beach County Classroom Tchrs. Assn., Phi Delta Kappa, Alpha Phi (former pres. alumni assn.). Roman Catholic. Avocations: reading, bicycling, walking, travel. Home: 18755 Cape Sable Dr Boca Raton FL 33498-6377 Office: Calusa Elem Sch Boca Raton FL 33446

KNAPP, LONNIE TROY, elementary education educator; b. Charles City, Iowa, Dec. 2, 1948; s. Troy Leroy and Anna Mildred (Conner) K.; m. Nancy Maureen Godfrey, Aug. 19, 1972; children: Eric Lonnie, Jamie Troy, Dusty Mack. BA, U. No. Iowa, 1972. Elem. tchr., Clear Lake, Iowa, 1972-92, Palm Springs (Calif.) Unified Sch. Dist., 1992—. Contbr. articles to profl. jours. Recipient Outstanding Tchr. award, Conservation Tchr. award, Iowa, North Cen. U.S. Mem. NEA, Iowa Edn. Assn., Calif. Tchrs. Assn., Clear Lake Edn. Assn. (various offices). Home: 42360 Minto Way Hemet CA 92544-9038

KNAPP, ROBERT STANLEY, English language educator; b. Alamosa, Colo., Mar. 29, 1940; s. Stanley Osgood and Pearl (Betts) K.; m. Christine Knodt, June 17, 1965. BA, U. Colo., 1962; MA, U. Denver, 1963; PhD, Cornell U., 1968. Instr. Princeton U., 1966-68, asst. prof., 1968-74; asst. prof. English Reed Coll., Portland, 1974-77, assoc. prof. English, 1977-83, prof. English, 1983—. Author: Shakespeare - the Theater and the Book, 1989; contbr. articles to profl. jours. NEH fellow, 1979-80. Mem. MLA, Shakespeare Assn. Am. Home: 3735 SE Woodstock Blvd Portland OR 97202-7537 Office: Reed Coll 3203 SE Woodstock Blvd Portland OR 97202-8138

KNAPP, VIRGINIA ESTELLA, retired secondary education educator; b. Washington, May 11, 1919; d. Bradford and Stella (White) Knapp; BA, Tex. Tech. U., 1940; MA, U. Tex. 1948; postgrad. Sul Ross Coll., 1950, Stephen F. Austin U., 1964-68. Tchr. journalism, high schs., Silverton, Tex., 1940-41, Electra, Tex., 1941-42, Joinerville, Tex., 1942-60, Carthage, Tex., 1961-69; tchr. history and journalism Longview (Tex.) High Sch., 1969-80; instr. Trinity U., San Antonio, summer 1972; fellowship tchr. Wall St. Jour., Tex. A&M U., College Station, summers 1964-67. Chmn., Rusk County (Tex.) Hist. Commn., 1980—2002; pres. Rusk County Hist. Found.; mem. Henderson Main St. Bd. Recipient Wall St. Jour. award Outstanding Journalism Tchrs. of Yr., 1965-66; Trail Blazer award Tex. High Sch. Press Assn., 1980; Woman of Yr. award, 1983. Mem. Tex. State Tchrs. Assn., Classroom Tchrs. Assn., Tex. Assn. Jour. Dirs., Rusk County Heritage Assn., Rusk County Hist. Commn., Women in Communications (pres. Longview chpt. 1972-74, Service award 1975), Tex. Press Women, bd-.member Gaston Mus. (finance chmn.) . Episcopalian. Contbr. hist. writing to Ala. Rev., Progressive Farmer, Rusk County C. of C. Brochure, Rusk County Heritage, numerous others. Home: 1802 Elm St Apt 301 Henderson TX 75652-6256 Office: 514 N High St Henderson TX 75652-5912

KNAPP-PHILO, JOANNE, school system administrator; b. Charleston, W.Va., Aug. 12, 1947; d. Denver H. and Theresa (Griffin) Knapp; m. John S. Philo, June 27, 1970; 1 child, Evan. BA in Elem. Edn., Mt. St. Agnes Coll., 1969; MA in Spl. Edn., Calif. State U., San Francisco, 1971; diploma in adminstrn. of spl. edn., U. Conn., 1983, PhD in Spl. Edn., 2001. Tchr. Hughson Union Sch. Dist., Hughson, Calif., 1969-70, Joseph McKinnon Sch., San Jose, Calif., 1971-73; instr. U. Calif., Santa Cruz, 1974; program mgr./tchr. Fremont (Calif.) Unified Sch. Dist., 1975-77; instr. early childhood studies dept. Ohlone Community Coll., Fremont, 1977-78; co-tchr., dir. presch. diagnostic and devel. skills class. Alum Rock Union Sch. Dist., San Jose, 1978; ednl. program supr. Unifed Sch. Dist. 3, Seaside Regional Ctr., Waterford, Conn., 1978-84; clin. faculty mem. Conn. Infant-Toddler Devel. Assessment Project, New Haven, 1989—; ednl. program supr. Unified Sch. Dist. 3, Region 3 Dept. Mental Retardation, Willimantic, Conn., 1984-92; program specialist Ventura County Superintendent Schs., Calif., 1992-96, prin., 1996; 1998infant/toddler specialist Head Start Resource Access Project Region IX, 1996; spl. quest dir. Hilton/EHS tng. program Calif. Instn. Human Svcs. Sonoma State U., 1998—. Instr. St.

Joseph's Coll., Hartford, Conn., 1991, Dept. Spl. Edn., Calif. No. U.; ednl. cons. early childhood spl. edn. Positive Behavior Support; core cons. SEEDS project Calif. Dept. Edn.; trainer Project CRAFT, Calif. State U., Northridge. Contbg. author Profiles of Women, Part 2, 1996. Rotary Internat. fellow, Birmingham, Eng., 1974-75. Mem. AAUW (co-chair women's history and pub. policy), Coun. for Exceptional Children (coun for adminstrn. spl. edn., divsn. cultural & linguistic diversity, exec. bd. Conn. divsn. early childhood), Nat. Assn. for Edn. Young Children, Soc. for Rsch. in Child Devel., Assn. Severely Handicapped. Office: # Sonoma 1 University Dr Camarillo CA 93012-8599

KNAUFF, HANS GEORG, physician, educator; b. July 8, 1927; arrived in Can., 1984; s. Friedrich and Sophie (Sauer) K.; m. Sigrid W. Keppner, Aug. 28, 1956; children: Ursula v. Wrangel, Barbara K. Student, U. Erlangen, 1947-49, U. Freiburg, 1949, U. Basel, 1949-51, U. Heidelberg, 1951-52, MD, 1953. Asst. pharmacology dept. Heidelberg U., 1953; with pharmacology dept. Univ. Coll., London, 1953, Royal Coll. Surgeons, London, 1954; with Pathol. Inst., Heidelberg U., 1955, Med. Clinic, U. Munich, 1955-63; privat dozent for internal medicine Munich and Marburg, 1967-83; prof. U. Marburg, 1967-83. Prof. internal medicine, Marburg. Contbr. articles to sci. jours. Lutheran. Mem. German Soc. for Internal Medicine. Home: 2155 Westhill Wynd West Vancouver BC Canada V7S 2Z3 E-mail: 1steinway@home.com.

KNAUST, CLARA DOSS, retired elementary school educator; b. Freistatt, Mo., Feb. 18, 1922; d. John Fredrick and Hedwig Louise (Brockschmidt) Doss; m. Donald Knaust, July 7, 1946 (dec.); children: Karen Louise, Ramona Elizabeth, Heidi Marie. BS in Edn., S.W. Mo. State U., 1969. Elem. tchr. Trinity Luth. Sch., Freistatt, 1942-46; tchr. kindergarten Trinity Luth Ch., Springfield, Mo., 1961-65, Redeemer Luth Ch., Springfield, 1962-63, 66-69, Springfield R-12 Sch. System, 1969-70, 73-84, elem. tchr., 1970-73; elem. and kindergarten tchr. Springfield Luth. Sch., 1984-88. Mem. planning bd. Early Childhood Conf., U. Mo., Columbia, 1977-80. Pres. Springfield Gen. Hosp. Guild, 1969-71; local and zone pres. Luth. Women's Missionary League, Springfield, 1986-94; historian Trinity Luth. Ch., 1985-94; chair bd. edn. Grace Luth. Ch., Tulsa. Mem. Assn. for Childhood Edn. Internat. (br. state pres. 1980-84, president's coun. 1983-85, Hall of Fame plaque 1988, state pres. 1989-93), Springfield Edn. Assn. (life), Springfield Luth. Sch. Assn. (pres. 1992-94), S.W. Dist. Kindergarten Assn. (pres. 1978-79), Alpha Delta Kappa. Avocations: painting, crafts, collecting, music. Home: Univ Club 1722 S Carson Ave Apt 1710 Tulsa OK 74119-4641

KNECHTGES, MARY KAY, retired coach; b. Elyria, Ohio, Jan. 4, 1945; d. Edwin Jospeh and Geneva Mae (Swan) K. BS, Bowling Green State U., 1967; postgrad., Wayne State U., 1968-70. Educator L'Anse Creuse H.S., Harrison Twp., Mich., 1967—2003, cheerleading coach, 1968-76, basketball coach, 1968-80, softball coach, 1976-78, basketball coach, 1990—, Bishop Gallagher H.S., Harper Woods, Mich., 1981-83; asst. basketball coach U. Mich., Dearborn, 1985-87. Contbr. articles to profl. jours. Mem. Clinton Twp. (Mich.) Youth Svc. Com., 1973-75. Named Coach of Yr., Macomb County Coaches, 1977, 78, 79, Mich. Coach of Yr., Detroit Free Press, 1978, Dist. 4 Coach of Yr., Nat. H.S. Coaches, 1981; nominated Sportswoman of Yr., United Found., 1981; named to Macomb County Coaches Hall of Fame, 1997. Mem. NEA, Nat. H.S. Athletic Assn. (state rep. 1980-83), Mich. High Sch. Athletic Assn. (ofcls. com. 1979, summer basketball com. 1981, volleyball ofcl. 1981-82, women in sports leadership com. 1994—), Mich. H.S. Basketball Coaches (regional chairperson 1980-82), Mich. H.S. Coaches Assn. (dist. rep. 1980-83), Mich. Edn. Assn., L'Anse Creuse Edn. Assn. Roman Catholic.

KNEE, RUTH IRELAN (MRS. JUNIOR K. KNEE), social worker, health care consultant; b. Sapulpa, Okla., Mar. 21, 1920; d. Oren M. and Daisy (Daubin) Irelan; m. Junior K. Knee, May 29, 1943 (dec. Oct. 1981). BA, U. Okla., 1941, cert. social work, 1942; MA in Social Svcs. Adminstrn., U. Chgo., 1945. Psychiat. social worker, asst. supr. Ill. Psychiat. Inst., U. Ill., Chgo., 1943-44; psychiat. social worker USPHS Employee Health Unite, Washington, 1944—49; social work assoc. Army Med. Ctr., Walter Reed Army Hosp., Washington, 1949-54; psychiat. social work cons.. HEW, Region III, Washington, 1955-56; with NIMH, Chevy Chase, Md., 1956-72; chief mental health care adminstrn. br. Health Svcs. and Mental Health Adminstrn., 1967-72, USPHS assoc. dep. adminstr., 1972-73; dep. dir. Office of Nursing Home Affairs, 1973-74; long-term mental health care cons.; mem. com. on mental health and illness of elderly HEW, 1976-77; mem. panel on legal and ethical issues Pres.'s Commn. on Mental Health, 1977-78; liaison mem. Nat. Adv. Mental Health Coun., 1977-81. Mem. editl. bd. Health and Social Work, 1979-81. Bd. dirs. Hillhaven Found., 1975-86, governing bd. Cathedral Coll. of the Laity, Washington Nat. Cathedral, 1988-94, Cathedral Fund Com., 1997—,bd. of visitors sch. of social work, Univ. of Okla., 2000— Recipient Edith Abbott award, U. Chgo. Sch. Social Svc. Adminstrn., 2001, Disting. Alumna award, U. Okla. Coll. Arts and Scis., 1999. Fellow APHA (sec. mental health sect. 1968-70, chmn. 1971-72), Am. Orthopsychiat. Assn. (life), Gerontol. Soc. Am., Am. Assn. Psychiat. Social Workers (pres. 1951-53); mem. Nat. Conf. Social Welfare (nat. bd. 1968-71, 2d v.p. 1973-74), Inst. Medicine/NAS (com. study future of pub. health 1986-87), Coun. on Social Work Edn., Nat. Assn. Social Workers (sec. 1955-56, nat. dir. 1956-57, 84-86, chmn. competence study com., practice and knowledge com. 1963-71, presdl. award for exemplary svc. 1999), Acad. Cert. Social Workers (NASW Found. co-chair social work pioneers 1993—), Am. Pub. Welfare Assn., DAR, U. Okla. Assocs., Woman's Nat. Dem. Club (mem. gov. bd. 1992-95, ednl. found. bd. 1992-2000), Cosmos Club (Washington, chair program com. 1998-2001), Phi Beta Kappa (fellow), Psi Chi. Address: 8809 Arlington Blvd Fairfax VA 22031-2705

KNEEDLER, RICHARD (ALVIN KNEEDLER), former academic administrator; b. Ruffsdale, Pa., Apr. 8, 1943; s. Alvin Raymond and Louise (Mac Innes) Kneedler; m. Suzette Gallagher, June 17, 1967; children: Eric, Rebecca. AB, Franklin and Marshall Coll., 1965; MA in French Lang. and Lit., U. Pa., 1967, PhD in French Lang. and Lit., 1970; cert. in Ednl. Mgmt., Harvard U., 1975; DHL (hon.), Tohoku Gakuin U., 1993. Instr. French Franklin and Marshall Coll., Lancaster, Pa., 1968—70, asst. prof. French, 1970—72, asst. to dean, 1971—74, asst. to pres., 1974—77, sec. coll., 1977—79, v.p. adminstrn., 1979—84, v.p. devel., 1984—88, sec. bd. trustees, 1974—88, pres., 1988—2002; cons. Coun. of Ind. Colleges, 2002—. Mem. exec. com. Assn. Ind. Colls. and Univs. Pa., 1989—98, 2000—, chmn., 1996—97; exec. com. Nat. Assn. Ind. Colls. and Univs., 1999, chair policy & pub. rels. com., 99, mem. coun. ind. coll. dir., 2000—. Mem. Lancaster City Planning Commn., 1980—85, chmn., 1983—85; v.p., bd. dirs. Hist. Preservation Trust, Lancaster, 1984—87; sec., bd. dirs. Pa. Sch. Arts, 1985—89; bd. dirs. St. Joseph Hosp., 1991—95, Lancaster Area Arts Coun., 1967—91, Louise Von Hess Found. for Med. Edn., 1990—, Urban League Lancaaster County, 1991—93, United Way, 1993—98, Urban Alliance, 1998—; chmn. Cmty. Cultural Planning Com., 1989—90; mem. Downtown Task Force, 1989—90; trustee Kiski Sch., 1988—95; chmn. exec. bd. Commonwealth Partnerships, 1997—98; mem. adv. bd. PRIME, Inc., 1991—98. Mem.: Am. Soc. 18th Century Studies, Am. Assn. Tchrs. French, Lancaster C. of C. and Industry (bd. dirs. 1990—92), Phi Alpha Theta, Phi Beta Kappa. Republican. Presbyterian. Home: 1416 Newton Rd Lancaster PA 17603-2461

KNEELAND, TIMOTHY WILLIAM, historian, researcher; b. Buffalo, N.Y., Nov. 25, 1962; s. Thomas Francis and Margaret Ann (Cronin) K.; m. Laura Grace Goodnough, July 30, 1988; children: Adam, Aaron, Benjamin, Anna. BA in History, SUNY, Buffalo, 1987, MA in History, 1989; MA in History of Sci., U. Okla., Norman, 1992, PhD in History, 1996. Instr. Okla. Jr. Coll., Oklahoma City, 1989-90, social and behavioral sci. chair, 1990-93; instr. Okla. State U., Oklahoma City, 1994-96; asst. prof. history Greenville Coll., Ill., 1996—2000, Nazareth Coll., Rochester, NY, 2000—. Adj. prof. So. Nazarene U., Bethany, Okla., 1993-96. Author: (Book) Pushbutton Psychiatry, 2002. Mem. Orgn. Am. Historians, So. Hist. Soc., History of Sci. Soc., Assn. Asian Studies. Presbyterian. Home: 93 Montaine Park Rochester NY 14617-1518 Office: Nazareth Coll 4245 East Ave Rochester NY 14618 E-mail: twkneela@naz.edu.

KNESTRICK, JANICE LEE, art educator; b. Ft. Belvoir, Va., Sept. 5, 1953; d. Bernard Paul and Mary (Ryan) Yurchik; m. Joseph Collins Knestrick, July 5, 1980; children: Mary Bridgette, Brittany Megan. BS in Art Edn., Radford (Va.) U., 1975; postgrad., U. Va., 1980, George Mason U., 1980. Tchr., fine arts chmn. Manassas Park (Va.) High Sch., 1976-91; tchr., art dept. chmn. Brentsville Dist. Mid.-Sr. High Sch., Nokesville, Va., 1991-92. Mem. vis. self-study com. Powhatan County High Sch., 1982; developer art program for elem. children Fairfax County Park Authority, Providence Recreation Ctr., 1982-83. Recipient Grants Wash. Post, 1989, Prince William County Pub. Schs. Edn. Found., 1991, Agnes Meyer Most Outstanding Tchr. award Wash. Post, 1990, Mem. NEA, Va. Art Edn. Assn. (No. Va. Oustanding Art Tchr. of Yr. 1991), Manassas Park Edn. Assn., Prince William Edn. Assn. Home: 3473 Country Walk Dr Port Orange FL 32129-3156 Office: Volusia County Schs South Daytona Elem Sch Elizabeth Ave Daytona Beach FL 32119

KNIERIEM, BEULAH WHITE, retired elementary school educator, minister; b. Appomattox, Va., Oct. 31, 1930; d. George Harrison and Virgie Ade (Kestner) White; m. Robert William Knieriem, July 11, 1953; children: Shawn, Roxanne (dec.), Roberta. AA, Mars Hill (N.C.) Coll., 1950; BA, Lynchburg (Va.) Coll., 1952; student, Baldwin-Wallace Coll., 1964-69, Ashland Sem., 1992-93. Lic. elem. tchr., Ohio; lic. to ministry, 1995. Tchr. Bd. Edn., Cleve., 1966-79; lifetime Stephen min. United Ch. of Christ, Cleve., 1990—; interim min., 1997—99; pastor Litchfield United Ch. of Christ, Ohio, 1999—. Min. nursing homes, Cleve., 1990—; chaplain Ky. Cols., 1990—. Democrat. Avocation: running. Home: 7324 Grant Blvd Cleveland OH 44130-5351

KNIERIM, WILLIS M. secondary school educator; b. Sept. 20, 1940; BA, U. Colo., 1963; MPA, U. Colo., Denver, 1971; postgrad., Northwestern U.; JD, Am. U., 1990; postgrad., Johns Hopkins U., U. Wyo. Tchr., curriculum coord. Boulder Valley Schs., 1963-96. Tchr., adminstr. Colegio Bolivar, Cali, Colombia, 1964-65; pres. Boulder Valley Edn. Assn., 1987-91; bd. dirs. Learning to Read; cons. democracy edn. Ea. Europe, NIS. Bd. dirs. United Way. Mem. Colo. Edn. Assn., C. of C. Home: 2290 Nicholl St Boulder CO 80304-2753 E-mail: knierim1@aol.com.

KNIESER, CATHERINE, music educator; b. Seoul, Republic of Korea, Aug. 12, 1974; d. Thomas and Susan Knieser. MusB, U. Del., 1997; MusM, Ithaca Coll., 2000. Cert. tchr. N.Y., Nat. Bd. Early Adolescent through Young Adulthood, 2003. Tchr.-in-charge, secondary music Wappingers Ctrl. Sch. Dist., Wappingers Falls, NY, 1999—. Grantee Latin Percussion Mini grant, Wappingers Ctrl. Sch. Dist., 1998—99, African Music Mini grant, Mid Hudson Tchr. Ctr., 1999—2000, Tech. Digital grant, Wappingers Ctrl. Sch. Dist., 2002—. Mem.: N.Y. State Sch. Music Assn., Music Educators Nat. Conf., Am. Orff-Schulwerk Assn., Sigma Alpha Iota (life). Personal E-mail: krabaple@vh.net.

KNIFFEN, DONALD AVERY, astrophysicist, educator, researcher; b. Kalamazoo, Apr. 27, 1933; s. Frederick Bowerman and Eva Virginia (Arp) Kniffen; m. Janis Kay Nesom, June 14, 1952; children: Karyol Kniffen Poole, Donald Avery Nesom Jr., Kimberly Kniffen Giesbrecht. BS magna cum laude, La. State U., 1959; AM, Washington U., St. Louis, 1960; PhD, Cath. U. Am., 1967. Astrophysicist Goddard Space Flight Ctr., Greenbelt, Md., 1960-91; lectr. physics U. Md., College Park, 1978-87; project scientist Compton Gamma Ray Obs., 1979-91; William W. Elliott prof., chmn. dept. physics and astronomy Hampden-Sydney Coll., Va., 1991-2001; rsch. prof. George Mason U., 2002—. Vis. scientist NASA/USRA, Greenbelt, 1997—98; astrophysics cons. NASA/HSTX, NASA/USRA, 1991—98; program scientist NASA Hdqrs., 1999—. Contbr. articles to profl. jours. Served with USN, 1952-56. Recipient Medal for Outstanding Leadership NASA, 1992, Laurel award Space/Missiles, Aviation Week & Space Tech., 1991. Fellow Royal Astron. Soc.; mem. AAUP, Am. Phys. Soc., Am. astron. Soc., Internat. Astron. Union, Sigma Xi. Democrat. Avocations: travel, reading, gardening. Home: 2814 Andy Ct Crofton MD 21114-3157 also: Code SE NASA Hdqs Office Space Scis Washington DC 20546-0001 Personal E-mail: donk@annapolis.net. E-mail: donald.a.kniffen@nasa.gov.

KNIGHT, ARTHUR WINFIELD, English educator; b. San Francisco, Dec. 29, 1937; s. Walter Arthur and Irja Blomquist K.; m. Glee Marquardt, Sept. 27, 1966 (dec. Oct. 1975); m. Kit Duell, Aug. 25, 1976; 1 child, Tiffany Carolyn. BA, San Francisco State U., 1960, MA, 1962. Tchr. English Anderson (Calif.) Union H.S., 1963-64; instr. journalism Riverside (Calif.) City Coll., 1964-65; instr. English Delta Coll., University Center, Mich., 1965-66; prof. English California U. Pa., 1966-93; film critic Anderson Valley Advertiser, Boonville, Calif., 1992—. Adj. prof. profl. studies U. San Francisco, 1995—2000; adj. prof. English Western Career Coll., 2001—02; co-entertainment editor Am. River Sentinel, 2003—. Author: All Together, Shift, 1972, Who Moved Among the Others as They Walked, 1974, The Secret Life of Jesse James, 1996, The Darkness Starts Up Where You Stand, 1996, The Cruelest Month, 1997, Johnnie D., 2000, Blue Skies Falling, 2001, The Erotic Life of Billy the Kid, 2003; contbr. articles to profl. jours.; author poems; author (plays): King of the Beatniks, 1985, 1988, 1993, Blue Earth, 1986, The Abused, 1986, Burning Daylight, 1987. Recipient 1st Pl. prize Joycean Lively Arts Guild, East Douglas, Mass., 1982. Mem. Western Writers Am. Avocation: photography. Office: PO Box 544 Citrus Heights CA 95611

KNIGHT, AUBREY KEVIN, vocational education educator; b. Oxford, Miss., May 2, 1947; s. Kenneth and Katherine (Bishop) K.; m. Bonnie Faye Cagle, Jan. 9, 1970; children: Aubrey Kenneth, Allen Keith. Grad., NRI Sch. Electronics, Washington, 1980; student, Itawamba C.C., Tupelo, Miss., 1987, Miss. State U., Starkville, 1988, 89, Northwest C.C., Oxford, Miss., 1988-89, 93-94. Owner and technician Yocona Electronics, Oxford, 1979-87; electronics instr. Oxford-Lafayette Bus. and Indsl. Complex, 1987-97; instr. info. tech. Millsaps Career & Tech. Ctr., Starkville, Miss., 1997—. Mem. Miss. Assn. Electronics Instrs. (pres. 1990-92), Miss. Trade and Tech. Assn. (2d v.p. 1991-92, 1st v.p. 1992-93, pres. 1993-94), Miss. Vocat. Indsl. Clubs of Am. (pres., Miss. bd. dirs. 1994-95), Miss. Assn. Vocat. Educators, Miss. Career & Tech. Educators Assn., Mississippians for Emergency Medicine, Miss. Emergency Med. Tech. Assn., Miss. Law Enforcement Officers Assn. Baptist. Avocations: gardening, computers. Office: Millsaps Career and Tech Ctr 803 Louisville Rd Starkville MS 39759-3798 E-mail: kevinknight457@hotmail.com.

KNIGHT, DIANE, special education educator; b. De Ridder, La., Dec. 2, 1955; BS, McNeese State U., 1976; MEd, Northwestern State U., Natchitoches, La., 1980, EdD, 1986. Cert. tchr., La., Ga. Tchr. English Vernon Parish Sch. Bd., Leesville, La., 1976-77; tchr. spl. edn. Natchitoches Parish Sch. Bd., La., 1978-80, ednl. diagnostician, 1985-88; tchr. spl. edn. Sabine Parish Sch. Bd., Many, La., 1983-85; dir. pupil appraisal Red River Parish Sch. Bd., Coushatta, La., 1988-89; asst. prof. Ga. Southwestern Coll., Americus, 1989-90, U. Southwestern La., Lafayette, 1990-95; assoc. prof. U. Ga., Athens, 1995-96; ednl. diagnostician Spl. Sch. Dist. 1, 1996—2002; assoc. prof. La. State U., Shreveport, 2002—03. Ednl. cons. and evaluator, Lafayette, 1990-95, Athens, Ga., 1995-96, Baton Rouge, 1996-2002, Shreveport, 2002—; presenter in field. Contbr. articles to profl. jours., chapters to books. Mem.: Coun. for Exceptional Children (learning disabilities divsn., tchr. edn. divsn., La. state sec., v.p., pres., past pres.), La. Assn. Evaluators, Am. Coll. Forensic Examiners, Rotary, Phi Delta Kappa, Kappa Delta Pi, Phi Kappa Phi. Republican. Mem. Unity Ch. Home: 9000 W Wilderness Way Apt 24 Shreveport LA 71106

KNIGHT, DOUGLAS MAITLAND, educational administrator, optical executive, writer; b. Cambridge, Mass., June 8, 1921; s. Claude Rupert and Fanny Sarah Douglas (Brown) K.; m. Grace Wallace Nichols, Oct. 31, 1942; children: Christopher, Douglas Maitland, Thomas, Stephen. AB, Yale U., 1942, MA, 1944, PhD, 1946; LLD (hon.), Ripon Coll., Knox Coll., Davidson Coll., 1963, U. N.C., 1965, Ctr. Coll., 1973, Ohio Wesleyan U., 1971; LHD (hon.), Lawrence U., 1964, Carleton Coll., 1966, Emory U., 1968; LittD (hon.), St. Norbert Coll., Wake Forest Coll., 1964. Instr. English, Yale U., 1946-47, asst. prof., 1947-53; vis. asst. prof. English, U. Calif., Berkeley, summer 1949; Morse rsch. fellow, 1951-52; pres. Lawrence U., Appleton, Wis., 1953-63, Duke U., Durham, N.C., 1963-69, pres. emeritus, 1992—; v.p. divsn. ednl. devel. RCA, N.Y.C., 1969-71, v.p. divsn. edn. svcs., 1971-72, staff v.p. edn. and community rels., 1972-73, cons., 1973-75; pres. RCA Iran, 1971-72, dir., 1971-73; pres. Social Econ. and Ednl. Devel., Inc., 1973-76, Questar Corp., 1976-99, chmn., 1999—2001, sr. cons. R & D, 2001—. Assoc. fellow Saybrook Coll., Yale U., 1954—; U.S. del. SEATO Conf. Asian U. Pres., Pakistan, 1961; mem. nat. commn. UNESCO, 1965-67; chmn. Nat. Adv. Commn. Librs., 1966-68; advisor Imperial Orgn. for Social Svc., Govt. of Iran; mem. Nat. Commn. Sci. and Engring. Manpower, 1959-61. Author: Pope and the Heroic Tradition, 1951, (poetry) The Dark Gate, 1971, Journeys in Time, 1993, Close Encounters, 2003; editor, contbr.: The Federal Government and Higher Education, 1960, Iliad and Odyssey, Twickenham edit., 1967, Medical Ventures and the University, 1967, Libraries at Large, Tradition, Innovation and the National Interest, 1970, Street of Dreams: The Nature and Legacy of the 1960's, 1989, Education and the Civil Order: A Memoir of the Woodrow Wilson National Fellowship Foundation, 1996, The Dancer and the Dance, One Man's Chronicle 1938-2001, 2003; co-inventor the Questar long-distance microscope, 1981; co-patentee the Questar stereo microscope, 2001. Trustee Edward W. Hazen Found., 1951-63; corp. mem. MIT, 1965-70; bd. dirs., chmn. Woodrow Wilson Nat. Fellowship Found., 1957-93, emeritus, 1993—; bd. dirs. CEEB, 1955-59, Catalyst, 1961-73, United Negro Coll. Fund, 1967-72, Near East Found., 1975-84, Internat. Schs. Svcs., 1976-82, Solebury Sch., 1975-83; program chmn. Salzburg Seminar, 1971, mem. adv. coun., 1997; founding trustee Questar Libr. Sci. and Art, 1982—, pres., 1996-99, 2002—; pres. Delaware River Mill Soc., 1992-97, emeritus, 1997. Mem. Am. Assn. Advancement of Humanities (bd. dirs. 1979-83), Grolier Club, Century Assn. (N.Y.C.), Cosmos Club (Washington), Elizabethan Club, Berzelius (New Haven), Phi Beta Kappa. Home: Heritage Towers #816 200 Veterans Ln Doylestown PA 18901 Office: Questar Corp 6204 Ingham Rd New Hope PA 18938-9663

KNIGHT, FRANKLIN W. history educator; b. Mile Gully, Manchester, Jamaica, Jan. 10, 1942; came to U.S., 1964; s. Willis Jefferson and Irick May (Sanderson) K.; m. Ingeborg Bauer, June 11, 1965; children: Michael, Brian, Nadine. BA with honors, U. West Indies, Jamaica, 1964; MA, U. Wis., 1965, PhD, 1969. From asst. to assoc. prof. SUNY, Stony Brook, 1968-73; assoc. prof. Johns Hopkins U., Balt., 1973-77, prof., 1977-91, Stulman prof. History, 1991—, dir. Latin Am. Studies Program, 1992-95; v.p. Latin Am. Studies Assn., 1997-98; pres., 1998-00. Author: Slave Society in Cuba, 1970 (Black Acad. award 1971), The Caribbean, 1990; co-editor: The Modern Caribbean, 1989, Atlantic Port Cities, 1991; editor: Caribbean Slave Societies, 1997. Active Md. Quincentenary Com., 1992. Named Disting. Grad. U. West Indies, Jamaica, 1992. Mem. The Hist. Soc., Latin Am. Studies Assn., Assn. Caribbean Historians. Office: Johns Hopkins U 3400 N Charles St Baltimore MD 21218-2680 E-mail: fknight@jhu.edu.

KNIGHT, IDA BROWN, retired elementary educator; b. Macon, Ga., Aug. 8, 1918; d. Morgan Cornelius and Ida (Moore) Brown; m. Dempsey Lewis Knight, Apr. 11, 1942; children: Lavera Knight Hughes, Eugene Charles. BS, Spelman Coll., 1940; MS, SUNY, Fredonia, 1958; postgrad., SUNY, 1974, U. Manchester, Eng., 1974. Cert. tchr. home econs. Clothing tchr. Bibb County Vocat. Sch., Macon, 1940-42; tchr. home econs. Ballard Normal Sch., Macon, 1943-45; elem. tchr. Jamestown (N.Y.) Pub. Schs., 1955-77; ret., 1977. Bd. dirs. Jamestown Girls Club, 1970-78, Jamestown Cmty. Schs., 1989-97; ch. organist, 1974-82; jr. bd. Elizabeth Marvin Cmty. House, 1994-2001, gov. bd. dirs., 1998-2000. Mem. AAUW, Chautauqua County Ret. Tchrs. Assn., N.Y. State Congress Parents and Tchrs. (hon. life), Links, Inc. (past pres. Jamestown chpt.), Delta Kappa Gamma (corr. sec. 1963-64). Avocations: flower gardening, hand crafts, playing piano, reading. Home: 5573 Place Dr South Bend IN 46614

KNIGHT, JANET ANN, elementary education educator; b. Covina, Calif., July 22, 1937; d. Arnold M. and Thelma (Lyle) Ostrum; m. Ronald L. Knight, Sept. 14, 1957; children: Barbara Lynne, Susan Kaye. BA in Edn., Cen. Wash. U., 1979; MA in Edn., Heritage Coll., 1992. Cert. elem, secondary tchr., Wash. 2nd grade tchr. Kennewick (Wash.) Pub. Schs., 1980-81, 1st grade tchr., 1981-85, 3rd grade tchr., 1985-93, 4th grade tchr., 1993—. Lang. arts dist. com. Kennewick Sch. Dist., 1985-89, curriculum, instrn. com., 1989-92, dist. curriculum and instruction renewal cycle for learning excellence, 1992-94, dist. assessment com., 1992-95. Mem. Richland (Wash.) Light Opera Co., 1963-75. Mem. NEA, ASCD, Wash. Edn. Assn., Kennewick Edn. Assn., Wash. Orgn. Reading Devel., Benton County Coun. of Internat. Reading Assn., Order of Rainbow for Girls, Sigma Tau Alpha. Episcopalian. Avocations: petit basset griffon vendeen show dogs, ceramics, golf, photography, reading. Home: 120 Heather Ln Richland WA 99352-9155 Office: Westgate Elem Sch 2514 W 4th Ave Kennewick WA 99336-3115

KNIGHT, MARGARET ELIZABETH, music educator; b. Biddulph, Staffordshire, Eng., July 3, 1938; came to U.S., 1972; d. William Bateman and Amy Elizabeth (Willshaw) Whitehurst; m. Richard Alan Scudder, Apr. 5, 1972 (div. Mar. 1979); m. Rev. Arthur James Knight, May 26, 1979. Grad., No. Sch. of Music, Manchester, Eng., 1959; Assoc. in Piano Teaching, Royal Coll. Music. Lic. in voice culture, aural tng., sch. music and psychology. Asst. to head dept. music Thistley Hough Sch., Stoke, Eng., 1959-65; head dept. music Macclesfield (Eng.) H.S., 1966-72; pvt. piano tchr. Shamong, N.J., 1972—. Adj. mem. faculty dept. music Crewe (Eng.) Tchrs. Coll., 1963-72; dir. student activities South Jersey Music Tchrs. Assn., 1986-88; N.J. state rep. for Assoc. Bd. Royal Schs. Music, London, 1993—, developmental cons., 1994—; presenter in field. Sec. Conservative Party, Congleton, Eng., 1968-71; active Town Coun., Congleton, 1971-72. County Music scholar Cheshire County Coun., Chester, Eng., 1955. Mem. Music Tchrs. Nat. Assn., Nat. Guild Piano Tchrs. (judge 1987—), N.J. Music Tchrs. Assn. (dir. student activities 1988-92, pres. 1992-94). Episcopalian. Avocation: travel. Home: 3 Blueberry Rd Shamong NJ 08088-8627 E-mail: margaretknight@prodigy.net.

KNIGHT, MARGARET L. librarian, educator; b. Rochelle, Ill., Feb. 13, 1920; d. Burton Eugene and Viola Amelia (Harter) K. BS in Edn., No. Ill. U., 1943; MLS, U. Ill., 1956. Rural sch. tchr. Ogle County, Rochelle, 1939-42; tchr. 6th grade, librarian Lee County, Dixon, Ill., 1943-56; librarian jr. high sch. Cook County, Park Ridge, Ill., 1956-57, dist. supr. libr.-media ctrs., 1957-75; librarian elem. sch. Ogle County, Lindenwood, Ill., 1994—, piano, organ tchr., 1976—. Mem. bd. dirs. League of Women Voters, Rochelle, Ill., 1977—, mem. bd. dirs., sec.-treas. Lindenwood Water Assn., 1977—. Mem. No. Ill. Botanical Soc. (librarian 1990—), Ogle County Hist. Soc. (bd. dirs. 1977—), Ogle County Genealogical Soc.,

Prairie Preservation Soc. of Ogle County (treas. 1980—), Des Plaines Valley Geological Soc. (librarian 1994-98, treas. 1998—), Flagg Twp. Hist. Soc. (bd. 1990—). Avocations: creation of jewelry, geology, music, gardening.

KNIGHT, REBECCA JEAN, secondary education educator; b. Oklahoma City, Nov. 8, 1949; d. G.B. and Lillian Pearl (Wright) Williams; m. Ronnie Dean (Knight), Mar. 1, 1968; children: Ronald Chad, Dustin Ryan. BS, U. Tex., East Tex., 1972, post grad., 1989-92. Cert., in teaching, Tex. Teachers aide Bailey Inglish Elem., Bonham, Tex., 1971; tchr. Bonham HS, Bonham, Tex., 1973—. Mem. ins. com. Bonham Ind. Sch. Dist., 1975—, dist. site based com., 1992-93, campus site based com., 1993-98; English Dept. Chair 2001-; tchr. adult Sunday sch. Ch. of God, Lannius, Tex., 1990—, tchr. teenage Sunday sch., 1969-90. Mem. NEA, Assn. Tex. Profl. Educators, Nat. Coun. Tchr. of English, Tex. State Tchrs. Assn., Alpha Chi. Avocations: gardening, computers, walking, sewing, decorating.

KNIGHT, WANDA BRIDGES, art educator; b. Reidsville, N.C., July 23, 1957; d. Major Lee and Mary Jane (Neal) Bridges; m. Julius Francis Knight, July 22, 1978; children: Franchesca Elise, Mark Ellington. BA, N.C. Ctrl. U., 1979; MEd, Saginaw Valley State U.; postgrad., Ohio State U., 1994—. Substitute tchr., coach gymnastics Makiminato Mid. Sch., Okinawa, Japan, 1980; staff layout artist United Svcs. Orgn., Okinawa, Japan, 1980; art specialist mid. sch. Stafford (Va.) County Schs., 1981-84; art specialist elem. sch. Camp Lejeune Dependents Schs., Jacksonville, N.C., 1984-87; asst. registrar & curatorial Albany (Ga.) Mus. Art., 1987-88; art specialist elem. sch. Dougherty County Schs., Albany, 1987-90, Chippewa Valley Schs., Clinton Twp., Mich., 1990-93, art specialist youth adults, 1993; teaching assoc., univ. supr. Ohio State U., Columbus, 1994—. Mem. dist.-wide strategic planning com. Chippewa Valley Schs., 1992-93; pres. Grad. Art Edn. Assn./Ohio State U.; mem. Profl. Devel. Sch. Editl. Bd., Ohio State U., 1994—, mem. grad. studies coms.; presenter in field. Chair officers' wives group Marine Wing Support Group 47, Selfridge, Mich., 1992-93. Univ. Dean's fellow The Ohio State U., 1994. Mem. NEA, Nat. Art Edn. Assn., Ohio Art Edn. Assn. Avocations: jogging, horseback riding, raising tropical fish, drawing. Home: 424 Kemmerer Rd State College PA 16801-6407

KNOELL, NANCY JEANNE, kindergarten educator; b. Boone, Iowa, Dec. 12, 1941; d. Wallace Knute and Dorothy Althea (Walker) Johnson; m. Gerald Dwain Brown, June 21, 1970 (div. Dec. 1987); children: Renae Jeanne, Arlan Gerald; m. Lawrence Hubert Knoell, Oct. 19, 1991. BS, Gustavus Adolphus Coll., 1963; postgrad., Hamlin U., U. Minn., Coll. St. Thomas. Cert. tchr. elem. K-6, Minn. Tchr. kindergarten Rochester (Minn.) Pub. Schs., 1963-66, Robbinsdale Area Ind. Sch. Dist. 281, New Hope, Minn., 1966—. Mem. sci. design team Robbinsdale Area Ind. Sch. Dist. 281, New Hope; mentor to 1st year tchr., 1995-96. Mem. Delta Kappa Gamma (co-treas.). Lutheran. Avocations: ballroom dancing, golf, roses, baking, travel. Home: 8209 Toledo Ave N Brooklyn Park MN 55443-2228 Office: Neill Elem Sch 6600 27th Ave N Minneapolis MN 55427-3042

KNOLES, GEORGE HARMON, history educator; b. Los Angeles, Feb. 20, 1907; s. Tully Cleon and Emily (Walline) K.; m. Amandalee (Barker), June 12, 1930; children: Ann Barker (Nitzan), Alice Laurane (Simmons). AB(hon.), Coll. of Pacific, 1928, AM, 1930; PhD, Stanford U., 1939. Instr. history union High Sch., Lodi, Calif., 1930-35; history asst. Stanford, 1935-36; history instr., 1937-41; asst. prof., 1942-46; assoc. prof., 1946-51; prof. history, 1951-72; Margaret Byrne, prof. Am. history, 1968-72; emeritus, 1972—; chmn. history dept., 1968-72. Dir. Inst. Am. History, 1956-72; prof. history; chmn. div. social sci. State Coll. Edn., Greeley, Colo., 1941-42; summer tchr. Central Wash. Coll. Edn., Ellensburg, 1939, State Coll., Flagstaff, Ariz., 1940, 1941, U. Calif. at Los Angeles, 1947; Stanford U., Tokyo U.; Am. Studies Seminars, Tokyo, 1950-52, 56, U. Wyo., 1955; Fulbright distinguished lectr., Japan, 1971 Author: The Presidential Campaign and Election of 1892, 1942; Readings in Western Civilization, (with Rixford K. Snyder), 1951; The Jazz Age Revisited, 1955, The New United States, 1959; Editor: The Crisis of The Union, 1860-61, 1965; Sources in American History, 10 vols, 1965-66, The Responsibilities of Power, 1900-1929, 1967; Essays and Assays: California History Reappraised, 1973; Contbg. articles to profl. jour. Lt., USNR, 1944-46. Mem. Am. So. Hist. Assn.; Orgn. Am. Historians (exec. com. 1950-54, bd. editors rev. 1955-58); Am. Studies Assn. (council 1952-54); Soc. of Am. Historians. Clubs: Commonwealth. Methodist. Home: 850 Webster St Apt 220 Palo Alto CA 94301-2878

KNOLL, ANDREW HERBERT T. biology educator; b. West Reading, Pa., Apr. 23, 1951; s. Robert Samuel and Anna Augusta (Meyer) K.; m. Marsha Craig, June 22, 1974; children: Kirsten C., Robert A. BA with highest honors, Lehigh U., 1973; MA, Harvard U., 1974, PhD, 1977; PhD (hon.), Uppsala U., Sweden, 1996; DSc (hon.), Lehigh U., 1998. Asst. prof. geology Oberlin Coll., Ohio, 1977-82; assoc. prof. Harvard U., Cambridge, Mass., 1982-85, prof. biology, 1985-2000, curator bot. mus., 1985—, prof. earth and planetary sci., 1985—, chmn. dept. organismic and evolutionary biology, 1992-98, Fisher prof. natural history, 2000—, assoc. dean faculty Arts and Scis., 2000—03. Mem. com. on planetary biology U.S. Space Sci. Bd., 1982-88, NRC Bd. on Earth Scis., 1987-88, 92-95, space studies bd., 1989-90, 97-2000; Crosby vis. lectr. MIT, 1999; mem. sci. team NASA MER 2003 Mars Mission. Assoc. editor Paleobiology, 1980-92, Precambrian Rsch., 1985—, Trends in Ecology and Evolution, 1987-92, Rev. of Palaeobotany and Palynology, 1987—, Am. Jour. Sci., 1990—, Geology, 1992-98, Palaios, 1996-2002, Palaeography Palacoclimatology Palaeocology, 1997—, Internat. Jour. Plant Scis., 1998—; contbr. articles to profl. publs. Bd. dirs. U.S. Nat. Mus. Nat. Hist., 1993-97. Named one of Time/CNN America's Best Scientists, 2002; recipient Walcott medal, Nat. Acad. Scis., 1987, Chang prize in paleontology, Am. Mus. Natural History, 2001; fellow, Geol. Soc. Am., Linnean Soc., London, Am. Acad. Arts and Scis., 1987, Guggenheim, 1987, AAAS; Vis. fellow, Gonville and Caius Coll., Cambridge, Eng., 1991—92. Fellow AAAS, European Union Geoscis. (hon.); mem. NAS, Bot. Soc. Am., Am. Philos. Soc., Paleontol. Soc. (Schuchert award 1987), Soc. Study Evolution, Phi Beta Kappa, Sigma Xi. Avocations: travel, reading, cooking, choral music. Office: Harvard Univ Botanical Museum 26 Oxford St Cambridge MA 02138-2902

KNOPF, BARRY ABRAHAM, lawyer, educator; b. Passaic, N.J., May 11, 1946; s. Edward and Sonia (Sameth) K.; children: Elisa, Scott. Student, Rutgers U., 1968, JD, 1972. Bar: N.J. 1972, U.S. Dist. Ct. N.J. 1972, U.S. Tax Ct. 1975, U.S. Supreme Ct. 1975, U.S. Ct. Appeals (3d cir.) 1981; cert. civil trial atty. Nat. Bd. Trial Advocacy, N.J. Supreme Ct. Assoc. Cohn & Lifland, Saddle Brook, N.J., 1972-75, ptnr., 1975—. Instr. N.J. Inst. for Continuing Legal Edn., 1982—, Nat. Inst. Trial Advocacy, 1989—; adj. faculty Hofstra U. Sch. of Law, 2000. Co-author: Professional Negligence, Law of Malpractice in New Jersey, 1979, 5th edit., 2001, Personal Injury Litigation Practice in New Jersey, 1990, Civil Trial Preparation, Practical skills Series, 1992, 2d edit., 1996, New Jersey Product Liability Law, 1994. V.p. Temple Beth Tikvah, Wayne, N.J., 1985-93, pres. 1993-95. Mem. Morris Pashman Inn of Ct. (master 1998—). Home: 1014 Smith Manor Blvd West Orange NJ 07052-4227 Office: Cohn Lifland Pearlman Herrmann & Knopf Park 80 West 1 Saddle Brook NJ 07663 E-mail: bak@njlawfirm.com.

KNOPF, KENYON ALFRED, economist, educator; b. Cleve., Nov. 24, 1921; s. Harold C. and Emma A. (Underwood) K.; m. Madelyn Lee Siddy Trebilcock, Mar. 28, 1953 (dec. June 1999); children— Kristin Lee, Mary George. AB magna cum laude with high honors in Econs., Kenyon Coll., 1942; MA in Econs.; PhD, Harvard U., 1949; LLD (hon.), Kenyon Coll., 1993. Mem. faculty Grinnell Coll., 1949-67, prof. econs., 1960-67, Jentzen prof., 1961-67, chmn. dept., 1958-60, chmn. div. social studies, 1962-64, chmn. faculty, 1964-67; dean coll. Whitman Coll., Walla Walla, Wash., 1967-70, prof. econs., 1967-89, Hollon Parker prof. econs., 1985-89, prof. emeritus, 1989—, provost, 1970-81, dean faculty, 1970-78, acting pres., 1974-75; pub. interest dir. Fed. Home Loan Bank, Seattle, 1976-83. Mem. council undergrad. assessment program Ednl. Testing Service, 1977-80 Author: (with Robert H. Haveman) The Market System, 4th edit, 1981; A Lexicon of Economics, 1991; editor: Introduction to Economics Series (9 vols.), 1966, 2d edit., 1970-71; co-editor: (with James H. Strauss) The Teaching of Elementary Economics, 1960. Mem. youth coun. City of Grinnell, 1957—59; mem. Walla Walla County Mental Health Bd., 1968—75, Walla Walla Civil Svc. Commn., 1978—84, chmn., 1981—84; mem. Grinnell City Coun., 1964—67; pres. Walla Walla County Human Svcs. Adminstrv. Bd., 1975—77; mem. Ia. adv. coun. SBA; tax aide AARP/IRS Tax Counseling for Elderly, 1987—98, local coord., 1990—91, assoc. dist. coord. S.E. Wash., 1991—94, assoc. dist. coord. tng., 1994—98; mem. planning commn. Swinomish Indian Tribal Cmty., 2002—; bd. dirs. Skagit County Boys & Girls Club, 2001—; mem. planning commn. Swinomish Indian Trial Cmty., 2002—; bd. dirs. Walla Walla United Fund, 1968—76, pres., 1973; bd. dirs. Shelter Bay Cmty., Inc., 1995—2003, v.p., 1995—97, pres., 1997—2003; bd. dirs. La Conner Cmty. Scholarship Found., 1997—, La Conner Boys and Girls Club, 1999—, pres., 2001—03; bd. dirs. Skagit County Boys and Girls Club, 2003—. With USAF, 1942—46, PTO. Social Sci. Rsch. Coun. grantee, 1951-52. Mem.: Am. Conf. Acad. Deans (exec. com. 1970—77, chmn. 1975), Am. Assn. Ret. Persons, LaConner Club, Kiwanis (pres. 2003—), Phi Beta Kappa. Office: 223 Skagit Way La Conner WA 98257-9602

KNOPF, TANA DARLENE, counselor, music educator; b. Des Moines, Oct. 19, 1951; d. Charles D. Sr. and Edith D. Smith; m. James E. Knopf, Aug. 7, 1982; children: Daniel P., Chandra D. BA, Met. State Coll., Denver, 1974; MEd, U. Colo., Denver, 1983. Instrumental music tchr. Denver Pub. Schs., 1974—2000, counselor, 2001—.

KNORR, GINNY WALTON, health and physical education educator; b. Washington, Feb. 6, 1950; d. Clarence Hixon and Dorothy Nell (Butcher) Walton; m. Roger William Knorr, Mar. 15, 1975; children: Dorothy Christine, David Walton, Michael William. BS, U. Tenn., Chattanooga, 1972; MS, U. Tenn., 1973. Cert. tchr., Ga. Instr. Armstrong State Coll., Savannah, Ga., 1973-76, asst. prof., 1976—. Author: Aquatic Skills and Safety, 1983, 2d edit., 1993. Named H. Dean Propst Outstanding Faculty Mem., 1980. Mem. AAHPERD, Assn. Am. Cheerleader Coaches and Advisors, Ga. Assn. Health, Phys. Edn., Recration and Dance. Republican. Methodist. Avocations: reading, running, roller blading, swimming. E-mail: (office) (home). Home: 1702 Stillwood Dr Savannah GA 31419-2428 Office: Armstron State Coll 11935 Abercorn St Savannah GA 31419-1909 E-mail: knorrgin@mail.armstrong.edu., fiveknorr@home.com.

KNOTT, BILL, poet, literature educator; MFA, Norwich U. Instr. Columbia Coll., 1972—75, Thomas Jefferson Coll., 1975, Emerson Coll., 1975—77, 1981—83, poet, assoc. prof. writing, 1984—; instr. Wright State U., 1978, New Eng. Coll., 1979, Centrum Arts Ctr., 1980, YHMA/WA Poetry Ctr., 1981; instr. Writers Workshop U. Iowa, 1983—84; instr. U. Ala., 2001. Author: The Naomi Poems, 1968, Auto-necrophilia, 1971, Rome in Rome, 1976, Selected and Collected Poems, 1977 (Elliston prize, 1979), Becos, 1983, Poems 1963-1988, 1989, Outremer, 1989, The Quicken Tree, 1995, Laugh at the End of the World, 2000. Fellow, John Simon Guggenheim Meml. Found., 2003; grantee, Nat. Endowment for the Arts, 1980, 1985. Office: Emerson Coll 120 Boylston St Boston MA 02116-4624*

KNOTT, KENNETH, engineering educator, consultant, expert witness; b. Dudley, Worcestershire, Eng., Mar. 6, 1929; came to U.S., 1977; s. John Peter Grainger and Sarah (Turner) K.; m. Margaret Knott, Apr. 22, 1957; children: DiLwyn John, Tracy James. Diploma in Grad. Studies, Engrng. Prodn., U. Birmingham at Edgbaston, Eng., 1956; MS in Indsl. Engrng., Pa. State U., 1966; PhD in Engrng. Prodn., Tech. U. Loughborough, Eng., 1983. Apprentice British Thompson Houston Co. Ltd., Birmingham, 1944-48, Coventry, Eng., 1948-50; design draftsman New Conveyor Co. Ltd., Smethwick, Eng., 1952-53; tech. asst. to gen. mgr. N. Hingley and Sons, Netherton, Eng., 1953-55; prodn. engr. Chubb and Sons, Ltd., Wolverhampton, Eng., 1955-56; plant mgr. John Morris Electrical Engring., Bilston, Eng., 1956; lectr. in prodn. engring. Dudley and Staffordshire Tech. Coll., Dudley, Eng., 1956-63; instr. in indsl. engring. Pa. State U., State College, 1963-66; mng. dir. Maynard Tng. Ctr., Birmingham, 1966-70, Kenneth Knott Ltd., Birmingham, 1966-77, Work Study Contract Svcs., Birmingham, 1970-77; asst. prof. indsl. and mgmt. systems engring. Pa. State U., 1977-84, assoc. prof. indsl. and mgmt. engring., 1984-87, prof. indsl. and mgmt. engring., 1987-95, emeritus prof. indsl. engring., 1996—. Mem. editorial bd. Internat. Jour. Prodn. Rsch., Loughborough, 1984—; mem. robotics sub-com. Welding Rsch. Coun., N.Y.C., 1977-79, welding processes sub-com., 1977-83; mem. com. maintenance in mfg. Nat. Mfg. Engring. Ctr., Ann Arbor, Mich., 1989-90. Author: Job Analysis Procedure Manual, 1970, (with others) A Comparison of Alternative Time Slotting Systems for Indirect Time Standards Work Measurement, 1986, An Analytical Approach to Designing and Testing Time Slotting Systems, 1986; co-author: Laboratory Manual Manufacturing Processes, 1965, Principles and Practice of MTM-2, 1970, Principles and Practice of MTM-3, 1971, Manufacturing Processes Associate Degree Program, 1980; editor Metods Time Measurement Jour., 1982-90; contbr. tech. papers to profl. jours. Recipient AT&T Found. Outstanding Teaching award Am. Soc. Engring. Edn., 1991, Lenhard Teaching fellowship Lenhardt Ctr. Innovative Teaching Pa. State U., 1992. Fellow Inst. Indsl. Engrs. (panel rsch. in work measurement work measurement and methods engring. divsn. 1981-83, assoc. editor IIE Transactions 1982-92, program chmn. 1983-87, rsch. chmn. 1984-89, reorganization com. 1988, divsn. dir. 1982-83, honors chmn. 1991—, pres. Ctrl. Pa. chpt. 1982-83, Phil Carroll award 1986, Tech. Innovation in Indsl. Engring. award 1993), World Acad. Productivity Sci.; mem. NSPE, Am. Soc. Quality Control. Soc. Am. Magicians, Pa. Soc. Profl. Engrs., Fedn. Productivity Scis. (hon., London), Methods Time Measurement Assn. (editor Methods Time Measurement Jour., chmn. midland region United Kingdom divsn. 1967-72, internat. com. investigation into Application Handbook Requirements 1970, tech. panel United Kingdom divsn. 1969-77, tng. and qualifications com.), Soc. Mfg. Engrs. (continuing edn. chmn. Ctrl. Pa. chpt. 1987, sec. 1993—), Internat. Brotherhood Magicians (mem. Magic Circle), Kano Soc., Sigma Xi, Alpha Pi Mu. Avocations: magic, Judo. Home: PO Box 234 Pine Grove Mills PA 16868-0234 Office: Pa State U 207 Hammond Bldg University Park PA 16802-1401 E-mail: kok@psu.edu., k.knott@fimexpert.com.

KNOWLES, CAROLYN SUE EDWARDS, secondary education educator; b. May 14, 1947; d. Lewis and Willie Inez (Ford) Edwards; m. William Limbret Knowles, Aug. 1, 1970; children: Cory Limbret, Heather Shantay. BS, Alcorn State U., 1968; MA, Fisk U., 1974. Tchr. Hunter High Sch., Drew, Miss., 1968-70, North Scott Sch., Forest, Miss., 1970-71, Morton (Miss.) Attendance Ctr., 1971-87, Forest Mcpl. Sch., 1987—99; h.s. tchr. biology Choctaw Tribal Schs., 1999—; chmn. dept. sci. Choctaw Ctr. H.S., 2002. Chmn. sci. dept Forest Mcpl. Sch. Dist., 1992-94. Sec. East Ctrl. Health System Agy., Newton, Miss., 1978-80, Scott County Dem. Exec. Com., Forest, 1972—; chmn. East Ctrl. Cmty. Action Agy., Forest, 1988-92; active VFW Women Aux., Forest, Scott County Colored Women Federated Club, Forest, 1992; leader Girl Scouts U.S., svc. unit co-chmn. Scott County; youth dir. Concord Bapt. Ch.; youth dir. 3d New Hope Dist.; vol. leader 4-H Club, coord. Capitol regional vol., 1993-94. NSF grantee, 1971-74; named Star Tchr. MS Econ. Coun. by Star Student Darryl Harvey Morton Attendance Ctr. Mem. NEA (pres. Scott/Forest Assn. Educators 1968), Miss. Assn. Educators (bd. dirs. 1993—), Miss. Sci. Tchr. Assn., Nat. Sci. Tchrs. Assn., Zeta Phi Beta. Avocations: singing, creative cooking, craft making, writing. Home: 430 George St Forest MS 39074-3412 Office: Hawkins Mid Sch 803 E Oak St Forest MS 39074-4699

KNOWLES, ELIZABETH ANNE, educator, counselor, assistant principal; b. Hyannis, Mass., June 30, 1948; d. George A. and Winifred (Rolfe) K. MusB, U. Mass., 1970, MEd in Counseling, 1990, EdD in Adminstrn., 1997. Cert. K-12 music tchr., K-12 guidance counselor, K-12 prin., asst. prin., supr., dir. guidance, pupil pers. svc., Mass. Dir. bands Springfield (Mass.) Pub. Schs., 1971-86, 89-95, alcohol and drug counselor, 1986-89, guidance counselor, grades 9-12, 1995-98, asst. prin., grades 9-12, 1998—2000, asst. prin. grades 6-8, 2000—. Cons. Mass. Gov.'s Alliance Against Drugs Sch./Community Adv. Coun., 1986-90. Mem. adv. bd. Springfield Spirit Women's Basketball Team (Nat. Women's Basketball League). Named Tchr. of Yr., Springfield Rotary Club, 1988. Mem. NEA, Mass. Tchrs. Assn., Springfield Adminstrs. Assn. Office: Springfield Pub Schs PO Box 1410 Springfield MA 01102-1410

KNOWLES, MARJORIE FINE, lawyer, educator, dean; b. Bklyn., July 4, 1939; d. Jesse J. and Roslyn (Leff) Fine; m. Ralph I. Knowles, Jr., June 3, 1972. BA, Smith Coll., 1960; LLB, Harvard U., 1965. Bar: Ala., N.Y., D.C. Teaching fellow Harvard U., 1963-64; law clk. to judge U.S. Dist. Ct. (so. dist.), N.Y., 1965-66; asst. U.S. atty. U.S. Atty.'s Office, N.Y.C., 1966-67; asst. dist. atty. N.Y. County Dist. Atty., N.Y.C., 1967-70; exec. dir. Joint Found. Support, Inc., N.Y.C., 1970-72; asst. gen. counsel HEW, Washington, 1978-79; insp. gen. U.S. Dept. Labor, Washington, 1979-80; assoc. prof. U. Ala. Sch. Law, Tuscaloosa, 1972-75, prof., 1975-86, assoc. dean, 1982-84; law prof., dean Ga. State U. Coll. Law, Atlanta, 1986-91, law prof., 1986—. Cons. Ford Found., N.Y.C., 1973-98, 2000-03, trustee Coll. Retirement Equities Fund, N.Y.C., 1983-2002; mem. exec. com. Conf. on Women and the Constn., 1986-88; mem. com. on continuing profl. edn. Am. Law Inst.-ABA, 1987-93. Contbr. articles to profl. jours. Am. Council Edn. fellow, 1976-77, Aspen Inst. fellow, Rockefeller Found., 1976. Mem. ABA (chmn. new deans workshop 1988), Ala. State Bar Assn., N.Y. State Bar Assn., D.C. Bar Assn., Am. Law Inst., Tchrs. Ins. Annunity Assn. (trustee Coll. Equities Ret. Equities Fund 2002—). Office: Ga State U Coll Law University Plz Atlanta GA 30303

KNOWLES, RICHARD JAMES ROBERT, medical physicist, educator, consultant; b. McPherson, Kans., Aug. 2, 1943; s. Richard E. and Pauline H. (Worland) K.; m. Stephanie R. Closter, May 14, 1970; 1 child, Guenevere Regina. BS, St. Louis U., 1965; MS, Cornell U., 1969; PhD, Poly. U., N.Y., 1979. Diplomate Am. Bd. Sci. in Nuclear Medicine, Am. Bd. Radiology. Chief med. physicist L.I. Coll. Hosp., Bklyn., 1977-81; dir. radiation physics lab. Downstate Med. Ctr., Bklyn., 1981-82; sr. med. physicist N.Y. Hosp. Cornell U. Med. Ctr., N.Y.C., 1982—; assoc. prof. physics in radiology Cornell U. Med. Coll., N.Y.C., 1989—. Author: Quality Assurance and Image Artifacts in Magnetic Resonance Imaging, 1988; contbr. articles to profl. jours. Mem. Am. Phys. Soc., Soc. Nuclear Medicine, Health Physics Soc., Am. Assn. Physicists in Medicine, N.Y. Acad. Scis., Soc. for Computer Applications in Radiology, Soc. Magnetic Resonance in Medicine, Sigma Xi. Office: NY Hosp-Cornell Med Ctr 525 E 68th St New York NY 10021-4885

KNOX, DIANNE MEDLIN, mathematics educator; b. Dallas, Sept. 18, 1953; d. Homer Lewis and Dorothy A. (Jordan) Medlin; 1 child, Colin Tyrel. BS in Edn., Tex. Tech. U., 1975. Substitute tchr. Folsom-Cordova Sch. Dist., Sacramento, 1975-76; purchasing coord. Raldon Homes, Dallas, 1977; membership officer/teller Luke Fed. Credit Union, Glendale, Ariz., 1978-79; tchr. Garland (Tex.) Ind. Sch. Dist., 1980—. Mem. Nat. Coun. Tchrs. of Math., Tex. State Tchrs. Assn., Garland Edn. Agy. Avocations: softball, piano, reading. Home: 1505 Savannah Pl Garland TX 75041-4914

KNOX, GEORGE CHARLES, college dean; b. Mt. Vernon, N.Y., Aug. 9, 1951; s. Maitland Brooks and Barbara Charlton (Moore) K.; m. Carol Lee Allen, Dec. 19, 1970; children: Steven Christopher, Adam Gregory. BS, Nova U., 1981, MS in Criminal Justice, 1982, postgrad., 1990—. Traffic homicide investigator Hollywood (Fla.) Police Dept., 1973-83; accident reconstructionist Nat. Hwy. Traffic Adminstrn., Washington, 1983-84; asst. dept. chmn. criminal justice Asheville (N.C.) - Buncombe Tech. C. C., 1984-87; assoc. dean Laf Enforcement Tng. Ctr. Western Piedmont C. C., Morganton, N.C., 1987—. Bd. dirs. Options, Inc., Morganton. Author: (manuals) Introduction to At-Scene Accident Investigation, 1991, Physical Evidence From Accident Vehicles, 1991, Satanic Influences on the Youth of Today, 1990. Mem. Burke County Bd. Edn., Morganton, 1992; bd. dirs. Morganton Planning Commn., 1990. With USAF, 1969-75. Recipient award for Outstanding Contbns., Internat. Assn. Juv. Officers, Greensboro, N.C., 1990, Disting. Acad. Achievement award Nova U., Ft. Lauderdale, Fla., 1982, Commendation for Bravery, Hollywood Police Dept., 1974. Mem. ASCD, Burke County C. of C. (bd. dirs.), N.C. Sch. Bds. Assn., Nat. Sch. Bds. Assn., N.C. Assn. Curriculum Deans, Internat. Assn. Campus Law Enforcement Adminstrs., N.C. Criminal Justice Assn. (past pres.), Catawba Valley Lodge, Masons (Master Mason). Republican. Methodist. Avocation: furniture making. Home: 302 New Orleans Blvd Morganton NC 28655-2776 Office: Western Piedmont Comm Coll 1001 Burkemont Ave Morganton NC 28655-4504

KNOX, JOHN, JR., philosopher, educator; b. Nashville, Mar. 5, 1932; s. John and Lois Adelaide (Bolles) K.; m. Alida van Bronkhorst, June 30, 1962 (div. 1978); children— Trevor McTaggart, Amethy Alida; m. Lois Marie Starner Uhlman, Jan. 7, 1990. Student, Cambridge U., 1952; BA, Emory U., 1953; PhD, Yale U., 1961. Instr. philosophy C.W. Post Coll., L.I. U., 1960, asst. prof. philosophy, 1961-67; from assoc. prof. philosophy to prof. emeritus Drew U., Madison, NJ, 1967—2002, prof. emeritus, 2002—. Vis. prof. philosophy U. Miami, spring 1981 Contbr. articles to philos. publs. Served to lt. (j.g.) USNR, 1953-56. Nat. Endowment for Humanities fellow, 1973-74 Mem. Am. Philos. Assn., Phi Beta Kappa, Phi Sigma Tau. Home: 4 Shadewood Ln Hilton Head Island SC 29926-2582

KNUDSEN, DEAN DEWAYNE, sociology educator; b. Harlan, Iowa, July 9, 1932; s. Arthur Stephen and Nina Surina (Christensen) K.; m. Ruth Lucille Dalton, June 9, 1956; children: Karen Elizabeth, Stephen Brent. BA, Sioux Falls Coll., 1954; BD, Berkeley Bapt. Div. Sch., 1957; MA, U. Minn., 1961; PhD, U. N.C., 1964. Instr. sociology Augsburg Coll., Mpls., 1960-61; asst. prof. Ohio State U., Columbus, 1964-69; assoc. prof. Purdue U., West Lafayette, Ind., 1969-88, prof., 1988—, head dept. sociology/anthropology, 1992-98. Cons. Tippecanoe County Welfare Dept., Lafayette, Ind., 1973-74. Author: Spindles and Spires, 1975, Child Protective Services, 1990, Abused and Battered, 1991, Child Maltreatment, 1992. Pres. bd. dirs. Cmty. and Family Resource Ctr., Lafayette, 1977-83; bd. dirs. United Way, Lafayette, 1980-81; mem. adv. bd. Cmty. Health Clinic, Lafayette, 1990-93; coord. child protection team State of Ind.-Tippecanoe County, 1979-83. NIMH postdoctoral fellow U. N.H., 1983-84. Mem. Am. Sociol. Assn. (sect. sec. 1961), Internat. Assn. Child Abuse, Soc. for Study of Social Problems (chairperson of chairpersons 1993-95), Soc. for Sci. Study of Religion (sec. 1972-73), North Ctrl. Sociol. Assn. (pres. 1977-78). Democrat. Baptist. Avocations: gardening, playing squash, woodworking. Home: 1805 Sheridan Rd West Lafayette IN 47906-2225 Office: Purdue Univ Dept Sociology/Anthropology 1365 Stone Hall West Lafayette IN 47907-1365

KNUDSON, RUTH ESTHER, education educator; b. Phila., June 29, 1945; d. Robert J. and Ruth M. (Weisner) Rodisch; m. Karl J. Knudson, June 15, 1968; children: Robert K., Richard K. BA, Bryn Mawr Coll., 1967; MS, U. Wis., 1968; PhD, U. Calif., Riverside, 1988. Cert. secondary tchr., Calif. Tchr. English and reading, Calif., La., and Mass., 1969-77; supr. tchr. edn. Sch. Edn., U. Calif., Riverside, 1985-88, asst. head tchr. edn., 1988-89, mem. edn. faculty, 1989-95; assoc. prof. Calif. State U., Long Beach, 1995-99, prof., 1999—. Chair single subject com. Calif. State U., Long Beach, 1995—97, mem. human subjects rsch. rev. com., 1997—99, chair faculty merit increase com., 2000—01, chair retention, tenure and promotion com. Coll. Edn., 2002—03; cons. pub. sch. dists., Calif., 1984—92; chair tchr. edn. com. U. Calif., Riverside, 1992—94, mem. retention, tenure and promotion com., 1999—; local arrangements chair Nat. Reading Conf., 1991; evaluator Mid. Schs. Demonstration Programs, 1997—2000. Contbr. articles to profl. jours. Woodrow Wilson fellow, 1967-68; recipient Spencer award Spencer Found., Chgo., 1989-90. Mem. Nat. Conf. of Rsch. on Lang. and Literacy, Nat. Coun. of Tchrs. of English, Am. Ednl. Rsch. Assn. (program reviewer 1989—, Dissertation of Yr. award 1989), Internat. Reading Assn., Phi Delta Kappa. Avocations: reading, family vacations. Office: Calif State U Long Beach Coll Edn 1250 N Bellflower Blvd Long Beach CA 90840-0006 E-mail: rknuded@aol.com., knudson@csulb.edu.

KNUPPEL, ROBERT ALAN, obstetrics-gynecology educator, healthcare consultant; b. Newark, June 7, 1947; s. Herman D. and Marion Knuppel; m. Evelyn Frieswyk, Aug. 7, 1971; children: Eric, Kurt, Kyle. BS, Georgetown U., 1969; MD, U. Medicine and Dentistry N.J., 1973; MPH, Harvard U., 1979. Diplomate Am. Bd. Ob-Gyn, Am. Bd. Med. Examiners (maternal-fetal medicine). Chief resident in ob-gyn Tufts Affiliated Hosps., Boston, 1974-76; asst. prof. ob-gyn Tufts U. Sch. Medicine, Boston, 1976-79; assoc. prof. U. S. Fla. Sch. Medicine, Tampa, 1979-84, prof. ob-gyn, maternal-fetal medicine, 1984—, dir. maternal-fetal medicine, s1979—. Chmn. ob/gyn Robert Wood Johnson Med. Sch.; bd. dirs. Obstet. Component Children's Med. Svc., Tampa; bd. dirs. Nat. Perinatal Info. Ctr., Medici Healthcare Consulting Princeton, Women's Integrated Network. Author: High Risk Pregnancy, 1986; editor Jour. Perinatology, 1986; obstet. editor Perinatal Press, 1984-86. Hon. chmn. Fla. Bay chpt. March of Dimes, 1986; chmn. Georgetown U. Alumni Admission Program, Tampa area, 1986—; admissions com., Georgetown U., Washington, 1983-84, mem. dean's adv. bd. Fellow Am. Coll. Obstetrics and Gynecology (sci. award 1980); mem. Assn. Profs. Gynecology and Obstetrics, Com. for Instnl. Grant Adminstrn., Fla. Obstet. and Gynecol. Soc., Maternal Mortality Soc. Roman Catholic. Avocations: sculpting, scuba diving, golf. Office: Saint Peters U Hosp 254 Easton Ave New Brunswick NJ 08903

KNUTH, MARYA DANIELLE, special education educator; b. Bowling Green, Ohio, Apr. 27, 1971; d. Kerry Lee and Sandra Jean Knuth. BEd, U. Toledo, 1997; MEd (hon.), U Toledo, 2002; cert. in reading (hon.), U. Toledo, 2002. Cert. in tchg. Tchr. spl. edn. Jefferson Jr. H.S., Toledo, 1997—98, Washington Jr. H.S., Toledo, 1998—; promotion coord. J&L Mktg., 2002—. Coach intramurals Washington Local Schs., Toledo, 1998—2002; chairperson bldg. beautification com. Washington Jr. H.S., Toledo, 2001—, chairperson best practice com.; dem. exch. program Ohio - Ukraine- Hungary Ednl. Exch. Program in the Pub. Sch. Setting, Toledo, 1999—2000; reading tutor Read for Lit., Toledo, 2000—; co-chairperson 100% Homework Club, Washington Jr. High, 2002—03; promotion coord. J&L Mktg., 1999—; head coach freshman girls Whitmer HS. Author (editor): A Netherland Tour, 1998. Mem. Build Your Sch. Garden Com., 2003—; head coach freshman Broomball Team, Toledo, 2003—; mem. Sister Cities of Toledo, 2000—. Recipient Best Lesson Plans award, Teachers Orgn., 2000. Mem.: ASCD, Coun. Exceptional Children. Republican. Avocations: tutoring, travel, rollerblading. Home: 4812 W Bancroft St Apt 30 Toledo OH 43615 Office: Washington Jr HS 5700 Whitmer Dr Toledo OH 43613 Personal E-mail: MaryaK1999@aol.com.

KNUTSON, AMANDA, art educator, artist; b. Pitts., Feb. 21, 1973; d. JEffrey and Bonita (Layne) Zdrale; married. BS in Art Edn., U. Wis., 1995. Cert. art tchr. K-12, Wis. Clk., framing cons. The Hang Up Gallery, Neenah, Wis., 1989-93; photostylist JanSport, Inc., Appleton, Wis., 1994; gallery shop asst. Madison Art Ctr., 1995—; elem. art edn. tchr., art specialist Adams Elem. Sch., Janesville, Wis., 1996—. Artist, designer Adams Sch. Logo, 1998—. Artist Works include watercolors, acrylics, metalwork, painted wood furniture, jewelry design and baby room wall murals. Learning Links grantee Janesville Found., 1998, Thompson Internat. Edn. grantee Wis. Found. Ind. Colls., 1999. Mem. Nat. Art Edn. Assn., Wis. Art Edn. Assn. Avocations: biking, painting, photography, travel. Home: 109 Pine View Dr Madison WI 53704 E-mail: sabrina_draw@yahoo.com.

KNUTSON, RICHARD DEAN, physical education educator; b. Glendale, Calif., Nov. 22, 1948; s. Harold Melvin Knutson and Viola Tucking; m. Beverly Anne Hammond, Aug. 27, 1977; children: Matthew Eric, David Andrew. BA in Phys. Edn., Calif. State U., Northridge, 1972; std. secondary credential, U. So. Calif., 1976; adminstrv. svcs. credential, MA in Ednl. Orgn. and Leadership, U. S.F., 1981. Std. elem. credential, Nat. Tchrs. Exam., 1979. Jr. high sch. tchr., dean, athletic dir. Archdiocese L.A., 1973-76; substitute tchr. William S. Hart Union High Sch. Dist., 1976-78; phys. edn. tchr., chairperson, advisor, dir., coord. Sierra Vista Jr. High Sch., 1978-89, 90—; interim dean students Canyon High Sch., 1989-90. Mem. Dist. Phys. Edn. Curriculum Com., Dist. Interdistrict Articulation Com., Dist. Planning Com. for New Jr. High # 4. State coord. Am. Heart Assn. (jump rope for heart 1984-88, task force com. mem. 1984-90). Recipient Cert. of Appreciation, City of L.A., 1978, Service award Valley Plaza Sports Bd. Dirs., 1978, Service award Sunland-Tujunga Golden State Basketball League Bd. Dirs., 1980, National Intramural Sports Council Service award Nat. Assn. Sport and Phys. Edn., 1985, Community Service award Sunland-Tujunga Kiwanis, 1978, award of Merit, Canyon Country Rotary, 1986, award of Merit, Newhall Rotary, 1989, 91. Mem. AAHPERD, Nat. Intramural-Recreation Sports Assn., Calif. Assn. Health, Phys. Edn., Recreation and Dance (co-founder and sec./treas. unit # 415 1982-90, mem. state membership com. 1986-87, state long range planning com. 1989—, v.p. athletic and sports so. dist. 1986-88, state level boys' and men's athletics 1987-88, co-mgr. state conf. 1989-90), Phi Delta Kappa (treas. 1988-90, bd. dirs. 1991, v.p. membership 1991-92, historian 1992-93). Home: 23470 Glenridge Dr Newhall CA 91321-3955

KNUTSON, RONALD DALE, economist, educator, academic administrator; b. Montevideo, Minn., July 12, 1940; s. Claus and Alice (Peterson) K.; m. Sharron DeGree, Sept. 16, 1961; children: Scott, Ryan, Nicole. BS, U. Minn., 1962, PhD, 1967; MS, Pa. State U., 1963. Prof. Purdue U., 1967-73; staff economist Agrl. Mktg. Svc., USDA, Washington, 1971-73; adminstr. Farmer Coop. Svc., 1973-75; prof. dept. agrl. econs. Tex. A&M U., Coll. Station, 1975—2001, dir. Agrl. Food Policy Ctr., 1989—2000, prof. emeritus, 2002—. Econ. cons. Kraft, Borden Inc., Sun-Diamond, Am. Bankers Assn., Milk Industry Found., GAO, U.S. Dept. Justice, Am. Farm Bur. Fedn., White House Food and Nutrition Study, NAS, U.S. Congress, Nat. Commn. on Productivity Exec. Office Pres.; project leader Rural Devel. Policy; chmn. milk pricing adv. com. U.S. Dept. Agr.; mem. Pres. Reagan's Transition Task Force for Agr., 1980-81; mem. agrl. policy adv. com. Sec. Agr. and Trade Rep., 1980-87; mem. agrl. group White House Partnership for Prosperity Conf., 2002; co-dir. Partnership for Prosperity, 2002- . Author: (with J.B. Penn and B.L. Flinchbaugh) Agricultural and Food Policy, 5th edit., 2003. Bd. dirs. Farm Found., vice chmn., 2000, chmn., 2001. Recipient Lifetime Achievement award So. Agrl. Econs. Assn., 1995, Faculty Disting. Achievement award in Ext., 1984, Former Students of Tex. A&M U., Faculty Disting. Achievement award in Tchg., 1998 Assn. Former Students of Tex. A&M U., Regents Prof. Svc. award The Tex. A&M U. Sys., 1999; Rsch. grantee Govt. of Trinidad and Tobago, 1999-2001. Mem. Am. Agrl. Econs. Assn. (bd. dirs. 1999-2002), So. Agrl. Econ. Assn. Home: 1011 Rose Cir College Station TX 77840-2327 Office: Tex A&M U Agrl Food Policy Ctr College Station TX 77843-2124

KOACH, LYNNE M. private school educator; b. Phila. d. Walter and Mary (Snyder) K. BS in Elem. Edn., East Stoudsburg U., 1973; MEd, Trenton State Coll., 1977. Tchr. to tech. coord. Assumption B.V.M. Sch., Feasterville, Pa., 1973—. Sci. coord., Assumption B.V.M. Sch., 1974-86, math. coord., 1986-99, libr. advisor, 1980-94. Named Tchr. of Yr., Ednl. Tutoring Ctr., 1988, Adminstr. of Yr., 1991; recipient Long Term Svc. award 1992. Mem. Nat. Cath. Edn. Assn. Office: Assumption BVM Sch 55 E Bristol Rd Langhorne PA 19053-2357

KOBAK, THERESA BERNICE, secondary education educator; b. Cleve., Aug. 22, 1944; d. Joseph Anthony and Helen Catherine (Dentkos) Kobak; m. John R. Bird, July 22, 2000; children: Jeannette, Irene, Wanda, Mary Ann, Theresa, Christine, Helen. BA, Ursuline Coll., 1967; cert. Theol. Studies, Jesuit Sch. Theology, Berkeley, Calif., 1978; M in Theol. Studies, Franciscan Sch. Theology, Berkeley, Calif., 1982. Tchr. French, history, religion Marymount H.S., Garfield Heights, Ohio, 1967-73, St. Vincent H.S., Vallejo, Calif., 1973-77; tchr., chair dept. French, counselor St. Patrick-St. Vincent H.S., Vallejo, 1982—, chmn. fgn. lang. dept., 1995-96. Mentor tchr. Cleve. State U., 1970-71; humanities divsn. leader St. Vincent H.S., Vallejo, 1975-76; leader student groups to Europe, 1975, 92, 95, 97, 99-2001; mem. campus ministry bd. St. Patrick-St. Vincent H.S., 1992—. Music minister for mental patients Turney Rd. State Hosp., Ohio, 1968-69; summer camp asst. Inner City Project, Cleve., 1970; asst. summer camp for mentally handicapped Cath. Charities, Oakland, Calif., 1973. Recipient Tchr. of Yr. award Elks #559, Vallejo, 1992. Mem. Am. Assn. Tchrs. French, Fgn. Lang. Assn. No. Calif., Calif. Lang. Tchrs. Assn., Sierra Club, Am. Council Tchrs. Foreign Languages. Avocations: gardening, hiking, reading, cross country skiing, travel. Office: St Patrick-St Vincent HS 1500 Benicia Rd Vallejo CA 94591-7523

KOBAYASHI, HISASHI, computer scientist, dean; b. Tokyo, June 13, 1938; arrived in U.S., 1965; m. Masaye Okubo. BS, U. Tokyo, 1961, MS, 1963; MA, Princeton U., 1966, PhD, 1967. Radar system designer Toshiba, Kawasaki, Japan, 1963-65; mem. rsch. staff IBM, Yorktown Heights, NY, 1967-86; dir. Japan Sci. Inst. IBM Japan Ltd., 1982-86; Sherman Fairchild U. prof. elec. engring., computer sci. Princeton (N.J.) U., 1986—, dean Sch. Engring. and Applied Sci., 1986-91. Vis. asst. prof. UCLA, 1969—70; vis. prof. U. Hawaii, 1975, Tech. U. Darmstadt, Germany, 1979—80, U. Victoria, Canada, 1998, U. Tokyo, 1991—92; cons. prof. Stanford U., 1976; internat. prof. U. Libre de Bruxelles, Belgium, 1980; mem. computer sci. panel NRC, 1981—82; mem. adv. bd. Inst. Sys. Sci., Nat. U. Singapore, 1986—, Advanced Sys. Found., Vancouver, Canada, 1986—98; mem. adv. bd. dep. elec. engring. U. Pa., 1986—91; mem. sci. adv. com. Stanford Rsch. Inst. Internat., Menlo Park, Calif., 1986—91; sci. adv. bd. NASA, Washington, 1990—92; external examiners rev. bd. Ctr. Sys. Sci. Simon Fraser U., 1990—92; mem. Premier's Coun., Ont., Canada, 1990—91; bd. advisors Bower award and prize Franklin Inst., Phila., 1990—; bd. dirs. gov. Internat. Coun. Computer Comms., Washington, 1992—. Author: (book) Modeling and Analysis, 1978; assoc. editor: IEEE Trans Info. Theory, 1980—83, editor-in-chief: Performance Evaluation, 1981—86; contbr. articles to profl. jours. Recipient David Sarnoff RCA award, 1960, Invention award, IBM, 1971, 1973, Outstanding Contbn. award, 1975, 1984, Humboldt award, 1979, Silver Core award, IFIP, 1980. Fellow: IEEE (chmn. Richard Hamming award 1990—91); mem.: Engring. Acad. Japan, Internat. Coun. Computer Comm. (gov. 1993—), Internat. Fedn. Info. Processing (chmn. working group 1982—86), Internat. Union Radio Sci. (vice chmn. commn. C 1978—81). Achievements include patents in field. Home: 21 Russell Rd Princeton NJ 08540-6729 Office: Princeton U B323 Engring Quadrangle Princeton NJ 08544-5263 E-mail: hisashi@ee.princeton.edu.

KOBAYASHI, RIKI, chemical engineer, educator; b. Webster, Tex., May 13, 1924; s. Mitsutaro and Moto (Shigeta) K.; m. Barbara Joan Stevens, June 1, 1957; children: James Brock, Alec Stevens; m. Lee Mary Parker Lovejoy; children: Susan, Anne. BSChemE, Rice U., 1944; MS, U. Mich., 1947, PhD in Chem. Engring., 1951. Faculty dept. chem. engring. Rice U., Houston, 1951-94, Louis Calder prof., 1967-94, prof. emeritus, 1994—. D.L. Katz disting. lectr. U. Mich., 1975; hon. chmn., honoree Symposia on Thermodynamics, Chromatography & Transport Phenomena, Am. Inst. Chem. Engrs. Spring Meeting, 1987; plenary lectr. Chemicon '89 Trivandrum, India; Lindsay disting. lectr. Tex. A&M U., 1985; cons. in field. Author: (with others) Handbook of Natural Gas Engineering, 1959; Contbr. over articles to profl. jours. Served with AUS, 1945-46. Recipient Meritorious award Cyrogenic Engring. Conf. Com., 1966, 1st Donald L. Katz award Gas Processors Assn., 1985, Outstanding Engring. Alumni award Rice U., 1985; Japan Soc. Promotion of Sci. fellow, 1985. Fellow AICE, Am. Inst. Chemists; mem. AIME, NAE, Am. Inst. Physics, Am. Chem. Soc., Japan Inst. Chem. Engring. (hon.), Nat. Acad. Engring., Sigma Xi, Alpha Chi Sigma, Tau Beta Pi, Phi Lambda Upsilon, Phi Kappa Phi. Unitarian Universalist. Achievements include co-invention of diffl. kinetics. Home: 348 Piney Point Rd Houston TX 77024-6506 Office: Rice U MS 362 PO Box 1892 Houston TX 77251-1892

KOBER, ARLETTA REFSHAUGE (MRS. KAY L. KOBER), supervisor; b. Cedar Falls, Iowa, Oct. 31, 1919; d. Edward and Mary (Jensen) Refshauge; m. Kay Leonard Kober, Feb. 14, 1944; children: Kay Mary, Karilyn Eve. BA, State Coll. Iowa, 1940; MA, U. No. Iowa. Tchr. HS, Soldier, Iowa, 1943—50, 1965—67; coord. Office Edn. Waterloo (Iowa) Cmty. Schs., 1967—84; head dept. coop. career edn. West HS, Waterloo, 1974—84. Mem. Waterloo Sch. Health Coun.; mem. nominating com. YWCA, Waterloo; Black Hawk County chmn. Tb Christmas Seals; ward chmn. ARC, Waterloo; co-chmn. Citizen's Com. Sch. Bond Issue; pres. Waterloo PTA Coun., Waterloo Vis. Nursing Assn., 1956—62, 1982—, Kingsley Sch. PTA, 1959—60; v.p. Waterloo Women's Club, 1962—63, pres., 1963—64, trustee bd. clubhouse dirs., 1957—58; mem. Gen. Fedn. Women's Clubs, Nat. Congress Parents and Tchrs.; bd. dirs. United Svcs. Black Hawk County, Broadway Theatre League, St. Francis Hosp. Found., Black Hawk County Rep. Women, 1952—53; del. Iowa Rep. Convs., 1996, 1998; Presbyterial world svc. chmn. Presbyn. Women's Assn.; deacon Westminister Presbyn. Ch., 1995—98. Mem.: LWV (dir. Waterloo 1951—52), NEA, AAUW (v.p. Cedar Falls 1946—47), Black Hawk County Hist. Soc. (charter), Internat. Platform Assn., Town Club (dir.), P.E.O., Elklets, Dleta Kappa Gamma, Delta Pi Epsilon (v.p. 1966—67). Home: 3436 Augusta Cir Waterloo IA 50701-4608 Office: 503 W 4th St Waterloo IA 50701-1554

KOBLINER, RICHARD, secondary school educator; b. Bronx, N.Y., May 29, 1935; s. Meyer and Celia (Kantner) K.; m. Suzanne, July 11, 1965. BA, CCNY, 1959, MS in Edn., 1962; postgrad., U. Wis. Cert. adminstr. and supr., social studies tchr., N.Y. Secondary sch. educator DeWitt Clinton, Bronx, N.Y., Hillcrest, Jamaica, N.Y., Cardozo, Bayside, N.Y. Mem. Nat. Coun. for Accreditation of Tchr. Edn.; supr., student tchr. Queens Coll., N.Y.C.; lectr. Elderhostel, Ret. Tchrs. Program. Author: Handbook for the Teaching of Social Studies, Middle Ages Workbook, History of Black Americans; mem. adv. bd. Wall St. Jour.; classroom edit., social studies publs.; contbr. Ency. of N.Y.C. Mem. ASCD, AFT, N.Y. SUT, UFT (chair innovations com.), ATSS, NCSS. Home: PO Box 740425 Boynton Beach FL 33474-0425

KOBYLARZ, JOSEPH DOUGLAS, secondary education educator; b. Garfield, N.J., Dec. 18, 1948; s. Joseph H. and Josephine (Rys) K.; m. Joyce Ann Metzger, July 15, 1978; children: Lauren Ann, Kristen Ann. BS, Northwestern State Coll., 1970; MA, Montclair State Coll., 1976. Cert. tchr. indsl. arts, coord. C.I.E., supr., prin., N.J. Tchr. Garfield Bd. Edn., 1970—, master tchr., 1974-76, dept. chmn., 1976—, adminstrv. asst. to the supt., 1991—. Mem. Am. Indsl. Arts Safety Com., 1978-81, adv. Am. Indsl. Arts Student Assn., Garfield, 1980-85; adj. instr. Montclair State Coll., Upper Montclair, N.J., 1982-86; transcript reviewer Bennett Pub. Co., Peoria, Ill., 1985-87; mem. com. practitioners State N.J. Dept. Edn., 1996—. Co-author: (safety guide) New Jersey Industrial Arts Safety Manual, 1982; author (safety guide) Garfield District Safety Manual, 1981. County committeeman Garfield Dem. Orgn., 1972-75; bd. govs. Ocean Beach and Yacht Club, Lavallette, N.J., 1972-78, dir. beach security, 1989—; mem. Garfield Housing Authority, 1979-84, chmn., 1984; mem. Kinnelon Cmty. Edn. Adv. Com., 1994—, N.J. State Dept. Edn. Com. Practitioners, 1996—. Mem. Vocat. Edn. Assn. N.J. (rec. sec. 1982-88, pres.-elect 1986-87, pres. 1987-88, editor newsletter 1991, region I rep. to Am. Vocat. Assn. 1992—, focus and task force com. State Vocat. Safety Manual 1991-92), Am. Vocat. Assn. (N.J. rep. region I 1990-91), N.J. Vocat. Adminstrs. and Suprs. Assn. (pres. 1997-98, sec. 2000—, Supr. of Yr. 1993), Kinnelon Edn. Found., Phi Delta Kappa. Roman Catholic. Avocations: windsurfing, jogging, racquetball, hiking, wave riding. Home: 97 Miller Rd Kinnelon NJ 07405-3003 Office: Garfield High Sch 500 Palisade Ave Garfield NJ 07026-2546

KOCAOGLU, DUNDAR F. engineering management educator, industrial and civil engineer; b. June 1, 1939; came to U.S., 1960; s. Irfan and Meliha (Uzay) K.; m. ALev Baysak, Oct. 17, 1968; 1 child, Timur. BSCE, Robert Coll., Istanbul, Turkey, 1960; MSCE, Lehigh U., 1962; MS in Indsl. Engring., U. Pitts., 1972; PhD in Ops. Rsch., 1976. Registered prof. engr., Pa., Oreg. Design engr. Modjeski & Masters, Harrisburg, Pa., 1962-64; ptnr. TEKSER Engring. Co., Istanbul, Turkey, 1966-69; project engr. United Engrs., Phila., 1964-71; rsch. asst. U. Pitts., 1972-74; vis. asst. prof., 1974-76; assoc. prof. indsl. engring., dir. engring. mgmt., 1976-87; prof., chmn. engring. and tech. mgmt. dept. Portland State U., 1987—. Pres., CEO TMA-Tech. Mgmt. Assocs., Portland, Oreg., 1973—; pres, CEO Portland Internat. Conf. Mgmt. Engring. and Tech., 1990—. Editor: Management of R&D and Engineering, 1992; co-editor: Technology Management-The New International Language, 1991, Technology and Innovation management, 1999, Innovation in Technology Management-The Key to Global Leadership; series editor: Wiley Series in Engring, and Tech. Mgmt., 1984-98; contbr. articles on tech. mgmt. to more than 100 profl. jours. Lt. C.E., Turkish Army, 1966-68. Fellow IEEE (Centennial medal 1984, Millenium medal, 2000); editor-in-chief trans. on engring. mgmt. 1986—, Millennium medal, 2000); mem. Informs (chmn. Coll. Engring. Mgmt. 1979-81), Am. Soc. Engring. Edn. (chmn. engring. mgmt. div. 1982-83), IEEE Engring. Mgmt. Soc. (fellow, publs. dir. 1982-85), ASCE (mem. engring. mgmt. bd. govs. 1988-93), Muhendis, Ilim Adamlari ve Mimarlar Dernegi Soc. Turkish Engrs. and Scientists (hon.), Am. Soc. Engring. Mgmt. (dir. 1981-86), Omega Rho (pres. 1984-86). Office: Portland State U Engring Mgmt Program PO Box 751 Portland OR 97207-0751

KOCH, CATHERINE ANN, music educator, musician; b. Manchester, N.H., July 27, 1953; d. David Milton and Clarice Joyce Cargill; children: Christopher Lawrence, Gretchen Renate. B in Music Edn., Bucknell U., Lewisburg, Pa., 1975; MS in Music Edn., Syracuse U., 1976. Cert. tchr. N.Y. Pvt. piano, voice and guitar tchr., Fayetteville, NY, 1975—; choral and gen. music tchr. Smith Rd. Sch., N. Syracuse, NY, 1976—81, Manlius Pebble Hill Sch., DeWitt, NY, 1981—89, Eagle Hill Middle Sch., Manlius, NY, 1989—. Substitute organist, soloist various chs., NY, 1993—; organist U. Meth. Ch., Manlius, 1976—93; jr. choir dir. DeWitt Cmty. Ch., 1993—2000; accompanist Syracuse U. Oratorio Soc., 1975—82; mgr., accompanist Jr. High All-County Chorus, Onondaga County, NY, 1992, Onondaga County, 95, Onondaga County, 98, Onondaga County, 2001; chmn. elem. and jr. high vocal task com. Elem. and Jr. High Schs., Onondaga County, 2001—03. Author: (pocket card) Student's Prayer, 1995; musician (pianist): Purely Percussion, 1993, 1995. Recipient Music Masters Harmony award, Soc. Preservation and Encouragement Barbershop Quartet Singing in Am., 2003. Mem.: Am. Choral Dirs. Assn., Onondaga County Music Educators Assn. (pres.-elect), N.Y. State Sch. Music Assn. (presenter 1997, Presdl. Citation for Fayetteville-Manlius music program 1997), Music Educators Nat. Conf. Avocations: reading, swimming, biking. Home: 320 Highbridge St Fayetteville NY 13066 Office: Eagle Hill Middle Sch 4645 Enders Rd Manlius NY 13104

KOCH, DONALD LEROY, retired geologist, state agency administrator; b. Dubuque, Iowa, June 3, 1937; s. Gregory John and Josephine Elizabeth (Young) K.; m. Celia Jean Swede, July 5, 1962; children: Kyle Benjamin, Amy Suzanne, Nathan Gregory. BS, U. Iowa, 1959, MS in Geology, 1967, postgrad., 1971-73. Research geologist Iowa Geol. Survey, Iowa City, 1959-71, chief subsurface geology, 1971-75, asst. state geologist, 1975-80, state geologist and dir., 1980-86; state geologist and bur. chief Geol. Survey Bur., Iowa City, 1986—2002; ret., 2002—. Contbr. articles to profl. jours. Fellow Iowa Acad. Sci. (bd. dirs. 1986-89); mem. Geol. Soc. Iowa (pres. 1969), Iowa Groundwater Assn. (pres. 1986), Rotary, Sigma Xi. Avocations: bicycling, camping, chess, numismatics. Home: 1431 Prairie Du Chien Rd Iowa City IA 52245-5615 E-mail: statefossil@aol.com.

KOCH, JAMES VERCH, academic administrator, economist; b. Springfield, Ill., Oct. 7, 1942; s. Elmer O. and Wilma L. K.; m. Donna L. Stickling, Aug. 20, 1967; children: Elizabeth, Mark. BA, Ill. State U., 1964; PhD, Northwestern U., 1968. From asst. prof. to prof. econs. Ill. State U., 1967-78, chmn. dept., 1972-78; dean Faculty Arts and Scis., R.I. Coll., Providence, 1978-80; prof. econs., provost, v.p. acad. affairs Ball State U., Muncie, Ind., 1980-86; pres. U. Mont., Missoula, 1986-90, Old Dominion U., Norfolk, Va., 1990-2001, prof. econs., 2001—. Author: Industrial Organization and Prices, 2d edit, 1980, Microeconomic Theory and Applications, 1976, The Economics of Affirmative Action, 1976, Presidential Leadership, 1996, The Entrepreneurial President, 2003. Mem. Am. Econ. Assn. Lutheran. Home: 240 Keith Ave Missoula MT 59801-4308 Office: Old Dominion U Dept Econs Norfolk VA 23529

KOCH, JANE ELLEN, secondary school educator; b. Evansville, Ind., Sept. 11, 1947; d. Mason Irwin and Mary Louise (Westfall) Price; m. Donald Lawrence Koch, Dec. 26, 1970; children: Christopher Evan, Darren Nicholas. BA in Edn., U. Evansville, 1970, MA in Edn., 1973. English tchr. Princeton (Ind.) Cmty. H.S., 1970-72, North Posey H.S., Poseyville, Ind., 1972-76; English tchr., libr. New Harmony (Ind.) Sch., 1989—. Roman Catholic. Avocations: reading, organ, piano. Home: 176 N Cale Poseyville IN 47633-0532 Office: New Harmony Sch 1000 E St New Harmony IN 47631 E-mail: kochj2@ccsi.tds.net., kochj@nharmony.k12.in.us.

KOCH, JOANNE ELLEN, guidance counselor; b. Paterson, N.J., Dec. 28, 1962; d. Walter Ernest and Karen Gambert. BA in Early Childhood Edn., William Paterson Coll., 1984, MA in Social Sci., 1987, MEd in Counseling, 1988, MEd in Ednl. Adminstrn., 1991. Cert. tchr., supr., dir. student pers. svcs., N.J. Tchr. St. Andrew Sch., Westwood, N.J., 1985-86; guidance counselor DePaul High Sch., Wayne, N.J., 1986-87; county 4-H agt. Rutgers Coop. Extension Svc., New Brunswick, N.J., 1987-88; guidance counselor High Point Regional High Sch., Sussex, N.J., 1988—. Mem.: Sussex County Guidance Assn. (pres.), N.J. Edn. Assn. Avocations: swimming, bicycling, rollerblading, animals, travel.

KOCH, KENNETH, poet, playwright; b. Cin., Feb. 27, 1925; s. Stuart J. and Lillian Amy (Loth) K.; m. Mary Janice Elwood, June 12, 1954 (dec. 1981); 1 child, Katherine; m. Karen Steinbrink, 1994. AB, Harvard U., 1948; MA, Columbia U., 1953, PhD, 1959. Lectr. Rutgers U., Newark, N.J., 1953-58, Brooklyn Coll., 1957-59; asst. prof. Columbia U., 1959-66, assoc. prof., 1966-71, prof. English and comparative lit., 1971—. Dir. poetry workshop New Sch. for Soc. Rsch., 1958-66. Author: (poetry) Poems, 1953, Ko; or, A Season on Earth, 1959, Permanently, 1960, Thank You and Other Poems, 1962, Poems from 1952 and 1953, 1968, The Pleasures of Peace and Other Poems, 1969, When the Sun Tries to Go On, 1969, Sleeping with Women, 1969, The Art of Love, 1975, The Duplications, 1977, The Burning Mystery of Anna in 1951, 1979, Days and Nights, 1982, Selected Poems, 1950-1982, 1985, On the Edge, 1986, Seasons on Earth, 1987, Selected Poems, 1991, One Train, 1994, On the Great Atlantic Rainway, 1994, Straits, 1998, New Addresses, 2000; (fiction) Interlocking Lives, 1970, The Red Robins, 1975, Hotel Lambosa, 1993; (non-fiction) Wishes, Lies and

Dreams: Teaching Children to Write Poetry, 1970, Rose, Where Did You Get That Red?: Teaching Great Poetry to Children, 1973 (Christopher Book award 1974, Ohioana Book award 1974), I Never Told Anybody: Teaching Poetry Writing in a Nursing Home, 1977, Les Couleurs des voyelles: Pour faire écrire de la poésie aux enfants, 1978, Desideri Sogni Bugie, 1980, (with Kate Farrell) Sleeping on the Wing, 1981, (with Farrell) Talking to the Sun, 1985, The Art of Poetry (criticism), 1996, Making Your Own Days/The Pleasures of Reading and Writing Poetry, 1998; (plays) Bertha and Other Plays, 1966, (a book of plays) The Gold Standard, 1996, A Change of Hearts Opera, 1973, The Red Robins, 1979, One Thousand Avant-Garde Plays, 1988 (Nat. Book Critics Circle award nomination 1988); plays produced include Little Red Riding Hood, 1953, Bertha, 1959, The Election, 1960, Pericles, 1960, George Washington Crossing the Delaware, 1962, The Construction of Boston, 1962, Guinevere, or the Death of the Kangaroo, 1964, The Tinguely Machine Mystery, or the Love Suicides at Kaluka, 1965, The Moon Balloon, 1969, The Artist, 1972, A Little Light, 1972, The Gold Standard, 1975, Rooster Redivivus, 1975, The Art of Love, 1976, The Red Robins, 1978, The New Diana, 1984, A Change of Hearts, 1985, Popeye Among the Polar Bears, 1986, The Banquet, 1998; mem. bd. editors lit. mag. Locus Solus, 1960-62. Recipient Harbison award for teaching, 1970, Frank O'Hara prize for poetry, 1973, Nat. Inst. Arts and Letters award, 1976, Award of Merit for poetry Am. Acad. of Arts and Letters, 1986, Contbn. to Poetry award Fund for Poetry, 1992, Disting. Work award Merrill Found., 1992, Bollingen prize for poetry Yale Univ. Libr., 1995, Bobbitt Nat. prize fo poetry, Libr. of Congress, 1996, Chevalier dans l'ordre des arts et des lettres, French Govt., 1999; Fulbright fellow, 1950-51, 78, 82; Guggenheim fellow, 1961-61; Nat. Endowment for Arts grantee, 1966; Ingram Merrill Found. fellow, 1969. Mem. Am. Acad. Arts and Letters. Home: 25 Claremont Ave New York NY 10027-6802 Office: Columbia U Hamilton Hall New York NY 10027

KOCH, NANCY JOY, music educator, choral director, vocal coach; b. Wellsboro, Pa., May 15, 1940; d. Alvan Robert and Irene Mildred (Howells) K. BS in Music Edn., Mansfield State Coll., 1962; postgrad., Mich. U., 1963; MA in Voice, Trenton State Coll., 1972; Fellowship, Oberlin Conservatory, 1967; pvt. vocal study with Emile Renan, Manhattan Sch. Music, N.Y.C., 1968-81; postgrad., Pa. State U., 1989. Cert. music educator, Pa. Tchr. vocal music, choral dir. East Strousburg (Pa.) Jr. Sr. H.S. Area, 1962-68, McDonald Elem. Sch., Warminster, Pa., 1968-72, Log Coll. Jr. H.S., Warminster, Pa., 1972-89, dept. chairperson, 1976-80; tchr. vocal music Log Coll. Mid. Sch., Warminster, Pa., 1989-99; choir dir. Warminster Presbyn. Ch., 1987-92. Dept. chmn. Log Coll. Jr. H.S., Warminster, 1976-80; founder, dir. New Beginning Youth Cmty. Choral Group, 1976-86. Soprano soloist (Bach cantata) Oberlin-Robert Fountain Dir., 1967, Verdi Requiem, Trenton State Coll., 1972; soprano soloist Schubert Mass in G, Nativity Cath. Ch., 1996, Vivaldi Gloria, 2000 Recipient Rockefeller Found. grant Oberlin Conservatory, 1967, 1st Place award-Log Coll. Vocal Ensemble, Music In The Pks., 1980-95, 97-99, Cmty. Svc. award Hatboro YMCA, 1981, Overall Outstanding Trophy, Music In the Pks., 1989, 91-94, 98, 99, Centennial/S.D. Tchr. of Yr. Achievement award, 1992. Mem. NEA, Pa. State Edn. Assn., Penn State Music Educators, Nat. Music Educators Assn., Pa. State Edn. Assn., Bucks County Music Educators, Bucks County Music Educators (treas. 1978-88), Order Ea. Star (Morning Light chpt. 312). Lutheran. Avocations: decorating, photography, gardening, choral performances for area nursing homes and cmty. orgns. Home: 1524 Mulberry Cir Warminster PA 18974-1871

KOCHERIL, ABRAHAM GEORGE, physician, educator; b. Alwaye, Kerala, India, Feb. 20, 1962; came to U.S., 1970; s. George Paul and Mary G. (Kallappara) K.; m. Elizabeth Kuruvilla, Jan. 3, 1988; children: George Stephen, Philip Abraham. AB, NYU, 1982, MD, 1986. Diplomate Am. Bd. Internal Medicine, Am. Bd. Cardiovascular Disease, Am. Bd. Clin. Cardiac Electrophysiology. Intern, resident, chief resident Miriam Hosp. Brown U., Providence, 1986—90; fellow Yale U., New Haven, 1990—93; dir. clin. electrophysiology, asst. prof. medicine Med. Coll. Ga., Augusta, 1993—95; head of cardiac electrophysiology Carle Heart Ctr., Urbana, Ill., 1995—; head of cardiology U. Ill. Coll. of Medicine, Urbana, 2001—. Assoc. prof. medicine U. Ill., Urbana, 1995—. Contbr. articles to profl. jours.; various TV appearances. Presdl. scholar N.Y.U., 1979-82. Fellow Am. Coll. Cardiology, ACP; mem. AMA, Am. Heart Assn., N.Am. Soc. Pacing and Electrophysiology, Phi Beta Kappa. Avocations: wine tasting, Tae Kwon Do, impressionist paintings. Office: Carle Heart Ctr 602 W University Ave Urbana IL 61801-2530

KOCIAN, NANCY JANE, elementary education educator; b. Allentown, Pa., May 5, 1950; d. Owen Bastian and Jean (Strauss); m. J. Nonnemacher, June, 1975 (div.); 1 child, Shari; m. S. Kocian, Mar. 1984 (div.). BS in Elem. Edn., Shippensburg State Coll., 1972; MEd, Kutztown State U., 1976; cert. elem. prin., Immaculata Coll. Cert. elem. tchr., Pa. Tchr. Brandywine Heights Sch. Dist., Topton, Pa., 1972—; dir. dist. Topton safety patrol Reading Berks AAA, 1990—, bldg. computer lab. coord., 1993—. Instr. grad. courses Performance Learning Systems, Inc., N.J., 1988-91; cooperating tchr. jr. prosem students and student tchrs. Kutztown U. Dir. family activities Parents Without Ptnrs., 1985-88; camp dir. Macungie Day Camp Girl Scouts U.S., 1989-90; instr. 4H, Berks County, Jr. Gt. Books; vol. coord. organize & share children's sermons. Mem. NEA, ASCD, Pa. Edn. Assn., Pa. Sci. Tchrs. Assn., Brandywine Heights Edn. Assn., Phi Delta Kappan. Avocations: gardening, singing, antique collecting, reading, yoga. Home: PO Box 275 Macungie PA 18062-0275

KOCSIS, JOAN BOSCO, elementary education educator, administrative assistant, assistant principal; b. Phillipsburg, N.J., Feb. 6, 1941; d. Frederick B. and Frances (Marina) Bosco; m. Gerald S. Kocsis Sr., Dec. 30, 1961; children: Gerald S. Jr., Jacqueline Kocsis Morgan. BA, Trenton State Coll., 1962; MEd, U. N.C., Charlotte, 1987. Cert. kindergarten-4 tchr., early childhood edn., lang. arts kindergarten-12, social studies 7-12, adminstrn., supervision and curriculum, N.C. Tchr. grades kindergarten, 1, 3 Hamilton Twp. (N.J.) Bd. Edn., 1962—68; tchr. grades kindergarten, talented and gifted Hopewell Valley Bd. Edn., Pennington, 1976—79; tchr. grades 4, 2, 3 Union County Pub. Schs., Monroe, 1981—88; tchr. grade 1 Charlotte (N.C.)-Mecklenburg Pub. Schs., 1988—89; tchr. grades 1, 2 Union County Pub. Schs., Monroe, 1989—. Presenter (TV show) "Positively for Parents", 1992. Recipient Presdl. award for excellence in tchg. sci. and math. NSF, 1994. Mem. NEA, NSTA, N.C. Sci. Tchrs. Assn., Assn. Presdl. Awardees in Sci. Tchg., Internat. Reading Assn. (Union-Monroe coun. treas. 1993—). Home: 309 Auckland Ln Matthews NC 28104-7867

KODISH, ARLINE BETTY, principal; b. Alliance, Ohio, Sept. 20, 1934; d. Edward J. and Frances Harris; m. Phillip Kodish, June 13, 1954; children: Douglas, Lori D. M in Ednl. Adminstrn., U. Akron, 1979. Cert. prin., tchr., Ohio. Owner Shatto Acad., Akron, 1973—. Mem. Nat. Assn. Elem. Sch. Prins., Ohio Assn. Elem. Sch. Adminstrs., Nat. Assn. for Early Childhood Edn., Assn. for Childhood Edn. Internat. Office: Shatto Acad 386 Wyant Rd Akron OH 44313-4254

KOEHLER, SISTER PATRICIA, elementary school administrator; b. Queens Woodhaven, N.Y., Feb. 4, 1949; d. Eugene Henry and Clara Catherine (Bradford) K. BS in Edn., St. John's U., Jamaica, N.Y., 1974; MS in Religious Edn., Fordham U., 1978. Cert. tchr. (life), adminstr., supr., N.Y. Sec. Sun Chem. Corp., N.Y.C., 1966-67, Old Republic Life Ins. Co., M.Y.C., 1967-68; tchr. St. Pancras Sch., Glendale, N.Y., 1974-79, St. Pius V Sch., Jamaica, N.Y., 1979-81; admistr. Presentation B.V.M. Sch., Jamaica, 1981-88; tchr. Sacred Heart Sch., Glendale, N.Y., 1988-89; adminstr. Long Beach (N.Y.) Cath. Sch., 1989—. Subsidy for Ministry Bd., Sisters of St. Dominic, Amityville, N.Y., 1991—. Tchr. arts and crafts handicapped program, KC, Maspeth, N.Y., 1979-82. Named Outstanding Vol. KC, Maspeth, 1982. Mem. ASCD, Nat. Cath. Edn. Assn. Democat. Roman Catholic. Avocations: tennis, arts and crafts, swimming, reading, running. Office: Long Beach Cath Sch 735 W Broadway Long Beach NY 11561-2864

KOEN, BILLY VAUGHN, mechanical engineering educator; b. Graham, Tex., May 2, 1938; s. Ottis Vaughn and Margaret (Branch) Koen; m. Deanne Rollins, June 3, 1967; children: Kent, Douglas. BA in Chemistry, BS in Chem. Engring., U. Tex., 1961; S.M. in Nuclear Engring., MIT, 1962, Sc.D. in Nuclear Engring., 1968; Diplome d'ingenieur en Genie Atomique, L'institut National des Scis. et Techniques Nucleaires, France, 1963. Registered profl. engr., Tex. Asst. prof. mech. engring. U. Tex., Austin, 1968-71, assoc. prof., 1971-80, Minnie S. Piper prof., 1980, prof., 1981—; dir. Bur. Engring. Teaching U. Tex.-Austin, 1973-76. Prof. Ecole Centrale, Paris, 1983; undergrad advisor mech. engring., 1988-92; vis. prof. Tokyo Inst. Tech., 1994 (summer), 1998-99, 2001 (summer); cons., lectr. in field. Author: Definition of the Engineering Method, 1985, Discussion of the Method, 2003; contbr. articles to profl. jours. Bd. dirs. Oak Ridge Associated Univs., 1975-76. Recipient Standard Oil Ind. award, 1970, W. Leighton Collins Distinguished and Unusual Service awd., Am. Soc. for Engineering Education, 1992. Fellow Am. Soc. Engring. Edn. (v.p. 1987-93, Chester Carlson award 1980, Ben Dasher best paper award 1985, 86, Helen Plants award 1986, William Elgin Wickenden best paper award 1986, Olmsted award, dir. 1982-84, W. Leighton Collins award 1992, Centennial medallion 1993), Am. Nuc. Soc.; mem. N.Y. Acad. Sci., Association des Ingenieurs en Genie Atomique, Rotary Club (Austin; Internat. fellow 1962), Phi Beta Kappa, Sigma Xi (disting. lectr. 1981-83), Tau Beta Pi. Mem. Soc. Of Friends. Achievements include development of computer algorithm for calculation of nuclear system reliability. Office: U Tex Dept Mech Engring Etc 5160 Austin TX 78712

KOENIG, DANIEL DEAN, college dean; b. Freelandville, Ind., Feb. 1, 1944; s. Walter G. and Ruby M. (Stone) K. BS in Edn., Ind. U., 1967; MS, Purdue U., 1973; postgrad. U. S.C.-Columbia, 1981-82; EdD in Higher Edn. Adminstrn. NOVA Univ., 1991. Tchr. math. and history Kankakee Valley Schs., Demotte, Ind., 1967-75; media specialist Eastern Handrock Schs., Charlottesville, Ind., 1975-77; dir., dean learning resources div. Piedmont Tech. Coll., Greenwood, S.C., 1977-87, dean gen. edn., 1988— . Contbr. articles to profl. jours. Counselor, Christian Haven Home for Boys, Wheatfield, Ind., 1968-69. Mem. Am. Libr. Assn. (co-chair standards com. 1987-90), Am. Tech. Edn. Assn. (S.E. region bd. dirs. 1993—), Kankakee Valley Tchrs. Assn. (pres. 1972-73), Ind. State Tchrs. Assn., S.C. Library Assn. (roundtable chmn. 1978-79), Assn. for Ednl. Communications and Tech. S.C. (pres. 1981-82, editor newsletter 1978-81, regional rep. 1984—, co-chair standards com. 1987-90). Recipient Outstanding Adminstr. award, S.C. Tech. Edn. Assn., 1985. Home: 101 Cypress Holw Greenwood SC 29649-8947 Office: Piedmont Tech Coll PO Drawer 1467 Emerald Rd Greenwood SC 29648

KOENIG, PETER LASZLO, artist, educator, curator, author; b. Miskolc, Hungary, Sept. 10, 1933; came to U.S., 1941; s. Zoltan T. and Klara E. (Bodnar) K.; m. Karen L. Weaver, July 11, 1964 (div. 1973); m. Jeane J. Jensen, Dec. 31, 1976. BFA, Mass. Coll. Art, 1959; MFA, Cranbrook Acad. Art, 1961; EdM, Harvard U., 1971. Instr. Kingswood Sch., Mich., 1961-63, R.I. Coll., Providence, 1963-67; asst. prof. Wheelock Coll., Boston, 1967-71; chmn. art dept. Weber State Coll., Ogden, Utah, 1971-76; dean of art Prahran Coll., Melbourne, Australia, 1976-79; chmn. art Dept. U. Ark., Little Rock, 1979-82; lectr. U. Colo., Colorado Springs, 1982-85; curator Art Complex Mus., Duxbury, Mass., 1985-89; art critic Enterprise Newspapers, Falmouth, Mass., 1985-95; dir. exhibns. Art Ctr. Sarasota, Fla., 1998—. Lectr. U. Hawaii, 1989-90; cons. Cape Mus. Fine Arts, Dennis, Mass., 1985—, Falmouth (Mass.) Sculpture Garden, 1989—; art critic Bradenton (Fla.) Herald, Art Review, Sarasota, Weekly Plantet, Sarasota, 1993—. Author: Falmouth-A Visual Legacy, 1987, New Horizons, 1988; exhibited in group shows at Worcester (Mass.) Mus., Detroit Inst. Art, Norfolk (Va.) Mus., Butler (Ohio) Inst. Am. Art, Salt Lake City Art Ctr., Boston Arts Festival, Harvard U., Pa. Acad. Fine Arts, Cape Mus. Fine Arts, numerous others. With U.S. Army, 1953-55. Fulbright grantee, 1964-65, MacDowell Found. grantee, 1964, U.S. Govt. Bicentennial grantee, 1976; Provincetown (Mass.) Workshop fellow, 1961. Mem. Am. Assn. Mus., New Eng. Mus. Assn., Falmouth Artists Guild, Harvard Club. Avocations: sailing, bicycling, hiking, swimming. Home and Office: PO Box 1223 Osprey FL 34229-1223

KOENIG, ROBERT AUGUST, clergyman, educator; b. Red Wing, Minn., July 14, 1933; s. William C. and Florence E. (Tebbe) K.; m. Pauline Louise Olson, June 21, 1962. BS cum laude, U. Wis., Superior, 1955; MA in Ednl. Adminstrn., U. Minn., 1965, PhD, 1973; MDiv magna cum laude, San Francisco Theol. Sem., 1969; postgrad. (John Hay fellow), Bennington Coll., summer, 1965. Ordained to ministry Presbyn. Ch., 1970. Supr. music Florence (Wis.) H.S., 1955—56; dir. instrumental music Chetek (Wis.) Pub. Schs., 1958—62; tchr. instrumental music and humanities Palo Alto (Calif.) Sr. H.S., 1962—65; asst. to min. St. John's Presbyn. Ch., San Francisco, 1964—65; min. Sawyer County (Wis.) larger parish, 1969—74; tchr. gen. music Jordan Jr. H.S., Palo Alto, 1966—69; instr. Coll. Edn. U. Minn., 1969—71; adminstv. asst. to pres. Lakewood State C.C., White Bear Lake, Minn., 1971—72; asst. to exec. dir. Minn. Higher Edn. Coord. Bd., St. Paul, 1972, coord. commn. and pers. svcs., 1972—74; instr. Inver Hills C.C., Inver Grove Heights, Minn., 1974; pastor First Presbyn. Ch. of Chippewa Falls (Wis.), 1974—85; sr. pastor Grove Presbyn. Ch., Danville, Pa., 1985—88, First Presbyn. Ch., South St. Paul, Minn., 1988—98; supply pastor Couderay and Radisson Presbyn. Chs., Wis., 1999—. Mem. study com. Presbytery of Chippewa, 1973-74, mem. min. rels. com., 1974-77; adj. asst. prof. ednl. adminstrn. U. Minn., Mpls., 1976-77; mem. faculty U. Wis. Ext., Eau Claire, 1977, chmn. 3d Ann. Bibl. Seminar, 1977, mem. faculty Communiversity, 1977-85; mem. internat. coord. com. ch. mission Synod of Lakes and Prairies, 1978-79; mem. ministerial rels. com. Presbytery of No. Waters, 1977-82, chmn. ministerial rels. com., 1981-82, moderator, 1983; chmn. Synod Designation Pastor Plan Cabinet, 1982-84; chmn. Presbytery Coun., 1982-84; chairperson Christian edn. com. Presbytery of Northumberland, 1987-88, mem. Presbytery coun., 1987-88; mem. Christian edn. com. Synod of the Trinity, 1987-88, mem. com. on ministry Presbytery of the Twin Cities Area, 1999-2001, chairperson subcom. on presbytery membership; mem. com. on ministry Danville-Riverside Area Ministerial Assn., 1985-88, pres., 1987-88; mem. South St. Paul Ministerial Assn., 1988-98, pres., 1989-90. Contbr. articles to profl. jours. Bd. dirs. North Ctrl. Career Devel. Ctr., Mpls., 1978-84, chmn. fin. com., 1979-84, bd. dirs. devel. found., 1983-85; pres. Chippewa Valley Ecumenical Housing Assn., 1984-85; mem. alumni bd. U. Minn., 1999—; bd. dirs. Coll. Edn. and Human Devel. Alumni Soc. U. Minn., 1999—, exec. com., v.p., 2001-2002, pres., 2002—. With U.S. Army, 1956-58, Korea. Mem. Masons (grand chaplain Wis. chpt. 1977-80, 83-85, pres. 2002—), Elks (Danville chpt.), Phi Delta Kappa Internat. (U. Minn. Twin Cities chpt.). Home: 6045 Bowman Ave E Inver Grove Heights MN 55076-1502

KOEPPEL, MARY SUE, communications educator; b. Phlox, Wis., Dec. 12, 1939; d. Alphonse and Emma Petronella Marx Koeppel; m. Robert B. Gentry, May 31, 1980. BA, Alverno Coll., 1962; MA, Loyola U., Chgo., 1968; postgrad., U. Wis., St. Louis U., U. N.H., U. Calif., U. North Fla., U. Minn., Jacksonville U. Tchr. St. Joseph H.S., Milw., 1962-68, Pius XI H.S., Milw., 1968-72; instr., head dept. comms., dir. learning ctr. Waukesha County Tech. Inst., Pewaukee, Wis., 1972-80; pres., exec. bd. West Suburban Coun. Tchg. Profession, 1976-80. Adv. Waukesha chpt. Parents Without Partners, 1975—80; cons. Learning Ctrs., 1976—, Coll. and Univ. Faculties; instr. comm. Fla. C.C., Jacksonville, 1980—; instr. (summers) Inst. for Tchrs. of Writing Westbrook Coll., Portland, Maine, 1980—84, instr. (summers) nat. master tchr. seminar, 1982—, TV interviewer, 1989—; instr. Nat. Inst. for Tchrs. Writing, Greenfield, Mass., 1987—94. Editor (-in-chief): Kalliope Jour. Women's Lit. and Art, 1988—, Lollipops, Lizards and Literature, 1994—; editor: Instructional Network Notes, 1982—85; co-editor: Women of Vision, 2000; author: Writing Resources for Conferencing and Collaboration, 1989, Writing Strategies Plus Collaboration, 1997, Writing Strategies Plus Collaboration. 3d edit., 2000, Write Your Life-The Memory Catcher, 1998, In the Library of Silences, Poems of Loss, 2001; contbr. ; contbg. editor: State St. Rev., 1992—. Mem. Sherman Park Cmty. Ctr., 1975—80; co-founder, bd. dirs. Instrnl. Network for coll. Faculty, 1981—85. Recipient Red Schoolhouse award for tchg. excellence, Assn. Fla. C.C., 1983, Faculty Excellence award, 2000, Frances Buck Sherman award, 2001, Educator of Yr. award, Cultural Coun. of Greater Jacksonville, 2001, Bd. Trustees award for Cmty. Svc., Fla. C.C. at Jacksonville, 2003; grantee, NDEA, 1968, Art Ventures, 1992, Tchg. and Learning Ctr., 1999; scholar, Fla. Humanities Coun., 1999. Mem.: Am. Pen Women, Nat. Coun. Tchrs. of English. Office: Kalliope 11901 Beach Blvd Jacksonville FL 32246 E-mail: skoeppel@fccj.edu.

KOEPPL, GERALD WALTER, chemistry educator; b. Chgo., Dec. 4, 1942; s. Walter Carl and Violet Beatrice (Groen) K.; m. Karen Constable Kitfield; children: Jacob Kitfield, Rebecca Carman. BS, Ill. Inst. Tech., 1965, PhD, 1969. NIH postdoctoral fellow Harvard U., Cambridge, Mass., 1969-70; from instr. to prof. Queens Coll., CUNY, Flushing, NY, 1970—90, prof., 1990—, dir. honors in math. and natural scis., 1994—2003; exec. officer PhD program in chemistry Grad. Sch. and Univ. CUNY, 1998—. Pres. New Eng. Wind Energy Conversion Svcs., Waterbury, Vt., 1978-82; cons. Green Mtn. Power, Inc., Burlington, Vt., 1978-82; vis. assoc. prof. Harvard U., 1975, U. Vt., 1978. Author: Putnam's Power From the Wind, 1982; contbr. articles to profl. jours. Com. mem. Boy Scouts Am., Vista, N.Y., 1992-96. Alfred P. Sloan fellow, 1975-76. Mem. Am. Chem. Soc., Am. Phys. Soc., Phi Lambda Upsilon (v.p. 1967, pres. 1968), Sigma Xi. Avocations: backpacking, hiking, mountain climbing. Home: 184 Elmwood Rd South Salem NY 10590-2202 Office: CUNY Grad Ctr 365 Fifth Ave New York NY 10016

KOEPSEL, WELLINGTON WESLEY, electrical engineering educator; b. McQueeney, Tex., Dec. 5, 1921; s. Wesley Wellington and Hulda (Nagel) K.; m. Dorothy Helen Adams, June 25, 1950; children: Kirsten Marta, Gretchen Lisa, Wellington Lief. BS in Elec. Engring., U. Tex., 1944, MS, 1951; PhD, Okla. State U., 1960. Engr. City Pub. Service Bd., San Antonio, 1946-47; research sci. Mil. Physics Research Lab., U. Tex., 1948-51; research engr. North Am. Aviation, Downey, Calif., 1951; asst. prof. So. Methodist U., 1951-59; assoc. prof. U. N.Mex., Albuquerque, 1960-63, Duke U., 1963-64; prof., head dept. elec. engring. Kans. State U., Manhattan, 1964-76, prof. elec. engring., 1976-84, prof. emeritus, 1984—; pres., owner, chief engr. Mutronic Systems, Austin, Tex. Contbr. articles profl. jours. Served from ensign to lt. (j.g.) USNR, 1944-46. Mem. IEEE (sr.), Sigma Xi, Eta Kappa Nu. Achievements include research on micro-computer simulation and modeling of electromagnetic (microwave) sensor systems; digital signal processing; development of R.F. wireless data transmission and computer software for systems simulation. Address: PO Box 26806 Austin TX 78755-0806 E-mail: wkoepsel@ieee.org..

KOERBER, DOLORES JEAN, music educator, musician; b. Martins Ferry, Ohio, Apr. 7, 1936; d. Clarence Donald and Bertha Gail (Palmer) K. B in Religious Edn., Malone Coll., 1958, BS, 1965; MEd, Kent State U., 1972; D in Religious Edn., Massillon Baptist Coll., 2000. Cert. tchr. music grades K-12, Ohio. Tchr. Coun. Religious Edn., North Canton, Ohio, 1958-60, Shelby, Ohio, 1960-62, Garaway Local, Sugarcreek, Ohio, 1965-71, Fairless Local, Justus, Ohio, 1971-73, Massillon (Ohio) Christian Sch., 1973-75; prof. Massillon Bapt. Coll., 1973—. Choir dir. Evang. United Brethren Ch., Sugarcreek, 1965-68, Westminster Presbyn., Canton, 1973-75, organist, 1981-85, Christ United Meth., Louisville, Ohio, 1985-92, St. Paul's United Meth., Canton, 1993—. Performer in programs for schs., clubs and chs. Named first native Cantonian to graduate from Malone Coll. after its relocation in Canton, 1958. Mem. Fortnightly Music Club (pres. 1970-71), MacDowell Club (rec. sec. 2001-03, 1st v.p. 2003—), Am. Guild Organists. Republican. Avocations: doll collecting, handwork, swimming.

KOERBER, MARILYNN ELEANOR, gerontology nursing educator, consultant, nurse; b. Covington, Ky., Feb. 1, 1942; d. Harold Clyde and Vivian Eleanor (Conrad) Hilge; m. James Paul Koerber, May 29, 1971. Diploma, Christ Hosp. Sch. Nursing, Cin., 1964; BSN, U. Ky., 1967; MPH, U. Mich., 1970. RN, Ohio, S.C.; cert. gerontologist. Staff nurse premature and newborn nursery Cin. Gen. Hosp., 1964-65; staff nurse, hosp. discharge planner Vis. Nurse Assn., Cin., 1967-69, asst. dir. Atlanta, 1976-78; instr. Coll. Nursing, U. Ky., Lexington, 1970-71; supr. Montgomery County Health Dept., Rockville, Md., 1971-74; asst. prof. Coll. Nursing, U. S.C., Columbia, 1979-86, instr., 1987-89; alzheimer's project coord. S.C. Commn. on Aging, Columbia, 1988-90; dir. edn. and tng. Luth. Homes S.C., White Rock, 1988-91; grad. asst. U. S.C. Sch. of Pub. Health, 1991-94; trainer for homemakers home health aides S.C. Divsn. on Aging, 1991-97; coord. to train homemakers home aides nursing assts. State Pilot Program, DSS and Divsn. on Aging, 1993-95; Alzheimer's trainer office aging, nurse mgr. Beaufort-Jasper Hampton Comprehensive Health, 1998—; allied health program mgr. Tech. Coll. of the Lowcountry, 1997—. Mem. utilization rev. bd. Palmetto Health Dist., Lexington, 1984-2000; test item writer, nurse aide cert. Psychol. Corp., San Antonio, 1989, 91, 92; bd. examiners Nursing Home Adminstrn. and Community Residential Care Facility Adminstr., chmn. of edn. com., Columbia, S.C., 1990-93; presenter gerontol. workshops and residential care facilities adminstrn. Contbg. editor: (handbook) Promoting Caregiver Groups, 1984; reviewer gerontology textbooks, 1983-91; contbr. tng. video and manuals on Alzheimers, 1988 (hon. mention Retirement Rsch. Found. 1989). Del. S.C. Gov. White House Conf. on Aging, Columbia, 1981; chmn. ann. meeting S.C. Fedn. for Older Ams., Columbia, 1989—91; v.p. Alzheimer's Family Services of Greater Beaufort, 1998—99, mem. adv. bd., 2002—; bd. dirs. Sr. Svcs. of Beaufort County, 1997—2002, Alzheimer's Family Services of Greater Beaufort, 1997—2002. USPHS trainee, 1965-67, Adm. on Aging trainee, 1969-70. Mem. ANA (cert. gerontol. nurse, cmty. health nurse), S.C. Nurses Assn., So. Gerontol. Soc., Gerontol. Soc. Am., S.C. Gerontol. Soc. (treas. 1989-91, Rosamond R. Boyd award 1986, Pres. award Mid State Alzheimers Chpt., 1993, Macy Scally Alzheimers award 2000), Soc. for Pub. Health Edn., Am. Soc. on Aging, Alzheimers Assn. (bd. dirs. Columbia chpt. 1988-93, sec. 1992, chmn. nominating com. 1991-92; bd. dirs. S.C. combined health appeal 1991-93), Nat. Coun. on Aging, Nat. Gerontol. Nursing Assn. Democrat. Unitarian Universalist. Avocations: interior decorating, wine tasting.

KOESTER, BERTHOLD KARL, lawyer, law educator, retired honorary German consul; b. Aachen, Germany, June 30, 1931; s. Wilhelm P. and Margarethe A. (Witteler) K.; m. Hildegard Maria (Buettner), June 30, 1961; children: Georg W., Wolfgang J., and Reinhard B. Doctor of Laws, U. Muenster, Fed. Republic Germany, 1957. Cert.in Real Estate Brokerage, Ariz. Asst. prof. civil and internat. law U. Muenster, Germany, 1957-60; v.p. Bank J. H. Vogeler and Co., Duesseldorf, Germany, 1960-64; atty. Ct. of Duesseldorf, Germany, 1960-82; pres. Bremer Tank-u, Kuehlschiffahrtsges, M.B.H., Germany, 1964-72; prof., internat. bus. law Am. Grad. Sch. Internat. Mgmt., Glendale, Ariz., 1978-81; of counsel Tancer Law Offices, Phoenix, 1978—86; chmn., CEO Arimpex, Inc., Phoenix, 1979—; ptnr. Applewhite, Laflin and Lewis, Real Estate Investments, Scottsdale, Ariz., 1981-88; atty., trustee internat. corp. Duesseldorf, Germany and Phoenix, 1983—; chief exec. officer, chmn. bd. German Consultants in Real Estate Investments, Phoenix, 1988—; prof., internat. bus. law, chmn. dept. Western Internat. U., Phoenix, 1996—. Bd. dirs. Ariz. Partnership for Air Transp., 1988-92; chmn. Finvest Corp., Phoenix, 1990—; hon. German cons. for Ariz., 1982-92. Author: The Refinancing of the Banking System,

1963, Long Term Finance, 1968, International Joint Ventures, 1974, History and Economy of the Middle East, 1975, Bauhaus and the Expresssionism, 1983; contbr. articles to profl. jour. Pres. Parents Assn., Humboldt Gymnasium, Duesseldorf, Germany, 1971-78; active German Red Cross, from 1977. Mem. Duesseldorf Chamber of Lawyers, Bochum, Fed. Republic Germany, Assn. Tax Lawyers, Bonn German-Saudi Arabian Assn. (pres. 1976-79), Bonn German-Korean Assn., Assn. for German-Korean Econ. Devel. (pres. 1974-78), Ariz. Consular Corp. (sec., treas. 1988-89), Nat. Soc. Arts and Letters (Greater Ariz. chpt., bd. dirs. 1997—), German-Am. C. of C., Phoenix Met., C. of C., Rotary, Scottsdale, Ariz. Home: 6201 E Cactus Rd Scottsdale AZ 85254-4409 Office: PO Box 15674 Phoenix AZ 85060-5674

KOETTER, LEILA LYNETTE, children's services administrator; b. McCook, Nebr., June 12, 1963; d. Larry Wayne and Leanna Lois (Leibrandt) Hoyt; m. Darin Koetter, May 29, 1993; children: Michaela Nichole, Logan Walter, Dalton Wayne. BS in Elem. Edn., BS in Early Childhood, U. Nebr., 1985; postgrad. in early childhood, U. Nebr. Lincoln at Kearney, 1987—. Asst. volleyball coach McCook (Nebr.) C.C., 1985-88; dir. nature camp YMCA, McCook, 1985-89; dir. nature camp child devel. ctr. McCook C.C., 1985-94, master tchr. child devel. ctr., 1985-90, faculty, instr., 1985—, adminstr. child devel. ctr., 1985—; instr. Kindermusik of S.W. Nebr., 1996—. Adv. bd. head child devel. ctr. McCook Community Coll., 1985—; advisor, instr. Coun. for Early Childhood Profl. Recognition, Washington, 1990—; founder, coord. Cmty. Children's Fair (instr. Cmty. Discovery Week for Elementary Sch. children 1995—) 1995—. Coord. Week of Young Child, McCook; youth coach YMCA, McCook, 1987—; program coord. Sidewalk Culture Fair and Children's Fair, 1996; organizer tchr. Kids Fun Fest, 1997-99, designer, coord. 1996—, editor Kaleidoscope Kids Newspaper pub., 1998-99, dir. Discovery Camps; mem. adv. com., ext. vol. Prairie Lakes Family and Consumer Scis. Mem. ASCD, Nat. Assn. Edn. Young Children, Nat. Coalition for Campus Childcare, Nebr. Assn. Edn. Young Children, Nebr. Edn. Assn. Avocations: coaching children sports, state and nat. softball, creating unique children's programs. Home: RR 1 Box 84 Mc Cook NE 69001-9705 Office: Kindermusik of SW Nebr RR 1 Box 84 Mc Cook NE 69001-9705

KOEVENIG, JAMES LOUIS, biology educator, artist; b. Postville, Iowa, Mar. 18, 1931; s. Louis O. and Mildred B. (Harrington) K.; m. Kathleen Ohloff, Aug. 15, 1954 (dec. May 1984); children: Kimberly K., Kurt Louis; m. Mary Sadler, Sept. 28, 1985. BA, U. Iowa, 1955; MA, U. No. Iowa, 1957; PhD, U. Iowa, 1961. Tchr. 8th grade, State Center, Iowa, 1955—56; rsch. assoc. U. Iowa, Iowa City, summer 1961; asst. prof. zoology San Diego State U., 1961-62; resident cons. Biol. Scis. Curriculum Study, Boulder, Colo., 1962-64; assoc. prof. botany, biology U. Kans., Lawrence, 1964-70, prof., 1970-72; prof. biology U. Ctrl. Fla., Orlando, 1972-96, prof. emeritus, 1997—. Vis. lectr. biology U. Colo., Boulder, 1963-64; mem. UNESCO panel on short biol. films, 1964, Am. Sci. Film Forum, India, 1965, commn. undergrad. edn. in biol. scis., 1965-1969; judge numerous art shows. Dir., writer, photographer, cons. ednl. films and videotapes; author, illustrator: History of Biology, 1996; contbr. articles to profl. jours. Recipient John Muir trophy for Best Ecology Film Nat. Ednl. Film Festival, 1977; NSF Faculty fellow Princeton (N.J.) U., 1967-68, numerous tchg. awards and awards for paintings. Mem. AAAS, Am. Inst. Biol. Scis., Nat. Watercolor Soc., Midwest Watercolor Soc., So. Watercolor Soc., Fla. Watercolor Soc., Sigma Xi, Phi Beta Kappa, Phi Kappa Phi, Beta Beta Beta, Phi Eta Sigma. Home: 845 Keystone Cir Oviedo FL 32765-9549

KOFF, ROBERT HESS, academic administrator; b. Chgo., June 5, 1938; s. Arthur Karl and Dorothy (Hess) K. BA, U. Mich., 1961; MA, U. Chgo., 1962, PhD, 1966. Lic. psychologist, Calif. Instr., counselor S. Shankman Orthogenic Sch. U. Chgo., 1961—64; tchr. U. Chgo. Lab. Sch., 1963—64; instr. U. Ill., Champaign, 1964, U. Chgo., 1964—66; vis. scientist, Lab. for Hypnosis Rsch., asst. prof. Stanford U., Calif., 1966—72; prof., dean Roosevelt U., Chgo., 1972—79; univ. dean SUNY, Albany, 1979—92; program dir., sr. v.p. Danforth Found., St. Louis, 1992—2003; prof. and dir. edn. skills initiative Washington U., St. Louis, 2003—. Vis. scholar Oxford U., Eng., 1965; chmn. N.Y. State Ednl. Conf. Bd., Albany, 1981-92. Mem. Nat. Adv. Coun. on Edn. of Disadvantaged Children, Washington, 1979-82, Gov.'s Adv. Commn. on Children and Youth, Albany, 1981-92. Mem. APA (com. chmn.), Am. Ednl. Rsch. Assn., Nat. Register Health Svc. Providers in Psychology. Home: 48 Kingsbury Pl Saint Louis MO 63112

KOHI, SUSAN, bilingual educator, translator; b. San Francisco, Nov. 28, 1948; d. Maurice Winkler Levinson and Fay Patricia (Lacey) Krier; m. Mahmoud Kohi, Mar. 24, 1973, (div. May 1993); children: Kamila, Samir, Kelly. BA, Holy Name Coll., 1970; MA, Middlebury Coll., 1973. Cert. French, Spanish, bilingual edn. tchr., Ariz. Tchr. fgn. lang. Marin Cath. H.S., Greenbrae, Calif., 1970-71; tchr. English Ecole Breguet, Paris, 1971-72; fgn. exch. teller Bank of Am., Paris, 1972-73; tchr. fgn. lang. Scottsdale C.C., Scottsdale, Ariz., 1974-75; translator Nat. Semiconductor Corp., Sidi-Bel-Abbes, Algeria, 1976-77; tchr., English Société Informatique, Aix-en-Provence, France, 1992; tchr. ESL Greenway Mid. Sch., Phoenix, 1994—98; ESL Spanish North Canyon H.S., Phoenix, 1998. Recipient scholarship, Pi Delta Phi. Mem. NEA, named to Who's Who Among America's Teachers; Nat. Assn. for Bilingual Edn., Ariz. Tchrs. of ESL. Avocations: tennis, swimming, gardening, day trips, with my children.. Home: 4114 E Union Hills Dr Unit 1189 Phoenix AZ 85050-3327

KOHL, HERBERT RALPH, education educator; b. Bronx, N.Y., Aug. 22, 1937; m. Judith Murdoch; children: Antonia, Erica, Joshua. AB in Philosophy magna cum laude, Harvard U., 1958; MA in Spl. Edn., Columbia U., 1962, postgrad., 1965-66. Tchr. Reece Sch. for Severely Disturbed, N.Y.C., 1961, N.Y.C. Pub. Schs., 1962-64; rsch. assoc., journalist Ctr. for Urban Edn., N.Y.C., 1965-67; dir. Tchrs. and Writers Collaborative, N.Y.C., 1966-67; rsch. assoc. Horace Mann-Lincoln Inst., N.Y.C., 1966-67; prin., tchr. Other Ways High Sch., Berkeley, Calif., 1968-71; co-dir. tchr. tng. Ctr. for Open Learning and Teaching, Berkeley, 1972-77; dir. ednl. devel. Coastal Ridge Rsch. and Ednl. Ctr., Point Arena, Calif., 1978—; tchr. Point Arean Pub. Schs., 1986-88; Gordon Sanders prof. edn. Hamline U., St. Paul, 1988-89; disting. prof. edn. Carlton Coll., Northfield, Minn., 1989—. Vis. assoc. prof. dept. English U. Calif.-Berkeley, 1967-68; vis. prof. edn. U. Alaska, Fairbanks, 1983; dir. software devel. Sci. Am. Books, N.Y.C., 1983-84; bd. dirs. Atari Inst., Calif. Poets in Schs., Childrens' Choice Book Club, Coastal Ridge Rsch. and Edn. Ctr., Computer Equity Project Nat. Women's Coalition, others; editorial bd. Learning Mag., The Lion and The Unicorn, Hungry Mind Rev., Interaction Mag., People's Yellow Pages, others; cons., lectr. pub., ednl. and profl. orgns. Author: The Age of Complexity, 1965, The Language and Education of the Deaf, 1967, Teaching the Unteachable, 1967, 36 Children, 1967, The Open Classroom, 1969, Fables: A Curriculum Unit, 1969, Golden Boy as Anthony Cool: A Photo Essay on Names and Graffiti, 1972, Reading: How To - A People's Guide to Alternative Ways of Teaching and Testing Reading, 1973, Games, Math and Writing in the Open Classroom, 1973, Half the House, 1974, On Teaching, 1976, A Book of Puzzlements, 1981, Basic Skills, 1982, Atari Games and Recreations, 1982, Insight: Reflections on Teaching, 1982, Conscience and Human Rights, 1983, Atari PILOT Games and Recreation for Learning, 1983, Atari Puzzlements, 1984, Commodore Puzzlements, 1984, 41 1/2 Things to do with your Atari, 41 1/2 Things to do with your Commodore, 1984, Growing Minds: On Becoming A Teacher, 1985, Mathematical Puzzlements, 1987, Making Theater: Developing Plays With Young People, 1988, The Question is College, 1989, I Won't Learn From You, 1991, From Archetype to Zeitgeist: An Essential Guide To Powerful Ideas, 1992, Powerful Mathematical Ideas, 1992, I Won't Learn From You and Other Thoughts on Maladjustment, 1994, Should We Burn Babar?, 1995; co-author: (with Judith Kohl) View From the Oak, 1977, Pack Band and Colony, 1983, (with Erica Kohl), Whatever Became of Emmett Gold, 1983, (with Myles Horton and Judith Kohl) The Long Haul, 1990; also numerous pamphlets, essays; columnist Teacher mag., 1968-82; editor: An Anthology of Fables (2 vols.), 1973, Stories of Sports and Society, 1973, Gamesmag, 1972-75, And Gladly Teach: A Dolores Kohl Education Foundation Anthology of Teaching and Learning Ideas, 1989, (with Victor Hernandez Cruz) Stuff, 1970; contbr. articles to profl. jours. Henry fellow in philosophy and logic Univ. Coll., Oxford, Eng., 1958-59; Woodrow Wilson Found. fellow Columbia U., 1959-60; recipient award for non-fiction article Nat. Endowment Arts, 1968, Nat. Book Award in CHildren's Lit., 1977, Robert Kennedy Book award, 1990; grantee Boehm Found., 1988, New World Found., 1988, Ford Found., 1970-71, Carnegie Corp. N.Y., 1968-70. Mem. PEN Am. Ctr., Nat. Assn. Devel. Educators, Authors Guild, Edn. Writers Assn. (Disting. Achievement award 1983, 84), Signet Soc., Phi Beta Kappa. Office: 1 N College St Northfield MN 55057-4001

KOHLER, PETER OGDEN, physician, educator, university president; b. Bklyn., July 18, 1938; s. Dayton McCue and Jean Stewart (Ogden) K.; m. Judy Lynn Baker, Dec. 26, 1959; children: Brooke Culp, Stephen Edwin, Todd Randolph, Adam Stewart. BA, U. Va., 1959; MD, Duke U., 1963. Diplomate Am. Bd. Internal Medicine and Endocrinology. Intern Duke U. Hosp., Durham, N.C., 1963-64, fellow, 1964-65; clin. assoc. Nat Cancer Inst., Nat Inst. Child Health and Human Devel., NIH, Bethesda, Md., 1965-67, sr. investigator, 1968-73, head endocrinology service, 1972-73; resident in medicine Georgetown U. Hosp., Washington, 1969-70; prof. medicine and cell biology, chief endocrinology divsn. Baylor Coll. Medicine, Houston, 1973-77; prof., chmn. dept. medicine U. Ark., 1977-86, interim dean, 1985-86; chmn. Hosp. Med. Bd., 1980-82, chmn. council dept. chmn., 1979-80; prof., dean Sch. Medicine, U. Tex., San Antonio, 1986-88; pres. Oreg. Health Scis. U., Portland, 1988—. Cons. endocrinology merit rev. bd. VA, 1985—86; mem. endocrinology study sect. NIH, 1981—85, chmn., 1984—85; mem. bd. sci. counselors NICHD, 1987—92, chair, 1990—92; mem. Nat. Adv. Rsch. Resources Coun. NIH, 1998—; chair task force on health care delivery AAHC, 1991—92; Inst. Medicine bd. dirs. Stds. Ins. Co.; bd. dirs. Portland br. Fed. Res. Bank of San Francisco; chair Task Force on Improving Quality of Long-Term Care, 1994; bd. dirs. Assn. Acad. Health Ctrs., chair, 1998—99; OHSU bd. Northwest Health Found., 1997—2001; mem. adv. bd. Loaves and Fishes, 1989—99; mem. Gov.'s adv. com. Commn. on Tech. Edn., 1989—92; chair Oreg. Health Coun., 1993—95; mem. bd. govs. Am. Bd. Internal Medicine, 1987—93, mem. endocrinology bd., 1983—91, chmn., 1987—91, 1997. Editor: Current Opinion in Endocrinology and Diabetes, 1994-97, Diagnosis and Treatment of Pituitary Tumors, (with G. T. Ross), 1973, Clinical Endocrinology, 1986; assoc. editor: Internal Medicine, 1983, 87, 90, 94, 98; contbr. articles to profl. jours. Mem. campaign cabinet United Way, 1999—; bd. dirs. Portland C. of C., 1997—. With USPHS, 1965-68. NIH grantee, 1973—; Howard Hughes Med. Investigator, 1976-77; recipient NIH Quality awrds, 1969, 71, Disting. Alumnus award Duke Med. Sch., 1992, MRF Mentor award, Med. Rsch. Found., 1994, Humanitarian award Am. Lung Assn., 1996, Jewish Nat. Fund Tree of Life award, 1998. Fellow ACP; mem. AMA (William Beaumont award 1988), Inst. Medicine, Am. Soc. Clin. Investigation, Am. Fedn. Clin. Rsch. (nat. coun. 1977-78, pres. so. sect. 1976), So. Soc. Clin. Investigation (coun. 1979-82, pres. 1983, Founder's medal 1987), Am. Soc. Cell Biology, Assn. Am. Physicians, Am. Diabetes Assn., Endocrine Soc. (coun. 1990-93), Raven Soc., Phi Beta Kappa, Sigma Xi, Alpha Omega Alpha, Omicron Delta Kappa, Phi Eta Sigma. Methodist. Office: Oreg Health Scis U Office of Pres 3181 SW Sam Jackson Park Rd Portland OR 97201-3011

KOHLER, SHEILA M. humanities educator, writer; b. Johannesburg, Nov. 13, 1941; arrived in U.S., 1981; d. Max Kohler and Sheila M. Bodley; m. William M. Tucker; children: Sasha T., Cybele, Brett. BA, Sorbonne, Paris; MA, Inst. Catholique, Paris; MFA, Columbia U., 1983. Prof. New Sch., N.Y.C., 1996—99, CCNY, 2001, Bennington Coll., 2001—03. Author: The Perfect Place, 1987, Miracles in America, 1990, The House on R Street, 1994, Cracks, 1999, The Children of Pithiviers, 2001, One Girl, 1999, Stories From Another World, 2002. Recipient O'Henry Prize, 1999; Lewis B. Cullman Libr. Fellowship, N.Y. Pub. Libr. Ctr. for Scholars and Writers, 2003—.

KOHN, ALAN J. zoology educator; b. New Haven, Conn., July 15, 1931; s. Curtis and Harriet M. (Jacobs) K.; m. Marian S. Adachi, Aug. 29, 1959; children: Lizabeth, Nancy, Diane, Stephen. AB. in Biology, Princeton U., 1953; PhD in Zoology, Yale U., 1957. Asst. prof. zoology Fla. State U., Tallahassee, 1958-61, U. Wash., Seattle, 1961-63, assoc. prof. zoology, 1963-67, prof., 1976-98, prof. emeritus, 1998—. Bd. dirs. Coun. Internat. Exchange Scholars, Wash., 1986-90. Author: A Chronological Taxonomy of Conus, 1758-1840, 1992, (with F.E. Perron) Life History and Biogeography: Patterns in Conus, 1994, (with D. Röckel and W. Korn) Manual of the Living Conidae, 1995, (with others) The Natural History of Enewetak Atoll, 1987; editor: (with F.W. Harrison) Microscopic Anatomy of Invertebrates, vol. 5, Mollusca I, 1994, vol. 6 II, 1997; mem. editl. bd. Am. Zoologist, 1973-77, Am. Naturalist, 1976-78, Malacologia, 1974—, Jour. Exptl. Marine Biology and Ecology, 1981-84, Coral Reefs, 1981-87, Am. Malacological Bull., 1983—; assoc. editor Am. Zoologist, 1999—; contbr. articles to profl. jours. Sr. postdoctoral fellow Smithsonian Inst., 1990, John Simon Guggenheim fellow, 1974-75, Nat. Rsch. Coun. fellow, 1967; numerous rsch. grants NSF, 1960-94. Fellow AAAS, Linnean Soc. London; mem. Internat. Soc. Reef Studies, Soc. for Integrative and Comparative Biology (treas. 1971-74, pres. 1997-98), Am. Malacol. Union (pres. 1982-83), Marine Biol. Assn. India, Marine Biol. Assn. U.K., Malacol. Soc. London, Malacol. Soc. Japan, Pacific Sci. Assn., Am. Microscopical Soc., Sigma Xi (pres. U. Wash. chpt. 1971-72). Home: 18300 Ridgefield Rd NW Shoreline WA 98177-3224 Office: U Wash Dept Zoology Seattle WA 98195-0001 E-mail: kohn@u.washington.edu.

KOHN, JOSEPH JOHN, mathematician, educator; b. Prague, Czechoslovakia, May 18, 1932; came to U.S., 1945, naturalized, 1953; s. Otto and Emilie (Schwarz) K.; m. Anna DiCapua, Dec. 15, 1966; children: Edward, Emma, Alicia. S.B., Mass. Inst. Tech., 1953; MA, Princeton, 1954, PhD, 1956; hon. degree, U. Bologna, 1990. Instr. Princeton U., 1956-57; mem. Inst. Advanced Study, 1957-58, 62-63, 76-77, 80-81, 88-89; mem. faculty Brandeis U., 1958-68, prof. math., 1965-68, chmn. dept., 1964-68, Henry Burchard Fine prof. math., 2002; prof. math. Princeton U., 1968—, chmn. dept., 1973-76, 93-96. Vis. prof. U. Florence, Italy, 1972-73, Harvard U., 1996-97; mem. U.S. pure and applied math. del. to People's Republic of China, 1976; chmn. com. math. NRC, mem. Bd. Math. Scis. Editor: Annals of Mathematics, 1977-88, University Series in Mathematics; contbr. articles to profl. jours. Bd. dirs. Am., Czech and Slovak Edn. Fund. Recipient L.P. Steele prize, 1979, Bolzano medal Czechoslovak Union Mathematicians and Physicists, 1990, first degree medal Union of Czech Mathematicians and Physicists, 1993; named NSF fellow, 1954, Sloan fellow, 1964, Guggenheim fellow, 1976-77; named to Bklyn. Tech. Hall of Fame, 2000. Mem. NAS, Am. Acad. Arts and Scis., Am. Math. Soc. (trustee 1976-81), Czechoslovak Soc. Arts and Scis. (v.p. 1992-94). Home: 32 Sturges Way Princeton NJ 08540-5335 E-mail: kohn@princeton.edu.

KOHN, MELVIN L. sociologist; b. N.Y.C., Oct. 19, 1928; s. Albert and Rose Kohn; m. Janet Goldrich, Oct. 3, 1952. BA, Cornell U., 1948, PhD, 1952. Research fellow Social Sci. Research Council, Ithaca, N.Y., 1951-52; research sociologist Lab. of Socio-environ. Studies, NIMH, Bethesda, Md., 1952-60, chief, 1960-85; prof. sociology Johns Hopkins U., Balt., 1985—, chair dept. sociology, 1996-99. Mem. sci. adv. bd. Max Planck Inst. für Bildungsforschung, Berlin, 1983-90; mem. Commn. on Humanities and Social Scis. of Am. Acad. Learned Soc. and Acad. Scis. of USSR, 1987-90; coord. Am. Sociol. Assn.-Soviet Sociol. Assn. Symposia in Sociology, 1985-90; bd. dirs. Am. Sociol. Found., 1987-92, pres., 1991-92. Author: Analysis of Situational Patterning in Intergroup Relations, 1952, 2d edit., 1980, Class and Conformity: A Study in Values, 1969, 2d edit., 1977, Personlichkeit, Beruf und soziale Schichtung, 1981; co-author: Work and Personality: An Inquiry into the Impact of Social Stratification, 1983, Praca a Osobowosc: Studium Wspolzalesnisci, 1986, Social Structure and Self-Direction: A Comparative Analysis of the United States and Poland, 1990, others; editor Cross-national Research in Sociology, 1989; editl. bd. mem. Am. Jour. Sociology, 1974-75, others; contbr. articles to profl. jours. With USPHS, 1952-60. Recipient Ernest Burgess award, Nat. Council on Family Relations, 1961; Guggenheim Found. fellow, 1987, Japan Soc. for Promotion of Sci. fellow, 1989. Fellow AAAS, Am. Acad. Arts. and Scis.; mem. Am. Sociol. Assn. (pres. 1987, Cooley-Mead award 1992), Internat. Sociol. Assn. (exec. com. 1982-90), Eastern Sociol. Soc. (pres. 1982-83, Merit award 1994), Sociol. Rsch. Assn. (pres. 1978-79), Polish Sociol. Assn. (hon.), D.C. Sociol. Soc. (Stuart A. Rice Merit award for career achievement 1996), Sociologists for Women in Soc., Soc. for Study of Social Problems (v.p. 1973-74). Office: Johns Hopkins U Dept Sociology Baltimore MD 21218

KOHUN, FREDERICK GREGG, information scientist, economist, educator; b. Cleve., Oct. 30, 1952; s. Alexander Fred and Elsie D. (Stanich) K.; m. Christine J. Marsek, June 4, 1977; children: Jordan Christine, Alex Janine. AB in Econs., Georgetown U., 1974; MA in Econs., U. Pitts., 1976, MS Info. Sci., 1986; PhD in Applied History, Carnegie-Mellon U., 1990. Instr. Econs. Pa. State U., Monaca, 1976-81; asst. prof. Computer Info. Scis. Robert Morris Coll., Coraopolis, Pa., 1981-86, assoc. prof., 1986-92, head dept., 1990—, prof., 1992—. Cons. Maintenance Svc. Corp., Milw., 1980—, Pietrogallo, Bosick & Gordon, Pitts., 1990— Contbr. articles to profl. jours. Mem. Am. Soc. Info. Sci., Decision Scis. Inst., Data Processing Mgmt. Assn., M Tech. Assn., Explorers Club Pitts. Avocations: mountain biking, mountaineering, climbing, adventure travel, cross country skiing. Office: Robert Morris Coll Narrows Run Rd Coraopolis PA 15108-1189 Home: 204 Trailside Dr Sewickley PA 15143-8933

KOLATTUKUDY, PAPPACHAN ETTOOP, biochemist, educator; b. Cochin, Kerala, India, Aug. 27, 1937; came to the U.S., 1960; m. Marie M. Paul. BS, U. Madras, 1957; B in Edn., U. Kerala, 1959; PhD, Oreg. State U., 1964. Prin. jr. high sch., India, 1957-58; high sch. chemistry tchr., 1959-60; asst. biochemist Conn. Agrl. Experiment Sta., New Haven, 1964-69; assoc. prof. Wash. State U., Pullman, 1969-73, prof. biochemistry, 1973-80, dir. inst. biol. chemistry, 1980-86; dir. Ohio State Biotech. Ctr., Columbus, 1986-95, dir. neurobiotech. ctr., dir. med. biotech., 1995—2003; dir. Biomolecular Sci. Ctr., chair dept. molecular biology and microbiology U. Ctrl. Fla., Orlando, 2003—. Cons. Analabs, New Haven, Allied Chem. Corp., Solvay, N.Y., Genencor Corp., South San Francisco, Calif., Monsanto Co., St. Louis; mem. Overseas Adv. Com., India; mem. Edison Bio-Tech. Ctr., Cleve., trustee; mem. adv. com. to MUCIA on Sci. and Tech., Nat. Agrl. Biotech. Consortium; Ohio rep. to Midwest Plant Biotech. Consortium. Contbr. over 300 articles to profl. jours.; patentee in field. Recipient Golden Apple award Wash. State Apple Commn., President's Faculty Excellence award Wash. State U.; grantee NIH, NSF, Am. Heart Assn., Am. Cancer Soc., DOE. Mem. Fedn. Am. Socs. for Exptl. Biology, Am. Soc. Plant Physiologists, Am. Soc. Microbiology. Home: 1112 Cherry Valley Way Orlando FL 32828 Office: U Ctrl Fla Biomolecular Sci Bldg Rm 136 4000 Central Florida Blvd Orlando FL 32816

KOLB, CHARLES CHESTER, humanities administrator; b. Erie, Pa., Sept. 4, 1940; s. John Christian and Edna Lucille (Church) K.; m. Joy Bilharz, June 3, 1972 (div. Mar. 1991); 1 child, Nancy Gwenyth; m. P. Jean Drew, July 20, 1991; 1 child, Catherine Claire Fraley. BA in History, Pa. State U., 1962, PhD in Archaeology and Anthropology, 1979. Instr. anthropology Pa. State U., University Park, 1966-69, Bryn Mawr (Pa.) Coll., 1969-73; from instr. to asst. prof. anthropology Pa. State U., Erie, 1973-84; dir. rsch. and grants Mercyhurst Coll., 1984-89, asst. dir. Hammermill Libr., 1989; humanities adminstr. program officer divsn. state programs NEH, Washington, 1989-91, program officer divsn. preservation and access, 1991-96, sr. program officer, 1997—. Manuscript reviewer Holt, Rinehart and Winston, Inc., 1977-89, Prentice-Hall, Inc., 1979-85, William C. Brown, Pubs., 1982-85, U. Tex. Press, 1988—, U. Utah Press, 1991—, U. Press of Fla., 1994—, AltaMira Press/Sage, 1995—, U. Pa. Mus. Applied Sci. Ctr. Archaeology, 1996—, Dover Pub., 1996—, U. Press of Colo., 2003—; grant proposal reviewer NEH, 1981-89, NSF, 1982—, Wenner-Gren Found. for Anthropol. Rsch., 1987-89; co-founder, ann. symposium co-organizer Ceramic Studies Interest Group, 1986—. Author: Marine Shell Trade and Classic Teotihuacan, 1987; editor: A Pot for All Reasons, 1988, Ceramic Ecology, 1988, 89, 97; contbr. articles to profl. jours., chpts. to books; book and film reviewer Sci. Books and Films, 1977—; manuscript reviewer Am. Antiquity, 1978—, Current Anthropology, 1979—, Ancient Mesoamerica, 1990—. Ethnohistory, 1995—, Jour. Material Culture, 1995—, Hist. Archaeology, 1995—, L.Am. Antiquity, 1995—, H-Net Revs., 1996-, Jour. Archaeol. Sci., 1998—, Jour. Am. Inst. for Conservation, 2001—; abstractor Ceramic Abstracts, 1990-96, Art and Archaeology Technical Abstracts, 1996—; regional editor La Tinaja: Newsletter of Archaeol. Ceramics, 1991—; N.Am. corr. Old Potter's Almanack, 1992—; reviewer CHOICE, 1992—, ScienceNETLinks, 1999—, Transoxiana: E-journal de Estudios Orientales, 2003—, Central Asian Rsch. Rev., 2003—; contbr. Encyclopedia of Modern Asia, 2002, Encyclopedia World's Minorities, 2003, Dictionary of American History, 2002. Mem. Commonwealth Pa., Gov.'s Conf. on Librs. and Info. Systems, 1989. Fellow AAAS (panelist sci. journalism awards 2003—), Royal Anthrop. Inst. Gt. Britain and Ireland, Am. Anthrop. Assn.; mem. Am. Ceramic Soc., Am. Chem. Soc., Am. Ethnological Soc., Am. Soc. Ethnohistory, Archaeol. Inst. Am., Assn. Field Archaeology, Coun. Mus. Anthropology, Materials Rsch. Soc., Prehist. Ceramic Rsch. Group, Soc. Am. Archaeology, Soc. Archaeol. Scis. (life, bd. dirs. 1998--, assoc. editor for archaeol. ceramics Bull. 1997—), Soc. Hist. Archaeology, Soc. Am. Archivists, Register Profl. Archaeologists, U.S. Naval Inst. (life), Soc. for Pa. Archaeology, N.Y. State Archaeol. Assn., Paleopathology Assn., Assn. Moving Image Archivists, Pearl Harbor History Assocs. (life), Naval Hist. Found., Ctrl. Eurasian Studies Soc., Sigma Xi, Alpha Kappa Delta, Phi Kappa Phi, Pi Gamma Mu. Achievements include rsch. in tech. and cultural interpretations of archaeol. ceramics by using physiochem. analyses and petrographic microscopy, ceramics from Afghanistan, Ctrl. Asia, Mexico, Guatemala, East Africa, Great Lakes Basin. Home: 1005 Pruitt Ct SW Vienna VA 22180-6429 Office: NEH Divsn Preservation & Access 1100 Pennsylvania Ave NW Washington DC 20004-2501 E-mail: ckolb@neh.gov.

KOLB, DOROTHY GONG, elementary education educator; b. San Jose, Calif. d. Jack and Lucille Gong; m. William Harris Kolb, Mar. 22, 1970. BA with highest honors, San Jose State U., 1964; postgrad., U. Hawaii, Calif. State U., L.A.; MA in Ednl. Tech., Pepperdine U., 1992. Cert. in elem. edn., edn. for mentally retarded, edn. for learning handicapped pre-sch., adult classes, resource specialist, English lang. devel., specially designed acad. instrn. in English, 2000. Tchr. Cambrian Sch. Dist., San Jose, 1964-66, Ctrl. Oahu Sch. Dist., Wahiawa, Hawaii, 1966-68, Montebello (Calif.) Unified Sch. Dist., 1968—. Recipient Very Spl. Person award, Calif. PTA, 1998, Hon. Svc. award, 2003; Walter Bachrodt Meml. scholar. Mem.: Tau Beta Pi, Pi Tau Sigma, Kappa Delta Pi, Pi Lambda Theta.

KOLB, HAROLD HUTCHINSON, JR., English language educator; b. Boston, Jan. 16, 1933; BA in English with honors, Amherst Coll., 1955; MA in Am. Studies, U. Mich., 1960; PhD in British and Am. Lit., Ind. U., 1968. Instr. English Valparaiso U., 1960-62; teaching assoc. Ind. U., 1962-65; from asst. prof. to prof. English U. Va., Charlottesville, 1967-99, prof. emeritus, 2000—, dir. Ctr. for Liberal Arts, 1984-99. Project dir. NEH, 1972-76, 85-99; dir. Canadian Judicial Writing Program, 1981-84; guest prof. Am. studies U. Bonn, 1982; chmn. MLA Delegate Assembly Steering Com., 1984-85. Author: The Illusion of Life-American Realism as a

Literary Form, 1969, A Field Guide to the Study of American Literature, 1976, A Writer's Guide: The Essential Points, 1980; co-author: A Handbook for Research in American Literature and American Studies, 1994; contbr. articles to scholarly and other publs. Naval aviator, 1955-59. Recipient Armstrong prize in English, Amherst Coll., 1952, James A. Work prize U. Ind., 1965, Guggenheim fellowship, 1970-71, Faculty Leadership award Am. Assn. Higher Edn., Carnegie Found. for Advancement of Teaching and Change mag., 1986, Citation for Leadership in Rejuvenation of Secondary and Elem. Edn., Va. Bd. Edn., 1987, Phillip E. Frandson award for Innovation and Creative Programming, Nat. U. Continuing Edn. Assn., 1988, Outstanding Faculty award Va. Coun. Higher Edn., 1988.

KOLBE, RONALD LYNN, research engineer; b. Washington, June 3, 1950; s. Casper Maul and Ruthlee (Cade) K.; m. Margaret Garret, Mar. 16, 1984; 1 child, Katharine Lynn. BSME, U. Md., 1973; MS in Nuclear Engring., Purdue U., 1976; PhD in ME, U. Tenn., 1986. Mech. engr. Burns & Roe, Oradell, NJ, 1981—84; asst. prof. engring. U.S. Mcht. Marine Acad., Kings Point, NY, 1984—87; asst. prof., dir. engr. Shepherd Coll., Sheperdstown, W.Va., 1987—88; staff scientist Berkeley Rsch. Assocs., Springfield, Va., 1989—91; mech. engr. Naval Rsch. Lab., Washington, 1991—97; sr. software engr. Mgmt. Tech., Lexington Park, Md., 1997—2000; sr. scientist Sci. Applications Internat. Corp., McLean, Va., 2000—. Mem.: ASME, AIAA, Sigma Xi. Republican. Methodist.

KOLBESON, MARILYN HOPF, holistic practitioner, educator, artist, advertising executive; b. Cin., June 9, 1930; d. Henry Dilg and Carolyn Josephine (Brown) Hopf; children: Michael Llen, Kenneth Ray, Patrick James, Pamela Sue Kolbeson Lang, James Allan. Student, U. Cin., 1947-48, 50. Cert. holistic memory release practitioner. Interior decorator Metro Carpet, 1971-77; sales and mktg. mgr. Cox Patrick United Van Lines, 1977-80; sales mktg. mgr. Creative Incentives, Houston, 1980-81; pres. Ad Sense, Inc., Houston, 1981-87, M.H. Kolbeson & Assocs., Houston, 1987, Seattle, 1987—, The Phoenix Books, Seattle, 1987-90, METASELF Healing, Seattle, 1999—. Bd. dirs. Umbrella Prodns.; cons. N.L.P. Practitioner and Cons.; Aircraft bus. mgmt. cons., Seattle, 1988—90; holographic memory release practitioner, 1996—; cooking demonstrator, nutritional advisor Puget Consumers Coop., Seattle, 1991—2002; lectr., cons. in field. Pub.: You Make the Difference in Nat. Lit. Poetry Anthology, Morning Song, 1996, : Moving On in Nat. Libr. Poetry, 1998; contbr. poetry to A Place at the Table, 1999; originator : Heart Button Technique, 1995; mgr., assoc. prodr. (mus. comedy) Times Three, 1999; prodn. mgr. Of a Certain Age, 2002; instrument keeper (group shows) Gentle Wind Project, 1999—. Vol. Seattle Pub. Schs., 1992—; mem. citizens adv. bd. Arcola (Ill.) Sch. Dist., 1964—66; charter mem. Rep. Task Force; mem. adv. bd. Alief Ind. Sch. Dist., 1981—87, pres., 1983—84; bd. dirs. Santa Maria Hostel, 1983—86, v.p., 1983—84; mem. citizen's adv. bd. Am. Inst. Achievement, 1986—87; bd. dirs. The Breighton Found. Sr. Housing Devel., Seattle, 2000—, S.E. Seattle Sr. Found., 2000—; founder, pres. Mind Force, Houston, 1978—87, Seattle, 1987—95; founder META Group, Seattle, 1991—, Meta-Self Healing Ministries, Seattle, 1997—. Mem. ARC (Seattle), Nat. Assn. Mentally Ill (Wash.), Internat. Platform Assn., Houston Advt. Splty. Assn. (bd. dirs. 1984-87, treas. 1985, v.p. 1986-87), Inst. Noetic Scis. (charter), Galleria Area C. of C. (bd. dirs. 1986-87), Toastmasters (area gov. 1978), Grand Club (v.p. 1986), Lakewood Seward Park Cmty. Club (bd. dirs.), Fair and Tender Ladies Book Group, Internat. Soc. Poets, World Future Soc. Republican. Universalist. Office: 5253 S Brandon St Seattle WA 98118-2522 E-mail: mhk9@attby.com.

KOLEILAT, BETTY KUMMER, middle school educator, mathematician; b. Houston, Aug. 18, 1948; d. Will Ernest and Nellie Kummer; m. Bashir M. Koleilat, Jan. 12, 1973; 1 child, Farah. BS in Edn., U. Houston, 1970, MEd in Adminstrn., 1973, EdD in Curriculum and Instrn., 1994. Cert. elem. and mid. sch. math. tchr., Tex.; cert. in mid.-mgmt., TEx. Elem. educator, math. specialist, asst. prin. Houston Ind. Sch. Dist., 1970-78; mid. math. tchr., team leader Singapore Am. Sch., 1978-80; tchr. 1st grad Spring Ind. Sch. Dist., Houston, 1980-85, gifted tchr. 3d to 5th grades, 1985-90; tchr. math. Aldine Ind. Sch. Dist., Houston, 1990—2002; ret., 2002; owner Koleilat Edn. Svc. Asst. prin. for curriculum/magnet program, Drew Acad.; presenter Coun. for Advancement of Math. Tchg., 1984-99; mem. Tex. Essential Knowledge and Skills Math Writing Team, Tex. Edn. Agy., 1995-97. Contbg. author: Helping Your Child at Home...With Mathematics, 1991. Recipient Austin High PTA Scholarship, 1966, Harris County PTA Scholarship, 1966, Tchr. Initiative Project award Spring Ind. Sch. Dist., 1983, 84, Link Elem. PTA Scholarship, 1990, Outstanding Math. Educator award, 1994-95; named Outstanding Asst. Prin. Region IV, Tex. Assn. Secondary Sch. Prins., 2002. Mem. ASCD, Nat. Coun. Tchrs. Math. (Arithmetic Tchr. Tchg. Math. in the Middle articles referee Reston chpt. 1987-99, materials reviewer 1995-99). Avocations: tennis, bridge.

KOLESON, DONALD RALPH, retired college dean, educator; b. Eldon, Mo., June 30, 1935; s. Ralph A. and Fern M. (Beanland) Koleson; children: Anne, David, Janet. BS in Edn., Ctrl. Mo. State U., 1959; MEd, So. Ill. U., 1973. Mem. faculty So. Ill. U., Carbondale, 1968—73; dean tech. edn. Belleville Area Coll., Ill., 1982—93; ret., 1993. Mem.: Nat. Assn. Two-Yr. Schs. of Constrn. (pres. 1984—85), Am. Welding Assn., Am. Vocat. Edn. Assn., Jesters, Shriners, Masons.

KOLJIAN, HOLLIS ANN, educational association administrator; b. Erie, Pa., Aug. 16, 1937; d. Robert McCormack Deckard and Marian (Silk) Goodman; 1 child, Kara Howard. BS, Edinboro State Tchrs. Coll., 1959; MS in Edn., U. Pa., 1991. Cert. permanent tchr., Pa. Tchr. Pennsbury Schs., Fallsington, Pa., 1959-93; facilitator Penn Literacy Network, Penn. and Del., 1993—. Adj. prof. U. Pa., 1993—. Scholar U. Pa., 1986. Avocations: yoga, swimming. Home: 122 N Main St New Hope PA 18938-1317

KOLL, KURTIS JAMES, physical and natural scientist, educator; b. Rock Rapids, Iowa, Dec. 28, 1948; s. Howard James and Lorayne Virginia (Winterfeld) K.; m. Sallie Mae Roedell, Aug. 2, 1975; children: Sara, Heather, Amanda. BS, Iowa State U., 1970; MEd, Southwestern Okla. U., 1978; PhD, U. Okla., 1993. Tchr. Eastwood Cmty. Sch. Dist., Correctionville, Iowa, 1971; prof. phys. sci. Cameron U., Lawton, Okla., 1974—. Facilitator Project Wild and Project Learning Tree, 1995—. Mem. supervisory com. Lawton Tchrs. Fed. Credit Union, 1985-92; continuing edn. presenter cmty. and adult continuing edn., Lawton, 1986—; scout leader Royal Rangers, Lawton, 1978-96. With U.S. Army, 1971-74. Mem. Am. Chem. Soc. (sec.-treas. 1994-96), Nat. Sci. Tchrs. Assn., Okla. Assn. for the Improvement of Devel. Edn. (chpt. sec. 1994—), Okla. Assn. Environ. Edn., Okla. Sci. Tchrs. Assn., Nature Conservancy, Phi Delta Kappa (chpt. pres. 1994-97), Beta Beta Beta. Assembly of God. Avocations: gardening, reading, astronomy, rock hound. Office: Cameron University 2800 W Gore Blvd Lawton OK 73505-6377

KOLLAR, EDWARD JAMES, retired biology educator; b. Forest City, Pa., Mar. 3, 1934; s. I. J. and Mary (Zaverl) K.; m. Catherine Ann Tobin, Feb. 23, 1963; children: Michelle, Elizabeth, Rachael, Brian, Rebecca. BS, U. Scranton, 1955; MS, Syracuse U., 1959, PhD, 1963. Instr., zoology, rsch. assoc. U. Chgo., 1963-66, asst. prof., biology, rsch. assoc., zoology, 1966-67, asst. prof., anatomy, biology, 1967-69, asst. prof., anatomy, 1969-71; assoc. prof., oral biology U. Conn. Health Ctr., 1971-76, prof., oral biology, 1976-97, prof. emeritus, 1998—, acting head, dept. oral biology, 1985-86, 96-98, oral biology grad. program dir., 1983-88, assoc. dean acad. affairs, 1988-98, program dir., dentist sci. award program, 1990-97. Vis. prof. Guy's Hosp. Med. Sch., London, 1978, Inst. Molecular Biology, Salzburg, Austria, prof., 1971-90; presenter in field. Editor-in-chief Archives of Oral Biology, 1978-97; mem. editl. bd. Saudi Dental Jour., Epithelial Cell Biology. Numerous exec. positions various ednl. coms. Grantee NIH; recipient Quantrell award, U. Chgo., 1968, Issac Schour Meml. Basic Sci. award, 1981, City of Paris medal, 1986. Mem. Am. Soc. Zoologists, Internat. Soc. Devel. Biologists, Cranofacial Group Internat. Assn. (pres. 1983), Internat. Soc. Differentiation, Devel. Biology, Tissue Culture Assn., Bone Tooth Soc., Sigma Xi (treas. Chgo. chpt. 1969, sec. 1970). Democrat. Roman Catholic. E-mail: kollar@nso.uchc.edu.

KOLODNER, ELLEN JAYNE LICHTENSTEIN, occupational therapy manager and educator; b. Phila., Dec. 26, 1947; d. Oscar S. and Anita (Dorfman) Lichtenstein; m. Bernard B. Kolodner, Dec. 29, 1968; children: Michael, Louis. BS, U. Pa., 1969; MSS, Bryn Mawr Coll., 1980. Lic. occupational therapist, Pa. Dir. therapeutic activities dept. Phila. Psychiat. Ctr., 1981-82; asst. prof. occup. therapy, asst. to dean, coord. fieldwork Thomas Jefferson U., Phila., 1982-92; dir. occupl. therapy dept. Magee Rehab. Hosp., 1992-94; neurorehab. program mgr. U. Pa. Health Sys., 1994-95; dir. clin. profl. devel. NovaCare, Inc., 1995-97; prof. and dir. occupl. therapy program Phila. U., 1997—2003, prof. healthcare mgmt., 2003—. Adj. asst. prof. Thomas Jefferson U., 1992—. Contbr. chpts. to books, articles to profl. jours. Fellow Am. Occupl. Therapy Assn. (cert., exec. bd. 1992, Outstanding Svc. award 1992, award of merit 1997, recognition of achievement award 1997); mem. NASW, Pa. Occupl. Therapy Assn. (Outstanding Achievement award 1985), World Fedn. Occupl. Therapy, Day Care Assn. Montgomery County, Fedn. Day Care Svcs., Alpha Eta. Home: 918 Frazier Rd Rydal PA 19046-2408 E-mail: kolodnere@philau.edu.

KOLODNER, RICHARD DAVID, biochemist, educator, geneticist; b. Morristown, N.J., Apr. 3, 1951; s. Ignace Izack and Ethel (Zelnick) Kolodner; m. Karin Ann Gregory, Aug. 6, 1983 (div. May 1991). BS, U. Calif., Irvine, 1971, PhD, 1975; MS (hon.), Harvard U., 1988. Rsch. fellow Harvard U. Med. Sch., Boston, 1975-78; asst. prof. Dana Farber Cancer Inst. and Harvard U. Med. Sch., Boston, 1978-83, assoc. prof., 1983-88, prof. biochemistry, 1988-97; chmn. divsn. cellular molecular biology Dana-Farber Cancer Inst., Boston, 1991-94, head x-ray crystallography lab., 1991-97, chmn. divsn. of human cancer genetics, 1995-97; prof. medicine, mem. Cancer Ctr. U. Calif. Med. Sch., San Diego, 1997—; mem. Ludwig Inst. for Cancer Rsch., San Diego, 1997—. Editor: PLASMID Jour., 1986—95; editor: (assoc.) Cancer Rsch. Jour., 1995—2000, Cell jour., 1996—; mem. editl. bd. Molecular Cellular Biology Jour., 1999—, Jour. Biol. Chemistry, 2000—, DNA Repair Jour., 2003—; contbr. articles to sci. jours. Recipient Jr. Faculty Rsch. award, Am. Cancer Soc., 1981, Faculty rsch. award, 1984, Merit award, NIH, 1993, Charles S. Mott prize, GM Cancer Rsch. Found., 1996; grantee rsch. grantee, Am. Cancer Soc., 1980—82, NIH, 1978—. Fellow: Am. Acad. Microbiology; mem.: NAS, Am. Assn. Cancer Rsch., Genetic Soc. Am., Am. Soc. Microbiology, Am. Soc. Biochemistry and Molecular Biology. Home: 13468 Kibbings Rd San Diego CA 92130-1231 Office: Ludwig Inst for Cancer Rsch CMME 3080 9500 Gilman Dr La Jolla CA 92093-0669 E-mail: rkolodner@ucsd.edu.

KOLODZIEJ, BRUNO JOHN, retired biology educator; b. Chgo., Aug. 27, 1934; s. John and Rose (Kryca) K.; m. Bernice Louise Kurka, Aug. 9, 1958 (dec. Mar. 1993); children: B. Allen, John, Joy; m. Wauketa Meyer, Sept. 3, 1994; stepchildren: Dinah, Mary Rose. BS in Biology, No. Ill. U., 1958; MS in Biology, Northwestern U., Evanston, Ill., 1960, PhD in Microbiology, 1963. Med. tech. West Suburban Hosp., Oak Park, Ill., 1953-54; NIH postdoctoral fellow U. Chgo., 1963-65; rsch. assoc. Albert Einstein Med. Ctr., Phila., 1965-66; asst. prof. biology Ohio State U., Columbus, 1966-71, assoc. prof., 1971-95, prof. emeritus, 1995—. Author: A Workbook for General Microbiology, 1980, Laboratory Procedures for General Microbiology, 1986. Mem. Downtown Sertoma Club. Avocation: stamps. Home: 3225 Atwood Ter Columbus OH 43224-4044

KOLOWSKI, RICHARD L. principal; BA in Govt., Lake Forest Coll., 1966; MS in History and Secondary Edn., U. Nebr., 1970, PhD in Secondary Edn., 1978. Cert. profl. adminstrv. and supervisory cert. Nebr., full supt., secondary prin., supr., full supt Minn., secondary prin. adminstr. Minn. Offensive lineman Omaha Mustangs, Continental Football League, 1967—69; instr. social studies St. Joseph's .S., Omaha, 1967—68; grad. asst. secondary edn. dept. Coll. Edn. U. Nebr., Omaha, 1968—70; instr. social studies, head social studies dept., head humanities dept. Millard South H.S., Omaha, 1970—77; grad. asst. secondary edn. dept. Tchr.'s Coll. U. Nebr., Lincoln, 1977—78; asst. prof. curriculum and instrn. Millard South H.S., Omaha, 1978—83; asst. commr. edn. Minn. State Dept. Edn., St. Paul, 1983—84; dir. secondary edn. Millard Pub. Schs., Omaha, 1984—93; prin. Millward West H.S., Millard Pub. Schs., Omaha, 1993—. Instr. continuing studies grad. level U. Nebr., Kearney, co-instr., Omaha, 1985. Contbr. articles to profl. jours. Sustaining mem. Boy Scouts Am., Nat. Eagle Scouts Assn., South/S.W. YMCA; past Sunday sch. supt., instr., mem. bd. Christian edn., mem. adult edn. com. and the diaconate 1st Covenant Ch. Omaha, past chmn. long-range planning com., 1984—87; bd. dirs. Omaha-Coun. Bluffs Met. YMCA, 1984—96. Named Nebr. Social Studies Educator of Yr., Nebr. State Coun. for Social Studies, 1982; recipient outstanding Young Educator award, Millard Jaycees, 1974, partial scholarship, Nat. Coun. for Social Studies, 1974, Disting. Svc. Adminstr.'s award, Nebr. Profl. Counselor Assn., 1986. Mem.: ASCD, NEA, Nebr. Assn. for Mid. Level Edn., Nat. Mid. Sch. Assn., Nebr. Assn. for Gifted, Nat. Assn. for Secondary Sch. Prins., Nebr. Assn. for Supervision and Curriculum Devel., Nebr. State Coun. for Social Studies, Nat. Coun. for Social Studies, Am. Vocation Assn., Nebr. Assn. for Humanities Edn., Nat. Assn. for Humanities Edn., Millard Edn. Assn., Nebr. State Edn. Assn., Phi Delta Kappa. Office: Millard West H S 5710 S 176th Ave Omaha NE 68135-2268*

KOLUMBA, KIM DALE, elementary education educator, speech and language pathologist; b. Marshfield, Wis., Dec. 11, 1954; d. Arthur and Helen (Mallek) K. BS, U. Wis., 1977; MS in Speech Pathology, U. Wis., 1978; cert. in teaching, U. Wis., 1990. Speech-lang. pathologist Sch. Dist. of Wis. Dells, Wis., 1978-90, tchr. early childhood and exceptional edn. needs, 1990—. Cooperating tchr. U. Wis., Stevens Point, 1990—. Exec. officer PTA, Wisconsin Dells, 1990—; mem., leader Wisconsin Dells Dist. Wellness com. Mem. NEA (early childhood divsn.), Wis. Edn. Assn., South Ctrl. Edn. Assn., Wisconsin Dells Tchrs. Assn. (rep. 1981—, chair com. 1997-98). Avocations: biking, football, gardening, travel, walking. Office: Sch Dist of Wisconsin Dells 300 Vine St Wisconsin Dells WI 53965-1826

KOM, AMBROISE, literature educator; b. Yogam, Cameroon, Dec. 15, 1946; s. Defomamotcha and Marguerite Wayou; m. Dorothée Njuidje; children: Nouepeyiô, Messà, Ghainsom. Lic in letters, U. Yaounde (Cameroon), l970, diploma higher studies, l97l; D 3d cycle, U. Pau (France), l975; D Letters, U. Sorbonne, Paris, l98l. Instr. Brown U., Providence, l972-75, asst. prof., 1975, Dalhousie U., Halifax, Canada, 1975—77; asst. prof., rschr. U. Sherbrooke, Canada, l978-82; assoc. prof. U. Rabat, l982-84; assoc. prof. lit. U. Yaounde, l984-88, prof., 1988-97, Coll. of the Holy Cross, Worcester, Mass., 1997—. Author: Le Harlem de Chester Himes, 1978, Dictionnaire des Oeuvres Littéraires Négro-Africaines de Langue Française, 1983, George Lamming et le destin des Caraïbes, 1986, Littératures of africaines, 1987, Le Cas Chester Himes, 1990, Mongo Beti. Présence francophone 42, 1993, Education et démocratie en Afrique, 1996, Dictionnaire des oeuvres littéraires de langue française en Afrique au sud du Sahara, vol. 2, 1996, La Malédiction francophone, 2000, Francophonie et dialogue des cultures, 2000, Mongo Beti parle, 2002, Remember Mongo Beti, 2003. Home: 17 Merlin Ct Worcester MA 01602-1363 Office: Coll Holy Cross Dept Modern Lang/Lit Box 89A Worcester MA 01610-2395 E-mail: akom@holycross.edu.

KOMARNENI, SRIDHAR, mineralogist, educator; b. Komarneni, India, Sept. 26, 1944; came to U.S. 1969; s. Veeraiah and Sambrajyamma (Vutla) K.; m. Sreedevi Nagabhyru, Nov. 25, 1979; 1 child, Jayanth. BSc in Agr., A.P. Agrl. U., Bapatla, 1968; MSc in Agr., Indian Agrl. Rsch. Inst., New Delhi, 1970; PhD, U. Wis., 1973. Rsch. asst. U. Wis., Madison, 1969-73, project assoc., 1973-76, Pa. State U., University Park, 1976-78, rsch. assoc., 1978-81, sr. rsch. assoc., 1981-87, assoc. prof. clay mineralogy, 1984-87, prof. clay mineralogy, 1987—. Contbr. articles over 400 to Nature, Sci., Clays Clay Minerals, and others. Recipient Gold Medals (4), A.P. Agrl. U., 1968. Fellow AAAS, Am. Ceramic Soc., Soil Sci. Soc. Am., Royal Soc. Chem., Am. Soc. Agronomy; mem. Clay Minerals Soc., Material Res. Soc., Sigma Xi. Patentee in field. Achievements include 9 patents in field. Home: 1112 Deer Brook Dr Port Matilda PA 16870-9461 Office: Pa State Univ Materials Rsch Lab University Park PA 16802

KOMMEDAHL, THOR, plant pathology educator; b. Mpls., Apr. 1, 1920; s. Thorbjørn and Martha (Blegen) K.; m. Faye Lillian Jensen, June 2, 1924; children: Kris Alan, Siri Lynn, Lori Anne. BS, U. Minn., 1945, MS, 1947, PhD, 1951. Instr. U. Minn., St. Paul, 1946-51, asst. prof. plant pathology, 1953-57, assoc. prof., 1957-63, prof., 1963-90, prof. emeritus, 1990—; asst. prof. plant pathology Ohio Agrl. Research and Devel. Ctr., Wooster, 1951-53, Ohio State U., Columbus, 1951-53; prof. Univ. Coll., U. Minn., St. Paul, 1990—. Cons. botanist and taxonomist Minn. Dept. Agr., 1954-60, Sci. Mus. Minn., 1990—; 7th A.W. Dimock lectr. Cornell U., 1979; external assessor U. Pertanian Malaysia, 1994-97. Author: Pesky Plants, 1989; co-author: Scientific Style and Format, 1994; editor Minn. Fulbright newsletter, 1995-2002, Procs. IX Internat. Congress Plant Protection, 2 vols., 1981, Corn Disease newsletter, 1970-76; assoc. editor The Boghopper, 1996—; cons. editor McGraw Hill Ency. Sci. and Tech., 1972-78; editor-in-chief Phytopathology, 1964-67; sr. editor: Challenging Problems in Plant Health, 1982, Plant Disease Reporter, 1979; contbr. articles to profl. jours. Bd. mem. Park Bugle, 1998—. Recipient Elvin Charles Stakman award, 1990, Award of Merit, Gamma Sigma Delta, 1994; Guggenheim fellow, 1961, Fulbright scholar, 1968. Fellow AAAS, Am. Phytopathol. Soc. (councilor 1958-60, pres. 1971, publs. coord. 1978-84, Disting. Svc. award 1984, 93, sci. adv. 1984—, adv. bd. office internat. programs 1987-93, editor Focus 1981—); mem. Am. Inst. Biol. Scis., Bot. Soc. Am., Coun. Sci. Editors, Internat. Soc. Plant Pathology (councilor 1971-78, sec.-gen. and treas. 1983-88, treas. 1988-93, editor newsletter 1983-93), Mycol. Soc. Am., Minn. Acad. Sci., N.Y. Acad. Scis., Weed Sci. Soc. Am. (award of excellence 1968), Fulbright Assn. (editor newsletter Minn. chpt. 1995-2002). Baptist. Home: 1666 Coffman St Apt 322 Saint Paul MN 55108-1340 Office: U Minn Dept Plant Pathology 495 Borlaug Hall 1991 Upper Buford Cir Saint Paul MN 55108-6030 Office Fax: 612-625-9728. E-mail: thork@umn.edu.

KONDEAS, ALEXANDER G. finance educator; b. Larissa, Greece, Jan. 11, 1965; s. George E. Kondeas and Irene V. Tsirimpa; m. Lisa Carol Vance; 1 child, George. BS in Acctg., Technol. Ednl. Inst. Larissa, Greece, 1988; MBA in Fin., U. South Fla., 1993, MA in Econs., 1994; PhD in Econs., Auburn U., 1998. Grad. tchg. asst. Auburn (Ala.) U., 1994—96, grad. rsch. asst., 1997—98, instr. fin., 1999; asst. prof. econs. and fin. Greensboro (N.C.) Coll., 1999—2002, assoc. prof. econs. and fin., 2002—. With Air Force Intelligence, Greek Air Force, 1988—90. Fellow Ctr. for Internat. Bus. Edn. and Rsch. fellow, U. of Memphis, 2000, acad. fellow, Greek Nat. Fellowship Found., 1985, Greek Nat. Fellowship Found., 1986; grantee Kathleen Price and Joseph M. Bryan family grantee, Greensboro Coll., 2000, 2002. Mem.: Am. Soc. of Bus. and Behavioral Scis., Sigma Beta Delta, Omicron Delta Epsilon. Avocations: reading, weight training, martial arts, basketball. Home: 3205 Coronet Ct Greensboro NC 27410 Office: Greensboro Coll 815 W Market St Greensboro NC 27401-1875 Office Fax: 336-271-6634. Personal E-mail: agkondeas@hotmail.com. Business E-Mail: akondeas@gborocollege.edu.

KONDONASSIS, ALEXANDER JOHN, economist, educator; b. Greece, Feb. 8, 1928; arrived in US, 1948, naturalized, 1960; s. John I. and Eve (Hatzistylianou) K.; m. Patricia Mundorff, Feb. 2, 1956; children: John, Yolanda. AB with distinction, DePauw U., 1952; MA, Ind. U., 1953, PhD, 1961. Teaching assoc. Ind. U., 1954-56, lectr., 1956-58; mem. faculty U. Okla., 1958—, prof. econs., 1964—, David Ross Boyd prof. econs., 1970—, chmn. dept., 1961-71, dir. div. econs., 1979-86, dir. advanced program in econs. bus. coll., 1971—, chmn. faculty senate, 1976-77, Regents prof., 1993. Lectr. Am. participant program U.S. Info. Agy., Iceland, Greece, Yugoslavia, 1986; Fulbright prof. Athens (Greece) Sch. Econs. and Bus. Sci., 1965-66, vis. prof., 1971; assocs. disting. lectureship U. Okla., 1988; bd. dirs. Am. Bank of Commerce; mem. Gov. Okla. Adv. Coun. Export Expansion, 1964-65;adv. council Inst. E. Mediterranean Affairs, 1967-68; chmn. editorial policies com. S.W. Soc. Sci. Quar., 1974-77. Author: Concepts of Economic Development with Special Reference to Underdeveloped Countries, 1963, Monetary Policies of the Bank of Greece, 1949-1951, Contributions to Monetary Stability and Economic Development, 1961, (with others) An Economic Base Study of Lawton, Oklahoma, 1963, Economic Planning and Free Enterprise, 1966, The Role of Agriculture in a Developing Economy, 1973, The EEC and Her Association with Israel, Spain, Turkey and Greece, 1972, Some Recent Trends in Development Economics, 1972, Contributions of Agriculture to Economic Development: The Cases of U.K., U.S.A., Japan and Mexico, 1973, Mediterranean Europe and the Common Market, 1976, The European Economic Community in the Mediterranean: Developments and Prospects on a Mediterranean Policy, 1976, The European Economic Community and Greece: Toward a Full Membership, 1977, The Greek Inflation and the Flight from the Drachma: 1940-48, 1977, The Greek Economy: The Old and the New, 1979, The Bank of Greece, 1949-51: Credit Control Changes in An Inflationary Environment, 1979, The European Economic Community: Toward a Common Development Policy, 1980, Recent Trends in Development Assistance Committee Aid Programs, 1981, Economic and Non-Economic Aspects of Economic Development, the Less Developed Countries: A Synthesis, 1983, Some Internal Problems of Social Sciences with Special Emphasis on the Economics of Development, 1985, Agricultural Productivity and Economic Development: A Note on Japan and Taiwan, 1987 Approaches to Economic Development: Some Swings of the Pendulum, 1988, The European Economic Community and the Single European Act, 1989, The European Economic Community in 1992, 1991, The Economy of Cyprus, 1991, Major Issues of Global Development, 1991, German Unification: Problems and Prospects, 1993, Monetary Union and Economic Integration: The Less Developed Areas of the European Community. 1993, Toward Monetary Union of the European Community: History and Experiences of the European Monetary System, 1994, NAFTA: Old and New lessons from Theory and Practice with Economic Integration, 1996, The European Monetary Union in Transition, 1998, Strengthening the Global Financial Stability, 2001. Bd. dirs. Am. Friends Wilton Park, N.Y., 1967-68. Recipient U. Okla. Regents award excellence teaching, 1964, Merrick Found. Teaching award, 1977, DePauw U. Rector Scholar Alumni Achievement award, 1977; inducted Okla. Higher Edn. Hall of Fame, 1998. Mem. Am. Econ. Assn., So. Econ. Assn., Southwestern Econ. Assn. (pres. 1993-94), Mo. Valley Econ. Assn. (dir., exec. com. 1980—, pres. 1983-84), Southwestern Social Sci. Assn. (v.p. 1980-83, pres. 1983-84), AAUP (pres. 1977-78), Phi Beta Kappa, Omicron Delta Epsilon (pres.-elect internat. exec. bd. 1985-89, pres. 1989-92), Beta Gamma Sigma. Home: PO Box 695 Norman OK 73070-0695

KONECSNI, JOHN-EMERY, marketing company executive, philosophy educator, university official; b. Bklyn., Sept. 1, 1946; s. Benjamin Francis and Mary Elizabeth (Konecsni) Hannigan; m. Gail Maria DiLeonardo, Apr. 2, 1977; children: Margaret Eileen, John-Emery III. BSc, St. Johns U., Jamaica, N.Y., 1967, MA, 1968; PhD, NYU, 1972; hon. diploma pathologists asst. program, Cath. Med. Ctr., 1987. Clk. Bankers Trust Co., N.Y.C., 1963-67; microbiologist Kings County Hosp., Bklyn., 1967; prof. philosophy, chmn. dept. Caldwell (N.J.) Coll., 1968-78; chief exec. officer Declan Finn Career Mktg. Assocs., N.Y.C., 1978—; adj. assoc. prof. philosophy St.

John's U., 1977—; asst. dean Grad. Sch. Pharmacy and Allied Health St. Johns U., 1980—. Pastoral asst. St. Lucy-St. Patrick Roman Cath. Ch., Bklyn., 1976-77; mem. educators caucus Am. Assn. Pathologist Assts., 1982—; chmn. N.Y. State Coun. Physician Asst. Programs, 1986-92. Author: Metabiology and Metascience, 1973, Biology and the Philosophy of Science, 1978, Scotus to Kant, 1978, A Post Kantian Anthropology, 1978, A Philosophy for Living, 2d edit., 1986; also articles and revs. Trustee Queens Village Civic Assn., 1994; mem. allied health edn. com. Cath. Med. Ctr. Bklyn & Queens, 1993—. Mem. Am. Soc. for Med. Tech. (treas. polit. action com. 1990-92), Empire State Assn. for Med. Tech. (pres. 1988, Mem. of Yr. award 1989), Am. Cath. Philos. Assn. (life), Amici Thomae Mori (life), Rho Chi, Lambda Tau. Avocation: reading and writing murder mysteries. Home: 9320 222nd St Queens Village NY 11428-1940 Office: St John's U Coll Pharmacy Allied H Jamaica NY 11439-0001

KONG, JIN AU, electrical engineering educator; b. Kiangsu, China, Dec. 27, 1942; s. Chin-Hwu and Shue C. Kong; m. Wen-Yuan Yu, June 27, 1970; children— Shing, David S. BS, Taiwan U., Taipei, 1962; MS, Chiao Tung U., Hsinchu, Taiwan, 1965; PhD, Syracuse U., 1968. Research engr. Syracuse U., N.Y., 1968-69; Vinton Hayes postdoctoral fellow engring., asst. prof. elec. engring. MIT, Cambridge, 1969-71, asst. prof., 1969-73, assoc. prof., 1973-80, prof., 1980—, chmn. area IV on energy and electromagnetic systems, 1984—. Vis. scientist Lunar Sci. Inst., Houston, summers 1971, 72; vis. prof. elec. engring. U. Houston, 1981-82; cons. UN, 1977-80, Raytheon Co., 1979-82, Hughes Aircraft Co., 1981, Lockheed Missile and Space Co., 1984, Schlumberger-Doll Research, 1985, MIT Lincoln Lab., 1979—; pres. Electromagnetics Acad., 1989—; lectr. in field. Author: Theory of Electromagnetic Waves, 1975, Electromagnetic Wave Theory, 1986; co-author: Applied Electromagnetism, 1983, Theory of Microwave Remote Sensing, 1985; editor: Research Topics in Electromagnetic Wave Theory, 1981, Wiley Series in Remote Sensing, 1985—; editor-in-chief Jour. of Electromagnetic Waves and Applications, 1986—, Progress in Electromagnetics Research, 1989—; contbr. numerous articles to profl. jours.; reviewer numerous jours., govt. orgns., book cos. Recipient Teaching award Grad. Student Council, MIT, 1985 Fellow IEEE; mem. Internat. Union Radio Sci., Am. Phys. Soc., Am. Geophys. Union, Optical Soc. Am., Sigma Xi, Phi Tau Phi, Tau Beta Pi Home: 9 Kitson Park Dr Lexington MA 02421-8109 Office: 77 Massachusetts Ave Rm 26-305 Cambridge MA 02139-4301

KONG, XIANGLI (CHARLIE KONG), mechanical and control engineer, educator; b. Chifeng, China, Mar. 11, 1953; came to U.S., 1989; s. Fanxin Kong and Yuzhen Y.; m. Xiuxian H., Jan. 28, 1978; children: Ling Xin, Brian Lingyu. B of Engring., Shenyang (China) Poly. U., 1978; MSc, Xian (China) Jiaotong U., 1981, PhD, 1985. Lectr. Xian Jiaotong U., 1983-86, assoc. prof., 1986-89; engring. dir. Hill Equipment Corp., Whittier, Calif., 1990-92; pres., CEO MS-Tech Corp., La Mirada, Calif., 1992—. Vis. assoc. prof. UCLA, 1988-90, tchr. computer-controlled machines course, 1993-2000, team leader, key contbr. advanced PC-CNC sys. Contbr. articles to profl. jours. Named Outstanding Young Scientist, Chinese Sci. & Tech. Assn., 1987, Outstanding Young Educator, Fok Yingtong Found., 1988; recipient more than 10 rsch. achievement awards. Office: MS-Tech Corp 14770 Firestone Blvd Ste 208 La Mirada CA 90638-5944

KONIECKO, MARY ANN, elementary education educator; b. Canton, Ohio, Aug. 29, 1952; d. Alexander Joseph and Mary Therese (Jaglowski) K. BS in Edn., Kent State U., 1974. Cert. tchr., Ohio. Tchr. elem. sch. Louisville (Ohio) City Schs., 1974—. Republican. Roman Catholic. Avocations: reading, american history, world history, art history, sports. Home: 714 E 1st St Minerva OH 44657-1104

KONIOR, JEANNETTE MARY, secondary school educator; b. Bronx, N.Y., Jan. 7, 1947; d. Stephen Louis and Frieda Anna (Schmautz) Sirko.; m. Richard Henry Drago, Nov. 13, 1971 (div. Mar., 1989); 1 child, Christina Angelina; m. John Anthony Konior, Feb. 20, 1993; stepchildren: John Adalbert, Joseph Anthony. AA in Social Sci., Orange County C.C., Middletown, N.Y., 1983; BS in Elementary Edn., SUNY, New Paltz, 1985, MS in Elementary Edn., Secondary English, 1993. Cert. tchr. elementary, secondary English, N.Y. Sec. M.W. Kellogg Co., N.Y.C., 1964-69; legal sec. Kaye, Scholar et al., N.Y.C., 1969-72; records coord. Orange & Rockland Utilities, Pearl River, N.Y., 1975-76; personal sec. Hercules, Inc., Middletown, 1976-82; substitute tchr. various dists., Orange County, N.Y., 1986-87; tchr. Archdiocese of N.Y. Most Precious Blood Sch., Walden, N.Y., 1987-2001, ret., 2001. Student tchr. advisor Most Precious Blood Sch., 1992—98, editor-in-chief yearbook, 1988—2000, dir. Christmas play, 1987, coord. various classroom plays, 1987—99; ind. mannatech assoc., 2001—. Chmn. membership com. Village on Green I Homeowners' Assn., Middletown, 1980—81, v.p., sec., 1981—82, pres., 1982—84; mem. Parents without Ptnrs., 1990—91; Vol. religious edn. tchr. St. Matthew's Ch., Bklyn., 1969—70, Mt. Carmel Ch., Middletown, 1973—83, St. Mary's Ch., Montgomery, NY, 1992—93, St. John's Ch., Woodstock, NY, 1994—99, 2001—. Avocations: dressmaking, swimming, boating, walking, reading, writing. E-mail: jenniek47@aol.com.

KONISHI, MASAKAZU, neurobiologist, educator; b. Kyoto, Feb. 17, 1933; BS, Hokkaido U., Japan, 1956, MS, 1958, LLD (hon.), 1991; PhD in Zoology, U. Calif., Berkeley, 1963. Postdoctoral Alexander von Humboldt Found. fellow, 1963-64; Internat. Brain Rsch. Orgn. and UNESCO fellow, 1964-65; asst. prof. zoology U. Wis., 1965-66; asst. prof. to assoc. prof. biology Princeton (N.J.) U., 1970-75; prof. biology Calif. Inst. Tech., Pasadena, 1975-79, Bing Prof. behavioral biology, 1979—. Mem. Salk Inst., 1991—. Assoc. editor Jour. Neurosci., 1980-89, sect. editor, 1990-93; mem. editorial adv. bd. Jour. Comparative Physiology. Recipient Elliot Coues award Am. Ornithologists Union, 1983, F.O. Schmitt prize, 1987, Internat. prize for biology Japan Soc. for Promotion Sci., 1990, honoris causa Hokkaide Univ., 1991, Fondation Ipsen prize, 1999. Recipient David Sparks award in Integrative Neurophysiology U. Ala., 1992, Charles A. Dana award for Pioneering Achievements in Health and Edn., 1992, Sci. Writing prize Acoustical Soc. Am., 1994. Office: Calif Inst Tech Divsn Biology 1200 E California Blvd Pasadena CA 91125-0001

KONNAK, JOHN WILLIAM, surgery educator; b. Racine, Wis., June 28, 1937; s. William Frank and Ruth Viola Konnak; m. Betty LaFleur, June 9, 1962; 1 child, William. BS, U. Wis., 1959, MD, 1962. Diplomate Am. Bd. Urology. Intern Phila. Gen. Hosp., 1962-63; asst. resident Harbor Gen. Hosp., Torrance, Calif., 1965-66; resident U. Mich. Hosp., Ann Arbor, 1966-69, attending staff mem., 1969—99; prof. surgery U. Mich. Med. Sch., Ann Arbor, 1982—2001, emeritus prof. urology, 2001—. Served with USPHS, 1963-65. Fellow ACS; mem. Cen. Surg. Assn., Am. Urol. Assn., Mich. Urol. Assn. (pres. 1991-92), Transplantation Soc. Mich. (pres. 1981-83), Alpha Omega Alpha. Republican. Avocation: scuba diving. Home: 2906 Parkridge Dr Ann Arbor MI 48103-1737

KONRAD, AGNES CROSSMAN, retired real estate agent, retired educator; b. Rutland, Vt., Nov. 26, 1921; d. Warren Julius and Susan Anna (Cain) Crossman; children: Suzanne Martha, Dianna Marie; m. Henry Konrad, Nov. 27, 1954. Assoc. degree in Edn., Castelton Coll., 1943; BS in Edn., Castelton State Coll., 1951; postgrad., SUNY, New Paltz, 1969-70, Fla. Atlantic U., 1973; grad., Realtors Inst. Fla., 1981. Cert. realtor. Tchr. 1st to 8th grades Pittsford (Vt.) Pub. Schs., 1943-44, tchr. 1st grade, 1950-52; tchr. 3d grade Ralph Smith Sch.-Hyde Park (N.Y.) Ctrl. Schs., 1952-69, Violet Ave. Sch.-Hyde Park Sch. Sys., 1969-73; realtor Four Star Realty of Boca Raton (Fla.), 1974-93; ret., 1993. Inducted into Golden Alumni Soc. of Castleton State Coll., 2001. Mem. AAUW (life), N.Y. State Ret. Tchrs. Assn. (life), Castleton Vt. State Coll. Alumni. Avocations: painting, travel, reading, poetry, computer art painting. Home: 1229 SW 13th St Boca Raton FL 33486-5307 E-mail: Henag40@aol.com.

KONSIS, KENNETH FRANK, forester, educator; b. Danville, Ill., Dec. 3, 1952; s. Frank John and Regina Ann (Stefaniak) K.; m. Lorna Jean Wiesemann, May 6, 1978. AS, Danville Area Community Coll., 1972; BS in Forestry, So. Ill. U., 1974. Park ranger Vermilion County Conservation Dist., Danville, 1974-84, dist. forester, 1984-87, rsch. forester, instr. in outdoor edn., 1987-91, dep. dir., 1991-92, exec. dir., 1992—. State del. Ill. Conservation Congress, 1993, 94, 97; mem. Lake Vermilion Water Quality Coalition, 1996—, treas., 2000—; mem. Vermilion River Ecosys. Partnership, 1997—. Mem. VOTEC Agr. and Horticulture Adv Com.; mem. external adv. coun. dept. natural resources and environ. scis. U. Ill., 1993—; v.p. Walnut Coun. Found., 2001—; mem. retail task force com. City of Danville, 2001—, mem. river front task force com., 2001—; mem. Interstate 74 Corridor Planning Com.; mem. nat resources com. Danville Halo Project. Mem.: Ill. Assn. Conservation Dists. (v.p. 1995—96, pres. 1996—2000, Ill. trails and greenways coun. 1997—, v.p. 2001—), Am. Forestry Assn., Shiitake Growers' Assn. Wis., Ill. Tree Farm Com., Ill. Walnut Coun. (regional bd. dirs. 1989—92, v.p. 1991—92, pres. 1992—93, treas. 1994—), Soc. Am. Foresters (comm. chair 1997—98), Am. Chestnut Soc., Ill. Lake Mgmt. Assn. (charter), Ill. Woodland Owners and Users Assn., Internat. Walnut Coun. (nat. meeting program chair 1998, v.p. 1998, pres. 1999, immediate past pres. 2000, v.p. Walnut Coun. Found. 2000—), Ill. Native Plant Soc. (pres. 1986—93, exec. com. 1986—). Roman Catholic. Avocations: photography, gardening, travel, biking, nature. Home: 234 S Walnut St Westville IL 61883-1664 Office: Vermilion Co Conservation Dist 22296-A Henning Rd Danville IL 61834-5336 E-mail: kkonsis@vccd.org.

KONSTAN, DAVID, classics and comparative literature educator, researcher; b. N.Y.C., Nov. 1, 1940; s. Harry and Edythe (Wahrman) K.; m. Pura Nieto; children: Eve Anna, Geoffrey Theodore. Instr. Bklyn. Coll., 1965-67; prof. Wesleyan U., Middletown, Conn., 1967-87; prof. classics and comparative literature Brown U., Providence, R.I., 1987—. Author: Epicurean Psychology, 1973, Roman Comedy, 1983, Simplicius Physics 6, 1989, Sexual Symmetry, 1994, Greek Comedy and Ideology, 1995, Friendship in The Classical World, 1997, Philodemus on Frank Criticism, 1998, Pity Transformed, 2001. Mem. Am. Philol. Assn. (pres. 1999). Avocation: cooking. Home: 70 Westford Rd Providence RI 02906-2515 Office: Brown U 48 College St Providence RI 02912-1856 E-mail: dkonstan@brown.edu.

KONTOS, GEORGE, computer science educator; b. Athens, June 17, 1943; s. Emmanuel and Helen (Nossi) K.; m. Natasha Ziombola, Sept. 3, 1968 (div. Sept. 1987); children: Emmanuel, Kathy, Marilyn Diana, Jennifer Barbara. BA, U. Athens, 1966; MA, U. Tex., 1973; EdD, U. Houston, 1992. Cons. Computer Techniques Internat., Athens, 1976-77; instr., cons. Nat. Iranian Oil Co., Abadan, Iran, 1977-79, U. Basrah, Iraq, 1979; instr. Wharton (Tex.) County Jr. Coll., 1979-92; prof. computer sci. edn. program Nova SE U., Ft. Lauderdale, Fla., 1992—. Bd. dirs. computer sci. and tech. adv. bd. Wharton Jr. Coll., com. mem. learning ctr., 1984—, com. mem. institutional effectiveness, 1986-88. Contbr. articles to profl. jours. With USN, 1966-69. Mem. Phi Delta Kappa. Avocations: square dancing, international folk dancing, tennis, travelling. Office: Nova SE U Abraham S Fischler Ctr 3301 College Ave Fort Lauderdale FL 33314-7721

KONWINSKI, MAUREEN KAVANAUGH, secondary school educator; b. Columbus, Nebr., Mar. 5, 1948; d. Daniel Sebastian and Pauline Mary (Carson) Kavanaugh; m. Gene Thomas Konwinski, Dec. 27, 1969; children: Todd Allen, Kelly Ann, Erin Renee. BA, Creighton U., 1970; M degree, U. Nebr., Omaha, 1986. Cert. tchr., Nebr. Tchr. Sts. Peter & Paul Jr. H.S., Omaha, 1971-77, Millard South H.S., Omaha, 1978, Millard North H.S., Omaha, 1979—, sponsor History Club, 1994—, mem. mentor program, 1995—. Mem. Ralston Cmty. Redevel. Authority, 2000; key communicator Ralston Pub. Schs., 2000. City councilwoman Ralston (Nebr.) City, 1993—; bd. dirs. Ralston Soccer Club, 1992—, sec., 1992—; participant Gov.'s Conf. on Youth Violence, Omaha, 1993—; bd. dirs. Ralston After-Sch. Youth Program; mayors com. Early Childhood Devel. Recipient Econ. Labor scholarship Teamster's, 1986. Mem. Nat. Coun. for Social Studies, Nebr. Coun. Econ. Edn., Consortium Application Space Data Edn. Roman Catholic. Avocations: reading, sports, golfing. Office: Millard North HS 1010 S 144th St Omaha NE 68154-2801

KOO, DELIA Z.F. mathematics educator; b. Hankow, Wuhan, China, May 14, 1921; came to U.S., 1941; d. Wht and Hk (Zung) Wei; m. Anthony Koo, June 6, 1943; children: Victoria Hitchins, Margery Bussey, Emily Koo. BA, St. John's U., Shanghai, China, 1941; AM, Harvard U., 1942, PhD, 1947; MA, Mich. State U., 1954, HHD (hon.), 2002. Tchr. high sch. French St. Mary's Hall, Shanghai, China, 1940-41; tchr. Chinese langs. Mich. State U., East Lansing, 1951-52, math. teaching asst., 1954-55, instr., 1955-56, 57-58; lectr. math. Douglass Coll., Rutgers U., New Brunswick, N.J., 1956-57; asst. prof., assoc. prof., prof. math. Eastern Mich. U., Ypsilanti, 1965-85; prof. emeritus Ea. Mich. U., Ypsilanti, 1985—. Adj. prof. Bus. Coll. br. Va. Poly. U., Washington, 1981; vol. English lang. tchr., vol. coord. for internat. students Mich. State U., East Lansing, 1984—; vol. lang. tchr. Fla. State U., Tallahassee, 1990—. Author: First Course in Modern Algebra, 1963, Elements of Optimization, 1978. Evans fellow, Ann Radcliffe fellow Radcliffe Coll., Cambridge, 1942-43, 45-46; acad. wing is named Delia Koo Internat. Acad. Ctr., Mich. State U. Mem. Math. Assn. Am. (sec.-treas. Mich. sect. 1974-77, editor newsletter 1974-77, vice chair, chair, 1978-80, gov. 1980-83, disting. svc. award 1988, meritorious svc. award 1992).

KOOB, KATHRYN LORAINE, religious studies educator; b. Independence, Iowa, Oct. 8, 1938; d. Harold Frederick Koob and Elsie Muriel Woodward. BA, Wartburg Coll., 1962; MA, U. Denver, 1968; MA Religion, Lutheran Theol. Sem., Gettysburg, Pa., 1998; LHD (hon.), Gwynedd-Mercy Coll., Gwynedd Valley, Pa., 1981, Upsala Coll., 1983. Dist. parish worker Am. Luth. Ch., Denver, 1958—60; tchr. St. Paul's Luth. Sch., Waverly, Iowa, 1962—64, Newton (Iowa) Pub. Schs., Newton, 1964—68; fgn. svc. officer U.S. Info. Agy., Washington, 1969—96; motivational spkr. Waverly, Iowa, 1981—. Co-chair Nat. Adv. Bd. for Comm. Arts Dept. Wartburg Coll., Waverly, Iowa, 2001—. Author: Guest of the Revolution, 1982 (Gold Medallion Book Award presented by Evang. Christian Pub. Assn., 1984); contbr. chapters to books Heroes, 1983, articles to profl. jours. and newspapers. Bd. dirs. Iowa Divsn. UN Assn.-U.S.A., Iowa City, 1999—, ASPIRE-Therapeutic Riding Program, Waterloo. Recipient medal of valor, U.S. Dept. State, 1981, Governor's medal of valor, Iowa State Gov., 1981, Woman of Yr. award, Am. Legion Women's Aux., 2002. Mem.: AAUW (Waverly chpt.), U.S. Info. Agy. Alumni Assn. (life), Am. Fgn. Svc. Assn. (life), Rotary, Kappa Delta Gamma. Lutheran. Avocations: travel, opera, reading. Home: 608 3rd Ave NW Waverly IA 50677-2331 Office: Wartburg Coll 100 Wartburg Blvd PO Box 1003 Waverly IA 50677 Business E-Mail: kathryn.koob@wartburg.edu.

KOONCE, JOHN PETER, investment company executive, educator; b. Coronado, Calif., Jan. 8, 1932; s. Allen Clark and Elizabeth (Webb) K.; m. Marilyn Rose Campbell, Sept. 21, 1952; children: Stephen Allen, William Clark, Peter Marshall. BS, U.S. Naval Acad., 1954; postgrad., U. So. Calif., 1957, U. Alaska, 1961, U. Ill., 1968-69; MS in Ops. Rsch., Fla. Inst. Tech., 1970; postgrad., Claremont Grad. Sch., 1970. Indsl. engr. Aluminum Co. Am., Lafayette, Ind., 1954-56; electronic rsch. engr. Autonetics Divsn. N.Am. Aviation, Downey, Calif., 1956-57; sys. field engr. Remington Rand Univac, Fayetteville, N.C., 1957-59; project engr. RCA Svc. Co., Cheyenne, Wyo., 1959-60, project supr. Clear, Alaska, 1960-62, Yorkshire, Eng., 1962-64, re-entry signature analyst Patrick AFB, Fla., 1964-66; mem. tech. staff TRW Sys. Group, Washington, 1966-68; mgr. ops. rsch. sys. analysis Magnavox Co., Urbana, Ill., 1968-69; tech. advisor EDP, to USAF, Aerojet Electro Sys. Co., Azusa, Calif., Woomera, Australia, 1969-72; investment exec. Shearson Hammill, L.A., 1972-74, Reynolds Securities, L.A., 1974-75; v.p. investments Shearson Hayden Stone, Glendale, 1975-77; v.p. accounts Paine, Webber, Jackson & Curtis, Inc., L.A., 1977-82; pres. Argo Fin. Corp., Santa Monica, Calif., 1982-83, Fin. Packaging Corp., Flintridge, Calif., 1983—; dir. Republic Resources, Inc., 2001—02. Fin. lectr. Princess Line Cruise Ships; tchr. investments Citrus Coll., Azusa, Calif., Claremont (Calif.) Evening Sch.; host, commentator Sta. KWHY-TV, L.A., (weekly) West of Wall Street, 1986-87; bd. dirs. Republic Resources, Inc. Contbr. articles to bus. jours. V.p. Claremont Rep. Club, 1973, pres., 1974; chmn. Verdugo Hosp. Assos., 1979. Mem. Nat. Assn. Security Dealers, Santa Maria Valley C. of C., Navy League U.S., Naval Acad. Alumni Assn., La Can. Flintridge Tournament Roses Assn. (patron), Masons (32d degree, master 1987, pres. dist. officers assn.), Shriners, Kiwanis (pres. La Canada 1995-96, Hixson fellow 2001), Marbella Golf and Country Club (founding). Home: 415 Foxenwood Dr Santa Maria CA 93455-4228 Office: 15233 Ventura Blvd Ste 404 Sherman Oaks CA 91403-2218

KOOTI, JOHN G. economist, educator; married; three children. BS, Jundi Shapour, Iran, 1974; MS, PhD, Mich. State U., 1980. Asst. prof., assoc. prof. econs. and bus. Albany (Ga.) State Coll., 1981-92, prof. econs. and bus., 1992-98; dean Sch. Bus. Ga. Southwestern State U., Americus, 1998—. Office: Ga Southwestern State U 800 Wheatley St Americus GA 31709-4376

KOPECEK, JINDRICH, biomedical scientist, biomaterials and pharmaceutics educator; b. Strakonice, Bohemia, Czechoslovakia, Jan. 27, 1940; came to U.S., 1986; s. Jan and Herta Zita (Krombholz) K.; m. Marie Porcari, Aug. 11, 1962 (Div. 1984); 1 child, Jana; m. Pavla Hrušková, Apr. 27, 1985. MS in Polymer Chemistry, Inst. Chem. Tech., Prague, Czechoslovakia, 1961; PhD in Polymer Chemistry, Inst. Macromolecular Chemistry, Prague, 1965; DSc in Chemistry, Czechoslovak Acad. Scis., Prague, 1990. Rsch. sci. officer Inst. Macromolecular Chemistry, Prague, 1965-67, 68-72, head lab. of med. polymers, 1972-80; postdoctoral fellow NRC, Ottawa, Can., 1967-68; head lab. of biodegradable polymers Inst. Macromolecular Chemistry Czechoslovak Acad. of Scis., Prague, 1980-88; co-dir. Ctr. Controlled Chem. Delivery U. Utah, Salt Lake City, 1986—, prof. bioengring., pharmaceutics and phamaceutical chemistry, 1989—2001, chair dept. pharmaceutics and pharmaceutical chemistry, 1999—, disting. prof. bioengring., pharmaceutics and pharm. chemistry, 2002—. Vis. prof. U. Paris-Nord, Paris-Villetaneuse, 1983, 2000, U. Utah, 1986-88, Tokyo Med. Women's U., 1999; adj. prof. material sci. U. Utah, 1987—; disting. lectr. Nagai Found., Tokyo, 1997; lectr. in field. Mem. editl. bd. 13 sci. jours., U.S., U.K., The Netherlands, 1973—; contbr. over 300 articles to sci. publs. Recipient Best Sci. Paper award Presidia of the Czechoslovak and USSR Acads. of Sci., 1977, awards Chem. Sec. Czechoslovak Acad. Scis., 1972, 75, 77-78, 85, J. Heller award Jour. Controller Release, 1999, Millennial Pharm. Scientist award Millennial World Congress Pharm. Scis., 2000, Paul Dawson Biotech. award Am. Assn. Colls. Pharmacy, 2001, J. Heyrovsky hon. medal for merit in the chem. scis. Acad. Scis. Czech Republic, 2003; Rsch. grantee NIH, U. Utah, industry, 1986—, Czechoslovak Acad. Sci., 1970-88. Fellow Am. Assn. Pharm. Sci., Am. Inst. Med. and Biol. Engring.; mem. AAAS, Am. Chem. Soc., Am. Assn. Cancer Rsch., Soc. Biomaterials (Clemson award for basic rsch. 1995), Soc. for Molecular Recognition, Controlled Release Soc. (bd. govs. 1988-91, v.p. 1993-94, pres.-elect 1994-95, pres. 1995-96, Founders award 1999), Czech Learned Soc. (hon.). Achievements include 37 patents in biomedical field; formulation and development of comprehensive approach to the problems of designing macromolecular carriers to modulate the pharmacokinetics and tissue localization of therapeutic agents; research in synthesis and physical characterization of hydrogels, in biocompatibility of biomedical polymers; design of genetically engineered biomaterials. Office: U Utah Dept Pharm and Pharm Chemistry 30 S 2000 E Rm 301 Skaggs Hall Salt Lake City UT 84112-5820 E-mail: jindrich.kopecek@m.cc.utah.edu.

KOPLOWITZ, STEPHAN, choreographer; b. 1956; Choreographer and dance dir. Packer Collegiate Inst., 1983—. Founding mem. Webbed Feats. Choreographer (multimedia works) seen at Grand Ctr. Terminal, Lincoln Ctr., Bryant Pk., N.Y.C., Nat. History Mus., London, Brit. Libr., Germany. Recipient N.Y. Dance and Performance award for Sustained Achievement in Choreography, 2000; fellowship, John Simon Guggenheim Meml. Found., 2003.

KOPP, WENDY, teaching program administrator; b. Austin, Tex., June 29, 1967; BA, Princeton U., 1998; degree (hon.), Conn. Coll., Drew U. Pres. and founder Teach For America, 1989—. Bd. dirs. New Tchr. Project, The Learning Project, Kipp Acad. Recipient Nat. Acad. fellow, 1990, Jefferson Award for Pub. Svcs., Woodrow Wilson award, 1993, Aetna's Voice of Conscience award, 1994, Citizen Activist award, 1994, Kilby Young Innovator award; named to Time Mag. Roster of Am. Most Promising Leaders Under 40, 1994, Woman of Yr. Glamour mag., 1990. Office: Teach For America 315 W 36th St Fl 6 New York NY 10018-6404

KOPPELMAN, LEE EDWARD, regional planner, educator; b. NYC, May 19, 1927; s. Max and Madelyn Judith (Eisenberg) K.; m. Constance E. Lowinger, June 18, 1948; children: Leslie, Claudia, Laurel, Keith. BEE, CCNY, 1950; MS, Pratt Inst., 1964; D in Pub. Adminstrn., NYU, 1970; LLD, L.I. U., 1978; DHL, Dowling U., 1991. Cert. landscape architect, NY; cert. profl. planner, NJ. Cons. on site planning and landscape architecture, 1950-60; dir. planning Suffolk County Planning Dept., 1960-88; exec. dir. LI Regional Planning Bd., 1965—; leading prof. polit. sci., dir. ctr. regional policy studies SUNY, Stony Brook, 1967—. Adj. prof. environ. sci. Syracuse U., 1976-83; cons. US Dept. Housing and Urban Devel., 1972-78, UN on Land Use and Coastal Zone Planning; mem. Coastal Zone Mgmt. Adv. Com., 1973-75, Nassau/Suffolk Comprehensive Health Planning Council, Melville, NY, 1973-76, Nat. Shoreline Erosion Adv. Panel, 1974-81; exec. dir. tax relief on LI Bi-County State Commn., 1991-92; adv. coun. Sch. of Art, Architecture and Planning Cornell Univ., 1995—. Co-author: Planning Design Criteria, 1968 (3rd edit. 1981), Housing: Planning and Design, 1974, A Methodology to Achieve the Integration of Coastal Zone Science and Regional Planning, 1974, The Urban Sea: Long Island Sound, 1976, Site Planning Criteria, 1978, Long Island Comprehensive Waste Treatment Management Plan, Vol. 1 and 2, 1979, Time Saver Standards for Site Planning, 1982, Long Island Segment of the Nationwide Urban Runoff Program, 1982, Financing Government on Long Island, 1992, The Long Island Comprehensive Special Groundwater Protection Area Plan, 1992, Airport Joint Use Feasibility Study: Calverton Airport, 1993, Financing Government on Long Island, working paper, vols. 1, 2, and 3, 1993, Groundwater and Land Use Planning Experience from North Am., 1996, Town of East Hampton comprehensive Plan, 2002. Recipient cert. of tribute Temp. State Commn. on Water Resources Planning, 1964, career achievement medal Engring. and Archtl. Alumni CCNY, 1977, Disting Alumnus award NYU, 1985, medal of honor LI Assn., 1987, Lone Eagle award Pub. Rels. Soc. Am., 1987, Disting. Leadership award nat. honors program Am. Planning Assn., 1989, Disting. Svc. award NY met. chpt. Am. Planning Assn., 2000, Disting. Svc. medal Found. for LI State Parks, 2001; Paul Harris fellow, 2002; named Citizen of Yr. LI chpt. Nat. Soc. Profl. Engr., 1983. Mem. Am. Inst. Architects (hon.), Am. Inst. Planners, NY State County Planners Assn. (pres. 1967-68), Internat. Fedn. Planning and Housing, Assn. Architecture and Engr., Sigma Xi. Home: 2 Dune Ct East Setauket NY 11733-1527 Office: SUNY Ctr Regional Policy Studies Stony Brook NY 11794-0001

KOPYTOFF, IGOR, anthropology educator; b. Mukden, China, Apr. 16, 1930; came to U.S., 1951; s. Gregory I. and Maria C. (Schenkmann) K.; m. Barbara Joan Klamon, Sept. 1, 1967; 1 child, Larissa. BA, Northwestern U., 1955, PhD, 1960; MA, U. Pa., 1957. Instr. Brown U., Providence, 1960-62; asst. prof. anthropology U. Pa., Phila., 1962-66, assoc. prof., 1966-77, prof., 1977—. Editor: Slavery in Africa, 1977, African Frontier, 1987 (Choice award 1987); contbr. articles to profl. jours. Ford Found. fellow, 1957-60,

NSF fellow, 1969-71, NEH fellow, 1975-76, Guggenheim fellow, 1984-85. Fellow Am. Anthrop. Assn., African Studies Assn., Internat. African Inst., Royal Anthrop. Inst. Office: U Pa Dept Anthropology Philadelphia PA 19104-6398

KORB, CHRISTINE ANN, music therapist, researcher, educator; b. Milw., Aug. 9, 1943; d. Carl William and Lucille (Bell) Knoernschild; m. Mark Lee Korb, June 3, 1967 (div. May 1991); children: Tracy Lee, Amy Elizabeth. BS, Mt. Mary Coll., Milw., 1965; MMus in Music Therapy, Colo. State U., Ft. Collins, 1988. Registered and bd. cert. music therapist. Field dir. Girl Scouts of Am., Ill, Wis., 1965-69; contractual swimming tchr. YMCA, Janesville, Wis., 1970-76; contractual music tchr. YWCA, Janesville, Wis., 1971-76; music therapist inpatient/outpatient psychiat. unit Poudre Valley Hosp., Ft. Collins, 1989-92; music therapist Mary Hill Retirement Ctr., Milw., 1992-93, VA Med. Ctr., Milw., 1992-98; vis. asst. prof. music therapy Willamette U., Salem, Oreg., 1998—2000; dir of music therapy Marylhurst Univ., Oreg., 2000—. Composer (musical works) Namasté, 1988 (Art of Peace award 1985), We Are Your People of Love, 1981 (hon. mention Am. Song Festival 1981), Windseeker, 1988, Merry Christmas Day, 1994. Founding mem. Women in the Arts, Ft. Collins, 1987-88. Rsch. for music therapy grantee Helen Bader Found., Milw., 1994-95. Mem. Am. Music Therapy Assn., Music Tchrs. Nat. Assn., Amnesty Internat., Mu Phi Epsilon, Am. assoc. of univ. women. Democrat. Avocations: reading, spirituality, hiking, cross-country skiing, canoeing. Home: 13538 SW 63rd Pl Portland OR 97219-8122

KORBA, DONNA MARIE, art educator; b. Wilkes-Barre, Pa., Mar. 15, 1958; d. Harry Jr. and Regina Ann (Jachimiak) K. BA in Art Edn., Marywood Coll., 1982, MA in Studio Art, 1988. Tchr. art/religion Notre DAme H.S., East Stroudsburg, Pa., 1982-88, Holy Cross H.S., Delran, N.J., 1988-94; tchr. art, music, English Centro-Educativo Anunciata, Chichicastenango, Guatemala, 1994—; min. to Hispanic cmty., art tchr. St. Joseph Pro-Cathedral, Camden, NJ, 1997—99; tchr. art, religion, choir, parish catechetical trainer Chichicastenango, El Quiche, Guatemala, 1999—2002, tchr., pastoral worker, 2003—; min. to Hispanic cmty. Diocese of Scranton, 2002—03. Artist (book design) Paths of Daring-Deeds of Hope, 1993, (cover designs) Bon Venture Svcs., 1985-91, Diocesan Publs., 1988—, IHM Publs. (Lent-Easter Reflections, 2000-01, Advent & Christmas Reflections, 2000) 1982—, Mental Health Guide, Diocese of Quiche, 2000, Diocesan Design, Jubilee Yr., 2000; photographer Med. Missions Mag., 1993; editl. bd., layout/graphic artist Journey, 1994—; graphic artist, Sercap, Guatemala, 1995—. Music min. Christ the Redeemer Ch., Mount Holly, N.J., 1991-94; mem. Pax Christi, Camden, N.J., 1989—, Women for Guatemala, Chgo., 1993—, Maryknoll Affiliate, Phila., 1993-95; com. mem. Schs. for Escuela Walk-a-Thon, Phila., 1991-93. Mem. Nat. Cath. Edn. Assn., Nat. Art Edn. Assn., Kappa Gamma Pi, Zeta Omnicron. Avocations: running, guitar, singing. Home and Office: 5035 Route 130 Delran NJ 08075-1702 E-mail: dmkorba@yahoo.com.

KORBITZ, BERNARD CARL, retired oncologist, hematologist, educator, consultant; b. Lewistown, Mont., Feb. 18, 1935; s. Fredrick William and Rose Eleanore (Ackmann) K.; m. Constance Kay Bolz, June 22, 1957; children: Paul Bernard, Guy Karl. B.S. in Med. Sci., U. Wis.-Madison, 1957, M.D., 1960, M.S. in Oncology, 1962; LL.B., LaSalle U., 1972. Asst. prof. medicine and clin. oncology, U. Wis. Med. Sch., Madison, 1967-71; dir. medicine Presbyn. Med. Ctr., Denver, 1971-73; practice medicine specializing in oncology, hematology, Madison, 1973-76; med. oncologist, hematologist Radiologic Ctr. Meth. Hosp., Omaha, 1976-82; practice medicine specializing in oncology, hematology, Omaha, 1982-95, ret., 1995; sci. advisor Citizen's Environ. Com., Denver, 1972-73; mem. Meth. Hosp., Omaha, 1977—; dir. Bernard C. Korbitz, P.C., Omaha, 1983-96; bd. dirs., pres. B.C. Korbitz P.C., ret., 1996. Contbr. articles to profl. jours. Webelos leader Denver area Council, Mid. Am. Council of Nebr. Boy Scouts Am.; bd. elders King of Kings Luth. Ch., Omaha, 1979-80; bd. elders St. Mark Luth. Ch., Omaha, 1993-98; mem. People to People Del. Cancer Update to People's Republic China, 1986, Eastern Europe and USSR, 1987; mem. U.S. Senatorial Club, 1984, Republican Presdl. Task Force, 1984. Served to capt. USAF, 1962-64. Named Medford (Wis.) H.S. Athletic Hall of Fame, 1997. Fellow ACP, Royal Soc. Health; mem. Am. Soc. Clin. Oncology, Am. Soc. Internal Medicine, AMA, Nebr. Med. Assn., Omaha Med. Society, Omaha Clin. Soc., Phi Eta Sigma, Phi Beta Kappa, Phi Kappa Phi, Alpha Omega Alpha. Avocations: photography, fishing, travel. Home: 9024 Leavenworth St Omaha NE 68114-5150

KORCHA, LYNDA LEE, school system administrator; b. Wichita, Kans., June 19, 1952; d. Rodney Roy and Gloria June (Ross) Brosius; m. Brian Eugene McClintock, Dec. 19, 1976 (div. 1984); children: Ericka Lynn, Malinda Angeline, Alexis Antoinette; m. Kyle Anthony Korcha, July 15, 1989 (div. 1997). AA, Antelope Valley Jr. Coll., Lancaster, Calif., 1972; BS in Kinesiology, UCLA, 1974; postgrad., Calif. State U., Chico, 1976; MED, Columbus State U., 1997, grad. in leadership, 1999. Recreation leader/coach L.A. County Parks and Recreation, Lancaster, Calif., summers 1972-74; trach coach Paradise (Calif.) Unified Sch. Dist., 1975-76; tchr./coach Fall River (Calif.) Joint Unified Sch. Dist., 1976-79, Morongo Unified Sch. Dist., 29 Palms, Calif., 1979-84, Palm Springs (Calif.) Unified Sch. Dist., 1984-91, Eddy Middle Sch., Columbus, Ga., 1991—, P.E. dept. head, 1991—95, sci. dept. head, 2003. Dept. coord. phys. edn. Nellie N. Coffman Middle Sch., Cathedral City, 1988-91. Recipient Exemplary Teaching award Nellie N. Coffman Middle Sch., 1990. Mem. NEA, UCLA Alumni Assn., Kappa Delta Pi, Alpha Chi Omega. Republican. Presbyterian. Avocations: reading, travel, dance, sports. Home: 4125 Mayfield Dr Columbus GA 31907-2639 Office: Eddy Middle Sch 2100 S Lumpkin Rd Columbus GA 31903-2730

KORCHNAK, LAWRENCE C. educational administrator, consultant, writer; AB, Georgetown U., 1968; MSEd, Duquesne U., 1974; PhD, U. Pitts., 1987. Tchr., basketball coach St. Vincent Prep. Sch., Latrobe, Pa., 1968-70; tchr., counselor St. Mary of the Mount H.S., Pitts., 1970-76; dir. of edn. Median Sch., Pitts., 1983-85; vocat. guidance coord., drug & alcohol coord., counselor Hopewell Area Sch. Dist., Aliquippa, Pa., 1976-86; instr. Pa. State U., Beaver, 1990-99; adminstr., profl. devel. coord. Beaver (Pa.) Area Sch. Dist., 1986-98; asst. supt. Hampton Township Sch. Dist., 1998-2000, supt., 2000—. Cons. Ednl. Support Svcs., 1987—; lectr. U. Pitts. Grad. Sch. Edn., 1988—; continuing edn. adv. bd. Pa. State U., Beaver, 1993-99; student assistance adv. bd. Prevention Project, Monaca, Pa., 1990-99; sch. attendance task force Beaver County, 1996-99; mem. Teen Pregnancy Task Force of Beaver County; mem. Allegheny County Student Assistance Coordinating Coun., 1998—; mem. Hampton Alliance for Ednl. Excellence, 1998—, Spl. Edn. Family Tng. Task Force, 1999-2001; mem. early childhood edn. action com. Edn. Policy and Issues Ctr. Author: Case Law and Common Sense, 1998, 2002, Important Legal Issues..., 1987, Focus on Careers, 1978 (Outstanding Rsch. award, 1999); contbr. articles to profl. publs. Mem. Managed Care Task Force, Beaver County, 1996-99, Drug and Alcohol Planning Coun., Beaver County, 1991-96, chair, 1994-98; exec. bd. dirs. Ars Millenium, 1996—; mem. Exec. Com., 2001—, Tri-State Study Coun., 2001—; ednl. adv. bd C.C. of Allegheny County, 2002—; adv. bd. Health South, 2002—; adv. coun. Pa. State Student Assistance Program, 2003—; coord. Allegheny county schs. United Way. Mem. ASCD, Am. Assn. Sch. Adminstrs., Pa. Assn. Sch. Adminstrs. (state del. 2001—, Region 3 exec. com., Pa. Assn. for Supervision and Curriculum Devel. (legis. com. 1986—, pre-conf. inst. chair 1996-97, state conf. com. 1995—, Svc. award 1994-98), Nat. Assn. of Secondary Sch. Prins., Nat. Sch. Bds. Assn., Pa. Sch. Reform Network, Pa. Assn. of Elem. and Secondary Sch. Prins. (legis. liason 1986-98), Pa. Sch. Bds. Assn., Middle Level Prins. of Beaver County (pres., v.p. 1994-98), Pa. Assn. of Student Assistance Profls., Pa. Assn. Pupil Svcs. Adminstrs., Phi Delta Kappa (exec. bd. 2003—). Avocations: numismatic research, writing, antiquities. Home: 4245 Old New England Rd Allison Park PA 15101-1533 Office: Hampton Township Sch Dist 2919 E Hardies Rd Gibsonia PA 15044-8423

KORETSKY, SIDNEY, internist, educator, paper historian; b. Chelsea, Mass., Dec. 30, 1921; s. Harry and Rachel (Greenfield) K.; m. Elaine Ruth Stern, Feb. 22, 1953; children: Peter Austin, David Stuart, Donna Monel. AB, Harvard U., 1943; MD, Jefferson Med. Coll., 1946. Intern Springfield (Mass.) Hosp., 1946-47; resident Boston City Hosp., 1949-52, New England Med. Ctr., Boston, 1952-53; clin. instr. in medicine Tufts U. Sch. Medicine, Boston, 1953—; pvt. practice internist Boston, 1953—; sr. physician Beth Israel Deaconess Med. Ctr., Boston, 1992—. Rschr. in heart disease, Beth Israel Deaconess Med. Ctr., 1953-68. Contbr. numerous articles to profl. med. jours.; editor, graphic designer, photographer: The Goldbeater of Mandalay, 1991, and other books dealing with the history of hand papermaking. Former pres. Greater Boston Med. Soc. Capt., U.S. Army Med. Corps, 1947-49, Korea, Japan. Mem. AMA, Internat. Assn. Paper Historians, Dard Hunter Paper History Soc., Mass. Med. Soc., Mass. Horticultural Soc., Harvard Club of Boston. Avocations: horticulture, high adventure travel, photography. Home and Office: 756 Washington St Brookline MA 02446-2109

KORETZKI, PAUL RICHARD, secondary educator, coach; b. Bklyn., Mar. 10, 1940; s. Paul Arthur and Dorothy Helen (Edwards) K.; m. Mary Joan Stampf, July 10, 1965; children: Krista, Kevin. BA, Hofstra U., 1963, MS in Edn., 1965. Cert. tchr., N.Y. Tchr. Brentwood High Sch., N.Y., 1963—, soccer coach, 1965-80; track coach Shoreham Wading River High Sch., N.Y., 1980—; v.p. Brentwood Soccer Club, 1972-76, North Shore Police Athletic League, Rocky Point, N.Y., 1979—. Dir. Calvary Luth. Basketball Program, Hauppauge, N.Y., 1967-82, Trinity Luth. Basketball Program, Rocky Point, 1982-87; coach L.I. Soccer Team, Empire State Games, 1979-82; committeeman Rocky Point Liberal Party, 1968-70, Liberal Party State Com. 1st Assembly Dist., 1992—. Named Coach of Yr., Suffolk Luth. Basketball League, 1968, 69, 72, Runner of Yr., Bohemia Track Club, 1979, Man of Yr. in Athletics Beacon Newspapers, 1990; recipient Outstanding Coach award Brentwood Schs., 1981, Shoareham-Wading River High Sch. Varsity Club, 1991; elected to Brentwood Sch. Soccer Hall of Fame, 1989. Mem. N.Y. State Tchrs. Assn., N.Y. State Sportswriters and Coaches Orgn. for Girls Sports (Jack Ault Meml. award 1993), Suffolk County Soccer Coaches Assn. (pres. 1970-73; Coach of Yr. award 1978, 79), Suffolk County Winter Track Coaches Assn. (Coach of Yr. award 1983-93), Suffolk County Spring Track Coaches Assn. (Coach of Yr. award 1980-93), Suffolk County Cross Country Coaches Assn. (Coach of Yr. award 1985, 86, 87, 88, 90, 91, 92), N.Y. State Coaches Assn. (honor award 1988), Nat. Track and Field Officials Assn. (National Coaching award 1989), Rocky Point Joggers (pres.—), Suffolk County Police Athletic League (County Vol. of Yr. 1986). Democrat. Lutheran. Home: 81 Mahogany Rd Rocky Point NY 11778-9309 Office: Brentwood High Sch 1st St Brentwood NY 11717-6602

KORMONDY, EDWARD JOHN, retired academic administrator, retired science educator; b. Beacon, N.Y., June 10, 1926; s. Anthony and Frances (Glover) Kormondy; m. Peggy Virginia Hedrick, June 5, 1950 (div. 1989); children: Lynn Ellen, Eric Paul, Mark Hedrick. BA in Biology summa cum laude, Tusculum Coll., 1950, DSc (hon.), 1997; MS in Zoology, U. Mich., 1951, PhD in Zoology, 1955. Tchg. fellow U. Mich., 1952-55; instr. zoology, curator insects Mus. Zoology, 1955-57; from asst. prof. to assoc. prof. Oberlin (Ohio) Coll., 1957—67, prof., 1967-69, acting assoc. dean, 1966-67; dir. Commn. Undergrad. Edn. Biol. Scis., Washington, 1968-72; dir. Office Biol. Edn. Am. Inst. Biol. Scis., Washington, 1968-71; mem. faculty Evergreen State Coll., Olympia, Wash., 1971-79, interim acting dean, 1972-73, v.p., provost, 1973-78; sr. profl. assoc., directorate sci. edn. NSF, 1979; provost, prof. biology U. So. Maine, Portland, 1979-82; v.p. acad. affairs, prof. biology Calif. State U., L.A., 1982-86; sr. v.p., chancellor, prof. biology U. Hawaii-West, Oahu and U. Hawaii, Hilo, 1986-93, chancellor emeritus, 2000—; pres. U. West L.A., 1995-97; spl. asst. to pres. Pacific Oaks Coll., 2000—. Author: (book) Introduction to Genetics: A Program for Self Instruction, 1964, Readings in Ecology, 1965, General Biology, A Book of Readings, 1966, Concepts of Ecology, 1969, 1976, 1983, 1996, General Biology: The Integrity and Natural History of Organisms, 1977, Handbook of Contemporary World Developments in Ecology, 1981, International Handbook of Pollution Control, 1989, (textbook) Biology, 1984, 1988, Fundamentals of Human Ecology, 1998, University of Hawaii-Hilo: A College in the Making, 2001; contbr. articles to profl. jours. With USN, 1944—46. Postdoctoral fellow, U. Ga., 1963—64, Vis. Rsch. fellow, Georgetown U., 1978—79, Rsch. grantee, NAS, Am. Philos. Soc., NSF. Fellow: AAAS; mem.: So. Calif. Acad. Scis. (bd. dirs. 1985—86, 1993—97, v.p. 1995—96), Nat. Assn. Biology Tchrs. (pres. 1981), Ecol. Soc. Am. (sec. 1976—78), Sigma Xi (Rsch. grantee). E-mail: ekor@aol.com.

KORN, DAVID, educator, pathologist; b. Providence, Mar. 5, 1933; s. Solomon and Claire (Liebman) Korn; m. Phoebe Richter, June 9, 1955 (div. Dec. 1993); children: Michael Philip, Stephen James, Daniel Clair; m. Carol Scheman, Dec. 24, 1997. BA, Harvard U., 1954, MD, 1959. Intern Mass. Gen. Hosp., Boston, 1959—60, resident in Pathology, 1960—61; rsch. assoc. NIH, 1961—63, asst. pathologist, 1963—68; mem. staff Lab. Biochem. Pharmacology; prof. pathology Sch. Medicine, Stanford (Calif.) U., 1968—97, chmn. dept. pathology Sch. Medicine, 1968—84; physician-in-chief pathology Stanford Hosp., 1968—84, dean Sch. Medicine, 1984—85, v.p., dean, 1986—95; cons. pathology Palo Alto VA Hosp., 1968—84; sr. v.p. biomed. and health scis. rsch. Assn. Am. Med. Colls., 1997—. Sr. surgeon USPHS, 1961—66; mem. cell biology study sect. NIH, 1973—77, chmn., 1976—77; mem. bd. sci. counselors divsn. cancer biology and diagnosis Nat. Cancer Inst., 1977—82, chmn., 1980—82, Nat. Cancer Adv. Bd., 1984—91; disting. scholar-in-residence Assn. Am. Med. Colls., 1995—97; sr. fellow sci. and health policy Assn. Acad. Health Ctrs., 1995—97. Mem. editl. bd. Human Pathology, 1969—74, assoc. editor, 1974—88, mem. editl. bd. Jour. Biol. Chemistry, 1973—79. Recipient Young Disting. Scientist award, Md. Acad. Sci., 1967. Fellow: AAAS; mem.: Inst. of Medicine, Fedn. Am. Soc. Exptl. Biology (bd. dirs., mem. exec. com.), Am. Soc. Investigative Pathology, Am. Soc. Biochemistry and Molecular Biology. Home: 3827 Cathedral Ave NW Washington DC 20016 Office: AAMC 2450 N St NW Washington DC 20037-1167 E-mail: dkorn@aamc.org.

KORN, IRENE ELIZABETH, retired elementary education educator, consultant; b. Wellston, Mo., May 28, 1937; d. Nicholas Anthony and Myrtle Marie (Knowles) Kuntz; m. Dale Stanley Korn, Sept. 12, 1959; children: Kurt Lawrence, Kenneth Dale, Nancy Ann. BS in Edn., U. Mo., St. Louis, 1969, MS in Edn., 1972, MS in Spl. Edn., 1985. Cert. K-12 reading, social studies tchr., learning disabilities, behavior disorders, Mo. Elem. tchr. N.W. R-1 Sch. Dist., House Springs, Mo., 1969-96; ret., 1996. Tchr. cons. geography program adv. coun. U. Mo., 1989—, Advanced Summer Inst., summer 1990; writer test items Mo. Mastery Achievement Test, fall 1990; mem. social studies work group to write state stds. edn. Mo. Dept. Elem. and Sec. Edn., 1994-95; mem. task force to restructure cert. stds. for U. Mo., Coll. of Edn., 1994. Named Woman of Yr., George Khoury Baseball Leagues, St. Louis, 1987. Mem. ASCD, Nat. Coun. Social Studies, Nat. Coun. for Geog. Edn., Am. Geog. Soc., Mo. State Tchrs. Assn. (mem. professorial rights and responsibilities com. 1987-91, pres. N.W. 1984-86), Mo. Coun. Social Studies, Jefferson County Dist. Edn. Assn. (pres.-elect 1988-89, 91-92), Mo. Geog. Alliance (mem. steering com. 1991—, chmn. elem. curriculum materials 1991-92, tchr. cons. Columbia 1988—, Advanced Inst. P.R. 1992), Phi Delta Kappa. Home: 8185 Country Bay Blvd Navarre FL 32566-4000

KORN, NEAL MARK, painter, art educator; b. Nyack, NY, May 11, 1957; s. Jacob and Sylvia Korn; m. Patsy Anne Trine, Oct. 25, 1985; 1 child, Sasha Jaye. AA, Palm Beach Jr. Coll., Lake Worth, Fla., 1978; BS in Art, Bklyn. Coll./SUNY, 1983; MA in Studio Art, Kean U., 1998. One-person show Tomasulo Art Gallery, N.J., Arts Guild Rahway, N.J., 2000-02, Art Alliance, N.J., 2001, City Without Walls, N.J., 2001; exhibited in group shows Night Gallery, N.Y.C., 1987, La Mama's La Galleria, N.Y.C., 1988-89, Ape Gallery, N.Y.C., 1990, 92, Art et Industrie Gallery, N.Y.C., 1991, 148 Gallery, N.Y.C., 1992-95, City Without Walls, N.J., 1995-96, 99, Art Alliance, N.J., 1995-98, Art Ctr. No. N.J., 1998, Aljira, N.J., 1996, 98, Audart, N.Y.C., 1996, N.J. Ctr. for Visual Arts, 1997, Watchung Arts Ctr., N.J., 1997, William Paterson U., N.J., 1998, Gallery of South Orange, N.J., 1999, Kean U., N.J., 1998, Joan Prats Gallery, N.Y.C., 1998, Liquid Gallery, N.J., 1999, Art Alliance, N.J., 2000, N.J. Ctr. Visual Arts, N.J., 2000, Art Guild of Rahway, 2001 (Merit award), N.J. Ctr. Visual Arts, 2001 (Best of Show, Marian H. Anderson Award for Portraiture 2002), Art Alliance, 2002, Jersey City Mus., 2002, 2003. two person show, Arts Guild of Rahway, N.J. 2003. Recipient Shaw award for painting Bklyn. Coll., 1982, Best of Oil Painting-Book, Rockport Pubs., 1996, other awards; Heart grantee for Art, 1998, 2002; Geraldine R. Dodge fellow, 2000; recipient Geraldine R. Dodge scholarship, Fine Arts Works Ctr. Provincetown, 2002, minigrant, 2003. Address: 912 Pennsylvania Ave Union NJ 07083-6930 E-mail: Nealpaintbrush11@earthlink.net.

KORNATOWSKI, SUSAN CAROL, elementary education educator; b. Constableville, NY, Apr. 21, 1955; d. Anthony John and Estella Helen (Ward) K. BA, SUNY, Potsdam, 1977; MA, Cortland State U., 1984. Cert. elem. edn. tchr., N.Y. 2nd grade tchr. Adirondack Central Sch., West Leyden, N.Y., 1983—. Active PTA, Nat. Arbor Day, 1990—. Named to SUNY Potsdam Alumni Sports Hall of Fame, 1990, Excellent Tchr. of Yr., 1997, 99; recipient Nat. Citizenship Edn. Tchr. award VFW, 2002-03. Mem. VFW (Nat. Citizenship Ednl. Tchr. award 2002-03), West Leyden Free Reading Ctr. (librarian 1982-83, treas. 1983—). Roman Catholic. Avocations: ceramics, knitting, sewing, sports, volleyball. Home: PO Box 121 West Leyden NY 13489-0121 Office: West Leyden Elem Sch Fish Creek Rd West Leyden NY 13489

KORNECKI, ANDREW JAN, computer scientist, educator; b. Krakow, Poland, Dec. 27, 1946; came to U.S., 1983; s. Adam and Karolina (Selinger) K.; m. Lucyna Cialowicz, Apr. 19, 1974; children: Katherine, Adam. MEE, Acad. Mining & Metallurgy, Krakow, Poland, 1970; PhD, Acad. Mining & Metallurgy, 1975. Doctoral fellow Acad. Mining & Metallurgy, Krakow, 1971-74, sr. instr., 1974-75, asst. prof., 1975-80, Garyounes U., Benghaz, Libya, 1980-83, U. Ky., Lexington, 1983-85; prof. Embry-Riddle Aero. U., Daytona Beach, Fla., 1985—, rschr., 1987—. Cons. in field. Contbr. numerous articles to profl. jours. Mem. IEEE, Soc. for Computer Simulation Inc., Fla. Artificial Intelligence Rsch. Symposium. Roman Catholic. Avocations: music, bridge, chess. E-mail: andrew.kornecki@erau.edu.

KORNEL, LUDWIG, medical educator, physician, scientist; b. Jaslo, Poland, Feb. 27, 1923; came to U.S., 1958, naturalized, 1970; s. Ezriel Edward and Ernestine (Karpf) K.; m. Esther Muller, May 27, 1952 (div. 1996); children: Ezriel Edward, Amiel Mark; m. Barbara Konaszewska, Mar. 18, 1997. Student, U. Kazan Med. Inst., USSR, 1943-45; MD, Wroclaw (Poland) Med. Acad., 1950; PhD, U. Birmingham, Eng., 1958. Intern Univ. Hosp., Wroclaw, 1949-50, Hadassah-Hebrew U. Hosp., Jerusalem, 1950-51, resident medicine, 1952-55; Brit. Council scholar, Univ. research fellow endocrinology U. Birmingham, 1955-57, lectr. medicine, 1956-57; fellow endocrinology U. Ala. Med. Ctr., 1958-59, from asst. prof. to prof. medicine, 1961-67; dir. steroid sect. U. Ala. Med. Center, 1962-67, assoc. prof. biochemistry, 1965-67; postdoctoral trainee in steroid biochemistry U. Utah, 1959-61; prof. medicine U. Ill. Coll. Medicine, Chgo., 1967-71; dir. steroid unit Presbyn.-St. Lukes Hosp., Chgo., 1967-93, assoc. biochemist, 1967-70, sr. biochemist on sci. staff, 1970-71, attending physician, 1967-71; prof. medicine and biochemistry Rush Med. Coll., 1970-93, prof. emeritus of internal medicine and biochemistry, 1993—; sr. attending physician, sr. scientist Rush-Presbyn.-St. Lukes Med. Ctr., 1971-96, dir. steroid hypertension rsch. lab., 1971-95; sr. endocrinologist KHK Endocrinology and Diabetes Outpatient Clinic, Jerusalem, Israel, 1996-98. Hon. guest lectr. Polish Acad. Sci., Warsaw, 1965; vis. prof. Kanazawa (Japan) U., 1973, 82, 88, 93. Mem. editl. bd. Clin. Physiol. Biochemistry, 1975-94, Endocrinology, 1994-98; co-editor: Yearbook of Endocrinology, 1986-90; co-author: Ency. of Human Biology, 1991, 96; contbr. articles on endocrinology and steroid biochemistry to profl.jours.; contbr. chpts to textbooks. Recipient Physicians Recognition award AMA, 1969, 73, 76, 81, 86, Outstanding New Citizen award Citizenship Council Met. Chgo., 1970 Fellow Am. Coll. Clin. Pharmacology and Chemotherapy, Nat. Acad. Clin. Biochemistry (bd. dirs. 1982-86), Royal Soc. health; mem. AMA, AAAS, AAUP, Endocrine Soc., Am. Fedn. Clin. Rsch., N.Y. Acad. Scis., Am. Physiol. Soc., Cen. Soc. Clin. Rsch., Israel Soc. for Biochemistry and Molecular Biology, Am. Acad. Polit. and Social Scis., Fedn. Am. Socs. for Exptl. Biology (nat. corr. 1975—), Fedn. Israel Socs. for Exptl. Biology, Am. Soc. Hypertension, Israel Soc. Hypertension, Sigma Xi. Office: 1 Yitzchak Sadeh 53467 Givatayim Israel

KORNIEWICZ, DENISE M. nursing educator; b. Detroit, Dec. 21, 1951; d. Edward John and Roseline Marie (Luczak) K. BS, Madonna Univ., 1974; MS in Nursing, Tex. Woman's U., 1977; DNSc in Nursing, Cath. U. of Am., 1986; postdoctoral, Johns Hopkins U., 1989. RN, Mich., Md., D.C. Dir. nurse practitioner program East Carolina U., Greenville, N.C., 1978-82; rsch. assoc. Cath. U. of Am., Washington, 1984-87; postdoctoral fellowship Johns Hopkins U., Balt., 1987-89, dir. acute care program, 1989-92; assoc. dean for acad. devel. Georgetown U., Washington, 1992-98; rsch. prof. U. Md., Balt., 1999—. Adv. bd. Ansell Cares, Sydney, Australia, 1993—, Regent Hosp. Products, Greenville, 1992—; chair, cons. Johns Hopkins U., Balt., 1993-94. Author: Pocket Guide to Infection Control, 1995; contbr. articles to profl. jours. Vol. probation officer, Washington, 1991. Capt. U.S. Army, 1973-77. Fellow Am. Acad. in Nursing; mem. So. Coun. on Colls. and Edn. (mentor 1992-94, Cert. 1994), Madonna U. Alumni (Plaque 1992), Am. Nurse Assn. Coun. of Nurse Rsch., Sigma Xi. Democrat. Roman Catholic. Achievements include developing the standards for patient examination gloves, sterile and unsterile; achieved success in technology development of materials used for patient care practices. Home: 1569 Redhaven Dr Severn MD 21144-1032 Office: U Md Sch Nursing 655 W Lombard St Baltimore MD 21201-1512 E-mail: korniewd@erols.com.

KORNMAN, ELSIE FRY, retired elementary education educator; b. Kirkland Lake, Ont., Can., Jan. 17, 1933; arrived in U.S., 1969; d. Bert and Ethel May (Wilson) Fry; divorced; children: Scott Elbert, Stacy Marie Kornman Webb. AA, Graceland Coll., Lamoni, Iowa, 1953; cert. in teaching, North Bay (Ont.) Tchrs. Coll., 1955; BS in Edn., Memphis State U., 1973-77; MS in Edn., S.W. Mo. State U., 1982. cert. Ontario, Can., Mo., Utah, New Mexico. Tchr. Brethour (Ont.) Twp. Sch. Dist., 1951; tchr. 2d grade Burford (Ont.) Sch. Dist., 1955-57; tchr. Hamilton (Ont.) Sch. Dist., 1957-60; grad. asst. S.W. Mo. State U., Springfield, 1979-80; reading specialist Willard (Mo.) R-2 Schs., 1980-82; tchr. Granite Sch. Dist., Salt Lake City, 1985-88; tchr. grade 1 Aztec (N.Mex.) Sch. Dist., 1988—98, ret., 1998. Author ch. sch. material. Dir. craft and religious classes Cmty. of Christ, 1989-92; peer counselor New Horizons, Durango, Colo., 1989-92; tchr. craft Getaway Ft. Lewis Coll., Durango, summers 1990, 91, 93; dir. Camp Quality Internat., Western Colo., 1990-94. Avocations: knitting, quilling. Home: 8301 Poplar Grove Cir Waxhaw NC 28173

KORNOWSKI, ROBERT RICHARD, engineer, science educator; b. Green Bay, Wis., June 1, 1943; m. 1965 (div. 1991); children: Robert Merrill, Jenny Lynn, Jane Ann. B in Electronics Engring. Tech., DeVry Inst. Tech., 1972. Employed Motorola, 1965, microcircuits new product group leader land mobile products sector, 1981-86, microcircuits staff engr. Land Mobile Products Sector, 1986-89, materials orgn. sr. staff engr. comml., govt. and indsl. solutions sector, 1996—, materials orgn. prin. staff engr./inventor with Component Tech. Engring. Group, comml. govt. and indsl. solutions sector, 1996—. Instr. and tech. curriculm cons. electronics William Rainey Harper Coll., Palatine, Ill., 1972—, mem. electronics and mfg. adv. com., 1995—; lectr. in field. Mem. Internat. Microelectronics and Pkg. Soc. Achievements include research in modelling structures to derive new or improved design equations, primarily in support of advanced component development; patentee in field. Office: Motorola Comml Govt and Indsl Solutions Sector 1301 E Algonquin Rd Rm 3025 Schaumburg IL 60196-1078

KORNRUMPH, JOAN O. counseling administrator, educator; b. Duluth, Minn., Oct. 1, 1933; d. George and Hilia Sophia (Hemming) Yien; m. Ralph E. Kornrumph, Feb. 29, 1964; 1 child, Michael David. BA, Northland Coll., 1955; MA in Edn., U. Alaska, 1968; MBA U. Ala., 1969; Specialist in Edn., Rollins Coll., 1976. Life cert. English tchr. Wis., cert. counselor Fla. English tchr. Eagle River H.S., Wis., 1955—58; asst. to program dir. YMCA, Mpls., 1958—59; commd. 2d lt. USAF, 1959, advanced through grades to capt., 1966; comdr. Hdqrs. Squadron Hamilton AFB, Calif., 1959—61, Norton AFB, Calif., 1961—63; comdr. hdqrs. Alaskan Comm. Region sect. Elmendorf AFB, Alaska, 1965—67; substitute tchr. East Grand Forks, ND, 1969—70; guidance counselor Lyman H.S., Longwood, Calif., 1970—86, secondary sch. English tchr., 1986—92; tchr. pre-sch. Joy's Child Care, Orlando, Fla., 1998—. Mem. Seminole County Curriculum Com., Fla. State Homebound/Hospitalized Steering Com., 1983—86. Author: (History) 919 SOG (USAFR), 1980—84; editor: Lyman Guidance Newsletter, 1984—86. Named Hon. Admissions Counselor US Naval Acad., 1985. Mem.: NEA, ASCD, Nat. Coun. Tchrs. of English, Profl. Bus. Women, Seminole County Tchrs. Assn. (past sec.), Seminole County Assn. Counseling and Devel. (past pres.), Am. Assn. Counseling and Devel. (participant Counselors Role in Excellence in Edn., Orlando 1985), Mil. Officers Assn., WAF Ret. Officers Assn. Republican. Home: 10634 Eastview Dr Orlando FL 32825-6847

KOROLOGOS, ANN MCLAUGHLIN, public policy, communications executive; b. Newark, N.J., Nov. 16, 1941; d. Edward Joseph and Marie (Koellhoffer) Lauenstein; m. John McLaughlin, 1975 (div. 1992); m. Tom C. Korologos, 2000. Student, U. London, 1961-62; BA, Marymount Coll., 1963; postgrad., Wharton Sch., 1987. Supr. network comml. schedule ABC, N.Y.C., 1963-66; dir. alumnae relations Marymount Coll., Tarrytown, N.Y., 1966-69; account exec. Myers-Infoplan Internat. Inc., N.Y.C., 1969-71; dir. comm. Presdl. Election Com., Washington, 1971-72; asst. to chmn. and press sec. Presdl. Inaugural Com., Washington, 1972-73; dir. Office of Pub. Affairs, EPA, Washington, 1973-74; govt. rels. and comm. exec. Union Carbide Corp., N.Y.C. and Washington, 1974-77; pub. affairs, issues mgmt. counseling McLaughlin & Co., 1977-81; asst. sec. for pub. affairs Dept. of Treasury, Washington, 1981-84; under sec. Dept. of Interior, Washington, 1984-87; cons. Ctr. Strategic and Internat. Studies, Washington, 1987; sec. labor Dept. of Labor, Washington, 1987-89; vis. fellow Urban Inst., 1989-92; pres., CEO New Am. Schs. Devel. Corp., 1992-93. Mem. def. adv. com. Women in the Svcs., 1973—74; mem. Am. Coun. Capital Formation, 1976—78; mem. environ. edn. task force HEW, 1976—77; chair Pres.'s Commn. Aviation Security and Terrorism, 1989—90; bd. dirs. Fannie Mae, Kellogg Co., Host Marriott Corp., Vulcan Materials Co., AMR Corp., Harman Internat. Industries, Inc., Microsoft; pres. Fed. City Coun., 1990—95; chair Aspen Inst., 1996—2000, vice-chair, 1996; vice chair RAND. Bd. dirs. Charles A. Dana Found., Conservation Fund, Catalyst; trustee Urban Inst., 1989—96; mem. bd. overseers Wharton Sch. U. Pa. Mem.: Sulgrave Club, Met. Club, Cosmos Club. Republican. Roman Catholic.

KORPAL, CHARYL ELAINE, secondary education educator; b. Emo, Ont., Can., Nov. 16, 1946; came to U.S., 1946; d. Charles Sigard and Martha Edith (Ericksen) Mark; m. Donald Paul Korpal, July 7, 1967. BS in Teaching, Mankato State U., 1976, postgrad., 1988; MEd, U. Minn., St. Paul, 1991. Tchr. Ind. Sch. Dist. 77, Mankato, Minn., 1976-77; tchr. mktg., coord., DECA advisor New Ulm (Minn.) Cathedral, 1977-78; mktg. tchr. coord., advisor Mankato East High Sch., 1978—. Active March Dimes, Boyd Schuler's campaign for Minn. House Reps. Recipient PTA scholarship Indus High Sch., 1965, Bus. Econs. Edn. Foud. scholarship Olaf Coll., 1986; Minn. State Bd. Vocational Tech. Edn. scholar, 1987. Mem. NEA, Distributive Edn. Clubs Am. (bd. dirs. 1980-81, recipient scholarship 1975, Outstanding Sr. Service award 1976, Cert. Appreciation 1980—, hon. life, Minn. Secondary Mktg. Tchr. of Yr. 1983), Nat. Assn. Distributive Edn. Tchrs., Mktg. and Distributive Edn. Assn., Am. Vocat. Assn., Mktg. Educators Minn., Mktg. Edn. Assn., Nat. Fedn. Bus. and Profl. Women's Clubs, Mankato Bus. Profl. Women's Club. Lodges: Sons of Norway Elvesvingen. Home: 54 Camelot Ln Mankato MN 56001-6308 Office: Mankato W High Sch 1351 S Riverfront Dr Mankato MN 56001-6830

KORSTAD, JOHN EDWARD, biology educator; b. Woodland, Calif., July 4, 1949; s. Vernon E. and Jeanette (Beard) K.; m. Sally Diane Steffen, July 29, 1972; children: Shauna, Sarah, Joya, Janna. BA, BS, Calif. Luth. U., Thousand Oaks, 1972; MS, Calif. State U., Hayward, 1979, U. Mich., 1979, PhD, 1980. Postdoctoral fellow SINTEF, Trondheim, Norway, 1987-88; prof. biology Oral Roberts U., Tulsa, 1980—. Asst. dir., dir. collegiate acad. Okla. Acad. Sci., 1984-89. Bd. dirs. MEND Pregnancy Crisis Ctr. and Young Life, Broken Arrow, Okla., 1991—. Fulbright fellow in aquaculture rsch., Norway, 1993-94; named Carnegie Found. Prof. of Yr. for Okla., 1996. Mem. Am. Soc. Limnology and Oceanography, World Aquaculture Soc., Catfish Farmers of Okla., Am. Assn. of Zool. Parks and Aquariums (advisor marine fishes adv. com. 1991—), Beta Beta Beta (faculty advisor), Gamma Beta Phi (faculty advisor). Republican. Avocations: scuba diving, snow skiing, outdoor sports, basketball. Office: Oral Roberts U Dept Biology 7777 S Lewis Ave Tulsa OK 74171-0001

KORT, BETTY, secondary education educator; English tchr. Hastings (Nebr.) Sr. High Sch., 1979—. Named Nebr. State English Tchr. of Yr., 1993. Office: Hastings Sen High Sch 1100 W 14th St Hastings NE 68901-3064

KOSA, JAYMIE REEBER, middle school educator; b. N.J., Oct. 19, 1967; BA in English Lit., U. Md.; EdM, Rutgers U., 1991. Nat. bd. cert. tchr. 1999. Tchr. The Newgrange Sch., Trenton, NJ, 1991—92, West Windsor-Plainsboro Middle Sch., Plainsboro, NJ, 1991—99, Thomas Grover Middle Sch., West Windsor, NJ, 2001—; adj. prof. Fairleigh Dickinson U., Teaneck, NJ, 2000—01. Mem.: Nat. Bd. for Profl. Tchg. Stds. (bd. mem.), Phi Beta Kappa.

KOSARAJU, S. RAO, computer science educator, researcher; b. Pedapulivarru, Guntur, India, Feb. 20, 1943; came to U.S., 1966; s. Punnaiah and Dhanalakshmi K.; m. Padmaja Valluripalli, Aug. 20, 1970; children: Sheela, Akhila. B.E., Andhra U., (India), 1964; M.Tech., Indian Inst. Tech., Kharagpur, 1966; PhD, U. Pa., 1969. Vis. asst. prof. computer sci. Johns Hopkins U., Balt., 1969-70, asst. prof., 1970-75, assoc. prof., 1975-77, prof., 1977—, Kouwenhoven prof., 1981-87; Compere and Marcella Loveless prof. Purdue U., West Lafayette, Ind., 1986-87; Edward J. Schaefer prof. Johns Hopkins U., Balt., 1987—, chmn. computer sci., 2001—. Contbr. articles to profl. jours.; assoc. editor Jour. Computer Langs., 1976-89, Theory of Computing Systems, 1976—, Jour. Computer and System Scis., 1981—, Information and Computation, 1983-91. Fellow IEEE, Assn. for Computing Machinery; mem. Soc. Indsl. and Applied Math. (mng. editor SIAM Jour. on Computing 1980-89, assoc. editor 1975—). Home: 4 Woodward Ct Reisterstown MD 21136-1835 Office: Johns Hopkins U Dept Computer Sci Baltimore MD 21218 E-mail: kosaraju@cs.jhu.edu.

KOSEK, WAYNE RICHARD, secondary education educator; b. Chgo., Aug. 11, 1946; s. Louis Frank and Alice Lorraine (Jerabek) K.; m. Susan Jean Schikora, June 1971 (div. June 1980); 1 child, Kersten; m. Konnie Gale Lorenz Benedict, Mar. 19, 1982; children: Derek, Jenna. BS in Edn., Ill. State U., 1964; MS in Edn., No. Ill. U., 1986. Cert. secondary edn. tchr., Ill. Tchr. Cmty. High Sch., West Chicago, Ill., 1968—. Contbr. articles to profl. jours. Parent rep. Strikers-Fox Valley F.C., Batavia, Ill., 1992-94, bd. dirs., 1994; computer cmty. chair Louise White PTO, Batavia, 1993-94. Mem. NEA, Ill. Edn. Assn., West Chicago Sch. Tchrs. Assn. (v.p. 1989-93, pres. 1993-97), Nat. Coun. Tchrs. English/Interdisciplinary, Ill. Assn. Tchrs. English. Avocations: tennis, golf, cross country skiing, reading. Home: 1311 Davey Dr Batavia IL 60510-8626 Office: Cmty High Sch Dist 94 326 Joliet St West Chicago IL 60185-3142 E-mail: wkosek@d94.org.

KOSHLAND, CATHERINE PRESTON, mechanical engineer, educator; b. Phila., May 11, 1950; d. Edmond III and Elizabeth Miriam (Johnston) Preston; m. James Marcus Koshland, May 17, 1975; children: Sarah, Margrethe, Jacob. Student, Smith Coll., Northampton, Mass., 1968-70; BA in Fine Arts, Haverford (Pa.) Coll., 1972; MS in Mech. Engring., Stanford U., Palo Alto, Calif., 1978, PhD in Mech. Engring., 1985. Asst. prof. U. Calif., Berkeley, 1985-92, assoc. prof., 1992-97, prof., 1997—, Wood-Calvert chair in Engring., 1995—, chair acad. senate, 2002—03. Mem. Bay Area Air Quality Mgmt. Dist. Adv. Coun., San Francisco, 1988-94, chair, 1991-92; bd. mgrs. Haverford (Pa.) Coll., 1994—, vice chair, 2000—. Contbr. over 50 articles to profl. jours. Recipient base rsch. award Nat. Inst. Environ. Health Sci., 1988—. Mem. Combustion Inst. (dir. 1994—, sec. 1996—, mem. exec. bd. Western states sect. 1988—), Am. Chem. Soc. Achievements include research in post-combustion chemistry of chlorinated hydrocarbons; research in industrial ecology and air pollution. Office: U Calif 140 Warren Hall Berkeley CA 94720-7360 E-mail: ckosh@uclink4.berkeley.edu.

KOSIARA, MICHAEL ANTHONY, secondary education educator; b. Gaylord, Mich., Nov. 24, 1960; s. George Eugene and Naomi Jean (Osborne) K.; m. Anne Marie Durecki, Oct. 29, 1988. BA, Albion Coll., 1983; postgrad., Mich. State U., 1988-92, Western Mich. U., 1988-90, Ferris State U., 1990-91. Cert. tchr. Jr. high tchr. St. Therese Sch., Wayland, Mich., 1987-90; adult edn. tchr. Mesick (Mich.) Cmty. Schs., 1990-91, Lake City (Mich.) Cmty. Schs., 1990-92; substitute tchr. Wexford-Missaukee Ind. Sch. Dist., Cadillac, Mich., 1990-92; jr. high tchr. Rogers City (Mich.) Area Schs., 1992—. Asst. jr. varsity football coach Gaylord (Mich.) St. Mary's H.S., 1983, Manton (Mich.) H.S., 1987-89, vol. jr. varsity football coach, 1990-93; asst. varsity football coach Rogers City (Mich.) Area Schs., 1993—. Writer, editor No. Mich. Sports Mag., Manton, Mich., 1991. Adv. bd. Rogers City H.S. Natural Helpers. Mem. ASCD, Mich. H.S. Football Coaches Assn. Avocations: environ. and outdoor edn., camping, canoeing, hiking. Office: Rogers City HS 1033 W Huron Ave Rogers City MI 49779-1428

KOSKI, WALTER S. chemistry educator, scientist; b. Phila., Dec. 1, 1913; s. Bruno and Helen (Laskowska) Stankiewicz; m. Helen Ireton Tag, May 11, 1940; children— Carol Lee, Ann Louise, Nancy Cheryl, Phyllis Ireton. PhD, Johns Hopkins, 1942. Research chemist Hercules Powder Co., 1942-43; group leader Los Alamos Sci. Lab., 1944-47; physicist Brookhaven Nat. Lab., 1947-48; asso. prof. Johns Hopkins, 1947-55; prof. chemistry Johns Hopkins (Grad. Sch.), 1955—, B.N. Baker prof. chemistry, 1975—, chmn. dept., 1958-69. Fellow Am. Phys. Soc.; mem. Am. Chem. Soc. (merit award Md. sect), Phi Beta Kappa. Office: Johns Hopkins U 3400 N Charles St Baltimore MD 21218-2680

KOSS, MARY LYNDON PEASE, psychology educator, researcher; b. Louisville, Sept. 1, 1948; d. Richard Charles and Carol (Bade) Pease; m. Paul G. Koss, Aug. 3, 1968; children: John Bade, Paul Shanor. AB, U. Mich., 1970; PhD, U. Minn., 1972. Lic. psychologist, Ariz. Asst. prof. psychology St. Olaf Coll., Northfield, Minn., 1973-76; prof. psychology Kent (Ohio) State U., 1976-88; prof. dept. health promotion scis. Coll. Pub. Health, U. Ariz., Tucson, 1988—. Grantee NIMH, 1978-98, NIAAA, 1995—. Mem. APA. Democrat. Unitarian Universalist. E-mail: mpk@u.arizona.edu.

KOSSLYN, STEPHEN M. psychologist educator; b. Santa Monica, Calif., Nov. 30, 1948; s. S. Duke and Rhoda Kosslyn; m. Robin S. Rosenberg, Mar. 28, 1982; children: Justin Lewis, David Alan, Nathaniel Solté. BA in Psychology, UCLA, 1970; PhD in Psychology, Stanford U., 1974; DSc (hon.), U. Caen, France, 2003. Asst. prof. of Psychology The Johns Hopkins Univ., 1974-77; assoc. prof. of Psychology Harvard Univ., 1977-81; rsch. affiliate of the Ctr. for Cognitive Sci. M.I.T., 1980-94; assoc. prof. of Psychology Brandeis Univ., 1981-82; prof. of Psychology Harvard Univ., 1983—; co-dir. James S. McDonnell Found. Summer Inst. in Cognitive Neuroscience, 1987; assoc. psychologist in neurology Mass. Gen. Hosp., 1990—. Vis. asst. prof. psychology U. Calif., Berkeley, 1976; vis. prof. psychology The Johns Hopkins U., 1982-83, Maitre de Conference, Coll. de France, 1997-98; cons. Consulting Statisticians, Inc., 1977-83; gov. bd. Cognitive Sci. Soc., 1989-95. Author: Image and Mind, 1980, Ghosts in the Mind's Machine, 1983, Wet Mind: The New Cognitive Neuroscience, 1992, Image and Brain, 1994, Elements of Graph Design, 1994, (with R. Rosenberg) Psychology: The Brain, The Person, The World, 2001, 2d edit., 2003; editor: (with others) Tutorials in Learning and Memory: Essays in Honor of Gordon H. Bower, 1983, Quantitative Analyses of Behavior, Vol. 9: Computational and Clinical Approaches to Pattern Recognition and Concept Formation, 1989, An Invitation to Cognitive Science: Visual Cognition and Action, 1990, Essays in Honor of William K. Estes, 1992, Frontiers in Cognitive Neuroscience, 1992, The Neuropsychology of Mental Imagery, 1996; contbr. articles to profl. jours. Recipient Boyd R. McCandless Young Scientist award divsn. 7 APA, 1978, Initiatives in Rsch. award NAS, 1983, Cattell award for sabbatical leave, 1991, J-L Signoret prize Fondation Ipsen/Am. Acad. Arts and Scis., 1995. Mem. AAAS, APA, Am. Psychol. Soc., Mass. Neuropsychol. Soc., Cognitive Sci. Soc., Psychonomic Soc., Soc. for Neurosci., Am. Acad. Arts and Scis., Soc. Exptl. Psychologists. Avocations: classical music, French. Office: Harvard U 33 Kirkland St Cambridge MA 02138-2044

KOSTER-PETERSON, LOIS MAE, educational administrator; b. Carroll, Iowa, Aug. 31, 1957; d. Doyle John and Bernice Clare (Broich) Koster; m. Kent Roger Peterson, Sept. 3, 1988. AA, Iowa Ctrl. C.C., 1977; BA, Buena Vista Coll., 1979; MS, Iowa State U., 1984; EdD, No. Ariz. U., 1993; Ednl. Specialist, Piont Loma Coll., 1993. Cert. secondary tchr. and adminstr., Iowa, Kans, Wis., Calif. Tchr., coach Colo. (Iowa) Cmty. Sch., 1979-82; dean students, basketball coach Wahlert H.S., Dubuque, Iowa, 1982-83; rsch. asst. Iowa State U., Ames, 1983; prin., activities dir. North Winneshiek Cmty. Sch., Decorah, Iowa, 1985-88; asst. prin. jr. high Unified Sch. Dist. 443, Dodge City, Kans., 1988-89; prin. sr. high Wintereset (Iowa) Cmty. Sch., 1989-90; interim prin. mid. sch. Ramona (Calif.) Unified Sch. Dist., 1992; assoc. prin. Shawnee Mission (Kans.) North H.S., 1993—. Exec. sec. Upper Miss. Valley Conf., Garnavillo, Iowa, 1986-87; planning com. Teens in Distress Conf., Decorah, 1986-87. Lector, cathecism instr., sr. citizen asst. St. Mary's Ch., Colo, 1979-82; interview judge Iowa Academic Decathlon, Denison, 1990; mem. selection com. Chuck Burdick Scholarship, Des Moines, 1987. Recipient Thespian Kans. Adminstr. of Yr. award, 1995; named Adminstr. of Yr., Shawnee Mission Sch. Adminstrs., 1997; named to Buena Vista Athletic Hall of Fame, 1996. Mem. ASCD, Calif. Sch. Adminstrs. Assn., Ariz. Rsch. Assn., Sch. Adminstrs. Iowa (panel for Iowa selection of fine program 1989-90), Nat. Assn. Secondary Sch. Prins., Optimists, Phi Delta Kappa (v.p. Greater Kansas City chpt.). Roman Catholic. Avocations: sports, travel. Home: 5348 Albervan St Shawnee Mission KS 66216-1457

KOSTER VAN GROOS, AUGUST FERDINAND, geology educator; b. Leeuwarden, Friesland, The Netherlands, Jan. 9, 1938; came to U.S., 1962; MS, Leiden U., 1962, PhD, 1966. Lectr. Utrecht U., The Netherlands, 1968-70; asst. prof. U. Ill., Chgo., 1970-77, assoc. prof., 1977-90, prof., 1990—, head prof. dept. geol. sci., 1992—. Cons. in field. Contbr. articles to profl. jours. Mem. AAUP, AAAS, Am. Geophys. Union. Achievements include rsch. in liquid immiscibility between silicate and carbonate melts; high pressure differential thermal analysis of clay-water and salt-water systems.

KOSTIĆ, NENAD MIODRAG, chemist, educator; b. Belgrade, Yugoslavia, Nov. 18, 1952; arrived in U.S., 1978; s. Miodrag N. and Vera (Klujic) K.; m. Dragana J. Dimitrijevic, Jul. 18, 1976; children: Dimitrije N., Bogdan N. BS, U. Belgrade, 1976; PhD, U. Wis., 1982. Rsch. fellow Calif. Inst. Tech., Pasadena, Calif., 1982-84; prof. chemistry Iowa State U., Ames, 1984—. Vis. prof. Leiden U., Leiden, The Netherlands, 1994. Contbr. articles to profl. jours. Recipient Presidential Young Investigator award Nat Sci. Found., 1988, Sci. and Rsch. award Karić Found., Belgrade, 2001; rsch. fellow A.P. Sloan Found., 1991. Mem. Am. Chemical Soc., Serbian Chemical Soc. Achievements include many research publications in inorganic, organometallic biological, physical, organic, and bioinorganic chemistry and invited lectures in the U.S. and abroad. Home: 3108 Sycamore Rd Ames IA 50014-4510

KOSZEWSKI, BOHDAN JULIUS, retired internist, medical educator; b. Warsaw, Dec. 17, 1918; Came to U.S., 1952; s. Mikolaj and Helen (Lubienski) K.; children Mikolaj, Joseph, Wanda Marie, Andrzej Bohdan. MD, U. Zurich, Switzerland, 1946; MS, Creighton U., 1956. Resident in pathology U. Zurich, 1944-46, resident in internal medicine, 1946-50, assoc. in medicine, 1950-52; intern St. Mary's Hosp., Hoboken, N.J., 1953; practice medicine specializing in internal medicine Omaha, 1956-90. Mem. staff St. Joseph's Hosp., Mercy and Meth. Hosps.; instr. internal medicine Creighton U., 1956-57, asst. prof., 1957-65, assoc. prof. internal medicine, 1965-90; cons. hematology Omaha VA Hosp., 1957-90. Author: Prognosis in Diabetic Coma, 1952; contbr. numerous articles to profl. jours. Served with Polish Army, 1940-45. Fellow ACP, Am. Coll. Angiology; mem. AAAS, Am. Fedn. Clin. Research, Internat. Soc. Hematology, Polish-Am. Congress Nebr. (pres. 1960-68, 82-92). Home: 1400 Broadmoor Ave Lincoln NE 68506

KOT, MARTA VIOLETTE, artist, art educator; b. Hartford, Conn. d. Edward Anthony and Maria Kot. Fulbright student, Royal U. of Malta, 1985; BA in Graphic Design/Art, Ctrl Conn. State U., 1985; pvt. art studies Studio Antoine Camilleri, Valletta, Malta, 1985; pvt. art studies, Studio Adam Wsiolkowski, Cracow, Poland, 1988; studied with Zbylut Grzywacz, Cracow, 1988; MS in Adminstrn., Supervision and Curriculum Devel., Ctrl Conn. State U., 1988; cert. in Polish Art History, Jagiellonian U., Cracow, Poland, 1988; MA in Studio Art and Environ. Art, NYU, 1990; student, Acad. de la Grande Chaumiere, Paris, 1990-93; cert. French lang. and Civilization, U. Paris, Sorbonne, 1992; cert. Polish lang., Cath. U. of Lublin, Poland, 1993; EdM in Art and Art Edn., Tchrs. Coll., Columbia U., 1997; postgrad. in Polish lang., Warsaw U., 1997; postgrad., Columbia U., 1999—. Cert. art educator, N.Y. Art cons. gifted and talented programs Consol. Sch. Dist. of City of New Britain, Conn., 1987-88; art educator summer art program Consolidated Sch. Dist. City of New Britain, 1997; studio art instr. Harlem Sch. of Arts, N.Y.C., 1997—2002; art educator LaGuardia H.S. of Music and Art and Performing Arts, N.Y.C., 1996-97; art cons. parent/toddler program Henry Street Settlement/Arbor Arts Ctr., N.Y.C., 1997; collaborator with artist Charles Searles Harlem Sch. of the Arts, N.Y.C., 1996, art cons., educator Totem Spirits project, 1996; prin., chair dept. music and art Internat. Am. Sch., Warsaw, 1997-98; supr. Tchr. Coll. Dept. Art and Humanities Columbia U., 1998—2001. Invited artist lectr. New Britain Mus. Am. Art, Conn., 1996, Macy Gallery, Tchrs. Coll. Columbia U., 1996, Nat. Mus. of Fine Arts, Malta and Macy Gallery, Tchr. Coll. Columbia U., 1997, Marymount Manhattan Coll., N.Y.C., 1998, N.Y.C., 99, AKA Gallery, Belevidere, Tenn., 1999, Aldrich Mus. of Contemporary Art, Ridgefield, Conn., 2002; curator Ctrl. Conn. State U. Elihu Burritt Spl. Collections Gallery, 1997, 98, Macy Gallery, N.Y.C., 1997, City of New Britain City Hall, 1997, Internat. Am. Sch., Warsaw, 1998; Annenberg/Javitts edn. art cons. PS153 and the Harlem Sch. of the Art, N.Y.C., 1998—2001; art specialist project arts PS129, N.Y.C., 1999; studio art educator Silvermine Sch. of Art, New Caanan, Conn., 1999—; vis. artist Hudson River Mus., N.Y., 1999, N.Y., 2001; adj. instr. Marymount Manhattan Coll., N.Y.C., 1999—; master tchg. artist Silvermine/Conn. Commn. on the Arts, 1999—; art specialist, edn. cons. student conf. Sacred Heart U., 2000; workship facilitator Arts For All, Stamford, Conn., 2000; edn. cons. Ctr. Arts Edn., N.Y.C., 2000. One-woman shows include 80 Washington Sq. East Galleries, N.Y.C., 1990, Conn. Ho. of Reps., Hartford, 1995, City Hall, New Britain, Conn., 1996, Macy Gallery, N.Y.C., 1996, Ctrl. Conn. State U. Elihu Burritt Libr., 1996, New Britain Pub. Libr., 1997, Nat. Mus. Fine Arts, Malta, 1997, Harlem Sch. of the Arts, N.Y.C., 1997, City of N.Y. Divsn. of Legal Affairs, 1997, Tchrs. Coll., Columbia U., 1997, New Britain City Hall, 1997, Ctrl. Conn. State U. Elihu Burritt Libr. Spl. Collections Gallery, 1998, Lab. Gallery, Ctr. Contemporary Art, Warsaw, 1999, AKA Gallery, Belvidere, Tenn., 1999, Gharb, Gozo, 2001, exhibited in group shows at Ctrl. Conn. State U., New Britain, 1982, 1984—88, Slocumb Gallery, Tenn., 1985, Macy Art Gallery, N.Y.C., 1994—97, Presdl. Inauguration, Tchrs. Coll., Columbia U., 1994, Nat. Arts Club, N.Y.C., 1995, Pumphouse Gallery, Hartford, 1995, Student Lounge Tchrs. Coll., Columbia U., 1996, Bklyn. Brewery, John Jay Gallery, N.Y.C., 1996, MMC Gallery, 1997, Hudson River Barge Mus., Red Hook, N.Y., 1997, others. Corp. mem. Boys and Girls Club, New Britain; bd. dirs. Camp Schade Program Affiliated United Way, New Britain. Recipient award for graphic design Advt. Club Greater Hartford, 1984, mural project (with Dave Burke) Incarnation Ctr. for Children with AIDS Tamarand Found., N.Y.C., 1995. Mem. ASCD, AAUW, Coll. Art Assn., Nat. Art Edn. Assn., Bklyn. Waterfront Artists Coalition, Kappa Delta Pi. Home: PO Box 2697 New Britain CT 06050-2697

KOTECKI, JOANNA KRYSTYNA EMERLE, middle school educator; b. Chgo., Apr. 16, 1953; d. Joseph and Maria (Jazwinski) Emerle; m. Jeffrey David Kotecki, July 1, 1978; children: Andrew James, Elizabeth Anne. Student, U. Madrid, 1973-74; BA in Tchr. Edn. in Spanish, U. Ill., Chgo., 1974, MA in Hispanic Lit., 1980. Cert. 7-12 Spanish tchr., Conn. Tchr. Spanish, Elk Grove (Ill.) High Sch., 1975-79, Maine-Oakton-Niles (Ill.) Adult Continuing Edn., 1975-77; tchr. Spanish Brookfield (Conn.) High Sch., 1990-91; adj. instr. Sacred Heart U., Fairfield, Conn., 1980-82; tchr. Spanish Stratford (Conn.) Cath. Regional Sch. System, 1992-93, West Shore Mid. Sch., Milford, Conn., 1993—. Translator, 1986—. Mem., corr. sec. Stratford Newcomers Club, 1980-88; rep. Internat. Hospitality Com., Fairfield County, Conn., 1985—; mem. hospitality com. Newtown (Conn.) Welcome Wagon, 1988-92, Head O'Meadow PTA, 1988-95, Newtown Middle Sch. PTA. Mem. Conn. Coun. of Fgn. Lang. Tchrs., Am. Coun. on Teaching Fgn. Langs. Roman Catholic. Avocations: hosting foreign visitors, reading, travel, needlework, gardening. Home: 8 S Fiore Pkwy Vernon Hills IL 60061-3269

KOTINAS, DEMETRA, advocate, educator; b. Chicago, Mar. 4, 1942; d. Festus A. Johnson and Georgia (Filler) Kotinas. EdB, Nat. Coll. Edn., 1966; post grad., U. Ariz., 1980-82. Cert. tchr. in Ill. and Ariz. Exec. sec. World Book Ency., Chgo., 1961-62; advt. asst. Norge Sales Corp., Chgo., 1963-66; tchr. Arlington Heights Jr. High Sch., Arlington Hieghts, Ill., 1966-68,

Chgo. Pub. Sch., Chgo., 1968-78, Phoenix Indian High Sch., Phoenix, 1978-79; tchr. dist. one Phoenix Elem Sch., Phoenix, 1979-95, cons., 1984-90. Designer, dir. Animals Benefit Club of Ariz., a caring sanctuary for dogs and cats, Phoenix. Author: All About Love, 1984, fourth edit., 1999. Adv., Maricopa County Rabies Animal Control, 1984—, mem. Phoenix City Council, 1987—; creator Vet. Clinic, 1999. Recipient Golden Bell Award, Ariz. Sch. Bd. Assn., 1985; initiated and established the first Pet Partners and Pet Assisted Therapy Programs in Ariz., numerous grants for pet rescue and edn., including Ariz. Community Found., Holbrook-Pyle Fund, 1987, Nina Mason Pulliman Trust Fund, 2002, Virginia G. Piper Charitable Trust. Mem. Humane Soc. U.S., Animals Benefit Club Ariz. (founder and pres. 1984—), People for Ethical Treatment of Animals, Soc. Prevention Cruelty to Animals, Cousteau Soc., Delta Soc. Avocations: grand canyon river trips;, bringing people and animals together. Home: 1226 E Seldon Ln Phoenix AZ 85020-3261 Office: Animals Benefit Club Ariz 3111 E St John Rd Phoenix AZ 85032-1952

KOTLER, RONALD LEE, physician, educator; b. Pitts., June 10, 1956; s. Milton and Marion (Oppenheimer) K.; m. Jane Ellyn Cobin, Feb. 20, 1982; children: Jennifer, Rachel, Drew. BA, Emory U., 1978; MD, U. Pa., 1982. Diplomate Am. Bd. Internal Medicine, Am. Bd. Pulmonary Disease, Am. Bd. Critical Care Medicine, Am. Bd. Sleep Medicine. Intern Pa. Hosp., Phila., 1982-83, resident, 1983-85; fellow pulmonary disease, postdoctoral trainee and rschr. Hosp. U. Pa/U. Pa. Sch. Medicine, Phila., 1985-87; clin. assoc. in medicine U. Pa. Sch. Medicine, Phila., 1987-88, clin. asst. prof., 1988—95, 1997—2002, clin. assoc. prof. of medicine, 2002—; clin. asst. prof. Thomas Jefferson U., Phila., 1994—. Co-dir. hosp. sleep lab. Pa. Hosp., Phila., 1991—. Contbr. articles to profl. jours. Lectr. City Phila. Dept. Health, Phila., 1988, 89, Pa. Hosp., 1995. Fellow ACP, Am. Coll. Chest Physicians; mem. Am. Thoracic Soc., Phi Beta Kappa, Omicron Delta Kapp, Alpha Omega Alpha. Avocation: tennis. Office: Casey Lugano Kotler Assocs 700 Spruce St Ste 500 Philadelphia PA 19106-4027

KOTLER, WENDY ILLENE, art educator, social studies educator, grants coordinator; b. Chgo., Mar. 4, 1947; d. Robert and Florence (Rabin) Abrams; m. Neil G. Kotler, Dec. 17, 1971; 1 child, Jena Julianne. BFA, U. Ill., 1969; MEd, U. Va., 1982, PhD, 1991. Cert. NK-12 art tchr., gifted and talented edn., mid., elem. and secondary sch. supr. and prin. Tchr. Sch. Dist. 109 and 23, Cook County, Ill., 1969-71; tchr. art, supr. Supervisory Union 32, N.H., 1972-74; tchr., curriculum developer Austin (Tex.) Ind. Sch. Dist., Hanover, N.H., 1974-75; staff devel. trainer, program developer Fairfax County (Va.) Pub. Schs., 1975-76, tchr., curriculum developer, 1979-85, program coord., art and mid. sch. resource tchr., 1985-92; mem. adj. faculty No. Va. Ext., U. Va., Fairfax, 1985—; adj. faculty George Mason U. Program developer, tchr. trainer Regional Ctr. for Ednl. Tng., Wilson Mus., Dartmouth Coll., Hanover, N.H., 1972-74; workshop presenter in field to regional, state, nat. and sch. confs.; curriculum and instrn. cons.; adj. faculty George Mason U. Contbr. articles to profl. publs. Recipient commendation for profl. excellence Fairfax County Pub. Schs., 1989, 92. Mem. NEA, ASCD, NCSS, Va. Edn. Assn., Fairfax Edn. Assn., Nat. Art Edn. Assn. (Southeastern Elem. Art Educator of Yr. award 1991, Nat. Elem. Art Educator of Yr. award 1992), Va. Art Edn. Assn. (bd. dirs. 1989, 93, Va. Elem. Art Tchr. of Yr. award 1989, cert. of commendation 1990), No. Va. Art Edn. Assn. (pres. 1993, No. Va. Art Tchr. of Yr. award 1988, 89), Phi Delta Kappa. Home: 507 Roosevelt Blvd Apt C403 Falls Church VA 22044-3156

KOTNOUR, MARY MARGARET, physical education educator; b. Winona, Minn., Jan. 28, 1956; d. Thomas and Maxine (Herber) K. BS in Phys. Edn., Winona State U., 1978; MEd in Counseling, U. Idaho, 1983. Cert. tchr. Minn., Idaho, Wash. Elem. phys. edn. specialist Sch. Dist. #211, Coeur d'Alene, Idaho, 1979-85; elem. phys. edn. coord. Sch. Dist. #271, Coeur d'Alene, 1985-86, elem. phys. edn. specialist, 1986—. Reviewer of Phys. Edn. Books, Prentice Hall, Inc., Englewood, N.J. Author: Physical Fitness Games and Activities Kit, 1990. Bd. dirs. Big Brothers and Big Sisters, Coeur d' Alene; coach, clinician, tng. chmn. Spl. Olympics, Coeur d' Alene; vol. chaplain County Jail. Recipient Disting. Young Alumni award Winona State U., 1987; named to Outstanding Young Women of Am., 1984. Mem. AAHPERD, NEA, Idaho Assn. Health Phys. Edn., Recreation and Dance (nominated for Outstanding Phys. Edn. Tchr. of Yr., 1986, '92), Idaho Edn. Assn., Coeur d' Alene Edn. Assn. (negotiating team 1988—), Delta Kappa Gamma. Avocation: travel. Office: Ramsay Elem Sch 1351 W Kathleen Ave Coeur D Alene ID 83815-8339

KOTZ, SAMUEL, statistician, educator, translator, editor; b. Harbin, China, Aug. 28, 1930; s. Boris and Guta (Kahana) K.; m. Roselyn Greenwald, Aug. 6, 1963; children— Tamar Ann, Harold David, Pauline Esther. MSc with honors, Hebrew U., Jerusalem, 1956; PhD, Cornell U., 1960; Dr. honoris causa, U. Athens, 1995, Harbin Inst. Tech., 1984, Bowling Green State U., 1997. Rschr. Israel Meterol. Service, 1954-58; lectr. Bar-Ilan U., Israel, 1960-62; postdoctoral Ford fellow U. NC, 1962-63; asso. prof. U. Toronto, 1963-67; prof. math. Temple U., 1967-79; prof. stats. U. Md., Coll. Pk., 1979-97, disting. scholar-tchr., 1984-85. Disting. vis. prof. Bucknell U., 1977, Guelph (Can.) U., 1987; hon. prof. Harbin Inst. Tech., 1987; Eugene Lukacs disting. rsch. prof. Bowling Green (Ohio) State U., 1992; vis. prof. U. Luleå, Sweden, 1993, 95, Hong Kong U., 1994, U. Copenhagen, summer 1996, U. South Brittany, Vannes, France, 1998; vis. prof. econs. and fin. St. Petersburg (Russia) U., summer 1995; vis. rschr. Internat. Statis. Inst., The Hague, summer 1996, U. Paul Sabatier, Toulouse, France, summer 1998, U. York, Eng., U. Salford, Eng., 1999, 2000, Athens U. Econs., 1999, U. Lund, Sweden, 2000; vis. rsch. scholar George Washington U., 1997—, U. Trento, Italy, summers, 2001, 02, U. Padua, 2002. Author, editor 30 books, 4 Russian-English profl. dictionaries, also numerous rsch. papers; translator 18 books; co-editor-in-chief Encyclopedia of Statistical Sci., 9 vols. and supplement, 1982-89, editor-in-chief up-date vols. 1-3, 1994-98, Quality Control and Mgmt., 2000-; co-editor-in-chief Breakthroughs in Statistics, 3 vol., 1995-98; editor: Leading Statistical Personalities, 1997; co-author: Process Capability Indices, 1993, 98, Applied Bayesian Statistics (in Chinese), 2000, 2d edit., 2001, Extreme Value Distributions, 2000, Correlation and Dependence, 2001, Laplace Distribution and Applications, 2001, Strength-Stress Models, 2003, Statistical Size Distributions in Economics, 2003; mem. editl. bd. Soviet Jour. Applied Math. Stat., Jour. Quality Rsch. and Tech.; coord. editor Jour. Statis. Planning and Inference, AIEE Transactions. Served with Israeli Army, 1950-52. Fellow Am. Statis. Assn., Inst. Math. Stat., Royal Statis. Soc., Washington Acad. Sci. (hon.); mem. Internat. Statis. Inst. (elected mem.). Office: George Washington U Dept Engring Management Washington DC 20052-0001 E-mail: kotz@seas.gwu.edu.

KOTZEN, MARSHALL JASON, mathematics educator; b. Malden, Mass., Dec. 29, 1942; s. Bernard and Regina (Katz) K.; m. Elizabeth Claudia Magner, Aug. 24, 1980. BS in Math., Tufts U., 1964; MS in Math., U. N.H., 1967. Grad. asst. in math. U. N.H., Durham, 1967-69; instr. of math. Worcester (Mass.) State Coll., 1969-74, asst. prof. math., 1974-89, assoc. prof. math., 1989—. Mem. Am. Math. Soc., Math. Assn. Am. Office: Worcester State Coll 486 Chandler St Worcester MA 01602-2597

KOUDELKA, GEORGE JOHN, retired music educator; b. Hallettsville, Tex., Feb. 27, 1945; s. John William and Hilda Barbara (Stavinoha) K. B MusEdn., Southwest Tex. State U., 1968; MEd, Prairie View A&M U., 1972. Cert. tchr. music and band, Tex. Instr. in percussion and music Southwest Tex. State U., San Marcos, 1967-69; dir. bands and music Flatonia (Tex.) Ind. Sch. Dist., 1969-82, Moulton (Tex.) Ind. Sch. Dist., 1982-98; ret., 1998. Lectr. Czech music symposium U. Tex., 1998. Contbg. author: A Passion for Polka, 1992, church cookbook, 1985, others. Pres. PTA, Flatonia, 1972-73; mem. Knights of Dixie Orch., Sugar Land, Tex., 1996—, Gil Baca Orch., 1997. Named Flatonia Citizen of Yr., 2000. Mem. Tex. Music Edn. Assn., Music Edn. Nat. Conf., Woodmen of the World, KC (Grand Knight 1971-73), Sons of Hermann Ins. Soc. Avocations: old phonograph record collecting, stamp collecting, old book collecting, comic strips, comic book collecting. Home: PO Box 165 Flatonia TX 78941-0165

KOURKOUMELIS, NICK, financial analyst, consultant, finance educator; b. San Francisco, Mar. 1, 1948; s. Gerasimos A. and Ismini (Melissaratos) K.; m. Maria Demetriadou; 1 child, Effie Nicole. BS, Fairleigh Dickinson U., 1970, MBA with high honors, 1974; PhD in Bus. Adminstrn., Century U., 1990. Supr., fin. analyst comptr.'s office Texaco Inc., White Plains, N.Y., 1970-85, coord. human resources, 1986-88, sr. coord. human resource devel. comptr.'s office, 1988-93; fin. tng. cons. exec. dept., 1994-95; value analyst corp. planning and econs. dept. Texaco Inc., White Plains, N.Y., 1995-96, sr. fin. cons. human resources dept., 1997-98; pres., CEO The Melis Group, LLC, 1999—; mng. ptnr. Oher & Assocs., 2000—; mem. strategic planning program Calif. Inst. Tech., 1992; assoc. prof. bus. Am. Coll. Thessaloniki, 2002—. Adj. prof. econs. and fin. exec. MBA program Fairleigh Dickinson U., Teaneck, NJ, 1978—; fin. mgmt. cons. IBM Inst. for Advanced Bus., Calif. State Poly U., Bell Atlantic, USF&G Corp., Chase Manhattan Bank, Time, Inc., MCI Corp., Roche Lab., Allied Signal, Lockheed Martin, Pfizer, Fed. Home Loan Bank San Francisco, Hall Neighborhood House, Women and Minority Owned Bus., N.J. Ethnic Adv. Coun.; bus. mgr. various actresses; fin. cons. to celebrities and sports figures; exec. cons. The Sable Group, 1990—. Mem. nat. steering com. Clinton/Gore Presdl. Campaign, 1996; dir. Greek Orthodox Sunday Sch. Program; coun. mem., treas. St. Athanasios Ch. Texaco scholarship recipient Capitol award Nat. Leadership Coun., 1991, FDU Teaching Excellence award, 1994-96; named on Wall of Tolerance, 2002. Mem. ASTD (v.p. fin. Westchester chpt.), Internat. Econs. Honor Soc., Mgmt. Devel. Forum, The Planning Forum, Greek Am. Voters League N.J. (founder, dir.). Greek Orthodox. Home: 15 Fayette Pl Fair Lawn NJ 07410 Personal E-mail: nikolaos@ac.anatolia.edu.gr.

KOUSARI, EHSAN O. art educator; b. Hamadan, Iran, Sept. 23, 1939; came to U.S., 1964; s. Nadali and Roghi (Mostaghami) K.; m. Mary Jean Wills, July 19, 1948; children: Nadia, Roya, Kavon. BS in Edn., N.E. Mo. State U., 1967; MA, Ball State U., 1969, MS, 1971, EdS, 1976. Elem. art tchr. Anderson (Ind.) Cmty. Schs., 1970-76, H.S. art tchr., 1976—. Mem. ASCD.

KOUZES, RICHARD THOMAS, physicist, educator; b. Arlington, Virginia, July 8, 1947; s. Thomas and Thelma Virginia (Loss) K.; m. Janice Mary (Costantino), Feb. 28, 1970; children: Ross, Emily. BS, Mich. State U., 1969; MS, Princeton U., NJ., 1972, PhD, 1974. Sr. rsch. physicist Princeton U., NJ, 1976-91; sr. scientist Pacific N.W. Nat. Lab., Richland, Wash., 1991-95; prof. W.Va. U., Morgantown, W.Va., 1995-2000; lab. fellow Pacific N.W. Nat. Lab., Richland, Wash., 2000—. Author: Astrophysics Simulations, 1995; editor: Neural Network Applications in Energy, Environment and Health, 1996. Mem. IEEE, Am. Phys. Soc., Sigma Xi. Home: 1005 Country Ct Richland WA 99352-9500

KOVACIC-FLEISCHER, CANDACE SAARI, law educator; b. Washington, Mar. 19, 1947; d. Donald George and Martha Eleanora (Saari) K.; m. Walter H. Fleischer; 1 child, Ilona Saari Fleischer. AB, Wellesley Coll., 1969; JD, Northeastern U., 1974. Law clk. to Hon. James L. Oakes U.S. Ct. Appeals (2d Cir.), Brattleboro, Vt., 1974-75; law clk. to Hon. Warren Burger U.S. Supreme Ct., Washington, 1975-76; assoc. Wilmer, Cutler & Pickering, Washington, 1976-80, Cole & Groner, Washington, 1980-81; prof. Am. U. Coll. Law, Washington, 1981—. Vis. prof. UCLA, 1988; moot ct. panelist Nat. Assn. of Attys. Gen., Washington, 1986-90; mediator U.S. Ct. Appeals (D.C. cir.). Author: (with Leavell, Love and Nelson) Equitable Remedies, Restitution and Damages 5th edit., 1994, 6th edit., 2000; contbr. to profl. publs. Officer Eisenhower Found. for Prevention of Violence, 1977-81; mem. D.C. Cir. Com. on the Bicentennial of the Constn., 1986-92. Recipient U. Faculty award for outstanding tchg., Am. U., 1987, student award for outstanding tchg., 1994; Pauline Ruyle Moore scholar, Coll. Law Am. U., Washington, 1984, 1998, 2000, Wellesley scholar, Wellesley Coll., 1968, 1969. Mem.: AAUW, ABA, Am. Law Inst., Women's Bar Assn., Am. Assn. Law Schs. (chair remedies sect. 1990), Cosmos Club. Office: Am U Coll Law 4801 Massachusetts Ave NW Washington DC 20016-8196

KOVARIK, M. LEORA, elementary principal; b. Carroll, Mo., Apr. 18, 1935; d. James Thomas and Vesta Cecil (Houseworth) Ellis; m. Louis John Kovarik, Oct. 21, 1976. BS with honors, So. Ill. U., 1970, MS with high honors, 1971. Cert. tchr., supr., adminstr., Ill. Spl. edn. tchr. Wood River (Ill.) Sch Dist. 14, 1970-71, Edwardsville (Ill.) Sch. Dist. 7, 1971-74, elem. prin., 1976—; spl. end. coord. Region II Spl. Edn. Coop., Edwardsville, 1974-76. Adj. instr. So. Ill. U., Edwardsville, 1988-90; bd. dirs. Child Study project Danforth Found., St. Louis; coord. Young Authors Program, Edwardsville, 1984-93; cons Meridian Cons., Edwardsville, 1990-93. Sponsor Boy Scouts Am., 1987-93, St. Jude's Math-a-thon, 1989-93, PTO, 1985-93. IDEA fellow Kettering Found., 1980, 81, 82; Inst. for Ednl. Leadership fellow, 1981-82; fellow Prins.'s Roundtable Washington U., St. Louis, 1992; recipient Those Who Excel Plaque Ill. State Bd. Edn., 1992. Mem. ASCD, Ill. Prins. Assn., Coun. for Exceptional Children (pres.), Phi Delta Kappa. Avocations: reading, painting, camping, travel. Home: 617 Grandview Dr Edwardsville IL 62025-2013

KOVER, ARTHUR JAY, marketing educator, consultant; b. N.Y.C., June 16, 1932; s. Theodore and Anita Pearl (Robinson) K.; m. Eugenia Marie Wetzel, Jan. 16, 1971 (div.); children: Amy R., Ezra W.; m. Margaret Sater Lord, Mar. 23, 1991. BA, Cornell U., 1953; MA in Sociology, Yale U., 1954, PhD in Sociology, 1970. Sr. project dir. dept. of rsch. Kenyon & Eckhardt, Inc., N.Y.C., 1960-64, v.p., dir. rsch., 1979-81; v.p., mgr. dept. of rsch. Foote, Cone & Belding, N.Y.C., 1964-69; asst prof. orgnl. behavior Cornell U., Ithaca, N.Y., 1970-78; v.p., dir. rsch. devel. J. Walter Thompson Co., N.Y.C., 1978-79; dir. rsch. and strategy planning Cunningham & Walsh, Inc., N.Y.C., 1981-87; sr. v.p.- rsch. N.W. Ayer, Inc., N.Y.C., 1987-91; prof. mktg. grad. sch. bus. adminstrn. Fordham U., N.Y.C., 1991—2001, chair mktg. area, 1993—98; mgmt. fellow Yale Sch. Mgmt., New Haven, 2001—. V.p., assoc. rsch. dir. Benton & Bowles, Inc., N.Y.C., 1972-74; mem. corp. rsch. & devel. com., new bus. com. J. Walter Thompson Co., N.Y.C., 1978-79, strategy planning bd., N.Y. operating com. Kenyon & Eckhardt, Inc., 1979-81; v.p. Cunningham & Walsh, Inc., N.Y.C., 1981, sr. v.p., 1982, trustee profit sharing plan, 1985, mng. dir. bd. dirs. strategy & planning com., quality com., 1986; adj. prof. mktg. grad. sch. bus. adminstrn. NYU, 1985-90; ind. mktg. and orgnl. cons. in field. Author: (with others) America as a Mass Society, 1963; book rev. editor Adminstrv. Sci. Quar., 1971-73; mem. edit. rev. bd. Jour. Advt. Rsch., 1982-92, assoc. editor, 1991—98, editor in chief Jour. Advt. Rsch., 1998—; contbr. articles to profl. jours.; pub. papers; reviewer in field. 1st lt. U.S. Army, 1954—56. N.Y. State Regents scholar, Cornell State scholar, 1949-54, Univ. scholar Yale U., 1954-57; Wilson U. fellow Yale U., 1959, Spl. Rsch. fellow NIMH, Yale U., 1968-70. Fellow Acad. Mktg. Sci., Soc. Applied Anthropology; mem. Am. Mktg. Assn. (exec.), Am. Sociol. Assn., Comm. Rsch. Coun., Market Rsch. Coun. (councilman at large, 1986-87, pres. 1989-90), Assn. Consumer Rsch., Lotos Club, Elizabethan Club, Franklin Inn Club. Office: Fordham U Grad Sch Bus Adminstrn 113 W 60th St New York NY 10023-7484

KOWALSKA, MARIA TERESA, research scientist, educator; b. Wielun, Poland, June 8, 1932; arrived in U.S., 1982, naturalized, 1991; d. Jozef Ozmina and Zofia Elzbieta Pecherska; m. Wielislaw Kowalski, Apr. 19, 1954 (dec. Nov. 1991); children: Jacek Kowalski, Beata Kowalska-Ellington. BA, Lyceum Gen. Edn., Lodz, Poland, 1950; MS in Pharmacy, Med. Acad., Poznan, Poland, 1954, PhD in Pharmacy, 1964; Dr. Hab., Med. Acad., Lodz, 1978. Asst. prof. pharmacy Med. Acad., Poznan, 1955—69; postdoctoral fellow in pharmacy U. Paris, 1969—70; assoc. prof. Acad. Agr., Poznan, 1970—80; prof. pharmacognosy Nat. U. Kinshasa, 1980—82; rsch. assoc. Rsch. Ctr. Fairchild Frop Garden, Miami, Fla., 1985—90. Adj. asst. prof. dept. biochemistry and molecular biology Sch. Medicine U. Miami, 1990—2000; counselor students Acad. Agr., Poznan, 1975—80; prin. investigator on grant Internat. Palm Soc., Miami, 1986, Miami, 87, World Wildlife Fund, Washington, 1988. Appeared (TV) ABC Miami News, 1992, CNN News, 1993; contbr. articles to profl. jours. Avocations: music, skiing, mountain climbing. Home: 6421 SW 106 St Miami FL 33156

KOWALSKI, KAZIMIERZ, computer science educator, researcher; b. Turek, Poland, Nov. 7, 1946; arrived in U.S., 1986, naturalized, 1994; s. Waclaw and Helena K.; m. Eugenia Zajaczkowska, Aug. 5, 1972. MSc, Wroclaw (Poland) U. Tech., 1970, PhD, 1974. Asst. prof. Wroclaw U. Tech., 1970-76, assoc. prof., 1976-86, Pan Am. U., Edinburg, Tex., 1987-88; prof. computer sci. Calif. State U.-Dominguez Hills, Carson, 1988—, chmn. computer sci. dept., 1998—2001. Lectr. U. Basrah, Iraq, 1981-85; cons. XXCal, Inc., L.A., 1987-91; conf. presenter in field; rsch. fellow Power Inst. Moscow, USSR, 1978; info. sys. tng. UNESCO, Paris, 1978; cons. Tex. Instruments, Inc., 1999-2001. Co-author: Principles of Computer Science, 1975, Organization and Programming of Computers, 1976; also articles. Recipient Bronze Merit Cross, Govt. of Poland, 1980, Knights' Cross of the Order of Merit Republic of Poland, 1997. Mem. IEEE Computer Soc., Assn. for Advancement of Computing in Edn., Mensa, Sigma Xi. Avocations: travel, puzzles. Home: 3836 Weston Pl Long Beach CA 90807-3317 Office: Calif State U 1000 E Victoria St Carson CA 90747-0001 E-mail: kowalski@computer.org.

KOWALSKI, SUSAN DOLORES, critical care nurse, educator; b. Aurora, Ill., Dec. 20, 1944; d. George Bernard and Dolores Ida (Smith) Bockman; m. Edgar Peter Kowalski, July 9, 1988. BSN, No. Ill. U., 1971; MSN, Boston Coll., 1976; MBA, Rockford Coll., 1987; PhD, Tex. Woman's U., 1994. Staff nurse ICU St. Joseph Hosp., Bloomington, Ill., 1971-72, St. Francis Hosp., Peoria, Ill., 1972-73; nursing instr. St. Francis Hosp. Sch. Nursing, Peoria, 1973-75, St. Anthony Med. Ctr. Sch. Nursing, Rockford, 1976-85; staff nurse ICU St. Joseph Hosp., South Bend, Ind., 1986-89; clin. instr. Ind. Vocat. Tech. Coll., South Bend, 1986-89; asst. prof. St. Mary's Coll., Notre Dame, Ind., 1987-89; sr. lectr. U. Tex., Tyler, 1990-94; assoc. prof. U. Nev., Las Vegas, 1994—. Contbr. articles to nursing jours. Mem.: ANA, Sigma Theta Tau. Republican. Roman Catholic. Home: 7736 Rye Canyon Dr Las Vegas NV 89123-0752 Office: U Nev 4505 S Maryland Pkwy Las Vegas NV 89154-9900

KOWALSKI, TIMOTHY JOSEPH, child and adolescent psychiatrist, educator; b. Detroit, Apr. 14, 1956; 1 child, Allison Marie. BA in Biology, Wayne State U., 1979; DO, Mich. State U., 1983. Transitional internship Tripler Army Med. Ctr., Honolulu, 1983-84, gen. psychiatry resident, 1986-89, child psychiatry fellowship, 1989-91; gen. med. officer 3rd Gen. Dispensary, Karlsruhe, West Germany, 1984-85; comdr. 19th Med. Detachment, Germersheim, West Germany, 1985-86; divsn. psychiatrist 25th Light Inf. Divsn., Schofield Barracks, Hawaii, 1991-93; chief adolescent high mgmt. svc. William S. Hall Psychiatric Inst., Columbia, S.C., 1993-96; sr. psychiatrist Columbia Area Mental Health Ctr., 1996-98; dir. child and adolescent outpatient svc. William S. Hall Psychiat. Inst., Columbia, 1998—2001; dir. med. ctr. William S. Hall Psychiat. Inst. Clinics, Columbia, 2001—. Asst. prof. psychiatry and behavioral scis. U. S.C. Sch. Medicine, 1993—; osteo. rep. S.C. State Bd. Med. Examiners, 1997—. Mem. APA, Am. Osteo. Assn. (bur. of state govt. affairs), Am. Osteo. Coll. Neurologists and Psychiatrists (bd. govs. 1995-2003, past pres.—), Am. Acad. Child and Adolscent Psychiatrists, S.C. Psychiatric Assn., S.C. Soc. Child and Adolescent Psychiatrists, S.C. Osteo. Med. Soc., Am. Assn. Osteo. Examiners (v.p. 2003). Avocations: professional football, golf, sports, drumming. Home: 7 Veranda Ln Blythewood SC 29016-7602 Office: Wm S Hall Psychiat Inst 1800 Colonial Dr Columbia SC 29203-6827

KOWLESSAR, MURIEL, retired pediatric educator; b. Bklyn., Jan. 2, 1926; d. John Henry and Arene (Driver) Chevious; m. O. Dhodanand Kowlessar, Dec. 27, 1952; 1 child, Indrani. AB, Barnard Coll., 1947; MD, Columbia U., 1951. Diplomate Am. Bd. Pediatrics. Instr. Downstate Med. Ctr., Bklyn., 1958-64, asst. prof., 1965-66; asst. prof. clin. pediatrics Temple U., Phila., 1967-70; assoc. prof. Med. Coll. Pa., Phila., 1971-83, dir. pediatric group svcs., 1975-90, acting chmn. pediatrics dept., 1981-83, vice chair pediatrics dept., 1982-91, prof., 1983-91, prof. emeritus, 1991—. Contbr. articles to med. jours. Mem. Pa. Gov.'s Task Force on Spl. Supplemental Food Program for Women, Infants and Children, Harrisburg, 1981-83, Phila. Bd. Health, 1982-86; vol. Phila. Com. for Homeless, 1991-92, Gateway Literacy Program, YMCA, Germantown Bridge, Pa., 1992-93. Fellow Am. Acad. Pediatrics (emeritus); mem. Phila. Pediatric Soc., Cosmopolitan Club Phila., Phi Beta Kappa. Democrat. Avocations: ballroom dancing, opera.

KOYAMA, SHEILA H. elementary educator; BA in English, Chico State U.; MA in Linguistics, U. Calif., Davis. Cert. elem. tchr., Calif., Wash. Elem. tchr. Rescue (Calif.) Union Sch. Dist., 1970-71, Hawaii State Dept. Edn., Honolulu, 1971-73, Dept. Def., Alexandria, Va., 1974-77, Sumner (Wash.) Schs., 1980—99; reading coach/support specialist Bethel Sch., Spanaway, Wash., 1999—. Tchr. cons. Comprehensive Health Edn. Found., Federal Way, Wash., 1990-92; instr. Intensive English Lang. Inst., Parkland, Wash., summer 1991, 92. Mem. Internat. Reading Assn., NEA, nat. Staff Devel. Coun., Tchrs. English to Speakers Other Langs. Avocations: reading, curriculum integration and development, music, multi-cultural and general children's books. Office: Bethel Sch 517 176th St E Spanaway WA 98387-1926

KOYM, ZALA COX, elementary education educator; b. San Antonio, July 21, 1948; d. Bruce Meador and Ruby Esther (Jordan) Cox; m. Charles Raymond Koym, July 5, 1969; children: Carol Ann, Cathy Lynn, Suzie Kay. BS in Edn., SW Tex. State U., 1970; grad., Inst. Children's Lit., 2003. Cert. supervision of tchr. effective practices. Elem. tchr. Schertz (Tex.)-Cibolo Ind. Sch. Dist., 1970-71; substitute tchr. Alamogordo (N.Mex.) Pub. Schs., 1973-75; elem. tchr. Round Rock (Tex.) Ind. Sch. Dist., 1983-96, asst. prin., 1988-91, mentor tchr., 1993-96, 99—; 3-4th grade multiage tchr. Ft. Sam Houston Elem., San Antonio, 1996-98; 3rd grade tchr. Silver Creek Elem., Azle, Tex., 1998-99, 4th grade tchr., 1999—, looping grades 3 and 4, 1998—2003. Textbook advisor State of Tex., 1989; chair, coord. 5th grade level Round Rock Ind. Sch. Dist., 1986-90, 2d grade level chair, 1990-93; sci. lab. coord. Robertson Elem., Old Town Elem, 1983-89; Ft. Sam Houston Dist. Improvement Coun., 1996-97, campus gifted and talented com. 1997-99, dir. campus spelling bee, 1998-2003, campus sci. coord., 1999-2003 Active PTA, 1981-96, v.p. programs, 1994-95, PTO, 1996-2003, site-based decision making campus rep., 1993-95; dir. vacation Bible sch. FUMC, 1984-87, scholarship com., 1992-94; neighborhood capt. March of Dimes, 1990, Am. Heart Assn., 1994-95, Am. Inst. Cancer Rsch., 1999; mem. Campus Student Assistance Program Team, 1990-96, Old Town Bldg Leadership Team, 1991-92. Named Silver Creek Tchr. of Yr., 1999—2000. Mem. ASCD, Assn. Tex. Profl. Educators (campus rep. 1998-2003), Phi Delta Kappa (sec. 1991-93, assoc. historian 1994-95, v.p. programs 1995-96). Home: 2316 Walter Smith Rd Azle TX 76020-4333 Office: Silver Creek Elem Sch 10300 S FM Rd 730 Azle TX 76020-9801 E-mail: ckoym@aol.com.

KOZACHEK, JANET LYNNE, artist, educator; b. Princeton, N.J., July 27, 1957; d. Walter and Agnes Robb (Davies) Kozachek; m. Nathaniel Owen Wallace, May 26, 1979. BA, Douglass Coll., New Brunswick, N.J., 1980; Cert. Grad. Study, Beijing (China) Ctrl. Art Acad, 1983-85; MFA,

Parsons Sch. Design, N.Y.C., 1990. Tchr. English Hebei U., Baoding, China, 1981-82, Jilin U., Changchun, China, 1982-83; lectr. art European divsn. U. Md., 1986-87; arts-in-edn. artist S.C. State Arts Commn., 1993—. Adj. prof. art Mercer County C.C., Trenton, N.J., 1990-91; guest lectr. Penland Sch. Art, N.C., 1985, Bluefield (W.Va.) State Coll., 1991, Kutztown (Pa.) U., 1991. Organizer six-artist show Gibbes Mus. Art, 1995; artist retrospective I.P. Stanback Mus., 1993; solo exhbns. include Gallerie de Vierde Dimensie, Plasmolen, Netherlands, 1989, Johnson and Johnson World Hdqrs., 1993, I.P. Stanback Mus., 1993, Goin Gallery, Charleston, S.C., 1994, Greenville (N.C.) Mus. Art, 1997, Nina Liu Gallery, Charleston, Portfolio Gallery, Columbia; exhibited in group shows at Alexandria (La.) Mus. Art, 1992, Picolo Spoleto Exhbn., Charleston, 1993, Armory Art Ctr., West Palm Beach, Fla., 1993, Summer Olympic Games, Stone Mountain, Ga., 1996, numerous others; work in numerous pvt. collections and I.P. Stanback Mus. Permanent Collection, Columbia Mus. Arts; featured in publs. Helena Rubinstein scholar, 1989-90; Orangeburg Arts Ctr. Small Grants awardee, 1993, 95, Curator's Choice award Stage Gallery, 2000, Best of Show award S.C. State Fair, 2002. Mem.: Soc. Am. Mosaic Artists (pres. 1999—2002, cofounder). Democrat. Avocations: travel, gardening, reading. Home: 639 Wilson St NE Orangeburg SC 29115-4872

KOZAREK, RICHARD ANTHONY, gastroenterologist, educator; b. Duluth, Minn., Apr. 22, 1947; s. Clarence Edward and Patricia Ann (Koors) K.; m. Linda Jane Cooper, June 9, 1973; children: Katherine, Ellen. BA in Philosophy, U. Wis., 1969, MD, 1973. Diplomate Am. Bd. Internal Medicine; bd. cert. internal medicine and gastroenterology. Intern Dalhousie U., Halifax, N.S., Can., 1973-74; resident Good Samaritan Hosp., Phoenix, Ariz., 1974-76; fellow U. Ariz.-Phoenix VA Med. Ctr., Tucson, 1976-78; asst. chief gastroenterology Phoenix VA Med. Ctr., Tucson, 1978-83; asst. clin. prof. medicine U. Ariz., Tucson, 1978-83; with sect. gastroenterology Virginia Mason Med. Ctr., Seattle, 1983—; chief gastroenterology Va. Mason Med. Ctr., Seattle, 1989—; clin. prof. medicine U. Wash., Seattle, 1990—. Author 4 books, 65 book chpts., numerous sci. articles; mem. editl. bd. 8 med. jours., 1983—. Recipient Eddy D. Palmer award William Beaumont Soc., 1982. Fellow ACP, Am. Coll. Gastroenterology; mem. Am. Gastroenterology Assn., Soc. for Gastrointestinal Endoscopy (gov. bd. 1990-95, pres.-elect 1996-97, pres. 1998—), Pacific N.W. Gastroenterology Soc. (sec. 1990, pres. 1991), Federated Socs. Gastroenterology and Hepatology (chair 1998—), Orgn. Mondiale de GastroEnterologie (dep. sec.-gen. 2002--). Office: Virgina Mason Med Ctr 1100 9th Ave Seattle WA 98101-2756

KOZBIAL, RICHARD JAMES, retired elementary education educator; b. Toledo, Nov. 11, 1933; s. Phillip and Bernice Bronislawa (Durka) K.; m. Jane Ardys Verny, July 8, 1961 (dec. Nov. 1983); children: Ardys Jane, Beth Lynne. EdB, U. Toledo, 1957, EdM, 1976. Tchr. Toledo Pub. Schs., 1956-58, 1962-84, Van Dyke Sch. Dist., Warren, Mich., 1958-62; intern tchr. cons. Toledo Pub. Schs., 1984-87, cons., 1987-93; supr. student tchrs., course facilitator U. Toledo, 1987-97, vis. prof., 1997-99, mem. faculty, 1997-99; ESL tchr. Szeged, Hungary, 1993-95; supr. alt. plan U. Toledo, 1993-99, instr. integrated social studies/lang. arts/reading block, 1996-99, ret., 1999. Mem. textbook selection coms. Toledo Pub. Schs.; instr. student tchr. tng. programs Toledo U., 1962-84; instr. student tchr. tng. Bowling Green State U., 1962-84, Mich. State U., 1958-59; organizer Multi-Cultural Awareness Workshop Toledo Elem. Tchrs. Internat. Inst., 1986-90; organizer Outdoor Edn. Program; participant Multi Unit Edn. Plan; mem. U. Toledo Internat. Edn. Com., 1997-98; mem. Eng. tour Canterbury Singers, 1989, 95, 2000. Author Spelling Curriculum Guide Toledo Pub. Schs., 1968; prodr. (TV programs) WGTE Famous Ams. Born in Feb., Israel. Up with People Host Family, Ohio Arab Affairs Coun., 1989—, ISS, USIA Host Family, 1986—; mem. Planned Parenthood N.W. Ohio, Toledo Mus. Modern Art, Nat. Trust Historic Preservation, 1988—; vestry mem. Trinity Episc. Ch., 1984-87, sesquicentennial com., chmn. music; baritone soloist Canterbury Choir; vocalist Hospice Meml. Svc., 1984—2001; bereavement vol. Hospice N.W. Ohio, Nat. Hospice Assn.; exec. bd. Toledo/Poznan Alliance, mem. Dozynki com. 1990-2002, chmn. 1990, 95, 2000; mem. Bedford Polish Culture Club, 1989-99; sponsor, coord. host families Zulu Choir, Durham, South Africa, Poznan (Poland) Nightengales. Named Outstanding Young Educator, Toledo C. of C., 1965-66; Jennings Founder scholar, 1979-80; recipient Miss Peach award Toledo Blade, 1963, Award of Excellence, 1983, Internat. Inst. Hall of Fame Disting. Svc. award, 1994, Letter of Commendation, Gov. of Ohio, 1994. Mem. Am. Fedn. Tchrs., Ohio Fedn. Tchrs., Toledo Fedn. Tchrs. (life), Internat. Inst. Inc. (life, chmn. edn. com., bd. dirs. 1985-91, pres. 1988-89), Assn. Two Toledos (bd. dirs., 1st v.p. 1990-91), U. Toledo Alumni Assn. (life), U. Mich. Alumni Assn., Am. Assn. Ret. Persons, Lucas County Ret. Tchrs. (life), Mid. East Affairs Coun. (bd. dirs.), Ellis Island Found., Smithsonian Assocs., Nat. Coun. Sr. Citizens, Toledo Sister Cities Internat. (bd. dirs., chmn. entertainment Masked Bash 1996, com. English lang. camp for students from Poland 1995, 96, chmn. host families), Am. Ctr. Polish Culture, Inc., Greenpeace, Phi Delta Kappa, Kappa Delta Pi (various offices including corr. sec., treas., v.p., pres., Point of Excellence award 1992). Democrat. Avocations: gardening, travel, reading, stained glass, calligraphy. Home: 1011 Fifth Ave Eau Claire WI 54703 E-mail: rkozbia@pop3.utoledo.edu.

KOZLOSKI, LILLIAN TERESE D. museum educator, consultant, lecturer; b. Pitts., Sept. 11, 1934; d. Andrew and Juliana (Yevchak) Dzmura; m. Joseph Kozloski, May 22, 1956; children: Lisa, Cynthia, Charles, Christopher, Dolores Anne. AS, Mt. Aloysius Coll., 1954; BIS, George Mason U., 1981. Mus. technician Smithsonian Air & Space Instn., Washington, 1981-85, mus. specialist, 1985-95, ret., 1995; lectr. U.S. Space Gear Enterprises, Spotsylvania, Va., 1996—; docent James Monroe Mus., Fredericksburg, Va., 2001—. Cons. Smithsonian Instn., Washington, 1996, N.Y. Times, 1996; lectr. on living and working in space. Author: U.S. Space Gear History of Space Suit Technology, 1994, paperback edit., 2000; contbr. articles to profl. jours. Mem. AAUW, Am. Assn. Mus., N.Y. Acad. Scis., Soc. for History of Tech. Roman Catholic. Achievements include categorization and study of Nat. Air and Space Mus. collection of space suits; collected and organized space suit into loan collections and preservation and study collection. Home: 5035 Ridge Rd Spotsylvania VA 22553-6334 E-mail: lillkoz@rcn.com.

KOZLOWSKI, CHERYL M. principal; b. Boston, July 19, 1974; d. Leo Dennis and Angeles Zenaida BA, Middlebury Coll., 1996; postgrad., Harvard Bus. Sch., 2000—02. Lic. pilot. Fin. analyst Merrill Lynch, N.Y.C., 1996-1998; prin. Clayton, Dubilier & Rice, Inc., N.Y.C., 1998-2000. Equity analyst Am. Express, 2002—. Treas. The Friends of Tolstoy Found., 1998—; chmn. Young New Yorkers of N.Y. Philharmonic, 1999—2002; bd. dirs. Shackleton Schs., 2000—. Avocation: skiing. Home: 610 Park Ave Apt 14A New York NY 10021-7080 E-mail: ckozlowski@mba2002.hbs.edu.

KOZMA, HELENE JOYCE MARIE, adult educator; b. Bridgeport, Conn. d. Ernest A. and Helen C. (Skurski) K. BA in English, Adelphi U.; MBA in Bus. Mgmt., Sacred Heart U., 1986, postgrad., 1990. Cert. English and bus. tchr., Conn. Tchr. bus. Town of Stratford, Conn., 1986-87, 92, 96, Acad. of Our Lady of Mercy, Milford, Conn., 1987-88; Gateway Comty./Tech. Coll., New Haven, Conn., 1994-2000; Norwalk (Conn.) C.C., 2000—. Tchr. Sacred Heart U., 1998—, St. Vincent Coll., 1998—, Housatonic C.C., Bridgeport, 2001—. Eucharistic min. Holy Name of Jesus Ch., 1991, lectr., reader, 1991, catechist tchr., 1990-91; mem. Stratford town com., 1995-97; bd. dirs. Stratford Libr. Assn., 1995-97. Mem. AAUW, Nat. Coun. Tchrs. of English, Shakespeare Guild, Toastmasters (charter, treas. 1984, adminstrv. v.p. 1986).

KOZOL, JONATHAN, writer; b. Boston, Sept. 5, 1936; s. Harry Leo and Ruth (Massell) K. BA, Harvard U., 1958; Rhodes scholar, Magdalen Coll., Oxford U., 1958-59. Tchr. Boston pub. schs., 1964-65, Newton pub. schs., 1966-68; dir., trustee Store-front Learning Center, 1968-74; vis. lectr. Yale U., 1969, numerous univs., 1971-2001; prof. edn. Trinity Coll., 1980. Cons. U.S. Office Edn., 1965-66; inst. Ctr. for Intercultural Documentation, Cuernavaca, Mex., 1969, 70, 74. Author: Death At An Early Age, 1967 (Nat. Book award, 1968), Free Schools, 1972, The Night Is Dark and I Am Far From Home, 1975, Children of the Revolution, 1978, Prisoners of Silence, 1980, On Being A Teacher, 1981, Illiterate America, 1985, Rachel and Her Children, 1988 (Robert F. Kennedy Book award, 1989), Savage Inequalities, 1991 (New Eng. Book award, 1992, Amazing Grace, 1995 (Anisfield-Wolf Book award, 1996), Ordinary Resurrections, 2000 (Christopher award, Harry Chapin award, 2001, Wilbur award, 2001); corr.: Los Angeles Times, USA Today, 1982-83; contbr. to N.Y. Times Book Rev., 1968-85; reporter-at-large The New Yorker mag., 1988. Trustee New Sch. for Children, Roxbury, Mass.; bd. dirs. Nat. Literacy Coalition, 1980-83. Recipient Olympia Thousand Dollar award, 1962, Lannan Literary award, 1994; Saxton fellow in creative writing Harper & Row, 1964; Guggenheim fellow, 1970, 84; Field Found. fellow, 1972; Ford Found. fellow, 1974; Rockefeller Found. fellow, 1978, fellow in humanities, 1983. Mem. Nat. Coalition for the Homeless, Fellowship of Reconciliation. Address: PO Box 145 Byfield MA 01922-0145

KRA, PAULINE SKORNICKI, French language educator; b. Lodz, Poland, July 30, 1934; arrived in US, 1950, naturalized, 1955; d. Edward and Nathalie Skornicki; m. Leo Dietrich Kra, Mar. 10, 1955; children: David Theodore, Andrew Jason. Student, Radcliffe Coll., 1951-53; BA, Barnard Coll., 1955; MA, Columbia U., 1963, PhD, 1968; MA, Queens Coll., 1990. Lectr. Queens Coll., CUNY, 1964-65; asst. prof. French Yeshiva U., N.Y.C., 1968-74, assoc. prof., 1974-82, prof., 1982-99, prof. emerita, 1999—; sr. programmer analyst Dept. Biomed. Informatics Columbia U., N.Y.C., 1998—. Author: Religion in Montesquieu's Lettres persanes, 1970; contbr. articles to profl. jours. Mem. MLA, Am. Assn. Tchrs. French, Am. Soc. 18th Century Studies, Société Française d'étude du XVIII Siècle, Soc. Montesquieu, Assn. for Computers and Humanities, Assn. for Lit. and Linguistic Computing, Phi Beta Kappa. Home: 10914 Ascan Ave Forest Hills NY 11375-5370 E-mail: kra@ymail.yu.edu.

KRACKOW, KENNETH ALAN, orthopaedic surgeon, educator, inventor; b. Balt., Sept. 6, 1944; s. Eugene Howard and Audrey Ruth (Goldstein) K.; children: Sydney E., Andrea G.; m. Joan Nicole Darmstaedter, July 25, 1993. AB in Math. with honors, Johns Hopkins U., 1966; postgrad., Duke U., 1968-69, MD, 1971. Diplomate Am. Bd. Med. Examiners, Am. Bd. Orthopaedic Surgeries. Intern in gen. surgery Johns Hopkins Hosp., Balt., 1971-72, asst. resident in gen. surgery, 1972-73, successively asst. resident, sr. asst. resident, chief resident in orthopaedic surgery, 1973-76, mem. staff in orthopaedic surgery, Good Samaritan Hosp., Balt., 1976-92, Children's Hosp., Balt., 1976-92; mem. staff Union Meml. Hosp., Balt., 1986-92; pvt. practice Drs. Filtzer, Reichmister & Becker, P.A., Balt., 1976-78; instr. orthopaedic surgery Johns Hopkins U., Balt., 1976-78, asst. prof., 1978-84, assoc. prof., 1984-90, prof., 1990-92, acting chief div. arthritis surgery dept. orthopaedic surgery, 1986; chief dept. orthopaedic surgery Buffalo Gen. Hosp., 1992-98; prof. orthopaedic surgery SUNY at Buffalo, 1992—. Pres. med. staff Good Samaritan Hosp., Balt., 1985-88, v.p. med. staff, 1984-85, sec. med. staff, 1980-83, med. exec. com., 1980-87, utilization rev. com. orthopaedic sect., 1976-81, ethics com., 1978-79; chmn. tissue com. Balt. County Gen. Hosp., 1977-78, by-laws com., 1977-78; chief divsn. orthopaedic surgery VA Hosp., Balt., 1980-87, vis. prof. U. Buffalo, 1983; bd. examiner Am. Bd. Orthopaedic Surgery, Chgo., 1989—; cons. Johns Hopkins Hosp., 1976-78, lectr., presenter in field. Author: Technique of Total Knee Arthroplasty, 1990, (with others) Total Knee Arthroplasty: A Comprehensive Approach, 1983, Non-Cemented Total Hip Arthroplasty, 1988, Total Joint Replacement, 1991; editor Advances in Orthopaedic Surgery, 1982—, Jour. Arthroplasty, 1993—; reviewer Jour. Bone Joint Surgery, 1996—; asst. chief editor Jour. Arthroplasty, 1988-93; mem. editorial bd. Am. Jour. Knee Surgery, 1988-92, Sports Medicine News, 1991—; founding editor Jour. Orthopaedic Techniques; contbr. over 100 articles and abstracts to profl. jours. Active Md. br. Arthritis Found., 1977-92, Md. Soc. Rheumatic Diseases, 1977-92. Recipient Peer Rev. award Genucom, 1986-88; Instl. grantee Johns Hopkins U., 1980-81; grantee O'Neil Found., 1979-80, Orthopaedic Rsch. and Edn. Found., 1980-81, Howmedica, Inc., 1988-90. Mem. AMA, Am. Orthopaedic Assn., Am. Acad. Orthopaedic Surgery, Am. Knee Soc., Md. Orthopaedic Soc., Md. Soc. Med. Rsch.,, Johns Hopkins Med. Surg. Soc., Acad. Orthopaedic Soc., Orthopaedic Rsch. Soc., Assn. Arthritis Hip and Knee Surgery (pres. 1999—), Western N.Y. Orthopaedic Soc., Phi Beta Kappa. Home: 58 N Woodside Ln Williamsville NY 14221-5953 Office: Buffalo Gen Hosp 100 High St Ste B203 Buffalo NY 14203-1154

KRAEMER, ALFRED ROBERT, school librarian; b. N.Y.C., Dec. 25, 1948; s. Philip George and Bernadette (Klein) K.; children: Sarah McCall, Philip Joseph. BA, Beloit Coll., 1973; MSLS, U. N.C., 1978; MA, N.C. State U., 1983; PhD, U. N.C., Greensboro, 1997. Cert. pub. libr., N.C.; lic. elem. and secondary tchr., N.C. Libr. asst. Duke Med. Ctr., Durham, N.C., 1976-78; English tchr. Patterson Sch., Lenoir, N.C., 1978-80; asst. prof. English St. Mary's Coll., Raleigh, N.C., 1980-88; asst. dir. tchg. fellows N.C. State U., Raleigh, 1989-92; sch. libr. Guilford County Schs., Greensboro, N.C., 1995--. Author: Malory's Grail Seekers and 15th Century English Hagiography, 1999. With USN, 1967-70. Mem. MLA, ALA. Democrat. Episcopalian. E-mail: jack_kraemer@yahoo.com.

KRAEMER, KENNETH LEO, architect, educator, urban planner; b. Plain, Wis., Oct. 29, 1936; s. Leo Adam and Lucy Rose (Bauer) K.; m. Norine Florence, June 13, 1959; children: Kurt Randall, Kim Rene. BArch, U. Notre Dame, 1959; MS in City and Regional Planning, U. So. Calif., 1964, M of Pub. Adminstrn., 1965, PhD, 1967. From instr. to asst. prof. U. So. Calif., Los Angeles, 1965-67; asst. prof. U. Calif., Irvine, 1967-71, assoc. prof., 1971-78, prof., 1978—, dir. Pub. Policy Research Orgn., 1974-92, dir. Ctr. for Rsch. on Info. Tech. and Orgns., 1992—. Cons. Office of Tech. Assessment, Washington, 1980, 84-85; pres. Irvine Research Corp., 1978—. Author: Management of Information Systems, 1980, Computers and Politics, 1982, Dynamics of Computing, 1983, People and Computers, 1985, Modeling as Negotiating, 1986, Data Wars, 1987, Wired Cities, 1987, Managing Information Systems, 1989, Asia's Computer Challenge, 1998. Mem. Blue Ribbon Data Processing Com., Orange County, Calif., 1973, 79-80, Telecomm. Adv. Bd., Sacramento, 1987-92. Fellow Assn. for Info. Sys.; mem. Am. Soc. for Pub. Adminstrn. (Disting. Research award 1985), Internat. Conf. on Info. Systems, Am. Planning Assn., Assn. for Computing Machinery, Notre Dame Club. Democrat. Roman Catholic. Office: U Calif Ctr Rsch Info Tech & Orgns Berkley Pl N Ste 3200 Irvine CA 92697-0001 E-mail: kkraemer@uci.edu.

KRAEMER, LINDA GAYLE, associate dean; b. San Antonio, May 5, 1949; d. Joe K. and Johnnie H. Gibbons; m. Morton D. Kraemer, June 18, 1972; 1 child, Lauren E. BA, Ohio State U., 1971; MS, Columbia U., 1975; PhD, U. Pa., 1986. Dental hygienist pvt. practice, Austin, Tex., 1971-72, Austin Health Dept., 1972-74; rsch. asst. Columbia U., N.Y.C., 1974-75; cons. program planning Thomas Jefferson U., Phila., 1976, chmn., 1976-89, asst. dean, 1988-90, assoc. dean, 1990-92, sr. assoc. dean, 1992—. Com. mem. Inst. Medicine, Washington, 1992-94; mem. adv. panel PEW Health Professions Commn., San Francisco, 1991-92; mem. adv. bd. Oral-B Labs., Redwood City, Calif., 1989-90; cons. in field. Contbr. chpt. to book and articles to profl. jours. Bd. trustees Nat. Multiple Sclerosis Soc., Phila., 1994; mem. adv. bd. Phila. Higher Edn. Congress, 1992-94; com. mem. Women in Concert, Women's Way, Phila., 1990; fundraiser Am. Diabetic Assn., Cherry Hill, N.J., 1990-94. Recipient Acad. Achievement award Pa. Dental Hygienists's Assn., 1986. Mem. Am. Assn. Dental Schs. (coun. chair 1987-88), Am. Dental Hygienists Assn. coun. chair 1990-91, Warner Lambert award 1995), Am. Assn. Higher Edn., Internat. Assn. Dental Rsch., Assn. Sch. Allied Health (com. co-chair 1989-90), Sigma Phi Alpha (pres. 1991-92), Alpha Eta. Independent. Jewish. Avocations: travel, visual and performing arts, reading, biking, hiking.

KRAFT, KAREN ANN, secondary school educator; b. Bklyn., June 27, 1964; d. Michael John and Barbara Ann (DeMaio) Miele; m. John L. Kraft, June 17, 1989; children: Taylor Michael, Mason Genaro. BS, North Tex. State U., 1986; MA in Edn., U. North Tex., 1990. Lic. provisional tchr. English and Spanish, gifted and talented, Tex. Tchr. Westwood H.S., Palestine, Tex., 1987-88, Allen (Tex.) H.S., 1988-93, Coppell (Tex.) H.S., 1993—. Tchr. Nat. Honor Soc. Faculty Coun., Allen, 1989-93; Nat. Honor Soc. sr. sponsor Coppell H.S., 1994—; facilitator Student Mentorship Course. Mem. ASCD, Nat. Coun. Tchrs. English, Tex. Assn. for Gifted and Talented. Roman Catholic. Home: 1303 Laguna Vista Way Grapevine TX 76051-2829 E-mail: kkraft@coppellISD.com.

KRAFT, ROSEMARIE, dean, educator; b. Franklin, Pa., Nov. 18, 1936; d. Jack B. Harter and Romaine B. Shick; m. Louis R. Kraft; children: Louis W., Jack C. PhD, Ohio State U., 1976. Prof. U. Calif., Davis, 1977—, assoc. dean, 1994—. Dir., prof. for future fellowship U. Calif., Davis, 1995—. Author: Individual Differences in Cognition, 1998. Recipient McNair Scholars grant, U.S. Dept. Edn., 1995, 1999. Avocations: hiking, reading, traveling. Home: 1315 Lake Blvd Davis CA 95616 Office: U Calif Davis One Shields Ave Davis CA 95616

KRAFT, SUMNER CHARLES, physician, educator; b. Lynn, Mass., Aug. 21, 1928; m. Patricia F. Pink, June 23, 1963; children: Gary Andrew, Jennifer Rose Kraft-Horwich, Steven Russell. BS, Tufts U., 1948; AM, Boston U., 1949; MD, U. Chgo., 1955. Diplomate Am. Bd. Internal Medicine, Am. Bd. Gastroenterology; cert. med. rev. officer 1999. Intern Boston City Hosp., 1955-56; asst. resident U. Chgo. Hosp., 1956-57, jr. asst. resident, 1957-58, resident, 1958-59, fellow in gastroenterology, 1958-60, instr. medicine, 1959-61, USPHS spl. fellow, 1961-66; rsch. fellow immunology Scripps Clinic & Rsch. Found., 1964—66; asst. prof. medicine U. Chgo., 1961—68, assoc. prof. medicine, 1968—73; USPHS rsch. career devel. fellow Nat. Inst. Allergy and Infectious Diseases, 1967-72; prof. medicine, 1974—; prof. com. on immunology, 1974-93; staff mem. U. Chgo. Med. Ctr. Ad hoc cons. food allergy and gastrointestinal immunolgy; faculty lectr. Nat. Ctr. Advanced Med. Edn., Chgo., 1969-96; vis. prof. medicine, then affil. prof. medicine Uniformed Svcs. U. Health Scis., Bethesda, Md., 1979-87. Chmn. editl. bd. Jour. Medicine on the Midway, 1981-96 contbr. articles to med. jours. Merit badge counselor Calumet coun. Boy Scouts Am., former scoutmaster, troop com. chmn., 1966-81; judge Chgo. Non-Pub. Sch. Sci. Exposition, 1981-82. Col. USAR, 1957-96. Recipient William Beaumont award for clin. rsch., 1977, U.S. Army Order of Mil. Med. Merit, 1994, Disting. Mem. Regiment award U.S. Army Med. Dept. Regiment, 1997. Fellow ACP; mem. AAAS, Am. Assn. Immunologists, Am. Fedn. Clin. Rsch., Am. Gastroent. Assn. (editl. bd. 1976-81), Am. Bd. Internal Medicine (mem. subspecialty examining bd. gastroenterology 1978-83), Army Reserve Assn., Am. Soc. Gastrointestinal Endoscopy, Assn. Mil. Surgeons U.S., Ctrl. Soc. Clin., Chgo. Assn. Immunologists, Chgo. Soc. Gastroenterology (organizing com. 1967-68, exec. com. 1968-71, pres. 1969-70), Chgo. Soc. Gastrointestinal Endoscopy, Chgo. Soc. Internal Medicine, Gastroenterology Rsch. Group, Inst. Medicine Chgo., Sr. Army Reserve Comdrs. Assn. (life), Midwest Gut Club (steering com. 1969-72), N.Y. Acad. Scis., Res. Officers Assn. (life), Soc. Exptl. Biology and Medicine, U.S. Army War Coll. Alumni Assn., Nat. Eagle Scout Assn. (life), Sigma Xi, Alpha Epsilon Pi (life). Office: U Chgo Hosp Mail Code 4076 5841 S Maryland Ave Chicago IL 60637-1463

KRAHMALKOV, CHARLES RICHARD, social sciences educator; b. N.Y.C., June 6, 1936; s. Max and Molly (Kushner) K.; m. Karen Diane Lieberman; children: Laura Joanne, Michelle Catherine. BA, U. Calif., Berkeley, 1957; PhD, Harvard Coll., 1965. Asst. prof. UCLA, 1966-68, U. Mich., Ann Arbor, 1965-66, from asst. prof. to prof., 1968—. Contbr. articles to profl. publs. Republican. Avocations: hiking, climbing, reading. Home: 47813 Stratford Ct Canton MI 48187 Office: Univ Mich 105 S State St Ann Arbor MI 48109-1285

KRAINSKI, JOANNA DONNA, middle school educator; b. Boston, May 7, 1947; d. Walter Joseph and Josephine Catherine (Regolino) K. AA, Mass. Bay Community Coll., 1967; BS in Edn., Boston State Coll., 1969; MA in Edn., Northeastern U., 1974; Cert. Advanced Grad. Studies in Computers in Edn., Lesley Coll., 1988. Cert. elem., secondary, math. and sci. tchr., Mass. Tchr. Tewksbury (Mass.) Pub. Schs., 1969—. Mem. reading draft com. Curriculum Frameworks of Math., Sci. and Tech., State of Mass.; math. curriculum coord. Middle Sch.; align curriculum to Mass. Math. State Frameworks from elem. to mid. sch.; Partnerships Advancing The Learnings for Mathematics Scis. and Tech. (PALMS) tchr. leader for Mass. Dept. Edn.; presenter PALMS workshops in math., sci. and tech.; reviewer for pub. book Math. on Call; critiques articles for Nat. Coun. Tchrs. Math. Mem. NEA, ASCD, Nat. Coun. Tchrs. Math., Mass. Tchrs. Assn., Tewksbury Tchrs. Assn., Kappa Delta Pi. Avocations: jogging, swimming, aerobic dance, reading, cooking.

KRAIZER, SHERRYLL A. child safety and interpersonal violence prevention educator; b. San Antonio, June 12, 1948; d. Faye Burton and Phyllis Anne (Ringer) Graves; m. Alvin T. Kraizer, July 30, 1978; children: Charles, Ben. BS in Edn./Spl. Edn., Emporia State U., 1969, MS in Edn./Psychology, 1970; PhD in Edn., The Union Inst., 1991. Pres., exec. dir. Coalition for Children, 1983—. Presenter confs. in field; expert witness on child abuse, instnl. abuse, stds. and practices. Author: The Safe Child Book, 1985, 2d edit., 1995, Take A Stand: Prevention of Bullying and Interpersonal Violence, 2000; author (tng. programs) The Safe Child Program (pre-K-grade 3), 1989, 2d edit., 1994, Dating Violence: Prevention and Intervention, 1991, Domestic Violence Prevention and Intervention, 1991, Reach, 1992, Challenge, 1992, Recovery, 1992; adult mentor editor R.E.B.E.L. Youth Adv. Mag., 2001. Recipient Nat. Prog. award Child Abuse Prevention Coun., Houston, 1989, rsch. grant Nat. Ctr. on Child Abuse and Neglect, 1987, prog. devel. grant Small Bus. Adminstrn., 1988, Violence Against Women Act grantee, 1996-99, Aspen Inst. scholar, 1999. Mem. Internat. Soc. Prevention of Child Abuse and Neglect (peer reviewer). Office: Coalition for Children PO Box 6304 Denver CO 80206-0304 E-mail: kraizer@safechild.org.

KRAJEWSKI-JAIME, ELVIA ROSA, social worker; b. Saltillo, Coahuila, Mexico, Aug. 30, 1938; d. Alfredo and Florinda (Nanez) Jaime; m. Eugene D. Krajewski, Sept. 29, 1962; children: Colette, Michelle, Diana. BA in Psychology, U. Pa., 1977; MSW in Planning, Temple U., 1982; PhD in Clinical Social Work, U. Tex.-Austin, 1987. Rsch. developer Puerto Rican Congress N.J., Trenton, N.J., 1978-82; rsch. asst. U. Tex.-Austin, 1982-84, instr., 1984-85; assoc. prof. Ea. Mich. U., Ypsilanti, Mich., 1985—. Cons. Inst. Gerontology, Wayne State U., Detroit, 1989-90, Latino Family Svcs., Detroit, 1990-91. Contbr. articles to profl. jours. Advisor Hispanic Student Orgn. Ea. Mich. U., Ypsilanti, 1987-88. Named Outstanding Faculty Ea. Mich. U., 1987, 89, Doctoral Fellow Coun. on Social Work Edn. Md., 1982, Continuing Edn. Fellow U. Tex.-Austin, 1984; recipient Outstanding Achievement award Puerto Rican Congress N.J., 1982. Mem. Presdl. Commn. on the Learning Univ. (vice chair 1990-92), Commn. on Minority Affairs, Nat Assn. Social Workers, Coun. on Social Work Edn., Mexican-Am. Women's Assn., The Gray Panthers Am. Home: 3241 Oak Dr Ypsilanti MI 48197-3797 Office: Ea Mich U Dept Social Work King Hall # 411 Ypsilanti MI 48197-2239

KRAKER, DEBORAH SCHOVANEC, special education educator; b. Enid, Okla., May 28, 1960; d. Charles Raymond and Marcella Ruth (Mack) Schovanec; m. Kevin Mark Kraker, July 10, 1987. BS, U. Ctrl. Okla., 1982; postgrad., Okla. State U., Stillwater, 1995—. Cert. tchr. spl. edn., learning disability/mentally handicapped. Customer svc. mgr. Skaggs, Oklahoma City, 1982-92; tchr. spl. edn. Edmond (Okla.) Pub. Schs., 1993—. Tchr. Francis Tuttle Vocat. Tech. Ctr., Oklahoma City, 1993, 94, 95, mem. adv. bd., 1993-96. Mem. adv. bd. Francis Tuttle Vocat. Tech. Ctr., 1993—. Mem. NEA, Okla. Edn. Assn. (del. nat. assembly 1996), Edmond Assn. Classroom Tchrs. (v.p. 1997-98), Coun. for Exceptional Children, Assn. Classroom Mems. (exec. bd.), Okla. Commn. Tchr. Preparation (mem. portfolio rev. team, mem. accreditation rev. team, mem. program accreditation), Learning Disabilities Assn., Kappa Delta Pi. Republican. Roman Catholic. Avocations: reading, sewing, cooking, collecting antiques. Home: 2721 Berkshire Way Oklahoma City OK 73120-2704

KRAL, NANCY BOLIN, political science educator; b. St. Louis, Oct. 4, 1958; d. Alpha E. Jr. and Shirley Judith (Wiseman) Bolin; m. Kenneth Joseph Kral, June 12, 1982; 1 child, Kelly Ann. BS, U. Tex., 1979; MA, U. Houston, 1989. Tchr. govt. Round Rock Ind. Sch. Dist., Austin, Tex., 1980-84, Spring Ind. Sch. Dist., Houston, 1984-85, Klein Ind. Sch. Dist., Houston, 1985-88; instr. polit. sci. Houston Community Coll., 1987-88; prof. polit. sci., program coord. North Harris Montgomery Coll. Dist., Tomball, Tex., 1988—; asst. to chancellor North Harris Montgomery Coll. dist., Tomball, Tex., 1993. Edn. chair Tomball Regional Arts Coun., 1991-93, bd. dirs.; bd. dirs. Tri-Magna Industries, Waco; del. U.S. Inst. of Peace Seminar, Washington, 1996. Co-author: Texas Government, 1995. Bd. dirs. Champion Forest Civic Assn., Houston, 1986-88, North Area chpt. Houston Symphony League, 1989—, Performing Arts Coun. North Houston, 1994-96; chair Tomball Coll. Law Day; pres. Northampton Homeowners Assn., 1985-86; del. Tex. Rep. Conv., Ft. worth, 1990, Dallas, 1992; faculty advisor Coll. Reps., Tomball Coll.; panelist Nat. Inst. Staff and Orgnl. Devel. Conf., 1992; mem. March of Dimes Guild; charter mem. Houston Holocaust Mus.; legis. chair N.W. Rep. Women, 1988-90, campaign chair, 1990-92. Taft fellow Abilene Christian U., 1988. Mem. NOW, AAUW, Am. Assn. Women in C.C., Tex. C.C. Tchrs. Assn. (chair govt. sect. 1991-92, legis. com. 1992-96, sec. 1994, 95, chair membership svcs. 1996—), Tex. Women's Polit. Caucus, Soc. Prevention Cruelty to Animals, Midwest Polit. Sci. Assn., Ctr. for Study of Presidency, U. Houston Alumni Assn., U. Tex. Austin Ex-Students' Assn., LWV, Alpha Xi Delta North Houston Alumnae (pres. 1990-92). Presbyterian. Avocations: travel, photography, arts. Home: 8627 Asprey Ct Spring TX 77379-6829 Office: North Harris Montgomery Coll Dist 30555 Tomball Pky Tomball TX 77375-4096

KRALEWSKI, JOHN EDWARD, health service research educator; b. Durand, Wis., May 20, 1932; s. Joseph and Esther (Hetrick) K.; m. Marjorie L. Gustafson; Apr. 22, 1957; children: Judy, Ann, Sara. BS in Pharmacy, U. Minn., 1956, MHA, 1962, PhD, 1969. Asst. prof. U. Minn., Mpls., 1965-69, prof. health svcs. rsch., 1979—; prof. U. Colo., Denver, 1969-78. 1st lt. USAF, 1957-60. Kellogg fellow Kellogg Found., 1962-65, Valencia (Spain) Acad. Medicine fellow, 1993. Mem. APHA, Assn. Health Svcs. Rsch. Avocation: oenology. Office: U Minn Health Svc Rsch 420 Delaware St SE Box 729 Minneapolis MN 55455-0374

KRAMAN, STEVE SETH, physician, educator; b. Chgo., Aug. 30, 1944; s. Julius and Ruth (Glassner) K.; m. Lillian Virginia Casanova, May 29, 1972 (div. Apr. 1991); children: Theresa, Pilar, Laura, Seth. BS, U. P.R., 1968, MD, 1973. Asst. prof. U. Ky., Lexington, 1978-84, assoc. prof., 1984-90, prof., 1990—. Chief of staff VA Med. Ctr., Lexington, 1986-2003. Contbr. articles to profl. jours. Mem. Am. Coll. Chest Physicians. Achievements include patent for simple capsule pneumograph. Office: Univ of Kentucky Kentucky Clinic Rm J515 Lexington KY 40536

KRAMBERG, HEINZ-GERHARD, ecomomist, educator; b. Hagen, Westfalen, Germany, Mar. 2, 1924; s. Richard and Elisabeth (Schulte) K. Cert. administr., Fachhochschule, Hagen, Germany, 1947; cert. comm. official, Akademy, Wuppertal, Germany, 1948; Studium d. Rechts, U. Staatswissensch, Germany, 1945-51; LLD, DSc h.C., Univ. Technologica, San Salvador. Dir. city City of Borken, Germany, 1951-58; Verwaltungsdirektor Versicherungswirtschaft, Duesseldorf, Germany, 1960-68; mgr. econ. housing sect. City of Duesseldorf, Germany, 1968-93; prof. Universidad Francisco Marroquin, Guatamala City, Guatamala, 1978—. Author: Recht, Rechtsinstitutionen und Finanzgebaren einer Veste als döerfliche Gemeinschaft, 1952, Verfassungsrecht und Verfassungsreform, 1953, Gebietsneuordnung, 1955, Grundzuege der Gemeindlichen Aufgaben, 1956, Organisation Planung und Bauablauf-Die Erstellungleines Verwaltungsgebäeudes, 1964, Dokumentation ARAG-Haus Duesseldorf, Brehmstr., 1965, Ausbildung in Arbeitsunterweisung-Ein Leitfaden, 1967, Public and Business Administration, 1976-94, Bedenken und Anregungen-Buergerbeteiligung und Bürgerverantwortung, 1973, Entwurf eines Bebauungsplanes, 1975, Longinus und die heilige Lanze, 1977, Staatsverfassung, 1977, Zur Bedeutung der Systemvergleichung in der Verwaltungswissenschaft, 1979, Der öeffentliche Dienst in verschiedenen Staaten und Lanedern, 1979, Untersuchung üeber Universitäeten in privater Träegerschaft, 1980, Kreuzfahrerspuren im Heiligen Land Gespräche und Notizen, 1983, Paralipomena 1 zur Geschichte des Ordens der Tempelherren, 1986, Planerische Grundüeberlegung zur Freizeitpolitik-Raum Winterberg/Hochsauerland, 1990-91; editor: Non Nobis, 1984-88. Mem. Ordo Militiae Crucis Templi (vice chancellor 1982-88). Roman Catholic.

KRAMER, BURTON, graphic designer, educator; b. NYC, June 25, 1932; s. Sam and Ida (Moore) K.; m. Irene Margarite Therese Mayer, Feb. 22, 1961; children: Gabrielle Kimberly, Jeremy Jacques. BS in Graphic Design, Ill. Inst. Tech., Chgo., 1954; postgrad. (Fulbright scholar), Royal Coll. Art, London, 1955-56; M.F.A., Yale U., 1957; D (hon.), Ontario Coll. of Art and Design, 2003. Registered graphic designer Ont. Designer Will Burtin, NYC, 1957-58; asst. art dir. Arch. Record, NYC, 1959; pres., creative dir. Kramer Design Assoc., Ltd., Toronto, Canada, 1967—2001; designer Geigy Chem. Corp., NYC, 1959-61; dir. corp. graphics Clairtone Sound Corp., Toronto, Canada, 1967; chief designer Halpern Advt., Zurich, Switzerland, 1961-65; instr. Ont. Coll. Art & Design, Ont., Canada, 1978—. Guest lectr. Rochester Inst. Tech., 1976, 81, designer-in-residence, 1981; vis. lectr. U. Cin., 1980; guest lectr., Arnhem, The Netherlands, 1994, Mexico City U. Autonoma, 1995; spkr. 1st Internat. Biennial of Symbols/Logotypes, Ostend, Belgium, 1994; mem. faculty Seneca Coll. Book designer The Art of Norval Morrisseau, 1979, Passionate Spirits, 1980; author Can. sect. Trademarks and Symbols of the World, 1973; co-author: Report on Canadian Road Sign Graphics, 1968; work pub. in numerous nat. and internat. jours., annuals and books; contbr. articles to profl. jours.; major works include signing-info. sys. CBC Broadcast Ctr., Toronto, IBM Tng. Ctr., Centenary Hosp., Scarborough, St. Lawrence Ctr. for Arts, Eaton Ctr., Erin Mills New Town, Mississauga, Metro Ctrl. YMCA, Copps Coliseum, Union Sta.; designer visual identity programs for CBC, N.Am. Life Assurance, Can. Imperial Bank Commerce, Reed Paper, ONEX Packaging Inc., Gemini, Vincor Internat., Can. Sys. Group, Nat. Rsch. Coun. Can., Centrestage, Royal Ont. Mus., Teknion Furniture Sys., Inc., Decoustics, Chartwell I.R.M., Scarborough Bd. Edn., Ont. Edn. Comm. Authority, Can. Crafts Coun., Ont. Guild Crafts, Zoomit Corp.; exhbn. paintings Pekao Gallery, Toronto, 1999, Peak Gallery, 2002, Kahat Wrorel Gallery, Toronto, 2003, Found. for Constructive Art, Calgary, 2002; work on website Canadian Ctr. for Contemporary Art, www.ccca.ca, 2002. Bd. dir. Arts Toronto. Decorated Order of Ont.; recipient gold medal Internat. Typographic Composition Assn., 1971, gold medal Art Dir. Club Toronto, 1973, medal Leipzig BookFair, Toronto Arts Lifetime Achievement award 1999. Fellow Soc. Graphic Designers Can. (past pres.); mem. Alliance Graphique Internat., Royal Can. Acad. Arts, Assn. Registered Graphic Designers of Ont. (bd. dirs.), Nat. Yacht Club. Home: 101 Roxborough St W Toronto ON Canada M5R 1T9 Office: 103 Dupont St Toronto ON Canada M5R 1V4 E-mail: burton@kramerdesign.com.

KRAMER, CECILE E. retired medical librarian; b. NYC, Jan. 6, 1927; d. Marcus and Henrietta (Marks) K. BS, CCNY, 1956; MS in L.S., Columbia U., 1960. Reference asst. Columbia U. Health Scis. Library, N.Y.C., 1957-61, asst. librarian, 1961-75; dir. Health Scis. Libr. Northwestern U., Chgo., 1975-91, asst. prof. edn., 1975-91, prof. emeritus, 1991—. Instr. library and info. sci. Rosary Coll., 1981-85 ; cons. Francis A. Countway Library Medicine, Harvard U., 1974. Pres. Friends of Libr., Fla. Atlantic U., Boca Raton. Fellow Med. Libr. Assn. (chmn. med. sch. librs. group 1975-76, editor newsletter 1975-77, instr. continuing edn. 1966-75, mem. panel cons. editors Bull. 1987-90, disting. mem. Acad. Health Info. Profls. 1993—); mem. Biomed. Comm. Network (chmn. 1979-80). Home: 9184 Flynn Cir Apt 4 Boca Raton FL 33496-6675 E-mail: kramer@fau.edu.

KRAMER, JAY HARLAN, physiologist, researcher, educator; b. Bklyn., Dec. 26, 1952; s. Albert and Blossom K.; m. Aisar Atrakchi, Apr. 18, 1993; 1 child, Evan. BA with honors, Northeastern U., 1976; MS, Lehigh U., 1979, PhD, 1982. Clin. lab. technician Boston Med. Lab., Waltham, Mass., 1974-75; rsch. asst. Lehigh U., Bethlehem, Pa., 1979-81; rsch. assoc. Med. Coll. Va., Richmond, 1982-83; sr. rsch. assoc. Okla. Med. Rsch. Found., Oklahoma City, 1983-85; rsch. assoc. George Washington U., Washington, 1985-86, asst. rsch. prof. medicine, 1986-90, assoc. rsch. prof., 1990—, adj. assoc. prof. physiology, 1991—, assoc. rsch. prof. physiology, 1998—. Lectr. physiology George Washington U., Washington, 1987-89; cons. Squibb & Sons, Princeton, N.J., 1989, mem. George Washington U. Instl. Animal Care and Use Com., 1988—, mem. Basic Sci. Faculty Assembly and Inst. Biomed. Scis., 1996—. Contbr. more than 54 articles to profl. jours.; article referee profl. jours. Mem. basic sci. faculty assembly coun. George Washington U., 1992-94. Grad. sch. scholar Lehigh U., 1980; named one of Outstanding Young Men of Am., Jaycees, 1981, 82. Mem. Am. Heart Assn., Am. Physiol. Soc., N.Y. Acad. Scis. (invited speaker 1993, presenter various nat. scientific meetings), Internat. Soc. for Heart Rsch., Internat. Soc. for Free Radical Rsch., Soc. for Exptl. Biology and Medicine, Acad. Honor Soc., Phi Sigma. Achievements include first to demonstrate relationship between toxic free radical prodn. and severity of ischemia in heart; first to demonstrate superoxide anion prodn. in postischemic heart using ESR spin trapping; first to demonstrate free radical prodn. in regionally ischemic canine and post-ischemic swine heart models; first to demonstrate that excessive neuropeptide release during dietary magnesium restriction leads to reduced tolerance of animal hearts to ischemia/reperfusion injury; developed non-invasive ESR spin trapping technique for free radical detection; demonstrated occurrance of potentially toxic free radicals in human heart following open heart surgery. Office: George Washington U Dept Physiol and Exptl Med 2300 I St NW Washington DC 20037-2336 E-mail: phyjhk@gwumc.edu.

KRAMER, JUDITH ANN, elementary education educator; b. Atlanta, Ga., Jan. 17, 1945; d. William Walter and Sara Jane (Blount) Blanton (dec.); m. James Anthony Kramer, Oct. 13, 1973; children: Kristopher J., Rebecca S. BS in Journalism, U. Fla., 1969; MEd in Elem. Edn., U. Houston, 1983. Pub. info. officer Fla. Dept. Edn., Tallahassee, 1970-73; tchr. kindergarten, 1st and 2d grades Galena Pk. Ind. Sch. Dist., Houston, 1983-87; tchr. 1st grade DeSoto Ind. Sch. Dist., Tex., 1987-88; tchr. 2d and 3d grades Cedar Hill Ind. Sch. Dist., Tex., 1988-98, ESL tchr., 1998—; commdg. officer Coast Guard Res. Unit, Dallas, 1994-95, ret. officer, 1995. ESL instr. U. Tex., Arlington, 1998-2000; freelance writer, photographer Gainesville Sun, Houston, Post, Dallas Morning News, Houston Bus. Jour., S.W. Life Mag., others, 1974—. Founder, bd. dirs., vol. Cedar Hill Food Pantry, 1989—; active High Pointe Elem. Sch. PTA. Mem. Assn. Tex. Profl. Educators (sec./bldg. rep., treas., v.p., pres., co-pres.). Methodist. Avocations: reading, sewing, swimming, gardening, travel. Office: Cedar Hill Ind Sch Dist High Pointe Elem Sch 1351 High Pointe Ln Cedar Hill TX 75104-5067 E-mail: kramj@chisd.com.

KRAMER, PAMELA KOSTENKO, librarian; b. Mar. 5, 1944; d. Barry Michael and Helene (Ullrich) Kostenko; m. Claude Richard Kramer, Aug. 17, 1966. AB, U. Ill., 1966; MALS, Rosary Coll., 1973. Tchr. English United Twp. H.S., East Moline, Ill., 1966-70, audiovisual libr., 1970-76; instr. Marycrest Coll., Davenport, Iowa, 1973-75; libr. United Twp. H.S., 1976-81, libr., audio visual dept. head, 1981-87; asst. libr. Libertyville (Ill.) H.S., 1987-92, Barrington (Ill.) H.S., 1992; dep. exec. dir. Am. Assn. Sch. Librs., 1993-97; owner Pamela K. Kramer and Assocs., Sch. Libr. Cons., 1997—. Sch. libr. cons.; instr. Virtual Ill. LTA program Coll. DuPage, 1999-2000; dir. youth and sch. and acad. svcs. DuPage Libr. Sys., 2000—. Author audiovisual software revs. for Previews mag., Sch. Libr. Jour., 1973-80; contbr. articles to Ill. Librs. mag. and Ill. English Bull. mag., Sch. Libr. Media Activities monthly mag.; prin. writer Linking for Learning, The Illinois School Library Media Guidelines. Trustee River Bend Libr. Sys., 1986-87; chair alumni bd. libr. and info. sci. Dominican U. Recipient Polestar award ISLMA, 1992, Exemplary Svc. award Dominican U., 2000; Edmund J. James scholar, 1962-66. Mem. ALA, NEA, Ill. Sch. Libr. Media Assn. (state pres. 1990-91, editor ISLMA news 1992-2000), Ill. State Libr. (adv. com. 1991-94, chair subcom. Interlibr. coop. 1993-94), Ill. Libr. Assn., Ill. Edn. Assn., Am. Assn. Sch. Librs., Young Adult Libr. Svcs. Assn., Beta Phi Mu. Home: 326 Stillwater Ct Wauconda IL 60084-2908 E-mail: pkramer@dupagels.lib.il.us.

KRANKING, MARGARET GRAHAM, artist, educator; b. Dec. 21, 1930; d. Stephen Wayne and Madge Williams (Dawes) Graham; m. James David Kranking, Aug. 23, 1952; children: James Andrew, Ann Marie Kranking Eggleton, David Wayne. BA summa cum laude (Clendenin fellow), Am. U., 1952. Asst. to head publs. Nat. Gallery Art, Washington, 1952-53. Tchr. art Woman's Club, Chevy Chase, Md., 1976-88, 98—; guest instr. Amherst Coll., 1985, The Homestead, Hot Springs, Va., 1997; judge The Miniature Painters, Sculptors and Gravers Soc. Washington, 69th Ann. Internat. Exhbn., 2002, Bethesda, Md. One-woman shows include Spectrum Gallery, Washington, 1974, 76, 78-79, 83, 85, 87, 90, 92, 95, 97, 2000, Philip Morris, U.S.A., Richmond, Va., 1982-83, 86, Forence (S.C.) Mus., 1991, Lombardi Cancer treatment Ctr., Washington, 1992, Capital Gallery, Frankfort, Ky., 1993, Acad. Arts, Easton, Md., 1999, Warm Springs (Va.) Gallery, 1997-98; exhibited in group shows at Balt. Mus., 1974, 76, Corcoran Gallery Art, Washington, 1952, 72, USIA Traveling Exhbt., C.Am., 1978-79, AARP Traveling Exhbn., 1986; represented in permanent collections U. Va., Philip Morris U.S.A., USCG, AT&T, Freddie Mac, Florence Mus., S.C., Navy Fed. Credit Union Hdqs., Vienna, Va., Marsh and McClennan Co., Washington, The Washington Hilton, D.C.; traveling exhbn. Nat. Watercolor Soc., Watercolor U.S.A., Am. Watercolor Soc., Am. Artist mag., North Light mag., Adirondacks Nat. Exhbn. of Am. Watercolor, Artitude Internat. Art Competition, N.Y., Shada Gallery, Riyadh, Saudi Arabia, Belle Grove Plantation Invitational, Middletown, Va., Strathmore Hall Arts Ctr., North Bethesda, Md., Wash. Woman mag., Am. Speech-Lang. Hearing Assn., mag., Govt. House, Annapolis, Md. Invitational, 1997-99, Strathmore Hall Arts Ctr., North Bethesda, Md., Montgomery Coll. Invitational, Md., Glen View Mansion Invitational, Rockville, Md., 2000; ofcl. artist USCG; contbr. reproductions and text to numerous books. Recipient George Gray award USCG Art Program, N.Y., 1991, 98. Mem.: Am. Watercolor Soc., Washington Soc. Landscape Painters, Potomac Valley Watercolorists (pres. 1981—83), Washington Watercolor Assn., So. Watercolor Soc., Ga. Watercolor Soc., Southwestern Watercolor Soc., Midwest Watercolor Soc., Nat. Watercolor Soc. Roman Catholic. Home: 3504 Taylor St Chevy Chase MD 20815-4022

KRANTZ, STEVEN GEORGE, mathematics educator, writer; b. San Francisco, Feb. 3, 1951; s. Henry Alfred and Norma Oliva (Crisafulli) K.; m. Randi Diane Ruden, Sept. 7, 1974. BA, U. Calif., Santa Cruz, 1971; PhD, Princeton U, 1974. Asst. prof. UCLA, 1974-81; assoc. prof. Pa. State U., University Park, 1981-84, prof., 1984-86; prof. dept. math. Washington U., St. Louis, 1986—, chmn. dept. math., 1999—, divsn. head for sci. depts., 2002—. Adv. bd. Am. Inst. Math., Am. Math. Soc. book series; mng. editor Jour. Math. Analysis and Applications. Founder, mng. editor Jour. Geometric Analysis; editor-in-chief Jour. of Math. Analysis and Apps.; Author: Function Theory of Several Complex Variables (monograph), 1982, 2d edition, 1992, Complex Analysis: The Geometric Viewpoint, 1990, Real Analysis and Foundations, 1991, Partial Differential Equations and Complex Analysis, 1992, A Primer of Real Analytic Functions, 1992, Geometric Analysis and Function Spaces, 1993, How to Teach Mathematics, 1993, 2nd edit., 1999, A Tex Primer for Scientists, 1995, The Elements of Advanced Mathematics, 1995, 2d edit., 2002, Techniques of Problem Solving, 1996, Function Theory of One Complex Variable, 1997, A Primer of Mathematical Writing, 1996; (with H. R. Parks) The Geometry of Domains in Space, 1999, Contemporary Issues in Mathmatics Education, 1999, A Handbook of Complex Variables, 1999, A Panorama of Harmonic Analysis, 1999, Handbook of Typography for the Mathematical Sciences, 2000, The Implicit Function Theorem, 2002, Mathematical Apocrypha, 2002, Graduate School and Careers in Mathematics: A Survival Guide, 2003; cons. editor Birkhäuser Pub., 2002-, McGraw-Hill, 2002-; contbr. numerous rsch. articles to profl. publs. Recipient Disting. Tchg. award, UCLA Alumni Found., 1979:NSF rsch. grantee, 1975—, Kemper grantee, 1994. Richardson fellow Australian Nat. U., 1995; mem. Am. Math. Soc. (prin. organizer summer rsch. inst. 1989), Math. Assn. Am. (Chauvenet prize, Beckenbach prize 1994), Textbook Authors Assn. E-mail: sk@math.wustl.edu.

KRANZER, HERBERT C. mathematician, educator; b. N.Y.C., Apr. 10, 1932; s. Emanuel C. and Ruth (Lippner) K.; m. Claire Malkevitch, Aug. 20, 1958; children: Ellen, Naomi Penny, Harold. BA, NYU, 1952, PhD, 1957. Instr. math. NYU, N.Y.C., 1957-59; assoc. prof. Adelphi U., Garden City, N.Y., 1959-63, prof., 1963-97, prof. emeritus, 1997—. Cons. Los Alamos Sci. Lab., 1956-64, IBM Corp., 1959-63, FONAR Corp., 1983-89. Editor: Non-Strictly Hyperbolic Conservation Laws, 1987; contbr. over 25 articles to profl. jours. Sr. postdoctoral fellow NSF, 1966-67, grantee, 1968-71; grantee Office Naval Rsch., 1960-66. Mem. AAUP, Am. Math. Soc., Math. Assn. Am., Soc. for Indsl. and Applied Math, Am. Assn. Advancement Sci. Achievements include prediction of the magnitude of ocean waves which would be caused by nuclear explosion over deep water; co-founded the research field of non-strictly hyperbolic conservation laws; simulation of Magnetic Resonance Imaging machine. Office: Adelphi Univ Dept Math and Computer Sci Garden City NY 11530

KRASNA, ALVIN ISAAC, biochemist, educator; b. N.Y.C., June 23, 1929; s. Selig and Esther (Finer) K.; m. Elaine C. Cohen, Feb. 27, 1955; children— Susan Roni, Gary Marc, Allen Selig. BA, Yeshiva Coll., 1950; PhD, Columbia U., 1955. Mem. faculty Columbia U., 1956—, prof. biochemistry, 1970—, acting chmn., 1977-78, 88-90, vice chmn., 1978-88, 90—. Contbr. to profl. jours. Predoctoral fellow NSF, 1953; Guggenheim fellow, 1962; research grantee NSF; research grantee NIH; research grantee Am. Cancer Soc.; research grantee AEC, Dept. Energy Mem. Am. Chem. Soc., Am. Assn. Biol. Chemists, AAAS, Harvey Soc., Am. Soc. Microbiology, Sigma Xi. Home: 6 Arbor Dr New Rochelle NY 10804-1101 Office: 630 W 168th St New York NY 10032-3702

KRASNEY, RINA SUSAN, school librarian; b. Phila., Mar. 15, 1950; d. Myron and Lillian (Shiman) K. BA, Douglass Coll., 1971; MLS, Rutgers U., 1973. Libr. Austin (Tex.) C.C., 1977-80, U. Mo., St. Louis, 1980-85, St. Louis Pub. Libr., 1985-86, Ferguson-Florissant Sch. Dist., St. Louis, 1986—. Mem. NEA. Home: 8260 Audrain Dr Saint Louis MO 63121-4504

KRASNO, RICHARD MICHAEL, foundation executive, educator; b. Chgo., Jan. 20, 1942; s. Louis R. K. and Adeline G. (Glassman) Kaplan; children: Jeffrey Patrick, Eric Peter; m. Carin Blucher. BS, U. Ill., 1965; PhD, Stanford U., 1970; LittD (hon.), Coll. St. Rose, 1983; LLD (hon.), Sacred Heart U., 1984. Asst. prof. ednl. psychology U. Chgo., 1970-74; program advisor Brazil Ford Found., Rio de Janeiro, 1974-77, program advisor Latin Am. N.Y.C., 1977, program advisor Mid.-East & Africa, 1978-80; deputy asst. sec. of edn. U.S. Dept. Edn., Washington, 1980-81; exec. v.p. Inst. Internat. Edn., N.Y.C., 1981-83, pres., CEO, 1983-98; pres. Monterey (Calif.) Inst. Internat Stud, 1998-99, Kenan Charitable Trust, Chapel Hill, N.C., 1999—. Commr. U.S.-Brazil Fulbright Commn., 1975-77, U.S. Nat. Commn. UNESCO, 1983; chmn. Internat. Transition Team Dept. Edn., 1979, 80; mem. U.S.-Mex. Bilateral Commn., 1980, 84; sr. Fulbright lectr., 1973-74. Contbr. articles to profl. jours. Trustee Laspau, Cambridge, Mass., 1980—82, Eisenhower Exch. Program, 2002—. Nat. Defense Edn. fellow U.S. Govt., 1967-68. Mem. Coun. Fgn. Rels., Century Assn., Cosmos Club. Office: The Kenan Ctr PO Box 3858 Chapel Hill NC 27515-3858 E-mail: richard_krasno@unc.edu.

KRAU, EDGAR, psychologist, scientist, educator, researcher; b. Stanislau, Poland, Apr. 9, 1929; arrived in Israel, 1977; s. Adolf and Ella (Lam) K.; m. Mary Epure, Dec. 27, 1958; 1 child, Nicole. MA, U. Cluj, Romania, 1951, PhD, 1964. Lic. Psychologist, Israel. Chief rsch. fellow Inst. Pedagogical Scis., Cluj, Romania, 1961-63; with U. Cluj, Romania, 1963-77; head psychology dept. Acad. Romanian Republic, Cluj, 1968-77; prof. U. Haifa, Israel, 1977-81, Tel-Aviv U., Israel, 1981-97, prof. emeritus, 1997—; prof. Thames Valley U., Haifa, Israel, 1997—. Mem. Internat. Test Commn., 1971-73; chmn. Internat. Colloquium on Human Resources Devel., Jerusalem, 1984; mem. sci. com. XXI Internat. Congress of Applied Psychology, 1986; editor-in-chief (jour. of labor studies) Man and Work, 1987—. Author: The Contradictory Immigrant Problem, 1991, Social and Economic Management in the Competitive Society, 1998, (with P. Goguelin) Projet Professionnel - Projet de Vie, 1992, The Realization of Life Aspirations Through Vocational Careers, 1997, A Meta-Psychological Perspective on the Individual Course of Life, 2003; co-author: Treatise on Industrial Psychology, 1967 (Romanian Acad. Vasile Conta award 1972); co-author, editor: Self-realization, Success and Adjustment, 1989; author Jour. Vocational Behavior, 1981-89 (hon. mention award 1986). Recipient diploma of high ctr. for logic and comparative scis. award, Bologna, Italy, 1972, Homagial Biography-Bibliography, Revue Européenne de Psychologie Appliquée, 1993. Mem. APA (affiliate), Israeli Psychol. Assn. (instr. 1979—), N.Y. Acad. Scis., London Diplomatic Acad. (mem. acad. coun. 2002). Home: 2 Hess St 33398 Haifa Israel E-mail: edgark@internet-zahav.net.

KRAUSE, LOIS RUTH BREUR, chemistry educator; b. Paterson, N.J., Mar. 26, 1946; d. George L. and Ruth Margaret (Farquhar) Breur; m. Bruce N. Pritchard, 1968 (div. May 1982); children: John Douglas, Tiffany Anne,; m. Robert H. Krause, June 16, 1990. Student, Keuka Coll., 1964-65; BS in Chemistry cum laude, Fairleigh Dickinson U., 1980, MAT summa cum laude, 1994; postgrad., Stevens Inst. Tech.; PhD, Clemson U., 1996. With dept. R & D UniRoyal, Wayne, N.J., 1966-68, Jersey State Chem. Co., North Haledon, 1968-69, Inmont, Clifton, N.J., 1969; from chemist to sr. analyst Lever Bros., Edgewater, N.J., 1976-80; process engr. Bell Telephone Labs., Murray Hill, N.J., 1980-84, RCA, Somerville, N.J., 1984-86; sr. engr. electron beam lithography ops. Gain Electronics Corp., Somerville, 1986-88; ind. tech. cons. Pritchard Assocs., Budd Lake, N.J., 1988-92; tchr. of math. and scis. Mt. Olive Bd. Edn. (temporary assignments), 1990-92; tchr. chemistry Morris Hills Regional Dist., 1992-93; vis. asst. prof. edn. Clemson U., 1994—95, instr. chem. labs., 1994-96, vis. asst. prof. edn., 1995-96, vis. asst. prof. chemistry, 1996-98, lectr. phys. scis. dept. geol. scis., 1998—. Faculty fellow Office of Tchg. Effectiveness and Innovation Clemson U., 1999-2000; presenter workshops and profl. papers for profl.

confs. Author: How We Learn and Why We Don't: Student Survival Guide, 1999, 2003; contbr. articles to profl. jours. Troop leader, trainer, cons. Bergen County council Girl Scouts U.S., 1969-80, troop leader Morris Area council, 1980-83, head com. Mt. Olive twp., 1980-81; den leader, den leader coach, trainer Boy Scouts Am., 1973-76. Peter Sammartino scholar, 1994. Fellow: Soc. Antiquaries (Scotland), Am. Inst. Chemists; mem.: AAUW, APA, ASCD, NRA (endowment mem.), IEEE (sr.), AAAS, Nat. Sci. Tchrs. Assn., N.Y. Acad. Scis., Assn. Women in Sci., Law Enforcement Alliance Am. (life), Am. Chem. Soc., Soc. Women Engrs., Am. Soc. Quality Control, 2d. Amendment Sisters, Single Action Shooting Soc., Catawba Valley Scottish Soc. (life patron), Clan Farquharson U.S.A. (asst. commr. for S.C. 1997—98, commr. Carolinas region 1998—99, clan genealogist 1999), Arbor Day Found., Clan Morrison Soc. N.Am. (life), 2d Amendment Found. (life), Nat. Woodlot Owners Assn., Mensa (cert. proctor 1999—), Clan Stewart Soc. of Am., Scottish Am. Mil. Soc. (color guard), Marine Corps League Aux., Alpha Epsilon Lambda, Phi Delta Kappa (editor Clemson Kappan 1995—2000), Phi Omega Epsilon. Republican. Achievements include work in ultra fine line electron beam lithography, statis. process control, rsch. in learning and cognition; designed graduate course of student centered instruction. Home: 303 Cherokee Hills Dr Pickens SC 29671-8619 Office: Clemson U 442 Brackett Hl Clemson SC 29634-0001 E-mail: krause@clemson.edu., krause@cognitiveprofile.com., L_krause@bellsouth.net.

KRAUSE, MARCELLA ELIZABETH MASON (MRS. EUGENE FITCH KRAUSE), retired secondary education educator; b. Norfolk, Nebr.; d. James Haskell and Elizabeth (Vader) Mason; student Northeast C.C., 1928-30; B.S., U. Neb., 1934; M.A., Columbia, 1938; postgrad. summers U. Calif. at Berkeley, 1950, 51, 65, Stanford, 1964, Creighton U., 1966, Chico (Calif.) State U., 1967; m. Eugene Fitch Krause, June 1, 1945; 1 dau., Kathryn Elizabeth. Tchr., Royal (Nebr.) pub. schs., 1930-32, Hardy (Nebr.) pub. schs., 1933-35, Omaha pub. schs., 1935-37, Lincoln Sch. of Tchrs. Coll., Columbia, 1937-38, Florence (Ala.) State Tchrs. Coll., summer 1938, Tchrs. Coll., U. Nebr., 1938-42, Corpus Christi (Tex.) pub. schs., 1942-45, Oakland (Calif.) pub. schs., 1945-83. Bd. dirs. U. Nebr. Womens Faculty Club, 1940-42; mem. Nebr. State Tchrs. Conv. Panel, 1940—; mem. U. Nebr. Reading Inst., 1940; speaker Iowa State Tchrs. Conv., 1941; reading speaker Nebr. State Tchrs. conv., 1941; lectr. Johnson County Tchrs. Inst., 1942; chmn. Reading Survey Corpus Christi pub. schs., 1943; chmn. Inservice Reading Meetings Oakland pub. schs., 1948-57. Mem. Gov.'s Adv. Commn. on Status Women Conf., San Francisco, 1966; service worker ARC, Am. Cancer Soc., United Crusade, Oakland CD; Republican precinct capt., 1964-70; v.p. Oakland Fedn. Rep. Women. Ford Found. Fund for Advancement Edn. fellow, 1955-56; scholar Stanford, 1964; Calif. Congress PTA scholar U. Calif., 1965, Norfolk (Nebr.) Hall of Success Northeast C.C., 1990; recipient award of Excellence, U. Nebr. Tchrs. Coll., 1998. Mem. Nat. Council Women, AAUW (dir.), Calif. Tchrs. Assn., Oakland Mus. Assn., U. Nebr. Alumni Assn. (Alumni Achievement award 1984), Californians for Nebr., Ladies Grand Army Republic, 1960, 1986-87 Ruth Assn., Martha Assn. (pres. East Bay chpt. 1979), Sierra DAR (regent), Eastbay DAR Regents Assn. (pres.), Nebr. Alumni Assn. (life, alumni achievement award 1984), Grand Lake Bus. and Profl. Women, Internat. Platform Assn., Eastbay Past Matrons Assn., P.E.O., Pi Lambda Theta (pres. No. Calif. chpt.), Alpha Delta Kappa. Methodist. Mem. Order Eastern Star (past matron). Contbr. articles to profl. jours. Home: 5615 Estates Dr Oakland CA 94618-2725

KRAUSE, SONJA, chemistry educator; b. St. Gall, Switzerland, Aug. 10, 1933; came to U.S., 1939; d. Friedrich and Rita (Maas) K.; m. Walter Walls Goodwin, Nov. 27, 1970 BS, Rensselaer Poly. Inst., 1954; PhD, U. Calif., Berkeley, 1957. Sr. phys. chemist Rohm & Haas Co., Phila., 1957-64; vol. U.S. Peace Corps, Nigeria, 1964-65; asst. lectr. Lagos U.; asst. prof. Gondar Health Coll. U.S. Peace Corps, Ethiopia, 1965-66; vis. asst. prof. U. So. Calif., L.A., 1966-67; chemistry faculty Rensselaer Poly. Inst., Troy, N.Y., 1967—, prof., 1978—. Mem. coun. Gordon Rsch. Conf., 1981-83; mem. com. on polymers and engrng. NRC, 1992-94; sabbatical Inst. Charles Sadron, Ctr. Rsch. on Macromolecules, Strasbourg, France, 1987. Author: (with others) Chemistry of Environment, 1978, 2d edit., 2002; editor: Molecular Electro-Optics, 1981; mem. editorial adv. bd. Macromolecules, 1982-84 Bd. dirs. Nat. Plastics Ctr. and Mus., Leominster, Mass., 1996-2000. Fellow Am. Phys. Soc. (coun. divsn. biol. physics 1980-93); mem. IUPAC (assoc.), Am. Chem. Soc. (chmn. ea. N.Y. sect. 1981-82, councillor 1991-95, adv. bd. petroleum rsch. fund 1979-81, assoc. mem. com. on edn. 1993-95, assoc. mem. internat. com. 1996), Biophys. Soc. (coun. 1977), N.Y. Acad. Scis., Sigma Xi (pres. Rensselaer Poly Inst. chpt. 1984-85). Office: Rensselaer Poly Inst Dept Chemistry Troy NY 12180 E-mail: krauss@rpi.edu.

KRAUSE-DIAZ, MARY JEAN, educational administrator; b. Clintonville, Wis., Oct. 24, 1939; d. Eric and Mable (Nelson) Strutz; m. Gerald Lee Krause, July 27, 1957; children: Michael Andrew, Gerald Lee; m. Edward Thompson (Skippá) Diaz, Dec. 11, 1977. BS summa cum laude with high honors, U. Wis., Milw., 1970; student, U. Hawaii, 1979; MEd, U. Hawaii-Manoa, 1989. Cert. profl. tchr., tchr. spl. edn. and elem. edn., adminstr., Hawaii. Substitute tchr. Milw. Pub. Schs., 1968-70; dir. Waialua/Haleiwa Headstart program Hawaii Dept. Edn., 1970-72, dir. Title I Honors Presch. project, 1972-78, coord., tchr. Halau O'Hale'Iwa Hale'iwa, 1978-79, tchr. spl. edn., 1979-88; vice prin. Pearl Ridge Elem., Hawaii Dept. Edn., 1989, Waialua High and Intermediate Sch., Hawaii Dept. Edn., 1990—. Mem. Waialua High and Intermediate Sch. Found., 1989—. Mem. Hawaii Assn. for Retarded Citizens, Honolulu, 1978-85; mem. bd. edn. St. Paul's Luth. Ch., West Allis, Wis., 1962-68, mem. exec. bd., 1962-68, Sunday sch. tchr., 1962-70. Mem. ASCD, Nat. Assn. Secondary Sch. Prins., Hawaii Assn. Secondary Sch. Adminstrs., Waialua Bus. and Profl. Women, Alii Pauhi Hawaiian Civic Club, Phi Kappa Phi. Lutheran. Avocations: water and snow skiing, ice skating, handcrafts, reading, helping with school sports. Office: Waialua High/Intermed Sch 67-160 Farrington Hwy Waialua HI 96791-9605

KRAUSER, JANICE, special education educator; b. Chgo., Apr. 30, 1951; d. John Francis and June (Fogle) K. BS, U. Tenn., 1973; MEd, Fla. Atlantic U., 1979. Tchr. John Sevier Elem. Sch., Knoxville, Tenn., 1973-76; substitute tchr. Broward County Schs., Ft. Lauderdale, Fla., 1976-78; tchr. Broward Estates Elem. Sch., Ft. Lauderdale, 1978-79, Attucks Mid. Sch., Hollywood, Fla., 1979-81; tchr., spl. edn. specialist South Broward High Sch., Hollywood, 1981-92; spl. edn. specialist New River Middle Sch., Ft. Lauderdale, 1992—. Selected mem. Fla. Spkrs. Bur., 1997—; state-wide design team mem. of inclusion materials for sch.-based adminstrs.; mem. Fla. Comprehensive Sys. Pers. Devel., 1997—. Co-author: (curriculum) Fundamental Math I and II, Consumer Math, Applied English I, II, and III, Fundamental English I, II, III; published photographer. Zone chmn. U.S.Water Polo, Colorado Springs, 1984-92, 98-2000, bd. dirs. 1998-2000; treas. Fla. Water Polo, 1982-97; dist. del. U.S. Masters Swimming, 1987-95; mem. internat. congress Internat. Swimming Hall of Fame, Ft. Lauderdale, 1994—, (bd. dirs. 1989-93); water polo referee VII World Master's Swimming Championships, Casablanca, Morocco, 1998. Named Swimming Coach of Yr. Hollywood Sun-Tattle, 1984-85, Head Water Polo Coach U.S. Olympic Festival, 1986, 90, selected to Pine Crest Sch. Athletic Hall of Fame, 1998, U.S. Water Polo Hall of Fame, 1998. Mem. Coun. Exceptional Children (v.p. Broward County 1998-2000), U. Tenn. Alumni Assn. (sec. Dade Broward chpt., 2003—), Pine Crest Alumni Assn. (bd. dirs. 1993-2000, sec. 1995-97, v.p. 1999-2000, pres. 2000), Brain Injury Assn. of Fla. (event com. 2001—), Phi Delta Kappa. Avocations: needlepoint, reading, sewing, volunteering. Home: 1610 NE 43rd St Oakland Park FL 33334-5509

KRAUSS, JUDITH BELLIVEAU, nursing educator; b. Malden, Mass., Apr. 11, 1947; d. Leo F. and Dorothy (Conners) Belliveau; m. Ronald L. Krauss, Sept. 5, 1970; children: Jennifer Leigh, Sarah Elizabeth. BS, Boston Coll., 1968; MSN, Yale U., 1970. RN, Conn. Clinical specialist Conn. Mental Health Ctr., New Haven, 1971-73; clin. instr. Yale Sch. Nursing, New Haven, 1971-73; asst. prof. rsch. Yale U. Sch. Nursing, New Haven, 1973-78, assoc. dean, 1978-85, prof., dean, 1985-98, prof., 1998—; master Yale U. Silliman Coll., 2000—. Cons. pharm. and pub. cons., sch., govt. agys. Author: The Chronically Ill Psychiatric Patient and the Community, 1982 (Am. Jour. Nursing Book of Yr. 1982); editor Archives of Psychiat. Nursing, 1986—; mem. editl. bd. Psychiat. Rehab., Psychiat. Svcs.; contbr. articles to profl. jours. Trustee Boston Coll., 1991-99, trustee assoc., 2000—. Am. Nurses Found. scholar, 1978; recipient Chamberlain award Soc. Edn. and Rsch. in Nursing, 1994; named Disting. Alumna Yale Sch. Nursing, 1984; Am. Acad. Nursing/Inst. of Medicine sr. scholar in residence, 1998-99. Mem. ANA (Disting. Contbn. to Psychiat. Nursing award 1992, Leadership citation 2002), Am. Acad. Nursing, Conn. Nurses Assn. (mem. cabinet on edn. 1987-89, bd. dirs. 1988-91, rep. to ANA house of dels. 1988-91, Josephine Dolan award 1989), Sigma Theta Tau (Disting. Lectr. award 1987), Delta Mu (Founders award 1987). Avocations: tennis, golf, hiking, skiing. Office: Yale U Sch Nursing Ste 200 100 Church St S New Haven CT 06536-0740 E-mail: judith.krauss@yale.edu.

KRAUSS, LEO, urologist, educator; b. N.Y.C., Nov. 5, 1928; s. Moe and Marie (Shapiro) K.; m. Harriet Powell, Dec. 4, 1955; children: Robert, Jennifer. BA summa cum laude, Syracuse U., 1948; MD, NYU, 1953. Diplomate Am. Bd. of Urology. Attending urologist N. Shore U. Hosp., Plainview, N.Y., 1963—, Manhasset, N.Y., 1987—; chief of urology Syosset (N.Y.) Comty. Hosp., 1963-78; urologist pvt. practice, Plainview, 1963—. Consulting urologist USAF, Plattsburgh, N.Y., 1961-63, VA Hosp., Tupper Lake, N.Y., 1961-63; asst. prof. urology SUNY, Stony Brook, 1976—. Contbr. articles and abstracts to profl. jours. Bd. dirs. Long Island Cancer Coun., Huntington, N.Y., 1977-79. Capt. USAF, 1954-56, Korea. Named Attending Urologist of Yr., Nassau County Med. Ctr., E. Meadow, N.Y., 1981. Fellow Am. Coll. Surgeons; mem. AMA, N.Y. State Urolog. Soc., Am. Assn. Clin. Urologists, Am. Fedn. for Clin. Rsch., Am. Urolog. Assn., Phi Beta Kappa, Alpha Omega Alpha. Avocations: tennis, travel, reading. Home: 33 Orchard Dr Woodbury NY 11797-2827 Office: Leo Krauss MD PC 875 Old Country Rd Plainview NY 11803-4942

KRAVETZ, NATHAN, education educator, writer; b. NYC, Feb. 11, 1921; s. Louis and Anna (Thau) K. m. Evelyn Cottan, Dec. 10, 1944; children: Deborah Ruth, Daniel. BEd with hons., UCLA, 1941, MA, 1949, EdD, 1954. Cert. tchg., adminstrn., Calif. Tchr. Walnut Creek (Calif.) Elem Sch., 1941-42; tchr., prin. L.A. Unified Sch. Dist., 1946-64; dir. evaluation rsch. Ctr. for Urban Edn., N.Y.C. Schs., 1965-69; prof. Hunter/Lehman Coll., CUNY, N.Y.C., 1964-76, prof. emeritus, 1979; prof. internat. and gifted edn., dean Calif. State U., San Bernardino, 1976-91, prof. emeritus, 1991. Vis. prof. U. SC, 1985-87, UCLA, 1989, Calif. State U., Northridge, 1998—; fgn. svc. officer US Dept. State, Lima, Peru, 1958-60; staff officer UNESCO, Paris, 1969-72, cons. Venezuela, 1968; cons. Ford Found., Chile, 1964, UN Devel. Program, S.Am., 1973-74, US AID, Pakistan and Indonesia, 1974-75, Benin, 1977, Guatemala, 1992, Chulalongkorn U., Thailand, 1999; lectr. UCLA Humanities Ext., 2002 Author 10 children's books; editor Borgo Press, Calif., 1990-95. Sgt. Air Corps. U.S. Army, 1942—46. Univ. fellow Harvard U., 1951-52; grantee Fulbright Rsch. award, Argentina, 1980. Jewish. Avocation: reading history. E-mail: nathan.kravetz@csun.edu.

KRAVITZ, MICHELLE RAE, elementary educator; b. Oakland, Calif., Dec. 8, 1963; d. Malcolm Douglas and Marilyn Rae (Lutters) Towns; m. David Craig Kravitz, Aug. 1, 1987; children: Drew Craig, Alex Daniel, Trent Payton, Katie Lyn. BA, Calif. State U., Sacramento, 1986; credential, Calif. State U., Hayward, 1987. Tchr. San Ramon Valley Unified Sch. Dist., Danville, Calif., 1988—. Spelling bee coord. Montair Sch., Danville, 1989—, speech contest coord., 1988-89; advisor student coun., 1987-89, 91-92; Country Club PTA, 1995—, 2d v.p., 2001—, spellabration chmn., 2001, chmn. Country Club Affair, 2000-01. Recreation com. Glen Cove Homeowners Assn., Vallejo, Calif., 1989—; tchr. rep. Montair Parent Tchr. Assn., 1989-90, Sycamore Elem. Sch., 1992-93, founding bd. mem. Cougar Fund, 2001—; founder, coord. Breakfast Book Club, 2001—. Mem. San Ramon Valley Educators Assn. (site rep. 1989-90, Outstanding Svc. Bay Area Math Project 1990). Democrat. Presbyterian. Avocations: sports, reading, cross stitching, travel. Home: 540 Amherst Ct San Ramon CA 94583 Office: Country Club Sch 7534 Blue Fox Way San Ramon CA 94583

KRAYBILL, DONALD BRUBAKER, humanities educator, writer; b. Mt. Joy, Pa., Sept. 24, 1945; s. Wilmer Garber and Helen (Brubaker) K.; m. Frances Mellinger, Sept. 3, 1966; children: Sheila Lynn, Joy Louise. BA in Sociology and Religion, Ea. Mennonite U., Harrisonburg, Va., 1967; MA in Sociology, Temple U., 1972, PhD in Sociology, 1975. Prof. sociology Elizabethtown Coll., Pa., 1971-96, dir. Young Ctr., 1989—96, disting. prof., 2002—; provost Messiah Coll., Grantham, Pa., 1996—2002. Author: The Upside-Down Kingdom, 1978, 2003 (Nat. Religious Book award Religious Book Rev. 1979), The Riddle of Amish Culture, 2001, The Amish and the State, 2003(Outstanding Acad. Book award Choice 1994), Amish Enterprise, 1995, On the Backroad to Heaven, 2003, others. Sr. Rsch. fellow NEH, 1987. Office: The Young Ctr Elizabethtown Coll Elizabethtown PA 17022

KRAYNAK, HELEN, special education consultant; b. Jersey City, N.J., Mar. 28, 1936; d. Stephen and Irene (DanKovich) Ozimok; m. John Kraynak, June 23, 1956; children: Deborah Mary Fiocco, Lorie Elizabeth Kraynak. BS in Edn., Jersey City State Coll., 1958; student, Rutgers U., 1985-87; learning disabilities cert., Nova U., 1991. Cert. Elem., N.J., Fla., Specific Learning Disabilities, Fla. Kindergarten tchr., Old Bridge, N.J., 1962-63; 2nd grade tchr., 1963-65; 3rd grade tchr., 1965-66; resource tchr., 1966-67; reading tchr., 1968-89; learning disabilities tchr. Palm City, Fla., 989-92; mainstream cons. Palm City Elem. Sch. and Hidden Oaks Mid. Sch., Palm City, Fla., 1992—. Bd. dirs. Old Bridge (N.J.) Cath. Youth Orgn., 1972-75; Christian Cath. Doctrine tchr. Nativity of Our Lord Ch., 1972-85; leader Girl Scouts U.S., East Brunswick, N.J., 1966-72. Mem. NEA, Coun. Exceptional Children, Am. Fedn. Tchrs., N.J. Tchrs. Edn. Assn., Alpha Delta Kappa (pres. 1990-92). Avocations: world travel, walking on the beach, grandchildren, reading. Home: 9500 S Ocean Dr Apt 207 Jensen Beach FL 34957-2327

KREAR, GAIL RICHARDSON, elementary education educator, consultant; b. Little Rock, July 24, 1942; d. Floyd E. Richardson and Selmarie (Hart) VanDerGriff; m. Bill J. Eason, May 17, 1963 (dec. 1985); 1 child, Kari V.; m. J. David Krear, Feb. 14, 1993. BA, U. Ark., 1964; MS, George Washington U., 1974; PhD in Elem. Edn., Montgomery County Pub. Schs., 1976. Ednl. cons., 1976-77, 85—; acting prin. Montgomery County Pub. Schs., Rockville, Md., 1974-76; tchr. in an award sch. State Sch. of Excellence, Rockville, Md., 1991-92; tchr. Nat. Sch. Excellence, 1994-95. Mem. nat. com. to preserve social security and medicare, 1996. Coach Montgomery County Recreational Dept., Rockville, 1978-81, Olney Boys & Girls Club, 1982; founding mem. FDR, 1996; mem. Animal Advocates Howard County, 1997. Mem. Am. Contract Bridge League (life master), Washington Bridge League, Alpha Delta Pi. Republican. Avocations: bridge, swimming, traveling. Office: Montgomery County Pub Schs Rockville MD 20850

KRECKLOW, DOUGLAS EARL, secondary education educator, coach; b. Omaha, July 6, 1952; s. Earl Harold and Evelyn Florence (Hammer) K.; m. Leslie Tamisiea, Aug. 25, 1973; children: Rebecca Anne, Kyle Douglas. BA in Edn., Wayne State Coll., 1974; MS, Pa. State U., 1986. Interim instr. Wayne (Nebr.) State Coll., 1977-78; aquatics dir./coach Ames (Iowa) Parks and Recreation, 1978-79; aquatics dir., coach, chair Westside High Sch., Omaha, 1979—. Del. People to People Visit, Republic China, 1987; pres. Swim Omaha, Performance Enhancement Enterprises, Inc., Omaha, 1990—. Contbr. articles to profl. jours. Instr., trainer ARC; bd. dirs. U.S./USSR Fitness Testing Project for Nebr., 1988. Mem. AAHPERD, Nat. Interscholastic Coaches Assn. (Outstanding Svc. award 1995), Nat. Strength Coaches Assn., Am. Coll. Sports Medicine, Am. Swim Coaches Assn., Nat. High Sch. Athletic Coaches Assn., Nat. Fed. High Sch. Swimming Rules Commn., Nebr. Coaches Assn. (Coach of Yr. 1979-88, 90-95), Omaha Westside Swim Club (advisor 1979—). Republican. Presbyterian. Avocations: golfing, cycling, swimming. Home: 9711 Walnut St Omaha NE 68124-1159 Office: Westside High Sch 8701 Pacific St Omaha NE 68114-5298

KREEGAR, PHILLIP KEITH, educational administrator; b. Anderson, Ind., Aug. 3, 1937; s. James Forrest and Uva Maxine (Johnson) K.; m. Martha Ann Kreegar, Aug. 10, 1958; children: Gregory, Pamela, Deborah. BS, Purdue U., 1959. Asst. prin., tchr. Harrison Twp. Sch. Corp., Kitchel, Ind., 1959-60; gen. fieldman Madison County Farm Bur. Coop., Anderson, Ind., 1962-65; pub. rels. asst. Ind. Farm Bur. Coop., Indpls., 1965-77, communications specialist, 1977-79, asst. mgr. edn., 1979-83, mgr. mem. rels., 1983-89, edn. specialist, 1989-91, edn. mgr., 1991—. Rep. Ind. Youthpower Com., 1983-94; bd. dirs. Ind. FFA Found., Trafalgar; chmn. Ind. Coop. Edn. Com., Indpls., 1983—; mem. com. Nat. Coun. Farmer Coops., Washington, 1987—; mem. edn. com. Ohio Coun. Coops., Columbus, 1992—. Photographer, contbr. Coop. Ofcl. jour., 1967, Agrafacts mag., 1978; editor: Farm News newspaper, 1967. Chmn. advancement com. Bethany Boy Scouts of Am., Anderson, Ind., 1964; mem. activities com. Orchard Park Sch. PTO, Carmel, Inc., 1968; chmn. publicity com. Carmel Dad's Club, 1970. Capt. U.S. Army, 1960-62. Named Hon. Ind. Young Farmer, Ind. Young Farmers Assn., 1986, Disting. Svc. award, 1991, Hon. Commr. Agr. State of Ind., 1980; recipient Hon. Hoosier Farmer Degree, 1984, Hon. Am. FFA Degree, Nat. FFA Assn., 1989, Ohio Coop. Edn. award, 1995. Mem. Assn. Coop. Educators, Purdue Agr. Alumni Assn., Purdue Alumni Assn. Avocations: fishing, bowling, horticulture. Office: Countrymark Coop Inc 950 N Meridian St Indianapolis IN 46204-1077

KREIDER, KEVIN LEE, mathematician, educator; b. Balt., Mar. 15, 1959; s. Harold Nelson and Elsie Mae Kreider; m. Valerie Ann Lamberton, May 20, 1995. BA, Wittenberg U., 1981; MS, Purdue U., 1982, PhD, 1986. Postdoctoral fellow Ames (Iowa) Lab., 1987-89; from asst. prof. to prof. applied math. U. Akron, Ohio, 1989—. Mem. Soc. Indsl. Applied Mathematics. Avocations: woodworking, guitar. Office: U Akron Dept Math Scis Akron OH 44325-0001

KREIDER, LEONARD EMIL, economics educator; b. Newton, Kans., Feb. 25, 1938; s. Leonard C. and Rachel (Weaver) K.; m. Louise Ann Pankratz, June 10, 1963; children: Brent Emil, Todd Alan, Ryan Eric. Student, Bluffton Coll., 1956-58; BA, Bethel Coll., 1960; student, Princeton U., 1960-61; MA, Ohio State U., 1962, PhD, 1968. Economist So. Ill. U., Carbondale, 1965-70; asst. prof. Beloit (Wis.) Coll., 1970—, prof., 1978, chmn. dept. econs. and mgmt., 1984-89, acting v.p. acad. affairs, 1987-88, Allen Bradley prof. econs., 1991—. Chief of party Devel. Assocs., Asuncion, Paraguay, 1970; economist Deere and Co., 1973, Castle and Cooke, San Francisco, 1975-76, AmCore, Rockford, Ill., 1984, Rockford Meml. Hosp., 1990-91, Stone Container, San Jose, Costa Rica, 1996; cons. corps. and attys. Author: Development and Utilization of Managerial Talent, 1968; contbr. numerous articles, reports to profl. jours. Mem. Nat. Assn. Bus. Economists, Am. Econs. Assn., Am. Assn. Higher Edn., Soc. Internat. Devel. (pres. So. Ill. chpt. 1969), Indsl. Relations Research Assn. (elections com. 1974). Presbyterian. Home: 820 Milwaukee Rd Beloit WI 53511-5636 Office: Beloit Coll Dept Econ Mgmt Beloit WI 53511

KREISBERG, ROBERT A. dean, medical educator; Student, U. Ala., U. South Ala.; MD, Northwestern U., 1958. Vice chair dept. medicine U. Ala., Birmingham, prof.; interim dean Univ. of South Alabama Coll. of Med., 2000, dean, 2001—. Med. dir. Univ. Consortium Clin. Rsch. Fellow Am. Coll. Physicians (gov. Ala., regent, chair scientific program subcom., ednl. policy com., gen. chair, Disting. Tchr. award 1994); mem. Am. Fedn. Clin. Rsch. (pres. 1974-75). Office: Coll of Med Univ of South Alabama 307 Univ Blvd, 170 CSAB Mobile AL 36688*

KREISER, RAYMOND MICHAEL, secondary school educator; b. Lebanon, Pa., Apr. 11, 1963; s. Adam John Jr. and Geneva Elaine (Stickler) K.; m. Karen Lynne Crum, Nov. 7, 1987; 1 child, Matthew Alan. BS in Math., Elizabethtown Coll., 1985. Cert. tchr., Pa. Tchr. No. Potter School Dist., Ulysses, Pa., 1985-90; tchr. math. and computer sci. Annville (Pa.)-Cleona Sch. Dist., 1990—. Math. club advisor No. Potter High Sch., 1985-89, class advisor, 1986-90; math club advisor Annville-Cleona High Sch., 1990—. Named Soccer Coach of Yr., North Tier Coaches Assn., Potter-Tioga County, Pa., 1988; coach champion team Dist. 3 Pa. Inter Scholastic Athletic Assn., 1987, 88, 89; recipient Gift of Time award, 1992, Excellence in Edn. award Lebanon Valley C. of C., 1992, 93. Mem. Math. Assn. Am., Pa. Tchrs. Assn. Math., Pa. State Edn. Assn. Republican. Methodist. Avocations: bowling, working with computers, camping. Home: 215 S Gary St Cleona PA 17042-2448 Office: Annville-Cleona High Sch 500 S White Oak St Annville PA 17003-2298

KREISMAN, DEA ANN, principal; b. Wakeeney, Kans., Sept. 25, 1955; d. Joe Donald and Donna LaVelle (smith) Butcher; m. Steven Neal Kreisman, June 15, 1986; 1 step child, Mark Jason. BA in Edn., Wichita State U., 1977, MA in Edn., 1980; cert., U. Phoenix, 1992. Cert. elem. tchr., adminstr. 1st grade tchr. Derby (Kans.) Pub. Schs., 1977-80; tchr. 1st-2d grades Aurora (Colo.) Pub. Schs., 1980-84, classrm. support tchr., 1984-90, resource tchr., 1990-93, prin., 1993—. Course cons. Regis U., Denver, 1991—, Colo. Dept. Edn., Denver, 1988. Mem. ASCD, Internat. Reading Assn., Colo. Assn. for Supervision and Curriculum Devel., Phi Delta Kappa. Avocations: restoring and collecting 40's and 50's cadillacs, dollhouse miniatures. Office: Boston Elem Sch 1365 Boston St Aurora CO 80010-3033 Home: 10019 Boca Cir Parker CO 80134-3591

KREITLOW, BURTON WILLIAM, retired adult education educator; b. Howard Lake, Minn., Aug. 14, 1917; s. William Arthur and Esther Ingeborg (Nelson) K.; m. Doris J. Ounsworth, Sept. 13, 1944; children: Karen Neal, Candace Kreitlow. Tchg. cert., Cokato (Minn.) Normal, 1935; BS, U. Minn., 1941, MA, 1948, PhD, 1949. Rural tchr. Dist. 58, Montrose, Minn., 1935-37; county 4-H agt. Minn. Ext. Svc., Mankato, Minn., 1938-39, county agr. agt. Warren, Minn., 1941-42, dist. supr. 4H St. Paul, 1945-46; asst. prof. basic coll. Mich. State U., East Lansing, 1948-49; from asst. prof. to prof. U. Wis., Madison, 1949-81, prof. emeritus, 1981—. Vis. prof. Tex. A&M U., Fla. State U., Alaska-Pacific U., Wash. State U., Nat. Taiwan U., U. Hawaii (Hilo), U. Alaska, Anchorage; Disting. vis. prof. Ohio State U. Grad. Sch., 1975-76; workshop leader, lectr.; chmn. Commn. of Profs., 1961-63; bd. dirs. emeritus Coll. St. Scholastica, Duluth, Minn., 1992-93, Aging Trust Fund, Northland Found., Duluth, 1991-94. Author: Rural Education: Community Backgrounds, 1954, Leadership for Action in Rural Communities, 1960, (series) Steps to Learning, 1966-80; playwright (with others) Under the Stars and Stripes--Stories of World War II, 2002; editor: Examining Controversies in Continuing Education, 1981, Creative Planning for the Second Half of Life, 1997; contbr. column to (jour.) Adult Learning, 1989-91. Mem. Wisconsin Heights Sch. Bd., Mazomanie, Wis., 1959-62; pres. Homestead Coop. of Grand Marais (Minn.), 1992-94. Recipient Haight Travel fellowship U. Wis. Grad. Sch., 1967; named to Internat. Adult and Continuing Edn. Hall of Fame, Am. Assn. Adult and Continuing Edn., 1996. Mem. NEA (chair publs. com. rural dept. 1965-67), Minn. Gerontol. Soc., Lions (pres. 1959, 85), Phi Delta Kappa. Democrat. Mem. UCC Ch.

Avocations: community volunteer, leading memoir writing groups, continued teaching and learning. Home: PO Box 865 Grand Marais MN 55604-0865 also: 78-7039 Kam 111 Rd Unit 145 Kailua Kona HI 96740-2530

KREITZ, HELEN MARIE, retired elementary education educator; b. Taylor, Tex., Aug. 22, 1929; d. Joseph Jr. and Mary Lena (Miller) K. BA, U. Mary Hardin-Baylor, 1950; MEd, U. Tex., 1959. Cert. tchr., Tex. Bookkeeper Singer Sewing Machine Co., Taylor, 1950-51; advt. salesperson Taylor Times, 1951-52; tchr. Temple (Tex.) Ind. Sch. Dist., 1952-88. Lector, eucharistic min. St. Mary's Cath. Ch., Temple, 1974—. Mem. Tex. Ret. Tchrs. (life, treas. Temple chpt. 1991-2002), Tex. State Tchrs. Assn. (life, treas. Temple chpt. 1954-55), Tex. Classroom Tchrs. Assn. (life, pres. Temple chpt. 1967-69), U. Tex. Execs. (life), Pi Lambda Theta. Roman Catholic. Avocations: sewing, handcrafts. Home: PO Box 3446 Temple TX 76505-3446

KREMIN, DANIEL PAUL, clinical forensic psychologist; b. Bklyn., Sept. 26, 1946; s. Harry and Ruth Kremin; m. Diane Joyce Siesel, Mar. 18, 1972; children: Sean, Todd. BA, Fairleigh Dickinson U., 1967, MA, 1974; MS, Yeshiva U., 1976, SpC., 1977, PhD, 1978. Diplomate Am. Bd. Forensic Medicine, Am. Bd. Forensic Examiners, Am. Bd. Adminstrv. Psychology, Am. Bd. Psychol. Specialties, cert. specialties Profl. Acad. Custody Evaluators, registered custody evalator Am. Coll. Forensic Exmainers; cert. bd. cert. sch. and emergency crisis response, bd. cert. homeland security. Sr. psychologist Columbia Presbyn. Hosp., 1975-76; mem. com. on handicapped N.Y. Bd. Edn., 1977-81, psychologist, 1977-78, clin. coord., 1978-79, coord. learning disabilities identification program, 1979, asst. to regional coord., 1979-80, chmn., 1980-81; dir. spl. svcs. Teaneck (N.J.) Pub. Schs., 1981-89; dir. spl. edn. and pupil pers. svcs. Hicksville (N.Y.) Pub. Schs., 1989-92, asst. supt., 1992-2000; pvt. practice in psychology, 1992—. Fellow clin. psychology Rousso Ctr., Albert Einstein Coll. Medicine. Tchg. fellow Fairleigh Dickinson U., 1974. Fellow Am. Coll. Forensic Examiners, Am. Acad. Experts in Traumatic Stress; mem. ASCD, APA, Soc. Pediat. Psychology, Nat. Honor Soc. Psychology, Nat. Assn. Sch. Psychologists, N.Y. State Psychol. Assn., Nassau County Psychol. Assn., Coun. Exceptional Children. Avocation: skiing. Office: Ste 102 990 Westbury Rd Westbury NY 11590-5309 E-mail: dockrem@aol.com.

KREN, MARGO, artist, art educator; b. Houston; BS, U. Wis., 1966; MFA, U. Iowa, 1979. Instr. art Kans. State U., Manhattan, 1971-80, asst. prof., 1980-88, assoc. prof., 1988—95, prof., 1995—. Vis. artist Wichita (Kans.) State U., 1986, Kansas City Art Inst., 1987, Deakin U., Melbourne, Australia, 2003, No. Territory U., Darwin, Australia, 2003. Represented Morgan Gallery, Kans. City, Mo., Haydon Gallery, Lincoln, Nebr.; critical review articles and artwork to New Art Examiner, numerous others, 1981—; one-person shows include Mulvane Art Mus., Topeka, 1981-83, Reuben Saunders Gallery, Wichita, Kans., 1983, 85, Albrecht-Kemper Art Mus., St. Joseph, Mo., 1986, U. Ctrl. Fla., Orlando, 1991, Swen Parson Gallery, De Kalb, Ill., 1983, South Bend (Ind.) Regional Mus. Art, 1985; exhibited in group shows Downey Mus., L.A., 1985, Spiva Art Ctr., Joplin, Mo., 1986, Karl Oskar Gallery, Kansas City, 1986, Emporia State U., 1986, Deutsch-Amerikanishes Inst., Regensburg, Fed. Republic Germany, 1988, U. Neb., Lincoln, 1992, Port Elizabeth Technikon, Rep. of So. Africa, 1995, U. of Durham, Westville, Rep. of So. Africa, 1995, U. of S.C., 1997, Yunnan Art Inst., China, 1997, New Harmony (Ind.) Gallery of Contemporary Art, 1998, No. Mich. U., 2000, Beach Mus. of Art, Kans. State U., 2000, Iowa State U., 2001, Vanderbuilt U., Nashville, 2002, The Waiting Room, New Orleans, 2002, The Arts Ctr. of the Ozarks, Springdale, Ark., 2002, Jasper (Ind.)Art Ctr., 2002, The Arts Ctr., Orange, Va., 2002; represented in permanent collections U. Va., Charlottesville, Maytag, West Des Moines, Iowa, N.H. Inst. Art, Manchester, N.Y. Pub. Libr., print room, N.Y.C., Pioneer HiBred Internat., Des Moines, Va. Ctr. Creative Arts, Sweet Briar, Yunnan Art Inst., Kunming, Yunnan, China, Deakin U., Melbourne, McAllen (Tex.) Internat. Mus., South Bend (Ind.) Regional Mus. Art, Marianna Beach Mus. of Art, Kans. State U., Maytag, West Des Moines, Iowa, Monsanto Co., St. Louis, Nelson Gallery/Atkins Mus., Kansas City, Mo., N.H. Inst. Arts, Manchester, N.H., Pioneer Hi Bred Internat., Des Moines, Iowa, Springfield (Mo.) Art Mus., The Nat. Mus. of Women in the Arts, Washington, D.C., The Print Club of Albany, N.Y., Yunnan Art Inst., China, Topeka (Kans.) Pub. Libr., Yellow Freight Systems, Inc., Kansas City, Spencer Mus. Art, Lawrence, Kans., Mulvane Art Mus., Topeka, Sheldon Meml. Art Gallery, Lincoln, Monsanto, Saint Louis, El Paso (Tex.) Mus. Art, Hosp. Trust Tower, Providence, Mut. Benefit Life Ins. Co., Kansas City, Nebr. Wesleyan U., Lincoln, Western Mich. U., Kalamazoo, Albrecht-Kemper Art Mus., St. Joseph, Mo., Wichita (Kans.) State U., Steel and Pipe Supply Co., Manhattan, Kans., Williston (N.D.) Arts Coun., Williston (N.D.) State U, Nelson Gallery/ATKINS Mus., Kansas City, Mo., The Nat. Mus. of Women Artists, Washington, U. Spartansburg, S.C., Yunnam Art inst., Kunming, Yunnan, P.R. China, Kans. Arts Commn., Artist Fellowship award, 2000. Mid-Am. Visual Arts fellow panelist, 1992; recipient Faculty Rsch. award Kans. State U., 1980, 85, 88, Gov.'s Art award, 1989, Artist Fellowship, Kans. Arts Commn., 2000; Kans. Arts Commn. Profl. Devel. grantee, 1992, Nat. Endowment for Arts grantee, 1981. Mem. Kans. Arts Commn. (visual artists panelist 1984-85, Artist in Edn. panelist 1984-87, 89), ARTS Midwest (visual artists panelist for NEA reg. fellowships 1988), Kansas City Artist Coalition (pres. 1982-83), Artist Colony, Ragdale Found., Va. Ctr. for the Creative Arts, Yaddo. Home: 2912 Tatarrax Dr Manhattan KS 66502-1978 Office: Kans State U Dept Art Willard Hall # 322 Manhattan KS 66506

KREND, WILLIAM JOHN, secondary education educator; b. Chgo., Oct. 25, 1947; s. Patrick H. and Irene Krend; m. Marjorie J. Tow, Aug. 15, 1970; children: Andrew William, Kira Loren. BA, U. Calif., Santa Barbara, 1969; MA, Calif. State U., Fresno, 1978. Cert. secondary, community coll. tchr., Calif. Tchr. Avenal (Calif.) High Sch., 1970-73; tchr. history Lemoore (Calif.) High Sch., 1973—; faculty history West Hills Coll., Lemoore, 1978-86, 97—, Chapman U., Nas Lemoore, Calif., 1979—. Curriculum cons. Kings County Office of Edn., Hanford, Calif., 1990-91. Contbr. articles to profl. jours.; contbr: World History supplement, 1990. Coord. History Day, Kings County, 1987—, Am. Youth Competition, 1992, We the People for Calif. 20th Congl. Dist., 1992—; bd. dirs. Avenal Recreation Com., 1973-74. Named Calif. State History Day Tchr. of Merit, 1997; CLIO Project/U. Calif.-Berkeley fellow, 1986, Calif. History Project/Calif. State U.-Fresno fellow, 1990, Ctr. for Energy Edn. fellow, 1994. Mem. Nat. Coun. for Social Studies (presenter), Calif. Coun. for Social Studies (bd. dirs. 1992—, no. co-chmn. govt. rels. com., co-chair publs. com. 1995-96, conf. com. 1996-97, co-chair profl. standards com. 1997-99), Calif. Hist. Soc., Nat. Geog. Soc., Calif. Fedn. Tchrs., San Joaquin Coun. for Social Studies (bd. dirs. 1991—, pres. 1995—). Avocations: travel, stamp collecting, photography, guitar playing. Home: 14230 16th Ave Lemoore CA 93245-9517 Office: Lemoore High Sch 101 E Bush St Lemoore CA 93245-3601

KRENDEL, EZRA SIMON, systems and human factors engineering consultant; b. NYC, Mar. 5, 1925; s. Joseph and Tamara (Shapiro) K.; m. Elizabeth Spencer Malany, Aug. 20, 1950 (dec. Nov. 1983); children: David A., Tamara E. Krendel-Clark, Jennifer K. Hall; m. Janet Brownlee Allen, June 27, 1992. AB, Bklyn. Coll., 1945; Sc.M. in Physics, MIT, 1947; A.M. in Social Relations, Harvard, 1949; MA honoris causa, U. Pa., 1971. From research engr. to sr. staff engr. Franklin Inst. Research Labs., 1949-55, lab. mgr., 1955-63, tech. dir., 1963-66, sr. adviser, cons., 1961; dir. Mgmt. Sci. Ctr., Wharton Sch. U. Pa., Phila., 1967-69, prof. ops. research and stats., Wharton Sch., 1966-90, prof. emeritus, 1990—, prof. systems engrng. Sch. Engrng. and Applied Sci., 1983-93; prin. scientist Systems Tech., Inc., Hawthorne, Calif., 1987—89. Emeritus prof.; mem. rsch. adv. com. on control guidance and nav. NASA, 1964-65; various coms. Hwy. Rsch. Bd., NRC, 1964-74; vis. lectr. NATO, 1968, 71; mem. roster of arbitrators Fed. Mediation and Conciliation Svc.; cons. govt. agys., industry, legal profession. Author: Unionizing the Armed Forces, 1977; contbr. articles to profl. publs. Mem. Phila. Mayor's Sci. and Tech. Adv. Council. Recipient Louis E. Levy Gold medal Franklin Inst., 1960 Fellow IEEE, AAAS, APA, Am. Psychol. Soc., Human Factors Soc.; mem. Ergonomics Soc., Cosmos Club, Sigma Xi. Home: 211 Cornell Ave Swarthmore PA 19081-1933 E-mail: krendel@wharton.upenn.edu.

KRESS, GERARD CLAYTON, JR., psychologist, educator; b. Buffalo, New York, July 10, 1934; s. Gerard Clayton and Eleanor Amelia (Rupp) K.; m. Suzanne Ardys (Raloff), May 4, 1957 (div. 1980); children: Timothy, Peter, Jennifer; m. Gloria (Wilson), May 20, 1994. BA, U. Rochester, NY., 1956; PhD in psychology, State U. of N.Y., Buffalo, 1962. Assoc. rsch. scientist Am. Inst. for Rsch., Pitts., 1961-64, rsch. scientist, 1964-68; asst. prof. U. Pitts., 1968-71; asst. dean Harvard U., Boston, 1971-80, assoc. dean, 1980-88; prof., dir. behavioral sci. Baylor Coll. Dentistry, Dallas, 1988; ret. Cons. U.S. VA, Washington, 1982-85; Boston U., 1980-82; U. Minn., Mpls., 1973, 88, 90, 91. Author: Behavior Management in the Classroom, 1969; contbg. chpt., Dental Clinics of North Am., 1988; contbg. articles to profl. jour. Served in USAR, 1957-60. Mem. Am. Psychol. Assn.; Am. Assn. Dental Sch. (chair behavioral sci. sect. 1992); Internat. Assn. Dental Rsch. (pres. behavioral sci. group 1974); Am. Ednl. Rsch. Assn. Democrat. Home: 7942 Goodshire Ave Dallas TX 75231-4721

KRETSCHMER, INGRID BUTLER, elementary school educator; b. Port Jefferson, N.Y., Apr. 19, 1936; d. Arthur David and Clara (Anderson) Butler; m. Fred Kretschmer, Apr. 10, 1955; children: Arthur Frederick, Susan Elizabeth Kretschmer Leining, Cory. BA, Adelphi Suffolk Coll., 1966; MEd, Dowling Coll., 1977. Cert. elem. tchr., N.Y. Tchr. k-6 Rocky Point (N.Y.) Sch. Dist., 1966-86, tchr. compensatory math., 1986—. Grade level coord. Rocky Point Sch. Dist., 1975-80, co-creator, instr. in-svc. math course k-6, 1992—. Co-author: Developmental Reading Skills Record, 1969. Mem. Rocky Point PTA, 1966—; pres. bd. Trinity Nursery Sch., Rocky Point, 1978-80; mem. Ch. Coun. Trinity Luth. Ch., Rocky Point, 1978-83, Riverhead (N.Y.) Rep. Club, 1983—. Mem. Am. Fedn. Tchrs., N.Y. State United Tchrs. (del. 1983—, Svc. award 1990), Rocky Point Tchrs. Assn. (sec. 1967-69, bldg. rep. 1973-83, pres. 1983-94), L.I. Pres.' Coun. (treas. 1989-91). Avocations: reading, logic puzzles, gardening, travel. Home: 333 E Woodland Dr Wading River NY 11792-9604

KRETZMAR, MARY LYNN, vocational education and sign language interpreter, educator; b. Hawthorne, Calif., Sept. 13, 1957; d. Hugh Leeroy and Joell (Morgan) K. Cert. in sign lang. interpretation, El Camino Coll., Torrance (Calif.) Unified Sch. Dist., 1993. Sec. Casio-PhoneMate, Inc., Torrance, 1991-96; sign lang. interpreter El Camino Coll., 1993—2000, instrnl. ednl. aide, 1996—; vocat. specialist transition program Manhattan Beach Unified Sch. Dist., Torrance, Manhattan Beach, Calif., 1996—. Author: Benjamin and the Missing Body Parts; poet (collection) Snapshot, 1996; contbr. poetry to lit. publs.; editor newsletter Hands of Friendship, El Camino Coll., 1991-92. Supporter AIDS Project L.A., 1993—, Best Buddies, 1996—, Father Flannagan's Home for Boys, 1996—, Paralyzed Vets. of Am., 1996—, World Wildlife Found., 2002—, Disabled Vets. Am., Nat. Multiple Sclerosis Soc. Avocations: gardening, cross-stitch, crocheting, music, church.

KREUTER, GRETCHEN V. academic administrator; b. Mpls., May 7, 1934; d. Sigmund and Marvyl (Larson) von Loewe; m. Robert L. Sutton, 1993; children: David Karl, Betsy Ruth Rymes. BA, Rockford Coll., 1955; MA, U. Wis., 1958, PhD, 1961; LLD (hon.), Rockford Coll., 1992, Coll. St. Mary, 1994. Lectr. in Am. Studies Colgate U., Hamilton, N.Y., 1962-67; lectr. in history Coll. St. Catherine, St. Paul, 1969-71, Hamline U., St. Paul, 1971-72; prof. of history Macalester Coll., St. Paul, 1972-73, St. Olaf Coll., Northfield, Minn., 1975-80; asst. to pres. Coll. St. Catherine, St. Paul, 1980-84; asst. to v.p. acad. affairs U. Minn., Mpls., 1984-87; pres. Rockford Coll., Ill., 1987-92, Olivet (Mich.) Coll., 1992-93; sr. fellow Am. Coun. Edn., Washington, 1993-94; hon. fellow Inst. for Rsch. in Humanities U. Wis., Madison, 1994—; interim pres. Coll. of St. Mary, Omaha, 1995-96. Mem., chmn. Minn. Humanities Coun., St. Paul, 1974-83; mem. Mich. Humanities Coun., 1993; bd. dirs. Nat. Assn. State Humanities Commn., Washington, 1984-86. Author: An American Dissenter, 1969 (McKnight prize 1978), Running the Twin Cities: editor: Women of Minnesota, 1977, 2d edit., 1998, Two Career Family, 1978, Forgotton Promise: Race and Gender Conflict on a Small College Campus: A Memoir, 1996. Bd. dirs. Kobe Coll. Corp., Rockford Mus. Ctr., ACE Commn. on Minorities in Higher Edn., 1991-92, Mich. Humanities Coun., 1993-94. Address: 2402 Kendall Ave Madison WI 53705-3845 E-mail: gkreuter@facstaff.wisc.edu.

KREUTZER, RITA KAY, speech and language pathologist; b. West Point, Nebr., Jan. 19, 1966; d. Raymond G. and Genevieve C. (Stalp) Meiergerd; m. Mark Eugene Kreutzer, Aug. 19, 1988; children: Jonathan, Matthew, Nathan, Megan. BS in Communication Disorders, Kearney State Coll., 1988, MS, 1990. Cert. tchr., Nebr. Speech/lang. pathologist Holdrege (Nebr.) City Schs., 1989—. Active All Sts. Ch. Altar Soc., Holdrege, 1988—. Mem. Am. Speech/Lang./Hearing Assn., Nebr. State Speech/Lang./Hearing Assn. (conv. presenter 1990). Roman Catholic. Avocations: reading, sewing, family fun.

KREVANS, JULIUS RICHARD, university administrator, physician; b. N.Y.C., May 1, 1924; s. Sol and Anita Krevans; m. Patricia N. Abrams, May 28, 1950; children: Nita, Julius R., Rachel, Sarah, Nora Kate. BS Arts and Scis, N.Y. U., 1943, MD, 1946. Diplomate: Am. Bd. Internal Med. Intern, then resident Johns Hopkins Med. Sch. Hosp., mem. faculty, until 1970, dean acad. affairs, 1969—70; physician in chief Balt. City Hosp., 1963—69; prof. medicine U. Calif., San Francisco, 1970—, dean Sch. Medicine, 1971—82, chancellor, 1982—93, chancellor emeritus, 1993—. Contbr. articles on hematology, internal med. profl. jours. Served with M.C. AUS, 1948-50. Served with USMC, 1948—50, AUS. Mem. ACP, Assn. Am. Physicians. Address: 32 Birch Bay Dr Bar Harbor ME 04609

KRIDER, MARGARET YOUNG, art educator; b. Pitts., Aug. 20, 1920; d. Thomas Smith and Josephine Bridget (Connolly) Y.; m. Robert Arthur Krider, May 12, 1945; children: Karen L., Ann Noel, Darcie Ellen Robbins. BFA in Art Edn., Carnegie-Mellon U., 1942; MEd in Art Edn., Edinboro U., 1969. Tchr. art West Homestead (Pa.) Pub. Sch., 1942-44, Mt. Oliver (Pa.) Pub. Sch., 1942-44; recreational worker Valley Forge Gen. Hosp. ARC, Phoenixville, Pa., 1944-45; assoc. prof. Villa Maria Coll., Erie, Pa., 1950-87. Adj. instr. Pa. State U. Behrend Campus, Erie, Pa., 1981-87; presenter papers Ea. Arts Conv., N.Y.C., 1962, Kutztown (Pa.) State U., 1967, U. Pa. Art Conf., Pitts., 1980; condr. workshops Peterborough State Coll., Toronto, Ont., Can., 1972-73; presenter in field, 1962—. Exhibited in one and two-person shows at Chautauqua Art Gallery, William Penn Meml. Mus., Butler Mus., Patterson Gallery, Glass Growers Gallery, Kada Gallery, Erie, Sycamore Gallery, Cummings Gallery, Schuster Gallery, Adams Gallery, Dunkirk, N.Y., Schuster Gallery of Gannon Unit, others; juried and invitational shows incl. Erie Art Mus., Erie Summer Festivals, Agnon Fine Art and Crafts, Carlow Coll. Pa. Women's Art, Bruce Gallery, Forum Gallery, Nat. Mus. Women in Arts; contbr. articles to art jours. Bd. dirs., sec. Arts Coun. Erie, Pa., 1974-76, Erie Civic Ballet Co., 1970-75; bd. dirs. Erie County Hist. Soc., 1988-94; active LWV, 1950s; Girl Scout leader Cathedral Grade Sch., Erie, 1956-66; hist. restoration advisor Battles Mus., Girard, Pa., 1993-98. Recipient Community award Florence Crittenton Home, 1991; named Outstanding Tchr. Villa Maria Coll. Presdl. Award, 1987, Outstanding Art Educator PAEA, 1989. Mem. AAUW (bd. dirs., chair 1967-90, Found. Ednl. award 1984, Outstanding Woman finalist 1992), Women's Round Table, Nat. Art Edn., Northwestern Pa. Artists Assn. (chair membership), Pa. Soc. Art Edn., Erie County Hist. Soc. (hon., life), Women's Round Table, Delta Kappa Gamma (chmn. Book Alive). Republican. Roman Catholic. Home: 6130 Mistletoe Ave Fairview PA 16415-2702

KRIDLER, JAMIE BRANAM, children's advocate, social psychologist; b. Newport, Tenn., Jan. 23, 1955; d. Floyd A. and Mary Leslie (Carlisle) Branam; m. Thomas Lee Kridler, Mar. 19, 1989; children: Brittani Audra, Houston Scott, Clark Eaton, Sabrina Morrow. BS, U. Tenn., 1976, MS, 1977; PhD, Ohio State U., 1985; cert. interior design, retailing, profl. modeling, Bauder Fashion Coll., Atlanta, 1973. Fashion coord. Bill's Wear House, Newport, Tenn., 1969-77; buyer Shane's Boutique, Gatlinburg, Tenn., 1977-78; instr. Miami U., Oxford, Ohio, 1978-81; asst. prof. U. Tenn., Knoxville, 1985-89; mktg. dir. Profitt's Dept. Stores, Alcoa, Tenn., 1989-90; mktg. cons. Kridler & Kridler Mktg., Newport, Tenn., 1990-93; children's advocate Safe Space, Newport, Tenn., 1993-95. Adj. faculty U. Tenn., Knoxville, 1990-94, Walters State Coll., Morristown, Tenn., 1990-96, Carson Newman Coll., Jefferson City, Tenn., 1993-99; prof., FACS dept. chair East Tenn. State U., 1996—; founding mem. Cmty. House Coop., 1995—; mem., Tenn. evaluator Nation Funding Collaborative on Violence Prevention; participant Children's Def. Fund, Washington, 1992—; founding mem. Cmty. House Co-op; mem. Gov.'s Prevention Initiative and Family Needs Task Force. Costume designer Newport Theatre Guild: Guys and Dolls, Carousel, Fiddler on the Roof, Music Man, Crimes of the Heart, Rumors, Come Back to the Five and Dime, Jimmy Dean, Oliver, The Odd Couple, The Sunshine Boys, Harvey, Miami U. Dance Theatre, Ice Show. Bd. dirs. Safe Space, 1991-92; v.p. Newport Theatre Guild, 1991-92, pres., 1992-96, bd. dirs., 1990-97; dir. Cast and Crew Youth Theatre; creator Looking Glass Players. Named Outstanding Tchr., Miami U., Oxford, 1981, Outstanding Educator, U. Tenn., Knoxville, 1989; recipient numerous grants from univ. and non-profit orgns. Mem. NAACP, Lioness Club, Kappa Omicron Nu. Democrat. Lutheran. Avocations: yogi exercise, fashion design, dance, family activities. Home: 112 Woodlawn Ave Newport TN 37821-3031

KRIEG, JEFFREY JAMES, secondary education educator; b. Mosinee, Wis., Aug. 24, 1963; s. James P. and Jacqueline L. (Kaskavitch) K. BA, Cardinal Stritch Coll., Milw., 1985. Cert. secondary tchr., Wis. Substitute tchr. Wausau (Wis.) Sch. Dist., 1985-87; substitute tchr. D.C. Everest Sch. Dist., Schofield, Wis., 1985-87; tchr. St. Lawrence Sem. H.S., Mt. Calvary, Wis., 1987—, social studies dept. chair, 1988—. Mem. ASCD, Nat. Coun. Social Studies. Republican. Roman Catholic. Avocations: classical music, opera, theater, travel. Home: 1027 Primrose Ln Apt 15 Fond Du Lac WI 54935-1806 Office: St Lawrence Sem H S 301 Church St Mount Calvary WI 53057-9605

KRIEGER, DOLORES ESTHER, retired elementary education educator; b. Ft. Dodge, Iowa, Oct. 22, 1935; d. James William and Grace Dolores (Donovan) Carpenter; m. Duane Art Krieger, June 14, 1958; children: Danette Marie, Diane Ellen, Douglas Arthur. BS, Coll. St. Francis, Joliet, Ill., 1971; MS, No. Ill. U., 1975; student, Alfred Adler Inst., Chgo., 1984-88. Tchr. Jefferson (Iowa) Grade Sch., 1956-58, Rockdale Grade Sch., Joliet, Ill., 1971—, ret., 1994. Creative dramatics tchr. Coll. St. Francis, 1970-72, co-operating tchr., 1980—, adult edn., 1987—; lectr. in field. Author video Successful Parenting Skills. Chairperson Franciscana/Jubilation, St. Francis Acad., 1980's. Fellow AAUW; mem. St. Joseph Med. Ctr. Aux. (sec. 1965-66), Delta Kappa Gamma (corres. sec. 1988-90, membership chmn. 1990—). Democrat. Roman Catholic. Avocations: sailing, golf, writing children stories, bridge, reading. Home: 617 N William St Joliet IL 60435-5939

KRIEGER, MARTIN H. planning and design educator; b. Bklyn., Mar. 10, 1944; s. Louis and Shirley Krieger. BA, Columbia U., 1964, MA, 1965, PhD in Physics, 1969. Lectr., researcher U. Calif., Berkeley, 1968-73; asst. prof. U. Minn., Mpls., 1974-80; lectr., researcher MIT, Cambridge, 1980-84; assoc. prof. planning U. So. Calif., Los Angeles, 1985-92; prof. planning, 1992—. Vis. prof. entrepreneurship U. Mich., 1990-91. Author: Advice and Planning, 1981, Marginalism and Discontinuity, 1989, Doing Physics, 1992, Constitutions of Matter, 1996, Entrepreneurial Vocations, 1996, What's Wrong With Plastic Trees?, 2000, Doing Mathematics, 2003. Fellow: Am. Council Learned Societies, Ctr. for Advanced Study in Behavioral Scis., Nat. Humanities Ctr.; mem. Am. Phys. Soc., History of Sci. Soc., Am. Math. Soc. Office: Univ So Calif Sch Policy Planning & Devel Los Angeles CA 90089-0626

KRIEGER, WILLIAM CARL, English language educator; b. Seattle, Mar. 21, 1946; s. Robert Irving Krieger and Mary Durfee; m. Patricia Kathleen Callow, Aug. 20, 1966 (div. Jan. 2002); children: Richard William, Robert Irving III, Kathleen Elizabeth. BA in English, Pacific Luth. U., Tacoma, 1968, MA in humanities, 1973; PhD in Am. studies, Wash. State U., 1986. Instr. Pierce Coll., Tacoma, 1969-98, prof. English, 1969-98, chmn. English dept., 1973-79, 81-84, 95-98, chmn. humanities divsn., 1979-81, ombudsman, 1995-98; adj. prof., Hist. and English Ctrl. Wash. State U., Wash., 1980; vis. prof., Hist. and English So. Ill. U., Carbondale, Ill., 1981-84, Pacific Luth. U., Tacoma, 1981-84; head wrestling coach Gig Harbor HS, Wash., 1990-95; dean acad. edn., Walla Walla CC, Walla Walla, Wash., 1998—; instr., humanities and comm. Walla Walla CC, Walla Walla, Wash., 2002—. Bd. dir. Thoreau Cabin Project, Tacoma, 1979-98; project dir. Campus Wash. Centennial Project, Tacoma, 1984-89; spl. cons. Clover Park Sch. Dist., Tacoma, 1985; lang. arts cons., Inst. for Citizen Edn. in Law, U. Puget Sound Law Sch., 1990. Author: A Necessary Evil? Sports and Violence, 1998; contbr. Handbook of Pesticide Toxicology, 2nd edit., 2001. Apptd. Wash. State Centennial Commn., Constrn. Com., Pierce Couny Centennial Com.; mem. bd. dir. Tacoma Symphony; choir dir. Rosedale Ch.; mem. Peninsula Cmty. Chorus, 1993-97, pres., 1995; dir. Peninsula Madrigal Singers, 1995-97; active Tacoma Opera Chorus, 1997-98; co-prodr. summer musical Walla Walla Cmty. Coll. Found., 2001, 02, 03. Recipient: Disting. Achievement Award Wash. State Centennial Commn., 1989, Outstanding Achievement Award Pierce County Centennial Commn., 1989, Centennial Alumni recognition Pacific Luth. U., Tacoma, 1990; named Outstanding Tchr. Nat. Inst. Staff and Orgnl. Devel., 1992; NEH rsch. fellow Johns Hopkins U. and Peabody Conservatory of Music, 1994. Mem. (life) Thoreau Soc., Community Coll. Humanities Assn. (standing com. 1982-83), Am. Studies Assn., Wash. Community Coll. Humanities Assn. (bd. dir. 1982-84, grantee, 1984), Western Wash. Ofcl. Assn. Avocations: officiating high sch. and coll. football and wrestling, hiking, powerlifting, poetry, vocal music. Office: Walla Walla Comty Coll 500 Tausick Way Walla Walla WA 99362-9270 Home: 653 E Chestnut St Walla Walla WA 99362-3323 E-mail: blitz@bmi.net., william.krieger@wwcc.ctc.edu.

KRIEGMAN, SUSAN L. artist, art educator; d. Leonard W. and Frances K. BS in Art Edn., U. Vt., 1972; MFA, Washington U., St. Louis, 1976; postgrad., Columbia U. Cert. tchr. art K-12. Instr. art, metalsmithing and jewelry design Washington U., St. Louis, 1974-76; instr. art, metalsmithing and jewelry No. Mich. U., Marquette, 1976-77; art specialist N.J. Pub. Schs., Piscataway, Somerville, Roosevelt and Montgomery Twps., 1979-89, So. Brunswick (N.J.) Pub. Schs., 1989—. Vis. prof. Ctr. for Creative Studies, Detroit, 1987-88; adj. art edn. and jewelry prof. Kean U., Union, N.J., 1994-98; bd. dirs. Peters Valley Craft Ctr., Layton, N.J., 1988-94; cons. Ednl. Testing Svc., 1994-98; dir. The Craft Experience in Art Edn. Conf., 1993-96; adj. art educator Columbia U., 1993-96; dir., curator The Craft Experience in Art Edn. ann. nat. conf. at TC Columbia U., 1993, 94, 95, 96; art edn. del. People to People Internat., Australia and New Zealand, 1998. Exhbns. include No. Mich. U., 1977, U. So. Miss., 1978, U. Pa., 1978, Washington U. Sch. Art, 1979, Morris Mus., U. Ariz., 1980, Morristown, N.J., 1984, 91, 94, Noyes Mus., N.J., 1984, Monclair State Coll., N.J., 1984, 87, Coll. N.J., 1985, Downey Mus. Art, Calif., 1986, N.J.

State Mus., 1986, 92, 96, Montclair Art Mus., N.J., 1986, Nabisco Corp. Hdqs. Art Invitational, 1986, N.J. Arts Anns., 1986, 91, 92, 93, 95, 96, Nat. Ornamental Metal Mus., Memphis, 1989, 92, 93, San Francisco State U., 1989, U. Del., 1990, Johnson & Johnson Corp. Hdqs. Art Invitational, 1991, Schering-Plough Corp. Hdqs. Art Invitational, 1991, Pro Art Heikki Seppa Art Invitational, St. Louis, 1992, La. State U., 1992, Anderson Mus. Art, Miss., 1992, Brown U., 1992, Colombia U., 1993, Newark Mus., 1995, Zimmerli Art Mus., N.J., ; presenter of workshops and seminars in field. VISTA vol., early childhood curriculum specialist Honolulu Cmty. Action Program Head Start, 1972-73. Fellow Jewish Mus., 1986, N.J. State Coun. Arts, 1983, 86, 89; recipient Geraldine Dodge Found. Artist/Educator award, 1993, 94, 97, 98, 2000, 03, fellow, 1993, Craft Concepts award of distinction, 1986, Tchr. INst. fellow Nat. Gallery Art, 1999; Profl. Devel. grantee S. Brunswick Bd. of Edn., 1992, 93, 94, 95, 96, 98; named one of 50 Dist. Alumni Washington U. Sch. Art Centennial Celebration, 1979. Mem. NEA, Nat. Art Edn. Assn., Am. Craft Coun., Soc. N.Am. Goldsmiths (life disting.), N.J. Edn. Assn. Office: S Brunswick Bd Edn 4 Exec Dr Monmouth Junction NJ 08852

KRIEGSTEIN, HELENE LESLY, secondary education educator; b. L.A., July 10, 1967; d. Fred S. and Elaine (Ogulnick) K. BS, SUNY, Oneonta, 1989; MA, SUNY, Stony Brook, 1993. Cert. tchr., N.Y. Tchr. math. Ward Melville High Sch., East Setauket, N.Y., 1990-91, Plainedge High Sch., North Massapequa, N.Y., 1991—. In-svc. trainer Coop. Learning Plainedge Cen. Sch. Dist., 1992. Mem. ASCD, Nat. Coun. Tchrs. Math. Office: Plainedge Ctrl Sch Dist Peony And Wyngate Dr North Massapequa NY 11758

KRIER, JAMES EDWARD, law educator, writer; b. Milw., Oct. 19, 1939; s. Ambrose Edward and Genevieve Ida (Behling) Krier; m. Gayle Marian Grimsrud, Mar. 22, 1962 (div.); children: Jennifer, Amy; m. Wendy Louise Wilkes, Apr. 20, 1974; children: Andrew Wilkes-Krier, Patrick Wilkes-Krier. BS, U. Wis., 1961, JD, 1966. Bar: Wis. 1966, U.S. Ct. Claims 1968. Law clk. to chief justice Calif. Supreme Ct., San Francisco, 1966-67; assoc. Arnold & Porter, Washington, 1967-69; acting prof., then prof. law UCLA, 1969-78, 80-83; prof. law Stanford U., Calif., 1978-80, U. Mich. Law Sch., Ann Arbor, 1983—, Earl Warren DeLano prof., 1988—. Cons. Calif. Inst. Tech., EPA; mem. pesticide panel NAS, 1972—75, mem. com. energy and the environment, 1975—77. Author: (book) Environmental Law and Policy, 1971; author: (with Stewart) Environmental Law and Policy, 2d edit., 1978; author: (with Ursin) Pollution and Policy, 1977; author: (with Dukeminier) Property, 1981, Property, 5th edit., 2002; contbr. articles to profl. jours. Served to lt. U.S. Army, 1961—63. Mem.: Order of Coif, Artus, Phi Kappa Phi. Office: U Mich Law Sch 625 S State St Ann Arbor MI 48109-1215 E-mail: jkrier@umich.edu.

KRIMS, LES, artist; b. N.Y.C., Aug. 16, 1942; s. Leo and Sally (Leibowitz) K.; m. Patricia Louise O'Brien, Dec. 28, 1985; 1 child, Lauren. BFA, Cooper Union, 1964; MFA, Pratt Inst., 1967. Instr. Rochester (N.Y.) Inst. Tech., 1967-69; asst. prof. Buffalo State Coll., 1969-75, assoc. prof., 1975-79, prof., 1980—. Author: (books of photographs) Fictcryptokrimsographs, 1975, The Incredible Case of the Stack O'Wheats Murders, 1972, The People of America, 1971, The Deerslayers; (original print portfolio) Idiosyncratic Pictures, 1980; (32 offset prints) Les Krims: Kodalith Images, 1968-75; one-man shows include Pratt Inst., Bklyn., 1966, Focus Gallery, San Francisco, 1969, Il Diaframma Gallery, Milan, George Eastman House, Rochester, N.Y., 1971, Witkin Gallery, N.Y.C., 1972, Galerie Delpire, Paris, 1974, Galerie Die Brucke, Vienna, Austria, 1975, Light Gallery, N.Y.C., 1978, Oreg. Ctr. for Photographic Arts, Portland, 1990, Centre de la Photographie Geneve, Geneva, Switzerland, 1993, VI Biennale Internazionale de Fotografia, Torino, Italy, 1995, Monterey (Calif.) Mus. of Art, 1999; exhibited in group shows at Mus. Modern Art, N.Y.C., 1978, Nat. Mus. Modern Art, Kyoto, Japan, 1987, III Fotobienal-Vigo, Spain, 1988, Maison Européenne de la Photographie, Paris, 1996, Neue Galerie Graz, Austria, 2003, others. NEA grantee, 1971, 72, 76. Office: Buffalo State Coll 1300 Elmwood Ave Buffalo NY 14222-1004

KRISH, RAYMOND PETER, computer technology coordinator, educator; b. Bridgeport, Conn., Dec. 14, 1943; s. Peter Edward and Mary Veronica (Misencik) K.; m. Elaine Anne Winoski, June 17, 1967; children: Janice Anne, Kevin William. BS, U. Conn., 1967; MS, So. Conn. State U., New Haven, 1971, Edn. Specialist, 1975; PhD, NYU, 1994. Cert. K-12 tchr., intermediate adminstrn.-supervision, sch. dist. adminstrn. Elem. tchr. Monroe (Conn.) Pub. Schs., 1970-84; dist. computer coord. Locust Valley (N.Y.) Schs., 1984-90; dir. computers Byram Hills Sch. Dist., Armonk, N.Y., 1990-92; computer tchr., coord. Region #10 Schs., Burlington, Conn., 1994-95; mid. sch. tchr. sci. Bridgeport (Conn.) Pub. Schs., 1967-70, coord. computer tech., 1995—. Owner Aladdin Prodns., Southbury, Conn., 1980-2001, Club 2! In-Home Tutoring Franchise, 2001—. Leader, organizer Southbury Bus. Assn. 10-K Road Race, 1993, 94. Named Outstanding Tech. Educator N.Y. State Computer and Tech. Assn., 1989-90. Mem. NEA, Conn. Educators Computer Assn., Danbury Area Computer Soc. Avocations: skiing, travel, swimming.

KRISTENSEN, KATHLEEN HOWARD, music educator; b. Salt Lake City, May 10, 1939; d. Erin Neils and Verdis Eliza (Berrett) Howard; m. Karl G. Topham (div. 1968); children: Stephanie T. Fullmer, Amelia T. Curtis, Suzanne T. Jones, David Howard Topham; m. Paul Kristensen, June 21, 1983. Student, Brigham Young U., 1957-59, U. Utah, 1970-72. Mem. Mormon Tabernacle Choir, 1972-79, 87-2000. Mem. Am. Guild Organists (sub-dean), Nat. Assn. Tchrs. Singing, Nat. Assn. Music, Utah Music Tchrs. Republican. Mem. Lds Ch. Home: 2146 E 7420 S Salt Lake City UT 84121-4925

KRISTENSEN, MARLENE, early childhood education educator; b. Baudette, Minn., Sept. 1, 1932; d. Glenn Edward and Frances Emma (Wilson) Munson; m. Robert A. Kristensen, June 5, 1955; children: Mary Kristensen-Quinlan, Debra Kristensen-Anderson. BA, Concordia Coll., Moorhead, Minn., 1954; student, Everett Community Coll., 1973, Edmonds Community Coll., 1974—; postgrad., Cen. Wash. U. From asst. dir. to dir. Lynnwood (Wash.) Day Care, 1974-84; kindergarten tchr. Edmonds (Wash.) Sch. Dist., 1957-58; tchr. trainer Children's World Learning Ctr., Edmonds, 1984-93; ret., 1993. Honor roll tchr., 1987-91. Mem. tchrs.' adv. bd. Weekly Reader Publs., 1991-93. Mem. ASCD, Nat. Assn. for Edn. Young Children.

KRITCHEVSKY, DAVID, biochemist, educator; b. Kharkov, Russia, Jan. 25, 1920; came to U.S., 1923, naturalized, 1929; s. Jacob and Leah (Kritchevsky) K.; m. Evelyn Sholtes, Dec. 21, 1947; children: Barbara Ann, Janice Eileen, Stephen Bennett. BS, U. Chgo., 1939, MS, 1942; PhD, Northwestern U., 1948; DSc (hon.), Purdue U., 2001. Chemist Ninol Labs., Chgo., 1939-46; postdoctoral fellow Fed. Inst. Tech., Zurich, Switzerland, 1948-49; biochemist Radiation Lab., U. Calif. at Berkeley, 1950-52, Lederle Lab., Pearl River, N.Y., 1952-57, Wistar Inst., Phila., 1957—; prof. biochemistry Sch. Vet. Medicine U. Pa., Phila., 1965—; prof. emeritus, 1992—; prof. biochemistry Sch. Medicine U. Pa., 1970—81, chmn. grad. group molecular biology, 1972-84. Mem. USPHS study sect. Nat. Heart Inst., 1964-68, 72-76; chmn. rsch. com. Spl. Dairy Industry Bd., 1963-70; food and nutrition bd. NAS, 1976-82. Author: Cholesterol, 1958; editor: (with G. Litwack) Actions of Hormones on Molecular Processes, 1964; co-editor: (with R. Paoletti) Advances in Lipid Research, 1963-89, (with P. Nair) 1973, Bile Acids, 1971; Western Hemisphere editor Atherosclerosis, 1978-90, cons. editor, 1990—; contbr. articles to profl. jours. Recipient Rsch. Career award Nat. Heart Inst., 1962, Herman award Am. Soc. Clin. Nutrition, 1992, Disting. Svc. award U. N.C. Inst. Nutrition, 1993, Auenbrugger medal U. Graz, Austria, 1994, SUPELCO/AOCS award, 1996, Lifetime Achievement award Am. Inst. for Cancer Rsch., 1996; Caspar Wistar scholar, 1992. Fellow: AAAS, Am. Soc. Oil Chemists (chmn. methods com. 1963—64), Am. Coll. Nutrition (award 1978), Am. Inst. Nutrition (pres. 1979, Borden award 1974), Am. Oil Chemists Soc.; mem.: Am. Oil Chemistry Soc., Internat. Soc. Fat Rsch., Am. Heart Assn. (spl. recognition coun. on atherosclerosis 1993), Arteriosclerosis Coun., Soc. Exptl. Biology and Medicine (pres. 1985—87), Am. Chem. Soc. (award Phila. sect. 1977), Am. Soc. Biol. Chemists. Achievements include research on role vehicle when cholesterol and fat produces atherosclerosis in rabbits, effects of saturated and unsaturated fat, deposition of orally administered cholesterol in aorta of man and rabbit, caloric restriction and cancer. Home: 136 Lee Cir Bryn Mawr PA 19010-3724 Office: Wistar Inst 36th And Spruce St Philadelphia PA 19104-4268 E-mail: kritchevsky@wistar.upenn.edu.

KRITZMAN, LAWRENCE DAVID, humanities educator; b. N.Y.C. s. Melvin M. and Margy (Rosenstein) K.; m. Janie L. Kritzman; 1 child, Jeremy. BA, U. Wis., 1969; AM, Middlebury Coll., 1970; PhD, U. Mich., 1976. Lectr. Rutgers U., New Brunswick, N.J., 1976-77, asst. prof., 1977-82, assoc. prof., dir. grad. studies, 1982-87; prof. French civilization Ohio State U., Columbus, 1987-89; prof. French & comparative lit. Dartmouth Coll., Hanover, N.H., 1989—, Edward Tuck prof. French, 1994—, chair comparative lit. dept., 1992-95, Ted and Helen Geisel Third Century prof. in the humanities, 1995—2002, Pat and John Rosenwald rsch. prof. in Arts and Scis., 2002—. Chair Com. for Future of French Studies, French Embassy, N.Y., 1991—; vis. prof. U. Mich., Ann Arbor, 1991, 93, Duke NEH Inst., 1986, 90, Northwestern NEH Inst., assoc. dir., 1995; vis. prof. Stanford U., 1999, Harvard U., 2001, 2003. Author: Destruction/Découverte, 1980, Rhetoric of Sexuality and Literature fo French Renaissance, 1991; editor: Fragments, 1981, France Under Mitterand, 1984, Foucault: Politics, Philosophy, Culture, 1988, Le Signe et le Texte, 1989, Auschwitz & After: Race, Culture & The Jewish Question in France, 1995; mem. editl. bd.: Etudes Montaignistes, 1988, Montaigne Studies, Early Modern Culture, Studies in 20th Century Literature, Contemporary French Civilization Sites, French Forum, Sites, gen. editor: European Perspectives, 1989—, Columbia U. Press, —, mem. adv. bd.: French Politics and Society, —; contbr. numerous articles to profl. jours., numerous chpts. to books. Chair Com. Future of French Studies in U.S.; dir. Edward Morot-Inst. French Cultural Studies, 1994, 1997, 1999, 2001, 2003. Recipient Chevalier de l'Ordre des Palmes Academics, French Govt., 1991, Ordre National de Merite by Pres. France, 2000; Officier des Palmes des Palmes Academics, 1994; sr. fellow Am. Coun. Learned Soc., 1989; Andrew W. Mellon Found. grant Duke U., 1980. Mem. MLA, Am. Coun. French Social and Cultural Affairs, Nat. Writer's Union, Am. Comparative Lit. Assn., Acad. Lit. Studies. Home: 24 Warwick Rd Brookline MA 02445 Office: Dept French Dartmouth Coll Hanover NH 03755

KRIZEK, RAYMOND JOHN, civil engineering educator, consultant; b. Balt., June 5, 1932; s. John James and Louise (Polak) K.; m. Claudia Stricker, Aug. 1964; children— Robert A., Kevin J. BE, Johns Hopkins U., 1954; MS, U. Md., 1961; PhD, Northwestern U., 1963. Instr. U. Md., College Park, 1957-61; rsch. asst. civil engring. Northwestern U., Evanston, Ill., 1961-63, asst. prof. civil engring., 1963-66, assoc. prof. civil engring., 1966-70, prof. civil engring., 1970—, chmn. dept. civil engring., 1980-92, dir. Master of Project Mgmt. program, 1994—, Stanley F. Pepper chair prof., 1987—. Cons. to industry Editor books; contbr. numerous articles to profl. jours. Served to lt. U.S. Army, 1955-57 Decorated Palmes Academiques (France), 1993; recipient Hogentogler award ASTM, 1970; named disting. vis. scholar NSF, 1972. Mem.: ASCE (pres. GEO Inst. 1997—98, Huber Rsch. prize 1971, Karl Terzaghi award 1997, Ill. sect. Civil Engr. of Yr. 1999, Hon. mem. 2002, Wallace Hayward Baker award Geo-Inst. 2003), Internat. Soc. Soil Mechanics and Geotech. Engring., Nat. Acad. Engring., Spanish Acad. Engring. (corr.). Roman Catholic. Home: 1366 Sanford Ln Glenview IL 60025-3165 Office: Dept Civil Engring Northwestern U 2145 Sheridan Rd Evanston IL 60208-3109

KRNJEVIC, KRESIMIR IVAN, neurophysiologist; b. Zagreb, Croatia, Yugoslavia, Sept. 7, 1927; arrived in Canada, 1964; s. Juraj Krnjevic and Nada K. (Hirsl) Krnjevic Marullaz; m. Jeanne W. Bowyer, Sept. 27, 1954; children— Peter Juraj, Nicholas John M.B.Ch.B., Edinburg U., Scotland, 1949; BSc with honors, Edinburgh U., Scotland, 1951, PhD, 1953. Joseph Morley Drake prof. physiology, chmn. dept. McGill U., Montreal, Canada, 1978-87, dir. dept. anaesthesia research, 1965—. Contbr. articles to profl. jours.; editor Can. Jour. Physiology and Pharmacology, 1972-78 Bd. govs. Montreal Children's Hosp. Rsch. Inst., 1982-88. Named to Order of Can., 1987; recipient Sarrazin award Can. Physiol. Soc., 1984, Gairdner Found award, 1984; Beit Meml. fellow U. Edinburgh, 1952-54 Fellow Royal Soc. Canada; mem. Can. Physiol. Soc. (pres. 1979-80), Internat. Union of Physiol. Socs. (council mem. 1983—, chmn. admissions commn.) Avocations: mountaineering; skiing; swimming; reading; music. Office: McGill Univ Dept Anaesthesia Rsch 3655 Drummond St Montreal QC Canada H3G 1Y6

KROEBER, KARL, English language educator; b. Oakland, Calif., Nov. 24, 1926; s. Alfred Louis and Theodora Quinn (Kracaw) K.; m. Jean Taylor, Mar. 21, 1953; children— Paul Demarest, Arthur Romeyn, Katharine. AA, Coll. of Pacific, Stockton, Calif., 1945; AB, U. Calif., Berkeley, 1947; MA, Columbia U., 1951, PhD, 1956. Asst. prof. U. Wis.-Madison, 1956-61, asso. prof., 1961-63, prof., 1963-70; asso. dean U. Wis.-Madison (Grad. Sch.), 1963-65; prof. English and comparative lit. Columbia U., N.Y.C., 1970—, chmn. dept. English and comparative lit., 1973-76, Mellon prof. humanities, 1987. Author: Romantic Narrative Art, 1960, The Artifice of Reality, 1964, Studying Poetry, 1965, Backgrounds to British Romantic Literature, 1968, Styles in Fictional Structure, 1971, Romantic Landscape Vision, 1975, Images of Romanticism, 1978, Traditional Literatures of the American Indian, 1981, rev. edit. 1997, Wordsworthian Scholarship and Criticism, 1973-84, 1986, British Romantic Art, 1986, Romantic Fantasy and Science Fiction, 1988, Retelling/Rereading, 1992, Romantic Poetry: Recent Revisionary Criticism, 1993, Native American Persistence and Resurgence, 1994, Ecological Literary Criticism, 1994, Artistry in Native American Myths, 1998, Ishi in Three Centuries, 2003; emeritus editor Studies in American Indian Literatures; mem. editorial bd. The Wordsworth Circle, Native American Bibiliography Series, Studies in English Lit., Boundary 2, European Romantic Review. Served with USNR, 1944-46. Named Disting. Scholar, Keats-Shelley Assn., 1991; Fulbright Rsch. grantee Italy, 1960-61, U.S. Office Edn. Rsch. grantee, 1965-66; Guggenheim fellow, 1966-67; NEH fellow, 1991. Mem. MLA, Internat. Assn. Univ. Profs. English, N.Am. Soc. Study of Romanticism, Jane Austen Soc. N.Am., Acad. Lit. Studies, Byron Soc., Assn. for Study of Native Am. Lit., Keats-Shelley Assn. Home: 226 Saint Johns Pl Brooklyn NY 11217-3406 Office: Columbia U Dept English & Comparative Lit New York NY 10027 Business E-Mail: kk17@columbia.edu.

KROGSTAD, JACK LYNN, associate dean, accounting educator; b. Harlan, Iowa, Jan. 27, 1944; s. Chester Milo and Geraldine Elizabeth (Archibald) K.; m. Nancy Ellen Coffin, June 18, 1967; children: Kristine Ellen, Brian Lynn. BS, Union Coll., 1967; MBA, U. Nebr., 1971, PhD, 1975. Staff acct. Trachtenbarg & Grant CPAs, Lincoln, Nebr., 1967-68; asst. prof. U. Tex., Austin, 1975-78; assoc. prof. Kans. State U., Manhattan, 1978-80; John P. Begley prof. acctg. Crieghton U., Omaha, 1980-96, prof. acctg., 1997—, assoc. dean, 2000—. Vis. assoc. prof. U. Mich., Ann Arbor, 1980; vis. prof. U. Ill. 2000-; dir. rsch. Nat. Commn. Fraudulent Fin. Reporting, 1985-87. Editor: Auditing: A Journal of Practice and Theory; contbr. articles to profl. jours. With U.S. Army, 1968-70. Recipient Disting. Faculty Svc. award Crieghton U., 1988; Arthur Anderson & Co. doctoral fellow, 1974-75, Paton Acctg. Ctr. rsch. fellow, 1980, Barret Disting. Svc. award, 2002, Coll. Faculty of the Yr. award, 2001. Mem. AICPA, Nebr. Soc. CPAs (Acctg. Educator of Yr. award 1983), Am. Acctg. Assn. (regional v.p. 1984-85, auditing sect. chmn. 1984-85, Outstanding Auditing Educator award 1994), Beta Gamma Sigma, Beta Alpha Psi. Republican. Seventh-Day-Adventist. Home: 56717 Deacon Rd Pacific Junction IA 51561-4169 E-mail: jkrogstad@creighton..edu.

KROHN, KENNETH ALBERT, radiology educator; b. Stevens Point, Wis., June 19, 1945; s. Albert William and Erma Belle (Cornwell) K.; 1 child, Galen. BA in Chemistry, Andrews U., 1966; PhD in Chemistry, U. Calif., 1971. Acting assoc. prof. U. Wash., Seattle, 1981-84, assoc. prof. radiology, 1984-86, prof. radiology and radiation oncology, 1986—, adj. prof. chemistry, 1986—. Guest scientist Donner Lab. Lawrence Berkeley (Calif.) Lab., 1980-81; radiochemist, VA Med. Ctr., Seattle, 1982—; affiliate investigator Fred Hutchinson Cancer Rsch. Ctr., 1997—. Contbr. articles to profl. jours.; patentee in field. Recipient Aebersold award, 1996; fellow, NDEA. Fellow AAAS; mem. Am. Assn. for Cancer Rsch., Am. Chem. Soc., Radiation Rsch. Soc., Soc. Nuclear Medicine, Acad. Coun., Sigma Xi. Home: 550 NE Lakeridge Dr Belfair WA 98528-8720 Office: U Washington Imaging Rsch Lab Box 356004 Seattle WA 98195-6004 E-mail: kkrohn@u.washington.edu.

KROLIK, JULIAN HENRY, astrophysicist, educator; b. Detroit, Apr. 4, 1950; m. Elaine F. Weiss, Oct. 9, 1983; children: Theodore, Abigail. BS, MIT, 1971; PhD, U. Calif., Berkeley, 1977. Mem. Inst. for Advanced Study, Princeton, N.J., 1977-79; postdoctoral scientist MIT, Cambridge, Mass., 1979-81; rsch. assoc. Harvard U., Cambridge, Mass., 1981-84; asst. prof. Johns Hopkins U., Balt., 1984-86, assoc. prof., 1986-91, prof., 1991—. Office: Johns Hopkins Univ Dept Of Physics Astron Baltimore MD 21218

KROLL, DENNIS EDWARDS, industrial engineering educator; b. Chgo., June 7, 1947; s. Witold Charles and Lillian Mary (Zwic) K.; m. Susan Ann Michalski, May 26, 1973 (div. Dec. 1979); children: Steven Edward, Brian Christopher; m. Karen Elizabeth Wood, Jan. 13, 1990 (div. Sept. 1994); m. Carolyn S. Clark, Nov. 25, 2000. BS in Indsl. Engring., Bradley U., 1970; MS in Indsl. Engring., U. Wis., 1973; PhD, U. Ill., 1989. Devel. engr. Western Electric Co., Chgo., 1970-74; plant mgr. Junis Mfg. Co., Franklin Park, Ill., 1974-75; sr. indsl. engr. Sunbeam Appliance Co., Chgo., 1975-76; sr. mfg. engr. Victor Comptometer, Chgo., 1976; indsl. engr. Methode Mfg., Rolling Meadows, Ill., 1976-77; planning engr. Western Electric div. AT&T Tech., Lisle, Ill., 1977-81; prof. indsl. and mfg. engring. Bradley U., Peoria, Ill., 1981—. Founding editor Jour. Indsl. Engring. Design, 1995—; contbr. articles to profl. jours., chpts. to books. Precinct committeeman Peoria Rep. Com., 1981-82., Woodford County, 2002—; bd. dirs. West Peoria (Ill.) Street Light Dist., 1991-95; founding alderman City of West Peoria, 1993-2000; mem. Peoria Water Adv. Com., 1999-2000; mem. Eureka2000plus commn., 2001—; precinct committeeman Woodford Rep. Com., 2002—. Recipient lab. devel. award Soc. Mfg. Engrs., 1990, Simulation Lab. Devel. award St. Francis Med. Ctr., 1995, Bradley virtual course devel. award, 2001. Mem. Soc. Mfg. Engrs. (sr.), Inst. Indsl. Engrs. (sr.; cert. sys. integrator, chpt. pres. 1982-83, 94-95), Am. Legion, Planetary Soc., Am. Soc. for Engring. Edn. (IE Divsn. webmaster, sec., newsletter editor, chair). Roman Catholic. Avocations: fishing, gardening, cooking, history. Office: Bradley U IMET Morgan 110 1501 W Bradley Ave Peoria IL 61625-0003 E-mail: dek@bradley.edu.

KROLL, PAUL BENEDICT, insurance consultant; b. Ft. Ord, Calif., Oct. 24, 1954; s. Harry Gardner and Jane Ellen (Cornwell) K.; 1 child, Dane Garcia. BA, Kans. Wesleyan U., 1977; MS, Emporia State U., 1979, MBA, 1983; cert. tchr., Washburn U., 1990. Cert. tchr., Tex. Pension adminstr. Kansas City (Mo.) Life Ins., 1980-82; actuary Victory Life Ins. Co., Topeka, 1983-85; actuarial analyst Security Trust Life Ins., Macon, Ga., 1985-87; policy examiner Kans. Ins. Dept., Topeka, 1987-88; adj. instr. math. Highland (Kans.) C.C., 1991-93; premium auditor Mountain States Mus. Cos., Albuquerque, 1995—2001; rep. Farmers Ins. Group. Kroll Ins. Cons., 2002—. Author: The Student's T Distribution, 1979. Mem. Ins. Inst. Am. (assoc. premium auditor), Am. Inst. Cert. Property and Casualty Underwriters (cert. property and casualty underwriter). Avocations: short wave listening, bird watching, bicycling. Office: 4255 Irving Ave N Minneapolis MN 55412 E-mail: krollic@juno.com.

KROMM, DAVID ELWYN, geography educator; b. Grosse Pointe, Mich., Sept. 1, 1938; s. Elwyn Benjamin and Isabel Wilhemina (Henning) K.; m. Roberta Joan Retzel, Sept. 17, 1960; children: David, Randall, Christopher. BS cum laude, Eastern Mich. U., 1960; MA, Mich. State U., 1964, PhD, 1967. Prof. geography Kans. State U., Manhattan, 1967—2002. Author: World Regional Geography, 1981; editor, author: Groundwater Exploitation in High Plains, 1992; contbr. numerous articles to profl. jours. Capt. U.S. Army, 1960-67. Named Outstanding Tchr. at Kans. State U., 1972; Phi Kappa Phi scholar Kans. State U., 1999; recipient numerous grants in field. Mem. Assn. Am. Geographers, Nat. Coun. Geog. Edn. (exec. bd. 1986-88, Disting. Teaching award 1994), Kans. Acad. Sci. (coun. mem. 1976-77), Nat. Geog. Soc. Avocations: photography, fgn. travel. Office: Kansas State U Dept Of Geography Manhattan KS 66506

KROMMINGA, AN-MARIE, special education educator; b. Yakima, Washington, Mar. 23, 1936; d. Fred Henry and Edith Bessie Jackson; m. William Reynold Kromminga, Aug. 23, 1956. BA in Edn., Walla Walla College, 1958. Cert. profl. educator K-12 spl. edn., K-8 elem. edn., P-3 early childhood spl. edn., early childhood edn. Washington. Tchr. grades 1-7 Upper Columbia Conf. of Seventh-Day Adventist, Toppenish, Wash., 1955—56, tachr. grades 1-4 Wapato, Wash., 1959—60; tchr. grades 5-6 Ill. Conf. of Seventh-Day Adventist, Aurora, 1963—64, tchr. grades 1-8 Canton, 1972—74; substitute and homebound tchg. various schs., Ill., 1974—79; homemaking skills tchr. Ill. Dept. Children and Family Svcs., Sterling, 1979—81; home products ind. dealer, unit sales leader, to dist. leader Stanley Home Products Inc., Ill. and Wash., 1975—; presch./kindergarten tchr. Upper Columbia Conf. of Seventh-Day Adventists, Pasco, Wash., 1986—90; life skills spl. edn. tchr. Kiona-Benton Sch. Dist. 52, Benton City, Wash., 1990—. Chair Work Opportunities for Rural Kids, Benton City, 1990—96, Spl. Edn. Parent Group, Benton City, 1990—96; mem. Tri-Cities (Wash.) Transition Team, 1990—. Author: History of Benton City, Washington, 2000; contbr. articles to ch. newsletters and publs. Active disaster relief and cmty. svc. Seventh-Day Adventist Ch., 1963—79; leader for children's clubs and recreation programs for cmty. and ch., 1963—79. Recipient Tri City Crystal Apple award for excellence in edn., various cmty. svc. groups, bus., and orgns., 2002. Mem.: Coun. for Exceptional Children. Seventh Day Adventist. Avocations: dolls, music boxes, leathercraft, travel. Home: 1004 Frontier PR NE Benton City WA 99320

KRON, LEO, psychiatrist, educator; b. Aug. 1, 1946; m. Jill Rubin, Dec. 31, 1979; children: Joshua, Emily. MD, U. B.C., Vancouver, Can., 1971. Diplomate Am. Bd. Psychiatry and Neurology, Am. Bd. Child Psychiatry. Intern Queens Med. Ctr., Honolulu, 1971-72; resident in psychiatry Albert Einstein Coll. Medicine, N.Y.C., 1973-76; resident in child psychiatry Columbia U. Coll. Physicians and Surgeons, N.Y.C., 1976-78, asst. clin. prof. psychiatry, 1986—; tng. in psychoanalysis N.Y. Psychoanalytic Inst., N.Y.C.; pvt. practice, N.Y.C., 1976—. Dir. div. child and adolescent psychiatry St. Luke's Hosp. Ctr., N.Y.C., 1986-90; corp. dir. divsn. child and adolescent psychiatry St. Luke's-Roosevelt Hosp. Ctr., N.Y.C., 1990-93, dir. consultation and liaison, 1994—; psychiat. cons. Assn. To Benefit Children, N.Y.C., 1995—, Hunter Coll., CUNY, 1989—. Contbr. numerous articles to med. jours., chpts. to books. Fellow Royal Coll. Physicians Canada; mem. Am. Psychiat. Assn., Am. Acad. Child and Adolescent Psychiatry, Am. Soc. Clin. Psychopharmacology, Can. Med. Assn., N.Y. Psychoanalytic Soc. Office: 30 E 76th St Apt 3A New York NY 10021-2765

KRONIK, JOHN WILLIAM, Romance studies educator; b. Vienna, May 18, 1931; arrived in U.S., 1939, naturalized, 1944; s. Bernard and Melanie (Hollub) K.; m. Eva Kronik, Dec. 26, 1955; children: Theresa J., Geoffrey B. BA, Queens Coll., 1952; MA, U. Wis., 1953, PhD, 1960; DHL, Ill. Coll., 1979. Asst. prof. Romance lang. Hamilton Coll., Clinton, 1958-63; assoc. prof. Spanish, U. Ill., Urbana, 1963-66; prof. Romance studies Cornell U., Ithaca, N.Y., 1966-2000, prof. emeritus, 2001—. Vis. prof. Columbia U., 1968, Middlebury Coll., Vt., 1979, 80, 86, 91, Brigham Young U., 1982, U. Colo., 1989, U. Calif., Berkeley, 91, U. Calif., Irvine, 1994, U. Calif., L.A., 1999, 2000, U. Calif., Riverside, 2003; cons. NEH, 1973-92, Guggenheim Found., 1988—; corporator Internat. Inst. in Spain, Madrid, 1972—. Author: La farsa y el teatro espanol, 1971; co-editor: La familia de Pascual Duarte, 1961, Textos y Contextos de Galdos, 1994, Intertextual Pursuits: Literary Mediations in Modern Spanish Narrative, 1998; series editor Prentice-Hall, 1962-75; mem. editl. bd. MLA, N.Y.C., 1983-85; editor PMLA, 1985-92, Anales Galdosianos, 1986-90; contbr. articles to profl. jours. With U.S. Army, 1953—55. Fulbright fellow, 1960-61, 87-88; Rockefeller Found. rsch. resident, 1975; Guggenheim fellow, 1983-84; ACLS grantee, 1983-84. Mem. MLA, Internat. Assn. Hispanists, Internat. Galdos Assn. (pres.), Am. Assn. Tchrs. Spanish and Portuguese. Home: 1020 Highland Rd Ithaca NY 14850-1448 Office: Cornell U Dept Romance Studies Ithaca NY 14853-4701

KRONMAN, ANTHONY TOWNSEND, law educator, dean; b. 1945; m. Nancy I. Greenberg, 1982 BA, Williams Coll., 1968, PhD, 1972; JD, Yale U., 1975. Bar: Minn. 1975, N.Y. 1983. Assoc. prof. U. Minn., 1975-76; asst. prof. U. Chgo., 1976-79; vis. assoc. prof. Yale U. Law Sch., New Haven, 1978-79, prof., 1979—, Edward J. Phelps prof. law, 1985—, dean, 1994—. Editor: (with R. Posner) The Economics of Contract Law, 1979 (with F. Kessler and G. Gilmore) Cases and Materials on Contracts, 1986; past mem. editorial bd. Yale Law Jour.; author: Max Weber, 1983, The Lost Lawyer, 1993. Danforth Found. fellow, 1968-72 Fellow ABA, Am. Acad. Arts and Scis.; mem. Selden Soc., Conn. Bar Assn. (Cooper fellow), Coun. on Fgn. Rels. Office: Yale U Law Sch PO Box 208215 New Haven CT 06520-8215

KROOTH, RICHARD, sociology and political studies educator; b. Chgo., May 8, 1935; s. Arthur Louis Wolf and Helen Löwenrosen (Feldman/Wasservogel) K.; m. Ann Baxandall, Aug. 30, 1963; 1 child, Karl William. BS, DePaul U., 1958; JD, U. Wis., 1962; PhD in Sociology, U. Calif., Santa Barbara, 1981. Bar: Ga. 1964. Ptnr. Krooth & Krooth, Atlanta, 1962; editor in chief Harvest Pub., Berkeley, Calif., 1975—. Rsch. dir. Harvest Pubs., Berkeley, 1975—; econ. cons. Euro/Pacific Group, Berkeley and San Francisco, 1984—; jury cons. Jury Consulting Svcs., Santa Cruz, Calif., 1989—; assoc. and vis. scholar, prof., rschr. U. Calif., various locations, 1981—; prof. Calif. Inst. Mgmt., Berkeley, 1990-93; adj. prof. Golden Gate U., San Francisco, 1994—, U. San Francisco, 2003. Author: Empire: A Bicentennial Appraisal, 1975, Japan: Five Stages of Development, 1976, The Great Social Struggle, vols. 1-3, 1978-80, Arms & Empire: Imperial Patterns Before WWII, 1981, Common Destiny: Japan and U.S. in Global Age, 1990, Quest For Freedom: The Transformation of Eastern Europe in the 1990s, 1993, Race and the Jury: Inequality and Justice, 1993, The Middle East: A Geopolitical Study, 1995, Mexico, NAFTA and Hardships of Progress, 1995, Anatomy of the McMartin Child Molestation Case, 2001, Race in the Jury Box: Affirmative Action in Jury Selection, 2003, A Century Passing: Carnegie, Steel & The Fate of Homestead, 2003, Ecosystems in Distress, 2003; corr. Econ. Polit. Weekly, 1980-83; contbr. articles to profl. jours. and anthologies. Founder Wis. Alliance Party, 1968-73; founder, dir. Law and Labor Rsch. Group, Santa Barbara, Calif., 1978-81; acad. dir. Diversion Team: Criminal Youth, Riverside, Calif., 1980-82; coord. Media's Effect on Children, Riverside, 1982-83. Recipient Outstanding Book award for human rights in N.Am., Gustavus Myers Ctr., 1994; grantee Louis M. Rabinowitz Found., N.Y.C., 1973-80; Faculty Senate grantee U. Calif., Riverside, 1979-83. Mem. Am. Arbitration Assn. (arbitrator and comml. panel 1983—), Ga. Bar Assn., Smithsonian Inst. (assoc.), DePaul Alumni Assn., U. Calif. Alumni Assn., Phi Gamma Mu. Office: Harvest Pub PO Box 9515 Berkeley CA 94709-0515

KROPFF, PATRICIA ANN, private school educator; b. Travis AFB, Calif., May 12, 1954; d. Joseph James and Anna Mae (Patton) Grier; m. Douglas Alan Kropff, Mar. 19, 1977; children: Ryan Patrick, Matthew Richard. BS, California (Pa.) U., 1975, postgrad. Cert. tchr. elem.; speech pathologist. Therapist speech and lang. Capital Area United Cerebral Palsy Ctr., Camp Hill, Pa., 1975-77; tchr. elem. substitute Southmoreland Sch. Dist., Scottdale, Pa., 1987-88; tchr. kindergarten St. John the Bapt. Sch., Scottdale, 1988—. Mem. curriculum com. Greensburg (Pa.) Diocese. Advisor St. John the Bapt. Youth Ministry. Mem. Nat. Cath. Ednl. Assn., St. John the Bapt. Sch. PTO (pres. 1989-90), St. John the Bapt. Athletic Assn. (pres. 1992-94). Democrat. Avocation: walking. Home: 407 Fountain Mills Rd Scottdale PA 15683-1424 Office: St John the Baptist Sch 504 S Broadway St Scottdale PA 15683-2121

KROSS, BETTY ANN, elementary education educator; b. Cleve., June 19, 1935; d. Charles Alan and Emily Margaret (Rendsland) Seedhouse; m. David V. Kross, Nov. 18, 1967; children: David A., Hope, Dawn, Christopher, Mary, Monica. BS in Edn., St. John Coll., 1964, postgrad., 1964-66, Cleve. State U., 1976-92, Kent State U., 1989-95. Cert. elem. tchr., learning disabilities tchr., Ohio. Tchr. grades 2-6 Cleve. Cath. Diocese, 1955-66, elem. tchr., 1984-86; learning disabilities tutor, home tutor North Olmsted (Ohio) City Schs., 1976-84; elem. tchr. Cleve. City Schs., 1986—. Cub Scout leader Boy Scouts Am., North Olmsted, 1976-78; aide Girl Scouts U.S.A., North Olmsted, 1978-88. Avocations: reading, music, walking. Home: 24777 Mitchell Dr North Olmsted OH 44070-3466

KROTEE, LESLIE LATSHAW, special education educator; b. Boston, Jan. 26, 1943; d. Robert James and Alice Louise (Jenks) Latshaw; m. March Lee Krotee, Agu. 21, 1965; children: March Lee Jr., Robert Latshaw. BS, West Chester U., 1965; MEd, U. Minn., 1989. Phys. edn. tchr. Langley Park (Md.) Elem. Sch., 1965-67, Winchester Thurston Sch. for Girls, Pitts., 1967-69; substitute tchr. Wayzata Sch. Dist., 1985-88; spl. edn. tchr. Crest View Elem. Sch., Brooklyn Park, Minn., 1990-91, Maple Grove (Minn.) Jr. High Sch., 1991-93, Richfield Sr. HS, 1993—2000, East Cary (N.C.) Mid. Sch., 2001—. Rsch. asst. U. Minn., Mpls., 1988-89. Author: (rsch. project) Educational Services to Minnesota Students With Disabilities, 1990. Presbyterian. Avocations: travel, gardening. Home: 320 Whisperwood Dr Cary NC 27511-9124 Office: East Cary Mid School Cary NC 27511

KROTINGER, SHEILA M. educator; b. Pitts., May 28, 1930; d. Michael N. and Rose Irene Lutsky; m. Nathan J. Krotinger, Mar. 7, 1949; children— Eve, Michelle. A.A. summa cum laude, East Los Angeles Coll., 1956; B.A. magna cum laude, Calif. State U.-Fullerton, 1966. Cert. life credential, Calif. Tchr. Norwalk-La Mirada Unified Sch. Dist., Calif., 1968— . Contbr. articles to profl. jours. Editor, producer, dir. cable TV shows. Bd. dirs. La Mirada Festival of Arts, 1981, 82, publicity dir., 1982— ; publicity dir. La Mirada Friends of Theatre, 1982— ; v.p. La Mirada Democratic Club, 1983; bd. dirs. Friends of McNally Ranch, La Mirada, 1984; mem. by-laws com., co-chmn. Hist. Com. Friends of La Mirada Civic Theatre, 1983; mem. initiative com. Californians for Non-Smokers Rights, 1980; founder Temple Beth Shalom, Whittier, Calif., 1952, Temple Beth Ohr, La Mirada, 1960; chmn. City of La Mirada Hist. Heritage Commn., 1991-94; founder Heritage Coalition of South Calif., 1992, chmn., 1992-96, emeritus bd. dir.; bd. dir. Sr. Net Learning Ctr., La Mirada, Calif. Recipient Vol. in Action Award of Excellance, Innovation, 1998; founder Heritage Coalition of So. Calif., chair 1993-97. Mem. Mensa. Home: 15310 Talbot Dr La Mirada CA 90638-5469

KROTSENG, MARSHA VAN DYKE, higher education administrator; b. Indiana, Pa., May 10, 1955; d. Chester James and Helen Louise (Gibson) Van Dyke; m. Morgan Lee Krotseng, June 24, 1978. BA in Spanish, Coll. of William and Mary, 1977, MEd in Ednl. Adminstrn., 1981, EdD in Higher Edn., 1987. Spanish, journalism tchr. Lancaster County Pub. Schs., Irvington, Va., 1977-79; office mgr., computer programmer SEMCO, Inc., Newport News, Va., 1979-80; Spanish, German tchr. Newport News Pub. Schs., 1980-82; rsch. asst. Coll. of William and Mary, Williamsburg, Va., 1982-87; Gov.'s fellow Office of Sec. of Edn. Commonwealth of Va., Richmond, 1984; instnl. rsch. assoc., asst. prof. higher edn. U. Miss., Oxford, 1987-89; asst. dir., planning and inst. rsch. U. Hartford, West Hartford, Conn., 1989-91; dir. rsch. and info. systems State Coll. and Univ. Systems, Charleston, W.Va., 1991-98; assoc. provost Cleve. State U., 1998-99; vice provost, exec. asst. to pres. West Liberty State Coll., 1999—2002; chief planning officer Valdosta State Univ., 2002—. Proposal review panel mem. Assn. for Study of Higher Edn.-Ednl. Resource Info. Ctr. Higher Edn. Report Series, 1992—. Author: (chpt.) Politics and Policy in the Age of Education, 1990; co-editor: Developing Executive Information Systems in Higher Education, 1993; mem. editl. adv. bd. Ednl. Studies, 1990-93; assoc. editor Review of Higher Edn., 1991-94; editorial adv. bd. CASE Internat. Jour. Ednl. Advancement, 1999—. Unit coord. United Way Fund Drive, Hartford, 1989, 90; choir mem., soloist First Presbyn. Ch., South Charleston, 1998-99; mem. Charleston Women's Forum, 1994-98; mem. Leadership W.Va., 1995; mem. Valdosta Symphony Guild. Recipient Outstanding Doctoral Rsch. award Va. Poly. Inst., 1988; named one of Outstanding Young Women of Am., 1985, 86, Outstanding West Virginian, Gov. of W.Va., 1994, Leadership W.Va., 1995, Leadership Wheeling, 2001. Mem. Assn. for Study of Higher Edn. (bd. dirs. 1987-90, site selection com. chair 1990-93), Am. Assn. for Higher Edn., Am. Ednl. Rsch. Assn. (program co-chair divsn. J 1988-89), Am. Assn. Univ. Adminstrs., Assn. for Instnl. Rsch. (publs. bd. 1990-92, exec. com., forum chair 1992-94, v.p. 1998-99, pres. 1999-2000), Soc. for Coll. and Univ. Planning, Nat. Postsecondary Edn. Coop. Coun. on Postsecondary Edn. Stats., Valdosta Symphony Guild, Rotary Internat., Phi Beta Kappa, Kappa Delta Pi (Nat. Essay award 1987). Avocations: cantori montani choral ensemble, art, reading, travel. Office: Valdosta State U 1500 N Patterson St Valdosta GA 31698-0295 E-mail: krotseng@valdosta.edu.

KROUSE, JENNY LYNN, elementary school educator; b. Houston, Oct. 9, 1956; d. Thomas Raymond and Anna Margaret (Davis) K. BS, U. Houston, 1979, M Adminstrn., 2002. Cert. tchr., Tex. 4th grade tchr. Orange Grove Elem. Sch., Houston, 1979-86, pre-kindergarten tchr., 1986-88, 3rd grade tchr., 1988-89; 5th grade tchr. lang. arts Oleson Elem. Sch., Houston, 1989-93, pre-1st grade tchr., 1993-94, 4th grade tchr., 1994-95; 5th grade sci. tchr. Drew Magnet Sch. Acad. Math., Sci. and Arts, Houston, 1995-96, Title I coord., 1996-97, chair reading dept., 1997-98; skills specialist, assessment coord. Drew Magnet Sch., 1997—. Coop. learning facilitator Johns Hopkins U., Houston, 1993; GESA facilitator Gray Hill, Houston, 1995; mentor Region IV, Houston, 1996; critical friends group coach, Annenberg Initiative, 1998. Mem. Women's Action Coalition, Houston, 1992-95. Mem. ASCD, S.E. Tex. Legal Clin. (bd. dirs. 1998), Tex. PTA (life), Internat. Reading Assn., Tex. State Reading Assn. Avocations: camping, softball, cooking, travel, theater/movies. Home: 15421 Henry Rd Houston TX 77060-4542 Office: Drew Academy 1910 W Little York Rd Houston TX 77091-1914

KROW, JOYCE ANNE, secondary education eductor; b. Lewistown, Pa., July 7, 1960; d. William Arthur and Betty Jane (Ertley) T. BS in Edn., Shippensburg State Coll., 1981; MS, Shippensburg U., 1986. Cert. tchr., Pa. Tchr. maths. Middleburg (Pa.) High Sch., 1981-2000, West Snyder H.S., Beaver Springs, Pa., 2000—. Mem. NEA, Pa. Coun. Tchrs. Maths., Pa. Edn. Assn. Home: RR 2 Box 1175 Port Royal PA 17082-9660

KRUCENSKI, LEONARD JOSEPH, secondary education educator; b. Buffalo, June 15, 1931; s. Stanislous and Anna Victoria (Pyzanowska) K.; m. Estelle Ann Gaik, Oct. 19, 1957; children: Leonard S., Brian M., William G. BS cum laude, SUNY, Buffalo, 1976, MS in Edn., 1980, EdD, 2001. Electronics technician Bell Aero Space Inc., Niagara Falls, N.Y., 1953-62, Moog Valve Inc, East Aurora, N.Y., 1962-69; engring. aid Cornell Aero. Labs. Inc., Buffalo, 1969-75; jr. engr. Kistler Instruments Inc., Clarence, N.Y., 1975-79; tchr. electronics Buffalo Pub. Sch. System, 1979—2000; ret., 2000. Recipient 85th Anniversary Alumni Disting. Svc. award Hutchinson Cen. Tech. High Sch., 1989. Mem. ASCD, NEA, Am. Vocat. Assn., Nat. Assn. Indsl. and Tech. Tchr. Educators, N.Y. State Occupational Edn. Assn., Vocat. Tech. Guild Buffalo, Buffalo Tchrs. Fedn. Avocations: woodworking, philately. Home: 176 Lorelee Dr Tonawanda NY 14150-4325

KRUCK, DONNA JEAN, special education educator, consultant; b. Peoria, Ill., Jan. 26, 1930; d. Walter George and Lois Irene (Newburn) Hagemeyer; m. Michael Roy Kruck Jr., June 27, 1948; children: Pamela Ann Kruck Hokanson, Michael Roy III, Quentin Robert; m. Somran Sirironrong, May 19, 1998. BS, Ill. State U., 1961; MEd, U. Ill., 1968. Cert. spl. edn. tchr. and adminstr., Ill. Tchr. New Lenox Dist. 122, Ill., 1956-61; tchr. spl. edn. Lincoln Way Area Joint Agreement, New Lenox, 1961-66; tchr. spl. edn., coord. Joliet Twp. High Sch. Dist. 204, Ill., 1966-86; pvt. practice cons. and diagnostician New Lenox, 1986-92. Child adv. New Lenox Dist. 122, 1986-88; instr. Chapel Christian U., 1994-96; LCMS missionary, ESL tchr., Bangkok, 1997—. Author: Let's Learn to Cook, 1971. Pres. Joliet Twp. Edn. Assn., 1971-76; donar Aurora Area Blood Bank, Joliet, 1974-90; v.p. Island Lakes Homeowners Assn., 1994-96; v.p. Luth. Women's Missionary League, 1993, pres., 1994-97; pres. Aid Assn. for Luths., 1995-97. Mem. AAUW, NEA (life), Nat. Ret. Tchr. Assn., Am. Assn. Retired Persons, Am. Assn. Mental Retardation, Am. Bus. Women's Assn., Coun. Exceptional Children (life), Coun. Adminstrs. Spl. Edn., Christian Edn. Assn., Ill. Edn. Assn. (life), Ill. Div. Learning Disabilities, Coun. for Ednl. Diagnostic Svcs. (div. learning disabilities), Lutherans for Life, Kappa Delta Pi, Delta Kappa Gamma. Lutheran. Avocations: traveling, presenting travelogues. Office: Concordia Gospel Ministry 205/20 Soi Chairyakiat 1 Ngam Wong Wan 10210 Bangkok Thailand Home: 1/121 Soi Chinnakhet 1/21 Ngam Wong Wan Rd Bangkok 10210 Thailand

KRUCKEBERG, ARTHUR RICE, botanist, educator; b. L.A., Mar. 21, 1920; s. Arthur Woodbury and Ella Muriel K.; m. Mareen Schultz, Mar. 21, 1953; children— Arthur Leo, Enid Johanna; children by previous marriage— Janet Muriel, Patricia Elayne, Caroline. BA, Occidental Coll., Los Angeles, 1941; postgrad., Stanford U., 1941-42; PhD, U. Calif.-Berkeley, 1950. Instr. biology Occidental Coll., 1946; teaching asst. U. Calif.-Berkeley, 1946-50; mem. faculty U. Wash., Seattle, 1950—, prof. botany, 1964-88, emeritus, 1988—, chmn. dept., 1971-77. Cons. in field. Co-founder Wash. Natural Area Preserves system, 1966. Served with USNR, 1942-46. Mem. Wash. Native Plant Soc. (founder 1976), Calif. Bot. Soc. Rsch. edaphics of serpentines, flowering plants. Home: 20312 15th Ave NW Shoreline WA 98177-2166 Office: U Wash PO Box 351330 Seattle WA 98195-1330 E-mail: ark@u.washington.edu.

KRUEGER, DARRELL WILLIAM, academic administrator; b. Salt Lake City, Feb. 9, 1943; s. William T. and E. Marie (Nelson) K.; m. Verlene Terry, July 1, 1965 (dec. Jan., 1969); 1 child, William; m. Nancy Leane Jones, Sept. 2, 1969; children: Tonya, Amy, Susan. BA summa cum laude, So. Utah State Coll., 1967; MA in Govt., U. Ariz., 1969, PhD in Govt., 1971. Asst. prof. polit. sci. N.E. Mo. State U., Kirksville, 1971-73, v.p. acad. affairs, dean of instrn., 1973-89; pres. Winona State U., Minn., 1989—. Facilitator The 7 Habits of Highly Effective People, 1993, Crucial Conservations, 2003; mem. adv. bd. U.S. Bank, Rochester, Minn., 1989—. Mem. Gamehaven Coun. Boy Scouts Am., 1989—. Recipient Outstanding Alumnus award, So. Utah State, 1992. Mem.: Am. Assn. Higher Edn., Am. Assn. State Colls. and Univs., Rotary, Phi Beta Kappa. Mem. Lds Ch. Avocations: running, golf. Home: 1411 Heights Blvd Winona MN 55987-2519 Office: Winona State U Somsen 201 8th & Johnson Winona MN 55987

KRUEGER, JAMES HARRY, chemistry educator; b. Milw., May 18, 1936; s. Clarence A. and Helen. K.; children: Melanie A., Diane M., Carolyn J. BS, U. Wis., 1958; PhD, U. Calif., Berkeley, 1961. Asst. prof. chemistry Oreg. State U., Corvallis, 1961-66, assoc. prof., 1966-73, prof., 1973—97, prof. emeritus, 1997—. Mem. Am. Chem. Soc. Office: Dept Chemistry Oreg State U Corvallis OR 97331-4003

KRUEGER, KATHLEEN SUSAN, special education administrator; b. Cape Girardeau, Mo., Jan. 21, 1951; d. Robert Settle and Myldred Frances (Jones) K. BS in Edn., Athens Coll., 1973; MEd, Ala. A&M U., 1980. Classroom tchr. Limestone County Schs., Athens, Ala., 1973-74; spl. edn. tchr. Huntsville (Ala.) City Schs., 1974-95, spl. edn. coord., 1995—. Mem. city-wide policy com. Huntsville City Schs., 1987-89, profl. devel. coord., 1986-95, dept. chair for spl. edn., 1993-95. Bd. dirs. H-Vote, Huntsville, 1989; vol. ARC, 1981-82; tchr. Sunday Sch., First United Meth. Ch., Huntsville, 1983-85, sec., 1985-86, mem. choir, 1985-89, hon. treas. for State of Ala., 1988. Mem. NEA (PAC), Ala. Edn. Assn., Huntsville Edn. Assn. (bldg. rep. 1992-95, treas. 1989, sec. 1992-93), Coun. for Exceptional Children, Ala. Coun. for Sch. Adminstrn. and Supervision, Phi Delta Kappa, Phi Mu (membership dir. 1970-71, treas. 1971-72). Home: 7801 Regent Pl SW Apt 8 Huntsville AL 35802-1471

KRUEGER, LESTER EUGENE, pyschology educator; b. Chgo., Nov. 6, 1939; s. Carl and Helen (Milanowski) Krueger. PhD, Harvard U., 1969. Asst. prof. CCNY, 1969—72, assoc. prof., 1973—74; asst. prof. psychology Ohio State U., Columbus, 1974—76, assoc. prof., 1976—80, prof., 1980—. Cons. editor: Memory & Cognition, 1977—99, assoc. editor: Perception & Psychophysics, 1987—98; contbr. articles to profl. jours. With U.S. Army, 1957. Grantee NIH grantee, 1970—76, NIMH grantee, 1979—80. Fellow: Am. Psychol. Soc., Am. Psychol. Assn.; mem.: AAUP, Psychonomic Soc., Sigma Xi. Home: 2812 N Star Rd Columbus OH 43221-2959 Office: Ohio State U Dept Psychology 1885 Neil Ave Columbus OH 43210-1222 Business E-Mail: krueger.2@osu.edu.

KRUG, ADELE JENSEN (MRS. WALTER JOHN KRUG), library sci. ed.; b. Thief River Falls, Minn., Mar. 30, 1908; d. Anton Martin Hulbert and Tillie Manspand (Johnson) Jensen; BA, Gallaudet Coll., 1930; MS, Cath. U. Am., 1961; m. Walter John Krug, June 18, 1932 (dec. May 1962); children— Janice Krug Riley (dec.), Diana Krug Armstrong, Walter F., Warren J. Instr., RI Sch. for Deaf, 1930-32; instr. libr. sci. Gallaudet U., Washington, 1955-63, asst. prof., 1963-67, assoc. prof., 1967-75. Pres., Stuart Jr. HS PTA, Washington, 1954-56, McKinley HS PTA, 1956-57. Mem. Conv. Am. Instrs. Deaf, Nat. Assn. of Deaf, DC Women's Aux., Nat. Luth. Home, Phi Kappa Zeta (nat. alumnae pres. 1954-60). Contbr. to Am. Anns. of Deaf. Home: 3440 S Jefferson St Apt 726 Falls Church VA 22041-3126

KRUGER, CHARLES HERMAN, JR., mechanical engineering educator; b. Oklahoma City, Oct. 4, 1934; s. Charles H. and Flora K.; m. Nora Nininger, Sept. 10, 1977; children— Sarah, Charles III, Elizabeth, Ellen. S.B., M.I.T., 1956, PhD, 1960; D.I.C., Imperial Coll., London, 1957. Asst. prof. MIT, Cambridge, 1960; research scientist Lockheed Research Labs., 1960-62; prof. mech. engring. Stanford (Calif.) U., 1962—, chmn. dept. mech. engring., 1982-88, sr. assoc. dean engring., 1988-93, vice provost, dean rsch. and grad. policy, 1993—2003. Vis. prof. Harvard U., 1968-69, Princeton U., 1979-80; mem. Environ. Studies Bd. NAS, 1981-83; mem. hearing bd. Bay Area Air Quality Mgmt. Dist., 1969-83 Co-author: Physical Gas Dynamics, 1965, Partially Ionized Gases, 1973, On the Prevention of Significant Deteriorization of Air Quality, 1981; asso. editor: AIAA Jour, 1968-71; contbr. numerous articles to profl. jours. NSF sr. postodoctoral fellow, 1968-69; recipient Plasma Chemistr award Internat. Plasma Chemistry Soc., 2003, Cuthbertson Award, Stanford Univ., 2003. Fellow AAAS; mem. AIAA (medal, award 1979), ASME, Am. Phys. Soc., N.Y. Acad. Scis.

KRUGER, PAUL, nuclear civil engineering educator; b. Jersey City, June 7, 1925; s. Louis and Sarah (Jacobs) K.; m. Claudia Mathis, May 19, 1972; children: Sharon, Kenneth, Louis. BS, MIT, 1950; PhD, U. Chgo., 1954. Registered profl. engr., Pa. Rsch. physicist GM, Detroit, 1954-55; mgr. dept. chemistry Nuclear Sci. and Engring. Corp., Pitts., 1955-60; v.p. Hazleton Nuclear Sci. Corp., Palo Alto, Calif., 1960-62; prof. civil engring. Stanford (Calif.) U., 1962-87, prof. emeritus, 1987—. Cons. Elec. Power Rsch. Inst., Palo Alto, 1975-95, Los Alamos (N.Mex.) Nat. Lab., 1985-98. Author: Principles of Activation Analysis, 1973, Geothermal Energy, 1972. 1st lt. USAF, 1943-46, PTO. Recipient achievement cert. U.S. Energy R & D Adminstrn., 1975. Fellow Am. Nuclear Soc.; mem. ASCE (divsn. chmn. 1978-79). Home: 819 Allardice Way Stanford CA 94305-1050 Office: Stanford U Civil Engring Dept Stanford CA 94305

KRUGLY, ANDREW, elementary school principal; b. Chgo., May 9, 1966; s. Michael Krugly and Penny Hoyt Pollack. BS, U. Ill., 1988, MEd, 1992. Tchr. 2d grade Prairie Sch., Buffalo Grove, Ill., 1988-92, Westbrook Sch., Glenview, Ill., 1992-93; tchr. 4th grade Half Day Sch., Lincolnshire, Ill., 1993-94; prin. Willow Creek Sch., Woodridge, Ill., 1994—98, Dewey Elem. Sch., Evanston, Ill., 1998—. Adj. faculty Nat.-Lewis U., Evanston, Ill., 1993; presenter workshops. Bd. dirs. Kohl Acad. for Outstanding Educators, 1993-96. Recipient Kohl Internat. Teaching award Kohl Acad. Outstanding Educators, 1992. Mem. ASCD. Office: Dewey Elem Sch 1551 Wesley Ave Evanston IL 60201

KRULIK, GLORIA LEE ANCELL, guidance counselor, educator, retired; b. Bklyn., Dec. 29, 1926; d. Samuel and Thelma (Lerner) Ancell; m. David Krulik, Dec. 25, 1948 (dec. July 1988); 1 child, Eleanor Jane Krulik Levitt. BA in Art, Bklyn. Coll., 1948, MS in Guidance Counseling, 1972; MA in Art Edn., Tchr.'s Coll. Columbia Coll., 1950. Cert. tchr., N.Y. Elem. tchr. Ctr. Acad., Bklyn., 1950-54; tchr. jr. h.s. N.Y.C. Bd. Edn., N.Y.C., 1960-66, guidance counselor, 1966-86; retired, 1986. Lectr. Inst. of Retired Profls. & Execs. Bklyn. Coll., Bklyn., 1990-91. Co-contbr. numerous articles to Guidance mag., 1985. Founding mem. Bnai Brith Schoolwomen's Post, 1950-94; mem. East Medwood Jewish Ctr., 1989—; founding mem. Mus. of Women Artists, Washington, 1991—, Holocaust Mus., Washington, 1992—. Democrat. Avocations: traveling, painting, museums, theater.

KRUMBOLTZ, JOHN DWIGHT, psychologist, educator; b. Cedar Rapids, Iowa, Oct. 21, 1928; s. Dwight John and Margaret (Jones) K.; m. Helen Brandhorst, Aug. 22, 1954 (div. Aug. 1986); children: Ann, Jennifer; m. Betty Lee Foster, Nov. 8, 1987. BA, Coe Coll., Cedar Rapids, 1950; MA, Columbia Tchrs. Coll., 1951; PhD, U. Minn., 1955; PhD (hon.), Pacific Grad. Sch. Psychology, 1991. Counselor, tchr. W. Waterloo (Iowa) H.S., 1951-53; from teaching asst. to instr. U. Minn., 1953-55; from asst. prof. ednl. psychology to assoc. prof. Mich. State U., 1957-61; faculty Stanford U. Sch. Edn., 1961-66, prof. edn. and psychology, 1966—. Vis. sr. research psychologist Ednl. Testing Service, 1972-73; fellow Ctr. for Advanced Study in Behavioral Scis., 1975-76, Advanced Study Ctr., Nat. Ctr. for Research in Vocat. Edn., Ohio State U., 1980-81; vis. colleague dept. psychology Inst. Psychiatry, U. London, 1983-84 Author: (with others) Learning to Study, 1960; (with Helen B. Krumboltz) Changing Children's Behavior, 1972; editor: Learning and the Educational Process, 1965, Revolution in Counseling, 1966; (with Carl E. Thoresen) Behavioral Counseling: Cases and Techniques, 1969, Counseling Methods, 1976; (with Anita M. Mitchell and G. Brian Jones) Social Learning and Career Decision Making, 1979; (with Daniel A. Hamel) Assessing Career Development,

1982; contbr. articles to profl. jours. With USAF, 1955-57. Recipient Eminent Career award Nat. Career Devel. Assn., 1994; Guggenheim fellow, 1967-68. Mem. APA (pres. div. counseling psychology 1974-75, award for disting. profl. contbns. to knowledge 2002), Am. Ednl. Rsch. Assn. (v.p. div. E. 1966-68), Am. Pers. and Guidance Assn. (Outstanding Rsch. award 1959, 66, 68, Disting. Profl. Svcs. award 1974, Leona Tyler award 1990). Home: 933 Valdez Pl Stanford CA 94305-1008

KRUMMEL, DONALD WILLIAM, librarian, educator; b. Sioux City, Iowa, July 12, 1929; s. William and Leta Margarete (Fischer) K.; m. Marilyn Darlene Frederick, June 19, 1956; children: Karen Elisabeth, Matthew Frederick. Mus.B., U. Mich., 1951, Mus.M., 1953, MA in Library Sci, 1954, PhD, 1958. Instr. in music lit. U. Mich., 1952-56; reference librarian Library of Congress, Washington, 1956-61; head reference dept., asso. librarian Newberry Library, Chgo., 1962-69; asso. prof. library sci. U. Ill., 1970-71, prof. library sci. and music, 1971—, assoc. Center Advanced Study, 1974; univ. scholar, 1991; Centennial scholar, 1994. Middle mgmt. intern U.S. Civil Svc., 1960; scholar in residence Aspen Inst., 1969; mem. faculty Rare Book Sch. Columbia U., 1990-91, U. Va., 1993—; archival cons. Kneisel Hall, 1990-94. Author: Bibliotheca Bolduaniana, 1972, Guide for Dating Early Published Music, 1974, English Music Printing, 1553-1700, 1975, Bibliographical Inventory to the Early Music in the Newberry Library, 1977, Organizing the Library's Support, 1980, Resources of American Music History, 1981, Bibliographies, Their Aims and Methods, 1984, Bibliographical Handbook of American Music, 1987, The Memory of Sound, 1988, Grove-Norton Handbook of Music Printing and Publishing, 1990, The Literature of Music Bibliography, 1993, Fiat Lux, Fiat Latebra, 1999; contbr. numerous articles and revs. to profl. jours. Recipient awards Huntington Libr., 1965, Am. Coun. Learned Socs., 1966-77, Am. Philos. Soc., 1969, Coun. Libr. Resources, 1967; Newberry libr. travelling fellow, 1969-70; Univ. Coll. (London) hon. rsch. fellow, 1974-75; Guggenheim fellow, 1976-77. Mem. ALA (G.K. Hall award 1987, Beta Phi Mu award 1999), Music Libr. Assn. (pres. 1981-83, spl. citation award), Bibliog. Soc. (London), Bibliog. Soc. Am., Sonneck Soc. (Lowens award 1989), Am. Antiquarian Soc., Caxton Club (Chgo.), Grolier club. Home: 702 W Delaware Ave Urbana IL 61801-4807 Office: U Ill 501 E Daniel St Champaign IL 61820-6211

KRUPA, JOHN HENRY, English language educator; b. Cleve., Aug. 24, 1944; m. Cheryl J. Henninger, May 29, 1971; children: Megan, Chad. BSEd, Kent State U., 1966; postgrad., Goethe German Lang. Inst., Germany, 1967, NDEA German Inst., 1968; MDiv cum laude, Trinity Evang. Div. Sch., 1977. German tchr. Hampton (Va.) High Sch., 1966-69; tchr. Eli Whitney Elem. Sch., Chgo., 1969-70; mgmt. intern Def. Supply Agy., Alexandria, Va., 1970-71; field staff mem. Campus Crusade for Christ, U. Del., 1971-74; German tchr. Trinity Coll., Deerfield, Ill., 1974-78; pastor Grace Gospel Ch., Chgo., 1977-84; asst. pastor Christian edn. and adult ministries Des Plaines (Ill.) Bible Ch., 1984-89; tchr. ESL Harper Coll., Palatine, Ill., 1989-90, Motorola, Schaumburg, Ill., 1989-94, Oakton Coll., Monnacep-Des Plaines, 1992-95, Triton Coll., 1993-96, tchr. ESL and GED math., 1995-97; skills enhancement instr. AT&T Alliance, 1993-97; tchr. ESL, GED Arthur Andersen: Teach internat. businessmen, 1993-95. Asst. prof. math., writing, algebra, psychology, sociology English as a 2d lang. and orientation East West U., 1997—; instr. English as a 2d lang. Harold Washington Coll. Mem. Soc. for Accelerated Learning and Teaching, Tchrs. of English to Sprs. of Other Langs. Avocation: refinishing antiques. Home: 1039 Walter Ave Des Plaines IL 60016-3332

KRUSE, MARYLIN LYNN, retired foreign language educator; b. Kansas City, Mo., June 26, 1940; d. Mildred Marie Goetsch; m. Richard Lee Weinberg, Dec. 26, 1962 (div. Oct. 1988); children: Eric H., Kerstin I; m. Leon Edward Kruse, Dec. 28, 1998. BA, Cornell Coll., 1962; MA, Marycrest Coll., 1982. English tchr. Galesburg (Ill.) Community Schs., 1962-63, Grant Community Schs., Fox Lake, Ill., 1963-64, Saydel Community Schs., Des Moines, 1965-66; English instr. Grandview Coll., Des Moines, 1966-70; behavior disorders cons. Western Ill. Assn., Galesburg, Ill., 1976-77; prevocational coord. Knox-Warren Spl. Edn. Dist., Galesburg, 1977-78; Spanish tchr. Winola Community Schs., Viola, Ill., 1979-80; spl. edn. tchr. Pleasant Valley (Iowa) Community Schs., 1980-86; English instr. Ea. Iowa Community Coll. Dist., Davenport, 1983-86; spl. edn. tchr. Davenport Community Schs., 1986-94; fgn. lang. tchr. Davenport Cmty. Schs., 1994—2002, ret., 2002. Co-author: Parent Prerogatives, 1979. Recipient tchr. Incentive award State of Iowa Dept. Edn., 1982; chpt. II grant U.S. Office of Edn., Williams Jr. High, 1988. Mem.: Audubon Soc., Sierra Club. Republican. Lutheran. Avocations: home decorating, bird watching. Home: 4614 Hamilton Dr Davenport IA 52807-3427

KRUSE, NANCY CLARSON, retired elementary school educator; b. Flushing, N.Y., Aug. 19, 1946; d. Robert LeRoy Jr. and Julie Clarson; m. William Franz Kruse, Feb. 4, 1984. BS in Elem. Edn., Adelphi U., 1968, MA in Elem. Edn., 1970; student, postgrad., Nat. U. Ireland, U. Coll. Dublin, 1966, 69. Cert. tchr., N.Y. Rschr., developer use of microcomputers in elem. classroom Syosset (N.Y.) Ctrl. Sch. Dist., 1980-81; tchr. 4th, 5th and 6th grades South Grove Sch., Syosset, 1968—2003, ret., 2003. Leader Children's Internat. Summer Villages, 1979, 80; bd. dirs. Goudreau Mus. Math. in Art and Sci., New Hyde Park, store buyer, 1987-94, store mgr., 1988-92; instr. in calligraphy. Speaker, workshop presenter in field. Recipient with 6th grade class Norma Gold Human Rels. award, Syosset Cent. Sch. Dist., 1985. Mem. N.Y. State Union of Tchrs., Apples in Edn. Users Group (founder), Wives Info. Network of N.Y. State Park Police (co-founder), Mac Users Group. Avocations: calligraphy, boating, needlework, long-haired cats. Home: 68 Ketcham Rd Hicksville NY 11801-2023 Home (Winter): 3427 Pinetree St Port Charlotte FL 33952

KRYZAK, LINDA ANN, educational administrator; b. Oak Park, Ill., Nov. 3, 1951; d. Eugene Joseph and Helen (Vlahos) K.; children: Melissa Lynn, Heather Rae. BS in Edn., No. Ill. U., 1973, MS in Edn., 1977; cert. advanced study in ednl. tech., Nat.-Louis U., 1998. Cert. gen. adminstr., elem. tchr., spl. edn., early childhood spl. edn. tchr., social/emotional disordered tchr., learning disabled, educable and trainable mentally handicapped, supervisory endorsements. Dir. career/life tng., rsch. project leader, ednl. cons. Grove Sch., Lake Forest, Ill., 1974-81; pvt. practice Addison, Ill., 1981-82; tchr. spl. edn. Sch. Dist. 83, Franklin Park, Ill., 1982-85; coord. spl. edn. Leyden Area Spl. Edn. Coop., Franklin Park, Ill., 1985-94; prin. South Elem. Sch., Franklin Park, Ill., 1994-99; dir. instrn. and tech. Franklin Park Sch. Dist. 84, 1999—2001, prin. East Early Childhood Ctr., dir. tech., 2001—. Founder Creative Learning Choices, 1992—; adj. prof. tech. in edn. Nat. Louis U., 2000—. Pub. speaker on computers, assistive technology, software and integration of spl. edn. students into regular classrooms, 1988—. Mem. Ill. Computing Educators.

KU, YU H. electrical engineer, educator; b. Wusih, Kiangsu, China, Dec. 24, 1902; SB, MIT, 1925, SM, 1926, ScD, 1928; MA, LLD (hon.), U. Pa. Prof. emeritus Moore Sch. Elec. Engring., U. Pa., Phila., 1972—. Mem. U.S. Nat. Com. of Theoretical and Applied Mechanics; hon. prof. Shanghai Jiao Tong U., 1979—, Xi'an Jiao Tong U., 1984—, Southwestern and No. Jiao Tong U., 1985—, N.E. U. Tech., 1986—, N.W. Inst. Telecom., 1986—, S.E. U., 1988. Recipient Profl. Accomplishment award Chinese Inst. Engrs., 1959, Gold medal Ministry of Edn., Republic of China, 1960, Profl. Accomplishment award Chinese Engrs. and Scientists Assn. So. Calif., 1969, Gold medal Chinese Inst. Elec. Engrs., 1972, Gold medal Pro Mundi Beneficio, Brazilian Acad. Humanities, 1975. Fellow IEEE (Lamme Medal award 1972), Instn. Elec. Engrs. London, Academia Sinica; mem. Internat. Union Theoretical and Applied Mechanics (personal mem. gen. assembly); mem. United Poets Laureate Internat. (hon.), Am. Soc. Engring. Edn., Sigma Xi, Eta Kappa Nu, Phi Tau Phi. Office: University of PA Prof Moore Sch E/Emeritus Philadelphia PA 19104

KUBECKA, RONNA DENISE, English language and art educator, psychotherapist; b. Freeport, Tex., Oct. 31, 1960; d. Warren Melvin and Bernice (Maroney) K. BS in Edn., Baylor U., 1983; MEd, U. North Tex., 1996. Cert. educator, Tex., cert. peer assistance leadership tchr. Tchr. English and art Martin H.S., Arlington, Tex., 1983—; counselor Women's Haven, Ft. Worth, Tex., 1995—. Sponsor Young Life, Arlington, 1984-85, The Care Team, 1988-89, Peer Assistance Leadership, Arlington, 1994; founder, co-facilitator New Wings Coda, Irving, Tex., 1991-95. Active Women's Chorus of Dallas, 199598—; sponsor Christian Childrens Fund, B PTA scholar Martin High PTA, 1990. Mem. ACA, Internat. Assn. Marriage and Family Counselors, United Educators Assn., Womens Bus. Network, Womens Cmty. Assn. Republican. Home: 8620 Brushy Creek Trl Fort Worth TX 76118-7416 Office: Martin H S 4501 W Pleasant Ridge Rd Arlington TX 76016-3410

KUBEY, ROBERT WILLIAM, media educator, developmental psychologist, television analyst and researcher; b. Berkeley, Calif., July 20, 1952; m. Barbara Lewert Kubey, Nov. 14, 1981; children: Benjamin, Daniel. AB in Psychology with honors, U. Calif., Santa Cruz, 1974; MA in Behavioral Sci., U. Chgo., 1978, PhD in Behavioral Sci., 1984. NIMH postdoctoral fellow U. Calif., Irvine, 1984-85, vis. lectr., 1985; asst. prof. dept. comm. Rutgers U., New Brunswick, N.J., 1985-91, assoc. prof. dept. comm., 1991-99, assoc. prof. dept. journalism and media studies, 1999—, dir. Master's Comm. and Info. Studies, 1997—2000, dir. Ctr. for Media Studies, 1999—; dir. N.J. Media Literacy Project, 1999—. Mem. faculty Harvard U. Inst. on Media Edn., Cambridge, Mass., 1993, 94; vis. assoc. prof. dept. comm. Stanford (Calif.) U., 1995-96; rsch. dir. Media Edn. Lab. Rutgers U., Newark. Co-author: Television and the Quality of Life, 1990; editor: Media Literacy in the Information Age, Transaction, 1997; editor media edn. series Lawrence Erlbaum Assocs., 1994—; author: Creating Television, 2004; contbr. articles to profl. jours. Annenberg scholar in media edn. Annenberg Sch. Comm., U. Pa., 1993. Fellow Ctr. for Critical Analysis of Contemporary Culture, Gerontol. Soc. Office: Rutgers Univ Dept Jour/Media Studies 4 Huntington St New Brunswick NJ 08901-1071 E-mail: kubey@scils.rutgers.edu.

KUBIAK, JOHN MICHAEL, academic administrator; b. Pulaski, Wis., Jan. 15, 1935; s. Anton Joseph and Genevieve (McGuire) K.; m. Mary Dee Neville, Aug. 5, 1966; children: Michelle Jo, Leslie A. Welsh, Robert N. Welsh. BS in Mil. Engring., U.S. Mil. Acad., 1958; MBA, Washington U., St. Louis, 1976, M Data Processing, 1977; PhD, St. Louis U., 1981. Commd. 2d lt. USAF, 1958, advanced through grades to col., 1979; prof. aerospace studies Cornell U., Ithaca, N.Y., 1983-86; retired USAF, 1986; exec. dir. Emaudi Ctr. Internat. Studies, Cornell U., 1986-96; ret., 1997—. Trustee Boulder City Hosp., 2000—, v.p. bd. trustees, 2002—. Decorated Legion of Merit (2), Meritorious Svc. Medal (2), Air Force Commendation Medals (2), Air Medals (2). Mem. Air Force Assn., Rotary (pres. Boulder City 1998-99, asst. gov. dist. 5300 2001-02), Beta Gamma Sigma, Order Daedalians. Republican. Avocations: gardening, golf, aviation. E-mail: kubiak@west-point.org.

KUBISTAL, PATRICIA BERNICE, educational consultant; b. Chgo., Jan. 19, 1938; d. Edward John and Bernice Mildred (Lenz) Kubistal. AB cum laude, Loyola U., Chgo., 1959, AM, 1964, AM, 1965, PhD, 1968; postgrad., Chgo. State Coll., 1962, Ill. Inst. Tech., 1963, State U. Iowa, 1963, Nat. Coll. Edn., 1974-75. With Chgo. Bd. Edn., 1959-93, tchr., 1959-63, counselor, 1963-65, adminstrv. intern, 1965-66, asst. to dist. supt., 1966-69, prin. spl. edn. sch., 1969-75; prin. Simpson Sch., 1975-76, Brentano Sch., 1975-87, Roosevelt H.S., 1987, Haugan Sch., 1989; prin. Cook County Juvenile Temporary Detention Ctr. Sch. Jones Met. H.S. Bus. and Commerce, 1989-90, adminstr. dept. spl. edn., 1990-93; supr. Lake View Evening Sch., 1982-92, ednl. cons., 1993—. Lectr. Loyola U. Sch. Edn., Nat. Coll. Edn. Grad. Sch., Mundelein Coll., 1982-91, DePaul U., 1998-99; coord. Upper Bound Program of U. Ill. Circle Campus, 1966-68. Book rev. editor of Chgo. Prins. Jour., 1970-76, gen. editor, 1982-90. Active Crusade of Mercy; mem. con. Ill. Constnl. Conv., 1967-69; mem. Citizens Sch. Com., 1969-71; mem. edn. com. Field Mus., 1971; ednl. advisor North Side Chgo. PTA Region, 1975; gov. Loyola U., 1961-87; pres. St. Matthews Parish Coun., 1995-98. Recipient Outstanding Intern award Nat. Assn. Secondary Sch. Prins., 1966, Outstanding Prin. award Citizen's Sch. Com. of Chgo., 1986; named Outstanding History Tchr., Chgo. Pub. Schs., 1963, Oustanding Ill. Educator, 1970, one of Outstanding Women of Ill., 1970, St. Luke's Logan Sq. Cmty. Person of Yr., 1977; NDEA grantee, 1963, NSF grantee, 1965, HEW Region 5 grantee for drug edn., 1974, Chgo. Bd. Edn. Prins.' grantee for study robotics in elem. schs.; U. Chgo. adminstrv. fellow 1984. Mem. Ill. Personnel and Guidance Assn., NEA, Ill. Edn. Assn., Chgo. Edn. Assn., Am. Acad. Polit. and Social Sci., Chgo. Prins. and Adminstrs. Assn. (pres. aux.), Nat. Coun. Adminstrv. Women, Chgo. Coun. Exceptional Children, Loyal Christian Benevolent Assn., Kappa Gamma Pi, Pi Gamma Mu, Phi Delta Kappa, Delta Kappa Gamma (paliamentarian 1979-80, pres. Kappa chpt. 1988-90, Lambda state editor 1982-92, chmn. Lambda state comm. com. 1992, Internat. Golden Gift Fund award), Delta Sigma Rho, Phi Sigma Tau. Home and Office: 5111 N Oakley Ave Chicago IL 60625-1829

KUBON, WALTER JOSEPH, JR., bilingual history educator; b. Chgo., Nov. 21, 1945; s. Walter J. and Lottie R. (Kurowski) K.; m. Ellen Mary Procter (dec. Dec. 1989); children: W. Joseph III, Todd M., Kristyn N. BA in History, Alliance Coll., 1967; MEd, Edinboro U., 1970. Cert. tchr. Pa., Ill; cert. bilingual tchr. Chgo., ESL tchr. Ill. History tchr., cross country coach Cranberry High Sch., Seneca, Pa., 1969-73; history tchr., track coach E. Maine Sch. Dist. 63, Des Plaines, Ill., 1974-79; history tchr., soccer coach Erie (Pa.) Day Sch., 1985-87; computer tchr. Our Lady of Victory Sch., Chgo., 1987-90; tchr. bilingual history Chgo. Pub. Schs., 1990—. Asst. scoutmaster Lake in the Hills Troop 152 Boy Scouts Am. Internat. Studies Summer scholar State of Pa., Westminster Coll., 1970. Mem. ASCD, Tau Kappa Epsilon (hegemon 1966—). Roman Catholic. Avocations: camping, railroading, stamps, concerts. Home: 3229 N Newcastle Ave Chicago IL 60634-4639 Office: Foreman High Sch 3235 N Leclaire Ave Chicago IL 60641-4289

KUBY, LOLETTE, English educator, writer; b. Wadsworth, Ohio, July 6, 1939; d. Sally Miller; m. Donald J. Kuby, May 2, 1962 (div. 1981); children: Lauren Goldhamer, David Goldhamer. PhD, Case Western Res. U., 1970. Instr. English Cleve. State U., 1986-98. Author: (lit. criticism) An Uncommon Poet for the Common Man, 1977, (poetry) In Enormous Water, 1982, Set Down Here, 2002; (short stories) The Mama Stories, 1995, (non-fiction) God and the Placebo Effect: An Argument fo Self-Healing, 2001, (poetry) lnwit, 2004. Bd. dirs. Poets League Greater Cleve., 1979-81, Performers and Artists for Nuclear Disarmament, 1986-87, Nuclear Weapons Freeze Campaign, 1985-86; del. Dem. Nat. Conv., 1984. Avocations: tennis, pottery. Home: 8501 Bayview Ave #1009 Richmond Hill ON Canada L4B 3G7 E-mail: lokuby@aol.com.

KUBY, PATRICIA ANN WILLIAMS, early childhood education educator; b. Mobile, Ala., Aug. 19, 1944; d. Percy Lafayette and Bertha Ross (Ledbetter) Williams; m. Carl Joseph Kuby Jr., Aug. 30, 1965; children: Kathryn Amelia, Candace Ross, Carl Joseph III. BA in Elem. Edn., La. Coll., Pineville, 1966; MA in Reading, N.E. La. U., Monroe, 1972; PhD in Early Childhood Edn. and Devel., U. Ala., Birmingham, 1994. Cert. in elem. edn., early childhood edn., reading, principalship, Ala. Tchr. 4th grade Orleans Parish Schs., New Orleans, 1966-70, 7th grade remedial reading tchr., 1972-74; tchr. 5th grade Franklin Parish Schs., Winnsboro, La., 1970-71, reading specialist, 1971-72, Etowah County Schs., Gadsden, Ala., 1974-76; instr. devel. reading Calhoun Coll., Decatur, Ala., 1987-88; instr. child care Decatur City Schs. Continuing Edn., 1989-90; grad. asst. U. Ala., Birmingham, 1989-93; asst. prof. early childhood/elem. edn. Athens (Ala.) State Coll., 1993—. Cons. early childhood edn. Headstart, Morgan County, Ala., 1989, Women's Missionary Union, Birmingham, 1992; cons. Dept. Human Resources, Ala., 1988-89; cons. pre-sch. Ala. Bapt. Conv., Montgomery, 1981—. Contbr. articles to profl. jours. Key communicator Westlawn Elem. Sch. Decatur, 1992-94. U. Ala. at Birmingham grantee, 1989-93. Mem. ASCD, Nat. Assn. for Edn. Young Children, Ala. Assn. for Edn. Young Children, Tennessee Valley Assn. for Edn. Young Children (pres. 1989-91, 93-94), Assn. Childhood Edn. Interant., So. Early Childhood Assn., Internat. Reading Assn., Tennessee Valley Reading Coun., Kappa Delta Epsilon, Kappa Delta Pi, Pi Tau Chi. Baptist. Avocations: swimming, reading, needlework, gardening. Home: 2214 Essex Dr SW Decatur AL 35603-1015

KUCHNER, EUGENE FREDERICK, neurosurgeon, educator, neuroscientist; b. N.Y.C., 1945; s. Morton H. and Edna Estelle Kuchner; m. Joan Ruth Freedman, Sept. 2, 1968; children: Marc Jason, Eric Benjamin. AB, Johns Hopkins U., 1967; MD, U. Chgo., 1971. Diplomate Am. Bd. Neurol. Surgery, Am. Bd. Med. Examiners. Resident in surgery Yale U. Sch. Medicine, New Haven, 1971-72; resident in neurosurgery Montreal (Que., Can.) Neurol. Inst., McGill U., 1972-76, spine fellow, 1976; neurosurgeon SUNY Downstate Sch. Medicine, Bklyn., 1976-79, SUNY Sch. Medicine, Stony Brook, 1979—, assoc. prof., 1983—; cons. neurosurgeon North Shore U. Hosp./NYU Sch. Medicine, 1997—. Mem. staff North Shore U. Hosp.-Cornell Med. Ctr., 1977—97, cons. surgeon, 1977—97; mem. staff Univ. Hosp., Stony Brook, 1979—97, Nassau County Med. Ctr., 1977—2000, St. John's Episcopal Hosp., 1976—99, Mt. Sinai-NYU Health Sys., 1997—, Nassau U. Med. Ctr., 2000—. Contbr. articles to profl. publs.; specialist in microsurgery, magnetic resonance imaging, spinal trauma, pituitary surgery. Recipient K.G. McKenzie Meml. award, Royal Coll. Physicians and Surgeons Can., 1976, Open Scholarship award, John Hopkins U., yearly, 1963—66, Scholarship award, U. Chgo., yearly, 1967—70; fellow, NSF, Blackman-Hoffman Found., 1969—70, USPHS, Divsn. Epidemiology Columbia U. Sch. Pub. Health, N.Y., 1969; chemistry fellow, MIT, 1968. Mem. ACS, AMA, Am. Assn. Neurol. Surgeons, Congress Neurol. Surgeons, N.Y. Acad. Scis., L.I. Neurosci. Acad., Suffolk Acad. Medicine, Montreal Neurol. Ins. Fellows Soc., N.Y. State Neurosurg. Soc., N.Y. State Med. Soc., N.Y. State Soc. Surgeons, Am. Coll. Med. Quality, Healthcare Info. and Mgmt. Sys. Soc., Am. Epilepsy Soc., Am. Soc. Law Medicine and Ethics, Yale Surg. Soc., Yale Club N.Y.C., Sigma Xi. Office: Stony Brook Med Ctr PO Box 721 Stony Brook NY 11790-0721

KUCIEWSKI, PATRICK MICHAEL, music educator; b. Buffalo, Aug. 20, 1958; s. Donald Michael and Lillian Frances (Lewandowski) K. BFA in Music Pedagogy, SUNY, Buffalo, 1980, MFA in Music Pedagogy, 1981; MS in Ednl. Adminstrn., Niagara U., Lewiston, N.Y., 1992, profl. diploma in Ednl. Adminstrn., 1993. Cert. sch. dist. adminstr., sch. adminstr. and supr., music edn., N.Y. Tchr. music Niagara Falls (N.Y.) City Schs., 1981—. Staff percussionist Artpark, Inc., Lewiston, 1985—; guest writer, arranger Niagara U. Theatre, Lewiston, 1992—; exec. dir. Niagara Summer Fine Arts Program, Niagara Falls, 1994—. Author, writer, arranger: (mus. rev.) With Kander From Ebb, 1994. Parade chairperson Festival of Lights, Niagara Falls, 1990-93, Cmty. Faire, Niagara Falls, 1992-94; exec. dir. Niagara Summer Fine Arts Program, 1995; bd. dirs. Niagara Coun. of the Arts, 1996—. Mem. ASCD, Music Educators Nat. Conf., N.Y. State Sch. Music Assn., Niagara County Music Educators Assn. (pres. 1993-95), Phi Delta Kappa. Democrat. Roman Catholic. Avocations: tour biking, music. Home: 1337 99th St Niagara Falls NY 14304-2723 Office: Niagara Middle School 6431 Girard Ave Niagara Falls NY 14304-2223

KUCINKAS, KATHERINE ANN MANSUR, special education consultant, writer; b. Hartford, Conn., Mar. 17, 1941; d. Charles Paul Mansur and Marjorie Morrill (Attenborough) Carlson; m. Chris M. Kucinkas, Aug. 19, 1964 (div. May 1983); children: Susan, Christina. RN, Hartford Hosp Sch Nursing, 1964; BA in Media Comm., Our Lady of the Lake U., 1982, MA in Human Scis., 1984. RN, Wis.; cert. tchr., Tex. Sec. U. Tex. Health Scis. Ctr., San Antonio, 1978-79, adminstrv. clk., 1979-80; mgr. media svcs. Our Lady of the Lake U., San Antonio, 1980-85; nursing asst. instr. Mansfield Bus. Schs., San Antonio, 1986-92; spl. edn. tchr. Edgewood Sch. Dist., San Antonio, 1990-91, Northside Ind. Sch. Dist., San Antonio, 1991-99, John H. Wood Jr. Charter Sch., San Antonio, 1999—. Book reviewer Delmar Pubs., Albany, N.Y., 1988—. Named Tchr. of Yr. Southwestern Assn. Ind. Colls. and Schs., 1989. Mem. Coun. of Exceptional Children, Friendship Force. Avocations: traveling to Europe and Russia, Ctrl. and N.E. Asia, photography, gardening. Home: 11750 Spring Club Dr San Antonio TX 78249-2671 E-mail: kkucinkas@msn.com.

KUCZYNSKI, JOHN-MICHAEL MAXIME, humanities educator, writer; b. Washington, Aug. 21, 1972; s. Pedro-Pablo Godard Kuczynski. BA, UCLA, 1997. Author: Elements of Virtualism: A Study in the Philosophy of Perception, 2003; contbr. articles to profl. jours. Home and Office: PO Box 14163 Santa Barbara CA 93107 Personal E-mail: jsbach@jps.net.

KUDDES, KATHRYN M. fine arts director; b. Midland, Tex., July 11, 1960; d. Fred M. and Dale M. Springer; m. Kenton C. Kuddes. MusB, Millikin U., 1983; Master in Music Edn., U. North Tex., 1995. Cert. provisional all-level music tchr. Tex., tchr. Kodály tng. Tex., profl. supr. Tex. . Choral dir. 6-12 Stafford Mcpl. Sch. Dist., Stafford, Tex., 1983—86; elem. music specialist Killeen Ind. Sch. Dist., Killeen, Tex., 1986—89, Coll. Sta. Ind. Sch. Dist., College Station, Tex., 1989—94; grad. tchg. fellow U. North Tex., Denton, Tex., 1994—95; elem. music specialist Plano Ind. Sch. Dist., Plano, Tex., 1995—98, K-12 coord. vocal music, 1998—2000, dir. fine arts. V.p. Kodály Educators Texas, 1992—97; pres. so. divsn. Orgn. Am. Kodály Educators, 1997—2001. Editor: (profl. newsletter) KET Encounter, 1997. Mem. P.E.O. Sisterhood, Allen, 1987—2002. Named nationally registered music educator, Music Educators Nat. Conf., 1993. Mem.: Assn. Supervision and Curriculum Devel., Am. Orff-Schulwerk Assn., Texas Music Adminstrs. Conf., Orgn. Am. Kodály Educators (pres. so. divsn. 1997—2001), Kodály Educators Tex. (v.p. 1992—97), Am. Choral Dirs. Assn., Tex. Choral Dirs. Assn., Music Educators Nat. Conf., Tex. Music Educators Assn. Avocations: music, folk instruments, travel. Office: Plano Ind Sch Dist 2700 W 15th St Plano TX 75075 Office Fax: 469-752-8039. Business E-Mail: kkuddes@pisd.edu.

KUDRLE, ROBERT THOMAS, economist, educator; b. Sioux City, Iowa, Aug. 23, 1942; s. Chester John and Helen Marguerite (Crakes) K.; m. Venetia Hilary Mary Thomas, July 20, 1970; children: Paul John Reginald, Thomas David Chester. AB, Harvard U., 1964, AM, 1969, PhD, 1974; MPhil., U. Oxford, Eng., 1967. Grad. rsch. assoc. Ctr. Internat. Affairs Harvard U., Cambridge, Mass., 1969-71; instr. Tex. A & M Univ., College Station, 1971-72; asst., assoc. prof. Humphrey Inst. U. Minn., Mpls., 1972-83, asst., assoc. dir. Ctr. Internat. Studies, 1972-82, prof. Humphrey Inst., 1983—, dir. MA program pub. affairs, 1984-86, dir. Freeman Ctr. Internat. Econ. Policy, 1990-97, assoc. dean rsch. Humphrey Inst., 1992-96. Cons. U.S. Dept. Justice, U.S. AID, Urban Inst., UN Ctr. Transnat. Corps., Consumer and Corp. Affairs Can., WHO, others. Author: Agricultural Tractors: A World Industry Study, 1975; co-author State Evaluation of Foreign Sales Efforts, 1988; co-editor Reducing the Cost of Dental Care, 1983, The Industrial Future of the Pacific Basin, 1984, Jour. Internat. Studies Quarterly, 1980-84, 85; mem. editorial bd. Internat. Political Economy Yearbook, 1983—, Jour. Health Politics, Policy & Law, 1981-92; contbr. articles to profl. jours., chpts. to texts. First v.p. UN Assn. Minn., Mpls., 1976-78, mem. adv. coun., 1978-88. Graduate prize fellow Harvard U., 1967-69, Pew Faculty fellow in Internat. Affairs Harvard U., 1990-91; Nuffield Coll. studentship, Oxford, Eng., 1966-67; Rhodes scholar, Oxford, Eng., 1964-67. Mem. Assn. Pub. Policy Analysis and Mgmt. (instl. rep. 1988-97), Internat. Studies Assn. (v.p. 1998-99), Am. Econ. Assn., Harvard

Club Minn. Avocations: running, gardening. Home: 4650 Fremont Ave S Minneapolis MN 55409-2263 Office: Humphrey Inst Pub Affairs 301 19th Ave S Ste 300 Minneapolis MN 55455-0429

KUECHEL, REBECCA JUNE, elementary education educator; b. Santa Ana, Calif., Nov. 17, 1961; d. George Raymond and Barbara June (DeVault) K. BS, No. Ariz. U., 1983, MEd, 1994. Cert. elem., spl. edn. tchr., adminstr., Ariz. Tchr. C.W. McGraw Elem. Sch., Yuma, Ariz., 1984—. Mem. ASCD, ASA, Las Dedicadas Assistance League of Yuma, No. Ariz. U. Alumni Assn., Phi Kappa Phi. Republican. Lutheran. Home: 2227 E 26th Way Yuma AZ 85365-3261 Office: Yuma Sch Dist One 450 W 6th St Yuma AZ 85364-2973

KUECKER, LIZA LOUISE, sociology educator; b. La Crosse, Wis., Aug. 19, 1955; d. Duane Albert and Jacqueline Ardith (Major) K. BS in Sociology and Spanish, U. Wis., La Crosse, 1976; MA in Sociology, U. Oreg., 1979, PhD in Sociology, 1985. Asst., then assoc. prof. sociology U. S.C., Spartanburg, 1986-94; assoc. prof. Mont. State U., Billings, 1994—, mem. bd. career svcs., 1994—. Contbr. articles and book revs. to profl. jours. Mem., chmn. New Horizons Fask Force on Fair Housing, Spartanburg, 1988-93; presenter Spartanburg Human Rights Commn., 1993, Coun. Concerned Citizens, Billings, 1996; mem. minority edn. del. to China, Citizen Amb. Program, 1995. Mem. Am. Sociol. Assn., Sociologists for Women in Soc., Pacific Sociol. Assn., So. Sociol. Soc., Nat. Women's Polit. Caucus, Older Women's League. Avocations: knitting, gardening, walking, cycling.

KUEHNE, HELENIRENE ANNE, art educator; b. Douglasville, Pa., Nov. 7, 1941; d. John Julius Dusco and Helen Kathryn Rogosky; m. Paul Howard Kuehne, June 28, 1980; 1 child, John Paul. BS, Kutztown U., 1964, MEd, 1968; postgrad., U. No. Colo., 1978, LaSalle U., 1994. Tchr. elem. art Kutztown (Pa.) Area Schs., 1964-83, tchr. secondary art, 1983—, chair fine arts dept., mem. curriculum coun., 1993—. Tchr. coop. tchr. program Kutztown U., 1970—, mem. program adv. com., 1972. Works exhibited in various art shows, 1978-81. Sec. Muhlenberg Twp. Arts Bd., Laureldale, Pa., 1991—; merit badge counselor Boy Scouts Am., Laureldale, 1993—; active Friends of Reading Pub. Mus., 1991. Grantee Pa. Coun. Arts, 1993-94. Mem. AAUW (chair 1979-80, 88-89), Wyomissing Inst. Fine Arts, Delta Kappa Gamma. Avocations: gourmet cooking, music. Home: 3512 Kent Ave Laureldale PA 19605 Office: Kutztown Area Sr High 50 Trexler Ave Kutztown PA 19530-9700

KUENNE, ROBERT EUGENE, economics educator; b. St. Louis, Jan. 29, 1924; s. Edward Sebastian and Margaret (Yochum) K.; m. Janet Lawrence Brown, Sept. 7, 1957; children: Christopher Brian, Carolyn Leigh Jeppsen. Student, Harris Jr. Coll., St. Louis, 1941-42; B.J., U. Mo., 1947; AB, Washington U., St. Louis, 1948, A.M., 1949, Harvard, 1951, PhD, 1953; PhD (hon.), Umea U., 1985. Asst. prof. econs. U. Va., 1955; mem. faculty Princeton (N.J.) U., 1956—, assoc. prof., 1960-69, prof. econs., 1969—. Cons. U.S. Naval War Coll., 1954, 55, Inst. Def. Analyses, Arlington, Va., 1968—2001, Inst. for Energy Analysis, Washington, 1978-82; vis. prof. mil. systems analysis U.S. Army War Coll., 1967-85; mem. sci. and mgmt. adv. com. U.S. Army Computer Systems Command. Author: The Theory of General Economic Equilibrium, 1963, The Attack Submarine: A Study in Strategy, 1965, The Polaris Missile Strike: A General Economic Systems Analysis, 1966, Monopolistic Competition Theory: Studies in Impact, 1967, Microeconomic Theory of the Market Mechanism, 1968, Eugen von Böhm-Bawerk, 1971, Rivalrous Consonance, 1986, Economics of Oligopolistic Competition, 1992, General Equilibrium Economics, 1991, Economic Justice in American Society, 1993, Price and Nonprice Rivalry in Oligopoly: The Integrated Battleground, 1999. Served with AUS, 1943-46. Named Oliver Ellsworth Bicentennial preceptor, 1975-60; fellow European Econs. and Fin. Ctr., 1992—. Mem. Princeton Club (N.Y.C.). Home: 63 Bainbridge St Princeton NJ 08540-3901 Office: Princeton U Dept Econs Princeton NJ 08544-0001 E-mail: kuenne@princeton.edu.

KUH, ERNEST SHIU-JEN, electrical engineering educator; b. Peking, China, Oct. 2, 1928; came to U.S., 1948, naturalized, 1960; s. Zone Shung and Tsia (Chu) K.; m. Bettine Chow, Aug. 4, 1957; children: Anthony, Theodore. BS, U. Mich., 1949; MS, MIT, 1950; PhD, Stanford U., 1952; DEng (hon.), Hong Kong U. Sci. and Tech., 1997; D Eng. (hon.), Nat. Chiao Tung U., Taiwan, 1999. Mem. tech. staff Bell Tel. Labs., Murray Hill, N.J., 1952-56; assoc. prof. elec. engring. U. Calif., Berkeley, 1956-62, prof., 1962—, Miller rsch. prof., 1965-66, William S. Floyd Jr. prof. engring., 1990—, William S. Floyd Jr. prof. engring. emeritus, 1993—, chmn. dept. elec. engring. and computer sci., 1968-72, dean Coll. Engring., 1973-80. Cons. IBM Rsch. Lab., San Jose, Calif., 1957—62, NSF, 1975—84; mem. panel Nat. Bur. Stds., 1975—80; mem. vis. com. Gen. Motors Inst., 1975—79; mem. vis. com. dept. elec. engring. and computer scis. MIT, 1986—91; mem. adv. coun. elec. engring. dept. Princeton U., 1986—98; mem. bd. councilors Sch. Engring. U. So. Calif., 1986—91; mem. sci. adv. bd. Mills Coll., 1976—80. Co-author: Principles of Circuit Synthesis, 1959, Basic Circuit Theory, 1967, Theory of Linear Active Network, 1967; Linear and Nonlinear Circuits, 1987 Recipient Alexander von Humboldt award, 1980, Lamme medal Am. Soc. Endring. Edn., 1981, U. Mich. Disting. Alumnus award, 1970, Berkeley citation, 1993, C & C prize Japanese Found. for Computers and Comm. Promotion, 1996, 1998 EDAC, Phil Kaufman award; Brit. Soc. Engring. and Rsch. fellow, 1982. Fellow IEEE (Edn. medal 1981, Centenial medal 1984, Circuits and Systems Soc. award. 1988), AAAS; mem. NAE, Acad. Sinica, Chinese Acad. Scis. (fgn. mem.), Sigma Xi, Phi Kappa Phi. Office: U Calif Elec Engring & Computer Sci Berkeley CA 94720-0001

KUHL, DAVID EDMUND, physician, nuclear medicine educator; b. St. Louis, Oct. 27, 1929; s. Robert Joseph and Caroline Bertha (Waldemar) Kuhl; m. Eleanor Dell Kasales, Aug. 7, 1954; 1 child, David Stephen. AB, Temple U., Phila., 1951; MD, U. Pa., 1955; LHD (hon.), Loyola U. Chgo., 1992. Diplomate Am. Bd. Radiology, Am. Bd. Nuc. Medicine (a founder; life trustee 1977-). Intern, then resident in radiology Sch. Medicine and Hosp. U. Pa., 1955—56, 1958—63, mem. faculty, 1963—76, chief div. nuc. medicine, 1963—76, prof. radiology, 1970—76, vice chmn. dept., 1975—76; prof. bioengring. Moore Sch. Electrical Engring. U. Pa., 1974—76; prof. radiol. scis. UCLA Sch. Medicine and Hosp., 1976—86, chief div. nuc. medicine, 1976—84, vice-chmn. dept., 1977—86; prof. internal medicine and radiology U. Mich. Sch. Medicine, Ann Arbor, 1986—2000, chief divsn. nuc. medicine, dir. PET Ctr., 1986—2002, prof. radiology, 2000—. Disting. faculty lectr. in biomed. rsch. U. Mich. Med. Sch., 1992, Henry Russel lectr., 98; mem. adv. com. Dept. Energy, NIH, Internat. Commn. on Radiation Units and Measures, Max Planck Soc. Mem. editl. bd.: various jours.; contbr. articles to med. jours. Served as officer M.C. USNR, 1956—58. Recipient Rsch. Career Devel. award, USPHS, 1961—71, Ernst Jung prize for medicine, Jung Found., Hamburg, 1981, Emil H. Grubbe gold medal, Chgo. Med. Soc., 1983, Berman Found. award peaceful uses atomic energy, 1985, Steven C. Beering award for advancement med. sci., Ind. U., 1987, Disting. Grad. award, U. Pa. Sch. Medicine, 1988, William C. Menninger Meml. award, ACP, 1989, Javits Neurosci. Investigator award, NIH, 1989, Charles F. Kettering prize, GM Cancer Rsch. Found., 2001, Hon. Lifetime Mem. award, Einstein Soc., Nat. Atomic Mus. Found., 2001. Fellow: Nat. Inst. for Med. and Biol. Engring., Am. Coll. Nuc. Physicians, Am. Coll. Radiology; mem.: Inst. Medicine Nat. Aad. Scis., Soc. Neurosci., Am. Neurol. Assn. (Foster Elting Bennett Meml. lectr. 1981), Soc. Nuc. Medicine (ann. lectr. 1991, Nuc. Pioneer citation 1976, Herman L. Blumgart, M.D. Pioneer award 1995, Disting. Scientist award 1981, George Charles de Hevesy Nuc. Medicine Pioneer award 1995, Benedict Cassen prize for rsch. 1996), Radiol. Soc. N.Am. (ann. orator 1982, Outstanding Rschr. award 1996), Assn. Univ. Radiologists, Assn. Am. Physicians, Alpha Omega Alpha, Sigma Xi. Office: U Mich Hosp Divsn Nuc Medicine 1500 E Medical Center Dr Ann Arbor MI 48109-0005 E-mail: dkuhl@umich.edu.

KUHN, NANCY JANE, educator; b. Gettysburg, Pa., Feb. 27, 1946; d. Charles Elbert and Marie Jane (Sterner) K.; m. John P. Richards, Jan. 23, 1982 (div. Nov. 1991); m. Fred U. Mills, Jr., Dec. 30, 2000. BA, Roanoke Coll., 1968; MEd, U. Va., 1970. Asst. admissions dir. Roanoke Coll., Salem, Va., 1968-69, Chatham Coll., Pitts., 1970-72; assoc. prof. Community Coll. of Allegheny County, Pitts., 1972-80; sr. trainer Washington Hosp. Ctr., 1980-83; mgmt. tng. coordinator Equibank, Pitts., 1983-84; supr. ednl. devel. Alcoa, Pitts., 1984-87; mgr. edn. and tng. Alcoa Labs., Pitts., 1987-93; v.p. edn. Am. Red Cross, Washington, 1993—99; dir. edn. and tng. Nat. Rural Elect. Coop. Assn., Arlington, Va., 1999; pres. Orgnl. Learning, Alexandria, Va., 2000—. Bd. dirs. mgmt. program for execs. U. Pitts.; bd. dirs. Human Resources Leadership Forum, Washington. Bd. dirs. Hope Ctr., New Kensington, Pa., 1987-92; mem. exec. com. Nat. Tech. U., 1989-92. Gov.'s fellow, 1969-70. Mem. ASTD (nat. rsch. com. 1985-88, tech. and skills tng. conf. chair 1989, tech. profl. practice area bd. dirs. 1990—, chair 1993, Nat. Tech. Trainer of Yr. award 1990), Am. Soc. Engring. Edn. Pa., Fedn. Tchrs. (exec. bd. 1979-80), Coalition of Labor Union Women (exec. bd. 1979-80). Democrat. Avocation: sailing. Home and Office: Orgn Learning 1703 Russell Rd Alexandria VA 22301

KUHNS, LARRY J. horticulturist, educator; BS in Gen. Agr., Pa. State U., 1968; MS in Ornamental Horticulture, Ohio State U., 1975, PhD in Ornamental Horticulture, 1977. Prof. ornamental horticulture Pa. State U., University Park, 1977—97. Chmn. Pa. Nurserymen's and Allied Industries Conf., 1977—98. With U.S. Army, 1969—72. Recipient Outstanding Extension educator award, 1992. Office: Penn State U Dept of Horticulture 304 Tyson Bldg University Park PA 16802*

KUHNS, SALLY NELSON, trumpeter, music ensemble director, educator; b. West Chester, Pa., Oct. 19, 1952; d. Kenneth Nelson and Katharine (Rhoads) Foster; m. Thomas Joseph Kuhns, July 7, 1990. Student, Ithaca Coll., 1970; MusB in Performance, New Sch. Music, Phila., 1974; MusM in Performance, Northwestern U., 1981. Trumpeter Youth Orch. of Greater Phila., 1970-74; asst. prin. trumpeter Ft. Wayne (Ind.) Philharm., 1975-79, Oreg. Symphony, Portland, 1978—; founder, dir. Portland Unlimited Chamber Ensemble, 1979—; trumpeter Oreg. Coast Festival, Sunriver Music Festival, 1979-82; 1st trumpeter Met. Brass Co., Portland, 1981-84, Peter Britt Festival, Jacksonville, Oreg., 1982-86, Chamber Music NW, 2000, Chamber Music Soc. Lincoln Center, NY, 2001. Tchr. trumpet Warner Pacific U., Portland, 1983-84, U. Portland, 1985. Rec. artist: (with Met. Brass Co.) Made in Oregon, 1986, Christmas Past and Present, 1987; writer, contbr. Woodwind, Brass and Percussion World; soloist Oreg. Symphony, 1984, 96. Recipient Am. Brass Chamber Music award Aspen Music Festival, 1977; scholar New Sch. Music, 1969-74, Berkshire Music Festival, 1975, Aspen Festival 1976-79, Spoleto Festival, 1980. Mem. Internat. Trumpet Guild, Portland Brass Soc., Am. Fedn. Musicians. Home and Office: 4209 SW Downs View Ct Portland OR 97221

KUIPER, NICHOLAS AHLRICH, psychology educator; b. Chatham, Ont., Can., Jan. 5, 1953; s. Nicolas and Wilma (Herfst) K.; m. Linda Joan Olinger, Aug. 8, 1983; 1 child, Heather Nicole. BA with honors, U. Western Ont., London, 1975; MS in Psychology, U. Calgary, Alta., Can., 1976; PhD in Psychology, 1978. Registered psychologist. Asst. prof. dept. psychology U. Western Ont., 1978-83; assoc. prof., 1983-88; prof., 1988—; dir. clin. psychology program, 1984-89; exec. officer grad. affairs, 1989-91, 95-96; assoc. dean Faculty Grad. Studies, 1998—2002. Contbr. numerous articles on depression, sense of humor, mental health, emotion, personality and well being to profl. jours. Mem. Canadian Psychol. Assn. Home: 95 Orkney Crescent London ON Canada N5X 3R8 Office: U Western Ont, Dept Psychology London ON Canada N6A 5C2

KUKURA, RITA ANNE, pre-school educator; b. Tulsa, July 18, 1947; d. James Albert and Carmen Alberta (Parsons) Hayden; m. Joel Richard Graft, Oct. 28, 1967 (dec. Apr. 1969); m. Raymond Richard Kukura, Dec. 18, 1971 (div. 1981); children: Tiffany Carmen Noel, Austin Raymond. BS, Kent. State U., 1971; MS, Okla. State U., 1991. Cert. early childhood, nursery, elem. tchr., Okla., spl. edn. tchr. for emotionally disturbed. Tchr. kindergarten Southlyn Elem. Sch., Lyndhurst, Ohio, 1971-73; elem. tchr. Wakefield Acad., Tulsa, 1981-83, tchr. kindergarten, 1983-87; reg. early intervention coord. Okla. Dept. Edn., Tulsa, 1990-92; tchr. devel. delayed children, coord. integrated program Child Devel. Inst. Children's Med. Ctr., Tulsa, 1992-93; tchr. elem. sch. Prue (Okla.) Schs., 1993-95, Tulsa Pub. Schs., 1995—. Manuscript reviewer for profl. orgns., 1989-91; mem. human rights com. Ind. Opportunities of Okla., 1995—; Oklahoma Edn. Assn. Leadership Acad., 1998; del. Okla. Edn. Assembly, 1995; grant reviewer for spl. grants State Dept. Edn., 1996; presenter and lectr. in field. Den leader Cub Scouts Am., Tulsa, 1984-88; com. mem. Boy Scouts Am., Tulsa, 1984-88; vol. office worker Met. Tulsa Citizen Crime Commn., 1986; adv. com. Latchkey Project, Tulsa County, 1985; ad hoc task force on day care Interagy. Coord. Coun., 1989-91; nat. rep. Tourette Syndrome Assn. to Nat. Broadcasting Assn. AERho, 1990-93; mem. resource com. Ronald McDonald House, 1990-92, vol. Tulsa area, 1991-97, STARBASE, 1993—, Drug Edn. for Youth, 1994; mem. adv. bd. Tulsa Regional Coordinating Coun. for Svcs. to Children and Youth and Families, 1991-92; planning com. symposium Magic Coun. Girl Scouts Am., 1991-93; lt. sr. mem. Tulsa Composite Squadron CAP, 1992-94; presenter numerous confs.; workshop participant Alternatives to Violence Project, 1996. Recipient Den Leader Tng. award Boy Scouts Am., 1988, State Commendation medal Air N.G., 1993. Mem. AAUW (bd. dirs. Tulsa county chpt. 1991-93, mem., 1997-2000), Nat. Assn. Early Childhood Tchr. Educators, Nat. Tourette Syndrome Assn. (state pres. 1987-92, state dir. 1992-93, hon. mem. bd. dirs. 1993, area coord., fundraiser 1988-90), Gold Star Wives Am., Tulsa Classroom Tchrs. Assn. (bldg. del. 1997-98), Okla. Edn. Assn. (leadership acad. 1998), Okla. Edn. Assn. (mem. resolution com. 1998-2000), Kappa Delta Pi, Omicron Nu, Alpha Epsilon Rho (hon. mem. S.W. region 1990-93), Phi Delta Kappa. Roman Catholic. Avocations: piano, exercising, reading. Office: Burroughs Elem Sch 1927 N Cincinnati Tulsa OK 74106 E-mail: kukurri@tulsaschools.org.

KULESZA, CAROL MAY, principal, elementary school educator; b. Terre Haute, Ind., Apr. 28, 1946; d. Robert Leo and Harriet Alice (Dupuy) Akers; m. Stanley Anthony Kulesza, May 25, 1968; children: Brian Michael, Timothy John, Emily Kathryn. BA in Elem. Edn., St. Mary-of-the-Woods Coll., 1968; MA in Pvt. Sch. Adminstrn., U. San Francisco, 1990. Tchr. La Mesa Elem. Sch., Vandenberg Village, Calif., 1968-69, St. Philip Sch., Evansville, Ind., 1970-73; substitute tchr. St. Cyprian Sch., Long Beach, Calif., 1980-83, Paramount (Calif.) Unifed Sch. Dist., 1980-83; tchr. St. Barnabas Sch., Long Beach, 1983-88; prin. St. Pancratius Sch., Lakewood, Calif., 1988-93, tchr. 2nd grade, 1993-97, prin., 1997—. Catechist Archdiocese of L.A., 1983—. Grantee St. Mary-of-the-Woods Coll., 1967, Inst. for Cath. Ednl. Leadership, 1988. Mem. ASCD, Nat. Cath. Edn. Assn. Avocations: crocheting, sewing. Home: 5638 Hayter Ave Lakewood CA 90712-1607

KULIKOWSKI, CASIMIR ALEXANDER, computer science and engineering educator; b. Hertford, Herts, Eng., May 4, 1944; arrived in U.S., 1961; s. Victor A. and Isabel S. (Tuckett) Kulikowski; m. Christine A. Wilk, May 31, 1969; children: Michael Edward, Victoria Anne. BE with honors, Yale U., 1965, MS, 1966; PhD, U. Hawaii, 1970. From asst. prof. to assoc. prof. Rutgers U., New Brunswick, NJ, 1970—77, prof., 1977—97, chmn. dept. computer sci., 1984—90, dir. Lab. Computer Sci. Rsch., 1985—96, bd. govs. prof., 1997—. Mem. bd. sci. counselors Nat. Libr. Medicine, Bethesda, Md., 1984—87; mem. biomed. libr. rev. com. NIH, 1994—99, chair, 1997—99. Author: A Practical Guide to Designing Expert Systems, 1984, Computer Systems that Learn, 1992; editor: Artificial Intelligence Expert Systems and Languages in Modeling & Simulation, 1988; co-editor: Yearbook of Medical Informatics, 2001—; assoc. editor: Artificial Intelligence in Medicine Jour., 2001—; mem. editl. bd. Computers in Biology and Medicine, 1980—, Jour. Am. Med. Informatics Assn., 1993—98, Methods Info. in Medicine, 1999—, Iterations: An Interdisciplinary Jour. of Software History, 2001—. Pres. Highland Park (N.J.) Residents Assn., 1983—88. Fellow: IEEE, AAAS, Am. Inst. Med. and Biol. Engring., Am. Coll. Med. Informatics, Am. Assn. Artificial Intelligence; mem.: NAS Inst. Medicine. Office: Rutgers U Dept Computer Sci Hill Ctr Busch Campus New Brunswick NJ 08903

KULIS, ELLEN MAE, elementary education educator; b. Punxsutawney, Pa., Jan. 19, 1943; d. John Williams and Julia (Knopick) Johnson; m. Raymond Edward Kulis, July 2, 1983. BS in Elem. Edn., Ind. U., Pa., 1966; MS in Elem. Edn., Clarion U., Pa., 1970; principalship, Penn State U., University Park, Pa., 1988. First grade tchr. Ridgway Sch. Dist., Ridgway, Pa., 1966-67; head start tchr. Jefferson County, Syskesville, Pa., summers 1967-70; first grade tchr. Punxsutawney Areas Schs., Punxsutawney, Pa., 1970-85, third grade tchr., 1985—. Co-op tchr. Ind. U., Pa., 1979-90. Asst. Encore Group, Punxsutawney, Pa., 1978-81; mem. Sodality, 1958-64, Newman Ctr., Indiana, Pa., 1983-90. Mem. PTO, PSEA, NEA, PAEA, RAEA, Delta Kappa Gamma. Democrat. Byzantine Catholic. Home: 921 Lilac St Indiana PA 15701-3332

KULP, BETTE JONEVE, retired educator, wallpaper installation business owner; b. Pomona, Calif., Jan. 5, 1936; d. John M. and Eva Kathleen (Lynch) Beck; m. Edwin Hanaway Kulp, Sept. 12, 1957 (div. Apr. 1972); m. Frank Harold Little, Oct. 8, 1977. BS in Home Econs., UCLA, 1957, GPPS credential, 1972. Credential C.C. counselor, gen. pupil personnel svcs., tchr. homemaking. Social worker L.A. County DPSS, 1957-59; tchr., counselor L.A. City Sch. Dist., 1959-81; wallpaper installer West Los Angeles, Calif., 1981-87. Mem. UCLA Scholarship Com. West L.A., San Luis Obispo, Calif., 1978—; judge Acad. Decathalon, San Luis Obispo County, 1989-90, 92, 98-2003. Vol. Daffodil Days Am. Cancer Soc., San Luis Obispo, 1992—, Am. Heart Assn., San Luis Obispo, 1992, Sr. Nutrition Program, San Luis Obispo, 1993-2002; runner Spl. Olympics, San Luis Obispo, 1992; participant Audubon Bird-A-Thon, San Luis Obispo, 1993; locator nesting birds Audubon Breeding Bird Atlas, San Luis Obispo, 1992; fundraiser Womens Shelter Program, San Luis Obispo, 1993-94; precinct clk., judge San Luis Obispo County Election Bd., 1989—; mem. Sch. Dist. Orgn. Com. San Luis Obispo County Schs., 1995—; aide Dist. 3 San Luis Obispo County Bd. Suprs., 1994-96; campaign com. Marie Kiersch for Cuesta Coll. Bd. Trustees, 1994; vol. 22nd Congl. Dist., 1997, Neighborhood Vol. March of Dimes, 1998. Recipient Appreciation award Women's Shelter Program, 1993, Unsung Heroine award San Luis Obispo Commn. Status Women, 1995. Mem. AAUW (treas. San Luis Obispo br. 1989-91, pres.-elect 1991-92, pres. 1992-93, bylaws revision com. 1993, San Luis Obispo Interbr. chair 1993-94, chair state resolutions 1994-95, Grant Honoree 1994, 2000, membership co-v.p. 1994-95, herstory coord., 1995-96, Cuesta scholarship chair 1995-96,scholarship treas. 2000—, parliamentarian 1993-94,interbranch rep., 2003-04; dual mem. five cities Pismo 1994, endorsement com. 1995, scholarship com. 1995—, chair 1996-2002,2003-04, bylaws chair 1996-97, 99, 2001, co-pres. 1998-99, scholarship treas. 2000—, tech. trek com. 2001, scholarship fundraising v.p., 2002-03, interbranch rep., 2003—), Santa Lucia Bridge Club, Phi Mu Alumnae (founder Calif. Ctrl. Coast chpt.), Newcomers Club, Morro Coast Audubon Soc. Avocations: bridge, birding, travel, reading, puzzles. Home: 2362 Meadow St San Luis Obispo CA 93401-5628

KULP, JONATHAN B. retired secondary school educator; b. Norristown, Pa., July 18, 1937; s. Abraham Moyer and Frances Mann (Connelly) K.; m. Priscilla Lory June 20, 1959 (div. 1968); m. Carol Janice (Nabinger) Apr. 5, 1968; children: Julie E., Penny S. BA, Dickinson Coll., Carlisle, Pa., 1959; MA, Am. U., 1963. Cert. tchr., Pa. Tchr., coach The Mercersburg (Pa.) Acad., 1959-60, The Episcopal Acad., Merion, Pa., 1963—2002, head history dept., 1983-89, dir. curriculum and faculty devel., 1989-96, dean of faculty, 1996-2000, asst. head sch., 2000—02; ret., 2002; ednl. cons. and faculty trainer, 2003. Adv. com. Project Cares, Exton, Pa., 1979-82; mem. Dodge Found. seminar on Women in History, Bryn Mawr, Pa., 1985-86; reader for Am. History Advanced Placement Program of Coll. Bds., Princeton, 1987; participant study mission Basic Edn. Leaders Study, China, Hong Kong, 1993; cons. in field. Active ARC, Montrose, Pa., 1974-96; mem. Downingtown Area Sch. Bd., Downingtown, Pa., 1975-79, pres. 1978-79; The Exton Chorale, Exton, Pa., 1976-99, v.p., 1977-79, pres. 1981; trustee Susquehannock Camps Inc., 2003—. Served with USAR, 1960-66. Cert. of Achievement Teaching fellow Commonwealth Partnership, 1986; Fellowship award, 1986; ind. study in humanities fellow Coun. for Basic Edn. and Nat. Endowment, 1987, Woodrow Wilson fellow in Am. History, 1989. Mem. ASCD, Ind. Sch. Tchrs. Assn. Phila. (chmn. history program 1985-88, profl. devel. chair 1991—), Nat. Interscholastic Swim Coaches Assn. Am., Coun. Basic Edn., Orgn. Am. Historians, Phila. Area Coun. for Women in Ind. Schs. (co-chmn. 1987-88, mem. exec. com. 1986-90). Republican. Avocations: swimming, tennis, walking, woodworking. Home: 1230 Street Rd Chester Springs PA 19425-1606

KUMAR, ASHOK, operations management educator; s. Kewal Krishna and Shanti Devi Kulshrestha; m. Manjusha K. Kumar, Apr. 27, 1980; children: Abhinav, Abhijeet. BSc, Agra U., Dehradun, 1965; B in Tech., Indian Inst. Tech., Kanpur, India, 1970; MSc, U. Birmingham, U.K., 1978; PhD, Purdue U., 1990. Cert. quality mgr. Am. Soc. Quality. Sr. quality assurance mgr. Hindustan Aeronautics Ltd., Nasik, India, 1970—84; vis. asst. prof. ops. mgmt. Case Western Res. U., Cleve., 1990—92; assoc. prof. mgmt. Grand Valley State U., Grand Rapids, Mich., 1992—. Contbr. over 100 articles in ops. mgmt. to profl. publs. Bd. dirs. Asian Ctr., Grand Rapids, 1999—2002. Recipient numerous rsch. and tchg. awards. Mem.: Am. Soc. Quality. Office: Grand Valley State Univ 454C DeVos Hall 401 W Fulton Grand Rapids MI 49504 Office Fax: 616-336-7445. Personal E-mail: ashokumar@aol.com. E-mail: kumara@gvsu.edu.

KUMAR, KRISHNA, retired physics educator; b. Meerut, India, July 14, 1936; came to U.S., 1956, naturalized, 1966; s. Rangi and Susheila (Devi) Lal; m. Katharine Johnson, May 1, 1960; children: Jai Robert, Raj David. BSc in Physics, Chemistry and Math., Agra U., 1953, MSc in Physics, 1955; MS in Physics, Carnegie Mellon U., 1959, PhD in Physics, 1964. Rsch. assoc. Mich. State U., 1963-66, MIT, 1966-67; rsch. fellow Niels Bohr Inst., Copenhagen, 1967-69; physicist Oak Ridge (Tenn.) Nat. Lab., 1969-71; assoc. prof. Vanderbilt U., Nashville, 1971-77; fgn. collaborator AEC of France, Paris, 1977-79; Nordita prof. U. Bergen, Norway, 1979-80; prof. physics Tenn. Tech. U., Cookeville, 1980-83, univ. prof. physics, 1983-99, prof. physics emeritus, 1999—. Tax assoc. H&R Block, 2003—; disting. hon. fellow Manibal Acad. Higher Edn., India, 2002—; lectr. in field; cons. various rsch. labs. Author: Nuclear Models and the Search for Unity in Nuclear Physics, 1984, Superheavy Elements, 1989, (with J.R. Kumar) The Redhead From Alpha Centauri, 2003; contbr. articles to profl. jours., books. Sec. India Assn., Pitts., 1958-59; faculty advisor, 1990-99, assoc. mem. Triangle Fraternity, 1990-99; deacon Presbyn. Ch., 1991-93, elder, 2000-02; faculty advisor Indian Assn. of Cookeville, 1994-95; mem. exec. com. Putnam County Dem. Party, 1999-2002. Recipient Gold medal Agra U., 1955; NSF rsch. grantee, 1972-75; Paul Harris fellow Rotary Internat., 1995. Mem. Indian Phys. Soc., Am. Phys. Soc., Tenn. Acad. Scis., Internat. Cmty. Hospitality Assn. (pres. 1992-94), Planetary Soc., Phi Kappa Phi, Sigma Pi Sigma, Sigma Xi (bd. dirs. 1992-93, charter mem. chpt. installation 1994). Unity Ch. Home: 718 W 12th St Cookeville TN 38501-7788 E-mail: kkaadmi_99@yahoo.com.

KUMAR, MARY LOUISE, physician, educator; b. Chgo., Jan. 23, 1941; d. Donald Martin and Esther (Acton) Morrison; m. Unni P. K. Kumar, June 15, 1968; children: Krishna, Shanta, Ravi, Maya. BA, U. Colo., 1962; MD, Case Western Res. U., 1967. Intern, resident Cleve. Met. Gen. Hosp., 1967-70, chief resident, 1970-71, instr. pediatrics, 1971-75, asst. prof., 1975-85; assoc. prof. Case Western Reserve Sch. Medicine, Cleve., 1985—94, prof., 1995—. Office: Metro Health Med Ctr 2500 Metro Health Dr Cleveland OH 44109-1957

KUMAR, RAJENDRA, electrical engineering educator; b. Amroha, India, Aug. 22, 1948; came to U.S., 1980; s. Satya Pal Agarwal and Kailash Vati Agarwal; m. Pushpa Agarwal, Feb. 16, 1971; children: Anshu, Shipra. BS in Math. and Sci., Meerut Coll., 1964; BEE, Indian Inst. Tech., Kanpur, 1969, MEE, 1977; PhD in Electrical Engring., U. New Castle, NSW, Australia, 1981. Mem. tech. staff Electronis and Radar Devel., Bangalore, India, 1969-72; rsch. engr. Indian Inst. Tech., Kanpur, 1972-77; asst. prof. Calif. State U., Fullerton, 1981-83, Brown U., Providence, 1980-81; prof. Calif. State U., Long Beach, 1983—. Cons. Jet Propulsion Lab., Pasadena, Calif., 1984-91, Aerospace Corp., El Segundo, Calif., 1995—. Contbr. articles. Recipient Best Paper award Internat. Telemetering Conf., Las Vegas, 1986, 10 New Technology awards NASA, Washington, 1987-91. Mem.: AAUP, AIAA, NEA, IEEE (sr.), Inst. of Navigation, Calif. Faculty Assn., Inst. Navigation, Auto Club So. Calif. (Cerritos), Tau Beta Pi (eminent mem.), Eta Kappa Nu, Sigma Xi. Achievements include patents for efficient detections and signal parameter estimation with applications to hihg dynamic GPS receivers; multiusage estimation of received carrier signal parameters under very high dynamic conditions of the receiver; fast frequency acquisition via adaptive least squares algorithms; Kalman filter ionospheric delay estimator; method and apparatus for reducing multipath signal error using deconvolution; others. Avocations: gardening, walking, hiking, reading. Home: 13910 Rose St Cerritos CA 90703-9043 Office: Calif State U 1250 N Bellflower Blvd Long Beach CA 90840-0001

KUMAR, SHRAWAN, university educator physical therapy, ergonomics consultant; b. Allahabad, India, July 1, 1939; arrived in Can., 1974; s. Tribeni and Dhairyavati (Devi) Shankar; m. Rita Srivastava, July 7, 1965; chidlren: Rejesh, Sheela. BSc, U. Allahabad, 1959, MSc, 1962; PhD, U. Surrey (Eng.), 1971, DSc, 1994. Fellow in ergonomics U. Dublin, Ireland, 1971-73; rsch. assoc. in rehab. U. Toronto, Ont., Can., 1974-77; asst. prof. phys. therapy U. Alta., Edmonton, Can., 1977-79, assoc. prof. phys. therapy, 1979-82, prof. phys. therapy, 1982—, McCalla Rsch. prof., 1984-85, Killam ann. prof., 1997-98. Vis. prof. U. Mich., 1983-84; hon. prof. health and rehab. scis. U. Queensland, Australia, 1998; speaker in field. Recipient Am. Medal of Honor, Am. Biog. Inst., 2003. Fellow Ergonomics Soc. (Sir Frederic Bartlett medal 1997, Soc. lectr. 2003), Assn. of Can. Ergonomists, Human Factors and Ergonomics Soc. (Disting. Internat. Colleague 1997, Jack Kraft Innovator award, 2000), Internat. Ergonomics Assn. (Ergonomic Devel. award, 2000); mem. Am. Soc. Biomechanics, Internat. Soc. for Occupl. Ergonomics (pres. 1998-99). Office: U Alta 3-75 Corbett Hall Edmonton AB Canada T6G 2G4

KUMMEROW, ARNOLD A. superintendent of schools; b. Framingham, Mass., Mar. 25, 1945; s. Arnold A. Sr. and Elizabeth Patricia (Westfield) K.; m. Constance Booth, July 10, 1971. BME, Eastern Mich. U., 1968, MA, 1975; PhD, U. Mich., 1989. Cert. adminstrn., Mich. Instrumental music dir. Vandercook Lake Pub. Schs., Jackson, Mich., 1968-74; instrumental music dir., asst. prin., prin. L'Anse Creuse Pub. Schs., Mt. Clemens, Mich., 1975-89; asst. supt. curriculum and pers. Lincoln Consol. Schs., Ypsilanti, Mich., 1989-91; asst. supt. Ypsilanti Pub. Schs., 1991-93; mem. curriculum devel. staff Mich. Dept. Edn., 1993-94; supt. Carsonville-Port Sanilac (Mich.) Schs., 1994-97, Armada (Mich.) Area Schs., 1997—. Named Exemplary Sch. Prin., Mich. Dept. Edn. and U.S. Dept. Edn. Mem. AASA, MASA, ASCD. Home: 17201 Knollwood Dr Clinton Township MI 48038-2833 Office: Armada Area Schs 74500 Burk St Armada MI 48005-3314

KUMMETH, PATRICIA JOAN, nursing educator; b. Libertyville, Ill., Mar. 7, 1949; d. Francis Alphonse Kummeth, Elizabeth Claire Kummeth. BSN, Coll. St. Teresa, 1970; MSN, U. Wis., Eau Claire, 1988. Registered nurse. Staff RN med. Saint Marys Hosp., Rochester, Minn., 1970—72, clin. insvc. educator, 1972—76, head nurse med., 1976—78, staff RN hematology/nephrology, 1978—81; nursing edn. specialist Mayo Clinic Hosp., Rochester, 1982—. Nursing continuing edn. appraiser Am. Nurses' Credentialing Ctr., Washington, 1998—. Author: (booklet) Problem-Oriented Charting: A Study Guide, 1976; developer (nursing asst. model in jour.) Med.-Surg. Nursing, 2001. Sec. Rochester Women's Softball Assn., 1994—98. Recipient Breaking Barriers award, Minn. Coalition to Promote Women in Athletic Leadership, 2001. Mem.: ANA (congress on nursing practice and economics 1998—2002), Minn. Nurses Assn. (commn. nursing practice 1999—2003, sec. 1992—93, commn. on edn. 1991—92), Acad. Med.-Surg. Nurses (sec. Upper Miss. River Valley chpt. 1999—2001), Am. Soc.Healthcare Educators and Trainers (info. mgr. Minn. affiliate 1993—95), Minn. Nurses Assn. (pres. 6th dist. 1988—92, sec. 1995—99, dir. 2000—02), Sigma Theta Tau (Kappa Mu chpt.), American Nurses' Credentialing Center (Commn. Accreditation 1998—2002). Roman Catholic. Avocations: reading, golf, travel. Office: Mayo Clinic Hosp 1216 Second St SW - 7 Marian Hall Rochester MN 55902

KUMTA, PRASHANT NAGESH, materials science educator, engineering educator, consultant; b. Madras, India, Aug. 17, 1960; arrived in U.S., 1984; s. Nagesh Shanker and Soomathee Nagesh (Marballi) Kumta; m. Ujwala Prashant Kamath; children: Tanay, Aniket. BTech, Indian Inst. Tech., Bombay, 1984; MS, U. Ariz., 1987, PhD, 1990. Undergrad. rsch. asst. Indian Inst. Tech., Bombay, 1983-84; grad. work asst. Oreg. Grad. Ctr., Beaverton, 1984-85; grad. tchg. asst. U. Ariz., Tucson, 1985-87, grad. rsch. asst., 1987-88, grad. rsch. assoc., 1988-90; asst. prof. Carnegie Mellon U., Pitts., 1990-95, assoc. prof., 1995-99, prof., 1999—; editor Materials Sci. and Engring. B, 2001—. Prin. investigator Eveready Battery Co., Cleve., 1993-2000, Mitsubishi Chem. Co., Japan, 2000—; cons. Changs Ascending, Taiwan, 2000—; prin. investigator Jet Propulsion Lab., Pasadena, Calif., 1997-2000, Pitts. Plate Glass (PPG) Industries, 1998-2000, Mitsubishi Chem. Co., Japan, 2000—; cons. Timo Industry, Pitts., 1992-93, EIC, Mass., 2001-02; mem. summer rsch. faculty Air Force Office, Washington, 1993. Author: Role of Ceramics in Advanced Electrochemical Systems, 1996, Covalent Ceramics: Science and Technology of Non-Oxides, 1996, Chemical Processing Aspects of Electronic Ceramics, 1998, Processing and Characterization of Electrochemical Materials and Devices, 2000, 2001, 2002; contbr. articles; editor: Materials Science of Engineering B, 2001—. Recipient Rsch. initiation award NSF, Washington, 1993; grantee NSF, Air Force Office, Army Rsch. Office Def., Advanced Rsch. Projects Agy., Washington, 1993—, Office of Naval Rsch., Washington, 2000—. Mem. Am. Ceramic Soc., Materials Rsch. Soc., Electrochem. Soc. Achievements include pioneering development of thio-sol-gel and hydrazide sol-gel processes to synthesize transition and rare-earth chalcogenides and nitrides, ceramics, novel complexed precursor approaches to new non-oxide ceramics, mechanochemical synthesis of oxide and non-oxide ceramics and composites, patents awarded related to development of novel cathode materials for primary batteries, novel processes to fabricate lithium-ion electrodes and new biomaterials for bone tissue engineering and gene delivery; patent for new class of polymer-ceramic composites for bone tissue engineering and new class of stable cathodes for lithium-ion batteries. Office: Carnegie Mellon U Dept Science 4309 Wean Hall 5000 Forbes Ave Pittsburgh PA 15213-3890 E-mail: kumta@cmu.edu.

KUNC, JOSEPH ANTHONY, physics and engineering educator, consultant; b. Baranowicze, Poland, Nov. 1, 1943; came to U.S., 1978; s. Stefan and Helena (Kozakiewicz) K.; m. Mary Eva Smolska, May 24, 1979; 1 child, Robert. PhD, Warsaw Tech. U., 1974. Assoc. prof. Warsaw Tech. U., 1974-79; rsch. assoc. prof. U. So. Calif., L.A., 1980-84, assoc. prof., 1985-89, prof. dept. aerospace engring., dept. physics, 1990—. Rsch. affiliate Jet Propulsion Lab., Calif. Inst. Tech., 1982-83; vis. scholar Inst. Theoretical Atomic and Molecular Physics, Harvard U., Cambridge, Mass., 1991; vis. scholar dept. high-temperature plasma Nat. Inst. for Nuclear Studies, Warsaw, 1991; vis. scholar atomic and plasma radiation divsn. Nat. Bur. Stds., Washington, 1979; cons. Nat. Tech. Systems, L.A., 1984-86, Phys. Optics Corp., Torrance, Calif., 1988—, Wolfsdorf and Assocs., L.A., 1991; mem. com. on liquid phase kinetics NRC, 1985-86; mem. Dept. Def. Adv. Group on Electron Devices, 1985—; mem. internat. adv. bd. Internat. Symposia Rarefied Gas Dynamics, 1994—; chmn. adv. bd. numerous sci. workshops and symposia. Author: (with others) Advances in Pulsed Power Technology, 1991, Progress in Astronautics and Aeronautics, vol. 116, 1989; contbr. over 200 articles to profl. jours., confs., symposia. Recipient award of merit Nat. Bur. Stds., 1979; fellow Nat. Bur. Stds., 1978, Harvard/Smithsonian fellow Inst. Theoretical Atomic and Molecular Physics, Harvard U., 1991. Fellow AIAA (assoc., mem. thermophysics com. 1994—, chmn. thermophysics publs. com. 1995—), Am. Phys. Soc.; mem. IEEE (sr.), Phi Beta Delta (co-founder Beta Kappa chpt.). Achievements include patent for heat release in micromechanical actuators and engines; principal investigator numerous government-sponsored research programs. Office: U So Calif University Park Mc 1191 Los Angeles CA 90089-0001

KUNDEL, HAROLD LOUIS, radiologist, educator; b. N.Y.C., Aug. 15, 1933; s. John A. and Emma E. (Tolle) K.; m. Alice Marie Pape, Mar. 28, 1958; children: Jean, Catherine, Peter AB, Columbia U., 1955, MD, 1959; MS, Temple U., 1963; MA (hon.), U. Pa., 1980. Diplomate Am. Bd. Radiology. Asst. to assoc. prof. Temple U., Phila., 1967-73, prof. radiology, 1973-80; Matthew J. Wilson prof. research radiology U. Pa., Phila., 1980—2001, Matthew J. Wilson prof. emeritus radiology, 2001—. Dir. Pendergrass Diagnostic Imaging Labs. U. Pa., Phila., 1980—2001. Contbr. articles to profl. jours. Capt. USAF, 1963—65. Fellow: Am. Coll. Radiology; mem.: Soc. Thoracic Radiology, Am. Roentgen Ray Soc., Radiol. Soc. N.Am. (Honor award 1978), Assn. Univ. Radiologists (Meml. award 1963, Stauffer award 1982), Alpha Omega Alpha. Lutheran.

KUNES, JOSEF, science educator, consultant; b. Nechanice, West Bohemia, Czech Republic, Jan. 19, 1930; s. Alois and Josefa (Mareskovà) Kunes; m. Marie Vojtasová, Dec. 17, 1955; children: Ilja, Oleg. MSc, Tech. U., Pilsen, Czech Republic, 1953, PhD, 1964; DSc, Tech. U., Prague, Czech Republic, 1991. Asst. lectr. Tech. U., Pilsen, 1953-56, lectr., 1956-66, asst. prof., 1966-76; leading sci. worker Skoda Rsch., 1976-91; prof. U. West Bohemia, Pilsen, 1992—, Tech. U., Prague, 1994—, head dept. automatisation, sub-dean faculty mech. engring., 1969—70. Head divsn. thermomechanics Rsch. Ctr. New Techs., 2000—. Co-author: (book) Hybride Modeling of Thermal Processes, 1987, Fundamentals of Modeling, 1989; author: Modeling of Thermal Processes, 1989; contbr. articles to profl. jours. Recipient Regional prize for results in foundry thermomechanics rsch., 1988, Best Sci. Book prize, Czech Literal Fund, 1990, prize, Czech Found. Sci., 1995. Mem.: Czech Tech. Soc., Soc. Cybernetics, Soc. Mechanics. Avocations: theater, music, philosophy, nature. Home: Kardinala Berana 11 30125 Plzeň Czech Republic Office: U West Bohemia Fac App Sci Dept Physics PO Box 314 Plzeň 30614 Czech Republic E-mail: kunes@ntc.zcu.cz., kunes@kfy.zcu.cz.

KUNEY, GARY WALLACE, elementary school educator, real estate agent; b. Gridley, Calif., July 30, 1951; s. W. Loren and Tawana Jo (Yadon) K.; m. Nancy Ellen Borden, Aug. 22, 1974. BS with honors, Portland State U., 1980, MS in Tchg., 1983. Cert. tchr., Oreg., Wash. Adaptive specialist Beaverton (Oreg.) Sch. Dist., 1979-80; phys. edn. specialist Gresham (Oreg.) Grade Dist., 1980-81, Damascus (Oreg.) Union Dist., 1981-82; self def. instr. Clackamas Cmty. Coll., Milwaukie, 1983; phys. edn. specialist North Clackamas Dist., Milwaukie, 1982-83, Damascus Union Dist., 1983-86; grad. instr. Portland State Continuing Edn., 1991; instr. Portland Parks Bur., 1988-93; phys. edn. specialist Portland Pub. Schs., 1986—. U.S. fitness del. Citizen's Amb. Program, Hungary and Russia, 1991; wellness dir. Woodmere and Woodlawn Schs., Portland, 1986—; volleyball coach, 1980-86. Author: Fitness Success for Everyone, 1985 (Impact II award 1990), Body and Mind: The WRITE Way, 1986 (Impact II award 1989); co-author: School Wide Daily Sports Math, 1989 (Impact II award 1991), (with others) Goals and Strategies for Teaching Physical Education by Dr. Hellison, 1985. With U.S. Army, 1969-76. Mem. AAHPERD (chair com. '95 conv. 1994-95), Masons (32 degree, line officer lodge 55, sr. warden 1991—, pub. sch. employee outstanding svc. award 1991), Scottish Rite (line officer Rose Croix, wise master). Republican. Avocations: Tae Kwon Do, acting in plays, waterskiing, cross-country skiing. Home: 3806 SE Rural St Portland OR 97202-7839

KUNG, HAROLD HING-CHUEN, engineering educator; b. Hong Kong, Oct. 12, 1949; s. Shien C. and Kai Sau (Wong) K.; m. Mayfair Chu, June 12, 1971; children: Alexander, Benjamin. BS in chem. engring., U. Wis., 1971; PhD in chemistry, Northwestern U., 1974. Rsch. sci. ctrl. rsch. and devel. dept. E.I. duPont de Nemours & Co., Wilmington, Del., 1974-76; asst. prof. chem. engring. Northwestern U., 1976, asst. prof. chem. engring. and chemistry, 1977, assoc. prof., 1981, prof. chem. engring. and chemistry, 1985-97, chmn. chemical engring., 1986-92; dir. Ctr. for Catalysis and Surface Sci., 1993-97. Chmn. Gordon rsch. Conf. on Catalysis, 1995; tech. advisor UNIDO Mission, 1995; John McClanahan Henske Disting. lectr. Yale U., 1996; mem. com. to rev. PNGV program Nat. Rsch. Coun., 1996-2000; Olaf Hongen vis. prof. U. Wis., Madison, 1999. Author: Transition Metal Oxides, Surface Chemistry and Catalysis, 1989, Catalyst Modificaton-Selective Oxidation Processes, 1991; editor: Methanol Production and Use, 1994, Applied Catalysis A = General, 1996—; patents include Photolysis of Water Using Rhodate Semiconductive Electrodes, and Oxidative Dehydrogenation of Alkanes to Unsaturated Hydrocarbons. Japanese Soc. for Promotion of Sci. fellow, 1996. Mem. AIChE, Am. Chem. Soc., Chgo. Catalysis Club (program chair 1992, pres. 1993, Herman Pines award 1999), N.Am. Catalysis Soc. (Paul H. Emmett award 1991, Robert L. Barwell lectr. 1999), Phi Lambda Epsilon. Office: Dept of Chem Engring Northwestern University 2145 Sheridan Rd Evanston IL 60208-0834 E-mail: hkung@northwestern.edu.

KUNG, SHAIN-DOW, molecular biologist, academic administrator; b. China, Mar. 14, 1935; came to U.S., 1971, naturalized, 1977; s. Chao-tzen and Chih (Zhu) K. Grad., Chung-Hsing U., Taiwan, China, 1958; PhD, U. Toronto, Can., 1968. m. Helen C.C. Kung, Sept. 5, 1964; children: Grace, David, Andrew. Rsch. fellow Hosp. for Sick Children, Toronto, 1968-70; biologist UCLA, 1971-74; asst. prof. biology U. Md., Baltimore County, 1974-77, assoc. prof., 1977-82, prof., 1982-86, acting chmn. dept., 1982-84, assoc. dean arts and sci., 1985-86, prof. botany College Park, 1986-93; acting dir. U. Md. Ctr. for Agrl. Biotech., 1986-88, dir., 1988-93; acting provost Md. Biotech. Inst., 1989-91; dean sch. sci. Hong Kong U. Sci. and Tech., 1991-92, v.p. for acad. affairs, 1992-98, acting v.p. for acad. affairs, 2000; prof. emeritus U. Md., 1993—, Hong Kong U. Sci. and Tech., 2001—. Hon. prof. Fudan U., 1986, Beijing Agrl. U., 1987. Author 6 books; editor 14 books; contbr. chpts. to books, articles to profl. jours. Recipient Philip Morris award for disting. achievement in tobacco sci., 1979, Outstanding Alumni award, 1990, Outstanding Svc. award, 1990; named Disting. Scholar, Nat. Acad. Sci., 1981; Fulbright grantee, 1982-83, grantee NSF, NIH. Mem. AAAS, Am. Soc. Plant Physiologists. Office: Hong Kong U Sci and Tech Clear Water Bay Kowloon Hong Kong

KUNIHOLM, BRUCE ROBELLET, university administrator; b. Washington, Oct. 4, 1942; s. Bertel Eric and Berthe Eugenie (Robellet) K.; m. Elizabeth Fairbank, June 29, 1968 (div. July 1987); children: Jonathan, Erin; m. Donna Slawson, Jan. 19, 2001. AB in English, Dartmouth Coll., 1964; MA in History, Duke U., 1972, MA in Pub. Policy Sci., PhD in History, Duke U., 1976. Instr. English Robert Acad./Robert Coll., Istanbul, Turkey, 1964-67; Coun. Fgn. Rels./NEH fellow Dept. State, Washington, 1979, internat. rels. officer policy planning staff, 1979-80; from instr. to lectr. policy studies and history Duke U., Durham, N.C., 1975-77, asst. prof. pub. policy studies and history, 1977-78, 80-84, assoc. prof. pub. policy studies and history, 1984-87, prof. pub. policy studies and history, 1987—, chmn. dept. public policy studies, 1989-94, dir. Terry Sanford Inst. Pub. Policy, 1989-94. Vis. prof. Internat. Rels. Koc U., Istanbul, Turkey, 1995-96, 2002; prof. pub. policy studies and history, 1996—; vice-provost for acad. and internat. affairs, Duke U., Durham, N.C., 1996—2001; chmn. acad. com.Can.-U.S. Fulbright Program, 2000—; dir. Ctr. for Internat. Studies, 1999—2001; guest scholar Woodrow Wilson Internat. Ctr. Scholars, 1982; cons. NEH, USMC, Dept. State, U.S. Army, United Tech. Corp.; invited lectr. numerous orgns., colls., univs., fgn. countries including U.S. Senate Fgn. Rels.Com., CIA, State Dept., Chase Manhattan Bank, Harvard U., Brown U., Dartmouth Coll., Yale U., Princeton U., France, Eng., Germany, Italy, Kuwait, Saudi Arabia, Sudan, Can., Turkey, also others. Author: Origins of the Cold War in the Near East, 1980 (Stuart L. Bernath prize 1981), The Persian Gulf and United States Policy, 1984, The Palestine Problem and United States Policy, 1986; contbr. articles to profl. jours.; contbr. chpts. books. Bd. dirs., chmn. acad. com. Found. for Edni. Exch. between Can. and U.S., 2000—. Capt. USMC, 1967-71, Vietnam. Decorated Bronze Star with V device; recipient Disting. Teaching award Trinity Coll., Duke U., 1989; rsch. grantee Harry S. Truman Libr., 1984, Duke U. Rsch. Coun., 1985-86, Inst. Turkish Studies, 1986-87, travel grantee Ctr. Soviet and East European Studies, 1991; Fulbright sr. rsch. fellow, Turkey, 1986-87, Woodrow Wilson Internat. Ctr. Scholars fellow Smithsonian Instn., 1986-87, sr. fellow Nobel Inst., Oslo, 1994. Mem. Am. Hist. Assn., Fulbright Fellows, Coun. Fgn. Rels., Orgn. Am. Historians, Soc. Historians Am. Fgn. Rels., Middle East Inst., Middle East Studies Assn., Internat. Inst. Strategic Studies, Phi Beta Kappa. Democrat. Avocations: triathlons, bluegrass banjo, wine. Home: 613 Swift Ave Durham NC 27701 Office: Duke U Sanford Inst Public Policy Durham NC 27708

KUNIN, JACQUELINE BARLOW, art educator; b. Harrisburg, Pa., Apr. 20, 1941; d. Rodney Kipton and Marie (Trunk) Barlow; m. Richard Henry Kunin, June 17, 1967. BFA, Pratt Inst., 1963; MEd, Temple U., 1967. Comml. artist Dock and Kinney Co., N.Y.C., 1963-64; art libr. Norcross, Inc., N.Y.C., 1964; tchr. graphic arts Jones Jr. H.S., Phila., 1964-66; tchr. art John Bartram H.S., Phila., 1966-86; tchr. painting and drawing H.S. for Creative and Performing Arts, Phila., 1986—. Named Disting Tchr. White House Commn. Presdl. Scholars, Washington, 1994, Outstanding Educator award Phila. Coll. Textiles and Sci., 1997. Mem. AAUW, Pa. Art Edn. Assn., Victorian Soc. Am. (Phila. chpt. bd. dirs. 1986-96), Valley Forge Civic Assn. Avocations: painting, collecting american costumes 1850-1950.

KUNIYASU, KEITH KAZUMI, secondary education educator; b. Honolulu, Apr. 16, 1955; s. Hajime and Betty Mieko (Yamamoto) K. AA in Liberal Arts, AS in Graphic Arts, U. Hawaii, Pearl City, 1978; BS in Tech. Edn., Western Wash. U., 1982; MEd in Tech. Edn., Oreg. State U., 1987. Cert. vocat. adminstr. Instrumental music instr. Aiea (Hawaii) Intermediate Sch., 1978-88; spl. edn. instr. Highlands Intermediate Sch., Pearl City, 1983-84; visual comm. instr. Oak Harbor (Wash.) High Sch., 1982-83; photography instr. Olympic Coll., Bremerton, Wash., 1984-85; comm. techs. instr. North Kitsap High Sch., Poulsbo, Wash., 1984-93; instr. comm. techs. River Ridge High Sch., Lacey, Wash., 1993—. Edn. rep. curriculum/competency validation com. Wash. State Supt. Pub. Instrn., Olympia, 1988-93; cons. Wash. SkillsUSA- Vocat. Indsl. Clubs Am., 1990—; mem. Nat. SkillsUSA- Vocat. Indsl. Clubs of Am. Leadership Handbook Revision Team, 1995; pvt. woodwind instr., 1974-94; counselor, woodwind specialist Maui (Hawaii) Intermediate Select Band Camps, 1975-80; advisor Leeward C.C. Graphic Arts Club, Pearl City, 1978-80; sch. accreditation teams for various high schs. throughout Wash., 1988—; writing com. leadership curriculum Wash. State Supt. Instrn. Edn., Olympia, 1993—. Author: (pamphlet series) Care of Single Reeds, 1983, (brochures) Addressing Technology Education, 1988-92, Communication Technologies, 1995, What Is Hawk Communications?, 1995, VisCom Student Study Guide, 1987, 2nd edit., 1990, 3rd edit., 1993, 4th edit., 1996, From Goods to Services, 1988, Technology Education Facility, 1988, Communication Technologies at North Kitsap High School, 1989, Visual Communications, 1990, Bob's Law's (Robert's Rules of Order), 1995, 2nd edit., 1997. Organizer, pres. Pacific Islanders Club at Western Wash. U., Bellingham, 1981-82; organizer, bd. dirs. Leeward Fine Arts Coun., Pearl City, 1981-94. Named Olympic Region Advisor of Yr., Wash. Skills USA-Vocat. Indsl. Clubs Am., 2003, Wash. State Advisor of Yr., 2003. Mem. NEA, Internat. Tech. Edn. Assn. (affiliate rep. 1990-94), Internat. Graphic Arts Educators Assn., Graphic Arts Tech. Found., Am. Vocat. Assn., Wash. Vocat. Assn., Wash. Tech. Edn. Assn., SkillsUSA-Vocat. Indsl. Clubs Am. (advisor, regional coord. 1990-96, 99-2000, 2002—). Avocations: travel, cooking, music, reading, working with young adults. Office: River Ridge H S 8929 Martin Way E Lacey WA 98516-5932 E-mail: kkuniyasu@nthurston.k12.wa.us.

KUNKEL, DOROTHY ANN, music educator; b. Weeping Water, Nebr., Nov. 24, 1934; d. Lloyd Nelson and Dorothy Grace (Holman) K. Student, Nebr. Wesleyan U., 1952-54; MusB, Am. Conservatory of Music, Chgo., 1958, B of Music Edn., 1960, M of Music Edn. cum laude, 1970. Cert. music instr. K-12, Mich. Music supr., orch. dir. Sch. Dist. 48, Villa Park, Ill., 1960-80; orch.'condr. Nat. Music Camp, Interlochen, Mich., 1970-84; dir. of orchs. Traverse City (Mich.) Area Pub. Schs., 1983-96; pvt. violin studio, 1995—. Dir., founder Galena (Ill.) Music Acad., 1961-69; v.p. bd. dirs. Concord Acad., Petoskey, Mich., 1996-97; string methods instr. Sherwood Sch. of Music, Chgo., 1969-73, Am. Conservatory of Music, Chgo., 1978-79; guest condr. Ga. All-State Orch., 1976, 81, 93, Fla. All-State Orch., 1977, 82, Ill. All-State Orch., 1982, Mich. Youth Arts Honors Orch., 1995, Marquette Symphony Orch., 1998, Great Lakes Chamber Orch., 2002, 03; condr. Petito Promonades concerts Chgo. Symphony Orch., 1981, Old Town Playhouse, Traverse City, Mich., 1997—. Choir dir. Oakbrook (Ill.) Christian Ctr., 1977-80, Lake Ann (Mich.) Meth. Ch., 1981-90; condr. Benzie Area Symphony Orch., 1999—, Great Lakes Chamber Orch., 2002—; mem. chancel choir Ctrl. United Meth. Ch., Traverse City. Recipient They Are Making Am. Mus. award Sch. Musician, 1981, Best in Class award Adjudicators Nat. Invitational, Kennedy Ctr., Washington, 1992, 95. Mem. Am. String Tchrs. Assn. (pres. Ill. chpt. 1979-80), Nat. Sch. Orch. Assn., Mid-West Internat. Band and Orch. Clinic (bd. dirs. 1980—, Medal of Honor 1966, 70, 74, 2000), Mich. Sch. Band and Orch. Assn. (adjudicator 1990—, Orch. Tchr. of Yr. 1995), Music Educators Nat. Conf., Sigma Alpha Iota, Willard Sorority. Avocations: camping, cats, cross-country skiing, feeding birds and small animals. Home: 2426 E Kasson Rd Cedar MI 49621-8673 E-mail: dkmusic934@aol.com.

KUNTZ, BECKY JO, physical education educator; b. Champaign, Ill., Feb. 6, 1951; d. Virgil Lewis and Bernice Irene (Knop) K. BS, Ea. Ill. U., 1973. Tchr. Gifford (Ill.) Grade Sch., 1973—. Head softball coach, Gifford Grade Sch., 1973—, head basketball coach, 1973—, track coach, 1973-88, athletic dir., 1991—. Mem. softball state tournament team, Amateur Softball Assn. of Am., 1984. Mem. AAHPERD, Ill. Edn. Assn., Gifford Edn. Assn., NEA, Womens Basketball Coaching Assn., Panther Club of Ea. Ill. U., Ill. Elem. Sch. Assn., Courtsiders of Univ. Ill., Delta Psi Kappa. Office: Gifford Grade Sch Po Box 70 406 S Main St Gifford IL 61847-9786

KUNTZ, KAREN FRANCES, preschool education educator; b. Amery, Wis., May 22, 1952; d. Frank John and Frances Winifred (Carr) Merth; m. James Edward Kuntz, June 22, 1974; children: Sara Jo, Kelli Jean. BS in Elem. Edn., U. Wis., River Falls, 1974. Cert. tchr., Wis. Tchr. 5th grade Albany (Wis.) Pub. Schs., 1974-76; tchr. 2nd grade Clayton (Wis.) Pub. Sch., 1976-85, jr. kindergarten tchr., 1986—. Facilitator Student Assistance

Program, Clayton, Wis., 1991—; supr. Student Tchrs. U. Wis. Stout. Author, presenter jr. kindergarten curriculum. Bd. dirs. Presch. Playhouse, Turtle Lake, Wis., 1988-90, Dollars for Scholars, Clayton, 1992; mem. Clayton Coronation Com., 1987—, St. Ann's Coun. of Cath. Women, Turtle Lake, 1978—, St. Isadore Cir., Turtle Lake, 1978—, St. Ann Renew Com., Turtle Lake, 1988—. Named Dist. Elem. Tchr. of the Yr. Clayton Pub. Schs., 1991-92; Kohl fellow, 1993. Mem. ASCD, St. Croix Valley Early Childhood Assn., Wis. Early Childhood Assn., Nat. Assn. for Edn. Young Children, St. Croix Valley Reading Coun., Wis. Reading Assn., Internat. Reading Assn., Wis. Fedn. Tchrs., Am. Fedn. Tchrs. Avocations: reading, biking, piano, dancing. Home: 130 70th Ave Clayton WI 54004-3310 Office: Clayton Pub Sch Prentice St Clayton WI 54004

KUNTZ, LILA ELAINE, secondary business education educator; b. Decorah, Iowa, July 13, 1931; d. Arthur Lloyd and Alice Elene (Thompson) Dahle; m. Darrell Wayne Kuntz, Dec. 26, 1959 (div. 1979); 1 child, Barbara Lynn. BA, Luther Coll., 1954; postgrad., U. Iowa, 1957-58, U. Minn., 1961-75, Mankato State Coll., 1966-76. Cert. tchr., Minn. Tchr. business Flat Rock (Mich.) High Sch., 1954-55, Springville (Iowa) High Sch., 1955-58, Spring Lake Park (Minn.) High Sch., 1958-60, Lincoln High Sch., Bloomington, Minn., 1961-70, Jefferson High Sch., Bloomington, 1970—. Rep. del., Edina, minn., 1979-95; active Norwegian-Am. Mus., Decorah, Iowa, 1987—. Mem. NEA, Minn. Edn. Assn., Minn. Bus. Edn. Assn., Bloomington Edn. Assn., Delta Pi Epsilon. Lutheran. Avocations: concerts, photography, reading, traveling. Home: 5221 Abercrombie Dr Edina MN 55439-1466 Office: Jefferson High Sch 4001 W 102nd St Bloomington MN 55437-2699

KUNZE, LINDA JOYE, educator; b. Grand Rapids, Mich., Mar. 27, 1950; d. Elon George and Lillian (Wolbers) Benaway (dec.); children: Christopher Russel, Jason Scott. BS, Grand Valley State U., Allendale, Mich., 1971, MEd, 1990. Substitute tchr. Kent Intermediate Sch. Dists., Grand Rapids, 1972-76, 85; instr. YWCA, Grand Rapids, 1972-77, youth svcs. dir., 1977-79; CETA tng. specialist Grand Rapids Pub. Schs., 1977-79; student intern Cen. Elem. Sch., Sparta, Mich., 1986; tchr. Sparta High Sch., 1986, Hastings (Mich.) Mid. Sch., 1986-87; dir. Northview Extended Day Care, Grand Rapids, 1988-95; tchr. Mich. Reformatory, Ionia, Mich., 1995-97, Ionia Temp. Facility, 1997-2000; prin. Brooks Correctional Facility and Muskegon Temporary Facility, 2000—; tchr. Handlon Mich. Correctional Facility, 2001—. Cons. Forest Hills Pub. Schs., Grand Rapids, 1989, Rockford (Mich.) Pub. Schs., 1989—90, Godwin Pub. Schs., Grand Rapids, 1989—, Northview Child Care Network, Grand Rapids, 1989—; mem. Mich. Adult Edn. Profl. Devel. Instrnl. Leadership Team. Cons. Citizens League/Child Care Task Force, Grand Rapids, 1988-89, Campfire Inc., Grand Rapids, 1988-89. Recipient Funding awards Fed. Govt., 1977, State Mich., 1988. Mem. Mich. Reading Assn., Mich. Assn. for Adult and Cmty. Educators, Correctional Edn. Assn., Mich. Assn. Adult Basic Educators (founder), Mich. Dept. Corrections (mem. Adult Basics Edn. curriculum com., trainer Tchg. Adults with Learning Disabilities), Literacy 2000 Internat. Corrections Conf. (workshop presenter). Avocations: volleyball, softball, camping, tennis, swimming. Home: 2182 Daylor Dr NE Grand Rapids MI 49525-1520

KUPCHYNSKY, JERRY MARKIAN, orchestra conductor, educator; b. Stryj, Ukraine, Sept. 12, 1928; came to U.S., 1946; s. Jaroslav and Cecilia Elizabeth (Jurkiv) K.; m. Jean Estelle Brown, June 29, 1957 (dec.); children: Melanie Jean, Stephanie Joy; m. Joan M. Rear, Sept. 13, 1997. B in Music Edn., Murray State U., 1951, MA in Edn., 1952; MEd, Rutgers U., 1961. Cert. tchr., supr., N.J. Tchr. music Pub. Schs., Shawneetown, Ill., 1954-57, East Brunswick, N.J., 1957-68, supr. music, 1968-95; guest condr. youth orchs. various Eastern states, 1965—. Founder, condr. Middlesex Youth Symphony Orch., 1961, Imperial Symphony Orch., 1979; founder, dir. Summer Conf. String Tchrs., 1964—; founder, chair East Brunswick Young Musicians Project, 1985—. Contbr. articles to profl. publs. Bd. dirs. East Brunswick Arts Commn., 1979, N.J. Teen Arts Festival, 1976, Alliance Arts Edn., 1977. With U.S. Army, 1952-54, Korea. Recipient N.J. Gov.'s award Arts Edn. for Disting. Leadership Music Edn., 1989, Cert. of Merit, N.J. Coun. on Arts, 1970, Fay S. Mathewson award Friends of Recreation, Parks and Conservation, 2003; named to Order Ky. Cols., Commonwealth of Ky., 1978; selected for Wall of Honor, Brunswick Bd. Edn., 1998. Mem. N.J. String Tchrs. Assn. (Disting. Svc. award 1974, 78, 84, 89), Music Educators Nat. Conf., N.J. Music Educators Assn. (dir. Disting. Svc. award 1986), Am. String Tchrs. Assn. (nat. pres. 1976-78, Disting. Leadership award 1980), Nat. Sch. Orch. Assn. (nat. pres. 1984-86, Disting. Leadership award 1987, Merle J. Isaac Lifetime Achievement award 1994), N.J. Prins. and Suprs. Assn. Home: 38 Mason Ave East Brunswick NJ 08816-4837 E-mail: kupchynsky@aol.com.

KURATKO, DONALD F. entrepreneur, educator, consultant; b. Chgo., Aug. 27, 1952; s. Donald W. and Margaret M. (Browne) K.; m. Deborah Ann Doyle, Dec. 28, 1979; children: Christina Diane, Kellie Margaret. BA in Econs., John Carroll U., 1974; MS in Mortuary Sci. and Adminstrn., Worsham Coll., 1975; MBA in Mktg.-Mgmt., Benedictine U., 1979; DBA in Small Bus. Mgmt., Nova Southea. U., 1984. Lic. funeral dir., Ill. Prof. bus. Benedictine U., Lisle, 1979-83; prof., exec. dir. entrepreneurship program Ball State U., Muncie, Ind., 1983—, disting. prof., 1990—; funeral dir. Kuratko Funeral Home, North Riverside, Ill., 1975-83. Cons. Kendon Assocs., Riverside, 1983-88, Intrapreneurial Group, 1989—, Acordia, AT&T, GTE, United Techs., Ameritech, Union Carbide Corp.; dir. Pathologists Assocs., Acordia Ctrl. Ind., Ind. monument advisors, Beacon Venture Capital. Author: Management, 1988, 3rd edit., 1991, Effective Small Business Management, 1986, 7th edit., 2001, Entrepreneurship, 1989, 5th edit., 2001, Entrepreneurship and Innovation in the Corporation, 1987; Entrepreneurial Strategy, 1994, The Entrepreneurial Decision, 1997, The Breakthrough Experience, 1998, Strategic Entrepreneurial Growth, 2001, Human Resource Function in Emerging Enterprises, 2002, Corporate Entrepreneurship, 2002; mem. editl. bd. Mid-Am. Bus. Jour., 1985-95, Jour. Bus. Venturing; cons. editor Entrepreneurship Theory & Practice Jour., Small Bus. Forum; contbr. 150 articles in field to profl. jours. Named Outstanding Young Hoosier, Ind. Jaycees, 1985, one of Outstanding Young Men of Am., 1983, 84, #1 Entrepreneurship Program Dir. in USA, Entrepreneur Mag., Disting. Tchg. Professorship, 1990, Stoops Disting Prof. Bus., 1990, Outstanding Univ. Prof., 1996, Entrepreneur of Yr. in Ind., Ernst & Young, Inc. Mag. and Merrill Lynch, 1990; 21st Century Entrepreneurship Rsch. fellow; Disting. scholar U.S. Assn. for Small Bus. and Entrepreneurship, 2003; recipient George Washington medal of honor, 1987, Leavey Found., 1988, Excellence award N.F.I.B. Found., 1993, Nat. Outstanding Entrepreneurship Educator of Yr. award, 1993, Kauffman Found. Entrepreneurship Educator award, 1994, Entrepreneurial World of Differences award, 1998, Thomas W. Binford meml award, 2000, Outstanding Rschr. award, 1999; developed nationally-ranked entrepreneurship program, Top 20 Business Week, Top 25 Success Mag., Top 20 Entrepreneur Mag., Top 5 U.S. News and World Report, Nat. Model Prog. award, 1990, Nat. Model Prog. award, grad. level, 1998, Nat, Innovative Pedagogy award, 2001. Mem. U.S. Assn. Small Bus. and Entrepreneurship (pres. 1993-94), Nat. Acad. Mgmt., Internat. Coun. Small Bus., Midwest Bus. Adminstrn. Assn. (pres. entrepreneurship divsn. 1992-93), Nat. Consortium Entrepreneurship Ctrs. Roman Catholic. Avocations: weightlifting, jogging. Home: 2309 N Kensington Way Muncie IN 47304-2484 Office: Ball State U Coll Bus Muncie IN 47306-0001 E-mail: dkuratko@bsu.edu.

KURCZYNSKI, THADDEUS WALTER, neurologist, geneticist, educator; b. Hamtramck, Mich., Oct. 31, 1940; s. Walter and Helen (Michalczak) K.; m. Elizabeth Mickelsen, June 23, 1963 (div. 1978); children: Peter L., Karen L.; m. Margaret A. Gray, Sept. 12, 1992. BS in Zoology, U. Mich., 1962, MS in Human Genetics, 1964; PhD in Human Genetics, Case-Western Res. U., 1969, MD, 1970. Diplomate Am. Bd. Psychiatry and Neurology, Am. Bd. Med. Genetics. Intern in medicine U. Mich., Ann Arbor, 1970-71, resident in neurology, 1971-73; resident in pediatrics Children's Hosp. Mich., Detroit, 1973-74; fellow in child neurology Albert Einstein Coll. Medicine, Bronx, N.Y., 1974-76; asst. prof. Case-Western Res. U., Cleve., 1976-81; assoc. prof. Med. Coll. Ohio, Toledo, 1981-93, prof., 1994—. Former lt. comdr. Toledo Power Squadron. Mem. AMA, Am. Soc. Human Genetics, Am. Bd. Med. Genetics, Am. Acad. Neurology, Child Neurology Soc., Am. Coll. Med. Genetics (founding fellow). Avocation: sailing. Office: Mercy Childrens Hosp 2222 Cherry St Ste 2300 Toledo OH 43608

KUREPA, ALEXANDRA, mathematician, educator; b. Zagreb, Croatia, Dec. 31, 1956; came to U.S., 1985; d. Svetozar and Zora (Lopac) K.; m. Rodney Anthony Waschka II, June 24, 1988; children: Andre Kurepa Waschka, Lana Kurepa Waschka. BS, U. Zagreb, 1978, MS, 1982; PhD, U. North Tex., 1987. Asst. prof. math. U. Zagreb, 1987-88, Tex. Christian U., Ft. Worth, 1989-93, N.C. A&T State U., Greensboro, 1993-96, assoc. prof., 1996-2001, prof., 2001—. Author: Matematika 2, 1989, 2000, Matematika 4, 2001; contbr. articles to profl. jours. Rsch. grantee UNESCO, 1988, 89, U.S. Dept. Edn., 1995-2000, Assn. Women in Math.-Nat. Security Agy., 1997-2000, NSF, 1997-2000,2003-, Math. Assn. Am./Tensor Found., 2002, Office Naval Rsch., 2003--. Mem. Am. Math. Soc., Math. Assn. Am., Assn. for Women in Math., Nat. Coun. Tchrs. Math. Office: NC A&T State U Dept Math Greensboro NC 27411-0001 E-mail: kurepa@ncat.edu.

KURIAN, PIUS, nephrologist, educator; b. Arpookara, Kerala, India, May 9, 1959; s. Pylo and Mariamma Kurian; m. Sally Kurian, May 11, 1986; children: Michelle Maria, Matthew Paul, Catherine Tresa. BSc, Kuriakose (India) Elias Coll., 1979; MB, BChir, Kottayam (India) Med. Coll., India, 1986. Diplomate Am. Bd. Internal Medicine, Am. Bd. Nephrology, Am. Bd. Forensic Examiners; specialist clin. hypertension, Am. Soc. Hypertension. Resident in internal medicine Nassau County Med. Ctr., East Meadow, N.Y., 1988-91, fellow in nephrology, 1991-94; attending physician in nephrology Mercy Med. Ctr. and Cmty. Hosp., Springfield, Ohio, 1994—. Asst. prof. dept. medicine Wright State U., Dayton, Ohio, 1998; chief divsn. internal medicine Mercy Med. Ctr., Springfield, Ohio, 1999, chmn., dir. dept. medicine Mercy Med. Ctr., Springfield, Ohio, 2000; mem. governing bd. Covenant Health Sys.; med. dir. Cmty. Physicians Dialysis, Springfield, 2000—. Fellow ACP; mem. AAAS, AMA, Am. Soc. Hypertension (specialist in clin. hypertension), Am. Soc. Nephrology, Am. Coll. Physicians Execs., Internat. Soc. Nephrology, Renal Physicians Assn., N.Y. Acad. Scis, Am. Diabetes Assn., Nat. Kidney Found. Roman Catholic. Office: 247 S Burnett Rd Springfield OH 45505-2639

KURKUL, WENYI WANG, musician, educator, administrator; b. Taipei, Taiwan, Oct. 30, 1964; arrived in U.S., 1986; d. Shih-Ming and Hsieh-Chu Wang. MusM, Ohio U., 1988; MusD, U. Mo., 1995; D in Music Edn., Ind. U., 2000. Prof., adminstr. Sch. Music Tainan (Taiwan) Coll., 1989-92; prof. Nat. Taiwan Acad. Arts, 1989-92, Nat Sun Yat-Sen U., Kaohsiung, Taiwan, 1990-92; mem. vis. faculty Sch. Music Ind. U., Bloomington, 1999—2000; prof. dept. music George Mason U., 2000—03, dir. music edn. dept. music Coll. Visual and Performing Arts, 2001—03, exec. dir. Orff Schulwerk Tchr. Tng. and Cert. Program, 2001—03. Soloist-in-residence Nat. Chiang Kai Shek Cultural Ctr., Taipei, 1991-94; flutist Asian Composers League, Taipei, 1990-92; asst. prin. flutist Taiwan Symphony Orch., Taichung, 1984-86; contbr. articles to profl. publs. Nat. Art and Sci. Coun. scholar, Taiwan, 1989-92; Nat. rsch. grantee Ministry of Edn., Taiwan, 1989-92; named New Performing Star of Yr. Nat. Theatre and Concert Hall Planning and Mgmt. Coun., Taiwan, 1991. Mem.: APA, AAUP, Internat. Soc. Philosophy Music Edn. (founding), Pub. Rels. Soc. Am., Am. Edml. Rsch. Assn., Am. Orff-Schulwerk Assn., Internat. Soc. for Music Edn. (Eng.), European Recorder Tchrs. Assn., Soc. for Rsch. in Music Edn., Music Edn. Nat. Conf., Coll. Music Soc., Nat. Flute Assn. (life), Phi Kappa Lambda. Home: 10716 Kings Riding Way Ste 102 Rockville MD 20852 E-mail: wkurkul@gmu.edu.

KURLAN, MARVIN ZEFT, surgeon, educator; b. Wilkes-Barre, Pa., Feb. 20, 1934; s. Ephraigm Joseph and Fannye Lillian Kurlancheek; m. Eleanor Frank, June 21, 1964; 1 child, Todd. BA, Wilkes Coll., 1957; MS, U. Ill., 1958; MD, SUNY, Buffalo, 1964. Diplomate Nat. Bd. Med. Examiners, Am. Bd. Surgery. Intern then resident in surgery Millard Fillmore Hosp., Buffalo, 1964-69, dir. trauma svcs., 1974-82, sr. attending surgeon, 1984-95; surgeon emeritus, 1995—; plant surgeon Bethlehem (Pa.) Steel Corp., 1969-74; med. dir. Bros. of Mercy Health Facilities, Clarence, N.Y., 1974-82. Assoc. examiner Am. Bd. Surgery, Phila., 1987-95; chmn. James Platt White Soc., Sch. Medicine and Biomed. Scis., SUNY, Buffalo, 1992-94 (Dean's adv. coun., 1995-97); cons. in surgery Walter Reed Army Med. Ctr., Washington. Contbr. articles to profl. jours. Vol. Empire State Games, Buffalo, 1986; mem. Jack Kemp Forum, Buffalo, 1985-91; bd. dirs. Jewish Fedn. Allentown, Pa., 1972-74. Served AUS (res.) to lt. col. Med. Corps, 1965-91, active duty operation Desert Shield and Desert Storm. Decorated Army Svc. medal with Oak Leaf Cluster, Army Achievement medal. Fellow Am. Coll. Gastroenterology, Am. Trauma Soc. (founder), N.Y. Acad. Scis.; mem. ACS (life fellow leadership soc.), Assn. Mil. Surgeons U.S., Hastings on Hudson Bioethics Ctr., Buffalo Surg. Soc. (sec. 1986-88, v.p. 1988-89, pres. 1989-90), SUNY at Buffalo Found. (pres.'s assoc.), Grand Coun. World Parliament, Confedn. Chivalry, Knight of Humanity, Order White Cross Internat. (dist. comdr. N.Y., U.S.), Chevalier Grand Cross, Ordre Soverain et Militaire de Milice du St. Sepulcre, Phi Lambda Kappa (nat. pres. 1993), Nu Sigma Nu. Clubs: Sci. Progress Research (Buffalo) (v.p. 1983-84). Lodges: Masons, Shriners. Republican. Avocation: world travel. Home and Office: 413 Dan Troy Dr Buffalo NY 14221-3558

KURLANDER, HONEY WACHTEL, artist, educator; b. Bklyn. d. Charles Bernard and Sara F. (Alexander) Wachtel; m. Neale Kurlander, June 25, 1949; children: Harold Michael, Susan Laurie. Student, Parsons Sch. Design; cert. in illustration, Pratt Inst., 1948. Freelance textile designer, N.Y.C., 1948-58; freelance children's book illustrator, 1950-60; art instr. East Meadow (N.Y.) High Sch., 1958-60, Kurlander Studio, East Meadow, 1958-79, Kurlander Art Studio, Old Westbury, N.Y., 1979-2000. Exhibited in one-man shows at Garden City (N.Y.) Galleries Ltd., 1960-90, Robley Gallery, Roslyn, N.Y., 1971, Madison Ave. Gallery, N.Y.C., 1975, Salmagundi Club, N.Y.C., 1978, Gallerie Marcel Bernheim, Paris, Kaigado Gallery, Tokyo; executed mural Astoria Queens, 1985, mural Oyster Bay-East Norwich Libr., 1998, poster Centennial Celebration of Statue of Liberty; represented in permanent collections at Dietz Mus., Wasserberg, Germany, C.W. Post Coll. Art Ctr., Brookville, N.Y., DeSeversky Conf. Ctr., Greenvale, N.Y. Recipient 1st prize Heckscher Mus., 1966; 1st prize Eastern Regional Exhibit, 1968. Mem. Nat. League Am. Penwomen (Best in Show award 1978, 81, 84, 90, 95, awards 1962—, Nat. Biennial 2000), Art League Nassau County, Salmagundi Club (Williams award 1979). Avocations: photography, gardening, sewing, travel. Home: Kurlander Studio 6185 Wooded Run Dr Columbia MD 21044

KURLANDER, NEALE, accounting and law educator, lawyer; b. Bklyn., Jan. 1, 1924; s. Sol and Eleanor Kurlander; m. Honey Wachtel, June 25, 1949; children: Harold M., Susan L. BS, Long Island U., 1948; JD, N.Y. Law Sch., N.Y.C., 1951; MBA, Adelphi U., 1967. Bar: N.Y. 1952; CPA, N.Y. V.p., chief fin. officer Profit Motivation Svcs., Inc., Garden City, N.Y., 1967-71; cons.-reviewer Ernst & Ernst, Garden City, 1967-72; lectr. Practicing Law Inst., N.Y.C., 1974; chmn. dept. accting and law Adelphi U., Garden City, 1964-82; cons. Regent's External Degree, Albany, N.Y., 1974-87; pvt. practice law Old Westbury, N.Y., 1952—; pvt. practice acct., CPA, 1960—; prof. acctg. and law Adelphi U., Garden City, 1962—. Prof. developer Harris, Kerr, Forster & Co., N.Y.C., 1969-71; treas. Fin. Execs. Inst., Long Island, N.Y., 1974-76, chmn. acad. rels., 1975—, bd. dirs. 1975—; faculty Found. for Acctg. Edn., 1975—, bd. trustees, 1976-79. Author: Basic Accounting, 1962, Auditing, Vol. I and II, 1978; contbr. articles to profl. jours. Cmdr. post 6081 VFW, Bklyn., 1953-54; mem. Bd. Elections, Nassau County, N.Y., 1964-70, Citizens' Adv. Com. N.Y. State Dept. Taxation, Albany, 1975-87, Bd. Appeals, Old Westbury, 1988-93; legis. adv. coun. N.Y. State Assembly 15th Dist., 1991-93. Recipient cert. Delta Mu Delta, 1982, Dr. Emanuel Saxe Outstanding CPA in Edn. award N.Y. State Soc. Cert. Pub. Accts., 2000; named Outstanding Acctg. Educator, Found. for Acctg. Edn., N.Y., 1982, Acct. of Yr. Acctg. Soc., 1992. Mem. AICPA, N.Y. State Soc. CPA's (Dr. Emanuel Saxe Outstanding CPA in Edn. award 2000), Am. Acctg. Assn., Nassau County Bar Assn., N.Y. State Assembly 15th Dist. (legis. adv. coun.). Avocations: reading, woodworking, traveling, walking, swimming. Home: 6185 Wooded Run Dr Columbia MD 21044 E-mail: nkurlander@aol.com.

KURMAN, JUTA, music educator; b. Wändra, Parnu, Estonia, Nov. 7, 1912; d. August and Maria (Reier) Tomberg; m. Alexander Pooman, Sept. 17, 1938 (dec. 1938); m. Hugo Kurman, Jan. 18, 1940; children: Jaan, Juri-George. Tchrs. Lic., Tchrs. Sem., Estonia, 1934; Artist Dipl., State Conservatory of Music, Estonia, 1940, N.Y. Coll. of Music, 1952. Tchr. Tallinn (Estonia) Pub. Schs., 1934-38; performing artist concerts, state radio, and theater Estonia, 1932-40; TV voice soloist Maj. Bowes Original Amateur Hour, Radio City, N.Y., 1949-50; with Claire Mann Show, Channel 5, N.Y.C., 1952; pres. Estonian Music Ctr., N.Y.C., 1973—. Club and ch. soloist; lectr in field; music critic Free Estonian Word, 1948—, Baltic Papers. Co-editor: Haapsalu Shawl, 1972, Kompiling Mart Saar VocalAlbum, 1965, Kompiling Kaljo Raid Estonian Volksongs Album, 1991; contbr. articles to profl. jurs. Sustaining mem. Rep. Nat. Com., 1990—; sustaining sponsor Ronald Reagan Presdl. Found., 1987—. Decorated White Star with V, Order Estonian Republic; named Laureate of Estonian Letters and Scis. Found.; N.Y. Coll. Music grantee, 1948. Mem. Estonian Music Sorority (pres. 1951-63), Estonian Women's Club of N.Y. (pres.), Estonian Ednl. Soc. (hon. mem. elders coun.), World Fedn. Estonian Women's Clubs in Exile (West) (founding pres. 1966—). Republican. Lutheran. Avocations: music, poetry, writing, gardening. Home: 68-50 Juno St Forest Hills NY 11375-5728 Office: Estonian Music Ctr 243 E 34th St New York NY 10016-4852

KURRE, JAMES ANTHONY, economics educator; b. Cin., Nov. 20, 1951; s. Theodore and Cecilia Kurre. BA magna cum laude, U. Cin., 1973; MA, Wayne State U., 1975, PhD, 1982. Teaching asst. Wayne State U., Detroit, 1973-75, rsch. asst., 1975-76, univ. grad. fellow, 1976-77; instr. Pa. State U., Behrend Coll., Erie, 1977-83, asst. prof., 1983-89, assoc. prof., 1989—. Regional economist and co-dir. Econ. Rsch. Inst. of Erie, 1982—; expert witness in wrongful death/injury cases Erie, 1986-88; cons. in field. Contbr. articles to profl. jours. Economist Erie County Task Force on Property Tax Reassessment, Erie, 1986-87; pres. bd. dirs. Roadhouse Theatre, Erie, Pa., 2000—. Recipient Excellence in Teaching award Behrend Coll. Coun. Fellows, 1982, 86, Blum award Dept. Econs., Wayne State U., 1977, U. Grad. Fellowship, Wayne State U., 1976-77, Guy W. Wilson Excellence in Advising award Pa. State U.-Erie, 1990. Home: 8070 Gulf Rd North East PA 16428-4302 Office: Pa State-Erie Behrend Coll School of Business Station Rd Erie PA 16563-1400

KURTZ, KENNETH JOHN, physician, educator; b. Pitts., Feb. 20, 1944; s. John Edmund and Elizabeth (Weimer) K.; m. Patricia Mae Albright, Dec. 17, 1972; 1 child, Roger. BA in Biology with honors, Williams Coll., 1966; MD, Cornell U., 1970; postgrad., Naval Aerospace Med. Inst., 1972. Diplomate Nat. Bd. Med. Examiners; diplomate in internal medicine and geriatric medicine Am. Bd. Internal Medicine. Fellow in Endocrinology U. Wash., Seattle, 1970-71; intern U. Calif., San Diego, 1971-72, resident II, III in primary care internal medicine San Francisco, 1976-78; clin. prof. internal medicine U. Nev. Sch. Medicine, Reno, 1990—. Mem. active staff VA Med. Ctr., Reno, 1978—. Contbr. chpts. to books, articles to med. jours. Capt., flight surgeon MC USNR, 1988—. Recipient Dwight Bot. prize, 1966, Phi Beta Kappa, 1966, Seligman award for ob-gyn., 1970, citation for Outstanding Advocacy and Teaching, U. Nev. Med. Sch., 1992. Fellow ACP. Avocations: swimming, vintage neckwear. Home: 3235 Markridge Dr Reno NV 89509-3837 Office: VA Med Ctr 1000 Locust St Reno NV 89502-2597

KURTZ, PAUL, philosopher, educator, writer, publisher; b. Newark, Dec. 21, 1925; s. Martin and Sara (Lasser) K.; m. Claudine C. Vial, Oct. 6, 1960; children: Valerie L., Patricia A., Jonathan, Anne. BA, NYU, 1948; MA, Columbia U., 1949, PhD, 1952. Instr. Queens Coll., 1950-52; instr. philosophy Trinity Coll., Hartford, Conn., 1952-55, asst. prof., 1955-58, assoc. prof., 1958-59, Vassar Coll., Poughkeepsie, N.Y., 1960-61; vis. prof. New Sch. Social Rsch., N.Y.C., 1960-65; assoc. prof. Union Coll., Schenectady, 1961-64, prof., 1964-65; vis. prof. U. Besancon, France, 1965; prof. philosophy SUNY, Buffalo, 1965-91, prof. emeritus, 1992—. Moderator TV series. Author (with Rollo Handy): (book) A Current Appraisal of the Behavioral Sciences, 1964; author: Decision and the Condition of Man, 1965, The Fullness of Life, 1974, Exuberance, 1977, In Defense of Secular Humanism, 1983, A Skeptics Handbook of Parapsychology, 1985, The Transcendental Temptation, 1986, Forbidden Fruit, 1988, Eupraxophy, 1989, Philosphical Essays in Pragmatic Naturalism, 1990, The New Skepticism, 1992, Toward a New Enlightenment, 1994, The Courage to Become, 1997, Humanist Manifesto 2000, 1999, Embracing the Power of Humanism, 2000, Skepticism and Humanism: The New Paradigm, 2001; editor: American Thought Before 1900, 1966, American Philosophy in the Twentieth Century, 1966, Sidney Hook and the Contemporary World, 1968, Moral Problems in Contemporary Society, 1969; co-editor: International Directory of Philosophy and Philosophers, 4th edit., 1978—81, Tolerance and Revolution, 1970, Language and Human Nature, 1971, A Catholic/Humanist Dialogue, 1972, The Humanist Alternative, 1973, Idea of a Modern University, 1974, The Philosophy of the Curriculum, 1975, The Ethics of Teaching and Scientific Research, 1977, University and State, 1978, Sidney Hook: Philosopher of Democracy and Humanism, 1983, Building a World Community, 1989, Challenges to the Enlightenment, 1994, Skeptical Odysseys, 2001, The Humanist, 1967—78; author, co-editor (book) Science and Religion, 2003, mem. editl. bd. The Humanist, 1964—78, Philosophers Index, 1969—85, Question, 1969—81, The Skeptical Inquirer, 1976—, pres. Prometheus Books, 1970—, editor-in-chief Free Inquiry Mag., 1980—, pub. The Sci. Rev. of Alternative Medicine, 2002—. Chmn. Coun. for Secular Humanism, 1980—, Coun. on Internat. Studies and World Affairs, 1966-69, Ctr. for Inquiry, 1995—; trustee Behavioral Rsch. Coun., Great Barrington, Mass.; bd. dirs. U.S. Bibliography of Philosophy, 1958-70, Univ. Ctrs. for Rational Alternatives, 1969-96; bd. dirs. Internat. Humanist and Ethical Union, 1968—, co-chmn., 1986-94; chmn. Com. for Sci. Investigation Claims of Paranormal, 1976—2002. With AUS, 1944-46. Behavioral Rsch. Coun. fellow, 1962-63, French Govt. fellow, 1965, John Dewey fellow, 1986-87; recipient Bertrand Russell Soc. award, 1988, Internat. Humanist award, 1999, Chancellor Charles Norton award, 2001. Fellow: AAAS; mem.: U.K. Rationalists Press Assn. (v.p. 1990—), Acad. Humanism (Laureate, pres. 1983—). Office: Prometheus Books Inc 59 John Glenn Dr Amherst NY 14228-2197 E-mail: paulkurtz@aol.com.

KURTZ, THOMAS GORDON, mathematics educator; b. Kansas City, Mo., July 14, 1941; s. Paul Stanton and Ruth Corine (Kreikenbaum) K.; m. Carolyn Sue Neville, Aug. 24, 1963; children: Marcia Ann, Kevin Michael. BA, U. Mo., 1963; MS, Stanford U., 1965, PhD, 1967. Vis. lectr. U. Wis., Madison, 1967-69, from asst. prof. to assoc. prof., 1969-75, prof. math., 1975—, prof. stats., 1985—, Paul Levy prof., 1996—, chmn. dept., 1985-88, dir. Ctr. Math. Scis., 1990-96. Vis. prof. U. Strasbourg, France, 1977-78. Author: Approximation of Population Processes, 1981, Markov Processes: Characterization and Convergence, 1986; contbr. numerous articles to profl. jours. Mem. supervisory bd. Dane County, Madison, 1974-75; chmn. parking utility com. City of Madison, 1976-77. Romnes fellow U. Wis., 1976; NSF research grantee, 1968—. Fellow Inst. Math. Stats.; mem. Am. Math. Soc., Soc. Indsl. and Applied Math., Bernouli Soc., Ops. Research Soc. Am., Internat. Statis.Inst. Democrat. Presbyterian. Avocations: singing, canoeing. Home: 117 N Oak Grove Dr Madison WI 53717-1196 Office: U Wis Dept of Math 480 Lincoln Dr Madison WI 53706-1325

KURTZMAN, NEIL A. medical educator; b. Bklyn., June 18, 1936; s. Louis S. and Roselie (Yegla) K.; m. Sandra Sabatini, Feb. 14, 1976; children from previous marriage: Jonathan, Laura. BA with honors, Williams Coll., 1957; MD, N.Y. Med. Coll., 1961. Intern Robert Packer Hosp., Sayre, Pa., 1961-62; resident Ohio State U. Hosp., Columbus, 1962-63; asst. chief med. services Nobel Army Hosp., Ft. McClellan, Ala., 1963-64; med. resident William Beaumont Gen. Hosp., El Paso, Tex., 1964-65, chief med. resident, 1965-66; fellow in nephrology U. Tex. Southwestern Med. Sch., Dallas, 1966-68; chief renal div. Brooke Army Med. Ctr., Ft. Sam Houston, Tex., 1969-72; prof., chief nephrology sect. U. Ill. Coll. Medicine, Chgo., 1972-84; prof. Tex. Tech U. Health Scis. Ctr., Lubbock, 1985—99, chief nephrology divsn., 1985-94, chief of staff univ. med. ctr., 1990-92, chmn. dept. internal medicine, 1985-98, prof., 1999—. Mem. gen. medicine B study sect. Nat. Inst. Arthritis, Metabolic and Digestive Diseases, Bethesda, Md., 1978-83; mem. merit rev. bd. VA, Washington, 1979-82, chmn., 1981-82; mem. sci. adv. bd. Nat. Kidney Found., N.Y.C., 1981-92, chmn., 1988-90, v.p., 1990-92, pres., 1992-94; prin. investigator regulation urinary acidification NIH, Bethesda, 1978—. Author: Handbook of Urinalysis and Urinary Sediment, 1974, Pathophysiology of the Kidney, 1977, Doing Nothing, 2000; also more than 300 sci. papers, more than 600 sci. presentations; editor-in-chief Seminars in Nephrology, 1981—, Am. Jour. Kidney Diseases, 1997-2002; assoc. editor Am. Jour. Nephrology; mem. editorial bd. 7 sci. jours.; referee 16 sci. jours. Faculty advisor Alpha Omega Alpha, U. Ill., 1977-84, Tex. Tech U. Health Sci. Ctr., 1985-2002. lt. col. U.S. Army, 1963-72. Decorated U.S. Army Meritorious Svc. award; recipient Pres.'s award Nat. Kidney Found., 1990, Outstanding Acad. Achievement award N.Y. Med. Coll., 1993, So. Soc. for Clin. Investigation's Founder's award, 1996, Tex. chpt. Am. Coll. Physicians Laureate award, 1996, David M. Hume award Nat. Kidney Found., 1999, Headliner award, 2003. Fellow AAAS; mem. Am. Physiol. Soc., Am. Soc. Clin. Investigation, Assn. Am. Physicians, Ctrl. Soc. Clin. Research, So. Soc. Clin. Investigation, Alpha Omega Alpha. Office: Dept of Int Med TTUHSC 3601 4th St Lubbock TX 79430-0001 E-mail: neil.kurtzman@ttuhsc.edu.

KURUGANTY, SASTRY PRATAP, electrical engineering educator; b. Masulipatam, India, Jan. 12, 1941; came to U.S., 1989; s. Sastry A. and Lalitha (Jandhyala) K.; m. Lakshmi V. Bhagavatula, June 20, 1962; children: Saila, Padma, Saroja. B Engring., Birla Inst., Pilani, India, 1964; M. Engring., U. Andhra, Waltair, India, 1966; MSc in Engring., U. N.B., Fredericton, Can., 1974; PhD, U. Sask., Saskatoon, Can., 1979. Asst. prof. Jawaharlal Nehru Tech. Inst., Hyderabad, India, 1966-71; rsch. assoc. U. N.B., 1974-75, U. Sask., 1979-80; reliability specialist Man. Hydro, Winnipeg, Can., 1980-89; prof., chair elec. engring. dept. U. N.D., Grand Forks, 1989—96; DOE Samuel Massie chair excellence U. Turabo, PR, 1996—. Expert lectr. NSF USAID Summer Schs., Hyderabad, 1968; cons. Man. HVDC Rsch. Ctr., Winnipeg, 1985-88; mem. transp. reliability task force, mem. res. requirements task force Mid Continent Area Power Pool, Mpls., 1984-89; chmn., expert panelist in field. Author over 30 papers in field. Rsch. fellow Can. Nat. Rsch. Coun., 1975-79, N.B., 1971-74. Mem. IEEE (sr. mem., sec.-treas. Red River Valley chpt. 1994-95, reviewer 1983—), NSPE, Am. Soc. for Engring. Edn. Achievements include research in area of bulk power system security assessment and reliability; expert in HVDC transmission system reliability assessment and generation-transmission system planning using probabilistic techniques. Office: U Turabo Sch Engring PO Box 3030 Gurabo PR 00778-3030 E-mail: powerreleng@ieee.org.

KUSER, EDWIN CHARLES, educational administrator, retired; b. Pottstown, Pa., Apr. 27, 1939; s. Melvin S. and Virginia B. (DeLong) K.; m. Rose M. Fatzinger, Aug. 19, 1961 (div. Dec. 1994); children: Alison M., Eric C. BS in Edn., Bloomsburg (Pa.) U., 1961; MS in Edn., Temple U., 1965, EdD in Adminstrn., 1977. Bus. edn. tchr. Boyertown (Pa.) Area Sch. Dist., 1961-63, chair dept. bus. edn., 1963-65, sr. high asst. prin., 1965-71, sr. high prin., 1971-88, dir. pupil svcs., 1988-97; retired, 1997. Mem. state adv. com., chair vis. evaluation teams Middle States Assn. Colls. and Schs. Com. on Secondary Schs., 1988-93, piloted 6th ednl. evaluation criteria Nat. Study of Sch. Evaluation, Phila., 1987. Author radio series: Music Around the World, 1963-64. Bd. dirs. YMCA, Boyertown, 1968-72; charter mem. Pottstown (Pa.) chpt. Pa. Sports Hall of Fame, 1973; mem. planning com. Lehigh U. Nat. Honor Soc., Bethlehem, Pa., 1961-72; pres. Ches-Mont League, Pa. Interscholastic Athletic Assn., Southeastern Pa., 1978-80; charter mem. Child Abuse Coalition, 1991—, Boyertown Area Unity Coalition, 1994—. Mem. Am. Assn. Sch. Adminstrs., Nat. Assn. Pupil Svcs. Adminstrs., Pa. Assn. Pupil Svcs. Adminstrs., Kiwanis (charter mem., sec. 1988-90, pres. 1992-93, lt. gov. 1997—, Rockett Outstanding Pres. 1993). Avocations: model railroading, photography. Home: 184 Popodickon Dr Boyertown PA 19512-2042

KUSHINKA, JOYCE WILLIAMS, secondary education educator, retired; b. Roaring Spring, Pa., July 11, 1925; d. Carl Hurlbert and Hazel Evelyn (Kemberlin) Williams; m. Michael Kushinka, Mar. 17, 1951; children: Kerry Kushinka Swan, Candice Kushinka Douma, Jennifer. BA, Dickinson Coll., 1947; MA in Teaching summa cum laude, Monmouth Coll., 1972; EdD, Rutgers U., 1979. Cert. tchr., supr., N.J. Mem. fgn. svc. U.S. Dept. State, Frankfurt, Germany, 1948-50; substitute tchr. Somerville (N.J.) Pub. Schs., 1968-71; tchr. social studies Somerville High Sch., 1971-93. Mission and Sunday sch. tchr. Meth. Ch., New Providence and Somerville, mem. ofcl. bd., Somerville; mem. adv. bd. Holocaust and Genocide Studies; mem. bldg. com. Habitat for Humanity. Fellow Ea. coll., Fairleigh Dickinson U., Rutgers U., Inst. on constitution, Eagleton Inst., others. Mem. NEA, AAUW, Nat. Coun. Social Studies, N.J. Edn. Assn., N.J. Coun. Social Studies, Leonardo Alliance, Figaro Alliance, Kappa Delta Pi.

KUSHINSKY, JEANNE ALICE, SAT tutor; b. Reading, Pa, Jan. 12, 1937; d. Otis Jacob and Alice Elizabeth (Kurtz) Rothenberger; m. Sheldon Melvin Wallerstein, May 9, 1959 (div. July 1978); children: Seth, Gail Wallerstein Melichar; m. David Lazar Kushinsky, Apr. 11, 1987. BS, Cedar Crest Coll., 1958; postgrad., Kean U. NJ., 1978—92, Rutgers U., 1993. Tchr. East Orange Bd. Edn., NJ, 1958—60; editor Dept. Testing and Assessment State Dept. Edn., Trenton, NJ, 1974—76; tchr. Edison Township Bd. Edn., NJ, 1974—2000; pvt. tutor SAT verbal sect. Edison, NJ, 1980—. Mem. Citizen's Adv. Coun. Edn., Edison, NJ, 1991—93. Fashion show com. Rahway Hosp. Found., 2002—; chairperson gala Edison Arts Soc., 2003—, bd. trustees, 2000—; active Dist. VIII Middlesex County Bd. Atty. Ethics, Trenton, NJ, 2000—. Grantee grant, N.J. Coun. for Humanities, 1996. Mem.: Brandeis Univ. Nat. Women's Comm., NJ Edn. Assn., NEA, Metuchen-Edison Hist. Soc., Proprietary House, Nat. Trust for Hist. Preservation, Borough Improvement League. Democrat. Jewish. Avocations: historic preservation architecture, feminist issues, mentoring young people, film studies, reading. Home: 119 Turner Ave Edison NJ 08820 Home Fax: 732-225-2353.

KUSHNER, BORIS ABRAHAM, education educator; b. Krasnouralsk, Russia, Dec. 10, 1941; arrived in U.S., 1989; s. Abraham Isaak and Sinaida Boris (Meerovich) K.; m. Marina Vitaly Kameneva, Feb. 5, 1966; children: Julia, Alexandr. M in Math., Moscow U., 1964, PhD in Math., 1967. Sr. researcher Computing Ctr./Acad. of Scis. of USSR, Moscow, 1968-89; asst. prof. U. Pitts., Johnstown, Pa., 1990-94, assoc. prof., 1994-96, prof., 1996—. Vis. prof. Carnegie Mellon U., Pitts., 1989-90. Author: (monograph) Lectures on Constructive Math Analysis, 1984; author 5 books of poetry; contbr. more than 80 papers in field to nat. and Russian publs. Mem. Am. Math. Soc., Assn. Symbolic Logic, Internat. PEN Club. Home: 329 Theatre Dr Apt 2b24 Johnstown PA 15904-3277 Office: Dept Math Univ Pittsburgh Johnstown PA 15904

KUSHNER, HAROLD JOSEPH, mathematics educator; b. N.Y.C., July 29, 1933; s. Hyman and Harriet Kushner; m. Linda Rosen, Sept. 20, 1960; children: Diana, Nina. BA, CCNY, 1955; MS, U. Wis., 1956, PhD, 1958. Mem. staff Lincoln Lab., Lexington, Mass., 1955-63, Rias, Balt., 1963-64; prof. applied math. Brown U., Providence, 1964—, dir. Lefschtez Ctr. Dynamical Systems, 1980-87, 95-99, chmn. divsn. applied math., 1988-91. Cons. numerous govt. agys. and cos., 1964—. Author: Stochastic Stability and Control, 1967, Introduction to Stochastic Control Theory, 1972, Probability Methods for Approximations in Stochastic Control, 1977, Stochastic Approximation, 1978, Weak Convergence Methods and Applications to Stochastic Systems, 1984, Weak Convergence Methods and Singularly Perturbed Stochastic Control and Filtering Problems, 1991, Numerical Methods for Stochastic Control Problems in Continuous Time, 1992, Stochastic Approximation Algorithms and Applications, 1997, Heavy Traffic Analysis of Controlled Queuing and Communication Networks, 2001. Recipient numerous grants U.S. govt. agys., 1964—, Louis E. Levy award Franklin Inst., 1994. Fellow IEEE (Control Systems award 1992); mem. Inst. Math. Stats., Soc. Indsl. and Applied Math. (W.T. and Idalia Reid prize 2003), Ops. Rsch. Soc. Am., Inst. Mgmt. Sci. Home: 560 Lloyd Ave Providence RI 02906-5427 Office: Brown U Divsn Applied Math Providence RI 02912-0001

KUSIAK, ANDREW, manufacturing engineer, educator; b. Kozia Wola, Poland, June 14, 1949; came to U.S., 1988; s. Stanislaw and Maria J. (Biernacka) K.; m. Anna B. Rakoczy, July 14, 1974; children: Derek, Dagmar E., Eric N.A. BS, Warsaw Tech. U., 1972, MS, 1974; PhD, Polish Acad. Scis., 1979. Project mgr. Inst. Mgmt. and Orgn., Warsaw, 1979-81; asst. prof. Tech. U. Nova Scotia, Halifax, 1982-85; assoc. prof. U. Manitoba, Winnipeg, 1985-88; prof., chair U. Iowa, Iowa City, 1988-95, prof., 1995—. Cons. Rockwell Internat., Iowa City, 1989—, Motorola, Inc., Chgo., 1991—; editor in chief Chapman and Hall, London, 1990—; U.S. editor Taylor and Francis, London, 1990—; chmn. Artificial Intelligence Conf., London, 1990, Hybrid Systems Conf., Budapest, 1993, Prodn. Systems Conf., Winnipeg, 1987. Author: Intelligent Manufacturing, 1990, Engineering Design: Products, Processes, and Systems, 1999, Computational Intelligence in Design and Manufacturing, 2000; editor: Intelligent Design, 1992, Artificial Intelligence, 1988, Expert Systems, 1988, Concurrent Engineering, 1993, 94, Handbook of Design Manufacturing and Automation, 1994. Active Iowa City Sci. Ctr., 1992. Recipient Publ. award Internat. Soc. for Productivity Enhancement, 1988, Outstanding Publ. award Inst. Indsl. Engrs., 1993. Mem. Ops. Rsch. Soc. Am., Soc. Mfg. Engrs. (sr., Publ. award 1990), Internat. Fedn. Automation and Control, Internat. Fedn. Info. Processing. Roman Catholic. Avocations: jogging, tennis. Home: 2629 Hickory Trl Iowa City IA 52245-3522 Office: U Iowa Dept Indsl Engring Iowa City IA 52242-1527

KUSSMAN, ELEANOR (ELLIE KUSSMAN), retired educational superintendent; b. Bklyn., Mar. 17, 1934; d. Mortimer Joseph and Eleanor Mary (O'Brien) Gleeson; m. Karl Kussman, June 30, 1956 (dec. Oct. 1988); children: Katherine Ann, Kristine Sue. BA, Wheaton Coll., Norton, Mass., 1955; MS, LaVerne Coll., Claremont, Calif., 1974. Cert. tchr. K-C.C., cert. in pupil pers. and adminstrn., Calif. Tchr. sci. and math. Norwood (Mass.) Jr. H.S., 1955-56; tchr. phys. edn. Brawley (Calif.) Union H.S., 1956-58, Ctrl. Union H.S., El Centro, Calif., 1958-74, tchr. health careers, 1974-80, state and fed. project dir., 1980-85; instr. horse husbandry and equitation Imperial Valley Coll., Imperial, Calif., 1974-76; supr. Imperial Valley (Calif.) Regional Occupational Program, 1985-95. Cons. E.E. Kussman Cons., El Centro, 1992—, Calif. Joint Gender Equity Com., Sacramento, 1991-96, State of Calif. Gender Equity, Sacramento, 1986-96; grad. instr. program in counseling and guidance U.Calif., Redlands, 1989. Mem. fin. com. United Way, El Centro, 1987-93; sec.-treas. Pvt. Industry Coun., El Centro, 1985-95; past sec.-treas. Calif. Regional Occupational Ctrs./Programs, 1986-88; bd. dirs. Imperial Valley Coll. Desert Mus., 1998-2000. Named Educator of Yr. Imperial Valley Chpt. Phi Delta Kappa, 1995. Mem. AAUW, ASCD, Assn. Calif. Sch. Adminstrs. (past local and regional officer), Rotary Internat. (bd. dirs. 1994-97). Avocations: camping, travel, gardening, reading, horses. Home and Office: PO Box 83 El Centro CA 92244-0083

KUSSMAUL, DONALD, academic administrator; Bachelor's degree, Master's degree, So. Ill. U.; Doctorate, Loyola U. Supt. East Dubuque (Ill.) Unit Sch. Dist. 119, 1983—. Mem. adv. com. to state supt. Ill.; dir. ext. svcs. East Dubuque campus Hillside C.C.; dir. Family T.I.E.S. Early Childhood At Risk Program. Co-author: (book) Preparing Schools and School Systems for the 21st Century. Active Greater Dubuque Area Red Cross, Jr. Achievement Orgn. Mem.: Ill. Assn. Sch. Adminstrs., Am. Assn. Sch. Adminstrs. (pres.-elect 2003—, exec. bd. 2000—, former chmn. rural/small schs. com.), Horace Mann League, Lions. Office: East Dubuque Sch Dist 119 200 Park Lane Dr East Dubuque IL 61025-9568*

KUSSROW, NANCY ESTHER, educational association administrator; BA, Valparaiso U., 1952; MA, U. N.C., 1954. Exec. dir. Nat. Assn. prins. of Schs. for Girls; ret., 1996.

KUSTER, JANICE ELIZABETH, biology educator, researcher; b. Thunder Bay, Ont., Can., Nov. 22, 1951; d. Norman Walter Kuster and Anne Hill Allan; m. Robert J. Keenan, June 6, 1981; children: Melissa Kuster Keenan, Tyler Kuster Keenan. BSc in Biology, Lakehead U., Thunder Bay, 1973; PhD in Entomology, U. Alta., Can., 1978. Undergrad. lab. demonstrator dept. biology U. Lakehead, 1973; grad. student teaching asst. dept. entomology U. Alta., Edmonton, 1974-76, lectr., lab. coord. dept. zoology, dept. physiology, 1983-84; lectr. George Brown Coll., Toronto, Can., 1986; lectr., lab. instr. Ryerson Polytech. Inst., Toronto, Can., 1986; lab. instr. dept. biol. scis. U. Pitts., 1989-91, lectr. dept. biol. scis., 1994-95; instr. Williamson Rd. Elem. Sch., Toronto, 1992, Kerr Elem. Sch., Pitts., 1993, Boyd Cmty. Ctr., Fox Chapel, Pa., 1993, 1995, Fairview Elem. Sch., Pitts., 1994-95, 1996, Beechwood Farms Audubon Soc. Western Pa., 1993-95. Post-doctoral rsch. fellow York U., Toronto, 1978-80, U. Alta., 1980-84; mem. edn. enhancement awards com. Fairview Elem. Sch., 1993, coord. sci. fair, 1994, chmn. great expectations, 1995-96. Contbr. articles to profl. jours. Instr. Summer Sci. Safari Camp Good Shepherd Luth. Ch., Fox Chapel, 1994, coord. Harvest Fair, 1993; mem. Integra Family House Polo com., Pitts., 1993-96. Alta. Heritage Found. Med. Rsch. fellow, 1981-84; Lakehead U. Alumni scholar, 1972, Gulf Oil Can. Ltd. scholar, 1973. Mem. AAUW (edn. com. 1992-96). Presbyterian. Avocations: tennis, hiking, cycling. Home: 211 Timber Ridge Rd Pittsburgh PA 15238-2436

KUTLAR, FERDANE, genetics educator, researcher; b. Turkey, Apr. 15, 1945; came to U.S., 1984; d. Mehmet and Sidika Tanrikulu; m. Abdullah Kutlar, Feb. 7, 1975. MD, Istanbul (Turkey) Med. Sch., 1971. Bd. cert in internal medicine, Turkey, 1976. Resident in internal medicine Istanbul U. Sch. Medicine, 1972-76; chief resident dept. medicine Istanbul Hosp., 1977-81; rsch. fellow Med. Coll. Ga., Augusta, 1982; hematology fellow Istanbul U. Sch. Medicine, 1983; rsch. fellow Med. Coll. Ga., Augusta, 1984, asst. prof., 1985-99, assoc. prof. medicine, 1999—. Dir. DNA lab. Med. Coll. Ga., Augusta, 1994—; presenter in field. Contbr. articles to profl. jours. Mem. Am. Soc. Hematology, Am. Soc. Human Genetics, Med. Coll. Ga. Pres.'s Club. Avocations: oil painting, gardening, decorating, chess. Home: 623 Sawgrass Dr Martinez GA 30907-9137 Office: Med Coll Ga Dept Medicine 15th St AC-1000 Augusta GA 30912-2100 E-mail: fkutlar@mail.mcp.edu.

KUTLINA, MARY LOUISE, language educator; b. Niagara Falls, NY, Dec. 1, 1963; d. Joseph William and Frida Marlene (Reumel) K. BA in Communications, Niagara U., 1985, MS in Edn., 1988. Cert. elem. tchr., English tchr. Elem. tchr., jr. high English tchr. St. Joseph Elem. Sch., Niagara Falls, NY, 1988-90; sub. tchr. Niagara Falls Bd. of Edn., 1990—97, 1999—; Eng. tchr. St. Peter's Luth. Sch., 1997-99; sub. tchr. Grand Island Ctrl. Sch. Dist., 2001—. Lectr. St. Stanislaus Kostka, 1977—; newsroom intern Sta. WIVB-TV, Buffalo, 1984—; prodn. asst. Niagara Frontier Cable TV, 1986. Author: (teleplay) Friends of Blondin, 1985, (children's play) Silly Sarah Becomes Smart, 1990, (book of poetry) Friends of Mary, 1991, also numerous radio and TV commls., news stories, charcoal and ink drawings. Vol. Blind Info. Svc., 1978-87; fundraiser, clerical aide March of Dimes Birth Defects Found., 1981-85, YMCA, 1990-94, Music Sch. Niagara, 1992-96, Friends of Niagra Falls Pub. Libr., 1990—, Friends of Niagara U. Theater; mem. Niagara U. Alumni Admissions Program, 1994. Mem. Internat. Platform Assn., 1994-01, Substitute Tchrs. United (newsletter staff, bd. dirs.-sec. 1991-92, editor SUB NEWS 1994), Pi Lambda Theta. Avocations: aerobics, reading biographies, writing poetry, volunteer work. Home: 2634 Welch Ave Niagara Falls NY 14303-1956 Office: Grand Island Central Sch 1100 Ransom Rd Grand Island NY 14072

KUTSCHINSKI, DOROTHY IRENE, elementary education educator; b. Denison, Iowa, Feb. 19, 1922; d. Gustave Waldemar and Wilhelmina Louisa (Stahl) Wiese; m. Alvin Otto Kutschinski; children: Karen E. Kutschinski Christensen, Linda K. Kutschinski Nepper. BA, Morningside Coll., 1965, MA in Teaching, 1970. Tchr. Crawford County (Iowa) Rural Schs., 1940-53, Charter Oak (Iowa) Community Schs., 1953-90; substitute tchr., 1990—. Apptd. to Crawford County Coun. Local Govt. for Hist. Preservation, 1992—, chair 1996—; tchr. Bible class St. John Luth. Ch., Charter Oak, Iowa, 1956—; sec. Crawford County Rep. Ctrl. Com., 1980-91, 98—; pres. Crawford County Rep. Women, 1978-86 trustee Iowa N.W. Regional Libr., 1991-2001; co-founder, sec., charter Oak-Ute Cmty. Sch. Edn. Found., 1994—, apptd. to adv. com., sec., 1993-2001. Named Outstanding Elem. Tchr. of Am., 1973; recipient Tchr. of Yr. award, Denison Newspapers, 1985, Women of Excellence award, Women Aware, Inc., 2001. Mem. AAUW (treas. 1985-90, pres. 1991-93), Iowa State Hist. Soc., Crawford County Hist. Soc. (life), The Smithsonian Assocs., The Audubon Soc., Living History Farms, Iowa Natural Heritage, Crawford County Arts Assn. (pres. 1986-88, bd. dirs. 1972—, sec. 1996—), Delta Kappa Gamma, Alpha Delta (sec. 1984—). Avocations: reading, sewing, bird watching, walking, writing. Home: 103 Pine Ave Charter Oak IA 51439-7453

KUTTLER, CARL MARTIN, JR., academic administrator; b. Daytona Beach, Fla., Jan. 31, 1940; s. Carl M. and Winona (Ellis) K.; m. Evelyn Flathmann, June 29, 1963; children— Cindy, Carl Martin III, Erika. AA, St. Petersburg Jr. Coll., 1960; BS in Mgmt., Fla. State U., Tallahassee, 1962; JD, Stetson U., 1965. Bar: Fla. bar 1965. Research aide 2d Dist. Ct. Appeals, Lakeland, Fla., 1965-66; instr. St. Petersburg (Fla.) Jr. Coll. (now St. Petersburg Coll.), 1965-76; asst. to v.p. for adminstrn. St. Petersburg (Fla.) Jr. Coll., 1966-67, dean. adminstrv. affairs, 1967-78, pres., 1978—. Adj. instr., cons. grad. edn. program U. Tex., Austin; judge Templeton Prize in Religion. Co-author: 1,001 Exemplary Practices in America's Two-Year Colleges, 1994. Mem. pres.'s Coun. Div. Cmty. Colls., 1978—; candidate for Fla. Commr. Edn., 1974; mem. judging panel selecting outstanding high schs. in Am. for U.S. Sec. Edn.; apptd. by Pres. U.S. Nat. Adv. Coun. Ednl. Rsch. and Improvement; apptd. by U.S. Sec. VA to Adminstr.'s Ednl. Assistance Adv. Com. Named Most Disting. Alumnus, Stetson U. Alumni Assn., 1978, 1988, Hon. Father of C.C. Sys. in Russia, Assn. Edn. for Everybody, 1994, Outstanding C.C. Pres. in Am., Assn. of C.C. Trustees, 1998; recipient Disting. Floridian award, Phi Theta Kappa, 1986, Nat. Disting. Coll. Pres. award, 1991, Internat. Leadership award, 1990, vis. scholar award, 1987, master tchr. award, 1988, 1992, 1993, U. Tex. Disting. Pres.'s award, PTK Fla., 1991, Alumnus award, Fla. State U., 1981, 1988, Liberty Bell award, St. Petersburg Bar Assn., 1992, Werner Kubsch award for outstanding achievement in internat. edn., C.C. for Internat. Devel., Inc., 1997, top Phi Theta Kappa chpt. award of 1200 cmty. colls., 2001, Chmn.'s award, St. Petersburg C. of C., 2001, C.W. Bill Young Pinellas Pinnacle award, Dept. Econ. Devel., 2002, Pres. award Profl. Excellence, Fla. Assn. C.C., 2002. Mem.: Fla. Bar Assn., Fla. Assn. C.C.s (Pres.'s award for profl. excellence 2002), Am. Assn. C.C.s, Nat. Assn. Coll. and Univ. Attys. Republican. Presbyterian. Home: 8336 40th Ave N Saint Petersburg FL 33709-3935 Office: St Petersburg Coll PO Box 13489 Saint Petersburg FL 33733-3489 E-mail: kuttlerc@spcollege.edu.

KUYKENDALL, CRYSTAL ARLENE, educational consultant, lawyer; b. Chgo., Dec. 11, 1949; d. Cleophus Campbell and Ellen (Campbell) Logan; m. Roosevelt Kuykendall, Apr. 10, 1969 (dec. Aug. 1972); children: Kahlil, Rasheki, Kashif. BA, Southern Ill. U., 1970; MA, Montclair State U., 1972; EdD, Atlanta U., 1975; JD, Georgetown U., 1982; LHD (hon.), Lewis and Clark Coll., Portland, 2002. Bar: D.C. 1988. Instr. Seton Hall U., South Orange, N.J., 1971-73; adminstrn. intern D.C. Pub. Schs., 1974-75; dir. citizens tng. inst. Nat. Com. for Citizens in Edn., Washington, 1975-77; dir. urban and minorities rels. dept. Nat. Sch. Bd. Assn., Washington, 1977-79; edn. dir. PSI Assocs., Inc., Washington, 1979-80; exec. dir. Nat. Alliance of Black Sch. Educators, Washington, 1980-81; dir. mktg. Roy Littlejohn Assoc., Inc., Washington, 1983—; pres., gen. counsel K.I.R.K., Inc. (Kreative and Innovative Resources for Kids), Washington, 1981—. Cons. to Ministry of Sport and Recreation, Western Australia Govt., 1990; chmn. U.S. Pres. Nat. Adv. Coun. on Continuing Edn., Washington, 1978-81; cons. U. Pitts. Race Desegregation Assistance Ctr., 1982-87, J.H. Lowry Assn., Chgo., 1982, U.S. Dept. of Edn. Transition Team, Washington, 1980. Author: Developing Leadership for Parent/Citizen Groups, 1975, You & Yours: Making the Most of this School Year, 1987, Improving Black Student Achievement by Enhancing Self Image, 1989, From Rage to Hope: Strategies for Reclaiming Black and Hispanic Students, 1992, rev. edit., 2003, Dreaming of a PHAT Century, 2000, 2nd edit., 2003. Mem. adv. bd. Inst. of the Black World, Atlanta, 1975-81; mem. steering com. Nat Conf. on Parental Involvement, Denver, 1977-78; mem. edn. task force Martin Luther King Jr. Ctr. for Social Change, Atlanta, 1978-80; mem. bd. dirs. Health Power, Inc., 1995-2001, Shiloh Bapt. Ch. of Washington Family Life Ctr. Fedn., 1996—. Named Honorary Citizen of New Orleans, Mayor's Office, 1976; Ford found. fellow, 1973-74; Honorary Ky Colonel award, 1993, 99, 2002; Cert. Congl. Recognition, 2001. Mem. Nat. Bar Assn., Nat. Alliance of Black Sch. Edn., Alpha Kappa Alpha. Democrat. Baptist. Avocations: poetry writing, card playing, swimming, jogging, skiing. Office: KIRK Inc PO Box 60115 Potomac MD 20859-0115

KUYKENDALL, JOHN WELLS, academic administrator, educator; b. Charlotte, N.C., May 8, 1938; s. James Bell and Emily Jones (Frazer) K.; m. Nancy Adams Moore, July 15, 1961; children— Timothy Moore, James Frazer BA cum laude, Davidson Coll., 1959; BD cum laude, Union Sem., Richmond, Va., 1964; STM, Yale U., 1965; MA, Princeton U., 1972, PhD, 1975; DD (hon.), Hanover Coll., 1999; LHD (hon.), Wofford Coll., 1999. Ordained to ministry Presbyterian Ch., 1965. Campus minister Presbyn. Ch., Auburn, Ala., 1965-70; faculty Auburn U., 1973-84; pres. Davidson (N.C.) Coll., 1984—97, pres. emeritus, prof. religion, 1997—2003. Author: (with others) Presbyterians: Their History and Beliefs, 1978, Southern Enterprize: The Work of Evangelical Societies in the Antebellum South, 1982; contbr. articles to profl. jours. Recipient Algernon Sydney Sullivan award Auburn U., 1982 Mem. Am. Soc. Ch. History, Phi Beta Kappa, Omicron Delta Kappa, Phi Kappa Phi. Democrat.

KUZIEMSKI, NAOMI ELIZABETH, educational consultant, counselor; b. Phila., Dec. 22, 1925; d. Andrew Raymond and Elizabeth M. (Graham) Hartman; m. Walter William Kuziemski, Dec. 28, 1943 (dec. Feb. 2000); children: Nancy Kuziemski Simpson, Sandra Ruth McElroy. BS in Bus. Edn., Temple U., 1945, MS in Counseling, 1949. Tchr. Sch. Dist. Phila., 1945-58; coll. counselor Phila. H.S. for Girls, 1958-96; ednl. cons., 1996—. V.p. Nat. Assn. Coll. Admissions Counselors, Alexandria, Va., 1985-87, dir. Tools of the Trade workshop, 1992-95; pres. Pa. Assn. Coll. Admissions Counselors, 1991-93; focus group mem. U.S. News and World Report, Washington, 1995-96; panelist and presenter in field. Del., instnl. rep. Coll. Bd., N.Y., 1978-96. Recipient Bernard P. Ireland award Coll. Bd., Phila., 1996, Gayle C. Wilson award Nat. Assn. Coll. Admission Counselors, Alexandria, 1996, Recognition award PASSCAC, 1998; named Counselor of the Yr., Inroads, Phila., 1982. Mem. AAUW (Phila. br., v.p. 1997-99), Coll. Bd.-Middle States (planning com. 1995-97). Home: 7 Lawnside Rd Cheltenham PA 19012-1812 E-mail: naomikuz@aol.com.

KVALE, JANICE KELLER, nurse-midwifery educator; b. Slayton, Minn., June 15; d. Clifford Rufus and Fern Adeline (Schumann) Keller; m. James Noel Kvale, July 18; children: Sarah, Elizabeth, Jonathan, James, Brian. RN Diploma, St. Luke's Hosp., Duluth, Minn., 1957; BS, U. Minn., 1959; MSN, Catholic U., Washington, 1965; PhD, Case Western Res. U., 1995. RN, Ohio, Tex. Nurse-midwife Med. Ctr., Long Prairie, Minn., 1971-80; free-lance writer Ill., 1980-83; asst. prof. MacMurray Coll., Jacksonville, Ill., 1983-87; instr. Case Western Res. U., Cleve., 1987-94, asst. prof., 1994-96; dir. faculty nurse-midwifery ednl. program U. Tex. Sch. Nursing, Galveston, 1996—2001. Vis. prof. U. Zimbabwe, Harare, 1995; cons. Life Span Internat., Tex. Author: Crisis Intervention in Maternal Newborn Nursing, 1975. SPAN Internat. scholar. Fellow Am. Coll. Nurses-Midwives (cert., bd. dirs. 2000-2003); mem. ANA, APHA, So. Nursing Rsch. Soc., Sigma Theta Tau (Fulbright sr. scholar 2003—). Avocations: canoeing, cross-county skiing, gardening, reading. Home: 131 Creekside Dr League City TX 77573-1751 Office: U Tex Med Br Sch Nursing 301 University Rte 1029 Galveston TX 77555-1029

KVALSETH, TARALD ODDVAR, mechanical engineer, educator; b. Brunkeberg, Telemark, Norway, Nov. 7, 1938; married; 3 children. BS, U. Durham, King's Coll., Eng., 1963; MS, U. Calif.-Berkeley, 1966, PhD, 1971. Research asst. engring. expt. sta. U. Colo., Boulder, 1963-64, teaching asst. dept. mech. engring.; mech. engr. Williams & Lane Inc., Berkeley, 1964-65; research asst. dept. indsl. engring. and ops. research U. Calif.-Berkeley, 1965-71, research fellow, 1973; asst. prof. Sch. Indsl. and Systems Engring. Ga. Inst. Tech., Atlanta, 1971-74; sr. lectr. indsl. mgmt. div. Norwegian Inst. Tech. U. Trondheim, 1974-79, head indsl. mgmt. div., 1975-79; assoc. prof. dept. mech. engring. U. Minn., Mpls., 1979-82, prof., 1982—. Guest worker NASA Ames Research Ctr., Calif., 1973; mem. organizing com. 1st Berkeley-Monterey Conf. Timespan, Pay and Discretionary Capacity, 1973; mem. steering com. Internat. Conf. Human Factors in Design and Op. Ships, Gothenburg, Sweden, 1977; mem. bd. Norwegian Ergonomics Com., 1977-80; gen. session chmn. Conf. Work Place Design and Work Environ. Problems, Trondheim, 1978 Author book chpts., articles, presentations, reports in field; editor text books; mem. editl. bd., reviewer for numerous profl. jours., patentee in field. Fellow AAAS; mem. IEEE, Inst. Indsl. Engrs. (sr.), Human Factors and Ergonomics Soc. (pres. upper Midwest chpt.), Nordic Ergonomics Soc. (coun. 1977-80), Internat. Ergonomics Assn. (gen. coun. 1977-80, v.p. 1982-85), Ergonomics Soc., Psychonomic Soc., Am. Psychol. Soc., Am. Statis. Assn., Sigma Xi. Lutheran. Home: 4980 Shady Island Cir Mound MN 55364 Office: U Minn Dept Mech Engring Minneapolis MN 55455 E-mail: kvals001@umn.edu.

KVAPIL, DONNA LEE, secondary school educator; b. Monte Vista, Colo., June 7, 1948; d. Jose Milton and Agnes M. (Roybal) Trujillo; m. Edward Louis Kvapil Jr., Apr. 21, 1968; 1 child, George Allen. BBA, U. Tex., El Paso, 1983. Tchr. bus. edn. El Paso Ind. Sch. Dist., 1983—. Advisor Effective Sch. Project to various schs. in program; mem. El Paso C.C. Articulation of Acctg. Classes between H.S.s and EPCC, 1985-86, 94, mem. articulation plan and agreement com.; mem. open/closed campus task force El Paso Ind. Sch. Dist., dist. officer task force tchr. rep. mem., 1990; mem. open/closed campus task force Andress H.S., 1990, chair action plan team Effective Schs. Project, 1989-91, mem. action planning team, 1989-91, task force facilitator, 1989-91; mem. El Paso Ind. Sch. Dist. Bus. Edn./Office Edn. Program Rev. Com., 1990-91, bus. edn. tchr. rep., tchr. rep., 1992-93; adviser Andress Future Bus. Leaders of Am., 1986-95; adviser, founder El Paso chpt. Future CPAs at h.s.-level, 1992-95; mem. Andress Campus Improvement Com., 1991-95; chair bus. edn. dept. Andress H.S. 1985-95; mem. local area textbook com. El Paso Ind. Sch. Dist., 1994-95, dist. voting del. Recipient Nat. Future Bus. Leaders of Am. Phi Beta Lambda Adviser Svc. Recognition award, 1992. Mem. Nat. Bus. Edn. Assn., Tex. Bus. Edn. Assn. (rep. dist. 19 1985-88, pres. dist. 19 1989-90, reporter historian 1989-90, state nominating com. 1990-92, state co-chair membership com. 1992-93, state treas. 1994—, Tchr. of Yr. award 1987, dist. 19 Trans-Pecos Tchr. of Yr. 1994-95), Tex. State Tchrs. Assn., Andress Parents, Tchrs., and Students Assn. (faculty liaison 1990—, Membership award 1991-92). Home: 10416 Mccormick Ln El Paso TX 79924-2319 Office: Andress H S 5400 Sun Valley Dr El Paso TX 79924-3418

KVETKO, NELL PATTERSON, elementary school educator; b. Ft. Lee, Va., Nov. 2, 1950; d. Alford August and Pattie Ray (Chandler) Patterson; m. James George Kvetko, Nov. 18, 1989; 1 child, Emily Caitlann. AA, Richard Bland Coll., 1970; BA, Coll. of William and Mary, 1972; MEd, Va. State U., 1989. Cert. tchr., Va. Tchr. Petersburg Pub. Schs., Va., 1972—75, chpt. I reading specialist, 1975—89; reading specialist Chesterfield County Pub. Schs., Chester, Va., 1989—. Mem. Internat. Reading Assn., Va. State Reading Assn., Phi Delta Kappa. Avocations: crafts, sewing, reading. Home: 4803 Lynbrook Ln Richmond VA 23237-4101

KVINT, VLADIMIR LEV, economist, mining engineer, finance educator; b. Krasnoyarsk, Siberia, Russia, Feb. 21, 1949; s. Lev V. Kvint and Lidia E. Adamskaya; children: Liza, Valeria. MS in Mining Engring., Inst. Non-Ferrous Metals, Krasnoyarsk, 1972; PhD in Managerial Econs., Inst. Nat. Economy, Moscow, 1975; D of Econs., Inst. Econs., Acad. Scis., Moscow, 1988; life-title: Prof. Pol. Economy, Inst. Economy, Acad. of Scis., Moscow, 1989; HHD, U. Bridgeport, 1997. Asst. prof. Inst. of Non-Ferrous Metals, 1972; chief of dept. non-ferrous metals co., Norilsk, Russia, 1975—76; dep. chair, chief economist Automation of non-ferrous metals com., 1976—78; chief dept. sci.-tech. progress Siberian br. Acad. of Scis., Novosibirsk, 1978—82; part-time prof. various Russian univs., 1976—89; leading rschr., fellow Inst. Econs., Acad. Scis., Moscow, 1982—89; econ. adviser Govt. of Albania, 2002—; chmn. expert econ. coun. Ministry of Sport, Russia, 2002—. Cons. GE, N.Y.C., 1989—94, Cable & Wireless, London, 1989—97; econ. adviser Pres. of the UN, 1997—98, King of Bulgaria, 1996—2001; vis. prof. Vienna (Austria) Econ. U., 1989—90; prof. Fordham U. Grad. Sch., N.Y.C., 1990—; disting. prof. Babson Coll. Bus., Mass., 1991; mng. dir. emerging markets Arthur Andersen, 1992—97; dir. for govtl. affairs Metromedia Internat. Telecom. Inc., 1997—2000; adj. prof. Stern Grad. Sch. Bus. NYU, 1995—2000. Author: The Acceleration of Technological Development of Production, 1976, The Introduction and Use of Automation Systems, 1981, The Krasnoyarsk Experiment, 1982, Management of Scientific-Technical Progress, 1986, The Economic and Scientific-Technical Information, 1987, Development of Economy of Daghestan, 1988, The Barefoot Shoemaker: Capitalizing on the New Russia, 1993, A Different Perspective on Emerging Markets, 1995, Incorporating Global Risk Management in the Strategic Decision Making Process, 1997, The Global Emerging Market in Transition, 1999; co-author: Creating and Managing International Joint Ventures, 1996, International M&A, Joint Ventures and Beyond, 1998, Investing Under Fire: Winning Strategies, 2003; editor-in-chief: Emerging Market of Russia: Sourcebook for Investment and Trade, 1997; contbr. articles to CNN, Forbes, Harvard Bus. Rev., others. Bd. dirs. USSR Exporters Assn., Moscow, 1988-90; mem. internat. com. Muhlenberg Coll., Allentown, Pa., 1992-99; chmn. Summits Instl. Investors & Global Risk Management, World Econ. Devel. Congress, Washington, 1995-97. Recipient Silver medal for achievements in nat. economy, USSR Main Nat. Com., Moscow, 1986, Gold medal Hon. Lawyer of Russia, 2003; US Fulbright Scholar award, 2001. Fellow: Wexner Heritage Found. (N.Y.C.), New Eng. Ctr. for Internat. and Regional Studies (hon.); mem.: Internat. Acad. Emerging Markets (pres.), Bretton Woods Com. (Washington), Am. Econ. Assn., Russian Acad. Natural Scis. (life), Internat. Acad. Regional Devel. (life), Internat. Informatization Acad. of UN (hon.), Philos. Soc., N.Y. Acad. Scis., World Jewish Acad. Scis. (pres.). Achievements include devel. of theory of regionalization of scientific tech. progress; evaluation of role of scientific-technical strategy in devel. of regional economy; devel. of regional programs, developed a theory of global emerging market, developed a system of optimization models of business strategies in new emerging markets, economic solutions to poverty. Office: Fordham U 113 W 60th St Fl 6 New York NY 10023-7484 E-mail: drvkvint@hotmail.com.

KWAK, JIN-HWAN, molecular biologist, educator; b. Taegu, South Korea, Feb. 6, 1961; s. Eui-Sook Park; children: Christine, Yerin. BS, Seoul (Korea) Nat. U., 1983, MS, 1985, PhD, 1990. Lic. for pharmacy. Rsch. assoc. U. Wis. Med. Sch., Madison, 1990-92; sr. scientist LG Chem. Rsch. Park, Taejon, Korea, 1992-96; assoc. prof. molecular biology Handong U., Pohang, 1996—2003; prof. Handong Global U., Pohang, 2003—. Mem. Am. Soc. Microbiology. Achievements include 21 patents in field. Office: Handong U Heunghae Pohang 791-940 Republic of Korea

KWIRAM, ALVIN L. physical chemistry educator, university official; b. Riverhills, Man., Can., Apr. 28, 1937; came to U.S., 1954; s. Rudolf and Wilhelmina A. (Bilske) K.; m. Verla Rae Michel, Aug. 9, 1964; children: Andrew Brandt, Sidney Marguerite. BS in Chemistry, BA in Physics, Walla Walla (Wash.) Coll., 1958; PhD in Chemistry, Calif. Inst. Tech., 1963; DS (hon.), Andrews U., 1995. Alfred A. Noyes instr. Calif. Inst. Tech., Pasadena, 1962-63; research asso. physics dept. Stanford (Calif.) U., 1963-64; instr. chemistry Harvard U., Cambridge, Mass., 1964-67, lectr., 1967-70; assoc. prof. chemistry U. Wash., Seattle, 1970-75, prof., 1975—, chmn. dept. chemistry, 1977-87, vice provost, 1987-88, sr. vice provost, 1988-90, vice provost for rsch., 1990—2002. Bd. dirs. Seattle Biomed. Rsch. Inst., 1992—2002; mem. divsn. rev. com. Pacific N.W. Nat. Lab., Environ. and Health Scis. Divsn., 1998—2001; mem. adv. com. Pacific N.W. Nat. Lab., 2000—; mem. adv. bd. for univ. connections U. Hawaii, 1999—2001; exec. dir. NSF Ctr. for Materials and Devices for Info. Tech. Rsch., 2002—. Contbr. numerous articles to sci. jours. Bd. dirs. Seattle Econ. Devel. Commn., 1988-92, Wash. Rsch. Found., 1989-94, Seattle-King County Econ. Devel. Coun., 1989-98, Helen R. Whiteley Found., 1997-, Lumera Corp., 2001-03; mem. vis. com. divsn. chemistry and chem. engring. Calif. Inst. Tech., 1991-96; chmn. adv. bd. Sch. Engring., Walla Walla Coll., 1992—. Recipient Eastman-Kodak Sci. award, U.-Industry Relations award Council for Chem. Research, 1986; Woodrow Wilson fellow, 1958; Alfred P. Sloan fellow, 1968-70; Guggenheim Meml. Found. fellow, 1977-78 Fellow: AAAS (chmn.-elect, chmn., past chmn. sect. on chemistry 1991—94, program com. 1994—98), Am. Phys. Soc.; mem.: Worldwide Univ. Network (acad. adv. bd. 2002—, U.S. liaison 2003—), Coun. Chem. Rsch. (bd. dirs. 1980—84, chmn. 1982—83), Am. Chem. Soc. (sec.-treas. divsn. phys. chemistry 1976—86, divsn. councilor 1986—, com. on sci., chmn. subcom. on fed. funding for rsch. 1990—94, adv. bd. for grad. edn. 2000—), Nat. Assn. State Univs. and Land Grant Colls. (past chmn. 2000—03, exec. com., coun. rsch. policy and grad. edn., chmn.-elect, chmn.), Sigma Xi. Office: Univ Wash Dept Chem Seattle WA 98195-1700 E-mail: kwiram@u.washington.edu.

KWOK, REGINALD YIN-WANG, urban planning and development educator, architect; b. Hong Kong, Jan. 24, 1937; came to U.S., 1967; s. On and Yee Fong (Pun) K.; m. Annette Holmes, Aug. 29, 1964; 1 child, Zoe Song-Yi. Diploma in architecture, Poly., London, 1963; Diploma in tropical studies, Archtl. Assn., London, 1967; MS in Architecture, MS in Urban Planning, Colombia U., N.Y.C., 1969, PhD in Urban Planning, 1973. Asst. architect Chamberlin Powell and Bon, London, 1960-61; architect Denys Lasdun and Ptnrs., London, 1963-64, 65-66, Palmer and Turner, Hong Kong, 1965; ind. architect London, 1971; rschr. Inst. Urban Environment, 1968-69; asst. prof. divsn. urban planning Columbia U., 1972-76, assoc. prof., 1976-80, assoc. East Asian Inst., 1975-80; prof. Ctr. Urban Studies and Planning, U. Hong Kong, 1980-89; prof. Sch. Hawaiian/Asian/Pacific Studies, Coll. Social Sci. U. Hawaii at Manoa, Honolulu, 1989—. Vis. prof., Zhongshan (China) U., 1983—, Tsinghua (China) U., 1985—, Wuhan (China) Acad. Urban Constrn., 1985—; vis. fellow Princeton U., 1986, Inst. Urban and Regional Devel. U. Calif., Berkeley, 1987; adv. prof. Tongji U., Shanghai, 1987—; dir. planning program for developing nations Columbia U., 1976-80; dir. Ctr. Urban Studies and Urban Planning U. Hong Kong, 1980-89; chairperson internat. affairs planning coun. U. Hawaii at Manoa, 1990—, advisor MA in Chinese Studies program; vis. scholar Harvard U., 1996-97. Author: (with M. Castells and L. Goh) The Shek Kip Mei Sundrome: Economic Development and Public Housing in Hong Kong and Singapore, 1990, General Theories of Urban Planning (transl. and edited by H. Chen), 1992, (with Alvin Y. So) The Hong Kong-Guangdong Link, 1996; editor: (with W.L. Parish and A.G.O. Yeh) Chinese Urban Reforms: What Model Now?, 1990, . Mem. bldg. com. Hong Kong Housing Authority, 1982-83, mem. mgmt. com., 1983-88; mem. planning bd. Lands and Works Br., 1985-89; mem. met. study steering group Hong Kong, 1987-89; mem. spl. econ. zone Shenzhen (China) City Planning Com., 1986; bd. dirs. Chinatown Planning Coun., N.Y.C., 1976-80; mem. adv. com. to borough pres. Manhattan Overall Econ. Devel. Program, N.Y.C., 1978-80; mem., sec. econ. devel. com., Chinatown Improvement Com., N.Y., 1975-76. Rsch. and study grantee, most recently Min. des Affaires Etranges, France, and Consulat Gen. de France, Hong Kong, 1988, Hawaii Com. of Humanities, 1990, Eu Tong Sen Endowment, 1992-93, 98. Mem. Assn. Asian Studies, Internat. Fedn. Housing and Planning, Archtl. Soc. China (hon. mem. coun. 1983—), Royal Inst. Brit. Architects (assoc.), Ea. Regional Orgn. Planning and Housing (mem. coun., mem. exec. com. Kuala Lumpur 1984—, dep. pres. 1984-86, hon. pres. 1986—), Hong Kong Inst. Architects, Internat. Sociol. Assn., Regional Sci. Assn., Geog. Soc. China. Office: U Hawaii at Manoa Moore Hall 409 Honolulu HI 96822

KYHOS, M. GAITHER GALLEHER, private school educator; b. Durham, N.C., Sept. 17, 1955; d. Earl Potter Jr. and Martha Hungerford (Wheelwright) Galleher; m. Thomas Flynn Kyhos, Sept. 4, 1982; children: Jennifer Chalfant, Patrick Flynn, Justin Farleigh. BA in Polit. Sci. cum laude, St. Lawrence U., 1977. Layout and prodn. asst. Nat. Geographic Mag., Washington, 1977-80, illustrations rschr., 1980-82, sr. rschr., 1982-85, sr. rschr./writer, 1985-88, sr. rschr./compiler, 1988-94; asst. tchr., social studies-resource St. Patrick's Episcopal Day Sch., Washington, 1994-97, co-head tchr., 1997—. Mem. internat. adv. bd. Sellinger Sch., Loyola Coll. in Md., Balt., 1992-96; presenter in field. Author map supplements for Nat. Geographic Mag. Bd. dirs. Lt. Joseph P. Kennedy Inst., Washington, 1993-95; Vice Presdl. advance person The White House, Washington, in Ivory Coast, 1991, in Estonia, 1992. Mem. Nat. Coun. for Social Studies, Spinal Cord Injury Network, Ednl. Alliance/Nat. Geog. Soc., So. Poverty Law Ctr. Avocations: travel, biking, yoga, reading, golf. Office: St Patrick's Episc Day Sch 4700 Whitehaven Pkwy NW Washington DC 20007-1554

KYMAN, WENDY, sex therapist, health educator; b. N.Y.C., Mar. 29, 1947; d. Jack and Tess (Starman) K.; 1 child, Jesse. BS, CCNY, 1968; MS, Bklyn. Coll., 1971; PhD, NYU, 1984. Diplomate, cert. sex therapist and educator Am. Bd. Sexology. Tchr. N.Y.C. Bd. Edn., 1968-74; coord., supr. YWCA Women's Ctr., 1977-78; instr. health edn. SUNY, Old Westbury, 1980-81, instr. allied health Nanuet, 1982; family planning counselor NYU Health Svc., N.Y.C., 1984; asst. prof. health edn. CUNY Hunter Coll., 1984-85; sr. pub. health educator Gouverneur Hosp., 1984-87; assoc. prof. health edn. Baruch Coll., CUNY, 1985—. Pvt. practice sex therapy and sex educator, cons., N.Y.C.; teaching fellow NYU, 1980. Contbr. articles to profl. jours. Profl. Staff Congress of CUNY rsch. grantee, 1988-89. Mem. Am. Assn. Sex Educators, Counselors and Therapists (cert. sex educator), Am. Bd. Sexology. Office: CUNY Baruch Coll 55 Lexington Ave New York NY 10010

KYSOR, DANIEL FRANCIS, psychologist; b. Corry, Pa., Aug. 3, 1956; s. Darrell Francis and Louise Mary (Col) K.; m. Kate Galbraith Morrison, Sept. 7, 1991; children: Kenneth Jon Kron, Samuel Morrison, Charles Col. BS, Edinboro U., 1980; MS in Ednl. Psychology, Edinboro U., Pa., 1988; MEd in Secondary Sch. Adminstrn., Edinboro U., 1994; postgrad., Miss. State U., 1991—. Cert. elem. edn., guidance, elem. and secondary adminstr., sch. psychologist; lic. psychologist, Pa. Tchr. Calhoun County Schs., Grantsville, W.Va., 1982; counselor, tchr. Bradford (Pa.) Children's Home, Pa., 1983; residential program counselor Assn. for Retarded Citizens, Meadville, Pa., 1984-86; resident hall dir. Edinboro (Pa.) U., 1984-86, counselor Edinboro Summer Acad. for the Gifted, 1985-96; guidance counselor Cranberry Sch. Dist., Seneca, Pa., 1986; dropout prevention counselor Erie (Pa.) Sch. Dist., 1988; sch. psychologist Seneca Highlands IU #9, Coudersport, Pa., 1989—. Pvt. practice Addis & Assocs., Bradford, Pa., 1994-97; CEO, dir. psychol. svc. Por t Psychol. Svcs., Inc., 1996—. Pa. Rural Leadership Program scholar Pa. State U., 1989; Rsch. grantee St. Bonaventure (N.Y.) U.; recipient citations Pa. House of Reps., 1991, 93, 95. Mem. ACA (life), NASP, Am. Sch. Counselor Assn., Nat. Fedn. Interscholastic Ofcls. Assns., Pa. Interscholastic Athletic Assn., Ea. Wrestling League, Ea. Ind. Officials Wrestling Assn., Nat. Wrestling Officials Assn., Clowns of Am. Internat., Inc./POCO Clowns. Democrat. Presbyterian. Avocations: wrestling officiating, reading, biking, backpacking. Home: 109 Chestnut St Port Allegany PA 16743-1248 Office: Seneca Highlands IU #9 306 N Main St Coudersport PA 16915-1626 E-mail: kysor@adelphia.net.

KYZAR, OLLIE JEANETTE, educator; b. Brookhaven, Miss., Oct. 7, 1933; d. Marcel Wooden and Annie Leona (Brister) Grice; m. Reese Eugene Kyzar, June 16, 1953. BS in Edn., Delta State U., 1960, postgrad., 1972-74, 79-81, MEd, 1990; postgrad. U. So. Miss., 1960-61, 65-66, 69-70, U. Miss., 1961-63. Tchr. English, Fielding L. Wright High Sch., Rolling Fork, Miss., 1960-61; tchr. Fielding L. Wright Elem. Sch., Rolling Fork, 1961-70; homebound tchr. Rolling Fork Elem. Sch., 1970-73, tchr. reading and math., 1973-84, resource tchr. computer assisted instrn., 1984-88, asst. prin., 1988—; evaluator Nat. Council Accreditation Tchr. Edn., Washington, 1982-87, Miss. Performanced Based Accreditation Schs.; mem. supt.'s adv. bd., Rolling Fork, 1981-83; mem. steering com. on sch. evaluation So. Assn. Colls. and Schs., 1962-73. Sunday sch. tchr., former dir. Acteens, mem. Womens Missionary Union, 1st Baptis Ch. Rolling Fork, 1959; bd. dirs. Adult Bapt. Tng. Union, 1989—. Mem. NEA, Smithsonian Instn. (assoc.), Internat. Platform Assn., Nat. Trust Historic Preservation, Fielding L. Wright Tchrs. Assn. (pres. 1966-67), Rolling Fork Assn. Educators (pres. 1977-78, 81-82, Disting. Service award 1978, 82), Miss. Assn. Educators (workshop presenter 1982-84), Assn. Supervision and Curriculum Devel., Miss. for Ednl. Broadcasting, Nat. Assn. Elem. Sch. Prins., Miss. Assn. Elem. Sch. Prins., Miss. Assn. Supervision and Curriculum Devel., Miss. Assn. Women Ednl. Leadership, Kappa Delta Pi. Avocations: reading, listening to music, walking, riding bicycle. Home: 202 N Second St Rolling Fork MS 39159-2630 Office: Rolling Fork Elem Sch 600 Parkway Ave Rolling Fork MS 39159-3122

LAANANEN, DAVID HORTON, mechanical engineer, educator; b. Winchester, Mass., Nov. 11, 1942; s. Joseph and Helen Katherine (Horton) L.; m. Mary Ellen Storck, Sept. 9, 1967 (div. 1981); children: Gregg David, Robin Kaye; m. Delores Ann Talbert, May 21, 1988. BS in Mech. Engring., Worcester Poly. Inst., 1964; MS, Northeastern U., 1965, PhD, 1968. Project engr. Dynamic Sci., Phoenix, 1972-74; asst. prof. Pa. State U., State College, 1974-78; mgr. R&D Simula Inc., Phoenix, 1978-83; assoc. prof. Ariz. State U., Tempe, 1983-97, prof., 1997—, dir. aerospace rsch. ctr., 1992-93, dir. Airworthiness Assurance Ctr. of Excellence, 1997-2000. Referee: Jour. Aircraft, Jour. Composite Materials; contbr. articles to Jour. Aircraft, Jour. Am. Helicopter Soc., Jour. Thermoplastic Composite Materials, Composites Sci. and Tech., others. Fellow AIAA (assoc.; design engring. tech. com.); mem. ASME, Am. Helicopter Soc., Sigma Xi, Sigma Gamma Tau, Pi Tau Sigma. Democrat. Achievements include research in aircraft crash survivability, composite structures. Office: Ariz State U Dept Mech Aerospace En Tempe AZ 85287 E-mail: david.laananen@asu.edu.

LAATSCH, WILLIAM, geography educator; BA, Carroll Coll., 1960; MA in Geography, U. Okla., 1966; PhD in Geography, U. Alberta, 1972. Prof. urban and regional studies and geography U. Wis., Green Bay, Wis., 1966—, chmn. urban and regional studies and geography. Mem. Wis. Hist. Preservation Rev. Bd., chmn. Recipient Disting. Teaching award Nat. Coll. Geog. Edn., 1992, award Brown County Hist. Soc., 2000, Pershing E. MacAllister Disting. Alumni award Carroll Coll., 2002. Office: U of Wisconsin 2430 Nicolet Dr Green Bay WI 54311-7003*

LABAREE, BENJAMIN WOODS, history educator; b. New Haven, Conn., July 21, 1927; s. Leonard Woods and Elizabeth Mary (Calkins) L.; m. Linda Carol Prichard, June 27, 1959; children: Benjamin Woods Jr., Jonathan Martin, Sarah Calkins Churchill. BA, Yale U., 1950; AM, Harvard U., 1953, PhD, 1957. Instr. history Conn. Coll., New London, 1957-58; from instr. to asst. prof. history, Allston Burr Sr. tutor Harvard U., Cambridge, Mass., 1958-63; dean Williams Coll., Williamstown, Mass., 1963-67, assoc. to prof. history, 1963-77, Ephraim Williams Prof. Am. History, 1972-77; dir. Williams Coll.-Mystic Seaport Program/Mystic Seaport Mus., Mystic, Conn., 1977-89; dir. Ctr. for Environ. Studies Williams Coll., 1989-91, prof. history and environ. studies, 1989-92; prof. emeritus, 1992—. Vis. prof. Trinity Coll., Conn., 1993, Williams Coll., 1994, Clark U., 1997, Tufts U. Fletcher Sch. Law and Diplomacy, 1998; dir. Munson Inst. Am. Maritime Studies, Mystic, 1974-96; mng. editor Essex Inst. Hist . Collections, Salem, Mass., 1956-60; co-dir. summer inst. Am. and the Sea NEH, 1996. Author: Patriots and Partisans, 1962, The Boston Tea Party, 1964, America's Nation-Time, 1972, Colonial Massachusetts, 1979; co-author: New England and The Sea, 1972, The Atlantic World of Robert G. Albion, 1975, Empire or Independence, 1976, America and the Sea, 1998; editor: The William Gottlieb Schauttler Family in America, 2002; mem. editl. bd.: American Neptune, 1996—. Mem. Mt. Greylock Regional H.S. Com., Williamstown, 1971-74; bd. dirs. Newburyport Maritime Soc., 1991-99, Lowell's Boat Shop trust, 1992-99. With USNR, 1945-46. Recipient Wilbur Cross award Conn. Humanities Coun., 1990, Samuel Eliot Morison award USS Constitution Mus., 1993, Citation of Honour, Soc. Colonial Wars, 1978; co-recipient John Lyman award N.Am. Soc. Oceanic History, 1999. Mem. Am. Hist. Assn. (com. 1971-73), Am. Antiquarian Soc., Colonial Soc. Mass., Mass. Hist. Soc., Inst. for Early Am. History and Culture (coun. mem. 1983-86), others. Democrat. Unitarian-Universalist. Avocations: sailing, rowing, swimming. Home and Office: 2 Andrews Ln Amesbury MA 01913-4102

LA BARGE, WILLIAM JOSEPH, tutor, researcher; b. Portis, Kans., June 27, 1943; s. Louis Joseph and Mary Genevieve (Colton) La B. AB, Ft. Hays State U., Hays, Kans., 1966, postgrad., 1980, Cloud County C.C., Concordia, Kans., 1984. Cert. tchr., Kans. Depot agt. Mo. Pacific R.R., Lenora, Kans., 1971-77; correctional officer Kans. Dept. Corrections, Hutchinson, 1977; prodn. worker Becker Mfg. Co., Downs, Kans., 1978-79; ind. study Downs, 1983-88; pvt. tutor world, Am., ancient and military history grade

6 to adult, Downs, 1988—. With USN, 1966-70. Mem. ASCD, Archaeol. Inst. Am., U.S. Naval Inst. Roman Catholic. Avocations: archaeology, history, toy soldiers, travel. Home and Office: 519 Blunt St Downs KS 67437-1713

LABORDE, TERRENCE LEE, audit consultant, negotiator; b. DuBois, Pa., June 20, 1947; s. Donald Leo and Anna Lee (Wise) LaB.; m. Brenda Sue Roberts, May 16, 1970 (div. 1975); 1 child, Terrence Lee II; m. Elisa Jean Meenan, Sept. 12, 1975; children: Marc Elliott, Dawn Ann. BS, Nat. Coll., 1973. Sr. auditor Def. Contract Audit Agy., State Coll., Pa., 1973-84; contract negotiator Pa. State U., State Coll., 1984-88, subcontract adminstr., 1988-91, mgr. grant & subcontract adminstrn., 1991-92; pres., CEO Keystone for Future Decisions, Inc., Pennsylvania Furnace, Pa., 1992-98; sr. contract adminstr. Concurrent Technologies Corp., Johnstown, Pa., 2002—. Owner LaBorde Enterprises, 1984-98; subcontrats adminstr. United Def., Chambersburg, Pa., 1997-99—; fin. cons. mil. programs, Altoona, Pa., 2000-2002, sr. contact adminstr. Concurrent Techs. Corp., Johnstown, Pa., 2002—. Sgt. USAF, 1966-70. Democrat. Lutheran. Avocations: hunting, fishing, landscaping, financial and educational consulting. Home and Office: PO Box 325 121 N Bedford St Newry PA 16665-0325 E-mail: exfed17@cs.com.

LABUZ, RONALD MATTHEW, design educator; b. Utica, N.Y., Nov. 17, 1953; s. Emil John and Elsie (Pritchard) L.; m. Carol Ann Altimonte, Sept. 5, 1975. BA, SUNY, Oswego, 1975; MA, Ohio State U., 1977; MPhil, Syracuse U., 1993, MA, 1994, PhD, 1997. Acquisition dir. Collegiate Pub., Columbus, Ohio, 1977-78; pres. Advocate Pub. and Avatar Media Advt. Agy., Columbus, 1978-80; prodn. specialist Am. Ceramic Soc., Columbus, 1980-81; assoc. prof. advt. Mohawk Valley C.C., Utica, 1981-85, prof. dept. art, 1985—. Author: Typography and Typesetting, 1988, Contemporary Graphic Design, 1991, The Computer in Graphic Design, 1994, Digital Design, 2000, and 9 other books. Recipient Chancellor's award for excellence, SUNY, 1989, 2002, faculty exch. scholar, 1990. Mem. Printing History Soc., Am. Printing History Assn., Graphic Design Educators Assn. (bd. dirs. 1989-94, treas. exec. bd. 1992-94), Am. Ctr. for Design, Am. Inst. Graphic Arts, N.Y. State Assn. Two-Yr. Colls. (bd. dirs. 1990-91). Office: Mohawk Valley CC 1101 Sherman Dr Utica NY 13501-5308 E-mail: rmlabuz@cs.com., rlabuz@mvcc.edu.

LACER, ALFRED ANTONIO, lawyer, educator; b. Hammonton, N.J., Feb. 14, 1952; s. Vincent and Carmen (Savall) L.; m. Kathleen Visser, June 15, 1974; children: Margaret, James, Matthew. BA in Polit. Sci., Gordon Coll., 1974; JD, Cath. U. Am., 1977. Bar: Md. 1977, U.S. Dist. Ct. Md. 1980, U.S. Ct. Appeals (4th cir.) 1980, U.S. Supreme Ct. 1997. Law clk. to Honorable Joseph A. Mattingly, Sr. Cir. Ct. St. Mary's County, Leonardtown, Md., 1977-78; ptnr. Lacer, Sparling, Densford & Reynolds PA and predecessors, Lexington Park, Md., 1978-99; county atty. St. Mary's County, Md., 1999-2000, CEO, county adminstr., 2000—03. Adj. prof. bus. law Fla. Inst. Tech., Patuxent, Md., 1989-92, 95-99; vis. instr. St. Mary's Coll. of Md., 1988, 91; mem. bd. edn. St. Mary's County (Md.) Pub. Schs., 1989-94, pres., 1991-92; mem. inquiry panel Atty. Grievance Commn. of Md., 1984-90. Bd. dirs. St. Mary's Hosp., Leonardtown, 1982-88, v.p., 1985-88; bd. dirs. So. Md. Cmty. Action, Inc., Hughsville, Md., 1982-84, St. Mary's County Tech. Coun., 1997-99. Mem. ABA, Md. Bar Assn. (com. on jud. appointments 1982-85), St. Mary's County Bar Assn. (v.p. 1979-80, pres. 1980-81). Episcopalian. Office: PO Box 55 Park Hall MD 20667

LACEY, HUGH MATTHEW, philosophy educator; b. Sydney, Australia, Sept. 7, 1939; came to U.S., 1972; s. Owen Charles and Margaret Jane (Devine) L.; m. Maria Ines Rocha E. Silva, Aug. 14, 1966; children: Andrew David, Daniel Carlos. BA, U. Melbourne, Australia, 1962, MA, 1964; PhD, Ind. U., 1966. Tutor in math. U. Melbourne, 1961-63; lectr. history and philosophy of sci. U. Sydney, 1966-68; prof. philosophy U. São Paulo, Brazil, 1969-72; sr. rsch. scholar Swarthmore (Pa.) Coll., 1972, 2003, chmn. dept. philosophy, 1973-83, Eugene M. Lang Rsch. Prof. of Philosophy, 1993-97, The Scheuer Family prof. humanities, 2000—. Vis. prof. Temple U., Phila., 1983; vis. prof. Villanova U., 1984, Inst. de Teologia, São Paulo, 1988, 92, Ctrl. Am. U., El Salvador, 1991, U. Pa., 1995, 2002, U. Melbourne, 1996, U. São Paulo, 1996, 2000; Dyason lectr. Australasian Assn. History, Philosophy and Social Studies of Sci., 1996. Author: A Linguagem Do Espaco E do Tempo, 1972, Valores e Atividade Cientifica, 1998, Is Science Value Free? Values and Scientific Understanding, 1999, Psicologia Experimental e Natureza Humana, 2001; co-author: Behaviorism, Science and Human Nature, 1982; co-editor: Towards a Society That Serves Its People: The Thought of El Salvador's Murdered Jesuits, 1991; cons. editor: Jour. for Theory of Social Behavior, 1977—, Behavior and Philosophy, 1987—, Jour. for Peace and Justice Studies, 1987—. Bd. dirs. Chester-Swarthmore Coll. Cmty. Coalition, 1993—2001. NSF fellow, 1975, 79, 83, 2000; Fulbright grantee, 1963; Research Found. of State of São Paulo grantee, 1969, 73, 96, 2000. Mem. Philosophy of Sci. Assn., Am. Philos. Assn., Am. Psychol. Assn. (commn. on behavior modification 1974-77). Roman Catholic. Home: 336 Park Ave Swarthmore PA 19081-2013 Office: Dept Philosophy Swarthmore 500 College Ave Swarthmore PA 19081-1306 E-mail: hlacey1@swarthmore.edu.

LACEY, JOHN DEREK, university administrator, admissions counselor; b. Bichester, Eng., Feb. 5, 1959; came to U.S., 1970; s. Sidney George and Yvonne Faith (James) L. AS, La Guardia C.C., Long Island, N.Y., 1986; BS, Coll. at OLd Westbury, 1988; MS, Long Island U., 1992. Cert. tchr., N.Y. Tchr. gen. edn. Veterans Edn. Ctr., Long Island, N.Y., 1984-85; diploma instr., asst. to registrar State Coll. at Old Westbury, 1986-89; admissins officer Long Island U., Bklyn., 1989—. Campaign vol. Rep. Party, 1988. Chief warrant officer U.S. Navy, 1976-84. Mem. N.Y., N.J. Assn. Collegiate Registrars and Admissions Officers, Middle States Assn. Collegiate Registrars and Admission Officers, Nat. Heritage Trust Eng., Phi Delta Kappa. Republican. Episcopalian. Avocations: swimming, soccer, european history, travel. Office: Long Island U 1 University Plz Brooklyn NY 11201-5372

LACHANCE, PAUL ALBERT, food science educator, clergyman; b. St. Johnsbury, Vt., June 5, 1933; s. Raymond John and Lucienne (Landry) Lachance; m. Therese Cecile Cote; children: Michael P, Peter A, M-Andre, Susan A. BS, St. Michael's Coll., 1955; postgrad., U. Vt., 1955-57; PhD, U. Ottawa, 1960; cert. in pastoral counseling, N.Y. Theol. Sem., 1981; DSc (hon.), St. Michael's Coll., 1982. Ordained deacon Roman Cath Ch, 1977. Assigned to St. Paul's Ch., Princeton, N.J.; aerospace biologist Aeromed. Research Labs., Wright-Patterson AFB, Ohio, 1960-63; lectr. dept. biology U. Dayton, Ohio, 1963; flight food and nutrition coordinator NASA Manned Spacecraft Center, Houston, 1963-67; assoc. prof. dept. food sci. Rutgers U., New Brunswick, N.J., 1967-72, dir. Sch. Feeding effectiveness research project, 1969-72, prof., 1972—, faculty rep. to bd. trustees, 1988-90, dir. grad. program food sci., 1988-91, chmn. food sci. dept., 1991-97, chmn. univ. senate, 1990-93, faculty rep. to bd. govs., 1990-94, exec. dir. The Nutraceuticals Inst., 1997—. Consult Nutritional Aspects Food Processing, Nutraceuticals; mem nutrition adv comt Whitehall-Robins/Centrum Consumer div, 1989—2000; mem sci adv bd Roche chem div Hoffmann La Roche Co, 1976—88; mem nutrition policy comt Beatrice Food Co, 1979—86; trustee religious ministries comt Princeton Med Ctr; bd dirs J R Short Milling Co. Mem. editl. adv. bd.: Nutrition Reports Internat., 1963—83, Sch. Food Svc. Rsch. Rev., 1977—82, Profl. Nutritionist, 1977—80, mem. editl. adv bd.: Jour. Med. Consultation, 1985—2002, Jour. Medicinal Foods, 1998—, Food and Chem. Toxicology, 2000—, Jour. Nutraceuticals Functional & Health Foods, 2000—; contbr. articles to profl. jours. Served to capt USAF, 1960—63. Named to Academic Hall of Fame, St. Michaels Coll., 2002; recipient Endel Karmas award for excellence in tchg. food sci., 1988. Fellow: Am Soc Nutritional Sci, Am Col Nutrition, Inst Food Technologists (William Cruess award for excellence in tchg. 1991, Babcock-Hart award 2001); mem.: NY Inst Food Technologists (chmn 1977—78), AAAS, The Oxygen Soc., Sociedad Latino Americano de Nutricion, Nat Asn Cath Chaplains, Am Pub Health Asn, Soc Nutrition Educ, Am Dietetic Asn, NY Acad Sci, Am Soc Clin Nutrition, Am Asn Cereal Chemists, Delta Epsilon Sigma, Sigma Xi. Home: 34 Taylor Rd Princeton NJ 08540-9521 Office: Rutgers U Food Sci 65 Dudley Rd New Brunswick NJ 08901-8520 E-mail: lachance@aesop.rutgers.edu.

LACHENAUER, ROBERT ALVIN, retired school superintendent; b. Newark, Apr. 1, 1929; s. Alvin Frederick and Helen Louise (Bowers) L.; m. Patricia McConnell, June 14, 1952; children: Jane, Nancy, Robert. AB, Montclair State U., 1951, MA, 1956; EdS, Seton Hall U., 1983. Diplomate in sch. adminstrn., 1988; cert. sch. adminstr., N.J., sch. bus. adminstr., N.J., tchr., N.J., supr., N.J., secondary sch. prin., N.J. Tchr. Bd. Edn., Union, N.J., 1951-52, 54-57, asst. bd. sec., 1957-61; dep. supt. New Providence (N.J.) Sch. Dist., 1961-76, supt., 1976-91, interim dir. transp., 2002—03. Interim bus adminstr. Morris Union Joint Commn, 2000. Vice pres. Rigorous Ednl. Assistance Deserving Youth Found., 1991-93; treas. sch. monies Morris-Union Jointure Commn., 1987-93; pres. Union County Sch. Bus. Ofcls., 1967-68; chmn. Title IV State Adv. Coun., Trenton, N.J., 1976-78; pres. Morris-Union Jointure Commn., N.J., 1981-83, Union County Supts. Roundtable, 1983-84; adv. bd. Summit Bank, 1971-86; elder treas. Presbyn. Ch., New Providence, 1958-62; treas. New Providence Hist. Soc., 1966-76 pres. United Way, New Providence, 1978; property mgr. Providence Presbyn. Ch., Hilton Head Island, 1993-98, elder, 1995-97. Served as seaman USN, 1952-54. Named Disting. Scholar of the Acad., Nat. Acad. for Sch. Execs., 1990. Mem. N.J. Assn. Sch. Adminstrs. (exec. bd. 1986-91, Dedicated and Disting. Svc. 1991), N.J. Assn. Sch. Bus. Ofcls. (pres. 1974-75), Assn. Sch. Bus. Ofcls. U.S. (professionalization com. 1974, membership chmn. 1976), N.J. Assn. Ednl. Secs. (adv. bd. 1976=91, Outstanding Adminstr. of Yr. 1987), Rotary (pres. 1980-81). Home: Amherst Mews 17 Dickinson Rd Basking Ridge NJ 07920-4905

LACHOWICZ, FRANCISZEK, foreign language educator; b. Poland, July 12, 1908; came to U.S., 1951; s. Ignacy and Anastazja (Szarejko) L.; m. Helena M. Pogonowska, Dec. 8, 1944; children: Barbara, Lech. MA, U. Warsaw, 1935; MS in Edn., U. Bridgeport, 1962, profl. diploma, 1966, MS in Math., 1970. Asst. U. Warsaw, Poland, 1936-39; tchr. Polish Tchrs.' Coll., Univ. Edinburgh, Scotland, 1943-45; prin. Polish Bus. Coll., England, 1946-48; math. tchr. Masuk High Sch., Monroe, Conn., 1961-77, Housatonic Community Coll., Stratford, Conn., 1966-67; adj. assoc. prof. Sacred Heart U., Fairfield, Conn., 1978—. Contbr. articles to profl. jours. 2d lt. Polish Army, 1939-43. Mem. Polish Am. Hist. Soc., Polish Nat. Alliance, Kosciuszko Found., Polish Inst. Arts and Scis. Am., Polish Am. Edn. Soc. (first pres. 1973, pres. 1989), Jozet Pilsudski Inst., Polish Heritage Soc. (Man of the Yr. 1986), Polish Army Vet. Assn. Democrat. Roman Catholic. Avocation: chess. Home: 95 Houston Ave Bridgeport CT 06606-3041 Office: Sacred Heart Univ 5151 Park Ave Fairfield CT 06432-1000

LACHOWICZ, RACHEL, artist, art educator; b. San Francisco, 1964; BFA, Calif. Inst. Arts, 1988. Adj. faculty art Claremont (Calif.) Grad. U., 1996—. One-woman shows include Dennis Anderson Gallery, L.A., 1989, 1991, Krygier/Landau Contemporary Art, Santa Monica, Calif., 1989, 1990, Shoshana Wayne Gallery, Santa Monica, 1991, 1993, 1996, Fawbush Gallery, N.Y.C., 1992, 1995, Newport Harbor Art Mus., Newport Beach, Calif., 1992, Rhona Hoffman Gallery, Chgo., 1993, Magazin 4 Vorarlberger Kunstverein, Bregenz, Austria, 1995, Dogenhaus Galerie, Berlin, 1997, Cristinerose Gallery, N.Y.C., 1998, Peggy Phekps Gallery, Claremont (Calif.) Grad. U., 1999, Kapinos Galerie for Zeitgenossische Kunst, Berlin, 2000, Cryo-Field Snap, L.A., 2001, Represented in permanent collections Denver Art Mus., Israel Mus., Jerusalem, L.A. County Mus. Art, Mus. Fine Art, Boston, Mus. Contemporary Art, L.A., Mus. Moderner Kunst, Palais Lichtenstein, Vienna, Orange County Mus. Art, Newport Beach, Whitney Mus. Am. Art, N.Y.C. Recipient Louis Comfort Tiffany Found. award, 1997; fellow, Skowhegan Sch. Painting and Sculpture, John Simon Guggenheim Meml. Found., 2003. Office: Claremont Grad Univ Art Dept 251 E Tenth St Claremont CA 91711*

LACHS, JOHN, philosopher, educator; b. Budapest, Hungary, July 17, 1934; s. Julius and Magda (Brod) L.; m. Shirley Marie Mellow, June 3, 1967; children: Sheila Marie, James Richard. BA, McGill U., 1956, MA, 1957; PhD, Yale, 1961. From asst. prof. to prof. philosophy Coll. William and Mary, 1959-67; prof. philosophy Vanderbilt U., 1967—, Centennial Prof., 1993—. Chmn. faculty senate Vanderbilt U., 1990—91. Author: Marxist Philosophy: A Bibliographical Guide, 1967, The Ties of Time, 1970, Intermediate Man, 1981, Mind and Philosophers, 1987, George Santayana, 1988, The Relevance of Philosophy to Life, 1995, In Love With Life, 1998, A Community of Individuals, 2003, (with M. Hodges) Thinking in the Ruins, 2000; editor: Animal Faith and Spiritual Life, 1967, Physical Order and Moral Liberty, 1969; co-editor: The Human Search, 1981; co-translator: Fichte, Science of Knowledge, 1970; contbr. articles to profl. jours. Past chmn. Tenn. Com. for Humanities. Recipient Award for Advancement of Scholarship Phi Beta Kappa, 1962, Harris Harbison award for distinguished teaching Danforth Found., 1967, Chancellor's cup Vanderbilt U., 1970, Madison Sarratt prize excellence undergrad. tchg., 1972, Alumni Edn. award Vanderbilt U., 1991, Grad Tchg. award, 2000. Mem. Internat. Neoplatonic Soc., World Sociology Assn. (alienation rsch. com.), Am. Philos. Assn., Metaphys. Soc. Am. (past pres.), Soc. Advancement Am. Philosophy (past pres.), Soc. Health and Human Values, C.S. Peirce Soc. (past pres.), Va. Philos. Assn., Tenn. Philos. Assn., So. Soc. Philosophy and Psychology, Hasting Ctr. Episcopalian. Home: 1968 Edenbridge Way Nashville TN 37215-5809 Office: Vanderbilt U 2305 W End Ave Nashville TN 37240-1700

LACKAN, SIEWCHAN, principal, school system administrator; b. Couva, Caroni, Trinidad, Sept. 24, 1936; came to U.S., 1967; s. Bansee and Piaree (Jaga Dass) L.; m. Mona Ramdath, June 16, 1984; children: Denise, Debbie, Dianne, Darren. BS in Chemistry and Math., U. Manitoba, 1963; MA in Chemistry, St. Mary's U., San Antonio, 1972; MA in Edn. Adminstr., U. Tex., San Antonio, 1976, postgrad. Cert. tchr., adminstr., Tex. Chemist Shell Oil, Port Fortin, Trinidad, 1964-65, chief chemist, 1965-68; tchr. Pearsall (Tex.) Ind. Sch. Dist., 1968-70, Harlandale Ind. Sch. Dist., San Antonio, 1970-71, Northside Ind. Sch. Dist., San Antonio, 1971-80; prin. Lytle (Tex.) Elem. Sch., 1980—, curriculum dir., 1992-93, interim superintendent, 1993—. Part time lectr. Alamo C.C. Dist., San Antonio, 1973-92; instr. Alama C.C. Dist.-St. Phillips Coll., 1973—. Mem. ASCD, Tex. Elem. Prin. and Suprs. Assn. (life mem.), PTA. Avocations: tennis, reading, chess, calligraphy, music. Home: 7536 Linkside St San Antonio TX 78240-3032

LACKEY, DEBORAH K. art educator; b. Gainesville, Ga., Nov. 1, 1952; d. R.G. Jr. and Florine L. BS in Art Edn., U. Ga., 1978, M in Art Edn., 1985, EdS, 1992, EdD, 1997. Cert. elem. tchr., Ga. Elem. art specialist Clarke County Bd. of Edn., Athens, Ga., 1979-80, Fulton County Bd. of Edn., Atlanta, 1980—. Adj. instr. Ga. State U., Atlanta, 1983-91, Clayton State Coll., Morrow, Ga., 1985-86, Mercer U., Atlanta, 1986—; curriculum chair elem. art edn. curriculum for Fulton County Schs., 1986; mem. Ga. tchr. cert. test revision com., Atlanta, 1990-94; adj. prof. Brenau U., 1998—. Mem. Gov.'s Fine Arts Edn. Adv. Coun., 1993—; mem. tchr. adv. panel High Mus. Art, Atlanta, 1995—; chair Art Edn. & Tech. Com., Fulton County Bd. Edn., 1995—. Mem. Nat. Art Edn. Assn. (rep.-elect southeast region elem. divsn. 1991-93, dir. 1993-95, southeastern elem. art educator 1998, nat. elem. art educator 1999), Ga. Art Edn. Assn. (bd. dris. 1985—, pres. 1991-93, Ga. Art Educator of Yr. 1991, Ga. Elem. Art Educator of the Yr. 1997), Ga. Citizens for the Arts, Gold Key, Phi Kappa Phi, Kappa Delta Phi, Phi Lambda Theta. Office: Roswell North Elem 10525 Woodstock Rd Roswell GA 30075-2939

LACKEY, JOYCE, special education educator; b. Enid, Okla., Feb. 18, 1948; d. Robert Keith and Mildred Belle (Seely) Stormont; m. Paul Thomas Pingleton, Oct. 12, 1967 (div. Dec. 1980); 1 child, Tiffany; m. Andrew Jerry Lackey, May 1, 1982; 1 child, Matthew Ryan. Student, Okla. State U., Ctrl. State U., Payne Edn. Ctr., 1988-89. Tchr. pre-sch. South Childrens Ctr., Oklahoma City, Okla., 1972-74; tchr. learning disabilities Putnam City Ctrl. Jr. High Sch., Oklahoma City, Okla., 1976-89, Putnam City Ctrl. Intermediate Sch., Oklahoma City, Okla., 1990—. Mem. prins. adv. com. Putnam City Ctrl. Intermediate Sch., 1993—, co-chair ptnr. in edn., 1994, chair ptnr. edn. com., 1995-97, chair leadership ctrl. student coun., 1996—, chmn. sch. improvement com., 2000—; mem. supts. adv. com. Putnam City Schs., 1994; sponsor SADD, Oklahoma City, 1987-89. Block facilitator Am. Cancer Soc., Oklahoma City, 1990, 1994, 1996, 2000, 2001, Am. Heart Assn., Oklahoma City, 1989. Recipient Golden Apple award of Excellence Putnam City Found., 1992; named Heartland Rotary Tchr. of Month, Oct. 2002. Mem. NEA, Okla. Edn. Assn., Acad. and Lang. Therapy Assn., PTA. Republican. Methodist. Avocations: sewing, reading, crafts, waterskiing, sports. Home: 6449 N College Ave Oklahoma City OK 73132-7209 Office: Putnam City Ctrl Intermediate 5430 NW 40th St Oklahoma City OK 73122-3303 E-mail: jlackey@putnamcityschools.org.

LACKEY, KAYLE DIANN, elementary school educator; b. Willard, Ill., Oct. 22, 1937; d. Lon Edward and Eldora Grace (Pecord) Ogborn; m. Joseph Donald Lackey, Nov. 29, 1958; 1 child, Dana Lyn Embree. BA in History, Asbury Coll., Wilmore, Ky., 1958; MA with honors, Webster U., 1975, cert. reading specialist, 1977; cert. gifted and talented educator, So. Ill. U., Edwardsville, 1990. Ltd. cert. elem. edn., Ill; cert. pub. sch. tchr. (life), Mo.; cert. reading specialist, Mo.; registered profl. real estate salesperson, Mo. Tchr. kindergarten Dist. # 196, Dupo, Ill., 1959-63, reading specialist, 1973-79, tchr. 2d grade, 1979-84, tchr. 4th grade, 1985-93, tchr. gifted and talented, 1990-92; tchr. 1st grade Mehlville R-9 Dist., St. Louis, 1963-65, substitute tchr., 1965-72, 1993—. Clin. coop. tchr. So. Ill. U., Edwardsville, 1989; salesperson Coldwell Banker Real Estate, St. Louis, 1985-2000. Rep. for tchrs. Am. Fedn. Tchrs., Dupo, 1975-77, negotiation com., 1981; tchr. U.S. Divsn. Laubach Literacy Internat., St. Louis, 1987-89; author, tchr. gifted and talented enrichment summer program, 1991; participant Asbury Coll. travel seminar on Near-Eastern studies, 1985; rep. ecumenical com. Cmty. Resource Svcs., 1986-89, trustee 2000-02; chmn. bd. edn. presch. Zion United Meth., St. Louis, 1987-88, 2000-02, trustee, 1986-90, adminstrv. bd. religion and race, ch. and soc., 1989-93, fin. sec., 1999, bd. dirs., 2000; active Ill. Tchrs. Retirement Sys., 1993—, Met. Congregations United of St. Louis, 2001-03; active voter registration Gephardt for Congress, St. Louis, 1993-95; vol. Am. Cancer Soc., 2000. Recipient Appreciation for Tchg. Excellence award Bd. Edn., Dupo, 1993, Ill. Math. and Sci. Acad. award of Excellence, 1999. Mem. St. Louis Zoo Soc., Mo. Bot. Soc. Avocations: piano, travel, writing, reading, political campaign volunteerism. Home: 6511 Towne Woods Dr Saint Louis MO 63129-4521

LACKO, J. MICHELLE, physical education, health and science educator; b. San Diego, Nov. 2, 1968; d. John Michael and Betty Joyce (Chaplain) L. BS in Phys. Edn., Biology, Ea. N.Mex. U., 1991. Cert. tchr., leader level coach and sport sci., N.Mex., sci./health phys. edn. Tex. Supr. recreation Aztec (N.Mex.) Boys' and Girls' Club, 1988; courtesy clk. Smiths, Farmington, 1989; instr. recreation City of Farmington Recreation Dept., 1990; groundskeeper Ea. N.Mex. U., Portales, 1991; substitute tchr. Portales Sch. Dist., 1991-92, Canyon (Tex.) Ind. Sch. Dist., 1992-93; phys. edn. tchr., coach Amarillo (Tex.) Ind. Sch. Dist., 1993-97, tchr. 7th grade sci., 1997—. Drug and violence prevention coord. Travis M.S., head coach Machaira Fencing. Contbr. poems to profl. publs. Named N.Mex. State CDP/MM Champion, 1st Female 4 Gun Master-Marksman, 1st person to reclissify sharpshooter. Mem. Fellowship Christian Athletes, Internat. Def. Pistols Assn. Avocations: volleyball, softball, golf, fencing, competitive shooting. E-mail: mlacko@aol.com.

LACY, CAROLYN JEAN, elementary education educator, secondary education educator; b. Marshall, Ark., Apr. 6, 1944; d. Charles Ira Bolch and Edna Rebecca Cherry; 1 child, Kelli Jean. AA with distinction, Riverside City Coll., 1980; BA, U. Calif., Riverside, 1982, postgrad., 1983; MEd, U.S. Internat. U., 1993. Cert. social sci. tchr., Calif. Educator Perris (Calif.) Elem. Sch. Dist., 1984-89, Rialto (Calif.) Unified Sch. Dist., 1989—. Instr. Developing Capable People, Riverside, Calif., 1986-89; presenter, lectr. Jurupa Unified Sch. Dist., Riverside, 1990, Rialto Unified Sch. Dist., 1990; developer peer tutor program Perris Elem. Sch. Dist., 1989; dir. chess club Dollahan Elem. Sch., 1995-98, computer chmn., 1995-97; dir. chess club Rialto Mid. Sch., 1998—. Editor: (newsletter) Perris Lights, 1989. Active Students in Environ. Action, Riverside, 1978; mem. Riverside County Task Force for Self-Esteem. Named Mentor Tchr. State of Calif., 1988. Mem. AAUW, NEA, Calif. Tchrs. Assn., U. Calif. Alumni Assn., Phi Delta Kappa, Alpha Gamma Sigma. Democrat. Mem. Lds Ch. Avocations: painting, writing, gardening, reading, travel. Home: 4044 Wallace St Riverside CA 92509-6809

LACY, CLAUD HAROLD SANDBERG, astronomer, educator; b. Shawnee, Okla., June 5, 1947; s. Lester Claud and Leola Chrstine (Hinton) L.; m. Patricia Kathryn McCoy, Apr. 1, 1971 (div. 1984); m. Patricia Alison Sandberg, Dec. 19, 1988; children: Adrian R., Kathryn Mia Rose. MS in Physics, U. Okla., Norman, 1971; PhD in Astronomy, U. Tex., 1978. Vis. asst. prof. Tex. A&M U., College Station, Tex., 1978-80; asst. prof. astronomy U. Ark., Fayetteville, 1980-86, assoc. prof., 1986-99, prof., 1999—. Author: Astronomy Laboratory Exercises, 1981; contbr. articles to Astron. Jour. With U.S. Army, 1971-73. NSF grantee, 1981-84, 2000—. Mem. Am. Astron. Soc., Internat. Astron. Union. Achievements include determination of accurate absolute properties for stars in over 30 eclipsing binary star systems, photometric orbits of 611 eclipsing binary stars in the Large Magellanic Cloud; discovery of 40 new double-lined eclipsing binaries. Office: U Ark Dept Physics Fayetteville AR 72701 E-mail: clacy@uark.edu.

LACY, NORRIS J. literature educator; b. Hopkinsville, Ky., Mar. 8, 1940; s. Edwin V. Lacy and Lillian Louise Joiner; m. Susan Houston, Jan. 6, 1984. AB, Murray State U., 1962; MA, Ind. U., 1963, PhD, 1967. From asst. prof. to prof. French U. Kans., Lawrence, 1966-88; prof. French and comparative lit. Washington U., St. Louis, 1988-98; Edwin Erle Sparks prof. French and Medieval Studies Pa. State U., University Park, 1998—. Vis. assoc. French UCLA, 1975-76; editor-in-chief Summa Publs., Birmingham, Ala., 1981-86; editl. dir. Arthurian Studies, Cambridge, Eng., 1999—; editor: Arthurian Archives, Cambridge, 1996—, Arthurian Characters and Themes, N.Y.C., 1994—. Author: Craft of Chrétien de Troyes, 1980, Arthurian Handbook, 1988 (Choice Outstanding Book award), Reading Fabliaux, 1993, 99; editor Arthurian Encyclopedia, 1986, Lancelot-Grail, 1993-96, others; contbr. articles to profl. jours. Knighted French Govt., 1988. Mem. MLA, Am. Assn. French Tchrs., Medieval Acad. Am., Internat. Arthurian Soc. (hon. pres.). Office: Pa State U Dept French University Park PA 16802 E-mail: NJL2@psu.edu.

LADD, CHARLES CUSHING, III, civil engineer, educator; b. Bklyn., Nov. 23, 1932; s. Charles Cushing and Elizabeth (Swan) Ladd; m. Carol Lee Ballou, June 11, 1954; children: Melissa, Charles IV, Ruth, Matthew. AB, Bowdoin Coll., 1955; SB, MIT, 1955, SM, 1957, ScD, 1961. Asst. prof. MIT, Cambridge, 1961-64, assoc. prof., 1964-70, prof., 1970-94, dir. Ctr. Sci. Excellence Offshore Engring., 1983-94, Edmund K. Turner prof., 1994-2001, Edmund K. Turner prof. emeritus, 2001—. Gen. reporter 9th Internat. Conf. Soil Mechanics and Found. Engring., Tokyo, 1977; co-gen. reporter 11th Internat. Conf. Soil Mechanics and Found. Engring., San Francisco, 1985; mem. geotech. bd. NRC, 1992—94; casagrande lectr. 12th Pan-Am. Conf. Soil Mechanics and Geotech. Engring., Cambridge, Mass.,

2003. Contbr. articles to profl. jours. Commr. Concord Dept. Pub. Works, 1965—78, chmn., 1972—74; mem. Concord Rep. Town Com., 1968—82. Fellow: ASCE (hon.; Terzaghi lectr. 1986, mem. exec. com. geotechnical engring. divsn. 1989—96, chmn. 1993—94, Geo-Inst. bd. govs. 1996—98, Rsch. prize 1969, Croes medal 1973, Norman medal 1976, Middlebrooks award 1996, Karl Terzaghi award 1999, Middlebrooks award 2002); mem.: AAUP, NSPE, ASTM (Hogentogler award 1990), NAE, Can. Geotech. Soc., Brit. Geotech. Soc., Assn. Engring. Firms Practicing Geosci., Am. Soc. Engring. Edn., Internat. Soc. Soil Mechanics and Geotech. Engring., Transp. Rsch. Bd., Boston Soc. Civil Engr. (bd. govs. 1972—81, pres. 1977—78, Arthur Casagrande meml. lectr. 2000). Home: 7 Thornton Ln Concord MA 01742-4107 Office: MIT Dept Civil & Environ Engrng Cambridge MA 02139 E-mail: ccladd@MIT.edu.

LADD, CULVER SPROGLE, secondary school educator; b. Bismarck, ND, Nov. 15, 1929; s. Culver Sprogle and Eleanor (Pearson)L. BS, U. Md., 1953; MA, Am. U., 1963, PhD, 1984; postgrad., Harvard U., summer 1963, Oxford (Eng.) U., 1975-76; cert. by correspondence, Nat. Def. U., Thailand, 1972. Clk.-photographer Dept. Justice, FBI, Washington, 1946-54; intercept controller Dept. of Def., USAF, 1954-56; asst. office mgr. Covington & Burling, Lawyers, Washington, 1956-62; tchr. Internat. Sch. Bangkok, Thailand, 1964-66; lectr. U. Md., Thailand, 1966-67, 71-74; project dir. Bus. Rsch. Ltd., Thailand, 1966-67, 72-74; spl. lectr. Payap U., Chiang Mai, Thailand, 1974-75, 2000-2001; tchr. D.C. Pub. Schs., 1978-2000. Cons. USAID, Thailand, 1973-74; vis. scientist Brookhaven Nat. Labs., L.I., 1988; master tchr. Woodrow Wilson Fellowship Found., 1989; bd. dirs. Chesapeake Ranch Water Co. Rep. candidate Md. Senate 29th Legislative Dist., 1998; bd. dirs. Property Owners Assn. Chesapeake Ranch Estates, Inc., Chesapeake Ranch Water Co. Capt. USAFR, 1953-72. Recipient Appreciation award Payap U. 1987. Mem. Mid-Atlantic Region Assn. for Asian Studies, Nat. Capital Area Polit. Sci. Assn., Nat. Coun. Tchrs. Math., Mid. States Coun. Social Studies, Aircraft Owners and Pilots Assn., Experimental Aviation Assn., Omicron Delta Kappa, Pi Sigma Alpha. Republican. Presbyterian. Avocations: gardening, flying. Office: POACRE Airfield 845 Crystal Rock Rd PO Box 2084 Lusby MD 20657-1884 E-mail: csladd@juno.com.

LADNER, ANN-MARIE CALVO, special education educator; b. Hartford, Conn., Feb. 6, 1949; d. Vincent J. and Mary S. (Santangelo) Calvo; m. R. Martin Ladner, June 19, 1971; children: Mary-Lorraine Amy Cox, R. Vincent, Michelle A. AA in Speech and Theater, Belleville Area Coll., 1983; BS in Speech and Theater, So. Ill. U., Edwardsville, 1985, MS in Reading, 1986; EdS in Mild Learning Handicaps, Auburn U. Montgomery, 1993. Cert. specific learning disabilities, Ala., psychometrist, Ala., sch. adminstr., Ala. Tchr. merchandising Skadron Coll. Bus., San Bernardino, Calif., 1981-82; tchr. English as second lang. Turkish-Am. Assn., Ankara, Turkey, 1986; tchr. speech and computers Ozel Atilim Lisesi, Ankara, 1987-88; tchr. English and reading St. Jude H.S., Selma, Ala., 1989-90; tchr. spl. edn. Selma Sch. Dist., 1990-92, Montgomery (Ala.) County Schs., 1992—93, Dept. Youth Svcs., Jemison, Ala., 1993-95, Montgomery (Ala.) County Schs., 1995—98; founder, adminstr. Exploratorium Acad. Inc., Montgomery, Ala., 1999—. Libr. bd. dirs. City of Millbrook, Ala., 1992-94; bd. dirs. Turkish-Am. Assn., Ankara, 1987-88, Millbrook YMCA, 1993-95; judge, coach Nat. Forensics League, Belleville, Ill., 1985. Named Competent Toastmaster, Toastmasters Internat., 1985; mini-grantee Montgomery Area Comty. Found., 1992. Mem. Nat. Coun. Tchrs. Math., Assn. for Supervision and Curriculum Devel., Mensa, Kappa Delta Pi. Avocations: Internet, internet, reading, collecting educational materials. Home: 844 Brookland Curv Montgomery AL 36117-4548

LADUE, EDDY LORAIN, economist, educator; b. Middlesex, N.Y., June 23, 1939; s. George Jay and Ester (Eddy) LaDue; m. Lorraine Judith Frankish, June 27, 1964; children: Steven George, Scott Philip, Shelley Ester. BS, Cornell U., 1964, MS, 1966; PhD, Mich. State U., 1972. Farm owner, operator George LaDue and Sons, Canandaigua, NY, 1959—62; extension assoc. Cornell U., Ithaca, NY, 1965—67, asst. prof. agrl. econs., 1971—76, assoc. prof. agrl. econs., 1976—84, prof. agrl. econs., 1984—98, W.I. Myers Prof. Agrl. Fin., 1998—. Agrl. economist U.S. Dept. Agr., 1977—78; cons. Congl. Budget Office, Washington, 1979; cons. in field; assoc. editor Jour. Agrl. Fin. Rev., 1983—90, co-editor, 1992—96, editor, 1991, 1997—. Mem.: Northeastern Agr. and Resource Econs. Assn., Am. Agr. Econs. Assn., Phi Kappa Phi. Republican. Avocations: golf, fishing, gardening. Home: 1132 Snyder Hill Rd Ithaca NY 14850-8802 Office: Cornell U 357 Warren Hall Ithaca NY 14853-7801 E-mail: ell4@Cornell.edu.

LAFFERTY, JOYCE G. ZVONAR, retired middle school educator; b. Balt., July 9, 1931; d. George S. and Carolyn M. (Bothe) Greener; children: Barbara Z. Gunter, John G. Zvonar, David A. Zvonar. BS, Towson State, 1963; M. equivalent, Md. Inst. Coll. of Art, 1978. Cert. tchr., Md. Tchr., dept. chmn. Hampstead Hill. Jr. High Annex, Balt.; tchr. Forest Park Sr. High, Balt.; tchr., dept. chmn. Roland Park Mid. Sch., Balt. Mem. Nat. Art Edn. Assn., Internat. Soc. Artists, Balt. Tchrs. Union. Home: 1225 Tetbury Ln Austin TX 78748

LAFIELD, KAREN WOODROW, science educator, demographer; b. Fairfield, Ill., Oct. 14, 1950; d. Raymond and Margaret Ann (Simpson) Woodrow; m. William E. Mason, June 13, 1970 (div. July 1976); m. William L. Lafield, July 16, 1991. BA, U. Ill., Chgo., 1972; MA, U. Tenn., 1976; PhD, U. Ill., 1984. Demographic statistician U.S. Census Bur., Suitland, Md., 1983-92; adj. rsch. assoc. Ctr. for Social and Demographic Analysis SUNY, Albany, 1993-96; sr. rsch. analyst U.S. Commn. on Immigration Reform, Washington, 1994-95; rsch. scientist U. Tex., Austin, 1995-96; asst. prof. Miss. State U., Starkville, 1996-99, assoc. prof., 1999—2002; vis. faculty fellow Univ. of Notre Dame, 2002—. Cons. NIH, Washington, 1994-99; cons.-rschr. Mex.-U.S. Binat. Migration Study, 1995-97; expert U.S. Immigration and Naturalization Svc., Washington, 1999—. Contbr. chpts. to books Migration Between Mexico and United States, 1998, Illegal Immigration: A Reference Handbook, 1999; mem. editl. bd.: Population Rsch. and Policy Rev., Columbia, S.C., 1999—; contbr. articles to profl. jours. Rsch. grantee Nat. Insts. of Child Health and Human Devel., 1998-01 Mem. AAUS, Am. Sociol. Assn., Population Assn. Am., Am. Statis. Assn. (program com. 2000-01), So. Demographic Assn., N.Y. Acad. Scis. Office: U Notre Dame Inst Latino Studies PO Box 764 250 McKenna Hall Notre Dame IN 46556-0764 E-mail: klafield@nd.edu.

LAFLAMME-ZUROWSKI, VIRGINIA M. secondary school special education educator; b. Moosup, Conn., May 3, 1946; d. Wilfred A. and Palma R. (Potvin) LaFlamme; children: Laura P., Helena M., Timothy W. BA in English, R.I. Coll., 1988, MEd in Spl. Edn., 1989. Spl. edn. tchr. Burrillville (R.I.) Middle Sch., 1989-90; spl. edn. tchr., English tchr., tchr. of homebound Cumberland (R.I.) H.S., 1990—. With Cumberland Spl. Edn. Adv. Com.; lectr. R.I. Gov.'s Conf. on Children at Risk, 1985; guest speaker R.I. Coun. on Arts, 1990, 91; numerous leadership roles. Active Girls Scouts U.S.A., ch., numerous others; hon. mem. Cumberland Sch. Vols; literacy vol. "Read Write Now" Program, St. John Vianney Ch, Elizabeth Ministry. Mem. ASCD, NEA, R.I. Edn. Assn., Nat. Coun. Tchrs. English. Home: 22 Ryder Ln Cumberland RI 02864-4255 Office: Cumberland High Sch 2602 Mendon Rd Cumberland RI 02864-3726 E-mail: vginnie46@aol.com.

LA FORCE, JAMES CLAYBURN, JR., economist, educator; b. San Diego, Dec. 28, 1928; s. James Clayburn and Beatrice Maureen (Boyd) La F.; m. Barbara Lea Latham, Sept. 23, 1952; children: Jessica, Allison, Joseph. BA, San Diego State Coll., 1951; MA, UCLA, 1958, PhD, 1962. Asst. prof. econs. UCLA, 1962-66, assoc. prof., 1967-70, prof., 1971-93, prof. emeritus, 1993—, chmn. dept. econs., 1969-78, dean Anderson Sch. Mgmt., 1978-93; acting dean Hong Kong U. Sci. & Tech., 1991-93. Bd. dirs. Arena Pharms., The Black Rock Funds, Payden & Rygel Investment Trust, Providence Investment Coun. Mut. Funds; adv. Series Trust, Cancavax; chmn. adv. com. Calif. Workmen's Compensation. Author: The Development of the Spanish Textile Industry 1750-1800, 1965, (with Warren C. Scoville) The Economic Development of Western Europe, vols. 1-5, 1969-70. Bd. dirs. Nat. Bur. Econ. Rsch., 1975-88, Found. Francisco Marroquin, Lynde and Harry Bradley Found., Pacific Legal Found., 1981-86; trustee Found. for Rsch. in Econs. and Edn., 1970—, chmn., 1977—; mem. bd. overseers Hoover Inst. on War, Revolution and Peace, 1979-85, 86-93; mem. nat. coun. on humanities NEH, 1981-88; chmn. Pres.'s Task Force on Food Assistance, 1983-84. Social Sci. Research Council research tng. fellow, 1958-60; Fulbright sr. research grantee, 1965-66; Am. Philos. Soc. grantee, 1965-66 Mem.: Mont Pelerin Soc., Econ. History Assn., Phi Beta Kappa. Office: UCLA Anderson Grad Sch Mgmt 405 Hilgard Ave Los Angeles CA 90095-9000

LAFRAMBOISE, JOAN CAROL, middle school educator; b. Bklyn., June 23, 1934; d. Anthony Peter and Nellie Eva (Zaleski) Ruggles; m. Albert George Laframboise, Aug. 5, 1961; children: Laura J., Brian A. BS in Edn., Springfield (Mass.) Coll., 1956. Cert. tchr. social sci., and mid. sch.; cert. tchr. support specialist; cert. tchr. gifted. Tchr. Meml. Jr. H.S., Wilbraham, Mass., 1956-61, Midland Park (N.J.) Jr./Sr. H.S., 1961-63, Luke Garrett Middle Sch., Austell, Ga., 1983-93; tchr. lang. arts Pine Mountain Middle Sch., Kennesaw, Ga., 1993-2001; ret., 2001. Coun. pres. Knights of Lithuania, Westfield, Mass., 1973-75, Holyoke, Mass., 1975-76, New Eng. dist. pres., 1976-77; mem. Wistariahurst Mus. Assocs., Holyoke, 1975-77. Jr. League mini-grantee, 1991. Mem. ASCD, NEA, Ga. Assn. Educators, Cobb County Assn. Educators, Nat. Coun. Tchrs. English, Nat. Coun. Social Studies. Home: 2891 Dara Dr Marietta GA 30066-4009

LAGEMANN, ELLEN CONDLIFFE, history and education educator; b. N.Y.C., Dec. 20, 1945; d. John Charles and Jane Grace (Rosenthal); m. Jonathan Kord Lagemann, June 28, 1969; 1 child, Nicholas Kord. AB cum laude, Smith Coll., 1967; MA, Columbia U., 1968, PhD with distinction, 1978. Tchr. Roslyn H.S., Roslyn, NY, 1967-69; exec. dir. WMCA: Call for Action, N.Y.C., 1969-71; asst. dir. Bank Street Sch. for Children, N.Y.C., 1971-72; tching. and rsch. asst. Inst. Phil. and Politics of Edn., Tchrs. Coll. Columbia U., N.Y.C., 1974-78; asst. prof., then assoc. prof. Tchrs. Coll. Columbia U. Dept. Hist., N.Y.C., 1978-87, prof. history and edn., 1987-94, NYU, N.Y.C., 1994—2000; pres. Spencer Found., 2000—02; Charles Warren prof. history of edn., dean Harvard Grad. Sch. Edn., Cambridge, Mass., 2002—. Dir. Markle Found., N.Y.C.; trustee, Russell Sage Found., N.Y.C.; former trustee Center for Advanced Study in Behavioral Scis., Stanford, Calif.; mem. gov. coun. Rockefeller Archive Ctr.; former mem. adv. com. Ctr. Nonprofits and Philanthropy, Urban Inst., Washington; affiliate dept. history Faculty of Arts and Sci. Author: A Generation of Women: Education in the Lives of Progressive Reformers, 1979, Private Power for the Public Good (Outstanding Book award), 1983, The Politics of Knowledge, 1989, An Elusive Science: The Troubling History of Education Research, 2000; editor: Nursing History: New Perspectives, New Possibilities, 1983, Jane Addams on Education, 1985, Teachers College Record, 1990-95, Brown v. Bd. of Education: The Challenge for Today's Schools, 1996, Philanthropic Foundations: New Scholarship, New Possibilities, 1999, Issues in Educational Research, Problems and Possibilities, 1999; many articles and book chpts. Grantee Carnegie Corp., Spencer Found, Carnegie Found. for Advancement of Teaching, Kettering Found., Lilly Endowment, fellow Ctr. for Advanced Study in Behavioral Scis. Mem. Nat. Acad. Edn. (pres. 1998-2001), History of Edn. Soc. (pres. 1987-88), Am. Hist. Assn., Orgn. Am. Historians, Am. Ednl. Rsch. Assn., Century Assn., Cosmopolitan Club, Home: 61 Grozier Rd Cambridge MA 02138 Office: Harvard Grad Sch Edn Dean's Office Appian Way Cambridge MA 02138

LAGRANGE, CLAIRE MAE, librarian; b. Tarkio, Mo., Oct. 11, 1937; d. Floyd Gerald and Phyllis Geneva (Wilson) McElfish; m. Irving Joseph LaGrange, May 20, 1955; children: Raymond, Robert, Rhonda, Roger. BA, U. Southwestern La., 1983; MEd, Northwestern State U., 1990. Cert. English, spl. edn., K-12 mild and moderate, assessment tchr., libr. sci., La. Tchr.'s aide St. Martin Parish Sch. Bd., Cecilia, La., 1979-82; tchr. English Florien (La.) High Sch., 1984-86; tchr. Zwolle (La.) High Sch., 1986-90, Cecilia (La.) Jr. High Sch., 1990-92, Cecilia High Sch., 1992-96; libr. Teche Elem. Sch., Breaux, La., 1996—99, St. Martin Parish Librs., Cecilia and Arnaudville, La., 1999—2001; br. mgr. Arnaudville (La.) Libr., 2001—. Den mother Cub Scouts-Boy Scouts Am., Spokane, Wash., 1967-69; Sunday sch. tchr. First Friends Ch., Spokane, 1968-69. Fellow U. La. Alumni Assn., Northwestern State U. Alumni Assn.; mem. NEA, ALA, Nat. English Honor Soc., La. Assn. Educators, St. Martin Assn. Educators. Avocations: sketching, reading, writing, crossword puzzles, studying the Bible. Home: 1052 Charles Marks Rd Arnaudville LA 70512-3820

LAHANN, JEANNE MARIE, special education educator; b. Davenport, Iowa, July 2, 1956; d. Richard Theodore Siefers and Carolyn Jane (Summers) Sunstrom; m. Jim O. Lahann, Aug. 2, 1975; children: Sheri, Susanna. AA, Clinton (Iowa) C.C., 1987; BA, Crest Mary Coll., Davenport, Iowa, 1989; MA, St. Ambrose U., Davenport, 1993. Lic. tchr., Iowa. Elem. resource rm. tchr. North Scott Sch. System, Alan Shephard Elem., Eldridge and Long Grove, Iowa, 1990—. Mem. NEA, Coun. Exceptional Children (treas., sec. Great River coun. 1990—). Lutheran.

LAHIRI, DEBOMOY KUMAR, molecular neurobiologist, educator; b. Varanasi, Uttar Pradesh, India, Sept. 9, 1955; arrived in U.S., 1983; s. Benoy Kumar and Nilima Rani (Moitra) L.; m. Mithu Mukherjee, Dec. 15, 1991; 1 child, Nilay K. MS, Benaras Hindu U., India, 1975, PhD, 1980. Rsch. fellow Benaras Hindu U., Varanasi, 1975-79; jr. scientist Indian Coun. of Agrl. Rsch., New Delhi, 1979-81; postdoctoral fellow McMaster U. Sch. Medicine, Hamilton, Ont., Can., 1982; asst. rsch. scientist NYU, N.Y.C., 1983-86; rsch. assoc. N.Y. State Inst. for Basic Rsch., Staten Island, 1987; asst. prof. Mt. Sinai Sch. Medicine, N.Y.C., 1988-90; asst. prof., chief molecular neurogenetics lab. Inst. Psychiat. Rsch. Ind. U. Sch. Medicine, Indpls., 1990—96, asst. prof. med. & molecular genetics, 1996—2002, assoc. prof. med. neurobiology and med. & molecular genetics, 1996—2002, prof. med. neurobiology and med. and molecular genetics, 2002—. Mem. study sects. NIH; mem. sci. rev. bd. Inst. for the Study of Aging, NY. Assoc. editor: Jour. Alzheimer's Disease, 2002—, guest editor: Current Drug Targets, 2003; contbr. articles to profl. jours. U.P. Govt. Merit scholar, 1970-75; Univ. Grants Commn. New Delhi jr. rsch. fellow, 1975-79; grantee NIH, 1991—, Alzheimer's Assn., Chgo., 2000—. Mem. AAAS, Am. Soc. Cell Biology, Am. Soc. Human Genetics, Am. Soc. for Neurochemistry, Am. Soc. Biochemistry and Molecular Biology, Genetics Soc. Am., Internat. Soc. for Neurochemistry, Soc. Biol. Psychiatry, Soc. for Neurosci., N.Y. Acad. Scis. Democrat. Hindu. Achievements include the molecular cloning and sequencing a cDNA for a major hnRNP (heterogenous nuclear ribonucleoprotein particle) core protein; determination of the presence of beta amyloid precursor protein (APP) in different regions of human brain, and alternatively spliced APP transcripts in different tissues and various cell types; demonstration of a relationship between cholinergic agonists and the processing of APP; elucidation of the role of cholinesterase inhibitor on the processing of APP, first demonstration that tacrine can alter the secretion/metabolism of APP in cultured cells; first characterization of the beta amyloid gene promoter; and an enhancer like element in the beta amyloid gene promoter; research related to the origin and biogenesis of Alzheimer amyloid plaque and the general areas of gene regulation and genetics of Alzheimer's Disease, development of a rapid, economical, non-enzymatic and non-organic method for DNA extraction, elucidation of the genetic basis of neuropsychiatric disorders by the linkage studies using molecular genetic methods and PCR (polymerase chain reaction) based genotyping, RFLP (restriction fragment length ploymorphism) and candidate gene studies in families ascertained through the NIMH Genetics Initiative in order to confirm association between the inheritance of a molecular marker with the member of the family sharing the illness, development of a sensitive radioimmunoassay to measure melatonin in human plasma samples, bipolar patients have an increased sensitivity to the effects of light on the circadian rhythm of melatonin secretion, and the risk of mood disorder seems to be related to this hypersensitivity to light, the suppression of melatonin by light may be a trait marker for bipolar affective disorder; demonstration pineal hormone melatonin can regulate the processing of Alzheimer's amyloid precursor protein in cultured cells. Home: 5518 Rosewood Commons Dr Indianapolis IN 46254 Office: Inst Psychiat Rsch Ind Univ 791 Union Dr Indianapolis IN 46202-2873

LAHR, BETH M. college administrator; b. Fort Wayne, Ind., May 9, 1952; d. Wynne Kirklin and Gay (Cooper) Burford; m. Jay Robert Lahr, Feb. 25, 1972; children: Christopher Jay, Casey Andrew. BS, Huntington (Ind.) Coll., 1990. Sec. Utah-Am. Corp., Huntington, 1972-73, Gordon Bendall & Branham, Huntington, 1973-76; fin. aid sec. Huntington Coll., 1976-77; sales sec. IMCO, Inc., 1977-78; coord. adminstr., clerical svc. Pathfinder Svcs., 1978-81; adminstv. asst. to the pres. Huntington Coll., 1981-96, dir. donor rels., 1996—98, campaign dir., 1998—2002, mng. dir. devel. ops., 2002—. Presdl. search cons. Spring Arbor (Mich.) Coll., 1996-98. Mem. Huntington Sesquicentennial, 1997-98; bd. dirs. ARC, Huntington, 1994-99. Mem. Assn. of Profl. Rschs. in Advancement, Coun. for Advancement and Support of Edn. Republican. Nazarene. Avocation: piano. Office: Huntington Coll 2303 College Ave Huntington IN 46750-1237

LAI, ERIC PONG SHING, family physician, educator; b. Kowloon, Hong Kong, May 20, 1946; s. Man Hoi and Lai Ming (Chiu) L.; m. Mimi Maria Mak Lai, Sept. 11, 1972; children: Gordon, Jennifer. BSc, Acadia U., Wolfville, Nova Scotia, 1971; MB, B CH, LRCS, LLMRCP, U. Ireland, Dublin, 1977; DFM, Chinese U. Hong Kong, 1989. Med. diplomate, Ireland, UK, Hong Kong. Rsch. fellow Med. Sch. McGill U., Montreal, Can., 1971; resident in medicine Chesterton Hosp. Cambridge (Eng.) U., 1977; resident New Addenbrooke Hosp., Cambridge, 1978; resident in gynecology Princess Margaret Hosp., Kowloon, Hong Kong, 1979-81; pvt. practice family physician Hong Kong, 1981-2001. Bd. dirs. First Med. Mgmt. Ltd., Calgary, Alta., Can., 1989; found. dir. Chinese Recreation Assn., Calgary; lectr. Hong Kong U., 1986-92, Chinese U. Hong Kong, 1986-92; facilitator Hong Kong Coll. Gen. Practitioners, 1986-92; internat. dir. World Orgn. Health Promotion, 1993-2002; cons. G-Way Holdings Internat. Inc., 1993-2002; internat. med. dir. G-Way Health Centre, Can., 1995-2002. Mem. Hong Kong Dem. Found., 1990-92, Hong Kong Bd. Edn. Coll. Gen. Practitioners, 1986-92, chmn., 1991-92, com. chmn. refresher course, 1991-92; vice chmn. found. Kidney Ctr. Precious Blood Hosp., 1991; adviser S.E. Asia Rsch. Inst., 1992; mem. Pub. Edn. Com., 1993-95; med. cons. World Orgn. Health Promotion, Can., 1993-2002. Named Henry Burton De Wolfe scholar to McGill U., 1971. Mem. Internat. Lions Club (v.p. Mt. Cameron chpt. 1986-90, pres. 1990-91, zone chmn. Internat. Club 1991-92, Melvin Jones fellow 1991-2002). Democrat. Avocations: reading, meditation, writing poetry, walking, boxing.

LAI, FENG-QI, instructional designer, educator; b. Shanghai, Mar. 25, 1948; came to U.S., 1992; d. Zheng-Zhong Lai and Yao-Zhang Zhu; m. Qun Zhang, Oct. 22, 1984. BA, Changsha (China) Railway Inst., 1982; MS, Purdue U., 1994, PhD, 1997. Asst. lectr. Shanghai Tiedao U., 1982-86, lectr., assoc. dir., 1986-91; instrnl. designer Nat. Edn. Tng. Group, Naperville, Ill., 1998; sr. instr., dir. tng. Advanced Tech. Support, Inc., Schaumburg, Ill., 1998-2000; sr. instrnl. designer Cognitive Concepts, Inc., Evanston, Ill., 2000—02; asst. prof. Ind. State U., Terre Haute, Ind., 2002—. Transl.: Writing Scientific Papers in English, 1983; co-author: Applied Cryptography, 1999. Mem. Phi Kappa Phi. Avocations: music, reading, Chinese poetry, photography, crafts.

LAI, W(EI) MICHAEL, mechanical engineer, educator; b. Amoy, Fukien, China, Nov. 29, 1930; naturalized U.S. citizen, 1967; m. Linda Yu-ling Chu, Dec. 21, 1963. BSCE, Nat. Taiwan U., 1953; MS in Engring. Mech., U. Mich., 1959, PhD, 1962. Asst. prof. mechanics Renssalaer Poly. Inst., Troy, N.Y., 1961-66, assoc. prof., 1967-77, prof., 1978-87, acting dept. chmn., 1986-87; prof. mech. engring. and orthopaedic bioengring. Columbia U., N.Y.C., 1987—, acting chmn. dept. mech. engring., 1995-96, chmn. dept. mech. engring., 1996—2002. Author: Elements of Elasticity, 1965, Introduction to Continuum Mechanics, 1974, 3rd edit., 1993, Fundamentals of Surface Mechanics, 2002. Fellow: ASME (chmn. bioengring. divsn. 1996—97, Melville medal for best paper 1982, Best Paper award bioengring. divsn. 1991, Lissner medal for outstanding achievement in bioengring. 2001), Am. Inst. Med. and Biol. Engring. (founding); mem.: AAAS, Orthopaedic Rsch. Soc., Am. Soc. Biomechanics. Home: 215 W 95th St Apt 9H New York NY 10025-6355 Office: Columbia U Dept Mech Engring W 120th St Mail Code 4703 New York NY 10027

LAIBSON, DAVID ISAAC, economist, educator; b. Phila., June 26, 1966; s. Peter Robert and Ruth (Siegel) L. AB, Harvard U., 1988; MS, London Sch. Econs., 1990; PhD, MIT, 1994. Prof. econs. Harvard U., Cambridge, Mass., 1994—. Office: Harvard U Dept Econs Littauer Ctr Cambridge MA 02138

LAIDLER, KAYWESLEY SNEED, elementary school educator; b. Quincy, Fla., Mar. 2, 1961; d. John Clinton Sneed and Juanita (Sheffield) Austin; m. Gregory Alexander Laidler, Dec. 29, 1990. BS, Fla. A&M U., 1983; cert. in elem. edn., Nova U.; cert. in early childhood edn., Fla. Internat. U. Cert. early childhood, elem. and English to speakers of other langs. tchr., Fla. Tchr. kindergarten Dade County Sch. Bd., Miami, Fla., 1983—, tchr., counselor Saturday sch., 1990-91, grade sch. advisor, 1991-92. Alt. mem. Sch. Base Mgmt. Cadre, Miami, 1989-90. Mem. Assn. for Childhood Edn. Internat., United Tchrs. Dade, NACCP. Democrat. Baptist. Avocations: reading, crocheting, writing poetry, swimming, student tutoring. Office: Twin Lakes Elem Sch 6735 W 5th Pl Hialeah FL 33012-6600

LAINE, ELAINE FRANCES, school system administrator; b. Huntington, Ind., July 25, 1951; d. Howard James and Frances Mary (Graft) Harold; m. Rudolph Lewis Laine, Oct. 26, 1975; 1 child, Christina Elaine. BA, Purdue U., 1973; MA, George Mason U., 1985, PhD, 2000; adminstrv. cert., U. Va., 1989. Cert. tchr. French, Spanish, middle and high sch. prin., Va. Foreign lang. tchr. Fairfax County Pub. Schs., Springfield, Va., 1981-85, Thomas Jefferson Sch. for Sci and Tech., Alexandria, Va., 1985-86; resource tchr. foreign langs. and ESL area IV adminstrv. offices Fairfax County Pub. Schs., Fairfax, Va., 1986-91; foreign lang. dept. chairperson Ormond Stone Sch. Fairfax County Pub. Schs., Centreville, Va., 1991-93; asst. prin. Cooper Mid. Sch. Fairfax County Pub. Schs., McLean, Va., 1993-96, Langley H.S., McLean, 1996—. Mem. foreign lang. curriculum adv. bd. Fairfax Pub. Schs., Springfield, 1990-91, supt.'s adv. coun., 1991-93, chairperson foreign lang. dept. adv. coun., 1992-93, mem. fine arts curriculum adv. com., 1993-96, mem. lang. arts curriculum adv. com., 1995—; bd. Judges Columbia Scholastic Press Assn., 1992-93. Named Exemplary Tchr., Fairfax County Pub. Schs., Springfield, Va., 1988, '92, Outstanding Tchr., Fairfax County Sch. Bd., Springfield, 1992; recipient Medalist awards Columbia Scholastic Press Assn., N.Y.C., 1990, '91, Crown Nominee, 1991; invited speaker Annual Conv. Columbia Scholastic Press Assn., 1992. Mem. ASCD, Nat. Sch. Bd. Assn., Assn. Secondary Asst. Prins., Greater Washington Assn. of Tchrs. of Foreign Langs. (del. at large No. Va. 1983, '89. Disting. Educator 1985), Purdue Alumni Assn. Avocations: travel, gourmet cooking, piano, singing, hiking. Home: 12732 Oak Farms Dr Oak Hill VA 20171-2202 Office: Fairfax County Pub Schs Langley High Sch 6520 Georgetown Pike Mc Lean VA 22101-2222

LAING, PENELOPE GAMBLE, art educator; b. Dallas, July 24, 1944; d. William Oscar and Beth (Robertson) G.; m. Richard Harlow Laing, June 29, 1970; children: Scott Emerson, Lindsey Elizabeth. BA in Art, N. Tex. State U., 1966; MFA, Edinboro State Coll., 1979; N.C. Prin. fellow, 1997-99. Cert. tchr., Tex. (life), N.C. (Art all-level). Art cons. Lawrence (Kans.) Unified Sch. Dist., 1966-68; instr. art Ball State U., Muncie, Ind., 1969-71, Edinboro (Pa.) State U., 1976-77, Pitt C.C., Greenville, N.C., 1980-83; exec. dir. Pitt-Greenville Arts Coun., Greenville, 1983-84; free-lance designer, 1984-90; art tchr., head dept. art Pitt County Schs., 1990—. Assoc. prin. Pitt. Co. Schs., 1999—, adminstrv. intern asst. prin., Pitt County schs., 1998-99; seminar participant N.C. Ctr. for Advancement of Tchg., 1993, tchr.-scholar, 1994, 95; assoc. dir. S.E. Regional Tech. and Tchg. Conf., East Carolina U., 1998. Bd. dirs., v.p. Pitt-Greenville Arts Coun., 1979-82; mem. adv. bd. Pitt County Schs., Greenville, 1985-87; pres. PTA S. Greenville Sch., 1986-87. Ralph Brimley Ednl. Friend Scholarship, 2000, 01, 03, Chip and Diane Linville Scholarship, 2002, Tchr. Exec. Inst. fellow Pitts County Edn. Found., Greenville, 1992, N.C. Prin. fellow State N.C. Legis., 1997-98; grantee Pitt County Edn. Found., 1991-93; recipient cert. of merit, NAASP, 1998. Mem. Am. Ednl. Rsch. Assn., Nat. Art Edn. Assn., Nat. Assn. Secondary Sch. Prins., N.C. Art Edn. Assn. (bd. dirs., chmn. elem. divsn. 1992-94), Pitt County Prins. and Asst. Prins. Assn., Surface Design Assocs. (southeastern rep.), Phi Delta Kappa. Democrat. Avocations: travel, reading. Home: 204 Pineview Dr Greenville NC 27834-6434 Office: 1325 Red Banks Rd Greenville NC 27858-5315

LAING, STEVEN O. school system administrator; MEd in Ednl. Adminstrn., EdD in Ednl. Leadership, Brigham Young U. With Cedar City high sch., 1976—87; dir. secondary edn. Iron Sch. Dist.; supt. Box Elder Sch. Dist., 1990—97; assoc. supt. Utah State Office Edn., 1997—99; state suprt. pub. instrn. Utah State Bd. Edn., 1999—. Office: Utah State Superintendent Pub Instruction 250 E 500 S PO Box 144200 Salt Lake City UT 84111-4200*

LAINSON, PHILLIP ARGLES, dental educator; b. Council Bluffs, Iowa, Feb. 11, 1936; s. Donald Wesley and Olive Ione (Stageman) L.; m. Mary Margaret Tangney, June 18, 1960; children: David, Michael, Elizabeth. BA, U. Iowa, 1960, DDS, 1962, MS, 1968; dental intern cert., USAF Malcom Crow Hosp., 1963. Diplomate Am. Bd. Periodontology. Instr. dept. periodontics U. Iowa, Iowa City, 1965-69, asst. prof., 1969-71, assoc. prof., 1971-75, prof., 1975—, head dept. periodontics, 1976-98, grad. program dir., 1998—2001. Cons. in periodontics VA Hosp., Knoxville, Iowa, 1967—, Iowa City, 1976—, Ctrl. Regional Dental Testing Svc., Topeka, Kans., 1977-81, Commn. on Dental Accreditation, ADA, Chgo., 1985-90. Contbr. articles to profl. jours.; editor newsletter Midwest Soc. Periodontology, 1982-85; assoc. editor: Iowa Dental Jour., 1974-76. Chmn., bd. in control of athletics U. Iowa, 1984-86. Served to capt. USAF, 1962-65, Iowa Army N.G., 1973-91. Am. Coll. Dentists fellow, 1976; Internat. Coll. Dentists fellow, 1991; Pierre Fauchard fellow, 1991. Mem. Iowa Soc. Periodontology (pres. 1976-78), U. Dist. Iowa Dental Assn. (pres. 1979-80), Midwest Soc. Periodontology (pres. 1987-88), Am. Acad. Periodontology, Internat. Assn. Dental Rsch., Am. Dental Assn. (coun. on govtl. affairs and fed. dental svcs. 1989-93), Joint Commn. Nat Dental Exam. (test construction com. 1995-99), Am. Assn. Dental Schs., Rotary, Omicron Kappa Upsilon. Republican. Roman Catholic. Avocations: sailing, fishing, biking, tennis. Home: 16 Ridgewood Ln Iowa City IA 52245-1632 Office: U Iowa Coll Dentistry Iowa City IA 52242

LAIOU, ANGELIKI EVANGELOS, history educator; b. Athens, Greece, Apr. 6, 1941; came to U.S., 1959; d. Evangelos K. and Virginia I. (Apostolides) Laios; m. Stavros B. Thomadakis, July 14, 1973; 1 son, Vassili N. BA, Brandeis U., 1961; MA, Harvard U., 1962, PhD, 1966. Asst. prof. history Harvard U., Cambridge, Mass., 1969-72, Dumbarton Oaks prof. Byzantine history, 1981—; assoc. prof. Brandeis U., Waltham, 1972-75; prof. Rutgers U., New Brunswick, N.J., 1975-79, disting. prof., 1979-81; chmn. Gennadeion com. (Am. Sch. Classical Studies), Athens, Greece, 1981-84; dir. Dumbarton Oaks, 1989-98; prof. history Harvard U., Cambridge, 1998—. Mem. Greek Parliament, 2000-2002; dep. min. fgn. affairs, Greece, 2000. Author: Constantinople and the Latins, 1972, Peasant Society in the Late Byzantine Empire, 1977, Mariage, amour et parenté à Byzance, XIe-XIIIe siècles, 1992, Gender, Society and Economic Life in Byzantium, 1992, The Economic History of Byzantium, 2002. Guggenheim Found. fellow, 1971-72, 79-80, Dumbarton Oaks sr. fellow, 1983—, Am. Coun. Learned Socs. fellow, 1988-89. Fellow Am. Acad. Arts and Scis., Medieval Acad., Acad. Athens; mem. Am. Hist. Assn., Medieval Acad. Am., Greek Com. Study of South Eastern Europe. Office: Harvard U Dept History Cambridge MA 02138 E-mail: laiou@fas.harvard.edu.

LAIRD, DORIS ANNE MARLEY, humanities educator, musician; b. Charlotte, N.C., Jan. 15, 1931; d. Eugene Harris and Coleen (Bethea) Marley; m. William Everette Laird Jr., Mar. 13, 1964; children: William Everette III, Andrew Marley, Glen Howard. MusB, Converse Coll., Spartanburg, S.C., 1951; opera cert., New Eng. Conservatory, Boston, 1956; MusM, Boston U., 1956; PhD, Fla. State U., 1980. Leading soprano roles S.C. Opera Co., Columbia, 1951-53, Plymouth Rock Ctr. of Music and Art, Duxbury, Mass., 1953-56; soprano Pro Musica, Boston, 1956, New Eng. Opera Co., Boston, 1956; instr. Stratford Coll., Danville, Va., 1956-58, Sch. Music Fla. State U., Tallahassee, 1958-60, dept. humanities, 1960-68; tchr. Fla. State U., 1973-79; asst. prof. Fla. A&M U., Tallahassee, 1979-89, assoc. prof., 1990—2002; ret., 2002. Vis. scholar Cornell U., 1988; participant So. Conf. on Afro-Am. Studies, Inc. Author: Colin Morris: Modern Missionary, 1980; contbr. articles to profl. jours. Soprano Washington St. Meth. Ch., Columbia, S.C., 1951-53, Copley Meth. Ch., Boston, 1953-56; soloist Trinity United Meth. Ch., Tallahassee, 1983—; mem. Saint Andrews Soc., Tallahassee, 1986—; judge Brain Bowl, Tallahassee, 1981-84. Named subject of article in Glamour mag., 2001; recipient NEH award, 1988, Disting. Alumna award, Converse Coll., 2001; scholar Phi Sigma Tau, 1960. Mem. AAUP, AAUW, Nat. Art Educators Assn., Tallahassee Music Tchrs. Assn., Tallahassee Music Guild, Am. Guild of Organists, DAR (mus. rep. 1984-85), Colonial Dames of 17th Century (music dir. 1984-85), Nat. Assn. Humanities Edn., U. Wyo. Women's Club, Woman's Club Tallahassee. Democrat. Avocations: travel, dancing, music. Home: 1125 Mercer Dr Tallahassee FL 32312-2833 Personal E-mail: wlaird@garnet.acns.fsu.edu. Business E-Mail: dorislaird@famu.edu.

LAIRD, JEAN ELOUISE RYDESKI (MRS. JACK E. LAIRD), author, adult education educator; b. Wakefield, Mich., Jan. 18, 1930; d. Chester A. and Agnes A. (Petranek) Rydeski; m. Jack E. Laird, June 9, 1951; children: John E., Jayne E., Joan Ann P., Jerilyn S., Jacquelyn T. Bus. Edn. degree, Duluth (Minn.) Bus. U., 1948; postgrad., U. Minn., 1949-50. Tchr. Oak Lawn (Ill.) H.S. Adult Evening Sch., 1964-72, St. Xavier Coll., Chgo., 1974—. Lectr., commencement address cir.; writer newspaper column Around The House With Jean, A Woman's Work, 1965-70, Chicagotown News column The World As I See It, 1969, hobby column Modern Maturity mag., travel column Travel/Leisure mag., beauty column Ladycom mag., Time and Money Savers column Lady's Circle mag., consumerism column Ladies' Home Jour. Author: Lost in the Department Store, 1964, Around the House Like Magic, 1968, Around the Kitchen Like Magic, 1969, How to Get the Most from Your Appliances, 1967, Hundreds of Hints for Harassed Homemakers, 1971, The Alphabet Zoo, 1972, The Plump Ballerina, 1971, The Porcupine Story Book, 1974, Fried Marbles and Other Fun Things to Do, 1975, Hundreds of Hints for Harassed Homemakers: The Homemaker's Book of Time and Money Savers, 1979, Homemaker's Book of Energy Savers, 1981; also 427 paperback booklets; contbr. articles to mags. Mem.: Marist, Mt. Assissi Acad., St. Linus Guild, Queen of Peace Parents Clubs, Oak Lawn Bus. and Profl. Women's Club, Canterbury Writers Club Chgo. Roman Catholic. Home: 10540 Lockwood Ave Oak Lawn IL 60453-5161 also: Vista De Lago Lake Geneva WI 53147 also: Harbor Towers Yacht Club Siesta Key FL 34242

LAIRD, MARY See WOOD, LARRY

LAIRD, ROBERTA JANE, reading specialist; b. DuBois, Pa., Jan. 9, 1955; d. Robert and Jane Aldine (Syphrit) Laird; m. Stephen George Santus, July 9, 1994. BA magna cum laude, Westminster Coll., New Wilmington, Pa., 1976, MEd, 1978. Cert. elem. tchr., reading specialist, Pa. Kindergarten tchr. Cameron County Sch. Dist., Emporium, Pa., 1976-77; grad. asst. Westminster Coll., 1977-78; reading specialist Clarion (Pa.) Area Sch. Dist., 1978-98; ednl. coord. Clarion U. of Pa., 2000—02. Temporary instr. Clarion U. of Pa., 1989; mem. adv. coun. for redesign of grad. programs in edn., 1984; speaker Internat. Reading Assn. Annual Conv., 1995. Mem. Clarion Cmty. Choir, 1980-88; mother advisor Order of Rainbow for Girls, Clarion, 1986-87. Mem. Keystone State Reading Assn. (regional dir. 1985-90, sec. 1990-91, pres.-elect 1992-93, pres. 1993-94, IRA state coord. 1997—), Seneca Reading Coun. (dir. 1985—, pres. 1983-85), Westminster Coll. Alumni Coun. (pres.). Methodist. Avocations: sewing, reading, travel.

LAJEUNESSE, MARCEL, university administrator, educator; b. Mont-Laurier, Que., Can., June 28, 1942; s. Achille and Gertrude (Grenier) L.; m. Louise Beauregard, Dec. 20, 1975; 1 child, Anne. BA, U. Laval, Que., Can., 1963; B. Bibliotheconomie, U. de Montreal, Que., Can., 1964, Licence ès Lettres, 1967, MA, 1968; PhD, U. Ottawa, Can., 1977. Prof. Coll. L'Outaouais, Hull, 1968-70, U. de Montreal, 1970—. Prof., dir. Grad. Sch. Libr. and Info. Sci., 1987-94, assoc. dean for planning Faculty of Arts and Scis., 1994-98, assoc. dean for human resources and mgmt., 1998-2002; cons. Aupelf UREF, IDRC, Can. Internat. Devel. Agy., Agence de cooperation culturelle et technique, UNESCO. Author, co-author 17 books; contbr. numerous articles to profl. and scholarly jours. Mem. Conseil de la Langue Française, Que., 1987-91.— Mem. Assn. Libr. and Info. Sci. Edn., Assn. Internat. des Écoles de Scis. de l'Information, Assn. pour l'Avancement des Scis. et des Techniques de la Documentation, Corp. des Bibliothécaires professionnels de Québec, Inst. French Am. History, Bibliog. Soc. Can. Home: 126 Dobie Mont-Royal QC Canada H3P 1S4 Office: EBSI U Montreal CP 6128 Succ A Montreal QC Canada H3C 3J7

LAKAH, JACQUELINE RABBAT, political scientist, consultant; b. Cairo, Apr. 14, 1933; arrived in U.S., 1969, naturalized, 1975; d. Victor Boutros and Alice (Mounayer) Rabbat; m. Antoine K. Lakah, Apr. 8, 1951; children: Micheline, Mireille, Caroline. BA, Am. U. Beirut, 1968; MPh, Columbia U., 1974; cert., Mid. East Inst., 1975, PhD, 1978. Adj. asst. prof. polit. sci. and world affairs Fashion Inst. Tech., N.Y.C., 1978-88, asst. prof., 1988-93, assoc. prof., 1993-97, prof., 1997—, asst. chair dept. social scis., 1989-95, chair dept. social scis., 1995-97, acting dean liberal arts, 1998-2000. Asst. prof. grad. faculty polit. sci. Columbia U., N.Y.C., summer 1979, vis. scholar, 1982-83, also mem. seminar on Mid. East, 1978—; guest faculty Sarah Lawrence Coll., 1981-82; cons. on Mid. East; faculty rsch. fellow SUNY, summer 1982. Columbia Faculty fellow, 1970-73, NDEA Title IV fellow, 1971-72; Mid. East Inst. scholar, 1976; Rockefeller Found. scholar, 1967-69. Home: 41-15 94th St Flushing NY 11373-1745 E-mail: jlakah@nyc.rr.com.

LAKE, WESLEY WAYNE, JR., internist, allergist, educator; b. New Orleans, Oct. 11, 1937; s. Wesley Wayne and Mary McGehee (Snowden) L.; m. Abby F. Arnold, Aug. 1959 (div. 1974); children: Courtenay B., Corinne A., Jane S.; married Melissa Bowman, Mar. 1999. AB in Chemistry, Princeton U., 1959; MD, Tulane U., 1963. Diplomate Am. Bd. Internal Medicine, Am. Bd. Allergy and Immunology. Intern Charity Hosp. of La., New Orleans, 1963-64, resident internal medicine, 1966-69; NIH fellow allergy and immunology La. State U. Med. Ctr., 1969-70; instr. dept. medicine Tulane U., New Orleans, 1967-69; fellow dept. medicine La. State U., New Orleans, 1969-70, instr. dept. medicine, 1970-73, asst. clin. prof. medicine, 1973-77; chief allergy clinic La. State U. Svc. Charity Hosp. La., New Orleans, 1970-77; assoc. clin. prof. medicine Tulane U., 1978—93. Temp. staff positions various hosps., 1963-70, including Baton Rouge Gen. Hosp., Our Lady of the Lake Hosp., Glenwood Hosp., St. Francis Hosp., Monroe, La., Lallie Kemp Charity Hosp., Independence, La., Huey P. Long Hosp., Pineville, La.; gen. med. officer outpatient clinic Hunter AFB, Savannah, Ga., 1964-65, gen. med. officer internal medicine svc., 1965-66; cons. physician Seventh Ward Gen. Hosp., Hammond, La., 1971-77, Slidell (La.) Meml. Hosp., 1971-89, St. Tammany Parish Hosp., Covington, La., 1977-85; cons. physician East Jefferson Hosp., Metairie, La., 1971-77, staff physician, 1990—; asst. vis. physician Charity Hosp. New Orleans, 1970-75, staff physician, 1975-77, vis. phys. Tulane divsn., 1979-93; assoc. physician So. Bapt. Hosp., New Orleans, 1970-75, chmn. dept. medicine, chmn. internal medicine com., 1982-84, chmn. pharmacy and therapeutics, 1980-82, mem. investigative rev. com., 1984-85, mem. internal medicine quality assurance com., 1989-94; staff physician Kenner (La.) Regional Med. Ctr. (formerly St. Jude Med. Ctr.), 1985-99, chmn. quality assurance com., 1987-89; staff physician Drs. Hosp. of Jefferson, 1988—; mem. pharmacy and therapeutics com. and continuing med. edn. com. East Jefferson Gen. Hosp., 1997—. Author: (with others) Infiltrative Hypersensitivity Chest Diseases, 1975; contbr. articles to profl. jours. including Jour. Immunology, Internat. Archives Allergy and Applied Immunology, Jour. Allergy and Clin. Immunology; also chpts. in books concerning chest diseases. Fellow ACP, Am. Coll. Allergy, Sigma Xi; mem. New Orleans Acad. Internal Medicine, Musser-Burch Soc., S.E. Allergy Soc., La. Allergy Soc. (sec. 1975-76, v.p. 1976-77, pres. 1977-78). Republican. Episcopalian. Home: 4636 Perrier St New Orleans LA 70115-3920 Office: 4224 Houma Blvd Ste 250 Metairie LA 70006-2935 Home: 1850 Gause Blvd Slidell LA 70461

LAKIER, THELMA, child development specialist, librarian; b. Pietersburg, Transvaal, S. Africa, May 28, 1941; came to U.S., 1978; d. Abraham and Berthe (MIchelsohn) Perlmann; m. Jeffrey Lakier, Dec. 20, 1964; children: Beth, Louise. BA, U. Witaters, Johannesburg, S. Africa, 1962; Transvaal tchrs. higher diploma, Johannesburg Coll. Edn., S. Africa, 1963; postgrad., Erikson Inst., Chgo., 1988-91; MEd, Loyola U., Chgo., 1992. Cert. tchr., Mich. Tchr. Transvaal Edn. Dept., S. Africa, 1964, 66-72; libr. Libr. of Johannesburg, 1965; tchr. Hebrew Acad., San Francisco, 1972-74, Discovery Corner, Troy, Mich., 1982-88, Michael Reese Day Care, Chgo., 1988-89; child devel. specialist Luth. Gen. Children's Day Care Ctr., Des Plaines, Ill., 1989—, resource libr. for staff and parents, 1993—. Mem. Luth. Gen. Found Benefit Com., Chgo., 1989—. Mem. Nat. Assn. for Edn. of Young Children (workshop co-leader Chgo. chpt. 1992), Assn. for Childhood Edn. Internat. Avocations: music, reading, needlework. Home: 2751 The Mews Northbrook IL 60062-2617 Office: Luth Gen Children's Day Care 9375 W Church St Des Plaines IL 60016-4271

LAKNER, HILDA BUCKLEY, consumer behavior educator; b. Gondelsheim, Germany, Nov. 16, 1948; arrived in U.S., 1951; d. John and Mary (Zugaj) Mayer; 1 child, Aaron John Buckley; m. Edward William Lakner, July 9, 1983. BS, Mt. Mary Coll., 1970; MS, U. Wis., Madison, 1972, PhD, 1979. Asst. pers. mgr. Evans-Singer Women's Apparel, Milw., 1967-70; instr. U. Ill., Urbana, 1975-79, asst. prof., 1979-85, assoc. prof., 1985—, dir. undergrad. programs Dept. Agrl. & Consumer Econs., 1997—. Vis. prof. M.S. U. Vavadora, India, 1988, Egerton U., Njoro, Kenya, 1988-89; chair div. consumer scis. U. Ill., 1989-91; intern Agrl. Experimentaiton Sta., 1991-92. Editorial bd. Home Econs. Rsch. Jour., 1982-84, 86-88, Clothing and Textiles Rsch. Jour., 1983-89; contbr. articles to profl. jours. Grantee U. Ill. Rsch. Bd., 1980-81, 89-90, U.S. AID, 1988-89; recipient Rotary Internat. award, 1988-89. Mem. Internat. Textile and Apparel Assn. (various coms. 1977—, v.p. 2000-02, pres. cen. region 1984-85, counselor 1985-86, nat. sec. 1986-88, v.p. 2000-02), Am. Home Econs. Assn. (various coms. 1984—), Am. Psychol. Assn., Assn. Consumer Rsch., Soc. for Consumer Psychology, Costume Soc. Am., Omicron Nu. Roman Catholic. Avocations: reading, museum touring, travel. Office: U Ill 1301 W Gregory Dr Urbana IL 61801-9015

LAKSHMIKANTHAM, VANGIPURAM, mathematics educator; b. Hyderabad, India, Aug. 8, 1926; came to U.S., 1960, naturalized, 1966; s. Soroja Bukkapatnam, Feb. 22, 1942; children: Sreekantham, Neerada, Nirupama. MA, Osmania U., Hyderabad, 1955, PhD, 1958. Mem. faculty UCLA, 1960-61, Math. Rsch. Ctr., U. Wis., Madison, 1961-62; mem. Rsch. Inst. Advanced Studies, Balt., 1962-63; assoc. prof. U. Alta., Calgary, Can., 1963-64; prof., chmn. dept. math. Marathwada U., Aurangabad, India, 1964-66, U. R.I., Kingston, 1966-73, U. Tex., Arlington, 1973-88; prof., head dept. math. scis. Fla. Inst. Tech., Melbourne, 1989—. Author 35 books; founder, editor: Jour. Nonlinear Analysis, A-Series and B-Series, Nonlinear Studies, Stochastic Analysis and Applications, Mathematical Problems in Engring., Hybrid Systems and Applications; assoc. editor other jours.; contbr. over 400 rsch. articles to profl. publs. Mem. Am. Math. Soc., Indian Math. Soc., Soc. Indsl. and Aplied Math., Nat. Acad. Sci. India, Internat. Fedn. Nonlinear Analysts (founder). Office: Fla Inst Tech Dept Math Scis 150 W University Blvd Melbourne FL 32901-6975 E-mail: lakshmik@winnie.fit.edu.

L'ALLIER, JAMES JOSEPH, educational multimedia company executive, instructional designer; b. St. Paul, June 24, 1945; s. Charlemagne Joseph and Mildred Marie (LeVasseur) L'A.; m. Susan Kay Margulies, Apr. 28, 1973. BS magna cum laude, U. Wis., River Falls, 1969, MS, 1973; PhD, U. Minn., 1980. Instr. English, multimedia specialist River Falls Sr. High Sch., 1969-71; instr. English Stillwater (Minn.) Sr. High Sch., 1971-80; mgr. computer assisted instrn. Wilson Learning Corp., Mpls., 1980-83, dir. R&D, 1983-86; v.p. R&D Wilson Learning Interactive Tech. Group, Santa Fe, 1986-89; v.p. product devel. Nippon Wilson Learning, Tokyo, 1989-90; v.p. instructional design Whole Systems International, Cambridge, Mass., 1990-93; v.p. product devel. NETg, A Thomson Learning Co., Naperville, 1993-98; v.p. R&D NETg, A Harcourt Brace Co., Naperville, Ill., 1998-2000; chief learning officer, v.p. R&D NETg, A Thomson Learning Co., 2000—. Expert witness Universal Tng., Chgo., 1989-91; bd. dirs. Info. Tech. Tng. Assn., chair standards com. 2000—. Author: (video prodns.) Who Shot the Terminal?, 1984, The Tenth Woman, 1987, Working Toward the Future, 1991, America's Workforce: A Vision for the Future, 1992; mem. editorial bd. Learning Age, Mpls., 1987-89, CLO Mag., Chgo., 2002-; product reviewer Ednl. Tech., N.Y.C., 1981-83; assoc. editor Performance and Instrn., Washington, 1983-85; inventor Interactive Learning System-Skill Builder; holder 240 copyrights; inventor, patent for interactive learning sys. Skill Builder; inventor, patent holder Precision Skilling. Curriculum chair Total Info. Ednl. Systems, St. Paul, 1971-76; fund raiser U. Minn. Alliance, Mpls., 1983-89; contbr. Am. Cancer Soc., Washington, 1987—; mem. pub. svc. com. Instructional Systems Assn., Sunset Beach, Calif., 1988—; reviewer William H. Donner Found., Inc., N.Y.C., 1993—; mem. ednl. tech. adv. bd. Utah State U., Logan. U. Minn. Grad. Sch. Edn. sr. fellow, 1984; U.S. Dept. Labor grantee, 1991. Mem. U. Wis. Alumni Assn., Instructional Systems Assn. (conf. chair 1980, 84), U. Minn. Alumni Assn., Boston Computer Soc., Ednl. Tech. Adv. Bd., Utah Sate U., Pres.'s Club U. Minn., Heritage Soc. U. Wis. Avocations: reading, photography, music. Office: Thomson NETg 1751 W Diehl Rd Naperville IL 60563-1840

LALLY-GREEN, MAUREEN ELLEN, superior court judge, law educator; b. Sharpsville, Pa., July 5, 1949; d. Francis Leonard and Charlotte Marie (Frederick) Lally; m. Stephen Ross Green, Oct. 5, 1979; children: Katherine Lally, William Ross, Bridget Marie. BS, Duquesne U., 1971, JD, 1974. Bar: Pa. 1974, D.C., U.S. Dist. Ct. (we. dist.) Pa. 1974, U.S. Ct. Appeals (3d cir.) 1974, U.S. Supreme Ct. 1978. Atty. Houston Cooper, Pitts., 1974-75, Commodity Futures Trading Commn., Washington, 1975-78; counsel Westinghouse Electric Corp., Pitts., 1978-83; prof. law Duquesne U., Pitts., 1986-2000, adj. prof. law, 1983-86, 2000—; apptd. judge Superior Ct., 1998, elected judge, 2000—. Fed. dist. ct. arbitrator; mem. criminal procedure rules com. Supreme Ct. Pa., 1994-97; dir. European Union Law Conf., Dublin, 1995-97, Intellectual Law Conf., Italy, 1997; panel Disciplinary Bd. of Commonwealth of Pa. Chair Cranberry Twp. Zoning Hearing Bd., Pa., 1983-98; counsel Western Pa. Ptnrs. of Ams., 1987-90, pres. 1993-95, bd. dirs., 1995-99; active Elimination of World Hunger Project, 1977-85, Bishop's Com. on Dialogue with Cath. Univs., 1999-2001; co-chair Millenium com. Duquesne U., 1997-2000; bd. regents St. Vincent Sem., Latrobe, Pa., 2002—; bd. dirs. St. Francis U., Loretto, Pa., 2003—; chair Gender Bias Com., 2003—. Fellow Kellogg Found. (for Ptnrs. of Ams.), 1990-92. Mem. Pa. Bar Assn. (ethics com. 1987-94, commn. on women in the profession 1994—, chair quality of work life com. 2002, mem. exec. com. of women in the profession), Allegheny County Bar Assn. (women in law com., professionalism com., ethics com., sec. bd. dirs. 1992-2001), Duquesne U. Alumni Assn. (bd. dirs. 1982-89, sec. 1988-89), Duquesne U. Law Alumni Assn. (bd. dirs. 1987, treas. 1991, v.p. 1992), St. Thomas More Soc. (bd. dirs. 2002—). Republican. Roman Catholic. Avocations: children's activities, sports. Office: 2420 Grant Bldg 330 Grant St Pittsburgh PA 15219-2202

LAMANET LALONDE, SHARI, artist, art educator; b. San Francisco, Sept. 29, 1949; d. Alfred Paul and Marjorie Theodora (Hibschle) L.; m. Philip Martin Lalonde, Sept. 28, 1974; children: Sydney Lamanet, Paul Braque. BFA, San Francisco Art Inst., 1971, MFA, 1979. Mem. painting faculty San Francisco Art Inst., 1981—. Group shows include Emmanuel Walter Gallery San Francisco Art Inst., 1980, 83, 87, Rental Gallery San Francisco Mus. Modern Art, 1980, 93, 96, Sierra Nevada Mus. Art, Reno, Nev., 1980, Minot (N.D.) State Coll., 1981 (Hon. Mention), San Francisco Mus. Modern Art, 1981, Stedman Art Gallery Rutgers U., Camden, N.J., 1981-82, So. Exposure Gallery, San Francisco, 1983, Slant Gallery, San Francisco, 1984, Alternative Mus., N.Y.C., 1984, Ian Birkstad Gallery, London, 1985, Musavi Gallery, N.Y.C., 1985 (First Place Drawing), ARCO Visual Arts Ctr., Anchorage, Alaska, 1985-86, Fairbanks (Alaska) Art Assn., 1985-86, Alaska State Mus., Juneau, 1985-86, Koslow Gallery, L.A., 1988, 89, Camerawork Gallery, San Francisco, 1988 (Phelan award 1987), Downey Mus. Art, L.A., 1989, John Michael Kohler Arts Ctr., Sheboygan, Wis., 1990, U. San Diego, 1990, Redding (Calif.) Mus. Art and History, 1991, San Francisco Art Inst., 1992, 93, 96, Opts Arts, San Francisco, 1994, Ctr. Visual Arts, Oakland, Calif., 1994, Jernigan Wicker Gallery, San Francisco, 1997, numerous others; one person shows include Bruce Velick Gallery, San Francisco, 1984, 86, 88, Sheppard Gallery, U. Nev., Reno, 1984, Slant Gallery, 1985, Monterey (Calif.) Mus. Art, 1986. Bd. dirs. San Francisco Children's Art Ctr., 1990-92; mem. fine arts com. Schs. of the Sacred Heart, San Francisco, 1995-96. Home: 2475 Pacific Ave San Francisco CA 94115-1237 Office: San Francisco Art Inst 800 Chestnut St San Francisco CA 94133-2206

LAMAR, HOWARD ROBERTS, educational administrator, historian; b. Tuskegee, Ala., Nov. 18, 1923; s. John Howard and Elma (Roberts) L.; m. Doris Shirley White, Sept. 3, 1959; children: Susan Kent, Sarah Howard. BA, Emory U., 1944; MA, Yale U., 1945, PhD, 1951; LHD (hon.), Emory U., 1975; LLD (hon.), Yale U., 1993; LittD (hon.), U. Nebr., 1994. Instr. U. Mass., 1945-46, Wesleyan U., Middletown, Conn., 1948-49; mem. faculty Yale U., 1949-94, prof. Am. History and history Am. West, 1964-94, W.R. Coe prof. Am. history, 1979-87, Sterling prof. history, 1987—, chmn. history dept., 1962-63, 67-70, dir. history grad. studies, 1964-67, fellow Ezra Stiles Coll., 1961-94, dean, 1979-85, pres., 1992-93, Sterling prof. history emeritus, 1994—. Author: Dakota Territory, 1861-1889, 1956, 97, The Far Southwest, 1846-1912, A Territorial History, 1966, 2d edit., 2000; also articles, reviews.; Editor: (Joseph Downey) Cruise of the Portsmouth, 1958, Western Americana Series, 1961—, New Encyclopedia of the

American West, 1998, Gold Seeker: Adventures of A Belgian Argonaut in California, 1985, paperback 1998; co-author, co-editor The Frontier in History: North America and Southern Africa Compared, 1981, History of the American Frontier Series, 1976—. Alderman, New Haven, 1951-53. Mem. Orgn. Am. Historians, Western History Assn. (pres. 1971-72), Am. Antquarian Soc., Elihu Soc., Conn. Acad. of Arts and Scis., Phi Beta Kappa. Democrat. Home: 1747 Hartford Tpke North Haven CT 06473-1249 Office: Yale U Dept History New Haven CT 06520

LAMARCA, MARY MARGARET, elementary education educator; b. Pitts., Pa., Feb. 16, 1953; d. James Joseph and Elizabeth Jane LaMarca. BS in Sci., Slippery Rock U., 1975; MEd, California U. of Pa., 1985. Cert. elem. tchr., adminstr., Md., Pa. Kindergarten and 2d grade tchr. Conchita Espinosa Acad., Miami, Fla., 1975-77; 1st grade tchr. Nativity Sch., Pitts., 1977-80; 1st and 2d grade tchr. Westinghouse-Kori Day Sch., Pusan, Republic of Korea, 1980-82; 5th and 6th grade tchr. Lake Valley Sch., Dept. of Interior, Crownpoint, N.Mex., 1983; 1st and 2d grade tchr. Westinghouse-Philippine Day Sch., Bagac, 1983-84; head tchr. Bechtel Internat.-Kori Day Sch., Republic of Korea, 1984-86, Bechtel Internat.-Korea 7-8 Sch., Republic of Korea, 1986-87; kindergarten tchr. Prince George's Cty., Md., 1987-92, Beginnings II Daycare, Seattle, 1992-93; primary tchr. Ft. Washington Forest, Md., 1993-97, tchr. reading recovery, 1997-99, sch. instrnl. specialist, 1999—. Republican. Roman Catholic. Avocations: aerobic dancing, quilting, crocheting. Home: 801 Hoods Mill Rd, B-25 Woodbine MD 21797

LAMB, CHARLES MOODY, political science educator, researcher; b. Murfreesboro, Tenn., Mar. 1, 1945; s. Edward Clay and Opal Irene (Tune) L. B.S., Middle Tenn. State U., 1967; M.A., U. Ala., 1970, Ph.D., 1974. Adminstrv. specialist NASA, Washington, 1971; research scientist George Washington U., Washington, 1973-75; equal opportunity specialist U.S. Commn. on Civil Rights, Washington, 1975-77; asst. prof. polit. sci. SUNY-Buffalo, 1977-84, assoc. prof., 1984—; vis. assoc. prof. U. Wis., Madison, 1990-91; cons. U.S. Congress Office Tech. Assessment, Washington, 1974-75, 84. Co-editor, contbg. author: Supreme Court Activism and Restraint, 1982 (Choice Outstanding Acad. Book award 1983); Implementation of Civil Rights Policy, 1984; Judicial Conflict and Consensus, 1986; The Burger Court: Political and Judicial Profiles, 1991. Served to 1st lt. U.S. Army, 1972. Recipient awards in field; grantee NSF, 1974-75, Office Tech. Assessment, 1974-75, SUNY Research Found., 1982, Lyndon Baines Johnson Found., 1996, Gerald R. Ford Found., 1997. Mem. N.Y. State Polit. Sci. Assn. (pres. 1985-86), Am. Polit. Sci. Assn. (exec. com. sect. on law cts. and jud. process 1984-86, 92-94), N.E. Polit. Sci. Assn. (exec. council 1983-85), Common Cause, Law and Soc. Assn., Leadership Conf. on Civil Rights, Midwest Polit. Sci. Assn., Pi Sigma Alpha, Pi Gamma Mu, Pi Sigma Beta. Democrat. Presbyterian. Avocations: tennis; swimming. Home: 6331 Lakemont Ct East Amherst NY 14051-2055 Office: SUNY Dept Polit Sci 520 Park Hall Buffalo NY 14221-5013 Business E-Mail: clamb@acsu.buffalo.edu.

LAMB, STACIE THOMPSON, elementary school educator; b. Abilene, Tex., Nov. 9, 1965; d. George Lyman and Shirley Elizabeth (Burton) T.; m. Dennis A. Lamb; children: Lane, Logann. BS in Edn., Lubbock Christian Coll., 1986; postgrad., Tex. Tech U. Elem. Edn. grades 1-6, Tex. 1st grade tchr. Lubbock (Tex.) I.S.D. Brown Elem., 1986-87; 3rd grade tchr., chairperson Morton (Tex.) I.S.D., 1987-89; 5th grade lang. arts tchr. Whiteface (Tex.) C.I.S.D., 1990—98; pre-kindergarten tchr. White CISD, 1998—. Mem. ASCD, Classroom Tchrs. Assn. (sec. 1988-89, elem. rep. 1991-92). Office: PO Box 117 Whiteface TX 79379-0117 Home: 7324 93rd St Lubbock TX 79424-4938

LAMB, WENDY KAREN LAURENT, secondary school mathematics educator; b. N.Y.C., Mar. 26, 1952; d. Randolph William and Anne (Adam) Laurent; m. Gerald Elliot Lamb, Aug. 24, 1974; children: Jeremy Michael, Timothy Matthew. BA, SUNY, Oswego, 1974; MA, Montclair State Coll., 1979. Tchr. Grover Cleveland Jr. H.S., Caldwell, N.J., 1975-85, James Caldwell H.S., 1985—, coord. math. dept., 1994-95. Sunday sch. tchr. Cmty. Ch. of Cedar Grove, N.J., 1986-94, mem. Christian edn. com., 1999-2001; chair phone squad Meml. Middle Sch. Faculty Assn., Cedar Grove, 1992-94. Mem. N.J. Edn. Assn., Assn. Math. Tchrs. N.J., Nat. Coun. Tchrs. Math. Avocations: tennis, walking, sewing, crafts, baking. Office: James Caldwell HS Westville Ave Caldwell NJ 07006

LAMBERT, DANIEL MICHAEL, academic administrator; b. Kansas City, Mo., Jan. 16, 1941; s. Paul McKinley and Della Mae (Rogers) L.; m. Carolyn Faye Bright, Dec. 27, 1969; children: Kristian Paige, Dennis McKinley. AB, William Jewell Coll., 1963; MA, Northwestern U., 1965; postgrad., Harvard U., 1965-66; PhD, U. Mo., Columbia, 1977. Dean student affairs William Jewell Coll., Liberty, Mo., 1970-77, exec. asst. to pres., 1977-80, v.p., 1980-85; pres. College Hill Investments Inc., Liberty, 1985-87, Baker U., Baldwin City, Kans., 1987—. Bd. dirs. Ferrell Co., Liberty; dir. Kansas City Bd. of Trade, 1988-90; hon. trustee Dohto U., Japan. Bd. dirs. Nat. Assn. Intercollegiate Athletics, The Barstow Sch., Kans. Ind. Colls. Assn.; trustee Midwest Rsch. Inst. Capt. U.S. Army, 1966-70, Vietnam. Recipient Civic Leadership award Mo. Mcpl. League, 1986. Mem. KC. Home: 505 E 8th St Baldwin City KS 66006 Office: Baker U Office of Pres PO Box 65 Baldwin City KS 66006-0065

LAMBERT, DELORES ELAINE, secondary education educator; b. Fairmont, W.Va., Dec. 16, 1947; d. William Beuglas and Grace Marie (Dillon) Fletcher; m. Paul Edward Lambert, Aug. 20, 1966; children: Christopher, Abigail. BA in Edn., Fairmont (W.Va.) State Coll., 1980; MA, W.Va. U., 1989, postgrad., 1989—. H.s. English instr. Bd. Edn. Marion County, Fairmont, 1983—2000, chmn. dept. English, 1995—2000; h.s. English instr. Bd. Edn. Berkeley County, Martinsburg, W.Va., 2000—. Mem. NCTE, Alpha Delta Kappa. Avocations: reading, needlework. Home: 164 La Costa Blvd Martinsburg WV 25401 Office: Musselman High Sch 126 Excellence Way Inwood WV 25428

LAMBERT, ETHEL GIBSON CLARK, secondary school educator; b. Atlanta, Apr. 18, 1943; d. Robert Harold and Ethel (Gibson) Clark; m. Hugh Felder Lambert, June 27, 1964 (div. Nov. 3, 1988); children: Courtney, Elizabeth, Hugh Lambert Jr. BA, Oglethorpe U., Atlanta, 1965; MEd, Kennesaw State U., Marietta, Ga., 1992; EdS, State U. West Ga., Carrollton, 1997. Lic. tchr. T-6, Ga. Tchr. Clayton County Bd. Edn., Jonesboro, Ga., 1965-66, Fulton County Bd. Edn., Atlanta, 1966-67; tchr. pre-sch. weekday program First Bapt. Ch., Gainesville, Ga., 1984-88; tchr. remedial edn. program Riverdale H.S./Clayton County Bd. Edn., 1990—. Author: The Impact of Geography on the Campaigns of the Civil War Fought in Georgia, 1993, The Utilization of Georgia Historical Sites as Teaching Methodology in MIddle Grades Education, 1993, (juvenile) Obnoxious Bill, 1993, Research on Academic Motivation of Elementary, Middle and Secondary School Students in America, 1993, Reading Strategies that Address the Reluctant Reader in America's Public Middle and High Schools, 1995, Mathematics: Tying Together the World of School and the World of Work, 1996, A Martin Family History: An Interview of Aunt Clyde: "I look back..., 1999. Den leader Cub Scouts Am., Gainesville, 1980-83; mem. Christian Businessmen's Prayer Breakfast, Atlanta, 1990-95, 96. Mem. Profl. Assn. Ga. Educators, Order Ea. Star, College Park Women's Club, College Park Hist. Soc., Pi Lambda Theta. Baptist. Avocations: swimming, water skiing, reading, walking, genealogy. Home: 1881 Myrtle Dr SW Apt 711 Atlanta GA 30311-4919 Office: Riverdale High Sch 160 Roberts Dr Riverdale GA 30274-3302 E-mail: elambert@clayton.k12.ga.us.

LAMBERT, JOAN DORETY, elementary education educator; b. Trenton, N.J., Oct. 21, 1937; d. John William and Margaret (Fagan) Dorety; m. James E. Lambert Sr., June 25, 1960; children: Margi, Karen, James E., Kevin. BA, Georgian Ct. Coll., Lakewood, N.J., 1958. Cert. tchr., Pa., N.J. Tchr. 2d and 3d grades combined Washington Elem. Sch., Trenton, 1958-61; tchr. kindergarten music St. Genevieve Sch., Flourtown, Pa., 1968-78, tchr. 3d grade, 1978—. Producer, dir. musical shows for St. Genevieve Sch., 1970-78; demonstration classroom for writing process on computers Chestnut Hill Coll. Mem. Jr. League of Trenton, 1960-68, Jr. League of Phila., 1968-70. Teleflex Internat. grantee, 1989-92, Anna B. Stokes Meml. scholar, 1960, Met. Opera grantee, 1958-60. Mem. NEA. Republican. Roman Catholic. Avocations: walking, theater, reading, swimming, family activities. Home: 33 Coventry Ct Blue Bell PA 19422-2528 Office: St Genevieve Sch 1237 Bethlehem Pike Flourtown PA 19031-1902

LAMBERT, JOSEPH BUCKLEY, chemistry educator; b. Ft. Sheridan, Ill., July 4, 1940; s. Joseph Idus and Elizabeth Dorothy (Kirwan) L.; m. Mary Wakefield Pulliam, June 27, 1967; children: Laura Kirwan, Alice Pulliam, Joseph Cannon. BS, Yale U., 1962; PhD (Woodrow Wilson fellow 1962-63, NSF fellow 1962-65), Calif. Inst. Tech., 1965. Asst. prof. chemistry Northwestern U., Evanston, Ill., 1965-69, assoc. prof., 1969-74, prof. chemistry, 1974-91, Clare Hamilton Hall prof. chemistry, 1991—, Charles Deering McCormick prof., 1999—2002, chmn. dept., 1986-89, dir. integrated sci. program, 1982-85. Vis. assoc. Brit. Mus., 1973, Polish Acad. Scis., 1981, Chinese Acad. Scis., 1988. Author: Organic Structural Analysis, 1976, Physical Organic Chemistry through Solved Problems, 1978, The Multinuclear Approach to NMR Spectroscopy, 1983, Archaeological Chemistry III, 1984, Introduction to Organic Spectroscopy, 1987, Recent Advances in Organic NMR Spectroscopy, 1987, Acyclic Organonitrogen Stereodynamics, 1992, Cyclic Organonitrogen Stereodynamics, 1992, Prehistoric Human Bone, 1993, Traces of the Past, 1997, Organic Structural Spectroscopy, 1998, Nuclear Magnetic Resonance Spectroscopy, 2003; audio course Intermediate NMR Spectroscopy, 1973; editor in chief Journal of Physical Organic Chemistry; contbr. articles to sci. jours. Recipient Nat. Fresenius award, 1976, James Flack Norris award, 1987, Fryxell award, 1989, Nat. Catalyst award, 1993; Alfred P. Sloan fellow, 1968-70, Guggenheim fellow, 1973, Interacad. exch. fellow (U.S.-Poland), 1985, Air Force Office sci. rsch. fellow, 1990. Fellow AAAS, Japan Soc. for Promotion of Sci., Brit. Interplanetary Soc., Ill. Acad. Sci. (life); mem. Am. Chem. Soc. (chmn. history of chemistry divsn., 1996, F.S. Kipping award 1998), Royal Soc. Chemistry, Soc. Archaeol. Scis. (pres. 1986-87), Phi Beta Kappa, Sigma Xi (hon. lectr. 1997-98). Home: 1956 Linneman St Glenview IL 60025-4264 Office: Northwestern University Dept of Chemistry 2145 Sheridan Rd Evanston IL 60208-3113

LAMBERT, LINDA MARGARET, reading specialist; b. Livingston County, Ky., Jan. 17, 1941; d. Wiley Jackson and Florence Allie (Davidson) Stallions; m. Leland Dawson Lambert; children: Sharon Kay, Sheila Lynn, Wiley Lee. AA, Yuba Coll., 1970; BLS, Mary Washington Coll., 1980; MEd, U. Va., 1986. Cert. tchr., Va. Elem. tchr. Stafford (Va.) County Schs., 1979-91, reading specialist, 1991—, reading recovery tchr., 1997—. Mem. com. Devel. Elem. Counselors, Stafford, 1987-89, Devel. Appropriate Assessment, Stafford, 1993-94. Sponsor Ghostwriter Mystery Club, Garrisonwoods Estates, 1993-97; mem. Fairview Bapt. Ch., Stafford Dem. Com., 1996—; del. Va. State Dem. Convention. Mem. NEA, Reading Recovery Coun. N.Am., Va. Edn. Assn., Stafford County Edn. Assn., Internat. Reading Assn., Va. State Reading Assn., Rappahanock Reading Coun., Hist. Fredericksburg Antique Automobile Club. Democrat. Avocations: swimming, reading, antiques. Home: 203 Rumford Rd Fredericksburg VA 22405-3206 Office: Hampton Oaks Elem Sch 107 Northampton Blvd Stafford VA 22554-7660

LAMBERT, LYNDA JEANNE, humanities and arts educator, artist; b. Ellwood City, Pa., Aug. 27, 1943; d. William Joseph McKinney and Esther Louella Kirker; m. Charles Robert Lambert, April 14, 1961; children: Salome Yaromey, Heidi McClure, Victoria Jacques, Ilsa Barry, R. Andrew. BFA, Slippery Rock U. of Pa., 1989, MA in English, 1994; MFA, W.Va. U., 1991. Gallery mgr., instr. W.Va. U., Morgantown, 1989-91; grants specialist West Valley Coll., Saratoga, Calif., 1991-92; exec. dir. Hoyt Inst. of Fine Arts, New Castle, Pa., 1992-96; assoc. prof. fine art and humanities Geneva Coll., Beaver Falls, Pa., 1997—. Site surveyor Am. Assn. Mus., Washington, 1998-2001; panel mem. Pa. Ptnrs. in the Arts, Loretto, 1997-2000; presenter in field. Author: Concerti: Psalms for the Pilgrimage, 2002; Trunk Show. Active workshop on printmaking Girl Scouts, Geneva Coll., 1999. Recipient Woman of Distinction award Beaver Castle Girl Scouts, Pa., 1995, Cash award Carnegie Mus. Art, Pitts., 1999, 2000, award of excellence in scholarship Geneava Coll., 2000, award of excellence Beaver Valley Internat. Art Festival, 2002; permanent exhibit includes Ambassadors Residence, Papua New Guinea, 2001—. Mem. Nat. Assn. Women Artists, Womens Caucus for Art, Associated Artists Pitts. (mem. exhbn. com.). Avocations: antique collecting, viking glass research, riding motorcycles. Home: 104 River Rd Ellwood City PA 16117-2607 Office: Geneva Coll 3200 College Ave Beaver Falls PA 15010-3557 E-mail: lyndalambert@zoominternet.net., llambert@geneva.edu.

LAMBERT, NADINE MURPHY, psychologist, educator; b. Ephraim, Utah; m. Robert E. Lambert, 1956; children— Laura Allan, Jeffrey. PhD in Psychology, U. So. Calif., 1965. Diplomate Am. Bd. Profl. Psychology, Am. Bd. Sch. Psychology. Sch. psychologist Los Nietos Sch. Dist., Whittier, Calif., 1952-53, Bellflower (Calif.) Unified Sch. Dist., 1953-58; research cons. Calif. Dept. Edn., Los Angeles, 1958-64; dir. sch. psychology tng. program U. Calif., Berkeley, 1964—, asst. prof. edn., 1964-70, assoc. prof., 1970-76, prof., 1976—, assoc. dean for student svcs., 1988-94. Mem. Joint Com. Mental Health of Children, 1967-68; cons. state depts. edn., Calif., Ga., Fla.; cons. Calif. Dept. Justice; mem. panel on testing handicapped people Nat. Acad. Scis., 1978-81. Author: School Version of the AAMD Adaptive Behavior Scale, 3d edit., 1993; co-author: (with Wilcox and Gleason) Educationally Retarded Child: Comprehensive Assessment and Planning for the EMR and Slow-Learning Child, 1974, (with Hartsough and Bower) Process for Assessment of Effective Functioning, 1981, (with Windmiller and Turiel) Moral Development and Socialization — Three Perspectives, 1979; assoc. editor Am. Jour. Orthopsychiatry, 1975-81, Am. Jour. Mental Deficiency, 1977-80, (with McCombs) How Students Learn-Reforming Schools Through Learner-Centered Education, 1998, (with Hylander and Sanoval) Consultee-Centered Consultation, 2003, others. With Hartsough and Sandoval Children's Attention and Adjustment Survey, 1990. Recipient Dorothy Hughes award for outstanding contbn. to ednl. and sch. psychology NYU, 1990, Tobacco Disease Related Rsch. award U. Calif., 1990-94, NIDA, 1994-2001; grantee NIMH, 1965-87, Calif. State Dept. Edn., 1-72, 76-78, NHSTE Dept. Transportation, 1995. Fellow APA (coun. reps. divsn. sch. psychologists, bd. dirs. 1984-87, mem. bd. profl. affairs 1981-83, bd. ednl. affairs 1991-94, chmn. 1992-94, exec. com. divsn. sch. psychology 1994-96, mem. commn. for recognition of specialities in psychology 1993-97, Disting. Svc. award 1980, award for disting. profl. contbns. 1986, award for disting. career contbns. of applications of psychology to edn. and tng. 1999), Nat. Assn. of Sch. Psychologists (hon., Legend in Sch. Psychology 1998), Am. Orthopsychiat. Assn.; mem. NEA, Calif. Assn. Sch. Psychologists (pres. 1962-63, Sandra Goff award 1985). Office: U Calif Dept Education Berkeley CA 94720-1670 E-mail: nlambert@socrates.berkeley.edu.

LAMBERT, RICHARD WILLIAM, mathematics educator; b. Gettysburg, Pa., May 1, 1928; s. Allen Clay and Orpha Rose (Hoppert) L.; m. Phyllis Jean Bain, Sept. 2, 1949 (div. May 1982); children: James Harold, Dean Richard; m. Kathleen Ann Waring, Aug. 30, 1982; stepchildren: Gregory Scott Gibbs, LeAnn Marie Gibbs. BS, Oreg. State U., 1952; MA in Teaching Math., Reed Coll., 1962. Instr. Siuslaw High Sch., Florence, Oreg., 1954-55, David Douglas High Sch., Portland, Oreg., 1955-67, Mt. Hood Community Coll., Gresham, Oreg., 1967-87, ret., 1987. NSF grantee, 1959, 60, 62. Mem. Nat. Coun. Tchr. Math., Am. Math Soc., Math. Assn. Am., Am. Math. Assn. of Two Yr. Colls., Oreg. Coun. Tchrs. Math. Democrat. Methodist. Avocations: travel, camping, home improvements, reading. Home: 11621 SE Lexington St Portland OR 97266-5933

LAMBERT, WILLIE LEE BELL, mobile equipment company owner, educator; b. Texas City, Tex., Oct. 23, 1929; d. William Henry and Una Oda (Stafford) Bell; m. Eddie Roy Lambert, July 2, 1949; (dec. Mar. 1980); children: Sondra Kay Lambert Bradford, Eddie Lee. Degree in bus., Met. Bus. Coll., 1950; AAS, Coll. of Mainland, 1971; BS, Sam Houston U., 1976. Cert. hand and foot reflexologist, Hatha Yoga instr. Sec. Judges Reddell & Hopkins, Texas City, 1945-47, Union Carbide Chemicals, Texas City, 1947-48, John Powers Modeling, 1948—49, Charles Martin Petroleum, Texas City, 1948-50; acct. Goodyear Co., La Marque, Tex., 1968-70; instr. Coll. of the Mainland, Texas City, 1970—, serials libr., 1970-77, instr., 1970; exec. dir., office mgr. Mobile Air Conditioning, La Marque, 1977-80; owner Kivert, Inc., La Marque, 1982—; ptnr., exec. dir. A/C Mobile Equipment Corp., La Marque, 1988—94. Owner Star Bell Ranch, 1985—. Vol. Union Carbide Chems., Texas City, 1970—, Carbide Retiree Corp., Inc., Texas City, 1980—, Hospice, Galveston, Tex., 1985—, various polit. campaigns, Texas City, 1951-62, MD Anderson Cancer Inst., U. Tex., 1995—; v.p. Coalition on Aging Galveston County, Tex. City, 1990-92; vol. Baylor Coll. Medicine, Houston, 1990—; mem. adv. coun. bd. Galveston County Sr. Citizens, Galveston, 1990—; mem. planning bd. Heart Fund and Cancer Fund, Texas City, 1953-62, Santa Fe (Tex.) St. Citizens, 1990—; benefactor mem. Mainland Mus., Texas City, Tex., 1994—; sec. YMCA, 1947-55; sec. Ladies VFW, 1950-59; leader Girl Scouts Am., 1958-65; v.p. PTA, 1957-60; counselor Bapt. Ch. Camp, 1960-64; v.p. Santa Fe Booster Club, 1963-67; mem. Internat. Platform Assn., 1995—. Named Vol. of Yr., Heights Elem. Sch., Texas City Sch. Dist., 1959, Most Glamorous Grandmother, 1985, Mother of Yr., Texas City/La Marque C. of C., 1990, Unsung Hero award Texas City, 1995, 96, 97, 99, 2001, 02; named to Tex. Women's Hall of Fame, 1984. Mem. Internat. Platform Assn. Republican. Baptist. Avocations: making porcelain dolls and soft sculpture dolls, painting china portraits, sewing, needlework, volunteer work. Home: PO Box 1253 Santa Fe TX 77510-1253

LAMBERTI, GARY ANTHONY, biology educator; b. Oakland, Calif., Oct. 5, 1953; s. Antonio A. and Olga C. (Caviglia) L.; m. Donna Packer, June 2, 1990; children: Matthew Lewis, Sara Kathryn. BS, U. Calif., Davis, 1975; PhD, U. Calif., Berkeley, 1983. Postdoctoral assoc. U. Calif., Berkeley, 1983-84; rsch. assoc. Oreg. State U., Corvallis, 1984-86, asst. prof., 1986-89; asst. prof. dept. biol. scis. U. Notre Dame, Ind., 1989-95, assoc. prof., 1995—2000, prof., 2000—, asst. chair biol. scis., 2001—, dir. environ. biology grad. tng. program. Presenter at profl. confs. Editor: Methods in Stream Ecology, 1996; assoc. editor Jour. N.Am. Benthol. Soc., Lawrence, Kans., 1991-96, Ecological Applications, 2001-; author tech. reports, symposium papers; contbr. 15 chpts. to books, 60 articles to profl. jours. NIH fellow, U. Calif., 1977; grantee NSF, 1990, 95, 2000. Mem. AAAS, Am. Inst. Biol. Scis., Ecol. Soc. Am., N.Am. Benthological Soc. (chmn. exec. com. 1986-87, pres. 1997-98, Best Paper award 1982). Achievements include first demonstration of importance of plant-animal interactions in stream ecosystems. Office: Univ Notre Dame Dept Biol Scis Notre Dame IN 46556-0369

LAMBRIX, WINIFRED MARIE MCFARLANE, retired elementary education educator; b. Phoenix, June 5, 1947; d. James McFarlane and Alice Lucille (McFarlane) Nedoff; m. Leroy Edward Lambrix, May 28, 1976; 1 child, Michael John. Diploma, Grand Rapids Sch. Bible & Music, 1968; BA, Cedarville Coll., 1970; postgrad., Western Mich. U., 1971-72, Grand Valley State Coll., 1974-75, Bakersfield Coll., 1978-80, Calif. State U., Bakersfield, 1987; MS, LaVerne U., 1993. Cert. tchr. art and music K-12, Mich., Calif.; cert. tchr. multiple subjects, Calif.; cert. in pupil pers. svc., Calif.; cert. adminstr., Calif.; cert. resource specialist. Tchr. S.W. Sch., Wyoming (Mich.) Pub. Sch., 1970-75; substitute tchr. Bakersfield area schs., 1976-82; kindergarten tchr. Planz Sch., Greenfield Union Sch. Dist., Bakersfield, 1982-2000; resource specialist Planz Sch., 1994-2000; ret.; pres. Dollars & Sense, 2003—04. Adj. faculty Bakersfield Coll. Sign Lang. Lab., 2001—02; adv. bd. Bakersfield-Greater L.A. Coun. Deafness., 2003, sec., 03. Paintings exhibited in various group shows, 1977-82 (numerous awards). Bd. dirs., sec. Artisan's Guild, Bakersfield, 1977-82. Avocations: art, music, children's choirs, american sign language.

LAMM, HARRIET A. mathematics educator; b. Beeville, Tex., Dec. 4, 1948; d. James R. and Dorothy D. (Kendall) L. BA, Tex. Christian U., 1971; BS in Edn., S.W. Tex. State U., 1973, MEd, 1976; PhD, Tex. A&M U., 1993. Cert. secondary tchr., Tex. Instr. math. South San Antonio Ind. Sch. Dist., San Antonio, 1973-74; teaching asst. in math. S.W. Tex. State U., San Marcos, 1974-76; tchr. math. Seguin (Tex.) Ind. Sch. Dist., 1976-78, George West (Tex.) Ind. Sch. Dist., 1978-83, Lingleville (Tex.) Ind. Sch. Dist., 1983, Northside Ind. Sch. Dist., San Antonio, 1984-87, Beeville (Tex.) Ind. Sch. Dist., 1987-88; teaching asst. Tex. A&M U., College Station, 1991-92; instr. math. Coastal Bend Coll., Beeville, 1988-91, 1992-01; asst. project dir. Tex A&M U., Corpus Christi, 01—. Instr. math. Tarleton State U., Stephenville, Tex., 1983. Mem. Nat. Coun. Tchrs. Math., Tex. Coun. Tchrs. Math., Sch. Sci. and Math. Assn., Math. Assn. Am., Assn. Tex. Educators, Rsch. Coun. for Math. Learning. Avocations: ranching, sculpture, drawing.

LAMM, NORMAN, academic administrator, rabbi; b. Bklyn., Dec. 19, 1927; s. Samuel and Pearl (Baumol) L.; m. Mindella Mehler, Feb. 23, 1954; children: Chaye Lamm Warburg, Joshua B., Shalom E., Sara Rebecca Lamm Dratch. BA summa cum laude, Yeshiva Coll., 1949; PhD, Bernard Revel Grad. Sch., 1966; Dr. of Hebrew Letters (hon.), Hebrew Theol. Coll., 1977, Gratz Coll., 1999. Cert. Ordained rabbi 1951. Ordained rabbi, 1951; asst. rabbi Congregation Kehilath Jeshurun, N.Y.C., 1952—53; rabbi Congregation Kodimoh, Springfield, Mass., 1954—58, Jewish Center, N.Y.C., 1958—76; Erna and Jakob Michael prof. Jewish philosophy Yeshiva U., N.Y.C., 1966—, pres., 1976—2002, Rabbi Isaac Elchanan Theol. Sem., N.Y.C., 1976—; chancellor Yeshiva U., 2002—. Vis. prof. Judaic studies Bklyn. Coll., 1974-75; dir. Union Orthodox Jewish Congregations Am. Author: A Hedge of Roses, 1966, The Royal Reach, 1970, Faith and Doubt, 1971, Torah Lishmah, 1972 (rev. English edition 1989), The Good Society, 1974, Halakot ve'Halikhot: Essays on Jewish Law, 1990, Torah Umadda: The Encounter of Religious Learning and Worldly Knowledge in the Jewish Tradition, 1990, The Shema: Spirituality and Law in Judaism, 1998, The Religious Thought of Hasidism: Text and Commentary, 1999 (Nat. Jewish Book awrd); editor: Library of Jewish Law and Ethics, 1975—; co-editor: The Leo Jung Jubilee Volume, 1962, A Treasury of Tradition, 1967, The Joseph B. Soloveitchik Jubilee Vol., 1984, Halakhot ve'Halikhot (Heb.): Essays on Jewish Law, 1990, Torah Umadda: The Encounter of Religious Learning and Worldly Knowledge in the Jewish Tradition, 1990. Trustee-at-large Fedn. Jewish Philanthropies, N.Y.; mem. exec. com. Assn. for a Better N.Y.; bd. dirs. Am. Friends-Alliance Israelite Universelle; mem. Pres.'s Commn. on the Holocaust, 1978-89; chmn. N.Y. Conf. on Soviet Jewry, 1970; mem. Halakhah Commn., Rabbinical Council Am. Recipient Abramowitz Zeitlin award, 1972 Mem. Assn. Orthodox Jewish Scientists (charter; bd. govs.) Office: Yeshiva U Office of Pres 500 W 185th St New York NY 10033-3201 also: Rabbi Isaac Eichanan Theol Sem 2540 Amsterdam Ave New York NY 10033-2807

LAMONE, RUDOLPH PHILIP, business educator; b. Wellsburg, W.Va., Dec. 20, 1931; s. Dominic and Maria (Branch) L.; m. Linda A. Hefler, Jan. 29, 1970. BS, U. N.C., Chapel Hill, 1960, PhD, 1966. Instr. U. N.C., 1963-66; mem. faculty U. Md., College Park, 1966—, prof. mgmt. sci., 1971—, dean Coll. Bus. and Mgmt., 1973-92, prof., chair adv. bd. Michael

Dingman Ctr. Entrepreneurship, 1993—. Bd. dirs. Md. Ctr. Productivity and Quality of Working Life, EA Engring. Sci. and Tech. Inc.; chmn. govtl. rels. com. Am. Assembly Collegiate Schs. Bus., 1977-78; cons. Tatung Co., Taiwan; mem. adv. com. Md. Dept. Econ. and Cmty. Devel. Co-author: Linear Programming for Management Decisions, 1969, Marketing Management and the Decision Sciences, 1971, Production-Operations Management, 1972. Served with AUS, 1952-55. Mem. Acad. Mgmt., Inst. Mgmt. Scis., Am. Inst. Decision Scis., Md. C. of C. (dir.), Phi Beta Kappa, Beta Gamma Sigma. Clubs: Annapolis Yacht (bd. dirs.). Democrat. Roman Catholic. Office: U Md Dingman Ctr Entrepreneur Robert H Smith Sch Bus College Park MD 20742-0001

LAMPERTI, JOHN WILLIAMS, mathematician, educator; b. Montclair, N.J., Dec. 20, 1932; s. Frank A. and Louise (Williams) L.; m. Claudia Jane McKay, Aug. 17, 1957; children— Matthew, Steven, Aaron, Noelle. BS, Haverford Coll., 1953; PhD, Calif. Inst. Tech., 1957. Instr., then asst. prof. math. Stanford (Calif.) U., 1957-62; rsch. assoc. Rockefeller Inst., 1962-63; faculty Dartmouth Coll., Hanover, N.H., 1963-98, prof. math., 1968-98, prof. emeritus, 1998—. Sci. exch. visitor to USSR, 1970; vis. prof. U. Aarhus, Denmark, 1972-73, Nicaraguan Nat. U., 1990; cons. Am. Friends Svc. Com., 1980, 85, 91. Author: Probability: A Survey of the Mathematical Theory, 1966, 2d edit., 1996, Stochastic Processes: A survey of the Mathematical Theory, 1977, What Are We Afraid Of? An Assessment of the "Communist Threat" in Central America, 1988. Fellow Inst. Math. Stats.; mem. ACLU, War Resisters League, Peace Action, Amnesty Internat., Fedn. Am. Scientists. Home: Upper Loveland Rd Norwich VT 05055 Office: Dartmouth Coll Dept Math Hanover NH 03755 E-mail: j.lamperti@dartmouth.edu.

LAMSON, ROBERT WOODROW, retired school system administrator; b. L.A., Dec. 28, 1917; s. Ernest K. and Mabel (Mahoney) L.; m. Jeannette Juett, July 22, 1949; children: Robert Woodrow Jr., Nancy Virginia, Kathleen Patricia. BA, Occidental Coll., 1940; MA, U. So. Calif., 1955. Cert. tchr., prin., supt., Calif. Tchr. El Monte (Calif.) Sch. Dist., 1940-43, L.A. City Sch. Dist., 1945—78, prin., 1949-55, supr., 1955-57, adminstrv. asst., 1957-59, area supt., 1959-78; ret., 1978; agt. Keilholtz Realtors, La Canada, Calif. Instr. various colls. and univs. so. Calif.; one of founders, v.p., bd. dirs. U.S. Acad. Decathlon, Cerritos, Calif., 1981-86. Bd. dirs. 10th Dist. PTA, L.A., 1965-70; chmn. Scout-O-Rama, Gt. Western coun. Boy Scouts Am., 1980. Lt. comdr. USNR, 1943-46, mem. Res. ret. Mem. Am. Assn. Sch. Adminstrs., Assn. Adminstrs. L.A., Alumni Occidental Coll. in Edn. (a founder, past pres., bd. dirs.), Town Hall, Nat. PTA (hon. life), Calif. PTA (hon. life, bd. dirs. 1978-80), 31st Dist. PTA (hon. life, bd. dirs. 1965-78, auditorium named in his honor 1978), Phi Beta Kappa, Alpha Tau Omega. Republican. Avocations: gardening, reading. Home: 4911 Vineta Ave La Canada Flintridge CA 91011-2624 Office: Richard Keilholtz Realtors 727 Foothill Blvd La Canada Flintridge CA 91011-3405

LAMUN, JOANNE, theatre producer, writer, educator, director; b. Casper, Wyo., Apr. 20, 1939; d. Lloyd Kenneth and Anne (Dilso) Blower; m. John R. Lamun, June 17, 1961 (div. 1987); children: Laura Anne, Lisa Christine. BS in Speech, Northwestern U., 1961; MA in Theatre, U. Colo., 1965. Tchr. Boulder (Colo.) Valley Schs., 1962-66, 92—; tchr. Davidson (Mich.) H.S., 1966-67, Royal Oak (Mich.) Pub. Schs., 1968-72, St. Agatha H.S., Redford, Mich., 1980-91; founder, prodr., dir. Lathrup Youtheater, Lathrup Village, Mich., 1973-91, Peanut Butter Players, Lathrup Village and Boulder, 1987—. Author: (children's mus.) Once Upon a Rainbow, 1980 (Playwriting award), There's A Frog..., 1982, Double Dealing With the Devil, 1984, Wild, Wild Quest, 1985, Sandcastles, 1985, Listen to the Children, 1987, Peter Pandemonium, 1990, Snow White 2000, 1996, Beatrace, 2003. Active mem. theatre adv. bd. Denver Children's Mus., 1996—. Recipient Best of Boulder (Peanut Butter Players) Boulder Daily Camera, 1993, 94, 97, 98, 99, 2000, 01, 02, 03, Boulder Daily Camera Pacesetter, 1999. Avocations: needlepoint, knitting, reading, gardening. Home and Office: Peanut Butter Players 2445 Mapleton Ave Boulder CO 80304-3755

LANCASTER, ALDEN, educational and management consultant; b. Balt., Feb. 25, 1956; d. Henry Carrington and Martha (Roe) L. BA magna cum laude, Duke U., 1977; MA, George Washington U., 1979. Program designer, coord. Duke U. and George Washington U., 1977-79; mgr. profl. devel. and tng. programs Nat. Assn. Coll. and Univ. Bus. Officers, Washington, 1979-80; assoc. dir. refugee relief agy. Ch. of the Saviour, Bangkok, 1980-81; dir. cmty. svcs. U.S. Cath. Conf. Refugee Resettlement Agy., San Diego, 1981-82; nat. project dir. Bread for the World Ednl. Fund, Washington, 1982-83; edn. dir., exec. dir. Ptnrs. for Global Justice, Washington, 1983-85; dir. adult edn. programs, tchr. Spanish Ednl. Devel. Ctr., Washington, 1983-86; exec. dir., cons. Samaritan Ministry Greater Washington, 1985-87; career counselor, tng. cons. Rockport Inst., Washington, 1985—89; dir. nat. literacy tng., ednl. cons. Assn. for Community Based Edn., Washington, 1987—; mgmt. cons. Women's Tech. Assistance Project, Ctr. Cmty. Change, Washington, 1988-89; ednl. cons. George Washington U., Washington, 1989-93, Pub./Pvt. Ventures, Phila., Savannah, Ga., Ft. Lauderdale, Fla., 1990-91; sr. cons., dir. nat. literacy projects Wider Opportunities for Women, Washington, 1991-94. Mem. nat. adv. bd. Project Lifelong Learning, Pa. State for Study Adult Literacy, 1992—93; sr. ednl. cons. United Way of Am., 1992—95; curriculum devel. cons. Eckerd Family Youth Alternatives, Clearwater, Fla., 1993—94; sr. literacy staff devel. and evaluation cons. U.S. Nat. Inst. Literacy, 1993—; sr. program and staff devel. cons. Ramah Navajo Sch. Bd., Pine Hill, N.Mex., 1993—; adj. prof. George Washington U. Grad. Sch. Edn., 1993; sr. cons. State of Utah Dept. Edn., 1994; sr. contextual literacy cons. Friends of the Family, Inc., Balt., 1994—2000; sr. literacy staff devel. participatory evaluation cons. State of Maine, 1994—96; sr. contextual literacy cons. State of S.C. Literacy Resource Ctr., 1995—96; staff devel. cons. Centro de Estudios de Espanol Pop Wuj, Quetzaltenango, Guatemala, 1995; sr. adult literacy expert Atlantic Resources Corp., Manassas, Va., 1995—97; tng. of trainers cons. Neighborhoods, Inc., Battle Creek, Mich., 1995—96; sr. adult literacy advisor Am. Inst. for Rsch.-CIR, Roslyn, Va., 1996—; trainer of trainers, author, evaluator D.C. Literacy Resource Ctr., 1996—; ednl. TV outreach cons. Mars Hill and York TV Assocs., 1996—2000; sr. cons. mgmt. and orgnl. devel., tng. and career devel. McNeil Techs. U.S. Dept. Energy, Energy Efficiency and Renewable Energy, 1997—, U.S. Dept. of Commerce, Office of Civil Rights, 1999; new sch. proposal expert reviewer D.C. Pub. Charter Sch. Bd., Washington, 1997—2000; mgmt. devel. cons. Laubach Lit. Action/ Proliteracy Worldwide, Syracuse, NY, 1997—; evaluator U.S. Corp. Nat. and Cmty. Svc Literacy AmeriCorps Prog, 2001—02, Nat. Alliance Urban Literacy Coalitions, Houston, 2003, D.C. Literacy AmeriCorps program, 2002—; sr. trainer Voice Adult Literacy United Edn., Phila., 2003—, designer train the trainer, 2003—, tng. evaluator, 2003—; edn. soc. change cons. United Fair Economy/ Responsible Wealth, Boston, 2002—. Co-author: National Institute for Literacy 1992-93 National Literacy Grants Final Report, 1995; author: An Introduction to Intergenerational Literacy, 1992, Guidelines for Developing Adult Literacy Curriculum, 2003; co-author: (with Thomas G. Sticht) Functional Context Education: A Primer for Program Providers, 1992; editor, primary author (with Paulo Freire): Literacy for Empowerment: A Resource Handbook for Community Based Educators (with preface by Paulo Freire), 1989. Democrat. Mem. Soc. Friends. Home and Office: 6708 Poplar Ave Takoma Park MD 20912-4810

LANCASTER, CAROLYN HOHN, secondary school educator; b. Harrison/Allegheny County, Pa., July 24, 1952; d. Carl Maurice Sr. and Doris Myrtle (Gilday) Hohn; m. Walter T. Johnson, Sept. 4, 1971 (dec. Oct. 1979); 1 child, David Alan Johnson; m. Ronald Lee Lancaster, Mar. 31, 1988. AAS, Cape Fear Tech. Inst., Wilmington, N.C., 1986; BS, U. Ctrl. Fla., Orlando, 1981; MS, N.C. A&T State U., Greensboro, 1993. Cert. technology, electronics tchr., N.C. Computer technician Nat. Data Processing GE, Wilmington, 1986-88; electronics technician Applied Tech. Assn., New Bern, N.C., 1988-89; computer tchr. Onslow County Schs., Jacksonville, N.C., 1989-90; indsl. arts tchr. Person County Schs., Roxboro, N.C., 1992-93; technology tchr. Alamance County Schs., Graham, N.C., 1993—. Technology advisor Technology Student Assn., Graham, N.C., 1994—; chairperson Raleigh Regional Program Area Leadership Coun. for Tech., 1996-97; vice chair Raleigh region Program Area Leadership Coun. for Tech., 1995-96; advisor Am. Tech. Honor Soc., 1996—. Mem. Jaycees, Orlando, 1980. With USCG Res., 1985-88. Recipient Tandy Tchr. Award cert. 1995-96; Profl. Devel. scholar N.C. Technology Educators Assn., 1993. Mem. NEA, N.C. Edn. Assn., Am. Vocat. Assn., Internat. Tech. Educators Assn., N.C. Tech. Educators Assn., Nat. Assn. Underwater Instrs., Am. Tech. Honor Soc. Methodist. Avocations: swimming, computers. Home: 2605 White Pine Dr Mebane NC 27302-8133 Office: Graham HS 903 Trollinger Rd Graham NC 27253-1945

LANCOUR, KAREN LOUISE, secondary education educator; b. Cheboygan, Mich., June 2, 1946; d. Clinton Howard and Dorothy Marie (Passeno) L. AA, Alpena Community Coll., 1966; BA, Ea. Mich. U., 1968, MS, 1970. Teaching asst. Ea. Mich. U., Ypsilanti, 1968-70; tchr. sci. Utica (Mich.) Community Schs., 1970-98, ret., 1998. Editor Sci. Olympiad Nat. Dir.'s Man., 2000—. Nat. event supr. Sci. Olympiad, 1986—, mem. nat. rules com., 1987—, Mich. state event supr., 1986—, regional dir., 1987, state bd., 1998—. Recipient Disting. Svc. award Nat. Sci. Olympiad, 1995. Mem. Nat. Sci. Tchrs. Assn., Mich. Sci. Tchrs. Assn., Nat. Assn. Biology Tchrs., Met. Detroit Sci. Tchrs. Assn. (Outstanding Sci. Educator award 1997), Smithsonian Inst., Nat. Geographic Soc., Edison Inst., Mortar Bd., Internat. Biograph. Soc., Am. Biograph. Inst. Rsch. Assn. (dep. gov.), Internat. Platform Assn., Phi Theta Kappa, Kappa Delta Phi. Home: 312 W Bosley St Alpena MI 49707-2126

LAND, BETTY LOU JACKSON, reading educator, writer; b. Southern Pines, NC, Mar. 22, 1947; d. James Lamar and Hermione (Dannelly) Jackson; m. J. Philip Land, June 25, 1970; children: Helen, Philip. BA in Elem. Edn., Samford U., 1969; MA in Elem. Edn., U. Ala., 1970; EdS in Reading, Winthrop Coll., Rock Hill, S.C., 1979; PhD in Early Childhood Edn., U of S.C., 1983. Elementary sch. tchr. Birmingham (Ala.) Bd. Edn., 1970-72, 74-75; prof. reading edn. Winthrop U., Rock Hill, SC, 1975—; writer Sunday Sch. Bd., So. Bapt. Conv., Nashville, 1984—95. Cons. Ft. Mill (S.C.) Sch. Dist., Rock Hill Sch. Dist., Chester (S.C.) County Sch. Dist., Kershaw County Sch. Dist., Camden, S.C., Prime Time, Chester Co. Libr., J. Marion Sims. Found. Author: God Sends His Son, 1986, Finding Ways to Show Kindness, 1988, 2d edit., 1991, Discovering Ways to Learn, 1989, Learning About Families, 1990, Learning to Obey God, 1991, Worshiping God, 1992, God Helps Us Make Good Choices, 1993, Literacy Strategies, 2003; author Tchr.'s Guide for Sunday Sch. Curriculum, Pupils' Quar. Sunday Sch. tchr., dir., deacon Oakland Bapt. Ch., Rock Hill, 1975—. Named to Outstanding Young Women of Yr., Rock Hill Jaycees, 1981; recipient Kinard award, 1991; named Disting. prof. Winthrop U., 2003. Mem. Internat. Reading Assn., S.C. Coll. Assn. Reading Educators, Kappa Delta Pi (counselor 1983—), Phi Delta Kappa, Phi Kappa Phi (chmn. nominating com. 1988, Excellence in Tchg. award 1977-78, 84-87, 90-91, 97-98), Omicron Delta Kappa. Home: 3393 Tanglewood St Rock Hill SC 29732-8649 Office: Winthrop U Withers Bldg Rock Hill SC 29733-0001

LANDAU, MICHAEL B. law educator, musician, writer; b. Wilkes-Barre, Pa., July 3, 1953; s. Jack Landau and Florence (Rabitz) Simon. BA, Pa. State U., 1975; JD, U. Pa., 1988. Vis. prof. law Dickinson Sch. Law, Pa. State U., Carlisle; assoc. Cravath, Swaine and Moore, N.Y.C., 1988-90, Skadden, Arps, N.Y.C., 1990-92; assoc. prof. Coll. Law Ga. State U., Atlanta, 1992-99, prof. law, 1999—. Vis. prof. law U. Ga. Law Sch., 1998; guest lectr. Johannes Kepler U., Linz, Austria, summer 1994, 95, 96; vis. scholar Univ. Amsterdam, 2000. Contbr. articles to law jours. on copyright, art, patent, entertainment law. Mem. ABA, N.Y. State Bar Assn., Internat. Bar Assn., Vol. Lawyers for Arts, Am. Fedn. Musicians, Am. Intellectual Property Law Assn., Copyright Soc. U.S. Am., Phi Kappa Phi, Omicron Delta Epsilon. Democrat. Avocations: photography, jazz guitar, jazz piano. Office: Ga State U Coll Law University Pla Atlanta GA 30303 E-mail: mlandau@gsu.edu.

LANDAU, SARAH BRADFORD, fine arts educator, author; b. Raleigh, N.C., Mar. 27, 1935; d. Zachary Bowman and Lacy (Gaston) Bradford; m. Sidney I. Landau, June 19, 1959; children: Paul Stuart, Amy Bradford. BFA, U. N.C., Greensboro, 1957; MA, Inst. Fine Arts, NYU, 1959, PhD, 1978. Landmarks preservation specialist N.Y.C. Landmarks Preservation Commn., 1975-76; instr. dept. of fine arts NYU, N.Y.C., 1971-73, 76-78, asst. prof., 1978-84, assoc. prof., 1984-96, prof., 1996—; guest curator Art Inst. of Chgo., 1981-82, The N.Y. Hist. Soc., 1998-99; cons. in field. Author: Edward T. and William A. Potter: American Victorian Architects, 1979, P.B. Wight: Architect, Contractor, Critic, 1838-1925, 1981, (with Carl W. Condit) Rise of the New York Skyscraper, 1865-1913, 1996, George B. Post, Architect: Picturesque Designer and Determined Realist, 1998; editor: (with Jan Cigliano) The Grand American Avenue, 1850-1920, 1994; contbr. articles to profl. jours. Commr. N.Y.C. Landmarks Preservation Commn., 1987-96, vice chair, 1993-96. Recipient Lucy G. Moses Preservation Leadership award N.Y. Landmarks Conservancy, 1997; fellow Woodrow Wilson Found., 1958-59, AAUW, 1974-75, NEH, 1979-80, Graham Found., 1980-81, Am. Council Learned Socs., 1985-86; grantee Mellon Found, 1984, AIA Coll. Fellows, 1984-85, N.Y. State Council on the Arts, 1987-88. Mem. Coll. Art Assn., Soc. Archtl. Historians (v.p. local chpt. 1980-86, bd. dirs. 1989-92), Victorian Soc. Am. Office: NYU Dept Fine Arts 303 Silver Center Washington Sq New York NY 10003

LANDAUER, ELVIE ANN WHITNEY, humanities educator, writer; b. Detroit, Dec. 10, 1937; d. Augustus and Leona (Green) Moore; m. Thomas Whitney, 1963 (div. 1978); m. Ernest Landauer, Dec. 31, 1987. BA, Calif. State U., L.A., 1978; MA, San Francisco State U., 1989; postgrad., U. N.Mex. Dep. dir. Calif. Arts Coun., Sacramento, 1976-79; exec. dir. Mothers Emergency Svc., Sacramento, 1979-82; assoc. dir. San Francisco Cmty. Bds., 1982-83; adminstr. San Francisco Rsch. Project, 1983-86; exec. dir. East Bay Ctr. for Performing Arts, Richmond, Calif., 1987-89; instr. English Calif. C.C.s, Pittsburg, Fremont & Hayward, 1990-93; instr. Am. studies U. N.Mex., Alburg, 1993-94; instr. humanities New Coll., San Francisco, 1994-95. Bus. owner, pub. Academics of Course! Books, Vallejo, Calif., 1997—; rschr. L.A. Cmty. Arts Alliance, 1972. Author: (drama anthology) The Disinherited, 1971, The Uptown Mrs. Carrie, 1989; prodr.: Meat Theater Co., 1970—72. Bd. dirs. Richmond (Calif.) Arts Coun., 1986-89; workshop coord. L.A. Writers Workshop, 1966-69, Sacramento Civic Theater, 1980; project coord. City Spirit Project, Pasadena, Calif., 1972-75. With USN, 1958-61. Recipient Woman of Yr. award Iota Phi Lambda, Sacramento, 1981. Home: 100 Kathy Ellen Ct Vallejo CA 94591-

LANDEN, SANDRA JOYCE, psychologist, educator; b. L.A., May 8, 1960; married, Aug. 1981. BA, UCLA, 1982, MA, 1984, PhD, 1988. Lic. clin. psychologist, Calif. Rsch. asst. UCLA Autism Clinic, 1980-82, UCLA Teaching Homes for Devel. Disabilities Project, 1981-82; rsch. assoc. UCLA Project for Devel. Disabilities, 1982-87; co-coord. parent tng. program UCI-UCLA Program for ADHD Children, 1984; teaching assoc. psychology dept. UCLA, 1984-87; psychology intern Hathaway Home for Children, Lakeview Terrace, Calif., 1985-86, clin. staff, 1986-87; clin. postdoctoral fellow Childrens Hosp. L.A., 1987-88; adj. faculty Grad. Sch. Edn. and Psychology Pepperdine U., L.A., 1988—2000; psychologist L.A., 1987—. Contbr. articles to profl. jours. Recipient scholarship UCLA, 1978-82, fellowship UCLA, 1982-85, dissertation rsch. grant UCLA, 1985-87. Mem. APA (divsn. psychoanalysis), Calif. Psychol. Assn., L.A. Psychol. Assn., Am. Assn. Mental Retardation. Office: 11500 W Olympic Blvd Ste 625 Los Angeles CA 90064-1528

LANDERHOLM, ELIZABETH JANE, early childhood education educator; b. Oak Park, Ill. d. Daniel R. and Dorothy E. LaBar; m. Wayne A. Landerholm, June 6, 1964; 1 child, Arthur Scott. BA in Sociology, DePauw U., 1963; MS in Tech., U. Chgo., 1966; EdD in Curriculum and Instrn., No. Ill. U., 1980. Cert. early childhood and elem. edn., Ill. Tchr. Chgo. Bd. Edn., 1966-69; student tchg. supr. Nat. Coll. Edn., Chgo., 1970-79; asst. prof. Roosevelt U., Chgo., 1980-83; project dir. Children's Devel. Ctr., Rockford, Ill., 1984-86; assoc. prof. Northeastern Ill. U., Chgo., 1986-92, prof., 1993—. Therapist Theraplay Inst., Chgo., 1980—84; project dir. McCosh Even Start, 1994—; project coord. Early Childhood Cohort/Ill. Profl. Learning Ptnrships. (TQE grant), 1999—. Contbr. articles to profl. jours. McCosh Even Start grant Ill. State Bd. Edn., Chgo., 1994—, Ill. Profls. Learning Partnerships grant, 1999—. Home: 325 N Humphrey Ave Oak Park IL 60302-2516 Office: Northeastern Ill Univ 5500 N Saint Louis Ave Chicago IL 60625-4699

LANDES, WILLIAM M. law educator; b. 1939; AB, Columbia U., 1960, PhD in Econs., 1966. Asst. prof. econs. Stanford U., 1965—66; asst. prof. U. Chgo., 1966—69, Columbia U., 1969—72; assoc. prof. Grad. Ctr. CUNY, 1972—73; now prof. U. Chgo. Law Sch.; founder, chmn. Lexecon, Inc., 1977—98, chmn. emeritus, 1998—; mem. bd. examiners GRE in Econs., ETS, 1967—74. Author (with Richard Posner): The Economic Structure of Tort Law, 1987; editor (with Gary Becker): Essays in the Economics of Crime and Punishment, 1974; editor: Jour. Law and Econs., 1975—91, Jour. Legal Studies, 1991—. Mem.: Am. Law and Econ. Assn. (v.p. 1991—92, pres. 1992—93), Am. Econ. Assn., Mont Pelerin Soc. Office: U Chgo Sch Law 1111 E 60th St Chicago IL 60637-2776 also: Lexecon Inc 332 S Michigan Ave Ste 1300 Chicago IL 60604-4406

LANDGARTEN, HELEN BARBARA, art psychotherapist, educator; b. Detroit, Mar. 4, 1921; d. Samuel and Lena (Lindenbaum) Tapper; m. Nathan Landgarten, Oct. 10, 1942. BFA, UCLA, 1963; MA in Marriage, Family and Child Counseling, Goddard Coll., 1972; D in Art Therapy (hon.), Norwich U., 1998. Cert. art therapist Art Therapy Credentials Bd., Inc. Coord. art psychotherapy Cedars-Sinai Med. Ctr., L.A., 1967-90; chmn., dir. clin. art therapy Immaculate Heart Coll., L.A., 1972-80; chmn., prof. dept. clin. art therapy Loyola Marymount U., L.A., 1980-88, prof. emeritus, 1988—. Cons. U.S. Dept. Defense, Germany, 1982-86; pres. Internat. Art Therapy Consultation, L.A., 1989-92; staff rsch. assoc. Rsch. and Edn. Inst. Harbor UCLA Med. Ctr., Beit T'shuvah Residence for Addiction Behaviors, 1999—. Author: Clinical Art Therapy, 1980, Family Art Psychotherapy, 1988; editor Adult Art Psychotherapy 1991 Mag., Photo Collage, 1993; contbr. articles to profl. jours. Founder L.A. County Art Mus., 1983—, L.A. Contemporary Mus., 1983—; v.p. Calif. Beach Art Corp., 2000—. Fellow Soc. Psychopathology of Expression; mem. Am. Art Therapy Assn. (hon., life, registered art therapist, bd. dirs. 1969-71, 84-86, treas. 1984-86), So. Calif. Art Therapy Assn. (hon., life, pres. 1972-74). E-mail: tandelini@aol.com.

LANDGRAF, KURT M. chemicals executive; b. Oct. 12, 1946; BA in Econs./Bus. Adminstrn., Wagner Coll.; M in Econs., Pa. State U.; M in Adminstrn., Rutgers U.; M in Sociology, Western Mich. U. With Upjohn co., 1974-80; mgr. worldwide mktg. svcs. DuPont, 1980-83, mktg. dir. pharm., 1983-85, dir. pharms. divsn., 1988-89, dir. pharms. and imaging agts. divsn., 1989-90; with DuPont Merck, 1991-95; CFO DuPont, 1996-97, exec. v.p., 1997-99, COO, 1999—. Chmn. United Way Del., Del. Assn. Rights Citizens Mental Retardation; bd. dirs. U. Del. Rsch. Found., Wilmington Grand Opera Ho.; trustee Goldey-Beacom Coll., Wagner Coll. Mem. Pharm. Rsch. and Mfrs. Am. (bd. dirs.), European Assn. Bioindustries (bd. dirs.), Nat. Alliance Bus. (bd. dirs.). Office: E I DuPont de Nemours and Co 1007 Market St Wilmington DE 19898-0001

LANDI, DALE MICHAEL, industrial engineer, academic administrator; b. Cleve., July 8, 1938; s. Lawrence Roy and Lillian (Caramell) L.; m. Mary Margaret Lipke, Mar. 23, 1974; children: Michael Kenneth, Kristin Marie. BS, Northwestern U., 1960, MS, 1963, PhD, 1965. Systems analyst Gen. Electric Corp., Chgo., 1960-61; research specialist Rand Corp., Santa Monica, Calif., 1965-68, assoc. dept. head, 1968-70, program dir., 1973-78, v.p., chief scientist, 1978-87; asst. budget dir. N.Y.C., 1970-71; asst. police commr. N.Y.C., 1971-73; v.p. SUNY, Buffalo, 1987—. Home: 238 Brantwood Rd Buffalo NY 14226-4306 Office: SUNY at Buffalo 544 Capen Hall Buffalo NY 14260-1600 E-mail: landi@research.buffalo.edu.

LANDIS, FRED, mechanical engineering educator; b. Munich, Mar. 21, 1923; came to U.S., 1947, naturalized, 1954; s. Julius and Elsie (Schulhoff) L.; m. Billie H. Schiff, Aug. 26, 1951 (dec. Jan. 10, 1985); children: John David, Deborah Ellen, Mark Edward. B.Eng., McGill U., 1945; S.M., MIT, 1949, Sc.D., 1950. Design engr. Canadian Vickers, Ltd., Montreal, Can., 1945-47; asst. prof. mech. engring. Stanford U., 1950-52; research engr. Northrop Aircraft, Inc., Hawthorne, Calif., 1952-53; asst. prof. NYU, 1953-56, assoc. prof., 1956-61, prof., 1961-73, chmn. dept. mech. engring., 1963-73; dean, prof. mech. engring. Poly. U., Bklyn., 1973-74; dean Coll. Engring. and Applied Sci., U. Wis., Milw., 1974-83, prof. mech. engring., 1984-94; emeritus prof. U. Wis., Milw., 1994—. Staff cons. Pratt & Whitney Aircraft Co., 1957-88. Cons. editor, Macmillan Co., 1960-68; cons. editorial bd.: Funk & Wagnalls Ency., 1969-90, Compton's Ency., 1984-94; contbr. numerous rsch. articles to profl. jours. and encys., including Ency. Britannica. Mem. Dobbs Ferry (N.Y.) Bd. Edn., 1965-71, v.p. 1966-67, 70-71, pres., 1967-68; bd. dirs. Westchester County Sch. Bds. Assn., 1969-70, v.p., 1970, pres., 1970-71; bd. dirs. Engring. Found., 1988-94. Fellow AIAA (assoc.), ASME (hon. mem., divsn. exec. com. 1965-73, policy bd. 1973-89, v.p. 1985-89, 92-95, bd. govs. 1989-91), Am. Soc. Engring. Edn.; mem. Sigma Tau, Tau Beta Pi, Pi Tau Sigma. Home: 2420 W Acacia Rd Milwaukee WI 53209-3306

LANDIS, JEAN MYER, elementary education educator; b. Lancaster, Pa., Sept. 8, 1946; m. J. Richard Landis, June 8, 1968; children: Nathan, Deborah. Diploma, Lancaster Bus. Sch., 1969; BA, U. N.C., 1973; MA, U. Mich., 1979; early childhood endorsement, Ea. Mich. U., 1985. Tchr. Frank Porter Graham Elem. Sch. Chapel Hill (N.C.)-Carrboro City Schs., 1973-75; grad. rsch. asst. reading program Sch. Edn. U. Mich., Ann Arbor, 1981; presch. dir. Saline (Mich.) Christian Sch., 1983-84; presch. tchr. Little Folks Corner Nursey, Ann Arbor, 1984-85; devel. kindergarten tchr. South Lyon (Mich.) Community Schs., 1986-88; reading/early childhood chpt. 1 tchr. Lancaster City Schs., 1990—. Mem. Assn. Childhood Edn. Internat., Internat. Reading Assn., Nat. Assn. Edn. Young Children. Avocations: watercolor painting, creative writing, biking, hiking, swimming. Home: 821 S 48th St Philadelphia PA 19143-3501

LANDIS, LINDA KAY, music educator; b. Keyser, W. Va., May 2, 1950; d. Donald Avis L. and Uldene May Mongold Duke. BS, West Chester State U., 1972, MM in Voice, 1976. Registered music educator; cert. profl. II. Music educator Phoenixville (Pa.) Area Middle Sch., 1972—. Soprano soloist St. John's Lutheran Ch., Phoenixville, Pa., 1972—. Composer: As The Daisy Fields Grow, 1984, God's Rainbow, 1985, Wedding Song, 1995. Sunday sch. tchr. St. John's Luth. Ch., Phoenixville, Pa., 1966—, mem. Christian edn. com., 1983-93, Stephen ministry leader mem., 1990—, mem. ch. coun., 1985-93. Mem. NEA, Pa. State Edn. Assn., Phoenixville Area Edn. Assn., Music Educators Nat. Conf., Pa. Music Edn. Assn., Bus. and Profl. Women (past dist. dir., Dist. Ten Woman of Yr. 1996-97), Acad. Boosters Club, Order Eastern Star (past matron), Delta Kappa Gamma. Lutheran. Avocations: christian clowning, travel, counted cross-stitch, photography. Home: 514 W Pothouse Rd Phoenixville PA 19460-2242 Office: Phoenixville Area Middle Sch 1330 S Main St Phoenixville PA 19460-4452

LANDIS, SHARYN BRANSCOME, educator; b. New Castle, Pa., Feb. 13, 1942; d. Maynard R. and Irene (Calderwood) Branscome; m. Kenneth R. Landis, Feb. 17, 1961; children: Kenneth R. Jr., Michelle Landis Nielsen, Jonathan A. BS in Edn., Youngstown U., 1967; MBA, U. Phoenix, 1984. Cert. secondary tchr., Colo. Tchr. Butler (Pa.) Community Coll., 1979-81, Barnes Bus. Coll., Denver, 1981-82, Arapahoe Community Coll., Little, Colo., 1981-82, Met. State Coll., Denver, 1982-84; dean of students Nat. Coll., Aurora, Colo., 1984-86; dist. resource tchr. Aurora (Colo.) Pub. Schs., 1986-93; tchr. bus. edn. Highlands Ranch (Colo.) H.S., 1993—. Bd. dirs. Children's Diabetes Assn., Denver, 1981-85. Named Hon. Life Mem. PTA, Pa., 1980-81. Mem. AAUW, Nat. Bus. Edn. Assn., Colo. Vocat. Assn. (state sec. 1991-94), Colo. Educators for and about Bus., Mt. Plains Bus. Assn., Phi Delta Kappa, Delta Pi Epsilon. Republican. Methodist. Avocations: reading, music, skiing, traveling. Home: 9245 S Mountain Brush Ct Highlands Ranch CO 80130-5303 Office: Highlands Ranch H S Peoria St 9375 S Cresthill Ln Highlands Ranch CO 80130-4408

LANDON, JOJENE BABBITT, special education educator; b. Boise, Idaho, Feb. 7, 1940; d. Clarence Ray and Mary (McHenry) Babbitt; m. James Wallace Landon, Dec. 8, 1963; children: Sharon Jene, John Charles, Franklin Thomas, Jonathan Kennette. BA in Far Ea. History, U. Md., 1968; MEd in Spl. Edn., Bowie (Md.) State Coll., 1974; MS in Reading, Johns Hopkins U., 1978; postgrad., Calif. State U., Sacramento, 1987-92. Cert. tchr. for severely handicapped and learning handicapped, also reading specialist, resource specialist, multiple subject and social sci., Calif. Spl. edn. resource tchr. Anne Arundel County, Glen Burnie, Md., 1974-80; tchr. severely emotionally disturbed Leeward Dist., Ewa Beach, Hawaii, 1980-84, North Valley Schs. Inc., Stockton, Calif., 1984-85, Stockton Unified Sch.Dist., 1985-87, Serene Community Sch., Sacramento, 1987-90; tchr. spl. edn. Sacramento Unified Sch. Dist., 1990; tchr. spl. edn., dept. chair Rio Tierra Jr. High Sch., Sacramento, 1990—. Developer, presenter project Ho'okoho U. Hawaii and Hawaii Dept. Edn., Honolulu, 1982-84. Supt. protestant Sunday schs. Pearl Harbor (Hawaii) Naval Sta. Chapel, 1983; lay speaker United Meth. Ch., 1989—. With U.S. Army, 1961-64. Named Grant Dist. Tchr. of Yr., 1997. Mem. Coun. Exceptional Children. Republican. Avocations: biblical studies, ancient history. Home: 8941 Lake Grove Ct Elk Grove CA 95624-2722

LANDRETH, JAMES MACK, elementary school music educator; b. Anderson, S.C., May 29, 1948; s. Johnny Clinton Sr. and Bonnie Ruth (Owen) L.; m. Nelwyn Elaine Pruitt, Aug. 17, 1969; children: Alanna, Evan. B in Mus. Edn., Lee Coll., 1970; M in Mus. Edn., Western Carolina U., 1974. Cert. profl. and music tchr., S.C.; cert. kindermusik tchr. Choral dir. Pendleton (S.C.) H.S., 1971-77; tchr. music Pendleton Jr. H.S., 1971-77, Townville (S.C.) Elem. Sch., 1978-93, Pendleton Elem. Sch., 1973—. Author: Building a Sequential Orff Elementary Music Program, 1986. Min. of music La France (S.C.) Ch. of God, 1971-81, 87-97. Edn. Improvement Act Competetive grantee S.C. Dept. Edn. (3), 1985-86. Mem. NEA, S.C. Edn. Assn., Music Educator Nat. Conf., Am. Orff Sculwerk Assn. (bd. dirs. Foothills chpt.), Phi Kappa Phi. Avocations: walking, gardening. Home: 502 Woodland Cir Pendleton SC 29670-9438

LANDRUM-BITTLES, JENITA, artist, educator; b. Jackson, Mich., Dec. 25, 1959; d. Bennie C. Landrum and Maxine A. Johnson; m. Roland Bittles, June 28, 1995; 1 child, Cory Mychal. BFA, Ariz. State U., 1991; MFA, Ohio State U., 1997. Art coord., grad. tchg. asst. Ohio State U., Columbus, 1997-98, vis. lectr., 1997—. Instr. art Columbus State Coll., 1997—, Cultural Arts Ctr., Columbus, 1997, Columbus Mus. Art, 1997; artist in residence Fort Hays Visual Arts Sch., Columbus, 1997, Skowhegan, N.Y.C., 1996. Solo exhbns. include Maine Daily News, 1996, The Lantern, 1996, 97, Ft. Hayes Shot Tower Gallery, Columbus, 1997, ACE Gallery, Columbus, 1998; contbr. articles to profl. jours. Grantee Liquitex, 1995, Edith Fergus Gilmore, 1997; Albert Murray Family scholarship, 1995-97; Ohio State U. fellow, 1997. Mem. Nation Women's Art Caucus, Black Women's Task Force (chairperson 1994—), Coll. Art Assn. Address: 3789 Towne Center Blvd Columbus OH 43219-3106

LANDSBERG, JILL WARREN, lawyer, educator, arbitrator; b. N.Y.C., Oct. 11, 1942; d. George Richard and Evelyn (Schepps) Warren; m. Lewis Landsberg, June 14, 1964; children: Alison, Judd Warren. BA, George Washington U., Washington, 1964; MAT, Yale U., 1965; JD, Boston Coll., 1976. Bar: Mass., 1977, Ill., 1991. Assoc., dir. (ptnr.) Widett, Slater & Goldman PC, Boston, 1976-90; pvt. practice Chgo., 1991-94; faculty Med. Sch. Ethics and Human Values Dept. Northwestern U., Chgo., 1991-94; exec. asst. spl. counsel for child welfare svcs. Office of the Gov., Chgo., 1994-95, acting spl. counsel for child welfare svcs., 1995-96; cons. in field, 1996—2002; adj. prof. law Northwestern U., 2000—. Govt. agys. cons.; mem. Legis. Com. on Juvenile Justice, Chgo., 1995—96, Task Force on Violence Against Children, Chgo., 1995—99, Citizens Com. on the Juvenile Ct., Chgo., 1995—. Tutor Ptnrs. in Edn., 4th Presbyn. Ch., Chgo., 1993—; mem. steering com. Ill. Ct. Improvement Program, 1995-99; Ill. Jud. Inquiry Bd., 2000—; adv. bd. Libr. Internat. Rels., Chgo., 1993-94; bd. trustees Children's Home and Aid Soc. of Ill. Mem. Chgo. Bar Assn., Ill. State Bar Assn., Am. Arbitration Assn. (cons. 1989—),Phi Beta Kappa, Order of the Coif. Home and Office: 70 E Cedar St Chicago IL 60611-1179

LANE, ANN JUDITH, history and women's studies educator; b. N.Y.C., July 27, 1931; d. Harry A. and Elizabeth (Brown) Lane; children: Leslie Patricia, Joni Alexandra. BA, Bklyn. Coll., 1952; MA, NYU, 1958; PhD, Columbia U., 1968. Mng. editor Challenge Mag., NYU, 1953-56; asst. prof. Douglass Coll., Rutgers U., New Brunswick, N.J., 1968-71; prof. John Jay Coll., SUNY, 1971-83; vis. prof. Wheaton Coll., Norton, Mass., 1981-82; prof. history, dir. women's studies Colgate U., Hamilton, N.Y., 1983-90, U. Va., Charlottesville, 1990—. Author: To Herland and Beyond, 1990, Mary Ritter Beard: A Sourcebook, 1977, 2d edit., 1988, The Brownsville Affair, 1971; editor: Charlotte Perkins Gilman Reader, 1980, Herland: A Lost Utopian Novel, 1979. Chair Com. on Status of Women in the Profession, Orgn. of Am. Historians, 1992-95; dir. History Tchr. Inst., N.Y. Coun. for Humanities, summer 1985; mem. historians adv. com. Nat. Women's Hall of Fame, 1986—; bd. dirs. Louis M. Rabinowitz Found., 1972-76. Fellow, Berkshire Conf. Women Historians, 1988, Ford Found., 1981-82, Nat. Endowment for Humanities, 1980-81, Lilly Endowment, Inc., 1977-79, AAUW, 1959-60. Mem. AAUP (mem. com. on women 1987—), Orgn. Am. Historians (mem. Frederick Jackson Turner prize com. 1979), Women in Hist. Profession (exec. bd., coordinating com. 1971-74). Home: 2603 Jefferson Park Cir Charlottesville VA 22903-4133

LANE, BARBARA MILLER (BARBARA MILLER-LANE), humanities educator; b. N.Y.C., Nov. 1, 1934; d. George Ross Rede and Gertrude Miller; m. Jonathan Lane, Jan. 28, 1956; children: Steven Gregory, Eleanor. BA, U. Chgo., 1953, Barnard Coll., 1956; MA, Radcliffe Coll., 1957; PhD, Harvard U., 1962. Tutor history and lit. Harvard U., Cambridge, Mass., 1960-61; lectr. to prof. history Bryn Mawr Coll., Pa., 1962-75, dir. Growth and Structure of Cities Program, 1971-89, Andrew W. Mellon prof. humanities, 1981-99, Katherine McBride emeritus prof., 1999—2003. Vis. prof. Architecture, Columbia U., 1989; cons. NEH sr. fellowships, Washington, 1971-73, Time-Life Books, N.Y.C., 1975; advisor Macmillan Ency. of Architects, N.Y.C., 1979-82; vis. examiner U. Helsinki, 1991; vis. lectr. Technische Universität, Berlin, 1991, Royal Inst. Tech., Stockholm, Sweden, 2002. Author: (books) Architecture and Politics in Germany, 1968, 1985; co-author: Nazi Ideology Before 1933, 1978, National Romanticism and Modern Architecture in Germany and the Scandinavian Countries, 2000; author (contbg.): Growth and Transformation of the Modern City, 1979, Macmillan Encyclopedia of Architects, 1982, Urbanisierung im 19. und 20. Jahrhundert, 1983, Perspectives in American History, 1984, The Evidence of Art: Images and Meaning in History, 1986, Art and History, 1988, Nationalism in the Visual Arts, 1991, Moderne Architektur in Deutschland: Expressionismus und Neue Sachlichkeit, 1994, Ultra terminum vagari: Scritti in onore di Carl Nylander, 1997; contbg. editor: Urbanism Past and Present, 1980—85; bd. editors Archtl. History Found., 1988—, (journal) Ctrl. European History, 1992—97; contbr. articles to profl. jours. Co-founder, dir., chmn. bd. dirs. New Gulph Child Care Ctr., Bryn Mawr, 1971-75; mem. Middle Atlantic Regional Com., Mellon Fellowships in the Humanities, 1985-87; mem. vis. com. Harvard U. Dept. History, 1986-92, Berlin Stadtforum (adv. coun. to Senator for Urban Devel. and Environment), 1991-96; mem. nat. screening com. Inst. Internat. Edn., 1999-2004; mem. com. NEH sr. fellowships, 2002. Recipient Lindback award for excellence in tchg., 1988, medal of honor U. Helsinki, 1996; fellow AAUW, 1959-60, Fels Found., 1961-62, Am. Council Learned Socs., 1967-68, Guggenheim Found., 1977-78, sr. fellow Ctr. for Advanced Study in Visual Arts, Nat. Gallery Art, Washington, 1983; Am. Scandinavian Found. fellow, 1989, Wissenschaftskolleg zu Berlin fellow, 1990-91; NEH grantee, summer 1989; NEH sr. fellow, 1998. Mem. Soc. Archtl. Historians (bd. dirs. 1977-80, Alice Davis Hitchcock award 1968, chmn. awards coms. 1976, 82, chmn. jour. com. 1982-83), Conf. Group on Central European History (bd. dirs. 1977-79, chmn. awards com. 1987), Am. Hist. Assn. (mem. coun. 1979-82, chmn. com. on Popular Mag. of History 1982), Coll. Art Assn., Phi Beta Kappa. Office: Bryn Mawr Coll Bryn Mawr PA 19010

LANE, CAROL ANN, secondary school educator; b. Sayre, Pa., June 25, 1943; d. Harold J. and Evelyn (Ward) L. BS, East Stroudsburg State, 1965, MEd, 1972. Tchr. health, physical edn. Troy (Pa.) Area Sch. Dist., 1965—. Instr. sta. 1st aid ARC, Bradford, County. Recipient Outstanding Secondary Educators Am. award, 1973, Community Leaders & Noteworthy Ams. award, 1976, 300 Victory Club award, 1991. Mem. NEA, AAHPERD, Pa. Assn. Health, Phys. Edn., Recreation and Dance, Pa. Edn. Assn., Troy Area Edn. Assn., Women's Basketball Coaches Assn., Dist. IV Basketball Coaches Assn. (bd. dirs. 1990—), Delta Kappa Gamma. Republican. Methodist. Avocations: jogging, gardening. Home: RR 3 Box 4 Troy PA 16947-9401 Office: Troy High Sch 250 High St Troy PA 16947-1122

LANE, JERRY ROSS, alcohol and drug abuse service counselor; b. Pampa, Tex., June 3, 1944; s. Wilbur Howard and Christina Lavina (Hendrix) L.; m. Mary Lou Jetton, July 9, 1966; children: Jeffrey Ross, Tamara Noel. BS, McMurry U., 1968; MS in Counseling Psychology, Emmanuel Bapt. U., 1988, D in Counseling Psychology, 1991. Cert. and registered hypnotherapist, CHt. Tchr. Fannin Elem., Abilene, Tex., 1968-70, Tierra Blanca Elem., Hereford, Tex., 1970-72; acctg. and sales staff Lane and Co., Inc., Panhandle, Tex., 1972-74; min. music and edn. Memphis (Tex.) United Meth. Ch., 1974-75, First United Meth. Ch., McAllen, Tex., 1975-79; chaplain cancer treatment ctr. McAllen (Tex.) Br. M.D. Anderson Hosp., 1977-79; owner, counselor Snelling and Snelling Employment, Pampa, 1979-83; tchr. Travis Elem., Pampa, 1983-89; student asst. program coord. Pampa (Tex.) Ind. Sch. Dist., 1989-92; counselor, dir. drug/alcohol program Clarendon Coll. Pampa (Tex.) Ctr., 1992-96; owner dir., Hi-Plains Hypotherapy/Counseling Inst., 1997—. Trainer Developing Capable People, Provo, Utah, 1990—; trainer family cmty. leadership Tex. Extension Svc., Amarillo, Tex., 1990—; parenting cons. Region XVI Edn. Svc. Ctr., Amarillo, 1991—, adv. bd. drug/alcohol, 1992—; cons. Cal Farley's Family Living Ctr., Borger, Tex., 1992—. Bd. dirs. Pampa (Tex.) Fine Arts, 1980-83, Pampa United Way, 1996; chmn. bd. Salvation Army, Pampa, 1982; bd. pres. Civic Ballet, Pampa, 1984; choir mem., bd. dirs. First United Meth. Ch.; vol. grief counselor Hospice of Panhandle. Named Family of Yr., Mormon Ch., Pampa, 1981, Top Gun, Tex. Tech. Dads and Moms Assn., Lubbock, Tex., 1990; grantee Tex. Coun. Assn. Drug/Alcohol, Pampa (Tex.) Ind. Sch. Dist., 1989-93. Mem. Am. Assn. Christian Counselor, Nat. Christian Counselor Assn., Tex. Christian Counselors Assn., Panhandle Christian Counselors Assn., Tex. Jr. Coll. Tchrs. Assn., Pampa C. of C. Avocations: interior decorating, writing, horticulture. Home: 2007 Williston St Pampa TX 79065-3632 Office: Clarendon Coll Pampa Ctr 900 N Frost St Pampa TX 79065-5456

LANE, JOSEPH M. orthopedic surgeon, educator, oncologist; b. N.Y.C., Oct. 27, 1939; s. Frederick and Madelaine Lane; m. Barbara Greenhouse, June 23, 1963; children: Debra, Jennifer. AB in Chemistry, Columbia U., 1957; MD, Harvard U., 1965. Surg. intern Hosp. U. Pa., Phila., 1965-66, resident in gen. surgery, 1966-67, resident, 1969-72, chief resident, 1972-73, chief MBD sect., 1973-76; rsch. assoc. NIH, NIDR, Bethesda, Md., 1967-69; rsch. fellow Phila. Gen. Hosp., 1969-70; chief MBD unit Hosp. Spl. Surgery, N.Y.C., 1976-93, 96—, dir. rsch. div., 1990-93, dir. clin. rsch., assoc. dir. trauma, 1996—; asst. dean Med. Coll. Cornell U., N.Y.C., N.Y., 1997—; chief orthopedic oncology Meml. Sloan-Kettering Cancer Ctr., N.Y.C., 1977-90; prof., chmn. orthopaedic surgery UCLA Med. Sch., L.A., 1993-96; prof. orthopedic surgery Weill Med Coll. Cornell U., N.Y.C., 1980-93, 96—. Assoc. dir. MultiPurpose Arthritis Ctr., N.Y.C., 1988-93, 96—; cons. Genetics Inst., Andover, Mass., Orquest, Mountain Side, Calif., Exogen, Piscataway, N.J.; mem. VA Merit Grant Bd. Recipient N.Y. Mayoral Proclamation, 1988. Fellow Am. Acad. Orthopaedic Surgeons (Kappa Delta award 1973); mem. Acad. Orthopaedic Surgeons, Am. Orthopaedic Assn., Am. Soc. Bone and Mineral Rsch., Med. Soc. State N.Y., Internat. Soc. Fracture Repair, Musculoskeletal Tumor Soc. (pres. 1982-83), Orthopaedic Rsch. Soc. (pres. 1984-85). Office: Hosp Spl Surgery 535 E 70th St New York NY 10021-4872

LANE, MARK, lawyer, educator, writer; b. N.Y.C., Feb. 24, 1927; s. Harry Arnold and Elizabeth Lane; m. Patricia Ruth Erdner, 1987; children: Anne-Marie, Christina. LLB, Bklyn. Law Sch., 1951. Bar: N.Y. 1951, D.C. 1995. Mng. mem. The Lane Law Firm, LLC, Greenwich, NJ, pvt. practice, 1952—; founder Mid-Harlem Community Parish Narcotics Clinic, 1953, East Harlem Reform Dem. Club, 1959; prof. law Cath. U., Washington, 1975—76. Founder and dir. Citizens Commn. Inquiry; founder Wounded Knee Legal Def.-Offense Com., 1973, The Covered Wagon, Mountain Home, Idaho, 1971. Author: (books) Rush to Judgment, 1966, A Citizen's Dissent, 1968, Chicago Eye-Witness, 1969, Arcadia, 1970, Conversations with Americans, 1970, Executive Action, 1973, (with Dick Gregory) Code Name Zorro, 1977, The Strongest Poison, 1980, Plausible Denial, 1991, Murder in Memphis, 1993; prodr. films Rush to Judgment, 1967, Two Men in Dallas, 1987, 92; writer, prodr. plays Trial of James Earl Ray, 1978, Plausible Denial, 1992, Winds of Doctrine, 1994; writer, prodr. screenplays, Arcadia, 1992, Slay the Dreamer, 1992, Plausible Denial, 1993; founder publs. Citizens Quar., 1975, Helping Hand, 1971. Mem. N.Y. State Assembly, 1960-62. With AUS, 1945-47. Home and Office: 272 Tindall Island Rd Greenwich NJ 08323

LANE, NEAL FRANCIS, physics educator, former government official; b. Oklahoma City, Aug. 22, 1938; s. Walter Patrick and Harietta (Hattie) Charlotte (Hollander) Lane; m. Joni Sue Williams, June 11, 1960; children: Christy Lynn Lane Saydjari, John Patrick. BS, U. Okla., 1960, MS, 1962, PhD, 1964, DHL (hon.), 1995; DSc (hon.), U. Ala., 1994, Mich. State U., 1995; DHL (hon.), Marymount U., Arlington, Va., 1995; DSc (hon.), Ohio State U., 1996, Washington Coll., 1998, Mt. Sinai Sch. Medicine, 1999, U. Colorado, 1999, Queen's U., Belfast, No. Ireland, 2000, North Carolina State U., 2001, SUNY, 2002; DHL and Sc (hon.), Ill. Inst. Tech., 2000. NSF postdoctoral fellow, 1964—65; asst. prof. physics Rice U., Houston, 1966—69, assoc. prof., 1969—72, prof. physics and space physics and astronomy, 1972—84, chmn. dept. physics, 1977—82; dir. divsn. physics NSF, Washington, 1979—80; chancellor U. Colo., Colorado Springs, 1984—86; provost Rice U., 1986—93; dir. NSF, Washington, 1993—98; asst. to pres. for sci. and tech., dir. Office of Sci. and Tech. Policy, Washington, 1998—2001; sr. fellow Dept. Physics and Astronomy James A. Baker III Inst. Pub. Policy, Rice U., 2001—. Adj. fellow Joint Inst. for Lab. Astrophysics, U. Colo., Boulder, 2001—, vis. fellow, 1965—66, 1975—76; mem. commn. on phys. sci., math. and applications NRC, 1989—93; bd. overseers Superconducting Super Collider (SSC) Univs. Rsch. Assn., 1985—93; disting. Karcher lectr. U. Okla., Norman, 1983; disting. vis. scientist U. Ky., Lexington, 1980; mem. adv. com. math. and phys. sci. NSF, 1992—93. Co-author: Quantum States of Atoms, Molecules and Solids, Understanding More Quantum Physics; contbr. articles to profl. jours. Active Cath. Commn. Intellectual and Cultural Affairs, 1991. Recipient George Brown prize for superior teaching, Rice U., 1973—74, 1976—77, Brown Coll. Tchg. award, 1972—73, Disting. Svc. award, Nat. Assn. Biology Tchrs., 1997, Pres.'s award, ASME, 1999, Support Sci. award, Coun. Sci. Soc. Pres., 2000, Pub. Svc. award, Am. Math. Soc., Am. Astron. Soc. and Am. Phys. Soc., 2001; fellow Alfred P. Sloan Found., 1967—71. Fellow: AAAS (Philip Hauge Abelson award 2000, William D. Carey award 2001), Am. Acad. Arts and Sci., Am. Phys. Soc. (chmn. divsn. electron and atomic physics 1977—78, exec. com. 1981—83, councilor-at-large 1983, Pub. Svc. award 2001); mem.: Am. Assn. Physics Tchrs., Am. Inst. Physics (governing bd. 1984—87), Am. Chem. Soc. (Pub. Svc. award 1999), Sigma Xi (pres.-elect 1992, pres. 1993), Phi Beta Kappa. Roman Catholic. Avocations: tennis, squash. Office: Rice U Physics and Astronomy MS-108 PO Box 1892 6100 Main St Houston TX 77251-1892 E-mail: neal@rice.edu.

LANE, PEGGY LEE, elementary school educator; b. Ferndale, Mich., Jan. 13, 1948; d. Otto Gustave and Ruth Geraldine (Keyser) Kleve; m. Mark Lane, Sept. 7, 1978 (dec. June 1989). BA, Ctrl. Mich. U., 1969, MA, 1972; PhD, U. North. Colo., 1998. Tchr. Potterville (Mich.) Schs., 1969-76, Alpena (Mich.) Pub. Schs., 1976-78, 87-89, Anchor Bay Schs., New Baltimore, Mich., 1978-79; owner Park Lane Jewelry, Glasgow, Mont., 1979-87; county supt. Valley County, Glasgow, Mont., 1987; tchr. Littleton (Colo.) Pub. Schs., 1990-97, Cherry Creek Pub. Schs., Colo., 1997—. Mem. ASCD, Am. Psychol. Soc., Am. Edn. Rsch. Assn. Unitarian Universalist. Home: 2905 S Clermont Dr Denver CO 80222-6719

LANE, ROSALIE MIDDLETON, extension specialist; b. Savannah, Ga. d. Freddie and Willie Blanche (Jones) Middleton; m. Martin Luther Jones, Apr. 24, 1964 (div. July 1977); children: Regina Veronica, Sharon Yolanda; m. Woodie Lane, Sr., Dec. 6, 1985; 1 stepchild, Woodie M., Jr. BA, Western Mich. U., 1989; M in Urban and Regional Planning, Ala. A&M U., 1995. Exec. sec. Curtis Brown, Ltd., N.Y.C., 1959-64; adminstrv. sec. Bronx (N.Y.)-Lebanon Hosp. Ctr., 1971-76; adminstr. IBM Corp., Savannah, Ga. and Huntsville, Ala., 1980-95; ext. specialist, rschr., educator Coop. Ext. Sys., Ala. A&M U., Normal, 1995—. Past mem. customer interface task force USDA, Washington. Author: (with others) A Directory of Resource for Low Income, Elderly, and Homeless Citizens in North Ala., 1995; author poems. Vol. Coalition/On- At-Risk Minority Males, Huntsville, Ala., 1992; bd. dirs. ARC Minority Initiatives Com., Huntsville, 1994. Mem. NEA, Am. Planning Assn., Com. Minorities in Pub. Transp. Orgn., Alpha Zeta. Presbyterian. Avocations: creative writing, song writing. Office: Ala Cooperative Extension Sys Meridian St Normal AL 35762

LANE, SARAH MARIE CLARK, elementary education educator; b. Conneaut, Ohio, July 27, 1946; d. Robert George and Julia Ellen (Sanford) Clark; m. Ralph Donaldson Lane, May 28, 1977; children: Richard, Laura. BS in Edn., Kent State U., 1977; MS in Edn., Coll. Mt. St. Joseph, 1988. Cert. tchr., Ohio. Coord. newspaper in edn. Tribune Chronicle, Warren, Ohio, 1986-89; tutor MacArthur Found. Project, Warren, Ohio, 1988-89; tchr. chpt. I Lakeview Local Schs., Cortland, Ohio, 1989—. Freelance writer newspaper Conn. News Herald, 1963-64, Tribune Chronicle, 1980-89; contbr. articles to profl. jours.; author: A Walk Through Historic Cortland, 1994. V.p. Bazetta Cortland Hist. Soc., 1983-85; chmn. com. local history project Lakeview Schs., Cortland, 1992—; mem. Trumbull County Bicentennial Commn., 1996—. George Record Found. scholar, 1964-66. Mem. Internat. Reading Assn. (Ohio coun.), Cortland Community Concert Band (pres. 1991-92), Mem. Christian Ch. (Disciples Of Christ). Avocations: writing, historical research, genealogy, reading. Home: 298 Corriedale Dr Cortland OH 44410-1622 Office: Cortland Elem Sch 264 Park Ave Cortland OH 44410-1098

LANE, TED, literacy education educator; b. Albany, N.Y., June 24, 1928; BS in Elem. Edn., U. N.Mex., 1951; MS in Sch. Adminstrs. and Supervision, N.Y. State Coll. for Tchrs., 1953; EdD in Elem. Edn., NYU, 1970. 5th grade tchr. South Colonie (N.Y.) Sch. Dist., 1954-57; 5th and 6th grade tchr. Levittown (N.Y.) Sch. Dist., 1957-58; fellow NYU, N.Y.C., 1958-59; prof. literacy edn. Jersey City (N.J.) State Coll., 1959—. Cons. Title I various schs., N.J., 1964—; cons. adult edn. Jersey City State Coll. Adult Resource Cr., 1964—; cons. individualized lang. arts Weehawken (N.J.) Sch. Sys., 1965-75; cons. project read write Newark Sch. Sys., 1972-75. Mem. ASCD, Nat. Coun. Tchrs. English, Internat. Reading Assn., N.J. Reading Assn.; N.J. Edn. Assn. Office: Jersey City State Coll Dept Literacy Edn 2039 John F Kennedy Blvd Jersey City NJ 07305-1527

LANE, WILLIAM C., JR., principal; Prin. Gulf Mid. Sch., Cape Coral, Fla. Recipient Blue Ribbon Sch. award U.S. Dept. Edn., 1990-91. Office: Gulf Mid Sch 1809 SW 36th Ter Cape Coral FL 33914-5599

LANE, WILLIAM HARRY, JR., principal; b. Camden, N.J., Apr. 12, 1951; s. William Harry Sr. and Dorothy (Critchley) L.; 1 child, Kristen Jill. AA, Wesley Coll., 1975; BS in Edn., U. Del., 1976, MEd, 1980; EdD, Widener U., 1993. Cert. tchr., adminstrn., Del. Tchr. Appoquinimink Sch. Dist., Middletown, Del., 1977-82; asst. prin. Woodbridge Jr./Sr. High Sch., Bridgeville, Del., 1982-84; adminstrv. asst. Lt. Gov. Del., Dover, 1984-85; spl. edn. tchr. Smyrna (Del.) High Sch., 1985-89; asst. prin. Delmar (Del.) Jr./Sr. High Sch., 1989-96, Lewes (Del.) Mid. Sch., 1996—. Bd. dirs. Spl. Olympics, Del., 1985-89; com. mem. Blue-Gold All-Star Football Game, Dover, 1990—, chmn. 31st Dist., Dover, 1990—; pres. Jaycees, Dover, 1989-90; bd. dirs. YMCA Resource Ctr., Wilmington, Del., 1990-95; mem. jr. bd. Kent Gen. Hosp. With USN, 1969-73. Mem. Nat. Assn. Secondary Sch. Prin., Assn. for Gifted, Del. Assn. Sch. Adminstrs., Kiwanis, Friends Old Dover, Capital Grange, Ducks Unlimited, VFW, Elks. Presbyterian. Office: Lewes Mid Sch 820 Savannah Rd Lewes DE 19958-1598

LANEGRAN, DAVID ANDREW, geography educator; b. St. Paul, Nov. 27, 1941; s. Walter Bucannon and Lita Evangeline (Wilson) L.; children: Kimberley Rae, Elizabeth Ann, Erik David, Katherin Jane. BA, Macalester Coll., St. Paul, 1963; MA, U. Minn., 1966, PhD, 1970. John S. Holl prof. geography Macalester Coll., 1969—. Dean of social sci., 1999-01, pres. Minn. Landmarks, St. Paul, 1988-03, mng. dir., 1979-82; program assoc. Gen. Svc. Found., St. Paul, 1980-85; vis. prof. several univs., U.S., 1979-89; chmn. bd. dirs. Geographic Edn. Nat. Implementation Project, 1987-90; coord. Minn. Alliance for Geographic Edn., St. Paul, 1987—; v.p. Nat. Coun. Geographic Edn., 1995—; pres. Nat. Coun. Geographic Edn., 1998; chair test devel. com. Advanced Placement Human Geographoc, 2000-03. Author: The Saint Paul Experiment: Initiative of the Latimer Administration, 1989, St. Anthony Park: Portrait of a Community, 1987, Grand Avenue: Renaissance of an Urban Street, 1996, (with others) The Legacy of Minneapolis: Preservation Amid Change, 1983, (with Judith Martin) Where We Live: Residential Districts of the Twin Cities, 1983, (with Ernest Sandeen) The Lake District of Minneapolis: A Neighborhood History, 1979, (with P. Kane) St. Paul Omnibus, Images of the Changing City, 1979, (with Risa Palm) An Invitation to Geography, 1978, (with Patrice St. Peter) Geolinks: K-12 Geography Curriculum, 1994. Chmn. St. Paul City Planning Commn., 1982-87; dir. Northwest Area Found., 1988-90, St. Paul Progress Housing Corp., 1984-86. Named one of ten outstanding coll. or univ. tchrs. of geography Ednl. Change Mag., 1977; recipient Award for Excellence Minn. Soc. AIA, 1978, Burlington-No. award for teaching excellence Burlington No. Found., 1988, 96, Thomas Jefferson Teaching and Cmty. Svc. award Robert McConnell Found.; named to South St. Paul Hall of Excellence, 1989. Mem. Assn. Am. Geographers (treas. 1987-89, nat. councilor 1986-89), Nat. Coun. for Geographic Edn. (joint com. for geographic edn. 1983-85, exec. com., v.p. 1995-97, pres. 1998-99). Democrat. Presbyterian. Home: 140 Wheeler St S Saint Paul MN 55105-1925 Office: Macalester Coll 1600 Grand Ave Saint Paul MN 55105-1801

LANE-MAHER, MAUREEN DOROTHEA, marketing educator, consultant; b. West Point, N.Y., June 26, 1943; d. John Joseph and Dorothea (Fennell) L. BA, St. Louis U., 1965; MEd, U. Va., 1972, EdD, 1977. High sch. history tchr., Va., Okinawa, Japan, 1965-69; published products coord. 3M Bus. Products Sales, Inc., Springfield, Va., 1969-71; program mgr. U. Va., Charlottesville, 1971-77, asst. prof., 1977-78; mktg. svcs. mgr. Westinghouse, Iowa City, 1978-83; mktg. mgr. Nat. Computer Systems, Washington, 1983-87; prof. Nat.-Louis U., McLean (Va.) Acad. Ctr., 1989—. Gen. ptnr. The ML Group, Washington, 1987—; spl. asst. USIA, Washington, 1982-83. Contbg. editor, contbr. Ednl. IRM Quar., 1990-92. Exch. exec. class XIII Pres.'s Commn. on Exec. Exch., 1982. Mem. Global Bus. Assn., Am. Mktg. Assn., Mid-Atlantic Women Studies Assn. Roman Catholic. Avocations: tennis, photography. Office: Nat Louis U 8000 Westpark Dr Mc Lean VA 22102-3105

LANEVE, COSIMO RAFFAELE, humanities educator; b. Taranto, Puglia, Italy, Jan. 14, 1940; s. Giuseppe Laneve, Anna Salamino; m. Emilia Salvatore, May 3, 1946; children: Annamaria, Giuseppe. Degree in Pedagogy, U. Bari, Italy, 1964. Tchr. G. Galilei Sch., Taranto, Italy, 1958—62, Quinto Ennio Sch., Taranto, Italy, 1964—69; tchr. high sch. Dr. Aristosseno Sch., Taranto, 1969—72; rschr., prof. gen. didactic U. Bari, 1972—2000, dir. dept., 1992—2000. Author: (book) Rhetoric and Education, 1981, Language and Person, 1987, Elements of Didactic, 1998, Cultural Drifts and Pedagogic Criticism, 2001, Didactic Between Theory and Practice, 2003. With Italian Mil., 1967—68. Recipient Pescara, 1997, Abroedi, 1996. Avocations: music, football. Home: Via Ancona 23 74100 Taranto Italy Office: Univ of Bari Palazzo Ateneo-Piazza Umberto 1 70121 Bari Italy

LANEY, JAMES THOMAS, former ambassador, educator; b. Wilson, Ark, Dec. 24, 1927; s. Thomas Mann and Mary (Hughey) L.; m. Berta Joan Radford, Dec. 20, 1949; children: Berta Joan Vaughan, James T., Arthur Radford, Mary Ruth Laney Reilly, Susan Elizabeth Castle. BA, Yale U., 1950, BD, 1954, PhD, 1966; DD (hon.), Fla. So. Coll., 1977; LHD (hon.), Rhodes Coll., 1979; HHD (hon.), Mercer U., 1980; LLD (hon.), DePauw U., 1985; DD (hon.), Wofford Coll., 1986; LHD (hon.), Millsaps Coll., 1988, Austin Coll., 1990, W.Va. Wesleyan Coll., 1990, Yale U., 1993; DD (hon.), Emory U., 1994; LLD (hon.), U. St. Andrews, Scotland, 1994, Alaska Pacific U., 1994; DD (hon.), Yonsei U., Korea, 1997; LHD (hon.), U. S.C., 1997, Queens Coll., 1998; D in Internat. Affairs, Am. U., 1998; LLD (hon.), Piedmont Coll., 1999; DD (hon.), Kwansei Gakuin U., Japan, 2000; LHD (hon.), LaGrange Coll., 2000, U. Richmond, 2001, LLD (hon.), 2001. Chaplain Choate Sch., Wallingford, Conn., 1953-55; ordained to ministry Meth. Ch., 1955; asst. lectr. Yale Div. Sch., 1954-55; pastor St. Paul Meth. Ch., Cin., 1955-58; sec. student Christian movement, prof. Yonsei U., Seoul, Korea, 1959-64; asst. prof. Christian ethics Vanderbilt U. Div. Sch., 1966-69; dean Candler Sch. Theology, Emory U., 1969-77, pres. univ., 1977-93; US amb. to Republic of Korea, 1993-97. Vis. prof. Harvard Div. Sch., 1974. Author: The Education of the Heart, 1994; (with J.M. Gustafson) On Being Responsible, 1968; contbr. columns NY Times, Washington Post, LA Times. Fgn. Affairs pres. Nashville Cmty. Rels. Coun., 1968-69; mem. Yale Coun. Com., 1972-77; bd. dir. Fund Theol. Edn.; chmn. United Bd. Christian Higher Edn. in Asia, 1990-93; bd. dir. Atlanta Symphony, 1979-91; chmn. bd. overseers com. to visit Harvard Div. Sch., 1980-85; mem. Yale U. Coun. Exec. Com., 1990-93; mem. Carnegie Endowment Nat. Commn. on Am. and the New World; mem. adv. com. Atlanta Project; chmn. so. dist. Rhodes Scholarship Com., 1980-90; bd. dir. Atlantic Coun., 1987-93. With AUS, 1946-48; mem. tercentenary steering com. Yale U., 1998—2001; co-chmn. Faith & City, Atlanta, Ga. Selected for Leadership Atlanta, 1970-71; recipient Disting. Alumnus award Yale U. Div. Sch., 1979, 93, Kellogg award for leadership in higher edn., 1983, Wilbur Cross medal Yale Grad. Sch., 1996, James Van Fleet award, Korean Soc., 1996, Kangwa medal for disting. diplomatic svc., Rep. Korea, 1997, Dept. Defense medal for disting. pub. svc., U.S. Govt., 1997, 1st Internat. Human Rights award Inst. Human Rights, Korea, 1998; D.C. Macintosh fellow Yale U., 1965-66. Mem. Am. Soc. Christian Ethics, Soc. for Values Higher Edn. (pres. 1987-91), Coun. on Fgn. Rels. (co-chair task force on Korean Peninsula 1997—), Pilgrim Soc., Atlanta C. of C., Commerce Club, Phi Beta Kappa, Omicron Delta Kappa, Elihu Soc. (hon). Office: Emory U Pres Emeritus 1462 Clifton Rd NE Ste 302 Atlanta GA 30322-1000

LANEY, LEROY OLAN, economist, banker, educator; b. Atlanta, Mar. 20, 1943; s. Lee Edwin and Paula Izlar (Bishop) L.; m. Sandra Elaine Prescott, Sept. 3, 1966; children: Prescott Edwin, Lee Olan III. B Indsl. Engring., Ga. Inst. Tech., 1965; MBA in Fin., Emory U., 1967; MA in Econs., U. Colo., 1974, PhD in Econs., 1976. Budget analyst Martin-Marietta Corp., Denver, 1971-72; economist Coun. Econ. Advisers, Washington, 1974-75; internat. economist U.S. Treasury Dept., Washington, 1975-78; sr. economist Fed. Res. Bank Dallas, 1978-88; prof. econs., chmn. dept. Butler U., Indpls., 1989-90; sr. v.p. lst Hawaiian Bank, Honolulu, 1990-98; prof. econs. and fin. Hawaii Pacific U., Honolulu, 1998—. Chmn. Fed. Res. Com. on Internat. Rsch., Washington, 1981-83; vis. prof. U. Tex., Arlington and Dallas, 1978-85; adj. prof. So. Meth. U., Dallas, 1982-85. Editor bank periodicals, 1975-88; contbr. articles to profl. jours. Mem. Internat. Fin. Symposium, Dallas, 1982-85; Hawaii Coun. on Revenues. Lt. USN, 1967-71. Scholar Ga. Inst. Tech., 1961; rsch. fellow Emory U., 1965-67, teaching fellow U. Colo., 1972-73; rsch. grantee Butler U., 1989-90. Mem. Am. Econ. Assn., Western Econ. Assn., Indpls. Econ. Forum, Plaza Club, Honolulu Rotary, Omicron Delta Epsilon, Lambda Alpha, Kappa Sigma. Avocations: sailing, skiing, reading, fly-fishing. Office: Sch Bus Adminstrn Hawaii Pacific Univ Honolulu HI 96813 E-mail: L09_LANEY@hotmail.com.

LANG, GERHARD, psychology educator; b. Germany, Mar. 19, 1925; came to U.S., 1940; s. Bertold and Else Lang; m. Adell Lang, Dec. 27, 1951; children: Kenneth, Judith Lang Knutsen. BS in Psychology, CCNY, 1952, MA in Sch. Psychology, 1954; PhD in Devel. and Ednl. Psychology, Columbia U., 1958. Cert. psychologist, N.Y.; lic. psychology, N.J. Tchg. fellow, rsch. asst., cons., lectr. CCNY, 1954-60; instr., asst. prof. psychology Fairleigh Dickinson U., Rutherford, N.J., 1958-63, assoc. prof., 1963-64; assoc. prof. psychology and edn. Montclair State U., Upper Montclair, NJ, 1966-70, prof., 1970—2001, prof. emeritus, 2001—, chmn. dept. ednl. rsch. and evaluation, 1970-73, team leader, 1973-94. Cons. N.Y.C. Bd. Edn., 1966-90, rsch. assoc. bd. examiners, 1964-66; cons. Jewish Edn. Svc. N.Am., N.Y.C., 1960-84, Title I reading project Dist. 29, Queens, N.Y., 1973-77, Twp. of Montclair, 1991—; pvt. practice, 1971—. Author: A Practical Guide to Statistics for Research and Measurements, 6th edit., 1998, A Practical Guide to Research Methods, 6th edit., 1998; contbr. articles to profl. jours., also chpts. and pamphlets. Grantee James McKeen Cattel Fund, 1957, U.S. Dept. Edn., 1962-64, 65-67. Mem. APA, Am. Ednl. Rsch. Assn., Nat. Coun. on Measurements in Edn., Northeastern Ednl. Rsch. Assn. Avocations: playing piano, tennis, reading, eating. Home: 4-39 Lyncrest Ave Fair Lawn NJ 07410-1634 Office: Montclair State U Dept Psychology Montclair NJ 07043

LANG, HARRY GEORGE, vocational education researcher; b. Pitts., June 2, 1947; s. Harry George and Harriet Lang; m. Bonnie Meath, Aug. 25, 1973. BS in Physics, Bethany Coll., 1969; MSEE, Rochester Inst. Tech., 1974; EdD in Curriculum and Tchg., U. Rochester, 1979. Cert. secondary sci. tchr., N.Y. Physics tchr. Nat. Tech. Inst. for Deaf, Rochester (N.Y.) Inst. Tech., 1970-84, prof., 1984—, coord. Office Faculty Devel., 1984-90, ednl. rschr. dept. ednl. R&D, 1990—. Vis. prof. U. Rochester, 1981-89; vis. lectr. U. Leeds, Eng., 1988. Author: Silence of the Spheres: The Deaf Experience in the History of Science, 1994, (with Bonnie Meath-Lang) Deaf Persons in the Arts and Sciences: A Biographical Dictionary, 1995, A Phone of Our Own: The Deaf Insurrection Against Ma Bell, 2000, (with Marc Marschark and John Albertini) Educating Deaf Students: From Research to Practice; contbr. numerous articles to profl. publs. Trustee Western Pa. Sch. for Deaf, Pitts., 1988. Recipient Alumni award for Achievement in Edn., Bethany Coll., 1994, Outstanding Alumni award Western Pa. Sch. for Deaf, 1994; NSF grantee, 1994, 95, 2001, Fund in Postsecondary Edn. grantee, 2000. Home: 402 Keyes Rd Honeoye Falls NY 14472-9030 Office: Nat Tech Inst for Deaf Rochester Inst Tech 96 Lomb Memorial Dr Rochester NY 14623-5604 E-mail: hgl9008@rit.edu.

LANG, JAMES RICHARD, education consultant; b. Cleve., Feb. 7, 1945; s. Francis H. and Rachel L. (Boyce) L.; m. Marilyn F. Hosken, July 1, 1967; children: Christopher Charles, James Walter. Salesman Stas. WOHI-AM/WRTS-FM, East Liverpool, Ohio, 1967-68; gen. mgr. Sta. WEIR-AM, Weirion, W.Va., 1969-76; v.p. sales Paperwork Systems, Inc., Bellingham, Wash., 1976-78; v.p. market devel. Sta. Bus. Systems div. Control Date Corp., Greenwich, Conn., 1978-85; mgr. Eaglestone div. Siber Hegner N.Am., Inc., Milford, Conn., 1986-89; dir. mktg. MacMillan/McGraw-Hill, Avon, Conn., 1990-93; pres. Imagination Works, Trumbull, 1993—. Served with USN, 1968-69. Recipient Outstanding Service to Cmty. award Italian Sons and Dads Am., 1970. Mem. Instrument Soc. Am., Direct Mtkg. Assn., Jaycees (Cmty. Svc. award 1975), Internat. Brotherhood of Magicians (Wizard award 2003), Rotary (pres. 1996-97, area rep. 1997-98, asst. gov. dist. 7980, 1999-2001, dist. gov. 2002-2003, bequest soc. mem., Man of Yr. 1975, Paul Harris fellow dist. 1980, Norm Parsells award 2000), Fellowship of Rotary Magicians. Methodist. Office: Imagination Works 24 Primrose Dr Trumbull CT 06611-5043

LANG, MARVEL, urban affairs educator; b. Bay Springs, Miss., Apr. 2, 1949; s. Otha and Hattie (Denham) L.; m. Mozell Pentecost, Sept. 15, 1973; children: Martin E., Maya S. BA cum laude, Jackson State U., 1970; MA, U. Pitts., 1975; PhD in Urban/Social and Econ. Geography, Rural Settlement and Quantitative Methods/Computer Applications, Mich. State U., 1979; postgrad., St. John's Coll., Santa Fe, 1973, Miss. State U., 1979, Murray State U., 1980. Grad. teaching fellow dept. geography U. Pitts., 1970-72; instr. geography Jackson (Miss.) State U., 1972-74, asst. prof. geography, 1978-82, assoc. prof. geography, 1982-83; assoc. prof., dir. geography program Jackson (Miss.) State U. Ctr. Urban Affairs, 1983-84; grad. teaching & rsch. asst. dept. geography Mich. State U. Computer Inst. Social Sci. Rsch., East Lansing, 1974-76; grad. teaching fellow dept. geography Mich. State U., East Lansing, 1976-78; grad. asst. to dir. Mich. State U. Ctr. Urban Affairs, Coll. Urban Devel., East Lansing, 1977-78; dir. Ctr. Urban Affairs, assoc. prof. urban affairs programs Mich. State U., East Lansing, 1986-91, dir. Ctr. Urban Affairs, prof. urban affairs programs, 1991-93, prof. urban affairs programs, 1993—; profl. geographer Bureau of the Census, Washington, 1984-85, rsch. geographer, 1985-86. Instr. geography Lansing C.C., 1976-78, vis. prof., 1990-91; vis. prof. grad. sch. edn. & allied professions Fairfield (Conn.) U., 1990, 91, Egeler correctional facility prison edn. program Spring Arbor Coll., Jackson, 1990, McNair summer rsch. opportunity program, Mich. State U., 1989, 90, Wilberforce U., 1991, 92; rsch. cons. Mich. State U. Ctr. Urban Studies, 1978-79; prin. investigator NASA, 1979-81, Inst. Rsch., Devel. & Engring. in Nuclear Energy, 1980-81, U.S. Dept. Energy, 1980-82; co-prin. investigator & dir. U.S. Bureau of the Census, 1988—; mem. commn. geography & Afro-Am. fellowship U. Pitts, 1970-72; mem. numerous coms. Jackson State U., Mich. State U.; commentator on various radio and television programs; conductor seminars, workshops, and presentations; cons.; speaker in field. Author: (with others) The World at Your Fingertips: A Self Instructional Geography Handbook, 1991; editor: Contemporary Urban America: Problems, Issues and Alternatives, 1991, (with C. Ford) Black Student Retention in Higher Education, 1988, Strategies for Retaining Minorities in Higher Education, 1992; author (with others) Introduction to Remote Sensing of the Environment, 1982, Black Student Retention in Higher Education, 1988, Politics and Policy in the Age of Education, 1990, International Science, Technology, and Development: Philosophy, Theory and Policy, 1990, The Second Handbook of Minority Student Services, 1990, Contemporary Urban America: Problems, Issues, and Alternatives, 1991, The Guide to College Success: For Black Students Only, 1992, numerous tech. reports; mem. editorial bd. Jour. Urban Affairs, Urban Affairs Quarterly, 1992—; referee Urban Affairs Quarterly, Jour. Urban Affairs, Social Devel. Issues Jour., Econ. Devel. Quarterly, Urban Geography Jour.; contbr. articles and reviews to profl. jours. Mem. Gov.'s Coun. Selective Svc. in the State of Miss., 1969-80; bd. dirs. Boys and Girls Clubs of Lansing, 1986-89; chair bd. program com., bd. dirs. St. Vincent Children's Home/Catholic Social Svcs. of Lansing, 1986-89; mem. com. community rels. Tri-County Coun. Aging, 1987-89; mem. adv. com. Mich. Legis. Black Caucus Found., 1987—, hon. host Ann. Black History Month Celebration, 1989-91; mem. coordinating com. Friendship Baptist Ch. Acad. Enrichment Program, 1986-89; bd. dirs. Mich. Protection & Advocacy Svcs., 1991—; faculty advisor MSU Black Grad. Student's Assn., 1989-90; active CIC Acad. Leadership Devel. Program, 1989-90; co-founder, v.p. Black Men Inc. of Greater Lansing, 1992—. Acad. and Marching Band scholar Jackson State U., 1966-70; recipient Outstanding Leadership award Friendship Bapt. Ch. Laymen's League, 1988, Meritorious Svc. award Mich. Legis. Black Caucus Found., 1988; grantee Commn. on Geography and Afro-America and the Nat. Office of Edn., 1973, Jackson State U. Grad. Sch. Rsch. and Publ. Com., 1979, NASA, 1979-80, 80-81, U.S. Dept. Energy, 1980-81, 81-82, Inst. Rsch., Devel. & Engring. Nuclear Energy, 1980-81, NSF, 1980-82, Kellogg Found., 1981-84, Miss. Coun. Humanities, 1982-83, U.S. Bureau of the Census, 1988-90, C.S. Mott Found., 1990-93. Mem. Urban Affairs Assn. (nominating com. 1987-88, membership com. 1987—, site selection com. 1988-89, governing bd. 1989—, chair membership com. 1990-91, sec., treas. 1991-92, vice chair 1992—, chair 1993—), Assn. Am. Geographers (chair com. on the status of Afro-Am. geographers 1980-83, com. affirmative action 1983—, census adv. com. 1990—), Southeast Divsn. Assn. Am. Geographers (steering com. 1980-81, com. edn. 1981-86, program com. 1982), Nat. Coun. Geog. Edn. (remote sensing com. 1981-84), Assn. Advancement of Policy, Rsch. and Devel. in the Third World (conf. program planning com. 1988-89, chair health and population sect. 1988-89), Miss. Coun. Geog. Edn. (pres., chair program com. 1979-80), Population Assn. Am., Assn. Social and Behavioral Scientists, Mich. Acad. Scis., Sigma Rho Sigma Nat. Honor Soc., Gamma Theta Upsilon Nat. Honor Soc., Alpha Kappa Mu Nat. Honor Soc., Alpha Phi Alpha Frat., Inc. Home: 3700 Colchester Rd Lansing MI 48906-3418 Office: Mich State U Ctr Urban Affairs W-104 Owen Hall East Lansing MI 48824

LANG, MARY ANN, special education educator, administrator; b. N.Y.C., Sept. 9, 1941; d. Raymond Joseph and Frances Dorothy (Campbell) Haefner; children: Diane Elyse, Linda Ann. BA, Queens Coll., CUNY, 1963; MS, Hunter Coll., CUNY, 1969; MPhil, CUNY, 1983, PhD, 1984. Lic. psychologist, N.Y.; cert. in elem. edn. and blindness and visual impairment, N.Y. Tchr. N.Y.C. Bd. Edn., 1963-68; adj. faculty Hunter Coll., CUNY, 1969-76; dir. child devel. ctr. The Lighthouse Inc., N.Y.C., 1976-78, dir. profl. tng., 1983-85, dir. program devel., 1985-88, dir. Nat. Ctr. for Vision and Child Devel., 1988—, coord. internat. programs, 1993-96, dir. Internat. Ctr. on Low Vision, 1996—, v.p. internat. programs, 1998—. Vis. prof. U. Talca, Chile, 1983-85; mem. adv. bd. Head Start-Resource Access Project, N.Y., N.J., P.R., V.I., 1980-94. Author: (book and video) A Special Start, 1991; co-author: AIDS, Blindness, and Low Vision: A Guide for Service Providers, 1990, Getting in Touch with Play, 1991, AIDS, Blindness, and Low Vision: A Manual for Health Organizations, 1992, Technology for Tots, 1992, Toys and Play, 1995; editor-in-chief: Lighthouse Handbook on Vision Impairment and Vision Rehabilitation, 2000; editor: Rehabilitation: Assessment, Intervention and Outcomes, 2000. Recipient Elena Gall medal Hunter Coll., 1969. Mem. APHA, Assn. for Edn. and Rehab. of the Blind and Visually Impaired (N.Y. state bd. dirs. 1985-91, Meritorious Achievement award 1993), Assn. for Childhood Edn. Internat., Nat. Assn. Parents of the Visually Impaired, Nat. Head Start Assn. Home: 205 West End Ave Apt 14C New York NY 10023-4810 Office: Lighthouse Internat 111 E 59th St New York NY 10022-1202

LANG, MICHAEL BENJAMIN, law educator; b. Washington, 1951; m. Isa Allentuck, 1973; children: Leonard Abraham, Julie Rose. AB, Harvard U., 1972; JD, U. Pa., 1975. Bar: Pa. 1975, Ill. 1981. Asst. prof. law Ill. Inst. Tech./Chgo.-Kent Coll. Law, 1978-79; assoc. prof. law U. Utah, Salt Lake City, 1979-81; from assoc. prof. law to prof. U. Maine Law Sch., Portland, Maine, 1983—2002, assoc. dean, 1993—96; prof. law Chapman U., Orange, Calif., 2002—, dir. LLM in Taxation program, 2002—. Vis. prof. law U. San Diego, 1986, 87-88, Washington U., St. Louis, 1991-92, U. Miami, 2000; bd. editors and advisors The Rev. of Taxation of Individuals, N.Y.C., 1989-92. Article editor The Tax Lawyer, Chgo., 1987-90, ann. report editor, 1997-2000; collaborator multivol. treatise; Federal Taxation of Income, Estates and Gifts, 1981; co-author: Federal Tax Elections, 1991; co-compiler; (multivol. index) Index to Federal Tax Articles, 1982—. Mem. ABA (chair tax sect. com. on standards of tax practice 2003—), Order of the Coif, Am. Coll. Tax Counsel.

LANG, VICKI SCOTT, primary school educator; b. Phila., June 30, 1951; d. Daniel Scotty and Verna (Laret) L. BA, Elon Coll., 1972; Masters, Old Dominion U., 1984. Kindergarten tchr. Moyock N.C. Elem. Sch., 1974—. Recipient Tchr. of the Year award, Moyock Elem. Sch., 1981, Govs. award, RaleighN.C., 1990. Mem. NCAE, NCA of Young Educators. Avocations: walking, sewing, enjoying the beach. Home: 2217 Maple St Virginia Beach VA 23451-1307

LANGAN, JOHN PATRICK, philosophy educator; b. Hartford, Conn., Aug. 10, 1940; s. Eugene Edward and Sarah Cecilia (McCole) Langan. AB, Loyola U., Chgo., 1962; MA, Loyola U., 1966; BD, Woodstock Coll., N.Y.C., 1970; PhD, U. Mich., 1979. Ordained priest, Roman Cath. Ch., 1972. Instr. philosophy U. Mich., Ann Arbor, 1971-72; research fellow Woodstock Theol. Ctr., Washington, 1975-83; vis. asst. prof. social ethics Yale Div. Sch., New Haven, 1983; sr. fellow Woodstock Theol. Ctr., 1983-95, acting dir., 1986-87; Rose F. Kennedy prof. Christian ethics Kennedy Inst. Ethics, Georgetown U., Washington, 1987—99; Joseph Cardinal Bernardin prof. of Cath. Social Thought Georgetown U., Washington, 1999—. Bd. dirs. Georgetown U. Press, 1984—; vis. rsch. scholar Jesuit Inst. Boston Coll., 1993-94; mem. rsch. coun. Ctr. Strategic and Internat. Studies, 1993—; Wirtenberger prof. social ethics Loyola U. Chgo., 1995-97; cons. in field. Editor: The American Search for Peace, 1991, The Nuclear Dilemma and the Just War Tradition, 1986, Human Rights in the Americas: The Struggle for Consensus, 1982, Catholic Universities in Church and Society, 1993, A Moral Vision for America, 1998. Bd. dirs. Cath. Health Svcs. of L.I., Care Alliance, S.C., Bon Secours Health Sys., 1990-2000, Nat. Capital Presbytery, Health Care Ministries, Washington, 1989-92. Rackham Prize fellow, U. Mich., 1972-73. Mem. Am. Acad. Religion, Am. Philos. Assn., Cath. Theol. Soc. Am., Soc. Christian Ethics (v.p., pres.-elect 2003-04), Soc. Christian Philosophers, Soc. for Bus. Ethics, Internat. Studies Assn. Roman Catholic. Avocations: music, swimming. Office: Georgetown U Kennedy Inst Ethics Washington DC 20057-0001

LANGBEIN, JOHN HARRISS, lawyer, educator; b. Washington, Nov. 17, 1941; s. I. L. and M. V. (Harriss) L.; m. Kirsti M. Hiekka, June 24, 1973; children: Christopher, Julia, Anne. AB, Columbia U., 1964; LLB, Harvard U., 1968, Cambridge U., 1969, PhD, 1971; MA (hon.), Yale U., 1990. Bar: D.C. 1969, Fla. 1970; barrister-at-law Inner Temple, Eng., 1970. Asst. prof. law U. Chgo., 1971-73, assoc. prof., 1973-74, prof., 1974-80, Max Pam prof. Am. and fgn. law, 1980-90; Goodhart Prof. Legal Sci. Cambridge Univ., 1997-98, Chancellor Kent prof., 1990—2001; Sterling prof. law and legal history Yale U., New Haven, 2001—. Commr. Nat. Conf. Commrs. on Uniform State Laws, 1984—; reporter Uniform Prudent Investor Act; assoc. reporter Am. Law Inst., Restatement of Property (3d): Wills and Other Donative Transfers, 1990—. Author: Prosecuting Crime in the Renaissance, 1974, Torture and the Law of Proof: Europe and England in the Ancient Regime, 1977, Comparative Criminal Procedure, 1977, The Origins of Adversary Criminal Trial, 2003; author: (with L. Waggoner) Uniform Trusts and Estate Statutes, rev. edit., 2003; author: (with R. Helmholz et al.) The Privilege Against Self-Incrimination, 1997; author: (with B. Wolk) Pension and Employee Benefit Law, 1990; contbr. articles to profl. jours. Fellow Trinity Hall Cambridge U. (hon.); mem. ABA, Am. Acad. Arts. and Scis., Am. Coll. Trust and Estate Counsel, Am. Law Inst., Am. Soc. Legal History, Am. Hist. Assn., Selden Soc., Gesellschaft fuer Rechtsvergleichung, Internat. Acad. Estate and Trust Law, Internat. Acad. Comparative Law. Republican. Episcopalian. Office: Yale Univ Sch Law PO Box 208215 127 Wall St New Haven CT 06520-8215 E-mail: john.langbein@yale.edu.

LANGDON, KAREN SIMS, consultant; b. Washington, Aug. 13, 1951; d. William Pierce and Doris Jane (Hannigan) Sims; m. John Todd Langdon, Aug. 25, 1984; children: Kaitlin Marie, Jordan Alyssa. BS, Emory U., 1973; MEd, U. Ariz., 1975; doctoral student, U. S.C., 1982—. Clin. counselor Dept. Behavioral Medicine, Hilton Head (S.C.) Hosp., 1976-79; dir. behavior modification Diabetes Rsch. & Tng. Ctr., Birmingham, Ala., 1979-81; bd. mem. Medianet, Inc., Austin, Tex., 1986—. Vol. crisis counselor Endometriosis Assn., Milw., 1986—; founder, dir. Summer Wonders, Inc., 1999—. Mem. APA.

LANGE, LINDA DIANE, education educator, researcher; b. Muskegon, Mich., Jan. 28, 1950; AB in Edn., U. Mich., 1974, EdS in Edn. and Psychology, 1978, PhD in Edn., 1991. Cert. sch. psychologist, N.J. Dance coach Huron (Mich.) H.S., 1974-75; sch. psychologist Lenawee County Schs., Adrian, Mich., 1979-80; rsch. asst. The Psychol. Corp., San Antonio, 1986-88; asst. prof. edn. Marshall U., Huntington, W.Va., 1991-95. Vis. asst. prof. edn. Sacred Heart U. Fairfield, Conn., 1995-96; ednl. rschr. Collaborative Rsch. Bd. Marshall U., 1992-93; presenter in field. Contbr. articles to profl. jours. Mem. ASCD, APA, Am. Assn. Tchg. and Curriculum, Am. Ednl. Rsch. Assn., Assn. Tchr. Educators, Ea. Ednl. Rsch. Assn., Soc. Rsch. on Adolescence, Soc. for Study of Social Problems, Southeastern Assn. Ednl. Studies, New England Edn. Rsch. Orgn. Lutheran. Avocations: dance, music, art, water sports, skiing. Address: PO Box 416 Bridgeport CT 06601-0416

LANGEFOSS, HEATHER SMITH, elementary education educator; b. Boston, Jan. 28, 1947; d. Nelson Clare and Julia Mary (Richards) Smith; m. Curt Michael Langefoss, July 24, 1982. BA, Wheaton Coll., 1968; MA in Teaching, Simmons Coll., 1969. Cert. tchr., Mass. Tchr. elem. South River Sch., Marshfield, Mass., 1969-79, Governor Winslow Sch., Marshfield, Mass., 1979—. Exec. bd. mem. The Woman's Club of Norwell, Mass., 1985-92. Selected to participate in Mus. Inst. for Teaching Sci., NSF, 1988, 90, selected to participate in year long sci. program Seasons and Cycles funded by Eisenhower grant, 1991-92; recipient grant, 1991-92, Patriot Ledger Golden Apple award, 1992. Mem. Profl. Devel. Com. of Marshfield Pub. Schs., Delta Kappa Gamma. Unitarian Universalist. Avocations: sailing, travel, gardening. Home: 705 River St Norwell MA 02061-2702 Office: Gov Winslow Sch 60 Regis Rd Marshfield MA 02050-4299

LANGENHEIM, RALPH LOUIS, JR., geology educator; b. Cin., May 26, 1922; s. Ralph Louis and Myrtle (Helmers) L.; m. Jean C. Harmon, Dec. 23, 1946; m. Virginia A.M. Knobloch, June 5, 1963; children: Victoria Elizabeth, Ralph Louis III; m. Shirley B. Ate, May 1, 1970; stepchildren: Judy Grigg, Lynn Ate, Kathleen Majack; m. Casey Diana, Mar. 6, 1993; stepchildren: Eric Steckler, Matthew Diana. BS, U. Tulsa, 1943; MS, U.

Colo., 1947; PhD, U. Minn., 1951. Registered profl. geologist, Wyo. Teaching asst. U. Tulsa, 1941-43, U. Colo., 1947; fellow U. Minn., 1947-48, tchg. asst., 1948-50; asst. prof. Coe Coll., 1950-52; asst. prof. paleontology U. Calif., Berkeley, 1952-59, curator Paleozoic and early Mesozoic fossil invertebrates, 1952-59; from asst. prof. geology to prof. U. Ill., Urbana, 1959-92, prof. emeritus, 1993—; curator fossil invertebrates Mus. Nat. History, 1988-92, curator emeritus, 1993—; with Inst. Geologico Nac. de Colombia, summer 1953; Geol. Survey Can., summer 1958; Geol. Survey Iran, fall 1973; Geol. Survey Republic of China, fall 1981; ptnr. Lanman Assocs., Cons. Geologists, 1974—. Cons., mem. faculty geology and mining depts. Poly. U., Albania, fall 1992; vis. disting. prof. U. Nev., Las Vegas, 1994-2003; book rev. editor Jour. Geol. Edn., 1990-2003. Assoc. editor Jour. Paleontology, 1995-96. Mem. Champaign County (Ill.) Bd., 1998—. With USNR, 1943-46; lt. comdr. Res., ret. Recipient Rudolph Eric Raspe medal Inst. Geometaphysik Neue Schwanstein, 1973. Fellow AAAS, Paleontol. Soc. (sec. 1962-70), Geol. Soc. Am., Soc. Sedimentary Geology (formerly Soc. Econ. Paleontologists and Mineralogists), Am. Assn. Petroleum Geologists, Internat. Assn. Cnidaria Specialists (treas. 1977-79), Nat. Assn. Geology Tchrs., Ill. Acad. Sci., Rocky Mountain Biol. Lab., Explorers Club, Sigma Xi. Rsch. and publs. in stratigraphy and paleontology. Home: 401 W Vermont Ave Urbana IL 61801-4928 Office: U Ill Dept Geology 1301 W Green St # 245NHB Urbana IL 61801-2919 E-mail: rlangenh@uiuc.edu.

LANGE-OTSUKA, PATRICIA ANN, nursing educator; b. Sandusky, Ohio, June 25, 1959; d. James Henry and Elaine Elnora Lange; m. Lewis Masao Otsuka, Mar. 29, 1994; 1 stepchild, Katrina. Diploma in nursing, Providence Hosp. Sch. Nursing, 1981; BSN, Bowling Green State U., 1984; MSN in Cmty. Health, Med. Coll. Ohio Sch. Nursing, 1991; postgrad. in pharmacology, U. Hawaii, 1996; EdD in Higher Edn., Nova Southeastern U., 1999. RN, Hawaii, Ohio; clin. specialist in cmty. health, ANA; APRN, Hawaii, Ohio, AONE, Hawaii. RN Providence Hosp., Sandusky, Ohio, 1981-91; grad. tchg. asst. Med. Coll. Ohio, Huron, 1989-91; nursing supr. Bellevue (Ohio) Hosp., 1991; asst. prof. nursing Hawaii Loa Coll., Kaneohe, 1991-92, Hawaii Pacific U., Kaneohe, 1992—, acad. coord., 1993-98, nursing grad. program chair, 1998—, assoc. prof., 2000—. NCLEX rev. provider Med. Coll. Pa., Honolulu, 1993, Stanley Kaplan Corp., Honolulu, 1994, LBJ Tropical Med. Ctr., Pago Pago, 1996; freelance edn. cons., Hawaii, 1991—; vice chmn. Faculty Assembly, 2000-01, chmn., 2001—. Recipient Svc. awards Am. Diabetes Assn. Ohio Affiliate, Columbus and Sandusky, 1990. Mem. Assn. Nurse Execs. (treas. Hawaii chpt. 1999-2000), Providence Hosp. Sch. Nursing Alumnae Assn. (pres.-elect, pres. 1988-90), Sigma Theta Tau (Gamma Psi at large, counselor 1993-97, Excellence in Nursing Edn. award 1999), Nat. Orgn. Nurse Practioner Faculty, Hawaii League for Nursing (pres.-elect 2002-03, pres. 2003—). Office: Hawaii Pacific Univ 45-045 Kamehameha Hwy Kaneohe HI 96744-5297

LANGER, ELLEN JANE, psychologist, educator, writer; b. N.Y.C., Mar. 25, 1947; d. Norman and Sylvia (Tobias) L. BA, NYU, 1970; PhD, Yale U., 1974. Cert. clin. psychologist. Asst. prof. psychology The Grad. Ctr. CUNY, 1974-77; assoc. prof. psychology Harvard U., Cambridge, Mass., 1977-81, prof., 1981—. Cons. NAS, 1979-81, NASA; mem. div. on aging Harvard U. Med. Sch., 1979—, mem. psychiat. epidemiology steering com., 1982-90; chair social psychology program Harvard U., 1982-94, chair Faculty Arts and Scis. Com. of Women, 1984-88. Author: Personal Politics, 1973, Psychology of Control, 1983, Mindfulness, 1989, The Power of Mindful Learning, 1997; editor: (with Charles Alexander) Higher Stages of Human Development, 1990, (with Roger Schank) Beliefs, Reasoning and Decision-Making, 1994; contbr. articles to profl. and scholarly jours. Guggenheim fellow; grantee NIMH, NSF, Soc. for Psychol. Study of Social Issues, Milton Fund, Sloan Found., 1982; recipient Disting. Contbn. of Basic to Applied Psychology award APS, 1995. Fellow Computers and Soc. Inst., Am. Psychol. Assn. (Disting. Contributions to Psychology in Public Interest award 1988, Disting. Contributions of Basic Sci. to Applied Psychology 1995); mem. Soc. Exptl. Social Psychology, Phi Beta Kappa, Sigma Xi. Democrat. Jewish. Avocations: theater, horseback riding, tennis. Office: Harvard U Dept Psychology 33 Kirkland St Cambridge MA 02138-2044

LANGER, GLENN ARTHUR, cellular physiologist, educator; b. Nyack, N.Y., May 5, 1928; s. Adolph Arthur and Marie Catherine (Doscher) L.; m. Beverly Joyce Brawley, June 5, 1954 (dec. Nov. 1976); 1 child, Andrea; m. Marianne Phister, Oct. 12, 1977. BA, Colgate U., 1950; MD, Columbia U., N.Y.C., 1954. Diplomate Am. Bd. Internal Medicine. Asst. prof. medicine Columbia U. Coll. Physicians and Surgeons, N.Y.C., 1963-66; assoc. prof. medicine and physiology UCLA Sch. Medicine, 1966-69, prof., 1969-97, Castera prof. cardiology, 1978-97, assoc. dean rsch., 1986-91, dir. cardiovascular rsch. lab., 1987-97, emeritus prof., 1997—. Griffith vis. prof. Am. Heart Assn., L.A., 1979; cons. Acad. Press, N.Y.C., 1989-97; founder, dir. Partnership Scholars Program, 1996—. Author: Understanding Disease, 1999; editor: The Mammalian Myocardium, 1974, 2d edit., 1997, Calcium and the Heart, 1990; mem. editl. bd. Circulation Rsch., 1971-76, Am. Jour. Physiology, 1971-76, Jour. Molecular Cell Cardiology, 1974-97; contbr. more than 200 articles to profl. jours. Pres., dir. Partnership Scholars Program for disadvantaged youth, 1996—. Capt. U.S. Army, 1955-57. Recipient Disting. Achievement award Am. Heart Assn. Sci. Coun., 1982, Heart of Gold award, 1984, Cybulski medal Polish Physiol. Soc., Krakow, 1990, Pasarow Found. award for Cardiovascular Sci., 1993, Outstanding Acad. Title citation Choice mag., 2001; Macy scholar Josiah Macy Found., 1979-80. Fellow AAAS, Am. Coll. Cardiology, Internat. Soc. for Heart Rsch.; mem. Am. Soc. Clin. Investigation, Am. Assn. Physicians. Achievements include research on control of cardiac contraction. E-mail: glang@mcn.org.

LANGFORD, JACK DANIEL, elementary school educator; b. Cookeville, Tenn., Jan. 15, 1960; s. Sam Harley and Mary Delma (Carr) L.; m. Marilyn Patricia Poteet. BS in Secondary Edn., Tenn. Tech. U., 1983, MA in Ednl. Adminstrn. and Supervision, 1987, MA, 1993, postgrad. Lic. tchr., Tenn. Bus. tchr. Dekalb County H.S., Smithville, Tenn., 1984; social studies tchr. White County Mid. Sch., Sparta, Tenn., 1985-92; 1st-6th grade title I tchr. Findlay Elem. Sch., Sparta, Tenn., 1992—. Chmn. Findlay Improvement Team, Sparta, 1993—, co-chmn. discipline stds. com., 1996—. Vice-pres. White County Natural Resource Conservation Svc.; mem. Nat. Arbor Day Found.; trustee Almyra Meth. Co. Recipient Career Ladder II State of Tenn., 1995. Mem. ASCD, NEA, Tenn. Edn. Assn., Internat. Reading Assn., Nat. Geog. Soc., White County Edn. Assn., Tenn. Cattlemen's Assn., White-Van Buren Cattlemen's Assn., White County Farm Bur., Nat. Arbor Soc., Tenn. Assn. for Supervision and Curriculum Devel., Tenn. Reading Assn., Phi Delta Kappa. Avocations: reading, movies, sight seeing, conversing with friends, visiting. Home: 1404 Lawrence Hudgens Rd Sparta TN 38583-3703

LANGGOOD, JUDITH ANN, secondary level art educator; b. Buffalo, Feb. 2, 1950; d. Alfred Victor Canetti and Irma Frances (Oakes) Reitz. BA, Geneseo (N.Y.) State Coll., 1972; MS in Edn., SUNY, Buffalo, 2000. Cert. elem. and secondary sch. art tchr., N.Y. H.S. art tchr., Holland, 1995—2002, Christian Home & Bible Sch., Mount Dora, Fla., 2002—. Dir. art Camp Agape, Buffalo, 1978-80; cons. art activities Camp Fresh Horizons, Buffalo, 1995. Freelance jewelry designer and fabricator, 1975—; exhibited paintings in area art shows, 1977—. Mem. Nat. Art Edn. Assn., N.Y. State Art Tchrs. Assn., Buffalo Fine Arts Acad., Kappa Delta Pi, Alpha Sigma Lambda. Avocations: painting, ceramics, jewelry design, music, literature.

LANGHAM, NORMA E. playwright, educator, poet, composer, inventor; b. California, Pa. d. Alfred Scrivener and Mary Edith (Carter) L. BS, Ohio State U., 1942; B in Theatre Arts, Pasadena Playhouse Coll. Theatre Arts, 1944; MA, Stanford U., 1956; postgrad., Summer Radio-TV Inst., 1960, Pasadena Inst. Radio, 1944-45. Tchr. sci. California High Sch., 1942-43; asst. office pub. info. Denison U., Granville, Ohio, 1955; instr. speech dept. Westminster Coll., New Wilmington, Pa., 1957-58; instr. theatre. California U., Pa., 1959, asst. prof., 1960-62, assoc. prof., 1962-79, prof. emeritus, 1979—, co-founder, sponsor, dir. Children's Theatre, 1962-79. Founder, producer, dir. Food Bank Players, 1985, Patriot Players, 1986, Noel Prodns., 1993. Writer: (plays) Magic in the Sky, 1963, Founding Daughters (Pa., Nat. DAR awards 1991), Women Whisky Rebels (Pa. Nat. DAR awards 1992), John Dough (Freedoms Found. award 1968), Who Am I?, Hippocrates Oath, Gandhi, Clementine of '49, Soul Force, Dutch Painting, Purim, Music in Freedom, The Moon Is Falling, Norma Langham's Job Johnson; composer, lyricist: (plays) Why Me, Lord?, (text) Public Speaking; co-inventor (computer game) Highway Champion. Recipient Exceptional Acad. Svc. award Pa. Dept. Edn., 1975, Appreciation award Bicentennial Commn. Pa., 1976, Gregg award Calif. U. of Pa. Alumni Assn., 1992, Emeriti Faculty award California U. Pa., 2000. Mem. AAUW (co-founder Calif. br., 1st v.p. 1971-72, pres. 1972-73, Outstanding Woman of Yr. 1986, 97), DAR, Internat. Platform Assn. (poetry award 1993, 94, monologue award 1997), California U. Pa. Assn. Women Faculty (founder, pres. 1972-73), California 150, California Hist. Soc., Pa. Assn. Safety Edn., Washington County Hist. Soc., Dramatists Guild, Ctr. in Woods, Mensa, Alpha Psi Omega, Omicron Nu. Presbyterian (elder). Home: 204 Ellsworth St California PA 15419-1206

LANGHORNE, LINDA KAY, health and physical education teacher; b. Lynchburg, Va., July 19; d. Theodore R. Sr. and Carolyn (Payne) L. BS, Hampton Inst. (Hampton U.), 1977, MA, 1984. Tchr. Lynchburg City Schs., Linkhorne Mid. Sch., 1978—. Mem. AAHPERD, NEA, Va. Edn. Assn., Va. Assn. for Health, Phys. Edn., Recreation and Dance, Va. Assn. Driver Edn. and Traffic Safety. Home: 1214 19th St Lynchburg VA 24504-3418 Office: Lynchburg City Schs Linkhorne Mid Sch 2525 Linkhorne Dr Lynchburg VA 24503-3315

LANGLAND, OLAF ELMER, retired dental educator; b. Madrid, Iowa, May 30, 1925; s. Raymond F. and Minnie Margaret (Kinsey) L.; m. Carolyn Anderson, Oct. 1955 (div. 1973); children: Sara Mindell, Beth Langland (dec. Feb. 2002); m. Ruth Klabunde, July 1, 1975 (dec. Jan. 1985); children: Julie Van Delden, Gary Kablunde; m. Gwen E. Stokes, Apr. 25, 1991; children: Renée Williams, Richard Stokes, Deborah Fato, D. Scott Stokes. DDS, U. Iowa, 1951, MS, 1961. Diplomate Am. Acad. Oral Medicine. Prof., head dept. oral diagnosis U. Iowa Sch. Dentistry, Iowa City, 1963-68; prof., head dept. oral diagnosis, medicine and radiology La. State U. Med. Ctr. and Dental Sch., New Orleans, 1968-74; prof., head div. oral and maxillofacial radiology U. Tex. Health Sci. Ctr., San Antonio, 1975-99, prof. emeritus, 1999—. Rotator U.S. Hope Ship, Maceio, Brazil, 1973. Author: Textbook of Dental Radiology, 1984, Radiology for Dental Assistants and Dental Hygienists, 1987, Principles and Practice of Panoramic Radiology, 1989, Diagnostic Imaging of the Jaws, 1994, Principles of Dental Imaging, 1997, 2nd edit. 2001. With inf. AUS, 1943-45, ETO. Decorated Purple Heart, Combat Infantry badge with star, Bronze Star; recipient Outstanding Tchr. award U. Tex. Health Sci. Ctr., 1992. Fellow Am. Coll. Dentists, Internat. Assn. of Dental Maxillofacial Radiology (hon.); mem. Am. Acad. Oral and Maxillofacial Radiology (diplomate, pres. 1984-85), Am. Acad. Dental Schs. (pres. sect. oral radiology 1974-75), Orgn. Tchrs. Diagnosis (pres. 1975-76), Masons, Shriners, Mil. Order of Purple Heart, Am. Legion. Avocation: civil war medical history. Home: 1819 Babcock Rd Apt 207 San Antonio TX 78229-4630

LANGLEY, JOELLEN S. music educator; b. Rocky Mt., N.C., Mar. 12, 1950; d. John Sidney Jr. and Josephine Smith; m. John B. Langley; 1 child, Jillian Joelle Hamby. BA in Music Edn., Temple U., 1975. Cert. K-12 music tchr., N.J., Pa. Music dir. Runnemede (N.J.) Pub. Schs., 1978—. Co-owner children's music prodn. co. JJ Creations; spkr. in field. Composer, singer, tchr., adult and children's music; performer Phila. Civic Ctr., 1988; publ. children's music; author, developer, prodr. All Inclusive Related Arts Curriculum and Prodns., 2000-. U.S. rep. to Venezuela by spl. invitation of consul gen. Venezuela and min. fgn. affairs, 1995. Recipient Tchr. of Yr. award Gov. Tom Keane, N.J., 1988.

LANGRAN, ROBERT WILLIAMS, political scientist, educator; b. N.Y.C., Feb. 15, 1935; s. Robert Joseph and Leona Gertrude (Williams) L.; m. Eleanor Victoria Groh, Dec. 26, 1959; children: Irene, Elizabeth, Thomas. BS with honors, Loyola U., Chgo., 1956; MA, Fordham U., 1959; PhD, Bryn Mawr Coll., 1965. Prof. polit. sci. Villanova U., Pa., 1959—. Author: (book) The United States Supreme Court: An Historical and Political Analysis, 1989, 2d edit. 1992, 3d edit. 1995, 4th edit. 1999; co-author: Government, Business, and the American Economy, 2001; contbr. articles to profl. publs. Served to 1st lt. U.S. Army, 1956-58. Mem. Am. Polit. Sci. Assn., Supreme Ct. Hist. Soc. Office: Villanova Univ Political Sci Dept Villanova PA 19085

LANGSHINE-KISTLER, DONNA, elementary education educator; b. Paterson, N.J., Jan. 1, 1952; d. Theodore John and Dorothy Langstine; m. David Mahlon Kistler, Aug. 4, 1979; 1 child, Dana Megan. BA in Edn., Rider Coll., 1974. Cert. K-8 tchr., Md. Title I tchr. Pemberton Township (N.J.) Schs., 1974-79; daycare tchr. Kindercare, Framingham, Mass., 1979-83; tchr. kindergarten Palloti Early Learning Ctr., Laurel, Md., 1988. Mem. AAUW. Avocations: reading, gardening. Office: Palotti Early Learning Ctr 113 Saint Marys Pl Laurel MD 20707-4025

LANGSTAFF, ELEANOR MARGUERITE, retired library science educator; b. Washington, June 21, 1934; d. William Truman and Bernice Louise (Tharpe-Mecum) De Selms; m. David Knox Langstaff, June 19, 1970 (dec. 1984). BA, Colo. State U., Ft. Collins, 1958; MA, Fordham U., 1961; MS, Cath. U. Am., 1970; MPhil, CUNY, 1994, PhD, 1998; cert. in tropical edn., U. London/Makerere Coll., Uganda. Mem. Tchrs. for East Africa program Columbia U., N.Y.C., 1961-64; fgn. svc. officer USIA, 1965-69, acting country pub. affairs officer, 1967-68, regional books officer, 1968-69; libr. Sch. Libr. and Info. Sci., Pratt Inst., N.Y.C., 1970-72; assoc. prof. libr. sci. Bernard M. Baruch Coll., CUNY, 1973-95, prof., 1996—. Cons. on info. Langstaff-French Assocs., Manchester, Vt., 1982-88; dir. hypermedia devel. project Libr. Svc. and Constrn. Act, U.S. Dept. Edn., 1989-90. Author: Andrew Lang, 1978; (with Thomas V. Atkins) Access to Information: Library Research and Demonstration Methods, 1979, Panama, 1982; co-author: Access Information: Business, 1986, 90, Access Information: Social Sciences and Humanities, 1990; (with others) British Women Writers, 1988. Vol. ARC, Bklyn., 1972—. Recipient excellence in French lit. award French Govt., 1958, Fulbright Lecturing award U. Mauritius, 1992—. Mem. ALA, Libr. Assn. CUNY (v.p. 1974-75, pres. 1975-76), Assn. Coll. and Rsch. Librs., Phi Beta Mu. Episcopalian. Home: 100 Remsen St Brooklyn NY 11201-4256 E-mail: elang2@juno.com.

LANGWIG, JOHN EDWARD, retired wood science educator; b. Albany, N.Y., Mar. 5, 1924; s. Frank Irving and Arlene Stone (Dugan) L.; m. Margaret Jacquelyn Kirk, Aug. 31, 1946; 1 dau., Nancy Ann Langwig Davis. BS, U. Mich., 1948; MS, Coll. of Forestry, SUNY, Syracuse, 1968, PhD, 1971. Asst. to supt. Widdicomb Furniture Co., Grand Rapids, Mich., 1948-50; salesman John B. Hauf Furniture, Inc., Albany, N.Y., 1950-51; asst. mgr. furniture dept. Montgomery Ward Co., Menands, N.Y., 1951-52; office mgr. U.S. Plywood Corp., Syracuse, 1952-65; instr. wood products engring. SUNY Coll. Forestry, Syracuse, 1969-70; asst. prof. wood sci. Okla. State U., Stillwater, 1971-74, prof., head dept. forestry, 1974-81, prof. wood sci., wood products extension specialist, 1982-86, mem. faculty council, 1983-86; mem. Gov.'s Com. on Forest Practices, 1975-77. Contbr. articles to profl. jours. Served with AUS, 1943-45. NSF fellow, 1966-68 Mem. Soc. Am. Foresters, TAPPI, Forest Products Research Soc. (regional bd. dirs. 1983-89, regional rep. to nat. exec. bd. 1983-86), Soc. Wood Sci. and Tech., Okla. Acad. Sci., Okla. Forestry Assn. (bd. dirs. 1982-83), Council Forestry Sch. Execs., Sigma Xi, Xi Sigma Pi., Gamma Sigma Delta, Alpha Zeta, Phi Kappa Phi. Episcopalian. Home: 33 Liberty Cir Stillwater OK 74075-2015 Office: Okla State U Dept Forestry Stillwater OK 74078-0001

LANIER, ANITA SUZANNE, musician, piano educator; b. Talladega, Ala., May 21, 1946; d. Luther Dwight and Elva (Hornsby) L. BS in Music Edn., Jacksonville (Ala.) State U., 1969. Elem. music tchr. Talladega City Schs., 1969-81; librarian, elem. music tchr. Talladega Acad., 1981-84; tchr. piano and organ Talladega, 1981—. Organist Trinity United Meth. Ch., Talladega, 1981—. Recipient Commemorative Honor medallion, 1990, World Decoration of Excellence medallion, 1990; named Woman of the Yr., 1990, Rsch. Adv. of Yr., 1990, ABI, 1990. Mem. NAFE, AAUW, Am. Pianists Assn., World Inst. Achievement, Women's Inner Circle Achievement, Internat. Platform Assn., Delta Omicron. Home: 601 North St E Talladega AL 35160-2525

LANIER, WILLIAM JOSEPH, college program director; b. Great Falls, Mont., Dec. 20, 1963; s. Bolder Lanue and Nancy Jo (Kiszczak) L. AS, No. Mont. Coll., 1985, B Tech., 1987, MEd, 1989. Grad. asst. No. Mont. Coll., Havre, 1987-89; dir. residence life Mont. State U. -No. (formerly No. Mont. Coll.), Havre, 1989-95, dir. student life, 1995—. Bd. dirs. Havre Encourages Long Range Prevention, 1992-95, Hill County Crimestoppers, 1991-93; adv. bd. No. Ctrl. Mont. Upward Bound, Harlem, 1992-97. Recipient Golden N award student senate No. Mont. Coll., 1992. Mem. Am. Counseling Assn., Am. Coll. Pers. Assn., Nat. Assn. Student Pers. Adminstrs., Nat. Eagle Scout Assn., No. Mont. Coll. Alumni Assn. (bd. dirs 1990—). Avocations: reading, collecting baseball cards. Home: 1236 10th Ave Havre MT 59501 Office: Mont State U PO Box 7751 Havre MT 59501-7751

LANIER, WILLIAM LOVEL, JR., anesthesiologist, educator; b. Statesboro, Ga., June 8, 1955; s. William Lovel Sr. and Nancy (Jones) L.; m. Mary Duckworth, July 15, 1978; children: Elizabeth Brooke, William Hudson. BS, U. Ga., 1976; MD, Med. Coll. of Ga., 1980. Diplomate Am. Bd. Anesthesiology (examiner 1994—, cert. of recertification 2001-). Resident in anesthesiology Wake Forest U. Med. Ctr., Bowman Gray Sch. Medicine, Winston-Salem, N.C., 1980-83; fellow in neurosurg. anesthesia Mayo Grad. Sch. Medicine, Rochester, Minn., 1983-84; cons. in anesthesiology Mayo Clinic, Rochester, 1984—, prof. anesthesiology, 1995—. Aitken Meml. lectr. U. Western Ont., London, 1993; Marshall Meml. lectr. U. Toronto, 2000. Sect. editor: Jour. Neurosurg. Anesthesiology, 1988—92, editor-in-chief: Mayo Clinic Procs., 1999—; contbr. numerous articles and editls. to profl. publs, chapters to books. Grantee NIH, 1999—. Mem.: Coun. Sci. Editors, Am. Diabetes Assn., Assn. of Univ. Anesthesiologists (mem. sci. adv. bd. 1998—2001), Soc. Neurosurg. Anesthesiology and Critical Care (pres. 1993—94), Am. Soc. Anesthesiologists, First Families of Ga., Phi Kappa Phi, Phi Beta Kappa. Roman Catholic. Avocations: fishing, hunting, reading, boating. Office: Mayo Clinic 200 1st St SW Rochester MN 55905-0002 E-mail: lanier.william@mayo.edu.

LANKFORD, MARY ANNE, elementary school educator; b. Nashville, July 22, 1965; d. Sammy Dale and Peggy Elizabeth (Overall) Cooper; m. Charles Lee Lankford, Aug. 31, 1985. Student, David Lipscomb Coll., 1987, Tenn. Tech. U., 2001—. Tchr. Clarendon Sch. Dist. 1, Summerton, SC, 1988-90, Sumter Sch. Dist. 2, 1990-92, Putnam County Schs., Tenn., 2001—. Treas. Sumter Community Concert Band, 1989-90. Mem.: Pi Lambda Theta, Phi Kappa Phi. Mem. Ch. of Christ. Avocations: sewing, reading. Home: 3590 White Cemetery Rd Cookeville TN 38501-6736

LANNOM, JULIE CONWAY HUDSON, secondary education educator; b. Knoxville, Tenn., Dec. 8, 1950; d. Julius F. and Rhema Y. (Smith) Hudson; m. David C. Lannom, Oct. 7, 1972; children: Marcus David, Michael Franklin. BS, U. Tenn., 1972, MS, 1976. Tchr. Roane County Schs., Kingston, Tenn., 1975—. Mem. Nat. Coun. Tchrs. Maths. Avocations: quilting, reading, cooking. Office: Roane County High Sch 540 W Cumberland St Kingston TN 37763

LANOU, ROBERT EUGENE, JR., physicist, educator; b. Colchester, Vt., Feb. 13, 1928; s. Robert E. and Flora G. (Goyette) L.; m. Cornelia Rockwell Wheeler, May 14, 1960; children: Katharine, Gregory, Elizabeth, Steven. BS, Worcester Poly. Inst., 1952; PhD, Yale U., 1957. Physicist Lawrence Berkeley (Calif.) Lab., 1956-59; asst. prof. physicist Brown U., Providence, 1960-63, assoc. prof., 1963-67, prof., 1967—, chair dept. physics, 1986-92, prof. rsch., 2001—, prof., rschr., 2001—. Cons. Brookhaven Nat. Lab., Upton, N.Y., Los Alamos (N.Mex.) Nat. Lab.; sci. advisor Gov. State of R.I., Providence, 1986-88. Contbr. articles to profl. jours. With USN, 1946-48, ETO. Grantee Dept. Energy, 1960—, NSF, 1995—. Fellow AAAS, Am. Phys. Soc.; mem. Sigma Xi, Tau Beta Pi. Achievements include research in experimental particle physics and astrophysics. Home: 90 Keene St Providence RI 02906-1508 Office: Brown U Dept Physics Providence RI 02906

LANQUETOT, E. ROXANNE, retired special education educator; b. Kansas City, Nov. 29, 1933; d. Myron Lewis and Bonnie (Goldberg) Leiser; m. Guy Alfred Lanquetot, Oct. 3, 1958; 1 child, Serge Normand. Student, Stanford U., 1951-53; cert. in French Pronunciation, Inst. de Phonetique, Sorbonne, Paris, 1954; BS, Columbia U., 1956, MA, 1957, CCNY, 1976; postgrad., CUNY, 1980-83. Asst. tchr. English Lycee Fenelon, Paris, 1960-62; tchr. kindergarten Lycee Francais N.Y., N.Y.C., 1964-65; dir. nursery & kindergarten Lyceum Francais, N.Y.C., 1965-66; tchr. 2d grade Pub. Sch. 113 M, N.Y.C., 1966-69; tchr., jr. guidance counselor Pub. Sch. 87 M, N.Y.C., 1969-71; tchr. emotionally handicapped Pub. Sch. 106, Bellevue Hosp., N.Y.C., 1971-99; ret., 1999. Contbr. articles to profl. publs., Newsday, Wall St. Jour., France-Amerique, others. Fellow Am. Orthophychiatric Assn.; mem. Nat. Alliance for Rsch. on Schizophrenia and Depression (mem. leadership coun.). Avocations: classical music, theater, creative writing, travel, ballet, classical music, theatre. Home and Office: 315 W 106th St New York NY 10025-3445 E-mail: rglanquetot@yahoo.com.

LANSDOWNE, KAREN MYRTLE, retired English language and literature educator; b. Twin Falls, Idaho, Aug. 11, 1926; d. George and Effie Myrtle (Avotte) Martin; m. Paul L. Lansdowne, Sept. 12, 1948; children: Michele Lynn, Larry Alan. BA in English with honors, U. Oreg., 1948, MEd, 1958, MA with honors, 1960. Tchr. Newfield (N.Y.) H.S., 1948-50, S. Eugene (Oreg.) H.S., 1952; mem. faculty U. Oreg., Eugene, 1958-65; asst. prof. English Lane C.C., Eugene, 1965-82, ret., 1982. Cons. Oreg. Curriculum Study Center. Co-author: The Oregon Curriculum: Language/Rhetoric, I, II, III and IV, 1970; rsch., co-author: Lansdowne Family Genealogy Center Studies, 1995-99. Rep. Calif. Young Neighborhood Assn., 1978—; mem. scholarship com. First Congl. Ch., 1950-70. Mem. MLA, Pacific N.W. Regional Conf. C.C.s, Nat. Coun. Tchrs. English, U. Oreg. Women, AAUW (sec.) Jaycettes, Pi Lambda Theta (pres.), Phi Beta Patronesses (pres.), Delta Kappa Gamma. Home: 2056 Lincoln St Eugene OR 97405-2604

LANSING, KATHY ANN, elementary school educator; b. Plymouth, Mass., Jan. 16, 1952; d. Richard William and Mary Ann (Quintal) Correa; m. George Harding Warren, June 28, 1975 (div. Aug. 1979); m. Richard Francis Lansing, Aug. 4, 1981; children: Julie Noelle, Neil Christopher, Ben Richard, Brett Christian, Ashley Faith. Student, Emmanuel Coll., Boston, 1969-71; BA, U. Mass., Boston, 1973; MEd, Cambridge (Mass.) Coll., 1993. Computer programmer Liberty Mut. Ins. Co., Boston, 1973; elem.

tchr. Plymouth (Mass.) Pub. Schs., 1974—. Pres., Plymouth Lupus Support Group, Jordan Hosp., 1985-92; troop leader brownies Girl Scouts U.S., 1991-94; tchr. St. Joseph's Ch., Kingston, 1992-94. Roman Catholic.

LANTZ, JOANNE BALDWIN, academic administrator emeritus; b. Defiance, Ohio, Jan. 26, 1932; d. Hiram J. and Ethel A. (Smith) Baldwin; m. Wayne E. Lantz. BS in Physics and Math., U. Indpls., 1953; MS in Counseling and Guidance, Ind. U., 1957; PhD in Counseling and Psychology, Mich. State U., 1969; LittD (hon.), U. Indpls., 1985; LHD (hon.), Purdue U., 1994; LLD (hon.), Manchester Coll., 1994. Tchr. physics and math. Arcola (Ind.) High Sch., 1953-57; guidance dir. New Haven (Ind.) Sr. High Sch., 1957-65; with Ind. U.-Purdue U., Fort Wayne, 1965—, interim chancellor, 1988-89, chancellor, 1989-94, chancellor emeritus, 1994—. Bd. dirs., hon. dir. Ft. Wayne Nat. Corp.; bd. dirs. Foellinger Found. Contbr. articles to profl. jours. Mem. Ft. Wayne Econ. Devel. Adv. Bd. and Task Force, 1988-91, Corp. Coun., 1988-94; bd. advisors Leadership Ft. Wayne, 1988-94; mem. adv. bd. Ind. Sml. Bus. Devel. Ctr., 1988-90; trustee Ancilla System, Inc., 1984-89, chmn. human resources com., 1985-89, exec. com., 1985-89; trustee St. Joseph's Med. Ctr., 1983-84, pers. adv. com. to bd. dirs., 1978-84, chmn., 1980-84; bd. dirs. United Way Allen County, sec., 1979-80; bd. dirs. Anthony Wayne Vocat. Rehab. Ctr., 1969-75. Mem.: AAUW (internat. fellowship com. 1986—88, program com. 1981—83, Am. women fellowship com. 1978—83, chmn. 1981—83, trust rsch. grantee 1980), APA, Southeastern Psychol. Assn. (referee conv. papers 1987, 1988), Ft. Wayne Ind.-Purdue Alumni Soc. (hon. mem. 1987), Ind. Sch. Women's Club (v.p. program chair 1979—81), Delta Kappa Gamma (editl. bd. 1986—88, gen. chair conv. 1985—86, dir. N.E. region 1982—84, adminstrv. bd. 1982—84, exec. bd. 1982—84, leadership devel. com. 1978—82, bd. trustees ednl. found. 1996—2002), Sigma Xi, Pi Lambda Theta. Avocations: swimming, reading, knitting, boating. E-mail: joalantz@aol.com.

LANYON, SUSAN WENNER, special education educator; b. Kansas City, Mo., July 29, 1953; d. Herbert Allan and Ruth Wenner; m. Phillip D. Lanyon II; children: Alyson Jill, Ian Wenner. BS, U. Kans., 1975, MS in Edn., 1984. Lic. tchr. elem. edn., spl. edn., early childhood handicapped, severely multiply handicapped, physically impaired, Kans. Spl. health itinerant, lead tchr. multiple disabilities program Shawnee Mission (Kans.) Pub. Schs.; coord., lead tchr. early intervention program U. Kans., Kansas City, early childhood spl. edn. practicum coord. Lawrence. Adj. faculty instr. Kansas City (Kans.) C.C., cons., 1994. Author: Introduction to Inclusive Education for Paraprofessionals, 1994. Mem. Coun. Exceptional Children (divsn. early childhood), Nat. Assn. for Edn. of Young Children. E-mail: slanyon@ku.edu.

LANZA, ROBERT PAUL, medical scientist; b. Boston, Feb. 11, 1956; s. Samuel and Barbara (Corbett) L. BA, U. Pa., 1978, MD, 1983. Sr. scientist Biohybrid Techs., Shrewsbury, Mass., 1990-93, dir. transplantation biology, 1993-98; clin. assoc. prof. surgery Tufts U., 1994-95; sr. dir. tissue engring. and transplant medicine Advanced Cell Tech., Inc., Worcester, Mass., 1999-2000; med. dir., v.p. med. and sci. devel. Advanced Cell Tech. Group Inc., Worcester, 1999—. Rsch. Lab. of Richard Hynes, 1975, Gerald Edelman, 1976, Jonas Salk, 1978, B.F. Skinner, 1979-81, Christiaan Barnard, 1981-84; assoc. surgery Harvard Med. Sch., 1991-93. Author: Xeno, 2000; editor: Heart Transplantation, 1984, Medical Science and the Advancement of World Health, 1985, Procurement of Pancreatic Islets I, 1994, Immunomodulation of Pancreatic Islets II, 1994, Immunoisolation of Pancreatic Islets III, 1994, One World, 1996, Tissue Engineering/Cellular Medicine Series, 1995—, Yearbook of Cell and Tissue Transplantation, 1996—, Principles of Tissue Engineering, 1997, 2d edit., 2000, Encapsulated Cell Technology and Therapeutics, 1999, Methods of Tissue Engineering, 2001, Principles of Cloning, 2002; contbr. articles to profl. and lit. jours. Active Conservation Commn., Town of Clinton, 1998—, mem. open space com., 1996-98; founder and dir. South Meadow Pond and Wildlife Assn., 1998—; bd. dirs. Clinton Greenway Conservation Trust, 2001—. Prof. Howe Buck scholar, 1974-75, Benjamin Franklin scholar, 1975-78, Univ. scholar, 1976-83, Fulbright scholar, 1978-79; Hon. Christiaan Barnard fellow, 1981-84, Mry K. Iacocca Transplantation fellow, 1988-90. Achievements include cloned first endangered species; first to reverse aging using nuclear transfer; was part of team that cloned first human embryo for medical purposes; first to demonstrate "proof-of-principle" for therapeutic cloning. Home: South Meadow Pond Island 35 S Meadow Rd Clinton MA 01510-4327 Office: Advanced Cell Tech 1 Innovation Dr Worcester MA 01605-4307 E-mail: rlanza@advancedcell.com.

LANZINGER, KLAUS, language educator; b. Woergl, Tyrol, Austria, Feb. 16, 1928; arrived in U.S., 1971, naturalized, 1979; m. Aida Schuessl, June, 1954; children: Franz, Christine. BA, Bowdoin Coll., 1951; PhD, U. Innsbruck, Austria, 1952. Rsch. asst. U. Innsbruck, 1957-67; assoc. prof. modern langs. U. Notre Dame, Ind., 1967-77, prof., 1977-97, prof. emeritus, 1997—. Resident dir. fgn. study program, Innsbruck, 1969-71, 76-78, 82-85; acting chmn. dept. Modern and Classical Languages, U. Notre Dame, fall 1987, chmn. dept. German and Russian, 1989-96. Author: Epik im amerikanischen Roman, 1965, Jason's Voyage: The Search for the Old World in Am. Lit., 1989, (online) Amerika-Europa: Ein transatlantisches Tagebuch 1961-1989, 2003; editor: Americana-Austriaca, 5 vols., 1966-83; contbr. numerous articles to profl. jour. Bowdoin Coll. fgn. student scholar, 1950-51; Fulbright rsch. grantee U. Pa., 1961; U. Notre Dame summer rsch. grantee Houghton Libr., Harvard U., 1975, 81; named to Internat. Order of Merit, 2001. Mem. MLA, Deutsche Gesellschaft für Amerikastudien, Thomas Wolfe Soc. (Zelda Gitlin Lit. prize 1993). Home: 52703 Helvie Dr South Bend IN 46635-1215 Office: Dept German Russian Langs & Lits U Notre Dame Notre Dame IN 46556

LAOPODIS, NIKIFORDS-THEMISTOCLES, economic and business educator; b. Corfu, Greece, Apr. 22, 1961; came to U.S., 1984; s. Socrates and Helen (Tzoras) L. BSc, Grad. Indsl. Sch. Thessaloniki, 1983; MA, Morgan State U., 1985; PhD, Cath. U. Am., 1991. Lectr. Towson (Md.) State U., 1985; teaching asst. The Cath. Univ. Am., Washington, 1986-90; asst. prof. Wesley Coll., Dover, Del., 1990—. Adj. lectr. Loyola Coll. Md., 1989. Mem. Am. Econ. Assn., Am. Fin. Assn. Greek Orthodox. Avocations: hunting, fishing, swimming, hiking, foreign languages. Home: 706 Rappolla St Baltimore MD 21224-4602

LA PAGLIA, UMBERTO, secondary education educator, retired; b. Phila., Feb. 1, 1927; s. Ignazio and Concetta La P. BSEd, Temple U., 1952, MA in History, 1956. High sch. tchr. Sch. Dist. of Phila., 1952-90. Exch. tchr. Fitzmaurice Grammar Sch., Bradford-on-Avon, Eng., 1961-62. Author: Exploring World Cultures, 1974. With U.S. Army, 1946-47, Korea. Mem. Orgn. Am. History. Avocation: travel. Home: 216 Uxbridge Cherry Hill NJ 08034-3731

LAPALOMBARA, JOSEPH, political science and industrial management educator; b. Chgo., May 18, 1925; s. Louis and Helen (Teutonico) LaP.; m. Lyda Mae Ecke, June 22, 1947 (div.); children— Richard, David, Susan; m. Constance Ada Bezer, June, 1971. AB, U. Ill., 1947, AM, 1950; AM (Charlotte Elizabeth Proctor fellow), Princeton U., 1952, PhD, 1954; student, U. Rome (Italy), 1952-53; MA (hon.), Yale U., 1964. Instr., then asst. prof. polit. sci. Oreg. State Coll., 1947-50; instr. politics Princeton U., 1952; mem. faculty Mich. State U., 1953-64, prof. polit. sci., 1958-64, head dept., 1958-63; prof. polit. sci. Yale U., 1964-96, prof. polit. sci. and mgmt., 1996—2001, Arnold Wolfers prof., 1969—2001, Arnold Wolfers prof. polit. sci. and mgmt. emeritus, 2001—, chmn. dept. polit. sci., 1974-78, 82-85, prof. Sch. Orgn. and Mgmt., 1979—84, 1997—2001; sr. rsch. scholar Yale Ctr. for Comparative Rsch., 2001—; dir. Instn. for Social and Policy Studies, 1987-92; chmn. Coun. Comparative and European Studies, 1966-71; cultural attache, first sec. U.S. embassy, Rome, 1980-81. Vis. prof. U. Florence, Italy, 1957-58, U. Calif.-Berkeley, 1962, Columbia U., 1966-67, U. Turin, 1974, U. Catania, 1974; cons. FCDA, 1956, Carnegie Corp., 1959, Brookings Instn., 1962, Ford Found., 1965-76, Twentieth Century Fund, 1965-69, AID, 1967-68, Fgn. Svc. Inst., 1968-72, 74-76, Ednl. Testing Svc., 1970-75, Alcoa, 1978-80, Rohm & Haas, 1975-76, GE, 1978-80, Union Carbide, 1981-92, Montedison, 1984-85, Ente Nazionale Idrocarburi, 1983-93, Guardian Industries, 1990-93, Praxair, 1992—, Swiss Bank Corp., 1994-99, Athena, 1994-95, Richard Medley Advisors, 1995-2001, Telecom Italia, 1996-99, S.I.A.D., 1999—; sr. rsch. assoc. Conf. Bd. N.Y., 1976-81; pres. Italian-Am. Multimedia Corp. N.Y., 1988—; bd. dirs. Transparency Internat.-U.S.A., 1994—. Author: The Initiative and Referendum in Oregon, 1950, The Italian Labor Movement: Problems and Prospects, 1957, Guide to Michigan Politics, rev. edit, 1960, (with Alberto Spreafico) Elezioni e Comportamento Politico in Italia, 1963, Bureaucracy and Political Development, 1963, Interest Groups in Italian Politics, 1964, Italy: The Politics of Planning, 1966, (with Myron Weiner) Political Parties and Political Development, 1966, Clientela e Parentela, 1967, Burocracia y desarrolo politico, 1970, Crises and Sequences of Political Development, (with others), 1972, Politics Within Nations, 1974, Multinational Corporations and National Elites: A Study in Tensions, 1975, (with Stephen Blank) Multinational Corporations in Comparative Perspective, 1976, Multinational Corporations and Developing Countries, 1979, A Politica nos Interior das Nações, 1982, Democracy, Italian Style, 1987, Democrazia all'italiana, 1988, Die Italiener: oder Demokratie als Lebenskunst, 1988, Democratie à l'italienne, 1990, SIAD at Seventy Five, 2002; bd. editors Midwest Jour. Polit. Sci, 1956-57, Yale U. Press, 1965-72, 73-76, ABC-CL10, 1976—, Global Perspectives, 1983-2000; mem. editorial bd. Comparative Politics, 1968—, Jour. Comparative and European Studies, 1969—, Am. Jour. Polit. Sci, 1976-80, Italian Jour., 1988, Yale Rev., 1993—; editor series comparative politics Prentice-Hall Co., 1971-85; editor Jour. Internat. Bus. Edn., 2001-; mem. editorial adv. bd. Jour. Comparative Adminstrn, 1970-74, Adminstrn. and Soc, 1974— ; adv. bd. ABC Polit. Sci; N.Am. editor: Mediterranean Observer, 1981-86; editor in chief Italy, Italy, 1988—; contbr. articles to profl. jours. Mem. exec. com. Inter Univ. Consortium Polit. Rsch., 1966-70; mem. staff Social Sci. Rsch. Coun., 1966-73; chmn. West European fgn. area fellowship program Social Sci. Rsch. Coun.-Am. Coun. Learned Socs., 1972-74; bd. dirs. Mich. Citizenship Clearing House, 1955; mem. internat. coun. Ctr. for Strategic and Internat. Studies, 1990—; mem. Coun. on Fgn. Rels.; U.S. com. Am. Fgn. Policy, 1996—. Decorated knight comdr. Order of Merit, Republic of Italy, Fulbright scholar, 1952-53, 57-58, Penfield scholar U. Pa., 1953; fellow Social Sci. Rsch. Coun., 1952-53, Ctr. Advanced Study Behavioral Scis., 1961-62, Rockefeller Found., 1963-64, Ford Found., 1969, Guggenheim Found., 1971-72, European U. Inst., 1996, Wissenschaftszentrum Berlin, 1996; recipient Guido Dorso prize, Italy, 1984, Medal of Honor, Italian Constitutional Ct., 1993, Presidency of Italian Republic, 1993. Mem. Am. Acad. Arts and Scis., Conn. Acad. Arts and Scis., Am. Acad. in Rome (trustee 1984-90), Social Sci. Research Council (com. comparative politics 1958-72), Am. Polit. Sci. Assn. (exec. coun. 1963-65, exec. com. 1967-68, v.p. 1979-80, mem. conf. group on Italian politics and soc. 1978, conf. pres. 1984-85), Am. Acad. Polit. and Social Sci., Soc. for Italian Hist. Studies, Societá Italiana di Studi Elettorali, Consiglio Italiano di Scienze Sociali, Phi Beta Kappa, Phi Kappa Phi, Phi Eta Sigma. Clubs: Yale of N.Y., Elizabethan, Morys Assn. Home: 50 Huntington St New Haven CT 06511-1333

LAPHAM, LOWELL WINSHIP, physician educator, researcher; b. New Hampton, Iowa, Mar. 20, 1922; s. Percy Charles and Altha Theresa (Dygert) L.; m. Miriam Amanda Sellers, June 22, 1945 (div. 1982); children: Joan, Steven, Judith, Jennifer. BA, Oberlin Coll., 1943; MD cum laude, Harvard U., 1948. Diplomate Am. Bd. Pathology in neuropathology, Am. Bd. Psychiatry and Neurology in neurology. Instr. Case Western Res. U. Sch. Medicine, Cleve., 1955-57, asst. prof., 1957-64, assoc. prof., 1964, U. Rochester (N.Y.) Sch. Medicine, 1964-69, prof., 1969-92; prof. emeritus, 1992—. Cons. neuropathology Cleve. Met. Gen. Hosp., 1957-64, Cleve. VA Hosp., 1957-64, Genesee Hosp., Rochester, 1966-92, Rochester Gen. Hosp., 1966-92. Contbr. numerous articles to profl. jours. 1st lt. USAR, 1951-53. Fellow Nat. Multiple Sclerosis Soc., 1957-59; rsch. grantee NIH, USPHS. Mem. Am. Assn. Neuropathologists. Unitarian Universalist. Avocations: music, travel. Home: 121 Kendal Dr Oberlin OH 44074-1905

LAPINSKI, TADEUSZ ANDREW, artist, educator; b. Rawamazowiecka, Poland, June 20, 1928; s. Tadeusz Alexander and Valentina (Kwiatkowska) L. MFA, Acad. Fine Arts, Warsaw, Poland, 1955. Prof. U. Md., College Park, 1973—. One-man shows include Mus. Modern Art, N.Y.C., also mus. in Washington, São Paulo and Rio de Janeiro, Brazil, Turin, Italy, Belgrade, Yugoslavia and Vienna, Austria, Regional Mus. of Torun, Poland, 1992, Plock Mus. and Libr., Poland, 1993, Regional Mus. of Zyrardow, Poland, 1994, Sci. Soc. Plock, 1993, Dist. Mus. City of Zyrardow, Poland, 1994, Zyrardow Mus. of Art, Poland, 1994; group shows include Nat. Royal Acad., London, biennial exhbns. in Venice, Italy, Paris, Buenos Aires, Argentina, John Guggenheim Gallery Exhibition, Coral Gables, Fla., 1988, numerous others; retrospective exhibition Nat. Mus. Torun, Poland, 1956-92; represented in permanent collections Mus. Modern Art, N.Y.C., Libr. of Congress, Washington, Nat. Mus. Am. Art, Washington, mus. in São Paulo, Warsaw and Cracow, Poland, others. Recipient Gold medal Print Festival, Vienna, 1979, Silver medal World Print '80, Paris, medal City of Zamosc, Poland, 1980, UNESCO prize Paris, Statue of Victory 85 World prize, Italy, Achievement award Prince George's County, 1989, Cultural Achievement award Am. Polish Art award U. Md., 1991, Am. Polish Arts Assn. award, 1991, medal Am. Inst. Polish Culture, 1996, medal City of Konin, Poland, 1999; T. Lapinski day proclaimed by mayor of Washington, 1981; named Man of Yr. Md. Perspectives Mag., 1984, Internat. Man of Yr. Intern., Art award City Plock, Poland, 1994. Mem. Soc. Graphic Art, Painters and Sculptors Soc. N.J. Office: U Md Dept Art College Park MD 20742-0001

LAPP, SUSAN BOLSTER, learning disability educator; b. Washington, Nov. 23, 1945; d. Robert Fay and Nona (Peifly) Bolster; m. Richard Gordon Lapp, Apr. 22, 1967. BS in Edn., Miami U., Oxford, Ohio, 1967; MEd, Xavier U., Cin., 1977. Cert. tchr. English; cert. in learning disabilities and behavior disorders K-12. Sec. Penta Tech. Coll., Perrysburg, Ohio, 1965-67; tchr. 3d grade Toledo Pub. Schs., 1966-67; thcr. 7th and 8th grades Fairfield (Ohio) City Schs., 1967-78, 6th, 7th and 8th grade learning disabilities tchr., 1978—, spl. svcs. coordinator, 1984—, career edn. coordinator, 1987—. Career edn. coordinator Butler County Joint Vocat. Sch., Hamilton, Ohio, 1987—; student vol. dir. Fairfield Middle Sch., 1990—. Vice chair S.W. Ohio Profl. Devel. Ctr., 1993-94, co-sec., 1994. Named Spl. Edn. Tchr. of Yr., S.W. Ohio Spl. Edn. Regional Resource Ctr., 1989, Ohio Career Educator of Yr., Career Edn. Assn., 1991, Outstanding Sch. Vol.-Ptnr. award, 1991, Ohio Mid. Sch. Career Planning Team of Yr., 1994. Mem. NEA, S.W. Ohio Edn. Assn., Fairfield Classroom Tchrs. Assn., Ohio Mid. Sch. Assn., Nat. Assn. for Career Edn., Career Edn. Assn. (Ohio Career Planning Team of Yr. 1994), Orton Soc. Avocations: beach activities, reading, antiquing. Home: 7833 1st Ave S Saint Petersburg FL 33707-1001 Office: Fairfield Middle Sch 255 Donald Dr Fairfield OH 45014-3085

LARABEE, BRENDA J. secondary education educator; b. North Platte, Nebr., Mar. 21, 1966; d. Buster Joy and Patricia Jean (Hopkins) Fear; m. Keith Allen Larabee, July 15, 1989; children: Amanda Jean, Ryan Charles. BS in Edn., Chadron State Coll., 1988; MEd, Doane Coll., 2003. Cert. tchr. Nebr. English/speech/drama 7-12 tchr. Campbell (Nebr.) Pub. Sch., 1988-89, Stuart (Nebr.) Pub. Sch., 1989—. Speech team coach Stuart Pub. Sch., 1989—; dir. plays at dinner theater, 1993-95; one act play coach, 1988—; adj. faculty N.E. Cmty. Coll., Norfolk, Nebr., 1999—. V.p. Town & Country Ext. Club, Stuart, 1995, pres., 1996-97; ch. sch. supt. Stuart Cmty. Ch., 1994-2000, elder, 2003—; mem. Stuart Cmty. Action Team; sec. Stuart Stock Car Assn., Inc., 2000—; leader 4-H, 1998—. Mem. Nat. Coun. Tchrs. English, Stuart Edn. Assn. (sec./treas.), Atkinson-Stuart Arts Coun. (programming dir.), Nebr. State Edn. Assn., Nebr. Speech Comm. Theater Assn. Republican. Methodist. Avocations: gardening, parenting, computers, bicycling, reading, cooking. Home: PO Box 155 Stuart NE 68780-0155 Office: Stuart Pub Sch PO Box 99 Stuart NE 68780-0099 E-mail: blarabee@esu8.org.

LARAYA-CUASAY, LOURDES REDUBLO, pediatric pulmonologist, educator; b. Baguio, Philippines, Dec. 8, 1941; came to U.S., 1966; d. Jose Marquez and Lolita (Redublo) Laraya; m. Ramon Serrano Cuasay, Aug. 7, 1965; children: Raymond Peter, Catherine Anne, Margaret Rose, Joseph Paul. AA, U. Santo Tomas, Manila, Philippines, 1958, MD cum laude, 1963. Diplomate Am. Bd. Pediatrics. Resident in pediatrics U. Santo Tomas Hosp., 1963-65, Children's Hosp. Louisville, 1966-67, Charity Hosp. New Orleans-Tulane U., 1967-68; fellow child growth and devel. Children's Hosp. Phila., 1968-69; fellow pediatric pulmonary and cystic fibrosis programs St. Christopher's Hosp. for Children, Phila., 1969-71, rsch. assoc., 1971-72; clin. instr. Tulane U., New Orleans, 1967-68; asst. prof. pediatrics Temple Health Scis. Ctr., Phila., 1972-77; assoc. prof. pediatrics Thomas Jefferson Med. Sch., Phila., 1977-79, U. Medicine & Dentistry N. J. Robert Wood Johnson Med. Sch., New Brunswick, 1980-85, prof. clin. pediatrics, 1985-98, prof. pediat., 1998—. Dir. pediatric pulmonary medicine and cystic fibrosis ctr. U. Medicine and Dentistry, Robert Wood Johnson Med. Sch., New Brunswick, 1981—. Co-editor: Interstitial Lung Diseases in Children, 1988. Recipient Pediatric Rsch. award Mead Johnson Pharm. Co., Manila, 1965. Fellow Am. Coll. Chest Physicians (steering com., chmn. cardiopulmonary diseases in children 1976—), Airways Network, Am. Acad. Pediatrics (tobacco free generation rep. 1986-92); mem. Am. Ambulatory Pediatric Soc., Am. Thoracic Soc., Am. Sleep Disorder Assn., N.J. Thoracic Soc. (chmn. pediatric pulmonary com. 1986-91, governing coun. mem. 1981-94), European Respiratory Soc. Avocation: pianist. Home: 100 Mercer Ave Spring Lake NJ 07762-1208 Office: UMDNJ Robert Wood Johnson Med Sch One RWJ Place New Brunswick NJ 08903 E-mail: cuasaylr@umdnj.edu.

LARDY, NICHOLAS RICHARD, economist, educator; b. Madison, Wis., Apr. 8, 1946; s. Henry Arnold and Annrita (Dresselhuys) Lardy; m. Barbara Jean Dawe, Aug. 29, 1970; children: Elizabeth Brooke, Lillian Henry. BA, U. Wis., 1968; MA, U. Mich., 1972, PhD, 1975. Asst. prof. Yale U., New Haven, 1975-79, assoc. prof., 1979-83, asst. dir. econ. growth ctr., 1979-82, Frederick Frank adj. prof. in internat. trade and fin. Sch. Mgmt., 1997-2000; assoc. prof. U. Wash., Seattle, 1983-85, chair China program, 1984-89, prof., 1985-95, dir. The Henry M. Jackson Sch. Internat. Studies, 1991-95; sr. fellow Brookings Instn., Washington, 1995—2003, Inst. Internat. Econs., Washington, 2003—. Bd. dirs. Nat. Com. U.S.-China Rels., N.Y.C., 1986—, Comm. Internat. Rels. Studies with China, 1989—92, Program Internat. Studies in Asia, 1993—95; chmn. Com. Advanced Study in China; vice chmn. com. scholarly comm. China NAS, Washington, 1991—95; bd. mgrs. Blakemore Found., 1993—95; founding mem. Pacific Coun. Internat. Policy, 1995—; mem. Coun. Fgn. Rels. Author: (book) Economic Growth and Distribution in China, 1978, Agriculture in China's Modern Economic Development, 1983, Foreign Trade and Economic Reform in China, 1978-1990, 1992, China in the World Economy, 1994, China's Unfinished Economic Revolution, 1998, Integrating China into the Global Economy, 2002, (policy study) Economic Policy Toward China in the Post-Reagan Era, 1989; mem. editl. bd.: The China Quar. (London), China Econ. Rev., Jour. Asian Bus., Jour. Contemporary China. Rsch. fellow, Am. Coun. Learned Socs., 1976, 1978—79, 1989—90, Henry Luce Found., Inc., 1980—82, Faculty Rsch. grantee, Yale U., 1976, 1978. Mem.: Assn. Comparative Econ. Studies (mem. exec. com. 1986—88), Assn. Asian Studies (mem. nominating com. 1986—87), Am. Econ. Assn. Avocations: skiing, squash, tennis, sailing. Home: 2811 Albemarle St NW Washington DC 20008-1037 Office: Inst for Internat Econs 1750 Massachusetts Ave NW Washington DC 20036-1903 E-mail: nlardy@iie.com.

LARE, JAYNE LEE, elementary education educator; b. Phila., May 1, 1947; d. James Robert and Laura Jayne (Brown) Raudenbush; children: James Peter Ault Jr., Matthew Robert Ault. BS, Valparaiso U., 1970. Elem. tchr. La Porte (Ind.) Schs., 1970, Valparaiso (Ind.) Pub. Schs., 1970-71; tchr. 3rd, 4th, 5th grades gifted and talented Mid. Twp. Pub. Schs., Cape May Court House, NJ, 1979—. Staff rep. dist. newspaper The Panther Press. Adv., Odyssey of Mind Program (mem. Dist. Tech. com.); participant Hands Across the Water, 1992-93. Recipient N.J. Gov.'s Tchr. Recognition Program award. Mem. Mid. Twp. Edn. Assn. (v.p., pres., sec.), N.J. Edn. Assn. (del. assembly), Cape May County Edn. Assn. (sec.), Delta Kappa Gamma. Office: Mid Twp Pub Schs 211 S Main St Cape May Court House NJ 08210-2274

LARIC, MICHAEL VICTOR, management and marketing administrator; b. Split, Yugoslavia, Feb. 8, 1945; came to U.S., 1971; s. Joseph and Ljubica (Abraham) L.; m. Roberta Kine; children: Shai Samuel, Pnina Leora, Ari Nathaniel. BA in Econs. and Polit. Sci., Hebrew U. of Jerusalem, 1968, MA in Bus., 1971; PhD, CUNY, 1976. Economist Israel Hotel & Motel Owners, Tel Aviv, 1968-69; gen. mgr. Galia Laundries, Jerusalem, 1969-71; economist Risk Analysis Corp., Alpine, N.J., 1971-72; lectr. CUNY, N.Y.C., 1972-73; asst. prof. Rutgers U., State U. N.J., Newark, 1974-75, U. Conn., Storrs, 1975-81; prof. mktg. U. Balt., 1981—, acad. assoc. dean, 1992-95, area coord. mktg., 1995-2000, co-dir. Ctr. Tech. Comm., 1995—, chair mktg., 2000—, div. dir. mgmt. & marketing, 2001—. Course dir. Data Tech. Inst., Clifton, N.Y., 1986-92, Frost & Sullivan, N.Y.C. and Eng., 1990—; cons. Ecomares Internat., Ellicott City, Md., 1981—. Author: Marketing Management: Analysis Using Spreadsheets, 1988, Lotus Exercises for Principles of Marketing, 1986, 14 other books; contbr. numerous articles, monographs and cases to profl. jours. Named Outstanding Young Man of The Yr. Jaycees, 1979, 80. Mem.: Acad. Mgmt., Am. Econs. Assn., Product Devel. and Mgmt. (charter, bd. dirs. 1981, 1982), Am. Mktg. Assn. (bd. dirs. Balt. chpt. 1976—82, Outstanding Contbr. of Conn. 1978), Beta Gamma Sigma. Home: 4609 Morning Ride Ct Ellicott City MD 21042-5927 Office: U Balt 1420 N Charles St Baltimore MD 21201-5720 E-mail: mlaric@ubmail.ubalt.edu.

LARIVIERE, JANIS WORCESTER, biology educator; b. Stamford, Conn., Oct. 3, 1949; d. Francis Harry Worcester and Evelyn M. Howson Rapp; m. Richard Wilfred Lariviere, June 5, 1971; 1 child, Anne. BS, U. Iowa, 1971; MS in Biology, Drexel U., Phila., 1979. Biology, chemistry tchr. English Valleys High Sch., North English, Iowa, 1971-72; biology, ecology tchr. Maple Shade (N.J.) High Sch., 1972-76; teaching asst. Drexel U., Phila., 1977-78; rsch. asst. Thomas Jefferson U. Microbiology Dept., Phila., 1978-79; rsch. asst. biochemistry U. Iowa, Iowa City, 1980-82; biology tchr. Anderson High Sch., Austin, Tex., 1982-92, Westlake High Sch., Austin, Tex., 1992—98; preparation tchr. The U. of Tex., 1998—. Mem. curriculum writing team Tex. Edn. Agy., Austin, 1990-91; bd. dirs. IBM/AISD Project A+ Austin, 1989-92; nat. design team Ctr. for Occupational Rsch. and Devel., Waco, 1988-90. Author textbook: BioCom, 1993-94; contbg. writer: Biology textbook, 1991; curriculum specialist textbook: Biology, 1986; author article and software revs. for The Science Teacher, 1987-88. Com. mem. Project A+ Zero Drop-Out Momentum Team, Austin, 1989-90; vol. Mother Teresa's Orphanage, Calcutta, India, 1976-77. Tandy Tech. scholar, 1991; Access Excellence fellow, 1994; grantee GTE, 1988, Toyota Tapestry, 1993, Eleanor Roosevelt grantee AAUW, 1995. Mem. NSTA (Ohaus award for innovation 1987, manuscript reviewer 1987-90), NEA, Nat. Assn. Biology Tchrs. (state rep. 1987-91, Outstanding Biology Tchrs. 1988), Tex. Assn. Biology Tchrs. (pres. 1996). Lutheran. Home: 3415 Cactus Wren Way Austin TX 78746-6636 Office: U of Tex Coll of Natural Scis Mailcode 2550 Austin TX 78712 E-mail: jlariviere@mail.utexas.edu.

LARIVIERE, RICHARD WILFRED, university administrator, educator, consultant; b. Chgo., Jan. 27, 1950; s. Wilfred Francis and Esther Irene Lariviere; m. Janis Anne Worcester, June 5, 1971; 1 child, Anne Elizabeth. BA, U. Iowa, 1972; PhD, U. Pa., 1978. Lectr. U. Pa., Phila., 1978-79; asst. prof. U. Iowa, Iowa City, 1980-82; prof. U. Tex., Austin, 1982—, Ralph B. Thomas Regents prof. Asian studies, 1993—, assoc. v.p., 1995-99, dean Coll. Liberal Arts, 1999—. Dir. Sinha & Lariviere Ltd., Austin; founder Doing Bus. in India seminar; cons. Perot Sys. Corp., Dallas, 1993—; bd. dirs. HCL/Perot Sys., Amsterdam; chmn. Coun. Am. Overseas Rsch. Ctrs., Washington. Author: Ordeals in Hindu Law, 1981, Narada Smrti, 1989; gen. editor Studies in South Asia. Fellow NEH, 1979-83. Fellow Royal Asiatic Soc.; mem. Am. Oriental Soc., Am. Inst. Indian Studies (sr.fellow 1989, 95, v.p. 1990), Assn. Asian Studies. Lutheran. Home: 3415 Cactus Wren Way Austin TX 78746-6636

LARMORE, CATHERINE CHRISTINE, university official; b. West Chester, Pa., Apr. 8, 1947; d. Ashby Morton and Catherine (Burns) L.; m. Thomas Henry Beddall, May 2, 1994 BA, Earlham Coll., 1969. Tchr. Westtown (Pa.) Sch., 1969-75, asst. dean girls, 1971-73, dean girls, 1973-75; sec. U. Pa., Kennett Square, 1976-78; media coord. New Bolton Ctr U. Pa. Sch. Vet. Medicine, Kennett Square, 1978-83, dir. external affairs, 1983-88, dir. devel., 1988-99; dir. devel. for equine programs Va. Tech. U., 1999—. Mem. London Grove (Pa.) Twp. Planning Commn., 1990-2000, Chester County (Pa.) Women's Task Force, 1992-93, Chester County Women's Commn., 1994-95; v.p. White Clay Watershed Assn., Landenburg, Pa., 1994-95, pres., 1997-2000; sec. White Clay Creek Bi-State Preserve Adv. Coun. Commonwealth of Pa., 1996-98, v.p. 1998-99, pres. 1999-2000; chmn. steering com. for Ad Hoc Task Force on White Clay Creek, 1990; bd. dirs. Coalition for Natural Stream Valleys, 1996—, Pa. Vet. Med. Hist. Soc., 1997-99. Recipient Take Pride in Pa. award Commonwealth of Pa., 1991. Mem. Nat. Soc. Fund Raising Execs., So. Chester County C. of C. (bd. dirs. 1989-91). Avocations: gardening and horticulture, equine carriage driving, environment and open space. Office: Va Tech Middleburg Agrl Rsch and Extension Ctr 5527 Sullivans Mill Rd Middleburg VA 20117-5207

LAROCCA, PATRICIA DARLENE MCALEER, middle school mathematics educator; b. Aurora, Ill., July 12, 1951; d. Theodore Austin and Lorraine Mae (Robbins) McAleer; m. Edward Daniel LaRocca, June 28, 1975; children: Elizabeth S., Mark E. BS in Edn./Math., No. Ill. U., 1973, postgrad., 1975. Tchr. elem. sch. Roselle (Ill) Sch. Dist., 1973-80; instr. math. Coll. DuPage, Glen Ellyn, Ill., 1988-90; tchr. math. O'Neill Mid. Sch., Downers Grove, Ill., 1995—. Pvt. cons., math. tutor, Downers Grove, Ill., 1980-88, 90-95. Bd. dirs. PTA, Hillcrest Elem. Sch., Downers Grove; active Boy Scouts Am.; mem. 1st United Meth. Ch. Ill. teaching scholar, 1969. Methodist. Avocations: antiques, softball, organ, dance. Home and Office: 5648 Dunham Rd Downers Grove IL 60516-1246

LARRICK, PHYLLIS DALE, retired elementary school educator; b. Stockton, Calif., May 31, 1930; d. Allen Dale and Lucile Genevieve (Copeland) Perry; m. James Milton Larrick, May 3, 1953; children: Michele Dale, Marcia Louise Boer, James Matthew. AS, Modesto Jr. Coll., 1949; BS, U. Calif., Davis, 1951; postgrad., Calif. State U., Turlock, 1985-88. Cert. clear multiple subject teaching credential, Calif., 1989. Seed analyst Calif. Crop Improvement Assn., Davis, 1951-53; comml. egg producer Waterford, Calif., 1957-85; horsemanship instr., 1976—96; sec. horse dept. 38th Dist. Agrl. Assn., Turlock, Calif., 1976-82, supt., 1983—; tchr. Hickman Elem. Sch., Hickman, Calif., 1984—2003, ret., 2003. Mem. Calif. Agrl. Literacy Project, 2000—02; mem. curriculum com. Agrl. Pavilion and Mus. Stanislaus County, 2003—. Adv. com. Oakdale HS Agrl. Dept., 1986—; 4-H and resource leader, U. Calif. Extension Svc., 1965—, 1975—; mem. Stanislaus County Farm Bur. Agrl. Edn. Com. Recipient outstanding service award Flying W Riding Club, 1980, service to youth award Waterford Pomona Grange, 1981, Vol Service to Community and Youth award, Soroptomists Internat. of Waterford, 1986, Youth award Waterford Dist. C. of C., 1970. Mem. AAUW, Calif. Women for Agr. (Stanislaus County chpt.), Nat. Sci. Tchrs. Assn., Future Farmers Amn. (Oakdale chpt. hon. mem., chmn. conservation/environ. com.), Calif. Christmas Tree Assn. (sec. bd, 1998—). Republican. Avocations: horses, camping, swimming. Home: 14849 Yosemite Blvd Waterford CA 95386-8718

LARSEN, DAVID CARL, school system administrator; b. Hanover, N.H., Oct. 4, 1948; m. Kathryn Britton; 1 child, Christopher. BA, U. Vt., 1970; MEd (hon.), Marlboro Coll., Vt., 1986. Tchr. social studies Wilmington Mid./H.S., Vt., 1972—; mem. Vt. Ho. of Reps., Montpelier, 1987—97, Vt. State Bd. of Edn.; vice chair; chair Vt. State Bd. of Edn.; edn. commr. Vt. Dept. of Edn., 2003—. Trustee U. Vt., Pettee Meml. Libr., Deerfield Valley Health Ctr.; bd. dirs. Wilmington (Vt.) Civil Authority, Deerfield Valley Affordable Housing; founder, pres. VAMARR. Named Tchr. of Yr., U. Vt., 1982, 1995; Toll fellow for outstanding achievement and svc. to state govt., Coun. State Govts., 1991. Address: Vermont Dept Education 120 State St Montpelier VT 05620-0001*

LARSEN, GLEN ALBERT, JR., finance educator; b. St. Louis, Nov. 9, 1947; s. Glen Albert Sr. and Jane (Steuby) L.; m. Nancy Ann McMahon, Mar. 30, 1980; children: Erik Paul, Colleen Elizabeth. BS in Ceramic Engring., U. Mo., Rolla, 1970; MS in Materials Engring., Purdue U., 1973; MS in Bus. Adminstrn., Ind. U., 1982, DBA in Fin., 1989. Registered profl. engr., Ill.; CFA. Plant ceramic engr. U.S. Steel Corp.-South Works, 1971-73, gen. foreman constrn. svcs., 1973-74; mgr. tech. svc. Merkle Engrs., Inc., 1974-76; gen. foreman U.S. Steel-Gary (Ind.) Works, 1976-80, asst. supt., 1980-83; pres. G.A. Larsen Co., Homewood, Ill., 1983-86; instr. Ind. U., Bloomington, 1986-89, vis. asst. prof. fin., 1989-90; asst. prof. fin. U. Tulsa, 1990-94, assoc. prof. fin., 1994-96; chairperson undergrad. program, assoc. prof. fin. Ind. U., Kelley Sch. Bus., 1996—. Presenter in field. Contbr. articles to profl. jours. 2nd lt. USAR N.G., 1970-76. Mem. Am. Fin. Assn., Fin. Mgmt. Assn. Home: 115 Lynn Ct Zionsville IN 46077-1026 Office: Ind Univ Kelley Sch Bus 801 W Michigan St Indianapolis IN 46202-5199

LARSEN, KAREN LYNN, principal; b. Fergus Falls, Minn., Jan. 22, 1949; d. Hans Peder and Garnette Imogene (Strissel) L. BA in English Edn., U. No. Colo., Greeley, 1971; M in English, Gonzaga U., 1990. Cert. prin., program adminstr. Tchr. Peace Corps, Bangkok, 1971-74; tchr. English Gordon (Nebr.) H.S., 1974-76, Joliet (Mont.) H.S., 1976-88; Costello fellow in English Gonzaga U., Spokane, 1988-90; tchr. English Lake Elsinore (Calif.) H.S., 1990-91, Temescal Canyon H.S., Lake Elsinore, 1991-95, Lake Stevens (Wash.) H.S., 1995—2001; asst. prin. San Benito H.S., Hollister, Calif., 2001—03; prin. Gustine (Calif.) H.S., 2003—. Named Tchr. of Yr. Joliet/Lake Elsinore, Wash., 1986, 87, 92, 94, 2001; Danforth Leadership Program scholar U. Wash., 2000-01. Mem. ASCD, ACSA (sec. San Benito chpt.), Nat. Assn. Secondary Sch. Prins. Democrat. Lutheran. Avocations: travel, writing, reading, gourmet cooking. Home: 1585 Via Del Pettoruto Gustine CA 95322 Office: 501 North Gustine CA 95322

LARSEN, LILA DUNCAN, curator, educator; b. Neola, Utah, Nov. 18, 1929; d. Joseph Roger and Katie (Petersen) Duncan; m. Richard Bryce Larsen, Dec. 20, 1950 (dec. Nov. 1990); children: Nancy Ann, David, Bryce, Kathryn, Samuel. Student, Brigham Young U., 1947-50; BS in Comm./English/Bus., Weber State U., 1979; MA in Art History, U. Utah, 1987. Asst. dir. Springville (Utah) Mus. of Art, 1987-92; curator of edn. Eccles Cmty. Art Ctr., Ogden, Utah, 1992-98. State mus. rep., bd. mem. Utah Art Educators Assn., 1990-92; bd. mem. arts commn. City of Ogden, 1992-98; mem. visual arts adv. bd. Utah Arts Coun., Salt Lake City, 1993—; curator edn. Eccles Cmty. Art Ctr., 1992-98. Bd. dirs. Eccles Cmty. Art Ctr., Ogden, 1974-78, Utah Mus. Vols. Assn., Salt Lake City, 1987-93; bd. mem., arts & crafts chmn. Federated Women's Clubs, Utah, 1992-94; bd. mem. Acad. Lifelong Learning-Weber State U., Ogden, 1992-96. Ednl. Outreach grantee Marriner S. Eccles Found., 1988, 89, 90, 91; named Utah Art Educator of Yr., Utah Art Educators Assn., 1992. Mem. Nat. Art Educators Assn. (Utah rep. lifelong learning 1992—), Kiwanis Club, Mystae Lit. Club (pres., sec.), Fine Arts Club. Mem. Lds Ch. Avocations: travel, cross country skiing, square dancing. Office: 4835 S 850 E Ogden UT 84403-4792

LARSEN, MARY ANN INDOVINA, counselor, educator; b. Chgo., Aug. 9, 1929; d. Michael and Mary Rosalie (Tamiazzo) Indovina; m. Arthur F. Larsen, Jan. 28, 1956 (dec. June 1989); children: Deborah M. Larsen McIlvain, Michael A., Suzanne M. Larsen Channell. BA, DePaul U., 1951, MA, 1986. 1st grade tchr., music tchr. Whittier Sch., Blue Island, Ill., 1951—57, Graham Sch., Chgo., 1958—59; kindergarten tchr. Twain Sch., Chgo., 1958—88; dental bus. asst. Glenwood, Ill., 1964-88; counselor Glenwood (Ill.) Sch. for Boys, 1987-89; counselor, coord. for special needs South Suburban Coll, South Holland, Ill., 1989-96, instr. English, 1988-93, counselor, instr., 1995—. Mem. Chgo. Archdiocesal Choral Festival, ch. choir. Mem. Ill. Counseling Assn. (writer critiques for manuscripts 1987-90), AACD (book reviewer 1988-91), Ill. Sch. Counselors Assn. (membership com. 198-91—), Phi Kappa Delta, Kappa Delta Pi. Roman Catholic. Avocations: singing, piano, reading, music, opera. Office: South Suburban Coll 15800 State St South Holland IL 60473-1200 E-mail: mlarsen@ssc.cc.il.45.

LARSON, ALLAN LOUIS, political scientist, educator, lay church worker; b. Chetek, Wis., Mar. 31, 1932; s. Leonard Andrew and Mabel (Marek) L. BA magna cum laude, U. Wis., Eau Claire, 1954; PhD, Northwestern U., 1964. Instr. Evanston Twp. (Ill.) High Sch., 1958-61; asst. prof. polit. sci. U. Wis., 1963-64; asst. prof. Loyola U., Chgo., 1964-68, assoc. prof., 1968-74, prof., 1974—. Author: Comparative Political Analysis, 1980, Soviet Society in Historical Perspective: Polity, Ideology and Economy, 2000, (essay) The Human Triad: An Introductory Essay on Politics, Society, and Culture, 1988; (with others) Progress and the Crisis of Man, 1976; contbr. articles to profl. jours. Assoc. mem. Paul Galvin Chapel, Evanston, Ill. Norman Wait Harris fellow in polit. sci. Northwestern U., 1954-56 Mem. AAAS, ASPCA, AAUP, Humane Soc. U.S., Northwestern U. Alumni Assn., Am. Polit. Sci. Assn., Am. Acad. Polit. and Social Sci., Acad. Polit. Sci., Midwest Polit. Sci. Assn., Spiritual Life Inst., Anti-Cruelty Soc., Nat. Wildlife Fedn., N.Am. Butterfly Assn., Acad. of Am. Poets (assoc.), Policy Studies Orgn., Noetic Scis. Inst., Humane Soc. U.S., Kappa Delta Pi, Pi Sigma Epsilon. Roman Catholic. Home: 4169 112th St Chippewa Falls WI 54729-6626 Office: Loyola U 6525 N Sheridan Rd Damen Hall Rm 915 Chicago IL 60626

LARSON, BEVERLY ROLANDSON, elementary education educator; b. Oklee, Minn., May 30, 1938; d. Orville K. and Belle A. (Anderson) Rolandson; m. Roland K. Larson, June 29, 1962; children: Amy Jo, Ann Marie, Carl Lee. BS, Concordia Coll., 1962; MA, Mankato State U., 1984. Cert. elem., spl. edn. tchr., Minn. Tchr. Hudson Sch. Dist., LaPuente, Calif., 1961-62, Thief River Falls (Minn.) Sch. Dist., 1962-63, Sch. Dist. 271, Bloomington, Minn., 1964-69, 71-72, Valley View Sch., Bloomington, Minn., 1989—; spl. edn. tchr. Sch. Dist. 271, Bloomington, Minn., 1975-79, 86-89. Youth leader, Sunday sch. tchr. Christ the King Luth. Ch., Bloomington, 1969-82; precinct co-chair Rep. Party, Bloomington, alt., del. Recipient Svc. award Walk for Mankind, 1976, Golden Apple Achiever award Ashland Oil, 1994. Mem. NEA, Assn. Childhood Edn. (pres. Bloomington br. 1992-94), Minn. Edn. Assn., Nat. Learning Disabilities Assn., Minn. Learning Disabilities Assn., Bloomington Edn. Assn. Republican. Lutheran. Avocations: crafts, reading, plays and musicals, golf. Home: 7800 Pickfair Dr Bloomington MN 55438-1380

LARSON, BRUCE ROBERT, lawyer, educator; b. Whittier, Calif., Jan. 14, 1955; s. Robert Edward and Ruth Marie Larson; m. Judith Elaine Sword, 1982; children: Seth Julius, Gregory Bruce. BA magna cum laude, Gustavus Adolphus Coll., 1977; JD cum laude, U. Minn., 1980. Bar: Minn. 1980, U.S. Dist. Ct. Minn. 1980, U.S. Ct. Appeals (8th cir.) 1980, Ga. 1986, Va. 2000. Immigration officer U.S. Immigration & Naturalization Svc., Mpls., 1977-81; atty. Bd. Immigration Appeals U.S. Dept. Justice, Washington, 1981-85; assoc. Powell, Goldstein, Frazer & Murphy, Atlanta, 1986-89, ptnr., 1990-96, Littler, Mendelson, Atlanta, 1996-98; hon. consul of Sweden Atlanta, 1996-2000; ptnr. Paul, Hastings, Janofsky, Walker, Atlanta, 1998-99, Flippin, Densmore, Morse & Jessee, Roanoke, Va., 1999—2001, of counsel, 2001—; dir. internat. pers. office, atty. legal dept. Mayo Found., Rochester, Minn., 2001—. Adj. prof. immigration law U. Ga., 1991-99; legal advisor Tonka Babe Ruth Baseball League, Minnetonka, Minn., 1980-81. Asst. organist Apostles Luth. Ch., Atlanta, 1986-99, mem. coun., 1994-96, pres. 1995; coach Tonka Babe Ruth and Little Leagues, Minnetonka, 1973-81; bd. govs., Scandinavian Am. Found. Ga., Atlanta, 1992-2000, chmn., 1993-97; bd. dirs. Scandinavian Festival, Inc., 1994-96; asst. dir. Masterworks Chorale, Atlanta, 1988-95; bd. dirs. Swedish Coun. Am., 1998— (sec., exec. com. 2002—) ; mem. bd. advs. Atlanta Internat. Museum, 1997-99; asst. organist, choir dir. St. John Luth. Ch., Roanoke, 1999-2001, interim dir. Praise Ministry, 1999-2000; bd. dirs. Roanoke Symphony Orch., 2000-2001; state coord. for musicians serving Evangelical Luth. Ch., 2001; asst. organist, choir dir. Good Shepherd Luth. Ch., Rochester, 2002 —, chair long-range planning com., 2003—. Recipient Cert. of Merit, U.S. Atty. Gen., 1982-85. Mem. Am. Immigration Lawyers Assn. (chpt. pres. 1991-93, nat. bd. govs.), Swedish-Am. C. of C., Vasa Order of Am., Iota Delta Gamma. Avocations: music, tennis, bridge, baseball. Office: Mayo Found Internat Pers Office Plummer 7 200 First St SW Rochester MN 55905 E-mail: larson.bruce@mayo.edu.

LARSON, CAROLE ALLIS, library and information scientist, educator; b. Dayton, Ohio, Aug. 31, 1945; d. Harold Arthur and Myra Barbara Larson; m. Lowell Wilson Eyer, Jr., Nov. 16, 1985. BA in Sociology, Carleton Coll., 1967; MA in Edn., Washington U., 1968; MA in Asian Studies, U. Oregon, 1975; MA in Libr. Sci., U. Denver, 1977. Reference libr. instrnl. svcs. U. Nebr., Kearney, 1978-80; campus libr. Met. Comty. Coll., Omaha, 1980-81; asst. prof. social scis., reference libr. U. Nebr., Omaha, 1981-85, assoc. prof., 1985—2001, ret., 2001. Cons. Bellevue Coll. Libr., Omaha, 1982-83 Contbr. articles to profl. jours. Co-recipient Reference Svc. Press award ALA Reference and Adult Svcs. Divsn., 1995; Washington U. fellow. Mem. ALA, Assn. Coll. and Rsch. Librs., Nebr. Libr. Assn. Democrat. E-mail: researchercl@yahoo.com.

LARSON, DIANE LAVERNE KUSLER, principal; b. Fredonia, N.D., July 28, 1942; d. Raymond Edwin and LaVerne (Mayer) Kusler; m. Donald Floyd Larson, Aug. 14, 1965. BS, Valley City (N.D.) State U., 1964; MS, Mankato (Minn.) State U., 1977; EdS, U. Minn., 1987. Cert. tchr., Minn. Tchr. elem. Cokato (Minn.) Elem. Sch., 1962-64, Lakeview Elem. Sch., Robbinsdale, Minn., 1964-66; vocal tchr. Wheaton (Minn.) High Sch., 1966-67; tchr. Owatonna (Minn.) Elem. Sch., 1967-88, prin., 1988—. V.p. Cannon Valley Uniserv, Mankato, 1981-83; NEA del. World Confederation of Orgns. of the Teaching Professions, Melbourne, 1988. Named Woman of Yr., Owatonna Bus. and Profl. Women, 1990. Mem. NEA (bd. dirs. 1986-88), Minn. Edn. Assn. (bd. dirs. 1983-88, Outstanding Woman in Leadership award 1983), Minn. Reading Assn. (bd. dirs. 1983-97, Pres. award 1984), Internat. Reading Assn. (coord. for Minn. 1990-97, bd. dirs. 1997-2000, Celebrate Literacy award 1998), Minn. Elem. Prins. Assn., Valley City State U. Alumni Assn. (Cert. of Merit 1998), Delta Kappa Gamma (legis. chmn. 1986-88, pres. 1992, Woman of Achievement award 1989, Tau leadership chair, Tau State 1st v.p. 1997-99). Congregationalist. Home: 19654 Bagley Ave Faribault MN 55021-2246 Office: Washington Sch 338 E Main St Owatonna MN 55060-3096 E-mail: pianodl@clear.lakes.com.

LARSON, G. STEVEN, coach, athletic director; b. Washington, Mar. 11, 1951; s. J. Stanford and Dorothy Madeline (Schwaller) L.; m. Debra Ann Roemer Larson, Mar. 11, 1972; children: Jennifer, Joshua, Jacqueline, Ryan. BS in English, U. Wis., Oshkosh, 1974, MS in Edn. Adminstrn., 1980; postgrad. Sports Mgmt., U.S. Sports Acad., 1993—. Cert. Edn. Adminstrn. Basketball coach, athletic dir., math tchr. St. Patrick Sch., Menasha, Wis., 1967-70, 73-76; j.v. basketball coach, tchr. English St. Mary's Ctrl. H.S., Menasha, Wis., 1970-71, head varsity basketball coach, athletic dir., devel. dir., 1982-86; head varsity basketball coach Riverside Milit. Acad., Gainesville, Ga. and Hollywood, Fla., 1976-78; grad. asst. basketball coach, grad. asst. to dean of students U. Wis., Oshkosh, Wis., 1978-79; head varsity basketball coach, dean of students St. Mary's Springs H.S., Fond Du Lac, Wis., 1979-82; head men's basketball, athletic dir. Edgewood Coll., Madison, Wis., 1986—. Dir. Steve Larson Basketball Sch., Madison, 1979—; dir., cons. Winning Images Network, Madison, 1988—; commr., pres. Lake Mich. Conf., Madison, 1992—, Midwest Classic Conf., 1987-89 Author: (booklet) The Motion Offense, 1993, Basketball Drills: Fundamentals, 1994, Individual Basketball Instruction, 1979-95; contbr. articles to profl. jours. Basketball com. NAIA, Dist. 14, 1991-95; pres. Queen of Peace Sch. Bd., Madison, 1995; fund raising chair Cystic Fibrosis Found., Neenah, Wis., 1982-86; commr. Badger State Games-Basketball, Madison, 1987-88; v.p. Catholic Boys League, 1974-76. Capt. faculty ROTC, 1976-78. Recipient Award of Merit NAIA, 1993, State of Wis. Gov.'s award for athletic leadership, 1988, Gold Medal Wis.-USA Friendship Games, 1986, City of Menasha Mayor & Common Coun. Resolution of Commendation, 1986, Fond du Lac City Coun. Resolution award, 1982, State of Wis. Assembly Citation, 1982; named Coach of the Year NAIA dist. 14/Affiliatied Conf. Men's Basketball, 1991-92, 92-93, 93-94, 94-95, Lake Mich. Conf. Men's Basketball, 1991-92, 92-93, 93-94, 94-95, North Ctrl. Dist. Men's Basketball, 1987-88, 88-89, 89-90, 89-91, Dist. Basketball, 1977-78. Mem. Nat. Assn. Basketball Coaches, Nat. Assn. Dirs. Athletics, Madison Pen & Mike Club (Sportsman of the Month 1992, Hall of Fame Spl. Achievement award 1994), Red Smith (Outstanding Coaching award 1992), Fox Valley Christian Conf. (All Star Coach 1981, 82, 86, Coach of the Year 1981-82, 85-86), Wis. Basketball Coaches Assn. (Fall clinic demonstration chair, 1986-94, Appreciation award 1990, Outstanding achievement award 1986, 89, 90, 95, Recognition award 1988, 89), Fellowship Christian Athletes, Kappa Delta Pi (pres. 1978-79). Roman Catholic. Avocations: reading, movies, chess, biking, collecting pins, video movies, caps and glasses. Office: Edgewood Coll 855 Woodrow St Madison WI 53711-1958

LARSON, JANICE TALLEY, computer science programmer; b. Houston, Sept. 29, 1948; d. Hiram Peak Talley and Jennie Edna Donahoo; m. Harold Vernon Larson, Apr. 8, 1977; children: Randall Neil, Christopher Lee. AA in Computers, San Jacinto Coll., 1981; BA in Computer Info. Systems, U. Houston, Clear Lake, 1984, MA in Computer Info. Systems, 1988; EdD in Instrnl. Tech., U. Houston, 1999. Programmer Control Applications, Houston, 1985-86, Tex. Eastern Pipeline, Houston, 1988-90; instr. computer sci. San Jacinto Coll., Houston, 1990-94; computer sci. reader Ednl. Testing Svc., Clear Lake, 1996—2000; programmer for shuttle cockpit avionics upgrade United Space Alliance, 2000—02; programmer Creative Process Cons., League City, Tex., 2003—. Adj. instr. U. Houston, Clear Lake, Tex., 1996, 99, 2003; sponsor Computer Sci. Club, Houston, 1992-94. Mem.: IEEE (assoc.), U. Houston Alumni Assn., Kappa Delta Pi, Phi Delta Kappa. E-mail: burnwuffie@aol.com.

LARSON, JEANETTE CAROLYN, librarian; b. Ft. Dix, N.J., Sept. 16, 1952; d. Wilbur Arthur and Carolyn Linda (Baker) Pawson; m. James Warren Larson, Jan. 31, 1975. BA, U. N.Mex., 1974; MS in Libr. Sci., U. So. Calif., 1979. Libr. Anaheim (Calif.) Pub. Libr., 1977-79; children's libr. Irving (Tex.) Pub. Libr., 1979-80, Mesquite (Tex.) Pub. Libr., 1980-85, supr. pub. svc., 1985-91; mgr. continuing edn. and cons. Tex. State Libr., Austin, 1991—98, dir. libr. devel. divsn., 1998—2000; youth svcs. mgr. Austin Pub. Libr., 2000—. Cons. Author Promotions, Austin, 1991—. Author: Animal Antics, 1987, Secret Code is READ, 1990; co-author: Model Policies for Small and Medium-Sized Public Libraries, 1996, Color Your World...Read!, 2004, Bringing Mysteries Alive, 2004; reviewer: Booklist, 1985—, Mostly Murder, Sch. Libr. Jour.; contbr. articles to libr. jours.; mem. editl. bd.: Book Links, 2003—. Active nat. adv. bd. Grolier Pub., 1996—; v.p. bd. dirs. Connections Resources Ctr., Austin, 1998—2000; bd. dirs., prodrs. Vols. for USA, Film Fest Dallas, 1989—91; vol. Reading is Fundamental, Austin, 1992—, Humane Soc., Austin, 1991—93. Mem.: ALA (Shirley Olofson award 1982), U. N.Mex. Alumni Assn. (pres. Austin chpt. 1994—95), Dallas County Libr. Assn. (pres. 1985—86), Tex. Libr. Assn. (Outstanding New Libr. award 1987, Libr. of Yr. 1998, Siddie Joe Johnson award 2002), Beta Phi Mu. Avocations: counted cross-stitch, animation art, animal welfare, films, travel. Home: 7300 Geneva Dr Austin TX 78723-1515 Office: Austin Pub Libr 800 Guadalupe Austin TX 78701

LARSON, KERMIT DEAN, accounting educator; b. Algona, Iowa, Apr. 7, 1939; s. Loren L. and Hansena Laurena (Andersen) L.; m. Nancy Lynne Weber, June 17, 1961; children: Julie Renee, Timothy Dean, Cynthia Lynne. AA, Ft. Dodge Jr. Coll., 1960; BBA, U. Iowa, 1962, MBA, 1963; PhD, U. Colo., 1966. CPA, Tex. Faculty U. Tex., Austin, 1966-94, Arthur Andersen & Co. Alumni prof. emeritus, 1994—, chmn. dept. acctg., 1971-75. Vis. assoc. prof. Tulane U., New Orleans, 1970-71; cons. sales tax audit litig., pvt. anti-trust litig., expropriation ins. arbitration. Author: (with John Wild and Barbara Chiappetta) Fundamental Accounting Principles, 1978, 16th edit., 2002, Financial Accounting, 7th edit., 1997, (with Charlene Spoede and Paul Miller) Fundamentals of Financial and Managerial Accounting, 1994; contbr. articles to profl. jours. Mem. AICPA, Am. Acctg. Assn. (v.p. 1978-79), Tex. Soc. CPAs, Beta Gamma Sigma, Beta Alpha Psi. Baptist. Home: 1310 Falcon Ledge Dr Austin TX 78746-5120

LARSON, L. JEAN, educational administrator; b. Sioux City, Iowa, Jan. 27, 1934; d. Marion A. and Lola J. (Willenborg) Robey; m. Herbert L. Larson, June 25, 1955; 1 child, Joan Irene. BA with honors, U. No. Iowa, 1954; MEd, U. Ariz., 1959. Cert. adminstr., elem. tchr., Ariz., cert. speech therapist, K-12 tchr., Iowa. Tchr. Tucson Unified Sch. Dist., counselor, prin.; dir. Tucson Hebrew Acad. Dir. Children's Ministries. Mem. Internat. Reading Assn., Ariz. Reading Assn., Tucson Reading Assn., ASCD, PTA, NEA, NAFE, Altrusa, Delta Kappa Gamma, Kappa Delta, Delta Sigma Rho, Kappa Delta Pi (Purple Arrow award). Home: 7041 E Hawthorne St Tucson AZ 85710-1232

LARSON, MARILYN J. retired elementary music educator; b. Lindstrom, Minn., July 20, 1933; d. Reuben and Dorothy (Holm) L.; m. Harold P. Cohen, Aug. 4, 1957 (div. Dec. 1975); children: Paul, Morrie, Robert. BS with distinction, U. Minn., 1955, MA with honors, 1957. Nat. cert. tchr. music; cert. tchr., Minn.; lic. realtor. Tchr. U. Minn., Mpls., 1955-57, Mpls. Jr. High Sch., 1957-60; piano tchr. pvt. studio, Fridley, Minn.; tchr. Mpls. Pub. Schs., 1976-78, St. Paul Pub. Schs., 1978-97. Designed music curriculum Mpls. Pub. Schs.; mem. INS Roundtable, 2000-03; accompanist Adult Day Care, St. Mary's Home, 2001-03; piano music for vets., 2000-03. Accompanist U. Minn. Chorus, 1953-56, Berkshire Music Ctr. at Tanglewood, Mass., 1953. Mem. Music Tchrs. Nat. Assn., Fedn. for Am. Immigration Reform, Minnesotans for Immigration Reform (founder, exec. dir. 1999—). Independent. Luth. Avocations: reading, music. Home: 5890 Stinson Blvd Fridley MN 55432-6002 E-mail: marilynmusic@webtv.net.

LARSON, MARK EDWARD, JR., lawyer, educator, financial advisor; b. Oak Park, Ill., Dec. 16, 1947; s. Mark Edward and Lois Vivian (Benson) L.; m. Patricia Jo Jekerle, Apr. 14, 1973; children: Adam Douglas, Peter Joseph, Alex Edward, Gretchen Elizabeth. BS in Acctg., U. Ill., 1969; JD, Northwestern U., 1972; LLM in Taxation, NYU, 1977. Bar: Ill. 1973, N.Y. 1975, D.C. 1976, Minn, 1982, Tex. 1984, U.S. Dist. Ct. (no. dist.) Ill. 1973,

U.S. Dist. Ct. (so. dist.) N.Y. 1975, U.S. Ct. Appeals (2d cir.) 1975, U.S. Ct. Appeals (7th cir.) 1976, U.S. Dist. Ct. D.C. 1977, U.S. Ct. Appeals (D.C. cir.) 1977, U.S. Dist. Ct. Minn. 1982, U.S. Ct. Appeals (8th cir.) 1982, U.S. Tax Ct. 1976, U.S. Supreme Ct. 1976; CPA, Ill. Acct. Deloitte & Touche (formerly Haskins & Sells), N.Y.C., 1973—76, Chgo., 1978—81; atty., ptnr. Larson, Perry & Ward, P.C. and former firms, Chgo., 1983—; prin. Winfield Fin. Svcs. and affiliates, Houston, Austin and Chgo., 1986—. Adj. faculty U. Minn., Mpls., 1982—83, Aurora (Ill.) U., 1990—98, St. Xavier U., Chgo., 2000—; exec. dir. UFG Ins. for Profl. Edn., 1996—; bd. dirs. Rush-wood Imaging Ptnrs., Ltd. Contbr. articles to profl. jours. Mem.: AHLA, AICPA, ABA, Am. Acctg. Assn., Acad. Fin. Svcs., Acad. Molecular Imaging, Am. Assn. Atty.-CPAs. Office: 1212 S Naper Blvd Ste 119-131 Naperville IL 60540-7349 E-mail: larsgen@usa.net.

LARSON, MARY BEA, elementary education educator; b. Brookings, S.D., Apr. 19, 1946; d. Theodore Orville and Doris Rose (Conway) Larson; children: Christie DiRé, Corey DiRe. BA, Wash. State U., 1968, Portland State U., 1973; MA, U. Guam, 1975; postgrad., Seattle Pacific U., 1980-85, Western Wash. U., Oxford U. Cert. tchr., Wash. Tchr. early childhood and creativity Chemeketa C. C., Salem, Oreg., 1971-73; tchr. kindergarten-1st grade Govt. Guam, Agana, 1973-75; tchr. kindergarten, 3rd grade Canal Zone Govt., Balboa, Panama, 1975-78; tchr. kindergarten, 2d-4th grades, elem. art specialist Marysville (Wash.) Sch. Dist., 1978-2001, ret., 2001. Mem. profl. adv. bd. coll. edn. Western Wash. U., 1989-96. Active Snohomish County Arts Coun. Mem. NEA (del. to Nat. Rep. Assembly, Washington 1992, San Francisco 1993), Wash. Edn. Assn., Marysville Edn. Assn. (pres. 1990-92), Nat. Mus. Women in Arts (founder), Seattle Art Mus. (landmark), Alpha Delta Kappa (state sgt.-at-arms 1990-92, state chaplain 1992-94, state v.p. 1994-96). Address: PO Box 11216 Hilo HI 96721

LARSON, PAUL THEODORE, elementary school educator; b. Mankato, Minn., Aug. 6, 1947; s. Theodore E. and Ruth M. (Peterson) L.; m. Kay I. Larson, Aug. 14, 1971; children: Kristine, Kari. BS, Mankato State U., MS in Elem. Reading, 1973. Cert. elem. edn., elem. remedial reading. Tchr. grade 6 Sch. Dist. 241, Albert Lea, Minn. With U.S. Army, 1970-71. Finalist Tchr. of Yr., 2003. Mem. NEA, Edn. Minn., Albert Lea Edn. (field rep., v.p.). Home: 1606 Southview Ln Albert Lea MN 56007-1860

LARSON, RICHARD BONDO, astronomy educator; b. Toronto, Jan. 15, 1941; came to U.S., 1963; s. Carl Johan and Elsie (Bondo) L. B.Sc., U. Toronto, 1962, MA, 1963; PhD, Calif. Inst. Tech., 1968. Asst. prof. astronomy Yale U., New Haven, 1968-73, assoc. prof., 1973-75, prof., 1975—, dir. undergrad. studies astronomy, 1971-81, 2001—, chmn. dept., 1981-87. Tinsley vis. prof. U. Tex., 1990. Editor: Evolution of Galaxies and Stellar Populations, 1977; contbr. numerous articles and revs. to tech. jours. Mem.: Royal Astron. Soc. Can., Royal Astron. Soc., Am. Astron. Soc., Internat. Astron. Union, Sigma Xi. Office: Yale Univ Dept Astronomy New Haven CT 06520-8101

LARSON, ROBERT WILLIAM, education educator, consultant; b. Iowa City, Feb. 8, 1935; s. Robert William and Mary Alice (Scannell) Larson; m. Linda Louise Carolan, Nov. 30, 2002. BS, U. Wyo., Laramie; MA, EdD, U. N. Colo., Greeley. Pres. Media, Inc., 1967—72; dir. Title 1 and fed. programs Greeley Sch., Colo., 1972—74; advt., pub. rels. dir. Blue Cross/Blue Shield, Cheyenne, Wyo., 1976—83; mktg. cons. Stress Mgmt. Inst., Cheyenne, Wyo., 1983—86; asst. prof. Minn. State U., Moorhead, 1986—90; mktg. cons. Ad Pro, Duluth, Ga., 1990—92; assoc. prof. Breneau U., Gainesville, Ga., 1990—92; asst. prof. Pitts. State U., 1992—98, Northwestern Okla. State, 1998—2002; adj. assoc. prof. Washburn U. of Topeka, Kans., 2002—. Editor: Campaign Cooking, 2000; contbr. Wild Horses, 1963. Dir. Joplin (Mo.) AdFedn., 1996-98; county coord. Sally Thompson Senate, Pittsburg, Kans., 1996; states coord., Kathy Karpan Sec. of State, Cheyenne, Wyo., 1996. Maj. USMC, 1958-62, USMCR, 1963-85. Mem. Pittsburg C. of C., Moorhead C. of C. Democrat. Methodist. Avocations: triathlons, waterskiing, basketball, remodeling houses, racquetball.

LARUSSO, ANTHONY CARL, company executive, educator; b. May 5, 1949; s. Nicholas and Rose (Ruspini) LaR.; m. Marianne Elizabeth Baviello, Apr. 4, 1971; children: Anne, Tony. BA, Fordham U., 1971; MBA, NYU, 1972. Cert. mgmt. acct. Sr. project mgr. Office Mgmt. and Control N.Y.C. Dept. Human Resources, 1972-73; mgr. econ. planning Trans World Airlines, N.Y.C., 1973-76; mgr. planning and analysis AMAX, Inc., Greenwich, Conn., 1976-81, mgr. corp. devel., 1981-84, v.p. planning and mktg. metals, 1984-86, from v.p. to pres. metal refining ops., 1986—89, pres. climax performance materials corp., 1990-93; gen. mgr. CRI-MET, White Plains, N.Y., 1994-95; pres. Elkem Metals Co., Pitts., 1996—2003; instr. Ctr. for Profl. Edn., Inc., 2003—, AICPA, 2003—. Adj. prof. mgmt. Pace U., 1975—95. Contbr. articles to profl. jours. Officer local homeowners assn., Pa.; former chmn. local homeowners assn., Mahopac, N.Y.; asst. to chmn. ann. cookie sale Girl Scouts USA, Shrub Oak, N.Y.; coach/safety dir. Am. Youth Soccer Orgn., Yorktown, N.Y. Mem. Acad. Mgmt., Am. Mgmt. Assn., Chief Exec. Network, Inst. Mgmt. Acctg., Orgn. Devel. Inst., Soc. Mining Engrs., Strategic Mgmt. Soc., Ferroalloys Assn. (officer 1996—2003), Soc. for Advancement of Mgmt., Inc. Republican. Roman Catholic. Avocations: racquetball, swimming, fishing. Home: PO Box 7548 Naples FL 34101

LARZELERE, MICHAEL LOUIS, elementary education educator; b. Northville, Mich., Aug. 30, 1948; s. Charles Theodore and Virginia Margaret (Valentine) L.; m. Bonnie Beth Breen, Aug. 12, 1972; 1 child, Lisa Lynn. AS, Oakland Community Coll., Farmington, Mich., 1971; BS, Ea. Mich. U., 1974; MA, Oakland U., 1978; cert. in adminstrn., Wayne State U., 1994. Tchr. St. Clair County Intermediate Sch. Dist., Maryville, Mich., 1974-80; tchr. learning disabled Capac (Mich.) Sch. Dist., 1980-88; tchr. spl. edn. severely emotionally impaired Port Huron (Mich.) Schs., 1988-94, tchr. 3rd grade, 1994—. Supr., tchr. summer tng. edn. program, Port Huron, 1990—; tchr. sch. year support, Port Huron, 1989, 90—. Mem. Bluewater Coun. for Emotionally Impaired (Golden Nugget 1987), Bluewater Reading Coun., Bluewater Assn. for Young Children (pres. 1977-78), Bluewater Writers Club, Mich. Assn. for Tchrs. of Emotionally Impaired Children, KC (mem. at large), Elks, So. Thumb Assn. (coach 1984-88). Roman Catholic. Avocation: golf. Home: 1130 Pine St Port Huron MI 48060-5257

LA SALA, CAROLANN MARIE, elementary, secondary and academic administrator, educator; b. Bklyn., Apr. 25, 1957; d. Vincent Joseph and Carole (Tricomi) La S.; divorced; children: Lisa Michelle, Gina Maria. BA, Adelphi U., Garden City, N.Y., 1978; MS in Edn., L.I. U., Brookville, N.Y., 1989, Profl. Diploma, 1996. Cert. elem. tchr., sch. dist. adminstr. Elem. tchr., L.I., N.Y., 1988-94, L.I. U.-C.W. Post Campus, L.I., 1994—, sr. adj. prof. edn. Brookville, 1994—. Nat. cons. edn., pub. sch. administr., L.I., N.Y. Author: (ednl. rsch.) Alternatives to Pull-Out Programs, 1995. Vol. Am. Cancer Soc., L.I., NY, 1988—. Mem.: ASCD, AAUW, L.I. Schs. Pub. Rels. Assn., Nat. Coun. Tchrs. Math., Phi Delta Kappa. Avocations: art, music, extensive travel.

LASH, TIMOTHY DAVID, chemistry educator, researcher; b. Salisbury, Eng., Oct. 13, 1953; came to U.S., 1979; s. David and Judith (Spence) L.; m. Susan Shirkey Lash, Feb. 23, 1981. BSc with honors, U. Exeter, Eng., 1975; MSc, U. Wales, Cardiff, 1977, PhD, 1979. Postdoctoral assoc. U. Tex., Arlington, 1979-81; vis. asst. prof. U. Wis., River Falls, 1981-82; asst. prof. Northern State U., Aberdeen, S.D., 1982-84, Ill. State U., Normal, 1984-88, assoc. prof., 1988-93, prof., 1993—2000, disting. prof., 2000—. Grantee NSF, NIH, Petroleum Rsch. Fund, Camille and Henry Dreyfus Found. Fellow Am. Inst. Chemists; mem. AAAS, Am. Chem. Soc., Royal Soc. of Chemistry, Internat. Soc. Heterocyclic Chemistry, Ill. State Acad. Sci. (chair chemistry div. 1988-90), Sigma Xi. Achievements include research on the synthesis, biosynthesis and geochemistry of porphyrins. Office: Ill State Univ Dept Chemistry Normal IL 61790-4160

LASHBROOK, VELMA JANET, research and development executive; b. Pipestone, Minn., May 26, 1948; d. August Jacob and Lorita Belle (Swift) W.; m. William Bradshaw Lashbrook, Sept. 4, 1971; children: Nicole Maurine, Christopher Cromwell. BS, Iowa State U., 1970; MS, Ill. State U., 1971; EdD, W.Va. U., 1976. Tchr., dir. debate Woodruff High Sch., Peoria, Ill., 1971-73; instr., rsch. asst. W.Va. U., Morgantown, 1973-76, asst. prof., 1976-77, Auburn (Ala.) Univ., 1977-79; dir. rsch. Wilson Learning Corp., Eden Prairie, Minn., 1979-84, v.p., 1984-91, Wilson Learning R&D Corp., Tokyo, 1991-93, Eden Prairie, 1993—98; pres. Strategy Implementation Assocs., Prairie Eden, 1998—. Cons. Wilson Learning Corp., 1977—79; adj. faculty U. Minn., 1999—, Augsburg Coll., 2000—, internal evaluator, 2001—; adj. faculty U. Phoenix Online, 2001—; cons., evaluator The Collaboration, 2002—. Contbr. articles to profl. jours.; devel. measurement systems and learning programs used in global bus. Vol. Community Resource Pool, Edina, 1993—. Mem. ASTD, Acad. of Mgmt., Am. Ednl. Rsch. Assn., Internat. Comm. Assn. (editl. bd., task forces), Internat. Soc. for Performance Improvement, Nat. Comm. Assn., Western Speech Comm. Assn. (divsn. officer), Planning Forum. Democrat. Avocations: music, international travel, art, reading, writing. Home and Office: 8986 Westhill Pt Eden Prairie MN 55347-5324

LASHINGER, GENROSE MULLEN, retired elementary school music educator; b. Jackson, Miss., Oct. 25, 1945; d. John DeWitte and Nelle Sue (Fly) Mullen; m. Donald R. Lashinger, July 10, 1976. BA in Music Edn. and Voice, Millsaps Coll., 1967; MA in Elem. Edn., Coll. William and Mary, 1974. Cert pre-K-12 music tchr., Va. Tchr. music Matthew Whaley Sch., Williamsburg, Va., 1967—. Assoc. choirmaster Bruton Parish Ch., Williamsburg, 1982-92; lectr. music Coll. William and Mary, Williamsburg, 1984-89; founding dir. Rainbow Connection, Williamsburg, 1987—; music coord. Williamsburg-James City County Schs., 1989-93; mem. del. to study music and dance to China and Commonwealth Ind. States, 1988, 90, 92. Performer with Robert Shaw Workshop Choir at Mostly Mozart Festival, N.Y.C., St. Cere Music Festival, France. Named Tchr. of Yr., Daily Press, 1993, Music Educator of Yr., Va. Music Educators Assn., 1992. Mem. Am. Choral Dirs. Assn., Music Educators Nat. Conf. (state chmn. 1984-86), Soc. for Gen. Music (chmn. 1990-94), Va. Music Educators Assn. (elem. pres. 1984-86). Episcopalian. Avocations: travel, gardening. Home: 2513 Campbell Close Williamsburg VA 23185-8072

LASHLEY, VIRGINIA STEPHENSON HUGHES, retired computer science educator; b. Wichita, Kans., Nov. 12, 1924; d. Herman H. and Edith M. (Wayland) Stephenson; m. Kenneth W. Hughes, June 4, 1946 (dec.); children: Kenneth W. Jr., Linda; m. Richard H. Lashley, Aug. 19, 1954; children: Robert H., Lisa Lashley Van Amberg, Diane Lashley Tan. BA, U. Kans., 1945; MA, Occidental Coll., 1966; PhD, U. So. Calif., 1983. Cert. info. processor, tchr. secondary and community coll., Calif. Tchr. math. La Canada (Calif.) High Sch., 1966-69; from instr. to prof. Glendale (Calif.) Coll., 1970-92, chmn. bus. div., 1977-81, coord. instructional computing, 1974-92, prof. emeritus, 1992—; sec., treas., dir. Victory Montessori Schs., Inc., Pasadena, Calif., 1980—; pres. The Computer Sch., Pasadena, 1983-92, ret., 1992—; real estate investor, 1992—. Pres. San Gabriel Valley Data Processing Mgmt. Assn., 1977-79, San Gabriel Valley Assn. for Systems Mgmt., 1979-80; chmn. Western Ednl. Computing Conf., 1980, 84. Editor Jour. Calif. Ednl. Computing, 1980. NSF grantee, 1967-69, EDUCARE scholar U. So. Calif., 1980-82; John Randolph and Dora Haynes fellow, Occidental Coll., 1964-66; student computer ctr. renamed Dr. Virginia S. Lashley Ctr., 1992. Mem. AAUP, AAUW, DAR (scholarship chair, 1994-2002, vice regent 2002—), Calif. Edn. Computing Consortium (bd. dirs. 1979—, v.p. 1983-84, pres. 1985-87), Orgn. Am. Historians, San Marino Women's Club, Colonial Dames, XVII Century (scholarship chair, 1997-99), Nat. Geneal. Soc., New Eng. Hist. Geneal. Soc. (life mem.), Town Hall, World Affairs Coun., Phi Beta Kappa, Pi Mu Epsilon, Phi Alpha Theta, Phi Delta Kappa, Delta Phi Upsilon, Gamma Phi Beta. Republican. Congregationalist. Home: 1240 S San Marino Ave San Marino CA 91108-1227 E-mail: vslash@aol.com.

LASHOF, CAROL SUZANNE, literature educator; b. Chicago, Aug. 8, 1956; d. Richard Kenneth and Joyce (Cohen) Lashof; m. William Tobin Newton Jr., Aug. 20, 1983; children: Elisabeth, Erica. BA, U. Calif., Santa Barbara, 1976; PhD, Stanford U., 1984. Asst. prof. St. Mary's Coll., Moraga, Calif., 1983—89, assoc. prof., 1989—96, prof. English and drama, 1996—. Author: (plays) The Story, 1981, Fräulein Dora, 1989, Medusa's Tale, 1991, Nora's Daughter, 1994, Persephone Underground, 1999, The Minotaur, 2001, The Melting Pot II, 2002, The Melting Pot (II), 2002. Mem.: Assn. Theater in Higher Edn., Dramatists Guild. Office: St Mary's Coll of Calif Moraga CA 94575 E-mail: clashof@stmarys-ca.edu.

LASICH, VIVIAN ESTHER LAYNE, secondary education educator; b. Hopewell Twp., Pa., Dec. 17, 1935; d. Charles McClung and Harriette Law (George) Layne; m. William G. Lasich, Apr. 10, 1958; children: C. Laurence, Celeste M., Michelle R. AB, Geneva Coll., 1956; MA in Edn., No. Mich. U., 1970, postgrad. Secondary tchr. Freedom (Pa.) High Sch., 1956-57; elem. educator Gilbert Elem. Sch., Gwinn, Mich., 1967-69; lang. arts educator Gwinn Mid. Sch., 1970-99, ret., 1999. Adv. bd. panel Mich. Dept. Edn./Arts, 1976-79; mem. sch. improvement team, 1988-91, 93-94, co-chair, 1995-98; mid sch. concept team, 1992-98, mid sch. at-risk coord. dist. curriculum coord. coun., 1995-96; dist. curriculum strategy action team, 1993-94; dist. profl. devel. strategy action team, 1993-94; mem. sounding bd. Mid. Sch., 1994-98, dist. sch. improvement team, 1994-98; lang. arts curriculum design com., 1997-98; rep. Gwinn Edn. Assn. Mid. Sch., 1995-98. Author: Prophets Without Honor: Teachers, Students, & Trust, 1991. V.p. Marquette (Mich.) Community Theatre, 1962-63 bd. dirs. 1963-74, mem. 1961-92; pres. Marquette Arts Coun. 1973-74, v.p. 1972-73, bd. dirs. 1970-78, mem. 1970-84; pres. Upper Peninsula Arts Coordinating Bd. 1976-78, v.p. 1974-76, bd. dirs. 1978-84; bd. dirs. Mich. Community Theatre Assn. 1972-73; bd. dirs. Mich Community Arts Agys., 1976-79. Recipient Committment to Excellence award Marquette Community Theatre, 1965. Devotion to Arts Development award Upper Peninsula (Mich.) Arts Coord. Bd. 1979. Mem. ASCD, NEA, AAUW, Mich. Edn. Assn., Phi Delta Kappa. Presbyterian. Avocations: rsch., writing, theatrical direction and performance, vocal music. Home: 508 Pine St Marquette MI 49855-3838 Office: Gwinn Area Community Schs Gwinn MI 49841

LASINSKI, KATHLEEN ZELLMER, elementary principal; b. Cleve., Jan. 5, 1948; d. Warren Creath and Kathleen (O'Toole) Zellmer. AB, High Point (N.C.) Coll., 1970; MA in Edn., George Washington U., 1974; PhD, The Am. U., Washington, 1992. Cert. tchr., counselor, prin., supr., Md. Elem. tchr. Montgomery County Pub. Schs., Rockville, Md., 1970-80, area-based tchr. for gifted/talented, 1980-83, elem. counselor, 1983-85, elem. prin., 1985—. Mem. Am. U. Coun. on Tchr. Edn., Washington, 1992-93. Mem. ASCD, Elem. Sch. Adminstrs. Ass., Montgomery County Assn. Adminstrv. and Supervisory Pers. Office: Carderock Springs Elem 7401 Persimmon Tree Ln Bethesda MD 20817-4511

LASKIN, DANIEL M. oral and maxillofacial surgeon, educator; b. Ellenville, NY, Sept. 3, 1924; s. Nathan and Flora (Kaplan) L.; m. Eve Pauline Mohel, Aug. 25, 1945; children: Jeffrey, Gary, Marla. Student, NYU, 1941-42; BS, Ind. U., 1947; MS, U. Ill., 1951; DSc (hon.), Ind. U., 2001. Diplomate Am. Bd. Oral and Maxillofacial Surgery, Am. Dental Bd. Anesthesiology. Faculty U. Ill., Chgo., 1949-84, prof. dept. oral and maxillofacial surgery, 1960-84, head dept., 1973-84, clin. prof. surgery, 1961-84, dir. temporomandibular joint and facial pain research center, 1963-84; prof., chmn. dept. oral and maxillofacial surgery Med. Coll. Va., Richmond, 1984—2002, chmn. emeritus, 2003, dir. temporomandibular joint and facial pain rsch. ctr., 1984—2002; head dept. dentistry MCV Hosp., Richmond, 1986—2002; former attending oral surgeon Edgewater, Swedish Covenant, Ill. Masonic, Skokie Valley Cmty. hosps., Chgo.; former chmn. dept. oral surgery Cook County Hosp., Chgo. Cons. oral surgery to Surgeon Gen. Navy, 1977-83; dental products panel FDA, 1988-92, cons., 1993-95; Francis J. Reichmann Lectr., 1971, Cordwainer lectr., London, 1980, Donald B. Osborn Meml. lectr., 1999. Author: Oral and Maxillofacial Surgery, Vol. I, 1980, Vol. II, 1985; contbr. articles to profl. jours.; editor-in-chief: Jour. Oral and Maxillofacial Surgery, 1972-2002; mem. editl. bd. Internat. Jour. Oral and Maxillofacial Surgery, 1978-88, Topics in Pain Mgmt., Densat, Internat. Jour. Oral and Maxillofacial Implants, Quintessence Internat., Revista Latino America Cirugia Traumatologia Maxilofacial, Va. Dental Jour., Jour. Dental Rsch.; mem. internat. editl. bd. Headache Quar.; mem. editl. bd. Greek Jour. Oral and Maxillofacial Surgery, Electronic Jour. Dentistry; assoc. editor Odontology. Nat. hon. chmn. peer campaign A.A.O.M.S. Edn. and Rsch. Found., 1990; bd. dirs. Internat. Assn. Oral and Maxillofacial Surgeons Found.; chmn. Nat. Acad. Dentistry, 1997-99; pres.-elect Nat. Acad. of Practice, 1999, pres., 2002—. Recipient Disting. Alumni Svc. award, Ind. U., 1975, William J. Gies editl. award 1st prize, 1978—79, 1984, 1987, 1989, 1992, 1996, 2001, spl. editl. citation, Internat. Coll. Dentists, 1999, Simon P. Hullihen Meml. award, 1976, Arnold K. Maislen Meml. award, 1977, Thomas P. Hinman medallion, 1980, W. Harry Archer Achievement award for rsch., 1981, Heidbrink award, 1983, Disting. Alumnus award, Ind. U. Sch. Dentistry, 1984, U. Ill. Coll. Dentistry, 2003, Rene Lefort medal, 1985, Semmelweis medallion, Semmelweis Med. U., 1985, Golden Scroll award, Internat. Coll. Dentists, 1986, Internat. award, Friends Sch. Dental Med., U. Conn. Health Ctr., Donald B. Osbon award, 1991, Achievement medal, Alpha Omega, 1992, Norton M. Ross Excellence in Clin. Rsch. award, 1993, Va. Commonwealth U. Faculty award of excellence, 1994, named Zendium Lectr., 1989, Edward C. Hinds Lectr., 1990, Disting. Practitioner Nat. Acads. Practice, 1992, Hon. Diplomate Am. Soc. Osseointegration, 1992; fellow in dental surgery, Royal Coll. Surgeons Eng., Glasgow Royal Coll. Physicians and Surgeons (hon.). Fellow: AAAS, Am. Acad. Implant Prosthodontists (academia), Internat. Coll. Dentists, Am. Coll. Dentists, Acad. Internat. Dental Studies (hon.), Internat. Assn. Oral and Maxillofacial Surgeons (hon.; exc. com. 1980—95, pres. 1983—86, sec. gen. 1989—95, exec. dir. 1995—99, gen. chmn. 14th Internat. Conf. on Oral and Maxillofacial Surg. 1999); mem.: ADA (adv. com. advanced edn. in oral surgery 1968—75, cons. Coun. on Dental Edn. 1968—82, mem. Commn. on Accreditation 1975—76), Odontographic Soc., William F. Harrigan Soc., Nat. Chronic Pain Outreach Assn. (adv. bd.), Am. Dental Bd. Anesthesiology (pres. 1983—92), Royal Soc. Medicine, Can. Assn. Oral and Maxillofacial Surgeons (hon.), Brazilian Coll. Oral and Maxillofacial Surgery and Traumatology (hon.), Chilean Soc. Oral and Maxillofacial Surgery (hon.), Hellenic Assn. Oral Surgery (hon.), Sadi Fontaine Acad. (hon.), Internat. Congress Oral Implantologists (hon.), Soc. Maxillofacial and Oral Surgeons South Africa (hon.), Japanese Soc. for Temporomandibular Joint (hon.), Am. Soc. Laser in Dentistry (hon.), Internat. Study Group for Advancement of TMJ Arthroscopy (hon.), Japanese Soc. Oral and Maxillofacial Surgeons (hon.), Am. Assn. Dental Editors, Am. Soc. Exptl. Pathology, Am. Dental Soc. Anesthesiology (pres. 1976—78), Internat. Assn. Dental Rsch., Am. Assn. Oral and Maxillofacial Surgeons (editor Forum 1965—96, pres. 1976—77, editor AAOMS Today 1996—, Disting. Svc. award 1972, rsch. recognition award 1978, William J. Gies award 1979, dedication 73d ann. meeting and sci. sessions 1991), Ill. Splty. Bd. Oral Surgery, Sigma Xi, Omicron Kappa Upsilon. Rsch. and publs. on connective tissue physiology and pathology, particularly cartilage and bone metabolism, craniofacial growth, oral maxillofacial surgery, and pathology of temporomandibular joint. Office: Va Commonwealth U Dept Oral/Maxillofac Surg PO Box 980566 Richmond VA 23298-0566 E-mail: dmlaskin@vcu.edu.

LASKIN, OSCAR LARRY, clinical pharmacology educator, virologist; b. Phila., Sept. 11, 1951; s. Bernard and Blanche (Friedman) L.; m. Christine Ann Goril, Apr. 4, 1981; children: Matthew Benjamin, Joshua Christopher, Jennifer Bonnie, Heather Rose. AB summa cum laude, Temple U., 1972, MD with honors, 1976. Diplomate Am. Bd. Internal Medicine. Intern Johns Hopkins Hosp., Balt., 1976-77, resident in medicine, 1977-79, fellow in medicine, 1979-82, fellow in pharmacology, 1981-82; asst. prof. clin. pharmacology Cornell U. Med. Coll., N.Y.C., 1982-88, asst. prof. pharmacology and medicine, 1982-88; asst. attending physician N.Y. Hosp., 1982-88; adj. assoc. prof. med. and clin. pharmacology Cornell U. Med. Coll., 1988; dir. clin. pharmacology Merck, Sharp, & Dohme Rsch. Labs., 1988-91, Sandoz Rsch. Inst., 1991-92, exec. dir. clin. pharmacology, 1993-96, global head clin. pharmacology, 1994-96; v.p. clin. pharmacology Novartis Pharm. Co., 1997-99; U.S. dir. clin. pharmacology Glaxo Wellcome, Inc., 1999—2001; v.p. clin. R&D Kyowa Pharm., Inc., 2001—02; exec. dir. pre-clin. devel. Celgene Corp., Warner, NJ, 2003—. Contbr. articles to profl. jours. NIH fellow, 1981, Hartford Found. fellow, 1983; clin. scholar Rockefeller Bros. Fund, 1982; recipient rsch. prize Am. Heart Assn., 1975; pharm. Mfrs. Assn. Found. rsch. starter grantee, 1984-86. Fellow ACP, Infectious Disease Soc. Am., Am. Coll. Clin. Pharmacology (bd. regents); mem. Am. Fedn. Clin. Rsch., Am. Soc. Microbiology, Am. Soc. Pharmacology and Exptl. Therapeutics (Young Investigator award 1987), Am. Soc. for Clin. Pharmacology and Therapeutics, Am. Bd. Clin. Pharmacology, Alpha Omega Alpha. Home: 183 Carriage Way Princeton NJ 08540-7320 Office: Celgene Corp 7 Powder Horn Dr Warren NJ 07059

LASPINA, PETER JOSEPH, computer resource educator; b. Bay Shore, N.Y., June 28, 1951; s. Peter Celestine and Barbara Elizabeth (Rodee) L.; 1 child; Joseph Peter. BMus with high honors, Performer's Cert. on Piano, N.Y. State Coll., Potsdam, 1973; MS in Music Edn., L.I. U., 1978; MS in Tech. Sys. Mgmt., SUNY, Stony Brook, 1987; postgrad., Nova Southeastern U., 1995-97. Tchr. music E. Meadow (N.Y.) pub. schs., 1974-75, Northport-East Northport Pub. Schs., 1975-86, computer resource tchr., 1986—. Adj. faculty SUNY, Stony Brook, 1991—; writer master trainer N.Y. State Edn. Dept., Albany, 1987-88; cons. ednl. tech., Smithtown, N.Y., 1987—; invited del. U.S./China Joint Conf. on Edn., Beijing, 1992, 95-96, and conf. presenter. Contbr. articles to profl. jours. Mem. Am. Fedn. Tchrs., N.Y. State United Tchrs., Suffolk County Music Educators Assn., Nat. Assn. Sci., Tech. and Soc., N.Y. State Assn. Computers and Techs. (mem. conf. com. 1994), Internat. Soc. for Tech. in Edn., Assn. Ednl. Comm. and Tech., Assn. for Advancement of Computers in Edn. Presbyterian. Avocations: reading, oenology, home repair, travel. Home: 21 Knolltop Dr Nesconset NY 11767-2221 Office: SUNY Tech And Soc Program Stony Brook NY 11794-0001 E-mail: plaspina@notes.sunysb.edu.

LASS, TERESA LEE, secondary school and special education educator; b. Atlanta, Aug. 30, 1958; d. Houston Lee and Carolyn (Cowan) L.; m. William Gary Carpenter, Oct. 1, 1983 (div. Sept. 1995). BA in German, Studio Art, Art History, Agnes Scott Coll., 1980; MEd, Ga. State U., 1994. Art gall. dir. TPS/Decor Corp., Atlanta, 1978-88; instr. adult literacy State Ga., Dept. Continuing Edn., Atlanta, 1990—; instr. New Tchr. Inst. Ga. State U., Atlanta, 1990-91; instr. staff devel. Dekalb Schs., Decatur, Ga., 1996—; tchr. prodn. and distbn. Warren Tech. Sch., Chamblee, Ga., 1988—, Ptnr. in Edn. liaison, 1994—, chair human rels., 1996—. Cons. Ga. Learning Resource Svcs., Atlanta, 1993—. Chmn. Peachtree Arts, High Mus. of Art, Atlanta, 1996-97, sec./liaison 1991-95, sec., 1999—, chair-elect, 2000-01, chair, 2001-02, membership chair, 2003—; artistic coord. Habitat for Humanity Artfest, Atlanta, 1996—. Named Tchr. of Yr., 1994-95, Tchr. Support Specialist, 2001—. Mem. Phi Beta Kappa, Kappa Delta Pi. Baptist. Avocations: travel, reading, art collecting, cooking, writing. Home: 2155 Morris Ave Tucker GA 30084-4510 Office: Warren Tech Sch 3075 Alton Rd Chamblee GA 30341-4301

LASSER, GAIL MARIA, psychologist, educator; b. Saddle River, N.J., Feb. 29, 1960; d. Dominick A. and Genevieve M. Sanzo; children: Michael, Jason, Jonathan. B.A., Seton Hall U., 1971; postgrad., Seton HaLL u., 1975—77; tchg. cert., William Paterson Coll., 1973; M.A., Montclair State Coll., 1975. Cert. staff psychologist N.J., 1977; lic. real estate agt. N.J., 1977, notary pub. Pub. rel. rep. European Health Spa, 1970—71; med. asst. Sci. Prevention and Rehab. Assn., 1973; grad. tchg. and rsch. asst. Montclair State Coll., 1973—74; clin. asst. Dr. Brower, 1974; instr. psychology Essex County Coll., 1976—77; clin. psychologist intern Cmty. Mental Health Ctr., Mt. Carmel Guild, Newark, 1976—77; lectr. St. Michaels Med. Ctr.-N.J. Coll. Medicine, 1977—80; instr. psychology Bergen Cmty. Coll., Paramus, NJ, 1977—. Asst. to ct. adminstr. Bergen County Cts., 1977—78; cons. telecom., 1994. Vol. Am. Heart Assn. Mem.: Am. Soc. Phy. Rsch., Am. Psychol. Assn., Psi Chi, Pi Lambda Theta. Home: 234 E Saddle River Rd Saddle River NJ 07458-2614

LASSITER, BETTIE WATFORD, retired elementary education educator; b. Colerain, N.C., Nov. 12, 1941; d. Hunter and Mary (Freeman) Watford; m. James Lassiter Jr., Dec. 30, 1963; children: Kimberly Arnet Lassiter, Tracy Arnez Lassiter. BS, Fayetteville (N.C.) State U., 1963. Cert. elem. tchr., N.C. Tchr. Bertie County Sch. Sys., Powellsville, N.C., 1963-64, 65-67; tchr. Hertford County Sch. Sys., Winton, N.C., 1967-95, ret., 1995. Mem. NEA (ret.), N.C. Ret. Sch. Pers., N.C. Assn. Educators. Democrat. Baptist. Avocations: reading, cooking, gardening, shopping. Home: 110 Doll Hill Rd PO Box 374 Powellsville NC 27967-0374

LASSLO, ANDREW, medicinal chemist, educator; b. Mukacevo, Czechoslovakia, Aug. 24, 1922; came to U.S., 1946, naturalized, 1951; s. Vojtech Laszlo and Terezie (Herskovicova) L.; m. Wilma Ellen Reynolds, July 9, 1955; 1 child, Millicent Andrea. MS, U. Ill., 1948, PhD, 1952, MLS, 1961. Rsch. chemist organic chems. div. Monsanto Chem. Co., St. Louis, 1952-54; asst. prof. pharmacology, divsn. basic health scis. Emory U., 1954-60; prof. and chmn. dept. med. chemistry Coll. Pharmacy, U. Tenn. Health Sci. Ctr., 1960-90, Alumni Disting. Svc. prof. and chmn., dept. medicinal chemistry, 1989-90; ret. as prof. emeritus, 1990. Cons. Geschickter Fund for Med. Research Inc., 1961-62; rsch. contractor U.S. Army Med. R&D Command, 1964-65; dir. postgrad. tng. program sci. librarians USPHS, 1966-72; chmn. edn. com. Drug Info. Assn., 1966-68, bd. dirs., 1968-69; dir. postgrad. tng. program organic medicinal chemistry for chemists FDA, 1971; exec. com. adv. council S.E. Regional Med. Library Program, Nat. Library of Medicine, 1969-71; chmn. regional med. library programs com. Med. Library Assn., 1971-72; mem. pres.'s faculty adv. council U. Tenn. System, 1970-72; chmn. energy authority U. Tenn. Center for Health Scis., 1975-77, chmn. council departmental chmn., 1977, 81; chmn. Internat. Symposium on Contemporary Trends in Tng. Pharmacologists, Helsinki, 1975. Producer, moderator (TV and radio series) Health Care Perspective, 1976-78; author: Travel at Your Own Risk-Reflections on Science, Research and Education, 1998, Molecules, Miracles and Medicine, 2000; editor: Surface Chemistry and Dental Intequments, 1973, Blood Platelet Function and Medicinal Chemistry, 1984; contbr. numerous articles to sci. and profl. jours.; mem. editl. bd. Jour. Medicinal and Pharm. Chemistry, 1961, U. Tenn. Press, 1974-77; composer (work for piano) Synthesis in C Minor, 1968; patentee in field. Trustee 1st Bohemian Meth. Ch., Chgo., 1951-52, mem. bd. stewards, 1950-52; mem. ofcl. bd. Grace Meth. Ch., Atlanta, 1955-60; mem. adminstrv. bd. Christ United Meth. Ch., Memphis, 1964-72, 73-75, 77-79, 81-83, 88-90, chmn. commn. on edn., 1965-67, chmn. bd. Day Sch., 1967-68. 1st lt. USAR, 1953-57, capt., 1957-62. Recipient Research prize U. Ill. Med. Ctr. chpt. Sigma Xi, 1949, Honor Scroll Tenn. Inst. Chemists, 1976, Americanism medal DAR, 1976; U. Ill. fellow, 1951-52; Geschickter Fund Med. Research grantee, 1959-65, USPHS Research and Tng. grantee, 1958-64, 66-72, 82-89, NSF research grantee, 1964-66, Pfeiffer Research Found. grantee, 1981-87. Fellow AAAS, Am. Assn. Pharm. Scientists, Am. Inst. Chemists (nat. councilor for Tenn. 1969-70), Acad. Pharm. Rsch. and Sci.; mem. ALA (life), Am. Chem. Soc. (sr.), Am. Pharm. Assn., Am. Soc. Pharmacology and Exptl. Therapeutics (chmn. subcom. pre and postdoctoral tng. 1974-78, exec. com. ednl. and profl. affairs 1974-78), Sigma Xi (pres. elect U. Tenn. Ctr. for Health Sci. chpt. 1975-76, pres. 1976-77, Excellence in Rsch. award 1989), Beta Phi Mu, Phi Lambda Sigma, Rho Chi. Methodist. Achievements include 7 U.S. and 11 foreign patents in field; identification of platelet aggregation-inhibitory specific functions in synthetic organic molecules; design and synthesis of novel human blood platelet aggregation inhibitors, novel compound for mild stimulation of central nervous system activity; research on relationships between structural features of synthetic organic entities, their physicochemical properties and their effects on biologic activity. Home and Office: 5479 Timmons Ave Memphis TN 38119-6932

LAST, SUSAN WALKER, training developer; b. Waterbury, Conn., Sept. 26, 1962; d. Harold Alfred and Mary (Alferie) Hull; m. Michael Allen Walker, Feb. 11, 1984 (div. July 1988); 1 child, Cassandra Mary; m. Robert Lee Last, Sept. 26, 1992. BS, Ind. U., 1983. Cert. franchise exec. Internat. Franchise Assn., 2003. Ctr. dir. Sylvan Learning Corp., Arlington, Tex., 1984-88, franchise cons., 1988-89, dist. mgr., 1989-90; coord. of program devel. Sylvan Learning Systems, Arlington, Tex., 1991-96; dir. tng. devel. Am. Fastsigns, Inc., Carrollton, Tex., 1996-97, v.p. tng., 1997—99, sr. v.p. franchise svcs., 1999—. Trainer, cons. Charles R. Hobbs Corp., Salt Lake City, 1989-96; cons. Highpointe, Arlington, 1988-94. Author: (curriculum) Study Skills Program, 1990, Study Power Video, 1991, Basic Math Program (K-8), 1994, Adult Reading Program, 1993, ESL program, 1995. Mem., speaker Parents Without Ptnrs., Arlington, 1991. Mem. ASCD, ASTD, Children and Adults with Attention Deficient Disorder, Nat. Coun. Tchrs. of Math., Nat. Coun. Tchrs. of English, Meeting Planners Internat., Internat. Franchise Assn., Internat. Sign Assn. Avocations: reading, writing, gardening, swimming. Home: 1316 Willow Wood Dr Carrollton TX 75010-1304 Office: FASTSIGNS International Inc 2550 Midway Rd Ste 150 Carrollton TX 75006-2372

LASYS, JOAN, medical nurse, writer, educator, publisher; b. Siauliai, Lithuania, Sept. 1, 1924; arrived in Can., 1948; came to U.S., 1960; d. Joseph-Apolinarius and Elena (Šlapokaite) Barcevičius; m. Bill Lasys, July 31, 1949. RN degree, Lithuanian Red Cross Sch. Nursing, 1945; student, Ariz. State U., 1981—86, Ea. Ariz. Coll., 1981—86. RN, Can., Nebr.; cert. nursing tchr., Ariz.; C.C., occupl. tchg. cert. Ariz. Staff RN St. Mary's Hosp., Montreal, Can., 1949-51, Montreal Gen. Hosp., 1951-53, 1959-60; pvt. duty Nurses Registry, Montreal, 1953-56; Can. civil svc. RN R.H.O. Ctr. Dept. Vets. Affairs, Ottawa, Can., 1956-57, Queen Mary Vets. Hosp., Montreal, 1957-58; staff RN St. Joseph's Hosp., Omaha, 1968-69, Meryvale Hosp., Phoenix, 1969-71, Valley View Hosp., Youngtown, Ariz., 1971-72, Boswell Hosp., Sun City, Ariz., 1972-76; RN Kivel Care Ctr., Phoenix, 1986—93, 2000—02. Past v.p. and officer Pine-Strawberry (Ariz.) Health Svcs.; columnist/reporter Payson (Ariz.) Roundup. Pub. (mag.) Small Town U.S.A.; prodr. audio tapes: Time Management, Nursing Communications. Life mem. Pine-Strawberry and Gila County Homemakers, Payson Regional Med. Ctr. Aux. Mem.: AAUW, Libr. Congress, Nat. Mus. Women in the Arts, Payson Libr., Rep. Presidential Task Force, Kivel Geriatric Ctr. Aux. (life), County Attys. and Sheriffs Assn. (hon.), Arbor Day Found., Nature Conservancy, Cooking Club of Am. (charter). Republican. Roman Catholic. Avocations: cooking, writing poetry, public speaking, arts and crafts. Home: 506 N William Tell Cir Payson AZ 85541-4050

LATANISION, RONALD MICHAEL, materials science and engineering educator, consultant; b. Richmondale, Pa., July 2, 1942; s. Stephen and Mary (Kopach) L.; m. Carolyn Marie Domenig, June 27, 1964; children: Ivan, Sara. BS, Pa. State U., 1964; PhD in Metall. Engring., Ohio State U., 1968. Postdoctoral fellow Nat. Bur. Standards, Washington, 1968-69; research scientist Martin Marietta, Balt., 1969-73, acting head materials sci., 1973-74; dir. H.H. Uhlig Corrosion Lab. MIT, Cambridge, 1975—, Shell Disting. prof. materials sci. and engring., 1983-88, dir. Materials Processing Ctr., 1984-91; co-founder ALTRAN Materials Engring. Corp., Boston, 1992—. Mem. tech. adv. bd. Modell Devel. Corp., Framingham, Mass., 1987-94; sci. advisor com. on sci. and tech. U.S. Ho. of Reps., 1982-83; chmn. ad hoc com. Mass. Advanced Materials Ctr., Boston, 1985—; mem. adv. bd. Mass. Office Sci. and Tech.; co-PI, NSF/SSI project PALMS; chmn. MIT Coun. on Primary and Secondary Edn. Editor: Surface Effects in Crystal Plasticity, 1977, Atomistics of Fracture, 1983, Chemistry and Physics of Fracture, 1987, Advances in Mechanics and Physics of Fracture, 1981, 83, 86; contbr. articles to profl. jours. Recipient sr. scientist award Humboldt Found., 1974-75, David Ford McFarland award Pa. State U., 1986; named Henry Krumb lectr. AIME, 1984, Disting. Alumnus, Ohio State U. Coll. Engring., 1991, hon. alumnus MIT, 1992; Centennial fellow Coll. Earth and Mineral Scis., Pa. State U., 1996. Fellow Am. Soc. Metals Internat. (govt. and pub. affairs com. 1984), Nat. Assn. Corrosion Engrs. (A.B. Campbell award 1971, Willis R. Whitney award 1994); mem. New Eng. Sci. Tchrs. (founder, co-chmn.), Nat. Acad. Engring., Am. Acad. Arts and Scis., Nat. Materials Adv. Bd., Masons. Roman Catholic. Office: MIT Materials Sci & Engring 77 Mass Ave Rm 16-206 Cambridge MA 02139-4307

LATHAM, LAVONNE MARLYS, physical education educator; b. Garrison, Iowa, Mar. 17, 1942; d. Harry August and Vona Irene (Loveless) Hilmer; m. Robert Allen Latham Jr., July 21, 1979. BA, U. Iowa, 1964; postgrad., No. Ill. U., 1985, Western Ill. U., 1970-88, Bemidji State U., 1979. Cert. tchr., Ill. Tchr. phys. edn., elem. computer coord. Erie (Ill.) Community Unit 1, 1964—. Head counselor Camp Lenore Owaissa, Hinsdale, Mass., 1964-85. Mem. NEA, AAHPER, Ill. Assn. Health, Phys. Edn. and Recreation, U. Iowa Alumni Assn., Ill. Edn. Assn., Erie Tchrs. Assn. (pres. 1982-83), Nat. Audubon Soc., Nature Conservancy, Delta Kappa Gamma. Baptist. Avocations: violin, computers, photography, travel, outdoor activities. Home: 1002 6th St Erie IL 61250 Office: Erie Community Unit 1 605 6th Ave Erie IL 61250-9452

LATHROP, THOMAS ALBERT, language educator, educator; b. L.A., Apr. 18, 1941; s. Donald C. and Ethel M. (Challacombe) L.; m. Constance Ellen Cook, Aug. 30, 1969; 1 child, Aline. BA, UCLA, 1964, MA, 1965, PhD, 1970. Mem. faculty Romance langs. UCLA, 1964-66, U. Wyo., 1966-68, Transylvania U., 1973-76, Lafayette Coll., 1976-80; prof. Romance langs. U. Del., Newark, 1980—. Founding editor Juan de la Cuesta Hispanic Monographs, 1978—; co-editor The Cabrilho Press, 1974-89; pres. Linguatext, Ltd., 1989—; asst. editor Cervantes Bull. of the Cervantes Soc. Am., 1980-90. Author: The Legend of the Siete Infantes de Lara, 1972; (with F. Jensen) The Syntax of the Old Spanish Subjunctive, 1973, La Vie Saint Eustace, 2000; Espanol--Lengua y cultura de hoy, 1974; The Evolution of Spanish, 1980; De Acuerdo! and Tanto Mejor, 1986; (with E Dias) Portugal, Lingua e Cultura, 1978, 2d edit., 1995, Curso de gramatica historica espanola, 1984, 89, (with E. Dias) Brasil: Lingua e Cultura, 2002, student edit. Don Quijote, others; editor: European Classics, 2001-. AID grantee, 1968; Nat. Endowment for Humanities grantee, 1976, 81; Gulbenkian Found. grantee, 1973; Del Amo Found. grantee, 1972. Mem. MLA, Cervantes Soc. Am., Internat. Assn. Hispanists, Am. Coun. on Tchg. of Fgn. Lag., Am. Assn. Tchrs. Spanish and Portugues. Home: 270 Indian Rd Newark DE 19711-5204 Office: U Del Dept Lang Newark DE 19716 E-mail: lathrop@udel.edu.

LATHROPE, DANIEL JOHN, law educator; BSBA, U. Denver, 1973; JD, Northwestern U., 1977; LLM, NYU, 1979. Bar: Ariz. 1977, Calif. 1978. Assoc. Evans, Kitchel & Jenckes, Phoenix, 1977-78; instr. law NYU, 1979-80; assoc. prof. U. Calif. Hastings Coll. Law, San Francisco, 1980-86, prof., 1986—. Assoc. acad. dean U. Calif. Hastings Coll. Law, San Francisco, 1986-87, acting dean, 1987-88, acad. dean, 1988-90; prof., assoc. dean, dir. grad. tax program U. Fla. Coll. Law, Gainesville, 1995-96. Co-author: (with Lind, Schwarz and Rosenberg) Fundamentals of Corporate Taxation, 5th edit., 2002, (with Lind, Schwarz and Rosenberg) Fundamentals of Business Enterprise Taxation, 2d edit., 2002, (with Lind, Schwarz and Rosenberg) Fundamentals of Partnership Taxation, 6th edit., 2002, (with Schwarz) Black Letter on Federal Taxation of Corporations and Partnerships, 4th edit., 2003, (with Freeland, Lind and Stephens) Fundamentals of Federal Income Taxation, 13th edit., 2004; author: The Alternative Minimum Tax-Compliance and Planning with Analysis, 1994. Mem. Order of Coif, Beta Gamma Sigma.

LATIMER, MARGARET PETTA, retired nutrition and dietetics educator; b. Sacramento, Aug. 17, 1932; d. Rosario and Helen (Sclafani) Petta; m. Westford Ramos Latimer, June l8, l978. BS, U. Calif., Berkeley, l954; MA, Calif. State U., Sacramento, l982. Registered dietitian, Calif.; life teaching credential, Calif. Therapeutic dietitian U. Calif. Med. Ctr., San Francisco, 1955—65; dietitian Roseville (Calif.) Cmty. Hosp., 1966—67, Mercy San Juan Hosp., Carmichael, Calif., 1967—69; substitute tchr. San Juan Unified Sch. Dist., Sacramento, 1970—75, tchr. adult edn., 1971—74; instr. dietetics American River Coll., Sacramento, 1975—77, San Joaquin Delta Coll., Stockton, Calif., 1975—95; ret., 1995. Cons. dietitian, Sacramento, l973-78. Mem.: AAUW (gourmet chmn. 1981—82, editor AAUW Book of Favorite Recipes 1982, membership treas. 1999—2003), Calif. Dietetic Assn. (pres. Golden Empire dist. 1974—75), Nutrition Today, Am. Dietetic Assn. Republican. Roman Catholic. Avocation: travel.

LATINI, NANCY JANE, special education administrator; b. Buhl, Minn., Mar. 20, 1943; d. Nazzareno Thomas and Josephine (Pervenanze) L. BS, U. Minn., 1965; MS, St. Cloud State U., 1975; PhD, U. Minn., 1985. Cert. adminstr., Minn., Oreg. Spl. edn. tchr., trainer, adminstr. Mpls. Pub. Schs., 1965-90; spl. edn. adminstr. North Clackamas Sch. Dist., Milwaukie, Oreg., 1990—. Cons. to univs.; mem. adv. bd. Spl. Edn. Adv. State Edn. Agy., Minn., 1985-88, Assn. for Retarded Citizens, Clackamas, 1990. Editor: Special Education Learning Disabilities Research, 1985. Mem. Coun. for Exceptional Children, Coun. of Adminstrs. in Spl. Edn., Delta Kappa Gamma, Phi Delta Kappa. Office: North Clackamas Sch Dist 1903 SE Oak Grove Blvd Portland OR 97267-2621

LATORRE, ROBERT GEORGE, naval architecture and engineering educator; b. Toledo, Jan. 9, 1949; s. Robert James and Madge Violette (Roy) L.; m. Iryna Koroe, 2000; 1 child, Marie-Elise. BS in Naval Architecture and Marine Engring. with honors, U. Mich., 1971, MS in Engring., 1972; MSE in Naval Architecture, U. Tokyo, 1975, PhD. in Naval Architecture, 1978. Asst. prof. U. Mich., Ann Arbor, 1979-83; assoc. prof. U. New Orleans, 1984-87, prof. naval architecture and marine engring., 1987—, chmn. dept., 1989-95. assoc. prof. mech. engring., U. Tokyo, 1986-87; rsch. scientist, David Taylor Naval R & D Lab., Bethesda, Md., 1980, 81, Bassin d'Essais des Carenes, Paris, 1983; cons. in field. Contbr. to profl. publs. Mem. ASME, Soc. Naval Architects, Royal Inst. Naval Archtects Gt. Britain, Soc. Naval Architects Japan, Am. Soc. engring. Edn. (program chmn. ocean engring. divsn. 1989-90, Japan Club New Orleans. Roman Catholic. Office: U New Orleans 911 Engring Bldg New Orleans LA 70148-0001 E-mail: rglna@uno.edu.

LATOVICK, PAULA R(AE), lawyer, educator; b. Detroit, Feb. 17, 1954; d. Raymond and Marjorie Camille (Peters) L.; m. William P. Weiner, Aug. 17, 1985; children: Jeffrey Devon, Robert Stirling. BA in Personnel with high honor, Mich. State U., 1976; JD cum laude, U. Mich., 1980, LLM, 1999. Bar: Mich. 1980, U.S. Dist. Ct. (ea. dist.) Mich. 1980, U.S. Dist. Ct. (we. dist.) Mich. 1981, U.S. Ct. Appeals (6th cir.) 1985. Assoc. Fraser, Trebilcock, Davis & Foster P.C., Lansing, Mich., 1980—86, ptnr., 1986—92, chmn. hiring com., 1987—92, chmn. govt. law dept., 1988—90; assoc. prof. Thomas M. Cooley Law Sch., 1992—97, prof., 1998—2001, chair property law dept., 2000—01; ret., 2001. Adj. prof. Thomas M. Cooley Law Sch., Lansing, 1984-86. V.p. YWCA, Lansing, 1988, pres., 1989—91, chmn. bldg. com., 1989—91; head advisor law explorers Boy Scouts Am., Lansing, 1982—84; mem. Capitol Area Women's Network, Lansing, 1988; rec. sec. Friends of Kresge Art Mus., 1992—93, corr. sec., 1993—94, 1st v.p., 1994—95, pres., 1995—96; treas. Cub Scouts Pack 107, Boy Scouts Am., 1998—2002; co-chair Friends Greater Lansing Symphony, 2000—01; pres. William Donley Elem. Sch. Parent Coun., 2001—. Named One of Outstanding Young Women of Am., 1985. Fellow Mich. State Bar Found.; mem. NOW, Mich. Bar Assn. (mem. young lawyers exec. coun. 1984-86, mem. com. character and fitness dist. F 1991-2000, subcom. chairperson 1994-2000), Women Lawyers Assn. Mich., Ingham County Bar Assn. (chairperson hist. com. 1984-87, mem. young lawyers bd. 1981-84, pres. 1983, mem. com. on jud. qualifications 1990-93, bd. dirs. 1990-92), Thomas M. Cooley Legal Authors Soc., U. Mich. Alumni Assn. (life), Mich. State U. Alumni Assn., Zonta (rec. sec. local club 1985-86, chmn. membership com. 1988-89). Democrat. Roman Catholic.

LATT, PAMELA YVONNE, school system administrator; b. Mineola, N.Y., Mar. 24, 1952; d. Michael and Irene (Pearlman) Vuicich; m. James Michael Latt, Aug. 31, 1974; 1 child, Jeremy Jacob. BA in Secondary Edn./English, SUNY, Fredonia, 1973, MA in English, 1974. Lectr. Adam Mickiewicz U., Poznan, Poland, 1970-72; English/reading specialist Halifax County (Va.) Pub. Schs., 1974-76; ESL tchr., grades K-6 Fairfax County (Va.) Pub. Schs., Baileys X-Roads, 1976-79, ESL tchr., grades 7-8 Vienna, 1979-80, coord. of cen. registration Falls Church, 1980-89, dir. of student svcs., 1989-92, subsch. prin./Lake Braddock Secondary Burke, Va., 1992-93; prin. Centreville H.S., Clifton, Va., 1993—. Spl. adjunct to U. Va., Falls Church, 1979-85; cons. State Dept., Arlington, Va., 1990—; mem. adv. bd. Am. Overseas Sch.; cons. Coll. Bd., Washington and N.Y., 1989—. Author/editor: School Health Care Emergencies, 1990, Handbook for School Health Risks, 1990; contbg. author/cons. Cross-Cultural Learning in K-12 Schools: Foreign Students as Resources, 1982. Cons., focus group Human Svcs./Fairfax County, 1988—. Adam Mickiewicz U. scholar, Poznan, 1970-72; named one of Outstanding Young Women of Am., 1979, Super Boss of Yr., Fairfax Assn. Ednl. Office Pers., 1989; nom. Prin. Yr., 1998, 99, 2001, 03. Mem. ASCD, Nat. Assn. Sch. Prins. Secondary Schs., Nat. Assn. Fgn. Student Affairs (region 8 rep. 1987-89). Democrat. Roman Catholic. Avocations: sculpting, golf, reading and writing poetry. Office: Centreville High Sch 6001 Union Mill Rd Clifton VA 20124-1128

LATTIN, VERNON EUGENE, academic administrator; b. Winslow, Ariz., Nov. 7, 1938; s. Eli Voil and Betty (Rubi) L.; m. Karen Conti, Aug, 29, 1962 (div.); 1 child, Tanya R.; m. Patricia Hopkins, June 1, 1973; 1 child, Carlos V.; stepchildren: Mark, Kim, John. BBA, U. N.Mex., 1960, MA in English, 1965; PhD in English, U. Colo., 1970. Instr. English Wright State U., Dayton, Ohio, 1965-67; asst. prof. English U. Tenn., Chattanooga, 1970-74; coordinator communication skills and English No. Ill. U., De Kalb, 1974-77, assoc. prof. English, 1974-81, dir. Ctr. Latino and Latin Am. Studies, 1978-81; assoc. v.p. acad. affairs U. Wis. system, Madison, 1982-88; provost, prof. English Ariz. State U., Phoenix, 1989-92; pres. Bklyn. Coll. CUNY, 1992-2000, pres. emeritus, 2000—. Editor: Contemporary Chicano Fiction: A Critical Study, 1986, Tomas Rivera, 1935-84: The Man and His Work, 1988. Mem. policy com. Phoenix Futures Forum, 1989; pres. Midwest Latino Coun. on Higher Edn., 1980-83. Recipient Disting. Hispanic Educator award Midwest Chicano Studies Assn., 1981; named one of 100 Influential Hispanics, Hispanic Bus. Mag., 1987; fellow Modern Lang. Seminar, 1976. Mem. MLA, Nat. Assn. Chicano Studies, Am. Assn. Higher Edn., Internat. Assn. Univ. Pres.', Phi Kappa Phi, Sigma Tau Delta. Democrat. Avocations: raquetball, running, reading. Home: Apt 5J 155 E 38th St New York NY 10016-2663

LATTMAN, LAURENCE HAROLD, retired academic administrator; b. N.Y.C., Nov. 30, 1923; s. Jacob and Yetta (Schwartz) L.; m. Hanna Renate Cohn, Apr. 12, 1946; children— Martin Jacob, Barbara Diane. BSChemE, Coll. City N.Y., 1948; MS in Geology, U. Cin., 1951, PhD, 1953. Instr. U. Mich., 1952-53; asst. head photogeology sect. Gulf Oil Corp., Pitts., 1953-57; asst. prof. to prof. geomorphology Pa. State U., 1957-70; prof., head dept. geology U. Cin., 1970-75; dean Coll. of Mines U. Utah, 1975-83, dean Coll. Engring., 1978-83; pres. N.Mex. Tech., Socorro, 1983-93, pres. emeritus, 1993—. Bd. dirs. Pub. Svc. Co. of N.Mex.; cons. U.S. Army Engrs., Vicksburg, Miss., 1965-69, also major oil cos. Author: (with R.G. Ray) Aerial Photographs in Field Geology, 1965, (with D. Zillman) Energy Law; Contbr. articles to profl. jours. Mem. N.Mex. Environ. Improvement Bd., 1995—. With AUS, 1943-46. Fenneman fellow U. Cin., 1953. Fellow Geol. Soc. Am.; mem. Am. Assn. Petroleum Geologists, Am. Soc. Photogrammetry (Ford Bartlett award 1968), Soc. Econ. Paleontologists and Mineralogists, AIME (Disting. mem. 1981, Mineral Industries Edn., award 1986—), Assn. Western Univs. (chmn. bd. dirs. 1986-87), Sigma Xi. Home: 11509 Penfield Ln NE Albuquerque NM 87111-6526

LAU, LAWRENCE JUEN-YEE, economics educator, consultant; b. Guizhou, China, Dec. 12, 1944; came to U.S., 1961, naturalized, 1974; s. Shai-Tat and Chi-Hing (Yu) Liu. BS with great distinction, Stanford U., 1964, MA, U. Calif., Berkeley, 1966, PhD, 1969; D.Social Sci. honoris causa, Hong Kong U. Sci. and Tech. From acting asst. prof. econs. to assoc. prof. Stanford U., Palo Alto, Calif., 1966-76, prof., 1976—, Kwoh-Ting Li prof. econ. devel., 1992—; dir. Stanford Inst. Econ. Policy Rsch., 1997—99. Co-dir. Asia/Pacific Rsch. Ctr., Stanford U., 1992-96; dir. Bank of Canton of Calif., San Francisco, 1979-85, 99-2002, Property Resources Equity Trust, Los Gatos, 1987-88; cons. The World Bank, Wash., 1976-; vice chmn. Bank of Canton of Calif. Bldg. Corp., San Francisco, 1981-85, Complete Computer Co. Far Eat Ltd., Hong Kong, 1981-89; bd. dirs. Taiwan Fund, Inc., BOC Internat. Holdings Ltd., Hong Kong, Media Ptnrs. Internat. Holdings Inc., Hong Kong. Co-author: (with D.T. Jamison) Farmer Education and Farm Efficiency, 1982, Models of Devlopment: A Comparative Study of Economic Growth in South Korea and Taiwan, 1986, rev. edit., 1990, Econometrics and the Cost of Capital: Essays in Honor of Dale W. Jorgenson, 2000, (with C.H. Yoon) North Korea in Transition: Prospects for Economic and Social Reform, 2001; contbr. articles to profl. jours. Adv. bd. Self-Help for Elderly, San Francisco, 1982—; bd. dirs. Chiang Ching-Kuo Found. for Internat. Scholarly Exch., 1989—; govs. coun. econ. policy advisors State of Calif., 1993-99; mem. Asian Art Commn., San Francisco, 1998-2001; mem. adv. coun. Innovation and Tech., Hong Kong, 2000-02. John Simon Guggenheim Meml. fellow, 1973, fellow Ctr. for Advanced Study in Behavioral Scis., 1982, Overseas fellow Churchill Coll., Cambridge U., Eng., 1984 Fellow Econometric Soc.; mem. Academia Sinica (academician), Conf. Research in Income and Wealth, Chinese Acad. Social Scis. (hon.), Internat. Eurasian Acad. Scis. (academician). Episcopalian. Office: Stanford U Dept Econs Stanford CA 94305-6072 E-mail: LJLAU@stanford.edu.

LAU, PATRICK HING-LEUNG, radiologist, educator; b. Hong Kong, May 21, 1945; m. Peggy Lau; children: Eric, Chad. BS, St. Louis U., 1970; DO, Midwestern U., 1974. Diplomate Am. Bd. Radiology. Intern Grandview Hosp. Med. Ctr., 1974-75; pvt. practice family medicine, 1975—80; resident Mt. Sinai Med. Ctr., 1981-84; fellow Coll. Medicine U. Ill., 1984-85, radiology instr., 1984-85; asst. prof. radiology Phila. Coll. Osteo. Medicine, 1985-86; chief imaging svcs. VA No. Ind. Healthcare Sys., Marion, 1988—; med. dir. radiology tech. program Ivy Tech. State Coll., 2001—. Contbr. articles to profl. jours. Dep. med. examiner, Monroe County, Mich., 1977-80; police surgeon Am. Law Enforcement Officers Assn., 1979-80. Recipient Abbie Norman Prince award for Outstanding Svc., Mt. Sinai Med. Ctr., 1984, cert. of appreciation, Midwestern U., 1984, 1999, cert. recognition, Am. Osteo. Coll. Radiology, 1985, award of appreciation, SME Boy Scouts Am., 1991, Hands and Heart award VA Affairs, 1995, 2000, Exceptional Svc. award, VFW, 1999. Mem. Am. Coll. Radiology, Radiol. Soc. N.Am. Office: VA No Ind Healthcare Sys 1700 E 38th St Marion IN 46953-4568

LAUB, MARY LOU, elementary education educator; m. James H. Laub, Aug. 18, 1973. BS in Elem. Edn., Kutztown U., 1973, M in Elem. Edn., 1976; EdD, Temple U., 1993. Cert. elem. edn., instrnl. I and II, reading specialist. Tchr. Kutztown Area Sch. Dist., 1973—; asst. prof. Kutztown U., Pa., 2000—. Adj. prof. Muhlenberg Coll., Allentown, Pa., 1994-95; cons., presenter Kutztown German Festival, 1996—; cons., rschr., presenter Elderhostel, Inc., Boston, 1997—. Mem., sec. of consistory Zion United Ch. of Christ, Maxatawny, Pa., 1996—. Mem. Internat. Reading Assn., Keystone State Reading Assn. (bd. dirs.), Assn. Childhood Edn. Internat., Nat. Coun. Social Studies, Nat. Coun. Tchrs. English, Tri-County Reading Coun. (v.p., pres.-elect, pres., Celebrate Literacy award), Orgn. Tchr. Educators in Reading (del.), Kappa Delta Pi, Phi Kappa Phi. Avocations: gardening, fishing, reading. Home: 331 Leiby Ln Kutztown PA 19530-9667

LAUCK, LYNNE RUTH, retired elementary and secondary school educator; b. Plainfield, N.J., Oct. 2, 1939; d. William Donald and Helen Mae (Kuhfahl) Boettger; m. George Bernard Lauck, Aug. 2, 1959; children: George Matthew, Nancy Elizabeth, James Francis. BA, Glassboro State Coll., (now Rowan Coll.), 1962. Cert. elem. tchr., secondary math tchr., tchr. of handicapped N.J. Elem. tchr. Janvier and Coles Mill Rd. Schs., Franklinville, N.J., 1960-62, Parker Sch., Middlesex, N.J., 1962-64; middle sch. tchr. Samuel Fleming Sch., Flemington, N.J., 1966-68; tchr. GED prep. Correctional Inst. for Women, Clinton, N.J., 1970-93, ret., 1993. Pres. Delaware Valley Regional High Sch. Bd. Edn., Frenchtown, N.J., 1979-85, Hunterdon County Sch. Bd. Assn., Flemington, 1979-84. Mem. N.J. Sch. Bds. Assn. (bd. dirs. 1981-84), Alexandria Twp. Hist. Soc., Nat. Running Data Ctr. (nat. age record 15, 20, 25 km., 10 mi.), Triathlon Fedn. Republican. Baptist. Avocations: running, woodworking, historic restoration, gardening.

LAUER, JAMES LOTHAR, physicist, educator; b. Vienna, Aug. 2, 1920; came to U.S., 1938, naturalized, 1943; s. Max and Friederike (Rapaport) L.; m. Stefanie Dorothea Blank, Sept. 4, 1955; children: Michael, Ruth. AB, Temple U., 1942, MA, 1944; PhD, U. Pa., 1948; postgrad., U. Calif., San Diego, 1964-65. Scientist Sun Oil Co., Marcus Hook, Pa., 1944-52, spectroscopist, 1952-64, sr. scientist, 1965-77; asst. prof. U. Pa., 1952-55; lectr. U. Del., 1952-58; rsch. fellow mech. engring. U. Calif., San Diego, 1964-65; rsch. prof. mech. engring. Rensselaer Poly. Inst., Troy, N.Y., 1978-85, prof. mech. engring., 1985-93, prof. mech. engring. emeritus, 1993—; rsch. sci. Ctr. Magnetic Recording Rsch. U. Calif., San Diego, 1993-95, vis. scholar applied mechanics and engring. sci., 1995—. Sr. faculty summer rsch. fellow NASA-Lewis Rsch. Ctr., 1986-87; vis. prof. Ctr. for Magnetic Rec. Rsch., U. Calif., San Diego, 1991; cons. Digital Equipment Corp., 1992-94, NASA-Lewis Rsch. Ctr., 1993-95. Author: Infrared Fourier Spectroscopy--Chemical Applications, 1978; co-author: Handbook of Raman Spectroscopy, 2001; mem. editl. bd. Tribology Letters, 1995--; contbr. articles to profl. jours.; patentee in field. Active Penn Wynne Civic Assn., 1959-77, Country Knolls Civic Assn., 1978-93. Sun Oil Co. fellow, 1964-65, Air Force Office Sci. Rsch. grantee, 1974-86, NASA Lewis Rsch. Ctr. grantee, 1974-86, Office Naval Rsch. grantee, 1979-82, Army Rsch. Office grantee, 1985-89, NSF grantee, 1987-95, Innovative Rsch. award Soc. Mech. Engrs., 1991, Discovery awards NASA, 1993, 96. Fellow: Inst. Physics (U.K.); mem.: AAAS (life), Optical Soc. Am. (emeritus), Soc. Applied Spectroscopy, Am. Phys. Soc. (emeritus), Am. Chem. Soc. (emeritus), Materials Rsch. Soc., Sigma Chi. Jewish. Home: 7622 Palmilla Dr Apt 78 San Diego CA 92122-4710 Office: U Calif San Diego La Jolla CA 92037

LAUER, JEANETTE CAROL, college dean, history educator, writer; b. St. Louis, July 14, 1935; d. Clinton Jones and Blanche Aldine (Gideon) Pentecost; m. Robert Harold Lauer, July 2, 1954; children: Jon, Julie, Jeffrey. BS, U. Mo., St. Louis, 1970; MA, Washington U., St. Louis, 1973, PhD, 1975. Assoc. prof. history St. Louis C.C., 1974-82, U.S. Internat. U., San Diego, 1982-90, prof., 1990-94, dean Coll. Arts and Scis., 1990-94, rsch. prof., 1997—. Author: Fashion Power, 1981, The Spirit and the Flesh, 1983, Til Death Do Us Part, 1986, Watersheds, 1988, The Quest for Intimacy, 5th edit., 2002, No Secrets, 1993, The Joy Ride, 1993, For Better of Better, 1995, True Intimacy, 1996, Intimacy on the Run, 1996, How to Build a Happy Marriage, 1996, Sociology: Contours of Society, 1997, Windows on Society, 1999; Becoming Family: How to Build a Stepfamily that Works, 1999, How to Survive and Thrive in an Empty Nest, 1999, Troubled Times: Readings in Social Problems, 1999, Love Never Ends, 2002, The Play Solution: How to Put the Fun Back into your Relationship, 2002. Woodrow Wilson fellow, 1970, Washington U. fellow, 1971-75. Mem. Am. Hist. Assn., Orgn. Am. Historians. Democrat. Presbyterian. Home: 18147 Sun Maiden Ct San Diego CA 92127-3102

LAUER, SUSAN PARKER, personal trainer, writer; b. Boston, Mar. 31, 1965; d. Lee Merkel and Dorothy Joan (Montgomery) P.; m. Carl Nyden Lauer, Feb. 16, 1992; children: Elizabeth Lee, Kathleen Jordan, Sarah Kighley. AB in Govt., Coll. of William and Mary, 1987; MEd in Early Childhood, U. N.C., 1989. Cert. kindergarten tchr., Va., personal trainer. Tchr. hearing impaired Fairfax (Va.) County Pub. Schs., 1990; tchr. kindergarten Rappahannock County Sch. Bd., Sperryville, Va., 1990-93; presch. tchr. Fredericksburg United Meth. Ch., 1994-97; personal trainer, 1998—2000; writer Nurturing Parent, 2000—. Contbr. Nurturing Parent Mag., 2000. Delta Delta Delta fellow, 1987-88. Mem. Warrenton (Va.) Fauquier Jaycees. Episcopalian. Avocations: running, tennis, cross stitching, poetry, reading. Home: 204 Barrows Ct Fredericksburg VA 22406-6447

LAUGHLIN, FAITH ANN, language educator; b. Oscoda County, Mich., Apr. 30, 1959; d. Roger Alzner and Pauline Ann (Densmore) Gardner; m. Kenneth Gene Laughlin, June 7, 1981; children: Kaitlin Ann, Kenneth James. BA, Andrews U., 1982; MA, Pacific Union Coll., 1989. Cert. tchr. K-12, Calif. Tchr. K-1 San Fernando Valley Acad., Northridge, Calif., 1984-88; tchr. grades 2 and 3 White Meml. Adventist Sch., L.A., 1988-89, tchr. 3-4, 1989-90, tchr. 7-8, 1990-93, reading tchr. K-8, 1993-94, tchr. K-1, 1994-96, tchr. multi-grade magnet room, 1996-98; with Learning Resource Ctr. Highland View Acad., Md., 1998-2000; tchg. prin. Fair Oaks SDA Christian Sch., 2000—01; tchr. Spanish Loudoun County Pub. Schs., 2001—. Contbr. articles to profl. jours. Recipient Zapara award for Excellence in Edn., So. Calif. Conf. of Seventh-day Adventists, 1992 Mem. Nat. Coun. of Tchrs. of English. Avocations: music, travel, genealogy, scrapbooking. Home: 12893 Shady Ln Purcellville VA 20132

LAUGHLIN, JO ANN, elementary school educator; b. Faucett, Mo., Aug. 8, 1939; d. Louis and Mary Evelyn (Horton) Smither; m. Robert Everett Laughlin, June 21, 1959; children: Mary Ruth, Ann Kathryn, Jonathan Everett. BS in edn., U. Mo., 1961. Tchr. Moberly Sch. Dist., Mo., 1961-63, Miami Sch. Dist., Amoret, Mo., 1966-67, Rich Hill Sch. Dist., Mo., 1969—. Project leader 4-H, Foster, Mo., 1968-87; lay leader Hume Meth. Ch., 1998—; sponsor Jeff Laughlin Meml. Scholarship. Recipient Bates County Ext. Coun. Leaders Honor Roll cert., 1995. Mem. Cmty. Tchr. Assn. (pres. 1977-78, 98-99,2002-03, chmn. health ins. com. 1995-2001, Tchr. of Yr. 1990-91), Mo. State Tchr. Assn., Alpha Delta Kappa (sec. 1994-95, treas. 2002-2004). Methodist. Home: RR I Box 276 Rich Hill MO 64779 Office: Rich Hill R-IV Sch Dist 3rd & Poplar Rich Hill MO 64779

LAULE, GERHARD HELMUT, chemistry educator, researcher; b. Wilhelmshaven, Germany, June 24, 1949; came to U.S., 1951; s. Helmut Adolph and Rosemarie Luci (Hoffmann) L.; m. Danielle Jeane Guyer, Aug. 17, 1991. BS in Chemistry, U. Ctrl. Ark., 1976; MS in Instrumental Scis., U. Ark., 1986. Lab. supr. Ark. Dept. Health, Little Rock, 1977-81; grad. rsch. asst. U. Ark., Little Rock, 1984-86; grad. tchg. fellow U. Oreg., Eugene, 1986-88; instr. chemistry Seminole (Okla.) State Coll., 1988—, pres. faculty senate, 1992-93. Rsch. assoc. Okla. State U., Stillwater, 1993—; chair math./sci. engring. divsn., Seminole State Coll., 1998-02. With USAF, 1968-72, Vietnam. Mem. Am. Chem. Soc. Avocations: bicycling, sailing, camping. Office: Seminole State Coll 2701 State St Seminole OK 74868-1901

LAUMANN, EDWARD OTTO, sociology educator; b. Youngstown, Ohio, Aug. 31, 1938; m. Anne Elizabeth Solomon, June 21, 1980; children: Christopher, Timothy; children by previous marriage: Eric, Lisa. AB summa cum laude, Oberlin Coll., 1960; MA, Harvard U., 1962, PhD, 1964. Asst. prof. sociology U. Mich., Ann Arbor, 1964-69, assoc. prof., 1969-72; prof. sociology U. Chgo., 1973—, George Herbert Mead Disting. Service prof., 1985—, dean divsn. of social scis., 1984—92, provost, 1992—93, chmn. dept., 1981—84, 1997—99, 2002—03. Bd. govs. Argonne Nat. Lab., 1992-93. Author: Prestige and Associations in an Urban Community, 1966, Bonds of Pluralism, 1973, (with Franz U. Pappi) Networks of Collective Action, 1976, (with John P. Heinz) Chicago Lawyers, 1982, (with David Knoke) The Organizational State, 1987, (with John P. Heinz, Robert Nelson and Robert Salisbury) The Hollow Core, 1993, (with John Gagnon, Robert Michael, Stuart Michaels) The Social Organization of Sexuality, 1994, (with Robert Michael, John Gagnon, Gina Kolata) Sex in America, 1994, (with Robert T. Michael) Sex, Love and Health, 2001, (with Stephen Ellison, Jenna Mahay, Anthony Pain, Yoosik Youm), The Sexual Organization of the City, 2004; editor Am. Jour. Sociology, 1978-84, 95-97. Mem. sociology panel NSF, Washington, 1972-74; commr. CBASSE, NRC, 1986-91; chair, bd. trustees NORC, 2001--; trustee U. Chgo. Hosps., 1992-93; mem. Panel on Elder Mistreatment, 2000-2002. Fellow AAAS (chmn. sect. K 2001—), Soc. Sci. Study of Sexuality; mem. Internat. Acad. Sex Rsch., Sociol. Rsch. Assn., Am. Sociol. Assn., Population Assn. Am. Office: U Chgo 5848 S University Ave Chicago IL 60637-1515 E-mail: ob01@midway.uchicago.edu.

LAURENCE, ROBERT LIONEL, chemical engineering educator; b. West Warwick, RI, July 13, 1936; s. Lionel Gerard and Gertrude Sara (Lefebvre) L.; m. Carol Leah Jolicoeur, Sept. 7, 1959; children: Jonathan, Lisa, Andrew. BSChemE, MIT, 1957; MSChemE, U. R.I., 1960; PhD-ChemE, Northwestern U., 1966; DSc (honoris causa), Inst. Nat. Poly., Toulouse, France, 1989. Rsch. engr. Gen. Dynamics, Groton, Conn., 1957-59, E. I. du Pont de Nemours, Wilmington, Del., 1960-61, field svc. engr. Beaumont, Tex., 1961-63; asst. prof. chem. engring. Johns Hopkins U., Balt., 1965-68; rsch. engr. Monsanto Co., Springfield, Mass., 1968; assoc. prof. U. Mass., Amherst, 1968-73, head dept. chem. engring., 1982-89, prof., 1973-2001, prof. emeritus, 2001—. Vis. prof. Imperial Coll., London, 1974-75, Coll. de France, Paris, 1982-83, Rijks U. Gent, 1996; invited prof. ENSIGC, Toulouse, France, 1990; vis. rsch. fellow GE, Schenectady, 1989; cons. UN Devel. Program, Argentina, 1978, 80, Beijing, 1982; mem. Conseil Technologique Groupe Rhone-Poulenc, Paris, 1988-96. Fellow Am. Inst. Chem. Engrs., Am. Inst. Chemists; mem. Am. Chem. Soc., Tau Beta Pi. Roman Catholic. Avocation: rugby. Home: 5 Ashley Terr Waterville ME 04901 E-mail: rlaurence@ecs.umass.edu.

LAURENSON, DAVID JAMES, academic director; b. Te-kuiti, New Zealand, Nov. 22, 1941; came to the U.S., 1989; s. James Neil and Mary Gentles (Rodger) L.; m. Doris Elizabeth Hepburn, Aug. 21, 1982; children: Natasha, Mary. BSc, U. Auckland, New Zealand, 1966; M in Math., U. Waterloo, Can., 1976; PhD, U. Ariz., 1992. Diploma in tchg., New Zealand; honors specialist math. tchg. cert., Ont. Elem. tchr. South Auckland (New Zealand) Bd. Edn., 1962; actuarial asst. Prudential Life, Wellington, New Zealand, 1967; market rschr. Charles Haines Advert, Auckland, 1968; secondary tchr. Bayview Secondary Sch., Toronto, Can., 1969-72, Grand River Coll., Waterloo, Can., 1972-76; asst. prin., tchr. U. Toronto (Can.) Schs., 1976-89, prin. continuing math. edn., 1992-94; exec. dir. Ala. Sch. Math. and Sci., Mobile, 1994—2001; dir. Hunter Coll. Campus Schs., N.Y.C., 2001—. Cons. for pvt. schs. math. curriculum Toronto, 1978-82. Author: Mathematics, 1993. Lt. New Zealand Army, 1962-66. Recipient Higher Edn. bursary New Zealand Govt., Auckland, 1964-66; grad. scholar U. Ariz., 1989-90, Packenham scholar, 1990-91. Mem. Nat. Assn. Secondary Prins., Nat. Coun. Tchrs. Math., Am. Ednl. Rsch. Assn. Mobile United. Avocations: skiing, tennis, water sports, music, automobiles. Office: Hunter Coll Campus Schs 71 E 94th St New York NY 10128 E-mail: david.laurenson@hunter.cuny.edu.

LAURENT, JEROME KING, economics educator; b. Knoxville, Tenn., Jan. 8, 1940; s. Francis William and Grace Ruth (King) L.; m. Virginia Spencer Huggins, Aug. 20, 1966; children: Katherine Harvie, Thomas King. BA cum laude, U. Wis., Eau Claire, 1961; MA, Ind. U., 1963, PhD, 1973. Grad. asst. Ind. U., Bloomington, 1961-62, teaching assoc., 1962-65; instr. econs. U. Wis., Whitewater, 1965-67, asst. prof., 1967-76, assoc. prof., 1976-81, prof., 1981—. Vis. assoc. prof. U. Wis., Madison, 1980. Contbr. book Internat. Trade and Fin., 1988, book Mgmt. Edn. and Tng.: An Ea. European Dilemma, 1994, articles to profl. jours., book revs. to Jour. Econ. History and other academic jours.; external reviewer: numerous jours., manuscript reviewer: numerous books. Lay dep. Diocese of Milw. coun. Episcopal Ch., 1968—, trustee of funds, 1983-92, pres., mem. fin. com., 1991-92, combined mut. fund Diocese of Milw.; jr. warden St. Luke's Episcopal Ch., Whitewater, 1981-83, sr. warden, 1984, treas., 1988-90, chmn. fin. com., 1991—; mem. edn. com. Wis. Fed. of Coops., Madison, 1983-99. Faculty fellow Inst. on Latin Am., Hamline U., St. Paul, 1977; recipient Editor's Best Essay on N.Am. Transp. prize Manchester U. Press, 1982. Mem.: Lexington Group in Transp. History, Assn. Gt. Lakes Maritime History (mem. rsch. and publs. com. 2000—), Wis. Econs. Assn. (mem. exec. bd. 1977—79, pres. 1983—85), Assn. for Comparative Econ. Studies, Econ. History Assn., Am. Econs. Assn., Kiwanis (treas. Whitewater Breakfast club 1978—83, mem. fin. com. 1983—, mem. audit com. 1996—), Omicron Delta Epsilon, Beta Gamma Sigma. Avocations: reading, hiking, travel. Home: 1268 W Court St Whitewater WI 53190-1625

LAURENT, PIERRE-HENRI, history educator; b. Fall River, Mass., May 15, 1933; s. Henri and Harriet (Moriarty) L.; m. Virginia Brayton, 1958; children: Paul-Henri, Bradford Webb, Nicole, Alexa. AB, Colgate U., 1956; AM, Boston U., 1960, PhD, 1964. Instr. polit. economy Boston U., 1961-64; asst. prof. history Sweet Briar Coll., 1964-66; vis. asst. prof. history U. Wis., Madison, 1966-67; asst. prof. history Tulane U., New Orleans, 1967-68, assoc. prof., 1968-70; assoc. prof. history Tufts U., Medford, Mass., 1970-75, prof., 1975—, chmn. dept., 1987-89, adj. prof. diplomatic history/Fletcher Sch. Law and Diplomacy, 1977, 84, chmn. Exptl. Coll., 1973-75, acting dir. internat. relations program, 1979, dir. internat. relations program, 1984-88, co-dir. Internat. Relations Inst., 1979-80; acad. dir. Tufts European Ctr., France, 1996. Mem. history devel. bd. Ednl. Testing Svc. of Princeton, 1979-82; instr. JFK Inst. Polit., Harvard U., Cambridge, 1989; mem. nat. screening com. Fulbright-Hays program Inst. Internat. Edn., 1988-91; rsch. assoc. Ctr. for Internat. Affairs, Harvard U. Mem. editorial bd. Jour. Social History, 1966-74; sect. editor Am. Hist. Rev., 1967-77; co-editor: The State of the European Union: Deepening and Widening, 1998, NATO and the European Union: Confronting the Challenges of European Security and Enlargement, 1999; contbr. chpts. to books, articles to profl. jours., mags., encys. Served with USAF, 1956-58. NATO fellow, 1967, NEH fellow, 1969, Paul-Henri Spaak Found. fellow, 1976-77; Sweet Briar Faculty rsch. grantee, 1965, Tufts Faculty rsch. grantee, 1972, 1994, Inst. European Studies-Exxon Ednl. Fund grantee, 1983; Fulbright Rsch. scholar, 1992-93; Fulbright chair Coll. of Europe, Bruges, 1998. Fellow Inst. des Rels. Internationales, Acad. Assoc. Atlantic Coun.; mem. AAUP (exec. com. Mass. State Conf. 1974-76, pres. Tufts U. chpt. 1982-84, 2000-2002), European Cmty. Studies Assn. (exec. com. 1988-92, 95-99, chmn. 1991-92, vice-chmn. 1997-99). Office: Tufts Univ Dept History Medford MA 02155 E-mail: plaurent@tufts.edu.

LAURIE, ALISON MARGARET, retired school librarian; b. Glossop, Derbyshire, England, Jan. 5, 1935; d. Kenneth Somerville and Kathleen Mary (Thatcher) Laurie. MA, Glasgow U., Scotland, 1956, BMus, 1958; PhD, Cambridge U., England, 1962. Sr. asst. libr. Glasgow U., England, 1960—63; music libr. Reading U., England, 1963—99; ret., 1999. Editor: Dioclesian, Purcell Soc. edit., vol. 9, 1961, (short score) Dido and Aeneas, 1961, King Arthur, vol. 26, 1971, Dido and Aeneas, vol. 3, 1979, (vocal score) Dioclesian, 1983, Secular Songs for Solo Voice, vol. 25, 1985, The Indian Queen, vol. 19, 1994, (facsimile) The Gresham Autograph, 1995; contbr. author Musik in Geschichte und Gegenwart, 1973, New Grove Dictionary of Music and Musicians, 1980, Music and Bibliography: Essays in Honour of Alec Hyatt King, 1980, Source Material and the Interpretation of Music: A Memorial Volume to Thurston Dart, 1981, Music in Britain: The Seventeenth Century, 1992, Henry Purcell, Dido and Aeneas: An Opera, 1986, Purcell Studies, 1995; contbr. articles to profl. jours. Chairwoman Purcell Soc. Trust., England, 1989—; mem,. Religious Soc. of Friends. Mem.: Internat. Assn. Music Librs. Mem. Soc. Of Friends. Avocations: singing, walking.

LAURSEN, FINN, education educator; b. Romlund, Denmark, June 17, 1944; s. Laurits and Hedvig (Kristensen) L.; m. Berenice Lara, May 10, 1962; children: Jannik, Itzel. Grad., Aarhus (Denmark) U., 1974; PhD, U. Pa., 1980. Rschr. European U. Inst., Florence, Italy, 1977-80; vis. fellow Princeton (N.J.) U., 1980-81; asst. prof. Odense (Denmark) U., 1981-82, assoc. prof., 1982-84; vis. fellow Woods Hole (Mass.) Oceanographic Inst., 1984-85; lectr. London Sch. Econs., 1985-88; assoc. prof. European Inst. Pub. Adminstrn., Maastricht, The Netherlands, 1988-90, prof. internat. politics, 1990-95; prof., dir. Thorkil Kristensen Inst., South Jutland U. Ctr., Esbjerg, Denmark, 1995-98. Vis. prof. U. Tsukuba, Japan, 1998-99, Schuman prof. Fudan U., China, 1998-99; prof. internat. politics dept. polit. sci. U. So. Denmark, Odense, 1999—, dir. Ctr. for European Studies, U. So. Denmark, 2002—, pres. Danish Soc. for European Studies, 2002—. Author: Superpower at Sea, 1983, L'Europe Bleue, 1987, Danmark og Havretten, 1988, Small Powers at Sea, 1993; editor: Toward a New International Marine Order, 1982, Efta and the EC: Implications of 1992, 1990, Europe, 1992, World Partner?, 1991, The Intergovernmental Conference on Political Union, 1992, The Ratification of the Maastricht Treaty, 1994, The Political Economy of European Integration, 1995, The EU and Central Europe: Status and Prospects, 1996, The Amsterdam Treaty, 2002, Comparative Regional Integration, 2003. Recipient Am. Studies award, Fulbright Commn., Copenhagen, 1975, Penfield scholar U. Pa., Phila., 1977, J.P. Compton fellow Princeton U., 1980. Office: Syddansk Univ Inst Statskundskab Campusvej 55 DK 5230 Odense Denmark E-mail: fla@sam.sdu.dk.

LAUTERBACH, EDWARD CHARLES, psychiatric educator; b. Chgo., Mar. 21, 1955; s. Edward G. and Virginia C. (Pochelski) L. AB cum laude, Augustana Coll., Rock Island, Ill., 1977; MD, Wake Forest U., 1982. Lic. psychiatrist, Mo., Pa., N.J., N.C., Ga.; diplomate Nat. Bd. Med. Examiners, Am. Bd. Psychiatry and Neurology with qualifications in geriat. psychiatry. Intern Washington U. Sch. Medicine/Barnes Hosp., St. Louis, 1982-83, resident in psychiatry, 1983-86, clin. asst., 1982-86; instr. neurology movement disorder fellow U. Medicine and Dentistry of N.J., New Brunswick, 1986-87; asst. prof. Mercer U. Sch. Medicine, Macon, Ga., 1988-92, chief div. adult and geriatric psychiatry, dept. psychiatry and behavioral scis., 1988-98, coord. grand rounds dept. psychiatry and behavioral scis., 1989-98, assoc. prof., 1992-96, prof., 1996—, prof. internal medicine/neurology, 1996—, prof. radiology, 1987-88; pvt. practice Charlotte, NC, 1987-88. Chair free comm. IVth World Congress Biol. Psychiatry, Phila., 1985; mem. neurology staff Lyons VA Hosp., 1986; med. staff privileges in neurology Mercy Hosp., Charlotte, 1987, cons., 1987; privileges in psychiatry Med. Ctr. Ctrl. Ga., 1994—, Coliseum Psychiat. Hosp., 1994—, dir. med. staff continuing edn., 1994-96, Middle Ga. Hosp., 1997-2002; med. dir. geropsychiatry program The Sr. Ctr., Middle Ga. Hosp., 1997-2002. Editor: Psychiatric Management in Neurological Disease, 2000; guest editor Psychiatric Annals, 2002, editl. reviewer Neuropsychiatry, Neuropsychology and Behavioral Neurology, Biological Psychiatry, Movement Disorders, assoc. editor Jour. Neuropsychiatry and Clin. Neuroscis., 1999—; contbr. articles to profl. jours. Recipient Med. Dir. of Yr. award S.E. region, Horizon Mental Health Mgmt., Inc., 1999—2001; scholar Rock Sleyster scholar, Wake Forest U., 1981. Fellow: Am. Psychiat. Assn. (course dir. 1990—92, 1994—95, symposium chmn. 1995—97, co-dir. 1998—2001, symposium chmn. 2001), Am. Neuropsychiat. Assn. (rsch. com. 1992—, vice-chair 1998—99, chmn. 1999—); mem.: Charlotte Psychiat. Soc., Movement Disorder Soc., Med. Assn. Ga., Mecklenburg County Med. Soc., N.C. Psychiat. Assn., Bibb County Med. Soc., Ga. Psychiat. Physicians Assn. (state com. on contg. med. edn.), Am. Acad. Neurology, AMA.

LAUZON, LAURA M. middle school educator; b. Chgo., Apr. 16, 1951; d. John Anthony and Barbara Jean (Bunche) Lauzon; children: Melissa Jean, Kimberly Anne. BS in Biology, DePaul U., 1973. Cert. tchr., Ill. Tchr. St. Viator H.S., Arlington Heights, Ill., 1973-76; sales rep. E.R. Squibb & Sons, Princeton, N.J., 1976-77; fin. analyst Motorola, Inc., Schaumburg, Ill., 1978-81; substitute tchr. Palatine, 1990; substance abuse prevention coord. Lake Zurich (Ill.) Schs., 1991-94; tchr. earth sci. and chemistry Grant Cmty. H.S., Fox Lake, Ill., 1994-97; sci. tchr. Lake Zurich Mid. Sch. North, 1997—2000; asst. ch. sec. St. Matthew Luth. Ch., Hawthorn Woods, Ill., 2003—. Bd. dirs. Lake Zurich Mid. Sch.-North PTO, 1991-98, sec., 1994-95, pres., 1995-97, hospitality chmn., 1997-98; music parent coord. Seth Paine Sch. PTO, 1993-94, vol. coord., 1992-93; vol. coord. Thomas Jefferson Sch. PTA, 1985-90; vol. tchr. Palatine and Lake Zurich Schs., 1989-98; vol. Bear Boosters, 1995-99; project co-dir. Ela Area Cmty. Partnership, Lake Zurich, 1991; referendum co-chmn. Citizens for New Schs., 1990-91, head spkrs. com., 1991; vol. St. Matthew Luth. Ch., 2000—. Co-recipient Partnership award Lake County Fighting Back Project, 1991. Avocations: children's soccer, crocheting, reading, amateur radio operator.

LAVALLEE, DAVID KENNETH, chemistry educator, researcher; b. Malone, New York, Oct. 1, 1945; s. Bernard Martin and Eleanor Jane (Magoon) Lavallee; m. Eileen Marie (Gilmartin); children: Jeffrey Michael, Gregory James, Jocelyn Marie. BS, St. Bonaventure U., 1967; MS, U. Ill., Chgo., 1968, PhD, 1971. Asst. prof. Colo. State U., Ft. Collins, Colo., 1972—78; assoc. prof. Hunter Coll., City Univ. of N.Y., N.Y.C., 1978—82; prof. chemistry Hunter Coll., City Univ. of N.Y., N.Y.C., 1983—94; assoc. provost Hunter Coll., City Coll. of N.Y., N.Y.C., 1990—94; provost, v.p. acad. affairs City Coll. of N.Y., N.Y.C., 1994—99, State Univ. of N.Y., New Paltz, NY, 1999—. Edn. adv. bd. Chemtech, Washington, 1978—84. Author: The Chemistry and Biochemistry of N-substituted Porphyrins, 1987; author: (with others) Chemistry, 1978. Bd. dir., v.p. Croton Free Libr., Croton On Hudson, NY, 1988—93, pres., 1992—93. Named USPHS Fellow, Anatomy Dept. U. Ill., Chgo., 1971—72; recipient NATO Rsch. Award, Ecole Normale, Superieure, Paris, 1983—85, Fulbright Rsch. Scholar Award, U. Rene Descartes, Paris, 1985—86, Catalyst Award, Chem. Mfr. Assn., 1986. Mem.: AAAS, Soc. Nuclear Medicine, Am. Chem. Soc. (chair Internat. Chemistry Olympiad 1986—93, soc. com. chem. edn. 1990—96, bd. publs. divsn. chem. edn. 1986—99, chair 1993—97). Democrat. Achievements include patents for N-substituted metalloporphyrins as anti-tumor agents; synthesis of radiolabelled metalloporphyrins via N-substituted precursors. Home: 97 Old Post Rd S Croton On Hudson NY 10520-2401 Office: State Univ NY 75 S Manheim Blvd Ste 1 New Paltz NY 12561-2499 E-mail: lavallee@newpaltz.edu.

LAVALLEY, THOMAS RICHARD, principal; b. Burlington, Vt., Dec. 31, 1948; s. Richard Earl and Pearl Margaret (Hammond) LaV.; m. Mary Lou Goulet, Jan. 13, 1973; children: Eric Thomas, Christopher Scott, Jason Richard; m. Lynne C. Schulte, July 19, 1997. AS in Bus. Adminstrn.,

Champlain Coll., Burlington, Vt., 1967; BA in Elem. Edn., Johnson (Vt.) State Coll., 1973, MA in Reading and Lang. Arts, 1977, MA in Ednl. Adminstrn., 1981. Cert. elem. educator, ednl. adminstr. Tchr. grades 3 and 5-8 Orange-Washington Supervisory Union, Websterville, Vt., 1973-76; tchr. grade 3 Internat. Sch. of Warsaw, Poland, 1976-77; tchr. grade 5 Hyde Park (Vt.) Elem. Sch., 1977-80; prin., tchr. grades 4-6 Greensboro (Vt.) Elem. Sch., 1980-85; prin. Ludlow (Vt.) Elem. Sch., 1985-88; asst. supt. Bennington-Rutland Supervisory Union, Manchester, Vt., 1988-89; prin. Barnard (Vt.) Ctrl. Sch., 1990-96, Woodsville (N.H.) Elem. Sch., 1996-99, Johnson Sch., Nahant, Mass., 1999—2001, Bates Sch., Salem, Mass., 2001—. Mem. local standards bd. for tchr. relicensing Windsor Ctrl. Supervisory Union, Woodstock, Vt., 1990-96; pres. Am. Field Svc. adult chpt. Lamoille Union H.S. Mem., treas. Bd. Libr. Trustees Town of Hyde Park; trustee Bliss Fund, Hyde Park. With Army Nat. Guard, 1970-76, 80-2000; mem. Army Res., 2000—. Joint Resolution in his honor Vt. Senate and Ho. of Reps., Montpelier, Vt., 1994. Mem. ASCD, NAESP (Nat. Disting. Prin. 1994), Internat. Reading Assn., Nat. Staff Devel. Coun., Vt. Prins. Assn. (mem. profl. devel., curriculum, spelling competition coms. 1980-96), Mass. Elem. Sch. Prins. Assn. Home: 192 Kennedy Dr Apt 601 Malden MA 02148 Office: Bates Sch 53 LibertyHill Ave Salem MA 01970

LAVELLE, MARY LEE DEMETRE, psychiatric nursing educator; b. Charleston, S.C., May 30, 1945; m. John L. Lavelle Jr., Aug. 4, 1973; children: Paul, Rachelle. Diploma nursing with honors, Med. Coll. S.C. 1966, BSN with high honors, 1974, MSN in Psychiat. Nursing with highest honors, 1990. RN, S.C.; cert. BCLS. Staff nurse coronary care unit Med. U. S.C., 1966-68; staff nurse Charleston County Hosp., Charleston, S.C., 1969, head nurse med. fl., supr., 1969-72, supr., 1972-75; coord. alumni affairs Med. U. of S.C., Charleston, 1974-76; with Family Planning Clinic, Charleston County Health Dept., Charleston, 1975-76; instr. med. terminology Trident Tech. Coll., Palmer Campus, Charleston, 1975-79; coord. alumni affairs Med. U. of S.C., Coll. of Nursing, Charleston, 1982-88; emergency med. system auditor Palmetto Lowcountry Health System, Charleston, 1986; curator Ruth Chamberlin Hist. Nursing Libr., Charleston, 1988-92; instr. psychiat. nursing Trident Tech. Coll., Charleston, 1990—, part-time instr. LPN program, 1991—; mem. nursing pool transitional care unit Med. U. S.C., 1996-98, mem. clin. faculty, 1998—. Asst. intern coord. staff devel. dept., diabetic instr. patient edn. dept. Roper Hosp., Charleston, 1985, clin. instr. psychiat. nursing practical nursing program, 1995—; staff nurse Inst. Psychiatry, Med. U. S.C., 1990-91; instr. psychiat. nursing Med. U. S.C., 1994—, instr. nursing, 1997—, instr. synthesis practicuum 2003; med. surg. nursing, Health Promotion, mem. nursing pool in psychiatry Charleston Meml. Hosp., 1991-96; presenter in field. Mem. S.C. Heart Assn., 1967-78. Recipient Outstanding Alumnus award Med. U. S.C. Coll. of Nursing, 2000; Saul Alexander Ednl. scholar, 1973, scholar Bus. and Profl. Women's Club, 1972, Am. Bus. Women's Assn., 1972. Fellow Nightingale Soc. (hon.); mem. Coll. Nursing Alumni Assn. Med. U. S.C. (v.p. 1967-69, pres. 1969-74, bd. dirs. 1974-75, ex-officio bd. mem. 1982-88, nominating com. 1992-93), Med. U. S.C. Alumni Assn. (councilor 1971-74, sec. 1974-75, v.p. 1977-79, pres. 1979-80, bd. dirs. 1981-88, 92-95), Sigma Theta Tau. Home: 694 Fort Sumter Dr Charleston SC 29412-4336

LAVIGNE, PETER MARSHALL, environmentalist, lawyer, educator; b. Laconia, N.H., Mar. 25, 1957; s. Richard Byrd and D. Jacquiline (Cobleigh) L.; m. Nancy Gaile Parent, Sept. 20, 1979; 1 child, Rhiannon Genevra Lavigne Parent. BA, Oberlin Coll., 1980; MSEL cum laude, Vt. Law Sch., 1983, JD, 1985. Bar: Mass. 1987. History tchr. Cushing Acad., Ashburnham, Mass., 1983-84; rsch. writer Environ. Law Ctr., Vt., 1985; lobbyist Vt. Natural Resources Coun., Montpelier, 1985; exec. dir. Westport (Mass.) River Watershed Alliance, 1986-88, Merrimack River Watershed Coun., West Newbury, 1988-89; environ. cons. Mass., N.H., Vt., and Oreg., 1990—2001; N.E. coord. Am. Rivers, Washington, 1990-92; dir. river leadership program River Network, Portland, Oreg., 1992-95, dir. spl. programs, 1995-96; dep. dir. For the Sake of the Salmon, Portland, 1996-97; pres. Watershed Cons., Portland, 1997-2001; pres., CEO Rivers Found. of the Ams., 2001—. Adj. prof. Antioch New Eng. Grad. Sch., Keene, N.H., 1991-92; mem. Portland Willamette River Task Force, 1997-99; chair adv. bd. Cascadia Times, Portland, 1995-99, Amigos Bravos, Taos, N.Mex., 1993-98; trustee Rivers Coun. Washington, Seattle, 1993-98; bd. dirs. Alaska Clean Water Alliance, 1995-98, acting pres. 1997-98; adv. bd. Glen Canyon Inst., 2000-01, bd. dirs., 2002—; Watershed adv. group Natural Resources Law Ctr. U. Colo., 1995-96; coastal resources adv. bd. Commonwealth of Mass., Boston, 1987-91; adj. assoc. prof. Portland State U., 1997—; Watershed Mgmt. Profl. program dir., Portland State U., 1999-01, sr. fellow exec. leadership inst., 2001—; pres. Cascadia Times Rsch. Fund, 1998-99. Co-author: Vermont Townscape, 1987; contbr. articles to profl. jours. Dir. Mass. League of Environ. Voters, Boston, 1988-92; mem. steering com. N.H. Rivers Campaign, 1988-92; co-founder, co-chair New England Coastal Campaign, 1988-92; EMT South Royalton (Vt.) Vol. Rescue Squad, 1982-86; dir., chairperson Vt. Emergency Med. Svcs. Dist. 8, Randolph, 1984-86; co-founder, v.p. Coalition for Buzzards Bay, Bourne, Mass., 1987; housing renewal commn. City of Oberlin, Ohio, 1980-81; mem. properties com. First Unitarian Ch., 1995. Recipient Environ. Achievement award Coalition for Buzzards Bay, 1988; land use rsch. fellow Environ. Law Ctr., Vt. Law Sch., 1984-85; Mellon found. rsch. grantee Oberlin Coll., 1980. Mem. Natural Resources Def. Coun., River Alliance of Wis., River Network, Idaho River United, League of Conservation Voters, Amigos Bravos, Glen Canyon Inst. Democrat. Unitarian-Universalist. Avocations: sea kayaking, mountaineering, woodwork, reading, photography. Home: 3714 SE 11th Ave Portland OR 97202-3724 Office: Rivers Found of Ams 3619 SE Milwaukie Ave Portland OR 97202-3858 Fax: (503) 232-2887. E-mail: watershed@igc.org.

LA VILLA, SILVIA J. early childhood educator; b. Havana, Cuba, Feb. 8, 1953; d. Miguel A. and Silvia (Betancourt) La V. AA, Miami Dade C.C., 1972; BEd, U. Miami, 1976; MEd, Fla. Internat. U., 1984. Tchr. pre-sch. Holy Cross Day Care Ctr., Miami, Fla., 1976-78, supr. curriculum, 1978-89; ctr. dir. KIDCO Child Care, Inc., Miami, 1989—. Adult edn. instr. Dade County Pub. Schs., Miami, 1978-88; cons. Redland's Christian Migrant Assn., Homestead, Fla., 1986—; instr. Miami Dade C.C., 1987-89; adj. prof. Fla. Internat. U., Miami, 1988—; presenter at profl. confs. Mem. ASCD, Am. Ednl. Rsch. Assn., Assn. Childhood Edn. Internat., Nat. Assn. Edn. Young Children (v.p. South Fla. chpt., membership chair), Under Six South Fla. Affiliation (bd. dirs., program com.), U. Miami Alumni Assn., Fla. Internat. U. Alumni Assn., Fla. Child Devel. Assn. (past v.p.), Phi Delta Kappa, Delta Kappa Gamma (chpt. program com.). Home: Apt 42 10317 NW 9th Street Cir Miami FL 33172-3283 Office: KIDCO Child Care Inc 3630 NE 1st Ct Miami FL 33137-3610

LAVINE, JOHN M. journalism educator, management educator; b. Duluth, Minn., Mar. 20, 1941; s. Max H. and Frances (Hoffman) L.; m. Meryl Esta Lipton, June 1, 1980; children: Miriam, Marc, Max. BA, Carleton Coll., Minn., 1963; postgrad., U. Minn., 1963; LL.D. (hon.), Emerson Coll., Boston, 1975. Pub., editor Lavine Newspaper Group, Chippewa Falls, Wis., 1964-89; pub. Ind. Media Group, Profl. Publs., Inc., 1984-94; Cowles prof. media mgmt. and econs. U. Minn., Mpls., 1984-89; prof., dir. Media Mgmt. Ctr., a joint program Northwestern U. Kellogg Grad. Sch. Mgmt./Medill Sch. Journalism, Evanston, Ill., 1989—. Cons., lectr. in field, vis. prof. numerous profl. and ednl. instns.; participant numerous profl. confs. Author: China, 1980; The Constant Dollar Newspaper, 1980; Managing Media Organizations, 1988; contbr. chpts. to books, articles to profl. jours. Recipient numerous awards for excellence in mgmt. and journalism. Mem. Newspaper Assn. Am., Am. Soc. Newspapers Editors, Inter Am. Press Assn., Inland Daily Press Assn. (chmn., pres. 1984-85), Wis. Newspaper Assn. (life). Home: 335 Greenleaf St Evanston IL 60202-1365 Office: Media Mgmt Ctr Rm 301 1845 Sheridan Rd Evanston IL 60208-0815

LAVINE, LEROY STANLEY, orthopedist, surgeon, consultant; b. Jersey City, Oct. 28, 1918; s. Max and Katherine (Miner) L.; m. Dorothy Kopp, Feb. 14, 1946; children: Michael, Nancy. AB, NYU, 1940, MD, 1943. Diplomate Am. Bd. Orthopedic Surgery. Intern Morrisania City Hosp., Bronx, N.Y., 1944; resident Jewish Hosp., Bklyn., 1949-51, Ind. U. Med. Ctr., Indpls., 1951-52; emeritus dir., prof. orthopedic surgery Health Scis. Ctr., SUNY, Bklyn., 1964-80; hon. orthopedic surgeon Mass. Gen. Hosp., Boston, 1983—; emeritus dir. rehab. svcs. Spaulding Rehab. Hosp., Boston, 1983—. Prof. emeritus Health Scis. Ctr., SUNY, Bklyn., 1980—; lectr. Harvard Med. Sch., Boston, 1983—; mem. adv. panel FDA, Rochville, MD, 1988-91, cons. 1992-95; cons. Dept. Health and Human Svcs., NIH, Bethesda, Md., 1992—. Contbr. more than 100 articles to profl. jours. Mem. coun. MIT, Cambridge, 1991—. Capt. U.S. Army, 1946-48. Grantee NIH, 1968-80, AEC, 1968-80. Fellow AAAS, ACS, N.Y. Acad. Scis., Am. Acad. Orthopedic Surgeons; mem. Cosmos Club. Achievements include initial performance clinical case of elec. bone stimulation. Office: Mass Gen Hosp Dept Orthopedic Surger Boston MA 02114

LAVINE, STEVEN DAVID, academic administrator; b. Sparta, Wis., June 7, 1947; s. Israel Harry and Harriet Hauda (Rosen) L.; m. Janet M. Sternburg, May 29, 1988. BA, Stanford U., 1969; MA, Harvard U., 1970, PhD, 1976. Asst. prof. U. Mich., Ann Arbor, 1974-81; asst. dir. arts and humanities Rockefeller Found., N.Y.C., 1983-86, assoc. dir. arts and humanities, 1986-88; pres. Calif. Inst. Arts, Valencia, 1988—. Cons. Wexner Found., Columbus, Ohio, 1986-87; selection panelist Input TV Screening Conf., Montreal, Can., and Granda, Spain, 1985-86; cons.; faculty chair Salzburg Seminar on Mus., 1989; co-dir. Arts and Govt. Program, The Am. Assembly, 1991; mem. arch. selection jury L.A. Cathedral, 1996, Arch. L.A., 1998-2001; adv. com. The Asia Soc., So. Calif. Ctr., 1998-; co-chair The Arts Coalition for Acad. Progress, L.A. Unified Sch. Dist., 1997-; vis. com. J. Paul Getty Mus., 1990-1997. Editor: The Hopwood Anthology, 1981, Exhibiting Cultures, 1991, Museums and Communities, 1992. Bd. dirs. Sta. KCRW-FM (NPR), KCET-Pub. TV, L.A. Philharm. Assn., Endowments, Inc., Cotsen Family Found., Villa Aurora Arts Internat., Inc. Recipient Class of 1923 award, 1979, Faculty Recognition award, 1980 U. Mich.; Charles Dexter traveling fellow Harvard U., 1972, Ford fellow, 1969-74. Jewish. Office: Calif Inst Arts Office Pres 24700 McBean Pkwy Santa Clarita CA 91355-2397

LAVIS, VICTOR RALPH, internist, educator; b. LA, Dec. 8, 1938; s. Salvo and Stella (Amado) L.; m. Adrianne Lewis, Sept. 10, 1978; children: Salvo A., Sheldon A. AB in Biology, Stanford U., 1959, MD, 1962. Diplomate Am. Bd. Internal Medicine. Instr. fellow endocrinology U. Wash., Seattle, 1967-70; asst. prof. U. Wash. Med. Sch., Seattle, 1970-76; assoc. prof. U. Tex. Med. Sch., Houston, 1976-96, prof., 1996—. Mem. editorial bd. Diabetes, 1989-92; rsch. peer rev. com. Tex. Affiliate Am. Diabetes Assn., Austin, Tex., 1986-90. Contbr. articles to Jour. Biol. Chemistry, Metabolism, Biochem. Biophysics. Bd. dirs. South Tex. Affiliate Am. Diabetes Assn., Austin, 1978-80, chmn. patient edn. com., 1984-86. Grantee Juvenile Diabetes Edn., 1987-89, Am. Diabetes Assn., 1987-89. Mem. AAAS, Am. Diabetes Assn., Endocrine Soc., Am. Fedn. Clin. Rsch. Office: U Tex Med Sch Dept Internal Medicine 6431 Fannin St Houston TX 77030-1501

LAVISTA, DANIEL J. educational association administrator; m. Rosemary LaVista; 2 children. BA in English, Siena Coll.; M in English Lit., U. Dayton; PhD in Speech and Dramatic Arts, Syracuse U. Assoc. prof. theater Ill. State U., Ill., 1976; v.p. acad. affairs Cuyahoga C.C., Cleve., 1985—87; pres. Coll. Lake County, 1987—95; chancellor C.C. Balt. County, 1995—97; pres. McHenry County Coll., 1997—2002; exec. dir. Ill. Bd. Higher Edn., Springfield, 2002—. Chair Ill. C.C. Pres. Coun.; presenter in field. Office: Ill Bd Higher Edn 2nd Fl 431 E Adams Springfield IL 62701-1418*

LAVOIE, DENNIS JAMES, secondary education educator; b. Syracuse, N.Y., Aug. 31, 1955; s. James Jay and Mary (Gadwood) L.; m. Allegra Ann Beahan, Oct. 11, 1980. BA in Spanish, St. John Fisher Coll., 1977; MA in Spanish Lang. and Lit., Middlebury Coll., 1982. Cert. tchr. Spanish, French, N-12, N.Y.; cert. secondary sch. adminstr., sch. dist. adminstr., N.Y. Fgn. lang. educator Fairport (N.Y.) Cen. Sch., 1977—, mentor tchr., 1990-91, 99-2000. Mem. Pacesetter Spanish spl. task force Ednl. Testing Svc., 1993-94, test devel. com., 1995—, Pacesetter trainer, Pacesetter standing com. Recipient N.Y. Coun. for the Humanities scholarship, Colgate U., 1991, MCES scholarship N.Y. State Edn. Dept. and the Spanish Govt., Universidad de Salamanca, 1989, NEH grant, U. Va., 1989. Mem. Fgn. Lang. Assn. of Tchrs. of the Rochester Area (pres. 1980-81, v.p. 1979-80), Am. Assn. Tchrs. of Spanish and Portuguese (pres. Rochester chpt. 1990-92, v.p. 1988-90, treas. 1984-86). Democrat. Roman Catholic. Avocations: skiing, golf, travel. Office: Fairport H S 1358 Ayrault Rd Fairport NY 14450-8939 E-mail: dlavoie@rochester.rr.com.

LAVOIE, NORMA YOLANDA BERBERIAN, education educator; b. Buenos Aires, Nov. 8, 1959; d. Roberto and Yolanda (Blanco) Berberian; m. Joseph Moril LaVoie, Dec. 31, 1981. AA, Briarwood Coll., Southington, Conn., 1980; BS, Cen. Conn. State U., New Britain, 1984, MS, 1993. Tchr. Burr Sch., Hartford, Conn., 1984-85, Betances Sch., Hartford, 1985-86, Notre Dame Sch., Saco, Maine, 1986-87, Kinsella Sch., Hartford, 1987-88, Parkville Sch., Hartford, 1988-92, Kennelly Sch., Hartford, 1992—. Mem. Alpha Mu Gamma, Gamma Theta Upsilon. Democrat. Roman Catholic. Avocations: dancing, aerobics, reading, cooking, fashion. Home: PO Box 331112 Hartford CT 06133-1112

LAW, JANET MARY, music educator; b. East Orange, N.J., Mar. 8, 1931; d. Charles and Mary Ellen (Keavy) Maitland; m. William Howard Law, Dec. 13, 1952; children: Robert Alan, Gail Ellen. Lic. Practical Nurse, St. Barnabas Sch., 1971; BA magna cum laude, Fairleigh Dickinson U., Rutherford, N.J., 1981; tchr. tng. course, Westminster Choir Coll., 1990—, Queens U., Canada, 1993. Registered Suzuki tchr., Suzuki piano tchr., traditional piano tchr. Staff nurse psychiat. unit St. Barnabas Med. Ctr., Livingston, N.J., 1972-78; office nurse, asst. to pvt. physician North Arlington, N.J., 1978-79; dir., owner B Sharp Acad., Rutherford, N.J., 1979-83; founder, tchr. piano music preparatory div. Fairleigh Dickinson U., Rutherford, 1983-89; founder, coord. piano divsn. Garden State Acad. Music, Rutherford, N.J., 1989-94, tchr. piano divsn., 1989-95; Suzuki piano coord., tchr. Suzuki piano program, coord. Suzuki piano divsn. Montclair (N.J.) State U., 1994—. Author: Keyboard Kapers, 1983; inventor music games, 1983. Mem. Music and Performing Arts Club, Profl. Music Tchrs. Guild N.J. Inc., Suzuki Assn. of the Ams. Avocation: concerts. Home: 169 Hillcrest Dr Wayne NJ 07470-5629 also: Montclair State U Valley Rd and Normal Ave Upper Montclair NJ 07043

LAW, NANCY ENELL, school system administrator; b. South Gate, Calif., Jan. 12, 1935; d. Frank Ronald Cruickshank and Grace Margaret (Wright) Brotherton; m. George Otto Enell, Aug. 26, 1955; children: George, Grace; m. Alexander Inglis Law, Feb. 1, 1987. BS, U. So. Calif., 1956, MEd, 1961, PhD, 1977. Tchr. El Monte (Calif.) City Schs., 1956-58, Pasadena (Calif.) City Schs., 1958-62; from tchr. to project cons. Fullerton (Calif.) Elem. Sch. Dist., 1966-76; evaluation specialist San Juan Unified Sch. Dist., Carmichael, Calif., 1976-84; from dir. evaluation svcs. to adminstr. accountability Sacramento (Calif.) City Schs., 1984—; officer divsn. H Am. Ednl. Rsch. Assn., 1995—. Mem. Phi Delta Kappa. Avocations: creative handiwork, piano. Home: 9045 Laguna Lake Way Elk Grove CA 95758-4219 Office: Sacramento City Schs 520 Capitol Mall Sacramento CA 95814-4704

LAWES, PATRICIA JEAN, art educator; b. Mathis, Tex., June 28, 1940; d. Thomas Ethan and Alma Dena (Pape) Allen; m. Elmer Thomas Lawes, Apr. 9, 1960; children: Linda Lee, Tracy Dena. BA in Art Edn., U. Wyo., 1976; MA in Curriculum and Instruction, Leslie Coll., 1988. Cert. tchr., Wyo. Elem. art tchr. Laramie County Sch. Dist. # 1, Cheyenne, Wyo., 1977—, facilitator elem. art. and gifted edn., 1979-87; ret. Laramie County Sch. Dist. #1, 1994, storyteller, 1995; owner, sec. Dundele Ltd. Liability Co., Mesa, Ariz., 1994-95; artist in the sch. Mesa, Ariz., 1994-95; ednl. cons. gifted edn. Bozman, Mont., 1995-96. Judge F.W. Warren AFB Artist Craftsman Show, Cheyenne, 1988-92; adjudicator for music festival for Assn. Christian Schs. Internat., Tempe, Ariz., 1995-97; storyteller Laramie County Sch. Dist. 1, 1995-96; presenter in field; artist in the sch., Tempe; instr. Smith Driving Sys. Salt River Project, Phoenix, 1996; ednl. cons. Assn. Christian Schs. Internat., Phoenix, 1995. Author, mem. visual arts task force various curricula; Author, dir: The Apron Caper, 1989 (recognition 1990), Oh Where Oh Were Have Those Little Dawgs Gone, 1989 (recognition 1990); exhibitions include Wyoming Artists Assn., Wyo., 1977, Washington Congressional Exhibit, 1977-78. Mem. state bd. dirs. Very Spl. Arts Wyo., 1995—. Recipient Cert. of Appreciation Mayor Erickson, Cheyenne, 1986, MWR Vol. Recognition F.E. Warren Moral, Welfare, Recreation Dept., Cheyenne, 1988-93; grantee Coun. on Arts, Cheyenne, 1987-91. Mem. NEA, Am. Fedn. Tchrs., Nat. art Edn. Assn., Wyo. Assn. Gifted Edn. (bd. dirs., W.E. rep. 1986—, presenter, chmn. state ass. award 1992—), Wyo. Arts Alliance for Edn. (presenter, bd. dirs. 1987—, sec. 1988-91, visual arts task force, chmn. state arts award 1990-92), Wyo. Coun. Arts (slide bank 1986—), Wyo. Odessey of Mind (bd. dirs. 1991-92), Wyo. Women's Fedn. Club (chmn. state safety 1972-75), Order of Eastern Star (presiding officer, worthy matron 1984-85, grand officer 1990-91), Daughters of Nile, Assn. of Christian Schs. Internat. Music Festival (adjudicator 1995). Avocations: art, hiking, traveling, photography, storytelling. Address: 460 S Sunnyvale Mesa AZ 85206-2257

LAWLER, JOHN GRIFFIN, graphic designer, educator; b. Albany, N.Y., June 11, 1936; s. John Griffin and Elizabeth Moore (Elder) L.; m. Priscilla Jury, 1961 (div. 1974); children: Dawn, Erin; m. Mary T. Flynn, Mar. 4, 1948; 1 child, Sean Flynn. BFA, Pratt Inst., Bklyn., 1963, MFA, 1968. Co-owner Comart, Ayer, Mass., 1957-59; pvt. practice John Lawler & Assocs., N.Y.C., 1959-68, Eau Claire, Wis., 1968-74; pres., CEO Greendoor Graphics & Advt., Eau Claire, 1974—; creator, head graphic design program U. Wis., Eau Claire, 1968-96, prof. emeritus, 1996—. Cons. Eau Claire Sch. Dist. Creator sculptures, 1961—. Mem. adv. bd. United Way of Greater Eau Claire, bd. dirs., 2001—; mem. adv. bd. Eau Claire Main St Assn.; pres., chmn. bd. Cmty. Learning Ctr., 1971-75; founder Chippewa Valley Communicators Club, 1975; co-founder Western Wis. Ad Club, 1982, pres., 1985-87; chair Neighborhood Plan Commn., 1998-2000. Recipient awards Ad Clubs, Soc. for Mktg. Profl. Svcs., Small Space Newspaper Advt. awards, Internat. Assn. Bus. Communicators, Univ. Design Assn., Wis. Credit Union League and Affiliates, Nat. Health Info. Awards, Smithsonian, 1969—, Vol. of Yr. award Gov. Tommy Thompson, 1994, award Wis. Credit Union League. Avocations: photography, architecture, furniture design, sculpture. Home: 1349 S Farwell St Eau Claire WI 54701-3948 E-mail: ggraphic@ecol.net.

LAWLER, SUSAN GEORGE, elementary education educator; b. Evergreen Park, Ill., Jan. 20, 1940; d. Louis Lawrence and Elsie Marie (Velk) George; m. Jerome Charles Lawler, Feb. 23, 1963; children: Susan Elizabeth, Kathleen Marie. BS in Edn., Mt. Mary Coll., 1961; MEd, Nat. Louis U., Evanston, Ill., 1991. Tchr. Oak Lawn (Ill.) Sch. Dist. 123, 1961-65, Palos Community Sch. Dist. 118, Palos Park. Ill., 1975—. Pres. Parent-Faculty Orgn. Sch. Dist. 230, Orland Park, Ill., 1982-85. Sec. Ishnala Homeowners Assn., Palos Heights, Ill., 1972-75; active Neighborhood Watch, City of Palos Heights, 1988—. Mem. AAUW (chair hist. 1975-77), Internat. Reading Assn., Nat. Coun. Tchrs. English, Ill. Reading Assn., Palas Edn. Assn. (pres. 1992—), Mt. Mary Coll. Alumni Assn. (co-chair Chgo. chpt. 1992—), Phi Delta Kappa. Avocations: reading, bridge, taking classes, golf, walking. Office: Palos Community Sch Dist 118 8800 W 119th St Palos Park IL 60464-1004 Home: 113 Augusta Dr Palos Heights IL 60463-2906

LAWLOR, SUZANNE KATHRYN, elementary school educator; b. Teaneck, N.J., Apr. 15, 1951; d. James Joseph and E. Margaret (Seymour) L. BA in Elem. Edn., Caldwell Coll., 1973; postgrad., Montclair State Coll., 1990—. Cert. elem. tchr., N.J. 2d, 3d and 5th grade tchr. Ringwood (N.J.) Pub. Schs., 1973-92; basic/supplemental skills instr. K-5 Robert Erskine Sch., Ringwood, 1992—. Piano accompanist Ringwood Pub. Schs., 1980-86, 91-92; ednl. TV panelist County Supt.'s Office, Passaic County, N.J., 1990; theatrical set designer Bergen C.C., Paramus, N.J., 1992. Recipient Gov.'s Tchr. Recognition award N.J. State Dept. Edn., 1990. Mem. ASCD, NEA, Am. Alliance for Theatre and Edn., N.J. Edn. Assn. Roman Catholic. Avocations: set design, painting, flute, piano, guitar. Address: 644 Lafayette Ave Apt L19 Hawthorne NJ 07506-2396

LAWRENCE, ALICE LAUFFER, artist, educator; b. Cleve., Mar. 2, 1916; d. Erwin Otis and Florence Mary (Menough) Lauffer; m. Walter Ernest Lawrence, Sept. 27, 1941 (dec. Dec. 2001); 1 child, Phillip Lauffer. Diploma in art, Cleve. Inst. Art, 1938; BS in Art Edn., Case Western Res. U., 1938. Grad. asst. in art edn. Kent (Ohio) State U., 1939-40; art tchr. Akron (Ohio) and Cleve. Pub. Schs.; comml. artist B.F. Goodrich Co., Akron, 1942-44; sub. art tchr. Akron Pub. Schs.; sketch artist numerous events Akron, 1945-91. Portrait sketch artist for various cos., including Estée Lauder, O'Neil's Dept. Store, Polsky's, Summit, Rolling Acres, Chapel Hill, Walden Books, K-Mart. Contbr. poetry to anthologies. Mem. Cuyahoga Valley Art Ctr., Women's Art Mus., Akron Art Mus., 1963-94, Rep. Nat. Com., 1998, New Rep. Nat. Fund. Recipient 2d pl. in drawing, Butler Mus. Am. Arts, 1940-41, recipient 1st pl. drawings and prints, Cleve. Mus. Art, 1944. Mem. Woman's Art League Akron (sec. 1962), Ohio Watercolor Soc., Internat. Soc. Poets (life, Outstanding Achievement in Poetry Silver award 2003). Republican. Avocation: writing poetry. Address: Walnut Hills Retirement Cmty PO Box 127 Walnut Creek OH 44687

LAWRENCE, FRANCIS LEO, former university president, language educator; b. Woonsocket, R.I., Aug. 25, 1937; BS, St. Louis U., 1959; PhD in French and Italian, Tulane U., 1962. Mem. faculty Tulane U., New Orleans, 1962—90, chmn. dept. French and Italian, 1969—76, acting dean Newcomb Coll., 1976—78, dep. provost, 1978—81, acting provost, grad. dean, 1981—82, prof. French, 1971, acad. v.p., provost, 1982—90; pres. Rutgers U., New Brunswick, 1990—2002; prof. Rutgers U. at Camden, 2002—. Author numerous publs. on French 17th century lit; contbr. articles, revs. and essays to profl. publs. Decorated Chevalier, Palmes Academiques, 1977 Mem. Am. Assn. Tchrs. French, N.Am. Soc. 17th Century French Lit., MLA. Office: Provost Office Rutgers U 325 Cooper St Camden NJ 08102*

LAWRENCE, JAMES DAVID, school system administrator; b. Lancaster, Pa., Apr. 7, 1945; s. Jacob Decker and Florence Ethel Lawrence; m. Janet Carol Artymovicz, Dec. 23, 1967; children: Jason Daniel, Michael Joseph. BS in Elem. Edn., Millersville U., 1967, MEd in Elem. Edn., 1970; EdD in Ednl. Adminstrn., Pa. State U., 1977. Cert. tchr., Pa.; cert. prin., sch. supt., Pa. Tchr. West York (Pa.) Sch. Dist., 1967, Conestoga Valley Sch. Dist., Lancaster, Pa., 1967-73; asst. prin. Donegal Sch. Dist., Mt. Joy, Pa., 1973-75, prin., 1975—2002, supr. curriculum and instrn., 2002—. Mem. Jaycees (pres. Conestoga chpt. 1975). Office: Donegal Sch Dist 366 S Market Ave Mount Joy PA 17552 E-mail: jlawrence@donegal.k12.pa.us.

LAWRENCE, JOHN R. academic administrator; Bachelor's degree, Master's degree, EdS, N.E. Mo. State U.; EdD, U. Mo., Columbia. Supt. Troy (Mo.) R-3 Schs., Mo., 1984—, Schuyler County R-I Pub. Schs., Lancaster, Mo. Mem.: Mo. Assn. Sch. Adminstrs. (pres.), Assn. Sch.

Adminstrs. (mem. exec. com. 1999—, pres.-elect 2002, pres. 2003). Office: Lincoln County R-III Sch Dist 951 W College St Troy MO 63379*

LAWRENCE, JOYCE WAGNER, health facility administrator, educator; b. N.Y.C., Apr. 3, 1942; d. Edward William and Bertha Beatrice (Merz) Wagner; m. William Robert Lawrence, Feb. 9, 1969; 1 child, Rebecca Suzanne. Diploma, Washington Hosp. Ctr., 1963; BS, St. Joseph's Coll., Windham, Maine, 1990. Cert. health care mgr., Va. Supr. Profl. Support Svcs., Virginia Beach, Va.; supr., asst. dir. nursing Med. Staff Svcs., Virginia Beach; supr. Health Care Resources, Inc., Norfolk, Va.; corp. dir., instr., coord. med./cna programs Tidewater Tech, Virginia Beach, Va. Instr. nurse aide program LTH, Norfolk. Lt. (j.g.) USNR, 1968-70. Recipient South Hampton Rds. Women-In-Transition award YWCA, 1991. Mem. Oncology Nurses Assn. (chmn., sec. local chpt.), Hampton Roads Home Health Assn. (chmn. com.), Southeastern Va. Am. Soc. Tng. and Devel., ABWA. Home: 1617 Ashton Dr Virginia Beach VA 23464-7717

LAWRENCE, LINDA HIETT, retired school system administrator, writer; b. Phoenix, July 26, 1939; d. Lydle and Hazeldell (Sutton) Hiett; children: Pamela Lee Reardon, Annabel Virginia Urrea. BA, U. Ariz., 1961; MA, Ariz. State U., 1985, EdD, 1986. Cert. sch. supt., prin., tchr., Ariz. Prin. Washington Elem. Sch. Dist. 6, Phoenix, 1980-83, Dysart Unified Sch. Dist. 89, Peoria, Ariz., 1985-87, asst. supt., 1987-88; supt. Cottonwood Ariz. Oak Creek Sch. Dist. 6, 1988-91; cons., 1991—; owner Lawrence Properties and Publs. Adj. prof. No. Ariz. U., 1990-91. Author: Adventures in Arizona, 2002, Crosswords for Kids; co-author: History of Jerome and Verde Valley, 1991. Trustee Marcus J. Lawrence Hosp.; past pres. bd. dirs. Children's Advocacy Ctr. NSF grantee for Math; recipient (twice) USC's 100 Outstanding Supts. award. Mem. AAUW, Ariz. Hist. Soc., Ariz. Ctr. for the Book, Sacred Heart Alumni Assn., Ariz. State U. Alumni Assn. Ariz. Humanities Coun., Phoenix Zoo, Friends of Our Bros. and Sisters, Phi Delta Kappa.

LAWRENCE, LOIS MARIE, art educator; b. Slaton, Tex., Jan. 6, 1928; d. Brent Gaston and Octavia Lois (Satterwhite) Thompson; m. Troy Odel Lawrence, Sept. 27, 1945; children: Teresa, Joni. BS, Tex. Tech U., 1970, MS, 1977. Art tchr., 1970-90. Art textbook advisor, 1989. One woman shows include Sand Hills Mus., Monahans State Pk., 1965, South Plains Coll., Levelland, Tex., 1980, YWCA, Lubbock, Tex., 1996, Garden and Art Ctr., Lubbock, 1998. Mem. Western Fedn., S.W. Watercolor, West Tex. Watercolor Soc. (pres., sec. 1985, news editor 1986, nat. show chmn. 1980, program com. 1995-96,, chair, 1997, 98-90, Top Watercolor award 1998), Lubbock Art Assn. (scholarship chair 1995-98). Avocations: sewing, travel, art history, golf.

LAWRENCE, LU, educator, photographer; b. Massillon, Ohio; d. Carl Wynn and Ruth Wynetta (Moser) L.; m. Altus Leon Simpson, Dec. 20, 1970; children: Candace, Susan. BA, MA, Calif. State U., Fullerton, 1968. Tng. cons. Host Internat., Los Angeles, 1961-77, Western Airlines, Los Angeles, 1961-67; prof. Cypress (Calif.) Coll., 1967-84; adj. faculty U. Puget Sound, Tacoma, 1984—94. Lectr. cruise ships, 1984—. Author: Airline and Travel Career, 1979, 1993, 1998, A Bird's Eye View of Bainbridge Island, 1989, 3d edit., 1998; contbr. articles and photographs to mags., jours. and newspapers; patentee in field. Home: PO Box 11170 Bainbridge Island WA 98110-5170

LAWRENCE, SALLY CLARK, academic administrator; b. San Francisco, Dec. 29, 1930; d. George Dickson and Martha Marie Alice (Smith) Clark; m. Henry Clay Judd, July 1, 1950 (div. Dec. 1972); children: Rebecca, David, Nancy; m. John I. Lawrence, Aug. 12, 1976; stepchildren: Maia, Dylan. Docent Portland Art Mus., Portland, Oreg., 1958-68; gallery owner, dir. Sally Judd Gallery, Portland, Oreg., 1968-75; art ins. appraiser, cons. Portland, Oreg., 1975-81; interim dir. Mus. Art Sch. Pacific NW Coll. Art, Portland, Oreg., 1981—82, asst. dir., 1982—83, acting dir., 1983—84, dir., 1984—94, pres., 1994—2003, ret., 2003. Bd. dir. Art Coll. Exch. Nat. Consortium, 1982-91, pres., 1983-84. Bd. dir. Portland Arts Alliance, Portland, Oreg., 1987—2003, Assn. Ind. Coll. of Art and Design, 1991—2003, pres., 1995—96, sec., 1996—2001. Fellow: Nat. Assn. Sch. Art and Design (life; bd. dirs. 1984—91, 1994—2002, pres. 1996—99); mem.: Oreg. Ind. Coll. Assn. (bd. dirs. 1981—2003, exec. com. 1989—94, pres. 1992—93, v.p. 2001—03), Pearl Arts Found. (chair bd. dirs. 2000—03).

LAWS, KAREN SUE, elementary school educator; b. St. Louis, Nov. 25, 1960; d. Trentis Risco and Janice Marlene Laws. BA in Elem. Edn., Mo. Bapt. Coll., St. Louis, 1982; M.Elem. Edn., U. Mo., St. Louis, 1992. Cert. elem. edn. K-8 Mo., spl. reading K-12, gen. sci. 4-8, cross-catagorical K-12. Sr. quality assurance examiner Cmty. Fed. Savs. and Loan, St. Louis, 1985-88; foreclosure processor Gershman Investment Corp., Clayton, Mo., 1989; substitute tchr. Ritenour Sch. Dist., Overland, Mo., 1989; tchr.'s asst. Spl. Sch. Dist. of St. Louis County, St. Louis, 1989-90; Chpt. I reading tchr. Wellston (Mo.) Sch. Dist., 1990-96; elem. tchr. Parkway Sch. Dist., Chesterfield, Mo., 1996-98; spl. edn. tchr. Spl. Sch. Dist. of St. Louis County, 1998—. Bd. govs. Mo. Bapt. Coll., St. Louis, 1993-96. Recipient Pres.'s citation Mo. Bapt. Coll., 1980, 81, 82. Mem. NEA, Mo. Edn. Assn., Parkway Edn. Assn., Internat. Reading Assn., St. Louis Suburban Internat. Reading Assn. (dist. contact person 1995-96). Baptist. Avocations: home computers, photography, walking, arts and crafts. Office: Spl Sch Dist 12110 Clayton Rd Saint Louis MO 63131

LAWS, PRISCILLA WATSON, physics educator; b. N.Y.C., Jan. 18, 1940; d. Morris Clemens and Frances (Fetterman) Watson; m. Kenneth Lee Laws, June 3, 1965; children: Kevin Allen, Virginia. BA, Reed Coll., 1961; MA, Bryn Mawr Coll., 1963, PhD, 1966. Asst. prof. physics Dickinson Coll., Carlisle, Pa., 1965-70, assoc. prof., 1970-79, prof. physics, 1979—, chmn. dept. physics and astronomy, 1982-83. Cons. in field. Author: X Rays: More Harm than Good?, 1977, The X-Ray Information Book, 1983, The Workshop Physics Activity Guide, 1997, Real Time Physics Laboratory Guides in Mechanics and Thermodynamics, Explorations in Physics, 2003; contbr. numerous articles to profl. jours.; assoc. editor Am. Jour. Physics, 1989—. Vice-pres. Cumberland Conservancy, 1972-73, pres. 1973; bd. dirs. Pa. Alliance for Returnables, 1974-77; asst. sec., treas. Carlisle Hosp. Authority, 1973-76; pres. bd. Carlisle Day Care Ctr., 1973-74. Fellow NSF, 1963-64, grantee, 1989-95, Commonwealth of Pa., 1985-86, U.S. Dept. Edn. Fund for Improvement of Post-Secondary Edn., 1986-89, 89-93, AEC; recipient Innovation award Merck Found., 1989, Educom NCRIPTAL award for curriculum innovation in sci. labs., 1989, award Sears Roebuck and Co., 1990, Ednl. Software Devel. awards Computers in Physics Jour., 1991, 97, Pioneering Achievement in Edn. award Dana Found., 1993. Mem. Am. Assn. Physics Tchrs. (Disting Svc. citation 1992, Robert A. Milliken award for Outstanding Contbns. to Physics Tchg., 1996), Am. Phys. Soc., Fedn. Am. Scientist, Sigma Xi, Sigma Pi Sigma, Omicron Delta Kappa. Democrat. Home: 10 Douglas Ct Carlisle PA 17013-1714 Office: Dickinson Coll PO Box 1773 Carlisle PA 17013-2896

LAWSON, BILLIE KATHERINE, elementary school educator; b. Cleveland, Tenn., Jan. 15, 1943; d. William Taylor and Katherine Beatrice (Kelley) L. BS in Elem. Edn., Lee Coll., 1970; postgrad., Exeter (Eng.) U., 1975; MEd, U. Tenn., 1975; postgrad., Trevecca Nazarene Coll., Nashville, 1989. Cert. elem. tchr., Tenn. Tchr. Prospect Sch., Cleveland, 1970-76, Trewhitt Elem. Sch., Cleveland, 1976-2000, ret., 2000. Mem. Gov.'s Coun. Gore del. 3rd Congl. Dist. Conv., Tenn., 1988. Recipient 4-H Leader award, 1985. Mem. NEA (local rep. to nat. conv.), Nat. Coun. Tchrs. of Math., Tenn. Edn. Assn. (local rep. to state conv.), Bradley County Edn. Assn. (treas., sch. rep., mem. coms.), U. Tenn. Alumni Assn., Lee Coll. Alumni Assn. Democrat. Baptist. Avocations: reading, travel. Home: 190 Bridgewater Dr Mc Donald TN 37353-5476

LAWSON, BILLY JOE, educational administrator; b. Longview, Tex., Sept. 15, 1941; s. Roy Lawson, Sr.; m. Velma Pryor, Jan. 20, 1963 (div. 1988); children: Keely N., Billy J., Jr. BS, Wiley Coll., 1965; M Natural Sci., Okla. U., 1968; M of Sci. Teaching, Tex. So. U., 1974. Tchr. chemistry and biology, coach Luling (Tex.) Ind. Sch. Dist., 1963-65, Palestine (Tex.) Ind. Sch. Dist., 1965-78; tchr. chemistry and biology, coach to asst. prin. Tyler (Tex.) Ind. Sch. Dist., 1978-92. Pres. Tyler Area Alliance of Black Sch. Educators, 1989-92. Steering com. Leadership Tyler, 1992-93; mentor Martin Luther King Scholars, U. Tex., Tyler, 1992-93. Recipient award of Recognition, Tex. High Sch. Coaches Assn., 1986, Tex. Assn. Basketball Coaches, 1985; named Coach of Decade, Tyler Courier Times, 1975-85. Mem. Nat. Assn. Secondary Sch. Prins., Tex. Assn. Secondary Sch. Prins., ASCD, NAACP, Phi Delta Kappa, Kappa Alpha Psi (life mem.), others. Avocations: golf, basketball, travel. Office: Tyler ISD 1120 NNW Loop 323 Tyler TX 75702

LAWSON, ELIZABETH LOUISE, special education educator; b. New London, Conn., May 2, 1945; d. V. Francis and Susan Louise (Spilman) Reynolds; m. Vernon Grady Lawson, Aug. 24, 1968; children: Mary Elizabeth Lawson Omar, Steven Raymond. BS in Home Econs., U. Ariz., 1967; MEd summa cum laude, N.C. Ctrl. U., 1993. Clerical and ad layout technician Impressive Advt., Waynesboro, Va., 1959-67; tchr. Augusta County (Va.) Schs., 1967, Waynesboro (Va.) City Schs., 1967-68; skin care cons. Luzier Cosmetics, Titusville, Fla., 1970-72; kindergarten aide Wake County Schs., Raleigh, N.C., 1979-81; spl. edn. tchr. Spring Hill Sch., Raleigh, 1984—, mentor tchr., 1994—. Tchr. of deaf adults Raleigh 1st United Pentecostal Ch., 1993—, interpreter for deaf, 1981—. Author model for interpretive dance for U. Meth. Ch. Leadership Mag., 1969. Recipient Appreciation award Brevard County coun. Girl Scouts U.S.A., 1971. Mem. Coun. for Exceptional Children (sec. N.C. fedn. of mental retardation/developmentally disabled divsn. 1995—), N.C. Registry of Interpreters for the Deaf. Republican. Avocations: knitting, crocheting, singing, musical instruments, tatting. Office: Spring Hill Sch/Dorothea Dix Hosp 820 S Boylan Ave Raleigh NC 27603-2246

LAWSON, FRANCES GORDON, child guidance specialist; b. Lexington, Ky., Oct. 20, 1949; d. George Frank and Novella (Thomas) G.; m. Frank Darryl Lawson (div. Sept. 1974); children: Alisa Lynnette, Darlene Lawson-Barber. BA, Ea. Ky. U., 1971, MA, 1979, Rank I cert., 1987. Cert. tchr., counselor, Ky. Tchr. Mary Todd Elem Sch., Fayette County Pub. Schs., Lexington, 1971-82, child guidance specialist Johnson Elem. Sch., 1982-92, child guidance specialist Booker T. Washington Elem., 1992—. Dir. social svc. Madeline McDowell Breckridge Camp Found. Inc., Lexington, 1987-98. Mem. Ky. Sch. Counselors Assn., Fayette County Guidance Assn., Phi Delta Kappa, Delta Sigma Theta. Democrat. Baptist. Home: 1795 Timber Creek Dr Lexington KY 40509-2393

LAWSON, JANICE RAE, retired elementary education educator; b. Chgo., Jan. 22, 1938; d. Ramon Joseph and Anne Joan (Seaquist) Wallenborn; m. Ralph Dreben Lawson, Jr. BEd, Beloit Coll., 1960; MEd, The George Washington U., 1966; postgrad., George Mason U., 1987-88, U. Va., 1965-85; Degree in Theol. Edn., U. of South, 1989. Cert. tchr. Va. Tchr. Quantico (Va.) Marine Base, 1960-62; elem. tchr. Pearl Harbor Elem. Sch., Honolulu, 1962-64, Quantico Dependents Sch. System, 1964-95, ret., 1995. Counselor Diet Ctr., Springfield, Va., 1979—89; lay Eucharistic min. Kingston Parish, vestry-stewardship warden, 2000—03. Mem. NEA (life), Quantico Edn. Assn. (treas. 1968-72), Va. Edn. Assn., Pi Lambda Theta (life), Kappa Alpha Theta (treas. 1979-81, pres. North Va. chpt. 1981-85, alumni dist. pres. 1989-95, historian 2000—). Republican. Episcopalian. Avocations: golf, crafts, cooking, aerobics, traveling. Home: PO Box 427 Cobbs Creek VA 23035-0427

LAWSON, JONATHAN NEVIN, academic administrator; b. Latrobe, Pennsylvania, Mar. 27, 1941; s. Lawrence Winters and Mary Eleanor (Rhea) L.; m. Leigh Farley (div.); children: Paul, Joshua, Jacob; m. Pamela (Cross)L. AA, York Coll., Penn., 1962; BFA, Tex. Christian U., Tex., 1964, MA, 1966, PhD, 1970. Dir. composition U. Minn., St. Cloud, Minn., 1971—77, assoc. dean, 1977-81; asst. vice chancellor Minn. State U. Sys., St. Paul, 1980-81; dean liberal arts U. Minn., Winona, Minn., 1981-84; dean arts and sci.. U. Hartford, West Hartford, Conn., 1984-86, sr. v.p., dean of faculty, 1986-95; v.p. acad. affairs Idaho State U., Idaho, 1995—. Mem. S.E. Id. Works Bd., 2000—. Author: Robert Bloomfield, 1980; editor: Collected Works: Robert Bloomfield, 1971; contbr. articles and papers to scholarly pub.; assoc. editor Rhetoric Soc. Quar., St. Cloud,Minn., 1974-79. Mem. regional adv. bd. Greater Hartford C.C., 1992-94; trustee Hartford Coll. for Women, 1992-94; mem. acad. affairs com. Idaho Bd. Edn., 1995—; bd. dirs. Bannock County Devel. Corp., 1998—, sec., treas., 2001—; bd. govs. The Rennaisance Group, 2003—. Mem. Am. Coun. Edn., Coun. Fellows Alumni, Coun. Liberal Learning, Assn. Gen. and Liberal Studies, Assn. Am. Colls., N.E. Assn. Schs. and Colls. (chmn. commn. on instns. higher edn. 1992-95), Asian Studies Consortium (chmn. bd. 1991-94), Pocatello C. of C. (bd. dirs., v.p.), Lambda Iota Tau (hon.), Alpha Chi (hon.). Episcopalian. Avocations: fishing, camping, writing, walking. Home: 1401 Juniper Hill Rd Pocatello ID 83204-4921 Office: Idaho State U PO Box 8063 Pocatello ID 83209-0001 E-mail: lawsona@isu.edu.

LAWSON, LOLITA AGNES, academic administrator; b. Pitts., Dec. 12, 1956; d. Robert D. and Elizabeth Jayne Ann (Styen) L.; m. Robert Dale Pratt, Aug. 11, 1990. BS, Emerson Coll., Boston, 1978; MS Edn., Lesley Coll., Cambridge, Mass., 1979. Dir. Comm. Apprehension Lab. Div. Social and Behavioral Scis., Emerson Coll., Boston, 1977-78; elem. counselor Lesley Schs. for Children, Cambridge, Mass., 1978-79, Reynolds Sch. Dist., Troutdale, Oreg., 1979-81; dir. Christian edn. St. Michael and All Angels Episcopal Ch., Portland, Oreg., 1980-81, chmn. adult enrichment commn., 1986-88; head tchr. Kinderland Child Devel. Ctr., Portland, 1982-88; exec. dir. Alberta Park Children's Ctr., Portland, 1988-89; coord. student parent svcs. Portland State U., 1989—. Various presentations and workshops throughout Oreg.; mem. Metro Child Care Resource Network, 1989—; mem. Multnomah County Child Care Coun., 1992—; mem. child care and devel. task force for prevention com. Multnomah County Children and Youth Svcs. Commn., 1991-92; participant Child Care Summits I and II, Oreg. Child Care Commn., 1991-92; mem. Consortium for Children and Families, Portland State U. Mem. Assn. Edn. Young Children. Democrat. Episcopalian. Avocations: writing poetry and short stories, cooking, reading. Office: Portland State U Student Parent Svcs PO Box 751 Portland OR 97207-0751

LAWSON, MARY BIRCHWOOD, elementary education educator; b. Tampa, Fla., Sept. 2, 1947; d. Archie William and Mary June (Hinson) Birchwood; m. Marcus E. Lawson, Dec. 13, 1969; children: Mary Louise, Birch. BA, U. Cen. Fla., 1979, MEd, 1986. Cert. elem. tchr., Fla.; ESOL endorsed. Elem. tchr. Osceola Dist. Schs., St. Cloud, Fla., 1979—. Cons. Fla. Ednl. Tech. Leadership Inst.; facilitator ESOL endorsement program Osceola Dist. Schs. Named Social Studies Tchr. of Yr., 1986; recipient tchr. merit award Walt Disney World Co., 1990, Michigan Ave. Elem. Tchr. of Yr. award, 2000. Mem. Fla. Assn. for Staff Devel., Fla. Coun. for Social Studies, Fla. Geog. Alliance (tchr. cons., adv. bd. 1994—), Edn. Ctr. Coun. (chmn.), Osceola Reading Coun., Osceola County Tchr. Assn. (rep.). Home: 2445 Toucan Ct Saint Cloud FL 34771-9511 Office: Michigan Ave Elem Sch 2015 Michigan Ave Saint Cloud FL 34769-5297

LAWSON, MELANIE KAY, management administrator, early childhood consultant; b. Fort Valley, Ga., Feb. 8, 1955; d. William C. and Mamie Nell (Brown) Chapman; m. Robert Scott Lawson, Dec. 18, 1975; children: Robert Scott Jr., Joshua Cody, Ashley Jeanell. AA, Cisco Jr. Coll., 1984; BE in Elem./Spl. Edn., Hardin-Simmons U., 1988, MEd in Reading, 1990; MEd in Sch. Adminstrn., Abilene Christian U., 1992; MEd in Higher Edn., Tex. Tech. U., 1996, postdoctoral. Cert. reading specialist, supr., mid-mgmt. tchr. Speech pathology asst. Head Start/Abilene Ind. Sch. Dist., Abilene, Tex., 1983-84; assoc. tchr. Head Start/AISD, Abilene, Tex., 1984-88, cert. tchr., 1988-90; English as second lang. tchr. AISD-Curriculum div., Abilene, Tex., 1990-92; kindergarten tchr. AISD-Long Elem. Sch., Abilene, Tex., 1992-93; asst. dir. Child Devel. Ctr., Dyess AFB, Tex., 1993-94; tng. mgr. 7 SVS Squadron, Dyess AFB, Tex., 1994-97; reading specialist North Kansas City Sch. Dist., Kansas City, Mo., 1997-99; 1st grade tchr. Lubbock (Tex.) Ind. Sch. Dist., 1999—. Tchr. Set Point multicultrual program Tex. Tech U. Mem. Youth Task Force, Abilene City Govt., 1994-95, Higher Edn. Working Group, Tex. Head Start Collaboration Project, local conf. corrd., Abilene Work/Family Planning Series Conf. Recipient Key City Reading award Reading Coun., 1988; Pres. Trust Fund scholarship Tex. Assn. for the Edn. of Young Children, 1996. Mem. AAUW, Internat. Reading Assn., Nat. Assn. Edn. of Young Children (Membership Affiliate grant 1994, academy mentor 1995—, validator 1993—), Tex. Assn. Edn. of Young Children (at-large, Tex. Affiliate grant, 1993, 94, exec. bd., chair accreditation, Pres.'s Trust Fund Scholarship 1996), Big Country Assn. for Edn. of Young children (membership chair 1988-90, pres. 1992-94, state repl 1992-94), Tex. Assn. for Gifted/Talented (grant 1991), U.S. Tennis Assn., Coun. Profl. Recognition (rep. 1993—), Golden Key Honor Soc., Kappa Delta Phi, Phi Delta Kappa. Avocations: reading, sewing, walking, ceramics, wood crafts. Home: PO Box 98693 Lubbock TX 79499

LAWSON, PATRICIA GILLY, secondary education English educator; b. Texarkana, Ark., Aug. 13, 1950; d. Norbert Sidney Jr. and Ora Marie (Chiasson) Gilly; m. James Patrick Lawson Jr., May 4, 1973; children: Ryan Patrick, Christopher Michael, Colin Timothy. BA in English Edn., U. New Orleans, 1972, MEd, 1979, cert. reading cons., 1984; cert. in supervision and adminstrn., Ctrl. Conn. State U., 1993. Cert. 7-12 English tchr., K-12 reading cons., adminstr. and supr., Conn. English tchr. Cohen Sr. H.S., Orleans Parish Sch., New Orleans, 1973; chpt. 1 reading tchr. Toulminville H.S., Mobile County Sch., Mobile, Ala., 1973-74; English and reading tchr. Orleans Parish Sch., 1974-76; 5th-8th grade English and reading tchr. St. Pius X Sch., New Orleans, 1976-77; 7th-8th grade English and reading tchr. St. Rita Sch., Harahan, La., 1978-79; 6th grade reading tchr. Ellender Mid. Sch., Jefferson Parish Schs., Marrero, La., 1983-84; 9th-12th grade English tchr. RHAM H.S., Region # 8 Schs., Hebron, Conn., 1985—, 7th-12th grade coord reading, English, language arts, 1993—. State assessor State of Conn. Best Program, Hartford, 1993—; mem. com. RHAM Profl. Devel. Com., Hebron, 1991—. Publicity/sports writer Glastonbury (Conn.) H.S., 1992-98, Ctrl. Conn. Youth Hockey Assn., Glastonbury, 1986-92. Mem. ASCD, Conn. ASCD, RHAM Edn. Assn. (rep. coun. mem. 1992—), Nat. Coun. Tchrs. English (mem. conf. on ednl. leadership 1993—), Conn. Coun. Tchrs. English, Conn. Reading Assn., Conn. Heads of English Depts. Roman Catholic. Avocations: reading, landscaping, interior decorating, needlecrafts. Office: RHAM HS 67 Rham Rd Hebron CT 06248-1500

LAWSON, WILLIAM, otolaryngologist, educator; b. N.Y.C., Nov. 23, 1934; s. Alexander and Sophia (Elkind) L.; m. Miriam Patkin, Nov. 7, 1965; 1 child, Vanessa Ann. BA, NYU, 1956, DDS, 1961, MD, 1965. Diplomate Am. Bd. Otolaryngology, Am. Bd. Cosmetic Surgery, Am. Bd. Facial Plastic Surgery. Intern Mt. Sinai Hosp., N.Y.C., 1965-66, rsch. fellow in otolaryngology, 1969-70, resident in otolaryngology, 1970-73; resident in gen. surgery Bronx (N.Y.) VA Hosp., 1966-67, chief otolaryngology, head and neck surgery, 1974—2003, cons., 2003—; prof. Mt. Sinai Sch. Medicine, N.Y.C., 1980—; vice chmn., 1996—. Co-dir. Paranasal Sinus Rsch. Lab.; dir. facial plastic surgery clini Mt. Sinai Hosp., N.Y.C.; cons. Nat. Space Biomed. Rsch. Consortium. Author: Paraganglionic Chemoreceptor Systems, 1982, Surgery of the Paranasal Sinuses, 1988, 2d edit., 1992, External Ear, 1995; contbr. over 200 articles to med. jours., chpts. to books. Capt. M.C., U.S. Army, 1967-69. Fellow ACS, Am. Acad. Facial Plastic and Reconstructive Surgery (svc. awrd), Am. Soc. Head and Neck Surgery, Am. Soc. Maxillofacial Surgeons, Am. Rhinologic Soc., Otologic and Laryngologic Soc., Am. Laryngol. Soc.; mem. Am. Acad. Otolaryngology (svc. award), Am. Bronchoesophagologic Soc. (included in Best Drs. Am., Best Drs. in N.Y.). Avocations: photography, art history, horology. Office: Mt Sinai Med Ctr 1 Gustave L Levy Pl New York NY 10029-6500

LAWSON, WILLIAM HAROLD, college dean, labor economist; b. San Jose, Calif., Nov. 2, 1934; s. Minster Bryan and Ruth Josephine (Hill) L.; m. Patricia Marguerette O'Carroll, Aug. 15, 1958 (div. Apr. 1979); children: Ronald W., Brian T., Thomas W.; m. Patricia Jeanne Prevedello, Feb. 6, 1982; children: Kathleen Ann Clark, George T., Tim J. BS in Civil Engring., San Jose State U., 1958, MBA, 1961; PhD in Labor Econs., Claremont Grad. Sch., 1969. Engr. Pacific Telephone, San Francisco, 1957-60; mgmt. intern U.S. Dept. Labor, Washington, 1961, pers. officer, 1962-64; instr. bus. San Bernardino (Calif.) Valley Coll., 1964-67, chmn. bus. dept., 1965-67; from tech. div. chmn. to asst. dean instrn. Moorpark (Calif.) Coll., 1967-72; dist. asst. supt. Ventura (Calif.) County Community Coll., 1972-83; dean vocat. edn. & econ. devel. Oxnard (Calif.) Coll., 1983-95, ret., 1995, tchr. credentialling mentor, 1995—. Cons. Evaluation Tech. Corp. and Lawson Cons. Group, Ventura, Calif., 1968—, Chancellor's office Calif. Cmty. Colls., Sacramento, 1977-83, with spl. assignments Calif. State Dept. Edn., Sacramento, 1977-80. Producer TV shows U.S. Dept. Edn., San Bernardino Valley Coll., 1975. Legis. cons. Calif. Adv. Com. Vocat. Edn., Sacramento, 1974-76; joint com. chmn. Joint Community Coll. Dept. Edn. Plan for Vocat. Edn., Sacramento, 1977-78; chmn. community adv. bd. Calif. Conservation Corps, Camarillo, 1987-94 Mem. Am. Vocat. Assn., Calif. C.C. Adminstrn. Occupational Edn. (v.p. 1991-94), Oxnard Coll. Ctr. Internat. Trade Devel. (dir. 1989-95), Oxnard Coll. Workplace Learning Ctr. (dir. 1992-94), Econ. Devel. Network (co-counder 1987-94), Econ. Devel. Network Internat. (trade devel. com. chmn. 1988-91, chair resorce devel. com. Calif. State U. Northridge-Ventura Campus 1993-95). Republican. Roman Catholic. Avocations: stamp collecting, racquetball, reading, computers. Home: 4496 Pomona St Ventura CA 93003-1920

LAWTON, BARBARA, lieutenant governor; b. Wis. m. Cal Lawton; children: Joseph, Amanda Krupp. BA summa cum laude, Lawrence U., 1987; MA, U. Wis., 1991. Lt. gov. State of Wis., Madison, 2003—. Founding mem. Ednl. Resource Found.; founding trustee Cmty. Found.; founding mem. Latinos Unidos; mem. adv. bd. Green Bay Multicultural Ctr., Women's Polit. Voice; mem. bus. planning and resource team Entrepreneurs of Color; bd. mem. Planned Parenthood Advs. Wis., Northeastern Wis. Tech. Coll. Edn. Found. Named Feminist of the Yr., Wis. Chpt. NOW, 1999; recipient Ft. Howard Founds. Humanitarian award. Mem.: AAUW, LWV, Nat. Women's Polit. Caucus. Office: Rm 19 East State Capitol Madison WI 53701

LAWTON, DEBORAH SIMMONS, library director, educational media specialist; b. Dover, N.J., Sept. 14, 1950; d. Coryden Jerome Simmons and Marjorie Lynd (Jewell) Weber; children: Catherine Randall, Christopher James. BA, Lebanon Valley Coll., 1972; tchr. cert., Coll. St. Elizabeth, 1974; MLS, Rutgers-The State U., 1994. Cert. ednl. media specialist, profl. libr., supr. Confidential ratings analyst Martindale-Hubbell, Summit, N.J., 1972-74; tchr. St. Rose Sch., East Hanover, N.J., 1975-77, St. Paul Sch., Princeton, N.J., 1977-78; libr. Mary Jacobs Libr., Rocky Hill, N.J., 1988-92, South Brunswick H.S., Monmouth Junction, N.J., 1994—. Reviewer Infolink, 1995—; chair press rev. com. Am. Assn. Univs. Author: Knowledge Quest, Book Report; co-author: Authentic Assessment in South Brunswick, Partnerships at Work in the Library. Chair Montgomery jointure com., Montgomery Twp., N.J., 1985; coach/dir. Montgomery Girls Softball, 1988-91; v.p., exec. bd. Montgomery Twp. PTSA, 1986-90; pres., treas. Lawrenceville (N.J.) Presbyn. Coop. Nursery Sch., 1981-84; ranking chair jrs. N.J. Tennis Dist.; mem. INFOLINK Book Evaluation Criteria Com., KidsConnect, INFOLINK Youth Svcs. Com.; deacon Blawenburg Reformed Ch., elder. Internet grantee N.J. State Libr., 1994, Instrnl. Coun. grantee South Brunswick Instrnl. Coun., 1995, 96, 97; recipient Pres.'s award N.J. Tennis. Mem. ALA, Am. Assn. Sch. Librs. (assn. Am. univ. presses com. 1996—, legis. com., chair youth svcs. com., intellectual freedom com., bd. tristees), Assn. for Libr. Svc. to Children, Young Adult Libr. Svcs. Assn., Intellectual Freedom Round Table, Ednl. Media Assn. N.J. (legis. chair, intellectual freedom chair), Assn. of Am. Univ. Presses (rev. com.), N.J. Libr. Assn., Beta Phi Mu, Pi Gamma Mu. Avocations: water sports, quilting. Office: South Brunswick HS 750 Ridge Rd Monmouth Junction NJ 08852-0183 E-mail: dlawton@sbschools.org.

LAWVERE, F. WILLIAM, mathematician, educator; b. Muncie, IN, Feb. 9, 1937; s. Francis William and Margaret Delight (Moorman) L.; m. Fatima Fenaroli, Sept. 9, 1966; children: Marco, John, Philip, Danilo, Silvana. BA, Ind. U., 1960; PhD, Columbia U., 1963. Asst. prof. Reed Coll., Portland, Oreg., 1963-64, U. Chgo., 1966-67; assoc. prof. CUNY Grad. Ctr., N.Y.C., 1967-68; Killam prof. Dalhousie U., Halifax, Nova Scotia, 1969-71; prof. SUNY, Buffalo, 1974—2000, prof. emeritus, 2000—. Vis. prof. ETH, Zurich, 1964—66, Zurich, 1968—69, Aarhus (Denmark) U., 1971—72, Perugia U., Italy, 1972—74, IHES, Paris, 1980—81, Sydney U., 1988. Co-author: (with S.H. Schanuel) Conceptual Mathematics, 1997, (with R. Rosebrugh) Sets for Mathematics, 2003. Recipient Sloan fellowship, 1969; Killam professorship, 1969-71, Martin professorship, 1977-82. Achievements include research in logic, differential geometry, continuum thermomechanics, simplified topos theory and enriched category theory. Office: SUNY Math Bldg Buffalo NY 14260-2900

LAXMINARAYANA, DAMA, geneticist, researcher, educator; b. Hyderabad, India, Apr. 20, 1953; came to U.S., 1990; s. Kishtaiah and Sathyamma; m. Dara Jayalakshmi; children: Dama Bhargavi, Dama Sriharsha, Dama Vishnupriya. BSc, Osmania U., Hyderabad, 1974, MSc, 1976, PhD, 1982. Jr. sci. asst. dept. genetics Osmania U., 1977-78, lectr. dept. zoology, 1985-90; jr. rsch. fellow Indian Dept. Atomic Energy, 1978-81, postdoctoral fellow, 1982-83, rsch. assoc., 1983-85; postdoctoral fellow dept. medicine Case Western Res. U. Sch. Medicine, Cleve., 1990-91; rsch. assoc. dept. internal medicine Wake Forest U. Sch. Medicine, Winston-Salem, N.C., 1991-94, rsch. instr., 1994-98, rsch. asst. prof., 1998—. Conf. presenter in field. Contbr. articles to sci. jours., chpts. to books. Mem. AAAS, Environ. Mutagen Soc. India, India Soc. Cell Biology, Soc. Geneticists and Cytologists India, N.Y. Acad. Scis. Home: 444 Lynn Ave Winston Salem NC 27104 Office: Wake Forest U Sch Medicine Dept Internal Medicine Medical Center Blvd Winston Salem NC 27157 E-mail: dlaxmina@wfubmc.edu.

LAY, ANDREW SEAN, secondary school educator, elementary school educator; b. Petersburg, Va., May 20, 1969; s. Michael Jamieson and Marilyn Elizabeth Lay; m. Colleen Scherrie Thompson, July 11, 1999. MusB in Music Edn., Atlantic Union Coll., 1993; MusM in Conducting, Andrews U., 1997. Tchr. music, ESL Pensionado Adventista 'Ciudad de Quito', Ecuador, 1989—90; music tchr. Modesto Adventist Acad., 1994—96; tchr. music, Spanish I Ind. Acad., Cicero, Ind., 1996—. Mem. steering com. Commitment 2002 Capital Campaign Ind. Acad., 2001—02. Mem.: ASCD, Internat. Adventists Musicians Assn., Nat. Assn. Music Edn., Am. Choral Dir. Assn., Am. Guild English Handbell Ringers, Pi Lambda Theta. Republican. Seventh Day Adventist. Avocations: reading, tennis, philanthropy, performing music. Office: Ind Acad 24815 State Rd 19 N Cicero IN 46034 Fax: 317-984-5081.

LAYCOCK, HAROLD DOUGLAS, law educator, writer; b. Alton, Ill., Apr. 15, 1948; s. Harold Francis and Claudia Anita (Garrette) L.; m. Teresa A. Sullivan, June 14, 1971; children: Joseph Peter, John Patrick. BA, Mich. State U., 1970; JD, U. Chgo., 1973. Bar: Ill. 1973, U.S. Dist. Ct. (no. dist.) Ill. 1973, Tex. 1974, U.S. Dist. Ct. (we. dist.) Tex. 1975, U.S. Ct. Appeals (5th and 11th cirs.) 1975, U.S. Supreme Ct. 1976, U.S. Ct. Appeals (6th cir.) 1987, U.S. Ct. Appeals (8th cir.) 1994, U.S. Ct. Appeals (10th cir.) 1997, U.S. Ct. Appeals (3rd cir.) 2003. Law clk. to judge U.S. Ct. Appeals (7th cir.), Chgo., 1973-74; pvt. practice Austin, Tex., 1974-76; asst. prof. U. Chgo., 1976-80, prof., 1980-81, U. Tex., Austin, 1980—, endowed professorships, 1983-88, assoc. dean for acad. affairs, 1985-86, endowed chair, 1988—, assoc. dean for rsch., 1991—. Vis. prof. U. Mich., 1990; reporter com. on motion practice Ill. Jud. Conf., 1977-78. Author: Modern American Remedies, 1985, 3d edit., 2002, The Death of the Irreparable Injury Rule, 1991; mem. bd. advisors Religious Freedom Reporter, 1990-2001; contbr. articles to profl. jours. Adv. bd. Consumer Svcs. Orgn., Chgo., 1979-80; exec. bd. Ctr. for Ch./State Studies, DePaul U., Chgo., 1982-87; adv. com. on religious liberty Presbyn. Ch. U.S.A., 1983-88, advisor restatement of restitution, 1984-85, 97—; v.p. St. Francis Sch., 1990-92, bd. dirs., 1990—, pres. 1992-2001; bd. adv. J.M. Dawson Inst. Ch./State Studies, Baylor U., 1990—; judicial speech adv. com., Supreme Ct. of Tex., 2002. Fellow AAAS, Internat. Acad. for Freedom of Religion and Belief; mem. AAUP (mem. com. on status of women in acad. profession 1982-85), Am. Law Inst. (mem. coun. 2001—), Chgo. Coun. Lawyers (v.p. 1977-78), Assn. Am. Law Schs. (chmn., sec. on remedies 1983, 94), chmn., sec. on constitutional law, 2000). Home: 8819 Chalk Knoll Dr Austin TX 78735 Office: U Tex Law Sch 727 E Dean Keeton St Austin TX 78705-3224 E-mail: dlaycock@mail.law.utexas.edu.

LAYCOCK, MARY CHAPPELL, gifted and talented education educator, consultant; b. Jefferson City, Mo., Jan. 11, 1915; d. Alvin E. and Ollie (Harris) Chappell; m. James Charles Laycock, June 22, 1937; children: Charles, Ann, Donald E., Jane. AB, Judson Coll., 1937; MA in Math. Edn., U. Tenn., 1961. Math. tchr. various, 1938-41; math. tchr. Kingsport (Tenn.) Jr. High Sch., 1942; math. coord. Oak Ridge (Tenn.) City Schs., 1956-68, high sch. math. tchr., 1945-68; math. specialist Nueva Ctr. for Learning, Hillsborough, Calif., 1968-98; cons. Hayward, Calif., 1990-97. Author many books including Mathematics for Meaning, The Fabric of Mathematics, Algebra in Concrete, Focus on Geometry, Hands On Mathematics for Secondary Teachers, Weaving Your Way from Arithmetic to Mathematics, 1993, The Magician's Castle Fantasy, 1995; developed documentary Don't Bother Me, I'm Learning, 12 videotapes on teaching manipulatives; contbr. articles to profl. jours. Recipient Calif. Educator award, 1989, Elem. Math. Tchr. award Calif. Math. Coun. and State of Calif., 1989, Award of Recognition Calif. Assn. for the Gifted. 1984, Glenn Gilbert Nat. Leadership award for outstanding contbns. to math. edn. Nat. Coun. Suprs. Math., 2003, Mary Waycoch award for Outstanding Contbn. of Math. Edn.,2003. Mem. NEA, Nat. Coun. Tchrs. Math., Oreg. Math. Coun., Calif. Math. Coun. (life), Fla. Math. Coun., Greater San Diego Math. Coun., San Mateo County Math. Coun., Calif. Assn. for the Gifted. Avocation: geometric art. Home and Office: 20655 Hathaway Ave Hayward CA 94541-3740 E-mail: info@activityresources.com.

LAYCOCK, WILLIAM ANTHONY, range management educator; b. Ft. Collins, Colo., Mar. 17, 1930; s. John and Caroline (Freudenthal) L.; m. Charlotte E. Pulscher, June 19, 1955; children: Cody, Donice. BS, U. Wyo., 1952, MS, 1953; PhD, Rutgers U., 1958. Rsch. asst. Rutgers U., New Brunswick, N.J., 1955-58; range scientist Intermountain Forest and Range Exptl. Sta., Dubois, Idaho, 1958-61, rsch. project leader Provo, Utah, 1961-64, Logan, Utah, 1964-74; asst. dir. Rocky Mountain Forest and Range Exptl. Sta., Ft. Collins, Colo., 1974-76; rsch. leader Agrl. Rsch. Svc., USDA, Ft. Collins, 1976-85; head dept. range mgmt. U. Wyo., Laramie, 1985-96; prof emeritus, 1996—; cons., 1996—. Mem. continuing com. Internat. Rangeland Congresses, 1991-99. Co-editor: Secondary Succession and the Evaluation of Range Condition, 1989; contbr. over 100 sci. articles to profl. jours., symposium proceedings, chpts. to books. Pres. Colo. State High Sch. Rodeo Assn., Ft. Collins, 1978. 1st lt. U.S. Army, 1953-55. Fellow Soc. for Range Mgmt. (pres. Colo. sect. 1982, chmn. adv. coun. 1983, Outstanding Achievement award 1985, nat. pres. 1988-89, del., rep. to Internat. Rangeland Congress, 1988, 92, 95, Renner award 1993, 95). Home: 3415 Alta Vista Dr Laramie WY 82072-5046

LAYNE, CHARLES SHANNON, medical educator; b. Midland, Mich., Apr. 15, 1957; s. Gilbert Shannon and Betty Lou Layne; m. Connie Leigh Fox; children: Macy, Max. BS, U. Tex., 1979, MEd, 1982, PhD, 1987. Asst. prof. Kans. State U., Manhattan, 1988—92; lab. dir. Krug Life Scis., Houston, 1992—96; assoc. prof. U. Houston, 1997—; chair dept. health and human performance U. of Houston, 2002—. Mem. Mental Health Network, N.Y.C. Contbr. rsch. articles to profl. jours. Grantee Rsch. grantee, NASA, 1999—2001. Mem.: Soc. for Neurosci. Office: Dept Health and Human Performance Univ Houston 104C Garrision Houston TX 77204 Office Fax: 713-743-9860. Business E-Mail: clayne2@uh.edu.

LAZAR, LUDMILA, concert pianist, music educator, pedagogue; b. Celje, Slovenia; married; two children. MusB, Roosevelt U., 1963, MusM, 1964; D of Musical Arts, Northwestern U., 1987. Faculty Roosevelt U., Chgo., 1967—, prof. piano Chgo. Musical Coll., 1988—, prof. emerita, 2003—, chmn. keyboard dept., 1983—2003. Lectr., demonstrator in field. Roosevelt U. rsch. grantee, 1988, 96; recipient Goethe Inst. award, 1987; named to All Star Profs. Team Chgo. Tribune, 1993. Mem. AAUP, Music Tchrs. Nat. Assn. (master tchr. cert. 1991), European Piano Tchrs. Assn., Ill. State Music Tchrs. Assn., Soc. Am. Musicians (pres., v.p.), Coll. Music Soc., Mu Phi Epsilon (pres., v.p.). Office: Roosevelt U 430 S Michigan Ave Chicago IL 60605-1394

LAZAR, RAYMOND MICHAEL, lawyer, educator; b. Mpls., July 16, 1939; s. Simon and Hessie (Teplin) L; children: Mark, Deborah. BBA, U. Minn., 1961, JD, 1964. Bar: Minn. 1964, U.S. Dist. Ct. Minn. 1964. Spl. asst. atty. gen. State of Minn., St. Paul, 1964-66; pvt. practice Mpls., 1966-72; ptnr. Lapp, Lazar, Laurie & Smith, Mpls., 1972-86; ptnr., officer Fredrikson & Byron P.A., Mpls., 1986—. Lectr. various continuing edn. programs, 1972—; adj. prof. law U. Minn., Mpls., 1983-99. Fellow Am. Acad. Matrimonial Lawyers; mem. ABA (chair divorce laws and procedures com. family law sect. 1993-94), Minn. Bar Assn., Hennepin County Bar Assn. (chair family law sect. 1978-79). Home: 400 River St Minneapolis MN 55401 Office: Fredrikson & Byron PA 4000 Pillsbury Ctr Minneapolis MN 55402-3314 E-mail: rlazar@fredlaw.com.

LAZARE, AARON, dean, psychiatrist; b. Newark, Feb. 14, 1936; s. H. Benjamin and Anne (Storfer) L.; m. Louise Cannon; children: Robert, Jacqueline, David, Sam, Sarah, Hien, Thomas, Naomi. AB, Oberlin Coll., 1957; MD, Case Western Reserve U., 1961. Intern in medicine Bronx (N.Y.) Mcpl. Hosp. Ctr., 1961-62; resident in psychiatry Mass. Mental Health Ctr., 1962-65; asst. in psychiatry Mass. Gen. Hosp., Boston, 1967-68; chief day hosp. inpatient unit Yale-New Haven Hosp., 1967-68; assoc. dir. adult outpatient psychiatry Mass. Gen. Hosp., Boston, 1968-70, dir. adult outpatient psychiatry, 1970-75, acting dir. residency tng., 1972, dir. outpatient psychiatry, 1975-82, dep. chief psychiatry, 1976-82, clin. dir. psychiatry, 1978-82; prof., chmn. dept. psychiatry U. Mass. Med. Ctr., Worcester, 1982—90, interim dean, 1989-90, dean, 1990—, chancellor, 1991—. Prof. Harvard U., 1982. Editor: Outpatient Psychiatry, 1979, 1989, 2nd edit.; contbr. articles to profl. jours.; co-author of books in field. Capt. U.S. Army, 1965-67. Named for Disting. Pub. Svc. Commonwealth of Mass., honorable mention U. Mass., 1987, Commonwealth of Mass., U. Mass., Boston, 1988, Brotherhood award NCCJ, 1992, Maimonides award for outstanding commitment as a physician and educator Anti-Defamation League New Eng., 1993, Friend and Leader award Mass. Assn. Mental Health Inc., 2001. Mem. AAAS, AMA, Am. Psychiat. Assn. (Benjamin Rush award 1992), Mass. Psychiat. Soc. Office: U Mass Med Ctr Off Chancellor 55 Lake Ave N Worcester MA 01655-0002*

LAZARNICK, SYLVIA, secondary education educator; b. Bklyn., Feb. 6, 1949; d. Emanuel and Karin Lazarnick; m. Timothy Taylor Beaman, June 18, 1973. BA, Bklyn. Coll., 1969; MA, Pa. State U., 1971. Math. tchr. Class. High Sch., Springfield, Mass., 1971-72, Alternative High Sch., Lakewood, N.J., 1972-73, Broadmeadows (Australia) Tech. Sch., 1975-77, Neshaminy-Langhorne (Pa.) High Sch., 1979, Rice Meml. High Sch., Burlington, Vt., 1979-80, Bellows Free Acad., St. Albans, Vt., 1980—. Bd. dirs. Franklin County Food Coop., St. Albans; coach Vt. All Stars; coach BFA Math League Team. Mem. Nat. Coun. Tchrs. Math., Assn. Tchrs. Math. in New Eng. (program co-chair fall meeting 1994), Vt. Coun. Tchrs. Math. (pres. 1995-97, finalist Presdl. award for excellence in math. tchg. 1996). Avocations: reading, rock climbing, skiing, hiking, cycling. Home: 578 Swamp Rd Fairfield VT 05455-9733 Office: Bellows Free Acad 71 S Main St Saint Albans VT 05478-2297

LAZARUS, BRUCE I. restaurant and hotel management educator; b. Pitts. s. Arnold H. and Belle Lazarus. BS, Pa. State U., 1975; JD, U. Pitts., 1980. Bar: Pa. 1980. Ops. analyst ARA Services, Phila., 1976-77; legal intern Pa. Human Relations Commn., Pitts., 1978-79; food service dir. Martin's Run Life Care, ARA Services, Phila., 1980-81; asst. dir. dept. nutrition Bryn Mawr (Pa.) Hosp., ARA Services, 1981-84; prof. restaurant and hotel mgmt. Purdue U., West Lafayette, Ind., 1984—96, prof. emeritus, 1996—. Mem. membership com. Coun. Hotel, Restaurant and Instnl. Edn., 1984—, mem. paper rev. com. 1988—. Contbr. articles to profl. pubs. Nat. Inst. Food Service Industry grantee, 1986, Internat. Franchise Assn., 1987; recipient Mary Mathew award for Outstanding Undergraduate teaching Consumer anf Family Svcs., 1993, Purdue Univ. award Outstanding Undergraduate Teaching, 1993. Mem. ABA, Ind. Bar Assn., Pa. Bar Assn., Nat. Restaurant Assn., Phi Kappa Phi. Office: Purdue U 1266 Stone Hall Lafayette IN 47907-1266

LAZARUS, FRANCIS MARTIN, academic administrator; b. Elma, N.Y., Dec. 29, 1944; s. Edward Alois and Olivia Anne (Peters) L.; m. Carol Mary Scheminger, June 29, 1968, children: Catherine M., Julie A., James E. AB, Canisius Coll., 1966; MA, Cornell U., 1968, PhD, 1973. Asst. prof. English U.S. Mil. Acad., West Point, N.Y., 1970-73; asst. prof. Classics Salem Coll., Winston-Salem, N.C., 1973-78; adminstrv. fellow Memphis State U., 1978-79; assoc. acad. dean Salem Coll., Winston-Salem, 1979-80; dean Coll. Arts and Scis. U. Dayton, Ohio, 1980-88; v.p. acad. affairs Marquette U., Milw., 1988-96; v.p., provost U. San Diego, 1996—. Chair acad. consortium Gt. Midwest Conf., Chgo., 1992-95. Editor: Faith, Discovery, Service, 1991. Bd. trustees Youth Leadership Acad., Milw., 1993-96. Capt. U.S. Army, 1970-73. Recipient Pres.'s award Wis. Dental Assn., 1994; named Outstanding Young Man Am. U.S. C. of C., 1973. Mem. Am. Coun. Edn. (fellow 1978), Am. Philol. Assn., Classical Soc. Am. Acad. in Rome, Vergilian Soc., Assn. Cath. Colls. and Univs. Avocation: fishing. Office: U San Diego 5998 Alcala Park San Diego CA 92110-2476

LAZARUS, FRED, IV, college president; b. N.Y.C., Jan. 1, 1942; s. Fred and Irma (Mendelson) L.; m. Jonna Gane, Nov. 27, 1970; children: Anna Mendelson, Fred Lazarus V. BA, Claremont McKenna Coll., 1964; MBA, Harvard U., 1966. Staff assoc. Nat. Council for Equal Bus. Opportunity, Washington, 1969-71; pres. Washington Council for Equal Bus. Opportunity, 1971-74; exec. asst. to chmn. Nat. Endowment for Arts, Washington, 1975-78; pres. Md. Inst. Coll. Art, Balt., 1978—. Vice chmn. Assn. Ind. Colls. Art and Design, 1992-96; trustee Alliance for Ind. Colls. Art, 1978-91, chmn., 1984-86, 89-91; founding chmn. Nat. Coalition for Edn. in Arts, 1988-90. Trustee St. Paul's Sch., 1988—96, Am. Coun. for Arts, 1980—97, sec., 1991—94; trustee Ams. for the Arts, 1998—, Md. Art Place, 1988—96; trustee emeritus Ptnrs. for Livable Places; bd. dirs. Afro-Am. Newspapers, Balt., 1990—2003, Balt. Artists Housing Corp.; chmn. Balt. Coun. for Equal Bus. Opportunity, 1991—2000; trustee Md. Ind. Coll. and Univ. Assn., vice chmn., 1995—99, chmn., 1999—2023; mem. Thurgood Marshall Meml. Statue Commn., 1996—98; chmn. Greater Balt. Cultural Alliance, 2001—, trustee, chmn., 2002—. Recipient mayor's art award, City of Balt., 1988. Mem. Harvard Club (N.Y.C.) Office: Md Inst Coll Art 1300 W Mount Royal Ave Baltimore MD 21217-4134

LAZARUS-FRANKLIN, PAULA GUILLERMINA, vocational services administrator; b. Panama City, Dec. 10, 1950; came to the U.S., 1956; d. Paul and Hazel Lazarus; m. Donald Franklin; children: Geela, Jahred. BS in Art Edn., SUNY, New Paltz, 1973; MS in Guidance, CUNY, 1978. Cert. sch. counselor, N.Y. Art tchr. Wyandanch (N.Y.) Schs., 1973-76; caseworker Washington Heights Community Svc. N.Y. Psychiat Inst., N.Y.C., 1977-79; career counselor Nat. Puerto Rico Forum, Jersey City, N.J., 1980; vocat. counselor N.Y. Urban Coalition, N.Y.C., 1980-83, dir. vocat. svcs., 1983—. Active Citizens Budget Advice Coun., West Hempstead, N.Y., 1991-92; inspector Bd. Elections, Nassau County, N.Y., 1990—; active Harlem Literacy Adv. Coun., N.Y.C., 1988-92. Mem. Am. Counseling Assn., Assn. Vocat. Rehab. Advocates for Substance Abusers. Office: NY Urban Coalition/CASH 356 W 123rd St New York NY 10027-5123

LAZEAR, EDWARD PAUL, economics and labor relations educator, researcher; b. N.Y.C., Aug. 17, 1948; s. Abe and Rose (Karp) L.; m. Victoria Ann Allen, July 2, 1977; 1 child, Julia Ann AB, A.M., UCLA, 1971; PhD, Harvard U., 1974; LLD (hon.), Albertson Coll., 1997. Asst. prof. econs. U. Chgo., 1974-78, assoc. prof. indsl. relations, 1978-81, prof. indsl. relations, 1981-85, Isidore and Gladys Brown prof. urban and labor econs., 1985-92; sr. fellow Hoover Instn. Stanford (Calif.) U., 1985—2002, coord. domestic studies Hoover Instn., 1987-90, prof. econs. and human resource mgmt. Grad. Sch. Bus., 1992-95, Jack Steele Parker prof. econs. and human resource mgmt., 1995—, mem. steering com. Stanford Inst. for Econ. Policy Rsch., 1996—. Econ. advisor to Romania, Czechoslovakia, Russia, Ukraine, Georgia; rsch. assoc. Nat. Bur. Econ. Rsch., Econs. Rsch. Ctr. of Nat. Opinion Rsch. Ctr.; chmn. rsch. adv. bd. World at Work; fellow Inst. Advanced Study, Hebrew U., Jerusalem, 1977-8; lectr. Inst. Advanced Study, Vienna, 1983-84, Nat. Productivity Bd., Singapore, 1982, 85; vis. prof. Inst. des Etudes Politiques, Paris, 1987; Wicksell lectr., Stockholm, 1993; chmn. Am. Compensation Assoc. Adv. Bd., 1999—; Adam Smith lctr., Saville, Spain, 2003. Author: (with R. Michael) Allocation of Income Within the Household, 1988; (with J.P. Gould) Microeconomic Theory, 1989, Personnel Economics, 1995, Personnel Economics for Managers, 1998; editor: Economic Transition in Eastern Europe and Russia, 1995; founding editor Jour. Labor Econs., 1982—; assoc. editor Jour. Econ. Perspectives, 1986-89, German Econ. Rev., 2000—; co-editor: Jour. Labor Abstracts, 1996—; contbr. numerous articles to scholarly jours. Recipient Leo Melamed prize for outstanding scholarship, 1998; NSF grad. fellow, 1971-74, Morris Arnold Cox sr. fellow Hoover Instn., 2002. Fellow Am. Acad. Arts and Scis., Econometric Soc., Soc. Labor Economists (1st v.p. 1995-96, pres. 1997-98); mem. Am. Econs. Assn. Home: 277 Old Spanish Trl Portola Valley CA 94028-8129 Office: Stanford U Grad Sch Bus Stanford CA 94305-5015 Also: Stanford Univ Hoover Inst Stanford CA 94305-6010

LAZERSON, EARL EDWIN, academic administrator emeritus; b. Detroit, Dec. 10, 1930; s. Nathan and Ceil (Stashefsky) L.; m. Ann May Harper, June 11, 1966; children from previous marriage: Joshua, Paul. BS, Wayne State U., Detroit, 1953; postgrad., U. Leiden, Netherlands, 1957-58; MA, U. Mich., 1954, PhD, 1982. Mathematician Inst. Def. Analyses, Princeton, N.J., 1960-62; asst. prof. math. Washington U., St. Louis, 1962-65, 66-69; vis. asso. prof. Brandeis U., 1965-66; mem. faculty So. Ill. U., Edwardsville, 1969—, prof. math., 1973—, chmn. dept. math. studies, 1972-73, dean Sch. Sci. and Tech., 1973-76, univ. v.p., provost, 1977-79, pres., 1980-93; pres. emeritus, 1994—. Chmn. Southwestern Ill. Devel. Authority, City of East St. Louis Fin. Adv. Authority; active Leadership Coun. Southwestern Ill., Gateway Ctr. Met. St. Louis, Inc., St. Louis Symphony Soc.; trustee Jefferson Nat. Expansion Meml. Assn., Ill. Econ. Devel. Bd. Recipient Sr. Teaching Excellence award Standard Oil Found., 1970-71 Mem. Am. Math. Soc., Math. Assn. Am., European Math. Soc., London Math. Soc., Soc. Mathematique France, Fulbright Alumni Assn., Sigma Xi. Home: 122 Forest Grove Dr Glen Carbon IL 62034 E-mail: laze@charter.net.

LAZUR, JAMES JOSEPH, accounting educator; b. Toledo, Ohio, Mar. 26, 1946; s. Emery Joseph and Ethel Ann (Kerekgyarto) L. Assoc. Applied Bus., Owens Tech. Coll., Toledo, 1987; BS, U. Toledo, 1988. Cert. tax profl. Store mgr. Gladieux Food Svc., Toledo, 1975-77; exec. and shift mgr. Frisch's Big Boy, Toledo, 1977-82; asst. office supr. H & R Block, Toledo, 1982-85; acct., tax preparer Toledo, 1985—; computer lab. technician Owens Tech. Coll., Toledo, 1986-87; instr. Capital U., Dayton, Ohio, 1989-91; instr. various fields Owens Tech. Coll., Toledo, 1987—. Mem. Owens Coll. Alumni Bd., 1988—; tutor acctg. and basic programming, 1987—. Fin. cons., computer operator, team leader, drama minister, youth pastor Found. Stone Christian Ctr., Toledo, 1985—. Mem. Nat. Assn. Accts., Nat. Soc. Tax Profls., Assn. Supervision and Curriculum Devel., Smithsonian Inst., Ohio Soc. Enrolled Agts. Avocations: desktop pub., movie classics, reading. Home: 546 Pleasant Pl Toledo OH 43609-3368

LEADER, BRUCE ROBERT, secondary education educator; b. Buffalo, Mar. 9, 1967; s. Bennett and Fay (Broder) L. BA in History and Philosophy, SUNY, Binghamton, 1989; MA in History, SUNY, Buffalo, 1991. Programming asst. Sta.-WBFO Radio, NY, 1989-90; supr. computer lab. Williamsville Ctrl. Schs., NY, 1991; tchr. social studies Starpoint Ctrl. Schs., Lockport, NY, 1991—; head of history Anglican Interant. Sch., Jerusalem, 2000—02. Head coach soccer Starpoint Ctrl. Schs., 1992—; tchr. Bridges for Edn., Poland, summer 1995; mem. U.S. Bicycling Tour, summer 1991; English lang. tchr. Yew Wah Lang. Sch., Shanghai, China, summer 1999. Head coach Amherst Soccer Assn., 1989-92. Recipient Nat. Sallie Mae award outstanding first yr. tchr. Democrat. Jewish. Avocations: reading, bicycling, traveling, camping. Home: 650 Auburn Ave Buffalo NY 14222-1415 Office: Starpoint Ctrl Schs 4363 Mapleton Rd Lockport NY 14094-9652

LEAF, JOHN BRIAN, art instructor, elementary education educator; b. South Bend, Ind., July 27, 1963; s. William Arthur and Betty Lou (Gannon) L.; m. Ana Teresa Palerm Leaf, Nov. 1m 1985; children: Zane Brien, Eoin Benjamin, Shanah Bernadette. BA in Art Edn., Ctrl. State U., Edmond, Okla., 1986; MEd, U. Ctrl. Okla., Edmond, 1994. Tchr. Victor Schs., Victorville, Calif., 1987-89; art instr. Putnam City Schs., Oklahoma City, 1989-92, Oklahoma City Pub. Schs., 1992-93, Norman (Okla.) Pub. Schs., 1993-1998; edn. instr. Langston U., Tinker AFB Midwest City, Okla., 1994-1995; art instr. Okla. City pub. sch., 1998-2000, Acad. dist. 20, Colorado Springs, Colo., 2000—. Named Most Enthusiastic Tchr. Parkview Elem. Faculty, Victorville, Calif., 1988, Tchr. Who Cares, 1992, Above and Beyond, 1993 U.S. Grant Prin., Okla. Secondary Art Eduacator of the Yr., Okla. Art Edn. Assoc., 1997; grantee Fencing Program Putnam City Found., Oklahoma City, 1991, Advanced Placement Art, Okla. State Dept. Edn., 2000. Mem. Nat. Art Edn. Assn. Republican. Avocations: wrestling, coaching, painting, bridge, basketball. Home: 4116 Tumbleweed Dr Colorado Springs CO 80918 E-mail: leaf-familys@juno.com.

LEAFGREEN, LISA DIANE, education coordinator; b. Cheyenne, Wyo., Nov. 13, 1964; d. Lavern Edward and Errolene Ruth (Clark) L. BS, U. Wyo., 1987. Co-mgr. The Limited, Denver, 1987-89; student svcs. coord. Colo. Free U., Denver, 1989-91, tchr. coord., 1991-92; edn. coord. Arvada (Colo.) Cen. for Arts & Humanities, 1992—. Office: Arvada Ctr for Arts & Humanities 6901 Wadsworth Blvd Arvada CO 80003-3448

LEAHY, WILLIAM P. academic administrator, historian, educator; b. Omaha, July 16, 1948; s. Edward and Alice (McGinnis) Leahy. Student, Creighton U., 1966—67, Jesuit Coll., 1967—70; BA in Philosophy, St. Louis U., 1972, MA in U.S. History, 1975; MDiv in Theology, Jesuit Sch. Theology, Berkeley, Calif., 1978, STM in Hist. Theology, 1980; PhD in U.S. History, Stanford U., 1986. Ordained to ministry Cath. Ch., 1978. Tchr. Campion Jesuit H.S., Prairie du Chien, Wis., 1973—75; tchg. asst. Stanford U., 1981; instr. history Marquette U., Milw., 1985—86, asst. prof., 1986—91, acting asst. chmn., 1988—90, assoc. prof. history, exec. v.p., 1991—96; pres. Boston Coll., Chestnut Hill, Mass., 1996—. Author: Adapting to America: Catholics, Jesuits and Higher Education in the Twentieth Century, 1991; contbr. articles to profl. jours. Trustee Boston Coll., Loyola U., Chgo.; bd. dirs. Weston Jesuit Sch. Theology, Assn. Cath. Colls. and Univs., Nat. ASsn. Ind. Colls. and Univs; mem. pres. com. Bishops and Cath. Coll. and Univs. Mem.: History Edn. Soc. Office: Boston College Office of the President 18 Old Colony Road Chestnut Hill MA 02467 E-mail: leahy@bc.edu.

LEALI, SHIRLEY A. mathematician, educator; b. Adel, Ga. d. Rufus and Georgia R. (Hall) Wright; m. Robert M. Leali Jr., June 18, 1971. BA, U. Denver, 1973; MA, U. Colo., Denver, 1984; PhD, U. Denver, 1992. Instr., adminstr. Denver Pub. Schs., 1974-93; assoc. prof. math. Weber State U., Ogden, Utah, 1993—, U. No. Colo., Greeley, Colo., 1995-96. Cons. Ogden Sch. Dist., 1994—; nat. gender equity expert; presenter internat. confs. Contbr. articles to profl. jours. Vol. math. tchr. for incarcerated youth; bd. dirs. State of Utah Black Adv. Coun., 1997—. Ednl. Tech. Initiative grantee Weber State U., 1994, Thiokol, 1994. Fellow Nat. Coun. Tchrs. of Math.; mem. Assn. Math. Tchr. Educators, Internat. Study Group on Ethnomath., Utah Sci. Tchrs. Assn. Achievements include work and recognition for advancing gender equity and awareness. Office: Weber State U Ogden UT 84403 E-mail: saleali@weber.edu.

LEAPMAN, PHYLLIS LENORE, retired nursing educator; b. Providence, June 26, 1936; d. Samuel and Sadye (Sandler) Kirshenbaum; m. Herbert G. Leapman, Oct. 2, 1966; children: Scott, Sherry, Robert. Grad., Beth Israel Hosp. Sch. Nursing, Boston, 1957; BS, Columbia U., 1960, MA, 1965. RN, Fla.; cert. geriatrics nurse, oncology nurse ANCC. Pub. health nurse Palm Beach County, Delray, Fla.; sch. nurse Warwick (R.I.) Sch. Dist.; head nurse Beth Israel Hosp., Boston; sr. instr. Palm Beach C.C., Lakeworth, Fla., 1982-92. Vol. counselor Planned Parenthood; vol. Alzheimer tr. Fed. trainee grantee, 1964-65. Mem. ANA, Oncology Nurses Soc., Kappa Delta Pi. Home: 2625 Crabapple Cir Boynton Beach FL 33436-6640

LEAR, ERWIN, anesthesiologist, educator; b. Bridgeport, Conn., Jan. 1, 1924; s. Samuel Joseph and Ida (Ruth) L.; m. Arlene Joyce Alexander, Feb. 15, 1953; children: Stephanie, Samuel MD, SUNY, 1952. Diplomate Am. Bd. Anesthesiology, Nat. Bd. Med. Examiners. Intern L.I. Coll. Hosp., Bklyn., 1952-53; asst. resident anesthesiology Jewish Hosp., Bklyn., 1953-54, sr. resident, 1955, asst., 1955-56, adj., 1956-58, assoc. anesthesiologist, 1958-64; attending anesthesiologist Bklyn. VA Hosp., 1958-64, cons., 1977—; assoc. vis. anesthesiologist Kings County Hosp. Ctr., Bklyn., 1957-80, staff anesthesiologist, 1980-81; vis. anesthesiologist Queens Gen. Hosp. Ctr., 1955-67; dir. anesthesiology Queens Hosp. Ctr. Jamaica, 1964-67; chmn. dept. anesthesiology Catholic Med. Ctr., Queens and Bklyn., 1968-80; dir. anesthesiology Beth Israel Med. Ctr., N.Y.C., 1981-98; clin. instr. SUNY Coll. Medicine, Bklyn., 1955-58, from clin. asst. prof. to clin. prof., 1958-80, prof., vice-chmn. clin. anesthesiology, 1980-81; prof. anesthesiology Mt. Sinai Sch. Medicine, 1981-94, Albert Einstein Coll. of Medicine, 1994—. Cons. in field. Author: Chemistry Applied Pharmacology of Tranquilizers; contbr. articles to profl. jours. Served with USNR, 1942-45 Fellow: N.Y. Acad. Medicine (sec. sect. anesthesiology 1985—86, chmn. sect. anesthesiology 1986—87), Am. Coll. Anesthesiologists; mem.: AMA, SUNY Coll. Medicine Alumni Assn. (pres. 1983, trustee alumni fund 1980), N.Y. County Med. Soc., N.Y. State Med. Soc. (chmn. sect. anesthesiology 1966—67, sec. sect. 1977—81), N.Y. State Soc. Anesthesiologists (chmn. pub. rels. 1963—73, assoc. editor Bulletin 1963—77, chmn. com. local arrangements 1968—73, dist. dir. 1972—73, bd. dirs. 1972—94, v.p. 1974—75, pres. 1976, chmn. jud. com. 1977—81, editor Sphere 1978—87, Disting. Svc. award 1996), Am. Soc. Anesthesiologists (ho. of dels. 1973—94, dir. 1981—97, chmn. com. on by-laws 1982—83, editor newsletter 1984—98, chmn. adminstrv. affairs com. 1987—94), Alpha Omega Alpha. Address: 1 Harriman Dr Sands Point NY 11050-1246

LEARMANN, JUDITH MARILYN, secondary school educator; b. Charleston, Ill., Feb. 1, 1938; d. Charles P. and Estelle M. (DeWitt) Swan; m. Paul C. Learmann, Aug. 29, 1958 (dec.); children: Kevin L., Michael P.(dec.). BS, Wis. State Coll., Oshkosh, 1960; MA, Pacific Western U., 1994. Tchr. Monona (Wis.) Grove H.S., 1960-62, U.S. Army Coll. Program, Denver, 1967, Wood Mid. Sch., Ft. Leonard Wood, Mo., 1983-85, Waynesville (Mo.) H.S., 1985—, chmn. dept. lang. arts, 1987—. Presenter in field; chmn. North Ctrl. Philosophy Com., Waynesville, 1987—88; reviewer textbook Adventures in English Literature Harcourt, Brace, Jovanovich, 1994; reviewer sci. curriculum, 1994—96; reviewer math. curriculum, 1995; reviewer social studies curriculum, 96; reviewer bus. curriculum, 97; reviewer computer sci. curriculum, 97; mem. evaluation steering com. Mo. sch. improvement program, chair instrn. process com. Waynesville R-VI Sch. Dist., 1996—97; mem. strategic planning com. Edn. 2003, 1997—; mem. sch. to work Career Quest com., 1998, Vanguard tech. com., 1999—, Continued Sch. Improvement Plan Learning Environ. com., 2001, PBTE rev. com., 2002. Named Most Influential Tchr. award, U. Mo., 1991; recipient Influential Tchr. Recognition letter, Westminster Coll., 1992, 1995, Tex. A&M U., 1998. Mem.: Cmty. Tchrs. Assn. (chmn. legal svcs. 1991—95, health leave pool com. 1996—), Mo. State Tchrs. Assn., Cmty. Tchrs. English (meeting chmn. dist. conv. 1989, 1990, 1998), Mo. Tchrs. Assn., Nat. Coun. Tchrs. English, Phi Delta Kappa (officer nomination, constn. revision coms., tchr. awards). Avocation: reading. Home: 1737 J C St Waynesville MO 65583-2460 Office: Waynesville HS 1001 Historic Rt 66 West Waynesville MO 65583 E-mail: jlearmann@waynesville.k12.mo.us.

LEARN, RICHARD LELAND, corrections classification program manager; b. New Kensington, Pa., Nov. 29, 1955; s. Leland Leroy Learn and Gendolyn Leora (Furman) George; m. Rosamond Amelia Kautz, July 31, 1982; children: Rebecca Amelia, Benjamin Richard. BS in Music Edn., Indiana U. of Pa., 1977, MA in Adult/Community Edn., 1984; PhD in Edn., U. Pitts., 1991. Adult edn. instr. PIC of Westmoreland County, Greensburg, Pa., 1980-82; corrections edn. specialist Pa. State Correctional Instn., Greensburg, 1984-87; acad. support coord. Indiana U. of Pa., 1987-89; sch. prin. Pa. State Correctional Instn., Mercer, 1989-92, Cambridge Springs, 1992-2000; classification and program mgr., 2000—. Mem. Am. Correctional Assn., Corrections Edn. Assn. Democrat. Presbyterian. Avocations: archery, music. Office: State Correctional Instn 451 Fullerton Ave Cambridge Springs PA 16403-1238 E-mail: rlearn@alltel.net.

LEARNARD, JAMES MICHAEL, middle school educator, former finance company executive, special education educator; b. Worcester, Mass., June 13, 1947; s. James Felix and Katherine M. (Slater) L.; m. Mary Kathryn Douglas, Mar. 16, 1972 (div. June 1974); 1 child, Sean Patrick; m. Joyce Stanek Hogan, June 10, 1989 (div. Nov. 1991); m. Donna Cecile Courtney, Aug. 12, 1993 (div. Aug. 1995). AA, Fla. Jr. Coll., Jacksonville, 1968; BSBA, Century U., Beverly Hills, Calif., 1987, MBA, 1988; PhD (hon.), Century U., 2001, MA in Edn., 2002; BA, Augusta (Ga.) Coll., 1991. Cert. paralegal, Ga.; cert. nursing asst. Epidemiologist L.A. Dept. Health, 1972-73; credit collector supr. Levy-Wolf, Inc., Jacksonville, 1973-75; correctional officer S.C. Dept. Corrections, Aiken, 1975-76; v.p., office mgr. Nat. Auto Fin. Corp., Aiken, 1976-81; ins. agt. Security Life Ins. Co. of Ga., Augusta, 1981-82, United Ins. Co. of Am., Aiken, 1982-86, Life Ins. Co. of Ga., Atlanta, 1986-87, The Keller Agy., Aiken, 1992-94; collector ARC, Inc., Augusta, Ga., 1994; owner, collector CSRA Recovery Svcs., Inc., Aiken, 1994-99; collection mgr. Service Loan Co., Augusta, 1999—; tchr. Richmond County (Ga.) Bd. Edn. Collector Apex Fin. Co., Inc., Augusta, 1999; telemarketer So. Ind., Augusta, 1999, Hospitality Mktg. Concepts, Inc., Augusta, 1999, DialAm. Mktg., North Augusta, S.C., 1999; nursing asst. Anna Maria Nursing and Rehab. Ctr., North Augusta, 1999. Author: Words of Love, 1985, Thoughts of Love and Inspiration, 1988, Student Protests at Harvard College, 1766-1780, 1986, Catholic Hospitals in the American Healthcare System, 1988, I Praise Your Name, A Collection of Love Poems, 1998, Recipes from the Heart: Cooking for the One You Love, 1999, How Do I Love Thee? A Collection of Love Poems, 2000, Love Lasts Eternal--Love Poems to a Lovely Lady, 2000, The Not So Famous Quotations and Other Writings of James M. Learnard, 20 vols., 2000; musical compositions include: Tonight (soul ballad), 1982, (pop rock ballad), 1982, Friends (pop rock ballad), 1983, Do You Remember (soul ballad), 1983, Eastern Morn (hymn), 1983, Christmas Day, 1982, Sunset on Tampa Bay (soul ballad), 1982, 83, My Angel (soul ballad), 1983, What Will She Say? (pop rock ballad), 1983, Easter Morn, 1983; prodr. album: Michael Hicks/Love Songs, 1983. Past chmn. Animal Control Adv. Bd., Aiken. Recipient Golden Poet award World of Poetry, 1986, 87, Silver Poet award, 1988, Recognition by the S.C. House of Reps. for accomplishment as an author, poet and lycricist, 1986; commd. admiral S.C. Navy, 1986; recipient Medal of Honor commemorating disting. lifelong achievement Am. Biog. Assn., 1990; Eagle Scout with Bronze Palm, Boy Scouts Am., 1963. Mem. Assn. of MBA Execs., Healthcare Fin. Mgmt. Assn., Fedn. of Am. Health Svcs., Am. Hosp. Assn., Soc. for Hosp. Healthcare and Mktg., K.C. (4th degree). Roman Catholic. Home: 117 Green St Graniteville SC 29829 E-mail: jamesmlearnard@aol.com.

LEARY, DAVID EDWARD, psychologist, educator; b. L.A., May 5, 1945; married; 3 children. BA in Philosophy, San Luis Rey Coll., 1968; MA in Psychology, San Jose State Coll., 1971; PhD in History of Sci., U. Chgo., 1977. Instr. psychology Holy Names Coll., Oakland, Calif., 1972-74, U. Calif. Extension Svcs., Berkeley, 1972-74; counseling psychologist Howard Inst., Oakland, 1972-74; instr. psychology San Jose (Calif.) State U. Extension Svcs., 1973-74, San Francisco State U. Extension Svcs., 1973-74, U. Calif. at Santa Cruz Extension Svcs., Monterey, 1973-74, U. Chgo., 1975; asst. prof. history and philosophy of psychology U. N.H., Durham, 1977-81, co-dir. grad. program in history and theory psychology, 1977-89, assoc. prof. psychology and humanities, 1981-87, chmn. dept. psychology, 1986-89, prof. psychology, history and humanities, 1987-89; prof. psychology, dean arts and scis. U. Richmond, Va., 1989—2002, univ. prof., 2002—. Vis. asst. prof. psychology Grad. Theol. Union, Berkeley, 1971-72; fellow Ctr. Advanced Study in Behavioral Scis., Stanford, Calif., 1982-83, co-dir. summer inst. on history of social sci. inquiry, 1986; assoc. prof. humanities Summer Program Cambridge U., Eng., 1984; presenter in field. Editor: A Century of Psychology as Science, 2d rev. edit., 1992 (Assn. Am. Pub. award 1986), An Introduction to the Psychology of Guilt, 1975; editor: Metaphors in the History of Psychology, 1990; author: (with others) The Anatomy of Impact: What Makes The Great Works of Psychology Great?, 2003, Evolving Perspectives on The History of Psychology, 2002, Encyclopedia of Psychology, 2000, A History of Psychology: Original Sources and Contemporary Research, 2d edit., 1997, The Encyclopedia of Higher Education, 1992, Writing the Social Text: Poetics and Politics in Social Science Discourses, 1992, Annual Review of Psychology, 1991, Metaphors in the History of Psychology, 1990, Reflections on The Principles of Psychology: William James After a Century, 1990, Psychology in Twentieth-Century Thought and Society, 1987, Psychology in its Historical Context, 1985, Thinkers of the 20th Century, 1984, Studies in Eighteenth-Century Culture, 1984, The Problematic Science: Psychology in Nineteenth Century Thought, 1982; contbr. articles to profl. jours. Grantee NEH, 1982-83, 91-94, Social Sci. Rsch. Ctr. Faculty Support, U. N.H., 1988, Coll. Liberal Arts Faculty Rsch. Support, U. N.H., 1987-88, Ctrl. U. Rsch. Fund, U. N.H., 1979, 87, Mellon Found., 1986, NSF, 1980-82, 82-83; rsch. fellow History Psychology Found., 1980, summer fellow NEH, 1979, U. N.H., 1978, grad. fellow U. Chgo., 1975-77. Fellow Am. Psychol. Soc.; mem. APA (centennial lectr. on history of psychology 1979-80, 91-92, fellow divsn. 24 1988—, fellow divsn. 1 1983—, pres. divsn. 26 1983-84, fellow divsn. 26 1982—, pres. divsn. 24 1994-95), Am. Assn. Higher Edn., Am. Conf. Acad. Deans (bd. dirs. 1994-00, chair 1998-99), Am. Hist. Assn., Assn. Am. Colls. Univs. (grantee 1990-91), Soc. History of Sci. in Am., Cheiron: Internat. Soc. History of Behavioral and Social Scis., Forum History of Human Sci., History of Sci. Soc., Phi Beta Kappa (hon.). Office: Univ Richmond Ryland Hall 302 Richmond VA 23173

LEARY, ROSEMARY FRECH, science educator; b. Phila., June 28, 1951; d. Frank Robert and Mary Dorothy (O'Connell) Frech; m. Guy Henry Leary, Oct. 26, 1974; children: Jennifer, Brian, Glenn. BS, Pa. State U., 1973; MEd, Ariz. State U., 1989, PhD, 1993. Cert. tchr. c.c., Ariz., standard secondary cert., Ariz., cert. tchr. chemistry, Ariz. Rsch. asst. Fox Chase Cancer Ctr., Phila., 1973-78; grad. tchg. assoc. Ariz. State U., Tempe, 1990-91; instrnl. devel. specialist math. and sci. U. Wash., Seattle, 1994; rschr. Ariz. Sci. Ctr., Phoenix, 1995-96; chemistry prof. Estrella Mountain C.C., 1996—. Faculty leader Westside Impact Sci. Leadership Program Maricola Office of Pub. Sch. Programs; presenter in field. Reviewer Jour. of Coll. Sci. Tchg., 2000—, Sci. and Children, faculty senate pres., 2000-01; contbr. numerous articles to profl. jours. Nem. Mountain Pointe H.S. Boosters, Phoenix, 1992-95. Named Woman of Yr., Beta Sigma Phi; Maricopa Inst. of Learning fellow, 1990; MCLI learning grantee, 2001; China faculty fellow, 2002. Mem. AAUP, Nat. Assn. for Rsch. in Sci. Tchg. (mem. equity com. 1992-95), Coll. Sci. Tchrs. Assn., Phi Kappa Phi. Home: 14653 S Foxtail Ln Phoenix AZ 85048-4355

LEARY, WILLIAM JAMES, educational administrator; b. Boston, Oct. 1, 1935; s. John Gilbert and Josephine Marie (Kelley) L.; m. Joann Linda Parodi, June 25, 1960; children: Lorraine, Lisa, Linda. S.B., Boston Coll.; M.Ed., Boston State Coll.; postgrad. (Fulbright fellow), Sophia U., Tokyo, 1967; cert. advanced study, Harvard U., 1972, Ed.D., 1973, Boston U., 1971. Tchr. pub. schs., Boston, 1960—67; chmn. dept. social studies Dorchester High Sch., Boston, 1967—68; dir. curriculum Boston Dist. Pub. Schs., 1969—72, supt. schs., 1972—75; exec. dir. Met. Planning Project, Newton, Mass., 1975—77; supt. schs. Rockville Centre, NY, 1977—82, North Babylon, NY, 1982—84, Broward County, Ft. Lauderdale, Fla., 1984—88; supt. Gloucester (Mass.) Pub. Schs., 1989—93; assoc. prof. dept. ednl. leadership, dept. chair U. Miss., Oxford, 1993—98, dir. PhD Program; prof. coll. edn. Lynn U., Boca Raton, Fla., 1998—2000. Assoc. prof. dept. continuing studies Bsoton State Coll., 1970-72; assoc. in edn. Harvard U. Grad. Sch. Edn., 1972-75; adj. prof. edn. Boston U., 1973-75, C.W. Post Ctr., L.I. U., 1979-84, Fla. Internat. U., 1984-88, Salem (Mass.) State Coll., 1990-93; prof. Suffolk U., 1977-82; TV commentator Channel 5, Boston, 1975-76; prodr. edn. programs New Eng. Cablevision, 1989-93; keynote spkr. Harvard U. Grad. Sch. Edn., 1976, NYU, 1980; mem. faculty senate U. Miss., 1994-96, chair subcom. on athletics, 1994-95. Edn. columnist Boston Herald, 1975-78, L.I. News, 1982-84, Gloucester Times; edn. commentator New Eng. Cablevision, 1989-93; contbr. articles to profl. jours. Edn. coord. Boston chpt. United Way, 1974, Rockville Centre United Fund, 1979-80, Broward County chpt., 1985-87; trustee Mus. Fin. Arts, Boston, 1972-77; bd. dirs. Boston Youth Symphony, 1972-77, Edn. Devel. Ctr., 1972-77, Broward Com. of 100, Boys Club Broward County, 1985-88; mem. nat. alumni bd. Boston U., 1975—; mem. vis. com. Suffolk U., 1978-80; adv. bd. Harvard N.Y. Alumni Forums, 1980-84; mem. L.I. Regional Planning Bd., 1983-84, Gov.'s Task Force on Alt. Edn., Fla., 1986-88; mem. Atty. Gen.'s edn. adv. com., Mass., 1991-93; lector, Eucharistic min. Ascension Cath. Ch., Boca Raton; bd. dirs., Mill Pond Homeowners Assn., Boca Raton. Recipient Friend of Youth award Hayden Goodwill Boys' Home, 1973, Ida M. Johnston Outstanding Alumni award Boston U. Sch. Edn., 1976, Man of Yr. award Pope's Hill Assn., 1976, Jenkins Meml. award for ednl. leadership N.Y. State Coun., PTA, 1980, Ednl. Leadership award L.I. chpt. NCCJ, 1980, Broward County Med. Aux., 1984, Lifetime Achievement award Matignon H.S. Alumni, 1995, Civil Rights award NAACP Layfayette County, MS, 1996; selected as mem. Exec. Educator 100, Nat. Sch. Bd. Assn., 1987; named to Matignon H.S. Hall of Fame, 1995. Mem. ASCD (nat. commn. on supervision 1984-85), Am. Assn. Sch. Adminstrs. (del. assembly 1991, 92, 93, resolutions com. 1988-89, 93-94, 94-95, 95-96), Am. Hist. Assn., Horace Mann League, Assn. for Asian Studies, Nat. Coun. Social Studies (nat. urban affairs com. 1977-80), Large City Sch. Supts., Mass. Atty. Gen.'s Adv. Group, Harvard Club N.Y.C., Boston Coll. Alumni Club, Varsity Club, KC, Rotary, Harvard Club of Boston, Harvard Club of Palm Beach, Am. Legion, Phi Delta Kappa. Roman Catholic. Office: Lynn U Grad Sch Edn Boca Raton FL 33431 E-mail: billyjoj@email.msn.com., wleary@lynn.edu.

LEASOR, JANE, religion and philosophy educator, musician; b. Portsmouth, Ohio, Aug. 10, 1922; d. Paul Raymond Leasor and Rana Kathryn (Bayer) Leasor-McDonald. BA, Wheaton Coll., 1944; MRE, N.Y. Theol. Sem., 1952; PhD, NYU, 1969. Asst. prof. Belhaven Coll., Jackson, Miss., 1952-54; dept. chmn. Beirut Coll. for Women, 1954-59; asst. to pres. Wheaton (Ill.) Coll., 1961-63; dean of women N.Y. Theol. Sem., N.Y.C., 1963-67; counselor CUNY, Bklyn., 1967-74; assoc. prof. Beirut U. Coll., 1978-80; tchr. internat. sch., Les Cayes, Haiti, 1984-85; pvt. tutor, 1985—; tchr. Fayette County (W.Va.) Schs., 1993—; prof. religion dept. U. Charleston, W.Va., 1999—. Author religious text for use in Syria and Lebanon, 1960; editor books by V.R. Edman, 1961-63, Time and Life mags. Mem. Am. Assn. Counselors, Am. Guild Organists. Episcopalian. Avocations: reading, gardening, golf, travel, history Islam religion. Home and Office: 1429 1/2 Quarrier St Charleston WV 25301-3009

LEATH, KENNETH THOMAS, research plant pathologist, educator, agricultural consultant; b. Providence, Apr. 29, 1931; s. Thomas and Elizabeth (Wooten) L.; m. Marie Andreozzi, Aug. 1955; children: Kenneth, Steven, Kevin, Maria Beth. BS, U. R.I., 1959; MS, PhD, U. Minn., 1966. Rsch. plant pathologist U.S. Regional Pasture Rsch. Lab. USDA-ARS, 1966-94; prof. Pa. State U., 1966-94; pvt. agrl. cons. Boalsburg, Pa., 1994—. Advisor numerous state and nat. orgns. Contbr. numerous articles to profl. jours. and chpts. to books. With USN, 1951-55. Mem. Elks. Achievements include research on root diseases and systemic wilts of forage species.

LEATHER, VICTORIA POTTS, college librarian; b. Chattanooga, June 12, 1947; d. James Elmer Potts and Ruby Lea (Bettis) Potts Wilmoth; m. Jack Edward Leather; children: Stephen, Sean. BA cum laude, U. Chattanooga, 1968; MSLS, U. Tenn., 1978. Libr. asst. East New Orleans Regional Libr., 1969-71; libr. Erlanger Nursing Sch., Chattanooga, 1971-75; chief libr. Erlanger Hosp., Chattanooga, 1975-77; dir. Eastgate Br. Libr., Chattanooga, 1977-81; dir. libr. svcs. Chattanooga State Tech. Community Coll., 1981-95, dean libr. svcs., 1996—. Mem. Allied Arts, Hunter Mus., High Mus. Art. Mem. ALA, Southeastern Libr. Assn., Tenn. Libr. Assn. (past chair legislation com.), Chattanooga Area Libr. Assn. (pres. 1978-79), Tenn. Bd. Regents Media Consortium (chair 1994-95), Phi Delta Kappa. Episcopalian. Avocations: reading, needlework, traveling.

LEATHERS, KATHERINE ANNE, education educator; b. Lynn, Mass., July 13, 1950; d. William Charles and Grace Rena (Hobbs) L. AA, Miami (Fla.) Dade C.C., 1970; BA in Edn., Fla. Atlantic U., 1971, postgrad., 1974; MS in Edn., U. Miami, 1980, EdD in Elem. Edn., 1987. Cert. tchr., Fla. Tchr. South Miami Heights (Fla.) Elem. Sch., 1972-83; tchr. Ctr. for the Expressive Arts South Miami (Fla.) Elem. Sch., 1986—2003, curriculum writer, summer 1986, asst. program planner and implementer, 1983-87; grad. asst. U. Miami, Coral Gables, 1983-86; asst. prin. intern Dade County Pub. Schs., Miami, 1988; adj. prof. elem. edn. Fla. Internat. U., Miami, 1993—98, 2001, St. Thomas U., Miami, 1993—98. Presenter U. Ga., Athens, 1987, Dade County Reading Conf., Miami, 1994, Fla. Reading Assn. Conf., Orlando, 1994; tchr. Tchg. with Toys, Miami, summer 1984, Mus. of Sci., Miami, summer 1984, 85. Contbr. articles to profl. jours. Mem. Granada Presbyn. Ch., Coral Gables, Fla., 1976-78, 81, Sunday sch. tchr., Bible study tchr., jr. H.S. advisor, counselor, mem. coll.-career activities com.; mem. Youth for Christ, Miami and Ft. Lauderdale, Fla., 1977, 80, 81, Christmas counselor; info. table vol. Key Biscayne (Fla.) Presbyn. Ch., 1991-92; nursery fol. Old Cutler Presbyn. Ch., 2001-03. Mem. ASCD, Internat. Reading Assn., Dade County Reading Assn., United Tchrs. Dade, Nat. Coun. Tchrs. English, Phi Delta Kappa, Alpha Delta Kappa. Presbyterian. Home: 11837 SW 99th St Miami FL 33186-8516

LEAVELL, LANDRUM PINSON, II, seminary administrator, clergyman, educator; b. Ripley, Tenn., Nov. 26, 1926; s. Leonard O. and Annie Glenn (Elias) L.; m. Jo Ann Paris, July 28, 1953; children: Landrum Pinson III, Ann Paris, Roland Q. II, David E. AB, Mercer U., 1948; BD, New Orleans Bapt. Theol. Sem., 1951, ThD, 1954; DD, MIss. Coll., 1981, Campbell U., 1989. Pastor Union Bapt. Ch., Magnolia, Miss., Crosby Bapt. Ch., Miss., First Bapt. Ch., Charleston, Miss., Gulfport, Miss., Wichita Falls, Tex., 1963-75; pres. New Orleans Bapt. Theol. Sem., 1975-95; pastor emeritus First Bapt. Ch., Wichita Falls, 1995. Author: Angels, Angels, Angels, 1973, Sermons for Celebrating, 1978, Twelve Who Followed Jesus, 1975, The Devil and His Domain, 1973, For Prodigals and Other Sinners, 1973, God's Spirit in You, 1974, The Harvest of the Spirit, 1976, John's Letters: Light for Living, 1970, Evangelism: Christ's Imperative Commission, 1979, The Doctrine of the Holy Spirit, 1983, Parting Shots, 1995. Mem. Bapt. Joint Com. Pub. Affairs, 1986-91; bd. dirs. Bapt. Cmty. Ministries, New Orleans, 1985-95-2001. Recipient George Washington Honor medal Freedoms Found., Valley Forge, Pa., 1968. Mem. New Orleans C. of C., Rotary (past pres. Paul Harris fellow). Home: 2100 Santa Fe St #601-2 Wichita Falls TX 76309-3461 E-mail: lleavellii@aol.com.

LEAVEN, GLORIOUS SHARPLESS, special education educator, reading specialist; b. Hampstead, N.C., Sept. 27, 1941; d. James Edward Sr. and Lecola (Shepard) Sharpless; div.; children: Grady Funderburk, Bryan Funderburk. BS, Winston-Salem State U., 1964. Cert. tchr., N.C. Tchr. Annandale Elem. Sch., Hampstead, 1964-68; tchr. spl. edn. Topsail High Sch., Hampstead, 1968-72; reading specialist Topsail High Sch., Topsail Mid. Sch., Hampstead, 1972—. Mem. NEA, N.C. Assn. Educators, Internat. Reading Assn. (pres. Cafe Fear coun. 1992—), N.C. Reading Assn., South Pender Alumni Assn. (sec. tng. 1991-92), Winston-Salem State U. Alumni (fin. sec. 1989-92), Olivet Social Women Club (treas. 1990-92). Democrat. Baptist. Avocations: piano, drawing, writing, storytelling, singing. Home: 336 Shepards Rd Hampstead NC 28443-2928 Office: Topsail Mid Sch 17447 Us Highway 17 N Hampstead NC 28443-7320

LEAVITT, LEWIS A. pediatrician, medical educator; b. N.Y.C., Nov. 7, 1941; s. Isidore and Sarah (Fishkowitz) L.; m. Judith E. Walzer, July 2, 1966; children: Sarah Abigail, David Isaac. BS, U. Chgo., 1961, MD, 1965. Diplomate Am. Bd. Pediat. Intern, then resident Albert Einstein Coll. Medicine, Jacobi Hosp., Bronx, N.Y., 1965-68; prof. pediat. U. Wis., Madison, 1984—; head infant devel. lab. Weisman Ctr. Mental Retardation and Human Devel., U. Wis., 1973—. Editor books on Down's syndrome and children's exposure to violence; contbr. artcles to profl. jours. Lt. comdr. USN, 1968-70. Mem. Soc. Rsch. in Child Devel., Am. Acad. Pediat. Office: U Wis 1500 Highland Ave Madison WI 53705-2274

LEAVITT, MARY JANICE DEIMEL, special education educator, civic worker; b. Washington, Aug. 21, 1924; d. Henry L. and Ruth (Grady) Deimel; m. Robert Walker Leavitt, Mar. 30, 1945; children: Michael

Deimel, Robert Walker, Caroline Ann Leavitt Snyder. BA, Am. U., 1946; postgrad., U. Md., 1963-65, U. Va., 1965-67, 72-73, 78-79, George Washington U., 1966-67. cert. spl. edn. tchr. 1968. Tchr. Rothery Sch., Arlington, Va., 1947; dir. Sunnyside Children's House, Washington, 1949; asst. dir. Coop Sch. for Handicapped Children, Arlington, 1962; dir. Arlington and Springfield, Va., 1963-66; tchr. mentally retarded children Fairfax (Va.) County Pub. Schs., 1966-68; asst. dir. Burgundy Farm Country Day Sch., Alexandria, Va., 1968-69; tchr., substitute tchr. specific learning problem children Accotink Acad., Springfield, Va., 1970-80; substitute tchr. learning disabilities Children's Achievement Ctr., McLean, Va., 1973-82, Psychiat. Inst., Washington and Rockville, Md., 1976-82, Home-Bound and Substitute Program, Fairfax, Va., 1978-84. Asst. info. splst. Ednl. Rsch. Svc., Inc., Rosslyn, Va., 1974-76; docent Sully Plantation, Fairfax County (Va.) Park Authority, 1981-87, 88-94, Children's Learning Ctrs. Vol. Honor Roll, 1987, Walney-Collections Fairfax County (Va.) Park Authority, 1989-97; sec. Widowed PersonsSvc., 1983-85, mem., 1985-90; mem. ednl. subcom. Va. Commn. Children and Youth, 1973-74; den mother Nat. Capital Area Cub Scouts, Boy Scouts Am., 1962; troop and fundraising chmn. Nat. Capitol coun. Girl Scouts U.S.A., 1968-69; capt. amblyopia team No. va. chpt. Delta Gamma Alumnae, 1969; vol. Prevention of Blindness, 1980-95; fund raiser Martha Movement, 1977-78; mem. St. John's Mus. Art, Wilmington, N.C., 1989—, Corcoran Gallery Art, Washington, 1989-90, 94—, Brunswick County Literacy Coun., N.C., 1989—; Sunday sch. tchr. St. Andrews Episcopal Ch., Burke, Va., 1995-99, mem. search com., 1996, libr. project, 1999; mem. World Affairs Coun. Washington DC, 1998—. Recipient award Nat. Assn. Retarded Citizens, 1975, Sully Recognition gift, 1989, Ten Yr. recognition pin Honor Roll, 1990. Mem. AAUW (co-chmn. met area mass media com. DC chpt. 1973-75, v.p. Alexandria br. 1974-76, fellowship co-chmn., historian Springfield-Annandale br. 1979-80, 89-94, 94-95, name grantee ednl. found., 1980, cultural co-chmn. 1983-84), Assn. Part-Time Profls. (co-chmn. Va. local groups, job devel. and membership asst. 1981), Older Women's League, Nat. Mus. Women in the Arts (charter), Libr. Congress Assocs. (nat.), Mil. Dist. Washington Officer's Clubs (McNair, Ft. Myer), Delta Gamma (treas. No. Va. alumnae chpt. 1973-75, pres. 1977-79, found. chmn. 1979-81, Katie Hale award 1989, treas. House Corp. Am. U. Beta Epsilon chpt. 1994-97). Episcopalian. Home: 7129 Rolling Forest Ave Springfield VA 22152-3622 also: 325A Brunswick Ave W Holden Beach NC 28462-1903

LEAVITT, MAURA LYNN, elementary education educator; b. Buffalo, N.Y., Mar. 7, 1946; d. Joseph Richard and Hermina (Wagner) Takats; m. Henry Clark Leavitt, Jan. 22, 1984. BA, Elmira Coll., 1968; MA, George Wash. U., 1977. Elem. tchr. Candor (N.Y.) Cen. Schs., 1968-72; ednl. dir., coord. Prelude Drug Rehab. Program, Arlington, Va., 1972-76; ednl. coord., tchr. Arlington County Jail - GED program, 1974-77, Argus House - Juv. Detention Home, Arlington, 1977; founder, dir. Ednl. Diagnostic Svcs., Arlington, 1978-81; adminstrv. asst. Caldwell, Prothro & Wilson, Arlington, 1981-84; tchr., elem. Flint Hill Prep. Sch., Oakton, Va., 1984-87; tchr., secondary history/govt. Clay/Langston Alt. Schs., Arlington, 1977-81; tchr., elem. Drew Model Sch./Alt. Sch., Arlington, 1987-91; tchr. Arlington Pub. Schs., 1991-99, fed., state and local curriculum developer, 1992-94; tchr. McKinley Elem., Arlington, 1999—. Rev. panelist NSF, 2002. Bd. dirs., v.p. No. Va. Hot Line, Arlington, 1984-86. Mem. Greater Washington Reading Coun., Va. Coun. for Social Studies (bd. dirs. 1994-96), Nat. Coun. for Social Studies. Avocations: stained glass design, travel, sports.

LEBAN, CELESTE CASDIA, elementary school educator; b. Que., Can., July 24, 1953; d. Carl Vincent and Maria del Carmen (Rodriguez) Casdia; m. Brian John Leban, Oct. 29, 1976; children: Carla Casiopia, Brianne Gem. BE, U. Miami, 1975; MS, Nova Southeastern U., 1998. Cert. elem. tchr., Fla. Tchr. 4th and 6th grades Inter Am. Mil. Acad., Miami, Fla., 1975-76; legal investigator Lloyds of Legals & Property Searchers Inc., Miami, 1977-79; tchr. 1st and 2nd grades Shady Acres Sch., North Miami, Fla., 1982-83; med. receptionist Drs. Nichols, Phillips, Elias et al, Miami, 1983-86; tchr. 1st grade Archdiocese of Miami, 1976-77, tchr. 2nd, 5th and 6th grades, 1986-89, tchr. 6th grade, 1989-90, Dade County Pub. Schs., Miami, 1990-97, tchr. 4th grade, 1997—, tchr. 4th grade alternative edn., 2002—03. Mem. adv. com., co-writer sch. improvement plan Natural Bridge Elem. Sch., North Miami, 1991—, peer tchr., 1996-97; advisor Future Educators of Am. club Natural Bridge Elem. Sch./Dade County Pub. Schs. and State of Fla., 1993—, grade level chair, 1998-99, 2000-01; participant Buddy Reading grant program Dade County Pub. Edn. Fund, 1993-94, chair testing com., 1995-96; co-chair Multicultural com., co-planner Cultural Fair, 1994—; directing tchr. for student tchrs., 1992-93, 95-96, 99—, peer tchr. for beginning tchr., 1997-98, 99-2000. Avocations: reading, photography, travel, needlework, ceramics.

LEBANO, EDOARDO ANTONIO, foreign language educator; b. Palmanova, Italy, Jan. 17, 1934; came to U.S., 1957, naturalized, 1961; s. Nicola and Flora (Puccioni) L.; m. Mary Vangell, 1957; children: Tito Nicola, Mario Antonio. Student, U. Florence, Italy, 1955; MA, Cath. U. Am., 1961, PhD, 1966. Tchr. high sch., Florence, 1955-57; Italian lang. specialist Bur. Programs and Stds., CSC, Washington, 1958; lang. instr. Sch. Langs., Fgn. Svcs. Inst., Dept. State, Washington, 1959-61; lectr. Italian, U. Va., Charlottesville, 1961-66; asst. prof. Italian, U. Wis., Milw., 1966-69, assoc. prof., assoc. chmn. dept. French and Italian, 1969-71; assoc. prof. dept. French and Italian, Ind. U., Bloomington, 1971-83, prof., 1983—2000, prof. emeritus, 2000—. Dir. Sch. Italian, Middlebury Coll., Vt., 1987-95. Author: A Look at Italy, 1976, Buon giorno a tutti, 1983, L'Insegnamento dell'italiano nei colleges e nelle universita del nordamerica, 1983; author introduction and notes to Morgante by Luigi Pulci, 1998; contbr. articles to profl. jours. Decorated cavaliere Ordine al Merito della Repubblica Italiana; recipient Uhrig award U. Wis.-Milw. faculty, 1968. Mem. MLA, AAUP, Am. Assn. Tchrs. Italian (sec.-treas. 1980-84, pres. 1984-87, Disting. Svc. award 1994), Dante Soc. Am., Renaissance Soc. Am., Boccaccio Soc. Am., Nat. Italian Am. Found., Am. Italian Hist. Assn., Am. Assn. Italian Studies, Midwest MLA. Home: 4323 Falcon Dr Bloomington IN 47403-9044 Office: Ind U Ctr for Italian Studies Bloomington IN 47405

LEBARON, JOHN FRANCIS, education educator; b. Montreal, Can., Aug. 15, 1939; came to the U.S., 1974; s. Francis Gordon and Anna Frances (Van Buskirk) LeB.; m. Faith Trumbull McClellan, Nov. 18, 1967; children: Matthew Francis, Jessie McClellan. BA, McGill U., 1963; MEd, U. Mass., 1971, EdD, 1976. Asst. prof. edn. York U., Toronto, 1973-75; dir. non-print media unit Mass. Bd. Libr. Commrs., Boston, 1975-76; dir. planning and devel. Mass. Ednl. TV, Boston, 1976-81, exec. dir. Quincy, 1981-87; assoc. prof. U. Mass., Lowell, 1987-95, prof., 1995—97, faculty chair edn., 1994—97, prof. emeritus, 1997—. Staff assoc. U. Mass. Sys. Pres., Boston, 1994. Author: Making Television, 1981; editor, author: Innovations in Distance Learning, 1991, Technology in Its Place: Successful Technology Infusion in Schools, 2001. Spl. advisor on tech. Exec. Office of Edn., Boston, 1991-93; adv. coun. mem. Mass. Corp. for Ednl. Tech., Cambridge, 1992-1997; chair parents fund Amherst (Mass.) Coll., 1993; com. mem. tech. Acton (Mass.) Pub. Schs., 1994-2000. Recipient Disting. Svc. award Amherst (Mass.) Coll., 1993, Tech. Pathfinder award Mass., 1996; Sr. Fulbright scholarship, 1998, Gulbenkian Vis. Professorship, 2001. Mem.: NEA, ASCD, Fulbright Assn., Assn. for Advancement of Computing in Edn. Avocations: volunteer civic work, photography, antiques. Home: 35 Nashoba Rd Acton MA 01720-2331 Office: Sch Edn U Mass Lowell 61 Wilder St Lowell MA 01854

LEBBY, GLORIA C. history educator; b. Orangeburg, S.C., July 12, 1956; d. Clarence Vivian and Eddie (Mitchell) L. BA, St. Augustine's Coll., 1976; MEd, S.C. State Coll., 1978; EdS, U. So. Miss., 1981; EdD, Nova Southeastern U., 1994. Cert. tchr., S.C., N.C., Miss., La. Instr. history Denmark (S.C.) Tech. Coll., 1993—. Vis. instr. history S.C. State Coll., Orangeburg, 1991—. Cert. lay speaker U. Meth. Ch., Orangeburg, S.C., 1986-93. Named Outstanding Young Woman of Am., 1982, 84. Mem. AAUW (life), ASCD, S.C. Hist. Assn., Bamberg County Mental Health Assn., Nat. Coun. for Social Studies, U. So. Miss. Alumni Assn. (life), Order of Ea. Star, Order Golden Cir., Nat. Geographic Soc., Am. Legion Aux., Delta Sigma Theta (Denmark alumnae chpt. Dedicated Svc. award 1984, 90), Phi Alpha Theta. Methodist. Avocations: traveling, reading, collecting videos, listening to music. Office: Denmark Tech Coll Dept History Denmark SC 29042

LEBLANC, JEANETTE AMY, psychotherapist, educator, writer, consultant; b. Blytheville, Ark., Mar. 31, 1968; d. Bob Gene and Joan Ann (Hall) Ash; m. Robert Louis LeBlanc, May 27, 1987. BS in Liberal Arts and Psychology, SUNY, Albany, 1989; MS in Cmty. Counseling, Ga. State U., 1991; PhD in Adminstrn. and Mgmt., Walden U., 1994. Libr. technician Civil Svc., Munich, 1988-89; crisis counselor U.S. Army Community Svc., Munich, 1988-89; adolescent counselor Bradley Ctr. Hosp., Inc., Columbus, Ga., 1990-91; group therapist children of alcoholics, 1991-92; social svcs. coord., therapist Anne Elizabeth Shepherd Home, Inc., Columbus, 1991-93; instr. Upper Iowa U., Ft. Polk, La., 1993—; cons., trainer, speaker, 1995—. Group therapist for womens group Vernon Cmty. Action Coun., Leesville, La., 1994-96. With U.S. Army, 1986-88. Mem. ACA, NAFE, Assn. for Counselor Edn. and Supr., Internat. Assn. Marriage and Family Counselors, Sierra Club, Toastmasters. Avocations: writing, travel, reading.

LEBOFF, BARBARA, educator; b. Apr. 11, 1949; Children: Darcie, Cory. MS, Fla. State U., 1977; EdD, Tex. So. U., 1994. Tchr. various schs., Houston & Tallahassee, 1977—, MacArthur Elem. Sch., Houston, 1997—, math. lead tchr., 1999—. Presenter Tex. Computer Edn. Assn., Tex., 1999-2002, Nat. Coun. Tchrs. Math., 2003, Houston ISD workshops in Math. and Tech. Author: Affirmation Journal: Positive Thinking for Beginners, 1997. Sec., membership chmn., Cypress Falls Band Boosters, Tex., 1996-98, People to People Ambassadors Tching. Standards Del. to China, 2001. Outstanding Coll. Students of Amer., 1989, Master Tchr., Gregg Elementary Sch., 1994, Nominee Tchr. of Yr., 2002-03. Avocations: writing, sewing, alternative health, photography. Home: 7519 Andiron Cir Houston TX 77041-1516

LEBOWITZ, JOEL LOUIS, mathematical physicist, educator; b. May 10, 1930; came to U.S., 1946, naturalized, 1951; m. Estelle Mandelbaum, June 21, 1953 (dec. Dec. 1996); m. Ann Keay Beneduce, June 3, 1999. BS, Bklyn. Coll., 1952; MS, Syracuse U., 1955, PhD, 1956; hon. doctorate, Ecole Poly. Federale, Lausanne, Switzerland, 1977, Clark U., 1999. NSF postdoctoral fellow Yale U., New Haven, 1956-57; mem. faculty Stevens Inst. Tech., Hoboken, N.J., 1957-59, Yeshiva U., N.Y.C., 1959-77, prof. physics, 1965-77, acting chmn. Belfer Grad. Sch. Sci., 1964-67, chmn. dept., 1967-76; George William Hill prof math. and physics, dir. Ctr. for Math. Scis., Rutgers U., New Brunswick, N.J., 1977—. Co-editor: Phase Transitions and Critical Phenomena, 1980, editor Jour. Statis. Physics, 1975—, Studies in Statis. Mechanics, 1973—, Com. Math. Physics, 1973—; contbr. articles to profl. jours. Recipient Boltzmann medal Internat. Union Pure and Applied Physics, 1992, Max Planck Rsch. award, 1993, Delmar S. Fahrney medal Franklin Inst., 1995, Henri Poincare prize Internat. Assn. of Math. Physics/Daniel Iagolnitzer Found., 2000, Vito Volterra medal Academia Nazionale dei Lincei, 2001; Guggenheim fellow, 1976-77. Fellow AAAS (Sci. Freedom and Responsibility award 1998), Am. Phys. Soc., N.Y. Acad. Scis. (pres. 1979, A. Cressy Morrison award in natural scis. 1986, Heinz R. Pagels Human Rights of Scientists award 1996); mem. NAS, AAUP, Am. Math. Soc., Phi Beta Kappa, Sigma Xi. Office: Rutgers U Ctr Math Sci Rsch 110 Frelinghuysen Rd Piscataway NJ 08854-8019 E-mail: lebowitz@sakharov.rutgers.edu.

LEBURTON, JEAN-PIERRE, electrical engineering educator; b. Liege, Belgium, Mar. 4, 1949; came to U.S., 1981; s. Edmond Jules and Charlotte (Joniaux) L.; m. Lisette Defraisne, Sept.9, 1983. Lic. in Physics, U. Liege, 1971, PhD in Physics, 1978. E.S.I.S. research assoc. U. Liege, Belgium, 1978-79; research engr. Siemens AG, Munich, Fed. Republic Germany, 1979-81; vis. asst. prof. U. Ill., Urbana-Champaign, 1981-83, asst. prof., 1983-87, assoc. prof., 1987-91, prof., 1991—. Vis. Hitachi Ltd. Quantum Materials chair U. Tokyo, 1992; invited prof. Fed. Polytechnic Inst., Lauganne, Switzerland, 2000. Contbr. articles and research papers to profl. jours. Fellow IEEE (sr. mem.), Am. Phys. Soc. (APS), Am. Assn. Advanced Sci. (AAAS), Optical Soc. Am. (OSA); mem. N.Y. Acad. Scis., Electrochem. Soc., Chevalier Dans L'ordre des Palmes Academiques. Patentee semiconductor devices with controlled negative differential resistance characteristics.

LECAPITAINE, JOHN EDWARD, counseling psychology professor, researcher, writer; b. Nov. 21, 1950; s. Vincent Bernard and Evelyn Lucille LeCapitaine; m. Jessica Dale; 1 child, Katherine Briee. BS in math. and psychology, U. Wis., 1973, MS, 1975; PhD in counseling and psychology, Boston U., 1980, PhD in Metaphysics, 2000. Diplomate forensic psychologist, psychotherapist. Counseling and sch. psychologist Martin Luther King. Jr. Ctr., Boston, 1976-78; prof. Boston U., 1980-90; rsch. cons. Dept. Mental Health, 1985-90; prof. counseling psychology U. Wis., River Falls, 1990—. Contbr. chpts. to books, poetry, fiction, chapts. and acad. articles to profl. jours. Recipient Disting. award, Ed. Jour., 1999, Disting. Author award, Schools As Devel. Clinics. Mem. APA, ACA, Inst. Noetic Scis., Internat. Biographical Inst., Nat. Assn. Sch. Psychologists, Internat. Coun. Psychologists, Assn. Play Therapy, Assn. Multicultural Counseling and Devel., Assn. Humanistic Devel. and Edn., Internat. Soc. Poets, Phi Delta Kappa. Avocations: fiction writing, poetry. Home: 731 Lumphrey Ct River Falls WI 54022-3426 Office: U Wis Grad Dept Dept Couns/Sch Psych, Web 232, 410 S 3rd St River Falls WI 54022-5013

LECHNER, JON ROBERT, nursing administrator, educator; b. Detroit, Nov. 5, 1957; s. Monroe Stanley and Helen Cecelia (Schneider) L. Cert. in practical nursing, Oakland C.C., Southfield, Mich., 1983; ADN, Mercy Coll. Detroit, 1991, BSN, 1992; MSA, Ctrl. Mich. U., 1998. Cert. EMT; RN, ANCC, Mich. Coord. emergency med. svcs., paramedic William Beaumont Hosp., Royal Oak, Mich., 1979-84, nurse, 1986—, asst. nursing mgr., 1992-97, nursing mgr., 1997—; pastoral assoc. St. Mary's Parish & Sch., Toledo, 1984-86; adj. clin. instr. Oakland C.C., Waterford, Mich., 1993—. Cert. BLS instr. Am. Heart Assn., Southfield, 1986—. Vol. Project Health-O-Rama, 1992—, Wellness Networks, Inc., 1992—; voting mem. region I State of Mich. HIV Planning & Prevention Commn., Detroit, 1994—. Mem. Am. Assembly Men Nursing, Am. Assn. Neurosci. Nurses, Acad. Med. Surg. Nurses (charter), Assn. Nurses AIDS Care, Sigma Theta Tau. Democrat. Roman Catholic. Avocations: reading, hiking, walking, cycling, theatre. Home: 28450 Universal Dr Warren MI 48092-2441 Office: William Beaumont Hosp 3601 W 13 Mile Rd Royal Oak MI 48073-6712 E-mail: jlechner@beaumont.edu.

LECLAIR, BETTY JO COGDILL, special education and early childhood educator; b. Oklahoma City, Sept. 25, 1934; d. Mark Loffett and Elma Elizabeth (Wade) Cogdill; m. Charles E. LeClair, Feb. 23, 1957 (div. 1988); children: Rebecca, Joan, Charles III, Laura, Jill. BA, Okla. Bapt. U., 1957; postgrad., Cen. State U., Edmond, Okla., 1970-71, U. S.C., 1974-95; MEd, Columbia (S.C.) Coll., 1988. Cert. elem., spl. edn. tchr., S.C. Spl. edn. tchr. Children's Opportunity Ctr., Ft. Worth, 1960-62; lang. missionary with Indians So. Bapt. Home Mission Bd., Oklahoma City, 1964-67; spl. edn. tchr. Child Study Ctr., Ft. Worth, 1968-69, Midlands Ctr., Columbia, S.C., 1970, Mill Creek Elem. Sch., Richland Dist. No. 1, Columbia, 1970-71; spl. edn. and resource tchr. Ft. Jackson (S.C.) Elem. Schs., 1971—93, first grade tchr., 1993—99, ret., 1999; supr. MAT interns U. S.C., Columbia, 1999—. Former parent advisor for children ages birth-36 months S.C. Sch. for the Deaf and Blind; former mem. Coun. for Exceptional Children, hospitality chmn. chpt. 165, 1988-89, sec., 1989-90, historian, 1990-91. Vol. Help Line of Columbia, 1993—2000; active North Trenholm Bapt. Ch., Columbia, 1970—2001; mem. Kathwood Bapt. Ch., 2001—. Avocations: quilting, sewing, baking, piano, walking. Home: 1919 Stanley St Columbia SC 29204-4332

LE CLAIR, CHARLES GEORGE, artist, retired university dean; b. Columbia, Mo., May 23, 1914; s. Carl Amie and Marie (Fess) LeC.; m. Margaret Foster, May 30, 1945 (dec. Nov. 1991). BS, MS, U. Wis., 1935; posgrad., Acad. Ranson, Paris, 1937, Columbia U., 1940-41. Instr. art U. Ala., 1935-36, asst. prof., head dept., 1937-42; asst. prof. art, head dept. Albion Coll., 1942-43; tchr. painting and design Albright Art Sch., Buffalo, 1943-46; assoc. prof., head dept. Chatham Coll., 1946-52, prof., 1952-60; dean Tyler Sch. Art, Temple U., Phila., 1960-74, dean emeritus, 1981—, prof. painting, 1974-81, chmn. painting and sculpture dept., 1979-81. Founder Tyler Sch. Art, Rome, Italy, 1966. Author: The Art of Watercolor, 1985, rev. edit., 1994, expanded edit., 1999, Color in Contemporary Painting, 1991; contbg. author: Everything You Ever Wanted to Know About Oil Painting, 1994; works exhibited at Pa. Acad. Met. Mus. Art, Carnegie Inst., Whitney Mus., Corcoran Mus., Chgo. Art Inst., Richmond Mus., Butler Mus. Art, Am. Watercolor Soc., Bklyn. Mus.; one-man shows include Carnegie Inst., 1954, Salpeter Gallery, N.Y.C., 1956, 59, 65, Rochester Inst. Tech., 1958, Phila. Art Alliance, 1962, 73, 2000, Franklin and Marshall Coll., 1969, Galleria 89, Rome, 1970, Left Bank Gallery, Wellfleet, 1983, 87, 96, Temple U., 1978, Visual Images, Wellfleet, 1978-80, Gross-McCleaf Gallery, Phila., 1979, 81, 96, 98, 2002, More Gallery Phila., 1983, 87, 89, Villanova U., 1998, Carspecken-Scott Gallery, Wilmington, Del., 1999, Susquehanna Mus. Art, Harrisburg, Pa., 2003. Named Pitts. Artist of Yr., 1957; recipient Pennell medal Pa. Acad. Fine Arts, 1965, Achievement award Am. Artist mag., 1995, Lifetime Achievement award Watercolor Honor Soc., 1997; fellow Fund for Advancement Edn. Ford Found., 1952-53. Achievements include being subject of Elizabeth Leonard's book Painting Flowers, 1986, cover story Watercolor mag., 1999. Home: 1810 Rittenhouse Sq Apt 812 Philadelphia PA 19103-5816

LECLAIR, PETER R. state agency supervisor, mental retardation services professional; b. Southbridge, Mass., Nov. 22, 1952; s. George Samuel and Elizabeth Louise (Willett) LeC. AS, Quinsigamond C.C., 1975; BS, Annhurst Coll., 1977; MA, U. Conn., 1986. Cert. tchr., Conn.; cert. Reiki practitioner. Aide Conn. State Dept. Mental Retardation, Putnam, Conn., 1976-77, instr., 1977-78, tchr., 1978-90, pupil svcs. specialist, 1990-91, coord. specialized employment program, 1991-92, coord. demonstration team Oreg. project Region 3 Willimantic, Conn., 1990-91, supr. individual supports and planning unit, cons. Region 3, 1992-96, supr. individual resources and devel. day svcs. Norwich, Conn., 1996-97; supr. individual resources and devel. team Day Svcs. Conn. State DMR Ea. Region-Dempsey Ctr., Putnam, Conn., 1997—. Cons. in field; participant Conn. State Dept. Mental Retardation Peace Corps/Romania Tng., March, 1991. Assoc. editors newsletter U. Conn., 1985-86. Foster parent Christian Children's Fund, Honduras, 1985—; chmn. memory book com. John N. Dempsey Regional Ctr. 25th Anniversary, Putnam, 1989; bd. dirs. ARC Quinebaug Valley, Putnam, 1988-90; mem. Dem. Nat. Com., 1993. Mem. Am. Assn. Mental Retardation (Conn. Tchr. of Yr. award 1986), Coun. for Exceptional Children, Amnesty Internat., JFK Libr. Found., Pi Lambda Theta. Democrat. Avocations: rock music, concert, painting, gardening, reading. Home: 131 Old Turnpike Rd Quinebaug CT 06262 Office: Conn State Ea Region Dept Mental Retardation 376 Pomfret St Dept Mental Putnam CT 06260-1834

LECLAIR, SUSAN JEAN, hematologist, clinical laboratory scientist, educator; b. New Bedford, Mass., Feb. 17, 1947; d. Joseph A. and Beatrice (Perry) L.; m. James T. Griffith; 1 child, Kimberly A. BS in Med. Tech., Stonehill Coll., 1968; MS in Med. Lab. Sci., U. Mass., Dartmouth, 1977; PhD in Clin. Hematology, Walden U., 2001. Cert. clin. lab. scientist; cert. med. technologist. Med. technologist Union Hosp., New Bedford, Mass., 1968-70; supr. hematology Morton Hosp., Taunton, Mass., 1970-72; edn. coord., program dir. Sch. Med. Tech. Miriam Hosp., Providence, 1972-79; hematology technologist R.I. Hosp., Providence, 1979-80; asst. prof. med. lab. sci. U. Mass., Dartmouth, 1980-84, assoc. prof. med. lab. sci., 1984-92, prof. med. lab. sci., 1992—. Instr. hematology courses Brown U., Providence, 1978-80; cons. bd. Div. Clin. Hematology, Charlton Meml. Hosp., St. Luke's Hosp., 1984-2000, Nemasket Group, Inc., 1984-87, Gateway Health Alliance, 1985-87, Pawtucket Meml. Hosp., 1999-2001; chair hematology/hemostasis com. Nat. Cert. Agy. for Med. Lab. Pers. Exam. Coun., 1994-98. Editor-in-chief, Clin. Lab. Sci., 2000; contbr. articles to profl. jours.; contbr. articles to jours and chpts. to books; author computer software in hematology. Reviewer Nat. Commn. Clin. Lab. Scis., 1986-89; chairperson Mass. Assn. Health Planning Agys., 1986-87; bd. dirs. Southeastern Mass. Health Planning Devel. Inc., (1975-88, numerous other offices and coms.); planning subcom. AIDS Edn. (presentor Info Series). Mem. Am. Soc. Clin. Lab. Sci. (editor clin. practice sect. CLS jour. 1996-2000, editor-in-chief CLS jour. 2001—), Am. Soc. Med. Tech. Edn. and Rsch. Fund, Inc. (chair 1983-85), Mass. Assn. for Med. Tech. (pres. 1977-78), Southeastern Mass. Soc. Med. Tech. (pres. 1975-76), Alpha Mu Tau (pres. 1993-94). Avocations: choral singing, cooking, reading. Office: U Mass Dept Med Lab Sci Dartmouth MA 02747

LECLERC, LEO GEORGE, guidance counselor; b. Central Falls, R.I., May 27, 1945; s. Joseph A. and Laura (Dube) L.; children: Peter John, Eric James, Jessica Lee. AA, Roger Williams Jr. Coll., 1966; BA, Providence Coll., 1968, MA in Guidance and Counseling, 1972; Cert. Advance Grad. Studies, Bryant Coll., 1976. Counselor Central Falls Sch. Dept., 1976—, dir. elem. guidance. Amb. Cumberland Theatrical Co., Central Falls, R.I. Sec.-treas. Central Falls Crimestoppers; com. mem. Pawtucket Starwalk of Fame; bd. dirs. Central Falls Hist. Soc., Blackstone Valley Tourism Coun., Camp Ruggles, Nat. Youth Sports Camp, R.I. divsn.; chief Explorer Program; chmn. Internat. Steamboat Muster, 1995, Stage A Mgr. of Celebrate R.I. Com., 1995; charter mem. Pawtucket Steamboat Alliance; youth chmn. of 1995 Centennial of City of Central Falls; co-founder Channel 1 Substance Prevention Agy., Central Falls Police Dept.; state chmn. Youth Squire Program, 1995-98; bd. dirs. Blackstone Valley Tourism Coun.; chmn. Channel 1 Screening Com. Mem. Elks, KC (dir. youth program and squire program), R.I. KC (comdr. color guard state marshall R.I. 4th degree). Home: 91 Chestnut St Central Falls RI 02863-2007 Office: Central Falls Sch Dept 21 Hedley Ave Central Falls RI 02863-1900

LECLERC, PAUL, library director; b. Lebanon, N.H., May 28, 1941; s. Louis and M. Juliette (Trottier) LeC; m. Judith Ginsberg, Oct. 26, 1980; 1 child, Adam Louis. BS, Coll. Holy Cross, 1963; student, U. Paris, 1963-64; MA, Columbia U., 1966, PhD with distinction, 1969; LHD (hon.), L.I. U., 1994, Coll. of the Holy Cross, 1994, Hamilton Coll., 1995, Union Coll., 1997, Hunter Coll., 1997, Fordham U., 1997, U. Paris, 2000. Assoc. prof. French Union Coll., Schenectady, 1969-79, chmn. dept. modern langs. and lit., 1972-77, chmn. humanities div., 1975-77; univ. dean for acad. affairs CUNY, 1979-84; provost and acad. v.p. Baruch Coll., CUNY, 1984-88; pres. Hunter Coll., CUNY, 1988-93; pres., CEO New York Public Library, N.Y.C., 1994—. Bd. dirs. N.Y. Alliance for Pub. Schs., N.Y.C., 1981-84, El Museo del Barrio, The Feminist Press; pres. N.Y. Tchr. Edn. Conf. Bd., Albany, N.Y., 1983-84. Author: Voltaire and Crebillon Pere, 1972, Voltaire's Rome Sauvée, 1992; co-editor: Lettres d'André Moreliet, vol. I, 1991, vol. II, 1994, vol. III, 1996; contbr. articles to profl. jours. Decorated officier Palmes Académiques, chevalier Legion of Honor (France); grantee NEH, 1971, 79, Am. Coun. Learned Socs., 1973, Ford Found., 1979. Mem. MLA, Am. Soc. for 18th Century Studies Office: NY Pub Libr Fifth Ave & 42nd St New York NY 10018

LECTKA, THOMAS, education educator; PhD, Cornell U. Prof. Chemistry John Hopkins U., 2002—. Alexander von Humboldt postdoctoral fellow U. of Heidelberg; NIH postdoctoral fellow Harvard U. Recipient Merck Faculty Develop. award, 2002, NSF career award; fellowship, John Simon Guggenheim Meml. Found., 2003, Alfred P. Sloan fellow, Camille Dreyfus Tchr. Scholar, 1999, Duponte ATE grant, grant, Am. Cancer Soc., Eli Lilly Young Faculty grant. Office: John Hopkins U Dept Chemistry Dunning Hall 302 3400 N Charles St Baltimore MD 21218

LEDBETTER, DEIDRE LEDAY, special education educator; b. New Orleans, Oct. 16, 1959; d. Felton Clark Augusta and Frances Ada (Norman) Provost; m. Robert Leday, June 8, 1975 (dec. Aug. 1976); 1 child, Demetria Marie; m. George Dallas Ledbetter, Jr., Feb. 7, 1981. B Gen. Studies in Behavioral Scis., U. Southwestern La., 1982, BA in Spl. Edn., 1993, MEd in Guidance and Counseling, 1996. Resource tchr. Iberia Parish Sch. Bd., New Iberia, La., 1982-94, link cons., 1994—. Mem. core com. Very Spl. Arts Festival, New Iberia, 1990-94. Active Coun. for Exceptional Children. Named Tchr. of Yr., Lee Street Elem. Sch., 1994. Mem. NEA, La. Assn. Educators, Iberia Assn. Educators (sec. 1989-90), Order Ea. Star, Order of Cyrene (royal Magdalene 1991—), Heroines of Jericho (vice ancient matron 1990—). Democrat. Methodist. Avocations: travel, sewing, cooking, photography. Home: 1007 Bank Ave New Iberia LA 70560-6146 Office: Iberia Parish Spl Edn Dept PO Box 200 New Iberia LA 70562-0200

LEDBETTER, SHARON FAYE WELCH, retired educational consultant; b. L.A., Jan. 14, 1941; d. James Herbert and Verdie V. (Mattox) Welch; m. Robert A. Ledbetter, Feb. 15, 1964; children: Kimberly Ann, Scott Allen. BA, U. Tex., Austin, 1963; learning disabilities cert., Southwestern U., Tex., 1974; MEd, Southwest Tex. State U., 1979, prin. cert., 1980, supt. cert., 1984. Speech pathologist Midland (Tex.) Ind. Sch. Dist., Tex., 1963, Austin (Tex.) Ind. Sch. Dist., Tex., 1964-72; speech pathologist, asst. prin. Round Rock Ind. Sch. Dist., Tex., 1972-84; prin. Hutto Ind. Sch. Dist., 1984-88; asst. dir. divsn. med. sch. edn. Tex. Edn. Agy., 1989-94. Pres. Berkman PTA, 1983-84; v.p. Round Rock Women's Club, 1977, pres., 1978-79; sponsor Jr. Woman's Club, 1980-82; vol. Round Rock Ind. Sch. Dist., 1984; mistress ceremonies Hutto Beauty Pageant, 1986-87. Recipient Meritorious Svc. award Round Rock Ind. Sch. Dist., 1984, St. Judes Children's Rsch. Hosp., 1985, Soc. Disting. Am. H.S. Students, 1984, Disting. Svc. award Tex. Edn. Agy., 1994. Mem. ASCD, Phi Delta Kappa. Home: 43 Woodland Loop Round Rock TX 78664-9776 E-mail: sledbet338@aol.com.

LEDBURY, DIANA GRETCHEN, adult education educator; b. Denver, Mar. 7, 1931; d. Francis Kenneth and Gretchen (Harry) Van Ausdall; m. Chander Parkash Lall, Dec. 26, 1953 (div. Aug. 1973); children: Anne, Neil, Kris; m. Eugene Augustus Ledbury, Sept. 13, 1976; stepchildren: Mark, Cindy, Rob. BA in Sociology, Colo. U., 1953. Instr. Home and Family Life Seattle Pub. Schs. Adult Edn., 1957-62, Seattle C.C., Seattle, 1962-69, Green River C.C., 1969-71; asst. tchr. Renton Sch. Dist., Wash., 1974-83; adult edn. instr. Mental Health Network, Renton, 1984-85; coord. Inter-Study, Renton, 1984-85, 1985-86; program dir. Crossroads Child Care, 1985-86, family svcs. coord., 1986-87; program supr. Candyland Too Child Care Ctr., 1987—, Candyland Also, 1987-90; coord. child care staff Washington Fitness Ctr., 1991-93. Mem. Renton Area Youth Svcs. Bd., Sch. and Community Drug Prevention Program, Renton dist. coun. PTA, Renton Citizen's Com. on Recreation; vol. Griffin Home for Boys; coord. Modern Dance Prodn., Carco Theater; adult leader Camp Fire Girls' Horizon Club; mem. bd. Allied Arts of Renton; mem. Bicentennial Com. for a Cultural Arts, Edn. and Recreation Ctr.; PTA rep. Dimmit Jr. High Sch.; mem. Sch. and Community Recreation Com.; founder Handicapped Helping Themselves, Mental Health Network; precinct committeeperson 11th dist. Republican party, Wash., 1976-85. Recipient Golden Acorn award Wash. State Congress PTA, Renton, 1972. Mem. AAUW (legis. chair 1983-87, mem. com. on strategic sch. policy safety in schs. 1993-94, com. on getting parents involved 1994-95, pub. policy chair AAUW 1994-96), Assn. Social and Health Services (mem. com. 1984-85). Episcopalian. Avocations: arts, culture, recreation, child and family advocate.

LEDEEN, ROBERT WAGNER, neurochemist, educator; b. Denver, Aug. 19, 1928; s. Hyman and Olga (Wagner) L.; m. Lydia Rosen Hailparn, July 2, 1982. BS, U. Calif., Berkeley, 1949; PhD, Oreg. State U., 1953. Postdoctoral fellow in chemistry U. Chgo., 1953-54; rsch. assoc. in chemistry Mt. Sinai Hosp., N.Y.C., 1956-59; rsch. fellow Albert Einstein Coll. Medicine, Bronx, NY, 1959, asst. prof., 1963-69, assoc. prof., 1969-75, prof., 1975-91; prof., dir. div. neurochemistry U. Medicine and Dentistry N.J., Newark, 1991—. Contbr. articles to profl. jours.; dep. chief editor Jour. Neurochemistry. Mem. neurol. scis. study sect. NIH; mem. study sect. Nat. Multiple Sclerosis Soc. NIH grantee, 1963—; Nat. Multiple Sclerosis Soc. grantee, 1967-74, 97-2003; recipient Humboldt prize, Javits Neurosci. Investigator award. Mem. Internat. Soc. Neurochemistry, Am. Soc. Neurochemistry, Am. Chem. Soc., Am. Soc. Biol. Chemists, N.Y. Acad. Sci. Jewish. Achievements include discoveries in the biochemistry of brain glycolipids and myelin. Home: 8 Donald Ct Wayne NJ 07470-4608 Office: U Medicine and Dentistry NJ Dept Neuroscis 185 S Orange Ave Newark NJ 07103-2757

LEDER, SANDRA JUANITA, retired elementary school educator; b. Stuttgart, Ark., Apr. 17, 1942; d. Everett Samuel and Lorene (Payer) L. BS, U. Cen. Ark., 1963; MEd, McNeese State U., 1976, EdS, 1979; PhD, Fla. State U., 1984. Cert. elem. tchr., supr., prin., aerospace edn., supr. student tchrs., La.; cert. pvt. pilot. Elem. tchr. DeWitt (Ark.) Pub. Schs., 1963-66, Gillett (Ark.) Pub. Schs., 1966-69; math. tchr. Tulsa County, Tulsa, Okla., 1970; tchr. Calcasieu Parish, Lake Charles, La., 1971-94, Episcopal Day Sch., Lake Charles, La., 1994-99; asst. prof. McNeese State U., Lake Charles, 1999—, asst. dept. head, 2003, NCATE std. II com. chair, 2002—. Condr., dir. numerous aerospace camps, 1980—2001; mem., chmn. self-study com. So. Assn. Colls. and Schs., 1985—86; guest instr. McNeese State U., Lake Charles, La., 1995, Lake Charles, 96, asst. dept. head, 2003, NCATE std. II com. chair, 2002—; chmn., judge sci. fairs; presenter, organizer tours and workshops in field. Manuscript rev. panel Sci. Scope, 1988-91, writer, 1992; TV interviews, 1991—; radio and ednl. TV appearances, Tchr. in Space applicant, 1985; contbr. Metric Curriculum Guide for La., 1978; contbr. articles to profl. jours. Vol. reader NEA; pres. Lake Charles Regional Airport Authority, 1989, 1998, 1991, 1995, 2000, v.p., 1990, 1994, 1999, sec., 1990, 1993, 2003; mem. gen. adv. coun. Sowela Tech. Inst., 1990—91; acive Mayor's Commn. for Women, 1986—91, fall conf. chmn. resource fair, 1988; founder Lake Charles Ninety-Nines, pres., 1993—2002, sec. South Ctrl. sect., 2002; pres., sec. La. Nat. Airsh Bd.1993, 1993—98; outreach com. vestry Episcopal Ch. of Good Shepherd, 1994, 2000—03; bd. mem. Lake Charles Symphony, 2000—02. Recipient S.W. Region Frank Brewer Aerospace Edn. award CAP, 1990, Excellence in Aviation Edn. Championship award S.W. region FAA, 1989, Acad. Edn. award Women's History Month, Lake Charles, Great Expectations Tchr. award Sta. KPLC-TV, 1993, Pinnacle award, 1993, NEWMAST award NASA, 1986, STEP award, 1993, Outstanding Young Astronaut Chpt. Leader award, 1993, award State of La. Blue Ribbon Commn. on Tchr. Quality, 2000; grantee Space Acad., 1988, South Ctrl. Bell, 1991, 93, Olin Corp., 1994, 95, 96, 97, 98. Mem. Nat. Sci. Tchrs. Assn., Nat. Space Soc., Nat. Coun. Accreditation Tchr. Edn. (com. chair 2003), La. Assn. Educators (del. to convs. 1977-79, 84, 86), Aircraft Owners and Pilots Assn., Delta Kappa Gamma (pres. 1992-94, legis. com. 1985-86, chair social com. 1987-89, comms. com. chair 1990, 94-95), Kappa Kappa Iota (pres. 1975, 86, 99), Phi Delta Kappa (v.p. 2002). Episcopalian. Office: McNeese State U Dept Tchr Edn PO Box 92300 Lake Charles LA 70609-0001 E-mail: sleder@mail.mcneese.edu.

LEDERBERG, JOSHUA, geneticist, educator; b. Montclair, N.J., May 23, 1925; s. Zwi Hirsch and Esther Lederberg; m. Marguerite S. Kirsch, Apr. 5, 1968; children: David Kirsch, Anne. BA, Columbia U., 1944; PhD, Yale U., 1947. With U. Wis., 1947-58; prof. genetics Sch. Medicine, Stanford (Calif.) U., 1959-78; pres. Rockefeller U., N.Y.C., 1978-90, univ. prof. Sackler Found. scholar, 1990—. Mem. adv. com. WHO, 1971; chmn. adv. bd. Ellison Med. Found., 1997—; mem. bd. sci. advisors Antigenics, N.Y.C., Pharmeonics, N.Y.C., Maxygen, Palo Alto, Calif., CombinatoRx, Boston; cons. U.S. Def. Sci. Bd., NSF, NIH, NASA, Arms Control and Disarmament Agy. Trustee Camille and Henry Dreyfus Found. With USN, 1943—45. Named Sr. Scholar, Stanford U. Ctr. Internat. Security and Arms Control, 1998; recipient Nobel prize in physiology and medicine for rsch. in genetics of bacteria, 1958, U.S. Nat. medal of sci., 1989, Alan Newell award, Assn. Computing Machinery, 1996, John Stearns award, N.Y. Acad. Medicine, 1996, Maxwell Finland award, NCIH, 1997, Morris Collen award, Am. Med. Info. Assn., 1999. Fellow: AAAS, Am. Acad. Arts and Scis., Am. Philos. Soc. (Benjamin Franklin medal 2002); mem.: NAS, N.Y. Acad. Scis. (hon. life gov.), Royal Soc. London (fgn.), Inst. Medicine (David Rall medal), Coun. Fgn. Rels. Office: Rockefeller U 1230 York Ave Stop 174 New York NY 10021-6399 E-mail: lederberg@mail.rockefeller.edu.

LEDERER, C. MICHAEL, energy researcher, academic administrator; b. Chgo., June 6, 1938; s. Philip C. Lederer and Jane (Bernheimer) Newburger; children: Laura Jane, Mark Edward; m. Christina Heather Taylor, Aug. 4, 2001. AB in Chemistry, Harvard U., 1960; PhD in Nuclear Chemistry, U. Calif., Berkeley, 1964. Head isotopes project and sr. staff scientist Lawrence Berkeley Lab., 1964-78, dir. info. and data analysis dept., 1978-80; dep. dir. U. Calif. Energy Inst., Berkeley, 1980—2001, dep. dir. emeritus, 2001—. Mem. U.S. Nat. Nuclear Data com., Washington, 1970's. Author, editor: Table of Isotopes, 6th edit., 1967, 7th edit. 1978; contbr. over 35 articles to profl. jours. Chmn. bd. Windrush Sch., El Cerrito, Calif., 1990-92. Mem. AAAS, Am. Phys. Soc., Am. Nuclear Soc., Sigma Xi. Home: 3040 Buena Vista Way Berkeley CA 94708-2020 Office: U Calif Calif Energy Inst 2510 Channing Way Berkeley CA 94720-5180 E-mail: lederer@uclink.berkeley.edu.

LEDERMAN, LEON MAX, physicist, educator; b. N.Y.C., July 15, 1922; s. Morris and Minna (Rosenberg) Lederman; m. Florence Gordon, Sept. 19, 1945; children: Rena S., Jesse A., Heidi R.; m. Ellen Carr, Sept. 17, 1981. BS, CCNY, 1943, DSc (hon.), 1980; AM, Columbia U., 1948, PhD, 1951; DSc (hon.), No. Ill. U., 1984, U. Chgo., 1985, Ill. Inst. Tech., 1987; 35 additional hon. degrees. Assoc. in physics Columbia U., N.Y.C., 1951, asst. prof., 1952—54, assoc. prof., 1954—58, prof., 1958—89, Eugene Higgins prof. physics, 1972—79; Frank L. Sulzberger prof. physics U. Chgo., 1989—92; dir. Fermi Nat. Accelerator Lab., Batavia, Ill., 1979—89, dir. emeritus, 1989—; Pritzker prof. sci. Ill. Inst. Tech., Chgo., 1992—; resident scholar Ill. Math. and Sci. Acad., 1998—. Dir. Nevis Labs., Irvington, NY, 1962—79; guest scientist Brookhaven Nat. Labs., 1955; cons. Nat. Accelerator Lab., European Orgn. for Nuc. Rsch. (CERN), 1970—; mem. high energy physics adv. panel AEC, 1966—70; mem. adv. com. to divsn. math. and phys. scis. NSF, 1970—72; sci. advisor to gov. State of Ill., 1989—93; chmn. XXIV Internat. Physics Olympiad, 1991—93; co-chair com. on capacity bldg. in sci. Internat. Sci. Unions, 1994—2001; pres. bd. sponsors Bull. Atomic Scientists, 2000—; mem. adv. com. to dean U. Chgo., 2000—; pres.'s coun. The Cooper Union, 2002—. Author: Quarks to the Cosmos, 1989, The God Particle, 1993; editor, contbr.: Portraits of Great American Scientists, 2001; editor: Science Education (NATO Sci. series), 2002; contbr. articles over 200 to profl. jours. including. Commr. White House Fellows Program, 1997—2000; Univ. Rsch. Assocs., 1967—71, 1992—; mem. sci. adv. bd. Sec. of Energy, 1991—2001; bd. dirs. Mus. Sci. and Industry, Chgo., 1989—, Weizmann Inst. Sci., Israel, 1988—. Named Hon. Prof., Beijing Normal U.; recipient Nat. medal of Sci., 1965, Townsend Harris medal, CUNY, 1973, Elliot Cresson medal, Franklin Inst., 1976, Wolf prize, 1982, Nobel prize in Physics, 1988, Enrico Fermi prize, 1992, Rosenblith lectr. in Sci. and Tech., NAS, Joseph Priestly award, Dickinson Coll., 1996, Pres.'s medal, CCNY, 1993, Heald prize, Ill. Inst. Tech., 2000, Pupin Med. award, Columbia U., 2000, Faraday award, NSTA, Discover, 2002, Dedication of Science Literacy in the 21st Century, to him and including one of his articles; fellow Guggenheim, 1958—59, Ford Found., European Ctr. for Nuc. Rsch., Geneva, 1958—59, NSF, 1967, Presdl., World Bank, 1996—99; scholar Great Minds program, Ill. Math. Sci. Acad. Fellow: AAAS (pres. 1990—91, chmn. 1991—92, Abelson award 2001), Am. Phys. Soc. (mem. coun.); mem.: IEEE, NAS (U.S., Argentina, Finland, Mex., Russia), Russian Acad. Scis. (fgn. mem.), Coun. Advancement of Sci. Writing, Tchrs. Acad. for Math. and Sci. in Chgo. (co-chmn. 1990—), Italian Phys. Soc. (hon.), Ill. Math. Sci. Acad. (founding vice chmn. 1985—98), Aspen Inst. Physics (pres. 1990—92). E-mail: Lederman@fnal.gov.

LEDIN, GEORGE, JR., computer science educator; b. Seekirchen, Austria, Jan. 28, 1946; came to U.S., 1962; naturalized, 1967; s. George Sr. and Helen (Folwarkow) L.; m. Suzánne Marie Fisher Smith Scudder, June 15, 1968; children: Kathryn E., Alexander M. BS in Engring. Math., U. Calif., Berkeley, 1967; JD, U. San Francisco, 1982. Sec., co-founder Scind Reserch and Devel. Co., Inc., San Francisco, 1966-69; info. scis. dir. Automated Health Systems, Inc., Burlingame, Calif., 1969-71; exec. v.p. More of Calif., Inc., San Francisco, 1971-73, also chmn. bd. dirs.; lectr. computer sci. and math. dept. U. San Francisco, 1968-75, chmn. dept. computer sci., 1976-83, project dir., sr. research assoc. Inst. Chem. Biology, 1973-75, asst. prof. computer sci., 1975-80, assoc. prof. computer sci., 1980-84, prof. computer sci., 1984-87. Legal cons., 1973-84; prof. computer sci. Sonoma State U., Rohnert Park, Calif., 1984—, chmn. dept. computer sci., 1994—; chmn. bd. dirs., CEO Micromental, Inc., NYC, 1985-95. Author books; contbr. articles to profl. jours. Avocations: light athletics, ping pong, baseball, tennis, golf. Office: Sonoma State U Computer Sci Dept Rohnert Park CA 94928

LEDING, ANNE DIXON, artist, educator; b. Fort Smith, Ark., Jan. 29, 1947; d. Charles Victor Dixon and Elizabeth Johanna (Mitchell) Dixon Roderick; m. Larry Joseph Peters (dec), Jan. 6, 1967; m. John Thomas Leding, June 24, 1978; children: Jonathan Brian (Peters) Leding, Caroline Kristen Leding. Student, Memphis State U., Memphis, 1964-66, Westark C.C., Fort Smith, 1976-78. Cert. custom framer. Art instr. Fort Smith (Ark.) Art Ctr., 1976; pvt. practice art instr. Fort Smith, 1977-78; classical guitar instr. Paul Mendy Guitar Studio, Fort Smith, 1978-79; framing merchandise mgr. MJDesigns, 1983-98; sr. cert. framer, framing supr. Michael Arts and Crafts, 1999—2001; cert. art instr. Robert Garden Sch. Art, 2002. Cmty. svc. classical guitar instr. Westmark C.C., 1976. One-woman shows include Ariel Gallery, Fort Smith Art Ctr., Cafe Bliss, La Cima Club; group shows include Del Mar Coll., Ariel Gallery, N.Y.C.; featured in Ency. of Living Artists in Am., 1986-87; listed in N.Y. Art Rev., S.W. Art Rev., 1990-91; critiqued in Artspeak, N.Y., 1990. Mentor Grapevine (Tex.) Mid. Sch. Recipient 1st place Fort Smith Sch. Dist., 1955; letter of recognition Seventeen Mag., 1963; hon. mention Fort Smith Art Ctr. Bicentennial, 1976, Del Mar Coll., 1985, Trinity Arts Competition, 1992, Mid Cities Fine Artists Competition, 1994. Mem. Nat. Mus. Women in the Arts, Nat. Watercolor Soc., Am. Watercolor Soc., Dallas Mus. Art, Kimbel Art Mus., Trinity Arts Guild, Ft. Smith Art Ctr., Toastmasters Internat. (advanced toastmaster bronze competant leader, v.p. pub. rels. local chpt., 1998-99, 99-2000, v.p. edn. 2002-03, pres. 2003-), Dallas/Ft. Worth Writer's Workshop. Republican. Anglican. Avocations: photography, music. Home and Office: Anne Leding Illustrations 402 Walden Trl Euless TX 76039-3870

LEDNUM, FLORENCE NASH, biological sciences educator; b. Abington, Pa., May 11, 1941; d. Charles Edgar and Jane (Gessner) N.; m. Allan Alfred Rieken, June 17, 1966 (div. Dec. 1976); children: Dawn Elizabeth, Holly Raina; m. Charles Wendell Lednum, Aug. 17, 1993. BS, Wash. Coll., 1962; MS, U. Del., 1964; EdD, U. Md., 1993. Biol. oceanographer U.S. Naval Oceanographic Office, Washington, 1964-69; anatomy, physiology and microbiology instr., recruiter Macqueen Gibbs Willis Sch. Nursing, Easton, Md., 1969-82; assoc. prof. biol. scis. WOR-WIC C.C., Salisbury, Md., 1982-92; prof. biol. scis., dept. chair Chesapeake Coll., Wye Mills, Md., 1992—, coord. sci. adv. com., 1994—. Coord., editor (cookbook) Trinity's Table, 1992-93. Recipient Excellence in Tchg. award Md. State Bd. for C.C.'s, 1990. Mem. Assn. for Advancement of County Coll. Tchg., Md. Assn. Sci. Tchrs., Soc. for Coll. Sci. Tchrs. Episcopalian. Avocations: quilting, gardening, sewing. Home: 31751 Tappers Corner Rd Cordova MD 21625-2133 Office: Chesapeake Coll PO Box 8 Wye Mills MD 21679-0008

LEDONNE, DEBORAH JANE, secondary education educator; b. Darby, Pa., Mar. 4, 1956; d. Peter Anthony and Camella Jean (Perrone) LeD. Undergrad. credits in Spanish, U. Madrid, 1977; BA in Modern Langs., BS in Edn., Villanova U., 1978; Sorbonne U. Paris, U. Paris, 1979; MA in Modern Langs., Villanova U., 1982. Tchr. French/Spanish Marple Newtown Sch. Dist., Newtown Square, Pa., 1978—. Tutor Phila. area, 1978—; sec. Faculty Adv. Coun., 1990—. Mem. Phila. Mus. Art, Annenberg Ctr. of Phila. Recipient Maria Rosa award for Excellence Am. Inst. Italian Culture, 1978; chosen to attend Nat. Debutante Ball, N.Y.C., 1974, Internat. Debutante Ball, Vienna, 1975; named a Woman of Yr. Am. Biog. Inst., 1993, one of 2,000 Notable Am. Women, 1994. Mem.: NEA, Pa. State Modern Lang. Assn., Alliance Francaise, Pa. State Edn. Assn., Kappa Delta Pi. Avocations: tennis, swimming, dancing, gourmet cooking. Office: Marple Newtown Sch Dist 120 Media Line Rd Newtown Square PA 19073-4614

LEDUC, KAREN LORAIN LEACU, elementary and middle school education educator; b. Ashland, Mass., July 30, 1956; d. John Michael and Eileen Francis (Hill) Leacu; m. Jacques V. LeDuc, Oct. 27, 1979; children: Laura Marie, Jeanne Michelle. BS in Edn., Framingham State Coll., 1978; MEd, Lesley Coll., 1995; PhD in Ednl. Studies, Lesley U., 2002. Cert. supt., elem. educator, supr., Mass. 6th grade math./reading tchr. Fuller Mid. Sch., Framingham, Mass., 1994-97; literacy specialist grades 6, 7, 8, 1997-99; mentor program facilitator, 1998-99; math curriculum coord. Framingham (Mass.) Pub. Schs., 1999—2003; asst. supt. Cirriculm, Instruction, and Assessment, Natick, Mass., 2003—. Sr. assoc. prof. Framingham State Coll., 1996—, Lesley U., 2000—; strategic planning co-leader Framingham Pub. Schs., 1996, Fuller sch. coun., 1994-98, coach Math Counts, 1995. Religious edn. tchr. St. Cecilia's Ch., Ashland, 1982-96, eucharistic minister, 1977-96. Mem. ASCD, NEA, Nat. Coun. Tchrs. English, Nat. Coun. Tchrs. Maths. Roman Catholic. Office: Walsh Middle Sch 301 Brook St Framingham MA 01701-4371 E-mail: karen_leduc@natick.kiz.ma.us.

LEDUY, ANH, engineering educator; b. Vietnam, Feb. 6, 1946; s. Thach and Tam (BuiThi) LeD.; m. Suzanne Roger, Sept. 24, 1977; children: Isabelle, Dominic. BS in Mech. Engring., U. Sherbrooke, Que., Can., 1969, MS in Chem. Engring., 1972; PhD in Biochem. Engring., U. Western Ont., Can., 1975. Registered profl. engr., Que. Research asst. CNRC Univ. Sherbrooke, Que., Can., 1975-77; asst. prof. chem. engring. Universite Laval, Sainte-Foy, Que., 1977-81, assoc. prof., 1981-85, prof., 1985—. Mem. grant selection coms.; cons. in field. Presenter symposiums, confs. Contbr. numerous articles to profl. jours. Mem. order of Engrs. of Que., N.Y. Acad. Scis. Office: Universite Laval Dept Chem Engring Sainte-Foy QC Canada G1K 7P4 E-mail: anh.leduy@gch.ulaval.ca.

LEDVOROWSKI, THOMAS EDMUND, secondary education educator; b. Milw., Feb. 11, 1960; s. Richard Joseph and Dorthy (Dymerski) L. BS in Math., Mercy Coll., Detroit, 1982; MS in Math. Edn., Purdue U., West Lafayette, Ind., 1985; postgrad., Cath. Theol. Union, Chgo., 1987-89, U. So. Calif. Grad. asst. Purdue U., West Lafayette, 1983-85; tchr. math. Roger Bacon High Sch., Cin., 1986-87; student mem. Franciscan Friars, Cin., 1987-89; tchr. math. Chino (Calif.) Unified Sch. Dist., 1985-86, 89-96, dept. chmn., 1993-96, swimming coach, 1991-93; secondary sch. math. mentor tchr., 1994-96; tchr. math. Roosevelt High Sch. N.E. Ind. Sch. Dist., San Antonio, 1996—, chmn. dept., 1999—. Reader Advanced Placement Calculus Exam., 1995, 96, 97, 98, 99, 2000. Mem. Nat. Coun. Tchrs. Math., Am. Math. Assn. Roman Catholic. Avocations: drawing, computers, swimming, photography, travel. Home: 4943 Timber Farm San Antonio TX 78250-4449 Office: T Roosevelt High Sch 5110 Walzem Rd San Antonio TX 78218-2194 E-mail: tledv004@neisd.net.

LEDWITCH, GRACE EVELYN, elementary school educator, principal; b. Crosshore, N.C., Dec. 15, 1938; m. John William Ledwitch Jr., June 11, 1960; children: lynn, Lisa, John William III. AA, Darton Coll., Albany, Ga., 1972; BA, Ga. Southwestern U., 1973, MEd, 1975; EdS. Ednl. Leadership, Albany State U., 1993. Lic. elem. tchr., Ga. Tchr. grade 3 St. Teresa Sch., Albany, 1973—78, libr. media specialist, 1974—97, tchr. grade 5, 1978—93, asst. prin., 1987—97, tchr. grade 6, 1993—97. Advisor Parent Tchr. Orgn. Bd., Albany, 1987—, St. Teresa's Sch. Bd., Albany, 1987—, Acad. Com., St. Teresa's Sch., Albany, 1987—; curriculum coord. St. Teresa's Sch., Albany, 1987—. Coord. donations neighborhood fund Am. Cancer Soc., Albany, 1990, Easter Seal, 1991-92, Am. Diabetes Assn., Albany, 1991; bd. dirs. Albany/Dougherty Cmty. Partnership for Edn., 1993—. Mem. Nat. Cath. Edn. Assn. Roman Catholic. Avocations: reading, travel, gardening, crossword puzzles, grandparenting. Office: St Teresa Sch 417 Edgewood Ln Albany GA 31707-3991

LEDYARD, JOHN ODELL, economics educator, consultant; b. Detroit, Apr. 4, 1940; s. William Hendrie and Florence (Odell) L.; m. Bonnie Higginbottom, May 23, 1970; children: Stephen, J. Henry, Meg. BA, Wabash Coll., 1963; PhD, Purdue U., 1967; PhD (hon.), Purdue U./Ind. U., 1993. Asst. prof. Carnegie-Mellon U., Pitts., 1967-70; prof. Northwestern U., Evanston, Ill., 1970-85, Calif. Inst. Tech., Pasadena, 1985—, exec. officer for social sci., 1989-92, chmn. div. humanities and social scis., 1992—2002. Contbr. articles to profl. jours. Fellow Am. Acad. Arts and Scis., Econometric Soc.; mem. Pub. Choice Soc. (pres. 1980-82), Econ. Sci. Assn. (exec. com. 1986-88). Office: Calif Inst Tech Dept HHS Pasadena CA 91125-0001

LEE, ANN MCKEIGHAN, curriculum specialist; b. Harlan, Iowa, Nov. 18, 1939; d. Earl Edward and Dorothy Elizabeth (Kaufman) McK.; m. Duane Edward Compton, Aug. 13, 1960 (div. 1985); children: Kathleen, David, Anne-Marie, John. Cert. in med. tech., Creighton U., 1960; BA in Art History, Ind. U., 1984; MA, U. South Fla., 1992, PhD, 2002. Cert. secondary tchr., Fla.; cert. med. technologist. Realtor Savage/Landrian Realty, Indpls., 1978-84; lectr. Marian Coll., Indpls., 1987-88; tchr. Sarasota (Fla.) County Schs., 1989-92, rep. faculty coun., 1991-92; lectr. curriculum & instrn. U. South Fla., 1993—2000. Vis. prof. U. South Fla., 2001—03; docent Historic Spanish Point, Osprey, Fla., 1989—93, Ringling Mus. Art, 1993—; presenter panel Bibliographic Instrn. Art History. Contbr. articles to profl. jours. V.p. fin. LWV, Indpls., 1971-73; v.p. dist. IV aux. ADA, 1976-78, comptroller, 1978-89; coord. Gold Coun. and Ambs. U. South Fla., 1990-92. Recipient Silver Svc. award Crossroads Guild, 1981. Mem.: Sarasota Arts Coun., Gulf Coast Heritage Assn. (ch-chmn. pub. rels.), Soc. Archtl. Historians (tchr. rep. 1990), Coll. Art Assn., Phi Delta Kappa, Phi Kappa Phi. Roman Catholic. Avocations: photography, tennis, landscape architecture, swimming. Home and Office: 3617 Shady Brook Ln Sarasota FL 34243-4840

LEE, ANNE, music educator; b. Taipei, Taiwan, July 19, 1951; d. William Chiang and Su-Chen Wu; married, Jan. 20, 1979; children: Joseph, Matthew. Degree, Shih Chien Univ., 1972. Tchr. Yamaha Music Found., Taipei, Taiwan, 1974—81; co-founder Polyphony Chamber Orch., Cupertino, Calif., 1998—. Music judge Taiwan TV music program, Taipei, 1978, Cupertino Sch. Dist., 1998—99. Ch. organist. Recipient 1st prize Composition, Shih Chien U., 1972. Mem.: Nat. Guild Piano Tchrs. (tchr. divsn. am. coll. musicians, Nat. Honor Roll Piano Tchr. 1999, 2000, 2001), Music Tchr. Nat. Assn., Music Tchr. Assn. Calif., Chinese Music Tchr. Assn. Calif. (music judge internat. music competition 1999, chmn. bd. dir. 1997—99, pres. 1996—97), Calif. Assn. Profl. Music Tchr. Avocations: chamber music, shopping, movies, church choir.

LEE, BARBARA ANNE, educator, lawyer; b. Newton, N.J., Apr. 9, 1949; d. Robert hanna and Keren (Dalrymple) L.; m. James Paul Begin, Aug. 14, 1982; 1 child, Robert James. BA, U. Vt., 1971; MA, Ohio State U., 1972; JD, Georgetown U., 1982; PhD, Ohio State U., 1977. Bar: N.J. 1983, U.S. Dist. Ct. N.J. 1983. Instr. Franklin U., Columbus, Ohio, 1974-75; rsch. asst. Ohio State U., Columbus, 1975-77; policy analyst U.S. Dept. Edn., Washington, 1978-80; dir. data trands Carnegie Found., Princeton, N.J., 1980-82; asst. prof. Grad. Sch. Edn. Rutgers U., Brunswick, N.J., 1982-84, asst. prof. Sch. Mgmt. and Labor Rels., 1984-88, assoc. prof., 1988-94, prof., 1994—, assoc. provost, 1995-96, dean, 2000—. Mem. Study Group on Excellence in Higher Edn., Nat. Inst. Edn., 1983-84; project dir. Carnegie Corp., N.Y.C., 1982-84. Author: Academics in Court, 1987; co-author: The Law of Higher Education, 3d edit., 1995; contbr. numerous articles to profl. jours. Corse fellow U. Vt., 1971; recipient John F. Kennedy Labor Law award Georgetown U., 1982; grantee Bur. Labor-Mgmt. Rels. and Coop. Programs, 1985-86. Mem. ABA, N.J. Bar Assn. (mem. exec. com. labor and employment law sect. 1987—, women's rights sect.), Am. Ednl. Rsch. Assn., Indsl. Rels. Rsch. Assn., Acad. Mgmt., Assn. Study Higher Edn. (legal counsel 1982-88), Nat. Assn. Coll. and Univ. Attys. (vice chair editl. bd. 1986-89, chair 1995-96, chair publs. com. 1988-91, bd. dirs. 1990-93). Office: Rutgers U Office of Dean Sch Mgmt and Labor Rels 94 Rockafeller Rd Piscataway NJ 08854-8054

LEE, BARBARA CATHERINE, career counselor; b. Augusta, Ga., Apr. 30, 1931; d. Walter Charles and Dorothy Fulgum (Sasser) L.; married, Dec. 23, 1951 (div. Feb. 1959); 1 child, William Lee Hooton. BS in Vocat. Hom Econs., Winthrop Coll., 1952; MEd, U. Ga., 1960, MS in Family and Child Devel., 1968; EdS in Counselor Edn., Ga. Southern U., 1991. Nat. bd. cert. counselor, 1994; nat. bd. cert. career counselor, 1997. Vocat. hom econs. tchr. Evans (Ga.) High Sch., 1955-56; vocat. home econs. tchr. Murphey Jr. High Sch., Augusta, Ga., 1956-63; vocat. consumer home econs. tchr. Butler High Sch., Augusta, 1963-75, Josey High Sch., Augusta, 1975-81; vocat. child devel. tchr. Hephzibah High Sch., Augusta, 1981-85; elem. and middle sch. counselor Ridge Spring-Monetta Elem. and Middle schs., 1986-87; part-time grad. rsch. asst. Ga. Southern U., Statesboro, 1990; career counselor St. John's High Sch., Charleston, S.C., 1991-96. Part-time tchr. Augusta Coll., 1972-73; part-time child devel. tchr. Augusta Tech. Sch., 1985-86; part-time edl. dir. adolescent program Human Hosp., 1988-89. Recipient Ga. Six-Yr. Study scholarhips Richmond County Bd. Edn., 1958; recipient Augusta Woman's Club scholarship, 1990. Mem. AAUW (scholarship chmn. Ga. chpt. 1983), Am. Counseling Assn., Nat. Career Devel. Assn., Ga. Career Devel. Assn., Kappa Delta Pi, Phi Upsilon Omicron, Phi Kappa Phi. Avocations: reading, swimming, painting, riding, remodeling and redecorating homes and offices occupied.

LEE, BETTY JANE, nursing educator; b. Chester, Pa., Oct. 6, 1928; d. Harvey and Elizabeth Mary (Edwards) Warner; children: Barton Warner, Barry Court (dec.), Byron Tucker. BS in Nursing, Keuka Coll., 1950; MS in Nursing, W.Va. U., 1979. Instr. Salem (W.Va.) Coll., 1973-78, Albright Coll., Reading, Pa., 1979-86, York (Pa.) Coll. Pa.; staff nurse Med. Pers. Pool, Reading, 1987-89; instr. St. Joseph Hosp., Reading, 1987-88; dir. nursing Lehigh Carbon C.C., Schnecksville, Pa., 1988-95; ret., 1995. Mem. ANA, Nat. League Nurses, Sigma Theta Tau Internat. Home: Box 153 408 Cambridge Ave Cape May Point NJ 08212

LEE, CARLTON K. K. clinical pharmacist, consultant, educator; PharmD, U. of the Pacific, 1985; MPH, Johns Hopkins U., 1994. Hosp. pharmacy resident Johns Hopkins Hosp., Balt., 1985-86, clin. staff pharmacist pediatrics dept. pharmacy, 1986-88, sr. clin. pharmacist pediatrics dept. pharmacy, 1988-90, clin. coord. pediatrics dept. pharmacy, 1990—, post doctoral fellow pharmacokinetics and pharmacodynamics Sidney Kimmel Comprehensive Cancer Ctr., 2002—03. Asst. prof. Sch. Pharmacy, Howard U., Washignton, 1987-88; clin. asst. prof. Sch. Pharmacy, U. Md., Balt., 1989-99, clin. assoc. prof., 1999—; instr. pediatrics Sch. Medicine, Johns Hopkins U., Balt., 1992-95, asst. prof., 1995—; cons. Nat. Med. Care Inc., Columbia, Md., 1994, Home Intensive Care Inc., Hunt Valley, Md., 1992-93; founder, pres. Mid-Atlantic Pediatric Pharmacotherapy Specialists, 1993—; dir. pediat. specialty pharmacy residency program Johns Hopkins Hosp., 1993—; presenter in field. Contbg. author: Harriet Lane Handbook, 1990, 93, 96, 99, 2002; investigational drug advisor Med. Sci. Bull., 1992-96; contbr. articles to profl. jours. Fellow Am. Soc. Health Systems Pharmacists; mem. Am. Coll. Clin. Pharmacy, Am. Assn. Pharmaceutical Scientists, Am. Soc. Clin. Pharm. and Therapeutics. Office: Johns Hopkins Hosp Dept Pharmacy Svcs 600 N Wolfe St Dept Pharmacy Baltimore MD 21287-0005

LEE, CATHERINE A. librarian, educator; b. Jersey City, N.J., Dec. 4, 1961; d. Peter John and Catherine (Powell) Apicella; m. Roger Alan Lee, Sept. 10, 1988. BA in English, U. South Fla., 1988, MLS, 1990; MA in English, Eastern Ky. U., 1993. Crisis counselor Alternative Human Svcs., St. Petersburg, Fla., 1985-90; libr. dir. Greenbrier C.C., Lewisburg, W.Va., 1990-91; pub. svcs. libr. Eastern Ky. U., Richmond, 1991-94; head libr. Pa. State U., DuBois, 1994—. Mem. libr. adv. bd. DuBois Bus. Coll., Pa., 1995—. Contbr. articles to profl. jours., chpts. to books; editor: Nat. Coun. Learning Resources Newsletter, 1996—. Friend DuBois Pub. Libr., 1994—. Recipient Acad. Excellence grants Pa. State DuBois Ednl. Found., 1995, 96; Continuing Edn. scholarship Pa. State Libr., 1994. Mem. AAUW (program chair 1995—, woman of yr. award 1996), ALA, Assn. Coll. & Rsch. Librs., Golden Key Nat. Honor Soc., Phi Kappa Phi (pres. eastern Ky. U. br.), Sigma Tau Delta. Republican. Office: Pa State U DuBois Campus College Pl Du Bois PA 15801

LEE, CHAN-YUN, physicist, process engineer, educator; b. Hwa-Liang, Taiwan, July 19, 1952; came to U.S., 1983; s. Hsiao-Feng and Shu-Yun (Huang) L.; m. Chia-Li Yang, Jan. 13, 1983; children: Yifan E., Ethel Y., Elias Y. BS in Physics, Soochow U., Taipei, Taiwan, 1974; MS, U. So. Calif., 1980; PhD, U. Notre Dame, 1988. Cert. assoc. prof., lectr. Dept. Edn. Asst. prof. physics Tatung Inst. Tech., Taipei, 1982-86, assoc. prof., 1986-88, chmn. physics sect., 1986-88; cons. Tatung Semiconductor Divsn., Taipei, 1985-88; dir. Tatung Natural Sci. Mus., Taipei, 1986-88; lab. instr. U. Notre Dame, Notre Dame, Ind., 1988-94; process engr. Lam Rsch. Co., Fremont, Calif., 1994-96, sr. process engr., 1996-99, mgr. metal etch key accounts, 1998-99; assoc. prof. physics San Jose City Coll., Calif., 1998-99; reginal chief process technologist Silicon Valley Group, 1999-2000; West Coast process coord., tech. staff Tokyo Electron Am., Santa Clara, Calif., 2000—. Rsch. asst. U. So. Calif., L.A., 1977-79. Contbr. numerous articles to profl. jours. 2d lt. Chinese Artillery, 1974-76. Recipient Excellent Rschrs. prize Chinese Nat. Sci. Coun., Taipei, 1986-88, Outstanding Acad. Pub. prize Hsieh-Tze Indsl. Revival Com., Taipei, 1987, 88, Sci. & Tech. Pers. Rsch. & Study award Chinese Nat. Sci. Coun., 1989. Mem. Chinese Physics Assn. Achievements include development of model of relativistic corrections to semiconducting properties of selected materials, simulated and calculated the dynamical syсceptibility of square lattice antiferromagnets; successfully developed the first large size SAC process in the world on high density plasma TCP etcher with satisfactory yields; designed and developed the single chamber dry clean process with a MW downstream and RF plate chamber for metal via applications; designed and constructed a spectrophotometer to measure the absolute photoabsorption cross section of atomic potassium in VUV region. Home: 471 Via Vera Cruz Fremont CA 94539-5325 Office: Tokyo Electron Am Inc 2953 Bunker Hill Ln Santa Clara CA 95054 E-mail: cylee9334@aol.com.

LEE, CORINNE ADAMS, retired English teacher; b. Cuba, N.Y., Mar. 18, 1910; d. Duston Emery and Florence Eugenia (Butts) Adams; m. Glenn Max Lee, Oct. 30, 1936 (dec.). BA, Alfred U., 1931. Cert. tchr. N.Y. Tchr. English Lodi (N.Y.) H.S., 1931—36, Ovid (N.Y.) Ctrl. Sch., 1936—67. Author: (light verse) A Little Leeway, 1983, (anecdotes, light verse, quips) A Little More Leeway, 1984, (essays, short stories, poems) Still More Leeway, 1986. Trustee Montour Falls Meml. Libr. Mem.: LWV, Elmira and Area Ret. Tchrs. Assn., Schuyler County Ret. Tchrs. Assn., N.Y. State Ret. Tchrs. Assn., Nat. Ret. Tchrs. Assn., PTA (life). Avocations: reading, travel, writing.

LEE, DEBORA ANN, elementary school educator, reading specialist; b. Beckley, W. Va., May 2, 1958; d. David Lavon and Edith (Graham) L. AB in Bus. Adminstrn., Beckley Coll., 1978; AB in Arts, Beckley Coll. (Coll. W. Va.), 1982; BS, Concord Coll., 1984; MA, U. W. VA., 1990. Cert. tchr. elem. edn. 1-8, reading specialist k-12, adult. Sec. United Mine Workers Assn., Mullens, W. Va., 1978; receptionist, sec. Ashland Fin., Mullens, 1978-79; tchr. Wyoming County Bd. Edn., Pineville, W. Va., 1984—. Mem. NEA, W. Va. Edn. Assn., Internat. Reading Assn., W. Va. State Reading Coun., Wyoming County Reading Coun. (charter, pres. 1990), Kappa Delta Pi. Democrat. Baptist. Avocations: reading, cooking, needlepoint, music, travel. Office: Mullens Elem Sch 300 Front St Mullens WV 25882-1304

LEE, DOUGLAS A. music educator; b. Carmel, Ind., Nov. 3, 1932; s. Ralph Henley and Flossie Ellen (Chandler) Lee; m. Beverly Ruth Haskell, Sept. 2, 1961. MusB with High Distinction, DePauw U., 1954; MusM, U. Mich., 1958, PhD, 1968; postgrad., U. Md., 1985. Instr. Nat. Mus. Camp, Interlochen, Mich., 1959-62, Mt. Union Coll., Alliance, Ohio, 1959-61, chmn. keyboard instrn., 1959-61; asst. prof. Music Wichita (Kans.) State U., 1964-68, assoc. prof., 1968-74, coord. Music History and Lit., 1968-71, coord. grad. studies in Music, 1969-70, chmn. dept. Musicology, 1971-74, prof. Music, 1974-86, administrv. intern, v.p. bus. affairs, 1983; pvt. practice event coord., 1974-85; prof. Musicology Vanderbilt U., Nashville, 1986—, chmn. Music History and Lit., advisor, 1987—98, prof. of musicology emeritus, 1998. Radio commentator Sta. KMUW-FM, 1969-76; judge various competitions, Mu Phi Epsilon, 1980, Kans. Music Tchrs. Assn., 1975-83, Baldwin Found. awards, 1979, 80; program annotator Nashville Symphony Orch., 1988-2001; cons. U.S. Dept. Edn. Jacob Javits fellowship program, 1988, 89, United Meth. Publishing Ho., 1988, Mayfield Pub. Co., 1990, Prentice-Hall, Inc., 1993, 97. Author: The Instrumental Works of Christoph Nichelmann: The Thematic Index, 1971, Franz Benda: A Thematic Catalogue of His Works, 1984, Franz Benda: A Musician at Court, 1998, Masterworks of 20th-Century Music, 2002; editor: Christoph Nichelmann: Clavier Concertos in E Major and A Minor, 1977, Six Sonatas for Violin and Bass by Franz Benda, with Embellishments, 1981; contbr. articles to The New Grove Dictionary of Music and Musicians, 1980, The New Grove Dictionary of Music in the United States, 1986; contbr. articles to profl. jours., chpts. to books. With U.S. Army, 1955-57, Japan. Rector Scholar Found., 1950-54; Rackham fellow U. Mich., 1961-65, fellow NEH, 1980, 85, Am. Philos. Soc., 1980, Kans. Arts Coun., 1985, Tenn. Arts Coun., 1988, 89, Packard Humanities Inst., Cambridge, Mass., 2002. Mem. Am. Musicological Soc. (program chmn. Midwest chpt. 1984, South-Ctrl. chpt. 1989, nat. coun. 1986, pres. South-Ctrl. chpt. 1990-91), Music Tchrs. Nat. Assn. (editor 1971-90), Am. Soc. Eighteenth Century Studies, Coll. Music Soc., Sonneck Soc. Am. Music (program coord. 1987-88, editor The Sonneck Soc. Bull. 1988-90. Episcopalian. Avocation: photography. Office: 6517 Cornwall Dr Nashville TN 37205-3041 E-mail: douglas.lee@vanderbilt.edu.

LEE, DRENNA O'REILLY, kindergarten educator; b. Advance, Mo., Apr. 22, 1948; d. Willard and Frances (Moore) Lee; m. Edward John O'Reilly, Jr., Sept. 12, 1970 (div.); children: Jennifer Anne, Heather Lee. BA in Edn., Lambuth U., 1970; MA in Edn., Southeast Mo. State U., 1984. Cert. K-9 tchr., Mo. Tchr. med.-dental assts. St. Louis Bus. Coll., 1970; tchr. Bell City (Mo.) R-2 Schs., 1971-74; tchr. 1st grade Delta (Mo.) R-5 Schs., 1974-81, tchr. kindergarten, 1981—. Adv. bd. Parents as Tchrs.; adj. faculty Coll. Edn., Southeast Mo. State U., Cape Girardeau. Active Delta R-5 PTO. Mem. Mo. State Tchrs. Assn., Community Tchrs. Assn. (sec., treas., v.p.). Office: Delta R-5 Elem Sch 3066 State Hwy N Delta MO 63744-0219

LEE, EARL WAYNE, library science educator; b. Rockford, Ill., Nov. 8, 1954; s. Earl Ray and Opal (Sharp) L.; m. Kathleen R. DeGrave, Mar. 10, 1978; children: Nathan, Cambria, Erin. BA, Lyon Coll., 1975; MA, U. Ark., Fayetteville, 1978, U. Wis., 1985. Instr. English No. Ill. U., DeKalb, 1979-80; lectr. English U. Wis., Green Bay, 1983-84; info. specialist Dept. of Transp., Madison, Wis., 1985-86; libr. Phillips U., Enid, Okla., 1986-87, Pittsburg (Kans.) State U., 1987—. Author: Drakulya, 1994, Libraries in the Age of Mediocrity, 1998, Drakulya: The Vampire Play, 2001; contbr. articles to profl. jours. Shrenk scholar U. Wis., 1985, McCain scholar Lyon Coll. Mem. ALA, Kans. Libr. Assn. Unitarian Universalist. Office: Axe Bldg Pittsburg State U Pittsburg KS 66762

LEE, ELIZABETH A. art educator; b. Joliet, Ill., Dec. 23, 1955; d. Kurt W. and Shirley R. (Wendt) Schmid; m. Robert R. Lee, June 16, 1979; children: Christiann E., Brian C. BS in Edn., Ill. State U., Normal, 1978, MS in Edn., 1993. Art tchr. K-4 N. B. Galloway Elem. Sch., Channahon (Ill.) Sch. Dist. 17, 1978—; instr. U. St. Francis, Joliet, 2002—. Founding mem. art tchr. edn. adv. bd. Ill. State U., 1994—. Lutheran. Avocations: painting, ceramics, sculpting, sewing, outdoor activities.

LEE, EVELYN MARIE, elementary and secondary education educator; b. Germantown, Ohio, Dec. 17, 1931; d. Robert Orlandus and Edna Cathern (Durr) Stump; m. John Henry Lee, Dec. 16, 1956; children: Mark Douglas, David Matthew, Lori Ann Lee Delehoy. BS in Edn., Otterbein Coll., 1954; EdM with emphasis in reading, U. Alaska, 1979. Dept. store tng. supr., asst. mdse. mgr. The Home Store, Dayton, Ohio, 1954-55; tchr. Parma Pub. Sch., Ohio, 1955-56; math aide civil svc. Nat. Adv. Com. for Aeros. Ames Lab., Moffett Field, Calif., 1956-57; substitute tchr. Warren Pub. Sch., Ohio, 1957-59, tchr., 1959-60, Gwinn Pub. Sch., Mich., 1960-64, Anchorage Sch. Dist., 1964-65, 68-87, substitute tchr., 1987-96. Hon. life mem. Alaska PTA; vol. City of Loveland, The Lincoln Ctr., Fort Collins Mem. NEA (ret.; life), NEA-Alaska (ret.; life), Alaska Hist. Soc. (life), Tulpehocken Settlement Hist. Soc., Hist. Soc. Germantown, The Alaskans, Queen Mother of the Loveland Red Hattitudes (Red Hat Soc.), Loveland New Friendship Club, Order Eastern Star. United Methodist. Avocations: travel, reading, arts and crafts, genealogy. Home: 1521 Park Dr Loveland CO 80538-4285

LEE, EVERYISCH HIENRIK, secondary and adult education educator; b. Kingston, Jamaica, Mar. 3, 1954; came to U.S., 1969; s. Ronald S. and Ruby R. (Chin) L. BS, Eastern Mich. U., 1977, MA, 1979; postgrad., U. Nev. Las Vegas, 1981-82; PhD in Edn., La Salle U., 1993. Cert. educator, Nev., Tex., La. Social worker Peace Corp, Philippines, 1980-81; tchr. reading Christ the King Sch., San Antonio, 1984-86, St. Leo Sch., New Orleans, 1986-87; tchr. ESL El Alba Sch., Comayagua, Honduras, 1987-88; tchr. reading So. Nev. Community Coll., Las Vegas, 1989-90; tchr. ESL Clark County Sch. Dist., Las Vegas, 1990—. Recipient Employee Excellent award CDE Adult Edn., 1990-91, Dedicated Community Svc. award Christ the King Sch., 1986, Outstanding Hurricane Crisis award Red Cross, 1986, Outstanding Tchr. award El Alba Sch., 1987, Appreciation award Clark County Sch. Dist. Attendance Enforcement Program, 1992, Edn. Excellence award Hot Line Electric Co., 1993, Amb. Courtesy award Las Vegas C. of C., 1993, 95, Edn. Excellence award Clark County Sch. Dist. RAVE, 1995, 96. Mem. Calif. Tchr. ESL, Tchrs. of ESL, Phi Delta Kappa. Avocations: reading, travel, dancing, gardening.

LEE, GLORIA DEANE, artist, educator; b. Council Bluffs, Iowa, Feb. 10, 1937; d. Carroll and Margaret Kathleen (Morse) Hamilton; m. Robert Dean Lee, June 29, 1962. BFA, U. Iowa, 1959; postgrad., Long Beach State U., 1964-68. Tchr. Garden Grove (Calif.) Unified Sch. Dist., 1959-64, Las Vegas (Nev.) Unified Sch. Dist., 1964, Compton Unified Sch. Dist., 1964-72, Manhattan Beach (Calif.) Unified Sch. Dist., 1984-95, L.A. Unified Adult Sch., 1993—; pvt. tutor academics and Positive Parenting, Manhattan Beach, 1978—; tutor Keys to Learning, Redondo Beach, Calif., 1984-96. Tchr. painting Beverly Hills (Calif.) Recreation, 1995-98, Palos Verdes (Calif.) rt Ctr., 1990—, El Segundo (Calif.) Recreation Sr. Ctr., 1996-98; dir. Palos Verdes (Calif.) Artists, 1985-89; mem. edn. com. Palos Verdes Art Ctr., 1986-90; represented by Artist's Studio Galleries, Palos Verdes Peninsula, 1987-99, Gail's Frames Gallery; juried assoc. Watercolor West, 1992, 96—, Women Artists of the West, 1992—, Women Painters West, 1992—, Fine Arts Inst., San Bernardino, Calif., 1995—. One woman shows at Collectors Gallery, Palos Verdes Art Ctr., 1995, Norris Theater, Rolling Hills Estates, Calif., 1995; exhibited in group shows at Malaga Cove Libr., Palos Verdes Estates, 1993, Beckstrand Gallery, Rancho Palos Verdes, 1993, 94, 95, 96, Artists' Studio, Rolling Hills Estates, 1993, 94, 96, Taos (N.Mex.) Convention Ctr., 1993, Stewart Gallery, Rancho Palos Verdes, 1993, 94, 96, 97, Petropavlovsk (Russia) Mus./Gallery, 1993, Gate Gallery, San Pedro, Calif., 1993, Palos Verdes Art Ctr., 1994, 95, 96, 97, 98, Lancaster (Calif.) Art Mus., 1994, Millennium Show, Montrose, CA, 2000, Square One Finegood Gall., West Hills, CA, Village Square Gall., Riverside (Calif.) Art Mus., 1995, 96, Long Beach (Calif.) Arts, 1995, 97, Joslyn Fine Arts Gallery, Torrance, Calif., 1995, 96, 97, 98, San Bernardino County Mus., 1996, Janet Turner Print Gallery, Chico, Calif., 1997, Brand Libr., 1997, Royal Birmingham (Eng.) Soc. Artists Gallery, 1997, Women Artists West, Biloxi, Miss., 1997, Lankersham Art Ctr. Gallery, Calif., 1997, Printmaking Coun. N.J., Cerritos Art Gallery/Cerritos Coll., Calif., 1998, Met. Life, Bridgewater, N.J., 1998, Monoprints and Books, Rancho Palos Verdes, 1998, Gallery 825, L.A., Lankersham Art Gallery, L.A., 1998, 99, NAPA 3d Ann. Exhbn., Covington, La., 1998, 99, Brand XXVIII Works on Paper, Glendale, Calif., 1998, 99, Brand XXIX Works on Paper, 1999-00, WAOW Membership Exhbn., Rancho Capistrano, Calif., 1998, 99, UCLA Med. Ctr., 1998, Lancaster (Calif.) Art Mus., 1999, Finegood Gallery, West Hills, Calif., 2000, Charles Borman Gallery, Montrose, Calif., 2000, Soleil, Manhattan Beach, 2000, others; represented in various pvt. collections; watercolors added to UCLA Med. Ctr. collection, 1998. Mem. South Bay Watercolor Soc. (bd. dirs. 1995-97, pres.), Nat. Acrylic Painters Assn., L.A. Printmaking Soc., Calif. Watercolor Assn., Pacific Art Guild (past officer), Paletteers, Women Artists of the West, Women Painters West. Avocations: singing, playing musical instruments, writing poetry, sailing, gardening. Home: 461 28th St Manhattan Beach CA 90266-2126

LEE, GREGORY PRICE, neuropsychology educator; b. Orange, N.J., July 3, 1952; s. John Landon and Olga (Squeo) Lee. BA in Psychology, U. No. Colo., 1975; MA in Clin. Psychology, Lone Mountain Coll., 1975; PhD in Clin. Psychology, Fla. Inst. Tech., 1980. Diplomate Am. Bd. Clin. Neuropsychology, Am. Bd. Profl. Psychology; lic. psychologist, Ga. Predoctoral intern Harlem Valley Psychiat. Ctr., White Plains, N.Y., 1977-78; instr. dept. psychology Coll. V.I., St. Thomas, 1981-82; rsch. assoc. Tex. Rsch. Inst. Mental Sci., Tex. Med. Ctr., Houston, 1983-84; postdoctoral fellow dept. psychology, sect. neuropsychology U. Houston, Baylor Coll. Medicine, 1983-84; postdoctoral fellow dept. neurology U. Wis. Med. Sch., Milw., 1984-86; dir. neuropsychology svc. sect. neurosurgery Dept. Psychiatry Med. Coll. Ga., Augusta, 1986—, mem. student ednl. enrichment program faculty to prof., 1987—2003, prof. dept. neurology, 2003—. Reviewer work samples Am. Bd. Clin. Neuropsychology, 1989—; cons. editor Jour. of the Internat. Neuropsychol. Soc., 1994-97, Archives of Clin Neuropsychology, 2002—; course dir. Med.Coll. Ga., Applied Pathophysiology, 2002—03, clin. rsch.I and II, 2001—03, Applied Neurosci., 2001—03. Co-author: Amobarbital Effects and Lateralized Brain Function: The Wada Test; contbr. numerous articles to profl. jours.; contbr. chpts. to books. Mem. med. adv. com. Alzheimer's Disease and Related Disorders Assn., 1986-97; bd. dirs. Red Devil, Inc., 1985-92. Fellow APA (divsn.40, membership program com., 2000—, awards com., 2000—), Nat. Acad. Neuropsychology (chair publs. com., mem.award com. 2001-04, program com., 2000-04); mem. Internat. Neuropsychol. Soc. (com. for dictionary neuropsychology 1987-98, editor neuroanatomy and neuropsychiatry sect. dictionary neuropsychology), Am. Acad. Neurology, Am. Epilepsy Soc., Sigma Xi. Office: Med Coll Ga EF 102 1120 15th St Augusta GA 30912-4010

LEE, GWENDOLIN KUEI, retired ballet educator; b. Shanghai, The People's Republic of China, Nov. 17, 1932; came to U.S., 1978; d. Din-Yuan and Ching (Chu) L.; m. C.T. Yu, May 1955 (div. 1965); children: Aldin, Marline. Diplomate, St. Mary's Hall, Shanghai, 1952; cert., Shanghai Inst. Arts, 1955. Instr. Shanghai People's Acad. Arts, 1954-56; dir. The Lee Sch. Ballet, Shanghai, 1955-66, dir., instr. Champaign, Ill., 1981-99; instr. Shanghai Gymnastic Inst., 1960-63, Shanghai Children's Palace, 1970-78, Parkland Coll., Champaign, 1979-80, McKinley YMCA, Champaign, 1979-81; ret., 1999; instr. Refinery Ballet, Champaign, Ill., 2003—. Cons. Chgo. City Ballet, 1984-85; artistic dir. Ill. Children's Expo, sponsored by Mercy Hosp., Champaign, 1986-88. Participant, Dayton Ballet, Tulsa Ballet, Cincinnati Ballet, North Carolina Ballet's Nutcracker, The Night Before Christmas; choreographer, artistic dir. numerous ballet recitals including Grandmother's Fairy Tales, 1982, An Evening of Children's Ballet, Cinderella, Faust-The Walpurgis Night Scene, 1984, Magic Key, Swan Lake Act II, 1986, Little Red Riding Hood, The Beautiful Blue Danube, 1988, Persian Market, The Dream Scene from Don Quixote, 1990, It's a Small World, The Nutcracker, 1992, An Enchanting Evening of Children's Ballet, 1994, Grandma's Golden Book, 1996, Don Quixote, 1996; photographer sch. calendars. Mem. Vintage Champaign Coun., 1983-87. Avocations: photography, opera, drama, music.

LEE, HAMILTON H. education educator; b. Zhouxian, Shandong, China, Oct. 10, 1921; s. Beiyuen and Huaiying Lee; m. Jean Chang, Aug. 14, 1945; children: Wei, Clarence, Karen, Kate. BA, Nat. Beijing Normal U., 1948; MA, U. Minn., 1958; EdD, Wayne State U., 1964. Rsch. assoc. Wayne State U., Detroit, 1958-64; asst. prof. Moorhead (Minn.) State U., 1964-65; assoc. prof. U. Wis., LaCrosse, 1965-66; prof. edn. East Stroudsburg (Pa.) U., 1966—, now prof. emeritus. Vis. prof. Seton Hall U., summer 1964; vis. scholar Harvard U., summer 1965, 66; vis. fellow Princeton U., 1976-78; hon. mem. adv. coun. Internat. Biog. Ctr., Cambridge, Eng., 1995. Author: Readings in Instructional Technology, 1970, (chapbook I) Reflection, 1989, (chapbook II) Revelation, 1991; contbg. editor Edn. Tomorrow, 1972-74; contbr. articles and poetry to profl. jours. and anthologies. Recipient numerous poetry contest awards; fellow World Lit. Acad. Mem. World Future Soc. (profl.), Acad. Am. Poets, Poetry Soc. Am., Pa. Poetry Soc., Internat. Soc. Poets (life, adv. panel), Am. Biol. Inst. (rsch. bd.), Phi Delta Kappa. Home: 2694-4 Lenox Rd Atlanta GA 30324 Address: PO Box 980 Los Altos CA 94023-0980 also: 30 Hacienda Dr Woodside CA 94062-2420

LEE, HEI WAI, finance educator, researcher; b. Hong Kong, Jan. 10, 1960; came to U.S., 1982; s. Po On and Yuk Wa (Ching) L.; m. Kamee Angela Lee, May 23, 1988; children: Jonathan Ian, Isabella Jaclyn. B in Social Sci., Chinese U. of Hong Kong, 1982; MBA, U. Okla., 1984; MS in Fin., U. Ill., Champaign, 1986; PhD in Fin., U. Ill., 1989. Cert. cash mgr., CFA. Vis. asst. prof. U. Miami, 1989-90, U. South Fla., Tampa, 1990-94; assoc. prof. corp. fin. and investments U. Mich., Dearborn, 1994—, dir. internat. programs. Contbr. articles to profl. jours. Mem. Am. Fin. Assn., Internat. Fin. Mgmt.

Assn., Assn. Investment Mgmt. and Rsch., Inst. CFAs, Midwest Fin. Assn., Ea. Fin. Assn., Investment Analysts Soc. Detroit, Beta Gamma Sigma, Phi Kappa Phi. Home: 44071 Darthmouth St Canton MI 48188-1015 Office: U Mich-Dearborn 4901 Evergreen Rd Dearborn MI 48128-2406

LEE, HON CHEUNG, physiology educator; b. Hong Kong, May 7, 1950; came to the U.S., 1967; s. Chai Chong and Yee Chin (Ng) L.; m. Miranda Wong, Aug. 1981; 1 child, Cyrus W. BA, U. Calif., Berkeley, 1971, MA, 1973, PhD, 1978; hon. degree in medicine and surgery, U. Genoa, Italy, 1997. Postdoctoral rschr. U. Calif., Berkeley, 1978-79, Stanford U., Pacific Grove, Calif., 1979-81; asst. prof. U. Minn., Mpls., 1981-86, assoc. prof., 1986-90, full prof., 1990—, Disting. McKnight univ. prof., 1996—. Mem. Reproductive Biology Study Sect., NIH, Bethesda, Md., 1993-97; chmn. Reproductive Biology Spl. Emphasis Panel, NIH, Bethesda, 1994. Contbr. articles to profl. jours. Rsch. grantee NIH, Bethesda, 1983—, 94—, NSF, Washington, 1986-89. Mem. AAAS, Am. Soc. for Cell Biology. Achievements include discovery of Cyclic ADP-ribose and NAADP, messenger molecules for regulating cellular calcium; patents for Cyclic ADP-ribose antagonists and novel caged nucleotides. Office: Univ Minn Dept Pharmacology 321 Church St SE Minneapolis MN 55455-0250 E-mail: leehc@tc.umn.edu.

LEE, HOWARD DOUGLAS, academic administrator; b. Louisville, Ky., Mar. 15, 1943; s. Howard W. and Margaret (Davidson) L.; m. Margaret Easley, Nov. 20, 1965; children: Gregory Davidson, Elizabeth Anna. BA in English, U. Richmond, 1964; ThM, Southeastern Seminary, Wake Forest, N.C., 1968; PhD in Religion, U. Iowa, Iowa City, 1971. Prof. religion, devel. dir. Va. Intermont Coll., Bristol, 1971-73; dir. univ. relations Wake Forest (N.C.) U., 1973-78; v.p. devel. Stetson U., DeLand, Fla., 1978-80, v.p. planning and devel., 1980-83, exec. v.p., 1984-86, pres.-elect, 1986-87, pres., 1987—. Contbr. articles to profl. jours. Founding dir. Atlantic Ctr. for Arts, New Smyrna Beach, Fla., 1978—; chmn. DeLand C. of C., 1994; chair Volusia Vision Com., 1994-96. Mem. So. Assn. Colls. and Schs. (exec. coun. 1993-94), Rotary, Deland Country Club, Omicron Delta Kappa. Avocations: running, golf, wood carving, woodworking/antiques, reading. Office: Stetson U Campus Box 8258 421 N Woodland Blvd Deland FL 32720-3761

LEE, HOWARD N. state senator, concessions company executive; b. July 28, 1934; m. Lillian Lee; 3 children. BA, Ft. Valley State Coll., 1959; MSW, U. N.C., 1966. Mem. faculty U. N.C., Chapel Hill; pres. Lee Airport Concessions, Raleigh, NC; mem. N.C. Senate, Raleigh, 1990—94, 1997—2003; chmn. N.C. State Bd. of Edn., Raleigh, 2003—. Chmn. appropriations on edn. and higher edn. com., edn. and higher edn. com., mem. appropriations/base budget com., fin. com., inf. tech. com., judiciary II com., vice chmn. commerce com., transp. com. Mayor, Chapel Hill, NC, 1969—75; sec. N.C. Dept. Environment and Natural Resources, 1977—81. With U.S. Army, 1959—61, with USAR, 1961—63. Democrat. also: 109 Glenview Pl Chapel Hill NC 27514-1948 also: Lee Airport Concessions Rm 406 Raleigh NC 27601 Office: NC State Bd of Edn 301 N Wilmington St 6302 Mail Svc Ctr Raleigh NC 27699-6302

LEE, ISAIAH CHONG-PIE, social worker, educator; b. Ma-kung, Taiwan, Jan. 31, 1934; s. Ju-Nie Chen and Chioh L.; m. Ho-Mei Chen, Feb. 8, 1960; children— Jense, Jenfei. Dr.P.H., UCLA, 1972. Lic. clin. social worker, family, marriage and child counselor. Dist. dir. public health social work Los Angeles County Health Dept., 1970-72; assoc. prof. social work Calif. State U., Long Beach, 1972-78, prof. social work, 1978-97, chmn. dept., 1980-86, dir. Internat. Inst. Social Work, 1982—, prof. emeritus, 1997—. Vis. prof. social work Tunghai U., Tai Chung, 1986-87; vis. prof. family medicine Kaoshiung Med. Coll., 1989, med. sociology, 1993-94; vis. prof. Nat. Pintung U. of Sci. and Tech., 1997-2000; dean Coll. Human Ecology, dir. Ctr. Gerontological Health Study, Shih-Chien U., Taipei, 2002-. Author: Medical Care in a Mexican American Community, 1972, Health Care Need of the Elderly Chinese in Los Angeles, 1979, Youth Leadership in Immigrant Communities, 1986, Yin-Yang Theory in Chinese Medicine, 1987, Selective Readings in Social Work, 1988, Community Organizing--Chinese-American Perspectives, 1992, The Proceedings of the Conference on Health and Social Policy Research at Kaohsiung Medical College, 1993, The Proceedings of the Conference on Medical Care and Welfare Policy for the Elderly at Kaohsiung Medical College, 1994, The Proceedings of the National Conference on the Medical Care and Social Policies for the Elderly, 1997, Modern Social Work, 2000, Community Development and Elderly Care, 2002. Sec. bd. dirs. Oriental Healing Arts Inst., Calif.; founder Formosan Presbyterian Ch. of Orange County, 1978; pres. bd. dirs. Formosan Presbyn. Ch. Orange County, 1978-79; chmn. Asian Presbyn. Council So. Calif., 1980-81; chmn. Internat. Task Force Nat. Comm. on Self-Devel. of People United Presbyn. Ch., 1980-84; advisor social econ. group World Coun. on Chs., Geneva, 1980-84; adv. bd. Asian Am. Community Mental Health Tng. Center, Los Angeles, 1972-77; v.p. Pacific Asian-Am. Center, Santa Ana, Calif., 1981-82, pres., 1982-84; founder Calif. Inst. of Human Care, 1988. 2d lt. Chinese Army, 1954-55. Fellow Soc. Clin. Social Work; mem. Oriental Social Health Soc. (founder, pres. 1970-72), AAUP, Council Social Work Edn., Chinese-Am. Social Workers Assn. USA, (founder, pres. 1985-88), Nat. Assn. Social Workers, Acad. Cert. Social Workers, Taiwanese-Am. Profl. Assn. USA (pres. 1993—). Democrat. Office: Calif State U Dept Social Work Long Beach CA 90840-0001

LEE, JAMES EDWARD, JR., educational consultant; b. Pitts., Mar. 9, 1939; s. Willard and Gladys Hilda (Jenkins) L.; m. Daisy Mae Tibbs, June 29, 1977; children: Stephen Michael, Monica Michelle, Brian Patrick, Priscilla Demone. BS, Wayne State U., 1962, EdS, 1969; MA, U. Mich., 1964; postgrad., Mich. State U., Wayne State U., U. Minn., U. Colo., 1964—65, Ctrl. Mich. U. Cert. tchr., adminstr., Mich. Tchr. Miller, Durfee and Michael Jr. High Schs., Detroit, 1962—67; team leader Nat. Tchr. Corps, Detroit, 1967—69; dept. head Noble Jr. High Sch., Detroit, 1969—74; asst. prin. MacKenzie High Sch., Detroit, 1974—80, Drew Mid. Sch., Detroit, 1980, prin., 1980—97, Chandler Park Acad., 1997—98; ops. supr. Detroit Mfg. Partnership, 1999—2000; exec. dir. Detroit Pub. Schs., 2000—01; prin. Rivers Mid. Sch., Charleston, SC, 2001—02, ednl. cons., 2002—. Instr. Wayne State U., Detroit, 1967-69, edn. cons., 1970-71; instr. Wayne C.C., 1967-81; prin. adult evening sch., 1974-80, summer gifted program, Detroit, 1986-92; profl. stds. commn. for sch. adminstrs. Mich. Dept. Edn., 1992-96, adminstrv. waiver com., 1992-94; mem. sch. improvement team Wayne County Regional Ednl. Svc. Agy., 1996-97. Contbg. author: The Development of Micro Teaching as an Evaluative Instrument in Teacher Training, 1969, (manual) The Principalship, 1990. Co-chair ednl. audit com. Oak Park (Mich.) Sch., 1988-90; bd. dirs. Scott Community Ctr., Detroit, 1988-97; adv. bd. Adrian/Scott program to inspire readiness for ednl. success, Detroit, 1990-97; adv. coun. Christ Child House, Detroit, 1990-92. With USMC, 1956-58. Recipient Prins. and Educators award Booker T. Washington Bus. Assn., Detroit, 1986, 90, Citation for Outstanding Leadership Detroit Bd. Edn., 1986; named finalist Boss of Yr., Detroit chpt. Am. Bus. Women's Assn., 1987. Mem. Nat. Assn. Secondary Sch. Prins., Nat. Mid. Sch. Assn., Mich. Assn. Supervision and Curriculum Devel., Mich. Assn. Secondary Sch. Prins. (exec. bd. 1986-88, Outstanding Mid. Level Prin. of Yr. 1991), Mich. Assn. Mid. Sch. Educators (bd. dirs. 1988-91). Avocation: tennis. Home: 16500 North Park Dr Apt 1117 Southfield MI 48075

LEE, JAMES JIEH, environmental educator, computer specialist; b. I-Lan, Taiwan, Aug. 27, 1939; came to U.S.A. 1968; s. Yun Ping and Lien Hwa (Kuo) L.; m. Margie J. Feng, March 31, 1965; 1 child: Jean H. BA, Taiwan Normal U., Taipei, 1962; MA, U. Minn., 1970; PhD in Environ. Scis., Greenwich U. Cert. high sch., univ. tchr., Taiwan. Tchr. I-Lan High Sch., 1962-64; instr. Ta-Tung & Taiwan Normal U., 1964-68; rsch. asst. U. Minn., Mlps., 1968-71, rsch. assoc., 1971-77; computer specialist U.S. Dept. Commerce, Silver Spring, Md., 1977-83; sr. computer system analyst U.S. Pub. Health Svc., Rockville, Md., 1983-92; planning dir. Ctr. for Taiwan Internat. Rels., Washington, 1990—; pres. World Fedn. Taiwanese Assns., 1995-99; deputy adminstr. EPA, Taiwan, 2000—. With Internat. Environ. Protection Assn., Washington, 1988-90, also bd. dirs. 1986—; bd. dirs. Asia Resource Ctr., Washington, 1993—; exec. dir. Constitution Movement for Taiwan, Washington, 1993—; chmn. Formosan Human Rights Assn. Washington chpt., 1976—. Co-author: (with others) Introduction to Human Geography, 1966, Yun-Wu Social Sci., 1971; author: Minnesota Taxing Jurisdictions, 1976, Back to Nature, 1991, Taiwan's Ecological Series, Vols. 1-4, 1995. Bd. dirs. Formosan Assn. Pub. Affairs, Washington, 1982-92. Recipient automation data processing/extramural rsch. USPHS, 1991. Mem. World Watch, Nat. Resource Def. Coun., Am. Solar Energy Soc., Union of Concerned Scientists, World Fedn. Taiwanese Assns. (pres. 1995-99), Sierra Club. Avocations: traveling, hiking. Home: 14306 Parkvale Rd Rockville MD 20853-2530

LEE, JAMES MICHAEL, religious education educator, publisher; b. Bklyn., Sept. 29, 1931; s. James and Emma (Brenner) L.; m. Marlene Mayr, Oct. 16, 1976; children: James v, Michael F.X., Patrick John. AB, St. John's U., 1955; A.M., Columbia U., 1956, Ed.D., 1958. Tchr. gen. sci. N.Y.C. secondary sch., 1955-56, chmn. sci. dept. and coordinator audio-visual aids, 1956-59, substitute tchr. adult edn., 1955-60; lectr. Hunter Coll. Grad. Sch., N.Y.C., 1959-60, Sch. Edn. Seton Hall U., South Orange, N.J., 1959; asst. prof. grad. dept. edn. St. Joseph Coll., West Hartford, Conn., 1959-62, U. Notre Dame, South Bend, Ind., 1962-65, assoc. prof., 1965-68, prof., 1968-77, chmn. dept. grad. studies in edn., 1966-71, dir. religious edn. program, 1967-77; prof. U. Ala. at Birmingham, 1977—, chmn. dept. secondary instrn. and ednl. founds., 1977-79. Lectr. Chaplain's Sch., Air U., 1985-88; subject matter expert, lectr. GS-16 Chaplain Corps, USN, 1990-91, hon. chaplain, 1991; mem. Birmingham Diocesan Bd. Edn., 1981-89; founder, pub. Religious Edn. Press, 1974—; cons. in field. Author: Principles and Methods of Secondary Education, 1963, sr. author Guidance and Counseling in Schools, Foundations and Processes, 1966, Purpose of Catholic Schooling, 1968, Shape of Religious Instruction, 1971, The Flow of Religious Instruction, 1973, Forward Together, 1973, The Content of Religious Instruction, 1985; sr. author: The Delivery of Religious Education in the Sea Services, 1991, The Sacrament of Teaching, Vol. I: Getting Ready to Enact The Sacrament, 1999; editor, contbr.: Seminary Education in a Time of Change, 1965, Readings in Guidance and Counseling, 1966, Catholic Education in the Western World, 1967, Toward a Future for Religious Education, 1970, The Religious Education We Need, 1977, The Spirituality of the Religious Educator, 1985, Handbook of Faith, 1990, Forging A Better Religious Education in the Third Millennium, 2000; corr. editor Panorama: An Internat. Jour. Religious Edn. and Values. Fulbright sr. research scholar U. Munich, 1974-75; Religious Edn. Assn. Lilly research tng. fellow, 1974-75, Fellow Soc. for Sci. Study Religion; mem. NEA, N.Am. Profs. of Christian Edn., Assn. Profs. and Rschrs. in Religious Edn. (exec. com. 1972-73, 78-80), Religious Edn. Assn. (rsch. com. 1970-76, bd. dirs. 1979-89, 1997-), K.C. (4th degree 1996). Home: 5316 Meadow Brook Rd Birmingham AL 35242-3315

LEE, JAN LOUISE, nursing educator; b. Grundy Center, Iowa, Oct. 30, 1953; d. Robert L. and B. Lucille (Frey) Thede; m. Henry M. Lee (div.). BSN, U. Iowa, 1975; MN, UCLA, 1980; PhD, U. So. Calif., 1988. Patient care coord. Queen of the Valley Hosp., West Covina, Calif., 1977-78; rsch. clin. nurse specialist Wadsworth VA Med. Ctr., L.A., 1980-83; asst. prof. nursing U. So. Calif., L.A., 1983-88, UCLA, 1988-95; dir. undergrad. and non-traditional programs U. Mich. Sch. Nursing, Ann Arbor, 1995—2003; prof., assoc. dean U. Tenn. Coll. Nursing, Knoxville, 2003—. Mem. ANCC Commn. on Cert. Contbr. articles to profl. jours. Grantee NIH, U. So. Calif., UCLA, others. Mem. Mich. Nurses Assn., Sigma Theta Tau (past chpt. pres.). Home: 9746 Dawn Chase Way Knoxville TN 37931 Office: U Tenn Knoxville Coll Nursing 1200 Volunteer Blvd Knoxville TN 37996-4180

LEE, JENNIFER MORITA, secondary school educator; b. Fairfield, Calif., Aug. 30, 1949; d. Harry Hideo and Takako M.; children: Jessica Mayumi, Jordan Minoru. BA, UCLA, 1971. Tchr. L.A. Unified Sch. Dist., 1973—. Mentor tchr., facilitator Nat. Bd. Cert.; lectr. UCLA. Vol. Boy Scouts Am., Hacienda Heights, Calif., 1987-91, Girl Scouts U.S., Hacienda Heights, 1989-91. Grant Ahmanson Found. Mem. United Tchrs. L.A., So. Calif. Paleontol. Soc. (sec.). Democrat. Avocations: archaeology, anthropology, antiques. Office: 725 S Indiana St Los Angeles CA 90023-1840

LEE, JOAN ROBERTA, elementary education educator; b. Everett, Mass., Dec. 3, 1939; d. Clifford Waldo and Harriet Alice (Goodridge) Mattsen;m. Robert Edward Lee, Nov. 3, 1962; children: Laura, Scott, Julie. BS in Edn., Bridgewater State U., 1962; MEd in Reading and Language, U. Lowell, 1989. Cert. cons. tchr. of reading, Mass. Tchr. elem. Chelmsford (Mass.) Pub. Schs., 1962-64, Tyngsboro (Mass.) Pub. Schs., 1979-98, reading specialist, 1990-98, Title I dir., 1992-98; retired, 1998. Tchr. rep., reading, writing and acad. coms., Tyngsboro, 1987—, chmn. reading com., 1992—; co-chairperson MA curriculum Frameworks-English-Lang. Study Group, Tyngsboro, 1995-96. Leader Girl Scouts U.S., Chelmsford, 1971-79, Boy Scouts Am., 1973-75; tchr. liaison Parent Vol. Orgn., Tyngsboro, 1988—; Sunday Sch. tchr., Chelmsford, 1970-79; tchr. pub. libr. story hours, Chelmsford, 1973-75. Mem. ASCD, NEA, Internat. Reading Assn., Mass. Reading Assn., Mass. Tchrs. Assn., Merrimack Valley Reading Assn. Avocations: traveling, needlework, crafts, reading. Home: 5 Draycoach Dr Chelmsford MA 01824-1003 Office: Pub Sch 135 Coburn Rd Tyngsboro MA 01879-1703 E-mail: Joanrlee@worldnet.att.net.

LEE, JOHN LAWRENCE, JR., educational administrator; b. Pitts., Oct. 4, 1956; s. John Lawrence Sr. and Helen Marie (Kenny) L. BS in Edn., Duquesne U., 1978, MS in Edn., 1982; prin. cert., Indiana U. of Pa., 1989. Cert. reading specialist, elem. prin. Tchr. Assumption Sch., Pitts., Avonworth Sch. Dist., Pitts.; tchr. grade 5 Seneca Valley Sch. Dist., Mars, Pa.; prin. Southmoreland Sch. Dist., Alverton, Pa. Mem. ASCD, NAESP, Pa. ASCD, Pa. Assn. Elem. Sch. Prins. Office: Scottdale Elem Sch 421 N Chestnut St Scottdale PA 15683-1058 Home: 121 N Mulberry Dr Mount Pleasant PA 15666-3401

LEE, JOHN THOMAS, finance educator, financial planner; b. Cleve., May 31, 1942; s. Harry C. and Lucille B. (Varnell) L.; m. Treasa (Susie) Leming, Dec. 28, 1996; children: Andrea, Joanne. BS in Econs., Tenn. Tech U., 1964; MS in Fin., U. Tenn., 1966; PhD in Fin., U. Ga., 1977. CFP. Instr. fin. Tenn. Tech U., Cookeville, 1966-71, asst. prof., 1973-78, assoc. prof., 1978-84; prof. fin. Mid. Tenn. State U., Murfreesboro, 1984—, Weatherford prof. fin., 1984-91, chmn. dept. econs. and fin., 1991—. Mem. faculty 5th Ann. Cash Mgmt. Inst. Nat. Forum, 1984, Grad. Sch. Banking of South, La. State U., 1986, 88, 89, Tenn. Bankers Sch., Vanderbilt U., 1985; spkr., discussant, moderator, presenter numerous profl. orgns. Contbr. numerous articles to profl. jours. Recipient Outstanding Faculty award Tenn. Tech. U. Coll. Bus. Found.; named Prof. of Yr. Coll. of Bus. Mid. Tenn. State U., 1988, 91; Ayers fellow ABA Stonier Grad. Sch. Banking, summer 1987. Mem. Financial Planning Assn. (Mid. Tenn. chpt. pres., 2001), Internat. Assn. Fin. Planning (pres. greater Tenn. chpt. 1995-96, bd. dirs. 1997-99), Fin. Mgmt. Assn., So. Fin. Assn., Ea. Fin. Assn., Midwest Fin. Assn., Southwestern Fin. Assn., Mid-South Acad. Econs. and Fin. (2d v.p. 1990-91, 1st v.p. 1991-92, pres. 1993-94), Mid. Tenn. Chpt. FPA (bd. dirs. 1996-99, pres. 2001), Civitan (pres. Cookeville 1983-84, Stones River 1990-91, lt. gov. Valley dist. 1984-85, 88-89, 89-90, 94-95), Beta Gamma Sigma (pres. Mid. Tenn. State U. chpt. 1986-87, 92-94), Omicron Delta Epsilon, Sigma Iota Epsilon, Alpha Kappa Psi, Phi Delta Theta. Baptist. Office: Mid Tenn State U E Main St Murfreesboro TN 37132-0001 Home: 2114 Creekwalk Dr Murfreesboro TN 37130-1803

LEE, JOLI FAY EATON, elementary education educator; b. Holdredge, Nebr., Sept. 24, 1951; d. Ray Lee and Lois Illeen (Willoughby) Larkins; m. James Edward Eaton, Aug. 16, 1969 (div. Jan. 1979); children: Threva, James, Beth; m. Chris Lee, Aug. 13, 1991; stepchildren: Michael Lee, Robyn Lee. BS in Elem. Edn., N.Mex. State U., Las Cruces, 1980, MA in Curriculum and Instruction, 1984. Cert. elem. tchr., N.Mex. Tchr. elem. Alamogordo (N.Mex.) Pub. Schs., 1980—. Co-chmn. City Elem. Sci. Fair, Alamogordo, 1989-90, chmn., 1990-92; with Summer Sci. Pilot Program, 1992-94. Contbr. articles to profl. jours. Nat. conv. co-chmn. Nat. Speleological Soc., Tularosa, N.Mex., 1986; joint venturer Cave Rsch. Found., 1983—; person. dir., Guadalupe Area Cave Rsch. Found., N.Mex., 1987-90; del. Cave Exploration Del. to People's Republic of China, 1993. Crimson scholar N.Mex. State U., 1980. Mem. NEA, Nat. Speleological Soc. (sec. Southwestern region 1984, 91-92, 93, Southwestern regional chmn. 1985-86). Republican. Episcopalian. Home: 1405 Saint Frances Dr Tularosa NM 88352-2003 Office: North Elem Sch 1300 Florida Alamogordo NM 88310

LEE, JOSEPH KING TAK, radiologist, medical educator; b. Shanghai, Mar. 17, 1947; came to U.S., 1968; s. S.Y. (Zee) Lee; m. Christina Y.M. Tsai, June 2, 1973; children: Alexander, Betsy, Catherine. BSc, Chinese U. of Hong Kong, 1968; MD, Washington U., St. Louis, 1973. Diplomate Am. Bd. Radiology. Intern Washington U. Sch. Medicine, St. Louis, 1973-74, resident, 1974-77, instr. radiology, 1977-78, asst. prof. radiology, 1978-82, assoc. prof. radiology, 1982-86, prof. radiology, 1986-91; prof. radiology, chair dept. radiology U. N.C., Chapel Hill, 1991—. Editor Topics in MRI, 1988-96. Author, editor: Computed Body Tomography, 1983, Computed Body Tomography with MRI Correlation, 1989, Pocket Atlas of Normal CT Anatomy, 1984, Manual of Clinical Magnetic Resonance Imaging, 1985, Computed Body Tomography with MRI Correlation, 3rd edit., 1998; asst. editor Am. Jour. Roentgenology. Fellow Am. Coll. Radiology; mem. Am. Roentgen Ray Soc. (mem. exec. coun. 1998—, sec., mem. exec. com. 2003—), Soc. Uroradiology (bd. dirs. 1988-90), Soc. Computed Body Tomography/MR (pres. 1993-94), Soc. of Chairmen of Acad. Radiology (exec. coun. 1997—, pres.-elect 1998, pres. 1999-2000), Radiology Soc. N.Am. Protestant. Office: Univ North Carolina Cb 7510 Chapel Hill NC 27599-0001

LEE, KANG-WON WAYNE, engineer, educator; b. Seoul, Nov. 15, 1947; came to U.S., 1976; s. Chong-Keuk and Jung-Ki (Baik) L.; m. Jee-Bock Hong, July 21, 1979; children: J. Stephen, J. Harold, Grace E. BS, Seoul Nat. U., 1974; MS, Rutgers U., 1978; PhD, U. Tex., Austin, 1982. Civil engr. Lyon Assocs., Inc., Seoul, 1974-76; structural engr. TAMS-Engrs. and Architects, Seoul, 1976; hwy. constrn. inspector N.J. Dept. Transp., East Brunswick, N.J., 1978; rsch. engring. asst. U. Tex., Austin, 1978-82; asst. prof. King Saud U., Riyadh, Saudi Arabia, 1982-85; from asst. prof. to prof. dept. civil engring. U. R.I., Kingston, 1985—. Vis. rsch. assoc. U. Calif., Berkeley, 1991; vis. prof. Seoul Nat. U., 1991, Korean Advanced Inst. of Sci. and Tech., Daejon, 1992; engring. cons. Lee Engring., Kingston, 1987—; dir. grad. studies, dept. civil engring., U. R.I., Kingston, 1996-99, dir. Transp. Rsch. Ctr., 1992—; mem. adv. com. New Eng. Transp. Consortium, Rocky Hill, Conn., 1986—; mem. policy com. Region I Univ. Transp. Ctr., Cambridge, Mass., 1988—; mem. R.I. Transp. Joint Rsch. Coun., Providence, 1994—, NSF Proposal Rev. Panel, 2002--. Contbr. articles to profl. jours. including ASCE Jour. Transp. Engrs., ASCE Jour. of Materials in Civil Engring., Transp. Rsch. Record, ITE Jour., ASTM spl. publ., several others. Recipient Program Devel. award U. R.I., 1987, Murphy Award for faculty excellence, 1990, Meritorious Svc. award RIDOT, 1996, Murphy Rsch. award, 1999. Mem. ASCE (chmn. bituminous materials com. and mem. pavement com.), ASTM, Transp. Rsch. Bd., Assn. of Asphalt Paving Technologists, Inst. Transp. Engrs., Chi Epsilon. Mem. United Ch. of Christ. Achievements include teaching and research in areas of pavement and transportation engineering. Office: U RI Dept Civil Engring Kingston RI 02881

LEE, KENNETH, secondary education educator; Tchr. Highlands Intermediate Sch., Pearl City, Hawaii, 1986—. Recipient Tchr. Excellence award Internat. Tech. Edn. Assn., Hawaii, 1992. Office: Highlands Intermediate Sch 1460 Hoolaulea St Pearl City HI 96782-2198

LEE, KENNETH STUART, neurosurgeon, educator; b. Raleigh, N.C., July 23, 1955; s. Kenneth Lloyd and Myrtie Lee (Turner) L.; m. Cynthia Jane Anderson, May 23, 1981; children: Robert Alexander, Evan Anderson. BA, Wake Forest U., 1977; MD, East Carolina U., 1981. Diplomate Nat. Bd. Med. Examiners, Am. Bd. Neurol. Surgeons; med. lic. N.C., Ariz. Intern, then resident in neurosurgery Wake Forest U. Med. Ctr., Winston-Salem, N.C., 1981-88; fellow Barrow Neurol. Inst., Phoenix, 1988-89; clin. asst. prof. neurosurgery East Carolina U., Greenville, NC, 1989-93, clin. assoc. prof. neurosurgery, 1994—2001, clin. prof. neurosurgery, 2001—, adj. assoc. prof. health edn., 1997—. Assoc. editor Current Surgery, 1990—; contbr. 30 articles to profl. jours. and 5 chpts. to books. Mem. Ethicon Neurosurgical Adv. Panel, 1989-95. Bucy fellow, 1988. Fellow ACS, Am. Heart Assn. (stroke coun.); mem. AMA, N.C. Med. Soc., Am. Assn. Neurol. Surgeons, Am. Soc. Stereotactic and Functional Neurosurgery, So. Med. Assn., Congress Neurol Surgeons, N.C. Neurosurg. Soc. (sec.-treas. 1991-93, pres. 1994-95), So. Neurosurg. Soc., Alpha Omega Alpha. Republican. Baptist. Achievements include research on the efficacy of certain surgical procedures, particularly carotid endarterectomy, in the prevention of strokes. Home: 792 Lexington Dr Greenville NC 27834 Office: Ea Carolina Neurosurg 2325 Stantonsburg Rd Greenville NC 27834-7534

LEE, KEUN SOK, business educator, consultant; b. Pusan, Korea, May 12, 1954; came to the U.S., 1981; s. Namho and Okki (Ryo) L.; m. Youn Bin Lee, Apr. 15, 1980; children: Grace, Danny. BA, Hankuk U. of Fgn. Studies, Seoul, 1979; MBA, U. No. Iowa, 1983; DBA, U. Ky., 1987; postgrad., Columbia U. Rsch. cons. U. No. Iowa, Cedar Falls, 1982-83; rsch. asst. U. Ky., Lexington, 1983-84, tchg. asst., 1984-85; instr. Hofstra U., Hempstead, N.Y., 1986-87, asst. prof., 1987-93, assoc. prof., 1998—. Author numerous publs. in mktg. jours. and confs. Recipient best article award Mu Kappa Tau, 1989, Acad. Mktg. Sci., 1991, best paper award AMS, 1991. Mem. Acad. Mktg. Svc., Am. Mktg. Assn. (assoc.). Avocation: tae kwon do (2d degree black belt). Home: 1503 John St Fort Lee NJ 07024-2560 Office: Hofstra U 141 Weller Hall Hempstead NY 11550

LEE, KYO RAK, radiology educator; b. Seoul, Korea, Aug. 3, 1933; s. Ke Chong and Ok Hi (Um) L.; came to U.S., 1964, naturalized, 1976; MD, Seoul Nat. U., 1959; m. Ke Sook Oh, July 22, 1964; children: Andrew, John. Intern, Franklin Sq. Hosp., Balt., 1964-65; resident U. Mo. Med. Center, Columbia, Mo., 1965-68; instr. dept. radiology U. Mo., Columbia, 1968-69, asst. prof., 1969-71; asst. prof. dept. radiology U. Kans., Kansas City, 1971-76, assoc. prof., 1976-81, prof., 1981—. Served with Republic of Korea Army, 1950-52. Diplomate Am. Bd. Radiology (cert. added qualification in pediat. radiology). Recipient Richard H. Marshak award Am. Coll. Gastroenterology, 1975. Fellow Am. Coll. Radiology; mem. Radiol. Soc. N.Am., Am. Roentgen Ray Soc., Assn. Univ. Radiologists, Kans. Radiol. Soc., Greater Kansas City Radiol. Soc., Wyandotte County Med. Soc., Korean Radiol. Soc. N.Am., Soc. Pediat. Radiology. Contbr. articles to med. jours. E-mail: klee@kumc.edu. Home: 9800 Glenwood St Shawnee Mission KS 66212-1536 Office: U Kans 39th St and Rainbow Blvd Kansas City KS 66103 E-mail: klee@kumc.edu.

LEE, LELA A. dermatology educator, researcher; b. Gorman, Tex., Sept. 7, 1950; d. J.H. and Pauline (Lemaster) L.; m. Norman Erling Wikner, June 24, 1984. BA, Rice U., 1972; MD, Southwestern Med. Sch., Dallas, 1976. Diplomate Am. Bd. Internal Medicine, Am. Bd. Dermatology. Resident in medicine Temple U. Hosp., Phila., 1976-79; resident in dermatology U. Colo., Denver, 1980-83, immunodermatology fellow, 1983-85, asst. prof.

dermatology and medicine, 1985-91; staff physician V.A. Hosp., Denver, 1985-91; prof. dermatology U. Okla. Sch. of Medicine, 1991-97; chief dermatology Denver Health Med. Ctr., 1997—. Mem. test com. Am. Bd. Dermatology, 1993-97, dir., 2001—; prof. dermatology and medicine U. Colo. Sch. Medicine, 1997—; vis. lectr. Kyoto U., 1991, Keio U. Sch. Medicine, Tokyo, 1991, Tyndale lectr. U. Utah, 1994; mem. adv. bd. Neonatal Lupus Nat. Registry, N.Y.C., 1995—; dir. Am. Bd. Dermatology, Neonatal Lupus Internat. Symposium, Aspen, Colo., 1996. Contbr. articles to med. jours.; chief assoc. editor: Jour. Investigative Dermatology, 1990-92. Mem. adv. com. Lupus Found. Colo., Denver, 1999—2002. Recipient Stelwagon award Coll. Physicians of Phila., 1983, Clin. Investigator award NIH, 1985-90; VA merit rev. grantee, 1991-97; fellow Exec. Leadership in Acad. Medicine, Phila., 2000-01; Bill Reed Traveling fellow Friends of Bill Reed Com., 1984; named Carl Herzog Prof. of Dermatology, 1991. Fellow: Am. Acad. Dermatology; mem.: Am. Bd. Dermatology (bd. dirs. 2001—), Colo. Dermatol. Soc., Am. Dermatol. Assn., Soc. Investigative Dermatology (bd. dirs. 1985—87), Med. Dermatology Soc. (pres. 1998—99), Southwestern Med. Sch. Alumni Assn., Assn. Rice Alumni. Avocations: puzzles, music, hiking. Office: U Colorado Sch Medicine Box B-153 Dermatology 4200 E 9th Ave Denver CO 80220-3706

LEE, NANCY T. human services administrator, educator; b. Washington, May 19, 1939; d. Robert D. and Marie (Burden) Thompson; m. Orlando W. E. Lee, July 7, 1967; children: Anthony Lester, William Edward. Diploma, Bellevue Sch. Nursing, N.Y.C., 1962; BS summa cum laude, Bowie State U., 1988; MA, Marymount U., 1991; MA in Religious Studies, Howard U., 1999, postgrad., 2002—. Cert. gerontol. nursing; ordained deacon African Meth. Episcopal Ch., 2002. Sch. nurse HHS, Washington; dir. clin. svcs. Staff Builders Temp. Svcs., Washington; instr. U. DC, Washington; dir. staff devel. Washington Home, Washington; dir. nursing Health Care Inst., Washington; instr. Prince George's CC, Alzheimer's Assn. Instr. divsn. nursing Howard U., Washington, chapel asst. advisor Andrew Rankin Meml. Chapel; cons. in field; clin. educator II Vis. Nurses Assn., Hyattesville, Md. Mem. task force nurse asst. competency exam. Ednl. Testing Svc. Fellow Diversity fellow, Nat. Interfaith Coun. on Aging, 2002—. Mem.: Alzheimer's Assn. (bd. dirs. local chpt.), LPN Assn., Nat. Gerontol. Nurses Assn., DC Nursing Assn., Nat. Black Nurses Assn., Nat. Nurses Staff Devel. Assn., Sigma Theta Tau, Delta Epsilon Sigma.

LEE, PATRICIA TAYLOR, pianist, music educator; b. Portland, Oreg., Aug. 22, 1936; d. James Russell and Helen A. (Sherman) Taylor; m. Richard Diebold Lee, June 17, 1957; children: Elizabeth, Deborah, David. BA, Mills Coll., 1957; MA, Yale U., 1959; D in Mus. Arts, Temple U., 1979. Instr. piano U. Calif., Davis, 1969-75; prof. music West Chester (Pa.) U., 1978-88, dean grad. studies, 1984-85, dean of faculty of profl. studies, 1986-87, assoc. v.p. acad. affairs, 1987-88; prof. music San Francisco State U., 1988—, chair dept. music, 1988—2002. Pianist Sacramento Symphony, 1963-75. Contbr. articles to Clavier mag., 1981-87, Am. Music Tchr., 1996; pianist (rec.) Stanley Weiner Trio for Violin, Clarinet and Piano, 1975. V.p. Sacramento Regional Arts Coun., 1969-71; pres. Sacramento Symphony League, 1952-54; trustee Mills Coll., 1990-96, Women's Philharm., San Francisco Community Music Ctr., Irving Klein Internat. String Competition, San Francisco Performing Arts Libr. and Mus., 1999-2003, San Francisco Friends of Chamber Music, 1999—, Ross McKee Found.; judge Gina Bachauer Internat. Piano Competition. Mem. Music Tchrs. Nat. Assn. (master tchr.), Nat. Assn. Sch. Music (mem. commn. accreditation 1998-), Coll. Music Soc., Calif. Assn. Profl. Music Tchrs., Mills Coll. Alumnae Assn. (exec. com., bd. govs.), Sacramento Symphony Assn. (sec. 1962-67), Phi Beta Kappa, Sigma Alpha Iota. Democrat. Episcopalian. Home: 2001 Sacramento St # 4 San Francisco CA 94109-3342 Office: San Francisco State U Sch Music and Dance 1600 Holloway Ave San Francisco CA 94132-1722

LEE, PHILIP RANDOLPH RANDOLPH, medical educator; b. San Francisco, Apr. 17, 1924; 5 children. AB, Stanford U., 1945, MD, 1948; MS, U. Minn., 1956; DSc (hon.), MacMurray Coll., 1967; PhD (hon.), Ben Gurion U., Israel, 1995, St. George U., 1998. Diplomate Am. Bd. Internal Medicine. Asst. prof. clin. phys. medicine and rehab. NYU, 1955—56; clin. instr. medicine Stanford (Calif.) U., 1956—59, asst. clin. prof., 1959—67; asst. sec. health and sci. affairs Dept. HEW, Washington, 1965—69; chancellor U. Calif., San Francisco, 1969—72, prof. social medicine, 1969—93. dir. inst. health policy studies, 1972—93; asst. sec. U.S. Dept. HHS, Washington, D.C., 1993-97; prof. emeritus, sr. advisor Inst. Health Policy, San Francisco, 1997—; cons. prof. human biology program Stanford U., 1997—. Mem. dept. internal medicine Palo Alto Med. Clinic, Calif., 1956—65; cons. bur. pub. health svc. USPHS, 1958—63, adv. com., 1978, 1978, nat. commn. smoking & pub. policy, 1977—78; dir. health svc. office tech. cooperation & rsch. AID, 1963—65; dep. asst. sec. health & sci. affairs HEW, 1965, mem. nat. coun. health planning & devel., 1978—80; co-dir. inst. health & aging, sch. nursing U. Calif., San Diego, 1980—93; pres. bd. dirs. World Inst. Disability, 1984—93; mem. population com Nat. Rsch. Coun.- Nat. Acad. Sci., 1983—86; mem. adv. bd. Scripps Clinic & Rsch. Found., 1980—86. Author (or coauthor): 15 books; contbr. more than 100 articles to profl. jours. Chmn. bd. trustees Jenifer Altman Found., 1992—93; trustee Kaiser Family Found., 1991—93, Mayo Found., 1971—75, Carnegie Fedn., 1971—79. Recipient Hugo Schaefer medal, medal Am. Pharm. Assn., 1976. Mem.: APHA, ACP, AMA, AAAS, Inst. Medicine-Nat. Acad. Sci., Assn. Am. Med. Colls., Am. Geriatric Soc., Am. Fedn. Clin. Rsch., Alpha Omega Alpha. Achievements include research in arthritis and rheumatism, especially Rubella arthritis; cardiovascular rehabilitation; academic medical administration; health policy. Home: 101 Alma St mt 805 Palo Alto CA 94301 Office: U Calif Inst Health Policy Studies 3333 California St Ste 265 San Francisco CA 94143-0001

LEE, ROLAND ROBERT, radiologist, educator; b. Cleve., July 18, 1954; s. Chia Huan and Ellen Lee. BS in Physics, Calif. Inst. Tech., 1975; MA in Physics, U. Calif., Berkeley, 1977; MD, UCLA, 1985. Diplomate Am. Bd. Radiology (added qualifications in neuroradiology). Physicist Lawrence Livermore Nat. Lab., Livermore, Calif., 1975-77; intern Harbor-UCLA Med. Ctr., Torrance, Calif., 1985-86; resident in radiology Brigham & Women's Hosp.-Harvard U., Boston, 1986-90; fellow MRI Meml. Magnetic Resonance Ctr., Long Beach, Calif., 1990-91; fellow neuroradiology U. Calif., San Francisco, 1991-92; asst. prof. radiology Johns Hopkins Hosp., Balt., 1992-97; assoc. prof. radiology U. N.Mex. and VA Med. Ctr., Albuquerque, 1997—2003; prof. radiology U. N.Mex., 2003—, dir. magnetic source imaging, 1997—. Cons. radiology, neuroradiology, and magnetic source imaging, functional neuroimaging Balt., 1992-97, Albuquerque, 1997—. Author, editor: Spinal Imaging, 1995; co-author: Spinal Cord Medicine: Principles and Practice, 2003; contbr. articles to profl. jours. Mem. AMA, Am. Soc. Neuroradiology (sr.), Am. Coll. Radiology, Radiolog. Soc. N.Am. Avocations: tennis, classical music. Office: Dept Radiology U NMex Sch Medicine Albuquerque NM 87131-0001 E-mail: rrlee@unm.edu.

LEE, RONALD DEMOS, demographer, economist, educator; b. Sept. 5, 1941; s. Otis Hamilton and Dorothy (Demetracopoulou) L.; m. Melissa Lee Nelken, July 6, 1968; children: Sophia, Isabel, Rebecca. BA, Reed Coll., 1963; MA, U. Calif., Berkeley, 1967; PhD, Harvard U., 1971. Postdoctoral fellow Nat. Demographic Inst., Paris, 1970-71; asst. prof. to prof. U. Mich., Ann Arbor, 1971-79; prof. demography and econs. U. Calif., Berkeley, 1979—. Dir. Berkeley Ctr. on Econs. and Demography of Aging; chair com. on population, NAS, 1993-97; cons. in field. Author, editor: Econometric Studies of Topics in Demographic History, 1978, Population Patterns in the Past, 1977, Population, Food, and Rural Development, 1988, Economics of Changing Age Distributions in Developed Countries, 1988, others; editor: Population Change in Asia: Transition, Development, and Aging, 2000, Demographic Change and Fiscal Policy, 2000, United States Fertility: New Patterns, New Theories, 1996; contbr. over 150 articles to profl. jours. Peace Corps. vol., Ethiopia, 1963-65. Recipient Mindel C. Sheps award Population Assn. of Am. and U. N.C. Sch. Pub. Health, 1984, MERIT award Nat. Inst. Aging, 1994-03, Taeuber award Population Assn. of Am. and Princeton U., 1999; NIH fellow, 1965-67; NSF fellow, 1968-69, fellow Social Sci. Rsch. Council, 1970-71; NIH grantee, 1973—; Guggenheim fellow, 1984-85. Fellow Brit. Acad. (corr.); mem. NAS, Population Assn. Am. (pres. 1987), Am. Econ. Assn., Internat. Union Sci. Study of Population. Democrat. Home: 2933 Russell St Berkeley CA 94705-2333 Office: U Calif Dept Demography 2232 Piedmont Ave Berkeley CA 94720-2120 E-mail: rlee@demog.berkeley.edu.

LEE, SUSAN JOYE, minister, educator; b. Pensacola, Fla., Apr. 2, 1947; Lifetime provisional tchg. cert. K-8, Tex., cert. K-12 in guidance and counseling; lic. profl. counselor. BA in Edn., Baylor U., 1968; MRE, Southwestern Bapt. Theol. Sem., 1978; MEd in Guidance and Counseling, S.W. Tex. State U., 1998. Cert. tchr. Tchr. Spring Br. Ind. Sch. Dist., Houston, 1968-71; curriculum developer West Meml. Bapt. Ch., Houston, 1970; spl. edn. min. Tallowood Bapt. Ch., Houston, 1971-74; leadership trainer Minn.-Wis. Baptist Ch., Rochester, Minn., 1979-84; dir., counselor Christian Lifestyle Counseling, Pewaukee, Wis., 1979-85; min. to mid. schs. Westburg Bapt. Ch., Houston, 1985-87; presch.-children's-women's min. Harpeth Heights Bapt. Ch., Nashville, 1987-92; presch.-children cons., curriculum writer Bapt. Sunday Sch. Bd., Nashville, 1992-96; tchr. T.H. Johnson Elem. Taylor (Tex.) Ind. Sch. Dist., 1996—. Vol. New Hope FBC, Cedar Park, Austin Health Svcs.; friend Cedar Park Libr. Named Southwesterner of Yr., Southwestern Bapt. Theol. Sem., 1982. Mem. ACA, Nat. Assn. for Edn. of Young Child, Tenn. Assn. for Young Child, Tex. Counseling Assn., Tex. Marriage and Family Counselors, Tex. Assn. Play Therapists, Christian Counselors of Tex., Christian Women's Club (Nashville bd. dirs. 1991-92). Avocations: camping, painting. Home: 1239 Lacey Oak Loop Round Rock TX 78681-2184

LEE, THOMAS LINDSEY, JR., business educator; b. Vicksburg, Miss., Feb. 18, 1947; s. Thomas Lindsey Sr. and Annetta A. (Allen) L.; m. Loraine Hintson Lee, Aug. 4, 1968; Thomas Howard, Lurlinda Wray Lee Soignier, guardian to Lurline M. Lawrence, Alisha E. Lawrence. BS, U. Southern Miss., 1969. Lic. vocat. teacher Miss. Asst. pers. dir. Miss. Industry for the Blind, Jackson, 1969-70, Marathon Letourneau Corp., Vicksburg, 1970-76; diversified occupations coord. Hinds Community Coll., Vicksburg, 1976--. Advisor Vocat. Indsl. Clubs, Vicksburg, 1976-94; cons. Delmar Pub. Co., Vicksburg, 1989-90; bd. dirs. Vocat. Indsl. Clubs Am. Supt. Sunday sch. Redwood (Miss.) Meth. Ch., 1987-92; mem. Miss. Farm Bur., 1972-92, Redwood PTO, 1975-92, Warren Cmty. Property Owners, 1985-92. Named Outstanding Secondary Tchr., Hinds Coll., 1991, Outstanding Vica Advisor, State Miss., 1991, Macvet Outstanding Tchr. of Yr., 1993-94. Mem. Miss. Assn. Vocat. Educators (2d v.p. 1990, v.p. 1991, pres. 1992, bd. dirs. and exec. bd. 1993-94, outstanding svc. award), Miss. Assn. Coop. Vocat. Edn. Tchrs. (2d v.p. 1991, v.p. 1992, pres. 1993), Hinds C.C. Edn. Assn. (pres. 1993), Am. Vocat. Assn., Vocat. and Indsl. Clubs Am. Republican. Methodist. Avocations: hunting, fishing, farming, football, baseball. Home: 10550 Highway 3 Redwood MS 39156-9771 Office: Hinds CC 755 Highway 27 Vicksburg MS 39180-8615

LEE, TSOUNG-CHAO, education educator; b. Taipei, Taiwan, Oct. 25, 1935; came to U.S., 1963; s. Chiou-Chin and Yu-Ing (Chen) L.; m. Chung-lien Shih, Jan. 25, 1964; children: Tony Jay, Jean May. BS, Nat. Taiwan U., 1958; MS, U. Ill., 1965, PhD, 1967. Teaching asst. Nat. Taiwan U., 1960-63; rsch. asst. U. Ill., Urbana-Champaign, 1963-65, Wright fellow, 1965-67; vis. scholar U. Wis., Madison, 1966; asst. prof. U. Conn., Storrs, 1967-71, assoc. prof., 1971-75, prof., 1975—2003, prof. emeritus, 2003—. Rsch. scientist U. Ga., Athens, 1977-78; vis. prof. Nat. Taiwan U., 1989; vis. rsch. full prof. Nat. Sci. Coun., Taipei, 1989. Author: Estimating the Parameters of the Markov Probability Model from Aggregate Time Series Data, 1970, 2d edit., 1977, Theory and Practice of Econometrics, 1980, 2d edit., 1985, Introduction to the Theory and Practice of Econometrics, 1982, 2d edit., 1988; reviewer articles for profl. jours. 2nd lt. Army, 1958-60, Taiwan. Recipient scholarship Cooperative Bank of Taiwan, Taipei, 1958, Book award Nat. Taiwan U., 1958, Cert. of Statistician Nat. Civil Svc. Gen. Exam, 1960, Travel fellowship Agr. Devel. Coun., N.Y., 1963-67, Cert. Gamma Sigma Delta, Storrs, 1972, sr. award Gamma Sigma Delta, 1996, Excellence in Teaching award Alumni Assn. Coll. Agr. and Natural Resources U. Conn., 1997, Outstanding Educators of Am. Award cert. (A divsn. of Fuller & Dees), 1975. Mem. Am. Agr. Econ. Assn., Econometric Soc., Northeastern Agr. and Resource Econs. Assn., Am. Stat. Assn. (editorial collaborator 1969-76). Avocations: photography, music, computer programming. Home: 127 Beech Mountain Rd Mansfield Center CT 06250 Office: U Conn U 4021 1376 Storrs Rd Storrs Mansfield CT 06269-4021 E-mail: tsoung@uconnvm.uconn.edu.

LEE, YOUNG BIN, psychiatry educator, neurologist; b. Seoul, Korea, Mar. 21, 1937; came to U.S., 1964; s. Suksin and Insik (Kim) L.; m. Moon Chin Cho, Apr. 24, 1965; children: Edward S., Susan E., Ellen M. Pre-med. study coll. sci. and engring., Yonsei U., Seoul, 1955-57, MD, 1961. Diplomate Am. Bd. Neurology and Psychiatry, Am. Bd. Profl. Psychiatry Cons., Am. Bd. Geriatric Psychiatry, Am. Bd. Profl. Disability. Rotating intern Sibley Meml. Hosp., Washington, 1964-65; neurology resident Pa. Hosp., Phila., 1965-68; psychiatry resident Ancora Psychiat. Hosp., Hammonton, N.J., 1968-70, neurologist in charge, 1970-97, asst. med. dir., 1972-88; clin. asst. prof. Robert Wood Johnson Med. Sch., Camden, N.J.; asst. prof. clin. psychiatry U. Medicine and Dentistry N.J., Newark, 1997—. Cons. in neurology West Jersey Hosp., Berlin, 1971, Vineland (N.J.) Devel. Ctr., 1971-87; cons. in neuropsychiatry Cumberland County Guidance Ctr., Millvile, N.J., 1971-86. With Korean Army, 1962-63. Named Outstanding Asian Am. N.J. Asian Am. Heritage Counsel, Hackketstown, N.J., 1994. Mem. Am. Acad. Neurology, Am. Psychiat. Assn., Am. Electroencephalography Assn., The Capitol Hist. Soc., Korean Am. Assn. So. N.J. (pres. 1988-91), The Fedn. of Korean Am. Assn. N.J. (pres. 1991-93). Achievements include establishment of Korean Language Course at Rutgers U. Home: 7 Pine Acres Dr Medford NJ 08055-9578 Office: U Medicine and Dentistry NJ 150 Bergen St Newark NJ 07103-2406

LEE, YUNG-KEUN, physicist, educator; b. Seoul, Korea, Sept. 26, 1929; came to U.S., 1953, naturalized, 1968; s. Kwang-Soo and Young-Sook (Hur) L.; m. Ock-Kyung Pai, Oct. 25, 1958; children: Ann, Arnold, Sara, Sylvia, Clara. BA, Johns Hopkins, 1956; MS, U. Chgo., 1957; PhD, Columbia, 1961. Research scientist Columbia U., N.Y.C., 1961-64; prof. physics Johns Hopkins U., Balt., 1964—. Vis. mem. staff Los Alamos Sci. Lab., 1971; vis. researcher Institut Scis. Nucléaires, Grenoble, France, 1975; cons. Idaho Nat. Engring. Lab., 1988-91; mem. Brahms collaboration Brookhaven Nat. Lab., 1996—. Contbr. articles to profl. jours. Mem. Am. Phys. Soc. Clubs: Johns Hopkins. Democrat. Methodist. Home: 1318 Denby Rd Baltimore MD 21286-1627 Office: Johns Hopkins U 34th and Charles Sts Baltimore MD 21218 E-mail: yklee@jhu.edu.

LEEBRON, DAVID WAYNE, dean, law educator; b. Phila., Feb. 12, 1955; BA, Harvard U., 1976, JD, 1979. Bar: Hawaii 1980, Pa. 1981, N.Y. 1982. Law clk. Judge Shirley Hufstedler, L.A., 1979—80; assoc. Cleary, Gottlieb, Steen & Hamilton, N.Y.C., 1981—83; prof. Sch. Law NYU, 1983—89, Columbia U., N.Y.C., 1989—, dean, Lucy G Moses prof. law, 1996—. Adj. prof. law UCLA, 1980; vis. fellow Max Planck Inst. Fgn. and Internat. Pvt. Law, Hamburg, Germany, 1988; Jean Monnet vis. prof. law, Bielefeld, Germany, 92. Author: (with others): Human Rights, 1999, Human Rights Documentary Supplement, 2000, Supplement to Human Rights, 2003. Pres. Columbia Cmty. Svc. Recipient Wickersham award for exceptional pub. svc. and dedication to the legal profession, 1997. Office: Columbia U Sch Law Box B12 801 Jerome Greene Hall 435 W 116th St New York NY 10027-7297*

LEEDS, MARGARET ANN, assistant principal; b. Memphis, Tex., Sept. 14, 1934; d. Roy Alvin and Abbie Cordelia (O'Neal) Massey; m. Charles Stanton Leeds, Nov. 3, 1959 (div. 1965). BA, Baylor U., 1956; MLA, U. So. Calif., 1976. Cert. tchr. secondary theatre arts, French, phys. edn., English. Tchr. Rexford Jr. and Sr. H.S., Beverly Hills, Calif., 1958-60; substitute tchr. Beverly Hills Unified Sch. Dist., 1960-66; tchr. phys. edn. Beverly Hills H.S., 1966-89, chair dept. phys. edn., 1981-89, asst. prin., 1989—, coach various sports incl. volleyball, gymnastics, fencing, 1966-89. Cons. Calif. Dept. Edn., 1986—; ofcl. volleyball ofcl. Nat. Assn. Girls and Women's Sports, 1975-80; presenter sessions to various confs., 1985—; conductor insvc. tng. workshops. Author: Beverly Hills Unified School District Physical Education Scope and Sequence, 1988, Beverly Hills High School Health Fitness Manual, 1987, Fight Back: A Woman's Guide to Self Defense, 1978; contbr. articles to profl. jours.; prodr. video tapes: Implementing Health Fitness in Schools, 1987, Physical Education is Alive and Well in Beverly Hills, California, 1986. Cons. Calif. Gov.'s Coun. on Phys. Fitness and Sports, 1993—; adv. bd. L.A. UNICEF, 1993—; ham radio operator Beverly Hills Disaster Comm. Sys. Vol., 1994—, L.A. County Disaster Comm. Sys. Vol., 1994—. Recipient Calif. Educator award Calif. Dept. Edn., 1987. Mem. NEA, AAHPERD (reviewer Jour. Health, Phys. Edn., Recreation and Dance 1989—, Calif. phys. best coord. 1988—, pub. rels. coord. 1987-91), Calif. Tchrs. Assn., Beverly Hills Edn. Assn. (pres. 1969-70), Calif. Assn. Health, Phys. Edn., Recreation and Dance (pres. unit 401 1986-88, dir. CORE Project 1987-91, pub. rels. chair 1987—, adminstrn. and supervision chair phys. edn. adv. com. 1994—, Honor award 1993, Outstanding Secondary Phys. Educator 1987, Calif. Phys. Educator of Yr. 1985). Baha'i Faith. Avocations: travel, folk art collecting, marathon running/jogging, backpacking, reading. Home: 1557 S Beverly Glen Blvd Los Angeles CA 90024-6163 Office: Beverly Hills High Sch 241 S Moreno Dr Beverly Hills CA 90212-3698

LEEDY, EMILY L. FOSTER (MRS. WILLIAM N. LEEDY), retired education educator, consultant; b. Jackson, Ohio, Sept. 24, 1921; d. Raymond S. and Grace (Garrett) Foster; MEd, Ohio U., 1957; postgrad. Ohio State U., 1956, Mich. State U., 1958-59, Case Western Res. U., 1963-65; m. William N. Leedy, Jan. 1, 1943; 1 son. Dwight A. tchr. Frankfort (Ohio) schs., 1941-46, Ross County Schs., Chillicothe, Ohio, 1948-53; elem. and supervising tchr. Chillicothe City Schs., 1953-56; dean of girls, secondary tchr. Berea City Schs., 1956-57; vis. tchr. Parma City Schs., 1957-59; counselor Homewood-Flossmoor High Sch., Flossmoor, Ill., 1959-60; teaching fellow Ohio U., 1960-62; asst. prof. edn., 1962-64; assoc. prof., counselor Cuyahoga Community Coll., 1964-66; dean of women Cleve. State U., 1966-67, assoc. dean student affairs, 1967-69; guidance dir. Cathedral Latin Sch., 1969-71; dir. women's service div. Ohio Bur. Employment Svcs., 1971-83; cons. in edn., 1983-87. Mem. adv. com. S.W. Community Info. Svc., 1959-60; youth com. S.W. YWCA, 1963-70, chmn., 1964-70, bd. mgmt., 1964-70; group svcs. coun. Cleve. Welfare Fedn., 1964-66; chmn. Met. YWCA Youth Program study com., 1966, bd. dirs., 1966-72, v.p., 1967-68; chmn. adv. coun. Ohio State U. Sch. Home Econs., 1977-80, chmn., 1978-80. Named Cleve. area Woman of Achievement, 1969; named to Ohio Women's Hall of Fame, 1979, Chillicothe Ross Women's Hall of Fame, 1988; recipient Outstanding Contbn. special award Nat. Assn. Commns. for Women, 1983, Meritorious Svc. award Nat. Assn. Women Deans, Adminstrs. and Counselors, 1984. Mem. AAUW (Berea-Parma br. v.p. 1995-97), Am., Northeastern Ohio (sec. 1958-59, exec. com. 1963-64, pub. rel. chmn. 1962-64, newsletter chmn., editor 1963-64, del. nat. assembly 1959-63) personnel and guidance assns., LWV, Am. Assn. Retired Persons (Ohio women's initiative spokesperson 1987-89, state legis. com. 1989-90, AARP/VOTE state coord. Ohio 1990-94), Nat. Assn. Women Deans and Counselors (publs. com. 1967-69, profl. employment practices com. 1980-82, Meritorious Svc. award 1984), Ohio (program chmn. 1967, editor Newsletter 1968-71), Cleve. Counselors Assn. (pres. 1966), Zonta Internat. (exec. bd. 1968-70, treas. 1970-72, chmn. dist. V Status of Women 1980-81), Nat. Assn. Commns. for Women (dir. 1980-81, sec. 1981-83), Rio Grande Coll. Alumni Assn. (Atwood Achievement award 1975), Bus. and Profl. Women's Club (Nike award 1973, Berea treas. 1996-97), Ohio Retired Tchrs. Assn., Svc. Corps of Retired Execs. Delta Kappa Gamma, Women's City Club (Cleve.). Home: 580 Lindberg Blvd Berea OH 44017-1418 Office: 699 Rocky Rd Chillicothe OH 45601-9469

LEEGE, DAVID CALHOUN, political scientist, educator; b. Elkhart, Ind., May 18, 1937; s. Harold Martin and Nellie Josephine (Bliss) L.; m. Patricia Ann Schad, June 8, 1963; children— David McChesney, Lissa Maria, Kurt Johannes BA, Valparaiso U., 1959; postgrad., U. Chgo., 1959-60; PhD, Ind. U., 1965. Instr. social sci. Concordia Coll., River Forest, Ill., 1962-64; asst. prof. polit. sci., dir. pub. opinion survey unit U. Mo., Columbia, 1964-68; assoc. prof., dir. survey research center SUNY, Buffalo, 1968-70; assoc. prof. U. Ill., Chgo., 1970-72, prof., 1972-76, head dept., 1972-73; prof. govt. and internat. studies U. Notre Dame, Ind., 1976—2002, dir. center for study of contemporary society, 1976-85, dir. London program, 1982, dir. program for research on religion, church and society, 1984—2002, prof. emeritus, 2002—; dir. Hesburgh Program in Pub. Service, 1987-92. Program dir. for polit. sci. NSF, 1974-76; mem. vis. faculty York U., Toronto, Ont., Can., 1970, U. Mich., 1971, 73, U. Leuven, Belgium, 1980, Cath. U. Am., 1985-86, U. Ariz., 2001—. Author: (with Wayne Francis) Political Research, 1974, (with Lyman Kellstedt) Rediscovering the Religious Factor in American Politics, 1993, (with K. Wald, B. Krueger and P. Mueller) The Politics of Cultural Differences, 2002; editor: The Missouri Poll, 1965-68, (with Joseph Gremillion) The Notre Dame Study of Catholic Parish Life Report Series, 1984-89; co-editor: Cambridge Studies in Social Theory, Religion, and Politics, 2003—; contbr. articles to profl. jours. Mem. bd. overseers Am. Nat. Election Studies, 1991-99, chair, 1994-97; mem. coun. ICPSR, 1966-69; bd. dirs. Luth. Music Program, Inc. Recipient numerous profl. prizes. Mem.: Soc. Scientific Study Religion, Midwest Polit. Sci. Assn. (chair nominating com., coun., program co-chair), Am. Polit. Sci. Assn. (sect. officer, program com., chmn. task force). Lutheran. Home: 2155 W Via Nuevo Leon Green Valley AZ 85614

LEEKLEY, MARIE VALPOON, secondary education educator; b. Honolulu, Mar. 28, 1941; d. Amil Richard and Florence Haruko (Soken) V.; m. John Darwin Leekley, Jr., June 26, 1965; children: Katherine Joan, Tracy Ann Kehaunani. BS, Carroll Coll., Waukesha, Wis., 1963; MEd, Nat. Coll. Edn., Evanston, Ill., 1990; PhD, Marquette U., 2002. Dir. Christian edn. Kamehameha Sch. for Girls, Honolulu, 1963-64; elem. tchr. Milw. Pub. Schs., 1965-67; vol. Marianas Edn. Dept. Peace Corps, Saipan, Mariana Islands, 1967-69, dist. coord. tchr. edn., 1969-71; tchr. Ethan Allen Sch. for Boys, Wales, Wis., 1977-96. Tchr. adult basic edn. Waukesha County Tech. Coll., Pewaukee, Wis., 1977—. Mem. Menomonee Falls (Wis.) Pub. Schs. Bd. Edn., 1990—; bd. dirs. Comprehensive Ednl. Svcs. Agys., West Allis, Wis., 1991-96. Recipient vol. appreciation award Greater Menomonee Falls Com., 1991, Boardmanship award Wis. Assn. Sch. Bds., 1991, 92, 93; named Edn. Leader of Yr. AAUW, 1996. Mem. ASCD, Correctional Edn. Assn., Nat. Sch. Bd. Assn., Wis. Assn. Adult and Continuing Edn., Wis. Vocat. Assn., Wis. Edn. Assn. Methodist. Home: W148N7590 Woodland Dr Menomonee Falls WI 53051-4522 Office: Waukesha County Tech Coll 327 E Broadway Waukesha WI 53186-5008

LEERABHANDH, MARJORIE BRAVO, chemist, educator; b. Negros Occidental, Philippines; came to U.S., 1982. d. Rustico Ginese and Monica Tolosa (Tolosa) Bravo; m. J. Victor S. Corpuz, Oct. 19, 2002. BS in chemistry cum laude, U. Santo Tomas, 1979; PhD in chemistry, U. So. Calif., 1990; MBA in Fin., Calif. Luth. U., 2000. Rsch. teaching asst. chem.

dept. U. So. Calif., L.A., 1984-89; faculty mem. chem. dept. Moorpark (Calif.) Coll., 1992—; project mgr. Med. Analysis Sys., Inc., Camarillo, Calif., 1989-93, rsch. team leader, 1993-94, mgr. rsch. and devel., 1994-2000, dir. tech. product support, interim dir. logistics, 2000—01. Author: Nitrogen Tixation Research Progress, 1985, Nitrogen Fixation: 100 Years After, 1988; contbr. articles to profl. jours. Mem. Am. Chem. Soc., Am. Assn. for Clin. Chemistry, Chem. Soc. U. Santo Tomas Manila (pres., 1979). Achievements include patents for Fructosamine Reagent and Calibrator Systems, Stabilization of Functional Proteins. Office: Med Analysis Sys Inc 5300 Adolfo Rd Camarillo CA 93012-8661

LEEVY, CARROLL MOTON, medical educator, hepatology researcher; b. Columbia, S.C., Oct. 13, 1920; s. Isaac S. and Mary (Kirkl) L.; m. Ruth S. Barboza, Feb. 4, 1956; children: Carroll Barboza, Maria Secora. AB, Fisk U., 1941; MD, U. Mich., 1944; ScD (hon.), N.J. Inst. Tech., 1973, U. Nebr., 1989; HHD (hon.), Fisk U., 1981. Intern Jersey City Med. Ctr., 1944-45, resident, 1945-48, dir. clin. investigation, 1947-57; fellow Banting-Best Inst., U. Toronto, Ont., Can., 1953; research assoc. Harvard U. Med. Sch., Cambridge, Mass., 1959; assoc. prof. U. Medicine and Dentistry of N.J., 1960-64, prof., 1964, Disting. prof., 1990—; chief of medicine EOVA Hosp., 1966—77; physician in chief Univ. Hosp., 1975-91; dir. Liver Ctr. U. Medicine and Dentistry N.J., 1983-85; dir. div. hepatology and nutrition N.J. Med. Sch., 1959-75, acting chmn. dept. medicine, 1966-68, chief of medicine, 1968-71, chmn. dept. medicine, 1975-91; disting. prof. medicine Univ. Hosp., physician in chief, 1975-91; acting chmn. Sammy Davis Jr. Nat. Liver Inst., 1984-86, pres., sci. dir., 1989—, dir., 1991—, N.J. Med. Sch. Liver Ctr., 1991—. Chief medicine VA Hosp., East Orange, N.J., 1966-71; cons. NIH, 1965-, FDA, 1970-80, VA, 1971-, Alcohol and Nutrition Found., 1970-80, Am. Liver Found., 1979-84; cons. Health Care Fin. Adminstrn., 1990-, mem. adv. com. on liver transplantation, 1991-; mem. Nat. Commn. on Digestive Disease, 1975-78; mem. expert com. on chronic liver disease WHO, 1978; mem. nat. adv. com. digestive disease HHS, 1989-93; chmn. monitoring com. VA Coop. Study on Alcoholic Hepatitis, 1989-94, VA Rsch. Study on Colchicine Alcoholic Cirrhosis, 1994-; med. dir. Univ. Hosp. Liver Transplant Program, 1989-; disting. prof. U. Medicine and Dentistry N.J., 1991-; chmn. Newark Hepatitis C Study Group, 2000-; mem. N.J. State Commn. on Viral Hepatitis C, 2002-; med. dir. Medicare Liver Transplant Program, 1991-. Author: Practical Diagnosis and Treatment of Liver Disease, 1957, Evaluation of Liver Function in Clinical Practice, 1965, 2d edit., 1974, Liver Regeneration in Man, 1973, The Liver and Its Diseases, 1973, Diseases of the Liver and Biliary Tract, 1977, Guidelines for Detection of Drug and Chemical-Induced Hepatotoxicity, 1979, Alcohol and the Digestive Tract, 1981, Standardization of Nomenclature, Diagnostic Criteria and Prognosis for Diseases of the Liver and Biliary Tract, 1994; contbr. numerous articles to med., sci. jours.; patentee in field. Bd. dirs. U. Cape Town, South Africa Fund, 1984-2001; active Pilgrim Congl. Ch. Comdr. USNR, 1954-59. E.V. Gabriel scholar, 1938, Kellog Med. scholar, 1942; recipient Modern Med. award, 1972, Edward Ill award, 1973, United Negro Coll. Fund award, 1980, Key to City of Newark, 1981, Key to City of Columbia, S.C., 1987, Key to City of Secaucus, N.J., 1981, 50th N.J. Achievement award U. Medicine and Dentistry N.J., 1995, Honor and Commendation for viral hepatitis rsch. N.J. State Senate and Gen. Assembly, 1999, Disting. Achievement award U. Mich. Med. Ctr. Alumni Soc., 1999; 40th Anniversary Faculty Honoree, U. Medicine and Dentistry N.J., 1995; comdr. chief pulmonary disease USN Disease Sect., developer liver ctr., 1954-56; chmn. organizing com. for establishing med. sch. in NJ. Mem. AAAS, ACP (publs. com. 1969-74, master), AMA (vice-chmn., chmn. program com. sect. on gastroenterology 1971-74), NAACP, Am. Assn. for Study Liver Diseases (pres. 1967-68, chmn. steering com. 1968-74, Disting. Svc. award 1991), Internat. Assn. for Study Liver (pres. 1970-74, chmn. criteria com. 1972—), Am. Gastroenterol. Assn. (edn. and tng. com. 1967-71), Assn. Profs. Medicine (Robert Williams Disting. Chmn. award 1991), Assn. Am. Physicians, Soc. Exptl. Biology and Medicine, Am. Soc. Clin. Nutrition, Am. Inst. Nutrition, Nat. Med. Assn. (award 1987, Centenial award 1995), Am. Fedn. Clin. Rsch., Assn. Acad. Minority Physicians (pres. 1986-88, chmn. bd. trustees 1988—, Disting. Achievement award 1995), Internat. Com. on Informatics in Hepatology (chmn. 1986—), Internal Hepatology Informatics Group (chmn. 1984-01, UNOS cert. transplant hepatologist med. dir. 1989—), N.J. Acad. Medicine, N.J. Liver Study Group (chmn. 1996—), Detection Counseling on Treatment Hepatitus Cir. Inner City Residents (chmn., 1986-2001, chmn. exec. com. 1986-2003), N.J. Commn. on Hepatitis, 2002—, Phi Beta Kappa, Alpha Omega Alpha, Sigma Pi Phi. Home: 35 Robert Dr Short Hills NJ 07078-1525 Office: UMDNJ Med School 100 Bergen St Newark NJ 07103-2484 E-mail: Leevyc.m.@umdng.edu.

LEE-WILLINGHAM, ANITA MARIE, school system liaison; b. Sanford, N.C., Apr. 29, 1951; d. Julian Cornell and Ruth Agnes (Stewart) Lee; m. Alfred Willingham; 1 child, Alfred Randolph. BS, Cheyney (Pa.) State U., 1973; Masters Degree, West Ga. Coll., 1993. Cert. tchr., Ga. Tchr. Archdiocese of Phila., 1973-76, Phila. Bd. Edn., 1976-77; dir. edn. Lou Hudson Youth Devel. Program, Atlanta, 1982-83; cons., 1983; asst. dir. Nat. Football League Players Assn., Washington, 1979-83; tchr. Fulton County Bd. Edn., Atlanta, 1977-92, home and sch. liaison, 1992—. Asst. prin., sch. system liaison Banneker High Sch., Coll. Park, Ga. pharm. rep., Ga., 1983-85; employment counselor Pvt. Industry Coun., Atlanta, 1983-91; tchr. Fulton County Summer Sch. Program, 1989-93; mem. leadership team, East Point, 1988-93, Paul D. West Local Sch. Adv. Bd., 1989-93, PTSA Exec. Bd., 1989. Contbr. articles to profl. jours. Bd. dirs. Ga. Assn. Retarded Citizens, Atlanta, 1983; active So. Christian Leadership Women, Atlanta, 1986. Recipient award of appreciation Nat. Football League Players Assn., 1980, Leadership award Paul D. West Mid. Sch., 1988-92, cert. of appreciation Mayor Maynard Jackson, Atlanta, 1981. Mem. ASCD, NAACP, NEA, AAUW, Nat. Alliance Black Educators, Nat. Assn. Black Educators, Ga. Assn. Educators, Metro-Atlanta Cheyney U. Alumni, Phi Delt Kappa, Alpha Kappa Alpha. Democrat. Methodist. Avocations: reading, travel, shopping. Office: Banneker High Sch 5439 Feldwood Rd Atlanta GA 30349-2860

LEFEBER, EDWARD JAMES, SR., medical educator, physician; b. Wauwatosa, Wis., June 1, 1911; s. Cornelius George and May (McCord) L.; m. Ellie Hancock Weisiger, June 4, 1938; children: Edward James, jr., Robert Randolph, John Courtney, Ann Elizabeth, Donald Louis, Nancy Ellen. B.S., U. Wis., 1934, M.D., 1936. Intern, resident in medicine Med. Coll. Va. Hosps., Richmond, 1936-40; mem. faculty Med. Br., U. Tex., Galveston, 1940-88, clin. assoc. prof. medicine, 1951-83, clin. prof. medicine and family practice, 1983-88, dir. Student Health Service, 1943-46; practice medicine, specializing in internal medicine Internal Medicine Assocs., Galveston, 1948-88; chief out-patient service Galveston office Houston Regional Office, VA, 1946-48; cons. gastroenterology USPHS Hosp., Galveston, 1952-53; pres. staff St. Mary's Infirmary, Galveston, 1961; mem. adv. com. on nursing home affairs Tex. Dept. Health, 1976-82. Bd. dirs. Galveston chpt. ARC, 1958-78; mem. Galveston Civic Orch., 1957-60; mem. Tex. Bd. Licensure for Nursing Home Adminstrs., 1979-88; bd. dirs. Moody House, 1964-65, 67-71, med. dir. Diplomate Am. Bd. Internal Medicine. Fellow ACP; mem. Galveston County Med. Soc. (pres. 1954, sec.-treas. 1948-53), AMA, Tex., So. med. assns., Am., Tex. (pres. 1977) socs. internal medicine, Am. Soc. Gastro-Intestinal Endoscopy, Tex. Club Internists, Phi Chi. Episcopalian (past vestryman). Club: Masons. Died Jan. 3, 1988. Office: 200 University Blvd Galveston TX 77550-2712 Address: PO Box 1149 Baytown TX 77522-1149

LEFEBVRE, GREN GORDON, school superintendent; b. Buffalo, May 2, 1943; s. Gordon and Anne B. (Finch-Noyes) L.; m. Mary Margaret Hill, Aug. 20, 1966; children: Lisa Jackman, Christopher. BS, Purdue U., 1966, MS, 1967, EdS, 1982. Lic. sch. supt., Ind. Tchr./coach Darlington (Ind.) High Sch., 1967-70, Coal Creek Cen. High Sch., New Richmond, Ind., 1970-71, North Montgomery High Sch., Crawfordsville, Ind., 1971-76; prin. Waynetown (Ind.) Elem.-Jr. High Sch., 1976-87, Northridge Mid. Sch., Crawfordsville, 1987-91; supt. North Montgomery Community Sch. Corp., Linden, Ind., 1991-96; prin. Lester B. Sommer Elem. Sch., 1996—. Cons. on stress mgmt. Mem. Town of Darlington Town Bd., pres., 1977-85; bd. dirs. Montgomery County United Fund, 1984—, Youth Svcs. Bur., Crawfordsville, 1986-92, Montgomery County Boys Club, 1978-84, Montgomery County coun. Boy Scouts Am., 1980-82. Mem. Am. Soc. Notaries, Ind. Assn. Pub. Sch. Supts., Darlington Community Assn., Ind. High Sch. Athletic Assn., Am. Legion, Darlington Conservation Club, Lions, Elks, Phi Beta Kappa. Republican. Episcopalian. Avocations: antiques, travel, raising cats, reading. Home: PO Box 176 Darlington IN 47940-0176 Office: North Montgomery Cmty Sch Corp PO Box 70 Linden IN 47955-0070

LEFKOWITZ, MARY ROSENTHAL, Greek literature educator; b. N.Y.C., Apr. 30, 1935; d. Harold L. and Mena (Weil) Rosenthal; m. Alan L. Lefkowitz, July 1, 1956 (div.); children: Rachel, Hannah; m. Hugh Lloyd-Jones, Mar. 26, 1982. BA, Wellesley Coll., 1957; AM, Radcliffe Coll., 1959, PhD, 1961; LHD (hon.), Trinity Coll., Hartford, Conn., 1996, Grinnell Coll., 2000; PhD (hon.), U. Patras, Greece, 1999. Instr. Greek Wellesley (Mass.) Coll., 1960-63, asst. prof. Greek and Latin, 1964-69, assoc. prof. Greek and Latin, 1969-75, prof. Greek and Latin, 1975-79; Andrew W. Mellon prof. in the humanities Wellesley (Mass.) Coll, 1979—. Vis. prof. U. Calif., Berkeley, 1978; vis. fellow St. Hilda's Coll., 1979-80, Corpus Christi Coll., 1991. Author: Heroines and Hysterics, 1981, Lives of the Greek Poets, 1981, Women in Greek Myth, 1986, First Person Fictions, 1991, Not Out of Africa, 1996, 2d edit., 1997, greek gods, Human Lives, 2003; co-editor: Women's Life in Greece and Rome, 1982, 2d edit., 1992, Black Athena Revisited, 1996. Fellow NEH, 1979-80, 91, ACLS, 1972-73, Hon. fellow St. Hilda's Coll., Oxford, 1994—. Mem. Am. Philol. Assn. (bd. dirs. 1974-77); Class Assn. New Eng. (pres. 1972-73). Home: 15 W Riding St Wellesley MA 02482-6914 Office: Wellesley Coll 106 Central St Wellesley MA 02481-8203 E-mail: mlefkowitz@wellesley.edu.

LEFT, JOAN MARILYN, principal; b. Bayonne, N.J., Aug. 21, 1940; d. William A. and Amelia P. (Jakowicz) Lapinski; m. Anthony Patrick Left, Aug. 4, 1962; children: Susan, Carol, Barbara, Patricia. BA in Sci. Edn., Jersey City State Coll., 1962; MA, U. Ala., Birmingham, 1981, EdS, 1992, EdD in Ednl. Leadership, 1994. Cert. elem. tchr., Ala. Sci. tchr. Point Pleasant (N.J.) Elem. Sch., 1962-63; biology tchr. Lakewood (N.J.) High Sch., 1964-67; lab. instr. Georgia Ct. Coll., Lakewood, 1968-67; tchr. St. Francis Xavier Sch., Birmingham, Ala., 1974-85, Phileo Sch., Birmingham, 1985-86, Pinson (Ala.) Elem. Sch., 1986-90; asst. prin. Cahaba Heights Elem. Sch., Birmingham, 1991-93, Leeds (Ala.) Elem., 1993-94; prin. Greystone Elem. Sch., Birmingham, 1994—. Cons., presenter in field; mentor tchr. First-Yr. Tchr. Scholar Program. Author papers in field. Grantee Nat. Sci. Tchrs Assn., Gen. Aviation Mfrs. Assn., Ala. Dept. Econ. & Conservation Affairs, Am. South Bank. Mem. NAESP, NEA, ASCD, Ala. Edn. Assn., Ala. Sci. Tchrs. Assn., Nat. Coun. Tchrs. Math., Women Educator's Network (v.p. 1991-93, pres. 1993—), Jefferson County Edn. Assn., Phi Delta Kappa (v.p.), Kappa Delta Pi. Home: 5291 Amber Hills Rd Birmingham AL 35210-3728 Office: Greystone Elem Sch Birmingham AL 35242

LEFTWICH, ROBERT EUGENE, oncological and adult nursing educator; b. Lubbock, Tex., July 2, 1940; s. Eugene L. and Georgia (Kirkpatrick) L. BSN, Baylor U., 1963; MS, Northern Ill. U., 1970; PhD, Clayton U., 1977. Head nurse Baylor U. Med. Ctr., Dallas, 1963-64; supr. U.S. Air Force Nurse Corps, Fla., Tex., 1964-67; instr. nursing Cameron State Coll., Lawton, Okla., 1967-68, Rock Valley Coll., Rockford, Ill., 1968-70; dir. ADN program Kankakee (Ill.) Community Coll., 1970-71, dean health edn., 1971-72; chmn. dept. adult nursing Med. Coll. Ga., Augusta, 1972-75; asst. prof. U. Louisville, 1975-77; prof. nursing Governors State U., University Park, Ill., 1977—. Bd. mem. Community Health Planning Bd., Kankakee, 1970-72; curriculum cons. Purdue U., Westville, Ind., 1983; oncology nursing cons. Ingalls Hosp., Harvey, Ill., 1979-85; grievance chairperson Univ. Profls. of Ill., University Park, 1981-83. Author: Nursing, Nutrition and the Adult Client, 1974, Humanistic Teaching Strategies and Nursing Students' Attitudes about Death and Dying, 1977, Self-Care Guide for the Cancer Patient, 1989; primary rschr.: Acuity Levels in an Adult Oncology Unit, 1981, Sexual Harrassment in Nursing Education, 1995; contbr. articles to profl. jours. Organist Trinity United Meth. Ch., Chgo., 1985—87; organist, choirmaster Bethel Covenant Ch., Flossmoor, Ill., 1987—96; organist Immanuel Ch., Evergreen Park, Ill., 1996—99, 1st Presbyn. Ch., Homewood, Ill., 1999—2001; mus. dir., organist Presbyn. Ch., Orland Park, Ill., 2001—. 1st lt. U.S. Air Force, 1963-67. Mem. Univ. Profls. Ill., Am. Guild Organists, Sigma Theta Tau. Avocations: ch. organist, choirmaster, concert organist, pianist, tenor soloist. Office: Governors State U Dept Nursing University Park IL 60466 E-mail: r-leftwich@govst.edu.

LEGER, PAMELA DENISE, secondary education educator; b. Ft. Lee, Va., Aug. 20, 1966; d. Daniel Joseph and Donna (Regan) L.; m. Darryl Mark Morgan, July 8, 1989 (div.); children: Tybor Mark, MeLani Suzette. BS, La. Tech. U., 1988. Summer sch. tchr. Lincoln Parish, Ruston, La., 1988; geometry/algebra tchr. Springhill (La.) High Sch., 1988-89; algebra and 8th grade tchr. East Beauregard Sch., Drycreek, La., 1990; tchr. math., chair dept. Fairview Sch., Grant, La., 1990-94; gifted math. tchr. Fairview Sch./Elizabeth Sch., Grant, 1994—. Tchr. Ruston Cath. Ch., 1985-86. Named High Sch. Math. Tchr. of Yr., Fairview Sch., 1992; Fairview H.S. Tchr. of Yr., 1993. Mem. ASCD, Math. Assn. Am., Assn. of Profl. Educators of La., Nat. Coun. Tchrs. Math., La. Assn. Tchrs. Math. Roman Catholic. Avocations: gourmet cooking, crocheting, crafts. Office: Fairview High Sch Highway 377 Grant LA 70644

LEGEYT, PATRICIA ANN, elementary education educator; b. Phila., Nov. 26, 1947; d. Vito Joseph and Anna (Cardinale) Mina; m. Charles Howard LeGeyt, Sept. 27, 1969; 1 child, Shelley Ann. BA in Applied Arts and Scis., San Diego U., 1980. Cert. collegiate profl. tchr. Va., career tchr. status Va. Beach Supt. Sch., 1989, tagged Va. Beach Supt. Sch., 2000. Flight attendant Am. Airlines, Washington, 1968-69; elem. sch. tchr. Sacred Heart Parochial Sch., Manoa, Pa., 1973-74; media ctr. asst. Solana Beach (Calif.) Elem. Sch., 1977-79; elem. sch. tchr. Brubaker Acad., Va. Beach, Va., 1981-82, Ryan Acad., Norfolk, Va., 1982-83, Shelton Park Pub. Sch., Va. Beach, 1983-86, Kempsville Meadows Pub. Sch., Va. Beach, 1986—94, Larkspur Mid. Sch., Va. Beach, 1994-96, Kempsville Meadows Pub. Sch., 1997—, mem. sch. planning coun., 2000—03, sci. lead tchr., 2001—, gr. level chairperson, 2002—. Data analyst Harris Pub. Co., 1996, 97; coord. Ptnr.-in-Edn., 1997—; organizer after-sch. clubs; condr. city-wide insvcs. in math. Co-author curriculum guides. Recipient Tchr. of Yr. award Kempsville Meadows Elem. Sch., 1990, Dist. Svc. award PTA, 2001. Mem. NEA, Va. Edn. Assn., Virginia Beach Edn. Assn. (sch. rep. 1984-86), Nat. Coun. Tchrs. Math., Virginia Beach Reading Coun., Tidewater Assn. Sci. Educators, Nat. Coun. Tchrs. English (faculty coun. 1992-94). Avocations: dancing, travel, gardening, reading, cooking. Home: 4016 Dillaway Ct Virginia Beach VA 23456-1257 Office: Kempsville Meadows Elem Sch Edwin Dr Virginia Beach VA 23462

LEGGE, JEAN MARY, secondary school educator; b. Jamestown, N.D., Apr. 26, 1951; d. Alvin and Caroline Steckler; children: Jennifer, Zachary, Erin. BS in Edn., Valley City (N.D.) State U., 1987. Legal sec. Bruce Britton Law Office, Jamestown, 1973-74; bookkeeper, vol. coord. South Ctrl. Mental Health, Jamestown, 1974-75; high sch. sci. tchr. Kathryn (N.D.) Pub. Sch., 1987-89, Marion (N.D.) Pub. Sch., 1989—. Mem. Breeding Bird Survey U.S. Fish & Wildlife, Valley City, 1988—, vol. neotropical migrant bird census on Arrowwood Nat. Wildlife Refuge, 1994; outdoor skills workshop facilitator N.D. Game & Fish Dept., Bismarck, 1992-95; HIV/AIDS workshop facilitator N.D. Dept. Pub. Instrn., Bismarck, 1991-93; sci. educator, panelist insvc. Valley City State U., 1989-99; reviewer Nat. Sci. Edn. Standards, 1995. Author curriculum material to use newspapers in class. Coach 4-H Wildlife Judging Team-Barnes County, Valley City, 1989; com. chair camp registratsion Barnes County Wildlife Fedn., Valley City, 1991-99; project facilitator WET, WILD; vol. bird population census project U.S. Geol. Svc., 1997; seasonal birding guide Dakota Birding Bus., vol. web page author, mem. steering com., Save Sheyenne. Recipient 1st pl. N.D. Wildlife Judging Team - 4H, 1989, Commendation U.S. Dept. Army C.E., Mpls., 1992; named N.D. Outstanding Biology Tchr. Nat. Assn. Biology Tchrs., 1992, Merit award, VCSU Alumni Assn., 1995, Excellence in Sci. Math. Teaching, 1998, ND Water Curriculum award Nat. Geog., Outstanding Water Conservationist award ND Wildlife Fedn., 2002.. Mem. NSTA, N.D. Sci. Tchrs. Assn., N.D. Orienteering Alliance (sec. 1993—, coach), Marion Edn. Assn. (v.p. 1990, sec. 1993, pres. 1994), Am. Birding Assn., Nat. Assn. of Biol. Tchr., Barnes County Wildlife Fedn., Water Edn. Tchrs. (curriculum field tchr. 1994), Sierra Club (conservation chair 2001—). Avocations: reading, gardening, camping, hunting, birding, butterfly collecting. Home: 3212 115th Ave SE Valley City ND 58072-9492

LEGGETT, NANCY PORTER, university administrator; b. Greenville, N.C., Aug. 14, 1952; d. Earl Lindeburgh and Louise (Adams) Porter; m. Ted Clayton Johnston, Nov. 19, 1971 (div. Dec. 1979); 1 child, Clayton Porter; m. Donald Yates Leggett, Aug. 17, 1980. Student, East Carolina U., 1971-73, Pitt C.C., Greenville, 1975-76. Sec./coord. grad. ext. and tchr. edn. programs Divsn. Continuing Edn., East Carolina U., Greenville, 1971-80; sect. sec. ambulatory pediat. Sch. Medicine, East Carolina U., Greenville, 1981-83; adminstrv. sec. to chmn. dept. pediat. East Carolina U., Greenville, 1983-94; resource person dept. pediat. Sch. Medicine, East Carolina U., Greenville, 1984-94, exec. asst. to chmn. dept. pediat., 1994—. Traffic appeals com. East Carolina U., Greenville, 1995-96, chair benefits com., 1995-97, parking and traffic com., 1996-2002, staff forum, 1999-2000. Active Greenville Mus. Art, 1980-82, Nat. Scleroderma Found., 1987-88, Hist. Hope Found., Windsor, N.C., 1990-96, Greenville Cmty. Appearance Commn., 1990-94; com. mem. N.C. Symphony, Greenville, 1988-89; steering com. Children's Miracle Network Telethon, Greenville, 1986-90; vol. Friends of Children's Hosp. Greenville, 1986-88; bd. dirs. Rose H.S. Acad. Boosters, 1994-95. Mem. Greenville Country Club, Kiwanis (charter mem., bd. dirs. 1990-91). Baptist. Avocations: gardening, reading, walking, birdwatching. Home: 113 Bells St Greenville NC 27858-8498 Office: East Carolina Univ Sch of Medicine Dept Pediat Greenville NC 27834 E-mail: leggettn@mail.ecu.edu.

LEGINGTON, GLORIA R. middle school educator; BS, Tex. So. U, Houston, 1967; MS, U. So. Calif., L.A., 1973. Cert. adminstr. (life). Tchr., mentor L.A. Unified Sch. Dist., 1991-93. Tchr. insvc. classes for area colloquim, parents, tchrs., faculty shared decision making coun., 1993-94, mem. faculty senate, 1992-93, mem. sch. improvement, 1993-94; del. U.S. Spain Joint Conf. on Edn., Barcelona, 1995; coord. ESEA, 2001. Sponsor 8th grade, 1994-97. Named semi-finalist Nat. Libr. Poetry, 1997, recipient Editor's Choice award, 1997. Mem. NEA, Internat. Reading Assn., United Tchrs. L.A., Calif. League of Mid. Schs., Internat. Libr. Poetry. Avocations: painting, writing, collecting black memorabilia, reading, traveling.

LEHAN, RICHARD D'AUBIN, English language educator, writer; b. Brockton, Mass., Dec. 23, 1930; s. Ralph A. and Mildred L.; m. Ann Evans, June 11, 1960; 1 son, Edward Scott. BA, Stonehill Coll., 1952; MA, Boston Coll., 1953; PhD, U. Wis., 1958. Mem. faculty U. Wis.-Madison, 1953-57, U. Tex.-Austin, 1958-62; mem. faculty dept. English UCLA, 1962—, prof. English, 1969—, chmn. dept. English, 1971-73. Fulbright exchange prof. Moscow State U., USSR, 1974-75. Author: F. Scott Fitzgerald, 1966, Theodore Dreiser, 1969, Literary Existentialism, 1973, The Great Gatsby: The Limits of Wonder, 1990, The City in Literature, 1998, Sister Carrie Critizues, 2000. Recipient Disting. Teaching award U. Tex., 1961, UCLA, 1970; Fulbright award, 1975; Guggenheim fellow, 1978-79, Pres.'s Rsch. fellow U. Calif., 1988-89 Home: 11876 Coral Reef Ln Malibu CA 90265-2251 Office: UCLA Dept English Los Angeles CA 90095-1530

LEHMAN, BARBARA ALBU, foreign language educator, translator; b. Vineland, N.J., July 7, 1950; d. Kurt Gunther and Ruth (Landau) Albu; children: David, Kara. BA, Douglass Coll., 1972; MS, Rutgers U., 1983; degree in Holocaust Edn. (hon.), Hebrew U., Jerusalem, 1994. Cert. educator French and German. French/German lang. educator Mount Olive Township Schs., Flanders, N.J., 1973-81; French lang. educator Upper Freehold Schs., Allentown, N.J., 1984—. Translator Internat. Congress on Glass, Albuquerque, 1980, Hamburg, Germany, 1983; travel guide EF Tours, Europe, 1984—; mem. N.J. Adv. Commn. on Status of Women, 1998; bd. dir. Nat. Assn. for Commn. on Status of Women. Vice-chmn. Somerset County Commn. on Women, Somerville, N.J., 1985—; apptd. mem. N.J. Adv. Commn. on Status of Women, 1998--; elected bd. mem. Nat. Assn. Commns. for Women, 2001--. Meml. scholar Lihn Family, 1968, Grauel scholar Brookdale Holocaust Studies, 1994. Mem. Kappa Delta Pi.

LEHMAN, DONALD RICHARD, physicist, educator, academic administrator; b. York, Pa., Dec. 13, 1940; s. Frederick Hinkle and Wilhelmina Emma (Ruesskamp) Lehman; m. Elyse Joan Brauch, Aug. 24, 1962. BA in Physics, Rutgers U., 1962; PhD in Theoretical Physics, George Washington U., 1970. NAS NRC postdoctoral rsch. assoc. Nat. Bur. Stds., Gaithersburg, Md., 1970-72; from asst. to assoc. prof. physics George Washington U., Washington, 1972-82, prof., 1982—2002, George Gamow prof. theoretical physics, 2003—, dep. chair physics, 1986-87, chair physics, 1987-93, dir. ctr. nuclear studies, 1990-93, assoc. v.p. rsch. and grad. studies, 1993-96, v.p. acad. affairs, 1996—2002, exec. v.p. acad. affairs, 2003—. Guest worker Nat. Bur. Stds., Gaithersburg, 1972—89, program analyst, 1974; vis. staff mem., collaborator Los Alamos (N.Mex.) Nat. Lab., 1973—2001; spkr. internat. confs. Contbr. articles to profl. jours. Grantee, Rsch. Corp., N.Y., 1974—76, Dept. Energy, Germantown, Md., 1979—98, NATO, Belgium, 1987—91. Fellow: Am. Phys. Soc.; mem.: Southeastern Univs. Rsch. Assn. (chair bd. trustees 2002—). Achievements include elucidation of the physics of the 3 body structure of 6Li; unraveling of the physics underlying the role of exact three body continuum states in the photodisintegration of 3He. Office: George Washington U Academic Affairs 2121 I St NW Washington DC 20037-2353

LEHMAN, JEFFREY SEAN, academic administrator, educator; b. Bronxville, N.Y., Aug. 1, 1956; s. Leonard and Imogene (McAuliffe) L.; children: Rebecca Colleen, Jacob Keegan, Benjamin Emil. AB, Cornell U., 1977; M of Pub. Policy, U. M of Pub. Policy, JD, U. Mich., 1981. Bar: D.C. 1983, U.S. Ct. Appeals (fed. cir.) 1984, U.S. Ct. Appeals (D.C. cir.) 1987, U.S. Supreme Ct. 1987. Law clk. to chief judge U.S. Ct. Appeals (1st cir.), Portland, Maine, 1981-82; law clk. to assoc. justice U.S. Supreme Ct., Washington, 1982-83; assoc. Caplin & Drysdale, Chartered, Washington, 1983-87; asst. prof. U. Mich. Law Sch., Ann Arbor, 1987-92, prof., 1992-93, prof. law and pub. policy, 1993—2003, dean, 1994—2003; pres. Cornell U., Ithaca, NY, 2003—. Vis. prof. Yale U., 1993, U. Paris II, 1994. Co-author: Corporate Income Taxation, 1994; editor-in-chief: Mich. Law Rev., 1979-80. Trustee Skadden Fellowship Found., 1995—. Mem. Am. Law Inst., Order of Coif. Office: Cornell University Office of the President 300 Day Hall Ithaca NY 14853 E-mail: president@cornell.edu.

LEHMAN, LISA MARIE, elementary education educator; b. Oklahoma City, Feb. 18, 1966; d. Wayne and Rowena Sue Wilson; m. Craig Lehman; children: Lindsey, Leah. BS in Early Childhood/Elem. Edn., U. Mo., 1988; MS in Edn., S.W. Bapt. U., Bolivar, Mo., 1991. Kindergarten tchr., Bolivar, Mo. Leader 4-H Club; mem. Positive Action Coun., Carl Junction, Mizzou Alumni Bd., Jasper County Fair Bd.; adv. CJ Young Farmer Orgn.; chmn. Earth Day Com., Carl Junction. Mem. MSTA (pres.), Federated Women's

Club (pres.), Beta Sigma Phi. (svc. com.). Democrat. Methodist. Avocations: showing horses, reading, cross-stitch, photography, water skiing. Home: 3620 S Springfield Ave Bolivar MO 65613-9111

LEHMAN, PAUL ROBERT, retired music educator; b. Athens, Ohio, Apr. 20, 1931; s. Harvey C. and Vera Marjorie (Simmons) L.; m. V. Ruth Wickline, June 27, 1953; children: David Alan, Laura Ann. BS in Edn. with honors, Ohio U., 1953; MusM, U. Mich., 1959, PhD in Music, 1962. Tchr. Jackson Twp. Sch. Dist., Massillon, Ohio, 1953-55; from instr. to asst. prof. U. Colo., Boulder, 1962-65; from assoc. prof. to prof. U. Ky., Lexington, 1965-70; music specialist U.S. Dept. Edn., Washington, 1967-68; prof. Eastman Sch. Music, Rochester, N.Y., 1970-75, U. Mich., Ann Arbor, 1975-96, assoc. dean sch. music, 1977-89, sr. assoc. dean, 1989-96; ret., 1996. Cons. NEA, U.S. Dept. Edn., Coun. of Chief State Sch. Officers, Nat. Assessment of Ednl. Progress, various univs., sch. systems, state depts. of edn., corps. Author: The Class of 2001, 1985, Music in Today's Schools: Rationale and Commentary, 1987; contbr. articles to profl. jours. Served to 1st lt. USAF, 1955-57. Recipient Cert. Merit Found. Advancement Edn. in Music, 1986, Nat. Fedn. of Music Club, 1993, Phi Mu Alpha, 1996, Music Industry Conf., 1997; named to Music Educators Hall of Fame, 2000. Mem. Music Educators Nat. Conf. (pres. 1984-86, Music Educators Hall of Fame 2000), Coll. Music Soc. (exec. bd. 1981-83), Internat. Soc. Music Edn. (hon. life, bd. dirs. 1988-92).

LEHMAN, WILLIAM JEFFREY, physiology educator; b. N.Y.C., June 20, 1945; s. Karl and Lisa Lehmann; m. Diana Carol Martin, Oct. 6, 1982; children: Frank Martin, John Marshall Lisle. BS, SUNY, Stony Brook, 1966; PhD, Princeton U., 1969. Postdoctoral fellow Brandeis U., Waltham, Mass., 1969-72; higher sci. officer Oxford (Eng.) U., 1973; asst. prof. physiology Sch. Medicine Boston U., 1973-78, assoc. prof., 1978-89, prof., 1989—. Contbr. articles to profl. jours. Charles Osgood Grosvenor fellow Princeton U., 1968, Muscular Dystrophy Assn. fellow, 1969-71; recipient Whitaker Health Sci. award Whitaker Found., 1983-85, Shannon award NIH, 1992-94. Mem. Soc. Gen. Physiologists, Biophys. Soc., Am. Soc. Cell Biology, Biochem. Soc. (U.K.), Am. Heart Assn. (established investigator 1982-87). Office: Boston U Sch Medicine Dept Physiology 715 Albany St Boston MA 02118-2307

LEHMANN, DORIS ELIZABETH, elementary education educator; b. Ramsey, N.J., Aug. 17, 1933; d. Alfred Harrison and Anna Elizabeth (Gerhold) Rockefeller; m. Victor S. Lehmann, June 25, 1955; children: Joanne E. Cathy Lynn, Victor A., Kristie Sue. BS in Edn. magna cum laude, Wagner Coll., 1955; student in edn., Columbia U., summers 1988-91, Jersey City State, 1990—, William Paterson, 1971. Elem. tchr. Sch. St. Sch., Ramsey, 1955-56; bedside instr. N. Bergen County schs., N.J., 1966-71; elem. tchr. Edith A. Bogert Sch., Upper Saddle River, N.J., 1971-2000. Author numerous poems; author: (with others) Curriculum for Values Education in New Jersey, 1991. Indian cons. Bergen County Mus. of Art and Sci., Paramus, N.J., 1983—. Recipient Fellowship of Life award Luth. Layman's Movement, 1955. Fellow Upper Saddle River Edn. Assn. (social sec. 1972-73, v.p. 1974-75, 84-85, liaison to USR hist. soc. 1986—) N.J. Edn. Assn., N.J. North Edn. Assn., Alpha Omicron Pi (life, treas. 1954, v.p. 1955). Republican. Lutheran. Office: Edith A Bogert Sch 395 W Saddle River Rd Saddle River NJ 07458-1622 E-mail: vlcco@aol.com.

LEHMANN-CARSSOW, NANCY BETH, secondary school educator, coach; b. Kingsville, Tex., Sept. 9, 1949; d. Valgene William and Ella Mae (Zajicek) Lehmann; m. William Benton Carssow, Jr., Aug. 1, 1981. BS, U. Tex., 1971, MA, 1979. Freelance photographer, Austin, Tex., 1971-99; geography tchr., tennis coach Austin Ind. Sch. Dist., 1974-98, geography tchr., instrnl. specialist, girls' wrestling coach, 1999—. Founder Custom Pet Wheels, 1997; salesperson, mgr. What's Going On-Clothing, Austin, 1972-78; area adminstr. Am. Inst. Fgn. Study, Austin, 1974-81; area rep. World Encounters, Austin, 1981—, tour guide, Egypt, Kenya, 1977, 79, 81, 87, 92, 97, 98, 99, 2000; participant 1st summer inst. Nat. Geog. Soc., Washington, 1986; tchr., cons. Nat. Geog., 1986—; tchr. Leader for People in Soviet Union, 1989, 90; vol. First Internat. Environ. Expedition to Antarctica, 1995; presenter Populaton Education, 1995—. Author curriculum materials; photographer (book) Bobwhites, 1984. Co-chair Peace-Works. Recipient Merit award Nat. Coun. Geog. Edn., 1975, Creative Tchg. award Austin Assn. Tchrs., 1978, study grant to Malaysia and Indonesia, 1990, Excellence award for outstanding H.S. tchr. U. Tex., 1997, Edn.'s Unsung Heroes award No. Life, 1998, Outstanding Tchg. of the Humanities award, 1998, Excellence award Tex. State Bd. Edn., 1995, Peacemaker award Austin Dispute Resolution Ctr., 1998; Fulbright scholar, Israel, 1983. Mem. NEA, Nat. Coun. Geog. Edn., Earthwatch (participant archaeol. dig in Swaziland 1984, Romania 2003), World Wildlife Fund, Rotary, Delta Kappa Gamma (pres. 1986-88), Phi Kappa Phi. Democrat. Roman Catholic. Avocations: stained glass, photography, tennis, gardening, needlepoint. Home: 1025 Quail Park Dr Austin TX 78758-6749 Office: Lanier High Sch 1201 Payton Gin Rd Austin TX 78758-6699 E-mail: nlehmann@ev1.net.

LEHNERT, HERBERT HERMANN, foreign language educator; b. Luebeck, Germany, Jan. 19, 1925; came to U.S., 1958, naturalized, 1971; s. Bernhard Alfred and Elisabeth (Doemel) L.; m. Ingeborg Poth, Aug. 13, 1952; children— Bernard (dec.), Brigitte, Bettina. PhD, U. Kiel, Germany, 1952. Lectr. U. Western Ont., Can., 1957; faculty Rice U., 1958-68, prof. German, 1966-68, U. Kans., 1968-69, U. Calif., Irvine, 1969-94, rsch. prof. German, 1994—, chmn. dept., 1974-76. Vis. prof. Harvard U., 1970. Author: Thomas Mann: Fiktion, Mythos, Religion, 1965, Struktur und Sprachmagie, 1966, Thomas Mann Forschung, 1969, Geschichte der deutschen Literatur: Vom Jugendstil zum Expressionismus, 1978, Nihilismus der Menschenfreundlichkeit: Thomas Manns Wandlung (with Eva Wessell), 1991; editor: Doctor Faustus: A Novel at the Margin of Modernism (with Peter C. Pfeiffer) 1991; contbr. articles to profl. jours. Nat. Endowment for Humanities fellow, 1973, 78; Guggenheim fellow, 1978-79 Mem. MLA, Am. Assn. Tchrs. German. Home: 8 Harvey Ct Irvine CA 92612-4033 Office: U Calif Dept German Irvine CA 92697-3150

LEHRHAUPT, KAREN, elementary and secondary education educator; b. Detroit, Feb. 4, 1942; d. Karl M. and Evelyn (Hubbell) Kuechenmeister; m. James Allen Youngling, Aug. 22, 1964 (div. 1976); 1 child, Lisa Youngling Howard; m. Michael Lehrhaupt, Aug. 25, 1978; stepchildren: Gwen, David, Nancy, Amy (dec.). BA, Hood Coll., 1964; MA, Fairleigh Dickinson U., 1977. Tchr. Old Bridge (N.J.) Bd. of Edn., 1968-97, Aiken County (S.C.) Bd. Edn., 1997—. Avocations: running, golf. Home: 31 Veranda Ln Aiken SC 29803-4943 Office: Aiken Middle Sch 1 Gator Ln Aiken SC 29801-7804

LEIBENSPERGER, PHILIP WETZEL, secondary education educator; b. Kutztown, Pa., July 15, 1945; s. Harold and Frances (Wetzel) L.; m. Alexis Anne Lamanna, June 27, 1970. B in Edn., Kutztown U., 1967; MEd, U. Va., 1972. Educator Prince William County Schs., Manassas, Va., 1967-72; child devel. counselor Arlington County Schs., Arlington, Va., 1972-76, educator, 1976—2000; ret., 2000. Producing ednl. CD study guides and historical virtual fieldtrips for classroom tchrs. Mem. NEA, Va. Edn. Assn., Arlington Edn. Assn. (bd. dir. 1985), Prince William Edn. Assn. (faculty rep. 1968-72). Democrat. Lutheran. Avocation: model train collecting. Home: 2020 Freedom Ln Falls Church VA 22043-1809 Office: Swanson Mid Sch 5800 Washington Blvd Arlington VA 22205-2906

LEIBOW, LOIS MAY, secondary education educator; b. Newark, Jan. 4, 1937; d. Samuel and Sada (Rothman) Applebaum; m. Sheldon G. Leibow, Aug. 11, 1963; children: Philip, Frances, Brian. BA, Douglass Coll., 1959; MA in Sociology, CCNY, 1962. Substitute tchr. Monmouth County Registry, N.J., 1983—; telemarketer Target Teleconcepts, Inc., Hazlet, N.J., 1991—, Prudential Ins. Co., Red Bnnk, N.J., 1991—. Newspaper columnist Atlanticville, Long Branch, N.J., 1984—; contbr. Am. String Tchr., 1979. Mem. Hadassah (life, program v.p. Woodbridge, N.J. chpt. 1972-74), Sisterhood of Temple Beth El (bd. dirs.), Jewish War Vets., Woman's Club Perth Amboy N.J. Republican. Avocations: aerobics, ballroom dancing, studying languages, gardening.

LEIBY, BRUCE RICHARD, secondary education educator, writer; b. Media, Pa., Aug. 30, 1947; s. Edward Charles and Margaret Ellen (Strawbridge) L.; m. Linda Pauline Flounders, June 26, 1971. BSBA, Tusculum Coll., Greeneville, 1969; postgrad. West Chester U., 1970, 72. Tchr. Interboro Sch. Dist., Prospect Park, Pa., 1969-70, Delaware County C.C., Media, 1974; acct., tchr. info. processing Upper Darby (Pa.) Adult Sch., 1970-88, Upper Darby Sch. Dist., 1970—. Staff asst. Upper Darby H.S., 1987—, mem. bus. edn. adv. bd., co-sponsor Bus. Club, 1987-88; mem. bus. edn. curriculum com., 1992—. Author for Greenwood Press, Westport, Conn., 1988—; author: Gordon Macrae--A Bio-Bibliography, 1991, Howard Keel--A Bio-Bibliography, 1995; co-author: A Reference Guide to Television's Bonanza, 2001. Co-lay leader Meth. ch.; mem. Voices of Praise Choir. Mem. NEA, Pa. Edn. Assn., Upper Darby Edn. Assn. (past membership chmn.), Am. Film Inst., Suburban Phila. Bus. Edn. Assn., Internat. Friends of Gordon Macrae, Internat. Doris Day Soc., Shirley Jones Fan Club, Michael Ball Fan Club. Republican. Avocations: music, reading, collecting performing arts memorabilia, acting. Home: 13 E 6th St Media PA 19063-2501 Office: Upper Darby HS Lansdowne Ave Upper Darby PA 19082-5410

LEIDINGER, WILLIAM JOHN, federal official; b. Chgo., Feb. 1, 1940; s. Arthur George and Anna (Choisek) L.; m. Karen Aldinger, Sept. 1, 1962; children: Michael, Steven. BA, Loras Coll., Dubuque, Iowa, 1962; MA, State U. Iowa, 1963. Adminstrv. asst. to city mgr., Pk. Forest, Ill., 1963—65; asst. to city mgr. Alexandria, Va., 1965—71; asst. city mgr. Richmond, Va., 1971—72; city mgr., 1972—78; v.p. Rolm/Atlantic Corp., 1979—81; exec. dir. McGuire Clinic, Richmond, 1981—86; exec. v.p., chief lending officer Security Fed. Savs., Richmond, Va., 1986—91; county executive Fairfax County, Fairfax, Va., 1992—96; instr. Purdue U., No. Va. CC; sr. mgr. Price Waterhouse Coopers, 1996—2003; asst. sec. for mgmt. US Dept. Edn., 2002—, chief info. officer, 2003—. Guest lectr. U. Richmond, mem. bd. assos., Va. Commonwealth U. Bd. dirs., pres. Greater Richmond Transit Co., 1973-78; mem. Richmond City Planning Commn., 1971-78; bd. dirs. Richmond Eye Hosp., 1979—, St. Luke's Hosp, Richmond Cerebral Palsy Ctr; mem. Richmond City Council, 1980— ; bd. dirs. Port of Richmond. Mem. Internat. City Mgmt. Assn. (chmn. labor/mgmt. relations com. 1974-75), Nat. League Cities, Va. Municipal League, Am. Soc. Pub. Adminstrn. Roman Catholic. Mailing: Chief Information Officer US Dept of Education 400 Maryland Ave SW Washington DC 20202*

LEIGH, HOYLE, psychiatrist, educator, writer; b. Seoul, Korea, Mar. 25, 1942; came to U.S., 1965; m. Vincenta Masciandaro, Sept. 16, 1967; 1 child, Alexander Hoyle. MA, Yale U., 1982; MD, Yonsei U., Seoul, 1965. Diplomate Am. Bd. Psychiatry and Neurology. Asst. prof. Yale U., New Haven, 1971-75, assoc. prof., 1975-80, prof., 1980-89, lectr. in psychiatry, 1989—. Dir. Behavioral Medicine Clinic, Yale U., 1980-89; dir. psychiat. cons. svc. Yale-New Haven Hosp., 1971-89; chief psychiatry VA Med Ctr., Fresno, Calif., 1989—; prof., vice chmn. dept. psychiatry U. Calif., San Francisco, 1989—, head dept. psychiatry, 1989—; cons. Am. Jour. Psychiatry, Archives Internal Medicine, Psychosomatic Medicine. Author: The Patient, 1980, 2d edit., 1985, 3d edit., 1992; editor: Psychiatry in the Practice of Medicine, 1983, Consultation-Liaison Psychiatry: 1990's & Beyond, 1994, Biopsychosocial Approaches in Primary Care: State of the Art and Challenges for the 21st Century, 1997. Fellow ACP, Internat. Coll. Psychosomatic Medicine (v.p.), Am. Acad. Psychosomatic Medicine; mem. AMA, AAUP, World Psychiat. Assn. Avocations: reading, music, skiing. Office: U Calif Dept Psychiat 2615 E Clinton Ave Fresno CA 93703-2223

LEIGH-MANUELL, ROBERT ALLEN, training executive, educator; b. Bay Shore, NY, Oct. 4, 1942; s. Darrell B. and Rose A. (Sanders) L.-M.; m. Diane W. Frisbee, Mar. 28, 1964 (div. May 1982); children: Nancy D., Timothy J., Charles R.; m. Donna M. McGrath, Oct. 25, 1982; children: Michael N., David A. Student, Kans. State U., 1960-61; BS, SUNY, Oswego, 1964; postgrad., Hofstra U., 1965-66; MA, NYU, 1977. Cert. secondary sch. tchr., N.Y.; cert. sch. adminstr., N.Y. Tchr. Sachem Cen. Sch. Dist., Holtsville, N.Y., 1964-67; tng. mgr. Deutsch Relays, North Port, N.Y., 1967-68; instructional systems engr. Sperry Gyroscope, Great Neck, N.Y., 1968-74; cons. Mind, Inc., N.Y.C., 1974; tchr. Wantagh Sch. Dist., Wantagh, N.Y., 1974-76; adminstrv. intern Mamaroneck (N.Y.) Sch. Dist., 1976; adminstr. Westchester B.O.C.E.S., Port Chester, N.Y., 1976-79; tng. mgr. Data Communication, Farmingdale, N.Y., 1979-84; mgr. program devel. The Southland Corp., Dallas, 1984-92; ind. cons., owner Monarch Assocs., Dallas, Tex., 1992—. Com. mem. Commr.'s Task Force for technology in edn. Tex. Edn. Agy., Austin, 1987-88. Mem. Huntington (N.Y.) Sch. Dist. Bd. Edn., 1973-79, pres., 1975-77; vol. fireman West Sayville (N.Y.) Fire Dept., 1960-70. Named Outstanding Young Man in Am., Jaycees, 1974. Republican. Baptist. Avocations: fishing, hunting. Home: 3439 Meadow Creek Ln Sachse TX 75048-4181 Office: Monarch Assocs Ste 122 102 N SHiloh Garland TX 75042

LEIGHTY, DIANE CAROL, secondary education educator; b. East Orange, N.J., Feb. 21, 1951; d. Paul and Miriam Ruth (Thrall) Kraeuter; m. James Larry Leighty, June 24, 1972; children: Jocelyn Rebecca, Steven James. BA in Math. magna cum laude, Grove City (Pa.) Coll., 1973; MA in Math., U. Va., 1993. Cert. secondary math. instr., Va. Tchr. math. Stonewall Jackson H.S., Charleston, W.Va., 1973-74, Cleve. City Schs., 1974-75; substitute tchr. Spotsylvania (Va.) Schs., 1981-83, tchr. math., 1983-84, Manchester H.S., Chesterfield County, Va., 1984-95; tchr. math., curriculum writer Math and Sci. H.S. at Clover Hill, Midlothian, Va., 1995—2002; math. coord. K-12 Powhatan County Pub. Schs., 2003—. Adj. prof. John Tyler C.C., Midlothian, Va., 2001—; tech. trainer Chesterfield County Schs., 1993-2002; presenter in field. Author: The Statistical Analysis of Compositional Data, 1993. Cmty. adv. coun. mem. Manchester H.S., Midlothian, 1990-92; youth dir. Christ King Luth. Ch., Richmond, Va., 1993-96, mem. ch. coun., 1993-95; mem. ch. choir. Recipient Grove City Coll., 1969—72, Manchester H.S. PTA scholar, 1992, Presdl. Award for Excellence in Tchng. Math., 1997, Tandy Tech. Scholar, 2000, Gifted Tchr. award, Chesterfield County Schools, 2001. Mem. Nat. Coun. Tchrs. Math., Va. Coun. Tchrs. Math., Greater Richmond Coun. Tchrs. Math. (mem. com. 1984—). Lutheran. Avocations: travel, reading, music. Home: 11930 Silbyrd Dr Midlothian VA 23113-2139 Office: Powhatan County Pub Schools 4135 Old Buckingham Rd Powhatan VA 23139

LEIJA, ANITA LEIJA, elementary school educator; b. Mathis, Tex., Sept. 15, 1959; d. Erasmo and Oralia (Gonzales) Huerta; m. Jose M. Leija, Nov. 21, 1987; children: Marivel Elis, Amadeus. AA, Bee County Coll., 1980; BEd, Corpus Christi State U., 1982; MEd, Tex. A&I U., 1985. Cert. elem. tchr., Tex. Kindergarten tchr. Sinton Schs., 1982—96, Mathis Ind. Sch. Dist., 1996—. Mem. Tex. State Tchrs. Assn., Assn. Tex. Profl. Educators. Roman Catholic. Office: Weber-Hardin Elem Sch 500 St Marys St Mathis TX 78368

LEINO, DEANNA ROSE, business educator; b. Leadville, Colo., Dec. 15, 1937; d. Arvo Ensio Leino and Edith Mary (Bonan) Leino Malenck; 1 adopted child, Michael Charles Bonan. BSBA, U. Denver, 1959, MS in Bus. Adminstrn., 1967; postgrad., C.C. Denver, U. No. Colo., Colo. State U., U. Colo., Met. State Coll. Cert. tchr., vocat. tchr., Colo. Tchr. Jefferson County Adult Edn., Lakewood, Colo., 1963-67; tchr. bus., coord. coop. office edn. Jefferson HS, Edgewater, Colo., 1959-93, ret., 1993; sales assoc. Joslins Dept. Store, Denver, 1978—; mem. ea. team. clk. office automation Denver Svc. Ctr., Nat. Pk. Svc., 1993-94; wage hour tech. US Dept. Labor, 1994—. Instr. C.C. Denver, Red Rocks, 1967-81, U. Colo., Denver, 1976-79, Parks Coll. Bus. (now Parks Coll.), 1983—, Front Range C.C., 1998-2000; dist. advisor Future Bus. Leaders Am. Author short story. Active City of Edgewater Sister City Project Student Exch. Com., Opera Colo. Assocs. and Guild, I Pagliacci; pres. Career Women's Symphony Guild; treas. Phantoms of Opera, 1982—;ex-officio trustee Denver Symphony Assn., 1980-82. Recipient Disting. Svc. award Jefferson County Sch. Bd., 1980, Tchr. Who Makes a Difference award Sta. KCNC/Rocky Mountain News, 1990, Youth Leader award Lakewood Optimist Club, 1993; named to Jefferson HS Wall of Fame, 1981, Jefferson County Hist. Commn. Hall of Fame, 2000, countess of the Wheat Ridge Carnation Festival, 2001. Mem. NEA (life), Colo. Edn. Assn., Jefferson County Edn. Assn., Colo. Vocat. Assn., Am. Vocat. Assn., Colo. Educators for and about Bus., Profl. Sec. Internat., Career Women's Symphony Guild, Profl. Panhellenic Assn., Colo. Congress Fgn. Lang. Tchr., Wheat Ridge C. of C. (edn. and scholarship com.), Federally Employed Women, Tyrolean Soc. Denver, Delta Pi Epsilon, Phi Chi Theta, Beta Gamma Sigma, Alpha Lambda Delta. Republican. Roman Catholic. Avocations: decorating wedding cakes, crocheting, sewing, music, world travel. Home: 3712 Allison St Wheat Ridge CO 80033-6124 E-mail: Leino.Deanna@dol.gov.

LEISEY, DONALD EUGENE, educational materials company executive, educator; b. Pa., Sept. 23, 1937; s. Alvin L. and E. Marie L.; m. Patricia M. Leisey; children: Kristen, Kendra. BS in Edn., West Chester (Pa.) U., 1959; MA in Adminstrn., Villanova U., 1962; cert. in bus. adminstrn., U. So. Calif., 1970, EdD in Adminstrn., 1973. Cert. gen. adminstrv., gen. secondary, gen. elem., Calif. Tchr., Coatesville, Pa., 1959-62; prin. Downingtown, Pa., 1962-64, Dept. Def. Dependent Schs., Japan, 1964-67; asst. sup. Lennox Schs., Inglewood, Calif., 1967-71; dir. adminstrv. svcs. San Rafael (Calif.) City Sch. Dist., 1971-73; sup. schs., 1973-79; instr. Dominican Coll., 1973-79; v.p., regional mgr. Am. Learning Corp., Huntington Beach, Calif., 1979-80; v.p., treas. Kittredge Sch. Corp., San Francisco, 1980-83; instr. Calif. State U., Hayward, 1981; chmn., CEO Merryhill Schs., Inc., Sacramento, 1981-89; pres., chmn. bd., CEO The Report Card, Citrus Heights, Calif., 1990—; co-dir. Internat. Acad. Ednl. Entrepreneurship, 2000—. Apptd. bd. councilors U. So. Calif., Rossier Sch. Edn., 1999; trustee Fund West Chester U., 2000. Co-author: The Educational Entrepreneur: Making a Difference, 2000. Apptd. to Gov.'s Child Care Task Force, Calif., 1984, Gov.'s Child Devel. Program Adv. Com., Calif., 1985—. Recipient Disting. Alumnus award West Chester U., 1983, Disting. Svc. award L.A. County Sheriff, 1969, Hon. Svc. award PTA, 1970. Home and Office: 21 Silk Oak Cir San Rafael CA 94901-8301 Office: 6366 Tupelo Dr Citrus Heights CA 95621-1700 E-mail: DELAPLUS@aol.com.

LEISTNER, MARY EDNA, retired secondary education educator; b. Evanston, Ill., Apr. 13, 1929; d. Joseph W. and Edna C. (Moe) Cox; m. Delbert L. Leistner, Sept. 30, 1950; children: David, Martha, Joseph. BS in Chemistry, Purdue U., 1950; MEd, Miami U., Oxford, Ohio, 1964. Tchr. sci. and math. Ctrl. Jr. H.S., Sidney, Ohio, 1962-66; tchr. chemistry, biology, advanced chemistry Sidney H.S., 1966-93; ret., 1993. Mem. high sch. chemistry test com. Nat. Sci. Tchrs. Assn., Am. Chem. Soc., 1983-85. Exec. com. Ohio Dist. Luth. Women's Missionary League, Columbus, 1978-82, convention chmn., 1988; pres. Miami Valley zone, 1985-87; pres. Redeemer Ladies Soc., Sidney, 1980-91, 94-98, treas., 1998-2003; mem. gift shop com. Wilson Meml. Hosp., Sidney, 1994-96, aux. sec., 1997-98, membership chair, aux. v.p., 1999, aux. pres., 2000. Mem. Nat. Sci. Tchrs. Assn. (Cadre 100 award), Wstn. Ohio Sci. Tchrs. Assn. (pres. 1972-73), Sci. Edn. Coun. Ohio (dist. rep. exec. bd. 1984-86, treas. 1986-90, pres. elect 1991-92, pres. 1992-93, immediate past pres. 1993-94, ch. retirees/hist. com. 1995-2000), Sidney Edn. Assn. (treas. 1980-82, 85-86, tchr. of yr. 1988), Ohio Acad. Scis. (Jerry Acker outstanding tchr. of yr. award 1988-89, Exemplar 1993), Shelby Co. Ret. Tchrs. Assn. (v.p. 2003—), Delta Kappa Gamma (2d v.p. 1992-94, 1st v.p. 1994-96, pres. 1996-98, past pres. 1998—). Republican. Lutheran.

LEITCH, VINCENT BARRY, literary and cultural studies educator; b. Hempstead, N.Y., Sept. 18, 1944; s. Eugene Vincent and Lucile Jean (Amplo) L.; m. Jill Robin Berman, May 20, 1970 (div. May 1987); children: Kristin M., Rory G. BA, Hofstra U., 1966; MA, Villanova U., 1967; PhD, U. Fla., 1972. Postdoctoral fellow Sch. Criticism and Theory, U. Calif., Irvine, 1978; interim asst. prof. U. Fla., Gainesville, 1972-73; from asst. prof. to prof. English Mercer U., Macon, Ga., 1973-86; prof. English Purdue U., West Lafayette, Ind., 1986-97, co-dir. English and philosophy doctoral program, 1986-93; Paul and Carol Daube Sutton chair English U. Okla., Norman, 1997—. Mem. adv. bd. Modern Fiction Studies, 1992—97, Symploke, 1995—; reviewer NEH, 1985—88; Moss chair of excellence U. Memphis, 1991; sr. Fulbright lectr. U. Tampere, Finland, 1979; vis. prof. U. Debrecen, Hungary, 2002. Author: Deconstructive Criticism, 1983, American Literary Criticism from the 1930s to the 1980s, 1988, Cultural Criticism, Literary Theory, Poststructuralism, 1992, Postmodernism-Local Effects, Global Flows, 1996, Theory Matters, 2003; mem. editl. bd. lit. and film series Fla. State U. Press, 1983—, Purdue Univ. Press, 1988—90, South Atlantic Rev., 1985—87, Genre, 1997—, Project for Discourse and Theory U. Okla. Press, 1998—2002, mem. adv. bd. Minn. Review, 1996—, South Crtl. Review, 1999—2002. Recipient Outstanding Acad. Book award Assn. Coll. and Rsch. Librs., 1988; Am. Philos. Soc. grantee, 1974; fellow NEH, 1980, Mellon Found., 1981, Am. Coun. Learned Socs., 1985-86, Ctr. for Humanistic Studies, Purdue U., 1989, 96, Okla. Humanities Coun., 2002. Mem. MLA (publs. com. 1990-93, assembly del. 1990-92, 93-95, chair organizing com. 1995, chair ad hoc com. on governance issues 1995, mem. 1996, exec. com. lit. criticism divsn. 1994-98), Cultural Studies Assn., Soc. for Critical Exch. (bd. dirs. 1978-83), PEN Am. Ctr., Internat. Assn. for Philosophy and Lit., Am. Comparative Lit. Assn., South Ctrl. Modern Lang. Assn. Office: U Oklahoma Dept English Norman OK 73019 E-mail: vbleitch@ou.edu.

LEITES, BARBARA L. (ARA LEITES), artist, educator; b. Hamilton, Ohio, June 3, 1942; d. Wilbur Frank and Alice Marie (Butts) Mayer; m. William Michael Whitley, Oct. 29, 1972 (div. Nov. 1977); 1 child, Rachel; m. Andre Leo Leites, Dec. 15, 1981 (div. Mar. 2000); chldren: David, Bevin; 1 stepchild, Daniella. BFA, Miami U., Oxford, Ohio, 1964, MFA, 1967. Tchr. Madison Elem. Sch., Hamilton, 1964-65; tchr. art and humanities Key West (Fla.) H.S., 1967-70, tchr. adult edn. in art, 1968-70; isntr. Fla. Keys Jr. Coll., Key West, 1969-70; co-dir. Kleinert Gallery, Woodstock, N.Y., 1977-80; self employed artist under the name Ara Leites, 1981—. Bd. dirs. Woodstock Guild of Craftsmen, 1978—79; instr. drawing and painting, divsn. head visual arts Georgiana Bruce Kirby Preparatory Sch., Santa Cruz, Calif., 1998—2001, ret., 2001; owner Ara Fine Art Giclee Studio; workshop instr. painting, Tuscany, 2001, ARA Fine Art Studio, Tuscany, 2003. Exhibited at Gallery El Ciruello, Tepoztlan, Mex., Club 209 Gallery, Cuernavaca, Mex., Black Sheep Art Gallery, Eng., Westminster Gallery, London, Cin. Art Mus., Dayton Art Inst., Springfield (Mo.) Art Mus., Miami U.; U.S. nat. exhbns. of over 200 shows and 70 awards including Rocky Mountain Nat., Watercolor USA, Adirondacks Nat., Nat. Watercolor Soc., Am. Watercolor Soc., Audubon Artists, Phila. Watercolor Club, Allied Artists, N.Y.C., Calif. Nat. Watercolor Soc.; subject of articles in publs. Mem. AAUW, Internat. Soc. Exptl. Artists (signature), Am. Artists Profl. League (signature), Nat. Watercolor Soc. (signature), Nat. Soc. Painters in Casein and Acrylic (signature), Nat. Acrylic Painters Assn. (signature), Watercolor USA Honor Soc. (signature), Ky. Watercolor Soc. (signature), Tex. Watercolor Soc. (signature), Ga. Watercolor Soc. (signature), Mo. Watercolor Soc. (signature), Miss. Watercolor Soc. (signature), Phila. Watercolor Club Soc. (signature), Audubon Artists (signature), Mont. Watercolor Soc. (signature), Rocky Mountain Nat. Watercolor Soc. (signature), Fedn. of Can. Artists (signature), Soc. Layerists in Mixed Media (signature), Watercolor Soc. Ala. (signature), Pa. Watercolor Soc. (signature), Taos Nat. Watercolor Soc. (signature), Ea. Washington Watercolor Soc., Delta Delta Delta Alumnae Assn. Democrat. Avocations: gardening, carpentry, skiing, snowboarding, surfing. Home: 168 Oxford Way Santa Cruz CA 95060-6447 E-mail: araleites@sbcglobal.net.

LEITH, EMMETT NORMAN, electrical engineer, educator; b. Detroit, Mar. 12, 1927; s. Albert Donald and Dorothy Marie (Emmett) Leith; m. Lois June Neswold, Feb. 17, 1956; children: Kim Ellen, Pam Elizabeth. BS, Wayne State U., 1950, MS, 1952, PhD, 1978; DSc (hon.), U. Aberdeen, Scotland, 1996. Mem. rsch. staff U. Mich., 1952—, prof. elec. engring., 1968—. Cons. several indsl. corps. Contbr. articles to profl. jours. With USNR, 1945—46. Named Man of Yr., Indsl. Rsch. mag., 1966; recipient Gordon Meml. award, SPIE, 1965, citation, Am. Soc. Mag. Photographers, 1966, Achievement award, U.S. Camera and Travel mag., 1967, Excellence of Paper award, Soc. Motion Picture and TV Engrs., 1967, Daedalion award, 1968, Stuart Ballantine medal, Franklin Inst., 1969, Alumni award, Wayne State U., 1974, cited by Nobel Prize Commn. for contbns. to holography, 1971, Holley medal, ASME, 1976, Nat. medal of Sci., 1979, Russel lecture award, U. Mich., 1981, Denins Gabor medal, Soc. Photo-Instrumentation Engrs., 1983, Gold medal, 1990, Mich. Trailblazer award, 1986. Fellow: IEEE (Liebmann award 1967, Inventor of Yr. award 1976), Optical Soc. Am. (Wood medal 1975, Herbert Ives medal 1985), The Royal Photographic Soc. of Great Britain (hon.), Engring. Soc. Detroit (hon.); mem.: NAE, Sigma Pi Sigma, Sigma Xi. Achievements include patents in field; first demonstrating (with colleague) capability of holography to form high-quality 3-dimensional image. Home: 51325 Murray Hill Dr Canton MI 48187-1030 Office: Univ Mich Inst Sci and Tech PO Box 618 Ann Arbor MI 48106-0618 E-mail: leith@umich.edu.

LEITH, KAREN PEZZA, psychologist, educator; b. Providence, Sept. 27, 1948; d. Henry and Lucy Maria (Bevilacqua) P.; m. James Robert Leith, June 6, 1970; children: Douglas Clay, Cara Beth. BA, Brown U., 1970; MA in Religious Studies, John Carroll U., 1988; MA in Psychology, Case Western Res. U., 1995, PhD, 1997. Substitute elem. tchr. City of Chgo., 1970; math. tchr. Lane Tech. HS, Chgo., 1971; instr. preschool art and coordination programs Pk. Dist. Deerfield, Ill., 1973-75, coord. preschool day camp, 1975-80; jr. high religious edn. coord., catechist trainer Holy Cross, Deerfield, 1975-80; H.S. religious edn. coord. St. Mary parish, Hudson, Ohio, 1981-85, youth min., dir. religious edn., 1985-88, pastoral assoc., 1988-91; pvt. math. tutor Hudson, Aurora sch., Ohio, 1980-88; cons. for ministry devel. Diocese of Cleve., 1989—, steering com., instr., Faith and Justice Leadership Inst., 1995—; adj. faculty John Carroll U., 1988—97, 1998—99; rsch. asst. Case Western Res. U., 1993-97; adj. faculty Baldwin Wallace Coll., 1997—. Editor and contbr., chair com. manual on parish and sch. partnerships, Diocese of Cleve., 1997; adv. bd. Office on Women in Ch. and Soc., Diocese of Cleve., chair 1993-97; steering com. Cath. Diocese of Cleve. Social Justice Leadership Inst., 1995-98; coord. tng. Justice Tng. Diocese of Cleve., 2000—; exec. dir. Call to Renewal of Summit County, 2001--; presenter in field. Contbr. articles to profl. jours. Recipient Bishop Anthony M. Pilla Leadership award Roman Cath. Diocese Cleve., 1998, 2002; faculty rsch. grantee Baldwin Wallace Coll., 1997, grad. alumni travel grantee Case West Res. U., 1993-95. Mem. APA (grad. student travel award 1994), Am. Psychol. Soc., Midwestern Psychol. Assn., Soc. for Personality and Social Psychology, Cath. Commn. (bd. dir. 1984-2001, chair 1997-2001), Hudson LWV (bd. dir. 1980-92, v.p., treas.), Holy Ground (founder, spiritual dir.), mem., FutureChurch Leadership Coun., 2000-. Avocations: reading, needlework.

LEITMANN, GEORGE, mechanical engineer, educator; b. Vienna, May 24, 1925; arrived in U.S., 1940; s. Josef and Stella (Fischer) Leitmann; m. Nancy Lloyd, Jan. 28, 1955; children: Josef Lloyd, Elaine Michèle. BS, Columbia U., 1949, MA, 1950; PhD, U. Calif., Berkeley, 1956; D Engring. honoris causa, Tech. U. Vienna, 1988; D honoris causa, U. Paris, 1989, Tech. U. Darmstadt, 1990. Physicist, head aeroballistics sect. U.S. Naval Ordnance Sta., China Lake, 1950-57; mem. faculty U. Calif., Berkeley, 1957—, prof. engring. sci., 1963—, prof. grad. sch., 1995—, assoc. dean acad. affairs, 1981-90, assoc. dean rsch., 1990-94, acting dean, 1988, chair faculty, 1994-98, assoc. dean internat. rels., 2003—. Cons. to aerospace industry and govt. Author: (book) An Introduction to Optimal Control, 1966, Quantitative and Qualitative Games, 1969, The Calculus of Variations and Optimal Control, 1981; contbr. articles to profl. jours. With AUS, 1944—46, ETO. Decorated Croix de Guerre France, Fourragere Belgium, Comdr.'s Cross, Order of Merit Germany, commendatore Order of Merit Italy; named Miller Rsch. prof., 1966; recipient Pendray Aerospace Lit. award, AIAA, 1979, Mechanics and Control of Flight award, 1984, Von Humboldt U.S. Sr. Scientist award, Von Humboldt Found., 1980, Levy medal, Franklin Inst., 1981, Berkeley citation, U. Calif.-Berkeley, 1991, Von Humboldt medal, Von Humboldt Found., 1991, Rufus Oldenburger medal, ASME, 1995, Distng. Engring. Alumni award, 2002; Berkeley fellow, 2002. Mem.: NAE, Georgian Acad. Sci., A. V. Humboldt Assn. Am. (pres. 1994—97), Bavarian Acad. Sci., Georgian Acad. Engring., Russian Acad. Natural Sci., Argentine Nat. Acad. Engring., Internat. Acad. Astronautics, Acad. Sci. Bologna. Office: U Calif Coll Engring Berkeley CA 94720-0001 E-mail: gleit@uclink4.berkeley.edu.

LE JEUNE, JEAN MARIA, administrator, educator; b. Coon Valley, Wis., Apr. 11, 1963; d. William John and Rosemarie Katherine (Mlsna) LeJ. BS, U. Wis., La Crosse, 1985, postgrad., 1990—. Substitute tchr. Onalaska (Wis.) High Sch., 1986-87, Bangor (Wis.) High Sch., 1986-88; tchr. upper elem. grades St. Mary's Ridge Sch., Norwalk, Wis., 1989-92, prin., 1991-92. Grad. asst. U. Wis., La Crosse, 1993—; cook Ridge View Inn, La Crosse, Wis., 1980—; cook, waitress Bluff View, La Crosse, 1986-88; cook, waitress, bartender, Likelee Spot, Bangor, Wis., 1992; mem. Edn. Com., St. Mary's Sch., Norwalk, 1992-93. Vol. Miss. Valley Archeol. Soc., La Crosse, 1992, 93. Recipient Dane, Eileen Nash Grant for Spl. Students, U. Wis., La Crosse, 1990. Mem. ASCD, Mem. Wis. Assn. for Middle Level Edn., Nat. Cath. Edn. Assn. Avocations: tennis, reading, cooking, bicycling. Office: St Mary's Ridge Sch RR 1 Box 1250 Norwalk WI 54648-9746

LELAND, HENRY, psychology educator; b. N.Y.C., Feb. 13, 1923; s. Ida (Miller) L.; m. Helen D. Faitos (div. 1979); children: Colombe, David Jean, Daniel Louis; m. Sherrie Lynn Ireland, Dec. 7, 1980. AB, San Jose State Coll., 1948; PhD, Université de Paris, Paris, 1952. Lic. psychologist, Ohio. Clin. psychologist with Dr. Jean Biro, Paris, 1949-52; sr. clin. psychologist N.Y. State Mental Health Commn., Syracuse, 1952-54; dir. dept. psychol. svc. Muscatatuck State Sch., Butlerville, Ind., 1954-57; chief clin. psychologist Parsons (Kans.) State Hosp. and Tng. Ctr., 1957-63, coord. profl. tng., edn. and demonstration, 1963-70; assoc. in child rsch. Kansas U. Bur. child Rsch., Lawrence, 1963-70; assoc. prof. psychology Ohio State U., Columbus, 1970-72, prof., 1972-93, prof. emeritus, 1993—, mem. senate, 1985-88; chief psychology Herschel W. Nisonger Ctr., Columbus, 1970-93. Tchg. asst. Ind. U. Extension Svc., 1956-57; assoc. prof. Kansas State Coll., 1958-70; dist. vis. lectr. U. So. Calif., L.A., 1969; prin. investigator Adaptive Behavior Project, Ohio Dept. Mental Health and Mental Retardation, 1972-75, cons., 1972-76; examiner State Bd. Psychology Ohio, 1987-88, 92-94, sec., 1988-89, pres., 1989-90, 94-95, active, 1986-95; cons. Cen. Ohio Psychiat. Hosp., 1986-93; com. on acad. misconduct Ohio State U., 1990-93; mem. Kans. State Bd. Examiners of Psychologists, 1967-70, chair, 1968-69; prin. investigator demonstrating adaptive behavior, psychiat. problem NIMH, 1964-70. Author: (with D. Smith) Play Therapy with Mentally Subnormal Children, 1965, (with others) Brain Damage and Mental Retardation, 1967, (with others) Handbuch der Kinderpsychotherapie, Vol. II, Germany, 1968, (with others) Social Perceptual Training Kit for Community Living, 1968, Impairment in Adaptive Behavior: A Community Dimension, Tracks, Vols. II, 12, 1960-67, (with others) Social Inference Training of Retarded Adolescents at the Pre-Vocational Level, 1968, (with others) Mental Health Services for the Mentally Retarded, 1972, (with others) Sociobehavioral Studies in Mental Retardation, 1973, (with D. Smith) Mental Retardation: Current and Future Perspectives, 1974, (with others) Research to Practice in Mental Retardation and Education and Training, II, 1977, (with others) International Encyclopedia of Psychiatry, Psychology, Psychoanalysis and Neurology, II, 1977, (with others) Psychological Management of Pediatric Problems, 1978, (with Deutsch)Abnormal Behavior, 1980, (with others) Pscychoeducational Assessment of Preschool and Primary Age Children, 1982, (with others) Comprehensive Handbook of Mental Retardation, 1983, (with others) The Foundations of Clinical Neuropsychology, 1983, (with others) Institutions for the Mentally Retarded: A Changing Role in Changing Times, 1986, (with others) Encyclopedia of Human Intelligence Vol. I, 1994, AAMR Adaptive Behavior Scale-Residential and Community, 1995, AAMR Adaptive Behavior Scale-School, 1993; cons. editor Am. Jour. Mental Deficiency, 1965-70, Profl. Psychology, 1977-95, Mental Retardation, 1980-84; contbr. articles to profl. jours. Mem. Franklin County Bd. Mental Retardation/Devel. Disabilities, 1980—82; trustee Goodwill Rehab. Ctr., 1975—, mem. exec. com., 1985—; trustee, treas. Shalom House, Inc., 2000—. Recipient Disting. Svc. in Mental Deficiency award, Am. Assn. on Mental Deficiency, 1985; NIMH grantee, 1964-70 Fellow AAAS, APA (councilor 1986-90, Edgar A. Doll Meml. award div. 33 1990), Am. Assn. on Mental Retardation (councilor 1964-68), Ohio Psychol. Assn., Soc. for Pediatric Psychology, Kans. Psychol. Assn. (pres. 1966), Ctrl. Ohio Psychol. Assn. (pres. 1996). Democrat. Jewish. Avocations: stamp collecting, gourmet cooking. Home: 2120 Iuka Ave Columbus OH 43201-1322 E-mail: irelandleland@columbus.rr.com.

LEMA, JO-ANNE S. academic administrator; b. Worcester, Mass., Nov. 5, 1947; d. James Patrick and Florence Marie (Howard) Sullivan; m. Luis E. Lema, Sept. 25, 1971; children: Maria, James. BA, Merrimack Coll., 1969; EdM, Boston U., 1975; EdD, Harvard U., 1981. Researcher MIT, Cambridge, Mass., 1969-71, 79-81; tchr. Colegio Bolivar, Cali, Columbia, 1971-73; contracts adminstr. Educators Cons. Svc., Shrewsbury, Mass., 1973-75; tchr., rsch. asst. Harvard Univ., Cambridge, 1977-79; dir. inst. rsch. Bryant Coll., Smithfield, R.I., 1982-89, asst. v.p., 1989—. Rep. town mtg. mem. Town Govt., North Attleboro, Mass., 1990-93; scholarship com. mem. Harvard Radcliffe Club of R.I., Providence, 1991—, exec. com., 1992—; trustee, chmn., North Attleboro Heights Assn. Mem. Soc. for Coll. and Univ. Planning (regional rep. 1991—, bd. dirs. 1991—), Harvard Radcliffe Club of R.I. (scholarship com. 1991—, exec. com.). Home: 106 Blackberry Rd North Attleboro MA 02760-6400 Office: Bryant Coll 1150 Douglas Pike Smithfield RI 02917-1291

LEMAITRE, LOUIS ANTOINE, secondary education educator; b. Monagas, Venezuela, May 27, 1946; came to U.S., 1964; s. Leon A. and Teodosia M. (Urbaez) Aumaitre. BA, Don Bosco Coll., 1973; MA, St. John's U., 1974; MS in Secondary Edn., CUNY, 1978, MS in Supervision and Adminstrn., 1984; PhD in Edn., NYU, 1980. Cert. adminstr., N.Y. Instr. bilingual/ESL N.Y.C. Sch. System, 1975—. Adj. prof. NYU, Adelhi U. Author: Between Flight and Longing, a Life of Teresa de la Parra, 1988, Mujer Ingeniosa, a Life of Teresa de la Parra, 1992, Venezolana y Universal, Rosario Blanco, 1993 (Spl. Commendation 1993). Mem. MLA Assn. Republican. Roman Catholic. Avocations: golf, tennis. Address: 405 E Sinto Ave Spokane WA 99202-1849

LEMIEUX, RON, education and youth minister; m. Val Lemieux; 3 children. BA, BEd, U. Winnipeg; Cert. in Edn., U. Manitoba. Profl. hockey player Pitts. Penguins, Pitts.; coach Lorette H.S. Girls' Hockey Team, Lorette; tchr. Lorette Pub. Schs.; elected minister Manitoba Legis. Assembly, Winnipeg, appointed minister of edn. and youth. Minister culture, heritage and tourism Manitoba Legis. Assembly, Winnipeg, minister responsible for sport, minister consumer and corp. affairs; mem. treasury bd Cabinet Providence of Manitoba, Winnipeg, comty. and econ. devel. com., mem. healthy child and neighborhoods com. Office: 168 Legis Bldg 450 Broadway Winnipeg MA RC3 0V8 Canada

LEMISH, DONALD LEE, university athletics director; b. Auburn, Ind., Oct. 4, 1943; s. Anthony G. and Dorothy (Palmer) L.; m. Sue Ann Schwartz, June 26, 1965; children: Michael Lee, Kyle Patrick. BS in Edn., Ball State U., 1965, MA, 1968; postgrad. cert., Harvard U., 1986. Assoc. and asst. dir. alumni and devel. programs Ball State U., Muncie, Ind., 1968-74, dir. devel., 1974-77; asst. v.p. devel. U. Ala., Birmingham, 1977-79; vice chancellor advancement and planning East Carolina U., Greenville, N.C., 1979-82; v.p. advancement Longwood Coll., Farmville, Va., 1982-87; v.p. univ. advancement James Madison U., Harrisonburg, Va., 1987-94; pres. James Madison U. Found., Harrisonburg, 1987-94; dir. athletics James Madison U., Harrisonburg, Va., 1994—; owner City Motors Co. Tchr. journalism Elmhurst High Sch., Fort Wayne, Ind., 1965-68. Author: Establishing a University Foundation, 1989, The Foundation Handbook, 1981. Treas. Constn. Bicentennial Commn., Prince Edward Co., Va., 1985-87; chmn. adv. coun. Harrisonburg Police Citizens, 1994; chair Harrisonburg/Rockingham County Crime Solvers, 1994—; bd. dirs. Shenandoah Valley Econ. Edn., Inc. Recipient CASE Alumni Giving Incentive award Coun. Advancement of Support Edn., 1975-81, 84-85. Mem. Bus. Edn. Assistance Corp. (dir., sec. 1991-92), Harrisonburg C. of C. (bd. dirs. 1990—, v.p. 1994-96, pres. 1997), Farmville C. of C. (pres. 1986-87, dir. 1983-87), Rotary Club, Elks. Roman Catholic. Avocations: athletic officiating, collecting baseball memorabilia. Office: James Madison U Godwin Hall 206 Harrisonburg VA 22807-0001 Home: 523 Paul St Harrisonburg VA 22801-3229

LEMKE, HERMAN ERNEST FREDERICK, JR., retired elementary education educator, consultant; b. Argo, Ill., July 13, 1919; s. Herman and Augusta Victoria (Statt) L.; m. Geneva Octavene Davidson, Sept, 5, 1942 (dec.); children: Patricia, Herman E.F. III, Gloria, John, Elizabeth. BA, George Peabody Coll., 1949, MA, 1952. Cert. social sci. tchr., Tenn., elem. tchr., Calif. Tchr. Cadd Parish Sch., Shreveport, La., 1950-55, Pacific Sch. Dist., Sacramento, 1956-58, Sacramento (Calif.) Sch. Dist., 1958-89; part-time tchr. Sacramento (Calif.) County Sch., 1974-84, ret., 2002—. Substitute tchr., 1989—. Co-author: Natural History Guide, 1963, (field guide) Outdoor World of Sacramento Region, 1975; contbr. articles to profl. jours. Asst. dist. Commn. Boys Scouts Am., Shreveport, 1954, cubmaster, 1954; leader 4-H Club, Shreveport, 1950-54; elder Faith Luth. Ch., Fair Oaks, Calif., 1981-88. Recipient Scouter award, Boy Scouts Am., Shreveport, 1954, Honorary Svc. award Am. Winn Sch. PTA, 1982, Calif. Life Diploma Elem. Schs., 1961. Mem. Calif. Congress Parents Tchrs. Inc. (life). Democrat. Avocations: backpacking, coin collecting, stamp collecting, antiques, fishing. Home: 7720 Magnolia Ave Fair Oaks CA 95628-7316

LEMKE, LAURA ANN, language educator, principal; b. Hollis, L.I., N.Y., May 4, 1964; d. Ronald Louis Zarobinski and Donna Jean (Strayer) Williams; m. David Michael Lemke, Aug. 25, 1984; children: Kelsey Marie, Kayla Nicole. BA in French and Bus. with honors, Mich. State U., 1987, M in Edn. Adminstrn., 1993, EdS, 2002. Cert. secondary tchr., vocat. and adminstrn., ednl. specialist 2002. Teaching asst. East Lansing (Mich.) Pub. Schs., 1985-87, French and bus. tchr. comty. edn., 1985-87; tchr. French and bus. Grand Blanc (Mich.) Comty. Schs., 1987&, coord. elem. fgn. lang., 1990-91, coord. K-12 fgn. lang., 1991-94. Chair North Cen. accreditation Grand Blanc Mid. Sch., 1990-96. Vol. Flint Internat. Inst., 1987-91, United Way, Flint, 1992. Mem. Nat. Bus. Edn. Assn. (Award of Merit 1987), Am. Assn. of Tchrs. of French, Mich. Fgn. Lang. Assn. (presider's chair 1994-95), Mich. Bus. Edn. Assn. (Outstanding Bus. Educator award 1986-87), Phi Kappa Phi. Avocations: reading mysteries, camping, traveling. Home: 2128 Perlin Ct Grand Blanc MI 48439-7312 Office: Flushing Jr High Sch 409 Chamberlain Flushing MI 48433 E-mail: lauralemke@flushing.k12.mi.us.

LEMOINE, PAMELA ALLYSON, principal; b. Mansura, La., Sept. 6, 1945; d. Levy Paul and Iva Rae (Paul) L. BA in English, Libr. Sci., Nicholls State U., 1967; MEd in Ednl. Tech., McNeese State U., 1976; postgrad., Pepperdine U., 1978-80, Boston U., 1980-82. Libr. Evergreen Jr. High Sch., Houma, La., 1967-69, Zukiran Elem. Sch., Okinawa, Japan, 1969-70, Goose Bay High Sch., Labrador, Can., 1970-72, Matthew Perry Sch., Iwakuni, Japan, 1972-76; head libr., audio-visual specialist Kubasaki High Sch., Okinawa, 1978-80; libr. Bamberg (Germany) Am. High Sch., 1980-82; tchr. Evergreen Jr. High Sch., Houma, 1982-83; libr. Lisa Park Elem. Sch., Houma, 1983-84; audio-visual specialist H.L. Bourgeois High Sch., Houma, 1984-85; asst. prin. Lisa Park Elem. Sch., Houma, 1985—. Cons. librarian Dept. Def. Schs., Bamberg, 1980-82. Contbr. articles to mags. Pres. Friends of the Libr., Houma, 1988, Houma-Terrebonne Arts and Humanities Coun., 1992-93, treas., 1989-91; bd. dirs. Terrebonne Libr. Bd. Control., Houma, 1990—. Named Outstanding Tchr. of Yr. Dept. Def. Schs., 1979, 81. Mem. NEA, Terrebonne Prin.'s Assn. (corr. sec. 1991), Phi Delta Kappa, Delta Kappa Gamma. Avocations: gardening, sewing, crafts, writing. Home: 116 Westview Dr Houma LA 70364-2534 Office: Lisa Park Sch 1900 Willie Lou Ave Houma LA 70364-2556

LEMONS, L. JAY, academic administrator; b. Chadron, Nebr., Aug. 30, 1959; s. Larry Dean and LaVana Lee (Smith) L.; m. Marsha Louise Shone, May 27, 1984; children: Olivia Jaye, Magdalene Marie, Thomas Potter. BS, BA, Nebr. Wesleyan U., 1983; MEd, U. Nebr., 1985; PhD, U. Va., 1991. Cert. phys. edn. tchr., health edn. tchr. Hall dir. office residence life Nebr. Wesleyan U., Lincoln, 1982-84; grad. asst. to dir. admissions office admissions and advising U. Nebr., Lincoln, 1984-85; asst. area coord. dept. student affairs Tex. A&M U., College Station, 1985-86, area coord. dept. student affairs, 1986-88; grad. asst. to dean Curry Sch. Edn. U. Va., Charlottesville, 1988-89, intern Curry Sch. Edn. Found., 1989, intern office of pres., 1989-90, asst. to pres., 1990—, chancellor Wise, Va., 1992—. Summer conf. program chair divsn. student svcs. Tex. A&M, 1987; presenter S.W. Assn. Coll. Univ. Housing Officers Conf., 1987, ann. minority student recruitment and retention conf. Tex. Higher Edn. Coord. Bd., 1988; bd. dirs. S.W. Va. Higher Edn. Ctr., Abingdon, S.W. Va. Pub. Edn. Consortium, Wise, Clinch Valley Coll. Found. Contbr. articles to profl. jours. Recipient Outstanding Young Men of Am. award, 1986, Gov.'s fellowship, 1988-90, Annette Gibbs Rsch. and Publ. award, 1990. Mem. Am. Assn. Counseling and Devel., Am. Coll. Personnel Assn. (presenter nat. conf. 1986), Nat. Assn. Student Personnel Adminstrs. (participant new profl.'s inst. region III 1987, local arrangements com. mem. fall conf. 1988, registration chair Tex. state conf. 1988, program coord. state conf. 1989, 90, presenter region IV west conf. 1986, nat. conf. 1988, region III chief student affairs officers workshop 1988, ann. conf. 1991, Outstanding New Profl. award region III 1987), Assn. Study Higher Edn., So. Assn. Coll. Student Affairs (registration chair devel. theories workshop 1988, presenter ann. conf. 1987), Blue Key Nat. Honor Soc., Kappa Delta Pi (Outstanding Edn. Student award 1983). Office: Univ Va Coll at Wise 1 College Ave Wise VA 24293-4400

LEMOS, RAMON MARCELINO, philosophy educator; b. Mobile, Ala., July 7, 1927; s. Marcelino and Marie Louise (Moore) L.; m. Mamie Lou McCrory, Dec. 26, 1951 (dec. Apr. 1990); children: Noah Marcelino, William Ramon, Christopher Tait, John Paul; m. Anne Craft, Aug. 7, 1994. BA, U. Ala., 1951; MA, Duke, 1953, PhD, 1955; Fulbright scholar, U. London, Eng., 1955-56. Mem. faculty U. Miami, 1956—, prof. philosophy, 1967—99, chmn. dept., 1971-84, prof. emeritus, 1999—. Author: Experience, Mind and Value, 1969, Rousseau's Political Philosophy, 1977, Hobbes and Locke: Power and Consent, 1978, Rights, Goods, and Democracy, 1986, Metaphysical Investigations, 1988, The Nature of Value: Axiological Investigations, 1995, A Neomedieval Essay in Philosophical Theology, 2001. Served with USMC, 1945-49. Named Outstanding Tchr. U. Miami, 1968 Mem. Am. Philos. Assn. (program chmn. Eastern div. meeting 1983), Fla. Philos. Assn. (pres. 1963), Phi Beta Kappa, Phi Kappa Phi, Omicron Delta Kappa. Home: 6960 SW 82nd Ct Miami FL 33143-2509 Office: U Miami Dept Philosophy Coral Gables FL 33124

LEMPERT, RICHARD OWEN, lawyer, educator; b. Hartford, Conn., June 2, 1942; s. Philip Leonard and Mary (Steinberg) L.; m. Cynthia Ruth Willey, Sept. 10, 1967 (div.); 1 child, Leah Rose; m. Lisa Ann Kahn, May 26, 2002. AB, Oberlin Coll., 1964; JD, U. Mich., 1968, PhD in Sociology, 1971. Bar: Mich. 1978. Asst. prof. law U. Mich., Ann Arbor, 1968-72, assoc. prof., 1972-74, prof. law, 1974—, prof. sociology, 1985—, Francis A. Allen collegiate prof. law, 1990—2001, acting chair dept. sociology, 1993-94, chair dept. sociology, 1995-98, dir. life scis., values and soc. program, 2000—, Eric Stein Disting. Univ. prof. law and sociology, 2001—; dir. divsn. social and econ. scis. NSF, 2002—. Mason Ladd disting. vis. prof. U. Iowa Law Sch., 1981; vis. fellow Centre for Socio-Legal Rsch., Wolfson Coll., Oxford (Eng.) U., 1982; mem. adv. panel for law and social sci. div. NSF, 1976-79, mem. exec. com. adv. com. for social sci., 1979; mem. com. law enforcement and adminstrn. of justice NRC, vice chmn., 1984-87, chmn., 1987-89; mem. adv. panel NSF program on Human Dimensions of Global Change, 1989, 92-94; mem. com. on DNA technology in forensic sci. NRC, 1989-92, com. on drug testing in workplace, 1991-93; vis. scholar Russell Sage Found., 1998-99; vis. scholar Russell Sage Found., 1998-99. Author: (with Stepehn Saltzburg) A Modern Approach to Evidence, 1977, 2d edit., 1983, 3d edit. (with Sam Gross and James Liebman), 2000; (with Joseph Sanders) An Invitation to Law and Social Science, 1986, Under the Influence, 1993; editor: (with Jacques Normand and Charles O'Brien) Under the Influence? Drugs and the American Work Force, 1994; editorial bd. Law and Soc. Rev., 1972-77, 89-92, 98—, editor, 1982-85; mem. editl. bd. Evaluation Rev., 1979-82, Violence and Victims, 1985—, Jour. Law and Human Behavior, 1980-82; contbr. articles to profl. jours. Fellow Ctr. for Advanced Study in Behavioral Scis., 1994-95; vis. scholar Russell Sage Found., 1998-99. Fellow Am. Acad. Arts and Scis.; mem. Am. Sociol. Assn. (chair sect. sociology of law 1995-96), Law and Society Assn. (trustee 1977-80, 90-93, exec. com. 1979-80, 82-87), Order of Coif, Phi Beta Kappa, Phi Kappa Phi. Office: U Mich Law Sch 625 S State St Ann Arbor MI 48109-1215 E-mail: rol25@hotmail.com.

LEMS, KRISTIN, English language educator, songwriter; b. Evanston, Ill., Dec. 2, 1950; d. William Lems and Carol Silver Lems-Dworkin; m. A. Daoudi (div.); children: Karima, Kennan. BA in English Lit. and Creative Writing with honors, U. Mich., 1972; MA in W. Asian Studies, U. Ill., 1975, MA in TESOL with honors, 1983; EdD, Nat. Coll. Edn., 2003. Cert. secondary tchr., Ill.; portapak video recording and editing. Adj. prof. Nat.-Louis U., Chgo., 1985-93, asst. prof., 1993-99, assoc. prof., 1999—. Tchr. piano, guitar children and adults, 1966—; with Movement Ctr., Nat.-Louis U., 1990-91; music coord. Latino Outreach Program, Evanston, 1992-93; instr. St. Augustine Coll., 1991, Ill. Inst. Tech., 1990-93, North Park U., 2002-03, U. Chgo., 2003; lectr. in field. Writer numerous ednl. and inspirational songs; affiliated writer, pub. BMI; pub. Kleine Ding Music Inc.; rec. artist with Carolsdatter Prodns., Smithsonian/Folkways, Rounder Records; contbr. articles to profl. jours. and newsletters. Founder Nat. Women's Music Festival, Champaign-Urbana, Ill., 1974; commr. Ridgeville Pk. Dist., 1995-2000. Recipient Woman Ill. Repute award Ill. Women's Agenda, 1989, Pres. award Ill. NOW, 1990, Humanist Heroine award Am. Humanist Assn., 1994; Fulbright scholar U.S. Info. Svc., U. Algiers, Algeria, 1983-85. Mem. TESOL (ann. presenter 1989—, feature writer newsletter). Avocations: songwriting, swimming, learning languages. Home and Office: Carolsdatter Prodns 221C Dodge Ave Evanston IL 60202-3667 E-mail: kristinlems@yahoo.com.

LENARD, MARY JANE, accounting and information systems educator; b. York, Pa., July 8, 1955; d. Martin and Anne Ruth (Zimmerman) Kondor; m. Robert Louis Lenard, July 9, 1977; children: Kevin, Kelsey. BS in Econ.

and Adminstrv. Sci., Carnegie Mellon U., 1977; MBA in Fin., U. Akron, 1982; PhD in Bus. Adminstrn., Kent State U., 1995. Cert. mgmt. acct. Mgmt. trainee Equibank, NA, Pitts., 1977-78; acct., auditor Goodyear Tire and Rubber Co., Akron, Ohio, 1978-86; instr. U. Akron, 1986-93; mem. adj. faculty Cleve. State U., 1994-97; assoc. prof. Barton Coll., Wilson, NC, 1997—2001; asst. prof. U. N.C., Greensboro, 2001—. Author procs.; contbr. articles to profl. jours. Pres. Hillcrest Elem. PTA, Richfield, Ohio, 1992—93; v.p. Summit County PTA, Akron, 1994—96; mem., newsletter dir. Wakefield Mid. Sch. PTSA, 2000—02; coord. Vol. Income Tax Assistance, Barton Coll., Wilson, 1998—2001; active Revere Schs. Computer Curriculum Com., 1994—95; mem. Wakefield H.S. PTSA, 2002—; mem. and chair IT Com. for Acctg. Dept. at UNC, 2001—; mem. Bryan Sch., UNC Greensboro Planning Com., 2002—, Bryan Sch., UNC Greensboro Faculty Develop. Com., 2002—. Grantee Faculty Devel. grant, Barton Coll., 1997, 1999. Mem.: Decision Scis. Inst., Akron Women's Network, Assn. for Info. Systems, Inst. Mgmt. Accts. (dir. mem. retention 1994—96), Am. Acctg. Assn. (Best Paper award 1998), Beta Gamma Sigma. Office: U NC Bryan Sch Bus & Econ Greensboro NC 26165 E-mail: mjlenard@uncg.edu.

LENDERMAN, JOANIE, elementary school educator; b. Medford, Oreg., Jan. 20, 1946; d. Jay Lenderman and Vivian Spencer. BS in Edn., So. Oreg. Coll., Ashland, 1969; MS in Edn., Portland State U., 1972; postgrad., U. Va., 1985. Elem. tchr. Beaverton (Oreg.) Schs., 1972-76, Internat. Sch. Svcs., Isfahan, Iran, 1976-78; ESL instr. Lang. Svcs., Tucker, Ga., 1983-84; tchr. Fairfax (Va.) Schs., 1985-86; elem. tchr. Beaverton (Oreg.) Schs., 1990-96. Home: 4105 Jefferson Pkwy Lake Oswego OR 97035-1479

LENING, JANICE ALLEN, physical education educator; b. Topeka, Mar. 10, 1946; d. John Otis and Bertha May (Simon) Allen; m. Jay Ridley Lening, Dec. 26, 1976; children: Brooke Michelle, Chad Allen. BA in Phys. Edn., U. Denver, 1968; MA in Elem. Edn., U. No. Colo., 1980. Lic. tchr. phys. edn., elem. edn., Colo. Tchr. Denver Pub. Schs., 1968-69; phys. edn. tchr. Jefferson County Schs., Lakewood, Colo., 1969—, gymnastics coach, 1969, 76-79, gymnastics judge, 1970-75. Mem. budget com. Shaffer Elem. Sch., Littleton, 1985-86, accountability com., 1985-86; wellnes rep. Shaffer, Colorow, Gov. Racn Elem., Littleton, 1985-98; mem. social com. Lasley, Green Gables, Shaffer, Gov. Ranch Elem. Lakewood and Littleton, 1970-98; student coun. supr. Green Gables Elem., Lakewood, 1978-85, credit union rep., 1980-85. Leader Girl Scouts, Littleton, 1986-87; coach Columbine Soccer Assn., Littleton, 1986-91; judge Odyssey of the Mind, Littleton, 1986-98. Recipient Gold medal Am. Heart Assn., Denver, 1991, Bronze award, 1994-97 State Champion award sch. Pres. Coun. on Phys. Fitness, 1990-98; chairperson Precedures Com., 1994-97. Mem. AAPHERD, NEA, PAC, Colo. Edn. Assn. (mentor tchr. 1997-99), JCEA. Republican. Avocations: softball, swimming, volleyball, golf, tennis. Home: 6546 W Hoover Pl Littleton CO 80123-3632 Office: Govs Ranch Elem Sch 5354 S Field St Littleton CO 80123-7800

LENNERS, COLLEEN RENEE, secondary education educator; b. Beatrice, Nebr., Aug. 31, 1956; d. Virgil M. and Edith B. (Fritzen) L. BS in Bus. Edn., U. Nebr., 1978, MEd in Bus. Edn., 1982. Tchr. bus. edn. Council Bluffs (Iowa) Pub. Schs., 1978-89; tchr. trainer Tchr. Effectiveness Tng. II Program, Council Bluffs, 1988-89; instr. bus.-vocat. edn., supr. student tchrs., project dir. U. Nebr., Omaha, 1990-91; tchr. bus. edn. Omaha Pub. Schs., 1991—. Tchr. sunday sch. Kountze Meml. Luth. Ch., Omaha, 1983—, mem. ch. coun., 1987-90, mem. youth com., 1987-94, mem. edn. com., 1994—; vol. Honey Sunday Greater Omaha Assn. for Retarded Citizens and Madonna Sch., 1991—; vol. Toys for Tots, USMCR, Omaha, 1992—; vol. Camp Quality HEartland, 1995. Recipient Belong Excel Study Travel in Nebr. award Nebr. Dept. Edn., 1994, 95. Mem. NEA, Nebr. Edn. Assn., Omaha Edn. Assn., Nat. Bus. Edn. Assn., Nebr. Bus. Edn. Assn. (co-coord. fall conf. 1993), Delta Pi Epsilon (past newsletter editor, corr. sec., v.p., pres., editor Tchg. Tips for Classroom 1985). Republican. Avocations: cooking, travel, reading. Home: 8817 Monroe St Omaha NE 68127-4435 Office: Central HS 124 N 20th St Omaha NE 68102-4801

LENNON, JOANNA LESLIE, conservation organization executive; b. L.A., May 5, 1948; d. John Joseph and Ethel Anne (White) L.; m. G. Craig Meacham, July 13, 1975 (div. 1982); m. Gene Knauer, Dec. 26, 1984; children: Nicholas Lennon Knauer, James Braden Knauer. BA in Social and Polit. Philosophy, U. Calif., Berkeley, 1970, secondary teaching credential, 1979, MS in Forestry & Resource Mgmt., 1981, postgrad. Cert. tchr., Calif. Teaching assoc. U. Calif., Berkeley, 1978-79, rsch. dept. forestry, 1979-80, rsch. asst., 1980, teaching assoc., 1980, 1981; project dir. Ecological Analysts, Inc., Concord, Calif., 1981, CYNEFIN Edn. Conf., Wales, U.K., 1982; exec. dir. Nat. Resources Inst., San Francisco, 1983; founder, exec. dir. East Bay Conservation Corps, Oakland, Calif., 1983—. Mgr., dir. Royal Gorge Ski Touring Sch., Alpine Meadows Cross Country Ski Sch., Squaw Valley Nordic Ctr. and Big Chief Guides, winters 1974-80; dist. naturalist, visitor info. specialist Tahoe Nat. Forest, U.S. Forest Svc., Nevada City, Calif., summers 1974-80; project dir. Nature Conservancy Coun., London, 1982-83; bd. mem. Youth Svc. Calif., L.A., 1989—; cons. Corp. on Nat. and Cmty. Svc., Washington, 1992—, Nat. Assn. Experiential Edn., 1993—; bd. mem., pres. Nat. Assn. Svc. and Conservation. Author: Highway 80 Interpretive Plan-U.S. Forest Service, 1976, Highway 20 Interpretive Plan-U.S. Forest Service, 1977, (U.S. Forest Svc. Interpretive Guide) Overland Emigrant Trail Through the Tahoe National Forest, 1978, Interpretive Handbook for Forest Naturalists, Resource Recycling-Recycling, California-Style: Urban, Creative and Young, 1992; contbr. articles to profl. jours. Bd. dirs. Nat. Assn. Svc. and Conservation Corps, Washington, 1985-91, Human Environment Ctr., Washington, 1986-91, Coastal Resources Ctr., San Francisco, 1990—, vice chair bd. dirs. Mus. of Children's Art, Oakland, 1988—. Office: East Bay Conservation Corps 1021 3rd St Oakland CA 94607-2507

LENOIR, GLORIA CISNEROS, consultant, educator; b. Monterrey, Nuevo Leon, Mex., Aug. 18, 1951; came to U.S., 1956, naturalized; d. Juan Antonio and Maria Gloria (Flores) Cisneros; m. Walter Frank Lenoir, June 6, 1975; children: Lucy Gloria, Katherine Judith, Walter Frank IV. Student, Inst. Am. Univs., 1971-72; BA in French Art, Austin Coll., 1973, MA in French Art, 1974; MBA in Fin., U. Tex., 1979, postgrad. in Ednl. Policy and Planning, 2001—03. French tchr. Sherman (Tex.) H.S., 1973-74; French/Spanish tchr, dept. chmn. Lyndon Baines Johnson H.S., Austin, 1974-77; legis. aide Tex. State Capitol, Austin, Tex., 1977-81; stock broker Merrill Lynch, Austin, 1981-83, Schneider, Bernet and Hickman, Austin, 1983-84; bus. mgr. Holleman Photographic Labs., Inc., Austin, 1984-87, 88-90; account exec., stock broker Eppler, Guerin & Turner, 1987-88; ind. distbr. Austin, 1990-93; owner, cons. Profl. Cons. Svcs., Austin, 1991—2001; adj. faculty Spanish for internat. trade St. Edwards U., 1991-99; bilingual interviewer The Gallup Orgn., 1997-98; Spanish tchr., club sponsor Hyde Park Bapt. Schs., 1997-99; tchr. computer applications Travis H.S. Comm. Acad., 1999-2000, 9th grade coord., 2000—01; tchr. langs. Travis HS Comm. Acad., 2001—. Group counselor, organizer Inst. Fgn. Studies, U. Strasbourg, France, 1976; mktg. intern IBM, Austin, 1978; mktg. cons. Creative Ednl. Enterprises, Austin, 1980-81; hon. speaker Mex.-Am. U. Tex., Austin, 1984; coord. small bus. workshops, 1985; group sponsor, advisor Travel Selections, 1997—; mem. campus adv. coun. Travis H.S., 1999-2002, partnership for behavioral success com., 2003—; Southwest area rep. Travel Selections from Campbell, Calif., 2000—; spkr. in field. Photographs pub. in Women in Space, 1979, Review, 1988; exhibited in group shows, Tex., 1979, 88-89, 99. Neighborhood capt. Am. Cancer Soc., Austin, 1982-86, 90, Am. Heart Assn., 1989; active PTA, 1989—, Advantage Austin, 1988; mem. Bryker Woods Elem. PTA Bd., 1990-92, pres., 1990-91, mem. Austin City coun. PTA Bd., 1991-96, Kealing Jr. H.S. PTA Bd., 1992-94, chair 50th anniversary celebration com., 1990, hospitality chmn., 1st grade coord., Austin, 1986, legis. com. Tex. State, 1990-92; vol. liaison leads program Austin Coll., 1983-2000; peer panelist Maj. Art Insts., Austin; elder Ctrl. Presbyn. Ch., 1988-90, 2000-02, mem. ch. choir, 1975-78, 2003—, renovation and implementation com., 2002—, H.S. Sunday sch. tchr., 2002-03; Megaskills leader Austin Ind. Sch. Dist., 1991-96; bd. dirs. Magnet Parents Coalition, 1995-98; cultural arts chair Dist. 13 PTA Bd., 1996-97; participant NASA Urban and Rural Cmty. Enrichment Program, 2002; mem. smaller learning communities com. Travis H.S., Austin, Tex., 2002—, mem. partnership for behavioral success com., 2003—. Recipient Night on the Town award IBM, 1978. Mem.: NEA, Edn. Austin, Tex. Fgn. Lang. Assn., Am. Assn. French Tchrs., Pi Lambda Theta. Republican. Home and Office: 1801 Lavaca St Apt 11E Austin TX 78701-1331 E-mail: mrs_lenoir@hotmail.com.

LENT, JOHN ANTHONY, journalist, educator; b. East Millsboro, Pa., Sept. 8, 1936; s. John and Rose (Marano) L.; children: Laura, Andrea, John, Lisa, Shahnon. BS, Ohio U., 1958, MS, 1960; PhD, U. Iowa, 1972; cert., Press Inst. of India, Sophia U., Tokyo, Japan, U. Oslo, Guadalajara, Mex., Summer Sch. Dir. public relations, instr. English W.Va. Tech., Montgomery, 1960-62; Newhouse research asst. and asst. to dir. communications research Syracuse (N.Y.) U., 1962-64; lectr. De La Salle Coll., Manila, 1964-65; asst. prof. W.Va. Tech., 1965-66; asst. prof. journalism U. Wis., Eau Claire, 1966-67; asst. prof. journalism, head tchrs.' journalism sequence Marshall U., Huntington, W.Va., 1967-69. Vis. assoc. prof. U. Wyo., Laramie, 1969—70; asst. editor Internat. Comm. Bull., Iowa City, 1970—72; coord. mass comm. U. Sains Malaysia, Penang, 1972—74; assoc. prof. comm. Temple U., Phila., 1974—76, prof. comm. journalism, 1976—95, prof. comm. broadcasting, telecomm. and mass media, 1995—, Benedum vis. disting. prof., 1987; Rogers disting. prof. U. Western Ont., Canada, 2000; guest prof. Shanghai U., 2002—. Author: Asian Newspapers Reluctant Revolution, 1971, Asian Mass Communications: A Comprehensive Bibliography, 1975, Asian Mass Communications: A Comprehensive Bibliography, 2d edit., 1978, Third World Mass Media and Their Search for Modernity, 1977, Broadcasting in Asia and Pacific, 1978, Topics in Third World Mass Media, 1979, Caribbean Mass Communications: A Comprehensive Bibliography, 1981, Asian Newspapers: Contemporary Trends and Problems, 1982, Videocassettes in the Third World, 1989, Asian Film Industry, 1990, Caribbean Popular Culture, 1990, Caribbean Mass Communications, 1990, Transnational Communications, 1991, Women and Mass Communications: An International Annotated Bibliography, 1991, Bibliographic Guide to Caribbean Mass Communications, 1992, Bibliography of Cuban Mass Communications, 1992, Cartoonometer, 1994, Animation, Caricature, and Gag and Political Cartoons in the U.S. and Canada: An International Bibliography, 1994, Comic Art of Europe: An International, Comprehensive Bibliography, 1994, Comic Books and Comic Strips in the United States: An International Bibliography, 1994, Asian Popular Culture, 1995, A Different Road Taken, 1995, Comic Art in Africa, Asia, Australia and Latin America: A Comprehensive, International Bibliography, 1996, Global Productions, 1998, Themes and Issues in Asian Cartooning, 1999, Pulp Demons, 1999, Women and Mass Communications in the 1990's, 1999, Illustrating Asia, 2001, Animation in Asia and the Pacific, 2001, Comic Art of Europe Through 2000: An Internat. Bibliography, 2 vols., 2003, others; founding editor: Berita, 1975—2002, Internat. Jour. Comic Art, 1998—, founding mng. editor: WittyWorld, 1987—; editor: Westview Press Internat. Comm. series, 1992—95, Asian Cinema, 1994—, Hampton Books Popular Culture series. Anchor Hocking scholar, 1954-59, U. Oslo scholar, 1962, Fulbright scholar, The Philippines, 1964-65; recipient Benedum award, 1968, Broadcast Preceptor award (2), 1979, Paul Eberman Outstanding Rsch. award, 1988, Ray and Pat Browne Nat. Book award, 1995, Temple U. Exceptional award, 1995, John A. Lent Travel award ICAF, 2003; decorated Chapel of Four Chaplains' Legion of Honor. Mem. Malaysia/Singapore/Brunei Studies Group (founding chmn. 1975-82), Caribbean Studies Assn., Assn. Asian Studies, Internat. Assn. Mass Comm. Rsch. (visual and comic art organizer, chair 1984—), Asian Cinema Studies Soc. (chmn. 1994—), Popular Culture Assn. (founding chmn. Asian popular culture group 1996—), Sigma Delta Chi, Sigma Tau Delta, Kappa Tau Alpha, Phi Alpha Theta. Home: 669 Ferne Blvd Drexel Hill PA 19026-3110 Office: Temple Univ Broadcasting/Telecomm Dept Philadelphia PA 19122

LENTZ, BERNARD FREDERIC, university administrator; b. Denver, Aug. 20, 1948; s. Jerome Henry and Elizabeth (Bails) L.; m. Carol DiCresce, Aug. 28, 1976; children: Corina, Jesse. BA, Oberlin Coll., 1970; MA, M.Phil., Yale U., 1972, PhD, 1976. Asst. prof. SUNY, Albany, 1972-77, Va. Poly. Inst. and State U., Blacksburg, 1977-82; assoc. prof. econs. Ursinus Coll., Collegeville, Pa., 1982-96, prof., 1989-96, chmn. dept., 1985-96; dir. inst. rsch. U. Pa., Phila., 1997—. Author: State Government Productivity, 1976, Roots of Success, 1985, Sex Discrimination in the Legal Profession, 1995. Grad. fellow NSF, Yale U., 1970-73. Mem. Am. Econ. Assn., Assn. Indsl. Rels. Rsch. Assn., Phi Beta Kappa. Office: U Pa Office Inst Rsch Philadelphia PA 19104-6228

LENTZ, THOMAS LAWRENCE, biomedical educator, dean, researcher; b. Toledo, Mar. 25, 1939; s. Lawrence Raymond and Kathryn (Heath) L.; m. Judith Ellen Pernaa, June 17, 1961; children: Stephen, Christopher, Sarah. Student, Cornell U., 1957-60; MD, Yale U., 1964. Instr. in anatomy Yale U. Sch. Medicine, New Haven, 1964-66, asst. prof. anatomy, 1966-69, assoc. prof. cytology, 1969-74, assoc. prof. cell biology, 1974-85, prof. cell biology, 1985—, asst. dean for admissions, 1976-2000, assoc. dean for admissions, 2000—03, assoc. dean admissions and fin. aid, 2003—, vice chmn. cell biology, 1992—. Mem. cellular and molecular neurobiology panel NSF, 1987-88, mem. cellular neurosci. panel, 1988-90; mem. neurology B-1 study sect. Nat. Inst. Neurol. Disorders and Stroke, NIH, 1996, 98; mem. exptl. virology study sect. Nat. Inst. Allergy and Infectious Disease, NIH, 1997, 98. Author: The Cell Biology of Hydra, 1966, Primitive Nervous Systems, 1968, Cell Fine Structure, 1971; contbr. over 100 articles to sci. publs. Vice chmn., chmn. Planning and Zoning Commn., Killingworth, Conn., 1979—; active Killingworth Hist. Soc. Recipient Conn. Fedn. Planning and Zoning Agys. award, 1995, Citizen of Yr. award Killingworth Lions Club, 1993, Pub. Svc. award Sec. of State, 2002; fellow Trumbull Coll., Yale U.; grantee NSF, 1968-92, Dept. Army, 1986, NIH, 1987-2000. Mem. AAAS, Am. Soc. Cell Biology, Soc. for Neurosci., Appalachian Mountain Club (trails com., Warren Hart award, Pychowska award, White Mountain Four Thousand Footer Club), Fla. Trail Assn., Appalachian Trail Conf., Mt. Washington Obs., Alpha Omega Alpha. Republican. Mem. United Ch. of Christ. Achievements include study of primitive nervous systems, identification of neurotoxin binding site on the acetylcholine receptor, identification of cellular receptor for rabies virus. Office: Yale U Sch Medicine Dept Cell Biol 333 Cedar St PO Box 208002 New Haven CT 06520-8002

LEOGRANDE, WILLIAM MARK, political science educator, writer; b. Utica, N.Y., July 1, 1949; s. John James and Patricia Ann (Ryan) LeoG; m. Martha J. Langelan AB, Syracuse U., 1971, MA, 1973, PhD, 1976. Asst. prof. Hamilton Coll., Clinton, NY, 1976-78; dir. polit. sci. Am. U., Washington, 1980-82, asst. prof. polit. sci., 1978-83, assoc. prof., 1984-89, prof., 1989—, chair dept. govt., 1992-96, dean Sch. Pub. Affairs, 1997-99, 2002—. Mem. profl. staff U.S. Senate, 1982-83, cons., 1984-85 Author: Cuba's Policy in Africa, 1980; editor: (with Morris Blachman) Confronting Revolution; Security Through Diplomacy in Central America, 1986, (with Louis Goodman) Political Parties and Democracy in Central America, Our Own Backyard: The United States in Central America, 1998; dir. Latin Am. Rsch. Rev., 1982-86, World Policy Jour., 1983-93. Dir. svc. com. Unitarian-Universalist Ch., Boston, 1983-86; mem. staff Michael Dukakis Presdl. Campaign, 1988. Council Fgn. Relation Internat. Affairs fellow, 1982-83, Pew Faculty fellow, 1994-95. Mem. Coun. Fgn. Rels., Am. Polit. Sci. Assn., Latin Am. Studies Assn. (exec. council 1984-87) Democrat. Home: 7215 Chestnut St Bethesda MD 20815-4051 Office: Am U Sch Pub Affairs Ward Cir Washington DC 20016 E-mail: wleogra@AMERICAN.edu.

LEONARD, BARBARA BALLARD, retired secondary school educator; b. Opelousas, La., July 18, 1938; d. Albert Louis Sr. and Lauvenia (Ventress) Ballard; m. Joseph F. Richard Jr., June 4, 1960 (div. Apr. 1970); children: Boroskie James Richard, Joseph F. Richard III; m. David Walter Leonard, Mar. 5, 1977; stepchildren: Ina L. Collins, Sheryll. BS, So. U., 1960; postgrad., Dillard U., 1966, La. State U., 1969, Tulane U., 1968-69; MAT, Ind. U., 1971; postgrad., Nicholls State U., 1973, Cornell U., 1974, Loyola U., 1974, U. So. Miss., 1978, St. Bernard Coll., 1983, Delgado Jr. Coll., New Orleans, 1984. Tchr. home econs. Evangeline Prish Sch. Bd., Ville Platt, La., 1961, St. Landry Parish Sch. Bd., Opelousas, 1960, 62-64, tchr. sci., 1964-65, Orleans Parish Sch. Bd., New Orleans, 1965-99. Workshop presenter to sci. orgns., 1970—. Contbr. numerous articles to newspapers. Leader 4-H Club, New Orleans, 1985—; mem. adv. bd. Orleans Parish 4-H, 1987—; dir. Vacation Bible Sch., New Orleans, 1975-80. Named Tchr. of Yr. Orleans Area III Schs., 1992, Outstanding 4-H Leader, 1990; Shell Merit fellow Cornell U., 1970. Mem. NAACP, AAUW, Nat. Sci. Tchrs. Assn., Am. Fedn. Tchrs., La. Fedn. Tchrs., Nat. Coun. Negro Women, African Am. Genealogy Connection, Inc., Am. Assn. of Univ. Women, Alpha Kappa Alpha. Democrat. Bapt. Avocations: reading, sewing, arts and crafts, golf, travel. Home: 2127 Saint Maurice Ave New Orleans LA 70117-1742 E-mail: endure101@aol.com.

LEONARD, JACQUELYN ANN, retired elementary school educator; b. Hollister, Okla., Apr. 2, 1931; d. Alex and Dolly M. (McCurty) McKinney; m. Malvin Paul Leonard, Feb. 6, 1952 (div. Apr. 1993); children: Diana, Andrea. BA in Art Edn. and Pub. Sch. Music, Ctrl. State U., 1955; postgrad., U. Mich., 1955—62, Mich. State U., 1955—62. Pres. Jacquelyn-Jackie Leonard Corp., Lake Orion, Mich., 1994—. Contbr. articles to profl. jours. Mem.: AAUW, Nat. Trust. Avocations: reading, singing, piano, swimming. Home: 3091 Oakridge Lake Orion MI 48360

LEONARD, JUDITH PRICE, educational advisor; b. Milw., July 10, 1941; d. Ralph H. and Sylvia (Shames) Price; m. Richard Black Leonard Jr., Dec. 15, 1962 (dec. Dec. 1978); m. Norman Crasilneck, Aug. 31, 1991. BS in Math., Antioch U., 1963; MS in Math., St. Louis U., 1970. Tchr. math. Ferguson Florissant (Mo.) Schs., 1963-94, coord., 1971-73; mentor, co-dir., faculty advisor Engelmann Math. & Sci. Inst., U. Mo., St. Louis, 1988-96; supr. student tchrs. U. Mo., St. Louis, 1995, 96; coord. Regional Inst. Sci. Edn., St. Louis, 1996-2000; cons., evaluator math. programs St. Louis Pub. Schs., 1994—2003; faculty advisor NSF Young Scholars, U. Mo., St. Louis, 1997, NSF Students & Tchrs. as Rsch. Scientists, U. Mo., St. Louis, 1998—99. Co-dir. Post Dispatch and Monsanto Greater St. Louis Sci. Fair, 1998—99; adv. bd. Post Dispatch and Monsanto Greater St. Louis Sci. Fair, 1997—2003, Intel Internat. Sci. and Edn. Fair, 1996—99, adults in charge, 1997—99, fair dir., 1999; chair Discovery Young Scientist Challenge, St. Louis, 1999—2003; sec. exec. bd. Math Educators Greater St. Louis, 2001—03; mem. Math. Sci. Network of Greater St. Louis (Expanding Your Horizons), 1995—2003; math. cons. U. Mo., St. Louis, 2002—03; presenter, judge, chmn. judges for math. computer sci., physics and engring. Jr. Sci., Engring. and Humanities Symposium, 1995—2001, 2003. Author: Word Problems, Basic Skills Instructional Fair, 1996; author, editor: (brochure) Teacher Linking Collaborative, 1997, 2002; editor 3 Math Books, 2002, 5th and 6th Pre Algebra, 2002. Hon. Engelmann scholar Engelmann Math. and Sci. Inst., St. Louis, 1993, NSF Young scholar U. Mo., St. Louis, 1997; recipient Math. Edn. award Math. Educators Greater St. Louis, 1994, NSF STARS award U. Mo., St. Louis, 2000. Mem. NEA, Nat. Coun. Tchrs. Math., Mo. Coun. Tchrs. Math. (life), Ferguson Florissant NEA (life). Avocations: tennis, biking, walking. Home: 22 Bellerive Acres Saint Louis MO 63121-4321 E-mail: judy@judyleonard.net.

LEONARD, KURT JOHN, plant pathologist, retired university program director; b. Holstein, Iowa, Dec. 6, 1939; s. Elvin Elsworth and Irene Marie (Helkenn) L.; m. Maren Jane Simonsen, May 28, 1961; children: Maria Catherine, Mary Alice, Benjamin Andrew. BS, Iowa State U., 1962; PhD, Cornell U., 1968. Plant pathologist Agrl. Rsch. Svc. USDA, Raleigh, N.C., 1968-88, dir. Cereal Disease Lab. U. Minn. St. Paul, 1988—2001. Author: (with others) Annual Review of Phytopathology, 1980; co-editor: Plant Disease Epidemiology, vol. 1, 1986, vol. 2, 1989, Fusarium Head Blight of Wheat and Barley, 2003; editor-in-chief: Phytopathology, 1981-84, Am. Phytopathol. Soc. Press, 1994-97; contbr. over 100 articles to profl. jours., chpts. to books. Fellow Am. Phytopathol. Soc. (coun. 1981-84, 94-97); mem. Am. Mycol. Soc., Internat. Soc. Plant Pathology (councilor 1982-93), Brit. Soc. Plant Pathology, Phi Kappa Phi, Sigma Xi, Gamma Sigma Delta. Achievements include description of new species and genera of plant pathogenic fungi; research on spread of disease through crop mixtures, on relationships between virulence and fitness in plant pathogenic fungi. Office: U Minn Dept Plant Pathology Saint Paul MN 55108

LEONARD, MARY BETH, principal; b. Fond du Lac, Wis., Aug. 11, 1946; BA in Sociology, Cardinal Stritch Coll., 1971, MA in Reading, 1980. Cert. elem. tchr., Wis. Tchr., reading specialist, coord. gifted and talented, drug edn., chtp. I Sch. Dist. Campbellsport, Wis., 1972-92; prin. elem. Wrightstown (Wis.) Community Sch. Dist., 1992—. Mem. Fond du Lac County Drug Abuse Coun., 1989-92; speaker Chpt. 1 Parents Coalition, Milw., 1989. Mem. ASCD, Wis. ASCD, Wis. Reading Assn., Assn. Wis. Sch. Adminstrs., Nat. Staff Devel. Coun., Coun. for Exceptional Children, Optimist. Avocations: reading, traveling, music, theater, art. Office: Wrightstown Community Sch Dist 351 High St Wrightstown WI 54180-1131

LEONARD, THOMAS J. biologist, department chairman; BA, Clark U.; PhD, Ind. U. Instr. U. Ky., U. Wis.; prof. biology Clark U., Worcester, Mass., chmn. Dept. Biology. Rschr. and dir. various MA and PhD programs. Office: Clark Univ Biology Dept 950 Main St Worcester MA 01610*

LEONARD, VIRGINIA WAUGH, history educator, writer, researcher; b. Willimantic, Conn., Dec. 9, 1941; d. William Norris and Elizabeth Flora (Waugh) L.; m. James Madison Ewing, May 14, 1978. BA in Internal. Rels., U. Calif., Berkeley, 1963; MA in Social Scis., Hofstra U., 1967; PhD in History, U. Fla., 1975. Cert. social studies tchr., N.Y.; cert. bilingual social studies tchr., N.Y.; lic. pvt. pilot. Civilian recreation officer U.S. Army Spl. Svcs., Nuremburg, West Germany, 1963-64; tchr. social studies Colegio Lincoln, La Lucila, Argentina, 1970, Seward Park H.S., N.Y.C., 1975-77; asst. prof. history Western Ill. U., Macomb, 1977-83, assoc. prof. history, 1983-90, prof. history, 1990—. Sr. program mgr. Nat. Faculty Exchange-Dept. of Edn., Washington, 1986-87; chairperson Univ. Personnel Commn., Western Ill. U., 1990-91; mem. internat. adv. bd. 5th Internat. Interdisciplinary Congress on Women, San Jose, 1992-93; mem. nat. screening com. U.S. Grad. Student Fulbright Program, 1999, 2002-03. Author: Politicians, Pupils and Priests: Argentine Education since 1943, 1989; author: (chpt.) Los Ensayistas, 1989, (chpt.) Women in the Thrd World: An Encyclopedia of Contemporary Issues, 1998; contbr. articles to profl. jours. Treas. Bus. and Profl. Women, Macomb, 1994-95; seminar leader Project Democracy, LWV, Dubna, Russia, summer 1995; coord. Grassroots, LWV, McDonough County, Ill., 1995. Recipient grant Orgn. Am. States, 1971-72, Fulbright Rsch. award Fulbright Office-Argentina, 1983, Grassroots Democracy grant LWV/USAID, 1995, NEH Summer Inst., Mystic Seaport, Conn., 1996. Mem. Am. Hist. Assn., Midwest Assn. for Latin Am. Studies (pres. 1984-85, Tchg. award 1997), North Ctrl. Coun. Latin Am. (chair nominating com. 1990-91, Tchg. award 1990), Berkshire Conf. of Women Historians (book prize com. 1990-95), Charlevoix Hist. Soc., Phi Kappa Phi, Delta Kappa Gamma (legis. com. 1993-94, 2002--), Nat. Screening Com. for the

U.S Grad. Student Fulbright Program, 2002-03. Unitarian Universalist. Avocations: skiing, swimming, tennis, reading, travel. Office: Western Ill Univ Dept History Macomb IL 61455

LEONE, MICHELE CASTALDO, secondary education educator; b. Bethpage, N.Y., July 10, 1956; d. Raime Andrew and Rose Marie (Salegna) Castaldo; m. James Blase Leone, July 25, 1992. AS, Nassau C.C., 1976; BA, Hofstra U., 1978, MA, 1982. Tchr. math. St. Dominic High Sch., Oyster Bay, N.Y., 1978-99, chair dept. math., 1988-99; math. tutor Bethpage, N.Y., 1999—. Adj. prof. math. Nassau C.C., Garden City, N.Y., 1990—; tchr. Cath. Edn. Coop. Exam. prep. class, SAT prep. class St. Dominic H.S., 1999—. Mem. ASCD, Nat. Coun. Math. Tchrs., N.Y. State Math. Tchrs. Assn., Nassau County Tchrs. Assn. Roman Catholic. Avocations: computers, cooking, dance. Home and Office: 3939 Hahn Ave Bethpage NY 11714-5010 E-mail: mcleone@aol.com.

LEONETTI, EVANGELINE PHILLIPS, retired nursing educator; b. Judith Gap, Mont., Sept. 29, 1924; d. Henry Harrison and Florence Elizabeth (Bascom) Phillips; m. Joseph Leonetti, Aug. 5, 1955 (dec. July 1989); 1 stepchild, Doris Leonetti Dwork. BSN, Loma Linda (Calif.) U., 1955, postgrad., 1985-93; MEd, UCLA, 1968; postgrad., U. So. Calif., L.A., 1971-83. Nursing instr. East L.A. Coll., 1959-64; DON Golden Age Convalescent, Covina, Calif., 1985, Mission Convalescent, San Gabriel, 1985; supr. Med. Home Care, Alhambra, Calif., 1985-87; nursing instr. med. and dental careers Concord Career Coll., North Hollywood, Calif., 1987-90; nursing instr. Pacific Coast Coll., Encino, Calif., 1992-94, St. Clare's Home Health, 1994, ret., 1994. House mother to oriental student's exchange, 2000—. Contbr. articles to profl. jours. Vol. ARC, 1997-98; mem. Tabitha Henken's and Robert Gates Julliard Sch. of Mus. SDA Choir, Alhambra; house mother Internat. Students Am. English Sch. Mem. U. Calif. Alumni Assn., Loma Linda U. Alumni Assn., UCLA Grad. Alumni Assn.

LEONG, G. KEONG, operations management educator; b. Georgetown, Penang, Malaysia, Mar. 10, 1950; s. Eng Loong Leong and Mee Lan Chiew; m. C. Lin Khong; 1 child, Michelle P.Y. BEngring., U. Malaya, Kuala Lumpur, 1973; MBA, U. S.C., 1984, PhD in Bus. Adminstrn., 1987. Trainee exec. Fraser and Neave Co., Kuala Lumpur, 1973-74; project engr. Behn Meyer Engring, Shah Alam, Malaysia, 1974-76, export mgr., 1977; tech. mgr. Behn Meyer Engring., Shah Alam, Malaysia, 1980-82; gen. mgr. Hanseatic Engring. and Trading Co., Bangkok, 1978-80; rsch. asst., teaching asst. U. S.C., Columbia, 1983-87; asst. prof. ops. mgmt. Ohio State U., Columbus, 1987-93, assoc. prof. ops. mgmt., 1993—2001; prof., chair mgmt. dept. UNLV, 2001—. Advisor Ohio State U. chpt. Am. Prodn. and Inventory Control Soc., 1989-90, 91-2000, acad. liaison, 1995-2000; assoc. dir. Ctr. Excellence in Mfg. Mgmt., 1995-2000. Coord. United Way Cen. Ohio, Columbus, 1988, 89, 90, 91. Internat. rsch. fellow Internat. Ctr. for Electronic Commerce, Seoul, Korea; named Educator Yr., Las Vegas Asian C. of C., 2001. Fellow Inst. of Engrs. Malaysia; mem. Decision Scis. Inst. (chair innovative edn. com. 1994-95, track chair in strategic mgmt. 3d internat. mtg., co-track chair Prodn. and Ops. Mgmt. Mfg. 1996, v.p. 1997-99, coord. doctoral student consortium 1998, chair doctoral student affairs com. 1999, editor Decision Line 2002-04, co-chair mfg. mgmt. track 2003, Best Paper award 1990, Stan Hardy Best Paper award 1994, 96), Acad. of Mgmt. (co-chair doctoral colloquium 2003, chair profl. develop. workshop 2004), Beta Gamma Sigma. Avocation: golf. Office: U Nev Las Vegas Coll Bus 4505 Maryland Pkwy Box 456009 Las Vegas NV 89154-6009 Home: 2041 Rose Cottage Way Henderson NV 89052 Business E-Mail: Keong.Leong@ccmail.nevada.edu.

LEONG, LAMPO (LANBO LIANG), artist, educator; b. Guangzhou, Guangdong, China, July 3, 1961; came to U.S., 1983; BFA in Chinese Brush Painting, Guangzhou Fine Arts Inst., 1983; MFA in Painting with high distinction, Calif. Coll. Arts & Crafts, 1988. Instr. art Calif. Coll. Arts and Crafts, Oakland, 1986-87, U. Calif. Ext., Berkeley, 1989; lectr. San Francisco State U., 1988-95, asst. prof., 1996—2001, U. Mo., Columbia, Mo., 2001—. Guest spkr. Asian Art Mus. San Francisco, 1985, 90, 92, 92, 94, 1996—2001, Stanford U., Palo Alto, Calif., 1999—2000; guest spkr. dept. art history U. Calif., Berkeley, Calif., 1997—98, guest spkr., 2001. Solo shows include Markings Gallery, Berkeley, 1984, Calif. Coll. Arts & Crafts, 1985, Rosicrucian Egyptian Mus., San Jose, 1986, U. Utah, Salt Lake City, 1986, Patrick Gallery, Regina, Sask., Can., 1986, Mus. Macao Luis De Camoes, Macao, 1986, Kai Ping County Mus., Guangdong, 1987, Guangzhou Fine Arts Mus., 1988, Moy Ying Ming Gallery, Chgo., 1990, Chinese Culture Ctr., San Francisco, 1991, Sanuk Fine Asian Collectables, San Francisco, 1992, The Univ. Gallery, San Francisco, 1994, Michael Thompson Gallery, San Francisco, 1995, China Art Expo '95, Guangzhou, China, 1995, Galerie du Monde, Hong Kong, 1997, d.p. Fong Galleries, San Jose, Calif., 1997, 2000, Instituto Cultural de Macau, 1998, Santa Catalina Gallery, Monterey, Calif., 1999, Legacy Art, Columbia, Mo., 2002, We. Ill. U., Macomb, Ill., 2002, Kotinsky Gallery, Pompton Lakes, N.J., 2003, Ea. Ky. U., Richmond, 2003, St. Louis U. Mus. Art, 2003, Suburban Fine Arts Ctr., Highland Park, Ill., 2003; exhibited in group shows at Hong Kong Arts Ctr., 1980, Chinese Painting Exhibit Guangdong Province, 1981 (3d Prize award 1981), Macao Artists Assn. Exhbn., 1982-96, Mus. Guangzhou Fine Arts Inst., 1983, Nat. Mus. Art, Beijing, 1985, Macao Young Artist Exhbn. (Excellence award, 1st prize), Pacific Art Ctr., Seattle, 1985, Chinese Culture Ctr., 1986, Faculty Show Calif. Coll. Arts & Crafts, San Francisco Campus, 1986, Sullivan Galleries, Salt Lake City, 1987, Oriental Gallery, N.Y., 1987, Santa Cruz Art League (Spl. award 1988, 1st prize 1990), Nat. Mus. Fine Arts, Beijing, 1988, 90, Chinese Art Gallery, San Leandro, Calif., 1989, Stanwood Gallery, 1989, Gallery Imago, San Francisco, 1990, Sun Gallery, Hayward, 1990, N.Y. Art Expo, N.Y.C., 1991, Gallery 5, Santa Monica, Calif., 1991, Butterfield & Butterfield Auction, San Francisco, 1992, 95-96, Asian Art Mus., San Francisco, 1992, Ke Shan Art Gallery, Taipei, 1993, Wan Fung Art Gallery, Hong Kong, 1993, Gallery On The Rim, San Francisco, 1994, Macao Art Expo, 1988-96, Acad. Art Coll., San Francisco, 1996, Shanghai Arts Mus., 1997, Pacific Heritage Mus., San Francisco, 1998, Ethan Cohen Fine Art, N.Y., 1998, 99, Chinese Culture Ctr., San Francisco, 2000, Zhuhai Mus., Guaungdong, China, 2000, Am. Inst. Taiwan,, 2001, U. Mo., Columbia, Mo., 2001, U. Wis.- Parkside, Kenosha, Wis., 2002, Bismarck Art & Galleries Assn., N.Dak., 2002, New City Gallery, Taipei, Taiwan, 2002, Legacy Art, Columbia & Capitol Rotunda, Jefferson City, Mo., 2002, Columbia Art League, Columbia, Mo., 2002, Rosenthal Gallery, Fayetteville State U., N.C., 2002, Fredericksburg Ctr. Creative Arts, Fredericksburg, Va., 2002, Watercolor Art Soc., Houston, Tex., 2002, La. State U., Baton Rouge, La., 2002, SUNY, Stony Brook, N.Y., 2002, Period Gallery Internat., Omaha, 2002, Juliana Kunst Academie, Utrecht, Holland, 2002, Ohr-O'Keefe Mus. Art, Biloxi, Miss., 2002, Taller Galeria Fort, Barcelona, 2002, Ctrl. Wyo. Coll. Gallery, Riverton, 2002, Wingfield Arts and Music Festival, Eng., 2002, Galerie L'Etang d'Art, Bages, France, 2002, Boscue Conservatory Art Coun., Clifton, Tex., 2002, Juliana Kunst Adavdemie, Utrecht, Holland, 2002, Puna Contemporary Art Ctr., Pahoa, Hawaii, 2002, Ctrl. Wyo. Coll. Gallery, Riverton, 2002, Masur Mus. Art, Twin City Art Found., Monroe, La., 2002, Pittsburg State U., Kans., 2002, Castle Theater, Maui Arts and Cultural Ctr, Kahului, Hawaii, 2003, Eccles Ctr. for Performing Art, Park City, Utah, 2003, Fayetteville State U., U. N.C., 2003, Machine Shop Gallery, Washington, Mo., 2003, Mus. Outdoor Arts, Englewood, Colo., 2003, Fort Hays State U., Kans., 2003, Ea. Washington U., Cheney, 2003, Adams State Coll., Alamosa, Colo., 2003, Maude Kerns Art Ctr., Eugene, Oreg., 2003, Arts Coun. SE Mo., Cape Girardeau, 2003, Art Guild Burlington, Iowa, 2003, Quincy Art Ctr., Ill., 2003, Memphis/Germantown Art League, Tenn., 2003, Period Gallery, Omaha, Nebr., 2003, Seaside Art Gallery, Nags Head, N.C., 2003, Strathmore Arts Ctr., N. Bethesda, Md., 2003,Fort Smith Art Ctr., Ariz., 2003; work represented in various mus., corp. and pvt. collections including Stanford Mus. Art (Cantor Ctr. for Visual Arts), St.Louis U. Mus. Art, We. Ill. U. Mus. Art, Macomb, Guangzhou Arts Mus., Macao Camoes Mus., Mus. Guangzhou Fine Arts Inst., Asian Art Mus., Macao Mus. Art, San Francisco, United Savs. Bank, Calif., Hotel East 21, Tokyo, The Tokyo Westin Hotel, Comml. Bank, San Francisco, Westin Surabaya, Indonesia; author: Brush Paintings of Lam-Po Leong, 1986, Journey of the Heart, 1994, Lampo Leong: Contemplation.Forces, 1997, The Common Ground of Light and Gravity: Lampo Leong's Contemplation/Forces, 1998; illustrator: Brushstrokes-Styles and Techniques of Chinese Painting, 1993, The Tao of Power, 1986; designer (granite medallion) Woh Hei Yueh Pk., San Francisco, 1993; designer (multi-image projection) Ctr. Arts Yerba Buena Gardens, San Francisco, 1996. Recipient Outstanding Merit award Young Art Now Competition, 1980, Decade of Achievement award Asian/Pacific Heritage Week, 1988, 2d prize Zunyi Internat. Brush Painting Competition, 1989, Gold Medal award 15th Macao Painting and Calligraphy Exhbn., 1998, Bronze Medal Forte Cup 20th Century Asian Pacific Art Competition, Washington, 1999, Mayoral Proclamation: Lempo Leong Day (Nov. 19th), City of San Francisco, 1999, art contest winner, Tulane Rev. Art Contest, 2002, 2d Place award Mo. Theater, Columbia, 2002, Juror's award Sumi-e Soc. Am., McLean, Va., 2002, 1st Juried award Bismarck Art and Galleries Assn., 2002, Juror's award Fort Hays State U., 2003, 3d Place award Arts Coun. SE Mo., 2003; inductee Pan-Pacific Asian Hall of Fame at San Francisco Internat. Expo., 1987; grantee City of Oakland Cultural Arts Divsn., 1994-96, San Francisco Art Commn., 1999, U. Mo.-Columbia, 2003. Mem. Nat. Oil and Acrylic Painters Soc., Nat. Sumi-e Soc. Am., Asian Artists Assn. Am., Oriental Art Assn., U.S.A. (v.p.), Macao Soc. Social Scis., Hai-Ri Artists Assn. (China), Nat. Modern Meticulous Painting Soc. (China), Chinese Am. Culture Exch. Assn. (co-founder, dir. 1992—). Avocations: film, ballroom dance, travel, photography. Office: Univ Mo Columbia A126 Fine Arts Columbia MO 65211-6090 Fax: 573-884-6807. E-mail: L@lampoleong.com.

LEONTIADES, MILTON, dean; b. Athens, Greece, Nov. 25, 1932; came to U.S., 1935; s. Chris and Eftihia (Vayanos) L.; m. Susan Tornstrom, Feb. 2, 1968; children: Lora, James. BA, Ind. U., 1954, MBA, 1957; PhD, Am. U., 1966. Fiscal economist U.S. Treasury, Washington, 1957-60; sr. analyst N.Y. Stock Exch., N.Y.C., 1960-64; dir. fiscal analysis Nat. Assn. Mfrs., N.Y.C., 1964-66; mgr., cons. Touche Ross, N.Y.C., 1966-70; dir. econ. devel. IU Internat., phila., 1970-73; sr. planner GE, N.Y.C., 1973-74; prof. Rutgers U., Camden, N.J., 1974-89, dean, 1989—. Cons. in field. Author: Strategies for Diversification and Change, 1980, Management Policy, Strategy and Plans, 1982, Policy, Strategy and Implementation, 1983, Managing the Unmanageable, 1986, Myth Management, 1989. 1st lt. Art., 1954-56. Home: 14 Tallowood Dr Voorhees NJ 08043-4208 Office: Rutgers U Sch Bus Camden NJ 08102 E-mail: miltonl@crab.rutgers.edu.

LEOPOLD, RICHARD WILLIAM, middle school educator; Tchr. (tech.) Wallkill (N.Y.) Middle Sch. Recipient Tchr. Excellence award Internat. Tech. Edn. Assn., 1992. Office: Wallkill Mid Sch PO Box 310 109 Bona Ventura Ave Wallkill NY 12589-3745

LEOVY, JANET SEITZ, elementary education educator; b. San Francisco, Jan. 19; d. George Francis and Grace Louise (Jackson) Seitz; m. Conway Barbour Leovy, Dec. 20, 1968; children: Joanne Grace, Steven Conway, Jill Adair, Suzanne Gail. AA, Coll. San Mateo, Calif., 1952; BA, San Jose State U., 1954; MEd, Seattle Pacific U., 1985. Cert. tchr., reading resource specialist, Wash. Elem. tchr. Walnut Creek (Calif.) Sch. Dist., 1954-58, Weston (Mass.) Sch. Dist., 1958-61; learning disabilities tutor and substitute Shoreline and Northshore Sch. Dists., Seattle, 1972-75; elem. lang. arts and reading enrichment and remediation specialist Northshore Sch. Dist., Bothell, Wash., 1975—. Literacy chair, past pres. Northshore Reading Coun. Mem. Wash. Orgn. for Reading Devel. (bd. dirs., coun. coordination chair 1987—, Pres.'s award 1989); Internat. Reading Assn., Kappa Delta Pi, Alpha Delta Kappa (co-pres. 1992—). Avocations: reading, walking, backpacking, sailing, theater.

LEPAGE, EILEEN MCCULLOUGH See MCCULLOUGH, EILEEN

LEPKE, CHARMA DAVIES, musician, educator; b. Delavan, Wis., Oct. 1, 1919; d. Ithel B. and Florence Mary (Jones) Davies; m. John Richard Lepke, Dec. 22, 1949 (div. July 1974). BA, Wellesley Coll., 1941, MA, 1942; MMusic, Am. Conservatory of Music, Chgo., 1946. Piano tchr., organist Fairfax Hall Jr. Coll., Waynesboro, Va., 1942-44; piano tchr. U. Nebr., Lincoln, 1946-50; ch. organist Trinity Methodist, Unitarian, Lincoln, 1946-50; missionary Am. Bd. Congl. Ch., Durban, Johannesburg, South Africa, 1950-56; ch. organist, choir dir. Congl. United Ch. of Christ, Oconomowoc/Sheboygan, Wis., 1957-70; organist Coloma, Mich., 1970-73; ch. organist Brick Bapt. Ch., Walworth, Wis., 1974, United Meth. Ch., Delavan, 1974-77, Congl. United Ch. of Christ, Delavan, 1977—. Music editor revised Zulu hymnal Amagama Okuhlabalela, South Africa, 1951-56; composer preludes for organ, piano pieces, song and anthem. Recipient 1st prize for song Wis. Fedn. Music Clubs, 1960, others. Mem. Am. Guild of Organists, Music Tchrs. Nat. Assn., Wis. Alliance for Composers, Delavan Musical Arts Soc. (founder, pres.), Phi Beta Kappa. Congregationalist. Home: 223 W Geneva St Delavan WI 53115-1626

LEPLEY, CHARMAINE GUNNOE, special education educator; b. Charleston, W.Va., Dec. 20, 1939; d. Arnold Leo and Ruth Louise (Fleck) Thomas; m. William Delano Lepley; children: Timothy, Pamela. BA, Glenville State Coll., 1961; MA, W.Va. U., 1970, EdD, 1993. Cert. spl. edn., reading, coop. learning tchr. Educator Kanawha County Schs., Charleston, 1961-92; adj. instr. Coll. of Grad. Studies U. W.Va., Institute, 1985-92; prof., head tchr. edn. U. Rio Grande, Ohio, 1992—. Curriculum cons. W.Va. Dept. Edn., Charleston, summer 1985-87; session speaker W.Va. Reading Assn., White Sulphur Springs, 1988-92; workshop cons., speaker U. W.Va. Coll. of Grad. Studies, Institute, 1989-92, U. Rio Grande, 1992—. Co-author (class text) Ideophobia, 1990; guest editor newspaper articles, 1991; contbr. articles to newsletters and jours. Pres. Pilot Club, St. Albans, W.Va., 1994. Mem. ASCD, Internat. Reading Assn. (session speaker 1988, 94), Coun. for Exceptional Children (co-founder student chpt. 1994), Ohio Assn. Tchr. Edn., Ohio Assn. Pvt. Colls. for Tchr. Edn. (trustee), Phi Delta Kappa. Democrat. Avocations: reading, volunteer work, cooking, gardening. Home: 105 Cedar Ln Saint Albans WV 25177-3401 Office: Univ Rio Grande 210 N College Rio Grande OH 45674

LEPP, STEPHEN HENRY, physicist, educator; b. Duluth, Minn., June 7, 1956; s. Henry and Maxine (Foster) L. BS in Physics, U. Minn., Duluth, 1978; PhD in Physics, U Colo., 1984. Postdoctoral fellow Harvard U., Cambridge, Mass., 1984-87, rsch. assoc., 1987-91; asst. prof. physics U. Nev., Las Vegas, 1991-95, assoc. prof., 1995—2002, prof., 2002—. Contbr. articles to profl. jours. Recipient Coll. of Sci. Disting. Rschr. award, 1998. Mem. Am. Astron. Soc., Internat. Astron. Union (Young Astronomer grant 1991). Office: U Nev Physics Dept 4505 S Maryland Pky Las Vegas NV 89154-9900

LEPPER, MARK ROGER, psychology educator; b. Washington, Dec. 5, 1944; s. Mark H. and Joyce M. (Sullivan) L.; m. Jeanne E. Wallace, Dec. 22, 1966; 1 child, Geoffrey William. BA, Stanford U., 1966; PhD, Yale U., 1970. Asst. prof. psychology Stanford (Calif.) U., 1971-76, assoc. prof., 1976-82, prof., 1982—, chmn., 1990-94, 2000—. Fellow Ctr. Advanced Study in Behavioral Scis., 1979-80; chmn. mental health behavioral scis. research rev. com. NIMH, 1982-84, mem. basic sociocultural research rev. com., 1980-82. Co-editor: The Hidden Costs of Reward, 1978; cons. editor Jour. Personality and Social Psychology, 1977-85, Child Devel., 1977-86, Social Cognition, 1981-84, Jour. Ednl. Computing Research, 1983—, Media Psychology, 1999—; contbr. articles to profl. jours. Recipient Hoagland prize Stanford U., 1990, Cattell Found. award, 1999; Woodrow Wilson fellow, 1966-67, NSF fellow, 1966-69, Sterling fellow, 1969-70, Mellon fellow, 1975, fellow Stanford U., 1988-90; grantee NSF, 1978-82, 86-88, NIMH, 1978-86, 88—, Nat. Inst. Child Health and Human Devel., 1975-88, 90-98, U.S. Office Edn., 1972-73. Fellow APA, AAAS, Am. Psychol. Soc., Soc. Personality and Social Psychology, Soc. Psychol. Study Social Issues; mem. Am. Ednl. Rsch. Assn., Soc. Exptl. Social Psychology, Soc. Rsch. in Child Devel. Home: 1544 Dana Ave Palo Alto CA 94303-2813 Office: Stanford U Dept Psychology Jordan Hall Bldg 420 Stanford CA 94305-2130

LEREW, EVERETT DUANE, special education administrator, poet, writer; b. Faulkton, S.D., May 20, 1941; s. Buster E. and Cecile (Elliott) L.; m. Sandra L. Sebade, Feb. 4, 1962; children: Shari Lerew Schutte, Jolene, Brett. BA, Black Hills State U., 1971, MA, 1978; specialist cert., Kearney State Coll., 1989. Elem. tchr. Kadoka (S.D.) Pub. Schs., 1971-74, Superior (Nebr.) Pub. Schs., 1974-87, head tchr., 1976-80; psychologist, dir. preschs. Ednl. Svc. Unit 7 Nebr. Dept. Edn., Columbus, 1987-89; dir. spl. edn. Valley (Nebr.) Pub. Schs., 1989—. Author: (textbooks) Superior Spelling I, 1986, Superior Spelling II, 1987. Active Parent-Tchr.-Student Orgn., pres., 1986. Sgt. USAF, 1960-67. Named Outstanding Educator, Jaycees, Kadoka, 1973, Disting. Educator, U. Nebr., 1986, Nebr. Tchr. of Yr., Nebr. Dept. Edn., Lincoln, 1987. Mem. NASP, Coun. for Exceptional Children, Coun. for Adminstrs. of Spl. Edn., Nebr. State Edn. Assn., Assn. of Childhood Edn. Internat., Assn. for Edn. of Young Children (pres. Superior chpt. 1981-85), Valley Edn. Assn. (chmn. grant com.), Superior Edn. Assn. (pres. 1985), Ednl. Svc. Unit 7 Edn. Assn. (pres. 1988). Democrat. Methodist. Avocations: writing, reading, painting, gardening, travel. Home: 710 S Mayne St Valley NE 68064-2012 Office: Valley Pub Schs 401 S Pine St Valley NE 68064-9720

LERNER, VLADIMIR SEMION, computer scientist, educator; b. Odessa, Ukraine, Sept. 12, 1931; arrived in U.S., 1990; s. Semion N. and Manya G. (Grosman) L.; m. Sanna K. Gleyzer, Sept. 28, 1954; children: Alex, Tatyana, Olga. BSEE, Odessa Poly. Inst., 1954; MEE, Inst. Problem's Controls, Moscow, 1959; PhD in Elec. Engring., Moscow Power Inst., 1961; D Sci. in Systems Analysis, Leningrad State U., 1974. Prof. elec. engring. Kishinev (Moldova) State U., 1962-64; prof. elec. engring. and control systems Kishinev Poly. Inst., 1964-79; sr. scientist in applied math. Acad. Sci., Kishinev, 1964-79; dir. math. modeling and computer sci. lab. Rsch. Inst., Odessa, 1979-89; sr. lectr. UCLA, 1991-93, rschr., 1993—; chmn. computer sci. dept. West Coast U., L.A., 1993-97, Nat. U., L.A., 1997-99. Mem. adv. bds. Acad. Sci., Kishinev, 1964—79, Poly. Inst. Kishinev, 1964—79; vis. prof. Leningrad State U., 1971—73; cons., mem. adv. bd. Poly. Inst. Odessa, 1979—89. Author: Physical Approach to Control Systems, 1969, Superimposing Processes in Control Problems, 1973, Dynamic Models in Decision Making, 1974, Special Course in Optimal and Self Control Systems, 1977, Lectures in Mathematical Modelling and Optimization, 1995, Mathematical Foundations of Informational Macrodynamics, 1996, Lectures in Informational Macrodynamics, 1996, Information Systems Analysis and Modelling: An Informational Microdynamics Approach, 1999, Variation Principle in Informational Macrodynamics, 2003. Recipient Silver medal for rsch. achievements, Moscow, 1961, outstanding achievements in edn., Kishinev, 1975. Achievements include development of new scientific discipline Informational Macrodynamics. Avocations: bicycling, travel. E-mail: vslerner@yahoo.com.

LEROUX, BETTY VON MOORE, elementary education educator; b. Rockingham County, N.C., Oct. 18, 1938; d. J. Melvin and Callie M. (Edens) Moore; m. Daneel Leon leRoux, July 25, 1959; 1 child, Anna Elizabeth. Student, Appalachian State U., 1957-59, Longwood Coll., 1959-61, U. N.C., Greensboro, 1962; BS, East Carolina U., 1966. English tchr. Appomattox (Va.) County Schs., 1959-61; middle sch. tchr. Madison (N.C.)-Mayodan City, 1961-65; tchr. Pitt County Schs., Greenville, N.C., 1966—. Chmn. Middle Sch. Comm., Greenville, 1986—; com. mem. Pitt County Middle Sch. Task Force, Greenville, 1992-93, Pitt County Writing Handbook, Greenville; chmn. Chicod Sch. So. Assn., Greenville. Treas. Rockingham County (N.C.) Dem. Women's Orgn., 1961-65; mem. Jr. Svc. League, Madison, N.C., 1961-65; corr. sec. Bus. and Profl. Women, Greenville, 1972-80. Named Outstanding Young Women of Am., Bus. and Profl. Women's Club, Greenville, 1972. Mem. ASCD, Delta Kappa Gamma Internat. (membership chmn.), Women's Ministries (pres. 1978-81). Avocations: traveling, piano, gardening, antiquing, reading.

LEROY, ELIZABETH REICHELT, retired adult education educator; b. Chgo., Dec. 17, 1939; d. Walter Glen and Dorothy Catherine (Hoffman) Reichelt; m. Robert Edward LeRoy, June 8, 1963; children: Robert Scott, Mary Beth, Linda Ann, Jeffrey Alan. BS in Edn., Ball State U., 1961, MA in Spl. Edn., 1965. Tchr. St. Victor's Sch., Calumet City, Ill., 1958-59, Hoover Sch., Calumet City, 1961-63, Michigan City (Ind.) Schs., 1964, LaPorte (Ind.) Comty. Schs., 1973-75, Dept. Corrections, Westville, Ind., 1977—99, ret., 1999. Coord. Promising Practices Adult Edn., Indpls., 1992—. Fellow AAUW (br. pres. 1977-79, 91-93, state chair women's issues 1977-81, state chair cultural issues 1981-83, edn. found. br. chair 1985—, state ednl. Found. chmn., 1997-2001, state libr., 2001—, grantee 1991), Am. Assn. Adult Continuing Edn. (charter), Ind. State Tchrs. Assn. (pres. 1986—99, instnl. tchr. task force 1989—1999), Correctional Edn. Assn., Correctional Edn. Assn. Ind. Roman Catholic. Avocations: swimming, cross-stitch, reading, weightlifting. Home: 701 W 11th St La Porte IN 46350-5709 Office: Westville Correctional Ctr PO Box 473 Westville IN 46391-0473

LESACK, BEATRIZ DIAZ, secondary education educator; b. Arequipa, Peru, Dec. 2, 1948; came to U.S., 1977; d. Jésus Heradio Díaz Vargas and Elisa (Huamán) Díaz Peralta; m. Federico Vera Ponce de León, May 22, 1965 (div. 1977); 1 child, Edson Giovanni; m. Leo Pap Dorn, Oct. 27, 1977. BS in Spanish, San Agustin U., 1974; MS in Gen. Edn., SUNY, New Paltz, 1978-81, postgrad. Cert. elementary and secontary tchr., French and Spanish lang. tchr., N.Y. Tchr. Spanish Huguenot Nursery Sch., New Paltz, N.Y., 1983; tchr. elem. bilingual Ellenville (N.Y.) Sch. Dist., 1984-85; tchr. Spanish Poughkeepsie (N.Y.) Sch. Dist., 1985-86, Liberty (N.Y.) Sch. Dist., 1986-88, Fla. Unified Sch. Dist., Fla., N.Y., 1988-89; tchr. Spanish-French Hyde Park (N.Y.) Sch. Dist., 1989-91; tchr. Spanish Greenburgh Eleven Unified Sch. Dist., Dobbs Ferry, N.Y., 1991—, Copake-Taconic Hills Sch., Hillsdale, N.Y., 1995-96, FDR Sch., Bristol Twp., Pa., 1996-97; tax examiner U.S. Treasury, 1998-99, rschr., 1999—. Substitute tchr. Newburgh, Wallkill, Onteora Sch. Dists., Poughkeepsie, N.Y., 1982-83; exec. sec. Hotels and Restaurants Assn., Arequipa, 1972-73; mem. asst. Radio Club Dr. Oscar Guillen, Arequipa, 1971; tax examiner U.S. Treasury, 1998-99, rsch., 1999-2000. Fund chairman Dem. Com., New Paltz, 1991-92; mem. fundraising com. Multicultural Edn., New Paltz, 1992; mem. Mid. Sch. Steering Com., 1989-91, Multicultural Edn. Com., 1991—, steering com. Maurice Hinchey Nat. Bilingual Edn., 1980—; candidate for Phila. Bd. Edn., 2000. Fulbright Hays fellow to Dominican Rep., 1991; faculty grantee SUNY, 1978, 83-84. Mem. NAFE, Am. Assn. Tchrs. Spanish, N.Y. Fgn. Lang. Tchrs. Assn. (pres.), N.Y. Union Tchrs., Faculty Wives and Women (pres. 1989-92). Avocations: photography, video production, handicrafts, reading, golf. Home: 5411 Vicaris St Philadelphia PA 19128-2823 Office: Greenburgh Eleven Unified Sch Dist PO Box 501 Dobbs Ferry NY 10522-0501

LESAGE, JANET BILLINGS, elementary school principal; b. Oak Park, Ill., Apr. 3, 1947; d. John Joseph and Lorna Betsy (Scott) Billings; m. Richard Alan LeSage, Dec. 6, 1969; children: Laureen, Justin. BS in Edn., No. Ill. U., 1968; MEd, So. Ill. U., 1972, U. Mo., St. Louis, 1994; EdD, St. Louis Univ., 2001. Tchr. Sch. Dist. 57, Mt. Prospect, Ill., 1968-70; sect. head Morris Libr., So. Ill. U., Carbondale, 1971-72; dir. St. Martin's Sch. for Spl. Children, Ellisville, Mo., 1981-87; tchr. Spl. Sch. Dist. St. Louis

County, Town and Country, Mo., 1987-96; asst. prin. Ritenour Sch. Dist., St. Louis, 1996—98, prin., 1998—. Active Midwestern Braille Vols., 1974-80. Mem. Mo. Coun. for Exceptional Children (v.p. 1989-90, pres.-elect 1990-91, pres. 1991-92, Tchr. of Yr. 1993), Mo. Divsn. for Early Childhood (founding pres. 1987-90), Pi Lambda Theta.

LESAK, DAVID MICHAEL, safety engineer, educator, consultant; b. Phila., July 5, 1952; s. Joseph Michael and Charlotte (Rockel) L.; m. Lora Jean Schmoyer, June 12, 1976; children: Jana Bryn, Scott David. BS, Kutztown U., 1976. Lab. technician Air Products and Chems. Inc., Trexlertown, Pa., 1976-78; sci. tchr. Parkland Sch. Dist., Orefield, Pa., 1978-79, Quakertown (Pa.) Sch. Dist., 1980; owner, pres. Hazard Mgmt. Assocs., Allentown, Pa., 1981—. Adj. prof. Nat. Fire Acad., Allentown, Pa., 1981—, devel. team mgr. Hazmat courses, course developer for emergency response to terrorism, Dept. of Justice; adj. prof. Emergency Mgmt. Inst., Emmitsburg, 1985—; contract instr., course developer FBI Hazmat Programs; contract instr. U.S. Dept. State Diplomatic Security Svc.; mem. Hazardous Materials Transp. Uniform Safety Act, Nat. Hazardous Materials Curriculum Devel. Com. Nat. Response Team; chief Lehigh County Hazmat Team, 1990—2001; mem. state and local adv. group U.S. Dept. Justice Nat. Domestic Preparedness Office; instr. internat. anti-terrorism assistance program U.S. State Dept. Author: Chemistry of Hazardous Materials, 1983, (study guide) Fire Chemistry I and II, 1991; author, prodr., narrator: (videotape) Fire Fighter Safety, 1984, (text) Hazardous Materials Strategies and Tactics, 1998; author, presenter: (videotape) Oxidizers, 1991; author GEDAPER emergency ops. decision-making process Nat. Fire Acad.; prodr.: (videos) Container Damage Assessment, 1993, Spill Control, Stop It, Confine It, 1993, Flammable Liquids and Gases, 1993, Flammable Solids and Dusts, 1993, Explosives and Other Unstable Substances, 1993, Alkali and Alkali Earth Metals, 1993. Chmn. Lehigh County Hazardous Materials Adv. Commn., Allentown, 1990-93; fire chief Lower Macangie Twp., Pa., 1984-86. Mem. Am. Soc. Safety Engrs., Pa. Assn. Hazardous Material Techs. (sec. 1994-97, 2d v.p. 1998-2000). Home and Office: Hazard Mgmt Assocs PO Box 3004 Allentown PA 18106-0004

LESCH, ANN MOSELY, political scientist, educator; b. Washington, Feb. 1, 1944; d. Philip Edward and Ruth (Bissell) Mosely. BA, Swarthmore Coll., 1966; PhD, Columbia U., 1973. Rsch. assoc. Fgn. Policy Rsch. Inst., Phila., 1972-74; assoc. Middle East rep. Am. Friends Svc. Com., Jerusalem, 1974-77; Middle East program officer Ford Found., N.Y.C., 1977-80, program officer Cairo, 1980-84; assoc. Univs. Field Staff Internat., 1984-87; prof. Villanova U., 1987—, assoc. dir. ctr. Arab and Islamic studies, 1992-95. Author: The Politics of Palestinian Nationalism, 1973, Arab Politics in Palestine, 1979, Political perceptions of the Palestinians on the West Bank and Gaza, 1980, (with Mark Tessler) Israel, Egypt and the Palestinians, 1989, Transition to Palestinian Self-Government, 1992, (with D. Tschirgi) Origins and Development of the Arab-Israeli Conflict, 1998, The Sudan: Contested National Identities, 1998, (with Steven Wondu) Battle for Peace in Sudan, 2000; contbr. articles to profl. jours. Co-chair Middle East Program Com., Am. Friends Svc. Com., 1989—94; mem. Quaker UN Com., 1979—80; U.S. adv. com. Interns for Peace, 1978—82; bd. dirs. Am. Near East Refugee Aid, 1980—86, Middle East Report, 1989—93, Human Rights Watch/Middle East, 1989—. Fellow Catherwood Found., 1965; NDFL, 1967-71; Am. Rsch. Ctr. grant Egypt, 1988, U.S. Inst. of Peace Rsch. grants, 1990-91, 97, 2002-03, Wilson Ctr. Guest scholar Smithsonian, 1990, Rockefeller Fdn. Bellagio Ctr., 1996, Fulbright scholar, Cairo, 1999-2000, Beirut, 2003. Mem.: Palestinian Am. Rsch. Ctr. (co-chair 1998—2001, U.S. dir. 2001—), Coun. on Fgn. Rels., Sudan Studies Assn. (sec. 1993—96, pres. 1998—2000), Am. Polit. Sci. Assn., Mid. East Inst., Mid. East Studies Assn. (bd. dirs. 1988—91, pres. 1993—96, bull. editor 1997—99). Unitarian Universalist. Office: Villanova U Dept Polit Sci Villanova PA 19085

LESHER, WILLIAM RICHARD, retired academic administrator; b. Carlisle, Pa., Nov. 14, 1924; s. David Luther and Carrie LaVerne (Adams) L.; m. Veda E. Van Etten, June 16, 1946; children— Eileen Fern, Martha Zoe Lesher Keough Th.B., Atlantic Union Coll., South Lancaster, Mass., 1946; MA, Andrews U., 1964; PhD, NYU, 1970. Ordained to ministry Seventh-day Adventist Ch., 1951. Pastor No. New Eng. Conf. Seventh-day Adventists, 1946-56; pastor, mission dir. Delta sect. Nile Union Seventh-day Adventists, Alexandria, Egypt, 1957-58; prin. Nile Union Acad., Cairo, Egypt, 1959-61; sec. Middle East Div. Seventh-day Adventists Beirut, Lebanon, 1962-64; assoc. prof. religion, dir. summer sch., asst. to pres. Atlantic Union Coll., 1964-71; assoc. dir. Sabbath sch. dept. Gen. Conf. Seventh-day Adventists, Washington, 1971-79; dir. Bibl. Research Inst., Gen. Conf. Seventh-day Adventists, Washington, 1979-84; gen. v.p. Gen. Conf. Seventh-day Adventists, Washington, 1981-84; pres. Andrews U., Berrien Springs, Mich., 1984-94; ret., 1994. Author: Tips for Teachers, 1979; editor adult Sabbath Sch. lessons, 1971-79, studies in sanctuary and atonement, 1980-81; contbr. articles to religious jours. Recipient Founders Day award NYU, 1970 Home: 4703 Greenfield Dr Berrien Springs MI 49103-9566

LESLIE, LOTTIE LYLE, retired secondary education educator; b. Huntsville, Ala., Aug. 5, 1930; d. James Peter and Amanda Lacy Burns; children: Thomas E. Lyle Jr., Theodore Christopher Leslie, DeMarcus Miller Leslie. BS, Ala. A and M U., 1953, student, 1960-83; training cert., Learning Ctrs. of Am., 1985. Cert. secondary tchr. Social studies, English, Music. Tchr. Madison County Bd. Edn., Huntsville, Ala. Author: Teaching the Importance of Character Through Poetry, 1968-69, Ways to Teach Language Composition and Literature, Versatility Versus Violence, Families and Foreign Relationships, Musical Instruments of the World From K-12 and Undergraduate to Graduate; contbr. poetry to profl jours. Active St. Joseph's Cmty., 1959—; organist Antioch AME Zion Ch., 1995—; mem. Huntsville Lit. Assn. (poetry divsn.), 1997—; sponsor Arts Festival for Madison County Schs., 1966; dir. voters edn. Project for Youth, 1977; consulting sponsor Ednl. Expo, 2000. Recipient Miss Liberty trophy, 1986, Victory pin, 1987, Medal of Honor Commemorating Disting. Lifelong Achievements, 1993, cert. appreciation Indian Creek P.B. Ch., 1994. Mem. NEA, ASCD, NAACP, Ala. Edn. Assn., Madison County Music Edn. Assn., Internat. Black Writers and Artists, Inc., N.Y. Poetry Soc., Am. Poetry Assn. (vol. IV no. 2 summer 1985), Huntsville Literary Assn. (poetry divsn. 1997—). Home: 3207 Farriss Dr NW Huntsville AL 35810-3342

LESLIE, LYNN MARIE, secondary education educator; b. Lake City, Fla., Nov. 17, 1948; d. Billy Verlyn Spooner and Dorothy Marie (Odom) Loomis; m. Roy Hamner Leslie, Nov. 25, 1967; children: Kim Ball, Billy Leslie, Dodi Leslie. BS in Edn., Trevecca U., 1970; ME in Spl. Edn., Tenn. State U., 1987, postgrad. in adminstrn./supervision, 1998; postgrad. in Edn., Cumberland U., 1996; cetr. in supervision and adminstrn., Tenn. State U., 1998. Cert. career ladder III, Tenn. Tchr. Leesburg (Fla.) Elem. Sch., 1970-71, Wessington Pl. Elem. Sch., Hendersonville, Tenn., 1974-87, Knox Doss Mid. Sch., Hendersonville, 1987—2000, Spring Run Elem. Sch., Midlothian, Va., 2000—. Mem. Sumner County Ins. Trust, Gallatin, Tenn., 1991-96; tchr, Hall of Fame Jr. Achievement, 1993. Mem. 5 year goal planning com. Sumner County, extended contract procedures com., 1992. Mem. NEA (del.), Va. Edn. Assn., Chesterfield Edn. Assn., Sumner County Edn. Assn. (pres. 1991-92, 95-96, sec. 1992-95, sec./treas. 1996—, calendar com. 1992, 96, 98, numerous coms. chair, tchr. welfare com. 1990-91). Mem. Ch. of Nazarene. Avocations: reading, travel. Home: 15825 Fox Marsh Drive Moseley VA 23120

LESLIE, NAN S. nursing educator, womens' health nurse; b. Pitts. d. Peter E. and Verda S. (Sill) Scolere; m. David C. Leslie, Aug. 13, 1966; children: Erin Lyn, Scott David. Nursing diploma, Presbyn. U. Hosp. Sch. Nursing, 1965; BSN summa cum laude, U. Pitts., 1971, MN, 1973, PhD, 1989. RN, Pa., W.Va.; registered nurse practitioner. Staff nurse ICU Presbyn. U. Hosp., Pitts., 1965-66, Temple U. Hosp., Phila., 1966-68, asst. head nurse ICU, 1968-69; staff nurse ICU Montefiore Hosp., Pitts., 1971; founder, bd. dirs., various positions Circle Cmty. Food Pantry, Wash., Pa., 1978-83; grad. rsch. asst. U. Pitts., 1985-86; lectr. nursing rsch. Carlow Coll., Pitts., 1987-89; assoc. prof. Sch. Nursing W.Va. U., Morgantown, 1990—. Mem. rev. bd. Perspectives in Psychol. Care, 1989-91. Bd. dirs. Family Svcs., Wash., 1979-82; dist. coord. U.S. Pony Club, Brush Run, Pa., 1989-90. NIMH trainee U. Pitts., 1971-73; rsch. grantee W.Va. U., 1992-93, grantee CDC Cancer Screening, 1991-93, NIH/NINR, 1997, Kornfeld, 1997, ONS Found., 2000-01. Mem. ANA, AWHONN (cert. registered nurse practitioner), So. Nursing Rsch. Soc., Oncology Nursing Soc., Presbyn. Univ. Hosp. Nurses Alumnae Assn., Sigma Theta Tau. Avocations: painting, horses, classical music. Home: 2262 S Main Street Ext Washington PA 15301-3259 Office: WVa U Sch Nursing Byrd Health Scis Ctr Morgantown WV 26506 E-mail: nleslie@wvu.edu.

LESLIE, RICHARD MCLAUGHLIN, lawyer, educator; b. Chgo., Oct. 31, 1936; s. Richard S. and Belle (McLaughlin) L.; m. Nancy Elizabeth Lomax; children: Saralynn, Richard W., Lance T. BA, U. Fla., 1958; JD, U. Mich., 1961. Bar: Ill. 1961, Fla. 1962, U.S. Dist. Ct. (no. dist.) Ill., U.S. Dist. Ct. (so. and mid. dists.) Fla., U.S. Ct. Appeals (5th cir.), U.S. Ct. Appeals (11th cir.), U.S. Supreme Ct. 1970. Assoc. Jacobs & McKenna, Chgo., 1961-63, Louis G. Davidson, Chgo., 1963; assoc., then ptnr. Shutts & Bowen, Miami, Fla., 1964—. Adj. prof. trial advocacy program U. Miami Law Sch., 1979-89. Chmn. bd. trustees Plymouth Congl. Ch., Miami, 1978. Capt. USAR, 1961-67. Mem.: Average Adjustors Assn., Ill. Bar Assn., Fla. Bar Assn. (trial lawyers com.), Maritime Law Assn. U.S. (bd. dirs. 2002—), Dade County Bar Assn. (bd. dirs. 1987—90, 1994—97, 1999—2002), Fedn. Def. and Corp. Counsel (v.p. 1987, bd. dirs. 1988—93), Fla. Def. Lawyers Assn. (pres. 1987), ABA (torts trial and ins. practice sect. coun. 1998—2001, mem. ho. of dels. 1999—), Riviera Country Club, Miami City Club, Delta Theta Phi, Phi Delta Theta. Avocations: tennis, skiing, travel. Home: 4116 Pinta Ct Coral Gables FL 33146-1119 Office: Shutts & Bowen Miami Ctr 201 S Biscayne Blvd Ste 1500 Miami FL 33131-4308 E-mail: rleslie@shutts-law.com.

LESSER, LAURENCE, musician, educator; b. Los Angeles, Oct. 28, 1938; s. Moses Aaron and Rosalyne Anne (Asner) L.; m. Masuko Ushioda, Dec. 23, 1971; children— Erika, Adam AB, Harvard U., 1961; student of Gaspar Cassadó, Germany, 1961-62; student of Gregor Piatigorsky, 1963-66. Mem. faculty U. So. Calif., Los Angeles, 1963-70, Peabody Inst., Balt., 1970-74, New Eng. Conservatory Music, Boston, 1974—, pres., 1983-96, pres. emeritus, 1997—. Former vis. prof. Eastman Sch. Music, Rochester, NY; vis. prof. Toho Gakuen Sch. Music, Tokyo, 1973—95; performed with New Japan Philharm., Boston Symphony, London Philharm., L.A. Philharm. and Marlboro, Spoleto, Casals, Santa Fe and Banff festivals; rec. artist. Trustee emeritus WGBH Ednl. Found.; mem. adv. coun. Chamber Music Am. Recipient prize Tchaikovsky Competition, Moscow, 1966; Fulbright scholar, 1961-62; Ford Found. grantee, 1972. Mem. Am. Acad. Arts and Scis., Harvard Mus. Assn., Phi Beta Kappa, Pi Kappa Lambda, Sigma Alpha Iota. Jewish. Home: 65 Bellevue St Newton MA 02458-1918 Office: New Eng Conservatory Music 290 Huntington Ave Boston MA 02115-5018 E-mail: llesser@rcn.com.

LESSER, WILLIAM HENRI, marketing educator; b. N.Y.C., Dec. 19, 1946; s. Arthur and Ethel (Boissevain) L.; m. Susan Elizabeth Bailey, Dec. 27, 1975; children: Andrew, Jordan. BA in Geography, U. Wash., 1968; MS in Resource Econs., U. R.I., 1974; PhD in Agrl. Econ., U. Wis., 1978. From asst. to assoc. prof. mktg. Cornell U., Ithaca, NY, 1978-91, prof., 1991—, dir. undergrad. program, 1998—99, dept. chmn., 2003—. With Internat. Acad. Environ., Geneva, 1993-94, FAO vis. scientist, 2002; grad. field rep. Dept. Agrl. Econs., Ithaca, 1985-88; dir. Cornell Western Socs. Program, 1991-93; cons. World Bank, Washington, US/AID, Winrock Internat., Morrilton, Ark. Editor: Animal Patents: The Legal Economic and Social Issues, 1990; author: Equitable Patent Protection in the Developing World, 1991, Marketing Livestock and Meat, 1993, Sustainable Use of Genetic Resources under the Convention on Biological Diversity, 1998. Zone capt. Dem. com. Town of Ithaca, 1985-90, mem. planning bd., 1987-93, councilman, 1999—. Nat. fellow Kellogg Found., 1988-91. Mem. Am. Agrl. Econ. Assn., Patent & Trademark Office Soc. Avocations: gardening, painting, antique cars. Home: 406 Coddington Rd Ithaca NY 14850-6012 Office: Cornell U Dept Applied Econs & Mgmt 154 Warren Hall Ithaca NY 14853-7801 E-mail: whl1@cornell.edu.

LESSICK, MIRA LEE, nursing educator; b. Hazleton, Pa., Jan. 25, 1949; d. Jack H. and Shirley E. (Frumkin) Lessick. Diploma in nursing, Albany (N.Y.) Med. Ctr., 1969; BSN, Boston U., 1972; MS, U. Colo., 1973; PhD, U. Tex., 1986. Staff nurse Boston City Hosp. and Mass. Gen. Hosp., 1969-72; instr. to asst. prof. nursing, genetics clinician U. Rochester, N.Y., 1973-79; asst. prof. nursing, practitioner Rush U. Coll. Nursing, Chgo., 1986-91, assoc. prof. nursing, 1992—2001, project dir. genetic health nursing program, 1993—2001; assoc. prof. U. Toledo, 2001—. Mem. human genome rsch. initial rev. group, ethical, legal, and social implications subcom. Nat. Human Genome Rsch. Inst., NIH, 1996-99; peer reviewer Bur. Health Professions, HHS, 2001-02. Mem. editl. adv. bd. AWHONN Lifelines, 1999—, Manuscript Review Panel, Rsch. in Nursing and Health Jour.; genetics column editor Medsurg Nursing: The Jour. of Adult Health, 2001—; contbr. articles to profl. jours. and textbooks. Recipient Bd. of Govs. award, Excellence in Pediatric Nursing award Albany Med. Ctr., 1969, Outstanding Nurse Recognition award March of Dimes Birth Defects Found., 1991, Recognition award for Individual Contbn. to Maternal-Child Health Nat. Perinatal Assn., 1993, Founders Award in Edn., Internat. Soc. Nurses in Genetics, 1997. Mem. AAAS, ANA, APHA, Internat. Soc. Nurses in Genetics (chair rsch. com. 1993-2002, Founders award in Edn. 1997), Assn. Women's Health, Obstetric, and Neonatal Nurses, Am. Soc. Human Genetics, Chgo. Nurses Assn. (legis. com. 1990-91), N.Y. Acad. Scis., Midwest Nursing Rsch. Soc., Sigma Theta Tau (Luther Christman award for excellence in published writing 1993, Luther Christmas award Excellence Pub. Writing, 1998), Phi Kappa Phi. Achievements include development of a genetic health area of concentration within a graduate level nursing program. Office: U Toledo Coll Health and Human Svcs Scott Park Campus Toledo OH 43606-3390 E-mail: mlessic@utnet.utoledo.edu.

LESTER, JUNE, library information studies educator; b. Sandersville, Ga., Aug. 25, 1942; d. Charles DuBose and Frances Irene (Cheney) L.; 1 child, Anna Elisabeth Engle. BA, Emory U., 1963, M in Librarianship, 1971; D in Libr. Sci., Columbia U., 1987, cert. in advanced librarianship, 1982. Asst. prof., cataloger U. Tenn. Libr., Knoxville, 1971-73; libr. divsn. libr. and info. mgmt. Emory U., Atlanta, 1973-81, asst. prof. div. libr. and info. mgmt., 1976-80, assoc. prof., 1980-87; accreditation officer Am. Libr. Assn., 1987-91; assoc. dean, assoc. prof. Sch. Libr. and Info. Scis. U. Okla., Norman, 1991—93, dir., Sch. Libr. and Info. Scis., 1993—2000, prof., 1993—. UCLA sr. fellow, 1987. Mem. ALA (coun. mem. 1987), Assn. for Libr. and Info. Sci. Edn. (bd. dirs. 1985-87, 94-97, pres. 1995-96), Am. Soc. Info. Sci. and Tech., Okla. Libr. Assn., Phi Beta Kappa, Beta Phi Mu. Unitarian Universalist. Home: 2006 Trailview Ct Norman OK 73072-6654 Office: U Okla Sch Libr and Info Studies 401 W Brooks St Norman OK 73019-6030 E-mail: jlester@ou.edu.

LESTER, LANCE GARY, education educator, researcher; b. Wausau, Wis., Sept. 12, 1943; s. Lawrence Harold and Joanna Susan (Martin) L.; m. Rochelle Damson McDermott, Sept. 25, 1973 (div.); stepchildren: Barbara Ann Brady, John Patrick McDermott. BA in English, St. John's U., 1965, MS in Secondary Edn., 1967; MA in Cinematography, NYU, 1969. Prof. football player N.Y. Jets/Titans, N.Y.C., 1960-61; educator Newtown H.S., Elmhurst, N.Y., 1965—; mgr. B. S. Klein Real Estate, Bayside, N.Y., 1974-92, track coach, 1973—; prof. film St. John's U., Jamaica, N.Y., 1981—; prof. White Magic Moving Pictures & Video, Glendale, N.Y., 1986—. Lectr., pres. N.Y. Jet Parking & Chowder Soc., N.Y.C., 1986, Queensborough Coll. Film Forum, Bayside, 1988-95. Named N.Y.C. Track Coach of Yr., 1986, Tchr. Who Made a Differance, N.Y. Times, 1999. Mem. United Fedn. of Tchrs., N.Y.C. Coun. of English, Cinephiles. Roman Catholic. Avocations: Karate, track, travel agent. Office: Newtown High Sch 48-01 90th St Elmhurst NY 11373

LESTER, ROBIN DALE, education educator, writer, former headmaster; b. Holdrege, Nebr., Mar. 1, 1939; s. Earl L. and Evelyn Grace (Robinson) L.; m. Helen Sargent Doughty, Aug. 26, 1967; children: Robin Debevoise, James Robinson. Student, St. Andrews U., Scotland, 1960—61; BA, Pepperdine U., 1962, MA, 1963; MAT, U. Chgo., 1966, PhD, 1971. Resident head, dean students office U. Chgo., 1964-72, Ferdinand Schevill fellow dept. history, 1966-68; asst. prof. history Columbia Coll., Chgo., 1966-70, chmn. social scis. dept., 1970-72; chmn. history dept. Collegiate Sch., N.Y.C., 1972-75; headmaster Trinity Sch., N.Y.C., 1975-86, San Francisco U. Sch., 1986-88, Latin Sch. of Chgo., 1989-92; tchr. Francis W. Parker Sch., Chgo., 1994-97. Adj. prof. Columbia Coll., Chgo., 1992-95; interim head Blake Sch., Mpls., 1997-98. Author: Stagg's University, 1995, Wuzzy Takes Off, 1995, Roy Foy, 1996, Going to School and Awww!, 1997; contbg. author: Problems in American Sports History, 1997; contbr. to N.Y. Times, Jour. Am. History, Chgo. Tribune, Jour. Sports History, History Edn. Quar., U. Chgo. mag. Mem. Manhattan Borough Dem. Com., N.Y.C., 1977-86; commr. Commn. on Ednl. Issues, 1980-84; mem. edn. com. Chgo. Hist. Soc., 1991-95; mem. Chgo.-Prague Sister Cities Com., 1991-97; trustee, treas. St. Andrews U. Am. Found., 1985—; precinct capt. Dem. Party, Chgo., 1964. Lauder fellow Aspen Inst., 1985. Mem. Am. Hist. Assn., Am. Studies Assn., N.Am. Soc. Sport Historians (Book of the Yr. award 1995), Orgn. Am. Historians, Headmaster's Assn., University Club (N.Y.C.), Quadrangle Club (Chgo.). Episcopalian. E-mail: rl1709@hotmail.com.

LESZCZYNSKI, JERZY RYSZARD, chemistry educator, researcher; b. Tomaszow, Poland, May 26, 1949; arrived in U.S., 1986; s. Leslaw and Hanna (Kaptur) L.; m. Danuta, June 25, 1972; children: Rafal, Magda. MS, Tech. U. Wroclaw (Poland), 1972, PhD, 1975. Lectr. chemistry Tech. U. Wroclaw, 1976-86; vis. sci. U. Fla., Gainesville, 1986-88; rsch. assoc. U. Ala., Birmingham, 1988-90; from asst. to assoc. prof. Jackson (Miss.) State U., 1990-95, prof., 1995—, Pres.'s Disting. fellow, 2001. Conf. chmn. organizing com. Current Trends in Computational Chemistry, 1992-2002, So. Schs. on Computational Chemistry, 2001-02; dir. Computational Ctr. for Molecular Structure and Interactions, NSF, 1998—; mem. rsch. adv. bd. Am. Biog. Inst.; guest prof. Chin. Acad. Sci., 2002; presenter in field. Author chpts. to books; editor: Computational Chemistry, Reviews of Current Trends, 1995-2002, Computational Molecular Biology, 1999; co-author: Computational Quantum Chemistry, 1988, Combustion Efficiency and Air Quality, 1995, Interaction of DNA Bases and the Structure of DNA, 1996, Molecular Structure and Infrared Spectra of DNA Bases and Their Derivatives: Theory and Experiment, 1997, Tautomeric Properties of Nucleic Acid Bases: Abnitio Study, 1998, Chemistry of the Liquid State: Current Trends in Quantum-Chemical Modeling, 1999, Computational Approaches to the Studies of the Interactions of Nucleic Acid Bases, 1999, Current Trends in Modeling Interactions of DNA Fragments with Polar Solvents, 1999, Aromatic DNA Base Stacking and H-bonding, 2000, Binding in Clusters with Closed-subshell Atoms, 2001, Imperfect Fullerene Molecules, An Ab initio Study, 2002; editor-in-chief Internat. Jour. Molecular Sci.; editor Electronic Jour. Theoretical Chemistry; sr. editor Asian Jour. Spectroscopy; guest editor: Structural Chemistry, 1995, 2002, Jour. Molecular Structure Theochem., 1996-2002; guest ed. Biopolymers Nucleic Acid Sci., 2001-02, Parallel Computing, 2000; ref.: Jour. Am. Chem. Soc., Internat. Jour. Quantum Chemistry, Chem. Physics Letters, Structural Chemistry, Jour. Organic Chemistry, Jour. Phys. Chemistry, Jour. Molecular Structure, Jour. Computational Chemistry, Jour. Biomolecular Structure and Dynamics, Chem. Physics, Computers Chemistry, Jour. Phys. Organic Chemistry, Vibrational Spectroscopy, Inorganic Chemistry, Jour. Chem. Soc. Perkin Transaction 2, Jour. Computer-Aided Design, Theoretical Chemistry Accts., Jour. Organic Chemistry, Collection Czechoslovak Chem. Comm.; mem. editl. bd. Structural Chemistry; contbr. articles profl. jours., contbr. chpts. to books. Recipient Outstanding Faculty award, AT&T, 1992, White Ho. Millennium HBCU award for Sci. and Tech., 2001. Mem. European Acad. Scis. (corres.), Am. Chem. Soc., Internat. Soc. Quantum Biology and Pharmacology (exec. com. 1995-98), Miss. Acad. Sci. Office: Jackson State U Dept Chemistry 1400 Lynch St Jackson MS 39217-0001 E-mail: jerzy@ccmsi.us.

LETCHER, NAOMI JEWELL, quality engineer, educator, counselor; b. Belle Point, W. Va., Dec. 29, 1924; d. Andrew Glen and Ollie Pearl (Meadows) Presley; m. Frank Philip Johnson, Oct. 5, 1945 (div. Dec. 1953); m. Paul Arthur Letcher, Mar. 6, 1954; children: Frank, Edwin, Richard, David. AA, El Camino Jr. Coll., 1964; BA, Calif. State U., 1971. Inspector N. Am. Aviation, Downey, Calif., 1964-71; substitute tchr. ABC Unified sch. Dist., Artesia, Calif., 1971-72; recurrence control rep. Rockwell Internat., Downey, Calif., 1972-80, quality engr., 1981-86; counselor Forest Lawn Cemeteries, Cerritos, Calif., 1980-81; tech. analyst Northrop, Pico Rivera, Calif., 1986-89. Gov. divsn. D-2 area T.M. Internat., Downey, Calif., 1978-79. Author: History of the Letcher Family, 1995. Docent Temecula (Calif.) Valley Mus., 1994—. Mem. AAUW, Nat. Mgmt. Assn., NOW, Srs. Golden Yrs. Club, Alpha Gamma Sigma. Democrat. Baptist. Avocations: genealogy, needlework, stamp collecting, dancing, bowling. E-mail: OMIE8@aol.com.

LETENDRE, BRENDA GUENTHER, educational consultant; b. Snyder, Tex., Mar. 15, 1949; d. Robert Otmar and Leona Mae (Jansky) Guenther; m. Dana LeTendre, May 29, 1970; 1 child, Danielle. BS, U. Tex., 1971; MEd, Tex. Woman's U., 1974; EdS, Pitts. State U., 1982; EdD, Stanford U., 1989. Cert. tchr., Tex., Kans., Mo., adminstr., Mo. Tchr. Dallas Ind. Sch. Dist., 1971-75, North Kansas City (Mo.) Schs., 1975-76, Unified Sch. Dist. 457, Garden City, Kans., 1977; ctrl. office Joplin (Mo.) R-8 Sch. Dist., 1977-85; instr. Pitts. (Kans.) State U., 1989-91; ednl. cons., 1989-94; coord. staff devel. Joplin (Mo.) Pub. Schs., 1994-95; mem. faculty Sch. Edn. Pittsburg (Kans.) State U., 1995—. Bd. dirs. S.W. Mo. Spl. Olympics, Joplin, 1983-85, S.W. Mo. Kidney Found., Joplin, 1984-85, Lafayette House, Joplin, 1992—. Mem. ASCD, Am. Ednl. Rsch. Assn., Phi Delta Kappa. Avocation: internat. travel. Home and Office: 404 E 33rd St Joplin MO 64804-3909

LETENDRE, JACQUELYN LEE, special education consultant; b. Charlottesville, Va., Apr. 8, 1941; d. Jesse Francis and Elizabeth Constance (Campbell) Richardson; m. Charles Richard Letendre, July 13, 1960; children: Constance Allyn, Brian Richard. BS, Westfield State Coll., 1975, MEd, 1977. Cert. tchr. elem. edn., spl. edn.; adminstr. spl. edn. Clin. tchr. nursery sch. State Dept. Mental Health, Boston, 1973-75; tchr., coord. So. Worcester County Edn. Collaborative, Southbridge, Mass., 1975-83; pvt. practice various orgns., Wales, Mass., 1985—. Author: (series) Circus Approach to Parenting, 1993; columnist Southridge News, 1985-94; editor: (newsletter) Drug Concerns Program, 1972-86, AARP, 1987-89. Mem. Coun. Exceptional Children, Coun. Learning Disabilities. Avocations: oil painting, gardening, piano playing. Home and Office: 116 Union Rd Wales MA 01081-9793

LETICHE, JOHN MARION, economist, educator; b. Uman, Kiev, Russia, Nov. 11, 1918; came to U.S., 1941, naturalized, 1949; s. Leon and Mary (Grossman) L.; m. Emily Kuyper, Nov. 17, 1945; 1 son, Hugo K. BA, McGill U., 1940, MA, 1941; PhD in Econs, U. Chgo., 1951. Rockefeller fellow Council Fgn. Relations, N.Y.C., 1945-46; Smith-Mundt vis. prof. U. Aarhus and U. Copenhagen, Denmark, 1951-52; spl. tech. econ. adv. UN

ECA, Africa, 1961-62; prof. U. Calif. at Berkeley, 1960—. Cons. AID, U.S. Depts. State, Labor, HUD and Treasury, 1962—; emissary to Japan and Korea, Dept. State, 1971; cons. Econ. Coun. Can., 1972—, World Bank, 1981—, Bank of Eng., London, Bundesbank, Frankfurt, Germany; lectr. Stockholm, Paris, Uppsala, Hamburg, Kiel, Oxford (Eng.), 1973—, Vancouver, Toronto, Montreal, Zagreb, 1983, Frankfurt, Bonn, Moscow and Nakhodka Acad. Scis. USSR, 1986, Hong Kong, Shanghai, Wuhan, Beijing, London, Bonn, Frankfurt, De Hague, 1987, Bundesbank, 1992, 93, 99, China, Beijing, Shanghai, 1988, 90, 94, New Delhi, Addis Ababa, Kuala Lumpur and Seoul, 1996, 99, U.S. War Coll., Quintico, Va., 1997, Acad. Scis., Taipei, 1989, Moscow, 2001, joint session Calif. legis., 1975; ext. examiner adv. degrees U. Hong Kong, U. Calcutta, India. Author: Reciprocal Trade Agreements in the World Economy, 1948, in Japanese, 1951, System or Theory of the Trade of the World, 2d edit., 1957, Balance of Payments and Economic Growth, 2d edit., 1976, A History of Russian Economic Thought, 2d edit., 1977, The Key Problems of Economic Reconstruction and Development in Nigeria, 1970, Dependent Monetary Systems and Economic Development, 1974, Lessons of the Oil Crisis, 1977, Gains from Trade, 1979, Controlling Inflation, Recession, Federal Deficits and the Balance of Payments, 1980, The New Inflation and Its Urban Impact, 1980, Monetary Systems of Africa in the 1980s, 1981, International Economic Policies and Their Theoretical Foundations, 1982, 2d edit., 1992; Russian Statecraft: An Analysis and Translation of Iuril Krizhanich's Politika, 1985, Economics of the Pacific Rim, 1989; editor Royer Lectures, 1980-90, Toward a Market Economy in China, 1992, China's Emerging Monetary and Financial Markets, 1995, India's Economic Reforms, 1996, Causes of the Financial and Economic Crisis in Southeast Asia, 1998, Lessons from the Euro Zone for the East Asian Economies, 2000; contbr. articles to encys., congl. coms. and profl. jours. Supervisory bd. Sch. Econs., St. Petersburg, Russia, 1994—. Recipient certificate merit Ency. Brit., certificate merit Inst. World Affairs, certificate merit Internat. Legal Center, U. Mich., U.S. Office Personnel Mgmt. Sr. Fed. Govt. Execs. and Mgrs., U. Calif.-Berkeley, Adam Smith medal U. Verona, 1977, Medal, Ioffe Inst. Physics and Tech., 1998; nominee Internat. Scientist of Yr., 2002, Cambridge, England; Guggenheim fellow, 1956-57 Mem. Am. Econ. Assn. (nominating com. 1968-69), Econometric Soc., Royal Econ. Soc., U.S.-Asian Econ. Com. (bd. dirs. 1983—), African Studies Assn., Am. Soc. Internat. Law (bd. 1969-72). Home: 968 Grizzly Peak Blvd Berkeley CA 94708-1549 E-mail: letiche@econ.berkeley.edu.

LETIZIA, DOROTHY, nursing educator; b. Dover, N.J., Dec. 20, 1938; d. Max and D. Marie (McManus) Meichsner; m. Carl Letizia, July 2, 1960; children: Karen, Janie. BSN, U. Pa., 1960, MSN, 1970; EdD, Rutgers U., 1989. RN, N.J. Clin. adj. faculty mem. Gloucester County Coll., Sewell, N.J., 1982-88; clin. assoc. prof. Camden County Coll., Blackwood, N.J., 1990—; assoc. dean, curriculum coord. Our Lady of Lourdes Sch. Nursing, Camden, N.J., 1990-2000, dean, 2000—. Mem. adv. bd. coop. programs in nursing Camden County Coll., 1990—, med.-surg. nursing coord., 1970—90; mem. Colleagues in Caring Project, 1996—2002. Mem. AACN, AAUW, Acad. Med. Surg. Nurses, Fedn. for Accessible Nursing Edn. and Licensure, Nat. League Nursing, Nat. Coalition Hosp. Based Schs. and Colls. Nursing, Am. Assn. Adult and Continuing Edn., Assn. Diploma Schs. Profls. Nursing (bd. dirs. 1999—), Sigma Theta Tau. Home: 209 Crest Rd Marlton NJ 08053-7133

LETKI, ARLEEN, secondary school educator; b. Pitts., Sept. 30, 1949; d. Henry S. and Monica (Kocinski) K. BS, Lambuth Coll., 1971; MA, Glassboro State Coll., 1989; postgrad., Widener U., 1991—. Cert. social studies, English, elem., spl. edn., pupil pers. svcs., supr., prin., N.J., elem. and secondary prin., Pa. 3d, 5th and 6th grade tchr. St. Mary Sch., Camden, N.J., 1971-72; 7th grade tchr. Annunciation Sch., Belmawr, N.J., 1972-74; 7th and 8th grade tchr. St. Rose Sch., Haddon Heights, N.J., 1974-84; spl. edn. tchr. Glassboro (N.J.) Intermediate Sch., 1984-87, lang. arts tchr., 1987-89; social studies tchr. Glassboro (N.J.) H.S., 1989-96; asst. prin. Washington Twp. H.S., 1996—. Mem. ASCD, AAUW, Nat. Coun. for Social Studies. Republican. Roman Catholic. Avocations: calligraphy, gardening, reading, walking. Home: 18 Bells Lake Dr Turnersville NJ 08012-1532 Office: Washington Twp HS Sewell NJ 08080

LETOURNEAU, DUANE JOHN, retired biochemist, educator; b. Stillwater, Minn., July 12, 1926; s. John Peter and Olga Margaret (Lange) LeTourneau; m. Phyllis Jean Kaercher, June 22, 1947; children: Bruce Duane, Diane Elaine, Keith George. BS, U. Minn., 1948, MS, 1951, PhD, 1954. Asst. prof., asst. agrl. chemist U. Idaho, Moscow, 1953-58, assoc. prof., assoc. agrl. chemist, 1958-63, prof., biochemist, 1963-91, asst. dept. head, 1988-89, sec. faculty, 1990-91, ret., 1991. Vis. prof. botany U. Sheffield (Eng.), 1973; vis. scientist Nat. Research Council Can., Saskatoon, 1981; Bd. dirs. Idaho Inst. Christian Edn., 1958-62, 73-75, v.p., 1959-62 Author research publs. on plant biochemistry. Bd. dirs. U. Idaho Luth. Campus Coun., 1962-64, 73-75, chmn., 1963-64; trustee FarmHouse Internat. Found., 1974-80, chmn., 1976-80; trustee Gritman Meml. Hosp., 1969-82, v.p., 1977-80; bd. dirs. Gritman Med. Ctr., 1991—, Palouse Regional Health Corp., 1992-96; bd. dirs. Latah County Hist. Soc., 1982-89, 92-96, 99, pres. bd. dirs., 1984-87; trustee Idaho Hist. Soc., 1992-98. With USAAF, 1945. Recipient Outstanding Faculty award Asso. Students U. Idaho, 1960-62, 87, Coll. Agr. Outstanding Instr. award, 1962, R.M. Wade Excellence in Teaching award, 1968, 78, Disting. Faculty award, 1982, Prof. of Yr. award, 1983; Citation for Disting. Achievement, U. Idaho, 1984; Nat. Acad. Scis.-NRC sr. postdoctoral fellow, 1964-65 Fellow AAAS, Am. Inst. Chemists; mem. AAUP (v.p. U. Idaho chpt. 1959-60, sec. 1984-87), Am. Chem. Soc., Am. Soc. Plant Physiologists, Am. Inst. Biol. Scis., Am. Phytopath. Soc., Idaho Acad. Sci. (v.p. 1985-86, pres. 1986-87, editor jour. 1983-89), Mycol. Soc. Am., Phytochem. Soc. N.Am., Am. Soc. Plant Physiologists, Iron Wedge, FarmHouse (dir. Idaho chpt. 1957-62, 72-75, 82-90, pres. 1957-62, 74, 82-85, 90; nat. dir. 1960-64, nat. v.p. 1962-64), Lions (bd. dirs. Moscow Central club 1971-74, 90-91, pres. 1973-74), Sigma Xi, Alpha Zeta, Gamma Alpha, Gamma Sigma Delta (pres. U. Idaho chpt. 1979-80), Phi Kappa Phi (v.p. U. Idaho chpt., pres. 1990-91), Phi Sigma (regional v.p. 1993—). Lutheran (chmn. ch. council and congregation, 1966-69). Home: 479 Ridge Rd Moscow ID 83843-2521

LETOURNEAU, MARK STEPHEN, English language educator, researcher; b. Idaho Falls, Idaho, Apr. 11, 1955; s. Joseph Richard Louis and Janet Marie (Casavant) LeT.; m. Georgette Samuel Faraj, June 5, 1982; children: Annette, Sarah. BA, U. Vt., 1977; MA, Purdue U., 1979, PhD, 1986. Teaching asst. Purdue U., West Lafayette, Ind., 1977-86, instr., 1986-87; asst. prof. English Weber State U., Ogden, Utah, 1987-89, 90-92, assoc. prof., 1992-98, prof., 1998—. Vis. prof. Purdue U., summer 1987, U. Khartoum, Sudan, 1989-90. Contbr. articles and papers to profl. jours. Rsch. grantee Purdue U., 1984, 85, Weber State U., 1988, 91, Fulbright grantee Coun. for Internat. Exchange of Scholars, Khartoum, 1989-90. Mem. Linguistic Soc. Am., Nat. Coun. Tchrs. of English, Conf. on Coll. Composition and Communication. Democrat. Episcopalian. Avocations: playing guitar, reading. Office: Weber State U 3750 Harrison Blvd Ogden UT 84408-0001

LETTON, ALVA HAMBLIN, surgeon, educator; b. Tampa, Fla., May 23, 1916; s. James Hervey and Minerva (Hamblin) L.; m. Roberta Rogers, Oct. 7, 1938; children: Robert Hamblin (dec.), Alice Roberta Zachodski. Student, U. Tampa, 1933-35, U. Fla., 1935-37; MD, Emory U., 1941. Diplomate Am. Bd. Surgery. Intern Ga. Baptist Hosp., Atlanta, 1941-42, resident, 1942-43; pvt. practice medicine specializing gen. surgery (oncology) Atlanta, 1946—; chief staff, attending surgeon Ga. Bapt. Hosp., 1965-73; sr. mem. Letton and Mason Surgery, Atlanta, 1980-95; dir. breast cancer demonstration project Bapt. Med. Ctr., 1972-78, chmn. exec. com. oncology dept.; clin. prof. surgery Med. Coll. Ga.; A. Hamblin Letton chair surg. oncology Ga. Bapt. Med. Ctr., 1990—95; founder Atlanta Cancer Ctr. Vis. prof. Egypt Cancer Inst., 1985, Med. and Dental Sch. N.J., 1986, Coll. Medicine U. Ill., Peoria, 1990; cons. Cobb. Gen. Grady Meml., Scottish Rite hosps.; chmn. cancer task force a. Regional Med. Program, 1966—71; mem. Ga. Sci. and Tech. Com., 1969—70; active Am. Cancer Soc., 1947—, nat. chmn. pub. edn., 1965—68, nat. chmn. svc. com., 1968—69, nat. chmn. med. and sci. com., 1969—70, v.p., nat. pres. elect, 1970—71, nat. pres., 1971—72, hon. bd. dirs. life, 1979—; pres. Atlanta Med. Ctr., 1965—90, Atlanta Health Evaluation Ctr., 1973—82; mem. Gov.'s Sci. Adv. Coun., 1972—75, U.S. nat. com. NAS, 1976—79; Roswell Park Meml. lectr., 1983; A. Hamblin Letton ann. lectr. Southeastern Surg. Congress, 1985—; bd. judges Criss Award; mem. Ethicon Gen. Surg. Adv. Panel, 1975—85; mem. cancer control adv. com. Nat. Cancer Inst., 1975—79; chmn. first cancer postgrad. course USA/USSR/ Union Internat. Contre Cancer, Leningrad, Former Soviet Union, 1999; mem. profl. edn. com. Union Internat. Contre Cancer, 1966—78; cons., Budapest, Hungary, 1986; cons. to exec. sec., Budapest, 72; cons. to forming Russian Cancer Soc., 1991—93; vis. prof. Pacific N.W. Cancer Found., 1998; mem. adv. bd. Ga. U. Sys., 1999—. Mem. editorial bd. Internat. Advances in Surg. Oncology, Jour. Cancer Prevention and Detection, 1985—; chmn. editorial bd. Oncology Times, 1979-90; guest editor Seminars in Surg. Oncology; contbr. articles to profl. jours., films. Deacon Bapt. ch. With M.C. USNR, 1943-46. Recipient Presdl. citation, 1944, Aven Citizenship award Fulton County Med. Soc., 1960, Honor Alumnus award Emory U., 1973, Hardman award Med. Assn. Ga., 1973, highest award John Muir Med. Film Festival, 1978; Disting. Svc. award Am. Cancer Soc., 1980, Nat. divsn. award, 1986, Vaughn award Ga. divsn., 1987; Atlanta Cmty. Svc. award, 2000. Fellow: ACS, Southeastern Surg. Congress (hon.; sec.-dir 1960—86, Disting. Svc. award 1982); mem.: Letton Cancer Found. (pres. 1999), Soc. Internat. de Chirugie, Am. Thyroid Assn., Soc. Nuclear Medicine, So. Surg. Assn., Soc. Surg. Oncology, Univ. Yacht Club (Flowery Branch, Ga.), Capital City Club (Atlanta). Baptist. Home: 3747 Peachtree Rd NE Apt 1508 Atlanta GA 30319-1374 Office: 315 Boulevard NE Atlanta GA 30312-1200

LETTS, LINDSAY GORDON, pharmacologist, educator; b. Warragul, Victoria, Australia, Jan. 9, 1948; came to U.S., 1987; m. Barbara Dawn Hawkey, Sept. 13, 1969; children: Michelle Maree, Kathryn Jane, David Gordon. BS, Monash U., Australia, 1971; PhD, Sydney U., 1980. Tutor Sydney (Australia) U., 1976-80; rsch. scientist Royal Coll. Surgeons Eng., London, 1980-82; sr. rsch. fellow Merck Frosst Can. Inc., 1982-87; dir. pharmacology Boehringer Ingelheim Pharms., Inc., Ridgefield, Conn., 1987-93; v.p. rsch. NitroMed Inc., Cambridge, Mass., 1993-96, chief sci. officer, sr. v.p. R&D, 1997—. Adj. assoc. prof. Yale U. Sch. Medicine, New Haven, 1991-94. Editor Mediators of Inflammation, 1992-98, Pulmonary Pharmacology and Therapeutics, 1992—; sect. editor Prostaglandins, 1986—; editor Inflammation Rsch., 1994-2002. Bd. dirs. Nat. Inst. for Community Health Edn., Quinnipiac Coll., Hamden, Conn., 1990-94, Conn. United Rsch. Excellence, Wallingford, 1991-94. Mem.: Internat. Assn. Inflammation Socs. (v.p. 2001—), Inflammation Rsch. Assn. (bd. dirs. 1992—2000, pres. 1996—98). Office: NitroMed Inc 12 Oak Park Dr Ste 2 Bedford MA 01730-1426 E-mail: gletts@nitromed.com.

LEUCHS, JOHN JAMES, JR., elementary gifted education educator; b. Greenwich, Conn., Mar. 23, 1947; s. John James and Louise Elizabeth (Schulze) L. BA in Elem. Edn., Kean Coll., Union, N.J., 1969; MA in Curriculum and Teaching, Columbia U., 1974, EdM, 1981. Cert. elem. tchr., supr., curriculum devel., N.J. Elem. tchr. Hudson Street Sch., Newark, 1969-71, South Mountain Sch., South Orange, N.J., 1971-82, Jefferson Sch., Maplewood, N.J., 1982-85; tchr. gifted edn. South Orange-Maplewood Sch. Dist., 1985—. Coord. After-Sch. Gifted Program for Minority Students, South Orange-Maplewood Sch. Dist., 1991-94; math. cons., curriculum evaluator, 1980-85; founder, owner, mgr. Creative Ednl. Materials Co., N.Y.C., 1975; mem. Community Schs. Task Force To Promote Racial Harmony. Creator math. bd. games. Chairman polit. action com. Coalition for Unity, South Orange-Maplewood, 1985-87; co-organizer South Orange-Maplewood Harmony Day, 1986; planned parenthood. Mem. ASCD, ACLU, Nat. Coun. Tchrs. Math., N.J. Edn. Assn., Essex County Steering Com. for Gifted and Talented, Mensa (coord. gifted children No. N.J. chpt. 1991—, nat. gifted coords. award 1993, nat. chmn. elem., mid. and high sch. groups 1992—, chmn. women and minorities advocacy group 1991-94), Amnesty Internat. Avocations: weightlifting, deltiology, jogging, reading, travel. Office: South Orange-Maplewood Bd Edn 232 Academy St Maplewood NJ 07040-1312

LEULIETTE, CONNIE JANE, secondary educator; b. Buckhannon, W.Va., Mar. 07; d. Audie Nelson and Sadie Laura (Gregory) Ware; m. Charles Benjamin Leuliette, Jr., Sept. 5, 1964; 1 child, Eric Wesley. BS, W.Va. U., 1963, MA, 1965. Tchr. grades 1-4 Point Mountain Elem. Sch., Webster Springs, W.Va., 1959-60; tchr. gen. sci. Webster Springs (W.Va.) High Sch., 1963-64; tchr. 2d grade Norwood Elem. Sch., Clarksburg, W.Va., 1965-66, tchr. 6th grade, 1966-67; circulation clk., librarian Clarksburg-Harrison Pub. Library, 1981-83, reference librarian, 1983-89; tchr. sci. South Harrison High Sch., Lost Creek, W.Va., 1989-90, Roosevelt-Wilson Middle Sch., Nutter Fort, W.Va., 1990-96, Washington Irving Mid. Sch., Clarksburg, W.Va., 1996—2003. Pres. Nutter Fort PTA, 1978-79; elder Presbyn. Ch. NSF grantee, 1964-65. Mem. NEA, AAUW (sec. W.Va. divsn. 1981-83, conv. chmn. 1978-80, treas. 1992-96, br. pres. 1983-85, chair W.Va. Ednl. Found. 2000-02), W.Va. Sci. Tchrs. Assn., W.Va. Assn. Parliamentarians (unit sec. 1986-90, treas. 1991-94, 1999-2001), W.Va. Fedn. Woman's Club (chmn. edn. dept. 1982-86, continuing edn. divsn. 1990-92, cmty. improvement program 1992-94, dist. edn. dept. 1990-92, dist. treas. 1994-98, dist. 2d v.p. 1998-2000, dist. 1st v.p. 2000-02, dist. pres. elect 2002—), Woman's Club Nutter Fort (pres. 1990-92), Alpha Delta Kappa (W.Va. chpt. v.p. 1992-94, chpt. pres. 1994-96, state historian 2000-02, state treas. 2002—). Democrat. Presbyterian. Avocations: reading, crosswords, walking, photography, stamp collecting. Home: 107 Arbutus Dr Clarksburg WV 26301-4301

LEUNG, CHRISTOPHER CHUNG KIT, anatomy educator; b. Hong Kong, Jan. 3, 1939; came to U.S., 1960; s. Nai Kuen and Sau Wah (Chan) L.; m. Stella M. Tang, May 11, 1970; children: Jacquelyn, Therese. PhD, Jefferson Med. Coll., 1969. Instr. Jefferson Med. Coll., Phila., 1969-71, asst. prof., 1971-74, assoc. prof., 1974-75; asst. prof. U. Kans. Med. Sch., Kansas City, 1975-79; assoc. prof. La. State U. Med. Sch., Shreveport, 1979-85, N.J. Med. Sch., Newark, 1985—. Cons. study section NIH, 1986. Contbr. 25 articles to Am. Jour. Anatomy, Devel. Biology, Jour. Immunology, Jour. Exptl. Medicine, Am. Jour. Zoology, Anatomical Record. Recipient Golden Apple Best Tchg. award, NJ Med. Sch., 1993, 1995, 2000; Rsch. grant, NIH, 1978—89. Mem. Am. Assn. Immunologists, Am. Assn. Anatomists, Am. Soc. Cell Biology, Teratology Soc. Office: NJ Med Sch Dept Surgery 185 S Orange Ave Newark NJ 07103-2757

LEUNG, JOSEPH Y. computer science educator, researcher; b. Hong Kong, June 25, 1950; came to U.S., 1970; s. Kun and Fung (Tse) L.; m. Maria Y. Mo, Jan 21, 1973; 1 child, Jonathan. BA in Math., So. Ill. U., 1972; PhD in Computer Sci., Pa. State U., 1977. Asst. prof. Va. Tech., Blacksburg, 1976-77; from asst. to assoc. prof. Northwestern U., Evanston, Ill., 1977-85; prof. U. Tex., Dallas, 1985-90, U. Nebr., Lincoln, 1990-98, chmn. dept. computer sci., 1990-96; disting. prof. N.J. Inst. Tech., Newark, 1999—, chmn. dept. computer and info. sci., 1999—2001. Assoc. program head U. Tex., Dallas, 1987-90. Editor Jour. Combinatorial Math and Combinatorial Computing, 1992—; assoc. editor Jour. Computing and Info., 1995—; contbr. articles to profl. jours. Rsch. grantee NSF, Evanston, 1979, Tex. Instruments, Lincoln, 1989-90, Office Naval Rsch., Lincoln, 1987—97, Fed. Avionics Adminstrn., Newark, N.J., 2001—, NSF, Newark, 2003—. Mem. AAAS, IEEE (sr.), Assn. Computing Machinery, N.Y. Acad. Sci. Home: 4 Jill Ct Edison NJ 08817-5301 Office: NJ Inst of Tech Dept Computer and Info Sci Newark NJ 07102

LEUPP, EDYTHE PETERSON, retired education educator; b. Mpls., Nov. 27, 1921; d. Reynold H. and Lillian (Aldridge) Peterson; m. Thomas A. Leupp, Jan. 29, 1944 (dec.); children: DeEtte(dec.), Patrice, Stacia, Roderick, Braden. BS, U. Oreg., 1947, MS, 1951, EdD, 1972. Tchr. various pub. schs., Idaho, 1941-45, 1945-55; dir. tchr. edn. N.W. Nazarene Coll., Nampa, Idaho, 1955-61; sch. adminstr. Portland Pub. Schs., 1963-84; dir. tchr. edn. George Fox Coll., Newberg, Oreg., 1984-87; ret., 1987. Vis. prof. So. Nazarene U., Bethany, Okla., 1988—95, Asia Pacific Nazarene Theol. Sem., 1996, prof., 2000; adj. prof. Warner Pacific Coll., Portland, 1996—97; pres. Portland Assn. Pub. Sch. Adminstrs., 1973—75; dir.-at-large Nat. Coun. Adminstrv. Women Edn., Washington, 1973—76; state chmn. Oreg. Sch. Prins. Spl. Project, 1978—79; chair Confdn. Oreg. Sch. Adminstrs. Ann. Conf.; rschr. 40 tchr. edn. programs in colls. and univs.; designer tchr. edn. program George Fox Coll. Author: tchr. edn. materials. Pres. Nampa PTA, 1958, Idaho State Aux. Mcpl. League, 1957. Named Honored Tchr. of Okla., 1993; recipient Golden Gift award, 1982; fellow, Charles Kettering Found., 1978, 1980, 1987, 1991, 1992, 1993, 1994; scholar Hazel Fishwood, 1970. Mem.: Am. Assn. Colls. Tchr. Edn., Pi Lambda Theta, Phi Delta Kappa, Delta Kappa Gamma (pres. Alpha Rho State 1986—88). Republican. Nazarene. Avocations: travel, crafts, photography. Home: 8100 SW 2nd Ave Portland OR 97219-4602

LEUTZE, JAMES RICHARD, academic administrator, television producer and host; b. Charleston, S.C., Dec. 24, 1935; s. Willard Parker and Magdalene Mae (Seith) L.; m. Kathleen Shirley Erskine, Feb. 13, 1960; children— Magdalene Leigh, Jay Er BA, U. Md., 1957; MA, U. Miami, 1959; PhD, Duke U., 1968. Legis. asst. U.S. Senator Hubert Humphrey, Washington, 1963-64; prof. history U. N.C., Chapel Hill, 1968-87, chmn. curriculum peace, war, and def., 1979-87, Bowman and Gordon Gray prof., 1982, Dowd prof. Peace and War, 1986; TV host-producer N.C. Ctr. for Pub. TV, Chapel Hill, 1984—; pres. Hampden-Sydney (Va.) Coll., 1987-90; chancellor U. N.C. at Wilmington, 1990—. Author: Bargaining for Supremacy: Anglo-American Naval Collaboration, 1937-41, 1977 (Bernath prize 1978), A Different Kind of Victory: The Biography of Admiral Thomas C. Hart, 1981 (John Lyman Book award 1981); editor: London Journal Gen. Raymond E. Lee, 1972, The Role of the Military in a Democracy, 1974; contbr. articles to profl. jours. Served to capt. USAF, 1960-63 Recipient Standard Oil award for teaching U. N.C., 1971, Tanner award for teaching, 1978, Order of Golden Fleece award, 1983, J.W. Pate award for creating environ. awareness, 1995. Mem. Orgn. Am. Historians, Royal U.S. Inst. (London), Am. Hist. Assn., Univ. Club (N.D.), George C. Marshall Found., Phi Beta Kappa. Democrat. Episcopalian. Avocations: sportsman, hunting, fishing. Office: U NCW 601 S College Rd Wilmington NC 28403-3297 E-mail: leutzej@uncwil.edu.

LEVASSEUR, SUSAN LEE SALISBURY, secondary education educator; b. Wyandotte, Mich., Nov. 20, 1967; d. David Henry and Lynda Lee (Macaulay) Salisbury; m. John Peter LeVasseur, Dec. 19, 1992. BS in Edn., Ctrl. Mich. U., 1990; MEd in Counseling, Wayne State U., 1997. Cert. secondary tchr., Mich. Substitute tchr. Dearborn (Mich.) Schs., 1991, Allen Park (Mich.) Schs., 1991; tchr. sci. Berkley (Mich.) Schs., 1991—. Instr. Mich. Red Cross, Detroit, 1983—; deacon Allen Park Presbyn. Ch., 1991-93; mem. Colitis Found. Am. Mem. ASCD, AAUW, Nat. Counseling Assn., Am. Kennel Club, Nat. Sci. Tchrs. Assn., Mich. Sci. Tchrs. Assn., Mich. Counseling Assn., Mich. Edn. Assn., Kappa Delta Pi, Alpha Phi Omega. Presbyterian. Avocations: figure skating, swimming, dog training. Home: 22436 Cobb St Dearborn MI 48128-1313

LEVEN, CHARLES LOUIS, economics educator; b. Chgo., May 2, 1928; s. Elie H. and Ruth (Reinach) R.; m. Judith Danoff, 1950 (div. 1970); m. Dorothy Wish, 1970 (div. 1999); children: Ronald L., Robert M., Carol E., Philip W., Alice S. Student, Ill. Inst. Tech., 1945-46, U. Ill., 1947; BS, Northwestern U., 1950, MA, 1957, PhD, 1958. Economist Fed. Res. Bank of Chgo., 1950-56; asst. prof. Iowa State U., 1957-59, U. Pa., 1959-62; asso. prof. U. Pitts., 1962-65; prof. econs. Washington U., St. Louis, 1965-91, chmn. dept. econs., 1975-80, prof. emeritus, 1991—; dir. Inst. Urban and Regional Studies, 1965-85. Disting. prof. U. Mo., St. Louis, 1991-2001; cons. EEC, Ill. Auditor Gen., Polish Ministry of Planning and Constrn., St. Louis Sch. Bd., Ukrainian Ctr. for Markets and Entrepreneurship, Joel Popkin & Co. Author: Theory and Method of Income and Product Accounts for Metropolitan Areas, 1963, Development Benefits of Water Resource Investment, 1969, An Analytical Framework for Regional Development Policy, 1970, Neighborhood Change, 1976, The Mature Metropolis, 1978. Served with USNR, 1945-46. Recipient Disting. Alumni award Sullivan H.S., Chgo., 2002; Ford Found. fellow, 1956; grantee Social Sci. Rsch. Coun., 1960; grantee Com. Urban Econ., 1965; grantee NSF, 1968, 73, Merc. Bancorp., 1976, HUD, 1978, NIH, 1985, 2001. Mem. Am. Econ. Assn., Regional Sci. Assn. (pres. 1964-65, Walter Isard award for distig. scholarship 1995), Western Regional Sci. Assn. (pres. 1974-75, Disting. fellow 1999), So. Regional Sci. Assn. (disting. fellow 1991). Home: 151 Marigold Ln Milford PA 18337-7322 Office: Washington U Box 1208 1 Brookings Dr Saint Louis MO 63130-4899

LEVENSON, DAVID JEFFREY, nephrologist, educator; b. Pitts., July 6, 1950; m. Debra Caplan. AB summa cum laude, Amherst (Mass.) Coll., 1972; MD, Harvard U., 1976. Diplomate Am. Bd. Internal Medicine, Am. Bd. Nephrology, Am. Bd. Critical Care Medicine, 1999, cert. clin. specialist in hypertension Am. Soc. HBP. Intern in medicine Brigham Hosp., Boston, 1976-77; resident in medicine Peter Bent Brigham Hosp., 1977-79; clin. fellow in medicine Sch. Medicine Harvard U., Boston, 1976-79; chief med. resident W. Roxbury VA Hosp., Boston, 1978; rsch. fellow in nephrology Brigham and Women's Hosp., Boston, 1979-81, clin. fellow in nephrology, 1981-82, assoc. physician, 1982-87; asst. in medicine Beth Israel Hosp., Boston, 1982-87; staff physician Harvard Cmty. Health Plan Hosp., Boston, 1982-85, consulting nephrologist, 1987; mem. staff New England Sinai Hosp., Boston, 1985-87, Brockton (Mass.) Dialysis Unit, 1985-87, Medford (Mass.) Dialysis Ctr., 1985-87; mem. affiliate staff Waltham (Mass.)/Weston Hosp. and Med. Ctr., 1985-87; mem. provisional assoc. staff Carney Hosp., Boston, 1985-87, New England Baptist Hosp., Boston, 1985-87; mem. assoc. staff Boston Dialysis Ctr., 1985-87; mem. provisional staff Leonard Morse Hosp., Boston, 1986-87; mem. affiliate staff St. Elizabeth's Hosp., Pitts., 1986-87; mem. staff Renal-Endocrine Assocs., Pitts., 1987—; assoc. dir. med. tchg. svc. dept. medicine Western Pa. Hosp., Pitts., 1987—, dir. Hypertension Consultation Ctr., 1991—; mem. staff Shadyside Hosp., Pitts., 1987—, co-chief divsn. renal, 1989—; mem. courtesy staff Broddock Gen. Hosp., Pitts., 1987-90, St. Margaret's Meml. Hosp., New Kensington, Pa., 1987—, med. dir. Dialysis Clin., Inc., Dialysis Ctr., 1992—; mem. courtesy staff Citizens Gen. Hosp., New Kensington, Pa., 1987—; mem. staff Forbes Health Sys., Monroeville, Pa., 1988—; mem. cons. staff HealthSouth, Monroeville, Pa., 1990—, Rehab. Inst., Pitts., 1996—; clin. specialist in hyptension Am. Soc. of Hypertension, 2001. Instr. medicine Sch. Medicine Harvard, Boston, 1982—87, liaison officer biomed. rsch. programs, 1984—86; clin. instr. Sch. Medicine U. Pitts., 1987—94, clin. asst. prof. medicine, 1994—99, clin. assoc. prof., 1999—; adj. clin. asst. prof. dept. internal medicine Lake Erie (Pa.) Coll. Osteo. Medicine, 1996—; mem. med. adv. com. Nat. Kidney Found., 1997—; mem. active staff Allegheny Gen. Hosp., 1997—. Chmn. Kidney Ball Nat. Kidney Found., 1995, 96. Fellow ACP; mem. Am. Soc. Nephrology, Am. Heart Assn., Am. Soc. Hypertension, Internat. Soc. Nephrology, Phi Beta Kappa, Sigma Xi (assoc.). Office: Renal-Endocrine Assocs PC 5140 Liberty Ave Pittsburgh PA 15224-2215

LEVENTHAL, BENNETT LEE, psychiatry and pediatrics educator, administrator; b. Chgo., July 6, 1949; s. Howard Leonard and Florence Ruth (Albert) L.; m. Celia G. Goodman, June 11, 1972; children: Matthew G., Andrew G., Julia G. Student, Emory U., 1967-68, La. State U., 1968-70, BS, 1972, postgrad., 1970-74, MD, 1974. Diplomate Am. Bd. Psychiatry and Neurology in Psychiatry, Am. Bd. Psychiatry and Neurology, Child Psychiatry; lic. physician N.C., La., Ill., Va. Undergrad. rsch. assoc. Lab. Prof. William A. Pryor dept. chemistry, La. State U., 1968-70; house officer I Charity Hosp. at New Orleans, 1974; resident in psychiatry Duke U. Med. Ctr., Durham, N.C., 1974-78, chief fellow divsn. dept. psychiatry, 1976-77, chief resident dept. psychiatry, 1977-78, clin. assoc. dept. psychiatry, 1978-80; staff psychiatrist, head psychiatry dept. Joel T. Boone Clinic, Virginia Beach, Va., 1978-80; staff psychiatrist, faculty mem. dept. psychiatry Naval Regional Med. Ctr., Portsmouth, Va., 1978-80; asst. prof. psychiatry and pediats. U. Chgo., 1978-85, dir. Child Psychiatry Clinic, 1978-85, dir. Child and Adolescent Psychiatry Fellowship tng. program, 1979-88, Irving B. Harris prof. child and adolescent psychiatry, 1998—, dir. Sonia Shankman Orthogenic Sch., 2002—. Psychiat. cons. Caledonia State Prision/Halifax Mental Health Ctr., Tillery, N.C., 1976-77, Fed. Correctional Inst., Butner, N.C., 1977-78; cons. Norfolk Cmty. Mental health Ctr., 1978-80; adj. prof. psychology, biopsychology, and devel. psychology U. Chgo., 1990, adj. assoc. prof. dept. psychology and com. on biopsychology, 1987-90; meed. dir. Child Life and Family Edn. program Wyler Children's Hosp. of U. Chgo., 1983-95; dir. child and adolescent programs Chgo. Lakeshore Hosp., 1986—; Pfizer vis. prof. dept. psychiatry U. P.R., 1992; examiner Am. Bd. Psychiatry and Neurology in Gen. Psychiatry and Child Psychiatry, 1982—; mem. steering com. Harris Ctr. for Devel. Studies, U. Chgo., 1983—; mem. com. on evaluation of GAPS project AMA, 1993—; treas. Chgo. Consortium for Psychiat. Rsch., 1994; pres. Ill. Coun. Child and Adolescent Psychiatry, 1992-94; vis. scholar Hunter Inst. Mental Health and U. New Castle, NSW, Australia, 1995; mem. Gov.'s Panel on Health Svcs., 1993-94; prof. psychiatry & pediats. U. Chgo., 1990—, chmn. dept. psychiatry, 1991-98, Irving B. Harris prof. child & adolescent psychiatry, 1998—; presenter in field. Mem. editl. bd. Univ. Chgo. Better Health Letter, 1994-96; cons. editor: Jour. Emo tional and Behavioral Disorders, 1992-96; reviewer: Archives of Gen. Psychiatry, 1983—, Biol. Psychiatry, 1983—, Am. Jour. Psychiatry, 1983—, Jour. AMA, 1983—, Jour. Am. Acad. Child and Adolescent Psychiatry, 1983—, Sci., 1983—; book rev. editor Jour. Neuropsychiatry and Clin. Neuroscis., 1989-92, mem. editl. bd., 1989-92; contbr. articles to profl. jours. Lt. comdr. M.C., USNR, 1978-80. Recipient Crystal Plate award Little Friends, 1994, Individual Achievement award Autism Soc. Am., 1991, Merit award Duke U. Psychiat. Resident's Assn., 1976, Bick award La. Psychiat. Assn., 1974; Andrew W. Mellon Found. faculty fellow U. Chgo., 1983-84; John Dewey lectr. U. Chgo., 1982. Fellow Am. Acad. Child and Adolescent Psychiatry (Outstanding Mentor 1988, dep. chmn. program com. 1979—, chmn. arrangements com. 1979—, new rsch. subcom. for ann. meeting 1986—, mem. work group on rsch. 1989—), Am. Psychiat. Assn. (Falk fellow, mem. Ittleson Award Bd. 1994-97, mem. Am. Psychiat. Assn./Wisniewski Young Psychiatrists Rsch. Award Panel 1994—), Am. Acad. Pediats., Am. Orthopsychiat. Assn.; mem. AAAS, Am. Coll. Psychiatrists, Brain Rsch. Inst., Ill. Coun. Child and Adolescent Psychiatry, Ill. Psychiat. Soc., Soc. for Rsch. in Child Devel., Soc. of Profs. of Child and Adolescent Psychiatry, Soc. Biol. Psychiatry, Nat. Bd. Med. Examiners, Mental Health Assn. Ill. (profl. adv. bd. 1991—), Sigma Xi. Office: U of Chgo Pritzker Sch of Medicine 5841 S Maryland Ave Chicago IL 60637-1463 E-mail: b-leventhal@uchicago.edu.

LEVENTHAL, RUTH, retired parasitology educator, university official; b. Phila., May 23, 1940; d. Harry Louis Mongin and Bertha (Rosenberg) Mongin Blai; children: Sheryl Anne, David Alan. BS, U. Pa., 1961, PhD, 1973, MBA, 1981; HHD (hon.), Thomas Jefferson U., 1995; student, Pa. Acad. Fine Arts, 2000—03. Cert. med. technologist, clin. lab. scientist. Trainee NSF, 1971, USPHS, 1969-70, 73; asst. prof. med. tech. U. Pa., Phila., 1974-77, acting dean, 1977-81; dean Hunter Coll., CUNY, 1981-84; provost, dean, prof. biology Capital Coll., Pa. State U., Middletown, 1984-95; prof. biology Pa. State U. Hershey Med. Ctr., 1996—2002; ret., 2002. Site visitor Mid. State Assn. Colls. and Secondary Schs., Phila., 1983—98. Author (with Creadle): Medical Parasitology: A Self Instructional Text, 1979; author: 5th edit., 2002. Chmn. founds. Tri-County United Way, South Central Pa., 1996, 97; mem. health found. bd. Harrisburg Hosp., Pa., 1984-92; pres. bd. dirs. Open Stage Harrisburg, 1996-97, bd. dirs. 1996-2000; bd. dirs. Tri-County Planned Parenthood, 1984-87, Harrisburg Acad., Wormleysburg, Pa., 1984-88, Metro Arts of Harrisburg, 1984-87, Tech. Coun. Ctrl. Pa., 1996-99; founding chmn. Coun. Pub. Edn., 1984-99. Recipient Alice Paul award Women's Faculty Club, U. Pa., 1981; Recognition award NE Deans of Schs. of Allied Health, 1984, Athena award Capital Region C. of C., 1992, John Baum Humanitarian award Am. Cancer Soc., 1992, Lifetime Achievement award Family and Children's Svcs., 1996, Coll. and Cmty. Svc. award Harrisburg Area C.C., 1993; named Disting. Dau. Pa. by Gov. of Pa., 1995. Avocations: painting, sculpture.

LEVENTIS, NICHOLAS, chemist, research scientist; b. Athens, Greece, Nov. 12, 1957; came to U.S., 1980; s. Spyro and Ephrosine (Nenou) L.; m. Chariklia Sotiriou, Nov. 12, 1988; children: Theodora E., Helen A., Julia S. BS in Chemistry, U. Athens, Greece, 1980; PhD in Chemistry, Mich. State U., 1985; grad. cert. in adminstrn. and mgmt., Harvard U., 1992. Grad. asst. Mich. State Univ., East Lansing, 1980-85; rsch. assoc. MIT, Cambridge, Mass., 1985-88; project dir. Molecular Displays, Inc., Cambridge, 1988-90, v.p. R & D, 1990-93; prof. chemistry U. Mo., Rolla, 1994—2002; civil servant NASA Glenn Rsch. Ctr., 2002—. Cons. Igen, Inc., Rockville, Md., 1987—94, Hyperion Catalysis Internat., Cambridge, 1988—94, Delta F Corp., Woburn, Mass., 1992—94, Moonwatch Inc., N.Y.C., 1995—2001, Pleotint LLP, 1998—2001. Contbr. articles on electrochromic phenomena and devices to Yearbook of Ency. of Sci. & Tech., Jour. Mat. Chem., Chem. of Materials, Jour. Electrochem. Soc., Polymer News, Jour. Phys. Chemistry, Analytical Chemistry, Jour. Organic Chem., Jour. Am. Chem. Soc. Recipient Greek Inst. State Scholarships awards Greek Govt. Dept. Edn., 1976-79, Katie Y. F. Yang prize Harvard U., Cambridge, 1992; named Ethyl Corp. fellow Mich. State U., East Lansing, 1983, Yates Meml. fellow Mich. State U., East Lansing, 1984, U.S. Naval Rsch. Lab. Summer Faculty fellow, 1998. Mem. Am. Chem. Soc. (Arthur K. Doolittle award 1993), Electrochemical Soc., Internat. Union Pure & Applied Chemistry (affiliate mem.), Soc. for Info. Display. Greek Orthodox. Achievements include patents for electrochromic, electroluminescent and electrochemiluminescent displays, apparatus for detecting moisture in garments; electrically conductive polymer composition, method of making same and device incorporating same; apparatus for conducting a plurality of simultaneous measurements of electrochemiluminescent phenomena; apparatus for detecting moisture in garments. Home: 25387 Brittany Cir Westlake OH 44145-3415 Office: NASA Glenn Rsch Ctr Materials Divsn 21000 Brookpark Rd MS 49-1 Cleveland OH 44135 E-mail: Nicholas.Leventis@grc.nasa.gov.

LEVERING, EMMA GERTRUDE, special education educator; b. Bryn Mawr, Pa., Feb. 17, 1946; d. William Joseph and Mary Kathryn (Smith) L. BA, Ursinus Coll., 1968; MEd, Millersville State Coll., 1973. Tchr. of socially/emotionally disturbed students Montomery County Intermediate Unit, Norristown, Pa., 1969—2003; tchr. learning/emotional support students Jarrettown Elem. Sch., 1993—. Recipient Annie Sullivan award Montgomery County Intermediate Unit, 1990. Mem. Coun. Exceptional Children (mem. chmn. chpt. 388 1988-93, Honor award 1988), Assn. Learning Disabilities, ASCD, Children with Attention Deficit Disorders. Avocations: gardening, embroidery, reading.

LEVI, ISAAC, philosophy educator; b. N.Y.C., June 30, 1930; s. Eliezer Asher and Eva (Lunenfeld) L.; m. Judith S. Rubins, Dec. 25, 1951; children: Jonathan Abram, David Isser. BA, NYU, 1951; student, Jewish Theol. Sem., 1947-52; MA, Columbia, 1953, PhD, 1957; PhD honoris causa, Lund U., 1988. Part-time instr. Rutgers U., 1954-56; lectr. CCNY, 1956-57, asst. prof. philosophy, 1962-64, Western Res. U., 1957-62, assoc. prof., 1964-67, prof., 1967-70, chmn. dept., 1968-70; prof. philosophy Columbia U., 1971—92, chmn. dept., 1973-76, 89-91; John Dewey prof. Columbus U., 1992—2003, prof. emeritus, 2003—. Vis. scholar Corpus Christi Coll., Cambridge (Eng.) U. 1973, vis. fellow Darwin Coll., 1980, 93; vis. rsch. fellow Australian Nat. U., 1987; vis. fellow All Souls Coll., Oxford (Eng.) U., 1988; vis. fellow Inst. Advanced Study, Hebrew U. Jerusalem, 1994, Wolfson Coll., Cambridge, 1997. Author: Gambling With Truth, 1967, The Enterprise of Knowledge, 1980 Decisions and Revisions, 1984, Hard Choices, 1986, The Fixation of Belief and Its Undoing, 1991, For the Sake of the Argument, 1996, The Covenant of Reason, 1997; contbr. articles to profl. jours. Fulbright scholar, 1966-67; Guggenheim fellow, 1966-67; NEH fellow, 1979-80. Fellow Am. Acad. Arts and Scis.; mem. AAUP, Am. Philos.Assn., Philosophy of Sci. Assn., Brit. Soc. Philosophy of Sci., Phi Beta Kappa, Pi Mu Epsilon. Democrat. Home: 25 Claremont Ave New York NY 10027-6802

LEVIN, A. LEO, law educator, retired government official; b. N.Y.C., Jan. 9, 1919; s. Issaachar and Minerva Hilda (Shapiro) L.; m. Doris Feder, Dec. 28, 1947; children— Allan, Jay Michael BA, Yeshiva Coll., 1939; JD, U. Pa., 1942; LLD (hon.), Yeshiva U., 1960, NY Law Sch., 1980, Quinnipiac Coll., 1995; PhD (hon.), Bar-Ilan U., Israel, 1990. Bar: N.Y. 1947, U.S. Supreme Ct. 1982. Instr., then asst. prof. law U. Iowa, 1947-49; law faculty U. Pa., Phila., 1949-69, 70-89, Meltzer prof. law, 1987-89, Meltzer prof. emeritus, 1989—, vice provost, 1965-68; v.p. for acad. affairs Yeshiva U., N.Y.C., 1969-70; dir. Fed. Jud. Ctr., Washington, 1977-87. Chmn. Pa. State Legis. Reapportionment Commn., 1971-73; founding dir. Nat. Inst. Trial Advocacy, 1971-73; conf. coord. Nat. Conf. on Causes of Popular Dissatisfaction with Adminstrn. of Justice (Pound Conf.); chmn. bd. cert. Circuit Execs., 1977-87; mem. adv. bd. Nat. Inst. Corrections, 1977-87. Author: (with Woolley) Dispatch and Delay: A Field Study of Judicial Administration in Pennsylvania, 1961; (with Cramer) Problems on Trial Advocacy, 1968; editor: (with Schuchman and Yablon) Cases on Civil Procedure, 1992, Supplement, 1997. Hon. trustee Bar Ilan U., Ramat Gan, Israel, 1967— ; hon. pres. (former pres.) Jewish Publ. Soc. Am. Served to 1st lt. USAF, 1942-46, ETO Recipient Mordecai Ben David award Yeshiva U., 1967, Disting. Svc. award U. Pa. Law Sch. Alumni, 1974, Bernard Revel award Yeshiva Coll., 1963, Justice award Am. Judicature Soc., 1995; White lectr. La. U., 1970, Jeffords lectr., N.Y. Law Sch., 1980, Murrah Lectr. U. Pa. Law Sch., 1989. Fellow Am. Acad. Arts and Scis.; mem. Am. Law Inst., Am. Judicature Soc. (pres. 1987-89), Order of Coif (nat. pres. 1967-70) Jewish. Office: U Pa Law Sch 3400 Chestnut St Philadelphia PA 19104-6204

LEVIN, CAROLE, history educator; b. Chgo. d. Frank Kern and Charlotte (Goodman) L. BA, So. Ill. U., Edwardsville, 1970; MA, Tufts U., 1972, PhD, 1976. Vis. asst. prof. Ariz. State U., Tempe, 1979-80, U. Iowa, Iowa City, 1982-84; coord. women's studies U. Wis., La Crosse, 1980-82; mem. faculty dept. history SUNY, New Paltz, 1984-98, prof., 1993-98; prof. dept. history U. Nebr., Lincoln, 1998—2002, Willa Cather Prof., prof. history, 2002—. Author: Propaganda in the English Reformation, 1988, The Heart and Stomach of a King, 1994; author: (with others) Extraordinary Women of the Medieval and Renaissance World, 2000, The Reign of Elizabeth I, 2002; editor: Ambiguous Realities, 1987, Sexuality and Politics in Renaissance Drama, 1991, Political Rhetoric, Power, and Renaissance Women, 1995. Office: U Nebr Dept History 612 Old Father Hall Lincoln NE 68588-0327

LEVIN, FRANK S. physicist, educator; b. N.Y.C., Apr. 14, 1933; s. James J. and Celia (Aronovitch) L.; m. Madeline Carol McMurrough, Apr. 1973; 4 children. BA, Johns Hopkins U., 1955; PhD, U. Md., 1961. Rsch. assoc. Rice U., Houston, 1961-63, Brookhaven Nat. Lab., Upton, N.Y., 1963-66, U.K. Atomic Energy Authority, Harwell, Eng., 1965-67; mem. faculty Brown U., Providence, 1967—, prof. physics, 1977-98, emeritus prof., 1998—. Co-organizer 9th Internat. Conf. on Few-Body Problems, 1980. Author: An Introduction to Quantum Theory, 2002; co-editor (series): Finite Systems and Multiparticle Dynamics. Recipient Sr. U.S. Scientist award Alexander von Humboldt Stiftung, 1979. Fellow Am. Phys. Soc. (founder, 1st chmn. topical group on few body systems and multiparticle dynamics) Office: Brown U Physics Dept PO Box 1843 Providence RI 02912-1843

LEVIN, HENRY MORDECAI, economist, educator; b. N.Y.C., Dec. 7, 1938. B.S. cum laude, NYU, 1960; M.A., Rutgers U., 1962, Ph.D., 1966. assoc. research scientist, Grad. Sch. Pub. Adminstrn., NYU, 1965-66; research assoc. social econs. Econ. Studies div. Brookings Inst., Washington, 1966-68; asst. prof. edn. and econs. Stanford U., Calif., 1968-69, assoc. prof. econs., 1969-75, prof. econs. and edn., 1975—, David Jacks Prof. of Higher Edn. and Econs., 1992—, William Heard Kilpatrick prof. econ. and edn., Tchrs. Coll., Columbia U.; fellow Ctr. for Advanced Studies in Behavioral Scis., 1976-77, dir. Inst. Research on Ednl. Fin. and Governance, 1978-84; Fulbright prof. U. Barcelona, 1989; vis. scholar Russell Sage Found., 1996-97. Office: Tchrs Coll Columbia U Box 181 525 W 120th St New York NY 10022 E-mail: hl361@columbia.edu.

LEVIN, MARLENE, human resources executive, educator; b. Detroit, Oct. 7, 1934; d. Louis and Cele (Drapkin) Bertman; m. Jerome J. Goodman, Apr. 4, 1954 (dec. Mar. 1962); children: Bennett J., Marc R.; m. Herbert R. Levin, June 7, 1967. Student, U. Miami, 1952-53; BA, Coll. of New Rochelle, 1975; MPA, NYU, 1978. Cert. human resource mgr. Asst. adminstr. Richmond Children Ctr., Yonkers, N.Y., 1973-74; research assoc. Westchester Country Dept. Mental Health, N.Y., 1975-80, clinic adminstr., 1980-82; founder, pres. The Phoenix Group, Armonk, N.Y., 1982-88; v.p. human resources and adminstrn. Ensign Bank, N.Y.C., 1988-92. Adj. prof. Iona Coll., New Rochelle, NY, 1978—88; lectr. trainer Volvo of Am., Inc., Rockleigh, NJ, 1983—84, Lederle Labs., Spring Valley, NY, 1984—88; docent trainer Mus. Art, Ft. Lauderdale, Fla., 1993—; program coord. Art Travels, 1995—; chair, Collector's Forum Boca Raton (Fla.) Mus. Art, 1996—; cons., lectr. in field; art lectr. and program coord. Boca Raton Mus. of Art, Boca Raton, Fla., 1991—. Home: 2576 NW 63rd St Boca Raton FL 33496-2029

LEVIN, NORMAN LEWIS, biology educator; b. Hartford, Conn., Mar. 31, 1924; s. Joseph and Fannie (Sosin) L.; m. Shirley Alleen Ginsberg, Sept. l950; children: Faye Deborah, Alan Jeffrey. BS, U. Conn., 1948, MS, l949; PhD, U. Ill., l956. Tchg. asst. U. Ill., Champaign, l953-56, instr. zoology, l956-57; vis. asst. prof. biology Westminster Coll., Fulton, Mo., l957-58, asst. prof., l958-60; fellow in tropical medicine La. State U. Sch. Medicine, 1959; instr. biology Bklyn. Coll., l960-64, asst. prof., l964-7l, assoc. prof., l97l-76, prof., 1976—, dep. chmn. dept., 1983—, emeritus prof., 1996. Evaluation panel NSF, Washington, 1968, 7l, 74; reader advanced placement exams. Ednl. Testing Svc., Princeton, N.J., l978-84. Contbr. articles to profl. jours. With AUS, l942-45, PTO. Fellow AAAS; mem. Am. Soc. Parasitologists, Am. Soc. Zoologists, Am. Soc. Tropical Medicine and Hygiene, Am. Microscopical Soc., Helminthological Soc. Wash., Sigma Xi, Phi Sigma. Avocations: photography, reading, hiking. Home: PO Box 142 Becket MA 01223-0142 Office: CUNY Bklyn Coll Ave H and Bedford Ave Brooklyn NY 11210 E-mail: manatee186@cs.com.

LEVIN, RICHARD CHARLES, academic administrator, economist; b. San Francisco, Apr. 7, 1947; s. Derek and Phylys M. (Goldstein) Levin; m. Jane Ellen Aries, June 24, 1968; children: Jon, Daniel, Sarah, Rebecca. BA, Stanford U., 1968; LittB, Oxford U., Eng., 1971; PhD, Yale U., 1974; LLD (hon.), Princeton U., 1993, Harvard U., 1994; D in Civil Law (hon.), Oxford U., 1998. With Yale U., New Haven, 1974—, pres., 1993—, chmn. econs. dept., 1987—92, Frederick William Beinecke prof. econs., 1992—, dean Grad. Sch., 1992—93. Rsch. assoc. Nat. Bur. Econ. Rsch., Cambridge, Mass., 1985—90; program dir. Internat. Inst. Applied Sys. Analysis, Vienna, 1990—92; trustee Tanner Lectures on Human Values; cons. numerous law and bus. firms. Trustee Hopkins Sch., New Haven, 1988—95, Yale-New Haven Hosp., 1993—, Univs. Rsch. Assn., 1994—99; bd. dirs. Yale-New Haven Health Svcs. Corp., Inc., 1993—; mem. bd. sci., tech. and econ. policy Nat. Rsch. Coun.; mem. The William and Flora Hewlett Found.; mem. presdl. commn. U.S. Postal Svc., 2003. Fellow, Merton Coll. Oxford U., 1996. Fellow: Am. Acad. Arts and Scis.; mem.: Satmetrix, Econometric Soc., Am. Econ. Assn. Democrat. Jewish. Office: Yale U Office of Pres 105 Wall St New Haven CT 06511-6608 also: Yale University Office of Public Affairs 265 Church Street, Suite 901 New Haven CT 06511

LEVIN, RICHARD LOUIS, English language educator; b. Buffalo, Aug. 31, 1922; s. Bernard and Meta (Block) L.; m. Muriel Abrams, June 22, 1952; children: David, Daniel. BA, U. Chgo., 1943, MA, 1947, PhD, 1957. Mem. faculty U. Chgo., 1949-57, asst. prof. English, 1953-57; prof. English, SUNY at Stony Brook, 1957—, acting chmn. English dept., 1960-63, 65-66. Mem. adv. bd. World Center for Shakespeare Studies.; mem. acad. adv. council Shakespeare Globe Ctr.; Fulbright lectr., 1984-85 Author, cons. in field.; Editor: Tragedy: Plays, Theory and Criticism, 1960, The Question of Socrates, 1961, Tragedy Alternate, 1965, (by Thomas Middleton) Michaelmas Term, 1966, The Multiple Plot in English Renaissance Drama, 1971, New Readings vs. Old Plays: Recent Trends in the Reinterpretation of English Renaissance Drama, 1979, Looking for an Argument: Critical Encounters with the New Approaches to the Criticism of Shakespeare and His Contemporaries, 2003. Served to lt. (j.g.) USNR, 1943-46, ETO. Recipient Explicator award, 1971; Am. Council Learned Socs. fellow, 1963-64; research fellow State U. N.Y., 1961, 65-68, 71, 73; NEH sr. fellow, 1974; Guggenheim fellow, 1978-79, Nat. Humanities Ctr. fellow, 1987-88; SUNY faculty exchange scholar. Mem. MLA (mem. adv. com. publs., mem. del. assembly), Internat. Shakespeare Assn., Shakespeare Assn. Am. (trustee), Joseph Crabtree Found., Medieval and Renaissance Drama Soc. (mem. coun.), Columbia U. Shakespeare Seminar. Democrat. Jewish. Home: 26 Sparks St Melville NY 11747-1727 Office: SUNY English Dept Stony Brook NY 11794-5350 E-mail: rlevin@ms.cc.sunysb.edu.

LEVIN, SIMON ASHER, mathematician, ecologist, educator; b. Balt., Apr. 22, 1941; s. Theodore S. and Clara G. L.; m. Carole Lotte Leiffer, Aug. 4, 1964; children: Jacob, Rachel. BA in Math., Johns Hopkins U., 1961; PhD in Math. (NSF fellow), U. Md., 1964; DSc (hon.), Ea. Mich. U., 1990. Teaching asst. U. Md., 1961-62, research assoc., 1964, visitor, 1968; NSF fellow U. Calif., Berkeley, 1964-65; asst. prof. math. Cornell U., 1965-70, assoc. prof. applied math., ecology, theoretical and applied math., 1971-77, prof. applied math. and ecology, 1977-92, Charles A. Alexander prof. biology, 1985-92, adj. prof., 1992—, chmn. sect. ecology and systematics div. biol. scis., 1974-79, dir. Ecosystems Rsch. Ctr., 1980-87, dir. Ctr. for Environ. Rsch., 1987-90; George Moffett prof. biology Princeton U., 1992—, associated faculty applied math., 1992—; dir. Princeton Environ. Inst., 1993-98, Del. Ctr. for Biocomplexity, 2001—. Vis. scholar U. Wash., 1973-74, Inst. for Advanced Study, 1999; vis. scientist Weizmann Inst., Rehovot, Israel, 1977, 80; hon. prof. U. B.C., 1979-80; Lansdowne lectr. U. Victoria, 1981; disting. vis. scientist SUNY, Stony Brook, 1984; vis. fellow All Souls Coll., U. Oxford, 1988; vis. scientist, Woods Hole Oceanographic Instn., Geophysical Fluid Dynamics Summer Prog., 1994; Ostrom lectr. Wash. State U., Pullman, 1994; lectr. Third Annual Stanislaw Ulam Meml., Santa Fe Inst., 1996; The Per Brinck Lecture, U. Lund, Sweden, 1999, Chesley Lecture, Carleton Coll., 2002; co-chmn. Gordon Conf. on Theoretical Biology, 1970, chmn. Gordon Conf. on Theoretical Biology and Biomath., 1971; chmn. Am. Math. Soc./ Soc. Indsl. and Applied Maths. Com. on Maths. in Life Scis., 1973-79; mem. core panel on math. in biol. scis., program com. Internat. Congress Mathematicians, 1977-78; co-convenor Biomath. Conf., Oberwolfach, West Germany, 1978; co-dir. Internat. Ctr. for Theoretical Physics Autumn Course on Math. Ecology, Trieste, Italy, 1988, 92, 96, 2000; mem. adv. com. divsn. environ. scis. Oak Ridge Nat. Lab., 1978-81; vice chmn. math. Com. Concerned Scientists, N.Y.C., 1979—; mem. sci. panel Hudson River Found., 1982-86, chmn., 1985-86, bd. dirs., 1986-96; mem. Commn. on Life Scis., NRC, 1983-89, mem. com. ecosys. mgmt. of sustainable marine fisheries ocean studies bd., 1995-98; mem. Health and Environ. Rsch. Adv. Com. Dept. of Energy, 1986-90; prin. lectr. Conf. Bd. on Math. Scis. course on math. ecology, 1985; mem. oversight rev. bd. U.S. Nat. Acid Precipitation Assessment Program; spkr. commencement address Ea. Mich. U., 1990; sci. bd. Santa Fe Inst., 1991—. Inst. Med. Bio Math., Bene Ataroth, Israel, 1999—; bd. dirs. Beijer Inst., 1994-99, chmn. 1997-99; The H. John Heinz III Ctr. for Sci., Econs. and the Environment, 1994-99; tech, adv. bd. Brit. Petroleum, 2001—. Author: Fragile Dominion: Complexity and the Commons, 1999; editor: Lectures on Mathematics in Life Sciences, vols. 7-12, 1974-79, Ecosystem Analysis and Prediction, 1974, (with R.H. Whittaker) Niche: Theory and Application, 1975, Studies in Mathematical Biology, 2 vols., 1978, New Perspectives in Ecotoxicology, 1983, Mathematical Population Biology, 1984, Mathematical Ecology, 1984, Math Ecology: An Introduction, 1986, (with others) Mathematical Ecology, 1988, Ecotoxicology: Problems and Approaches, 1989, Perspectives in Theoretical Ecology, 1989, (with T. Hallam and L. Gross) Applied Mathematical Ecology, 1989, (with T. Powell and J.H. Steele) Patch Dynamics, 1993, Frontiers in Mathematical Biology, 1994, (with Abe and Higashi) Biodiversity: An Ecological Perspective, 1997 (with A. Okuba) Diffusion and Ecological Problems,2d edit.2001, (with P. Kareiva) The Importance of Species, 2003; editor-in-chief Ecological Applications, 1988-95, Ency. of Biodiversity, 1997-2000; Mathematical and Computational Biology Book Series, 1997-2000; editor: Ecology and Ecol. Monographs, 1975-77, Princeton Series in Theoretical and Computational Biology, 2000; editor Jour. Math. Biology, 1976-79, mng. editor, 1979-95; mng. editor Biomath., 1976-95, Lecture Notes in Biomath., 1973-95; mng. editor Princeton U. Press, Monographs in Population Biology, 1992—; assoc. editor Theoretical Population Biology, 1976-84; mem. editl. bd. Evolution Theory, 1976—, Ecol. Issues, 1995—, Conservation Ecology, 1995—, Discrete Applied Math., 1978-87, Internat. Jour. Math. and computer Modelling, 1979—, SIAM Rev., 1997—, Santa Fe Inst., 1998—, Philosophical Transactions of the Royal Soc., Series B, 1998—, Jour. Biomath., 1999, Procs. Nat. Acad. of Scis., 2000— ; mem. editl. bd. Princeton U. Press, Complexity series, 1992—; mem. adv. bd. Jour. Theoretical Biology, 1977—, Ecological Rsch., 1996—, Ecosystems, 1996—; also various other editl. positions. Bd. dirs. N.J. chpt. Nature Conservancy, 1995-97. Guggenheim fellow, 1979-80, Japanese Soc. for Promotion of Sci. fellow, 1983-84; recipient Disting. Statis. Ecologist award Internat. Assn. Ecology, 1994. Fellow AAAS (bd. dirs. 1994-98), Am. Acad. Arts and Scis.; mem. Ecol. Soc. Am. (chmn. Mercer awards subcom. 1976, mem. coun. 1975-77, ad hoc com. to evaluate ecol. consequences of nuclear war 1982-83, pres. 1990-91, MacArthur award 1988, Disting. Svc. citation 1998, chmn. MacArthur award com. 1999-2000), Soc. and Indsl. and Applied Math. (mem. coun. 1977-79, coun. exec. com. 1978-79, coun. rep. to bd. trustees 1978-79, chmn. human rights com. 1980-83, mng. editor Jour. Applied Math. 1975-79), Am. Inst. Biol. Scis., Am. Soc. Naturalists, Soc. Math. Biology (pres. 1987-89), Soc. for Conservation Biology, Brit. Ecol. Soc., Soc. Study Evolution, Japaneses Soc. Theoretical Biology (Okuba Lifetime Achievement award), U.S. Com. for Israel Environ., Sigma Xi. Jewish. Home: 11 Beechtree Ln Princeton NJ 08540-7428 Office: Princeton U Dept Ecology & Evolutionary Biology Eno Hall Princeton NJ 08544-1003

LEVINE, BARBARA GERSHKOFF, primary school educator, consultant; b. Providence, June 2, 1950; d. Aaron and Miriam Charlotte (Blackman) Gershkoff; m. Alan Marshal Levine, Aug 22, 1971 (div. Sept. 1986); children: Adam Jonathan, Matthew Corey Gershkoff; m. H. Michael Mogil, Feb. 6, 1988. BS in Early Childhood Edn., Wheelock Coll., 1972; MA in Elem. Sci. and Math. Edn., Hood Coll., 1995. Head tchr. Town & Country Schs., College Park, Md., 1973-74, head tchr., supr., 1974-75; head tchr. Early Childhood Ctr., Rockville, Md., 1987-95; tchr. 2d/3d grade, elem. sch. sci./math coord. Sandy Spring Friends Sch., 1995—2000; math resource tchr. John Eaton Elem. Sch., Washington, 2000—. Cons. How the Weatherworks, Rockville, 1987—; co-chair Project Sky Awareness Week, Think Weather, Inc., Rockville, 1991—. Co-author: (videotape, tchr.'s guide) Our Sea of Clouds, 1992, (videotape, tchr.'s manual) A Hurricane: Through the Eyes of Children, 1993, Weather Study Under a Newspaper Umbrella, 1989, (books) The Amateur Meteorologist, 1993, Anytime Weather Everywhere, 1996; contbr. articles to profl. jours. Mem. Nat. Assn. for Educating Young Children, Nat. Sci. Tchrs. Assn., Nat. Coun. Tchrs. Maths. Avocations: bridge, bicycling, travel, reading, cross country skiing. Home and Office: How the Weatherworks 301 Creek Valley Ln Rockville MD 20850-5604

LEVINE, DANIEL, historian, educator; b. N.Y.C., Dec. 31, 1934; s. Morris Simeon and Margaret (Hirsch) L.; m. Susan Rose, July 29, 1954; children— Timothy, Karen. BA in History, Antioch Coll., 1956; PhD in History (Woodrow Wilson fellow, Social Sci Research Council fellow), Northwestern U., 1961. Asst. prof. history Earlham Coll., 1960-63; asst. prof. Bowdoin Coll., Brunswick, Maine, 1963-66, assoc. prof., 1966-72, prof., 1972—, Thomas Bracket Reed prof. history and polit. sci., 1974—. Fulbright sr. lectr., Munich, 1979-80; vis. prof. U. Copenhagen, 1991. Author: Varieties of Reform Thought, 1964, Jane Addams and the Liberal Tradition, 1971, Poverty and Society, 1988, Bayard Rustin and the Civil Rights Movement, 2000; contbr. articles to profl. jours; editl. bd.: Explorations in Entrepreneurial History, 1962-70. Bd. dirs. Maine Civil Liberties Union, 1988-94. Fulbright lectr. Denmark, 1969-70; mem. jury Ralph Waldo Emerson prize Phi Beta Kappa, 1973-74; Guggenheim fellow, 1972-73. Mem. Am. Hist. Assn., Orgn. Am. Historians, AAUP, Social Welfare History Group (v.p. 1975-76), Arbeitskreis: Geschichte Sozialer Sicherung un Sozialer Disziplinierung. Democrat. Home: 785 Mere Point Rd Brunswick ME 04011 Office: Bowdoin Coll History Dept Brunswick ME 04011

LEVINE, DANIEL BLANK, classical studies educator; b. Cin., July 22, 1953; s. Joseph and Elizabeth (Blank) L.; m. Judith Robinson, Aug. 14, 1984; children: Sarah Ruth, Amy Elizabeth. Student, Am. Sch. Classical Studies, Athens, 1974, 78-89; BA in Greek and Latin magna cum laude, U. Minn., 1975; PhD in Classics, U. Cin., 1980. Seymour fellow Am. Sch. Classical Studies, 1978-79; asst. prof. U. Ark., 1980-84, assoc. prof., 1984-98, prof., 1998—. Dir. Summer Session Am. Sch. Classical Studies, Athens, 1987, 95; dir. study tour in Greece Vergilian Soc., 1990, Greece Univ. Ark., 2000, 01, 03; referee Classical Jour., 1984-88, Helios, 1984-88, Cornell U. Press, 1988-89, 91—, Classical Outlook, 1988-89; panelist NEH, Washington, 1986; co-dir., instr. gifted and talented H.S. students summer program State of Ark. Dept. Edn. Grant, 1988; mem. mng. com. Am. Sch. Classical Studies Athens, 1991—. Contbr. articles to profl. jours. Grantee NEH 1981, 82, 83, 84, 92; recipient Outstanding Tchr. award Mortar Bd. Sr. Honor Soc., U. Ark., 1991, Master Tchr. award Fulbright Coll., 1995. Mem. Am. Philological Assn. (Excellence in Teaching Classics award 1992), Am. Classical League, Classical Assn. Mid. West and South (Ovatio 1996, v.p. com. promotion Latin in Ark. 1980-86, 91-95, chmn. regional rep. com. for promotion Latin, Outstanding State V.P. for 1982-83), U. Ark. Teaching Acad., Golden Key, Phi Beta Kappa. Home: 904 Park Ave Fayetteville AR 72701-2027 Office: U Ark Dept Fgn Langs 425 Kimpel Hall Fayetteville AR 72701

LEVINE, FELICE, educational association administrator; AB in Sociology and Psychology, AM in Sociology and Psychology, PhD in Sociology and Psychology, U. Chgo. Sr. rsch. social scientist Am. Bar Found., 1974—79; program dir. NSF, 1979—91; exec. officer Am. Sociol. Assn., Washington, 1991—2002; exec. dir. Am. Ednl. Rsch. Assn., Washington, 2002—. Mem. nat. human rsch. protections adv. com. U.S. Dept. Health and Human Svcs., co-chair social and behavioral sci. working group; exec. com. Consortium of Social Sci. Assns., chair, 1997—2000; mem. adv. com. Decennial Census; bd. mem. Nat. Humanities Alliance; mem. adv. com. Nat. Consortium of Violence Rsch. Fellow: AAAS, Am. Psychol. Soc. Office: Am Ednl Rsch Assn 1230 Seventeenth St NW Washington DC 20036*

LEVINE, GEORGE LEWIS, English language educator, literature critic; b. N.Y.C., Aug. 27, 1931; s. Harris Julius and Dorothy Sara (Podolsky) L.; m. Margaret Bloom, Aug. 19, 1956; children: David Michael, Rachel Susan. BA, NYU, 1952; MA, U. Minn., 1953, PhD, 1959. Instr. Ind. U., Bloomington, 1959-62, asst. prof., 1962-65, assoc. prof., 1965-68; prof. English Rutgers U., New Brunswick, N.J., 1968—, chmn. dept., 1979-83, Kenneth Burke prof., 1985—. Vis. prof. U. Calif.-Berkeley, 1968, Stanford U., Calif., 1974-75; vis. rsch. fellow Girton Coll., Cambridge U., Eng., 1983; Avalon prof. lit. Northwestern U., 1998; dir. Ctr. for Critical Analysis of Contemp. Culture. Author: Boundaries of Fiction, 1968, The Endurance of Frankenstein, 1975, The Realistic Imagination, 1981, One Culture, 1987, Darwin and the Novelists, 1988, Lifebirds, 1995, Dying to Know, 2002; author, editor: The Art of Victorian Prose, 1968, Mindful Pleasures, 1975, Constructions of the Self, 1992, Realism and Representation, 1993, Aesthetics and Ideology, The Politics of Research, 1994, Cambridge Companion to George Eliot; editor Victorian Studies, 1959-68. With U.S. Army, 1953—55. Guggenheim Found. fellow, 1971-72; NEH fellow, 1978-79; Rockefeller Found. fellow, 1983; Rockefeller Found. Bellagio fellow, 1996, Bogliasco Found. fellow, 1999. Mem. MLA, AAUP Democrat. Jewish. Home: 108 Wesley Ave Atlantic Highlands NJ 07716 Office: Rutgers U Ctr Critical Analysis Cont Culture New Brunswick NJ 08903

LEVINE, GEORGE RICHARD, English language educator; b. Boston, Aug. 5, 1929; s. Jacob U. and Rose Lillian (Margolis) L.; m. Joan Adler, June 8, 1958 (div. 1977); children— David, Michael; m. Linda Rashman, Apr. 17, 1977. BA, Tufts Coll., Medford, Mass., 1951; MA, Columbia, 1952, PhD, 1961. Lectr. English Columbia, 1956-58; instr. Northwestern U., 1959-63; mem. faculty SUNY, Buffalo, 1963—2001, prof. emeritus, 2001—; prof. English State U. N.Y., 1970—, dean faculty arts and letters, 1975-81. Author: Henry Fielding and The Dry Mock, 1967; editor: Harp on the Shore: Thoreau and the Sea, 1985, Jonathan Swift: A Modest Proposal and Other Satires, 1995; contbr. articles to profl. jours. Chmn. bd. dirs. Youth Orch. Found., Buffalo, 1974-75; trustee Buffalo Chamber Music Soc., Arts Devel. Svcs.; bd. dirs. Buffalo Philharm. Orch., 1992-97; pres. Arts in Edn. Inst. Western N.Y. With AUS, 1952-54. Univ. fellow Columbia U., 1958-59, Faculty Research fellow SUNY, 1966-67; Fulbright lectr. W. Ger., 1969-70; recipient Chancellor's award excellence in teaching SUNY, Buffalo, 1973-74. Mem. MLA, Am. Soc. 18th Century Studies, Internat. Assn. Univ. Profs. English, Adirondack Mountain Club. Jewish. Home: 18 Saint Andrews Walk Buffalo NY 14222-2010 Office: SUNY Dept English 306 Clemens Hall Buffalo NY 14260-4600 E-mail: grlevine@acsu.buffalo.edu.

LEVINE, MAITA FAYE, mathematics educator; b. Cin., Oct. 17, 1930; d. Aaron and Jessie (Byer) L. BA, U. Cin., 1952, BE, 1953, MA in Tchg., 1966; PhD, Ohio State U., 1970. Tchr. Woodward H.S., Cin., 1953-63; instr. math. U. Cin., 1963-70, asst. prof., 1970-76, assoc. prof. math. edn., 1976-86, prof. math. sci., 1986-96, prof. emeritus, 1996—. Lectr. NSF Inst., 1962-94, Ohio Bd. Regents Insts., 1988-93. Writer Nat. Longitudinal Study Math. Abilities, 1963, Am. Coll. Testing Program, 1973, 81, 88-89; contbr. articles to profl. jours. Fellow NSF. Mem. AAUP (mem. coun., 1st v.p., chair com. W), Math. Assn. Am., Sch. Sci. and Math. Assn., Assn. Women in Math., Nat. Coun. Tchrs. Math., Ohio Coun. Tchrs. Math., Phi Beta Kappa, Sigma Xi, Delta Kappa Gamma. Democrat. Jewish. E-mail: maita.levine@uc.edu.

LEVINE, MICHAEL STEVEN, science educator; b. L.A., Mar. 5, 1955; married; 2 children. BA, U. Calif., Berkeley, 1976; PhD, Yale U., 1981. Postdoctoral staff U. Basel, 1982—83, U. Calif., Berkeley, 1983—84; asst. prof. dept. biol. scis. Columbia U., 1984—86, assoc. prof. dept. biol. scis., 1986—88, prof. dept. biol. scis., 1988—90; prof. dept. biology U. Calif., San Diego, 1991—96, prof. divsn. genetics Berkeley, 1996—, Frances Williams prof. genetics, 2002—, dir. Ctr. for Integrative Genomics. Mem. devel. biology study sect. NSF, 1988—90, genetics study sect. NIH, 1990—94; co-dir. MBL Embryology, Woods Hole, Mass., 1991—96; vis. prof. Zoology Inst., U. Zürich, 1999—2000. Editor: (jours.) Mech. Devel., 1990—95, Devel., 1995—; mem. editl. bd. (jours.) Sci., Genes & Devel., —, Current Opinion Cell Biology, —, Procs. Nat. Acad. Sci., —; contbr. more than 120 articles to profl. jours. Recipient award in molecular biology, NAS, 1996, Singer medal, SBD, 2003; fellow Jane Coffin Childs postdoctoral, 1982—84, Alfred P. Sloan Rsch., 1985—87, Searle Scholars, 1985—88. Fellow: Am. Acad. Arts and Sci.; mem.: Nat. Acad. Scis. Office: Univ Calif Dept MCB Divsn Genetics 401 Barker Hall Dept Mcb Berkeley CA 94720-3208

LEVINE, MURRAY, psychology educator; b. Bklyn., Feb. 24, 1928; s. Israel and Birdie Levine; m. Adeline Gordon, June 15, 1952; children: David Israel, Zachary Howard. BS, CCNY, 1949; MA in Psychology, U. Pa., 1951, PhD in Psychology, 1954; JD, SUNY, Buffalo, 1983. Bar: N.Y. 1984; lic. psychologist, N.Y.; diplomate in clin. psychology Am. Bd. Profl. Psychology. Psychologist VA, Phila., 1949-57, Devereux Schs., Devon, Pa., 1957-63; from asst. to assoc. prof. psychology Yale U., New Haven, 1963-68; prof. SUNY, Buffalo, 1968—, disting. svc. prof., 1995-2000, prof. emeritus, 2000—. Author: Community Psychology, 1987, 2d edit., 1997, Helping Children, 1992, Psychological Problems, Social Issues and Law, 2002; contbr. articles to profl. jours. Chmn. bd. dirs. Ctr. for Health, Environment and Justice, Falls Church, Va., 1983—; U.S. adv. bd. Child Abuse and Neglect. Recipient Seymour Sarason award Soc. for Cmty. Rsch. and Action, 1997, Kurt Lewin award N.Y. State Psychol. Assn., 1997. Mem. APA (fellow sects. 12, 27, 41, disting. contbns. award 1987, teaching and mentoring award 1992), Am. Psychology and Law Soc. (pres. 1999-2000). Home: 74 Colonial Cir Buffalo NY 14213-1467 E-mail: psylevin@acsu.buffalo.edu.

LEVINE, NAOMI BRONHEIM, academic administrator; b. N.Y.C., Apr. 15, 1923; d. Nathan and Malvina (Mermelstein) Bronheim; m. Leonard Levine, Apr. 11, 1948; 1 child, Joan. BA, Hunter Coll., 1944; LLB, Columbia, 1946, JD, 1970. Bar: N.Y. 1946. With Scaadrett, Tuttle & Chalaire, N.Y.C., 1946-48, Charles Gottleib, N.Y.C., 1948-50, Am. Jewish Congress, 1950-78, exec. dir., 1972-78; v.p. to sr. v.p. external affairs NYU, N.Y.C., 1978—2002, spl. advisor to pres., 2002—; chmn., dir. Heyman Ctr. for Philanthropy and Fund Raising, 2002—. Asst. prof. law and police sci. John Jay Coll., N.Y.C., 1969—73, L.I. U., 1965—69. Author: (book) Schools in Crisis, 1969, The Jewish Poor-an American Awakening, 1974, Politics, Religion and Love, 1990; mem. editl. bd. Columbia Law Rev., 1945—46. Chmn. N.Y.U. Bronfman Ctr., N.Y.U. Ctr. for Israeli Studies; bd. dirs. Jewish Cmty. Rels. Coun., N.Y. Ctr. Philanthropy and Fund Raising. Named to Hunter Coll. Hall of Fame, 1972. Office: NYU 29 Washington Square West New York NY 10011

LEVINE, ROBERT JOSEPH, secondary school administrator; b. Bklyn., Jan. 7, 1945; s. Robert J. Sr. and Thelma Lillian (Myatt-Coates) L.; m. Marilyn Barbara Sokol, Dec. 24, 1965 (div. Apr. 1970); m. Martha Klein Levine, May 24, 1981; children: Justin David, Ryan Michael. BA in Anthropology, U. Ariz., 1967; MS in Edn., CUNY, 1974, advanced cert. edn. adminstrn./super., 1976. Cert. adv. prof., Md.; supr. and prin., guidance, social studies, N.Y.; supr., prin. Tchr. social studies Intermediate Sch. 128M, N.Y.C., 1968-70, Prospect Heights H.S., Bklyn., 1970-71; tchr. social studies, English, Spanish, TESOL John Jay H.S., Bklyn., 1971-76; guidance counselor Lake Clifton H.S., Balt., 1976-79, Ea. H.S., Balt., 1980-83, Francis M. Wood Alternative H.S., Balt., 1983-85, Balt. Poly. Inst., 1988-92, asst. prin., 1992—. Dir. summer opportunity program Friends Sch. of Balt., 1978-86; chmn. guidance adv. panel Balt. City Pub. Schs., 1981-85; chmn. Balt. Nat. Coll. Fair, 1989-96. Author: (curriculum document) The History of Brooklyn, 1975. Mem. exec. bd. Hist. Balt. Soc., 1989-92; parent com. Cub Scout Pack 18, Balt., 1990-92; referee U.S. Soccer Fedn. Mem. Nat. Assn. Secondary Sch. Prins., Nat. Assn. Coll. Admission Counselors, Soc. for Applied Anthropology, Pipe Club of Gt. Britain (life). Avocations: bicycling, music, chess. Home: 14 Strongwood Rd Owings Mills MD 21117-2442 Office: Balt Poly Inst 1400 W Cold Spring Ln Baltimore MD 21209-4904

LEVINE, STEVEN Z, humanities educator, department chairman; Leslie Clark prof. of Humanities Byrn Mawr Coll., 1975—; dir., ctr. for visual culture Bryn Mawr Coll. Author: (book) Monet, Narcissus, and Self-Reflection: The Modernist Myth of the Self, 1994, several essays on art history. Fellowship, John Simon Guggenheim Meml. Found., 2003. Office: Bryn Mawr Coll 101 N Merion Ave Bryn Mawr PA 19010

LEVINE, STUART GEORGE, editor, English literature educator, author; b. N.Y.C., May 25, 1932; s. Max and Jean (Berens) L.; m. Susan F. Matthews, June 6, 1962; children: Rebecca, Aaron, Allen. AB, Harvard U., 1954; MA, Brown U., 1956, PhD, 1958. Teaching fellow Brown U., 1956-57; instr. in English U. Kans., Lawrence, 1958-61, asst. prof., 1961-64, assoc. prof. Am. studies, 1964-66, prof., 1966—, founder, chmn. dept. Am. Studies, 1963-70, prof. English, 1976-92, Exxon intra-univ. vis. prof. dept. music history, 1981-82, prof. emeritus, 1992—; Fulbright disting. lectr., Naples chair U. Federico II, Italy, 1994-95. Fulbright prof. U. La Plata (Argentina), 1962, U. Costa Rica, 1965, 67, Nat. Autonomous U. Mexico, 1973, several univs. in Chile, 1985; exch. professorship U. West Indies, 1988; scholar-in-residence U. Ariz., 1972-73; profl. concert musician, 1955-58, 69—, also artist; dir. NEH Summer Seminar for Coll. Tchrs., 1978; also cons. panels; vis. prof. various univs. Author: (with N.O. Lurie) The American Indian Today, 1968, Caffin's The Story of American Painting, 1970, Edgar Poe: Seer and Craftsman, 1972, (fiction) The Monday-Wednesday-Friday Girl and Other Stories (Gross-Woodley competition winner 1994); also author short stories pub. in various mags.; editor in chief Am. Studies, 1960-89, founding editor, 1989—; editor (with Susan F. Levine) The Short Fiction of Edgar Allan Poe: An Annotated Edition, 1976, 90; one-man shows include Regents Ctr. Gallery, Kansas City, 1983, Lawrence Arts Ctr., 1984; French horn player Lawrence Woodwind Quintet, Lawrence Symphony Orch., Lawrence Mcpl. Band, CottonWood Winds. Recipient Anisfield Wolf award (with others) Saturday Rev., 1968, citation NCCJ, 1969; grantee Kans. Com. for Humanities, 1982-83, 83-84 Mem. Am. Studies Assn. (exec. com. nat. meeting 1965-66, publs. com. nat. meeting 1965-66, Gabriel and Bode prize coms. 1983, chmn. both coms. 1984-85), Mid-Am. Am. Studies Assn. (exec. and editorial bds. 1960—), MLA, Am. Fedn. Musicians. Home: 1644 University Dr Lawrence KS 66044-3150

LEVINS, JOHN RAYMOND, investment advisor, management consultant, educator; b. Jersey City, Aug. 4, 1944; s. Raymond Thomas and Catherine (Kelly) L. BS in Acctg., U. N.H., 1973; MBA, U. N.H., Plymouth, 1976. Registered investment advisor; cert. mgmt. cons., enrolled to practice IRS; cert. licensing instr., real estate and multiple lines ins. broker, comml. arbitration panelist; accredited tax advisor; cert. mediator; registered securities prin. Office Supervisory Jurisdiction. Mgmt. risk analyst Express Treaty Mgmt. Corp., N.Y.C., 1962-67; asst. risk mgr. Bigelow-Sanford, Inc., N.Y.C., 1967-71; cons., broker BYSE, Inc., Laconia, N.Y., 1971-74; asst. prof. Nathaniel Hawthorne Coll., Antrim, N.H., 1975-82, Keene (N.H.) State Coll., 1982—; prin. Levins & Assocs., Concord, N.H., 1986—; investment advisor Reality Techs., Internat. Fin., Concord, 1991—. Dir. Small Bus. Inst. Keene State Coll., 1982-86; exec. seminar leader Strategic Mgmt. Group, Inc., 1986—, Boston U., 1976—; mem. bd. advisors Am. Biog. Inst.; pvt. practice real estate, ins. cons., Concord, 1981; panelist securities arbitration Nat. Assn. Security Dealers, Am. Stock Exch., N.Y. Stock Exch., Gen. Securities Prin.; consumer affair mediator Dept. Justice, Office of Atty. Gen., N.H.; mortgage banker; comml. financing broker; mem. SEC, spkr., seminar leader in field; fin. faculty grad. programs Boston U., 1996 fin. and investment provider Dun & Bradstreet, 1997; exepert witness investments and securities WestLaw.com, FindLaw.com, Martindale and Hubbelle Author: Finance and Accounting, 1979 (Excellence award 1980), Financial Analysis, 1981 (Excellence award 1980), Managing Cash Flow, 1988 (Excellence award 1988), Finance and Management, 1989. Incorporator Spaulding Youth Ctr., Tilton, N.H., 1990; colleague Found. for Acctg. Edn., assoc., profl. standing, 1988; mem. Nat. Consortium Edn. and Tng., Madison, Wis., 1989. With USN, 1969-71, S.E. Asia. Named Outstanding Support Leader U.S. Small Bus. Adminstrn., Concord, 1985, Oustanding Svc. Leader Community Leaders Am., N.H., 1990, One of Outstanding Young Men Am. U.S. Jaycees Bd. Adv.'s, 1983. Mem. AICPA (mem. Profl. Devel. Inst., sponsor trainer 1988-89), Found. Acctg. Acctg., Investment Co. Inst. (assoc., nat. standing 1987), Inst. Mgmt. Cons. (assoc., nat. standing 1985, cert. profl. cons. to mgmt.), Nat. Soc. Pub. Accts. (del., profl. standing 1985), Nat. Soc. Non-Profit Orgns. (svc. provider 1989, colleague), Accreditation Coun. for Accountancy (fed. taxation accreditation 1987, colleague). Avocations: boating, teaching, community service, athletics. Home and Office: Levins & Associates Wall St Tower 555 Canal St 812 Manchester NH 03101 Fax: 603-629-0056. E-mail: Levins.john@verizon.net.

LEVINS, RICHARD, biologist, educator; b. N.Y.C., June 1, 1930; s. Ruben and Ruth (Sackman) L.; m. Rosario Morales, June 10, 1950; children: Aurora, Ricardo, Alejandro. AB, Cornell U., 1951; PhD, Columbia U., 1965; PhD in Environ. Sci. (hon.), U. Havana, 2000. Farmer, P.R., 1951-56; research assoc. U. Rochester, N.Y., 1960-61; assoc. prof. biology U. P.R., 1961-66; assoc. prof. biology and math. biology U. Chgo., 1967-68, prof., 1969-75; John Rock prof. population sci. Harvard Sch. Pub. Health, 1975—. Mem. sci. adv. council natural resources P.R. Dept. Pub. Works, 1970-72; mem. adv. bd. N.Y. Marxist Sch. Author: Evolution in Changing Environments, 1968; co-author: (with R.C. Lewontin) The Dialectical Biologist, (with C. Puccia) Qualitative Modeling of Complex Systems, (with Yrjo Haila) Humanity and Nature, 1992; editorial bd.: La Escalera, 1965-72, Am. Naturalist, 1968-71, Theoretical Population Biology, 1970— . Coffee region organizer P.R. Communist Party, 1952-54; mem. Partido Socialista Puertorriqueño; bd. dirs. Concilo Hispano, 1986-94, Oxfam Am., 1988-95, Grassroots Internat., 1996-97. Recipient Arthur Felberbaum award Brecht Forum, 1995; Edinburgh medal The Wider Soc., 1996, Award Inst. of Fundamental Rsch. in Tropical Agrl., 1996, Robert H. Ebert lectureship, Wichita, 1998. Mem. Am. Acad. Arts and Sci., New World Agr. and Ecol. Group, Sci. for Vietnam, N.E. Organic Farmers Assn., Cuban Botanical Assn. (corr. mem.). Home: 107 Amory St Cambridge MA 02139-1229

LEVINSKY, NORMAN GEORGE, physician, educator; b. Boston, Apr. 27, 1929; s. Harry and Gertrude (Kipperman) Levinsky; m. Elena Sartori, June 17, 1956; children: Harold, Andrew, Nancy. AB summa cum laude, Harvard U., 1950, MD cum laude, 1954. Diplomate Am. Bd. Internal Medicine. Intern Beth Israel Hosp., Boston, 1954—55, resident, 1955—56; commd. med. officer USPHS., 1956; clin. assoc. Nat. Heart Inst., Bethesda, Md., 1956—58; NIH fellow Boston U. Med. Center, 1958—60; practice medicine, specializing in internal medicine and nephrology Boston, 1960—; chief of medicine Boston City Hosp., 1968—72, 1993—97; physician-in-chief, dir. Boston U. Med. Ctr. Hosp., Boston, 1972—97; asst. prof., then assoc. prof. medicine Boston U., 1960—68, Wesselhoeft prof., 1968—72, Wade prof. medicine, 1972—97, chmn. medicine, 1972—97, prof. medicine, assoc. provost, 1997—. Mem. drug efficacy panelNRC; mem. nephrology test com. AM. Bd. Internal Medicine, 1971—76; mem. gen. medicine B rev. group NIH; mem. comprehensive test com. Nat. Bd. Med. Examiners, 1986—89; chmn. com. to study end-stage renal disease program NAS/Inst. Medicine, 1988—90, chmn. com. on Xenografts, 1995. Editor (with R.W. Wilkins): Medicine: Essentials of Clinical Practice, 3d edit., 1983; editor: (with R. Rettig) Kidney Disease and the Federal Government, 1991; editor: Ethics and the Kidney, 2001; contbr. chapters to books, sci. articles to med. jours. Master: ACP (Disting. Tchr. award 1992); mem.: AAAS, Interurban Clin. Club (pres. 1985—86), Inst. Medicine NAS, Am. Soc. Nephrology, Assn. Profs. Medicine (sec., treas. 1984—87, pres.-elect 1987—88, pres. 1988—89), Am. Physiol. Soc., Assn. Am. Physicians, Am. Heart Assn., Am. Soc. Clin. Investigation, Am. Fedn. Clin. Rsch., Alpha Omega Alpha, Phi Beta Kappa. Home: 20 Kenwood Ave Newton MA 02459-1439 Office: Boston U Med Ctr 75 E Newton St Boston MA 02118-2340 E-mail: nlevinsk@bu.edu.

LEVINSON, WARREN EDWARD, physician, microbiologist, educator; b. N.Y.C., Sept. 28, 1933; s. Jay Raymond and Claire (Grossman) L.; m. Barbara Boykin, Aug. 12, 1965. BS, Cornell U., 1953; MD, U. Buffalo, 1957; PhD, U. Calif., Berkeley, 1965. Diplomate Nat. Bd. Med. Examiners. Commd. lt. USN, 1957, flight surgeon, 1958; faculty Sch. of Med. U. Calif., San Francisco, 1967—. Author: Medical Microbiology and Immunology, 1989, 7th edit. 2002. Mem. Planning Commn., Mill Valley, Calif., 1978-80, 1988-90; mem. Mill Valley City Coun., 1990-97, vice mayor, 1991-92, mayor, 1992-93. Mem. AAAS, Am. Soc. Microbiology, Calif. Acad. Scis., Alpha Omega Alpha (med. hon. soc.). Home: 183 Molino Ave Mill Valley CA 94941-2742 Office: U Calif Dept Microbiology PO Box 414 San Francisco CA 94143-0001

LEVINTHAL, ELLIOTT CHARLES, physicist, educator; b. Bklyn., Apr. 13, 1922; s. Fred and Rose (Raiben) L.; m. Rhoda Arons, June 4, 1944; children— David, Judith, Michael, Daniel. BA, Columbia Coll., 1942; MS, Mass. Inst. Tech., 1943; PhD, Stanford U., 1949. Project engr. Sperry Gyroscope Co., N.Y.C., 1943-46; research assoc. nuclear physics Stanford (Calif.) U., 1946-48, sr. scientist dept. genetics Sch. Medicine, 1961-74, dir. Instrumentation Research Lab., 1961-80, assoc. dean for research affairs, 1970-73, adj. prof. genetics Sch. Medicine, 1974-80, research prof. mech. engring., dir. Inst. Mfg. and Automation Sch. Engring., 1983-90, assoc. dean for research Sch. Engring., 1986-90, assoc. dean spl. programs, 1990-91, prof. emeritus, 1991—; research physicist Varian Assocs., Palo Alto, Calif., 1949-50, dir. research, 1950-52; chief engr. Century Electronics, Palo Alto, 1952-53; pres. Levinthal Electronics, Palo Alto, 1953-61; dir. def. scis. office Def. Advanced Projects Agy., Dept. Def., Arlington, Va., 1980-83. Mem. NASA Adv. Coun., 1980-84, space studies bd., NRC, 1989-91, mem. human exploration, 1991-92, army sci. bd., 1989-91; cons. HEW; chmn. bd. dirs. Eunoe, Inc. Recipient NASA Public Service medal, 1977 Mem. AAAS, IEEE, Am. Phys. Soc., Optical Soc. Am., Biomed. Engring. Soc., Sigma Xi. Democrat. Jewish. Home: 59 Sutherland Dr Atherton CA 94027-6471 E-mail: levinthal@stanford.edu.

LEVIS, DONALD JAMES, psychologist, educator; b. Cleve., Sept. 19, 1936; s. William and Antoinette (Stejskal) L.; children: Brian, Katie. PhD, Emory U., 1964. Postdoctoral fellow clin. psychology Lafayette Clinic, Detroit, 1964-65; asst. prof. psychology U. Iowa, Iowa City, 1966-70, assoc. prof., dir. research and tng. clinic, 1970-72; prof. SUNY-Binghamton, 1972—. Author: Learning Approaches to Therapeutic Behavior Modification, 1970, Implosive Therapy, 1973; cons. editor: Jour. Abnormal Psychology, 1974-80, Jour. Exptl. Psychology, 1976-77, Behavior Moedifications, 1977-81, Behavior Therapy, 1974-76, Clin. Behavior Therapy Rev., 1978— ; contbr. articles to profl. jours. Served to capt. AUSR, 1958-66. Fellow Behavior and Therapy Research Soc. (charter, clin.), Am. Psychol. Assn.; mem. Assn. Advancement Behavior Therapy (publ. bd. 1979-82), AAAS, Psychonomic Soc., N.Y. State Psychol. Assn., Sigma Xi Home: 48 Riverside Dr Binghamton NY 13905-4402 Office: SUNY at Binghamton Dept Psychology Binghamton NY 13901

LEVIS, RICHARD GEORGE, secondary school educator; b. Kenosha, Wis., Nov. 20, 1946; s. Elso R. and Valentina (Maraccini) L.; m. Diane Rose Christie, June 12, 1971; 1 child, Maureen R. BS, U. Wis., 1968, MS, 1973. Tchr. social studies Parker Jr. H.S., Janesville, Wis., 1969, Washington Jr. H.S., Kenosha, 1969-98, Mary D. Bradford H.S., Kenosha, 1998—2002. Mem. com. on vandalism and mid. schs. Kenosha Unified Schs., social studies benchmarks and stds. com.; jr. h.s. rep. Kenosha Ednl. Found., 1994; KABA bowl coach Bradford H.S., 1999—. Co-author: (with James Hansen) United Nations Resource Materials and Bibliographies, 1974. V.p. Kenosha Tchrs. Union, 1971-73; exec. bd. Kenosha Dem. Party, 1969-86; mem. canvass bd., Kenosha; rep. United Fund, 1985—; mem. City of Kenosha Bd. Tax Rev., 2003—. Mem. NEA, Nat. Coun. Social Studies, Wis. Social Studies Coun., Wis. Edn. Assn., Kenosha Edn. Assn. (bd. dirs. 1975-77), Phi Delta Kappa. Democrat. Roman Catholic. Avocations: golf, reading, watching sports, politics, travel. Home: 3520 14th Pl Kenosha WI 53144-2939 Office: Mary D Bradford HS 3700 Washington Rd Kenosha WI 53144-1641

LEVISAY, LEESA DAWN, music educator, composer; b. Fort Worth, Tex., Mar. 30, 1959; d. Earl Lee and Dawn Estelle (Langley) Hall; m. Charles Glen Levisay, Apr. 14, 1984; children: Laura, Leah, Chad. MusB, Tarleton State U., 1982, MBA, 1983. Grad. asst. dept. fine arts and speech, asst. condr. choirs Tarleton State U., Stephenville, 1982-83, piano tchr., 1983; ins. underwriter Carter, Metsger, & Jones, Inc., Stephenville, 1984-85; piano, vocal instr. Stephenville, 1985—; co-owner A Musical Spectrum - Sch. Music, Stephenville, 1999—. Mem. Cross Timbers Fine Arts Coun. Bd. Dirs., Stephensville, 1989-90; adjuctor piano competition Music Tchrs. Assn., Weatherford, Tex., 1990-96, Ft. Worth, 1991-92, Abilene, Tex., 1992-93; composer Concert Master Pub. Co., Dallas, 1993—; condr., composer Nat. Group Piano Tchrs. Assn., 1994; guest condr. The Keynote Studio, Dallas, 1996-97; guest composer, condr. Nat. Piano Tchrs. Inst., So. Meth. U., Dallas, 1997; adjudicator vocal judge Tarleton State U., 1998. Composer, arranger Christmas Collection, 1993, Canon in D-Pachelbel, 1996; composer Laura's Song, 1994. Singer Cross Timbers Civic Chorale, Stephenville, 1982-99; com. mem. Cross Timbers Habitat for Humanity, Stephenville, 1997-99. Mem. Nat. Piano Tchrs. Guild, Music Tchrs. Nat. Assn. (cert. profl. music tchr.), Tex. Music Tchrs. Assn., Cross Timbers Music Tchrs. Assn. (ensemble dir. 1985-97), Early Childhood Music and Movement Assn. (cert. early childhood music level 1), Stephenville C. of C. Presbyterian. Avocations: crafts, church work, gardening, reading. Office: A Musical Spectrum - Sch Music 495 N Harbin Dr Stephenville TX 76401-2861

LEVI-SETTI, RICCARDO, physicist, director; b. Milan, July 11, 1927; married; 2 children. Doctor Degree in Physics, U. Pavia, Italy, 1949; Libera Docenza in Physics, U. Rome, 1955. Asst. prof. U. Pavia, Italy, 1949-51; rsch. mem. Nat. Inst. for Nuclear Rsch. U. Milan, 1951-56; rsch. assoc. Enrico Fermi Inst. U. Chgo., 1956-57, asst. prof., 1957-62, assoc. prof., 1962-65, prof. physics, 1965—, emeritus prof. physics, 1992—; Guggenheim fellow CERN, Geneva, 1963. Hon. rsch. assoc. Field Mus. Natural History, Chgo., 1976—. Decorated Commendatore dell'Ordine al Merito (Italy); John Simon Guggenheim fellow, 1963, Angelo della Riccia fellow Italian Phys. Soc., 1954. Fellow Am. Phys. Soc.; mem. Phi Beta Kappa. Office: U Chgo Enrico Fermi Inst 5640 S Ellis Ave Chicago IL 60637-1433

LEVIT, MIKHAIL, mathematician, statistician, educator; b. Leningrad, Russia, Nov. 20, 1945; came to U.S., 1993; s. Vladimir and Valentina (Dementyeva) L.; m. Anna Mochkina; 1 child, Catherina. BS in Math., Leningrad State U., 1967, PhD in Math., 1974. Asst. prof. Leningrad Elec. Engring. Inst., 1974-82, assoc. prof., 1982-93; adj. assoc. prof. N.Y. Inst. Tech., N.Y.C., 1993—. Statis. analyst Adminstrs. for the Proffessions, Manhasset, N.Y., 1995—. Contbr. articles to profl. publs. Achievements include research on control theory; stability and spectral analysis of systems with stochastic coefficients numerical methods; fixed point prediction algorithms and optimum lyapunov functions. Office: Adminstrs for Professions 111 E Shore Rd Manhasset NY 11030-2902

LEVITAN, DAVID M(AURICE), lawyer, educator; b. Tver, Lithuania, Dec. 25, 1915; (parents Am. citizens); m. Judith Morley; children: Barbara Lane Levitan, Stuart Dean Levitan. BS, Northwestern U., 1936, MA, 1937; PhD, U. Chgo., 1940; JD, Columbia U., 1948. Bar: N.Y. 1948, U.S. Dist. Ct. (so. dist.) N.Y. 1948, U.S. Supreme Ct. 1953. Various U.S. Govt. adminstrv. and advisory positions with Nat. Youth Adminstrn., Office Price Adminstrn., War Prodn. Bd., Fgn. Econ. Adminstrn. Supreme Hdqrs. Allied Expeditionary Force, and Cen. European div. Dept. State, 1940-46; cons., sec. joint-com. of 5th and 6th coms., 2d Gen. Assembly, dir. com. of experts for establishing adminstrv. tribunal UN, 1946-47; cons. pub. affairs dept., producer series of pub. affairs programs on TV and radio ABC, 1946-53; pvt. practice N.Y.C., 1948-66; counsel Hahn & Hessen, N.Y.C., 1966-68, ptnr., 1968-86, counsel, 1986-96; instr. U. Chgo., 1938-41; adj. prof. public law Columbia U., 1946-65; adj. prof. John Jay Coll. Criminal Justice, CUNY, 1966-75; adj. prof. polit. sci. Post Coll., 1964-66; adj. prof. law Cardozo Sch. Law, 1978-82; pvt. practice, N.Y.C., 1996—. Asst. to Ill. state adminstr. Nat. Youth Adminstrn., chief budget sect., Washington, 1940-41; mgmt. analyst Office of Price Adminstrn., 1941; spl. asst. to chmn. War Prodn. Bd., 1942-43; chief property control divsn. Fgn. Econ. Adminstrn., Washington, 1944-45; with U.S. Group of Control Coun. for Germany at SHAEF, London, 1944; advisor Ctrl. European divsn. U.S. Dept. State, 1945; cons. UN, 1946-47, Sect. Joint Com. 5th and 6th Coms., 1946-47, 2d session of 1st Gen. Assembly, 1946-47; dir. Com. of Experts on Establishment of Adminstrn. Tribunal, 1946-47; cons. pub. affairs dept. ABC, 1946-53. Contbr. articles to legal jours. Mem. Nassau County (N.Y.) Welfare Bd., 1965-69; chmn. Planning Bd., Village of Roslyn Harbor, N.Y., 1965-66; chmn. Bd. of Zoning Appeals, Village Roslyn Harbor, 1967-86. Recipient Demobilization award Social Sci. Rsch. Coun., 1946-48. Fellow Am. Coll. Trust and Estate Counsel; mem. ABA, Am. Polit. Sci. Assn., Am. Soc. Internat. Law, Am. Law Inst., Assn. Bar City N.Y. Home: 103 NE 19th Ave Deerfield Beach FL 33441-6106 Office: Ste 704 455 North End Ave New York NY 10282

LEVITT, GREGORY ALAN, education educator; b. Memphis, Jan. 12, 1952; s. Robert Riley and Martha Lorraine (Swincher) L.; m. Billie Diane Tomblin (div. June 1985); 1 child, Joshua Paul; m. Yueping Guo, June 3, 1994; 1 child, Maya Guo. BA, Capital U., Columbus, Ohio, 1975; MA, Ohio State U., 1988, PhD, 1990. Cert. secondary sch. tchr., adminstr., Ohio; cert. tchr. Chinese lang. Beijing Lang. Inst. Tchr. Wehrle H.S., Columbus, 1975-85; grad. teaching assoc. Ohio State U., Columbus, 1985-90; cons./rschr. CBS News, Beijing, China, 1989; dir. fgn. tchrs. Beijing U. of Aero. and Astron. Engring., 1988-90; assoc. prof. U. New Orleans, 1990—. Assoc. dir. Ctr. for the Pacific Rim, New Orleans, 1990—; dir. A World of Difference Inst., New Orleans, 1994—. Mem. editl. rev. bd. Teaching About Asia Jour., 1993—; contbr. articles to profl. jours., chpts. to books and computer software. Bd. dirs. Tyomey Ctr. for Peace Through Justice, New Orleans, 1994—; mem. cmty. bd. Success Dropout Prevention, New Orleans, 1990—; coll. organizer AIDS Walk, U. New Orleans, 1993-94. Grantee U.S. Dept. Edn., 1994, East-West Ctr., Honolulu, 1994, La. Endowment for Humanities, 1993. Mem. ASCD, Nat. Coun. for the Social Studies, Assn. for Asian Studies, Nat. Assn. for Multicultural Edn., La. Coun. for the Social Studies, La. Ednl. Rsch. Assn., Phi Beta Delta, Phi Delta Kappa (advisor 1994—). Avocations: golf, racquetball, tennis, snorkeling, swimming. Office: Univ of New Orleans Coll of Edn Dept Of C&i New Orleans LA 70148-0001 Home: 11004 Desert Dove Ave Las Vegas NV 89144-1451

LEVITT, RAYMOND ELLIOT, civil engineering educator; b. Johannesburg, Republic of South Africa, Aug. 7, 1949; came to U.S., 1972; s. Barnard and Riva Eleanor (Lazarus) L.; m. Kathleen Adele Sullivan, Nov. 26, 1976; children: Benjamin John, Joanna Maurine, Zoë Ellen. BSCE, U. Witwatersrand, Johannesburg, 1971; MSCE, Stanford U., 1973, PhDCE, 1975. Project engr. Christiani & Neilsen, Cape Town, South Africa, 1971-72; asst. prof. civil engring. MIT, Cambridge, 1975-79, assoc. prof., 1979-80, Stanford U., Calif., 1980-88, prof., 1988—, acad. dir. advanced project mgmt. program, 1999—, dir. collaboratory for rsch. on global projects, 2003—. Bd. dirs. Visual Network Design, Burlingame, Calif.; chmn. bd. Vité, Palo Alto, Calif.; advisor U.S. Dept. Labor, Washington, 1976-77, Calif. Pub. Utilities Commn., San Francisco, 1982-84, U.S. Dept. Energy, 2002-2003. Co-author: Union and Open-Shop Construction, 1978, Construction Safety Management, 1987, 2d edit., 1993, Knowledge-Based Systems in Engineering, 1990. Pres. Stanford Homeowners Assn., 1981-83. Recipient Marksman award Engring. News Record, N.Y.C., 1985, Commitment to Life award Nat. Safe Workplace Inst., 1987. Mem. ASCE (Huber Prize award 1982, Computing Civil Engring. award 2000), INFORMS, Project Mgmt. Inst. Unitarian Universalist. Avocations: swimming, trout fishing, music, surfing. Office: Stanford U Dept Civil Engring # 4020 Stanford CA 94305

LEVITZ, I. S. artist, educator, curator; b. Bklyn., Aug. 24, 1943; d. Irving Jacob and Mary (Matts) Steiner; m. Martin N. Levitz, June 19, 1965; children: Robin, David, Jodi. Student, Vesper George Sch. Art, Boston, Hartford Art Sch., Trinity Coll., Hartford, Wesleyan U., Middletown, Conn. Artist-in-residence Brandeis U. Women's Commn.,1994. Juried exhibits include Mattatuck Mus. "Conn. Vision", 1992, Silvermine Guild, Norwalk, Conn., 1983, New Britain Mus. Am. Art, 1982, 85, 87, 90, Conn. Acad. Fine Arts, 1988-91, 95, 96, Three Women Artists - Chase Freedom Gallery, Hartford Jewish Ctr., 1994, Women in the Arts, Wave Gallery, New Haven, 1995, Yale-New Haven Hosp. The Arts in Health Care, 1995. Vol. Toys for Tots, Bloomfield, 1989-92; active Hartford Arts Coun., 1976; chmn. Ann Randall Arts Com., 1978-80. Recipient Purchase award Town of Bloomfield, 1991. Mem. West Hartford Art League (chmn. selection com. for exhbns. 1983-84), Conn. Watercolor Soc.(mem.), Conn. Acad. Fine Arts (bd. dirs. 1995-96), New Britain Mus. Am. Art. Avocations: hiking, skiing, ice skating, travel, family. Home: 869 Farmington Ave Apt 205 West Hartford CT 06119-1404

LEVY, CHARLOTTE LOIS, law librarian, educator, consultant, lawyer; b. Cin., Aug. 31, 1944; d. Samuel M. and Helen (Lowitz) Levy; m. Herbert Regenstreif, Dec. 11, 1980; 1 child, Cara Rachael Regenstreif. BA, U. Ky., 1966; MS, Columbia U., 1969; JD, No. Ky. U., 1975. Bar: Colo. 1979, NY 1985, Ky. 1985, U.S. Ct. Appeals (6th cir.) 1986. Law libr. No. Ky. U., 1971—75; law libr., assoc. prof. law Pace U., 1975—77; mgr. Fred B. Rothman & Co., Littleton, Colo., 1977—79; law libr., prof. Bklyn. Law Sch., 1979—85; adj. prof. Pratt Inst. Grad. Sch. Libr. and Info. Sci., 1982—85; atty. Cabinet for Human Resources, Frankfurt, Ky., 1985—87; atty., pres. Vantage Info. Cons., Inc., Frankfurt, 1983—. Cons. to various librs., pubs. Author: The Human Body and the Law, 1974 (Am. Jurisprudence Book award in domestic rels., 1974, in trusts, 1975), 2d edit., 1983, Computer-Assisted Litigation Support, 1984; mem. editl. bd.: No. Ky. U. Law Rev., 1974—75. 1st v.p. Ohavay Zion Synagogue; pres. bd. trustees Syncopated, Inc. Mem.: ABA, Fayette County Bar Assn., Ky. Bar Assn., Am. Assn. Law Librs. (cert. law libr.). Democrat. Jewish. Home: 200 McDowell Rd Lexington KY 40502-1896

LEVY, DANIEL, economics educator; b. Tschakaia, Georgian Republic, Georgia, Nov. 13, 1957; came to U.S., 1983; s. Shabtai and Simha (Leviashvili) L.; m. M. Sarit Adler, Spet. 10, 1981; children: Avihai, Eliav. BA, Ben-Gurion U., Beer-Sheva, Israel, 1982; MA, U. Calif., Irvine, 1989, PhD, 1990. Lectr. U. Minn., Mpls., 1983-88, St. Olaf Coll., Northfield, Minn., 1986-88, The Coll. St. Catherine, St. Paul, 1987-88; prof. Pepperdine U., Irvine, 1989-90, U. Calif., Irvine, 1990-91, Union Coll., Schenectady, N.Y., 1991-92, Emory U., Atlanta, 1992—, Bar-Ilan U., 1999—. Computer software programmer Mac Cartuli, 1989. Contbr. articles to profl. jours. Treas. Minn. Student Orgn., 1984-85. Mem. Am. Econ. Assn., Soc. Econ. Dynamics and Control, Econometric Soc., Western Econ. Assn., Mensa. Avocations: basketball, tennis, chess, computers, piano. Office: Emory U Dept Economics Atlanta GA 30322-0001 E-mail: econdl@emory.edu., levyda@mail.biu.ac.il.

LEVY, DAVID CORCOS, museum director; b. N.Y.C., Apr. 10, 1938; s. Edgar Wolf and Lucille (Corcos) L.; m. Janet Meyer, June 7, 1959 (div.); children: Jessica Anne, Thomas William; m. Carole L. Feld, May 19, 1992; 1 child, Alexander Wolf. BA, Columbia U., 1960; MA, NYU, 1969, PhD, 1979; DFA (hon.), New Sch. for Social Rsch., 1989, Cedar Crest Coll., 1998. Asst. dir. admissions Parson Sch. Design, N.Y.C., 1961-62, dir. admissions, 1962-67, v.p., 1967-70, dean, chief adminstrv. officer, 1970-79, exec. dean, chief adminstrv. officer, 1979-89; chancellor New Sch. for Social Rsch., N.Y.C., 1989-90; pres., dir. The Corcoran Gallery of Art, Washington, D.C., 1991—. Photographer of works exhibited in Guggenheim Mus., Mus. Modern Art, State Mus., Dortmund, Germany; art dir. jours., books, posters; contbr. articles to jours. and newspapers. Decorated Chevalier des Arts et des Lettres (France). Home: 2556 Massachusetts Ave NW Washington DC 20008-2822 Office: Corcoran Gallery of Art 500 17th St NW Washington DC 20006-4804

LEVY, GAD, atmospheric scientist, educator, statistician; b. Tel Aviv, Nov. 22, 1954; came to U.S., 1981; s. Rudi and Zipora Loewy; m. Felice S. Tiu, July 8, 1990; children: Tal Adam, Kai Tiu. BSc, Hebrew U., 1980; MS, Colo. State U., 1982; PhD, U. Wash., 1987. Rsch. asst. Hebrew U., Jerusalem, 1979-80, Colo. State U., Ft. Collins, 1981-82; rsch. asst./assoc. U. Wash., Seattle, 1982-88, sr. rsch. scientist, 1993—2000; rsch. assoc. Oreg. State U., Corvallis, 1988-89, asst. prof., 1989-96, assoc. prof., 1996—. Co-chair flux modeling group TOGA-COARE Internat. Data Workshop, Toulouse, France, 1994; mem. radarsat sci. adv. team NASA, Washington, 1995—, mem. atmospheres panel, Mission to Planet Earth, 1989-94; cons. applied stats. Boeing Co., Seattle, 2001-2002; prin. investigator Northwest Rsch. Assocs., Bellevue, Wash., 2002—; adj. faculty U. Phoenix, 2002—; spkr. in field. Editor: Remote Sensing of the Pacific Ocean By Satellites, 1998; contbr. articles to profl. jours. Coord. edn. task force Amnesty Internat., 1984-94; charter mem. Com. for Israeli Palestinian Peace, Seattle, 1983-86; bd. dirs. Found. for Internat. Understanding Through Students, Seattle, 1987. Recipient Elizabeth Gould award for Internat. Understanding, Found. for Internat. Understanding Through Students, 1987, Pres. Fund for Innovative Rsch., Calif. Inst. Tech., 1990. Mem. Am. Meteorological Soc. (Travel award 1989), Am. Geophys. Union (Travel award 1991). Achievements include innovative research on the marine atmosphere boundary layer and the use of satellite based observations to develop and test hypotheses about the dynamics of the marine atmosphere, maritime atmospheric fronts, and equatorial climate dynamics of the atmosphere.

LEVY, GERALD DUN, nonprofit organization administrator; b. N.Y.C., May 11, 1924; s. Robert Louis and Beatrice (Straus) L.; m. Marion Fennelly, Dec. 27, 1952; children: Alison, Elizabeth, Robert. BS, Harvard U., 1945, MBA, 1947. From asst. buyer to mdse. v.p. R.H. Macy & Co. Inc., N.Y.C., 1947—73; v.p. Roosevelt Hosp., N.Y.C., 1973—77; assoc. exec. dir. Vis. Nurse Svc., N.Y.C., 1977—81; various mgmt. positions, bd. dirs. Nat. Exec. Svc. Corps, N.Y.C., 1981—. Chmn. bd. World Edn., Inc., Boston, 1980-95; vice chmn. bd. U.S Com. for UNICEF, N.Y.C., 1975-85; v.p. bd. dirs. N.Y. Heart Assn., N.Y.C., 1975-85; vice chmn. bd. Fund for Peace, 1990—. 1st lt. field arty. U.S. Army, 1943-46, ETO. Avocations: fly fishing, gardening, reading, tennis. Home: 333 E 68th St New York NY 10021-5693 Office: Nat Exec Svc Corps 120 Wall St New York NY 10005

LEVY, LESLIE ANN, application developer; b. N.Y.C., Dec. 25, 1941; d. Paul and Ruth Candace (Tachna) Bauman; m. Marc Gersan Gerard Levy, Oct. 1962 (div.); children: Benjamin Gerard, Remy Marcel Gerard. BA summa cum laude in philosophy and history, Smith Coll., 1962; MBA, Harvard U., Boston, 1976, DBA, 1980. Cert. French Fashion Acad., 1964. Tchg. asst. in philosophy UCLA, 1962-63; pres. Commonwealth Collaborative, Inc., Cambridge and Sarasota, Fla., 1976—99; sr. rsch. assoc. Harvard Sch. Bus. Adminstrn., Boston, 1979-81; asst. prof. mgmt. policy, industry analysis Case Western Res. U., Cleve., 1981-84; pres., CEO Acad. for Corp. Governance, Fordham U. Grad. Sch. Bus., 1990-91; pres., dir., treas., sec. Directors, Data, Inc., 1999—; pres., sec. Life Choices and Death Wishes, 2000—. Sr. advisor, pres., dir. Inst. Rsch. on Bd. Dirs., 1998-; with Honeywell Info. Sys., Boston, 1971-75; former cons. and lectr. in field. Author: Director Motivation: Incentives and Disincentives to Board Service, 1996, Separate Chairmen of the Board: Their Roles, Legal Liabilities, and Compensation; editor, co-author: Boards of Directors Part II; columnist: Directors and Boards, 1996-97; contbr. aricles to profl. jours. Mem. Boston and Tampa Bay Com. on Fgn. Rels. Acad. Corp. Governance rsch. fellow; Fulbright scholar. Mem. Am. Soc. Corp. Secs., Nat. Assn. Corp. Dirs., Acad. Mgmt. (article reviewer), Nat. Investor Rels. Inst., Inst. of Dirs., Federalist Soc., Women in Pensions, So. Fin. Assn., Harvard Club of Sarasota, Am. Jewish Com., Am. Jewish Congress, Nat. Coun. Jewish Women. Avocations: hiking, art history, construction, whitewater canoeing. E-mail: dirsdata@drleslielevy.com., irbd@drleslielevy.com.

LEVY, ROBIN CAROLE, elementary guidance counselor; b. Berlin, Apr. 13, 1964;, parents Am. citizens; d. Kenneth and Henrietta Nan (Weithorn) Kaplan; m. Guy Glickson Levy, July 27, 1986; children: Clare Sydney, Frankie Hannah. BS, Fla. State U., 1986; MEd, Coll. William and Mary, 1991. Cert. tchr. Va. Presch. tchr. Talent House Pvt. Sch., Fairfax, Va., 1986-87; 4th grade tchr. Mt. Vernon Elem. Sch., Tabb, Va., 1987-92; elem. counselor Bethel Manor Elem. Sch., LAFB, Va., 1992-95. Family mediator Dispute Settlement Ctr., Norfolk, Va., 1993—2000, Richmond, Va., 1994—95; contract mediator EEOC, 2001—. Past pres., v.p. Denbigh Jaycees (Project Mgr. of Yr. 1991, 93, Outstanding Local Pres. 1994), Va., 1987—94; sec., treas. Denbigh Jaycees. Democrat. Jewish. Avocation: Avocations: jogging, swimming, reading. Home: 463 Cheshire Ct Newport News VA 23602-6404

LEVY, STEVEN Z. elementary education educator; b. St. Louis, Mar. 13, 1949; s. Marvin Bernard and Alice Ruth (Plattner) L.; m. Joanna Levy, July 30, 1975; children: Noah, Mariam, Susannah, Naomi. BA, Colgate U., 1971; MA, Adelphi U., 1973. Tchr. Wellston (Mo.) High Sch., 1971-73, Bowman Sch., Lexington, Mass., 1987—, Waldorf Sch., Lexington, 1974-87, headmaster, 1974-84; pres. Waldorf Sch., Inc., Lexington, 1976-79. Cons. Sta. WGBH-TV, Cambridge, Mass., 1993, JFK Libr., Boston, 1993. Author: Starting From Scratch, 1996. Recipient JFK Tchg. of History prize JFK Libr., 1991; named Mass. State Tchr. of Yr. Mass. Dept. Edn., 1993, Outstanding Elem. Tchr. Walt Disney Co. Am. Tchr. Awards, 1994. Home: 11 Fletcher Ave Lexington MA 02420-3721 Office: Bowman Sch 9 Philip Rd Lexington MA 02421-6099

LEWANDOSKI, SUZANNE TAYLOR, English educator; b. Hoboken, N.J., Mar. 21, 1967; d. Patrick Bernard and Elinor Mary (Sartori) Taylor; m. Eric John Lewandoski, Aug. 19, 1994; children: Sean Patrick, Jillian Elinor. AAS, Berkeley Coll. Bus., 1987; BA in English Edn., Montclair State U., 1990, MA in Reading, 1993. Tchr. secondary English Belleville (N.J.) Pub. Schs., 1990—. Mem. Nat. Coun. Tchrs. English. Avocations: theatre, dance, reading. Office: Belleville Pub Schs 100 Passaic Ave Belleville NJ 07109-1807

LEWARK, CAROL ANN, special education educator; b. Fort Wayne, Ind., Mar. 8, 1935; d. Lloyd L. and Elizabeth J. (Arthur) Meads; m. Paul N. Lewark, Aug. 20, 1955; children: David P., Laura, Beth, Daniel A. BA, St. mary of Woods, 1978; MS, Ind. U., 1981. Cert. elem. educator, spl. educator mentally retarded K-12, learning disabilities K-12, Ind.; cert. home tng. specialist, Wis. Home tng. specialist Madison Wis. ARC, Madison, 1968-70; nursery sch. cons. Arc N.E. Ind., Ft. Wayne, 1971-73, early childhood spl. edn. dir., 1973—; v.p. ARC of N.E. Ind., Fort Wayne, 1996-99; sr. v.p. Easter Seals ARC of N.E. Ind., 1999—. Cons. in field; presenter in field; apptd. by Ind. Gov. to State Interagy. Coordinating Coun. for Infants and Toddlers, 1992-95; apptd. to Higher Ed Coun. for Early Childhood and Spl. Edn. Contbr. articles to profl. jours. Apptd. to Leadership Ft. Wayne, 1994; v.p. N.E. Ind. chpt. ARC, 1995; apptd. chairperson Citizens Adv. Bd., Cmty. Devel. Block Grant, Mayor of Ft. Wayne, 1999. Named Model Project Site 99-457 Early Intervention Ind. State Dept. Mental Health, 1987; Tech. Assistance grantee Georgetown U., 1991-93. Mem. Ind. Coun. for Exceptional Children (sec. 1990-94), First Steps of Allen County (facilitator 1989—), Leadership Fort Wayne. Avocations: painting, music, needle work, travel. Home: 910 Kensington Blvd Fort Wayne IN 46805-5312 Office: Easter Seals ARC of NE Ind 2542 Thompson Ave Fort Wayne IN 46807-1051 E-mail: clewark@esarc.org.

LEWELLEN, WILBUR GARRETT, management educator, consultant; b. Charleroi, Pa., Jan. 21, 1938; s. Anthony Garrett and Cozie Harriett (Watson) L.; m. Jean Carolyn Vanderlip, Dec. 8, 1962 (div. 1982); children— Stephen G., Jocelyn A., Jonathan W., Robyn E.; m. Eloise Evelyn Vincent, Mar. 5, 1983 BS, Pa. State U., University Park, 1959; MS, MIT, Cambridge, 1961, PhD, 1967; LhD (hon.), Budapest U. of Econ. Scis., 1996. Asst. prof. mgmt. Purdue U., West Lafayette, Ind., 1964-68, assoc. prof. mgmt., 1968-72, prof., 1972-83, Loeb prof. mgmt., 1983-88, Krannert disting. prof. mgmt., 1988—, dir. exec. edn. programs, 1985—. Cons. Bank Am., San Francisco, 1975—90, Ind. Bell Tel. Co., Indpls., 1976—90, Am. Water Works Co., Wilmington, Del., 1978—94, Indpls. Power and Light Co., 1993—99, NiSource, Inc., 2000—; bd. dirs. Indsl. Dielectrics, Inc. Author: Executive Compensation in Large Industrial Corporations, 1968, Ownership Income of Management, 1971, The Cost of Capital, 1981, Financial Management: An Introduction to Principles and Practice, 2000. Recipient Salgo-Noren award as Outstanding Tchr. in Grad. Profl. Programs, Salgo-Noren Found., 1973, 77, 79, 84. Mem. AAUP, Fin. Mgmt. Assn. (v.p. 1973-74), Am. Fin. Assn., Western Fin. Assn., Lafayette Country Club. Methodist. Office: Purdue Univ Grad Sch Mgmt West Lafayette IN 47907

LEWES, ULLE ERIKA, English educator; b. Tallinn, Estonia, Europe, Mar. 22, 1942; d. Karl Erik Allik and Ella (Vaher) Laaman; m. Kenneth Lewes, June 1967 (div. June 1975); m. Allen Dunlap, Jr., June 17, 1988 (dec. Sept. 1997). BA, Cornell U., 1964; MA, Harvard U., 1965, PhD, 1972. Asst. prof. Temple U., Phila., 1971-78; assoc. prof. Ohio Wesleyan U., Delaware, Ohio, 1978-83, full prof., 1983—. Cons. Ohio Bd. Regents, 1995-97, Mellon Found., Ohio Wesleyan Grant, 1979-82, Jefferson County Schs., Ohio, 1989-97, numerous writing projects in Ohio, 1982-98. Author: (books) Life in Forest, 1979, Writing as Learning, 1990; contbr. articles to Tristania jour. Life supporter So. Poverty Law Ctr., Montgomery, Ala. Mem. NOW, MLA, Amnesty Internat., Nat. Coun. Tchrs. English, Conf. on Coll. Composition and Comms., Medieval Acad. Am., Coun. of Writing Program Adminstrs., Tristan Soc., Shakespeare Soc. Avocations: photography, travel, ethnic cuisines, prisoners' rights struggle. Office: Ohio Wesleyan Univ Corns 325 Delaware OH 43015-1937

LEWICKE, CATHERINE PEARL, retired education educator; b. Lowell, Mass., Aug. 29, 1917; d. John P. and Anna G. (O'Reilly) Cryan; m. Edward Lewicke, Apr. 8, 1945 (dec. Mar. 1991); children: Edward Thomas, John Arthur, Jane Frances, Peter Paul, Anna Maria. BS in Edn., Lowell Tchrs. Coll., 1939; EdM, Boston U., 1956, CAGS, 1964; EdD, U. Lowell (Mass.), 1991. Cert. tchr., sch. psychologist, reading cons., Mass. Prin. elem. sch., Wilmington, Mass., 1941—44; tng. specialist U.S. Army, Ft. Devens, Mass., 1944—45; reading and test cons. pub. schs., Uxbridge, Mass., 1956—61, reading supr. Westford, Mass., 1961—66; assoc. prof.

edn. Worcester (Mass.) State Coll., 1966—82, supr. student tchrs., 1967—82, prof. emerita, 1982—2002. Adj. prof. grad. program Children's Literature, Linguistics, undergrad. supervision of student tchrs., Worcester (Mass.) State Coll., 1982-91, supervision practicum for grad. students, 1990—; storyteller pub. schs. Mem. Internat. Reading Assn., Nat. Coun. Tchrs. English, Assn. Tchr. Educators. Roman Catholic. Avocations: reading, writing, sewing, camping, travel. Home: Uxbridge, Mass. Died July 8, 2002.

LEWIS, ANNICE MOORE, middle school language arts educator; b. Dallas, Sept. 18, 1947; d. Eugene T. and Darlene (Sanford) Moore; m. Olan H. (Bud) Lewis, Aug. 23, 1969; children: Dane, Lora. BA, East Tex. Bapt. U., 1969. Cert. secondry sch. tchr. English, Music, Tex. Tchr. English, reading (high sch.) White Oak (Tex.) Ind. Sch. Dist., 1969-71, tchr. English, reading, speech (middle sch.), 1975-77; tchr. English Marshall (Tex.) Ind. Sch. Dist., 1972-73; tchr. English, reading, speech Sequoyah Middle Sch., Broken Arrow, Okla., 1979-81; music sec., coord. children.s choir 1st Bapt. Ch., Texarkana, Tex., 1981-83; tchr. lang. arts, reading, Tex. studies Hawkins (Tex.) Ind. Sch. Dist., 1986—. Coord. UIL, coach Middle Sch., Hawkins, 1987—, lang. arts coord., mentor, 1989—; mem. Dist. Wide Improvement Coun., Hawkins, Tex., 1991—, Outcome Based Edn. Curriculum Devel. Com., 1992—; presenter Middle Sch. Kaleidescope Conf., Henderson, Tex., 1990—. Author: lang. arts planning guides (middle schs.), 1969—; asst. producer (religious drama) The Promise, 1984. Soloist adult choir 1st Bapt. Ch., Tex., Okla., Ark., 1969—; mem. handbell choirs, 1969-94; dir. 1st-3rd grade choir 1st Bapt. Ch., Gladewater, Tex., 1984-86. Mem. Tex. Assn. Supervision and Curriculum Devel., Assn. Tex. Profl. Educators (pres. 1992-94, region 7 v.p.), Nat. Coun. Tchrs. English (N.E. Tex. chpt.), Internat. Reading Assn. (local pres. region 7 1992-94, v.p., bd. dirs. 1995—), Home: PO Box 1592 Gladewater TX 75647-1592 Office: Hawkins Mid Sch Drawer L Hawkins TX 75765

LEWIS, CHERIE SUE, lawyer, English language and journalism educator; b. Chgo., Feb. 6, 1951; d. Samuel D. and Evelyne P. L. BA, U. Mich., 1973; MS, Boston U., 1975; PhD, U. Minn., 1986; JD, Southwestern U., L.A., 1996. Cert. ESL tchr., Calif. Prof. Pa. State U., State College, 1988-89, Nat. Chengchi U., Taipei, Taiwan, 1989-91, Syracuse U., 1992-93, Nat. U., L.A., 1993—; atty.-advisor U.S. Social Security Adminstrn., L.A., 1998—. Cons. Pacific Rim Inst., L.A., 1992-95. Author: (book chpt.) Disability Rights, International, 1994, ednl. brochures, 1994; mng. editor Southwestern U. Jour. Law and Trade, 1995-96. Mem. AAUP, ABA. Avocations: music, skiing, internat. travel. Office: 6 Kenwood Ct Beachwood OH 44122-7501 E-mail: Cherie0206@hotmail.com.

LEWIS, CHRISTINA LYNN, human services administrator; b. Brook Park, Ohio, June 19, 1963; d. Albert Joseph and Gail Ann (Kohler) Urbas; m. Timothy Allen Lewis, Aug. 3, 1989; 1 child, Cherie Ann. AA, Pasco Hernando C.C., Brooksville, Fla., 1996; BA in Social Svcs., MA, Columbia State U., 1998. Owner, operator Spl. Touch Day Care, Olmsted Twp., Ohio, 1986-89, Spring Hill, Fla., 1989-94; dir., tng. coord. United Cerebral Palsy, Brooksville, 1994-96, mentor, tng. advisor child care outreach program, 1993—. Advisor, instr. Child Devel. Assn. Credential Program, Brooksville, 1991—; coun. mem. Pre-K Interagy. Coun., Brooksville, 1994—; CPR, First Aid instr. ARC, 1994—; area supr. Head Start, Inverness, Fla., 1996—; trainer/mentor Fla. Brain Rsch. Project, 1997—. Author (tng. packet) CDA: Everything You Need to Know to Get Started, 1992. Dep. registrar Supr. Elections, Hernando County, 1994; vol. instr. ARC. Recipient Resolution 91-70 award Hernando County Commr., Brooksville, 1991. Mem. Nat. Assn. for the Edn. Young Children, Assn. for Better Child Care (founding mem., newsletter editor 1990, sec., resource and referral 1989-93, Tchr. of Yr. 1990), Phi Theta Kappa. Republican. Avocations: snorkeling, pottery, camping. Home: 9063 Spring Hill Dr Spring Hill FL 34608-6241 Office: Childhood Devel Svcs 5641 W Gulf To Lake Hwy Crystal River FL 34429-7562

LEWIS, CLEOTRICE O. NEY TILLIS, retired elementary education educator; b. Dallas, Oct. 2, 1933; d. Christopher Columbus and Ida Bell Tillis; divorced; 1 child, Glenn Eric. BS in Elem. Edn., Prairie View A&M U., 1955; MEd, Tex. so. U., 1964; postgrad., U. Nebr., 1978, U. Houston, 1988. Cert. tchr., Tex. Tchr. Drew Elem. Sch.-Crosby (Tex.) Ind. Sch. Dist., 1955-57, Wesley Elem. Sch.-Houston Ind. Sch. Dist., 1958-60, Osborne Elem. Sch.-Houston Ind. Sch. Dist., 1960-84, chpt. I coord., 1985-93; substitute tchr. Houston Ind. Sch. Dist., 1993—. Presenter in field. Mem. Foster Pl. Civic Club, Houston, 1990—, YWCA, Houston, 1991—, Greater Houston Area Writing Project; sponsor writing lab., Osborne Elem. Sch., Houston, 1991—, life mem. Nat. Congress PTA. Mem. Greater Houston Area Reading Assn., Tex. Tchrs. Assn., Houston Assn. Childhood Edn. Internat., Assn. Tex. Profl. Educators, Internat. Reading Assn. Methodist. Avocations: reading, weaving, bowling, writing, knitting. Home: 6504 Sherwood Dr Houston TX 77021-4032

LEWIS, CORINNE HEMETER, psychotherapist, educator; b. N.Y.C., Nov. 28, 1925; d. Leslie Hall and Frances Pope Hemeter, m. Aug. 22, 1947 (div. 1984); children: Anne Marie, Richard Allyn, Timothy Hall; m. Ceylon S. Lewis Jr., Aug. 6, 1999. BSN, U. Pitts., 1947; MSW, U. Okla., 1978. Diplomate in clin. social work. Staff nurse St. Joseph's Hosp., Buckhannon, W.Va., 1947; head nurse Myer's Clinic, Phillipi, W.Va., 1948; clin. instr., supr. Allegheny Valley Hosp., Tarentum, Pa., 1949; coord. psychiat. nursing edn. Hillcrest Med. Ctr., Tulsa, 1966-67; clin. staff mem. Tulsa Psychiat. Ctr., Tulsa, 1968-77; tchr. principles personality devel. Hillcrest Med. Ctr., Tulsa, 1966-75; supr., interns in psychotherapy Tulsa Psychiat. Ctr., 1971-77; pvt. practice psychotherapist Tulsa, 1978—. Dir. Drug Day Hosp., Tulsa Psychiat. Ctr., 1969, dir. nursing, 1970-71; adminstrv. cons. Family and Children's Svcs., Tulsa, 1978; renal dialysis unit cons. Hillcrest Med. Ctr., 1978; dir. Am. Cancer Soc. funded program Tulsa Psychiat. Ctr., 1977-79, cons. to dept. internal medicine, Tulsa Med. Coll., 1977-98. Jr. bd. mem. Women's Assn., Tulsa Boys Home, 1957-59; mem. Mental Health Assn. Tulsa, 1968-83, bd. dirs., 1982-83; vol. Jr. Assn., Tulsa Boys Home, 1958-59, Children's Med. Ctr., 1953-56; bd. dirs. Nursing Svc. Inc., Tulsa, 1982-83. Mem. Nat. Assn. Social Workers, Acad. Cert. Social Workers, Sigma Theta Tau. Democrat. Presbyterian. Avocations: classical music, reading. Home: 2300 Riverside Dr Apt 8F Tulsa OK 74114-2403

LEWIS, DAN ALBERT, education educator; b. Chgo., Feb. 14, 1946; s. Milton and Diane (Sabath) L.; m. Stephanie Riger, Jan. 3, 1982; children: Matthew, Jake. BA cum laude, Stanford U., 1968; PhD, U. Calif., Santa Cruz, 1980. Rsch. assoc. Arthur Bolton Assocs., Sacramento, 1969-70; survey contr. Sci. Analysis Corp., San Francisco, 1971; dir. Stanford Workshops on Polit. and Social Issues Stanford (Calif.) U., 1971-74; projects adminstr. Ctr. Urban Affairs and Policy Rsch., Northwestern U., Evanston, Ill., 1975-80, asst. prof. edn., 1980-86, assoc. prof. edn., 1986-90, assoc. dir., chair grad. program human devel./social policy, 1987-90, prof. edn., 1990—. Vis. scholar Sch. Edn., Stanford U., 1990-91; mem. task force on restructuring mental health svcs. Chgo. Dept. Health, 1982; mem. human rights authority Ill. Guardianship and Advocacy Commn., 1980-82; adv. mem. com. on planning and inter-agy. coordination Commn. Mental Health and Devel. Disabilities, 1979; interim adv. com. on mental health City of Chgo., 1978; adv. mem. Gov.'s Commn. to Revise Mental Health Code Ill., 1975-77;dir. Univ. Consortium on Welfare Reform, 1999-2003; presenter at profl. confs.; presenter workshops. Editor: Reactions to Crime, 1981; co-author: Fear of Crime: Incivility and the Production of a Social Problem, 1986, The Social Construction of Reform: Crime Prevention and Community Organizations, 1988, The Worlds of the Mentally Ill, 1991, The State Mental Patient in Urban Life, 1994, Race and Educational Reform, 1995; contbr. articles, book revs. to profl. pubs. Bd. dirs. Designs for Change, Ill. Mental Health Assn.; rsch. adv. com. Chgo. Urban League, Chgo. Panel Pub. Sch. Finances, 1989-91; needs assessment tech. com. United Way Chgo., 1989-90; ednl. coun. Francis W. Parker Sch., Chgo., 1988-90; task force on restructuring mental health svcs. Chgo. Dept. Health, 1982; com. on mentally disabled Ill. State Bar Assn., 1983-89; dir. U. Consortium on Welfare Reform, 1999-2002; rsch. policy com. Ill. Dept. Mental Health, 1978; bd. dirs. Mental Health Assn. Greater Chgo., 1977-84, v.p. pub. policy, 1979-83 Recipient Excellence in Tchg. award Northwestern U. Alumni Assn., 1998; named to Faculty Honor Roll Associated Student Govt., 2001-02. Office: Northwestern Univ 2040 Sheridan Rd Evanston IL 60208-0855 E-mail: dlewis@northwestern.edu.

LEWIS, EDWARD B. biology educator; b. Wilkes-Barre, Pa., May 20, 1918; s. Edward B. and Laura (Histed) L.; m. Pamela Harrah, Sept. 26, 1946; children: Hugh, Glenn(dec.), Keith. BA, U. Minn., 1939; PhD, Calif. Inst. Tech., 1942; Phil.D., U. Umea, Sweden, 1982; DSc, U. Minn., 1993. Instr. biology Calif. Inst. Tech., Pasadena, 1946—48, asst. prof., 1949—56, prof., 1956—66, Thomas Hunt Morgan prof., 1966—87, prof. emeritus, 1988—. Rockefeller Found. fellow Sch. Botany, Cambridge U., England, 1948—49; mem. Nat. Adv. Com. Radiation, 1958—61; vis. prof. U. Copenhagen, 1975—76; rschr. in developmental genetics, somatic effects of radiation. Editor: Genetics and Evolution, 1961. Capt. USAF, 1942—46. Recipient Gairdner Found. Internat. award, 1987, Wolf Found. prize in medicine, 1989, Rosenstiel award, 1990, Nat. Medal of Sci., NSF, 1990, Albert Lasker Basic Med. Rsch. award, 1991, Louisa Gross Horowitz prize, Columbia U., 1992, Nobel Prize in Medicine, 1995. Fellow: AAAS; mem.: NAS, Am. Philos. Soc., Royal Soc. (fgn. mem.; London), Am. Acad. Arts and Scis., Genetics Soc. Am. (sec. 1962—64, pres. 1967—69, Thomas Hunt Morgan medal), Genetics Soc. Japan (hon.), Genetical Soc. Great Britain (hon.). Home: 805 Winthrop Rd San Marino CA 91108-1709 Office: Calif Inst Tech Divsn Biology 1201 E California Blvd Pasadena CA 91125-0001

LEWIS, ELISAH BLESSING, university official; b. Coral Gables, Fla., Feb. 14, 1961; d. James Lowell and Jean Sara (Mechlouitz) L. BFA, EdB, U. Miami, 1983, MEd, 1985, PhD, 1990. Art tchr. U. Miami, Coral Gables, Fla., 1979-89, Lowe Art Mus.; grad. asst. fin. assistance dept. U. Miami, Coral Gables, 1983-88, grad. asst. to acad. advisor, 1985-88, master tutor coord., 1988-89, testing examiner, 1988—, coord. transfer, pre-law acad. advisor, 1989—. Mem. Fairchild Tropical Garden, Parrot Jungle and Garden, Lowe Art Mus. Recipient Silver Knight award in Art, 1979, Hibiscus award Fairchild Tropical Garden, 1993, Rose award, 1994; named Outstanding Young Women in Am., 1988. Mem. Nat. Acad. Adv. Assn. (grantee 1990, award 1991), Nat. Geog. Soc., Audubon Soc., Omicron Delta Kappa, Rho Lamda, Alpha Epsilon Phi (officer 1980-83, award 1983). Avocations: painting, tennis, gardening. Office: U Miami Coll Arts & Scis PO Box 248004 Coral Gables FL 33124-8004

LEWIS, ELLEN CLANCY, assistant principal; b. Hartford, Conn., Feb. 18, 1945; d. Thomas Gerard and Hedwig Ann (Kondrasiewicz) Clancy. BA, Barry U., Miami, Fla., 1967; EdM, U. S.C., 1988, EdS, 1992, PhD, 1995. Cert. adminstr./supr. elem. grades, English, middle grades, data collection. Tchr. math. Bayvale Elem. Sch., Augusta, Ga., 1967-70; tchr. sci./math. Terrace Manor Elem. Sch., Augusta, 1970-72; tchr. sci. Wheeless Rd. Elem. Sch., Augusta, 1972-74; tchr. social studies/sci./math. Grovetown (Ga.) Elem. Sch., 1974-88; JTPA coord./tchr. Harlem (Ga.) H.S., 1988-92, asst. prin., 1992—. Editor: HHS At-Risk Manual, 1991. Commr. Profl. Stds. Com., Atlanta, 1991-95. Named Columbia County Tchr. of Yr. Columbia County Bd. Edn., 1988, Augusta C. of C. Tchr. of Yr., 1988; grantee Job Tng. Partnership Act, 1989-96. Mem. Profl. Assn. Ga. Educators. Avocations: horse breeding, reading, stamp collecting. Home: 3994 Evans To Locks Rd Evans GA 30809-4034 Office: Harlem High School 1070 Appling Harlem Rd Harlem GA 30814-5319

LEWIS, ENID SELENA, elementary school educator, special education educator; b. Jamaica, W.I., Aug. 6, 1928; arrived in U.S., 1989; d. Thomas Vivian and Carlena Agatha (Hemmings) Davis; m. George Nathaniel Lewis, Aug. 12, 1953; children: Patrick, Heather, Peter, Charmaine, George Jr., Suzanne. BA in Early Childhood Edn., Univ. Coll. W.I., 1983. Primary sch. tchr. Ministry of Edn., Jamaica, 1949-70, trainer tchr. early childhood and spl. edn., 1970-80, edn. officer early childhood and spl. edn., 1980-83, edn. officer spl. edn., 1983-88; tchr. Archdiocese of N.Y., 1989—. Field work in edn. Swasiland, Africa, 1976; adv. bd. Edn., Jamaice, 1986-88. Recipient Nat. award scholarships Jamaica Gov., 1982, Israel Assn. Internat Coop. to Israel, 1974-75, U. Kans., 1983, U. West Indies, 1979, 80. Baptist. Avocations: cooking, music, church activities, reading. Home: 391A Decatur St Brooklyn NY 11233-1507 Office: Sacred Heart of Jesus Sch 456 W 52nd St New York NY 10019-6302

LEWIS, GARY ALAN, radiologic technologist, educator; b. Syracuse, Kans., Nov. 22, 1956; s. Donald Eugene Lewis and Maxcine Campbell Shetterly. AS, Hutchinson Community Coll., Kans., 1977. Staff radiographer Hertzler Clinic, Halstead, Kans., 1977-79; staff radiographer/instr. St. Joseph Med. Ctr., Wichita, Kans., 1979-81; clin. instr., diagnostic supr. Comanche County Meml. Hosp., Lawton, Okla., 1981-88; clin. dir. and instr. Great Plains Area Vocat. Tech. Sch., Lawton, Okla., 1988—. Radiologic tech. rep. State Dept. of Okla. Vo-Tech., Stillwater, 1990-91. Mem. Okla. Soc. Radiologic Technologists (seminar speaker 1990, 92, pres.-elect 1993-94), Am. Soc. Radiologic Technologists, Great Plains Soc. Radiologic Technologists, Am. Registry Radiologic Technologists, Am. Vocat. Assn., Okla. Vocat. Assn., Okla. Health Occupational Educators Tchrs. Assn. Democrat. Methodist. Avocations: golf, fishing, painting, woodworking, gardening. Office: Great Plains Area Vo-Tech 4500 SW Lee Blvd Lawton OK 73505-8399

LEWIS, KATHLEEN F. special education educator; b. Albuquerque, Jan. 22, 1950; d. James R. and Alice T. (Gardner) Craig; m. Brian D. Lewis, Aug. 24, 1968; children: Christopher Scott, Tanya Renee. AA with honors, Amarillo Coll., 1978; BS cum laude, West Tex. State U., 1980, MEd, 1983, cert. in mid-mgmt., 1992. Cert. elem. tchr., generic spcl. edn., counseling, mid. mgmt. adminstr. Tchr., counselor Amarillo Ind. Sch. Dist., Tex., staff devel. instr., instructional and parental involvement specialist, asst. prin., prin. elem. sch. Contbr. articles to profl. jours. Mem. ASCD, Nat. Staff Devel. Coun., North Plains Assn. Children with Learning Disabilities (Meritorious Svc. award 1984, Outstanding Coun. award), Spl. Edn. Adv. Bd. (pres.).

LEWIS, LINDA SUE, elementary education educator; b. San Francisco, Sept. 16, 1947; d. Harry John and Virginia Ruth (Benbow) Walter; m. Danny Morton Lewis, June 28, 1969; children: Mark, Geoffrey. BA in Polit. Sci., U. Calif., 1969; MS in Edn. Curriculum, So. Ill. U., 1998. Cert. elem. edn. tchr. Tchr. Effingham Community Unit #40, Edgewood, Ill., 1971—. Assessor Summit Twp., Effingham County, 1986-93; chair Effingham County Edm. Women, 1985; bd. dirs. Effingham Child Devel. Ctr., 1975-78; bd. dirs., adminstrv. bd. Centenary United Meth. Ch., Effingham, 1989-92, trustee, 1992-95, adminstrv. bd. 1999-2001, missions com., 2001—. Mem. AAUW (bd. dirs. Ill. state 1981-87, treas. 1990-92, pres.-elect 1992, pres. 1993-95, mgr. e-mail network 1998—), Ill. Edn. Assn. (membership chair region #7 1985-86, membership com. region #7 1982-86), Effingham Classroom Tchrs. Assn. (sec. 1974-76, regional coun. del. 1990-92, exec. com. 2002—). Democrat. United Methodist. Avocations: reading, counted cross-stitch. Home: 9337 E Nees Ave Effingham IL 62401-7629 Office: Edgewood Sch PO Box 207 Edgewood IL 62426-0207

LEWIS, MARK RICHARD, aerospace engineer, educator; b. Spokane, Feb. 4, 1962; s. Robert Mead and Patricia Ruby Jane (Gation) L. AA, Highline Coll., 1982; BS, U. Wash., 1986, MS, 1991. Performance engr. Boeing Aerospace, Seattle, 1987-88; assoc. U. Wash., Seattle, 1991-92; adj. prof. Bellevue (Wash.) Coll., 1994-95; sr. propulsion engr. Boeing Comml. Airplane Group, 1996—. Adj. prof. Shoreline (Wash.) Coll., 1992, Highline (Wash.) Coll., 1993. Mem. AIAA, Seattle Profl. Engring. Employees Assn., Golden Key, Tau Beta Pi Assn., Phi Theta Kappa. Democrat. Avocation: weight lifting. Office: Propulsion Sys Divsn BCAG PO Box 3707 Seattle WA 98124-2207

LEWIS, MARTHA NELL, Christian educator, minister, expressive arts therapist; b. Atlanta, Mar. 4, 1944; d. Clifford Edward and Nell (Shropshire) Wilkie; m. Jeffrey Clark Lewis, Aug. 20, 1966 (div. Aug. 1986); children: John Martin, Janet Michelle Teal. BA, Tex. Tech. U., 1966; massage therapy, The Winters Sch., 1991; MA, Norwich U., 1994; MTS, Ch. Divinity Sch. Pacific, 2000. Cert. music practitioner, expressive therapist, massage therapist, music instr. Geophys. analyst Shell Oil Co., Houston, 1966-68; photography specialist Photogravity, Inc., Houston, 1972-80; tchr. music Little Red Sch. House, Houston, 1974-75; sec., treas. Lewis Enterprises, Inc., Houston, 1976-83; regulatory supr. Transco Energy Co., Houston, 1983-92; expressive arts therapist Shalom Renewal Ctr., Splendora, Tex., 1995—, River Oaks Health Alliance, Houston, 1995-96; co-founder, past nat. exec. dir., pres., tchr. Music for Healing and Transition Program, 1994—. Massage therapist, expressive therapist, Houston, 1991—, Calif., 1996—; adj. prof. Holy Names Coll., Oakland, Calif., 1998-99; Sunday sch. coord. St. Stephen's Episc. Ch., Belvedere, Calif., 2000; min. Christian edn. St. Paul's Episc. Ch., Waco, Tex., 2000—. Advisor youth Corpus Christi Ch., Houston, 1970-80; vocalist, instrumentalist Sounds of Faith Folk Group, Houston, 1978—; harpist Houston Harpers Harp Ensemble, 1990-92; liturgical dancer Random Dance, Berkeley, Calif., 1997-2000; instr. exercise, body awareness Transco Energy Co. Fitness Ctr., Houston, 1990-92; vol. The Inst. for Rehab. and Rsch., Houston, 1989-90, Houston Hospice, 1992-96, Houston Healing Healthcare Project, 1993-96; vol. Healing Environ. Coun. St. Luke's Episc. Hosp., 1993-96; lay chaplain Cmty. of Hope, 1994—; founder The Winters Sch. Massage Therapy Care Team, Houston, 1991-96; vol. Ctr. for AIDS Svcs., Oakland, 1996-2000, Hillcrest Hospice, 2003—. Mem.: Nat. Assn. for Episcopal Edn. Dirs., Nat. Network Lay Profls., Christian Dance Fellowship USA, Nat. Sacred Dance Guild, Am. Massage Therapy Assn., Internat. Folk Harp Assn., Internat. Expressive Arts Therapy Assn., Sigma Kappa Alumnae Sorority (pres. Houston chpt. 1974—76, nat. collegiate province officer 1981—85, Houston Alumnae of Yr. 1981, Tex. Alumnae of Yr. 1980, Pearl Ct. award 1991), Houston Sigma Kappa Found. (bd. dirs.), Space City Ski Club (asst. trip coord. 1991—92). Roman Catholic. Episcopalian. Avocations: harp, piano, voice, dance, travel. Home: 1625 Wooded Acres #115 Waco TX 76710 E-mail: mlewis3444@aol.com., marthal@stpaulswaco.org.

LEWIS, MARY ANN, nursing educator; b. Kansas City, Mo., Aug. 1, 1937; m. Charles Edwin Lewis, Dec. 27, 1963; children: Kevin, David, Matthew, Karen. BS in Nursing, U. Kans., 1962; MS in Nursing, Boston U., 1963; DrPH, UCLA, 1984. cert. adult nurse practitioner. Instr. pub. health nursing U. Kans., Kansas City, Mo., 1963-66; coordinator pub. health nursing Children's Mercy Hosp., Kansas City, 1966-68; research health specialist UCLA, 1971-73, project dir. Primex Family Nurse Practicioner, 1972-76, adj. asst. prof. nursing, 1976-80, adj. prof. nursing and medicine, 1980-86, asst. prof. nursing, 1986—, prof., 1989—; chair faculty UCLA Sch. Nursing, 1992-96, chair primary care sect., 1996—2002. Cons. internat. health Health Resources Adminstrn., Washington, 1978—; bd. dirs. Maxicare Rsch. and Edn. Found., L.A.; cons. Asthma and Allergy Found. Am., L.A., Washington; ad hoc reviewer NIH, Robert Wood Johnson Found. Author: Health Decision-Making, 1980; bd. dirs., editl. bd. The Nurse Practitioner, 1981—; contbr. articles to profl. jours. Com. mem. AIDS Project, L.A., 1986-88. Fellow Am. Acad. Nursing; mem. AAUW, ANA, APHA, Assn. for History of Nursing, Chironians of UCLA Sch. Nursing (co-chmn. 1987-2002), Sigma Theta Tau. Office: UCLA Sch Nursing PO Box 956919 5-266 Factor Bldg Los Angeles CA 90095-6191 E-mail: mlewis@ucla.edu.

LEWIS, NANCY LOUINE LAMBERT, school counselor; b. Austin, Tex., Jan. 28, 1938; d. Claud Standard and Audrey Louine (Jackson) Lambert; m. Raymond Clyde Lewis, Dec. 27, 1958; children: Laura Beth, John Lambert. BA in English with highest honors, U. Tex., 1958, MEd in Guidance and Counseling, 1964. Lic. tchr. secondary English, counselor; lic. profl. counselor. Tchr. English Allan Jr. High Sch. Austin Ind. Sch. Dist., 1958-62, counselor Univ. Jr. High Sch., 1963-65; counselor Gary Job Corps Ctr., San Marcos, Tex., 1965-67; supr. student tchrs. English dept. curriculum and instrn. U. Tex., Austin, 1968-69, editor, writer, group leader Ctr. Pub. Sch. Ethnic Studies, 1969-76; counselor Allan Jr. High Sch. Austin Ind. Sch. Dist., 1976-80, counselor Martin Jr. High Sch., 1980-86, counselor Fulmore Mid. Sch., 1986-87, counselor Mendez Mid. Sch., 1987—. Instr. corr. studies U. Tex., Austin, 1968—. Contbr. articles to profl. jours. Vol. Dem. party, Austin, 1973—, First United Meth. Ch., Austin, 1955—; mem. Mayor's Task Force on Gangs, Crime and Drugs, City of Austin, 1990-91. Recipient Optimist Internat. Achievement in Edn. award, 1996, Presdl. citation State Bar Tex., 2002. Mem. NEA, ACA, Am. Sch. Counselors Assn. (editl. bd. Sch. Counselor 1989-96), Tex. State Tchrs. Assn., Tex. Sch. Counselors Assn. (senator 1981-84, pres. 1985-86, chair counseling advocacy com. 1991-93, Mid. Sch. Counselor of Yr. 1993, Mid. Sch./Jr. HS v.p. 2000-02, senator 2002—), Tex. Counseling Assn. (senator 1981-84, publs. com. chair 1981-84, membership com. chair 1994-96), Tex. Mid. Sch. Assn., Capital of Tex. Counseling Assn. (pres. 1982-83), Edn. Austin (cons. com. 1990-93, Human Rels. award 1989-90), Pathways (bd. dirs.), Delta Kappa Gamma (pres. Lambda Iota chpt. 1990-92), Phi Beta Kappa. Avocations: travel, reading, playing bridge. Home: 1427 Salem Meadow Cir Austin TX 78745-2911 Office: Mendez Mid Sch 5106 Village Square Dr Austin TX 78744-4462 E-mail: nlewis1427@aol.com.

LEWIS, NATHAN SAUL, chemistry educator; b. L.A., Oct. 20, 1955; BS in Chemistry with highest honors, MS in Chemistry, Calif. Inst. Tech., 1977; PhD in Chemistry, MIT, 1981. Asst. prof. chemistry Stanford (Calif.) U., 1981-86, assoc. prof., 1986-88, Calif. Inst. Tech., 1988-90, prof., 1990—. Cons. Lawrence Livermore (Calif.) Nat. Lab., 1977-81, 84-88, Solar Energy Rsch. Assocs., Santa Clara, Calif., 1981-85, Am. Hosp. Supply, Irvine, Calif., 1983-85, Molecular Devices, Palo Alto, Calif., 1983-88; mem. U.S. Japan Joint Conf. Photochemistry and Photoconversion, 1983, Chem. Revs. Adv. Bd., 1989-92, long range planning com. Electrochem. Soc., 1991-94, Adv. Bd. Progress Inorganic Chemistry, 1992-94, vis. com. dept. applied sci. Brookhaven Nat. Lab., 1993—. Divisional editor Jour. Electrochemical Soc., 1984-90; mem. editorial adv. bd. Accounts Chem. Rsch., 1993—. Recipient Presdl. Young Investigator award, 1984-88, Fresenius award Phi Lambda Upsilon, 1990, Pure Chemistry award Am. Chem. Soc., 1991; Achievement Rewards Coll. Scientists Found. scholar Calif. Inst. Tech., 1975-77, Calif. State scholar, 1976-77, Carnation Co. Acad. Merit scholar, 1976-77, Camille and Henry Dreyfus Tchr. scholar, 1985-90; Fannie and John Hertz Found. fellow MIT, 1977-81, Alfred P. Sloan Rsch. fellow, 1985-87. Office: Calif Inst Tech Dept Chem 127 72 Pasadena CA 91125-0001 E-mail: nslewis@caltech.edu.

LEWIS, PAUL LE ROY, pathology educator; b. Tamaqua, Pa., Aug. 30, 1925; s. Harry Earl and Rose Estella (Brobst) L.; m. Betty Jane Bixby, June 2, 1953; 1 child, Robert Harry. AB magna cum laude, Syracuse U., 1950; MD, SUNY, Syracuse, 1953. Diplomate Am. Bd. Pathology. Intern Temple U. Hosp., Phila., 1953-54; resident in pathology Hosp. of U. Pa., Phila., 1954-58, asst. instr., 1957-58; instr. pathology Thomas Jefferson U. Coll. Medicine, Phila., 1958-62, asst. prof., 1962-65, assoc. prof., 1965-75, prof., 1975-93, hon. prof., 1993—; pathologist Thomas Jefferson U. Hosp., 1958-91; attending pathologist Meth. Hosp., Phila., 1975-93, dir. clin. labs., chmn. dept. pathology, 1975-92, consulting pathologist, 1993—; pathologist pvt. practice Phila., 1993—. Pres. Penndel Labs. Inc., Ardmore, Pa., 1974-85; cons. VA Hosp., Coatesvillle, Pa., 1976-85; mem. med. adv. com.

ARC Blood Bank, Phila., 1978—. Contbg. author: Atlas of Gastrointestinal Cytology, 1983; contbr. articles to med. jours. 2d lt. USAAF, 1943-46. Fellow Am. Soc. Clin. Pathologists, Coll. Am. Pathologists; mem. AMA, Pa. Med. Soc., Philadelphia County Med. Soc., Internat. Acad. Pathology, Am. Soc. Cytology, Masons, Phi Beta Kappa, Alpha Omega Alpha, Nu Sigma Nu. Republican. Methodist. Avocations: photography, hiking. Home and Office: 521 Baird Rd Merion Station PA 19066-1301

LEWIS, PHILIP, educational and technical consultant; b. Chgo., Oct. 23, 1913; s. Solomon and Fannie (Margolis) L.; m. Geraldine Gisela Lawenda, Sept. 1, 1947; 1 child, Linda Susan. BS, DePaul U., Chgo., 1937, MA, 1939; EdD, Columbia Tchrs. Coll., 1951. Chmn. dept. edn. Chgo. Tchrs. Coll.; also asst. prin., tchr. South Shore High Sch., Chgo., 1940-51; prin. Herman Felsenthal Elementary Sch., Chgo., 1955-57; dir. Bur. Instructional Materials, Chgo. Pub. Schs., 1957-63, Bur. Research Devel. and Spl. Projects, 1963-67; pres. Instructional Dynamics Inc., Chgo., 1967-89, ret., 1989; ednl. and tech. cons., 1991—. Nat. cons. TV and instructional techniques, 1955— ; ednl. cons. to accrediting bur. Health Edn. Schs., 1971-89; chmn. adv. com. U.S. Office Edn., Title VII, 1964-67 Author: Educational Television Guidebook for Electronics Industries Association, 1961, also numerous articles.; mem. editorial bd. Nation's Schs. and Colls; multimedia tech. editor: Tech. Horizons in Edn; cons.: Jour. Ednl. Tech. and Communications; producer ednl., multimedia, tng. and mental health and human devel. materials. Served to lt. comdr. USNR, 1942—45. Mem. Soc. Programmed and Automated Learning (pres. 1960-65), NEA (v.p. dept. audiovisual instrn., chmn. commn. on tech. standards dept. audiovisual instrn. 1965-85), Nat. Assn. Ednl. Broadcasters, Am. Legion, Council for Ednl. Facilities Planners (editorial adv. bd. 1972-80) Ill. C. of C. (edn. com. 1970-77), Chgo. Assn. Commerce and Industry (chmn. edn. com. 1970-80), Nat. Audio-Visual Assn. (profl. devel. bd. 1969-76, chmn), Chgo. Press Club, Masons, Shriners, Rotary, Phi Delta Kappa.

LEWIS, PHYLLIS MARIE NORTH, retired secondary school educator; b. Denison, Iowa, June 17, 1937; d. Ray F. North and Adelaide Potter; m. Leslie Alan Lewis, July 2, 1965; 1 child, Marie Ann; m. Gerald R. Anderson, Aug. 2, 1958 (div. May 1964); 1 child, LaVon Marie. BA cum laude in Edn., Drake U., 1959. Cert. tchr. Tex., Iowa. Tchr. Des Moines Pub. Sch., Des Moines, 1959—60; debate & speech coach Amarillo Pub. Sch., Amarillo, Tex., 1960—62; tchr. Des Moines Pub. Sch., 1963—65; cons. urban edn. State Dept. Edn., Des Moines, 1971—72; tchr. IKM Pub. Sch., Manilla, Iowa, 1979—88; writer Am. Media Film Co., Des Moines, 1988—89; tchr. IKM Pub. Sch., 1990—99, ret., 1999, substitute tchr., 1999—. Cons. Dept. Edn., Des Moines, 1971—73; state gov. affairs com. Iowa State Edn. Assn., Des Moines, 1995—99. Contbr. Change Mag., 1972; co-author: (films) Coping with Difficult People, 1989. Publicity chmn. Dem. Candidate Iowa House Rep., Denison, Iowa, 2000; bd. dir. Crawford County Hosp., Denison, 1987—89. Mem.: PEO, AAUW (membership chmn. 1999—2002), Crawford County Arts Assn. (co-chmn. 2000—02), Federated Women's Club, Zeta Phi Eta (pres. Des Moines chpt. 1974, nat. by-laws chmn. 2001). Democrat. Presbyterian. Avocations: antiques, trail riding, bridge, writing, refinishing antiques. Home: 2884 Hwy 30 Denison IA 51442

LEWIS, R. BARRY, archaeology educator; b. Searcy, Ark., Aug. 7, 1947; s. Lloyd Jones and Anna Ruth (Campbell) L.; m. Shelia Dale Landreth, Aug. 12, 1969 (div. 1976); 1 child, Amanda; m. Susan Murphy, Nov. 19, 1977; children: Molly Ruth, Hannah Maureen. BA, U. Miss., 1969; MA, U. Mo., 1973; postgrad., U. N.Mex., 1973-74; PhD, U. Ill., 1979. Rsch. assoc. Ill. State Mus. Soc., Springfield, 1973-78; staff archaeologist Miss. State Hwy. Dept., Jackson, 1974-75; archaeologist Office of State Archaeology, Lexington, Ky., 1979-80; asst. prof. U. Ill., Urbana, 1980-86, assoc. prof., 1986-2000, prof., 2000—. Vis. lectr. U. Ill., Urbana, 1977; adv. bd. ann. editions Phys. Anthropology, Dushkin Pub. Group, Inc., Guilford, Conn., 1995—. Editor: Mississippi Towns of the Western Kentucky Border, 1986, Kentucky Archaeology, 1995, Mississippian Towns and Sacred Spaces, 1998; co-editor: Cahokia and the Hinterlands, 1991; contbr. articles to profl. jours. Pres. Friends of Champaign Pub. Libr., 1995-96. With U.S. Army, 1971-73. Rsch. grantee Ky. Heritage Coun., 1983-91, U. Ill. Rsch. Bd., 1981-99, NSF. Mem. Soc. for Am. Archaeology, Ill. Archaeolog. Survey (pres. 1985-87), Assn. Asian Studies, Am. Statis. Assn., Southeastern Archaeol. Conf., Sigma Xi. Democrat. Avocations: kids, southern writers 1860-1950, cooking. Home: 1309 Old Farm Rd Champaign IL 61821-5947 E-mail: blewis@uiuc.edu.

LEWIS, RICHARD A. educational association administrator, writer; b. N.Y.C., May 15, 1935; BA, Bard Coll., 1958. Tchr. Art Ctr. of No. N.J., Englewood, 1961-64, Walden Sch., N.Y.C., 1963-64; instr. New Sch. for Social Rsch., N.Y.C., 1964-73; drama and writing tchr. Manhattan-Country Sch., N.Y.C., 1967-93; dir., founder Touchstone Ctr. for Children, N.Y.C., 1969—. Adj. instr. Bank St. Coll. of Edn., N.Y.C., 1972-73; adj. prof. Rutgers U., New Brunswick, N.J., 1976-78, Western Wash. State U., Bellingham, 1980-82, Lesley Coll. Grad. Sch., Cambridge, Mass., 1981-84, Queens Coll., N.Y.C., 1988. Author: The Bird of Imagining, 2002, In the Space of The Sky, 2002, Each Sky Has its Words, 2000, Living By Wonder: Essays on the Imaginative Life of Childhood, 1998, German, 1999, Japanese, 2003, When Thought Is Young: Reflections on Teaching and the Poetry of the Child, 1992, All of You Was Singing: A Retelling of an Aztec Myth, 1994, In the Night Still Dark: A Retelling of the Hawaiian Creation Chant, 1988, The Park, 1968; editor: The Luminous Lanscape: Chinese Art and Poetry, 1981, I Breathe a New Song: Poems of the Eskimo, 1971, There are Two Lives: Poems by Children of Japan, 1970, The Way of Silence: Prose and Poetry of Basho, 1981, Still Waters of the Air: Three Modern Spanish Poets, The Poetry of Lorca, Machado and Jimenez, 1981, Muse of the Round Sky: Greek Lyric Poetry, 1969, Journeys: Prose by Children of the English-Speaking World, 1969, 2d edit., 1977, Of This World: A Poet's Life in Poetry-Poetry of Issa, 1969, In A Spring Garden, 1965; author, editor: (video) In the Spirit of Play, 1998, To Make A World, 1997; contbr. articles to profl. jours. Recipient Art Educator award N.Y. State Art Tchrs., 1997, Sch. and Cultural award Alliance for the Arts, 1988, Disting. Svc. award Assn. Tchg. Artists, 2002. Office: The Touchstone Ctr 141 E 88th St New York NY 10128

LEWIS, RICHARD JEFFREY, special education administrator; b. Amityville, N.Y., Feb. 10, 1954; s. Geoffrey John and Daphne Eileen (Antrobus) L.; m. Lyn Joanne Worley, July 11, 1987. BA in Psychology, SUNY, Stony Brook, 1976; MS in Edn., U. Ky., 1979, EdD in Spl. Edn. Adminstrn., 1994. Cert. dir. spl. edn., edn. of severely/profoundly handicapped. Spl. edn. tchr. Franklin County Pub. Schs., Frankfort, Ky., 1978-82; exec. dir. PUSH Infant/Presch. Program, Frankfort, 1982-87; dir. early childhood, spl. edn. Jefferson County Pub. Schs., Louisville, 1987-97; assoc. dir. Mid-South Regional Resource Ctr., U. Ky., Lexington, 1997—. Govtl. rels. chair Internat. Divsn. for Early Childhood, Reston, Va., 1994-97, tchr., 1997-99, chair com. on info. and tech., 1999-2002; pres. Ky. Divsn. for Early Childhood, Frankfort, 1986-87, polit. action chair, 1989-94; v.p. Ky. Assn. for Edn. Young Children, Louisville, 1990-92, 93-95; presenter confs. in field. Chair Ky. Early Intervention Com., Frankfort, 1993-94; treas./founding bd. dirs. Metro disAbility Coalition, Louisville, 1993-96. Named Spl. Edn. Adminstr. of Yr., Ky. Coun. for Exceptional Children, 1988, Contbr. of Yr. Ky. Divsn. Early Childhood Edn., 1994. Mem. Coun. Exceptional Children. Democrat. Methodist. Avocations: whitewater kayaking, technology, reading. Home: 680 Biddle Pike Georgetown KY 40324-9570 Office: Mid-South Regional Resource Ctr U Ky 1 Qyality St Ste 722 Lexington KY 40506-0051

LEWIS, ROBERT ENZER, lexicographer, educator; b. Windber, Pa., Aug. 12, 1934; s. Robert Enzer and Katharine Torrence (Blair) L.; m. Julie Fatt Cureton, May 14, 1977; children: Perrin Lewis Rubin, Torrence Evans Lewis; stepchildren: Sarah Cureton Kaufman, James S. Cureton. BA, Princeton U., 1959; MA, U. Pa., 1962, PhD, 1964. Tchr. English Mercersburg (Pa.) Acad., 1959-60; teaching fellow U. Pa., Phila., 1961-63; lectr. Ind. U., Bloomington, 1963-64, asst. prof., 1964-68, assoc. prof., 1968-75, prof. English, 1975-82, U. Mich., Ann Arbor, 1982—. Author: (with A. McIntosh) Descriptive Guide to the Manuscripts of the Prick of Conscience, 1982, (with others) Index of Printed Middle English Prose, 1985; editor: De Miseria Condicionis Humane (Lotario dei Segni), 1978; co-editor: Middle English Dictionary, 1982-83, editor-in-chief: vols. 8, 9, 10, 11, 12, 13, 1984-2001; gen. editor: Chaucer Libr., 1970—, chmn. editl. com., 1978-89, 97—. Bd. regents Mercersburg Acad., 1975-87. U.S. Army, 1954-56. Vis. rsch. fellow Inst. Advanced Studies in the Humanities, U. Edinburgh, 1973-74; Am. Coun. Learned Socs. fellow, 1979-80. Mem. Medieval Acad. Am. (mem. publs. com. 1987-92), Dictionary Soc. N.Am., New Chaucer Soc. Episcopalian. Office: U Mich Dept English 3187 Angell Hall Ann Arbor MI 48109-1003 E-mail: relewis@umich.edu.

LEWIS, STEPHEN RICHMOND, JR., economist, educator, academic administrator; b. Englewood, N.J., Feb. 11, 1939; s. Stephen Richmond and Esther (Magan) Lewis; m. Judith Frost, 1996; children from previous marriage: Virginia, Deborah, Mark. BA, Williams Coll., 1960, LLD, 1987; MA, Stanford U., 1962, PhD, 1963; LHD, Doshisha U., 1993, Macalester Coll., 2002; LLD, Carleton Coll., 2002. Instr. Stanford U., 1962—63; research advisor Pakistan Inst. Devel. Econs., Karachi, 1963—65; asst. prof. econs. Harvard U., 1965—66, Williams Coll., 1966—68, assoc. prof., 1968—73, prof., 1973—76, Herbert H. Lehman prof., 1976—87, provost of coll., 1968—71, 1973—77, spl. asst. to pres., 1979—80, dir. Williams-Botswana Project, 1982—88, chmn. dept. econs., 1984—86; vis. sr. research fellow Inst. Devel. Studies, Nairobi, Kenya, 1971—73; econ. cons. to Ministry of Finance and Devel. Planning, Govt. of Botswana, 1975—; vis. fellow Inst. Devel. Studies, Sussex, England, 1986—87; pres., prof. econs. Carleton Coll., Northfield, Minn., 1987—2002, pres. emeritus, 2002—. Cons. econs. Ford Found., Edna McConnell Clark Found., World Bank, Orgn. Econ. Coop. and Devel., Govts. of Kenya, Philippines, Botswana; trustee Carnegie Endowment for Internat. Peace, 1988—; dir. Am. Express Funds, 2002—, XDX, Inc., 2002—, Xenomosis, LLC, 2002—, Valmont Industries, Inc., 2002—. Author (with others): Relative Price Changes and Industrialization in Pakistan, 1969; author: Economic Policy and Industrial Growth in Pakistan, 1969, Pakistan: Industrialization and Trade Policy, 1970, Williams in the Eighties, 1980, Taxation for Development, 1983, South Africa: Has Time Run Out?, 1986, Policy Choice and Development Performance in Botswana, 1989, The Economics of Apartheid, 1989; mem. editl. bd.: Jour. Econ. Lit., 1985—87; contbr. chapters to books, articles to profl. jours. Exec. com. Indianhead coun. Boy Scouts Am., 1989—. Decorated Presdl. Order of Meritorious Svc. Botswana; recipient Disting. Eagle Scout award, 1993; fellow, Danforth Found., 1960—63, dissertation, Ford Found., 1962—63. Mem.: Am. Econ. Assn., Nat. Tax Assn., Coun. on Fgn. Rels., Phi Beta Kappa. Office: Ste 440 222 S Ninth St Minneapolis MN 55402

LEWIS, THOMAS ROBERT, elementary school educator; b. Chgo., Sept. 29, 1954; s. Robert Oliver and Daisy Ann (Anderson) L.; m. Catherine Halbur, Dec. 27, 1977; children: Zachary Halbur, Mark Halbur. BS in Elem. Edn., No. Ill. U., 1977; MS in Elem. Edn., Western Ill. U., 1992. 1st grade tchr. Moline (Ill.) Pub. Sch. Dist. 40, 1978-93, 5th grade tchr., 1994—2000, 3d grade tchr., 2002—; vis. math. educator Nat. Coun. Tchrs. Math., Reston, Va., 1993-94; educator in residence Ill. State Bd. Edn., 2000—02. Adv. bd. Numbers Alive!, Md. Pub. TV, Owings Mills, 1993—; ednl. adv. bd. Disney Channel Am. Tchr. Awards, Burbank, Calif., 1993—; instr. Western Ill. U., 1998-2001. Editor: Teaching Children Mathematics. Mem. NEA, Nat. Coun. Tchrs. Math. (bd. dirs. 1998-2001), Ill. Coun. of Tchrs. of Math. (bd. dirs. 1997-2000), Ill. Coun. of Tchrs. of Math., West Ctrl. Coun. of Tchrs. of Math. Office: Logan School 1602 25th St Moline IL 61265

LEWIS-KAUSEL, CECILIA, interior design educator; b. Santiago, Chile; came to U.S., 1970; d. Wilfred Philip and Ximena (Silva) Lewis; m. Edward Kausel, Apr. 9, 1967; 1 child, Christoph. BA, U. Mass., Boston, 1977; SM, MIT, 1982. Prof. interior design Chamberlayne Sch. Design, Mount Ida Coll., Newton Centre, Mass., dir. interior design dept., 2001—. Rsch. affiliate dept. civil and environ. enging. MIT, 1999—; guest prof. Bauhaus U., Weimar, Germany, 1996; spkr. 8 confs., 1996-98. Contbr. articles to profl. jours., illustrations to profl. jours.; author: Santiago Calatrava-Conversations with Students: The MIT Lectures, 2002. Recipient rsch. funds Bauhaus U. Spain's Ministry Edn. & Sci., 1992, 96, Patronato de la Alhambra and Mount Ida Coll., 1998. Mem. AIA (bd. dirs. IFRAA 1992-94, regional dir. 1994-96, 96-98, adv. group 1998—), Internat. Facility Mgmt. Assn., Interior Design Educators Coun. Office: Chamberlayne Sch Design Mt Ida Coll 777 Dedham St Newton MA 02459-3323

LEWIS-WHITE, LINDA BETH, elementary school educator; b. Fresno, Calif., June 30, 1950; d. Lloyd Ernest and Anne Grace (Barkman) Lewis; m. Francis Everett White, Feb. 15, 1975; children: Anna Justine, Christopher Andrew Arthur. BA in Home Econs., Calif. State U., Sacramento, 1972, MA in Social Scis., 1973; postgrad., Tex. Women's U., 1976-79; PhD in Reading, East Tex. State U., 1994. Cert. bilingual and elem. edn. tchr., Tex. Tchr. bilingual Arlington Sch. Dist., 1977-96; assoc. prof. reading Eastern Mich. U., 1996—. Adj. prof. reading Tex. Women's U., Denton, 1989, adj. prof. ESL East Tex. State U., 1993; mem. tchr. trainer cadre, Dallas Ind. Sch. Dist., 1985-92; freelance cons., 1987—; presenter TESOL Internat. Conf., San Antonio, 1989. Cons., writer (book) Ciencias-Silver Burdett, 1988. Troop leader Girl Scouts U.L.S., Dallas, 1980-82. Mem. Nat. Reading Conf., Nat. Writing Project, Internat. Reading Assn., Tchrs. of English to Spkrs. of Other Langs. (nominating com. 1990-91), TEXTESOL V (chair elem. edn. com. 1989-91), Tex. Assn. Bilingual Edn., Phi Delta Kappa, Phi Mu. Mem. Christian Ch. Avocations: sewing, knitting, quilting, reading, gourmet cooking. Office: Eastern Mich U 313A Porter Bldg Ypsilanti MI 48197-2210

LEWITT, MICHAEL HERMAN, physician, educator; b. Hartford, Conn., Nov. 27, 1948; s. Bernard and Celeste (Garfunkel) LeW.; m. Lynne Rubin, Apr. 1, 1979; children: Mattea, Jeremy, Rachel. BA, Lafayette Coll., 1970; MD, Jefferson Med. Coll., 1974; MPH, Med. Coll. Wis., 1997. Diplomate Am. Bd. Preventive Medicine, Am. Bd. Emergency Medicine, Am. Bd. Family Practice. Intern Misericordia Hosp., Phila., 1974-75; resident U. Cin., 1982, 83; med. dr. FMC Group, 1975-78; physician U.S. Steel Corp., 1978-81, Jeanes Hosp., 1981-84; emergency medicine physician Chester County Hosp., 1984-90; asst. prof. dept. surgery Jefferson Med. Coll., Phila., 1983—, pvt. practice, 1990—. Cons., 1990—. Fellow Am. Acad. Emergency Medicine, Phila. Coll. Physicians, Am. Coll. Emergency Physicians, Am. Coll. Occupational and Environ. Medicine, Am. Acad. Family Practice; mem. ACP. Fax: 610-993-0288. E-mail: DoctorMike@aol.com.

LEWTER, HELEN CLARK, elementary education educator, retired; b. Millis, Mass., Jan. 14, 1936; d. Waldimar Kenville and Ida Mills (Currier) Clark; m. Alvin Council Lewter, June 18, 1966; children: Lois Ida, David Paul, Jonathan Clark. BA, U. Mass., 1958; MS, Old Dominion U., 1978. Tchr. Juniper Hill Sch., Framingham, Mass., 1960-63, Aragona Elem. Sch., Virginia Beach, Va., 1963-65, Park Elem., Chesapeake, Va., 1965-67; edn. specialist Riverview Sch., Portsmouth, Va., 1977-78; reading tchr. Truitt Jr. H.S., Chesapeake, 1979-83; reading resource tchr. Southeastern Elem., Chesapeake, 1983-86; tchr. Deep Creek Elem. Sch., Chesapeake, 1986-99, ret., 1999. Pers. task force, textbook adoption com. Chesapeake Pub. Schs., Va., 1984—85, employee handbook com., Va., 1986—87, K-6 writing curriculum com., Va., 1988—89. Active PTA, 1979—99; mem. mayor's adv. coun. City of Chesapeake, Va., 1988—89; tchr., workshop leader, dir., mem. various coms. Fairview Heights Bapt. Ch., Deep Creek Bapt. Ch., Va. So. Bapt. Retreats, 1968—; mem. summer missionary Va. So. Bapts., 1993. Mem.: NEA, Va. Reading Assn., Internat. Reading Assn., Chesapeake Reading Assn. (v.p., pres., honor and merit coun., chmn. various coms.), Chesapeake Edn. Assn., Va. Edn. Assn., Phi Kappa Phi, Kappa Delta Pi, Delta Kappa Gamma (legis. chmn.). Republican. Avocations: church related activities, reading. Home: 428 Plummer Dr Chesapeake VA 23323-3116

LEWY, JOHN EDWIN, pediatric nephrologist; b. Chgo., Apr. 22, 1935; s. Stanley B. and Lucile (Mayer) L.; m. Rosalind Portnoy, June 9, 1963; children— Karen, Steven. BA, U. Mich., 1956; MD, Tulane U., 1960. Diplomate Am. Bd. Pediat. (oral examiner 1985-89, oral exam com. 1987-89, certifying exam. com. on clin. problems 1989-92, com. on rsch. and rev. 1992-98), Am. Bd. Pediatric Nephrology. Intern Michael Reese Hosp. Med. Center, Northwestern U., 1960-61, resident in pediatrics, 1961-62, Michael Reese Hosp. Med. Center, 1963-64, chief resident, 1964, pediatric nephrology fellow, 1965, dir. sect. pediatric nephrology, 1967-70; fellow dept. pediatrics Cornell U. Med. Coll., N.Y.C., 1966, research fellow physiology, 1966-67, asst. prof. pediatrics, 1970-71, assoc. prof., 1971-75, prof., 1975-78, dir. div. pediatric nephrology, 1970-78; Reily prof., chmn. dept. pediat. Tulane U. Sch. Medicine, New Orleans, 1978—; physician-in-chief Tulane Hosp. for Children, New Orleans, 1993—. Pediatrician La. Handicapped Children's Program; mem. exec. com., sci. adv. com. La. End Stage Renal Disease Coun.; mem. life options adv. bd. Rehab. Digest for Nephrologists, 1999—; mem. sci. adv. bd. Nat. Kidney Found., 1979—86, mem. health and sci. affairs com., 1989—95, mem. pub. policy com., 1990—96, chmn. pub. policy com., 1994—96, bd. dirs., 1994—96, mem. task force on early intervention and prevention, 1996—; mem. clin. sci. coun. Tulane U., chmn., 1980—90, 1995—, mem. exec. com. of clin. sci. coun., 1978—, mem. faculty senate, 1987—90; mem. task force on cmty. health care Tulane Sch. Pub. Health and Tropical Medicine, 1993—; bd. dirs. Kidney Found. La., 1984—, mem. med. adv. bd., 1981—, mem. sci. adv. bd., 1982—, rep., regional dir., 2000—, task force early intervention and prevention, 1996—. Contbr. over 200 articles and abstracts to profl. jours. Mem. profl. adv. com. Nat. Found. March of Dimes; sci. adv. com. U.S. Renal Data System, HHS, 1990—93; mem. com. on future of pediat. nephrology NIDDK, 1991—; spl. com. on ctrs. of excellence in kidney and urology diseases HHS Nat. Kidney and Urology Diseases Adv. Bd., 1994—96. Served with M.C. USAF, 1962—63. Named Intern of Year, Michael Reese Hosp. Med. Ctr., 1961; recipient award, La. Pediatric Soc., 1960, Ronald McDonald Children's Charities Gift of Love award, 1996, Disting. Svc. award, Nat. Kidney Found., 1996, Julio Figueroa Gift of Life award, Nat. Kidney Found. La., 1999, Disting. Svc. award, Tulane U. Med. Alumni Assn., 1999. Mem.: AAAS, APHA, Nat. Assn. Children's Hosps. (liason from comm. on Federal Gov. Affairs 2002), So. Soc. Pediatric Rsch. (Founder's award 2003), Greater New Orleans Pediatric Soc., Orleans Parish Med. Soc. (pub. health com. 1981—, media resource panel 1999—, Award for excellence in rsch. 2003), Am. Soc. Artificial Internal Organs, Assn. Med. Sch. Pediatric Dept. Chairmen, La. State Med. Soc., Internat. Pediatric Nephrology Assn. (asst. sec. gen. 1977—78), Internat. Pediatric Chairs Assn., N.Y. Acad. Scis., Midwest Soc. Pediatric Research, Internat. Soc. Nephrology, Am. Soc. Nephrology, Am. Soc. Pediatric Nephrology (sec.-treas. 1974—80, pres. 1980—81, pub. policy com. 1991—94, 1996—2000, Founder's award 2000), Am. Pediatric Soc. (co-chair work group on pub. policy), Soc. Pediatric Rsch., Am. Acad. Pediat. (liaison from AMSPDC 1992—95, coun. fed. govt. affairs 1992—, task force on access 1999—, coun. on coms. 2002—, rsch./edn./orgn. action group 2002—, chmn. 2002, Henry L. Barnett award 1999), Am. Soc. Transplant Physics, Inst. Medicine (end stage renal disease com. 1989—91), Salt and Water Club, Alpha Omega Alpha (faculty advisor 1987—92). Home: 700 S Peters St New Orleans LA 70130-1663 Office: Tulane U Sch Medicine 1430 Tulane Ave New Orleans LA 70112-2699

LEWY, PHYLLIS, English educator; d. Leonard and Rosalie (Solomon) L. BA, Temple U., 1968, MA, 1971, reading specialist cert., 1979. Cert. secondary tchr., Pa. English instr. Mercer C.C., Trenton, N.J., 1971; English tchr. Lansdowne (Pa.) Aldan H.S., 1972-74; English instr. C.C. of Phila., 1975; reading specialist, grades K-12 Montgomery County Intermediate Unit, Norristown, Pa., 1979—. Part-time English instr. Delaware County C.C., 1991-94, Villanova U., Pa. State U., 1979-83, Temple U., 1968-71; pvt. tutor. Freelance editor for Lea & Febiger, Amsco Sch. Publs. Recipient teaching assistantship Temple U., 1968-71, summer fellowship Temple U., 1980. Avocations: movies, dance, exercise classes, writing.

LEWYN, ANN SALFELD, retired English as a second language educator; b. N.Y.C., Dec. 1, 1935; d. Henry and Betty (Ahrens) Salfeld; m. Thomas Mark Lewyn, July 15, 1955; children: Alfred Thomas, Mark Henry. BA, Hunter Coll., 1967, MA, 1982. Mem. faculty UN Hospitality Extension Lang. Program, N.Y.C., 1974-86; adj. instr. ESL NYU, 1986-90, adj. asst. prof., 1990-95, adj. assoc. prof., 1995-2000, adj. prof., 2001—02; ret., 2003—. Editor-in-chief (Newsletter) UN Hospitality Com., 1967-86. Mem. exec. bd. Small Press Ctr., N.Y.C., 1990-98; mem. adv. coun. Hospitality Com. for UN Dels. Inc., 1991-98; bd. dirs. Hunter Coll. Scholarship and Welfare Fund, N.Y.C., 1992—, sec., 1998-2000, 3d v.p., 2000-2001, 2d v.p., 2001—. Mem. Teachers of English as Second Lang. (author in Aug. 1990 newsletter), N.Y. State Tchrs. of English as Second Lang., Pi Sigma Alpha, Kappa Delta Pi. Avocations: travel, tennis, needlepoint, photography, golf. Home: 911 Park Ave New York NY 10021-0337

LEYBOLD-TAYLOR, KARLA JOLENE, college official; b. Lincoln, Nebr., Mar. 18, 1969; d. Norman Alfred and Marcella Ann (Stander) Leybold; m. Cameron Craig Taylor, May 28, 1994; 1 child, Amelia L. BA, Nebr. Wesleyan U., Lincoln, 1991; M in Theol. Studies cum laude, So. Meth. U., 1993. Assoc. registrar Thomas Nelson C.C., Hampton, Va., 1993-96; registrar Wells Coll., Aurora, N.Y., 1996—. Mem. Am. Assn. Collegiate Registrars and Admissions Officers, Mid. States Assn. Collegiate Registrars and Admissions Officers (new mems. orientation, mentoring and membership com. 1998—, chairperson 2000-2001, program com. 2001—, v.p. for profl. devel. and chair profl. activities com. 2002—), Va. Assn. Collegiate Registrars and Admissions Officers (hon., chmn. local arrangements 1995, mem. publs. com. 1995-96, Disting. Young Profl. award 1995), Assn. Internat. Educators, N.Y./N.J. Assn. Collegiate Registrars and Admissions Officers. Democrat. Roman Catholic. Avocations: travel, hiking, pets, reading. Office: Wells Coll PO Box 500 Aurora NY 13026-0500 E-mail: kleybold@wells.edu.

L'HUILLIER, VALERIE ELIZABETH, elementary education educator; b. Little Rock, Apr. 4, 1959; d. Kenneth Leroy and Mary Elizabeth (Hogan) Schuck; m. Steven Paul L'Huillier, June 4, 1982; children: Kara Ann, Bradley Javin. BS in Edn. cum laude, North Tex. State U., 1981, MEd, 1985. Spl. edn. aide Lewisville (Tex.) Ind. Sch. Dist., 1982-83, tchr. 4th grade, 1983-85, Flower Mound, 1985—, chair 4th grade, 1985-91, 1998—2002, mentor tchr., 1992—. Mem. supts. adv. com. FLower Mound Elem. Sch., 1986-89; mem. reading textbook adoption com. Lewisville Ind. Sch., 1992-94, social studies textbook adoption com., 2002-2003, mem. dist. study skills com., 1988; mem. bldg. leadership team FLower Mound Elem. Sch., 1990. V.p. Flower Mound Elem. Sch. PTA; mem. Youth Protection, 1994-96, 8th v.p.; Brownie troop leader Crosstimbers coun. Girl Scouts U.S., 1994-98; dir. Flower Mound Youth Sports Assn., 1997—. Recipient Flower Mound Elem. Tchr. Yr., 1999—2000. Mem. Assn. Tex. Profl. Educators (treas. 1983—), Phi Delta Kappa, Delta Kappa Gamma, Delta Kappa Gamma (chair contact com. 1999-2001). Avocations: bicycling, cooking. Office: Flower Mound Elem 4101 Churchill Dr Flower Mound TX 75028-1598

LI, CHING-CHUNG, electrical engineering and computer science educator; b. Changshu, Kiangsu, China, Mar. 30, 1932; came to U.S., 1954, naturalized, 1972; s. Lung-Han and Lien-Tseng (Hwa) L.; m. Hanna Wu,

June 10, 1961; children: William Wei-Lin, Vincent Wei-Tsin. BSEE, Nat. Taiwan U., 1954; MSEE, Northwestern U., 1956, PhD, 1961. Jr. engr. analytical dept. Westinghouse Electric Corp., East Pittsburgh, Pa., 1957; inst. fellow Northwestern U., Evanston, Ill., 1957-59; asst. prof. elec. engring. U. Pitts., 1959-62, assoc. prof., 1962-67; vis. assoc. prof. elec. engring. U. Calif.-Berkeley, 1964; vis. prin. scientist Alza Corp., Palo Alto, Calif., 1970; faculty rsch. participant Pitts. Energy Tech. Ctr., Dept. Energy, Pitts., 1982, 83, 85, 88, 89; prof. elec. engring. U. Pitts., 1967—, prof. computer sci., 1977—; mem. Ctr. Multivariate Analysis, 1982-87, Ctr. for Parallel and Distributed Intelligent Systems, 1986—96; sabbatical leave Lab. for Info. and Decision Systems, MIT, 1988, Robotics Inst., Carnegie Mellon U., 1999. Mem. sci. adv. com. Horus Therapeutics, Inc., 1995-97. Guest editor: Jour. Cybernetics and Info. Sci., 1979, Computerized Med. Imaging and Graphics, 1991, assoc. editor: Pattern Recognition, 1985—2001, mem. editl. bd.: Internat. Jour. Image and Graphics, 2000—; contbr. articles to profl. jours. Co-recipient cert. of merit Radiol. Soc. N.Am., 1979; rsch. grantee NSF, 1975-81, 85-87, Pa. Dept. Health, 1977-79, We. Pa. Advanced Tech. Ctr., 1983-84, 86-88, Health Rsch. and Svc. Found., 1985-86, Air Force Office Sci. Rsch., 1990-93, Pitts. Digital Greenhouse, Inc., 2000-02. Fellow IEEE (tech. com., com. chmn. 1967—); mem. Biomed. Engring. Soc., AAAS, Pattern Recognition Soc., Sigma Xi, Eta Kappa Nu. Home: 2130 Garrick Dr Pittsburgh PA 15235-5033 Office: U Pitts Dept Elec Engring Pittsburgh PA 15261-0001

LI, FU, electrical engineering educator, editor; b. Chengdu, Sichuan, China, Sept. 12, 1958; came to U.S., 1985; s. Zhi and Xiu-Juan (Ding) L.; m. Grace Hui Fang, Mar. 18, 1984; children: Susan J., Karen M. BS in Physics, Sichuan U., 1982, MS in Physics, 1985; PhD in Elec. Engring., U. R.I., 1990. Profl. engr., Oreg. Rsch./teaching asst. U. R.I., Kingston, 1986-89; rsch. staff Philips Labs., Briarcliff Manor, N.Y., summer 1987; tech. staff Prime Computer, Inc., Bedford, Mass., 1989-90; asst. prof. elec. engring. Portland (Oreg.) State U., 1990-94, assoc. prof. elec. engring., 1994—. Author chpts. to 4 books, 1991-94; contbr. articles to profl. jours. Recipient Faculty Devel. award Portland State U., 1991, Pew Teaching Leadership award 2d Nat. Conf. on Teaching Assts., 1989, Excellent Paper award Chinese Assn. Sci. and Tech., 1986. Mem. NSPE, IEEE (sr., assoc. editor Transactions on Signal Processing 1993—, organizer Oreg. chpt. 1993, chair 1993-95, exec. com. 1993—, session chair internat. conf. on acoustics, speech and signal processing 1993-96, session chair statis. signals and array processing workshop 1992, 94, tech. com. on statis. signals and array processing 1992—, chair tech. subcom. power spectrum estimation 1992—, chair 1994—, recognition award 1993, chpt. chmn. award 1994, outstanding counselor award 1995), Eta Kappa Nu. Avocations: thinking, reading, playing computer, swimming, investing. Office: Portland State Univ Dept Elec Engring 1800 SW 6th Ave Portland OR 97201-5204

LI, JAMES CHEN MIN, materials science educator; b. Nanking, China, Apr. 12, 1925; came to U.S., 1949; s. Vei Shao and In Shey (Mai) L.; m. Lily Y.C. Wang, Aug. 5, 1950; children: Conan, May, Edward. BS, Nat. Ctrl. U., China, 1947; MS, U. Wash., 1951, PhD, 1953. Rsch. assoc. U. Calif., Berkeley, 1953-55; supr. Mfg. Chemists Assn. project Carnegie Inst. Tech., Pitts., 1955-56; phys. chemist Westinghouse Elec. Co., Pitts., 1956-57; sr. scientist U.S. Steel Corp., Monroeville, Pa., 1957-69; mgr. strength physics Allied Chem. Co., Morristown, N.J., 1969-71; A.A. Hopeman prof. engring. U. Rochester (N.Y.), 1971—. Vis. prof. Columbia U., N.Y.C., 1964-65, adj. prof., 1965-71; adj. prof. Stevens Inst. Tech., Newark, 1971-72; vis. prof. Ruhr U., Bochum, Fed. Republic Germany, 1978-79. Author 1 book; editor 3 books; contbr. 340 articles to profl. jours.; holder 5 patents in 6 countries. Recipient Alexander Von Humboldt award, 1978, Acta Metallurgica Gold medal, 1990, Grad. Teaching award U. Rochester, 1993. Fellow TMS/AIME (Robert F. Mehl medal and lectr. 1978, Champion H. Mathewson Gold medal 1972, Structural Materials Divsn. luncheon spkr. 1993, chmn. phys. mutall. com. 1992-95), ASM Internat. (chmn. materials sci. divsn. 1982-84), Am. Phys. Soc.; mem. ASME, Materials Rsch. Soc., Chinese Soc. Materials Sci. (Lu Tse-Hon medal 1988). Office: U Rochester Dept Mech Engring PO Box 270132 Rochester NY 14627-0133 E-mail: li@me.rochester.edu.

LI, JIAN JIAN, medical educator; b. Xian, Shaanxi, China, July 19, 1954; m. Ming Fan; children: Leeanne, Robert. MD, Xian Med. Coll., Xian, China, 1979; MS, Fourth Med. U., Xian, China, 1984; PhD, U. Iowa, 1994. Vis. scholar U. Calif., San Francisco, 1988—89, rsch. fellow, 1989—90; IRTA rsch. fellow NIH, Frederick, Md., 1995—96, sr. rsch. fellow, 1996—99; asst. prof., sect. head Beckman Rsch. Inst. and City of Hope Nat. Med. Ctr., Duarte, Calif., 1999—. Contbr. articles to profl. jours. Named E. Roosevelt fellow, Internat. Union Against Cancer, 1988; recipient Radiation Rsch. award, N.Am. Hyperthermia Soc., 1992, fellows award for rsch. excellence, NIH, 1996, Cancer Rsch. Fellow award, 1998. Mem.: AAAS, Radiation Rsch. Soc., Internat. Union Against Cancer, Am. Assn. Cancer Rsch., Oxygen Soc. Office: City of Hope Nat Ctr 1500 Duarte Road Duarte CA 91010-3000 Personal E-mail: jjli999@hotmail.com.

LI, JING RONG, neurosurgeon, educator, consultant; b. Shang Hang, Fujian, China, Sept. 11, 1929; s. Kok Tai Li and Yu Chun Hwang; m. Xuan Mei Chen, Feb. 10, 1959 (dec. Feb. 1985); children: Gang, Qiang, Qiong Hui, Chen Peng; m. Zhi Ying Chen, Nov. 8, 1991. BS, Beijing Med. U., 1956. Neurologist Hsiang Ya Hosp. of Hunan Med. U., Changsha, China, 1956-60; neurosurgeon, lectr., asst. prof. Hsiang Ya Hosp. Zhong Nan U., Changsha, China, 1961-86; neurosurgeon Rsch. Inst. Neuroscis. Guangzhou (China) Med. Coll., 1986—, prof., 1988—, vice dir. neurosurg. dept., 1989-95. Cons. Hsiang-Qian Ry. Campaign Hdqs. Hosp., Zhijiang, China, 1971-74; editor, supr. neurology and neurosurgery Fgn. Med. Scis., Changsha, 1978-83, cons. editor, 1986. Editor, Supr. Neurology and Neurosurgery Fgn. Med. Scis., Changsha, Hunan, 1978-83, cons. editor, 1986-98; cons. editor Jour. Guangzhou Med. Coll., 1988-98, Chinese ENT and Skull Base Surgery Jour., 1995-98; contbr. articles to med. jours., including Chinese Med. Jour. and Chinese Neurosurgery Jour. Fellow Guangzhou Neurosurg. Assn.; mem. N.Y. NYAS, Chinese Med. Assn. in Guangdon, Guangzhou Overseas Chinese Assn. (vice chmn. 1988-98), Malaysia Ipoh Yok Choy and Perak Girl's Sch. Alumni Assn. (chmn. Guangzhou 1993—). Avocations: travel, exercise, chess, photography, reading. Office: Guangzhou Med Coll Neurosci Rsch Inst 250 Chang Gang Don Rd Guangdon Guangzhou 510260 China E-mail: lijgrg@163.net.

LI, KAM WU, mechanical engineer, educator; b. China, Feb. 16, 1934; came to U.S., 1959; s. Yang Chung and Oy Lan Li; MS, Colo. State U., 1961; PhD, Okla. State U., 1965; m. Shui Mui Chan, Aug. 30, 1956; children: Christopher, Charles. Asst. prof. mech. engring. Tex. A&M U., Kingsville, 1965-67; assoc. prof. N.D. State U., Fargo, 1967-73, prof., 1973—, assoc. dean engring. and arch., 1989-91, chmn. dept. mech. engring., 1994-96; cons. Charles T. Main Inc., Boston, 1973-80, Center for Profl. Advancement, East Brunswick, N.J., 1982-84. Recipient cert. appreciation U.S. Navy, 1974; NSF fellow, 1966; Ford Found. fellow, 1972. Mem. ASME, N.Y. Acad Scis., Sigma Xi, Tau Beta Pi, Pi Tau Sigma, Kappa Mu Epsilon. Author: Power Plant System Design and Applied Thermodynamics. Contbr. numerous articles to profl. jours.; govt. engring. research, 1965—. Home: 2516 18th St S Moorhead MN 56560-4811 Office: ND State U University Ave Fargo ND 58105

LI, MENGFENG, molecular biologist, virologist, educator; b. Guiyang, Guizhou, China, Oct. 4, 1964; came to U.S., 1993; s. Qiaoxin Li and Youchun Zhu; m. Qing Zeng, Feb. 20, 1992; 1 child, Cindy. MD, Sun Yat-Sen U. Med. Sci., 1986, PhD, 1991. Investigator Nat. Lab. Molecular Virology and Genetic Engring., Beijing, 1991-93; vis. rsch. investigator Cancer Inst. U. Pitts., 1993-97, asst. prof., 1997—. Author: Advances in Molecular Virology, E-C Dictionary of Molecular Biology and Biotechnology, Medical Molecular Virology and Application, Encyclopedia of Medical Diagnosis, Progress in Techniques of Medical Molecular Microbiology, Rsch. Trends in Immunology; contbr. articles to profl. jours. Mem. Am. Assn. Cancer Rsch., Soc. Natural Immunity. Achievements include discovering new members of human interferon family and making them applicable in medicine; discovering oncogenic effects of a retrovirus in melnocytes; designing and constructing encaphaline directed tumor-targeting interferon molecules; anti-angiogenic therapy of cancer. Office: Univ Pitts Cancer Inst 200 Lothrop St # W907 Bst Pittsburgh PA 15213-2546

LI, QINGDI QUENTIN, physician, research scientist, medical educator; b. Guilin, Guangxi, China, Apr. 18, 1956; m. Li Ding; 1 child, Julie. MA, MD, Guangxi Med. U., 1987; MS, PhD, U. Md., 2000. Microbiologist, immunologist Guangxi Med. U., Nanning, China, 1983—87; dermatologist Zhongshan Univ. Sch. Medicine, Guangzhou, China, 1987—91; postdoctoral fellow Nat. Cancer Inst., Bethesda, Md., 1996—98; rsch. assoc. Balt. VA Med. Ctr., Baltimore, Md., 1998—2000; asst. prof. W. Va. Univ. Health Sci. Ctr., Morgantown, W.Va., 2000—. Rsch. coord. W.Va. U. MBR Cancer Ctr., Morgantown, 2000—04; guest prof. Wuhan (China) U., 2002—04, Guangxi Med. U., 2002—04. Recipient Intramural Rsch. Award, Nat. Cancer Inst., 1996-1998, Nat. Svc. Award, NIH, 1998-2000. Mem.: NY Acad. Sci., Am. Assn. Advanced Sci., Am. Assn. Cancer Rsch., Chinese Med. Assn., Am. Soc. Microbiology (assoc.). Home: 216 Watkins Pond Blvd Rockville MD 20850 Office: W Va Univ Health Sci MBR Cancer Ctr PO Box 9300 Morgantown WV 26506-9300 Home Fax: 301-208-1945; Office Fax: 304-293-4667. Business E-Mail: qli@hsc.wvu.edu.

LI, YONGJI, chemistry educator; b. Beijing, Sept. 5, 1933; came to U.S., 1981; s. Li Zhi-Ping and Zhi-Zhang (Chen); m. Zhihua Yu, June 30, 1956; children: Zidan, Lisa. BS in Physics, Beijing U., 1955; PhD in Chemistry, SUNY, Buffalo, 1985. Instr., lectr. physics Jilin U., Changchun, Jiling, China, 1955-81; rsch. asst., teaching asst. SUNY, Buffalo, 1981-85; postdoctoral rsch. assoc. U. New Orleans, 1985-89; assoc. prof. chemistry U. P.R., San Juan, 1989-93, dir. X-Ray Lab., 1989-93; adj. assoc. prof. chemistry N.Y. Inst. Tech., L.I., 1994—. Contbr. articles to profl. jours. Grantee High Edn. Ministry, China, 1979, NSF, 1992. Mem. Am. Chem. Soc., Am. Crystallographic Assn. Achievements include construction of first Chinese ultra-high pressure mini-generator (diamond anvil cell, 300kb without a gasket); x-ray crystallographic studies on inorganic and/or biologically active compounds; accurate measurements of electron density distribution on organometallics and biologically active compounds. Home: 7 Royal Dr Coram NY 11727-2251 Office: NY Inst Tech Old Westbury NY 11568-8000 E-mail: yongii99_2000@yahoo.com.

LIAN, BONG H. mathematician, educator, mathematician, department chairman; BA, U. Toronto, Can., 1985; PhD in Physics, Yale U., 1991. Math. and sci. tutor Yale Coll. Yale U., 1988—90, postdoctoral fellow dept. math. and physics, 1993; postdoctoral instr. dept. math. U. Toronto, 1991—93; postdoctoral fellow dept. math. Harvard U., 1994—95; asst. prof. dept. math. Brandeis U., Waltham, Mass., 1995—97, assoc. prof., 1997—2001, full prof., 2001—, undergrad. advisor, 1997—99, grad. advisor, 2001—02, chmn. dept. math., 2002—. Vis. assoc. prof. Nat. U. Singapore, 2001. Contbr. articles to profl. jours. Fellow, John Simon Guggenheim Meml. Found., 2003; A.P. Sloan Grad. Dissertation fellow in math., 1990—91. Mem.: Internat. Congress Chinese Mathematicians (sci. com. mem. 1999—), Internat. Sci. Found. Cambridge (sec. 1998—). Achievements include research in representation theory and semi-infinite cohomology; mirror symmetry and Calabi-Yau geometry; string theory. Office: Brandeis Univ Goldsmith Bldg Rm 314 MS 050 415 South St Waltham MA 02454-9110*

LIANG, EDISON PARKTAK, astrophysicist, educator, researcher; b. Canton, Republic of China, July 22, 1947; came to U.S., 1964; s. Chi-Sen and Siu-Fong (Law) L.; m. Lily K. Yuen, Aug. 7, 1971; children: Olivia, James, Justin. BA, U. Calif., Berkeley, 1967, PhD, 1971. Rsch. scientist U. Tex., Austin, 1971-73; assoc. instr. U. Utah, Salt Lake City, 1973-75; asst. prof. Mich. State U., East Lansing, Mich., 1975-76, Stanford (Calif.) U., 1976-79; physicist, group leader Lawrence Livermore Nat. Lab., Livermore, Calif., 1980-88, assoc. div. leader, 1988-91; prof. space physics and astronomy Rice U., Houston, 1991-2001, Andrew Hays Buchanan prof. astrophysics, 2001—. Mem. NASA Rev. Panels, Washington, 1988—. Editor: (book) Gamma Ray Bursts, 1986. Named Sci. fellow and Anthony scholar U. Calif., Berkeley, 1967-69. Fellow Am. Phys. Soc. (chair topical group in plasma astrophysics 2003); mem. Am. Astron. Soc., Internat. Astron. Union, Phi Beta Kappa, Sigma Xi. Office: Rice U Herman Brown Hall 6100 Main St MS108 Houston TX 77005-1892 E-mail: liang@spacsun.rice.edu.

LIANG, JEROME ZHENGRONG, radiology educator; b. Chongging, China, June 23, 1958; arrived in U.S., 1981; BS, Lanzhou U., China, 1982; PhD, CUNY, 1987. Rsch. instr. Albert Einstein Coll. Medicine, Bronx, NY, 1986—87; rsch. assoc. Duke U. Med. Ctr., Durham, NC, 1987—89, asst. med. rsch. prof., 1990—92; asst. prof. SUNY, Stony Brook, 1992—97, assoc. prof., 1997—2000, prof., 2000—, co-dir. biomed. engring., 1996—. Mem. adv. bd. MDOL, Inc., 1999—; bd. dirs., v.p. R&D, founder Viatronix, Inc., 2000—. Contbr. articles to profl. jours.; mem. editl. bd.: IEEE Transactions on Med. Imaging, 1999—. Recipient NIH awards, 1990—, AHA award, 1996—2001, N.Y. State Biotech. award, 1996—98, E-Z-EM award, 1997—98; grantee, Soc. Thoracic Radiology, 1994—95, ADAC Rsch. Lab., 1994—95. Achievements include development of Bayesian image processing, quantitative emission computed tomography, tissue segmentation from magnetic resonance images, virtual endoscopy, virtual realities in radiology. Avocations: swimming, fitness, tennis. Office: SUNY Stony Brook Dept Radiology 4th Fl Rm 120 Stony Brook NY 11794-8460

LIANG, JUNXIANG, retired aeronautics and astronautics engineer, educator; b. Hangzhou, Zhejiang, China, Aug. 17, 1932; s. Yigao and Yunruo (Yu) L.; m. Junxian Sun, Jan. 27, 1960; 1 child, Song Liang. Grad., Harbin Inst. Tech., 1960. Head control dept. Shenyang (Liaoning, China) Jet Engine R&D Inst., 1960-70, China Gas Turbine Establishment, Jiangyou, Sichuan, China, 1970-78, assoc. chief engr., 1978-83; vis. scientist MIT, Cambridge, Mass., 1984-86; prof. China Aerospace Inst. Systems Engring., Beijing, 1986—; grads. supr. Beijing U. Aero-Astronautics, Beijing, 1986—; chief engr. Full Authority Digital Elec. Engine Control China Aerospace Industry Ministry, Beijing, 1986-93; now ret. Mem. China Aerospace Sci. and Tech. Com., Beijing, 1983-94, Aero-engine R&D Adv. Bd., Beijing, 1991-95; bd. dirs. China Aviation Ency. Editl. Bd., Beijing, 1991-95; tech. support supr., mgmt. info. svc. dir. Am. PC, Inc., Union City, Calif., 1993—. Author: Nonlinear Control System Oscillation, 1964; contbr. articles to Jour. Aeronautics and Astronautics, Jour. Propulsion Tech., Internat. Aviation, Acta Aeronautica et Astronautica Sinica. Recipient Nat. Sci. and Tech. 2d award, China Nat. Sci. and Tech. Com., Beijing, 1965, Sic. and Tech. Progress award, China Aerospace Industry Ministry, 1991, Nat. Outstanding Sci. and Tech. Contbn. award, 1992. Mem. AIAA (sr.), Chinese Soc. of Aeronautical, Astronautical Engine Control (mem. commn. 1987—). Achievements include solution of oscillation problem on nonlinear control system; formulation of aircraft overall strategy, study and control of High Thrust/Weight Engine Rsch. Program.

LIANG, LANBO See **LEONG, LAMPO**

LIBBY, JOSEPH ANTHONY, physician, educator; b. Phila., Dec. 3, 1965; s. Joseph Adolph and Marie Elaine Libby; m. Maria Angela Froio, Sept. 18, 1993. BS, St. Joseph's U., Phila., 1987; MD, UMDNJ, 1991. Diplomate Am. Bd. Internal Medicine. Resident in internal medicine Cooper Hosp., Camden, N.J., 1991-94; attending physician Cooper Physician Offices, Cherry Hill, NJ, 1994—98, Sewell, NJ, 1998—; clin. instr. medicine UMDNJ-Robert Wood Johnson Med. Sch., Camden, 1994-97, asst. prof. medicine, 1997—2003, assoc. prof. medicine, 2003—. Contbr. articles to profl. jours. Mem. ACP, AMA, Am. Med. Students Assn. (chpt. pres. 1988-89), Sigma Xi (assoc.). Avocations: physical fitness, astronomy, computers, model rocketry. Office: Cooper Physician Offices 1 Plaza Dr Sewell NJ 08080

LIBBY, RONALD THEODORE, political science educator, consultant, researcher; b. L.A., Nov. 20, 1941; s. Theodore Harold and Patricia Mildred (Griswold) L.; m. Kathleen Christina Jacobson, June 3, 1982; children: Kathleen Elizabeth Libby, Erin Kristin Jenne. BA, Wash. State U., 1965; MA, U. Wash., 1966, PhD, 1975. Lectr. U. Bostwana, Lesotho and Swaziland, 1973-75, U. Malawi, Zomba, 1975-76, U. Zambia, Lusaka, 1976-79; asst. prof. U. Notre Dame, South Bend, Ind., 1981-83; sr. lectr. U. W.I., Kingston, Jamaica, 1983-85; assoc. prof. Northwestern U., Evanston, Ill., 1985-86; sr. rsch. fellow Australian Nat. U., Darwin, 1986-87; sr. lectr. Victoria U., Wellington, New Zealand, 1987-89; prof. S.W. State U., Marshall, Minn., 1989-96; prof., chmn. dept. St. Joseph's U., Phila., 1996-2000; prof. polit. sci. U. North Fla., Jacksonville, 2000—. Treas. New Zealand Polit. Sci. Assn., Wellington, 1988-89. Author: Towards an Africanized U.S. Policy for Southern Africa, 1980, The Politics of Economic Power in Southern Africa, 1987, Hawke's Law, 1989 (Choice award 1991), Protecting Markets: U.S. Policy and the World Grain Trade, 1992, ECO-WARS: Political Campaigns and Social Movements, 1999; contbr. articles to profl. jours. With U.S. Army, 1962-64. Rsch. grantee Carnegie Endowment, 1971. Mem. Am. Polit. Sci. Assn., Internat. Studies Assn., Australian Polit. Sci. Assn. Roman Catholic. Avocations: tennis, handball, piano, singing. Office: U North Fla Dept Polit Sci 4567 St Bluff Rd S Jacksonville FL 32224 Home: 117 Turtle Bay Ln Ponte Vedra Beach FL 32082 E-mail: rlibby@unf.edu., rt12129@aol.com.

LIBKA, ROBERT JOHN, educational director, consultant; b. Pigeon, Mich., Sept. 19, 1951; s. Neil August and Joan Lois (Frank) L.; m. Bonnie Rae Borcher, June 16, 1973; children: Michelle, Kimberly, Jennifer. Cadet, U.S. Coast Guard Acad., 1969-71; BA in Edn., Concordia U., River Forest, Ill., 1975, MA in Edn., 1978. Cert. tchr. elem. & secondary schs., Ill., spl. guidance cert. Dir. residence hall Concordia U., River Forest, Ill., 1975-79, dir. student activities, 1975-87; dir. student ctr. dir. Koehneke Community Ctr., River Forest, 1975-88; project coord. Khusrau translation Harvard U. and Smithsonian Instn., Boston, Washington, 1988-89; pres. Attitudinal Dynamics Internat., Inc., Maywood, Ill., 1970—; dir. guidance Walther Lutheran High Sch., Maywood, Ill., 1989—; exec. dir. Luth. H.S. Assn. Kane and DuPage Counties, St. Charles, Ill., 1993-99; tchr. algebra Proviso West H.S., St. Charles, Ill., 2000—02; dir. aux. programs Dist. 209 Proviso Township HS, 2002—. Cons. Harvard U., Smithsonian Instn., Century Insur., Cook Cty. Sheriff's Officeand others, 1970—. Author: (Book) India: Price of Adventure, 1990; producer: Many videos of Internat. Religions and Cultures, 1988—; contbr. numerous articles to profl. and religious jours. Leader ARC, Chgo., 1975-85; mem. N. Maywood (Ill.) Community Orgn., 1975-85; pres. St. Paul Luth. Ch., 1987-88. Recipient Rsch. grant Smithsonian Instn., New Delhi, India, 1988. Mem. Am. Mgmt. Assn., Am. Personnel & Guidance Assn., Ill. Assn. Coll. Admissions Counselors, Luth. Edn. Assn. (life mem.), Gospel Music Assn., Nat. Assn. Campus Activities (bd. dirs. 1985-87). Avocations: travel, video production, distance running, photography. Home: 97 Hilltop Dr Lake In The Hills IL 60156-1168 Office: HS Dist 209 807 S First Ave Maywood IL 60153

LIBRERA, WILLIAM, education commissioner; m. Nancy Libera; children: Kelly Anne, Sally, William (Billy). BS, U. Vermont, 1968, MA in History, 1971; EdM, Rugers U., New Brunswick, 1977, EdD, 1982. Tchr. social studies West Morris, Park Ridge H.S.s, NJ, 1970—77; asst. to prin. West Morris H.S., Chester, NJ, 1977—78; asst. prin. Vernon Twp. H.S., Vernon, NJ, 1978—80; prin. Columbia H.S., Maplewood, 1980—83; supt. Wallkill Valley Regional H.S., NJ, 1983—87, Bernardsville Pub. Schs. Dist., 1987—92, Montclair Pub. Schs., 1992—97, Allamuchy Elem. Sch. Distr., NJ, 1997—2001; commr. N.J. Dept. Edn., Trenton, 2002—. Office: of the Commr PO Box 500 100 River View Plz Trenton NJ 08625-0500

LIBRO, ANTOINETTE CHRISTINE, university dean; b. Somers Point, N.J., May 24, 1938; d. Salvatore Anthony and Concetta (La Rosa) L.; m. Louis Braca, Jr., Apr. 20, 1963; 1 child, Aimèe Lee. BA, Glassboro State Coll., 1960, MA, 1967; PhD, NYU, 1983. Tchr. English, Ocean City (N.J.) H.S., 1960-61; tchr. art Sea Isle City (N.J.) Elem. Sch., 1968; prof. English, Glassboro (N.J.) State Coll., 1968-96; interim dean Rowan U., Glassboro, 1996—98, dean, 1998—2001, prof. emeritus, 2002—. Editor, pub. Blackbird Press, Asphodel, N.J., 1978-89; poetry cons. South Jersey Poetry Festival, Haddonfield, N.J., 1995— Author: (one-act plays) Out of Bounds, 1988, Out of the Cradle, 1990, Out of the Shadows, 1991 (chapbooks) Kokoro: Seasons of the Heart, 1982, Women without Wings, 1986, 2d edit., 1992, The House at the Shore, 1997 (full length plays) Dwellers Above the Clouds, 1986, Watchfire for Freedom, 1992; mem. editl. bd. Transformations Jour.; contbr. poetry to numerous lit. mags. and jours. Named Outstanding Woman of Edn., Gloucester County Bus. and Profl. Women, 1989; recipient poetry award Soc. N.J. Poets; faculty fellow Princeton U., 1992-93. Mem. Poets and Writers, Haiku Soc. Am., Am. Italian Hist. Soc., Sea Isle City Hist. Assn., Questers, People Organized Against Spouse Abuse, NYU Alumni Club. Avocations: travel, gardening, reading, antiques. Office: Rowan U 201 Mullica Hill Rd Glassboro NJ 08028-1702

LICATA, DAVID PAUL, chemistry educator; b. Chgo., Jan. 24, 1954; s. Alfonso and Carmela (Castrogiovanni) L.; m. Gale Lynn (Lieggi) Fetzer, Dec. 17, 1988; children: Nathan Dean Fetzer, Allison Nicole Licata. BS in Chemistry, U. Calif., Irvine, 1976, MS in Adminstrn., 1981. Cert. adminstrv. services tchr., single subject tchr., community coll., tchr., Calif., Ariz. Tchr. Garden Grove (Calif.) Unified Sch. Dist., 1977-78, 91-93, Huntington Beach (Calif.) Union High Sch. Dist., 1978-86; assoc. prof. Coastline C. C., Fountain Valley, Calif., 1981-86, 92—; mgr. precoll. sci. Am. Chem. Soc., Washington, 1986-90; v.p. prodn. and product devel. World Organics Corp., Huntington Beach, Calif., 1993—. Cons., mem. curriculum adv. bd. Nat. Inst. Nutritional Edn., 1984-87, Coastline Community Coll., 1985-86; cons., workshop dir. Chevron Petroleum Tech. Co., La Habra, Calif., 1991—. Author: Advanced Placement Chemistry Student Handbook, 1983, Basic Chemistry in Microscale, 1992, Chemistry Labs for Distance Learners, 1994, (manual) Chemistry Kit for Distance Learners, 1994; editor: Chemunity (magazine), 1986-90; designer chemistry and advanced placement chemistry lab. software. Recipient Orange County award for tchg. excellence, 1986. Mem. Nat. Sci. Tchrs. Assn. (Gustav-Ohaus award 1985), Am. Chem. Soc. (edn. com Orange County (Calif.) sect. 1990-93), Calif. Assn. Chem. Tchrs., Calif. Sci. Tchrs. Assn., Orange County Sci. Educators Assn. Republican. Protestant. Avocations: track, cross country, photography, computers. Office: World Organics Corp 5242 Bolsa Ave Ste 3 Huntington Beach CA 92649-1054

LICH, GLEN ERNST, writer, business executive, public education consultant; b. Fredericksburg, Tex., Nov. 5, 1948; s. Ernst Perry and Thelma Olive (Woolfley) L.; m. Lera Patrick Tyler, Sept. 5, 1970; children: James Ernst Lich-Tyler (dec.), Stephen Woolfley Lich-Tyler, Elizabeth Erin Lich-Tyler. Student, U. Vienna, Austria, 1969-70; BA, Southwestern U., 1971; MA, U. Tex., 1976; MA, S.W. Tex. State U., 1978; PhD, Tex. Christian U., 1984; grad., U.S. Army Command and Gen. Staff Coll., 1984. Instr. U. New Orleans, 1979-80; asst. prof. Schreiner Coll., 1980-87; assoc. prof. and dir. regional studies Baylor U., 1987-90; prof. and chair U. of Winnipeg, 1990-93; exec. dir. Hill Country Inst., 1992—; dir. World Heritage Tours, 1978—; pres., CEO The Sagres Group Inc., Kerrville, Tex., 1996—; adj. faculty U.S. Army Command and Gen. Staff Coll., 1987-97; vis. fellow Yale U., 1987, German Fgn. Ministry, 1983; rsch. fellow Mosher Inst. Internat. Policy Studies, Tex. A & M U., 1988-93; sr. rsch. fellow Ctr.

Socioeconomic Rsch. U. Coahuila, Mexico, 1990-95; coord. Standing Conf. Ethnic Chairs and Professorships in Can., 1991-92; cons. in field. Author: The German Texans, 1981, The Humanities and Public Issues, 1990, Fred Gipson at Work, 1990, The Women of Viscri, 1997; editor: (with Dona Reeves-Marquardt) Retrospect and Retrieval: The German Element in Review: Essays on Cultural Preservation, 1978, German Culture in Texas: A Free Earth, 1980, The Cabin Book, 1985, (with Dona Reeves-Marquardt) Texas Country: The Changing Rural Scene, 1986, (with Joseph A. McKinney) Region North America: Canada, United States, Mexico, 1990, Regional Studies: The Interplay of Land and People, 1992; assoc. editor Jour. German-Am. Studies, 1977-80, Yearbook of German-Am. Studies, 1981-93; editor: Jour. Am. Studies Assn. Tex., 1988-90; contbr. articles to profl. publs. Served with U.S. Army, 1972-75, lt. col. USAR, asst. attache to Portugal, 1987-92, asst. attache to Germany, 1992-94; project officer U.S. Embassy, Bucharest, Romania, 1993, Ljubljana, Slovenia, 1993-94; dir. internat. programs Adj. Gen.'s Dept. of State of Tex., 1994-95. Recipient Gold Def. Medal Republic of Slovenia, 1994; NEH rsch. grantee, 1978, 86-87; Fed. Republic Germany, 1983, 87; Swiss Humanities Acad., 1988; Tex. Com. Humanities, 1988, 89; Am. Coun. of Learned Socs., 1988; Embassy of Can., 1988; Max Kade Found., 1989-92; Joint Econ. Com. of U.S. Congress, 1989-91; Ministry of Multiculturalism and Citizenship of Can., 1991-92; Soc. Scis. and Humanities Rsch. Coun. Can., 1991-92, Interactivity Found., 1996—; Mem. MLA, Am. Studies Assn., Assn. Am. Geographers, Am. Folklore Assn., Am. Assn. Tchrs. German, Nat. Coun. Tchrs. English, Soc. for Romanian Studies, Assn. for Can. Studies in U. S., Can. Ethnic Studies Assn., Oral History Assn., Tex. Folklore Soc., Tex. State Hist. Assn., German Studies Assn., Pi Kappa Alpha. Office: Hill Country Inst PO Box 1850 Kerrville TX 78029-1850

LICHTEN, WILLIAM L. physics educator; b. Phila., Mar. 5, 1928; s. Harold and Goldie (Rosenbaum) L.; m. Susan Lurie, June 18, 1950; children: Michael, Stephen, Julia. BA in Physics, Swarthmore Coll., 1949; MS in Physics, U. Chgo., 1953, PhD in Physics, 1956. Rsch. physicist, postdoctoral fellow Columbia U., N.Y.C., 1956-58; from. asst. prof. to assoc. prof. U. Chgo., 1958-64; prof. Yale U., New Haven, 1964—2003, prof. emeritus, 2003—. Contbr. articles to sci. jours. Fellow Am. Phys. Soc. Office: Dept Physics Yale University PO Box 208120 New Haven CT 06520-8120 E-mail: williamlichten@yale.edu.*

LICHTENBERG, ALLAN JOSEPH, science educator; b. Passaic, N.J., Sept. 22, 1930; s. Milton and Ida (Krulewitz) L.; m. Elizabeth Anne Lind, Sept. 15, 1959. AB, Harvard U., 1952; MS, MIT, 1954; PhD, Oxford (England) U., 1961. Asst. prof. U. Calif., Berkeley, 1959-65, assoc. prof., 1965-71, prof. science, 1971—. Rsch. prof. Japan Inst. Fusion Sci., Nagoya, 1991. Author: Phase Space Dynamics of Particles, 1969; co-author: Regular and Stochastic Motion, 1983, Regular and Chaotic Dynamics, 2nd Edition, 1991, Principles of Plasma Discharges and Materials Processing, 1994. Fellow Guggenheim Found., 1965-66, Miller Inst., 1968-69, U.S.-Australia fellow NSF, 1984, 91. Home: 1560 Hawthorne Ter Berkeley CA 94708-1806

LICHTENBERG, JUDITH A. philosophy educator; b. N.Y.C., Apr. 19, 1948; d. Al and Friedel (Rothschild) L.; m. David J. Luban, Mar. 5, 1983; children: Daniel, Rachel. BA, U. Wis., 1968, MA, 1971; PhD, CUNY, 1978. Asst. prof. philosophy U. N.C., Chapel Hill, 1978-81; rsch. scholar Inst. Philosophy and Pub. Policy U. Md., College Park, 1981—, assoc. prof., 1991—. Editor: Democracy and the Mass Media, 1990; contbr. articles to profl. jours. Mem. Am. Philos. Assn., Am. Soc. Polit. and Legal Philosophy. Office: U Md Dept Philosophy College Park MD 20742-0001

LICHTENWALNER, PAMELA SMITH, special education educator, consultant; b. Spokane, Wash., June 28, 1946; d. Gerald Alfred and Marjorie Evelyn (McKee) Smith; m. John Lichtenwalner, Aug. 20, 1977 (div. Aug. 1983); 1 child, Arwen Harmony. BA, Ea. Ky. U., 1967; MA, San Francisco State U., 1983, U. Calif., Berkeley, 1992, postgrad., 1992-93. Cert. spl. edn. tchr.; Bayley Scales of Infant Devel. assessor; Brazelton assessor. Spl. edn. tchr. Napa State Hosp., Calif., 1980-84; learning disabled and gifted tchr. Hong Kong Internat. Sch., 1986-87; spl. edn. tchr. Napa County Office Edn., 1987-88, San Francisco Unified Sch. Dist., 1988—. Created 1st coll. course on pediatric HN issues, 1991; HIV pediatric specialist; cons. psychol. corp. on validity study for BSID II on HIV infants; mem. AIDS coord. com. SFSU, 1990—; mem. children and youth HIV network. Mem. Am. Himalyan Found., San Francisco, 1989—; steering com. Marin family Action, 1990—, co-founder, 1991. Named Star Tchr. in San Francisco, 1989-90. Mem. Coun. Exceptional Children, Pi Lambda Theta (v.p. Omega chpt., pres.; treas. region V). Buddhist. Avocations: gardening, reading, traveling. Home: PO Box 473 Stinson Beach CA 94970-0473 Office: San Francisco State Univ Dept Spl Edn 1600 Holloway Ave San Francisco CA 94132-1722

LICHTER, PAUL RICHARD, ophthalmology educator; b. Detroit, Mar. 7, 1939; s. Max D. and Buena (Epstein) L.; m. Carolyn Goode, 1960; children: Laurie, Susan. BA, U. Mich., 1960, MD, 1964, MS, 1968. Diplomate Am. Bd. Ophthalmology. Asst. to assoc. prof. ophthalmology U. Mich., Ann Arbor, 1971-78, prof., chmn. dept. ophthalmology and visual scis., 1978—. Chmn. Am. Bd. Ophthalmology, 1987. Editor-in-chief Ophthalmology jour., 1986-94. Served to lt. comdr. USN, 1969-71. Fellow: Am. Acad. Ophthalmology (bd. dirs. 1981—97, pres. 1996, sr. hon. award 1986, Lifetime Achievement award 2001); mem.: Acad. Ophthalmologica Internat., Internat. Coun. Ophthalmology, Assn. Univ. Profs. Ophthalmology (trustee 1986—93, pres. 1991—92), Mich. Ophthalmol. Soc. (pres. 1993—95), Washtenaw County Med. Soc., Mich. State Med. Soc., Pan Am. Assn.Ophthalmology (bd. dirs. 1988—, sec.-treas. English-speaking countries 1991—95, pres. 1999—2001), Am. Ophthalmol. Soc. (pres. 2000—01), AMA, Alpha Omega Alpha. Office: U Mich Med Sch Kellogg Eye Ctr 1000 Wall St Ann Arbor MI 48105-1912 E-mail: Plichter@umich.edu.

LICHTMAN, LILLIAN MARGARET YAEGER, special education educator; b. Munich, Mar. 16, 1947; d. Bernard and Pearl (Saks) Yaeger; div.; 1 child, Carrie Elizabeth. BS in Edn., Case-Western Res. U., 1969; MEd, Cleve. State U., 1979, postgrad., 1990. Cert. tchr., spl. edn. tchr., supr., reading, Ohio. Tchr. East Meadow (N.Y.) Bd. Edn., 1969; substitute tchr. N.Y.C. area, 1969-70; tchr. pre-sch. Universal Edn. Corp., N.Y.C., 1970; tchr. spl. kindergarten class Jewish Day Nursery, Cleve., 1970-72; learning disabilities tutor Euclid (Ohio) Bd. Edn., 1976-77, East Cleveland (Ohio) Bd. Edn., 1977-79; tchr. severely behaviorally handicapped Shaker Heights (Ohio) Bd. Edn./Shaker Heights Mid. Sch., 1979—, chair dept. spl. edn. Presenter workshops. Rep. tchr., mentor Tchrs. Assn. Named Spl. Edn. Tchr. of Month, Cuyahoga Spl. Edn. Svc. Ctr. Parent Coun., 1993. Mem. ASCD, Coun. Exceptional Children, Coun. Children with Behavioral Disorders, Assn. Children with Learning Disabilities. Office: Shaker Heights Mid Sch 20600 Shaker Blvd Shaker Heights OH 44122-2698

LICHTWARD, FRED, headmaster; b. St. Paul, Apr. 27, 1950; s. Fred Whitmore and Violet (Hunter) L.; m. Deborah Ann Schultz, Jan. 13, 1973; 1 child, Fred. BS, Mercy Coll., Dobbs Ferry, N.Y., 1973; MA, U. North Fla., Jacksonville, 1974; EdS, U. Fla., 1979; EdD, U. Sarasota, 1981. Cert. in spl. edn., elem. edn., ednl. adminstrn., Fla. Tchr. Nassau County Schs., Fernandina Beach, Fla., 1974-79; headmaster St. Andrew's Episc. Sch., Jacksonville, 1979-82, Assumption Sch., Jacksonville, 1982-87; exec. dir. Hope Haven Children's Clinic, Jacksonville, 1987-90; headmaster Arlington Country Day Sch., Jacksonville, 1990—. Author ednl. games Games for Remediation, 1975; contbr. articles to ednl. jours. Bd. dirs. YMCA, Jacksonville, 1984-86; pres., bd. dirs., umpire Assumption Athletic Assn., Jacksonville, 1988-90; bd. dirs. Southside Youth Athletic Assn., Jacksonville, 1984-87, Arlington Child Devel. Ctr., Jacksonville, 1990-92; vol. coach YMCA, Arlington, 1984—. Named Tchr. of Yr., West Jacksonville Jaycees, 1974, Vol. of Yr., YMCA, Jacksonville, 1984; U. North Fla. grad. fellow, 1973. Avocations: reading, walking, tutoring. Office: Arlington County Day Sch 5725 Fort Caroline Rd Jacksonville FL 32277-1799

LICK, DALE WESLEY, educational leadership educator; b. Marlette, Mich., Jan. 7, 1938; s. John R. and Florence M. (Baxter) L.; m. Marilyn Kay Foster, Sept. 15, 1956; children: Lynette (dec.), Kitty (dec.), Diana, Ronald. BS with honors, Mich. State U., 1958, MS in Math, 1959; PhD in Math, U. Calif., Riverside, 1965. Research asst. physics Mich. State U., East Lansing, 1958, teaching asst. math., 1959; instr., chmn. dept. math. Port Huron (Mich.) Jr. Coll., 1959-60; asst. to comptroller Mich. Bell Telephone Co., Detroit, 1961; instr. U. Redlands, 1961-63; teaching asst. math. U. Calif., Riverside, 1964-65; asst. prof. math. U. Tenn., Knoxville, 1965-67; postdoctoral fellow Brookhaven Nat. Lab., Upton, N.Y., 1967-68; assoc. prof. U. Tenn., 1968-69; assoc. prof., head dept. math. Drexel U., Phila., 1969-72; adj. assoc. prof. dept. pharmacology Med. Sch., Temple U., Phila., 1969-72; v.p. acad. affairs Russell Sage Coll., Troy, N.Y., 1972-74; prof. math. and computing scis. Old Dominion U., Norfolk, Va., 1974-78; also dean Old Dominion U. (Sch. Scis. and Health Professions); pres., prof. math. and computer sci. Ga. So. Coll., Statesboro, 1978-86; pres., prof. math. U. Maine, Orono, 1986-91, Fla. State U., Tallahassee, 1991-93, univ. prof. Learning Sys. Inst. and Dept. Edn. Leadership, 1993—. Cert. in tng. and cons., mng. orgnl. change. Author: Fundamentals of Algebra, 1970, (with C. Murphy) Whole-Faculty Study Groups: A Powerful Way to Change Schools and Enhance Learning, 1998, (with C. Mullen) New Directions in Mentoring: Creating a Culture of Synergy, 1999, (with C. Murphy) Whole-Faculty Study Groups: Creating Student-Based Professional Development, 2001; contbr. articles to profl. jours. Bd. dirs. Statesboro/Coll. Symphony, 1978-86, Statewide Health Coordinating Coun. Va., 1976-78, United Way of the Big Bend, 1992-98; chmn. higher edn. adv. bd. Cmty. of Christ, 1986—; mem. planning com. Bulloch Meml. Hosp., 1979-86; active Coastal Empire coun. Boy Scouts Am., 1982-86, Katalidin coun., 1986-91; bd. dirs. Health Care Ctrs. Am., Virginia Beach, Va., 1978, Ea. Va. Health Systems Agy., 1976-78; chmn., bd. dirs. Assembly Against Hunger and Malnutrition, 1977-78, pres., 1977-78; mem., high priest Cmty. of Christ. Mem. AAUP, AAAS, Am. Math. Soc., Math. Assn. Am., Am. Assn. Univ. Adminstrs., Am. Soc. Allied Health Professions, Am. Assn. State Colls. and Univs. (chmn. com. agr. resources and rural devel. 1981-86), Am. Assn. Higher Edn., Sigma Xi, Phi Kappa Phi, Pi Mu Epsilon (governing coun. 1972-77), Beta Gamma Sigma, Pi Sigma Epsilon. Office: Fla State U Learning Systems Inst C-4600 University Ctr Tallahassee FL 32306-2540 E-mail: dlick@lsi.fsu.edu., dlick@mailer.fsu.edu.

LIDTKE, VERNON LEROY, history educator; b. Avon, S.D., May 4, 1930; s. Albert William and Aganeta (Boese) Lidtke; m. Doris Eileen Keefe, Apr. 21, 1951. BA, U. Oreg., 1952, MA, 1955; PhD, U. Calif., Berkeley, 1962. Tchr. high sch., Riddle, Oreg., 1953-55; instr. social sci. U. Calif., Berkeley, 1960-62; asst. prof. history Mich. State U., 1962-66, asso. prof., 1966-68; vis. asst. prof. U. Calif., Berkeley, 1963; asso. prof. Johns Hopkins U., 1968-73, prof., 1973—2001, chmn. dept. history, 1975-79, prof. emeritus, 2001—; pres. Friends of the German Historical Inst., Washington, 1991-94. Author: (book) The Outlawed Party: Social Democracy in Germany, 1878-1890, 1966, The Alternative Culture: Socialist Labor in Imperial Germany, 1985; mem ed bd: Jour Modern Hist, 1973—76, Cent European Hist, 1982—89, Int Labor and Working Class Hist, 1984—89; contbr. articles to profl jours. Fellow Fulbright Research, 1959—60, 1966—67, Nat Endowment Humanities, 1969—70, Davis Ctr Hist Studies, Princeton Univ, 1974—75, Wissenschaftskolleg zu Berlin, 1987—88, Max-Planck-Institut für Geschichte, Göttingen, 1996. Mem.: AAUP, Conf Group German Polit (officer 1975—83), Conf Group Cen European Hist (vpres 1985, pres 1986), Col Art Asn, Am Hist Asn (chair modern European sect 1992, Eugene Asher Distinguished Teaching Award 1999), Johns Hopkins Club. Home: 4806 Wilmslow Rd Baltimore MD 21210-2328 Office: Johns Hopkins U Dept History Baltimore MD 21218 Business E-Mail: Lidtke@jhu@edu.

LIEB, ELLIOTT HERSHEL, physicist, mathematician, educator; b. Boston, July 31, 1932; s. Sinclair M. and Clara (Rosenstein) L.; m. Christiane Fellbaum; children: Alexander, Gregory. BSc, MIT, 1953; PhD, U. Birmingham, Eng., 1956; DSc (hon.), U. Copenhagen, 1979; Dr. (hon.), Ecole Poly. Fed. Lausanne, Switzerland, 1995. With IBM Corp., 1960-63; sr. lectr. Fourah Bay Coll., Sierra Leone, 1961; mem. faculty Yeshiva U., 1963-66, Northeastern U., 1966-68, MIT, Cambridge, 1968-75, prof. physics, 1963-68, prof. math., 1968-73, prof. math. and physics, 1973—, Princeton (N.J.) U., 1975—. Author: (with D.C. Mattis) Mathematical Physics in One Dimension, 1966, (with B. Simon and A. Wightman) Studies in Mathematical Physics, (with M. Loss) Analysis; also articles. Recipient Boris Pregel award chem. physics N.Y. Acad. Scis., 1970, Dannie Heineman prize for mathematical physics Am. Inst. Physics and Am. Phys. Soc., 1978, Prix Scientifique, Union des Assurances de Paris, 1985, Birkhoff prize Am. Math. Soc. and Soc. Indsl. Applied Math., 1988, Max-Planck medal German Phys. Soc., 1992, Boltzmann medal Internat. Union of Pure and Applied Physics, 1998, Onsager medal Norwegian U. Sci. and Tech., 1998, Rolf Schock prize in math. Swedish Acad. Scis., 2001, Levi L. Conant prize of Am. Math. Soc., 2002; Guggenheim Found. fellow, 1972, 78. Fellow AAAS, Am. Phys. Soc.; mem. NAS, Austrian Acad. Scis., Danish Royal Acad., Am. Acad. Arts and Scis., Internat. Assn. Math. Physics (pres. 1982-84, 97-99). Office: Princeton U Jadwin Hall-Physics Dept PO Box 708 Princeton NJ 08544-0001

LIEBER, ROBERT JAMES, political science educator, writer; b. Chgo. m. Nancy Lieber; 2 children. BA in Polit. Sci. with high honors, U. Wis., 1963; postgrad. in Polit. Sci., U. Chgo., 1963-64; PhD in Govt., Harvard U., 1968. Asst. prof. Polit. Sci. U. Calif., Davis, 1968-72, assoc. prof., 1972-77, chmn. dept. Polit. Sci., 1975-76, 77-80, prof., 1977-81; postdoctoral rschr. St. Antony's Coll. Oxford (Eng.) U., 1969-70; prof. Georgetown U., Washington, 1982—, chmn. dept. govt., 1990-96, acting chmn. dept. psychology, 1997-99. Vis. prof. Oxford U., 1969, Fudan U., Shanghai, 1988; rsch. assoc. Ctr. Internat. Affairs, Harvard U., 1974-75; cons. U.S. Dept. State and Dept. Def., 1975—. Author: British Politics and European Unity, 1970, Theory and World Politics, 1972, Oil and the Middle East War: Europe in the Energy Crisis, 1976, The Oil Decade: Conflict and Cooperation in the West, 1983, No Common Power: Understanding International Relations, 1988, 4th edit., 2001; co-author: Contemporary Politics: Europe, 1976; editor, contbg. author: Eagle Adrift: American Foreign Policy at the End of the Century, 1997, Eagle Rules? Foreign Policy and American Primacy in the 21st Century, 2002; co-editor, contbg. author: Eagle Entangled: U.S. Foreign Policy in a Complex World, 1979, Eagle Defiant: U.S. Foreign Policy in the 1980s, 1983, Eagle Resurgent? The Reagan Era in American Foreign Policy, 1987, Eagle in a New World: American Grand Strategy in the Post-Cold War Era, 1992; editor: Will Europe Fight for Oil?, 1983; contbr. articles to Harper's Commentary, Politique étrangère, N.Y. Times, Washington Post, Christian Sci. Monitor, L.A. Times, others, and profl. jours. Advanceman nat. campaign staff McCarthy for Pres., 1968; fgn. policy advising presdl. campaigns of Sen. Edward Kennedy, 1979-80, Walter Mondale. 1984, Bill Clinton, 1991-92; coord. Mid. East Issues presdl. campaign Michael Dukakis, 1988. Woodrow Wilson fellow, 1963, fellow NDEA, 1963-64, grad. prize fellow Harvard U., 1964-68, Social Sci. Rsch. Coun., 1969-70, Coun. Fgn. Rels., 1972-73, Guggenheim fellow, 1973-74, Rockefeller Found., 1978-79, Wilson Ctr. Smithsonian Inst., 1980-81, 99-00, Ford Found., 1981; vis. fellow Atlantic Inst. Internat. Affairs, Paris, 1978-79; guest scholar Brookings Inst., 1981. Mem. Coun. on Fgn. Rels., Internat. Inst. for Strategic Studies, Phi Beta Kappa. Office: Georgetown U Dept Of Government Washington DC 20057-1034 E-mail: lieberr@georgetown.edu.

LIEBERMAN, FREDRIC, ethnomusicologist, educator, composer; b. N.Y.C., Mar. 1, 1940; s. Stanley and Bryna Lieberman. MusB, U. Rochester, 1962; MA in Ethnomusicology, U. Hawaii, 1965; PhD in Music, UCLA, 1977; diploma in Electronics, Cleve. Inst. Electronics, 1973; cert. Inst. for Ednl. Mgmt., Harvard U., 1984. Asst. prof. music Brown U., 1968—75; assoc. prof. U. Wash., Seattle, 1975-83, chmn. dept. ethnomusicology, 1977—80, dir. sch. music, 1981-83; prof. U. Calif., Santa Cruz, 1983—, dir. divsn. arts, 1983-85, provost Porter Coll., 1983-85, chmn. dept. music, 1988-92; expert witness and forensic musicology cons. Virgin Records and others, 1991—. Fieldworker, Taiwan and Japan, 1963-64, Sikkim, winter 1970, Madras, India, winters 1977, 78, 82, 83; mem. folk arts panel Nat. Endowment for Arts, 1977-80, internat. panel, 1979-80; panelist basic rsch. divsn. NEH, 1982-84, Calif. Arts Coun., 1993, Mass. Cultural Coun., 1995; fieldworker, presenter Smithsonian Instn. Festival Am. Folklife, 1978-82; reviewer Ctr. for Scholarly Comm. with China, 1979-91; exch. lectr. U. Warsaw, Poland, spring 1980; co-dir. summer seminar for coll. tchrs. NEH, 1977; dir. Am. Mus. Heritage Found., 1991-96. Author: Chinese Music: An Annotated Bibliography, 1970, 2d edit., 1979, A Chinese Zither Tutor: The Mei-An Ch-in-P'u, 1983, (with Mickey Hart) Drumming at the Edge of Magic, 1990, Planet Drum: A Celebration of Percussion and Rhythm, 1991, (with Leta Miller) Lou Harrison: Composing a World, 1998, (with Mickey Hart) Spirit into Sound: The Magic of Music, 1999; editor: (with Fritz Kuttner) Perspectives on Asian Music: Essays in Honor of Lawrence Picken, 1975; gen. editor Garland Bibliographies in Ethnomusicology, 1980-86; mem. editl. bd. Musica Asiatica, 1984—; contbr. numerous articles and revs. to profl. publs.; composer: Suite for Piano, 1964, Sonatina for Piano, 1964, Two Short String Quartets, 1966, Leaves of Brass (for brass quartet), 1967, Psalm 136: By the Rivers of Babylon (for chorus), 1971; records include China I: String Instruments, 1969, China II: Amoy Music, 1971, Music of Sikkim, 1975; ethnomusicology cons. 360 Degrees Prodns., 1988—; filmer, editor (with Michael Moore) Traditional Music and Dance of Sikkim, Parts I and II, 1976; prodr., dir., editor videotape Documenting Traditional Performance, 1978, South Indian Classical Music House Concert, 1994, At Home with Master Musician T.N. Krishnan, 2000. Mem. exec. bd. Pub. Radio Sta. KRAB-FM, Seattle, 1977-78; mem. King County Arts Commn., Seattle, 1977-80; bd. dirs. Young People's Symphony Orch., 1997—2000. Grantee Nat. Endowment for the Arts, 1978, NEH, 1978, 80, 95-97, N.Y. State Regents fellow, 1958-62, East-West Ctr. fellow and travel grantee, 1962-65, UCLA Chancellor's tchg. fellow, 1965-69, John D. Rockefeller 3d Fund rsch. fellow, 1970-71. Mem. NARAS, Soc. for Ethnomusicology (editor Ethnomusicology 1977-81, nat. coun. 1970-72, 74-76, 78-81, 83-86, 2003-05), Soc. for Asian Music (editorial bd. Asian Music 1968-77, editor publs. series 1968-83), Assn. Rsch. Chinese Music (mem. adv. bd. 1987—), Coll. Music Soc. (nat. coun. 1973-75, exec. bd. 1974-75, 76-77), Conf. on Chinese Oral and Performing Lit. (exec. bd. 1971-74, 78-80), ASCAP, Internat. Coun. Traditional Music, Phi Mu Alpha Sinfonia. Avocations: amateur radio n7ax, photography. Office: U Calif Dept Music Santa Cruz CA 95064 E-mail: gagaku@ucsc.edu.

LIEBERMAN, JANET ELAINE, academic administrator; b. N.Y.C., Oct. 21, 1921; d. Samuel and Ida (Schubert) Rubensohn; m. Allen L. Chase, July 9, 1940 (div. 1954); children: Gary Andrew, Randolph H.; m. Jerrold S. Lieberman, June 30, 1957. Student, Vassar Coll., 1939-40; BA, Barnard Coll., N.Y.C., 1943; MA, City Coll., N.Y.C., 1946; PhD, NYU, N.Y.C., 1965. Asst. prof. Hunter Coll., N.Y.C., 1965-70; prof. LaGuardia C.C., Long Island City, N.Y., 1970-72, asst. dean faculty, 1972-74, prof. psychology, 1974-86, asst. to pres., 1986—. Recipient Innovation in Higher Edn. award Charles A. Dana Found., N.Y.C., 1989, Break the Mold award U.S. Dept. Edn., Washington, 1992, LaGuardia medal of honor, 2002, Disting. Alumni award NYU, 2003. Mem. Am. Assn. Higher Edn. Avocation: tennis. Office: LaGuardia CC 31-10 Thomson Ave Long Island City NY 11101-3071

LIEBERMAN, JOSEPH ALOYSIUS, III, physician, educator; b. Oct. 15, 1938; s. Joseph Aloysius and Marie Catherine (McDermott) Lieberman; m. Judith Ann Dees, July 23, 1966; children: Lila, Lucy, Joseph Lieberman IV, Karl. BS, Georgetown U., 1960; MD, Jefferson Med. Coll., Phila., 1964; MA in Pub. Health, Rutgers U., 1989. Family physician Sr/Jr Partnership, Allentown, 1967—68; pvt. practice Allentown, 1968—71; sr. ptnr. West End Med. Group, Allentown, 1971—77; faculty mem. Robert Wood Johnson Med. Sch., Piscataway, NJ, 1977—91; prof. family medicine Jefferson Med. Coll. Thomas Jefferson U., 1991—. Prof., chmn. dept. family medicine Robert Wood Johnson Med. Sch., Piscataway, 1982—91; chmn. dept. family and cmty. medicine Christiana Care Health Sys., 1991—2001. Contbr. Capt. USAF, 1965—67. Recipient Exceptional Merit award, U. Medicine and Dentistry of N.J., 1979—82; fellow Health Policy fellow, Inst. Medicine NAS, 1988—89. Republican. Roman Catholic. Office: Med Soc Delaware Ste 405 131 Continental Dr Newark DE 19713-1668 E-mail: jlieberman@jalmd.com.

LIEBERMAN, MORRIS BARUCH, psychologist, educator, researcher; b. Warsaw, Nov. 8, 1925; came to U.S., 1959, naturalized, 1964; s. Aaron and Pearl D. (Orlinsky) L.; m. Bilha Reichberg, Jan. 26, 1948; children: Aaron, Shiloh I., Pearl T. Student, London U., 1943-44; diploma Indsl. Psych. and Bus. Adminstrn., I.C.S.U.S., 1961; RN, Geha Hosp., Pardes Katz, Israel, 1947; cert. pharmacology, Bklyn. Coll. Pharmacy, 1960; MS in Indsl./Sch. Psychology, L.I. U., 1965; PhD in Clin. Psychology, LIU, 1974. Diplomate Am. Acad. Behavioral Medicine, Am. Acad. Pain Mgmt., Am. Bd. Psychol. Examiners, Am. Coll. Forensic Examiners, Am. Coll. Advance Practice Psychologists; cert. Nat. Register Health Care Providers in Psychology; lic. psychologist, N.Y. Psychiat. nurse Kupat Holim, Israel, 1944-50, regional dir. Holon dist., 1952-59; pub. health educator N.Y. State Dept. Health, 1964; rschr. neuropsychol. labs. Einstein Coll. Medicine, N.Y., 1965-66; resident neurology and psychiatry dept. Kingsbrook Med. Ctr., Bklyn., 1966-68; sr. clin. psychologist, dir. neuro-psychiat. unit Bronx Psychiat. Ctr./Einstein Coll. Medicine, N.Y., 1968-72; dir. Heights Hill inpatient svcs., prin. psychologist South Beach Hosp. N.Y. State, SUNY, 1975-76; coord. psychiat. divsn. Workman Cir. Med. Dept., N.Y.C., 1976-85; prof. dept. psychology L.I. Univ. and Coll. Pharmacy, N.Y., 1976—. U.S. rep. Til Israel Inst. Orgnl. and Indsl. Psychology, N.Y., 1978-85; exec. dir. Psychol. Consulting Assocs., N.Y., 1978—; sr. staff mem. Nassau Pain and Stress Ctr., N.Y., 1985-87; tng., supervising and chief psychologist Am. Inst. Creative Living, S.I., N.Y., The Sklar and Gingerbread Learning Ctrs., S.I., 1986—. Author: (with others) Pscyhological Aspects in Physical Rehab. Regional dir. Am. Mental Health Affiliation with Israel, Israel Assn. Academicians and Students in Am., MDA Israeli Ambulance Emergency Svcs., Mapleton-Midwood Cmty. Mental Health Bd., N.Y. Maj. Israeli Def. Force, 1946-48, Israeli Def. Force Reserves, 1948-59. Decorated Haganah medal War of Independence medal, Sinai campaign medal, granted by IDF (Israel Defense Force); postgrad. fellowship analytic psychotherapist N.Y. Dept. Mental Hygiene/Advanced Inst. Psychoanalytic Psychotherapy, N.Y.C., 1969-72. Fellow Am. Assn. Marriage and Family Therapy, Am. Assn. Prescribing Psychologists, Am. Orthopsychiat. Assn.; mem. APA (Amer. Psychol. Assn.), AAAS (Amer. Assn. Advancement in Sci.), Am. Soc. Group Psychotherapy and Psychodrama, Am. Assn. Sex, Counselors and Therapists, Assn. Advancement Behavior Therapy, Am. Soc. Clin. Hypnosis, N.Y. Soc. Clin. Psychologists, Amer. Assn. Marriages and Family Therapy. Achievements include developer of psychological instrumentation, scales for assessment of cognitive and perceptual functioning. Home and Office: 114 Avenue N Brooklyn NY 11230-5507 also: 146 Hilltop Rd East Otto NY 14729

LIEBMAN, JUDITH RAE STENZEL, operations research educator; b. Denver, July 2, 1936; d. Raymond Oscar and Mary Madelyn (Galloup) Stenzel; m. Jon Charles Liebman, Dec. 27, 1958; children: Christopher Brian, Rebecca Anne, Michael Jon. BA in Physics, U. Colo., Boulder, 1958;

PhD in Ops. Rsch., Johns Hopkins U., 1971. Successively asst. prof., head indsl. systems, assoc. prof. U. Ill., Urbana, 1972-84, prof., 1984-96, prof. emerita, 1996—, acting vice chancellor for rsch., 1986-87, vice chancellor for rsch., 1987-92, acting dean Grad. Coll., 1987-92, dean, 1987-92. Vis. prof. Tianjin (China) U., 1985; charter mem. Ill. Gov.'s Sci. Adv. Com., Ill. Exec. Com., 1989-92; mem. adv. com. for engring. NSF, 1988-92, chmn., 1991-92; mem. NRC Bd. Engring. Edn., 1997-2001, Army Sci. Bd., 1997-99. Author: Modeling and Optimization with GINO, 1986; author numerous articles in field. Bd. dirs. United Way, Champaign, Ill., 1986-91, U. Colo. Found., 1999-2003; bd. dirs. East Cen. Ill. Health Systems Agy., Champaign, 1977-82, pres., 1980-82. Mem. Ops. Rsch. Soc. Am. (pres. 1987-88), Nat. Assn. State Univs. and Land Grant Colls. (exec. bd. 1990-92), Rotary, Sigma Xi, Sigma Pi Sigma, Alpha Pi Mu, Phi Kappa Phi. Home: 110 W Whitehall Ct Urbana IL 61801-6664

LIEBMAN, LANCE MALCOLM, law educator, lawyer; b. Newark, Sept. 11, 1941; s. Roy and Barbara (Trilinsky) L.; m. Carol Bensinger, June 28, 1964; children: Jeffrey, Benjamin. BA, Yale U., 1962; MA, Cambridge U., 1964; LLB, Harvard U., 1967. Bar: D.C. 1968, Mass. 1976, N.Y., 1995. Asst. to Mayor Lindsay, N.Y.C., 1968-70; asst. prof. law Harvard U., 1970-76, prof., 1976-91, assoc. dean, 1981-84; dean, Lucy G. Moses prof. law Columbia U. Sch. Law, N.Y.C., 1991-96, prof., dir. Parker Sch. Fgn. Law, 1996—, Williams S. Beinecke prof. law, 1998—; dir. Am. Law Inst., 1998—. Successor trustee Yale Corp., 1971-83 Office: Columbia U Sch Law 435 W 116th St New York NY 10027-7297

LIEBSON, MILT, sculptor, educator, author; b. N.Y.C., Dec. 12, 1923; s. Ely and Gertrude (Kern) L.; m. Lila Jacobs, Mar. 5, 1944; children: Richard, Ellen Liebson Porges, Donald. BS, St. John's U., 1948; MS, L.I. U., 1960. Tchr. Mercer Community Coll., West Windsor, N.J., 1987-99, Artworks, Princeton, N.J., 1989-96. One-man shows include Gallery 100, Princeton, N.J., George B. Markle Gallery, Hazelton, Pa., Bergen Mus., Paramus, N.J., Rutgers U., New Brunswick, N.J., Baron Art Ctr., Woodbridge, N.J., Monmouth Mus., Lincroft, N.J., AT&T Corp. Gallery, Hopewell, N.J., Ellarslie Mus., Trenton, N.J., Strand Gallery, Summit, N.J., Trenton City Mus., Mus. of Artists, Moscow, Delann Gallery, Plainsboro, N.J., Golden Door Gallery, New Hope, Pa., The Sculpture Showcase, New Hope, others; represented in various permanent collections; author: Direct Stone Sculpture, 1991, Direct Stone Sculpture II, 1992, Printmaking with Clay, 1996, Direct Wood Sculpture, 2001; video: Sculpting in Stone, 1995. With U.S. Army, 1942-44. Mem. Internat. Sculpture Ctr., Trenton Artists Workshop Assn., Allied Artists of Am. (assoc. mem.), Rho Chi. Avocations: tennis, golf, music. Home and Office: 69B Picea Plz Monroe Township NJ 08831-4143 E-mail: mil-lil@worldnet.att.net.

LIEM, DARLENE MARIE, secondary education educator; b. Lorain, Ohio, June 25, 1941; d. Frederick August and Mary Jane (Derby) Kubishke; m. Frans Robert Liem; children: Dorothea Saliba, Frans Liem, Raymond Liem, Bryan Liem, Shannon Daniel. BS in Edn., Ohio State U., 1963; ME, Wright State U., 1980. Cert. secondary tchr., Ohio. Sci. tchr. Southwestern City Schs., Grove City, Ohio, 1963-66, Greeneview High Sch., Jamestown, Ohio, 1973—. Advisor Quick Recall Team, Jamestown, 1984—, NASA Student Shuttle Projects, Regional winners, 1981, 82; dir. Ramblers Drill Team, Jamestown, 1973-77; adv. TEAMS, 1991—. Contbr. articles to profl. jours. Mem. Huber Heights (Ohio) Community Chorus, 1989-90; girl scout leader Huber Heights Girl Scout Troop, 1976-78; children's choir dir., Huber Heights, 1980-84, Sunday sch. tchr., Huber Heights, 1978-83; summer camp dir. Kirkmont Presbyn. Camp, Bellefontaine, Ohio, 1978-83; ordained elder Presbyn. Ch. Named Outstanding Educator Green County Bd. Edn., 1988-89, 92, Woman of Yr. Am. Bus. Women's Assn., 1988, West Region Project Discovery Tchr.-Leader, 1992—, Tandy Tech. Hon. Mention Tchr., 1994; named to Hall of Fame, Miami Valley Sci. and Engring., 1994. Mem. Nat. Sci. Tchrs. Assn., Sci. Edn. Coun. Ohio (bd. dirs. 1981-83), Am. Assn. Physics Tchrs. (South Ohio sect.), Western Ohio Sci. Tchrs. Assn. (pres. 1981-83), Delta Kappa Gamma, Phi Delta Kappa, Kappa Delta Pi. Avocations: chorus, crafts, camping, gardening, reading. Home: 7056 Montague Rd Dayton OH 45424-3044 Office: Greeneview High Sch 53 N Limestone St Jamestown OH 45335-1599

LIENHARD, JOHN HENRY, IV, mechanical engineer, educator; b. St. Paul, Aug. 17, 1930; s. John Henry and Catherine Edith Lienhard; m. Carol Ann Bratton, June 20, 1959; children: John Henry V, Andrew Joseph. AS, Multnomah Jr. Coll., 1949; BS, Oreg. State Coll., 1951; MSME, U. Wash., 1953; PhD in Mech. Engring., U. Calif., Berkeley, 1961; DHL (hon.), U. Houston, 2002, Sacred Heart U., 2002. Assoc. prof. mech. engring. Wash. State U., Pullman, 1961-67; prof. mech. engring. dept. U. Ky., Lexington, 1967-80; prof. mech. engring. U. Houston, 1980-89, M.D. Anderson prof. mech. engring. and history, 1989—2000, prof. emeritus, 2000—. Clyde chair prof. U. Utah, Salt Lake City, 1981. Author (with C. L. Tien): Statistical Thermodynamics, 1971, 1979; author: (with J. H. Lienhard V) A Heat Transfer Textbook, 1981, 1987; author: (with E. T. Layton) History of Heat Transfer, 1988; author: The Engines of Our Ingenuity, 2000, Inventing Modern, 2003; author, host (radio) The Engines of Our Ingenuity; contbr. articles to profl. jours. Mem.: ASME (hon. Heat Transfer Meml. award, Charles Russ Richards award, Engr. Historian award 1998), Nat. Acad. Engring., Am. Soc. Engring. Edn. (Ralph Coates Roe Tchg. medal). Episcopalian. Home: 3719 Durhill St Houston TX 77025-4006 Office: U Houston Dept Mech Engring Houston TX 77204-4006 E-mail: jhl@uh.edu.

LIETZ, JEREMY JON, educational administrator, writer; b. Milw., Oct. 4, 1933; s. John Norman and Dorothy B. (Drew) L.; m. Cora Fernandez, Feb. 24, 1983; children: Cheryl, Brian, Angela, Andrew, Christopher, Jennifer. BS, U. Wis., Milw., 1961; MS, U. Wis., Madison, 1971; EdD, Marquette U., 1980. Tchr. Milw. Pub. Schs., 1961-63, diagnostic counselor, 1968-71, sch. adminstr., 1971-95, hearing panel ombudsman, 1999—, acting student svcs. coord., 1999—; tchr. Madison Pub. Sch., Wis., 1964-65; rsch. assoc. U. Wis., Madison, 1965-67; instr. Marquette U., Milw., 1980-82, Milw. U. Sch., 2000—02. Lectr. HEW Conf. on Reading, Greeley, Colo., 1973, NAESP Conf. on Reading, St. Louis, 1974, various state and nat. orgns.; co-founder, bd. dirs., cons. Ednl. Leadership Inst., Shorewood, Wis., 1980—; dir. Religious Edn. Program, Cath. Elem. East, Milw., 1985-86. Author: The Elementary School Principal's Role in Special Education, 1982; contbr. numerous articles, chpts., tests, revs. to profl. jours. V.p. PTA, 1961-62. With U.S. Army, 1954-56, ETO. Recipient Cert. of Achievement award NAESP, 1974. Mem. AAAS, Assn. Wis. Sch. Adminstrs. (mem. state planning com. 1977-79, lectr. 1982), Adminstrs. and Suprs. Coun. (mem. exec. bd. dist. 1977-79, mem. contract negotiations com. 1991-95), Filipino Am. Assn. Wis., U. Wis. Alumni Assn. (Madison), Milw. Mcpl. Chess Assn., U.S. Chess Fedn., Phi Delta Kappa. Home: 424 Susan Ln Thiensville WI 53092-1451 Office: Ednl Leadership Inst PO Box 11411 Shorewood WI 53211-0411 E-mail: dcphil@prodigy.net.

LIGGETT, TWILA MARIE CHRISTENSEN, academic administrator, public television executive; b. Pipestone, Minn., Mar. 25, 1944; d. Donald L. Christensen and Irene E. (Zweigle) Christensen Flesher. BS, Union Coll., Lincoln, Nebr., 1966; MA, U. Nebr., 1971; PhD, 1977; DHL (hon.), Marymount Manhattan Coll., 2000. Dir. vocal and instrumental music Sprague (Nebr.)-Martell Pub. Sch., 1966-67; tchr. vocal music pub. schs., Syracuse, Nebr., 1967-69; tchr. Norris Pub. Sch., Firth, Nebr., 1969-71; cons. fed. reading project pub. schs., Lincoln, Nebr., 1971-72; curriculum coord. Westside Cmty. Schs., Omaha, 1972-74; dir. state program Right-to-Read Nebr. Dept. Edn., 1974-76; asst. dir. Nebr. Commn. on Status of Women, 1976-80; asst. dir. project admisntrn./devel. Great Plains Nat. Instructional TV Libr. U. Nebr., Lincoln, 1980-97; sr. v.p. for edn. Lancit Media Ent., Ltd. a Junior Net Co., N.Y., 1998-2001. Exec. prodr. Neb. ETV Network/GPN a nat. PBS children's series Reading Rainbow, 1980—; cons. U.S. Dept. Edn., 1981; cons. Far West Regional Lab. Nebr. Edn. TV Network, San Francisco, 1978—79; panelist, presenter in field; Blue Ribbon panelist NATAS, 1991—2003; final judge Nat. Cable Ace Awards, 1991—92, 1997. Author: Reading Rainbow's Guide to Children's Books: The 101 Best Titles, 1994, rev. edit., 1996. Bd. dirs. Planned Parenthood, Lincoln, 1979-81. Recipient Grand award, N.Y., 1993, Gold medal, Internat. Film and TV Festival, 1996, 1999, World Gold medal, N.Y. Internat. Film and TV, 1995, Golden Eagle award, Coun. on Non-theatrical Events, 1995, Image award, NAACP, 1994, 1996, 1999, 2002, 20 Nat. Emmy awards, 8 for Outstanding Children's Series, 1985—2003. Mem. NATAS, Internat. Reading Assn. (panelist, presenter, Spl. award Contbns. Worldwide Literacy 1992), Am. Women in Film and TV, Phi Delta Kappa. Presbyterian. Home: 37 Crescent Pl Matawan NJ 07747 E-mail: Rrainbow1@aol.com.

LIGGIO, JEAN VINCENZA, adult education educator, artist; b. NYC, Nov. 5, 1927; d. Vincenzo and Bernada (Terrusa) Verro; m. John Liggio, June 6, 1948; children: Jean Constance, Joan Bernadette. Student, N.Y. Inst. Photography, 1965, Elizabeth Seton Coll., 1984, Parsons Sch. of Design, 1985. Hairdresser Beauty Shoppe, N.Y.C., 1947-65; instr. watercolor N.Y. Dept. Pks., Recreation and Conservation, Yonkers, 1985-89, Bronxville (N.Y.) Adult Sch., 1989—. Substitute tchr. cosmetology Yonkers Bd. Edn., 1988-89; tchr. watercolor painting J.V.L. Watercolor Workshop of Fine Arts, Jakes Art Ctr., Mt. Vernon, N.Y. Paintings pub. by Donald Art Co., C.R. Gibson Greeting Card Co., Enesco Corp., 1996; paintings for Avon Calendar, Avon Cosmetics Co., 1994, 96, Avon-Can. Publ., 1996-97; greeting cards published by C.R. Gibson Co. Publ., 1996-1997, boxed notecards by C.R. Gibson; painting on cover of C.R. Gibson Jour., 2000, C.R. Gibson Inspirational Jour.; pub. Friends Jour. Mag., Phila. Mem. Mt. Vernon Art Assn. (pres. membership com. 1983—, 215 awards), Scarsdale Art Assn. (publicity chmn. 1984-89, 215 awards), New Rochelle Art Assn., Hudson Valley Art Assn., Art Soc. Old Greenwich. Avocation: antiques. Home and Office: 166 Helena Ave Yonkers NY 10710-2524

LIGHTELL, KENNETH RAY, education educator; b. Oak Park, Ill., Nov. 13, 1944; s. Ray and Mildred (Miller) L.; m. Charlotte Hawkins, Aug. 3, 1989. BA, North Ctrl. Coll., Naperville, Ill., 1966; grad. studies in edn., U. Mo., 1969; grad. studies in computers, Depaul U., 1983; MLA, Houston Bapt. U., 1995. Tchr., coach Roycemore Sch., Evanston, Ill., 1966-68; dir. middle sch. Bklyn. Friends Sch., 1969-81; dir. Olympia (Wash.) Ind. Sch., 1982-83; tchr., coach The Lexington (Ky.) Sch., 1984-88; prin. Charles Wright Acad., Tacoma, 1988-89; dir. of mid. sch. John Cooper Sch., Woodlands, Tex., 1989-92; headmaster St. James Episcopal Sch., Houston, 1993-94, The McClelland Sch., Pueblo, Colo., 1995—. Owner, dir. Washinee Woods Camp, Taconic, Conn., 1975-81, Wilderness Adventures, Bklyn., 1970-75; pres., CEO S.L.K. Inc., N.Y.C., 1975-83. Editor: N.C.C. Spectrum, 1966; dir. Festival of the Arts, 1986. Pres. NCC Young Rep., Naperville, Ill., 1964-65; trustee Assn. Colo. Ind. Schs., Pueblo Day Nursery Found. Mem. B.P.O.E. Elks, Nat. Mid. Sch. Assn., Alpha Sigma Lambda. Avocations: sailing, wooden boat building, photography, travel. Home: 415 S Pin High Dr Pueblo CO 81007-6036

LIGHTMAN, ALAN PAIGE, writer, physicist, educator; b. Memphis, Nov. 28, 1948; s. Richard Louis and Jeanne (Garretson) L.; m. Jean Greenblatt, Nov. 28, 1976; children: Elyse, Kara. AB, Princeton U., 1970; PhD in Physics, Calif. Inst. Tech., 1974. Postdoctoral fellow Cornell U., Ithaca, N.Y., 1974-76; asst. prof. Harvard U., Cambridge, Mass., 1976-79; staff scientist Smithsonian Astrophys. Obs., Cambridge, 1979-88; prof. sci. and writing MIT, Cambridge, 1988-95, John E. Burchard prof. humanities, 1995—2001, adj. prof. humanities, 2001—. Chair sci. panel NRC Astron. and Astrophys. Survey for 1990's. Author: Problem Book in Relativity and Gravitation, 1974, Radiative Processes in Astrophysics, 1976, Time Travel and Papa Joe's Pipe, 1984, A Modern Day Yankee in Connecticut Court, 1986, Origins: The Lives and Worlds of Modern Cosmologists, 1990, Ancient Light, 1991, Great Ideas in Physics, 1992, Time for the Stars, 1992, Einstein's Dreams, 1993, Good Benito, 1995, Dance for Two, 1996, The Diagnosis, 2000, Reunion, 2003. Recipient Most Outstanding Book in Phys. Sci., Assn. Am. Pubs., 1990 (Origins); Runner up PEN New England/Boston Globe Book Award, 1993 (Einstein's Dreams); Lit. Light of Boston Pub. Libr., 1995; Gemant award Am. Inst. of Physics, 1996, Gyorgy Kepes prize in the arts, MIT, 1998; Finalist Nat. Book Award in Fiction, 2000 (The Diagnosis); Disting. Alumnus Award Calif. Inst. Tech., 2003. Fellow AAAS, Am. Acad. Arts and Scis., Am. Phys. Soc.; mem. Am. Astron. Soc. (chmn. high energy astrophysics divsn. 1991).

LIGHTNER, PATRICIA PAYNE, elementary education educator; b. Danville, Va., May 8, 1953; d. William Harvey and Viola Agnes (Tenney) Payne; m. John Steven Rotz, May 31, 1975 (div. June 1990); children: Jason Andrew Rotz, Cory Adair Rotz; m. Bruce Wayne Lightner, Apr. 12, 1991. BA in Elem. Edn., Va. Poly. Inst. and State U., 1975; MS in Libr. Sci., Shippensburg U., 1992. Cert. K-8, Va. Tchr. 4th grade Caroline County, Bowling Green, Va., 1975-76; tchr. 7th grade English Clarke County, Berryville, Va., 1976-77, tchr. 5th and 6th grade, 1977-79; tchr. 3d grade Frederick County, Winchester, Va., 1986—2000, tchr. 8th grade, 2000—. Mem. Va. Edn. Assn. (pres. dist. 21), Frederick County Edn. Assn. (pres. 1992-94), Phi Delta Kappa. Methodist. Avocations: reading, crafts. Home: 271 Deer Creek Rd Winchester VA 22602-1648 Office: James Wood Mid Sch 1616 Amherst St Winchester VA 22601

LIKENS, JAMES DEAN, economics educator; b. Bakersfield, Calif., Sept. 12, 1937; s. Ernest LeRoy and Monnie Jewel (Thomas) L.; m. Janet Sue Pelton, Dec. 18, 1965 (div.); m. Karel Carnohan, June 4, 1988 (div.); children: John David, Janet Elizabeth; m. Christine Irons, Feb. 8, 2003. BA in Econs., U. Calif., Berkeley, 1960, MBA, 1961; PhD in Econs., U. Minn., 1970. Analyst Del Monte Corp., San Francisco, 1963; economist 3M Co., Mpls., 1968-71; asst. prof. econs. Pomona Coll., 1969-75, assoc. prof. econs., 1975-83, prof. econs., 1983-85, Morris B. and Gladys S. Pendleton prof. econs., 1989—, dept. chair, 1998-2001. Vis. asst. prof. econs. U. Minn., 1970, 71, vis. assoc. prof., 1976-77; pres., dean Western CUNA Mgmt. Sch., Pomona Coll., 1975—; chmn. bd. 1st City Savs. Fed. Credit Union, 1978—; coord. So. Calif. Rsch. Coun., LA, 1980-81, 84-85; adv. coun. Western Corp. Fed. Credit Union, 1993—; cons. in field. Author: (with Joseph LaDou) Medicine and Money, 1976, Mexico and Southern California: Toward A New Partnership, 1981, Financing Quality Education in Southern California, 1985; contbr. articles to profl. jours. Served with USCG, 1961-67. Named Dir. of Yr., Calif. Credit UnionLeague, 1997, Credit Union Exec. Soc., 2001; recipient Leo H. Shapiro Lifetime Achievement award, Calif. Credit Union League, 2001; grantee rsch. grantee HUD-DOT, Haynes Found. Mem.: ABA, Western Econ. Assn., Am. Econ. Assn. Home: 725 W 10th St Claremont CA 91711-3719 Office: Pomona Coll Dept Econs Claremont CA 91711 E-mail: jlikens@pomona.edu.

LIKINS, PETER WILLIAM, university administrator; b. Tracy, Calif, July 4, 1936; s. Ennis Blaine and Dorothy Louise (Medlin) L.; m. Patricia Ruth Kitsmiller, Dec. 18, 1955; children: Teresa, Lora, Paul, Linda, Krista. BCE, Stanford U., 1957, PhD in Engring. Mechanics, 1965; MCE, MIT, 1958; PhD (hon.), Lafayette Coll., 1983, Moravian Coll., 1984, Med. Coll. Pa., 1990, Lehigh U., 1991, Allentown St. Francis de Sales, 1993, Czech Tech U., 1993. Devel. engr. Jet Propulsion Lab., Pasadena, Calif., 1958-60; asst. prof. engring. UCLA, 1964-69, assoc. prof., 1969-72, prof., 1972-76, asst. dean, 1974-75, assoc. dean, 1975-76; dean engring. and applied sci. Columbia U., N.Y.C., 1976-80, provost, 1980-82; pres. Lehigh U., Bethlehem, Pa., 1982-97, U. Ariz., Tucson, 1997—. Cons. in field. Author: Elements of Engineering Mechanics, 1973, Spacecraft Dynamics, 1982; Contbr. articles to profl. jours. Mem. US Pres.'s Coun. Advisors Sci. and Tech., 1990-93. Ford Found. fellow, 1970-72; named to Nat. Wrestling Hall of Fame Fellow AIAA; mem. Nat. Acad. Engring., Phi Beta Kappa, Sigma Xi, Tau Beta Pi. Office: U Ariz PO Box 210066 Tucson AZ 85721-0066 E-mail: plikins@arizona.edu.

LILIEN, ELLIOT STEPHEN, secondary education educator; b. Maplewood, N.J. s. Bernard Banner and Judith Batson (Mulally) L.; m. Louise Anne Hoehl, Jan. 29, 1965 (div. July 1968); m. Nancy Goddard Pierce, July 21, 1985. BA, U. Chgo., 1961; JD, Columbia U., 1964; MAT, Harvard U., 1965. Tchr. Concord (Mass.)-Carlisle H.S., 1965—, head coach fencing, 1965-85, head coach tennis, 1989—; curriculum coord. social studies K-12 Concord-Carlisle Schs., 1997. Head coach fencing Brown U., Providence, 1987-93; dir. Concord-Acad. Fencing Camp, 1975—; fencing coach Harvard U., 2000—. Author: German History 1815-1945, 1972, History of Greece and Rome, 1979, Competition Experiment, 1986. Commr. Northeast Fencing Conf., Boxboro, Mass., 1993—. Grantee Coun. for Basic Edn., 1983; elected to Concord-Carlisle Athetic Hall of Fame, 1996. Mem. Four Sch. Consortium (founder, pres. 1987), Concord-Carlisle Tchrs. (pres. 1972-94). Avocations: tennis, wwi poster collecting, swords, beer steins, autographs. Home: 62 Chester Rd Boxboro MA 01719-1808 Office: Concord-Carlisle H S 500 Walden St Concord MA 01742-3699

LILJESTRAND, HOWARD MICHAEL, environmental engineering educator; b. Houston, July 29, 1953; s. Walter Emmanuel and Frances Newland (Lane) L.; m. Blinda Eve McClelland, Aug. 19, 1986; children: Emily Morgan, Frasier Lane. BA, Rice U., 1974; PhD, Calif. Inst. Tech., 1980. Registered profl. engr., Tex. Asst. prof. civil engring. Calif. State U., L.A., 1979-80, U. Tex., Austin, 1980-85, assoc. prof., 1985-92, prof., 1992—. Reviewer U.S. Nat. Acid Precepitation Assessment Program, 1983-90; mem. adv. bd. Alta. (Can.) Acid Deposition Rsch. Program, Calgary, 1987-88. Contbr. articles to Jour. Environ. Sci. and Tech., Atmospheric Environ., Water Sci. and Tech. Mem. ASCE, Am. Chem. Soc., Sigma Xi, Tau Beta Pi. Achievements include initial documented existence of acid rain in the western U.S., importance of nitric acid in acid rain in the west, and importance of dry deposition of acids in the west. Office: U Tex Civil Engring 1 Univ Sta C 1786 Austin TX 78712

LILLEGRAVEN, JASON ARTHUR, paleontologist, educator; b. Mankato, Minn., Oct. 11, 1938; s. Arthur Oscar and Agnes Mae (Eaton) L.; m. Bernice Ann Hines, Sept. 5, 1964 (div. Feb. 1983); children: Brita Anna, Ture Andrew; m. Linda Elizabeth Thompson, June 5, 1983. BA, Long Beach State Coll., 1962; MS, S.D. Sch. Mines and Tech., 1964; PhD, U. Kans., 1968. Professional geologist, Wyo. Postdoctoral fellow Dept. Paleontology U. Calif., Berkeley, 1968-69; from asst. prof. to prof. zoology San Diego State U., 1969-75; from assoc. prof. to prof. geology and zoology U. Wyo., Laramie, 1975—. Program dir. NSF Systematic Biology, Washington, 1977-78; assoc. dean U. Wyo. Coll. Arts and Scis., 1984-85, temporary joint appointment Dept. Geography, 1986-87; U.S. sr. scientist Inst. for Paleontology Free U., Berlin, 1988-89; mem. adv. panel geology and paleontology program NSF, 1997-2000. Author, editor: Mesozoic Mammals the First Two Thirds of Mammalian History, 1979, Vertebrates, Phylogeny and Philosophy, 1986; mem. editl. bds. of Research and Exploration (Nat. Geographic Soc.), Jour. of Mammalian Evolution, Jour. of Vertebrate Paleontology, Cretaceous Rsch., Palaios; co-editor Contbns. to Geology, Rocky Mountain Geology; contbr. articles to profl. jours. Recipient numerous rsch. grants NSF, 1970-2001, George Duke Humphrey Disting. Faculty award, Humboldt prize. Mem. Am. Soc. Mammalogists, Am. Assn. Petroleum Geologists, Paleontol. Soc., Soc. Vertebrate Paleontology (pres. 1985-86), Linnean Soc. London, Soc. Mammalian Evolution, Sigma Xi. Avocations: computer graphics, outdoor activities. E-mail: bagpipe@uwyo.edu.

LILLEHEI, KEVIN OWEN, neurosurgeon, educator; b. Mpls., July 6, 1953; m. Anne Cheryl Hofmann; 1 child, Kira Anne. BS, Cornell U., 1975; MD, U. Minn., 1975-79. Diplomate Am. Bd. Neurol. Surgery. Intern in surgery U. Mich., 1979—80, resident, 1980—85; asst. prof. surgery neurosurgery divsn. U. Colo. Health Scis. Ctr., Denver, 1985—2000, prof. neurosurgery, 2000—, chief sect. neuro-oncology, 1990—, vice chmn. dept. neurosurgery, 2001—; dir. neurosurgery intensive care unit Denver Gen. Hosp., 1986-87; chief neurosurgery Denver VA Hosp., 1987-90. Mem. AMA, Denver Med. Soc., Colo. Med. Soc., Colo. Neurosurg. Soc., Congress Neurol. Surgeons, Denver Acad. Surgery. Office: U Colo Health Scis Ctr 4200 E 9th Ave # 307C Denver CO 80262

LILLER, KAREN DESAFEY, public health educator; b. Pitts., Nov. 18, 1956; d. Thomas and Irene (Cenderelli) DeSafey; m. David Allen Liller, Aug. 30, 1980; children: Matthew Thomas Allen, Rebecca Irene Rose. BS, W.Va. U., 1978; MA, U. South Fla., 1982, EdS, 1986, PhD, 1988. Med. technologist Fla. Hosp., Altamonte Springs, 1978-81; lab. instr. Tampa (Fla.) Med. Coll., 1982-83; edn. dir. Sch. Med. Tech. Tampa Gen. Hosp., 1983-85; sci. advisor Mylan Pharms., Inc., Tampa, 1986-87; postdoctoral fellow Coll. Pub. Health, U. South Fla., Tampa, 1988-90, asst. prof., 1990-96, assoc. prof., 1996—. Contbr. articles to profl. jours. Home: 16509 Cayman Dr Tampa FL 33624-1065 Office: U South Fla Coll Pub Health 13201 Bruce B Downs Blvd Tampa FL 33612-3805 E-mail: kliller@hsc.usf.edu.

LILLEY, JOHN MARK, academic administrator, dean; b. Converse, La., Mar. 24, 1939; s. Ernest Franklin and Sibyl Arrena (Geoghagan) L.; children: Sibyl Elizabeth, Myles Durham; m. Geraldine Murphy; stepchildren: Benjamin Murphy, Jason Murphy. B in Music Edn., Baylor U., 1961, MusB, 1962, MusM, 1964; D of Musical Arts, U. So. Calif., 1971. Mem. faculty Claremont McKenna, Harvey Mudd, Pitzer and Scripps Colls., Claremont, Calif., 1966-76; asst. dean faculty Scripps Coll., 1973-76; asst. dean arts and scis. Kans. State U., Manhattan, 1976-80; provost, dean Pa. State U., Erie, 1980—2001; pres. U. Nev. Bd. dirs. Erie Conf., 1997-01, Erie Plastics Corp., 1994—; mem. N.W. Pa. Indsl. Resource Ctr., 1987-01, Forum for a common Agenda, 2001—, Econ. Devel. Auth. of W. Nev., 2001—. Condr. 1st performances Kubik, 1972, 76, Ives, 1974, (recording) Kubik, 1974. Bd. dirs., v.p. So. Calif. Choral Music Assn., L.A., 1971-76; mem. Archtl. Commn., Claremont, 1974-76; bd. dirs. Erie Philharm., 1980-86, Sta. WQLN Pub. Broadcasting of N.W. Pa., 1992-01; bd. dirs. United Way of Erie County, 1981-01, chair, 1998-99; mem. Regents Commn. on Nursing Edn., Kansas City, Kans., 1978-79; pres. Pacific S.W. Intercollegiate Choral Assn., L.A., 1969-70. NEH grantee, 1978. Mem. Am. Assn. Higher Edn., Coll. Music Soc., Am. Choral Dirs. Assn., Am. Assn. State Colls. and Univs. (vice chair confs. and profl. devel. com. 1989, 97, chair 1990, bd. dirs. 1995—, govs. tuition account program adv. bd. 1996—), Erie Club, Kahkwa Club, Rotary (bd. dirs. Manhattan club 1979-80, Erie club 1981-88), Phi Mu Alpha Sinfonia, Omicron Delta Kappa. Republican. Presbyterian. Avocation: golf. Home: 3103 Marble Ridge Ct Reno NV 89511-5383 Office: U Nev Reno Office Pres MS 001 Reno NV 89557-0061

LILLIE, MARSHALL SHERWOOD, college safety and security director, educator; b. Corry, Pa., May 23, 1953; s. Lloyd G. and Jalean R. (Sherwood) L.; m. Anita M., Aug 16, 1975; children: Amanda M., Sarah N., Rebekah L., Reuben L. ASB, Erie Bus. Ctr., Pa., 1974; BA, Olivet Nazarene U., Kankakee, Ill., 1980; MS, Mercyhurst Coll., Erie, Pa., 1984. Cert. mcpl. police officer trainer, EMS technician. Dir., security Olivet Nazarene U., Kankakee, Ill., 1977-81; administr. asst. Mercyhurst Coll., Erie, Pa., 1981-86; dir. security Thiel Coll., Greenville, Pa., 1986—2002; owner Lillie Tng. Enterprises; sr. pastor Springboro Ch. of the Nazarene, Pa., 2001—. Chmn. Western Pa. Security Dirs., 1989-90; instr. Thiel Coll., Greenville, Pa., 1990—, Mercyhurst Coll., Erie, 1992—; defensive tactics instr. Pressure Point Control Sys., 1995—; defensive driving instr. Nat. Safety Coun.; EMT, hazardous materials technician, ARC emergency response instr. Master Sunday Sch. Supr. Ch. of Nazarene, 1991; Mayor's Adv. com., Greenville, Pa., 1990. Mem. NRA, N.E. Coll. and Univ. Security Assn. (editor The Clipboard 1993-94, bd. dirs. 1992-96), Western Pa. Coll., Security Dirs. Assn., Am. Soc. Law Enforcement Trainers, Am. Soc. Indsl. Security (chmn. Lake Erie chpt. 1990-91). Republican. Mem. Ch. of Nazarene. Office: Springboro Ch of the Nazarene 139 S Main St Springboro PA 16435 E-mail: servant@infonline.net.

LILLY, LUELLA JEAN, academic administrator; b. Newberg, Oreg., Aug. 23, 1937; d. David Hardy and Edith (Coleman) L. BS, Lewis and Clark Coll., 1959; postgrad., Portland State U., 1959-61; MS, U. Oreg., 1961; PhD, Tex. Woman's U., 1971; postgrad., various univs., 1959-72. Tchr. phys. edn. and health, dean girls Cen. Linn Jr.-Sr. High Sch., Halsey, Oreg., 1959-60; tchr. phys. edn. and health, swimming, tennis, golf coach Lake Oswego (Oreg.) High Sch., 1960-63; instr., intramural dir., coach Oreg. State U., Corvallis, 1963-64; instr., intercollegiate coach Am. River Coll., Sacramento, 1964-69; dir. women's phys. edn., athletics U. Nev., Reno, 1969-73, assoc. prof. phys. edn., 1971-76, dir. women's athletics, 1973-75, assoc. dir. athletics, 1975-76; dir. women's intercollegiate athletics U. Calif., Berkeley, 1976-97. Organizer, coach Lue's Aquatic Club, 1962-64; v.p. PAC-10 Conf., 1990-91. Author: An Overview of Body Mechanics, 1966, 3d rev. edit., 1969. Vol. instr. ARC, 1951; vol. Heart Fund and Easter Seal, 1974-76, Am. Heart Assn., 1991-95, ofcl. Spl. Olympics, 1975; mem. L.A. Citizens Olympic Com., 1984; bd. dirs. Las Trampas, 1993-98, sec. 1996-98. Recipient Mayor Anne Rudin award Nat. Girls' and Women's Sports, 1993, Lifetime Sports award Bay Area Women's Sports Found., 1994, Golden Bear award Vol. of Yr., 1995; inducted Lewis and Clark Coll. Athletic Hall of Fame, 1988; named to U. Calif. First 125 Yrs. Women of Honor, 1995 Mem. AAHPER (life), AAUW, Nat. Soc. Profs., Women's Sports Found. (awards com. 1994-2000), Nat. Assn. Coll. Women Athletic Adminstrs. (divsn. I-A women's steering com. 1991-92, Lifetime Achievement award 1999), Women's Athletic Caucus, Coun. Collegiate Women Athletics Adminstrs. (membership com. 1989-92), Western Soc. Phys. Edn. Coll. Women (membership com. 1971-74, program adv. com. 1972, exec. bd. 1972-75), Western Assn. Intercollegiate Athletics for Women (exec. bd. dirs. 1973-75, 79-82), Oreg. Girls' Swimming Coaches Assn. (pres. 1960, 63), Ctrl. Calif. Bd. Women Ofcls. (basketball chmn. 1968-69), Calif. Assn. Health, Phys. Edn. and Recreation (chmn.-elect jr. coll. sect. 1970), Nev. Bd. Women Ofcls. (chmn. bd., chmn. volleyball sect., chmn. basketball sect. 1969), No. Calif. Women's Intercollegiate Conf. (sec. 1970-71, basketball coord. 1970-71), No. Calif. Intercollegiate Athletic Conf. (volleyball coord. 1971-72), Nev. Assn. Health Phys. Edn. and Recreation (state chmn. 1974), No. Calif. Athletic Conf. (pres. 1979-82, sec. 1984-85), Soroptimists Club (bd. dirs. 1988-02, 2000-2003, v.p. 1989, 92-93, sec. 1993-95, 2001-02, 1st v.p. 1996-97, corr. sec. 1997-98, pres. 1998-2000, Women Helping Women award 1991, Women of Distinction award 2002), Phi Kappa Phi, Theta Kappa. Avocation: Held Am. records in swimming, 1950's. Home and Office: 60 Margrave Ct Walnut Creek CA 94597-2511

LIM, ALEXANDER RUFASTA, neurologist, clinical investigator, clinical neurophysiologist, educator, writer; b. Manila, Philippines, Feb. 20, 1942; s. Benito Pilar and Maria Lourdes (Cuyegkeng) Lim; m. Norma Sue Hanks, June 1, 1968; children: Jeffrey Allen, Gregory Brian, Kevin Alexander, Melissa Gail. AA, U. Santo Tomas, Manila, Philippines, 1959, MD, 1964. Intern Bon Secours Hosp., Balt., 1964-65; resident in internal medicine Scott and White Clinic Tex A&M U., Health Sci. Ctr. Coll. Medicine, Temple, Tex., 1965-67; resident in neurology Cleve. Clinic, 1967-69, chief resident in neurology, 1969-70, fellow clin. neurophysiology, 1970-71; clin. assoc. neurologist Cleve. Clinic Hosp., 1971-72; neurologist-in-chief, co-founder, co-mng. ptnr. Neurol. Clinic, Corpus Christi, Tex., 1972—; pres., CEO Neurology, P.A., Corpus Christi, 1972-92. Chief neurology dept. Meml. Med. Ctr., Corpus Christi, Tex., 1975—90, Spohn Hosp., Corpus Christi, 1974—90, Reynolds Army Hosp., Ft. Sill, Okla., 1990—91; clin. assoc. prof. Sch. Medicine U. Tex. Health Sci. Ctr., San Antonio; cons., reviewer Tex. Medicine, 1995—. Mem. editl. bd. Coastal Bend Medicine, 1988—95, NEURO Ctrl., 1999—. Active mentorship program for gifted and talented srs. South Tex. Area H.S. Lt. col. med. corps U.S. Army, 1990—91, Desert Shield/Desert Storm. Recipient Army Commendation medal, 1991, Nat. Def. medal, U.S. Army, 1991. Mem.: KC, AMA, Tex. Neurol. Soc. (sec. 1986—88, pres. 1989—90), Tex. Med. Assn. (chmn. neurology 1985—86), Am. Acad. Pain Mgmt., So. Electroencephalographic Soc., Soc. Behavioral and Cognitive Neurology, Am. Acad. Immunotherapy, Am. Clin. Neurophysiology Soc., Am. Acad. Clin. Neurophysiology, Am. Epilepsy Soc. (editl. bd. mem. Neurocentral), Am. Acad. Neurology (spkrs. bur.), Internat. Soc. Poets, Acad. Am. Poets, Internat. Platform Assn. Republican. Roman Catholic. Avocations: tennis, philately, travel, skiing, bonsai. Home: 4821 Augusta Cir Corpus Christi TX 78413-2711 Office: The Neurological Clinic Christus Spohn Med Plaza 1415 3d St Ste 101 Corpus Christi TX 78404-2175 E-mail: anlim8@hotmail.com., alim@neurological_clinic.neurohub.net.

LIM, JEANETTE J. federal agency administrator; b. July 23, 1940; BS in chem., U. Mich., 1962; M in med. genetics, U. Wis. Med. Sch., 1965; JD, Temple U. Law Sch., 1978. Dep. asst. sec. US Dept Edn., Mgmt. and operations, Wash., 2002—; atty. US Dept. Edn., Off. Civil Rights, Wash., acting asst. sec, 1992—93, 2000—01; spec. asst. to pres. Wes Chester State U., Pa., 1976—79; med. geneticist; rschr. and bench scientist. Office: US Dept Edn Mgmt and Operations 400 Maryland Ave SW FOB-6 Rm 3W314 Washington DC 20202 E-mail: jeanette.lim@ed.gov.*

LIM, LARRY KAY, university official; b. Santa Maria, Calif., July 4, 1948; s. Koonwah and Nancy (Yao) L.; m. Louise A. Simon, Aug. 15, l988. BA, UCLA, l970, teaching cert., l97l. Asst. engr. Force Ltd., L.A., 1969; tchg. asst. UCLA, l970-7l; tchr. L.A. Sch. Dist., l97l-82; dir. pre-coll. programs Sch. Engring., U. So. Calif., L.A., 1979—. Presenter minority math.-based intervention symposium U. D.C., Washington, l988; presenter NEMEPA/WEPAN nat. conf., l997, ASEE conf., 2003. Newsletter editor, l98l-92. Bd. dirs. Developing Ednl. Studies for Hispanics, L.A., 1983-88. Named Dir. of Yr., Math., Engring., Sci. Achievement Ctr. Adv. Bd., 1986, 91, 92. Fellow Inst. Advancement Engring. (educator award); mem. Nat. Assn. Pre-Coll. Dirs., Nat. Assn. Minority Engring. Program Adminstr., Lotus/West Club (pres. l98l-92). Avocation: automobile racing. Office: U So Calif Sch Engring Ohe 104 Los Angeles CA 90089-0001

LIM, RAMON (KHE-SIONG LIM), neuroscience educator, researcher; b. Cebu City, The Philippines, Feb. 5, 1933; came to U.S., 1959, naturalized, 1973; s. Eng-Lian and Su (Yu) L.; m. Victoria K. Sy, June 21, 1961; children: Jennifer, Wendell, Caroline. AB, U. Santo Tomas, Manila, 1953; MD cum laude, U. Santo Tomas, 1958; PhD in Biochemistry, U. Pa., 1966. Diplomate Am. Bd. Psychiatry and Neurology. Rsch. neurochemist U. Mich., Ann Arbor, 1966-69; asst. prof. biochemistry U. Chgo., 1969-76, assoc. prof. Brain Rsch. Inst., 1976-81; prof. dept. neurology U. Iowa, Iowa City, 1981—, dir. divsn. neurochemistry and neurobiology, 1981—. Career investigator VA, 1983; adv. internat. writing program U. Iowa, 2002—. Mem. editl. bd. Internat. Jour. Devel. Neurosci., 1984-91, Neurochem. Rsch., 1997—; contbr. numerous articles to sci. jours. Grantee NIH, 1971—, NSF, 1979—, VA, 1981—; recipient 3d prize Art Assn. Philippines, 1957; named Outstanding Overseas Young Chinese, Fedn. Overseas Chinese Orgns., 1961. Mem. Am. Soc. Biochem. Molecular Biology, Internat. Soc. Neurochemistry (vis. lectureship 1986), Am. Soc. Neurochemistry, Soc. Neurosci., Am. Soc. Cell Biology. Achievements include research in isolation and characterization of regulatory brain proteins; growth and differentiation of brain cells; brain chemistry and molecular biology. Avocations: calligraphy, painting, writing, music. Home: 118 Richards St Iowa City IA 52246-3516 Office: U Iowa Iowa City IA 52242 E-mail: ramon-lim@uiowa.edu.

LIM, SHUN PING, cardiologist, educator; b. Singapore, Jan. 12, 1947; came to U.S., 1980; s. Tay Boh and Si Moi (Foo) L.; m. Sock Kian Ng, Dec. 9, 1972; children: Corinne Xian-Li, Damien Xian-Ming, Justin Xian-An. MB, BS with honors, Monash U., Melbourne, Australia, 1970, PhD, 1982. Diplomate Am. Bd. Internal Medicine, Am. Bd. Cardiovasc. Disease. Chief non-invasive cardiovasc. imaging U. Cin.-VA Med. Ctr., 1982-86; pvt. practice, Bismarck, N.D., 1986-89, Terre Haute, Ind., 1989-91, Marion, Ohio, 1991—; assoc. prof. cardiology Ohio State U., Columbus, 1994—. Chief cardiology U. N.D., Fargo VA Med. Ctr., N.D., 1991-93; pres. Inst. for Advanced Med. Tech., Marion, 1989—. Vol. physician Marion Free Med. Clinic, 1997—. Rsch. scholar Australian Nat. Health and Med. Rsch. Coun., 1978; rsch. grantee VA, Cin., 1985. Fellow ACP, Am. Coll. Cardiology, Am. Heart Assn. (rsch. grantee 1984), Royal Australasian Coll. Physicians, Acad. Medicine (Singapore), N.Y. Acad. Scis. (life); mem. Marion Acad. Medicine (pres.). Achievements include patent for in-vivo lactate sensor. E-mail: 1011168002@webmd.com.

LIMA, MARILYNNE, foreign language educator, consultant; b. Murray, Utah, Aug. 20, 1938; d. John William and Mary Elsie (Barr) Fitzgerald; m. Marco Antonio Lima, Aug. 22, 1959 (div. 1986); children: Maria Lorraine, Shawn Antonio. BA, Brigham Young U., Provo, Utah, 1962, MA, 1972. Cert. tchr. Utah. Tchr. Spanish/English Jordan Sch. Dist, West Jordan (Utah) Jr. High, 1962-67; supr. student tchrs. Brigham Young U., 1967-68; tchr. Spanish/English Granite Sch. Dist., Evergreen Jr. High, Salt Lake City, 1968-69; tchr. Spanish Brigham Young U., 1978-79, Granite Sch. Dist., Cottonwood High Sch., Salt Lake City, 1969—. Sales cons. Scott Foresman Pub., Salt Lake City, 1993-96; presider, presenter numerous adv. placement seminars in Spanish, 1976-86. Mem. Am. Fedn. Tchrs., Utah Fgn. Lang. Assn., Sigma Delta Pi. Mem. Ch. Latter Day Saints. Avocations: traveling and living in spanish-speaking countries, reading, family events. Office: Cottonwood HS 5717 S 1300 E Salt Lake City UT 84121-1023

LIN, ALICE LEE LAN, physicist, researcher, educator; b. Shanghai, Oct. 28, 1937; came to U.S., 1960, naturalized, 1974; m. A. Marcus, Dec. 19, 1962 (div. Feb. 1972); 1 child, Peter A. AB in Physics, U. Calif., Berkeley, 1963; MA in Physics, George Washington U., 1974. Statis. asst. dept. math. U. Calif., Berkeley, Calif., 1961-63; rsch. asst. in radiation damage Cavendish Lab. Cambridge U., England, 1965-66; info. analysis specialist Nat. Acad. Sci., Washington, 1970-71; tchng. fellow, rsch. asst. George Washington U., Cath. U. Am., Washington, 1971-75; physicist NASA /Goddard Space Flight Ctr., Greenbelt, Md., 1975-80, Army Materials Tech. Lab., Watertown, Mass., 1980—. Contbr. articles to profl. jours. Mencius Ednl. Found. grantee, 1959-60. Mem. AAAS, N.Y. Acad. Scis., Am. Phys. Soc., Am. Ceramics Soc., Am. Acoustical Soc., Am. Men and Women of Sci., Optical Soc. Am. Democrat. Avocations: rare stamp and coin collecting, art collectibles, home computers, opera, ballet. Home: 28 Hallett Hill Rd Weston MA 02493-1753

LIN, PING-WHA, engineering educator, consultant; b. Canton, China, July 11, 1925; BS, Jiao-Tong U., Shanghai, China, 1947; PhD, Purdue U., 1951, MS, 1950. Instr. Lingnan U., Canton, China, 1947—47; engr. various, 1951-61; cons., engr. WHO, Geneva, 1962-66, 84, project mgr., 1980-82; prof. Tri-State U., Angola, Ind., 1966-90, Laurence L. Dresser chair prof., 1991-95, prof. emeritus, 1995—. Pres. Lin Techs Inc., Angola, 1989—; presenter; spkr. at internat. confs. on environment and energy. Contbr. articles to profl. jours. Grantee Dept. of Energy, 1983-84. Fellow ASCE (past pres. Ind. chpt.); mem. AAAS, Am. Chem. Soc., Am. Water Works Assn. (life), N.Y. Acad. Sci., Sigma Xi. Achievements include 15 patents in the fields. Home: 506 S Darling St Angola IN 46703-1707

LIN, STEVEN AN-YHI, economics educator, consultant; b. Taipei, Republic of China, Apr. 19, 1933; s. Ching-Ho Lin-Sheh and Wen (Chen) Lin; m. Yen-Yen Yeh, Jan. 27, 1961 (dec.); 1 child: Anthony; m. Ning Gu, Mar. 26, 1993. BS, Nat. Taiwan U., Taipei, 1956; MS, Iowa State U., 1965, PhD, 1967. Asst. prof. U. Wis., River Falls, 1967—68, So. Ill. U., Edwardsville, 1968—71, assoc. prof., 1971—75, prof. econs., 1975—. Vis. prof. U. Chgo., 1975. Editor: Theory and Measurement of Economic Externality, 1975; editor Jour. Econs., 1974-76; contbr. numerous articles to profl. jours. Mem. Am. Econ. Assn., Mo. Valley Econ. Assn. (pres. 1978-79, sec. 1975-76). Home: 112 Sherwood Dr Glen Carbon IL 62034-1046 Office: So Ill Univ Dept Econs Edwardsville IL 62026-1102

LIN, THOMAS WEN-SHYOUNG, accounting educator, researcher, consultant; b. Taichung, Republic of China, June 3, 1944; arrived in U.S., 1970; s. Ju-chin and Shao-chin (Tseng) L.; m. Angela Kuei-fong Hou, May 19, 1969; children: William Margaret. BA in Bus. Adminstrn., Nat. Taiwan U., Taipei, 1966; MBA, Nat. Chengchi U., Taipei, 1970; MS in Acctg. and Info. Systems, UCLA, 1971; PhD in Acctg., Ohio State U., 1975. Cert. mgmt. acct., Calif. Internal auditor Formosa Plastics Group, Taipei, 1967-69, spl. asst. to the pres., 1969-70; asst. prof. U. So. Calif., L.A., 1975-80, assoc. prof., 1980-86, prof. acctg., 1986-90, acctg. cir. prof., 1990—, dir. doctoral studies acctg., 1982-86, MBA program China country desk officer, 1997—, amb., 2000—. Cons. Intex Plastics, Inc., Long Beach, Calif., 1979-81, Peat, Marwick, Mitchell, L.A., 1982, City of Chino, Calif., 1982; bd. dirs., audit com. chmn. FCB Taiwan Calif. Bank, 1997-2001. Author: Planning and Control for Data Processing, 1984, Use of Mathematical Models, 1986, Advanced Auditing, 1988, Using Accounting Information in Business Planning, Product Costing, and Auditing, 1991, Cost Management: A Strategic Emphasis, 1999, 2d edit., 2002; assoc. editor Internat. Jour. Bus., 1997—; mem. editl. bd. Taiwan Mgmt. Acctg., Quarterly Jour. Bus. and Econs., Am. Jour. Math. and Mgmt. Scis., Taiwan Acctg. Rev., Chinese Bus. Horizon, 1988—; contbr. articles to profl. jours. Bd. dirs. U. So. Calif. Acctg. Circle, L.A., 1986-88, 93-99, Taiwan Benevolent Assn. Am., Washington, 1986-89; pres. Taiwan Benevolent Assn. Calif., L.A., 1986-88, Chinese Am. Faculty Assn. So. Calif., 2000—2001. 2d lt. China Army, 1966-67. Recipient cert. appreciation L.A. City Mayor Tom Bradley, 1988, Congressman Martinez award for outstanding community svc., 1988, Best Paper award 3rd Biennial Internat. Acctg. Rsch. Conf., 2000, Best Paper award 9th World Congress Acctg. Educators, 2002; Faculty Rsch. scholar U. So. Calif. Bus. Sch., L.A., 1984-87. Mem. Am. Acctg. Assn. (we. region dir. 1986-88), Chinese Acctg. Profs. N.Am. (founding pres. 1976-80), Chinese Am. Faculty Assn. So. Calif. (pres. 2000-01, Svc. award 2003), Inst. Cert. Mgmt. Accts. (cert. of disting. performance 1978), Inst. Mgmt. Accts. (coord. 1984-96, Author's trophy 1978, 79, 81, 87), Inst. Mgmt. Scis. Republican. Baptist. Avocation: gardening. Home: PO Box 8023 Rowland Heights CA 91748-0023 Office: U So Calif Leventhal Sch Acctg Univ Park Acc 109 Los Angeles CA 90089-0441 E-mail: wtlin@marshall.usc.edu.

LIN, TU, endocrinologist, educator, researcher, academic administrator; b. Fukien, China, Jan. 18, 1941; came to U.S., 1967; s. Tao Shing and Jan En (Chang) L.; m. Pai-Li, July 1, 1967; children: Vivian H., Alexander T., Margaret C. MD, Nat. Taiwan U., Taipei, 1966. Diplomate Am. Bd. Internal Medicine, Am. Bd. Endocrinology and Metabolism. Intern Episcopal Hosp.-Temple U., Phila., 1967-68; resident in medicine Berkshire Med. Ctr., Pittsfield, Mass., 1968-70; fellow in endocrinology Lahey Clinic, Boston, 1970-71, Roger Williams Gen. Hosp.-Brown U., Providence, 1971-73; rsch. fellow in med. sci. Brown U., 1971-73; chief, endocrine sect. WJB Dorn Vet. Hosp., Columbia, S.C., 1975—; asst. prof. U. S.C. Sch. Medicine, Columbia, 1976-80, assoc. prof., 1980-84, prof. medicine, 1984—, prof., dir. divsn. endocrinology, diabetes and metabolism, 1992—. Merit review bd. endocrinology Dept. Vet. Affairs, 1990-94. Co-author: Disorders of Male Reproductive Function, 1996; mem. editl. bd. Biology of Reproduction, 1990-95, Jour. of Andrology, 1993-96; contbr. articles to profl. jours. Recipient Disting. Investigator award U. S.C. Sch. Medicine, 1981, 88, 95. Fellow ACP; mem. Endocrine Soc., Am. Soc. Andrology (chmn. ann. meeting, coun. 1993-96), Soc. for the Study of Reproduction, Am. Diabetic Assn., Am. Soc. Hypertension. Office: U SC Sch Medicine Med Library Bldg Ste 316 Columbia SC 29208-0001 E-mail: lin@med.sc.edu.

LINCOLN, ANNA, company executive, foreign languages educator; b. Warsaw, Dec. 13, 1932; came to U.S., 1948; d. Wigdor Aron and Genia (Zalkind) Szpiro; m. Adrian Courtney Lincoln Jr., Sept. 22, 1951; children: Irene Anne, Sally Linda, Allen, Kirk. Student, U. Calif., Berkeley, 1949-50; BA in French and Russian with honors, NYU, 1965; student, Columbia Tchrs. Coll., 1966-67. Tchr. Waldwick (N.J.) H.S., 1966-69; chmn. Tuxedo Park (N.Y.) Red Cross, 1969-71; pres. Red Cross divsn. Vets. Hosp.; pres. China Pictures U.S.A. Inc., Princeton, N.J., 1994—; prof. fgn. rels. Fudan U., Shanghai, 1994—, prof. English and humanitarian studies, 1996—. Adv. bd. guidance dept. Waldwick (N.J.) H.S., 1966-69; hon. bd. dirs. Shanghai Fgn. Lang. Assn., 1994; hon. prof. Fudan U., Shanghai, 1994; leader seminars, China at top univs., 1996—; pub. spkr., human rels., China, 2003—. Author: Escape to China, 1940-48, 1985, Chinese transl., 1985, The Art of Peace, 1995, Anna Lincoln Views China, 2000; publ.: China Beyond the Year 2000 and the Nature of Love, 1997, Anna Lincoln Views China, 1999; co-dir. (TV docudrama) Escape to China 1941-48, 1998. Hon. U.S. Goodwill amb. for peace and friendship, China, 1984, 85, 86, 88; founder Princeton-Lincoln Found., Inc., 1985—. Named Woman of Yr. Am. Biog. Soc., 1993; recipient Peace Through the Arts prize Assn. Internat. Mujeres en las Artes, Madrid, 1993. Mem. AAUW, Women's Coll. Club (publicity chmn. 1991-96), Lit. Coll. Princeton, Present Day Club. Avocations: reading, swimming, bridge, seminars, ballroom dancing. Home and Office: China Pictures USA Inc 550 Rosedale Rd Princeton NJ 08540-2315

LINCOLN, BRUCE KENNETH, anthropology and history of religions educator; b. Phila., Mar. 5, 1948; s. William D. Lincoln and Geraldine (Kovsky) Grossman; m. Louise Hassett Lincoln, Apr. 17, 1971; children: Martha, Rebecca. BA, Haverford Coll., Pa., 1970; MA, U. Chgo., 1973, PhD, 1976; PhD (hon.), U. Copenhagen, 2001. Asst. prof. Humanities and religious Studies U. Minn., Mpls., 1976-79, assoc. prof., 1979-84, prof., 1984-94; prof. history of religion, anthropology, classics U. Chgo., 1993—, Caroline E. HAskell prof. history religions, 2000—. Vis. prof. U. Siena, 1984-85, U. Uppsala, 1985, Novosibirsk State Pedagogical Inst., 1991, U. Copenhagen, 1998, Coll. de France, 2003. Author: Priests, Warriors and Cattle: A Study in the Ecology of Religions, 1981, Emerging from the Chrysalis: Studies in Rituals of Women's Initiation, 1981, Myth, Cosmos, and Society: Indo-European Themes of Creation and Destruction, 1986, Discourse and the Construction of Society: Comparative Studies of Myth, Ritual and Classification, 1989, Death, War, and Sacrifice: Studies in Ideology and Practice, 1991, Authority: Construction and Corrosion, 1994, Theorizing Myth: Narrative, Ideology and Scholarship, 1999, Holy Terrors: Thinking about Religion after September 11, 2002; editor: Religion, Rebellion, Revolution, 1985; contbr. articles to profl. jours. Grantee Am. Coun. Learned Soc. Travel, 1979, Rockefeller Found. Rsch. Conf. 1981, A,. Coun. of Learned Soc. Rsch., 1982-83, Guggenheim Meml. Found. Rsch., 1986. Office: Univ of Chgo 1025 E 58th St Chicago IL 60637-1509 E-mail: blincoln@midway.uchicago.edu.

LINCOLN, WALTER BUTLER, JR., marine engineer, educator; b. Phila., July 15, 1941; s. Walter Butler and Virginia Ruth (Callahan) L.; m. Sharon Platner, Oct. 13, 1979; children: Amelia Adams, Caleb Platner. BS in Math., U. N.C., 1963; Ocean Engr., MIT, 1975; MBA, Rensselaer Poly. Inst., 1982; MA, Naval War Coll., 1994. Registered profl. engr., N.H.; chartered engr., U.K. Ops. rsch. analyst applied physics lab. Johns Hopkins U., Silver Spring, Md., 1968-70; grad. asst. MIT, Cambridge, 1971-75; ocean engr. USCG R&D Ctr., Groton, Conn., 1976-78, chief marine systems divsn., 1983-97; program mgr. R&D, 1997—2002; prin. engr. Sanders Assocs., Nashua, N.H., 1978-83; lectr. U. Conn., Avery Point, 1986-95; prin. Lincoln Maritime, LLC, 2002—. Master, U.S. Mcht. Marine; comdg. officer res. unit U.S. Naval War Coll., 1999-2001. Contbr. articles to profl. jours. Capt. USNR, ret. Mem. SAR, Am. Soc. Naval Engrs., Nat. Assn. Underwater Instrs. (instr. 1971—), Royal Inst. Naval Architects, Soc. Naval Architects & Marine Engrs. (chmn. New Eng. sect. 1996-97), Marine Tech. Soc. (exec. bd. New Eng. sect. 1980), Navy League, Naval War Coll. Found., Navy Sailing Assn. (ocean master), Pi Mu Epsilon. Achievements include discovery of rev. war ship Defense; rsch. in integrated systems modeling and engring. of deep ocean systems; devel. of algorithms for simulation of hydromechs. of ocean systems and ships; fuel cell power systems; engring. mgmt. of ship and marine environmental response and security systems, rsch., devel., test and evaluation. Home: 189 Avery Hill Rd Ledyard CT 06339 Office: 14 Holmes St Mystic CT 06355 E-mail: waltnebula@aol.com.

LINDAHL, THOMAS JEFFERSON, retired university dean; b. Norwalk, Wis., July 4, 1937; s. Gust Adolf and Mabel Louise (Zietlow) L.; m. Lee Ann Snowberry, Dec. 22, 1962; children: Gary, Mark. BS, U. Wis., 1960; MEd, U. Ill., 1970; PhD, Iowa State U., 1977. Instr. Stockton (Ill.) Community High Sch., 1968-74, Highland Community Coll., Freeport, Ill., 1968-74; instr. Iowa State U., Ames, 1974-75; chmn. dept. Area I Vocat.-Tech. Sch., Calmar, Iowa, 1975-77; assoc. prof., chmn. agrl. bus. dept. U. Minn., Waseca, 1977-83, vice chancellor, 1983-90, acting chancellor, 1990-91; dean Coll. Agriculture U. Wis., Platteville, 1991-94, dean Coll. Bus. Industry, Life Sci. and Agr., 1994-98, sr. advancement officer, 1998-2000; higher edn. and agr. cons., 2000—. Cons., evaluator North Ctrl. Assn. Commn. on Instns. Higher Edn., Chgo., 1985-2000; cons. Citizens Network for Fgn. Affairs, Ukraine, 1999-2001; numerous presentations in field. Author: (with Bennie L. Byler) Professional Education In-Service Needs of Agriculture Instructors in Iowa Post Secondry Area Vocational Schools, 1977, (with Wayne Robinson and N.J. Guderon) Cooperative College of Kenya Feasibility Study for Expansion, 1980, (with Myron A. Eighmy) An Individualized Course in Getting Started, 1980, (with James L. Gibson) Associate Instructor Handbook, 1980; also articles and curr. courses. Lay speaker United Meth. Ch., 1980—; pres. Wis. Rural Leadership Program Bd., 1995-97. Recipient hon. state degree Wis. Future Farmers Am., 1993. Fellow Nat. Assn. Coll. Tchrs. Agr. (exec. com., v.p. 1991-92, pres. 1992-93, Disting. Educator award 1997); mem. NEA, Nat. Vocat. Agrl. Tchrs. Assn., Am. Vocat. Assn., Wis. Vocat. Assn., Minn. Vocat. Agrl. Tchrs. Assn. (25-yr. Tchg. award 1985), Iowa Vocat. Agrl. Tchrs. Assn. (15-yr. Membership award), Wis. Assn. Inst. Agr., Am. Assn. Colls. and Schs. Agr. and Renewable Resources (v.p. 1995-96, pres. 1996-97), Phi Delta Kappa, Alpha Delta Pi, Phi Kappa Phi. Home: 295 Flower Ct Platteville WI 53818-1915 E-mail: lindahl@uwplatt.edu.

LINDBERG, DONALD ALLAN BROR, library administrator, pathologist, educator; b. N.Y.C., Sept. 21, 1933; s. Harry B. and Frances Seeley (Little) L.; m. Mary Musick, June 8, 1957; children: Donald Allan Bror, Christopher Charles Seeley, Jonathan Edward Moyer. AB, Amherst Coll., 1954, ScD (hon.), 1979; MD, Columbia U., 1958; ScD (hon.), SUNY, 1987; LLD (hon.), U. Mo., Columbia, 1990. Diplomate Am. Bd. Pathology, Am. Bd. Med. Examiners (exec. bd. 1987-91). Rsch. asst. Amherst Coll., 1954-55; intern in pathology Columbia-Presbyn. Med. Ctr., 1958-59, asst. resident in pathology, 1959-60; asst. in pathology Coll. Physician and Surgeons Columbia U., N.Y.C., 1958-60; instr. pathology Sch. of Medicine U. Mo., 1962-63, asst. prof. Sch. of Medicine, 1963-66, assoc. prof. Sch. of Medicine, 1966-69, prof. Sch. of Medicine, 1969-84, dir. Diagnostic Microbiology Lab. Sch. of Medicine, 1960-63, dir. Med. Ctr. Computer Program Sch. of Medicine, 1962-70, staff, exec. dir. for health affairs Sch. of Medicine, 1968-70, prof., chmn. dept. info. sci. Sch. of Medicine, 1969-71; dir. Nat. Libr. of Medicine, Bethesda, Md., 1984—. Adj. prof. pathology U. Md. Sch. Medicine, 1988—, clin. prof. pathology U. Va., 1992—; dir. Nat. Coord. Office for High Performance Computing and Comms., exec. office of Pres., Office Sci. & Tech. Policy, 1992-95; mem.

LINDBERG, computer sci./engring. bd. Nat. Acad. Sci., 1971-74, chmn. Nat. Adv. Com. Artificial Intelligence in Medicine, Stanford U., 1975-84; U.S. rep. to Internat. Med. Info. Assn./Internat. Fedn. Info. Processing, 1975-84; bd. dirs. Am. Med. Info. Assn., 1992—, Health on the Net Found.; adv. coun. Inst. Medicine, 1992—. Author: The Computer and Medical Care, 1968; The Growth of Medical Information Systems in the United States, 1979; editor: (with W. Siler) Computers in Life Science Research, 1975; (with others) Computer Applications in Medical Care, 1982; editor Methods of Info. in Medicine, 1970-83, assoc. editor, 1983—; editor Jour. Med. Systems, 1976—, Med. Informatics Jour., 1976—; chief editor procs. 3d World Conf. on Med. Informatics, 1980; editorial bd. Jour. of AMA, 1991—; contbr. articles to jours. Recipient Silver Cord award Internat. Fedn. for Info. Processing, 1980, Walter C. Alvarez award Am. Med. Writers Assn. 1989, PHS Surgeon Gen.'s medallion, 1989, Nathan Davis award AMA, 1989, Presdl. Disting. Exec. Rank award, Sr. Exec. Svc., Outstanding Svc. medal Uniformed Svcs. U. Health Scis., 1992, Computers in Healthcare Pioneer award, 1993, recognition award High Performance Computing Industry, 1995, silver award U.S. Nat. Commn. on Librs. and Info. Scis., 1996, meritorious award Coun. Biol. Editors, 1996; Simpson fellow Amherst Coll., 1954-55; Markle scholar in acad. medicine, 1964-69; recipient pres.'s award Med. Libr. Assn., 1997, Morris F. Collen, M.D. award of excellence Am. Coll. Med. Informatics, 1997, Info. Frontier award N.Y. Acad. Medicine, 1999, Ranice W. Crosby Disting. Achievement award Johns Hopkins U. Sch. Medicine, 1998, Spl. Recognition award Coll. P&S Columbia U. Alumni, 2001. Fellow: AAAS; mem.: Am. Med. Informatics Assn. (pres. 1988—91), Gorgas Meml. Inst. Tropical and Preventive Medicine (bd. dirs. 1987—), Am. Assn. Med. Systems and Informatics (internat. com. 1982—89, bd. dirs. 1982, editor conf. procs. 1983, 1984), Salutis Initas (Am. v.p. 1981—91), Assn. for Computing Machines, Mo. Med. Assn., Coll. Am. Pathologists (commn. on computer policy and coordination 1981—84), Inst. Medicine of NAS, Cosmos Club (38th Cosmos Club award 2001), Sigma Xi. Democrat. Avocations: photography, riding. Home: 13601 Esworthy Rd Germantown MD 20874-3319 Office: Nat Libr of Medicine 8600 Rockville Pike Bethesda MD 20894-0002*

LINDBERG, STEPHEN, secondary education educator; Sci. tchr. Westmont Hilltop High Sch., Johnstown, Pa. Summer tchr. Pa. Appalachia Intermediate Unit 8; tchr. Summer Fun Program, Sci. on Saturday Univ. Pittsburg. Recipient Outstanding Earth Sci. Tchr. of the Year award, 1992. Westmont Hilltop Education Assn. (pres.). Office: Westmont Hilltop High Sch 200 Fair Oaks Dr Johnstown PA 15905-1316

LINDBOE, BERIT ROBERG, language educator, literature educator; b. Stavanger, Norway, July 28, 1944; arrived in U.S., 1947; d. Odd and Ingbjorg Roberg. BA, Wellesley Coll., 1966; MA, Yale U., 1967. English tchr. Daniel Hand H.S., Madison, Conn., 1967—69; tchg. asst. U. Va., Charlottesville, 1971—73; asst. prof. English Humboldt State U., Arcata, Calif., 1973—77; grad. instr. U. Va., 1979—83; English tchr. Barstow Sch., Kansas City, Mo., 1983—. Cons. Ednl. Testing Svc., Princeton, NJ, 1991—2002; panelist NEH, Washington, 1991. Contbr. articles to profl. jours. Grantee, NEH, London and Oxford, Eng., English-Speaking Union, Mo. Humanities Coun. Mem.: Lychnos Honor Soc., Cum Laude Soc., Mensa.

LINDELL, TERRENCE JON, history educator; b. Mitchell, SD, Nov. 8, 1954; s. Earl Eugene and Erma Mary (Mizener) L.; m. Lois Ann McElroy, May 8, 1982. BA in History, Augustana Coll., 1978; MA in History, U. Nebr., 1982, PhD in History, 1987. Instr., history dept. chair Wartburg Coll., Waverly, Iowa, 1984-85, asst. prof., history dept. chair, 1985-90, assoc. prof., history dept. chair, 1990-96, prof., 1996—. Pres. McCook County Hist. Soc., Salem, S.D., 1978-79; mem., bd. dirs. Bremer County Hist. Soc., Waverly, 1993—; mem. Waverly Historic Preservation Commn., 1999—. Mem. State Hist. Soc. Iowa, Orgn. Am. Historians, Immigration History Soc., Nebr. State Hist. Soc., S.D. State Hist. Soc., Soc. Mil. Historians. Republican. Lutheran. Avocation: collecting wwii memorabilia. Office: Wartburg Coll Dept History Waverly IA 50677 Business E-Mail: terrence.lindell@wartburg.edu.

LINDEN, BLANCHE MARIE GEMROSE, history educator; b. Battle Creek, Mich., July 4, 1946; d. George and Lauretta (Cate) Gemrose; m. Thomas Elwood Lindow, Aug. 2, 1968 (div. 1976); children: Julia C. Lindow, Marc T. Lindow; m. Alan Lester Ward, June 26, 1982. BA, U. Mich., 1968; M.A. U. Cin., 1976; PhD, Harvard U. 1981. Teaching asst. U. Cin., 1974-76; teaching fellow Harvard U., Cambridge, Mass., 1977-79; instr. Brandeis U. Waltham, Mass., 1979-81; vis. asst. prof. Middlebury (Vt.) Coll., 1981-82; asst. prof. history Brandeis U., Waltham, 1982-83, assoc. prof., 1993-94; asst. prof. history Emerson Coll., Boston, 1985-90, assoc. prof., 1990-93, U. N.H., Durham, 1993—. Hist. cons. Mt. Auburn Cemetery, Cambridge, 1981—, Soc. Preservation of New Eng. Antiquities, African Meetinghouse, Arnold Arboretum, all Boston, 1991-93. Author: Silent City on a Hill: Landscapes of Memory, 1989; co-author: American Women in the 1960's: Changing the Future, 1993; assoc. editor: Encyclopedia New Eng. Culture, 1999—; contbr. articles to profl. jours. Mem. Am. Studies Assn., New Eng. Am. Studies Assn. (pres. 1985-87, sec., newsletter editor 1989—), Am. Hist. Assn., Orgn. Am. Historians, Am. Culture/Popular Culture Assn., New Eng. Hist. Assn. (chair exec. com. 1992-94). Democrat. Avocations: photography, travel in france. Home: 3019 NE 20th Ct Fort Lauderdale FL 33305-1807 Office: U NH Ctr Humanities Murkland Durham NH 03824-3596

LINDEN, CAROL MARIE, special education educator; b. Pitts., Dec. 24, 1953; d. Enio P. and Mary C. (Santollo) Cardone; m. Frank J. Miller Jr., Nov. 21, 1974 (div. 1989); children: Emily, Karl, Richard; m. James Anthony Linden, Dec. 9, 1989; children: Shiloh, Shane, Shasta, Shelby (dec.). BS, California (Pa.) State U., 1974; MS, Youngtown State U., 1981. Cert. moderate, severe, profoundly retarded, educable mentally retarded, learning disabled/behavior disordered, speech and hearing. Tchr. multi-handicapped Youngstown (Ohio) City Schs., 1987—; tchr. multihandicapped Trumbull County Bd. Edn., Lordstown, Ohio, 1986-87; spl. vocat. edn. coord. Trumbull County Joint Vocat. Sch., Warren, Ohio, 1985-86; lang. devel. specialist Fairhaven Sheltered Workshop, Niles and Champion, Ohio, 1976-85. Grantee N.E. Ohio Spl. Edn. Resource Ctr., 1989-92, Ohio Bell and Ameritech Impact II, 1991-92, 95, Consumer/Econ. grantee, 1989-95; Wolves Club Carapolis scholar, 1971. Mem. Ohio Speech and Hearing Assn., Coun. for Exceptional Children, Nat. Soc. for Autistic Citizens (sec. 1986-87). Roman Catholic/Baptist. Avocations: reading, crafts, camping. Home: 432 Hunter Ave Niles OH 44446-1625

LINDENBERG, MARY K. artist; b. N.Y.C., Feb. 21, 1921; d. David and Ida (Goodman) Kostezky; m. Martin S. Lindenberg, Feb. 21, 1942. AB magna cum laude, Hunter Coll., 1942. Cert. secondary tchr., Mass. Actuarial asst. Nat. Coun. Compensation Ins., N.Y.C., 1943-44; engring. asst. Babcock & Wilcox Co., N.Y.C., 1944-45; statistician Harvard Optical Rsch. lab., Cambridge, Mass., 1945-46; sec. Am. Math. Soc., N.Y.C., 1946-48; statistician Cornell-Dubelier Corp., New Bedford, Mass., 1948-49; tchr. math. local schs., New Bedford, Mass., 1955-63; tchr. of watercolor YWCA, New Bedford, Mass., 1978-92. One-woman shows include Bierstadt Art Soc., Cape Cod Art Assn., Copley Soc. Boston; exhibited in group shows at Brick Market Gallery, Newport, Dryden Gallery, Providence, Edgartown Art Gallery, James Barker Gallery, Nantucket, Heritage Gallery, Swansea, Providence Watercolor Club, Providence Art Club, Cape Cod Art Assn., Copley Soc. Boston; paintings appeared in books, calendars, mags., greeting cards, newspapers and movie program booklet; appeared on TV shows as co-founder Mass. Art Week, 1957, Bob Bassett, 1964-79; calendar referee and contbr. to Math. Tchr. Mag., 1994—; contbr. articles to profl. jours. Co-founder, co-leader Great Books Discussion Group, New Bedford, 1948-2000; pub. rels. dir. New Bedford Power Squadron, 1962-2000; mem. Dartmouth Town Meeting, 1976-2000; mem. com. Artists Community Task Force, New Bedford, 1993—. Recipient numerous exhibition awards including 18 first prizes, Bierstadt Art Soc. Fall River Art Assn., Newport Art Assn., Brockton Art Mus., 1954—;named to New Beford Women of Yr., 1995-2003. Mem. Marion Art Ctr., Westport Art Group, Nat. Coun. Tchrs. Maths., Phi Beta Kappa, Pi Mu Epsilon. Avocations: reading, sailing, painting, photography, writing. Home: 20 Emerald Dr North Dartmouth MA 02747-3511

LINDENMEYER, MARY KATHRYN, secondary education educator, psychologist; b. Denver, Dec. 9, 1952; d. Edward L. and Margaret Mary (Hogan) L. BA in English and History, St. Mary Coll., Leavenworth, Kans., 1975; MA in History, U. No. Colo., 1990; grad. reading specialist, U. Phoenix, 1997; MA in Counseling, Western N.Mex. U., 2003. Cert. tchr., Mo., Colo., N.Mex., Okla., Ariz. Tchr. Bishop Hogan H.S., Kansas City, Mo., 1976-82; tchr. St. Pius X H.S., Kansas City, Mo., 1982-84, Machebeuf Cath. H.S., Denver, 1984-89; prin. Trinidad (Colo.) Cath. H.S., 1989-90; tchr. Navajo Pine H.S., Navajo, N.Mex., 1990-99, chair dept. lang. arts, 1998-99, Breadloaf Sch. English, Middlebury, Vt., 1999—; psychologist Gallup McKinley Schs., 2003—. Adj. faculty Navajo C.C., Window Rock, Ariz., 1991—98; social studies tchr. Window Rock H.S., Ft. Defiance, Ariz., 1998—, social studies chair, 2000—03; dir. writing ctr. Gallup Grad. Studies Ctr. Western N.Mex. U., 2001—; sch. psychologist, Gallup, N.Mex., 2003—, Gallup/McKinley Co., 2003—. Recipient Dickerson award U. No. Colo. History Fellowship, 1989; named Disting. Tchr., Gallup-McKinley County, 1993; NEH scholar, 1985, 89. Mem. ASCD, Nat. Coun. Tchrs. English. Roman Catholic. Avocations: writing, reading, yard work, photography.

LINDER, BEVERLY L. elementary school educator; b. Kansas City, Mo., Mar. 12, 1951; d. William B. and Una M. (Dishman) Reese; m. John H. Linder, Feb. 24, 1979; 1 child, Elaine M. BSEd, Cen. Mo. State U., 1972; MA in Reading, U. Mo., Kansas City, 1975. Cert. elem. edn., reading. Elem. tchr. Ft. Osage Sch. Dist., Independence, Mo., tchr. 4th grade chpt. I reading. Mem. Internat. Reading Assn., Nat. Coun. Tchrs. Math. Home: 1317 NE Buttonwood Ave Lees Summit MO 64086-8438

LINDERMAN, CHARLENE RUTH, media specialist; b. Charleroi, Pa., May 25, 1955; d. C. Cecil and Louise E. (Annis) L. AA, Delta Coll., 1974; BA, Mich. State U., 1975; MA, Cent. Mich. U., 1981; postgrad., various univs. Cert. tchr. and libr. sci., Mich. Exec. sec. Marshall Appraisal & Co., Midland, Mich., 1972-73; tchr. 2d-5th grades Midland Pub. Schs., 1975-87, media specialist K-6th grades, 1987—. Instr. adult edn. Meridian Pub. Schs., Sanford, Mich., 1984-86; presenter confs. Co-author and producer video Antarctica, 1992; co-producer photography Antarctica Photographs, 1993; co-author: Midland Public Schools' Media Handbook. Grantee Midland Jaycees, 1992, Rotary, 1992, Midland Found., 1992, J.C. Penney Co., Inc., 1992, Target Stores, 1993; recipient Women's Book Project award AAUW, Celebrate Literacy award Midland County Reading Coun., 1995. Mem. NEA, Mich. Edn. Assn. (life; rep. assembly del. alt. 2002—), Mich. Assn. for Media Edn., Mich. Assn. for Computer-Related Tech. Users in Learning, Midland City Edn. Assn. (bldg. rep. 1988-95, exec. com. 1995-2003), Friends of the Libr., Delta Kappa Gamma (sec. 1994-96, 2000—, Woman of Distinction 1994). Avocations: traveling, photography, reading. Office: Midland Pub Schs 600 E Carpenter St Midland MI 48640-5417 E-mail: lindermanc@mps.k12.mi.us.

LINDER WARD, DEBRA SUSAN, secondary school educator; b. Beebe, Ark., Mar. 24, 1960; d. James P. and Sibyl (Baty) L. BS in Edn., U. Cen. Ark., 1981, MS in Edn., 1985. Cert. elem. tchr., mid. sch. math., sci. and social studies tchr., Ark. Mid. sch. tchr. sci. and math. Osceola (Ark.) Pub. Schs., 1981-83; elem. tchr. Carlisle (Ark.) Pub. Schs., 1983—99, tchr. sci., math, math. specialist, 1999—. Presenter in field. Recipient Prsdl. award for excellence in elem. sci. teaching, 1991. Mem. Nat. Coun. Tchrs. Math., Ark. Coun. Tchrs. Math., Ark. Sci. Tchrs. Assn., Sigmma Beta Phi, Alpha Chi. Home: 693 Joe Baty Rd Lonoke AR 72086-9801 Office: Wilbur D Mills Edn Svc Coop PO Box 850 Beebe AR 72012

LINDGREN, CARL EDWIN, educational consultant, antiquarian, historian; b. Coeburn, Va., Nov. 20, 1949; s. Carl and Ruby (Corder) L. AA in Edn. with honors, N.W. Jr. Coll., 1970; BA in Edn., U. Miss., 1972, MEd, 1977, EdS, 1993; DEd, U. South Africa, 1999. FCP, Coll. of Preceptors, London, 1993. Coord. dept. edn. Delta Hills Edn. Assn., 1976-79; lectr. photography U. Miss., 1979-81; instr. health edn. Batesville Job Corps Ctr. U.S. Dept. Labor, 1980-82; pres., dir. Inst. for Ednl. and Hist. Rsch., London, England and Courtland, Miss., 1981—. Mem. faculty Am. Mil. U. Contbr. over 200 articles to profl. jours. and mags.; author 10 books; mem. several adv., rev. and editl. bds. including London Inst. Sci. Tech., Ednl. Forum, Introductions, others; one-man shows and exhbns. U.S., Eng. and India. Capt., historian Brit. N.Am. Command Legion of Frontiersmen, 1999; lay assoc. the Priesthood, Handmaids of the Precious Blood, Cor Jesu Monastery; mem. Internet Franciscan Fraternity, Italy, Confraternity of the Most Holy Rosary (Dominican 15th Century); oblate novice Order of St. Benedict; v.p. Decorated Order of St. Ignatius of Antioch (Vatican), Noble Compania de Ballesteros Hijosdalgo de San Felipe y Santiago; named professed brother Real Irmandade de Mais Santo Miguel da Ala, professed venerable brother Royal Brotherhood of the Most Holy Miracle of Eucharistic Shrine of Santarém, grand cross Imperial Order of Star of Honor of Ethiopian Empire, knight The Equestrian Order of Holy Sepulchre of Jerusalem, knight comdr. Order of St. Michael of the Wing, Knight Comdr., Order of Vila Vicosa, knight comdr. Cross of the Order of Civic and Cultural Merit, Brazil; recipient Acad. Achievement award, 1970; EDPA fellow, 1973, Robert A. Taft fellow, 1977; Hon. Life fellow (Jnana Ratna) World Jnana Sadhak Soc., Calcutta, 1978, Cert. of Excellence and Svc. Associateship award India Internat. Photog. Coun., New Delhi, 1991, Mahatma Gandhi Meml. award, 1994, Brotherhood of Blessed Gerard. Fellow Royal Soc. Arts, Royal Asiatic Soc., Soc. Antiquaries of Scotland, Coll. Preceptors of Essex; mem. Royal Hist. Soc., Am. History of Edn. Soc., Humanitarian Soc., Commissione Internazionale Pre Lo Studio Degli Ordini Cavallereschi, Cambridge U. Heraldic and Geneal. Soc., Am. Acad. Rsch. Historians of Medieval Spain, Soc. for Study of Crusades and the Latin East, Internat. Crusade for Holy Relics, Am. Acad. for Geneaol. and Heraldic Studies (founder, v.p.), Union of Napoleonic Nobility (U.S. del.), Academia Portuguesa de Ex Libris (academican), Hist. Geneal. Soc. Moscow (hon.), Medieval Acad. Am., Asiatic Soc. Calcutta (affiliate), Phi Alpha Theta, Phi Delta Kappa, Kappa Delta Pi, Phi Theta Kappa, KC. Republican. Home: Avalon Woods 10431 Highway 51 Courtland MS 38620-9425 Office: 10431 Highway 51 Courtland MS 38620-9425 E-mail: lindgren@panola.com.

LINDHOLM, RICHARD THEODORE, economics and finance educator; b. Eugene, Oreg., Oct. 5, 1960; s. Richard Wadsworth and Mary Marjorie (Trunko) L. m. Valaya Nivasananda, May 8, 1987. BA, U. Chgo., 1982, MA, 1983, PhD, 1993. Ptnr. Lindholm and Osanka, Eugene, 1986-89, Lindholm Rsch., Eugene, 1995—2001, owner, 1995—, The Lindholm Co., 1995—; ptnr. DBA Lindholm Rsch., Eugene, 2001—. Guest lectr. Nat. Inst. Devel. Adminstrn., Bangkok, Thailand, 1989; pres. Rubicon Inst., Eugene, 1988—; adj. asst. prof. U. Oreg., Eugene, 1988—. Campaign co-chmn. Lane C.C. Advocates, Eugene, 1988; coord., planner numerous state Rep. Campaigns, Oreg., 1988—; campaign mgr. Jack Roberts for Oreg. State Labor Commn., 1994; mem. staff Oreg. Senate Rep. Office, 1989-90; precinct committeeperson Oreg. Rep. Party, 1987-92, 1994—; bd. dirs. Rubicon Soc., Eugene, 1987—, pres., 1993-98. Republican. Lutheran. Home: 3335 Bardell Ave Eugene OR 97401-8021

LINDLEY, L. See POWERS, L. LINDLEY

LINDLY, DOUGLAS DEAN, elementary/middle school educator, administrator; b. San Diego, Aug. 22, 1941; s. George A. and Jessie V. L.; m. Brenda J., Oct. 22, 1971; children: Elizabeth, David. MA in Curriculum, Pepperdine U., 1967, student, 1975; credential edn., USC, 1971; student, U. Oreg., 1981-85, Oreg. State U., 1981-85; credential adminstrn., Calif. State U., Fullerton, 1991; cert. in spl. edn., Calif. State U., L.A., 1994. Cert. in profl. adminstry. svcs., Calif., gen. teaching, Calif., standard designated adult edn., Calif., standard elem. teaching, Oreg., standard adminstry., Oreg.; cert. lang. devel. specialist, Calif., Learning Handicapped and Resource Specialist credential. Supervising tchr. Imperial Schs., Pasadena, Calif., 1965-70; tchr. Charter Oak Unified Sch. Dist., Covina, Calif., 1970-78, Sweet Home (Oreg.) Unified Sch. Dist., 1978-81; prin. Lewis and Clark Sch. Dist., Astoria, Oreg., 1981-86, Barstow (Calif.) Unified Sch. Dist., 1986-88; spl. edn. dir. River Delta Unified Sch. Dist., Walnut Grove, Calif., 1988-89; resource specialist Los Angeles Unified Sch. Dist., 1990—. Tchr. motivational program Great Kids Club, 1982—. Author: A Handbook for Parents, 1967, Summer Education Handbook, 1970; contbr. numerous articles on ednl. programs to newspapers and mags., 1970-89. Vol. ARC, Pasadena/Covina, 1970-78; cubmaster Boy Scouts Am., Astoria and Barstow, 1982-88 (Outstanding Svc. award 1988); coach Little League, Astoria, 1985; leader youth group Ch. of God, 1975-81; Grantee Adventures in Success, 1976-78; scholar Future Tchrs. Am. and Eugene Tchrs. Assn. 1959; named San Gabriel Valley Outstanding Educator, San Gabriel Valley Endl. Consortium, 1977; recipient Outstanding Speaker award Toastmasters Internat., 1986, Outstanding Svc. award PTA, 1988. Mem. NEA, ASCD, Assn. Am. Educators, Calif. Assn. Gifted, Calif. Tchrs. Assn., Assn. Calif. Sch. Adminstrs. (assoc.), Kappa Delta Pi. Avocations: family, physical fitness, grandparenting, reading, travel. Home: 616 E Ghent St San Dimas CA 91773-1913

LINDNER, ERNA CAPLOW, dance educator, choreographer, movement therapist; b. N.Y.C., May 26, 1928; d. Abraham Murray and Mildred T. (Farb) Caplow; m. Norman Lindner, June 18, 1950 (dec. Sept. 1981); 1 child, Amy Beth; m. Seymour Gilbert, Sept. 1, 2003. AB, Bklyn. Coll., 1948; MS, Smith Coll., 1950; PhD, Columbia Pacific U., 1986. Instr. dance Brown U., 1950-54, Rutgers U., 1954-55; dance specialist Samuel Field YM-YWHA, Queens, N.Y., 1962-68, N.Y.C. Bd. Edn., 1963-69; asst. dance dir., choreographer Martin de Porres Center, Queens, 1967-70; dir. Saturday Cultural Program Rochdale Village Nursery Sch., Queens, 1964-73; dir.-choreographer Danceabouts Co., N.Y.C., 1966-80; prof. health, phys. edn. and recreation Nassau C.C. SUNY, N.Y., 1968-91, prof. emeritus, 1992; dance therapy cons. Fla. W.O.W., 1993—. Adj. prof. phys. edn. and dance Adelphi U., 1979—91; mem. faculty CUE program Queens Coll., CUNY, 1988—93; lectr. and trainer on dance for spl. populations. Contbr. chpts. on dance to Fun for Fitness; interviewer on dance Sta. WHPC-FM; (with others) selected music and wrote manual for recordings Special Music for Special People, Ednl. Act Rec. Co., 1977, special Dancing on Your Feet and in Your Seat, 1982, Come Dance Again, 1987, 2nd edit., 1993, Young and Old Together, 1994. Author: (with others) Therapeutic Dance/Movement, 1979; (monograph) Use of Dance in Sex Education and Counseling, 1974; also articles on geriatric dance therapy. Charter mem. Queens Council on Arts, exec. bd. dirs., 1970-74; sec., mem. exec. com. Nat. Ednl. Council Creative Therapies. Mem. AAHPERD (life, honoree Ea. dist. 1990, 91), Am. Dance Guild (charter mem., past nat. pres., nat. exec. bd.), Am. Dance Therapy Assn., Am. Assn. Sex Educators, Counselors and Therapists. Office: Lindner/Harpaz 4-8 Rolling Hills Lenox MA 01240

LINDO, SANDRA MARCELE, elementary school administrator; b. St. Thomas, V.I., Jan. 3, 1951; d. Isaac and Utah Lucilda (Abbott) Lindo; children: Osbert W. Liburd Jr., Austin L.D. Andrews Jr. BA, Coll. of the V.I., 1973, MA, 1980. Acting coord. basic skills Dept. of Edn., St. Thomas, supvr. intermediate grades Dept. Edn., St. Thomas-St. John Sch. Dist. Mem. ASCD, V.I. ASCD (past pres.), St. Thomas-St. John RC, St. Thomas-St. Johns TE, Early Childhood Assn., IRA, NCTE. Home: Princess Gade # 17A St Thomas VI 00802

LINDQUIST, EVAN, artist, educator; b. Salina, Kans., May 23, 1936; s. E.L. and Linnette Rosalie (Shogren) L.; m. Sharon Frances Huenergardt, June 8, 1958; children: Eric, Carl. BS, Emporia State U., 1958; MFA, U. Iowa, 1963. Prof. art Ark. State U., 1963—2003, emeritus prof., 2003—, Presdl. fellow, 1981—82, 1984—85. One-man shows include Mo. Arts Coun., 1973-75, Albrecht Art Mus., St. Joseph, Mo., 1975, 89, S.E. Mo. State U., 1977, Sandzen Gallery, Lindsborg, Kans., 1978, Galerie V. Kunstverlag Wolfbrum, Vienna, 1979, Poplar Bluff, Mo., 1987, Gallery V. Kansas Clty, Mo., 1988, Northwest Mo. State U., 1991, U. Iowa, Iowa City, 1995, WR Harper Coll., Palatine, Ill., 1996, Northwestern Coll., Orange City, Iowa, 1997, Art Ctr. of the Ozarks, Springdale, Ark., 1998, Fowler Ctr., Ark. State U., Jonesboro, 2001, Evan Lindquist: Master Printmaker, Ark. arts Ctr., Little Rock, 2002; group shows include Benjamin Galleries, Chgo., 1976, City of Venice, 1977, Boston Printmakers, 1971-87, Visual Arts Ctr. of Alaska, Anchorage, 1979, Western Carolina U., 1980, Pa. State U., 1980, Kans. State U., 1980, U. N.D., 1981, 92, Ariz. State U., 1981, 93, Barcelona, Cadaques, Girona, 1990, 93, 94, Tulsa, 1982, Jay Gallery, N.Y.C., 1983, Artists Books, German Dem. Rep., 1984, U. Tenn., Knoxville, 1985, Memphis State U., 1985, Ark. Arts Ctr., 1983, Miss. State U., 1986, Hunterdon Art Ctr., Clinton, N.J., 1986-87, 94, 95, Washington, 1988, Soc. Am. Graphic Artists/Printmakers, 1988-94, Boston, 1989-94, John Szoke Gallery, 1989, Woodstock, N.Y., 1990, 92, Silvermine Guild Galleries, New Canaan, Conn., 1992, 93, Woodstock Artists Assn., Littman Gallery, Portland State U., Galleria Brita Prinz, Madrid, Spain, 1992, U. Nebr., 1992, Parkside Nat., Kenosha, Wis., 1993, 95, 2000, 2001, Minot, N.D., 1994, Fla. C.C., Jacksonville, 1995, Stonemetal Press, San Antonio, Tex., 1995, San Diego Art Inst., 1995, Schenectady (N.Y.) Mus., 1995, Fla. Printmakers, Jacksonville, 1996, Clemson U., 1996, U. Tex., Tyler, 1996, Old Print Shop, N.Y.C., 1997, Frederick Baker Gall., Chgo., 1997, Krasdale Gall., N.Y., 1998, Memphis Brooks Mus., 1998, Webster U., St. Louis, 1999, Bradley U., Peoria, Ill., 1999, 2001, Soc. of Am. Graphic Artists, New York, 1999, Hunterdon Art Ctr., Clinton, NJ, 1999, Irving Arts Ctr., Irving Tex., 1999, Payne Gall., Bethlehem, Pa., 1999, U. Hawaii, Holo, 2000; represented in permanent collections Albertina, Vienna, Art Inst. Chgo., Nelson-Atkins, Kansas City, Phoenix Art Mus., Ufizi Gall., Florence, Mcpl. Gall., Dublin, San Francisco Art Mus., Whitney Mus. Am. Art, N.Y.C., St. Louis Art Mus., Museo Reina Sofia, Madrid, others; staff artist Emporia State U., 1958-60; dir. Delta Nat. Small Prints Exhbn. Ark. State U., 1996, 97. Mem. Soc. Am. Graphic Artists, Coll. Art Assn. Am., Mid-Am. Coll. Art Assn., Visual Artists and Galleries Assn. Office: PO Box 2782 State University AR 72467-2782 E-mail: elind@astate.edu.

LINDQUIST, KEITH NELSON, mathematics educator; b. Hayward, Wis., May 21, 1932; s. Lawrence Ernest and Rosamund Lucille (Nelson) L.; m. Margaret Ann Long, Oct. 10, 1955; children: Peter James, Thomas Matthew, John Andrew, Mary Rose, Kathleen Marie. BS in Edn., Wis. State Coll., 1960; MA in Teaching Math., Stanford U., 1966; postgrad., San Diego State U., 1969. Tchr. music, math. Cameron (Wis.) Sch. Dist., 1960-62; tchr. music, math. computer sci. Cumberland (Wis.) Sch. Dist., 1962-96; lectr. math. U. Wis., Barron County, 1998—. Adj. prof. U. Wis. River Falls, 1982-83; software cons. 3M Corp., Cumberland, 1990-92. Author newspaper column Cumberland Advocate, 1987—. Alderman Common Coun., Cumberland, 1990-98; dir. Cumberland Hosp. Bd., 1990—. With U.S. Army, 1953-55. Named Outstanding Educator Cumberland Jaycees, 1967, Outstanding H.S. Tchr. Wis. Soc. Profl. Engrs., Green Bay, 1986, Outstanding Music Person, Federated Music Club, Cumberland, 1987, Outstanding Citizen Cumberland C. of C., 1998. Mem. NEA, Nat. Coun. Tchrs. Math., Math. Assn. Am. (outstanding achievement award), Wis. Math. Coun., Cumberland Edn. Assn., KC (Grand Knight 1972).

Democrat. Roman Catholic. Avocations: crossword puzzles, theatre, music, reading, vol. work. Home: 1530 1st Ave Cumberland WI 54829-0172 E-mail: klindqui@uwc.edu., keithl@chibardun.net.

LINDQUIST, MARY LOUISE, special education educator; b. South St. Paul, Minn., May 30, 1925; d. Henry Emanuel and Hulda Laura Margaret (Brocker) L. BS in Edn., Minot State Coll., 1962; MS, U. Wis., 1964, PhD, 1969. Cert. psychologist N.D. Missionary in Japan Augustana Luth. Bd. Fgn. Missions, Mpls., 1952-56; elem. sch. tchr. Upham (N.D.) Pub. Schs., 1958-59, Vang Sch. Dist., Ryder, N.D., 1959-61, Minot (N.D.) Pub. Schs., 1961-63; sch. psychologist Madison (Wis.) Pub. Schs., 1966-69; prof. U. N.D., Grand Forks, 1969-90, prof. emeritus, 1990—. Cons. Multi-County Spl. Edn., New Rockford, N.D., 1982-85; vis. psychologist Turtle Mountain Schs., Belcourt, N.D., 1978-82; pvt. practice psychologist, Grand Forks, 1980—. Author: Sunday Sch. curriculum/Bd. of Parish Edn., Assn. Free Luth. Congregations. Grantee U.S. Office of Edn., 1984, 87. Mem. Am. Assn. Christian Counselors, Internat. Coun. Learning Disabilities (N.D. rep. 1992-95), Internat. Platform Assn., No. Lights Coun. Learning Disabilities (pres. 1993-94). Republican. Lutheran. Avocations: singing, reading. Home and Office: Apt 103 749 S 30th St Grand Forks ND 58201-4076

LINDSAY, BEVERLY, b. San Antonio, Dec. 21, 1948; d. of Joseph Bass Benson and Ruth Edna (Roberts) L. BA, St. Mary's U., San Antonio, 1969; MA, U. Mass., 1971, EdD, 1974; PhD, Am. U., 1986. Asst. prof. Pa. State U., University Park, 1974-79; Am. Coun. on Edn. fellow Nat. Inst. Edn., Washington, 1979-81, sr. rschr., sr. staff, 1981-83; spl. asst. to v.p. Pa. State U., University Park, 1983-86; adminstr., coord. USIA, Washington, 1983-86; assoc. dean, prof. edn. U. Ga., Athens, 1986-92; dean internat. edn. and policy studies, prof., exec. dir. Hampton (Va.) U., 1992-95; dean internat. programs and studies Pa. State U., University Park, 1996—2002; prof., exec. fellow Inst. Mulit-Track Diplomacy, Republic of Korea, 2002—; sr. Fulbright prof., sr. scientist. Mem. nat. adv. and rev. bd. Fulbright Programs, Washington, 1993—; mem. nat. adv. bd. So. Ctr. for Study in Pub. Policy, Atlanta, 1990; cons. AID, Washington, 1990—, Acad. for Ednl. Devel., Washington, 1990—. Editor: Comparative Perspectives of Third World Women, 1980, 83, Migration and National Development in Africa, 1985; co-editor: Political Dimension in Education, 1995, The Quest for Equity in Higher Education, 2001; mem. editl. bd. Comparative Edn., 1994—, New Edn.: Internat. Jour., 1994—; guest on radio and TV programs. Coord. United Way/Coll. Edn., Athens, 1989-92; treas., bd. dirs. Winston/Beers Cmty. Sch., Washington, 1979-84, aerobics instr., 1981-82. Grantee U. Ga., 1987, 90, Ministry of Edn./U. Montreal, 1989, Charles Sturt U., Australia, 1996; A Coun. on Edn. fellow, 1979-81, 90, fellow Inst. for Multi-Track Diversity, 2002—. Mem. NAACP (life), Comparative Internat. Edn. Soc. (pres. 1988-89), World Coun. on Comparative Edn. Socs. (bd. dirs., exec. coun. 1986-89), Am. Ednl. Rsch. Assn. (presdl. com. 1987-90), Am. Assn. Colls. for Tchr. Edn. (univ. rep. 1990-94, bd. comparative edn.), Coun. on Fgn. Rels. Avocations: jogging, running charity races.

LINDSAY, CAROL FRANCES STOCKTON, art specialist; b. Haileyville, Okla., Dec. 25, 1940; d. Buel Benjamin and Natalie Frances (Bailey) Stockton; m. Robert Carr Lindsay, Oct. 15, 1961; children: Matthew Robert, Mark Stockton, Michael George. AA, Stockton Coll., 1960; BA, Calif. State U., Sacramento, 1970; MEd, U. Nev., 1982, EdS, 1990. Cert. tchr., adminstr., Calif. Tchr. 2d grade Taft Elem. Sch., Stockton, Calif., 1966-67; tchr. 2d and 3rd grades Dry Creek Joint Elem. Sch., Roseville, Calif., 1967-69; tchr. 1st-5th grades Chartville Elem. Sch., Linden, Calif., 1970-77; tchr. 1st grade Northside Elem. sch., Fallon, Nev., 1977-80; tchr. 3rd grade West End Elem. Sch., Fallon, 1980-83; tchr. 5th-8th grades Roosevelt Roads Midd./High Sch., Ceiba, P.R., 1983-85, fine arts dept. coord., 1984-85; student svcs. coord., tchr. Stead Elem. Sch., Reno, 1986-89; student svcs. coord. Silver Lake Elem. Sch., Reno, 1989-93, dean students, 1993-94; art specialist Clark County Sch. Dist., 1994-95. Sch. rep. Antilles Consolidated Sch. System Curriculum Coun., Ceiba, P.R., 1983-85. Co-author: Art Goals and Objectives, 1989; author: Site Based Management, 1990. Co-chairperson Muscular Dystrophy Telethon, Fallon, 1980-82; neighborhood supr. Am. Heart Assn., Reno, 1985-86; mem. PTA. Named one of Outstanding Tchr. of Am., 1972. Mem. AAUW, ASCD, Linden Edn. Assn. (bldg. rep., exec. bd. dirs. 1970-77), Churchill County Edn. Assn. (bldg. rep., exec. bd. dirs. 1980-83), Nev. Assn. Sch. Adminstrs., Internat. Reading Assn., Washoe County Tchrs. Assn. (Disting. Svc. award 1988, Dedicated Svc. award 1992, bldg. rep. 1989-92), Clark County Classroom Tchrs. Assn., Nat. Art Edn. Assn. Avocations: art, music, golfing.

LINDSAY, DIANNA MARIE, educational administrator; b. Boston, Dec. 7, 1948; d. Albert Joseph and June Hazelton Raggi; m. James William Lindsay III, Feb. 14, 1981. BA in Anthropology, Ea. Nazarene Coll., 1971; MEd in Curriculum and Instrn., Wright State U., 1973, MA in Social Studies Edn., 1974, MEd in Edn. Adminstrn., 1977; EdD in Urban History, Ball State U., 1976; MA in Counseling, U. Dayton, 2000. Supr. social edn. Ohio Dept. Edn., Columbus, 1976-77; asst. prin. Orange City Schs., Pepper Pike, Ohio, 1977-79; prin. North Olmsted (Ohio) Jr. High Sch., 1979-81; dir. secondary edn. North Olmsted City Schs., 1981-82; supt. Copley (Ohio)-Fairlawn City Schs., 1982-85; prin. North Olmsted High Sch., 1985-89, New Trier High Sch., Winnetka, Ill., 1989-96, Worthington Kilbourne H.S., Columbus, Ohio, 1996-2001; headmaster Columbus Jewish Day Sch., New Albany, Ohio, 2001—. Bd. dirs. Harvard Prins. Ctr., Cambridge, Mass. Contbr. articles to profl. jours. Bd. dirs. Nat. PTA, Chgo., 1987-89 (Educator of Yr. 1989), Found. Human Potential, Chgo.,; bd. trustee Columbus Jewish Country Day Sch. Named Prin. of Yr. Ohio Art Tchrs., 1989, one of 100 Up and Coming Educators, Exec. Educator Mag., 1988, Milken Educator of the Yr. Ohio, 1999; recipient John Vaughn Achievements in Edn. North Cen. Assn., 1988; named Ohio Prin. of Yr, 2000. Mem. AAUW, Ill. Tchrs. Fgn. Lang., Rotary Internat., Phi Delta Kappa. Methodist. Avocations: stained glass, reading, travel, biking, harpist. Office: Ridgefield HS 700 N Samem Rd Ridgefield CT 06877

LINDSAY, JOHN, IV, principal; b. Trenton, N.J., Oct. 31, 1960; s. John III and Dolores (Hambright) L.; m. Mandy Jane Ablitt, Aug. 23, 1982; children: John V, James Stirling, Cameron Sinclair. BS, Trenton State Coll., 1982; MS, U. North Tex., 1993. Cert. tchr., adminstr., Tex., N.J. Tchr. Dallas Ind. Sch. Dist., 1984-91, asst. prin. Pearl C. Anderson Mid. Sch., 1991-95; prin.Aledo (Tex.) Elem. Sch. Aledo Ind. Sch. Dist., 1995-2000, prin. Willard R. Stuard Elem. Sch., 2000—03, prin. Aledo Mid. Sch., 2003—. Demonstration tchr. Project CARE, Dallas, 1985-88; team leader Leadership Devel. Acad. Dallas Ind. Sch. Dist., 1989. Mem. ASCD, Assn. Tex. Profl. Educators, Phi Delta Kappa. Avocations: reading, golf. Home: 606 Rolling Hills Dr Aledo TX 76008-4379 Office: Aledo Middle School 416 FM 1187 South Aledo TX 76008 E-mail: jlindsay@aledo.k12.tx.us.

LINDSAY, ROBBY LANE, English educator; b. West Monroe, La., May 5, 1963; s. Robert Lane and Ginger (Rainbolt) L.; m. Rhonda Lynne Stansbury, June 4, 1994; children: Gabriella Lynne, Caelin Robert, Ian Thomas, Morgan Cecile. AA in Gen. Studies, World Evangelism Bible Coll., 1988; BA in Religious Studies, Southwestern Coll., 1989; MA in English, La. Tech. U., 1993; EdD, Grambling State U., 2001. Mgr., asst. mgr. Family Dollar Stores, Inc., Dallas, Monroe, La., 1988-90; mgr. Kentwood Water Co., Monroe, 1990-92; tchr. Simsboro (La.) H.S., 1993-94, Delhi (La.) H.S., 1994-95; asst. prof. Grambling (La.) State U., 1995—2002; v.p., head dept. edn., assoc. prof. edn. Christian Inst. of West, Tex., 2002—. Mentor La. Nat. Guard Youth Challenge Program; youth min. New Prospect Bapt. Ch. Author: The Executioner's Journal, 1998; editor: Literature: An Introduction to Fiction, Poetry, Drama, and Non-Fiction, 2001; also short stories. Active faculty senate Grambling State U., 1997-99. Mem. La. Assn. Devel. Educators, Assn. Tchrs. Advanced Composition, Grambling State U. Doctoral Student Assn. (pres. 1998-99), Lambda Iota Tau, Sigma Tau Delta, Kappa Delta Pi. Avocations: reading, research, writing. Home: 2244 Locust St Amarillo TX 79109

LINDSAY, SUSAN RUCHTI, school director; b. Denver, Feb. 20, 1944; d. Ross Roy and Betty Lou Ruchti; 1 child, D. Michael. BS, Memphis U.; MEd, Miss. Coll. Cert. in adminstrn., counseling, social studies, Miss. Tchr. social studies North Little Rock (Ark.) Schs., 1969-70, Jackson (Miss.) Prep. Sch., 1970-85, chair dept. social studies, 1980-85, sr. high counselor, 1985-90, interim co-head of sch., 1997-98, jr. h.s. prin., 1990-99, dir. acad. affairs, 1999—, assoc. head of acadamics. Bd. dirs., mem. exec. com. Career Forum, Jackson, 1995—. Mem. Metro Jackson C. of C. (bd. youth leadership 1996—). Baptist. Avocation: travel. Home: 220 Azalea Ct Brandon MS 39047-7916 Office: 3100 Lakeland Dr Jackson MS 39232-8834 E-mail: slindsay@jacksonprep.net.

LINDSEY, LINDA LEE, sociology educator; b. St. Louis, Aug. 16, 1947; d. Robert Houston and Ruth Margaret (Weimert) L. BA in Sociology and Edn., U. Mo., 1969; MA, Case Western Res. U., 1972, PhD in Sociology, 1974; MA in Counseling, St. Louis U., 1983. Cert. secondary social sci. tchr., Mo. Asst. prof. sociology John Carroll U., Cleve., 1973-78; mktg. rsch. supr. Southwestern Bell, St. Louis, 1978-79; assoc. prof. St. Louis Coll. Pharmacy, 1979-86; prof. social thought and analysis Washington U., St. Louis, 1981—; prof. sociology Maryville U., St. Louis, 1986—. Cons. Fact Finders Mktg. Rsch., 1982-2002; rep., co-chair Women's Program Coun. St. Louis, 1983—; rschr. Women in the Developing World, Washington U. and Maryville U., 1990—; spokesperson Tobacco-Free Mo., St. Louis, 1996—; presenter World Congress Sociology, 1978, UN Conf. on Women, Beijing, 1995; program evaluator Asian Studies devel. program East-West Ctr., 1999-2002; fellowship coord. Asian Studies Devel. Program, Pearl River Delta, Hong Kong, 2001 Author: Gender Roles: A Sociological Perspective, 1997; contbr. articles to profl. jours. Trustee Children's Survival Fund, Carbondale, Ill., 1985-96; chair advocacy com., bd. dirs. Luth. Family and Children's Svcs., St. Louis, 1992—; feedback supr. health focus group Med. Sch. St. Louis U., 1986—. Japanese Culture fellow NEH, 1995, fellow Keizai Koho Ctr., Tokyo, 1990, NSF fellow Harvard U., 1989, Malone fellow Nat. Coun. U.S.-Arab Rels., Jordan, 1988, Fulbright fellow, India, 1981, Pakistan, 1986, India Inst., 1999, S.E. Asia Inst., 2002; grantee Freeman Inst./Japan Studies Assn., 2003; NEH summer Seminar awardee, Asian Studies Devel. Program summer Inst. award to Korea, 2000. Mem. Am. Sociol. Assn., Global Health Coun., Japan Studies Assn. (freeman fellow 2003), Sociologists for Women in Soc., Midwest Sociol. Soc. (presenter 1979—), Mo. State Sociol. Soc. (pres. 1994-95, conf. presenter 1997-99), Fulbright Assn. Democrat. Lutheran. Avocations: international travel, swimming, speaking, writing. Home: 29 Algonquin Wood Pl Saint Louis MO 63122-2013 Office: Maryville Univ 13550 Conway Rd Saint Louis MO 63141-7299 E-mail: lindsey@maryville.edu.

LINDSEY, LYDIA, education educator, researcher; b. Trenton, N.J., Jan. 10, 1951; d. Charles and Ollie S. Lindsey. BA, Howard U., 1972, MA, 1974; PhD, U. N.C., 1992. Asst. prof. N.C. Ctrl. U., Durham, 1974-92, archivist, 1992—; adj. prof. U. N.C., Chapel Hill, 1992—. Cons. A Philip Randolph Ednl. Found., 1975-78; rsch. assoc. U. Warwick, Coventry, Engr., 1985-86; Rockefeller doctoral fellow Duke-U.N.C. Women's Studies Rsch. Ctr., 1985-886; bd. dirs. Carolina Wren Press, Durham, Stagville Plantation, 1992—; minority postdoctoral fellow U. N.C., 1994-96, participant in nat. land interaction confs. Contbr. articles to profl. jours. Campaign mgr. Beverly Jones Sch. Bd., Durham, 1991-92; active People's Alliance, Durham, 1991-92, Durham Hist. Preservation Soc., 1991-92. Recipient DAR History award; N.C. Minority Postdoctoral fellow, 1994—, N.C. Bd. Gov.'s Doctoral fellow, 1986-87, NEH fellow for coll. tchrs. of historically black colls., 1985-86, U. N.C.-Chapel Hill Reynolds Overseas Grad. fellow, 1985-86, Rockefeller fellow from Duke-U. N.C. Women's Studies Rsch. Ctr. Doctoral fellow, 1985-86; N.J. State scholar, 1968-72, Fulbright scholar, 1995; NEH grantee, 1979. Mem. Assn. Black Women Historians, Assn. for Study African, Caribbean and Asian Culture in Britain, Assn. for Study of Afro-Am. Life and History, Assn. Caribbean Studies, Assn. So. Women Historians, Assn. Social and Behavioral Scis., Collegium for African Am. Studies, Am. Hist. Assn., Nat. Coun. Black Studies, Nat. Coun. Black Women, Carolina Symposium Brit. Study, So. Confs. Brit. Studies, Golden Key (hon.), Delta Sigma Theta, Pi Gamma Mu, Phi Alpha Theta. Democrat. Baptist. Avocations: reading, writing, gardening, swimming, travel. Home: 2210 Alpine Rd Durham NC 27707-3970 Office: NC Ctrl U Durham NC 27707

LINDSEY, RUTH, retired education educator; b. Kingfisher, Okla., Oct. 26, 1926; d. Lewis Howard and Kenyon (King) L. BS, Okla. State U., 1948; MS, U. Wis., 1954; D in Phys. Edn., Ind. U., 1965. Registered kinesiotherapist, 1970. Instr. Okla. State U., Stillwater, 1948-50, Monticello Coll., Alton, Ill., 1951-54, DePauw U., Greencastle, Ind., 1954-56; prof. Okla. State U., Stillwater, 1956-75; vis. prof. U. Utah, Salt Lake City, 1975-76; prof. phys. edn. Calif. State U., Long Beach, 1976-88, prof. emeritus, 1988—; ret. Cons. in field. Co-author: (originally titled Body Mechanics) Fitness for the Health of It, 6 edits., 1969-89, Concepts of Physical Fitness, 9 edits., 1997, Fitness for Life, 1st edit., 1979, 4th edit., 1997, Concepts of Physical Fitness and Wellness, 1st edit., 1994, 2d edit., 1997, The Ultimate Fitness Book, 1984, Survival Kit for Those Who Sit, 1989, A Menu of Concepts: Physical Fitness Concepts, Toward Active Lifestyles and Fitness and Wellness Concepts, Toward Healthy Lifestyles, 1996, Fundamental Concepts of Fitness and Wellness, 2000; contbg. author: Exercise and the Older Adult, 1998; editor, pub.: Why Don't You Salt the Beans, 1997, Kenyon's Songs, 1998; editor: Perspectives: Jour. of Western Soc. for Phys. Edn. Coll. Women, 1988-95; contbr. articles to profl. jours. Mem. Commn. on Aging, City of Westminster, 1998-2001 Amy Morris Homans scholar, 1964; recipient Disting. and Meritorious Svc. Honor award Okla. Assn. Health, Phys. Edn. and Recreation, 1970, Meritorious Performance award Calif. State U., 1987, Julian Vogel Meml. award Am. Kinesiotherapy Assn., 1988, Texty award Text and Acad. Authors Assn., 1997, William Holmes McGuffey award Tex. and Acad. Authors Assn., 1998. Fellow AAHPERD, Am. Kinesiotherapy Assn., Calif. Assn. Health, Phys. Edn., Recreation and Dance, Nat. Coun. Against Health Fraud, Western Soc. for Phys. Edn. of Coll. Women (Hon. Mem. award 1995), Phi Kappa Phi. Democrat. Baptist. Avocations: golf, travel, writing.

LINDSEY, STACEY JEAN, secondary education educator; b. Batesville, Ark., Jan. 31, 1967; d. Doyne and Charlotte (Tanner) Finney; m. Elbert W. Lindsey, May 28, 1988; children: William Tanner, Elley Adrianna. BA in Sci., Ark. Coll., 1990. Cert. tchr. biology. Tchr. Poughkeepsie (Ark.) H.S., 1990-92, Newark (Ark.) H.S., 1992—. Mem. NSTA, Ark. Sci. Tchrs. Assn. (Tchr. of Yr. 1992, 97). Home: 1160 Dogwood Dr Batesville AR 72501-7505 Office: Newark HS 1500 N Hill St Newark AR 72562-9544

LINDSEY, TANYA JAMIL, secondary education administrator; b. New Orleans, Tex., Sept. 10, 1961; d. Fredrick Jr. and Ruthie Lee (Leach) Lindsey. BS, Xavier U., New Orleans, 1985; MEd in Ednl. Adminstrn., U. North Tex., 1992. Cert. in sci., middle mgmt., Tex. Tchr. sci. Dallas Ind. Sch. Dist., 1988—. With Leadership Devel. Acad. Dallas Ind. Sch. Dist., 1993—. Youth vol. Voters League, New Orleans. Mem. ASCD, NAACP, Tex. Middle Sch. Assn., Profl. Adminstrs. and Suprs. Coun., Nat. Alliance of Black Sch. Educators, Alpha Kappa Alpha. Avocations: theatre, reading. Home: 2626 Duncanville Rd Dallas TX 75211-7400

LINDSKOG, MARJORIE OTILDA, elementary school educator; b. Rochester, Minn., Oct. 13, 1937; d. Miles Emery and Otilda Elvina (Hagre) L. BA, Colo. Coll., 1959, MA in Teaching, 1972. Field advisor/camp dir. Columbine council Girl Scouts U.S., Pueblo, Colo., 1959-65; staff mem. Wyo. Girl Scout Camp, Casper, 1966, dir., 1967; tchr. Sch. Dist. 60, Pueblo, 1966—; asst. dir. camp Pacific Peaks Girl Scouts U.S., Olympia, Wash., 1968, dir., 1969; instr. Jr. Gt. Books Program, 1981—; mem. adv. bd. Newspapers in Edn., 1988—; mem. supervisory com. Pueblo Tchr.'s Credit com.; lectr., instr. edn. U. So. Colo., 1990-96; instr. math. Adams State Coll., 1991; mem. adv. bd. ctr. for advancement teaching sci., math, and tech. U. So. Colo., 1992-94; apptd. by Gov. to Colo. Standards Assessment Devel. and Implementation Coun., 1993—. Author: (series of math. lessons) Bronco Mathmania, 1987, 88, 89, 90, 91, 92, 93, 94, 95, Welcome to Wall Street, 1992, 93, 94, 95, 96, Day to Day Math, 1994, Mental Math, 1995, Everyday Math, vol. 1 and 2, 1996, Word Problems, 1996; area co-chair Channel 8 Pub. TV Auction, Pueblo, 1983-87; contbr. articles to profl. jours. Bd. dirs. Columbine Girl Scout Council, 1983-85, Dist. #60 Blood Bank, 1985—; mem. Pueblo Greenway and Nature Ctr., 1981—. Recipient Thanks badge Girl Scouts U.S., Presdl. award for Outstanding Tchg. in Elem. Math., 1995. Mem. Nat. Council for Tchrs. Math., Colo. Coun. Tchrs. Math. (Outstanding Elem. Math Tchr. of Yr. 1989), Intertel, Mensa, Phi Delta Kappa, Alpha Phi. Lutheran. Club: Pueblo Country. Lodge: Sons of Norway. Home: 52 Country Club Vlg Pueblo CO 81008-1626 Office: Baca Elem Sch 2800 E 17th St Pueblo CO 81001-4741

LINDVIG, LEONA MINDELL, librarian, educator; b. Bremerton, Wash., Sept. 18, 1946; d. Edward and Adene Mindell (Lynum) Vig; m. James David Selin, Nov. 27, 1969 (div. 1977); 1 child: Korin Nicole; m. Paul Wallace Johnson, May 21, 1977 (div. 2000); children: Gunnar, Turi, Ole-Paul. BA in Psychology, Western Wash. U., 1969; forest technician cert., Peninsula Coll., 1975; MEd, Central Wash. U., 1994. Cert. tchr. K-8, Wash. Forest engr. Crown Zellerbach, Sekiu, Wash., 1975-77; forest tech. U.S. Forest Svc., Cle Elum, Wash., 1978; libr. Roslyn (Wash.) Pub. Libr., 1978-96, Carpenter Meml. Libr., Cle Elum, 1980-81; libr. II Clallam Bay (Wash.) Correctional Ctr., 1990; grad. asst. Ctrl. Wash. U., Ellensburg, Wash., 1992-93, libr. specialist, 1996—. Substitute tchr. Cle Elum (Wash.)-Roslyn Sch., 1994-96. Scholar AAUW, 1992. Office: Cen Wash U Library Ellensburg WA 98926

LINDZEN, RICHARD SIEGMUND, meteorologist, educator; b. Webster, Mass., Feb. 8, 1940; s. Abe and Sara (Blachman) L.; m. Nadine Lucie Kalougine, Apr. 7, 1965; children: Eric, Nathaniel. AB, Harvard U., 1960, SM, 1961, PhD, 1964. Research assoc. U. Wash., Seattle, 1964-65; Research asso. U. Oslo, 1965-66; with Nat. Center Atmospheric Research, Boulder, Colo., 1966-68; mem. faculty U. Chgo., 1968-72; prof. meteorology Harvard U., 1972-83, dir. Center for Earth and Planetary Physics, 1980-83; Alfred P. Sloan prof. meteorology MIT, 1983—. Lady Davis vis. prof. Hebrew U., 1979; Sackler prof. Tel Aviv U., 1992; Vikram Sarabhai prof. Phys. Rsch. Lab., Ahmendabad, India, 1985; Lansdowne lectr. U. Victoria, 1993; Haurwitz lectr. Am. Meteorol. Soc., 1997; cons. NASA, Jet Propulsion Lab., others; corr. mem. com. on human rights NAS. Author: Dynamics in Atmospheric Physics; co-author: Atmospheric Tides; contbr. to profl. jours. Recipient Macelwane award Am. Geophys. Union, 1968 Fellow NAS, AAAS, Am. Geophys. Union, Am. Meteorol. Soc. (Meisinger award 1969, councillor 1972-75, Charney award 1985, Haurwitz lectr. 1997), Am. Acad. Arts and Scis., Norwegian Acad. Scis. and Letters; mem. Internat. Commn. Dynamic Meteorology, Institut Mondial des Scis. (founding mem.). Jewish. Office: MIT 54 1720 Cambridge MA 02139

LINEBERRY, PAUL F., JR., secondary education music educator; b. Waynesville, N.C., Aug. 6, 1944; s. Paul F. and Elmorene L. Lineberry; m. Jane Bulla, Aug. 27, 1966; children: Scott Eric, Brittnay Anne. MusB Edn., East Carolina U., 1966, MusM Edn., 1967. Cert. music tchr. K-12, Pa., supvr. pub. sch. music, Pa. Adj. graduate faculty Music Dept., Trenton State Coll., N.J.; dist. coord. music edn. Coun. Rock Sch. Dist., Richboro, Pa.; instrumental music instr. Coun. Rock H.S., Newtown, Pa., 1991—, chairperson music dept., 1993—. Dir. sch. bands in performance in U.S. and Western Europe; cons. pub. sch. music programs, Bucks County, Pa.; lectr. in field. Curriculum devel. com. Coun. Rock Sch. Dist., Richboro, Bucks County Int. Unit Task Force on Music Edn., 1991—; mem. Pa. State Profl. Stds. Com. in Music Edn., 1990—. Recipient graduate study grant Fed. HEW Dept. Mem. NEA, ASCD, Music Educators Nat. Conf., Pa. Music Educators Assn. (com. chmn., Citation of Excellence in Teaching award 1991), Bucks County Music Edn. Assn. (past pres. and com. chmn.), Coun. Rock Edn. Asns., Pa. Edn. Assn., Phi Mu Alpha, Phi Beta Mu. Home: 221 Ridgecrest Rd Asheboro NC 27203-5837

LINER, RONALD SIMS, middle school administrator; b. Concord, N.C., Sept. 20, 1946; s. James Harold and Agnes Matilda (Sims) L.; m. Judy Ann Greene, June 7, 1969; 1 child, Matthew Scott. BS, Appalachian State U., 1968, MA, 1972, EdS, 1989. Cert. tchr., mentor, adminstr., N.C. Elem. tchr. Winston Salem (N.C.), Forsyth County Schs., 1968-72, 75-90, jr. high sch. tchr., coord., 1972-74; adminstr., 1990—; tchr., adminstr. Trinity High Sch., Winston Salem, 1974-75. Counselor N.C. Dept. Corrections, Winston Salem, N.C., 1969-74; mentor tchr. Winston Salemforsyth County Schs., 1966—, A.M.A. Task Force, 1981-82, supts. adv. com. mem., 1988-90, evaluation instr., 1989-90. Scoutmaster, Boy Scouts Am., Winston Salem, N.C., 1973-76. Named Tchr. of Yr. Oak Summit Elem. Sch., 1981, '82, Jefferson Elem. Sch. 1986, finalist for Tchr. of Yr. Winston Salem/ Forsyth County Schs., 1981, '86. Mem. ASCD, NEA, Internat. Reading Assn., N.C. Edn. Assn., Forsyth Assn. Classroom Tchrs. (bldg. rep.), Masons, Phi Delta Kappa (historian 1988-90, treas. 1992-95). Democrat. Presbyterian. Avocations: golf, fishing, bridge, dancing, carpentry. Home: 5555 Alma Dr Winston Salem NC 27105-9601 Office: Hanes Middle Sch 2900 Indiana Ave Winston Salem NC 27105-4426

LINEWEAVER, PAUL KELTON, retired secondary education educator; b. Berkeley Spring, W.Va., May 30, 1925; s. Allen Lee and Bessie May (Fredman) L.; m. Hilda Eloise Crane, Nov. 16, 1947; 1 child, Amanda Storm. BS in Econs., Ind. U., 1955; MEd, Shippensburg (Pa.) State Coll., 1962. With Fairchild Aircraft, Hagerstown, Md., 1942-43; hosp. tech. VA, Martinsburg, W.Va., 1947-51; project coordinator Fairchild Aircraft, 1955-59; tchr. social studies Chambersburg (Pa.) High Sch., 1961-86; ret. With U.S. Army, 1943-47. Mem. Ind. U. Alumni Assn., Chambersburg Club, NEA, Pa. Edn. Assn., Masons, Delta Sigma, Alpha Kappa Delta. Avocations: fishing, gardening, hiking, photography. Address: 5270 Milford Dr Zanesville OH 43701-7453

LING, NAM, educator; b. Singapore, Dec. 9, 1956; s. Yu-Chich Ling and Siew-Chee Chen; m. Mei-Yan Lu, Dec. 3, 1994; children: Grace, Sophia. PhD, U. La., 1989. Product, process engr. Hewlett Packard, Singapore, 1981—83; asst. prof. Santa Clara (Calif.) U., 1989—94, assoc. prof., 1994—2001, prof., 2001—, assoc. dean, 2002—. Author: Specification and Verification of Systolic Arrays, 1999; contbr. articles over 90 articles to profl. jours., chapters to books. Interpreter Chinese Ch. in Christ, Mountain View, Calif., 1996—2000. Named IEEE Disting. Lectr., 2002—; recipient Rsch. Initiation award, NSF, 1990—93, Rschr. of Yr. award, 2000, Recent Achievement in Scholarship award, 2002; grantee, Nortel Networks, 2000, New Japan Radio Corp., 1995—97, 1997—99, Medianix Semiconductor, Inc., 1997—98. Mem.: IEEE (sr.; assoc. editor 1990—, tech. com. chair 1993—95), Am. Soc. for Engrng. Edn., Assn. for Computing Machinery. Avocation: travel. Office: Santa Clara U Dept Computer Engring 500 El Camino Real Santa Clara CA 95053

LINGLE, CRAIG STANLEY, glaciologist, educator; b. Carlsbad, N.Mex., Sept. 11, 1945; s. Stanley Orland and Margaret Pearl (Ewart) L.; m. Diana Lynn Duncan, Aug. 21, 1972; 1 son, Eric Glenn. BS, U. Wash., 1967; MS, U. Maine, 1978; PhD, U. Wis., 1983. Nat. rsch. coun. resident rsch. assoc. Coop. Inst. for Rsch. in Environ. Scis., U. Colo., Boulder, 1983-84, rsch. assoc., 1984-86; program mgr. polar glaciology divsn. polar programs NSF, Washington, 1986-87; cons. Jet Propulsion Lab., Pasadena, Calif., 1987-88; nat. rsch. coun. resident rsch. assoc. NASA Goddard Space Flight

Ctr., Oceans and Ice Branch, Greenbelt, Md., 1988-90; rsch. assoc. prof. Geophys. Inst., U. Alaska, Fairbanks, 1990-2000, acting dir. Alaska synthetic aperture radar facility, 1997-98, rsch. prof. geophysics, 2000—. Contbr. articles to profl. jours. Recipient Antarctic Svc. medal of U.S., NSF, 1987, Rsch. Project of Month award Office of Health and Environ. Rsch., U.S. Dept. Energy, 1990, Group Achievement award NASA, 1992. Mem. AAAS, Internat. Glaciological Soc., Am. Geophys. Union, Sigma Xi. Avocations: downhill and cross-country skiing, canoeing, hiking. Office: U Alaska Geophys Inst PO Box 757320 Fairbanks AK 99775-7320

LINGLE, MURIEL ELLEN, retired elementary education educator; b. Sundown Twp., Minn., Sept. 15, 1927; d. Harold O. and Carrie H. (Ewald) Anderson; m. Dale A. Lingle, Aug. 21 (dec. June 1999); children: Barbara Jean, Tamara Jane. BS with distinction, Union Coll., Lincoln, Nebr., 1968; MA, U. Nebr., Lincoln, 1976. Cert. tchr., Nebr. Elem. tchr., Hallam, Nebr., 1959-62; tchr. Cen. Elem. and High Sch., Sprague-Martell, Nebr., 1963-67, Helen Hyatt Elem. Sch., Lincoln, 1968-70; elem. tchr. Crete (Nebr.) Sch. System, 1970-91; ret., 1991. Recipient award for excellence in teaching Cooper Found., 1990-91, Internat. Woman of Yr. award, 1993-94. Avocations: reading, sewing, music, antique cars, collecting plates and die-cast precision automobile and truck models. Home (Winter): # 27 530 S Alma Sch Rd Mesa AZ 85210 Home (Summer): 4730 Hillside St Lincoln NE 68506

LINGREN, WESLEY EARL, chemistry educator; b. Pasadena, Calif., Aug. 27, 1930; s. Lawrence Earl and Dorothy (Green) L.; m. Merrilyn Elizabeth Summer, Feb. 24, 1961; children: Eric, Leslie. BS, Seattle Pacific Coll., 1952; MS, U. Wash., 1954, PhD, 1962. Asst. prof. chemistry Pasadena Coll., 1956-58; asst. prof. Seattle Pacific U., 1962-65, assoc. prof., 1965-67, prof., 1968—98; NSF fellow Yale U., New Haven, 1967-68. Author: Inorganic Nomenclature, 1980, Essentials of Chemistry, 1986; contbr. articles to profl. jours. Served to sgt. M.C., U.S. Army, 1954-56. Fellow Am. Assn. Engring. Edn., Solar Energy Research, Golden, Colo., 1984. Mem. Am. Chem. Soc., Nat. Sci. Tchrs. Assn., U.S. Tennis Assn., Sigma Xi. Presbyterian. Avocation: tennis.

LINHART, JOSEPH WAYLAND, retired cardiologist, educational administrator; b. N.Y.C., Feb. 7, 1933; s. Joseph and Myrla Watson (Wayland) L.; m. Marilyn Adele Voight, Sept. 1, 1956; children: Joseph, Mary-Ellen, Richard, Jennifer, Donna-Lisa, Daria. BS, George Washington U., 1954, MD, 1958. Diplomate Am. Bd. Internal Medicine with subspecialty in cardiovascular diseases. Intern Washington Hosp. Ctr., 1958-59; resident George Washington U. Hosp., Washington, 1959-60, Duke U. Hosp., Durham, N.C., 1961, fellow, 1960, 62-63, Nat. Heart Inst./Johns Hopkins Hosp., Bethesda/Balt., Md., 1963-64; asst. prof. medicine U. Fla., Gainesville, 1964-67; clin. assoc. prof. U. Miami, Fla., 1967-68; assoc. prof. medicine U. Tex., San Antonio, 1968-71; prof., dir. cardiology Hahnemann Med. Coll., Phila., 1971-75; prof., chmn. dept. medicine Chgo. Med. Sch., 1975-79, Oral Roberts U., Tulsa, 1979-83; prof. medicine U. South Fla., Tampa, 1983-92; prof., regional chmn. medicine Tex. Tech. U., Odessa, 1992-93; prof. medicine La. State U., Shreveport, 1993-97; chief med. svc. VA Med. Ctr., Shreveport, 1993-97, acting chief of staff, 1996-97; ret., 1997. Cons. in cardiology and med./legal questions. Contbr. articles to profl. jours.; author 4 books. Mem. med. adv. com. YMCA, Niles, Ill., 1976-79; bd. govs. Phila. Heart Assn., 1972-75; mem. rsch. coun. Okla. Heart Assn., Tulsa, 1980-83. Fellow ACP, Am. Coll. Cardiology; mem. AAAS, Planetary Soc., Nat. Space Soc., Astron. Soc. of Pacific, Alpha Omega Alpha. Republican. Avocations: astronomy, history, model building, organ playing, music. Home: 625 Red Cedar Ct NE Saint Petersburg FL 33703-6203

LINK, DAVID THOMAS, dean, lawyer; b. 1936; BS magna cum laude, U. Notre Dame, 1958, JD, 1961; postgrad., Georgetown U., 1965—66. Bar: Ohio 1961, Ill. 1966, Ind. 1975, U.S. Supreme Ct. Trial atty. Office of Cjief Counsel, IRS, 1961—66; ptnr. Winston, Strawn, Smith & Patterson, Chgo., 1966—70; prof. U. Notre Dame Law Sch., Notre Dame, Ind., 1970—99, dean, 1975—99, dean, prof. emeritus, 1999—; founding dep. vice chancellor, provost St. Augustine U. Coll., South Africa, 1999—; pres., CEO Internat. Ctr. Healing and Law, 2001—; assoc. coun. Office Ind. Counsel. Cons. to GAO. Author (with Soderquist): Law of Federal Estate and Gift Taxation, Vol. 1, 1978, Vol. 2, 1980, Vol. 3, 1982. Mem. Ind. Gov.'s Com. on Individual Privacy; mem. pres.' task force New Methods for Improving the Quality of Lawyers' Svcs. to Clients; chair. Ind. State Ethics Commn., 1988—90; acad. coun., provost's adv. com., athletic affairs, acad. affairs, faculty affairs coms. of bd. trustees U. Notre Dame, founding pres., vice chancellor, 1990—92; bd. trustees, bd. govs., interim dir. U. Notre Dame Ctr. for Civil and Human Rights; chair World Law Inst. Served to lt. comdr. USN. Mem.: ABA (coun. on sci. and tech., com. on advt., sect. on legal edn., com. on professionalism 1993—97), Soc. for Values in Higher Edn.

LINK, E. G. (JAY LINK), corporate executive, family wealth counselor; b. Portsmouth, Va., Apr. 30, 1952; s. Edward and Hazel (Blalock) L.; m. Pamela Kay Kidwell, Jan. 19, 1955; children: Bethany, Anna, Kara, Lissa. BA, Cin. Bible Coll., 1974; MDiv, Cin. Christian Sem., 1979; BS, Am. Coll. Nutripathy, 1988; postgrad., Calif. Coast U., 1985-86. Ordained min. Chs. of Christ, 1974; cert. family wealth counselor. Min., Northern Ky., 1974-79; sales rep. Met. Life Ins., Joplin, Mo., 1979-81, sales mgr., 1981-82; founder, pres. E.G. Link Leasing Co., Inc., Franklin, Ind., 1982-87; founder, dir. Ind. Buying Club, Franklin, 1986-99; co-founder, pres. Co-op Svcs., Inc., Franklin, 1990-99; founder Shiloh Found., Franklin, 1993—; founder, pres., owner Philanthro Dynamics, Inc., Franklin, 1982-96, Family Wealth Counselors of Am., LLC, 1998—; founder, owner Thinking Beyond Technologies, LLC, 1998—2000. Nat. seminar spkr. on family wealth counseling; founder, pres. T.E.A.M. Products, Inc., 1993-2000; cons. to non-profit orgns.; founder Nat. Assn. Family Wealth Counselors; founder, pres. Profl. Mentoring Program, 1996-2000, Family Wealth Counselors Mgmt. Co., Inc., 1998-2000; founder, chmn. Family Wealth Counseling Cos., Inc., 1999-2000; lic. real estate cons., 2002—. Author: Family Wealth Counseling: Getting to the Heart of the Matter; editor Natural Alternatives, 1990-92, Thinking Beyond..., 1993-2000; contbr. articles to profl. jours. Founder, dir. Stewardship Ministries, Inc., Franklin, 1984-92. Mem. Nat. Assn. Family Wealth Counselors, Nat. Com. Planning Giving, Planned Giving Group Ind., Ind. Assn. Home Educators. Republican. Avocations: mission work, preaching, teaching bible study, outdoor living. Home: 4363 E State Road 252 Franklin IN 46131-8164 Office: Family Wealth Counselors of Am 4363 E SR 252 Franklin IN 46131 E-mail: jlink@thinkingbeyond.net.

LINK, ELEANOR ANN, elementary education educator; b. Salisbury, N.C., May 5, 1943; d. Rufus Edward and Alma Eleanor (Jordan) Scruggs; m. John Barry Link, Dec. 24, 1964; children: Leigh Ann Link Cross, John Edward. AB in Elem. Edn. and Home Econs., Catawba Coll., 1965. Cert. elem. tchr., N.C. Tchr. 3d grade Davidson County Sch. System, Lexington, N.C., 1965-66; tchr. asst. Guilford County Sch. System, Greensboro, N.C., 1984-88, tchr. 1st grade, 1988—. Mem. Sch. Improvement Team. Recipient Evon Dean Svc. award to Children, Guilford County PTA. Mem. NEA, N.C. Edn. Assn., Internat. Reading Assn., Greater Greensboro Reading Coun., N.C. Ctr. Advancement of Teaching. Democrat. Methodist. Avocations: reading, cross stitch, traveling, church work. Home: 8757 Snow Camp Rd Snow Camp NC 27349-8708 Office: Nathanael Greene Elem Sch 2717 Nc Highway 62 E Liberty NC 27298-9119

LINK, PHOEBE FORREST, educator, poet, author; b. Palmerton, Pa., Feb. 20, 1926; d. Phoebe Eleanor (Lewis) Forrest and John Nevins Forrest; m. Robert H. Link, July 13, 1962; children: David Forrest, Anne Harris. BA in Psychology, Pa. State U., 1947, MS in Child Devel. and Family Relationships, 1952; postgrad. U. Rochester, 1957-59, Harvard U., 1958. Dir. teen age program YWCA, Lansing, Mich., 1947-50, Rochester, N.Y., 1952-56; research asst. Pa. State U., State College, 1950-52; tchr. Rochester, 1956-60; demonstration tchr. William Antheil Sch., Trenton, N.J., 1960-63; mem. faculty Trenton State Coll., 1960-63; tchr. State College area schs., 1971-1993; lectr. Am. Home Econs. Assn. Conv.; cons. family studies, leader continuing edn. workshops Pa. State U., 1977, others; mem. staff dean women Harvard U., Cambridge, Mass., summer 1958; dir. Children's Program for Pa. Dist. Attys. Author: Small? Tall? Not At All, 1973, Passionate Realist, 1994; staff writer Horizon, 1985-87; author, creator Hearthrob series, Pa. State U., 1987; contbr. articles to profl. jours. Trustee Schlow Pub. Library, State College, Pa., 1980-83; founder, first chmn. poetry com. Cen. Pa. Festival Arts; founder Children's Link, Bar Harbor, Maine. AAUW Simmons grantee, 1984; recipient Excellence in Edn. award Pa. State Univ., 1993; featured author on TV series The Writing Life, featured speaker at 50th class reunion P.S.U., reader-editor for WPSX-TV, Mem. AAUW, NEA, Pa. Edn. Assn., State Coll. Area Edn. Assn.(scholarship com.), Mortar Board Alumni (founder, 1st pres., pres.), Pa. State U. Coll. Human Devel. Alumni (bd. dirs.). Phi Delta Kappa, Omicron Nu Alumni, Tau Phi Sigma, Peterson Society P.S.U. Home: 22 Cricklewood Cir State College PA 16803-2105

LINKE, ERIKA C. academic librarian; d. Heinz G. and Martha Linke; m. Henry A. Pisciotta, Feb. 22, 1979; 1 child, Rachel N. L. Pisciotta. BA, Miami U., 1970; MLS, U. Minn., Mpls., 1978; cert., ACRL Harvard Leadership Inst., 2000. Assoc. libr. Carnegie Mellon U., Pitts., 1985—. Bd. dirs. Oakland Libr. Consortium, Pitts., 1991—98. Treas. Carnegie Mellon U. Fed. Credit Union, Pitts., 1993—2003; adv. coun. Pitts. Bibliophiles, Pitts., 2001—. Recipient award, Mortar Bd., 1969, Sr. Fellow, UCLA, 2003. Mem.: Libr. Adminstrn. & Mgmt. Assn. (exec. com. stats. sect. 1999—2001), We. Pa./W.Va. Assn. Coll. & Rsch. Libr. (v.p./pres.-elect 2002—), Assn. Coll. & Rsch. Libr. (chair copyright con. 1995—97, exec. bd. 2001—, chair budget & fin. com. 2001—). Office: Carnegie Mellon Univ 5000 Forbes Ave Pittsburgh PA 15213

LINN, BRIAN M, education educator; BA with honors, U. of Hawaii at Manoa, 1978; MA, Ohio State U., 1981, PhD, 1985. Vis. asst. prof. U. Nebr., Dept. of History, 1986—87, Old Dominion U., Dept. of History, 1987—89; asst. prof. Tex. A&M U., Dept. History, 1989—95, assoc. prof., 1995—98; prof. history Tex. A&M U., 1998—. Harold K. Johnson vis. prof. of mil. history Army War Coll., 1999—2000; grad com. Tex. A&M U., 1997—99, grad. com., 2000—, Asian history search com., 1997—98; dir. Mil. Studies Inst., 2001; co-chair, program com. Soc. for Mil. History Ann. Conf., 2001—02; awards com. Soc. for Mil. History, 2001—. Mem. editl. bd. Jour. of Mil. History, 1998—2001. Recipient U.S. Army Mil. History Inst. Advanced Rsch. Assoc., 1982; fellowship, John Simon Guggenheim Meml. Found., 2003, grant, Tex. A&M U., 1993, 1997, Faculty Develop. grant, 1995—96, Susan Louise Dyer Peace fellowship, Hoover Inst. on War, Revolution and Peace, Stanford U.1993, 1993—94, John M. Olin postdoctoral fellowship, Yale U., 1990—91, Rsch. and Grad Studies Faculty Mini-Grants, Tex. A&M U., 1992, 1993, Mil. Studies Inst. Summer Rsch. grant, 1991, Rsch. and Grad Studies Faculty Mini-Grants, 1992, Nat. Endowment for the Humanities Summer Stipend, 1989, grant, U.S. Marine Corps Hist. Ctr. Rsch. grant, 1986—87, U.S. Army Ctr. of Mil. History Visiting Rsch. Fellow, 1984—85. Mem.: Inter-Univers Seminar on Armed Forces and Soc., Philippine Hist. Assn., U.S. Commn. on Mil. History, Soc. for Mil. History. Office: Tex A&M U 200A History Bldg College Station TX 77843-4236

LINN, DIANA PATRICIA, elementary education educator; b. Perth, Australia, Dec. 31, 1943; came to U.S., 1948; d. Evan Andrew and Grace Henrietta (Springhall) Jarboe; m. Jim F. Erlandsen, July 9, 1966 (div. Mar. 1989); children: Rebecca, Tim, Jenny; m. Richard George Linn, Mar. 31, 1990; 1 stepchild, Cristal. AA, Olympic Coll., 1963; BA in Elem. Edn., Western Wash. U., 1965; MA, U. Ariz., 1969. Cert. tchr., Wash. Tchr. Neomi B. Willmore Elem., Westminster, Calif., 1965-66; tchr. English and sci. Sunnyside Jr. H.S., Tucson, 1966-70; tchr. kindergarten All Seasons Sch., Tucson, 1972-74; tchr. St. Cyril's Sch., Tucson, 1974-77; elem. tchr. Grace Christian Sch., Tucson, 1977-80; kindergarten and elem. tchr. Ridgeview Christian Ctr., Spokane, Wash., 1983-85, Spokane Christian Schs., 1985-87; dir. Ridgeview Christian Learning Ctr., Spokane, 1987-88; tchr. kindergarten Arlington Elem. Sch., Spokane, 1988-96, Grant Elem. Sch., Spokane, 1996—. Mem. curriculum study com. Sunnyside Sch. Dist., Tucson, 1967-68; chmn. accreditation and sch. bd. St. Cyril's Sch., Tucson, 1976-77; chair faculty involvement group, chair staff devel., chair wellness com. Arlington Elem., Spokane, 1992-93, sch. reporter, 1994-95; instr. reading readiness Family Learning Fair, Home Schooling Seminar, Spokane Falls C.C., Spokane, 1988; chair, coord. pre-sch. coop. Arlington Elem. with Spokane Falls C. C. of Spokane C.C., 1992-93; chair faculty involvement group, Arlington Elem., Spokane, 1995-96, Grant Elem. Sch., 1996-97, also wellness chair, 1996-2001, site coun. faculty rep. 2001—, strategic plan equity com. Arlington Elem., Spokane, 1995-96, pres. site coun., 2003—. Coord. Christian edn. Valley Foursquare Ch., Spokane, 1982-87; coord. children's ch. Victory Faith Fellowship, Spokane, 1993-2003; Brownie troop leader Willmore Elem., Westminster, 1965-66; ednl. restructuring rep. for Arlington Elem., Spokane Sch. Dist. 81, 1992-93; mem. equity com., 1996-99, mem. early childhood com., 1996—, mem. strategic planning com., 1998—, wellness chmn., 1998-2000, mem. instrnl. team, 1999—; primary rep. Site Coun. Grant Elem., 2002. Scholar Naval Officer's Wives Club, 1961-62; recipient Eisenhower grant, 1990, 94, 96-97. Mem. ASCD, NEA, Wash. Edn. Assn., Spokane Edn. Assn. (Arlington Elem. rep. 1991-93), CPA Wives Club (sec., ball chair 1983-84), Alpha Delta Kappa (membership chair 1994-95, corr. sec. 1996-99). Republican. Avocations: collecting dolls, plates, swimming, quilt-making. Home: 1324 S Perry St Spokane WA 99202-3572 Office: Grant Elem Sch 1300 E 9th Ave Spokane WA 99202-2499 E-mail: dianaL.@sd81.k12.wa.us.

LINN, MARCIA CYROG, education educator; b. Milw., May 27, 1943; d. George W. and Frances (Vanderhoof) Cyrog; m. Stuart Michael Linn, 1967 (div. 1979); children: Matthew, Allison; m. Curtis Bruce Tarter, 1987. BA in Psychology and Stats., Stanford U., 1965, MA in Ednl. Psychology, 1967, PhD in Ednl. Psychology, 1970. Prin. investigator Lawrence Hall Sci. U. Calif., 1970-87, prin. investigator Sch. Edn., 1985—, asst. dean Sch. Edn., 1983-85, prof., 1989—; prin. investigator NSF Funded Ctr.- Tech.-Enhanced Learning in Sci. (TELS), 2003—08; chancellor's prof., 2003—. Fulbright prof. Weizmann Inst., Israel, 1983; exec. dir. seminars U. Calif., 1985-86, dir. instnl. tech. program, 1988-96, chair cognition and devel., 1996—98; cons. Apple Computer, 1983—; mem. adv. com. on sci. edn. NSF, 1978—85, Ednl. Testing Svc., 1986—, Smithsonian Instn., 1986—, Fulbright Program, 1983-86, Grad. Record Exam. Bd., 1990-94, adv. com. edn. and human resources directorate, NSF; chair Cognitive Studes Bd. McDonell Found., 1994-97; mem. computing svcs. adv. bd. Carnegie Mellon U., 1991-99; mem. steering com. 3d Internat. Math. and Sci. Study, U.S., 1991-2002. Author: Education and the Challenge of Technology, 1987; co-author: The Psychology of Gender--Advances Through Meta Analysis, 1986—, Designing Pascal Solutions, 1992—, Designing Pascal Solutions with Data Structures, 1996, Computers, Teachers, Peers-Science Learning Partners, 2000, Internet Environments for Science Education, 2003; contbr. articles to profl. jours. Sci. advisor Parents Club, Lafayette, Calif., 1984-87; mem. Internat. Women's Forum, Women's Forum West, 1992—, membership com., 1995-98; bd. dirs. Nat. Ctr. for Sci. Edn., 1997—, GIS and edn. com., 2000—; mem. bd. on behavioral, cognitive and sensory scis. Nat. Rsch. Coun., 1997—, mem. com. on info. tech. literacy, computer sci. and telecomms., 1997-2000; mem. nat. adv. bd. Nat. Ctr. for Improving Studnet Learning and Achievement in Math. and Sci., 1997—. Recipient fellow Ctr. for Adv. Study in Behavior. Scis. 1995-96, 2001-02, Excellence Ednl. Rsch. award Coun. Sci. Soc. Pres., 1998. Fellow AAAS (bd. dirs. 1996-2001), APA, AAUW (mem. commn. tech. and gender 1998-2001), Am. Psychol. Soc.; mem. Nat. Assn. Rsch. in Sci. and Teaching (bd. dirs. 1983-86, assoc. editor jour., Outstanding Paper award 1978, Outstanding Jour. Article award 1975, 83, Disting. Contbns. to Sci. Edn. Through Rsch. award 1994), Am. Ednl. Rsch. Assn. (chmn. rsch. on women and edn. 1983-85, Women Educators Rsch. award 1982, 88, edn. in sci. and tech. 1989-90, ann. mtg. program com. 1996, Willystine Goodsell award 1991), Nat. Sci. Tchrs. Assn. (mem. rsch. agenda com. 1987-90, task force 1993-94), Soc. for Rsch. in Child Devel. (editl. bd. 1984-89), Soc. Rsch. Adolescence, Sierra Club. Avocations: skiing, hiking. Office: U Calif Grad Sch Edn 4611 Tolman Hl Berkeley CA 94720-0001

LINN, ROBERT LEE, educational researcher; b. Denver, June 29, 1938; s. Thomas E. and Ruth L. (Connor) L.; m. Joyce E. Lester, Aug. 29, 1958; children: Stephen B., Michael C. AB, UCLA, 1961; MA, U. Ill., 1964, PhD, 1965. Rsch. psychologist Ednl. Testing Svc., 1965-73; prof. U. Ill., urbana, 1973-87, U. Colo., Boulder, 1987-96, disting. prof., 1996—. Editor: (book) Educational Measurement, 1989; author: (book) Educational Assessment in Teaching, 1995. Disting. Contbn. to Ednl. Measurement, Ednl. Testing Svc., 1989; recipient EL Thorndike award APA, 1992, EF Lindquist award Am. Ednl. Rsch. Assn., 1993. Fellow APA (pres. divsn. 5 1985—, disting. contbn. award 1998); mem. Nat. Assn. Measurement in Edn. (pres. 1985—, disting. contbn. award 1995), Am. Ednl. Rsch. Assn. (v.p. divsn. D 1985, pres. 2003-03, disting. contbn. award 1997), Nat. Acad. Edn. Office: U Colo PO Box 249 Boulder CO 80309-0249

LINOWES, DAVID FRANCIS, political economist, educator, corporate executive; b. N.J., Mar. 16, 1917; m. Dorothy Lee Wolf, Mar. 25, 1946; children: Joanne Linowes Alinsky, Richard Gary, Susan Linowes Allen (dec.), Jonathan Scott. Founder, ptnr. Leopold & Linowes (now BDO Siedman), Washington, 1946-62; cons. sr. ptnr. Leopold & Linowes, Washington, 1962-82; nat. founding ptnr. Laventhol & Horwath, 1965-76; chmn. bd, CEO Mickleberry Comm. Corp., 1970-73; chmn., CEO Perpetual Investment Co., Inc., 1950-88; dir. Horn & Hardart Co., 1971-77, Piper Aircraft, 1972-77, Saturday Rev./World Mag., Inc., 1972-77, Chris Craft Industries, Inc., 1958—, Work in Am. Inst., Inc.; prof. polit. economy, pub. policy, bus. adminstrn. U. Ill., Urbana, 1976—, Boeschenstein prof. emeritus, 1987—. Cons. DATA Internat. Assistance Corps., 1962-68, U.S. Dept. State, UN, Sec. HEW, Dept. Interior; chmn. Fed. Privacy Protection Commn., Washington, 1975-77, U.S. Commn. Fair Market Value Policy for Fed. Coal Leasing, 1983-84, Pres.'s Commn. on Fiscal Accountability of Nation's Energy Resources, 1981-82; chmn. Pres.' Commn. on Privatization, 1987-88; mem. Council on Fgn. Relations; cons. panel GAO; adj. prof. mgmt. NYU, 1965-73; Disting. Arthur Young Prof. U. Ill., 1973-74; emeritus chmn. internat. adv. com. Tel Aviv U.; headed U.S. State Dept. Mission to Turkey, 1967, to India, 1970, to Pakistan, 1968, to Greece, 1971; U.S. rep. on privacy to Orgn. Econ. Devel. Intergovtl. Bur. for Informatics, 1977-81, cons., N.Y.C., 1977-81; U.S. State Dept. mission to Chile, Argentina and Uruguay, July, 1988, Yugoslavia, May, 1991. Author: Managing Growth Through Acquistion, Strategies for Survival, Corporate Conscience; commn. report Personal Privacy in Information Society, Fiscal Accountablility of Nation's Energy Resources; editor: The Impact of the Communication and Computer Revolution on Society, Privacy in America, 1989, Creating Public Policy, 1998, Living Through 50 Years of Economic Progress with 10 Presidents-The Most Productive Generation in History 1946-1996, 2000; contbr. articles to profl. jours. Trustee Boy's Club Greater Washington, 1955-62, Am. Inst. Found., 1962-68; assoc. YM-YWHA's Greater N.Y., 1970-76; chmn. Charities Adv. Com. of D.C., 1958-62; emeritus bd. dirs. Religion in Am. Life, Inc.; former chmn. U.S. People for UN; chmn. citizens com. Combat Charity Rackets, 1953-58. 1st lt. Signal Corps, AUS, 1942-46. Recipient 1970 Human Relations award Am. Jewish Com., U.S. Pub. Service award, 1982, Alumni Achievement award U. Ill., 1989, CPA Distinguished Pub. Svc. award, Washington, 1989. Mem. AICPA (v.p. 1962-63), U. Ill. Found. (emeritus bd. dirs. 1), Coun. Fgn. Rels., Cosmos Club, Phi Kappa Phi (nat. bd. dirs.), Beta Gamma Sigma. Home (Summer): 5630 Wisconsin Ave 801 Chevy Chase MD 20815 Home (Winter): 120 SE 5th Ave 524 Boca Raton FL 33432-5072

LINTINGER, GREGORY JOHN, electrical engineer, educator; b. New Orleans, Oct. 8, 1946; s. Emile John Jr. and Lucy (Perez) L.; m. Barbara Gaudet, Mar. 14, 1965 (div. Sept. 1981); children: Gregory John Jr., Melissa Anne; m. Brenda Celeste Wambsgans, Dec. 12, 1981; 1 child, Emily Celeste. BS in Elec. Engring., U. New Orleans, 1985. Registered profl. engr., La., Tenn., Miss., Ark. Office mgr. Upper City Electric Co., New Orleans, 1967-72, elec. estimator, 1972-76, elec. designer, estimator, 1976-87, v.p. elec. design/estimating, 1987—; mgr., elec. and instrumental engring. dept. Wink Engring., New Orleans, 1994—. Instr. Associated Builders and Contractors, New Orleans, 1975-95. Pres. Young Men's Bus. Club of Greater New Orleans, 1975. Recipient Bush award Young Men's Bus. Club, New Orleans, 1973-75, Colomb award, 1975; named U. New Orleans Disting. Engring. Alumni, 1999. Mem. Illuminating Engrs. Soc. (sec. 1987-88), Inst. Electronic Engrs., Industry Application Soc. (exhibits chair 1997 annual meeting), Kiwanis (treas. 1986-87), A.B.C. (bd. dirs. New Orleans chpt. 1986-87). Republican. Roman Catholic. Avocations: piano, computers, music, philanthropy. Home: 639 Labarre Dr Metairie LA 70001-5442 Office: Wink Engineering Elect & Instrumental Engring Dept 4949 Bullard Ave Ste 100 New Orleans LA 70128-3147

LINTON, FRED ERNEST JULIUS, mathematics educator; b. Genova, Italy, Apr. 8, 1938; s. Martin and Melitta (Joel) L.; m. Barbara Mikolajewska, Dec. 18, 1990. BA, Yale U., 1958; MA, Columbia U., 1959, PhD, 1963; MA (hon.), Wesleyan U., Middletown, Conn., 1972. Asst. prof. Wesleyan U., Middletown, 1963-68, assoc. prof., 1968-72, prof. math., 1972—, chmn. math. dept., 1975. Mem. Am. Math. Soc., Math. Assn. Am. Home: 36 Everit St New Haven CT 06511-2208 Office: Wesleyan U Dept Math Middletown CT 06459-0001

LINTON, JOY SMITH, primary school educator; b. Scranton, Pa., Dec. 9, 1952; d. Burnley J. and Josephine (Sbaraglia) Smith; m. William Howard Linton Jr., May 28, 1972; children: Kristy, David, Shelby. BSEd, West Chester State Coll., 1973. Minister St. Leo the Great Parish, Lancaster, Pa.; tchr. Apostles Community Preschool, Lancaster. Mem. bio-med. ethics com., mem. bio-med. edn. com. Ephrata Community Hosp; mem. subcom. med. and legal affairs Lancaster County Bar Assn. Mem. nat. bd. dirs., head family affairs commn. Nat. Coun. of Cath. Women, 1994-96 (pub. in Cath. Woman mag., submissions pub. in Bulletin Bd. publ.). Named St. Leo Woman of Yr., 1993; Hannah Kent Shopf Meml. scholar; Pa. Higher Edn. grantee. Mem. Nat. Assn. Edn. Young Children, Lancaster Assn. Edn. Young Children, Zeta Tau Alpha. Home: 808 Hillaire Rd Lancaster PA 17601-2221 E-mail: joy.linton@att.net.

LIPAN, PETRUTA E. semiotician, curator, artist; b. Braila, Romania, Oct. 18, 1957; d. Ene and Maria C. L. BFA, Washington Univ., 1991; MFA, PhD in Semiotic Studies, Ind. Univ., 1995. Instr. sculpture Ind. U., Bloomington, 1993-94, instr. 3-dimensional design, 1994-95; instr. sculpture Laumeyer Sculpture Mus., St. Louis, 1995-96; prof. art appreciation St. Louis U., 1996, assoc. curator S. Cuples House and McNamee Gallery, 1996—; mem. faculty Washington U., St. Louis, 1996-99; prof. art history St. Louis U., 1999-2000. Vis. artist Laumeier Sculpture Park, 1997, 1996, artist in residence, 1996; assisted in curating, organization and mktg. of shows including Edward Boccia: The Eye of the Painter, 1996, Ads With A Conscience, 1997, A Voice of Their Own, 1997, Mev Puelo: Witness to Life, 1997, Iridescence, 1998; curator Enduring Light: Fragility and Persistence, 1998, Passion for Color: Frederick Carder at Steuben Glass Works, 1999; presenter 5th Argentinian congress on Color, APHRA Behn Soc., Phila., 1999, Can. Semiotic Assn. Conf., Que., 1999, 7th Congress of IASS-AIS, Dresden, Germany, 1999, Math. Connections in Art, Music, and Sci., Winfield, Kans., 1999. Group exhibitions include Sioux City Art Ctr.,

1997, Ind. Univ., 1996, Centre Interculturel Strathearn, 1996, The Editions Limited Gallery of Art, 1995, The Carver Cultural Ctr., 1995, Ind. Univ. Art Mus., 1995, Ind. Univ., 1993, 94, 95, San Diego Art Inst., 1993, Steinberg Gallery, 1991, Bixby Gallery, 1991, South Grand Gallery, 1986, numerous others. Mem. Nat. Sculpture Soc., Internat. Assn. for Semiotic Studies (presenter at confs.), Semiotic Soc. Am., Am. Assn. Mus., Assn. for Art History, Internat. Assn. for Visual Semiotics, Midwest Art History Soc. Home: 1129 Olivaire Ln Saint Louis MO 63132-3010 E-mail: lipanp@yahoo.com.

LIPETZ, BEN-AMI, dean, information science educator; b. Fargo, N.D., Mar. 14, 1927; s. Elijah Yekusiel and Ruth Dobrusya (Leavitt) L. BME, Cornell U., 1948, PhD, 1959. Editor Brookhaven Nat. Lab., Upton, N.Y., 1948-50; project leader, asst. divsn. chief Battelle Meml. Inst., Columbus, Ohio, 1953-59; project mgr., libr. dir. Itek Corp., Lexington, Mass., 1959-62; cons. Carlisle, Mass., 1962-66; head of rsch. dept. Yale U. Libr., New Haven, 1966-78; dean, prof. sch. of info. sci. and policy SUNY, Albany, 1978—95, prof. emeritus, 1995—. Editor, bus. mgr. Info. Sci. Abstracts, New Haven, 1966-81; bd. dirs. Documentation Abstracts, Inc., Wilmington, treas., 1988-96. Author: Measurement of Efficiency of Scientific Research, 1965, Guide to Case Studies of Scientific Activity, 1965; contbr. articles to profl. jours. With USN, 1945-46. Mem. ALA, Am. Soc. for Info. Sci. and Tech.(bd. dirs.), Am. Soc. Indexers (pres.), Spl. Librs. Assn., Cornell Soc. Engrs., Friends of Libr. SUNY-Albany (pres.). Home: 365 Woodward Rd Nassau NY 12123 Office: Sch Info Sci and Policy Suny Albany NY 12222-0001 E-mail: balipetz@albany.edu.

LIPHAM, WILLIAM PATRICK, principal, educator; b. Franklin, Ga., Oct. 15, 1950; s. William Taft and Claudie Evelyn (McCord) Lipham; m. Jane King, Aug. 11, 1973; children: Leslie Ann, William Brian. BA, West Ga. Coll., 1973, MEd, 1979, EdS, 1990. Cert. in secondary sci., adminstrn./supervision, Ga. Tchr. Heard County Bd. Edn., Franklin, Ga., asst. prin., prin. With U.S. Army Nat. Guard, 1972-78. Recipient Dave Edelson award, Boy Scouts Am., 1982, Dist. award of Merit, 1980. Mem. Ga. Assn. Educators, (v.p., pres., treas.), Ga. Assn. Edn. Leaders. Home: 2727 Ga Hwy 34 Franklin GA 30217 Office: Heard Elem Sch 150 Alford Dr Franklin GA 30217-6345

LIPINSKI, BARBARA JANINA, psychologist, psychotherapist, educator, writer; b. Chgo., Feb. 29, 1956; d. Janek and Alicja (Brzozkiewicz) L. (dec.); m. Bernard Joseph Burns, Feb. 14, 1976 (div. 1985). B of Social Work, U. Ill., Chgo., 1978; MFCC, MA, U. Calif., Santa Barbara, 1982; PhD, U. So. Calif., 1992. Diplomate Am. Bd. Forensic Medicine; cert. tchr., Calif., psychology tchr., Calif.; cert. adminstr., non-pub. agent; lic. marriage, family and child therapist; bd. cert. forensic examiner; lic. psychologist. Police svc. officer Santa Barbara (Calif.) Police Dept., 1978-79; peace officer Airport Police, Santa Barbara, 1979-80; emergency comms. Univ. Police, Santa Barbara, 1980-82; facilitator, instr. Nat. Traffic Safety Inst., San Jose, Calif., 1981-87; assoc. dir. Community Health Task Force on Alcohol and Drug Abuse, Santa Barbara, 1982-86; instr. Santa Barbara C.C., 1987-88; patients' rights adv. Santa Barbara County Calif. Mental Health Adminstrn., 1986-89; pvt. practice psychotherapist Santa Barbara, 1985—; faculty mem., chair Pacifica Grad. Inst., Carpinteria, Calif., 1989-2000; police psychologist L.A. Police Dept., 2000; evaluator mentally ill offender crime reduction grant Bd. Corrections, Ventura, 2002—03. Intern clin. psychology L.A. County Sheriff's Dept., 1991-92, cons. Devereaux Found., Santa Barbara, 1993-95, Ctr. for Law Related Edn., Santa Barbara, 1986; cons., trainer Univ. Police Dept., Santa Barbara, 1982, 89. Author: In The Best Interest of the Patient: Ethical and Legal Issues in the Practice of Psychotherapy, 1999, Wisdom of the Oracle, 2000m, Feng Shui Wisdom, 2001, Heed the Call: Psychological Perspectives on Child Abuse, 2001, The Tao of Integrity: Legal, Ethical and Professional Issues in Psychology, 2002. Vol. crisis work Nat. Assn. Children of Alcoholics, L.A., 1987; crisis intervention worker Women in Crisis Can Act, Chgo., 1975-76; vol. counselor Santa Barbara Child Sexual Assault Treatment Ctr.-PACT, Santa Barbara, 1981-82. Recipient Grad. Teaching assistanship U. So. Calif., 1990-92. Mem. APA, Am. Profl. Soc. on Abuse of Children, Am. Coll. Forensic Examiners, Calif. Assn. Marriage and Family Therapists, Am. Psychotherapy Assn. (exec. adv. bd. 1997-99). Avocations: horticulture, aviculture, ecology. Office: Pacific Meridian 301 Los Cabos Ln Ventura CA 93001-1183 E-mail: pacificmeridian@aol.com.

LIPKA, RITA ANN, retired elementary education educator; b. Buffalo, Nov. 10, 1929; d. Edward and Clara (Elvers) L. BS in Elem. Edn., Daemen Coll., Buffalo, 1963. Tchr. Buffalo Diocese, 1950-51, 56-57, 1957-58, Columbus Diocese, New Lexington, Ohio, 1951-52, Columbus, 1958-66, tchr., prin., 1968-72; tchr. Wheeling Diocese, Charleston, W.Va., 1952-56, Jesuit-Franciscan Boarding Sch., St. Francis, S.D., 1966-68, Todd County Schs., Parmelee, S.D., 1972-80, Clark County Sch. Dist., Las Vegas, Nev., 1981-97; ret. Vol. work among the Otomi Indians, Ixmiquilpan, Mex., 1967. Mem. NEA, Nev. Edn. Assn., Clark County Classroom Tchrs. Assn.

LIPMAN-BLUMEN, JEAN, public policy and organizational behavior educator; b. Brookline, Mass., Apr. 28, 1933; AB, Wellesley Coll., 1954, AM, 1956; PhD, Harvard U., 1970; postdoctoral study, Carnegie-Mellon U., 1970-71, Stanford U., 1971-72. Asst. dir., Nat. Inst. Edn., dir women's rsch. program, 1973-78; spl. asst., mem. domestic policy staff The White House Office of Asst. Sec. Edn.; mem. domestic policy staff The White Ho., Washington; fellow ctr. for adv. study in behavioral sci., 1978—79; pres. LBS Internat., Ltd., 1979-84; prof. orgnl. behavior Claremont (Calif.) Grad. U., Thornton F. Bradshaw prof. pub. policy, 1983—; mem. White House domestic policy staff, Washington. Vis. prof. sociology and orgnl. behavior U. Conn., 1979-80, U. Md., 1980-82; spkr. in field.; cons. Exec. Office of Pres., Dept. State, Dept. Labor, Dept. HHS, Dept. Agr., Dept. Edn., Bell Labs., Singapore Airlines, MarketIndex, Finland, also various fgn. govts.; tchr. exec. mgmt. and MBA programs. Author, editor: (with Jessie Bernard): Sex Roles and Social Policy, 1978; author: The Paradox of Success: The Impact of Priority Setting in Agricultural Research and Extension, 1984, Metaphor for Change: The USDA Competitive Grants Program, 1978-84, 1985, Gender Roles and Power, 1984, Women in Corporate Leadership: Reviewing a Decade's Research, 1996, The Connective Edge: Leading in an Interdependent World, 1996 (Pulitzer prize nomination), (with Harold J. Leavitt) Hot Groups: Seeding, Feeding, and Using Them to Ignite Your Organization, 1999 (Best Book award Assn. Am. Pubs. 1999), Connective Leadership: Managing in a Changing World, 2000. Fellow AAAS. Office: Drucker Grad Sch Mgmt 1021 N Dartmouth Ave Claremont CA 91711 E-mail: jeanlipman@earthlink.net.

LIPOFSKY, MARVIN BENTLEY, art educator; b. Elgin, Ill., Sept. 1, 1938; s. Henry and Mildred (Hyman) L.; 1 child, Lisa Beth; m. Ruth Okimoto, 1990. BFA in Indsl. Design, U. Ill., 1961; MS, MFA in Sculpture, U. Wis., 1964. Instr. design U. Wis., Madison, 1964; asst. prof. design U. Calif., Berkeley, 1964-72; prof., chmn. glass dept. Calif. Coll. Arts and Crafts, Oakland, 1967-87, pres. faculty assembly, 1984-87. Guest instr. Haystack Mountain Sch., Deer Isla, Maine, 1967, 73, 87, San Francisco Art Inst., 1968, Hunterdon Art Ctr., Clinton, N.J., 1973, Pilchuck Sch. Glass, Stanwood, Wash., 1974, 77, 81, 84, 88; vis. prof. Bazalel Acad. Art and Design, Jerusalem, 1971; pres. faculty assembly, 1984-87. One-man shows include Richmond (Calif.) Art Ctr., 1965, Anneberg Gallery, San Francisco, 1966, Crocker Art Gallery, Sacramento, 1967, San Francisco Mus. Art, 1967, Mus. Contemporary Crafts, N.Y.C., 1969, U. Ga., Athens, 1969, Utah Mus. Fine Arts, U. Utah, Salt Lake City, 1969, Calif. Coll. Arts and Crafts, 1970, Stedelijke Mus., Amsterdam, The Netherlands, 1970, Galerie de Enndt, Amsterdam, 1970, Baxter Art Gallery, Calif. Inst. Tech., Pasadena, 1974, Yaw Gallery, Birmingham, Mich., 1976, 78, Gallery Marionie, Kyoto, Japan, 1979, 87, U. Del., Newark, 1979, Greenwood Gallery, Washington, 1980, SM Gallerie, Frankfurt, Fed. Republic Germany, 1981, Galerie L. Hamburg, Fed. Republic Germany, 1981, Betsy Rosenfield Gallery, Chgo., 1982, Robert Kidd Gallery, Birmingham, Mich., 1984, Holsten Galleries, Palm Beach, Fla., Maurine Littleton Gallery, Washington, Union Bulgarian Artists, Sofia, 1991, Marvin Lipofsky: A World of Glass, 1994, Judah L. Magnes Mus., Berkeley, Calif., 1994, Marvin Lipofsky's World of Glass Show: A Hist. Retrospective, 1996, Kennedy Art Ctr. Gallery, 1996, Holy Names Coll., Oakland, Calif., 1996, Marvin Lipofsky: A Glass Odyssey, Retrospective, Oakland Mus. Calif., 2003; vis. artist, critic Gerriet Rietveld Academie, Amsterdam; vis. artist Atheneium Sch. Art and Design, Helsinki, Finland, 1970, UCLA, 1973, Sommervail, Battle Mountain Glass Symposium, Vail, Colo., Miasa (Japan) Bunka Ctr., 1987, Internat. Glass Symposium, Novy Bor, Czech Republic, 1982, 85, 88, 91. Trustee Calif. Coll. Arts and Crafts, Oakland, 1984-87. Named Calif. Living Treasure, 1985, Hon. Mem., Hungarian Glass Art Soc., 1996, Hon. Inspiration award Calif. Glass Exch., 2002; named to Coll. Fellows, Am. Craft Coun., 1991; NEA fellow, 1974, 76. Mem. Glass Art Soc. (hon. life, pres. 1978-80, jour. editor 1976-80, advisor 1980—), Am. Craft Coun. (trustee 1986-90, trustee emeritus 1998—), Bay Area Studio Art Glass (pres. 1993—).

LIPPE, PHILIPP MARIA, physician, surgeon, neurosurgeon, educator, administrator; b. Vienna, May 17, 1929; came to U.S., 1938, naturalized, 1945; s. Philipp and Maria (Goth) L.; m. Virginia M. Wiltgen, 1953 (div. 1977); children: Patricia Ann Marie, Philip Eric Andrew, Laura Lynne Elizabeth, Kenneth Anthony Ernst; m. Gail B. Busch, Nov. 26, 1977. Student, Loyola U., Chgo., 1947-50; BS in Medicine, U. Ill. Coll. Medicine, 1952, MD with high honors, 1954. Diplomate Am. Bd. Neurol. Surgery, Nat. Bd. Med. Examiners, Am. Bd. Pain Medicine. Rotating intern St. Francis Hosp., Evanston, Ill., 1954-55; asst. resident gen. surgery VA Hosp., Hines, Ill., 1955, 58-59; asst. resident neurology and neurol. surgery Neuropsychiat. Inst., U. Ill. Rsch. and Ednl. Hosps., Chgo., 1959-60, chief resident, 1962-63, resident in neuropathology, 1962, postgrad. trainee in electroencephalography, 1963; resident in neurology and neurol. surgery Presbyn.-St. Luke's Hosp., Chgo., 1960-61; practice medicine, specializing in neurol. surgery/pain medicine San Jose, Calif., 1963—. Instr. neurology and neurol. surgery U. Ill,. 1962-63; clin. instr. surgery and neurosurgery Stanford U., 1965-69, clin. asst. prof., 1969-74, clin. assoc. prof., 1974-96, clin. prof., 1996—; staff cons. in neurosurgery O'Connor Hosp., Santa Clara Valley Med. Ctr., San Jose Hosp., Los Gatos Cmty. Hosp., El Camino Hosp. (all San Jose area); chmn. divsn. neurosurgery Good Samaritan Hosp., 1989-97, chmn. dept. clin. neurosciis., 1997-99; founder, exec. dir. Bay Area Pain Rehab. Ctr., San Jose, 1979—; clin. adviser to Joint Commn. on Accreditation of Hosps.; mem. dist. med. quality rev. com. Calif. Bd. Med. Quality Assurance, 1976-87, chmn., 1976-77; cons., med. expert Med. Bd. Calif., 1996—. Assoc. editor Clin. Jour. Pain; contbr. articles to profl. jours. Capt. USAF, 1956-58. Fellow ACS, Am. Coll. PAin Medicine (bd. dirs. 1991-94, v.p. 1991-92, pres. 1992-93); mem. AMA (ho. of dels. 1981—, CPT editl. panel 1995-99, sr. adv. panel Guides to the Evaluation of Permanent Impairment 1997—), Am. Coll. Physician Execs., Calif. Med. Assn. (ho. of dels. 1976-80, sci. bd., coun. 1979-87, sec. 1981-87, Outstanding Svc. award 1987), Santa Clara County Med. Soc. (coun. 1974-81, pres. 1978-79, Outstanding Contbn. award 1984, Benjamin J. Cory award 1987), Chgo. Med. Soc., Congress Neurol. Surgeons, Calif. Assn. Neurol. Surgeons (dir. 1974-82, v.p. 1975-76, pres. 1977-79, Pevehouse Disting. Svc. award 1997), San Jose Surg. Soc., Am. Assn. Neurol. Surgeons (chmn. sect. on pain 1987-90, dir. 1983-86, 87-90, Disting. Svc. award 1986, 90), Western Neurol. Soc., San Francisco Neurol. Soc., Santa Clara Valley Profl. Stds. Rev. Orgn. (dir., v.p., dir. quality assurance 1975-83), Fedn. Western Socs. Neurol. Sci., Internat. Assn. for Study Pain, Am. Pain Soc. (founding mem.), Am. Acad. Pain Medicine (sec. 1983-86, pres. 1987-88, Philipp M. Lippe Disting. Svc. award 1995, exec. med. dir. 1996—), Am. Bd. Pain Medicine (pres. 1992-93, exec. v.p. 1994—), Am. Soc. Law, Medicine, and Ethics, Alpha Omega Alpha, Phi Kappa Phi. Achievements include pioneer med. application centrifugal force using flight simulator. Office: PO Box 41217 San Jose CA 95160-1217

LIPPERT, ROBERT J. administrator and culinary arts educator, consultant; b. Alma, Mich., May 17, 1932; s. Ackley William Matthew and Myrtle (Boddy) L.; m. Marie Alphonsine Mantei, Apr. 2, 1956; children: Robert Jr., Jeffrey Paul, Mark Edward. BS, Ctrl. Mich. U., 1959, MA, 1965, EdS, 1977. Exec. chef Mt. Pleasant (Mich.) Country Club, 1983-86, Riverwood Golf Course, Mt. Pleasant, 1986-90, The Embers, Inc., Mt. Pleasant, 1957-67; instr. Mt. Pleasant Pub. Schs., 1959-67; dir./ culinary arts instr. Mt. Pleasant Tech. Ctr., 1968-95; instr. Lansing C.C., 1982-84, Ferris State U., Mt. Pleasant, Mich., 1996. Exec. banquet chef The Embers, Inc., 1967—; pres. Lippert Consulting and Svc., Mt. Pleasant, 1983—; hon. prof. Mich. State U., 1997. Writer, editor, dir. TV program Ask The Chef, 1989-90; contbr. articles to profl. jours. Active ch. fund raisers, Mt. Pleasant, 1973—, State Spl. Olympics, 1982-87; chef banquets for sr. citizens. With USN, 1951-54, Korea. Inducted into Mt. Pleasant Pub. Schs. Hall of Fame, 1994. Mem. Internat. Food Svc. Execs. Assn., Am. Acad. Chefs (Svc. award 1990), Am. Culinary Fedn. (Ctrl. Regional Profl. Chef award 1990), Capitol Profl. Chefs (pres. 1985-89, chmn. of bd. 1990-91, Chef of Yr. award 1987), Food Svc. Tchrs. (pres. 1980, 81, 84, bd. dirs. 1979-89), Golden Toque (bd. dirs. 1995-97, sec. 1998—), Mich. Restaurant Assn. (bd. dirs. 1980-82, 84-85, 93—, Food Tchr. of Yr. award 1981, Disting. Svc. award 1996), Mich. Occupational Edn. Assn. (bd. dirs. 1980-87, Vocat. Tchr. of Yr. award 1986), Mich. Chefs (Jefferson medal 1986). Roman Catholic. Home: 1214 Greenwood Dr Mount Pleasant MI 48858-9582 Office: 1214 Glenwood Pl Mount Pleasant MI 48858-4328

LIPPINCOTT, JANET, artist, art educator; b. N.Y.C., May 16, 1918. Student Emil Bisttram, Taos., N.Mex., Colorado Springs Fine Art Ctr., Art Students League N.Y.C., San Francisco Art Inst. Artist in residence, Durango, Colo., 1968; guest artist Tamarind Inst., Albuquerque, 1973; participant TV ednl. programs, Denver, Albuquerque; art instr. Santa Fe Community Coll., N.Mex., 1984—. Participant juried exhbns. including: Denver Mus., 1968, N.Mex. Arts Commn. traveling shows, 1967, Chautauqua Exhbn. Am. Art, N.Y., 1967, High Mus., Atlanta, Butler Inst. Am. Art, Springfield, Ohio, Dallas Mus. Fine Art, Mid Am. Exhbn., Nelson Atkins Mus., Kansas City, Kans., Mus. Fine Arts, Houston, Denver Art Mus., U. N.Mex. Art Gallery, Albuquerque, Ball State Tchrs. Coll., Muncie, Ind., N.Mex. Painting Invitational, 1968, Colorado Springs Fine Art Ctr., 1968, N.Mex. Biennial, Santa Fe, 1969, 72, 73 (award 1962), Tyler Mus. Art, Tex, 1977, Santa Fe Arts Festival, 1978, 79, 80, Enthios Gallery, Santa Fe, 1987; participant invitation exhbns. including: Albuquerque Mus. Art, 1977, Bethune & Moore, Denver, 1969, Yellowstone Art Ctr., Billings, Mont., 1967, Tucson Fine Art Ctr., 1965, Hockaday Sch., Dallas, 1965, Hayden Calhoun Galleries, Dallas, 1966, Leone Kahl Gallery, Dallas, 1965, U. Utah, Salt Lake City, 1966, Roswell Mus. and Art Ctr., N.Mex., 1963, Lucien Labaudt Gallery, San Francisco, 1963, Denver U.S. Nat. Ctr., 1963, Muse d'Art Moderne, Paris, 1962, Instituto Cultural, Mexico City, 1957, Colo. State Coll., Greeley, 1961, Highland U., Las Vegas, N.Mex., 1960-70, St. John's Coll., Santa Fe, 1965, 75, 80, Coll. Santa Fe, 1968, 81, 4748 Galleries, Oklahoma City, 1965, Owen Gallery, Denver, 1970, New West Gallery, Albuquerque, 1970, 71, 72, 73, 74, Columbia Fine Arts Mus., S.C., 1972, Arts and Crafts Mus., Columbus, Ga., 1972, Dubose Gallery, Houston, 1972, Jamison Gallery, Santa Fe, 1972, Tex. Tech U., Lubbock, 1973 (award), Triangle Gallery, Tulsa, 1973, Gallery 26, Tulsa, 1974, West Tex. Mus., Lubbock, 1976, Britton Gallery, Denver, 1975, 77, 78, 79, 80, Osborne Gallery, Winnipeg, Ont., Can., 1979, Blair Gallery, Santa Fe, 1979, 80; works represented in pvt. and mus. collections; represented by Fletcher Gallery, Santa Fe, 1989-90; Day Star Internat. Galleries, Albuquerque, 1990; New Directions Gallery, Taos, N.Mex., 1995—; Laurel Seth Gallery, Santa Fe, N.Mex., 1995—; Tartan Pony Gallery, 1995—; New Directions Gallery, Taos N. Mex., 1996, Karen Ruhen Gallery, Santa Fe, 1996. With WAC, 1943-45, ETO. Purchase awards and prizes include: Southwestern Biennial, Santa Fe, 1966, N.Mex. Mus. Fine Arts, 1957, Roswell Mus., 1958, Okla. Art Ctr., Oklahoma City, 1962, Atwater Kent award, Palm Beach, Fla., 1963, Chautauqua Art Award Assn. prize, 1963, El Paso Mus. prize, 1962, 76. Home and Office: 1270 Upper Canyon Rd Santa Fe NM 87501-6189

LIPPINCOTT, WALTER EDWARD, law educator; b. Bronxville, N.Y., Aug. 15, 1959; s. Walter Edwin and Helen (Patterson) L.; m. Andrea Pratt, July 30, 1983; children: Brittany Marie, Matthew, Anna. BS, Roger Williams Coll., 1981; JD, Western New Eng. Coll., 1984; MS, Fla. Inst. Tech., 1995. Bar: Conn. 1984, D.C. 1985. Prosecutor State of Conn. Judicial Dept., Hartford, 1990-93; prof. Naugatuck Valley Cmty. Coll., Waterbury, Conn., 1993—, U. Conn., Storrs, 1996-97. Lt. col. U.S. Army, 1985-90, USAR, 1990—. Mem. ABA, Conn. Bar Assn., D.C. Bar Assn. Home: 613 Highland Ave Torrington CT 06790-4410

LIPPMAA, ENDEL, education educator, science educator; b. Tartu, Estonia, Sept. 15, 1930; s. Teodor and Hilja-Helene L.; m. Helle Raam, July 20, 1960; children: Jaak, Mikk. Chem. Engr., Tallinn (Estonia) Tech. U., 1953, PhD in Engring., 1956; DSc in Chem. Physics, Inst. Chem. Physics, Moscow, 1969. Lectr. Tallinn (Estonia) Tech. U., 1953-56, asst. prof., 1956-61; head dept. chem. physics Inst. Cybernetics, Tallinn, Estonia, 1961-80; prof. phys. chemistry and chem. physics Estonian Acad. Sci., Tallinn, 1971—; prof. Tartu (Estonia) U., 1993—. Divsn. head Estonian Acad. Scis., Tallinn, 1977-82, 99-; dir. Inst. Chem. Physics and Biophysics, Tallinn, 1980-2001; chmn. bd. Nat. Inst. Chemical Physics and Biophysics, Tallinn, 1999-. Patentee in field; contbr. articles to profl. jours. Rep. USSR Congress of Peoples' Deputies, Moscow, 1989-91; minister Eastern affairs Govt. Republic of Estonia, Tallinn, 1990-91, min. European affairs, 1995-96. Recipient R & D 100 award, 1989, Humboldt/Max-Planck Rsch. prize, 1992; named to Centenary Lectureship, Royal Soc. Chemistry, 1989; recipient Hon. Doctor degree Jyväskylä (Finland) U., 1975, Tallinn Tech. U., 1991, Tartu U., 1999. Fellow Am. Chem. Soc., Am. Phys. Soc., IEEE (Inst. Electrical and Electronics Engrs.; mem. Estonian Acad. Sci., Finnish Acad. Sci., Royal Swedish Acad. Engring. Scis., Finnish Chem. Soc. Coalition. Lutheran. Home: Sõbra 14-2 Tallinn 10920 Estonia Office: Estonian Acad Sci Rävala Puiestee 10 Tallinn 10143 Estonia

LIPPMAN, SHARON ROCHELLE, art historian, art therapist, filmmaker; b. NYC, Apr. 9, 1950; d. Emanuel and Sara (Goldberg) L. Student, Mills Coll., Columbia U., 1968; BFA, New Sch. Social Rsch., 1970, CCNY, 1972; MA in Cinema Studies, NYU, 1976, postgrad., 1987. Cert. secondary tchr., N.Y.; cert. in nonprofit orgn. mgmt. Instr., dir., founder Sara Sch. of Creative Art, Sayville, N.Y., 1976-85; founder, exec. dir., tchr. Art Without Walls, Inc., Sayville and N.Y.C., 1985—; curator art exhbn. Mus. Without Walls Heckscher State Park, East Islip, NY, 1985-87; exec. dir., curator Profl. Artist Network for Artists Internationally, 1991—; founder Art Without Walls, Inc., 1985—. Organizer Profl. Artist Network for Nat./Internat. Artists, 1994; curator Pub. Art in Pub. Spaces. Author: Patterns, 1968, College Poetry Press Anthology, 1970, America at the Millennium, 2000; exhibited in group shows at L.I. Children's Mus., Garden City, N.Y., 1995-97, Suffolk County Legislature, Hauppauge, N.Y., 1997, Bayport-Bluepoint Libr., 1997, East Islip Libr., 1997-98, U.S. Dept. Interior, Ft. Wadsworth, N.Y., 2001, Ellis Island Immigration Mus., N.Y., 2002, West Islip Libr., 2000-01, Battery Park, N.Y.C., 2002, Central Park, N.Y.C., 2003, Spirit Walk Gallery, Sayville, N.Y., 2003, others; pub. art mural History of L.I. Baymen, 1987, Immigration on the NYS Waterways, 2001, Art Therapy Program and Exhbn. at Leadership Tng. Inst., Hempstead, N.Y., 2003, Nassau County Detension Ctr., 2003; represented in permanent collection Devel. Disabilities Inst., Suffolk County Legis. Bldg., Polish Consulate, N.Y., West Islip Pub. Libr., East Islip Pub. Libr., Ctrl. Park Zoo, Coll. Art Assn. Bull. Conv. N.Y., Robert Moses State Park, N.Y., Smith Haven Mall Lake Grove, Garden City Mall, N.Y., Southside Hosp., Bayshore, N.Y.; art therapy program and exhbn. Leadership Tng. Inst., 2003, Suffolk Outreach Project, Art Therapy Wellness Program, 2003. Vol. Good Samaritan Hosp., 1984, Southside Hosp., 1983, U. Stony Brook Hosp., 1985, Schneider Children's Hosp., New Hyde Park, N.Y., 1992, New Light-AIDS Patients, Smithtown, N.Y., 1993, Helen Keller Svcs. for the Blind, Hempstead, N.Y., 1993-94, St. Charles Hosp. and Rehab. Ctr., 1996, Nat. Health Bill Pub. Forum, Sayville Mid. Sch., 1996, Art Puzzles-Art Therapy Geriatrics Ward, Brookhaven (N.Y.) Meml. Hosp., 1990, Art Therapy Program Original Dept. Disabilities, Suffolk County, N.Y., 1988, Din-o-Soar Art Therapy Southside Hosp.-Pediatrics Ward, Bayshore, N.Y., 1999, Art Box-Art Therapy, Pediat. Ward Southside Hosp., Bayshore, 2000, It Takes Two Art Therapy, St. Charles Hosp., Port Jefferson, N.Y., 2000; mem. Whitney Mus., Guggenheim Mus., Mus. Modern Art, Met. Mus. Art, Jewish Mus., Mus. of the City of N.Y., Art in Am., Art News, Am. Artist; trustee Sayville Libr. Bd., 1996; bd. dirs. Friends of the Arts St. Joseph's Coll., N.Y., 1997. Recipient Suffolk County New Inspiration award, 1990, Am. Artist Art Svc. award Am. Artists mag., 1993, Suffolk County Legis. proclamation, 1993, Newsday Leadership Vol. award Newsday newspaper, 1994, Nat. Women's Month award Town of Islip, 1996, Disting. Women's award Town of Islip, 1996, Nat. Poetry Press award, 1996, Cmty. Action award Suffolk County Ret./Sr. Vol. Program, 2002. Mem. Orgn. Through Rehab. and Tng., Coll. Art Assn., Met. Mus. Art, Mus. Modern Art Univ. Film Assn., Sayville C. of C. Avocations: fine art, books, cinema, political science, inventions. Office: Art Without Walls Inc PO Box 341 Sayville NY 11782-0341 E-mail: artwithoutwalls@webtv.net.

LIPPOLD, NEAL WILLIAM, criminal justice educator; b. Aurora, Ill., Dec. 30, 1946; s. Daniel Carl and Ada Louise (Knudson) L.; children: Neal William II, Cara Jo, Kenneth Franklin; m. Carol Ann Duckwiler, Dec. 31, 1988. A of Gen. Edn., Waubonsee C.C., 1972; BA, Aurora U., 1974; MS, Chgo. State U., 1978; ABD, No. Ill. U. Counselor, parole agt. State of Ill., Chgo., 1971-75; prof. criminal justice Waubonsee C.C., Sugar Grove, Ill., 1975—. Police officer/police chief Village of Sugar Grove, 1976-86; campus police chief Waubonsee C.C., Sugar Grove, 1976-82; police sgt. Fox Valley Park Dist., Aurora, 1987-92. Sgt. USAF, 1966-69. Recipient Award of Honor, Kane County Bar Assn., 1990. Mem. Ill. Assn. Police Planners (treas., past sec.), Midwest Criminal Justice Assn., Midwest Gang Investigations Assn. Avocations: camping, fishing, golf, computing. Home: 127 Mattek Ave Dekalb IL 60115-4647

LIPPS, DELORIS JEAN, secondary school educator; b. Buckhannon, W.Va., Jan. 27, 1949; d. Kenna Monroe and Martha Jane (Pringle) L. BA in Edn., Glenville State Coll., 1971; MS in Teaching, U. N.H., 1978; postgrad., Marshall U., 1973, 74, W.Va. U., 1976-77, 82. Cert. secondary tchr., W.Va. Math. tchr. Wirt County High Sch., Elizabeth, W.Va., 1971—, head math. dept., 1979—. County math. adminstr. Wirt County Schs., Elizabeth, 1978—, dir. math. field day, 1980—2000; dir. math. field day W.Va. Region V., 1990-91. Editor: WVCTM History Update, 1991, (newsletter) Math News, 1987—, (manual) Wirt County Math Field Day Manual, 1988. Recipient Presdl. award for Excellence in Math. Teaching, NSF, 1987. Mem. Nat. Coun. Tchrs. of Math., W.Va. Coun. Tchrs. of Math. (historian 1987-92), W.Va. Acad. Sci., Coun. Presdl. Awardees in Math., Delta Kappa Gamma (chapt. treas. Mich. U., 1996-2002, sec. 2002—). Methodist. Avocations: embroidery, bead crafts, reading. Home: PO Box 124 Elizabeth WV 26143-0124 Office: Wirt County High Sch PO Box 219 Elizabeth WV 26143-0219

LIPPS, JERE HENRY, paleontology educator; b. L.A., Aug. 28, 1939; s. Henry John and Margaret (Rosaltha) L.; m. Karen Elizabeth Loeblich, June 25, 1964 (div. 1971); m. Susannah McClintock, Sept. 28, 1973; children: Jeremy Christian, Jamison William. BA, UCLA, 1962, PhD, 1966. Asst. prof. U. Calif., Davis, 1967-70, assoc. prof., 1970-75, prof., 1975-88, Berkeley, 1988—, prof. paleontology, 1988-89, prof. integrative biology, 1989—; dir. Mus. Paleontology, Berkeley, 1989-97. Dir. Inst. Ecology U. Calif., Davis, 1972-73, chmn. dept. geology, 1971-72, 79-84, chmn. dept.

integrative biology, Berkeley, 1991-94. Contbr. articles to sci. publs. Dir. Cushman Found., pres., 1983—84, 2002—03. Recipient U.S. Antarctic medal NSF, 1975; Lipps Island, Antarctica named in his honor, 1979. Fellow: Com. for the Sci. Investigation of Claims of the Paranormal, AAAS, Cushman Found. (pres. 1983—84, 2001—02), Geol. Soc. Am., Calif. Acad. Scis.; mem.: Coun. for Media Integrity, Paleontol. Soc. (pres. 1996—97). Avocation: scuba diving. Office: U Calif Mus Paleontology #4780 1101 Valley Life Sciences Bldg Berkeley CA 94720-4780 E-mail: jlipps@uclink4.berkeley.edu.

LIPSCHULTZ, JEREMY HARRIS, communication educator; b. Chgo., Feb. 12, 1958; BA in Polit. Sci., U. Ill., 1980; MA in Reporting, Sangamon State U., 1981; PhD in Journalism, So. Ill. U., 1990. Adj. instr. U. Evansville, Ind., 1983; news dir., anchor-reporter Stas. WGBF-AM/WHKC-FM, Evansville, 1981-84; grad. asst., instr. So. Ill. U., Carbondale, 1985-88; prof. U. Nebr., Omaha, 1989—, chair grad. program com., 1995-2000, interim chair comm. dept., 2000, Robert Reilly prof., 2002—. Author: Broadcast Indecency: F.C.C. Regulation and the First Amendment, 1997, Free Expression in the Age of the Internet: Social and Legal Boundaries, 2000, Crime and Local Television News: Dramatic, Breaking and Live From the Scene, 2002; editl. asst. Journalism Monographs, 1986-87; book reviewer: Communications and the Law, Journal of Radio Studies; editl. bd. Jour. of Broadcasting and Electronic Media, Jour. and Mass Comm. Edn., Jour. of Radio Studies, Comm. and the Law; contbr. articles to profl. jours. Mem. Assn. for Edn. in Journalism (chair law dvsn. rsch. 1991-92, profl. freedom and responsibility 1992-93, tchr. 1993-94), Nebr. Writers Guild. Office: U Nebr Coll Arts & Scis Arts and Sci Hall 107-C 6001 Dodge St Omaha NE 68182-0112 Fax: 402-554-3836. E-mail: jlipschultz@mail.unomaha.edu.

LIPSCOMB, SHIRLEY RUTH, vocational education educator; b. Statham, Ga., Mar. 10, 1951; d. Rosevelt and Lucille (Barnette) Thurmond; children: Tyrish, Miranda; m. William Lipscomb. Master Lic. Cosmetology, Minosa Sch. Beauty, 1970-71; AA, Gainesville (Ga.) Coll., 1971-73; BS, Brenau Coll., 1973-75; MEd, Ga. State U., 1980-83. Cert. tchr., Ga. Owner, mgr. Shirley's Beauty Salon, Gainesville, 1971-79; vocat. tchr. Lanier Tech. Inst., Oakwood, Ga., 1977—. Faculty steering com. Lanier Tech. Sch., Oakwood, 1986-91, sec. adv. bd., 1991, in-svc. com., 1992. Author: Positional Papers Hair, 1981. Chmn. AKA Cotillion, Gainesville, 1975, AKA Scholarship Com., Gainesville, 1985-90; coord. Gen. Missionary Bapt. Ch., Ga., 1980-89; pres. PTO, Gainesville, 1990; vol. Project Find, 1972 (cert.), Summer Reading Program, 1974 (cert.); active Leadership Hall County, 1992, Exec. Leadership Ga. State U., 1990-91, Coalition on Teenage Pregnancy, Hall County, 1986; v.p. Angelic Voices Choir St. John Bapt. Ch., 1971—. Recipient Cert. of Merit award Kiwanis, Gainesville, 1969, Outstanding Svc. award St. John Bapt. Ch., Gainesville, 1986, Cert. of Appreciation award Girl Scouts, Gainesville, 1987. Mem. Ga. Vocat. Assn., Cultural Ednl. Tour Inst. (pres., cons.), Alpha Kappa Alpha (Soror of Yr. 1989, 90). Democrat. Methodist. Avocations: golf, swimming, reading, singing, community service. Home: 2079 Garden Rd Gainesville GA 30507-5019

LIPSCOMB, STEPHEN LEON, retired mathematician; b. Junior, W.Va., Jan. 31, 1944; s. David Leon and Dema Ann (Alkire) L.; m. Patrecia Ann Skidmore, Sept. 15, 1962; children: Stephen Leon, Darrin Joel. BE, Fairmont State Coll., 1965; MMath, W.Va. U., 1967; PhD in Math., U. Va., 1973. High sch. tchr. and coach, Rehoboth Beach, Del., 1965-66; sr. mathematician Naval Surface Weapons Ctr., Dahlgren, Va., 1967-83; eminent scholar in math. Mary Washington Coll., Fredericksburg, Va., 1983-84, chmn. dept. math. sci. and physics, 1984-86, chair dept. math., 1990-95; ret., 2003. Adj. prof. math. Va. Poly. Int. and State U., 1976-92; sr. fellow Navy-Am. Soc. Engring. Edn., 1994-95, 99-2001, 03. Contbr. articles to profl. jours. Mem. Am. Math. Soc. (author vol 46 in math. surveys and monograph series). Achievements include invention of Lipscomb's topological space, path notation in inverse semigroup theory, alternating semigroups; pioneering many mathematical concepts including first thurst integral programs for U.S. navy; chairing tiger team in the Tomahawk missile system prior to 1983 operational evaluation. Home: 8809 Robert E Lee Dr Spotsylvania VA 22553-3584 E-mail: slipscom@mwc.edu.

LIPSITT, LEWIS PAEFF, psychology educator; b. New Bedford, Mass., June 28, 1929; s. Joseph and Anna Naomi (Paeff) L.; m. Edna Brill Duchin, June 8, 1952; children: Mark, Ann. BA, U. Chgo., 1950; MS, U. Mass., 1952; PhD, U. Iowa, 1957. Instr. dept. psychology Brown U., Providence, 1957, asst. prof., 1958-61, assoc. prof., 1961-66, prof., 1966-96, dir. Child Study Ctr., 1967-92, Wriston lectr., 1993—, prof. emeritus psychology, med. sci. and human devel., 1996—, rsch. prof. psychology, 1996—. Mem. Gov.'s Adv. Commn. on Mental Retardation, 1963-66; cons. Nat. Inst. Health; edn. task force Model Cities Program, Providence, 1969-71; fellow Stanford Ctr. for Advanced Study in Behavioral Scis., 1979-80; vis. scientist Nat. Inst. Mental Health, 1986-87; chair steering com. nat. child care project Nat. Inst. for Child Health and Human Devel., 1994-99, adv. com., 1999-2001. Co-author: Child Development, 1979; founder, editor: Infant Behavior and Devel., 1978-82; founding co-editor: Advances in Child Development and Behavior, 1963-70, 78-82; co-editor: Research Readings in Child Psychology, 1963, Experimental Child Psychology, 1971, Advances in Infancy Research, 1981-99, Self-regulatory Behavior and Risk Taking, 1991, Progress in Infancy Research, 1991—; contbr. articles to profl. jours. Bd. dirs. Providence Child Guidance Clinic, 1960-63; trustee Butler Hosp., Providence, 1965-84; mem. bd. sci. counselors Nat. Ins. Child Health and Human Devel., 1984-88; nat. co-dir. Lee Salk Family Ctr., Kidspeace, Allentown, Pa., 1993—; participant White House Conf. on Child Care, 1998. Recipient Mentor award for lifetime achievement AAAS, 1995, Profl. Achievement citation U. Chgo., 1995; USPHS Spl. Rsch. fellow, 1966, Guggenheim fellow, 1972-73, USPHS fellow, 1973. Fellow AAAS (Lifetime Mentor award 1994), APA (exec. com. divsn. devel. psychology 1967-70, pres. divsn. devel. psychology 1980-81, bd. sci. affairs 1985-88, exec. dir. for sci. 1990-91, sci. officer 1991-92, Nicholas Hobbs award 1990, exec. com. divsn. gen. psychology 1997-2001, coun. of reps. 1997-2000, pres. divsn. gen. psychology 1999-2000, exptl. psychology coun. of reps. 2001—, Ernest R. Hilgard award for life achievement in gen. psychology 2004, Urie Bronfenbrenner award 2004); mem. AAUP, Soc. Rsch. in Child Devel., Internat. Soc. Study Behavioral Devel. (membership sec. 1981-83, exec. com. 1984-89), Am. Psychol. Soc. (founding mem., charter fellow, bd. dirs. 1989-90), Can. Inst. for Advanced Rsch. (chair adv. com. human devel. group 1995-2003, mem. adv. com. human devel. and population health 2000—), RI Psychol. Assn. (bd. dirs. 1995-98, Mental Health Svc. award 1998). E-mail: Lewis_Lipsitt@brown.edu.

LIPSMAN, RICHARD MARC, lawyer, educator; b. Bklyn., Aug. 17, 1946; s. Abraham W. and Ruth (Weinstein) L.; m. Geri A. Russo, 1979; children: Eric, Dara Briana. BBA, CCNY, 1968; JD, St. John's U., Jamaica, N.Y., 1972; LLM in Taxation, Boston U., 1976. Bar: N.Y. 1973, Mass. 1975, U.S. Dist. Ct. (ea. and so. dists.) N.Y. 1977, U.S. Supreme Ct. 1978, U.S. Tax Ct. 1979; CPA, N.Y., Mass. Tax atty. Arthur Young & Co., N.Y.C., 1972-74; assoc. Gilman, McLaughlin & Hanrahan, Boston, 1974-76, Lefrak, Fischer & Meyerson, N.Y.C., 1976-77; ptnr. Tarnow, Landsman & Lipsman, N.Y.C., 1978; pvt. practice N.Y.C., 1979—. Adj. faculty Baruch Coll. CUNY, 1984-86, curriculum specialist Rsch. Found. CUNY, 1977-78; adj. faculty Pratt Inst., Bklyn., 1974, Queensboro Coll., Bayside, N.Y., 1978-80. Author, producer book/cassette program Learning Income Taxes, 1978—. Mem. ABA, AICPA, N.Y. State Bar Assn., Assn. of the Bar of the City of N.Y., N.Y. State Soc. CPA's. Jewish.

LIPSON, ABIGAIL, psychologist; b. Washington, Mar. 6, 1956; d. Leon Samuel and Dorothy Ann (Rapoport) L.; m. Craig Nicholson, 1996. BA, Hampshire Coll., 1977; PhD, Duke U., 1981. Lic. clin. psychologist. Instr., teaching asst. Duke U., Durham, N.C., 1977-79; staff psychotherapist Duke Psychol. Svcs., Durham, N.C., 1977-81; clin. psychology intern Harvard U., Cambridge, Mass., 1981-82; sr. counselor Harvard U. Bur. Study Counsel, Cambridge, Mass., 1982-97; pvt. practice Cambridge, Mass., 1983-97; dir. psychol. svcs. Am. U., Washington, 1997—. Vis. faculty Cambridge Coll., 1984, Kennedy Sch. Govt., Cambridge, 1985, 91; rsch. assoc. U. Mass., Amherst, 1989-91. Co-author: BLOCK, 1990; contbr. articles to psychology and edn. jours. Mem. APA, Am. Ednl. Rsch. Assn., Mass. Psychol. Assn.

LIPSON, CHARLES HENRY, political scientist, educator; b. Clarksdale, Miss., Feb. 1, 1948; s. Harry Mason Jr. and Dorothy (Kohn) L.; m. Susan Linda Bloom, July 13, 1980; children: Michael H., Jonathan S. BA, Yale Coll., 1970; MA, Harvard U., 1974, PhD, 1976. Rsch. assoc. Harvard Ctr. for Internat. Affairs, Cambridge, Mass., 1976-77; asst. prof. U. Chgo., 1977-84, assoc. prof., 1984—2002, prof., 2003—. Vis. scholar Harvard Ctr. for Internat. Affairs, 1979-80; founding dir. program on internat. politics, econs. and security U. Chgo., 1987—, chair com. on internat. rels., 1992-95; vis. fellow London Sch. Econs, 1988-89; mem. Chgo. Com.; ptnr. Capstone Entertainment; fgn. affairs analyst NBC 5, Chgo. Author: Standing Guard: Protecting Foreign Capital in the 19th and 20th Centuries, 1985, Reliable Partners: How Democracies Have Made a Separate Peace, 2003; editor: Theory and Structure in International Political Economy, 1999, Issues and Agents in International Political Economy, 1999; mem. bd. editors Internat. Orgn., 1984-90, 96-2001, World Politics, 1998—; contbr. articles to profl. jours. Bd. dirs. Newberger Hillel Found. of U. Chgo., 1990—, mem. exec. com., 1993—, chmn. bd. dirs., 1994-99; bd. dirs. K.A.M. Isaiah Israel Congregation, Chgo., 1992-2001. Recipient Faculty Achievement award Burlington-No. Found., 1986; grantee German Marshall Fund U.S., 1983-84; fellow Rockefeller Found., 1979-81. Mem. Am. Polit. Sci. Assn. (sec. 1990-91), Am. Soc. for Internat. Law, Brit.-Am. Conf. for Successor Generation, Chgo. Com., Chgo. Coun. on Fgn. Rels., Internat. Inst. for Stratetic Studies, Internat. Studies Assn., Royal Inst. for Internat. Affairs. Jewish. Home: 5809 S Blackstone Ave Chicago IL 60637-1855 Office: U Chgo Dept Polit Sci 5828 S University Ave Dept Polit Chicago IL 60637-1515 E-mail: c-lipson@uchicago.edu.

LIPUT, ANDREW LAWRENCE, lawyer, educator; b. Trenton, N.J., June 28, 1962; s. Andrew and Bernice Helen L.; m. Jacquelyn Anne Liput, Jan. 11, 1997; children: Mallory, Sloane. BA, Drew U., 1984; JD, Fordham U., 1987. Bar: N.J., 1987, N.Y., 1988, Conn., 1996. V.p., gen. cousel Parssine Group, Inc., NYC, 1988-91; sr. lawyer Hartman, Buhrman & Winnicki, Paramus, NJ, 1991-93; v.p., gen. counsel Marjam Supply Co., Inc., Bklyn., 1993-96; ptnr. Liput, Ricca, Donner LLP, Huntington, NY, 1996—; adj. prof. Felician Coll., Lodi, NJ, 1994-97; assoc. prof. Suffolk C.C., Long Island, NY, 1998—, Briarcliff Coll., Bethpage, NY, 2001—; prof. St. Joseph's Coll., 2001—. Trust officer, Neighborhood Cleaners Assn., N.Y.C., 1998—, Metropolitan Package Store Assn., Westchester, N.Y., 1997—. Author: Long Lost Tales of the Legendary Snarfdoodle, 2001; contbr. articles to profl. jours. Pres., dir. Bridge the Gap!, Long Island, 1999—, councilman, No. Plainfield, N.J., 1988-89. Mem. U.S. Rowing Assn., Aircraft Owners & Pilots Assn., N.Y. State Bar Assn., N.J. State Bar Assn., Conn. Bar Assn. Republican. Avocations: rowing, flying, reading, world travel. Office: Liput & Sperengen PC 790 New York Ave Huntington NY 11743-4499

LISANDRELLI, CARL ALBERT, social studies educator; b. Rome, Mar. 18, 1952; s. Nello and Annetta (Ragnacci) L.; m. Elaine Marie Slivinski, June 20, 1980. BS in History/Govt., East Stroudsburg U., 1973. Masters Equivalency. Substitute tchr. North pocono, Moscow, Pa., 1973-75, freshmen football coach, 1975-80; dept. chmn. North Pocono Mid. Sch., Moscow, 1985—, social studies tchr., 1975—. Mem. Nat. Coun. Social Studies. Avocations: golf, reading, landscaping, exercise, film buff. Office: North Pocono Sch Dist 701 Church St Moscow PA 18444-9391

LISENKO, EMILIE DIERKING, secondary school educator; b. Rolla, Mo., May 6, 1955; d. Edward Fritz Carl Dierking and Dorothy Marie (Anderson) Brown; m. Alexander Ivanovich Lisenko, May 20, 1979; children: Daniel, Timothy. BA, Coe Coll., 1977; MATS, Sch. of Theology, Claremont, Calif., 1983. Religion and social studies educator Pilgrim Sch., LA, 1983-88; social studies educator Immaculate Heart HS, 1988—95; religion instr. Ctrl. Meth. Coll. at Mineral Area Coll., Park Hills, Mo., 1995—97; campus min. Immaculate Heart of Mary HS, Westchester, Ill., 1997—. Interreligious dialogue facilitator Nat. Conf. of Christians and Jews, LA, 1986-87. Mem. AAUW, Nat. Cath. Ednl. Assn., So. Poverty Law Ctr., Phi Beta Kappa, Phi Kappa Phi. Mem. Eastern Orthodox. Avocations: music, reading, justice issues, movies. Office: Immaculate Heart of Mary HS 10900 W Cermak Rd Westchester IL 60154

LISK, EDWARD STANLEY, musician, educator, conductor; b. Oswego, N.Y., Feb. 1, 1934; s. Edward Andrew and Jennie (Segal) L.; m. Doris E. Thornber, Sept. 1, 1956; children: Janice, Carol, Jean. B Music Edn., Syracuse (N.Y.) U., 1956; postgrad., Ithaca (N.Y.) Sch. Music, 1965, Oswego State Coll., 1980. Cert. tchr., adminstr. Tchr. music Red Creek (N.Y.) Cen. Schs., 1958-70; band dir., K-12 music supr. Oswego (N.Y.) City Sch. Dist., 1970-91. Clarinetist Syracuse Symphony Orch., 1963-67; profl. musician Syracuse orchs., bands, 1960-90; clinician, lectr. Australian Nat. Band and Orch. Assn., Perth, Melbourne and Sydney, 1990, condr./clinician, 1995; clinician numerous convs., 1980—. Author: The Creative Director, 1987, Alternative Rehearsal Techniques Student Supplement, Books 1 and 2, 1993, A.R.T. Teaching Accessories, 1994, (video) A.R.T. and the V.C. University Wind Ensemble, 1994, Intangibles of Musical Performance, 1996, The Creative Director: Beginning and Intermediate Levels, 2001; co-author: Teaching Music Through Performance in Band-Vol. 1,2,3 & 4; contbr. articles to profl. jours. Sgt. U.S. Army, 1956-58. Named Tchr. of Yr., Oswego Classroom Tchrs. Assn., 1974, 83, Disting. Bandmaster Am., First Chair of Am., 1981, Area Educator of Yr., Phi Delta Kappa, 1983, Adminstr. of Yr., Oswego Bd. Edn./Adminstrn., 1989; recipient Sudler Order of Merit John Philip Sousa Found., 1997. Mem. Music Educators Nat. Conf., Nat. Band Assn. (1st v.p. 1988-90, pres. 1990-92, news editor 1992—, Citation of Excellence 1977), Am. Bandmasters Assn. (v.p. 1998-99, pres. 2000—), N.Y. State Band Dirs. Assn. (bd. dirs. 1981-96, named Outstanding Band Dir. 1995), N.Y. State Sch. Music Assn., World Assn. for Symphonic Bands and Ensembles, John Philip Sousa Found. (v.p.), Phi Beta Mu. Roman Catholic. Avocations: computers, golf, travel. Home: 836 County Route 25 Oswego NY 13126-5716

LISLE, MARTHA OGLESBY, retired mathematics educator; b. Charlottesville, Va., June 29, 1934; d. Earnest Jackson and Lucy Elizabeth (Berger) Oglesby; m. Leslie M. Lisle, June 18, 1955 (div. June 1997); children: Lucie Austin, Karen B., John D. BA, Randolph-Macon Woman's Coll., 1955; MA, Fla. State U., 1957. Instr. various univ., 1957-69; tchr. Am. Sch., Khartoum, Sudan, 1971-72, Holton-Arms, Bethesda, Md., 1974-78, Rabat Am. Sch., Morocco, 1978-81, Stone Ridge Sch., Bethesda, 1981-82; instr. part-time Montgomery Coll., Takoma Pk., Md., 1982-83; assoc. prof. Prince George's Community Coll., Largo, Md., 1983-97. Adj. prof. Md. Coll. Art and Design, 1997-99. Mem. DAR, Am. Math. Assn. Two Yr. Coll., Math. Assn. Am., Md. Math Assn. Two Yr. Coll., Assn. Women in Math., Pi Mu Epsilon. Democrat. Mem. Unitarian Ch. Avocations: sewing, working crafts, playing flute, singing in choir, quilting. Home: 11108 Woodson Ave Kensington MD 20895-1607 E-mail: martha.lisle@verizon.net.

LISMAN, ELIAS, pediatric dentist, educator; b. Newark, Sept. 15, 1919; s. William and Celia (Levowitz) L.; m. Ruth Shapiro, Dec. 18, 1949; children: Clifford G., Susan R., Sharon J., Joel I. BA, NYU, 1939, DDS, 1942. Diplomate Am. Bd. Pediatric Dentistry. Pvt. practice, Irvington, N.J., 1946-88; instr. pediatric dentistry NYU Coll. Dentistry, N.Y.C., 1951-56; clin. prof. pediatric dentistry Fairleigh S. Dickinson, Jr. Coll. Dental Medicine, Hackensack, N.J., 1983-90; retired. Cons. N.J. Bd. Dentistry, 1983-92; lectr. to profl. socs. and convs. Contbr. articles to dentistry jours. Capt. AUS, 1942-46, PTO; major army res. Fellow Am. Acad. Pediatric Dentistry, Am. Coll. Dentists; mem. ADA, N.J. Dental Assn., Am. Soc. Dentistry for Children (past pres. N.J. chpt.), Toastmasters (past treas. Westfield, N.J. chpt.), N.J. Table Tennis Club, Masons, Omicron Kappa Upsilon, Alpha Omega, Phi Beta Epsilon. Democrat. Jewish. Avocations: astronomy, juggling, race walking, jewelry fabrication, table tennis. Home: 9 Lamberts Cir Westfield NJ 07090-3501

LISOWY, DONALD C. conservation and science educator; b. Hempstead, N.Y., July 26, 1960; s. Stephen and Alice (Lyddon) L.; m. Susan M. Riordan; 1 child, Alexander George. B of Forest Biology, SUNY, Syracuse, 1982; MS in Edn., Syracuse U., 1986. Zool. instr. N.Y. Zool. Soc., Bronx, 1983-87, sr. instr., 1987-88, project coord., 1988—. Life sci. cons. Macmillan-McGraw Hill Pub., Columbus, Ohio, 1991; mem. Nat. Diffusion Network, U.S. Dept. Edn., 1988—, N.Y. State Sharing Successful Programs, N.Y. State Dept. Edn., 1988—; wildlife researcher N.Y. State Coun. on Arts, 1987-88. Contbr. articles to profl. publs. Helena Rubinstein fellow, 1983. Mem. Nat. Sci. Tchrs. Assn., Am. Assn. Zool. Parks and Aquariums, Quoque Beach Club. Avocations: mountaineering, nordic and alpine skiing, backpacking, baseball. Office: NY Zool Soc Edn Dept Bronx Zoo Bronx NY 10460

LISS, IVAN BARRY, dean, computer science educator; b. Lebanon, Ky., June 21, 1938; s. Samuel and Edna (Allen) L.; m. Frances Carol Mitchell, July 29, 1977; children: Barry, David. BA, Georgetown Coll., 1960; MA in Edn., U. Ky., 1963; PhD in Chemistry, U. Louisville, 1973; MA in Computer Sci., U. Ill., Springfield, 1985. Chemistry tchr. Shelby County H.S., Shelbyville, Ky., 1960-65; faculty mem. chemistry Blackburn Coll., Carlinville, Ill., 1974-84; faculty mem., chair computer sci. Radford (Va.) U., 1985-93, assoc. dean, prof. computer sci., 1993-96, dean Coll. Arts and Scis., 1996—. Contbr. articles to various computer sci. jours. Mem. Am. Assn. Higher Edn., Assn. Computing Machinery, Coun. Colls. Arts and Scis., Sigma Xi. Office: Radford Univ PO Box 6940 Radford VA 24142-6940 E-mail: iliss@radford.edu.

LISSKA, ANTHONY JOSEPH, humanities educator, philosopher; b. Columbus, Ohio, July 23, 1940; s. Joseph Anthony and Florence (Wolfel) L.; m. Marianne Hedstrom, Mar. 16, 1968; children: Megan Catherine, Elin Elizabeth. BA in Philosophy cum laude, Providence Coll., 1963; AM in Philosophy, St. Stephen's Coll., Dover, Mass., 1967; PhD in Philosophy, Ohio State U., 1971; Cert., Harvard U., Cambridge, 1979. Asst. prof. Denison U., Granville, Ohio, 1969-76, assoc. prof., 1976-81, dean of coll., 1978-83, prof. philosophy, 1981—, dir. honors program, 1987—2002, Charles and Nancy Brickman disting. svc. chair, 1998-2001. Vis. scholar U. Oxford, Eng., 1984; Aquinas lectr. Providence Coll., 2002; project reviewer NEH, Washington, 1979-90, evaluator; adv. bd. Midwest Faculty Seminar, Chgo., 1981-90; mem. scholarship com. Sherex Chem. Co., Dublin, Ohio, 1984-92; cons. Franklin Pierce Coll., Ringe, N.H., 1991, Hampden-Sydney (Va.) Coll., 1998; referee various philosophy jours. Author: Philosophy Matters, 1977, Aquinas's Theory of Natural Law, 1996, paperback edit. 1997, 2002; co-editor: The Historical Times, 1988—; contbr. numerous articles to profl. jours., chpts. to books. Bd. mgmt. Granville Hist. Soc., 1987-2002; precinct rep. Dem. Party, Granville, 1994—; convener Civil War Roundtable, Granville, 1989-95; v.p. The Granville Found., 2003—; mem. Granville Bicentennial Commn., 1996—. Named Carnegie Prof. of Yr., Carnegie Found., 1994, Sears Found. Teaching award, 1990; NEH grantee, 1973, 77, 85; R.C. Good fellow, 1990, 96, 2002. Mem. Am. Philos. Assn. (program com. 2003, Tchg. award 1994), Am. Cath. Philos. Assn., Nat. Collegiate Honors Coun., Soc. for Ancient Greek Philosophy, Soc. for Medieval and Renaissance Philosophy, Internat. Thomas Aquinas Soc. Democrat. Roman Catholic. Avocations: local history, photography. Home: 285 Burtridge Rd Granville OH 43023-1214 Office: Denison U Dept Pilosophy Knapp Hall Granville OH 43023 E-mail: lisska@denison.edu.

LISTON, MARY FRANCES, retired nursing educator; b. N.Y.C., Dec. 17, 1920; d. Michael Joseph and Ellen Theresa (Shaughnessy) L. BS, Coll. Mt. St. Vincent, 1944; MS, Catholic U. Am., 1945; EdD, Columbia, 1962; HHD (hon.), Allentown Coll., 1987. Dir. psychiat. nursing and edn. Nat. League for Nursing, N.Y.C., 1958-66; prof. Sch. Nursing, Cath. U. Am., Washington, 1966-78, dean, 1966-73; prof. Marywood Coll., 1984-87. Spl. assignment Imperial Med. Center, Tehran, Iran, 1975-78; dep. dir. for program affairs Nat. League for Nursing, N.Y.C., 1978-84 Mem. Sigma Theta Tau. Home: 182 Garth Rd Scarsdale NY 10583-3863

LITMAN, GEORGE IRVING, physician, educator; b. Mass., Oct. 15, 1939; children: Scott, Amy, Kimberly, Megan. BS, Boston Coll., 1960; MD, Boston U., 1964. Intern Phila. Gen. Hosp., 1964-65; resident Univ. Hosp., Boston, 1965-66, Boston Vet.'s Hosp., 1966-67; fellow cardiology Emory U., Atlanta, 1967—69; unit head cardiology Genessee Hosp., Rochester, N.Y., 1969-71; assoc. physician Morton F. Plant Hosp., Clearwater, Fla., 1971-72; chief cardiology Akron Gen. Med. Ctr., Akron, Ohio, 1972—, med. dir. The Heart Ctr., 2002—; prof. medicine NE Ohio U., Rootstown, Ohio, 1982—. Recipient Disting. Svc. award Ohio Heart Assn., 1988. Fellow Am. Coll. Cardiology, ACP, Am. Coll. Chest Physicians; mem. AMA, Summit County Med. Soc., Am. Heart Assn. (trustee Ohio 1974—, research rev. com. 1975—, chmn. 1981-83), Ohio Heart Assn. (Disting. Service award 1983), Akron Heart Assn. (Sauvageot Vol. Services award 1984). Office: Akron Gen Med Ctr 400 Wabash Ave Akron OH 44307-2463

LITMAN, ROSLYN MARGOLIS, lawyer, educator; b. N.Y.C., Sept. 30, 1928; d. Harry and Dorothy (Perlow) Margolis; m. S. David Litman, Nov. 22, 1950; children: Jessica, Hannah, Harry. BA, U. Pitts., 1949, JD, 1952. Bar: Pa. 1952; approved arbitrator for complex comml. litigation and employment law. Practiced in Pitts., 1952—; ptnr. firm Litman Law Firm, 1952—; adj. prof. U. Pitts. Law Sch., 1958—. Permanent del. Conf. U.S. Circuit Ct. Appeals for 3d Circuit; past chair dist. adv. group U.S. Dist. Ct. (we. dist.) Pa., 1991-94, mem. steering com. for dist. adv. group, 1991—; chmn. Pitts. Pub. Parking Authority, 1970-74; mem. curriculum com. Pa. Bar Inst., 1986—, bd. dirs., 1972-82. Bd. dirs. United Jewish Fedn., 1999—, cmty. rels. com., co-chair ch./state com.; bd. dirs. City Theatre, 1999—. Recipient Roscoe Pound Found. award for Excellence in Tchg. Trial Advocacy, 1996, Disting. Alumnus award U. Pitts. Sch. Law, 1996; named Fed. Lawyer of Yr., We. Pa. Chpt. FBA, 1999. Mem. ABA (del., litigation sect., anti-trust health care com.), ACLU (nat. bd. dirs., Marjorie H. Matson Civil Libertarian award Greater Pitts. chpt. 1999), Pa. Bar Assn. (bd. govs. 1976-79), Allegheny County Bar Assn. (bd. govs. 1972-74, pres. 1975, Woman of Yr. 2001), Allegheny County Acad. Trial Lawyers (charter), Order of Coif. Home: 5023 Frew St Pittsburgh PA 15213-3829 Office: One Oxford Centre 34th Fl Pittsburgh PA 15219

LITT, IRIS FIGARSKY, pediatrics educator; b. N.Y.C., Dec. 25, 1940; d. Jacob and Bertha (Berson) Figarsky; m. Victor C. Vaughan, June 14, 1987; children from previous marriage: William M., Robert B. AB, Cornell U., 1961; MD, SUNY, Bklyn., 1965. Diplomate Am. Bd. Pediatrics (bd. dirs. 1989-94), sub-specialty bd. cert. in adolescent medicine. Intern, then resident in pediat. N.Y. Hosp., N.Y.C., 1965-68; assoc. prof. pediat. Stanford U. Sch. Medicine, Palo Alto, Calif., 1982-87, prof., 1987—, dir. divsn. adolescent medicine, 1976—, dir. Inst. for Rsch. on Women and Gender, 1990-97. Editor Jour. Adolescent Health; contbr. articles to profl. jours including Jour. Am. Med. Assn., Pediatrics. Mem. Soc. for Adolescent Medicine (charter), Am. Acad. Pediatrics (award sect. on adolescent health),

Western Soc. Pediatric Rsch., Soc. Pediatric Rsch., Am. Pediatric Soc., Inst. of Medicine/NAS. Office: 750 Welch Rd Ste 325 Palo Alto CA 94304-1510 E-mail: iris.litt@stanford.edu.

LITTELL, FRANKLIN HAMLIN, theologian, educator; b. Syracuse, N.Y., June 20, 1917; s. Clair F. and Lena Augusta (Hamlin) L.; m. Harriet Davidson Lewis, June 15, 1939 (dec. 1978); children: Jennith, Karen, Miriam, Stephen; m. 2d Marcia S. Sachs, 1980; children: Jonathan, Robert, Jennifer. BA, Cornell Coll., 1937, DD, 1953; BD, Union Theol. Sem., 1940; PhD, Yale U., 1946; Dr. Theology (hon.), U. Marburg, 1957; ThD (hon.), Thiel Coll., 1968; other hon. degrees, Widener Coll., 1969, Hebrew Union Coll., 1975, Reconstructionist Rabbinical Coll., 1976, Gratz Coll., 1977, St. Joseph's U., 1988, Stockton State Coll., 1991, U. Bridgeport, 1996, U. of New England, 2001. Dir. Lane Hall, U. Mich., 1944-49; chief protestant adviser to U.S. High Commr., other service in Germany, 1949-51, 53-58; prof. Chgo. Theol. Sem., 1962-69; pres. Iowa Wesleyan Coll., 1966-69; prof. religion Temple U., 1969-86. Adj. prof. Inst. Comtemporary Jewry, Hebrew U., Israel, 1973-94; Ida E. King disting. prof. Holocaust studies Richard Stockton Coll., 1989-91, 96-98; disting. prof. Holocaust and Genocide Studies, 1998—; Robert Foster Cherry disting. vis. prof. Baylor U., 1993-94; guest prof. numerous univs. Author numerous books including The Anabaptist View of the Church: an Introduction to Sectarian Protestantism (Brewer award Am. Soc. Ch. History), 1952, rev. edit., 1958, 64, 99, From State Church to Pluralism, 1962, rev., 1970; (with Hubert Locke) The German Church Struggle and the Holocaust, 1974, 90; The Crucifixion of the Jews, 1975, 86, 96, The Macmillan Atlas History of Christianity, 1976, German edit., 1976, 89, (with Marcia Sachs Littell) A Pilgrim's Interfaith Guide to the Holy Land, 1981; A Half-Century of Religious Dialogue: Amsterdam 1939-1989, 1989, Historic Atlas of Christianity, 2001, Christian Response to Holocaust: Addresses and Papers 1952-2002, 2003; editor or assoc. editor numerous jours. including Jour. Ecumenical Studies, A Jour. of Ch. and State and Holocaust Genocide Studies; author weekly syndicated columns, also over 300 major articles or chpts. of books in field of modern religious history. Cons. NCCJ, 1958-83; mem. exec. com. Notre Dame Colloqium, 1961-68; vice chmn. Ctr. for Reformation Research, 1964-77; nat. chmn. Inst. for Am. Democracy, 1966-69, sr. scholar, 1969-76; co-founder, pres. Ann. Scholars' Conf. on Ch. Struggle and Holocaust, 1970—; pres. Christians Concerned for Israel, 1971-78, Nat. Christian Leadership Conf. for Israel, 1978-84, pres. emeritus 1985—; founder, chmn. ecumenical com. Deutscher Evangelischer Kirchentag, 1953-58; co-founder, cons. Assn. Coordination Univ. Religious Affairs, 1959—; mem. U.S. Holocaust Meml. Council, 1979-93; founder, pres. Nat. Inst. on Holocaust, Temple U., 1975-83, Anne Frank Inst., Phila., 1983-89; co-founder, pres. Phila. Ctr. on Holocaust, Genocide and Human Rights, 1989—; mem. exec. com. Remembering For The Future, Oxford and London, 1988, Berlin, 1994, hon. chmn. Oxford and London, 2000; named observer to Vatican II; mem. Internat. Bd. of Yad Vashem, Jerusalem, 1981—. Decorated Grosse Verdienstkreuz (Fed. Republic Germany); recipient Jabotinsky medal, Israel, Ladislaus Laszt Internat. Ecumenical award Ben Gurion U. of Negev, 1991, Buber Rosenzweig medal, Germany, 1996. Mem. European Assn. Evang. Acads. (co-founder 1965), Pen and Pencil Club, Phi Beta Kappa, Phi Beta Kappa Assocs. Home: PO Box 10 Merion Station PA 19066-0010

LITTELL, MARCIA SACHS, Holocaust and genocide studies educator; b. Phila., July 12, 1937; d. Leon Harry Sobel and Selma Fisher Goldstein Lipson; children: Jonathan R., Robert L. Jr., Jennifer Sachs-Dahnert; m. Franklin H. Littell, Mar. 23, 1980. BS in Edn., Temple U., 1971, MS in Edn., 1975, EdD, 1990. Internat. exec. dir. Anne Frank Inst., Phla., 1981-89; exec. dir. Ann. Scholars' Conf. on the Holocaust & the Chs., Merion, Pa., 1980—; prof., founding dir. MA program Holocaust & genocide studies The Richard Stockton Coll. N.J., 1997—. Adj. prof. Temple U., Phila., 1990-97; vis. prof. Phila. C.C., 1974-76; dir. Phila. Ctr. on the Holocaust, Genocide and Human Rights, 1989—; exec. com. Remembering for the Future, Oxford, Eng. and Berlin, 1986—; mem. edn. com. U.S. Holocaust Meml. Mus., Washington, 1987-89, chmn.'s adv. com., 1985. Mem. editl. bd. Holocaust & Genocide Studies, Oxford U. Press, 1987—, Bridges: An Interdisciplinary Journal of Theology, Philosophy, History and Science, 1995—; editor: Holocaust Education: A Resource for Teachers and Professional Leaders, 1985, Liturgies on the Holocaust: An Interfaith Anthology, 1986, rev. edit., 1996 (Merit of Distinction award), The Holocaust: Forty Years After, 1989, The Netherlands and Nazi Genocide, 1992, From Prejudice to Destruction: Western Civilization in the Shadow of Auschwitz, 1995, Remembrance and Recollection: Essays on the Centennial Year of Martin Neimoller and Reinhold Niebuhr, 1995, The Uses and Abuses of Knowledge: The Holocaust and the German Church Struggle, 1997, The Holocaust: Lessons For the Third Generation, 1997, Holocaust and Church Struggle: Religion, Power and the Politics of Resistance, 1996, Confronting the Holocaust: A Mandate for the 21st Century, part 1, 1997, part 2, 1998, A Modern Prophet, 1998, Hearing the Voices: Teaching the Holocaust to Future Generations, 1999, Women in the Holocaust, 2001, The Century of Genocide, 2002. Exec. com. YM/YWHA Arts Coun., Phila., 1980—; adv. bd. Child Welfare, Montgomery County, 1975-80, Am. Friends the Ghetto Fighters House; bd. govs. Lower Merion Scholarship Fund, 1972-80. Named Woman of the Yr., Brith Sholom Women, Phila., 1993; recipient Eternal Flame award Anne Frank Inst., 1988; named to Hall of Fame Sch. Dist. of Phila., 1988. Fellow Nat. Assn. Holocaust Educators, Assn. of Holocaust Orgns. (founding sec. 1985-88), Nat. Coun. for the Social Studies. Democrat. Jewish. Avocations: walking, travel, reading. Office: PO Box 10 Merion Station PA 19066-0010 E-mail: Drlittell@aol.com.

LITTKY, DENNIS, educational association administrator; PhD in Psychology, PhD in Edn., U. Mich. Co-dir. The Big Picture Co., Providence, 1995—; co-founder, co-prin. The Met. Ctr. H.S., Providence. Recipient McGaw prize in edn., 2002. Office: The Big Picture Co Ste 500 275 Westminster St Providence RI 02903*

LITTLE, ANGELA CAPOBIANCO, nutritional science educator; b. San Francisco, Jan. 12, 1920; d. Alfredo Agosto and Elizabeth (Kruse) Capobianco; m. George Gordon Little, Nov. 8, 1947; 1 child, Judith Kristine. BA, U. Calif., Berkeley, 1940, MS, 1954, PhD, 1969. Specialist jr. to asst. to assoc. U. Calif., Berkeley, 1958-69, food scientist, 1969-85, assoc. prof. to prof, 1977-85, prof. emeritus, 1985—, acad. ombudsman, 1985-87, 89-91. Cons. in field; v.p., bd. dirs. Math/Sci. Network, Berkeley; vis. scholar U. Wash., Seattle, 1976-77, Kans. State U., Manhattan, 1972; mem. faculty Fromm Inst., U. San Francisco, 1992-96; pres. bd. dirs. Laguna Heights Co-op Corp., 1999-2001. Author: Color of Foods, 1962. Nutritional adv. bd. Project Open Hand, San Francisco, 1989—91, vol., 1988—91, UNICEF, San Francisco, 1986—89, Saint Francis Hosp., 1992—; mem. San Francisco Museum of Modern Art, Calif. Palace of the Legion of Honor, Asian Art Museum, Yerba Buena Ctr. of the Arts, Museo Italo-Am. Rsch. grantee Robert Woods Johnson Found., 1989-90, others 1960-85. Mem. AAUW, San Francisco Acad. Sci., San Francisco Mus. Soc., U. Calif. Berkeley Emeritii Assn. (pres. 1991-93), Am. Assn. for History of Medicine, Exploratorium, Bay Area History of Medicine Club (pres. 1995-97), Laguna Heights Co-op Corp. (pres., bd. dirs. 1999-2001), Sigma Xi. Avocations: music, books, travel, exercising, walking. Home: 85 Cleary Ct Apt 3 San Francisco CA 94109-6518 Office: U Calif Dept Nutritional Scis Berkeley CA 94720-0001 E-mail: aclittle@uclink.berkeley.edu.

LITTLE, CLAIRE LONG, education educator, humanities educator; b. Caswell County, N.C. d. William McKinley and Rachel (Garland) Long; m. Clarence Little, June 19, 1965; children: Cedric Ty, Cerise Jeanyne. BS, Barber-Scotia Coll., 1964; MS, Hofstra U., 1973, CAS in Edn. Adminstrn., 1983, EdD in Reading, Lang. and Cognition, 1993; postgrad., CUNY. Cert. tchr., English, reading, sch. dist. adminstrn., N.Y., sch. adminstr./supr. Lang. arts tchr. Levittown (N.Y.) Pub. Schs., 1967-70; adj. instr. SUNY, Westbury, 1975-77, lectr. Jamaica; reading and lang. specialist Hicksville (N.Y.) Sch. Dist., 1973—. Advisor, organizer to numerous civic and charitable orgns. Mem. NEA, ASCD.

LITTLE, DANIEL EASTMAN, philosophy educator, university program director; b. Rock Island, Ill., Apr. 7, 1949; s. William Charles and Emma Lou (Eastman) L.; m. Ronnie Alice Friedland, Sept. 12, 1976 (div. May 1995); children: Joshua Friedland-Little, Rebecca Friedland-Little. BS in Math. with highest honors, AB in Philosophy with high honors, U. Ill., 1971; PhD in Philosophy, Harvard U., 1977. Asst. prof. U. Wis.-Parkside, Kenosha, 1976-79; vis. assoc. prof. Wellesley (Mass.) Coll., 1985-87; vis. scholar Ctr. Internat. Affairs Harvard U., 1989-91, assoc. Ctr. Internat. Affairs, 1991-95; asst. prof. Colgate U., Hamilton, N.Y., 1979-85, assoc. prof., 1985-92, prof., 1992-96, chmn. dept. philosophy and religion, 1992-93, assoc. dean faculty, 1993-96; v.p. academic affairs Bucknell U., Lewisburg, Pa., 1996-2000, prof. philosophy, 1996-2000; chancellor U. Mich., Dearborn, 2000—, prof. philosophy, 2000—; faculty assoc. Inter-U. Consortium for Social and Political Rsch., 2000—. Teaching fellow Harvard U., 1973-76; participant internat. confs. Ctr. Asian and Pacific Studies, U. Oreg., 1992, Social Sci. Rsch. Coun./McArthur Found., U. Calif., San Diego, 1991, Budapest, Hungary, 1990, Morelos, Mex., 1989, Rockefeller Found., Bellagio, Italy, 1990, U. Manchester, Eng., 1986; mem. screening com. on internat. peace and security Social Sci. Rsch. Coun./MacArthur Found., 1991-94; manuscript reviewer Yale U. Press, Cambridge U. Press, Princeton U. Press, Oxford U. Press, Westview Press, Harvard U. Press, Can. Jour. Philosophy, Philosophy Social Scis., Synthese, Am. Polit. Sci. Rev.; grant proposal reviewer NSF, Social Sci. Rsch. Coun., Nat. Endowment for Humanities; tenure and promotion reviewer U. Tenn., Bowdoin Coll., Duke U., U. Wis.; faculty assoc. Inter-Univ. Consortium for Social and Polit. Rsch., 2000—. Author: The Scientific Marx, 1986, Understanding Peasant China: Case Studies in the Philosophy of Social Science, 1989, Varieties of Social Explanation: An Introduction to the Philosophy of Social Science, 1991 (Outstanding Book award Choice 1992), On the Reliability of Economic Models, 1995, Microfoundations Method and Causation: On the Philosophy of the Social Sciences, 1998, The Paradox of Wealth and Poverty: Mapping the Ethical Dilemmas of Global Development, 2003; contbr. articles to profl. jours., books. Social Sci. Rsch. Postdoctoral fellow MacArthur Found., 1989-91, Rsch. grantee NSF, 1987, Woodrow Wilson Grad. fellow, 1971-72. Mem. Am. Philos. Assn., Assn. Asian Studies, Internat. Devel. Ethics Assn., Social Sci. History Assn., Soc. for the History of Tech., Phi Beta Kappa. Office: Chancellor U Mich Dearborn 4901 Evergreen Rd Dearborn MI 48128 E-mail: delittle@umich.edu.

LITTLE, H. MAURICE, vocational educator; b. Brenham, Tex., July 31, 1947; s. Hoxie and Bert Estelle (Jameson) L. BS, Tex. So. U., 1972; MEd, Prairie View A & M U., 1974, Tex. So. U., 1985. Office adminstrn. coop. coord. M.B. Smiley High Sch., Houston, 1972—. Devel. reading instr. Houston Cmty. Coll., 1985—; bus. edn. prof. Tex. So. U., Houston, 1987—. Mem. Bus. Profls. of Am. Baptist. Office: MB Smiley HS 10726 Mesa Dr Houston TX 77078-1402

LITTLE, JOHN DUTTON CONANT, management scientist, educator; b. Boston, Feb. 1, 1928; s. John Dutton and Margaret (Jones) L.; m. Elizabeth Davenport Alden, Sept. 12, 1953; children: John Norris, Sarah Alden, Thomas Dunham Conant, Ruel Davenport. SB in Physics, MIT, 1948, PhD, 1955; PhD (hon.), U. Liege, Belgium, 1992, Cath. U. of Mons, 1997; PhD (hon.), U. London, 2002. Engr. Gen. Electric Co., Schenectady, 1949-50; asst. prof. ops. research Case-Western Res. U., 1957-60, assoc. prof., 1960-62; research asst. MIT, 1951-54, assoc. prof. mgmt., 1962-67, prof., 1967-78, George M. Bunker prof. mgmt., 1978-89, Inst. prof., 1989—, dir. Ops. Research Ctr., 1969-76, head mgmt. sci. group Sloan Sch. Mgmt., 1972-82, head behavioral and policy scis. area, 1982-88, chmn. undergrad. program, 1990—; pres. Mgmt. Decision Systems, Inc., 1967-80, chmn. bd. dirs., 1967-85; dir., advisor to bd. dirs. Info. Resources, Inc., 1985—. Cons. ops. rsch. indsl. govtl. orgns., 1958—; vis. prof. mktg. European Inst. Bus. Adminstrn., Fontainebleau, France, fall 1988; researcher math. programming, queuing theory, mktg., traffic control, decision support systems, e-commerce; bd. dirs. InSite Mktg. Technology, Inc., 1997-99. Assoc. editor: Mgmt. Sci, 1967-71; contbr. articles to profl. jours. Trustee Mktg. Sci. Inst., 1983-89. Served with AUS, 1955-56. Fellow AAAS (mem. coun. 2000—); mem. NAE, Ops. Rsch. Soc. Am. (coun. 1970-73, pres. 1979-80), Inst. Mgmt. Scis. (v.p. 1976-79, pres. 1984-85), Fellow Inst. for Ops. Rsch. and the Mgmt. Scis. (pres. 1995), Am. Mktg. Assn., Sigma Xi. Home: 37 Conant Rd Lincoln MA 01773-3912 Office: MIT Sloan Sch Mgmt Cambridge MA 02142-1347

LITTLE, JOHN WILLIAM, plastic surgeon, educator; b. Indpls., Mar. 12, 1944; s. John William Jr. and Naida (Jones) L.; m. Patricia Padgett Lea, May 26, 1969 (div. 1974); m. Teri Ann Tyson, Feb. 28, 1981 (div. 1982). AB, Dartmouth Coll., 1966, B in Med. Scis., 1967; MD, Harvard U., 1969. Diplomate Am. Bd. Med. Examiners, Am. Bd. Surgery, Am. Bd. Plastic Surgery. Intern Case Western Res. U., Cleve., 1969-70, resident in surgery, 1970-74, resident in plastic surgery, 1973-75; fellow in plastic surgery U. Miami, 1975-77; asst. prof. Georgetown U., Washington, 1977-82, assoc. prof., 1982-87, prof., 1987-92, clin. prof., 1992—, dir. div. plastic surgery, residency tng. program, plastic surgeon-in-chief univ. hosp., 1979-92; dir. Nat. Capital Tng. Program in Plastic Surgery affiliated hosps. Georgetown U. and Howard U., 1988-92; dir. Georgetown Plastic Surgery Fellowship in Breast and Aesthetic Surgery, 1990-92; pvt. practice Washington, 1992—. Prof. postgrad. edn. in plastic surgery Internat. Soc. Aesthetic Plastic Surgery, 1999—; chief plastic surgery Medlantic Ctr. for Ambulatory Surgery, Inc., 1993—, mem. med. adv. bd., 1993—; cons. Nat. Cancer Inst., NIH, Bethesda, Md., 1977-92, Washington VA Med. Ctr., 1981-92, Reach to Recovery program Nat. Capital chpt. Am. Cancer Soc., 1981—, RENU program in breast reconstrn., 1982; specialist site visitor plastic surgery residency rev. com. Accreditation Coun. for Grad. Med. Edn., 1982-95; vis. lect. various insts.; bd. govs. Nat. Endowment for Plastic Surgery, 1995—. Adv. editor Plastic and Reconstructive Surgery, 1997—, manuscript reviewer Plastic and Reconstructive Surgery, Annals of Plastic Surgery; assoc. editor Surgery of the Breast: Principles and Art, 1998; contbr. numerous articles to med. jours., numerous chpts. to books. Bd. dirs. Triann reconstructive surgery teams to Caribbean and S.Am., Georgetown Tissue Bank, 1986-88, Operation Luz del Sol; founder, pres., med. dir. Reconstructive Surgeons Vol. Program; bd. dirs. Washington Summer Opera Theater; trustee Washington Opera, 1993—, artistic com., 1994—; Domingo Circle, 1995—, Laureates' medal, 1999. Recipient Laureate medallion Domingo Cir., 1999, Mem. AMA, ACS (coord. plastic surgery audiovisual program Ann. Clin. Congress 1988-90, 92-93, bd. govs., Met. Washington chpt. councillor 1985-94, chmn. sci. program com. 1990-91, v.p. 1991-92, pres. 1992-93, bd. govs. 1998—), Nat. Capital Soc. Plastic Surgeons (sec. treas. 1982-83, pres. 1984-85), Am. Soc. Plastic Surgeons (audiovisual program dir. ann. meeting 1984-86, strategic planning com. 1987-96, fin. com. 1989-94, conv. policy com. 1993-96, ops. com. 1993-96, chmn. 1994-95, spokesperson network steering com. 1994-96, bd. dirs. 1994-96, exec. com. 1995-96, spokesperson 1998—, rep. to IPRAS 1999—), Am. Assn. Plastic Surgeons (co-chmn. various coms.), Plastic Surgery Ednl. Found. (bd. dirs. 1985-97, devel. com. 1991—, chmn. 1997-2000, chmn. various coms., rep. to Coun. Plastic Surg. Orgns. 1989-95, parliamentarian 1992-93, v.p. 1993-94, pres. adv. coun. 1993-96, commr. various commns., pres.-elect, 1995, pres. 1995-96, Maliniac fellow 1998—, Disting. Svc. award, 2000), Med. Soc. D.C. (chmn. plastic surgery sect. 1985), D.R. Millard Surg. Soc. and Ednl. Found. (pres. 1985-87), Am. Cleft Palate Assn., Am. Soc. Maxillofacial Surgeons, Washington Acad. Surgeons (coun. 1988-90), Am. Soc. Aesthetic Plastic Surgery (In Chun Sung award philanthropic svc. 2000), NE Soc. Plastic Surgeons (chmn. various coms., v.p. 1991-92, pres. 1992-93, historian 1994-99), Internat. Soc. Aesthetic Plastic Surgery (chmn. bylaws com. 1990-93, 95-97, parliamentarian 1990-93, mem. membership com. 1993-97, chmn. 1993-95, sec. gen. 1997-2000, rep. to IPRAS 1997-2000, prof. postgrad. edn. in aesthetic plastic surgery, others), Am. Alpine Workshop in Plastic Surgery (founder, pres. 1991-92, historian 1995—), Internat. Confedn. Plastic Reconstructive and Aesthetic Surgery (mem. exec. com. 1997-2000, coun. dels. 1999—), Nat. Endowment Plastic Surgeons (bd. govs. 1995—), Internat. Plastic, Reconstructive and Aesthetic Surgery Found. (bd. dirs. 1999—, ednl. program com. chmn. 1999—, vice chmn. devel. com. 1999—, publs. and videotape com.), European Assn. Plastic Surgeons (corr.), Turkish Soc. Plastic Surgeons (hon.), Argentine Soc. Plastic, Reconstructive and Aesthetic Surgeons (assoc.), Atlantic Soc. Plastic Surgeons (hon.), Soc. Am. and Italian Plastic Surgeons (founding mem. 1988—), Turkish Soc. Plastic Surgeons (hon. mem. 1996—), Argentina Soc. Esthetic Plastic Surgery and Repair (corr. mem. 1999—), European Assn. Plastic Surgeons (corr. mem 2000—), Atlantic Soc. Palstic Surgeons (hon. mem. 2000—), Mediterranean Soc. Plastic and Aesthetic Surgery (active mem. 2001—); fellow Am. Israeli Plastic Surgeons (charter mem. 1997—), Republican. Presbyterian. Home: 3030 K St NW Ph 212 Washington DC 20007-5107 Office: 1145 19th St NW Ste 802 Washington DC 20036-3700

LITTLE, RICHARD ALLEN, mathematics and computer science educator; b. Cochocton, Ohio, Jan. 12, 1939; s. Charles M. and Elsie Leanna (Smith) L.; children from previous marriage: Eric, J. Alice, Stephanie; m. Laura Ann Novosel, June 15, 1991. BS in Math. cum laude, Wittenberg U., 1960; MA in Edn., Johns Hopkins U., 1961; EdM in Math., Harvard U., 1965; PhD in Math. Edn., Kent State U., 1971. Tchr. Culver Acad., Ind., 1961-65; instr., curriculum cons. Harvard U., Cambridge, Mass. and Aiyetoro, Nigeria, 1965-67; from instr. to assoc. prof. Kent State U., Canton, Ohio, 1967-75; from assoc. prof. to prof. Baldwin-Wallace Coll., Berea, Ohio, 1975—, dept. chair, 1978-83. Mathematician/educator Project Discovery Ohio Bd. Regents, 1992-96; vis. prof., math. Ohio State U., Columbus, 1987-88, 92-95; lectr. various colls. and univs.; pres. Cleve. Collaborative on Math. Edn., 1986-87, bd. dirs. 1985-2002; mem. policy bd. Ohio Resource Ctr. for Math. Sci. and Reading, 2000—, mem. exec. com. policy bd., 2001—, chair exec. com., 2002-03. Contbr. articles to profl. jours. Bd. dirs. Canton Symphony Orch., 1973-75; Sunday sch. tchr. Bethany English Luth. Ch., Cleve., 1991—; bd. deacons Holy Cross Luth. Ch., Canton, 1968-74, chmn., 1971-74. Recipient Strosacker Excellence in Tchg. award and Student Senate Faculty Excellence award Baldwin-Wallace Coll., 1999. Mem. Nat. Coun. Tchrs. Math. (profl. devel. and status adv. com. 1987-90, program com. ann. meeting 1997), Ohio Coun. Tchrs. Math. (pres. 1974-76, v.p. 1970-73, sec. 1982-84, dir. state math. contest 1983-92, Christofferson-Fawcett award 1990), Ohio Math. Educators Leadership Coun. (pres. 1990-91, bd. dirs. 1988-92), Greater Canton Coun. Tchrs. Math. (pres. 1969-70), Math. Assn. Am. (pres. Ohio sect. 1983-84, editor 1977-83). Avocations: hiking, tennis, handball. Office: Baldwin-Wallace Coll Dept Math & Computer Sci 275 Eastland Rd Berea OH 44017-2005 E-mail: rlittle@bw.edu.

LITTLE, ROBERT DAVID, library science educator; b. Milw., July 11, 1937; s. Kenneth Edwin and Grace Elizabeth (Terwileger) L. BA, U. Wis., Milw., 1959; MA, U. Wis., 1964, PhD, 1972. Tchr., sch. librarian Sevastapol Pub. Schs., Sturgeon Bay, Wis., 1959-62; sch. librarian Highland Park (Ill.) High Sch., 1962-63; supr. sch. libraries Sevastapol/Gilbraltor Pub. Sch., Sturgeon Bay, 1963-65; state sch. library supr. Wis. Dept. Pub. Instrn., Madison, 1965-69, program adminstr., 1969-70; asst. prof. libr. sci. U. Wis., Milw., 1970-71, acting dir. Sch. Libr. Sci., 1971; assoc. prof. libr. sci. Ind. State U., Terre Haute, 1971-77, prof., 1977-97, chmn. dept., 1971-93. Cons. Ind. Nat. Network Study, Terre Haute, 1978-79; cons., researcher Nat. Ctr. Edn. Stats., Washington, 1978-79; mem. Ind. State Libr. Adv. Coun., Indpls., 1981-91. Co-author: Public Library Users and Uses, 1988; editor: Cataloging, Processing, Administering AV Materials, 1972; contbr. articles to profl. jours. Pres. West Cen. Ind. chpt. Ind. Civil Liberties Union, 1988-92. Edn. Act fellow U. Wis., Madison, 1967, 68. Mem. ALA, Am. Assn. Sch. Librs., Assn. Ind. Media Educators (pres. 1981-82, Peggy Leach Pfeiffer Svc. award 1987). Methodist. Avocations: reading, travel. Home: 500 W 43rd St Apt 22H New York NY 10036-4335

LITTLE, ROBERT EUGENE, mechanical engineering educator, materials behavior researcher, consultant; b. Enfield, Ill., May 24, 1933; s. John Henry and Mary (Stephens) L.; m. Barbara Louina Farrell, Feb. 4, 1961; children: Susan Elizabeth, James Robert, Richard Roy, John William. BSME, U. Mich., 1959; MSME, Ohio State U., 1960; PhDME, U. Mich., 1963. Asst. prof. mech. engring. Okla. State U., Stillwater, 1963-65; assoc. prof. U. Mich., Dearborn, 1965-68, prof., 1968—. Author: Statistical Design of Fatigue Experiments, 1975, Probability and Statistics for Engineers, 1978 Mem. ASTM, Am. Statis. Assn. Home: 3230 Pine Lake Rd West Bloomfield MI 48324-1951 Office: U Mich 4901 Evergreen Rd Dearborn MI 48128-1491

LITTLE, WILLIAM ARTHUR, physicist, educator; b. South Africa, Nov. 17, 1930; came to U.S., 1958, naturalized, 1964; s. William Henry and Margaret (Macleod) L.; m. Annie W. Smith, July 15, 1955; children— Lucy Claire, Linda Susan, Jonathan William. PhD, Rhodes U., S. Africa, 1953, Glasgow (Scotland) U., 1957. Faculty Stanford, 1958—, prof. physics, 1965-94; prof. emeritus, 1994—. Cons. to industry, 1960— ; co-founder, chmn. MMR Techs. Inc., 1980—, 3L&T, Inc., 1999—. Recipient Deans award for disting. teaching Stanford U., 1975-76, Walter J. Gores award for excellence in teaching, Stanford U., 1979, IR-100 award Indsl. Rsch. and Devel., 1981; NRC Can. postdoctoral fellow Vancouver, Can., 1956-58, Sloan Found. fellow, 1959-63, John Simon Guggenheim fellow, 1964-65, NSF sr. postdoctoral fellow, 1970-71 Fellow Am. Phys. Soc.; mem. Am. Chem. Soc. Achievements include spl. research low temperature physics, superconductivity, neural network theory, cryogenics; holder 14 patents in area of cryogenics and med. instrumentation. Home: 15 Crescent Dr Palo Alto CA 94301-3106 Office: Stanford U Dept Physics Stanford CA 94305 E-mail: bill@mmr.com.

LITTLEFIELD, ROY EVERETT, III, association executive, legal educator; b. Nashua, NH, Dec. 6, 1952; s. Roy Everett and Mary Ann (Prestipino) L.; m. Amy Root; children: Leah Marie, Roy Everett IV, Christy Louise. BA, Dickinson Coll., 1975; MA, Catholic U. Am., 1976, PhD, 1979. Aide U.S. Senator Thomas McIntyre, Democrat, N.H., 1975-78, Nordy Hoffman, U.S. Senate Sergeant-at-arms, N.H., 1979; dir. govt. rels. Nat. Tire Dealers and Retreaders Assn., Washington, N.H., 1979-84; exec. dir. Svc. Sta. and Automotive Repair Assn., Washington, NH, 1984—2003; exec. v.p. Svc. Sta. Dealers of Am., 1994—2003; exec. dir. Tire Industry Assn., 2003—. Faculty Cath. U. Am., Washington, 1979—; cons. Internat. Tire and Rubber Assn., 1984-2003. Author: William Randolph Hearst: His Role in American Progressivism, 1980, The Economic Recovery Act, 1982, The Surface: Transportation Assistance Act, 1984; editor Nozzle mag.; contbr. numerous articles to legal jours. Mem. Nat. Dem. Club, 1978—. Mem. Am. Soc. Legal History, Md. Hwy. User's Fedn. (pres.), Nat. Hwy. User's Fedn. (sec.), Nat. Capitol Area Transp. Fedn. (v.p.), N.H. Hist. Soc., Kansas City C. of C., Capitol Hill Club, Phi Alpha Theta. Roman Catholic. Home: 1707 Pepper Tree Ct Bowie MD 20721-3021 Office: 9420 Annapolis Rd Ste 307 Lanham Seabrook MD 20706-3061

LITTLETON, JESSE TALBOT, III, radiology educator; b. Corning, N.Y., Apr. 27, 1917; s. Jesse Talbot and Bessie (Cook) L.; m. Martha Louise Morrow, Apr. 17, 1943 (dec. 1994); children: Christine, Joanne, James, Robert, Denise; m. Mary Lou Durizch, Mar. 25, 1995. Student, Emory and Henry Coll., 1934-35, Johns Hopkins U., 1935-39; MD, Syracuse U., 1943. Diplomate Am. Bd. Radiology. Intern Buffalo Gen. Hosp., 1943; resident in medicine, surgery and radiology Robert Packer Hosp., Sayre, Pa., 1946-51, assoc. radiologist, 1951-53, chmn. dept. radiology, 1953-76; prof. radiology U. South Ala., Mobile, 1976-87, prof. emeritus, 1987—. Cons. in field. Author 4 textbooks; contbr. chpts. to books and articles to profl. jours., sci. exhibits to profl. confs. Served with M.C., U.S. Army, 1944-46, PTO. Fellow Am. Coll. Radiology; mem. AMA, Radiol. Soc. N.Am., Am. Roentgen Ray Soc., Ala. Acad. Radiology, Med. Assn. Ala., French Soc. Neuroradiology, Country Club of Mobile, Sigma Xi, Alpha Omega Alpha. Republican. Methodist. Achievements include research on conventional tomography, physical principles, equipment development and testing and clinical applications; transportation and radiology of acutely ill and traumatized patient; development of patient litter with removable top leading to placement of backboards in ambulances; development of dedicated trauma x-ray machine; angiography, development of first sheet film serialograph; development of equipment for sectional radiographic anatomy with Durizch. Home: 5504 Churchill Downs Ave Theodore AL 36582-9601 Office: U South Ala Med Ctr 2451 Fillingim St Mobile AL 36617-2238

LITTLETON, NAN ELIZABETH FELDKAMP, psychologist, educator; b. Covington, Ky., Oct. 23, 1942; d. William Albert and Norma Elizabeth (Smith) Feldkamp; m. O.W. Littleton, Oct. 4, 1969 (div. 1979). AAS, No. Ky. U., 1976, BS, 1978; MACE, Morehead State U., 1981; MA, U. Cin., 1986, PhD, 1995. Prof. No. Ky. U., Highland Heights, 1976—, dir. mental health and human svcs. program, 1989—. Officer, pres. Holly Hill Children's Home, Cold Spring, Ky., 1980-86; cons. Attituding Healing Ctr., Cin., 1990-94. Treas., editor So. Orgn. Human Svcs. Edn. Link, 1997-2002. Bd. dirs. Coun. for Stds. in Human Svc. Edn., Chgo., 1990-98—, Cancer Family Care, Cin., 1992-96. Mem. APA, Am. Psychol. Soc., Nat. Orgn. Human Svc. Edn., Am. Coun. Assn., So. Orgn. Human Svc. Edn. (state rep. 1991—, treas., 1999-2002), Nat. Women's Studies Assn., Assn. Humanistic Psychologists. Home: 333 W 17th St Covington KY 41014-1007

LITTLEWOOD, THOMAS BENJAMIN, retired journalism educator; b. Flint, Mich., Nov. 30, 1928; s. Thomas Nelson and Louise Engela (Grebenkemper) L.; m. Barbara E. Badger, June 9, 1951; children: Linda S. Johnson, Lisa L. Ratchford, Thomas S., Leah J. Hamrick. Student, DePauw U., 1948-51; BS, Northwestern U., 1952, MS, 1953. Reporter Chgo. Sun-Times, 1953-76, chief Springfield State Capital Bur., 1955-64, corr. Washington Bur., 1965-76; prof. journalism U. Ill., Urbana-Champaign, 1977-96; prof. emeritus, 1996—; head dept. U. Ill., Urbana-Champaign, 1977-87. Author: Bipartisan Coalition in Illinois, 1959, Horner of Illinois, 1969, The Politics of Population Control, 1977, Coals of Fire, 1988, Arch, 1990, Calling Elections, 1999, The True Picture in the PR Age, 2002.. Fellow John F. Kennedy Inst. Politics fellow, Harvard U., 1975. Mem. Soc. Profl. Journalists (SDX Nat. award 1988), Ill. State Hist. Soc., Kappa Tau Alpha. E-mail: tbbblittlewood@prodigy.net.

LITTMAN, MARLYN KEMPER, information scientist, educator; b. Mar. 26, 1943; d. Louis and Augusta (Jacobs) Janofsky; m. Bennett I. Kemper, Aug. 1, 1965 (dec. June 1987); children: Alex Randall, Gari Hament, Jason Myles; m. Lewis Littman, Apr. 22, 1990. BA, Finch Coll., 1964; MA in Anthropology, Temple U., 1970; MA in Info. Sci., U. South Fla., 1983; PhD in Info. Sci., Nova Southeastern U., 1986. Dir. Hist. Broward County Preservation Bd., Hollywood, Fla., 1979—87; automated systems libr. Broward County Main Libr., Ft. Lauderdale, Fla., 1984—86; assoc. prof. info. sci. Nova U., Ft. Lauderdale, Fla., 1987—94, dir. info. sci. doctoral program, 1987—94; prof. info. sci. Nova Southeastern U., Ft. Lauderdale, Fla., 1995—. Weekly columnist Ft. Lauderdale News, 1975—79; contbg. editor Hyper Nexus-Jour. Hypermedia and Multimedia Studies, 1996—2000; assoc. editor Jour. On-Line Learning, 1997—2002. Author: A Comprehensive Documented History of the City of Pompano Beach, 1982, A Comprehensive History of Dania, 1983, A Comprehensive History of Hallandale, 1984, A Comprehensive History of Deerfield Beach, 1985, A Comprehensive History of Plantation, 1986, A Comprehensive History of Davie, 1987, Networking: Choosing a LAN Path to Interconnection, 1987, Building Broadband Networks, 2002; author: (with others) Mosaics of Meaning, New Ways of Learning, 1996; contbr. articles to profl. jours., chapters to books. Pub. info. officer Broward County Hist. Commn., 1975—79; vice chmn. Broward County Adv. Bd., 1987—92; bd. dirs. Ctrl. Agy. Jewish Edn., 1992—94. Recipient Judge L. Clayton Nance award, 1977, Broward County Hist. Commn. award, 1979. Mem.: IEEE, Assn. Computing Machinery, Internat. Soc. for Tech. in Edn., Phi Kappa Phi, Beta Phi Mu. Home: 2845 NE 35th St Fort Lauderdale FL 33306-2007 Office: Nova Southeastern U Grad Sch Computer and Info Sci 6100 Guffin Rd Fort Lauderdale FL 33314 E-mail: marlyn@nova.edu.

LITTON, DAPHNE NAPIER RUDHMAN, special education educator; b. Schenectady, July 28, 1952; d. James Napier and Mary (Stathas) Rudhman; m. John Shelby Litton, Oct. 5, 1984; children: Christian Napier, Erin Elizabeth. BS in Elem. Edn., Ind. U., South Bend, 1974, MS in Elem. Edn., cert. learning disabled, Ind. U., South Bend, 1978; cert. emotionally disturbed, Ind. U.-Purdue U., Indpls., 1982. Tchr. remedial reading, dir. motor skills, tchr. summer sch. Olive Twp. Elem. Sch., New Carlisle, Ind., 1976; tchr. learning disabled, gifted, remedial reading Ox Bow Elem. Sch., Elkhart, Ind., 1976-85, dir. motor skills, 1976-85; tchr. learning disabled Stafford (Va.) Community Schs., 1985-87; tchr. emotionally disturbed Elvin Hill Elem. Sch., Columbiana, Ala., 1987-88; dir., adminstr. Riverchase Presbyn. Presch./Mother's Day Out, Birmingham, Ala., 1989-90; tchr. learning disabled Yorkshire Elem. Sch., Manassas, Va., 1993-95, Piney Grove Elem. Sch., Kernersville, N.C., 1995—. Mem. Ind. State Com. for Svc. Personnel Devel., Elkhart, 1979-85; asst. girl's volleyball coach Ox Bow Elem. Sch., Elkhart, 1985-87; asst. dir. Sports Medicine 10K Run Vols., South Bend, 1986. Contbr. poetry to lit. jours. Active Am. Cancer Soc., South Bend, 1975, Girl Scouts. Recipient Editor's Choice award, Nat. Libr. of Poetry, 1997. Mem. Coun. Exceptional Children. Republican. Presbyterian. Avocations: musical instruments, choir, travel, swimming, genealogy. Home: 1820 Glenridge Dr Kernersville NC 27284-8666

LITTON, NANCY JOAN, education educator; b. Baton Rouge, Mar. 26, 1952; d. Gilbert Dupre and Mell Baynard Litton. BS in Elem. Edn., La. State U., 1973, MEd in Elem. Edn., 1977, MA in History, 1986. Tchr., various grades various sch., Baton Rouge area, Eng. and Switzerland, 1974—94; tchg. assoc., Learning Assistance Ctr. La. State U., Baton Rouge, 1994—96, instr. for Coll. Edn., 1996—. Evaluator for talented drama students East Baton Rouge Parish Pub. Sch. Actor: over 70 plays. Christmas caroler for benefit Gilbert and Sullivan Soc., Baton Rouge, 2000—01; lector Our Lady of Mercy Cath. Ch., Baton Rouge, 1989—. Recipient Best Actress in a Play award, Baton Rouge Little Theater, 1998, Actress of Yr. award, Baker Little Theatre, 1995, Supporting Actress of Yr. award, 1997. Roman Catholic. Avocations: public speaking, singing, travel, acting. Home: 4900 Claycut Rd Apt 52 Baton Rouge LA 70806 Office: La State U Coll of Edn Baton Rouge LA 70803 E-mail: nlitto@lsu.edu.

LITVIN, FAYDOR LEIBA, education educator, researcher; b. Belarus, Jan. 21, 1914; came to U.S., 1979; s. Leiba I. and Rebecca B. (Golman) L.; m. Shifra Gershenovich, Mar. 30, 1938; children: Boris, Julia. MS, Polytech. Inst., Leningrad, Russia, 1937; PhD, Polytech. Inst., Tomsk, Russia, 1944; D of Tech. Scis., Polytech. Inst., Leningrad, 1954; DHC, Miscolc U., Hungary, 1999. Prof. Polytech. Inst., Leningrad, 1947-64; prof., dept. head Inst. Precision Mechs. & Optics, Leningrad, 1964-78; prof. U. Ill., Chgo., 1979—92, emeritus prof., 1999—; Engring. Disting. Prof. emeritus U. Chgo., 2000—. Cons. in field. Author: Theory of Gearing, 1988, Gear Geometry and Applications, 1994, Development of Gearing, 1998, others; contbr. articles to profl. jours.; inventor in field (Inventor of the Yr., 2001). Fellow ASME; mem. AGMA. Jewish. Avocations: research, reading, music. Office: U Ill 842 W Taylor St Chicago IL 60607-7021 E-mail: flitvin@uic.edu.

LIU, ALICE Y. C. biology educator; b. Hunan, China, July 12, 1948; came to U.S., 1970; d. Tin-Kai and Te-Ming (Young) L.; m. Kuang Yu Chen, Aug. 26, 1978; children: Andrew T-H, Winston T-C. BS, Chinese U., Hong Kong, 1969; PhD, Mount Sinai Sch. Med., 1974. Postdoctoral fellow Yale U. Med. Sch., New Haven, Conn., 1974-77; asst. prof. Harvard Med. Sch., Boston, 1977-84; assoc. prof. Rutgers U., Piscataway, N.J., 1984-89, prof., 1989—; dir. grad. program in cell and devel. biology Rutgers U.-U. Medicine-Dentistry N.J.-R.W. Johnson Med. Sch., 1994-99. Mem. pharmacological scis. rev. com. NIH, 1984-88, scientific rev. spl. emphasis panel, 1999, 2000, 2003; mem. cell biology panel NSF, 1989-93, 94-95; mem. basic rsch. adv. group N.J. Commn. on Cancer Rsch., 1989-93, 94—. Author: Receptors Again, 1985; mem. editl. bd. Biol. Signals, 1991—2001. Recipient N.Y.C. Bd. of Higher Edn. award, 1972, Am. Cancer Soc. Scholar award, Boston, 1982-85; NIH postdoctoral fellow, 1974-77, Medical Found. fellow, Boston, 1977-79. Mem.: Am. Soc. Biochemistry and Molecular Biology. Home: 4 Silverthorn Ln Belle Mead NJ 08502-5549 Office: Rutgers Univ Nelson Biology Labs 604 Allison Rd Piscataway NJ 08854-8000

LIU, BEDE, electrical engineering educator; b. Shanghai, Sept. 25, 1934; arrived in U.S., 1954, naturalized, 1960; s. Henry and Shan (Yao) L.; m. Maria Agatha Sang, Jan. 31, 1959; 1 child, Beatrice Agatha. BS in Elec. Engring., Nat. Taiwan U., 1954; MEE, Poly. Inst. Bklyn., 1956, DEE, 1960. Equipment engr. Western Electric Co., N.Y.C., 1954-56; intermediate engr. A.B. DuMont Lab., Clifton, NJ, summer 1956; mem. tech. staff Bell Telephone Labs., Murray Hill, NJ, 1959-62, summers 1957, 58, 66; mem. faculty Princeton U., 1962—, prof. elec. engring., 1969—; dept. chmn., 1994-97. Vis. prof. Nat. Taiwan U., 1970—71, U. Calif., Berkeley, 1971, Shanghai Jiao Tong U., 1979; hon. prof. Acad. Sinica, 1988, Chinese U. Electronics, Sci. and Tech., 1997. Co-author: (Book) Digital Signal Processing, 1976, Multamedia Data Hiding, 2002; editor: Digital Filters and the Fast Fourier Transform, 1975. Mem.: IEEE (pres. Cir. and Systems Soc. 1982, bd. dirs. 1984—85, Centenniel medal 1984, Millenium medal 2000, Achievement award Signal Processing Soc. 1985, Soc. award Signal Processing Soc. 1997, Edn. award Cir. and Systems Soc. 1988, Mac Van Valkenburd award Cir. and Systems Soc. 1997), Nat. Acad. Engring. Achievements include patents in field. Home: 248 Hartley Ave Princeton NJ 08540-5656 Office: Princeton Univ Dept Elec Engring Princeton NJ 08540 E-mail: liu@ee.princeton.edu.

LIU, KEH-FEI FRANK, physicist, educator; b. Beijing, Jan. 11, 1947; came to U.S., 1969; s. Hsien-Chang and Juihua (Wang) L.; m. Yao-Chin Ko, Apr. 6, 1974; children: Helen, Alexander. BS, Tunghai U., Taichung, Taiwan, 1968; MS, SUNY, Stony Brook, 1972, PhD, 1975. Vis. scientist C.E.N. Saclay France, Paris, 1974-76; from rsch. assoc. to adj. asst. prof. UCLA, 1976-80; assoc. prof. U. Ky., Lexington, 1980-86, prof. physics, 1986—. Vis. prof. SUNY, Stony Brook, 1985-86, 1990; univ. rsch. prof. U. Ky., 1992. Editor: Chiral Solitons, 1987; assoc. editor World Scientific Pub. Co., Singapore, 1985—; contbr. articles to profl. jours. Recipient First Prize in Theoretical Physics Academia Sinica, China, 1987, Grand Challenge award DOE, 1988, 1989, Alexander Von Humboldt Sr. Scientist award Humboldt Found., Germany, 1990. Fellow Am. Phys. Soc.; mem. European Phys. Soc., Overseas Chinese Physicists Assn. (pres. 2003—). Office: U Ky Dept Physics & Astronomy Lexington KY 40506-0001

LIU, MIN, technology educator; b. Shanghai, July 15, 1959; d. Ding-Wu and Zong-Wu (Zheng) L.; m. Jia-Ming Qian, Jan. 1, 1987; 1 child, Michael F. BA, East China Normal U., 1982; MA, W.Va. U., 1990, EdD, 1992. Instr. East China Normal U., Shanghai, 1982-86; computer cons. W.Va. U., Morgantown, 1986-90, rsch. asst., 1987-90, asst. dir. HRE micro lab., 1990-93; assoc. prof. instrnl. tech. U. Tex., Austin, 1993—. Editor: (with others) Multimedia and Megachange: New Roles for Educational Computing, 1994; contbr. articles to profl. jours. Fellow Judith Spencer Tate fellow. Mem. Am. Ednl. Rsch. Assn., Assn. for Advancement of Computing Edn., Assn. Ednl. Comm. and Tech., Internat. Soc. Tech. in Edn., Ea. Ednl. Rsch. Assn. (Meritorious Rsch. award 1993), Phi Delta Kappa. Avocations: reading, traveling, swimming, movie watching. Office: U Tex Dept Curriculum and Instrn Austin TX 78712

LIU, MING WEI, cardiologist, educator; b. Fong-shang, Taiwan, Nov. 10, 1955; came to U.S., 1982; s. Ching-Lang and I-Ing (Huang) L.; m. Carole Su-Yen Chen, Mar. 29, 1981; children: John, Jonathan. MD, Taipei Med. Coll., 1980. Diplomate Am. Bd. Internal Medicine, Am. Bd. Cardiovascular Disease. Intern then resident in internal medicine Vets. Gen. Hosp., Taipei, Taiwan, 1980-82; resident in internal medicine Creighton U., Omaha, 1982-85; fellow in cardiology U. Ill., Chgo., 1985-87; fellow in interventional cardiology Emory U., Atlanta, 1987-89; attending cardiologist Vets. Gen. Hosp., Taipei, 1989-91; assoc. prof. cardiology U. Ala., Birmingham, 1991—2001; assoc. prof. medicine U. So. Calif., LA, 2001—. Co-author: Interventional Cardiovascular Medicine, 1994; contbr. articles to med. jours. Fellow Am. Coll. Cardiology; mem. ACP. Office: U So Calif 1355 San Pablo St Ste 117 Los Angeles CA 90089

LIU, VI-CHENG, aerospace engineering educator; b. Wu-ching, China, Sept. 1, 1917; came to U.S., 1946, naturalized, 1973; s. Bi-Ching and Shu-Fung (Keng) L.; m. Hsi-Yen Wang, Mar. 1, 1947. BS, Chiao Tung U., 1940; MS, U. Mich., 1947, PhD, 1951. Instr. Tsing-Hua U., Kunming, 1940-46; research engr. Engring. Research Inst., U. Mich., Ann Arbor, 1951-59; prof. aerospace engring. U. Mich., 1959-89, prof. emeritus, 1989—; vis. prof. Inst. of Mechanics, Chinese Acad. Sci., Peking, 1980—. Ministry edn., vis. chair prof. Nanjing Aero. Inst., China, 1989-91, hon. prof., 1991—; cons. NASA, 1964-65; vis. prof. Nat. Def. U. Sci. and Tech., Changsha, China. Contbr. articles to profl. jours. Ministry of Edn. China rsch. fellow, 1946-49; NASA rsch. grantee, 1964-80, USAF Geophys. Rsch. grantee, 1958-64. Achievements include research in rarefied gas dynamics; ionospheric physics; space physics; geophysical fluid dynamics. Home: 2104 Vinewood Blvd Ann Arbor MI 48104-2762

LIU, WING KAM, mechanical engineering educator; b. Hong Kong, May 15, 1952; came to U.S., 1973, naturalized, 1990; s. Yin Lam and Siu Lin (Chan) L.; m. Betty Hsia, Dec. 12, 1986; children: Melissa Margaret, Michael Kevin. BSc with highest honors, U. Ill., Chgo., 1976; MSc, Calif. Inst. Tech., 1977, PhD, 1981. Registered profl. engr., Ill. Asst. prof. mech. and civil engring. Northwestern U., Evanston, Ill., 1980-83, assoc. prof., 1983-88, prof., 1988—, Walter F. Murphy Prof. Mech. Engring., 2003—; dir. NSF Summer Inst. on Nano Mechanics and Materials, 2003—. Prin. cons. reactor analysis and safety div. Argonne (Ill.) Nat. Lab., 1981—, Dir. of NSF Summer Inst. on Nano Mechanics and Materials. Co-author: Nonlinear Finite Elements for Continua and Structures, 2000; co-editor: Innovative Methods for Nonlinear Problems, 1984, Impact-Effects of Fasts Transient Loadings, 1988, Computational Mechanics of Probabilistic and Reliability Analysis, 1989. Recipient Thomas J. Jaeger prize Internat. Assn. for Structural Mechanics in Reactor Tech., 1989, Ralph R. Teetor award Soc. Automotive Engrs., 1983, Computational Mechanics award Internat. Assn. for Computational Mechanics, 2002; named among 93 most highly cited rschrs. in engring. Inst. for Sci. Info., 2001; grantee USF, Army Rsch. Office, NASA, AFSOR, ONR, GE, Ford Motor, Chrysler. Fellow ASCE, ASME (exec. mem. applied mechanics divsn. 2001, Melville medal 1979, Pi Tau Sigma gold medal 1985, Gustus L. Larson Meml. award 1995), U.S. Assn. Computational Mechanics (pres. 2000—, Computational Structural Mechs. award 2001), Am. Acad. Mechanics, Internat. Assn. Computational Mechanics (exec. 2002—, Computational Mechanics award 2002). Office: Northwestern U Dept Mech Engring 2145 Sheridan Rd Evanston IL 60208-0834 E-mail: w-liu@northwestern.edu.

LIU, Y. A. engineering educator; BS, Nat. Taiwan U., 1967; MS, Tufts U., 1970; PhD, Princeton U., 1974. Frank C. Bilbrandt prof. chem. engring. Va. Polytech. Inst. and State U., Blacksburg, 1983—. Sr. tech. advisor UN Devel. Program; hon. prof. chem. engring. Qingdao Inst. Chem. Tech., Ministry Chem. Industry, China, 1993—. Editor: Recent Developments in Chemical Process and Plant Design, 1987; contbr. articles to profl. jours. Recipient Nat. Catalyst award 1986, Fred Merryfield Design award, 1993, Internat. award Aspen Tech., Cambridge, Mass., 1996, Nat. Friendship award State Coun., People's Republic China, 2000, Outstanding Faculty award State Coun. Higher Edn. Va., 2000. Mem.: ASEE (George Washington award 1990, Western Electric Fund award 1984). Office Fax: 540-231-5022. E-mail: design@vt.edu.*

LIU, YUAN HSIUNG, drafting and design educator; b. Tainan, Taiwan, Feb. 24, 1938; came to U.S., 1970; s. Chun Chang and Kong (Wong) L.; m. Ho Pe Tung, July 27, 1973; children: Joan Anshen, Joseph Pinyang. BEd, Nat. Taiwan Normal U., Taipei, 1961; MEd, Nat. Chengchi U., Taipei, 1967, U. Alta., Edmonton, 1970; PhD, Iowa State U., 1975. Cert. tchr. Tchr. indsl. arts and math. Nan Ning Jr. H.S., Tainan, Taiwan, 1961-64; tech. math. instr. Chung-Cheng Inst. Tech., Taipei, 1967-68; drafter Sundstrand Hydro-Transmission Corp., Ames, Iowa, 1973-75; assoc. prof. Fairmont (W.Va.) State Coll., 1975-80; per course instr. Sinclair C.C., Dayton, Ohio, 1985; assoc. prof. Miami U., Hamilton, Ohio, 1980-85, Southwest Mo. State U., Springfield, 1985—. Cons. Monarch Indsl. Precision Co., Springfield, 1986, Gen. Electric Co., Springfield, 1988, Fasco Industries, Inc., Ozark, Mo., 1989, 95, Springfield Remfg. Corp., 1990, 92, Ctrl. States Indsl., Intercont Products, Inc., L&W Industries, Inc., ZERCO Mfg. Co., 1994-95, Paul Mueller Co., 1996. 2d lt. R.O.C. Army, 1962-63. Recipient Excellent Teaching in Drafting award Charvoz-Carsen Corp., Fairfield, N.J., 1978. Mem. Am. Design Drafting Assn. Avocations: walking, tv. Office: SW Mo State U Dept Indsl Mgmt 901 S National Ave Springfield MO 65804-0094 E-mail: yhl045f@smsu.edu.

LIUZZO, JOSEPH ANTHONY, food science educator; b. Tampa, Fla., Dec. 16, 1926; s. Joseph and Annie (Minardi) L.; m. Elaine Grammer, Nov. 30, 1951; children: Paul Arthur, Patricia Joyce, Jolaine Marie. BS, U. Fla., 1950, MS, 1955; postgrad., U. So. Calif., 1952-53; PhD, Mich. State U., 1958. Microbiologist Stokely-Van Camp Co., Tampa, 1950; head divsn. microbiology Nutrilite Products, Inc., Buena Park, Calif., 1951-54; asst. prof. biochemistry La. State U., Baton Rouge, 1958-62, assoc. prof. food sci., 1962-69, prof., 1969-97, prof. emeritus, 1997—, faculty chmn. athletics, 1979-83, prof. emeritus, 1997—. Chmn. Am. Legion Baseball Program, 1976-82, 97-2002. Contbr. articles to profl. jours. With U.S. Army, 1945-46. Recipient Outstanding Alumnus award Food Sci. and Human Nutrition, Mich. State U., 1994. Fellow AAAS, Am. Inst. Chemists, Inst. of Food Technologists; mem. Am. Inst. Nutrition, Am. chem. Soc., Kiwanis (pres. 1988-89, div. lt. gov. 1990-91), Sigma Xi, Phi Tau Sigma, Gamma Sigma Delta, Phi Sigma, Omicron Delta Kappa. Republican. Mem. Ch. of Christ. Office: La State U Dept Food Science Baton Rouge LA 70803-0001 E-mail: jluizzo@agcenter.lsu.edu.

LIVINGSTON, BARBARA, special education educator; BA in Elem. Edn., Bklyn. Coll., 1955; MA in Early Childhood Edn., Adelphi U., 1975. Cert. elem. edn. tchr., N.Y., early childhood edn., N.Y., spl. edn., N.Y. Reading tchr. P.S. 182, Dist. 19, Bklyn., 1974-76; spl. edn. tchr. self-contained classroom P.S. 13, East N.Y., Bklyn., 1976-81; resource room tchr. P.S. 128, Middle Village, Queens, N.Y., 1981-86; spl. edn. lang. coor./tchr. trainer/ staff developer Dist. Office 24Q, Middle Village, N.Y., 1986-90; VAKTS (reading system)/lang. coord. Dist. 24 Queens, Corona, N.Y., 1988-90; resource room tchr., staff developer Intermediate Sch. 61Q, Corona, N.Y., 1990—. Group leader Centre for Creative Arts Saturday Morning Program, Adelphi U., Garden City, 1972-75; dir. adult edn. program Temple Judea Howard Beach, 1974-76. Recipient Educator of Yr. award, Assn. Tchrs. NY, 1985. Mem. Orton Dyslexia Soc., Coun. for Exceptional Children (Master Tchr. award 1987), ASCD, Internat. Reading Assn., United Fedn. Tchrs., Am. Fedn. Tchrs., Jewish Tchrs. Assn., Lincoln Ctr. Inst. (cert.). Home: 15506 86th St Howard Beach NY 11414-2404

LIVINGSTON, SAMUEL ALTON, statistician; b. Chgo., Feb. 9, 1942; s. David Abraham and Ruth Jessie Livingston; m. Judith Ann Gilbert, Jan. 7, 1968; children: Amy Ruth, Melanie Faye. AB in Polit. Sci., U. Chgo., 1962; EdM in Secondary Edn., U. Pitts., 1964; PhD in Edn., Johns Hopkins U., 1974, AM in Math. Scis., 1975. Social studies tchr. Perry High Sch., Pitts., 1964-65; computer programmer U.S. Steel Corp., 1965; rsch. asst. Ctr. Social Orgn. of Schs. Johns Hopkins U., Balt., 1968-73; assoc. examiner Ednl. Testing Svc., Princeton, N.J., 1974-76, assoc. program rsch. scientist, 1976-79, program rsch. scientist, 1979-82, assoc. measurement statistician, 1982-83, measurement statistician, 1983-87, sr. measurement statistician, 1987—2000, prin. measurement statistician, 2002—. With U.S. Army, 1966-67, Germany. Office: Ednl Testing Svc Princeton NJ 08541-0001

LIVINGSTON, WILLIAM SAMUEL, university administrator, political scientist; b. Ironton, Ohio, July 1, 1920; s. Samuel G. and Bata (Elkins) L.; m. Lana Sanor, July 10, 1943; children: Stephen Sanor, David Duncan. BA, MA, Ohio State U., 1943; PhD, Yale U., 1950. Asst. prof. U. Tex., Austin, 1949-54, asso. prof., 1954-61, prof. govt., 1961—, chmn. dept. govt., 1965-69, Jo Anne Christian centennial prof. Brit. studies, 1982-95, asst. dean Grad. Sch., 1954-58, chmn. Grad. Assembly, 1965-68, chmn. faculty senate, 1973-79, chmn. comparative studies program, 1978-79; vice chancellor acad. programs U. Tex. System, 1969-71; v.p., dean grad. studies U Tex. Austin, 1979-95; acting pres. U. Tex. Austin, 1992-93; sr. v.p., 1995—. Vis. prof. Yale U., 1955-56, Duke U., 1960-61; sec.-treas. Assn. Grad. Schs., 1982-85; bd. dirs. Council Grad. Schs. in U.S., 1983-86. Author: Federalism and Constitutional Change, 1956; contbg. author: World Pressures on American Foreign Policy, 1962, Teaching Political Science, 1965, Federalism: Infinite Variety in Theory and Practice, 1968, Britain at the Polls 1979, 1981; editor: The Presidency and Congress: A Shifting Balance of Power, 1979; co-editor: Australia, New Zealand and the Pacific Islands Since the First World War, 1979; editor, contbr. author: Federalism in the Commonwealth, 1963, A Prospect of Liberal Democracy, 1979, The Legacy of the Constitution: An Assessment for the Third Century, 1987; book rev. editor: Jour. Politics, 1965-68, editor-in-chief, 1968-72; mem. editl. bd. Publius: Jour. of Federalism, 1971-95; mem. bd. editors: P.S, 1976-82, chmn., 1978-82. Served to 1st lt. FA AUS, 1943-45. Decorated Bronze Star, Purple Heart.; Recipient Teaching Excellence award, 1959; Ford Found. fellow, 1952-53; Guggenheim fellow, 1959-60; USIS lectr. in U.K. and India, 1977 Mem. Am. Polit. Sci. Assn. (exec. coun. and adminstrv. com. 1972-74, chmn. nominating com. 1973-74, 78-79), So. Polit. Sci. Assn. (exec. coun. 1964-67, pres. 1974-75), Southwestern Polit. Sci. Assn. (pres. 1973-74), Hansard Soc. (London), Philos. Soc. Tex., Austin Soc. for Pub. Adminstrn. (pres. 1973-74), Southwestern Social Sci. Assn. (pres. 1977-78), Phi Beta Kappa, Omicron Delta Kappa, Phi Gamma Delta, Pi Sigma Alpha (nat. coun. 1976-84, nat. pres. 1980-82). Home: 3203 Greenlee Dr Austin TX 78703-1621 Office: U Tex Office Sr VP Austin TX 78712

LIVINGSTONE, TRUDY DOROTHY ZWEIG, dancer, educator; b. N.Y.C., June 9, 1946; d. Joseph and Anna (Feinberg) Zweig; m. John Leslie Livingstone, Aug. 7, 1977; 1 child, Robert Edward. Student, Charles Lowe Studios, N.Y.C., 1950-52, Nina Tinova Studio, 1953-56, Ballet Russe de Monte Carlo, 1956-57, Bklyn. Coll., 1964-66; BA in Psychology cum laude, Boston U., 1968, MEd, 1969; postgrad., Serena Studios, Carnegie Hall Ballet Arts, N.Y.C., 1973-74. Tchr. Millis (Mass.) Pub. Schs., 1969-72, Hebrew Acad. Atlanta, 1974-76; profl. dancer various orgns. including Rivermont Country Club, Jewish Community Ctr., Callanwolde Performing Arts Ctr., Atlanta, 1974-84; founder, owner, instr. dance Sasha Studios, Atlanta, 1974-77; owner Trudy Zweig Livingstone Studios, Wellesley, Needham, Mass., 1987-88, Palm Beach, Fla., 1989—. Judge dance competition Atlanta Council Run-Offs, 1976. Vol. League Sch., Bklyn., 1965, Kennedy Meml. Hosp., Brighton, Mass., 1969, Nat. Affiliation for Literacy

Advances, Santa Monica, Calif., 1982. Mem. Am. Alliance for Health, Phys. Edn., Recreation and Dance, Poets of the Palm Beaches, L.A. Athletic Club, Wellesley Coll. Club, Governor's Club (West Palm Beach). Avocation: writing poetry.

LLANUSA, STEVEN MICHAEL, elementary education educator; b. Burbank, Calif., Feb. 26, 1960; s. Louis Henry and Margaret Mary (Ferruzza) L.; life ptnr. Glenn Miya; children: Aaron, Alex, Eric. AA, L.A. Valley Coll., Van Nuys, Calif., 1982; BA, UCLA, 1985. Cert. tchr., Calif. Tchr. nursery sch. Child Devel. Ctr., L.A. Valley Coll. Campus, 1979-82; asst. tchr. UCLA Child Devel. Ctr., 1982-85; tchr. L.A. Unified Sch. Dist., Lincoln Heights, Calif., 1987-89, Colton Unified Sch. Dist., Bloomington, Calif., 1989—. Curriculum specialist Gerald Smith Sch., Bloomington, 1993—, NASA, 1998—. Chmn. diversity com. UCLA, 1992-94. Recipient cmty. svc. award ARC, 1981; scholar Tau Alpha Epsilon, 1982. Mem. ASCD, San Bernardino Humane Soc., UCLA Alumni Assn. (bd. dirs.-at-large 1992-94, co-chmn. Lambda alumni 1993-94, beginning tchr. support mentor), U. So. Calif. Lambda Alumni Assn. (edn. com. 1993-94), Sigma Phi Epsilon. Roman Catholic. Avocation: computer philanthropy theatre. Home: 2627 San Andres Way Claremont CA 91711-1556 Office: Gerald Smith Sci Magnet Sch 9551 Linden Ave Bloomington CA 92316-1430

LLEWELLYN, RALPH ALVIN, physics educator; b. Detroit, June 27, 1933; s. Ralph A. and Mary (Green) L.; m. Laura Diane Alsop, June 12, 1955; children: Mark Jeffrey, Rita Annette, Lisa Suzanne, Eric Matthew. BS in Chem. Engring. with high honors, Rose-Hulman Inst. Tech., 1955; PhD in Physics, Purdue U., 1962. Mem. faculty Rose-Hulman Inst. Tech., Terre Haute, Ind., 1961-70, assoc. prof. physics, 1964-68, prof., 1968-70, chmn. dept. physics, 1969-70; prof., chmn. dept. Ind. State U., Terre Haute, 1970-72, 74-80; dean Coll. of Arts and Scis. U. Ctrl. Fla., Orlando, 1980-84, prof., 1980—, chmn. dept. physics, 2003—, interim chair, 2003—. Exec. sec. Energy Bd., staff officer environmental Studies Bd. NAS/NRC, Washington, 1972-74; vis. prof. Rensselaer Poly. Inst., Troy, N.Y., 1964; cons. Commn. on Coll. Physics, 1987-89, NSF, 1965-66; mem. Ind. Lt. Gov.'s Sci. Adv. Coun., 1974-80; adv. bd. Ind. Gov.'s Energy Extension Svc., Fla. Solar Energy Ctr., policy coun. Fla. Inst. Govt., Fla. Radon Adv. Coun., 1988-96; mem. environ. adv. com. Fla. Inst. Phosphate Rsch.; mem. grievance com. Fla. Bar, nat. adv. coun. Nat. Commn. on Higher Edn. Issues, 1982. Author: (with others) Physics 3E, 1991, Elementary Modern Physics, 1992, Modern Physics 3E, 1999, Modern Physics 4E, 2003; assoc. editor: Modern Physics 4E, 2003; contbr. articles to profl. jours.; producer instructional films and TV. Trustee Merom (Ind.) Inst. Recipient Tchg. Incentive award Fla. State Univ. Sys., 1994, 97; NSF Coop. fellow, 1959-60, Am. Coun. Edn. Acad. Adminstrn. Internship Program fellow. Fellow Ind. Acad. Sci. (chmn. physics divsn. 1969-70, Spkr. of Yr. award 1975, pres.-elect 1980); mem. AAAS, AAUP, Am. Phys. Soc., Am. Assn. Physics Tchrs. (pres. Ind.), N.Y. Acad. Scis., Fla. Acad. Scis. (endowment com.), Internat. Oceanographic Found., Ind. Acad. Sci., Sigma Xi, Tau Beta Pi. Home: 1463 Palomino Way Oviedo FL 32765-9304 Office: U Cen Fla Dept Physics Orlando FL 32816-0001 E-mail: ral@physics.ucf.edu.

LLOYD, JACQUELINE, English language educator; b. N.Y.C., Aug. 21, 1950; d. R.G. and Hortense (Collins) L. BA, Fisk U., 1972; MEd, U. North Fla., 1989. Instr. English, dir. Writing Ctr. Edward Waters Coll., Jacksonville, Fla., 1983, 90—. Mem. Nat. Coun. Tchrs. English. Democrat. Presbyterian. Avocation: movies. Home: 5006 Andrew Robinson Dr Jacksonville FL 32209-1002

LLOYD, JEAN, early childhood educator; b. Montgomery, Ala., Mar. 3, 1935; d. James Jack and Dorothy Gladys (Brown) L.; 1 child, Jamie Angelica. BA, Queens Coll., 1957; MA, NYU, 1960, PhD, 1976. Tchr. jr. HS NYC Bd. of Edn., 1961, dir. head start ctr., 1966, 67 summer, tchr. early childhood, 1961-69, tchr. kindergarten, 1984—; instr., asst. prof. U. Coll. Rutgers U., Newark, 1969-83. Cons. Bd. Examiners, N.Y.C., 1982, Dept. of Pers., N.Y.C., 1985; rsch. cons. Seymour Laskow CPA, 1983; chmn. bd. dirs. Your Family Inc., N.Y.C., 1989—; prodr. New Ventures cable TV show (Manhattan), 1987—. Author: Sociology and Social Life, 1979; contbr. over 10 articles to profl. jours. Recipient Ed Press award Ednl. Press Assn., 1968; Project Synergy fellow Tchrs. Coll., Columbia, 1991-93. Mem. ASCD, United Fedn. of Tchrs., Delta Kappa Gamma. Democrat. Methodist. Avocations: writing poetry and related articles, singing in church choir. Home: 180 W End Ave New York NY 10023-4902 Office: PS 149 41 W 117th St New York NY 10026-1901

LLOYD, LILA G. business educator; b. Laurens, S.C., Mar. 10, 1937; d. Shellie and Alberta Barksdale Garrett; m. Clifton H. Lloyd Sr.; children: Clifton H. Jr., William P. BS, Benedict Coll., 1957; MEd, U. N.C., Greensboro, 1971; PhD, Columbia Pacific U., 1999. H.S. tchr., Bath, SC, 1958—59, Siler City, NC, 1963—84; tchr. S.E. H.S., Greensboro, NC, 1984—92; instr. bus. edn. A&T State U., Greensboro, NC, 1992—. Mem. sch. leadership team, Greensboro, 1988—91; chmn. recruiting com. N.C. A&T State U., Greensboro, 1986—91, Greensboro, 1992—. Author: Lloyds: Refresher Course in Computer and Office Skills, 2002. Pres. Friends of McGirt-Horton Libr., Greensboro, 1989—94; v.p. precinct 19 Dem. Party, Greensboro, 1986—90; treas. United Meth. Ch., 1996—; bd. dirs. Claremont Housing Project, 1988, vice chmn. edn. program, 1988. Mem.: AAUW (contbr. newsletter 1997—99, pres. 1997—99, Outstanding Leadership award 1999), N.C. Assn. Educators (Human Rels. award 1990), Young Womens Christian Assn. Methodist. Avocations: amateur photography, reading, viewing old classical movies. Home: 1702 Woodbriar Ave Greensboro NC 27405

LLOYD, MARGARET ANN, psychologist, educator; b. Weiser, Idaho, Sept. 14, 1942; d. Laurance Henry and Margaret Jane (Patch) L. BA, U. Denver, 1964; MS in Edn., Ind. U., 1966; MA in Psychology, U. Ariz., 1972, PhD in Psychology, 1973. Asst. prof. psychology Suffolk U., Boston, 1973-76, assoc. prof., 1976-79, prof., 1979-88, chair dept., 1981-88; prof. Ga. So. U., Statesboro, 1988—, head dept., 1988-93. Author: Adolescence, 1985; author: (with others) Psychology Applied to Modern Life, 1991, 1994, 1997, 2000, 2003; contbr. articles to profl. jours. Mem. AAUP, APA (bd. ednl. affairs 2000-2002, sec.-treas. divsn. 2 1990-93, pres. 1994-95, coun. rep. 2003—), New Eng. Psychol. Assn. (steering com. 1984-86), Mass. Psychol. Assn. (sec. 1979-81, chair bd. acad. and sci. affairs 1981-82), Coun. Undergrad. Psychology Programs (chmn. 1990-91). Home: 805 Shelter Pointe Rd Statesboro GA 30458-9113 Office: Ga So U Statesboro GA 30460-8041

LLOYD, ROBERT ANDREW, art educator; b. Boston, Mar. 10, 1934; s. Claude T. and Dorothy (Clarkson) L.; m. Susan M. McIntosh, Jan. 28, 1956; children: Benjamin, Seth, Thomas. BA, Harvard U., 1956, MArch, 1959. Cert. nat. bd. for profl. tchg. stds. Tchr. art Phillips Acad., Andover, Mass., 1962-97, dean Visual Studies Inst., 1978-95. Mem. accreditation com. Taft Acad., Stoneleigh-Burnham Acad., Deerfield Acad., Baylor Acad., Westminster Schs., coun. acad. affairs The Coll. Bd., 1978-81, steering com. 1996 Nat. Assessment Ednl. Progress Arts Edn. Consensus Project; pres. Vt. Coverts: Woodlands for Wildlife, Inc., 2000, mentor Poultney H.S., 2002-03. Author: Images of Survival, 1973. Chmn. bldg. com. Bancroft Sch., Andover, 1965-70, Greater Lawrence (Mass.) Habitat for Humanity, 1991-95; mem. Andover Hist. Commn., 1982-85; bd. dirs. Vt. Accomplished Teaching Collaborative, 2003—; vice chmn. Rutland Regional Planning Commn., 2003—. Klingenstein fellow Columbia U., N.Y.C., 1981-82. Avocations: singing, writing, land conservation. Home: 430 Gulf Rd RR Tinmouth Middletown Springs VT 05757-4279

LLOYD, SUSAN ELAINE, middle school educator; b. Sioux Falls, S.D., Aug. 25, 1942; d. Travis Monroe and Lois Elaine (Herridge) Hetherington; m. Jerry Glynn Lloyd, Mar. 13, 1982; children: Joseph Sanders Rogers III, Melissa Elaine Withaeger. BS in Edn., SW Tex. State U., 1965; MA, U. Tex., San Antonio, 1979; AA, Stephens Coll., 1962. Cert. reading specialist, supervisory, art (all levels), secondary English, elem. edn. Art tchr. South Park Ind. Sch. Dist., Beaumont, Tex., 1965-68; reading specialist John Jay High Sch., San Antonio, 1979-84; reading dept. coord. Sul Ross Mid. Sch., Northside Ind. Sch. Dist., San Antonio, 1984-98, remedial reading tchr., 1990; reading dept. coord. Barbara Bush Middle Sch. N.E. Ind. Sch. Dist., San Antonio, 1998—. Developer, reading curricula, cons.; advisor Scholastic TAB Book Club, 1992—94; presenter Tex. Mid. Sch. Conf., 1998—2001. Author: Reading Education in Texas, 1992, 93. Named Sul Ross Middle Sch. Tchr. of Yr., 1993, Trinity U. Disting. Educator, 1993. Mem. ASCD, Internat. Reading Assn. (hon. chmn. 14th ann. SW regional meeting, presenter 19th 1991, 20th 1992), Tex. Reading Coun., Tex. Mid. Sch. Assn., Alamo Reading Assn., Assn. Tex. Profl. Educators, San Antonio Watercolor Group, Mid. Sch. Assn. Home: 7614 Tippit Trl San Antonio TX 78240-3627 Office: Barbara Bush Mid Sch 1500 Evans Rd San Antonio TX 78258-6900

LOACH, PAUL ALLEN, biochemist, biophysicist, educator; b. Findlay, Ohio, July 18, 1934; s. Leland Oris and Dorothy Elizabeth (Davis) L.; m. Patricia A. Johnson, Dec. 27, 1957; children: Mark, Eric, Jennifer; m. Pamela Sue Parkes, Apr. 19, 1986; children: Matthew, Sarah, Andrew. BS, U. Akron, 1957; PhD (NIH fellow), Yale, 1961. Research assoc. Nat. Acad. Scis.-NRC; postdoctoral fellow U. Calif. at Berkeley, 1961-63; asst. prof. chemistry Northwestern U., 1963-68, assoc. prof., 1968-73, prof., 1973-74, prof. biochemistry and molecular biology, and chemistry, 1974—. Mem. BBCA study sect. NIH, 1978-82. Assoc. editor: Photochemistry and Photobiology, 1973-80, Biophysics of Structure and Mechanism, 1973-82; Contbr. articles, revs. to profl. jours. Recipient C.P. award U. Akron, 1957, Research Career Devel. award USPHS, 1971-76. Fellow AAAS; mem. Am. Soc. Biol. Chemists, Am. Soc. Photobiology (pres. 1985-86). E-mail: p-loach@northwestern.edu.

LOBAY, IVAN, mechanical engineering educator; b. Koltuny, Ukraine, Oct. 4, 1911; came to U.S., 1961, naturalized, 1968; s. Stephan and Clementina (Maret) Lobay; m. Halyna Makarenko, Apr. 25, 1943; children: Maria Ivanna, Halyna Blahoslava. Mech. Engr., Inst. Tech., Brno, Czechoslovakia, 1940, Cen. U. Venezuela, Caracas, 1956. Registered profl. engr., Conn. Engr., designer Erste Bruenner Maschinenfabriksgesellschaft, Brno, 1940-41; asst. prof. dept. mech. engring. Inst. Tech., Lviv, Ukraine, 1942-43, sci. asst. dept. mech. engring. Brno, 1943-45; engr. san. and civil engring. Ministry San. Affairs, Caracas, Venezuela, 1948-59; prof. dept. civil engring. U. Santa Maria, Caracas, 1957-60; prof., chmn. divsn. tech. machines & prodn Cen. U. Venezuela Mech. Engring. Sch., Caracas, 1956-62; prof. dept. mech. engring. U. New Haven, West Haven, 1963-77, 83-84, prof. emeritus, 1984—; prof. gas sect. Inst. Algerien du Petrole, Boumerdes, Algeria, 1977-82. Cons. Ministry of Edn., Ukraine, Kyiv, 1993. Author: Lecciones de Elementos de Maquinas, No. 3, 1960, No. 2, 1961, Estudio Sobre Descarga de Aguas de Lluvia, 1962, Free Lateral Discharge from an Open Triangular Channel, 1993, Education of Engineering Squads in USA, 1996, Workload of University Professors in USA, 1996, Faculty in Higher Education in USA, 1997, Governance in Higher Education in USA, 1999, Memoirs, 1999. With U.S. Army, 1945-47. Decorated Hramota and Cross of Merit Bukovynian Battalion, 1995; recipient Hramota award Govt. in Exile of Ukrainian Nat. Republic, 1992. Mem. AAUP, AAAS, ASME, NSPE, Conn. Soc. Profl. Engrs., N.Y. Acad. Scis., Ukrainian AAUP, Ukrainian Engrs. Soc. Am., Coll. Engrs. Venezuela, Assn. Profs. U. Ctrl. Venezuela, Acad. Engring. Scis. Ukraine. Home: 873 Orange Center Rd Orange CT 06477-1712

LOBIG, JANIE HOWELL, special education educator; b. Peoria, Ill., June 10, 1945; d. Thomas Edwin and Elizabeth Jane (Higdon) Howell; m. James Frederick Lobig, Aug. 16, 1970 (dec. Dec. 2001); 1 child, Jill Christina. BS in Elem. Edn., So. Ill. U., 1969; MA in Spl. Edn. Severely Handicapped, San Jose State U., 1989. Cert. elem. tchr., Calif., Mo., Ill., handicapped edn., Calif., Mo.; ordained to ministry Presbyn. Ch. as deacon, 1984. Tchr. trainable mentally retarded children Spl. Luth. Sch., St. Louis, 1967-68; tchr. trainable mentally retarded and severly handicapped children Spl. Sch. Dist. St. Louis, 1969-80, head tchr., 1980-83; tchr. severly handicapped children San Jose (calif.) Unifed Sch. Dist., 1983-86; tchr. autistic students Santa Clara County Office Edn., San Jose, 1986—; tchr. Suzanne Dancers, 1991-92. Vol. Am. Cancer Soc., San Jose, 1986—89, 1992, Am. Heart Assn., 1985—, Multiple Sclerosis Soc., 1990—, Wildlife Ctr. Silicon Valley, 1998—; moderator bd. deacons Evergreen Presbyn. Ch., 1986—89. Mem. Council for Exceptional Children, Assn. for Severly Handicapped, Nat. Edn. Assn., Calif. Tchrs. Assn. Avocations: golf, motor home travel, bridge, needlework. Office: James Franklin Smith Elem Sch 2220 Woodbury San Jose CA 95121 Home: 3211 Bracciano Ct San Jose CA 95135 E-mail: JanieAngel@aol.com.

LOBOSCO, ANNA FRANCES, state program development specialist; b. Binghamton, N.Y., Nov. 13, 1952; d. James H. and Marie A. (Wilcox) Mee; m. Charles M. Lobosco, Apr. 27, 1974; children: Charles Jr., Amanda, Nicholas, Dennis. BA in History, Marist Coll., Poughkeepsie, N.Y., 1974; MS in Edn./Spl. Edn., Coll. St. Rose, Albany, 1978; PhD in Curriculum and Instrn., SUNY, Albany, 1989. Cert. tchr. elem., secondary and spl. edn., N.Y. Diagnostic remedial tchr. Orange County Assn. for Help of Retarded Children, Middletown/Newburgh, N.Y., 1973-78; instr., supr. student tchrs. Mt. St. Mary Coll., Newburgh, 1980-82; rsch. asst., assoc. dir. evaluation consortium SUNY, Albany, 1985-89; devel. disability program planner/prevention specialist N.Y. State Developmental Disabilities Planning Coun., Albany, 1989-2001, dep. exec. dir., 2001—. Cons. N.Y. State Edn. Dept. Edn., 1987-89, N.Y. State Unified Tchrs., 1988-89, N.Y. State Coun. on Children's Families, 1986-88, N.Y. State Assn. Counties, 1987-88; instr. Coll. St. Rose, Albany, 1989-90; adj. faculty dept. ednl. theory and practice U. Albany/SUNY, 1997-2000. Contbr. articles to profl. jours.; exec. producer vieedeos Mary's Choice: The Effects of Prenatal Exposure to Alcohol and Other Drugs, 1992, Its Up to You, 1995. Mem. sch. bd. Saratoga Ctrl. Cath. H.S., 1996—2002, v.p., 1998—2000, pres., 2000—02. Named Advocate of the Yr., N.Y. Libr. Assn., 1993. Mem. Coun. Exceptional Children, Am. Evaluation Assn., Am. Ednl. Rsch. Assn., Am. Assn. Mental Retardation, Kappa Delta Pi. Avocations: needlework, sports, reading. Bus. Office: NYS Devel Disabilities Planning Coun 155 Washington Ave Fl 2 Albany NY 12210-2329 E-mail: alobosco@ddpc.state.ny.us.

LOCH, JOHN ROBERT, university administrator; b. Aug. 25, 1940; s. Robert Addison and Mary Virginia (Beck) L. Student, Waynesburg Coll., 1958; AB, Grove City Coll., 1962; postgrad., Pitts. Theol. Sem., 1962; MEd, U. Pitts., 1966, PhD, 1972, Harvard U., 1984. Asst. to dean of men U. Pitts., 1963—64, dir. student union, 1964—70, dir. student affairs rsch., 1970—71, dir. suburban ednl. svcs. Sch. Gen. Studies, 1971—75; dir. continuing edn. and pub. svc. Youngstown (Ohio) State U., 1975—82, dir. univ. outreach, 1990—. Chief adminstrv. officer Metro Coll., 1996-98; assoc. mem. grad. faculty, 1980-95; rsch. assoc. Pres.'s Commn. on Campus Unrest, 1970; trustee program com. Park Vista Retirement Cmty., 1993-99, chmn. 1994-95, vice chair bd. dirs., 1995-96, mktg. com., 1999—; trustee Ohio Presbyn. Retirement Cmtys., 1993-99, program com., 1993-99. Trustee Mahoning Shenango Area Health Edn. Network, 1976-91, Career Devel. Ctr. for Women, 1978-80; trustee Youngstown Area Arts Coun., 1980-85, pres., 1981-83; bd. dirs. Protestant Family Svcs., 1981-83; active Older Adults Task Force, Mahoning County, 1992-96; trustee Mahoning County RSVP, 1983-89, chmn. evaluation com., 1983-84, chmn. pers. com., 1984-85, chmn. bd. trustees, 1986-87; coord. fund raising Nat. Unity Campaign, Mahoning County, 1980; state chmn. Young Rep. Coll. Coun. Pa., 1960; elder First Presbyn. Ch., Sharon. Mem. AAUW, Assn. Continuing Higher Edn. (chair-elect region VI 1997-98, chair 1998-99), Adult Edn. Assn. USA, Nat. U. Continuing Edn. Assn., Ohio Coun. Higher Continuing Edn. (pres. 1979-80), Ohio Continuing Higher Edn. Assn. (hon. life, co-chmn. constn. com. 1982, v.p. state univs. 1984-85, pres.-elect 1985-86, pres. 1986-87, historian 1988-96, chmn. awards and honors com. 1989-92, editor Voluntary Continuing Edn. Requirements 1993-95, Spl. Svc. award 1989), Ohio-Pa. Higher Edn. Network (chmn. 1989-90), Learning Resources Network (cert. program planner, Univ. Coun. Gt. Lakes rep. 1996-2003, emeritus mem. Lern U. Coun., Lifetime Achievement award, 2002), Youngstown Traffic Club (hon. life mem.), Youngstown Club, Kiwanis (dir. 1981-82), Youngstown Dist., Purchasing Mgrs. Assn., Omicron Delta Kappa, Kappa Kappa Psi, Phi Kappa Phi (pres. 1980-81, pres. 1994-95, 96-97, Disting. Mem. award 2000), Alpha Phi Omega, Alpha Sigma Lambda, Phi Delta Kappa. Home: 242 Upland Ave Youngstown OH 44504-1849 Office: Met Coll Southwoods Commons 100 De Bartolo Pl Youngstown OH 44512 E-mail: jrloch@ysu.edu.

LOCHER, ELIZABETH AIKEN, elementary education educator, reading specialist; b. N.Y.C., Oct. 10, 1943; d. Richard Eustace Jr. and Marjorie Armstrong (Siebers) Aiken; m. Peyton Ring Neal Jr., June 20, 1964 (div.); children: Melissa Davis Neal Reed, Peyton Ring Neal III; m. Baldwin Gerard Locher Jr., Dec. 21, 1979; 1 child, Baldwin Locher III. AA, Peace Coll., 1964; BA, Mary Baldwin Coll., 1980; MEd, U. Va., 1991, PhD, 2002. Cataloger, asst. libr. Georgetown Law Ctr., Washington, 1965-71; asst. libr. Lexington (Va.) High Sch., 1976-79; reading specialist, tchr. Nat. Bridge Elem./Rockbridge County Schs., Lexington, 1989—. Presenter in field. Editor: Union List of Legal Periodicals, 1971; contbr. articles to newspapers and jours. Bd. dirs. Rockbridge Regional Libr., Lexington, 1994-98, rec. sec., 1997-98; corr. sec. Colonial Dames XVII Century, Lexington, 1993-94; bd. dirs., sec. Lexington Downtown Devel., 1985-91; bd. dirs. Habitat, 2003—; libr., docent Stonewall Jackson House, Lexington, 1979-89. U. Va. fellow, Charlottesville, 1991. Mem. ASCD, NEA, DAR, Internat. Reading Assn., Nat. Coun. Tchrs. English, Va. Edn. Assn., Va. State Reading Assn., Rockbridge Edn. Assn. (treas. 1995-98), Shenandoah Valley Reading Coun. (rec. sec. 1994-96, membership chmn. 1997-98, Tchr. of Yr. 1994), Internat. Dyslexia Assn., Coun. for Exceptional Children, Va. ASsn. for the Gifted, Phi Alpha Theta, Delta Kappa Gamma (rec. sec. 1996-98). Episcopalian. Avocations: quilting, needlepoint, collecting and sharing children's literature, teachers' stories. Home: 26 Beatty Holw Lexington VA 24450-4040 Office: Natural Bridge Elem PO Box 280 Natural Bridge Station VA 24579-0280

LOCKAMY, ARCHIE, III, operations management educator; b. El Paso, Tex., July 24, 1957; s. Archie Jr. and Corrine Ann Lockamy; m. Vicki G. Glover, Dec. 19, 1981. B of Chem. Engring., Ga. Inst. Tech., 1979; MBA, Atlanta U., 1983; PhD, U. Ga., 1990. Cert. in prodn. and inventory mgmt.; cert. fellow in prodn. and inventory mgmt.; acad. Jonah. Corp. mgmt. intern TRW, Inc., Cleve., 1983-85; prodn. supt. TRW Motor Divsn., Dothan, Ala., 1985-87; asst. prof. ops. mgmt. U. Mich., Ann Arbor, 1990-92; interim asst. v.p. for acad. affairs Fla. A&M U., Tallahassee, 1996-97, prof. ops. mgmt., 1992-2000, Samford U., Birmingham, Ala., 2000—. Mem. bd. examiners Malcolm Baldridge Nat. Quality Award, 1997-2002; acad. quality improvement project design cons. North Cen. Assn. Colls. and Schs., 1999-2000. Co-author: (book) Reengineering Performance Measurement, 1994; contbr. articles to profl. jours.; mem. editl. rev. bd. Benchmarking: An Internat. Jour., 1995—, Jour. Ops. Mgmt., 1994—; referee Mfg. Rev., 1991, Internat. Jour. Prodn. Rsch., 1992—, Jour. Sys. Improvement, 1994—, Ann. Advances in Bus. Cases, 2000—, Prodn. and Inventory Mgmt. Jour., 2000—; contbr. APICS Dictionary, 1992-97. Bd. dirs. Innovation Investment Program, Tallahassee, 1996, APICS E&R Found., 1998-2000, sec., 1999, v.p., 2000. Recipient Cert. of Appreciation for Outstanding Svc. to the Nation, U.S. Dept. Commerce, 1997-2002. Mem. APICS, AIChE, Decision Scis. Inst., Prodn. and Ops. Mgmt. Soc., Performance Measurement Assn., Beta Gamma Sigma (pres. Sanford U. chpt. 2001-03). Avocations: chess, racquetball, music. Office: Samford U 800 Lakeshore Dr Birmingham AL 35229 Office Fax: 205-726-2464. E-mail: aalockam@sanford.edu.

LOCKE, CARL EDWIN, JR., academic administrator, engineering educator; b. Palo Pinto County, Tex., Jan. 11, 1936; s. Carl Edwin Sr. and Caroline Jane (Brown) L.; m. Sammie Rhae Batchelor, Aug. 25, 1956; children: Stephen Curtis, Carlene Rhae. BSChemE, U. Tex., 1958, MSChemE, 1960, PhDChemE, 1972. Rsch. engr. Continental Oil Co., Ponca City, Okla., 1959-65; prodn. engr. R.L. Stone Co., Austin, Tex., 1965-66; prodn. rsch. engr. Tracor Inc., Austin, 1966-71; vis. assoc. prof. U. Tex., Austin, 1971-73; from asst. prof. to prof., dir. chem. engring. U. Okla., Norman, 1973-86; dean engring. U. Kans., Lawrence, 1986—2002, prof. chem. and petroleum engring., 1986—. Co-author: Anodic Protection, 1981; contbr. articles to profl. jours. Recipient Disting. Engring. Svc. award U. Kans. Sch. Engring., 2002; named Disting. Engring. grad. U. Tex., 1993, Kansas Engr. of Yr. Kansas Engring. Soc., 1996. Fellow AIChE, NSPE; mem. ASTM, Nat. Assn. Corrosion Engrs. (regional chair 1988-89, Eben Junkin award South Cen. region 1990), Am. Soc. Engring. Edn. (vice-chair engring. deans coun. 1999-2001, chair 2001-02), Lawrence C. of C., Rotary (pres. 2001-02). Democrat. Presbyterian. Office: U Kans Sch Engring 1530 W 15th St Rm 4006 Lawrence KS 66045-7526 E-mail: lok@ku.edu.

LOCKE, MICHAEL, zoology educator; b. Nottingham, Eng., Feb. 14, 1929; came to U.S., 1961; s. R.H. and K.N. L.; m. J. V. Collins; children by previous marriage, Vanessa, John, Timothy, Marius. BA, Cambridge U., 1952, MA, 1955, PhD, 1956, Sc.D., 1976. State scholar, found. scholar St. John's Coll., 1949-56; lectr. zoology Univ. Coll. W.I., 1956-61; guest investigator Rockefeller Inst., N.Y.C., 1960; assoc. prof. biology Case Western Res. U., Cleve., 1961-67, prof. biology, 1967-71; prof., chmn. dept. zoology U. Western Ont., London, Can., 1971-85, prof. zoology, 1985-94; prof. emeritus, 1994—. Raman prof. U. Madras, India, 1969; vis. dir. rsch. Internat. Ctr. Insect Physiology and Ecology, Nairobi, Kenya, 1977-81; chmn. Gordon Conf. on Lysosomes, 1970. Editor Monographs on Ultrastructure, 1970—; mem. editorial bd. Tissue and Cell, 1968—, Jour. Insect Physiology, 1978—, Insect Sci. and Its Applications, 1979-89; former editor: Growth Soc. Symposia; editor, contbr. vols. 11 A, B, C, Insecta-Microscopic Anatomy of Invertebrate, 1998; contbr. over 200 articles to profl. jours. Served with No. 3 Med. Parachute Team RAF, 1947—49. Recipient Disting. Internat. award in insect morphology and embryology gold medal, 1988, Wigglesworth medal and lectr., Internat. Entomol. Congress, Brazil, 2000, Cert. of Distinction, 2000, Helmuth Prize, U.W.O., 2001;, Killam fellow, 1988—90. Fellow Royal Soc. Can., AAAS, Am. Soc. Entomol. (hon.), Royal Entomol. Soc. London (hon.); mem. Am. Soc. Cell Biology. Avocations: lapidary, gemologist, bone, ivory, horn antiquities. Office: U Western Ont Dept Biology London ON Canada N6A 5B7 Home Fax: 519-433-4166. Business E-Mail: mlocke@uwo.ca.

LOCKERBY, WILLIAM H. secondary education educator, administrator; b. Chattanooga, June 5, 1945; s. Charles Herbert and Mae (Wallace) Lockerby; m. Nikki Bowman, June 23, 1979; children: Abby, Katie, Teddy, Charlie. BA in History and Secondary Edn., Tenn. Wesleyan Coll., 1967; MEd, Supervision, U. Tenn. at Chattanooga, 1975. Cert. history instr., Tenn.; cert. Sch. Administr., Tenn. History instr. Cleveland Day Sch., Tenn.; prin. Senter Sch. Found., Chattanooga, 1973—. Mem. Christ United Meth. Ch. Home: 5004 Alabama Rd Apison TN 37302-9714

LOCKETTE, DAPHNEY D. elementary education educator; b. N.Y.C., Sept. 30, 1973; BA, Va. State U., 1995; M in Elem. Edn., Fairleigh Dickinson U., 2001; postgrad. studies in instructional tech., Farleigh Dickinson U., Teaneck, N.J., 2001—; postgrad. in human svcs., 2003—. Technology coord. Americorps/Project First, N.Y.C., 1995—97; substitute tchr. Bergen County Bd. of Edn., Englewood, NJ, 1997; adminstrv. asst.

Silver Palate, Cresskill, NJ, 1997; kindergarten tchr. My Friend's Day Sch., Teaneck, NJ, 1997—99; tchr. asst. First Grade Englewood on the Palisades Charter Sch., Englewood, NJ, 1999—. Tutor computer tech. and lang. arts Esteem Acad., Englewood. Author: Secrets from the Depths of My Soul, 2000. Treas., Praise Ministries, 2000—. Mem. Alpha Kappa Alpha.

LOCKHART, MADGE CLEMENTS, educational organization executive; b. Soddy, Tenn., May 22, 1920; d. James Arlie and Ollie (Sparks) Clements; m. Andre J. Lockhart, Apr. 24, 1942 (div. 1973); children: Jacqueline, Andrew, Janice, Jill. Student, East Tenn. U., 1938-39; BS, U. Tenn., Chattanooga and Knoxville, 1955, MEd, 1962. Elem. tchr. Tenn. and Ga., 1947-60, Brainerd H.S., Chattanooga, 1960-64, Cleveland (Tenn.) City Schs., 1966-88; owner, operator Lockhart's Learning Ctr., Inc., Cleveland and Chattanooga, 1966-2003; co-founder, pres. Hermes, Inc., 1973-79; co-founder Dawn Ctr., Hamilton County, Tenn., 1974; apptd. mem. Tenn. Gov.'s Acad. for Writers. Author poetry, short stories and fiction; contbr. articles to profl. jours. and newspapers. Pres. Cleveland Assn. Retarded Citizens, 1970, state v.p., 1976; pres. Cherokee Easter Seal Soc., 1973-76, Cleveland Creative Arts Guild, 1980; bd. dirs. Tenn. Easter Seal Soc., 1974-77, 80-83; chair Bradley County Internat. Yr. of Child; mem. panel for grants Coun. Govts. S.E. Tenn. Devel. Dist., 1990-92; mem. Internat. Biog. Centre Adv. Coun., Cambridge, Eng., 1991-92; mem. mayor's com. Mus. for Bradley County, Tenn., 1992—. Recipient Service to Mankind award Sertoma, 1978, Gov.'s award for service to handicapped, 1979; mental health home named in her honor, Tenn., 1987. Mem. NEA (life), Tenn. Edn. Assn., Am. Assn. Rehab. Therapy, S.E. Tenn. Arts Coun., Cleveland Edn. Assn. (Service to Humanity award 1987). Mem. Ch. of Christ. Clubs: Byliners, Fantastiks. Home: 3007 Oakland Dr NW Cleveland TN 37312-5281

LOCKHART, PATRICIA ANN, elementary school educator; b. Bklyn., N.Y., Jan. 7, 1961; d. Grace Copp; 1 child, Dana. AAS, Coll. Staten Island, 1988, BA, 1993, MS in Spl. Edn., 1996. Cert. tchr. N.Y. Life skills specialist Cath. Guardian Soc., N.Y.C., 1980; asst. tchr. Soc. Devel. Disabilities & Autism, Staten Island, NY, 1988—94; elem. sch. tchr. PS 57, Staten Island, 1994—. Vol. coord. Staten Island Tough Love, 1997—2001; outreach spkr. United Fedn. Tchrs., 2000—01. Named woman of achievement, Staten Island Advance, 2001; grantee, HUD, 2002. Home: 50 Dongan Hills Ave 2B Staten Island NY 10306

LOCKHART, VIRGINIA KING, reading specialist; b. Glen Ridge, N.J., Mar. 4, 1948; d. Oliver Kingdon and Margaret Louise (Bowers) King; m. James Cobert Belsches Jr., Nov. 20, 1971 (div. 1981); m. Stephen Donald Lockhart, Nov. 21, 1981; children: Travis Jefferson, Margaret Sharon. BA, Longwood Coll., 1970; MEd, Duke U., 1977. Cert. Spanish tchr., reading specialist, Md. Spanish tchr. Stonewall Jackson Jr. High Sch., Mechanicsville, Va., 1970-73; math. and reading tchr. Franklin County Pub. Schs., Louisburg, N.C., 1973-78; reading instr. Louisburg Coll., 1975-78; reading and English tchr. Montgomery County Pub. Schs., Rockville, Md., 1978-2000, instrnl. specialist, 2000—02, vertical articulation specialist, 2002—03; faculty assoc. Johns Hopkins U., 2002—, h.s. instructional specialist, 2003—. Author: Success in Every Class, 1977. Mem. Internat. Reading Assn., Md. Internat. Reading Assn., Montgomery County Internat. Reading Assn., Nat. Coun. Tchrs. English, Montgomery County Tchrs. English Lang. Arts, Md. Coun. Tchrs. of English Lang. Arts (1992 Tchr. of Yr. 1992). Presbyterian. Avocation: calligraphy. Office: Montgomery County Pub Schs 850 Hungerford Dr Rockville MD 20850

LOCKLAIR, GARY HAMPTON, computer science educator; b. Sacramento, May 1, 1956; s. Oliver Hampton and Frances Eleanor (Snyder) L.; m. Karen Ann Kellar, Aug. 13, 1977; children: Joshua, Sabrina, David, Daniel, Valerie. BA in Chemistry, Calif. State U., Sacramento, 1979, BS in Computer Sci., 1980; MS, U. Idaho, 1986; PhD in Computer Sci., Nova Southeastern U., 2002. Programmer, analyst Calif. Dept. Transp., Sacramento, 1977-79; mem. tech. staff Hewlett-Packard Co., Cupertino, Calif., 1980-81, software quality engr. Corvallis, Oreg., 1981-83, software program mgr. Boise, Idaho, 1983-86; prof. Concordia U. Wis., Mequon, 1986—, chair computer sci. dept., 1986—, dir. computer ctr., 1986-93. Computing cons., Milw., 1986—. Author: All of the Above, 1992; contbr. articles to profl. jours. Dist. computer cons. Philomath (Oreg.) Sch. Dist., 1981-83. Recipient HP Customer Svc. award Hewlett-Packard and Exxon Corp., 1985. Mem. IEEE, Assn. for computing Machinery. Lutheran. Avocation: photography. Office: Concordia U Wis 12800 N Lake Shore Dr Mequon WI 53097-2418 E-mail: locklair@luther.cuw.edu.

LOCKLEAR, BRENDA LOUISE, mathematics educator; b. Laurinburg, N.C., Apr. 22, 1950; d. Glassie and Emma Bell (Jones) L.; m. Edward Arnold Locklear, Apr. 29, 1973; children: Glendoria, Margaret Joyce. Early childhood cert., Fayetteville State U., 1987. Tchr. Robeson County Schs., N.C., 1987—. Mem. NEA, N.C. Assn. Educators. Republican. Baptist. Avocations: writing children stories, programming computer student activities, cooking.

LOCKLIN, GERALD IVAN, language educator, poet, writer; b. Rochester, NY, Feb. 17, 1941; s. Ivan Ward and Esther Adelaide Locklin. BA, St. John Fisher Coll., 1961; MA, U. Ariz., 1963, PhD, 1964. Instr. Calif. State U., L.A., 1964-65, prof. English Long Beach, 1965—. Author: Down and Out, 1999, Go West, Young Toad: Selected Writings, 1999, A Simpler Time A Simpler Place: Three Mid-Century Stories, 2000, Candy Bars: Selected Stories, 2000, The Life Force Poems, 2002, The Pocket Book: A Novella and Nineteen Short Fictions, 2003; (novella) The Case of the Missing Blue Volkswagen, 1984; (short stories) The Gold Rush, 1989; co-editor: A New Geography of Poets, 1992; featured in The Oxford Companion to Twentieth Century Literature in English, 1996; author numerous poems; contbr. more than 3000 poems and stories to periodocals. Mem.: Western Lit. Assn., Assoc. Writing Programs, Hemingway Soc., E.E. Cummings Soc., PEN USA/West. Avocations: swimming, jazz, travel, yankees, lakers. Office: Calif State U English Dept Long Beach CA 90840-0001 E-mail: glocklin@csulb.edu.

LOCKWOOD, JOANNE SMITH, mathematician educator; b. Quebec City, Can., Nov. 9, 1946; d. Donald William MacKay and Sylvia Eleanor (Howard) Smith; m. Bryce M. Lockwood Jr., Aug. 10, 1968; children: Daren MacKay, Keith McLellan. BA in English, St. Lawrence U., 1968; MBA, Plymouth State Coll., 1980, BA in Math., 1985. Editor Houghton Mifflin Co., Boston, 1969-86; tchr. New Hampton (N.H.) Sch., 1974-76, 80-81; lectr. Plymouth (N.H.) State Coll., 1988—. Author: (textbooks) Beginning Algebra with Applications, 1989, 92, 96, Intermediate Algebra with Applications, 1989, 92, 96, Business Mathematics, 1988, 94, Introductory Algebra with Basic Mathematics, 1989, 96, Algebra with Trigonometry for College Students, 1991, A Review of Geometry, 1993, Prealgebra, 1994, Algebra for College Students: A Functions Approach, 1994. Mem. Am. Math. Assn. of Two Yr. Colls., Text and Acad. Authors Assn. Home: RR 1 Box 180 New Hampton NH 03256-9717

LOEB, SUSANNA, education educator; BSCE, BA in Polit. Sci., Stanford U., 1988; MPP in Pub. Policy Studies, U. Mich., 1994, PhD in Econs., 1998. Rsch. asst. U. Mich. Sch. Edn., 1991—93; rsch. asst. dept. econs. U. Mich., 1993—96; rsch. fellow Population Studies Ctr., U. Mich., 1995—; rsch. asst. U. Mich. Sch. Edn., 1996—; asst. prof. U. Calif., Davis, 1998—99; asst. prof. edn. Stanford (Calif.) U., Calif., 1999—. Rsch. cons. Inst. for Rsch. on Women and Gender, U. Mich., 1997—. Office: Stanford U Sch Edn 485 Lasuen Mall Stanford CA 94305-3096*

LOEFFLER, GARRY ANTONE, principal, municipal official; b. Lewiston, Idaho, Mar. 12, 1941; s. John Antone and Germaine Agnes (Meyer) L.; m. Bonnie Louise Ferguson, Dec. 28, 1968; children: Stacey Anne, Brian John, Bradley Scott. BS in Edn., U. Idaho, 1963; MS in Sch. Adminstrn., Calif. State U., Hayward, 1983. Tchr. Roosevelt Sch., San Leandro, Calif., 1965-70, vice prin., 1970-74; prin. Wash. Sch., San Leandro, Calif., 1975-80, Wilson Sch., San Leandro, Calif., 1980-85, Garfield Sch., San Leandro, Calif., 1985-97, facilitator conversion to yr.-round edn., 1994. Mem. city coun. City of San Leandro, 1994—; co-chair San Leandro Collaborative for Youth and Families. Lt. U.S. Army, 1963-65, Res., 1965-83. Mem. ASCD, Am. Assn. Sch. Adminstrs., Assn. Calif. Sch. Adminstrs., San Leandro Adminstrs. Assn. (pres. 1991, Outstanding Sch. Adminstr. award 1992), World Future Soc., Phi Delta Kappa. Democrat. Roman Catholic. Avocations: model railroading, reading, writing, cartooning, travel. Home: 235 Begier Ave San Leandro CA 94577-2813 Office: City San Leandro 835 E 14th St San Leandro CA 94577-3782 E-mail: gloeffle@ricochet.net.

LOEUP, KONG, cultural organization administrator; b. Battambang, Cambodia, May 26, 1944; s. Kong Niem and Chhit Roeun; m. Ly Keo Thim, Aug. 1968; children: Kong Bandaul, Kong Panlauk. Diploma in edn., U. Phnom Penh, 1965; BA, Antioch U., 1983; MA, U. Colo., Denver, 1987; PhD, Columbia Pacific U., 1987. Tchr. Ministry Edn., Phnom Penh, 1964; counselor, community case worker Internat. Refugee Ctr., Denver, 1983; refugee program coord./counselor Refugee Camps, Thailand; cons. Cambodian Buddhist Soc. of Colo., Denver; counselor Cambodian Community Colo., Denver; pres. Cambodian Cultural Ctr., Denver, 1992—. Pres. Cambodian Fine Arts Preservation Group Colo.; mem. Asian Edn. Adv. Coun., Rep. Presdl. Task Force, 1986. Mem. ASCD. Home and Office: 1804 S Eliot St Denver CO 80219-4904

LOEWENTHAL, NESSA PARKER, intercultural communications consultant; b. Chgo., Oct. 13, 1930; d. Abner and Frances (Ness) Parker; m. Martin Moshe Loewenthal, July 7, 1951 (dec. Aug. 1973); children: Dann Marcus, Ronn Carl, Deena Miriam; m. Gerson B. Selk, Apr. 17, 1982 (dec. June 1987). BA in Edn. and Psychology, Stanford U., 1952. Faculty Stanford Inst. for Intercultural Communication, Palo Alto, Calif., 1973-87; dir. Trans Cultural Svcs., San Francisco, 1981-86, Portland, Oreg., 1986—. Dir. dependent svcs. and internat. edn. Bechtel Group, San Francisco, 1973-81, internat. edn. cons., 1981-84; mem. adv. com. dept. internat. studies Lesley Coll., Cambridge, Mass., 1986—; mem. Oreg. Ethics Commns., 1990—; mem. Bay Area Ethics Consortium, Berkeley, 1985-90; chmn. ethics com. Sietar Internat., Washington, 1987—, mem. governing bd., 1992-95; mem. faculty Summer Inst. for Internat. Comms., Portland, Oreg., 1987-97; core faculty Oreg. Gov.'s Sch. Svc. Leadership, Salem, 1995-97. Author: Professional Integration, 1987, Update: Federal Republic of Germany, 1990, Update: Great Britain, 1987; author, editor book series Your International Assignment, 1973-81; contbr. articles to profl. jours. Mem. equal opportunity and social justice task force Nat. Jewish Coun. on Pub. Affairs; bd. dirs. Kids on the Block, Portland, Portland Jewish Acad., 1996—, Portland Ashkalon Sister City Assn., Portland Jewish Fedn., 1999—, Coalition to Eliminate Bias and Hate Crimes in Oreg., 1999—; bd. dirs., co-chair ethics com. Soc. Humanistic Judaism, 1996-99; task force on Racism and Violence, Portland, Oreg.; mem. Lafayette (Calif.) Traffic Commn., 1974-80; bd. dirs. Ctr. for Ethics and Social Policy, 1988-91; mem. exec. bd. and planning com. Temple Isaiah, Lafayette, 1978-82; bd. dirs. Calif. Symphony, Orinda, 1988-90; mem. exec. com. overseas schs. adv. com. U.S. Dept. State, 1976-82; bd. dirs. Jewish Fedn. Oregon; mem. cmty. rels. com. Portland Jewish Fedn.; mem. Nat. Jewish Cmty. Rels.; mem. Task Force on Racism, Ethnicity and Pub. Policy, 1998—. Named Sr. Interculturalist, Sietar Internat., 1986. Mem. ASTD (exec. bd. internat. profl. performance area 1993-97, 99), Soc. for Intercultural Edn. Tng. and Rsch. (chmn. 1986-87, nomination com. 1984-86, co-chmn. 1989-90, chmn. ethics com. 1989-98, governing bd. 1992-95), World Affairs Coun. Democrat. Avocations: photography, swimming. Office: 2399 NW Hosmer Lake Dr Bend OR 97701-5475 E-mail: nessa@transport.com.

LOFGREN, CHARLES AUGUSTIN, legal and constitutional historian, history educator; b. Missoula, Mont., Sept. 8, 1939; s. Cornelius Willard and Helen Mary (Augustin) L.; m. Jennifer Jenkins Wood, Aug. 6, 1986. AB with great distinction, Stanford U., 1961; AM, 1962, PhD, 1966. Instr. history San Jose State Coll., 1965-66; asst. prof. Claremont McKenna Coll., 1966-71; assoc. prof., 1971-76; prof., 1976—; Roy P. Crocker prof. Am. history and politics, 1976—. Author: Government from Reflection and Choice, 1986, The Plessy Case, 1988, Claremont Pioneers, 1996; contbr. articles to profl. jours. Served with USAR, 1957-63. Mem. Am. Soc. Legal History, Orgn. Am. Historians, Am. Hist. Assn. Republican. Roman Catholic. Office: Claremont McKenna Coll Dept History 850 Columbia Ave Claremont CA 91711-6420

LOFLAND, PATRICIA LOIS, secondary school educator, travel company executive; b. New Orleans, Apr. 18, 1937; d. Willie and Philomene (Foster) Seymore; m. Eugene Joseph LeBeauf, Apr. 24, 1954 (div. 1967); children: Valentino, Renee, Merlin, Tammy, Gina; m. Trusten P. Causey Lofland, Jan. 21, 1974. AA, Long Beach City Coll., 1972; BA in Sociology, Calif. State U., Dominguez Hills, 1972; MA Early Childhood Edn., Calif. State U., 1974. Cert. tchr., Calif. Community/liaison tchr. Long Beach (Calif.) Community Improvement League, 1964-70; dep. probation officer Orange County, Orange, Calif., 1972-74; substitute tchr. Compton (Calif.) Unified Sch. Dist., 1974-76; tchr./pers.commr. Long Beach Unified Sch. Dist., 1976—96; customer service rep. Western/Delta Airlines, L.A., 1978-87; travel agt./sales cons., 1986—. Mem. exec. bd. Westside Neighborhood Assn., Long Beach, 1981, Long Beach Fair Housing Found., 1987—; sec. L.A. County Grand Jury, 1982-83; pres. St. Luke Mission Soc., Long Beach, 1978-88; mem. Christian bd. edn. St. Luke Baptist Ch., Long Beach, 1986-88.,mem., State Calif. Sch. Pers. Commn. Assn., 1999; cmty. development advisor, Long Beach, 1993-2002; Relocation Appeals Bd., 1988-1995, Elected Trustee, Long Beach Cmty. Coll. Bd., 1996-2000, Christ Second Bapt. Ch., mem. Youth Worker Missionary Soc., Fin. Comm., New Members Counselor and Dept. sec., 1995- Recipient cert. of appreciation Westside Neighborhood Assn., 1981, cert. of appreciation Lutheran U., 1996; Long Beach City Coll. recognition for commitment and outstanding svc.to the EOPS and CARE program, 1999, cert. of appreciation for outstanding leadership in the Long Beach Cmty., 1996, 1999, recognition as the first african mem. of the Long Beach City Coll. Bd. of Trustees, 1997, cert. of appreciation, Bd. of Trustees, 2000, cert. of appreciation from the Calif. Senate and Assembly, 1999, State of Calif. Senate and Assembly, 1999, Pearl award Alpha Kappa Alpha, 2000, cert. of appreciation L.A. county Bd. Suprs., 2002. Mem. Calif. Tchrs. Assn., Calif. Personnel Commrs. Assn., Nat. Coun. Negro Women, NAACP, Delta Phi Upsilon (v.p. Nu chpt. 1973-77). Democrat. Avocation: world-wide travel. Home: 1281 W Cameron St Long Beach CA 90810-2209

LOFSTROM, ARLENE KATHERINE, primary school educator; b. Jersey City, N.J., July 28, 1946; d. Edward and Dorothy Staats McClain; children: Courtney Lynne, Derek Jason. BA, Jersey City State Coll., 1968. Tchr. 4th to 6th grade Jersey City Bd. Edn., 1968—75; tchr. 3d grade Union Beach (N.J.) Bd. Edn., 1989—. Remedial reading tchr. Union Beach Meml. Sch., 1985—89, Latch Key tchr., 1987—88, Gifted and Talented tchr., 1988—89, summer sch. tchr., 1987—; ESL tchr. Union Beach Adult Sch., 2000—01. Mem.: NEA, N.J. Edn. Assn., Highlands Hist. Soc., Highlands Rep. Club. Avocations: golf, travel, book discussion groups. Home: A-12 Oceanview Terr Highlands NJ 07732

LOFT, BERNARD IRWIN, education educator, consultant; m. Sadye Loft; 1 child, Richard Dale. BS, West Chester (Pa.) U., 1939; MA in Edn., U. Fla., 1949; Directorate in Health and Safety, Ind. U., 1956, D of Health and Safety, 1957. Ednl. advisor Civilian Conservation Corps, Branchville, N.J., 1940-42; dir. phys. edn., coach Lower Paxton Twp. H.S., Harrisburg, Pa., 1942; field rep. in safety svcs. ARC, Atlanta, 1946; instr. in biology and phys. edn., coach Andrew Jackson H.S., Jacksonville, Fla., 1946-48; chmn. safety edn. program, instr. phys. edn., faculty, coach U. Fla., Gainesville, 1948-51; asst. prof. edn. and continuing edn. Mich. State U., East Lansing, 1951-55; fgn. assignment Cultural Exch. Program Americans Abroad U.S. Dept. State, Cambodia, 1961-62; prof. Sch. of Health, Phys. Edn. and Recreation, dir. health and safety Ind. U., Bloomington, 1956—, assoc. prof. health and safety, 1957-65, dir. Ctr. for Safety Studies, prof. health safety edn., 1962-63, prof. emeritus Applied Health Sci., dir., 1981, prof. emeritus health and safety, 1981—. Ednl. cons. Am. Automobile Assn., Washington, Am. Trucking Assn., Washington; vis. lectr. U. Md., U. N.C., U. Ga., Syracuse (N.Y.) U., Kent (Ohio) State U., U. Miami, Fla. State U., S.C. A&M Coll., Purdue U.; faculty advisor doctoral studies and PhD and EdD degrees, chair health svcs. track Walden U., acad. policies bd.; participant The White House Conf. on Health, 1965, White House Conf. on Occupl. Safety, 1956; participant cultural exch. program to Phnom Penh, Cambodia, U.S. Dept. State, Voice of Am. Author: How to Prevent Accidents in the Motor Home, 1978; contbr. articles to profl. jours. Head counselor Camp Ridgedale, Sumneytown, Pa., waterfront dir., counselor; athletic dir. Camp Arthur, Zieglersville, Pa.; waterfront dir. Pocono Highland Camp, Marshall's Creek, Pa., Blue Mountain Camps, East Stroudsburg, Pa., Kitatinny Camps, Dingman's Ferry, Pa., head counselor. Lt. comdr. USN, 1942-46, USNR, 1946-65, World War II, ret., 1965. Recipient Cert. of Appreciation, Ind. U. Student Found., 40 Yr. Svc. Pin, ARC; decorated Cheva'Lier de L'Order du Monisaraphon (Cambodian Govt.). Fellow AAHPERD, Am. Acad. Safety Edn. (charter, pres.), Am. Sch. Health Assn.; mem. NEA, Ind. Mobile Home Assn. (hon. Cert. of Appreciation 1966), Nat. Safety Coun. (gen. chmn. higher edn. sect. 1960-61 Plaque), Ind. Assn. for Health, Phys. Edn. and Recreation (v.p.), Am. Sch. Health Assn. (chmn. sch. safety edn. com., and others), Ind. Coll. Health Assn. (pres. 1958-59), Ind. Tchr.'s Assn., Am. Acad. Safety Edn. (pres., v.p., chmn. membership com., pres. 1967-68), Mid-Am. Coll. Health Assn., Ind. Assn. Health Educator Avocations: soccer, football, swimming, boxing, lacrosse. Office: Walden University Liaison Rep to Ind Univ 801 Anchor Rode Dr Naples FL 34103-2751

LOFTUS, STEPHEN EDWARD, elementary art educator; b. Stoughton, Wis., Sept. 17, 1949; s. Edward Henry and Gladys Lillian (Lange) L. BS, U. Wis., Platteville; M in Art Edn., U. Wis., 1995. Cert. tchr., Wis. Art tchr. Wausau (Wis.) Pub. Schs., 1981—. Sculpture judge State Visual Arts Classic Competition, Madison; presenter in field. Contbr. Jour. on Japan's Edn. in Art, 1991; sculptor; songwriter. Vol. tchr. Ctr. for the Visual Arts; sculpture judge State Visual Arts Classic Competition MATC, Madison; citizen amb. Japan art educators, People to People Program, Wausau, summer 1991; soapbox derby judge, art advisor Boy Scouts Am.; vol. Meals on Wheels; councilor, choir mem. United Meth. Ch.; representer WAEA Cranbrook Estate western region state's ann. meeting art edn. issues, Mich. Recipient Award of Excellence for mixed media painting, State Wis. Art. Edn. Assn. Conf., 2000, Award of Excellence for sculpture, Ctr. Visual Arts Wausau, Resolution of Commendation, Pres. Philip R. Albert, MD, Wausau Pub. Schs. Sch. Bd., 2000, 2d Resolution Commendation bringing recognition to Wausau Pub. Schs., Christine A. Bremer Pres. Bd. Edn., Wausau, Wis. . Mem. Nat. Art Edn. Assn. (v.p. North Ctrl. region bd. 1993-95, pres.-elect del. at dels. assembly nat. spring conf. 2002, 03), NEA, State Edn. Assn., Wis. Art Edn. Assn. (pres., 2003-05, Art Educator of Yr. 2000), Wis. Alliance Arts Edn. (Disting. Svc. award within the arts edn. profession 2000). Home: 1243 Sunset Dr Wausau WI 54401-4256 Office: 2701 Robin Ln Wausau WI 54401

LOGAN, JOYCE POLLEY, education educator; b. Providence, Ky., Sept. 18, 1935; d. Vernon and Hattie Alice Polley; m. Jewell Wyatt Logan (dec.), June 4, 1956; 1 child, James Edward. BS, Murray State U., 1956, MA, 1960; EdD, Vanderbilt U., 1988. Cert. bus. tchr., vocat. adminstrn. Student sec. Murray (Ky.) State U., 1954-56; bus. tchr. Hopkins County Schs., Madisonville, Ky., 1956-68; regional coord. Vocational Region 2 Ky. Dept. Edn., Madisonville, 1968-83; prin. Health Occupations Sch., Madisonville, 1983-88; voc., tech. administr. Ky. Dept. Edn., Frankfort, 1988-90; asst. prof. dept. adminstrn. and supervision Coll. Edn. U. Ky., Lexington, 1991—99; state dir. Ky. Com. for Secondary and Middle Schs. So. Assn. Colls. and Schs., 1995-98; assoc. prof. dept. adminstrn. and supervision Coll. Edn. U. Ky., Lexington, 2000—. Evaluator Distance Edn. Training Coun., Washington, 1981—; field coord. military evaluations, Am. Coun. on Edn., Washington, 1984—. Author: (with A.C. Krizan) Basics of Writing, 1993, 2000; contbg. author: Records Management and Business Communication. Mem. alumni bd. Murray (Ky.) State U. Coll. Bus., 1988-2001; fundraiser Ky. Spl. Olympics, Madisonville, 1983, YMCA, Madisonville, 1984; mem. edn. com. Greater Leadership Program Madisonville, Ky. C. of C., 1987-88. Recipient Exceptional Svc. award Coll. Edn., U. Ky., 1999; named FFA Hon. State Farmer, Ky. FFA., 1979, Woman of the Year, Lion's Club, Madisonville, Ky., 1987, Outstanding Tchr. Educator, 1992, Exceptional Achievement award for svc. U. Ky., 1999. Mem. Nat. Bus. Edn. Assn., Am. Vocat. Assn., Ky. Vocat. Assn., Southern Assn. of Colls. and Schs. (trustee 1973, 1976-78, chmn. Commn on Occupational Ednl. Insts. 1973), Ky. Assn. for Sch. Adminstrs., Assn. for Supervision and Curriculum Devel., Phi Delta Kappa, Omicron Delta Kappa (hon.). Avocations: jogging, tennis, reading, piano playing. Home: 2956 Tabor Oaks Ln Lexington KY 40502-2898 Office: U Ky 111 Dickey Hall Coll of Edn Lexington KY 40506

LOGAN, LINDA JO, secondary school educator; b. Houston, May 3, 1968; d. Earl Roger and Louise Delphine (Meyer) L. BS in Secondary English Edn., U. Tex., 1990. Cert. English and reading tchr., Tex. Tchr. reading Northside Ind. Sch. Dist., San Antonio, 1990—. Counselor Master Sch., Austin, Tex., summers 1989—. Mem. ASCD, NEA, Tex. Mid. Sch. Assn., Ex-Students Assn. U. Tex. Republican. Roman Catholic. Avocations: reading, horseback riding, writing poems, dancing. Office: HB Zachry Mid Sch 9410 Timber Path San Antonio TX 78250-4900

LOGAN, LINDA MARY, art education educator; b. Detroit, Dec. 28, 1942; d. Ervin John Moore, Joseph R. Sanson (stepfather) and Helen (Kolczynski) Moore Sanson; divorced; 1 child, Stephen Kelly. BA, Wayne State U., 1965, MA in Tchg., 1971; postgrad., Oakland C.C., 1989—. Cert. tchr., Mich. Instr. art Detroit Bd. Edn., 1967—, instr. gifted art, 1971—. Audio-visual asst. Wayne State U., Detroit, 1960-62; clk. Wayne County Treas., Detroit, summers, 1960-63; pvt. decorative painter, Mich., 1962—; pvt. graphic designer logos, Mich., 1971—; tchr. workshops Detroit Schs., 1988—, Children's Mus., Detroit, 1995; advisor Davis Publs., 1990—; developer core curriculum Detroit Art Edn.; judge Free Press Editl. contest. Co-author art appreciation guide; photographer Detroit Zoo Jour., 1991; cons. Art Edn. Text Books, 1988—; exhibited at group shows at Biagus Gallery, Scarab Club, 1995, Oakland C.C., Mich. Coun. of Arts, Mich. Art Edn. Conf., Focus Gallery, 1980—. Vol. Detroit Inst. of Arts, 1992. Mem. Am. Fedn. Tchrs., Mich. Art Edn. Assn., Detroit Art Tchrs. Assn. (treas.), Nat. Art Edn. Assn., Founder's Soc., Greenpeace, Earthwatch. Avocations: painting, drawing, photography, ancient history, water sports. Home: 10705 Nadine Ave Huntington Woods MI 48070-1519

LOGAN, LYNDA DIANNE, elementary education educator; b. Detroit, June 22, 1952; d. Horatio Bernard and Ruby (Newsom) Graham; m. Keith L. Logan, Aug. 16, 1980 (div); 1 child, Lauren Nicole. BS, Ea. Mich. U., 1974, MA, 1980. Cert. tng. program quality rev., Calif.; cert. tchr., Calif., Miss., Mich.; cert. Lang. Devel. Specialist (CLAD), 1996; lic. guidance counselor basic related edn., Miss.; cert. counselor pupil pers. svc. credential, Mich., Calif. Substitute tchr. Detroit Pub. Schs., 1974-76; mid. sch. tchr. Inkster (Mich.) Pub. Schs., 1976-80; CETA vocat. counselor Golden

Triangle Vocat.-Tech. Ctr., Mayhew, Miss., 1980-82, basic related educator, 1980-82; elem. tchr. Inglewood (Calif.) Unified Sch. Dist., 1982-93, reading resource specialist, 1993-96; tchr. Crozier Magnet Mid. Sch., Inglewood, Calif., 1996—. Advisor Assn. Student Body, 2000-2001; tchr.-mentor The Gear-Up Program, 2000—, counselor, 2003; mem. forecast adv. bd. COED Mag., N.Y.C., 1979-80; advisor/founder Newspaper Club Fellrath Mid. Sch., Inkster, 1979-80; mem. interviewing com. Golden Triangle Vocat.-Tech. Ctr., Mayhew, 1980-82, evaluation and follow-up com., 1980-82; pronouncer spelling bee Inglewood Unified Sch. Dist., 1991, 94; organizer student study team meetings Worthington Sch., Inglewood, 1993-96, coord. reading program, 1993-96; mem. interviewing com., 1987-95; co-chair yearbook com., 1993-94, prin. adv. bd., 1987-92, ct.-liaison and child welfare attendance rep. L.A. County Edn., 1995-96, sch. leadership team mem., 1991—, supt. adv. coun., 1995-96, reading is fundamental coord., 1993-96, mem. team earthquake preparedness com., 1994-96, coord. after-sch. tutoring program, 1998-99, curriculum coun. rep. 1998-99, mentor tchr.-gear up program, 2000—, grant proposal writer, 2000-01, mem. sch. site coun.; adult edn. tchr. CBET ESL Program, 2001—; supervising tchr. Calif. State U., Dominguez, 1987, 94, 2002, Nat. U., 1987, 94, 2003, UCLA, 2001-02, mem. bldg. fund com. West Angeles Ch. of God in Christ, 2001—. Youth co-chair March of Dimes, Detroit, 1976-80; com. mem. Nat. Coun. Negro Women, L.A. chpt., 1982-84; com. mem. Cmty. Action Program, Eternal Promise Bapt. Ch., L.A., 1991, pres. choir, 1991, v.p. hospitality com., 1987-88; co-chmn. women's com., 1990; mem. parent adv. com. Knox Presbyn. Ch. Nursery Sch., L.A., 1988-89; co-chair higher learning parent com. West Angeles Ch. of God in Christ, 2003—; v.p., mem. fin. com. Fairview Gardens Homeowner Assn., 2003; mentor, tchr. UCLA. Mem. ASCD, AAUW, NAFE, Black Women's Forum, Ladies Aux. Knights of St. Peter Claver, Ea. Mich. U. Alumni Assn., Phi Gamma Nu. Avocations: bike riding, community organizational activities, travel, movies, theater. Office: Highland Elem Sch 430 Venice Way Inglewood CA 90302 E-mail: pontiaclyn@aol.com.

LOGAN, SANDRA JEAN, retired economics and business educator; b. Dayton, Ohio, Jan. 3, 1940; d. Max B. and Edna E. (Sanderson) Parrish; m. John E. Logan, Apr. 25, 1964. BA, Drew U., 1962; MBA, Columbia U., N.Y.C., 1964; PhD, U. S.C., 1976. Piano tchr., Whippany, N.J., 1957-64; lab. analyst Bear Creek Mining Co., Morristown, N.J., summer 1957, 58; rsch. asst. Drew U., Madison, N.J., summer 1962; staff asst. N.J. Bell Telephone Co., Newark, summer 1963, 64-67; instr. bus. U. Toledo, 1967-69; asst. prof. econs. and bus. S.C. State Univ., Orangeburg, 1970-76; prof. econs. and bus. Newberry (S.C.) Coll., 1976—2002, emeritus, 2002—, acting v.p. acad. affairs, 1993-95. Cons. econs., Ohio and S.C., 1967—, N.J. Bell Telephone Co., Newark, 1968; lectr. bus. Ea. Mich. U., Ypsilanti, spring 1969. Active Coldstream Home Owners Assn., Columbia, S.C., 1972-80; officer St. Andrews Woman's Club, Columbia, 1969-76. Rsch. grantee U. S.C. and S.C. State U., 1974-75. Mem. Am. Econs. Assn., So. Econs. Assn. Republican. Presbyterian. Home: 112 Smiths Market Ct Columbia SC 29212-1923

LOGAN-GENERETTE, CHARLETTA LEE, elementary education educator; b. Balt., Nov. 13, 1954; d. Randolph Jr. and Alice (Johnson) Logan; m. Tyrone Marcellous Generette, May 15, 1983; children: Jonel Alicia, Jerrod Tyrone. BS, Coppin State Coll., Balt., 1976; postgrad., Morgan U., Balt., 1988. Cert. advanced profl. tchr., Md.; lic. manicurist. Elem. tchr. Balt. City Pub. Schs., 1976—, demonstration tchr., 1978—, mem. supt.'s tchr. addv. group, 1988-90. Writer Md. State Dept. Edn./Health Edn. Evaluation Project, 1992; coord. Just Say No to Drugs Club, 1989-92; curriculum writer Balt. City Pub. Sch. System, 1992; family math. instr., 1988—. Trainer Hist. Balt. Day, Women's Civic Group, 1983-88. Named Tchr. Yr., Balt. City Coun. PTA, 1984, 87. Avocations: sewing, nail artistry. Home: 1201 Ramblewood Rd Baltimore MD 21239-2638

LOGAN-SUTTON, FLORETTA R. elementary school educator; b. Elizabeth City, N.C., Mar. 13, 1930; d. Ivy Hillard and Rosa Lillian (Stewart) Roach; m. Chester C. Sutton, Sept. 19, 1949 (dec. 1988); children: Gwen Omari, Chester Jr., Karen Bailey, Fred, Renee, Verona Dunn; m. Ben L. Logan; stepchildren: Tyrone, Karen Graham, Kathy, Darryl, Victor, Christopher. BA, Elizabeth City State U., 1955; MA, Glassboro (N.J.) State Coll., 1962. Tchr. grades 1-5 Bd. Edn., Atlantic City, N.J., tchr. basic skill improvement program. Contbr. rsch. to profl. jours. Mem. NEA, NAACP, Internat. Assn. Ministers' Wives and Ministers' Widows, Inc., N.J. Ret. Edn. Assn. Atlantic County, N.J. Edn. Assn., Atlantic City Edn. Assn., Phi Delta Kappa, Alpha Bettes. Home: 1910 Marmora Ave Atlantic City NJ 08401-2014

LOGEMANN, JERILYN ANN, speech pathologist, educator; b. Berwyn, Ill., May 21, 1942; d. Warren F. and Natalie M. (Killmer) L. BS, Northwestern U., 1963; MA, 1964, PhD, 1968. Grad. asst. dept. communicative disorders Northwestern U., 1963-68; instr. speech and audiology DePaul U., 1964-65; instr. dept. communicative disorders Mundelein Coll., 1967-71; rsch. assoc. dept. neurology and otolaryngology and maxillo, 1970-74; asst. prof., 1974-78; dir. clin. and rsch. activities of speech and lang., 1975—; assoc. prof. depts. neurology, otolaryngology and comm. scis, 1978-83; prof., 1983; chmn. dept. comm. scis. and disorders, 1982-96; Ralph and Jean Sundin Prof. of Comm. Scis. and Disorders, 1995—; mem. assoc. staff Northwestern meml. Hosp., 1976—; N. Chgo. VA Hosp., 1983—; Evanston (Ill.) Hosp., 1988—. Cons. in field; assoc. dir. cancer control Ill. Comprehensive Cancer Coun., Chgo., 1980-82; mem. rehab. com. Ill. divsn. Am. CAncer Soc., 1975-79, chmn., 1979—; mem. upper aerodigestive tract organ site com. Nat. Cancer Inst., 1986-89; postdoct. fellow Nat. Inst. Neurologic Disease, Communicative Disorders and Stroke,Northwestern U., 1968-70. Author: The Fisher-Logeman Test of Articulation Competence, 1971, Evaluation and Treatment of Swallowing Disorders, 1983, 2nd edit., 1998, Manual for the Videofluorographic Evaluation of Swallowing, 1985, 93; assoc. editor: Jour. Speech and Hearing Disorders, Jour. Head Trauma Rehab., Dysphagia Jour., 1978—. Fellow Inst. Medicine Chgo., 1981—; grantee Nat Cancer Inst., 1975—, Am. Cancer Soc., 1981-82, Nat. Inst. Dental Rsch., 1996—, Nat. Inst. Deafness and Other Comm. Disorders, 1997—; recipient Honors award Conn. Speech Lang. Hearing Assn., 1995, Am. Acad. Otolaryngology-Head Neck Surgery, 1997, Appreciation award Coun. Grad. Prgrams in Comms. Scis. and Disorders, 1995, Cellular One award Vanderbilt U., Am. Special Lang. Hearing Assn., 2003. Fellow Speech, Lang. and Hearing Assn. (pres. 1994, 2000, Honors award 2003), Inst. Medicine; mem. Internat. Assn. Logopedics and Phoniatrics, AAUP, Acoustic Soc. Am. (program com. Chgo. regional chpt.), Linguistic Soc. Am., Speech Comm. Assn., Am. Cleft Palate Assn., Ill. Speech and Hearing Assn. (DiCarlo award 1988), Chgo. Heart Assn., Chgo. Speech Therapy and Auditory Soc. Office: Northwestern U Med Sch 303 E Chicago Ave Chicago IL 60611-3072 also: Northwestern U Dept Comm Sci and Disorder 2240 Campus Dr Evanston IL 60208-0001

LOGSDON, RICHARD M. English language educator, magazine editor; b. Boise, Idaho, June 2, 1948; s. Richard M. and Eula Jane (Randall) L.; m. Juliet Anne de Neufuille, Dec. 27, 1968; children: Tobias, Heather. BA, U. Oreg., 1970, MA, 1972, PhD, 1976. English prof. C.C. So. Nev., Las Vegas, 1975—. Author: (textbooks) Community College Reader, 1984, 4th edit., 1991, Red Rock Reader, 2003; editor-in-chief Red Rock Rev., 1995—; editor: In the Shadow of the Strip, 2003; author: (short stories) Alex the Wolfgod, 1999, Valley of the Shadow, 2000, Sweet Darkness, 2002. Coach boys and girls teams Nev. State Youth Soccer, 1981-93; head soccer coach men's team Las Vegas Premiere Soccer League, 1991—, coll. men's team, 1999—. Avocations: soccer, writing fiction, fishing, sports. Home: 3090 El Camino Rd Las Vegas NV 89146-6620 Office: CC So Nev 3200 E Cheyenne Ave North Las Vegas NV 89030-4228

LOHMAN, LORETTA CECELIA, social scientist, consultant; b. Joliet, Ill., Sept. 25, 1944; d. John Thomas and Marjorie Mary (Brennan) L. BA in Polit. Sci., U. Denver, 1966, PhD in Am. History, 1996; MA in Social Sci., U. No. Colo., 1975. Lectr. Ariz. State U., Tempe, 1966-67; survey researcher Merrill-Werthlin Co., Tempe, 1967-68; edn. asst. Am. Humane Assn., Denver, 1969-70; econ. cons. Lohman & Assocs., Littleton, Colo., 1971-75; rsch. assoc. Denver Rsch. Inst., 1976-86; owner, rsch. scientist Lohman & Assocs., Littleton, 1986-99; affiliate Colo. Water Resources Rsch. Inst., Ft. Collins, Colo., 1989-91; Colo. Nonpoint source info./edn. coord. coop. ext. Colo. State U., 1999—. Tech. adv. com. Denver Potable Wastewater Demo Plant, 1986—90; cons. Constrn. Engring. Rsch. Lab., 1984—; peer reviewer NSF, 1985—86, Univs. Coun. Water Resources, 1989; WERC consortium reviewer N.Mex. Univs.-U.S. Dept. Energy, 1989—, Co-Alliance Environ. Edn. Adv. Bd., 2000—; course cons. Regis Coll., Denver, 1992—. Contbr. articles to profl. jours. Vol. Metro Water Conservation Projects, Denver, 1986-90; co-coord. AWARE Colo., 2003--; vol. handicapped fitness So. Suburban Parks and Recreation. Recipient Huffsmith award Denver Rsch. Inst., 1983; Nat. Ctr. for Edn. in Politics grantee, 1964-65. Mem. ASCE (social and environ. objectives com.), Orgn. Am. Historians, Pub. Hist. Assn., Sigma Xi, Pi Gamma Mu, Phi Alpha Theta. Avocations: vegetable and xeriscape gardening, traveling, miniature boxes. Home and Office: 3375 W Aqueduct Ave Littleton CO 80123-2903 E-mail: llohman@juno.com.

LOHMANN, JACK R. engineering educator; b. Stillwater, Okla., Feb. 7, 1951; AS in engring., Ea. Okla. State Coll., 1971; BS in mech. engring., Okla. State U., 1974; MS in indsl. engring., Stanford U., 1975, PhD, 1979. Lic. profl. engr., Mich. Asst. prof. indsl. and ops. engring. U. Mich., Ann Arbor, 1979-85, assoc. prof., 1985-91, assoc. dean grad. and undergrad. studies, 1987-89; sr. program dir. NSF, Washington, 1989-91; prof. indsl. and systems engring. Ga. Inst. Tech., Atlanta, 1991—, assoc. dean acad. affairs, 1991—. Vis. assoc. prof., U. So. Calif., L.A., 1985; professeur associé, École Centrale des Arts et Manufactures, Paris, 1986; EHR adv. com. NSF, Washington, 1994-96; nat. adv. bd. mem. Synthesis Engring. Edn. Coalition, Ithaca, N.Y., 1991—; witness Subcom. on Sci., U.S. House Reps., Washington, 1992, Com. on HUD, VA Ind. Agys., Washington, 1993. Editor: The Engineering Economist, Atlanta, 1991—; dept. editor IIE Tranactions, Atlanta, 1982-87; contbr. articles to profl. jours. Recipient Presdl. Young Investigator award, White House, Washington, 1984, Dirs. Award for Excellence, NSF, Washington, 1991. Mem. Am. Soc. Engring Edn. (chair engring. economy divsn. 1984-85, centennial cert. 1993), Inst. Indsl. Engrs. (program chair engring. economy divsn. 1984-85), Accreditation Bd. Engring. and Tech. Achievements include research in econ. decision analysis, replacement econs., risk and engring. and sci. edn. Office: Ga Inst Tech Coll Engring Atlanta GA 30332-0001

LOMAS, CHARLES GARDNER, engineering educator, retired, psychotherapist; b. Ft. Peck, Mont., Dec. 5, 1934; s. George Edward and Evelyn Gardner (Carr) L.; m. Arletta Pelekaluhi Akamine, Apr. 27, 1957; 1 child, Kathleen Pelekaluhi Lomas. BS in Edn., U. Md., 1957, BSME, 1964, MS in Mech. Engring., 1975; MA in Psychotherapy, Naropa U., 2000. Instr. U. Md., College Park, 1971-77; engr. Dantec Electronics, Ramsey, N.J., 1977-80; instr. Lafayette Coll., Easton, Pa., 1980-82; freelance writer Greenbelt, Md., 1982-85; asst. prof. Rochester (N.Y.) Inst. Tech., 1985-86; assoc. prof. Northampton Community Coll., Bethlehem, Pa., 1986-88, Calif. Poly. State U., San Luis Obispo, 1988-92, Oreg. Inst. Tech., Klamath Falls, 1992-97; owner Big Sage Counseling, LLC, Klamath Falls, Oreg., 2001—. Author: Fundamentals of Hot Wire Anemometry, 1985. Achievements include patents for fluidic pressure regulator, sonic detector. Home and Office: 3881 Rio Vista Way Klamath Falls OR 97603

LOMAX, KENNETH MITCHELL, agricultural engineering educator; b. Wilmington, Del., Nov. 4, 1947; s. Ernest S. and Martha W. (Mitchell) L.; m. Nancy R. Beltz, Oct. 16, 1971. BS in Chem. Engring., Lafayette Coll., Easton, Pa., 1969; MS in Entomology, U Del., Newark, 1971; PhD in Agrl. Engring., U. Md., College Park, 1976. Registered profl. engr., Del. Asst. prof. Horn Point Environ. Labs. U. Md., Cambridge, 1976-80; asst. prof. agrl. engring. U. Del., Newark, 1980-85, assoc. prof. agrl. engring., 1985—, dept. chairperson, 1998—2003. Pres. faculty senate U. Del., 1992-93. Contbr. articles to profl. jours. Recipient Excellence In Teaching award U. Del. and Lindbach Found., 1988; named Faculty Mem. of Yr., Panhellenic Coun., 1993. Mem. ASHRAE, Am. Soc. Agrl. Engrs., Am. Mushroom Inst. (dir. 1987-90). Avocation: outdoor activities. Office: U Del Bioresources Engring Dept Newark DE 19716-2140 E-mail: kml@udel.edu.

LOMAX, PEGGY QUARLES, gifted and talented education educator; b. Bradenton, Fla., Dec. 21, 1941; d. Archie Eugene and Katherine Louise (Stowe) Q.; m. David W. Ridge, Dec. 27, 1958 (div. July 1972); m. Robert T. Lomax, Nov. 23, 1978; children: Anita Ann, Michael Wade. MA in Mid. Sch. Edn., Appapachian State U., 1977; MA im Mid. Sch. Edn., Lenoir Rhyne Coll., 1987. Cert. tchr., sch. adminstr. gifted edn., N.C. Media asst. J.B. Little Elem. Sch., Arlington, Tex., 1969-72; pub. info. officer Appalachian State U., Boone, N.C., 1974-77; tchr. academically gifted Gamewell Mid. Sch., Lenoir, N.C., 1977-89, William Lenoir (N.C.) Mid. Sch., 1989-93; tchr., coord. gifted and talented Mayflower (Ark.) Pub. Schs., 1993-95; secondary gifted and talented tchr. Vilonia (Ark.) Pub. Schs., 1995—. Pres. Lenoir Bus. and Profl. Orgn., 1984-85; spl. registration commr. Caldwell County, 1985-87; bd. dirs. Caldwell County Libr., 1985-87; mem. N.C. Commn. on Youth and Children, 1987-89; mem. youth com. Mt. Grove Bapt. Ch. Recipient Caldwell County Human Rels. award, 1987=88; grantee Caldwell County C. of C., 1992, Z. Smith Reynolds Found., 1993. Mem. NEA, ASCD, N.C. Assn. Educators (v.p. 1985-86, 90-91, pres. 1986-87, 92-93), N.C. League Mid. Schs. (bd. dirs. 1981-84, v.p.), N.C. Assn. Gifted Educators, Caldwell County Assn. Educators (pres. 1984-85), Arkansans for Gifted and Talented Edn., Caldwell County Parents for Academically Gifted Edn., Nat. Mid. Sch. Assn., Arkansans Assn. Gifted Adminstrs., Kappa Delta Pi. Office: Vilonia Pub Schs PO Box 160 Vilonia AR 72173-0160

LOMBARDI, GIANCARLO, Italian language educator; b. Rome, Mar. 6, 1965; s. Fernando Lombardi and Maria Luisa Basili. PhD, Cornell U., 1996. Asst. prof. Italian, Smith Coll., Northampton, Mass., 1996-99, CUNY, Staten Island, 1999—. Author: Rooms With a View: Feminist Diary Fiction, 2002; contbr. articles to profl. jours. Mem.: MLA. Office: Coll Staten Island CUNY 2800 Victory Blvd Staten Island NY 10314 E-mail: lombardi@mail.csi.cuny.edu.

LOMBARDI, LINDA CATHERINE, health facility administrator, educator; b. Bronx, N.Y., Apr. 12, 1953; d. Maurice and Catherine (Reidy) L. BA, Herbert H. Lehman Coll., 1975; MA in English, Columbia U., 1976; MA in Psychology, New Sch. for Social Rsch., 1980; MPhil, CUNY, N.Y.C., 1994, PhD, 1995. Assoc. exec. dir. Bellevue Hosp. Ctr., N.Y.C.; assoc. dir. Met. Hosp. Ctr., N.Y.C. Adj. asst. prof. scis. NYU, N.Y.C. Recipient award for tchg. excellence NYU Sch. Continuing Edn., 1995. Mem. AAUW, Nat. Assn. Healthcare Access Mgrs., Crisis Prevention Inst. (cert. instr.), Columbia U. Alumni Assn., New Sch. for Social Rsch. Alumni Assn., Grad. Sch. CUNY Alumni Assn. Office: 462 1st Ave New York NY 10016-9196

LOMBARDO, FREDRIC ALAN, pharmacist, educator; b. New Castle, Pa., May 11, 1948; s. Valentine Frank and Clara Eleanor (Cugini) Lombardo; m. Loretta D. Patts, May 22, 1971; children: Alan John, Lauren Beth, Leslie Anne. BS in Pharmacy, Duquesne U., 1971, PharmD, 1974; MS, Fla. Inst. Tech., 1979. Lic. pharmacist Pa., Va., D.C., Tex., cert. Am. Coll. Clin. Pharmacists. Resident in hosp. pharmacy Mercy Hosp., Pitts., 1973; commd. 2nd lt. U.S. Army, 1974, advanced through grades to lt. col., 1993; chief clin. pharmacy support svc. Brooke Army Med. Ctr., Ft. Sam Houston, Tex., 1980-85; chief outpatient pharmacy svc. Walter Reed Army Med. Ctr., Washington, 1985-86, chief cancer treatment sect., chief hematol.-oncol. pharmacy, 1986-92; resigned active duty entered U.S. Army reserve, 1993; sr. clin. pharmacy supr. Nat. Heart, Lung and Blood Inst., NIH, Bethesda, Md., 1992-95; asst. prof. clin. and adminstrv. pharmacy sci. Howard U., Washington, 1995—, asst. prof. psychiatry Coll. Medicine, assoc. prof. cmty. medicine and family practice; asst. prof. U. Md. Asst. prof. pharmacology Cath. U., Washington, 1995—, H. Lee Med. Sch., USUHS, Bethesda, Md., 1995—; asst. prof. pharmacology Cancer Ctr., Ctr. Sickle Cell Disease Howard U., 1995—, asst. dir. Cancer Ctr., 1997; prof. Found. Advancement Edn. Sci., Grad. Sch. NIH, 1996—; mem. Mid-Atlantic Oncology Adv. Group, Washington, 1997; mem. coun. experts com. Oncologic Diseases USP. Co-host Ask the Pharmacy Doctor program Sta. WRC-980, Washington, 1997—, guest various TV and radio programs. Active Urban Health U., Urban Family Inst., Washington, 1996—97. Lt. col. USAR, 1993—. Grantee Rsch., Ortho-McNeil Pharm., Washington, 1996—97. Fellow: Am. Soc. Cons. Pharmacists; mem.: Nat. Pharm. Assn., Am. Soc. Health Professions, Am. Pharm. Assn. (bd. cert. in pharmacotherapy nutrition support, oncology, psychopharmacology, and geriatrics), KC, Am. Legion. Democrat. Roman Catholic. Avocations: military history, mathematics. Home: 13503 Apple Barrel Ct Herndon VA 20171-4006 Office: Howard Univ Coll Pharmacy and Pharm Sci 2300 4th St NE Washington DC 20002-1220

LOMELI, MARTA, elementary education educator; b. Tijuana, Baja Calif, Mex., Oct. 1952; came to U.S. 1954; d. Jesus and Guadalupe (A.) Lomeli; m. Rudolph Benitez, 1978 (div. 1982); children: Pascual Lomeli Benitez; m. David E. Miller, Aug. 16, 1991. BA, San Diego State U., 1977. With M & N Tree Nursery, Vista, Calif., 1957-70; libr. Vista Boys Club, 1969-70; vol. tutor MECHA U. Calif. San Diego, La Jolla, 1971-73; tchr. aide San Diego City Schs., 1976-77; educator National City (Calif.) Schs., 1978—. Mem. restructuring com. Lincoln Acres Sch., 1991. Author: Cuentos from the House on West Connecticut Avenue. Mem. Lincoln Acres Com. to Advise the Prin., National City, 1986—88, Com. to Advise the Supt., National City, 1986—88; art editor Third World U. Calif., San Diego, 1970—73; mem. Lincoln Acres Sch. Site Coun., 1988—89, 1994—96; mem. high tech. com. Nat. Sch. Dist., 1993—94; vol. tchr. St. Vincent de Paul's Ctr. for Homeless, San Diego, 1991—93, Shaolin Kempo Karate (black belt 2d degree); mem. Paradise Hills Citizens Patrol, 1994—2000; vol. in policing San Diego Police Dept., 1999—; founder, mem. The Learning Club, 1999—2002; mem. MANA spkrs. bur., 1999—. Mem.: Learning Club, Nat. Assn. Bilingual Edn., Calif. Assn. Bilingual Edn. (sec. 1986), Calif. Tchrs. Assn. (site rep. Nat. City 1985), La Raza Club (pres., co-founder 1970), Learning Club (founder). Independent. Avocations: drawing cartoons, Karate, writing. Home: PO Box 880007 San Diego CA 92168-0007

LOMEN, DAVID ORLANDO, mathematician, educator; b. Decorah, Iowa, May 11, 1937; s. Erlin Reuben and Ellen Dorthea (Jensen) L.; m. Constance Sylvia Trecek, Dec. 25, 1961; 1 dau., Catherine Ellen. BA, Luther Coll., 1959; MS, Iowa State U., 1962, PhD, 1964. Rsch. asst. Socony Mobil Rsch. Lab., Duncanville, Tex., summer 1960; design specialist Gen. Dynamics/Convair Co., San Diego, 1963-66; asst. prof. math. U. Ariz., Tucson, 1966-69; assoc. prof., 1969-74, prof., 1974—, univ. disting. prof., 1996--; vis. scientist dept. applied math. and theoretical physics U. Cambridge (Eng.), 1972-1994; vis. scientist Inst. voor Cultuurtechniek en Waterhuishouding, Wageningen, The Netherlands, summer 1978; vis. prof. U. Oslo, 1980; cons. in field. Bd. dirs. Tucson chpt. Cystic Fibrosis Found., 1975-80. Recipient Creative Teaching award U. Ariz. Found., 1978; Marshall Fund Rsch. award Am. Assn., Norway, 1980, 84, Disting. Teaching award Faculty of Sci., 1988, Disting. Svcs. award Luther Coll., 1989, Burlington No. Teaching award, 1989. Mem. Am. Math Soc., Soc. Indsl. and Applied Math., Soil Sci. Soc. Am., Geophys. Union, European Geophys. Soc., Consortium for Math. and Application, Nordmanns Forbundet Club. Lutheran. Research in math. modeling of water flow in soils and developing math. lessons for computer aided instrn. Author: (with others) Calculus, 1992, 94, 98, 2002, (with James Mark) Ordinary Differential Equations with Linear Algebra, 1986, Differential Equations, 1988, (with David Lovelock) Exploring Differential Equations via Graphics and Data, 1996, Differential Equations: Graphics, Models, Data, 1999, (with others) Applied Calculus, 1999, 2003; contbr. numerous articles and rsch. reports to Applied Math. Home: 6945 E Blue Lake Dr Tucson AZ 85715-3216 Office: Math Dept U Ariz Tucson AZ 85721-0001 E-mail: lomen@math.arizona.edu.

LOMON, EARLE LEONARD, physicist, educator, consultant; b. Montreal, Nov. 15, 1930; came to U.S., 1951, naturalized, 1965; s. Harry and Etta (Rappaport) L.; m. Ruth Margaret Jones, Aug. 4, 1951; children: Martha Glynis, Christopher Dylan, Deirdre Naomi. B.Sc., McGill U., Montreal, 1951; PhD, MIT, 1954. NRC Can. overseas research fellow Inst. Theoretical Physics, Copenhagen, 1954-55; fellow Weizmann Inst., Rehovoth, Israel, 1955-56; research assoc. lab. nuclear studies Cornell U., Ithaca, N.Y., 1956-57; assoc. prof. theoretical physics McGill U., Montreal, 1957-60; assoc. prof. physics MIT, Cambridge, 1960-70, prof., 1970-99, prof. emeritus, 1999—; program dir. NSF, 2002—. Vis. staff mem. Los Alamos Nat. Lab., 1968—; project dir. Unified Scis. and Math. for Elem. Schs., Cambridge, 1970-77; adj. prof. U. Louvain-la-Neuve, Belgium, 1980; vis. prof. U. Paris, 1979-80, 86-87, UCLA, 1983, U. Wash., 1985, Nanjing U., 2002; vis. rschr. Kernforschungsanlage Jülich, 1986-92, U. Geneva, 1993, CERN, Geneva, 1994, IPN, Orsay, 1994; Lady Davis vis. prof. Hebrew U., Jerusalem, 1993-94; vis. rschr. U. Tübingen, 1997; vis. fgn. scientist KEK (Tanashi br.), Tokyo, 1999-2000, vis. rschr. and lectr. Nanjing U., 2002. Contbr. articles to profl. jours. Guggenheim Meml. Found. fellow CERN, Geneva, 1965-66; Dupont fellow, 1952-53; Ossabaw Island Project fellow (Ga.), 1978; Sci. Research Council fellow U. London, 1980 Fellow Am. Phys. Soc.; mem. Can. Assn. Physicists Office: MIT 6-302 77 Mass Ave Cambridge MA 02139-4307 E-mail: lomon@mitlns.mit.edu.

LONCHAR, PATRICIA PAULETTE, English educator; b. Greensburg, Pa., Oct. 13, 1944; d. George Michael and Anne Lee (Shirley) Lonchar; m. Michael Wayne Fite, June 21, 1969 (div.). BA, U. St. Thomas, 1967; MEd, U. Houston, 1972; PhD, Tex. A&M U., 1995. Cert. tchr., Tex. English, history tchr. Marian H.S., Bellaire, Tex., 1967-68; English tchr. M.B. Smiley H.S., Houston, 1968-72, Marian H.S., 1972-75; English, social studies tchr. Gilmary Sch. Girls, Coraoplis, Pa., 1975-76; asst. prin. Marian H.S., 1976-78; adminstrv. asst. Tex. Paralyzed Veterans, Houston, 1978; dir. religious edn. St. Elizabeth Ann Seton Ch., Houston, 1979-80; English tchr., counselor Incarnate Word Acad., Houston, 1980-83; prof. English U. Incarnate Word, San Antonio, 1983—, Moody prof. English, 1999-2000; reader Rising Young Writers Nat. Coun. Tchrs. English, 2000—; chair English U. Incarnate Word, 2001—. Evaluator Nat. Exam. Svc., Austin, 1997—. Co-author: Union in Christ, 1974. Oversight rev. com. United Way San Antonio, 1996—. Mem. Nat. Coun. Tchrs. English, Internat. Reading Assn., Coll. Coun. Tchrs. English, Tex. Coun. Tchrs. English, San Antonio Area Coun. Tchrs. English, Phi Kappa Phi, Sigma Tau Delta. Roman Catholic. Avocations: gardening, sewing, photography. Office: U Incarnate Word 4301 Broadway St San Antonio TX 78209-6318

LONDEREE, RAMONA GAYLE, art educator; b. Hammond, Ind., Apr. 22, 1949; d. Virgil Raymond and Emma Ettalene (Ford) Howard; m. William Patrick Londeree, July 6, 1969; children: James William, Kimberly Sarette. BA in Edn., U. Fla., 1971; MA in Edn., U. South Fla., 1981. Cert. art educator; cert. early adolescence through young adulthood/art Nat. Bd. Profl. Tchg. Standards. Tchr. art Jewett Jr. High Sch., Winter Haven, Fla., 1973-84, Winter Haven High Sch., 1984-95, Lake Region High Sch., Eagle Lake, Fla., 1995—. Contbr. photos: Design Standards for Art Facilities. Grantee Fla. Arts for a Complete Edn., 1993-94. Mem. NEA, Nat. Art Edn.

Assn., Fla. Art Edn. Assn., Polk Edn. Assn., Polk Art Edn. Assn. Avocations: reading, painting, gardening. Home: 584 Somerset Dr Auburndale FL 33823-9570 Office: Lake Region HS 1995 Thunder Rd Eagle Lake FL 33839-3086

LONDON, CHARLOTTE ISABELLA, secondary education educator, reading specialist; b. Guyana, S.Am., June 11, 1946; came to U.S., 1966, naturalized, 1980; d. Samuel Alphonso and Diana Dallett (Daniels) Edwards; m. David Timothy London, May 26, 1968 (div. May 1983); children: David Tshombe, Douglas Tshaka. BS, Fort Hays State U., 1971; MS, Pa. State U., 1974, PhD, 1977. Elem. sch. tchr., Guyana, 1962-66; secondary sch. tchr., 1971-72; instr. lang. arts Pa. State U., University Park, 1973-74; reading specialist/ednl. cons. N.Y.C. C.C., 1975; dir. Skills Acquisition and Devel. Ctr. Stockton (N.J.) State Coll., 1975-77; reading specialist Pleasantville (N.J.) Pub. Schs., 1977—, supr. English dept., supr. gifted and talented program, 1999—, supr. world langs., 2002—. Ind. specialist United Nations Devel. Programme, Guyana, 1988—; v.p. Atlantic County PTA, 1980-82; del. N.J. Gov.'s Conf. Future Edn. N.J., 1981; founder, pres. Guyana Assn. Reading and Lang. Devel., 1987. Sec. Atlantic County Minority Polit. Women's Caucus. Mem. Internat. Reading Assn., Nat. Coun. Tchrs. English, ASCD, AAUW, Pi Lambda Theta, Phi Delta Kappa (sec.). Mem. African Meth. Episcopal Ch. Home: 6319 Crocus St Mays Landing NJ 08330-1107 Office: Pleasantville Pub Schs W Decatur Ave Pleasantville NJ 08232

LONDON, DOUGLAS, English educator; b. N.Y.C., May 30, 1952; s. Robert David and Ellin (Naumburg) L.; m. Kathy Ellin Kilroy, June 19, 1977; children: Kevin, Katie, Lindsay, Charlie. BA, Kenyon Coll., 1974; MA, U. Md., 1984, Johns Hopkins U., 1993. Cert. advanced profl., Md. Prin. Bullis Sch., Potomac, Md., 1975-97, coach varsity soccer team, 1978-97; chair English dept. Dawson Sch., Lafayette, Colo., 1998—, coach varsity soccer, dir. summer programs, 1998—, dean of students, 2002—. Home: 228 Wildwood Ln Boulder CO 80304-0400 Office: Alexander Dawson Sch 10455 Dawson Dr Lafayette CO 80026

LONDON, HERBERT IRA, humanities educator, institute executive; b. N.Y.C., Mar. 6, 1939; s. Jack and Esta (Epstein) L.; m. Joy Weinman, Oct. 13, 1942 (div. 1974); children: Staci, Nancy; m. Vicki Pops, Nov. 18, 1950; 1 child, Jaclyn. BA, Columbia U., 1960, MA, 1961; PhD, N.Y. U., 1966; DL, U. Aix.-Marseille, Aix-en-Provence, France, 1982, Grove City Coll., 1993. Teaching fellow N.Y. U., N.Y.C., 1963-64, instr., 1964-65, asst. prof., 1967-68, univ. ombudsman, 1968-69, assoc. prof., 1969-73, prof., 1973—, dean Gallatin div., 1972-92, John M. Olin U. Prof. Humanities, 1992—; instr. New Sch. for Social Research, N.Y.C., 1964-65; research scholar Australian Nat. U., Canberra, Australia, 1966-67; pres. Hudson Inst., 1997—. Bd. overseers Ctr. for Naval Analysis, Washington, 1983-93; trustee Hudson Inst., Indpls., 1979—, research fellow 1974—; sr. fellow Nat. Strategy Info. Ctr. Created TV programs: Myths That Rule America, The American Character; contbr. numerous articles to profl. jours. Bd. dirs., former chmn. Nat. Assn. Scholars, N.Y.C., 1986; bd. advisors Coalition for Strategic Def. Initiative, Washington, 1986; candidate for mayor of N.Y.C., 1989; conservative candidate for gov., N.Y., 1990, 94; candidate for comptroller of N.Y. State, 1994. Named Danforth Assoc., Danford Found., 1971; recipient Anderson award, NYU, 1965, Fulbright award, U.S. Govt., 1966—67, Def. Sci. award, Def. Sci. Jour., 1985, Martin Luther King award, Congress of Racial Equality, 1995, Peter Shaw Meml. award, Exemplary Writing Nat. Assn. Scholars, 1996, Jacques Maritain Humanitarian award, Am. Maritain Assn., 1996, Ellis Island Medal of Honor, 2000, Am. Jewish Congress award, 2001, Libery and Media award, 2002. Mem. Freedom House, Am. Hist. Assn., Edn. Excellence Network, Heritage Found (assoc. scholar 1983—), Ethics and Pub. Policy Ctr. (assoc. scholar 1985—), Nat. Strategy Info. Ctr., Coun. Fgn. Rels. Republican. Jewish. Avocations: writing, tennis. Home: 10 West St New York NY 10004 Office: NYU 113 University Pl New York NY 10003-4527

LONDON, IRVING MYER, physician, educator; b. Malden, Mass., July 24, 1918; s. Jacob A. and Rose (Goldstein) London; m. Huguette Piedzicki, Feb. 27, 1955; children: Robert L.J., David T. B in Jewish Edn., Hebrew Coll., 1938; AB summa cum laude, Harvard U., 1939, MD, 1943; DSc (hon.), U. Chgo., 1966. Sheldon Traveling fellow Harvard U., 1939—41, Delamar research fellow med. sch., 1940—41; intern Presbyn. Hosp., N.Y.C., 1943, asst. resident, 1946—47, asst. physician, 1946—52, assoc. attending physician, 1954—55; Rockefeller fellow in medicine Coll. Physicians and Surgeons, Columbia U., 1946—47; instr. Columbia U., 1947—49; asso. in medicine Coll. Phys. and Surg., Columbia U., 1949—51; asst. prof. Coll. Phys. and Surg., Columbia, 1951—54, assoc. prof., 1954—55; prof., chmn. dept. medicine Albert Einstein Coll. Medicine, N.Y.C., 1955—70, vis. prof. medicine, 1970—; prof. biology MIT, 1969—89, prof. emeritus, 1989—; vis. prof. medicine Harvard Med. Sch., 1969—72, prof. medicine, 1972—89, prof. emeritus, 1989—; dir. div. health scis. and tech. Harvard and MIT, 1969—85, prof. medicine, 1972—, Grover M. Hermann prof. health scis. and tech., 1977—89, prof. emeritus, 1989—; dir. Whitaker Coll. Health Scis., Tech. and Mgmt., MIT, 1978—83; dir. med. service Bronx Mcpl. Hosp. Center, 1955—70. Delta Epsilon lectr. U. Colo., 1962, Harvey lectr., 61; Jacobaeus lectr., Stockholm, 64; vis. scientist Pasteur Inst., Paris, 1962—63; Commonwealth Fund fellow, 1962—63; Alpha Omega Alpha lectr. Yale, Boston U., Columbia, SUNY Downstate Med. Ctr., U. Chgo.; Harry L. Alexander vis. prof. Washington U., St. Louis, 1968; Alpha Omega Alpha vis. prof. Johns Hopkins U., 1970; Eugene A. Stead Jr. vis. lectr. Duke Med. Ctr., 1970; cons. to Surgeon Gen. AUS, 1957—60; chmn. metabolism study sect. USPHS, 1961—63; Med. fellowship bd. NAS, NRC, 1955—64; mem. bd. sci. cons. Sloan Kettering Inst., 1960—72; bd. sci. counselors Nat. Heart Inst., 1964—68; exec. com. Health Rsch. Coun., City N.Y., 1958—63; mem. sci. adv. coun. Pub. Health Rsch. Inst., N.Y.C., 1958—63; mem. adv. com. to dir. NIH, 1966—70, nat. cancer adv. bd., 1972—76; physician Brigham and Women's Hosp., 1972—83, sr. physician, 1983—; chmn. rsch. group Nat. Commn. on Arthritis, 1975—76; chmn. adv. com. Divsn. Health Scis., Inst. Medicine, 1979—82; mem. Bd. Sci. Counselors, NIADDK, 1979—83; bd. dirs., cons. Johnson and Johnson, 1982—89; founder Genetix Pharms., 1996. Assoc. editor: Jour. Clin. Investigation, 1952—57, mem. editl. bd.: Am. Jour. Medicine, 1965—79. Bd. trustees Hebrew Coll., 2000—; bd. dirs. Philippe Found. Capt. U.S. Army, 1944—46. Recipient Bloomfield medal and lectr., Lady Davis Inst., 1986. Fellow: Am. Acad. Arts and Scis., Am. Assn. Advanced Scis. (Theobald Smith award in med. scis. 1953); mem.: NAS (med. bd. medicine 1967—70, founding mem. Inst. Medicine 1970), Assn. Am. Physicians, Internat. Soc. Hematology, Am. Soc. Hematology, Am. Soc. Clin. Investigation (pres. 1963—64), Am. Soc. Biol. Chemists, Alpha Omega Alpha, Phi Beta Kappa. Office: Harvard U-MIT Div Health Scis and Tech 77 Massachusetts Ave Cambridge MA 02139-4301 E-mail: imlondon@mit.edu.

LONDRÉ, FELICIA MAE HARDISON, theater educator; b. Ft. Lewis, Wash., Apr. 1, 1941; d. Felix M. and Priscilla Mae (Graham) Hardison; m. Venne-Richard Londré, Dec. 16, 1967; children: Tristan Graham, Georgianna Rose. BA with high honors, U. Mont., 1962; MA, U. Wash., 1964; PhD, U. Wis., 1969. Asst. prof. U. Wis. at Rock County, Janesville, 1969-75; asst. prof., head theatre program U. Tex. at Dallas, Richardson, 1975-78; assoc. prof. U. Mo., Kansas City, 1978-82, prof. theatre, 1982-87, curators' prof., 1987—; women's chair in humanistic studies Marquette U., 1995. Dramaturg Mo. Repertory Theatre, Kansas City, 1978-2001, Nebr. Shakespeare Festival, 1990—; guest dramaturg Gt. Lakes Theater Festival, 1988; mem. archives task force Folly Theatre, 1982-83; artistic advisor New Directions Theatre Co., 1983-90; hon. lectr. Mid.-Am. State Univs. Assn., 1986-87; mem. U.S.-U.S.S.R. Joint Commn. on Theatre Historiography, 1989; mem.adv. bd. Contemporary World Writers, 1991—; lectr. univs. Budapest, Pecs, Debrecen, Hungary, 1992; vis. prof. Hosei U., Tokyo, 1993; vis. scholar Wabash Coll., 2003. Author: Tennessee Williams, 1979, Tom Stoppard, 1981, Federico Garcia Lorca, 1984, Love's Labour's Lost: Critical Essays, 1997; (play) Miss Millay Was Right, 1982 (John Gassner Meml. Playwriting award 1982), The History of World Theater: From the English Restoration to the Present, 1991 (Choice Outstanding Acad. Book award 1991), Chow Chow Pizza, 1995 (Kansas City Gorilla Theatre First Prize, winner Stages '95 Competition, Dallas); (opera libretto) Duse and D'Annunzio, 1987; (with Daniel J. Watermeier) The History of North American Theater: The United States, Canada, and Mexico from Pre-Columbian Times to the Present, 1998; co-editor: Shakespeare Companies and Festivals: An International Guide, 1995; book rev. editor: Theatre Jour., 1984-86; assoc. editor: Shakespeare Around the Globe: A Guide to Notable Postwar Revivals, 1986; mem. editl. bd. Theatre History Studies, 1981-87, 89—, Studies in Am. Drama, 1945 to the present, 1984-93, 19th Century Theatre Jour., 1984-95, Bookmark Press, Tennessee Williams Rev., 1985-87, Jour. Dramatic Theory and Criticism, 1986—, On-Stage Studies, The Elizabethan Rev., 1992-99, Theatre Symposium, 1994—, The Oxfordian, 1998—, Estreno Contemporary Spanish Plays, 1998—, So. Ill. U. Press Theater in the Americas series, 2000—; contbr. articles to profl. jours. Hon. co-founder, bd. dirs. Heart of Am. Shakespeare Festival, 1991—, v.p., 2000—; bd. dirs. Edgar Snow Meml. Fund, 1993-2002; active UMKC Grad. Coun., 2001—, acad. stds. com. Coll. Arts and Scis., 2001—; elected Nat. Theatre Conf., 2001; sec. Coll. Fellows Am. Theatre, 2001-03.. Fulbright grantee U. Caen, Normandy, France, 1962-63, NEH grantee, 1971, 80, Faculty Rsch. grantee U. Mo., 1985-86, 90-91, tchr. seminar grantee Mo. Humanities Coun., 1993, 96; recipient Disting. Alumni award U. Mont., 1998, winner Amy and Eric Burger Essay on Theatre Competition, U. Wyo., 2003; grad. fellow U. Wis., 1966-67, Trustees fellow U. Kansas City, 1987-88; inductee Coll. Fellows Am. Theatre. Fellow Mid-Am. Theatre Conf. (chair grad. rsch. paper competition 1985); mem. Am. Soc. Theatre Rsch. (exec. com. 1984-90, program chair 1995), Shakespeare Theatre Assn. Am. (sec. 1991-93), Internat. Fedn. for Theatre Rsch. (del. gen. assembly 1985), Am. Theatre Assn. (commn. on theatre rsch. 1981-87, chmn. 1984-86), Theatre Libr. Assn., Dramatists Guild, Literary Mgrs. and Dramaturgs Am., Shakespeare Oxford Soc., Am. Theatre and Drama Soc. (v.p. 1995-97, pres. 1997-99), Nat. League of Am. PEN Women (v.p, 2002—, bd. dirs. Kansas City-Westport br.), Assn. for Theatre in Higher Edn. (v.p. for awards 2001-03, Outstanding Tchr. award 2001), Internat. Al Jolson Soc., Lewis and Clark Heritage Found. Roman Catholic. Avocations: travel, theatre, continental cuisine. Home: 528 E 56th St Kansas City MO 64110-2769 Office: Mo Repertory Theatre Dept Theatre 5100 Rockhill Rd Kansas City MO 64110-2481 Fax: 816-235-6562. Business E-Mail: londref@umkc.edu.

LONERGAN, WALLACE GUNN, economics educator, management consultant; b. Potlatch, Idaho, Mar. 18, 1928; s. Willis Gerald and Lois (Gunn) L.; m. Joan Laurie Penoyer, June 1, 1952; children: Steven Mark, Kevin James. BA, Coll. Idaho, 1950; MBA, U. Chgo., 1955, PhD, 1960. Asst. dir., asst. prof. bus. Indsl. Relations Ctr. U. Chgo., 1960-70, assoc. dir., assoc. prof., 1970-74, dir., prof., 1974-84; vis. prof. Rikkyo U., Tokyo, 1985; vis. fellow Merton Coll. Oxford (Eng.) U., 1986; chair, prof. bus. econs. divsn. Albertson Coll. Idaho, Caldwell, 1987—. V.p. Human Resources Research Cons., Chgo., 1980-87. Author: Leadership and Morale, 1960, Group Leadership, 1974, Performance Appriasal, 1978, Leadership and Management, 1979. Chmn. Episcopal Commn. on Higher Edn., Chgo., 1970-80, mgmt. com. United Way Chgo., 1982-85. 1st lt. U.S. Army, 1950-53, Korea. Named Disting. Alumni Coll. Idaho, 1962; vis. scholar Internat. Anglican Exchange, N.Y.C., 1976, Tokyo, 1986. Mem. Internat. House Japan, Internat. Indsl. Relations Research Assn., Acad. Mgmt., Rotary. Avocations: power walking, hiking. Home: 812 E Linden St Caldwell ID 83605-5335 Office: Albertson Coll Idaho Bus Econs Divsn 2112 Cleveland Blvd Caldwell ID 83605-4432

LONG, ANDRE EDWIN, law educator, lawyer; b. San Francisco, Dec. 28, 1957; s. Edwin John and Anna (Suss) L.; m. Michele Jean Dubinsky, Oct. 4, 1986; children: Christian Andre, Katrina Marie. BA, U. Pacific, 1979; MBA, Golden Gate U., 1981; JD, Southwestern U., 1982. Bar: Hawaii 1984, D.C. 1990, Wash. 2001, U.S. Ct. Appeals (9th cir.) 1984. Legal counsel Pure Water, Ltd., Manama, Bahrain, 1982-84; pvt. practice Honolulu, 1984-85; sr. contracts negotiator Litton Data Systems Corp., Van Nuys, Calif., 1985-87; contracts mgr. Eaton, Am. Nucleonics Corp., Westlake Village, Calif., 1987-92; owner, broker A. Long Realty, Ridgecrest, Calif., 1989—; asst. prof. contract law Air Force Inst. Tech., Dayton, 1992-99; assoc. counsel Navy Office of Gen. Counsel, China Lake, 1999—. Lectr. Tech. Tng. Corp., 1991-92; instr. Oxnard Coll., 1990-92, George Washington U. Law Sch./ESI Govt. Contract Law Program; asst. adj. prof. Embry-Riddle U. Author: U.S. Immigration and Visa Laws Made Simple, 1985, 2d edit., 1991, Government Contract Law, 1995, 96, 98, 99, Negotiating Government Contracts, 1996; editor The Clause, 1995-2000, Contract Mgmt. Jour., 1998-2000; contract mgmt. editor Jour. Pub. Procurement.. Fellow Nat. Contract Mgmt. Assn. (pres. China Lake chpt. 2001-02, bd. dirs.); mem. Hawaii Bar Assn., D.C. Bar Assn., Aircraft Owners and Pilots Assn., Bd. Contracts Appeals Bar Assn. (chmn. publs. com. 1995-2000, bd. govs. 1997-2000), Canyon Ranch Assn. (chmn. 2000—). Avocations: scuba diving, snow skiing, sailing, flying. Office: NAWCWD Code 111000D 1 Administration Cir Ridgecrest CA 93555 E-mail: andre.long@navy.mil.

LONG, ANTHONY ARTHUR, classics educator; b. Manchester, Eng., Aug. 17, 1937; came to U.S. 1983; s. Tom Arthur and Phyllis Joan (LeGrice) L.; m. Janice Calloway, Dec. 30, 1960 (div. 1969); 1 child, Stephen Arthur; m. Mary Kay Flavell, May 25, 1970 (div. 1990); 1 child, Rebecca Jane; m. Monique Marie-Jeanne Elias, Mar. 22, 1997. BA, U. Coll. London, 1960; PhD, U. London, 1964. Lectr. classics U. Otago, Dunedin, N.Z., 1961-64; lectr. classics U. Nottingham, Eng., 1964-66; lectr. Greek and Latin U. Coll. London, 1966-71; reader in Greek and Latin U. London, 1971-73; Gladstone prof. Greek U. Liverpool, Eng., 1973-83; prof. classics U. Calif., Berkeley, 1982—; pub. orator U. Liverpool, Eng., 1981-83; Irving Stone prof. lit. U. Calif., Berkeley, 1991—, chmn. dept. classics, 1986-90. Mem. Inst. Advanced Study, Princeton, N.J., 1970, 79; vis. prof. U. Munich, 1973, Ecole Normale Supérieure, Paris, 1993, 2001; Cardinal Mercier prof. philosophy U. Louvain, Belgium, 1991; Belle van Zuylen prof. philosophy, U. Utvecht, Netherlands. mem. Mellon Fellowships Selection Com., 1984-90; mem. selection com. Stanford U. Humanities Coun., 1985-86; Corbett lectr. U. Cambridge, 1998-99; Faculty Rsch. lectr. U. Calif., Berkeley, 1999-2000; Breckenbridge prof., U. Tex., San Antonio, 2003. Breckenridge lectr., U. Tex., San Antonio, 2003. Author: Language and Thought in Sophocles, 1968 (Cromer Greek prize 1968), Problems in Stoicism, 1971, 96, Hellenistic Philosophy, 1974, 2d edit., 1986, (with Fortenbaugh and Huby) Theophrastus of Eresus, 1985, (with Sedley) The Hellenistic Philosophers, 1987, (with Dillon) The Question of Eclecticism, 1988, 96, (with Bastianini) Hierocles, 1992, (with others) Images and Ideologies, 1993, Stoic Studies, 1996, 2d edit., 2001, Cambridge Companion to Early Greek Philosophy, 1999, Epictetus, 2002; editor: Classical Quar., 1975-81, Classical Antiquity, 1987-90; gen. editor: (with Barnes) Clarendon Later Ancient Philosophers, 1987—. Served to lt. Royal Arty., Eng., 1955-57 Named hon. citizen City of Rhodes, Greece; sr. fellow humanities coun. Princeton U., 1978, short-term fellow, 2002, Bye fellow Robinson Coll., Cambridge, 1982, Guggenheim fellow, 1986-87, sr. fellow Ctr. for Hellenic Studies, 1988-93, fellow NEH, 1990-91, Wissenschaftskolleg fellow, Berlin, 1991-92, William Evans fellow U. Otago, New Zealand, 1995. Fellow Am. Acad. Arts and Scis., Brit. Acad. (corr.); mem. Classical Assn., Aristotelian Soc., Am. Philol. Assn., Phi Beta Kappa (hon.). Avocations: music, walking, travel, bridge. Home: 32 Sunset Dr Kensington CA 94707-1139 Office: U Calif Dept Classics Berkeley CA 94720-0001 E-mail: aalong@uclink4.berkeley.edu.

LONG, ASHLEY DIANE, finance educator, technology educator; b. Dallas, Tex., June 2, 1970; d. Mary Margaret Dodd, Lavon Couch Dodd, Jr.; m. Michael Graham Long; children: Tyler Graham, Shelby Jordan. BS in Sociology, East Tex. State U., 1995. Registered finl. rep. 1997, cert. tchr. Tex., 2001, spl. edn. tchr. Tex. Finl. sales asst. Lehman Brothers, Dallas, 1996—2000; dir. spl. edn. dept. Aubrey Indep. Sch. Dist., Aubrey, 2000—02; educator bus. and tech., UIL coach Archer City ISD, 2002—. Instr. Nat. Cheerleaders Assn., 1988—92, cheerleader coach, 2000—01. Baptist. Office: 600 S Ash St Archer City TX 76351 E-mail: ashley.long@esc9.net.

LONG, CARL FERDINAND, engineering educator; b. N.Y.C., Aug. 6, 1928; s. Carl and Marie Victoria (Wellnitz) L.; m. Joanna Margarida Tavares, July 23, 1955; children: Carl Ferdinand, Barbara Anne. S.B., MIT, 1950, S.M., 1952; D.Eng., Yale U., 1964; A.M. (hon.), Dartmouth Coll., 1971. Registered profl. engr., N.H. Instr. Thayer Sch. Engring., Dartmouth Coll., Hanover, N.H., 1954-57, asst. prof., 1957-64, assoc. prof., 1964-70, prof., 1970-94, assoc. dean, 1970, dean, 1972-84, dean emeritus, 1984—; prof. emeritus, 1994—; dir. Cook Design Ctr. Thayer Sch. Engring., Dartmouth Coll., 1984-94. Engr. Western Electric Co., Alaska, 1956-57; v.p. ops., dir. Controlled Enivronment, 1975-81; pres., dir. Q-S Oxygern Processes, Inc., 1979-84; N.H. Water Supply and Pollution Control Com., U.S. Army Small Arms Systems Agy.; mem. New Eng. Constrn. Edn. Adv. Coun., 1971-74; mem. adv. com. U.S. Patenta and Trademark Office, 1975-79; mem. ad hoc vis. com. Engrs. Coun. for Profl. Devel., 1973-81; pres., dir. Roan of Thayer, Inc., 1986-93; bd. dirs. Micro Tool Co., Inc., Micro Weighing Systems, Inc., 1986-91, Roan Ventures, Inc., 1987-91; pres., dir. Hanover Water Works Co., 1989-97. Mem. Hanover Town Planning Bd., 1963-75, chmn., 1966-74; trustee Mt. Washington Obs., 1975-92; bd. dirs. Eastman Community Assn., 1977-80; mem. corp. Mary Hitchcock Meml. Hosp., 1974—. NSF Sci. Faculty fellow, 1961-62; recipient Robert Fletcher award Thayer Sch. of Engring., 1985, Fellow Members awd., Am. Soc. for Engineering Education, 1992. Fellow AAAS, ASCE, Am. Soc. Engring. Edn. (chmn. New Eng. sect. 1977-78, chmn. council of sects. Zone 1, dir. 1981-83); mem. Sigma Xi, Chi Epsilon, Tau Beta Pi. Republican. Baptist. Home: 25 Reservoir Rd Hanover NH 03755-1311

LONG, CHARLES THOMAS, lawyer, history educator; b. Denver, Dec. 19, 1942; s. Charles Joseph and Jessie Elizabeth (Squire) L.; m. Susan Rae Kircheis, Aug. 9, 1967; children: Brian Christopher, Lara Elizabeth, Kevin Charles. BA, Dartmouth Coll., 1965; JD cum laude, Harvard U., 1970. Bar: Calif. 1971, U.S. Dist. Ct. (cen. dist.) Calif. 1971, U.S. Ct. Appeals (9th cir.) 1975, D.C. 1980, U.S. Dist. Ct. D.C. 1981, U.S. Ct. Claims 1995. Assoc. Gibson, Dunn & Crutcher, Los Angeles, 1970-77, ptnr., 1977-79, Washington, 1979-83; dep. gen. counsel Fed. Home Loan Bank Bd., Washington, 1984-85; ptnr. Jones, Day, Reavis & Pogue, Washington, 1985-98; grad. tchg. asst. hist. dept. George Washington U., 1998—. Bar: Calif. 1971, U.S. Dist. Ct. (ctrl. dist.) Calif. 1971, U.S. Ct. Appeals (9th cir.) 1975, D.C. 1980, U.S. Dist. Ct. 1981, U.S. Ct. Fed. Claims 1995. Contbr. articles to profl. jours. Mem. Chesapeake Bay Maritime Mus., Friends of the Nat. Maritime Mus., Greenwich, Eng.; pres. Leigh Mill Meadows Assn., Great Falls, Va., 1980. Served to lt. USNR, 1965-67. Mem. ABA, Calif. Bar Assn., D.C. Bar Assn., Coun. for Excellence in Govt., Women in Housing and Fin., Dartmouth Lawyers Assn., Herrington Harbour Sailing Assn. (sec.-treas. 1996), Soc. for Mil. History, N.Am. Conf. on Brit. Studies, Navy Records Soc. (London), U.S. Naval Inst., Orgn. Am. Historians, Omohundro Inst. Early Am. History and Culture, Chesapeake Bay Maritime Mus., Friends of the Nat. Maritime Mus. (Greenwich, Eng.), Westwood Country Club (Vienna, Va.), Am. Hist. Assn.. Republican. Methodist. Avocations: sailing, photography, computers, naval history.

LONG, DAVID RUSSELL, academic program director; b. Worcester, Mass., Feb. 12, 1942; s. Wendell Russell and Eleanor May (Ohlund) L.; children: Daphne Ruth Evdokia, Payson David Cheslov. BA, Emerson Coll., 1965; MS in Ednl. Communication, U. Albany, 1970, MS in Ednl. Adminstrn., 1977. TV producer-dir. U. Albany, N.Y., 1968-69, dir. audio-visual svc., 1969—. Pres., cons. Media Assocs., Scotia, N.Y., 1982—; asst. to dir. White Funeral Home, Scotia, 1982—. Creator slide programs for fire chiefs, police, children's mus.; author: (videotape) Children's Participation Play (selected for inclusion in Libr. of Congress). Fin. sec., mem. pub. rels com. Scotia Fire Dept., 1975-85, commr., 1985-88; bd. dir. Scotia-Glenville Children's Mus., 1980-84, Schenectady Acess Cable Coun., 1980-84. With U.S. Army, 1966-67, Vietnam. Recipient Chancellor's award for excellence in profl. svc. U. Albany, 1982. Mem. Capital Dist. Media Assn., Hudson-Mohawk Vol. Fireman's Assn., Glenville Fire Fighters Assn. (pub. rels. com. 1978-86). Republican. Methodist. Avocations: walking, swimming, reading, travel, exercise. Home: 144 Van Aernem Rd Ballston Spa NY 12020-3800 Office: U Albany 1400 Washington Ave Albany NY 12222 E-mail: drl14@albany.edu.

LONG, EARLINE DAVIS, elementary education educator; b. Chgo., Mar. 31, 1944; d. Augustus (step father) and Eddie Virginia (Long) Grant; children: Tommie A. Grant, Virginia C. Sears. BS in Edn., Chgo. State U., 1971, MA in Adminstrn., 1983. Cert. tchr., adminstr., Ill. Electronic order writer Spiegels, Chgo., 1962-65; sr. clk. Chgo. Police Dept., 1966-72; tchr. Chgo. Bd. Edn., 1972—. Consulting tchr. Teachers' Union, Chgo., 1990-92; continuing edn. courses in computer literacy, alcohol and drug edn., improving tchr. effectiveness, immersion week-end in Spanish. Home: 9608 S Eggleston Ave Chicago IL 60628-1106

LONG, ELLEN JOYCE, accounting/business educator; b. Clarence, Mo., Apr. 28, 1938; d. Paul L. and Phoebe M. (Hill) Baker; m. Everett Lee Long, June 10, 1961; children: Paula Dawn, Laura Ruth, Jay Douglas. BS, U. Mo., 1960, MS in Bus. Edn., 1963; MS in Acctg., U. Wis., 1986. Bus. edn. tchr. Warren County R-111, Warrentown, Mo., 1960-62, Sturgeon (Mo.) Sch. Dist. No-RV, 1962-64; staff acct. Virchow Krause & Co., Whitewater, Wis., 1987; cost acct. Albert Trostel Packing, Ltd., Lake Geneva, Wis., 1988; sec.-treas. BL Farms, Inc., Whitewater, 1982—. Lectr. U. Wis., Whitewater, 1965-92, mem. cultural affairs com., 1991—. Pres., treas., bd. dirs., newsletter editor Cmty. of Christ Ch., 1986-2003; bd. dirs. Habitat for Humanity; chair devel. com. City of Whitewater, 1994-2002, v.p. 1995-96. Mem. Wis. Inst. CPAs, PEO (pres., v.p., newsletter editor), LWV, Delta Pi Epsilon (v.p. 1980, corr. sec. 1979), Phi Kappa Phi. Avocations: cross country skiing, collecting, cookbooks, aerobic dancing. Home: 1259 W Satinwood Ln Whitewater WI 53190-1601

LONG, HARVEY SHENK, retired computer educational consultant; b. Cornwall, Pa., May 14, 1933; s. Harvey I. L.; m. Constance Mareen Root, June 14, 1956; children: Bradford, Dean, Jody. BS in Edn., Millersville State Tchrs. Coll, 1955; MS in Math., Carnegie Inst. Tech., 1957; PhD in Math. Edn., NYU, 1969. Tech. pioneer of the 20th cent. 1999. Assoc. adv. engr. IBM, Poughkeepsie, N.Y., 1957-70, sr. adminstr. San Jose, 1971, White Plains, N.Y., 1971-72; edn. systems cons. DiscoVision Assocs., Washington, 1979-82, IBM, Washington, 1972-79, edn. applications cons. Boca Raton, Fla., 1982-85, edn. cons. Washington, 1985-92, ret. Cons. Am. Fedn. Tchrs., Washington, 1992-95, Tech. in Edn., 1992—; faculty George Mason U. Grad. Sch., 1990-95, Montgomery Coll., 1996-2000. Contbr. to books and articles to profl. jours. Pres. Somers (N.Y.) PTA, 1973, Music Assn., Rockville, Md., 1976-80. Assn. Devel. Computer Based Inst. fellow, 1986 Fellow Am. Tomorrow. Avocations: gardening, walking, model building, bridge. Home: 11025 Rosemont Dr Rockville MD 20852-3650

LONG, JOHN MADISON, elementary music educator; b. Brookhaven, Miss., Nov. 26, 1964; s. Troy Maxwell and Anna Lee (Madison) L.; m. Sheryl Ann Rogers, Dec. 16, 1995. MusB, East Tex. Bapt. U., 1988. Tchr. Roosevelt Elem. Sch., West Palm Beach, Fla., 1988—. Mem. curriculum com. Sch. Dist. Palm Beach County, West Palm Beach, 1988-89; instrnl. innovation team Roosevelt Elem. Sch., West Palm Beach, 1992—, vice-chmn. sch. adv. coun., 1994—, chmn. tech. team, 1993—; grant writer. Author: (tech. plan) RESTECH, 1993; designer, implementor: Tech Tools for Our School, 1993. Republican. Baptist. Avocations: travel, music, science fiction, disney memorabilia. Home: 1475 Forest Hill Blvd Apt 5 West Palm Beach FL 33406-6030 Office: Roosevelt Elem Sch 1220 15th St West Palm Beach FL 33401-2498

LONG, KENNETH MAYNARD, chemistry educator; b. Nappanee, Ind., July 10, 1932; s. G. Maurice and Mabel A. (Bechtel) L.; m. Nancy Y. Long, Aug. 27, 1952; children: Gregory, Steven, Jeffrey, Kristen, Kevin. BS, Goshen Coll., 1954; MAT, Mich. State U., 1960; PhD, Ohio State U., 1967. Tchr. Bethel Springs Sch., Culp, Ark., 1954-56, Lakeshore H.S., Stevensville, Mich., 1956-61; rsch. asst. Whirlpool Corp., St. Joseph, Mich., 1961; instr. Westminster Coll., New Wilmington, Pa., 1962-65, asst. prof., 1967-70, assoc. prof., 1970-79, prof., 1979—2002, chair chemistry, 1983-99, asst. dean, 1971-75, prof. emeritus. Bd. overseers Goshen (Ind.) Coll., 1972-81; vis. scholar Northeastern U., Shenyang, China, 1988-89. Contbr. articles to profl. jours. Mem. Am. Chem. Soc., Nat. Speleological Soc., Nat. Assn. Geosci. Edn., Field Conf. Pa. Geologists. Mennonite. Avocations: geology, caving, hiking, gardening. Office: Dept Chemistry Westminster Coll New Wilmington PA 16172-0001 Home: 5897 Parfet Ct. Arvada CO 80004-4748 E-mail: longkm@westminster.edu.

LONG, KIM MARTIN, language and literature educator; b. Denton, Tex., Oct. 23, 1955; d. William Matheson Martin and Wando Jo (Foster) Sparks; m. Mark Dale Mayo, Aug. 13, 1977 (div. June 1987); children: Scott, Bryan, Kyle; m. David Harrison Long, Feb. 14, 1988. BA in English, U. North Tex., Denton, 1978, MA in English, 1986, PhD in English, 1993. Cert. secondary English and history tchr. Tchr. Irving (Tex.) Ind. Sch. Dist., 1978-90; instr. North Lake Coll., Irving, 1992-93; teaching fellow U. North Tex., Denton, 1990-93; instr. Tex. Woman's U., Denton, 1991-94, U. Tex.-Dallas, Richardson, 1992-94; tchr. Nimitz H.S. Irving Ind. Sch. Dist., 1993—95; assoc. prof. English Shippensburg (Pa.) U. Author: American Eve, 1993. Mem. MLA, Am. Lit. Assn., Coll. English Assn., Melville Soc., Poe Soc., Nat. Coun. Tchrs. English, Multi-Ethnic Lits. of U.S. (treas.) Democrat. Home: 217 E King St Shippensburg PA 17257-1426 Office: 1871 Old MainDr Shippensburg PA 17257 E-mail: kmlong@ship.edu.

LONG, LELAND TIMOTHY, geophysicist educator, seismologist; b. Auburn, N.Y., Sept. 6, 1940; s. Walter K. and Carmalita Rose Long; m. Sarah Alice Blackard, Mar. 1970; children: Sarah Alice, Katherine Rose, Amy Virginia. BS in Geology, U. Rochester, 1962; MS in Geophysics, N.Mex. Inst. Mining and Tech., 1964; PhD in Geophysics, Oreg. State U., 1968. Registered profl. geologist, Ga. From asst. to assoc. prof. Sch. Earth and Atmosphere Scis. Ga. Inst. Tech., Atlanta, 1968-81, prof., 1981. Cons. in seismology, near-surface seismic imaging, seismic road vibrations, blast vibrations and gravity data analysis. Contbr. articles to profl. jours. Office: Ga Inst Tech Earth And Atmospheric Scis Atlanta GA 30332-0340 E-mail: tim.long@eas.gatech.edu.

LONG, LEVITHA OWENS, special education educator; b. Washington, Aug. 5, 1951; d. Otha and Lola Mary (Robinson) Owens; m. Johnnie Edward Long, Aug. 22, 1987 (div.); 1 child, Owen Edward Robinson; m. James P. Lowery, Jr., Oct. 10, 1999. BS, Va. State U., 1980; MA, U. D.C., 1983. Tchr., adminstrv. asst. Friendship House Inc., Washington, 1980-82; spl. edn. educator Prince George's County (Md.) Pub. Sch., 1982-84, Davis Elem. Sch., Washington, 1984-86, Weatherless Elem. Sch., Washington, 1986-92, co-chmn. gifted and talented com., 1989-92; spl. edn. educator Ketcham Elem. Sch., Washington, 1992-95, Roper Middle Sch. of Science and Math Technology; coord. spelling bee Ketcham Elem. Sch., Washington, 1992-94, chairperson music/drama club; spl. edn. educator Charles Hart Mid. Sch., Washington, 1996—. Sponsor Hart's Young Ladies Club, 1997-98, Best Friends Mentor. Dir. summer program Girl Scouts Am., Washington, 1985-93; mem. voter registration com. Prince George's County, 1991-94, voter registration ward 7 Rylan-Epworth Civiv Assn., Washington, 1977-85; mem. polit. action com., Kaypark Civic Assn., Sutland, Md., 1985—. Mem. ASCD, Coun. for Exceptional Children, Black Child Devel. Inst., Va. State U. Alumni Assn. (chair 1991-93), Va. State U. Alumni Assn. (chair scholarship fundraising), Alpha Kappa Alpha (co-chair 1985-87, cotillion co-chair). Democrat. Methodist. Avocations: piano, gardening. Home: 2846 Fort Baker Dr SE Washington DC 20020-7220 Office: Charles Hart Mid Sch 601 Mississippi Ave SE Washington DC 20032-3899

LONG, LINDA SUE, special education educator; b. Marshall, Mo., Oct. 14, 1947; d. Thomas Arnet and Helen Louise (Ray) Meads; m. Robert Earl Long, Aug. 7, 1999; 1 child from previous marriage, Lisa Susanne Meads Casey. Student, Mo. Valley Coll., Marshall, Mo., 1966-67; AA, Longview C.C., Lee's Summit, Mo., 1987; BS in Edn. cum laude, Cen. Mo. State U., Warrensburg, 1990; MS in Edn., 1996. Technician AT&T, Lee's Summit, Mo., 1969-87; tchr. spl. edn. Lee's Summit Sch. Dist., 1990, Midway Sch. Dist., Cleveland, Mo., 1990—. Dist. coord. HIV/AIDS edn. Midway Sch. Dist.; guest speaker on the impact of HIV/AIDs on families. Recipient Crystal Apple award for excellence in teaching, 1995. Mem. Coun. Exceptional Children, Learning Disabilities Assn., Kappa Delta Pi, Phi Kappa Phi. Home: 5613 NW Hutson Rd Kansas City MO 64151-2831 Office: Midway Sch Dist Cleveland MO 64734

LONG, MARK CHRISTOPHER, English educator; b. LaJolla, Calif., Nov. 30, 1959; s. Wendell Oliver and Mary Ellen (Ricketts) L.; m. Rebecca Elizabeth Todd, Sept. 10, 1994; children: Nathaniel Carroll Todd Long, Ellinore Ruth Todd Long. BA, Ithaca (N.Y.) Coll., 1990; MA, U. Wash., 1992, PhD, 1996. Profl. ski instr., back-country guide Profl. Ski Instrs. of Am., Calif., 1980-86; tchg. asst. U. Wash., Seattle, 1991-96, asst. dir. writing ctr., 1992-93, asst. dir. expository writing program, 1993-95, acting instr. dept. English, 1996-98; asst. prof. English and Am. studies Keene State Coll., NH, 1998—2002, assoc. prof. English and Am. studies, 2003—, chair dept. English, 2003—. Author: U.S. Marine Corps Ski Instruction Manual, 1994; contbr. articles to profl. jours. Mem. MLA, Nat. Coun. Tchrs. English, Assn. for Study of Lit. and the Environment, Phi Alpha Theta, Phi Kappa Phi. Democrat. Unitarian Universalist. Avocations: nordic skiing, climbing, sea kayaking, wilderness travel. Home: 123 Coyote Canyon Rd PO Box 12 Chesterfield NH 03443-0012 Office: Keene State Coll Dept English Keene NH 03435-1402 E-mail: mlong@keene.edu.

LONG, PATRICIA GAVIGAN, elementary education educator, English language educator; b. Bryn Mawr, Pa., Mar. 5, 1942; d. Thomas and Martha Mary Gavigan; m. James Robert III, Nov. 22, 1978; children: Jon Rhys Long, Martha Lucille Long. AA, AssumptionColl., Mendham, N.J., 1964; BS in Elem. Edn., St. Joseph's Coll., Phila., 1970; MEd, Pa. State. U., 1975. Cert. Tchr. grades 1-7, mid. sch., 6-8. Reading Specialist, K-12, Pa., Va. Grade 2 tchr. St. Nicholas Elem. Sch., Jersey City, N.J., 1962-64; grade 1 and 2 tchr. St. Lawrence Elem. Sch., Harrisburg, Pa., 1964-66, Holy Trinity Elem. Sch., Hazelton, Pa., 1966-68; grade 3 tchr. St. Margaret's Elem. Sch., Narberth, Pa., 1968-75; reading resource tchr. K-5 Arrowhead Elem. Sch., Virginia Beach, Va., 1975-84; reading tchr. grade 8-9 Stonewall Jackson Jr. High, Mechanicsville, Va., 1984-89; grade 6 tchr., chair English dept. Stonewall Jackson Middle Sch., Mechanicsville, Va., 1989—2003; ret., 2003. Mem. PTA Stonewall Jackson Middle Sch. (reflection chair), Richmond Area reading Coun., Va. State Reading Coun., Hanover Edn. Assn. Va. Edn. Assn., NEA, Richmond Area English Coun., Va. Area Tchr. of English, Arrowhead PTA Bd. (life.). Republican. Roman Catholic. Avocations: reading, walking, wallpapering, painting, helping others. Office: Stonewall Jackson Mid Sch Lee Davis Rd Mechanicsville VA 23111-4699

LONG, RUSSELL CHARLES, academic administrator; b. Alpine, Tex., Oct. 9, 1942; s. Roy Joel and Lovis Lorene (Graham) L.; m. Elaine Gresham, May 8, 1964 (div. Jan. 1986); 1 child, Mark Roy; m. Natrelle Hedrick, Mar. 28, 1986. BS, Sul Ross State U., Alpine, 1965; MA, N.Mex. State U., 1967; PhD, Tex. A&M U., 1977. Assoc. prof. Schreiner Coll., Kerrville, Tex., 1967-69; instr. Tarleton State U., Stephenville, Tex., 1969-72, asst. prof., 1972-77, assoc. prof., 1977-85, prof., 1985-92, asst. v.p. acad. adminstrn., 1987-90, chair dept. English and Lang., 1990-92; provost and v.p. acad. adminstrn. West Tex. A&M U., Canyon, 1992-94, interim pres., 1994-95, pres., 1995—. Office: West Texas A&M Univ Wt Sta 2501 4th Ave Canyon TX 79016-0001 E-mail: rlong@mail.wtamu.edu.

LONG, SHERI SPAINE, foreign language educator; b. Waterloo, Iowa, Dec. 2, 1958; d. Richard Clifton Jr. and Dorothea Knarr Spaine; m. John A. Long, May 24, 1980; children: Morgan Taylor, John Richard. BA in Spanish, U. Iowa, 1980, MA in Spanish, 1983; PhD in Hispanic Langs. and Lit., UCLA, 1990. Asst. prof. Spanish Samford U., Birmingham, 1991-92, U. Ala., Birmingham, 1993-98, assoc. prof. Spanish, 1998—2002, chair dept. of fgn. lang. and lit., 2003—. Pres. bd. dirs. Children's Dance Found., Birmingham, 1998—2000; acad. dir. Nat. Collegiate Honors Coun. Spain Semester, Alcalá, 2000; assoc. bd. dirs. Nat. Mus. Langs., 2001—; appointee task force profl. devel. New Visions in Fgn. Langs. Project, 2001—. Co-author: En train d'écrire, 1993, Redacción y revisión, 1993, Hacia la literatura, 1998. Global adv. Concordia Lang. Villages, Minn., 1997—; mem. exec. coun. Am. Coun. Tchg. Fgn. Langs., 2003—. Mem. MLA, Am. Coun. on the Tchg. of Fgn. Langs. (exec. coun. 2003) Am. Assn. Tchrs. Spanish and Portuguese (recipient Mead grant 2002), Ala. Assn. Fgn. Lang. Tchrs. (pres. 1998-99, Outstanding Fgn. Lang. Tchr. award 2000), Ala. Assn. Tchrs. Spanish and Portuguese (pres. 1994), Lang. Tchr. award 1999). Democrat. Episcopalian. Office: U Ala Birmingham Dept Fgn Langs Birmingham AL 35294-0001 E-mail: espanol@uab.edu.

LONG, STEPHEN JAMES, clergyman; b. Johnstown, Pa., July 14, 1948; s. Harry Ross Long and Mary Jane (Thomas) Horner; m. Cinda Ann Peck, May 25, 1974; children: Matthew J., Nathaniel J. Diploma, Buffalo Bible Inst., West Seneca, N.Y., 1970; BS, Houghton Coll., 1971; MRE summa cum laude, Grand Rapids Bapt. Theol. Sem., 1976; postgrad., Temple Bapt. Sem., Chattanooga, 1988—. Ordained to ministry Bapt. Ch., 1973. Draftsman Gen. Tel. Co., Johnstown, 1966-67; pastor Christian edn. Emmanuel Bapt. Ch., Johnstown, 1971-73; min. Christian edn., assoc. pastor North Syracuse (N.Y.) Bapt. Ch., 1976—. Seminar leader Walk through Bible Ministries, Atlanta, 1988—; dir. Ministry Devel. Inst., North Syracuse, 1990—; mem. adv. bd. youth div. Syracuse Rescue Mission Alliance, 1992—. Contbr. articles to profl. jours. Recipient Christian Edn. cert. Evang. Tchr. Tng. Assn., 1971, cert. of achievement Walk through Bible Ministries, 1988. Mem. ASCD, Profl. Assn. Christian Educators, Greater Syracuse Dirs. Christian Edn. (pres. 1985-87), Christian Svc. Brigade (Herald of Christ award 1968), Syracuse U. Libr. Assocs. Republican. Avocations: backpacking, running, collecting civil war relics and autographs, rare books and bibles. Office: North Syracuse Bapt Ch 420 S Main St North Syracuse NY 13212-2861

LONG, THOMAS LAWRENCE, English educator; b. Washington, Jan. 29, 1953; s. Thomas Lawrence Sr. and Lucy Ann (McVey) L. BA in English, Cath. U. Am., 1975, MA in Theology, 1981; MA in English, U. Ill., 1977; PhD in English, Indiana U. of Pa., 1997. Pastoral intern Cath. Diocese Richmond, Va., 1977-81, pastor, 1981-88; from asst. prof. to full prof. English Thomas Nelson C.C., Hampton, Va., 1989—, full prof. English, 2000—, head English dept., 2000—. Chairperson Cath. Comm., Richmond, 1981-87; pres. Writing Program Assocs., Norfolk, 1991-93; vis. prof., Coll. of William & Mary, 1999-2000. Author: Let the Children Come to Me, 1988, AIDS and American Apocalypticism, 2003; prodr., dir. (video) Voyagers to a New World, 1985, writer, prodr. (theater performance) Our Kind, 1977; editor: Harrington Gay Men's Fiction Quar., 2000—. Sec. Lesbian and Gay Pride Coalition, Norfolk, Va., 1989-93, pres., 1993-94; mem. Virginians for Justice, Richmond, 1990—; bd. mem., adv. coun. Tidewater AIDS Taskforce, Norfolk, 1994—. Mem. ASTD, Modern Lang. Assn., Nat. Coun. Tchrs. English, Assn. Tchrs. Tech. Writing, Modern Lang. Assn./Gay Caucus. Avocations: travel, cooking, gardening, music. Office: Thomas Nelson CC PO Box 9407 Hampton VA 23670-0407 E-mail: longt@tncc.vccs.edu.

LONG, WILLIAM MCMURRAY, physiology educator; b. Greenville, S.C., Nov. 9, 1948; s. William McMurray and Cecile Mae (Ariail) L.; m. Kathleen Webb, Mar. 18, 1971 (dec. Oct. 1990); m. Marianne Castrén, July 22, 1992. BA, Tulane U., 1970, BS, 1974; PhD, La. State U., 1980. Rsch. assoc. Med. Ctr. La. State U., New Orleans, 1974-75; pathology extern Charity Hosp. of La., New Orleans, 1975-80; Nat. Rsch. Svc. Award fellow Pa. State Med. Ctr., Hershey, 1980-82; rsch. assoc. Mt. Sinai Med. Ctr., Miami Beach, Fla., 1983-89; rsch. physiologist VA Med. Ctr., Miami, Fla., 1982-89; asst. prof. medicine U. Miami, 1982-89; asst. prof. physiology U. N.D., Grand Forks, 1989-94; CFO OBI Lab. Co., 1994-2000, dir., 2000—. Cons. VA Med. Ctr., Miami, 1991; ad hoc reviewer Am. Jour. Physiology, Bethesda, Md., 1990-91, Va. Ctrl. Office, 1987-90; dir. Minority Access to Rsch. Careers, U. N.D., Ah'jo'gun to the Baccalaureate. Author: Non-Steriodal Agents in Sepsis Syndrom, 1989, (with others) Airways: Asthma, Bronchietasis and Emphysema, 1992; contbr. articles to profl. jours. Chmn. Nat. Letter-In Com., New Orleans, 1968, Cliff Solar Fund, New Orleans, 1973; cood. Spring Jazz Festival, New Orleans, 1970. Recipient Rsch. award Bush Found., 1990, Nat. Rsch. Svc. award NIH, 1980-82; grantee NIH, 1986-89, Fla. Lung Assn., 1984-85, VA, 1986-90, Am. Heart Assn. Dakota affiliate, 1991-93, Nat. Inst. Gen. Med. Scis., 1992—. Mem. Am. Physiol. Soc., Am. Thoracic Soc., N.Y. Acad. Scis., Da Vinci Soc. (sec. 1987-88). Achievements include research in modification of cardiac proteolysis with amino acid methyl esters, in inefficacy of steroids in treatment of septic shock syndrome, in differentiation of histamine effects on bronchial flow and bronchomotor tone, on protein profiles in differentiating mechanisms of pulmonary edema, in role of bronchial blood flow in allergic airway disease and pharmacologic modification of that response; establishment of research and science education program for minorities and statewide tribal colleges; differential accumulation in brain of radon daughters in Alzheimer's Disease and Parkinson Disease. Home: 1339 Clara Brown Rd Prosperity SC 29127 Office: OBI Labs 1339A Clara Brown Rd PO Box 718 Prosperity SC 29127-0718

LONGACRE, LINDA S. school administrator; b. Sommerset, Ky., Aug. 1, 1948; d. Quentin and Nell (Hoyle) Cooper; m. John D. Longacre, Dec. 18, 1971. BA, U. South Fla., 1971; MA, U. West Fla., 1984. Cert. tchr., adminstr., Fla. Tchr. Hillsborough Dist. Schs., Tampa, Fla., 1971-72, Escambia Dist. Schs., Pensacola, Fla., 1973-74, 78-89, West Bath Sch. Dist., Bath, Maine, 1975-78; prin. Pensacola Beach Elem. Sch., Gulf Breeze, Fla., 1989—. Trainer Onward to Excellence sch. improvement model Northwest Regional Ednl. Lab., Portland, Oreg., 1991—. Mem. Community Drug and Alcohol Commn., Pensacola, 1990. Mem. ASCD, Nat. Assn. Elem. Sch. Prins., Escambia Edn. Assn., Alpha Delta Kappa. Democrat. Avocations: reading, fabric painting, calligraphy, snorkeling. Office: Pensacola Beach Elem Sch 900 Via De Luna Dr Pensacola Beach FL 32561-2262

LONGAN, SUZANNE M. retired elementary school educator; b. San Francisco, June 8, 1936; d. Walter Emerson Murfee and Ferne Inez Nelson; m. George B. Longan III, Aug. 27, 1958 (div. June 7, 1965); 1 child, Nancy Ann. BA with distinction, U. Ariz., 1958; postgrad., Calif. State U., 1987—89. Elem. sch. tchr. Johnson County Sch. Dist., Leawood, Kans., 1958—60; corp. sec., CEO Villa Chartier-Lanai, Inc., San Mateo, Calif., 1965—84. Dir. San Mateo County Hotel and Restaurant Assn., 1971—79. Treas. Pre-Sch. for the Visually Handicapped, Kans. City, Mo., 1961—62, chmn. advisory bd., 1963—65; div. chmn. Heart of Am. United Campaign, Kans. City, 1962; chair sch. solicitation Johnson County (Kans.) United Funds, 1963; mem. adv. bd. Children's Mercy Hosp., Kans. City, 1963—65; treas. Music in the Mountains, Nev. City, Calif., 1986—90; mem. bd. trustees Foothill Theatre Co., Nev. City, Calif., 1990—92; treas. Nev. County Land Trust, Nev. City, 1995—97; mem. Emmanuel Episc. Ch. Choir, Grass Valley, Calif., 1981—91; treas., CFO Emmanuel Episc. Ch., Grass Valley, Calif., 1988—91; mem. bd. dirs. Twin Cities Concert Assn., Grass Valley, 1984—86. Named Vol. Nurse Aide, Am. Red Cross, 1964, Concessionaire Extraordinaire, Foothill Theatre Co., 1986—87, Master Gardener, U. Calif., 1990; recipient Cmty. Svc. award, United Funds Coun., Inc., 1963. Mem.: Jr. League, Gamma Phi Beta. Republican. Episcopalian. Avocations: gardening, wildlife habitat maintenance. Home: 13350 Wildwood Heights Dr Penn Valley CA 95946

LONGANECKER, DAVID A. educational association administrator; BA in Sociology, Wash. State U., 1968; MA in Student Personnel Work, George Washington U., 1971; EdD in Adminstrn. and Policy Analysis in Higher Edn., Stanford U., 1978. With student affairs and residence life dept. George Washington U., Washington; with Congl. Budget Office, Washington, 1977-81, Minn. Higher Edn. Coordinating Bd., 1981-84, exec. dir., 1984-88; exec. dir., exec. dir. dept. higher edn., officer Gov. Roy Romer's cabinet Colo. Commn. Higher Edn., 1988-93; asst. sec. postsecondary edn. U.S. Dept. Edn., Washington, 1993—99; exec. dir. Western Interstate Commn. Higher Edn., Boulder, Colo., 2000—. Past. pres. State Higher Edn. Exec. Officers orgn.; commr. We. Interstate Commn. Higher Edn.; mem. postsecondary edn. and tng. for workplace com. Nat. Acad. Scis., commn. on ednl. credit and credentials Am. Coun. Edn.; mem. various bds. and coms. including Exec. Com. Minority Edn. Coalition Colo., Gov.'s Commn. Families and Children, Math., Sci. and Tech. Commn. Office: Western Interstate Commission Higher Edn PO Box 9752 Boulder CO 80301-9752*

LONGHENRY, JOHN CHARLES, social studies educator, human resources specialis; b. Rockford, Ill., Oct. 27, 1948; s. Helen Janice (Weingartner) Willfong; m. Carol Ann Carroll, Dec. 18, 1971; 1 child, Ethan R. AA, Rock Valley Coll., 1972; BA, No. Ill. U., 1976; MBA, Rockford Coll., 1993. Cert. human resources specialist. Major assembler Chrysler Corp., Belvidere, Ill., 1969-75; social studies tchr. Belvidere H.S., 1975-76, Rockford Luth. H.S., 1977-79; sales/human resources Sundstrand Corp., Rockford, 1979-92; world/U.S. history/govt. tchr. Rockford Auburn H.S., 1992—. Class of 1995 advisor Auburn H.S., 1992-95, co-sponsor Key Club, 1993-03, Jr. Engring. Tech. Soc. coach, 1993-94, class of 2000 advisor; capital fund drive bd. dirs. Barbara Olson Sch. of Hope, Rockford, 1989. Exec. bd. mem.-at-large Blackhawk Area coun. Boy Scouts Am., Rockford, 1988-95, chmn. Nat. Eagle Scout Assn., 1985-88, cubmaster Pack 21, 1988-92, scoutmaster troop 21, 1994-98, commr. dist. and unit, 1977-85, mem. com., 1998-03. Served with U.S. Army, 1967-69, Vietnam. Recipient Disting. Svc. award Jaycees, 1982, Silver Wreath award Nat. Eagle Scout Assn., 1983, Silver Beaver award Boy Scouts Am, 1997, Caring to Challenge award Ill. Math Sci. Acad., 2003, numerous other awards. Mem.: NEA, World History Assn. Presbyterian. Avocations: visiting civil war battlefields, reading, photography, travel. Office: Auburn HS 5110 Auburn St Rockford IL 61101-2402

LONGMAN, ANNE STRICKLAND, special education educator, consultant; b. Metuchen, N.J., Sept. 17, 1924; d. Charles Hodges and Grace Anna (Moss) Eldridge; m. Henry Richard Strickland, June 22, 1946 (dec. 1960); m. Donald Rufus Longman, Jan. 20, 1979 (dec. 1987); children: James C., Robert H. BA in Bus. Adminstrn., Mich. State U., 1945; teaching credentials, U. Calif., Berkeley, 1959; postgrad., Stanford U., 1959-60; MA in Learning Hand, Santa Clara U., 1974. Lic. educator. Exptl. test engr. Pratt & Whitney Aircraft, East Hartford, Conn., 1945-47; indsl. engr. Marchant Calculators, Emeryville, Calif., 1957-58; with pub. rels. Homesmith, Palo Alto, Calif., 1959-62; cons. Right to Read Program, Calif., 1978-79; monitor, reviewer State of Calif., Sacramento, 1976-79; tchr. diagnosis edn. Cabrillo Coll., Aptos, Calif., 1970-79; lectr. edn. U. Calif., Santa Cruz, 1970-79; cons. Santa Cruz Bd. Edn., 1970-79; reading rschr. Gorilla Found., Woodside, Calif., 1982—. Bd. mem. Western Inst. Alcoholic Studies, L.A., 1972-73; chmn. Evaluation Com., Tri-County, Calif., 1974; speaker Internat. Congress Learning Disabilities, Seattle, 1974; ednl. cons. rsch. on allergies, 1993—. Author: Word Patterns in English, 1974-92, Cramming 3D Kids, 1975—, 50 books for migrant students, 1970-79; contbr. articles on stress and alcoholism and TV crime prevention for police, 1960-79. Founder Literacy Ctr., Santa Cruz, 1968-092; leader Girl Scouts U.S.A., San Francisco, 1947-50; vol. Thursday's Child, Santa Cruz, 1976-79, Golden Gate Kindergarten, San Francisco, 1947-57; vol. Yosemite Nat. Pk. Recipient Fellowships Pratt & Whitney Aircraft, 1944, Stanford U., 1959. Mem. Internat. Reading Assn. (pres. Santa Cruz 1975), Santa Clara Valley Watercolor Soc., Los Altos Art Club (v.p. 1992), Eichler Swim and Tennis Club. Republican. Episcopalian. Avocations: drawing, watercolor, watercolor painting, travel, drama. Home and Office: 651 Sinex Ave #J211 Pacific Grove CA 93950

LONG-MIDDLETON, ELLEN, family nurse practitioner, educator, researcher; b. Danville, Pa., June 14, 1954; d. Samuel Murray and Dorothy Morgan (Wasley) Long; m. Jeffrey Long-Middleton, Sept. 5, 1981; children: Matthew, Andrew, Douglas, Samuel. BS, U. Vt., 1976; MN, U. Wash., 1982; PhD, Boston Coll., 2001. Cert. family nurse practitioner. Nurse practitioner emergency dept. Hosp. of U. Pa., Phila., 1985—88, nursing dir. admission evaluation ctr., 1988—90; nursing dir. family practice Family Health Svcs., Worcester, Mass., 1990—94; family nurse practitioner U. Mass. Meml. Health Care, 1990—2001; instr. Boston Coll., 1994-98; project co-dir. MassHealth Workforce Devel. Project U. Mass. Med. Sch., 1998—2001; nursing fellow Children's Hosp. of Boston, 1999—2000; asst. prof., coord. family nurse practitioner specialty Mass. Gen. Hosp. Inst. Health Professions, 2001—; family nurse practitioner Family Health Ctr. of Worcester, 2002—. Lectr. U. Pa., 1985-89 Recipient Nat. Rsch. Svc. award Nat. Inst. Nursing Rsch., 1997-2000. Mem. Sigma Theta Tau. E-mail: elongmiddleton@mghihp.edu.

LONGSTREET, WILMA S. curriculum and instruction educator; b. N.Y.C., July 3, 1935; d. Hyman Steinberg and Estelle Rosa; widowed; stepchildren: Patricia, Robert, Richard Engle. BA, Hunter Coll., 1956; MS, Ind. U., 1968, PhD, 1970. Cert. tchr., N.Y.C. Asst. prof. U. Ill., Champaign/Urbana, 1970-72; from assoc. prof. to prof. edn. U. Mich., Flint and Ann Arbor, 1972-78; dean, prof. edn. DePaul U., Chgo., 1978-82; dean edn. U. New Orleans, 1982-85, prof. curriculum and instrn., 1982—. Mem. Coll. and Univ. Faculty Assembly, 1970—, pres., 1999; cons. to sch. sys., Gary, Ind., Flint, Mich., New Orleans, State of Ind. Author: Aspects of Ethnicity, 1978, The Leaders and the Led, 1979; co-author: A Design for Social Education, 1972, (with Shirley H. Engle) Curriculum for a New Millennium, 1993; contbr. over 70 articles to profl. jours. Mem. Profs. of Curriculum (factotum, chair nominating com. 2001), Phi Delta Kappa. Democrat. Unitarian-Universalist. Home: 49 Gull St New Orleans LA 70148 Office: U New Orleans Coll Edn New Orleans LA 70148 E-mail: wlongstr@uno.edu.

LONIGAN, PAUL RAYMOND, language professional, educator; b. New York, May 27, 1935; s. William Raymond Maloy and Irene Rita (Hickman) Lonigan; m. Cynthia Ann (Hartley), June 5, 1965; children: Jennifer, Cynthia. BA(hon.), Queens Coll., N.Y., 1960; PhD, Johns Hopkins U., 1967. Instr. Russell Sage Coll., Troy, NY, 1963-65; assoc. prof. State Univ. of N.Y., Oswego, NY, 1963-65, Queens Coll., City Univ. of N.Y. Grad. Ctr., N.Y.C., 1967-83, prof., 1983—, dep. exec. officer PhD program in French, 1969-72, coord. French program, 1982-85, 91-96. Author: Gormont et Isembart, 1976; Chrétien's Yvain, 1978; The Early Irish Church, 1989; The Druids, 1996; editor: Respuetas del Corazón by Maria Carreño; contbg.

editor: Oidhreacht. Sponsor Le Cercle Français. Served in U.S. Marine Corps, 1954-62. Decorated chevalier L'Ordre Des Palmes Académiques (France), Internat. Order of Merit; recipient Commemorative medal of Honor. Mem. Phi Beta Kappa, and Delta Phi Alpha (Commemorative Medal Hon. award). Avocations: numismatics, philately, writing poetry, hunting, fishing. Office: Queens Coll King 207 6530 Kissena Blvd Flushing NY 11367

LOO, MARCUS HSIEU-HONG, urologist, physician, educator; b. N.Y.C., Aug. 12, 1955; s. David Wei and Patricia (Pai) L.; m. Donna C. Wingshee, Oct. 3, 1987; children: Christopher, Courtney. BSEE with distinction, Cornell U., 1977, MD, 1981. Diplomate Am. Bd. Urology. Asst. attending urologist N.Y. Hosp.-Cornell Med. Ctr., N.Y.C., 1988—; clin. asst. prof. urology Cornell U. Med. Coll., N.Y.C., 1994-2000, clin. assoc. prof. urology, 2000—. Admissions com. Cornell U. Med. Coll.; mem. univ. coun. Cornell U.; mem. operating bd. Columbia Cornell Care, LLC.; cons. Chinatown Health Cilnic; clin. dir. Asian Am. Cancer Awareness Rsch. and Tng. grant. Author: The Prostate Cancer Source Book, 1998. Mem. oper. bd. Columbia Cornell Care L.L.C.; mem. Univ. Coun. Cornell U., 2002—, trustee, 2003—. Fellow: ACS; mem.: IEEE, AMA, Fedn. Chinese Am. and Chinese Can. Med. Socs. (bd. dirs., v.p.), Chinese Am. Med. Soc. (pres., bd. dirs. 1990—97), Soc. Internat. d'Urologie, Am. Urological Assn., Am. Assn. Clin. Urologists, Cornell U. Med. Coll. Alumni Assn. (bd. dirs.), Tau Beta Pi, Phi Tau Phi, Eta Kappa Nu. Office: 58 A East 7955 New York NY 10021-4941

LOOCKERMAN, WILLIAM DELMER, educational administrator, retired; b. Phila., Feb. 24, 1939; s. William Delmer and Kathleen (Cullen) L.; m. Alice Clara Winnemore, June 9, 1962; 1 child, Alice B. BS in Health and Phys. Edn., West Chester (Pa.) State U., 1962, MS in Health and Phys. Edn., 1967; EdD in Phys. Edn., Temple U., 1970; cert. sch. dist. adminstr., Niagara U., 1974. Tchr. Upper Darby (Pa.) Schs., 1965-68; teaching assoc. Temple U., Phila., 1968-70; asst. prof. SUNY, Buffalo, 1970-73; dir. health, phys. edn. and recreation Orchard Park (N.Y.) Cen. Schs., 1973-81; registered sch. bus. adminstr. Springville (N.Y.) Griffith Inst. Cen. Sch. Dist., 1981-2001, ret., 2001, adminstr. emeritus, 2001—. Adj. asst. prof. Niagara U., Niagara Falls, NY, 1975—77; adj. prof. Canisius Coll., Buffalo, 1979—81; statewide rep. Group 491 Ins. Safety Program, Albany, NY, 1983—2001, trustee, 1991—2001, mem. exec. com., 1991—2001, chair, 1996—2001; spkr. local, state, nat. and internat. meetings. Contbr. articles to profl. jours. Capt. USNR ret. Recipient spl. honor award N.Y. State Coaches Assn., 1980, honor award N.Y. State Assn. Health, Phys. Edn. and Recreation, 1979, conf. dedication, 1980. Mem. Internat. Assn. Sch. Bus. Ofcls. (mem. choir 1989—, song leader Opening Gen. Session 1997, appreciation award 1990, 94), N.Y. State Sch. Bus. Ofcls. (chpt. exec. com. 1983-85), AMVETS, Naval Order U.S. (chpt. comdr. 1987-96, 2000-2001, companion to gen. coun. 1997-99), Naval Res. Assn. (chpt. pres., nat. budget/fin. com. 1995—, nat. v.p. 1997-99, 2001—, treas. 1999-2001, mem. nat. adv. com . 1987—, Nat. award of Merit 2001), Am. Legion; mem. WNY Armed Forces Week com. 1980—), Springville Cmty. Choir 1997. Republican. Episcopalian. Avocation: woodworking. Home: 7643 Lewis Rd Holland NY 14080-9625

LOOMIS, REBECCA C. psychology educator; b. New London, Conn., Nov. 9, 1959; d. Aubrey Kingsley and Marillyn Louise (Dirks) Loomis; m. DeWitt Montgomery Smith, Nov. 24, 1984 (div. Sept. 1997); children: Adrienne Kingsley Smith, Walker Loomis Smith. BA in Sociology and Polit. Sci., Vanderbilt U., 1981; MEd, U. Houston, 1990, student, 1993—. Group rep. Home Life Ins., Houston, 1981—83; sr. account exec. CNA Ins. Co., Houston, 1983—87; rsch. asst. dept. ednl. psychology U. Houston, 1988—90, 1991—93, tchg. asst., 1993, rsch. asst. Clearwater, Tex., 1993, rsch. assoc., 1999—; acad. advisor Montclair (N.J.) State U., 2001—02; psychology intern Assn. Help of Retarded Children, N.Y.C., 2002—03, clinician, 2003—. Group facilitator children div. parents, counselor Houston Child Guidance, 1990; counselor learning support svcs. U. Houston, 1990, counselor counseling and testing svcs., 1994—95; facilitator mentorship program Wildwood Elem. Sch., Mountain Lakes, NJ, 1996. Contbr. articles to various profl. jours. Hospice aid Casa de Ninos Hospice, Houston, 1986—87; vol. Houston Area Women's Ctr., 1992—93, 1994—95; cmty. aid Mountain Lakes, 1999—; vol. organizer grief workshop for September 11, 2001 attacks Cmty. Ch. Mem.: APA, N.J. Psychol. Assn. Democrat. Home and Office: 82 Briarcliff Rd Mountain Lakes NJ 07046 E-mail: beckyloomis@earthlink.net.

LOONEY, JOANN MARIE, learning disabilities consultant, educator; b. N.Y.C., Mar. 18, 1954; d. Jack A. and Ann (Shaw) Lowney; m. Dennis M. Looney, Nov. 19, 1977; children: Matthew, Kathryn. BA, Rosemont (Pa.) Coll., 1976; MEd, William Paterson Coll., 1979; postgrad., Seton Hall U., 1989—. Tchr. grade 2 Holy Rosary Sch., Edgewater, N.J., 1978-79; tchr. grades 4 and 5 Mt. Carmel Sch., Tenafly, N.J., 1979-83; pvt. practice Maywood, N.J., 1984—; co-dir. religious edn. program Our Lady Queen of Peace Parish, Maywood, 1988-89. Instr. Felician Coll., Lodi, N.J., 1988—. Mem. N.J. Assn. Tchr. Educators, N.J. Round Table of Tchr. Educators, N.J. Assn. Learning Cons., Coun. for Exceptional Children, Assn. Suprs. Curriculum Devel., Coun. Learning Disabilities, Pi Lambda Theta, Kappa Delta Pi. Office: Felician Coll 262 S Main St Lodi NJ 07644-2117

LOOSE, VICKY DIANNE, special education educator; b. Bethesda, Md., Dec. 22, 1953; d. Josiah Arthur and Frances Maxine (Richeson) L. BS in Health and Phys. Edn., East Carolina U., 1977, MEd in Adapted Phys. Edn., 1983, MEd in Spl. Edn., 1985. Cert. tchr., N.C. Tchr. health, phys. edn. Craven County Schs., Havelock, N.C., 1978-80; adapted phys. edn. specialist O'Berry Ctr. Mentally Retarded/Devel. Disabled Facility, Goldsboro, N.C., 1980-82, asst. coord. therapeutic recreation, 1982-84, outreach svc. specialist, 1984-85; rsdl. srs. coord. Wake County Mentally Retarded/Devel. Disabled Svcs., Raleigh, 1985-88; devel. disabled specialist Wilson-Green Mentally Retarded/Devel. Disabled Svcs., N.C., 1988-89; crisis tchr. Wilson County Schs., 1989-90, tchr. behavioral emotionally handicapped, 1990-92; program dir. Adolescent Partial Hosp. Program, Wilson, 1992—; tchr. behavioral emotional handicapped Johnston County Schs., 1994-95; program svcs. dir. QDDP/QMAP Health Svcs. Personnel, 1995-97. Ednl. cons. Nash-Wilson-Wake-Green county schs., 1988—; faculty Wake-Nash-Wilson Tech. Coll., 1988—; tutor Wilson County schs., 1990—; cons. Health Svcs. Personnel. Author counseling game: Word Up, 1989. Named Tchr. of the Yr. Wilson County Schs., 1991. Mem. NCABA, CEC, NCCCBD, Phi Kappa Phi. Avocations: running, biking, camping, hiking, reading. Home: 4514 Virginia Rd Wilson NC 27893-8541 Office: North Johnston Mid Sch Micro NC 27555

LOPARDO, SUSAN JOAN, special education educator; b. Flushing, N.Y., Dec. 29, 1948; d. Patrick Sylvester and Virginia Lulu (Kleber) Hannigan; m. Bruce Edward Powers, June 19, 1971 (div. Feb. 1981); children: Michelle, Danielle. BS, U. Conn., 1970; postgrad., U. Western Conn., 1970-71, 71-74. Tchr. Wassaic (N.Y.) Devel. Ctr., 1970-74; rehab. asst. Harlem Valley Psychiat. Ctr., Wingdale, N.Y., 1983-85; tchr. Webutuck Ctrl. Sch., Amenia, N.Y., 1985—. Tchr. adult edn. BOCES, Salt Point, N.Y., 1987-94; instruction coord. Webutuck Ctrl. Sch., Amenia, N.Y., 1994-96, network systems operator, 1994-98, Webutuck tech. com., 1995—; mem. adv. bd. Ednl. Products Svcs., 1999, 2000. Pres. Gaylordsville (Conn.) Fire Dept. Aux., 1978-81, Gaylordsville Civic Assn., 1981-83; treas. Webutuck Tchrs. Assn., 1994, bldg. rep., 1987-94. Mem. Nat. Learning Differences Network, Danbury Music Ctr., Webutuck Tchrs. Assn. (v.p. 1999—). Roman Catholic. Avocations: bowling, crafts. Home: 26 Poplar Ln Wassaic NY 12592-9710 Office: Webutuck Elem Sch Haight Rd Amenia NY 12501

LOPER, CARL RICHARD, JR., metallurgical engineer, educator; b. Wauwatosa, Wis., July 3, 1932; s. Carl Richard S. and Valberg (Sundby) Loper; m. Jane Louise Loehning, June 30, 1956; children: Cynthia Louise Loper Koch, Anne Elizabeth. BS in Metall. Engring., U. Wis., 1955, MS in Metall. Engring., 1958, PhD in Metall. Engring., 1961; postgrad., U. Mich., 1960. Metall. engr. Pelton Steel Casting Co., Milw., 1955-56; instr., rsch. assoc. U. Wis., Madison, 1956-61, asst. prof., 1961-64, assoc. prof., 1964-68, prof. metall. engring., 1968-88, prof. materials sci. and engring., 1988-2001, ret. prof. materials sci. and engring., 2001, assoc. chmn. dept. metall. and mineral engring., 1979-82; pres. CRL Corp., 1979—. Rsch. metallurgist Allis Chalmers, Milw., 1961; adj. prof. materials U. Wis., Milw., 2002—; cons., lectr. in field. Author: (book) Principles of Metal Casting, 1965; contbr. articles to profl. jours. Chmn. 25 Anniversary Ductile Iron Symposium, Montreal, Canada, 1973; pres. Ygdrasil Lit. Soc., 1989—90. Recipient Adams Meml. award, Am. Welding Soc., 1963, Howard F. Taylor award, 1967, Svc. citation, 1969, 1972, others, Silver medal award, Sci. Merit Portuguese Foundry Assn., 1978, medal, Chinese Foundrymen's Assn., 1989, E.J. Walsh Award, 2002; fellow Foundry Ednl. Found., 1953—55, Wheelbrator Corp., 1960, Ford Found., 1960. Fellow: AIM, Am. Soc. Metals (chmn. 1969—70); mem.: Tau Beta Pi, Foundry Ednl. Found. (E.J. Walsh award 2002), Korean Inst. Metals and Materials (hon.), Am. Welding Soc., Am. Foundrymen's Soc. (bd. dirs. 1967-70, 76-79, Foundry Ednl. Found. dirs. award 1994, Best Paper award 1966, 67, 85, John A. Penton gold medal 1972, Hoyt Meml. lectr. 1992, Aluminum Divsn. award sci. merit 1995), Blackhawk Country Club, Torske Klubben (bd. dirs., co-founder 1978—, Foundry Hall of Honor 2001), Gamma Alpha, Alpha Sigma Mu, Sigma Xi. Lutheran. Achievements include significant contributions to understanding the solidifcation and metallurgy of ferrous and non-ferrous alloys; recognized authority of solidification and cast iron metallurgy, and on education in metallurgy and materials science. Office: U Wis Cast Metals Lab 1509 University Ave Madison WI 53706-1538 E-mail: loper@engr.wisc.edu.

LOPER, GEORGE WILSON, JR., physical education educator; b. Phila., Sept. 1, 1927; s. George Wilson Sr. and Emma Margaretta (Davis) L.; m. Eleanor Ruth Shell, mar. 10, 1951 (div. Aug. 1967); children: George Wilson III, Carol Ann Loper Cloud; m. Jeanne Ann Lodeski, Aug. 12, 1967; children: Lynn Jeanne Loper Sakers, Anne Marie Loper Todd, John Vincent. BS, W. Chester State U., 1954; MEd, Temple U., 1957. Cert. tchr. Fla. Tchr., coach Media (Pa.) Pub. Schs., 1954-63, Duval County Sch. System, Jacksonville, Fla., 1963-67; tchr., dept. chmn., coach Bradford County Sch. System, Starke, Fla., from 1967. Dir. March Dimes Walkathon, Starke, 1970; coord. Spl. Olympics, Starke, 1970-89; chmn. Adminstrv. Bd. First Meth. Ch., Starke, 1970; co-chmn. Toys for Tots USMC, Starke, 1976, 78. With USMC Res., 1945-87. Named Coach of Yr. Fla. Times Union, 1966, 67, Coach of Yr. Cross Country Gainesville Sun, 1985, 86; recipient Lifetime Achievement award Govs. Coun. on Phys. Fitness and Sports, 1997, Award Hartwell Conklin Golden South Classic, 1997. Mem. AAHPERD (life), NEA, Nat. Health Assn. (life), Nat. High Sch. Coaches Assn., Fla. Athletic Coaches Assn. (state vice chmn. 1972—, Meritorious Svc. awrd 1988, Nat. Boys Track Coach of Yr. 1991, Life Membership award 1992), The Athletic Congress (lead instr. 1987—, internat. level track ofcl. 1983—, Track Hall of Fame 1987), Fla. Ofcls. Assn. (high sch. games com. 1964—, state vice chmn. track 1972—), Bradford Edn. Assn. (v.p. 1977-79) Democrat. Methodist. Avocations: reading, music, art, swimming and track officiating. Home: Starke, Fla. Died Sept. 18, 2000.

LOPER, LINDA SUE, special collections librarian; b. Wakefield, R.I., Jan. 28, 1945; d. Delmas Field and Dora Belle (Hanna) Sneed; children: Matthew Lee Mathany, Amanda Virginia Mathany Van DerHeyden, Morgan Lynnclare Loper. BA, Peabody Coll., Nashville, 1966, MLS, 1979; EdD in Ednl. Adminstrn., Vanderbilt U., Nashville, 1988. Tchr. Parkway Sch., Chesterfield, Mo., 1966-68, Charlotte Mecklenburg Schs., Charlotte, N.C., 1968-71; dir. city libr. Jackson George Regional Libr. System, Pascagoula, Miss., 1979-82; media ctr. specialist Pascagoula Mcpl. Sch. Dist., 1982-83, Moore County Sch. System, Lynchburg, Tenn., 1983-91; ref. libr. Motlow State C.C., Tullahoma, Tenn., 1983-85; dir. learning resource ctr. Columbia (Tenn.) State C.C., 1991-99; CEO Grant Seekers, Inc., 1996-99; CEO Loper Literary Agy., 1999—2001; accounts svcs. mgr. E.B. Stephens Co. (EBSCO), 1999-2001; spl. collections divsn. mgr. Nashville Pub. Libr., 2001—. Presenter TLA Ann. Conv., Knoxville, 1998, Am. Assn. Women in C.C.s Regional Conf., 1997, LEAP State Dept. Edn. Conf. for Libr., Chattanooga; career ladder participant Tenn. Edn. Dept. Level II; TIM trainer Dept. Edn., Nashville; exec. dir. Tenn. Bd. of Regents Media Consortium, 1993-96; chair profl. staff orgn. Columbia State C.C., 1998-99; presenter, judge 6th Ann. Cumberland Writers Conf., Cookeville, Tenn. Author: Bibliography for Tennessee Commission on Status of Women, 1979; contbr. article to profl jour. Pres. Moore County Friends of Libr., Lynchburg, Tenn., 1991; bd. dirs. Moore County Hist. and Geneal. Soc., Lynchburg, 1991; mem. Tenn. Bicentennial Com., Giles County, 1996; co-dir. So. Tapestry, a Bicentennial oral history project; sec., mem. exec. bd. Hope Ho. Domestic Violence Shelter, 1993—96, mem. adv. bd., 1996—99; mem. steering com. Bus., Industry, Edn. Partnership, 1994—99. Recipient Gov.'s Acad. award State Dept. of Edn., U. Tenn., 1988, Inst. for Writing Tenn. History, U. Tenn., 1990, Gov.'s Conf. on Info. Sci., Nashville, 1990. Mem. ASCD, ALA, S.E. Libr. Assn., Tenn. Libr. Assn. (co-chair strategic planning com. 1996-99), TENNSHARE (chair collection devel. com. 1996-99), Moore County Edn. Assn. (treas., chair tchrs. study coun., chair polit. action commn. 1989-91), Giles County Edn. Found. UDC, DAR (historian), Tenn. Acad. Libr. Collaborative (exec. coun. 1996-99), Phi Delta Kappa, Beta Phi Mu, Delta Kappa Gamma. Democrat. Episcopalian. Avocations: french hand sewing, crosstitch, sewing, reading, gardening. Office: Nashville Pub Libr Spl Collections Divsn 615 Church St Nashville TN 37219 E-mail: sue.loper@nashville.gov.

LOPER, LUCIA ANN, retired elementary school educator; b. Albany, Ga., Nov. 11, 1937; d. Andrew and Elizabeth Francis (Bacon) Wurst; m. Leo Gerald Loper (div. Oct. 1984); children: Valecia Ann, Sheri Lee. MusB, Wesleyan Coll., Macon, Ga., 1959. Lic. tchr. music edn. elem., high sch., Fla. Music tchr. Mil. Trail Sch., Palm Beach County Bd., West Palm Beach, Fla., 1959, Cen. Elem. Instrn. Sch., Palm Beach County Bd., West Palm Beach, 1961-65, Jupiter (Fla.) Elem. Sch., Palm Beach County Bd., 1966-70, Eisenhower Elem. Sch., Palm Beach County Bd., Lake Park, Fla., 1970-95, ret., 1995. Gen. chmn. Devel. of Opera for Schs. with Opera Lyrica, West Palm Beach, 1961-62; co-chmn. North County Music in Our Schs. Performance, Lake Worth, Fla., 1984. Active Music Team for Devel Palm Beach County Music Unified Curriculum, 1984, Palm Beach County Arts Council, 1975-76. Recipient Spotlight award Fla. Music Dir. mag., 1986. Mem. Music Educators Nat. Conf., Fla. Elem. Music Educators Assn. (hostess workshop Tampa), Palm Beach County Elem. Music Educators Assn., Am. Orff Schulwerk Assn., Sigma Alpha Iota. Republican. Home: PO Box 571 Jupiter FL 33468-0571

LOPES, MYRA AMELIA, writer; b. Nantucket, Mass., July 9, 1931; d. Leo Joseph and Mary Ellen (Moriarty) Powers; m. Curtis Linwood Lopes, June 25, 1955; children: Dennis, Sherry, Kathy, Curtis, Becky. BS, Bridgewater, 1954; diploma, Inst. Children's Lit., 1982, N.Y. Inst. Journalism, 1984. Cert. elem. educator Mass. Tchr. Fairhaven (Mass.) Sch. Sys., 1954-58; prin. Sheri Ka Kindergarten, Fairhaven, 1960-76; tchr. Oxford Sch., 1977—78, tchr. Title I, 1978—80; writer, 1984—. Author: (novels) Look Around You, 1990, Looking Back, 1991, Seeing It All, 1992, But Then There Was More, 1993, (book) Captain Joshua Slocum: A Centennial Tribute, 1994, Captain Slocum's Life Before and After the Spray, 1997, The Rogers Legacy, 1997, The Castle on the Hill, 1998, My Town, 1999, (documentary) Joshua Slocum: New World Columbus, 2001, Around the Kitchen Table, 2002, Architectural Treasures from the Rogers Mansion: The Michell House, 2002, Pa's Magic Pillow, 2003. Bd. dirs. Fairhaven Improvement Assn., 1986—, chair membership, 1986—96, pres., 1990—93; bd. dirs. YWCA, New Bedford, 1982—88, chair cmty. rels., 1982—83, nominating chair, 1983—84, chair pers. bd., 1984—88; trustee Millicent Libr., 1993—; bd. govs. Am. Biog. Instn., 1997—; bd. dirs. Fairhaven HS Hall of Fame, 1999—. Named Woman of the Yr., New Bedford Std.-Times and cmty., 1999; named to Hall of Fame, Fairhaven H.S., 1997. Mem.: Joshua Slocum Soc. Internat. (historian 1997—, bd. dirs.), Rotary (bd. dirs. 1998—99, v.p. 2000—, pres.-elect 2001, pres. Fairhaven chpt. 2002—03, Paul Harris fellow 2000, Internat. Peace prize 2003, Internat. Pres. citation 2003, Dist. 1090 Significant Achievement award 2003, Gt. Women of the 21st Century). Democrat. Roman Catholic. Avocations: gardening, reading, walking, crafts, music. Home: 71 Fort St Fairhaven MA 02719-2811 Personal E-mail: clopes7081@aol.com.

LOPEZ, DAVID TIBURCIO, lawyer, educator, arbitrator, mediator; b. Laredo, Tex., July 17, 1939; s. Tiburcio and Dora (Davila) L.; m. Romelia G. Guerra, Nov. 20, 1965; 1 child, Vianei López Robinson. Student, Laredo Jr. Coll., 1956-58; BJ, U. Tex., 1962; JD summa cum laude, South Tex. Coll. Law, 1971. Bar: Tex. 1971, U.S. Dist. Ct. (so. dist.) Tex. 1972, U.S. Ct. Appeals (5th cir.) 1973, U.S. Dist. Ct. (we. dist.) Tex. 1975, U.S. Ct. Claims 1975, U.S. Ct. Appeals (fed. cir.) 1975, U.S. Supreme Ct. 1976, U.S. Dist. Ct. (ea. dist.) Tex. 1978, U.S. Dist. Ct. N.Mex. 2000, U.S. Ct. Appeals (11th cir.) 1981, U.S. Ct. Appeals (9th cir.) 1984; cert. internat. com. arbitrator Internat. Ctr. for Arbitration; mediator tng. Atty.-Mediator Inst. Reporter Laredo Times, 1958-59; cons. Mexican Nat. Coll. Mag., Mexico City, 1961-62; reporter Corpus Christi (Tex.) Caller-Times, 1962-64; state capitol corr. Long News Svc., Austin, Tex., 1964-65; publs. dir. Interam. Regional Orgn. of Workers, Mexico City, 1965-67; nat. field rep. AFL-CIO, Washington, 1967-71, publs. dir. Tex. chpt. Austin, 1971-72; pvt. practice Houston, 1971—. Adj. prof. U. Houston, 1972-74, Thurgood Marshall Sch. Law, Houston, 1975-76; mem. adv. com. nat. Hispanic ednl. rsch. project One Million and Counting Tomas Rivera Ctr., 1989-91; mem. adv. bd. Inst. Transnat. Arbitration; charter mem. Resolution Forum Inc.; mem. adv. bd. South Tex. Ctr. Profl. Responsibility; mem. nat. panel of neutrals JAMS/ENDISPUTE, 1996-2000. Bd. dirs. Pacifica Found., N.Y.C., 1970-72, Houston Community Coll., 1972-75; mem. bd. edn. Houston Ind. Sch. Dist., 1972-75. With U.S. Army. Mem. ABA, FBA, Tex. Bar Assn. (com. on pattern jury changes), Houston Bar Assn. (com. on alternative dispute resolution), Internat. Bar Assn., Interam. Bar Assn., Bar of U.S. Fed. Cir., Mex.-Am. Bar Assn., Inter-Pacific Bar Assn., Tex.-Mex. Bar Assn., Hispanic Bar Assn., World Assn. Lawyers (chair internat. lab. sect.), Am. Judicature Soc., Indsl. Rels. Rsch. Assn., Sigma Delta Chi, Phi Alpha Delta. Democrat. Roman Catholic. Home: 28 Farnham Ct Houston TX 77024 Office: 3900 Montrose Blvd Houston TX 77006-4959 E-mail: dtlopez@lopezlawfirm.com.

LOPEZ, FRANCISCA UY, elementary education educator; b. Leyte, The Philippines, Mar. 9, 1925; d. Juan and Perpetua (Loyola) Uy; m. Elias Espiritu Lopez, Apr. 10, 1955; 1 child, Maria Elisa Lopez Stevens. BSE, Philippine Normal Coll., Manila, Philippines, 1952; MEd, Pa. State U., 1961; MA, Nat. Tchr. Coll., Manila, 1955. Cert. life standard tchr., Calif., tchr. (life cert.), Tex. Instructional resource tchr. El Tejon Union Sch. Dist., Mettler, Calif.; reading specialist Saudi Arabia Internat. Sch., Dhahran; facilitator staff devel. unit, instr. indsl. tng. ctr. Arabian Am. Oil Co., Dhahran; tchr. Dallas Ind. Sch. Dist. Leader Girl Scouts U.S. Fulbright Smith-Mundt grantee, 1960-61. Mem. NEA, Classroom Tchrs. Dallas (sch. rep., Tex. State Tchrs. Assn. Home: 1816 Tawakoni Ln Plano TX 75075-6732 Office: Dallas Ind Sch Dist 4200 Met Ave Dallas TX 75210

LOPEZ, GUILLERMO, obstetrician-gynecologist, educator; b. Bogota, Colombia, Oct. 3, 1919; came to U.S., 1944; s. Pedro P. and Sofia (Escobar) L.; m. Jeannie Pareja, July 16, 1955; children: Monica, Diana, Roberto, John G. MD, U. Nacional, Bogota, 1943; MS in Ob-Gyn, St. Louis U., 1947; asst. etranger, U. Paris, 1954. BE Am. Bd. Ob-Gyn. Intern Hosp. San Juan de Dios, U. Nacional, Bogota, 1942-43; resident in ob-gyn St. Louis U. Group Hosps., 1944-47; head gynecol. svc. San Juan de Dios Hosp., U. Nacional, Bogota, 1949-53, prof. of ob-gyn, 1951, assoc. dean clin. scis., 1965-66; head dept. gynecol. Inst. Nacional Cancer, Bogota, 1950-68; rsch. assoc. UCLA Harbor Gen. Hosp., 1967-68; head population div. Colombian Assn. Med. Schs., Bogota, 1969-73; head dept. gynecology, obstetrics and reproduction Centro Medico de los Andes, Fundacion Santa Fe, Bogota, 1981-88; rsch. prof. dept. community and family health Coll. Pub. Health, U. South Fla., Tampa, 1989—. Seminar cons., tchr. mother and child care Peruvian Assn. Acad. Med. programs, Paracas, Peru, 1970; pres. Corp. Cen. Regional Population, Bogota, 1973-89; cons. Pan-Am. Health Orgn. (WHO), UN Fund for Population Activities (UNFPA), 1989—; bd. dirs. Bogota Health Div., 1981-82; presenter in field. Editor: Reproduction, 1979, editor Reproductive Health in Americas, 1992; contbr. articles to profl. jours., including Am. Jour. Ob-Gyn., Med. Cir., Panamerican Health Orgn., Editorial Fotolito Garcia e Hijos, others. Bd. dirs. Floridians for a Sustainable Population. Fellow ACS, Am. Coll. Ob-Gyn.; mem. N.Y. Acad. Scis., Am. Fertility Soc., Nat. Acad. Medicine Colombia, Fla. Ob-Gyn. Soc., Am. Pub. Health Assn. Office: U South Fla Coll Pub Health 13201 Bruce B Downs Blvd Tampa FL 33612-3805 Home: 5918 Bayview Cir S Gulfport FL 33707-3930

LOPEZ, HERMINIA G. bilingual educator; Nominated Tchr. of Yr. Tex. Assn. Bilingual Edn., 1992. Office: Baytown Assn Bilingual Educators 16442 Brookford Dr Houston TX 77059-4707

LOPEZ, LINDA CAROL, social sciences educator; b. NYC, Dec. 26, 1949; d. Ralph B. and Miriam (Tayor) L. BA, U. Wis., Madison, 1972; MA, Ohio State U., 1974, PhD, 1976. Vis. asst. prof. U. Wis., Eau Claire, 1976-77; instr., asst. prof. SUNY, Oneonta, 1977-83; assoc. prof. Rockford (Ill.) Coll., 1983—89; prof. dept. social scis. Western N.Mex. U., Silver City, 1989—, dir. field experience, 1989-91. Contbr. articles to profl. jours., including Psychol. Reports, Internat. Jour. Addiction, Hispanic Jour. Behavioral Scis., Jour. Genetic Psychology, Jour. Employment Counseling, Perceptual and Motor Skills, Reading Improvement, Counseling and Values, Social Studies Jour. Recipient Best Paper award New Eng. Ednl. Rsch. Orgn., 1979; postdoctoral faculty fellow Northeastern U., Boston, 1980-81. Mem.: Midwestern Ednl. Rsch. Assn., Am. Assn. Behavioral and Social Scis., Phi Delta Kappa. Avocations: walking, reading. Home: PO Box 1479 Bayard NM 88023

LOPEZ, MARIA ELENA CHELALA, principal, educator; b. Miami, Fla., Aug. 18, 1963; d. Rosendo and Dora (Mestril) Chelala; m. William John Lopez, Mar. 2, 1985. BS, U. Miami, 1984; MS, Nova U., 1989; postgrad. in Edn., Greenwich U., 1990—. Cert. elem. edn., middle grade edn., tchr., Fla.; cert. childcare trainer; notary. Tchr.'s aide Children's Garden, Miami, 1983-84; 7th and 8th grade lit. tchr. Sts. Peter & Paul Sch., Miami, 1984-86; K-5 fgn. lang. tchr. Williams Elem., Gainesville, Fla., 1988-90; 2d grade tchr. Epiphany Sch., Miami, 1990-91, asst. prin., 1991-94, prin., 1994-95; project developer, prin. Our Lady of Lourdes Elem. Sch., Miami, 1995-96, Dade County Pub. Schs., 1996—. Bd. dirs. Sch. Tech. Adv. Bd., Miami; adj. prof. Miami Dade C.C., 1994—. Fellow ASCD, South Fla. Assn. for Young Children, Nat. Assn. for Edn. of Young Children, Rotary. Office: Miami Dade CC 11011 SW 104th St Miami FL 33176-3330

LOPEZ, RALPH IVAN, pediatrics educator; b. San Juan, P.R., Jan. 3, 1942; s. Ralph and Aida (Miranda) L.; m. Paula, July 30, 1964; 1 child, Abigail Jennifer. AB cum laude, Fordham Coll., 1963; MD, NYU, 1967. Intern pediatrics NYU Bellevue Hosp., N.Y.C., 1967-68, resident pediatrics, 1968-69, Boston Children's Hosp., Harvard Med. Ctr., 1969-70; asst. prof. pediatrics N.Y. Hosp., N.Y.C., 1973-79, assoc. prof. pediatrics, 1979-83, clin. assoc. prof. pediatrics, 1983—. Cons. physician The Dalton Sch., N.Y.C., 1973-86, Nightingale Bamford, N.Y.C., 1986-90. Editor: Adolescent Medicine Topics, 1976, 2d edit. 1980; author: The Teen Health Book,

2002; contbr. articles to profl. jours. Bd. dirs. Louis August Jones Found., Rhinebeck, N.J., 1973-91, chmn. bd. dirs., 1990—; bd. dirs. Covenant House, N.Y.C., 1990-92; mem. nominating com. Girl Scouts U.S., N.Y.C., 1991. Lt. comdr. USNR, 1971-73. Mem. Phi Beta Kappa. Office: 418 E 71st St New York NY 10021-4894

LOPEZ DE MENDEZ, ANNETTE GISELDA, education educator; b. Santurce, P.R., July 13, 1949; d. Frank and Ana Maria (Vale) López; m. Héctor Méndez, Feb. 15, 1971; 1 child, Nannette. BA in Humanities, U. P.R., Rio Piedras, 1970; MA in Early Childhood Edn., NYU, 1978; EdD, Harvard U., 1994. Rsch. asst. Mt. Sinai Hosp., N.Y.C., 1972-73; founder, elem. educator Humacao (P.R.) Montessori Sch., 1973-76; dir., tchr. Montessori Sch. P.R., San Juan, 1976-78; supr., trainer head start insvc. program U. P.R., Rio Piedras, 1978-80; assoc. prof. U. P.R. Coll. Edn., Rio Piedras, 1980-85, 87—; tchg. fellow Harvard U., Cambridge, Mass., 1985-86; dir. ednl. rsch. U. P.R., 1992—. Cons. Gen. Coun. Edn., San Juan, 1992-95, Commn. Women's Affairs, San Juan, 1990—; dir. Edn. Rsch. Ctr. U. P.R., 1992—; mem. Educators' Forum Harvard U., 1990—; mem. systemwide ednl. reform com. Dept. Edn., P.R., 1992-94; mem. Action Rsch. for Ednl. Change Com., 1993—; dir. project for devel. cmty. schs. Cambridge U., U.K., 1995—; dir. revision project Tchg. Edn. Program for Secondary Sch. in Area of Sci., 1996—; pub. rels. dir. collaborative project on acad. achievement of Puerto Rican circular migration Students, Brown U., 1997—. Editor Cuaderno de Investigaciones Educativas Rsch. Jour. of U. P.R. Faculty of Edn., 1995—. Pres. Isla Verde Residence Assn., P.R., 1992-95; mem. U. P.R. Com. to Protect Human Rights in Rsch., 1995—. Recipient Excellence and Productivity award U. P.R., 1996-97. Mem. ASCD, Am. Montessori Soc., Assn. Childhood Edn. Internat., Nat. Assn. Edn. Young Children, N.Am. Montessori Soc., Montessori Internat. Assn., Am. Ednl. Rsch. Assn. (tchg. and curriculum dissertation award com. 1996—, mem. divsn. K awards com. 1998). Democrat. Roman Catholic. Avocations: swimming, travel. Office: Univ PR Sch Edn PO Box 23304 Rio Piedras PR 00931-3304

LOPEZ-REID, NORMA ALICIA, elementary school prinicpal; b. El Paso, Tex., Aug. 25, 1953; d. Frank and Josefina (Sapien) López; 1 child, Kris Reid. BA in Spanish, Sociology, Calif. State U., L.A., 1974; MA in Edn., Calif. State U., 1978. Cert. secondary sch. tchr., reading specialist, bilingual tchr., cc. tchr., adminstr., Calif. Bilingual tchr. Westminster (Calif.) High Sch., 1975-77; ESL tchr., Spanish tchr., reading specialist Marina High Sch., Huntington Beach, Calif., 1977-81; resource tchr. Mark Keppel High Sch., Alhambra, Calif., 1981-82; tchr. 1st and 4th grades Eastmont Elem. Sch., Montebello, Calif., 1983-85; bilingual 7th grade tchr. Montebello Intermediate Sch., 1985-86; bilingual resource tchr. Wilson Elem. Sch., Lynwood, Calif., 1986-87; spl. assignment tchr. Immigrant Program Lynwood Sch. Dist., 1987-88; asst. prin. Lindbergh Elem. Sch., Mark Twain Elem. Sch., Lynwood, 1988-90; prin. Lindbergh Elem. Sch., Lynwood, 1990-91, Kenmore Elem. Sch., Baldwin Park, Calif., 1991—. Presenter edn. confs. statewide in Calif., 1976—; mem. bilingual cert. of competency panel Orange County Dept. Edn., 1977-78, State Dept. Edn. Program Quality Rev., 1982—; planner, coord. Parent Conf., 1982. Mem. Montebello H.E.L.P. Steering Com., P.T.A. Montebello Sch. Dist.; block capt. Montebello Police Dept. Neighborhood Watch. Mem. Kappa Delta Pi. Avocations: travel, theater, music. Office: Kenmore Elem Sch 3822 Kenmore Ave Baldwin Park CA 91706-4038

LOPRESTI, MARILYN ANGELA, school system administrator; b. N.Y.C., Oct. 11, 1944; d. Mario Vincent and Theresa (Capalbi) Caccioppoli; m. Anthony C. LoPresti, Feb. 12, 1966; children: Vincent Joseph, Christine Marie. BA, St. Johns U., 1966; MA, SUNY, Stony Brook, 1974; PhD, NYU, 1986. Cert. dist. adminstr., sch. adminstr. and supr., elem. tchr., 7-12 social studies tchr., N.Y. From social studies tchr. to asst. prin. Longwood High Sch., Middle Island, N.Y., 1974-85; asst. prin. Kings Park (N.Y.) High Sch., 1985-87; pers. adminstr. Kings Park Sch. Dist., 1987-88; asst. prin. William T. Rogers Middle Sch., Kings Park, 1988-91; elem. and sec. curriculum and instruction adminstr. Kings Park Ctrl. Sch. Dist., 1991—. Contbr. articles to profl. jours. Impartial hearing officer N.Y. State Edn. Dept., 1992—. Mem. Phi Delta Kappa (v.p. 1983-85, pres. 1985-87). Home: PO Box 715 Miller Place NY 11764-0715 Office: Kings Park Ctrl Sch Dist 101 Church St Kings Park NY 11754-1770

LORANCE, ELMER DONALD, organic chemistry educator; b. Tupelo, Okla., Jan. 18, 1940; s. Elmer Dewey and Imogene (Triplett) L.; m. Phyllis Ilene Miller, Aug. 30, 1969; children: Edward Donald, Jonathan Andrew. BA, Okla. State U., 1962; MS, Kansas State U., 1967; PhD, U. Okla., 1977. NIH research trainee Okla. U., Norman, 1966-70; asst. prof. organic chemistry So. Calif. Coll. (now Vanguard U. of So. Calif.), Costa Mesa, 1970-73; assoc. prof. So. Calif. Coll., Costa Mesa, 1973-80, prof., 1980—, chmn. div. natural scis. and math., 1985-89, chmn. chemistry dept., 1990-93, chmn. divsn. natural scis. and math., 1993-99, chmn. dept. chemistry, 1999—. Contbr. articles to profl. jours. Mem. AAAS, Am. Chem. Soc., Internat. Union Pure and Applied Chemistry (assoc.), Am. Inst. Chemists, Am. Sci. Affiliation, Phi Lambda Upsilon. Republican. Mem. Ch. Assembly of God. Avocations: reading, gardening, music. Office: Vanguard U So Calif 55 Fair Dr Costa Mesa CA 92626-6520 E-mail: dlorance@vanguard.edu.

LORCH, MARISTELLA DE PANIZZA, medieval and Renaissance scholar, writer; b. Bolzano, Italy, Dec. 8, 1919; came to U.S., 1947, naturalized, 1951; d. Gino and Giuseppina (Cristoforetti) de Panizza Inama von Brunnenwald; m. Claude Bové, Feb. 10, 1944 (div. 1955); 1 child, Claudia; m. Edgar R. Lorch, Mar. 25, 1956; children: Lavinia Edgarda, Donatella Livia. Ed., Liceo Classico, Merano, 1929-37; Dott. in Lettere e Filosofia, U. Rome, 1942; DHL (hon.), Lehman Coll., CUNY, 1993. Prof. Latin and Greek Liceo Virgilio, Rome, 1941-44; assoc. prof. Italian and German Coll. St. Elizabeth, Convent Station, N.J., 1947-51; faculty Barnard Coll. and Columbia U., 1951-90; prof. Barnard Coll., 1967—, chmn. dept., 1951-90, co-founder, chmn. medieval and renaissance program, 1972-90. Founder, dir. Ctr. for Internat. Scholarly Exch., Barnard Coll., 1980-90; dir. Casa Italiana, Columbia U., 1969-76, chmn. exec. com. Italian studies, 1980-90, founding dir. Italian Acad. Advanced Studies in Am., 1991-96, founding dir. emerita and dir. external rels., 1996—. Author: Critical edit. L. Valla, De vero falsoque bono, Bari, 1970, (critical edit.) Michaelida (with W. Ludwig), 1976, On Pleasure (with A. K. Hieatt), 1981, A Defense of Life: L. Valla's Theory of Pleasure, 1985, Folly and Insanity in Renaissance Literature, 1986, (with E. Grassi) All' America, 1990, Italy at the Millennium, 2001; editor: Il Teatro Italiano del Renascimento, 1981, Humanism in Rome, 1983, La Scuola, New York, 1987; mem. editorial bd. Italian jour. Romanic Review; also articles on Renaissance lit., philosophy and theater. Chmn. Am. Ariosto Centennial Celebration, 1974; chmn. bd. trustees La Scuola NY, 1986-92; trustee Lycée Française NY, 1986—; adv. bd. Marconi Found., 1998. Decorated Cavaliere della Repubblica Italiana, Commendatore della Repubblica Italiana, Grande Ufficiale della Republica Italiana; recipient AMITA award for Woman of Yr. in Italian Lit., 1973, Columbus '92 Countdown prize of excellence in humanities, 1990, Elen Cornaro award Sons of Italy Woman of Yr., 1990, Father Ford award, 1994, hon. mem. Legendary Women, 1997. Mem. Medieval Acad. Am., Renaissance Soc. Am., Am. Assn. Tchrs. Italian, Am. Assn. Italian Studies (hon. pres. 1990-91), Internat. Assn. for Study of Italian Lit. (Am. rep., assoc. pres. 8th Congress 1973), Acad. Polit. Sci. (life), Pirandello Soc. (pres. 1972-78), Arcadia Acad. (Asteria Aretusa 1976). Home: 445 Riverside Dr New York NY 10027-6801 Office: Columbia Univ Italian Acad Adv Study Casa Italiana New York NY 10027

LORD, JERE JOHNS, retired physics educator; b. Portland, Oreg., Jan. 3, 1922; s. Percy Samuel and Hazel Marie (Worstel) L.; m. Miriam E. Hart, Dec. 30, 1947; children— David, Roger, Douglas. Physicist U. Calif. Radiation Lab., Berkeley, 1942-46; research asso. U. Chgo., 1950-52; asst. prof. physics U. Wash., Seattle, 1952-57, assoc. prof., 1957-62, prof., 1962-92, prof. emeritus, 1992—. Fellow AAAS, Am. Phys. Soc.; mem. Am. Assn. Physics Tchrs. Home: 720 Seneca St Apt 1004 Seattle WA 98101 Office: U Wash Dept Physics Box 351560 Seattle WA 98195-1560

LORD, JEROME EDMUND, education administrator, writer; b. Waterbury, Conn., Dec. 24, 1935; s. James Andrew and Mary Frances (Hayes) L.; m. Eleanor Louise Collins, Apr. 22, 1967; children: Hayes Alexander FitzWarin, Stavely Hampston deHodnet, Savile Collins de Montenay, Dorian Warfield d'Amours, Wallis Jennings dePantulf. BA, Georgetown U., 1957; MA, Boston Coll., 1962, Columbia U., 1963, PhD, 1969; diploma (hon.), U. Madrid, 1962. Tchr. The Taft Sch. Peekskill Mil. Acad., 1957-60; editor, lang. recs. supr. Allyn and Bacon Inc., Boston, 1961-62; adminstrv. assoc. internat. programs and services Tchrs. Coll. Columbia U., N.Y.C., 1963-65, assoc. in higher edn., 1965-66; asst. prof. edn., exec. asst. to dean acad. devel. CUNY, 1965-67, assoc. prof. edn., exec. asst. to vice chancellor exec. office, 1967-69; dir. rsch. Ford and Carnegie Study of Fed. Politics of Edn. Brookings Instn., Washington, 1969-70; program officer Nat. Ctr. for Ednl. Tech., U.S. Dept. Edn., Washington, 1971-73; sr. assoc. Nat. Inst. Edn., Washington, 1973-86, Office Ednl. Rsch. and Improvement, Dept. Edn., Washington, 1986—. Pres. Jerome Lord Enterprises, Inc., Washington; advisor to vol. edn. policy group Office Dir. Def. Edn., U.S. Dept. Def., 1975-76; chmn. Fed. Interagy. Panel for Rsch. on Adulthood; mem. World Affairs Coun., Washington, other various nat. panels and coms.; cons. in field; lectr. in field. Playwright: Teresa, 1971, The Election, 1972, Audition!, 1973, Decent Exposure, 1979, Amazing Grace, 1987, Heads You Win, 1991, Making Believe, 1996, My One and Only, 1997; author: Perfectly Proper, 1993, Teacher Training Abroad: New Realities, 1993, Adult Literacy Programs: Guidelines for Effectiveness, 1995; contbr. articles to profl. jours. Trustee St. John's Child Devel. Ctr., Washington, 1978-83; mem. nat. bd. sponsors Protestant and Orthodox Ctr., N.Y. World's Fair, 1964; mem. adv. bd. N.Y.C. Urban Corps, 1965-69, others; mem. coun. of friends Folger Shakespeare Libr.; sponsor Nat. Symphony Orch.; mem., donor reception rooms Dept. State. Named Coakley scholar, 1953-57, M.T. Runyan scholar, 1967-68; fellow W.T. Kellogg Found., 1968-69, Rinehart Found., 1970-71, others. Mem. Soc. Friends St. George's and Desc. Knights of Garter, Acad. Am. Poets, Pilgrims of the U.S., World Affairs Coun., The Lansdowne Club (London), Met. Club, Kappa Delta Pi, Phi Delta Pi, Eta Sigma Phi. Episcopalian. Avocations: historic preservation, music, art history, architecture, antiques. Office: 555 New Jersey Ave NW Washington DC 20001-2029 Home (Summer): 10000 Coastal Hwy # 1103 Ocean City MD 21842 : 2500 S Ocean Blvd Palm Beach FL 33480

LORD, RICHARD NEWELL, JR., science educator; b. Fort Fairfield, Maine, Nov. 1, 1943; s. Richard Newell and Phyllis Evelyn (Deane) L.; m. Marcia Evelyn Valliere, July 13, 1974; 1 child, Andrew Scott. BS, U. Maine-Orono, 1965, MEd, 1971. Tchr. chemistry Presque Isle H.S., Maine, 1965-66, tchr. biology, 1966—, chair sci. dept., 1999—. Online tutor Acad. Assistance Ctr., Am. Online, 1996—; mem. adv. bd. Science Works for Maine, Scarborough, Maine, 1992—; ednl. cons. Chances'Choices, 1994-97. Time Warner cable tchr. adv. bd., 1994—. Pres. Bethany Bapt. Ch., Presque Isle, 1984-89. Named Maine award winner Presdl. award NSF, 1984; recipient Gustav Ohaus award Ohaus Scale Corp.-Nat. Sci. Tchrs. Assn., 1983, Presdl. award (from Maine), NSF, 1986, First Pl. Nat. Tchrs. Grant Competition A&E Network, 1991, Crystal Apple Nat. Tchr. award Time Warner Cable, 1993, 94, 95, 96, 2003, Tchr. Recognition award Discovery Network, 1995, Tandy prize Outstanding Tchr. Tandy Corp., 1995, Regl. winner Tchg. Excellence award Chevy Malibu, 2001, Presdl. Scholars Tcrh. Recognition award, 2002, Edn.'s Unsung Heroes award ING No. Annuity, 2001, SEED Devel. award Ctr. Ednl. Svcs., Auburn, Maine, 2002. Mem. Nat. Assn. Biology Tchrs. (Outstanding Biology Tchr.-Maine 1975, 94), Nat. Sci. Tchrs. Assn., NEA, Maine Educators Assn., Maine Sci. Tchrs. Assn., Assn. of Presdl. Awardees in Sci. Tchg., Maine Presdl. Awardees in Math and Sci. Republican. Avocations: genealogy, music. Home: 114 Fleetwood St Presque Isle ME 04769-3032 Office: Presque Isle High Sch 16 Griffin St Presque Isle ME 04769-2445

LORD, THOMAS REEVES, biology educator; b. Alexandria, Va., Mar. 14, 1943; s. Arthur Roberts and Dorothy (Reeves) L.; m. Jane Tompkins, June 17, 1967; children: Erik Thomas, Andrea Margaret, Elizabeth Jane. BS in Biology, Rutgers U., 1965, D Sci. Edn., 1983; MS in Biology, Trenton State Coll., 1969. Tchr. biology Rancocas Valley Regional High Sch., Mt. Holly, N.J., 1965-69; instr. biology Frankfurt (Germany) Internat. Sch., 1969-73; prof. Burlington County Coll., Pemberton, N.J., 1973-89; prof. biology, sci. edn. Indiana U. Pa., 1989—. Cons. Innovative Community Colls., Kansas City, Kans., 1989-91, Zero Population Growth, Inc., Washington, 1989—; fellow, cons. Dept. Higher Edn., Trenton,1985-89; fellow Birmingham (Eng.) U., 1980-81. Author: Stories of Lake George--Fact and Fancy, vol. I, 1986, Vol. II, 1993, Vol. III, 1999, Poems of Lake George--Prose and Poesy, 1995; contbr. articles to profl. jours. Instr. swimming, life saving, canoeing, sailing, first aid, CPR ARC, Burlington County, 1975—. Grantee Biol. Scis. Curriculum Studies, 1990-92, Pa. Acad. for Provession of Teaching, 1991-92, NSF-Biology Sci. Curriculum Studies, 1991-92, Pa. Dept. Environ. Resources, 1994, 95. Mem. Nat. Assn. for Rsch. in Sci. Teaching (jour. reviewer 1988-93), Nat. Assn. Biology Tchrs. (coll. com. 1989-2003), Soc. for Coll. Sci. Tchrs. (bd. dirs. 1998-2003), Sigma Xi. Mem. Soc. Of Friends. Avocations: jogging, swimming, canoeing. Home: 92 Valley Rd Indiana PA 15701-3624 Office: Indiana U Pa Weyandt Hall Indiana PA 15705

LORD, WILLIAM HERMAN, performing arts educator, theatre consultant; b. Providence, Feb. 28, 1931; s. Herman Maurice and Gertrude Elizabeth (Thompson) L.; m. Catherine Lynn Ball, Sept. 14, 1957; children: Jennifer Lynn, Louise Giovanna. BA, Evansville Coll., 1953; MA, Northwestern U., 1961. Installation/sales R.H.M. Stage Equipment, Indpls., 1955-57; scenic carpenter WFBM-TV, Indpls., 1957-58; prodn. supr. Avondale Playhouse, Indpls., summer 1957-63; tchr. tech. theatre North Ctrl. H.S., Indpls., 1958-96, dept. chmn., 1985-96; theatre cons. William H. Lord, Inc., Indpls., 1960—; pres. Theatre Assocs., Inc., Indpls., 1958-96. Author: (textbook) Stagecraft 1: Your complete guide to backstage work, 1978, 2nd edit., 1991, 3rd edit., 2000, (manual) Installing a Stage Lighting System, 1977, (workbook) Stagecraft 1, 1985, 2nd edit., 2000, tchrs. guide, 2000; contbr. articles to profl. jours. Deacon Northminster Presbyn. Ch., Indpls., 1958-60, elder, 1971-73, 90-93. Served to sgt. U.S. Army, 1953-55. Mem. Ednl. Theatre Assn. (inducted into Hall of Fame 1995), Ind. Theatre Assn. (v.p. 1990-92), Sagamore of the Wabash, 1996. Avocations: electronic and electrical work, boating. Home and Office: William H Lord Inc 9210 N College Ave Indianapolis IN 46240-1031

LORENZ, ANNE PARTEE, special education educator, consultant; b. Nashville, Aug. 6, 1943; d. McCullough and Mary Elizabeth (Shemwell) Partee; m. Philip Jack Lorenz, Jr., Nov. 26, 1970 (dec. Aug. 2002); stepchildren: Brenna Ellen, Philip Jack III. Student, Rhodes Coll., 1961-63, 64; BS, George Peabody Coll., 1966; postgrad., Ga. State U., 1967-68; MS, George Peabody Coll., 1969. Clerk Tenn. State Libr. Archives, Nashville, 1963-64; tchr. learning disabilities Howard Sch., Atlanta, 1966-68; prin., tchr. learning disabilities Sewanee (Tenn.) Learning Ctr., 1969-78; tchr. learning disabilities Clark Meml. Sch., Winchester, Tenn., 1978-79; tutor, cons. learning disabilities Anne Partee Lorenz Tutoring Consultation Svc., Sewanee, 1979—. Psychol. cons. U. of South, 1974-78; cons. St. Andrew's-Sewanee Sch., Tenn., 1980—, coord. tutoring program, 1993—; vol. presenter Effective Adv. for Citizens With Handicaps, Inc. workshop, 1986. Active Coun. for Exceptional Children, 1968-79; treas. Franklin County Dem. Party; sec. Sewanee Precinct Dem. Party, 1974-76; del. dist. and state Dem. Conf.; judge John M. Templeton Laws of Life Essay Contest, 1995; vol. Cordelle-Lorenz Obs., U. of the South, 1970-94; bd. dirs. Franklin County Adult Activities Ctr., 1979-82; vol. presenter E.A.C.H., Inc. (Effective Advocacy for Citizens with Handicaps), 1986. Recipient letter of commendation Gov. Tenn., 1974. Mem. Tenn. LWV (pres., bd. dirs.), Franklin County LWV (pres.), Learning Disabilities Assn. Tenn. (1st Tchr. Yr. 1975), Children and Adults with Attention Deficit Disorders. Avocations: wild flowers, bird and wild animal watching, walking, reading, crocheting. Home and Office: 390 Onteora Ln Sewanee TN 37375-2639

LORENZ, LATISHA JAY, elementary education educator; b. Uniontown, Pa., June 16, 1967; d. Lou Jean Lorenz and Mary Lou (Sesler) Rupp; m. Donald Raye Shetley, May 25, 1991 (div. Oct. 1993). AA, U. S.C., Union, 1987; BS in Edn., Lander U., 1989. Cert. elem. edn. 6th grade tchr. Union (S.C.) Acad., 1990-93; 7th grade lang. arts tchr. Sims Jr. H.S., Union, 1993—. Mem. S.C. State Coun. of the Internat. Reading Assn., Union Jr. Charity League. Republican. Baptist. Avocations: cats, reading stephen king, watching the buffalo bills, going to movies. Office: Sims Jr High 200 Sims Dr Union SC 29379-7398

LORENZ, SARAH LYNNE, secondary education educator; b. Ann Arbor, Mich., June 19, 1971; d. Robert Charles and Nancy Ruth (Davis) Birk; m. Craig Steven Lorenz, Apr. 3, 1972. BS in Edn., Ea. Mich. U., 1993, MA, 2000. Cert. tchr., Mich. Head dept. English Franklin Ed. Christian Sch., Novi, Mich., 1993—. Coach jr. varsity and varsity cheerleading Franklin Rd. Christian Sch., 1993-98, chair comm. target com., 1995-97, sr. project/block coord. 1996—; steering chair North Ctrl. Assn., 1996-2000; cons. and presenter in field. Contbr. articles to profl. jours. Campaign vol. Rep. Ctrl. Com. Washtenaw County, Ann Arbor, 1994. Mem. Nat. Coun. Tchrs. English. Avocations: interior decorating, writing, art. Office: 40800 W 13 Mile Rd Novi MI 48377

LORENZEN, LOUIS OTTO, art educator; b. Akron, Ohio, Apr. 20, 1935; s. Lorenz Jack and Anne (Strampher) L.; m. Veronica Ann Lorenzen, Dec. 10, 1978; children: Michelle Melody Raitt, Teresa Ann Hopkins, Lisette Marie Jackson, Anthony Frederick, Nicholas Joseph. BSEd in Art, Bowling Green (Ohio) State U., 1959; MEd in Adminstrv. Counseling, Bridgewater State Coll., 1964; MAT, Assumption Coll., 1970; MFA, Syracuse (N.Y.) U., 1982. Cert. art tchr., Mass.; cert. secondary English, counseling and guidance, secondary adminstrn., Mass. Art tchr. K-12 Bluffton (Ohio) City Schs., 1959; dir. pubs. Illustrator, graphic designer Greater Cleve. Regional Rsch. Coun., 1959; English tchr. DUEL Vocat. Inst. Calif. Dept. Corrections, Tracey, 1960-61; spl. needs tchr. Old Rochester Regional High Sch., Mattapoisett, Mass., 1961-62; English tchr. Roosevelt Jr. High Sch., New Bedford, Mass., 1962-63, New Bedford Vocat. High Sch., 1963-65; full prof. art Fitchburg (Mass.) State Coll., 1965—. Chair program rev. com. Mass. Dept. Edn. Certification, Quincy, Mass., 1991, program rev. com., 1987-90; artist-in-residence Mt. Washington Hotel, 1981. One man shows include LaGardina Gallery, San Francisco, 1960, Fitchburg State Coll., 1968, 80, 82, Jaffrey Civic Ctr., 1972, The Elms Coll., 1985, Borgia Gallery; exhibited in group shows at Rockport Art Assn., 1980-82, 84, Fitchburg Art Mus., 1978, 79, 81-83, 90, Fitchburg State Coll. Faculty Shows, 1982-89, Brick House Gallery, Boothbay Harbor, Maine, 1984-90 (3 ann. shows), New Eng. Art Educators Conf. Show, 1983, also represented in permanent collections. Adv. bd. dirs. Boston Globe Art awards, 1980-85; judge ann. show Westfield (Mass.) State Coll. Dept. Art, 1985. Mem. NEA (life), Mass. Tchrs. Assn., State Coll. Edn. Assn. (local bd. dirs. 1989-90, promotion com. 1988-90, curricula com. 1991—), Mass. Art Edn. Assn. (recording sec. 1968-69, corr. sec. 1970-72, chmn. nominations com. 1972-74, v.p. 1981-83, pres. 1983-86), Mass. Art Edn. Assn., Nat. Art Edn. Assn. (chair authored coee of ethics 1985, ea. rep. to exec. com. for the com. of minority concerns 1986-90, Cert. of Apprecation), Internat. Soc. for Edn. Through Art (ea. alt. rep. nat. chpt. 1989-91), Amnesty Internat., Phi Delta Kappa Office: Fitchburg State Coll 160 Pearl St Fitchburg MA 01420-2631

LORING, MILDRED ROGERS, retired elementary educator, reading specialist; b. N.Y.C., Mar. 28, 1924; d. Herman and Frances (Posner) Rogers; m. Murray Loring, Mar. 15, 1945 (dec.); children: Arthur S., Sasha Trudy, Sondra E. BA, Hunter Coll., 1945; M in Reading Edn., Coll. William and Mary, 1976. Cert. reading specialist biology K-4, Va. Bacteriologist, lab. technician Bklyn. Jewish Hosp., 1945-46; 4th grade tchr. Norge Elem. Sch., Williamsburg, Va., 1967-73; 4th-5th-6th grade tchr., chpt. 1 reading specialist Berkeley Elem. Sch., Williamsburg, 1987-89; 1st, 2d, 3rd chpt. I reading specialist Norge Elem. Sch., Williamsburg, 1989-94; supr. student tchrs. Coll. of William and Mary, Williamsburg, 1997-98, ret., 1999. Religious sch. cons. Temple Beth El of Williamsburg, 1994—, religious sch. prin., 1994-96. Co-author: Bicentennial of U.S. Constitution Ideas Package for Elementary Schools, 1987 (Leadership award 1987). Pres. Women's Club of Williamsburg, 1965-66, Birchwood Garden Club, Williamsburg, 1962-63; bd. dirs. Williamsburg Cmty. Ctr., 1965; pres. Home Demonstration Club, Williamsburg, 1961-62; v.p. James Blair H.S. PTA, Williamsburg, 1961-62; pres. Temple Beth El Sisterhood, Williamsburg, 1965-69. Recipient Ea. Bicentennial of the U.S. Constitution Leadership award Justice Earl Warren Bicentennial Project, 1987, Jr. Am. Citizens Thatcher award Nat. Soc. of DAR Coun. for the Advancement of Citizenship, 1987. Jewish. Avocations: writing, walking, reading.

LORIO, KATHRYN VENTURATOS, lawyer, law educator; b. Pitts., Feb. 15, 1949; d. George Stellios and Aphrodite (Bon) Venturatos; m. Philip D. Lorio III, Nov. 16, 1974; children: Elisabeth Bon, Philip D. IV. BA magna cum laude, Tulane U., 1970; JD, Loyola U., New Orleans, 1973. Bar: La., 1973. Atty. Deutsch, Kerrigan & Stiles, New Orleans, 1973-76; asst. prof. law Loyola U. Law Sch., New Orleans, 1976-79, assoc. prof., 1979-83, prof., 1983—, Leon Sarpy prof. law, 1992—, assoc. dean acad. affairs, 1996-97. Mem. adv. com. joint legis. com. on Forced Heirship and Illegitimate Children State of La., Baton Rouge, 1981; vice chair La. Task Force on Assisted Conception and Artificial Means of Reproduction. Author: Louisiana Successions, Donations and Trusts, 2002, (with others) Louisiana Civil Law Treatise on Successions and Donations, 1995; contbr. articles to profl. jours. Bd. dirs. Mental Health Advocacy Bd., New Orleans and Baton Rouge, 1984-88, Trinity Episcopal Sch., New Orleans, 1998-2001. Fellow Am. Coll. Trust and Estate Counsel; mem. Am. Assn. Law Schs. (chmn. sect. on women in legal edn. 1990), Am. Law Inst., La. State Bar Assn. (bd. govs. 1995-97, 2003—), La. Law Inst. (marriage-persons com. 1982—, coun. 1989—, successions-donations com. 1993—), Phi Beta Kappa, Phi Delta Phi. Greek Orthodox. Home: 23 Richmond Pl New Orleans LA 70115-5019 Office: Loyola U Law Sch 7214 Saint Charles Ave New Orleans LA 70118-3538

LORO, LAUREN MARGUERITE, secondary education educator; b. New Haven, Mar. 14, 1948; d. Anthony S. and Marguerite (Belviso) L. BS, Western Conn. State Coll., Danbury, 1970; MS, U. Bridgeport (Conn.), 1977. Instrumental music dir. Sleeping Giant Jr. High, Hamden, Conn., 1970-77, Hamden High Sch., 1977—. Flute with New Haven Symphony Orch., 1971, 72; music dir. Hamden H.S. Concert Band, Orch., Marching Band, 1977—, Hamden H.S. Dance Band, 1982—, Theatre Dept., 1972—, Hamden Summer Theatre, 1974—, Michael J. Whalen Theatre Dept., 1975-84, Sleeping Giant Jr. High, Hamden, 1972-83, Quinnipiac Coll., Hamden, 1980, dist. so. region CMEA All Mid. Sch. Band, 1994; profl. devel. chairperson Hamden H.S.; profl. devel. co-chair Town of Hamden. Mem. Hamden Edn. Assn., Conn. Music Educators Assn. Avocations: photography, french gourmet cooking. Office: Hamden High Music Dept 2040 Dixwell Ave Hamden CT 06514-2404

LOS, CORNELIS ALBERTUS, financial economist, portfolio risk manager, educator; b. Purmerend, The Netherlands, Dec. 14, 1951; arrived in U.S., 1977, naturalized, 1994; s. Klaas and Adriaantje (Nieuwland) Los; m. Diane Nichols, June 10, 1979 (div. 1984); 1 child, Francesca R. E.; m. Elizabeth M. Ten Houten, June 18, 1986 (div. 1991); 1 child, Marguerita E.

A.; m. Rose Lee Haubenstock, May 5, 1994. Candidatus cum laude (BA Hon), U. Groningen, 1974, Doctorandus (MPhil), 1976; diploma, Inst. Social Studies, The Hague, 1977; MPhil, Columbia U., 1980, PhD, 1984. Tchg. asst. Columbia U., N.Y.C., 1978-80, preceptor, 1979, instr., 1980-81; economist Fed. Res. Bank of N.Y., N.Y.C., 1981-85, sr. economist, 1985-87, Nomura Rsch. Inst. (America) Inc., 1987—90; chief U.S. economist NMB Postbank Group/ING Bank/ING Capital, N.Y.C., 1991-93; assoc. prof. banking and fin. Nanyang Tech. U., Singapore, 1995-99; assoc. prof. fin. U. Adelaide, Australia, 2000; vis. assoc. prof. fin. Deakin U., 2001; assoc. prof. fin. Kent State U., 2001—. Adj. lectr. Hunter Coll., N.Y.C., 1980, CCNY, 1980—81; adj. prof. Baruch Coll., N.Y.C., 1985—86; rsch. assoc. Ctr. Math. Sys. Theory U. Fla., Gainesville, 1986—92; pres. EMEPS Assocs. Inc., 1986—; lectr. numerous profl. confs., U.S. and fgn. countries; cons. Worldbank, 1994—, Inter-Am. Devel. Bank, 1994—, Asian Devel. Bank, 1996—. Author: (books) Computational Fin.-A Sci. Perspective, 2001, Financial Market Risk-Measurement & Analysis, 2003; contbr. articles to profl. jours., chapters to books. Mem. acad. bd. Nanyang Tech. U., 1997—99; bd. dirs. The Netherland-Am. Found., Inc., 1991—95. Recipient Lady Van Renswoude of The Hague Found. awards, 1974—75, MAOC Countess Van Bylandt Found. award, 1976, Scholten Cordès Found. awards, 1976—77; Fulbright-Hays scholar, 1977. Fellow: Soc. Columbia Scholars, Australasian Inst. Banking and Fin., Am. Coll. Forensic Examiners (life); mem.: AIMR, IEEE (sr.), Singapore Soc. Fin. Analysts, Nat. Econ. Club, N.Y. Acad. Sci., Am. Math. Soc., Am. Fin. Assn., Am. Econ. Assn., Am. Statis. Assn., Internat. Assn. Math. and Computer Modeling, Internat. Assn. Fin. Engrs., Econometric Soc., Math. Assn. Am., London Goodenough Trust, World Coun. Alumni Internat. Ho. (N.Y.C.), Grad. Faculties Alumni Columbia U., Nanyang Bus. Sch. Alumni Assn., Columbia U. Club (Singapore) (found. treas.). Republican. Avocations: history of the Silk Road, Am. Revolution, French-Indian War, Lewis and Clark Expedition, War of 1812, travel, hiking, collecting and shooting black powder muzzle loaders, photography. Office: Kent State U Coll Bus Adminstrn & Grad Sch Mgmt Dept Fin Rm 416 Kent OH 44242-0001 Fax: 330-672-9806. E-mail: clos@kent.edu.

LOSACCO, LESLEY HERDT, supervisor, educator; b. Pitts., Mar. 31, 1936; d. Leslie Weyman and Grace Langhans Henig (Lauterbach) Herdt; m. Raymond B. Losacco, July 31, 1964. BMFA-BMFAME, Carnegie-Mellon U., 1959, MFA-MFAME, 1969; PhD, Duquesne U., 1983. Cert. AGO-FAGO, tchr. music, supr. music. Supr., music tchr. North Hills Sch. Dist., Pitts. Author: The Music Course of Study. Recipient Community Leadership in Music awards, Gift of Time tribute Am. Family Inst., 1990. Mem. ASCD, Music Educators Nat. Conf., Pa. Music Educators Assn., North Hills Edn. Assn., Am. Guild of Organists, Orff-Shlwerk Assn., Phi Kappa Phi, Sigma Alpha Iota. Home: 161 Lakewood Ave Pittsburgh PA 15229-1729 Office: 135 6th Ave Pittsburgh PA 15229-1291

LOSCHI, RICHARD PAUL, middle school educator; b. Medford, Mass., Feb. 18, 1949; s. Leo Francis and Frances Rita (Forti) L. BS in Edn., U. Mass., 1970, MAT, 1971. Elem. tchr. grades 4-6 West Elem. Sch., Andover, Mass., 1971-88; mid. sch. tchr. West Middle Sch., Andover, 1988—, team leader grade 6, 1989—. Mem. NEA, Andover Edn. Assn., Mass. Tchrs. Assn., Nat. Soccer Coaches Assn., Ea. Mass. Soccer Coaches Assn. (treas., Coach of Yr. 1987, 95, 99, 2001), Mass. State Soccer Assn. (treas.). Roman Catholic. Avocations: golf, hockey, soccer, travel. Home: 40 Lowell St Andover MA 01810 Office: West Middle Sch Shawseen Rd Andover MA 01810 E-mail: Rloschi@aps1.net.

LOSER, JOSEPH CARLTON, JR., dean, retired judge; b. Nashville, June 16, 1932; s. Joseph Carlton and Pearl Dean (Gupton) L.; m. Mildred Louise Nichols, May 25, 1972; 1 child, Joseph Carlton III. Student, U. Tenn., 1950-51, Vanderbilt U., 1952-55; LLB, Nashville YMCA Night Law Sch., 1959. Bar: Tenn. 1959. Pvt. practice, 1959-66; judge Gen. Sessions Ct., Davidson County, Tenn., 1966-69, Cir. Ct. 20th Jud. Dist. Tenn., 1969-86; dean Nashville Sch. Law, 1986—. Mem. ABA, Tenn. Bar Assn., Nashville Bar Assn., Am. Legion, Masons, Shriners, Sigma Delta Kappa, Kappa Sigma. E-mail: jcloser@prodigy.net.

LOSS, JOHN C. architect, retired educator; b. Muskegon, Mich., Mar. 6, 1931; s. Alton A. and Dorothy Ann (DeMars) Forward; m. LaMyrna Lois Draggoo, June 7, 1958. B.Arch., U. Mich., 1954, M.Arch., 1960. Registered architect, Md., Mich. Architect Eero Saarinen & Assocs., Bloomfield Hills, Mich., 1956-57; owner John Loss & Assocs, Detroit, 1960-75; prof., acting dean Sch. Architecture, U. Detroit, 1960-75; prof., head dept. architecture N.C. State U., Raleigh, 1975-79; assoc. dean. Sch. Architecture U. Md., College Park, 1981-83, prof. architecture, 1979-93, prof. emeritus architecture, 1993—; dir. Architecture and Engring. Performance Info. Ctr., 1982-93; pvt. practice, Annapolis, College Park, 1979-93, Whitehall, Mich., 1993—. Mem. com. NRC-NAS, 1982-93; bldg. diagnostics com. Adv. Bd. on Build Environ., 1983-93; com. on earthquake engring. NRC, 1983-93; leader survey team for tornado damage in Pa. and Ohio, 1985. Author: Building Design for Natural Hazards in Eastern United States, 1981, Identification of Performance Failures in Large Structures and Buildings, 1987, Analysis of Performance Failures in Civil Structures and Large Buildings, 1990, Performance Failures in Buildings and Civil Works, 1991; works include med. clinic, N.C.; Aldersgate Multi Family Housing, Oscoda, Mich. Advisor Interfaith Housing Inc., Detroit, 1966-74; advisor Detroit Mayor's Office, 1967-69, Interim Housing Com. Mich. State Housing Devel. Authority, Lansing, 1969-71, Takoma Park Citizens for Schs., Md., 1981-82; advisor, cons. Hist. Preservation Commn., Prince George's County, Md.; planning commn. Blue Lake Twp., Mich., 1994—; art and environ. commn. Grand Rapids Diocese of Cath. Ch., 1996-2002; vol. tchr. St. James Sch., Montague, Mich., 2001-. With U.S. Army, 1954-56. NSF grantee, 1978-84, 86-90; named one of Men of Yr., Engring. News Record, 1984. Fellow AIA; mem. K.C. (charter Grand Knight 2001-). Democrat. Roman Catholic.

LOSSE, CATHERINE ANN, pediatric nurse, critical care nurse, educator, clinical nurse specialist, family nurse practitioner; b. Mount Holly, N.J., Mar. 12, 1959; d. David C. and Bernice (Lewis) Losse. Diploma, Helene Fuld Sch. Nursing, 1980; BSN magna cum laude, Thomas Jefferson U., 1986; MSN, U. Pa., 1989; Family Nurse Practitioner Cert., Widener U., 1997. RN N.J., Pa. Staff nurse adult med.-surg. Meml. Hosp. Burlington County, Mount Holly, N.J., 1980-81; staff nurse pediatric home care Newborn Nurses, Moorestown, N.J., 1986-87; clin. nurse II surg. intensive care Deborah Heart & Lung Ctr., Browns Mills, N.J., 1986-87, clin. nurse III pediatric cardiology, 1981-86, 87-97; ednl. nurse specialist critical care The Children's Hosp., Phila., 1992-94; instr. nursing of families, maternal-child health, pediat., geriatrics Burlington County Coll., 1994-96; staff nurse pediatric home care Bayada Nurses, Burlington, N.J., 1995; family nurse practitioner Alliance Family Medicine Ctr. Fam. Med. Res. Prog., Mt. Holly, N.J., 1997-99; nurse practitioner long term care The Masonic Home of N.J., Burlington, 1999—. Clin. instr. pediat. Thomas Jefferson U., 1990; clin. instr. adult med. surg. Burlington County coll., 1991. Rep. Congress on Policy and Practice: Gerongol. Health rep., 2001—03. Mem.: ANA, Congress on Policy and Practice (rep. gerontologic health 2001—03), Am. Geriatrics Soc., N.J. State Nurses Assn. (cabinet on continuing edn. rev. team III 1992—96, advanced practice forum 1994—). Home: 253 Spout Spring Ave Lumberton NJ 08048-2041 Fax: 609-386-0414. E-mail: cal@njmasonic.org.

LOTAN, RACHEL, education educator; BA in English Lit. and French Lang., Lit. and Civilization, Tel Aviv U., 1971; MA in Edn., Stanford U., 1981, MA in Sociology, 1983, PhD in Edn., 1985. Assoc. prof. edn. Stanford (Calif.) U., 1999—; tchr. jr. and sr. h.s., 1969—80; rsch. asst. Ctr. for Ednl. Rsch., Stanford U., Calif., 1982—85. Vis. asst./assoc. prof. Inst. for Advancement of Social Integration in Schs., Bar-Ilan U., Israel, 1986—91. Mem. editl. bd.: European Jour. for Intercultural Edn. Office: Stanford U Sch Edn 485 Lasuen Mall Stanford CA 94305-3096*

LOTSPEICH, ELLIN SUE, elementary education educator; b. Spring Valley, Ill., July 2, 1952; d. Donald Robert and Mary Rita (Smith) Mason; m. Thomas Grant Weaver, Jan. 26, 1974 (dec. July 1989); children: Jennifer, Michelle, Patrick; m. Michael Charles Lotspeich, Apr. 9, 1994; children: Michael Charles II, Charles David. BS, Western Ill. U., 1974, M Ednl. Adminstrn., 1995. Unit art specialist Winola Unit Dist., Viola, Ill., 1974-84, Al Wood Unit Dist., Woodhull, Ill., 1984—; discipline based art cons. Getty Ctr. for Edn. in Arts, 1989—; prin. Apollo Elem. Sch., Carbon Cliff, Ill., 1998-2001; ednl. specialist Western Ill. U., 2001—; prin. Irving Elem. Sch., Kewanee, Ill. Exec. bd. Commn. on Edn. Diocese of Peoria, Ill., 1993—, exec. chmn. Religious Edn. Com., 1994—. Mem. Nat. Art Edn. Assn., Ill. Art Edn. Assn. (exec. bd. 1980—, state youth art chmn. 1990-93), Ill. Rembrandt State Assn. (editor newsletter 1987-90, bd. dirs.), Ill. Alliance for Arts, Henry Stark H.S. Art Tchrs. (pres. 1984-96). Home: 621 E Prospect St Kewanee IL 61443-3021 Office: Irving Elem 609 W Central Blvd Kewanee IL 61443

LOTT, MELINDA JO, special education and secondary education educator; b. Detroit, July 16, 1954; d. Frank Norris and Nellie Virginia (Shumaker) L. AA, Mitchell Coll., 1974; BS, Pfeiffer Coll., 1978; M in Elem. Edn., Francis Marion U., 1993. Cert. learning disabilities, mental retardation, secondary, social studies, spl. edn. tchr. Spl. edn. educator Millers Creek (N.C.) Intermediate Sch., 1978-86, Kingstree (S.C.) Elem. Sch., 1986-89, Savannah Grove Elem. Sch., Effingham, S.C., 1989-94, Moore Intermediate Sch., Florence, S.C., 1994—. Faculty adv. coun. rep. Florence Sch. Dist. 1, 1992—; student tchr. supr. Coker Coll., Hartsville, S.C., 1992-93; student placement adv. bd. Savannah Grove Elem. Sch., 1989-94, Moore Intermediate Sch., 1994—. Active First Bapt. Ch., Florence, 1989, Nat. Trust for Hist. Preservation, Washington, 1994, Wildlife Action, Inc., Florence, 1992. Mem. AAUW, S.C. Coun. for Exceptional Children, Children with Attention Deficit Disorders, Orton Dyslexia Soc. (Ednl. Conf. grant 1992, 93), Palmetti State Tchrs. Assn., Internat. Reading Assn., Phi Delta Kappa. Office: Moore Intermediate Sch 1101 Cheraw Dr Florence SC 29501-5619 Home: 2247 Inverness Dr Florence SC 29505-3782

LOTT, VERA NAOMI, artist, educator; b. Allentown, Pa., Oct. 26, 1923; d. Russell Edgar and Tivilia Landis (Gerhart) Kemmerer; m. Jack Edward Lott (dec. Nov. 1998); children: Dennis Michael, Jack Andrew(dec.), Gary Randall, Timothy Blair, Bruce Edward. Grad. h.s., Phila. Art tchr., 1960—, YWCA, Ohio. Judge Ohio State Fair for Childrens Art Show; pvt. art tchr., Westerville, Ohio; pvt. dance instr. Singer for 3 ch. choirs; singer for 2 sr. ctrs. With U.S. Coast Guard, 1940—42. Recipient 1st place for pencil portraits of children, Graceland. Mem.: Westerville Art League (past pres., sec.). Lutheran. Home: 7000 Lee Rd Apt3R Westerville OH 43081-9557

LOU, DAVID YEONG-SUEI, mechanical engineering educator; b. Yuncom, China, Nov. 12, 1937; came to U.S., 1961; s. Yeh Ting and Mo Kwan (Wu) L.; m. Marjorie Feng, Mar. 28, 1964; children: Eugene Chunlin, Derek Chuntao. BSME, Nat. Taiwan U., Taipei, 1959; MSME, MIT, 1963, Mech. Engr., 1966, ScD, 1967. Asst. prof. U. Del., Newark, 1967-70, assoc. prof., 1970-77, prof. mech. engring., 1977-79; prof., chmn. U. Tex., Arlington, 1979-90, Syracuse (N.Y.) U., 1990-92, U. Nebr., Lincoln, 1993—. Vis. prof. Nat. Taiwan U., Taipei, 1973-74. Co-editor: Mechanical Engineering Handbook, 1974; editor Procs. Internat. Power Conf., 1990, Procs. Internat. Conf. on Power Engring., 1992; contbr. articles to profl. jours. Grantee NSF, Dept. of Energy, Dept. of Def., 1967. Mem. ASME (com. chair 1974—, assoc. editor Jour. Engring. for Gas Turbines and Power 1994—2002), Am. Soc. Engring. Edn. Achievements include research in areas of rarefied gases, thermodynamics, heat transfer, fluid mechanics and materials processing. Office: U Nebr N104 WSEC Lincoln NE 68588-0656

LOUGHRAN, JAMES NEWMAN, philosophy educator, college administrator; b. Bklyn., Mar. 22, 1940; s. John Farley and Ethel Margaret (Newman) L. AB, Fordham U., 1964, MA, 1965, PhD in Philosophy, 1975; PhD (hon.), Loyola Coll., Balt., 1985; PhD (hon.), Mt. St. Mary's Coll., 2002. Joined S.J., 1958; ordained priest Roman Catholic Ch., 1970. Instr. philosophy St. Peter's Coll., Jersey City, 1965-67; asst. dean Fordham U., Bronx, N.Y., 1970-73, tchr. philosophy, 1974-79, 82-84, dean, 1979-82; pres. Loyola Marymount U., L.A., 1984-91; acting pres. Bklyn. Coll., 1992; Miller Prof. Philosophy John Carroll U., Cleve., 1992-93; interim pres. Mount St. Mary's Coll., Emmitsburg, Md., 1993-94; interim acad. v.p., Fordham U., Bronx, N.Y., 1994-95; pres. St. Peter's Coll., 1995—. Contbr. numerous articles and revs. to popular and scholarly jours. Mem. (ex-officio) N.J. Commn. for Higher Edn., 2000—02; trustee St. Peter's Coll., Jersey City, 1972—78, 1994—, Xavier U., Cin., 1981—84, Canisius Coll., Buffalo, 1994—2001, Fordham U., 2000—; chair N.J. Presidents' Coun., 2000—02. Mem. Am. Philos. Assn. Avocation: tennis. E-mail: loughran_j@spc.edu.

LOUIE, STEVEN GWON SHENG, physics educator, researcher; b. Canton, China, Mar. 26, 1949; came to U.S., 1961; s. Art and Kam Shui (Lau) L.; m. Jane Yuk Wong, Aug. 3, 1975; children: Jonathan S., Jennifer Y., Sarah W. AB in Math. and Physics, U. Calif., Berkeley, 1972, PhD in Physics, 1976. IBM postdoctoral fellow IBM Watson Rsch. Ctr., Yorktown Heights, N.Y., 1977-79; mem. vis. tech. staff AT&T Bell Labs., Murray Hill, N.J., 1979; asst. prof. U. Pa., Phila., 1979-80; NSF postdoctoral fellow physics dept. U. Calif., Berkeley, 1976-77, assoc. prof., 1980-84, prof., 1984—, Miller rsch. prof., 1986, 95. Faculty scientist Lawrence Berkeley Lab., 1980-93, sr. faculty scientist, 1993—; cons. Exxon Rsch. & Engring. Co., Annandale, N.J., 1981-87. Editor Solid State Comm., 1994—; contbr. over 300 articles to sci. jours. Recipient sustained outstanding rsch. in solid state physics award Dept. Energy, 1993; fellow A.P. Sloan Found., 1980, Guggenheim fellow, 1989. Fellow Am. Phys. Soc. (Aneesur Rahman prize 1996, Davisson-Germer prize 1999); mem. Materials Rsch. Soc. Baptist. Avocations: gardening, skiing, tennis. Office: U Calif Dept Physics 366 LeConte Hall 7300 Berkeley CA 94720-7300

LOUNSBURY, HELEN MARIE, education educator, consultant; d. Joseph and Helen Golden; m. Patrick Lounsbury Sr., Jan. 30, 1960; children: Patrick Jr., Elaine Teresa, Amy Jo. BS with distinction, SUNY, 1960; MA in Lit., Vt. Coll., 1993. Tchr. Mohanasen Ctrl. Sch., Rotterdam, N.Y., 1960-62, Berne-Knox-Westerlo Ctrl. Sch., Berne, N.Y., 1962-96; clin. edn. regional supr. SUNY, Oneonta, 1996—; instr. Coll. St. Rose, Albany, N.Y., 1996-98; themes advisor Albany Sch. Humanities, 1997—2001; scorer Nat. Eral Svc., 2001—; clin. edn. supr. SUNY Potsdam, 2003—; clin. edn. regional supr. SUNY, Potsdam, NY, 2003—. Presenter in field; cons. U.S. Dept. Edn.; pres. bd. edn. Berne-Knox-Westerlo Ctrl. Sch. Dist.; reviewer N.Y. State Dept. Edn., 1997—, CTB McGraw-Hill, 1999--, WESTAT, 1998-; mem. NY Dept. Ed. Commnr. Dist. Adv. Com., 1998-. Co-author: DeBeers, A Factory Family, 1985, Chances Are: Investigations in Probability, 1995. Bd. dirs. Hilltown Cmty. Rsch. Ctr., Berne, 1982-94, Albany County (N.Y.) Rural Housing Alliance, 1984-99, Albany City Reading Coun.; coord. Arts Connection Learning Partnership, Albany, 1992-95, coord. BERNE Heritage Days, 2003. Named N.Y. Tchr. of Excellence, 1993; grantee NEH Masterworks Study, 1995, N.Y. Found. of the Arts, 1993, 94, Pioneering Partner Found., 1996, 98, NY Coun. Humanities, 2003. Mem. ASCD, PTA (hon. life, Disting. Svc. award 1996)), N.Y. State Reading Assn., N.Y. State Math. Assn., Internat. Reading Assn., Assn. Math. Tchrs. N.Y. State, N.Y. State English Tchrs., Hodge Podge Soc., Civil War Roundtable, Kiwanis, Kappa Delta Pi. Avocations: travel, reading, genealogy. Office: Lounsbury Cons East Berne NY 12059

LOURWOOD, DAVID LEE, JR., pharmacotherapist, educator; b. St. Louis, Nov. 20, 1956; s. David Lee Sr. and Nancee Joan (Spradling) L.; m. Betty Jane McClure, May 19, 2001. BS in Pharmacy, St. Louis Coll. Pharmacy, 1979; PharmD, Wayne State U., 1982. Bd. cert. pharmacotherapy specialist, 1992. Pharmacy intern Jewish Hosp., St. Louis, 1976-79; pharmacist Hutzel Hosp., Detroit, 1980-81; clin. pharmacist Cook County Hosp., Chgo., 1981-85, clin. pharmacy coord., 1985-89; asst. dir. pharmacy Edgewater Med. Ctr., Owen Healthcare Inc., Chgo., 1989-90; pharmacotherapist Columbia/ Michael Reese Hosp. and Med. Ctr.-Columbia/HCA, Chgo., 1990-97; clin. pharmacy coord. St. James Hosp. Health Ctr., Chicago Heights, Ill., 1997—99; clin. pharmacist Corum Healthcare, 1999—2001; dir. pharmacy Kindred Hosp., St. Louis, 2002—03; clin. pharmacy coord. Jefferson Meml. Hosp., Crystal City, Mo., 2003—. Clin. asst. prof. dept. pharmacy practice Coll. Pharmacy, U. Ill., Chgo., 1990-97, clin. asst. prof. dept. pharmacy practice Chgo. Coll. Pharmacy, Midwestern U., 1998-2002, St. Louis Coll. Pharmacy, 1999-; cons. Profl. Drug Systems, Inc., St. Louis, 1982—. Author: Antibiotic Drug Interactions in Evaluations of Drug Interactions, 1982—; mem. editl. bd. Annals of Pharmacotherapy, 1986-94, Jour. Am. Pharm. Assn., 1999-2003. Dist. commr. Boy Scouts Am., Oak Park, Ill., 1982-85, La Grange, Ill., 1985-89; pres. Lombard (Ill.) Park Dist. Swim and Dive Team, 1994-96, chmn. water park adv. com., 1996-99. O.J. Cloughly Grad. fellow St. Louis Coll. Pharmacy, 1979. Mem. Am. Soc. Health-Systems Pharmacists, Am. Coll. Clin. Pharmacy, Am. Pharm. Assn., Gateway Coll. Clin. Pharmacy, Mo. Soc. Health-Systems Pharmacists, St. Louis Coll. Pharmacy Alumni Assn., St. Louis Soc. Hosp. Pharmacists, Masons. Avocations: personal computers, baseball, science fiction, jogging. Home: 10078 Stonell Dr Saint Louis MO 63123-5214 Office: Jefferson Meml Hosp PO Box 305 Crystal City MO 63019

LOUTHIAN, BRENDA JENNINGS, elementary music educator; b. Galax, Va., Apr. 30, 1948; d. Thomas Ralph and Blanche Catherine (Galyean) Jennings; m. Jerry Wayne Louthian, Aug. 2, 1972; children: Lindsay, Todd, Brett. BA in Music, Mary Washington Coll., 1970. Music specialist Back Creek/Conehurst Sch., Roanoke, Va., 1970-72, Penn Forest Sch., Roanoke, 1972-73, Mt. Vernon/Roland E. Cook Sch., Roanoke, 1973-81, W.E. Cundiff Sch., Vinton, Va., 1981—. Mem. Music Educators Nat. Conf., Am. Orff-Schulwerk Assn., Va. Highlands Orff-Schuelwerk Assn. (historian 1994-96, v.p. 1997—). Avocations: music, reading, sewing, crafts. Home: 705 Rock Lily Rd Wirtz VA 24184-4012 Office: WE Cundiff Sch 1200 Hardy Rd Vinton VA 24179-2206

LOVAS, SANDOR, chemist, researcher, educator; b. Kunmadaras, Hungary, Apr. 28, 1958; came to the U.S., 1990; s. Sándor and Mária (Diószegi) L.; m. Éva Acs, Apr. 19, 1980; 1 child, Veronika Éva. MS in Chemistry, József Attila U., Szeged, Hungary, 1982, PhD in Organic Chemistry, 1985. Rsch. asst. Biol. Rsch. Ctr., Szeged, 1982-85, rsch. fellow, 1985-90; postdoctoral fellow Creighton U., Omaha, 1990-93, asst. prof., 1994—. Contbr. articles to profl. jours. Grantee State of Nebr., 1991. Mem. Am. Chem. Soc., Am. Peptide Soc., Hungarian Chem. Soc., World Assn. Theoretically Oriented Chemists. Achievements include patent for specific anticancer activity of GNRH-III analogs; research in conformationally constrained peptides and molecular dynamics simulations of peptides. Office: Creighton Univ Dept Biomed Sci 2500 California Plz Dept Biomed Omaha NE 68178-0001

LOVE, GAYLE MAGALENE, special education educator; b. New Orleans, July 25, 1953; d. Lowell F. Sr. and Nathalie Mae (Adams) L.; children: Nathanael Dillard, Raphael. BMEd, Loyola U., New Orleans, 1975, MMEd, 1981; postgrad., U. New Orleans. Cert. learning disabled, emotionally disturbed, gifted-talented, adult edn., mild-moderate, elem.-secondary vocal music, prin., spl. sch. prin., parish/city sch. supr. instrn., supervision of student tchg., supr. adult edn. & spl. edn., child search coord. Asst. prin., dean student svcs. Jefferson Parish Sch. Bd., Harvey, La., chmn. spl. edn. dept., 1990-94; adult educator instr. Chmn. Sch. Bldg. Level Com., 1994-96, 97; presenter St. Joseph the Worker Cath. Ch., 1988, Very Spl. Arts Week Jefferson Parish Pub. Sch. Sys., 1988-2003, Harvest Ripe Ch., 1998; mem. spl. edn. alternative curriculum com., 1990—, Urban Ctr. Tchrs. Devel. com. U. New Orleans, 1990-91. Author: Good Morning, God: Prayers and Reflections and Meditations for Early Morning, 2003. Mem. adv. bd. Jefferson Parish Litter; mem. parish coun. St. Joseph Worker, Grand Lady Knights Peter Claver; mem. Hazel Rhea Hurst Scholarship Com., City Citizens Involved with Today's Youth. Recipient Trailblazer award, Jefferson Parish, La., 2003. Mem.: ASCD, Jefferson Assn. Pub. Sch. Adminstrs., La. Assn. Sch. Execs. Home: 1740 Burnley Dr Marrero LA 70072-4522

LOVE, MILDRED ALLISON, retired secondary school educator, historian, writer, volunteer; b. Moultrie, Ga., Mar. 12, 1915; d. Ulysees Simpson Sr. and Susie Marie (Dukes) Allison; m. George Alsobrook Love, Aug. 24, 1956 (dec. 1978). BSEd, U. Tampa (Fla.), 1941; MS in Home Econs., Fla. State U., 1953; MA in History, U. Miami, Coral Gables, Fla., 1969. Cert. tchr., Fla. Vocat. home econs. tchr. Hamilton County Pub. Schs., Jasper, Fla., 1941-43, Pinellas County Pub. Schs., Tarpon Springs, Fla., 1946-51, Dade County Pub. Schs., Miami, Fla., 1951-61, history tchr., 1961-73; supr. food svcs. Ft. Jackson (S.C.), 1944-46. Chmn. subcoun. for crime prevention Brickell Area, City of Miami, 1983-87; mem. Crisis Response Team, Miami Police Dept., 1983—; vol. VA Hosp., Miami, 1987—; historian, vol. vets affairs VFW Aux., Miami, 1988-89; precinct worker presdl. election, 1976, 80; sponsor history honor soc. Miami Edison Sr. H.S., 1961-73; mem. Mus. of Sci., St. Stephen's Episc. Ch., Coconut Grove, Fla.; mem. Dade Heritage Trust; charter mem. Libr. Congress Assocs.; mem. Arthritis Found., Consumer Union. Mem. AAUW, VFW (aux. post 471 Miami, Fla.), Am. Assn. Ret. Persons, Hist. Assn. S. Fla., U. Miami Alumni Assn., Fla. Ret. Educators Assn., Nat. Wildlife Fedn., Am. Legion (aux. post 29 Miami, Fla.), Nat. Trust Hist. Preservation, Coll. of Arts and Scis. Assn. U. Miami, Fla. Vocat. Home Econs. Tchrs. (pres. 1947), Fla. Vocat. Home Econs. Assn. (pres. 1948-49), Dade Heritage Trust, Woman's Club of Miami Beach, Sierra Club, Phi Alpha Theta. Democrat. Episcopalian. Avocation: foreign languages. Home: 2411 S Miami Ave Miami FL 33129-1527

LOVE, SARA ELIZABETH, retired elementary school educator; b. Detroit, Nov. 5, 1914; d. Gustav John and Florence Marian (Keller) Scherling; m. Harold O. Love, June 12, 1937 (dec. 1986); children: Robert Evans, Barbara Lynn. AB, U. Mich., 1936. Tchg. cert., Mich. Pres. Tombstone (Ariz.) Historama Corp., 1986—, Tombstone Epitaph, 1986—. Pres. Grosse Pointe (Mich.) Womens Rep. Club, 1952-54, Women's Assn. for the Detroit Symphony Orch., 1956-58; chmn. vol. com. Detroit Mus. Art, 1958-60; founder Detroit Assn. of the Soc. of Contbrs. of the Archives of Am. Art, 1960-62. Recipient Hon. award in French studies French Govt., 1936. Mem. Skytine Country Club. Avocations: golf, travel.

LOVE, SHARON IRENE, elementary education educator; b. Pontiac, Mich., July 27, 1950; d. James and Ethlyn (Cole) M.; div.; 1 child, Sheralyn Reneé. BS, Western Mich. U., 1964; postgrad., Oakland U., Rochester, Mich. Cert. elem. educator, early childhood educator, Mich. Tchr. kindergarten Pontiac Bd. Edn., 1964-69, 76-83, 87—, tchr. 1st grade, 1965-66, tchr. 4th grade, 1983-84, tchr. 2d grade, 1984-87. Tchr. trainer triple I.E. classroom instruction Emerson Elem. Sch., Pontiac, 1988-89; trainer Math Their Way, Pontiac Sch. Sys., 1989, leadership, 1990; trainer Mich. Health Model Oakland Schs., Waterford, 1987; co-chair com. for developing and writing new Fine Arts curriculum for Pontiac Sch. Dist., 1993-94; chmn. coordinating coun. Webster Elem. Sch., 1994-95; head tchr. kindergarten pilot Bethune Elem. Sch., 1995-96. Co-author: kindergarten sci. curriculum for Pontiac Sch. Dist., 2000—02. Chair coord. coun. Walt Whitman Elem. Schs., Pontiac, 1987-91; mem. PTA, 1970-90; chair coord. coun. Webster Elem. Sch., 1993-94, Bethune Elem. Sch., 1999-2000, mem. sch. improvement com., 1999-2000, mem. tech. com., 1999-2000. Creative Art grantee Pontiac PTA, 1965; recipient cert. Appreciation Pontiac Blue Ribbon Com.,

1991, cert. for outstanding educator Mich. Gov. Engler, 1991, Mark Twain Elem. cert. for excellence, 2001, AIDS Awareness cert. City of Pontiac, 2001, others. Mem. NAACP, Mich. Edn. Assn., Pontiac Edn. Assn. (del. 1965-66). Avocations: art, writing poetry, sewing. Office: Pontiac Bd Edn 350 Wide Track Dr E Pontiac MI 48342-2243

LOVEJOY, JEAN HASTINGS, social services counselor; b. Battle Creek, Mich, July 1, 1913; d. William Walter and Elizabeth (Fairbank) H.; m. Allen Perry, March 27, 1912; children: Isabel L. Best, Linda L. Ewald, Elizabeth L. Fulton, Margaret L. Baldwin, Helen L. Battad. BA, Mt. Holyoke Coll., So. Hadley, Mass., 1935. Traveling sec. Student Vol. Movement, NYC, 1935; bookkeeper Hartford Consumers Co-op, Conn., 1944; tchr. Pre-School, Congl. Ch., West Hartford, Conn., 1944-45; instr. St. John's U., Shanghai; tchr. Edn., 1st Congl. Ch., Berkeley, Calif., 1958-59; instr. Tunghai U., Taiwan, 1960-63; sec. Pres. Tunghai U., Taichung, Taiwan, 1960-63. Pres. Ecumenical Assn. for Housing, San Rafael, 1971, 78-80; founding mem. Hospice of Havasu, 1982, pres. bd. dir., 1985-87, vol. trainer, 1987-92; bereavement vol. Cmty. Hospice, Tucson, 1993-96; vol. friendly visitor N.W. Interfaith Ctr., Tucson, 1995—; vol. libr. La Rosa Health Ctr., Tucson, 1998-2003. Recipient OACC Sr. Achievement award, 1991; named Vol. of Yr., Marin County, Calif., 1970, 79; street named Lovejoy Way in her honor Novato (Calif.) City Coun., 1980. Mem. LWV (program v.p. Pierce County chpt. 1967, pres. cen. Marin County chpt. 1973-75, legis. analyst land use 1979-80, Calif. chpt.). Mem. United Ch. of Christ (Stephen min.) Home: Apt 8208 7500 N Calle Sin Envidia Tucson AZ 85718-7363

LOVELAND, CHRISTINE ANN, anthropology educator; b. Watertown, S.D., July 28, 1946; d. Earl Joseph and Grace Leanore (Philp) Brown; m. Franklin Olds Loveland III, Nov. 22, 1969; children: Elizbeth Rachel, David Franklin. BA, Carleton Coll., 1968; MA, Duke U., 1973, PhD, 1975. Adj. instr. Wilson Coll., Chambersburg, Pa., 1976-84; asst. prof. sociology and anthropology Shippensburg (Pa.) U., 1985-86, assoc. prof. anthropology, 1986-91, prof., 1991—. Mem. nat. panel profl. advisors Nat. Multiple Sclerosis Soc., N.Y.C., 1994—. Editor, author: Sex Roles and Social Change in Native Lower Central American Societies, 1982; contbg. author: End Results and Starting Points: Expanding the Field of Disability Studies, 1996; contbr. articles to profl. jours. Vol. Pa. Assn. for Blind, Gettysburg, 1984-91. Named Vol. of Yr., Gettysburg chpt. Pa. Assn. for Blind, 1988; Title VI fellow NDEA, 1968-70; grantee Shippensburg U., 1987-91, Nat. Multiple Sclerosis Soc., 1992-93. Fellow Am. Anthrop. Assn.; mem. Soc. for Disability Studies, Am. Ethnol. Soc., Soc. for Med. Anthropology. Avocations: travel, computers, reading. Office: Shippensburg U 1871 Old Main Dr Shippensburg PA 17257-2299

LOVELESS, JAMES KING, art educator; b. Saginaw, Mich., Apr. 24, 1935; s. James Clifton and Edris Maureen (King) L.; m. Ruthann Speer, Oct. 5, 1974; children— Elizabeth, Ellen, Karen, Douglas, David. A.B., DePauw U., 1957; M.F.A., Ind. U., 1960. Asst. prof. art Hope Coll., Holland, Mich., 1960-64; asst. prof. U. Ky., Lexington, 1964-66; prof. Colgate U., Hamilton, N.Y., 1966— . One-man shows include: Everson Mus., Syracuse, N.Y., 1978, Fine Arts Gallery, SUNY, Oneonta, 1984; exhibited in group shows: Munson-Williams-Proctor Inst., Utica, N.Y., 1979, traveling exhbn. sponsored by Mus. Am. Art, Washington; 1981-83; represented in permanent collection: Munson-Williams-Proctor Inst., Utica, Picker Gallery, Colgate U., Hamilton, N.Y., Chase Manhattan Bank, N.Y.C., Gettysburg (Pa.) Coll. Fellow Yaddo, Millay Colony. Home: 2759 E Lake Rd Hamilton NY 13346-9737 Office: Colgate Univ Art and Art History Dept Hamilton NY 13346

LOVELL, KATHRYN SHEEHY, elementary education educator; b. Butte, Mont., Sept. 16, 1948; d. Michael Joseph and Frances Marie (Boyle) Sheehy; m. Willard Francis Lovell, Dec. 27, 1980. BS, Western Mont. Coll., 1970; MEd, Lesley Coll., 1993. 3d grade tchr. Sherman Sch., Butte, 1970-73, kindergarten tchr., 1973-77, McKinley Sch., Butte, 1977-80, 3d grade tchr., 1980-86, West Elem. Sch., Butte, 1986—; 2d grade tchr. Margaret Leary Sch., Butte, 1988-93, tchr. STEP lead, 1993—2002. Mem. student tchg. partnership We. Mont. Coll., 1992—; Keystone mentor, 1995-2001. Keystone grantee NSF, 1995-2000, volunteer & substitute, Montessori Sch. Mem. AAUW, S.W. Mont. Reading Coun., Alpha Delta Kappa. Home: 21 Wathena Dr Butte MT 59701-3179 E-mail: kbvell@montana.com.

LOVELL, WALTER BENJAMIN, secondary education educator, radio broadcaster; b. Cottonwood, Ariz., Jan. 7, 1947; s. Walter William Lovell and Mary Katherine (MacDonald) Bruce; m. Patsy Nichols, July 16, 1965 (div. Nov. 1986); children: Katherine Vi, Walter Kenneth, Karen Jennifer, Kristin Diane; m. Karen Lynn Bird, Mar. 3, 1990. AA, Ea. Ariz. Coll., 1966; B of Music Edn., No. Ariz. U., 1969, MusM, 1975; PhD in Music Edn., Hamilton U., 2002. Dir. of bands Kingman (Ariz.) High Sch., 1968-70; asst. dir. bands Phoenix Union High Sch., 1970-71; dir. bands Carl Hayden High Sch., Phoenix, 1971-73, Mohave High Sch., Bullhead City, Ariz., 1973-78, Elko (Nev.) High Sch., 1978—. Condr. competitive performances with Elko H.S. Band, including Grand Champions Holiday Bowl Parade, Field and Jazz competition, 1994, Nat. Freedom Bowl, Anaheim, Calif., 1988, 90, Disneyland Parade, Anaheim, 1990, Weber State U., Ogden, Utah, 1990-97, 2002, U. Utah, 1995, Boise (Idaho) State U., 1990-97, 2000-01, U. Nev.-Las Vegas Band Competition, 1988, Fiesta Bowl Parade, Phoenix, 1985, Tournament of Roses Parade, Pasadena, 1983, 95, 99, Presdl. Inaugural Parade, Washington, 1981, No. Nev. Youth Band Tour of Great Britain, 1982, Macy's Thanksgiving Day Parade, 1979, 2000, Performances in Washington, 1981, 2000, Hollywood Christmas Parade, 2002; assoc. dir. All-Ariz. Bi-Centennial Band, 1976. Composer: (concert band compositions) Suite For Band, 1975, Tranquility, 1988, (jazz band compositions) Maybe Tuesday, 1974, Sunday Afternoon, 1987. Recipient Gubernatorial Proclamation for Elko H.S. Band, 1981, 83, 86, 88, 90, 92, 94, 96, 98, Proclaimed The Pride of Nev., 1995, 96, 2000, Proclaimed Nev.'s Mus. Amb., 1998, 2000; Gubernatorial Proclamation No. Nev. Youth Band, 1982, Nat. Sch. Band Achievement awards, 1981, 82; recipient Disting. Svc. award U. Nev.-Reno Bands, 1986, Citation of Excellence Nat. Band Assn., Nev. State Bd. Edn., 1983, Disting. Bandmaster of Am. award, 1981, Nev. State Marching Band Champion award, 1983-86, 92-94, 97, 99, 2001, Holiday Bowl Jazz Festival Grand Champion award, 1992, Nev. Music Educator of Yr., 1999; named to Nev. Broadcasters Hall of Fame, 2001; regional finalist Bands of Am., 1999, Class AA Regional Champion, 2001. Mem. Nat. Band Assn. (citation of Excellence 1987), Am. Sch. Band Dirs. Assn., Nev. Music Educators Assn., Music Educators Nat. Conf., Ariz. Band and Orchestra Dir.'s Assn., Internat. Assn. Jazz Educators, Nat. Assn. Jazz Educators, Ariz. Music Educators Assn. Office: Elko High Sch 987 College Ave Elko NV 89801-3419 E-mail: bandguy@elko-nv.com.

LOVERIDGE-SANBONMATSU, JOAN MEREDITH, communication studies and women's studies educator, poet; b. Hartford, Conn., July 5, 1938; d. Gilbert Thomas and Rosabel Frances (Nowry) Loveridge; m. Akira Sanbonmatsu, Aug. 29, 1964; children: James Michael, Kevin Yosh. BA, U. Vt., 1960; MA, Ohio U., 1963; PhD, Pa. State U., 1971. Writer, programming radio/tv WRUV, WCAX, Burlington, Vt., 1956-60, WOUB, Athens, Ohio, 1962-63, AFKN, Korea, 1960-61; unit head ARC, Japan, Korea, 1960-61; asst. prof. SUNY, Brockport, 1963-77, prof. comm. studies and women's studies Oswego, 1977-98, prof. emerita, 1999—, instr. intensive English summer program, 1993—2001, co-coord. women's studies program, 1978-80, 82, instr. internat. studies infusion program, 1985-91. Vis. prof. Rochester (N.Y.) Inst. Tech., 1971; assoc. adj. prof. Monroe C.C., Rochester, 1972-76; instr. Pa. State, State College, 1966-67; cons. for oral history project ARC Overseas Assn., 1994—; cons. Cazenovia Coll., N.Y., 1988-89; pres. bd. dirs. Woman's Career Ctr. Inc., Rochester, 1975-76; invited Japan Lecture Tour, 1997. Author: Winged Odyssey: Poems and Stories, 2002; co-author: Feminism and Woman's Life, 1995; contbg. author: Public Speakers in the US, 1925-1993, Vol. 2, 1994, Life in a Fishbowl: A Call to Serve, 2003; contbr. poetry to publs., 1986—; poetry editor/editl. bd.: Lake Effect, 1985-92; contbr. articles to profl. jours. including Howard Jour. Comms., Comm. Edn., Phoebe and Feminist Jour. Religious edn. team tchr. May Meml. Unitarian Universalist Soc., Syracuse, 1979-81; mem. adv. parent com., Oswego H.S., 1986-87. Recipient Unsung Heroine award Ctrl. N.Y. NOW, Syracuse, 1987, presdl. citation for social change ARC Overseas Assn., 1998; rsch. grantee Pa. State U., 1970, SUNY, Oswego, 1978, 91, 92, 94, 95, 96, N.Y. State United Univ. Professions Profl. Devel. and Quality of Working Life grantee, 1985, 87, 93, 94, 98, SUNY Oswego Women's Ctr. award, 1996, 98, SEED award for outstanding work with disabled students, 1998, Internat. Awareness and Peace award Coalition for Peace Edn., 2000; fellow U. Ill., Chgo., 1983. Mem. N.Y. Asian Studies Assn., Nat. Comm. Assn. (women's caucus job placement dir., exec. bd. 1977-78), Ea. Comm. Assn., N.Y. Nat. Comm. Assn., Soc. for Intercultural Edn., Tng. and Rsch., Nat. Women's Studies Assn., Speech Comm. Assn. P.R., N.Y. State Women's Studies Assn., ARC Overseas Assn. (v.p. 1999-2001), Nat. Assn. Poet and Writers, Inc. Avocations: poetry, Spanish, walking. Home: 23 McCracken Dr Oswego NY 13126-6011

LOVETT, CLARA MARIA, university administrator, historian; b. Trieste, Italy, Aug. 4, 1939; came to U.S., 1962; m. Benjamin F. Brown. BA equivalent, U. Trieste, 1962; MA, U. Tex., Austin, 1967; PhD, U. Tex., 1970. Prof. history Baruch Coll. CUNY, N.Y.C., 1971-82, asst. provost, 1980-82; chief European divsn. Libr. of Congress, Washington, 1982-84; provost, v.p. acad. affairs George Mason U., Fairfax, Va., 1988-93; on leave, dir. Forum on Faculty Roles and Rewards Am. Assn. for Higher Edn., 1993-94; pres. No. Ariz. U., Flagstaff, 1994-2001, pres. emerita, 2001—; sr. fellow, dir. Ctr. for Competency-Measured Edn. The Oquirah Inst., 2002—03; pres., CEO, Am. Assn. for Higher Ed., 2003—. Vis. lectr. Fgn. Svc. Inst., Washington, 1979-85. Author: Democratic Movement in Italy 1830-1876, 1982 (H.R. Marraro prize, Soc. Italian Hist. Studies); Giuseppe Ferrari and the Italian Revolution, 1979 (Phi Alpha Theta book award); Carlo Cattaneo and the Politics of Risorgimento, 1972 (Soc. for Italian Hist. Studies Dissertation award), (bibliography) Contemporary Italy, 1985; co-editor: Women, War, and Revolution, 1980, (essays) State of Western European Studies, 1984; contbr. sects. to publs., U.S., Italy. Organizer Dem. clubs Bklyn., 1972-76; mem. exec. com. Palisades Citizens Assn., Washington, 1985-87; vestry mem. St. David's Episc. Ch., Washington, 1986-89; bd. dirs. Blue Cross Blue Shield Ariz., 1995—; trustee Western Govs. U., 1996—; mem. Ariz. State Bd. Edn., 1999-2001. Fellow Guggenheim Found., 1978-79, Woodrow Wilson Internat. Ctr. for Scholars, 1979 (adv. bd. West European program), Am. Coun. Learned Socs., 1976, Bunting Inst. of Radcliffe Coll., 1975-76, others; named Educator of Yr. Va. Fedn. of Bus. and Profl. Women, 1992. Mem. Am. Assn. Higher Edn. (cons. 1979—), Soc. for Italian Hist. Studies, Assn. Am. Coll. and Univs. (bd. dirs. 1990-93). Avocations: choral singing, swimming. Office: One Dupont Cir Ste 360 Washington DC 20036 E-mail: clara.lovett@nau.edu.

LOVETT, FRANCIS WILLIAM, JR., adult education educator; b. Northampton, Mass., July 9, 1922; s. Francis William Lovett and Elizabeth Claire Costello; m. Shirley Virginia Green, June 19, 1948; children: Francis William Lovett III, Jane L. Schenderlein, Susan L. Dahl. BS with distinction, Wesleyan U., Middletown, Conn., 1948; MS, Northwestern U., 1953. Cert. tchr. N.Y., Ohio. Prin. Latin Sch. of Chgo., 1948—57; headmaster Hillsdale Sch., Cin., 1957—66; counselor Culver Mil. Acad., Ind., 1966—69; headmaster Moravian Acad., Bethlehem, Pa., 1971—74; dir. Duluth Cathedral Sch., Minn., 1974—77; curriculum dir. Univ. Sch., Milw., 1979—86; lectr SUNY, Plattsburgh, 1987—94; lectr. Ohio U., Chillicothe, Ohio, 1996—2000; ret., 2000. Author (literary drama): Intempestuous Storm, 1948 (award of Distinction, 1948); author: (historical novel) Six Colors for a Champion, 2002; contbr. articles to profl. jours. Pfc 10th Mt. Divsn. U.S. Army, 1942—45, Italy. Decorated Bronze Star with 2 oak leaf clusters. Mem.: Am. Conf. for Irish Studies, 10th Mt. Divsn. Nat. Assn., Int. Fed. Mt. Soldiers. Avocations: writing, lecturing, travel in Ireland, travel in Greece. Home: 304 Robin Rd Waverly OH 45690-1521

LOVETT, WENDELL HARPER, architect, educator; b. Seattle, Apr. 2, 1922; s. Wallace Herman and Pearl (Harper) L.; m. Eileen (Whitson), Sept. 3, 1947; children: Corrie, Clare. Attended, Pasadena Jr. Coll., 1943-44; BArch, U. Wash., 1947; MArch, M.I.T., 1948. Arch., designer Naramore, Bain, Brady, and Johanson, Seattle, 1948; arch. assoc. Bassetti and Morse, Seattle, 1948-51; instr. architecture U. Wash., 1948-51; pvt. practice, arch. Seattle, 1951—; asst. prof. U. Wash., 1951-60, assoc. prof., 1960-65, prof., 1965-83, prof. emeritus, 1983—. Lectr. Technische Hochschule, Stuttgart, 1959-60. Prin. works include nuclear reactor bldg., U. Wash., 1960; Villa Simonyi Medina, Wash., 1989; patentee in field. Pres. Citizen's Planning Coun., Seattle, 1968-71; bd. dir. Seattle Baroque Orch., 1998-2002. Served in AUS, 1943-46. Recipient 2d prize Progressive Architecture U.S. Jr. C. of C., 1949; Internat. design award Decima Triennale di Milano, 1954; Arch. Record Homes awards, 1969, 72, 74; Interiors award, 1973; Sunset-AIA awards, 1959, 62, 69, 71; Fulbright grantee, 1959; AIA fellow, 1978 Mem. AIA (sec. Wash. chpt. 1953-54, bd. dirs. Found. Seattle chpt. 1991-92, Seattle chpt. medal 1993, pres. sr. coun. 1991-92, Plestcheeff Inst. bd. dir. 1992; bd.dir., Soc. of Architectural Historians, MDRC, 2002-03. Home and Office: 420 34th Ave Seattle WA 98122-6408

LOVETTE, LILLIE FAYE, education educator; b. Magee, Miss., May 18, 1951; d. Barnett L. and Margaret Smith AA, Hinds Community Coll., 1978; B of Edn., U. Miss., 1980, M of Social Sci., 1981. Social worker, tchr. Sunnybrook Children's Home, Ridgeland, Miss., 1982-83; prof. Holmes Community Coll., Ridgeland, Miss., 1983—. Co-author: (with Dr. Leroy Gruner) Sociology: As You Like It, 1988, Interaction, Conflict and Change, 1989. Fulbright scholar, 1989; NEH fellow; recipient Internat. Fulbright Rsch. award, 1985, Pub. Achievement award Miss. Pub. Humanities, 2003; named Outstanding Educator Miss. Legis., Jackson, 1990, Outstanding Coll. Educator Madison County Chamber of Conn., Ridgeland, 1991. Mem. Am. Sociological Assn., Ala.-Miss. Sociological Assn., Miss. Assn. Univ. Women (internat. rels. chmn. 1991). Episcopalian. Avocation: florist. Home: 204 Royal St Edwards MS 39066-8943 Office: Holmes Community Coll 412 W Ridgeland Ave Ridgeland MS 39157-1815

LOVIN, KEITH HAROLD, academic administrator, philosophy educator; b. Clayton, N.Mex., Apr. 1, 1943; s. Buddie and Wanda (Smith) L.; m. Marsha Kay Gunn, June 11, 1966; children: Camille Jenay, Lauren Kay BA, Baylor U., 1965; postgrad., Yale U., 1965-66; PhD, Rice U., 1971. Prof. philosophy Southwest Tex. State U., San Marcos, 1970-77, chmn. dept. philosophy, 1977-78, dean liberal arts, 1978-81; provost, v.p. acad. affairs Millersville U., Pa., 1981-86; provost, v.p. acad. and student affairs U. So. Colo., Pueblo, 1986-92; pres. Maryville U. St. Louis, 1992—. Adv. bd. Southwest Studies in Philosophy, 1981—90. Contbr. articles to profl. jours. Bd. dirs. St. Louis Symphony Orch., 1995-2001, United Way Greater St. Louis, 1992-99, Boys Hope, Jr. Achievement Mississippi Valley, Inc., 1992-2001, Nat. Coun. Alcohol and Drug Abuse Adv. Bd., St. Louis Intercollegiate Athletic Conf., Higher Edn. Coun., St. Luke's Hosp., vice-chmn., 2001-03, chmn., 2003—; bd. dirs., pres. Ind. Colls. and Univs. Mo., 1999-2002; vice-chair pres.'s adv. com. Mo. Coordinating for Bd. Higher Edn., 2002-03; bd. trustees TV Sta. KETC, 2003—; bd. dirs. KETC Channel 9, 2003—. Mem.: Chesterfield C. of C., Gov. Bus. Edn. Roundtable, Media Club, Univ. Club. Avocation: fly fishing. Home: 13664 Conway Rd Saint Louis MO 63141-7234 Office: Maryville U 13550 Conway Rd Saint Louis MO 63141-7299 E-mail: klovin@maryville.edu.

LOVINGOOD, REBECCA BRITTEN, elementary school educator; b. Bethlehem, Pa., June 5, 1939; d. Clyde Robert and Helen Cauffiel (Britten) L. BS, Syracuse U., 1961; MA, Guildhall Sch. of Music, London, 1962; cert., Jagiellonian U., Krakow, Poland, 1985. Cert. tchr., N.Y., Pa., N.J. Del.; LPN, Pa. Newspaper reporter The Christian Sci. Monitor, Boston, 1963-65; music tchr. Devereux Found., Devon, Pa., 1965-66; elem. sch. tchr. The Episcopal Acad., Merion, Pa., 1966-90; tchr. Diocese of Wilmington Schs., 1991-92; tchr. 2d grade King of Peace Italian Sch. Archdiocese of Phila., Phila., 1992—; 3d grade tchr., music tchr. West End Cath. Sch., Johnstown, Pa. Edn. tchr. U. Ala., Tuscaloosa, 1988; dir. children's theater, Saratoga Performing Arts, Saratoga Springs, N.Y., 1969; dir. music events, Aldeburgh Music Festival, Suffolk, Eng., 1970. Author numerous children's plays. Vol. The Musical Fund Soc., Phila., The Coll. of Physicians. Recipient Legion of Honor, Chapel of Four Chaplains, Phila., 1981; travel grant, Kosciuszko Found., N.Y.C., 1985. Mem. Am. Assn. for the History of Medicine. Democrat. Roman Catholic. Avocations: masters swimming, piano and cello concerts, miniature dachshunds, johnstown symphony. Home: 165 Dartmouth Ave Johnstown PA 15905-2306 Office: West End Catholic Sch 317 Power St Johnstown PA 15906-2730

LOW, BOON CHYE, physicist; b. Singapore, Feb. 13, 1946; came to U.S., 1968; s. Kuei Huat and Ah Tow (Tee) Lau; m. Daphne Nai-Ling Yip, Mar. 31, 1971; 1 child, Yi-Kai. BSc, U. London, Eng., 1968; PhD, U. Chgo., 1972. Scientist High Altitude Observatory Nat. Ctr. for Atmospheric Rsch., Boulder, Colo., 1981-87, sect. head, 1987-90, 97—, acting dir., 1989-90, sr. scientist, 1987—. Mem. mission operation working group for solar physics NASA, 1992-94; vis. sr. scientist Princeton Plasma Physics Lab., 1998-99. Mem. editl. bd. Solar Physics, 1991—. Named Fellow Japan Soc. for Promotion of Sci., U. Tokyo, 1978, Sr. Rsch. Assoc., NASA Marshall Space Flight Ctr., 1980. Mem. Am. Physical Soc., Am. Astron. Soc., Am. Geophysical Union. Office: Nat Ctr for Atmosph Rsch PO Box 3000 Boulder CO 80307-3000 E-mail: low@hao.ucar.edu.

LOW, DONALD GOTTLOB, retired veterinary medicine educator; b. Cheyenne Wells, Colo., May 14, 1925; s. John Louis and Marie (Gabriel) L.; m. Jeanette Maxine Reedy, Dec. 4, 1948 (div. Feb. 1972); children: Ronald, Raymond, Richard, Christine, Cheryl; m. Jane M. Herschler, May 12, 1973. D.V.M., Kans. State U., 1947; PhD, U. Minn., 1956. Pvt. practice vet. medicine, 1947-49; dist. veterinarian U.S. Dept. Agr., 1949-50; instr. U. Minn., 1950-53, 55-56, asso. prof., 1956-60, prof., 1960-65, head dept. vet. hosps., 1965-70; prof., head dept. clin. scis. Colo. State U., 1971-74; prof. vet. medicine, dir. teaching hosp. U. Calif.-Davis, 1974-80, assoc. dean instrn., 1982-83, assoc. dean pub. programs, 1983-93; ret., 1993. Author: (with Osborne, Finco) Small Animal Urology, 1972; Contbr. articles to tech. jours. Active Boy Scouts Am., PTA; established Don Low/Calif. Vet. Med. Assn. Practitioner Fellowship, 1995. Served with AUS, 1943-44; as capt. 1953-55. Recipient Disting. Teaching award U. Minn., 1965, Disting. Svc. award, 1990, 91, Robert W. Kirk award for Disting. Svc., Am. Coll. Vet. Internal Medicine, Disting. Alumnus award Kans. State U. and the Vet. Med. Alumni Assn., 1994. Mem. AVMA, Am. Coll. Vet. Internists (founder), Colo. Vet. Med. Assn., Am. Animal Hosp. Assn. (Veterinarian of Yr. award 1970), Nat. Acad. Practice-Vet. Medicine, Calif. Vet. Med. Assn. (pres. award 1988), Calif. Acad. Vet. Medicine (excellence in Continuing Edn. award 1989, disting. svc. award Wild West Vet. Conf. 1995, Mark Morris Lifetime Achievement award 1998), Phi Zeta. Methodist. Home: 26778 County Road 34 Winters CA 95694-9064

LOW, EMMET FRANCIS, JR., mathematics educator; b. Peoria, Ill., June 10, 1922; s. Charles Walter and Nettie Alys (Baker) Davis; m. Lana Carmen Wiles, Nov. 23, 1974. BS cum laude, Stetson U., 1948; MS, U. Fla., 1950, PhD, 1953. Instr. physics U. Fla., 1950-54; aero. research scientist NACA, Langley Field, Va., 1954-55; asst. prof. math. U. Miami, Coral Gables, Fla., 1955-60, assoc. prof., 1960-67, prof., 1967-72, chmn. dept. math., 1961-66; acting dean U. Miami (Coll. Arts and Scis.), 1966-67, assoc. dean, 1967-68, assoc. dean faculties, 1968-72; prof. math. Coll. at Wise, U. Va., 1972-89, dean Coll. at Wise, 1972-86, chmn. dept. math. scis. Coll. at Wise, 1986-89, emeritus prof. math. Coll. at Wise, 1989—. Vis. research scientist Courant Inst. Math. Scis., NYU, 1959-60 Contbr. articles to profl. jours. Mem. Wise County Indsl. Devel. Authority, 1992—, chmn., 1996—. Served with USAAF, 1942-46. Recipient William P. Kanto award for significant contbns. to pub. edn. Forum on Edn., 1998; hon. Ky. Col.; established endowed chair in physics U. Va. Coll. at Wise, 1999. Mem. Am. Math. Soc., Math. Assn. Am., Soc. Indsl. and Applied Math., Nat. Council Tchrs. of Math., Southwest Va. Council Tchrs. of Math. (Outstanding Svc. award 1999), AAUP, AAAS, Sigma Xi, Delta Theta Mu, Phi Delta Kappa, Phi Kappa Phi. Clubs: Univ. Yacht (Miami, Fla.); Kiwanis.

LOW, MORTON DAVID, physician, educator, policy consultant; b. Lethbridge, Alta., Can., Mar. 25, 1935; s. Solon Earl and Alice Fern (Litchfield) L.; m. Cecilia Margaret Comba, Aug. 22, 1959 (div. 1983); children— Cecilia Alice, Sarah Elizabeth, Peter Jon Eric; m. Barbara Joan McLeod, Aug. 25, 1984; 1 child, Kelsey Alexandra MD, C.M., Queen's U., 1960, M.Sc. in Medicine, 1962; PhD with honors, Baylor U., 1966. From instr. to asst. prof. Baylor Coll. Medicine, Houston, 1965-68; assoc. prof. medicine U. B.C., Vancouver, Can., 1968-78, prof. medicine, 1978-89, clin. assoc. dean, 1974-76, assoc. dean rsch. and grad. studies, 1977-78, coord. health scis., 1985-89, creator Health Policy Rsch. Unit, 1987; Alkek-Williams Disting. Prof. and pres. U. Tex. Health Sci. Ctr., Houston, 1989-2000, disting. mem. faculty Grad. Sch. Biomed. Scis., 1989—, dir. Health Policy Inst., 1990—; Rockwell chair in soc. and health, dir. Ctr. Soc./Population U. Tex., Houston, 2000—; prof. neurology U. Tex. Med. Sch., Houston, 1989—2001; prof. health policy and mgmt. Sch. Pub. Health U. Tex., 1989—. Cons. in neurology U. Hosp. Shaughnessy site, Vancouver, 1971-89, U. B.C. site, Vancouver, 1970-89; dir. dept. diagnostic neurophysiology Vancouver Gen. Hosp., 1968-87; cons. in EEG, 1987-89; exec. dir. Rsch. Inst., 1981-86; med. sci. adv. com. USIA, 1991-93; adj. prof. Health Informatics Sch. Allied Health Scis.; mem. Premier's Adv. Coun. on Health, Alta., Can., 2000-2002; strategic adv. Calgary Regional Health Auth., 2002—. Mem. editorial bd. numerous jours.; contbr. articles to profl. jours. Bd. dirs. Tex. Inst. for Rehab. and Rsch. Found., Greater Houston Ptnrship., 1994-2000, Episcopal Health Charities Found., 1997—, Houston Ind. Sch. Dist. Found., 2002—; governing bd. Houston Mus. Natural Sci., 1991-97; trustee Kinkaid Sch., Houston, 1991—, Meml.-Hermann Hosp. Sys., 1997-2000. Med. Rsch. Coun. Can. grantee, 1968-80; recipient Tree of Life award Jewish Nat. Fund, 1995, Caring Spirit award Inst. Religion, 1995. Fellow Am. EEG Soc., Royal Coll. Physicians (Can.), Royal Soc. Medicine (London); mem. AMA, Tex. Med. Assn. (coun. on med. edn. 1990-2000), Tex. Found. Soc. & Health (founding chmn. 1999), Can. Soc. Clin. Neurophysiology, Internat. Fedn. Socs. for EEG and Clin. Neurophysiology (rules com. 1977-81, sec. 1981-85), Assn. Acad. Health Ctrs. (task force on access to care and orgn. health svcs. 1988-95, chmn. 1992, task force on instnl. values 1989-95), Harris County Med. Soc., Am. Coun. Edn., Forum Club of Houston (governing bd. 1991-96). Avocations: sailing instructing, photography, youth soccer coach, vol. ski-patrol, flying. Office: U Tex-Houston Health Sci PO Box 20036 Houston TX 77225-0036 E-mail: david.low@uth.tmc.edu.

LOW, SETHA MARILYN, anthropology and psychology educator, consultant; b. L.A., Mar. 14, 1948; BA in Psychology and Biology, Pitzer Coll., Claremont, Calif., 1969; MA in Anthropology, U. Calif., Berkeley, 1971, PhD in Anthropology, 1976; MA (hon.), U. Pa., 1983. Instr. anthropology San Francisco State U., 1971; lectr. dept. landscape architecture and regional planning U. Pa., Phila., 1974-76, asst. prof. Sch. Allied Med. Professions, 1976-77, asst. prof. dept. anthropology, 1976-82, assoc. prof. dept. anthropology, 1982-88, mem. grad. group Sch. Social Work, 1977-87; prof. PhD programs in anthropology and environ. psychology CUNY Grad. Sch. and Univ. Ctr., 1987—, dir. pub. space rsch. group Ctr. for Human Environs., 1988—. Hon. prof. U. Costa Rica, 1986-87; cons. Andropogon Assocs., Phila., 1978, Nat. Trust for Hist. Preservation, Washington, 1981-92, U. del Valle Guatemala, 1982-86, Hanna/Olin Assocs., Phila.,

1983-89, Carnegie Assocs., Princeton, N.J., 1983-89, Office Tech. Assessment, Washington, 1986, Am. Folklife Ctr., Washington, 1988-90, Central Park Conservancy, N.Y.C., 1992, Columbia U., 1993, State of Pa., Harrisburg, 1994, Nat. Park Svc., 1995-96, N.Y.C. Dept. Parks and Recreation, 1996—; also others; vis. lectr. dept. landscape arch. and regional planning U. Pa., Phila., 1992—; vis. adj. prof. N.Y.U., 1995; cons. Nat. Park Svc., 1994-95; cons. Dept. Parks and Recreation, N.Y.C., 1996-98, Getty Ctr., 1998-99; cons. Granada Television, England, 1999. Corr. editor Med. Anthropology Quar., 1976-82, Practicing Anthropology, 1977-86; editor med. anthropology series SUNY Press, 1983—; editor Cultural Aspects of Design Newsletter, 1985—; assoc. editor Med. Anthropology Jour., 1986—, Advances in Environ., Behavior and Design Series, 1989-91, Gordon and Breach, 1992—, Medical Anthropological Quarterly, 1994—, City and Society, 1995—; contbg. editor unit news Anthropology Newsletter, 1986-89; contbr. articles to profl. jours. Mem. design com. Parks Coun., N.Y.C., 1992—, Citizens Commn. N.Y.C., 1995-97, Nat. Heritage Coalition, 1993?—, Mcpl. Arts Soc., 1992—; active Phila. Mayor's Commn. on Health in Eighties, 1982-83, Pinelands' Commn. N.J., 1983-84; com. advisor Comprehensive Town Planning. Recipient Robert Textor and Family award for excellence in Anticipatory Anthropology, 2000; grantee Hunter-Grubb Found., El Salvador, 1968-69, U. Calif., Costa Rica, 1973-74, NIMH, 1976-78, Ctr. for Environ. Design and Planning, 1981-82, U. Pa., Guatemala, 1982-83, 85-86, Wenner-Gren Found. for Anthrop. Rsch., 1987-88, 95-96, NSF, Zagreb, Yugoslavia, 1988, Rsch. Found. CUNY, 1989-90, CUNY Caribbean Exch. Program, 1992-93, Wenner-Gren Found. Grant-In-Aid, 1994-96; fellow Ctr. for L.Am. Studies, 1972-74, NIMH, 1972-74, Fulbright rsch. fellow, San Jose, Costa Rica, 1986-87, NEH, John Carter Brown Libr. fellow, 1989-90, John Simon Guggenheim fellow, 1996-97; Getty Conservation Inst. Guest scholar, 2003. Fellow Am. Anthrop. Assn. (exec. bd. 1993-96), Soc. for Gen. Anthropology, Wenner Gren Found., 1997-98, Soc. for Applied Anthropology (exec. bd. 1993-96), Soc. for Cultural Anthropology; mem. Environ. Design Rsch. Assn. (bd. dirs. 1987-90, vice chmn. 1987-88, chmn. 1988-89), Soc. for L.Am. Anthropology (sec. 1986-88), Soc. for Med. Anthropology (exec. bd. 1986-89), Am. Ethnol. Soc., Soc. for Urban Anthropology (exec. bd. 1992—, program editor), Soc. Urban, Nat. and Trnasnat. Anthropology (pres.), Soc. for Psychol. Anthropology, L.Am. Studies Assn., Internat. Assn. People and Their Phys. Surroundings. Office: CUNY The Grad Ctr 365 5th Ave New York NY 10016-4334 E-mail: slow@gc.cuny.edu.

LOW, WALTER CHENEY, neuroscience and physiology educator; Madera, Calif., May 11, 1950; s. George Chen and Linda Quan (Gong) L.; m. Margaret Mary Schwarz, June 4, 1983; children: Matthew Mangan, Elizabeth Catharine. BS with honors, U. Calif.-Santa Barbara, 1972; MS, U. Mich., 1974, PhD, 1979. Postdoctoral fellow U. Cambridge, Eng., 1979-80, U. Vt., Burlington, 1980-83; asst. prof. physiology Ind. U. Sch. Med., Indpls., 1983-84, asst. prof. physiology, biophysics and med. neurobiology, 1984-89, assoc. prof. physiology, biophysicis and medical neurobiology, 1989-90; assoc. prof. physiology, neurosurgery, physiology & neurosci. U. Minn. Med. Sch., Mpls., 1990-93; dir. lab. for Neurol Transplantation, 1990—; prof. Neurosurgery, Physiology and Neurosci., 1993—; dir. Lab for Cell and Gene Therapies, 1995—; assoc. dir. Alzheimer's Disease Ctr., 1995—; dir. grad. program in physiology and biophysics, Sch. Medicine Ind. U., 1985-88. Contbr. numerous publs. to profl. jours. on brain rsch. Established Investigator Award Am. Heart Assn., 1990—. Recipient Individual Nat. Rsch. Svc. award Nat. Heart, Lung and Blood Inst., 1981-83, Nat. Inst. Neurol., Communicative Disorders and Stroke, 1979, Bank of Am. Lab. Scis. award, 1968; grantee NIH, 1984, 85, 87-92, Alzheimers Disease Assoc. award, 1988-89, Am. Parkinsons Disease Assoc. award, 1993-94, Am. Cancer Soc. award, 1994-95, Am. Heart Assn., 1987-90; Rackham U. Mich., 1976-78; internat. programs travel Ind. U., 1984; AGAN rsch. fellow Am. Heart Assn., 1980-81; Rotary scholar, 1968-69. Mem. AAAS, Soc. for Neurosci. (pres. Indpls. chpt. 1985-87), Am. Soc. for Neural Transplantation (sec. elect. 1994-95, pres. 1995-96), Internat. Brain Rsch. Orgn., Calif. Scholastic Fedn. (life), N.Y. Acad Sci., Sigma Xi. Avocations: tennis, cross-country skiing, sailing. Office: U Minn Med Sch Dept Neurosurgery Box 96 UMHC 420 Delaware St SE Minneapolis MN 55455-0374

LOWDER, MARY KATHERINE, school system administrator; b. Asheville, N.C., Sept. 11, 1943; d. William Robert Jr. and Iris Myrtle (Holden) Sherrill; m. Marcus William Sumner, Oct. 26, 1962 (div. June 1973); 1 child, Marcus Kevin; m. Frank Pearson Robinson, Jr., Oct. 26, 1974 (div. Jan. 1997); m. Charles Douglas Lowder, Aug. 5, 1999. BS in Edn., Western Carolina U., Cullowhee, N.C., 1968, MA in Edn., 1983. Cert. tchr., N.C. Tchr. reading Jackson County Bd. Edn., Sylva, N.C., 1968-69, elem. tchr., 1970-76; instr. reading Western Carolina U., 1968, instr. remedial reading, 1972; Reading Program developer Haywood County Bd. Edn., Waynesville, N.C., 1976-82, Resource and Program developer, 1982—. Cons. divsn. health, safety and phys. edn. N.C. Dept. Pub. Instrn., Raleigh, 1974-75; mem. adv. bd. Haywood Tech. Inst., Clyde, N.C., 1978-79; mem. N.C. Textbook Commn., Raleigh, 1989-93; mem. curriculum rev. com. in mktg. edn., bus. edn. N.C. Dept. Pub. Instrn., 1992, health edn., 1993. Compiler: Robert Lee Holden Family, 1993; contbr. to periodical; creator vocabulary game Jaw Breakers, 1977. Vol. Reading Is Fundamental project Haywood County Libr., 1978-79; treas. PTO, 1971-72; active Haywood County Found. Bd., 1995—. Recipient Gold Key award N.C. State Supt., 1991. Mem. NEA, ASCD, N.C. Assn. Educators (sec. 1977, v.p./pres. elect 1994-95, pres. 1995-96), Internat. Reading Assn. (v.p. 1978-79, pres. 1979-80), Bus. and Profl. Women's Orgn., Friends of Haywood County Libr., Delta Kappa Gamma (corr. sec. 1988-90, v.p. 1990-92, pres. 1992-94), Phi Delta Kappa, Kappa Delta Pi. Democrat. Avocations: genealogy, travel. Home: PO Box 336 Hazelwood NC 28738-0336

LOWE, CLAYTON KENT, radio film critic, educator; b. Endicott, N.Y., July 10, 1936; s. Clayton Edwin and Loretta Arlene (Terry) L.; m. Janet E. Snider, 1957 (div. 1977); children: Steven Scott, Kim Ann Parker, David William, Rebecca Michelle Sobel; m. Robin S. McKell, 1980 (div. 1993). BA, Bethany Coll., 1958; MS, Butler U., 1967; PhD, Ohio State U., 1970; BD, Christian Theol. Sem., Indpls., 1962. Pastor Bellaire (Ohio) Christian Ch., 1957-58, Beallsville (Ohio) Christian Ch., 1958, Russellville (Ind.) Christian Ch., 1958-60, Montclair (Ind.) Christian Ch., 1960-61; youth dir. St. Paul United Ch. of Christ, Columbus, 1967-70; asst. prof. journalism U. Ga., 1970-72; asst. prof. comm. Ohio State U., Columbus, 1972-73, asst. prof. photography and cinema, 1973-74, assoc. prof., 1974—, chairperson photography and cinema, 1974-78, assoc. prof. emeritus, 1992—. Comml. TV prodr., dir., writer Sta. WISH-TV, 1960—66, Sta. WLWI-TV, 1966—67, Sta. WOSU-TV, 1967—70; moderator World Film Classics, Educable TV-25, 1991—97, also bd. dirs.; part-time faculty Franklin U., 2000—; film critic It's Movie Time WCBE FM, 2001—; part-time faculty Denison U., 2003. Editor: The Movies on Media Catalog, 1995, 2000, Movies on Media Video Collection Bd. dirs. Columbus Friends of the Libr.; trustee Met. Libr., 1997—2002. Nominee Regional Emmy award, Lucasville, 1970, High Street, 1975; recipient Casper award for A Thing Called Hope, WISH-TV, 1966, Regional Emmy award for A Tribute to Dr. King, 1968, Leadership award, Ohio State U. Outstanding Alumni Soc., 1997, Communicator award of excellence for It's Movie Time New Yr.'s Spl., Sta WCBE-FM, 2002; grantee, Eli Lilly Found., 1961—63, Ohio State U. Devel. of media on media Study Collection, 1985, Ohio Humanities Coun., 1996—97, 1999. Mem.: Ohio State U. Dept. Photography and Cinema Alumni Assn. (pres. 1994—95, 2001—02, bd. dirs. 1994—). Home: 68 Walhalla Rd Columbus OH 43202-1441

LOWE, FORREST GILBERT, mechanical engineering educator; b. Gilman City, Mo., Mar. 27, 1927; s. Forrest Ray and Alice (Mather) L.; m. Joan Blaine, Aug. 15, 1948. BS in Edn., N.W. Mo. State U., 1951; MS, Tex. Christian U., 1962; EdD, Nova U., 1989. Registered profl. engr., Mo. Tchr. Maryville (Mo.) Sch. Dist., 1950-53, Kansas City (Mo.) Sch. Dist., 1953-56; nuclear engr. Convair divsn. Gen. Dynamics, Ft. Worth, 1956-59; instr. Kansas City Jr. Coll., 1959-64, Met. C.C. Dist., Kansas City, 1964-93; vis. assoc. prof. mech. engring. dept. U. Mo., Kansas City, 1982—. Past pres. Mid Am. Engr. Guidance Coun. With USCG, 1944-45. Recipient award Sci. Pioneers, 1974, 79, 84, 95. 2000. Mem. NSPE, Am. Soc. Engring. Edn., Soc. Mfg. Engrs., Am. Assn. Physics Tchrs., Mo. Soc. Profl. Engrs. (sec., chmn. profl. engring. in edn. Western chpt. 1982-92, pres. 1995—), Mo. Acad. Sci., Robotics Internat., Compter and Automated Sys. Assn., Am. Math. Assn. 2-Yr. Colls. (conv. chmn. 1987), Nat. Assn. Indsl. Tech. (accrediting bd.), Order of Engr., Masons, York Rite MO., Shriners, Sigma Phi Sigma, Epsilon Pi Tau. Republican. Baptist. Home: 8412 E 49th St Kansas City MO 64129-2104 Office: UMKC 5100 Rockhill Rd Kansas City MO 64110-2823 Business E-Mail: lowef@umkc.edu.

LOWE, LISA, education educator, department chairman; BA in history, Stanford U., 1977; PhD in lit., U. of Calif., Santa Cruz, 1986. Prof. comparative lit. U. Calif. at San Diego, 1986—, chmn., lit. dept., 1998—2001. Exec. com. Divsn. on Sociol. Approaches to Lit. of the Modern Lang. Assn., 2001—; adv. bd. U. of Calif. Humanities Rsch. Inst., U. of Calif. President's Humanities Commn.; disting. faculty vis. Ctr. for Ideas and Soc. at U. of Calif., Riverside. Author: (book) Critical Terrains: French and British Orientalisms, 1991, Immigrant Acts: On Asian American Cultural Politics, 1996 (Book award in Cultural Studies from the Assn. for Asian Am. Studies, 1997); co-editor: The Politics of Culture in the Shadow of Capital, 1997. Fellowship, John Simon Guggenheim Meml. Found., 2003. Mem.: Nat. Coun. of the Am. Studies Assn. Office: U of Calif, San Diego Lit Dept 9500 Gilman Dr La Jolla CA 92093

LOWELL, JEANNE, nursing educator, psychiatric-mental health nurse; b. Duncan, Okla., July 3, 1946; d. E.O. and Abbie Louise (Wood) Meeks. AS in Nursing, Cameron U., Lawton, Okla., 1970; BS in Edn., U. Cen. Okla., Edmond, Okla., 1976; MS in Nursing, Tex. Woman's U., 1981; postgrad., U. Okla. Cert. psychiat. nurse. Instr. nursing Cameron U., 1980-82; asst. prof. nursing U. Okla., Oklahoma City, 1982-86; dir. nursing Community Mental Health Ctr., Norman, Okla., 1986-89; prof. nursing Oklahoma City Community Coll., 1989—2002. Contbr. articles to profl. jours. Mem.: Am. Assn. Legal Nurse Cons. (cert.). Home: 213 Skylark Ct Norman OK 73069-8664

LOWENBERG, GEORGINA GRACE, retired elementary school educator; b. El Paso, Tex., Feb. 15, 1944; d. Eduardo Antonio and Grace Elizabeth (Fletcher) Orellana; m. Edward Daniel Lowenberg, June 14, 1968, (div. 1985); 1 child, Jennifer Anne. BSEd, U. Tex., El Paso, 1965, postgrad., 1965-66, U. St. Thomas, 1983. Permanent profl. teaching cert., Tex. Tchr. 5th grade El Paso Pub. Sch. Dist., 1965-70; tchr. 3d grade gifted, talented Ysleta Ind. Sch. Dist., El Paso, 1980—2002. Mem. com. Tex. State Textbook Selection Com., Austin, 1984-85, Tex. State TEAMS Math Adv. Com., Austin, 1986-87; sci. presentor Silver Burdett, Albuquerque, 1985-86; critic reader Scott-Foresman, Dallas, 1986; pres., v.p. Scotsdale Elem. Sch. PTA, El Paso, 1976-83; v.p. Eastwood Middle Sch. PTA, El Paso, 1984-85; mem. Eastwood Heights Elem. Sch. PTA, 1985-87; sec. Eastwood High Sch. Band Boosters, El Paso, 1985-89, Speech Boosters, 1986-88; life mem. Tex. State PTA, 1981—. Troop leader Brownie and Jr. Girl Scouts Am., El Paso, 1977-82; dir. Eaglette Dance Team, 1994—. Named Tchr. of Yr., Eastwood Heights Elem., 1983, Top Ten Dist. Tchr. of Yr., 1983. Mem. Assn. Tex. Profl. Educators (regional treas. 1987-88). Roman Catholic.

LOWENFELD, ANDREAS FRANK, law educator, arbitrator; b. Berlin, May 30, 1930; s. Henry and Yela (Herschkowitsch) L.; m. Elena Machado, Aug. 11, 1962; children: Julian, Marianna. AB magna cum laude, Harvard U., 1951, LLB magna cum laude, 1955. Bar: N.Y. 1955, U.S. Supreme Ct. 1961. Assoc. Hyde and de Vries, N.Y.C., 1957-61; spl. asst. to legal adv. U.S. State Dept., 1961-63, asst. legal adviser for econ. affairs, 1963-65, dep. legal adviser, 1965-66; fellow John F. Kennedy Inst. Politics Harvard U., Cambridge, Mass., 1966-67; prof. law Sch. Law NYU, N.Y.C., 1967—, Charles L. Denison prof. law, 1981-94, Herbert and Rose Rubin prof. internat. law, 1994—. Arbitrator internat. comml. panels Internat. C. of C., Am. Arbitration Assn., Internat. Ctr. for Settlement of Investment Disputes. Author (with Abram Chayes and Thomas Ehrlich): International Legal Process, 1968—69; author: Aviation Law, Cases and Materials, 1972, 2d edit., 1981, International Economic Law, vol.I, 1975, 3d edit., 1997, vol. II, 1976, 2d edit., 1982, vol. III, 1977, vol. IV, 1977, 2d edit., 1984, vol. VI, 1979; : 2d edit., 1983, Conflict of Laws, Federal, State and International Perspectives, 1986, 2d rev. edit., 2002, International Litigation and Arbitration, 1993, 2d edit., 2002, International Litigation: The Quest for Reasonableness, 1996, The Role of Government in International Trade: Essays Over Three Decades, 2000, International Economic Law, 2002; editor, co-author Expropriation in the Americas: A Comparative Law Study, 1971; assoc. reporter: Am. Law Inst. Restatement on Foreign Relations Law; co-reporter Am. Law Inst. Project on Internat. Jurisdiction and Judgments; contbr. articles and book revs. on pub. internat. law, internat. econ. law, air law, conflict of laws, arbitration, history and politics to profl. jours. Mem.: ABA, Internat. Acad. Comparative Law, Inst. de Droit Internat., Coun. Fgn. Rels., Am. Law Inst., Am. Arbitration Assn. (arbitrator), Am. Soc. Internat. Law, Assn. of Bar of City of N.Y., Gray's Inn (assoc.). Home: 5776 Palisade Ave Bronx NY 10471-1212 Office: NYU Sch Law Sch Law 40 Washington Sq S New York NY 10012-1005 E-mail: andreas.lowenfeld@NYU.edu.

LOWENSTEIN, HENRY, business educator, dean; b. Danville, Va., Jan. 29, 1954; s. Murray H. and Jacqueline D. (Gerson) L.; divorced; children: Jennifer Anne, Sarah Helen. BSBA with hons., Va. Commonwealth U., 1975; MBA Transp., George Washington U., 1976; PhD Labor/Indsl. Rels., U. Ill., 1984. V.p. Americana Furniture, Inc., Richmond, Va., 1977-80; asst. mgmt. analyst U.S. Office Mgmt. and Budget, Washington, 1975-76; instr. mgmt. Va. Commonwealth U., Richmond, 1977-78; grad. rsch. asst. U. Ill. Urbana/Champaign, Urbana, 1978-80; asst. prof. mgmt. U. Ill. Chgo., Chgo., 1980-85; dir. corp. edn. Kemper Group, Long Grove, Ill., 1985-89; v.p., dir. edn. Dominion Bankshares Corp., Roanoke, Va., 1989-90; chairperson, prof. pub. adminstrn. Gov.'s State U., University Park, Ill., 1990-94; chairperson, prof. bus. W. Va. U. Parkersburg, 1994-2000; prof. mgmt., dean Sch. Bus. and Pub. Adminstrn. Calif. State U., Bakersfield, 2000—. Transp. cons. Ill. Gen. Assembly, Springfield, 1981-85, Chgoland C. of C., 1982-93, Mid-Ohio Valley C. of C., Parkersburg, 1994-2000; cons. editor Harper and Row Pubs., N.Y.C., 1982; cons. editor MacMillian Pubs., N.Y.C., 1984; higher edn. cons. W.Va. Gen. Assembly, 1994-2000. Assoc. editor/co-founder: Jour. of Mgmt. Case Studies, 1984; cons. editor: Strategy Formulation: Power and Politics, 1984, Strategic Management: Planning and Implementation, 1982; co-author: An Act to Reorganize the Regional Transportation Authority, 1983; guest reviewer Jour. Ethics and Behavior, 2000; contbr. articles to profl. pubs. Recipient grad. fellowship U. Ill.-Urbana/Champaign, Urbana, 1978-80, Scottish Rite Found. fellowship George Washington U., Washington, 1975-76; cited for Svc. to the State, Gov. of Ill., Springfield, 1985. Mem. Transp. Rsch. Forum of Chgo., Ill. Assn. Grad. Programs on Pub. Adminstrn. (bd. dirs. 1990-94), Omicron Delta Epsilon, Sigma Beta Delta. Jewish. Avocations: reading, classical music, opera. Office: Calif State U Bakersfield Sch Bus & Pub Adminstrn 9001 Stockdale Hwy Bakersfield CA 93311-1099

LOWENTROUT, PETER MURRAY, religious studies educator; b. Salinas, Calif., Mar. 14, 1948; m. Christine Ione, Sept. 30, 1980; children: Mary, Brandon. AB, U. Calif., Riverside, 1973; PhD, U. So. Calif., L.A., 1983. Prof. religious studies Calif. State U., Long Beach, 1981—, chair dept. religious studies, 1999—. Contbr. articles to profl. jours. Capt. Orange County Fire Dept., Orange, Calif., 1977-94. Mem. Am. Acad. Religion (regional pres. 1989-90), Ctr. for Theology and Lit. U. Durham (Eng.), Sci. Fi. Rsch. Assoc. (pres. 1991, 92). Office: Calif State U Dept Religious Studies 1250 N Bellflower Blvd Dept Long Beach CA 90840-0001 E-mail: plowentr@csulb.edu.

LOWERY, LAWRENCE FRANK, mathematic science and computer educator; b. Oakland, Calif., June 26, 1932; AA, U. Calif., Berkeley, 1952, BA, 1954, MA, 1962, EdD, 1965. Assoc dean Sch. Edn. U. Calif., Berkeley, 1980-84, prof., 1965—. Contbr. articles to profl. jours.; also, books, videos and films; prolific writer. Numerous leadership roles in field. With U.S. Army, 1954-56. Mem. AAAS, ASCD, Am. Edn. Rsch. Assn. (res. rev. bd.), Assn. for the Edn. Tchrs. Sci., Phi Delta Kappa. Home: 650 Diablo Rd Danville CA 94526-2802

LOWI, THEODORE J(AY), political science educator; b. Gadsden, Ala., July 9, 1931; s. Alvin R. and Janice (Haas) L.; m. Angele M. Daniel, May 11, 1963; children: Anna Amelie, Jason Daniel. BA, Mich. State U., 1954; MA, Yale U., 1955, PhD, 1961; HLD (hon.), Oakland U., 1972; LittD (hon.), SUNY, Stony Brook, 1988; Doctorate (hon.), Nat. Found. Polit. Scis., Paris, 1992. Mem. faculty dept. govt. Cornell U., 1959-65, 72—, asst. prof., 1961-65, John L. Senior prof. Am. insns., 1972—; assoc. prof. U. Chgo., 1965-69, prof., 1969-72. Fellow Ctr. Advanced Study in Behavioral Scis., 1977-78; chair Am. civilization U. Paris, 1981-82. Author: At the Pleasure of the Mayor, 1964, The End of Liberalism, 1969, 2d edit., 1979, Japanese edit., 1981, French edit., 1987, The Politics of Disorder, 1971, Incomplete Conquest: Governing America, 1981, The Personal President: Power Invested, Promise Unfulfilled, 1985, The End of the Republican Era, 1995, La Scienza del Politiche, 1999; author: (with others) Poliscide - Big Government, Big Science, Lilliputian Politics, 1976, 1990, Nationalizing Government: Public Policies in America, 1981 Spanish edit., 1993; author: (with B. Ginsberg and Kenneth Shepsle) American Government: Power and Purpose, 1990, 7th edit., 2002; author: (with B. Ginsberg) Embattled Democracy, 1995; author: (with B. Ginsberg and M. Weir) We the People, 1997, 4th edit., 2003; author: (with J. Romance) A Republic of Parties? Debating the Two-Party System, 1998; author: (with Robert Kennedy) The Pursuit of Justice, 1964. Recipient Richard Neustadt award for Best Book on Presidency, 1986; Social Sci. Rsch. Coun. fellow, 1963-64; Guggenheim Found. fellow, 1967-68; NEH fellow, 1977-78; Ford Found. fellow, 1977-78; Fulbright 40th Anniversary Disting fellow, 1987. Mem. Am. Polit. Sci. Assn. (v.p. 1985-86, pres. 1991), Am Acad. Arts and Sci., Policy Studies Orgn. (pres. 1977), Internat. Polit. Sci. Assn. (1st v.p. 1994-97, pres. 1997-2000). Home: 101 Delaware Ave Ithaca NY 14850-4707 E-mail: TJL7@cornell.edu.

LOWMAN, ROBERT PAUL, psychology educator, academic administrator; b. Lynwood, Calif., Jan. 23, 1947; s. Hubert Alden and Martha Guynn (Howard) L.; m. Kathleen Marie Drew, June 25, 1972; children: Sarah Guynn, Amy Katherine. AB, U. So. Calif., 1967; MA, Claremont U., 1969, PhD, 1973. Asst. prof. U. Wis., Milw., 1972-76; adminstrv. officer APA, Washington, 1976-81; asst. dean Kans. State U., Manhattan, 1981-86, assoc. dean grad. sch., 1986-90, assoc. vice provost, 1990-91; dir. rsch. svcs. U. N.C., Chapel Hill, 1991—2002, adj assoc. prof. psychology, 1991—, assoc. vice chancellor for rsch., 1994-96, 2001—, assoc. vice provost for rsch., 1996-2001. Editor: APA's Guide to Rsch. Support, 1981; contbr. over 30 articles to profl. jours. Recipient numerous grants. Mem. APA (sec. bd. sci. affairs 1976-81, sec. com. on internat. rels. in psychology 1978-81), AAAS, Am. Psychol. Soc., Soc. for Psychologists in Mgmt. (newsletter editor 1994-96, bd. dirs. 1996-2001, pres. 2000), Nat. Coun. Univ. Rsch. Adminstrs., Soc. Rsch. Adminstrs., Phi Beta Kappa, Phi Kappa Phi, Phi Eta Sigma, Psi Chi. Democrat. Methodist. Home: 104 Chesley Ln Chapel Hill NC 27514-1459 Office: Univ NC Office of Vice Chancellor for Rsch CB # 4100 Chapel Hill NC 27599-4100 E-mail: lowman@unc.edu.

LOWRANCE, RITA GALE HAMRICK, elementary school educator; b. Chattanooga, Sept. 27, 1951; d. Thomas Austin and Alma Lucille (Horne) Hamrick; m. Bill R. Hilliard, Jan. 11, 1974 (div. Aug. 1980); stepchildren: Terri Feraghat, Renee Beaumont; m. James Karnenik, June 27, 1981 (div. Feb. 1994); m. Charles L. Lowrance, Jr., Mar. 30, 2000. BS in Band and Choral Music Edn., U. Tenn., Chattanooga, 1975, elem. and spl. edn. endorsement, 1981, MEd in Spl. Edn., 1984; postgrad., W. Ga. Coll., 1986-87; cert. edn. specialist, U. Ala., 1996; postgrad., Walker Tech. C.C., 1996—. Cert. tchr. spl. edn., Ga., band and choral music, spl. edn., Tenn. Tchr. spl. edn. Chattanooga City Schs., 1981-83, Walker County Schs., Lafayette, Ga., 1983-93; dir., owner Sterling Learning Ct., Ft. Oglethorpe, Ga., 1991-93; tchr. partial hospitalization program for children Cumberland Hall Psychiat. Hosp., 1993-94; music tchr. Daisy Elem. Sch., Chattanooga, 1994-2000; tchr. Birchwood (Tenn.) Elem. Sch., 2000—. Founder, dir. Sterling Learning Found., Ft. Oglethorpe, 1992-93. Singer Rita G. Hamrick Southern Belle album, 1995. Pres. Bradley County Rep. Women, Cleveland, Tenn., 1975; leader Girl Scouts U.S.A., Chattanooga, 1981-82; mem., choir soloist, dir. youth handbells St. Timothy's Episcopal Ch., Signal Mountain, Tenn. Named Hon. Sgt. at Arms Tenn. Ho. of Reps., Nashville, 1975. Mem. NEA, Nat. Story League, Tenn. Edn. Assn., Hamilton County Edn. Assn., Tenn. Aquarium, Ladies Oriental Shrine N.Am., Order of Amaranth (life, royal matron 1978-79, grand musician 1992-93), Kappa Delta Pi. Episcopalian. Avocations: scuba diving, underwater photography, writing, music, riding motorcycles. Home: 910 Irongate Ct NE Cleveland TN 37312-4703 Office: Birchwood Elem Sch Hwy 60 Birchwood TN 37408

LOWREY, ANNIE TSUNEE, retired cultural organization administrator; b. Osaka, Japan, Mar. 3, 1929; naturalized U.S. citizen, 1963; d. Shigeru Takahata and Kuniko Takahata Takahashi; m. Lawrence K. Lowrey, Mar. 17, 1953; children: Kristine K. Ricci, Jay. BS in Lit., Wakayama (Japan) Shin-Ai, 1949; BS in Art Edn., Kans. State U., 1957; MA in Indsl. Tech., Wichita State U., 1976. Cert. instr. Wichita-Tchr. Assessment and Assistance Program, 1987. Tchr. Minoshima Elem. Sch., Wakayama, Japan, 1945-46, Wakayama Jr. H.S., 1948-49, Truesdell Jr. H.S., Wichita, Kans., 1967-69; tchr., coord. dept. fine arts Wichita H.S. East, 1969-92, instr. Japanese, 1991-92; lectr. dept. art and indsl. tech. Wichita State U., 1974-88, instr. computer applications in industry, 1990-91; tchr. Woodman Elem. Sch., Wichita, summer 1987; instr. art appreciation Butler County C.C., McConnell and Wichita, 1988-92; dir. edn. and exhbn. Wichita Ctr. for Arts, 1992-95; ret., 1995. Asst. to fine arts photographer Charles Phillips, Wichita, spring 1989; judge Sister City Art Contest, 1991, Wichita Botanica Photography Competition, painting competition Wichita Painter's Guild, design competition Kans. Aviation Mus., 1991-92; instr. art instrnl. strategy to elem. and secondary art tchrs. Ft. Collins and Loveland, Colo. sch. dists., 1989; presenter many profl. confs. and workshops, most Nat. Art Edn. Conf., Phoenix, 1992, Kans. Accessible Arts, 1994, Kans. State U., 1994. Chairperson writing team for Kans. Plan for Indsl. Edn.-TV, 1974-75; co-author tech. edn. curriculum Kans. State Bd. Regents, 1989. Judge Miss Asia contest 10th Ann. Asian Festival, Wichita, 1990; pres. pub. art adv. bd. City of Wichita, 1991—. Carnegie grantee for development of interdisciplinary program on cultural literacy, 1984, Matsushita Electronic Co. grantee for curriculum devel., 1986; inductee Kans. Tchrs. Hall of Fame, 1994. Mem. NEA (presenter nat. conv. 1985), ASCD, Nat. Art Edn. Assn.Western Region Secondary Outstanding Educator of Yr. 1988), Kans. Alliance for Arts Edn. (bd. dirs. 1987-89), Phi Delta Kappa (pres. Wichita State U. chpt. 1983-84), Delta Phi Delta. Home: 2727 S Linden St Wichita KS 67210-2423

LOWRIE, PAMELA BURT, educator, artist; b. Geneva, Ill., May 12, 1937; d. Morris Nathan and Helyn (Beetlestone) B.; children: Edmund Gale, Matthew Burt; m. Michael Hammer, Aug. 14, 1982. BA, U. Mich., 1959; MS in Edn., No. Ill. U., DeKalb, 1970; MA, Claremont Grad. Sch. (Calif.), 1979. Art cons. Sch. Dist. 41, Glen Ellyn, Ill., 1970-72; prof. art Coll. DuPage, Glen Ellyn, 1972-94; ret., 1994; curator Olcott Gallery,

Wheaton, Ill., 1994—. Dir., staff Nat. Great Tchrs. Seminars, Williams Bay, Wis., 1976-94; staff Calif. Great Tchrs. Seminar, Santa Barbara, 1979, Hawaii Great Tchrs. Seminar, 1990; vis. prof. Christ Ch. Coll., Canterbury, Eng., 1990. One-woman shows include Loyola U. Gallery, Chgo., U. Ill. Med. Ctr. Gallery, 1978, Elmhurst (Ill.) Coll. Gallery, 1980, Kankakee (Ill.) Coll. Gallery, 1982, The Edge Gallery, Villa Park, Ill., 1984, Gahlberg Gallery Coll. of DuPage, 1986, 87, 92, Elmhurst Art Mus., 1994, Am. Hdqs. of Theosophical Soc., Wheaton, Ill., 1995, 2000, Schafer Gallery, 1995, NICOR, Naperville, Ill., 1996, 97, 2001, Olcott Gallery, Wellness Ctr., 1997, Zurich AM Bldg., Schaumberg, Ill., 1998, DuPage Art League, Wheaton, Ill., 1999, Unilever Corp. Office, Rolling Meadows, Ill., 1999, City Hall, Wheaton, Ill., 2000, Roosevelt U., Schaumberg, Ill, 2001; group shows include Five Women Artists from Ill., Notre Dame U., 1979, Springfield (Ill.) Art Assn. Gallery, 1981, Am. Cultural Ctr., Taipei, Taiwan, 1982, Campanille Gallery, Chgo., 1986, Limelight-Abstract Art, Riverwalk Gallery, Naperville, 1987, David Adler Cultural Ctr., Libertyville, Ill., Norris Gallery, St. Charles, Ill., Gov. State U., Park Forest, Ill., 1982-91, Woman Made Gallery, Gallery Egg, Chgo., Claremont Grad. Sch. Gallery, Calif., 1994, Kohn Turner Gallery, L.A., 1995, N.W. Cultural Coun. Corp. Gallery, 1996-97, Helene Curtis Corp. Ctr., 1997, Unilever Corp., 2000, 2002, Bloomigdale Art Mus., 2001, Roosevelt U., 2001, TLD Design Ctr. and Gallery, 2001, Zurich AM Bldg., 2002, Am. Hdqs. of Theosophical Soc., 2002, 2003; represented in permanent collections Coll. DuPage, Glen Ellyn, AT&T, Naperville, Eastman Pharms., Malvern, Pa., Getty Synthetic Fuel, Chgo., Monte Christo Condominiums, Fla., Nara Jr. Coll., Japan, No. Trust Bank, Chgo., Plan Corp., Wheaton, Nat. Hdqs. Theosophical Soc., Wheaton, Zurich-Am. Ins. Co., Schaumberg. Bd. dirs. Fine Arts Rev. Com., DuPage County, Ill., 1982. Home: 926 N Scott St Wheaton IL 60187-3862 E-mail: pmblowrie@aol.com.

LOWRY, RALPH JAMES, SR., retired history educator; b. Pitts., Dec. 30, 1928; s. Robert William and Elizabeth (Carter) L; 1 son. AB with hons., Lincoln U. of Pa., 1955; MA, Temple U., 1957; PhD, U. N.Mex., 1972; postgrad., Carnegie-Mellon U., 1980. History tchr. William Penn High Sch. for Girls, Phila., 1957-58; asst. prof. dept. history So. Univ., Baton Rouge, La., 1959-64, Md. State U., Princess Anne, 1965-69; tchr. sixth grade John Marshall Elem. Sch., Albuquerque, 1969-70; assoc. prof. dept. history/geography Va. State U., Petersburg, 1970-78; tchr. English/social studies Schenley High Sch., Pitts., 1978-80; assoc. prof. history and geography Bishop Coll., Dallas, Tex., 1980-83; asst. prof. philosophy and history Alcorn State U., Lorman, Miss., 1983-90; assoc. prof. history and geography Lincoln Univ., Pa., 1991; ret. Lincoln Univ. of Pa., Pa., 1995. Adj. prof. Black history, John Tyler C.C., Chester, Va., 1971-72, U. Va., Danville, 1972-74; substitute tchr. Dallas Ind. Sch. System, 1983; history scholar U.S. Mil. Acad., West Point, N.Y., summer 1985. Contbr. articles to profl. jours./publs. With USN, 1948-52, Korea. John Hay Whitney fellow, Jessie Smith Noyes scholar, others. Mem. Am. Hist. Soc., Miss. Polit. Sci. Assn., Western Pa. Psychiat. Clinic, Smithsonian Assocs., Western Pa. Rsch. and Hist. Soc., Phi Delta Kappa, Phi Alpha Theta, Alpha Phi Omega, Beta Sigma Tau, Pi Gamma Mu, Alpha Kappa Mu, Alpha Mu Gamma, Shriners. Democrat. Episcopalian. Home: # 425 4511 Walnut St Philadelphia PA 19139-4559

LOW-WESO, DENISE LEA, writing educator; b. Emporia, Kans., May 9, 1949; d. William Francis and Dorothy Lea (Bruner) Dotson; m. Donald Andrew Low, Jan. 10, 1972 (div.); children: David Andrew, Daniel Lee; m. Anthony Thomas Allard, Dec. 18, 1983 (div.); m. Thomas Francis Weso, Dec. 7, 1994. BA in English, U. Kans., 1971, MA in English, 1974; MFA in Creative Writing, Wichita State U., 1984; PhD in English, U. Kans., 1997. Part-time instr. Kans. State U., Manhattan, 1975-77; lectr. U. Kans., Lawrence, 1977-84, 88, Washburn U., Topeka, 1982, 84; instr. Haskell Indian Nations U., Lawrence, 1984—. Editor, reader Cottonwood Press, Lawrence, 1977-84; bd. dirs. Woodley Meml. Press, Topeka, 1986—. Author: Dragon Kite, 1981, Spring Geese, 1984, Starwater, 1988; editor: Kansas Poems of William Stafford, 1990, Tulip Elegies: An Alchemy of Writing, 1993, Touching the Sky: Essays, 1995, New and Selected Poems, 1999, Thailand Journal, 2003. Recipient Poetry Prize Roberts Found., 1989; fellow Nat. Endowment Humanities, 1987, 90; recipient Kans. Arts Commn. Lit. fellow, 1991. Mem. MLA, Associated Writing Programs. Democrat. Congregationalist. Office: Haskell Indian Coll Lawrence KS 66046

LOXLEY, KATHRYN, retired elementary school educator; b. Darke County, Ohio, Mar. 25, 1918; d. Fred and Henrietta (Hosier) Harleman; m. Orval B. Loxley, Mar. 15, 1935; children: Connie K. Wharton, Ted, Cheryl E., Carolyn L. Loxley. BS in Edn., Miami U., Oxford, Ohio, 1962; postgrad., Ohio U., 1980. Lic. minister 1993. Elem. tchr. Milton-Union Dist., West Milton, Ohio, Jackson (Ohio) City Dist.; ret., 1995—. Named State Tchr. of Yr. nominee, 1984-85, Regional Conservation Tchr., State Social Studies Tchr. of Yr., State Econs. Tchr., Ohio Alliance Environ. Tchr. of Yr.; recipient Gov. Arbor Day award, Community Svc. award; Martha Holden Jennings grantee. Mem. NEA, Ohio Edn. Assn. (human rels.), Jackson City Edn. Assn. (pres., del. to conv.). Home: State Route 788 Wellston OH 45692

LOYD, JUDY, special education educator; b. Scottsbluff, Nebr., Feb. 10, 1956; d. David Carl Jr. and Dorothy Maria Kaufman; m. Richard Eugene Chrisman, Aug 23, 1973 (div. Oct. 1991); children: Matthew, Elisabeth, Kathy; m. Marvin Ray Loyd, July 29, 1994; children: Jenene, Brian. AA, Nebr. Western Coll., Scottsbluff, 1988; BS, Chadron State Coll., 1990. Cert. tchr., Colo., Nebr. Tchr. 4th grade Bridgeport (Nebr.) Pub. Sch., 1990—91; severe/profound tchr. Meridian Sch., Scottsbluff, 1991—93; jr. high, h.s. resource tchr. Morrill (Nebr.) Pub. Sch., 1993-95; mild/moderate tchr. Scottsbluff Pub. Sch., 1995-97; elem. resource tchr. Genoa-Hugo Sch., Hugo, Colo., 1998—2000, Limon Sch., 2000—02, Southwest Mid. Sch., 2002—. Mem. choir Church Zion, Scottsbluff, 1992-97, Meth. Ch., Limon, Colo., 1998—. Mem. NEA, Genoa-Hugo Edn. Assn. (pres. 1998-2000), Ladies Music Club (Limon). Republican. Methodist. Avocations: sewing, crafts.

LU, HUIZHU, computer scientist, educator; m. Yin Ming Wang; children: Serkuang, Qiang. BS in Physics, Fudan U., Shanghai; MS in Computer Science, U. Okla., 1983, PhD in Computer Science, 1988. Lectr. Shanghai U., China, 1961-80; vis. rsch. assoc., scientist U. Okla., Norman, 1981-85; asst. prof. Okla. State U., Stillwater, 1985-92, assoc. prof., 1992-98, prof., 1998—. Prin. investigator of projects Okla. Dept. Health, Okla. Dept. Environ. Quality, others. Co-author: Digital Measurement Techniques, 1980; contbr. numerous rsch. articles to profl. jours. Recipient numerous rsch. grants. Mem. Assn. for Computing Machinery, IEEE Computer Soc., Sigma Xi. Office: Oklahoma State U 213 Mathematical Sci Bldg Stillwater OK 74078

LU, JOHN KUEW-HSIUNG, physiology educator, endocrinologist; b. Miaoli, Taiwan, Republic of China, Sept. 16, 1937; came to U.S., 1967; s. En-Gie and Jan-Mei (Wu) L.; m. Marianne Mann Wang, Dec. 29, 1969; children: Judith Maria, John Lawrence. BS, Nat. Taiwan Normal U., Taipei, 1961; MS, Nat. Taiwan U. Med. Sch., 1967; PhD, Mich. State U., 1972. Postdoctoral fellow U. Pitts., 1972-74; rsch. assoc. Mich. State U., East Lansing, 1974-75; asst. prof. U. Calif.-San Diego, La Jolla, 1975-77; asst. prof. depts. ob-gyn. and neurobiology UCLA Sch. Med., 1977-82, assoc. prof., 1982-88, prof., 1988—. Mem. biochem. endocrinology study sect. NIH, Bethesda, 1990-94, Health Reviewers Res., NIH, 1994-98. Mem. editl. bd. Procs. Soc. Exptl. Biology and Medicine, N.Y.C., 1987—93, mem. publ. com., 1996—2001; contbr. articles to profl. jours., chpts. to books. Recipient Methods to Extend Rsch. in Time award, NIH, 1987—97; Rsch. grantee on reproductive senescence, Nat. Inst. Aging, 1980—91, Rsch. grantee on oocyte physiology, NICHD, 2003—. Mem. Soc. for Study Reprodn., Endocrine Soc., Am. Physiol. Soc., Soc. for Gynecologic Investigation, Soc. Exptl. Biology and Medicine. Home: 1129 Iliff St Pacific Palisades CA 90272-3830 Office: D Geffen Sch Medicine at UCLA Dept Ob-Gyn 22-172 CHS 10833 Le Conte Ave Los Angeles CA 90095-1740 E-mail: jlu@mednet.ucla.edu.

LU, MI, computer engineer, educator; b. Chongqing, Sichuan, China, July 22, 1949; d. Chong Pu Lu and Shu Sheng Fan. MS, Rice U., 1984, PhD, 1987. Registered profl. engr. From asst. prof. to assoc. prof. Tex. A&M U., Coll. Sta., 1987-98, prof., 1998—. Stream chmn. 7th Internat. Conf. Computing and Info., Peterborough, Ont., Can., 1995; conf. chmn. 5th Internat. Conf. Computer Sci. and Informatics, 2000, 6th Internat. Conf., 2002. Assoc. editor Jour. Computing and Info., 1995—, Info. Sci., 1996-97. 2002--; contbr. articles to profl. jours. Mem. Computer Soc. of IEEE (sr.). Office: Tex A&M U Dept Elec Engring College Station TX 77843

LUBATTI, HENRY JOSEPH, physicist, educator; b. Oakland, Calif., Mar. 16, 1937; s. John and Pauline (Massimino) L.; m. Catherine Jeanne Berthe Ledoux, June 29, 1968; children: Karen E., Henry J., Stephen J.C. AA, U. Calif., Berkeley, 1957, AB, 1960; PhD, U. Calif., 1966; MS, U. Ill., 1963. Research assoc. Faculty Scis. U. Paris, Orsay, France, 1966-68; asst. prof. physics MIT, 1968-69; assoc. prof., sci. dir. visual techniques lab. U. Wash., 1969-74, prof., sci. dir. visual Techniques lab., 1974-98. Vis. lectr. Internat. Sch. Physics, Erice, Sicily, 1968, Herceg-Novi, Yugoslavia Internat. Sch., 1969, XII Cracow Sch. Theoretical Physics, Zapokane, Poland, 1972; vis. scientist CERN, Geneva, 1980-81; vis. staff Los Alamos Nat. Lab., 1983-86; guest scientist SSC Lab., 1991-93; mem. physics editl. adv. com. World Sci. Pub. Co. Ltd., 1982-93; guest scientist Fermilab., 1999-2000; vis. scientist U. Rome, summers 2001-03. Editor: Physics at Fermilab in the 1990's, 1990; contbr. numerous articles on high energy physics to profl. jours. Alfred P. Sloan research fellow, 1971-75 Fellow AAAS, Am. Phys. Soc.; mem. Sigma Xi, Tau Beta Pi. Office: Elem Particle Experiment Group U Wash PO Box 351560 Seattle WA 98195-1560 E-mail: lubatti@u.washington.edu.

LUBBERS, AREND DONSELAAR, retired academic administrator; b. Milw., July 23, 1931; s. Irwin Jacob and Margaret (Van Donselaar) L.; m. Eunice L. Mayo, June 19, 1953 (div.); children— Arend Donselaar, John Irwin Darrow, Mary Elizabeth; m. Nancy Vanderpol, Dec. 21, 1968; children— Robert Andrew, Caroline Jayne. AB, Hope Coll., 1953; AM, Rutgers U., 1956; LittD, Central Coll., 1977; DSc, U. Sarajevo, Yugoslavia, 1987; LHD, Hope Coll., 1988; DSc, Akademia Ekonomiczna, Krakow, Poland, 1989, U. Kingston Univ., Eng., 1995. Rsch. asst. Rutgers U., 1954-55; rsch. fellow Reformed Ch. in Am., 1955-56; instr. history and polit. sci. Wittenberg U., 1956-58; v.p. devel. Central Coll., Iowa, 1959-60, pres., 1960-69, Grand Valley State U., Allendale, Mich., 1969-2001; ret., 2001. Mem. Am. Assn. State Colls. and Univs. seminar in India, 1971, Fed. Commn. Orgn. Govt. for Conduct Fgn. Policy, 1972; USIA insp., Netherlands, 1976; mem. pres.'s commn. NCAA, 1984-87, 89—, chmn. pres.'s commn., 1998-2002; bd. dirs. Grand Bank, Grand Rapids, Mich., Macatawa Bank; cons. Olivet Coll., Hackley Hosp., Muskelow, Mich.; cons. in field. Sutdent Cmty. amb. from Holland (Mich.) to Yugoslavia, 1951; bd. dirs. Grand Rapids Symphony, 1976-82, 99, Butterworth Hosp., 1988; chmn. divsn. II NCAA Pres.'s Commn., 1992-95, 98-99, mem. pres.'s coun., 1997; mem. Michigan Cmty. Svc. Commn., 2001--. Recipient Golden Plate award San Diego Acad. Achievement, 1962, Golden-Emblem Order of Merit Polish Peoples Republic, 1988, trustee's award cmty. leadership Aquinas Coll., 1998, Lifetime Achievement award Econ. Club Grand Rapids, 2001; named 1 of top 100 young men in U.S. Life mag., 1962. Mem. Mich. Coun. State Univs. Pres. (chmn. 1988, 2000—), Grand Rapids World Affairs Council (pres. 1971-73), Phi Alpha Theta, Pi Kappa Delta, Pi Kappa Phi. Home: 4195 N Oak Pointe Ct Grand Rapids MI 49525 E-mail: njdelta@aol.com.

LUBERDA, GEORGE JOSEPH, lawyer, educator; b. N.Y.C., Apr. 27, 1930; s. Joseph George and Mary Loretta (Koslowski) L. Bar: D.C. 1959, U.S. Ct. Appeals (D.C. cir.) 1959, Mich. 1970, Mo. 1973. Washington rep. Ford Motor Co., Washington, 1955-59; atty. FTC, Washington, 1960-64; trial atty. Antitrust Div. Dept. Justice, Washington, 1965-69; sr. atty. Bendix Corp., Mich., 1970-71; assoc. Butzel, Long, Gust, Klein & Van Zile, Detroit, 1972; antitrust counsel Monsanto Co., St. Louis, 1973-88; assoc. Herzog, Crebs and McGhee, 1988-93; ptnr. Luberda & Carp, St. Louis, 1993—2002, Luberda, Gusdorf & Weir, LLC, St. Louis, 2002—. Adj. prof. St. Louis U., 1985-96. Mem. Mo. Bar Assn., Bar Assn. Met. St. Louis. Republican. Roman Catholic. Home: 716 Ridgeview Circle Ln Ballwin MO 63021-7810 Office: Luberda Gusdorf & Weir LLC Ste 1220 225 S Meramec Ave Saint Louis MO 63105-3511

LUBETZKY, CAROLE DIANE, elementary education educator, math-science specialist; b. L.A., Oct. 4, 1942; d. Lawrence and Bessie (Gursky) Schneider; m. David H. Lubetzky, Aug. 27, 1967; 1 child, Darren H. BS, San Jose State U., 1965; postgrad., U. Calif., Berkeley, UCLA. Cert. elem. tchr., Md. Tchr. Ascot Elem. Sch., L.A., 1966-67, Greenbelt (Md.) Elem. Sch., 1967—. Recipient 1st Pl Md. State Bicentennial, 1st Pl. Nat. Statistics Contest (grades 4-6), 1992. Mem. NEA, ASCD, Nat. Sci. Tchrs. Assn., Nat. Coun. Tchrs. Math., Am. Statis. Soc., Med. Coun. Tchrs. Math. Republican.

LUBLINER, IRVING, mathematics educator, consultant; b. Oakland, Calif., Aug. 29, 1952; s. Abram and Felicia (Bornstein) L.; m. Joanne C. May Kliejunas. BA, U. Calif., Berkeley, 1974; MA in Teaching, U. Calif., Davis, 1988. Cert. tchr., Calif. Tchr. math. and computer programming, chmn. math. dept. Novato (Calif.) Unified Sch. Dist., 1976-85; program dir., math. specialist Black Pine Circle Sch., Berkeley, 1985-90; math specialist, tchr. Bentley Sch., Oakland, 1990-95, head middle sch., 1995-98, dean of students, 1998—2001, math. splist., 1998—. Instr. U. calif., Davis, 1975-76; dir. Kindercamp, Oakland, 1972-76, Camp Kee Tov, Berkeley, 1980-83; tchr. Marin County Office Edn., San Rafael, Calif., 1982-83; speaker Bur. of Edn. and Rsch., 1992—; speaker, cons., Oakland, 1974—. Contbr. articles to profl. jours. Recipient Hon. Svc. award Calif. Congress Parents and Tchrs., 1985, Spl. Honors award for contbn. to tchg. highly talented youth Johns Hopkins U. Calif. Tchr. Recognition Program, 1991, 94, 97, 98, 2000; Sarah D. Barton's Mark Taper Found. fellow Johns Hopkins U.'s Ctr. for Talented Youth, 1994. Mem. Nat. Coun. Tchrs. Math., Calif. Math. Coun., Alameda and Contra Costa Counties Math. Educators. Avocations: blues harmonica, table tennis. Home: 878 Longridge Rd Oakland CA 94610-2445 Office: Bentley Sch 1 Hiller Dr Oakland CA 94618-2301

LUBMAN, RICHARD LEVI, physician, educator, research scientist; b. Bklyn., Dec. 10, 1956; m. Sue Ann Feinberg, Dec. 14, 1986; children: Rachel, Louisa. BA, Cornell U., 1977; MD, SUNY, Bklyn., 1981. Diplomate Am. Bd. Internal Medicine, Am. Bd. Pulmonary Diseases; cert. in critical care medicine. Intern, then resident in internal medicine SUNY Downstate Med. Ctr., 1981-84; chief resident SUNY-Bklyn. VA Hosp., 1984-85; fellow in pulmonary and critical care medicine N.Y. Hosp.-Cornell U. Med. Ctr., N.Y.C., 1985-88, instr. medicine, 1988-91; asst. prof. U. So. Calif., L.A., 1991-99, assoc. prof. medicine, 1999—. Expert reviewer Med. Bd. Calif., 1996—. Parker B. Francis fellow Francis Families Found., 1988-91, J. Burns Amberson fellow N.Y. Lung Assn., 1986-88. Fellow ACP, Am. Coll. Chest Physicians; mem. Am. Thoracic Soc., Am. Heart Assn. (initial investigator Greater L.A. affiliate 1993-95), Am. Physiol. Soc., Internat. Union Against Tb and Lung Disease, Western Soc. Clin. Investigation, Am. Soc. Matrix Biology. Office: HMR 900 2011 Zonal Ave Los Angeles CA 90089-0903 E-mail: rlubman@usc.edu.

LUCAS, BILLY JOE, philosophy educator; b. Houston, Jan. 7, 1942; s. Joseph Cuthel and Billie Louise (Smith) L.; m. Diana Stephens, July 13, 1965 (div. 1976); children: Lisa Ann, Deborah Lynn; m. Shelby Hearon, Apr. 19, 1981 (div. 1995). BA, U. Houston, 1970; MA, McMaster U., 1972; PhD, U. Tex., 1981. Instr. Houston Community Coll., 1973-77; asst. instr. U. Tex., Austin, 1978-81; asst. prof. Manhattanville Coll., Purchase, N.Y., 1981-86, assoc. prof., 1986-89, prof., 1989—. Edn. policy cons. to the pres. Manhattanville Coll., 1990-91, 92-93; invited del. Citizem Amb. Program Philosophy Del., People's Rep. China, 1993. Assoc. editor Internat. Jour. for Philosophy of Religion, 1990—; contbr. articles to profl. jours. Mem. AAAS, Soc. for Philosophy of Religion (exec. coun. 1986-93, v.p. 1989-90, pres. 1990-91), Assn. for Symbolic Logic, Computer Soc. of IEEE (tech. com. on multiple valued logic 1987—), Am. Acad. Religion, Am. Philos. Assn. (logic sect. adv. com. 1990-93), N.Am. Soc. for Social Philosophy (exec. coun. 1986-93, co-chair Eastern div. 1986-90), Am. Math. Soc., N.Y. Acad. Scis., Phi Kappa Phi. Achievements include complete axiomatization of the minimal modal logic in which each formula is provably equivalent to a formula of finite degree, related work on reduction laws in deontic and other modal logics, applications of formal logic to philosophy, and logic curriculum development. Office: Manhattanville Coll 2900 Purchase St Purchase NY 10577-2131

LUCAS, CAROL MCCANN, vocational education educator; b. Ferrellsburg, W.Va., Feb. 9, 1945; d. Mason and Essie (Adkins) McCann; m. Lonnie C. Lucas, Feb. 20, 1965; 1 child, Joshua Tad. AB, Marshall U., 1968, MS, 1978, postgrad., 1990. Cert. home economist, W.Va. Tchr., prin. Francis Creek Elem. Sch., Harts, W.Va., 1965-66; tchr. Cammack Jr. High Sch., Huntington, W.Va., 1968-75; tchr. home econs. Barboursville (W.Va.) Mid. Sch., 1979-80, 87—, Barboursville High Sch., 1980-87; ret., 2001. Adviser Future Homemakers Am., Barboursville, 1980—. Adviser Future Homemakers Am., Barboursville, 1980—, Outstanding chpt., 1991. Huntington, 1987-89, v.p., 1990-92. Named one of Top Ten Teachers of Yr., AAFCS, 2001. Mem. NEA, Am. Home Baking Assn. (Top 40 Home Econs. Tchr. 1994), Am. Vocat. Assn., Am. Home Econs. Assn. (cert. home economist), W.Va. Edn. Assn., W.Va. Vocat. Assn., W.Va. Home Econs. Assn. (Outstanding Consumer and Homemaking Program 1991), Cabell County Edn. Assn. Republican. Avocations: needlecrafts, painting, piano, writing. Office: Barboursville Mid Sch Main St Barboursville WV 25504

LUCAS, DEAN HADDEN, retired home economics educator; b. Avera, Ga., June 2, 1931; d. Thomas Clayton and Lonice Ethyl (Williams) Hadden; m. Ben F. Lucas, June 27, 1953 (dec. Mar. 1992); children: Jon Gregory, Barry Hadden, Angela d'Arcy; m. Ray Ninche Renbarger, Sept. 10, 1994. Student, U. Ga., 1951; BS in Home Econs. Edn., Berry Coll., 1952; MAT in Home Econs. Edn., Winthrop Coll., 1969; postgrad., Clem. U., 1976-77, U. S.C., 1977, 80, 81, 88, S.C. State Coll., 1985, 87. Asst. home demonstration agt. Ga. Extension Svc., Calhoun, 1952, home demonstration agt. Alma, 1952-53; 1st grade tchr. Tenn. Edn. Dept., East Ridge, 1953-54; 4th grade tchr. Kershaw County Sch. Dist., Camden, S.C., 1954-55, home econs. tchr., 1955-57; asst. home dem. agt. Clemson Extension Svc., Camden, 1958-61, home dem. agt., 1963-69, assoc. home economist, 1970-74, assoc. county extension leader Sumter, S.C., 1974-76; home econs. instr. Kershaw County Sch., Camden, 1976-93, ret., 1994. Writer curriculum guides for home econs. courses. Mem. adv. bd. Dist. Home Econs., Kershaw County, S.C., 1985-92, Supt. Adv. Coun., Camden, 1989-90, Teen Coalition, Camden, 1989-92, Teen Pregnancy Prevention, Kershaw County, 1985-89; mem. Kershaw County Jr. Welfare League, Camden, 1959-92; co-sponsor, organizer SADD Chpt. at North Central, Kershaw, 1988; Clemson U. del. Nat. 4-H Conf., Chgo., 1974, Home Econs. Educators Citizens Amb. Program, Russia, Hungary, 1992; tchr. Sunday sch. Bapt. Ch. Named for Nat. Disting. Svc., Nat. Extension Home Econs. Assn., 1973, S.C. Home Econs. Tchr. of Yr., S.C. Home Econ. Assn., 1990. Mem. NEA, Am. Vocat. Assn. (del. to policy seminar), S.C. Vocat. Assn. (v.p. 1989-90, 92), S.C. Assn. Home Econs. Tchrs. (pres. 1989-90), Am. Home Econs. Assn. (legis. contact 1988-91, Vocat. Home Econs. Tchr. of Yr. 1993, Vocat. Tchr. of Yr. 1993), S.C. Edn. Assn. Cert. Home Economists. Avocations: running, work-outs, boating, cooking, golf. Home: 202 Point Place Dr Westminster SC 29693-6441 Office: North Cen High Sch 3000 Lockhart Rd Kershaw SC 29067-9661

LUCAS, GEORGETTA MARIE SNELL, retired educator, artist; b. Harmony, Ind., July 25, 1920; d. Ernest Clermont and Sarah Ann (McIntyre) Snell; m. Joseph William Lucas, Jan. 29, 1943; children: Carleen Anita Lucas Underwood, Thomas Joseph, Joetta Jeanne Lucas Allgood. BS, Ind. State U., 1942; MS in Edn., Butler U., 1964; postgrad., Herron Sch. of Art, 1961-65, Ind. U., Indpls. and Bloomington, 1960-62, 65. Music, art tchr. Jasonville City Schs., Ind., 1942-43, Van Buren H.S., Brazil, Ind., 1943-46, Plainfield City Schs., Ind., 1946-52, Met. Sch. Dist. Wayne Twp., Indpls., 1952-56, 59-68; art tchr. Met. Sch. Dist. Perry Twp., Indpls., 1968-81. Lectr. Art Educators Assn. Ind., Ind. U.-Bloomington, 1976. Illustrator: (book) Why So Sad, Little Rag Doll, 1963; artist (painting) Ethereal Season, 1966, (lithograph) Bird of Time, 1965-66; exhibited in group shows Hoosier Salon Art Exhibit, 1954, 56, 60, 62-65, 67, 68, 70, 72, 87, 94, N.Y. Lincoln Ctr., N.Y.C., 1994; represented in permanent collections Ind. State U., Ind.-Purdue U.-Indpls. Jane Voorhees Zimmerli Art Mus., Rutgers U., N.J., Indpls. Pub. Sch. Collection; drummer with Hendricks County Ramblers, 1986—. Mem. NEA (life), Nat. Assn. Women Artist, Ind. Artist Craftsmen, Inc. (hon., pres. 1979-85, 87, 88, scholarship chmn. 1986—, bd. dirs. 1986—), Ind. Fedn. Art Clubs (hon., pres. 1986-87, counselor 1988-91, bd. dirs. 1991—, parliamentarian 1992-94, conv. mgr. 1999, Best of Show 1997), Hoosier Salon, Ind. State U. Mortar Bd., Art Edn. Assn. Ind. (life), Nat. League Am. Pen Women (Ind. state art chmn. 1984-96, Best of Show award 1983, 97, pres. Indpls. br. 1994-96, Ind. State Assn. pres. 1998-2000, front cover drawing Pen Women Nat. Mag. 1994), Fine Art for State Ind. (Internat. Women's Yr. fine art chmn. 1977), Ctrl. Ind. Artists (hon.), Alpha Delta Kappa (life, Ind. state chmn. of art 1973-77, pres. 1972-74, represented by painting in nat. hdqrs.-Kansas City, Mo., Fidelis Delta first v.p.), Retired Educators Sorority (1st v.p., pres. 1997-99), Order of Eastern Star. Republican. Methodist. Avocations: genealogy, travel, numismatics. Home and Office: 3192 E Main St Plainfield IN 46168-2721

LUCAS, HARRY DAVID, secondary education educator; b. Mahanoy City, Pa., July 22, 1960; s. Victor J. and Mary Jane (Davies) L. BA in Humanities, Pa. State U., 1984; MEd, Kutztown U., 1990. Cert. tchr., Pa. Substitute tchr. St. Clair (Pa.) Area Sch. Dist., 1984-85, Pottsville (Pa.) Area Sch. Dist., 1985-86; tchr. English Tamaqua (Pa.) Area Sch. Dist., 1987-89, North Schuylkill Sch. Dist., Frackville, Pa., 1986-87, 89—. Trustee Mahanoy City (Pa.) Pub. Libr.; vol. tchr. St. Clair Religious Edn. Program, 1986-92. Mem. Elks. Office: North Schuylkill Jr and Sr H S Rte 61 Ashland PA 17921

LUCAS, LINDA LUCILLE, dean; b. Stockton, Calif., Apr. 22, 1940; d. Leslie Harold Lucas and Amy Elizabeth (Callow) Farnsworth. BA, San Jose State Coll., 1961, MA, 1969; EdD, U. San Francisco, 1982; JD, John F. Kennedy U., 2002. Dist. libr. Livermore (Calif.) Elem. Schs., 1962-64; libr. Mission San Jose High Sch., Fremont, Calif., 1964-69; media reference libr. Chabot Coll., Hayward, Calif., 1969-75; asst. dean instrn. Chabot-Las Positas Coll., Livermore, 1975-91; assoc. dean instrn. Las Positas Coll., Livermore, 1991-94, dean acad. svcs., 1994-2000, dean emeritus, 2000—. Participant Nat. Inst. for Leadership Devel., 1991. Bd. dirs. Tri-Valley Community TV, Livermore, 1991-98, Valley Choral Soc., 1993-98, Chabot-Las Positas Colls. Found., Pleasanton, Calif., 1991-94; mem. needs assessment com Performing Arts Coun., Pleasanton. Mem. ALA, Coun. Chief Librs., Assn. Calif. Community Coll. Adminstrs., Calif. Libr. Assn. Avocations: choral music, photography. Home: 4848 Golden Rd Pleasanton CA 94566-6038

LUCAS, MELINDA ANN, pediatrician, educator; b. Maryville, Tenn., June 27, 1953; d. Arthur Baldwin and Dorthy (Shields) L. BA, Maryville Coll., 1975; MS, U. Tenn., 1976, MD, 1981, postgrad., 1992-93, U. Mich., 1995-97. Diplomate in pediat. critical care Am. Bd. Pediat., 2002, lic. physician Mich., N.Y., Tenn. Intern U. Rochester, N.Y., 1981-82, resident in pediat., 1982-84; pvt. practice, Maryville, 1984-85; clin. fellow U. Tenn. Genetics Ctr., 1988-89; emergency room pediatrician U. Tenn. Med. Ctr., Knoxville, 1985-90, dir. child abuse clinic, 1985—90, pediat. intensivist, 1985—, acting dir. pediat. ICU, 1987-88, 90-92, faculty, 1988—2002; fellow in pediat. critical care U. Mich., Ann Arbor, 1995-96; emergency dept. pediatrician U. Tenn. Med. Ctr., Knoxville, 2001—; pediatrician ABC Pediatrics, 2000—; adj. asst. prof. U. Tenn., 2001—02. Mem. Pediatric Cons., Inc., Knoxville, 1985—99; physician rep. Project Search Working Symposium, 1990—91, Regional Tenn. Early Intervention Sys., 1992—; adj. asst. prof. dept. theory and practice in tchr. edn. Coll. of Edn., U. Tenn., Knoxville, 2000—02. Contbr. articles to profl. jours. Mem. child watch com. Children's Def. Fund, 1977—99; mem. Blount County Foster Care Rev. Bd., Maryville, 1985—93, Blount County Exec. Bd. Maryville Coll. Alumni Assn., 1988—92; mem. adv. bd. Safe Kids of Tenn., 1998—2002, Knoxville Area Safe Kids, 1998—2002, ABC Pediat., 2000—; physician coord. Knoxville Area Project Delivery of Chronic Care; child passenger safety techican Am. Acad. Pediats. and U. Tenn Med. Ctr., Knoxville, 1999—2002, child passenger coord., 1997—2001, Children's Def. Fund, 1997—2001. Recipient Spl. Achievement award Am. Acad. Pediatrics/Tenn. Pediatric Soc., 2001, 2002, Spl. Achievement award Am. Acad. Pediatrics; United Presbyn. Ch. scholar, 1971, Mary Lou Braly scholar, 1971-74; grantee AAP-Nat. Hwy. Traffic Safety Adminstrn. for Safe Ride Program, 1993. Fellow: Am. Acad. Pediat. (Spl. Achievement award Tenn. chpt.); mem.: Soc. Critical Care Medicine (abstract reviewer 1991, 1992, 1993, 1994, 1995, 1996, 1997, 1998, 1999), Knoxville Area Pediat. Soc., Tenn. Pediat. Soc. (co-chmn. accident and injury prevention com. 1993—95, 1996—97, chmn. accident and injury prevention com. 1997—2002), Am. Profl. Soc. Abuse of Children, AMA (Physician Recognition award 1984—87, 1988—91, Spl. Achievement award Tenn. chpt. 1991—94, 1994—97, 1997—2000). Methodist. Avocations: basketball, tennis, piano. Office: ABC Pediatrics PO Box 419 Alcoa TN 37701

LUCAS, PANOLA, elementary education educator; b. Pikeville, Ky., Nov. 18, 1932; d. Robert Lee and Trulie Ann (Pinson) Fields; m. Kenneth R. Lucas, Dec. 7, 1956 (div. Apr. 1984); 1 child, Nathan Wade. BS in Vocat. Home Econs., Marshall U., 1971; elem. teaching cert., W.Va. State Coll., 1976; cert. prin., W.Va. Coll. Grad. Studies, elem., mid., jr. and sr. high sch. prin., supt., supr. gen. instrn., vocat. admnstr., 1986. Tchr. Buffalo (W.Va.) High Sch., 1972; tchr. homebound Putnam County Bd. Edn., Winfield, W.Va., 1972-86; tchr. Poca (W.Va.) Elem. Sch., 1986-91, Scott Teays Elem. Sch., Scott Depot, W.Va., 1991—. Mem. W.Va. Profl. Educators, Kappa Delta Pi. Democrat. Baptist. Avocations: reading, travel, gardening, bowling, dancing. Home: 205 Hillside Dr # B Nitro WV 25143-2327 E-mail: panolal@msn.com.

LUCAS, ROBERT EMERSON, JR., economist, educator; b. Yakima, Wash., Sept. 15, 1937; BA, U. Chgo., 1959, PhD, 1964, U. Paris-Dauphine, 1992, Athens U. Econ. and Bus., 1994; DSc (hon.), Technion-Israel Inst. Tech., 1996; PhD (hon.), U. Montréal, 1998. Lectr. U. Chgo., 1962-63; asst. prof., economics Carnegie-Mellon U., Pittsburgh, 1963-67; assoc. prof., 1967-70; prof., 1970-75; prof., economics U. Chgo., 1975-80, vice chmn. Dept. Econs., 1975—83, John Dewey Disting. Svc. prof., 1980—, chmn. Dept. Econs., 1986—88. Ford Found. vis. rsch. prof. U. Chgo., 1974-75; vis. prof. econ. Northwestern U., Chgo., 1981-82. Author: Studies in Business-Cycle Theory, 1981, Models of Business Cycles, 1987, Lectures on Economic Growth, 2001; co-author: Recursive Methods in Economic Dynamics, 1989; co-editor: Rational Expectations and Econometric Practice, 1981; assoc. editor Jour. Econ. Theory, 1972-78, Jour. Monetary Econs., 1977—; editor Jour. Polit. Theory, 1978-81, 1988-; contbr. articles to profl. jours. Woodrow Wilson fellow, 1959-60, Brookings fellow, 1961-62, Woodrow Wilson Dissertation fellow, 1963, Ford Found. Faculty fellow, 1966-67, Guggenheim Found. fellow, 1981-82; Proctor and Gamble scholar, 1955-59; recipient Nobel Prize in Econ., 1995. Fellow AAAS, Econometric Soc. (2nd v.p. 1995, pres. 1997), Am. Acad. Arts and Scis.; mem. NAS, Econometric Soc. (2nd v.p., v.p. 1995, pres. 1997), Am. Econ. Assn. (v.p. 1987, pres. 2001), European Acad. Arts, Scis. and Humanities, Am. Philosophical Soc., Phi Beta Kappa. Office: U Chgo Dept Econs 1126 E 59th St Chicago IL 60637-1580*

LUCAS, TAMMI MICHELLE, music educator; b. Tifton, Ga., Nov. 27, 1971; d. Louis Elvin Lucas and Faye Wynema Allmond; m. Clayton Arthur Priest, July 22, 1995 (div. July 1999). B of Music Edn., Troy State U., 1995. Tchr. music W. Bainbridge Elem., Ga., 1995—96, Potter St. Elem., Bainbridge, 1996—97; dir. band Hutto Mid. Sch., Bainbridge, 1997—. Active ch. choir. Mem.: Profl. Assn. Ga. Educators, Ga. Music Educators Assn. (sec. 1999—). Republican. Baptist. Home: 1634 Longleaf Dr Bainbridge GA 39819

LUCAS, THERESA EILEEN, elementary education educator; b. Bellingham, Wash., Jan. 6, 1948; d. John M. and Lillian Sigrid (Westford) Cairns; m. Paul T. Lucas, 1970 (div. June 1987); children: Jeffrey Thomas, Aimee Michelle. BA, U. No. Colo., 1970, MA, 1985. Cert. elem. edn. grades K-6, spl. edn. grades K-12, Colo. Tchr. spl. edn. Baker Elem. Sch. Adams County Sch. Dist. 50, Westminster, Colo., 1970-77, tchr. 1st grade Berkeley Gardens Elem. Sch., 1978-84, tchr. kindergarten Harris Park Elem. Sch., 1984-87, tchr. kindergarten Tennyson Knolls Elem. Sch., 1987—. Mem. sch. coms. Baker Elem. Sch., Berkeley Gardens Elem. Sch., Harris Park Elem. Sch., Tennyson Knolls Elem. Sch., Adams County Sch. Dist. 50, Westminster, 1970—; co-author literacy grant Adams County Ednl. Found., 1994, Gov.'s Creativity grant Tennyson Knolls Elem. Sch., 1989-90. Vol. Rainbows for All God's Children, Spirit of Christ Ch., Arvada, Colo., 1988-90, vol. crisis hotline, 1990-91; campaign vol. pro-edn. candidates, Arvada, 1992. Mem. ASCD, NEA, Internat. Reading Assn., Colo. Edn. Assn., Colo. Coun. Internat. Reading Assn., West Adams County Coun. Internat. Reading Assn., Westminster Edn. Assn. (membership rep. Tennyson Knolls Elem. Sch. 1990-95). Democrat. Avocations: reading, biking, dancing, walking, crafts. Home: 8279 Iris St Arvada CO 80005-2136

LUCATORTO, HELEN ANN, elementary education educator; b. Pitts., Feb. 17, 1952; d. Michael and Alice Josephine (Zimbicki) Wittas; m. Eugene Carl Lucatorto, July 30, 1977; children: Sara Elizabeth, Eugene Michael. BS, Indiana (Pa.) U. Pa., 1974; MEd, U. Pitts., 1977. Cert. instrnl. level II, elem. K-8. Tchr. various grades Chartiers Valley Sch. Dist., Pitts., 1974-81; tchr. St. Mary's Presch., Cecil, Pa., 1983-84, Chartiers Valley Sch. Dist., Pitts., 1984—85, Sts. Simon and Jude, Pitts., 1985-89; dept. head Chartiers Valley Primary Sch., Bridgeville, Pa., 1996—; tchr. Chartiers Valley Sch. Dist., Pitts., 1989—. Forensics coach Sts. Simon and Jude, Pitts., 1986-89; tchr. liason rep. PTO, Pitts., 1990-92, 94-95; primary transition team mem. Chartiers Valley Sch. Dist., Pitts., 1994-96. Mem. ASCD, Chartiers Valley Fedn. Tchrs., Pa. Lit. Framework Network. Avocations: sewing, reading, writing children's poetry, swimming, baking. Office: 125 Thoms Run Rd Bridgeville PA 15017-2800

LUCCA, CAROLE CELIBERTI, secondary school educator; b. N.Y.C., Mar. 25, 1941; d. James Salvatore and Lucy (Panico) Celiberti; m. Thomas George Lucca, Dec. 15, 1962; children: Carolynn, Thomas, James. BS, St. John's U., 1962; postgrad., Hofstra U., St. John's U.; MA, SUNY, Stony Brook, 1992. Tchr. East Woods Sch., Oyster Bay, L.I., 1984-91; tchr. English Meml. Jr. High Sch., Valley Stream, Ill., 1962-67; tchr. spl. edn. BOCES III, Dix Hills, L.I., 1979-84; prin. Homework Help, 1992—; pres., founder All Around L.I. Tchrs., 1993—. Pres. Half Hollow Oaks Civis assn., 1984—, Manasquan PTA, 1978-79; co-chmn., co-founder Huntington PTA legis. coalition, 1986—; mem. Conservative Com., 1984—; 1st v.p. United Italian Ams. for Progress, 1986-88, LIDC task force, 1993—; mem. by-laws com. Citizens Def. Fund Suffolk County, 1987-88. Mem. Half Hollow Hills Swim Club (sec. 1981-83), Sweet Adelines Club, Toastmasters Internat. Roman Catholic. Home: 19 Newfoundland Ave Huntington NY 11743-4942 E-mail: clucca@juno.com.

LUCENKO, LEONARD KONSTANTYN, sport, recreation management, and safety educator, coach, consultant; b. Ukraine, Aug. 2, 1937; came to U.S., 1949; s. Konstantyn and Pauline Lucenko; m. Larissa Rohowsky, June 7, 1963; children: Leonard Jr., Kristina. BA, Temple U., 1961; MA, NYU, 1962; PhD, U. Utah, 1972. Instr. Lehman Coll., N.Y.C., 1962-62; athletic dir. Eron Prep Sch., N.Y.C., 1962-65; coach, trainer Pratt Inst., Bklyn., 1965; prof. sport, recreation mgmt., and safety, coach, administrator Montclair (N.J.) State Coll., 1966—. Mem. com. N.J. Vol. Coaches Com., Trenton, 1988-91; cons. soccer Pres.'s Coun. Phys. Fitness, Washington; bd. dirs. All Am. Soccer Camp, South Orange, N.J., 1966—, Montclair State Coaching Acad., 1980—. Author: (with others) U.S. Soccer Federation Official Book, 1982; contbr. articles to profl. jours. Named Coach of Yr. Met. Conf., N.Y., 1971, N.J. State Athletic Conf. Mem. Ea. N.Y. Soccer Assn. (bd. dirs. coaching sch. 1972—, Most Valuable Player 1983). Office: Montclair State Coll Normal Rd Montclair NJ 07043

LUCENTE, GREGORY L. humanities educator; b. Evanston, Ill., Apr. 10, 1948; s. Martin M. and Verle (Straus) L.; m. Gloria Lauri-Lucente. BA, Yale U., 1970. With Johns Hopkins U., Balt., 1979-88; prof. Dept. Romance Langs. U. Mich., Ann Arbor, 1988—.*

LUCENTE, ROSEMARY DOLORES, retired educational administrator, consultant; b. Renton, Wash., Jan. 11, 1935; d. Joseph Anthony and Erminia Antoinette (Argano) Lucente. BA, Mt. St. Mary's Coll., 1956, MS, 1963. Tchr. pub. schs., L.A., 1956-65; supr. tchr., 1958-65; asst. prin., 1965-69; prin. elem. sch., 1969-85, 86-99; dir. instrn., 1985-87; ret., 1999. Nat. cons., lectr. Dr. William Glasser's Educator Tng. Ctr., 1968—; nat. workshop leader Nat. Acad. for Sch. Execs.-Am. Assn. Sch. Adminstrs., 1980; L.A. Unified Sch. Dist. rep. for nat. pilot of Getty Inst. for Visual Arts, 1983-85, 92-98, site coord., 1983-86, team leader, mem. supt.'s adv. cabinet, 1987-98. Recipient Golden Apple award Stanford Ave. Sch. PTA, Faculty and Cmty. Adv. Coun., 1976, resolution for outstanding svc. South Gate City Coun., 1976, resolution for commitment to youth L.A. city Coun., 1996; named Woman of Yr., Calif. State Senate, 1997. Mem. NAESP, L.A. Elem. Prins. Orgn. (v.p. 1979-80), Assn. Calif. Sch. Adminstrs. (charter mem.), Assn. Elem. Sch. Adminstrs. (vice chair chpt. 1972-75, 79-80), Assn. Adminstrs. L.A. (charter mem.), Pi Theta Mu, Kappa Delta Pi (v.p. 1982-84, Hon. Educator award 1998), Delta Kappa Gamma, Phi Delta Kappa (Cert. of Recognition of Svc. on Membership Com. 2000). Democrat. Roman Catholic. Home: 6501 Lindenhurst Ave Los Angeles CA 90048-4733

LUCKETT, JERRY LYNNE, business administration educator; b. Rapid City, S.D., July 10, 1956; d. Patricia (Knutson) Lindstrom; m. Douglas Howard Bechen, Aug. 14, 1976 (div. Sept. 1980); children: Travis Douglas, Trevor Howard; m. Gary Rae Luckett, Nov. 28, 1981 (div. 1997); children: Teri Lynne, Tricia Rose Ann. Diploma, Mitchell Vocat. Tech. Inst., 1975; BA, Dakota Wesleyan U., 1989; MA in Tchg., No. State U., 1992. Cert. bus. edn. Owner, mgr. South Gulch Western Wear, Wessington Springs, S.D., 1978-79; pvt. sec., payroll staff, acct. Syncom Techs., Mitchell, 1979-81; mgr. Boots 'n More Western Wear, Mitchell, 1994-95; owner Cowboy Corral Western Wear & Tack, Mitchell, 1995-97; asst. prof. bus. adminstrn. and econs. Dakota Wesleyan U., Mitchell, 1994—. Profl. rodeo queen, seminar judge, pageant coord., Mitchell, 1990—; state and local advisor Phi Beta Lambda, Mitchell, 1990—; rodeo coach Dakota Wesleyan U. Rodeo Club, Mitchell, 1994-2000; timer Profl. Rodeo Cowboys Assn., 2003. Author: Ms. Jerry L. Luckett Rodeo Queen Seminars, 1992. Mem. Corn Palace Stampede Rodeo Com. (sec. 1994—). Democrat. Roman Catholic. Avocations: rodeo, horse training, arts and crafts. Home: 1200 W University Ave Mitchell SD 57301-4358 Office: Dakota Wesleyan Univ 1200 W University Ave Mitchell SD 57301-4398 E-mail: jelucket@dwu.edu.

LUDDINGTON, BETTY WALLES, library media specialist; b. Tampa, Fla., May 11, 1936; d. Edward Alvin and Ruby Mae (Hiott) L.; m. Robert Morris Schmidt, Sept. 20, 1957 (div. Dec. 1981); children: Irene Schmidt-Losat, Daniel Carl Schmidt. AA, U. South Fla., 1979, BA in Am. Studies and History, 1980, MA in Libr., Media and Info. Studies, 1982, EdS in Gifted Edn., 1986. Cert. tchr. media and gifted edn., Fla. Media intern Witter Elem. Sch., spring 1982; media specialist Twin Lakes Elem. Sch., 1982-84, Just Elem. Sch., 1984-87, Blake Jr. H.S., 1987-88, Dowdell Jr. H.S. (now Dowdell Mid. Sch.), 1988—. Educator Saturday enrichment program for gifted children U. South Fla., springs 1980, 84, 85; participant pilot summer program in reading and visual arts Just Elem. Sch., 1987; educator gifted edn. program in visual and performing arts Kingswood Elem. Sch., summers 1985, 86, gifted edn. program in video camera Apollo Beach Elem. Sch., summer 1989, Gifted Enrichment Prog. Imagi-lympics 2012, Maniscalco Elem. Sch., 1998, others. Author: (book of poetry) Aaron Tippin: A Hillbilly Knight, 1993; contbr. articles and poems to various books and periodical publs., 1986—. Parent vol. media ctr. Witter Elem. Sch., 1976-78; tchr. sponsor Storytelling Club, Dowdell Jr. H.S., 1994-95; news media liaison, tchr. vol. Dowdell Jr. H.S., 1993-96. Recipient Student Affairs Golden Signet award U. South Fla., 1980, Parent award for continuing support of Fla. chpt. # 39 Am. Indsl. Arts Student Assn., 1987-88, Editor's Choice awards for outstanding achievement in poetry Nat. Libr. of Poetry, 1996; nominee Tchr. of Month, Sta. WTSP-TV, 1994; recognized for contbn. of motivational activity for Sunshine State Young Reader's Award program Fla. Assn. for Media in Edn., Inc., 1985; named to Internat. Poetry Hall of Fame, 1996. Mem. Internat. Soc. Poets (Disting. mem. 1995), Hillsborough Classrm. Tchrs. Assn. (grantee 1988, 90), Hillsborough Assn. Sch. Libr. Media Specialists, Clan Wallace Soc. (life), Phi Kappa Phi, Kappa Delta Pi, Phi Alpha Theta (pres., v.p., rep. to honors coun. 1980, 81, Outstanding Student award), Omicron Delta Kappa (treas., chairperson, del., mem. selection com. 1981, Leslie Lynn Walbolt book award), Pi Gamma Mu. Episcopalian. Avocations: poetry, books, cats, country music. Home: 1032 E Robson St Tampa FL 33604-4344

LUDDY, PAULA SCOTT, nursing educator; b. Plymouth, MA, May 29, 1945; d. James Bernard Scott and Margaret Elizabeth Legge Scott; m. Robert Thomas Luddy, May 20, 1944; children: Scott, Shawn. BSN, Bowie State U., 1993, MSN, 1996. RN Mass., 1966, Md., 1970. Educator Group Health Assn., Washington, 1983—87; ob/lactation cons. Dr. Rafiq Mian, Cheverly, Md., 1984—94; childbirth educator Childbirth Edn. Assn., Washington, 1971—95; staff nurse Prince George Hosp. Ctr., Cheverly, Md., 1981—87, patient educator, 1987—2002; coord./home interviewer Prince George Med. Soc., Prince George County, 1994—2002. Mem. adj. faculty dept. nursing Prince George's C.C., 1997—. Recipient Award of Excellence in Health Care, Assn. Women's Health, 2000, Hero for Babies, March of Dimes, 2002, Excellence in Edn. award, Prince George's C. of C. Bd. Edn., 2001.

LUDINGTON, TOWNSEND, English and American studies educator; b. Bryn Mawr, Pa., Jan. 31, 1936; s. Charles Townsend and Constance (Cameron) L.; m. Jane Ross, Feb. 22, 1958; children: David, Charles, James, Sarah. BA, Yale U., 1957; MA, Duke U., 1964; PhD, Duke U, 1967. Tchr. English Ransom Sch., Miami, Fla., 1960-62; from asst. prof. to prof. English U. N.C., Chapel Hill, 1967-78, Cary C. Boshamer prof. English and Am. Studies, 1982—, chair Am. studies curriculum, 1986—2001. Part-time instr. Duke U., 1963-66; resident scholar U.S. Internat. Communication Agy., 1980-81; vis. prof. U.S. Mil. Acad., West Point, N.Y., 1988-89 Author: John Dos Passos, 1980 (Mayflower award 1981), Marsden Hartley, 1992, Seeking the Spiritual: The Paintings of Marsden Hartley, 1998; Editor: The Fourteenth Chronicle, 1973, U.S.A., John Dos Passos, 1996, Three Soldiers, John Dos Passos, 1997, The Devil and Daniel Webster and Other Stories and Poems by Stephen Vincent Benet, 1999, A Modern Mosaic: Art and Modernism in the United States, 2000. Mem. adv. com. Florence Griswold Mus.; elector Wadsworth Atheneum. Capt. USMC, 1957—60. Recipient Outstanding Svc. medal U.S. Army, 1988-89; Fulbright fellow, 1971-72, Nat. Humanities Ctr. fellow, 1985-86, Wurlitzer Found. fellow, 1996, Beinecke Libr. Yale U. fellow, 1998. Mem.: PEN, Am. Studies Assn. Democrat. Avocations: golf, reading. Office: U NC Curriculum in Am Studies Greenlaw Hall Clb # 3520 Chapel Hill NC 27599-0001

LUDWICK, KATHLEEN, special education educator; b. Hannibal, Mo., Mar. 22, 1947; d. Harry Richard and Anna Mary (Morriss) Snyder; m. Boyd Reed Ludwick, Oct. 11, 1981 (dec. Mar. 1990); children: Deanna Marie, Mark William, Deidre Michelle; m. David C. Daggett, June 23, 2000. BA, Avila Coll., 1978; M in Edn., U. Kans., 1990. Cert. special edn./learning disabilities K-12. Tchr. Belton Sch. Dist., Mo., learning disability resource tchr. Former bldg. coord. Belton H.S., Mo. Office: Belton Sch Dist 107 Pirate Pkwy Belton MO 64072 E-mail: kludwick@beltonschools.org.

LUDWIG, KURT JAMES, residence director; b. Bristol, Pa., July 10, 1964; s. Lee Edward Sr. and Pauline Marcella (Stallone) Danis. BA, East Stroudsburg U., 1990; MA, Indiana U. Pa., 1993. Substitute tchr. Montpelier (Vt.) Sch. Dist., 1990-91; residence dir. Thiel Coll., Greenville, Pa., 1991-93; counselor, residence dir. U. Rio Grande, Ohio, 1993-95; residence dir. SUNY, Brockport, 1997-99; coord. residential programs, complex coord. Green Mountain Coll., Poultney, Vt., 1999-2000, dir. residence life, 2000—01; residence halls dir. Restaurant Sch. Walnut Hill Coll., Phila., 2002—. Home: 200 S 42d St Apt 2R Philadelphia PA 19104

LUECKENHOFF, MARK ALBERT, elementary school educator; b. Jefferson City, Mo., Sept. 24, 1955; s. Albert and Nancy (Hohenstreet) L.; m. Linda K. King, Jan. 8, 1977; children: Bethany, Phillip. BA, Ill. State U., 1977; MA, N.E. Mo. State U., 1982. Tchr. Lewis County C-1 Schs., Ewing, Mo., 1978—. Author: U.S. Neighbors, 1993; co-author: United States, 1993. Recipient Milken Family Found. award, 1996; named Mo. Elem. Social Studies Tchr. of the Yr., Mo. Coun. Social Studies, 1992. Mem. Mo. Geog. Alliance (newsletter editor 1993—). Home: 5 Lakeview Drive Ewing MO 63440-9445 Office: Highland Elem Sch PO Box 366 Ewing MO 63440-0366

LUEDECKE, SHARON ANNETTE, special education educator, speech therapist; b. Austin, Tex., July 25, 1957; d. William Orval Jr. and Adeline Mariann (Richter) Flynn; m. Garland Lee Luedecke, May 31, 1980; children: Heather Katherine, Phillip Ryan. BS in Elem. Edn., Tex. A & I U., 1979; postgrad., Trinity U., 1980. Cert. tchr., Tex.; lic. speech-lang. pathologist, Tex. Self contained resource Midland (Tex.) Ind. Sch. Dist., 1981-82, speech therapist, 1982-83; chpt. I reading Austin Ind. Sch. Dist., 1983-86, self contained resource, 1986-87; with resource dept. Round Rock (Tex.) Ind. Sch. Dist., 1987-89, with spl. edn. content mastery and inclusion, 1989—. Mem. Assn. Tex. Profl. Educators, Tex. Speech, Lang. and Hearing Assn., Tex. Assn. for the Improvement of Reading, Austin Area Assn. Speech-Lang. Pathologists. Republican. Methodist. Avocations: writing, arts and crafts. Home: 11007 Country Knls Austin TX 78750-3437

LUEDEKE, J. BARTON, academic administrator; Pres. Westminster Choir Coll., Princeton, N.J., Rider Coll., Lawrenceville, NJ, 1990—2003.

LUEKE, DONNA MAE, yoga instructor, Reiki practitioner, instructor; b. Toledo, Sept. 18, 1946; d. Herbert Henry and Margery Alberta (Welsh) L. BA, Adrian Coll., 1968. Tchr. Anchor Bay Schs., New Baltimore, Mich., 1968-74; salesperson Jacobson's, Birmingham, Mich., 1974-76; sales rep. Stark & Co., Detroit, 1976-80; regional retail supr. Norwich-Eaton Consumer Pharms., Louisville, 1980-83; territory rep. Procter & Gamble, Louisville, 1983-84; dir. Progressive Retail, Raleigh, N.C., 1984-89; nat. retail mgr. CIBA Consumer Pharms. and CIBA Vision Corp., Wayne, Pa., 1989-92; mem. apprentice program Holistic Options, 1997-98. Student govt. v.p. Adrian Coll., 1966, 67. Mem. Nature Conservancy. Avocations: creative writing, gardening, fishing.

LUENBERGER, DAVID GILBERT, electrical engineer, educator; b. Los Angeles, Sept. 16, 1937; s. Frederick Otto and Marion (Crumley) L.; m. Nancy Ann Iversen, Jan. 7, 1962; children: Susan Ann, Robert Alden, Jill Alison, Jenna Emmy. BSE.E., Calif. Inst. Tech., 1959; MSE.E., Stanford U., 1961, PhD in Elec. Engring., 1963. Asst. prof. elec. engring. Stanford (Calif.) U., 1963-67, assoc. prof. engring.-econ. systems, 1967-71, prof., 1971—, dept. chmn., 1980-91, prof. mgmt. sci. & engring., 2000—. Tech. asst. dir. U.S. Office Sci. and Tech., Exec. Office of Pres., Washington, 1971-72; vis. prof. MIT, Cambridge, 1976; guest prof. Tech. U. of Denmark, Lyngby, 1986. Author: Optimization by Vector Space Methods, 1969, Linear and Nonlinear Programming, 1973, 2d edit., 1984, Introduction to Dynamic Systems, 1979, Microeconomic Theory, 1995, Investment Science, 1998; contbr. articles to tech. jours. Recipient Hendrik W. Bode Lecture prize Control Systems Soc., 1990, Rufus Oldenburger medal, 1998. Fellow IEEE; mem. Econometric Soc., Soc. for Advancement Econ. Theory, Soc. for Promotion of Econ. Theory, Inst. Mgmt. Sci., Soc. Econ. Dynamics and Control (pres. 1987-88), Math Programming Soc., Palo Alto Camera Club, Sigma Xi, Tau Beta Pi. Lutheran.

LUEPKER, RUSSELL VINCENT, epidemiology educator; b. Chgo., Oct. 1, 1942; s. Fred Joseph and Anita Louise (Thornton) L.; m. Ellen Louise Thompson, Dec. 22, 1966; children: Ian, Carl. BA, Grinnell Coll., 1964; MD with distinction, U. Rochester, 1969; MS, Harvard U., 1976; PhD (hon.), U. Lund, Sweden, 1996. Intern U. Calif., San Diego, 1969-70; resident Peter Bent Brigham Hosp., Boston, 1973-74; cardiology fellow Peter Bent Brigham Hosp./Med., Boston, 1974-76; asst. prof. divsn. epidemiology med. lab. physiol. hygiene U. Minn., Mpls., 1976-80, assoc. prof., 1980-87, prof. divsn. epidemiology and medicine, 1987—, dir. divsn. epidemiology, 1991—, Mayo prof. pub. health, 2000—. Cons. NIH, Bethesda, Md., 1980—, U. So. Calif., L.A., 1985—, Armed Forces Epidemiology Bd., 1993-97; vis. prof. U. Goteborg, Sweden, 1986, Ninewells Med. Sch., Dundee, Scotland, 1995. With USPHS, 1970—73. Harvard U. fellow, 1974-76, Bush Leadership fellow, 1990; recipient Prize for Med. Rsch. Am. Coll. Chest Physicians, 1970, Nat. Rsch. Svc. award Nat. Heart, Lung and Blood Inst., Bethesda, 1975-77, Disting. Alumni award Grinnell Coll., 1989. Fellow ACP, Am. Coll. Cardiology, Am. Heart Assn. (chmn. coun. on epidemiology 1992-94, chair program com. sci. sessions 1995-97, award of merit 1997), Am. Coll. Epidemiology; mem. Am. Epidemiol. Soc., Am. Soc. Preventive Cardiology (Joseph Stokes award 1999), Delta Omega Soc. (Nat. Merit award 1988). Office: Univ Minn Sch Pub Health Div Epidemiology 1300 S 2nd St Minneapolis MN 55454-1087 E-mail: luepker@epi.umn.edu.

LUFT, CECILE E. music educator; b. Brooklyn, NY, May 14, 1925; d. Jacob and Sophie Burrows; m. Morris Luft; children: Tamara, Leslie Noymer. Diploma in piano, Juilliard School of Music, N.Y.C., 1946; MA, C.W. Post U., Brookville, N.Y., 1985—87. Choir dir. Temple Beth El, Bellmore, NY, 1953—56; music dir. Reform Jewish Congregation, Westbury, NY, 1960—68; music tchr. Pvt. Lessons, Merrick, NY, 1950—2001; music dir. Camp Rosemont & Roselake, Honesdale, Pa., 1967—68. Choir dir. Evangelical Covenant Ch., Floral Park, NY, 1986—2001. Mem.: Assn. Piano Tchrs. Long Island Inc. Avocations: travel, swimming.

LUHTA, CAROLINE NAUMANN, airport manager, flight educator; b. Cleve., Mar. 26, 1930; d. Karl Henry and Fannie Arletta (Harlan) Naumann; m. Fred Harlan Jones, July 2, 1955 (div. 1961); m. Adolph Jalmer Luhta, Dec. 12, 1968 (dec. 1993); 1 child, Katherine Louise. BA, Ohio Wesleyan U., 1952; BS magna cum laude, Lake Erie Coll., Painesville, Ohio, 1977. Rsch. chemist Standard Oil Co. Ohio, Cleve., 1952-68; office mgr. Adolph J. Luhta Constrn. Co., Painesville, 1968-83; acct. Thomas Y. Ellis, CPA, Painesville, 1978; bd. dirs. Painesville Flying Svc., Inc., 1968—, flight instr., 1970—, pres., 1993—. Bd. dirs. Concord Air Park, Inc., Painesville, 1968—, pres. 1993—; accident prevention counselor FAA, Cleve., 1975-85. Contbr. articles to profl. jours. Trustee Northeastern Ohio Gen. Hosp., Madison, 1973-83, chmn. bd. 1980-82; trustee Internat. Women's Air and Space Mus., Cleve., 1989—, treas. 1991-95, pres., 1997—; trustee Concord Twp., 1992—. Recipient Aerospace award Cleve. Squadron, Air Force Assn., 1966, Woman of Achievement award Lakeland C.C., 1999, Harvey High Sch. Alumni Assn. Hall Fame, 2001. Mem. Nat. Assn. Flight Instrs., Exptl. Aircraft Assn., Aircraft Owners and Pilots Assn., Ninety-Nines (life, chmn. All-Ohio chpt. 1969-70, Achievement award 1965, Amelia Earhart Meml. scholar 1970), Silver Wings (life), Order Ea. Star, Alpha Delta Pi (life). Avocations: air racing (Powder Puff Derby, All Women's Internat. Air Race). Office: Painesville Flying Svc Inc 12253 Concord Hambden Rd Painesville OH 44077-9566 E-mail: cluhta@iwasm.org.

LUI, ERIC MUN, civil engineering educator, practitioner; came to U.S., 1977; BS in Civil and Environ. Engring., U. Wis., 1980; MS in Civil Engring., Purdue U., 1982, PhD, 1985. Teaching asst. Purdue U., W. Lafayette, Ind., 1981-82, rsch. asst., 1983-85, post-doctoral rsch. asst., 1985-86, lectr., 1985-86; asst. prof. Syracuse (N.Y.) U., 1986-91, assoc. prof., 1992, dept. chair, 2003. Engring. cons. in field; advisor ASCE Student Chpt., 1992—, Hong Kong Cultural Assn., 1997—. Co-author: Structural Stability-Theory and Implementation, 1987, Stability Design of Steel Frames, 1991; editor (assoc.): ASCE Jour. Structural Engring., 1994—97; editor: (book), 1997—2000; author: monographs; contbr. more than 70 articles to profl. jours., papers to sci. procs., chapters to books. Recipient Bleyer scholarship U. Wis., 1979, Bates & Rogers Found. scholarship, 1980, David Ross fellowship Purdue U., 1982, 83; recipient Nellie Munsion award 1982, Crouse Hinds award for Excellence in Edn. Syracuse U., 1997. Mem. ASCE, AAUP, Am. Concrete Inst., Am. Acad. Mechanics, Am. Inst. Steel Constrn., Am. Soc. Engring. Edn., Coun. Tall Bldgs. and Urban Habitat, Structural Stability Rsch. Coun., Tau Beta Pi, Phi Kappa Phi, Sigma Xi. Avocations: painting, classical music, piano playing. E-mail: emlui@syr.edu.

LUIGART, CRAIG, federal official; m. Connie Rose Trammell; children: Kristen, Alyssa. BS in Biology and Chemistry, U. Louisville, Ky.; MS in Mgmt. Info. Systems cum laude, Naval Postgrad. Sch. Commd. U.S. Navy; chief info. officer Naval Air Systems Command; chief info. officer Naval Info. Systems Infrastructure for the Pentagon, Washington; chief tech, officer Just Medicine, Inc., Norcross, Ga.; chief info. officer U. S..Dept. Edn., Washington, 1999—; chief tech. officer U.S. Dept. Edn., Washington, 2003—. Decorated 2 Legion of Merit awards Sec. of the Navy; named Chief Info. Officer of Yr., Microsoft, 1992; named one of Premier Info. Tech. Leaders in The Country and Top Visionary Chief Info. Officer of Yr., Computerworld, 2002; recipient Exec. Mgmt. award, Dept. Edn., 2000, Fed. 100 award, Fed. Computer Week, 2001. Office: US Dept Edn 400 Maryland Ave SW Washington DC 20202

LUJAN, ROSA EMMA, bilingual specialist, trainer, consultant, assistant principal, assistant principal; b. El Paso, Tex., May 17, 1949; d. Rosendo G. and Petra (Rubalcava) López; m. Daniel Lujan, Feb. 21, 1976; children: Lorena Janel, Daniel Omar, Carina Viani, Crystal Rose. BA in Elem. Edn., U. Tex. El Paso, 1972, MS in Edn., 1978, postgrad., 1988, N.Mex. State U. Tchr. Ysleta Ind. Sch. Dist., El Paso, 1972-74, bilingual tchr., 1974-90, immigrant tchr., 1990—, now bilingual program supr. project mariposa. Cons. Internat. Acad. Coop. Learning, 1994; mem. Tex. Task Force on Profl. Preparation and Profl. Devel.; nat. bd. dirs. profl. tchg. stds. com. English as a New Lang., 1994; cooperating tchr. U. Tex. El Paso, 1978—; tchr. tnr. Ysleta Ind. Sch. Dist., 1980—; rschr. tnr. Johns Hopkins, U. Tex. El Paso, Haifa U., Israel, 1988—; mentor tchr. U. Tex. El Paso, El Salvador C.A., Boise, Idaho, 1990—; bd. dirs. Nat. Bd. for Profl. Tchg. Stds. Editor: (bilingual newsletter) El Chisme Bilingüe, 1986—. Pres. Ysleta Assn. Bilingual Edn., 1975-76, SW Assn. Bilingual Edn., El Paso, 1990-91; mem. Mt. Carmel Sch. Bd., El Paso, 1991-94, Tex. Com. Student Learning, Austin, 1992—. Named Tex. Tchr. of Yr., Tex. Edn. Agy., 1991-92, Tex. Elem. Tchr. of Yr., 1991-92. Mem. Nat. Assn. Bilingual Edn., Tex. Assn. Bilingual Edn., Phi Kappa Phi, Delta Kappa Gamma, Kappa Delta Pi. Democrat. Roman Catholic. Avocations: reading, sewing, traveling, dancing. Office: Ysleta Ind Sch Dist 9600 Sims Dr El Paso TX 79925-7200

LUKE, ROBERT GEORGE, nephrologist, medical educator; b. Sept. 4, 1935; s. Henry and Jemima (McCracken) L.; m. Catriona Mary MacDonald, Mar. 10, 1964; children— Colin Henry, Margaret Ann M.B., Ch.B., U. Glasgow, Scotland, 1959. Intern, then resident Univ. Hosps., U. Glasgow, 1959-63; Dir. renal div. U. Ky. Med. Ctr., Lexington, 1968-79; dir nephrology rsch. and tng. ctr. U. Ala., Birmingham, 1979-88; chmn. dept. medicine U. Cin. Med. Ctr., 1988—. Contbr. articles to profl. jours. Grantee NIH, 1972-91; fellow Yale U. Med. Ctr., 1964-65. Mem. Assn. Am. Physicians, Am. Soc. Clin. Investigation, Nat. Kidney Found., Am. Soc. Nephrology (former pres.), Clin. and Climatol. Assn. (sec.-treas.). Presbyterian. Avocation: tennis.

LUKEHART, CHARLES MARTIN, chemistry educator; b. DuBois, Pa., Dec. 21, 1946; s. David Blair and Grace Dorothy L.; m. Marilyn Orleana McKinney, Aug. 4, 1973; children: Mark, Brian, Laura. BS in Chemistry, Pa. State U., 1968; PhD in Inorganic Chemistry, MIT, 1972. Postdoctoral assoc. Tex. A&M U., College Sta., 1972-73; asst. prof. chemistry Vanderbilt U., Nashville, 1973-77, assoc. prof. chemistry, 1977-82, prof., 1982—. Author: Fundamental Transition Metal Organometallic Chemistry, 1985. Rsch. fellow Alfred P. Sloan Found., 1979-81. Mem. Am. Chem. Soc. (chmn. Nashville sect. 1979, 92), Materials Rsch. Soc. Office: Vanderbilt U Dept Chemistry Box 1822 Sta B Nashville TN 37235

LUKER, JEAN KNARR, school system administrator; b. St. Petersburg, Fla., May 4, 1944; d. Harry M. Jr. and Mary M. (Insley) Knarr; m. Maurice S. Luker Jr., Mar. 1, 1976; children: Maurice S. III, Amy Luker Cloud, Marc A. Miller. AA, Manatee Jr. Coll., 1964; BS in Edn., Fla. State U., 1966; MS in Edn., U. Va., 1982. Tchr., 1st grade Sarasota (Fla.) County Pub. Schs., 1966-70, tchr. emotionally disturbed, 1974-76; tchr. mentally retarded Washington County Schs., Abingdon, Va., 1978-82, tchr. learning disabled, 1982-89; coord. gifted secondary Washinton County Schs., 1990-91, coord. instructional technology, gifted, 1991—. Chair, bd. dirs. Southwest Va. Edn. & Tng. Network, Abingdon, 1993—; founding mem. Electronic Village of Abingdon; mem. VESIS Bd., Richmond, Va., 1993—. Co-author, illustrator: Of Clay Metal and Stone: Objects for Life and Death in Ancient Palestine, 1979. Mem. Va. Assn. Edn. of Gifted, Delta Kappa Gamma (scholar com. chair 1991—, AK7 Founders scholar), Phi Delta Kappa, Kappa Delta Pi, Phi Theta Kappa. Methodist. Avocations: reading, gardening. Home: 216 Stonewall Hts NE Abingdon VA 24210-2924 Office: Washington County Schs 220 Stanley St Abingdon VA 24210-2324

LUKSHA, ROSEMARY DOROTHY, art educator; b. Wilkes-Barre, Pa., Jan. 5, 1952; d. William Peter and Julia Catherine (Zavislak) L.; 1 child, Mary Rose. BS in Art Edn., Kutztown (Pa.) U., 1973, MEd, 1991; postgrad., Skidmore Coll., 1978, Marywood Coll., 1975, Wilkes U. Cert. instrnl. II art K-12. Art educator Wyoming Valley West Sch. Dist., Kingston, Pa., 1973-84; co. dancer Wilkes-Barre (Pa.) Ballet Theatre, 1973-80; dance instr. Coll. Misericordia, Dallas, Pa., 1980-81; art educator N.W. Area Sch. Dist., Shickshinny, Pa., 1988—; co. dancer Scranton (Pa.) Ballet Theatre, 1980-84. Art cons. Wilkes U. Polish Rm. Com., Wilkes-Barre, 1976-92; mem. planning com. Wilkes-Barre Fine Arts Fiesta, 1980-82; illustrator Wilkes-Barre Ballet Theatre, N.E. Ballet, 1977-85, Wyo. Valley Oratorio, Wilkes-Barre, 1979. Choreographer: (dance work) Continue the Balance We Hold, Sisters, Young Choreographer's Performance inN.E. Regional Ballet Festival, 1979. Mem., cantor St. Anthony of Padua Roman Cath. Ch.; advisor St. Anthony of Padua Youth Group, Larksville, Pa. Recipient Dance Scholarship N.E. Regional Ballet Festival, Melissa Hayden Ballet Sch., N.Y.C., 1979. Mem. Nat. Art Edn. Assn., N.W. Area Edn. Assn., Pa. Edn. Assn., Osterhout Libr. Soc., Phi Delta Kappa. Republican. Roman Catholic. Avocations: reading, gardening, travel, bicycling, calligraphy. Office: NW Area Jr/Sr HS RR 2 Box 2271 Shickshinny PA 18655-9201

LULL, ROBERT JOHN, nuclear medicine physician, educator; b. Buffalo, Aug. 23, 1940; s. Joseph J. and Margaret L.; m. Dorothy Lee Murtha, Feb. 2, 1965 (div. 1987); children: Jonathan C., Benjamin D. AB in Biochemistry, Canisius Coll., 1962; MD, Albany Med. Coll., 1966. Diplomate Nat. Bd. Med. Examiners, Am. Bd. Internal Medicine, Am. Bd. Nuclear Medicine; lic. Calif., Tex., N.Y. Commd. U.S. Army, 1966, advanced through ranks to col., 1980; rotating intern Brooke Army Med. Ctr., San Antonio, Tex., 1966-67, resident in internal medicine, 1967-70; fellow in nuclear medicine William Beaumont Army Med. Ctr., El Paso, Tex., 1970-72; chief nuclear med. svc. Brooke Army Med. Ctr., San Antonio, 1972-76, Letterman Army Med. Ctr., San Francisco, 1976-90; ret., 1990; assoc. dir. nuclear medicine dept. San Francisco Gen. Hosp., 1990-91; clin. prof. radiology and lab. medicine U. Calif., San Francisco, 1990—, dir. nuclear medicine residency, 1991—; dir. nuclear medicine dept. San Francisco Gen. Hosp., 1991—. Bd. dirs. Calif. Radioactive Materials Mgmt. Forum, Sacramento, Calif., chmn., 1989-90; cons., adv. com. FDA, Washington, 1991-97. Editor San Francisco Medicine, 1997-99, mem. editorial bd., 1995—; contbr. 30 peer rev. articles med. jours., chpts. to 7 med. books; reviewer for 8 med. jours.; editor (audio visual med. series) AIMS program, 1987-89. Nuclear medicine cons. Surgeon Gen., U.S. Army, Washington, 1977-90; senate appointee Citizen's Adv. Com. on Nuclear Emergencies, Calif., 1989-92; commr. Calif. Southwestern Low Level Radioactive Waste Compact, 1994—; bd. dirs. Nat. Assn. Cancer Patients, 1995-99. Recipient Boss of Yr. award No. Calif. chpt. Am. Bus. Women's Assn., 1979, Legion of Merit award U.S. Army, Presidio of San Francisco, 1990. Fellow: ACP, Am. Coll. Nuc. Physicians (bd. dirs. 1988—, pres. Calif. chpt. 1990—93, nat. pres. 1992—93, Pres. award 1995); mem.: San Francisco Med. Soc. (bd. dirs. 1996—, editor, chmn. editl. bd. 1998—2000, exec. com. 1998—, sec. 2000—, pres.-elect 2001—02, pres. 2002—03, immediate past pres. 2003—), Calif. Med. Assn. (chmn. nuc. medicine sect. 1996—, nuclear medicine rep. to coun. on scientific affairs 1996—, del. 2000—, pres. coun. 2001—, mem. editl. bd. Calif. medicine), Soc. Nuc. Medicine (pres. north Calif. chpt. 1986—87, Silver medal 1972—83), Radiol. Soc. N.Am., Am. Coll. Radiology (com. mem. 1990—95). Avocations: trombone, tennis, sailing, horseback riding, skiing. Office: San Francisco Gen Hosp Nuclear Medicine Dept NH 1001 Potrero Ave Rm G100 San Francisco CA 94110-3594

LUM, JEAN LOUI JIN, nursing educator; b. Honolulu, Sept. 5, 1938; d. Yee Nung and Pui Ki (Young) L. BS, U. Hawaii, Manoa, 1960; MS in Nursing, U. Calif., San Francisco, 1961; MA, U. Wash., 1969, PhD in Sociology, 1972. Registered nurse, Hawaii. From instr. to prof. Sch. Nursing U. Hawaii Manoa, Honolulu, 1961-95, acting dean, 1982, dean, 1982-89, prof. emeritus, 1995—. Project coordinator Analysis and Planning Personnel Svcs., Western Interstate Commn. Higher Edn., 1977; extramural assoc. div. Rsch. Grants NIH, 1978-79; mem. mgmt. adv. com. Honolulu County Hosp., 1982-96; mem. exec. bd. Pacific Health Rsch. Inst., 1980-88; mem. health planning com. East Honolulu, 1978-81; mem. rsch. grants adv. coun. Hawaii Med. Svcs. Assn. Found., Nat. Adv. Coun. for Nursing Rsch., 1990-93. Contbr. articles to profl. jours. Trustee Straub Pacific Health Found., Honolulu; bd. dirs. Friends of the Nat. Inst. of Nursing Rsch., 1994-97. Recipient Nurse of Yr. award Hawaii Nurses Assn., 1982; named Disting. Practitioner in Nursing, Nat. Acads. of Practice, 1986; USPHS grantee, 1967-72. Fellow Am. Acad. Nursing; mem. Am. Nurses Assn., Am. Pacific Nursing Leaders Conf. (pres. 1983-87), Council Nurse Researchers, Nat. League for Nursing (bd. rev. 1981-87), Western Council Higher Edn. for Nurses (chmn. 1984-85), Western Soc. for Research in Nursing, Am. Sociol. Assn., Pacific Sociol. Assn., Assn. for Women in Sci., Hawaii Pub. Health Assn., Hawaii Med. Services Assn. (bd. dirs. 1985-92), Western Inst. Nursing, Mortar Bd., Phi Kappa Phi, Sigma Theta Tau (Kupuna award 2003), Alpha Kappa Delta, Delta Kappa Gamma. Episcopalian. Office: U Hawaii Manoa Sch Nursing Webster Hall 2528 The Mall Honolulu HI 96822

LUMB, SANDRA JAYNE, elementary school educator; b. Lawrence, Mass., June 1, 1955; d. William Taylor and Virginia Ruth (Peate) L. BS, U. Lowell, 1977. Cert. tchr., Mass. Instl. asst. Title 1 (Chpt.1), Methuen, Mass., 1978-80; grade 1 tchr. Our Lady of Mt. Carmel Sch., Methuen, Mass., 1980-86, grade 3 tchr., 1986-91, 92-94, tchr. 4th grade, 1994—; asst. adminstr. Our Lady of Mt. Carmel, Methuen, 1991-92. Mem. Nat. Catholic Edn. Assn. Avocations: bowling, stamp collecting, ch. activities.

LUMBARD, ELIOT HOWLAND, lawyer, educator; b. Fairhaven, Mass., May 6, 1925; s. Ralph E. and Constance Y. L.; m. Jean Ashmore, June 21, 1947 (div.); m. Kirsten Dehner, June 28, 1981 (div.); children: Susan, John, Ann, Joshua Abel, Marah Abel. BS in Marine Transp., U.S. Mcht. Marine Acad., 1943-45; BS in Econs., U. Pa., 1949; JD, Columbia U., 1952. Bar: N.Y. 1953, U.S. Supreme Ct. 1959, Pa. 1983. Assoc. Breed, Abbott and Morgan, N.Y.C., 1952-53; asst. U.S. atty. So. Dist. N.Y., 1953-56; assoc. Chadbourne, Parke, Whiteside & Wolff, N.Y.C., 1956-58; ptnr. Townsend & Lewis, N.Y.C., 1961-70, Spear and Hill, N.Y.C., 1970-75, Lumbard and Phelan, P.C., N.Y.C., 1977-82, Saul, Ewing, Remick & Saul, N.Y.C., 1982-84; pvt. practice law N.Y.C., 1984-86; ptnr. Haight, Gardner, Poor & Havens, N.Y.C., 1986-88; pvt. practice law N.Y.C., 1988-92; ret. Chief counsel N.Y. State Commn. Investigation, 1958-61; spl. asst. counsel for law enforcement to Gov. N.Y., 1961-67; organizer N.Y. State Identification and Intelligence Sys., 1963-67; chair Oyster Bay Conf. on Organized Crime, 1962-67; criminal justice cons. to Gov. Fla. and other states, 1967; chief criminal justice cons. to N.J. Legis., 1968-69; chmn. com. on organized crime N.Y.C. Criminal Justice Coordinating Coun., 1971-74; organizer schs. of criminal justice at SUNY Albany and Rutgers, Newark; mem. departmental disciplinary com. First Dept., N.Y. Supreme Ct., 1982-88; trustee bankruptcy Universal Money Order Co., Inc., 1977-82, Meritum Corp., 1983-89; spl. master in admiralty Hellenic Lines Ltd., 1984-86; chmn. Palisades Life Ins. Co. (former Equity Funding subs. 1974-75); bd. dir. RMC Industries Corp.; chair Am. Maritime History Project, Inc., Kings Point, N.Y., 1996—; lectr. trial practice NYU Law Sch., 1963-65; mem. vis. com. Sch. Criminal Justice, SUNY-Albany, 1968-75; adj. prof. law and criminal justice John Jay Coll. Criminal Justice, CUNY, 1975-86; arbitrator Am. Arbitration Assn. and N.Y. Civil Ct.-Small Claims Part, N.Y. County; mem. Vol. Master Program U.S. Dist. Ct. (so. dist.) N.Y. Contbr. articles to profl. jours. Bd. dirs. Citizens Crime Commn. N.Y.C., Inc., Big Bros. Movement, Citizens Union; trustee Trinity Sch., 1964-78, N.Y.C. Police Found., Inc., 1971-92, chmn., 1971-74, emeritus. Lt. j.g. USNR, 1943-52. Recipient 1st Disting. Svc. award SUNY-Albany, Disting. Svc. award U.S. Merchant Marine Acad. Alumni, 2000. Mem. Assn. Bar City N.Y., N.Y. County Lawyers Assn., ABA, N.Y. State Bar Assn., Maritime Law Assn., Down Town Assn. Club. Republican. Home: 39B Apple Ln Hollis NH 03049-6311

LUMELSKY, VLADIMIR JACOB, engineering educator; b. Kharkov, Russia, Jan. 21, 1939; s. Jacob and Rachel (Polonsky) L.; m. Nadya Katsman, June 1973; children: Michael Leon, Anna Esther. BS in Elec. and Computer Engring., Inst. Precision Tech., Leningrad, Russia, 1960, MS in Elec. and Computer Engring., 1962; PhD in Applied Math., Nat. Acad. Scis., Moscow, 1970. Design engr. Computer Tech. Bur., Ioshkar-Ola, Russia, 1962-64; sr. rschr. Inst. Control Scis., Nat. Acad. Scis., Moscow, 1964-75; adj. prof. Inst. Radio Electronics, Nat. Acad. Scis., Moscow, 1970-75; rsch. engr. Ford Motor Co. Sci. Labs., Dearborn, Mich., 1976-80; rsch. scientist GE Rsch. Ctr., Schenectady, N.Y., 1980-85; assoc. prof. Yale U., New Haven, Conn., 1985-90; Consolidated Paper prof. engring. U. Wis., Madison, 1991—. Vis. program dir. NSF, Washington, 1999—. Contbr. over 160 articles to profl. jours. Fellow IEEE (bd. govs. Soc. Robotics and Automation 1986—, editor Transactions on Robotics and Automation 1987—, Disting. lectr. Soc. Robotics and Automation 1992-94). Office: Univ Wis 1513 University Ave Madison WI 53706-1539

LUMPKIN, MARGARET CATHERINE, retired education educator; b. Franklinton, N.C., Apr. 13; d. Willie Lee Lumpkin and Margaret (Ray) Pollock. BS, U. N.C., Greensboro, 1944; MS, Wellesley Coll., 1945; EdD, Oreg. State U., 1956. Instr. Mary Washington Coll., Fredricksburg, Va., 1945-48; from asst. prof. to prof. edn. Oreg. State U., Corvallis, 1948-87; co-owner, dir. The Reading Place, Corvallis, 1990-97; ret., 1997. Owner, co-dir. Camp Tamarack, Deschutes Nat. Forest, Sisters, Oreg., 1953-80; v.p. Britton & Assocs., Corvallis, 1972-2003; pres. Lake Creek Lodge, Inc., Sisters, 1974—2003; condr. workshops on lang. simplification, 1978-87; cons. on textbook selection criteria and lic. readability program Oreg. Legislature, Oreg. Edn. Dept.; resource person, cons. on lang. simplification pub. documents State of Oreg., 1979-89. Co-author: A Consumers Guide to Sex, Race and Career Roles in Public School Texts, 1977, Readability—A Consumers Guide, 1976-80, 17 Consumers Guides to Readability of Text Book Series; contbr. articles on reading improvement, devel. and psychology to profl. jours. Founding mem., bd. dirs. Youth Outreach., Inc., Corvallis, 1971-77; treas., sec., v.p., pres. Linn Benton Womens Polit. Caucus, Corvallis, 1977-87; founding voter, mem. Oreg. Womens Polit. Caucus, 1972—. Recipient meritorious award for rsch. in reading Project Innovation, Chula Vista, Calif., 1977, svc. award Oreg. Womens Polit. Caucus, 1980, nat. award for rsch. in reading Reading Improvement jour., 1978; grantee U.S. Office Edn., 1985-88, also other small grants. Mem. AAUW, ACLU (Liun-Benton bd. dirs. 1992-96), Phi Kappa Phi. Avocations: world travel, charities. Home and Office: 7565 NW Mountain View Dr Corvallis OR 97330-9751

LUMSDAINE, EDWARD, mechanical engineering educator; b. Hong Kong, China, Sept. 30, 1937; came to U.S., 1953; s. Clifford Vere and Miao Ying Lumsdaine; m. Monika Amsler, Sept. 8, 1959; children: Andrew, Anne Josephine, Alfred, Arnold BS in Mech. Engring., N.Mex. State U., Las Cruces, 1963, MS in Mech. Engring., 1964, ScD, 1966. Research engr. Boeing Co., Seattle, 1966-67, 68; asst. prof. to assoc. prof. S.D. State U., Brookings, 1967-72; assoc. prof. to prof. U. Tenn., Knoxville, 1972-77; prof., sr. research engr. phys. sci. lab., dir. N.Mex. solar energy inst. N.Mex. State U., Las Cruces, 1977-81; prof., dir. energy, environ. and resources ctr. U. Tenn., Knoxville, 1981-83; dean engring., prof. U. Mich., Dearborn, 1982-88, U. Toledo, 1988-93; dean of engring. Mich. Technol. U., Houghton, 1993-95, prof. mech. engring., 1993—; mgmt. cons. Ford Motor Co., 1995—. Vis. prof. Cairo U., Egypt, 1974, Tatung Inst. Tech., Taipei, China, 1978, Qatar U., Doha, 1983, Inst. Enterprise and Innovation U. Nottingham, Eng., 1999-00; spl. prof. bus. U. Nottingham, 2000—; UNESCO expert cons. to Egypt, 1979-80; dir., cons. E&M Lumsdaine Solar Cons., Hancock, Mich., 1979-97; cons. Oak Ridge (Tenn.) Nat. Lab., 1979-82, BDM Corp., Albuquerque, 1984, Ford Motor Co., Dearborn, Mich., 1984-95, Am. Supplier Inst., Dearborn, 1986-95. Author: Industrial Energy Conservation for Developing Countries, 1984, (with Monika Lumsdaine) Creative Problem Solving: An Introductory Course for Engineering Students, 1990, Creative Problem Solving: Thinking Skills for a Changing World, 1995, (with Monika Lumsdaine and J. William Shelnutt) Creative Problem Solving and Engineering Design, 1999, (with Martin Binks) Keep On Moving! Entrepreneurial Creativity and Effective Problem Solving, 2003; contbr. software packages, articles to profl. jours. Served with USAF, 1954-58 Recipient Am. Soc. Engring. Edn./Xerox Chester F. Carlson award for innovation in engring. edn., 1994; NASA faculty fellow, 1969, 70; grantee NSF, NASA, U.S. Dept. Energy, Dept. Navy, ASHRAE, AID, Ford Motor Co. Fellow AIAA, ASME, Royal Soc. Arts; mem. Am. Soc. Engring. Edn., Am. Creativity Assn. Baptist. Office: Mich Tech U Dept Mech Engring Houghton MI 49931 E-mail: lumsdain@mtu.edu.

LUNA, CHARALINE, superintendent; b. Feb. 7, 1955; d. Earle Russell and Edith (Gibbs) Vaughan; m. Robert E. Luna; children: Elizabeth, Michele, Gabrielle. AA in Early Childhood Adminstrn., Santa Ana (Calif.) Coll., 1977; BA in Liberal Studies and Elem. Edn., Calif. State U., L.A., 1985; MSEd in Adminstrn., Pacific We. U., L.A., 1991, EdD, 1992. Cert. tchr., Calif., Fla. Tchr.'s aide Page Pvt. Schs., L.A., 1970-72, team kindergarten tchr., 1972-75, pre-sch. tchr., 1976-78, dir., prin., 1978-86, dir. Sanford, Fla., 1986, supr., 1988—. Mem. Fla. Tri-County Prekindergarten Interagy. Coun., 1994-97; mem. Seminole County health Start Coalition, 1994—; mem. Seminole County Health Adv. Bd., 1995—; mem. adv. county Seminole County DARE, 1996—; mem. Gov.'s Children's Summit, 1996-97. Recipient Pres.'s award Page Pvt. Sch., 1990, Appreciation award Desert Storm Support Group, 1992, Outstanding Svc. award Assn. Ind. Schs. of Fla., 1995, Spl. Recognition award for svc. Assn. Ind. Schs. Fla., 1998. Mem. DAR (regent 1991-92), Assn. Ind. Schs. of Fla. (bd. dirs. 1990—, rep. to Nat. Coun. Pvt. Sch. Accreditation 1994—), Cen. Fla. Assn. Non-Pub. Schs. (sec. 1988-89), Sanford C. of C. (edn. com. 1987-93), Sanford Woman's Club, Zeta Tau Alpha (collegiate pres. 1974). Office: Page Pvt Schs 650 E Airport Blvd Sanford FL 32773-8020

LUNA PADILLA, NITZA ENID, photography educator; b. San Juan, P.R., Mar. 13, 1959; d. Luis and Carmen Iris (Padilla) Luna. BFA, Pratt Inst., 1981; MS, Brooks Inst., 1985. Instr. U. P.R., Carolina, 1981-82, Cultural Inst., San Juan, 1988; prof. photography U. Sacred Heart, Santurce, P.R., 1987—; assoc. dir. communication ctr. U. Sagrado Corazon, Santurce, P.R., 1989-90. Contbr. articles to profl. publs.; one-woman shows P.R. Inst. Culture, 1988, Art and History Mus., San Juan, 1989, 94, 96, U. P.R., 1989, 90, Brooks Inst. Phototography, Santa Barbara, Calif., 1990, Miriam Walsh Gallery, Glenwood Springs, Colo., 1991, Mus. Ponce, 1991, Spokane (Wash.) C.C., 1994, Centro Europa, San Juan, 1996, Galería de Arte, P.R., 1996; exhibited in group shows Santa Barbara Mus. Art, 1987, Coll. of Santa Fe, N.Mex., 1988, Durango (Colo.) Arts Ctr., 1988, 90, Laband Art Gallery, L.A., 1989, Cultural Ctr., Vercelli, Italy, 1989, Univ. Union Gallery Calif. Poly. State U., 1990, Coconino Ctr. Arts, Flagstaff, Ariz., 1990, Centro Cultural Washington Irving, Madrid, 1991, L.A. County Fair, 1991, Museo del Grabado Latinoamericano, San Juan, 1992, 93, 94, P.R. Inst. Culture, 1994, Hostos Art Gallery, N.Y.C., 1996, The Platinum Gallery, Sante Fe, 1996, Gallería Botello, San Juan, 1996, The Queens Mus., N.Y.C., 1997, The Platinum Gallery, N.Y.C., 1997, Arsenal, San Juan, 1997, Wis. Union Art Gallery, U. Wis., 1998; in permanent collections; juror Fotografía de prensa "Mandin," 1991-92. MacDowell Colony grantee, Instituto de Cultural Puertorriqueña grantee, 1993, 94, 96. Mem. Soc. Photog. Edn., Friends of Photography. Roman Catholic. Avocations: painting, aerobics. Office: U Sagrado Corazón PO Box 12383 San Juan PR 00914-8505

LUNARDINI, CHRISTINE ANNE, writer, historian, school administrator; b. Holyoke, Mass., Jan. 27, 1941; d. Virgil Joseph and Christine Hildegarde (Cavanaugh) L. AA, Holyoke C.C., 1973; BA, Mt. Holyoke Coll., 1975; MA, Princeton U., 1979, PhD, 1981. Instr. history Princeton (N.J.) U., 1981-85; adminstrv. asst. Refco Inc., N.Y.C., 1985-87; assoc. prof. Pace U., N.Y.C., 1987-91; freelance writer, N.Y.C., 1991—; exec. asst. to pres. Lynn Chase Designs, Inc., N.Y.C., 1999-2000; dir. devel. St. Michael Acad., N.Y.C., 2000—. Vis. assoc. prof., Barnard Coll., Columbia U., N.Y.C., 1984-85; project mgr., sr. editor Carlson Pub., Bklyn., 1992-93.

Author: From Equal Suffrage to Equal Rights: Alice Paul and the National Woman's Party 1910-1928, 1986, The American Peace Movement in the 20th Century, 1994, What Every American Should Know About Women's History, 1996, Women's Rights, 1996; editor, project mgr.: Black Women in America, An Historical Encyclopedia, 2 vols., 1993 (Dartmouth medal 1994), Columbia Guide to American Women: The Nineteenth Century, 1999; mem. editl. adv. bd. Am. Heritage Multi Media, Am. Heritage: Women in Am., 1994—. Princeton U. fellow, 1975-79, Woodrow Wilson nat. fellow, 1980, AAUW nat. fellow, 1980-81. Mem. NOW, Women's Bond Club N.Y., Phi Beta Kappa. Democrat. Episcopalian. Home: 26 Beaver St New York NY 10004-2311 Office: 425 W 33rd St New York NY 10001 E-mail: lunar127@aol.com.

LUND, DARYL BERT, food science educator; b. San Bernardino, Calif., Nov. 4, 1941; married June 15, 1963; children: Kristine, Eric. BS in Math., U. Wis., 1963, MS in food Sci., 1965, PhD in Food Sci., 1968. Rsch. asst. in food sci. U. Wis., Madison, 1963-67, instr., 1967-68, asst. prof., 1968-72, assoc. prof., 1972-77, prof. food sci., 1977-87, chmn. dept. food sci., 1984-87; chmn. dept. food sci., assoc. dir. agrl. experiment sta. Rutgers, the State U., New Brunswick, 1988-89, interim exec. dean agr. and natural resources, 1989-91, exec. dean agr./natural resources, 1991-95, exec. dir. N.J. Agrl. Experiment Sta., dean Cook Coll., 1991-95; Ronald P. Lynch dean of agr. and life scis. Cornell U., Ithaca, N.Y., 1995-2000; exec. dir. North Ctrl. Regional Assn., U. Wis., Madison, 2001—. Vis. engr. Western Regional Rsch. Lab., Berkeley, Calif., 1970-71; advisor for evaluation of food tech. dept. Inst. Agr., Bogor, Indonesia, 1973; mem. four-man evaluation team to review grad. edn. programs Brazilian univs., 1976; vis. prof. food process engring. Agrl. U., Wageningen, The Netherlands, 1979; invited vis. prof. food process engring. Univ. Coll., Dublin, 1982; invited advisor Inter-Univ. Ctr. on Food Sci. and Nutrition, Bogor, 1991; advisor Agrl. U., Bogor, 1992; lectr. in field. Contbr. over 200 articles to profl. jours.; editor 5 books; co-author text book. Recipient Food Engring. award Dairy and Food Industries Supply Assn. and Am. Soc. Agrl. Engring., 1987. Fellow Inst. Food Technologists (Wis. sect. 1968-87, N.Y. sect. 1988-95, ctrl. N.Y. 1995-2000, Travel award as promising young scientist to Internat. Congress on Food Sci. and tech., Madrid 1974, pres. 1990-91, Internat. award 1995,Carl L. Fellers aard 2003), Internat. Union Food Sci. and Tech. (charter fellow); mem. AIChE, Am. Inst. Nutrition, Am. Soc. Agrl. Engrs., Sigma Xi, Gamma Sigma Delta, Phi Tau Sigma. Avocations: golf, travel, wood working. Home: 151 E Reynolds St Cottage Grove WI 53527

LUNDE, DOLORES BENITEZ, retired secondary education educator; b. Honolulu, Apr. 12, 1929; d. Frank Molero and Matilda (Francisco) Benitez; m. Nuell Carlton Lunde, July 6, 1957; 1 child, Laurelle. BA, U. Oreg., 1951, postgrad., 1951-52, U. So. Calif., L.A., 1953-54, Colo. State U., 1957-58, Calif. State U., Fullerton, 1967-68. Cert. gen. secondary tchr., Calif.; cert. lang. devel. specialist. Tchr. Brawley (Calif.) Union High Sch., 1952-55; tchr. Fullerton (Calif.) Union High Sch. Dist., 1955-73; tchrs. aide Placentia (Calif.) Unified Sch. Dist., 1983-85; tchr. continuing edn. Fullerton Union High Sch. Dist., 1985-91; tchr. Fullerton Sch. Dist., 1988, Fullerton Union H.S. Dist., 1989-94. Presenter regional and state convs., so. Calif., 1986-88. Innovator tests, teaching tools, audio-visual aids. Vol. Luth. Social Svcs., Fullerton, 1981-82, Messiah Luth., Yorba Linda, Calif., 1981-88, 91-2001. Recipient Tchr. of Yr. award Fullerton Union High Sch. Dist., 1989. Mem. NEA, AAUW (life, bull. editor 1979-80, corr. sec. 1981-83, program v.p. 1983-84, gift honoree Fullerton br. 1985), Calif. State Tchrs. Assn., Fullerton Secondary Tchrs. Assn., Internat. Club/Spanish Club (advisor La Habra, Calif. 1965-72), Tchrs. English to Speakers Other Langs., Calif. Assn. Tchrs. English to Speakers Other Langs. Avocations: singing, folk and interpretive dance, guitar, reading, travel. Home: 4872 Ohio St Yorba Linda CA 92886-2713

LUNDELIUS, ERNEST LUTHER, JR., vertebrate paleontologist, educator; b. Austin, Tex., Dec. 2, 1927; s. Ernest Luther and Hazel (Halton) L.; m. Judith Weiser, Sept. 28, 1953; children— Jennifer, Rolf Eric. BS in Geology, U. Tex., 1950; PhD in Paleozoology, U. Chgo., 1954. Postdoctoral Fulbright scholar to Western Australia, 1954-55; postdoctoral research fellow Calif. Inst. Tech., 1956-57; mem. faculty U. Tex., Austin, 1957—, prof. vertebrate paleontology, 1969; John Andrew Wilson prof. vertebrate paleontology, 1978-98; prof. emeritus, 1998. Served with AUS, 1946-47. Fulbright sr. scholar to Australia, 1976. Home: 7310 Running Rope Austin TX 78731-2132 Office: U Tex Dept Geol Scis Austin TX 78712

LUNDGREN, LEONARD, III, retired secondary education educator; b. San Francisco, June 22, 1933; s. Leonard II and Betty (Bosold) L.; m. Jane Gates, June 12, 1976. AA, City Coll. San Francisco, 1952; AB, San Francisco State U., 1954, MA, 1958, postgrad., 1958-71. Cert. tchr., Calif. Phys. edn. tchr., athletic coach Pelton Jr. High Sch., San Francisco, 1958-59; social studies tchr., dept. chair, phys. edn. tchr., athletic coach Luther Burbank Jr. High Sch., San Francisco, 1959-78; history, govt. econs., geography tchr. George Washington High Sch., San Francisco, 1978-93. Water safety instr. ARC, San Francisco, 1946-61; mem. Calif. Quality Teaching Ctr. Conf. Bd., 1965-67. Author: Guide for Films and Filmstrips, 1966, Teacher's Handbook for Social Studies, 1966, Guide for Minority Studies, 1968. V.p. Lakeside Property Owners Assn., San Francisco, 1986—88, legis. advocate, 1988—95; v.p. West of Twin Peaks Coun., San Francisco, 1986—87; pub. affairs polit. econ. cons. Calif. Fulbright scholar, Greece, 1963; recipient Svc. Pin, ARC, 1961. Mem.: AARP (cmty. coord. San Francisco 1996—97, rep. 2001—), PTA (sch. v.p. 1980—81), NEA (life; del. 1970, 1972—76), San Francisco Classroom Tchrs. Assn. (pres. 1972—73, Gavel award 1973), Calif. Coun. Social Studies (v.p. San Francisco chpt. 1969—70), Nat. Coun. Social Studies, Calif. Tchrs. Assn. (state coun. rep. 1963—74), Calif. Assn. Health, Phys. Edn., Recreation and Dance (life; treas. San Francisco chpt. 1959—60), Calif. Ret. Tchrs. Assn. (life; legis. chmn. San Francisco divsn. 1995—99, 1st v.p. 1997—99, pres. 1999—2000, legis. co-chmn. 2001—), World Affairs Coun. No. Calif., Nat. Geog. Soc. (life), San Francisco State U. Alumni Assn. (life; treas. 1959), Commonwealth Club of Calif., Phi Delta Kappa (life; pres. chpt. 1965—66). Avocations: travel, swimming, gardening, research, service.

LUNDIN, NORMAN KENT, artist, educator; b. Los Angeles, Dec. 1, 1938; s. John R. and Louise A. (Marland) L.; m. Sylvia Johnson; children: Kelly Jean, Christopher David. BA, Sch. Art Inst. Chgo., 1961; M.F.A., U. Cin., 1963. Asst. to dir. Cin. Art Mus., 1962-63; instr. art U. Wash., Seattle, 1964-66, asst. prof., 1966-68, assoc. prof., 1968-75, prof., 1976—. Vis. artist Hornsey Coll. Art, London, 1969-70; vis. prof. Ohio State U., Columbus, 1975; prof. San Diego State U., 1978; vis. prof. U. Tex.-San Antonio, 1982, Chelsea Coll. Art, London, 1996. Exhibited one-man shows, Francine Seders Gallery, Seattle, Space, L.A., Jack Rasmussen Gallery, Washington, Allen Stone, N.Y.C., Adams Middleton Gallery, Dallas, Allport Gallery, San Francisco, Stephen Haller Fine Art, N.Y.C., 1987-94, Schmidt-Bingham Gallery, N.Y.C., 1997, Koplin Gallery, L.A., 1997; group shows include Mus. Modern Art, N.Y.C., Whitney Mus. Am. Art, N.Y.C., Denver Art Mus., Seattle Art Mus., San Francisco Mus. Modern Art Nat. Endowment Arts grantee; Fulbright-Hays grantee Norway, 1963-64; Tiffany Found. grantee, 1968; Ford. Found. grantee Soviet Union, Eastern Europe, 1978-79 Office: U Wash Sch Art Seattle WA 98105

LUNDY, SHERMAN PERRY, secondary school educator; b. Kansas City, Mo., July 26, 1939; s. Loren F. and O. Metta (Brown) L.; m. Beverly J., Feb. 25, 1960; children: Paul, Carolyn. BA, U. Okla., 1963; MA, So. Meth. U., 1966; EdS, U. Iowa, 1975. Cert. tchr., Iowa. Tchr. Platte Canyon High Sch., Bailey, Colo., 1964-65, Lone Grove (Okla.) High Sch., 1966-68, Ardmore (Okla.) High Sch., 1968-69; tchr., sci. dept. chair Burlington (Iowa) High Sch., 1969—. Geologist Basic Materials Corp., Waterloo, Iowa, 1983—, Raid Quarries, Burlington, 1975-80. Contbr. articles to profl. jours.; author curriculum guide: Environmental Activities, 1975. Mem., commr. Regional Solid Waste Commn., Des Moines County, 1990—; mem., pres. Conservation Bd., Des Moines County, 1978-88; bd. dirs. Iowa Conservation Bd. Assn., 1984-85; mem. Civil Rights Commn., City of Burlington, 1970-76; pres. Burlington Trees Forever, 1998-99. With USMC, 1960-64. Recipient Silver Beaver Boy Scouts Am., 1975, Service Recognition, Des Moines County Conservation Bd., 1988, Project ESTEEM agt., Harvard/Smithsonian, 1992, Soil Conservation Water Shed Achievement award State of Iowa, 1998, DAR Award for Conservation, 1998, Environ. Educator of Yr. award U.S. EPA, Region 7, Iowa, 1998. Mem. Geol. Soc. Am. (North Cen. edn. com. 1989—), Iowa Acad. Sci. (edn. com. 1990-91, chair earth sci. tchrs. sect. 1993-94, exec. bd. 1992-94), Nat. Assn. Geology Tchrs. (Outstanding Earth Sci. Tchr. 1992, v.p. ctrl. sect. 1994-95, pres. ctrl. sect. 1996-98), Soc. Econ. and Sedimentary Geology, Geol. Soc. Iowa, Am. Chem. Soc. (Excellence in Sci. Tchg. award consortiums 1996, Chem. Cos. award), Unitarian Fellowship, Sons of Confederate Vets. (comdr. Camp 1759 1998—), SE Iowa Civil War Round Table (chair 1992-94). Unitarian Universalist. Avocations: civil war, stamp collecting, fossil collecting. Home: 4668 Summer St Burlington IA 52601-8985

LUNN, PAMELA KELLOGG, elementary education educator; b. Bossier, La., Oct. 3, 1954; d. Ronald Robert and Janet Lucille (Zinnel) Kellogg; m. Raymond Cortez Lunn, Jr., June 10, 1974. BA, Southeastern La. U., 1976, MEd, 1982, postgrad., 1987. Cert. spl. educator, prin., elem. educator, academically gifted educator, reading specialist, La. Tchr. Ascension Parish-Donaldsonville (La.) Jr. High Sch., 1976-77, St. John Parish-John L. Ory, LaPlace, La., 1977-78, St. John Parish-East St. John Middle Sch., Reserve, La., 1978-81, tchr. gifted edn., 1981-83; tchr. spl. edn. St. Martin Parish-St. Martinville (La.) Elem. Sch., 1983-84; tchr. gifted edn. St. Martin Parish-Breaux Bridge (La.) Jr. High Sch., 1984-85; tchr. spl. edn. St. John Parish-John L. Ory, LaPlace, 1985-87, tchr. chpt. I reading Reserve, 1987-93; tchr. Mandeville (La.) Middle Sch., 1994—. Coord. Parishwide Spelling Bee, 1987-91, parish judge, 1991-93; steering com. mem. Chpt. I, 1989-93; mem. Process Evaluation Com., 1989-93, Chpt. I Selection of Materials Com., 1989-93; leader 4-H Club, 1985-90; student coun. leader, 1978-83; coord. Parent Adv. Coun., 1989-93. Recipient Crystal Apple Community Svc. award, 1986-87; nominated for Tchr. in Residence for Southeastern La. U., 1990-91; named Tchr. of the Yr. for Reserve Middle Sch., 1978. Mem. Nat. Assn. Educators, Internat. Reading Assn., Nicholl's Reading Coun., La. Reading Assn., La. Assn. Educators. Democrat. Baptist. Avocations: sand painting, cooking, boating, camping. Home: 1149 Hillsboro Mile Apt 212N Hillsboro Beach FL 33062-1724 Office: Mandeville Middle Sch 2525 Soult St Mandeville LA 70448-6228

LUO, HONG YUAN, biomedical scientist, educator; b. Shengyang, Liaoning, China, June 29, 1951; d. Xin Luo and Rong K. Ren; children: Patrick Yj, Michael Yl. MD, Zhongshan Med. Sch., Guangzhou, China, 1976; M Medicine, Chinese Acad. Med. Scis., Beijing, 1982; PhD, McMaster U., 1993. Tchg. asst. Zhongshan Med. U., 1976-78; rsch. assoc. Beijing Nutrition, 1982-85; vis. scholar McMaster U., Hamilton, Ont., Can., 1985-87; postdoctoral fellow U. Tex. Med. Br., Galveston, 1993-95, instr. biomed. scis., 1995-99; rsch. specialist U. Pa., Phila., 2000—03; rsch. asst. prof. Boston U. Med. Ctr., 2003—; asst. dir. Lab. Hemoglobin, Ctr. of Excellence for Sickle Cell Disease, Boston, 2003—. Mem. Am. Soc. Hematology. Achievements include development of 2 monoclonal antibodies for human embryonic hemoglobin zeta chain, which have been used for identifying Alpha-thalassemia (Southeast Asian deletion) carriers in population; this deletion causes hydrops fetalis syndrome that leads to fetal death; these antibodies have also been used to identify the fetal cells in maternal blood for non-invasive prenatal diagnosis. Home: 230 W Squantum St Quincy MA 02171

LUOMA, GARY A. accounting educator; b. Pequaming, Mich., June 14, 1936; s. Otto Samuel and Ruth Eleanor (Braeger) L.; m. Evelyn Marie Gervais, July 7, 1956; children: Gary Jr., Valerie, Steven, Patricia. BA, Northern Mich. U., 1958; MA, Western Mich. U., 1959; D of Bus. Adminstrn., Washington U. St. Louis, 1966. CPA, CMA, CFM. Lectr., instr., asst. to dean Washington U., St. Louis, 1959-64; asst. prof., assoc. prof., prof., dir. BBA program Emory U., Atlanta, 1964-77; dir. Sch. Acctg., prof. Ga. State U., Atlanta, 1977—86; prof. U. SC, Columbia, SC, 1986—, dir. Sch. Acctg., 1986—93. Cons. in field. Author: Financial Aspects of Contract Negotiation and Administration, 1972, Fund Accounting for Colleges and Universities, 1973, Accounting and Record Keeping for Small Business, 1982, Cases on Business Ethics, 1988; contbr. articles to profl. jours. With USNR, 1954-58. Office: U SC Sch Bus Columbia SC 29208-0001

LUPULESCU, AUREL PETER, medical educator, researcher, physician; b. Manastiur, Banat, Romania, Jan. 1, 1923; came to U.S., 1967, naturalized, 1973; s. Peter Vichentie and Maria Ann (Dragan) L. MD magna cum laude, Sch. Medicine, Bucharest, Romania, 1950; MS in Endocrinology, U. Bucharest, 1965; PhD in Biology, U. Windsor, Ont., Can., 1976. Diplomate Am. Bd. Internal Medicine. Chief lab. investigations Inst. Endocrinology, Bucharest, 1950-67; rsch. assoc. SUNY Downstate Med. Ctr., 1968-69; asst. prof. medicine Wayne State U., 1969-72, assoc. prof., 1973—. Vis. prof. Inst. Med. Pathology, Rome, 1967; cons. VA Hosp., Allen Park, Mich., 1971-73. Author: Steroid Hormones, 1958, Advances in Endocrinology and Metabolism, 1962, Experimental Pathophysiology of Thyroid Gland, 1963, Ultrastructure of Thyroid Gland, 1968, Effect of Calcitonin on Epidermal Cells and Collagen Synthesis in Experimental Wounds As Revealed by Electron Microscopy Autoradiography and Scanning Electron Microscopy, 1976, Hormones and Carcinogenesis, 1983, Hormones and Vitamins in Cancer Treatment, 1990, Cancer Cell Metabolism and Cancer Treatment, 2001; reviewer various sci. jours.; contbr. chpts., numerous articles to profl. pubs. Recipient Lifetime Sci. Achievement award, 2003. Fellow Fedn. Am. Socs. for Exptl. Biology; mem. AMA, AAAS, Electron Microscopy Soc. Am., Soc. for Investigative Dermatology, N.Y. Acad. Scis., Am. Soc. Cell Biology, Soc. Exptl. Biology and Medicine. Republican. Achievements include research on hormones and tumor biology; studies regarding role of hormones and vitamins in carcinogenesis. Home: 21480 Mahon Dr Southfield MI 48075-7525 Office: Wayne State U Sch Medicine 540 E Canfield St Detroit MI 48201-1928

LURENSKY, ELEANOR GOLDMAN, humanities educator; b. Boston, Aug. 28, 1926; d. Harry R. and Jennie A. (Himmelstein) Goldman; m. Robert Lee Lurensky, Oct. 15, 1961; children: Harriet Claire, Steven Michael. BA, Northeastern U., Boston, 1947, EdM, 1962. Adj. prof. reading vocabulary and comprehension Southeastern U., Washington, 1975—90; tutor Kingsbury Ctr., Washington, 1975—93. Den mother Boy Scouts Am., Bethesda, Md., 1974-76; troop co-leader Girl Scouts Am., Bethesda, 1972-75. Jewish. Home: 7520 Holiday Ter Bethesda MD 20817

LURENSKY, ROBERT LEE, economist, educator; b. Roxbury, Mass., May 5, 1928; s. Abraham and Celia (Kamm) L.; m. Eleanor Vivian Goldman, Oct. 15, 1961; children: Harriet Claire, Steven Michael. BA, Syracuse U., 1950; MBA, Wharton Sch. U. Pa., 1952; MA, Harvard U., 1954. Economist, loan officer Export-Import Bank of U.S., Washington, 1961-67; internat. fin. economist Office Internat. Fin., U.S. Dept. Commerce, Washington, 1967-84, Office of Internat. Major Projects, Washington, 1984-93, Office of Energy, Environment and Infrastructure, Washington, 1993—94; ret., 1994. Assoc. prof. fin. Southeastern U., Washington, 1966-91, dir. dept. fin. and banking, 1966-88, asst. to acad. v.p., 1988-89. Comdr. USNR, 1953-73. Mem. Am. Econ. Assn., Phi Beta Kappa. Jewish.

LURIA, ZELLA HURWITZ, psychology educator; b. N.Y.C., Feb. 18, 1924; d. Hyman Hurwitz and Dora (Garbarsky) H.; m. Salvador Edward Luria, Apr. 18, 1945; 1 child, Daniel David. BA, Bklyn., 1944; MA, Ind. U., 1947, PhD, 1951. lic. clin. psychologist, Mass. Ford Found. post-doctoral fellow U. Ill., Urbana, 1951-53, Russell Sage found. fellow, 1953-56, clin. researcher, 1954-58; asst. prof. psychology Tufts U., Medford, Mass., 1958-62, assoc. prof., 1962-70, prof., 1970—2003, prof. emerita, 2003. Psychiatry lectr. Mass. Gen. Hosp., Boston, 1970-79; vis. scholar Stanford U., 1977, 83; vis. prof. UCLA, 1992, U. Mich., 1993. Sr. author: Psychology of Human Sexuality, 1979, Human Sexuality, 1987. Pro-bono psychol. assessment Physicians for Human Rights, 1997—; state bd. dept. edn. Planned Parenthood of Mass., 2001—. Postdoctoral fellow USPHS, Paris, 1963-64, Bunting fellow Radcliffe Coll., 1989-90; Mellon Found. Faculty grantee Wellesley Coll., 1979-80. Mem.: AAUP (Tufts U. pres. 1986—), New Eng. Psychol. Assn. (pres. 1971—72). Office: Tufts Univ Dept Of Psychology Medford MA 02155

LUSTIG, ROBERT HOWARD, pediatrician, educator; b. Bklyn., May 24, 1957; s. Richard Simon and Judith Ellen (Marcus) L.; m. Julie Kay Plumb, Mar. 25, 1995. BS, MIT, 1976; MD, Cornell U., 1980. Diplomate in pediat. endocrinology Am. Bd. Pediat. Resident St. Louis Children's Hosp., 1980-83; fellow pediatric endocrinology U. Calif., San Francisco, 1983-84; rsch. assoc. Rockefeller U., N.Y.C., 1984-90; asst. prof. pediat. U. Wis., Madison, 1990-95; assoc. prof. pediat. U. Tenn., Memphis, 1999—2001; prof. clin. pediat. U. Calif., San Francisco, 2001—. Adj. clin. faculty St. Jude Children's Rsch. Hosp., Memphis, 1999-2001. Mem. Endocrine Soc., Soc. Neurosci., Soc. Pediatric Rsch., Lawson Wilkins Pediat. Endocrine Soc., N.Am. Assn. Study Obesity. Office: U Calif San Francisco Dept Pediat S 672D San Francisco CA 94143 E-mail: rlustig@peds.ucsf.edu.

LUSZTIG, PETER ALFRED, university dean, educator; b. Budapest, Hungary, May 12, 1930; s. Alfred Peter and Susan (Szabo) L.; m. Penny Bicknell, Aug. 26, 1961; children: Michael, Cameron, Carrie. B in Com., U. B.C., Vancouver, Can., 1954; MBA, U. Western Ont., London, Can., 1955; PhD, Stanford U., 1964. Asst. to comptroller B.C. Electric, Vancouver, 1955-57; instr. fin. U. B.C., 1957-60, asst. prof. fin., 1962-64, assoc. prof., 1965—68, Killam sr. research fellow, 1968-69, prof., 1968—95, dean faculty commerce, 1977-91, dean emeritus, 1995—. Chair, bd. trustees BC Health Benefit Trust; bd. dirs. Canfor Corp.; fed. commr. BC Treaty Commn., 1995-2003; vis. prof. IMEDE, Switzerland, 1973-74, London Grad. Sch. Bur. Studies, 1968-69, Pacific Coast Banking Sch., 1977—1982; sr. advisor B.C. Ministry of Econ. Devel., Small Bus. and Trade, 1991. Author: Report of the Royal Commission on Automobile Insurance, 2 vols., 1968, Financial Management in a Canadian Setting, 6th rev. edit., 2001, Report of the Commission on the B.C. Tree Fruit Industry, 1990. Ford Found. faculty dissertation fellow, Stanford U., 1964. Lutheran. E-mail: p.lusztig@shaw.ca.

LUTEN, KAREN A. English language educator; b. N.Y.C., Nov. 8, 1955; d. Colby John and Carol Ann (Green) L. BA, U. Pa., 1977; MA, Columbia U., 1984, PhD, 1992. From asst. to assoc. editor Metro. Opera Guild, N.Y.C., 1977-83; tchg. asst. Columbia U., N.Y.C., 1985-90; English tchr. Dalton Sch., N.Y.C., 1990—. Recipient Excellence in Tchg. award, Dalton Sch., 1996—97. Mem. Phi Beta Kappa. Avocations: theater, opera, ballet, guitar, reading. Home: 240 Cabrini Blvd Apt 1F New York NY 10033-1113

LUTHER, JOHN STAFFORD, biology educator, consultant; b. Apr. 5, 1943; s. John Andrew and Marcia (Stafford) L.; div.; 1 child, David. BA, Beloit (Wis.) Coll., 1965; MA, Calif. State U., Hayward, 1968. Mem. faculty dept. biology Merritt Coll., Oakland, Calif., 1968-70; mem. faculty Coll. of Alameda, Calif., 1970—. Chmn. sci. and math. div., Coll. of Alameda, 1973-75; cons. Environ. Impacts Reports, 1972—; leader natural history trips, 1978—; mem. Ednl. Use Adv. Com., East Bay Regional Park Dist., 1981-90. Contbr. articles to Western Birds; mem. editl. bd. Western Birds. Tchr. natural sci. docent program Oakland Mus., 1987-2000. Mem. Western Field Onithologists (pres. 1978-81, dir. 1975-91), Calif. Bird Records Com. (sec. 1976-81), Sierra Club, Am. Birding Assn., Golden Gate Audubon Soc. (bd. dirs., 2002-), Nature Conservancy, Point Reyes Bird Obs., Alameda County Breeding Bird Atlas (bd. dirs.), Oakland Zoo-East Bay Zool. Soc., San Francisco Bay Bird Obs. Home: 6511 Exeter Dr Oakland CA 94611-1641 Office: Coll of Alameda 555 Atlantic Ave Alameda CA 94501-2109

LUTHER-LEMMON, CAROL LEN, elementary school educator; b. Waverly, N.Y., May 8, 1955; d. Carl Rose and Mary Edith (Auge) Luther; m. Mark Kevin Lemmon, June 21, 1986; children: Mattew C. Lemmon, Cathryn M. Lemmon. BS, Ithaca Coll., 1976; MS in Edn., Elmira Coll., 1982. Cert. elem. and secondary tchr. Pa., N.Y. Reading aide Waverly Ctrl.I Schs., 1978-80; tchr. reading N.Y. State Divsn. Youth, Lansing, 1981-82; tchr. title I reading, mem. student assistance program and instrnl. support team Rowe Mid. Sch., Athens (Pa.) Area Sch. Dist., 1982-94; tchr. Title I reading Lynch Elem. Sch., 1995—. Robotics team advisor Waverly HS, 2003. Basketball coach Youth Activities Dept., Athens, 1982—85, asst. softball coach, 1990—91; mem. ad hoc com. Waverly Sch. Dist., 1990—91; mem. Goal G parents & edn. mid sch. implementation team WINGS-Waverly in Global Soc., Waverly Ctr. Sch. Dist. Strategic Plan; active Girls' Softball League, Waverly, 1978—80, commr., 1980; mem. Valley Chorus, Pa. and N.Y., 1983—86, 1998—2002, Village of Waverly Recreation Commn., 1999—; robotics advisor Waverly H.S., 2003—; bd. dirs. Waverly Cmty. Ch., 1976—78; choir mem. Meth. Ch., Waverly, 1976—90, 1997—, adminstrv. bd., 1995, trustee, 1996, chmn. bd. trustees, 2001—03; bd. dirs. SACC, 1995—96. With USAR, 1977—83. Mem.: AAUW (v.p. Waverly br. 1982—83, pres. 1992—97), ASCD, N.Y. State Reading Assn., Chemung Area Reading Coun., Am. Legion Aux. (girl's state rep. 1972, girl's state chmn. 1976—80, Waverly post counselor 1977). Republican. Home: 490 Waverly St Waverly NY 14892-1102 Office: Athens Area Sch Dist Pennsylvania Ave Athens PA 18810-1440 E-mail: ccmml@stny.rr.com.

LUTHY, JOHN FREDERICK, management consultant; b. Kansas City, Mo., Dec. 12, 1947; s. Walter Frederick Luthy and Loraine Florence Tramill; children: Roslyn, Bryan, John Paul. BA, Baker U., 1969; MS, U. Mo., 1973; MPA, Boise State U., 1978; EdD, U. Idaho, 1991. Mgr. State Com. Disease Edn., Topeka, 1973; dir. Divsn. Health Edn., Johnson County, Kans., 1973-75; state dir. Bur. Health Edn., Boise, Idaho, 1975-80; dir. Gen. Svcs. Adminstrn., Boise, 1980-84; dir. bus. devel. Morrison Knudsen Tech. Inc., Boise, 1984-86; pres. The Futures Corp., Boise, 1986—. Pres. Exec. Mgmt. Devel. Inst., Boise, 1991—; del. to China People to People, 1994. Author: (manual) Grantsmanship--A Time of Plenty, 1988; contbr. articles to profl. jours. Staff sgt. USAR, 1969-75. Recipient Nat. Early Career award APHA, 1978; named one of Outstanding Young Men of Am., U.S. Jaycees, 1977. Mem. ASTD, Am. Mgmt. Assn., U.S. Powerlifting Fedn. (exec. bd. dirs., regional chmn. 1981-86), Phi Delta Kappa. Avocations: mountain biking, power lifting, backpacking. Office: The Futures Corp 1109 Main St Ste 299A Boise ID 83702-5642 E-mail: futurescorp@aol.com.

LUTSKY, SHELDON JAY, financial and marketing consultant, writer; b. New Kensington, Pa., Jan. 13, 1943; s. Hyman I. and Rose S. (Schwartz) L. BS, Kent State U., 1967; postgrad., U. Colo., 1969-70. Chemist B.F. Goodrich, Akron, Ohio, 1966; with United Bank of Denver, 1968-75; founder Mountain States Ski Assn., pub. Mountain States Recreation, Denver, 1976-81; pres. Dolphin Assocs., Denver, 1981—; sec.-treas. Millennium Ballast, L.L.C., 2000—. Pres. Eagle Venture Acquisitions, Inc., 1986-90; pres. Sunburst Acquisitions I, Inc., 1997—. Co-patent developer (patent) power factor correction circuit for power supplies and electronic ballasts, 2001. Recipient Burr Photog. Achievement award Kent State U., 1965. Mem. Nat. Ski Writers Assn. Achievements include development of Slope Scope, ski slope evaluation system; patent for control cir. for power factor correction, 2001. Home: 4807 S Zang Way Morrison CO 80465-1630 Office: Dolphin Assocs 2124 S Dayton St Denver CO 80231-3425

LUTTON, JOHN DUDLEY, medical educator, cell biology/hematology-immunology educator; b. Sioux City, Iowa; s. John D. and Leona (Phelps) L. BS, U. Nebr., 1961, MS, 1963; PhD, NYU, 1969. Damon Runyon cancer rsch. predoctoral fellow NYU, 1966—69, Damon Runyon cancer rsch. postdoctoral fellow, 1969—71; instr., rsch. scientist cell biology NYU Sch. Medicine, N.Y.C., 1970—73; asst. prof. physiology Mt. Sinai Sch. Medicine, N.Y.C., 1973-77; asst. prof. medicine SUNY Downstate Med. Ctr., Bklyn., 1977; assoc. prof. medicine N.Y. Med. Coll., Valhalla, 1977-88, assoc. prof. anatomy, cell biology, 1978-96, prof. medicine, 1989-96, assoc. prof. immunology, 1990-94, rsch. prof. pharmacology, 1997—2002; with Inst. Human Genetics and Biochemistry Cabrini Med. Ctr., N.Y.C., 2001—. Guest investigator, adj. faculty Rockefeller U., N.Y.C., 1994—2001. Mem. editorial bd. Procs. Soc. Exp. Biol. Med., 1986—; contbr. articles to profl. jours. Grantee NIH, 1977—. Mem. Am. Soc. Hematology, Internat. Soc. Exptl. Hematology, Reticuloendothelial Soc., AAAS. Home: 42 Redwood Dr Highland Mills NY 10930-2813 Office: Cabrini Med Ctr New York NY 10003

LUTZ, CARLENE, educational association administrator; b. Chgo., Feb. 4, 1946; d. John Calvin Sr. and Helen (Kwast) L. BS in Edn., No. Ill. U., 1967; MA in Edn., U. Conn., 1971; adminstrv. endorsement, Chgo. State U., 1988. Cert. early childhood edn., tchr. kindergarten-grade 9. 2d grade tchr. Chgo. Pub. Schs., 1967-73, reading resource tchr., 1973-79, ESEA coord., 1979-80, upper grade lang. arts, 1980-89, reading resource tchr., 1989-92; asst. dir. Chgo. Tchrs. Union Quest Ctr., 1992—. Trainer ednl. rsch. and dissemination and critical thinking programs, Chgo., 1986—. Editor (pamphlet) EPDA Project, Pictorial Report, 1971. Ill. State scholar Ill. State Scholarship Commn., 1964; EPDA fellow U.S. Dept. Edn., 1971. Mem. ASCD, Internat. Reading Assn., Am. Fedn. Tchrs., Chgo. Tchr. Union, Ella Flagg Young Assn., Delta Kappa Gamma, Phi Delta Kappa. Home: 125 Acacia Cir Apt 613 Indianhead Park IL 60525-9037 Office: Chgo Tchrs Union Quest Ctr 222 Merchandise Mart Plz Ste 400 Chicago IL 60654-1103

LUTZ, MYRON HOWARD, obstetrician, gynecologist, surgeon, educator; b. N.Y.C., June 26, 1938; s. Morris David and Rose (Greenblatt) L.; m. Judy Cohen, Aug. 6, 1963; children: Mark Steven, Sheri Lutz Barnett, Kenneth Ian. BA, Columbia U., 1960; MD, NYU, 1964. Diplomate Am. Bd. Ob-Gyn., Am. Bd. Gynecologic Oncology. Intern Phila., Gen. Hosp., 1964-65; resident in ob-gyn. Albert Einstein Coll. Medicine, Bronx, NY, 1965-69; fellow M.D. Anderson Hosp., Houston, 1971-72, U. Miami Sch. Medicine, Fla., 1972-73; asst. prof. ob-gyn. Med. U. S.C., Charleston, 1973-76, co-dir. gynecology oncology, 1973-77, clin. assoc. prof. ob-gyn., 1977—, clin. assoc. prof. surgery, 1986—; pvt. practice, Charleston, 1973—. Mem. cancer adv. bd. Roper Hosp., Charleston, 1993—; star TV mid-day talk show, 1990—. Mem. editl. bd. House Calls mag., 1992—. Bd. dirs. Am. Cancer Soc., Charleston, 1974-75, v.p., 1975-76, pres., 1976-78; bd. dirs. Trident Acad., Charleston, 1982-86, Hospice, Charleston, 1984-86. Maj. M.C., U.S. Army, 1969-71. Named a Top Obstetrician and Gynecologist, Consumers Rsch. Coun. of Am., 2002—03; named one of Best Doctors in Am., 1999—2002. Fellow ACOG, ACS; mem. AMA, Am. Radium Soc., Am. Soc. Clin. Oncology, Soc. Gynecologic Oncologists, Felix Rutledge Soc., S.C. Med. Soc., S.C. Oncology Soc., Charleston Med. Soc. Avocations: water and snow skiing, archery, biking. Home: 1205 Wisteria Rd Charleston SC 29407 Office: 1205 Wisteria Dr Charleston SC 29407-5902 E-mail: jmlutz@home.com.

LUTZ, WENDY S. elementary school educator; b. Toledo, Apr. 15, 1966; d. John Thomas and Marie Louise Brewer; m. Dusty L. Lutz, July 20, 1984; children Aaron Charles, Brandon Thomas. BA, Ind. State U., 1987; MA in Curriculum and Supervision, Wright State U., 1991. Cert. elem. edn., behavior disorders, and learning disabilities tchr. Ga., gifted endorsement 2002. Tchr. elem. Gwinnett County Schs., Dacula, Ga., 1992—. Recipient numerous scholarships. Mem. Alpha Lambda Delta, Kappa Delta Pi. Lutheran. Avocation: traveling. Home: 3490 Mill Valley Dr Dacula GA 30019-1299 Office: Duncan Creek Elem 4500 Braselton Hwy 124 Hoschton GA 30548

LYALL, KATHARINE C(ULBERT), academic administrator, economics educator; b. Lancaster, Pa., Apr. 26, 1941; d. John D. and Eleanor G. Lyall. BA in Econs., Cornell U., 1963, PhD in Econs., 1969; MBA, NYU, 1965. Economist Chase Manhattan Bank, N.Y.C., 1963-65; asst. prof. econs. Syracuse U., 1969-72; prof. econs. Johns Hopkins U., Balt., 1972-77, dir. grad. program in pub. policy, 1979-81; dep. asst. sec. for econs. Office Econ. Affairs, HUD, Washington, 1977-79; v.p. acad. affairs U. Wis. Sys., 1981-85; prof. of econ. U. Wis., Madison, 1982—; acting pres. U. Wis. Sys., Madison, 1985-86, 91-92, exec. v.p., 1986-91, pres., 1992—. Bd. dirs. Kemper Ins. Cos., Marshall & Ilsley Bank, Wis. Power & Light, Alliant, Carnegie Found. for Advancement of Teaching. Author: Reforming Public Welfare, 1976, Microeconomic Issues of the 70s, 1978. Mem. Mcpl. Securities Rulemaking Bd., Washington, 1990-93. Mem. Am. Econ. Assn., Assn. Am. Univs., Phi Beta Kappa. Home: 6021 S Highlands Ave Madison WI 53705-1110 Office: U Wis Sys Office of Pres 1720 Van Hise Hall 1220 Linden Dr Madison WI 53706-1559 E-mail: klyall@uwsa.edu.

LYBARGER, JOHN STEVEN, human resources development consultant, trainer; b. Yuba City, Calif., June 13, 1956; s. Rodger Lee and Phyllis Ruth (Roseman) L.; m. Marjorie Kathryn Den Uyl, Aug. 22, 1981; children: Ashley Ann, Ryan Christopher. AA, Yuba Community Coll., 1977; BS in Christian Edn., Biola U., La Mirada, Calif., 1980; MS in Counseling, Calif. State U., Fullerton, 1984; PhD in Psychology, Calif. Coast U., 1985, MBA in Bus. Adminstrn., 1999. Lic. marriage family and child counselor; cert. alternative dispute resolution educator/practitioner. Assoc. dir. Concept 7 Family Svcs., Tustin, Calif., 1981-85; exec. dir. Family Life Ctr., Tustin, 1984-86; pres. Marriage & Family Counseling, La Habra, Calif., 1985-89; clin. dir. New Life Treatment Ctrs., Inc., Laguna Beach, Calif., 1988-89; faculty Loma Linda (Calif.) U. Sch. Medicine, 1990; dir. partial hospitalization programs CPC Brea Canyon Hosp., 1991-93; clin. dir. Oasis Counseling Ctr., Denver, 1993-95; pres. Lybarger & Assocs., Westminster, Colo., 1995—. Tng. cons. Dale Carnegie Tng., Denver, 1995-96; pres., CEO Nat. Coun. on Sexual Addiction, Atlanta, 1990-94. Mem. Am. Assn. for Marriage and Family Therapy (clin.). Republican. Avocations: skiing, tennis, racquetball. Home: 8489 W 95th Dr Broomfield CO 80021-5330 Office: 9975 Wadsworth Pkwy Ste K2-414 Broomfield CO 80021-4296

LYDON, KERRY RAINES, elementary school educator; b. Urbana, Ill., Dec. 31, 1948; d. Irving Isaac and Charlotte Austine (Butler) Raines; m. Michael Mario Lydon, Aug. 17, 1970; children: Scott Michael, Heather Anne. BA, U. Md., 1970; early childhood Montessori credential, Ctr. for Montessori Tchr. Edn., 1984. Exec. dir. Cumberland County Mental Health Assn., Fayetteville, N.C., 1980-82; dir. Montessori Sch. Fayetteville, 1983—, adminstr., 1990—2001, bd. dirs. Workshop presenter in field. Author: A Birthday for Blue, 1989; editor, creator (newsletter) Connections, 1980-82; author, illustrator (activity newsletter) Montessori Mailbox, 1985, Montessori Mailbox-Parents Pages, 1998. Mem. Am. Montessori Soc., Authors Guild. Office: Montessori Sch Fayetteville 1201 Cape Ct Fayetteville NC 28304-4404

LYDON, MARY C. physical education educator; b. Boston, May 12, 1931; d. Patrick J. and Annie (O'Neill) L. BS in Edn., Bridgewater State Coll., 1955; EdM, Northeastern U., 1963; EdD, Boston U., 1978. Cert. tchr., Mass. Tchr. phys. edn. Chelsea (Mass.) Pub. Schs., 1955-57, Quincy (Mass.) Pub. Schs., 1959-63, 70—, Buffalo (N.Y.) Pub. Schs., 1963-66; field worker Girl Scouts U.S., Boston, 1957-59; instr. phys. edn. Boston State Coll., 1966-70, adj. prof., Boston Coll., 1983-89. Clin. instr. U. Mass., Boston, 1994; presenter at profl. confs.; sec. Coun. Sch. Adminstrs. Health & Phys. Edn., 1994—. Trustee Bridgewater Found., 1990-92. Mem. NEA, AAHPERD (conv. planning com. 1988-89, coun. for svcs. Ea. Dist. 1984-88), Mass. Assn. Health, Phys. Edn., Recreation and Dance (pres. 1986-87, exec. bd. 1987—), Quincy Edn. Assn., Mass. Tchrs. Assn., Bridgewater State Coll. Alumni Assn. (pres. 1990-92), Women's Sports Found., Hyannis-Bridgewater Phys. Edn. Alumni Assn. (exec. com. 1980—, pres. 1985-89). Office: Quincy Pub Schs 70 Coddington St Quincy MA 02169-4501

LYDON, PATRICIA DIANE, secondary education educator; b. Parkersburg, W.Va., Sept. 29, 1946; d. Forrest Woodrow and Hazel Virginia (Bell) Walcutt; m. James Patrick Lydon, Nov. 10, 1967; children: Michael, Pamela. Student, Glenville State Coll., 1968; Master's degree, W.Va. U., 1984. Tchr. Marshall County Bd. of Edn., Moundsville, W.Va., 1967, Wirt County Bd. Edn., Elizabeth, W.Va., 1979—. Trainer Appalachian Edn. Lab., Charleston, W.Va.; ptnr. in edn. Wesvaco, Parkersburg, W.Va. Mem. Am. Fedn. Tchrs., Nat. Geography Alliance, Delta Kappa Gamma (legis. chair), Woman's Club (past pres.), Alpha Sigma Alpha. Roman Catholic. Avocations: reading, traveling, painting. Home: PO Box 657 Elizabeth WV 26143-0657 Office: Wirt County H S PO Box 219 Elizabeth WV 26143-0219

LYLES, ADELE HEMPHILL, secondary school educator; b. Toccoa, Ga., May 3, 1948; d. Horace and Ruth Boyette Hemphill; m. Samuel Clair Lyles; 1 child, Heath. MA in Edn., North Ga. Coll. and State U., 1985. Cert. secondary English tchr. Secondary English tchr. Stephens County H.S., Toccoa, 1981—. Participant Yonah Cmty. Chorus, Toccoa, 1974—99. Recipient Blue Ridge Leadership award, Blue Ridge Leadership Conf., 2000. Mem.: Nat. Coun. Tchrs. English. Baptist. Avocations: swimming, singing, piano. Office: Stephens County HS 6438 White Pine Rd Toccoa GA 30577

LYMAN, CHARLES EDSON, materials scientist, educator; b. Willimantic, Conn., Mar. 7, 1946; s. Edson Hunt and Sylvia (Hill) L.; m. Valerie Ann Livingston, Aug. 30, 1984. BS, Cornell U., 1968; PhD, MIT, 1974. Postdoctoral fellow dept. metallurgy Oxford (England) U., 1974-76; asst. prof. Rensselaer Poly. Inst., Troy, N.Y., 1976-80; staff scientist E.I. DuPont de Nemours, Wilmington, Del., 1980-84; assoc. prof. Lehigh U., Bethlehem, Pa., 1984-90, prof., 1990—. Electron microscopy steering com. Argonne (Ill.) Nat. Lab., 1984—. Author, editor: Scanning Electron Microscopy, X-Ray Microanalysis, and Analytical Electron Microscopy: A Laboratory Workbook, 1990; co-author: Scanning Electron Microscopy and X-ray Microanalysis, 2003; editor-in-chief: Microscopy and Microanalysis; contbr. articles to profl. jours. Mem. Microscopy Soc. Am. (pres. 1991), Microbeam Analysis Soc. (pres. 2000), Am. Soc. Materials Internat., Am. Chem. Soc., Burnside Plantation Inc. (pres. 1993), Historic Bethlehem, Inc. (pres. 1996-98). Home: 444 N New St Bethlehem PA 18018-5814 Office: Lehigh U Whitaker Lab 5 E Packer Ave Bethlehem PA 18015-3102 E-mail: charles.lyman@lehigh.edu.

LYMBERIS, MARIA T. psychiatrist, psychiatric educator; b. Athens, Greece, Aug. 7, 1938; came to U.S., 1956; m. Pedro de Cordoba, Sept. 14, 1963; children: Jason Richard, Anthony Triantaphyllos, Alexander Patrick. BA in Philosophy, Rutgers U., New Brunswick, N.J., 1960; MD, U. So. Calif., 1964. Diplomate Am. Bd. Psychiatry and Neurology (examiner in adult psychiatry and child psychiatry, 1984—); cert. psychiatry, cert. child psychiatry. Intern Mt. Sinai Hosp., L.A., 1964-65, resident in neurology N.Y.C., 1965-66; resident in psychiatry Albert Einstein Bronx Mcpl. Hosp., N.Y.C., 1966-68; fellow in child psychiatry Neuropsychiatric Inst. UCLA Sch. Medicine, 1968-70, clin. prof. psychiatry, 1996—; grad. psychoanalyst L.A. Psychoanalytic Inst., 1978, sr. faculty, dir. psychotherapy program, 1996-2000; med. dir. Marianne Frostig Ctr. for Ednl. Therapy, 1969-77; pvt. practice in adult and child psychiatry, 1970—; pvt. practice in psychoanalysis for adult and child, 1972—. Chief psychiatry Westwood Hosp., 1987-89, v.p. med. staff, 1989-90; expert cons. Med. Bd. Calif., 1978—; mem. Calif. Senate Task Force on Psychotherapist Patient Sexual Contact, 1986-87. Contbr. chpts. to books; presenter in field. Recipient Soroptimist scholarship award, 1961-63. Fellow Am. Psychiat. Assn. (mem. assembly task force on pvt. practice 1978-79, cons. assembly task force 1979-82, mem. com. misuse and abuse of psychiatry in U.S., 1980-86, assembly liaison to the com. on misuse and abuse of psychiatry in U.S. 1983-84, cons. ethics com. 1986-89, mem. subcom. edn. psychiatrists on ethical issues, chair subcom. on edn. psychiatrists on ethical issues 1989-91, mem. com. on continuing edn. 1991-94, mem. membership com. 1993-96, trustee at large 1994-97, treas., 1998-2000), Am. Coll. Psychiatrists; mem. Internat. Psychoanalytical Students Orgn. (hon.), Am. Acad. Psychiatry and Law, Psychiat. Edn. and Rsch. Found. (founder, pres. 1990—), Calif. Psychiatric Assn. (chair ann. meeting program com. 1990-91, mem. G.A. com. 1990—, area IV rep. to Am. Psychiat. Assn. joint commn. on pub. affairs 1993-96, others), Southern Calif. Psychiat. Soc. (mem. program com. 1972-74, treas. 1973-74, co-chair ethics com. 1976-77, councilor 1975-79, chair ethics com. 1977-86, mem. ethics com. 1977—, mem peer rev. com. 1977-90, mem. awards and fellowship com. 1983-85, cons. awards and fellowship com. 1985-88, chair subcom. on edn. of psychiatrists on ethical issues 1986-90, chair ad hoc com. on ethics procedures 1986-88, pres.-elect 1988-89, pres. 1989-90, state legis. rep. 1990-94, appreciation award 1984, 91, disting. svc. award 1992, others), Southern Calif. Soc. for Adolescent Psychiatry, So. Calif. Soc. for Child Psychiatry, L.A. Psychoanalytic Soc., L.A. County Med. Assn. (mem. ctrl. com. on ethics 1984—), Hellenic Am. Psychiat. Assn. (founder, pres. 1999-2001). Office: 1500 Montana Ave Ste 204 Santa Monica CA 90403-1849 Fax: 310-454-1039. E-mail: mlymberi@ucla.edu.

LYNAM, GLORIA, elementary school educator; d. Abraham and Diana Beatrice Gerber; m. Roger Lynam. B Arts and Scis. with honors, U. Conn., 1973; MEd, Coll. St. Joseph Vt., 1991. Vt. profl. educator. Tchr. middle sch. lang. arts Rutland (Vt.) Town Sch., 1998—. Editor: student poetry anthologies, comic books. Grantee, Chapbooks for Learning, 1999, Excellence in Edn. grantee, SHOPA Found., 1999—2000, No strings art, Chaffee Art Gallery, 1999, Nat. writing project, Vt., 1999. Mem.: New Eng. League of Middle Schs. Assn., Vt. Assn. Middle Level Edn., Nat. Coun. Tchrs. Eng., Northern Vt. Artists Assoc., Vt. Watercolor Soc. Avocations: writing, reading, mountain biking, walking, watercolors.

LYNCH, CAROL, director special services, psychologist; b. Passaic, N.J., Sept. 22, 1943; d. Joseph Louis and Ellen (Birish) Dobkowski; 1 child, Eric Alexander. BA, William Paterson Coll., 1966; MA, NYU, 1970, PsyD, 1984. Lic. psychologist, N.J., N.Y. Tchr. Bloomfield (N.J.) Pub. Schs., 1966-68, psychologist, 1970-87; dir. spl. svcs. Waldwick (N.J.) Pub. Schs., 1987—, acting supt. schs., 1995-96, 98. Adj. clin. prof. NYU, N.Y.C., 1983-86 adj. prof. Montclair (N.J.) State Coll., 1984-85. Mem. prof. alumni coun. Sch. Edn., Health and Nursing, NYU, 1989—91; alumni coun. chair Sch. Edn., NYU, 1991—93, sec., 2002—03; sec., bd. trustees First Church of Religious Sci., New York, NY, 2001—. NYU fellow, 1981-82; recipient Best Practice award N.J. State Dept. Edn. for Fast Families Program, 1995, Disting. Grad. Brian E. Tomlinson Meml. award NYU, 1995, Exemplary Practice award N.J. Adminstrs. Assn./N.J. Sch. Bds. "Crisis Response Initiative," 2002. Mem. APA (sch. psychology task force 1989-90), N.J. Psychol. Assn. (treas. 1985-86, Sch. Psychologist of Yr. 2003), Nat. Assn. Sch. Psychologists (del. 1984-88), N.J. Assn. Sch. Psychologists (pres. 1982-83, Sch. Psychologist of Yr. 2003), Ea. Ednl. Rsch. Assn. (pres. 1993-95), Bergen County Assn. Lic. Psychologists (bd. dirs. 1991-93), NYU Sch. Psychology Alumni Assn. (founder 1988-92), Ramapo Valley Adminstrs. (v.p. 1996-98, pres. 1998—). Avocations: skiing, antiques collecting, tennis, gourmet cooking. Home: 124 Frank Ct Mahwah NJ 07430-2963 Office: Waldwick Pub Schs 155 Summit Ave Waldwick NJ 07463-2133 E-mail: drcarollynch@msn.com.

LYNCH, CHARLES THEODORE, SR., materials science engineering researcher, consultant, educator; b. Lima, Ohio, May 17, 1932; s. John Richard and Helen (Dunn) L.; m. Betty Ann Korkolis, Feb. 3, 1956; children: Karen Elaine Ostdiek, Charles Theodore Jr., Richard Anthony, Thomas Edward. BS, George Washington U., 1955; MS, U. Ill., 1957, PhD in Analytical Chemistry, 1960. Group leader ceramics div. Air Force Materials Lab., Wright-Patterson AFB, Ohio, 1962-66; lectr. in chemistry Wright State U., Dayton, Ohio, 1964-66; chief advanced metall. studies br. Air Force Materials Lab., Wright-Patterson AFB, Ohio, 1966-74, sr. scientist, 1974-81; head materials div. Office of Naval Rsch., Arlington, Va., 1981-85; pvt. practice cons. Washington, 1985-88; sr. engr. space ops. Vitro Corp., Washington, 1988-95, 96-98; cons. Burke, Va., 1996—; sr. cons. space ops. Marconi Systems Techs., Washington, 1998—99; v.p. RSC&L, Inc., Grayling, Mich., 1996—. USAF liaison mem. NMAB Panels on Solids Processing, Ion Implantation and Environ. Cracking, Washington, 1965-68, 78, 81; U.S. rep. AGARD structures and materials panel NATO, 1983-85. Co-author: Metal Matrix Composites, 1972; editor, author: Practical Handbook of Materials Science, 1989; editor: (series) Handbook of Materials Science, vol. I, 1974, vol. II, 1975, vol. III, 1975; vice chmn. editorial bd. Vitro Corp. Tech. Jour., 1989-92, chmn., 1993; contbr. articles to profl. jours. including Jour. Am. Ceramics Soc., Analytical Chemistry, Sci., Transactions AIME, Corr. Jour., Jour. Inorganic Chemistry, SAMPE, Jour. Less Common Metals. Mem., soloist George Washington U. Traveling Troubadours, Washington, 1950-55; choir dir. Trinity United Ch. of Christ, Fairborn, Ohio, 1966-81, Univ. Bapt. Ch., Champaign, Ill., 1957-60, Chapel II, Wright-Patterson AFB, Ohio, 1960-64; bd. dirs. Southport Home Owners' Assn., Burke, Va., 2002—; pres. Pub. Sch. PTO, 1967-69. 1st lt. USAF, 1960-62. Bailey scholar U. Ill., 1958-60; recipient Commendation medal USAF, 1962, Outstanding Achievement cert. NASA, 1992, award Soc. for Tech. Comm. Publ., 1993. Mem. Am. Chem. Soc. (treas. 1966-67, chmn. audit sect. 1967-68), ASM Internat. (sec. oxidation and corrosion com. 1980-81, chmn. 1981-82). Methodist. Achievements include patents for new corrosion inhibitors including encapsulated types, and for alkoxides and oxides; co-development of the refractory ceramic Zyttrite, the first high density translucent zirconia made from thermal or hydrolytic decomposition of mixed alkoxides followed by hot pressing; pioneered general approach of organometallic compounds as precursors of high purity, fine particulate, materials. Office: 5629 Kemp Ln Burke VA 22015-2041

LYNCH, DAVID WILLIAM, physicist, retired educator; b. Rochester, N.Y., July 14, 1932; s. William J. and Eleanor (Fouratt) L.; m. Joan N. Hill, Aug. 29, 1954 (dec. Nov. 1989); children: Jean Louise, Richard William, David Allan; m. Glenys R. Bittick, Nov. 14, 1992. BS, Rensselaer Poly. Inst., 1954; MS, U. Ill., 1955, PhD, 1958. Asst. prof. physics Iowa State U., 1959-63, assoc. prof., 1963-66, prof., 1966—2003, chmn. dept., 1985-90, disting. prof. liberal arts and scis., 1985—; on leave at U. Hamburg, Germany; and U. Rome, Italy, 1968-69; sr. physicist Ames Lab. of Dept. of Energy; acting assoc. dir. Synchrotron Radiation Ctr., Stoughton, Wis., 1984. Vis. prof. U. Hamburg, summer 1974; dir. Microelectronics Rsch. Ctr., Iowa State U., 1995-99. Fulbright scholar U. Pavia, Italy, 1958-59. Fellow: Am. Phys. Soc.; mem.: AAAS. Achievements include research on solid state physics. Home: 2020 Elm Cir West Des Moines IA 50265-4294 E-mail: dwl@ameslab.gov.

LYNCH, EDWARD CONOVER, hematologist, educator; b. Fayette, Mo., Feb. 24, 1933; s. Edward Clel and Mary Elizabeth (Sessen) L.; m. Nell Ruth Robinson, June 18, 1955; children: Edward Douglas, David Robinson, Deborah Ruth, Stephen Russell. BA, Washington U., 1953, MD, 1956. Diplomate in internal medicine and hematology Am. Bd. Internal Medicine. Intern, asst. resident in internal medicine Barnes Hosp., St. Louis, 1956-58; resident in internal medicine Strong Meml. Hosp., Rochester, N.Y., 1958-60; instr. Baylor Coll. Medicine, Houston, 1962-64, asst. prof. medicine, 1964-68, assoc. prof. medicine, 1968-72, prof. medicine, 1972—, assoc. dean, 1971-76, assoc. chmn. dept. medicine, 1977—2000. Adj. prof. biomed. engring., dept. chem. engring. Rice U., Houston, 1973-99. Contbr. 12 chpts. to books and 56 articles to profl. jours. Capt. U.S. Army, 1960-62. Master ACP; mem. Am. Soc. Hematology, So. Soc. Clin. Investigation, Tex. Med. Assn. (internal medicine sect., pres. 1983-84), Sigma Xi, Phi Beta Kappa, Alpha Omega Alpha. Home: 311 Wilchester Blvd Houston TX 77079-7326 Office: Baylor Coll of Medicine Texas Med Ctr Houston TX 77030

LYNCH, SISTER ELIZABETH, elementary school principal; b. Chgo., May 3, 1931; d. Charles John and Alice Annette (O'Neil) L. MEd, DePaul U., 1968. Cert. tchr., adminstr., supr., K-14, Ill. Tchr. St. Bridgid Sch., Detroit, 1952-54, Queen's Sch., Jackson, Mich., 1954-59, St. John Sch., Albion, Mich., 1959-60, St. Joseph Sch., Homewood, Ill., 1960-63; prin. St. James Sch., Maywood, Ill., 1963-69; sec. Adrian Dominicans, Hometown, Ill., 1969-71; prin. St. Denis Sch., Chgo., 1971-2001. Mem. ASCD, Nat. Cath. Edn. Assn.

LYNCH, GERALD WELDON, academic administrator, psychologist; b. N.Y.C., Mar. 24, 1937; s. Edward Dewey and Alice Margaret (Weldon) L.; m. Eleanor Gay Sherry, Dec. 5, 1970; children: Timothy, Elizabeth. BS, Fordham Coll., 1958; PhD, N.Y. U., 1968. Tech. employment rep. Bell Telephone Labs., N.Y.C., 1958-63; psychologist VA Hosp., NY, 1966—68; asst. prof. psychology John Jay Coll. Criminal Justice, N.Y.C., 1967-71, dir. student activities, 1968-70, asso. prof., 1971-74, prof., 1974—, dean students, 1968-71, v.p., 1971-76, pres., 1976—. Chmn. Use of Force in Jails, N.Y.C., 1987—; mem. internat. curriculum com. Internat. Law Enforcement Acad., Budapest, Hungary, 1996—; mem. Ind. Commn. on Policing No. Ireland, 1998-2000; coord., co-chair Biennial Conf. Series, St. Petersburg, 1992, N.Y., 1994, Dublin, Ireland, 1996, Budapest, 1998, Bologna, 2000. Editor: Human Dignity and the Police, 1999; contbr. articles to profl. jours. Chmn. N.Y.C. Police Found., 1979-92; chmn. N.Y. State Casino Gambling Study Panel, 1979, N.Y. State Fire Fighting Pers. Edn. and Stds. Com., 1980—, Westchester County Spl. Task Force on Dept. Pub. Safety Svcs.; mem. N.Y. State Fire Safety Task Force, 1981, N.Y. State Crime Control Planning Bd., 1979-86; chmn. bd. advisors Channel 13, 1984-87; chmn. N.Y.C. Fire Safety Found., 1984—; vice chmn. U.S. Marshals Found., 1987—; pres. Cath. Interracial Coun., 1990—; chmn. Mayoral Search Com. for Police and Fire Commn., 2002. Recipient Criminal Justice award N.Y. State Bar Assn., 1977; Disting. Alumni award in edn. Fordham Coll. Alumni Assn., 1978; Brotherhood award NCCJ, 1985; named Person of Yr., N.Y.C. chpt. Indsl. Security Soc., 1987, N.Y.C. Police Dept. Patrolwomen's Endowment Assn., 1987, Man of Yr., Police Self Support Group, 1989. Mem. Acad. Criminal Justice Scis., Am. Soc. Criminology, Am. Assn. State Colls. and Univs., AAAS, Am. Psychol. Assn. Democrat. Roman Catholic. Office: CUNY John Jay Coll Criminal Justice 899 10th Ave New York NY 10019-1069 E-mail: president@jjay.cuny.edu.

LYNCH, JAMES WALTER, mathematician, educator; b. Cornelia, Ga., Mar. 28, 1930; s. Ulysses Samuel and Ida Dell (Woodall) Lynch; m. Monika Antonie Fehrmann, May 2, 1959; children: Steve, David, Judith. AB, U. Ga., 1952, MA, 1956. Math. statistician Proving Ground, Aberdeen, Md., 1956-61; asst. prof. math. Ga. So. U., Statesboro, 1961-92, prof. emeritus math., 1992—; ret. prof. emeritus of math. Contbr. articles to profl. jours., Crux Mathematicorum, 1982—92. Grantee, NSF, 1964. Mem.: AAAS, Can. Math. Soc., Ga. Coalition for Excellence in Tchg. Math., Ga. Coun. Tchrs. Math. (life), Sigma Xi (life). Lutheran. Achievements include discovery of that American Indians designed their projectile points to conform to the golden section ratio. Avocations: coin collecting, gardening, shooting. Home and Office: 172 Thornhill Dr Athens GA 30607-1743 E-mail: jamwallyn@aol.com.

LYNCH, JOHN PATRICK, classics educator, university official; b. Great Barrington, Mass., Aug. 30, 1943; s. John Joseph and Sophia (Pruhenski) L.; m. Sheilah Eileen Fulbright, Sept. 21, 1973; children— Bernadette, Brendan BA with high honors, Harvard U., 1965; MA, Yale U., 1968, M.Phil., 1969, PhD, 1970. Cert. in archaeology, Am. Sch. Classical Studies, Athens, Greece, 1967. Asst. prof. classics U. Calif., Santa Cruz, 1970-73, assoc. prof., 1974-85, prof., 1985—, acting dean humanities, 1993, provost Cowell Coll., 1983-89, assoc. dir. Edn. Abroad Program, U. Calif. Study Ctr. in London, 1979-81. Jr. fellow Harvard U. Ctr. Hellenic Studies, Washington, 1976-77; mem. Inst. Advanced Study, Princeton, N.J., 1989-90. Author: Aristotle's School, 1972; contbg. author: The Cambridge Ancient History, Vol. 6, 1994; editor: Second World and Green World, 1989. Fellow NEH, summer 1973, U. Calif. Humanities Inst., summer 1972, NDEA Title IV, 1967-70, Rotary Internat., 1966-67, Woodrow Wilson, 1965-66; Harvard Coll. scholar, 1961-65. Mem. Am. Philol. Assn. (Excellence in Teaching Classics award 1992), Calif. Classical Assn., Hellenic Soc. (U.K.), Petronian Soc., Virgilian Soc. Democrat. Roman Catholic. Home: 204 King St Santa Cruz CA 95060-3408 Office: U Calif Cowell College Santa Cruz CA 95064

LYNCH, LAURA ELLEN, elementary education educator; b. Chgo., June 25, 1965; d. Edgar Lewis and Loretta Ann (Sheehar) Hield; m. Terrence Michael Lynch, June 22, 1991; children: Dennis Edgar, Ellen Rose. BA in Edn., St. Xavier U., 1987. Cert. tchr., Ill. Tchr. Queen of Martyrs Sch., Chgo., 1987-92; tutor, 1992—; co-owner Histories for Kids, 2002—.

LYNCH, LILLIAN, retired secondary education educator; b. Cairo, Ga., Aug. 28, 1937; d. Dave Royal Sr. and Georgie Ann (Walker) Cochran; m. William Howard Lynch, Dec. 17, 1960. BS, Ft. Valley State Coll., 1960; MEd, U. Ga., 1972. Cert. tchr. Ga. Tchr. home econs. Carver High Sch., Monroe, Ga., 1960-74, Monroe Area Comprehensive High Sch., 1974-92; ret., 1992. Mem. adv. bd. mental health Monroe, Ga., 1980-85. Jury commr.City/Walton County Govt., Monroe, 1991—. Mem. Am. Vocat. Assn., Nat. Assn. Vocat. Home Econs. Tchrs., NAACP, Ga. Vocat. Assn., Ga. Assn. Home Econs. Educators, Alpha Kappa Alpha. Democrat. Baptist. Avocations: recipes, aerobics, wedding cons., interior design. Home: 1620 Peters Cemetary Rd Monroe GA 30655-6162

LYNCH, LINDA LOU, reading and language arts specialist, educator; b. L.A., Feb. 9, 1941; d. Alexander Alfred and Gizella Mary (Bajus) Laszloffy; m. John Joseph Lynch, June 13, 1964; children: Valerie Ann, Colinda Lee, Lee Anne Ellen. BS, Calif. State U., Northridge, 1964; MEd, Loyola Marymount U., L.A., 1990; EdD, Pepperdine U., 1995. Cert. tchr., Calif. Computer programmer Union Bank, L.A., 1962-64; substitute tchr. various sch. dists. Calif., 1964-68, 79-80; tchr. Richard H. Dana Mid. Sch., Hawthorne, Calif., 1980-88; reading specialist Wiseburn Sch. Dist., Hawthorne, 1988-91; elem. sch. tchr. Juan de Anza Elem. Sch., Hawthorne, 1991-93; reading specialist Wiseburn Sch. Dist., 1994-99; tchr. 1st grede Juan de Anza Elem. Sch., Hawthorne, 1999—. Adj. faculty mem. Loyola Marymount U., L.A., 1991—, dir. reading program Grad. Sch., 1992; rsch. asst. Pepperdine U., L.A., 1992-94, teaching asst., 1993, asst. dir. student tchrs., 1993, adj. prof., 1994—; adj. prof. Chapman U., L.A., 1995—. Mem. NEA, AAUW, ASCD, Am. Edn. Rsch. Assn., Internat. Reading Assn., Calif. Reading Assn., Ventura County Reading Assn., Calif. Tchrs. Assn., Wiseburn Faculty Assn., Phi Delta Kappa. Democrat. Roman Catholic.

LYNCH, LUANN JOHNSON, business educator; b. Raleigh, N.C., June 20, 1962; d. James Vinson and Eloise (Edwards) Johnson; m. Byron Claude Lynch III, Oct. 3, 1987. BS in BA, Meredith Coll., Raleigh, 1984; MBA, Duke U., 1986; PhD, U. N.C., 1998. Fin. analyst Procter & Gamble, Cin., 1985; fin. mgmt. program No. Telecom, Inc., Research Triangle Park, N.C., 1986-89; mgr. corp. pricing Roche Biomed. Labs., Inc., Burlington, N.C., 1989-91, asst. v.p., 1991-93; Joseph E. Pogue doctoral fellow U. N.C., Chapel Hill, 1993-97; asst. prof. bus. adminstrn. Darden Sch. Bus., U. Va. Am. Acctg. Assn. Doctoral Consortium fellow, 1995, AICPA Doctoral fellow, 1993-95; Fuqua scholar, 1986. Mem. AAUW, NAFE, Inst. Mgmt. Accts., Am. Acctg. Assn., Healthcare Fin. Mgmt. Assn. Avocations: golf, running. Home: 3200 Sandown Park Rd Keswick VA 22947-9166 Office: U NC Kenan-Flagler Bus Sch Chapel Hill NC 27599

LYNCH, MARIA ROSARIA, mathematics educator, private tutor; b. Darby, Pa., Jan. 17, 1962; d. Giuseppe and Olga M. (DeStefano) Dragonetti; m. James F. Lynch, Mar. 24, 1984; children: Kevin J., Michael J., Mary E., David F., Kathryn E. BA in Math., Rosemont Coll., 1983; MA in Math., Villanova U., 1989. Cert. math tchr., Pa. Tchr. math. Rosemont (Pa.) Sch. of the Holy Child, 1983-91; math tchr. Del. Community Coll., 1992—, St. Francis Sch., Springfield, Pa., 1997—; math. tchr. Merion Mercy Acad., 2002—. Pvt. tutor Catechist St. Alice Ch., Upper Darby, Pa., 1984-89, St. Francis Ch., Springfield, Pa., 1989-91. Republican. Roman Catholic. Avocation: embroidery. Home: 236 N Rolling Rd Springfield PA 19064-1425

LYNCH, NITA MARIE SMITH, vocational curriculum developer, ballroom dancer; b. Portland, Oreg., Aug. 11, 1952; d. Jay Harvey Jr. and Harriet Smith; m. Paul Michael Lynch (dec.). AAS, C.C. of Air Force, 1987, AAS, 1989; BS with highest honors, U. So. Miss., 1991, MS, 1992, postgrad., 1992—. Cert. tchr., Miss. Enlisted USAF, 1979, tech. tng. instr., 1985-89, curriculum developer, 1989-95, ret., 1995; ednl. cons., 1995—. Contbr. articles to profl. jours. Mem. Fed. Women's Program, 1992-95; bd. dirs. Portland Computer Tng. Inst., 1999—. Mem. Am. Vocat. Assn., Am. Assn. Adult and Continuing Edn., Fed. Info. Sys. Security Edn. Assn., Soc. Applied Learning Tech., Info. Sys. Security Assn., Phi Kappa Phi. Home and Office: 7815 SE Carlton St Portland OR 97206-6320

LYNCH, PATRICIA MARIE, elementary education educator; b. Columbus, Ohio, Dec. 2, 1950; d. Ralph F. E. and Betty Lou (Rogers) Nicol; m. James Robert Lynch, June 17, 1972; children: Jason, Christopher. BEd, Capital U., 1972; MEd, Ashland U., 1997. Cert. tchr., Ohio. Tchr. Marion (Ohio) City Schs., 1972—. Instr., worshop leader Portland (Oreg.) State U., summer, 1992—; math tchr. leader Cen. Ohio Reg. Profl. Devel. Ctr.; co-author math. pre-sch. curriculum Ohio State Math Model, State Dept. Edn.; reviewer Coll. Eisenhower Grants for Ohio Bd. Regents. Den leader Boy Scouts Am., Ohio. Recipient Presdl. award for excellence in math., NSF, 1994-96; named Educator of Yr., PTA, 1993, 2003. Mem. Internat. Reading Assn., Ohio Coun. Tchrs. Math. (Outstanding Math. Tchr. Cen. Dist. 1993), Nat. Coun. Tchrs. of Math. (Nat. Presdl. award 1996), NEA, Ohio Edn. Assn., Marion Edn. Assn., DAR, Craft Club, OES, Delta Kappa Gamma. Republican. Lutheran. Avocations: crafts, volunteer activities. Home: 1065 Barks Rd E Marion OH 43302-6718

LYNCH, PETER ROBIN, physiology educator; b. Phila., July 18, 1927; s. Harold Vincent and Elsa C. (Richter) L.; m. Linda R. Roller, 1953 (div. 1976); children: Christopher R., Jonathan David, Elizabeth Ann; m. Eileen Patricia Thomas, June 1978; stepchildren: Elizabeth Ann and Cathleen Ellen (twins). BS, U. Miami, Fla., 1950; MS, Temple U., 1954, PhD, 1958. Instr. of physiology Temple U. Sch. Medicine, Phila., 1958-60, asst. prof., 1960-66, assoc. prof. of physiology and radiology, 1966-70, prof. of physiology and radiology, 1970—, prof. of internal medicine, 1986—, chmn. physiology dept., 1987—, George H. Stewart prof. of physiology, 1991—. Adj. prof. Druckkammerlab., Kantonssital, Zurich, 1977-78. Contbr. over 150 articles to sci. jours. With USN, 1944-46. Mem. Am. Physiol. Soc., Physiol. Soc. Phila. (pres.), Am. Heart Assn., Undersea Med. Soc. Mem. Soc. Of Friends. Office: Temple U Sch Medicine Dept Physiology 3420 N Broad St Philadelphia PA 19140-5104

LYNCH, PRISCILLA A. nursing educator, therapist; b. Joliet, Ill., Jan. 8, 1949; d. LaVerne L. and Ann M. (Zamkovitz) L. BS, U. Wyo., 1973; MS, St. Xavier Coll., Coll., 1981. RN, Ill. Staff nurse Rush-Presbyn.-St. Luke's Med. Ctr., Chgo., 1977-81, psychiat.-liaison cons., 1981-83, asst. prof. nursing, unit dir., 1985—. Mgr. and therapist Oakside Clinic, Kankakee, Ill., 1987—; mem. adv. bd. Depressive and Manic Depression Assn., Chgo., 1986—; mem. consultation and mental health unit Riverside Med. Ctr., Kankakee, 1987—; speaker numerous nat. orgns. Contbr. numerous abstracts to profl. jours., chpts. to books. Bd. dirs. Cornerstone Svcs., ARC of Ill. Recipient total quality mgmt. award Rush-Presbyn.-St. Luke's Med. Ctr., 1991, named mgr. of the quarter, 1997, Wayne Lerner Leadership award, 1998. Mem. ANA, Ill. Nurses Assn. (coms.), Coun. Clin. Nurse Specialists, Profl. Nursing Staff (sec. 1985-87, mem. coms.). Presbyterian. Home: 606 Darcy Ave Joliet IL 60436-1673

LYNCH, ROSEMARY G. secondary school educator; b. Fairmont, W.Va., Nov. 18, 1951; d. Okey James and Iva Marie (Seccuro) Moore; m. John Paul Lynch Sr., June 6, 1970; children: John Paul Jr., Scott, Ryan. AB, Shepherd Coll., 1985; MA, W.Va. U., 1990. Family and consumer svcs. tchr. Berkeley County Pub. Schs., Martinsburg, W.Va. Adj. faculty Shepherd Coll. Webmaster Martinsburg H.S. Band and South Middle Sch. Named. W.Va.'s Outstanding New Home Econs. Tchr., 1988, Outstanding Young Educator Martinsburg, 1988. Mem. NEA, Am. Assn. Family Consumer Sci., Assn. Career Tech. Edn., W.Va. Edn. Assn., Berkeley County Edn. Assn., Shepherd Coll. Alumni Assn., W.Va. U. Alumni Assn., Cath. Daus. Ams., Kappa Omicron Nu.

LYNCH, TIMOTHY JEREMIAH-MAHONEY, lawyer, educator, theologian, realtor, writer; b. June 10, 1952; s. Joseph David and Margaret Mary (Mahoney) L. MS, JD in Taxation, Golden Gate U., 1981; MA, PhD in Modern European History, U. San Francisco, 1983; Licentiate, Inter-Am. Acad., Rio de Janeiro, 1988; PhD in Classics and Divinity/Theology, Harvard U., 1988; JSD in Constl. Law, Hastings Law Ctr., 1990. Bar: D.C. 1989, Calif., U.S. Ct. Appeals (2d cir.) 1989, U.S. Ct. Appeals (4th cir.) 1990; mem. Bar/Outer Temple/Comml. Bar of U.K.; European Econ. Ct. of 1st Instance. Legal bus., tax, counsel Lynch Real Estate, San Francisco, 1981-85; researcher, writer Kolb, Roche & Sullivan, San Francisco, 1986-88; chmn. internat. law dept. Timothy J.M. Lynch & Assocs., San Francisco, 1987-88, chmn., mng. dir. law dept., 1988—. Chmn., pres., CEO Lynch Real Estate Investment Corp., San Francisco, 1989—; ptnr. Lynch Investment Corp.; bd. lawyer/arbitrators Pacific Coast Stock Exch., NASD, 1994—; chmn. bd. Lynch Holdings Corp. Group; corp. counsel, sr. ptnr. L.A. Ctr. Internat. Comml. Arbitration, 1991—; vis. fellow classics, Inst. of Classical Studies, U. London; rsch. prof. Canon law and ecumenical ch. history grad. Theological Union U. Calif. Berkeley, 1992—; vis. scholar Patristic theology and classical philosophy of ecumenical doctrines, U. Laval, Quebec, Can., 1993—; vis. scholar Medieval ch. history U. Leeds, Eng., 1993-95; del. lectr. 24th Internat. Congress Arts Comms., Kreble Coll., Oxford U., 1997; arbitrator Iran-U.S. Claims Tribunal, The Hague, 1993; mem. internat. corp. adv. bd. J.P. Morgan and Co., N.Y.C.; bd. dirs. Morgan-Stanley Corp., N.Y.C.; chmn. Latin Am., African and Middle East Corp. Groups J.P. Morgan Internat., Corp.; adv. bd. Morgan Stanley Corp., N.Y.C.; mem. Orgn. Econ. Cooperation and Devel., mem. adv. com. Internat. Labor Orgn.; participant Forum/A Group of Internat. Leaders, Calif., 1995, mem. adv. bd. U.S.-Saudi Arabia Bus. Coun., OECD on Industry and Fin., Paris, 1995, others; apptd. U.S. amb. Spl. Del. to Commn. Security/Coop. in Europe on Econ. and Pub. Reforms in Russian Republics; participant World Outlook Conf. on 21st Century, 1995; mem. Nat. Planning Assns., Washington, Brit.-North Am. Com. on Econ. and Pub. Policy Planning, Global Econ. Coun.; mem. adv. bd. Nat. Bus. Leadership Coun., Washington; mem. Arbitration Tribunal, Geneva; judge World Intellectual Property Orgns.; selected arbitrator, mem. tribunal; mem. arbitration bd., panel of arbitrators NAFTA Trade Policy; mem. adv. com. on private internat. law U.S. State Dept., Washington; mem. Dead Sea Scrolls Rsch. Project, 1998; mem. author and writers group on multi-vol. transl. series classical works from late Roman, medieval near eastern, patristic and early Christian ch. periods Princeton U., 1998, Cath. U. Am., 1998, U. Calif., Berkely, 1998; rsch. prof. Old and New Testament bibl. lit. commentary, 1998. Author: (10 vol. manuscript) History of Ecumenical Doctrines and Canon Law of Church; editorial bd. Internat. Tax Jour., 1993; author: Publishers National Endowment for Arts and Humanities Classical Translations: Latin, Greek, and Byzantine Literary Texts for Modern Theological-Philosophical Analysis of Social Issues; Essays on Issues of Religious Ethics and Social, Public Policy Issues, 1995, 96, others; editorial bd. Internat. Tax Jour., 1993, Melrose Press: Internat. Firm; contbr. articles to profl. jours. Dir., vice chmn. Downtown Assn. San Francisco; councillor, dir. Atlantic Coun. U.S., 1984—; corp. counsel, chmn. spl. arbitrator's tribunal on U.S.-Brazil trade, fin. and banking rels. Inter-Am. Comml. Arbitration Commn., Washington; chmn. nat. adv. com. U.S.-Mid. East rels. U.S. Mid. East Policy Coun., U.S. State Dept., Washington, 1989—; mem. Pres. Bush's Adv. Commn. on Econ. and Public Policy Priorities, Washington, 1989; mem. conf. bd. Mid. East Policy Coun., U.S. State Dept., Washington, 1994—; elected mem. Coun. of Scholars U.S. Libr. Congress, Washington; bd. dirs. Internat. Diplomacy Coun., San Francisco Opera, Ballet, Symphony Assns. Recipient Cmty. Svc. honors Mayor Dianne Feinstein, San Francisco, 1987, Leadership awards St. Ignatius Coll. Prep., 1984, Calif.'s Gold State award, 1990, AU-ABA Achievement award, 1990, Medal of Honor Order Internat. Ambs. Com. U.S. State Dept. and Foreign Svc. Inst., Washington D.C., World Lifetime Achievement award, Induction 20th Century Millenium Hall Fame and Dist. Leadership Hall Fame Am. Acad. Achievement, 1998, award Superior Talent in Bus. and Arts, Century Dist. Acheivement award, Am. Acad. Achievement, 1998, Internat. Cultural award, 1997, Presdl. Seal Honor, 1997, Decree Internat. Cultural Letters, 1997; named Civic Leader of Yr., Nat. Trust for Hist. Preservation, 1988, 89; named to Presdl. Order of Merit, 1991., Induction U.S. Lib. Congress 500 Leaders of Influence Hall Fame, 1998, Noble Installation Orders of Knighthood Royal British Legions by Queen Elizabeth II, 1998. Fellow World Jurist Assn., World Assn. Judges (Washington); mem. ATLA, Internat. Bar Assn. (various coms., internat. litigation, taxation, labor issue), Am. Arbitration Assn. (panelist, internat. decree), Am. Fgn. Law Assn. (various coms.), Am. Soc. Ch. History, Am. Inst. Archaeology (Boston), Pontifical Inst. Medieval Studies (Toronto, Can.), Am. Hist. Assn., Am. Philol. Assn., Inst. European Law, Medieval Acad. Am., U.S. Supreme Ct. Hist. Soc. (presdl. seal of honor, cultural diploma honor), J Canon Law Soc. U.S., Nat. Planning Assn., Nat. Assn. Scholars (Eminent Scholar of Yr. 1993), Netherlands Arbitration Inst. (mem. Gen. Panels of Arbitrators, mem. Permanent Ct. Arbitration), Calif. Coun. Internat. Trade (GATT com., tax com., legis. com.), Practicing Law Inst., Am. Fgn. Law Assn. (mem. editl. bd. Working Groups on Rsch. Jour. for Legal systems of Africa, Mid. East, Latin Am., EEC and Soviet Union), U.S.-China Bus. Coun. (export com., GATT com., banking and fin. com., import com.), Bay Area Coun. (corp. mem.), Nat. Acad. Conciliators (Spl. award), Internat. Bar (mem. U.S. Group on Model on Insolvency Corp. Acts), Ctr. Internat. Comml. Arbitration, Comml. Club (various positions), Am. Venture Capital Assn., Pacific Venture Capital Assn., Am. Soc. Internat. Law, Washington Fgn. Law Soc., Asia-Pacific Lawyers Assn., Soc. Profls. in Dispute Resolution, British Inst. Internat. and Comparative Law, Internat. Law Assn. (U.S. br.), Commercial Bar Assn. of United Kingdom (London), Inter-Pacific Bar Assn. (Tokyo; mem. arbitration intellectual property, consitutional taxation, labor, legal groups), Inst. European Law Faculty of Laws (United Kingdom), Urban Land Inst. Internat., Mid. East Inst. (Am.-Arab Affairs Coun.), Inter-Am. Bar Assn., 1987—, Calif. Trial Lawyers Assn., Ctr. Reformation Rsch. (co-chmn. Calif. State Com. on U.S-Mid. East Econ. and Polit. Rels.), Soc. Biblical Lit., Am. Acad. Arts and Letters, Am. Acad. Religion, World Lit. Acad., Coun. Scholars, Am. Com. on U.S.-Japan Rels., Japan Soc. No. Calif., Pan-Am. Assn. San Francisco, Soc. Indsl./Office Realtors, Assn. Entertainment Lawyers London, Royal Chartered Inst. Arbitrators (London), Soc. Indsl. and Office Realtors, Urban Land Inst., San Francisco Realtors Assn., Calif. Realtors Assn., Coun. Fgn. Rels., Chgo. Coun. Fgn. Rels., Conf. Bd., San Francisco Urban and Planning Assn., U.S. Trade Facilitation Coun., Asia Soc., Am. Petroleum Inst., Internat. Platform Assn., San Francisco C. of C. (bus. policy com., pub. policy com., co-chmn. congl. issues study group), Am. Inst. Diplomacy, Overseas Devel. Coun. (Mid. East, Russian Republics, Latin Am. studies group), Internat. Vis. Ctr. (adv. bd.), Fin. Execs. Inst., Nat. Assn. Corp. Dirs., Heritage Found. (bd. dirs.), Archaeological Inst. Am. (fellow coun. near east studies, Egyptology), Am. Literature Judicature Soc., Soc. of Biblical, Nat. Assn. Indsl. and Office Properties, World Literary Acad. (Cambridge, Eng.), Am. Acad. Arts & Letters, Am. Acad. Religion, Pres. Club, Nat. Assn. Bus. Economists, Villa Taverna Club, Palm Beach Yacht Club, Pebble Beach Tennis Club, Calif. Yacht Club, Commonwealth Club, City Club San Francisco, British Bankers Club, London, San Diego Track Club (registered athlete), Crow Canyon Country Club (bd. dirs.), Western Venture Capital Assn., Am. Venture Capital Assn., Authors Guild, Internat. Pen Soc., diplomate-delegate World Econ. Summit Conf., Paris, 1998, IOSECC Conf. Internat. Org. Securities Conf., Paris, 1998. Republican. Roman Catholic; Clubs: Crow Canyon Country Club, The Players. Avocations: theater, social entertainment events, opera, ballet, fine arts. Home: 501 Forest Ave Palo Alto CA 94301-2631 Office: 540 Jones St Ste 201 San Francisco CA 94102-2008

LYNCH, WILLIAM FRANCIS, JR., secondary mathematics educator; b. Sharon Hill, Pa., July 9, 1956; s. William Francis Sr. and Patricia Claire Marie (Kilpatrick) L.; m. Marian Grace Geiger, Nov. 11, 1985. BS in Social Studies Edn., Temple U., 1978, postgrad., 1980-81; MA in Edn. in Math., Beaver Coll., 1984; postgrad., U. of the Arts, Phila., 1992-93. Social studies tchr. Ben Franklin H.S., Phila., 1978-79; math., English, reading, TV tchr. William Penn H.S., Phila., 1979; math., English, reading, social studies tchr. Stetson Jr. H.S., Phila., 1980-84; secondary sch. math. tchr. CAPA, Phila., 1984-85, Phila. H.S. for Girls, 1985, Kensington H.S., Phila., 1985, Edison H.S., Phila., 1985-86; math., sci., reading tchr. Jones Mid. Sch., Phila., 1986-90; math. tchr., head dept. LaBrum Mid. Sch., Phila., 1990-96, Phila. H.S. Girls, 1996—2001; math., social sci. tchr., asst. disciplinarian, acad. tutor Central H.S., 2001—. Acad. tutor, student advisor Phila. Sch. Dist., 1978—. Author curriculum in field. Mem. Phila. Fedn. Tchrs. Avocations: woodwork, music, sports, art, reading. Office: Ctrl HS Ogontz & Olney Aves Philadelphia PA 19141

LYNCH-FIRCA, DIANA JOAN, secondary education educator; b. Kearny, N.J., Sept. 7, 1954; d. Joseph Daniel and Eleanor L. Lynch; m. John Nicholas Firca, Dec. 18, 1993. BA in Art History and Italian, U. Colo., 1976; MA in Art History, Rosary Coll. at Villa Schifanoia Grad. Sch. of Fine Arts (Italy), River Forest, Ill., 1979; BFA in Painting, Acad. Fine Arts, Milan, Venice, Bari, Italy, 1987; cert. in English as fgn. lang., Internat. House, London, 1990; postgrad., Monmouth Coll., 1990-91, Kean Coll. Cert. art, Italian, elem. edn. tchr. Tchr. English as foreign lang. Am. Inst., Florence, Italy, 1978-79, Brit. Sch., Venice, 1984-85, Am. Lang. Ctr., Matera, Italy, 1986-90; lectr. English U. Inst. Modern Langs., Milan, 1980-84, U. Studi di Bari, 1985-90; tchr. Italian Matawan Regional High Sch., Aberdeen, N.J., 1991—. Tchr. art and ESL, Am. Sch., Montagnola, Switzerland, summers 1983-89; tchr. English as fgn. lang. Lord Byron Coll., London, summer 1990, Anglo Continental West Long Branch, N.J., 1990—; mem. adj. faculty ESL, fine art and art history Brookdale C.C., Lincroft, N.J., 1990— Mem. N.J. Edn. Assn., Nat. Art Edn. Assn., Fgn. Lang. Educators N.J., Guild Creative Art, Art Educators N.J. Roman Catholic. Avocations: art, photography, languages, irish dancing, music. Office: Matawan Regional High Sch Atlantic Ave Matawan NJ 07747

LYNE, DOROTHY-ARDEN, educator; b. Orangeburg, N.Y., Mar. 9, 1928; d. William Henry and Janet More (Freston) Dean; m. Thomas Delmar Lyne, Aug. 16, 1952 (div. June 1982); children: James Delmar, Peter Freston, Jennifer Dean. BA, Ursinus Coll., 1949; MA, Fletcher Sch. Law and Diplomacy, 1950. Assoc. editor World Peace Found., Boston, 1950-51; editorial assoc. Carnegie Endowment Internat. Peace, N.Y.C., 1951-52; dir. Assoc. of Internat. Rels. Clubs, N.Y.C., 1952-53; editor The Town Crier, Westport, Conn., 1966-68; editorial assoc. Machinery Allied Products Inst., Wash., 1959-63; tchr. Helen Keller Mid. Sch., Easton, Conn., 1967-89. Vice chmn. Cooperative Ednl. Svcs., Fairfield, 1983-85. Editor: Documents in American Foreign Rels., 1950, Current Rsch. in Internat. Affairs, 1951. Chmn. Westport Zoning Bd. of Appeals, 1976-80, Westport Bd. of Edn., 1985-87; vice chmn. Westport Bd. of Edn., 1980-85; mem. Westport Charter Revision Commn., 1966-67. Republican. Episcopalian.

LYNN, CHRISTOPHER KENNETH, internist, educator; b. Seattle, Dec. 18, 1956; s. Kenneth Clyde and Bettylu (Hines) L.; m. Elloise Carol Gard, Oct. 1990. BS, Duke U., 1978; MD, Med. Coll. of Ohio, 1983. Diplomate Am. Bd. Internal Medicine. Intern Med. Coll. Ohio, Toledo, 1983-84, resident, 1984-86, asst. prof. internal medicine, 1986-91, assoc. prof., 1992—, clerkship dir. internal medicine, 1987—, co-chief divsn. gen. internal medicine, 1995—2003, chief divsn. gen. internal medicine, 2003—. Dir. phys. exam course Med. Coll. Ohio, 1988—, curriculum com., 1990-2000, chmn. subcom. on 3d and 4th yr. curriculum, 1990-2000. Mem. ACP, Soc. of Gen. Internal Medicine, Clerkship Dirs. Internal Medicine. Office: Med Coll Ohio Dept Medicine Box #10008 3000 Arlington Ave Toledo OH 43699

LYNN, GWENDOLYN RENAYE, physical and health education educator; b. Monticello, Fla., Nov. 12, 1958; d. Elder Joe Gray and Beatrice W. Lynn-Gray. BS, Fla. A&M U., 1980, MEd, 1984. Cert. profl. educator, Fla. Playground dir. Tallahassee Parks & Recreation Dept., 1978-84, instr. and recreation leader, 1978-82; tchr. phys. edn. Leon County Schs., Tallahassee, 1984-89, tchr. health edn., 1990—; team leader Griffin Mid. Sch., Tallahassee, 1993-95, sch.-based mgmt. mem., 1995, Newton/learner profile trainer, 1994—. Bd. dirs., treas. New Hope New Faith Ministries, Tallahassee, 1993—; co-sponsor Fellowship of Christian Athletes, Tallahassee, 1994—. Mem. NEA, Fla. Alliance Health, Phys. Edn., Recreation, Dance. Avocations: reading, writing, public speaking. Office: Griffin Middle School 800 Alabama St Tallahassee FL 32304-2298

LYNN, NAOMI B. academic administrator; b. N.Y.C., Apr. 16, 1933; d. Carmelo Burgos and Maria (Lebron) Berly; m. Robert A. Lynn, Aug. 28, 1954; children: Mary Louise, Nancy Lynn Francis, Judy Lynn Chance, Jo-An Lynn Cooper. BA, Maryville (Tenn.) Coll., 1954; MA, U. Ill., 1958; PhD, U. Kans., 1970. Instr. polit. sci. Cen. Mo. State Coll., Warrensburg, Mo., 1966-68; asst. prof. Kans. State U., Manhattan, 1970-75, assoc. prof., 1975-80, acting dept. head, prof., 1980-81, head polit. sci. dept., prof., 1982-84; dean Coll. Pub. and Urban Affairs, prof. Ga. State U., Atlanta, 1984-91; chancellor U. Ill., Springfield, 1991-2001, chancellor emerita, 2001—. Cons. fed., state and local govts., Manhattan, Topeka, Altanta, 1981-91; bd. dirs. Bank One Springfield; bd. trustees Maryville Coll., 1997—. Author: The Fulbright Premise, 1973; editor: Public Administration, The State of Discipline, 1990, Women, Politics and the Constitution, 1990; contbr. articles and textbook chpts. to profl. pubs. Bd. dirs. United Way of Sangamon County, 1991-98, Ill. Symphony Orch., 1992-95; bd. dirs. Urban League, 1993-99. Recipient Disting. Alumni award Maryville Coll., 1986; fellow Nat. Acad. Pub. Adminstrn. Mem. Nat. Assn. Schs. Pub. Affairs and Adminstrn. (nat. pres.), Am. Soc. Pub. Adminstrn. (nat. pres. 1985-86), Am. Polit. Sci. Assn. (mem. exec. coun. 1981-83, trustee 1993—96, Am. Assn. State Colls. and Univs. (bd. dirs.), Midwest Polit. Sci. Assn. (mem. exec. coun. 1976-79), Women's Caucus Polit. Sci. (pres. 1975-76), Greater Springfield C. of C. (bd. dirs. 1991-99, accreditation task force 1992), Cosmos Club, Pi Sigma Alpha (nat. pres.). Presbyterian.

LYNN, WALTER ROYAL, civil engineering educator, university administrator; b. N.Y.C., Oct. 1, 1928; s. Norman and Gussie (Gdalin) L.; m. Barbara Lee Campbell, June 3, 1960; children: Michael Drew. BS, U. Miami, 1950; MS, U. N.C., 1955; PhD, Northwestern U., 1963. Registered profl. engr., N.Y. State registered land surveyor, Fla. Land surveyor Ehly Constrn. Co., Miami, Fla., 1950-51; chief party Rader Engring. Co., Miami, 1951; supt. sewage treatment, lectr. civil engring. U. Miami, 1951-53, asst. prof. mech. engring., 1954-55, asst. prof. civil engring., 1955-57, research asst. prof. marine lab., 1957-58, assoc. prof. civil and indsl. engring., 1959-61; dir. research Ralph B. Carter Co., 1957-58; assoc. prof. san. engring. Cornell U., Ithaca, N.Y., 1961-64, prof. civil and environ. engring., 1964—, dir. Center Environ. Quality Mgmt., 1966-76, dir. Sch. Civil and Environ. Engring., 1970-78, dir. Program on Sci., Tech. and Society, 1980-88, dean univ. faculty, 1988-93; sr. fellow Ctr. for the Environ., 1992-97, 2000—, dir., 1996-97, univ. ombudsman, 1998—; adj. prof. pub. health Med. Coll. Cornell U., 1971-80. Mem. spl. adv. commn. on solid wastes NRC, 1968-76, mem. com. to rev. Washington met. water supply, 1976-84, chmn., 1980-84, mem. bd. water sci. and tech., 1982-86, chmn., 1982-85, mem. com. on water resources rsch., 1987-90, chmn., 1988-90; mem. U.S. Nat. Com. for the Decade on Nat. Disaster Reduction, 1991-96, chmn., 1991-96; cons. WHO, 1969—, Rockefeller Found., 1976-81, SEARO, 1978; chmn. N.Y. State Water Resources Planning Coun., 1986—, NRC Bd. on Nat. Disasters, 1992-96 (chmn. 1992-96). Editor: (with A. Charnes) Mathematical Analysis of Decision Problems in Ecology, 1975; assoc. editor: Jour. Ops. Research, 1968-76, Jour. Environ. Econs. and Mgmt, 1972-88; contbr.: chpt. to Human Ecology and Public Health, 1969; author articles. Chmn. Ithaca Mayor's Citizens Adv. Com., 1964-65, Ithaca Urban Renewal Agy., 1965-68; trustee Cornell U., 1980-85, Village of Cayuga Heights, 2000-02, mayor, 2002—; bd. dirs. Cornell Research Found., 1978-96; commr. So. Cayuga Lake Intergovtl. Water Commn., 1997—. Served with AUS, 1946-48. Recipient Disting. Alumnus award U. Miami, 1985, U. N.C., 1996, Pub. Svc. award Universities Coun. on Water Resources, 1991, Conservation Svc. award U.S. Dept. Interior, 1994. Fellow ASCE (life), AAAS; mem. Nat. Acad. Engrs. Mex. (corr.), Sigma Xi, Phi Kappa Phi., Chi Epsilon Home: 102 Iroquois Pl Ithaca NY 14850-2221 E-mail: WRL1@cornell.edu.

LYON, BARBARA BROOKS, educational administrator; b. Galax, Va., Nov. 6, 1946; d. Reeves Mack and Hazel (Maines) Brooks; m. Danny Dean Lyon, Sept. 21, 1965; children: Noah Christopher, Danna Dianne. BS, Appalachian State U., 1972, MA, 1982. Cert. tchr., prin., N.C. Tchr Glade Creek Sch., Ennice, N.C., 1972-92; asst. prin. Alleghany H.S., Sparta, NC, 1992—2002, prin., 2002—. Active Work First, Sparta, 1994—. Named to Outstanding Young Women in Am., 1983. Mem. NEA, N.C. Assn. Educators, (sec. Alleghany County 1974), Boosters Club of Alleghany H.S., Delta Kappa Gamma, Phi Delta Kappa. Baptist.

LYON, JAMES HUGH, education specialist, legislative consultant; b. Clarksburg, W.Va., Apr. 17, 1936; s. James M. and Mildred E. Lyon; m. Marilyn Jean Lyon. BA in English, Salem Internat. U., 1960; MA, W.Va. U., 1967. Cert. English tchr., Ohio. Tchr. coll. preparatory English Harrison County (W.Va.) Schs., 1960-64, Urbana (Ohio) City Schs., 1964-70; edn. cons., lobbyist Ohio Edn. Assn., Columbus, 1970-93; edn. cons. Lyon Assocs., Canton, Ohio, 1993—. Mem. Nat. Assn. Lobbyists for Sch. Employees, Ohio Edn. Assn. (edn. specialist in Ohio state legislature 1981-93, Outstanding Svc. award 1986), Elks. Home and Office: 6627 Avalon St NW Canton OH 44708-1084

LYON, MARINA, secondary school educator, translator; b. Chapaevsk, Russia, Mar. 15, 1967; arrived in U.S., 96; d. Nicholas Nuzhdin and Antonina Nuzhdina; m. Charles Lyon, July 20, 1963; 1 child, Anastasia. MA in Fgn. Langs., Kuibyshev State U., Samara, Russia, 1989. Cert. English/ESL tchr. English tchr. secondary sch., Chapaersk, Russia, 1989—90, vice prin., 1989—91; interpreter, translator U. Ky., Lexington, 1996—99; tchr. Russian, ESL Henry Clay H.S., Lexington, 1996—. Recipient Fame award for tchg., Fayette County Bd. Edn., 1999. Mem.: Ky. Fgn. Lang. Tchrs. Assn. Avocations: skiing, skating, gymnastics, dancing. Home: 1004 Winding Cir Lexington KY 40517 Office: Henry Clay HS Fontain Rd 2100 Lexington KY 40502 E-mail: marina.lyon@usa.net.

LYON, MARY LOU, educator; b. Wichita, Kans., Sept. 18, 1926; d. Theodore Joseph and Hazel Pearl (Johnson) Cochran; m. William Madison Lyon, Mar. 15, 1944 (div. July 1970); children: William Madison, Jr., Theodore Richard. AA, Coll. San Mateo, Calif., 1958; BA with distinction and honors, San Jose (Calif.) State U., 1960, lifetime secondary credential, 1961, MA, 1967. Cert. secondary edn. tchr., Calif. Tchr. Los Gatos (Calif.) HS, 1961, Blach Jr. HS Los Altos (Calif.) Elem. Dist., 1961-62, Homestead High, Fremont Union HS Dist., Cupertino, Calif., 1962—93, Metropolitan Adult educator program, San Jose, 1986—. Tchr. San Jose State U. Extension, Cupertino, 1974-76, Fremont Union High Sch. Adult Edn., 1977; various offices Calif. Coun. for Social Studies, Sacramento, 1962-80; historian, photographer Anza Trek Observance Bicentennial, Santa Clara County (Calif.) Bicentennial Commn., 1975-76; cons. Calif. map Hearne Bros. Map Co., 1981; speaker Genealogical Soc., San Jose Hist. Mus., Calif. Hist. Soc., Menlo Park Hist. Soc., Tulare County Hist. Soc., others. Author, editor (pamphlet) Social Sci. Rev., 1975-76, San Francisco Westerners News from Telegraph Hill 1995-, Santa Clara County Trailblazers, 1997-2002; ; author, numerous books on Santa Clara County, photographer (one-woman show) Cupertino Hist. Soc., 1975; photographer: (textbook) Addison Wesley, 1980, Chair of site & times Conf. Calif. hist. soc., 1985—; commr. Santa Clara County Hist. Heritage, 1994—2003; delegate Calif. State Sesquicentennial commn. for CCHS, 1998—2000. Recipient history honor, Phi Alpha Theta, 1959—60, Award of excellence for tchng. Calif. history, Conf. of Calif. Hist. Soc., 1973, Honored as an Achiever, Santa Clara County Penwomen, 1976, Coke Wood award, Conf. of Calif. Hist. Soc., 1994, Coke wood award, 1997, award of merit, Calif. Pioneers of Santa Clara County, 1999, Pres. award, Conf. of Calif. Hist. Soc., 1999, 2002. Mem. Conf. Calif. Hist. Soc. (various offices 1973—, pres. 1983-84), Oreg.-Calif. Trail Assn. (publicity com. Calif.-Nev. Hawaii br. 1985—), Nat. Oreg.-Calif. Trail Assn., Westerners Internat. (bd. dirs.); mem. Cupertino Hist. Soc., San Jose Hist. Soc. (cons.), Santa Clara County Hist.Heritage Commn., Santa Clara County Pioneers, Golden Gate Park Assoc., Heritage Coun. of Santa Clara County, Lewis & Clark Hist. Assoc., Nat. Parks & Conservation Assoc., Menlo Park Hist. Soc., San Jose Hist. Mus. Assoc., Santa Fe Trail Assoc., Tulare County Hist. Soc., San Franciso Corral of Westerners sheriff, 1995, others. Democrat. Presbyterian. Avocations: photography, traveling, lecturing, western history. Home: 879 Lily Ave Cupertino CA 95014-4261

LYON, RICHARD HAROLD, physicist educator; b. Evansville, Ind., Aug. 24, 1929; s. Chester Clyde and Gertrude Lyon; m. Jean Wheaton; children: Katherine Lyon Davis, Geoffrey Cleveland, Suzanne Marie Riggle. AB, Evansville Coll., 1952; PhD in Physics (Owens-Corning fellow), MIT, 1955; DEng, U. Evansville, 1976. Asst. prof. elec. engring. U. Minn., Mpls., 1956-59; Mem. research staff Mass. Inst. Tech., 1955-56, lectr. mech. engring., 1963-69, prof. mech. engring., 1970-95, prof. emeritus, 1995—, head mechanics and materials div., 1981-86. NSF postdoctoral fellow U. Manchester, Eng., 1959-60; sr. scientist Bolt Beranek & Newman, Cambridge, 1960-66, v.p., 1966-70; chmn. Cambridge Collaborative, Inc., 1972-90; v.p. Grozier Pub., Inc., 1972; pres. Grozier Tech. Systems, 1976-82, RH Lyon Corp., 1976—. Author: Transportation Noise, 1974, Theory and Applications of Statistical Energy Analysis, 1975, 2d edit. (with R. DeJong), 1994, Machinery Noise and Diagnostics, 1987, Designing for Product Sound Quality, 2000; mem. editl. bd. Acoustical Soc. Japan, 1996—. Bd. dirs. Boston Light Opera, Ltd., 1975; mem. alumni bd. U. Evansville, 1988-94, trustee, 1995-98, chmn. ann. fund, 1996-97. Recipient Rayleigh medal Brit. Inst. Acoustics, 1995, Nat. Acad. Engring. award 1995, Disting. Alumni award U. Evansville, 1997, medal of Honor, U. Evansville, 2002, Gold medal Indian Acoustical Soc., 2003. Fellow: AAAS, Acoustical Soc. Am. (assoc. editor jour. 1967—74, exec. coun. 1976—79, v.p. 1989—90, pres. 1993—94, Silver medal in engring. acoustics 1998, Gold medal 2003), Internat. Inst. Acoustics and Vibrations (hon.); mem.: Brit. Inst. Acoustics (Rayleigh medal 1995), Nat. Acad. Engring., Sigma Xi, Sigma Pi Sigma. Achievements include research and publications in fields of nonlinear random oscillations, energy transfer in complex structures, sound transmission in marine and aerospace vehicles, building acoustics, environmental noise, machinery diagnostics, home theater audio systems. Home: 60 Prentiss Ln Belmont MA 02478-2021 Office: RH Lyon Corp 691 Concord Ave Cambridge MA 02138-1002 E-mail: rhlyon@lyoncorp.com.

LYON, WILLIAM JAMES, sociology educator; b. El Paso, Tex., Feb. 22, 1957; s. James William and Ana (Mendez) L.; m. Brandi A. Ferrari; children: Kim, Aaron. BA, U. Tex., El Paso, 1982, MA, 1984. Therapist Cath. Soc. Svc., Phoenix, 1989—99; prof. sociology, social work, adminstrn. of justice Paradise Valley C.C., 1992—. Mem. adj. faculty Lewis-Clark State Coll., Lewiston, Idaho, 1989. Nat. Hispanic Fund scholar, 1985-86, 87-88. Office: Paradise Valley CC 32nd St and Union Hills Phoenix AZ 85032

LYONS, CHERIE ANN, researcher, writer; b. Denver, Dec. 15, 1948; d. Clair Leroy and Mary Margaret (Benner) Case; m. David Greer Lyons, Aug. 22, 1970; children: Michael Greer, Andrea Christine. BS, U. Colo., 1971, MA, 1975, PhD, 1992. Profl. tchr. cert., adminstr., cert. Colo. Dept. Edn. Tchr. English Cherry Creek Schs., 1971—76; tchr. English, health edn. Jefferson County Schs., Lakewood, Colo., 1971—76, curriculum writer, 1975—78, project dir., career edn., 1976—81, staff devel. specialist, 1981—87, jr. h.s. prin., 1987—88, coord. prevention program, 1989—90; exec. dir., dir. grants devel. Jefferson Found., 1990—; cons. Region VII Tng. Ctr., U.S. Dept. Edn., Ctr. Substance Abuse Prevention; dir. Sch. Team Approach to Substance Abuse Prevention Jefferson County; coord. Jefferson County Prevention Task Force; exec. dir. rsch. and resource devel. Jefferson County Schs., 1995—96; exec. dir. planning, rsch. and resource devel. Jefferson County Sch. Dist., 1996—2001; prof. ednl. adminstrn. U. Colo., Denver, 2001—; rsch. assoc. RMC Rsch. Corp., Denver, 2002—. Author: The Writing Process: A Program of Composition and Applied Grammar, Book 12, 1982. Mem.: Nat. Soc. for Study of Edn., Assn. Supervision and Curriculum Devel., Am. Soc. for Quality, Jefferson County Adminstrs. Assn., Phi Delta Kappa. Home: 7584 Taft Ct Arvada CO 80005-3294 Office: RMC Rsch Corp 1512 Larimer St Ste 540 Denver CO 80202

LYONS, HARVEY ISAAC, mechanical engineering educator; b. N.Y.C., Sept. 26, 1931; s. Joseph and Betty L.; m. Rebecca Anne Szeman, June 10, 1978; children: Neal Joshua, Leslie Eve. Cert. in indsl. design, Pratt Inst., 1952; BSME, The Cooper Union, 1962, MS in Mech. Engring., 1971; PhD in Mech. Engring., Ohio State U., 1978. Registered profl. engr., N.Y., Ohio, Wis., Wash., Mont., N.H., Mich. From design engr. to sr. mech. engr. various orgns., N.Y.C., 1954-72; assoc. prof. mech. engring. Mont. State U., Bozeman, 1978-79, U. Wis.-Parkside, Kenosha, 1979-81, U. N.H., Durham, 1981-84, Seattle U., 1984-85; chmn. dept. mech. engring. Alfred (N.Y.) U., 1985-88; assoc. prof. mech. engring. Union Coll., Schenectady, 1988-92, Ind. Inst. Tech., Ft. Wayne, 1992-95; cons. engr. in pvt. practice Ft. Wayne, Ind., 1995-98; assoc. prof. mech. engring. Ea. Mich. U., 1998—. Contbr. articles to profl. jours. Sgt. 2d inf. divsn. U.S. Army, 1952-54, Korea. Mem. ASME, NSPE, Nat. Assn. Indsl. Tech., Am. Soc. Engring. Edn., Soc. Mfg. Engrs. Achievements include development of methods to investigate tribological phenomenon of Fretting-Wear in-situ, towards development of failure prediction criteria, development of mechanical engineering departments in industry and academe. Home: 2787 Page Ave Ann Arbor MI 48104 E-mail: harvey.lyons@emich.edu.

LYONS, JOHN DAVID, French, Italian and comparative literature educator; b. Springfield, Mass., Oct. 14, 1946; s. John Joseph and Loretta Francis (Feighery) L.; m. Patricia Stuart, July 31, 1971; 1 dau., Jennifer Catherine. AB, Brown U., 1967; MA, Yale U., 1968, PhD, 1972. Asst. prof. French, Italian and comparative lit. Dartmouth Coll., Hanover, NH, 1972-78, assoc. prof., 1978-82, prof., 1982-87, chmn. comparative lit. program, 1981-84, chmn., prof. dept. French and Italian, 1987; dir. Am. Univ. Ctr. for Film and Critical Studies, Paris, 1984-85; prof. French U. Va., Charlottesville, 1987-92, Commonwealth prof. French, 1993—, chmn. dept., 1989-92, 98-99. Author: A Theatre of Disguise, 1978, The Listening Voice, 1982, Exemplum, 1989, The Tragedy of Origins, 1996, Kingdom of Disorder, 1999; co-editor: Mimesis: Mirror to Method, 1982, Dialectic of Discovery, 1983, Critical Tales, 1993; editor: Art, Architecture, Text: The Late Renaissance, 1985; assoc. editor Continuum, 1987-93; editor Academe, 1994-97; editl. adv. bd. Philosophy and Literature, 1992-2002, French Forum. Recipient Robert Fish award for teaching Dartmouth Coll., 1978, Outstanding Tchr. award U. Va., 1996; Woodrow Wilson fellow, 1967, ACLS study fellow, 1978, NEH fellow, 1985-89, 92-93, ACLS contemplative practice fellow, 2002, J.S. Guggenheim fellow, 2002-03, Ctr. for Advanced Studies U. Va. fellow, 1987-89. Mem.: N.Am. Soc. for Seventeenth-Century French Lit. (pres. 2002). Office: U Va Dept French Lang & Lit Charlottesville VA 22903

LYONS, MARY E. academic administrator; BA, Sonoma St. Univ., 1971; MA, San Diego St. Univ., 1976; Ph.D, Sonoma St. Univ., 1983. Prof. Franciscan School of Theology, Berkeley, Calif., 1984—90; pres. Calif. Maritime Acad., Vallejo, 1990-96, Coll. of St. Benedict, St. Joseph, Minn., 1996—2003, Univ. San Diego, 2003—. Office: Office of the President Univ San Diego 5998 Alcala Pk San Diego CA 92110-2492*

LYONS, PATRICK JOSEPH, management educator; b. NYC, Dec. 12, 1943; BEE, Manhattan Coll., 1965; MS in Applied Math., Case Western Res. U., 1967; PhD in Applied Math., Adelphi U., 1973. Systems analyst Grumman Aerospace, Bethpage, N.Y., 1967-75, asst. mgr., 1975-76; prof. mgmt. St. John's U., Jamaica, N.Y., 1976—. Cons. in field. Contbr. articles to profl. jours. Adult edn. instr. Sacred Heart Ch., Bayside, N.Y., 1983—. Mem. IEEE, Inst. Ops. Rsch. and Mgmt. Sci., N.Y. Acad. Scis. Roman Catholic. Avocations: photography, jogging. Office: St John's U Coll Bus Jamaica NY 11439-0001

LYONS, THOMAS TOLMAN, history educator; b. Stoneham, Mass., June 21, 1934; s. Louis Martin and Margaret Wade (Tolman) L.; m. Eleanor Frances Coneeney, Aug. 31, 1958; children: John Louis, Kathleen Margaret, David Tolman, Joseph Charles. BA, Harvard U., 1957, MAT, 1958. Tchr. history Mount Herman Sch., Gill, Mass., 1958-63, Phillips Acad., Andover, Mass., 1963-68, 69—, Dartmouth Coll., Hanover, N.H., 1968-69. Creater, dir., tchr. seminar NEH-Phillips Acad., 1987. Author (with others) Presidential Power in the Era of the New Deal, 1963, Realism and Idealism in Wilson's Peace Program, 1965, Reconstruction and the Race Problem, 1968, Black Leadership in American History, 1971, The Supreme Court and Individual Rights in Contemporary Society, 1975, The Expansion of the Federal Union, 1801-1848, 1978, (with others) After Hiroshima: America since 1945, 1979, 3d edit. 1993; author: President: Preacher, Teacher, Salesman, Presidential Speeches, 1933-1983, 1985. Found. chair John M. Kemper, 1980-82, Independence Teaching Found., 1980-82, Phillips Acad., Andover, 1982—. Recipient Disting. Secondary Sch. Tchr. award Harvard U., 1966; Social Sci. fellow Wesleyan U., Middletown, Conn., Coe History fellow Stanford U., 1963, Coun. for Basic Edn. fellow, 1986. Mem. Orgn. Am. Historians, New Eng. History Tchrs. Assn. (Kidger award 1985), Orgn. of History Tchrs. Democrat. Roman Catholic. Avocations: reading, writing, sports. Home: 8 Oak St Newburyport MA 01950-3206

LYSUN, GREGORY, artist, educator; b. Yonkers, N.Y., Oct. 24, 1924; s. John and Paraska (Petryszyn) L. Student, Art Students League, N.Y., 1947-53. Instr. painting and drawing Westchester C.C., White Plains, N.Y., 1969—; art dir., instr. Fairview Greenburgh Cmty. Ctr., White Plains, N.Y., 1972—; artist-in-residence, instr. painting and drawing Pelham Art Ctr., 1978—. Instr. painting and drawing Hudson River Mus., Yonkers, 1978-79, SUNY, Purchase, 1982—. One-man shows include Berkshire Mus., Pittsfield, Mass., 1971; exhibited in group shows at Am. Artists Profl. League, N.Y.C., 1997, Mystic Art Assn. Galleries, 1995, Allied Artists Am., 1993, Nat. Arts Club, N.Y.C., 1988, Conn. Acad. Fine Arts, 1988, William Benton Mus., 1988, Berkshire Mus., 1980, Knickerbocker Artists Am., 1979, Nat. Arts Club, 1979; represented in permanent collections Butler Inst. Am. Art, Youngstown, Ohio, New Britain (Conn.) Mus. Am. Art, Pittsfield, De Cordova Mus., Lincoln, Mass.; works featured in Best of Oil Painting, 1996; contbr. articles to mags. Restorer paintings Jefferson County Hist. Soc., Oskaloosa, Kans., 1982, St. Joseph's Ch., Bronxville, N.Y., 1991. With USCG, 1942-45, ETO, NATOUSA. Recipient Gen. Telephone and Electronics Corp. award, 1972. Fellow Am. Artists Profl. League (Dir. award 1992); mem. Conn. Acad. Fine Arts (Best Landscape award 1977, Best Portrait award 1983, prize 1986), Allied Artists Am., Art Students League N.Y.C. (life). Address: 481 Winding Rd N Ardsley NY 10502-2701

LYTAL, PATRICIA LOU, art educator; b. Ft. Wayne, Ind., Sept. 11, 1936; d. George F. and Geraldine (Beck) Heingartner; m. Wayne Earl Lytal; Sept. 16, 1956; children: Michael Wayne, Patrick Allen (dec.), Terry Lee, Shawn David. Tchr. oil painting Ft. Wayne Park Sch. Bd, 1980-83, Ind. U.- Purdue U. Continuing Edn., Ft. Wayne, 1986-90; ind. tchr. oil painting Ft. Wayne, 1976-95. Instr. Ft. Wayne Sr. Ctr., Decatur (Ind.) Park Bd., Ft. Wayne Park and Recreation Dept.; tchr. oil painting for Chpt. 2 through St. Joseph Med. Ctr.; tchr. South Bay Adult Sch., 1996-97, 98; judge art contest Ft. Wayne Women's Club, 1989-90, 94. Artist: (murals) Diehm Mus. Natural History, 1981, Grace United Meth. Ch. Home, 1983, La Margarita Restaurant. Recipient 3d pl. china painting State of Ind., Best of Show award Ft. Wayne Woman's Club Ind. Artist Show, award Montpelier Brass Latch Art Show, 1993, 94, 95, Judges award Huntington Coll. Arts Contest, 1993. Mem. Brown Country Art Soc., Park County Art Soc., Ft. Wayne Artist Guild, Torrence Artist Guild, Niguel Art Assn., San Clemente Arts and Crafts Club. Democrat. Avocations: china painting, silverpoint drawing, fishing, swimming, traveling. Home and Office: PO Box 1416 Sugarloaf CA 92386-1416

LYTLE, ELLEN JUANITA WILSON, special education educator; b. Port Arthur, Tex., Jan. 26, 1941; d. Walter Dean and Velma Juanita (Henry) Wilson; m. Donald L. Lytle, Jr., Apr. 12, 1963 (div. Jan. 1979); children: David Anthony, Shannon Wilson. BA in Elem. Edn., U. Southwestern La., 1963, MEd, 1972; spl. edn. cert., McNeese State U., 1992, postgrad., 1992-94; D of Psychology, Kennedy-Western U., 1994. Cert. tchr., spl. edn. assessor, computer lit., La. Tchr. Duson (La.) Elem. Sch. Lafayette Parish, 1963-65, N.P. Moss Elem. Sch. Lafayette Parish, Lafayette, 1965-70, St. Antoine Elem. Sch. Lafayette Parish, Lafayette, 1970-72; substitute tchr. French and band Merryville (La.) High Sch. Beauregard Parish, 1987; tchr. spl. edn. Pickering Elem. Sch. Vernon Parish, Leesville, La., 1989-92; alt. spl. edn. H.S. classes Pickering H.S. Vernon Parish, Leesville, 1992-94; ednl. diagnostician Vernon Parish Spl. Edn. Ctr., Leesville, 1994—. Officer, pres. La. Divsn. Career Devel. and Transition, 1993—; spkr. spl. edn. super conf., 1992, 94. Author: (juvenile) Tales of the Circus, 1990, Histories of Louisiana Fairs, Festivals, and Historic Places, Book 1, 1993, Book 2, 1994, Louisiana: Festival of Color Coloring Book, 1994; illustrator: Chad and the Mighty Dragon, 1992; author and illustrator: Tales; creator classroom games. Officer Homemakers Club, Beauregard Parish, 1975-88; sec. La. Assn. Fairs and Festivals, 1985-89; sec.-treas. Beauregard Parish Fair Assn., DeRidder, 1980—. Mem. Coun. for Exceptional Children (sec. La. fedn. coun. 1995), Assn. Profl. La. Educators, La. Ednl. Diagnosticians Assn., Kappa Kappa Iota (pres. 1993-94). Methodist. Avocations: arts and crafts, sewing, travel, writing. Home: 3570 Neale Oilfield Rd Deridder LA 70634-2526 Office: Vernon Parish Spl Edn Ctr 201 Belview Rd Leesville LA 71446-2904

LYTLE, RICHARD, artist, educator; b. Albany, N.Y., Feb. 14, 1935; s. Ralph Dudley and Mary (Putnam) L.; m. Berit Ore Lytle, June 16, 1959; children: Mara, Claudia, Dorian. Diploma, Cooper Union, N.Y.C., 1955; BFA, Yale U., 1957, MFA, 1960. Instr. Yale Sch. Art, New Haven, 1960-63, assoc. prof., 1966-80, acting dean, 1980—81, 1990, 1994, prof. art, 1980—2002; dean Silvermine Coll. Art, New Canaan, Conn., 1963-66, prof. emeritus painting, 2002—. Cons. Rockefeller Fund, N.Y.C., 1970; dir. Yale Summer Sch., Norfolk, Conn., 1976, 77; vis. artist-in-residence Dartmouth Coll., Hanover, N.H., 1986. One-man shows in N.Y.C., New Haven and other locales; exhibited in group shows at Mus. Modern Art, N.Y.C., 1959, Whitney Mus. Art, 1963, Pa. Acad. Art, 1983, Bruce Mus., Greenwich, Conn., 1989; works in permanent collections of Kykuit (Rockefeller home), Yale Art Gallery, New Haven, Mus. Modern Art, N.Y.C., Mpls. Inst. of Art, Nat. Mus. Art, Washington, many other pub. and pvt. collections. Chmn. Region 5 Bd. Edn., Woodbridge, Conn., 1988-97. Fullbright fellow, 1958-59; recipient St. Gaudens award Cooper Union, N.Y.C., 1985. Avocations: windsurfing, gardening. Home: 14 Sperry Rd Woodbridge CT 06525-1234

LYTTON, ROBERT LEONARD, civil engineer, educator; b. Port Arthur, Tex., Oct. 23, 1937; s. Robert Odell and Nora Mae (Verrett) L.; m. Eleanor Marilyn Anderson, Sept. 9, 1961; children: Lynn Elizabeth, Robert Douglas, John Kirby. BSCE, U. Tex., 1960, MSCE, 1961, PhD, 1967. Registered profl. engr., Tex., La., land surveyor, La. Cowhand Slaughter Ranch, Douglas, Ariz., 1963; assoc. Dannenbaum and Assocs., Cons. Engrs., Houston, 1963-65; U.S. NSF fellow U. Tex., Austin, 1965-67, asst. prof., 1967-68; NSF fellow Australian Commonwealth Sci. & Indsl. Rsch. Orgn., Melbourne, Australia, 1969-70; assoc. prof. Tex. A&M U., College Station, 1971-76, prof., 1976-90, Wiley chair prof., 1990-95, dir. ctr. for infrastructure engring., 1991—, Benson chair prof., 1995—; divsn. head Tex. Transp. Inst., 1982-91, head infrastructure and transp. divsn. civil engring. dept., 1993-95. Bd. dirs. MLA Labs., Inc., Austin, Lyric Tech., Llc., Houston; v.p. bd. dirs. MLAW Cons., Inc., Austin, 1980—, ERES Cons., Inc., Champaign, Ill., 1981-95, Geostructural Tool Kit, Inc., 1995—, Concho St., Inc., 2002; prin. investigator strategic hwy. rsch. program A005 rsch. project, 1990-93; Disting. lectr. Transp. Rsch. Bd., 2000. Patentee sys. identification and analysis of subsurface radar signals. Active St. Vincent de Paul Soc., Houston, 1963-65, Redemptorist Lay Mission Soc., Melbourne, Australia, 1969-70. Capt. U.S. Army, 1961-63. Recipient SAR medal of honor St. Mary's U., 1957, Soc. Am. Mil. Engrs. Outstanding Sr. cadet U. Tex., 1959, Disting. Mil. grad. award, 1960, Hamilton Watch award Coll. Engring., 1960, Everite Bursary award Coun. for Sci. and Indsl. Rsch., South Africa, 1984, Disting. Achievement award Tex. A&M U. Assn. Former Students, 1996, Zachry Sr. Rschr. award Tex. Transp. Inst., 1996. Fellow ASCE (John B. Hawley award Tex. sect. 1966); mem. NSPE, Transp. Rsch. Bd. (chmn. com. A2LO6 1987-93), Internat. Soc. for Soil Mechanics and Geotech. Engring. (U.S. rep. tech. com. TC-6 1987—, keynote address 7th internat. conf. on expansive soils 1992, keynote address 1st internat. conf. on unsaturated soils 1995), Assn. Asphalt Paving Technologists, Post-Tensioning Inst. (adv. bd.), Tex. Soc. Profl. Engrs., Internat. Soc. Asphalt Pavements, Sigma Xi, Phi Kappa Delta, Chi Epsilon, Tau Beta Pi, Phi Kappa Phi. Roman Catholic. Office: Tex A&M U 503A CE Tex Transp Inst Bldg College Station TX 77843-3136 E-mail: rllytton@mail.com.

LYYTINEN, KALLE JUHANI, computer scientist, educator; b. Helsinki, Aug. 19, 1953; arrived in U.S., 2001; s. Veli Kaarlo and Raili Annikki (Lehto) Lyytinen; m. Pirjo-Riitta Taipale, Sept. 6, 1974; children: Joonas, Juho, Markus. BA, U. Jyväskylä (Finland), 1976, MA, 1977, PhD, 1986. Rschr. U. Stockholm, 1981-82; prin. rschr. Acad. Finland, Jyväskylä,

1983-85; vis. rschr. London Sch. Econs., 1986; prof. U. Jyväskylä, 1987—, Hong Kong U. Sci. and Tech., 1993-94; G.E. Smith vis. prof. Ga. State U., 1997, dean, mem. faculty info. tech., 1998-2000; Iris S. Wolstein prof. Case Western Res. U., Cleve., 2001—. Editor: several profl. and acad. jours.; contbr. articles to profl. jours. Served to 3d st. inf. Finnish Army, 1972—73. Mem.: Internat. Fedn. Info. Processing (tech. com. 8, 2d chair 1991—93, chair internat. conf. on info. sys. com. 1998—99). Avocation: literature. Home: 2926 Torrington Rd Shaker Heights OH 44122 Office: Dept Info Sys Weatherhead Sch Mgmt Western Res U 10900 Euclid Ave Cleveland OH 44106-7235 E-mail: kalle@cwru.edu.

MA, FAI, mechanical engineering educator; b. Canton, People's Republic of China, Aug. 6, 1954; came to U.S., 1977, naturalized, 1988; s. Rui-Qi and Shao-Fen (Luo) M. BS, U. Hong Kong, 1977; MS, PhD, Calif. Inst. Tech., 1981. Sr. rsch. engr. Weidlinger Assocs., Menlo Park, Calif., 1981-82; rsch. fellow IBM, Yorktown Heights, N.Y., 1982-83; sr. engr. Standard Oil Co., Cleve., 1983-86; prof. mech. engring. U. Calif., Berkeley, 1986—. Vis. scholar Oxford U., Eng., 1992, U. Stuttgart, Germany, 1993. Co-author: Probabilistic Analysis, 1983, Computational Mechanics, 1989; co-editor Advances in Engring., 1995--; contbr. articles to profl. jours. Young Investigator award NSF, 1987; Humboldt fellow, 1992; Fulbright awardee, 2002. Fellow ASME, Instn. Diagnostic Engrs. Office: U Calif Dept Mech Engring Berkeley CA 94720-0001

MA, JING-HENG SHENG, East Asian languages educator; b. Beijing, Mar. 15, 1932; came to U.S., 1963; d. Xue Shu and Guo Ying (Yin) Sheng; m. Wei-Yi Ma, Sept. 28, 1958; children: Lyou-fu, Syau-fu. BEd, Taiwan Normal U., 1958; MA, Philippine Women's U., 1963; MA in Applied Linguistics, U. Mich., 1971, PhD in Linguistics, 1983. Instr. Chinese Cornell U. Extension Program, Taipei, Taiwan, 1959-62; lectr. Chinese U. Mich., Ann Arbor, 1963-84; assoc. prof., chairperson dept. East Asian langs. Williams Coll., Williamstown, Mass., 1984-88. Vis. prof. Chinese dept. Wellesley Coll., 1988-89, prof., chair dept., 1989-92, 95-98, Mayling Soong prof. Chinese studies, 1997, chair dept., 2000—. Author: Chinese Language Patterns, 1985, A Study of the Mandaring Chinese Verb Suffix Zhe, 1986, At Middle Age: A Learning Guide for Students of Chinese, 1988, 2nd edit. 1991, Strange Friends: A Learning Guide for Students of Chinese, 1989, 2nd edit. 1991, Great Wall: A Learning Guide for Students of Chinese, 1990, 2d edit., 1993, The True Story of Ah Q: A Learning Guide for Students of Chinese, 1992, Difficult Points in Chinese Grammar, 1992, others; co-author: HyperChinese: The Grammar Modules (CD), 1993, Chinese Unmasked: Grammatical Principles and Applications, 1994, HyperChinese: The Pronunciation Modules, 1995, Drills and Quizzes in Mandarin Chinese Pronunciation, 1999, Keys to Chinese Character Writing, 2000, (book and CD) Learning Through Listening: An Introduction to Chinese Proverbs and Thin Origins, 2002. Mem. Chinese Lang. Tchrs. Assn. (exec. bd. 1990-93), Assn. for Asian Studies, Internat. Soc. for Chinese Lang. Tchg. (bd. dirs. 1997—). Home: 10 Nonesuch Dr Natick MA 01760-1041

MA, TSO-PING, electrical engineering educator, researcher, consultant; b. Lan-Tsou, Gan-Su, China, Nov. 13, 1945; arrived in U.S., 1969; s. Liang-Kway and Zwey-Yueen (Liu) Ma; m. Pin-fang Lin, June 10, 1972; children: Mahau, Jasmine. BS, Nat. Taiwan U., 1968; MS, Yale U., 1972, PhD, 1974. Tchg. asst. Yale U., New Haven, 1971—74, asst. prof. elec. engring., 1977—80, assoc. prof., 1980—85, prof., 1985—. Chmn. dept. elec. engring. Yale Chinese Student Svc., 1991—95, acting chmn. dept. elect. engring., 1988, vis. lectr., 1976—77, advisor, 1977—; staff engr. IBM, Hopewell Junction, NY, 1974—77; Whitney Symposium lectr. GE, 1985; hon. prof. Chinese Acad. Scis., 1994—; cons. in field. Contbr. articles to profl. jours. Bd. dirs. New Haven Chinese Sch. Recipient Conn. Yankee Ingenuity award, 1991, Nat. Collegiate Inventor's Advisor award, B.F. Goodrich, 1993, Harding Bliss prize, 1975; grantee, Rsch. Corp., 1978, Mobil Found., 1981—84, GE Found., 1984. Fellow: IEEE (officer semiconductor interface specialists vond. 1986—88, chmn. various coms. 1986—); mem.: Yale Sci. and Engring. Assn., Conn. Acad. Sci. and Engring., Electrochem. Soc., Am. Phys. Soc., Materials Rsch. Soc., Nat. Acad. Engring., Orgn. Chinese Ams. (pres. New Haven chpt. 1988—90, bd. dirs.), Yale Figure Skating Club (v.p. 1991—93, 2000—), Sigma Xi (v.p. Yale chpt. 1986, pres. Yale chpt. 1987—88). Achievements include patents in field. Avocations: music, violin, ice skating. Home: 169 Northford Rd Branford CT 06405-2823

MA, TSU SHENG, chemist, educator, consultant; b. Guangdong, China, Oct. 15, 1911; came to U.S., 1934, naturalized 1956; s. Shao-ching and Sze (Mai) M.; m. Gioh-Fang Dju, Aug. 27, 1942; children: Chopo, Mei-Mei. BS, Tsinghua U., Peking, 1931; PhD, U. Chgo., 1938. Faculty U. Chgo., 1938-46; prof. Peking U., 1946-49; sr. lectr. U. Otago, New Zealand, 1949-51; mem. faculty NYU, 1951-54, CUNY, 1954—, prof. chemistry, 1958—, prof. emeritus, 1980—. Vis. prof. Tsinghua U., 1947, Lingnan, 1949, NYU, 1954-60, Taiwan U., 1961, Chiangmei U., 1968, Singapore U., 1975; hon. prof. Hangzhou Tchrs. Coll., 1998—; specialist Bur. Ednl. and Cultural Affairs State Dept., 1964, Hong Kong, Philippines, Burma, Sri Lanka; Fulbright lectr., 1961-62, 68-69. Author: Small-Scale Experiments in Chemistry, 1962, Organic Functional Group Analysis, 1964, Microscale Manipulations in Chemistry, 1976, Organic Functional Group Analysis by Gas Chromatography, 1976, Quantitative Analysis of Organic Mixtures, 1979, Modern Organic Elemental Analysis, 1979, Organic Analysis Using Ion-Selective Electrodes, 1982, Trace Element Determination in Organic Materials, 1988; editor: Mikrochimica Acta, 1965-89; contbr. articles to profl. jours., chpts. to 10 books. Recipient Benedetti-Pichler award in microchemistry, 1976. Fellow N.Y. Acad. Sci., AAAS, Royal Soc. Chemistry, Am. Inst. Chemists; mem. Am. Chem. Soc., Soc. Applied Spectroscopy, Am. Microchem. Soc., Sigma Xi. Achievements include 1 patent; research in trace element analysis, microchemical investigation of medicinal plants, organic analysis and synthesis in the milligram to microgram range, and the use of small-scale, inexpensive equipment to teach chemistry. Office: CUNY Dept Chemistry Brooklyn NY 11210 Home: 7900 Creedmoor Road #224 Raleigh NC 27613

MA, YAN, information science educator; b. Hangzhou, China, Apr. 27, 1957; came to U.S., 1986; d. Ru-jin Chen and Chao-ying Ma. BA in English, Zhejiang U., 1982; MLS in LS, Kent State U., 1988; postgrad., U. Wis., 1990, PhD in Curriculum and Instrnl and Ednl. Tech., 1993. Instr. English Zhejiang (China) Med. U., 1982-86; grad. asst. Kent (Ohio) State U., 1986-88; tchg. asst. U. Wis., Madison, 1989-91; cataloging libr. Northwestern U., Chgo., 1991-94; asst. prof. U. Wis., Milw., 1994-96, U. R.I., Kingston, 1996—98, assoc. prof., 1999—2003, prof., 2003—. Presenter in field at local, nat., and internat. confs. Editor Jour. Ednl. Media Libr. Sci., 1999-; contbr. articles to profl. jours. Grantee in field. Mem. Internat. Visual Lit. Assn. (bd. dirs. 1994—, pres. 2003-2004), Am. Ednl. Rsch. Assn., Assn. for Ednl. Comm. and Tech., Assn. for Libr. and Info. Sci. Edn., Chinese Am. Librs. Assn. Med. Libr. Assn., Am. Soc for Info. Sci. Office: U RI Grad Sch Libr and Info Sci 94 W Alumni Ave Kingston RI 02881-2016 Home: 142 Vista Cir North Kingstown RI 02852

MABEE, JOHN RICHARD, physician assistant, educator; b. San Francisco, Sept. 18, 1956; s. Robert John and Mary Sachiko (Nose) M.; m. Cheryl Ann Saxton, June 24, 1978 (div. Aug. 1995); children: Jonathan, Alan; m. Carol Mendez, 1998. BS, Regents Coll., 1981; MS, Calif. State U., L.A., 1991; PhD, Union Inst., Cin., 2001. Cert. physician asst., Nat. Commn. Cert. Physician Assts. Physician asst. resident dept. emergency medicine LA County/U. So. Calif. Med. Ctr., 1984-85, emergency medicine physician asst., 1985—. Rsch. asst. dept. biology Calif. State U., L.A., 1987—88, lectr., 1988—91, physician asst., 1992; rsch. physician asst. U. So. Calif. Emergency Medicine Assocs., L.A., 1993—95, clin. instr. dept. emergency medicine, 1994—, conscious sedation adv. com., 1995—, lectr. sch. medicine, 1995—2000, asst. prof. clin. family medicine, 2001—. Contbr. articles to profl. jours. Named Alumnus of Yr., Emergency Medicine Physician Asst. Residency, 1994. Fellow Am. Acad. Physician Assts., Calif. Acad. Physician Assts. (Educator of Yr. 1998); mem. AAAS, N.Y. Acad. Scis., Soc. Emergency Medicine Physician Assts. (founding, election com., 1988—). Democrat. Avocations: reading, watching videos, horseback riding, chess, cooking, Tae Kwon Do. Home: 302 Pamela Kay Ln La Puente CA 91746-2726 Office: U So Calif Keck Sch Medicine 1000 S Fremont Ave Bldg 6 Alhambra CA 91803 E-mail: mabee@email.usc.edu.

MABIE, SUSAN (SUSSE MABIE), secondary education educator; b. Rockville Centre, N.Y., Nov. 13, 1946; d. James Spencer and Marjorie Janet (Van Fleet) Rothston; m. Howard Evon Mabie, June 22, 1968; 1 child, Robin Marie Boyette. AAS in Graphic Arts, SUNY, Farmingdale, 1966; BS in Art Edn., SUNY, Buffalo, 1969; MEd in Art Edn., U. Ctrl. Fla., 1972. Artist, account exec. Graphics III, Inc., N.Y.C., 1966-67; tchr. art Lyman High Sch., Longwood, Fla., 1970-85; tchr. photography and graphic arts, yearbook advisor Oviedo (Fla.) High Sch., 1985-997; sales and svc. rep. Taylor Pub. Co., Dallas, 1997—. Instr. seminars Taylor Pub. Co., 1988—, Sunshine Journalism Workshop, 1991-94. Mem. Fla. Scholastic Press Assn. (coord. state conv. spkrs. 1991, pres. 1995-97, Fla. Journalism Tchr. of Yr. award 1992), Seminole County Art Edn. Assn. (sec. 1991-93), So. Interscholastic Press Assn. (spkr.), Columbia Scholastic Press Assn. (judge), Journalism Edn. Assn., Nat. Scholastic Press Assn. Republican. Home and Office: 1697 Sparkling Water Cir Ocoee FL 34761-9132

MABRY, BETSY, elementary education educator; Tchr. Dewitt Waller Jr. High Sch., Enid, Okla. Named Okla. State Tchr. of Yr., 1993. Office: Dewitt Waller Jr High Sch 2604 W Randolph Ave Enid OK 73703-4031

MABRY, CATHY DARLENE, elementary school administrator; b. Atlanta, Dec. 9, 1951; d. German William and Erma Isabel (Lyons) M. BA in Sociology and Psychology, U. Ga., 1975; Cert. in Edn., Oglethorpe U., Atlanta, 1983, MA in Elem. Edn., 1990; MA in Adminstrn. & Supv. Edn., Ga. State U., 1997. Cert. in early childhood edn., Ga. Charge account svcs. staff C&S Nat. Bank, Atlanta, 1974-75; with Rich's, Decatur, Ga., 1975-76, 79-84; mgr. trainee sales Sears Roebuck & Co., Decatur, 1974-75, 76-78; intermediate clk. Superior Ct. of DeKalb County, Decatur, 1978-81; paraprofl. kindergarten DeKalb County Sch. Sys., Decatur, 1979-81, tchr., 1984-98. Mem. sch.-based mgmt. com. Hooper Alexander Sch., Decatur, 1991-92, strategic planning com., 1990-96; mem. social studies curriculum com. DeKalb County Sch. Sys., 1990-91, tchr. forum rep., 1992-95. Author poetry in Am. Poetry Anthology, 1986. Sec. Lithonia Civic League, Inc., 1987-94, Teen Scene, Inc., Lithonia, 1993-94; chair bd. dirs. DeKalb Econ. Opportunity Authority, Decatur, 1991-92, 93-94; mem. Teach Well Wellness Program, Emory U. Sch. Pub. Health, 1994; active PTA. Mem. NAACP, Nat. Coun. of Negro Women, Inc., Nat. Geog. Soc., DeKalb Assn. Educators, Zeta Phi Beta. Democrat. Baptist. Avocations: reading, cooking, nature walks, writing poetry, listening to gospel/jazz. Home: 1430 Smithson Dr Lithonia GA 30058-6156 Office: Edward L Bouie Theme Sch 5100 Rock Springs Rd Lithonia GA 30038-2328

MABUS, BARBARA JEAN, secondary science educator; b. Cleve., Nov. 6, 1950; d. Elmer Wilhelm and Florence Pauline Witzke; m. Stephen Michael Mabus, June 29, 1974; 1 child, Mark Samuel. BS in Edn., Bowling Green U., 1973, postgrad., 1991, 94, 98, Baldwin-Wallace Coll., 1991, U. Toledo, 1997, Ashland U., 2002—03. Lic. English and earth sci. educator 7-12, spl. learning disabilities K-12 Ohio. Tchr. lang. arts Bellefontaine (Ohio) City Schs., 1973-74; substitute tchr. Bryan (Ohio) City Schs., 1974-76, 90-93, spl. needs tutor, 1993-96, tchr. sci., 1996—, vol. art appreciation tchr., 1988-91. Substitute tchr. Williams County Schs., Bryan, 1974-76, 90-92; tchr. sci., health and phys. edn. St. Patrick Sch., Bryan, 1991. Leader 4-H, Bryan, 1987-96; mem. Clowns of Grace, Bryan, 1991-94; youth leader Grace Cmty. Ch., Bryan, 1992-93; prayer coord. Celebrate Life Christian Fellowship, 2002—. Mem.: NEA, Nat. Sci. Tchrs. Assn., Ohio Mid. Sch. Assn., Bryan Edn. Assn. (scholarship com. 1993—94), Ohio Edn. Assn., Nat. Multiple Sclerosis Soc., Academic Booster Club. Avocations: quilting, collecting memories, writing, hiking, clown ministry. Home: 219 Lakeview Dr Bryan OH 43506 Office: Bryan Mid Sch 1301 Center St Bryan OH 43506-9125

MACARTNEY, NORMAN SCARBOROUGH, retired middle school educator; b. Pt. Washington, N.Y., Oct. 29, 1938; s. Horace Bramwell Macartney and Jean Sheila MacPhail; m. Armena Virginia Dolloff, June 15, 1968; children: Lisa Kimberly, Jennifer Lynn, David Cameron. Bachelor's, Colby Coll., 1961. Field geologist Core Labs., Bogota, Colombia, 1964-65; asst. geophysicist Atlantic Refining Co., Dallas, Tex., 1965-66; tchr. sci. and math. Cardigan Mountain Sch., Canaan, N.H., 1966-68, Selwyn Sch., Denton, Tex., 1968-69, Cistercian Prep. Sch., Irving, Tex., 1969-71, Rippowam Cisqua Sch., Bedford, N.Y., 1971-81, head sci. dept., 1974-81; pres., owner Dalijen Landscaping Design, Katonah, N.Y., 1985-94; ret. Author: Probing the Heart, 2000, Seasons of Value, 2003. With USN, 1961-63. Mem. U.S. Master's Swimming (Top 10, 1998, nat.). Avocations: motorcycling, swimmng, writing. Home: 729 Comet Dr Beaufort NC 28516

MACCINI, LOUIS JOHN, economic educator; b. Cambirdge, Mass., Aug. 3, 1942; s. Joseph and Jennie (Leccacorvi) M.; m. Carol Monterisi, June 25, 1965; children: Michael S., Sharon L. BS in Economics, Boston Coll., 1965; PhD in Economics, Northwestern U., 1970. From asst. prof. to assoc. prof. economics The Johns Hopkins U., Balt., 1969-86, prof., 1986—, chair, 1992—. Ad hoc com. mem. graduate fin. aid, Johns Hopkins U., editorial bd., public interest investment adv. com., law sch. com., med. sch. com., and other coms.; mem. recruting chair dept. grad. student advisor dept., and other depts. Referee Am. Econ. Review, Jour. Econ. Dynamics and Control, Oxford Econ. Papers, and others; contbr. articles to profl. jours. Grantee NSF. Mem. Am. Econ. Assn., The Econometric Soc., Internat Soc. Inventory Rsch. Office: Johns Hopkins U 3400 N Charles St Baltimore MD 21218-2680 E-mail: maccini@jhu.edu.

MACCONI, MARY DAVIS, secondary education educator; b. Birchleaf, Va., May 16, 1942; d. Albert H. and Gaynell Davis; m. Horace R. Macconi; children: Beth, Richard, Gina Sue. BA in Arts and Scis., U. Del., 1978; EdM, Wilmington Coll., 2002. Owner, operator RiGi's Amusement Ctrs., Stone Harbor, N.J., 1978—; English tchr. Penns Grove (N.J.) H.S., 1985—. Mem. Nat. Coun. Tchrs., N.J. Edn. Assn. Avocation: restoration of antiques. Home: 9 Jefferson Ave Pennsville NJ 08070-1309 Office: 321 96th St Stone Harbor NJ 08247-1405

MACCREERY, NEAL JOSEPH, education educator; b. Phila., Aug. 9, 1941; s. Joseph R. and Sophia (Pawluk) MacC.; m. Kathleen Marie MacCreery, Dec. 23, 1977; 1 child, Joshua Neal. BS in Edn., SUNY, Brockport, 1969; MEd, U. Rochester, 1972, CAS, 1982, EdD, 1992. Lic. elem. tchr., sch. prin., supt., N.Y. Elem. tchr. SUNY, Brockport, 1969-71; reading tchr. 7th-9th grade Rush-Henrietta (N.Y.) City Sch. Dist., 1971-73; dir. reading, spl. programs Marion (N.Y.) City Sch. Dist., 1973-76; elem. prin., dir. spl. edn. Herkimer (N.Y.) City Sch. Dist., 1976-84; dir. spl. edn. Utica (N.Y.) City Sch. Dist., 1984-87; asst. prof. Roberts Wesleyan Coll., Rochester, N.Y., 1987-88, SUNY, Oneonta, 1989—. Right to read regional cons. N.Y. State Edn. Dept., Albany, 1973-78, test exam writer, 1978-82, 90; chairperson adv. bd. N.Y. State Devel. Disabilities Community Program, Herkimer, 1978-82. Contbr. articles to profl. jours. Coord. Spl. Olympics, Oneonta, 1990-92, vol. Holiday Project, Oneonta, 1990-91; v.p., mgr., exec. bd. mem. Oneonta Little League, 1990—; founder Kards for Kids, Oneonta, 1991-94. Profl. Devel. grantee N.Y. State United Tchrs., 1990. Mem. N.Y. State Assn. Tchr. Educators, N.Y. State Reading Assn., Assn. N.Y. State Educators of Emotionally Handicapped Students, Catskill Area Reading Coun., Phi Delta Kappa (chpt. pres., rsch. rep. 1985—, Outstanding Dissertation award). Avocations: desk-top publishing, computer technology, collecting sport cards, traveling, working with young children. Home: PO Box 636 Oneonta NY 13820-0636 Office: SUNY 420 Fitzelle Hall Oneonta NY 13820

MACDIARMID, ALAN GRAHAM, metallurgist, educator; b. Masterton, New Zealand, Apr. 14, 1927; married, 1954; 4 children. BSc, U. New Zealand, 1948, MSc, 1950; MS, U. Wis., 1952, PhD in Chemistry, 1953, Cambridge U., 1955. Asst. lectr. in chemistry St. Andrews U., 1955; from instr. to assoc. prof. U. Pa., Phila., 1955-64, Sloan fellowship, 1959-63, prof. chemistry, 1964—, Blanchard prof. chemistry, 1998—. Recipient Frederic Stanley Kipping award, 1970, Marshall award, 1982, Doolittle award, 1982, Chemical Pioneer award, 1984, Royal Soc. of Chem. Centenary Medal, Francis J. Clamer medal, Franklin Inst., 1993, Nobel Prize in Chemistry, 2000. Mem.: Royal Soc. Chemistry, Am. Chem. Soc. Achievements include preparation and characterization of organosilicon compounds; preparation and charachterization of derivatives of sulfur nitrides and quasi one-dimensional semiconducting and metallic covalent polymers such as polyacetylene and its derivatives. Office: U Pa Dept Chemistry Rm 343 231 S 34th St Philadelphia PA 19104-3803*

MACDONALD, DIGBY DONALD, scientist, science administrator; b. Thames, New Zealand, Dec. 7, 1943; came to U.S., 1977; s. Leslie Graham and Francis Helena (Verry) M.; m. Cynthia Lynch, 1969; m. Mirna Urquidi, July 6, 1985; children: Leigh Vanessa, Matthew Digby, Duncan Paul, Nahline. BS in Chemistry, U. Auckland, New Zealand, 1965; MS in Chemistry with honors, U. Auckland, 1966; PhD, U. Calgary, Alta., Can., 1969. Asst. research officer Atomic Energy of Can., Pinawa, Man., Can., 1969-72; lectr. Victoria U., Wellington, New Zealand, 1972-75; sr. research assoc., assoc prof. Alta. Sulfur Research U. Calgary, 1975-77; sr. metallurgist SRI Internat., Menlo Park, Calif., 1977-79; prof. metall. engring. Ohio State U., Columbus, Ohio, 1979-84; lab dir., dep. dir. phys. scis. divsn. SRI Internat., Menlo Park, 1984-91; prof. material sci. engring., dir. Ctr. Advanced Materials Pa. State U., 1991-98, 99—; v.p. pure and applied phys. sci. SRI Internat., 1998-99. Adj. prof. Ohio Stae U., 1984; W.B. Lewis Meml. lectr. Atomic Energy Can., 1993; mem. USAF Sci. Adv. Bd., 1993-97; cons. in field; A.B. Lewis lectr. Atomic Energy Can., Ltd., 1993. Author: Transient Techniques in Electrochemistry, 1977; contbr. numerous articles to profl. jours.; patentee in field. Nat. Rsch. Coun. scholar, Ottawa, Can., 1967-69; recipient Rsch. award Ohio State U., 1983, Wilson Rsch. award Pa. State U., 1994, 96. Fellow Nat. Assn. Corrosion Engrs. Internat. (pub. com. 1982-85, Whitney award), Electrochem. Soc. (divsn. editor 1982-84, C. Wagner Meml. award 1991), Royal Soc. Can., Royal Soc. of New Zealand. Avocation: sailing. Office: Pa State U 517 Deike Bldg University Park PA 16802-2714

MACDONALD, JANE CRONIN, elementary school educator, supervisor; b. Bklyn., June 12, 1950; d. Joseph Victor and Edith Rita (Ferrari) Cronin; m. Kenneth Francis MacDonald, Dec. 22, 1973; 1 child, Amanda Jane. BA, Georgian Ct. Coll., 1971; MA, Kean Coll. N.J., 1975; EdD, Nova Southeastern U., 1984. Cert. elem. tchr., reading tchr., reading specialist, nursery sch. tchr., adminstr./supr., N.J. Elem. sch. tchr. Toms River (N.J.) Regional Schs., 1971—. Instr. reading Brookdale C.C., Lincroft, N.J., 1994; instr. humanities Ocean County Coll., Toms River, 1992—; cons. DJ Mac Assocs., Island Heights, N.J., 1984—; internat. cons. Creative Publs.; N.E. regional mgr. Creative Publ./Chgo. Tribune. Prodr., host Going Strong! Growing Straight! series, Toms River, 1982-85, Parent Express TV show, Toms River, 1994; rschr. in field. Bd. dirs. Parent Kid Tips, South Toms River, 1992-94; mem. com. N.J. Edn. Assn., 1984-86; assembly del. NEA, Washington, 1980-85. Hilda Maehling fellow NEA, 1984. Mem. AAUW, ASCD, Assn. for Childhood Edn. Internat., Nat. Assn. for Edn. of Young Children, Georgian Ct. Coll. Alumni Assn. (v.p. of clubs 1981-87), Phi Delta Kappa, Alpha Delta Kappa. Republican. Roman Catholic. Avocations: reading, baking, travel, creating rainbows. Home: 720 Dunedin St Toms River NJ 08753-4514 Office: DJ Mac Assocs PO Box 908 Island Heights NJ 08732-0908 E-mail: djmacassoc@aol.com.

MACDONALD, JOHN THOMAS, educational administrator; b. Utica, N.Y., Nov. 21, 1932; s. Gerald Clement and Mildred (Hayes) MacD.; m. Marcia Sprague Gallup; children: Terrence (dec.), Anthony, Elizabeth, Michele, Elise, Denise. BS, Northeastern U., 1958, MEd, 1960; PhD, U. Conn., 1970. Cert. elem. and secondary sch. tchr., prin., supt., Mass., Conn. Supervising prin. Noank, Ft. Hill. and Poquonnock Elem. Schs., Groton, Conn., 1962-66, Robert E. Fitch Jr. High Sch., Groton, 1966-70; rsch. asst. Ednl. Resources and Devel. Ctr. U. Conn., Storrs, 1969-70; supt. schs. Wallingford (Conn.) Pub. Schs., 1970-73, Walpole (Mass.) Pub. Schs., 1973-78, Dartmouth (Mass.) Pub. Schs., 1978-86; commr. edn. State Dept. Edn., Concord, N.H., 1986-90; asst. sec. for elem. and secondary edn. U.S. Dept. Edn., Washington, 1990-93; dir. state leadership ctr. Coun. of Chief State Sch. Officers, Washington, 1993-99, sr. advisor, 2000-01; prof. of ednl. policy and leadership Neag Sch. Edn., U. Conn., 2001—; dir. NE Ctr. for Ednl. Policy and Leadership. Mem. Postsecondary Edn. Commn., Concord, 1986-90, Coun. for Tchr. Edn., Concord, 1986-90, Profl. Standards Bd., Concord, 1986-90; trustee Univ. System of N.H., Durham, 1986-90; mem. Surgeon Gen's Task Force, 1990-93; mem. White House Conf. on Indian Edn., 1990-93; mem. Interagy. Com. on Sch. Health, 1990-93, others; mem. dean's adv. coun. U. Conn., 1999—, Coll. Arts and Scis., Northeastern U., 1999—; mem. adv. coun. Va. Edn. Policy Inst., Va. Commonwealth U., 2000—; mem. adv. bd. ERIC, Washington, 1998—. Contbr. articles to profl. jours. Co-chmn. Emergency Sch.-Aide Proposals, U.S. Office Edn., 1973—75; mem. adv. com. external program rev. CDC, 1992—; mem. nat. adv. bd. ERIC Clearinghouse, 1999—; mem. Mass. Adv. Commn. for Ednl. TV, 1983—86, N.H. Task Force on Child Abuse, 1987—90; mem. nat. adv. coun. Northeastern U., 1990—; mem. Galaxy Classroom Nat. Adv. Coun. Galaxy Inst. for Edn., 1992—; mem. sch. health policy initiative Ctr. for Population & Family Health Columbia U., 1992—; mem. Packard roundtable to children Ctr. for Health Policy George Washington U., 1992—; mem. adv. bd. Va. Commonwealth Policy Inst., 1999—; mem. Dean's adv. council Neag Sch. Edn. U. Conn., 1999—, Coll. Arts & Scis. Northeastern U., 1999—. Recipient Sears B. Condit award, 1958, Alumni award Northwestern U., 1973, Recognition award Coun. of Chief State Sch. Officers, 1990. Fellow Phi Delta Kappa, Phi Alpha Theta; mem. N.H. Sch. Bldg. Authority, Mass. Assn. Sch. Supts. (pres. 1985-86). Office: U Conn Neag Sch Edn Dept Ednl Leadership 249 Glenbrook Rd Box U-2093 Storrs Mansfield CT 06269-2064 E-mail: macmarjack@aol.com.

MACDONALD, KAREN HOPE COWART, educator, reading specialist; b. Denver, Dec. 10, 1942; d. John Roscoe Cowart and Wanda Lorraine (Johnson) Cook; m. Charles Monte Dennis, Aug. 26, 1961 (div. 1979); children: Van Loren, Jon Charles, Kit Emery, Wanda Renee Dennis McGuire. BS in Edn., N.Mex. State U., 1975; MA in Edn., Ea. N.Mex. U., 1983. Cert. tchr., Tex., N.Mex. Tchr. 1st grade Carlsbad (N.Mex.) Mcpl. Schs., 1975-76; tchr. reading, 1st grade Hobbs (N.Mex.) Mcpl. Schs., 1976-87; reading tchr., dept. chair Bel Air High Sch., El Paso, 1987-94. Instr. reading workshops Ea. N.Mex. U., Portales, 1982-86; reading instr. El Paso C.C., 1990—. Mem. ASCD, MADD, Internat. Reading Assn. (pres. Hobbs coun. 1985-86, bd. dirs. El Paso coun. 1989-92), Civitan, Women in Politics, Phi Delta Kappa. Democrat. Methodist. Avocations: reading, physical fitness. Home: 4651 Oakwood Dr Apt 43 Odessa TX 79761-2023

MACDONALD, ROBERT ALAN, language educator, educator; b. Salamanca, N.Y., Mar. 25, 1927; s. Guy E. and Hildur V. (Helene) MacD. BA, U. Buffalo, 1948; MA, U. Wis., 1949, PhD, 1958. Asst. prof. U. Richmond, Va., 1955-61, assoc. prof., 1961-67, prof. Spanish, 1967-95, prof. emeritus, 1995; ofcl. project reviewer NEH, Washington, 1977-95; mem. Social Sci.

and Humanties Rsch. Coun., Ottawa, Ont., Can., 1981-95. Author: Espéculo, texto juridico atribuido a Alfonso X, 1990, Alfonso X, Libro de las Tahurerias, 1995, Alfonso X, Libro de los Adelantados Mayores, 2000; editor Bull. of Fgn. Lang. Assn. Va., 1962-67, 72-86; contbr. articles to profl. jours. With U.S. Army, 1946-47, 51-53. A.L. Markham traveling fellow U. Wis., 1958-59, Am. Coun. Learned Socs. fellow, 1976; fellow, grantee U. Richmond, 1958-94; named Cultural Laureate of Va., 1977; recipient Disting. Svc. award Fgn. Lang. Assn. Va., 1981. Mem. Acad. Am. Rsch. Historians on Medieval Spain, Am. Assn. Spanish and Portuguese (past pres. state chpt.), AAUP (past pres. local chpt.), Am. Coun. on Tchg. Fgn. Langs., Medieval Acad. Am. MLA, Torch Club (Richmond).

MACDONALD, WILLIAM BURKE, secondary education educator, education consultant; b. Chgo., Dec. 19, 1942; s. William C. nad Jane (Burke) MacD.; m. Mary E. Kotre, Dec. 1968; children: Colleen, Kevin. AB, Regis U., Denver, 1964; MEd, Loyola U., Chgo., 1968. Nat. cert. counselor. Tchr. Lindop Sch., Broadview, Ill., 1964-68; guidance dir. Miner Jr. H.S., Arlington Heights, Ill., 1968-70; tchr. Addison Trail H.S., Addison, Ill., 1970—94, guidance dir., 1982-94; crises counselor Alexian Bros. Med. Ctr., 1996-99; field reporter Heartbeat Schaumburg Park Dist. Cable Access, 2000—. Mem. parish coun. Ch. of the Holy Spirit, Schaumburg, 1993—. Mem. AFT (pres. DuPage Coun. 1981-84), Suburban Dirs. Guidance (pres. 1993-94). Avocations: photography, computers. Home: 430 Greenhill Ln Schaumburg IL 60193-1764 Office: 430 Greenhill Ln Schaumburg IL 60193-1764

MACDOUGALL, JOHN DOUGLAS, environmental scientist educator, science administrator, academic administrator; b. Toronto, Ont., Can., Mar. 9, 1944; s. Lorn Graham and Grace A. (Virtue) MacD.; m. Shiela Dawn Ward, June 8, 1968; children: Christopher David, Katherine Heather. BS, U. Toronto, 1967; MS, McMaster U., 1968; PhD, U. Calif.-San Diego, 1972. Asst. rsch. geologist U. Calif., Berkeley, 1972-74; prof. earth scis. Scripps Inst. Oceanography U. Calif.-San Diego, La Jolla, 1974—, chmn. geol. rsch. divsn., 1985-89, dir. program in earth scis., 1995-99; dir. U. Calif. Edn. Abroad Office (Edinburgh), 1999—2001. Contbr. articles to profl. jours. Fellow Am. Geophys. Union and Meteoritical Soc.; mem. AAAS, Geochem. Soc. Home: 534 Bonair St La Jolla CA 92037-6112 Office: Scripps Inst Oceanography # 0220 La Jolla CA 92093

MAC DOWELL, SAMUEL WALLACE, physics educator; b. Camaragibe, Brazil, Mar. 24, 1929; came to U.S., 1963; s. Samuel Wallace and Maria Anita (Amazonas) Mac D.; m. Myriam Ramos Da Silva, Feb. 2, 1953; children: Ana Myriam, Samuel Wallace, Maria Dolores. BSc in Engring., U. Pernambuco, Brazil, 1951; PhD in Math. Physics, Birmingham (Eng.) U., 1958. Rsch. assoc. Princeton (N.J.) U., 1959-60; assoc. prof. Centro Brasileiro De Fisicas Pesquisas, Rio de Janeiro, 1960-63; fellow Inst. for Advanced Study, Princeton, 1963-65; assoc. prof. Yale U., New Haven, 1965-67, prof., 1968—. Fellow Am. Phys. Soc.; mem. Brazilian Acad. Scis. Roman Catholic. Office: Yale U Sloane Physics Lab PO Box 208120 New Haven CT 06520-8120

MACDUFF, ILONE MARGARET, music educator; b. Berwyn, Ill., Jan. 30, 1938; d. Albert Kenneth Hinckle and Dorothy Lydia Ardina Lange; m. James Donald Macduff, Jr., Apr. 2, 1959; children: Gordon Scott, James Alexander, Charles Colin. MusB, U. Idaho, 1976. Internat. rep. Boy Scouts Am., 1983—93; mem. Thurston County (Wash.) Hist. Commrs., 1984—98; active Boy Scouts Am., Tumwater, Wash., 1968—93, dist. Cub Scout program chmn., 1973—75, mem. coun. Pow Wow staff, 1973—76; founder Cub Scout Day Camp, Tumwater Area Coun., 1973; chmn. Coun. Scout-O-Rama, 1979, 1980, 1981; mem. coun. Eagle bd. Boy Scouts Am., 1985—90; dir. monthly musicales State Captial Mus., 1970—74. Recipient Single and Double awards, Nat. Fedn. Music Clubs, 1969, 1977, Silver Beaver award, Boy Scouts Am., 1981, Disting. Commr. award, 1981, Lamb award, 1987. Mem.: Olympia Music Tchrs. Assn. (pres. 2003—), Music Tchrs. Nat. Assn. (Olympia chpt. voice auditions chair 2001), Gordon Setter Club Am. (chmn. nat. dog show 2003), Puget Sound Gordon Setter Club (treas. 1998—2000, show chmn. 2003). Lutheran. Avocation: photography. Home: 8524 Delphi Rd SW Olympia WA 98512

MACEWAN, BARBARA ANN, middle school educator, historian; b. Adams, Mass., Apr. 22, 1938; d. Thomas Lawrence and Vera (Ziemba) Gaskalka; m. George Louie MacEwan, Feb. 16, 1963; children: Rebecca, Debra. BS in Edn. cum laude, North Adams State Coll., 1959; MEd with honors, Plymouth State Coll., 1994. Cert. K-8, secondary social studies tchr., sch. libr., Mass. Tchr. Town of Valatie, N.Y., 1959-61, 62-63, Dept. Def., Aachefensburg, Germany, 1961-62, Town of East Longmeadow, Mass., 1964; asst. children's libr. Springfield (Mass.) Libr., 1964; tchr. history Southwick (Mass.)-Tolland Regional Schs., 1971—2001. State coord. Nat. History Day, 1989-92; curriculum coord. mid. sch. Southwick-Tolland Regional Schs., 1995-96, 97—, vice chair Cmty. Preservation Com. 2003, chair New Haven/Northampton Canal Nat. Register Com. 2002-. Author: The Old Cemetery: Southwick, 1977, Shays Rebellion, 1987, The Princess, 1995, Indian Images, Text for Traveling Indian Images Display. Sec. Southwick Hist. Soc., 1976-79, treas., 1979-86, pres., 1986-94; trustee Moore House, Southwick, 1989—; chair Southwick Hist. Commn., 1994—; Mass. Curriculum Framework Focus Group, 1994-96; mem. Southwick Master Plan com., 1996-98; bd. dirs. Pioneer Valley Inst., 2001—; mem. Cmty. Preservation Com., Southwick, 2003—, vice chmn. 2003—. Recipient recognition New Eng. League Mid. Schs., 1991, Recognition for Cmty. Svc. Southwick Selectmen, 1998; Horace Mann grantee Southwick Sch. Com., 1982, Southwest Regional Alliance grantee. Mem. ASCD, NEA, Mass. Tchrs. Assn., New Eng. Oral History Assn., New Eng. Hisotry Tchrs. Assn., Nat. Coun. for Social Studies, Mass. Coun. Social Studies (recognition 1992), Western Mass. Coun. for Social Studies (bd. dirs. 1987-95), Mass. Assn. Ednl. Media, Nat. Mus. Am. Indian, New Eng. Native Am. Inst., Pioneer Valley Inst., Historic Mass., Nat. Women's Hall Fame, Nat. Trust Historic Preservation, Phi Delta Kappa. Roman Catholic. Avocations: gardening, walking, reading, travel. Office: Town Hall 454 College Hwy Southwick MA 01077-9324

MACFARLAND, MARY HARRIS, home economics educator; b. Lincoln, Maine, Jan. 9, 1954; d. Jerrold Earnest and Helen Elizabeth (Wakefield) Harris; m. James Issac MacFarland, Feb. 14, 1976; children: Martha Anne, Michelle Rae. BS, U. Maine, 1975. Tchr. home econs. SAD #13, Bingham, Maine, 1976-78, Erskine Acad., South China, Maine, 1978—. Student coun. advisor Erskine Acad., 1984—. Leader Kemebee coun. Girl Scouts Am., Maine, 1990-2000; mem., chair China Sch. Com., 1988-91. Mem. Nat. Assn. State Student Coun. Exec. Dirs., Nat. Assn. Secondary Sch. Advisors, Nat. Assn. Workshop Dirs., Maine Assn. Student Coun. Dirs. (exec. dir. 1992—). Avocation: sewing. Home: PO Box 116 South China ME 04358-0116

MACGREGOR, BONNIE LYNN, school administrator; b. Buffalo, Apr. 18, 1948; d. John Stevenson and Sylvia Marie (Bailey) MacG.; m. Franklin H. McCulloch, July 28, 1976. AAS, Erie County Tech. Inst., Buffalo, 1968; BS, SUCABNY, Buffalo, 1971, MS, 1976; postgrad, Nova Southeastern U., 1993—. Cert. bus. and distributive edn. and workstudy tchr., N.Y. Asst. bus. mgr. Sta. WKBW-TV-AM, Buffalo, 1968-75; tchr., chmn. dept. bus. Cheektowaga Cen. High Sch., Buffalo, 1975-82; lectr. D'Youville Coll., Buffalo, 1982-87; curriculum coord. Bryant and Stratton Bus. Schs., Buffalo, 1987-90, acad. dean, 1990-91, dir. edn., 1991-93, sch. dir., 1993-94; edn. dir., 1994—. Contbr. numerous articles to profl. jours. Mem. BTANYS (past pres.), Am. Vocat. Assn., BEAWNY (Post-Secondary Tchr. of Yr. 1986), NYSOEA, NYSCEA, EBEA, NBEA, ASCD, NAFE, Nova Doctoral PHE Candidates (grad. student coun. 1993), Alpha Lambda.

MACHAMER, SYLVIA GERALDINE, special education educator; b. Visalia, Calif., Oct. 3, 1939; d. Henry Ross and Lucille Marian (Alvarez) Mata; m. Milton Lynn Machamer, June 17, 1962; children: Jonathan (dec.), Leah, Anne Marie, Jill, Ryan, Daniel. AA, Coll. of Sequoia, Visalia, Calif., 1959; BA, San Jose State U., 1961, spl. edn. cert., 1977. Cert. elem. tchr., spl. edn. elem. and secondary, Calif. Tchr. 2nd and 3rd grade Noble Sch. Berryessa Dist., San Jose, Calif., 1961-62; 3rd grade tchr. L.A. Sch. Dist., 1962-63; 2nd and head start tchr. Toyon Sch. Berryessa Dist., San Jose, 1963-67; supplemental educator grade 1, 4, 6. Garden Gate Sch., Cupertino, Calif., 1969—, educator learninc handicapped students, 1969—, educator severely handicapped students, 1969—. Cons. and workshop presenter to sch. dists. state and nationwide, 1988—; video mentor tchr., Cupertino Union Sch. Dist., 1991-93; intervention specialist, 1994—. Developer Gift of Reading Program, Computerized I.E.P. Program. Chmn. Indian Edn. Parent Com. Fremont High Sch. Dist., 1991-93. Recipient Continuing Svc. award Garden Gate PTA, Cupertino, 1989, Eagle Feather award Title U Coalition, 1993. Mem. De Anza Coll. Cable TV, Computer Using Educators, Parents Helping Parents (Outstanding Educator 1991), Coastal Band of Chumash Nation. Avocations: video, computers, walking, reading, Native Am. affairs. Office: Garden Gate Sch 10500 Ann Arbor Ave Cupertino CA 95014-1697 Home: 1 Mt Rose Ln Petaluma CA 94952-5268

MACHEN, ETHEL LOUISE LYNCH, retired academic administrator; b. Chgo., July 16, 1938; d. Samuel Thomas and Louise (Brown) Lynch; m. Robert Caldwell Jr., Sept. 7, 1957 (div. 1968); m. Ronald C. Machen, July 27, 1997. BS in Bus. Edn., DePaul U., 1976; MS in Counseling Psychology, MS in Adminstrn., George Williams Coll., Downers Grove, Ill., 1979. Lic. tchr., Ill. Sec. Inland Steel Co., Chgo., 1957-68; adminstrv. asst. 1st Nat. City Bank, St. Thomas, V.I., 1968-71; pers./purchasing mgr. Peoples Bank of V.I., St. Thomas, 1971-73; bus. edn. tchr. Ctrl. YMCA Coll., Chgo., 1976, Chgo. Profl. Coll., 1976-78; rsch. asst. U. Ill., Chgo., 1978-79, rsch. assoc., 1980-81, asst. dir. early outreach, 1981-83, dir. early outreach, 1983-98; ret. Pres. Lynch Enterprises, Summit, Ill., 1987—; cons. Chgo. Pub. Schs. Monitoring Commn. for Desegregation Implementation, 1996-97; mem. adv. bd. Ctr. for Ednl. R&D U. Ill., Chgo., 1989-98, Project Canal, Chgo. Pub. Schs., 1990-92; mem. exec. bd. Chgo. Coun. Postsecondary Edn., 1989-91; lectr. African-Am. Studies Ctr., Smithsonian Inst., Washington, 1992; mem. counselor articulation bd. DePaul U., 1993-97; field reader U.S. Dept. Edn., 1993—, U.S. Dept. Energy, 1995; mem. adv. coun. Greater Chgo. Youth Behavior Project, 1993-97. Active Chgo. Urban League, Lulac Coun. 5201, 1988-91, Ill. Com. on Black Concerns in Higher Edn., 1989-98. Recipient Health Careers Opportunity Program award U.S. Dept. HHS, 1987-80, 93-95, Dept. HHS Pub. Health Svcs., 1994, 95, Disting. Alumna award Argo Community High Sch., 1993, Dean's Merit award Coll. of Edn., 1998, Early Outreach Eagle award, 1998. Mem. Am. Assn. for Higher Edn. (Achievement award 1991), Nat. Assn. for Coll. Admissions Counselors, Assn. Black Women in Higher Edn. (founding mem. Chgo. chpt.). Baptist. Avocations: horticulture, reading, walking, travel.

MACHLIN, EUGENE SOLOMON, metallurgy educator, consultant; b. N.Y.C., Dec. 29, 1920; s. Gershon and Rose (Kaplan) M.; m. Edda Servi, May 21, 1960; children: Rona Susan, Argia Debora; m. Gertrude Green, Oct. 15, 1943 (dec. May 1959); 1 child, Chester Elia. BME, CCNY, 1942; MS, Case Inst. Tech., 1948; ScD, MIT, 1950. Aero. rsch. scientist Nat. Adv. Commn. Aeronautics, Cleve., 1942-48; rsch. assoc., asst. prof. MIT, Cambridge, 1948-50, 50-51; asst. prof. Columbia U., N.Y.C., 1951-54, assoc. prof., 1954-58, prof. metallurgy, 1958-89, Howe prof., 1989-91, Howe prof. emeritus, 1991—. Cons. Spl. Metals Corp., Utica, N.Y., 1951-76; cons., dir. UV Industries, N.Y.C., 1966-79; summer faculty fellow IBM T.J. Watson Res. Lab., 1984-90. Author: An Introduction to Aspects of Thermodynamics and Kinetics Relevant to Materials Science, 1990, Materials Science in Microelectronics—The Relationships Between Thin Film Processing and Structure, 1995, Materials Science in Microelectronics—The Effects of Structure on Properties in Thin Films, 1998; editor: Synthesis of Metastable Phases, 1980; inventor Udimet 700, 1960. Chmn. solid state scis. adv. com. Office Sci. Rsch. USAF, Washington, 1954-59. Recipient C.H. Mathewson Gold medal AIME, 1954; Guggenheim fellow, 1965 Fellow AIME; mem. Am. Soc. Metals (Achievement award 1961, Edn. award 1974). Democrat. Jewish. Office: Columbia U 500 W 120th St New York NY 10027-6623

MACIAS, EDWARD S. chemistry educator, university official and dean; b. Milw., Feb. 21, 1944; s. Arturo C. Macias and Minette (Schwenger) Wiederhold; m. Paula Wiederhold, June 17, 1967; children: Matthew Edward, Julia Katherine. AB, Colgate U., 1966; PhD, MIT, 1970. Asst. prof. Washington U., St. Louis, 1970-76, assoc. prof., 1976-84, prof. chemistry, 1984—, chmn. dept., 1984-88, provost, 1988-95, interim dean Faculty Arts and Scis., 1994-95, exec. vice chancellor and dean Faculty Arts and Scis., 1995—. Cons. Meteorology Rsch., Inc., Altadina, Calif., 1978-81, Salt River Project, Phoenix, 1980-83, Santa Fe Rsch., Bloomington, Minn., 1985-88, AeroVironment, Inc., Monrovia, Calif., 1986-88. Author: Nuclear and Radiochemistry, 1981; editor: Atmospheric Aerosol, 1981; contbr. numerous articles to profl. jours. Bd. dirs. Mark Twain Summer Inst., St. Louis, 1984-87, 88-90, The Coll. Sch., St. Louis, 1984-88, Colgate U., 1997—. Grantee NSF, EPA, Electric Power Rsch. Inst., So. Calif. Edison Co., Dept. Energy, AEC. Mem. Am. Chem. Soc., Am. Assn. Aerosol Rsch. (editorial bd.), Am. Phys. Soc., AAAS. Home: 6907 Waterman Ave Saint Louis MO 63130-4333 Office: Washington U Campus Box 1094 One Brookings Dr Saint Louis MO 63130

MACINNES, SALLY ACKERMAN, computer education educator; b. Columbus, Ind., Nov. 12, 1946; d. Louis L. and Josephine K. Ackerman; m. James C. MacInnes, June 13, 1981; children: Todd Keenan, Jennifer Mangel, Christopher Keenan, Daniel Keenan. BA, U. Iowa, Iowa City, 1968; MS, No. Ill. U., Dekalb, 1989; postgrad., Nat. Coll. Edn., Evanston, Ill., DePaul U., Chgo., St. Xavier Coll. Cert. tchr. Computer lab. asst. York High Sch., Elmhurst, Ill.; tchr. 2nd grade Cossitt Sch., LaGrange, Ill.; library-media coord. Unit Sch. 205, Elmhurst; tchr. computer edn. Dist. 93, Hillside, Ill. Home: 915 Saylor Ave Elmhurst IL 60126-4762

MACINTYRE, ALASDAIR, philosophy educator; b. Glasgow, Scotland, Jan. 12, 1929; came to U.S., 1969; s. Eneas John and Margaret Emily (Chalmers) MacI. BA, Queen Mary Coll., U. London, 1949; MA, Manchester U., 1951, Oxford U., 1961; D.H.L. (hon.), Swarthmore Coll., 1983; DLitt (hon.), Queen's U., Belfast, Ireland, 1968; D.O.E. (hon.), Essex (Eng.) U. Lectr. Manchester (Eng.) U., 1951-57, Leeds (Eng.) U., 1957-61; research fellow Nuffield Coll. Oxford (Eng.) U., 1961-62; sr. fellow Council Humanities, Princeton, 1962-63; fellow Univ. Coll., Oxford U., 1963-66; D.U.E. (hon.) U. Essex, Eng., 1966-69; prof. history of ideas Brandeis U., Waltham, Mass., 1969-72; dean Coll. Liberal Arts, Boston U., 1972-73, prof. philosophy and polit. sci., 1972-80; Henry Luce prof. Wellesley (Mass.) Coll., 1980-82; W. Alton Jones prof. Vanderbilt U., Nashville, 1982-88; Henry Luce scholar Whitney Humanities Ctr. Yale U., 1988-89; McMahon/Hank prof. U. Notre Dame, Ind., Ind., 1988-94; prof. arts & scis. Duke U., Durham, 1995—2000; rsch. prof. U. Notre Dame, 2000—. Riddell lectr. U. Newcastle on Tyne, Eng., 1964, Bampton lectr. Columbia U., 1966, Gifford lectr. U. Edinburgh, 1988. Author: Marxism and Christianity, 1953, Th Unconscious, 1957, A Short History of Ethics, 1966, Against the Self-Images of the Age, 1971, After Virtue, 1981, Whose Justice? Which Rationality?, 1988, Three Rival Versions of Moral Enquiry, 1990. Queen Mary Coll. fellow, 1984 Fellow Am. Acad. Arts and Scis., Brit. Acad. (corr.); mem. Royal Irish Acad. Office: U Notre Dame Dept Philosophy Notre Dame IN 46556 Home: 1405 S Lake george Dr Mishawaka IN 46545

MACINTYRE, PATRICIA COLOMBO, middle school educator; b. San Diego, Jan. 20, 1955; d. Vincent Christopher Colombo and Ellen Louise (Johnson) David; m. John Malcolm MacIntyre, July 25, 1981; children: Ann Marie, Katherine Christine. BA, San Diego State U., 1977; MA in Computer Edn., U.S. Internat. U., 1987. Cert. tchr., Calif. Math. and art tchr. Adams Jr. High Sch., Richmond, Calif., 1979-80; math. and computer tchr. Piedmont (Calif.) Middle Sch., 1980-81, La Jolla (Calif.) Country Day Sch., 1982-85; adminstrv. asst. to headmaster St. Michael's Sch., Newport, R.I., 1981-82; math. tchr. Kubasaki High Sch., Dept. Def. Dependents Sch., Okinawa, Japan, 1989-90; compuer tchr., tech. coord. Palm Middle Sch., Lemon Grove, Calif., 1985—. Local telementor Calif. Tech. Project, 1994-95. Selected for KUSI TV's Class Act, 1995, One of 20 Top Tchrs. in San Diego County, 1995; recipient Honoring Our Own award San Diego Sch. Bds. Assn., 1995. Mem. San Diego Computer-Using Educators (grantee 1991), Phi Kappa Phi. Republican. Roman Catholic. Avocations: children, family activities. Office: Palm Middle Sch 8425 Palm St Lemon Grove CA 91945-3314

MACISAAC, ANGUS, education minister; b. London, June 4, 1943; m. Mary Ann MacIsaac; 2 children. Grad., Nova Scotia Tchrs. Coll.; BA, St. Francis Xavier U. Tchr. h.s. Calgary, Canso, Guysborough and Antigonish.; owner, farmer Woodlot, Christmas Tree, maple syrup products, also blueberries; elected min. Nova Scotia Legis. Assembly, 1969—71, elected min, 1999—, minister housing and mcpl. affairs, 1999, minister education, 2003—. Past chmn. Strait of Canso Indsl. Devel. Authority; vol. Can. Assn. for Comty. Living, Antigonish Minor Hockey Assn., Nova Scotia Minor Hockey Assn.; past pres. Nova Scotia Progressive Conservative Assn.; vol. St. Ninian's Roman Catholic Ch. Office: Dept Edn 4th Fl Trade Mart PO Box 678 2021 Brunswick St Halifax NS B3J 2S9 Canada

MACIUSZKO, KATHLEEN LYNN, librarian, educator; b. Nogales, Ariz., Apr. 8, 1947; d. Thomas and Stephanie (Horowski) Mart; m. Jerzy Janusz Maciuszko, Dec. 11, 1976; 1 child, Christinia Alexsandra. BA, Ea. Mich. U., 1969; MLS, Kent State U., 1974; PhD, Case Western Res. U., 1987. Reference libr. Baldwin-Wallace Coll. Libr., Berea, Ohio, 1974-77, dir. Conservatory of Music Libr., 1977-85; dir. bus. info. svcs. Harcourt Brace Jovanovich, Inc., Cleve., 1985-89; staff asst. to exec. dir. Cuyahoga County Pub. Libr., Cleve., 1989-90; dir. Cleve. Area Met. Library System, Beachwood, Ohio, 1990; media specialist Cleve. Pub. Schs., 1991-93, Berea (Ohio) City Sch. Dist., 1993—. Author: OCLC: A Decade of Development, 1967-77, 1984; contbr. articles to profl. jours. Named Plenum Pub. scholar, 1986. Mem. Spl. Librs. Assn. (pres. Cleve. chpt. 1989-90, v.p. 1988-89, editor newsletter 1988-89), Baldwin-Wallace Coll. Faculty Women's Club (pres. 1975), Avocation: music. Office: Midpark HS 7000 Paula Dr Middleburg Heights OH 44130

MACK, CINDY STEIGERWALT, early childhood educator; b. Lehighton, Pa., June 1, 1956; d. Burdell Clark and Florence Mabel (Hoffman) Steigerwalt; m. Bruce D. Mack, Aug. 27, 1977; children: Shawn Matthew and Jeanna Maria (twins). BS cum laude, East Stroudsburg State Coll., 1978, MEd in Elem. Edn., 1984. Cert. tchr., Pa. Substitute tchr. various pub. schs., Pa., 1979-80; head tchr. Mekeel Child Care Ctr. East Stroudsburg (Pa.) U., 1981-92; owner, dir. Child Care Express, Gilbert, Pa., 1992—. Coord. Monroe County Early Childhood Task Force, 1992—; presenter workshops on edn. of young children. Organist, choir dir. Trinity Luth. Ch., Bowmanstown, Pa. Mem. Monroe County Assn. Edn. Young Children (program chair 1990—). Office: Child Care Express PO Box 43A Gilbert PA 18331-0043

MACK, JANE LOUISE, early childhood education educator, administrator; b. Drexel Hill, Pa., Nov. 23, 1926; d. George Schober and Estelle Marie (Heyland) Cridland; m. Charles Lawrence Mack, June 10, 1950; children: Jacqueline Judith, Nancy David. BS in Nursing, U. Pa., 1949. Instr. nursing arts U. Pa. Hosp., Phila., 1949-53; nurse Mass. Gen. Hosp., Boston, 1953-55; instr. in nursing Emerson Hosp., Concord, Mass., 1954-55; tchr. kindergarten Reading Clinic, Concord, 1959-62; tchr. 3d grade Bartlett Pvt. Elem. Sch., Arlington, Mass., 1962-63; asst. tchr. Lexington (Mass.) Montessori Sch., 1963-64, tchr., administr., 1964-80, prin., 1980-91, tchr., 1991—, headmistress emerita, 1991—, toddler tchr., 1992—. Advisor to elem. newspaper, 1991—. Contbr. articles to profl. jours. Tchr. mother and baby care ARC, Lexington, 1970-72; pres. Lexington Family Counseling Bd., 1976-81; bd. dirs., admissions chair Dana Home of Lexington, 1992—. Jane Mack Bldg. named in her honor Lexington Montessori Sch., 1990. Mem. Am. Montessori Soc. (chairperson Montessori tchrs. 1972-76), N.Am. Montessori Tchrs. Assn., Montessori Schs. Mass. (pres. 1987-91). Republican. Avocations: research, running, cooking, volunteer work, parent education. Home: 7 Parker St Lexington MA 02421-4906

MACK, JUDITH COLE SCHRIM, political scientist, educator; b. Cin., Aug. 9, 1938; d. James Douglas and Cathleen (Cole) Schrim; m. Thomas H. Mack, Jan. 3, 1968; children: Robert Michael, Cathleen Cole. AB with high distinction, U. Ky., 1960; AM, Radcliffe Grad. Sch., 1962; MPhil, Columbia U., 1988, postgrad., 1986—. Tchr. Lexington (Ky.) Sch., 1962-63; instr. Russian Emory U., Atlanta, 1963-64, Kent (Ohio) State U., 1964-65; instr. Hunter Coll., N.Y.C., 1988-90; adj. lectr. Barnard Coll., N.Y.C., spring 1991, 92; instr. Douglass Coll. Rutgers U., New Brunswick, NJ, 1992-93. Rsch. asst. sociology dept. U. Ky., 1961; rsch. asst. Russian and E. European Studies Ctr. UCLA, 1965—67, rsch. asst. Security Studies Ctr., 1967—68; adj. lectr. Hunter Coll., N.Y.C., 1988; presenter in field. Chmn. state pub. affairs com. N.J. Jr. Leagues, 1979—80; bd. dirs. Children's Aide Adoption Soc., Hackensack, NJ, 1979—90, v.p., 1985—90; bd. dirs. Assn. Children N.J., Newark, 1982—, v.p., 1983—88, chair spl. events, 1999; trustee Divsn. Youth and Family Svcs., Trenton, NJ, 1982—91, v.p., 1983—88; others; trustee Dumbarton Ho., Washington; mem. Millburn-ShortHills County Rep. Com., 1994—, corr. sec., 1994—96, chmn., 1996—98. Woodrow Wilson fellow, Radcliffe Coll., 1960—61, Nat. Def. fellow, 1961—62. Mem.: Mortar Bd., Nat. Soc. Colonial Dames Am. (N.J. treas. 1995—2001), Phi Sigma Iota, Phi Beta Kappa. Episcopalian. Avocations: bridge, cooking, ballet, theater, movies. Home: 657C Del Parque Dr Santa Barbara CA 93103

MACK, ROBERT WILLIAM, secondary school educator; b. Elizabeth, N.J., Oct. 25, 1941; s. Edward A. and Genevieve Emma (Kollar) M.; m. D. Nadine Hixson, June 25, 1966; children: Timothy Robert, Gregory Dennis, Katherine Ann. AA, Union Jr. Coll., Cranford, N.J., 1961; BA, Rutgers U., Newark, 1963; MEd, Rutgers U., New Brunswick, N.J., 1970. Cert. tchr. secondary sch. history, English. Tchr. Readington (N.J.) Twp. Pub. Schs., 1963-70; tchr. social studies Bridgewater-Raritan (N.J.) Pub. Schs., 1970—, asst. wrestling coach, 1975-78. ESL GED instr. Somerville Adult Sch., 1968-82. Mem. Hillsborough Twp. (N.J.) Bd. Edn., 1994—, committeeman, 1999-2000; com. mem. Hillsborough Dem. Party, 1975-82. NDEA Inst. grantee in econs. Colo. State U., 1969, in urban studies San Diego State U., 1970, East-West Inst. grantee, 1972, NEH Summer Seminar grantee, 1994. Mem. NEA, N.J. Edn. Assn., Somerset County Edn. Assn., Bridgewater Edn. Assn., Nat. Coun. Social Studies, N.J. Coun. Social Studies. Democrat. Roman Catholic. Avocations: reading, computers, photography. Office: Bridgewater-Raritan Bd Edn 836 Newmans Ln Bridgewater NJ 08807 Home: 100 Flanders Dr Hillsborough NJ 08844-4616

MACK, SANDRA LEE, secondary school educator; b. Charleston, S.C., Feb. 8, 1953; d. Arthur and Lucille (Brown) M. BS in Edn., Knoxville Coll., 1976; MA in Edn., Western Ky. U., Bowling Green, 1977. Cert. tchr., Va. Tchr. Richmond (Va.) Public Schs., 1977—. 4-H vol. Va. Coop. Ext. Svcs., Richmond, 1984—, svc. award, 1990; spl. event coord. West End Svc. unit Commonwealth Girl Scout Coun. of Va., Inc., 1994—, svc. award, 1990, vol. of yr. award, 1995; pres. new mem. com. Trinity Bapt. Ch., Richmond, 1984; head judge Miss Black Am. Richmond pageant, 1990, 91; mem. local

PTA; vol. Black History instr. Minority Youth Appreciation Soc., Inc. Learning Ctr., Richmond. Recipient Creighton Ct.'s Youth Sponsor award Richmond Redevel. and Housing Authority, 1990, Cmty. Svc. award, 1994, Vol. of Yr. Gardner-Robinson Youth Svc. award, 1994, Outstanding Vol. award Girl Scout Coun. Va., Inc., 1991, J.C. Penney Golden Rule award for Vol. Excellence in Edn., 1994. Mem. NEA (Va. and Richmond chpts.), Va. Geographic Soc., Va. Socal Studies Coun. (Tchr. of Yr. award 1988), Alpha Kappa Mu. Avocations: stage and set designer, arts and crafts exhibitor, singing, reading.

MACKAY, CYNTHIA JEAN, music educator; b. Kane, Pa., Apr. 30, 1943; d. Theodore Elmer and Frances Agnes (Bertch) Johnson; m. Angus James Mackay, Dec. 30, 1972; children: Shannon Leslie, Brendan Douglas. BS, Mansfield (Pa.) State Coll., 1965; cert., U. Calif., San Diego, 1972. Cert. basic tchg., Oreg.; std. life tchg. credential, Calif; cert. music educator K-12, Tex. Instr. vocal music Camp Curtin Jr. H.S., Harrisburg, Pa., 1965-69, Lincoln Jr. H.S., Oceanside, Calif., 1969-73, Poynter Jr. H.S., Hillsboro, Oreg., 1973-75; tchr. piano Collingswood, N.J., 1976-94, Spring, Tex., 1976-94; tchr. music Holmsley Elem. Sch., Houston, 1995—. Organist 1st Meth. Ch., Kane, 1958-61; part-time organist 1st Presbyn. Ch., Mansfield, 1961-65; piano accompanist, 1958—. Ednl. docent Houston Symphony League, 1985-92, creator Alice Flores Scholarship Competition, 1988; dist. vol. music coord., Klein, Tex., 1987-88; mem. Cypress Woodlands Jr. Forum, North Houston, Tex., 1988-94; pres. PTO Haude Elem., Spring, Tex., 1988-89, Strack Intermediate, Spring, 1991-92; 1st v.p. Klein Oak Strutters Booster Club, 1992-93. Mem. Tex. Music Educators Assn., Cypress Creek Music Tchrs. Assn. (corr. sec.). Republican. Presbyterian. Avocation: travel. Home: 3419 Blue Cypress Dr Spring TX 77388-5808

MACKAY, GLADYS GODFREY, adult education educator; b. Buffalo, N.Y., Sept. 17, 1915; d. Joseph Edwin and Hazel Winifred (Brown) Godfrey; m. James Albert MacKay, July 11, 1944 (wid. June 1997); children: Michael Paul, Cynthia Louise. BS, Cornell U., 1936; MA, Tchrs. Coll., Columbia U., 1940; postgrad., Case Western Res. U., Cleve., 1948-50. Cert. tchr. N.Y. Asst. home demonstration agt. Cornell U., N.Y., 1936-38; tchr. rural vocat. home econs. Consolidated Schs., Gilbertsville, N.Y., 1938-39; jr./sr. h.s. home econs. tchr. City Pub. Sch., Peekskill, N.Y., 1940-42; home econs. instr. Mather Coll./Cleve. Coll., Western Res. U., Cleve., 1946-48; marriage counselor/probation officer Lucas County Ct of Domestic Rels., Toledo, 1950-51; tchr./psychologist, spkr.'s bur. Family Health Assn. and Cen. Sch. of Practical Nursing, Cleve., 1951-54. Rep. to nat. consumer-retailer coun. for AAUW, Am. Stds. Assn., N.Y.C., 1940-42; mem. com. setting textile color-fastness stds. for FTC, Am. Stds. Assn., 1941; mem. task force to develop health edn. curriculum, Cleve. Heights Bd. of Edn., Ohio, 1967-69; mem. adv. bd. Children's Svcs., Cleve., 1963-65; mem. mental health com. Fedn. for Cmty. Planning, Cleve., 1977-78, others. Active Coun. on World Affairs, Cleve., 1960-76, in chg. fgn. doctors at Univ. Hosp., VA Hosp.; presenter Cleve. Growth Assn., 1964, Ohio Citizen's Coun., Columbus, 1974-77, others; presenter Met. Health Planning Corp., Cleve., 1978, chair Health Edn. Conf., 1978. Lt. USNR, 1942-46, WWII. Recipient Navy Commendation; named to Nat. Inst. of Pub. Affairs Conf. on Met. Problems, Washington, 1968. Mem. AAUW (life, honoree Ohio Wall of Fame 2000), Case Western Res. Univ. Women's Club (bd. mem. Sch. Medicine), Cleve. Acad. of Medicine Aux., Pi Lambda Theta. Presbyterian. Avocations: travel, reading, creative thinking. Achievements include being one of first 2 women to fly Navy antisubmarine Patrol NAS, Norfolk, Va., 1943. Home: 162 Kendal Dr Oberlin OH 44074-1907

MACKEN, DANIEL LOOS, physician, educator; b. Rochester, New York, May 7, 1933; s. Daniel Edward and Mary Frances (Loos) M.; children: Elizabeth Redford, Diana Loos; m. Maria Luisa (Medina de Palma), Nov. 16, 1979. BA, Holy Cross Coll., Worcester, Mass., 1955; post grad., Yale U., 1956-57; MD, U. Mass, Boston, 1960. Resident Roosevelt and Columbia-Presbyn. Hosp., N.Y.C., 1960-63; fellow Am. Heart Assn., 1964-65; dir., coronary care unit Walter Reed Gen. Hosp., Washington, 1968; staff rsch. physician Walter Reed Army Inst. of Rsch., Washington, 1970; instr. Columbia U., N.Y.C., 1966-78, asst. clin. prof., 1979—. Pres. Medica Found., Inc., N.Y.C., 1971—; bd. dir. Medica Endowment Fund, N.Y.C.; vis. lectr. U. saigon, Vietnam, 1969. Contbr. chpts. in book and articles to profl. jours.; student editor Jour. of History of Medicine and Allied Scis., 1956-57. Lt. Col., U.S. Army Med. Corp, 1967-70; Vietnam. Decorated Bronze Star and Vietnam Cross. Fellow Am. Coll. Cardiology; Royal Soc. Medicine; N.Y. Acad. Medicine; Harvey Soc.; mem. AMA; Assn. Mil. Surgeons of U.S.; Am. Heart Assn.; Met. Gov. Island Officers Club. Republican. Roman Catholic. Home: 570 Park Ave New York NY 10021-7370 Office: Columbia-Presbyn Med Ctr 161 Ft Washington Ave New York NY 10032-3713 E-mail: DLM1@columbia.edu.

MACKENZIE, CHARLES SHERRARD, academic administrator; b. Quincy, Mass., Aug. 21, 1924; s. Charles Sherrard and Dorothy (Eaton) MacK.; m. Florence Evelyn Phelps Meyer, Aug. 28, 1964 (dec. 1981); 1 child, Robert Walter Meyer; m. Lavonne Rudolph Gaiser, Mar. 30, 1985. Student, Boston U., 1942-43; BA, Gordon Coll., 1946; M.Div., Princeton Theol. Sem., 1949, Th.D., 1955, PhD, 1957; LHD, Grove City Coll., 1997; postgrad., U. Paris, 1953. Ordained to ministry Congl. Christian Ch., 1949. Pastor Carversville (Pa.) Christian Ch., 1948-51; fellow faculty Princeton Theol. Sem., 1949-51, 53-54, Princeton U., 1954-64; pastor First Presbyn. Ch., Avenel, N.J., 1954-64, Broadway Presbyn. Ch., Columbia U., N.Y.C., 1964-67, First Presbyn. Ch., Stanford U., San Mateo, Calif., 1967-71; pres. Grove City (Pa.) Coll., 1971-91, chancellor, 1991-92; advisor to pres., prof. philosphy Reformed Seminary, Orlando, Fla., 1992—; sr. min. Eastminster Presbyn. Ch., Wichita, Kans., 1993. Bd. dirs. Covenant Life Ins. Co., C.S. Lewis Inst.; cons. Oxford Project, 1992—, Provident Mutual Ins. Co.; lectr. Oxford U., 1965, U. Hamburg, 1968, Columbia U., 1964-67, Stanford U., 1967-71, U. Pitts., 1990-93; adv. Provident Mutual Ins. Co. Author: The Anguish and Joy of Pascal, 1973, Freedom, Equality, Justice, 1980, The Trinity and Culture, 1985. Bd. dirs. Knox Fellowship, Frontline, Orlando; mem. Human Relations Commn., San Mateo, 1968-70; mem. Indsl. Devel. Council, Grove City, 1972-75. Served with USAF, 1951-53. Mem. Presbyn. Coll. Union, Am. Assn. Pres.'s Ind. Colls. and Univs. (dir., pres.), Nat. Assn. Ind. Colls. and Univs. (mem. secretariat 1985-91), Freedoms Found. (nat. jury), Soc. Christian Philosphers, Duquesne Club (Pitts.), Univ. Club Boston, Citrus Club (Orlando), Evangelical initiative Notre Dame U., Rockford Inst. Main St. com. (De Toqueville award 1998). Republican. Address: 1231 Reformation Dr Oviedo FL 32765-7197

MACKEY, RUTH ELIZABETH (BETTY MACKEY), nutrition and food educator, real estate broker; b. Haskins, Ohio, Sept. 30, 1918; d. Paul Ernest and Dora Fern (McColley) Schutzberg; m. Gage R. Mackey, Apr. 4, 1942; children: Linda Louise Mackey Buroker, Sue Ellen Mackey Burrey, Betsy Lee, Carol Ann Mackey Bowens BS, Bowling Green State U., 1939; MS, Ohio State U., 1965. Lic. real estate, Ohio, 1979. Instr. home econs. McComb (Ohio) Secondary Sch., 1939-41; home demonstration agt. Ohio Extension Svc., 1941-42; instr. home econs. Marseilles (Ohio) Secondary Sch., 1943, Mt. Victory (Ohio) Secondary Sch., 1955-63, Ridgemont Secondary Sch., Ridgeway, Ohio, 1963-64; grad. teaching asst. Ohio State U., 1964-65; asst. state vocat. edn. home econs. Ohio State Dept. Edn., 1965-67; instr. food and nutrition Bowling Green State U., 1967-69, asst. prof., 1969-74, assoc. prof., 1974-78, prof. emerita, 1978—; owner Betty Mackey Real Estate. Vis. prof. Bluffton Coll., 1980-81, 86-87; broker/owner Mackey Real Estate; co-owner Bur-Mac Devel. Ltd.; tchr. real estate Continuing Edn. Ohio, High Point; treas. Glasgo Mackey Farms Inc.; apptd. acad. rev. bd. Rep. Michael Oxley, U.S. Congressman, 4th dist. Ohio; cons., spkr. in field. Mem. Hardin Meml. Hosp. Guild, Mt. Victory Child Study League; past mem. Nutrition for Today Soc.; trustee Sullivan Johnson Mus., Kenton, Ohio, 1982-90, pres. bd. trustees, 1984-86; past exec. bd. mem. Coll. Home Econs., Ohio State U.; past mem. advminstrv. bd. Dist. United Meth. Ch.; pres. United Meth. Women, 1st United Meth. Ch., Kenton, Ohio; past mem. adv. com. nutrition edn. divsn. Ohio Dept. Edn., Hardin County Extension Svc., Ohio Sch. Food Svc., Penta County Vocat. Sch.; past pres. Hardin County Rep. Women; mem. of founding com. Health Coll., Bowling Green State Univ., others. Recipient Golden Paradigm award Women of Achievement, Appleseed Ridge Girl Scouts, 1998; State honoree Ohio Fedn. Rep. Women, 1996. Mem. Nat. Bd. Realtors, Ohio Home Econs. Assn. (state exec. com.), Am. Home Econs. Assn., Ohi Dietetic Assn., Am. Dietitic Assn. (life), Ohio Acad. Sci., Ohio Nutritional Coun. (state exec. com.), Soc. Nutrition Edn., Future Homemakers Am. (state), Heartland Bd. Realtors, Ohio Bd. Realtors, Fortnightly Literary Club (treas., v.p., pres.), Ohio Ret. Tchrs., DAR (regent, state com. mem.), Pi Kappa Delta, Sigma Delta Epsilon, Kappa Delta Pi, Alpha Lambda Delta (Tchr. of Yr. 1968, 78). Methodist. Home and Office: 635 N High St Kenton OH 43326-1353

MACKINNON, CATHARINE ALICE, lawyer, law educator, legal scholar, writer; d. George E. and Elizabeth V. (Davis) MacKinnon. BA in Govt. magna cum laude with distinction, Smith Coll., 1969; JD, Yale U., 1977, PhD in Polit. Sci., 1987. Vis. prof. Harvard U., Stanford U., Yale U., others, Osgoode Hall, York U., Canada, U. Basel, Switzerland; prof. of law U. Mich., 1990—. Long term vis. prof. U. Chgo., 1997—; co-dir. project equality now Legal Alliance Women, 2001—. Author: Sexual Harassment of Working Women, 1979, Feminism Unmodified, 1987, Toward a Feminist Theory of the State, 1989, Only Words, 1993, Sex Equality, 2001; co-author: In Harm's Way, 1997. Office: U Michigan Law School Ann Arbor MI 48109-1215

MACKINNON, ROGER ALAN, psychiatrist, educator; b. Feb. 13, 1927; Student, Princeton U., 1944-46; MD, Columbia U., 1950, cert. in psycoanalytic medicine, 1957. Diplomate Am. Bd. Psychiatry and Neurology. Intern E.W. Sparrow Hosp., Lansing, Mich., 1950-51; resident in psychiatry N.Y. State Psychiatric Inst., N.Y.C., 1951-52, 52-54; chief psychiatry Vanderbilt Clinic, Presbyn. Hosp., N.Y.C., 1959-77; prof. clin. psychiatry Coll. Physicians & Surgeons, Columbia U., N.Y.C., 1986-97, prof. emeritus, 1997—; tng., supervising analyst Columbia U. Psychoanalytic Ctr., 1970—, asst. dir. for selection, 1981-91, dir., 1991-97; attending psychiatrist Presbyn. Hosp., N.Y.C., 1972—, N.Y. State Psychiatric Inst., N.Y.C., 1972—. Asst. examiner Am. Bd. Psychiatry and Neurology, 1960-70; cons., lectr. in field. Co-author textbook: The Psychiatric Interview, 1971, The Psychiatric Evaluation, 1986; contbr. articles to profl. jours., chpts. to books. Lt. USNR, 1952-54. Fellow Am. Psychiat. Assn. (life), N.Y. Acad. Medicine; mem. Am. Psychoanalytic Assn., Assn. Psychoanalytic Medicine (George E. Daniels Merit award 1995), N.Y. Psychiat. Soc. (pres. 1987-88), N.Y. Psychiat. Inst. (Centennial award 1996). Avocations: woodworking, boating, hiking. Home: 11 Edgewood St Tenafly NJ 07670-2909 Office: 11 E 87th St New York NY 10128-0527

MACKLIS, ROGER MILTON, physician, educator, researcher; b. Stratford, Conn., Mar. 12, 1956; m. Carol Clark, July 25, 1987; children: Andrew Clark, Paul Clark. BS, MS, Yale U., 1978; MD, Harvard U., 1983. Diplomate Am Bd Radiation Oncology. Instr. Harvard Med. Sch., Boston, 1988-89, asst. prof. radiation oncology, 1989-93; dep. div. chief Children's Hosp., Boston, 1990-93; chmn. dept. radiation oncology Cleve. Clinic Found., 1993—. Biomedical consult, Boston, 1989—; prof radiology/radiation oncology Ohio State Univ, 1995—; assoc prof hist med Case Western Res Univ, 1995—. Author: (book) Manual of Introductory Clinical Medicine, 1984; contbr. articles to profl jours. Recipient Resident Research Award, ASTRO, 1988, Jr Faculty Research Award, Am Cancer Soc, 1990. Mem.: Soc Chairs of Acad Radiation Oncology Programs (treas, vpres, pres), Am Soc Therapeutic Radiology and Oncology, Am Soc Clin Oncology (Young Investigator Award 1987), Radiation Research Soc. Achievements include research in research on new approaches to cancer treatment involving radioactively labeled molecules and novel technologies for minimizing medical errors in oncology. Office: Cleve Clinic Found Dept Radiation Oncology 9500 Euclid Ave Cleveland OH 44195-0001 Business E-Mail: macklis@radonc.ccf.org.

MACKNIGHT, CAROL BERNIER, educational administrator; b. Quincy, Mass., Apr. 12, 1938; d. Harold Nelson and Marguerite (Norris) Bernier; m. William J. MacKnight, Aug. 19, 1967. BS, Ithaca Coll., N.Y., 1960; MM, Manhattan Sch. Mus., N.Y.C., 1961; Dipl., Fontainebleau Sch. Music/Art, France, 1963; EdD, U. Mass., 1973. Asst. to supt. Falmouth (Mass.) pub. schs., 1975-76; dir. bus., mgmt., engring. prog. Sch. Bus. Adminstrn. U. Mass., Amherst, 1976-79, assoc. dir. continuing edn., 1979-82, dir. Office Instructional Tech., 1982—. Trustee New Eng. Regional Computer Program, Inc., 1986—92; bd. dirs. Info. Sys. and Bus. Exch., 1992—93; keynote spkr. Australian Soc. for Computers in Learning In Tertiary Edn. Conf., Adelaide, 1996; conf. chair Transforming Practice with Tech., 2002. Editor: Jour. Computing in Higher Edn., 1988—, Jour. Info. Sys. for Mgrs., 1992—93; mem. editl. rev. bd.: Jour. of Computer-Based Instrn., 1988—2002, author/editor: computer progs.; contbr. articles to profl. jours. CDC grantee, 1986, Regents of Boston grantee, 1988, Lilly Fellow Mentor, 1991-92. Mem. ACM, Assn. for Computing Machinery, Educom, Soc. Applied Learning Techs. (bd. dirs. 2003—), New England Regional Computer Program. Avocations: music, photography, tennis, hiking, skiing. Office: Norris Consulting and Pub PO Box 2593 Amherst MA 01004

MACKO, STEPHEN ALEXANDER, education educator; b. Mobile, Ala., Sept. 21, 1951; s. John and Dorothy Caroline (Kruppa) M.; m. Faylene Gail Moors, Dec. 21, 1977; children: Rebekah, Nikolas, Christopher. BS in Chemistry, Carnegie-Mellon U., 1973, BA in Psychology, 1973; MS in Oceanography, U. Maine, 1976; PhD in Chemistry, U. Tex., 1981. Asst. prof., assoc. prof. Meml. U., St. John's', Can., 1983-90; lectr. Marine Biol. Lab., Woods Hole, Mass., 1991; assoc. prof., prof. U. Va., Charlottesville, 1990—. Guest assoc. scientist Brookhaven Nat. Lab., Upton, N.Y., 1982-88; invited guest rschr. U. Que., Montreal, Can., 1989-90; vis. investigator Geophys. Lab., Washington, 1990; mem. sedimentary geochemistry processes panel Ocean Drilling Program, 1989-90, 93-97. Guest editor Organic Geochemistry, 1997, Isotope Geoscience, 1992, Geochimica et Cosmochimica, 1996; assoc. editor Geochimica Cosmochimica Acta, 1989-97, Organic Geochemistry, 1991-97, Amino Acids, 1996—; mem. editl. adv. bd. Geochimica et Cosmochimica Acta, 1996—. Recipient President's medal for outstanding rsch. Meml. U. Nfld., 1987, Meritorious Svc. award Geochimica Cosmochimica Acta, 1994. Mem. Am. Geophys. Union, European Assn. Organic Geochemists, Geochem. Soc. (councilor 1991—, best paper award organic geochemistry divsn. 1996), Sigma Xi. Avocations: stamp collecting, mushroom hunting, chess.

MACLAURY, BRUCE KING, financial institution executive; b. Mount Kisco, N.Y., May 7, 1931; s. Bruce King and Edith Mae (Wills) MacL.; m. Virginia Doris Naef, Jan. 8, 1955; children— John, David. BA, Princeton, 1953; MA, Harvard, 1958, PhD, 1961. Successively mgr., v.p. fgn. dept. Fed. Res. Bank N.Y., N.Y.C., 1958-69; dep. under sec. for monetary affairs U.S. Treasury Dept., Washington, 1969-71; pres. Fed. Res. Bank of Mpls., 1971-77, Brookings Instn., Washington, 1977-95, pres. emeritus, 1995—. Bd. dirs. Am. Express Bank Ltd., Nat. Steel Corp., St. Paul Cos., The Vanguard Group. Trustee Nat. Com. for Econ. Devel., 1978—; mem. Coun. on Fgn. Rels., N.Y.C., 1962-; chair emergency trustees D.C. Pub. Schs., 1996-98. Recipient Exceptional Service award U.S. Treasury Dept., 1971 Mem. Phi Beta Kappa, Cosmos. Home: 5109 Yuma Pl NW Washington DC 20016-4309 Office: Brookings Instn 1775 Massachusetts Ave NW Washington DC 20036-2103

MACLEOD, STUART MAXWELL, health science administrator, educator, pharmacologist, physician; b. Toronto, Ont., Can., June 20, 1943; s. Ellis Maxwell and Irene Constance (Howlett) M.; m. Patricia Ann Marontate, 1967 (div. 1986); children: Andrew, Virginia; m. Helen Nancy McCullough, 1987. BSc, MD, U. Toronto, 1967; PhD, McGill U., 1972. Clinician, scientist Addiction Rsch. Found. Ont., Toronto, 1973-78; sr. scientist Rsch Inst. Hosp. for Sick Children, Toronto, 1979-86; prof. medicine, pediat., pharmacology, clin. biochemistry U. Toronto, 1984-86; prof. medicine, pediats., clin. epidemiology and biostats. McMaster U., Hamilton, Ont., 1987—, dean faculty health scis., 1987-92; dir. Father Sean O'Sullivan Rsch. Ctr., Hamilton, 1992—2002, Ctr. for Evaluation of Medicines, 1992-97; v.p. med. affairs Innovus Rsch. Inc., Burlington, Ont., Can., 1996—; exec. dir. BC Rsch. Inst. Children's and Women's Health, Vancouver, Canada, 2003—. Mem. Premier's Coun. on Health Strategy, Ont., 1987-91; chmn. Coun. Ont. Faculties Medicine, Ont., 1989-91; mem. sci. adv. bd. Health Can., 2000-03; asst. dean rsch. Faculty Medicine, U. BC, Vancouver, Can., 2003—; v.p. academic devel., Provincial Health Svcs. Authority of BC, Can., 2003—. Clin. rsch. scholar Ont. Ministry of Health, 1978-83; recipient sr. investigator award Can. Soc. Clin. Pharmacology, 1987, Disting. Svc. award, 2001. Fellow Royal Coll. Physicians (Can., Edinburgh, Glasgow); mem. European Soc. Devel. Pharmacology Therapy, Am. Soc. for Clin. Pharmacology and Therapeutics, Can. Soc. for Clin. Investigation (pres. 1984-85, Disting. Svc. award 1999), Can. Pharmacol. Soc., Am. Soc. for Pharmacology and Exptl. Therapeutics, Soc. for Pediat. Rsch., Assn. Can. Med. Colls. (exec. com. 1988-91), Alpha Omega Alpha. Office: Innovus Rsch Inc 1016-A Sutton Dr Burlington ON Canada L7L 6B8 Fax: 905-331-9912. E-mail: smacleod@innovus.com.

MACLISE, JAMES RAYMOND, educator, writer; b. Newark, Dec. 14, 1935; s. Deming Gerow and Vivian Ruth (Jackson) M.; m. Lura Elizabeth Geyser, Aug. 24, 1968; children: James Deming, Daniel Ross. B.A., U. Calif.-Davis, 1957; M.A., U. San Francisco, 1971. Cert. secondary and community coll. tchr., Calif. Lectr. U. San Francisco, 1971-72; tchr. English, Lodi High Sch., Calif., 1972-96. Author radio mystery articles. Served with U.S. Army, 1959-60. Mem. Soc. to Preserve Hist. Radio Program Materials.

MACMANUS, SUSAN ANN, political science educator, researcher; b. Tampa, Fla., Aug. 22, 1947; d. Harold Cameron and Elizabeth (Riegler) MacM. BA cum laude, Fla. State U., 1968, PhD, 1975; MA, U. Mich., 1969. Instr. Valencia C.C., Orlando, Fla., 1969-73; rsch. asst. Fla. State U., 1973-75; asst. prof. U. Houston, 1975-79, assoc. prof., 1979-85, dir. MPA program, 1983-85; rsch. assoc. Ctr. Pub. Policy, 1982-85; prof., dir. PhD progam Cleve. State U., 1985-87; prof. pub. adminstrn. and polit. sci. U. South Fla., Tampa, 1987—, chair dept. govt. and internat. affairs, 1987-93, disting. univ. prof., 1999. Vis. prof. U. Okla., Norman, 1981—; field rsch. assoc. Brookings Inst., Washington, 1977—82, Princeton (N.J.) U., 1979—, Cleve. State U., 1982—83, Westat, Inc., Washington, 1983—; summer field rsch. assoc. Columbia U., N.Y.C., 1979, Nat. Acad. Pub. Adminstrn., Washington, 1980. Author: Revenue Patterns in U.S. Cities and Suburbs: A Comparative Analysis, 1978, Federal Aid to Houston, 1993; author: (with others) Governing A Changing America, 1984; author: (with Francis T. Borkowski) Visions for the Future: Creating New Institutional Relationships Among Academia, Business, Government, and Community, 1989; author: Reapportionment and Representation in Florida: A Historical Collection, 1991, Doing Business with Government: Federal, State, Local and Foreign Government Purchasing Practices for Every Business and Public Institution, 1992, Young v. Old: Generational Combat in the 21st Century, 1996; author: (with Elizabeth R. MacManus) Citrus, Sawmills, Critters & Crackers: Life in Early Lutz and Central Pasco County, 1998; author: Targeting Senior Voters, 2000; author: (with Elizabeth R. MacManus) The Lutz Depot, 2000; editor: Mapping Florida's Political Landscape: The Changing Art and Politics of Reapportionment and Redistricting, 2002; editor: (with Thomas R. Dye) Politics in States and Communities, 11th edit., 2003; writer: manuals in field, mem. editl. bd.: various jours; contbr. articles to jours., chpts. to books. Bd. dirs. Houston Area Women's Ctr., 1977, past pres., v.p. fin., treas.; mem. LWV, Gov.'s Coun. Econ. Advisers, 1988-90, Harris County (Tex.) Women's Polit. Caucus, Houston; bd. dirs. USF Rsch. Found., Inc.; chair Fla. Elections Commn., 1999-2003; mem. Fla. Gov.'s Coun. Econ. Advisers, 2000—. Recipient U. Houston Coll. Social Scis. Tchg. Excellence award, 1977, Herbert J. Simon award for best article in 3d vol., Internat. Jour. Pub. Adminstrn., 1981, Theodore & Venette Askounes-Ashford Disting Scholar award U. South Fla., 1991, Disting. Rsch. Scholar award, 1991, Tchg. Excellence award, 1999; Ford Found. fellow, 1967-68; grantee Valencia C. C. Faculty, 1972, U. Houston, 1976-77, 79, 83; Fulbright Rsch. scholar, Korea, 1989; Choice mag. award, 1996; named Disting. Univ. Prof., 1999; rsch. fellow Fla. Inst. of Govt., 2000—. Mem. Am. Polit. Sci. Assn. (program com. 1983-84, chair sect. intergovtl. rels., award 1989, mem. exec. coun. 1994—, pres.-elect sec. urban politics 1994-95, pres. sect. urban politics 1995-96), So. Polit. Sci. Assn. (v.p. 1990-91, pres.-elect 1992-93, pres. 1993-94, V.O. key award com. 1983-84, best paper on women and politics 1988, Diane Blair award 2001), Midwest Polit. Sci. Assn., Western Polit. Sci. Assn., Southwestern Polit. Sci. Assn. (local arrangements com. 1982-83, profession com. 1977-80), ASPA (nominating com. Houston chpt. 1983, bd. mem. Suncoast chpt., pres.-elect 1991, Lilly award 1992), Policy Studies Orgn. (mem. editl. bd. jour. 1981—, exec. coun. 1983-85), Women's Caucus Polit. Sci. (portfolio pre-decision rev. com. 1982-83, projects and programs com. 1981, fin.-budget com. 1980-81), Fla. Polit. Sci. Assn. (pres. 1997-98, Manning Dauer Disting. Fla. Polit. Sci. award 2001), Acad. Polit. Sci., Mcpl. Fin. Officers Assn., Phi Kappa Phi (Artist/Scholar award U. South Fla. 1997), Phi Beta Kappa, Pi Sigma Alpha (mem. exec. coun. 1994-96, pres. 2000-02), Pi Alpha Alpha. Methodist. Home: 2506 Collier Pky Land O Lakes FL 34639-5228 Office: U South Fla Dept Polit Sci Tampa FL 33620 E-mail: samacmanus@aol.com.

MAC MASTER, HARRIETT SCHUYLER, retired elementary school educator; b. Maxbass, ND, Nov. 5, 1916; d. Hugh Riley and Christine (Park) Schuyler; m. Jay Myron Mac Master, May 27, 1944; children: Jay Walter, Robert Hugh, Anne Schuyler. BS, postgrad., Coll. N.J., 1971; grad., Inst. for Children's Lit., 1993. With staff spl. govt. WWII project Office Sci. R & D, 1943-44; tchr. Woodfern Elem. Sch., Neshanic, N.J., 1972-87; ret., 1987. Freelance writer elem. sci. program Silver Burdett Co., 1983. Elite mem. Nat. Rep. Congl. Com.; active Grace United Meth. Ch. Named Republican of Yr. from Fla., 2001. Fellow AAUW, LWV. Republican. Home: 230 NE 22nd Ave Cape Coral FL 33909-2820

MACMILLAN, ROSS, sociology educator; b. Peterhead, Scotland, Mar. 8, 1968; arrived in U.S., 1998; s. Ian Reid Anderson Macmillan and Joan Elizabeth Cummings Roberts; m. Annette Marie Nierobisz, Sept. 1, 1998. BA with honors, U. Winnipeg, Man., Can., 1991; MA, Queen's U., Kingston, Ont., Can., 1994; PhD, U. Toronto, Ont., 1998. Lectr. Queen's U., 1997-98; asst. prof. dept. sociology U. Minn., Mpls., 1998—. Contbr. articles to profl. jours. Doctoral fellow Social Sci. and Humanities Rsch. Coun. Can., 1994-98. Office: U Minn Dept Sociology 909 Social Scis 267 19th Ave S Minneapolis MN 55455 E-mail: macmilla@atlas.socsci.umn.edu.

MACMURREN, MARGARET PATRICIA, secondary education educator, consultant; b. Newark, Nov. 4, 1947; d. Kenneth F. and Doris E. (Lounsberry) Bartro; m. Harold MacMurren, Nov. 21, 1970. BA, Paterson State U., 1969; MA, William Paterson Coll., 1976; postgrad., Jersey City State Coll., 1976—. Tchr. Byram (N.J.) Twp. Schs., 1969-77; learning cons., child study team coord. Andover Regional Schs., Newton, N.J., 1977—. Mem. NEA, N.J. Edn. Assn., N.J. Assn. Learning Cons., Sussex Coutny Assn. Learning Cons. (pres. 1982-83, 93-94, sec.-treas. 1991-92, v.p. 1992-93), Andover Regional Edn. Assn. (pres. 1986-87). Avocations: skiing, dancing, weight training, travel, reading. Home: 4 Systema Pl Sussex NJ 07461-2833 Office: Andover Regional Schs 707 Limecrest Rd Newton NJ 07860-8801

MACOVSKI, ALBERT, electrical engineer, educator; b. N.Y.C., May 2, 1929; s. Philip and Rose (Winogr) Macovski; m. Adelaide Paris, Aug. 5, 1950; children: Michael, Nancy. BEE, City Coll. N.Y., 1950; MEE, Poly. Inst. Bklyn., 1953; PhD, Stanford U., 1968. Mem. tech. staff RCA Labs., Princeton, NJ, 1950—57; asst. prof., then assoc. prof. Poly. Inst. Bklyn., 1957—60; staff scientist Stanford Rsch. Inst., Menlo Park, Calif., 1960—71; fellow U. Calif. Med. Center San Francisco, 1971—72; prof. elec. engring. and radiology Stanford U., 1972—, endowed chair, Canon USA prof. engring., 1991—. Dir. Magnetic Resonance Sys. Rsch. Lab.; cons. to industry. Author. Recipient award for color TV cirs., Inst. Radio Engrs., 1958; fellow spl., NIH, 1971. Fellow: IEEE (Zworykin award 1973), Internat. Soc. Magnetic Resonance in Medicine (trustee 1991—94, gold medal 1997), Optical Soc. Am., Am. Inst. Med. Biol. Engring.; mem.: NAE, Am. Assn. Physicists in Medicine, Inst. Medicine, Eta Kappa Nu, Sigma Xi. Jewish. Achievements include patents in field. Home: 2505 Alpine Rd Menlo Park CA 94025-6314 Office: Stanford U Dept Elec Engring Stanford CA 94305 E-mail: macovski@stanford.edu.

MACWILLIAMS, DEBRA LYNNE, language arts consultant; b. Buffalo, June 6, 1952; d. Charles Edward and Dorothy Elizabeth (Whitton) Fields; m. Thomas Michael MacWilliams, Aug. 18, 1979; children: Amy Claire, Matthew Brandon. BA in Liberal Arts, SUNY, Albany, 1977; cert. elem. teaching, SUNY, Geneseo, 1987, MS in Edn., 1988. Cert. elem. tchr., reading specialist, N.Y. Tchr. gifted and talented, reading specialist Letchworth Ctrl. Sch., Gainesville, N.Y., 1988—. Reading cons., N.Y., 1988—. Sch. coord. Am. Cancer Soc. (Outstanding Svc. award 1992), Wyoming County Unit, 1988—; parent network coord. Assn. for Pediatric Patients, Buffalo, 1987; vol. Candlelighters Childhood Cancer Found., Washington, 1986—, Camp Good Days and Spl. Times, Rochester, N.Y., 1986—; exec. com. Cub Scouts Genesee Region, Batavia, N.Y., 1991-92. Mem. Internat. Reading Assn., N.Y. State Reading Assn., N.Y. State Assn. Compensatory Educators, Advocacy for Gifted and Talented Edn., Mary Jemison Reading Coun., Inst. for Children's Lit., Phi Delta Kappa. Avocations: writing, boating, woodworking, traveling. Home: 180 Wyoming St Warsaw NY 14569-9580 Office: Letchworth Central Sch 5567 Jordon Rd Gainesville NY 14066-9700

MADAMA, PATRICK STEPHEN, academic official; b. Rochester, N.Y., Jan. 4, 1951; s. Anthony L. and Mary S. (Silvio) M. AS, Monroe Community Coll., Rochester, 1971; BS, SUNY, Brockport, N.Y., 1977, MS Edn., 1987. Cert. fund raising exec. Acct. Monroe Community Coll. Assn., Inc., Rochester, 1973—81; dir. alumni affairs & devel. SUNY, Brockport, 1981—87, exec. dir. for coll. devel., 1987—96; pres. Brockport Coll. Found. Inc., 1993—96; chief devel. officer York Coll. Pa., 1996—99; v.p. for inst. advancement N.Y.C. Coll. Tech., 1999—. Bd. dirs. SUNY Coun. for Univ. Affairs & Devel., Albany, 1982-90; senator alt. SUNY faculty senate, Albany, 1985-89; senator SUNY, Brockport Coll. Faculty Senate, 1983-87. Contbr. articles to profl. jours. Exec. committeeman Monroe County Dem. Party, Rochester, 1988-92; bd. dirs. Edgerton Child Care Ctr., Rochester, 1988-93, Monroe C.C. Alumni Assn., Rochester, 1971-86; chmn. Holy Family Parish Coun., Rochester, 1971-75. Recipient Monroe Community Coll. Disting. Alumnus award, 1983, Outstanding Svc. award SUNY Coll. Brockport Alumni Assn., 1996, cert. appreciation SUNY. Mem. Assn. Fundraising Profls. (pres. ctrl. Pa. chpt. 1998-99, pres. Genesee Valley chpt., found. bd. dirs. 1998—), Coun. for Advancement and Support of Edn. Democrat. Roman Catholic. Avocations: gardening, numismatics, reading. Office: NYC Coll Tech 300 Jay St Namm 325 Brooklyn NY 11201 Home: Apt 1K 279 Prospect Park W Brooklyn NY 11215-6273 E-mail: pmadama@citytech.cuny.edu.

MADDEN, ANTOINETTE LIADIS, special education educator; b. Warren, Ohio, May 10, 1957; d. Peter James and Mary (Mougianis) Liadis; m. William Thomas Madden, July 22, 1989; 1 child, Stephen Peter. BS in Edn., Kent State U., 1979, MEd, 1986. Cert. elem., learning disabilities and behavior disorders tchr., Ohio. Learning disabilities tutor Warren City Schs., 1979-80; learning disabilities tchr. Niles (Ohio) City Schs., 1980-89; tutor learning disabilities Cleveland Heights/Univ. Heights Schs., 1989-90; learning disabilities tchr. Solon (Ohio) City Schs., 1990—2001, 4th grade tchr., 2001—. Mem. NEA, Ohio Edn. Assn., Learning Disabilities Assn., Warren Jaycees (sec. 1984, chmn. for area teenager of month program 1986). Avocations: playing piano, aerobics, golf, tennis, painting, gardening. Office: Lewis Elem Sch 32345 Cannon Rd Cleveland OH 44139-1698

MADDEN, DAVID WILLIAM, English language educator; b. San Francisco, Sept. 10, 1950; s. John Joseph and Esther Calvert (Pearce) M.; m. Mary Virginia Davis, Mar. 19, 1977; children: Anne Elizabeth, Margaret Kathleen. Student, St. Mary's Coll., Moraga, Calif., 1968-70; BA, U. Calif., Davis, 1972, MA, 1974, PhD, 1980. Lectr. U. Calif., Davis, 1980-82; asst. prof. Calif. State U., Sacramento, 1982-85, assoc. prof., 1985-90, prof., 1990—. Author: Understanding Paul West, 1993; editor: Critical Essays on Thomas Berger, 1995; guest editor: Review of Contemporary Fiction XI, 1991, Review of Contemporary Fiction XVII, 1997; contbr. articles to profl. jours. Active Am. Cancer Soc., Sacramento, 1986-87, site coun. Jefferson Sch., Sacramento, 1987-94. Recipient Capital Svc. Ctr. Coun. award, 1992, Outstanding Tchr. award Calif. State U., Sacramento, 1999; Fulbright grantee, 1977-78, Rsch. grantee Calif. State U., Sacramento, 1989-93. Mem. Am. Com. Irish Studies, Irish Am. Cultural INst., Phi Kappa Phi. Democrat. Home: 3201 Lemitar Way Sacramento CA 95833-2756 Office: Calif State U Dept English 6000 J St Sacramento CA 95819-2605 E-mail: maddendw@csus.edu.

MADDEN, JAMES A. gifted and talented educator; b. Butler, Pa., Jan. 27, 1947; s. James Henry and Josephine Grace (Zagst) M.; m. Mary Ellen Adamcin, July 16, 1977; children: Joann Marie, Jamie Elyse. BS, U. Ariz., 1970, MEd, 1973. Cert. jr. coll. tchr. Tchr. Tucson Unified Sch. Dist., 1972—, tchr. of gifted, 1976—. Developer ednl. games and computer programs for math. and computer sci. Named Ariz. Tchr. of Yr., IBM, 1990, Honored Educator Flinn Scholars, 1998. Home: 4442 E Cooper Cir Tucson AZ 85711-4260 Office: University High Sch 421 N Arcadia Ave Tucson AZ 85711-3097

MADDEN, PAUL HERMAN, education educator; b. Adairsville, Ga., Sept. 18, 1924; s. William Herbert and Bessie Rosanna (Green) M.; m. Marion Ghiz, July 31, 1954; children: Michael Peter, Kenneth Robert. BS in Edn., W. Ga. Coll., 1967; MEd in Adminstrn/Supervision, Univ. Ga., 1969, EdD in Adminstrn/Supervision, 1976. Enlisted USN, 1941-45; advanced through grades to maj. U.S. Army, 1949-65, ret., 1965; employment interviewer Ga. State Employment Svc., Cedartown, 1947-48; prin. Fish Creek Elem. Sch./Polk County Schs., Cedartown, 1966-67; asst. prin. jr. high Clark County Schs., Athens, Ga., 1970-72; dir. child care Ga. Mountains Plan Commn., Gainesville, 1972-74; assoc. prof. ednl. adminstrn. Tenn. State U., Nashville, 1976—. Cons. elem. and mid. sch. coms., Tenn., 1977-93; pres. Nat. Adult Literary Coun., 1983-84. Pres. Gaines Sch. Civitan Club, Athens, 1976. Decorated combat ribbons USN. Mem. NAESP, NEA, Nat. Mid. Sch. Assn., Nat. Elem. Prin. Assn., Tenn. Elem. Prin. Assn., Tenn. Edn. Assn., Phi Delta Kappa (pres. local chpt. 1972-73, 83-85, Leadership award 1986, 88, 92). Democrat. Avocations: reading, sports. Office: Dept Ednl Adminstrn 3500 John A Merritt Blvd Nashville TN 37209-1500

MADDEN, THERESA MARIE, elementary education educator; b. Phila., Feb. 12, 1950; d. James Anthony and Marie Margaret (Clark) Madden. BA in Social Sci., Neumann Coll., 1977; postgrad., Beaver Coll., Immaculata Coll. Cert. tchr. Pa., prin. Pa. Tchr. elem. grades St. Anthony Sch., Balt., 1971-73, St. Mary-St. Patrick Sch., Wilmington, Del., 1973-74, Queen of Heaven Sch., Cherry Hill, N.J., 1974-77, St. Bonaventure Sch., Phila., 1977-78, 79-83, St. Stanislaus Sch., Lansdale, Pa., 1978-79; substitute tchr. various schs. Phila., 1983-84; tchr. 8th grade math. St. Cecilia Sch., Phila., 1984-94; tchr. math., vice prin. Corpus Christi Sch., Lansdale, Pa., 1994-99; tchr. grades 6-8 St. Maria Goretti Sch., Hatfield, Pa., 1999—. Mem. vis. team Mid. States Assn., Phila., 1992, Phila., 97, Phila., 99, Phila., 2000, Phila., 02, chair, 03; presenter workshops. Mem.: Assn. Tchrs. Math. Phila. and Vicinity, Pa. Coun. Tchrs. Math., Nat. Coun. Tchrs. Math. Roman Catholic. Avocations: crocheting, cross stitch, baking, horseback riding, walking. Office: St Maria Goretti Sch Cowpath Rd Hatfield PA 19440

MADDOCK, LAWRENCE HILL, retired language educator; b. Ogden, Utah, July 14, 1923; s. Lawrence J. and Nellie (Hill) Maddock. Student, U. Fla., 1941-42; BA, George Peabody Coll., 1946, PhD, 1965; MA, U. So. Calif., 1949. Tchr. pub. schs., Jacksonville, Fla., 1949-52; instr. U. Fla., Gainesville, 1952-53; asst. prof. California (Pa.) State Coll., 1955-56, assoc. prof., 1956-64, N.E. La. State Coll., Monroe, 1964-67, U. West Fla., Pensacola, 1967-90. Author: The Door of Memory, 1974, revised, 2003, John Maddock: Mormon Pioneer, 1996; contbr. chpts. to books and articles to profl. jours. Mem. MLA (bibliographer 1978-93), Thomas Wolfe Soc., Mormon History Assn. Republican. Mem. Lds Ch. Home: 1012 Gerhardt Dr Pensacola FL 32503-3222

MADDOX, IRIS CAROLYN CLARK, secondary education educator; b. Wardell, Mo., Apr. 20, 1936; d. Newman Walter and Mary Elizabeth (Edney) Clark; m. James P. Maddox, June 4, 1954; children: James Steven, Sandra Jean. BS cum laude, Prairie View A&M U., 1983, MEd in Indsl. Edn., 1984, MEd in Counseling., 1990. Cert. counselor and tchr., Tex. Tchr. Spring Branch Ind. Sch. Dist., Houston, 1982—. Sec. Bus. Office Svcs. Adv. Com., Houston, 1991-92. Mem. Am. Vocat. Assn., Tex. Assn. Continuing Adult Edn., Nat. Assn. Classroom Educators in Bus. Edn., Chi Sigma Iota. Avocations: gardening, collecting antiques and coins. Home: 1902 Mapleton Dr Houston TX 77043-2409

MADDOX, NANCY L, elementary school educator, special education educator; b. Marion, Ind., July 3, 1950; d. William Vaughn and Verlie Uldene (Craig) Hutchison; m. Brian Wayne Maddox, Dec. 12, 1981; stepchildren: Noelle, Travis. BS in Edn., Ind. U., 1972; MA in Edn., Ball State U., Muncie, Ind., 1980. Lic. tchr. spl. edn., mentally retarded. 2nd grade tchr. Met. Sch. Dist., Martinsville, Ind.; tchr. 3rd, 4th and 6th grade Marion (Ind.) Community Schs., 2nd grade tchr; tchr. reading recovery, Title I coord. Coord., peer tchr. Tchr. Expectations and Student Achievement; involved in curriculum writing for Marion Community Schs.; tchr. pub. sch. tchrs., Ryazan, Russia, 1994-95 Mem. Internat. Reading Assn., Ind. Marion Educators (bd. dirs.). Home: 5225 E 300 S Marion IN 46953-9179

MADDOX, UTRICIA ANTOINETTE, English educator, communications educator; b. New England; d. Curtis Anthony and Penolope Rotha (Sabusan) M. BA, New Rochelle Coll.; MA, Herbert H. Lehman U.; cert. advanced study, NYU. Cert. sch. dist. adminstr., sch. adminstr., supr., English tchr. Spl. asst. to deputy supt. N.Y.C. Bd. Edn.; prof. English SUNY, Westchester, 1985—; trainer communication skills GM, Westchester, 1987—. Mem. Mid. States Rev. Fin. Com., Westchester, Fgn. Born Program Com., Westchester, policy making com. Learning Disabled Students, Westchester, freshman study skills Coll. Success Com., Westchester; speaker in field. Producer, host (radio broadcast mag.) Platinum Plus, 1986—. Mgr. advt. SSACIA, Westchester; co-host tv program Parenting, N.Y.C.; mem. Senate Homelessness Fact Finding Com., Westchester. Mem. ASCD, Nat. Pub. Radio, Nat. Coun. of Tchrs. of English, Lit. Soc. (past v.p.). Avocations: equestrian arts, field hockey, badminton, cryptograms, oil painting. Office: PO Box 95 Bronx NY 10467-0095

MADDOX-ADAMS, SHERRY, secondary school educator; Tchr. E.L. Connally Sch., Atlanta. Recipient Excellence Tchg. award, Nat. Coun. Negro Women, 2001, Chevy Malibu Tchg. Excellence award, Atlanta Jour.-Constitution Honor Roll Tchr. award; fellow, Earth Watch Inst.; Fulbright Meml. Fund Tchr. scholar, Japan. Mem.: Nat. Bd. for Profl. Tchg. Stds. (bd. mem.). Office: EL Connally Sch 1654 S Alvarado Terr SW Atlanta GA 30311*

MADDREY, WILLIS CROCKER, medical educator, internist, academic administrator, consultant, researcher; b. Roanoke Rapids, N.C., Mar. 29, 1939; s. Milner Crocker and Sara Jean (Willis) M.; m. Ann Marie Matt; children: Jeffrey, Gregory, Thomas. BS, Wake Forest U., 1960; MD, Johns Hopkins U., 1964. Diplomate: Am. Bd. Internal Medicine. Intern Osler Med. Service Johns Hopkins Hosp., Balt., 1964-65, asst. resident, 1965-66, 68-69, chief resident, 1969-70; fellow in liver disease Yale U., 1970-71; asst. prof. medicine Johns Hopkins U., Balt., 1971-75, assoc. prof., 1975-79, prof., 1980—82, asst. dean Sch. Medicine, 1975-79, assoc. dir. dept. medicine, 1979-82; prof., chmn. dept. medicine Jefferson Med. Coll., Phila., 1982-90; v.p. clin. affairs U. Tex. Southwestern Med. Ctr., Dallas, 1990-93, exec. v.p. clin. affairs, 1993—. Assoc. editor: Medicine, 1972-82, Hepatology, 1988-95, mem. editl. bd., 1981-84, 86-87, Gastroenterology, 1982-87, Am. Jour. Medicine, 1978-88; contbr. articles to profl. jours. Bd. dirs. Am. Liver Found., 1978-81, Dallas County Med. Soc., 1996-98; trustee Magee Rehab. Hosp., Phila., 1982-87. With USPHS, 1966-68. Mem. ACP (bd. regents 1986-92, pres. 92-93), Am. Soc. Clin. Investigation, Am. Gastroenterol. Assn., Am. Assn. Study Liver Disease (pres. 1981). Republican. Office: U Tex Southwestern Med Ctr 5323 Harry Hines Blvd Dallas TX 75390-8570

MADDY, JANET MARIE, retired physical education educator, dean; b. Crestline, Ohio, Feb. 20, 1939; d. Hubert Franklin and Mabel May (Hotelling) M. AA, Pasadena City Coll, 1959; BA, Calif. State U., L.A., 1965, MA, 1972. Instr. Calif. State Coll., L.A., fall 1965; tchr. phys. edn. Irving Jr. High, L.A. Unified Sch. Dist., spring 1966, Bret Harte Jr. High Sch., L.A. Unified Sch. Dist., 1966-67; tchr., phys. edn. tchr., dept. chair Walton Jr. High Sch.-Compton (Calif.) Unified Sch. Dist., 1967-72; tchr. phys. edn./coach Dominguez H.S., Compton, 1972-78; prin. Westchester Luth. Schs., L.A., 1978-84; tchr. phys. edn., dept. chair Nimitz Middle Sch., L.A. Unified Sch. Dist., Huntington Park, Calif., 1985-94, dean of students-C Track, 1994-97. Mem. shared decision making coun. Nimitz Middle Sch., Huntington Park, 1992-96; mentor tchr. selection com. L.A. Unified Sch. Dist., 1993-94; women in sports delegation to China, Citizen Amb. Program, Spokane, Wash., 1994, U.S. China Joint Conf. on Women's Issues, China, 1995, Internat. Conf. on Domestic Violence, Singapore, 1998. Chair cmty. com. Police Activity League, Ingelwood, Calif., 1990—93; co-chair Neighborhood Watch, Ingelwood, 1988—97, Crestline City Coun., 2001—; vol. Turning Point, Marion, Ohio, 1998—, Crawford Park Dist.; mem. Crawford County Bicentennial Com.; synod womens orgn. bd. ECLA Women, L.A., 1990—93, 1994—96, chair references and counsel com. triennial nat. conf., 1993, del. triennial conv. Mpls., 1996, v.p. Southeastern conf. N.W. Ohio Synod, 2000—01, pres. S.E. Conf., 2001—; sec. Luth. Social Svcs. Ctrl. Ohio, 1998—2000, v.p., 2001—02; adminstrv. coun. mem. Trinity Luth. Ch., Crestline, Ohio, 2000—01, congl. pres., 2002—03. Comdr. ret. USNR, 1960—83. Mem. CAHPER, AAHPER, CTA, UTLA. Democrat. Lutheran. Avocations: reading, sports, travel. Home: 501 E Bucyrus St Crestline OH 44827-1509

MADEIRA, FRANCIS KING CAREY, conductor, educator; b. Jenkintown, Pa., Feb. 21, 1917; s. Percy Childs and Margaret (Carey) M.; m. Jean E. Browning, June 17, 1947. Grad., Avon Old Farms, 1934; student, Julliard Grad. Sch., 1937-43; DFA (hon.), Providence Coll., 1966; DHL, R.I. Coll., 1969; MusD (hon.), Brown U., 1976. Instr. music Brown U., 1943-46, asst. prof. music, 1946-56, assoc. prof. music, 1956-66. Founder, condr. R.I. Philharm. Orch., 1945-78; concert pianist recitals and condr. concerts, U.S. and Europe; also guest condr. U.S. and fgn. orchs. World premiere Trilogy (JFK-MLK-RFK) (by Ron Nelson), R.I. Philharmonic Orch., 1969. Mem. music panel Maine State Arts Commn., 1987-90; bd. trustees Saco River Festival Assn., 1988-94; mem. adv. bd., trustee Portland (Maine) Symphony Orch., 1996—. Recipient Gov.'s award for excellence in arts, 1972; John F. Kennedy award for svc. to cmty., 1978, Maestro award R.I. Philharm. Orch., 1998, Millennium Reflections award R.I. Philharm. Orch., 1999, John Hazen White Sr. Leadership award R.I. Philharm. Orch., 2003, Citizen Citation award Mayor or Providence, R.I., 2003.

MADIGAN, RITA DUFFY, career education coordinator; b. N.Y.C., Jan. 22, 1919; d. Anthony E. and Mary (Feichter) Duffy; m. John Callanan Madigan, May 1, 1943; children: John C., James A., Paul F. BA in English History, Our Lady of Good Counsel Coll., 1940; M of Adminstrn., U. Bridgeport, 1963, postgrad., 1970. Tchr. English City of Bridgeport (Conn.), 1961-63, Birkshire Jr. High Sch., Birmingham, Mich., 1963-66; career counselor East Side Mid. Sch., Bridgeport, 1969-71; coord. career edn. Ctrl. HS, Bridgeport, 1972—99, ret., 1999. Recipient State SCOVE award, 1986, CCCA Meritorious award, 1993, Meritorious award Teikyo Post Univ, 1993, Meritorious award for svc. to cmty. Girl Scouts of Am., 1996. Mem. AAUW, NEA, Conn. Edn. Assn., Conn. Career Counselors Assn., Bridgeport Edn. Assn., St. Joseph's Ladies League (bd. dirs. 1992-94), Bridgeport U. Alumnae Assn. Republican. Roman Catholic. Avocations: skiing, golf, tennis, sailing, travel. Home: 44 Chatham Dr Trumbull CT 06611-3262

MADIGAN, SHARON MAY, physical education and health educator; b. Beaver Dam, Wis., May 5, 1947; d. Russell George and Orabell Rose (Mayr) M. BS, U. Wis., Oshkosh, 1969; postgrd., Marion Coll., 1980—. Tchr. high sch. Kiel (Wis.) Area Sch. Dist., 1969—. Instr. in CPR, ARC, Kiel, 1974—, instr. in first aid, 1975—; coach volleyball, basketball and track in field. Recipient Svc. award ARC, 1974, 75. Mem. AAPHERD, Wis. chpt. AAHPERD. Republican. Roman Catholic. Avocation: cooking. Home: 539 Millersville Ave Howards Grove WI 53083-1400 Office: Kiel Pub Sch Dist 210 Raider Hts Kiel WI 53042-1747

MADISON-COLMORE, OCTAVIA DIANNE, adult education educator; b. Lynchburg, Va., Mar. 28, 1960; d. Raymond Barlow Sr Madison and Dorothea Madison Anderson. BA, Hampton U., 1982; MEd, Lynchburg Coll., 1983; postgrad., George Mason U., Fairfax, Va., 1989-94; EdD, Va. Poly. Inst. and State U., 1997. Lic. prof counselor, marriage and family therapist, clinically cert. forensic counselor. Resource counselor Lynchburg Community Action Group, 1983, placement specialist, 1984; program mgr. Lynchburg 70001 Program, 1985; therapist, case mgr. Cen. Va. Community Svcs., Lynchburg, 1985-88; substance abuse counselor II Fairfax County Govt., 1988-94; therapist Women's Ctr. No. Va., Vienna, 1990-93; psychotherapist Dr. Carolyn Jackson-Sahni-Assocs., 1993; mental health therapist Arlington County Dept. Human Svcs., 1994-97; grad. asst. Va. Poly. Inst. and State U., 1994-97; asst. prof. Va. Tech., 1997—2003. Bd examiners Profl Counselors, 1991—; asst secy Southern Christian Leadership Conf, Lynchburg, Va., 1983—84; mem single ministry, asst chair youth adv bd Mt Pleasant Bapt Ch, Alexandria, Va., 1991—. Recipient 2-Star Award, United Way, 1989. Mem.: ACA, Assn. for Multicultural Counseling and Devel. (pub. policy chair), Nat. Bd. Cert. Counselors, Va. Counselors Assn. (sec.-treas. multicultural and devel. divsn. 1999), Chi Sigma Iota, Beta Kappa Chi, Psi Chi. Avocations: reading, swimming, sports, viewing mountains. Home: 6341 Mary Todd Ct Centreville VA 20121-3547 E-mail: omadison@vt.edu., colmore1@juno.com.

MADIX, ROBERT JAMES, chemical engineer, educator; b. Beach Grove, Ind., June 22, 1938; s. James L. and Marjorie A. (Strohl) M.; children: Bradley Alan, David Eric, Micella Lynn, Evan Scott. BS, U. Ill., 1961; PhD, U. Calif., 1964. NSF postdoctoral fellow Max Planck Inst., Göttingen, Fed. Republic of Germany, 1964-65; asst. prof. chem. engr. Stanford (Calif.) U., 1965-72, assoc. prof., chem. engr., 1972-77; prof. chem. engring. Stanford U., 1977—, chmn., chem. engr., 1983-87, prof. chemistry, 1981—. Cons. Monsanto Chem., St. Louis, 1975-84, Shell Oil Co., Houston, 1985-86; Peter Debye lectureship Cornell U., 1985; Eyring lectr. chemistry Ariz. State U., 1990; Barnett Dodge lectr. Yale U., 1996; disting. prof. lectr. U. Tex., Austin, 1980; Walter Robb Disting. lectr. Penn State U., 1996; chmn. Gordon Rsch. Conf. on Reactions on Surfaces, 1995. Assoc. editor Catalysis Rev., 1986—, Catalysis Letters, 1992—, Rsch. on Chem. Intermediates, 1994—; contbr. articles to profl. jours. Recipient Alpha Chi Sigma award AIChemE, 1990, Paul Emmett award Catalysis Soc. N.Am., 1984, Humboldt U.S. Sr. Scientist prize, 1978; Ford Found. fellow, 1969-72. Mem. AIChE, Internat. Precious Metal Inst. (Henry J. Alber award 1997), Am. Chem. Soc. (Irving Langmuir Disting. Lectr. award 1981, Arthur Adamson award 1997, Am. Phys. Soc., Am. Vacuum Soc., Calif. Catalysis Soc.

MADRID, OLGA HILDA GONZALEZ, retired elementary education educator, association executive; b. San Antonio, May 4, 1928; d. Victor A. and Elvira Ardilla Gonzalez; m. Sam Madrid, Jr., June 29, 1952; children: Ninette Marie, Samuel James. Student, U. Mex., San Antonio, St. Mary's U.; BA, Our Lady of Lake U., 1956, MEd, 1963. Cert. bilingual tchr., adminstr., Tex. Sec. Lanier HS San Antonio Ind. Sch. Dist., San Antonio, 1945-52; tchr. Collins Garden Elem. Sch., Storm Elem. Sch., San Antonio Ind. Sch. Dist., San Antonio, 1963-92; tutor Dayton, Ohio, 1952-54. Bd. dir., sch. rep. San Antonio Tchr. Coun., 1970-90; chair various coms. Collins Garden Elem., 1970-92. Elected dep. precinct, senatorial and state Dem. Conv., San Antonio, 1968—; apptd. commr. Keep San Antonio Beautiful, 1985; life mem., past pres. San Antonio YWCA; bd. dir. Luth. Gen. Hosp., Nat. Conf. Christians and Jews, Cath. Family and Children's Svc., St. Luke's Luth. Hosp.; nat. bd. dir. YWCA, 1985-96, also mem. exec. com.; mem. edn. commn. Holy Rosary Parish, 1994—; mem. bus. assoc. com. Our Lady of the Lake U., 1995—. Recipient Outstanding Our Lady Lake Alumni award Our Lady Lake U., 1975, Guadalupana medal San Antonio Cath. Archdiocese, 1975, Yellow Rose Tex. citation Gov. Briscoe, 1977; Olga H. Madrid Ctr. named in her honor, YWCA San Antonio and San Antonio City Coun., 1983; Lo Mejor De Lo Nuestro honoree San Antonio Light, 1991, honoree San Antonio Women's History Month Coalition, 1996; named Our Lady of Lake Outstanding Alumna, 1999, one of five women honored for promoting literacy and cultural hertiage with a sch. wall mural titled "Mis Palabras, Mi Poder", 2002. Mem. San Antonio Bus. and Profl. Women, Inc. (mem. exec. com.), Salute Quality Edn. (honoree 1993), Delta Kappa Gamma (Theta Beta chpt., mem. exec. com.). Avocations: reading, gardening. Home: 2726 Benrus Blvd San Antonio TX 78228-2319

MADRY-TAYLOR, JACQUELYN YVONNE, educational administrator; d. Arthur Chester and Janie (Cowart) Madry; 1 child, Jana LeMadry. BA, Fisk U., 1966; MA, Ohio State U., 1969; EdD, U. Fla., 1975. Cert. Inst. for Ednl. Mgmt., Harvard U., 1981. Tchr. Spanish Terry Parker Sr. High Sch., Jacksonville, 1967-72; instr. U. Fla., Gainesville, 1972-75; asst. to v.p. for acad. affairs. Morris Brown Coll., Atlanta, 1975-76; dean for instructional svcs. No. Va. Community Coll., Annandale, Va., 1976-83; dean undergrad. studies Bridgewater (Mass.) State Coll., 1983-92, exec. asst. to acting pres., 1988, acting v.p. acad. affairs, 1988-90; dir. Acad. Leadership Acad. Am. Assn. State Coll. and Univs., Washington, 1992-94; dir. ednl. programs and svcs. United Negro Coll. Fund Hdqs., 1994-97; pres. JYM Assocs., 1999—.

Cons. to colls., univs. and orgns., 1997-99; cons. W.K. Kellog Found., 1993-97; bd. dirs. Bridgewater State Coll. Early Learning Ctr., 1984-88; evaluator U.S. Dept. State/Fgn. Svc., Washington, 1982—, U.S. Dept. Edn., 1989—; pres. JYM Assocs., 1999—. Vice chmn. No. Va. Manpower Planning Coun., Fairfax County, Va., 1981. Recipient Cert. Achievement Bridgewater State Coll. Black Alumni, 1988, Women Helping Women award Soroptimist Internat., 1983, Outstanding Young Women Am. award, 1976, 78; named Personalities of South, 1977; recipient Outstanding Tchr./Student Rels. Humanitarian award B'nai B'rith, 1972. Mem. Pub. Mem. Assn. U.S. Fgn. Svc., Soroptimist Internat., Boston Club (v.p. 1986-88), Jack and Jill of Am., Inc., Pi Lambda Theta, Phi Delta Kappa, Alpha Kappa Alpha, Links Inc. (Reston, Va. chpt.). Methodist. Avocations: playing piano, bike riding. Home and Office: 12274 Angel Wing Ct Reston VA 20191-1119 Fax: 703-716-4364. E-mail: jkemt@aol.com.

MADSON, PAULETTE KAY, secondary school educator; b. Spencer, Iowa, Mar. 26, 1957; d. Harry Martin and Marjorie Elizabeth Nielsen; m. Larry Lee Madson, Aug. 3, 1990; 1 child, Gabriel Paul. BS, Iowa State U., 1979. Family and consumer sci. tchr. Walnut (Iowa) Community Sch., 1979—. Treas. Patterns for Progress, Des Moines, 1986-89; cons. Shelby County Econ. Devel. Coun., Harlan, Iowa, 1988; active Rep. Women, Walnut, 1989—, Questers, 1990—, Danish Immigrant Mus., 1987—, Future Homemakers Am. Hero-Master Advisor, 1993; mem. planning com. for Home Econs. Educators Conf., 1993, 94; fair judge 4-H, 1981—, state fair judge, 1991—; county voting del. Rep. Ctrl. Com., 1994. Recipient 4-H Alumni award Shelby County, 1993, Outstanding H.S. Tchr., Optimists, 1995. Mem. ASCD, FHA (hon.), Am. Vocat. Assn., Family and Consumer Sci. Edn. Assn., Iowa State U. Alumni Assn., Coll. Family and Consumer Scis. Alumni Assn., Delta Kappa Gamma. Republican. Lutheran. Avocations: gardening, sewing, entertaining. Home: 512 Quince Rd Harlan IA 51537-6524

MAEHL, WILLIAM HARVEY, historian, educator; b. Bklyn., May 28, 1915; s. William Henry and Antoinette Rose (Salamone) M.; m. Josephine Scholl McAllister, Dec. 29, 1941; children: Madeleine, Kathleen. BSc, Northwestern U., 1937, MA, 1939; PhD, U. Chgo., 1946. Asst. prof. history St. Louis U., 1941-42, Tex. A&M U., College Sta., 1943, De Paul U., Chgo., 1944-49; historian Dept. of Def., Karlsruhe, Stuttgart, Fed. Rep. Germany, 1950-52; chief briefing office U.S. hdqrs. U.S. Hdqs. European Command, Frankfurt, Germany, 1952-53; chief historian Arty. Sch., Okla., 1954; with War Plans Office, Hdqs. No. Air Materiel Area for Europe, Burtonwood, Eng., 1954-55; assoc. prof. European history Nebr. Wesleyan U., Lincoln, 1955-57, prof., 1958-62, 65-68; prof. German history Auburn (Ala.) U., 1968-81, prof. emeritus, 1981—. Vis. prof. U. Nebr., 1962, U. Auckland, New Zealand, 1963-64, Midwestern U., Wichita Falls, Tex., 1965. Author: German Militarism and Socialism, 1968, History of Germany in Western Civilization, 1979, A World History Syllabus, 3 vols., 1980, August Bebel, Shadow Emperor of the German Workers, 1980, The German Socialist Party: Champion of the First Republic, 1918-33, 1986; author monographs for U.S. Army in Europe, chpts. in books, atomic, biol. and emergency war plans for No. Air Materiel Area for Europe; contbr. poetry to Question of Balance, Tears of Fire, Disting. Poets Am., Best Poems of 1995, Journey of Mind; contbr. articles to profl. jours. Grantee Nebr. Wesleyan U., 1959, Auburn U., 1969-73, 79-80, Am. Philosophical Soc., 1973-74, Deutscher Akademischer Austauschdienst, 1978. Mem. Am. Hist. Assn., Phi Kappa Phi, Phi Alpha Theta.

MAESAKA, MARTHA H. special education educator; b. Honolulu, Apr. 28, 1940; d. Robert I. and Toshiko (Okasako) Tanaka; m. John K. Maesaka, July 21, 1962; children: Alan K., Robert K. BA, Washington U., 1962; MS, Bank Strett Coll., 1992. Cert. special edn. educator, elem. edn. educator. Kindergarten tchr. Ritenour Sch. Dist., St. Louis, 1962-63, Ft. Sill (Okla.) Army Sch., 1963-64; substitute teaching N.Y.C. Pvt. Schs., 1968-69; tchr. Collegiate Sch., N.Y.C., 1983-87, dept. chair spl. edn., 1987—. Grantee Collegiste Sch., 1990, Oxford U., 1991. Mem. ASCD, Nat. Coun. Tchrs. English, N.Y. C. Orton Soc. Episcopalian. Avocations: reading, writing, tennis, classical music. Home: 1212 5th Ave New York NY 10029-5210 Office: Collegiate Sch 370 W End Ave New York NY 10024-6505

MAGANZINI, BROTHER JOHN BERNARD, academic administrator; b. Somerville, Mass., Nov. 11, 1947; s. Bernard Louis and Eva (Alo) M. BS, St. Francis Coll., 1982; MS, Fordham U., 1987, postgrad., 1987—. Named to Order of Friars Ninor. Tchr. spl. religious edn. Kennedy Meml. Hosp. Day Program, Brighton, Mass., 1980-81; parish asst. Our Lady Queen of Peace, Hewitt, N.J., 1981; tchr. Holy Cross Sch., Bronx, N.Y., 1982, St. Anthony's Grade Sch., Washington, 1982-83; dir. religious edn. Holy Cross Parish & Sch., Bronx, 1983-84, tchr., 1984-88, dept. chmn., tchr., 1990-93, asst. prin., 1993—; tchr. East Boston (Mass.) Ctrl. Cath. Sch., 1988-90. With U.S. Army, 1967-69. Recipient John J. Duffy award Archdiocese of N.Y., 1987. Mem. Nat. Assn. Elem. Sch. Prins., Assn. Supervision and Curriculum Devel., Cath. Sch. Adminstrs. Assn. N.Y. State, Nat. Cath. Edn. Assn., 11th Armored Cavalry's Vets. Vietnam and Cambodia. Avocations: music, theater, youth work. Address: Saint Anthony Shrine 100 Arch St Boston MA 02110-1111

MAGAZINER, IRA, government agency administrator; b. N.Y.C. s. Louis and Sylvia M.; m. Suzanne Magaziner, 1981; children: Seth, Jonathan, Sarah. Grad., Brown U. With Boston Consulting Group; co-founder Telesis, 1979-88; issues advisor Clinton campaign, 1992; sr. advisor policy devel. The White House, 1993—98; bd. mem. Internet Policy Inst., Washington, 1998—. Chief architect Health Security Act, 1993. Rhodes scholar Oxford U. Office: Internet Policy Inst 1600 Pennsylvania Ave NW Washington DC 20004-2601*

MAGEE, STEPHEN PAT, economics and finance educator; b. Wichita, Kans., Mar. 17, 1943; s. Lawrence Patrick and Edna Willard (Brock) M.; m. Naneska Nall, Aug. 20, 1965 (div. Dec. 1987); children: Christopher Sean Patrick, Theodore Parker; m. Frances Jean Toepperwein, July 28, 1988. BA in Econs., Tex. Tech. U., 1965, MA in Econs., 1966; PhD in Econs., MIT, 1969. Asst. prof. U. Calif., Berkeley, 1969-71; assoc. prof. U. Chgo., 1971-76; economist The White House, Washington, 1972-73; rsch. fellow Brookings Insts., Washington, 1973-74; prof. fin. and econs. U. Tex., Austin, 1976—, chmn. fin., 1980-84, McDermott prof., 1980-84, Fred H. Moore prof., 1984-92, Charles and Sarah Seay prof., 1992-94; Bayless/Enstar Corp. chairholder, 1994—. Mem. econ. adv. bd. U.S. Sec. Commerce, Washington, 1978-79, NSF, 1979; expert witness Mesa Petroleum, Avis Rent-a-Car, El Paso Natural Gas, Kodak, Proctor & Gamble, AB Dick, Exxon; acad. lectr. in 11 fgn. countries for U.S. govt., 1977-88; vis. prof. bus. U. Chgo., 1990-91, 1997; expert effects of lawyers on U.S. economy and microeconomics and intellectual property and internat. econs. Author: International Trade (transl. to Japanese, Chinese, Korean), 1980, Black Hole Tariffs and Endogenous Policy Theory, 1989; mem. editorial bd. Rev. Econs. and Stats., 1972-79, Jour. Internat. Econs., 1977-79, Econs. and Politics, 1988-94, Rev. Internat. Econs., 1992-94; contbr. articles to scholarly publs., fin. publs. including Fortune Mag., Wall St. Jour. Grantee NSF, 1972-77; recipient Joe Beasley Teaching award U. Tex. Grad. Sch. Bus., 1979, Outstanding Career Rsch. Contbn. award, 1990, named Top-Core MBA prof., 1986. Avocations: soccer, drag racing, photography. Home: 1219 Castle Hill St Austin TX 78703-4125

MAGEE, THOMAS HENRY, medical doctor, medical educator; b. Newport, Rhode Island, Nov. 26, 1958; s. Francis Robert and Anne Louise (Moriarty) M.; m. Christina Marie (Lapolla), June 7, 1987. BA, Wesleyan Univ., 1977-81; MD, NY. Med. Coll., 1982-86. Diplomate, Am. Bd. Radiology. Staff radiologist Bethesda Naval Hosp., Md., 1991-94; asst. prof. medicine Uniformed Svc. Sch. of Med., Bethesda, Md., 1991-94, Kans. U. Sch. of Med., Kans. City, Kans., 1994—; staff radiologist Menorah Med. Pk., Overland Pk., Kans., 1994—; asst. prof. radiology U. Mo., Kans. City, Mo., 1997—. Pres. Rockhill Radiology, 1999. Contbg. articles to profl. journals including Radiology; Jour. of Computer Assisted Tomography, and others. Lt. comdr. USNR, 1991-94. Recipient: Jonas N. Muller Award, NY. Med. Coll., 1986. Mem. Am. Roentegen Ray Soc.; Radiologic Soc. of North Am. (cert. of merit 1990); Kansas City Roentegen Ray Soc. (pres.). Avocations: stamp collecting, tennis. Home: 185 Lanternback Island Dr Satellite Beach FL 32937-4704 Office: Neuroimaging Inst Melbourne FL

MAGEE, WAYNE EDWARD, biochemistry educator, researcher; b. Big Rapids, Mich., Apr. 11, 1929; s. William Fredrick and Elsie E. (Gifford) M.; m. Nannette A. Pierce, June 11, 1951; children: Lawrence, William, John. BA magna cum laude in Chemistry, Kalamazoo Coll., 1951; MS in Biochemistry, U. Wis., 1953, PhD in Biochemistry, 1955. Sci., then sr. sci. Upjohn Co., Kalamazoo, 1955-71; prof. life sci. Ind. State U., 1971-74; prof. biology, head divsn. allied health and life sci. U. Tex., San Antonio, 1975-80; prof. biochemistry, head dept. bacteriology and biochemistry U. Idaho, 1981-85; dir. divsn. Life. Scis., prof., head dept. biosci./biotech. Drexel U., Phila., 1985-92, prof. biosci., 1985-95, W.R. Nes prof. bioscience, 1995-99; prof. emeritus, 1999—. Adj. prof. biology Western Mich. U., 1970-71; adj. prof. molecular and cellular biology U. Ariz., 2000—. Contbr. articles and abstracts to profl. jours., chpts. in books. Wis. Alumni Found. Grad. fellow, 1951-52; Predoctoral fellow NSF, 1952-55. Fellow AAAS, Am. Chem. Soc., Am. Inst. Biol. Sci., Am. Soc. Biochemistry and Molecular Biology, Am. Soc. Microbiology. Achievements include research in phospholipid membranes, liposomes as drug carriers, immune modulation, monoclonal antibodies; improving under grad. edn. Home: 7672 S Galileo Ln Tucson AZ 85747 Office: U of Ariz Dept Molec and Cell Biology PO Box 210106 Tucson AZ 85721-0106 E-mail: mageewe@aol.com.

MAGER, MARGARET JULIA ECKSTEIN, special education educator; b. Belleville, Ill., May 4, 1954; d. Wilbert Frank and Therese Rose (Holdmeyer) Eckstein; m. Stephen Charles Mager, Oct. 1, 1983; children: Julia, Therese, Elizabeth. BA summa cum laude, St. Louis U., 1976; MEd in Spl. Edn. summa cum laude, U. Mo., St. Louis, 1983. Cert. tchr., spl. edn. tchr., Mo. Tchr. spl. edn. Cen. Sch.-Francis Howell Dist., St. Charles, Mo., 1975-85, Castlio Sch.-Francis Howell Dist., St. Charles, 1985-95, John Weldon Elem. Sch. Francis Howell Dist., St. Charles, 1995—2002, Independence Elem. Sch., 2002—. Troop leader St. Charles area coun. Girl Scouts U.S.; coach St. Charles Spl. Olympics, 1976-85; bd. dirs. Willows Way, 1995-00, bd. dirs. St. Monica Sch., 1998-01. Recipient St. Anne award Cath. Girl Scouting, 2001, Daisy award, Outstanding Leader award, Promise award, Girl Scouts. Mem. Coun. Exceptional Children, Learning Disabilities Assn., St. Charles Assn. Retarded Citizens (recording sec. 1982-83, Vol. of Yr. 1983), Am. Guild English Handbell Ringers, Choristers Guild, Mo. Citizens for Life, Bread for the World, Right to Life, Am. Assn. on Mental Retardation, Phi Beta Kappa. Roman Catholic. Avocations: music, photography, gardening. Home: 767 Montmartre Dr Saint Louis MO 63141-6121 Office: Independence Elem Sch 4800 Meadows Pkwy Saint Charles MO 63304 E-mail: mrsmager@aol.com.

MAGILL, DODIE BURNS, early childhood education educator; b. Greenwood, S.C., July 10, 1952; d. Byron Bernard and Dora Curry B.; children: Charles Towner II, Emily Curry. BA, Furman U., 1974; MEd, U. S.C., 1978. Cert. tchr., early childhood, elementary, elementary principal, supv., S.C. Kindergarten tchr. Sch. Dist. Greenville County, 1974-83; early childhood edn. instr. Valdosta (Ga.) State Univ., 1983-84; dir. lower sch. Valwood Sch., Valdosta, 1984-86; kindergarten tchr. Sch. Dist. Greenville County, 1986—. Tchr.-in-residence S.C. Ctr. for Tchr. Recruitment, Rock Hill, 1993, mem. policy bd.; workshop presenter and lectr. in various schs. and sch. dists. throughout U.S., 1974—; chmn. S.C. Pub. Kindergarten Celebration, 1994; giv. S.C. State Readiness Policy Group; mem. Southeastern Region Vision for Edn. Adv. Bd., S.C. Coun. Ednl. Collaboration. Demonstration tchr. S.C. ETV (TV show) Sch. Begins with Kindergarten. Mem. Gov. of S.C.'s State Readiness Policy Group, Southeastern Regional Vision for Edn. Adv. Bd., South Carolina Ctr. Tchr. Recruitment Policy Bd. Recipient Ralph Witherspoon award S.C. Assn. for Children Under Six; named Tchr. of Yr., Greenville County, 1992, 93, State of S.C., 1993, S.C. Tchr. of Yr. Coun. of Chief State Sch. Officers, 1993, 94. Mem. Assn. for Childhood Edn. Internat., S.C. Tchr. Forum (chmn. 1993-94), S.C. Early Childhood Assn., Alpha Delta Kappa. Presbyterian. Office: Partee Elem Sch 4350 Campbell Rd Snellville GA 30039-6922 Fax: 770-982-6923.

MAGILL, SAMUEL HAYS, academic administrator, higher education consultant; b. Decatur, Ga., July 19, 1928; s. Orrin Rankin and Ellen Howe (Bell) M.; children: Samuel Hays Jr., Katherine Magill Walters, Suzanne Magill Weintraub. AB, U. N.C., 1950; BD, Yale U., 1953; PhD, Duke U., 1962; LHD (hon.), Stockton State Coll., 1990. Ordained to ministry Congl. Christian Ch., 1953; gen. sec. Davidson Coll. YMCA, 1953-55; dir. student activities U. N.C., Chapel Hill, 1955-58, asst. dean student affairs, 1958-59; chaplain Dickinson Coll., 1962-63, asst. prof. religion, 1962-66, asso. prof. religion, 1966-68, dean coll., 1963-68; pres. Council Protestant Colls. and Univs., Washington, 1968-70; exec. asso., chief office acad. affairs Assn. Am. Colls., 1971-76; pres. Simon's Rock Early Coll., Great Barrington, Mass., 1976-79, Monmouth U., West Long Branch, N.J., 1980-93, pres. emeritus, 1993—; higher edn. cons., 1993-98; assoc. dir. gift planning U. N.C., 1999—. Adj. prof. Duke U., 1996. Trustee Jersey Shore Med. Ctr., 1985-93; bd. overseers N.J. Gov.'s Schs., 1986-93. Guerney Harris Kearns fellow in religion, 1960-61; Danforth Found. spl. grad. fellow, 1959-61. Fellow Soc. Values in Higher Edn. (dir. 1969-81); mem. Am. Assembly Collegiate Sch. Bus. (accreditation task force 1989-90), NCAA (pres.'s commn. 1990-93), Am. Coun. Edn. (commn. leadership devel. 1982-85, commn. on minority affairs 1986-89), Harvard Inst. Ednl. Mgmt., Assn. Ind. Colls. and Univs. N.J. (dir. 1980-93, exec. com. 1983—, chair 1987-89), Order of Golden Fleece U. N.C., Fearrington Dem. Club (co-chair 1997-98). Home: 1 Weybridge Pl Chapel Hill NC 27517-8938 E-mail: Smagill@nc.rr.com.

MAGLEBY, FLORENCE DEMING, special education educator; b. Porterville, Utah, Apr. 15, 1912; d. Vernon and Lydia (Florence) Deming; m. McRay Magleby, June 1, 1938; children: McRay, Jr., Susan D., Tom D. BS in Elem. and Secondary Edn., U. Utah, 1954, MS in Ednl. Psychology, 1969; EdD in Ednl. Psychology, Western Colo. U., 1977. Cert. early childhood edn., elem., secondary, spl. edn. and learning disabilities tchr., Utah, adminstr./supr., Utah, Orton-Gillingham therapist. Psychoednl. diagnosis, therapy practice, Salt Lake City, 1980-83, 88-00; psychol. evaluator Wash. County Sch. Dist, 1984-88; postdoctoral U. Utah; state specialist learning disabilities Utah State Office Edn., 1969-77; grant proposal field reader U.S. Office Edn.; dir. Utah State Learning Disability Ctr., 1971-73; clinic coord., demonstration tchr. Exemplary Ctr. Reading Instrn., 1967-69. Mem. Internat. Learning Disabilities Assn., Learning Disabilities Assn. Utah, (profl. adv. bd.), Internat. Reading Assn., Utah Coun Internat. Reading Assn., Orton Dyslexia Soc. (life), Coun. Exceptional Children (life), Delta Kappa Gamma, Utah Reading Resource Network Ctr. (adv. bd.). Home: 109 E South Temple Apt 3G Salt Lake City UT 84111-1106

MAGNANTI, THOMAS L. management educator, engineering educator; b. Omaha, Oct. 7, 1945; s. Leo A. and Florence L. Magnanti; m. Beverly A. McVinney, June 10, 1967; 1 child, R. Randall. BS in Chem. Engring., Syracuse U., 1967; MS in Stats., Stanford U., 1969, MS in Math., 1971, PhD in Ops. Rsch., 1972; Doktor honoris causa, Linköping U., 1995. Asst. prof. Alfred P. Sloan Sch. Mgmt. MIT, Cambridge, Mass., 1971-75; rsch. fellow, vis. prof. Ctr. for Ops. Rsch. and Econometrics Univ. Catholique de Louvain, 1976-77, 89; assoc. prof. Alfred P. Sloan Sch. Mgmt. MIT, 1975-79, prof., 1979-85, George Eastman prof. of mgmt. sci., 1985—, head mgmt. sci. area, 1982-88, co-dir. Ops. Rsch. Ctr., 1986—, founding co-dir. Leaders for Mfg. Program, 1988-94, prof. dept. elec. engring. and computer sci., 1995—; founding co-dir. System Design and Mgmt. Program, 1995—; now dean Sch. Engring., Inst. prof. MIT. Vis. scientist Bell Labs., 1977, GTE Labs., 1989; vis. scholar Grad. Sch. Bus. Adminstrn., Harvard U., 1980-81; mem. corp. mfg. staff Digital Equipment Corp., 1990; mem. editl. bd. Jour. Computational Optimization and Applications; mem. adv. bd. North Holland Handbooks in Ops. Rsch. and Mgmt. Sci. Author: Applied Mathematical Programming, 1977, Network Flows, 1993; editor: Jour. Ops. Rsch., 1983-87; co-editor: Math. Programming, 1981-83; assoc. editor SIAM Jour. Algebraic and Discrete Methods, 1981-83, Mgmt. Sci., 1978-81, Ops. Rsch., 1978-81, SIAM Jour. Applied Math., 1976-81, Math. Programming, 1988—; adv. editor Transp. Sci., 1985—, Mktg. Sci., Math. of Artificial Intelligence, 1987-91; contbr. numerous articles to profl. jours. Mem. NSF Sci. and Tech. Exchange Delegation to Soviet Union, 1977, NSF Rsch. Initiation Grant panels, 1985, 90; advisor NSF program on decision, risk and mgmt. sci., 1988, 89; mem. mfg. studies bd. Nat. Rsch. Coun., 1993—. Recipient Gordon Billard award MIT, 1992; Mgmt. Program Exch. grantee IREX, Curriculum Devel. grantee Sloan Found., 1990-94. Mem. IEEE (com. on large scale systems 1979-83), TIMS (mem. and chmn. various coms.), Nat. Acad. Engring., Ops. Rsch. Soc. Am. (pres. 1988-89, mem. and chmn. various coms., coun. mem. computer sci. tech. sect. 1983-87, co-organizer 1st doctoral consortium 1983, plenary speaker conf. on telecom. 1983, Lanchester prize 1993, Kimball medal 1994), Tau Beta Pi, Pi Mu Epsilon, Phi Kappa Phi. Achievements include research in network analysis and optimization, network design and combinatorial optimization, and applications in manufacturing, telecommunications, and transportation; development of new engineering/management programs. Home: 33 School St Hopkinton MA 01748-2003 Office: MIT Ops Rsch Ctr 77 Massachusetts Ave Cambridge MA 02139-4307

MAGNARELLI, SHARON DISHAW, Spanish language educator; b. Seneca Falls, N.Y., Oct. 3, 1946; d. Claude Nathan and Joyce Dishaw; m. Louis Magnarelli, June 28, 1969. BA, SUNY, Oswego, 1968; PhD, Cornell U., 1975. Prof. Spanish, Albertus Magnus Coll., New Haven, 1976-94, Quinnipiac U., Hamden, Conn., 1994—. Author: The Lost Rib, 1985, Reflections/Refractions, 1988, Understanding Jose Donoso, 1993; contbr. articles to profl. jours. Office: Quinnipiac U Hamden CT 06518 E-mail: sharon.magnarelli@quinnipiac.edu.

MAGNUSEN, OLGA CRISTINA, career planning and placement director; b. Havana, Cuba, Oct. 24, 1949; came to U.S., 1961; d. Pedro Jose and Olga (Wolter) Talavera; m. Karl Owen Magnusen, Aug. 7, 1982. BA in Spanish, Old Dominion U., 1971; MS in Guidance and Counseling, St. John's U., 1972. Counselor Bishop Kearney High Sch., Bklyn., 1972-73; career counselor Fla. Internat. U., Miami, 1974-77, coop. counselor, 1977-79, assoc. dir. career resource ctr., 1979-88, dir. career planning & placement, 1988—. Presenter in field. Hispanic Leadership fellow Woodrow Wilson Found., 1986; named to The Nat. Disting. Svc. Registry, 1989-90, Leadership Miami, 1987. Mem. Fla. Coop. Edn. Placement Assn. (pres. 1987-88), So. Coll. Placement Assn. (chair local arrangements 1989, chair orgn. com. 1990-91), Coop. Edn. Assn. (co-chair student affairs com. 1980-82, 90-91, chair 1991-92), Southeastern Assn. Colls. and Employers (v.p. fin. 1996—). Avocations: travel, cooking, doll collecting. Office: Fla Internat U Tamiami Trl Miami FL 33199-0001

MAGOON, DONALD W. retired business educator; b. Big Rapids, Mich., Mar. 1, 1910; s. Elbert Elvin Magoon and Edith Marie Whitsey; widowed, 1994; children: Elbert, Louise Libii, Carol Feakins. BSME, U. Mich., 1932, MS, 1934, MBA, 1941. Grad. gemologist Gemological Inst. Am. Instr. U. Findlay, 1932-33, asst. prof., 1934-37; rschr. L.A. Examiner, 1938-39; asst. prof. bus. La. State U., Baton Rouge, 1940-41; treas. Meijer Supermkts., Grand Rapids, Mich., 1946-60; cons. U.S. State Dept., Israel, Mex., 1961-64; prof. bus. Ea. Mich. U., Ypsilanti, 1965-80; prof. emeritus, 1980—. Tutor, Canton (Ohio) City Schs., 1996—. Capt., statis. officer, U.S. Army Signal Corps, 1941-46. Mem.: Rotary (com. mem. 1995—2001). Achievements include at 93 yrs. of age has sent out hundreds of letters with article 'World Scientists Warning to Humanity' on protecting the world environ. Avocation: gemology.

MAGRATH, C. PETER, educational association executive; b. N.Y.C., Apr. 23, 1933; s. Laurence Wilfrid and Giulia Maria (Dentice) M.; m. Deborah C. Howell, 1988; children: Valerie Ruth, Monette Fay. BA summa cum laude, U. N.H., 1955; PhD, Cornell U., 1962. Faculty Brown U., Providence, 1961-68, prof. polit. sci., 1967-68, assoc. dean grad. sch., 1965-66; dean Coll. Arts and Scis. U. Nebr., Lincoln, 1968-69, dean faculties Coll. Arts and Scis., 1969-72, interim chancellor, 1971-72, prof. polit. sci., 1968-72, vice-chancellor for acad. affairs, 1972; pres. SUNY, Binghamton, 1972-74, prof. polit. sci., 1972-74; pres. U. Minn., Mpls., 1974-84, U. Mo. System, 1985-91, Nat. Assn. State Univs. and Land Grant Colls., Washington, 1991—. Bd. dirs. Salzburg Seminar. Author: The Triumph of Character, 1963, Yazoo: Law and Politics in the New Republic, The Case of Fletcher v. Peck, 1966, Constitutionalism and Politics: Conflict and Consensus, 1968, Issues and Perspectives in American Government, 1971; (with others) The American Democracy, 2d edit., 1973; (with Robert L. Egbert) Strengthening Teacher Education, 1987; contbr. articles to profl. jours. Served with AUS, 1955—57. Mem. Assn. Am. Univs. (chmn. 1985-86, bd. dirs. Salzburg Sem. 2002—), Phi Beta Kappa, Phi Kappa Phi, Pi Gamma Mu, Pi Sigma Alpha, Kappa Tau Alpha. Office: Nat Assn State U and Land Grant Colls 1307 New York Ave NW Ste 400 Washington DC 20005-4722 E-mail: cmagrath@nasulgc.org.

MAGRINO, LISA ANN, elementary education educator; b. Syosset, N.Y., Apr. 8, 1967; d. Joseph William and Marie Clara (Trupo) M. BS in Edn., St. John's U., Jamaica, N.Y., 1990; MS in Early Childhood Edn., L.I. U., 1992. Cert. tchr., N.Y. Substitute tchr. Carle Place (N.Y.) Union Free Sch. Dist., 1990-92, Hicksville (N.Y.) Union Free Sch. Dist., 1990-92, Jericho (N.Y.) Union Free Sch. Dist., 1990-92, Syosset (N.Y.) Cen. Sch. Dist., 1990-92, tutor learning ctr., 1992-93; tchr. 6th grade Clarence E. Witherspoon Elem. Sch., South Ozone Park, N.Y., 1993—. Head tchr. Busy Bee Day Sch. and Camp, Amityville, N.Y., 1991. U.S. del. People to People Citizen Amb. Program, Reading Conf. to China. Mem. ASCD, Internat. Reading Assn. Home: 305 Southwood Cir Syosset NY 11791-5712

MAGRY, MARTHA J. elementary education educator; b. Paragould, Ark., Jan. 6, 1936; d. Burrell F. and Georgia M. (Watkins) Spence; m. James Magry, June 28, 1958; 1 child, David J. BS, Wheaton (Ill.) Coll., 1957; MS, Ind. U. Northwest, Gary, 1985; postgrad., Ark. State U., Jonesboro, 1964. Cert. elem., gen. sci. tchr. 4th grade tchr. Gary City Schs., sci. tchr.; 2d grade tchr. Merrillville (Ind.) Community Schs. Mem. NEA, Ind. State Tchrs. Assn., Merrillville Classroom Tchrs. Assn. Home: 5312 Pierce St Merrillville IN 46410-1364

MAGSIG, JUDITH ANNE, retired early childhood education educator; b. Saginaw, Mich., Nov. 9, 1939; d. Harold Howard and Catherine Louise (Barstow) Gay; m. George Arthur Magsig, June 22, 1963; children: Amy Catherine, Karl Joseph. BA, Alma Coll., 1961. Cert. tchr., early childhood tchr., Mich. 1st grade tchr. Gaylord (Mich.) Schs., 1961-64, spl. edn. tchr., 1965-67, kindergarten tchr., 1968-99; violin tchr. Concord Acad. Antrim, Mancelona, Mich., 2003—. Instr. Suzuki violin method; second violinist Traverse (Mich.) Symphony Orch., 1985-92, Cadillac (Mich.) Symphony Orch., 1999-2000, Gaylord Chamber Orch., 2001—, Great Lakes Chamber Orch., 2001—. Mem. ASCD, NEA, Mich. Edn. Assn., Gaylord Edn. Assn. (historian 1997-99), Assn. for the Edn. of Young Children, Assn. for Childhood Edn. Internat., Suzuki Assn. Am., Am. String Tchrs. Assn., Music Tchrs. Nat. Assn., Order Eastern Star (chaplain 1997-98, warder 1999-2000, electa 2000—), Spirits of the North, Alpha Delta Kappa (pres. Beta Rho chpt. 1980-82, 84-86, treas. 1996-2000, music chmn. Mich., v.p.

Beta Rho chpt. 2000-02, pres. 2002—). Methodist. Avocations: cross-stitch, camping, canoeing, sewing. Home: 2130 Evergreen Dr Gaylord MI 49735-9165 Office: Musik Haus 2300 S Otsego Ave Gaylord MI 49735-1869 E-mail: gjmagsig@avci.net.

MAGUIRE, JOHN DAVID, academic administrator, educator, writer; b. Montgomery, Ala., Aug. 7, 1932; s. John Henry and Clyde (Merrill) M.; m. Lillian Louise Parrish, Aug. 29, 1953; children: Catherine Merrill, Mary Elizabeth, Anne King. AB magna cum laude, Washington and Lee U., 1953, Litt.D. (hon.), 1979; Fulbright scholar, Edinburgh (Scotland) U., 1953-54; B.D. summa cum laude, Yale, 1956, PhD, 1960; postdoctoral research, Yale U. and U. Tübingen, Germany, 1964-65, U. Calif., Berkeley, 1968-69, Silliman U., Philippines, 1976-77; HLD (hon.), Transylvania U., 1990. Dir. Internat. Student Ctr., New Haven, 1956-58; mem. faculty Wesleyan U., Middletown, Conn., 1960-70, assoc. provost, 1967-68; vis. lectr. Pacific Sch. Religion and Grad. Theol. Union, Berkeley, 1968-69; pres. SUNY Coll. at Old Westbury, 1970-81, Claremont (Calif.) Grad. U., 1981-98. Sr. fellow Claremont Grad. U. Sch. Politics and Econs.; dir. nat. project Renewing Democracy through Interracial/Multicultural Comty. Bldg., 1998—. Author: The Dance of the Pilgrim: A Christian Style of Life for Today, 1967; also numerous articles. Mem. Conn. adv. comt. US Comn. Civil Rights, 1961—70; participant White House Conf. on Civil Rights, 1966; advisor Martin Luther King Cent. Social Change, Atlanta, 1968—, permanent trustee, 1968—, 1st chmn. bd. dirs., 1968—; bd. dirs. Nassau County Health and Welfare Coun., 1971—81, pres., 1974—76; trustee United Bd. Christian Higher Ed in Asia, 1975—81, Inst. Int. Ed., 1980—86; charter trustee Tomas Rivera Policy Inst., Claremont, Calif., 1984—, vice chmn., 1987—94, treas., 1995—; with Asn. Ind. Calif. Cols. and Univs., 1985—98; chmn. Asn. Ind. Calif. Cols. and Univs., 1990—92, mem. exec. comt., 1992—98; with Calif. Achievement Coun., 1985—94, chmn., 1990—94; with Transylvania Univ. Bingham Trust, 1987—, Lincoln Found. and Lincoln Inst. Land Policy, Inc., 1987—94; The JL Found., 1988—; with Bus. Enterprise Trust, 1989—99; with Educ. Found. African Ams., 1991—99; bd. dirs. Asn. Am. Cols. and Univs., 1981—86, chmn., 1984—85; bd. dirs. Legal Def. and Edu. Fund NAACP, 1991—, west coast div., 1981—91, Thacher Sch., Ojai, Calif., 1982—94, vice chmn., 1986—90; with Salzburg Seminar, 1992—96; charter mem. Pacific Coun. Int. Policy, 1995—; mem. Am. Comt. US-Soviet Rels., 1981—92, Blue Ribbon Calif. Comn. Teaching Profession, 1984—86; mem. gov. coun. Aspen Inst. Wye Faculty Seminar, 1984—94; mem. Coun. Fgn. Rels., 1983—; mem. adv. bd. RAND Cent. Research Immigration Policy, 1994—97, Peter F. Drucker Found. Non-Profit Mgt, 1990—, Andrew Young Sch. Policy Ga. State Univ., 1999—, The Eureka Communities, 1998—; mem. Pres.'s Adv. Coun. Comn. on Calif. Master Plan Higher Educ., 1986—87, Los Angeles Educ. Alliance Restructuring Now, 1992—98, Calif. Bus. Higher Educ. Forum, 1992—98; leader Idyllwild Sch. Summer Poetry Festival, 1998—. Recipient Julia A. Archibald High Scholarship award Yale Div. Sch., 1956; Day fellow Yale Grad. Sch., 1956-57; Kent fellow, 1957-60; Howard Found. postdoctoral fellow Brown U. Grad. Sch.., 1964-65; Fenn lectr., 7 Asian countries, 1976-77; recipient Conn. Prince Hall Masons' award outstanding contbns. human rights in Conn., 1965; E. Harris Harbison Gt. Tchr. prize Danforth Found., 1968 Fellow Soc. Values Higher Edn. (pres. 1974-81, bd. dirs. 1972-88); mem. Phi Beta Kappa, Omicron Delta Kappa Democrat. Office: Claremont Grad U Inst for Dem Renewal 170 E 10th St Claremont CA 91711-5909

MAGUIRE, MILDRED MAY, chemistry educator, magnetic resonance researcher; b. Leetsdale, Pa., May 7, 1933; d. John and Mildred (Sklarsky) Magura. BS in Chemistry, Carnegie-Mellon U., 1955; MS in Phys. Chemistry, U. Wis., 1960; PhD in Phys. Chemistry, Pa. State U., 1967. Devel. chemist Koppers Co., Monaca, Pa., 1955-58; rsch. chemist Am. Cyanamid Co., Stamford, Conn., 1960-63; asst. prof. chemistry Waynesburg (Pa.) Coll., 1967-70, assoc. prof., 1970-74, prof., 1974—. Leverhulme vis. prof. U. Leicester, Eng., 1980-81, summer 1989; cons. Pitts. Energy Tech. Ctr., summers 1978-86; faculty rsch. participant Oak Ridge Assoc. Univs., 1978-80, 82-85; U.S. del. Internat. Conf. Phys. Chemists, China, 1996, Sci. and Tech. Conf., India, 1997. Contbr. articles to sci. jours., chpt. to book. Sec. Waynesburg Women's Club, 1981-82; citizen amb. People to People Program, 1996, 97. Recipient Woman of the Yr. award AAUW, Waynesburg, 1983; Cottrell grantee Rsch. Corp. N.Y., 1970-71; Leverhulme vis. fellow U.K., 1980-81; Curie Internat. fellow AAUW, U.K., 1980-81; Robert West Superconductor Rsch. Grantee, Univ. Wis., 2001-02. Mem. AAUP, AAAS, Am. Chem. Soc.; Spectroscopy Soc. of Pitts.; Pitts. Soc. of Analytical Chemists. Avocations: gardening, painting, swimming, classical music, reading. Home: 1550 Crescent Hills Waynesburg PA 15370-1654 Office: Waynesburg Coll College St Waynesburg PA 15370 E-mail: mmaguire@waynesburg.edu.

MAGYARY, CYNTHIA MARIE, elementary school educator, music educator; b. New Brighton, Pa., June 3, 1956; d. Nicholas (m) Magyary and Mary Helen Bedo-Magyary. BS in Music Edn., BS in Elem. Edn., Geneva Coll., 1978. Elem. music tchr. Wilmington Area Sch. Dist., New Wilmington, Pa., 1983—. Youth choir dir. Neshannock Presbyn. Ch., New Wilmington, Pa., 2001. Mem.: Wilmington Area Educators Assn. (sec.), Pa. State Educators Assn., Pa. Music Educators Assn. Avocations: piano, golf, swimming, sewing, reading. Office: New Wilmington Elem 450 Wood St New Wilmington PA 16142 Home: 168 Orchard Terrace Dr New Wilmington PA 16142

MAHAFFEY, JAMES PERRY, education educator, consultant; b. Greenville, S.C., Sept. 29, 1935; s. Earl Perry and Flora Virginia (Painter) M.; m. Nora Dean Padgett, Dec. 22, 1961; 1 child, Janet E. BA cum laude, Furman U., 1957; MA, Vanderbilt U., 1958; PhD, U. S.C., 1974. Cert. edn. specialist-reading. Tchr. Greenville (S.C.) County Schs., 1958-61, reading supr., 1961-65; S.C. state reading supr. S.C. Dept. Edn., Columbia, 1965-69; asst. supt. for instrn. Anderson (S.C.) Pub. Schs., 1969-77; assoc. prof. edn. Furman U., Greenville, 1977-79; assoc. supt. for instrn. Horry County Schs., Conway/Myrtle Beach, S.C., 1979-91; prof. edn. Wofford Coll., Spartanburg, S.C., 1991—. Adj. prof. Converse Coll., Spartanburg, 1961-65; instr. U. S.C., Columbia, 1973-74; mem. S.C. Basic Skills Commn., Columbia, 1981-89; bd. trustees So. Assn. Colls./Schs., Atlanta, 1990-93. Author, editor: Teaching Reading in South Carolina Secondary Schools, 1969; contbg. author: Elementary School Criteria: Focusing on Student Performance, 1994; contbr. articles to profl. jours. Named Outstanding Sch. Adminstr., S.C. Assn. Sch. Adminstrs., Columbia, 1989, Outstanding Educator, So. Assn. Colls./Schs., Atlanta, 1990; Carnegie fellow Peabody Coll. of Vanderbilt U., Nashville, 1958. Mem. Internat. Reading Assn. (S.C. pres. 1977). Baptist. Avocation: gardening. Office: Wofford Coll Edn Dept 429 N Church St Spartanburg SC 29303-3612 Home: 1303 Cherokee St Conway SC 29527-4801

MAHER, SHEILA, secondary school principal; Prin. R. L. Turner High Sch., Carrollton, Tex., 1997, Creekview H.S., Carrollton, 1997—. Recipient Blue Ribbon Sch. award U.S. Dept. Edn., 1990-91. Office: Creekview HS 3201 Old Denton Rd Carrollton TX 75007-3957

MAHER, THOMAS GEORGE, academic administrator, producer, media educator; b. St. Louis, Feb. 18, 1947; s. Dale Russel and Dorothy Leone M.; m. (div.). AB, St. Louis U., 1969, MA, 1971; PhD, U. So. Calif., 1985. Cert. C.C. tchr. and supr., Calif. Tchg. fellow St. Louis U., 1969-71; assoc. prof. Chaffey Coll., Rancho Cucamonga, Calif., 1974-79, media dir., 1980-84; assoc. producer Corp. for C.C. TV, Orange, Calif., 1979-80; assoc. dir. instrnl. tech. Calif. State Poly. U., Pomona, 1984-89; dir. office media svcs. U. Ill., Chgo., 1989-94; dir. office instrnl. svcs. Colo. State U., Ft. Collins, 1994—, interim v.p. divsn. ednl. outreach, 2000—02. Cons. Rsch. Comm., Ltd., Boston, 1984—; book reviewer Focal Press, Inc., Boston, 1985—. Writer: (TV series) Project: Universe, 1978 (Emmy award nomination 1979), The Business of Management, 1981; assoc. producer, dir., writer (TV series) Oceanus: The Marine Environment, 1979 (Emmy award 1980); exec. producer (TV program) For the People: Local Gov. Budget Making, 1992 (Cert. Merit, Chgo. Internat. Film/Video Festival 1992); producer, dir. numerous refereed ednl. TV shows, 1974—. 1st lt. USAF, 1971-74. Mary Clemens scholar St. Louis U., 1965-67, Educare scholar U. So. Calif., 1983-84; grantee numerous competitive contracts. Mem. Acad. TV Arts and Scis., Am. Ednl. Research Assn., Assn. for Ednl. Comm. and Tech. Democrat. Roman Catholic. Avocations: reading spy novels, computers, running, theatre. Office: Colo State U A 71 Clark Bldg Fort Collins CO 80523-2023 E-mail: thomas.maher@colostate.edu.

MAHESWARANATHAN, PONN, physicist, educator, physicist, researcher; b. Colombo, Sri Lanka, Dec. 15, 1954; arrived in U.S., 1985, naturalized, U.S., 1998; s. Sithamparanathar and Kamalambikai Ponnampalam; m. Shyamala Navaratnam, July 2, 1987; children: Mithunan, Niruban. BS, Peradeniya U., Sri Lanka, 1978; MS, Purdue U., 1982, PhD, 1985. Asst. lectr. U. Peradeniya, 1978-79, U. Jaffna, Sri Lanka, 1979-80; asst. prof. physics Winthrop U., Rock Hill, SC, 1985-92, assoc. prof., 1992—2003, prof., 2003—. Contbr. articles to profl. jours. Grantee, Winthrop Rsch. Coun., 1992, 1998, 2000. Mem.: Am. Assn. Physics Tchrs., Am. Phys. Soc. Hindu. Achievements include discovery of of enhancement of electromechanical coupling; piezoelectric constant in Cd1-x MnxTe. Home: 1750 Colony Rd Rock Hill SC 29730-3810 Office: Winthrop U 101 Sims Rock Hill SC 29733-0001

MAHLA, MICHAEL E. anesthesiologist, educator; b. Wilmington, Del., Mar. 8, 1953; s. Elbert Myron and Mary Pauline (Tice) M.; m. Sno Ellen White, June 8, 1979; 1 child, Melody Joy. BS in Chemistry, Davidson Coll., 1975; MD, Jefferson Med. Coll., 1979. Diplomate Am. Bd. Anesthesiology. Intern Walter Reed AMC, Washington, 1979-80, resident in anesthesiology, 1980-83; fellow in neuroanesthesiology Johns Hopkins Med. Inst., Balt., 1983; mem. staff Shands Teaching Hosp., Gainesville, Fla.; assoc. prof. anesthesiology/neurosurgery U. Fla. Coll. Medicine. Program dir. anesthesiology residency Walter Reed AMC, Washington, 1986-88; assoc. prof., assoc. chair edn. dept. anesthesiology U. Fla. Coll. Medicine, Gainesville, 1995—. Author: (with others) Clinical Anesthesiology Practice, 1994, Clinical Neuroanesthesia, 1997. Fellow Am. Soc. Neurologic Monitoring; mem. AMA, Am. Soc. Anesthesiologists, Soc. Neurosurg. Anesthesia and Critical Care. Office: Box 100254 Dept Anesthesiology Gainesville FL 32610-0254

MAHLENDORF, URSULA RENATE, literature educator; b. Strehlen, Silesia, Germany, Oct. 24, 1929; came to U.S., 1953; Student, Oberschule an der Hamburgerstraße, Bremen, Fed. Republic Germany, 1950, U. Tübingen, Fed. Republic Germany, 1950-52, Brown U., 1953-57, MA in English Lit., 1956, PhD in German Lit., 1958; student, Bonn (Fed. Republic Germany) U., 1953, London U. Teaching asst. Brown U., Providence, 1953-57; from acting instr. to prof. German U. Calif., Santa Barbara, 1957—93, assoc. dir., campus coord. edn. abroad program, 1967—69, chmn. dept. Germanic and Slavic langs. and lits., 1980-83, assoc. dean Coll. Letters and Sci., 1986-89, emeritus, 1993—. Chmn. symposium in honor of Harry Slochower, 1977; campus coord. edn. abroad program U. Calif., 1967-69, assoc. dir., 1969-72; co-chair Nietzsche symposium Dept. Germanic and Slavic Langs. and Lits., U. Calif., Santa Barbara, 1981. Author: The Wellsprings of Literary Creation, 1985; editor: (with John L. Carleton) Man for Man: A Multi-Disciplinary Workshop on Affecting Man's Social and Psychological Nature through Community Action (Charles C. Thomas), 1973, Dimensions of Social Psychiatry, 1979, (with Arthur Lerner) Life Guidance through Literature, 1992; assoc. editor Am. Imago, Am. Jour. Social Psychiatry, Jour. Evolutionary Psychology; contbr. more than 90 articles to profl. jours. Recipient Alumni award, 1981; rsch. grantee U. Calif., 1974—; Fulbright fellow, 1951-52. Mem. MLA, Am. Assn. for Aesthetics and Art Criticism (past pres. Calif. div.), Assn. for applied Psychoanalysis (profl. mem.), Am. Assn. Social Psychiatry (councillor 1977-81), Internat. Assn. Social Psychiatry (treas. 1978-83). Avocations: sculpting, woodcarving. Home: 1505 Portesuello Ave Santa Barbara CA 93105-4626 Office: U Calif Dept Dept Germanic Semitic Slavic Studie Santa Barbara CA 93106

MAHLMANN, JOHN JAMES, music education association administrator; b. Washington, Jan. 21, 1942; s. Charles Victor and Mary Elizabeth (Deye) M.; m. Ning Ning Chang, Feb. 5, 1972; 1 son, Justin Geeng Ming. BFA, Boston U., 1962, MFA, 1963; postgrad., U. Notre Dame, summer 1962; EdD, Pa. State U., 1970; DM (hon.), Duquesne U., 1997. Grad. asst. Boston U., 1962-63, instr., supr. student tchrs., dir. masters degree candidates, 1964-66; grad. asst., research asst. Pa. State U., 1963-64, instr., 1966-67, dir. gallery, art edn. dept., 1966-67; asst. prof. Tex. Tech Coll., 1967-69; chmn. tenure and promotions com.; dir. publs., asst. exec. sec. Nat. Art Edn. Assn., Washington, 1969-71, exec. sec., 1971-82, also tour dir. to Japan and Orient; exec. dir. Music Educators Nat. Conf., 1983—. Instr. drawing Lubbock Art Assn.; asst. debate coach, asst. coord. forensics Boston U.; vis. instr., mem. staff George Washington U., No. Va. C.C., Tchrs. Coll. N.Y. Exhibited at, Boston U., Pa. State U., Harvard U., Tex. Tech. U., Salem (Mass.) State Coll., Botolph Gallery, Boston, Inst. Contemporary Art, Boston, Barncellar Gallery, Orleans, Mass., State Gallery, State College, Pa., Halls Gallery, Lubbock, Lubbock Art Assn., Loft Gallery, San Antonio, Llano Estacado Art Assn., Hobbs, N.Mex., Purdue U., Cushing Gallery, Dallas, Religious Art Exhbn., Cranbrook Acad. Art, Bloomfield Hills, Mich., Upstairs Gallery, Arlington, Tex., S.W. Tex. State Coll., San Marcos.; Editor: Art Edn., 1970-81, Art Tchr., 1971-80; contbr. articles to mags. Mem. adv. bd. Hartt Sch., 1997—. Mem. Music Educators Nat. Conf., Nat. Art Edn. Assn., Am. Soc. Assn. Execs., Washington Soc. Assn. Execs., Phi Delta Kappa. Home: 10703 Cross School Rd Reston VA 20191-5105 Office: Music Ed Nat Conf 1806 Robert Fulton Dr Reston VA 20191-4348

MAHMOUD, BEN, artist, art educator; b. Charleston, W.Va., Oct. 6, 1935; s. Ben Mahmoud and Ina (Lilly) Mahmoud-Waybright; m. Wendy Kravit, Aug. 1987; children: Jermy, Amanda, Kassandra. Cert., Columbus (Ohio) Art Sch., 1957; BFA, Ohio U., 1958, MFA, 1960. Instr. Columbus Coll. Art & Design, 1960-61; asst. prof. La. U. InterAm., San Germán, P.R., 1961-63, W.Va. State Coll., Institute, 1963-65; from asst. prof. to prof. No. Ill. U., DeKalb, 1965-88, pres., rsch. prof., 1988—92, Disting. rsch. prof., 1998, Disting. prof. emeritus, 1998—. One-man shows include Zaks Gallery; represented in permanent collections Art Inst. Chgo., Bklyn. Mus., Mus. Contemporary Art Chgo. Nat. Endowment for Arts fellow in painting, 1978. Home: 118 Ilehamwood Dr Dekalb IL 60115-1857 Studio: 1016 Market St Dekalb IL 60115-3527

MAHMOUDI, HODA, academic administrator, sociology educator; b. Tehran, Iran, Oct. 24, 1948; came to U.S., 1959; s. Jalil and Badri (Behnam) M.; m. Richard W. DaBell, June 21, 1975; 1 child, Bijan Mahmoudi DaBell. BA, U. Utah, 1972, MA, 1973, PhD, 1979. Instr. U. Utah, Salt Lake City, 1976-78, acting dir. Middle East libr., 1978-79; adj. prof. Santa Monica (Calif.) Coll., 1984-86; asst. prof. Westminster Coll., Salt Lake City, 1979-84; assoc. dean for acad. affairs Calif. Luth. U., 1987-93, assoc. prof., 1986-96, Olivet (Mich.) Coll., 1996—, assoc. v.p. for acad. affairs, 1997—. Sec. Women for Internat. Peace and Arbitration, Santa Monica, 1975-96; adv. bd. mem. Nat. Conf. of Christians and Jews, Santa Monica, 1991—, Jour. of Baha'i Studies, Ottawa, Can., 1988—; statis. cons. in field. Author: (book chpt.) Altruism and Extensivity in the Baha'i Religion, 1992, Tahira: An Early Iranian Feminist, 1985; contbr. articles to profl. jours. Recipient Prof. of the Yr. award Westminster Coll., 1982, Award for Jour. Article, Assn. for Baha'i Studies, 1990. Mem. AAUW, Am. Sociol. Assn., Consortium on Peace Rsch., Edn. & Devel., World Future Soc., Western Social Sci. Assn. Baha'I. Avocations: photography, music. Office: Olivet Coll Olivet MI 49076

MAHON, MARINNA FAIRBANK, secondary education educator, writer, consultant; b. Phila., Dec. 27, 1940; d. Joseph Aloysius and Marie Josephine (McMahon) McNulty; m. Robert L. Fairbank (div. 1980); children: Wendy Anne, Elsa Marie. BA in History and Polit. Sci., Rosemont (Pa.) Coll., 1963; postgrad., Spanish-Am. Bilingual Inst., Mexico City, 1974-79, John Carroll U., 1991-93, Case Western Res. U., 1995-96. Cert. secondary tchr., Ohio. Substitute tchr. Cleveland Heights-University Heights (Ohio) Bd. Edn., 1982-92, 97—; cons. in writing, manuscript rschr., copywriter Mahon Enterprises, Chagrin Falls, Ohio, 1988—. Substitute tchr. Shaker Heights (Ohio) Sch. Bd., 1989-94, Mayfield Heights (Ohio) Bd. Edn., 1990-92, Orange Village Sch. Dist., Beachwood, Ohio, 1996-97; tutor, mem. substitute faculty Beaumont Sch., Cleveland Heights, 1996-97; writer, coord. nat. newsletter on stress reduction Am. Mensa Ltd., Dallas, 1990-96, writer, rschr., coord. nat. newsletter on entrepreneurship, 1994-96. Contbr. poetry to various publs. Vol., capt. local fund raising Sta. WTTW, pub. TV, Chgo., 1969-70; fund raiser Humane Soc., Mexico City, 1976; vol. Natural History Mus., Cleve., 1987-89; vol. exhbn. tour guide Cleve. Art Mus., summer 1997. Recipient Sound of Poetry award Nat. Libr. Poetry, 1995; tchr. devel. scholr John Carroll U., 1990-93. Mem. NAFE, Am. Mensa (program chmn. Cleve. 1988-90), Smithsonian Assocs. Avocations: writing, abstract prints artist, hiking, swimming, reading. Office: Cleve Heights-Univ Heights Bd Edn 2155 Miramar Blvd University Heights OH 44118-3301

MAHONEY, CATHERINE ANN, artist, educator; b. Macon, Mo., Nov. 18, 1948; d. Joe H. and Berniece Joyce (Garnett) Dickson; m. Michael W. Mahoney, July 19, 1969; children: Karin Lynn Mahoney Broeker, Ryan Michael. BS in Edn. with honors, Truman U., Kirksville, 1969. Mo. state life cert. for tchg. art. Elem./secondary art instr. Bucklin (Mo.) R-I Schs., 1970-74; pvt. art instr. Groom (Tex.) Artist's Assn., 1974-75; substitute tchr. Gasconade R-I Schs., Hermann, Mo., 1977-89; pvt. art instr. Colorful Brushes Studio, Hermann, Mo., 1987—; elem./secondary art instr. Crosspoint Christian Schs., Union, Mo., 1994-98. Pres. City of Hermann Arts Coun., 1983-87, membership chmn., 1980-82; dir. Summertime Children's Watercolor Workshops, Colorful Brushes, Hermann, 1987—. One-woman shows at Truman U., Kirksville, 1969, Capitol City Art Guild, Jefferson City, Mo., 1983, Kolbe Gallery of Art, Hermann, 1984, Colorful Brushes Studio, Hermann, 1987-94; designer Sister Cities Emblem City of Hermann/Arolsen, Germany, 1989; works published in: Best of Watercolor: Texture, 1998. Pres. Hermann Parent-Tchr. Orgn., 1985—87; leader 4-H, Girl and Boy Scouts, Hermann, 1982—95; organist, pianist, tchr. Hermann Cath. and Bapt. Chs., 1977—97, E. Free Ch., 1997—2003. Named Outstanding Young Woman of Yr., Hermann Jaycees, 1984, 1st place award Mo. Artists Collection, Mo. Pub. Svc., Sedalia, Mo., 1992, 3d place award and purchase prize Watercolor USA, Springfield (Mo.) Art Mus., 1995, 1st place award Arts Rolla Art Show, 1999. Mem.: Mo. Watercolor Soc. (M. Graham Mdse. award 2003), Oil Painters Am., St. Louis Artist Guild (mem. art sect., Hon. Mention 1993, 1998, 2002), Watercolor USA Honor Soc. (hon. Art Show award 1995), Okla. Watercolor Assn. (assoc. included Art Show 1989), Nat. Watercolor Soc. (assoc. included Nat. Art Show 1995). Avocations: piano, reading, embroidery, sewing, knitting. Home: 1058 Old Stonehill Hermann MO 65041 Office: Colorful Brushes Studio 126 E 4th St Hermann MO 65041-1130 E-mail: camahoney@ktis.net.

MAHONEY, LINDA KAY, mathematics educator; b. Bay Shore, NY, June 8, 1951; d. James Nathaniel and Katherine Pauline (Booth) Palmer Jr.; m. Peter Allan Mahoney, Jr., June 5, 1976; children: Matthew J., Michael J., Patrick A. BS, U. Md., 1972; MEd, 1979; postgrad., R.I. Coll., 1988-89, Providence Coll., 1989-90. Tchr. math. Prince George's County Pub. Schs., Benjamin Tasker Jr. High, Bowie, Md., 1973-76; tchr. substitute Warwick (R.I.) Pub. Schs., 1987-90, tchr. math., 1990-91; instr. math. Ctrl. Tex. Coll., P.R., 1992-96, U. Tenn., Knoxville, 1996—. Vol. Sherman Elem. Sch., Warwick, 1989-90, Rohr Elem. Sch., Chula Vista, Calif., 1985-87. Mem.: Am. Math. Soc., Math. Assn. Am., Nat. Coun. Tchrs. Math. Republican. Lutheran. Avocations: gardening, baking. E-mail: mahoney@math.utk.edu.

MAHONEY, MAUREEN E. retired secondary education educator; b. Jersey City, Aug. 24, 1940; d. Michael J. and Margaret M. (Lynch) M. BA, Montclair State Coll., Upper Montclair, N.J., 1962, MA, 1964; postgrad., NYU, Fairleigh Dickinson U. Tchr. English Teaneck (N.J.) High Sch., Northern Highlands Regional High Sch., Allendale, N.J., 1994. N.J. state judge Nat. Coun. Tchrs. English Achievement awards in writing; critiquer in creative writing Bergen County Teen Arts Festival; supr. M.A. in Tchg. candidates Fairleigh Dickinson U. Dir. children's theater prodns., dramatic prodns. 2d lt. USAF, 1962. Mem. NEA, N.J. Edn. Assn., Bergen County Edn. Assn., Northern Highlands Edn. Assn., Nat. Coun. Tchrs. English, Bergen County Tchrs. English, N.J. Coun. Tchrs. English, N.J. Reading Coun./N.J. Reading Assn., Bergen County Ret. Tchrs. Assn., Affiliate of Internat. Reading Assn., Soc. Women Educators, Delta Kappa Gamma. Home: 115 Sherman Ave Teaneck NJ 07666-4120

MAHONEY, SHEILA IRENE, middle school educator; b. Dallas, Apr. 6, 1945; d. Raymond Francis and June Mary (Hoffman) M. BS in Edn., Ohio State U., 1970; MS in Adminstrn. Supervision, Nova U., Ft. Lauderdale, Fla., 1974-78. Tchr. 4th, 5th grades Avalon Elem. Sch. Collier County Schs., Naples, Fla., 1974-78; tchr. lang. arts, 11th grade Lely High Sch. Collier County Schs., Naples, 1978-80; tchr. lang. arts Gulfview Middle Sch. Collier County Schs., Naples, 1980—. Mem. adv. bd. Collier County Reading Coun., Naples, 1975-78. Mem. ASCD, Collier County Reading Coun., Ohio State Alumni Assn., Phi Delta Kappa (adv. bd., historian Naples, 1988-91). Republican. Roman Catholic. Avocations: reading, travel, politics. Home: 255 2nd Ave S Naples FL 34102-5957

MAHOOD, RAMONA MADSON, library science educator, financial consultant; b. Brigham City, Utah, June 7, 1933; d. Stanley Johnson and Effie (Webb) Madson; m. Harry Richard Mahood, Dec. 21, 1962. BS, Utah State U., 1955; MS, U. Ill., 1959, cert. advanced study, 1971. Cert. tchr., Utah. Reference librarian Weber State U., Ogden, Utah, 1955-62; asst. prof. libr. sci. U. Memphis, 1964—. Editor: Young Adult Literature, 1980; contbr. articles on libr. sci. edn. and investing to various publs. Mem. ALA, Tenn. Libr. Assn., Nat. Coun. Tchrs. English, Phi Kappa Phi, Beta Phi Mu, Delta Kappa Gamma. Avocations: reading, music, knitting.

MAIDIQUE, MODESTO ALEX, academic administrator; b. Havana, Cuba, Mar. 20, 1940; s. Modesto Maidique and Hilda Rodriguez; children: Ana Teresa, Mark Alex. BS, MIT, 1962, MS, 1964, PhD, 1970. Instr. MIT, Boston, 1976-79; v.p., gen. mgr. Analog Devices Semiconductor, Boston, 1970-76; asst. prof. Harvard U., Boston, 1976-81; assoc. prof. Stanford U., Palo Alto, Calif., 1981-84; sr. ptnr. Hambrecht and Quist Venture Ptnrs., Palo Alto, Calif., 1981-86; co-founder, dir. U. Miami (Fla.) Innovation and Entepreneurship Inst., 1984-86; pres. Fla. Internat. U., Miami, 1986—. Mem. Pres.'s Edn. Policy Adv. Com.; chmn. Beacon Coun., 1992-93. Recipient Citizenship award HEW, 1973, Teaching award Stanford U., 1983 Mem. IEEE, Assn. Cuban Engrs. Republican. Roman Catholic. Office: Fla Internat U Office of Pres Univ Park PC 528 Miami FL 33199-0001 Fax: 305-348-3660. E-mail: maidique@fiu.edu.

MAIER, CHARLES STEVEN, history educator; b. N.Y.C., Feb. 23, 1939; s. Louis and Muriel (Kraalsheimer) M.; m. Pauline Alice Rubbelke, June 17, 1961; children— Andrea Nicole, Nicholas Winterer, Jessica Elizabeth Heine. AB, Harvard U., 1960; postgrad., St. Anthony's Coll., Oxford, Eng., 1960-61; PhD, Harvard U., 1967. Instr. history Harvard U., Cambridge,

Mass., 1967-69, asst. prof., 1969-73, lectr., 1973-75; vis. prof. U. Bielefeld, Fed. Republic Germany, 1976; assoc. prof. history Duke U., Durham, N.C., 1976-79, prof., 1979-81; prof. history Harvard U., Cambridge, Mass., 1981-91, Krupp Found. prof. European studies, 1991—2002; Leverett Saltonstall prof. history, 2002; dir. Ctr. for European Studies, 1994-2001. Rsch. fellow Lehrman Inst., N.Y.C., 1975-76; mem. assoc. staff Brookings Instn., Washington, 1978-84; mem. coun. Fondation Jean Monnet pour l'Europe, Lausanne, Switzerland; mem. joint comm. on We. Europe Social Sci. Rsch. Coun. and Am. Coun. Learned Socs., 1978-84, chmn., 1979-81; mem. German Am. Acad. Coun., Bonn, Germany and Washington, 1998-2001. Author: Recasting Bourgeois Europe, 1975 (Am. Hist. Assn. George Louis Beer award 1976, Herbert Baxter Adams award 1977), In Search of Stability, 1987, The Unmasterable Past, 1988, Dissolution: The Crisis of Communism and the End of East Germany, 1997; editor: The Origins of the Cold War and Contemporary Europe, 1978, rev. edit., 1990, (with Dan S. White) The Thirteenth of May and the Advent of de Gaulle's Republic, 1967, (with Leon Lindberg) The Politics of Inflation and Economic Stagnation, 1985, Changing Boundaries of the Political, 1987, The Marshall Plan and Germany, 1991. Decorated comdr.'s cross Order of Merit (German Fed. Rep.); fellow NEH, 1977-78, German Marshall Fund, 1980-81, Guggenheim Found., 1984-85; rsch. grantee MacArthur Found., 1988-89; recipient Alexander von Humboldt Found. Rsch. prize, 2003; fellow Woodrow Wilson Ctr. for Scholars, Washington, D.C., 1989. Mem. Coun. on Fgn. Rels., Am. Hist. Assn., Soc. Italian Hist. Studies, Soc. Historians of Am. Fgn. Rels., Am. Acad. Arts and Scis., Phi Beta Kappa Home: 60 Larchwood Dr Cambridge MA 02138-4639 Office: Harvard U Ctr for European Studies Cambridge MA 02138 E-mail: csmaier@fas.harvard.edu.

MAIER, PAULINE, history educator; b. Apr. 27, 1938; d. Irvin Louis and Charlotte (Winterer) Rubbelke; m. Charles Steven Maier, June 17, 1961; children: Andrea Nicole, Nicholas Winterer, Jessica Elizabeth Heine. AB, Radcliffe Coll., 1960; postgrad., London Sch. Econs., 1960-61; PhD in History, Harvard U., 1968; LLD (hon.), Regis Coll., 1987; DHL (hon.), Williams Coll., 1993. Asst. prof. then assoc. prof. history U. Mass., Boston, 1968-77; Robinson-Edwards prof. history U. Wis., Madison, 1977-78; prof. history MIT, Cambridge, Mass., 1978—, William R. Kenan Jr. prof. history, 1990—. Dept. head, MIT, 1979-88, mem. coun. Inst. Early Am. History, 1982-84; trustee Regis Coll., 1988-93; trustee Commonwealth Sch., 1991-96; bd. mgrs. Old South Meeting House, 1987-97. Author: From Resistance to Revolution: Colonial Radicals and the Development of American Opposition to Britain, 1765-1766, 1972, The Old Revolutionaries: Political Lives in the Age of Samuel Adams, 1980, The American People: A History, 1986, American Scripture: Making the Declaration of Independence, 1997; co-author: Inventing America, 2002. Recipient Douglass Adair award Claremont Grad. Sch.-Inst. Early Am. History, 1976, Kidger award New Eng. History Tchrs. Assn., 1981; fellow Nat. Endowment Humanities, 1974-75, 88-89, Charles Warren fellow, 1974-75, Guggenheim fellow, 1990. Mem. Orgn. Am. Historians (mem. exec. bd. 1978-82), Am. Hist. Assn. (mem. nominations com. 1983-85, chmn. 1985), Soc. Am. Historians, Am. Antiquarian Soc. (mem. exec. coun. 1984-89), Colonial Soc. Mass. (mem. exec. coun. 1990-93), Mass. Hist. Soc., Am. Acad. Arts and Scis., The Hist. Soc. (bd. govs. 1998—). Home: 60 Larchwood Dr Cambridge MA 02138-4639 Office: MIT E51-279 77 Massachusetts Ave Cambridge MA 02139-4307 E-mail: pmaier@mit.edu.

MAIER, WILLIAM OTTO, martial arts, yoga and pilates instructor, author, seminar leader, consultant; b. Newark, July 15, 1949; s. Emil William Maier and Elizabeth Muriel Flader; children: William Wyatt, Kami Elizabeth. BA, Marietta (Ohio) Coll., 1971; MA, Coll. of Wooster (Ohio), 1973; grad., Citizens Police Acad., 1995. Lic. sr. mastr ninjutsu Internat. Bujinkan Dojo, Noda City, Japan, cert. lic. tactical master instr. CDT Non-Lethal Force Tng. Tchr. Howard County (Md.) Pub. Schs., 1975-78; dean Martial Arts Am., Columbia, Md., 1975—2002. Mem. faculty martial arts Am. Bus. Coll., Irvine, Calif., 1995; founder Modern Ninjutsu Sys. Author: Modern Ninjutsu; featured on (TV) on CNN, ABC, NBC and CBS. Named Sch. of Month Black Belt Mag., Sept. 1992, Master Instr. of Yr., Internat. Hall of Fame, 2000; recipient State Md. Govs. citation, 1992, Nat. Sch. of Yr. award U.S. Martial Arts Assn., 1992, 93, Cmty. Svc. award, 1993, Excellence award Martial Arts Bus. Info. Mag., 1996, recognition Md. Senate, 1995, County Exec. Proclamation, 1999. Mem. U.S. Marital Arts Assn. (cons., bd. dirs. 1986-95, named Man of Yr. 1991, recipient award for best student retention 1988-93, Top Sch. award 1994), Martial Arts Am. (cons., bd. dirs. 1995-2001, award Excellence 1997, 99, 2000). Address: 5702 E Justine Rd Scottsdale AZ 85254-1829 E-mail: willmaierseminars@yahoo.com.

MAIKOWSKI, THOMAS ROBERT, educational director, priest; b. Milwaukee, Wis., Oct. 20, 1947; s. Thomas Robert and Eugenia A. (Rogowski) M. BA, St. Francis Coll., Milw., 1970, MS in Edn., 1972; MA, Cardinal Stritch Coll., 1974; MDiv, Kenrick Sem., St. Louis, 1976; BA, Notre Dame Coll., St. Louis, 1976; MEd, Marquette U., 1977; PhD, St. Louis U., 1980; EdD, U. San Francisco, 1992. Ordained priest Roman Cath. Ch., 1976; cert. secondary sch. tchr. and adminstr., Ariz., N.Mex.; cert. elem. tchr., N.Mex. Tchr., adminstr. Cathedral High Sch., Gallup, N.Mex., 1976-78; supt. of schs. Diocese of Gallup, 1978-90; prin. tchr. The Cath. Acad., Farmington, N.Mex., 1980-90; dir. edn. Diocese of Gallup, 1990—. Contbr. articles to religious jours. Maj. USAFR. Mem. Nat. Cath. Ednl. Assn. (exec. com. 1978-81, 87-90), Religious Edn. Assn., Am. Assn. on Mental Retardation, Assn. for Supervision and Curriculum Devel., N.Mex. Assn. Non-pub. Schs. (bd. dirs. 1981-84), Phi Delta Kappa. Address: PO Box 1028 Gallup NM 87305-1028

MAIL, PATRICIA DAVISON, public health specialist; b. Kamloops, B.C., Can., Dec. 10, 1940; d. George Allen and Constance (Davison) M. BS, U. Ariz., 1963, MA, 1970; MS, Smith Coll., 1965; MPH, Yale U., 1967; postgrad., Seattle U., 1974; PhD, U. Md., 1996. Cert. health edn. specialist. Commd. officer USPHS, 1970-97; chief health edn. br. Portland Indian Health Svc., 1979-86; dep. chief field ops. Nat. Health Svc. Corps., 1986-87, dep. chief clin., prof. activities bd., 1987-88, br. chief Health Resources and Svcs. Adminstrn., 1988; dep. staff dir. Office Pub. Health Svc. Surgeon Gen., 1989; officer pers. specialist Alcohol, Drug Abuse and Mental Health Adminstrn., 1990—92; chief evaluation sect., divsn. clin. and prevention rsch. Nat. Inst. Alcohol Abuse and Alcoholism, 1991—93, extramural sci. adminstr., 1993-97; faculty Medicine Creek Tribal Coll., 1998—99. Mem. faculty Seattle U., 1974-78; commr. Nat. Commn. Health Edn. Credentialing, chair, 1993-94; accreditation site visitor Coun. on Edn. in Pub. Health, 1996—; vis. scientist Addictive Behaviors Rsch. Ctr., U. Wash., 1998-99, rsch. scientist, 1999—; pres. Dragon-Archer Cons., 1997—; asst. prof. Oreg. Health Scis. U., 1998-99. Author: (with D.R. McDonald) Tulapai to Tokay, 1980; editor: (with Heurtin-Roberts, Martin and Howard) American Indian Alcoholism: Multiple Perspectives on a Complex Problem, 2002; editor Soc. for Pub. Health Edn. Sounds, 1976-86; assoc. editor Health Promotion Practice; contbr. articles to profl. jours. Recipient Meritorious Svc. award Uniformed Svcs. U. Health Scis., 1991, Tom Drummy award Wash. State Pub. Health Assn., 2002; USPHS traineeship, 1965-67; grantee NDEA, 1968-70. Fellow Am. Sch. Health Assn., Soc. Applied Anthropology; mem. AAAS (life), APHA (chair pub. health edn. sect. 1995-96, chmn. continuing profl. edn. com. 1997, 98, exec. bd. 2001—, Early Career award Pub. Health Edn. sect. 1979, Judith Miller award 1998, Exec. Dir.'s citation 1999), Commd. Officers Assn. USPHS (life), Am. Assn. Health Edn. (life), Am. Acad. Health Behavior (bd. dirs. 2001), Soc. Pub. Health Edn., Med. Anthropology Soc., Assn. Mil. Surgeons U.S. (life), Res. Officers Assn. (life), Smith Coll. Alumnae Assn., Delta Psi Kappa, Eta Sigma Gamma. Episcopalian. Home: 35214 28th Ave S Federal Way WA 98003-7120 E-mail: pmail@sprynet.com.

MAIN, EDNA DEWEY (JUNE MAIN), education educator; b. Hyannis, Mass., Sept. 1, 1940; d. Seth Bradford and Edna Wilhelmina (Wright) Dewey; m. Donald John Main, Sept. 9, 1961 (div. Dec. 1989); children: Alison Teresa Main Ronzon, Susan Christine Main Leddy, Steven Donald. Degree in merchandising, Tobe-Coburn Sch., 1960; BA in Edn., U. North Fla., 1974, MA in Edn., 1979, M in Adminstrn. and Supervision, 1983; PhD in Curriculum and Instrn., U. Fla., 1990. Asst. buyer Abraham & Straus, Bklyn., 1960-61; asst. mdse. mgr. Interstate Dept. Stores, N.Y.C., 1962-63; tchr. Holiday Hill Elem. Sch., Jacksonville, Fla., 1974-86; instr. summer sci. inst., 1984-92; prof. edn. Jacksonville U., 1992—, dir.. masters program in integrated learning and ednl. tech. Instr. U. Fla., 1987—90, U. N. Fla., 1990—92; cons. Assn. Internat. Schs. Africa, 1994—97. Co-author: (book) Developing Critical Thinking Through Science, Book I, 2001, Developing Critical Thinking Through Science, Book II, 2002. Rep. United Way, 1981—86; tchr. rep., chpt. leader White Ho. Young Astronaut Program, 1984—85; team leader NSF Shells Elem. Sci. Project. Named Fla. Prof. of the Yr., Carnegie Found., 2002, Jacksonville U. Prof. of Yr., 2003; recipient Innovative Excellence in Tchg., Learning and Tech. award, Internat. Coll. Conf., 1999, Outstanding Alumni award, U. N. Fla., 1999, Eve award for Edn., 2001, Apple Disting. Educator award, 2003—04. Mem.: ISTE, ASCD, Nat. Sci. Tchrs. Assn. (Sci. Tchrs. Achievement Recognition award 1983), Kappa Delta Pi, Delta Kappa Gamma, Phi Delta Kappa, Phi Kappa Phi. Episcopalian. Office: Jacksonville U 2800 University Blvd N Jacksonville FL 32211-3394 E-mail: main750@bellsouth.net.

MAIN, MYRNA JOAN, retired mathematics educator; b. Kirksville, Mo., Oct. 31, 1947; d. Stanford H. and Jennie Vee (Nuhn) Morris; m. Carl Donet Main, Feb. 22, 1968; children: D. Christopher, Laura S. BSE, Northeast Mo. State U., 1968, MA, 1970. Instr. math. Callao (Mo.) Sch., 1968-73; tchr., chair dept. math. Macon (Mo.) R-I Schs., 1973—; regional dir. math. Mo. Middle Sch.; math. leadership coord. U. Mo., Columbia, Mo. math. leadership project coord., 1999—. Ext. staff Moberly (Mo.) Area C.C., 1983—, Cen. Meth. Coll., 1994; adj. faculty N.E. Mo. State U., Kirksville, 1987-93; mentor Mo. Math. Mentoring Project, Moberly, 1989-96; trainer Mo. Show-Me Stds. and Frame Works, 1997; Mo. Math. Leadership Project dir. U. Mo., Columbia; mgr. Midwest Bone & Joint Ctr. PC, Macon, Mo. Organist, UBS tchr. Crossroads Christian Ch., Macon, 1981—; mem. Macon County Watershed Adv. Bd., Long Br. Recipient Presdl. award for excellence in math., 1989; named Outstanding Secondary Tchr., Sigma Xi Truman State Univ. Chpt., 1999; semi-finalist The Disney Co. Presents the Am. Tchr., 1991. Mem. AAUW (chpt. pres. 1980-81), Nat. Coun. Tchrs. Math., Mo. Coun. Tchrs. Math. (treas. 1978-79, v.p. 1976), Mo. Alliance for Sci., Math. and Tech. Edn. (bd. dirs. 1988-92, mem. Mo. Framework writing team), Macon R-I Christian Club (co-sponsor). Democrat. E-mail: mainfarms@yahoo.com.

MAIN, ROBERT GAIL, communications educator, training consultant, television and film producer, former army officer; b. Bucklin, Mo., Sept. 30, 1932; s. Raymond M. and Inez L. (Olinger) M.; m. Anita Sue Thoroughman, Jan. 31, 1955; children: Robert Bruce, David Keith, Leslie Lorraine. BS magna cum laude, U. Mo., 1954; grad. with honors, Army Commd. Gen. Staff Coll., 1967; MA magna cum laude in Comm., Stanford U., 1968; PhD, U. Md., 1978. Commd. 2d lt. U.S. Army, 1954, advanced through grades to lt. col., 1968; mem. faculty Army Commd. Gen. Staff Coll., 1968-70; chief speechwriting and info. materials divsn. U.S. Army Info. Office, 1971, chief broadcast and film divsn., 1972-73; dir. def. audiovisual activities Office of Info. for Armed Forces, 1973-76; ret., 1976; prof. instrnl. tech. Calif. State U., Chico, 1976—, dept. chair, 1993-98. Cons. in field. Author: Rogues, Saints and Ordinary People, 1988; prodr. (TV documentary) Walking Wounded, 1983, Army Info. Films, Army Radio Series, 1972-73; contbr. articles on computer based tng. and telecoms. to scientific and profl. jours. Decorated Legion of Merit, Meritorious Svc. medal, Commendation medal with oak leaf cluster, combat Inf. Badge; Vietnamese Cross of Gallantry; recipient Freedom Found. awards, 1972, 73, 74; Bronze medal Atlanta Film Festival, 1972; Best of Show award Balt. Film Festival, 1973; Creativity award Chgo. Indsl. Film Festival, 1973; Cine gold award Internat. Film Prodrs. Assn., 1974; named an Outstanding Prof. Calif. State U., 1987-88. Mem. Phi Eta Sigma, Alpha Zeta, Phi Delta Gamma, Omicron Delta Kappa, Alpha Gamma Rho.

MAISEL, HERBERT, computer science educator; b. N.Y.C., Sept. 22, 1930; s. Hyman and Dora (Goldstein) M.; m. Millicent Sherry Kushner, Apr. 13, 1957; children— Scott Alan, Raymond Bruce. B.S., CCNY, 1951; M.S., NYU, 1952; Ph.D., Catholic U. Am., 1964. Mathematician, statistician Dept. Army, Aberdeen, Md., Washington, 1954-63; dir. acad. computer ctr. Georgetown U., Washington, 1963-76, prof. computer sci., 1963— ; systems advisor Social Security Adminstrn., Balt., 1976-84; cons. Nat. Bur. Standards, Gaithersburg, Md., 1968-72, Balt. Housing Authority, 1972-73, Social Security Adminstrn., Balt., 1966-73; mem. study group HHS, Washington, 1975-76. Author: An Introduction to Electronic Digital Computers, 1969; Simulation of Discrete Stochastic Systems, 1972; Computers for Social and Economic Development, 1974; Computers: Programming and Applications, 1975; also others. Contbr. articles to profl. jours. Mem. Community Housing Resources Bd., Montgomery County, Md., 1975. Recipient spl. service award Internat. Assn. Parents of Deaf, 1982. Fellow Assn. Computing Machinery (chmn. external activities bd. 1981-86, chmn. mems. and chpts. bd. 1978-80, chmn. nominating com. 1983-84, mem. council, chmn. Washington chpt. 1971-73, Outstanding Contribution award 1986); mem. Phi Beta Kappa (chmn. Georgetown chpt. 1974-76), Sigma Xi. Jewish.

MAITRE, JOAN, education educator; b. Aug. 30, 1943; BA, Bklyn. Coll., 1963, MS, 1970. Museums asst. U. Richmond, Va., 1990—. With Marsh Art Gallery, 1999. Office: U Richmond Univ Museums Richmond VA 23173

MAIZE, LINDA LOU, elementary education educator; b. Hazen, N.D., Aug. 30, 1952; d. F. Robert and Mary (Keller) Oestreich; m. Kirk Edward Maize, Aug. 10, 1974; 1 child, Allen Edward. BS in Elem. and Spl. Edn., U. Nebr., 1974; MS, Minot State U., 1998. Nat. bd. cert. tchr., 2002. Tchr. Naughton Sch., Bismarck, N.D., 1974-75; elem. tchr. Golden Valley (N.D.) Pub. Sch., 1975-78, Beulah (N.D.) Pub. Schs., 1978—. Tchr. Bible sch. Concordia Luth. Ch., Beulah, 1976-77, Wednesday sch. tchr., 1994—; vol. campaign for U.S. senator, Beulah, 1982, 84; past sec. Dist. 33 Dem. Com., Beulah; leader Boy Scouts Am.; leader 4-H, 1999; sec. Beulah Area Dollars for Scholars, Mercer County 4-H Coun. Mem. ASCD, Internat. Reading Assn., Nat. Coun. Tchrs. Math., Nat. Coun. Tchrs. English, N.D. Edn. Assn. (dist. 33 govt. rels. contact 1982-88, 93—), Beulah Edn. Assn. (treas. 1979-80, v.p. 1981-82, pres. 1982-83), Am. Quarter Horse Assn., Delta Kappa Gamma. Avocations: reading, riding, stamp art, photo albums, quarter horses. Office: Beulah Elem Sch 200 7th St NW Beulah ND 58523

MAJOR, PATRICK WEBB, III, principal; b. Wai, Maharastra, India, Mar. 12, 1947; s. Patrick W. Jr. and Alice (Seeland) M.; m. Daphnelynn Jantz, June 26, 1971; children: Mindy Joy, Matthew Patrick Webb. BA in BE, Columbia Internat. U., 1969; BA, Biola U., 1972; MA, Point Loma Nazarene U., 1979; postgrad., U. Calif., Irvine. Cert. secondary tchr., adminstr., Calif. Prin. Omega High Sch., Bakersfield, Calif., 1980-84; headmaster Bakersfield Christian Life Schs., 1984-86; prin. North Kern Christian Sch., Wasco, Calif., 1986-88; prin., adminstr. Yucaipa (Calif.) Christian Schs., 1988-2000; prin. Christian H.S., El Cajon, Calif., 2000—03; adminstr. First Bapt. Ch. of Lakewood (Calif.) Schs., 2003—. Chmn. ACSI So. Calif. Accreditation Commn., 1998-2003. Mem. ASCD, Assn. Christian Schs. Internat. (former dist. rep., exec. bd. 1992-2001), Ctrl. Redwood League (pres. 1985-86), CIF Ctrl Sect., Internat. Fellowship Christian Sch. Adminstrs.

MAJORS, SANDRA MARIE, elementary school educator; b. Boise, Idaho, July 17, 1945; d. Walter Alan and Phyllis Maxine (Lehrman) Buck; m. Wilburn Elmer Majors Jr., Aug. 27, 1965; children: Tyler, Tacee. Student, East Mont. Coll., 1963-65; BS in Edn., Ctrl. State U., 1968; postgrad., Kans. State U., 1976-77, Okla. City U., 1983, N.E. State U., 1986-87; M, Okla. State U., 2001. Cert. tchr., Okla., Kans. 3d grade tchr. Windsor Hills Elem. Sch., Putnam City, Okla., 1968-72; 2d grade tchr. Garfield Elem. Sch., Liberal, Kans., 1975; 4th grade tchr. McKinley Elem. Sch., Liberal, Kans., 1975-76; pre-sch. tchr. Children's House Montessori, Edmond, Okla., 1982-84; 4th grade tchr. Lynn Wood Elem. Sch., Broken Arrow, Okla., 1988-90, Arrow Springs Elem. Sch., Broken Arrow, Okla., 1990-91, Jenks (Okla.) East Elem. Sch., 1991—, gifted tchr., 1993-94, organizer, leader Bible club Trojans for Christ, 1992—. Mem. State Textbook Com., Broken Arrow, Okla., 1989; mem. Vision 21 Charter Com., Jenks, 1993; workshop instr. Reader's/Writer's Workshop, 1992, 94; telecom. intermediator TV Classroom Exch., Tulsa; mem. Okla. State U. Writing Project; assessor Nat. Boards 2001, 02. Producer: (play) Cricket & the Cracker Box Kid, 1993. Mem. Fellowship Bible Church. Recipient awards Jenks Found., 1992, 93, 94, 98, Vision of Excellence award, 2001, Leadership Certificate Conn. League of Nursing, 2002. Mem. Christian Educators Assn., Internat. Reading Assn., Kappa Delta Pi. Republican. Avocations: music, sports, physical fitness. Home: 9416 S 70th East Ave Tulsa OK 74133-5354 Office: Jenks Pub Sch 205 E B St Jenks OK 74037-3906

MAKAR, NADIA EISSA, secondary education educator, educational administrator; b. Cairo, Oct. 7, 1938; came to U.S., 1966. d. Michel and Yvonne (Bitar) Issa; m. Boshra Halim Makar, Jan. 1, 1960 (dec.); children: Ralph, Roger. Cert., Moscow U., 1964; BA, St. Peter's Coll., 1969, MA, 1981; postgrad., Hope Coll. and Brown U., 1972, 1973. Cert. tchr., supr., prin., N.J. Tchr. Hudson Cath. H.S., Jersey City, 1970-72, sci. dept. chairperson, 1972-79; coord. Convocation Model Project Union City N.J. Bd. Edn., 1979-81, tchr., coord. industry and coll. rels., 1989-96, sci. supr., 1996—. Mem. Bd. Edn., Jersey City; cons. Stevens Inst. Tech. Hughes Grant, Hoboken, N.J., 1989-94; cons./advisor Project RISE. Author: Health; Space; Environment, 1980; co-editor NSSA mag., 1974-76; contbr. articles to profl. jours. Co-founder N.J. Bus./Industry/Sci. Edn. Consortium, 1981; pres. Bus./Profl. Women, Jersey City, 1984-86, sec. N.J., 1985, dir. dist. III, 1995—; treas. Mental Health Assn., Hudson County, 1977-80; bd. dirs. N.J. Math. Coalition; U.S. del. 1st U.S./Russian Meeting for Math. Educators. Recipient Outstanding Secondary Educator Am. award U.S. Sec. Edn., 1973, award Mfg. Chemists Assn., 1975, recognition award Gov. State of N.J., 1988, Presdl. award for excellence in math. and sci. teaching, 1989, Sigma Xi award of encouraging rsch. at pre-coll. level, award parents Assn., 2001; named to Hall of Fame Hudson County Sci. Fair, 2001. Mem. Am. Chem. Soc. (chmn. Hudson-Bergen sect. 1980-82, sec. N.Y. sect. 1994—, reviewer for Chem. Edn. Jour., bd. dirs. Home PC Mag., Nicol award 1975, Outstanding Achievement award New Eng. region 1976), St. Peter's Coll. Alumni Assn. (v.p. 1982-88, treas.), Nat. Coun. Tchrs. Math (reviewer). Office: Union Hill High Sch 3808 Hudson Ave Union City NJ 07087-6020 E-mail: nmakar@union-city.k12.nj.us.

MAKARA, CAROL PATTIE, education educator, consultant; b. Norwich, Conn., Feb. 27, 1943; d. Howard G. and Ruth R. Robinson; m. Benjamin Makara, Feb. 19, 1966; children: Cheryl A., John J. AS, Three Rivers Community-Tech. Coll., 1988; BS, Cen. Conn. State U., 1965; MA, U. Conn., 1967. Cert. tchr., Conn. Tchr. Ledyard (Conn.) Bd. of Edn., 1965-66, Preston (Conn.) Bd. of Edn., 1974—; continuing edn. unit mgr. Preston (Conn,) Pub. Schs., 1993—. Computer analyst Clinton (Conn.) plant Stanley Bostitch, summers 1987-92; evening instr. Three Rivers Cmty. Tech. Coll., 1989—; evening mgr. AutoCad Tng. Ctr., 1990-95; coop. mentor tchr. Dept. Edn., Conn., 1988—; advisor Conn. Educators' Computer Assn., 1992—; tchr. assessor The Begining Educator Support and Tng. Program, Conn. State Dept. Edn., 1995—. Author: (with others) Pedagogical Guide: Strategies for Improving Instruction, 1992. Active Fellowship Program for Disting. Tchrs., 1987-94. Fellow Conn. Bus. and Industry Assn.; mem. NEA, Conn. Edn. Assn. Home: 89 Mathewson Mill Rd Ledyard CT 06339-1114 Office: Preston Plains Sch 1 Route 164 Preston CT 06365-8818

MAKAROWITZ, LLOYD, physics educator; b. Bronx, N.Y., Jan. 16, 1947; s. Sol and Frances (Levinson) M.; m. Kay Kramer, Aug. 10, 1969 (dec. Oct. 2000); children: Jonathan Michael, Seth Mathew; m. Wendy Katz, Aug. 3, 2003. BS, CUNY, 1967; MA, Columbia U., 1969; PhD, CUNY, 1974. Tchg. fellow Columbia U., N.Y.C., 1967-69, CUNY, 1969-74; instr. Kean Coll. N.J., Union, 1974-75; asst. prof. St. John's U., Jamaica, N.Y., 1975-78; project dir. N.Y.C. Sch. Dist. 6, 1978-79; asst. prof. SUNY, Farmingdale, 1979-84, assoc. prof., 1984-89, prof., 1989—, chairman dept. physics, 1981—. Mem. admissions and acad. stds. com. SUNY, Farmingdale, 1996-99, chair admissions and acad. stds. com., 1991-93, chair curriculum com., 1989-90, mem. Farmingdale exec. com., 1993-96, 99—, mem. curriculum com., 2000-; presiding officer faculty, SUNY, Farmingdale, 2001-. Lectr. physics and careers in physics local high schs., L.I., N.Y., 1980—. Mem. AAUP, Am. Phys. Soc., Am. Assn. Physics Tchrs., N.Y. Acad. Scis. Home: 8 Putnam Ave Jericho NY 11753-1926 Office: SUNY Farmingdale Farmingdale Melville Rd Farmingdale NY 11735 E-mail: makarolm@farmingdale.edu.

MAKE, ISABEL ROSE, multicultural studies educator, small business owner; b. Phila., Oct. 6, 1947; d. Aaron M. and Lillian (Simon) Rose; m. Barry Jay Make, June 13, 1970; children: Jonathan David, Jeremy Simon. BA, George Wash. U., 1969; EdM, Temple U., 1970; cert. advanced grad. studies, W.Va. U., 1975. Cert. tchr., Pa., Mich., W.Va., Mass. Dir. learning ctr. Kirkbride Elem. Sch., Phila., 1970-71, Huron High Sch., Ann Arbor, 1971-73; learning disabilities tutor Brookline (Mass.) Pub. Schs., 1976-82; ednl. cons. Newton, Mass., 1982-84; child care cons. Isabel Make Assocs., Newton, 1984-88; adj. prof. reading and multicultural studies Metro State Coll., Denver, 1989—; pres. Top Hat Gourmet, 1992—; bus. lectr. on The Art of Corp. Giving, 1993—. Ednl. counselor Phila. Home for Emotionally Disturbed Girls, 1970; cons. Ann Arbor Pub. Schs., 1971; child care cons. Newton Cmty. Schs., 1985; founding mem. Denver Parenting Ctr., 1989—; chair legis. and regulations subcom. Commonwealth of Mass., Boston, 1984-88; adj. prof. met. State Coll., 1992—, C.C. Denver, 1992—. Founder Temple Shalom Nursery Sch., Newton, 1975; chmn. childcare task force The U. Hosp., Boston U. Med. Ctr., 1985-88; bd. dirs. Greenwood Village Arts and Humanites Coun., 1991—; mem. at large Colo. Consortium Community Arts Couns., 1992, Greenwood Village Arts and Humanities Coun. (chair A Space of my Own, Parent-Child Art Day), 1991—; mem. steering com. Colo. Alliance for Arts in Edn., 1993; co-chair Teen Arts Adv. Bd., Greenwood Village, Colo., 1999—. Democrat. Jewish. Avocations: gourmet cooking, swimming. Home and Office: 9400 E Maplewood Ave Apt 8 Englewood CO 80111-5237

MAKINS, JAMES EDWARD, retired dentist, dental educator, educational administrator; b. Galveston, Tex., Feb. 22, 1923; s. James and Hazel Alberta (Morton) M.; m. Jane Hopkins, Mar. 4, 1943; children: James E. Jr., Michael William, Patrick Clarence, Scott Roger. DDS, U. Tex.-Houston, 1945; postdoctoral, SUNY-Buffalo, 1948-49. Lic. dentist, Tex. Practice dentistry specializing in orthodontics, Lubbock, Tex., 1949-77; dir. clinics Dallas City Dental Health Program, 1977-78; dir. continuing edn. Baylor Coll. Dentistry, Dallas, 1978-92, ret., 1992, prof. emeritus Baylor Coll. Dentistry. Author: (book chpt.) Handbook of Texas, 1986, The New Handbook of Texas, 1996. Chmn. profl. div. United Fund, Lubbock, 1958; pres. Tex. State Bd. Dental Examiners, Austin, Tex., 1968; instl. chmn. United Way, Dallas, 1983. Served to lt. comdr., USNR, 1945-47. Recipient Community Service award W. Tex. C. of C., Abilene, 1968, Clinic award Dallas County Dental Soc., 1981. Fellow Am. Coll. Dentists, Internat. Coll.

Dentists; mem. Tex. Dental Assn. (life, v.p. 1954, Goodfellow 1973), West Tex. Dental Assn. (pres. 1955), Am. Assn. Dental Examiners, Park City Club, Rotary, Omicron Kappa Upsilon. Methodist. Avocation: dental history.

MAKSI, GREGORY EARL, engineering educator; b. Wilkes-Barre, Pa., May 9, 1939; s. Stephen Cedric and Laura Victoria (Pytell) M.; children: Sabrina, Jared, Joshua. BSME, Ga. Inst. Tech., 1961, MS in Indsl. Mgmt., 1964; PhD in Edn. Adminstrn., U. Miss., 1983. Registered profl. engr., Tenn. Mech. engr. Ellicott Machine Corp., Balt., 1961-62; project engr. Celanese Corp., Rock Hill, S.C., 1964-67; assoc. prof. State Tech. Inst., Memphis, 1967-71, prof., 1971-73, program chmn. of indsl. engring., 1973-90, dept. chmn. mech. engring./indsl. engring., 1990—. Cons. Tenn. Ednl. Alliance, Nashville, 1994—, U. Ark., Millington, Tenn., 1988, instr., 1988—; curriclum coord. Memphis City H.S., 1993—; quality-productivity adv., 1990—; CAD/CAM cons., 1995—. Hon. sheriff Shelby County Sheriff's Office, 1991; hon. state legis. Tenn. Ho. Reps., Nashville, 1992. Named Disting. Engr. Memphis Engrs. Coun., 1986, Outstanding Tech. Tchr. Am. Tech. Edn. Assn., 1998, Leadership Excellence award Nat. Inst. of Staff and Orgnl. Devel., 1997. Mem. Soc. Mfg. Engrs. (Outstanding Engr. 1998), Inst. of Indsl. Engrs., World Future Soc., Tenn. Profl. Engrs. Soc., Epsilon Pi Tau. Avocations: computers, tennis, racquetball, fishing. Office: State Tech Inst Memphis 5983 Macon Cv Memphis TN 38134-7642

MALACHOWSKI, ANN MARY, elementary and secondary art educator; b. Chelsea, Mass., May 13, 1948; d. Bronislaw Paul and Stephanie (Mikolajewski) M. BS in Art Edn., Mass. Coll. Art, 1970; MEd, Lesley Coll., 1990; Cert. Fine Arts Dir., Fitchburg State Coll., 1990. Cert. art tchr., art supr., elem. edn. tchr. Art tchr., dept. chair 6-12 Norwood (Mass.) Pub. Schs., 1970—. Adj. faculty Fitchburg (Mass.) State Coll., 1991-95; focus group mem. Mass. Curriculum Frameworks for Arts, 1994; mem. sch. coun. J.P. Oldham Sch., Norwood, 1993-95; conf. presenter N.E. Art Edn. Bi-annual Conf., 1991; presenter Nat. Art Edn. Conv., 1994, 95 Recipient Horace Mann grant Mass. Dept. Edn., 1989, Disting. Tchr. award TEC Supts., 2003. Mem. Mass. Art Edn. Assn. (coun. 1991—, conf. presenter 1990, 94, Mass. Art Educator of Yr. 1994-95), Mass. Dirs. of Art Edn. (pres. 1994-96), Art Allstate (steering com. 1991-94), Polish Falcons of Am. (dist. sec. 1988—), Delta Kappa Gamma (corr. sec. Theta chpt. 1992-94, rec. sec. 2000—, co-pres. 2002—). Avocations: reading, computer graphics, interior decorating, travel, gardening. E-mail: a.malachowski@norwood.k12.ma.us., annm3@rcn.com.

MALAMUD, DANIEL, biochemistry educator; b. Detroit, June 5, 1939; s. Jack and Jennie (Ashe) M.; m. Judith Disner, Mar. 7, 1961; children: Randy, Lisa. BS, U. Mich., 1961; MA, Western Mich. U., 1962; PhD, U. Cin., 1965; MA, U. Pa., 1983. Postdoctoral fellow Temple U., Phila., 1966-68, asst. prof. pathology, 1968-69; asst. biologist Mass. Gen. Hosp., Boston, 1969-72, assoc. biologist, 1972-77; assoc. prof. biochemistry Sch. Dental Medicine, U. Pa., Phila., 1977-84, prof. biochemistry, 1984—, chmn. dept., 1985-92. Asst. prof. pathology Harvard U., Boston, 1970-77; vis. assoc. prof., Fulbright lectr. U. Philippines, Manila, 1975; vis. scientist Wistar Inst., Phila., 1985; affiliated scientist Monell Chem. Senses Ctr., Phila., 1985—; exch. scientist Hebrew U., Jerusalem, 1982. Author: Autoradiography, 1969, Saliva As a Diagnostic Fluid, 1993; contbr. over 120 articles to profl. jours., chpts. to books. Recipient Career Devel. award NIH, 1972-77. Mem. Am. Soc. Biol. Chemists, Am. Soc. Cell Biologists, Am. Soc. Microbiologists, Am. Soc. Biochem. Molecular Biology, N.Y. Acad. Scis. Office: U Pa Sch Dental Medicine 240 S 40th St Philadelphia PA 19104-4118 E-mail: malamud@pobox.upenn.edu.

MALASANOS, LOIS JULANNE FOSSE, nursing educator; b. LaPorte City, Iowa, Sept. 1, 1928; d. Lewis Reginald and Henrietta Marie Fosse; widowed; 1 child, Toree. BSN, U. Tex., 1948; BA in Gen. Sci., U. Iowa, 1952; MA in Nursing Edn., U. Chgo., 1959; PhD in Physiology, U. Ill., 1973. Assoc. dir. nursing U. Iowa Hosps., Iowa City, 1950-51, staff charge nurse, 1951; instr. operating room Sch. Nursing, Michael Reese Hosp., Chgo., 1951-58; charge nurse, med.-surg. U. Chgo., Billings Hosp., 1952-59; pvt. duty nurse Ill., 1959-63; charge nurse, maternal-infant nursing Weiss Meml. Hosp., Chgo., 1963-66; asst. prof. Loyola U., Chgo., 1966-69; teaching asst. in physiology U. Ill., Chgo., 1969-73, assoc. prof., assoc. head gen. nursing dept. Coll. Nursing, 1973-76, prof., assoc. head gen. nursing dept., 1976-80; prof., dean Coll. Nursing U. Fla., Gainesville, 1980-95, Disting. Svc. prof., 1995—. Instr. anatomy and physiology Cook County Hosp., Chgo., 1973; lectr. endocrinology Chgo. Coll. Osteopathic Medicine, 1973-80; active Pres. Clinton's Task Force on Health Care, 1993; cons. Am. Assn. Med. Colls., 1977-78, Am. Heart Assn., 1977-94, Am. Jour. Nursing, 1978-79, Gainesville (Fla.) Vets. Ctr., 1980-95, Lake Butler Receiving Ctr., 1980—; chair Deans and Dirs. of Fla. Colls. Nursing, 1981-89; chair edn. com. State Bd. Nursing, 1983-87, chair probable course com., 1984—; vis. prof. Dokuz Eylul U., Izmir, Turkey, 1995-96; cons., presenter in field. Co-author, editor: Manual of Medical Surgical Nursing, 1983, Translating Comitment to Reality, 1986, Health Assessment, 1977 (Am. Jour. Nursing Book of Yr. award 1977), 4th edit., 1989; editor: Vital Signs, 1981-90, Fla. Cancer Nursing News, 1983-84; co-editor: Fla. Nursing Rev., 1986-90; mem. editl. rev. bd. Image, 1980-96; editl. cons. Nursing, 1982-94; manuscript referee Rsch. in Nursing and Health, 1980-94, Jour. Profl. Nursing, 1985-94, Turkish Jour. Nurse Rshc.; chairperson adv. com. Nursing Outlook, 1986-91, Peer Rev., 1986-94; contbr. more than 100 articles, revs. to profl. jours. Nursing com., scholarship com. and rsch. rev. com. Am. Cancer Soc., Tampa, Fla., 1980-94. Recipient Bronze medal Fla. Heart Assn., 1986, Silver medal Fla. Heart Assn., 1989, 93; named Disting. Alumnus U. Tex. Med. Br., 1985; named to Disting. Faculty, Albany State U., 1988, Hall of Fame, U. Tex. Med. Br., 1992; NEH fellow, 1981; Fulbright awardee to Turkey, 1995-96, 2001-02. Mem. ANA (mem. coun. nurse rschrs.), AACN, AAAS, AAUP, Am. Acad. Nursing (mem. pub. com. 1986-89) Am. Assn. Higher Edn., Am. Assn. Colls. Nursing, Fla. Nurses Assn. (mem. dist. 10), N.Y. Acad. Sci., Fla. League Nursing, Nat. League Nursing (chair, mem. coun. baccalaureate and higher degree program, Dirs. award 1995, site visitor for program rev. 1980—, bd. rev. for accreditation 1993-2002, Outstanding Leadership in Nursing Edn. award 2002), Fla. State Bd. Nursing (probable cause com.), So. Regional Edn. Bd., Sigma Xi, Sigma Theta Tau (Outstanding Leadership award 2003), Phi Kappa Phi (pres. 1987-88). Office: U Fla Coll Nursing PO Box 100187 Gainesville FL 32610-0187 E-mail: malaslj@nursing.ufl.edu.

MALAYERY, NASRIN, educator, consultant; b. Tehran, Iran, Jan. 27, 1943; U.S. citizen, 1990; d. Mahmoud Malayery and Ghamar Narjis Kia. BA with spl. honors in history, George Washington U., 1964; EdM in Edn. and Social Studies, Boston U., 1967, EdM in Media and Tech., 1977, EdD in Media Tech., 1986. Editor in-house mgmt. jour. Oil Consortium, Employee Comm., Tehran, 1970-74; mgr. documents and publs. Iran-UNESCO Adult Literacy Program, Tehran, 1974-76; instr., instrnl. designer Shiraz (Iran) U. Med. Sch., 1977-81; ednl. cons. WHO Eastern Mediterranean Regional Orgn., Alexandria, Egypt, 1981-87; sr. ednl. cons. Compaq Computer Corp., Littleton, Mass., 1987—. Mem. Internat. Soc. for Performance Improvement, Nat. Mus. of Women in the Arts (assoc.), Libr. of Congress Assocs., Phi Beta Kappa. Avocations: writing, reading, gardening, ballet, yoga. Home: 7 Millstone Ct Cold Spring KY 41076-1861

MALCOLM, RICHARD WARD, academic administrator, consultant; b. Columbus, Ohio, July 27, 1933; s. Ralph James and Beatrice (Ward) M.; 1 child, Gwynn Malcolm Socolich. BS, U. Findlay (Ohio), 1956; MA, Ariz. State U., 1960; MEd, U. So. Calif., 1965, EdD, 1966. Acad. dean Martin Coll., Pulaski, Tenn., 1965-67; dean instrn. Arapahoe C.C., Littleton, Colo., 1967-71; chair edn. divsn. Chapman U., Orange, Calif., 1971-80; assoc. prof. U. So. Calif., 1976-77; dean instrn. Mesa (Ariz.) C.C., 1980-91; asst. to provost Chandler (Ariz.)/Gilbert C.C., 1991-92, chair divsn. social and behavioral scis., 1993-96; dir. R & D Williams campus Maricopa C.C., 1998-97; coord. Phoenix Ctr. U. Findlay, 1997—. Author: Mental Measurement Yearbook, 1972. Pres. Ariz. Rail Pasenger Assn., Phoenix, 1984-93. Mem. Am. Assn. Higher Edn., Ariz. Acad. Adminstrv. Assn. (treas. 1991—), Rotary. Methodist. Avocations: reading, travel, hiking, railroading, music. E-mail: pultolic@aol.com.

MALDONADO, THERESA MARY, elementary education educator; b. Chama, Colo., Oct. 26, 1949; d. Alfirio and Estella Maria (Vigil) Sanchez; m. Epifanio Mike Maldonado, July 3, 1971; children: Suzette, Mariano. AA in Elem. Edn., Trinidad St. Jr. Coll., 1971; BA in Elem. Edn., Adams State Coll., 1973, MA in Educationally Handicapped, 1977. Cert. tchr., Colo. With Centennial Sch. Dist. R-1, San Luis, Colo., 1973—, tchr. kindergarten, 1990—. Vol. voter registration Costilla County, 1978-79; instr. Costilla County 4-H, San Luis, 1980-85; eucharistic minister Sangre De Cristo Parish, San Luis, 1991—, Circle of Friendship, 1989—. Receipient Anthony Garcia Spirit award So. Peaks Officials, 1990. Mem. NEA, Colo. Edn. Assn., Colo. Coun. IRA, Centennial Edn. Assn. (sec.-treas. 1977-79), Coun. for Exceptional Children, Nat. Cursillo Movement. Republican. Roman Catholic. Avocations: reading, walking, camping. Home: PO Box 449 4th and Broad St San Luis CO 81152 Office: Centennial Sch Dist R-1 909 Main St San Luis CO 81152

MALDONADO-BEAR, RITA MARINITA, economist, educator; b. Vega Alta, P.R., June 14, 1938; d. Victor and Marina (Davila) Maldonado; m. Larry Alan Bear, Mar. 29, 1975. BA, Auburn U., 1960; PhD, NYU, 1969. With Min. Wage Bd. & Econ. Devel. Adminstr., Govt. of P.R., 1969-70; asst. prof. econs. Manhattan Coll., 1970-72; assoc. prof. econs. Bklyn. Coll., 1972-75; assoc. prof. fin. & econs., undergrad./grad. divsn. Stern Sch. Bus. NYU, 1975-81, prof., 1981—. Vis. assoc. prof. fin. Stanford (Calif.) Grad. Bus. Sch., 1973-74; acting dir. markets, ethics & law, NYU, 1993-94; cons. Morgan Guaranty Trust Co., N.Y.C., 1972-77, Bank of Am., N.Y.C., 1982-84, Res. City Bankers, N.Y.C., 1978-87, Swedish Inst. Mgmt., Stockholm, 1982-91, Empresas Master of P.R., 1985-90. Author: Role of the Financial Sector in the Economic Development of Puerto Rico, 1970; co-author: Free Markets, Finance, Ethics and Law, 1994; contbr. artiles to profl. jours. Bd. dirs. Medallion Funding Corp., 1985-87; mem. NYU Senate and Faculty Coun., 1995—, chair fin. com., 1996—; apptd. adv. bd. dirs. equity & diversity in ednl. environs. Mod. States Commn. Higher Edn., 1991—; trustee Securities Industry Assn., N.Y. Dist. Econ. Edn. Found., 1994—; chair NSF, Nat. Vis. Com. Curriculum Devel. Project Networked Fin. Simulation, 1995—; econ. cons. Inst. Women of Color, NAt. Coun. Black Women Cmty. Svcs. Fund, 2000—; trustee Bd. Edn., Twp. Mahwah, N.J., 1991-92. P.R. Econ. Devel. Adminstrn. fellow, 1960-65, Marcus Nadler fellow, NYU, 1966-67, Phillips Lods Dissertation fellow, 1967-68. Mem. Am. Econs. Assn., Am. Fin. Assn., Metro. Econ. Assn. N.Y., Assn. Social Econs. (trustee exec. coun. 1994-96). Home: 95 Tam O Shanter Dr Mahwah NJ 07430-1526 Office: Mgmt Edn Ctr 44 W 4th St Ste 9-190 New York NY 10012-1106

MALEFAKIS, EDWARD E. history educator; b. Springfield, Mass., Jan. 2, 1932; s. Emmanuel A. and Despina (Sophoulakis) M.; m. Cali Doxiadis, 1988; children from previous marriage: Michael, Laura. AB, Bates Coll., 1953; MA, Johns Hopkins U., 1955; PhD, Columbia U., 1965. Instr. Northwestern U., 1962-63, assoc. prof., 1968-71; asst. prof. modern European history Columbia U., 1964-67, prof., 1975—, U. Mich., Ann Arbor, 1971-74. Author: Agrarian Reform and Peasant Revolution in Spain, 1970, Southern Europe in the 19th and 20th Centuries, 1992; editor: Indalecio Prieto, 1975, La guerra de España, 1936-39, 1996, Franquismo: El juicio de la historia, 2000. Recipient Herbert Baxter Adams award Am. Hist. Assn., 1971, Faculty Teaching award Northwestern U., 1971, medal of honor U. Internacional Menendez Pelayo, 1982, Orden de Mérito Civico (Spain), 1988, Nebrija prize U. Salamanca, 2000; Social Scis. Rsch. Coun. grantee, 1967, NEH grantee, 1977; Guggenheim fellow, 1974, Inst. Juan March fellow, 1991. Mem. Modern Greek Studies Assn. (exec. com. 1981-87), Soc. for Spanish and Portuguese Hist. Studies (exec. council 1969-72), Spanish Inst. N.Y.C. (bd. dirs. 1982—). Democrat. Greek Orthodox. Home: 380 Riverside Dr New York NY 10025-1858 Office: Columbia Univ 524 Fayerweather Hall New York NY 10027

MALETTA, DIANE STANLEY, education educator; b. Fairmont, W.Va., July 1, 1960; d. Dan Jarrell and LaModa June (Forth) Stanley; m. Robert Thomas Maletta, May 22, 1993; children: Adam Robert, Derek Nathaniel, Jasmine Elizabeth, Robert Thomas II. BS in Edn. with honors and distinction, Valparaiso U., 1982; MS in Edn. summa cum laude, Butler U., 1986; PhD in Lang. Edn., Ind. U., 1996; gifted/talented endorsement, Purdue U., 1992. State of Ind. life license: gen. elem., reading minor, gifted/talented endorsement. Tchr. grade 1, Spanish tchr. grades 7-8, coach St. John's Luth. Sch., Indpls., 1983-86; tchr. grade 1 River Grove (Ill.) Sch., 1986-87; tchr. grades 2 and 4, intramural dir. Washington Twp. Sch., Valparaiso, Ind., 1987-89; asst. prof. edn. Valparaiso U., 1989-92, 96—; tchr. gifted and talented Valparaiso Cmty. Schs., 1992-97. Mem., rec. sec. Ind. Dist. Luth. Tchrs., Indpls., 1983-85; mem. Luth. Edn. Assn., Indpls., 1983-86, Nat. Orgn. Tchr. Educators in Reading, 1989-92, Ind. Reading Profs., Indpls., 1989-92; adv. bd. mem. The Learning Pl., Valparaiso, 1990-92; asst. planner Nat. Assessment Symposium, 1990; adj. prof. edn. Ind. U. N.W., Gary, 1995-98; tutor, spkr. and conf. presenter in field. Choir mem. St. John's Luth. Ch., Indpls., 1983-86, Immanuel Luth. Ch., Valparaiso, 1987-89; road race runner Lakeshore Striders, Chgo., N.W. Ind., 1989-94; mem. St. Patrick's Cath. Ch., 1999—; runner, phone vol. Dem. Election Com., Porter, 1994. Mem. ASCD, Internat. Reading Assn., Porter County Reading Assn. (past sec., bd. mem., com. chairperson), Kappa Delta Pi, Pi Lambda Theta, Phi Delta Kappa, Mortar Bd. Avocations: running, biking, swimming, traveling, reading. Home: 1140 Dune Meadows Dr Porter IN 46304-1286 Office: Valparaiso U Miller Hall Valparaiso IN 46383

MALEWITZ, JOAN, elementary school educator, library and information scientist; b. Dec. 15, 1947; d. Benjamin and Minnie Malewitz. B in Elem. Edn., Queens Coll., 1968, M in Elem. Edn., 1972, MLS, 1992. Cert. tchr. N-6 N.Y. Tchr., sch. libr. media specialist PS 160Q, Jamaica, NY, 1968—. Children's book reviewer Kirkus Revs., N.Y.C., 2000—. Recipient Success award, Citibank, N.Y.C., 1994. Mem.: ALA, Beta Phi Mu. Avocations: reading, travel, New York City history. Home: 62-95 Saunders St Rego Park NY 11374 Office: PS 160Q 109-59 Inwood St Jamaica NY 11435

MALHOTRA, ASHOK KUMAR, philosophy educator; b. Ferozepur, India, 1940; came to the U.S., 1963, naturalized, 1977. s. Nihal Chand and Vidya (Wanti) M.; m. Nina Judith Finestone, Oct. 24, 1966 (dec.); children: Raj Kumar, Ravi Kumar. BA, U. Rajasthan, 1961, MA, 1963; PhD, U. Hawaii, 1969. Asst. prof. SUNY, Oneonta, 1967-70, assoc. prof., 1970-80, prof., 1980—, chmn. philosophy dept., 1975-80. Vis. prof. SUNY-Buffalo, summer 1970, Kurukshetra U. and Birla Inst., Pilani, India, spring 1980; grants reviewer NEH, 1978—; bd. dirs. SUNY Press editorial, 1989-93, dir. SUNY study abroad, program to India, 1980—; cons. TV series Kung Fu: The Legend Continues., 1992. Author: Sartre's Existentialism in Nausea and Being and Nothingness, 1978, Sartre's Existentialsim as Literature and Philosophy, 1995, Pathways to Philosophy: A Multidisciplinary Approach, 1996, Culture and Self, 1997, Transcreation of the Bhagavad Gita, 1998, Instant Nirvana, 1999, An Introduction to Yoga Philosophy, 2001; TV appearances include ABC World News Now, NBC News, JAIN TV, Doordarshan TV, ZEE TV (India), Natraj TV (Holland), All India Radio, NPR. Founder Ninash Found. Oneonta; established Indo-Internat. Sch., Dundlod, Rajasthan and Kuran, Gujarat, India. Recipient Excellence in Tchg. award and Disting. Tchg. Prof. award United Univ. Profession; Friend of Ednl. award City of Oneonta, 1998, Disting. Alumni award East-West Ctr., 2000, Jewel of India award 2002, Bharat Excellence award Friendship Forum of India, 2002; East-West Ctr. fellow, 1963-65, 66-67; N.Y. State Dept. Edn. grantee, 1967-69, NEH grantee, 1979. Mem. Am. Philos. Assn., Soc. Asian and Comparative Philosophy, Assn. Asian Studies, N.Y. State Asian Studies Soc., Internat. Phenomenol. Soc. Home: 17 Center St Oneonta NY 13820-1445 E-mail: malhotak@oneonta.edu.

MALHOTRA, NARESH KUMAR, management educator; b. Ambala, Punjab, India, Nov. 23, 1949; arrived in U.S., 1975; s. Har Narian and Satya (Kakkar) M.; m. Veena Bahl, Aug. 13, 1980; children: Ruth Veena, Paul Naresh. BTech with honors, Indian Inst. Tech., Bombay, 1971; MBA, I.I.M., Ahmedabad, India, 1973; MS, SUNY, Buffalo, 1978, PhD, 1979. Mgmt. cons. ASCI, Hyderabad, India, 1971-73; asst. prof. Ga. Tech. Inst., Atlanta, 1979—, assoc. prof. mgmt., coord. mktg., 1982-87, 89—, prof., 1988, Regents' prof., 1992—. Organizer several nat. and internat. mktg. mgmt. confs. Author: Marketing Research: An Applied Orientation (N.Am., European, Internat., Australia and New Zealand, Spanish, Portuguese, Chinese, Russian and Hungarian edits.), Basic Marketing Research: Application to Contemporary Issues; contbr. articles to profl. jours. Lay preacher of the Gospel. Fellow Acad. Mktg. Sci. (disting., program chmn. 1984-85, 85-86, v.p. programs 1988-90, chmn. bd. 1990-92, pres. 1994-96, chmn. found. 1996-98, Top Rsch. Jour., Jour. Mktg. Rsch., Jour. Acad. Mktg. Sci., Jour. Healthcare Mktg.), Decision Scis. Inst. (track chmn. 1984-86); mem. Am. Mktg. Assn. (track chmn. 1983-84), Am. Statis. Assn. Republican. Baptist. Avocations: reading, writing, ch. activities, outdoor activities. Home: 1956 Lenox Rd NE Atlanta GA 30306-3035 Office: Ga Tech Inst Coll Mgmt Atlanta GA 30332-0520 E-mail: naresh.malhotra@dupree.gatech.edu.

MALI, PAUL, publisher, retired management educator; b. Hartford, Conn., July 6, 1926; m. Mary S. Mali; children: Faith, Dawn. BS in Engring., U. Conn., 1953, MS, 1962, PhD in Mgmt. and Engring., 1967; postgrad., Cornell U., 1964. Cert. mgmt. cons. Inst. Mgmt. Cons. Elec. engr. Gen. Dynamics, Groton, Conn., 1953—67, dir., 1961—67; prof. mgmt. Entrepreneurial, New London, Conn., 1961—67, U. Hartford, Conn., 1967—94; minister/co-pastor Bible Student ch., New London, Conn., 1994—; prof. Swiss Inst. Tech., Hebrew U.; pub. Horizon Publs.; mgmt. cons. to IBM, Westinghouse, U.S. Steel, United Tech., Aetna, Hanes, Alcan Aluminum, Combustion Engring. Founding fellow Acad. Disting. Engrs. and Hall of Fame of U. Conn. Author: various profl. books, including Writing and Word Processing for Scientists and Engineers, 1981, MBO Updated, 1986, (ministerial books) Magnetic Amplifiers, 1960, The Bible as a Rising Civilization, 1998, Ten Bad Mistakes About God, 2000, Terrorism and the Permission of Evil, 2002, Biblical View on Human Cloning, others, 2002. Pres. Good Samaritan Fund, New London, Conn., 1994—; bd. dirs. 12 state cmty. colls., Conn., 1981—88. Mem.: Am. Mgmt. Assn., Tau Beta Pi, Phi Delta Kappa, Eta Kappa Nu.

MALIK, DAVID JOSEPH, chemist, educator; b. Pittsburg, Calif., July 24, 1945; s. Joseph Elois and Marguerite Barbara (Jacopetti) M.; m. Sandra Louise Funk, Oct. 10, 1986; children: Stephanie Lauren, Stephen David, Michael Josef. BS, Calif. State U., Hayward, 1968; MS, Calif. State U., 1969; PhD, U. Calif., La Jolla, 1976. Post-doctoral rsch. chemist Dept. of Chemistry, U. Calif., La Jolla, Calif., 1976-77; post-doctoral rsch. assoc. Dept. of Chemistry, U. Ill., Urbana, 1977-80; asst. prof. dept. chemistry Ind. U.-Purdue U., Indpls., 1980-86, assoc. prof., 1986-95, prof., 1995—, dept. chmn., 1990-2000, Chancellor's prof. of chemistry, 2002—. Organizer Midwest Theoretical Chemistry Conf., Indpls., 1989, 96. Contbr. articles to profl. jours. Grantee Rsch. Corp., 1981, Petroleum Rsch. Fund, U.S. Dept. Edn.; P.A. Mack founding fellow, 2002-03. Mem. Am. Assn. Higher Edn., Am. Chem. Soc. (chmn. Ind. sect. 1986, tech. program chmn. joint Cen.-Great Lakes regional mtg. Indpls. 1991, councilor 1996—, com. on edn. 1998—), Am. Phys. Soc. (life), Sigma Xi. Democrat. Home: 30 Danbury Ct Zionsville IN 46077-3825 Office: Ind U Purdue U Sch Sci-Dept Chemistry 402 N Blackford St Indianapolis IN 46202-3274 E-mail: malik@chem.iupui.edu.

MALIK, HAFEEZ, political scientist, educator; b. Lahore, Pakistan, Mar. 17, 1930; m. Lynda P. Malik; children: Cyrus, Dean. BA, Government Coll., Lahore, Pakistan, 1949; grad. diploma in Journalism, U. Punjab, Lahore, 1952; MS in Journalism, Syracuse U., 1955, MA in Polit. Sci., 1957, PhD in Polit. Sci., 1961. Asst. prof. polit. sci. Villanova (Pa.) U., 1961-63, assoc. prof., 1963-67, prof., 1967—. Pub. rels. officer City of Lahore, 1950-53; White House corr. The Nawa-i-Waqt, 1958-61, The Shabaz, 1958-61; mem. grad. com. dept. Polit. Sci. Villanova U., 1961-67, chmn., 1967-78; vis. prof. Fgn. Svc. Inst., Washington, 1961-63, 66-68, 70-85, Syracuse U. 1964, 65, Drexel U., Phila., 1968-69; mem. grad. coun. com. rsch. and publs., 1969-70, mem. grad. adv. com. liberal arts and social studies, 1964-67, mem. faculty libr. com., 1964-67, mem. undergrad. com. polit. sci., 1980—, mem. rank and tenure com., 1991-92; pres. Am. Inst. Pakistan Studies, 1972-88, Pakistan Am. Found., 1972—; exec. dir. Am. Coun. Study of Islamic Socs., 1983—; cons. Soviet Acad. Scis., 1979, Dept. Def., 1980, Pakistan-U.S. subcommn. edn. and culture, 1985, 88, USIA, 1986; presenter in field. News editor The Daily Magharabi Pakistan, 1948-50; tech. editor: Meteorological and Geoastrophysical Abstracts, Am. Meteorological Soc. 1960-63; author: Muslim Nationalism in India and Pakistan, 1963, rev. edit. 1980, Sir Sayyid Ahmed Khan's History of the Bijnore Rebellion, 1972, rev. edit. 1980, Sir Sayyid Ahmad Khan and Muslim Modernization in India and Pakistan, 1980, Political Profile of Sir Sayyid Ahmad Khan: A Documentary Record, 1982, Sir Sayyid Ahmad Khan's Educational Philosophy: International Security in Southwest Asia, 1984, Domestic Determinants of Soviet Foreign Policy Towards South Asia and the Middle East, 1989, Dilemmas of National Security and Cooperation in India and Pakistan, 1993, Soviet-Pakistan Relations and Post-Soviet Dynamics, 1996, Central Asia: Its Strategic Importance and Future Prospects, 1994, U.S., Russia, China in the New World Order, 1996; editor: Iqbal: Poet-Philosopher of Pakistan, 1971, rev. edit., 1982, Soviet-American Relations with Pakistan, Iran, and Afghanistan, 1987; mem. editl. adv. bd. Islam and the Modern Age, Islam Awr Aser-i Jadid, 1969-79; editor Jour. South Asian and Middle Eastern Studies, 1977—; contbr. articles to profl. jours., encyclopedias, chpts. to books. Grantee Office Health, Edn. Welfare, 1974, 1978, Assn. Pakistan and Indic-Islamic Studies/Pakistan Am. Found, 1982. Office: Villanova U 416-421 SAC 800 E Lancaster Ave Villanova PA 19085-1603 E-mail: hafeez.malik@Villanova.edu.

MALIN, IRVING, English literature educator, literary critic; b. N.Y.C., Mar. 18, 1934; s. Morris and Bertha (Silverman) M.; m. Ruth Lief, Dec. 18, 1955; 1 child, Mark. BA, Queens Coll., 1955; PhD, Stanford U., 1958. Acting instr. English Stanford U., 1955-58; instr. Ind. U., 1958-60; from instr. to prof. CCNY, 1960-72, prof., 1972—. Cons. Jewish Publ. Soc., 1964, Am. Quar., 1964, NEH, 1972, 79, 80, 81, 82, B'nai B'rith, 1974-75, Yaddo, 1975-77, Jewish Book Coun., 1976, 79, PEN, 1978-82, Princeton U. Press, 1979, Fairleigh Dickinson Press, 1980, Wayne State U. Press, 1980, Internat. Coun. Exch. of Scholars, 1980-81, Duke U. Press, 1981, Jewish Daily Forward, 1981, U. Pitts. Press, 1981, Papers on Lang. and Lit., 1981, U. Ga. Press, 1983, UMI Rsch., 1989, Gordian Press, 1990, Ctr. for Study of Higher Edn., 1990, Mosiac, 1991, MacArthur Found., 1996, U. of S.C. Press, 1998, Purdue U. Press, Lafayette, Ind., 1999. Author: William Faulkner: An Interpretation, 1957, New American Gothic, 1962, Jews and Americans, 1965, Saul Bellow's Fiction, 1969, Nathanael West's Novels, 1972, Isaac Bashevis Singer, 1972; co-editor: Breakthrough: A Treasury of Contemporary American Jewish Literature, 1964, William Styron's The Confessions of Nat Turner: A Critical Handbook, 1970, The Achievement of William Styron, 1975, William Goyen, 1997, Into the Tunnel, 1998, Garrett's Elizabethan Trilogy, 1998; editor: Psychoanalysis and American Fiction, 1965, Saul Bellow and the Critics, 1967, Truman Capote's in Cold Blood: A Critical Handbook, 1968, Critical Views of Isaac Bashevis Singer, 1969, Contemporary American-Jewish Literature: Critical Essays, 1973, Conrad Alken's Prose, 1982; co-editor: Underwords: Perspectives on Don

DeLillo's Underworld, 2002; adv. editor: Studies in American Jewish Literature, Jour. Modern Literature, Review of Contemporary Fiction, Saul Bellow Jour., 20th Century Literature; reviewer: Hollins Critic, So. Quar.; co-editor Paul Bowles, 1986, Spl. Issue of 20th Century Lit., James Dickey Spl. Issue of S.C. Rev., 1994, Pynchon and Mason and Dixon, 2000, So. Novelists on Stage and Screen So. Quar., 1995, James Dickey's Fiction Spl. Tex. Rev., 1996, Leslie Fiedler and American Culture, 1999, Torpid Smoke: The Stories of Vladimir Nabokov, 2000. Fellow Yaddo, 1963, Nat. Found. for Jewish Culture, 1963-64, Huntington Libr., 1978. Mem. MLA, AAUP, Am. Studies Assn., Am. Jewish Hist. Soc., Melville Soc., Authors League Am., Soc. Study of So. Lit., Poe Studies Assn., English Inst., Nathaniel Hawthorne Soc., N.Y. Acad. Scis., Poetry Soc. Am., Popular Culture Assn., Nat. Book Critics Circle, Sherwood Anderson Soc., Internat. Assn. Univ. Prof. English, Kafka Soc., English-Speaking Union, Multi-Ethnic Lit. U.S. Soc., Hastings Ctr., Am. Jewish Congress, Assoc. Writing Programs, Nat. Coun. Tchrs. of English, Vladimir Nabokov Soc., Phi Beta Kappa. Jewish. Home: 96-13 68th Ave Forest Hills NY 11375-5039 Office: CCNY Dept English New York NY 10031

MALINOWSKI, PATRICIA A. community college educator; b. Buffalo, N.Y., Jan. 19, 1950; d. Raymond J. and Emily M. (Ferek) Cybulski; m. Leonard T. Malinowski, July 12, 1975; children: Adam, Christopher. BA, SUNY, Fredonia, 1971; MEd, Bowling Green State U., 1972. Asst. prof. devel. studies Finger Lakes C.C., Canandaigua, NY, 1987-92, assoc. prof., 1992-96, prof. devel. studies, 1996—, chair devel. studies dept., 1991—. Editor: Rsch. and Tchg. in Devel. Edn., 1990—; contbr. articles to profl. jours. Active Literacy Vols., Canandaigua, 1994—2000; counselor Boy Scouts Am., 1998—; active Canandaigua PTO, 1998—; youth adv. com. St. Mary's Ch., Canandaigua, 2000—; mem. sch. bd. St. Mary's Sch., Canandaigua, 1993—99; parish coun. youth adv. com. St. Mary's Ch., Canandaigua, 2002—, liturgy com., 2002—. Nominee ATHENA, 2002; recipient Excellence in Profl. Svc. award, N.Y. State Chancellor, 1993, Disting. Svc. award, Finger Lakes C.C., 1988, 2000, Pelican award, Boy Scouts Am., 2002. Mem.: NADE (edn. bd. 1994—, Outstanding Publ. award 1995), N.Y. Coll. Learning Skills Assn. (v.p., sec., conf. chair 1987—, Outstanding Profl. Svc. award 1995), N.Y. State English Coun., N.Y. State Reading Assn., Nat. Coun. Tchrs. English, Internat. Reading Assn. (editl. bd. 1994—), Nat. C.C. Chair Acad. (editl. bd. 1992—), Phi Delta Kappa. Avocation: Avocations: family, reading, travel, walking. Office: Finger Lakes CC 4355 Lakeshore Dr Canandaigua NY 14424-8347 E-mail: malinopa@flcc.edu.

MALKAWI, ALI MAHMOUD, architecture educator, researcher; b. Irbid, Jordan, Feb. 12, 1967; came to U.S., 1989; s. Mahmoud Ahmed and Safia (Khatib) M. BS in Archtl. Engring. with honors, Jordan U. Sci. and Tech., Irbid, 1989; MArch, U. Colo., Denver, 1990; PhD with honors, Ga. Inst. Tech., 1994. Project designer Malkawi Cons. Engrs., Amman, Jordan, 1989; instr. Ga. Inst. Tech., Atlanta, 1992-94, doctoral fellow, 1991-94, project coord., 1994; asst. prof. architecture U. Mich., Ann Arbor, 1994—; coord., asst. prof., 1994—; postdoctoral/Oberdick fellow U. Mich., Ann Arbor, 1994-95; assoc. prof. U. Pa., Phila., 2001—. Vis. prof. Harvard Grad. Sch., 2001—; pres. Intelligenet Energy Optimization Cons., Ann Arbor, 1995—. Mem. ASHRAE, Acoustical Soc. Am., Illumination Engring. Soc., Am. Solar Energy Soc. Achievements include copyrighted theory development and implementation of intelligent CAD software. Office: U Pa Dept Arch 207 Meyerson Hall Philadelphia PA 19104-6311 E-mail: malkawi@pobox.upenn.edu.

MALKIEL, BURTON GORDON, economist, educator; b. Boston, Aug. 28, 1932; s. Sol and Celia (Gordon) Malkiel; m. Judith Ann Atherton, July 16, 1954 (dec. 1987); 1 child, Jonathan; m. Nancy Weiss, July 31, 1988. BA, Harvard, 1953, MBA, 1955; PhD, Princeton, 1964. Assoc. Smith Barney & Co., N.Y.C., 1958—60; asst. prof. dept. econs. Princeton U., 1964—66, assoc. prof., 1966—68, prof., 1968—81, Rentschler prof. econs., 1969—81, chmn. dept. econs., 1974—75, 1977—81, Chem. Bank chmn.'s prof. econs., 1988—; dean Sch. Orgn. and Mgmt., Yale U., 1981—87. Mem. Pres.'s Coun. Econ. Advisors, 1975—77; dir. Jeffrey Co., Prudential Fin., BKF Capital, Vanguard Group. Author: The Term Structure of Interest Rates, 1966; author: (with others) Strategies and Rational Decisions in the Securities Options Market, 1969; author: The Inflation-Beater's Investment Guide, 1980, Global Bargain Hunting, 1998; author: (with others) The Index Fund Solution, 1999; author: A Random Walk Down Wall Street, 8th edit., 2003, The Random Walk Guide to Investing, 2003. 1st lt. U.S. Army, 1955—58. Mem.: Am. Fin. Assn. (dir., pres. 1978). Home: 76 North Rd Princeton NJ 08540-2430 Office: Princeton U Dept Econs Princeton NJ 08544-0001 E-mail: bmalkiel@princeton.edu.

MALKIEL, NANCY WEISS, dean, historian, educator; b. Newark, Feb. 14, 1944; d. William and Ruth Sylvia (Puder) Weiss; m. Burton G. Malkiel, July 31, 1988. BA summa cum laude, Smith Coll., 1965; MA, Harvard U., 1966, PhD, 1970. From asst. to assoc. prof. history Princeton (N.J.) U., 1969-82, prof., 1982—, master Dean Mathey Coll., 1982-86, dean coll., 1987—. Author (as Nancy J. Weiss): (book) Chalres Franis Murphy, 1858-1924: Respectability and Responsibility in Tammany Politics, 1968; author: (with others) Blacks in America: Bibliographical Essays, 1971, The National Urban League, 1910-1940, 1974, Farewell to the Party of Lincoln: Black Politics in the Age of FDR, 1983 (Berkshire Conf. of Women Historians prize, 1984), Whitney M. Young Jr., and the Struggle for Civil Rights, 1989. Trustee Woodrow Wilson Nat. Fellowship Found., 1975—, chmn. bd. trustees, 1999—; trustee Smith Coll., Northampton, Mass., 1984—94. Fellow, Woodrow Wilson Found., 1965, Charles Warren Ctr. Studies in Am. History, 1976—77, Radcliffe Inst., 1976—77, Ctr. Advanced Study Behavioral Scis., 1986—87. Mem.: So. Hist. Assn., Orgn. Am. Historians (chmn. status women hist. profession 1972—75), Am. Hist. Assn., Phi Beta Kappa. Democrat. Jewish. Office: Princeton U Office Dean Of College Princeton NJ 08544-0001

MALKINSON, FREDERICK DAVID, dermatologist, educator; b. Hartford, Conn., Feb. 26, 1924; s. John Walter and Rose Malkinson; m. Una Zwick, June 15, 1979; children by previous marriage: Philip, Carol, John. Student, Loomis Inst., 1937-41; 3 yr. cert. cum laude, Harvard U., 1943, DMD, 1947, MD, 1949. Intern Harvard-Beth Israel Hosp., Boston, 1949-50; resident in dermatology U. Chgo., 1950-54, from instr. to assoc. prof. dept. dermatology, 1954-68; prof. medicine and dermatology U. Ill., Chgo., 1968-71; chmn. dept. dermatology Rush Med. Coll. and Rush-Presbyn.-St. Luke's Med. Ctr., Chgo., 1968-92, Clark W. Finnerud, M.D. prof. dept. dermatology, 1981-95, 95—; trustee Sulzberger Inst. Dermatol. Comm. and Edn., 1976-96; pres. Sulzberger Inst. Dermatol. Communication and Edn., 1983-88, 93-96; prof. emeritus Rush Presbyn.-St. Luke's Med. Ctr., Chgo., 1995—. Editor: Year Book of Dermatology, 1971-78; chief editor: AMA Archives of Dermatology, 1979-83; bd. editors, 1976-84, Jour. AMA, 1979-83; editorial cons. World Book Medical Encyclopedia, 1991—; contbr. articles and abstracts to profl. jours., chpts. to books. Active Evanston (Ill.) Libr. Bd., 1988-94, pres., 1993-94. With M.C. USN, 1950-52. Grantee U.S. Army, 1955-61, USPHS, 1962-73 Fellow AAAS; mem. Am. Acad. Dermatology (v.p. 1987-89, dir. 1964-67), Am. Dermatol. Assn., Soc. Investigative Dermatology (v.p. 1978-79, dir. 1963-68), Am. Fedn. Med. Rsch., Cen. Soc. Clin. Rsch., Radiation Rsch. Soc., Assn. Profs. of Dermatology (dir. 1982-85), Dermatology Found. (trustee 1980-93, pres. 1983-85), Nat. Coun. on Radiation Protection and Measurements (mem. com. on cutaneous radiobiology 1986-92), Chgo. Dermatol. Soc. (pres. 1964-65, Gold Medal award 1992), Chgo. Lit. Club (v.p. 1997-99, 2000-03, pres. 1999-2000). Office: Rush-Presbyn-St Luke's Med Ctr Kidston 507b 1653 Congress Street Pkwy Chicago IL 60612 Office Fax: (312) 942-7778.

MALKUS, DAVID STARR, retired mechanics educator, applied mathematician; b. Chgo., June 30, 1945; s. Willem V.R. Malkus and Joanne (Gerould) Simpson; m. Evelyn R. (div.); children: Christopher, Annelise, Byron, Renata. AB, Yale U., 1968; PhD, Boston U., 1976. Mathematician U.S. Nat. Bur. Standards, Gaithersburg, Md., 1975-77; asst. prof. math. Ill. Inst. Tech., Chgo., 1977-83, assoc. prof., 1983-84; assoc. prof. mechanics U. Wis., Madison, 1984-87, prof., 1987—2002, chmn. Rheology Rsch. Ctr., 1991-94, prof. emeritus, 2002—. Chair prof. Nanjing (People's Republic China) Aero. Inst., 1986. Co-author: Concepts and Applications of Finite Element Analysis, 1989; contbr. articles to Computer Methods Applied Mech. Engring., Jour. Computational Physics. Achievements include research on finite element methods--reduced and selective integration techniques, a unification of concepts. Home: 2710 Mason St Madison WI 53705-3716 Office: U Wis Dept Engring Physics 1500 Engineering Dr Madison WI 53706-1609 E-mail: malkus@engr.wisc.edu.

MALL, SHANKAR, engineering mechanics educator, researcher; b. Varanasi, India, June 10, 1943; came to U.S., 1974; s. Hari Das and Methul Mall; m. Raj Kumari, Dec. 2, 1965; 1 child, Sharal. BSME, Banaras Hindu U., Varanasi, 1964, MS, 1966; PhD, U. Wash., 1977. Engr. in tng. Kisha Seizo Kaisha, Osaka, Japan, 1966-67; lectr. mech. engring. Banaras Hindu U., 1967-74; rsch. asst. U. Wash., Seattle, 1974-77; asst. prof. U. Maine, Orono, 1978-81, assoc. prof., 1981-83, U. Mo., Rolla, 1983-86; prof., head Air Force Inst. Tech., Wright-Patterson AFB, Ohio, 1986-98; prof., prin. materials rsch. engr. Air Force Rsch. Lab., Wright-Patterson AFB, 1998—. Rsch. engr. NASA Langley Research Ctr., Hampton, Va., 1981-82. Fellow ASME, AIAA (assoc.); mem. Sigma Xi, Tau Beta Pi. Home: 2374 N Knoll Dr Dayton OH 45431-2454 Office: Dept Aeronautics & Astronautics Air Force Inst Technol Wright Patterson Afb OH 45433 E-mail: shankar.mall@afit.edu.

MALLARD, JACQUELINE, secondary education educator; b. Mobile, Ala., Mar. 3, 1953; d. Willie Kiser and Dora Louise (Johnson) M. BA, Pepperdine U., 1973, MS, 1979; postgrad., Calif. State U., Dominguez Hills, 1988—. Tchr. math. L.A. Unified Sch. Dist., 1974-85, tchr.math. and spl. edn., 1987—, chmn. math. dept., 1979-80. Coord. sch. proficiency English program Bret Harte Prep. Sch., L.A., 1989-90. Dir. Evangelism Outreach, First Ch. of God, 1991—; active NAACP, juvenile prison fellowship program. Recipient Wall of Fame award, 1990. Mem. ASCD, Assn. United Tchrs. L.A., Assn. of American University Women. Avocations: travel, reading, writing, shopping, food. Home: 11730 Denver Ave Los Angeles CA 90044-4044 Office: Bret Harte Prep Sch 9301 S Hoover St Los Angeles CA 90044-4722

MALLERY, ANNE LOUISE, elementary education educator, consultant; b. Myersdale, Pa., June 14, 1934; d. Samuel Addison and Ruth Elizabeth (Meehan) M.; m. Richard Gwen Jones, Mar. 9, 1953 (div. 1974); children: Valerie Anne, Joseph Samuel, Richard Alan (dec.). BS in Edn., Calif. U., Pa., 1970, MEd, 1972; EdD, Pa. State U., 1980. From proficiency coord. to prof. elem. edn. Millersville (Pa.) U., 1980—; asst. to pres. for planning MobileVision Tech., Inc., Coral Gables, Fla., 1990—; editor Innovative Learning Strategy, Nat. Publ., 1989—; cons. East Brunswick Pub. Schs., 1995. Cons. Pequea Valley H.S., Lancaster, Pa., 1985, Cambridge Adult Edn. Co., 1987, Conawago Elem. Sch., York, Pa., 1991; co-dir. NEH grant, 1993-94. Co-author The Secret Cave Multimodal Reading Program; contbr. numerous articles to profl. jours. Judge Intelligencer Reg. Spelling Bee, Lancaster, 1990,91. Mem. Assn. Pa. State Coll. and U. Faculty, Internat. Reading Assn., Lancaster Lebanon Reading Assn., Assn. Tchr. Educators, Am. Assn. Colls. Tchr. Edn., Am. Reading Forum. Republican. Presbyterian. Avocations: swimming, walking, reading, films. Home: 4901 Saratoga Blvd Corpus Christi TX 78413-2265 Office: Millersville Univ Stayer Education Ctr Millersville PA 17551

MALLETT, DEBORAH GLENN, gifted talented education educator, coordinator; b. Beaumont, Tex., May 20, 1951; d. Gerald Gordon and Mildred (Long) Mallett; m. Eric Lee Newman, Aug. 10, 1985 (dec. Sept. 1987). BA in Elem. Edn., Baylor U., 1973; cert. in ins. mktg., U. Houston, 1983; MEd summa cum laude, U. Oreg., 1991. Cert. gifted edn. educator, Tex.; cert. tchr., Tex., N.Mex., Ala. Women's ministry coord. Campus Crusade for Christ, San Bernardino, Calif., 1973-79; tchr. Spring Br. Ind. Sch. Dist., Houston, 1979-81; paralegal Butler, Binion, Rice, Cook, Knapp, Houston, 1081-83, Fouts and Moore, 1983-84; owner fashion cons. bus. Design for Beauty, Houston, 1983-85, fashion cons., 1984-85; tchr. The Kinkaid Sch., Houston, 1985-89, Beaumont (Tex.) Ind. Sch. Dist., 1989-90; talented/gifted facilitator and coord. Alamogordo (N.Mex.) Pub. Sch. Sys., 1992-94. Ednl. cons., Houston, 1990-92; mem. adv. bd. Marrs Hill Prodns., Houston, 1991-92, South Ctrl. Aviation Ministries, Houston, 1985-87; cons. Gifted Edn. Task Force, Albuquerque; owner Ednl. Cons. Svcs. Author numerous short stories. Named one of Notable Women of Tex., State of Tex., 1984-85. Mem. NEA, ASCD, Nat. Assn. for Gifted Child, U.S. Water Fitness Assn. (cert. instr.), State Bar Tex. Legal Assts. Divsn. (charter mem.), Baylor Alumni Assn; Tex. Assn. for Gifted and Talented. Republican. Baptist. Avocations: writing, painting, aerobics, skiing, fashion.

MALLETT, HELENE GETTLER, retired elementary education educator; b. Goshen, N.Y., Aug. 20, 1937; d. John and Anna Gettler; m. Richard David Mallett, July 29, 1967; 1 child, Anna Alma. BS in Fgn. Svc., Georgetown U., 1959; MA, SUNY, Stonybrook, 1989. Supr. Fulbright Program/Europe Inst. Internat. Edn., N.Y.C., 1961-65; editor Am. Assn. Fund Raising Coun., N.Y.C., 1965-67; coord. adult GED/ESL programs BOCES 3, Deer Park, N.Y., 1973-85; tchr. UFSD #3 and UFSD #4, Huntington, N.Y., 1967-97; ret., 1997. Trustee Eastwood Sch., Oyster Bay, N.Y., 1977-83; alumni interviewer, Georgetown U., Washington, 1989—. Mem. ASCD, Nat. Coun. for the Social Studies, N.Y. State United Tchrs. (com. 100), Chemist Club. Avocations: travel, angora rabbits, diplomatic history, robots, geography. Home: 79 Little Neck Rd Centerport NY 11721-1615

MALLETTE, LILA GENE MOHLER (GURUDEV SRI RASALI-LANANDA), educator, writer, editor; b. Fort Lauderdale, Fla., June 7, 1931; d. Marvin Francis and Silvia Ione (Kenney) Mohler; divorced; children: Michael F., Polly A. Mallette McPeak, Jefferson A. Student U. N.Mex., 1963-65 Founder, dir. Coun. for World Community, Washington, 1975-82; coord. Arlington Visitor Ctr., 1982-93; dir., founder Metamorphosis, 1978—. Mem. Menninger Found., Acad. Religion and Psychical Rsch., Kundalini Rsch Network, Spiritual Emergence Network, Internat. Assn. of Yoga Therapists, Inst. Noetic Scis., World Federalists, NOW, World Future Soc., Assn. Humanistic Psychology, Sci. and Med. Network U.K., Mensa. Office: 6274 Edsall Rd Apt 108 Alexandria VA 22312-2639

MALLINSON, RICHARD GREGORY, chemical engineering educator; b. Indpls., Apr. 9, 1954; s. Harry and Susan Louise (Keckler) M. BSChemE, BS in Biomed. Engring., Tulane U., 1977; MSChemE, Purdue U., 1979, PhD, 1983. Rsch. asst. Purdue U., West Lafayette, Ind., 1977-83, Argonne Nat. Lab., Chgo., 1978; asst. prof. chem. engring. U. Okla., Norman, 1983-89, assoc. prof., 1989-99, dir. Inst. for Gas Utilization Techs., 1995—, prof., 1999—. Faculty fellow Lawrence Livermore Nat. Lab., Livermore, Calif., 1990; vis. prof. Tianjin (China) U., 1994—, Chulalongkorn U., Bangkok, 1994—; ptnr. OKKINETICS, Norman, 1996-2000; prin. investigator Univ. Technologists, Inc., Norman, 1988-91; Kerr McGee Disting. lectr. Kerr-McGee Found./U. Okla., 1989-94. Contbr. many articles on Energy. Bd. dirs. C.D. Mallory Found., Inc., Ala., 1994-99, Heartland Found., Inc., Okla., 1995—; mem. Okla. Found. for Excellence, 1993—. 1st lt. USAR, 1977-85. Mem. AIChE (dir. local sect. 1989, symposia organizer 1986-89), Am. Chem. Soc. (symposia organizer 1985-91), Am. Soc. Engring. Edn., Sigma Xi. Achievements include patents pending and patents in field for high density natural gas storage at high temperature, and chemical conversion of natural gas at low temperatures; other areas of exoertise such as natural gas utilization, clean production of N204, emulsion polymerization modeling, alkane cracking modeling, coal conversion modeling. Home: 4631 Ridgeline Dr Norman OK 73072-1700 Office: U Okla 100 E Boyd St Rm T335 Norman OK 73019-1028 E-mail: mallinson@ou.edu.

MALLORY, ELGIN ALBERT, business educator, management consultant, small business owner, school system administrator; b. Lake Arthur, N.Mex., Aug. 7, 1938; s. Albert Edgar and Thelma Ann (McCulley) M.; m. Shirley Jo Mallory, June 12, 1959 (dec. Oct. 1990); children: Brenda Sue Gottlieb, Linda Jo Saidla; m. Sarah Ann Mallory, Aug. 1, 1992; children: Lynn Janette Towne, Karen Kay Olson. BS, Ea. N.Mex. U., Portales, 1964; MEd, Ea. N.Mex. State U., Portales, 1969; PhD, Colo. State U., 1990. Cert. supt. schs., h.s. prin., math. and chemistry tchr., N.Mex., Colo. Tchr. h.s. math. Clovis (N.Mex.) Mcpl. Sch., 1964-71; jr. h.s. prin. Grants (N.Mex.) Mcpl. Sch., 1971-73; h.s. prin. Silver Consol. Sch., Silver City, N.Mex., 1973-75, Roswell (N.Mex.) Ind. Sch. Dist., 1975-78; dir. secondary edn. Mesa County Sch. Dist., Grand Junction, Colo., 1978-80, asst. supt., 1980-83; owner, mgr. House of Sleep, Grand Junction, 1983-87; prof. Mesa State Coll., Grand Junction, 1986-95. Mgmt. cons. to small businesses, Colo. and N.Mex., 1985—. Bd. dirs. Mesa County Econ. Coun., Grand Junction, 1983-87; pres. bd. Western Colo. coun. Boy Scouts Am., 1982-90; bd. dirs., campaign chair United Way, Grand Junction, 1980—. Recipient Silver Beaver award Boy Scouts Am., 1983. Mem. Am. Statis. Assn., Mountain Plains Mgmt. ASsn., Coop. Edn. Assn., Western Mgmt. and Mktg. Assn. Republican. Presbyterian. Avocations: golf, fishing, hunting, motorcycle riding, boating. Home: 2098 Hodesha Way Grand Junction CO 81503-1049 E-mail: malloryeands@aol.com.

MALLORY, LEE WESLEY, III, English and French language educator, poet; b. San Mateo, Calif., Mar. 16, 1946; s. Lee W. Mallory II and Mary Ann (Gadd) Rector; m. Adell J. Patterson, June 27, 1969 (div. Dec. 1989); children: Misty Ann, Natalee Adell. AA, Orange Coast Coll., 1966; Bachelor's degree, U. Calif., Santa Barbara, 1969; Master's degree, Calif. State U., Long Beach, 1978. Cert. prof. English and French, Calif. Prof. Santa Ana (Calif.) Coll., 1980—. Pres. acad. senate Santa Ana Coll., 1986-87, officer faculty bargaining unit, 1987—. Author: (books) 91739, 1970, I Write Your Name, 1990, Full Moon, Empty Hands, 1994, Holiday Sheer, 1997, Bettin' on the Come, 2002. Pres. Cen. Newport Beach (Calif.) Comty. Assn., 1976-78; co-prodr. Factory Poetry Readings, Costa Mesa, Calif., 1988—; prodr. Poetry at Alta, Newport Beach, 1992—. Capt. U.S. Army, 1973-76. Mem. Assn. Rancho Santiago Coll. Dist. (polit. action officer 1992-98), Phi Beta Kappa. Democrat. Avocations: poetry, long distance running. Office: Santa Ana Coll 17th at Bristol St Santa Ana CA 92706

MALLORY, SARA BROCKWELL, education educator; b. Newberry, S.C., Feb. 20, 1940; d. Charles Wilbur and Amelia Georgianna (Wideman) Brockwell; m. Buddy Lee Mallory, Feb. 4, 1967. BA, Columbia (S.C.) Coll., 1962; MS in Edn., Old Dominion U., 1986. Cert. collegiate profl., Va. Tchr. English, Ryan Schs., Inc., Norfolk, Va., 1979-86; adj. instr. reading Old Dominion U., Norfolk, 1986-88, instr. ednl. curriculum and instrn., 1988—. Tchr. Spanish, Norfolk Collegiate Sch., spring 1987; reading resource tchr., Virginia Beach, 1993. Sec.-treas. ch. sch. Miles Meml. United Meth. Ch., Norfolk, 1992-93, chmn. com. on higher edn. and campus ministry, 1993. Named Most Inspiring Faculty Mem., Coll. Edn., Old Dominion U., 1990, Most Outstanding Faculty Mem. Office Student Svcs., 1992. Mem. ASCD, Nat. Coun. Tchrs. English, Internat. Reading Assn., Va. Reading Assn., Va. Coll. Reading Educators, Dickens Fellowship. Avocations: reading, travel, playing piano, singing, sewing. Home: 8605 Meadow Brook Ln Norfolk VA 23503-5411 Office: Old Dominion U Edn Bldg Rm 244 Norfolk VA 23529

MALLORY HARRISON, GEORGE WILLIAM, education educator, consultant; b. Milw., July 29, 1951; s. George William and June Rose (Kinast) H.; m. Jacqueline Marie Patterson, Aug. 3, 1971 (div.); 1 child, Althaea Rachel; m. Carol Ruth Hershenson, Oct. 30, 1989; 1 child, George William. AA, Concorda Coll., Milw., 1971; BA, Marquette U., Milw., 1973; MA, U. Wis., 1976; PhD, Johns Hopkins U., Balt., 1984. Asst., assoc. prof. Xavier U., Cin., 1985—. Ptnr. Stupak and Mallory Harrison, Balt., 1984-85; pres. Werlong Edn. Comms., Inc., 2000—. Author: (poems) Cerrd Defod, 1970, The Romans and Crete, 1993; editor: Seneca in Performance, 2000; translator Cyclops; contbr. over 50 articles to profl. jours. Mem. Internat. Plutarch Soc. Jewish. Avocation: boating. Home: 134 William Howard Taft Cincinnati OH 45219-2128 Office: 3800 Victory Pkwy Cincinnati OH 45207-5181 E-mail: harrison@xu.edu.

MALLOW, ALISSA JANE, social worker, educator; b. Bklyn., Oct. 8, 1959; d. Gerald Mallow and Marcia (Bunkin) Edwards. BA, SUNY, Stony Brook, 1981; MSW, Adelphi U., 1983, postgrad., 1994—. Social worker Assn. for Advancement Blind and Retarded, Jamaica, N.Y., 1983-84, Syosset (N.Y.) Cmty. Hosp., 1984-87; social work therapist North Shore U. Hosp., Manhasset, N.Y., 1987-90, program coord. Glen Cove, N.Y., 1990-94, coord. outreach, edn. and tng., 1994—. Adj. instr. Adelphi U., Sch. Social Work, 1995—. Contbr. articles to profl. jours. Mem. NASW, Acad. Cert. Social Workers. Office: North Shore U Hosp Saint Andrews Lane Glen Cove NY 11542

MALLOY, EDWARD ALOYSIUS, academic administrator; b. Washington, May 3, 1941; s. Edward Aloysius and Elizabeth (Clark) Malloy. BA, U. Notre Dame, 1963, MA, 1967, ThM, 1969; PhD, Vanderbilt U., 1975. Ordained to ministry Cath. Ch., 1970. Instr. U. Notre Dame, South Bend, Ind., 1974—75, asst. prof., 1975—81, assoc. prof., 1981—88, prof. theology, 1988—, assoc. provost, 1982—86, pres. elect, 1986, pres., 1987—. Established chair Cath. Studes in name of Edward A. Malloy Vanderbilt U., 1997; bd. regents U. Portland, 1985—. Chmn. Am. Coun. Edn.; bd. dirs. NCAA Found., 1989—; mem. Pres. Adv. Coun. on Drugs, 1989—; mem. adv. bd. AmeriCorps and Nat. Civilian Cmty. Corps, 1994—97; interim chmn. Ind. Commn. Cmty. Svc., 1994—97; mem. Boys and Girls Clubs Am., 1997—; trustee St. Thomas U., 1967—, Vanderbilt U., 1999; bd. advisors Bernadin Ctr., 1997—; bd. dirs. Points of Light; past chmn. Campus Impact; mem. Bishopps and pres. com. Assn. Cath. Colls. and Univs., 1988—; bd. dirs. Internat. Fedn. Cath. Univs., 1988—. Mem.: Nat. Assn. Ind. Colls. and Univs. (bd. dirs. 1997), The Conf. Bd., Assn. Governing Bds. of Univs. and Colls. (vice chair 1996—), Bus.-Higher Edn. Forum, Am. Soc. Christian Ethics, Cath. Theol. Soc. Roman Catholic. Office: U Notre Dame Office Pres Notre Dame IN 46556*

MALLOY, JOHNN EDWARD, media artist, writer; b. Superior, Wis., Jan. 1, 1940; s. Robert Francis and Celestine Marie (Evenson) M. BS, U. Wis., LaCrosse, 1962; MS, Winona (Minn.) State U., 1967; MEd, Chgo. State U., 1970; EdS, Ea. Ill. U., 1977; D Arts, U. No. Colo., 1982. Cert. K-14 tchr., Ill., Wis., Colo. Tchr. speech and English Merrill (Wis.) Pub. Schs., 1962-65; tchr. radio and TV Harvey (Ill.) Sch. Dist., 1965-94; instr. speech and theatre, set designer So. Suburban Coll., South Holland, Ill., 1968-70, 75-77, 85; media lectr. Chgo. State U., 1970-72; supr. media lab. U. No. Colo., Greeley, 1980-82; news anchor Colo. Radio Info. Svc., Greeley, 1981-82. Actor College Street Players, LaCrosse, 1964, Summer Theatre Co., Charleston, Ill., 1974-78; actor, dir. Theatre 21 Co., South Holland, 1974-78; scene painter Sedona (Ariz.) Art Ctr. Theatre, 1996; tech. asst. Red Barn Playhouse, Saugatuck, Mich., 1996—; theater mgr. Thornton Auditorium, Harvey, Ill., 1976-96; art assoc. You'nique Internat. Gallery, Douglas, Mich., 1999—, Art Assoc. Discovery Art Ctr., Saugatuck, Mich., 2000—; stage designer, cons. Saugatuck Ctr. for the Arts, 2001—; cons. Mason St. Warehouse Theatre, 2003—. Author: Communication in the High School: Speaking and Listening, 1972, Instructional Guides to Media

Communication, 1982; prodr. TV mag. series Getting Around, 1981-94. Active CAP, Chgo., 1965—; participant in tchr.-in-space program NASA, 1985-86; charter sponsor, USAF Meml., Washington. Recipient degree of Diamond Key Coach, Nat. Forensic League, Ripon, Wis., 1994, Silver Medalist Canon USA Photo Contest, 1985, Publ. award Internat. Libr. Photography, 1999; Cert. of Recognition in CBS TV Worth Teaching Program, 1987. Mem. NEA, Ill. Speech and Theatre Assn., Ill. Edn. Assn., Am. Air Mus. Britain (founding mem.), Challenger Ctr. (founding mem.), Air Force Assn., Nat. Air & Space Soc. (founding mem.), Libr. of Congress Assocs. (founding mem.), Saugatuck-Douglas Hist. Soc. (Mich. chpt.), Brit. Interplanetary Soc., Saugatuck-Douglas Art Club. Lutheran.

MALLOY, MICHAEL PATRICK, law educator, consultant; b. Haddon Heights, N.J., Sept. 23, 1951; s. Francis Edward and Marie Grace (Nardi) Malloy; m. Susie Pieratos, Jan. 1992; children: Michael Emil, Nicholas Charles, Edward Francis, Theodora Marie, Sophia Grace, Elizabeth. BA magna cum laude (scholar), Georgetown U., 1973, PhD, 1983; JD (scholar), U. Pa., 1976. Bar: N.J. 1976, U.S. Supreme Ct. 1991. Rsch. assoc. Inst. Internat. Law and Econ. Devel., Washington, 1976—77; atty. advisor Office Fgn. Assets Control U.S. Dept. Treasury, Washington, 1977—80, spl. asst. Office Gen. Counsel, 1985; atty. advisor Office Fgn. Assets Control Office Comptr. Currency, Washington, 1981; spl. counsel SEC, Washington, 1981—82; asst. prof. N.Y. Law Sch., N.Y.C., 1982—83; assoc. prof. Seton Hall U. Sch. Law, Newark, 1983—86, prof., assoc. dean, 1986—87; prof. Fordham U. Sch. Law, N.Y.C., 1987—96, dir. grad. studies, 1990—94; prof. U. Pacific McGeorge Law Sch., Sacramento, 1996—2002, disting. prof. and scholar, 2003—. Law lectr. Morin Ctr. Banking and Fin. Law Studies Boston U. Law Sch., 1986—90, 1995—96, 2001; vis. prof. U. Salzburg, Austria, 2000, Suffolk U. Sch. Law, 2001—02; cons. bank regulation and pvt. internat. law matters. Author: (book) Corporate Law of Banks, 2 vols., 1988, Economic Sanctions and U.S. Trade, 1990, The Regulation of Banking, 1992, Banking Law and Regulation, 3 vols., 1994, Fundamentals of Banking Regulation, 1998, International Banking, 1998, Banking and Financial Services Law, 1999, Hornbook on Bank Regulation, 1999, 2d edit., 2003, U.S. Economic Sanctions: Theory and Practice, 2001; contbr. articles, revs. and comments to profl. jours. Mem.: L'Association des Auditeurs et Anciens Auditeurs de l'Academie de Droit International de la Haye, Hegel Soc. Am., Assn. Am. Law Schs. (chair-elect and program chair 2001—02, chair sect. fin. insts. and consumer fin. svcs. 2002—03), Internat. Law Assn. (com. chair Am. br. 1995—97), Am. Soc. Internat. Law (exec. coun. 1986—89), Phi Beta Kappa. Office: U of Pacific McGeorge Sch Law 3200 5th Ave Sacramento CA 95817-2705 E-mail: malloympm@aol.com.

MALMGREN, RICHARD AXEL, JR., art educator; b. Washington, July 7, 1950; s. Richard Axel and Elizabeth Olivia (Hanson) M.; m. Judith Eileen Burke, Sept. 5, 1981. BA in Sociology with distinction, Cornell U., 1972; MFA in Ceramics, Antioch U., 1977. Supr. Met. State Hosp., Waltham, Mass., 1972-73; instr. Providence Ctr., Annapolis, Md., 1974-75; studio potter Rick Malmgren Pottery, Severn, Md., 1975—; asst. prof. Anne Arundel C.C., Arnold, Md., 1991—. Artist in residence Old Mill (Md.) H.S., 1990 (Mar.). Artist: Unnamed Ceramic Art Piece, 1985 (award of excellence by Cynthia Bringle 1985); contbr. articles to Ceramics Monthly. Mem. Annapolis Potters Guild (pres. 1992-94), Washington Kiln Club (artist craftsman emeritus), Coll. Art Assn., Nat. Coun. for Edn. in Ceramic Arts. Democrat. Buddhist. Avocations: running, meditation. Home: 1357 Wrighton Rd Lothian MD 20711-9740 Office: Anne Arundel CC Art Dept 101 College Pkwy Arnold MD 21012 E-mail: rmalmgren@aacc.edu.

MALO, DOUGLAS DWANE, soil scientist, educator; b. Fairmont, Minn., May 1, 1949; s. Robert John and Laurel Marie (Musser) M.; m. Rosalie Kay Pitzen, Dec. 26, 1970; children: Robert Jason, Denise Michelle. BS in Agronomy/Plant Pathology, Iowa State U., 1971; MS in Soil Genesis, N.D. State U., 1974, PhD in Soil Genesis, 1975. Cert. prof. soil scientist, profl. soil classifier. Instr. soil scis. dept. N.D. State U., Fargo, 1974-75; asst. prof. plant sci. dept. S.D. State U., Brookings, 1975-80, assoc. prof., 1980-86, prof., grad. faculty, 1986-97, prof., prog. leader, teaching coord., 1990-93, disting. prof., 1998—. Chmn. acad. senate S.D. State U., 1981-82, 93-94, coord. Bolivia project, 1994-98, grad. faculty, 1986—, Biostress Ctr. of excellence coord., 1998-2001, program leader 1990-93, tchg. coord. 1990-93, 95-97. Author: (lab manual) Introductory Soils Lab Manual (32 edits.), 1976-99; author 15 videos for class instrn., 1992-20039; contbr. over 240 articles to profl. jours. and internet publs. Pres. Ascension Luth. Ch., Brookings, 1990-91; asst. scoutmaster Boy Scouts Am., Brookings, 1984-92; advisor Mortar Board, S.D. State U., 1987-90, advisor student senate, 1992-94. Named Tchr. of Yr., plant sci. dept. S.D. State U., 1981, 89, 91, 94, Charles Sewrey Lectr., 1989, 95, Tchr. of Yr./Grad. Sch., 1991, Tchr. of Yr. agrl./biol. scis., 1982; fellow Nat. Def. Edn. Act, 1971-74; named to Outstanding Young Men of Am., 1978, 82; recipient Religious Leader award Brookings Jaycees, 1981, Burlington No. Tchg. award, 1991, Nat. Award for Excellence in Coll. and Univ. Tchg. USDA, 1995, others. Mem. FarmHouse Fraternity (advisor/dir. 1980-83, Snyder Alumni Svc. award 1980, 91, H.M. Briggs Alumni award, 1992), Am. Soc. Agronomy/Soil Sci. Soc., Soil Water Conservation Soc. Am. (chair divsn. A-1 1996-98, assoc. editor jour. Nat. Resources Life Scis. Edn. 1996-2000, editor Jour. Nat. Resources Life Scis. Edn. 2001—, Nat. Achievement award 1979), Nat. Assn. Colls. and Tchrs. of Agr. (editl. bd. 1981—, Nat. Tchr. Fellow 1982), Gamma Sigma Delta (Teaching award 1992). Republican. Achievements include development of new system to estimate land productivity for land evaluation in S.D. (adopted by state govt.); providing detailed soils information to assist USDA-SCS in Cooperative Soil Survey Program and in definition of hydric soils, use of electromagnetic induction for soil identification and characterization. Home: 434 Dakota Ave Brookings SD 57006-2343 Office: S D State Univ Plant Sci No Plain Biostress Lab 247C PO Box 2140C Brookings SD 57007-2141 Fax: 605-688-4452. E-mail: douglas_malo@sdstate.edu.

MALONE, DAVID ROY, educational association administrator, director; b. Beebe, Ark., Nov. 4, 1943; s. James Roy and Ila Mae (Griffin) M.; m. Judith Kaye Huff, June 20, 1965 (div. Feb. 1990); 1 child, Michael David. BSBA, U. Ark., 1965, JD, 1969, MBA, 1982. Bar: Ark. 1969, U.S. Dist. Ct. (we. dist.) Ark. 1969, U.S. Tax Ct. 1972, U.S. Ct. Appeals (8th cir.) 1972, U.S. Supreme Ct. 1972. Pvt. practice, Fayetteville, Ark., 1969-72; atty. City of Fayetteville, 1969-72; asst. prof. bus. U. Ark., Fayetteville, 1972-76, asst. dean law, 1976-91; mem. Ark. Ho. of Reps., 1980-84, Ark. Senate, 1984—2002; exec. dir. U. Ark. Found., 1991—2002, Ark. Tchr. Ret. Sys., 2003—. Chair Senate edn. com., 1997-2002, co-chair legis. coun., 1999-2000; bd. dirs. Bank of Elkins, 1976-98, S.W. Edn. Devel. Lab., Austin, Tex., 1988-94; legal adv. coun. So. Regional Edn. Bd., Atlanta, 1991-2002. Contbr. articles to profl. jours.; bd. dirs. Ark. Law Rev., 1978-92; contbg. author U. Ark. Press, 1989. Mayor City of Fayetteville, 1979-80; mem. Jud. Article Task Force, Little Rock, 1989-91; chair Motor Voter task force, 1994-95; bd. dirs. Music Festival Ark., 1989-91, Washington County Hist. Soc., 1993-96; bd. dirs. Walton Arts Ctr. Found., 1994-2000, chmn., 1994-98; chmn. bd. dirs. Washington County Law Libr., 1970-84; chmn. Ark. Tuition Trust Authority, 1997-99. Recipient Svc. award Ark. Mcpl. League, 1980, Disting. Service award U. Ark., 1988, Lucas Svc. award, Ark. Alumni Assn., 1998. Mem. Ark. Bar Assn. (ho. of dels. 1977-81, award of merit 1980, exec. 1981-82, Outstanding Lawyer-Citizen award 1990), Washington County Bar Assn., Ark. Inst. Continuing Legal Edn. (bd. dirs. 1979-88), Fayetteville C. of C. (bd. dirs. 1984-99), Ark. Genealogy Soc. (bd. dirs. 1990-99). Democrat. Methodist. Avocations: genealogy, stamp collecting. Home: 804 N Arthur St Little Rock AR 72205-2902 Office: 1400 W Third St Little Rock AR 72201

MALONE, DEBRA BEATRICE, elementary education educator; b. Tulsa, July 15, 1945; d. Gene Joseph Dennehy Jr. and Maureen E. (Keaton) Haggin; m. Richard Malone, Nov. 20, 1971 (div. 1976); 1 child, Richard Jr. BS in Edn., U. Tex., El Paso, 1967, postgrad., 1968-88, Ea. N.Mex. U., 1988-89; MEd in computers, Lesley Coll., 1995. Cert. tchr., Tex., N.Mex. Tchr. art and music El Paso Ind. Sch. Dist., 1967-72, 82-88; tchr. grades 4 & 5 Ysleta Ind. Sch. Dist., El Paso, 1976-82; tchr. 1st grade Tularosa (N.Mex.) Pub. Schs., 1988-90, Clint Ind. Sch. Dist., El Paso, 1990-91, Sorocco Ind. Sch. Dist., El Paso, 1991-93. Houghton Mifflin pilot tchr. Sorocco Indt. Sch. Dist., 1991-92, intersession coord., 1991-93, GT coodr., 1994-95, mem. textbook and lang. arts coms. 1992-93; chair whole lang. Tularosa Pub. Schs., mem cirriculum com., 1989; mem. El Paso Collaborative Tchr. Ctr. Bd., Tchr. Edn. Curriculum Coun. Mem. Internat. Reading Assn., Tex. Reading Assn., Tchrs. Applying Whole Lang, Delta Kappa Gamma (scholarship chair 1992), Kappa Kappa Iota (v.p. 1993, Nat. Scholarship award 1994, Tex. Scholarship award 1994). Methodist. Avocations: art, golf, sewing, painting. Office: Sorocco Ind Sch Dist 2640 Robert Wynn St El Paso TX 79936-3380 Home: 110 W Riverside Dr Ruidoso NM 88345-7611

MALONE, JENNIFER CAROL SMITH, primary school educator; b. Key West, Fla., Sept. 3, 1968; d. Tommy Joe and Carolyn Ruth (Spaulding) Smith; m. Marshall Malone; 1 child, Noah. BS, Berea (Ky.) Coll., 1990; MS, Ea. Ky. U., 1994. Cert. tchr. early elem. edn., Ky. Primary tchr. Broughtontown Elem. Sch., Crab Orchard, Ky., 1992-94, Crab Orchard Elem. Sch., 1994-2000, McKinney (Ky.) Elem. Sch., 2000—. Home: 445 Redwood Dr Stanford KY 40484

MALONE, JOSEPH LAWRENCE, linguistics educator; b. N.Y.C., July 2, 1937; s. Joseph Timothy and Katherine Veronica (O'Connor) M.; m. Pamela Joan Altfeld, Jan. 31, 1964; children— Joseph Timothy II, Otis Taig BA, U. Calif.-Berkeley, 1963, PhD, 1967. Mem. faculty Barnard Coll., N.Y.C., 1967—2002, prof. linguistics, 1975—2002, chmn. dept., 1967—2002, prof. emeritus linguistics, 2002—. Vis. lectr. U. Pa., 1970; linguistics advisor Grolier Pub. Co. Author: The Science of Linguistics in the Art of Translation, 1988, Tiberian Hebrew Phonology, 1993, Carmina Gaiana, 1997, As Light Rises, 1999, Above The Salty Bay, 2001; editor, contbr. Acad. Am. Ency., Grolier Multimedia Ency.; mem. editorial bd. Hellas; contbr. articles to profl. jours. Served with U.S. Army, 1957-60 Grad. fellow U. Calif.-Berkeley, 1965-66, Am. Council Learned Socs., 1966-67 Mem. Linguistics Soc. Am., Am. Oriental Soc., AAUP, N.Am. Conf. Afro-Asiatic Linguistics, Phi Beta Kappa Democrat. Home: 169 Prospect St Leonia NJ 07605-1929 Office: Barnard Coll New York NY 10027-6598

MALONE, LAURENCE JOSEPH, economics educator, writer; b. Troy, NY, Apr. 4, 1957; s. Laurence Bernard and Barbara Ethel (McCormack) M.; m. Eva Trelease Davidson, June 25, 1983; children: Luke, Theo. BA in Econs., SUNY, 1979; PhD in Econs., New Sch. for Social Rsch., 1991. Sr. rsch. assoc. N.Y. State Assembly, Albany, N.Y., 1980-83; prof. econs. Hartwick Coll., Oneonta, NY, 1986—, chmn. dept., 1996—, Carnegie fellow, 2001—. Author: Opening the West, 1998; co-author: Learning Interdependence, 2001; co-editor: The Essential Adam Smith, 1986. Carnegie fellow, 2001—. Mem. Econ. and Bus. Hist. Soc. (chmn. bd. trustees 2001—), Econ. History Assn., Am. Econs. Assn., Order of the Omega. Avocations: tennis, basketball, debate society. Office: Hartwick Coll Bresee Hall Oneonta NY 13820

MALONE, ROBERT ROY, artist, art educator; b. McColl, S.C., Aug. 8, 1933; s. Robert Roy and Anne (Matthews) M.; m. Cynthia Enid Taylor, Feb. 26, 1956; 1 child, Brendan Trevor. BA, U. N.C., 1955; MFA, U. Chgo., 1958; postgrad., U. Iowa, 1959. Instr. art Union U., Jackson, Tenn., 1959-60, Lambuth Coll., 1959-61; asst. prof. art Wesleyan Coll., Macon, Ga., 1961-67, assoc. prof., 1967-68, W.Va. U., 1968-70, So. Ill. U., Edwardsville, 1970-75, prof., 1975—2000, prof. emeritus, 2000—. One-man shows at Gallery Illien, Atlanta, 1969, De Cinque Gallery, Miami, 1968, 71, Ill. State Mus., Springfield, 1974, U. Del., Newark, 1978, Elliot Smith Gallery, St. Louis, 1985, Merida Galleries, Louisville, 1985, Yvonne Rapp Gallery, Louisville, 1990, 92, 93, 96, 98, 2000, St. John's Coll., Santa Fe, 1991, Uzelac Gallery, Pontiac, Mich., 1997, others; group shows include Bklyn. Mus., 1966, Assoc. Am. Artists Gallery, N.Y.C., 1968, Musée d'Art Modern, Paris, 1970, DeCordova Mus., 1973, 74, St. Louis Art Mus., 1985, Wake Forest U., 1985, New Orleans Mus. Art, 1990, Dakota Internat., Vermillion, 1994; represented in numerous permanent collections including Smithsonian Instn., Washington, USIA, Washington, Library of Congress, Calif. Palace of Legion of Honor, San Francisco, N.Y. Pub. Library, N.Y.C., Victoria and Albert Mus., London, Chgo. Art Inst., Indpls. Mus. Art, Humana Inc., Louisville, State of Ill. Ctr., Chgo., Speed Mus., Louisville, N. Ill. Univ., Capital Devel. Bd., Ill.; co-editor: Contemporary American Printmakers, 1999 (English and Chinese edits.). Recipient numerous regional, nat. awards in competitive exhbns.; Ford fellow, 1977; So. Ill. U. at Edwardsville sr. research scholar, 1976, 84 Home: 600 Chapman St Edwardsville IL 62025-1260

MALONE, THOMAS FRANCIS, academic administrator, meteorologist; b. Sioux City, Iowa, May 3, 1917; s. John and Mary (Hourigan) M.; m. Rosalie Doran, Dec. 30, 1942; children: John H., Thomas Francis, Mary E., James K., Richard K., Dennis P. BS, S.D. Sch. Mines, 1940, D.Eng., 1962; Sc.D., MIT, 1946; L.H.D., St. Joseph Coll., West Hartford, Conn., 1965; Sc.D. (hon.), Bates Coll., 1988. Instr. MIT, 1942-43, asst. prof., 1943-51, assoc. prof., 1951-56; dir. Travelers Rsch. Ctr., Travelers Ins. Co., Hartford, Conn., 1955-56, dir. rsch., 1956-69, sr. v.p., 1968-70, chmn. bd., 1961-70; dean Grad. Sch., U. Conn., Storrs, 1970-73; chmn. bd. Ctr. for Environment and Men, 1970-71; dir. emeritus Holcomb Rsch. Inst., Butler U., Indpls., 1983—; scholar in residence St. Joseph Coll., 1983-91; Nat. Scis. fellow Resources for Future, 1983-84; Univ. Disting. scholar N.C. State U., 1991—98. Chmn. bd. Univ. Corp. for Atmospheric Rsch., 1973—76; mem. Conn. Weather Control Bd., 1959—73; mem. panel on sci. and tech. com. on sci. and astronautics U.S. Ho. of Reps., 1960—70; nat. adv. com. cmty. air pollution HEW, 1962—66; mem. sci. info. coun. NSF, 1962—66; rep. Am. Geophys. Union to U.S. Nat. Commn. for UNESCO, 1963—73, chmn. U.S. Nat. Commn., 1965—67; mem. nat. adv. com. on oceans and atmosphere, 1972—75; mem. Conn. Rsch. Commn., 1965—71; mem. com. application sci. and tech. New Eng. Coun.; chmn. Nat. Motor Vehicle Safety Adv. Coun., 1967—70; mem. sci. adv. com. climate impact assessment and response program UN Environ. Program, 1992—; mem. adv. com. on accreditation Conn. Dept. Higher Edn., 2000—; mem. acad. adv. bd. S.D. Sch. Mines and Tech., 1991—; bd. dirs. Conn. Acad. for Edn., 2001—. Editor: Compendium of Meteorology, 1951; contbg. editor: Environment, 1992-99; bd. editors: Jour. of the Marine Tech. Soc., 1995-99. Bd. dirs. Engrs. Joint Coun., 1968-70; bd. govs. Ins. Inst. Hwy. Safety, 1968-70; mem. oversight rev. bd. Nat. Acid Precipitation Assessment Program, 1990-96; corporator Hartford Sem., 2003—. Recipient Robert M. Losey award Inst. Aero. Sci., 1960, Charter Oak Leadership medal Greater Hartford C. of C., 1962, Charles Franklin Brooks award, 1964, Cleveland Abbe award Am. Meteorol. Soc., 1968, Conn. Conservationist of Yr. award, 1966, Guy E. March Silver medal S.D. Sch. Mines, 1976, Internat. Meteorol. Orgn. prize, 1984, Internat. St. Francis Assissi prize for environment, 1991, AAAS Internat. prize, 1994, Irving award Distance Edn. Consortium, 1997, Disting. Alumni award S.D. Sch. Mines, 1998, named to S.D. Hall of Fame, 2003; N.C. State U. disting. scholar, 1990-99, emeritus, 1999—. Fellow AAAS (internat. sci. coop., 1994), N.Y. Acad. Scis., Am. Meteorol. Soc. (pres. 1960-62), Am. Geophys. Union (past pres., sec. internat. participation 1964, Waldo E. Smith award 1986); mem. NAS (chmn. geophysics rsch. bd. 1969-76, chmn. bd. on internat. orgns. and programs, dep. fgn. sec. 1969-73, fgn. sec. 1978-82), NRC (space application bd. 1973-77), Am. Acad. Arts and Scis., Internat. Coun. Sci. Unions (v.p., sec.-gen. sci. com. problems environ. 1970-76, treas. 1978-82) Am. Geog. Soc. (coun. 1971-77), Royal Irish Acad. (hon.), Conn. Acad. Sci. and Engring. (exec. scientist 1987-91, 97-2000), Acad. Polit. Scis., Sigma Xi (bd. dirs. 1983-96, pres. 1988-89, dir. Sigma Xi Ctr. 1992-95, chief scientist 1996-98). Home: 275 Steele Rd Apt 504B West Hartford CT 06119 E-mail: tfmalone@aol.com.

MALONEY, EDWARD DENNIS, state senator, assistant principal; b. Chgo., May 22, 1946; s. John Frances and Lucille Veronica (Wiechern) M.; m. Norine Marie Smith, Oct. 26, 1968; children: Brian, Matthew, Daniel, Martin. BA in Polit. Sci., Lewis U., 1968; MEd, Chgo. State U., 1976. Tchr., counselor Oak Lawn HS, Ill., 1968—91, dept. chair, 1991—97; dep. dir. Chicago park dist., 1997—2001; asst. prin. Brother Rice HS, 2001—; senator, dist. 18 State of Ill., 2002—. Mem. S.W. Counselors Assn., Ill. Personel and Guidance Assn., Cen. Ofcls. Assn. Clubs: Bull Baseball (Chgo.) (commr.). Democrat. Roman Catholic. Avocations: triathlons, basketball officiating. Office: 311 Capitol Bldg Springfield IL 62706*

MALONEY, MILFORD CHARLES, retired internal medicine educator; b. Buffalo, Mar. 15, 1927; s. John Angelus Maloney and Winifred Hill; m. Dione Ethyl Sheppard. BS, Canisius Coll., 1947, postgrad., 1947-49; MD, U. Buffalo, 1953. Diplomate Am. Bd. Internal Medicine. Rsch. chemist Buffalo Electrochem. Co., 1947-49; intership Mercy Hosp./Georgetown U., 1953-54; med. residency Buffalo VA Hosp., 1954-56; cardiology fellow Buffalo Gen. Hosp., 1956-57; chmn. dept. medicine Mercy Hosp., 1969-94, program dir., internal medicine residency, 1972-89; with steering com. Assn. Program Dirs. in Internal Medicine, 1976, coun. mem., 1977-80; clin. prof. medicine SUNY, Buffalo, 1981-94; trustee Am. Soc. Internal Medicine, 1984-90, edn. leader, European seminar, 1987, edn. leader, So. Am. seminar, 1988; faculty instr. Christopher Wren Assn. Coll. William and Mary, Williamsburg, Va., 1997—. Bd. dirs. Internal Medicine Ctr. for Advancement and Rsch. Edn.; pres. Heart Assn. Western N.Y., Buffalo, 1969; sr. cancer rsch. physician Roswell Park Meml. Cancer Inst., 1959-62; mem. internal medicine liaison com. N.Y. State, 1980-90; faculty instr., mem. curriculum com. Christopher Wren Assn. Coll. William & Mary, Williamsburg, Va., 1997-99. Editor (newsletter) N.Y. State Soc. Internal Medicine, 1972-78. Bd. dirs. Health Sys. Agy. Western N.Y., Buffalo, 1981; mem. exec. com., bd. dirs. Blue Cross Western N.Y., Buffalo, 1987; mem. bd. regents Canisius Coll., Buffalo, 1987—; mem. pres. assocs. SUNY, Buffalo; founding mem. Greater Williamsburg Va. Symphony Soc., 1998; bd. dirs. Va. Symphony, Norfolk, 2001. Capt. M.C., U.S. Army, 1957-59. Recipient award of merit N.Y. State Soc. Internal Medicine, 1980, Man of Yr. award Heart Assn. Western N.Y., 1982, ann. honoree award Trocaire Coll., 1986, Disting. Alumni award Canisius Coll., 1991, Berkson Excellence award in tchg. and art of medicine, SUNY at Buffalo, 1992, Outstanding Med. Tchg. Attending award Mercy Hosp./SUNY Med. Residents, 1994, Lifetime Career Achievement award Med. Alumni Assn. SUNY, Buffalo, 1998; named to Sports Hall of Fame, Canisius Coll., 1978. Fellow ACP (Upstate Physician Recognition award 1989), fellow Am. Coll. Cardiology; mem. AMA (SUNY rep. 1986-94, rep. to sect. med. schs. at ann. meetings 1984-94, chmn. sect. on internal medicine 1990-91), Am. Soc. Internal Medicine (bd. dirs. Internal Medicine Ctr. for Advancement of Rsch. Edn. 1988-91, trustee 1984-90, pres. 1990-91, chmn. long range planning com., rep. to Federated Coun. on Internal Medicine 1990-91, rep. to AMA nat. practice parameters and guidelines com. 1989-91, Scroll of Honor benefactor for Internal Medicine Ctr. for Advancement of Rsch. and Edn. 1991), N.Y. State Soc. Internal Medicine (pres. 1974-75), Alumni Assn. SUNY (pres. 1975), Med. Soc. County Erie (pres. 1991-82), Va. Soc. Internal Medicine (hon.), Greater Williamsburg Va. Symphony Soc. (founding mem. 1998, editor newsletter 1998-2003). Home: 116 Cove Point Ln Williamsburg VA 23185-8613 E-mail: mcmaloney@widomaker.com.

MALONEY, PATSY LORETTA, nursing educator; b. Murfreesboro, Tenn., Feb. 19, 1952; d. Buford Leon Browning and Ina (Bush) DuBose; m. Richard J. Maloney, July 26, 1975; children: Katherine Nalani, Nathaniel Allen, Elizabeth Maureen. BS in Nursing, U. Md., 1974; MA, MS in Nursing, Cath. U., 1984; EdD, U. So. Calif., 1994. Commd. 1st lt. U.S. Army, 1974, advanced through grades to lt. col., 1989; asst. chief nurse evenings and nights DeWitt Army Hosp., Ft. Belvoir, Va.; chief nurse, tng. officer 85th EVAC Hosp., Ft. Lee, Va.; clin. head nurse emergency rm./PCU Tripler Army Med. Ctr., Honolulu, chief nursing edn.; chief surg. nursing sect. and acute care nursing sect. Madigan Army Med. Ctr., Tacoma, 1991-94; ret., 1994; dir. Ctr. for Continued Nursing Learning Pacific Luth. U., Tacoma, Wash., 1994—. Asst. prof., dir. continuing nursing edn. Pacific Luth. U., Tacoma, 1994—2000, assoc. prof., 2000—. Mem. Emergency Nurses Assn., Nat. Nursing Staff Devel. Orgn., Acad. Med. Surg. Nurses, Sigma Theta Tau, Phi Kappa Phi. Home: 7002 53rd St W Tacoma WA 98467-2214 Office: Pacific Luth U Continuing Nursing Edn Tacoma WA 98467 E-mail: malonepl@plu.edu.

MALONEY, ROBERT KELLER, ophthalmologist, medical educator; b. May 1, 1958; AB in Mathematics summa cum laude, Harvard U., 1979; MA in Philosophy, Politics and Econs., Oxford (Eng.) U., 1981; MD, U. Calif., San Francisco, 1985. Diplomate Am. Bd. Ophthalmology. Rsch fellow dept. physiology Cambridge (Eng.) U., 1985; intern U. Calif., L.A., 1985-86; resident Wilmer Ophthalmol. Inst. Johns Hopkins Hosp., Balt., 1986-89; Heed fellow cornea and refractive surgery Emory U., Dept. Ophthalmology, Atlanta, 1989-91; assoc. prof. ophthalmology UCLA Sch. Medicine, Jules Stein Eye Inst., 1991-98. Bd. dirs. Lasik Inst., Calhoun Vision. Contbr. numerous articles to profl. jours.; presenter and spkr. in field; assoc. editor (N.Am.) Jour. Refractive and Corneal Surgery, 1991-95; internat. editl. bd. European Jour. Implant and Refractive Surgery, 1995; reviewer Am. Jour. Ophthalmology, Ophthalmology, Archives of Ophthalmology, Jour. Cataract and Refractive Surgery, Ophthalmic Surgery and Lasers; editl. bd. Ophthalmology Times. Rhodes scholar, 1979, Heed Found. fellow, 1989-90, Heed/Knapp fellow, 1990-91, John Harvard scholar, 1978; recipient Detur and Edward Whitaker prizes, Harvard U., Rsch. to Prevent Blindness Career Devel. award, 1992, Mericos Whittier award, 1997, VISX Star Surgeon award, 1999, 2000, Sr. Achievement award Am. Acad. Opthalmology, 2002 . Mem. Am. Acad. Ophthalmology (long-range planning com. 1989-92, quality of care com. 1987-91, retina preferred practice pattern subcom., refractive errors preferred practice pattern subcom.; chmn. ann. meeting program com. for young ophthalmologists, 1990-92; adv. group to ad hoc com. on orgnl. design 1991, young ophthalmologists' com. 1992-94; Honor award 1993, 97), Assn. Rsch. in Vision and Ophthalmology, Internat. Soc. Refractive Surgery (Disting. Lans Refractive Surgery award 2001), Calif. Assn. Ophthalmology, Max Fine Corneal Soc., Phi Beta Kappa. Office: Maloney Vision Inst 10921 Wilshire Blve Ste 900 Los Angeles CA 90024

MALOOF, GILES WILSON, academic administrator, educator, author; b. San Bernardino, Calif., Jan. 4, 1932; s. Joseph Peters and Georgia (Wilson) M.; m. Mary Anne Ziniker, Sept. 5, 1958 (dec. Oct. 1976); children: Mary Jane, Margery Jo. BA, U. Calif., Berkeley, 1953; MA, U. Oreg., 1958; PhD, Oreg. State U., 1962. Petroleum reservoir engr. Creole Petroleum Corp., Venezuela, 1953-54; mathematician electronics divsn. rsch. dept. U.S. Naval Ordnance Rsch. Lab., Corona, Calif., 1958-59; asst. prof. math. Oreg. State U., Corvallis, 1962-68, rsch. assoc. dept. oceanography, 1963-68, vis. prof. math., 1977-78; prof. math. Boise (Idaho) State U., 1968—, head dept., 1968-75, dean grad. sch., 1970-75. Author, reviewer of coll. textbooks; contbr. to profl. jours. Served with Ordnance Corps, AUS, 1950, 54-56. Recipient Carter award, 1963, Mosser prize, 1966, Oreg. State U., Alumni Found. scholar Teaching award Boise State U., 2000. Mem. Math. Assn. Am., Am. Math. Soc., Soc. Indsl. and Applied Math., N.W. Coll. and Univ. Assn. for Sci. (dir. 1973—, pres. 1990-92), N.W. Sci. Assn. (trustee

1977-80), Assn. Western Univs. (mem. edn. and rsch. com. 1993-2001), Sigma Xi, Pi Mu Epsilon, Phi Kappa Phi. Home: 1400 Longmont Ave Boise ID 83706-3730 E-mail: giles@diamond.boisestate.edu.

MALOOLEY, DAVID JOSEPH, electronics and computer technology educator; b. Terre Haute, Ind., Aug. 20, 1951; s. Edward Joseph and Vula (Starn) M. B.S., Ind. State U., 1975; M.S., Ind. U., 1981, doctoral candidate. Supr., Zenith Radio Corp., Paris, Ill., 1978-79; assoc. prof. electronics and computer tech. Ind. State U., Terre Haute, 1979— ; cons. in field. Served to 1st lt. U.S. Army, 1975-78. Mem. Soc. Mfg. Engrs., Nat. Assn. Indsl. Tech., Nat. Fire Protection Assn., Instrument Soc. Am. (sr.), Phi Delta Kappa, Pi Lambda Theta, Epsilon Pi Tau. Democrat. Christian. Home: 11420 Spring Creek Rd Terre Haute IN 47805-9679 Office: Ind State U Dept Electronics and Computer Tech Terre Haute IN 47809-0001 E-mail: etmaloo@isugw.indstate.edu.

MALOON, CLEVE ALEXIS, music educator; b. St. Thomas, V.I., Sept. 22, 1965; came to U.S., 1989; s. Claude Devlin Sr. and Jaunita (Fahie) M.; m. Kimberly Louise Patton, Nov. 5, 1991. B in Music Edn., Augustana coll., 1987; MA in Music, U. Iowa, 1989. Cert. music tchr. K-12, Ill., Iowa. Tchr. instrumental music Rock Island (Ill.) Sch. Dist., 1989—, dist. music coord., tchr. alternative high sch., star pride, 1990—. Scholar Aid Assn. Luths.; Music Performance grantee U. V.I. Mem. NEA, Am. Fedn. Tchrs., Nat. Assn. Black Sch. Educators, Music Educators Nat. Conf. Internat. Trombone Assn., Internat. Assn. Jazz Educators, Nat. Band Assn., Rock Island-Milan Fedn. Tchrs. (v.p. 1993-94), Sinfonia Music Fraternity for Men in Music, Phi Mu Alpha, Kappa Alpha Psi (keeper records 1993). Office: Rock Island H S 1400 25th Ave Rock Island IL 61201-5356

MALOY, FRANCES, librarian; MLS, SUNY Albany. Leader of the access services divsn. Emory U. Gen. Libraries, 1992—; v.p. Assoc. Rsch. and Coll. Libraries, 2003—; dir., pub. services Hamilton Coll. Mem. bd. dirs. ACRL; chmn. ACRL Nominations Com. and ACRL Com. on Ethics. Office: 50 East Huron St Chicago IL 60611

MALSON, VERNA LEE, special education educator; b. Buffalo, Wyo., Mar. 29, 1937; d. Guy James and Vera Pearl (Curtis) Mayer; m. Jack Lee Malson, Apr. 20, 1955; children: Daniel Lee, Thomas James, Mark David, Scott Allen. BA in Elem. Edn. and Spl. Edn. magna cum laude, Met. State Coll., Denver, 1975; MA in Learning Disabilities, U. No. Colo., 1977. Cert. tchr., Colo. Tchr.-aide Wyo. State Tng. Sch., Lander, 1967-69; spl. edn. tchr. Bennett Sch. 29J, Colo., 1975-79, chmn. health, sci. social studies depts., 1977-79; spl. edn. tchr. Deer Trail Sch., Colo., 1979-98, chmn. careers, gifted and talented, 1979-87, spl. edn./presch. tchr., 1992-98, ret., 1998. Course cons. Regis Coll., Denver, 1990; mem. spl. edn. parent adv. com. East Central Bd. Coop. Ednl. Services, Limon, Colo. Colo. scholar Met. State Coll., 1974; grantee Colo. Dept. Edn., 1979, 81; recipient Cert. of Achievement, Met. State Coll., 1993. Mem. Coun. Exceptional Children, Bennett Tchrs. Club (treas. 1977-79), Kappa Delta Pi. Republican. Presbyterian. Avocations: coin collecting, reading, sports. Home: PO Box 208 Edgerton WY 82635-0208

MALTBY, FLORENCE HELEN, library science educator; b. Sumner, Iowa, Mar. 2, 1933; d. Harold George and Blanche Theresa (Gritzner) Garland; m. George Robert Maltby, June 3, 1964 (dec. Oct. 1985); 1 child, Patricia Garland Maltby Clark. BA, U. No. Iowa, Cedar Falls, 1954; MS in Libr. Sci., U. Ill., 1960, cert. advanced study librarianship, 1967. Elem. sch. libr. Barrington (Ill.) Pub. Sch., 1954-57, USAF Dependent Sch. Europe, Sculthorpe, Eng., 1957-58, Ramstein, Fed. Republic of Germany, 1958-59, Wiesbaden, Fed. Republic of Germany, 1960-61; grad. asst. U. Ill., Champaign, 1959-60; reference asst., instr. Libr. Cen. Mich. U., Mt. Pleasant, 1961-63; asst. prof. libr. sci. Southwest Mo. State U., Springfield, 1963-66, 67-80, assoc. prof. libr. sci., 1980-97; instr. libr. sci. U. Ill., Champaign, 1966-67; archivist Diocese of Springfield-Cape Girardeau, 2001—. Evaluator North Cen. Assn., Springfield, 1989, Dept. Elem. and Secondary Edn., Mo. Sch. Improvement, 1989; com. mem. Children's Lit. Festival, Springfield, 1990, treas., 1991. Contbr. to Masterplots II: Juvenile and Young Adult Fiction, 1991, 97. Mem. AAUP, ALA, Assn. Libr. and Info. Sci. Edn., Mo. Assn. Sch. Librs. (mem. standards rev. com. for state sch. libr. media standards 1994), Assn. Cath. Diocesan Archivists, Beta Phi Mu, Alpha Beta Alpha, Kappa Delta Pi. Roman Catholic. Avocations: reading, playing organ and piano, cert. literary braille transcriber.

MALTBY, SUE ELLEN, special education educator; b. Waterford, Ohio, Apr. 30, 1950; d. James Lawrence and Agatha Macel (Crosby) Starcher; m. Marshall Martin Maltby, Nov. 25, 1978; stepchildren: Laura Leigh Maltby Karanthasis, Lisa Michelle Maltby Atkinson. BA, Marietta Coll., 1972; MA, Ga. Coll., 1976. Cert. tchr., adminstr., W.Va. Psychology technician Cen. State Hosp., Milledgeville, Ga., 1972-74, psychologist, 1976-77, Ga. War Vets. Home, Milledgeville, 1974-76; mental retardation specialist Albany (Ga.) Mental Health/Mental Retardation Ctr., 1977-81; dir. residential program Colin Anderson Ctr., St. Marys, W.Va., 1981-84; tchr. spl. edn. W.Va. Dept. Edn., St. Marys, 1984-91, lead tchr. Waverly, 1991—. Tech. asst. cons. County Bds. Edn., W.Va., 1985—, insvc. presenter, 1985—. Recipient Outstanding Svc. award Ga. Assn. Retarded Citizens, 1978. Mem. Assn. Retarded Citizens, Assn. Severely Handicapped, Coun. Exceptional Children/Persons, Nat. Down Syndrome Assn. Republican. Methodist. Avocations: crafts, travel, volunteer work. Home: 3624 Gordon St Terrell NC 28682-9729

MALTIN, FREDA, retired university administrator; b. Calgary, Alta., Can., June 4, 1923; came to the U.S., 1958; d. Meyers Wolfe and Ida (Kohn) Rosen; m. Manny Maltin, Aug. 25, 1950; 1 child, Richard Allan. Diploma Garbutt's Bus. Coll., Calgary, 1942. Various secretarial and bookkeeping positions, 1951; mem. adminstrv. staff U. So. Calif., 1960-92, asst. to exec. dir. Davidson Conf. Ctr., 1987-92, Grad. Sch. Bus. Adminstrn., 1981-92. Recipient staff achievement award U. So. Calif., 1991. Mem. U. So. Calif. Staff Club (charter), U. So. Calif. Skull and Dagger (hon.), U. So. Calif. Town and Gown.

MALY, WOJCIECH P. engineering educator, researcher; b. Inowroclaw, Poland, Jan. 5, 1946; came to U.S., 1979; s. Feliks and Maria (Gordzialkowska) M.; m. Halina Zarembowska, Apr. 11, 1970; 1 child, Katarzyna. MSc, Tech. U. Warsaw, 1970; PhD, Polish Acad. Sci., Warsaw, 1975. Asst. prof. Tech. U. Warsaw, 1975-86; assoc. prof. dept. elec. and computer engrng. Carnegie Mellon U., Pitts., 1986-90, prof., 1990-96, Whitaker prof., 1996—. Author: Atlas of IC Technologies, 1986; contbr. chpts. to books, numerous articles to profl. jours. Recipient Teare Tchg. award Carnegie Mellon U., 1989; SRC Tech. Excellence award Semicondr. Rsch. Corp., 1993. Fellow IEEE. Roman Catholic. Achievements include development of methodologies of design for manufacturability of integrated circuits; patents in field. Office: Carnegie Mellon U ECE Dept 5000 Forbes Ave Pittsburgh PA 15213-3890

MALYUK, PATRICIA L. elementary school educator; b. Ashland, Wis., May 12, 1967; d. Michael M. and Arlene A. (Starry) M. BA, Northland Coll., Ashland, 1989; MS in Edn., U. Superior, 1997. Cert. elem. tchr., Wis. Student tchr. Glidden (Wis.) Sch. Nat. scholar. Mem. Alpha Delta Kappa. Home: 314 8th St W Ashland WI 54806

MAMER, JAMES MICHAEL, secondary education educator; b. L.A., Oct. 8, 1948; s. James Robert and Annette (Babue) M.; m. Jessica Puma, Aug. 31, 1963. BA in Polit. Sci., Calif. Poly. U., Pomona, 1970; MA in Internat. Studies, Immaculate Heart Coll., 1990. Tchr. Irvine (Calif.) Unified Sch. Dist., 1978—. Mentor tchr. Irvine Sch. Dist., 1988-95. Mem. editl. bd. Global Pages, L.A., 1991-96. Recipient Global Teaching award Western Internat. Studies Consortium, L.A., 1991, Am. Coun. Internat. Edn. award, 1998; Fulbright-Hays grantee, India, 1977; Coe fellow, 1984. Mem. Nat. Coun. Social Studies (Nat. Social Studies Tchr. of Yr. 1992), Irvine Tchrs. Assn. Democrat. Avocation: reading. Home: 29102 Kommers Ln Silverado CA 92676-9726

MAMMONE, RICHARD JAMES, engineering educator; b. N.Y.C., Sept. 3, 1953; s. Americo Anth and Helen (Kowalski) M.; m. Christine Podilchuk, Aug. 19, 1989; children: Robert, Jason, Richard, James Jr. BE, CCNY, 1975, ME, 1977; PhD, CUNY, 1981. Computer systems analyst Picatinny Arsenal, Dover, N.J., 1975-77; rsch. fellow CCNY, 1977-81; asst. prof. Manhattan Coll., Riverdale, N.Y., 1981-82; assoc. prof. engrng. Rutgers U., Piscataway, N.J., 1981-93, prof., 1993—. Co-founder Computed Anatonomy Inc., N.Y.C., 1982; founder SpeakEZ, Inc., N.J., 1992, chmn. of bd., 1995—; chief tech. advisor, bd. dirs T-NETIX, Inc., Colo., 1995—; founder, CEO Visionary Systems Inc. (VSI), 1999; cons. in field. Co-author: Image Recovery: Theory and Applications, Acad. Press Pubs., 1987, Computational Methods of Signal Recovery and Recognition, 1992; co-editor: Neural Networks: Theory and Applications, 1991; editor: Artificial Neural Networks for Speech and Vision, 1993; editor Pattern Recognition Jour., 1989—; series editor Chapman-Hall on Neural Networks, 1991—; editor artificial neural networks speech and vision Chapman-Hall Pubs., 1993—; asst. editor IEEE Transactions on Speech and Audio Processing, IEEE Transactions on Neural Networks; contbr. articles to profl. jours.; patentee in filed. Assoc. Whitaker Found. grant, 1982, NSF grant, 1992; Internat. Tel. & Tel. grant, 1984; CAIP Rsch. Ctr. grant, 1985; Henry Rutgers fellow, 1985-87; U.S. Nat. Security Agy. grant, 1986—, USAF grant, 1986—, Temeplex grant, 1986—. Mem. IEEE (sr., editor Comms. Jour. 1983-89), N.Y. Acad. Scis. Office: Rutgers U Dept Elec Engring Piscataway NJ 08854

MAN, CHI-SING, mathematician, educator; b. Hong Kong, Aug. 23, 1947; s. Yip and Sau-Ying (Leung) M.; m. May Lai-Ming Chan, July 5, 1973; children: Li-Xing, Yi-Heng. BSc, U. Hong Kong, 1968, MPhil, 1976; PhD, Johns Hopkins U., 1980. Tutor of math. and physics Hong Kong Bapt. Coll., 1970-72, asst. lectr. of physics, 1972-76; postdoctoral fellow Johns Hopkins U., Balt., 1980-81; asst. prof. civil engring. U. Manitoba, Winnipeg, 1981-85; rsch. assoc. Inst. for Math. and Its Applications U. Minn., Mpls., 1984-85; asst. prof. math. U. Ky., Lexington, 1985-88, assoc. prof., 1988-96, prof., 1996—. Vis. assoc. prof. U. Minn., 1991, 96, U. Manitoba, 1992. Mem. editl. bd. Jour. Elasticity, 1996—. Grantee Natural Scis. and Engring. Rsch. Coun. of Can., 1982-86, NSF, 1987—, AFOSR, 1994—. Mem. Am. Math. Soc., Soc. Natural Philosophy (svc. mem., sec. 1992-93, acting sec. 1998). Achievements include research on ultrasonic measurement of residual stress and crystallographic texture, effects of crystallographic texture on constitutive equations, elasticity with initial stress, stress waves in lungs, constitutive equation for creep of ice, foundations of continuum thermodynamics and Gibbsian thermostatics. Home: 348 Melbourne Way Lexington KY 40502-3202 Office: U Ky Dept Math Lexington KY 40506-0001

MANAHAN, JOAN ELSIE, health and physical education educator; b. Haskell, N.J., Jan. 18, 1940; d. Edward A. and Elsie G. (Beckmann) M. BA, Trenton State Coll., 1962; MA, Columbia U., 1966, EdD, 1975. Tchr., coach Bloomfield (N.J.) Bd. Edn., 1962-97. Cons. Nat. Dairy Coun., 1970s. Cons. (book): Basic Stuff: Motor Learning and Performance; contbr. articles to profl. jours. Grantee A+ For Kids Tchr. Network, Inc., 1992-93; recipient Proclamation, N.J. State Legislature, 1997. Mem. NEA, AAHPER (cons. 1980s, 1990s), Am. Archery Assn., N.J. AHPER, N.J. Athletic Assn. (treas. 1966-67, co-editor newsletter 1967-68, archery tournament chairperson 1965-75), N.J. Edn. Assn., Essex County Coaches Assn., Kappa Delta Pi, Pi Lambda Theta. Roman Catholic. Avocations: collecting playing cards and swizzle sticks, life master bridge.

MAÑAS, RITA, educational administrator; b. Newark, N.J., Dec. 6, 1951; d. John and Sofia Mañas. BA, Kean U., 1974; MA, Seton Hall U., 1977; PhD, Rutgers U., 1990. Cert. tchr. K-12, N.J. Ednl. counselor Aspira Inc. of N.J., Newark, 1974-75; student devel. specialist ednl. opportunity program Seton Hall U., South Orange, N.J., 1975-88; asst. dir. ednl. opportunity fund program Fairleigh Dickinson U., Madison, N.J., 1988-89; dir. office of minority edn. William Paterson U., Wayne, N.J., 1990-95; asst. prof. dept. modern langs. Coll. N.J., 1995-96; dir. ednl. opportunity fund program Centenary Coll., Hackettstown, N.J., 1996-99; world langs. tchr. Univ. H.S., Newark, 1999—. Adj. instr. Essex County Coll., Newark, N.J., 2000, Ctr. for African Am. Studies, English dept. Seton Hall U., South Orange, 1978-79, modern langs. dept., 1981-82, 85-91, 91-93; adj. instr. fgn. langs. dept. Bergen C.C., Paramus, N.J., 1990; adj. instr. langs. and cultures dept. William Paterson U., Wayne, N.J., 1991, 95. Bd. dirs. North End Nursery, Newark, 1993-94; mem. adv. bd. Sch. and Comty. Organized to Promote Edn. Program (S.C.O.P.E.), Paterson, N.J., 1993-95. Recipient Achievement award P.R. Inst. of Seton Hall U., 1977, Svc. award Black Student Assn. of William Paterson U., 1991, 92, Orgn. of Latin Am. Students of William Paterson U., 1991, 93, Tri State Disting. Alumni award Tri-State Consortium of Opportunity Programs in Higher Edn., 1993. Mem. MLA (del. 1993-95, P.R. Lit. and Culture com. 1995-99), Am. Assn. Tchrs. of Spanish and Portuguese, N.E. MLA, Mid. Atlantic Coun. Latin Am. Studies, N.J. Ednl. Opportunity Fund Profl. Assn. (20th anniv. conf. planning com. 1989, Svc. award 1989, 93), Hispanic Women's Task Force (Svc. award 1991), Hispanic Assn. Higher Edn. (conf. coord. N.J. chpt. 1999-2000). Avocations: crocheting, reading, traveling.

MANASSAH, JAMAL TEWFEK, electrical engineer, educator, management consultant; b. Haifa, Palestine, Feb. 23, 1945; s. Tewfek George and Alia Nasrallah (Kardoush) M.; m. Azza Tarek H.I. Mikdadi, Mar. 16, 1979; children: Tala, Nigh. BSc, Am. U., Beirut, Lebanon, 1966; MA, Columbia U., 1968, PhD, 1970. Mem. Inst. Advanced Study, Princeton, N.J., 1970-72, 74-79; asst. prof. Am. U. Beirut, 1972-75; chief sci. adviser Kuwait Inst. Sci. Rsch., 1976-81; COO Kuwait Found., 1979-81; prof. dept. elec. engrng. CUNY, N.Y.C., 1981—. Cons. Columbia Radiation Labs., N.Y.C., 1970-73, Ford Found., N.Y.C., 1973-79, NSF, Washington, 1978-83; chmn. Internat. Symposium Series, Kuwait, 1979-81; mng. dir. Khayatt and Co., Inc., N.Y.C., 1982; organizing com. Chem. Rsch. Applied to World Needs II, 1980-83; mem. Welfare Assn., Geneva, 1984-92; steering com. Internat. Workshop on Laser Physics, 1993-2000. Editor: Alternate Energy Sources (2 vols.) 1981; (with others) Advances in Food Producing Systems for Arid and Semiarid Lands (2 vols.), 1981, Innovations in Telecommunication (2 vols.), 1982, (with others) Transient Coherent Phenomena, 1995, Elementary Mathematical and Computational Tools for Electrical and Computer Engineering Using MATLAB, 2001, (with others) Coherent and Nonlinear Optics and Spectroscopy, 2002; mem. editl. bd. Internat. Jour. Laser Physics, 1994—; contbr. over 150 articles on statis. field theory, nonlinear and quantum optics, photonics, ultrafast phenomena and new techs. assessment. Commr. Lebanese Boy Scouts Assn., Beirut, 1972-75; adviser internat. program NSF, 1979-83; bd. dirs. CUNY Rsch. Found., 2001-03. Columbia U. faculty fellow, 1966-68, Pfister fellow, 1968-70; grantee NSF, 1982-87; recipient ABI Key award, 1987, Commemorative medal of honor, 1988; named Man of Yr., 1990. Mem. Assn. Mems. of Inst. for Advanced Study, Princeton Club. Christian Orthodox. Achievements include the theoretical discovery or co-discovery of resonant absorption coefficient frequency shift, collective Lamb shift, pion minus condensation in nuclear matter, blackbody frequency shift, dynamical Lorenz shift, reflectivity frequency shift, induced coherent pulse compression, induced spectral broadening, induced frequency shift, three-photons frequency shift, twin peaks in second harmonics generation, induced waveguiding and focusing, time-space superspike, non-linear compression of noise correlation time, soliton phases, coherently inhibited amplification, induced channeling, delayed reflectivity, two-color photon echos, superradiance without inversion, pressure induced optical cavities. Home: 55 E 87th St Apt 15G New York NY 10128-1051 Office: CUNY Dept Elec Engring Convent Ave New York NY 10031 E-mail: manassah@ccny.cuny.edu.

MANATT, RICHARD, retired education educator; b. Odebolt, Iowa, Dec. 13, 1931; s. William Price and Lucille (Taylor) M.; m. Sally Jo Johnson, Aug. 20, 1952; children— Tamra Jo, Ann Lea, Joel Price; m. Jacquelyn M. Nesset, Feb. 25, 1970; 1 child, Megan Sue. BSc, Iowa State U., 1953, MS, 1956; PhD, U. Iowa, 1964. Prin. Oskloosa (Iowa) Schs., 1959-62; rsch. assoc. U. Iowa, Iowa City, 1962-64; mem. faculty Iowa State U., Ames, 1964—, prof., 1972—, chmn. dept. ednl. adminstrn., 1970-80, 93-98, dir. Sch. Improvement Model Projects, 1980—, univ. prof., 1998—2002, univ. prof. emeritus, 2002—. Cons. performance evaluation for public and independent schs.; disting. vis. prof. Calif. State U., L.A. Author: Educator's Guide to the New Design, When Right is Wrong, Fundamentalists and the Public Schools, Clinical Manual for Teacher Performance Evaluation Compendias of Professional Growth Plans, (computer software program) Computer Assisted Teach Evaluation/Supervision. Served with AUS, 1953-55. Named Disting. Prof., Nat. Acad. Sch. Execs., 1979, Regents' Prof. Edn., 1994; recipient faculty citation Iowa State U. Alumni Assn., 1998, Margaret White Grad. Faculty award, 2001, Pres.'s award NAACP, 2002. Mem. NEA, NASSP, ASCD (Outstanding Cons. 1981), Am. Assn. Sch. Adminstrs., Phi Kappa Phi, Phi Delta Kappa, Delta Chi. Democrat. Methodist. Home: 2926 Monroe Dr Ames IA 50010-4362 E-mail: rmanatt@iastate.edu.

MANCALL, JACQUELINE COOPER, library science educator, information science educator; b. Phila., Mar. 31, 1932; d. Morris and Bertha Cooper; 1953; m. Elliott Lee Mancall, Dec. 27, 1953; children: Andrew Cooper, Peter Cooper. BA, U. Pa., 1954; MS, Drexel U. Sch. Libr. and Info. Sci., 1970, PhD, 1979. Adminstr., Miquon (Pa.) Sch., 1966-67, libr., 1967-76; teaching asst. Drexel U., Phila., 1976-78, rsch. assoc., 1979, asst. prof., 1979-85, assoc. prof., 1985-89, prof., 1989; chair Phila. Children's Reading Round Table, 1982-84, mem. steering com., 1979-89; mem. faculty coun. Drexel U., 1984-89, chair, 1987-89, senate, 2000-2003, chair senate 2001-2002; mem. sch. libr. survey com. State Libr. Pa., 1983; cons. Author: (with M. Carl Drott) Measuring Student Information Use: A Guide for Sch. Library Media Specialists 1983, (with Elizabeth S. Aversa) Management of Online Search Svcs. in Schools, 1989; rsch. editor Sch. Libr. Media quar., 1982-88; editl. bd. Jour. Libr. and Info. Sci. Edn., 1981-86; editl. adv. bd. Multimedia Schs.; contbg. editor Catholic Libr. World, 1981-85; contbr. chpts. to books, articles to profl. jours. Bd. dirs. Friends of William Jeannes Meml. Libr., Plymouth Meeting, Pa., 1976-79; pres. bd. dirs. Miquon Sch., 1964-66. Recipient Annual award Assn. Phila. Sch. Libr., 1994. Mem. ALA (chair Am. Assn. Sch. Librs. rsch. com. 1983-85, chmn. continuing edn. com. 1985-87, com. rsch. stats. 1988-92, v.p./pres.elect, 1993, pres. 1994, continuing edn. task force 1995-98, co-chair ICONect evaluation com. 1996-2000, adv. com. office info. tech. 1995-97, pub. awareness com. 1997-99, libr. congress nat. digital libr. adv. com. 1997, dir. KidsConnect 2000-2002), Pa. Sch. Librs. Assn. (bd. dirs. 1984-87, chmn. profl. standard com. 1980-82, 91—, tech. com. 1982-84 Outstanding Contbr. award 1997), Assn. Am. Libr. Schs. (Disting. Svc. award 1999), Pi Gamma Mu, Beta Phi Mu, Phi Delta Kappa. Democrat. Jewish. Office: Drexel U Coll Info Sci & Tech Philadelphia PA 19104

MANCHE, EMANUEL P. chemistry educator; b. N.Y., Apr. 30, 1931; s. Emanuel Manche and Carmela (Frate) Santaniello; m. Theresa Sheehan, June 18, 1961; children: Lisa, Edward, Robert. BS in Chemistry, CUNY, 1956, MA in Chemistry, 1959; PhD in Chemistry, Rutgers U., 1965. Rsch. chemist Am. Chicle Co., L.I., N.Y., 1956-57; advanced rsch. engr. Gen. Telephone and Electronics Rsch. Labs., Bayside, N.Y., 1965-68; asst. prof. York Coll., CUNY, Jamaica, N.Y., 1968-72, assoc. prof., 1973-80, prof. chemistry, 1981—. Fellow, lectr. Bklyn. Coll, CUNY, 1958-62; adj. lectr., instr., prof. Rutgers U., Newark, N.J., 1962-73 Patentee determination of the acceleration of gravity; contbr. articles to profl. jours. Sgt. U.S. Army, 1952-54. Recipient Outstanding Educator of Am. award, 1975; grantee Hewlett Packard, 1983, U.S. Dept. of Edn., 1982-85, 89-92, NSF, 1986-88, rsch. grant Profl. Staff Congress-Bd. of Higher Edn., 1978-80. Mem. Am. Chem. Soc., Phi Lambda Upsilon, Sigma Xi. Roman Catholic. Office: York Coll of CUNY Dept Natural Scis Jamaica NY 11451-0001 E-mail: manche@york.cuny.edu.

MANCINI, LOIS JEAN, elementary education educator; b. Pitts., May 1, 1944; d. Edward Walter and Margaret Jane Freidhof; m. George John Mancini, July 7, 1967; children: Robin Jennifer, Lori Jean. MEd, Rutgers U., 1988. Cert. elem. tchr. N.J., prin. N.J. Tchr. Moorestown (N.J.) Bd. Edn., Cinnaminson (N.J.) Bd. Edn., Andover (N.J.) Bd. Edn. Author: Mortimer Goose, 1998. Pres. Westampton N.J. Bd. Edn., 1993—. Named Tchr. of Yr., State of N.J., 1996. Mem. NEA, N.J. Edn. Assn., N.J. Sch. Bds. Assn. (pres. bd. dirs. 1993). Presbyterian. Avocations: reading, travel. Home: 57 Tarnsfield Rd Mount Holly NJ 08060-2363 E-mail: mancinil@mtps.middle.com.

MANDARINO, CANDIDA ANN, education educator, consultant; b. Buffalo, N.Y., July 26, 1944; d. Amerigo and Adelaide (Alfieri) Mandarino. BS in Edn., SUNY, Buffalo, 1966; MA in Ednl. Psychology, Calif. State U., Long Beach, 1974; postgrad. in interior and environ. design, 1980—85; PhD in Psychology, Berne U., Wolfboro Falls, N.H., 2000. Tchr. on spl. assignment Norwalk (Calif.)-La Mirada Unified Sch. Dist. Office, 1990—99; mentor/master tchr.; literacy and resource specialist Los Alisos Middle Sch., Norwalk, 1999—2000; prin. Escalona Elem. Sch., La Mirada, 2000; ednl. trainer, cons. K-12 and univs. Heuer Corp., N.Y.C., 2001. Spkr., presenter in field. Mem.: Tchrs. Assn. Norwalk-LaMirada Area, Calif. Tchrs. Assn., Assn. Supervision and Curriculum Devel., Pi Lambda Theta. Home: 178 Roycroft Ave Long Beach CA 90803

MANDEL, MAURICE, II, lawyer, educator, mediator; b. Hollywood, Calif. s. Maurice and Wynne Mandel. BSBA, U. So. Calif., 1971, MEd, 1972; JD, Western State U., 1979. Bar: Calif. 1980, U.S. Dist. Ct. (ctrl. dist.) Calif. 1982, U.S. Ct. Appeals (fed. and 9th cirs.) 1983, U.S. Dist. Ct. (we. dist.) Tenn. 1987, U.S. Dist. Ct. Ariz. 1990, U.S. Dist. Ct. (so. dist.) Calif. 1991, U.S. Supreme Ct. 1991, U.S. Ct. Appeals (5th cir.) 1995; cert. level I ski instr. PSIA Nat. Acad. 1998, child specialist 1999, settlement officer, USDC-CDCa. Tchr. Orange County (Calif.) Sch. Dist., 1972-82; pvt. practice law Newport Beach, Calif., 1982—; fed. settlement officer CDCA, 1998—. Instr. Coastline C.C., 1987-95, prof., 1995—, Coastline C.C. Acad. Senate, Coastline C.C. Parlimentarian 1996-99; prof. law Irvine (Calif.) U. Coll. of Law, 1994-98; instr. Orange County Bar Assn. Coll. of Trial Advocacy, 1994—; instr. Orange County Bar Assn. Mandatory Continuing Legal Edn., 1992—, Bear Mountain Calif. Ski Sch., 1996—, Ziet Maros, 1998—; FBA/OCC Mandatory Continuing Legal Edn. provider, 1994—, COURSE Vail Co. Alpine World Cup Finals, 1997, Alpine World Championships, 1999, World Cup, 1999, COURSE St. Anton am Arlberg, Alpine World Championships, 2001, COURSE Ladies' Norams, Snowbasin, Utah, 2001, COURSE XIX Olympic Games, Salt Lake City, 2002, Alpine Ski, COURSE St. Moritz, Switzerland, Alpine World Championships, 2003. Counselor Troy Camp, 1969-72; chmn. Legal Edn. for Youth, 1984-86; active Ctr. Dance Alliance, Orange County, 1986-97; JOC racing dir. So. Cal, 1998-2000; mem. Friends Am. Ballet Theatre, Opera Pacific Guild, Opera Pacific Bohemians, Calypso Soc., World Wildlife Found., L.A. County Mus. Art, Newport Beach Art Mus., Met. Mus. Art, Laguna Beach Mus. Art, Smithsonian Instn., Friend of Ballet Pacifica, Friends of Joffrey Ballet; assoc. U.S. Ski Team, 1975—; com. assoc. U.S. Olympics, 1988—; 100th Olympics vols., 1996, XIX Olympics, 2002; F.I.S. vol., 1997—, COURSE Alpine World Cup Finals, Vail, Colo., 1997, Alpine World Championships, 1999, 2001, 03, XIX Olympics, 2002; mem. alumni and scholarship com. Beverly Hills H.S.; Opera Pacific Bohemians, Friends of

Ballet Pacifica. Recipient cert. of appreciation U.S. Dist. Ct., L.A., 1985, U.S. Dist. Ct. Mediation award O.C., 2000, Thwarted Thwart award Newport Harbor C. of C., 1989, Tovarich award Kirov Ballet, 1989, 92, Perostroika award Moscow Classical Ballet, 1988-89, 94, Skrisivi Nogi award Bolshoi Ballet, 1990, Marinskii Dance award St. Petersburg, 1993; ABT Romeo & Juliet, 1996, Thwarted Thwart award Newport Harbor, 1996; Ziet Maros award Moscow Classical Ballet, 1998, 99, 2000, 2nd Place award JOC Slalom, 1998, 1st place award JOC Slalom, 2000, 2d place award Big Bear Instrs. Giant Slalom, 2000, 1st place award JOC Concourse, 2000, 14th pl. nat. standing JCNA Slalom, 1999. Mem. ABA, ATLA, Assn. Bus. Trial Lawyers, Fed. Bar Assn., (founding pres. Orange County chpt. 1986, nat. del. 1988-90, founder criminal indigent def. panel 1986, mem. numerous other coms., nat. chpt. activity award 1987, nat. membership award 1987, chpt. svc. award 1989, nat. regional membership chmn. 1990, spl. appointee nat. membership com. 1991), Calif. Bar Assn. (Pro Bono awards 1985-89), Pres.'s Coun. (founder 1996—), Orange County Bar Assn. (legal edn. for youth com. 1982-90, chmn, 1985, fed. practice com., sports com., mandatory fee arbitration com. 1985—, lawyer's referral svc. com. 1984-98, Merit award 1986), Orange County Bar Found. (trustee 1984-87), Women Lawyers of Orange County, U.S. Supreme Ct. Hist. Soc., 9th Jud. Cir. Hist. Soc., Am. Inns of Ct., Calif. Trial Lawyers Assn., Calif. Employee Lawyers Assn., Plaintiff Employee Lawyers Assn., Employees Rights Coun., Bar Leaders Coun. Dist. 8, Amicus Publico, U. So. Calif. Alumni Assn., Mensa, Cougar Club of Am., So. Calif. Cougar Club, San Diego Cougar Club, So. Calif. Jaguar Owners Assn. Clubs: Balboa Yacht. Avocations: skiing, yachting, tennis. Home: PO Box 411 Newport Beach CA 92662 Office: Ste 360 881 Dover Dr Newport Beach CA 92663-6929

MANDELKERN, LEO, biophysics and chemistry educator; b. N.Y.C., Feb. 23, 1922; s. Israel and Gussie (Krostich) M.; m. Berdie Medvedoff, May, 1946; children: I. Paul, Marshal, David. BA, Cornell U., 1942, PhD, 1949. Postdoctoral rsch. assoc. Cornell U., Ithaca, N.Y., 1949-52; phys. chemist Nat. Bur. Standards, Washington, 1952-62; prof. chemistry and biophysics Fla. State U., Tallahassee, 1962—, R.O. Lawton Disting. prof., 1984—. Vis. prof. U. Miami (Fla.) Med. Sch., 1963, U. Calif. Med. Sch., San Francisco, 1964, Cornell U., 1967; mem. biophysics fellowship com. NIH, 1967-70; mem. study panel crystal growth and morphology NRC, 1960; cons. in field. Author: Crystallization of Polymers, 1964, An Introduction to Macromolecules, 1972, 1983, Crystallization of Polymers, Vol. 1, 2002; contbr. numerous articles to profl. jours. 1st lt. USAAF, 1942-46, PTO. Recipient Meritorious Svc. award U.S. Dept. Commerce, 1957, Arthur S. Fleming award Washington Jaycees, 1958, Mettler award N.Am. Thermal Analysis Soc., Phila., 1984, Disting. Svc. in Advancement of Polymer Sci. award Soc. Polymer Sci., Japan, 1993. Fellow: AAAS, Biophys. Soc., Polymer Soc. Japan (sr.), Am. Chem. Soc. (Polymer Chemistry award 1975, Fla. award 1984, Rubber divsn. Whitby award 1988, Charles Goodyear medal 1993, Applied Polymer Sci. award 1989, Disting. Svc. in Advancement of Polymer Sci. 1993, Polymer Divsn. P.J. Flory award 1994, Polymer Materials Sci. & Engring. Divsn. Coop. Rsch. award 1995, Herman F. Mark award 2000), Am. Phys. Soc. (sr. Outstanding Educator of Am. 1973, 1975), Cosmos Club Washington, Alpha Epsilon Pi. Home: 1503 Old Ft Dr Tallahassee FL 32301-5637 Office: Fla State U Dept Chemistry Tallahassee FL 32306

MANDELL, ARLENE LINDA, communications educator; b. Bklyn., Feb. 19, 1941; d. George and Esther Kostick; m. Lawrence M. Mandell, May 23, 1982; children from previous marriage: Bruce R. Rosenblum, Tracey B. Grimaldi. BA magna cum laude, William Paterson U., 1973; MA, Columbia U., 1989. Newspaper reporter Suburban Trends, Riverdale, NJ, 1972-73; writer Good Housekeeping mag., N.Y.C., 1976-78; account exec. Carl Byoir & Assocs., N.Y.C., 1978-86; v.p. Porter/Novelli, N.Y.C., 1986-88; adj. prof. composition, lit., poetry, women's studies William Paterson U., Wayne, NJ, 1989-99; writer, collage artist Sonoma County, Calif., 1999—. Author: Variations on a Theme, a poetry chapbook, 2001; co-author: 7 anthologies; contbr. articles to profl. jours. and newspapers, poetry to N.Y. Times and poetry jours. Recipient 1st pl. women's interest writing, N.J. Press Assn., 1973.

MANDELL, BARBARA DEBORAH, clinical social worker, educator; b. Boston, Aug. 9, 1950; d. Leo and Helen (Steloff) M.; m. Edward Samuel Steinberg, June 12, 1983; children: Daniel, Jonathan. BA in Psychology, Carnegie-Mellon U., 1972; MSW, Smith Coll., 1975. Lic. ind. clin. social worker, Mass., Oreg.; diplomate Am. Bd. Examiners in Clin. Social Work. Adminstrv. asst. Psychol. Testing Lab., Peter Bent Brigham Hosp., Boston, 1972-73; psychiat. social worker Mass. Mental Health Ctr., Boston, 1977-80, Bath (Maine)-Brunswick Mental Health Ctr., 1975-77, Boston VA Med. Ctr., 1980-87; adj. asst. prof. Boston U. Sch. Social Work, 1987-89; pvt. practice, Sudbury and Brookline, Mass., 1980-89, Portland, Oreg., 1990—97; clin. social worker St. Vincent's Hosp., 1994—2000, lead clin. social worker, 2000—. Instr. Portland State U., 1990-91. Mem. NASW, Acad. Cert. Social Workers. Avocations: aerobic exercise, reading, travel.

MANDERSCHEID, LESTER VINCENT, agricultural economics educator; b. Andrew, Iowa, Oct. 9, 1930; s. Vincent John and Alma (Sprank) M.; m. Dorothy Helen Varnum, Aug. 29, 1953; children: David, Paul, Laura, Jane. BS, Iowa State U., 1951, MS, 1952; PhD, Stanford U., 1961. Grad. asst. Iowa State U., Ames, 1951-52, Stanford (Calif.) U., 1952-56; asst. prof. Mich. State U., East Lansing, 1956-65, assoc. prof., 1965-70, prof., 1970-73, prof., assoc. chmn., 1973-87, prof., chmn., 1987-92, prof., 1992-95, prof. emeritus, 1996—, coord. Grad. Sch., 1993—. Reviewer Tex. A&M Agrl. Econ. Program, College Station, 1989; cons. Consortium Internat. Earth Sci. Info. Network, Ann Arbor, 1990. Co-author: Improving Undergraduate Education, 1967; contbr. articles to jours. in field. Pres. parish coun. St. Thomas, East Lansing, 1984-87; coll. coord. United Way, East Lansing, 1983-84; pres. bd. dirs. Cristo Rey Cmty. Ctr., 1998-2001. Recipient Disting. Faculty award Mich. State U., 1977. Mem. Am. Agrl. Econ. Assn. (pres. 1988-89, bd. dirs. 1982-85, excellence in teaching award 1974), Am. Statis. Assn., Am. Evaluation Assn., Am. Econ. Assn., University Club, Sigma Xi (pres. 1986-87), Phi Kappa Phi (pres. 1979-80). Roman Catholic. Home: 2372 Burcham Dr East Lansing MI 48823-3885 Office: Mich State U Dept of Agrl Econs Circle Dr East Lansing MI 48824-1039 E-mail: mandersc@msu.edu.

MANDLE, EARL ROGER, design school president, former museum executive; b. Hackensack, N.J., May 13, 1941; s. Earl and Phyllis (Key) M.; m. Gayle Wells Jenkins, July 11, 1964; children: Luke Harrison, Julia Barnes. BA cum laude, Williams Coll., 1963; MA, cert. in Museum Training, NYU, 1967, postgrad.; DFA (hon.), U. Toledo, 1983, Kenyon Coll., 1986; PhD, Case Western Reserve U., 2002; DFA (hon.), Brown U., 2003. Intern in drawings Met. Mus. Art, N.Y.C.; intern in sculpture and architecture Victoria and Albert Mus., London, 1966-67; assoc. dir. Mpls. Inst. Arts, 1967-74, Toledo Mus. Art, 1974-76, dir., 1977-88; dep. dir. Nat. Gallery Art, Washington, 1988-93; pres. RISD, Providence, 1993—. Chmn. exec. com. Am. Fedn. Arts, 1987-93; mem. adv. panel New Zealand-U.S. Arts Found., Mus. Mgmt. Inst.; trustee Internat. Exhbns. Found., Sterling & Francine Clark Art Inst., Spanish Found. for Restoration of Toledo (Spain); mem. NEA, Nat. Com. Standards in Arts, 1992-94, steering com. 1993-94; mem. adv. council Nat. Mus. Act, Smithsonian Instn.; mem. adv. com. on mus. mgmt. J. Paul Getty Trust; adv. bd. Charles Hosmer Morse Found., Inc., Wexner Ctr., 1986, search com. dirs., 1988; chmn. U.S. Com. on Restoration of Toledo; cons. Nat. Mus. Western Art, Tokyo, Kerr Found., Oklahoma City; chair cultural adv. council Netherlands-Am. Amity Trust, Inc., Annual Coun. Retreats, 1990, 91, co-chmn. agenda com., 1992, cultural diversity task force, 1993, chair Clinton adminstrn. liaison com., 1993; mem., exec. Ohio Arts Coun.; mem. exec. adv. com. Williams Coll. Mus. Art; mem. arts adv. com. Barnes Found.; com. for the preservation of the U.S. Treasury Bldg., hist. advisor, 1989-93; vis. prof. Robert Sterling Clark Prof. of Art Williams Coll., Williamstown, Mass., 1993; mem. bd. trustees, sec. Art Mus. Assn., 1983, v.p. 1985, pres. 1986; com. mem. Art Against Aids, 1987, The Barnes Found. Conservation, 1992; founding trustee Coun. Mus. and Edn. in the Visual Arts, 1971; exec. com. Intermuseum Conservation Assn., 1977; appted. to Nat. Coun. Arts, Pres. Reagan, 1988, Pres. Bush, 1990-94; mem. search adv. com. U.S. State Dept. Curator, 1992; resource cons. Arts Edn. Partnership Working Group Subcommittee, Nat. Ctr. Arts Edn., 1992-93;bd. mem. Assn. Independent Coll. Art & Design (AICAD), Fraunhofer Gesellschaft; hon. bd. mem. Sterling & Francine Clark Art Inst., Toledo Mus. Art; testimony to the adv. bd. Nat. Mus. African Art, Smithsonian Instn., 1990; adv. session for bd. trustees The Textile Mus., Wash., D.C., 1993. Contbr. to profl. mags. and jours. Chmn., bd. dirs. Health and Edn. Leadership for Providence, 1996-99; trustee Providence Found., 1996, Toledo Arts Commn. 1975-78, Toledo Hosp., 1979, pub. rels. Com., 1979-88; mem. City Film Commn., 1995, Coun. Ambs; bd. dirs. Cranston Print Works, 1994-99; mem. adv. bd. Corp. Design Found., 1995, Alliance of Artists' Cmtys., chmn. com. on trustees, 1997-99; mem. nat. policy bd. Ams. for Arts, 1998; mem. steering com. Nat. Endowment for Arts, 1999; bd. trustees nom. com. Am. Red Cross, Toledo chpt., 1976, chmn. youth com.; founder English Speaking Union, Mpls. chpt., 1974; trustee long range planning com. Maumee Valley Country Day Sch., 1983-84, v.p., chmn. com. on trustees, 1987-88; Mayor's com. planning, City of Perrysburg, Ohio, 1985; mem. Rotary, vice-chmn. internat. svc. com., 1987, chmn. 75th anniversary sculpture com. 1987; design review bd. Toledo 1% for Art, 1978-88; mem. Toledo Bicentennial commn. 1974-76; mem. Toledo's com. of One Hundred, Cultural Task Force, 1987; bd. mem. Toledo's Cmty. And Cultural Arts Ctr., 1983; mem. Toledo Econ. Planning Coun., Cmty, and Cultural Programs Subcommittee, chmn. design com., 1981; mem. Toledo Exec. Forum, 1974-81, Toledo Mayor's Citizen Forum, 1975, Toledo Mayor's Com. on Renaissance Bldg. Redevelopment, 1983, Toledo Modern Art Group, 1974-1981, Toledo Sesquicentennial Commn., 1986-87, Young Pres. Org., Wash. Metro chpt., 1988-91, Greater Providence C. of C., 1994-; mem. task force com. Toledo Pub. Sch. "Partners in Edn.", 1981; coord. and speaker United Way Campaign Toledo, Company Program, 1975-81; mem. Warren/Sherman City Venture Project Mobility/Land Use Design Use com., 1977; mem. corp. bd. Trustcorp, Inc., audit, loan and nom. com., 1981-88. Decorated by the His Majesty Juan Carlos Knight of the Order of Isabel the Cath., Spain, 1985; Andover teaching fellow, 1963-64; Ford Found. fellow, 1966; Nat. Endowment Arts fellow, 1974; recipient Am. Hellenic Educational Progressive award, 1983, Distinguished Citizen for Art award Ohio Art Edn. Assn., 1983, Resolution for Leadership award Ohio Senate, 1983, Governor's award State of Ohio, 1983, Marketer of the Year award Am. Marketing Assn., 1983. Mem. Am. Assn. Mus. (trustee, v.p.), Art Mus. Assn. (pres.), Assn. Art Mus. Dirs., Am. Arts Alliance (trustee, policy com.), Coll. Art Assn. (mem. pres.' adv. bd.), Ohio Found. for Arts, Ohio Art Coun., Am. Assn. 18th Century Studies (treas.), Young Pres. Orgn., R.I. Ind. Higher Edn. Assn., Am. Fedn. Arts (chmn. exec. com., chmn. exhbn. com. 1985-93), R.I. Commodores, Confrerie des Chevaliers du Tastevin, Phi Kappa Phi. (hon. mem.), Providence Art Club, Univ. Club, Tile Club, Century Club (N.Y.C.), The Answer Club, Williams Club (N.Y.C.), Carranor Hunt and Polo Club, Catawba Island Yacht Club, The Toledo Club (mem, trustee 1977-88), Hope Club. Office: RISD Office of President 2 College St Providence RI 02903-2784

MANDRACCHIA, VIOLET ANN PALERMO, psychotherapist, educator; b. N.Y.C. d. Anthony and Anna (Yetto) Palermo; m. John J. Mandracchia (dec. 1979); children: Dona Williams, Anne Marino, Marisa, John, Matthew, Lisa Williams. Student, Coll. Mt. St. Vincent; BA, St. John's U.; MA, Bklyn. Coll.; cert. in ednl. adminstrn. & supervision, Hofstra U.; MSW, SUNY, Stony Brook, 1990; advanced study in psychotherapy, L.I. Gestalt Ctr., 1988-92. LCSW, registered RCSW N.Y.; cert. secondary sch. adminstr., supr., English and social studies, practitioner Eye Movement Desensitization and Restructuring. Tchr. English Bay Ridge H.S., Bklyn., Ctrl. Islip (N.Y.) H.S., Smithtown (N.Y.) H.S.; asst. prin. Shoreham-Wading River (N.Y.) H.S., 1977-81; prin. West Islip (N.Y.) H.S., 1981-83; pvt. practice as psychotherapist Stony Brook and Manhattan, 1990—. Satellite psychotherapist Health House, Islandia, N.Y., 1988-97, supr., 1990-97. Active Suffolk County (N.Y.) Human Rights Commn., 1979-84, 88-92; chair adv. bd. Office for Women, Suffolk County, 1986-89; treas. bd. dirs. Women's Ctr., SUNY, Farmingdale, N.Y., 1985-87; chair Women's Equal Rights Coalition, Suffolk County, 1979-84, 88-92; chair North Fork Task Force in Arts, Suffolk County, 1977-79. Recipient Woman of Yr. award Suffolk County Exec. Office for Women, 1989; named Citizen of Yr., Smithtown LWV, 1984, Educator of Yr., Suffolk County Exec. & Women's Equal Rights Coalition, 1982; practitioner writing grantee Harvard U. Grad. Sch. Edn., 1981. Mem. NASW, NOW, Nat. Assn. Secondary Sch. Prins. Avocations: writing, film, theater, travel, painting. Home: 15 Shore Oaks Dr Stony Brook NY 11790-1417 Office: 211 Thompson St New York NY 10012-1365 E-mail: vmandr6889@aol.com.

MANERA, ELIZABETH STURGIS, education educator emeritus; b. Atlanta, Nov. 27, 1929; d. Issac A. and Roberta (Roberts) Sturgis; m. Paul Allen, Jan. 3, 1959; children: Paul S., Melanie. BS, Towson State U., Ariz., 1951; MA, Ariz. State U., 1962, EdD, 1967. Cert.in secondary edn. tchr., Ariz. Grad. tchr. asst. phys. edn. Ariz. State U., 1961-62, instr. phys. edn., 1963-67, vis. lectr. secondary edn., 1967-72, asst. prof. secondary edn., 1972-79, assoc. prof. secondary edn., 1979, program coord. secondary edn., 1990—. Cons. edn. Bur. Indian Affairs, No. Ariz. U., Flagstaff, Ariz., summer 1968-69; vis. scholar edn. adminstrn. U. Victoria, Can., 1987-90, 92, 93. Gerneral editor and co author of chapters 3, 4, and 8, substitute Teaching: Planning for Success, West Lafayette, Ind.; editor: Substitute Teaching: Planning For Success, 1996; contbr. articles to profl. jours. Bd. dirs. World Coun. Curriculum and Instrn., 1987-90; speaker Peoria Elem. Sch. Dist., Phoenix, 1990, New Dawn Correctional Facility, Phoenix, 1991, Orangewood Retirement Cmty., Phoenix, 1991-94, Tauple High Tchr. Insvc., Phoenix, 1991. Mem. ASCD (chair publs. com.) 1989—, chair substitute tchr. commn., 1989-94, chair fiscal affairs com. 1988-91, nat. nominating com. 1986-89, conf. planning com. 1989-92, Outstanding Contbn. to Edn. in Ariz. Award 1985), Am. Ednl. Rsch. Assn., Assn. Tchr. Educators (bd. dirs. 1989-91), chair nat. conf. planning coms. 1982, 86, 88, 89, Phi Delta Kappa (pres. 1988-89). Kappa Delta Pi, 1996

MANESS, JEANIE JONES, secondary education educator, mathematics educator; b. Little Rock, Oct. 26, 1948; d. Robert Bryant and Lavonne (Griffin) Jones; m. RCliff Maness, May 11, 1996; 1 child, Sarah Kristen. BS, U. Ark., Little Rock, 1970; MS in Edn., U. Ark., 1983. Tchr. math. Little Rock Parkview High Sch., 1970-80, Darby Jr. High Sch., Ft. Smith, Ark., 1980-81, Ft. Smith Northside High Sch., 1981—99; instr. Westark Community Coll., Ft. Smith, 1987—99, ret., 1999. Mem. Ark. Ret. Tchrs. Assn.. Methodist. Avocation: woodworking.. Home: 8206 Valley Forge Rd Fort Smith AR 72903-5127

MANESS, MILDRED, reading specialist; b. Caldwell, N.J., Dec. 10, 1928; d. Joseph and Olympia (Gaito) Raimo; m. Frank W. Maness, Aug. 3, 1958. Masters, Kean Coll., 1975. Cert. elem. tchr., learning cons., reading specialist, N.J. Tchr. Piscataway Twp. (N.J.) Schs., 1951-59, Parsippany-Troy Hills Schls., Parsippany, N.J., 1959-94, reading specialist, 1978-93. Founder outdoor reading program, 1967-94; bd. dirs. Parsippany Day Care Ctr.; mem. awards com. Rudolph Rsch., Flanders, N.J. Co-author curriculum programs, 1968-94. Coord. Parsippany-Troy Hills Twp. Tree-Arbor, environ. projects and sr. citizen twp. parade, 1959-94. Named Outstanding Educator, Parsippany Rotary, 1975, one of Outstanding Elem. Tchrs. Am., 1973; recipient A+ for Tchrs. award Sta. 9 TV,, 1989, 92, Gov.'s Recognition, 1990, Disney Am. Tchr. award 1992. Mem. NEA, N.J. Edn. Assn., Alpha Delta Kappa. Home: PO Box 455 Caldwell NJ 07006-0455 Office: Intervale Sch PO Box 52 60 Pitt Rd Parsippany NJ 07054

MANEY, DANIEL B. elementary administrator; b. Great Falls, Mont., Mar. 9, 1947; S. Josephine (Taras) Maney. AA, Flathead Valley C.C., 1975; BEd, Eastern Mont. Coll., 1977, MEd, 1985. Classroom tchr. Lame Deer (Mont.) Elem. Sch., 1977-89, chpt. I dir., 1989—, adminstrv. asst., 1989-91, acting prin., acting supt., 1990-91. With U.S. Army, 1967-69. Mem. NEA, Mont. Edn. Assn., Mont. State Reading Assn.

MANFRA, JO ANN, history educator, lawyer; b. Schenectady, NY, Aug. 5, 1941; d. Joseph Manfra and Anne (Marrocoo) Frescatore; m. Robert R. Dykstra, Aug. 2, 1981. BS, SUNY, Cortland, 1963, MS, 1967; PhD, U. Iowa, 1975; JD, Suffolk U., 1977; LLM, Harvard U., 1979. Bar: Mass. 1977, U.S. Dist. Ct. Mass. 1982. English tchr. Notre Dame High Sch., Schenectady, N.Y., 1964; tchr. Am. and world history Kingston (N.Y.) High Sch., 1964-66; instr. history Ball State U., Muncie, Ind., 1966-67; asst. prof. history Worcester (Mass.) Poly. Inst., 1972-75, assoc. prof. history, 1976-82, prof. history, 1982—, head humanities dept., 1983-93. Co-editor: Law and Bioethics: Text with Commentary on Major U.S. Court Decisions, 1982; contbr. articles to profl. jours. and books. Recipient Summer Rsch. fellowship NEH, 1976, Rsch. fellowship Mary Ingraham Bunting Inst., 1977-79, Profl. Devel. grant Andrew U. Mellon Found., 1984-89, Lectureship Porgram GTE Found., 1985-86, Interpretive Rsch. grant NEH, Washington, 1988-90, JAH Binkley-Stephenson award. Mem.: Mass. Bar Assn. Home: 39 Waterford Dr Worcester MA 01602-3509 Office: Worcester Poly Inst 100 Institute Rd Worcester MA 01609-2247

MANGRU, BASDEO, secondary education educator; b. Guyana; came to U.S., 1987; m. Doreen Nadia Permaul, Aug. 4, 1965; children: Rajendra, Tricia Nadini (Mangru) Dhanraj. Tchr. cert., Tchrs. Coll., Guyana, 1964; BA, U. Guyana, 1970, MA in Guyanese, West Indian History, 1976; PhD in South Asian Studies, U. London, 1981. Cert. social studies tchr., NYC bd. edn.; grade I, class I, trained tchrs. cert., Guyana. Tchr. Guyana High Sch., 1959-74; lectr. U. Guyana, 1974-76, asst. prof., 1976-80, assoc. prof., 1980-84, also coord. Caribbean studies course for non-history majors; student evaluator, interviewer freshmen history majors; tchr., rscher., 1984-87; tchr. social studies N.Y.C. Bd. Edn., 1987—. Participant in seminars, symposiums, lectr. on East Indian Diaspora to ednl. and cultural groups; adj. assoc. prof. York Coll. Author: Benevolent Neutrality, Indian Government Policy and Labour Migration to British Guiana, 1854-1884, 1987, Indenture and Abolition, Sacrifice and Survival on the Guyanese Sugar Plantations, 1993; editor: (with others) The East Indian Diaspora: 150 Years of Survival, Contributions and Achievements, 1993, A History of East Indian Resistance on the Guyana Sugar Estates, 1996, Indians in Guyana: A Concise History From Their Arrival to the Present, 1999; asst. editor The East Indian Diaspora Newsletter; resident historian The East Indian Diaspora Com.; contbr. articles to profl. jours. Vol. civilian asst. to Richmond Hill police dept. working with youth and teenage problems; organizer remedial reading and citizenship classes for local residents. Recipient Bookers' Sugar Estates scholarship, Guyana, 1966-70, Commonwealth Acad. Staff fellowship, Commonwealth Scholarship Commn., UK, 1978-81, Ednl. Achievement award, Corentyne Comprehensive High Sch. Student-Tchr. Reunion Orgn., 1989, Rockefeller Residency fellowship in Humanities, Queens Coll. Asian-Am. Ctr., CUNY, 1990-91. Mem. Am. Hist. Assn. (Albert J. Beveridge Rsch. award 1990), Assn. Caribbean Historians, Assn. Caribbean Studies, Assn. Third World Studies, E. Indian Diaspora Com. (asst. sec., history cons., conf. coord.). Avocations: reading, writing, music, cricket, lawn tennis. Home: 10941 115th St Jamaica NY 11420-1112

MANGRUM, DEBRA KIRKSEY, elementary school educator; b. Jonesboro, Ark., May 17, 1955; d. Hayward Leon and Marguerite (Bailey) Kirksey; children: Wayne, Marissa, Martina. BS in Mktg., Ark. State U., Jonesboro, 1979, BSE in Edn., 1990, MSE in Counselor Edn., 1992; postgrad., Edn. Specialist in psychology and Counseling. Cert. elem. edn. tchr. Ark. Adminstrv. sec. to pres. Planters Prodn. Credit Assn., Jonesboro, 1983-85; owner, mgr. Goodship Lollipop Children's Shop, Jonesboro, 1985-88; grad. and rsch. asst. Ark. State U., Jonesboro, 1990-92. Mem. MSE in Counselor Edn. curriculum com. Ark. State U., 1990-91, mem. tchr. edn. program com., 1991-92; presenter papers ann. conf. Mid.-South Ednl. Rsch. Assn., ann. spring conf. Ark. Assn. Colls. of Tchr. Edn./Assn. Tchr. Educators, 1992. Mem. Valley View PTA, Jonesboro, 1979—, Valley View Athletic Booster Club, Jonesboro, 1979—; cert. judge Miss Ark. Pageant Sys., Hot Springs, 1989—; dir. Miss Mistletoe Pageant, Jonesboro, 1989-93. Mem. ASCD, Am. Sch. Counselor Assn., Ark. Edn. Assn., Phi Delta Kappa, Kappa Delta Pi. Avocation: reading. Home: 4507 Southwest Dr Jonesboro AR 72404-8929

MANIERI, MICHELE DAWN, musician, educator; b. Melbourne, Fla., Apr. 25, 1955; d. Ettore Don and June Laclaire (Spaur) Manieri. AA, U. Fla., 1976, B in Music Edn., 1978; M in Early Childhood and Elem. Edn., Nova U., 1983; M in Guidance and Counseling, U. South Fla., 1993. Cert. tchr., Fla. Profl. vocalist, Fla., 1973—; pvt. practice vocal tchr., 1978-80; substitute tchr. Alachua Sch. Bd., Gainesville, 1978-79; music specialist Levy County Sch. Bd., Williston, Fla., 1979-82, kindergarten tchr., 1982-83; tchr. 2d grade Hernando County/Moton Elem., Brooksville, Fla., 1983-84, tchr. 1st grade, 1984—86, music specialist with integrated counseling concepts and basic skills, 1986—2000; music specialist Hillsborough County Schs., 2000—. Chair calendar plus com. Moton, 1994-99; adj. prof. St. Leo U., 1984—; adj. prof. Pasco-Hernando C.C.; Fla. cert. observer and peer tchr., 1986—, master scheduling com., 1983-99; mem. Hernando County Fine Arts Curriculum Writing Team, 1994-96, accreditation steering com., chair music SAC com., Tchr. of Yr. selection com., 1994-2000; staff devel., trainer integrating music and counseling with academics Connections, Classroom Managed Assessment, Responsibility Tng., Coop. Learning, Multiple Intelligences, Profl. Study Groups, Music Integration; trainer and lessons, unit creator Beacon Learning Ctr.; mem. gala cast Hillsborough Edn. Found., 2002, 03. Featured vocalist Hernando Symphony Orch., Spring Hill, Fla., 1992, 95, 96; soloist Hillsborough Edn. Gala, Tampa, Fla., 2002, 2003, Hillsborough County Music Specialists ann. banquet, 2002, 2003; featured soloist with Nature Coast Festival Singers, 1994, 96, Brooksville Music Club Christmas Ho., 1985, 94; dir., prodr. 30 sacred cantata-dramas, 52 children's musicals. Music dir. 1st Bapt. Ch., Brooksville, 1989-98; mem., actress Playhouse 19, Crystal River, Fla., Stage West Cmty. Theater, Spring Hill, Richey Suncoast Theatre, New Port Richey, Fla.; min. of music 1st Bapt. Ch., Spring Hill, 1999-2001; pvt. concerts. Named 1994 Hernando County Tchr. of Yr., 1994, Best Musical Actress, Stage West, 1995, Best Musical Supporting Actress, Favorite Female Performer, 2000; named to Outstanding Young Women of Am., 1981; nominated Fla. Regional Tchr. of Yr.. Mem. Am. Fedn. of Tchrs., Fla. Elem. Music Educator's Assn., Greater Tampa Bay Orff Assn., Hillsborough County Elem. Music Tchrs. Assn. (entertainment com.), Hillsborough Classroom Tchrs. Assn., FTP-NEA, Nat. Music Educators Assn., Fla. Music Educators Assn., Fla. League Tchrs., Fla. Mental Health Counseling Assn., Fla. Counseling Assn., Fla. Assn. Staff Devel., Hernando Counseling Assn. (Counseling Advocate of Yr. 1994), Hernando County Bd. Fine Arts Coun., Hernando Edn. Found. (sec. 1995-96, Mini grantee), Hernando Classroom Tchrs. Assn. (exec. bd. 1985-86), Hernando Acad. Tchrs. (vice-chair 1994-95, chair 95-96, chair Crystal Apple Sem. 1996), Alpha Delta Kappa. Office: Sch Dist Hillsborough Co Muller Fine Arts Magnet 2421 East 138 Ave Tampa FL 33613 Business E-Mail: michele.manieri@sdhc.k12.fl.us.

MANIFOLD, REBECCA MARCH, elementary school art educator; b. Frederick, Md., Mar. 11, 1949; d. William Dean and June Lois (March) M. BA, W.Va. U., 1971; postgrad., Kutztown U., 1972-75, Shippensburg U.,

1976-77. Cert. art and comprehensive English tchr., Pa. Elem. and secondary art tchr. Fannett-Metal Sch. Dist., Willow Hill, Pa., 1971-73; elem. art tchr. Greencastle (Pa.)-Antrim Sch. Dist., 1973—. Vol. in fashion archives Shippensburg (Pa.) U., 1985—. Mem. NEA, Nat. Art Edn. Assn., Greencastle Area Arts Coun. Republican. Presbyterian. Avocations: collecting and studying historic costume, antique dolls, travel, reading. Office: Greencastle-Antrim Sch Dist 500 Leitersburg Rd Greencastle PA 17225-8332

MANKEL, FRANCIS XAVIER, former principal, priest; b. Knoxville, Tenn., Nov. 8, 1935; s. George Whitehead Sr. and Willia Frances (Duncan) M. BA, St. Ambrose U., 1957; STB, St. Mary's Sem. and U., Balt., 1959, STL, 1961; MEd, Loyola Coll., Balt., 1965. Ordained priest, Roman Cath. Ch., 1961. Assoc. pastor Holy Ghost Ch., Knoxville, 1962-67; prin. Knoxville Cath. High Sch., 1967-79; pastor Sacred Heart Ch., Lawrenceburg, Tenn., 1979-84, St. John Neumann Ch., Knoxville, 1984-87, Sacred Heart Cathedral, Knoxville, 1987-97, Holy Ghost Ch., Knoxville, 1997—. Chancellor Cath. Diocese Knoxville, 1988-96, vicar gen., 1988-98, 99—; supt. Cath. Schs., Diocese of Knoxville, 1989-92. Bd. dirs. Knoxville area chpt. ARC, 1986—; sch. bd. Knoxville Cath. HS, 1967—79, 1984—85, 1987—; com. mem. Sacred Heart Cathedral Sch., Knoxville, 1987—97, St. Joseph Sch., Knoxville, 1997—. Mem. Knoxville Ministerial Assn. Home and Office: 111 Hinton Ave Knoxville TN 37917-6418 E-mail: hgchurch@bellsouth.net.

MANKINS, DONNA KAY, primary school educator; b. Oklahoma City, Aug. 19, 1953; d. Floyd C. and Geraldine (Jackson) Howard; m. Harvey Dwayne Mankins, Dec. 21, 1973; 1 child, Jennifer Kate. BS in Elem. Edn., Ctrl. State U., Edmond, Okla., 1975; MEd in Reading, U. Ctrl. Okla., 1991, postgrad., 1991—. Cert. elem. tchr., reading, early childhood. Kindergarten tchr. Grace Christian Acad., Oklahoma City, 1975-76; tchr. 3rd grade Van Buren Elem. Sch. Oklahoma City Pub. Schs., 1976-77, tchr. 3rd grade Telstar Elem. Sch., 1979-80, tchr. 1st grade Hayes Elem. Sch., 1981—. Facilitator Kelwynn Effective Teaching bldg., sch. improvement program bldg. Inst. Devel. Ednl. Activity. Tchr. adult Sunday Sch., working with youth Assemblies of God Ch. Grantee Oklahoma City Pub. Sch. Found., 1986-93, State Dept. Edn., 1991-92; recipient Master Tchr. award, 1987-88; named Excellent Educator Oklahoma City Jr. League. Mem. NEA, Okla. Edn. Assn., Oklahoma City Reading Coun. (pres. 1987-88), Hayes PTA, Kappa Delta Pi. Office: Hayes Elem Sch 6900 S Byers Ave Oklahoma City OK 73149-1499

MANKIW, NICHOLAS GREGORY, federal agency administrator, economics educator; b. Trenton, N.J., Feb. 3, 1958; s. Nicholas and Dorothy (Sawchak) M.;m. Deborah Jean Roloff, June 16, 1984. AB, Princeton U., 1980; PhD, MIT, 1984. Staff economist Coun. Econ. Advisers, Washington, 1982-83; instr. MIT, Cambridge, 1984-85; asst. prof. Harvard U., Cambridge, 1985-87, prof. econs., 1987—; chmn., mem. Coun. of Econ. Adv., Washington, 2003—. Author: Macroeconomics, 1992, Principles of Economics, 1998; contbr. articles to profl. jours. Recipient Presidential Young Investigator award NSF, 1986. Office: Harvard U Dept Econs Littauer 223 Cambridge MA 02138 also: Eisenhower Exec Office Bldg 17th St and Pennsylvania Ave NW Rm 94 Washington DC 20502

MANLEY, FRANK, retired English language educator, writer; b. Scranton, Pa., Nov. 13, 1930; s. Aloysius F. and Kathryn L. (Needham) M.; m. Carolyn Mary Holliday, Mar. 14, 1952; children: Evelyn, Mary. BA, Emory U., 1952, MA, 1953; PhD, Johns Hopkins U., 1959. Instr., then asst. prof. Yale U., New Haven, 1959-64; assoc. prof., then prof. dept. English Emory U., Atlanta, 1964-2000, chmn. dept., 1968-70, Candler prof. English, 1982-2000, dir. creative writing program, 1990-2000, retired, 2000. Editor: The Anniversaries (John Donne), 1963, (with R. Sylvester) De Fauctu qui ex Dietrina Percipitur, 1967, A Dialogue of Comfort (St. Thomas More), vol. 12, 1977 and Epistola ad Pomeranum, vol. 7, 1990, Yale edit. More's complete works; author: Resultances, 1980 (Devins award for poetry 1980), Two Masters (co-winner Gt. Am. New Play Contest 9th Ann. Humana Festival New Am. Plays 1985), (with F. Watkins) Some Poems and Some Talk About Poetry, 1985, Within the Ribbons: 9 Stories, 1989, (play) The Trap, 1993, The Cockfighter: a Novel, 1998, Among Prisoners: Stories, 2000, (poems) The Emperors, 2001, True Hope: A Novel, 2002. With U.S. Army, 1953—55. Guggenheim Found. fellow, 1966-67, 78-79; recipient NEH transl. program fellowship, 1981-83, Nat. Endowment Arts Creative Writing Fellowship in Fiction, 1995-97, Disting. Teaching award, 1984, Univ. scholar/tchr. of yr. award, 1989, Disting. Alumnus award The Marist Sch., 1993. Roman Catholic. Home: 401 Adams St Decatur GA 30030-5207 also: Doublehead Gap Rd Ellijay GA 30540 Office: Emory U Dept Theater Studies 212 Rich Bldg Atlanta GA 30322-0001 E-mail: fmanley@emory.edu.

MANLEY, GERTRUDE ELLA, librarian, media specialist; b. Phila., Dec. 29, 1930; d. William Eugene and Anna G. (Price) Lomas; m. Harley E. Manley Jr., July 20, 1957; children: Marc Alan, Karen Sue Manley Thornton, Gail Ann Manley Rivera. BRE, Shelton Coll., 1955; MSEd, MS in Libr. Edn., Queens Coll., 1958; postgrad., various. Libr. tchr. Plainedge (N.Y.) Sch. Dist., 1955-60; libr. dir. Huntington (N.Y.) Christian Sch., 1968-70; libr./media specialist Connetquot Ctrl. Sch. Dist. of Islip, Bohemia, N.Y., 1970—. Editor: Manley Family Newsletter, 1983—; exec. prodr.: LomasLines Newsletter, 1996—. Adminstr. pre-sch. story time program E.J. Bosti Sch., Bohemia, 1972—, instr. sign lang., 1988—, Huffine award chairperson, 1985—, spell bee judge, 1984—, arranger spkes. program, 1988—, kindergarten screening participant, 1988—; numerous in-house site-base planning and mgmt. coms. New Life Cmty. Ch., 1990—93, mem. nursery sch. bd., 1985—89, mem. missions com., 1996—, missionary corresponder, 1997—; mem. family crisis ministry com. First Bapt. Ch., Patchogue, 2001—. Mem.: Connetquot Ret. Tchrs. Assn. (rec. and corr. sec. 1993—), Connetquot Tchrs. Assn. (chmn. scholarship com. 1978—93), N.Y. State United Tchrs., We. Suffolk Ret. Tchrs. Assn. (life), N.Y. State Ret. Tchrs. Assn. (life), Bapt./Reformed Ch. Am., Descs. and Friends of 51st Pa. Vol. Inf. (charter). Avocations: genealogy, reading, family history research, writing history articles. Home: 171 Nathan Dr Bohemia NY 11716-1319 Office: Connetquot Ctrl Sch Dist Islip 780 Ocean Ave Bohemia NY 11716-3631 E-mail: trugem@optonline.net.

MANLEY, JO ANN SEAGRAVES, education educator, consultant; b. Hull, Ga., June 17, 1930; d. George Thomas and Mary Magdalene (Wynn) Seagraves; children: Molly Manley, Myra M. Watkins, Thomas, George, Bruce. BS in Edn., U. Ga., 1955, MEd, 1958, EdS in Supervision and Curriculum Devel., 1966, EdD in Adminstrn. and Supervision, 1972. Tchr., counselor, prin. and curriculum dir. various Ga. schs., 1952-64; curriculum dir. Newton County Schs., Covington, Ga., 1964-66, Butts County Schs., Jackson, Ga., 1967-76; asst. supt. Hancock County Schs., Sparta, Ga., 1977-83; ednl. cons. Milledgeville, Ga., 1988—. Adj. asst. prof. Ga. Coll., Milledgeville, Ga., 1973—; chmn. bd. dirs. Baldwin Christian Learning Ctr. Mem. Oconee Mental Health Adv. Coun., 1980-90; N.E. Ga. Presbytery Adminstrv. com., 1986—ruling elder First Presbyn. Ch., 1972—. Recipient Disting. Svc. award Ga. Assn. of Curriculum and Supervision 6th Dist., 1975; named Outstanding Young Educator in Ga., Ga. Jaycees, 1966. Mem. AAUW (program chmn. 1985), Wesley Found. (bd. dirs., chmn. 1989-91), Milledgeville/Baldwin County C. of C. Avocations: reading, sewing, travel, theatre, cooking. Home: 1715 Briarcliff Rd Milledgeville GA 31061-2154 Office: PO Box 1482 Milledgeville GA 31059-1482

MANLEY, JOHN FREDERICK, political scientist, educator; b. Utica, N.Y., Feb. 20, 1939; s. John A. and Gertrude Manley; children from previous marriage: John, Laura; m. Kathy Lynn Sharp, 1991; 1 child, Cole Sharp Manley. BS, Le Moyne Coll., 1961; PhD, Syracuse U., 1966. Asst. prof. polit. sci. U. Wis., 1966, assoc. prof., 1969-71; prof., chmn. dept. polit. sci. Stanford U., 1977-80. Fellow Center for Advanced Study in Behavioral Scis., 1976-77; vis. prof. Stanford in Oxford, 1996. Author: The Politics of Finance, 1970, American Government and Public Policy, 1976; author, co-editor: The Case Against the Constitution, 1987. Congressional fellow, 1963-64; Brookings Instn. fellow, 1965-66; Guggenheim fellow, 1974-75; Fulbright fellow U. Bologna, 1992. Office: Stanford U Dept Polit Sci Stanford CA 94305

MANLEY, MARGARET EDWARDS, primary education educator; b. Somerset, Ky., June 24, 1938; d. Ellis Thomas and Edna May (Denton) Edwards; m. Charles Dudley Manley, June 21, 1959; children: Jennifer Manley Figg, Mary Manley Meininger. BA, Georgetown Coll., 1958, U. Ky., 1960, student, 1981-82, Georgetown Coll., 1982-84. Cert. tchr. Rank I, Ky. Com. chmn. sch. based decision making Fayette County Schs., Lexington, 1990—. Supr. student tchrs. U. Ky., Eastern U., Richmond, 1970-72, faculty assoc., 1989-90, Holmes profl. devel. team, 1988-91; presenter in-svc. seminars, 1990-93; mentor tchr. Tchr. Opportunity Program, 1993—. Vol. Southland Christian Ch., Lexington, 1983—. Mem. NEA, Ky. Edn. Assn., Fayette County Edn. Assn., Alpha Delta Kappa (v.p., sec. 1990-92, pres. 1992—). Republican. Avocations: reading, historic homes, children's literatures, walking, traveling. Office: Fayette County Schs Main St Lexington KY 40509

MANLEY, MOLLY ELIZABETH, special education educator, elementary school educator; b. Reno, Nev., Aug. 13, 1948; d. Francis E. and Irma A. (Mason) Bagley; m. Charles Douglas Manley, Oct. 25, 1980. BA in Speech, U. Nev., Reno, 1970, grad. spl., 1971, MA in Remedial Reading, 1979. Cert. remedial reading, speech therapy, spl. edn., alternative edn., elem. edn. Teaching asst. Truckee Meadows Community Coll., Reno, 1973-74; adult educator Washoe High Sch., Reno, 1975-76; alternative educator Sparks (Nev.) High Sch., 1976-80; sole proprietor tutoring bus. Reno, 1981-86; contract tutor Thompson Learning Ctr., Reno, 1985-86; edn. coord. Hosp. Corp. Am.-Truckee Meadows Hosp., Reno, 1986-87; spl. edn. tchr. Sparks (Nev.) High Sch., 1987-92, alternative edn. tchr., 1992—96; tchr. spl. edn. Greenbrae Elem. Sch., 1996—99; tchr. 3d grade Lincoln Park Elem. Sch., 1999—2001. Mem. Washoe County Tchrs. Assn., Sierra Nev. Coun. Avocations: ranching, horse tng., hunting, fishing. Home: 4951 Skyridge Ln Sparks NV 89431-1138

MANLEY, WALTER WILSON, II, lawyer, business educator; b. Gainesville, Fla., Mar. 16, 1947; s. Walter Wilson and Marjorie Iley (Watkins) M.; children: Marjorie, Benjamin. BA, Fla. So. Coll., 1969; JD, Duke U., 1972; MBA, Harvard U., 1975. Assoc. Blackwell, Walker & Gray, Miami, Fla., 1972-75; pvt. practice, Lakeland, Fla., 1975-84; prof. bus. adminstrn. Fla. State U., Tallahassee, 1985—; ptnr. MacFarlane, Ferguson, Allison & Kelly, Tallahassee, 1991-94. Vis. prof. bus. adminstrn. Ridley Hall Coll. and Cambridge Fedn. Theol. Colls., Eng., 1988-90, Cambridge U. Faculties of Mgmt. Studies, Philosophy, Law, Social and Polit. Scis. and Divinity, 1989-90; pres. Exeter Leadership Cos. Inst., Inc., Tallahassee, 1989-94, Fla. North Shore Tech. Ctrs., Inc., 1995-97. Author: Critical Issues in Business Conduct, 1990, Executive's Handbook of Model Business Conduct Codes, 1991, Handbook of Good Business Practice, 1992, What Florida Thinks, 1997, The History of the Supreme Court of Florida and Its Predecessor Courts, 1821-1917, 1997 (nominated Littleton Griswold prize in Am. Law & Soc. 1998) Chmn. Fla. Endowment Found. for Vocat. Rehab., 1991-93; bd. dirs. Fla. Real Property and Casualty Joint Underwriters Assn., 1987-91, Consumer Coun. Fla., 1992-99; bd. visitors Duke U. Sch. Law, 1991-98; trustee The Webb Sch., BellBuckle, Tenn., 1983-92, nat. fund chmn., 1982; trustee Ctr. for Fla. History; pres. Polk County Legal Aid Soc.; legal editor Harbus, ofcl. Class of 1975 rep. 350th anniversary Harvard U.; mem. Great Floridians Nominating Com., 2003—. Recipient Outstanding Alumnus award Fla. So. Coll., 1999. Fellow Fla. Supreme Ct. Hist. Soc. (disting. historian); mem. ABA, Fla. Bar Assn. (Pres.' Pro Bono Svc. award 1985), Lakeland Bar Assn. (pres.), Capital Duke Club (founder, past pres.), Tallahassee Quarterback Club Found. (past chmn., Biletnikoff award), Psi Chi, Omicron Delta Kappa, Sigma Alpha Epsilon (Nation's Outstanding Educator award 1998), Phi Delta Phi. Episcopalian. Avocations: hot air balloons, gliders, fly fishing, wing shooting. Home: 2804 Rabbit Hills Rd Tallahassee FL 32308-0837

MANLY, CAROL ANN, speech pathologist; b. Canton, Ohio, Nov. 21; d. William George and Florence L. (Parrish) M.; m. William Merget, Sept. 19, 1992; children: William, John. MA, U. Cin., 1970; PhD, NYU, 1988. Instr. U. Cin. Med. Ctr., 1970-72; asst. dir. Goldwater Hosp. NYU, 1972-83; pvt. practice N.Y.C., 1983—. Cons. Mary Manning Walsh Home, N.Y.C., 1974-85, Beth Israel Med. Ctr.-North Divsn., N.Y.C., 1983—; adj. asst. prof. NYU, 1989-90, C.W. Post campus L.I. U., Brookville, 1990—. Author: (with others) Current Therapy in Physiatry, 1984, Communication Disorders of the Older Adult: A Practical Handbook for Health Care Professionals, 1993; contbr. articles to profl. jours. Mem. N.Y. Acad. Scis., Am. Speech-Lang.-Hearing Assn., N.Y. State Speech-Lang.-Hearing Assn., N.Y. Neuropsychology Group, NOW. Achievements include development of new diagnostic and treatment procedures for oral-pharyngeal dysphagia in neurologically impaired adults. Office: 360 E 65th St Apt 21D New York NY 10021-6726

MANN, CHARLES FREDERICK, language educator, translator, author; b. Gloucester, Mass., July 27, 1946; s. John Jacob Mann and Evelyn Ann Salah. BA cum laude, U. Ottawa, Ont., Can., 1969; MA, Boston Theol. Inst., 1973; license-es-lettres, La Sorbonne, Paris, 1974; PhD, l'Inst. Catholique de Paris, 1978. Ordained priest Roman Cath. Ch., 1973. Admissions officer U. Ottawa, 1964-66; H.S. tchr. Ottawa schs., 1966-69; head religious edn. St. Mary's Parish, Marlborough, Mass., 1973-75; French interpreter Claude Davie Media, Paris, 1975-78; French translator, linguistic cons. Univers Pubs., Paris, 1978-80; French tchr. Boston Sch. Modern Langs., 1980-82; dir. students Tutoring Svc. of San Francisco, 1982-90; fgn. lang. tutor U. Calif., Berkeley, 1991—. ESL coord. Fgn. Lang. Inst., San Francisco, 1991—2001. Author: Madeleine Delbrêl: A Life Beyond Boundaries, 1996; translator: Jeanne Jugan, 1997, God Behind Bars, 1999, We, the Ordinary People of the Streets, 2000. Elections inspector San Francisco City Hall, 1982—; reading tutor San Francisco Pub. Libr., 1982—; vol. Project Head Start, San Francisco, 1995—; vol. literacy program Ctrl. YMCA of San Francisco, 1995—. Named Vol. of Yr., San Francisco Elections Office, 1995; recipient Favorite Book of Yr. award Nat. Cath. Reporter, 1999, Excellence in Translation award Paulist Press, 1999, Univers Media, 2000. Fellow Book Coun. San Francisco; mem. Amnesty Internat., Small Pubs. Assn. No. Calif., Fgn. Lang Tchrs. Assn. Am. Democrat. Roman Catholic. Avocations: writing, language research, weightlifting, global affairs, contemporary spirituality. Home: 954 Geary St Apt 55 San Francisco CA 94109

MANN, J. KEITH, retired law educator, arbitrator; b. May 28, 1924; s. William Young and Lillian Myrle (Bailey) M.; m. Virginia McKinnon, July 7, 1950; children: William Christopher, Marilyn Keith, John Kevin, Susan Bailey, Andrew Curry. BS, Ind. U., 1948, LLB, 1949; LLD, Monmouth Coll., 1989. Bar: Ind. 1949, D.C. 1951. Law clk. Justice Wiley Rutledge and Justice Sherman Minton, 1949-50; pvt. practice Washington, 1950; with Wage Stblzn. Bd., 1951; asst. prof. U. Wis., 1952, Stanford U. Law Sch., 1952-54, assoc. prof., 1954-58, prof., 1958-88, prof. emeritus, 1988—, assoc. dean, 1961-85, acting dean, 1976, 81-82, cons. to provost, 1986-87. Vis. prof. U. Chgo., 1953; mem. Sec. of Labor's Adv. Com., 1955-57; mem. Pres.'s Commn. Airlines Controversy, 1961; mem. COLC Aerospace Spl. Panel, 1973-74; chmn., mem. Presdl. Emergency Bds. or Bds. of Inquiry, 1962-63, 67, 71-72; spl. master U.S. vs. Alaska, U.S. Supreme Ct., 1980-97. Editor book rev. and articles Ind. U. Law Jour., 1948-49. Ensign USNR, 1944-46. Sunderland fellow U. Mich., 1959-60; scholar in residence Duke U., 1972. Mem. ABA, AAUP, Nat. Acad. Arbitrators, Indsl. Rels. Rsch. Assn., Acad. Law Alumni Fellows Ind. U., Order of Coif, Tau Kappa Epsilon, Phi Delta Phi. Democrat. Presbyterian. Home: 872 Lathrop Dr Stanford CA 94305-1053 Office: Stanford U Sch Law Stanford CA 94305-8610 E-mail: jkmann@leland.stanford.edu.

MANN, LESTER PERRY, mathematics educator; b. Milford, Mass., May 30, 1921; s. Lester P. and Viola E. (Tracy) M.; m. Dorothy M. Davis, Oct. 11, 1947; children: Kelly P., Leslie P. BS with high honors, U. Md., 1964; MEd, U. Alaska, Anchorage, 1974; EdD, Boston U., 1983. Cert. elem. tchr., reading specialist and supr., Mass.; cert. elem. tchr., reading specialist, Alaska. Commd. 2nd lt. USAAF, 1941; advanced through grades to maj. USAF, 1954, navigator, weather officer, 1941-64; ret., 1964; resident counselor OEO-Job Corps, 1965-66; flight navigator Südflug, Braniff, Capitol and Japan Air Lines, 1966-73; instr. math., adminstr., curriculum developer U. Alaska, 1974-86, adj. instr., 1987-99; instrnl. assoc. Mann Assocs., Applied Lifelong Learning, Anchorage, 1983-99. Instr. Anchorage Community Coll., 1974-86; asst. prof. Embry-Riddle Aero. U., Anchorage, 1987-98, acad. advisor, 1987-90; mem. for remedial reading Alaska Talent Bank; vis. adult educator German Adult Edn. Assn., 1984. Mem. Math. Assn. Am., Nat. Coun. Tchrs. Math., Internat. Reading Assn., Am. Assn. Adult and Continuing Edn. (profl., past mem. nomination and election com.), Am. Meteorol. Soc. (emeritus), Phi Alpha Theta, Phi Kappa Phi. Home and Office: 2304 Turnagain Pky Anchorage AK 99517-1124 Fax: 907-243-MANN. E-mail: lesmann@alaska.net.

MANN, MARY LOUISE, special education educator; b. Crawfordsville, Ind., Oct. 2, 1955; d. William Edward Biddle and Alice Marie (Lowe) Klemans; m. Rodney Mann, Aug. 23, 1975; children: Kathryn, Alice, Ryan. Student, Ball State U., 1973-77, postgrad., 1993—; BS, U. Indpls., 1991, student. Cert. elem. tchr., learning disabilities, non-departmental, Ind.; licensed seriously emotionally handicapped K-12, 1993. Tchr. seriously emotionally handicapped Clverdale (Ind.) Jr-Sr. High Sch., 1991—. Mem. Coun. Exceptional Children, Ind. Coun. Children with Behavioral Disorders, Kappa Delta Pi. Baptist. Avocation: camping. Home: PO Box 699 Cloverdale IN 46120-0699 Office: Cloverdale Jr Sr High Sch RR 3 Box 1A Cloverdale IN 46120-9803

MANN, OSCAR, retired physician, internist, educator; b. Paris, Oct. 13, 1934; arrived in U.S., 1953; s. Aron and Helen (Biegun) Mann; m. Amy S. Mann, July 19, 1964; children: Adriana, Karen. AA with distinction, George Washington U., 1958; MD cum laude, Georgetown U., 1962. Diplomate Am. Bd. Med. Examiners, Am. Bd. Internal Medicine, Am. Bd. Cardiovasc. Disease, cert. advanced achievement in internal medicine. Intern Georgetown U. Med. Ctr., Washington, 1962-63, jr. asst. med. resident, 1963-64, clin. fellow in cardiology with Proctor Harvey program, 1965-66; sr. asst. resident in medicine Georgetown svc. D.C. Gen. Hosp., Washington, 1964-65; clin. prof. medicine Georgetown U. Sch. Medicine, 1985—; nat. chmn. med. alumni fund Georgetown U. Med. Sch., Washington, 1993-95; pvt. practice internal medicine and cardiology, Washington, 1966-99. Mem. med. nursing com. Georgetown U. Med. Ctr., mem. adv. com. CME, mem. tchg. adv. com., opthalmology dept. rev. com., surgery dept. rev. com., faculty com., search com. for a new dean for acad. affairs; appointed coun. to the dean Georgetown U. Sch. Medicine, 1977—; mem. Instnl. Self Study Task Force. Contbr. articles to profl. jours. Nat. chmn. med. alumni fund Georgetown U., 1997—99. Served with U.S. Army, 1953—55, with U.S. Army, 1953—55. Recipient Mead Johnson Postgrad. Scholar ACP, 1964—65, Physicians Recognition award, AMA, 1987—96, Advanced Achievement in Internal Medicine, 1987, John Carroll award, Georgetown U., 1999. Fellow: ACP, Am. Coll. Chest Physicians, Am. Coll. Cardiology; mem.: AMA, Med. Soc. D.C., Am. Heart Assn. (coun. clin. cardiology), Am. Soc. Internal Medicine, Georgetown U. Alumni Assn. (bd. govs. 1993—, chair med. alumni bd. 1995—, nat. chmn. med. alumni fund 1997—99), Cosmos Club, Phi Delta Epsilon, Alpha Omega Alpha. Home: 5137 Yuma St NW Washington DC 20016 E-mail: oscarmann@peoplepc.com.

MANN, ROBERT WELLESLEY, biomedical engineer, educator; b. Bklyn., Oct. 6, 1924; s. Arthur Wellesley and Helen (Rieger) M.; m. Margaret Ida Florencourt, Sept. 4, 1950; children: Robert Wellesley, Catherine Louise. SB, MIT, 1950, SM, 1951, ScD, 1957. With Bell Telephone Labs., N.Y.C., 1942-43, 46-47; with U.S. Army Signal Corps, 1943-46; research engr. MIT, 1951-52, rsch. supr., 1952, mem. faculty, 1953—, prof. mech. engring., 1963-70, Germeshausen prof., 1970-72, prof. engring., 1972-74, Whitaker prof. biomed. engring., 1974-92, Whitaker prof. emeritus, sr. lectr., 1992—, head systems and design div., mech. engring. dept., 1957-68, 82-83, founder, dir. engring. projects lab., 1959-62; founder, chmn. steering com. Center Sensory Aids Evaluation and Devel., 1964-86, chmn. div. health scis., tech., planning and mgmt., 1972-74, founder, dir. Newman biomechanics and human rehab. lab., 1975-92; dir. bioengring. programs Whitaker Coll. MIT, 1986-89; dir. Harvard-MIT Rehab. Engring. Ctr., 1988-93. Mem. exec. com. Divsn. Health Scis. and Tech. Harvard U. MIT, 1972-85; prof., 1979—, mem. Com. on Use of Humans as Exptl. Subjects MIT, 1984-93, co-chair Pub. Svc. Ctr., 1988-92; lectr. engring. Faculty of Medicine, Harvard U., 1973-79; rsch. assoc. in orthopedic surgery Children's Hosp. Med. Ctr., 1973—; cons. in engring. sci. Mass. Gen. Hosp., 1969—; cons. in field, 1953—; mem. Nat. Commn. Engring. Edn., 1962-69; com. prosthetics rsch. and devel. NRC, 1963-69; chmn. sensory aids subcom., 1965-68, com. skeletal sys., 1969; mem. com. interplay engring. with biology and medicine Nat. Acad. Engring., 1969-73; mem. bd. health scis. policy Inst. Medicine, 1973-74, 82-86; mem. com. on nat. needs for rehab. physically handicapped Nat. Acad. Scis., 1975-76; mem.-at-large confs. com. Engring. Found., 1975-81; chair sensory aids panel scis. merit rev. bd. Rehab., R & D Svc., Dept. Vets. Affairs, 1983-95, 99—, mem. Visual/Hearing Impairment Rehab. Panel, 1999—; mem. Commn. on Life Scis. NRC, 1984-88, Com. on Strategic Tech. for U.S. Army, NRC, 1989-93; NRC Com. on Space Biology and Medicine, 1992-95. Consulting editor: Ency. Sci. and Tech., 1962-67; assoc. editor: IEEE Trans. in Biomed. Engring., 1969-78, ASME Jour. Biomech. Engring., 1976-82; mem. editl. bd. Jour. Visual Impairment and Blindness, 1976-80, SOMA, 1986-92; mem. editl. adv. bd. new liberal arts program Alfred P. Sloan Found., 1986-92; contbr. over 400 articles to profl. jours. Pres., trustee Amanda Caroline Payson Scholarship Fund, 1965—86; trustee Nat. Braille Press, 1982—, pres., 1990—94; trustee Mary Flannery O'Connor Charitable Trust, 2002—; bd. dirs. Carroll Ctr. Blind, 1967—74, pres., 1968—74; mem. corp. Perkins Sch. Blind, 1970—2000, Mt. Auburn Hosp., 1972—2000; mem. Cardinal's adv. com. on social justice Archdiocese of Boston, 1993—96; bd. overseers St. Marguerite D'Youville Found., Youville Lifecare Inc., 1994—98; chmn. Flannery O'Connor-Andalusia Found., Inc., 2002—. Recipient Sloan award for Outstanding Performance, 1957, Talbert Abrams Photogrammetry award, 1962, Assn. Blind of Mass. award, 1969, IR-100 award for Braillemboss, 1972, Bronze Beaver award MIT, 1975, UCP Goldenson Rsch. for Handicapped award, 1976, New Eng. award, 1979, J.R. Killian Faculty Achievement award MIT, 1983, Martin Luther King Leadership award MIT, 1995, Distng. Alumnus lectr. dept. mech. engring. MIT, 1997. Fellow Am. Acad. Arts and Scis., Am. Inst. Med. and Biol. Engring., IEEE (mem. editl. bd. Spectrum 1984-86), AAAS, ASME (gold medal 1977, H.R. Lissner award for biomed. engring. 1977); mem. NAS, Inst. Medicine NAS, NAE, Biomed. Engring. Soc. (bd. dirs. 1981-84), Orthopedic Rsch. Soc., Rehab. Soc. N.Am., MIT Alumni Asssn. (pres. 1983-84, Alumni Fund Bd. 1978-80, bd. dirs. 1980-86, 93-95, corp. joint adv. com. 1983-84, chair nat. selector com. 1985-88, awards com. 1992-94, chmn. 1994, bd. Tech. Rev. 1986-95, chmn. 1993-95), Sigma Xi (nat. lectr. 1979-81), Tau Beta Pi, Pi Tau Sigma, Sigma Xi. Roman Catholic. Achievements include patents on missile power units, founding of computer aided design in 1963, earliest braille translation software and hardware in 1962, cybernetic amputation prosthesis, 1966, in vivo measurements of human cartilage pressures, 1984. Home: 5 Pelham Rd Lexington MA 02421-5707 Office: MIT 77 Massachusetts Ave Rm 3-137 Cambridge MA 02139-4307 E-mail: rwmann@mit.edu.

MANNERS, PAMELA JEANNE, middle school educator; b. Holyoke, Mass., Mar. 20, 1951; d. Francis Edward and Helen Mary (Kurtyka) Herbert; div. 1985; children: Tracy, Kristen. BA, U. So. Miss., 1986, MEd, 1993. Cert. elem. edn. K-3, 4-8, secondary Eng., Social Studies; cert. elem. prin., secondary prin., elem. and secondary adminstrn. Registrar Michel Mid. Sch., Biloxi, Miss., 1987-88, tchr. Eng. and Social Studies, 1988-90, tchr. reading/law related edn., 1990-95; curriculum coord. Biloxi Pub. Schs., 1995-98; administrator Fernwood Jr. High Sch., Biloxi Pub. Schs., 1998-2000; dir. ABA Reading Curriculum Program, 1989-95; prin. Michel Jr. H.S., Biloxi Pub. Schs., 2000—. Law-related edn. trainer Miss. Law-Related Edn. Ctr., Jackson, 1990-2002; law-related trainer Ctr. Civic Edn., Calabasas, Calif., 1993; law-related trainer Constitutional Right Found., 1994-2002. Participant program Lawyer in Every Class Miss. Bar Assn., Jackson, 1990-93 On-site target grantee Miss. Bar/Dept. Justice, 1992; A+ Site recognition U.S. Dept. Edn. Mem. Leadership Gulf Coast C. of C. (edn. com. 1996—). Roman Catholic. Office: Biloxi Pub Schs 1400 Father Ryan Ave Biloxi MS 39530 E-mail: PamonCoast@aol.com.

MANNING, CHARLES W. university chancellor; b. Mar. 18, 1943; s. Charles Manning; m. Sharon Fischer; children: Shannon, Charles, Kelly. BS in Chemistry, McDaniel Coll., 1965; PhD in Analytical Chemistry, U. Md., 1969; postgrad., Johannes Gutenberg U., Mainz, Germany, 1969—70. Sr. staff assoc. Nat. Ctr. Higher Edn. Mgmt. Systems, Boulder, Colo., 1971-74; asst. provost, asst. prof. chemistry U. Mo., Kansas City, 1974-79; assoc. exec. dir. acad. affairs Colo. Commn. Higher Edn., Denver, 1979-81, dep. exec. dir., 1982-88; v.p. acad. affairs U. No. Colo., Greeley, 1981-82; exec. vice chancellor Okla. State Regents for Higher Edn., Oklahoma City, 1988-90; chancellor U. System W.Va., Charleston, 1991-2000, Tenn. Bd. Regents, Nashville, 2000—. Cons. as v.p. for planning and fin. Fed. U., Ceara, Brazil, 1976-77; presenter in field. Contbr. articles to profl. jours. Capt. U.S. Army, 1970-71. Office: Tenn Bd Regents 1415 Murfreesboro Pike Ste 350 Nashville TN 37217-2829

MANNING, CHRISTOPHER ASHLEY, finance educator, consultant; b. L.A., June 26, 1945; s. Ashley and Vivian LaVerne (Wagner) M.; m. Cathy Ann Nichols, July 30, 1977 (div. Sept. 1993). BS, San Diego State U., 1967; MBA, Northwestern U., 1971; PhD, UCLA, 1983. Corp. loan officer Security Pacific Nat. Bank, L.A., 1971-75; v.p. fin. Solitude Ski Resort, Bravo Ski Corp., Salt Lake City, 1975-78; pres. Sequoia Spa Co., L.A., 1976-79, Manning and Co., L.A., 1971-86, Manning's Little Red Piano Shop, L.A., 1971-86; instr. corp. fin. Pepperdine U., L.A., 1979-83; instr. corp. fin. and real estate Long Beach (Calif.) State U., 1983-86; assoc. prof. fin. Loyola Marymount U., L.A., 1986-92, prof. fin., 1992—. Mng. prin. Denver office Houlihan Valuation Advisors, 1993-94; founder, mng. prin. Manning Advisors. Mem. editl. bd. Jour. of Real Estate Rsch., 1988-90, 91-93, 94-96, 97-99, 2003—; contbr. articles to profl. jours. 1st lt. U.S. Army, 1967—70. Decorated Bronze Star. Mem.: Am. Real Estate Soc. (bd. dirs. 1994—96, 1997—99, v.p./program chair 2000—01, bd. dirs. 2000—, pres.-elect 2001—02, pres. 2002—03), Phi Eta Sigma, Beta Gamma Sigma. Republican. Episcopalian. Home: 29438 Quailwood Dr Palos Verdes Peninsula CA 90275-4929 Office: Manning Advisors 29438 Quailwood Dr Palos Verdes Peninsula CA 90275-4929

MANNING, J. FRANCIS, school administrator; b. Syracuse, N.Y., May 11, 1963; s. Thomas Michael and Elena Ann (Corbacio) M. BS, SUNY, Buffalo, 1986; MS, Syracuse U., 1987; CAS, SUNY, Cortland, 1991; postgrad., Century U., 1991—. Math. tchr. Huntington Elem. Sch., Syracuse, N.Y., 1987-91; adminstrv. intern Henniger High Sch., Syracuse, 1991; vice prin. Levy Middle Sch., Syracuse, 1991-92; asst. prin. West Genesee Mid. Sch., Camillus, N.Y., 1992—; grade level adminstr. Pine Grove Jr. H.S., East Syracuse, N.Y. La crosse coach Syracuse High Sch. Dist., 1987-90; cooperating tchr. SUNY at Cortland, 1987-91; resident mentor Syracuse Tchr. Ctr., 1990-93; supt.'s issue team, Syracuse City Sch. Dist., 1990-92; prin. Henniger High Sch. Summer Sch., 1991, '92; facilitator Syracuse City Sch. Dist., 1992-3 Recipient scholarship Syracuse U., 1986. Mem. N.Y. State Assn. for Supervision, Curriculum Devel., Sch. Adminstrs. Assn. N.Y., Nat. Assn. Secondary Prins., N.Y. State Middle Sch. Assn., N.Y. State Devel. Coun., Commn. on Adult Basic Learning. Avocation: tae kwon do karate black belt. Home: 8098 Mccamidge Dr Cicero NY 13039-9007 also: Pine Grove Jr HS Fremont Rd East Syracuse NY 13057

MANNING, KEVIN JAMES, academic administrator; b. N.Y.C., Nov. 8, 1944; s. James and Helen (Gurry) M.; m. Sara Garrity; children: Elizabeth Ann, Meagan Garrity, Kevin James. BA in Theatre, Webster U., St. Louis, 1967; MS in Pers., Shippensburg (Pa.) U., 1976; PhD in Ednl. Adminstrn., Ohio State U., 1982; attended, Inst. Ednl. Mgmt., Harvard U., 1989. Adminstr., intr. Webster U., St. Louis, 1967-68; mgmt recruiter L.S. Brady, Inc., St. Louis, 1969; adminstr. Washington U., St. Louis, 1969-71; admissions counselor Elizabethtown (Pa.) Coll., 1972-76, dir. admissions, 1976-80, spl. asst. to pres., 1982-83; rsch. asst. Ohio State U., Columbus, 1980-82; chief staff Gov.'s Commn. Higher Edn., Harrisburg, Pa., 1983-84; v.p. devel. Immaculata (Pa.) Coll., 1984-2000; pres. Villa Julie Coll., Md., 2000—. Workforce adv. panel Commonwealth of Pa. Mem. attractions com. Phila. Econ. Devel. Coalition, 1988—; bd. trustees Peirce Coll., 1998—2001; mem. oversight com. Vision 2030; bd. dirs. Chester County Export Ctr., Exton, Pa., 1990. Mem. Sr. Devel. Officers Phila. (chmn. 1995-96), Great Valley C. of C. (bd. dirs.). Avocations: reading, arts, film, golf. Home: 1907 Billy Barton Cir Reisterstown MD 21136 Office: Villa Julie Coll 1525 Greenspring Valley Rd Stevenson MD 21153-0641

MANNING, PETER KIRBY, sociologist educator; b. Salem, Oreg., Sept. 27, 1940; s. Kenneth Gilbert and Esther Amelia (Gibbard) M.; m. Victoria Francis Shaughnessy, Sept. 1, 1961 (div. 1981); children— Kerry Patricia, Sean Peter, Merry Kathleen; m. Betsy Cullum-Swan, Aug. 4, 1991 (div. 1997). BA, Willamette U., 1961; MA, Duke U., 1963, PhD, 1966; MA (hon.), Oxford U., Eng., 1983. Instr. sociology Duke U., 1964-65; asst. prof. sociology U. Mo., 1965-66, Mich. State U., East Lansing, 1966-70, assoc. prof. sociology and psychiatry, 1970-74, prof., 1974—; prof. criminal justice, 1993—. Beto chair lectr. Sam Houston State U., 1990; Ameritech lectr. E. Ky. U., 1993; vis. prof. U. Victoria, 1968, MIT, 1982, SUNY, Albany, 1982, U. Mich., 1990—91, York U., Toronto, 1999; vis. sr. scholar Northeastern U. Coll. Criminal Justice, 2001, E.V. and E.M. Brooks chair; cons. Nat. Inst. Law Enforcement and Criminal Justice, U.S. Dept. Justice, Rsch. Triangle Inst., NSF, Nat. Health and Med. Rsch. Coun., Australia, 1980—, Social Sci. Rsch. Coun. Eng., AID, Jamaica, 1991, Sheehy com. Police Pay and Performance, England, 1993. Author: Sociology of Mental Health and Illness, 1975, Police Work, 1977, 2d edit., 1997, The Narcs' Game, 1980, 2d edit., 2003, Semiotics and Fieldwork, 1987, Symbolic Communication, 1988, Organizational Communication, 1992, Private Policing, 1999, other books; also book chpts., articles in profl. jours.; cons. editor series: Principal Themes in Sociology; co-editor Sage Series in Qualitative Methods; mem. editorial bd. numerous jours. in social scis. Recipient Bruce Smith Sr. award Acad. Criminal Justice Scis., 1993, O.W. Wilson award, 1997, Charles H. Cooley award Mich. Sociol. Assn., 1994; NDEA fellow, 1962-64, NSF fellow, 1965, fellow Balliol Coll., Oxford U., 1982-83, vis. fellow Wolfson Coll., Oxford U., 1981, 82-83, fellow, 1984-86; Am. Bar Found. rsch. fellow, 1998; Rockefeller resident, Bellagio, Italy, 2000. Mem. Am. Soc. Criminology, Am. Sociol. Assn., Brit. Soc. Criminology, Internat. Sociol. Assn., Midwest Sociol. Soc., Soc. Study of Social Problems, Soc. for the Study of Symbolic Interaction (spl. recognition award 1990, v.p. 1992-93, program chair 1993), Internat. Soc. for Semiotics and Law. Office: Northeastern U Coll Criminal Justice Boston MA 02115 E-mail: manningpk@hotmail.com.

MANNING, RANDOLPH H. academic administrator; b. Bronx, Dec. 18, 1947; s. Ruthfoy M. and Gertrude (Webber) M.; m. Monica S. McEvilley, May 15, 1972; children: Randolph, Craig, Corey. AA, Suffolk Community Coll., 1969; BA, SUNY, Stony Brook, 1971, MALS, 1975, PhD, 1998. Owner, operator R.H. Manning Enterprises, Coram, N.Y., 1973—; counselor Suffolk County Community Coll., Riverhead, N.Y., 1971-80, prof. psychology and sociology, 1980-85, dean instrn., 1985—. Pres. emeritus Spl. Program Personnel Assn., SUNY, 1978-82; ednl. cons. Bds. Coop. Ednl. Svcs., Westhampton, N.Y., 1980; adv. bd. Re-Route Dept. Labor, Suffolk County Sheriff's Dept., 1980—; assoc. commr. N.Y. State Task Force on Race Rels. N.Y.; co-dir. Counsel Internat. Programs, 1990—; Mid. States evaluator, 1990—; cons. to N.J. Dept. Higher Edn., 1990—; curriculum and program evaluator. Pres. N.Y. State Program Personnel Assn., 1978-82; bd. dirs. Gordon Heights FCU, L.I., 1975-82, treas, bd. dirs. L.I. Sickle Cell Inc., Hempstead, 1981—, adv. bd. Suffolk County Farm Coop. Extension, USN. Named one of Outstanding Young Men Am., 1981; recipient Proclamation for Service, County of Suffolk, 1986. Mem. Am. Sociol. Assn., Black Faculty and Staff Assn., N.Y. State Bd. Profl. Med. Conduct, Cmty. Coll. Gen. Edn. Assn. (pres.). Home: 3 Indian Valley Rd East Setauket NY 11733-4037 Office: Suffolk County CC Crooked Hill Rd Brentwood NY 11717

MANNING, WINTON HOWARD, psychologist, educational administrator; b. St. Louis, Feb. 9, 1930; s. Winton Harry and Jane (Swanson) M.; m. Nancy Mercedes Groves, Aug. 1, 1959; children: Cecelia Groves Tazelaar, Winton H. III. AB with honors, William Jewell Coll., 1951; PhD in Psychology, Washington U., St. Louis, 1959. Instr. psychology William Jewell Coll., Liberty, Mo., 1954-55, asst. prof., acting head dept. psychology, 1955-56; rsch. psychologist Washington U., St. Louis, 1956-58, rsch. assoc., 1958-59; from asst. prof. to prof. psychology Tex. Christian U., Ft. Worth, 1959-65, assoc. dir. univ. honors program, 1962-65; from assoc. dir. rsch. to exec. dir. R & D Coll. Entrance Examination Bd., N.Y.C., 1965-69; from dir. devel. rsch. divsn. to sr. v.p. R & D Ednl. Testing Svc., Princeton, N.J., 1969-83, v.p., 1970-77, sr. v.p. devel. and rsch., 1977-83, sr. scholar, 1983-93; pres. Ednl. Devel. Svc., Princeton, 1993—2000. Vis. fellow Princeton U., 1982-83; cons. Gallup Internat. Inst., 1990—, Applied Ednl. Rsch., 1993-95; cons. Grad. Mgmt. Admissions Coun., 1992-95, Carnegie Found. for the Advancement of Tchg. 1993-95; vis. lectr. Washington U., St. Louis, summer, 1961. Author: The Pursuit of Fairness in Admissions to Higher Education, 1977; Student Manual for Essentials of Psychology, 1960. Contbr. articles on ednl. measurement and psychology of learning to profl. publs. Patentee in field U.S. and Europe. Trustee Assn. for Advancement of Mentally Handicapped, 1975-78, Nat. Chicano Coun. on Higher Edn., 1977-85, N.J. Arts Festival, 1980-85; vice-chmn. Found. for Books to China, 1980-98; chmn. bd. trustees Princeton Day Sch., 1981-93; trustee Princeton Area Found., 1991-94, Our House Found., 1991-92; bd. dirs. The Princeton Singers, 1992-99, Christian Renewal Effort in Emerging Democracies, 1992-94, George H. Gallup Internat. Inst., 1992-98; chmn., trustee Trinity-All Saints' Cemetery, 1993-98; chmn. Affordable Housing Bd. of Princeton Borough, 1987-89; chmn., commr. Princeton Pub. Housing Authority, 1995-99, 2000-03; sr. warden All Saints Episc. Ch., 1987-89; chmn. ins. com. Diocese N.J., 1993-95; coun. mem. Diocese of N.J., 1996-99, 2003—, mem. audit com., 1997-98, mem. standing com., 1998-2002, mem. fin. com., 2003—; adv. coun. U. Okla. Ctr. for Rsch. on Minority Edn., 1987-92, Ind. Sch. Chmn. Assn., 1987-92; trustee Friends of Princeton Open Space, 1995-98; trustee Russian Ministry Network, 1995-98; cons. Carnegie Found. for Advancement of Tchg., 1987-95; cons. The Coll. Bd., 1988-91; spl. cons. Commn. on Admission to Grad. Mgmt. Edn., 1987-89; chair Princeton Residents Traffic Safety Com., 1994—2002. Recipient Alumni Achievement citation William Jewell Coll., 1970; named Gallup Scholar in Edn., 1995. Fellow Am. Psychol. Soc. (charter), Eastern Psychol. Assn., Psychometric Soc., Nat. Assn. Scholars, Am. Ednl. Rsch. Assn., Nat. Coun. on Measurement in Edn. (mem. com. on legal issues in measurement 1977-79), N.Y. Acad. Scis., Nassau Club, Pendragon Soc., Old Guard of Princeton, Oratory of Good Shepherd, Phi Beta Kappa, Sigma Xi, Order of St. John of Jerusalem (comdr.). Home: 12 Morven Pl Princeton NJ 08540-3024 Office Fax: 609-924-9528. E-mail: win.manning@verizon.net.

MANNINO, EDWARD FRANCIS, lawyer, educator; b. Abington, Pa., Dec. 5, 1941; s. Sante Francis and Martha Anne (Hines) M.; m. Mary Ann Vigilante, July 17, 1965 (div. 1990); m. Antoinette K. O'Connell, June 25, 1993; children: Robert John, Jennifer Elaine. BA with distinction, U. Pa., 1963, LLB magna cum laude, 1966. Bar: Pa. 1967. Law clk. 3d cir. U.S. Ct. Appeals, 1966-67; assoc. Dilworth, Paxson, Kalish & Kauffman, Phila., 1967-71, ptnr., 1972-86, co-chmn. litigation dept., 1980-86, sr. ptnr., 1982-86; sr. prin. Elliott, Mannino & Flaherty, PC, Phila., 1986-90; chmn. Mannino Griffith PC, Phila., 1990-95; sr. ptnr. Wolf, Block, Schorr & Solis-Cohen, Phila., 1995-98; ptnr. Akin, Gump, Strauss, Hauer & Feld LLP, Phila., 1998—. Hearing examiner disciplinary bd. Supreme Ct. Pa., 1986—89, mem. adv. com. on appellate ct. rules, 1989—95; lectr. Temple U. Law Sch., 1968—69, 1971—72; mem. Phila. Mayor's Sci. and Tech. Adv. Com., 1976—79; project mgr. Pa. Environ. Master Plan, 1973; chmn. Pa. Land Use Policy Study Adv. Com., 1973—75; chmn. adv. com., hon. faculty history dept. U. Pa., 1980—85, lectr. Am. history, 2001—. Author: Lender Liability and Banking Litigation, 1989, Business and Commercial Litigation: A Trial Lawyer's Handbook, 1995, The Civil RICO Primer, 1996; mem. editl. bd. Litigation mag., 1985-87, Comm. Lending Litigation News, 1988-2001, Bank Bailout Litigation News, 1989-93, Bus. Torts Reporter, 1988-99, Practical Litigator, 1989—, Civil RICO Report, 1991-2001; contbr. articles to profl. jours. Pres. parish coun. Our Mother of Consolation Ch., 1977-79; bd. overseers U. Pa. Sch. Arts and Scis., 1985-89, chmn. recruitment and retention of faculty com.; commonwealth trustee Temple U., 1987-90, audit, bus. and fin. coms. Named one of Nation's Top Litigators Nat. Law Jour., 1990, Pa.'s Top Ten Trial Lawyers, 1999, listed in The Best Lawyers in Am., Am.'s Leading Bus. Lawyers. Fellow Am. Bar Found., ABA (chmn. various coms.), Am. Law Inst., Hist. Soc. U.S. Dist. Ct. Ea. Dist. Pa. (bd. dirs.), Pa. Bar Assn., Phila. Bar Assn. (gov. 1975), Pa. Soc., Order of Coif, Phi Beta Kappa, Phi Beta Kappa Assocs. Democrat. Office: Akin Gump Strauss Hauer Et Al 2005 Market St Fl 22 Philadelphia PA 19103-7014 E-mail: emannino@akingump.com.

MANNO, BRUNO VICTOR, foundation administrator; BA, U. Dayton, 1970, MA, 1972; PhD, Boston Coll., 1975. Mem. faculty U. Dayton, 1975-78; dir. rsch. Data Bank and In-svc. programs Nat. Cath. Edn. Assn., Washington, 1979-86; dir. planning Office of Ednl. Rsch. and Improvement Dept. Edn., Washington, 1986, chief staff, acting asst. sec., 1986-91, asst. sec. edn., 1991-93; sr. fellow edn. policy studies program Hudson Inst., Washington, 1993-98; sr. program assoc. edn. The Annie E. Casey Found., Balt., 1998-99; sr. program assoc. The Annie E. Carey Found., 1999—. Vis. sr. lectr. Cath. Tchrs. Coll., Sydney, Australia; vis. rsch. assoc. Nat. Opinion Rsch. Ctr., U. Chgo.; vis. lectr. Inst. for Cath. Ednl. Leadership, U. San Farncisco. Co-author: Charter Schools in Action: Renewing Public Education, 2000; co-editor book; author 150 articles and 30 book revs. Office: The Annie E Casey Found 701 Saint Paul St Baltimore MD 21202-2311

MANOS, CONSTANTINE THOMAS, geologist, educator; b. White Plains, N.Y., Jan. 2, 1933; m. Catherine Manos, June 19, 1971; children: Georgia, Andrew. BS, CCNY, 1958; MS, U. Ill., 1960, PhD, 1963. Rsch. asst. Ill. State Geol. Survey, Urbana, 1958-63; asst. prof. SUNY, Plattsburgh, 1963-64; instr. CCNY, summer 1964; asst. prof. SUNY, New Paltz, 1964-66, assoc. prof., 1966-70, geology coord., 1966-72, chmn. geology dept., 1969-72, 86-92, prof. geology, 1970—, grievance chmn., 1980-92. Contbr. articles to profl. jours. including Jour. Sedimentary Petrology, Jour. Am. Assn. Petroleum Geologists, and Am. Geol. Inst. (editl. com. for lab. exercises 1985). Fellow NSF, 1973. Fellow Geol. Soc. Am. (sr.); mem. Soc. Econ. Paleontologists and Mineralogists, Sigma Xi. Office: SUNY Dept Geology New Paltz NY 12561

MANOWITZ, PAUL, biochemist, researcher, educator; b. Monticello, NY, Dec. 13, 1940; s. Jacob M. and Rose (Levine) M.; m. Joyce L. Swartz, June 16, 1968; children: Neal J., Lauren H. BA in Chemistry with honors, Cornell U., 1962; PhD in Biochemistry, Brandeis U., 1967. Fellow NYU Sch. Medicine, 1967-70, instr., 1970-72; asst. prof. psychiatry U. Medicine and Dentistry N.J. Robert Wood Johnson Med. Sch., Piscataway, 1972-78, assoc. prof. psychiatry, 1978-96, prof. psychiaty, 1996—. Rsch. cons. VA Med. Ctr., Lyons, N.J., 1987—. Mem. editl. bd. Jour. of Studies on Alcohol, 1993—; contbr. articles to profl. jours. Grantee Nat. Inst. on Alcohol Abuse and Alcoholism. Mem. AAAS, Internat. Soc. for Biomed. Rsch. on Alcoholism, Am. Soc. Human Genetics, Am. Soc. Neurochemistry, Soc. Biol. Psychiatry, Rsch. Soc. on Alcoholism. Home: 7 Guernsey Ln East Brunswick NJ 08816-3506 Office: U Medicine and Dentistry NJ Robert Wood Johnson Med Sch 671 Hoes Ln Piscataway NJ 08854-5627

MANRIQUE, JAIME, writer, educator; b. Barranquilla, Atlantico, Colombia, June 16, 1949; came to U.S., 1966; d. Gustavo Manrique and Soledad (Ardila) Reina. BA in English Lit., U. South Fla., Tampa, 1972; student, Columbia U., 1977. Instr. The Poetry Project, N.Y.C., 1986, 90-92; vis. prof. writing The New Sch. U., Eugene Lang Coll., N.Y.C., 1988-2000; assoc. prof. MFA program Columbia U., 2002. Writer-in-residence Yaddo, Saratoga Springs, N.Y., 1983, The McDowell Colony, Peterborough, N.J., 1985, New Sch. for Social Rsch., 1989-91, Va. Ctr. for Creative Arts, 1990. Author: Los Adoradores de la Luna, 1976, Confesiones de un Critico Amateur, 1979, El Cadaver de Papa, 1980, Colombian Gold, 1983, Scarecrow, 1990, Latin Moon in Manhattan, 1992, Twilight at the Equator, 1997, My Night With Federico Garcia Lorca, 1999, Eminent Maricones: Arenas, Lorca, Puig, and Me, 1999, Mi Cuerpo Yotros Poemas, 1999, Tarzan, My Body, Christopher Columbus, 2001. Recipient Nat. Poetry award Instituto de Cultura Y Bellas Artes, Cucuta, Colombia, 1975; grantee Found. for Contemporary Performance Arts, 1999; John Simon Guggenheim fellow 2000-01. Mem. PEN Am. Cen. (prison writing com., 1988-90, chmn. PEN Am. Ctr. fund for writers and editors with AIDS 1990-92). Democrat. Avocations: going to movies, hiking, traveling. E-mail: JMardila@aol.com.

MANS, THOMAS CHARLES, academic administrator; b. Riceville, Iowa, Sept. 7, 1952; s. Reinhart Lawrence and Pauline Theresa (Bieniek) M.; m. Mary Kay Melcher, June 14, 1975; children: Jeremiah Michael, Jesse Reinhart, Janine Elizabeth, Rachel Elise. BA, St. John's U., Collegeville, Minn., 1974; MA, U. Iowa, 1975, PhD, 1981. Asst. prof. Berea (Ky.) Coll., 1978-83; asst./assoc. prof. Creighton U., Omaha, 1983-01, chair dept. polit. sci., 1993-96, asst. to dean, 1987-89, assoc. dean Coll. Arts and Scis., 1996-00; v.p. for academic affairs St. Vincent College, Latrobe, Pa., 2001—. Roman Catholic. Office: Office of Academic Affairs St Vincent College 300 Fraser Purchase Rd Latrobe PA 15650

MANSELL, DARREL LEE, JR., English educator; b. Canton, Ohio, Apr. 9, 1934; s. Darrel Lee and Virginia (Shepherd) M.; m. Elizabeth Meihack, Jan. 1957 (div. July 1970); 1 child, Benjamin Lloyd; m. Adriana Saviane, July 16, 1983. BA, Oberlin Coll., 1956; student, Oxford U., 1961—62; PhD, Yale U., 1963; MA (hon.), Dartmouth Coll., 1975. Instr. Dartmouth Coll., Hanover, N.H., 1962-64, asst. prof., 1964-68, assoc. prof., 1968-74, prof., 1974-99, prof. emeritus, 1999—. Author: The Novels of Jane Austen, 1973; contbr. articles to scholarly jours. Mem. Jane Austen Soc. N.Am. (founding patron), Phi Beta Kappa. Home: 2 Dana Rd Hanover NH 03755-2227 Office: Dartmouth Coll Dept English Hanover NH 03755 E-mail: darrel.mansell@dartmouth.edu.

MANSELL, JOYCE MARILYN, special education educator; b. Minot, N.D., Dec. 17, 1934; d. Einar Axel and Gladys Ellen (Wall) Alm; m. Dudley J. Mansell, Oct. 31, 1954; children: Michael, Debra Mansell Richards. BS, U. Houston, 1968; MEd, Sam Houston State U., 1980. Cert. provisional elem. tchr. 1-8, provisional mentally retarded tchr., provisional lang. and/or learning disabilities tchr., profl. elem. tchr. gen. 1-8, profl. reading specialist. From 1st grade tchr. to 3rd grade tchr. Johnson Elem. Sch., 1968-77; spl. edn. tchr. mentally retarded/learning disabled Meml. Parkway Jr. H.S., 1982-86, Waller Mid. Sch., 1986-90; spl. edn. tchr. mentally retarded Royal Mid. Sch., Tex., 1990-95, Royal H.S., 1995-96; ret., 1996. Tchr. Am. sign lang. for retarded students in pub. schs. Lutheran. Avocations: painting, bridge, reading, fishing, grandchildren and family, watercolor painting. Home: 2155 Paso Rello Dr Houston TX 77077-5622

MANSERGH, GORDON DWIGHT, health maintenance and prevention researcher; b. St. Paul, Aug. 7, 1962; s. Gerald Gordon and Nancy Helen (Stuessy) M. BA, Gustavus Adolphus Coll., 1984; MA, Mich. State U., 1986; MEd, Boston U., 1991; postgrad., U. So. Calif., 1992—. Substance abuse counselor NORCAP Lodge, Foxboro, Mass., 1986-87; asst. dir. student affairs Chamberlayne Coll., Boston, 1987; asst. dir. orientation, off-campus svcs. Boston U., 1987-90, founding dir. Wellness Ctr., 1990-92; rsch. asst. U. So. Calif. Inst. for Prevention Rsch., 1992—; grant writer, program evaluator. Cons. EMT Calif. State Drug Prevention Tech. Assistance Project; rsch. asst. Kaiser Permanente So. Calif., 1992—, U.S. Ctrs. Disease Control and Prevention, 1995; co-founder, coord. Pasadena Area Colls. Together in Drug Prevention, 1993—; dir. PREVENT Consortium, 1991-92; drug prevention planning com. U.S. Dept. Edn., 1991-94; dir. Project DART, 1990-92; mem. N.W. Pasadena Health Coalition, L.A. Adolescent HIV Consortium, Mass. Coun. on Compulsive Gambling Prevention Coalition; chair Boston U. Substance Abuse Task Force, 1989-92; founding chair Boston AIDS Consortium Coll. Cmty. Edn. Com., 1988-90. Editor, co-author: The Wellness Resource Book, 1991, Adventures in Prevention, 1992, Wellnews, 1990-92. Vol. community svc. AIDS Action Com. Mass., Calif. AIDS Ride, AIDS Project L.A., Calif. AIDS Ride. Named Outstanding Young Man of Am., 1986-87; recipient Nat. Disting. Svc. Registry award, 1989-90; honoree Guild of St. Ansgar Gustavus Adolphus Coll., 1984; fellow Mich. State U., 1984-85. Mem. Am. Coll. Pers. Assn. (dir. wellness com. 1990-92), Am. Coll. Health Assn., Am. Psychol. Assn., Am. Pub. Health Assn., Soc. for Behavioral Medicine, Pi Lambda Theta.

MANSON, LIONEL ARNOLD, immunology educator, researcher; b. Toronto, Ont., Can., Dec. 24, 1923; came to U.S., 1947; naturalized citizen, 1962; s. Max and Florence (Rachlin) M.; m. Rosalie Weisblatt, May 27, 1945; children: Aaron Nachum, Florence Natanya, David Sholom Eliezar. BA, U. Toronto, 1945, MA, 1947; PhD, Washington U., St. Louis, 1949. Rsch. asst. dept. biochemistry U. Toronto, summer 1944, 45; tchg. asst. dept. biol. chemistry Washington U., 1947-48; instr., sr. instr. dept. microbiology Western Res. U., 1950-54; from fellow to prof. Wistar Inst., 1954-89; from rsch. asst. prof. to prof. dept. microbiology U. Pa., Phila., 1954—. Mem. grad. group microbiology U. Pa., 1955—, mem. grad. group molecular biology, 1965—, mem. grad. group immunology, 1971—, chmn. grad. group immunology, 1974-81, mem. grad. group human genetics, 1977—, sr. fellow dept. biology, 1987—; cons. New Eng. Nuclear Corp., Newton, Mass., 1981-83, Creative Biomolecules, Hopkinton, Mass., 1983-85. Editor Jour. Cellular Physiology, 1966-76, Transplantation Procs., 1969—, Hazardous Materials Mgmt. Jour., 1979-81; assoc. editor Jour. Immunology, 1980-82; series editor Biomembranes, 1971—; sr. editor Immunologic Techniques, 1985—; contbr. over 125 articles to profl. jours. Fulbright scholar, France Dept. State, 1963-64; fellow Nat. Cancer Inst., Israel, 1971-72; recipient fellowship NRC Can., 1945-46, 46-47, rsch. fellowship NIH, 1948-49, Postdoctoral award NRC, 1949-50. Mem. AAAS, Am. Assn. Biol. Chemists, Am. Chem. Soc., Am. Soc. Cell Biology, Am.

Soc. Microbiology, Am. Acad. Microbiology, European Assn. Biol. Chemists, N.Y. Acad. Scis., Transplantation Soc., Israeli Immunological Soc., Am. Assn. Immunologists, Am. Assn. Cancer Rsch., Sigma Xi. Jewish. Achievements include development of oncotope hypothesis, to explain the progressive growth of tumors in the autochthonous host; a new paradigm for development of immunotherapeutic programs against cancer. Home: 103 Grasmere Rd Bala Cynwyd PA 19004-2906 Office: Univ Pa Dept Biology Philadelphia PA 19104 Office Fax: 215-898-8780.

MANSON, MALCOLM HOOD, educational consultant; b. Melton Mowbray, Leicester, Eng., May 31, 1938; s. James Milne and Williamina (Hood) M.; m. Snowden Sandra Johnston. BA, Oxford U., Eng., 1961, MA, 1964. Tchr. The Choate Sch., Wallingford, Conn., 1961-63, adminstr., 1963-69; headmaster Marin Country Day Sch., Corte Madera, Calif., 1969-82, Ore. Episcopal Sch., Portland, Oreg., 1982-90; canon headmaster Cathedral Sch. for Boys, San Francisco, 1990-99. Mem. Calif. Assn. Ind. Schs. (bd. dirs., v.p. 1976-80), Pacific N.W. Assn. Ind. Schs. (pres. 1985-86). Episcopal.

MANSOUR, TAG ELDIN, pharmacologist, educator; b. Belkas, Egypt, Nov. 6, 1924; came to U.S., 1951, naturalized, 1956; s. Elsayed and Rokaya (Elzayat) M.; m. Joan Adela MacKinnon, Aug. 6, 1955; children—Suzanne, Jeanne, Dean. DVM, Cairo U., 1946; PhD, U. Birmingham, Eng., 1949, DSc, 1974. Lectr. U. Cairo, 1950-51; Fulbright instr. physiology Howard U., Washington, 1951-52; sr. instr. pharmacology Case Western Res. U., 1952-54; asst. prof., assoc. prof. pharmacology La. State U. Med. Sch., New Orleans, 1954-61; assoc. prof., prof. molecular pharmacology Stanford U. Sch. Medicine, 1961—, chmn. dept. pharmacology, 1977-91, Donald E. Baxter prof., 1977-98, prof. emeritus, 1999—. Cons. USPHS, WHO, Nat. Acad. Scis.; Mem. adv. bd. Med. Sch., Kuwait U.; Heath Clarke lectr. London Sch. Hygiene and Tropical Medicine, 1981 Author: Chemotherapeutic Targets in Parasites, 2002; contrbr. sci. articles to profl. jours. Commonwealth Fund fellow, 1965; Macy Found. scholar NIMR, London, 1982. Fellow AAAS; mem. Am. Soc. Pharmacology and Exptl. Therapeutics, Am. Soc. Biol. Chemists, Am. Heart Assn., Sierra Club, Stanford Faculty Club. Office: Stanford Sch Medicine Dept Molecular Pharm CCSR 269 Campus Dr Rm 3155 Stanford CA 94305-5174

MANSUR, SHARIF SAMIR, counselor, education educator; b. Cleve., Feb. 26, 1963; s. Aasim and Fareeda Mansur. BA, Knox Coll., 1985; MA in Psychology, Valparaiso U., 1988, MEd, 1990. Cert. sch. counselor, cert. profl. counselor. Clin. therapist Christian Haven Homes, Wheatfield, Ind., 1988-92, Tri-City Cmty. Mental Health, East Chicago, Ind., 1988-92; instr. edn. and psychology Valparaiso (Ind.) U., 1989-91; lectr. psychology Chgo. (Ill.) State U., 1991-92; tchr., counselor Michigan City (Ind.) Area Schs., 1991-92; lectr. psychology Cardinal Stritch Coll., Milw., 1992-94; sch. counselor Menomonee Falls (Wis.) Sch. Dist., 1992-94; lectr. edn. Carroll Coll., Waukesha, Wis., 1994—; asst. dir. career svcs. Cardinal Stritch Coll., Milw., 1994-95. Counseling cons. Knox (Ind.) Elem. Sch.-Social Svc., 1989-92; ednl. cons. Our Lady Lourdes Sch., Chgo., 1991-92; human rels. cons. in field. Mem. Wis. Assn. for Counseling and Devel. (exec. bd. mem. 1994), Wis. Assn. for Multicultural Counseling and Devel. (pres. 1994-96), Met. Milw. Alliance Black Sch. Educators (co-chair higher edn. commn.), Cardinal Stritch Coll. Tchr. Edn. Adv. Coun. Home: N89w16045 Main St Menomonee Falls WI 53051-2939 Office: Carroll College Waukesha WI 53186

MANTHEY, ROBERT WENDELIN, retired secondary school educator; b. N.Y.C., Dec. 23, 1935; s. Frank A.J. and Josephine (Roth) M.; m. Marcia Christine Dampman; Dec. 27, 1958; children: Catherine, A. David, Jeffrey R. BA, SUNY, Albany, 1957; MA in Teaching, Brown U., 1962. Cert. secondary, sci. tchr., N.Y. Tchr. high. sch., Croton-on-Hudson, N.Y., 1957-94. Coord. Boy Scouts Am., Peekskill, N.Y., 1974-90; chmn. Conservation Adv. Coun., Peekskill, 1987. Recipient Excellence award Math. Soc. Am., 1953; fellow NSF, 1962; Rsch. Participation grantee Boyce Thompson Inst., Yonkers, N.Y., 1963-64. Mem. Sci. Tchrs. Assn. N.Y. State, N.Y. State Tchrs. Assn., Croton Tchrs. Assn. (v.p. 1972-74, treas. 1976-93, exec. com. 1972-94), Lions (pres. Peekskill chpt. 1992-93), Elks, KC. Republican. Roman Catholic. Avocation: running. Home: 405 Pelican Bay Dr Daytona Beach FL 32119-1309 also: PO Box 103 92 Fremont Ave Daytona Beach FL 32114-5520

MANTONI, PHILIP JOSEPH, principal; b. Springfield, Mass., Dec. 3, 1944; s. Adelino Philip and Mary (Barberis) M.; m. Susan Beth Hartley Mantoni, Aug. 4, 1973; 1 child, Christian Philip. BSE in Elem. Edn., North Adams (Mass.) State Coll, 1969; MEd in Edn., Springfield Coll., 1979; C.A.G.S. in Adminstrn., Westfield (Mass.) State Coll., 1988. Tchr. Washington Sch., Springfield, 1969-77, Ecology Ctr. of Springfield, 1977-89; asst. prin. New North Cmty. Sch., Springfield, 1989-90; prin. A.G. Zanetti Elem. Sch., Springfield, 1990-95, Alice B. Beal Sch., Springfield, 1995—. Exec. bd. South End Cmty. Ctr., 1992—; mem. chmn., exec. bd., bldg. rep. Springfield Fedn. Tchrs. Mem. Springfield Citywide Sch. Centered Decision Making Team, 1993-99; chmn. Springfield Park Commn., 1982-91; mem. Forest Park Zool. Soc. Edn. and Curriculum Com., 1981-89; mem. Olmstead grants Com. for Forest Park, 1986-88; mem. Springfield Schs. Sci. Curriculum Com., 1978-83; mem. Springfield Mcpl. Planning Bd., 1983-91. Mem.: Springfield Elem. Prins. Assn. (treas. 1992—93, sec. 1993—94, v.p. 1994—95). Home: 41 Texel Dr Springfield MA 01108-2637 Office: Alice B Beal Sch 285 Tiffany St Springfield MA 01108-3333 E-mail: pjmsiri@aol.com.

MANTOR-CLARYSSE, JUSTINE CLAIRE, fine arts educator; b. Neenah, Wis., Aug. 12, 1943; d. Jack Allen and Ann Elizabeth (Suchy) Mantor; m. John Allan Wantz, June 18, 1968 (div. 1983); m. Omer T. Clarysse, July 28, 1994. BFA, Sch. Art Inst. Chgo., 1967; MA, No. Ill. U., 1969, MFA, 1971. Assoc. prof. fine arts Loyola U., Chgo., 1971-93, dir. women's studies, 1982-83; represented by Artisimo Gallery, Scottsdale, Ariz. Instr. Coll. of DuPage, Glen Ellyn, Ill., 1971-72, North Shore Art League, Winnetka, Ill., 1972-73, DuPage Art League, Wheaton, Ill., 1972; gallery dir. Water Tower Gallery, Loyola U., Chgo., 1973-82; lectr. Ill. Conf. L.Am. Studies, U. Ill., 1990, Chantanqua Conf. Fgn. Lang. Tchrs., Pheasant Run, Ill., 1991, U. Wis., Madison, 1991, Mid-Am. Coll. Art Assn., Madison, Wis., 1991, 92, Mid-Am. South-East Coll. Art Assn., Birmingham, Ala, 1992, Nat. Coll. Art Assn., Seattle, 1993, N.Y., 94. Solo exhbns. include U. Ill. Med. Ctr., Chgo., 1979, Springfield (Ill.) Art Assn., 1979, John Nelson Bergstrom Art Ctr. and Mus., Neenah, Wis., 1980, Aurora (Ill.) Coll., 1980, Arc Gallery, Chgo., 1981, 83, Illini Union Gallery, Champaign, Ill., 1982, Fountain Hills Cmty. Ctr., Ariz., 1990, Downtown Gallery, Phoenix, 1994, others; permanent collections include Ill. State Mus., Rockford Mus., Kemper Ins. Co., Gillman Gallery, Chgo., Byer Mus., No. Ill. U. Student Ctr. and Fine Arts Dept., Loyola U. Gallery Coll., Chgo., others. Named Best of Show, Fountain Hills Art Fair, Ariz., 1993, 94, Best of Show and 1st Pl. Acrylic, Juried Competition, 1994, Fountain Hills Art Fair; grantee Ill. Arts Coun., 1978, Ill. Art Coun./Mellon Found., 1979, Nat. Humanities Assn., 1980, Ill. Humanities Coun., 1980-81. Mem. AAUP, Nat. Coll. Art Assn. (lectr. 1993), Mid-Am. Coll. Art Assn. (lectr. 1991, 92), Internat. Friends of Transformative Art (co-editor The Transformer newsletter) Fountain Hills Art League, Ariz. Artists' Guild, Chgo. Artists' Coalition, Sch. Art Inst. Chgo. Alumni Assn., Ariz. Women's Caucus for Art (pres. 1994). Democrat. Presbyterian. Avocations: painting, bookbinding, archaeology, mexican culture. Address: 16615 E Gunsight Dr Unit 101 Fountain Hills AZ 85268

MANTYLA, KAREN, distance learning consultant; b. Bronx, NY, Dec. 31, 1944; d. Milton and Sylvia (Diamond) Fischer; 1 child, Michael Alan. Student, Rockland Community Coll., Suffern, N.Y., 1962, NYU, 1967, Mercer U., 1981. Mktg. coordinator Credit Bur., Inc., Miami, Fla., 1973-79; dist. mgr. The Research Inst. Am., N.Y.C., 1979-80, regional dir., 1980-85, field sales mgr., 1985-86, nat. sales mgr., 1986-87; nat. accounts mgr. The Rsch. Inst. Am., N.Y.C., 1989; v.p. sales Bur. Bus. Practice/Paramount Comm., Inc., Waterford, Conn., 1989-93; pres. Quiet Power, Inc., Washington, 1993—. Author: Consultative Sales Power, 1995, Interactive Distance Learning Exercises That Really Work, 1999, The 2000/2001 ASTD Distance Learning Yearbook, 2000, Blending e-Learning: The Power is in the Mix, 2001; co-editor The 2001/2002 ASTD Distance Learning Yearbook; co-author: Distance Learning: A Step-By-Step Guide for Trainers, 1997, Blending E-Learning: The Power is in the Mix, 2001. Bd. dirs. Federal Govt. Distance Learning Assn. Named to Distance Learning Hall of Fame, Fed. Govt. Distance Learning Assn., 2003. Mem. ASTD, Sales and Mktg. Execs. (past bd. dirs. N.Y. chpt., v.p. Ft. Lauderdale chpt. 1979), U.S. Distance Learning Assn. (editor Distance Learning News, mem. tech. and comm. com. Fla. chpt.), Nat. Assn. Women Bus. Owners, U.S. C. of C., Women Entrepreneurs. Avocations: antiques, tennis, writing, swimming. Home: 6500 Majestic Prince Loop Gainesville VA 20155 Office: Quiet Power Inc 1201 Pennsylvania Ave NW Washington DC 20004-2401 E-mail: quietpower@aol.com.

MANUEL, JENNY LYNN, elementary education educator; b. Pomeroy, Ohio, Jan. 17, 1964; d. Charles Raymond and Osie Evelyn (Snyder) M. BS in Elem. Edn. magna cum laude, Rio Grande Coll., 1986; MA in Tcrh. Edn., U. Dayton, 1989. Cert. elem. tcrh., Ohio. Chpt. 1 reading tchr. So. Local Schs., Letart and Syracuse, Ohio, 1986-88; substitute tchr. Meigs County Schs., Pomeroy, Ohio, 1988-91, Mason County Schs., Point Pleasant, W.Va., 1988-91; tchr. 6th grade So. Local Schs., Racine, Ohio, 1991—2001, So. Elem., 2001—. Active So. Elem. Sch. PTO. Mem. NEA, U. Dayton Alumni Assn., Phi Alpha Theta, Alpha Lambda Delta. Avocations: reading, shopping, outdoor activities, community involvment. Home: 49115 Manuel Rd Racine OH 45771-9725 Office: Letart Elem Sch SR 338 Racine OH 45771-0407

MANUEL, NANCY WILLIAMSON, elementary education educator, special education educator; b. Ft. Hood, Tex., June 26, 1949; d. Coolidge and Cora J. (Ledoux) Williamson; m. Edlee S. Manuel, Jr., Dec. 21, 1968; children: Melissa Anne, Marla Melain, Marcelite Marie. BA, MeNeese State U., Lake Charles, La., 1973; MEd, La. State U., 1975, cert. supervisory edn. adminstrn., 1988, postgrad., 1988—. Tchr. St. Landry Parish Pub. Schs., Opelousas, La., 1973-80, St. Edmund Elem. Sch., Eunice, La., 1980-85, Acadia Parish Pub. Schs., Crowley, La., 1988—. Master tchr. LATIP and LATEP, 1990. Leader Camp Fire, Eunice. Named Leader of Yr., Camp Fire, 1985, Elem. Tchr. of Yr., Acadia Parish, 1990. Mem. Assn. Profl. Educators La. (rep. 1988—), Am. Ednl. Rsch. Assn., Phi Kappa Phi, Beta Sigma Phi. Democrat. Roman Catholic. Avocations: camping, antiques, plays. Address: 208 Denier Dr Lafayette LA 70508-6519

MANUEL, RALPH NIXON, former private school executive; b. Frederick, Md., Apr. 21, 1936; s. Ralph Walter and Frances Rebecca (Nixon) M.; m. Sarah Jane Warner, July 22, 1960; children: Mark, David, Stephen, Bradley. AB, Dartmouth Coll., 1958; M.Ed., Boston U., 1967; PhD, U. Ill., 1971. Assoc. dean Dartmouth Coll., Hanover, N.H., 1971-72, dean of freshmen, 1972-75, dean, 1975-82; pres. Culver (Ind.) Acad. and Culver Edn. Found., 1982-99. Bd. dirs. Ind. Sch. Cen. States, 1986-99, chair, 1993-95. Mem. Assn. Mil. Colls. and Schs. of U.S. (pres., bd. dirs.), Nat. Assn. Ind. Schs. (bd. dirs. 1995-99).

MANUELIAN, LUCY DER, art educator, architecture educator; b. Arlington, Mass. AB in English lit., Radcliffe Coll.; MA in Art History, Boston U., 1975, PhD in Art History, 1980. Head teaching fellow Boston U., 1975-76; vis. lectr. Framingham State Coll., 1979-80; archivist Armenian Archtl. Archives Project, 1979-84; lectureship in Armenian art and architecture Tufts U., Harvard U., McGill U., Boston U., Boston Coll., U. Mass., 1984—89; Arthur H. Dadian and Ara Oztemel prof. Armenian art and archtl. history Tufts U., Medford, 1989—. Mus. cons. Dartmouth Coll.; lectr. Poly Inst., U. Erevan, USSR, U. Aarhus, Denmark, Courtauld Inst., England, McGill U., U. Mich., U. Pa., Harvard U., Brown U., U. Chgo., Columbia U., Northeastern U., UCLA, Dartmouth Coll., Wellesley Coll., Mt. Holyoke Coll., Queens Coll., Rutgers U., London Sch. Econs.; Libr. Congress lectr. Met. Mus. N.Y., cultural and cmty. orgns. U.S. and abroad; author/narrator 4 TV documentaries on Armenian art. Author: Armenian Architecture, 4 vols., 1981—88, Dictionary of Middle Ages, 1982—89, Dictionary of Art, The Gregorian Collection-Armenian Rugs, 1983, Weavers, Merchants and Kings: The Inscribed Rugs of Armenia, 1984; contbr. chapters to books, articles to profl. jours. Fellow to USSR, 1977-78, fellow Bunting Inst., Radcliffe Coll., 1971-73; Samuel H. Kress grantee Boston U., 1975, 78, Rsch. grantee Nat. Assn. for Armenian Studies and Rsch. to USSR, 1972, 78; sr. scholar grantee Am. Coun. Learned Socs./Soviet Acad. Scis., 1983; recipient Jack H. Kolligian award Nat. Assn. Armenian Studies and Rsch., 1981, Boyan award Armenian Students Assn., Woman of Achievement award Armenian Internat. Women's Assn., 1994, Kohar award Armenian Rugs Soc.; named to Boston U. Acad. Disting. Alumni, 1986, Armenian of Yr., Masons, 1990. Mem. Armenian Acad. Sci. (cons. Art Inst. symposium 1990—), Nat. Assn. Armenian Studies and Rsch. (adv. bd. 1991—), Soc. Armenian Studies, Aga Khan Program Islamic Architecture (affiliate), Middle East Studies Assn., Coll. Art Assn., Medieval Acad. Accademia Tiberina Rome (assoc.), Assn. Internat. Etudes Armeniennes, Nat. Assn. Armenian Studies & Rsch. (hon. life), Phi Beta Kappa (hon. Radcliffe Coll.). Achievements include research in archaeological projects using ground penetrating radar technology. Avocations: music, piano, tennis, the restoration of Medieval Armenian churches. Business E-Mail: lucy.manuelian@tufts.edu. E-mail: ldm@world.std.com.

MANUES, PATRICIA ANN, elementary education educator; b. Omaha, Feb. 15, 1951; d. Vance John and Catherine Ann (McDonald) Henning; m. Patrick Manues; children: Heather Marie, Christopher James. BA, U. No. Iowa, 1973. Tchr. Gilmore City (Iowa) - Bradgate Cmty. Schs., 1973-76, Eagle Grove (Iowa) Cmty. Schs., 1977—. Mem. Iowa Reading Assn., Internat. Reading Assn. Avocations: fabric crafts, reading. Bus. Office: Eagle Grove Schs 1015 NW 2nd St Eagle Grove IA 50533-1034 E-mail: pmanues@eagle-grove.k12.ia.us.

MANZER, RACHAEL LEE ELIZABETH, early childhood education educator; b. Hartford, Conn., Mar. 19, 1970; d. Stanley Joseph and Bonnie Anne Zimnoch. BS cum laude, Cen. Conn. State U., 1991. Cert. tchr. pre-kindergarten through grade 8, Conn. Vol. tchr. 1st grade Smalley Elem. Sch., New Britain, Conn., 1990; pre-practicum kindergarten tchr. Mark Twain Elem. Sch., Hartford, 1991; student tchr. grade 3 Ann Antolini Sch., New Hartford, Conn., 1991, tchr. grade 3, 1993—; long term subsititute tchr. grade 2 New Hartford Elem. Sch., 1992, tchr. kindergarten, 1992-93. Vol. Four on the Floor Overnight Read-a-thon program Ann Antolini Sch., 1991, 92, Family Math. Night program New Hartford Elem. Sch., 1992, 93, 94; planner/organizer comty. spl. events Fitzgerald's Foods, Simsbury, Conn., 1986—; leader Lichtfield County 4-H, Litchfield, Conn., pres., 1988-89; capt. Northwestern Softball Team, 1987; mem. Winsted (Conn.) Comty. Band, 1990—; mem. curriculum grant com., regional sci. com. Ann Antolini Elem. Sch. PTA, regional sci. project leadership team. Recipient Excellence in Leadership award Litchfield County 4-H, 1990, Medal for Leadership, 1988. Mem. Acad. Supervision and Devel., Tchrs. Applying Whole Lang., Kappa Delta Pi. Avocations: playing flute, softball, gardening, hiking, canoeing. Home: 12 Meadow St New Hartford CT 06057-2313 Office: Ann Antolini Elem Sch 725 Litchfield Tpke New Hartford CT 06057-3107

MANZIONE, ARTHUR P. parochial schools administrator; b. Bklyn., May 20, 1943; s. Peter Anthony and Concetta Maria (Moscato) M. BA in Social Studies, St. Francis Coll., Bklyn., 1969; MS in Edn., Fordham U., 1978; postgrad., St. John's U., Queens, N.Y., 1977; postgrad. Catechical Inst., St. Joseph's Sem., 1978-79. Deacon, Roman Cath. Ch. Tchr. 6th grade St. Mary's Star of the Sea Sch., Bklyn., 1965-67; tchr. 7th grade Assumption Sch., S.I., 1967-72; asst. prin. Our Lady of Good Counsel Sch., S.I., 1972-74; prin. Sacred Heart Sch., Newburgh, N.Y., 1974-83; edn. specialist U.S. Army, West Point, N.Y., 1983-88; prin. Holy Family Sch., Bronx, N.Y., 1988-91; dist. supt. Archdiocese of N.Y., White Plains, 1991—. Mem. parish bd. edn. Sacred Heart Sch., Newurgh, N.Y., 1974-83; mem. parish coun. Holy Family Parish, Bronx, 1988-91. Named Support Person of Yr., U.S. Recruiting Bn. Newburgh, 1986. Republican. Avocations: reading, baseball, travel. Home: 15 Greenridge Ave Apt 14 White Plains NY 10605-1249 Office: Dist Supt Sch 950 Mamaroneck Ave White Plains NY 10605-3526

MAPEL, DOUGLAS WAYNE, epidemiologist, educator, health facility administrator; b. Torrejon U.S. AFB, Madrid, Spain, Apr. 14, 1961; m. Vesta Marie Mapel (div. 2001). BS in Chemistry, U. Tex., Arlington, 1984; MD, U. Tex., Galveston, 1988; MPH, U. N.Mex., 1996. Diplomate Am. Bd. Internal Medicine, Am. Bd. Pulmonary Diseases, Am. Bd. Critical Care Medicine. Resident Tex. Tech. U., Lubbock, 1988—92; fellow U. N.Mex., Albuquerque, 1992—96, asst. prof., 1996—2000, clin. prof., 2001—; med. dir. Lovelace Respiratory Rsch. Inst., Albuquerque, 2001—. Co-author: (book) Rom's Occupational Medicine, 1996, Occupational Pulmonary Disease, 2001. Fellow: Am. Coll. Chest Physicians; mem.: ACP, Am. Thoracic Soc. Home: PO Box 51537 Albuquerque NM 87181 Office: Lovelace Respiratory Rsch Inst 2441 Ridge Crest Dr SE Albuquerque NM 87108

MAPLE, MARILYN JEAN, educational media coordinator; b. Turtle Creek, Pa., Jan. 16, 1931; d. Harry Chester and Agnes (Dobbie) Kelley; 1 child, Sandra Maple. BA, U. Fla., 1972, MA, 1975, PhD, 1985. Journalist various newspaper including Mountain Eagle, Jasper, Ala., Boise (Idaho) Statesman, Daytona Beach (Fla.) Jour., Lorain (Ohio) Jour.; account exec. Frederides & Co., N.Y.C.; prodr. hist. films Fla. State Mus., Gainesville, 1967-69; writer, dir., prodr. med. and sci. films and TV prodns. for 6 medically related colls. U. Fla., Gainesville, 1969—. Pres. Media Modes, Inc., Gainesville. Author: On the Wings of a Butterfly; columnist Health Care Edn. mag.; contbr. Fla. Hist. Quar. Recipient Blakslee award, 1969, spl. award, 1979; Monsour lectr., 1979. Mem. Health Edn. Media Assn. (bd. dirs., awards 1977, 79), Phi Delta Kappa, Kappa Tau Alpha. Home: 1927 NW 7th Ln Gainesville FL 32603-1103 Office: U Fla PO Box 16J Gainesville FL 32602-0016 E-mail: mmaple@atlantic.net.

MAPLES, MARY LOU, elementary education educator; Tchr. kindergarten Lessie Moore Elem. Sch., Pineville, La., 1974-97; early childhood Title I supr. Media Ctr., Pineville, 1997—. Recipient La. Tchr. of Yr. award La. Dept. Edn., 1992. Office: Media Ctr PO Box 1230 Alexandria LA 71309-1230 E-mail: maplesm@rapides.k12.la.us.

MAPOTHER, DILLON EDWARD, physicist, university official; b. Louisville, Aug. 22, 1921; s. Dillon Edward and Edith (Rubel) M.; m. Elizabeth Beck, June 29, 1946; children: Ellen, Susan, Anne. BS in Mech. Engring, U. Louisville, 1943; D.Sc. in Physics, Carnegie-Mellon U., 1949. Engr. Westinghouse Rsch. Labs., East Pittsburgh, Pa., 1943-46; instr. Carnegie Inst. Tech., Pitts., 1946; mem. faculty U. Ill., Urbana, 1949-94, prof. physics, 1959-94, dir. acad. computing services, 1971-76, assoc. vice chancellor for rsch., 1976-94, acting dean grad. coll., vice chancellor research, 1977-78, assoc. dean grad. coll., 1979-94, assoc. vice chancellor rsch. emeritus, 1995—, assoc. dean emertus grad. coll., prof. emeritus physics, 1995—. Cons. in field. DuPont fellow, 1947-49; Alfred P. Sloan fellow, 1958-61; Guggenheim fellow, 1960-61 Fellow Am. Phys. Soc.; mem. AAAS, Assn. Univ. Tech. Mgrs., Am. Assn. Physics Tchrs., Sigma Xi. Achievements include research on ionic mobility in alkali halides, thermodynamic properties of superconductors, calorimetric study of critical points, administration of university research, commercialization of academic research technology. Home: 1013 Ross Dr Champaign IL 61821-6631 Office: U Ill Physics Dept Loomis Lab 1110 W Green St Urbana IL 61801-9013 E-mail: mapother@staff.uiuc.edu.

MAPP, ALF JOHNSON, JR., writer, historian; b. Portsmouth, Va., Feb. 17; s. Alf Johnson and Lorraine (Carney) M.; m. Hartley Lockhart, Mar. 28, 1953; 1 son, Alf Johnson III; m. Ramona Hartley Hamby, Aug. 1, 1971. AA, Coll. William and Mary, 1945, AB summa cum laude, 1961. Editorial writer Portsmouth Star, 1945-46, assoc. editor, 1946-48, editorial chief, 1948-54; news editor, editorial writer Virginian-Pilot, Norfolk, 1954-58; free-lance writer, 1958—; lectr. Old Dominion U., 1961-62, instr., 1962-67, asst. prof. English and history, 1967-73, asso prof. English, journalism, creative writing, history, 1973-79, prof., 1979-82, eminent prof., 1982-89, eminent scholar, 1989-92, eminent scholar emeritus, 1992—, Louis I. Jaffe prof. English, 1990-92; Louis I. Jaffe prof. emeritus, 1992—. Radio commentator WSAP, Portsmouth, Va., 1947-48; profl. lectr., 1984—; frequent analyst or guest on radio and TV including individual stas. and Universal Studio and BBC radio networks, CBS-TV, 1985—, C-SPAN, 1998—, PBS, 2001, NPR, 2001, CNN, 2001—; mem. Nat. Jefferson-Hemings Scholars commn., 2001-2002. Host TV series Jamestown to Yorktown, 1975-77; author: The Virginia Experiment, 1975, 3d edit., 1987, Frock Coats and Epaulets, 1963, 5th edit., 1996, America Creates Its Own Literature, 1965, Just One Man, 1968, The Golden Dragon: Alfred the Great and His Times, 1974, 4th edit., 1990, Thomas Jefferson: A Strange Case of Mistaken Identity, 1987, 3d edit., 1989 (Book-of-Month Club feature selection 1987), Thomas Jefferson: Passionate Pilgrim, 1991, 3d edit., 1993 (Book-of-Month Club feature selection 1991), (novel) Bed of Honor, 1995, 2d edit., 2000, Three Golden Ages: Discovering the Creative Secrets of Renaissance Florence, Elizabethan England, and America's Founding, 1998, Faiths of our Fathers: What America's Founders Really Believed, 2003; co-author: Chesapeake Bay in the Revolution, 1981, Portsmouth: A Pictorial History, 1989, Constitutionalism: Founding and Future, 1989, Constitutionalism and Human Rights, 1991, Great American Presidents, 1995; mem. editl. bd. Jamestown Found., 1967—; author lyrics for symphonic composition, world debut with Va. Symphony, 1998; author nationally distributed AP editl., 1998; contbr. to N.Y. Times, Wall St. Jour., other newspapers and mags. Mem. Portsmouth-Norfolk County Savs. Bond Com, 1948-51, Va. Com. on Libr. Devel., 1949-50; mem. publs. com. 350th Anniversary of Rep. Govt. in the Western World, 1966-69, War of Independence Commn., 1967-83; chmn. Portsmouth Revolutionary Bicentennial Com., 1968-81; chmn. awards jury Baruch award United Daus. Confederacy-Columbia U., 1976, mem., 1980; chmn. Portsmouth Mus. and Fine Arts Commn., 1983-85, Southeastern Va. Anglo-Am. Friendship Day, 1976, Bicentennial Commemoration of Cornwallis' Embarkation for Yorktown, 1981, World Premiere of Mary Rose Marine Archeol. Exhibit, 1985; mem. grant rev. com. Va. Commn. for the Arts, 1986-87; bd. dirs. Portsmouth Pub. Libr., 1948-58, v.p., 1954-56; bd. dirs. Va. Symphony, 1986-87, trustee, 1987—; mem. taxes and mandates com. City of Portsmouth, 1982-86; mem. adv. com. City Mgr. of Norfolk, 1988-94; bd. dirs. Portsmouth Area Cmty. Chest, 1948-52, Va. YMCA Youth and Govt. Found., 1950-52; mem. All-Am. cities com. for award-winning city Nat. League Municipalities, 1976; bd. advisors Ctr. Study Interactive Learning, Pasadena, Calif., 1993—; mem. steering com. Old Dominion U. Friends of the Libr., 1994-2002, dir., 1995-2002; trustee Coun. for Am.'s First Freedom, 1994-98; chair ad hoc com. Joint Portmouth-Suffolk Libr., 1999—; dir. Va. R.R. Mus., 2000--. Named Portsmouth Young Man of Year, 1951; recipient honor medal Freedoms Found., 1951, Disting. Rsch. award Old Dominion U., 1987, Great Citizen award Hampton Roads 8 Cities, 1987, Notable Citizen award Portsmouth, Va., 1987; English award Old Dominion Coll., 1961; Troubadour, Great Tchrs. award, 1969; Outsdanding Am. Educator award, 1972, 74; Nat. Bicentennial medal Am. Revolution Bicentennial Adminstrsn., 1976; medal Comité Francais du Bicentenaire de l'Independence des Etats-Unis, France, 1976; (with Ramona Mapp) Nat. Family Svc. award Family Found. Am., 1980; Laureate award Commonwealth of Va., 1981; Disting. Alumnus award Old Dominion U., 1982; Liberty Bell award Portsmouth Bar Assn., 1985; Old Dominion U. Triennial Phi Kappa Phi Scholar award, 1986, 91; History medal Daus. Am. Revolution; Portsmouth Downtown Merchants award, 1984, 85, Nat. Founders and Patriots award, 1995; Old Dominion U. Outstanding Achievement award, 1995; Gladstone Hill Friend of the Arts award (with Ramona H. Mapp), 1995, Richard Hakluyt award for Am. history, 1996; named to Order of the Crown of Charlemagne, 1993. Mem. Am. Hist. Assn., Va. Hist. Soc., Portsmouth Hist. Soc. (historiographer 1975-82, v.p. 1982-84, pres. 1985), Norfolk Hist. Soc. (dir. 1965-72), No. Neck Hist. Soc., Hist. Socs. Eastern Va. (dir. 1971—), SAR, Am. Assn. U. Profs., Authors Guild, Va. Library Assn. (legislative com. 1950-51), Poetry Soc. Va. (pres. 1974-75, adv. com. 1976—), Va. Writers Club, Assn. Preservation of Va. Antiquities, Order of Cape Henry (dir. 1970—, nat. pres. 1975-76), Jamestowne Soc. (chief historian 1975-77, internat. sec. state 1978-79), English Speaking Union (dir. 1976-77), Modern Lang. Assn., Order of First Families Va. 1607-1624 (councillor 1996-99), Nat. Historians Circle, Phi Theta Kappa, Delta Phi Omega (chpt. pres. 1961), Phi Kappa Phi. Baptist. Home: Willow Oaks 2901 Tanbark Ln Portsmouth VA 23703-4828

MARABLE, ROBERT BLANE, secondary school educator, agricultural studies educator; b. Athens, Ga., Jan. 7, 1959; s. Robert S. and Judy M.; m. Judy ANdrews Marable, July 20, 1985; 1 child, Mary Ashley Marable. BSA, U. Ga., 1981, MEd, 1982, EDS, 1985. Agr. edn. instr. Winder-Barrow High Sch., Winder, Ga., 1981-82, Greene-Taliaferro Comp. High Sch., Greensboro, Ga., 1982-89, Morgan County High Sch., Madison, Ga., 1989-98, Area Forestry Inst. Ga. Dept. Edn., 1998—. Named Young Agr. Tchr. of Yr., Ga., 1985, Tchr. of Yr. Morgan County Sch. System, 1992, Nat. Conservation Tchr. of Yr. Soil Conservation Svc., 1992, Youth Conservation Group of Yr., Ga. Wildlife Fedn., 1992. Mem. Ga. Vocat. Assn., Nat. Vocat. Assn., Ga. Vocat. Agr. Tchr's. Assn., Nat. Vocat. Agr. Tchr's Assn., profl. Assn. Ga. Educators Assn., Ga. Conservancy, Ga. Wildlife Fedn. Home: 1041 Buckeye Pointe Athens GA 30606-7617 Office: U Ga Four Towers Ga Dept Edn Athens GA 30602

MARAK, RANDY BARTON, computer educator; b. Waco, Tex., Feb. 26, 1962; s. Raymond J. and Rudy M. (Barton) M.; m. Judith Ross Standifer, Dec. 26, 1987 (div.); children: Eleanor, Michelle; m. Kelli Lynn Basye, May 13, 2002. BA, Baylor U., 1985; MBA, Tarleton State U., Stephenville, Tex., 1992; postgrad., U. North Tex., 1988-90. Cons. KRZI Radio, Waco, 1984-85; dir. KHBR Radio/Reporter Newspaper, Hillsboro, Tex., 1979-92; head computer sci. dept. Hill Coll., Hillsboro, Tex., 1985—, dir. info. sys. and computer ops., 1994-2000, divsn. dir. computer and info. tech., 2000—. Mem. ACM, SIGUCCS (spl. svcs.), Tex. C.C. Tchrs. Assn., Small Coll. Computing Consortium, Cleburne Lions Club, RVOS Soc., KJT Soc. Republican. Roman Catholic. Home: 2113 Pebblecreek Dr Cleburne TX 76033-7910 Office: Hill Coll Johnson County Campus PO Box 1899 Cleburne TX 76033-1899 E-mail: marak@hill-college.cc.tx.us.

MARANS, ROBERT WARREN, architect, planner; b. Detroit, Aug. 3, 1934; s. Albert and Anne Rose (Siegel) M.; m. Judith Ann Bloomfield, Jan. 24, 1956; children: Gayl Elizabeth, Pamela Jo. BArch, U. Mich., 1957; M in Urban Planning, Wayne State U., 1961; PhD, U. Mich., 1971. Reg. architect, Mich. Archtl. engr., planner Detroit City Planning Commn., 1957-61; planning cons. Blair & Stein Assocs., Providence, 1961-64; architect-urban designer Artur Glikson, Architect, Tel Aviv, Israel, 1964-65; regional planner Detroit Area Transp. Land Use Study, 1965-67; asst. prof. Fla. State U., Talahassee, 1967; rsch. assoc., sr. study dir. Inst. Social Rsch., Ann Arbor, Mich., 1968-74, sr. rsch. scientist, 1974—; from lectr. to assoc. prof. Coll. Architecture Urban Planning, Ann Arbor, 1971-78; prof. architecture and urban planning U. Mich., Ann Arbor, 1978—. Cons. TVA, 1972, UN, 1974; chmn. urban and regional planning program, 1987-98. Co-author: Planned Residential Environments, 1970, Quality of NonMetropolitan Living, 1978, Evaluating Built Environments, 1981, Retirement Communities: An American Original, 1984; co-editor: Methods of Environmental and Behavioral Research, 1987, Environmental Stimulation: Research and Policy Perspectives, 1993, Advances in Environment, Behavior and Design, vol. IV, 1997; contbr. articles to profl. jours. and tech. reports. Sec. Washtenaw County Parks Recreation Commn., Ann Arbor, 1972—; chmn. Huron-Clinton Met. Parks Authority, Brighton, Mich., 1986—. Recipient fellow Social Sci. Rsch. Coun., 1969-70; Fulbright Rsch. award Coun. Internat. Exchange Scholars, Israel, 1977; Progressive Architecture Applied Rsch. award Progressive Architecture Mag., 1982; Design Rsch. Recognition award Nat. Endowment for Arts, 1983. Mem. Am. Planning Assn., Nat. Recreation Pk. Assn., Environ. Design Rsch. Assn. Avocations: swimming, stamp collecting. Office: U Mich Coll Arch and Urban Planning Ann Arbor MI 48109 E-mail: marans@umich.edu.

MARASALCO, LYNNE CALLIS, elementary education educator; b. Grenada, Miss., Sept. 7, 1950; d. Woodrow Wilson and Ora Belle (Lott) Callis; m. Louis C. Marascalco, Aug. 16, 1970; children: Amanda Katherine, Louis C. III. B Elem. Edn., Delta State U., 1972, M Elem. Edn., 1978, specialist in elem. edn., 1993. Cert. tchr., Miss. Tchr. upper elem. grades Grenada Pub. Schs., 1972-79, tchr. primary grades, 1979—. Rep. supt.'s adv. com., Grenada Pub. Schs. Tchr. St. Peter's Cath. Ch., Grenada. Mem. Jaycettes. Republican. Roman Catholic. Avocations: reading, music, handcrafts. Home: PO Box 312 Grenada MS 38902-0312 Office: Grenada Pub Sch System Jackson Ave Grenada MS 38901

MARASHIO, PAUL WILLIAM, humanities educator; b. Woburn, Mass., May 30, 1941; s. Peter and Catherine (Danizio) M.; m. Nancy Feeney, June 24, 1967. BEd, Keene State Coll., 1963; MA, U. N.H., 1968; cert. advanced studies, Wesleyan U., 1977. Tchr., Somersworth, N.H., 1963-66; history dept. head Salem, N.H., 1966-69; supr. instrn. and curriculum, 1969-71; prin. Woodbury Sch., Salem, 1971-77; curriculum coord. Salem Sch. Dist., 1977-83, educator, 1983-86; prof. humanities N.H. Cmty. Tech Coll., Claremont, 1986—. Mem. N.H. Excellence in Edn. Commn., 1983-84. Editor: Myth in U.S. Culture; editor Pedagogy Jour.; contbr. articles to profl. jours. Pres. Salem Hist. Soc., 1977-80; mem. Salem Com. on Environ. Issues, 1977, Old Town Hall Restoration Com., Salem Mus. Com.; rschr. N.H. Bicentenial Celebration U.S. Constn., 1985. Recipient award N.H. Coun. Better Schs., 1974, Tchrs. Who Inspire award Lawrence Eagle Tribune, 1983; Ariz. State U. fellow, 1968; scholar U.S. Constn. Bicentenial, 1986—. Mem. Am. Hist. Assn., Orgn. Am. Historians, Coll. Humanities Assn., Nat. Assn. for Humanities Edn., Sunapee Yacht Club, Phi Delta Kappa. Roman Catholic. Address: PO Box 2211 Mount Sunapee NH 03255-2211

MARAZITA, ELEANOR MARIE HARMON, retired secondary education educator; b. Madison County, Ind., Oct. 25, 1933; d. William Houston Harmon and Martha Belle (Savage) Hinds; m. Philip Marazita; children: Mary Louise, Frank, Dominic, Vincent, Elizabeth Faye, Candice Marie, Daniel William. BS in Home Econs., Ctrl. Mich. U., 1955; MA in Human Ecology, Mich. State U., 1971. Cert. vocat. home econs. tchr., K-Jr. Coll., cert. speech correction tchr. Tchr. adult edn., Mt. Pleasant, Mich., 1956; substitute tchr. North Branch (Mich.) Schs., 1961-64; tchr. Pied Piper Coop. Nursery Sch., Lansing, Mich., 1964-69, Lansing C.C., 1971-81, Grand Ledge (Mich.) H.S., 1969-98. Mich. tchr. del. World Conf. Tchg. Profls., 1985, 98; adv. mem. Mich. Tchr. Competency Testing Program, 1992. Bd. dirs. Greater Lansing chpt. U.N., 1995-98; vol. St. Lawrence Mental Health Hosp., 1972-73, Listening Ear Crisis Intervention Ctr., 1973-77, Capital City Convalescent Home, 1969-73; chmn. study com. Delta Twp. Libr., 1969-73, Jr. League, 1969—; interviewer Youth for Understanding, 1978-83; active exch. student orientation program Mich. State U., 1977, exch. trips, 1979-82; mem. adv. bd. Mich. League Human Svcs., 1988-91, Eaton County Extension Svcs., 1988-91, Mich. Women's Assembly, 1986-91; mem. Friends of Waverly Libr., 1963—; participant 3rd Congress Educators Caucus, 1986-92; 4-H leader, 1950-65. Recipient State Tchr. Multicultural award, 1989, UN Global Educator award, 1991, State Tchr. Maureen Wyatt feminist award, 1996. Mem. AAUW, LWV, NEA (del. 1998, observer 2d ann. Ednl. Internat. Congress 1998), DAR (co-chair State Good Citizen 1999-2003), DAR (v.p. Cameo Club 2002—), PEO, Mich. Edn. Assn. (polit. action exec. bd. 1986-98, v.p. women's caucus 1986-93, Liz Siddell State Internat. Cultures award 1992), Circumnavigators Club (travel around world in one trip 1993), Century Club (travel in 100 countries outside U.S. 1994, Seven Continent award 2003, Globetrotter award 2003), Delta Kappa Gamma (co-chair State World Fellowship 1993-95, chair state legislation com. 1997-99, chpt. Women of Distinction award 1993), Phi Delta Kappa (Tchr. of Yr. Mich. State U. 1992). Avocation: travel. Home: 214 Farmstead Ln Lansing MI 48917-3015

MARBURGER, DARLA A. federal agency administrator; d. Maynard and Dawn Marburger. BS in agr. Journalism, Tex. A&M U.; MS in agr. econ., Tex. A&M. Dep. asst. sec. US Dept. Edn., Off. Elem. Sec. Edn. Policy, Wash., 2002—; sr. policy analyst Tex. Senate Edn. Com., Tex.; Congl. adv., agr. nat. resources issues Tex. Leg., Tex., 1994. Vol. tchr. ESL. Office: US Dept Edn Policy Dept FOB-6 Rm 3W305 400 Maryland Ave SW Washington DC 20202 Office Fax: 202-205-0303. E-mail: darla.marburger@ed.gov.

MARCEAU, JUDITH MARIE, retired elementary school educator, small business owner; b. Gardner, Mass., Aug. 10, 1946; d. George Joseph and Bernice Victoria (Johnson) Babineau; m. James Victor Krymowski, Aug. 20, 1976 (div. Mar. 1985); children: Kathryn Victoria, Kenneth James; m. Glenn Francis Marceau, Aug. 30, 1989. Grad., Sch. Worcester Art Mus., 1967; BFA, Clark U., 1971. Tchr. elem. art Quabbin Regional Pub. Schs., Barre, Mass., 1967-70, Gardner (Mass.) Pub. Schs., 1970—2003, ret., 2003. Author, editor: Fascinating Facts of Gardner, 1977, 2d edit., 1999, Hubbardston as Seen Through the Eyes of its Children, 1987; author numerous poems. Active Hubbarston Hist. Commn.; vol. Hubbarston Recycling Initiative; bd. dirs. Gardner Edn. Assn., 1975-86; bd. dirs. Youth Advocacy and Counseling Ctr., Gardner, 1979-82. Recipient Citation of Outstanding Edn. City of Gardner, 1994, 2000, Cert. of Commendation, Mayor of City of Gardner. Mem. Mass. Tchrs. Assn., Nat. Tchrs. Assn. Avocations: writing history, poetry, antiques, watercolor painting, sketching. Home: 221 Gardner Rd Hubbardston MA 01452-1655 Office: Elm Street Sch 160 Elm St Gardner MA 01440

MARCELLO, FRANK F. lawyer, educator, writer; b. Chgo., Aug. 11, 1961; s. Fred Anthony and Antoinette Marie (Colombo) M. BS, DePaul U., 1983; MBA, Dominican U., 1996; JD, The John Marshall Law Sch., 1986. Exec. legal coord. Office of Cook County Pub. Defender, Chgo., 1985-87, asst. dep. chief, 1987-89; v.p. exec. counsel Connaught Corp., Chgo., 1989-93; v.p. sr. counsel Internat. Cons. Group, Chgo., 1993-96; prof. law Northwestern Bus. Coll., Chgo., 1996—, Dominican U., River Forest, Ill., 1996—. Active Joint Civic Com. Italian Ams., Chgo. Mem. ABA, AAUP, Justiniam Soc., Nat. Italian Am. Bar Assn., Sons of Italy Found., Assn. Cath. Colls. and Univs. Office: Dominican U 7900 W Division St River Forest IL 60305 E-mail: ffm@abanet.org.

MARCH, CATHLEEN CASE, education educator; b. Port Jervis, N.Y., Dec. 8, 1942; d. Fred Baker Case and Elizabeth (Mayes) Allen; children: Elizabeth, Brian, Matthew, Melinda. BS, U. Pa., 1963; MS, SUNY, Buffalo, 1979, PhD, 1998. Cert. K-12 tchr., N.Y. 1st grade tchr. Anna Merritt Sch., Lockport, N.Y., 1964-65; kindergarten tchr. Dewitt Clinton Sch., Lockport, N.Y., 1966-69; asst. librarian Lockport Pub. Libr., 1970-72; reading tchr. Starpoint Ctrl. Sch., Lockport, 1975-78, Medina (N.Y.) Ctrl. Schs., 1979-98; prof. D'Youville Coll., 1998—. Adj. prof. Canisius Coll., Buffalo, 1992-98. Editor: Niagara Frontier Reading Coun., 1991-96. Named Educator of Excellence N.Y. State English Coun., 1994. Mem. Internat. Reading Assn., N.Y. State Reading Assn. (Svc. to Reading award 1996), Niagara Frontier Reading Coun. (pres. 1997-98). Avocations: reading, writing. Home: 6801 Lilac Dr Apt A Lockport NY 14094-6824 E-mail: Cathymarch@adelphia.net.

MARCHAND, SHEILA ANNE HALEY, special education educator, consultant; b. Hartford, Conn., Sept. 7, 1948; d. Edward Patrick and Ida (Sheehan) Haley; m. Gerald Francis Marchand, Feb. 8, 1975; children: David, Marcella, Christopher. BS cum laude, St. Bonaventure U., 1971; MS, Ctrl. Conn. State Coll., 1977. Cert. elem. edn. N-6, special edn. 1-12. Tchr. Eng. grades 6-8 Diocese of Niagara Falls, N.Y., 1971; elem. tchr. Hartford Pub. Schs., 1972-77; tutor special edn. Newington Pub. Sch., W. Hartford, 1978-79; tchr. special edn. W. Hartford Pub. Sch., 1980-81, tchr. Eng., 1982; kindergarten tchr. Hartford Pub. Schs., 1983-86, preschool special edn. tchr., 1986-90, cons., 1990—. Facilitator Learning/Teaching Inst. of Conn., 1992; cons. Head Start, Hartford Day Care, 1990—. Presenter in field. Mem. Nat. Assn. Edn. Young Children, Coun. of Exceptional Children Divsn. Early Childhood, Assn. Supervision and Curriculum Devel. Office: Hartford Pub Schs Simpson-Waverly Sch 55 Waverly St Hartford CT 06112-1625

MARCHANT, GREGORY JOHN, education educator; b. South Bend, Ind., Jan. 21, 1956; s. John and Lillian Marchant; m. Sharon E. Paulson, July 11, 1998. BS in Spl. Edn., Ind. U., South Bend, 1978, MS in Spl. Edn., 1982; PhD in Teaching and Learning, Northwestern U., 1988. Resource rm. tchr. Jimtown High Sch., Elkhart, Ind., 1978-82, Lake Ctrl. High Sch., Spl. Edn. Coop., Munster, Ind., 1983-84; coord., asst. prof. Moraine Valley Cmty. Coll., Palos Hills, Ill., 1982-86; psychology instr. Robert Morris Coll., Chgo., 1984; learning resource ctr. dir. Northwestern U., Evanston, Ill., 1986-87; adj. faculty edn. U. Wis.-Parkside, Kenosha, 1987-88; acad. staff ednl. psychology U. Wis.-Milw., 1988-89; prof. ednl. founds. U. Akron, Ohio, 1989-90; prof. ednl. psychology Ball State U., Muncie, Ind., 1990—. Com. of examiners Ednl. Testing Svc., Princeton, N.J., 1994-97. Contbr. articles to profl. jours. Sch. bd. selection com. Citizens Sch. Orgn., Indpls., 1994, 96. Mem. APA (divsn. 15, newsletter assoc. editor 1994-97), Am. Ednl. Rsch. Assn. (Lindquis award com. 1993-95, S.I.G. chair 1994-95), Midwest Assn. Tchr. Ednl. Psychology (program chair 1990), Mid-Western Ednl. Rsch. Assn. (pres. 1995—, editor 1991-93), Phi Delta Kappa. Office: Ball State U Ednl Psych Tc Muncie IN 47306-0595 E-mail: gmarchant@bsu.edu.

MARCHANT, MAURICE PETERSON, librarian, educator; b. Peoa, Utah, Apr. 20, 1927; s. Stephen C. and Beatrice (Peterson) M.; m. Gerda VaLoy Hansen, June 3, 1949; children: Catherine, Barrie, Alan, Roxanne, Claudia, David, Theresa. BA, U. Utah, 1949, MS, 1953; AM in Libr. Sci., U. Mich., 1966, MA, 1968, PhD, 1970. Tchr. area h.s., Altamont, Utah, 1949-50; libr. area h.s. Salt Lake City and Preston, Idaho, 1950-53; chief tech. libr. Dugway (Utah) Proving Ground, 1953-58; libr. Carnegie Free Libr., Ogden, Utah, 1958-66; mem. faculty Brigham Young U., Provo, Utah, 1969-92, prof. libr. and info. scis., 1976-92, dir. Sch. Libr. and Info. Scis., 1975-82; prof. emeritus libr. and info. scis. Brigham Young U. (Sch. Library and Info. Scis.), Provo, Utah, 1992—. Exec. dir. Nat. Libr. Week, Utah, 1961-62. Author: Participative Management in Academic Libraries, 1976, SPSS as a Library Research Tool, 1977, Books That Made a Difference in Provo, 1989, Why Adults Use the Public Library, 1994, also articles. Served with USN, 1945-46. Mid-career fellow Coun. Libr. Resources, 1972. Mem. AAUP, ALA (rsch. paper award Libr. Rsch. Round Table 1975), Utah Libr. Assn. (pres. 1964-65, Disting. Svc. award 1986). Address: 2877 N 220 E Provo UT 84604-3906

MARCHESE, MELISSA J. special education educator, director; b. Queens, N.Y., Nov. 2, 1959; d. James R. and Marilyn (Ackerina) M.; m. Kevin M. Dougherty, Feb. 4, 1989. BA, St. Joseph's Coll., Bklyn., 1981; MS, SUNY, Albany, 1982; postgrad., Queens Coll., 1991. Cert. sch. adminstrn., N.Y. Devel. specialist Builders for Family and Youth, Bklyn., 1982-83; spl. educator Brookdale Hosp. Bruner Devel. Disabilities Ctr., Bklyn., 1983-86, Interdisciplinary Ctr. for Child Devel., Queens, 1986-87, ednl. dir., 1988—. Grad. fellow Rsch. Found., SUNY, Albany, 1981. Mem. Coun. for Exceptional Children, Div. for Early Childhood., Nat. Assn. Edn. Young Children. Avocations: gardening, cycling, travel, cooking. Office: Interdisciplinary Ctr for Child Devel 98-02 62nd Dr Rego Park NY 11374-1741

MARCOCCIA, LOUIS GARY, accountant, university administrator; b. Syracuse, NY, Nov. 6, 1946; s. George A. and Rose J. (Misita) M.; m. Susan Evelyn Miller, June 21, 1974; 1 child: Rachel Kathryn. BS, Syracuse U., 1968, MS, 1969; EdD, U. Pa., 2003. CPA, N.Y. Acct. Price Waterhouse & Co., Syracuse, N.Y., 1969-75; dir. internal audit Syracuse U., 1975-76, comptroller, 1976-82, v.p., comptroller, 1982-95, sr. v.p. bus., and fin., 1985-95, sr. v.p. bus., fin. and adminstrv. svcs., 1995—. Bd. dirs. Syracuse Bd. Chase Manhattan Bank, Syracuse Divsn., 1985-2001, Lincoln Life and Annuity Co. N.Y., Univ. Hill Corp., Upstate Med. Univ. Found.; pres. Syracuse U. Hotel and Conf. Ctr., LLC; spkr. Harvard U. Inst. Ednl. Mgmt., 1984-88, 90-91. Pres. parish coun. St. Michael's Ch., Syracuse, 1985-88; pres. Syracuse U. Theatre Corp., 1987—; bd. dirs. Friends of Burnet Park Zoo, 1987-93, Syracuse U. Press., 1982—, Syracuse Sports Corp., 1990-91. Mem. AICPA, N.Y. Soc. CPA, Nat. Assn. Accts., Fin. Execs. Inst., Inst. Internal Auditors. Clubs: Drumlins (pres. 1976—); Century. Republican. Roman Catholic. Avocations: swimming, tennis. Home: Hedge Ln Cazenovia NY 13035 Office: Syracuse U Off of VP Bus Fin Adminstrv Svc Skytop Rd Syracuse NY 13244-0001 E-mail: lmarcocc@syr.edu.

MARCOPOULOS, GEORGE JOHN, history educator; b. Salem, Mass., June 30, 1931; s. John George and Urania Christou (Moustakis) M. BA, Bowdoin Coll., 1953; MA, Harvard U., 1955, PhD, 1966. Instr. Tufts U., Medford, Mass., 1961-66, asst. prof., 1966-71, assoc. prof., 1971-92, prof., 1992—. Contbr. articles to profl. jours. and Am. Ann. yearbooks. Bd. dirs. Gerondelis Found., Inc., Lynn, Mass., 1987—, treas., 1994—. Recipient Mellon Faculty Devel. grant Tufts U., 1983. Mem. AAUP, Am. Assn. Advancement Slavic Studies, Am. Hist. Assn., New Eng. Hist. Assn., Modern Greek Studies Assn., Phi Beta Kappa. Greek Orthodox. Avocations: music, films, reading, performing arts, excursions. Office: Tufts U Dept History East Hall Medford MA 02155

MARCUS, BERNARD ANDREW, biology educator; b. Springfield, Mass., Mar. 18, 1944; s. Martin and Rose (Buchman) M.; m. Joan Isabel Cushing, Aug. 19, 1967; children: Robert, Paul, Jerome, Justine. BS, Rider Coll., 1966; MA, Colgate U., 1967; MS, SUNY, Brockport, 1975; PhD, Columbia Pacific U., 1992. Instr. Genesee C.C., Batavia, N.Y., 1968-70, asst. prof., 1970-74, assoc. prof., 1974-78, prof. biology, 1978—. Mem. design com. Biol. Scis. Curriculum Study, Colorado Springs, Colo., 1995-96. Contbr. articles to profl. jours. Mem. Nat Edn Assoc, Soc of Sigma Xi, Nat. Assn. Biology Tchrs. Office: Genesee Cmty Coll 1 College Rd Batavia NY 14020-9703

MARCUS, CAROL A. counseling administrator, educator; b. St. Louis; d. Morton and Annabelle Adler; m. Daniel F. Marcus; 2 children. BA, Washington U., St. Louis, 1964, MA, 1967. History tchr. Mehlville H.S., St. Louis, 1965—66; guidance counselor High Point H.S., Beltsville, Md., 1967—68; fgn. student adv. Contra Costa (Calif.) Coll., 1968—69; career counselor U. Mo., St. Louis, 1969—70; counselor Marquette U., Milw., 1970—72; owner Regarding Women, Inc., Toledo, 1992—. Adv. bd. Womens Entreprenial Network, Toledo, 1996—2000, pres., 1999. Contbr. articles to local newspaper. Avocations: skiing, reading, sewing, knitting, genealogy. Office: Regarding Women Inc 1700 N Reynolds Rd Toledo OH 43615

MARCUS, H. LOUISE, special education educator, writer; b. Chgo., Apr. 10, 1928; d. Philip and Dora G. (Abraham) Moshel; m. Bernard Louis Marcus, Mar. 29, 1948; children: Bonnie Gail Marcus Graybill, Donald Lawrence, Leonard Michael, Sally Marcus Rodeman. AA, Wright Jr. Coll., Chgo., 1947; BA, U. Calif., Santa Barbara, 1967. Tchr. Temple B'nai B'rith, Santa Barbara, 1965-72; tutor handicapped Santa Barbara Adult Edn., 1991-94; aide Hollister Sch., Goleta, Calif., 1996—. Writer short stories. Program chmn. Orgn. for Rehab. Tng., 1990-93; pres. Hadassah, 1970-71. Mem. LWV, B'nai B'rith Sisterhood, Elderhostel. Democrat. Jewish. Avocations: writing, gardening, grandchildren.

MARCUS, HARRIS LEON, materials science educator; b. Ellenville, N.Y., July 5, 1931; s. David and Bertha (Messite) M.; m. Leona Gorker, Aug. 29, 1962; children: Leland, M'Risa. BS, Purdue U., 1963; PhD, Northwestern U., 1966. Registered profl. engr., Tex. Tech. staff Tex. Instruments, Dallas, 1966-68, Rockwell Sci. Ctr., 1968-70, group leader, 1971-75; prof. mech. engring. U. Tex., Austin, 1975-79, Harry L. Kent Jr. prof. mech. engring., 1979-90, Cullen Found. prof., 1980-95, dir. ctr. for Materials Sci. and Engring., dir. program, 1979-95; prof. metallurgy and materials engring., dir. Inst. for Material Sci., U. Conn., 1995—. Cons. numerous orgns. Contbr. numerous articles to profl. publs. Recipient U. Tex. faculty U. Tex. Engring. Found., 1983; Krengel lectr. Technion, Israel, 1983; Alumni Merit medal Northwestern U., 1988, Disting. Purdue Univ. Engring. Alumnus award, 1994. Fellow Am. Soc. Metals; mem. ASTM, ACS, AIME (bd. dirs. Metall. Soc. 1976-78, 84-86), Materials Rsch. Soc. Achievements include 22 patents. Home: 78 Ellise Rd Storrs Mansfield CT 06268-1424 Office: Inst Materials Scis 97 N Eagleville Rd Unit U-3136 Storrs Mansfield CT 06269-3136 E-mail: hmarcus@mail.ims.uconn.edu.

MARCUS, KAREN MELISSA, foreign language educator; b. Vancouver, B.C., Can., Feb. 28, 1956; came to the U.S., 1962; d. Marvin Marcus and Arlen Ingrid (Sahlman) Bishop; m. Jorge Esteban Mezei, Jan. 7, 1984 (div. Mar. 1987). BA in French, BA in Polit. Sci., U. Calif., Santa Barbara, 1978, MA in Polit. Sci., 1981; MA in French, Stanford U., 1984, PhD in French, 1990. Lectr. in French Stanford (Calif.) U., 1989-90; asst. prof. French No. Ariz. U., Flagstaff, 1990-96, assoc. prof. French, 1996—. Cons. Houghton Mifflin, 1993, Grand Canyon (Ariz.) Natural History Soc., 1994. Vol., letter writer Amnesty Internat. Urgent Action Network, 1991-95; vol. No. Ariz. Aids Outreach Orgn., Flagstaff, 1994-95. Recipient medal for outstanding achievement in French, Alliance Française, Santa Barbara, 1978; named Scholarship Exch. Student, U. Geneva, Switzerland, 1979-80; doctoral fellow Stanford (Calif.) U., 1981-85. Mem. MLA, Am. Assn. Tchrs. French, Am. Coun. on the Tchg. Fgn. Langs., Am. Literary Translators Assn., Women in French, Coordination Internat. des Chercheurs Sur Les Litteratures Maghrebines, Phi Beta Kappa, Pi Delta Phi, Alpha Lambda Delta. Democrat. Jewish. Avocations: walking, yoga, reading, writing short stories. Office: No Ariz Univ Modern Lang Dept PO Box 6004 Flagstaff AZ 86011-6004 E-mail: melissa.marcus@nau.edu.

MARCUS, LOLA ELEANOR, elementary and secondary education educator; b. Mass., Apr. 8, 1934; d. Wendel Phillip and Janice Eleanor (Padan) Shedd; m. Bruce Richard Marcus, May 30, 1953; children: Robert Bruce, Craig Donald, Brian Phillip. BS in Edn., Ohio State U., 1962; MA in Econs. Edn., Ohio U., 1982. Tchr. Columbus (Ohio) Pub. Schs., 1962—. Dir., cons. Sylvan Learning Ctr., Reynoldsburg, Ohio, 1984—. Elder Blvd. Presbyn. Ch., Columbus, 1990-93. Martha Holden Jennings Found. scholar, 1977-78. Mem. Columbus Edn. Assn. (bldg. rep. 1976), Order of Eastern Star, Alpha Delta Kappa Hon. Educators Sorority, Zeta Phi Eta, Alpha Chi Omega. Presbyterian. Home: 1177 Lincoln Rd Columbus OH 43212-3237

MARCUS, MARIA LENHOFF, lawyer, law educator; b. Vienna, June 23, 1933; came to U.S., 1938, naturalized, 1944; d. Arthur and Clara (Gruber) Lenhoff; m. Norman Marcus, Dec. 23, 1956; children: Valerie, Nicole, Eric. BA, Oberlin Coll., 1954; JD, Yale Law Sch., 1957. Bar: N.Y. 1961, U.S. Dist. Ct. (so. and ea. dists.) N.Y. 1962, U.S. Ct. Appeals (2d cir.) 1962, U.S. Supreme Ct. 1964. Assoc. counsel NAACP, N.Y.C., 1961-67; asst. atty. gen. N.Y. State, N.Y.C., 1967-78; chief litigation bur. Atty. Gen. N.Y. State, 1976-78; adj. assoc. prof. NYU Law Sch., 1976-78; assoc. prof. Fordham U. Law Sch., N.Y.C., 1978-86, prof., 1986—, Joseph M. McLaughlin prof., 1997—. Arbitrator Nat. Assn. Securities Dealers; chair subcom. interrogatories U.S. Dist. Ct. (so. dist.) N.Y., 1983-85. Contbr. articles to profl. jours. Recipient Teacher of Year award, Fordham Law School Students, 2001. Fellow N.Y. Bar Found.; mem. Assn. Bar City of N.Y. (v.p. 1995-96, long range planning com. 1996-2000, exec. com. 1976-80, com. audit 1988-95, labor com. 1981-84, judiciary com. 1975-76, chmn. civil rights com. 1972-75), N.Y. State Bar Assn. (exec. com. 1979-81, ho. dels. 1978-81, com. constitution and by-laws 1984-93), N.Y. Women's Bar Assn. (Pres.'s award 1999). Office: Fordham U Law Sch 140 W 62nd St New York NY 10023-7485

MARCUS, MARIANO NAKAMURA, secondary school principal; b. Weno Chuuk, Federated States Micronesia, Sept. 5, 1961; s. Teruo Ignacio and Machko Ursula (Nakamura) M.; m. Marcelly Kantito, Feb. 28, 1987; children: Antinina, Antinisi, Anter, Anterina, Ancher, Mariano, Mark Metek. BSW, U. Guam, Mangilao, 1986; MA, U. San Francisco, 1997. Registrar Xavier H.S., Weno Chuuk, 1979-80, dean students, 1981-83; rschr. Micronesian Seminar, Weno Chuuk, 1986-87; health educator Dept. Health, Weno Chuuk, 1987-89, mental health counselor, 1989-90; prin. Saramen Chuuk Acad., Weno Chuuk, 1990-96. Mem. rsch./devel. cadre Pacific Regional Ednl. Lab., Honolulu, 1992—. Sec.-treas. Mechitiw Village, Weno Chuuk, 1990—; chmn. Youth Commn., Weno Chuuk, 1992-94; bd. consultors Xavier H.S., Weno, 1992—; chmn. non-pub. schs., Weno, 1993—; mem. Close Up Washington Program, 1992-94. Mem. ASCD, Nat. Cath. Edn. Assn., Cath. Sch. Adminstrs. Roman Catholic. Office: Saramen Chuuk Academy PO Box 662 Chuuk FM 96942-0662

MARCUS, PAUL, law educator; b. N.Y.C., Dec. 8, 1946; s. Edward and Lillian (Rubin) M.; m. Rebecca Nimmer, Dec. 22, 1968; children: Emily, Beth, Daniel. AB, UCLA, 1968, JD, 1971. Bar: Calif. 1971, U.S. Dist. Ct. (cen. dist.) Calif. 1972, U.S. Ct. Appeals (D.C. cir.) 1972, U.S. Ct. Appeals (7th cir.) 1976. Law clk. U.S. Ct. Appeals (D.C. cir.), 1971-72; assoc. Loeb & Loeb, L.A., 1972-74; prof. law U. Ill., Urbana, 1974-83; dean Coll. Law U. Ariz., Tucson, 1983-88, prof., 1988-92; Haynes prof. law Coll. William and Mary, Williamsburg, Va., 1992—, interim dean, 1993-94, 97-98. Reporter, cons. Fed. Jud. Ctr. Commn. Author: The Entrapment Defense, 1989, 3d edit., 2003, The Prosecution and Defense of Criminal Conspiracy, 1978, 5th edit., 2002, Gilbert Law Summary, 1982, 7th edit., 2001, Criminal Law: Cases and Materials, 1982, 5th edit., 2003, Criminal Procedure in Practice, 2001, 2d edit., 2003; nat. reporter on criminal law Internat. of Comparative Law, 1978—. Nat. reporter on criminal law Internat. of Comparative Law, 1978—. Office: Coll William & Mary Law Sch PO Box 8795 Williamsburg VA 23187-8795 E-mail: pxmarc@wm.edu.

MARCUS, RICHARD LEON, lawyer, educator; b. San Francisco, Jan. 28, 1948; s. Irving Harry and Elizabeth (McEvoy) M.; m. Andrea June Saltzman, Apr. 26, 1981; 1 child, Ruth. BA, Pomona Coll., 1969; JD, U. Calif., Berkeley, 1972. Bar: Calif. 1973, U.S. Dist. Ct. (no. dist.) Calif. 1976, U.S. Dist. Ct. (cen. dist.) Calif. 1978, U.S. Ct. Appeals (9th cir.) 1981. Law clk. to judge Calif. Supreme Ct., San Francisco, 1972; assoc. Boalt Hall U. Calif., 1973-74; law clk. to judge U.S. Dist. Ct. Calif., San Francisco, 1974-75; from assoc. to ptnr. Dinkelspiel, Pelavin, Steefel & Levitt, San Francisco, 1976-81; assoc. prof. law U. Ill., Champaign, 1981-84, prof. law, 1984-89, U. Calif. Hastings Sch. Law, San Francisco, 1989-97, disting. prof. law, 1997-99, Horace O. Coil '57 prof. litigation, 1999—. Vis. prof. law U. Mich., 1986-87, U. Calif., Hastings, 1988; assoc. reporter Fed. Cts. Study Com., 1989-90; reporter com. civil motions Ill. Jud. Conf., Chgo., 1984, com. on evidence, 1985; cons. Nat. Commn. on Judicial Discipline and Removal, 1992-93; reporter Civil Justice Ref. Act Adv. Group No. Dist. of Calif., 1992-99, chair local rules adv. com. No. Dist. Calif., 1994-99; spl. reporter advisory commn. on the civil rules, jud. conf. of the U.S., 1996—; mem. 9th Cir. local rules and internal operating procedures com., 1996-2002, 9th Cir. task force on self-represented lit., 2002—. Author: Complex Litigation, 1985, 3rd edit., 1998, Civil Procedure: A Modern Approach, 1989, 3rd edit., 2000, Federal Practice and Procedure, vols. 8, 8A, and 12, 2d edit., 1994, 1997; rsch. editor U. Calif. Law Rev., 1971-72; contbr. articles to profl. jorus. Named Order of Coif. Mem. ABA, Am. Law Inst., Am. Assn. Law Schs. (chmn. sect. civil procedure 1988,chmn. complex litigation com. 1991). Democrat. Home: 70 Domingo Ave Berkeley CA 94705-2436 Office: U Calif Coll Law 200 Mcallister St San Francisco CA 94102-4707

MARCUS, RUDOLPH ARTHUR, chemist; b. Montreal, July 21, 1923; arrived in U.S., 1949, naturalized, 1958; s. Myer and Esther (Cohen) Marcus; m. Laura Hearne, Aug. 27, 1949 (dec. Jan. 2003); children: Alan Rudolph, Kenneth Hearne, Raymond Arthur. BS in Chemistry, McGill U., 1943, PhD in Chemistry, 1946, DSc (hon.), 1988, U. Chgo., 1983, Poly. U., 1986, U. Göteborg, Sweden, 1987, U. N.B., Can., 1993, Queens U., 1993, U. Oxford, Eng., 1995, Yokohama Nat. U., Japan, 1996, U. N.C., 1996, U. Ill., 1997, Technion-Israel Inst. Tech., 1998, Polytechnic U. Valencia, 1999, Northwestern U., 2000, U. Waterloo, Can., 2002. Rsch. staff RDX Project, Montreal, 1944—46; rsch. assoc. NRC of Can., Ottawa, 1946—49, U. N.C., 1949—51; asst. prof. Poly. Inst. Bklyn., 1951—54, assoc. prof., 1954—58, prof., 1958—64, acting head, div. phys. chem., 1961—62; prof. U. Ill., Urbana, 1964—78, head, div. phys. chem., 1967—68; Arthur Amos Noyes prof. chem. Calif. Inst. Tech., Pasadena, 1978—; vis. prof. theoretical chem. U. Oxford, 1975—76; Baker lectr. Cornell U., Ithaca, NY, 1991; Linnett vis. prof. chemistry Cambridge (Eng.) U., 1996; hon. prof. Fudan U., Shanghai, 1994—; hon prof. Inst. Chem. Chinese Acad. Scis., Beijing, 1995—; hon. fellow Univ. Coll., Oxford, 1995—; hon. prof. Tianjin U., China, 2002, China Ocean U., China, 2002. Professorial fellow Univ. Coll., Oxford, 1975—76; mem. Courant Inst. Math. Scis., NYU, 1960—61; trustee Gordon Rsch. confs., 1966—69; assoc. mem. Ctr. Advanced Studies, U. Ill., Urbana, 1968—69; chmn. bd. dirs. Gordon Rsch. confs., 1968—69, mem. coun., 1965—68; mem. rev. panel Brookhaven Nat. Lab., 1966—72, chmn., 1967—68; mem. rev. panel Brookhaven Nat. Lab., 1971—74; mem. rev. com.Radiation Lab., U. Notre Dame Radiation Lab., U. Notre Dame, 1975—80; mem. panel on atmospheric chemistry climatic impact com. NAS-NRC, 1975—78, mem. com. kinetics of chem. reactions, 1973—77, chmn., 1975—77, mem. com. chem. scis., 1977—79; lectr. in field, 1982; mem. com. to survey opportunities in chem. scis., 1982—86; mem. math. panel Internat. Benchmarking of U.S. Rsch. Fields, 1996—97; mem. panel on accountability of federally funded rsch. Com. on Sci., Engring. and Pub. Policy, 2000—01; adv. com. for chemistry NSF, 1977—80; external adv. bd. NAS Ctr. Photoinduced Charge Transfer, 1990—; mem. presdl. chairs com., Chile, 1994—96; advisor, Ctr. for Molecular Scis. Chinese Acad. Scis. and State Key Lab. for Structural Chemistry of Unstable and Stable Species, Beijing, 1995—; co-hon. pres. 29th Internat. Chemistry Olympiad, 1997; hon. visitor Nat. Sci. Coun., China, 1999. Former mem. editl. bd. Jour. Chem. Physics, Ann. Rev. Phys. Chemistry, Jour. Phys. Chemistry, Accounts Chem. Rsch., Internat. Jour. Chem. Kinetics Molecular Physics, Theoretica Chimica Acta, Chem. Physics Letters, Faraday Trans., Jour. Chem. Soc., editl. bd. Laser Chemistry, 1982—, Advances in Chem. Physics, 1984—, World Sci. Pub., 1987—, Internat. Revs. in Phys. Chemistry, 1988—, Progress in Physics, Chemistry and Mechanics (China), 1989—, Perkins Transactions 2, Jour. Chem. Soc., 1992—, Chem. Physics Rsch. (India), 1992—, Trends in Chem. Physics Rsch. (India), 1992—, hon. editor Internat. Jour. Quantum Chemistry, 1996—. Named Hon. Citizen, City of Winnipeg, 1994, Treasure of L.A., Ctrl. City Assn., 1995; recipient Anne Molson prize in chem., McGill U., 1943, Sr. U.S. Scientist award, Alexander von Humboldt-Stiftung, 1976, Electrochem. Soc. Lecture award, 1979, 1996, Robinson medal, Faraday divsn. Royal Soc. Chemistry, 1982, Centenary medal, 1988, Chandler medal, Columbia U., 1983, Wolf prize in Chem., 1985, Nat. medal of Sci., 1989, Evans award, Ohio State U., 1990, Nobel prize in Chem., 1992, Hirshfelder prize in Theoretical Chemistry, U. Wis., 1993, Golden Plate award, Am. Acad. Achievement, 1993, Lavoisier medal, French Chem. Soc., 1994, Oesper award, U. Cin., 1997, Key to City of Taipei, Taiwan, 1999, William Jost lectr. and medal, Deutsche Bunsenges and Acad. Sci., Göttingen, 1999; fellow Alfred P. Sloan, 1960—61, NSF sr. postdoctoral, 1960—61; scholar sr. Fulbright-Hays, 1972. Fellow: AAAS, Royal Soc. Can. (hon.), Internat. Acad. Quantum Molecular Sci. (hon.), Royal Soc. (London) (hon.), Royal Soc. Chemistry (hon.), Chinese Acad. Scis. (hon.), Internat. Soc. for Theoretical Chem. Physics (hon.), Am. Acad. Arts and Scis. (hon.; exec. com. western sect., co-chmn. 1981—84, rsch. and planning com. 1989—91), Internat. Soc. Electrochemistry (hon.); mem.: NAS (hon.), Am. Chem. Soc. (past divsn. chmn., mem. exec. com., mem. adv. bd. petroleum rsch. fund, Irving Langmuir award in chem. physics 1978, Peter Debye award in physic. chemistry 1988, Willard Gibbs medal Chgo. sect. 1988, S.C. Lind Lecture, East Tenn. sect. 1988, Theodore William Richards medal Northwestern sect. 1990, Edgar Fahs Smith award Phila. sect. 1991, Ira Remsen Meml. award Md. sect. 1991, Pauling medal Portland, Oreg., and Puget Sound sect. 1991, Auburn-Kosolapoff award 1996, Theoretical Chemistry award 1997, Top 75 Chem. & Engring. News award 1998), Am. Phys. Soc., Korean Chem. Soc. (hon.), Am. Philos. Soc. (hon.), Alpha Chi Sigma. Achievements include development of the Marcus Theory of electron transfer reactions in chemical systems and RRKM theory of unimolecular reactions. Home: 331 S Hill Ave Pasadena CA 91106-3405 E-mail: ram@caltech.edu.

MARCUS, STEVEN, dean, English educator; b. N.Y.C., Dec. 13, 1928; s. Nathan and Adeline Muriel (Gordon) M.; m. Gertrud Lenzer, Jan. 20, 1966; 1 son, John Nathaniel. PhD, Columbia U., 1961; D.H.L. (hon.), Clark U., 1985. Prof. English Columbia U., 1966—, George Delacorte prof. humanities, 1976—, chmn. dept. English and comparative lit., 1977-80, 85-89, v.p. Arts and Scis., 1993-95; dean Columbia Coll., 1993-95; dir. planning Nat. Humanities Center, 1974-76; chmn. exec. com. bd. dirs. Nat. Humanities Ctr., 1976-80, 96—, also bd. dirs.; chmn. Lionel Trilling Seminars, 1976-80. Author: Dickens: From Pickwick to Dombey, 1965, The Other Victorians, 1966, Engels, Manchester and the Working Class, 1974, Representations, 1976, Doing Good, 1978, Freud and The Culture of Psychoanalysis, 1984, Medicine and Western Civilization, 1995; assoc. editor: Partisan Rev. Co-dir. Heyman Ctr. for the Humanities. With AUS, 1954-56. Guggenheim Found. fellow, 1967-68; Nat. Humanities Ctr. fellow, 1980-82; Rockefeller Found. fellow in humanities, 1980-81; fellow Ctr. Advanced Studies in the Behavioral Scis., 1972-73. Fellow: Acad. Lit. Studies, Am. Acad. Arts and Scis. (editor of the Acad.); mem.: Am. Acad. Psychoanalysis (sci. assoc.), Am. Psychoanalytic Assn. (hon.), Inst. for Psychoanalytic Tng. and Rsch. (hon.), Columbia Soc. Fellows in Humanities (co-chmn.). Home: 39 Claremont Ave New York NY 10027-6802

MARCUSE, ADRIAN GREGORY, academic administrator; b. N.Y.C., Mar. 25, 1922; s. Maxwell Frederick and Mildred Ann (Hitter) M.; m. Janet Constance Radlo, Oct. 28, 1945 (dec. Mar. 22, 1980); children: Nancy Ruth Marcuse Marshall, Sally Ann Marcuse Crawford, Elizabeth Susan Marcuse; m. Betty Jane Lieberman Rossman, Jan. 11, 1985; 1 stepchild, Amy Beth Rossman Schurtz. BS, MIT, 1942, MS, 1946; LLD (hon.), Lab Inst. Merchandising, 1992. Registered profl. engr. N.Y., Fla. Rsch. assoc. MIT, Cambridge, Mass., 1945-46; rsch. scientist United Aircraft Co., E. Hartford, Conn., 1946-47; application engr. Westinghouse Electric Corp., Boston, N.Y.C., 1947-60; consulting engr. pvt. practice, N.Y.C., 1955-62; v.p. mktg. and sales Corrosion Control Corp., N.Y.C., 1960-62; sales and merchandising mgr. B. Altman & Co., N.Y.C., 1962; v.p., COO Lab. Inst. of Merchandising, N.Y.C., 1962-72, pres., CEO, 1972—2002, pres. emeritus, counsel to pres., 2002—. Pres. LIM Fashion Edn. Found., N.Y.C., 1978—; chmn. Assn. Regionally Accredited Prvt. Colls. and Univs., Washington, 1990-93. Charter commr. City of Glen Cove, N.Y., 1964, chmn. bd. engrs., 1964-68, mem. planning bd., 1980-87; past treas. Community Concert Assn., Glen Cove; past trustee and budget chmn. North Country Reform Temple, Glen Cove; past mem. YMCA Fund-Raising Coun., Glen Cove. 1st lt. USAAF, 1942-45, PTO. Mem.: N.Y. State Counselors Assn., Assn. Proprietary Colls., Am. Coun. on Edn., Am. Assn. Higher Edn., Sigma Beta Delta, Sigma Xi. Republican. Avocations: sailing, bicycling, travel, theater. Office: Lab Inst of Merchandising 12 E 53rd St Fl 2 New York NY 10022-5268 Home (Winter): 356 Golfview Rd #306 North Palm Beach FL 33408 E-mail: amarcuse@limcollege.edu.

MARCY, JEANNINE KOONCE, retired educational administrator; b. Lake City, S.C., Dec. 22, 1935; d. Alton Earle Sr. and Bernice Eva (Gerrald) K.; m. Shawn Marcy Fuentes, Vanessa Marcy Ruebel. BA, Winthrop Coll., 1957; MS, Barry Coll., 1976. Tchr. Florence (S.C.) County Schs., 1957-59, Kershaw County Schs., Camden, S.C., 1959-61; tchr., dept. chmn. Dade County Pub. Schs., Miami, Fla., 1961-82, asst. prin., 1982-86, coord. personnel staffing, 1986-89, dir. cert., 1989-92, pers. adminstr., 1993-97; ret., 1997. Mem. collective bargaining team Dade County Pub. Schs., 1983-84, trainer tchr. assessment devel. systems, 1983-85, trainer master tchr. program, 1984-85; panelist nat. conv. Assn. Supervision and Curriculum Devel., Altanta, 1980; presenter in field. Campaign worker Bob Graham for Gov., Miami, 1980's, Janet Reno for State Dist. Atty., Miami, 1980's. Mem. Kappa Delta Pi, Alpha Delta Kappa. Republican. Episcopalian. Avocations: piano, organ, guitar, reading. Home: 3250 Cypress Glen Way Apt 417 Naples FL 34109-3876

MARDIN-BURCHETT, KAREN JOAN, elementary education educator; b. Piqua, Ohio, Jan. 3, 1951; d. Pierre Vernon and Dorothy Joan (Christian) Coppess; m. William Louis Mardin, Feb. 17, 1973 (div. Jan. 1985); children: Jonathan David; m. Daniel William Burchett, Sept. 21, 1991; stepchildren: Brett, Ben. BS in Edn., Miami U., 1972; MEd, Wright State U., 1991; student, U. Dayton. Cert. tchr. Ohio. Tchr. various grades Woodland Hts. Elem. Sch. Greenville (Ohio) City Schs., 1973—. Active March of Dimes, Greenville, Heart Fund, Greenville, Cancer Soc., Greenville; tchr. Sunday Sch., mem. choir, mem. fellow com., St. Paul's Luth. Ch., 1969—. Mem. NEA, Ohio Edn. Assn., Tchr. Devel. Assn. West Ctrl. Ohio, Greenville Edn. Assn. (bldg. rep. 1991-92, 92-93), Phi Delta Kappa. Republican. Avocations: collecting antiques, cooking, gardening, reading, collecting children's books. Home: 1185 Howard Dr Greenville OH 45331-2656 Office: Woodland Hts Elem Sch 7550 State Route 118 Greenville OH 45331-9395

MARDIS, HAL KENNEDY, urological surgeon, educator, researcher; b. Lincoln, Nebr., Apr. 4, 1934; s. Harold Corson and Marie (Swaim) M.; m. Janet Reimers Schenken, June 22, 1956; children: Michael Corson, Anne Lucille, Jeanne Marie. BS, U. Nebr., Lincoln, 1955; MD, U. Nebr., Omaha, 1958. Diplomate Am. Bd. Urology. Intern Nebr. Meth. Hosp., Omaha, 1958-59, med. dir. The Stone Ctr., 1966—; resident in urology Charity Hosp. La., New Orleans, 1959-62, chief resident in urology, 1962-63; pvt. practice Omaha, 1965—; instr., asst. prof. La. State U. Sch. Medicine, New Orleans, 1963-65; asst. prof., assoc. prof. surgery U. Nebr. Med. Ctr., 1965-85, prof., 1985—. Investigator North Cen. Cancer Treatment Group, Rochester, Minn., 1988—, Technomed Internat., Inc., Danvers, Mass., 1988—; cons. Boston Sci. Corp., Watertown, Mass., 1988—. Assoc. editor Jour. Stone Disease; contbr. articles to Jour. AMA, So. Med. Jour., Jour. Urology, Urology, Urol. Clinics N.Am., Seminars in Interventional Radiology. Sec., pres. Omaha Symphony Assn., 1973-76; advisor United Arts Omaha, 1983-88. Recipient Outstanding Contbn. award dept. surgery U. Nebr. Med. Ctr., 1990. Fellow ACS; mem. AMa (del. med. staff sect. 1983-86), Am. Urol. Assn. (pres. South Cen. chpt. 1990-91, 1st prize 1976, best clin. exhibit award 1977, Gold Cane achievement award 2001), Am. Lithotripsy Soc. (pres. 1989-90), Alpha Omega Alpha (pres. 1991-92). Republican. Achievements include development of guidewire techniques for angiography and endourology, thermoplastic internal ureteral stent; description of benefits of hydrophilic polymers for endourologic devices. Office: The Urology Ctr 111 S 90th St Omaha NE 68114-3907 E-mail: hkmardis@urologycenterpc.net.

MARDIS, LINDA KEISER, educator, consultant, writer; b. New Haven, Jan. 9, 1937; d. Donald Eskil and Elizabeth Marie Hallsten; m. Gordon Delbert Craig, June 29, 1957 (dec. Jan. 1963); m. Harry Robert Keiser, June 11, 1964 (div.); children: Harry Rudolph, Robert Hungerford; m. Arthur Lowell Mardis, Dec. 29, 1990. BA, Mount Holyoke Coll., 1957; MA, Yale U., 1958. Chmn. dept. fgn. langs. Walter Johnson H.S., Bethesda, Md., 1960-65; music dir. Geneva United Presbyn. Ch., Rockville, Md., 1966-79; assoc. dir. ICM Tng. Seminars, Balt., 1979-85; facilitator, trainer Bonny Method of Guided Imagery and Music, 1980—; master Usui Sys. Reiki Healing, 1982—; pres., founder Archedigm, Inc., Olney, Md., 1985—; v.p. Archedigm Pubs., 1985—. Founder, dir. The Archedigm Collection, 1990—; workshop, retreat leader, 1959—; bd. dirs. Well-Springs Found., Madison, Wis., 1980—88; cons. LIND Inst., San Francisco, 1988—2001. Author: Conscious Listening, 1986, Light Search, 1987, Teaching Guided Imagery & Music, 1989, Program 33: A New Guided Imagery & Music Program and a New Programming Concept, 1996, Creativity I, II and III, Grieving, Expanded Awareness, Changing Patterns, 1984—88, Mythic Experience, 1989, Program 34: Labyrinth, 2000, Program 35: Peace, 2003, (music program series) Relax with the Classics series, Classical Spirit, Classical Harmonies, Classical Impressions, 1998. Deacon Christ Congl. Ch., Silver Spring, Md., 1981-84. Fellow Inst. Music and Imagery (bd. dirs. 1981-88, assoc. exec.-dir. 1986-89); mem. Soc. Noetic Scis., Assn. for Rsch. and Enlightenment, Assn. Music and Imagery, U. Holistic Healers Assn., Internat. Assn. Healthcare Practitioners, Associated Bodywork and Massage Profls., Mt. Holyoke Coll. Alumnae Assn. (bd. dirs. 1978-83). Democrat. Home: 17247 Sandy Knoll Dr Olney MD 20832-2036 Office: Archedigm Inc PO Box 1109 Olney MD 20830-1109 E-mail: linda@archedigm.com.

MARECEK, JEANNE, psychologist, educator; b. Berwyn, Ill., May 28, 1946; d. Frank J. and Josephine (Serio) M. BS, Loyola U., Chgo., 1968; MS, Yale U., 1971, PhD, 1973. From asst. prof. to prof. psychology Swarthmore (Pa.) Coll., 1972—, chmn. dept., 1986-91, 94-95, 98—, head women's studies program, 1996—. Fulbright sr. lectr., Sri Lanka, 1988. Co-author: Making a Difference: Psychology and the Construction of Gender; contbr. numerous articles to profl. jours. and chpts. to books. Bd. dirs. Women in Transition, Phila., 1980-86; vice patron Nest, Hendala, Sri Lanka, 1995—; bd. dirs. Women's Therapy Ctr., Phila., 1996—. Fellow Swedish Collegium for Advanced Study in Social Scis., 1997; various fed. research grants. Mem. APA, Ea. Psychol. Assn., Assn. for Asian Studies, Am. Inst. Sri Lanka Studies (sec. 1995—). Office: Swarthmore Coll Dept Psychology 500 College Ave Ste 2 Swarthmore PA 19081-1306

MARGED, JUDITH MICHELE, information technology educator; b. Phila., Nov. 27, 1954; d. Bernard A. and Norma Marged. Student, Drexel U., 1972-73; AA in Biology, Broward C.C., Ft. Lauderdale, Fla., 1975; BA in Biology, Fla. Atlantic U., 1977, BA in Exceptional Edn., 1980, MEd in Counseling, 1984; EdD in Early and Middle Childhood, Nova U., 1991; postgrad., Capella U., 2002—03. Cert. tchr., Fla.; cert. tech. trainer; Microsoft cert. sys. engr.; Microsoft cert. profl., trainer. Tchr. Coral Springs (Fla.) Mid. Sch., 1979-80, Am. Acad., Wilton Manors, Fla., 1980-83, Ramblewood Mid. Sch., Coral Springs, 1984-96; info. tech. prof. Am. InterContinental U., Plantation, Fla., 1999—2002. Creator programs for mid. sch. students. Author: A Program to Increase the Knowledge of Middle School Students in Sexual Education and Substance Abuse Prevention, An Alternative Education Program to Create Successful Learning for the Middle School Child At-Risk. Mem.: IEEE, Assn. for Career and Tech. Edn., Phi Delta Kappa. Home: 9107 NW 83d St Tamarac FL 33321-1509

MARGESSON, MAXINE EDGE, educator; b. Cordele, Ga., Aug. 29, 1933; d. Bryant Peak and Maxie (Grantham) Edge; m. Burland Drake Margesson, June 24, 1956; children: Anda Margesson Foxwell, Risa Margesson Carpenter. BS, Bob Jones U., 1958; MEd, SUNY, Buffalo, 1971; EdD, Western Mich. U., 1983. Elem. tchr. Cheektowaga (N.Y.) Cen. Sch. Dist., 1965-72; elem. prin. Grand Rapids (Mich.) Bapt. Acad., 1972-85; reading rsch. Wake Forest U., Winston-Salem, N.C., 1987-90; prof. Piedmont Baptist Coll., Winston-Salem, 1985-90; reading specialist Randolph (N.Y.) Ctrl. Sch. Dist., 1990-98; chair edn. dept. Cornerstone Coll., Grand Rapids, Mich., 1998—. Chair dept. edn. Cornerstone Coll., Grand Rapids; bd. dirs. Salem Day Sch., Winston-Salem. Mem. Forsyth County Coalition for Literacy Com. Mem. Assn. for Supervision and Curriculum Devel., Assn. Christian Schs. Internat. Republican. Baptist. Avocations: travel, reading, sewing. Office: Cornerstone Coll Grand Rapids MI 49525-5897

MARGOLIS, EMANUEL, lawyer, educator; b. Bklyn., Mar. 18, 1926; s. Abraham and Esther (Levin) M.; m. Edith Cushing; m. Estelle Thompson, Mar. 1, 1959; children: Elizabeth Margolis-Pineo, Catherine, Abby Margolis Newman, Joshua, Sarah. BA, U. N.C., 1947; MA, Harvard U., 1948, PhD, 1951; JD, Yale U., 1956. Bar: Conn. 1957, U.S. Dist. Ct. Conn. 1958, U.S. Supreme Ct. 1969. Instr. dept. govt. U. Conn., 1951-53; assoc. Silberberg & Silverstein, Ansonia, Conn., 1956-60, Wofsey Rosen Kweskin & Kuriansky, Stamford, Conn., 1960-66, ptnr., 1966-96, of counsel, 1996—. Arbitrator State of Conn., 1984-85; adj. prof. Quinnipiac U. Sch. Law, 1986—. Sr. editor Conn. Bar Jour., 1971-80, 83—, editor-in-chief, 1980-83; contbr. to profl. jours. Mem. nat. bd. ACLU, 1975-79; mem. Westport (Conn.) Planning and Zoning Commn., 1971-75; chmn. Conn. CLU, 1988-95, legal advisor, 1995—; exec. com. Yale Law Sch., 2000—. With U.S. Army, 1944-46. Decorated Purple Heart; recipient First Award for Disting. Svc. to Conn. Bar, Conn. Law Tribune, 1987. Fellow Conn. Bar Found. (James W. Cooper fellow 1996); mem. ABA, Conn. Bar Assn. (chmn. human rights sect. 1970-73), Nat. Assn. Criminal Def. Lawyers, Am. Arbitration Assn. (arbitrator 1998—, trial referee 1985—). Office: 600 Summer St Stamford CT 06901-1990 Home: 72 Myrtle Ave Westport CT 06880-3512 E-mail: emesq@optonline.net.

MARGOLIS, NADIA, foreign language educator, medievalist, translator; b. Neuilly-sur-Seine, France, Apr. 27, 1949; came to U.S., 1950; d. Morton Margolis and Diane Seyfort-Ruegg Kensler; m. Peter Kenneth Marshall, May 23, 1984. BA, U. N.H., 1971; PhD, Stanford U., 1977. Lectr. in French Stanford (Calif.) U., 1976-77; editorial asst. Medieval Acad. of Am., Cambridge, Mass., 1977-78; asst. prof. in French Amherst (Mass.) Coll., 1978-85; assoc. prof. French U. Utah, Salt Lake City, 1985-89; rsch. assoc. Inst. Advanced Study in Humanities/U. Mass., Amherst, 1993—. Asst. coord. Jr. World Cycling Championships, Trexlertown, Pa., 1978; adj. instr. French, U. Mass., 1992-93, vis. lectr. in comparative lit., 1993; panelist NEH, Washington, 1984, 86-87; cons. Garland Medieval Series, N.Y.C., 1992—, for composer Richard Einhorn, 1994, for Capella Films, 1994; rsch. prof. Ctr. Nat. Sci. Rsch., Paris, 1973—; vis. assoc. prof. French U. Calif., Santa Barbara, 2002, UCLA, 2003. Author: Joan of Arc in History, Literature and Film; co-author, co-editor: Christine de Pizan, 2000, 2000; co-translator: Book of the Duke of True Lovers, 1991, others. Author, panel mem. Bicycle Safety/Bike Path com., Amherst, 1984. Miner Crary fellow Amherst Coll., 1979, NEH Ind. fellow, 1981; Rsch. grant Am. Philos. Soc., 1982. Mem. Modern Lang. Assn., Soc. Rencesvals, Medieval Acad. of Am., Christine de Pizan Soc. (sec. 1991—, editor newsletter 1991-96), Internat. Courtly Lit. Soc. Democrat. Jewish. Avocations: cycling, gardening, drawing, painting. Home: 75 Amherst Rd Leverett MA 01054-9746

MARGON, BRUCE HENRY, astrophysicist, educator; b. N.Y.C., Jan. 7, 1948; s. Leon and Maxine E. (Margon) Siegelbaum; 1 dau., Pamela. AB, Columbia U., 1968; MA, U. Calif.-Berkeley, 1971, Ph.d., 1973. Asst. rsch. astronomer U. Calif.-Berkeley, 1973-76; assoc. prof. astronomy UCLA, 1976-80; prof. astronomy U. Wash., Seattle, 1980—, chmn., 1981-87, 90-95, sci. dir. Sloan Digital Sky Survey, 1998-99; assoc. dir. Space Telescope Sci. Inst., Balt., 2001—. Bd. govs. Astrophys. Rsch. Consortium, Inc., Seattle; chmn. bd. dirs. AURA, Inc., Washington; co-investigator Hubble space telescope NASA, Washington, 1977—. NATO postdoctoral fellow, 1973-74; Sloan Found. research fellow, 1979-83 Fellow AAAS, Am. Phys. Soc.; mem. Internat. Astron. Union, Am. Astron. Soc. (Pierce Prize 1981), Royal Astron. Soc. Office: Space Telescope Sci Inst 3700 San Martin Dr Baltimore MD 21218 E-mail: margon@stsci.edu.

MARGOTTA, MAURICE HOWARD, JR., management consultant; b. Tarrytown, N.Y. s. Maurice Howard Sr. and Mary (Hritz) M.; children: Maureen Rancourt, Gregory. BA, U. Hartford, 1974, MS, 1976; postgrad., U. Conn., 1979-80; MA, Columbia U., 1989, EdD, 1990. Cert. credit exec. Asst. mgr., br. mgr. Sperry Rand Corp., 1968—70; credit svcs., corp. credit mgr. RBM div. Litton Industries, Hartford, Conn., 1970-78; adj. prof. mgmt.continuing edn. div. U. Hartford, 1975-84, coord. div., 1978-84; credit mgr., trainer Mercantile Acceptance Corp., Hartford, 1978-84; dir. edn. Nat. Assn. of Credit Mgmt., N.Y.C., 1985-87, v.p., dir. edn. Columbia, Md., 1987-94, Credit Rsch. Found., Columbia, 1988-94; exec. officer Corp. Rsch. Assocs., Columbia, 1994-97; corp. credit mgr. Heath Cons., Inc., Houston, 1998—. Chmn. curriculum group Grad. Sch. Credit and Fin. Mgmt., Columbia, 1987-94, chief acad. officer, 1987, exec. officer, Corp. Rsch. Assoc., Inc., 1994. Author: Credit Management Review, 1987, rev. 2d edit., 1992; contbr. numerous articles on mgmt. topics to profl. jours. and mags.; presenter speeches on mgmt. and fin. at pub. forums. Town chmn. United Cerebral Palsy Assn., East Windsor, Conn., 1970—. With USMC, then res., Korea, Vietnam. Recipient merit award U. Hartford, 1979, Teaching Excellence award, 1985. Fellow Nat. Inst. Credit (assoc.); mem. ASTD, Internat. Platform Assn., Am. Assn. Adult Continuing Edn., Am. Soc. Assn. Execs., Nat. Econs. Club, Nat. Assn. Credit Mgmt. (cert. credit exec., bd. dirs. Conn. chpt. 1978-80, chmn. edn. com. 1978-84, nat. edn. com. 1985—, nat. accreditation bd. 1987—), Fin. Mgmt. Assn., Phi Delta Kappa. Roman Catholic. Avocations: hiking, fishing, tennis, walking, reading. Office: Heath Cons Inc 9030 Monroe Rd Houston TX 77061-5229 E-mail: credit@heathus.com., mauredn@cs.com.

MARGRAVE, JOHN LEE, chemist, educator, university administrator; b. Kansas City, Kans., Apr. 13, 1924; s. Orville Frank and Bernice J. (Hamilton) M.; m. Mary Lou Davis, June 11, 1950; children: David Russell, Karen Sue. BS in Engring. Physics, U. Kans., 1948, PhD in Chemistry, 1950. AEC postdoctoral fellow U. Calif. at Berkeley, 1951-52; from instr. to prof. chemistry U. Wis., Madison, 1952-63; prof. chemistry Rice U., 1963—, E.D. Butcher chair, 1986—, chmn. dept., 1967-72, dean advanced studies and rsch., 1972-80, v.p., 1980-86. V.p. rsch. Houston Advanced Rsch. Ctr., chief sci. officer, 1989—; vis. prof. chemistry Tex. So. U., 1993; vis. disting. prof. U. Wis., 1968, U. Iowa, 1969, Ga. Inst. Tech., 1970, U. Colo., 1975; dir. HARC Materials Sci. Ctr., 1986—93, Coun. Chem. Rsch., 1985—88, Woodlands Sci. and Art Ctr., 1999—; various nat. and internat. confs. on chem. vapor deposition of thin diamond films, 1989—98; advisor NROTC Assn., 1984—; mem. Wilhelm und Else Heraeus Stiffung Found. Symposium on Alkali Metal Reactions, Germany, 1988; mem. com. on stockpile of chem. weapons NRC, 2001—; Reilly lectr. Notre Dame, 1968; Patrick lectr. Kans. State U., 2002; Dupont lectr. U. S.C., 1971; Abbott lectr. U. N.D., 1972; Cyanamid lectr. U. Conn., 1973; Sandia lectr. U. N.Mex., 1981; Phi Lambda Upsilon lectr. Kans. State U., 1995; Seydel-Wooley lectr. Ga. Inst. Tech., 1970; lectr. NSF-Japan Joint Thermophys. Properties Symposium, 1983, Ohio Aerospace Inst., 1999; orgnl. com. NATO Conf. on Supercooled Metals, Il Ciocio, Italy, 1993, Internat. Symposia Fluorine Chemistry, Santa Cruz, 1988, Vancouver, B.C., 96, Durham, England, 2000, First, Second, Third and Fourth World Superconductivity Congresses, 1989, 90, 92, 94; chmn. com. chem. processes in severe nuc. accidents NRC, 1987—88, mem. com. on armor and armaments, 1994—, chmn. molten salt reactor panel, 1996—99, mem. com. alt. techs. demilitarization assembled chem. weapons, 1997—2000; cons. to govt. and industry, 1954—; dir. Rice Design Ctr., Houston Area Rsch. Ctr., U. Kans. Rsch. Found., Gulf Univs. Rsch. Consortium, Energy Rsch. and Edn. Found., Spectroscopic Assocs., World Congress on Superconductivity; mem. adv. coms. chem., materials sci., rsch. U. Tenn., Knoxville, Ohio State U., Tex. So. U., La. Bd. Regents; sci. adv. bd. SI Diamond Tech., 1992—96, BioNumerik, 1993—, Intrepid Tech., 1994—96; pres. Mar Chem., Inc., 1970—, High Temperature Sci., Inc., 1976—99. Editor: Modern High Temperature Sci., 1984; contbg. editor Characterization of High Temperature Vapors, 1967, Mass. Spectrometry in Inorganic Chemistry, 1968; editor High Temperature Sci., 1969-99, Procs. XXIII and XXIV Confs. on Mass Spectrometry, 1975, 76; author: (with others) Bibliography of Matrix Isolation Spectroscopy, 1950-85, 87; contbr. articles to profl. jours.; patentee in field. Served with AUS, 1943-46; capt. Res. ret. Sloan rsch. fellow, 1957-58; Guggenheim fellow, 1960; recipient Kiekhofer Teaching award U. Wis., 1957; IR-100 award for CFX lubricant powder, 1970, IR-100 award for Cryolink, 1986; Tex. Honor Scroll award, 1978; Disting. Alumni citation U. Kans., 1981, Sci. and Tech. award North Harris Montgomery Cmty. Coll., 1994. Fellow AAAS, Am. Inst. Chemists (Chem. Pioneer award 2002), Am. Phys. Soc., Tex. Acad. Sci.; mem. AAUP, NAS, Am. Chem. Soc. (Inorganic Chemistry award 1967, S.W. Regional award 1978, Fluorine Chemistry award 1980, S.E. Tex. Sect. award 1993, chem. edn. com. 1968-70, publs. com. 1973-74, patents and related matters com. 1994-96), Am. Ceramic Soc., Am. Soc. Mass Spectrometry (dir.), Am. Soc. Metals, Electrochem. Soc., Chem. Soc. London, Tex. Philos. Soc., Materials Rsch. Soc., Sigma Xi (Disting. Svc. award 1994), Omicron Delta Kappa, Sigma Tau, Tau Beta Pi, Alpha Chi Sigma. Methodist. Home: 4511 Verone St Bellaire TX 77401-5513 Office: Rice University Dept of Chemistry MS-60 6100 Main St Houston TX 77005-1892 Fax: 713-523-8236. E-mail: margrav@rice.edu.

MARGULIS, GREGORY A. mathematics educator, researcher; b. Moscow, Feb. 24, 1946; came to U.S., 1991; s. Alexander Y. Margulis and Tsilya M. Osherenko; m. Raisa T. Kristal, Aug. 30, 1972; 1 child, Boris. Diploma, Moscow U., 1967, PhD, 1970; DSc, Belorrussian Acad. Scis., Minsk, 1983. Rschr. Inst. Problems in Info. Transmission, Soviet Acad. Scis., Moscow, 1970-91; prof. math. Yale U., New Haven, 1991—. Scientific adv. coun. Math. Scis. Rsch. Inst., Berkeley, Calif., 1993-97. Author: Discrete Subgroups of Semisimple Lie Groups, 1991; mem. editl. bd. math. jours. Recipient prize for young mathematicians Moscow Math. Soc., 1968, Fields medal Internat. Math. Union, 1978, Humboldt Found. prize, 1995, Lobachevski prize Russian Acad. Scis., 1996. Mem. AAAS (fgn. hon.), NAS. Avocations: chess, jogging, swimming. Home: 20 Vista Ter New Haven CT 06515-2402 Office: Yale U Dept Math 10 Hillhouse Ave Dept Math New Haven CT 06511-6814

MARHIC, MICHEL EDMOND, engineering educator, entrepreneur, consultant; b. Ivry, Seine, France, June 25, 1945; came to U.S., 1968; s. Jean-Marie and Yvonne Marie (Nenez) M. Ingenieur, Ecole Sup. D'Electricite, Paris, 1968; MS, Case Western Res. U., 1970; PhD, UCLA, 1974. Asst. prof. Northwestern U., Evanston, Ill., 1974-79, assoc. prof., 1980-84, prof., 1985—98; consulting prof. Stanford (Calif.) U., 1998—. Vis. asst. prof. U. So. Calif., L.A., 1979-80; vis. prof. Stanford U., 1984-85, 93-94; bd. dirs. Holographic Industries, Lincolnshire, Ill. Contbr. and co-contbr. over 240 jour. articles and conf. publs.; holograhic portrait Ronald Reagan, 1991. Mem. IEEE (sr.), Optical Soc. Am., Tau Beta Pi. Achievements include 8 patents in field. Office: Stanford U Dept Elec Engring 374 Packard Bldg Stanford CA 94305

MARIANI, MARCIA ANNE, health and physical education educator; b. Pottstown, Pa., Apr. 8, 1961; d. Richard Eugene and Rita Theresa (Yonkovitch) M. BS, Westchester State Coll., 1983. Cert. tchr., Pa. Tchr., coach Pottstown (Pa.) Jr. High Sch., 1984-87; long term substitute tchr. Methacton Sch. Dist., Collegeville, Pa., 1987-88; teacher, coach Tredyffrin, Easttown Sch. Dist., Berwyn, Pa., 1988—. Coach Conestoga Field Hockey and Basketball, Berwyn, Pa., 1988—; faculty rep. Family Life Curriculum Coun., Tredyfferin, Easttown Schs., Berwyn, 1989—; mem health steering com., Tredyfferin, Easttown Schs., Berwyn, 1991—, Tredyffrin/Easttown Middle Sch. Student Assistance Program. Mem. AAHPERD, Pa. State Edn. Assn., U.S. Women's Field Hockey Assn., U.S. Women's Lacrosse Assn. (coach nat. tournament 1990-93). Avocations: singer, songwriter, guitar, field hockey, lacrosse. Office: Tredyffrin Easttown Mid Sch 840 Old Lancaster Rd Berwyn PA 19312-1270

MARINAS, CAROL ANN, mathematics educator; b. Indiana, Pa., Aug. 24, 1956; d. Peter John and Helen Mae (Adams) M. MS, Indiana U. of Pa., 1984; EdS, Barry U., 1987; PhD, Fla. State U., 1999. Cert. tchr. Instr. Indiana U. of Pa., 1984-85; assoc. prof. Barry U., Miami Shores, Fla., 1985—. Cons. Dade County Pub. Schs., Miami, Fla., 1986—; writer/editor Printice-Hall, Addison-Wesley, Key Publ. and Words and Numbers. Contbr. articles to math. jours. Named Outstanding Young Woman of Am., 1987. Mem. AAUP, Math. Assn. Am., Nat. Coun. Tchrs. Math., Fla. Assn. Computers in Edn. Avocations: computing, traveling. Office: Barry U 11300 NE 2nd Ave Miami FL 33161-6695

MARINE, SUSAN SONCHIK, analytical chemist, educator; b. Maple Heights, Ohio, Mar. 10, 1954; d. Stephen Robert and Gloria Ann (Hach) Sonchik; m. Michael David Marine; 1 child, Matthew Robert Marine. BS in Chemistry magna cum laude, John Carroll U., 1975; MS in Analytical Chemistry, Case Western Res. U., 1978, PhD in Phys. Chemistry, 1980. Asst. chemist Horizons Research Inc., Beachwood, Ohio, 1974-75; chemist specialist Standard Oil of Ohio, Warrensville Heights, Ohio, 1975-79; organic chemistry br. mgr. Versar, Inc., Springfield, Va., 1980-83; mgr. gas chromatography program IBM Instruments Inc., Danbury, Conn., 1983-87, radiation safety officer, 1985-87; expert witness, cons. Martin, Craig, Chester & Sonnenschein, Chgo., 1981-83; adv. engr. in advanced lithography IBM Corp., Essex Junction, Vt., 1987-95; vis. assoc. prof. chemistry Centre Coll., Danville, Ky., 1995-98; asst. prof. chemistry and biochemistry, coord. tech. program Miami U., Middletown, Ohio, 1998—; spl. term appointment energy sys. divsn. Argonne Nat. Lab., Ill., 2003—. Vis. asst. prof. chemistry and math. Heritage Coll., 1991—92; spkr. in field. Author: African Walking Safari, 1985; editl. adv. bd. Jour. Chromatographic Sci., 1977-93, guest editor, 1987. Mem. Danbury Conservation Commn., 1986-87, tchr. and tutor chemistry, 1985-89, 91-92, 94; troop leader Lake Erie coun. Girl Scouts U.S.A., 1971-80, Southwestern Conn., 1983-87; leader explorer post Cleve. coun. Boy Scouts Am., 1977-78; managerial advisor Jr. Achievement, Warrensville Heights, Ohio, 1977-78; judge State or Regional Sci. Fair, 1977, 80, 89-91, 99, 2000, Odyssey of the Mind, 1994; asst. leader Internat. Folk Dancers, Newtown, Conn., 1985-87; tchr. religion, 1981-84, 87-90, 93-94. Recipient Overall Best Paper award Eastern Analytical Symposium, 1984, First Gas Chromatograph award IBM Instruments Inc., 1985, contbn. award (tech. paper) 10th Internat. Congress of Essential Oils, Flavors, Fragrances, Washington, 1986. Mem. ASTM (exec. com. E-19 1985-2000, chmn. subcom. 1986-2000, vice chmn. arrangements 1994-98), Am. Chem. Soc. (chmn. membership com. Green Mountain sect. 1988-89, chair elect 1989-90, chmn. 1990-91, local coord. Nat. Chemistry Week 1991, 93-98, 2002-03, Phoenix award 1994, 97), Iota Sigma Pi (pres. N.E. Ohio chpt. 1978-79, mem.-at-large fin. mgr. 1993-97, nat. v.p. 1996-99, nat. pres. 1999-2002, immediate past pres. 2002-), No. Vt. Canoe Cruisers (treas. 1990-92), Green Mountain Steppers (sec. 1993-95), Centre Coll. Outdoors Club (faculty liaison 1996-98), Miami U. Middletown Chemistry Club (faculty liaison 2003—). Roman Catholic. Avocations: camping, dancing, travel. Home: 4667 Sebald Dr Franklin OH 45005-5328 Office: Miami U Middletown 4200 E University Blvd Middletown OH 45042-3458 E-mail: mariness@muohio.edu.

MARINELLI, DONALD, drama educator; b. Bklyn., June 9, 1953; s. Bernard and Teresa (Tiscione) M.; m. Jan Grice, June 26, 1982; 1 child, Olivia Teresa. BA in Speech, Drama and Psychology, U. Tampa, 1975; MA in Psychology, Duquesne U., Pitts., 1976; PhD in Theatre, U. Pitts., 1987. Mng. dir. The Floating Theatre, Pitts., 1979-81; asst. head drama dept. Carnegie Mellon U., Pitts., 1981-86, assoc. head drama dept., 1986-95, coord. pre-coll. program, 1984-95, rschr. informedia project Sch. Computer Sci., 1995, mng. dir. Repertory Theatre, 1984-85, co-dir. Entertainment Tech. Ctr., Sch. Computer Sci., 1996—, prof. drama and arts mgmt., 1997—; assoc. producer Carnegie Mellon Theatre Co., Pitts., 1986-89, co-producer Showcase of New Plays, 1989-95. Chmn. Am. Ibsen Theatre, Pitts., 1983-85; panel mem. Pa. Coun. on Arts, Harrisburg, 1983-84, 89-91; mem., adjudicator Am. Coll. Theater Festival, 1987-96. Critic High Performance Mag., 1985-91; book reviewer Pitts. Press, 1985-93; mng. editor Theatre Three, 1986-92; radio interviewer Sta. WQED-RM Arts Mag., 1986-88. Mem. Carnegie Mellon Affirmative Action Com., Pitts., 1984. Served with USAFR, 1980-86. Mem. Theatre Assn. Pa. (pres. 1986-90). Roman Catholic. Avocation: royalist - mem. numerous monarchist organizations. Home: 5505 5th Ave Pittsburgh PA 15232-2301 Office: Purnell Ctr Arts Rm 333 Pittsburgh PA 15213 E-mail: futurist@cs.cmu.edu., thedon@cmu.edu.

MARINI, JOHN JOSEPH, medical scientist, educator, physician; b. Syracuse, N.Y., Oct. 6, 1946; s. Warren John and Theresa Josephine (Palermo) M.. B in Engring. Sci., Johns Hopkins U., 1969, MD, 1973. Intern internal med. U. Wash., Seattle, 1973-74, resident internal med., 1974-76, fellow respiratory diseases, 1976-78, asst. prof., assoc. prof. medicine, 1978-83; assoc. prof. medicine Vanderbilt U., Nashville, 1983-89; prof. medicine U, Minn., Mpls., St. Paul, 1989—; dir. pulmonary and critical care medicine St. Paul-Ramsey Med. Ctr./Regions Hosp., 1989—; chief academic medicine Regions Hosp., 1997—2001, dir. physiologic translational rsch., 2001—. Chmn. critical care section Am. Thoracic Soc., 1989-90; mem. policy and exam writing com. Am. Bd. Internal Medicine, 1991-96; disting. Simmons lectr. UCLA, 1991; Eagan Sci. lectr. Am. Assn. for Respiratory Care, 1992. Author 9 books on pulmonary and intensive care; mem. editl. bds. 7 profl. jours.; contbr. numerous articles to profl. jours. Named one of Outstanding Pulmonologists/Critical Care Physicians in U.S., Town & Country, 1989, 95, One of Best Doctors in Am. Woodward Whyte, 1992, 95, 97, 99; recipient Lifetime Achievement award Am. Assn. Respiratory Care, 1998, Jimmie Young medal, 1998. Fellow Am. Coll. Chest Physicians (Cecil Lehman Mayer award 1980, 86), Am. Bd. Internal Medicine; mem. ACP, European Soc. Intensive Care, European Respiratory Soc., Am. Thoracic Soc., Soc. Critical Care Medicine. Avocations: skiing, tennis, foreign languages, computer science. Office: Regions Hosp 640 Jackson St Saint Paul MN 55101-2502

MARINO, IGNAZIO ROBERTO, transplant surgeon, educator, researcher; b. Genoa, Italy, Mar. 10, 1955; s. Pietro Rosario and Valeria (Mazzanti) M.; m. Rossana Parisen-Toldin, Sept. 15, 1990; 1 child, Stefania Valeria. Maturità-Classica, Coll. of Merode, Rome, 1973; MD, Cath. U., Rome, 1979. Diplomate Nat. Bd. Gen. Surgery, Nat. Bd. Vascular Surgery. Intern, then resident Gemelli U. Hosp., Rome, 1979-84; temp. asst. dept. surgery Cath. U., Rome, 1981, asst. prof. surgery, 1983-92; asst. prof. surgery Transplantation Inst. U. Pitts., 1991-95, assoc. prof. surgery Transplantation Inst./, 1995-99; prof. surgery postgrad. Sch. Microsurgery, Exptl. Surgery U. Milan, 1994—; prof. surgery Sch. Medicine U. Perugia, 1994—; attending surgeon U. Pitts. Med. Ctr., Pitts., 1991—2002; assoc. dir. transplant divsn. VA Med. Ctr., Pitts., 1992—2002; attending surgeon Children's Hosp. Pitts., 1993—; prof. surgery Transplantation Inst., U. Pitts., 1999—2002, Thomas Jefferson Med. Coll., Phila., 2002—; assoc. chief transplant divsn. Thomas Jefferson U. Hosp., Phila., 2002—, dir. liver transplantation and surgery, 2002—. Mem. surg. team 1st and 2d baboon to human liver transplants U. Pitts. Med. Ctr., 1992-93, dir. European med. divsn., 1995-2002; sci. journalist Agenzia Nazionale Stampa Associata, 1992—; nat. ad hoc donations com. United Network for Organ Sharing, 1995—; cons. Nat. Transplant Com. Italy, 1999—; regional com. Organ Procurement Orgn. for Sicily, 1999—; mem. Nat. Tech. Commn. for Informative Campaign on Organ Donation of Italy, 1999—, Nat. Ctr. for Transplantation of Italy, 2000—. Author: New Technique to Avoid the Revascularization Syndrome in Liver Transplantation, 1985 (Ann. prize Italian Soc. Surgery, 86), New Technique in Liver Transplantation, 1996 (De Angelis award, 86); mem. editl. bd.: Clin. Transplantation, Leadership Medica, Transplantation, Jour. Investigative Surgery; contbr. more than 550 articles to profl. jours. Grantee Italian Nat. Coun. Rsch., 1979, 86-93, Gastroenterology Soc., 1988; recipient award Inst. Nazionale Previdenza Dirigenti Aziende Industriali, 1982. Mem. ACS, Am. Soc. Transplantation Surgeons, Am. Soc. Transplant Physicians, Italian Soc. Surgery, Transplantation Soc. (grant 1988), European Soc. for Organ Transplantation, Soc. Surgeons Under 40 (ann. prize 1986), Cell Transplant Soc. (founding mem.), Acad. Surg. Rsch., Soc. Critical Care Medicine, Internat. Liver Transplantation Soc., Italian Order Journalists, Assn. Italian Corrs. in N.Am. (assoc.), Xenotransplantation Club (founding mem.), Internat. Coll. Surgeons, Assn. for Acad. Surgery, Nat. Assn. VA Physicians, Univ. Physician Practice Assn., Xenotransplantation Assn., Am. Assn. for the Study of Liver Diseases. Avocations: reading (history books), sailing, scuba diving, yoga, Annibale (pet cat). Home: Corso Italia 29 Rome 00198 Italy Office: Thomas Jefferson U Ste 605 Coll Bldg 1025 Walnut St Philadelphia PA 19107-5083 E-mail: ignazio.marino@jefferson.edu.

MARION, JOHN MARTIN, academic administrator; b. Fitchburg, Mass., Jan. 11, 1947; s. Don Louis and Violet Pearl Marion; m. Joann Elizabeth Trzcinski, Aug. 8, 1970; children: Benjamin Andrew, Jessica Noelle. BS in Edn., Fitchburg State Coll., 1969, MEd, 1971; postgrad., Pepperdine U. Tchr. Groton (Mass.) Dunstable Regional Schs., 1969-84; computer tchr. Littleton (Mass.) Pub. Schs., 1985-86; computer coord. K-12th grades Newburyport (Mass.) Pub. Schs., 1986-90; assoc. dean Acad. Computing Endicott Coll., Beverly, Mass., 1990—98; dir. tech. Reading (Mass.) Pub. Schs., 1998-00; media tech. specialist Dracut Pub. Schs., Mass., 2000—03; tech. edn. specialist Jefferson County (Colo.) Pub. Sch., 2003—. Instr. Merrimack Edn. Ctr., Chelmsford, Mass., 1980-90; trainer, cons. Logo Computer Sys., Inc., N.Y.C., 1984-90; tchr. trainer Lego-Decta, Lego Sys., Inc., Enfield, Conn., 1987-90; mem. adv. bd. Claris Software Co.; bd. dirs. Mass. Computer Using Educator, 1989-90. Bd. dirs. Reading Cmty. TV, Inc., 1998-99. Fulbright scholar tchr. exch., Southampton, Eng., 1973-74. Mem. Internat. Soc. Tech. in Edn., Mass. Computer Using Educators, Phi Delta Kappa. Office: Jeffco Schs 9201 W Columbine Dr Littleton CO 80128 Home: 29656 Buffalo Park Rd Unit 201 Evergreen CO 80439 E-mail: jmarion@aol.com.

MARION, SARAH KATHLEEN, music educator; b. Wenatchee, Wash., Mar. 31, 1974; d. John Alfred Braden and Diana Lee Black; m. Jim Johan Marion; children: Christina, Daniel. AAS, Wenatchee Valley Coll., Wenatchee, Wash., 1995. Pvt. piano instr., Wenatchee, 1990—; part-time instr. Wenatchee Valley Coll., Wenatchee, 2001. Sec. Family Issues and Awareness Team, Wenatchee, 2000—; at-large bd. mem. Wenatchee Free Meth. Ch., 2001. Mem.: Wenatchee Chpt. Wash. State Music Tchrs. Assn. (publicity chmn. 1997—99), Music Tchrs. Nat. Assn., Wash. State Music Tchrs. Assn., Phi Theta Kappa. Avocations: travel, languages, running, outdoor recreation. Home: 50-19th St NE East Wenatchee WA 98802

MARION, SUZANNE MARGARET, music educator; b. Hutchinson, Kans., May 6, 1938; d. Charles Myers and Margaret Lansden (Foster) Davis; m. Stuart Eli Marion, June 2, 1962; children: John Stuart, David Evan, Matthew Charles. BA in Psychology, U. Ariz., 1960; BA in Music, U. Houston, 1982. Psychiat. social worker Ariz. State Hosp., Phoenix, 1960-62; tchr. voice, theory, piano Houston Music Inst., 1978-81; pvt. practice Houston, 1970—. Performer Class Act, Houston, 1994—. Soloist Emerson Unitarian Ch. choir, Houston, 1983—2000. Voice scholarship Madrigal Club, 1964. Mem. Houston Tuesday Musical Club (pres. 1996-98), Treble Clef Club, Sigma Alpha Iota. Republican. Unitarian Universalist. Avocations: creative writing, study of spanish, computer, reading, working with dogs. Home: 910 Briarbrook Dr Houston TX 77042-2006

MARK, LILLIAN GEE, educational administrator; b. Berkeley, Calif., Mar. 18, 1932; d. Pon Gordon and Sun Kum (Wong) Gee; m. Richard Muin Mark, June 20, 1954; children: Dean, Kim, Faye, Glenn, Lynne. BA in Psychology, U. Calif., Berkeley, 1954; MS in Christian Sch. Adminstrn., Pensacola Coll., 1987; HHD (hon.), Shasta Bible Coll., 2002. Supt. Alpha Beacon Christian Sch., San Mateo, Calif., 1976—. CEO, Alpha Beacon Christian Ministries. Author: Handbook for Parents and Students, 1983, How To Encourage Your Staff. Mem.: Internat. Fellowship Christian Sch. Adminstrs., Assn. Christian Sch. Internat., Christian Ministries. Republican. Avocations: tennis, swimming, piano, Bible study. Home: 384 Montserrat Dr Redwood City CA 94065-2806 Office: Alpha Beacon Christian Sch 1950 Elkhorn Ct San Mateo CA 94405-4666 Office Fax: 650-212-1026. Business E-Mail: abcinfo@alphabeacon.org.

MARKEE, KATHERINE MADIGAN, librarian, educator; b. Cleve., Feb. 24, 1931; d. Arthur Alexis and Margaret Elizabeth (Madigan) M. AB, Trinity Coll., Washington, 1953; MA, Columbia U., 1962; MLS, Case Western Res. U., 1968. Employment mgr., br. store tng. supr. The May Co., Cleve., 1965-67; assoc. prof. libr. sci., data bases libr. Purdue U. Libr., West Lafayette, Ind., 1968—, libr. spl. collections, 1996—. Contbr. articles to profl. jours. Mem. ALA, AAUP, Spl. Librs. Assn., Ind. Online Users Group, Sigma Xi (Rsch. Support award 1986). Avocations: photography, sailing, gardening. Office: Purdue U Libr West Lafayette IN 47907-2058 E-mail: kmarkee@purdue.edu.

MARKEY, MARY HELEN, secondary education educator; b. Providence, Aug. 25, 1954; d. Raymond J. and Vivian (Vekeman) M. BA in Biology, BS in Secondary Edn., R.I. Coll., 1986. Tchr. biology Mt. Pleasant H.S., Providence, 1987—. Tchr. sci. R.I. Coll. Upward Bound, Providence, 1988; tchr. sci. Elmwood Cmty. Summer Sch., Providence, 1989-93; Fulbright lectr. biology, Hungary, 1992-93; G.E.D. instr. Adult Corrections Inst., Cranson, R.I., 1989-93; adv. mem. action team for ednl. reform Providence Sch. Dept., 1993—, mem. restructuring evaluation com., 1994—; Fulbright lectr. biology, Ankara, Turkey, 1998-99; Outreach program Rockefeller U., N.Y.C., 2000; sci. instr. Khartoum Am. Sch., Khartoum, Sudan, 2001-03. Treas. Elmwood Found. for Archtl. Preservation, 1980-85. Named Tchr. of Yr. by students Mt. Pleasant H.S., 1994. Mem. R.I. Sci. Tchrs. Assn. Address: 57 Metcalf Ave North Providence RI 02911-3147

MARKEY, WINSTON ROSCOE, aeronautical engineering educator; b. Buffalo, Sept. 20, 1929; s. Roscoe Irvin and Catherine L. (Higgins) M.; m. Phoebe Anne Sproule, Sept. 10, 1955; children: Karl Richard, Katherine Ilse, Kristina Anne. BS, MIT, 1951, Sc.D., 1956. Engr. MIT, 1951-57, asst. prof., 1957-62, assoc. prof., 1962-66, prof., 1966—, undergrad. officer, 1988-2000, dir. Measurement Systems Lab., 1961-89. Chief scientist USAF, 1964-65, mem. sci. adv. bd., 1966-69 Author: (with J. Hovorka) The Mechanics of Inertial Position and Heading Indication, 1961; Assoc. editor: AIAA Jour, 1963-66. Recipient Exceptional Civilian Service award USAF, 1965 Mem. Sigma Xi, Tau Beta Pi, Gamma Alpha Rho. Home: 11 Edgewood Rd Lexington MA 02420-3501 Office: MIT Bldg 33-208 Cambridge MA 02139 E-mail: wrmarkey@mit.edu.

MARKFERDING, GAIL MAUREEN, elementary school educator; b. Windber, Pa., July 20, 1947; d. William and Elaine June (Holsopple) Maggs; m. Dennis Robert Markferding, June 7, 1969 (div. 1986); children: Jennifer Nicole, Damian Russell. BS, U. Pitts., 1968, cert. reading specialist, 1977; postgrad., We. Md. U., 1970, Frostburg U., 1993; MEd, U. Md., 1973. Cert. tchr., reading specialist, Pa.; cert. acad. supr. Tchr. Greater Johnstown (Pa.) Sch. Dist., 1969, Prince George's County Sch. Dist., Upper Marlboro, Md., 1969-73, North Star Sch. Dist., Boswell, Pa., 1973—, fed. project coord., 1976—. Reading specialist Conemaugh Twp. Sch. Dist., Davidsville, Pa., 1985-86; tchr. Project Kids, Lewisburg, Pa., 1989; cons. Macmillan Pub. Co., Riverside, N.J., 1990. Fin. com. St. David's Luth. Ch., Davidsville. Grantee NSF, 1971. Mem. NEA, AAUW, Pa. State Edn. Assn., North Star Edn. Assn., Internat. Reading Assn., Somerset Reading Assn. (pres.), Keystone State Reading Assn., Pa. Assn. Fed. Program Coords. Republican. Avocations: swimming, reading, soccer, sewing. Home: 143 Hilltop Dr Davidsville PA 15928-9649 Office: North Star Sch Dist 1200 Morris Ave Boswell PA 15531-1297

MARKGRAF, J(OHN) HODGE, chemist, educator; b. Cin., Mar. 16, 1930; s. Carl A. and Elizabeth (Hodge) M.; m. Nancy Hart, Apr. 4, 1957; children: Carrie G., Sarah T. AB, Williams Coll., 1952; M.Sc., Yale U., 1954, PhD, 1957; postgrad., U. Munich, W. Ger., 1956-57. Research chemist Procter & Gamble Co., Cin., 1958-59; asst. prof. chemistry Williams Coll., Williamstown, Mass., 1959-65, assoc. prof., 1965-69, prof., 1969-98, Ebenezer Fitch prof. chemistry, 1977-85, 94-98, prof. emeritus, 1998—, provost, 1980-83, v.p. for alumni relations and devel., 1985-94, coll. marshal, 1995-98. Vis. prof. U. Calif., Berkeley, 1964—65, 1968—69, 1976—77, Duke U., 1983—84, 2001, U. Houston, 1999, Williams Coll., 2002, 2003—. Contbr. articles to profl. jours.; patentee in field. NSF sci. faculty fellow, 1964-65; NSF grantee, 1961-63, Am. Chem. Soc.-Petroleum Rsch. Fund grantee, 1965-68, 70-72, 93-95, Merck & Co. grantee, 1967, Rsch. Corp. grantee, 1963, 75, 90-92, Pfizer Inc. grantee, 1996, 97, 98, Camille and Henry Dreyfus Found. grantee, 2000-2001. Mem.: Am. Chem. Soc., Phi Beta Kappa, Sigma Xi. Home: 104 Forest Rd Williamstown MA 01267-2029 Office: Williams College Dept Chemistry Williamstown MA 01267-2692 E-mail: j.hodge.markgraf@williams.edu.

MARKHAM, J. DAVID, educator, writer, historical consultant; b. Austin, Tex., Dec. 26, 1945; s. James Walter and Myrtle (Sturges) M.; m. Barbara Ann Munson, May 14, 1983. BS, U. Iowa, 1971; MA, U. No. Iowa, 1972; postgrad., So. Ill. U., 1972-74, U. Wis., 1981-82; MEd, Ariz. State U., 1991; postgrad., Fla. State U., 1996—97, Oxford (Eng.) U., 1996. Instr. sociology U. Wis., Fond du Lac/Stevens Point, 1974-76; dir. Vietnam edn. grants Wis. Dept. Vet. Affairs, Madison, 1979-83; coordinator internat. edn. AFSCME, Phoenix, 1983-84; vets. svc. officer Ariz. Vets. Service Commn., Phoenix, 1984-86; asst. to dir. Commn. on Ariz. Environ., Phoenix, 1986-88; div. supr. Ariz. Dept. Liquor Lics. and Control, Phoenix, 1988-89; world history and English tchr. Tolleson Union H.S. Dist., 1990-92; world history tchr. Lake Worth H.S., Palm Beach, Fla., 1992-2000; history tchr. Tumwater H.S., 2000—01, Centralia H.S., 2001—02, Orting HS, 2002—. Instr. sociology and polit. sci., Maricopa C.C. Dist., Phoenix, 1985-91; instr. Palm Beach C.C., 1993-95; pres. Olympia (Wash.) World Affairs Coun. Co-author: Napoleon: The Final Verdict, 1996, Napoleon's Road to Glory: Triumphs, Defeats and Immortality, 2003; author: Imperial Glory: The Bulletins of Napoleon's Grand Armée, 2003; contbr. articles to profl. jours. Bd. dirs. World Affairs Coun. Ariz., 1987-90; v.p. Ariz. Com. for Bicentennial of the French Revolution, 1988-89; exec. v.p. Napoleonic Alliance, 1996—; pres. Olympia World Affairs Coun., 2003—. With U.S. Army, 1968-69, Vietnam. Decorated Bronze Star; recipient medal of Landtag of Badden-Württemberg, Germany, 1987, Spl. Svc. award Alliance Francaise of Phoenix, 1992, Marengo medal Province of Alessandria, Italy, 1997, medal City of Ajaccio, Corsica, France, 1997. Fellow Internat. Napoleonic Soc. (exec. v.p. and editor-in-chief 1995—, Legion of Merit 1996); mem. Napoleonic Alliance (exec. v.p. 1992—, editor conf. procs., editor bull., Pres. medal 1998), Inst. on Napoleon and the French Revolution, Western Soc. for French History, Am. Byron Soc., Sierra Club, Zero Population Growth, Alpha Kappa Delta, Phi Kappa Phi, Phi Alpha Theta. Democrat. Avocations: collecting Napoleonic items, writing history, outdoor activities, travel, music. Home: 1841 52nd Way SE Olympia WA 98501-8000 E-mail: imperialglory@comcast.net.

MARKLAND, FRANCIS SWABY, JR., biochemist, educator; b. Phila., Jan. 15, 1936; s. Francis Swaby Sr. and Willie Lawrence (Averritt) M.; m. Barbara Blake, Jun. 27, 1959 - April 5, 1996; children: Cathleen Blake, Francis Swaby IV. BS, Pa. State U., 1957; PhD, Johns Hopkins U., 1964. Postdoctoral fellow UCLA, 1964-66, asst. prof. biochemistry, 1966-73; vis. asst. prof. U. So. Calif., Los Angeles, 1973-74, assoc. prof., 1974-83, prof., 1983—, acting chmn. dept. biochemistry, 1986-88, vice-chmn., 1988-92. Cons. Clin. Lab. Med. Group, LA, 1977-88, Cortech, Inc., Denver, 1983-88, Maret Corp., Wayne, Pa., 1996-2000; mem. biochem., endocrinology study sect. NIH, 1986-90, mem FLAIR prog., rev. NIH ACI, 2002-2003, Contbg. editor: Toxicon, Jour. Natural Toxins; contbr. articles to profl. jours.. Mem. Angeles Choral, L.A. Capt. USNR, 1957-59, ret. Recipient NIH rsch. career devel. award USPHS, NIH, 1968-73; rsch. grantee Nat. Cancer Inst., 1979-86, 91-93, Nat. Heart Lung and Blood Inst., 1984-88, 95-2002, State of Calif. Breast Cancer Rsch. Program, 1995-2002, State Calif. Cancer Rsch. Program, 2000-2003; fellow study sec. reviewer, Am. Heart Assn. We. reg., 2003— . Mem. AAAS, Am. Soc. Biochem. and Molecular Biology, Am. Chem. Soc., Internat. Soc. on Toxinology, Soc. Fibronolysis & Proteolysis, Internat. Soc. on Thrombosis and Haemostasis (subcom. exogenous hemostatic factors, chair 1994-96, co-chair 1999-2003), Am. Assn. Cancer Rsch., Am. Soc. Hematology, Sigma Xi, Alpha Zeta. Avocations: singing, skiing, aerobics, golf. Office: U So Calif Keck Sch Medicine Cancer Rsch Lab Rm 106 1303 N Mission Rd Los Angeles CA 90033-1020 E-mail: markland@usc.edu.

MARKMAN, ARTHUR BRIAN, psychology educator; b. Plainfield, N.J., Feb. 28, 1966; s. Edward Steven and Sondra Rae (Gold) M.; 1 child, Lucas Gabriel. BS, Brown U., 1988; MA, U. Ill., 1990, PhD, 1992. Vis. asst. prof. Northwestern U., Evanston, Ill., 1991-93; asst. prof. psychology Columbia U., N.Y.C., 1993-98; assoc. prof. U. Tex., Austin, 1998—2003, prof., 2003—. Author: (book) Knowledge Representation, 1999, (with D.L. Medin and B.H. Ross) Cognitive Psychology, 2000; co-editor: Cognitive Dynamics, 2000, Human Factors in Remote Sensing Imagery; mem. editl. bd. Jour. Exptl. Psychology, Learning, Memory and Cognition, 1995-2000, Memory and Cognition, 1998—, Cognitive Science, 2000—, Psychonomic Bull. and Rev., 2003—; contbr. articles to profl. jours. Mem. APA, Am. Psychol. Soc., Cognitive Sci. Soc. (exec. officer), Am. Assn. for Artificial Intelligence, Psychonomic Soc., Sigma Xi, Phi Kappa Phi. Achievements include seminal research on parallels between analogy and similarity; research on the role of comparison in decision-making. Office: U Texas Dept Psychology 1 University Station A8000 Austin TX 78712 E-mail: markman@psy.utexas.edu.

MARKO, ANDREW PAUL, school system administrator; b. Kingston, Pa., Aug. 16, 1936; s. Andrew Paul and Anna (Stragis) M.; m. Janet Thimm, Aug. 10, 1988; 1 child, Danielle. BA, Kings Coll., Wilkes-Barre, Pa., 1962; MA, Scranton U., 1968, prin.'s cert., 1971; postgrad., Oxford (Eng.) U., 1988, Lehigh U., 1991, Widener U., 1991—. Cert. tchr., secondary prin., supt.'s letter of eligibility, Pa. Elem. tchr. Dundalk Elem. Sch., Balt., 1963-64; English tchr. Kingston (Pa.) High Sch., 1964-66, Wyoming Valley West High Sch., Plymouth, Pa., 1966-90, vice prin., 1980, 89; secondary curriculum adminstr. Wyoming Valley West Sch. Dist., Kingston, 1990, dir. instrnl. svcs. and pupil svcs., 1991-95, apptd. supt., 1995—. Wrestling coach Kingston High Sch., 1964-69; jr.-sr. class advisor Wyoming Valley West High Sch., Plymouth, 1968-88, newspaper advisor, 1970-90, literary mag. advisor, 1970-90, publs. bus. mgr., 1988-90. Councilman Kingston Borough Coun., 1969-77; pres. Holy Name Soc.; ward capt. Heart Fund and March of Dimes; bd. dirs. Childrens Svc. Ctr. United Way, Diversity Bd. Coll. Misricordia, Dallas, Pa.; exec. dir. Northeastern Health Trust Pa.; mem. adv. bd. Blue Cross/Blue Shield; chmn. Sch. to Work; bd. dirs. libr. bd. Leham campus Pa. State U.; exec. dir. Northeast Pa. Sch. Dist. Health Trust, 2001-04. With USN, 1954-57. Fellow Ednl. Policy and Leadership Pa.; mem. ASCD, Pa. Assn. Student Assistance Profls., Pa. Assn. for Supervision and Curriculum Devel., Pa. Assn. Pupil Svcs. Adminstrs., Nat. Assn. Pupil Svcs. Adminstrs., Pa. Staff Devel. Coun., Nat. Mid. Sch. Assn., Ptnrs. for Quality Learning, VFW, Am. Legion, KC. Democrat. Roman Catholic. Avocations: sports, gardening, building, reading. Home: 6 Halowich Rd Harveys Lake PA 18618-9629 Office: Wyoming Valley West Sch Dist 450 N Maple Ave Kingston PA 18704-3683

MARKOVITS, ANDREI STEVEN, political science educator; b. Timisoara, Romania, Oct. 6, 1948; came to U.S., 1960, naturalized, 1971; s. Ludwig and Ida (Ritter) M. BA, Columbia U., 1969, MBA, 1971, MA, 1973, MPhil, 1974, PhD, 1976. Mem. faculty NYU, 1974, John Jay Coll. Criminal Justice, CUNY, 1974, Columbia U., 1975; rsch. assoc. Inst. Advanced Studies, Vienna, Austria, 1973-74, Wirtschafts und Sozialwissenschaftliches Inst., German Trade U. Fedn., Düsseldorf, Germany, 1979, Internat. Inst. Comparative Social Rsch., Sci. Ctr. Berlin, 1980; asst. prof. govt. Wesleyan U., Middletown, Conn., 1977-83; assoc. prof. polit. sci. Boston U., 1983-92; prof., chair dept. politics U. Calif., Santa Cruz, 1992-99; prof. dept. Germanic langs. and lit. U. Mich., Ann Arbor, Mich., 1999—2003, Karl W. Deutsch Collegiate prof. comparative politics and German studies, 2003—; Fulbright prof. U. Innsbruck, Austria, 1996. Vis. prof. Tel Aviv U., 1986, Osnabruck U., 1987, Bochum U., 1991; vis. prof. com. degrees social studies Harvard U., 2002—03; sr. rsch. assoc. Ctrl. European Studies Harvard U., 1975—99; adj. prof. polit. sci. and sociology U. Mich., 1999—. Author, editor books and papers in field; TV and radio commentator. Univ. Pres.'s fellow Columbia U., 1969, B'nai B'rith Found. fellow, 1976-77, Kalmus Found. fellow, 1976-77, Ford Found. fellow, 1979, Hans Boeckler Found. fellow, 1982 Inst. for Advanced Study Berlin fellow, 1998-99; N.Y. State scholar Columbia U., 1969. Mem. N.Y. Acad. Scis., Am. Polit. Sci. Assn., Internat. Polit. Sci. Assn., AAUP. Home: 718 Onondaga St Ann Arbor MI 48104-2611 Office: Univ Mich 3110 Modern Lang Bldg 812 E Washington St Ann Arbor MI 48109-1275 Office Fax: 734-763-6557. E-mail: andymark@umich.edu., andreimarkovits@cs.com.

MARKOWITZ, PHYLLIS FRANCES, retired mental health services administrator, psychologist; b. Malden, Mass., Sept. 2, 1931; d. Abraham and Rose (Kaplan) Kalishman: children: Gary Keith, Carol Diane Donnelly. AB, Harvard U., 1972, EdM, 1974; EdD, Boston U., 1987. Lic. psychologist Health Svc. Provider; lic., cert. social worker, Mass.; cert sch. psychologist, secondary English and social studies tchr., Mass.; cert. health svc. provider Mass. Rsch. asst. Boston Coll., Newton, Mass., 1971-73; social worker Combined Jewish Philanthropies, Boston, 1973-74; instr. Harvard U., Cambridge, Mass., 1974-75, counselor, 1974-79; supr. Dept. Social Svcs., Newton and Marlborough, Mass., 1979-88; area dir. case mgmt. and tng. Dept. Mental Health, Boston, 1988-94, area coord. medically-mentally ill, 1988—, chair consumer/family empowerment project, 1992-96. Area dir. Svcs. Integration, 1994-95; project dir. Supported Employment Svcs., 1994-95; area dir. Clin. Affairs and Rehab., 1995-2000; area Ams. with Disabilities coord. Dept. Mental Health, Boston, 1995-2000; instr. human devel. U. Mass., Boston, 1990-97. Grantee Radcliffe Inst., 1972; recipient Rsch. scholar award Boston U., 1981-82. Mem. APA, Mass. Psychol. Assn. Avocations: music, opera, writing.

MARKOWITZ, SAMUEL SOLOMON, chemistry educator; b. Bklyn., Oct. 31, 1931; s. Max and Florence Ethel (Goldman) M.; children: Michael, Daniel, Jonah; m. 2d Lydia de Antonis, Oct. 31, 1993. BS in Chemistry, Rensselaer Poly. Inst., 1953; MA, Princeton U., 1955, PhD, 1957; postgrad., Brookhaven Nat. Lab., 1955-57. Asst. prof. chemistry U. Calif., Berkeley, 1958-64, assoc. prof., 1964-72, prof., 1972—. Faculty sr. scientist Lawrence Berkeley Lab., 1958—; vis. prof. nuclear physics Weizmann Inst. Sci., Rehovot, Israel, 1973-74. Mem. Bd. Edn. of Berkeley Unified Sch. Dist., 1969-73, pres. bd., 1971-72. Recipient Elizabeth McFeely D'Urso Meml. Pub. Ofcl. award Alameda County Edn. Assn., 1973; LeRoy McKay fellow Princeton U., 1955, Charlotte Elizabeth Proctor fellow Princeton U., 1956, NSF postdoctoral fellow U. Birmingham, Eng., 1957-58, NSF sr. postdoctoral fellow Faculte des Scis. U. Paris a Orsay, Laboratoire Joliot-Curie de Physique Nucleaire, 1964-65. Fellow AAAS; mem. Am. Chem. Soc. (bd. dirs. Calif. sect., chmn. 1991, 93-94, Walter Petersen award 2003), Am. Phys. Soc., Am. Inst. chemists, N.Y. Acad. Scis., Calif. Inst. Chemists, Sigma Xi. Home: 555 Pierce St # 245 Albany CA 94706 Office: U Calif Dept Chemistry Berkeley CA 94720-1460 Business E-Mail: markowit@cchem.berkeley.edu.

MARKOWSKY, GEORGE, computer science educator; BA, Columbia U., 1968; MA, Harvard U., 1969, PhD, 1973. Asst. prof. St. Mary's Coll. Md., St. Mary's City, 1969-72; postdoctoral researcher Harvard U., Cambridge, Mass., 1973-74; rsch. staff mem. IBM, Yorktown Heights, N.Y., 1974-84; chmn. computer sci. U. Maine, Orono, 1984-90, 96-97, 99—, prof. computer sci., 1984—, chmn. math./stats depts., 2001—03. Pres., founder Trefoil Corp. (computing and tech. svcs. firm), Orono, SciCloid LLC, Orono; co-founder Mindship Internat., Orono, Cybersea Seminar Series, 1997—. Author: A Comprehensive Guide to the IBM PC, 1984, The Downeast PC Course, 1991, The DOS/Windows Book, 1994; contbr. more than 60 articles to profl. jours. Dir. Maine Housing Found., Orono, 1990-93. Mem. Am. Math. Soc., Math. Assn. Am., Assn. Computing Machinery, Maine Software Developers Assn. (founder, pres. 1992—98), Bedford Audubon Soc. (pres. 1981-82). Achievements include patent (with other) for hash functions. Office: Dept Computer Sci Univ Maine Orono ME 04469-5752 also: Trefoil Corp PO Box 127 Orono ME 04473-0127

MARKS, ANN THRASHER, secondary and special education educator; b. Palo Alto, Calif., Feb. 2, 1946; d. J. Fred and Elizabeth (Chastain) Thrasher; m. Robert E. Marks, July 26, 1980; children: Bobby, Keith, Jared, Beth, Katie. BS, U. So. Miss., 1968; MA, U. Ala., Tuscaloosa, 1970, EdS, 1973. Tchr. Jefferson County Bd. Edn., Birmingham, Ala., 1968-70, Homewood (Ala.) Bd. Edn., 1970-71, Ctr. for Devel. and Learning Disorders, Birmingham, 1971-72; ednl. specialist Child Devel. Ctr., Mobile, Ala., 1972-73, Albert P. Brewer Devel. Ctr., Mobile, 1973, coord. insvc. tng., 1973-76, dir. edn. and tng., 1976-80; tchr. home econs. and spl. edn. Tuscaloosa County Bd. Edn., Tuscaloosa, 1980-95; ret., 1995. Ind. rep. Excel Telecoms., 1995—; adult edn. tchr. Tuscaloosa County Bd. Edn., 1997. Mem. Kappa Delta Pi. Home: 2420 Saint James Ldg Tuscaloosa AL 35406-3629 Office: Excel Telecoms PO Box 650582 Dallas TX 75265-0582

MARKS, ARTHUR, prosthodontist, educator; b. N.Y.C., June 5, 1920; s. Louis and Elizabeth (Levine) M.; AB, NYU, 1942, DDS, 1944; m. Ruth Flamberg, July 18, 1948; children: Pauline, Deborah, Frances. Practice dentistry, N.Y.C., 1947—; assoc. vis. oral surgeon Sydenham Hosp., N.Y.C., 1947-75; mem. speakers bur. N.Y. Oral Hygiene Com.; dental rep. inter-profl. socs. adv. com. on Medicaid to commr. health N.Y.C.; asst. clin. prof. removable prosthodontics, asst. clin. prof. dept. family practice NYU Coll. Dentistry, 1981-87, assoc. clin. prof. prosthodontics and occlusion, comprehensive care and practice adminstrn., 1987—. Hon. asst. chmn. Democratic State Conv., N.Y., 1966; mem. New Rochelle Dem. City Com.; mem. New Rochelle Columbus Day Com., 1981, 82. Served with Dental Corps, AUS, 1944-47. Recipient N.Y. U. Alumni Meritorious Service award, 1976. Fellow Am. Coll. Dentists, Acad. Gen. Practice, Am. Endodontic Soc., Internat. Coll. Dentists; mem. Am. Acad. Prosthodontics, ADA, Am. Soc. Advancement Gen. Anesthesia in Dentistry, Am. Soc. Childrens Dentistry, Am. Dental Soc. Anaesthesiology, N.Y. Inst. Clin. Oral Pathology, Alumni Assn. N.Y. U. Dental Sch. (dir. 1961—, chmn. installation dinner 1963-64, 65, 67, chmn. constl. by-laws com. 1964-66, sec. 1968-69, pres. elect 1970-71, pres. 1971-72), Alumni Fedn. N.Y. U. (past pres., dir., Great Teacher award 1990), N.Y. Hort. Soc., Am. Acad. Polit. and Social Sci., Eastern Dental Soc. (pres. 1978), First Dist. Dental Soc. (dir., chmn. govt. funded health care com.), Empire Dental Polit. Action Com. (sec. 1976-77), Sydenham Hosp. Dental Clin. Soc. (pres. 1971-72), Grand St. Boys Assn., Assn. Mil. Surgeons, Thomas Paine Hist. Soc. Democrat. Club: N.Y. University College of Dentistry Century (organizing com. N.Y.C., dir. 1961-66). Home: 85 Hilary Cir New Rochelle NY 10804-1805 Office: 601 W 139th St New York NY 10031-7312

MARKS, GERALD, surgeon, educator; b. Bklyn., Apr. 14, 1925; s. Maurice and Lee (Leib) M.; m. Barbara Ann Hendershot, Nov. 25, 1950; children: Richard M., James M., John H. Grad., Villanova U., 1945; MD, Jefferson Med. Coll., 1949. Diplomate: Am. Bd. Surgery, Am. Bd. Colon and Rectal Surgery (examiner). Intern Jefferson Med. Coll. Hosp., Phila., 1949-51, resident in surgery, 1952-57, resident in proctology, 1953-54, asst. dir. Tumor Clinic, 1959-68; practice medicine specializing in gen. and colorectal surgery Phila., 1957—; asst. chief surgery Phila. Gen. Hosp., 1957-70, chief Proctology Clinic, 1968-70, coordinator student surg. edn. Jefferson Surg. Service, 1960-70; asst. attending physician in surgery Thomas Jefferson U. Hosp., 1957-95, sec. med. staff, 1974-77, dir. Comprehensive Rectal Cancer Ctr., Colorectal Surgery Residency Program, exec. dir. Colorectal Surgical Found., 1984-95, co-dir. Colorectal Cancer Genetics Ctr.; dir. div. internat. surg. edn. and practice Ctr. for Research in Med. Edn. and Health Care; instr. surgery Jefferson Med. Coll., 1958-67, assoc. in clin. surgery, 1967-68, clin. assoc. prof. surgery, 1974-78, prof., 1978-95; chief sect. colorectal surgery, cons. in colon-rectal surgery Pa. Hosp.; cons. in colon-rectal surgery VA Hosp., Coatesville, Pa., 1959—, San Juan, P.R., 1968—, Wilmington, Del., 1977—; cons in colon-rectal surgery USN Regional Med. Ctr., Phila., 1977—; Edgar Deissler prof. surgery Allegheny U. Health Scis., 1995—2001, dir. comprehensive rectal cancer ctr., 1995—98, dir. GI surg. endoscopy, 1995. Adj. prof. surgery U. Pa. Sch. Medicine; sr. investigator, Lankenan Inst. for Med. Rsch.; dir. Internat. Network Comprehensive Rectal Cancer Ctrs., 1997-; chmn. Marks Colorectal Surg. Found. Sr. editor Surg. Endoscopy, Ultrasound and Interventional Techniques Jour.; assoc. editor Diseases of the Colon and Rectum Jour., 1977—; cons. editor Pa. Medicine; editl. cons. bd. mem. Gen. Surgery News, 1991, Jour. Surg. Techn.; contbr. articles to profl. jours.; developed colonscopic colon teaching model. Served with USN, 1943-46; served to capt. M.C. USAF, 1951-52. Recipient 7th Ann. Jonathan M. Wainwright award, Moses Taylor Hosp., Scranton, Pa., 1989. Mem. ACS (rep. to bd. govs. 1983, council Met. Phila. chpt.), AMA, Pa. Soc. Colon and Rectal Surgery (pres. 1981-82), Am. Soc. Colon and Rectal Surgeons (v.p. 1989), Am. Soc. Clin. Oncology, Internat. Soc. Univ. Colon and Rectal Surgeons, Coll. Physicians Phila., Internat. Fedn. Socs. Endoscopic Surgeons (pres. 1991-2000), Royal Soc. Medicine (affiliate), Ea. Surg. Soc., Phila. Acad. Surgery (mem. council), Pa. Med. Soc., Phila. County Med. Soc. (bd. dirs., v.p., chmn. publs. com., pub. affairs com., v.p. 1986—), Soc. Surgery Alimentary Tract, Am. Soc. Gastrointestinal Endoscopy, Italian Soc. Gastrointestinal Endoscopy (hon.), Soc. Am. Gastrointestinal Endoscopic Surgeons (founder, pres. 1980, bd. govs., honoree Annual Gerald Marks Lectureship, former chmn. internat. rels. com.), Italian Soc. Surgery (hon.), Northeastern Soc. Colon and Rectal Surgeons (past pres.), Jefferson Vol. Faculty Assn. (pres. 1973-74), Am. Soc. Colon and Rectal Surgeons (v.p. 1989—), Alpha Omega Alpha. Home: 45 Fairview Rd Narberth PA 19072-1328 Office: 100 E Lancaster Ave # 3-west Wynnewood PA 19096-3411 also: Allegheny U Health Scis Dept Surgery Broad and Vine Sts MS 413 Philadelphia PA 19102-1192

MARKS, LAWRENCE EDWARD, psychologist, educator; b. N.Y.C., Dec. 28, 1941; s. Milton and Anne (Parnes) M.; m. Joya Ellen Cazes, Dec. 24, 1963; children: Liza, Laura. AB, Hunter Coll., N.Y.C., 1962; PhD, Harvard U., Cambridge, Mass., 1965; PhD honoris causa, Stockholm U., 1994. Rsch.-assoc. prof. Yale U., New Haven, 1966-84; asst.-assoc. fellow John B. Pierce Lab., New Haven, 1966-84; prof. epidemiology and psychology Yale U., New Haven, 1984—; fellow John B. Pierce Lab., New Haven, 1984—, dir., 1999—. Author: Sensory Processes: The New Psychophysics, 1974, The Unity of the Senses, 1978. Named to Hall of Fame, Hunter Coll., N.Y.C., 1985; recipient Jacob Javits award NIH, Washington, 1987. Fellow AAAS, Am. Psychol. Assn., Am. Psychol. Soc., N.Y. Acad. Sci. Democrat. Jewish. Achievements include elucidation of common principles underlying sensory processes in various sense modalities; development of validational scheme for quantifying magnitudes of sensory experience; indication of role of cross-modal (synesthetic) perception in relation to language and literature. Home: 48 Maplevale Dr Woodbridge CT 06525-1118 Office: John B Pierce Lab 290 Congress Ave New Haven CT 06519-1403 E-mail: marks@jbpierce.org.

MARKS, LILLIAN SHAPIRO, secretarial studies educator, author; b. Bklyn., Mar. 16, 1907; d. Hayman and Celia (Merowitz) Shapiro; m. Joseph Marks, Feb. 21, 1932; children: Daniel, Sheila Blake, Jonathan. BS, NYU, 1928. High sch. tchr., N.Y.C., 1929-30; tchr. Evalina de Rothschild Sch., Jerusalem, 1930-31; social worker United Jewish Aid Bklyn., 1931-32; tchr. Richmond Hill High Sch., 1932-40, Andrew Jackson High Sch., Cambria Heights, N.Y., 1940-71; mem. faculty New Sch. Social Rsch., N.Y.C., 1977-87; staff Vassar Summer Inst., 1946. Vol. tchr. English Israel schs., 1987—2000. Am. editor: Teeline, A System of Fast Writing, 1970; author: College Teeline, 1977, College Teeline Self Taught, 1988, Touch Typing Made Simple, 1985; contbr. articles to profl. lit. jours. Mem. Am. Fedn. Tchrs. Democrat. Home and Office: 300 E46 St 17J New York NY 10017

MARKS, MARSHA KASS, history educator; b. NYC, May 6, 1935; d. Aaron and Edith (Malkin) K.; m. Henry S. Marks, June 8, 1965; 1 child, Barbara Carol. BA, Hunter Coll., 1956; MA, Yale U., 1957, postgrad., 1957-59. Instr. Ga. State Coll., Atlanta, 1960-65, J.C. Calhoun Jr. Coll., Decatur, Ala., 1965-67; asst. prof. Ala. A&M U., Normal, 1967-79, assoc. prof. history, 1979—97; adj. J.C Calhoun C.C., Huntsville, Ala., 1997—; ret., 1997. Co-author: Alabama Past Leaders, 1982; also contbr. articles to encys. and reference books. Mem. Friends of Library, Huntsville, 1986-87; chorus mem. Huntsville Opera Theater, 1983-84. Mem. So. Hist. Assn. (membership com. 1985-86), Ala. Hist. Assn., Ala. Assn. Historians, Popular Culture Assn. in South (exec. council 1980-81), The Humanities and Tech. Assn. (state coordinator 1978-79), Huntsville Lit. Assn. (exec. bd. 1980-81), Phi Beta Kappa. Lodges: Hadassah (exec. bd. Huntsville 1985-87). Democrat. Jewish. Avocations: reading, gardening. Home: 405 Homewood Dr SW Huntsville AL 35801-3432

MARKS, MICHAEL, association administrator; BS in Speech Comms./Edn., MS in Pub. Rels., U. So. Miss. Tchr. Perry County Schs., Lumberton Schs.; debate/drama coach Hattiesburg (Miss.) H.S., to 1997; pres. Miss. Assn. Educators, 1997—. State chair Miss. Forensic League, 1996-97. Recipient Miss. Tchr. of Yr. award, 1998, Milken Nat. Educator award, 1996, Disney/McDonald's Outstanding Tchr. of Performing Arts award, 1996. Office: Miss Assn Educators 775 N State St Jackson MS 39202-3086

MARKS, NORA MARALEA, retired secondary school educator; b. Tarentum, Pa., Aug. 17, 1939; d. Chauncey Holmes and Mary Hettie (Bartmas) Elliott; m. Donald Richard Jacobs, July 8, 1961 (div. June 1979); children: Matthew John Jacobs, Donna Marie Gentz; m. Carr Bishop Marks, June 24, 1989; 1 stepchild, Michele Binkley. BS in Edn., Temple U., 1961, MS in Music Edn., 1981, postgrad., Hofstra U., Westminster Choir Coll., Trenton, N.J. Choral dir. Upper Perkiomen Schs., East Greenville, Pa., 1961—67; music tchr. Valley Stream Schs., NY, 1973—79; choral dir. Gettysburg H.S., Gettysburg, Pa., 1979—2000. State sec. Pa. Rural Letter Carriers Assn., 1993—; handbell choir dir. Uriah United Meth. Ch.,

Gardners, Pa., 1984—, dir. instrumental ensemble, adult choir dir., asst. organist; music dir. Uriah United Meth. Ch. Daycare, Gardners, 2003—. Scholar, Berkshire Music Ctr., Mass., 1963. Mem.: NEA, Adams County Music Educators Assn., Am. Choral Dirs. Assn. Home: 1971 Shippensburg Rd Biglerville PA 17307

MARKS, PAUL ALAN, oncologist, cell biologist, educator; b. N.Y.C., Aug. 16, 1926; s. Robert R. and Sarah (Bohorad) Marks; m. Joan Harriet Rosen, Nov. 28, 1953; children: Andrew Robert, Elizabeth Susan Marks Ostrer, Matthew Stuart. AB with gen. honors, Columbia U., 1945, MD, 1949, DSc (hon.), 2000; D in Biol. Sci. (hon.), U. Urbino, Italy, 1982; PhD (hon.), Hebrew U., Jerusalem, Israel, 1987, U. Tel Aviv, 1992; DSc (hon.), Ben Gurion U., Beer Sheva, Israel, 2003. Fellow Columbia U. Coll. Physicians and Surgeons, 1952—53, assoc., 1955—56, mem. faculty, 1956—82, dir. hematology tng., 1961—74, prof. medicine, 1967—82, prof. human genetics and devel., 1969—82, dean faculty of medicine, v.p. med. affairs, 1970—73, dir. Comprehensive Cancer Ctr., 1972—80, v.p. health scis., 1973—80, Frode Jensen prof. medicine, 1974—80; prof. cell biology and genetics Cornell U. Coll. Medicine, N.Y.C., 1980—99, prof. medicine Grad. Sch. Med. Scis., 1983—; pres., CEO Meml. Sloan-Kettering Cancer Ctr., N.Y.C., 1980—99, pres. emeritus, 2000—. Instr. Sch. Medicine George Washington U., 1954—55; cons. VA Hosp., N.Y.C., 1962—66; attending physician Presbyn. Hosp., N.Y.C., 1967—82, Meml. Hosp. for Cancer and Allied Diseases, 1980—; prin. investigator, Devel. Cell Biology Sloan-Kettering Inst. for Cancer Rsch., 1980—; adj. prof. Rockefeller U., 1980—; vis. physician Rockefeller U. Hosp., 1980—; hon. staff N.Y. Hosp., 1981—; bd. sci. counselors divsn. cancer treatment Nat. Cancer Inst., 1980—83; mem. steering com. Nat. Cancer Inst. Frederick Cancer Rsch. Facility, 1982—86; chmn. program adv. com. Robert Wood Johnson Found., 1983—89; mem. Gov.'s Commn. on Shoreham Nuc. Plant, 1983, Mayor's Commn. Sci. and Tech. City of N.Y., 1984—87; mem. adv. com. on NIH to Sec. HHS, 1989—90, 1993—98; external adv. com. Intramural Rsch. Program Rev. NIH; mem. gov. com. NYPRHA, 1996; mem. Mayor's Task Force Biomed. Rsch. and Tech., N.Y.C., 1999; mem. tech. adv. group UN Assn. U.S.; mem. coun. biol. scis. Pritzker Sch. Medicine U. Chgo., 1977—88; first lectr. Nakasone Program for Cancer Control U. Tokyo, 1984; Ayrey fellow, vis. prof. Royal Postgrad. Med. Sch. U. London, 1985; William Dameshek vis. prof. hematology Mt. Sinai Med. Ctr., 1985; nat. vis. com. CUNY Med. Sch., 1986—89; trustee Feinberg Grad. Sch. Weizmann Inst. Sci., Rehovot, Israel, 1986—; William H. Resnick lectr. in medicine Stamford Hosp., 1986; disting. faculty lectr. M.D. Anderson Hosp. U. Tex., 1986; Maurice C. Pincoffs lectr. U. Md., Balt., 1987; vis. prof. Coll. de France, 1988; Alpha Omega Alpha vis. prof. N.Y. Med. Coll., 1990; Mario A. Baldini vis. prof. Harvard Med. Sch., 1991; mem. sci. adv. bd. City of Hope Nat. Med. Ctr., Duarte, Calif., 1987—92, Raymond and Beverly Sackler Found., Inc., 1989, Jefferson Cancer Inst., Phila., 1989; mem. Found. Biomed. Rsch., 1989—; sci. adv. com. Imperial Cancer Rsch. Fund, 1994; pres., CEO Meml. Sloan-Kettering Cancer Ctr., 1980—99; sr. adv. Lazard Freres, 2000—; dir. Tularik, San Francisco, 1993—2002, Pfizer, N.Y.C., 1978—96, Dreyfus Mutual Funds, 1977—; co-founder, sec. and vice chmn. Aton Pharma, Tarrytown, NY, 2001—. Author: 11 books; mem. editl. bd.: Blood, 1964—76, editor-in-chief:, 1978—82, mem. editl. bd.: Jour. Clin Investigation, 1970—71, editor-in-chief:, mem. editl. bd.: Cancer Treatment Revs., 1981—, Japanese Jour. Cancer Rsch., 1985—, Molecular Reprodn. and Devel., 1988—, Cancer Preventions, 1989, Sci., 1990, Current Opinion Oncologic Endocrine and Metabolic Drugs, 1998, expert analyst: Chemistry and Molecular Biology edit. of Chemtracts, 1990—92, mem. adv. bd.: Internat. Jour. Hematology, 1992, Stem Cells, bd. contbg. editors: Blood Cells, Molecules and Diseases, 1994, Comité des Sages, 1994; contbr. over 400 articles to profl. jours. Trustee St. Luke's Hosp., 1970—80, Roosevelt Hosp., 1970—80, Presbyn. Hosp., 1972—80, Metpath Inst. Med. Edn., 1977—79, Hadassah Med. Ctr., Jerusalem, 1996; mem. jury Albert Lasker Awards, 1974—82; bd. dirs. Revson Found., 1976—91, Am. Found. for Basic Rsch. Israel, Israel Acad. Scis., 1991; mem. tech. bd. Milbank Meml. Fund, 1978—85; bd. govs. Friends of Sheba Med. Ctr., Tel Hashomer. Recipient Charles Janeway prize, Columbia U., 1949, Joseph Mather Smith prize, 1959, 1995, Stevens Triennial prize, 1960, Swiss-Am. Found. award in med. rsch., 1965, Columbia U. Coll. Physicians and Surgeons Disting. Achievement medal, 1980, Centenary medal, Inst. Pasteur, 1987, Disting. Oncologist award, Hipple Cancer Ctr. and Kettering Ctr., 1987, Found. for Promotion of Cancer Rsch. medal (Japan), 1984, Disting. Svc. medal, Robert Wood Johnson Found., 1989, Outstanding Achievement award in hematopoiesis, U. Innsbruck, 1991, Pres.'s Nat. Medal Sci., 1991, Gold medal, Coll. Physicians and Surgeons, 1994, Japan Found. for Cancer Rsch. award, 1995, John Jay award, Columbia Coll., N.Y., 1996, Lifetime Achievement award, Greater N.Y. Hosp. Assn., 1997, Am. Italian Cancer Found., 1999, Katherine Berken Judd award, Meml. Sloan-Kettering Cancer Ctr., 1999, Humanitarian award, Breast Cancer Rsch. Found., 2000, Disting. Lifetime Achievement award, Healthcare Chaplaincy, NY, 2001, John Stearns award for lifetime achievement, NY Acad. Medicine, 2002, Annie Blount Storrs Humanitarian award, Calvary Hosp., NY, 2002; fellow Commonwealth Fund fellow, Pasteur Inst., 1961—62. Master: ACP, Coll. Phys. Surgeons; fellow: AAAS, Pasteur Inst. Paris (Commonwealth Fund fellow 1961—62), Am. Acad. Arts and Scis., Royal Soc. Medicine; mem.: NAS (chmn. sect. med. genetics, hematology and oncology 1980—83, chmn. Acad. Forum Adv. Com. 1980—81, coun. 1984—87, del. biol. warfare com. Internat. Security and Arms Control 1986—89), European Acad. Scis., UN Assn. U.S.A. (tech. adv. group), Health Scis. Adv. Coun. Columbia U., Weizmann Inst. Sci. (bd. govs. 1976—, gov. emeritus, Israel), Chinese U. Hong Kong, Sci. Adv. Bd. Hong Kong Cancer Inst., Third World Acad. Scis. (advisor), Soc. for Study Devel. and Growth, Internat. Leadership Ctr. on Longevity and Soc. Interurban Clin. Club, Japan Soc. Hematology (Disting. lectr. 1989, Disting. lectr. 1989), Soc. for Devel. Biology, Internat. Soc. Devel. Biologists, Harvey Soc. (pres. 1973—74), Assn. Am. Physicians, Am. Soc. Hematology (pres.-elect 1983, pres. 1984, chmn. adv. bd. 1985), Soc. Cell Biology, Assn. Am. Cancer Insts. (bd. dirs. 1983—88), Italian Assn. Cell Biology and Differentiation (hon.), Chinese Anti-Cancer Assn. (hon.), Japanese Cancer Assn. (hon.), Am. Assn. Cancer Rsch., Am. Soc. Human Genetics (past mem. program com.), Am. Soc. Biol. Chemists, Am. Soc. Clin. Investigation (pres. 1972—73), Am. Fedn. Clin. Rsch. (past councillor Ea. dist.), Red Cell Club (past chmn.), Inst. Medicine (coun. 1973—76, chmn. com. study resources clin. investigation with NAS 1988), Univ. Club (N.Y.C.), Century Assn., Econ. Club (N.Y.C.), Alpha Omega Alpha. Office: Meml Sloan-Kettering Cancer Ctr 1275 York Ave New York NY 10021-6094

MARKS, RICHARD HENRY LEE, biochemist, educator; b. Richmond, Va., Nov. 23, 1943; s. Henry Lee and Helen Campbell (Hutchison) M.; m. Lynne Evelyn Griffith, Aug. 21, 1966; children: Christopher Scott, Brian Stuart. BS, U. Richmond, 1965; PhD, Ind. U., 1969. Postdoctoral fellow U. Calif., Santa Barbara, 1969-72; asst. prof. U. of Medicine and Dentistry of N.J., Newark, 1972-76, East Carolina U. Sch. of Medicine, Greenville, N.C., 1976-77, assoc. prof., 1977-92, prof., 1992—. Mem.: Internat. Assn. Med. Sci. Educators, Am. Soc. for Biochemistry and Molecular Biology, Am. Chem. Soc. Home: 1226 Worthington Ln Greenville NC 27858-7952 Office: Sch of Medicine Dept of Biochemistry East Carolina U Greenville NC 27858 E-mail: marksr@mail.ecu.edu.

MARKS, STEPHEN J. neurologist, educator; b. Bklyn., Aug. 30, 1953; s. Ansel R. Marks and Frances L. Carpenter; m. Cindy G. Marks, Mar. 27, 1994; children: Jordan, Avery. BA, Colgate U., 1979. Diplomate Am. Bd. Neurology & Psychiatry. Intern Lenox Hill Hosp., NYC; resident Mt. Sinai Hosp., NYC; assoc. prof. N.Y. Med. Coll., Valhalla, 1987—. Team neurologist N.Y. Jets, Hempstead, 1986. Co-author: (chapter) Principle & Practice of Emergency Medicine, 1992, (book), 1997. Fellow: Am. Heart Assn. (mem. stroke coun.); mem.: Soc. Neuroscience, Nat. Stroke Assn., Am. Acad. Neurology. Avocations: skiing, windsurfing. Office: Dept Neurology Munger Pavilion, NYMC Valhalla NY 10595

MARKUSON, CIRA PROFIT, college administrator; b. Jersey City, Apr. 15, 1947; d. Joseph Francis and Aldona Frances (Novak) P.; m. Roger Alcide Masse, Aug. 23, 1976 (div. Mar. 1989); children: Jeanine Elizabeth, Crissa Marie, Paul Joseph; m. Stephen Harvey Markuson, Oct. 12, 1991. BA, Rosary Coll., River Forest, Ill., 1969; MS, Rutgers U., 1971. Cert. clin. competence Am. Speech & Hearing Assn.; cert. in health care mgmt. Rutgers U. Dir. speech and hearing ctr. Mercer Med. Ctr., Trenton, N.J., 1970-73, dir. vol. svcs., 1973-75, Friends Hosp., Phila., 1975-76; asst. dir. devel. Hartwick Coll., Oneonta, NY, 1986-88, dir. ann. fund, 1988—, dir. stewardship and event planning, 1995—2001, dir. alumni and coll. rels., 2001—. Pres. bd. dirs. Catskill Symphony Orch., Oneonta, 1992-94; entertainment chmn. Oneonta First Night, 2001, 2002. Mem. AAUW (pres. 1982-86, co-pres. 1988-90, corporate rep. for Hartwick Coll), Coun. for Advancement and Support of Edn., Assn. Performing Arts Presenters. Avocation: theatre. Home: PO Box 719 Oneonta NY 13820-0719 Office: Hartwick Coll Oneonta NY 13820

MARLAND, ALKIS JOSEPH, rental company executive, computer scientist, educator, financial planner; b. Athens, Greece, Mar. 8, 1943; arrived in U.S., 1961, naturalized, 1974; s. Basil and Maria (Pervanides) Mouradoglou; m. Anita Louise Malone, Dec. 19, 1970 (dec. Mar. 27, 2003); children: Andrea Weber, Alyssa. BS, Southwestern U., 1963; MA, U. Tex., Austin, 1967; MS in Engring. Adminstrn., So. Meth. U., 1971. CLU; cert. data processing, enrolled agt., fund specialist, ChFC, CFP, accredited tax preparer, accredited tax advisor. With Sun Co., Richardson, Tex., 1968-71, Phila., 1971-76; mgr. planning and acquisitions Sun Info. Svcs. subs. Sun Co., Dallas, 1976-78; v.p. Helios Capital Corp. subs. Sun Co., Radnor, Pa., 1978-83; pres. ALKAN Leasing Corp., Wayne, Pa., 1983—, also bd. dirs. Prof. dept. computer scis. and bus. adminstrn. Ea. Coll., St. Davids, Pa., 1985—87; prof. math. Villanova (Pa.) U., 1987—89. Bd. dirs. Radnor Twp. Sch. Dist., 1987—91, Delaware County Intermediate Unit, 1988—91. Mem.: IEEE, Assn. Investment Mgmt. and Rsch., Phila. Union League, World Affairs Coun. Phila., Fgn. Policy Rsch. Inst., Phila. Fin. Assn. (mem. award 1988, sec. 1989—92, bd. dirs. 1989—92), Fin. Planning Assn. (bd. dirs. Phila. Tri-State Area 2000—, treas. 2000—02, pres. elect 2002—03, pres. 2003), Fin. Analysts Phila., Nat. Assn. Pub. Accts., Nat. Assn. Tax Practitioners, Nat. Assn. Enrolled Agts., Inst. Cert. Fin. Planners (bd. dirs. Phila. Tri-State Area 1993—99, v.p. membership 1994—95, treas. 1995—99), Am. Assn. Equipment Lessors, Fin. Svc. Profls., Data Processing Mgmt. Assn., Assn. Computing Machinery, Main Line C. of C., Masons, Rotary (pres. 1989—90, asst. gov. 1990—92, pres. 1993—94, treas. dist. 7450 2002—, Wayne). Republican. Home: 736 Brooke Rd Wayne PA 19087-4709 Office: PO Box 8301 Radnor PA 19087-8301 E-mail: almarland@aol.com., marlandatalkan@aol.com.

MARLER, ADDIE KAREN, elementary school educator; b. Dothan, Ala., Nov. 5, 1950; d. James Luther and Beulah Lee (Clenney) Savell; m. Thomas Franklin Marler, June 15, 1967; children: Jeffery, Jamie, Pamela. AA, Pasco Hernado C.C., 1981; BA, St. Leo Coll., 1985, postgrad. 6th and 7th grade lang. arts tchr. Moore Mickens Mid. Sch., Dade City, Fla., 1985-86, 7th grade gifted class tchr., 1985-86; developmental kindergarten tchr. Pasco Elem. Sch., Dade City, 1986-88, tchr. 6th grade self-contained class, 1988-89, 1st grade tchr., 1989-90, 1st/2d grade tchr., 1990-91, primary house K-2d grade tchr., 1991-93, intermediate house 3d-5th grade tchr., 1993-94, ESOL resource tchr., 1994—. Migrant lead tchr. Pasco Elem. Sch., 1990-92, ESL tchr., 1994-95, ESOL resource tchr., 1994-96; dist. curriculum writer Pasco County Schs., 1991-93; ednl. cons., 1990—. Mem. adv. bd. Fla. League of Tchrs./Fla. Dept. Edn.; mem. Heritage Arts Assn., Dade City. Named 20th Anniversary Ambassador, Edn. Ctr. N.C., 1993-94. Mem. Fla. Assn. Childhood Edn., Alpha Delta Kappa (historian, scholarship chmn. 1990-93 Alpha Phi chpt.). Republican. Baptist. Avocations: interior decorating, shopping, audio books, elderly advocacy. Office: Pasco Elem 37350 Florida Ave Dade City FL 33525-4097

MARLER, CHARLES HERBERT, journalism educator, historian, consultant; b. Garfield, Ark., Apr. 13, 1933; s. William Owen and Velma Valentine (Poe) M.; m. Peggy Lucille Gambill, Dec. 30, 1954; children: David Owen, Todd Alan, Scott Ladd. BA, Abilene Christian U., 1955, MA, 1968; PhD, U. Mo., 1974. Publicity asst. Abilene (Tex.) Christian U., 1955-56, sports info. dir., 1958-63, assoc. dir. devel., 1963-64, dir. info. and pubs., 1964-71, prof. journalism, 1974—2003, chmn. dept. journalism and mass comm., 1987-98, prof. emeritus journalism and sr. faculty, 2003—; rsch. asst. U. Mo., Columbia, 1973-74. Editor: Horizons, 1963-71, Lone Star Christmas, 1989, No Ordinary University, 1998; cons. Parenting Today, Christian Woman, Gospel Advocate, IdeaShop, Christian Chronicle; mem. editl. bd. Am. Journalism, Southwestern Mass Comm. Jour.; contbr. articles to profl. jours. Elder Univ. Ch. Christ, Abilene, 1977—; trustee Christian Village of Abilene, 1981-2000, Members of Chs. of Christ for Scouting, Abilene, 1985—, nat. chmn., 1989-91; mem. coun. bd. Boy Scouts Am., Abilene, 1981-2001. With U.S. Army, 1956-57, Germany. Frank Luther Mott Hist. Rsch. fellow U. Mo., Columbia, 1972-74, Cullen Fund grantee, 1982-84, 85-87; recipient Improvement award Time/Life Alumni Mag., 1966, Journalism Excellence award 20th Century Christian Mag., 1968, Clinton H. Denman Freedom of Info. Writing award U. Mo., 1974, Scoutmaster's key Boy Scouts Am., 1981, Dist. Merit award, 1982, Keith Ware award U.S. Army Journalism Competition, 1985, Tchr. of Yr. Trustees award, 1987, Silver Beaver award Boy Scouts Am., 1988, Christian Journalism award The Christian Chronicle, 1993; named Advisor of Yr., Tex. Intercollegiate Press Assn., 1982, Faithful Servant, Chs. Christ for Scouting, 1990, Faculty Senate award, 2000, Coll. Arts and Scis. Career Achievement award, 2000, Charlie Marler scholarship, Southwestern Journalism Congress, 2001; named to Tex. Intercoll. Press Assn. Hall of Fame, 2003. Mem. Am. Journalism Historian Assn. (bd. dirs. 1985-88, chmn. pub. com. 1983-87, 95-96, chmn. election and site com. 1987-90), Nat. Conf. Editorial Writers, S.W. Edn. Coun. for Edn. in Journalism and Mass Comm. (pres. 1988-89), SW Journalism Congress (pres 1987-88, 1997-98, 1998-99, 99-2000), Texas Intercollegiate Press Assn. Advs. (pres. 1987-89), Soc. Newspaper Design, Soc. Profl. Journalists (dep. dir. journalism edn. 1988-90, mem. nat. journalism edn. com. 1988-90), Assn. for Edn. in Journalism and Mass Comm. and Religion and Media Interest Group (chair 1999-2000). Avocations: geneaology, newspaper coffee mug collecting, travel, research, camping. Home: 818 Radford Dr Abilene TX 79601-4613 Office: Dept Journalism and Mass Comm ACU Box 27892 Abilene Christian U Abilene TX 79699-7892 E-mail: charlie.marler@jmc.acu.edu.

MARLOW, LYDIA LOU, elementary education educator; b. Aledo, Ill., Aug. 21, 1954; d. Dwayne Elwood Irwin and Phyllis Jean (McKeown) Graff; m. Sidney G. Marlow Jr.; children: Erika Lynn, John Andrew. BA in Edn. with honors, Stephens Coll., 1976; MA in Reading, U. Mo., Kansas City, 1983. Cert. elem. tchr., Mo. Tchr. 2d grade Atlanta (Mo.) C-3 Sch. Dist., 1976-81; from tchr. headstart to tchr. 2d grade Independence (Mo.) Sch. Dist., 1982-92; reading clinician Santa Fe Trail & Procter Elem. Sch., Independence, 1993-99; Title 1 reading tchr. George Caleb Bingham 7th Grade Ctr., Independence, 1999-2000; gifted and talented tchr., 2001—. Adj. prof. children's lit. Webster U., Kansas City, Mo., 1994; developer program Focus on Reading, Independence, Mo., 1996; dept. chair, contbr. Missouri Reader, 1998—; presenter in field. Author: (novels) The Master Teacher: Memorable Moments, 2001; contbr. articles. Facilitator attention deficit hyperactivity disorder support group Caring Cmty. Santa Fe Trail Sch., Independence, 1996—97; rschr., author Truman Whistlestop Project, Independence, 1996—97; reading clinician Literacy Learning Ctr., Independence, 1997—2001. Recipient True Friend award Friends United Ednl. Support, Independence, 1994, Excellence in Tchg. award Govt. Employees Hosp. Assn., 1997, 2002. Mem.: Cmty. Assn. for the Arts, Children and Adults with Attention Deficit Disorder, Internat. Reading Assn. (local pres., publicity com. 1989—90, publicity co-chmn., editor Indep. IRA local 1991—93, editor Mo. state IRA 1992—95, Pres. award 1989), AAUW (publicity chair 1982—83), NEA (MNEA/Reliant grantee 1997), ASCD, Writers Club (coord. 1993—99, Editor's Choice 2001). Avocations: writing, gardening, reading, collecting antiques and elephant figurines. Home: 14609 E 44th St S Independence MO 64055-4810 Office: Christian Ott Elem School 1525 N Noland Rd Independence MO 64050 E-mail: Lydz14609@yahoo.com.

MARLOW, MARCIA MARIE, secondary school educator, publishing executive; b. Maywood, Calif., Jan. 24; d. George Murf Chandler and Zelda Marie Chandler; m. L. K. Higginbotham (dec. Dec. 23, 1998); children: Kevin Darrell Smith, Trisha Nicole Ailey Abbott, Shannon Marie Ailey Alexander, Bryan Chandler Ailey. A in Bus., No. Okla. Coll., 1980; BS in Edn., Mo. So. State Coll., 1984, cert. reading specialist, 1985, degree in art edn., 1993. Tchr. McDonald County Sch., Jane, Mo., 1984—88; owner Southwestern Steel, Inc., Grove, Okla., 1988—99, New Horizons Steel, Grove, Okla.; pub. Chandler Day Pub., Inc., Fairland, Okla., 1999—. Educator Wyandotte Pub. Sch., Okla., 2001—. Editor: (book) Murphy, The Littlest Elf, 2000; author: Love Verses, 2001; acrylic and oil paintings. Recipient Tchr. of the Yr., McDonald county Sch./ Grove, Okla., 1988. Mem.: Brush and Palette Club, Phi Theta Kappa (life). Baptist. Avocations: art, singing, reading, horseback riding, gardening.

MARMOR, MICHAEL FRANKLIN, ophthalmologist, educator; b. N.Y.C., Aug. 10, 1941; s. Judd and Katherine (Stern) M.; m. C. Jane Breeden, Dec. 20, 1968; children: Andrea K., David J. AB, Harvard U., 1962, MD, 1966. Diplomate Am. Bd. Ophthalmology. Med. intern UCLA Med. Ctr., 1967; fellow neurophysiology NIMH, 1967-70; resident in ophthalmology Mass. Eye and Ear Infirmary, Boston, 1970-73; asst. prof. ophthalmology U. Calif. Sch. Medicine, San Francisco, 1973-74; asst. prof. surgery (ophthalmology) Stanford (Calif.) U. Sch. Medicine, 1974-80, assoc. prof., 1980-86, prof., 1986—, head. div. ophthalmalogy, 1984-88, chmn. dept., 1988-92, dir. Basic Sci. Course Ophthalmology, 1993—. Faculty mem. program in human biology Stanford U., 1982—; chief ophthalmology sect. VA Med. Ctr., Palo Alto, Calif., 1974-84; mem. sci. adv. bd. No. Calif. Soc. to Prevent Blindness, 1984-92, Calif. Med. Assn., 1984-92, Nat. Retinitis Pigmentosa Found., 1985-95. Author: The Eye of the Artist, 1997, Degas Through his own Eyes, 2002; editor: The Retinal Pigment Epithelium, 1975, The Effects of Aging and Environment on Vision, 1991, The Retinal Pigment Epithelium: Function and Disease, 1998; editor-in-chief Doc. Ophthalmologica, 1995-99; history editor: Survey of Ophthalmology; editl. bd. Healthline; contbr. more than 200 articles to sci. jours., 50 chpts. to books. Mem. affirmative action com. Stanford U. Sch. Medicine, 1984-92. Sr. asst. surgeon USPHS, 1967-70. Recipient Svc. award Nat. Retinitis Pigmentosa Found., Balt., 1981, Rsch. award Alcon Rsch. Found., Houston, 1989; rsch. grantee Nat. Eye. Inst., Bethesda, Md., 1974-94. Fellow Am. Acad. Ophthalmology (bd. councillors 1982-85, pub. health com. 1990-93, rep. to NAS com. on vision 1991-93, Honor award 1984, Sr. Honor award 1996), Cogan Ophthalmology Hist. Soc. (pres. 2003—); mem. Internat. Soc. Clin. Electrophysiology of Vision (v.p. 1990-98, dir. stds.), Assn. Rsch. in Vision and Ophthalmology, Internat. Soc. for Eye Rsch., Macula Soc., Retina Soc. Democrat. Avocations: tennis, race-walking, chamber music (clarinet), art, medical history. Office: Stanford U Sch Medcine Dept Ophthalmology Stanford CA 94305-5308

MAROLDA, MARIA RIZZO, mathematics educator; b. Springfield, Mass., Aug. 15, 1943; d. Arthur R. and Frances M. (McLaughlin) Rizzo; m. Anthony J. Marolda, Oct. 10, 1970; children: Matthew D.A., Ria F.R. BA, Tufts U., 1965, MA, 1966. Math. tchr. Newton (Mass.) Pub. Schs., 1966-68, asst. math. coord., 1968-70; math. specialist Learning Disabilities Program: Children's Hosp., Boston, 1971—, assoc. dir., 1992—. Adj. assoc. prof. Simmons Coll., Boston, 1968-89; pvt. practice cons. in math. edn., assessment and learning, 1970—. Author: Cuisenaire Alphabet Book, 1976, Activities with Attributes, 1992; contbr. chpt. to (book) Windows of Opportunity: Math For Students With Special Needs, 1994; assoc. author Math in My World, 1996; editor: Perspectives: Summer Edit. Math Education, 2000. Chair bd. trustees Nashoba Brooks Sch., Concord, 1979-90; trustee Fenn Sch., Concord, 1980-91; mem. parents com. Middlesex Sch., Concord, 1989-91. Named Outstanding Young Woman of Am., 1970. Office: Learning Disabilities Prog Childrens Hosp Dept Neurol 300 Longwood Ave Boston MA 02115-5724

MARONI, DONNA FAROLINO, biologist, researcher; b. Buffalo, Feb. 27, 1938; d. Enrico Victor and Eleanor (Redlinska) Farolino; m. Gustavo Primo Maroni, Dec. 16, 1974. BS, U. Wis., 1960, PhD, 1969. Project assoc. U. Wis., Madison, 1960-63, 68-74; Alexander von Humboldt fellow Inst. Genetics U. Cologne, Fed. Republic Germany, 1974-75; Hargitt fellow Duke U., Durham, N.C., 1975-76, rsch. assoc., 1976-83, rsch. assoc. prof., 1983-87; sr. program specialist N.C. Biotech. Ctr., Research Triangle Park, 1987-88, dir. sci. programs div., 1988-92, v.p. for sci. programs, 1992-94, ret., 1995. Mem. adv. com. MICROMED at Bowman Gray Sch. Medicine, Winston-Salem, NC, 1988—94; mem. sci. adv. bd. NC Biosci. Fund, LLC, 1998—99, Minority Sci. Improvement Alliance for Instrn. and Rsch. in Biotech, Ala. A&M U., Normal, 1990—91. Contbr. over 20 articles and revs. to profl. jours. Grantee NSF, 1977-79, NIH, 1979-82, 79-83, 82-87. Mem. Genetics Soc. Am., N.C. Acad. Sci., Inc. (bd. dirs. 1983-86), Sigma Xi (mem. exec. com. Duke U. chpt. 1989-90). Achievements include research in electron microscopy, evolution of chromosomes, chromosome structure, evolution of mitosis, and mitosis and fungal phylogeny.

MAROVITZ, SANFORD E. English language and literature educator; b. Chgo., May 10, 1933; s. Harold and Gertrude (Luster) M.; m. Eleonora Dimitsa, Sept. 1, 1964. BA with honors, Lake Forest Coll., 1960; MA, Duke U., 1961, PhD, 1968. Instr. English Temple U., 1963-65; Fulbright instr. U. Athens, Greece, 1965-67; from asst. prof. English to prof. Kent State U., Ohio, 1967-96, prof. emeritus, 1996—. Vis. prof. English, Shimane U., Matsue, Japan, 1976-77, chair, 1987-92; co-dir. Melville Among the Nations, Greece, 1997. Co-editor: Artful Thunder: Versions of Romanticism in American Literature in Honor of Howard P. Vincent, 1975, Melville Among the Nations: Proceedings, 2001; co-author: Bibliographical Guide to the Study of the Literature of the U.S.A., 5th edit., 1984; author: Abraham Cahan, 1996; contbr. articles to profl. jours. Nat. trustee Lake Forest Coll., 1990-98. With USAF, 1953-57. Woodrow Wilson fellow, 1960-61; recipient Disting. Svc. Citation Lake Forest Coll., 1985, Disting. Tchg. award Kent State U., 1985, Presdl. Citation Shimane U., 1998. Mem.: MLA, Coll. English Assn. (Robert Miller award for best article 2000), R.W. Emerson Soc., Saul Bellow Soc., W.D. Howells Soc. (v.p. 2000—01, pres. 2002—03), Aldous Huxley Soc. (curator 1998—), Henry James Soc., Hawthorne Soc., Melville Soc. (sec. 1994—96, pres. 1998), Am. Studies Assn., Phi Beta Delta, Omicron Delta Kappa, Phi Beta Kappa. Democrat. Jewish. Home: 1155 Norwood St Kent OH 44240-3342 Office: Kent State U Dept English Kent OH 44242-0001 E-mail: smarovit@kent.edu.

MARQUAND, JEAN MACMURTRY, educational administrator; b. Schenectady, N.Y., Feb. 1, 1947; d. Louis Frederick Jr. and Eleanore Jean (Noyes) McM. BA in Edn. with honors, Simmons Coll., 1969; MEd, U. Vt., 1975; grad. cert. advanced studies in mgmt., Radcliffe Coll., 1993. Elem. tchr., Pittsford, N.Y., 1969-70; reading specialist Lincoln, Vt., 1971-73, Pembroke, Mass., 1976; grad. teaching asst U. Vt., 1975; elem tchr. Chatham, Mass., 1977-80; with Arthur D. Little, Cambridge, Mass., 1981-82; exec. sec. Meredith & Grew, Inc., Boston, 1982—2003. V.p. alumnae fund Simmons Coll., Boston, 1994-96. Bd. mgrs. Jr. League Boston, 1990-92, v.p. pres., 1993-94, sustainer com., 1997—; Boston chpt. Philanthropic Ednl. Orgn., 1983—, chair Mass. state bylaws com., 1998;

mem. Greater Boston Real Estate Bd., 2001—. Recipient Vol. Recognition award Jr. League Boston, 1989. Mem. The Coll. Club (pres. 1994-98, chair bylaws com. 1998—, parliamentarian 2001-), PEO, The Internat. Alliance, Chowder Soc. Home and Office: On Holiday 77 Barley Neck Rd Orleans MA 02653

MARQUARDT, LARRY DEAN, librarian; b. Hendricks, Minn., May 30, 1950; BS, S.D. State U., 1972, MEd, 1973; MLS, Vanderbilt U., 1985. Investigator Dept. Commerce and Consumer Affairs, Pierre, S.D., 1974-75; social worker Dept. Social Svcs., Brookings, S.D., 1975-84; aging program specialist, librarian Tenn. Commn. on Aging, Nashville, 1985-86; libr. dir. Des Moines U.-Osteo. Med. Ctr., 1986—. Vanderbilt U. scholar, 1984. Mem. ALA, Med. Libr. Assn. (instnl. mem. Midwest chpt.), Assn. Coll. and Rsch. Librs., Polk County Biomed. Consortium, Iowa Rsch. Edn. Network, Iowa Health Scis. Roundtable, Soc. for German-Am. Studies, Phi Kappa Phi, Kappa Delta Pi. Avocations: genealogy, travel, reading, gardening.

MARQUEZ, HOPE, school system worker, educator; b. Winters, Tex., Sept. 12, 1948; Bus driver, office asst., safety officer Ft. Worth Ind. Sch. Dist., 1977-90; ops.mgr., in charge bus driver tng. and cert. Ednl. Svc. Ctr., Ft. Worth, 1990—, coord., 1994. Vol. Ft. Worth Fire Dept. Relief, 1987, sec., 1991. Mem. Tex. Assn. for Pupil Transp. (region XI reporter 1995, 96, chmn. poster contest 1995). Office: Edn Svc Ctr Region XI 3001 North Fwy Fort Worth TX 76106-6526

MARQUEZ-MAGAÑA, LETICIA MARIA, biology educator; b. Sacramento, Aug. 15, 1963; d. Jesús José and Guadalupe María Márquez; married; children: Joaquín, Elías. BS,MS in Biol. Scis., Stanford U., 1986; PhD in Biochemistry, U. Calif., Berkeley, 1991. Postdoctoral fellow Stanford (Calif.) U., 1991-94; assoc. prof. biology San Francisco State U., 1994—, microbial geneticist, 1994—. Contbr. articles to profl. jours., including Jour. Bacteriology and Jour. Biol. Chemistry. Motivational spkr. to minority students, No. Calif., 1994—; mem. task force Hispanic-Serving Inst. Hispanic Assn. Colls. and Univs.; mentor to UC San Fransico Tchg. postdoctoral fellows, 2002—. Named Hispanic Powerhitter, Hispanic Engr. mag., 2003; named one of 100 Most Influential Hispanics, Hispanic Bus. mag., 1998. Mem.: AAAS (Mentor award 2001), Soc. Advancement of Chicanos and Native Americans in Sci. (e-mentor for K-12 educators 2001—, bd. dirs. 1989—91), Am. Soc. Microbiology. Office: San Francisco State U Dept Biology 1600 Holloway Ave San Francisco CA 94132

MARR, JO ANN, special education educator; b. Deadwood, S.D., July 13, 1945; d. James A. and Frances M. (Yonker) M.; divorced; children: Seth P. Hawken, Tyler U. Hawken, Sara F. Hawken. BS in Edn., Black Hills State U., 1966, postgrad., 1968-69, 86, U. Wyo., 1970—. Social studies tchr. Cheyenne-Eagle Butte (S.D.) High Sch., 1966-67; elem. tchr. Wakpala (S.D.) Pub. Sch., 1968-69, Moorcroft (Wyo.) Elem. Sch., 1969-79; substitute tchr. Riverton (Wyo.) Sch. Dist., 1984-86; spl. edn. tchr. Wyo. State Tng. Sch., Lander, 1986-88, Wind River Sch. Dist., Kinnear, Wyo., 1988-90; spl. edn. tchr., case mgr. Converse County Sch. Dist., Glenrock, Wyo., 1990—. Local hostess, facilitator CCLD/CDE sponsored Odyssey Program, Glenrock, 1992— Crook County rpe. Wyo. Right to Read Program, Moorcroft, 1978-79; coord. Crook and Weston County drug edn. program Wyo. State Dept. Edn., Moorcroft, 1973-77. Sec., bd. dirs. Sundance (Wyo.) Kids Day Care Ctr., 1971-75; county officer, mem. state com. Nat. Cattlewomen, Crook County, 1970-75. Mem. NEA, Wyo. Edn. Assn., Nat. Coun. Learning Disabilities, GEA, Colo. Coun. Learning Disabilities. Home: PO Box 104 Glenrock WY 82637-0104

MARR, KATHLEEN MARY, biologist, educator; b. Sheboygan, Wis., Sept. 20, 1954; d. David William Rath and Gloria Agnes (Carus) Otto; m. Philip Dean Marr, Jan. 3, 1976; children: Amanda, Samantha, Cornelius, Emerson. BS, Lakeland Coll., 1976; MS, Marquette U., 1986, PhD, 1999. Instr. U. Wis., Sheboygan, 1978-82, Manitowoc, 1982; teaching asst. Marquette U., Milw., 1982-85; asst. prof. Divine Word Coll., Epworth, Iowa, 1985-87; assoc. prof. Lakeland Coll., Sheboygan, 1987—, chair dept. biology, dir. pre-med. program. Author Lab Studies in Intro Biology, Lab Studies in Human Anatomy & Physiology. Educator Elderhostels, Lakeland Coll., 1989-91; accordionist Cedar Grove (Wis.) Klompen Dancers, 1982-91; ethicist Speakers Bur., Union of Concerned Scientists, Washington, 1990—; sec. bd. dirs. Maywood Environ. Park. Assoc. Prof. Underkofler Excellence in Tchg. Awd., 1999. Mem.: Assn. Coll. and Univ. Biology Educators (exec. sec.). Roman Catholic. Office: Lakeland Coll County Trunk M Sheboygan WI 53082 E-mail: rathmarrk@lakeland.edu.

MARRAFFINO, ELLEN TALENFELD, retired special education educator; b. Mia Beach, Fla., Feb. 10, 1959; d. Burton Hill and Phillis Hope (Levin) Talenfeld; m. Lawrence Joseph Marraffino, Aug. 1, 1982; children: Matthew David, Sarah Anne. BA in Edn., U. Fla., 1981; postgrad., Fla. Atlantic U. Spl. edn. tchr. Reddick (Fla.) Elem. Sch., 1981-84, J.C. Mitchell Elem. Sch., Boca Raton, Fla., 1984-91, Boca Raton Middle Sch., 1991—95; ret., 1995. Coach Spl. Olympics, 1981—; curriculum advisor Palm Beach City (Fla.) Sch. Bd., 1990—. V.p. Reddick Collier PTA, 1982-83; chmn. acad. com .Golf Coast Gator Club, Boca Raton, 1990-92. Mem. Coun. Exceptional Children. Avocations: swimming, biking, crafts, gardening. Office: Boca Raton Middle Sch 1250 NW 8th St Boca Raton FL 33486-2102

MARREN, MARYANN FAHY, primary school educator; b. Paterson, N.J., May 9, 1957; d. Thomas J. and Anna Helen (O'Hara) Fahy; m. Christopher J. Marren, July 22, 1995; children: Shannon Brianna, Kelsey Faye. BA, William Paterson Coll., 1979. Cert. tchr., nursery sch. tchr., N.J. Dir. recreational profl. Unirec, East Orange, N.J., 1979—; youth min. parish coun., eucharistic min. diocesan deanery coun., emmaus leader Blessed Sacrament Sch. and Ch., Paterson, N.J., 1979-92; tchr. Blessed Sacrament Sch., Paterson, N.J., 1979-92, mem. schoolwide discipline com., tchr. spelling coord., mem. math-a-thon coord.; religious edn. dir., youth min. St. Francis Sch., Haskell, N.J., 1992—. Spelling coord. Sch. #12, Paterson, mem. discipline com., schoolwide com. format tng.; cheerleading coach, softball coach; dir. religious edn. Antioch dir. St. Francis of Assisi, Haskell; math. coord., math-a-thon chairwoman St. Jude's Hosp. Mem. Nat. Cath. Educators Asn., N.J. Edn. Assn. (com. format learning), Early Childhood Edn. Assn. (steering com. Mid. states evaluation com.). Home: 593 Mcbride Ave West Paterson NJ 07424-2820

MARRIOTT, MARCIA ANN, health facility administrator, finance educator; b. Rochester, N.Y., Mar. 21, 1947; d. Coyne and Alice (Schleper) M.; children: Brian, Jonathan. AA, Monroe C.C., Rochester, 1967; BS, SUNY, Brockport, 1970, MA, 1975; PhD, S.W. U. La., 1985. Program adminstr. N.Y. Dept. of Labor, N.Y.C., 1970-75; employment mgr. Rochester Gen. Hosp., 1975-77, salary adminstr., 1982-98, compensation mgr., 1996—; corp. dir. wage and salary dept. Gannett Newspapers, Rochester, 1977-80; compensation and benefits adminstr. Sybron Corp., Rochester, 1980-82; compensation mgr. Rochester Gen. Hosp., 1996—; dir. compensation Via Health, Rochester, 1995-98; pres. Compensation Link, 1997—; prof. Grad. Sch. Bus. Rochester Inst. Tech., 1998—2003, SUNY, Brockport, 1998—2003. Instr. N.Y. State Sch. Indsl. Rels., Cornell U., N.Y.C., 1976-79; assoc. prof. Rochester Inst. Tech., 1978—, Monroe C.C., 1981—, dir. career adv. coun., 1989—; assoc. prof. SUNY, Brockport; assoc. prof. Nazareth Coll., 1998; dir. Rochester Presbyn. Home, 1987-91, 96—, v.p. bd. dirs., 1997-98, pres. bd. dirs., 1998—; dir. area hosp. coun. Kidney Svc. Ctrs., Rochester, 1988-91; cons. in field. Author: (pamphlets) Guideline for Writing Job Descriptions, 1983, (manual) Career Planning Manual, 1985, (booklet) Guideline for Writing Criteria-Based Job Descriptions, 1988, Skill-based Job Descriptions: A Quality Approach, 1994, Redesigning the Performance Appraisal Process, 1996. Campaign mgr. Carter Campaign Commn., Rochester, 1975; mem. coun. Messiah Luth. Ch., Rochester, 1991-94. Davenport-Hatch Found. grantee, 1973, Wegman Found. grantee, 1975. Mem. Am. Compensation Assn., Single Adopted Parents Group (pres. 1988-93). Avocations: tennis, hiking, reading, swimming, skiing. Office: Rochester Gen Hosp 1425 Portland Ave Rochester NY 14621-3095

MARRONE, DANIEL SCOTT, business, production and quality management educator; b. Bklyn., July 23, 1950; s. Daniel and Esther (Goodman) M.; m. Portia Terrone, Sept. 1, 1979; children: Jamie Ann. BA, Queens Coll., 1972, MLS, 1973; MBA, N.Y. Inst. Tech., 1975; PhD, NYU, 1988; diploma in Quality Engring., 1992, diploma in Mfg. Engring., 1993. Auditor/investigator N.Y. State Spl. Pros., N.Y.C., 1977-78; asst. prof. Delehanty Inst., N.Y.C., 1978-79, Ladycliff Coll., Highland Falls, N.Y., 1979-80, Am. Bus. Inst., Bklyn., 1980-82; asst. dir. Adelphi Inst., Bklyn., 1982-85; asst. prof. Coll. St. Elizabeth, Convent Station, N.J., 1986-88; prof. SUNY, Farmingdale, 1987—. Editor: Research Techniques in Business Education, NYU Business Education Doctoral Abstracts, 1981—, Agnew lecture by P.M. Sapre, 1989, NYU Symposium, 1989. Recipient Paul S. Lomax award, NYU, 1989, Bus. Edn. Leadership award, 1993. Mem. Am. Prodn. and Inventory Control Soc. (cert. prodn. and inventory mgmt., cert. integrated resource mgmt.), Inst. for Supply Mgmt. (cert. purchasing mgr.), Delta Pi Epsilon (Cert. of Merit 1988). Republican. Home: 493 Lariat Ln Bethpage NY 11714-4017

MARRS, SHARON CARTER, librarian; b. Andover, Va., May 7, 1943; d. Wallace Ralph and Dorothy (Stout) Carter; m. Glenn Robert Marrs, July 3, 1965. BS, East Tenn. State U., 1965; MLS, U. Pitts., 1974, postgrad., 1983—. Cert. libr. sci. and English, Pa. Tchr. English grades 8 and 10 Powell Valley H.S., Big Stone Gap, Va., 1964-65; libr. Coeburn (Va.) Elem., 1967-68, tchr. grade 2, 1968; libr. Wise (Va.) Elem., 1968-69; tchr. English grade 7 Christiansburg (Va.) Elem. Sch., 1969-70, libr., 1970-71, Myrtle, Vernridge and Kelton Schs., Pitts., 1972—. Apptd. to serve on Microcomputer in the Media Ctr. Award com., Am. Assn. Sch. Librs.; presenter workshops in field. Inventor games for children on use of card catalog, the Dewey Decimal System, various ref. books. Mem. ALA, Pa. State Libr. Assn. (mem. tech. com.), Internat. Assn. Sch. Librarianship, Beta Phi Mu. Home: 620 Broughton Rd Bethel Park PA 15102-3775

MARSALA-CERVASIO, KATHLEEN ANN, medical/surgical nurse, administrator; b. Mar. 22, 1955; d. James Patrick and Kathleen (McLoughlin) Waters. AAS with honors, S.I. Coll., 1974, BS in Nursing with honors, 1984; MSN with honors, CUNY, 1986; PhD in Pub. Adminstrn., Kensington U., 1997. RN, N.Y.; cert. CS, CCRN, CNAA. Staff nurse USPHS Hosp., S.I., 1974-80; head nurse MICU-critical care unit-surg. ICU Bayley Seton Hosp., N.Y., 1980-82; staff nurse surg. ICU, MICU, critical care unit East Orange (N.J.) VA Med. Ctr., 1982-86, critical care nurse specialist; clin. specialist, cons. Med. Ctr. Bklyn. VA Med. Ctr., 1989-95; dir. nursing svcs., asst. prof. nursing U. Hosp./SUNY Health Sci. Ctr., Bklyn., 1990-2000. Asst. clin. prof. SUNY Health Sci. Ctr.; adj. prof. L.I. U., 2001—; cmty. health nurse Met. Jewish Healthcare Sys.; early intervention evaluator, VNS of N.Y. Mem. ANA (coun. clin. nurse specialists), AACN (no. N.J. chpt., N.J. chpt.), Am. Coll. Healthcare Execs. (assoc.), N.Y. Orgn. Nurse Execs., Nat. League for Nursing, Sigma Theta Tau. Home: 8898 16th Ave Brooklyn NY 11214-5804

MARSH, BRUCE DAVID, geologist, educator; b. Munising, Mich., Jan. 4, 1947; s. William Roland and Audrey Jane (Steinhoff) M.; m. Judith Anne Congdon, Jan. 24, 1970; children: Hannah Eyre, William Noah. BS, Mich. State U., 1969; MS, U. Ariz., 1971; PhD, U. Calif.-Berkeley, 1974. Geologist, geophysicist Anaconda Co., Tucson, 1969-71; asst. prof. dept. earth/planet sci. Johns Hopkins U., Balt., 1974-78, assoc. prof., 1978-81, prof., 1981—. Chmn., 1989-93; vis. prof. Calif. Inst. Tech., Pasadena, 1985, U. Maine, 1992-93; co-chmn. Gordon Rsch. Conf. on Inorganic Geochemistry, Holderness, N.H., 1983-84; advisor NASA, Washington, 1975-84, NSF, Washington, 1978-90, NRC, 1985-91; Hallimond lectr. Mineral. Soc. Great Britain and Ireland, 1995. Assoc. editor Geology, 1981-83, Jour. Volcanology and Geothermal Rsch., 1978—, Jour. Petrology, 1986—; editor Jour. Volcanology and Geothermal Rsch., 1985—. Fellow Geol. Soc. Am. (assoc. editor Bulletin 1986-92), Royal Astron. Soc., Mineral. Soc. Am., Am. Geophys. Union (sec. sect. on volcanology, geochemistry and petrology 1984-86, pres. elect 1988-90, pres. 1990-92, Bowen award 1993, Daly lecture 2000); mem. Model A Ford Club Am. Office: Johns Hopkins U Dept Earth-Planetary Scis 322 Olin Hall Baltimore MD 21218 E-mail: bmarsh@jhu.edu.

MARSH, LYNN, elementary education educator; Tchr. Meridian (Idaho) Alternative Sch. Recipient Tchr. Excellence award Internat. Tech. Edn. Assn., Idaho, 1992. Office: Meridien Academy 2311 East Lanark Meridian ID 83642*

MARSH, OWEN ROBERT, education educator, researcher; b. Springfield, Ill., Oct. 4, 1935; s. Owen Rainey and Dorothea Nell (Frutiger) M.; m. Evelyn Joyce Mathews, Aug. 19, 1958; children: Jeffrey, John, Thomas. BS in Edn., Ill. State Normal U., 1957, MS in Edn., 1958; EdD, Ill. State U., Normal, 1967. Tchr. Galesburg (Ill.) Pub. Schs., 1958-61; instr. edn. Western Ill. U., Macomb, 1962-64, Ill. State U., Normal, 1967; rsch. assoc. Ill. Bd. Higher Edn., Springfield, 1967-69; registrar U. Ill., Springfield, 1969-72; dean of admissions and records Tex. Ea. U., Tyler, 1972-80; registrar U. Tex., Tyler, 1980-89, assoc. prof., 1989—. Author: Illinois Board of Higher Education, 1969; contbr. articles to mags. Treas. Assn. Retarded Citizens, Springfield, 1971-72; mem. Human Rights Com., Tyler, 1992—. With USAF, 1961-62. Roy A. Clark scholar Ill. State U., 1967. Mem. St. Louis Performance Coun., Lions (pres. Springfield 1967-72, Tyler 1979-80, 86-87, bd. dirs. 1995—), Kappa Delta Pi (counselor 1992-99, area rep. 1994-97). Methodist. Avocation: camping. Home: 3613 Glendale Dr Tyler TX 75701-8642 Office: Univ Tex Tyler 3900 University Blvd Tyler TX 75701-6699

MARSH, PETER JEROME, credit union officer, former educator; b. Boulder, Colo., Oct. 3, 1957; BA, Rockhurst Coll., 1980. Tchr. St. Vrain Valley Sch. Dist., Longmont, Colo., 1980-82; officer U. Colo. Fed. Credit Union, Boulder, Colo., 1982-88; mgr. fin. instn. rels., asst. v.p. mktg. 1st Am. Savs. Bank, Colorado Springs, Colo., 1988-89; mgr. student lending, mgr. Briargate (Colo.) br. Security Svc. Fed. Credit Union, 1990—. Bd. dirs. Pikes Peak Vineyard Christian Fellowship; mem. accountability and accreditation com. St. Vrain Valley Sch. Dist.; mem. examining bd. State Colo. Dept. Pers. for Adminstrv. Officer, Colo. Student Loan Program; chmn. classroom presentations com. of youth devel. Flatirons chpt. of Credit Unions; com. chmn. cub scout pack Longs Peak coun. Boy Scouts Am. Mem. Colo. Assn. Fin. Aid Adminstrs. Home: 1026 N Arcadia St Colorado Springs CO 80903-2637

MARSH, ROBERTA REYNOLDS, elementary education educator, consultant; b. Kokomo, Ind., June 2, 1939; d. Elwood Bert and Mildred Bell Reynolds; m. Ronald Dean Marsh Sr., Apr. 5, 1958; children: Ronald Jr., Bryan William, Joel Allen. BEd, Ind. U., Kokomo, 1970; MEd, Ind. U., Bloomington, 1971. Cert. tchr., spl. edn. tchr., Ind., Ariz. Tchr. spl. edn. Kokomo Ctr. Schs., 1970-77, Tempe (Ariz.) Elem. Dist. #3, 1978-86, tchr. civics, geography, English/lit., 1986-97, ret., 1997. Facilitator seminars and workshops with tchrs., 1997—. Local dir. Spl. Olympics, Kokomo, 1974-77, Tempe Assn. Retarded Citizens, 1978-2002; den mother Boy Scouts Am., Kokomo, 1967-73; leader 4-H Club, Kokomo, 1974-77. Recipient Excellence in Edn. award Tempe Diablo, 1991. Mem. Coun. for Exceptional Children (state pres. 1986-87, Tempe chpt. pres. 1994-95, outstanding leader award 1985, outstanding regular tchr., 1996, Tempe coun. 1995-96), Internat. Reading Assn., Assn. for Children with Learning Disabilities, Ind. U. Alumni Assn., Grand Computers Club (pres. 2000), Alpha Delta Kappa (corr. sec. 1986-88, Theta pres. 1990-92). Democrat. Avocations: bridge, traveling, reading, collecting apples and bells. Home: 16000 W Wildflower Dr Surprise AZ 85374-5053

MARSH, SUE ANN, special education educator; b. Marshall, Tex., Dec. 5, 1949; d. Orman and Della Florence (Floyd) M. BS in Edn., Stephen F. Austin State U., Nacogdoches, Tex., 1971, MEd, 1975. Cert. elem. tchr., reading tchr., spl. edn. in mental retardation, Tex. Tchr. Title 45 Dickinson (Tex.) Ind. Sch. Dist., 1971, tchr. Title I, 1971-72; tchr. trainable mentally retarded Conroe (Tex.) Ind. Sch. Dist., 1972-85, tchr. Option III, 1985—. Coach, asst. coach Vol. Spl. Olympics, Conroe, 1973—, advt. chmn for golf tournament, 1989-90. Editor: Almost Reader Series. Leader for mentally retarded boys and girls Boy Scouts Am., Conroe, 1990—; chmn. Crockett Cougars Year Book Advertisement 50th Anniversary Edit. Named Crockett Intermediate Tchr. of Yr., 1992; recipient Sam Houston Disting. Scouting award of merit, 1993, Sam Houston Disting. Scouting award of Merit, 1996; co-recipient State Centennial Farm award, Career Ladder, 1984-93. Mem. Assn. Tex. Profl. Educators (bldg. rep. 1983—), Classroom Tchrs. Assn. (bldg. rep. 1975-78), Floyd Family Assn. (sec.-treas. Plantersville, Tex.), River Plantation Lions (camp chmn. 1990-94, chmn. attendance 1990-91, bd. dirs. 1990-96, 3rd v.p. 1992-93, 2nd v.p. 1993-94, v.p. 1994-95, pres. 1995-96, treas. 1996). Democrat. Baptist. Avocations: travel, needlecrafts, plays, concerts. Office: Wash Intermediate Sch 507 Avenue K Conroe TX 77301-3881

MARSHAK, MARVIN LLOYD, physicist, educator; b. Mar. 11, 1946; s. Kalman and Goldie (Hait) M.; m. Anita Sue Kolman, Sept. 24, 1972; children: Rachel Kolman, Adam Kolman. AB in Physics, Cornell U., 1967; MS in Physics, U. Mich., PhD in Physics, 1970. Rsch. assoc. U. Minn., Mpls., 1970-74, from asst. prof. to assoc. prof., 1974-83, prof. physics, 1983-96, dir. grad. studies in physics, 1983-86, prin. investigator high energy physics, 1982-86, head Sch. Physics and Astronomy, 1986-96, sr. v.p. for acad. affairs, 1996-97, Morse-Alumni disting. tchg. prof. physics, 1996—, dir. residential coll., 1997—, faculty legis. liason, 1997—2001. Contbr. articles to profl. jours. Trustee Children's Theater Co., 1989-94. Mem. Am. Phys. Soc. Home: 2855 Ottawa Ave S Minneapolis MN 55416-1946 E-mail: marshak@umn.edu.

MARSHALL, ANNETTE, special education educator; b. Winchester, Mass., Dec. 4, 1942; d. Laurence Fredrick and Agnes Estelle (Hannegan) Sanford; m. Patrick Henry Marshall, Aug. 14, 1965; children: Peter Randolph, Natalie Jean, Daniel Patrick, Michael Laurence Cavins. BS in Elem. Edn., St. Joseph's Coll., 1964; MEd, Rivier Coll., 1992. Cert. tchr., spl. tchr., learning disabilities tchr. Grade 4 tchr. St. Mary's Elem. Sch., Waco, Tex., 1964-65; grade 6 tchr. Orlando, Fla., 1965-66; grade 4 tchr. St. Monica Elem. Sch., Indpls., 1969-71; vol. work sch. and cmty., 1971-85; substitute tchr., 1985-89; para-profl. behavior modification class, 1989-91; spl. needs tchr. 3rd and 4th grades Nottingham West Elem. Sch., Hudson, N.H., 1992—. Recipient award Children and Adults with Attention Deficit So. N.H., 1995. Mem. Internat. Reading Assn. (Granite State literary award 1993). Roman Catholic. Avocations: reading, sewing, craft projects. Home: 5 Beaver Path Hudson NH 03051-5101 Office: Nottingham West Elem Sch 10 Pelham Rd Hudson NH 03051-4830

MARSHALL, C. CHRISTINE, secondary education educator; d. William James and Janet E. (Witte) Shea; m. John Heath Marshall, July 24, 1965. BS, So. Ill. U., 1966, MA, 1972; MLA, Washington U., St. Louis, 1983, MA in Internat. Affairs, 1994. Cert. secondary tchr., Ill., Mo. Tchr. world and Am. history Pattonville Jr. High, Maryland Heights, Mo., 1982-70; tchr. history Pattonville Sr. High Sch., Maryland Heights, Mo., 1982—2002, John Burroughs Sch., St. Louis, 2002—. Participant seminars, workshops; advanced placement reader, 2001; cons. in field. Recipient Internat. Edn. Consortium's award Appreciation, 1988, Fulbright-Hays fellowship to China, 1992, Outstanding Tchr. award Pattonville Sr. High, 1987; delegation leader for Am.-Soviet Youth Exch. Program, People-to-People, 1989. Mem. Nat. Coun. Social Studies, NEA, Mo. Nat. Edn. Assn., Pattonville Nat. Edn. Assn. Roman Catholic. Office: John Burroughs School 755 South Price Rd Saint Louis MO 63124-1899

MARSHALL, CAK (CATHERINE ELAINE MARSHALL), music educator, composer; b. Nashville, Nov. 24, 1943; d. Dean Byron and Petula Iris (Bodie) M. BS in Music Edn., Ind. U. Pa., 1965; cert., Hamline U., 1981, 82, 83, Memphis State U., 1985; MME, Duquesne U., 1992. Nat. registered music educator, 1993; vocal music tchr., Pa. Tchr. music Mars (Pa.) Area Sch. Dist., 1965-66; music specialist Fox Chapel (Pa.) Area Sch. Dist., 1966—, Duquesne U. City Music Ctr., Pitts., 1994-98; ednl. dir. Peripole-Bergerault, Inc., Salem, Oreg., 2001—. Orff specialist Chatham Coll. Fine Arts Camp, Pitts., 1977-91; instrn. rep. elem. curriculum Dist. I, Pitts., 1986-92; arts curriculum project Pa. Dept. Edn., 1988; level one basic Orff tchr. U. Wis.-Milw., 2002, U. South Fla., 2002, U. Fla., Gainesville, 2003. Author: (plays) The Rainbow Recorder, 1988, The Gift Disk Dilemma, 1989; composer, author: (play) Pittsburgh-The City with a Smile on Her Face, 1986, (holiday musical) The Dove That Could Not Fly, 1986, (book) Seasons in Song, 1987, (play) The Search for Happiness, 1990; composer: What Color Was the Baby, 1990, Kaia, 1990, Sing Praises To His Name, 1990, Go In Peace, 1990, Sing Unto The Lord, 1990, Simple Gift, 1991, I Love America, 1992, The Cost Is Correct Caper, 1993, The Adventures of Arffie, 1997, The Greatest Snow on Earth, 1997, A Second Grade "Informance", 1998, Stopping by Woods, 1999, A Play-Party Play-in, 1999, Give Thanks, 1999. Actor North Star Players, Pitts., 1975-80; soloist Landmark Bapt. Ch., Penn Hills, Pa., 1981-86, Bible Bapt. Ch., 1987; performer Pitts. Camerata, 1977-89; group leader Pitts Recorder Soc., 1985-86; soloist Grace Bapt. Ch., Monroeville, 1991— Willamette Master Chorus, 2002—. Recipient Citation of Excellence award Pa. Dept. Edn., 1996. Mem. NEA, Am. ORFF-Schulwerk Assn., Pitts. Golden Triangle Chpt. (pres. 1985—), Music Educators Nat. Confl., Pa. Music Educators Assn. (elem. jour. 1986—), Am. Recorder Assn., Pi Kappa Lambda. Baptist. Avocations: cake decorating, bargello, needlework, swimming, folk dancing. Office: Peripole-Bergerault Inc PO Box 12909 Salem OR 97309 Home: 2494 Percheron Ct SE Salem OR 97301-6273

MARSHALL, GAILEN DAUGHERTY, JR., physician, scientist, educator; b. Houston, Sept. 9, 1950; s. Gailen D. and Evelyn C. (Gresham) M.; m. Elizabeth M. Marek, Nov. 5, 1978; children: Sarah Elizabeth, Jonathan David, Rebecca Marie. BS, U. Houston, 1972; MS, Tex. A&M U., 1975; PhD, U. Tex., 1979, MD, 1984. Rsch. sci. U. Tex., Galveston, 1981-84; rsch. fellow U. Iowa, Iowa City, 1985-86; lab. dir. Biotherapeutics Inc., Memphis, 1986-88; chief med. resident Bapt. Meml. Hosp., Memphis, 1988-89; assoc. dir. Rsch. for Health Inc., Houston, 1989-90; dir. divsn. allergy and immunology U. Tex., Houston, 1990—, clin. asst. prof. medicine, 1990-91, asst. prof. medicine, 1991—98, assoc. prof. medicine and pathology, 1998—2003, prof., 2003—. Mem. sci. adv. com. Carrington Labs., Dallas, 1992-94; mem. Merck Rhinitis Adv. Bd., 2002—, Genentech/Novartis Adv. Bd., 2003—. Mem. editl. bd. Molecular Biotherapy, 1992-93, Cancer Biotherapy, 1994-96, Allergy Proceedings, 1994—, Annals Allergy, Asthma and Immunology, 1995-99, Jour. Interferon Cytokin Rsch., 1999—, Clin. Immunology, 2001—, Jour. Clin. Immunology, 2002—, Cellular Molecular Allergy, 2003—; contbr. articles to profl. jours. Judge Greater Houston Sci. Fair, 1992—. Fellow ACP, Am. Coll. Allergy and Immunology, Am. Acad. Allergy-Immunology (chair com.); mem. Tex. Allergy-Immunology Soc. (chair com., bd. dirs. 1999-2002), Greater Houston Allergy Soc. Republican. Baptists. Avocations: classical music, fishing. Office: U Tex Houston Med Sch 6431 Fannin St Ste 4-202 Houston TX 77030-1501 E-mail: gmarshall@uth.tmc.edu.

MARSHALL, GRAYSON WILLIAM, JR., biomaterials scientist, health sciences educator; b. Balt., Feb. 12, 1943; s. Grayson William and Muriel Marie Marshall; m. Sally Jean Rimkus, July 4, 1970; children: Grayson W. III, Jonathan Charles. BS in Metall. Engring., Va. Poly. Inst., 1965; PhD in Materials Sci., Northwestern U., 1972, DDS, 1986; MPH, U. Calif., Berkeley, 1992. Rsch. assoc., design and devel. ctr. Northwestern U., Evanston, Ill., 1972-73, NIH fellow, 1973, instr. Dental and Med. Schs. Chgo., 1973-74, asst. prof. Dental Sch., 1974-78, assoc. prof. Dental Sch. and Grad. Sch., 1978-87; prof. preventive and restorative dental scis. U. Calif., San Francisco, 1987—, chief biomaterials sect., 1988-92, chmn. biomaterials and bioengring. divsn., 1992—. Chmn. oral and craniaofacial scis. program U of Calif., San Francisco, 2002—; guest scientist Lawrence Livermore Nat. Lab., 1989—, Lawrence Berkeley Nat. Lab., 1989—; cons. oral biology and medicine study sect. NIH, 1988-92; dir. Clin. Rsch. Unit, 1992-96, Dentist-Sci. Award Program, 1996—, Integrated DDS-PhD Program, 1996—, Comprehensive Oral Health Rsch. Tng. Program, 2001—. Contbr. articles to profl. jours. Recipient Spl. Dental Rsch. award Nat. Inst. Dental Rsch., 1975; vis. fellow U. Melbourne, Australia, 1981. Fellow: AAAS, Acad. Dental Materials (exec. sec. 1983—85, chmn. credentials 1984—91, bd. dirs. 1985—93, mem. editl. bd. Scanning Microscopy 1987—93, sec. 1988—91, pres. 1991—93, Cells and Materials 1992—2000, sect. editor 1993—2000, Jour. Oral Rehab. 1994—, Dent Mater 1998—), Am. Coll. Dentists, Internat. Coll. Dentists; mem.: Am. Assn. Pub. Health Dentistry, AIME, Am. Assn. Pub. Health Dentistry, APHA, ADA (assoc. editor Jour. ADA 2002—), U.S. Power Squadrons, U.S. Naval Inst., Calif. Pub. Health Assn.-North, Calif. Acad. Scis., N.Y. Acad. Scis., Am. Assn. Dental Rsch. (bd. dirs. 1996—98, San Francisco coun. 1997—), Microscopy Soc. Am., Am. Soc. Metals, Am. Coll. Sports Medicine, Internat. Assn. Dental Rsch. (Chgo. sect. officer 1978—80, dental materials coun. 1990—96, pres. 1998—99), Soc. Biomaterials, Am. Assn. Dental Schs. (sect. officer 1981—83), Omicron Kappa Upsilon, Sigma Gamma Epsilon, Sigma Xi, Alpha Sigma Mu. Office: U Calif Dept Preventive and Restorative Dental Scis San Francisco CA 94143-0001 E-mail: graymar@itsa.ucsf.edu., gwmarshall@lbl.gov.

MARSHALL, JOSIE, secondary school educator; b. American, Idaho, Dec. 26, 1942; BS, MS in Edn., U. Idaho. Nat. bd. cert. tchr. 1999. Tchr. Sacajawea Jr. H.S., Lewiston, Idaho. Recipient Idaho Middle Sch. Tchr. of the Yr. award, 1997—98; Tom Wright fellow. Mem.: Idaho Edn. Assn. (bd. mem.), Nat. Bd. for Profl. Tchg. Stds. (bd. mem.). Office: Sacajawea Jr HS 3610 12th St Lewiston ID 83501*

MARSHALL, LORETTA, elementary education educator; b. Pensacola, Fla., Aug. 20, 1957; d. Leon and Nettie Lucile (Franklin) M.; (div.); 1 child, Matthew Teliferro Smith Jr. BE, Tuskegee U., 1979; BS in Elem. Edn., U. Ga., 1980; student, Ga. State U., 1982; MEd, Ft. Valley (Ga.) State Coll., 1991. Cert. elem. tchr., Ga., Ala. 3rd grade tchr. Walker Park Sch., Monroe, Ga., 1979-81, Monroe Primary Sch., 1982-87, 2d grade tchr., 1987-95, 1st and 2nd grade Chpt. I and math. tchr., 1995—. Staff devel. coord., Monroe Primary Sch., 1983-87, 93—, student support team chairperson, 1987-90, sch. data collector and support tchr., 1982-90, textbook adoption com. mem., 1991-92. Mem. PTO, Monroe, 1991, PTA, Bogart, Ga., 1993. Mem. ASCD, NEA, Ga. Assn. Educators, Walton Assn. Educators (v.p., pres. 1984-86), Delta Sigma Theta (sec. 1981-82). Democrat. Seventh Day Adventist. Avocations: travel, music, reading. Home: 2175 Woodlake Blvd Monroe GA 30655-8370 Office: Monroe Primary School 109 Blaine St Monroe GA 30655-2403

MARSHALL, MARK DAVID, chemistry educator, researcher; b. West Hartford, Conn., Mar. 6, 1957; s. Frank Henry Marshall and Miriam Eve (Fox) Gabler; m. Helen Oi-Lun Leung, Nov. 21, 1987. BS, U. Rochester, 1979; AM, Harvard U., 1981, PhD, 1985; MA (hon.), Amherst Coll., 2000. Rsch. assoc. Nat. Rsch. Coun. Can., Ottawa, Ont., 1985-87; asst. prof. Amherst (Mass.) Coll., 1987-94, assoc. prof., 1994—2000, prof., 2000—. Vis. rsch. asst. prof. U. N.C., Chapel Hill, 1990-91; vis. rsch. prof. U. Pa., 2000-01, 03—; Dana vis. prof. U. Rochester, 1995-96. Contbr. articles to sci. jours. Recipient Rsch. Opportunity award, NSF, 1991; Henry Dreyfus Tchr. scholar, 1996. Mem. Am. Phys. Soc., Am. Chem. Soc. (John Burlew Conn. Valley Sect. award 1994). Office: Amherst Coll Dept Chemistry PO Box 5000 Amherst MA 01002-5000

MARSHALL, MARYANN RADKE, special education consultant; b. Pittsfield, Mass., July 15, 1955; d. Edward August Jr. and Elizabeth (Lysonski) Radke; m. Richard Joseph Marshall, Jr., July 3, 1982; children: J. Arif, Honnah, Steven, Micah, David. BA in Communication, Queens Coll., Flusing, N.Y., 1979; MA in Spl. Edn., Appalachian State U., 1981. Tchr. of autistic Priestly Sch. New Orleans Pub. Schs., 1981-82, St. Tammany Schs., Slidell, La., 1982; coord. Our Daily Bread Coop., Slidell, 1982-85; mgr. Harvest Moon Coop., Lynchburg, Va., 1986-88; newsletter coord. SpringHill Natural Foods Coop., Mobile, Ala., 1988-90; resource coord. Our Lady of Guadalupe Sch., 1990-94, also bd. dirs. Mem. steering com. Hawkins County Cmty. Christian Sch., 1994-98; cons. Grains of Hope, Slidell, 1983-85, Lynchburg, 1985-88, Mobile, 1988-94, Rogersville, 1994-98, Anderson, 1998—; Webmaster, Heart of Home, 1997—; workshop instr. The Birth Edn. Ctr., Mobile, 1989. Author: Out of Many One, 1985, (book and website) Waterways in the Heartland; contbg. editor: The Harvester: Staff of Life, 1986-88; editor Spring Hill Coop News, 1989-90; columnist The Peace Letter, 1993-94; Waterways in the Heartland, 2001, Grains of Hope News, 2003-. Lobbyist La. Midwives Assn., Slidell, 1983; presenter Consortium on Infant Mortality, Mobile, 1988, New Destiny Fedn., Fayetteville, Ark., 1984-85, Appatlantic Fedn., Durham, N.C., 1987; coord. Kids Club, Nativity of Our Lord Cath. Ch., Noel, Mo., 1999—. Recipient Grad. Assistanship Appalachian State U., 1979-81. Mem. Grains of Hope Coop., Frontier Coop. Herbs, Project Leader Indian Creek 4H, PARENT Home Sch. Group, McDonald County, Mo., Holy-Family Cath. Home Schoolers S.W. Mo. Republican. Roman Catholic. Avocations: gardening, herbology, nutrition, writing. E-mail: marshall@heartofhome.net.

MARSHALL, NAVARRE, retired secondary education educator; b. Stockton, Calif., Oct. 31, 1916; d. Winfield Scott and Elizabeth (Brophy) Baggett; m. Robert Frank Marshall, Aug. 10, 1947; 1 child, Roberta Navarre Marshall. BA, San Francisco State U., 1937; postgrad., U. Calif., Berkeley, 1945-47, U. Calif., Santa Cruz, 1970-72. Cert. elem.-jr. high tchr. Tchr. Pittsburg (Calif.) Sch. Dist., 1937-40, Martinez (Calif.) Sch. Dist., 1941-49, Pajaro Valley Sch. Dist., Watsonville, Calif., 1958-76; ret., 1976. Sec., sponsor Watsonville Friends of the Libr.; mem. Pajaro Valley Arts Coun., 1994, Pajaro Valley Hist. Assn. Mem. AAUW (sec. 1963-64, pres. Watsonville br. 1992-93, sec. 1994-95, publicity chair 1995-97), Calif. Tchrs. Assn., Order Ea. Star, Delta Kappa Gamma (charter pres. 1961-62), Libr. of Congress (nat. mem. 1995), Nat. Trust for Historic Preservation, Internat. Zeta Epsilon (charter pres. 1961-62, chpt. pres. 1986-88, scholarship chair 1984-86, 88-90, Woman Making History award 1994), Nat. Steinbeck Ctr. Democrat. Avocations: reading, bridge, travel.

MARSHALL, ROBERT CLIFFORD, economics educator; b. 1956; AB, Princeton U., 1977; PhD, U. Calif., San Diego, 1983. Asst. prof. econs. Duke U., Durham, N.C., 1983-88, assoc. prof. econs., 1988-95; prof. econs. Pa. State U., University Park, 1995—, head of econs. dept., 1995—. Cons., panel mem. NRC com. on nat. stats., Washington, 1994. Contbr. articles to profl. jours. Grantee NSF, 1985-91. Mem. Am. Econ. Assn., Econometric Soc. Mem. Soc. Of Friends. Avocations: golf, carpentry. Office: Pa State U 613 Kern Grad Bldg University Park PA 16802

MARSHALL, ROBERTA NAVARRE, middle school educator; b. Martinez, Calif., Sept. 26, 1949; d. Robert Frank and Navarre (Baggett) M. BS, Calif. Polytech. State U., 1971; MS in voc. edn., Calif. State U., 1981. Cert. secondary educator, Calif. Consumer-homemaking tchr. Hanford (Calif.) H.S., 1972-73, Eagle Mountain (Calif.) H.S., 1974-79, Solano Jr. H.S., Vallejo, Calif., 1980—. Co-chairperson applied acads. dept. Solano Jr. H.S., Vallejo; competitive recognition events coord. FHA-HERO Region 3, 1991-95; workshop presenter. Middle grades curriculum task force Calif. Dept. Edn., Sacramento, 1987-88. Recipient home econs. curriculum grants, 1985-86, 89-90; named Tchr. of Yr. Elks Lodge, 1988-89. Mem. Calif. Tchrs. Assn., Home Econs. Tchrs. Assn. Calif. (v.p. 1991-93), Am. Assn. Univ. Women, Am. Voc. Assn., Am. Assn. Family & Consumer Scis., Future Homemakers of Am. (adv. 1972), Home Econs. Related Occupations, Delat Kappa Gamma (Theta Iota chpt.). Avocations: reading, needlework, walking, traveling. Home: 5038 Brittany Dr Suisun City CA 94585-6855 Office: Solano Jr H S 1025 Corcoran Ave Vallejo CA 94589-1844

MARSHALL, SHARON BOWERS, nursing educator, director clinical trials; b. Alameda, Calif. d. Stanley Jay and Rosalie Kathryn (Soldati) Bowers; m. Lawrence F. Marshall; children: Derek, Kathryn, Samantha. BS in Nursing, San Francisco State U., 1970. Charge nurse med./surg. unit Mt. Zion Hosp., San Francisco, 1970-73, charge nurse med./surg. ICU, 1973-75; clin. nurse U. Calif. San Diego Med. Ctr., 1975-78, coordinator neurotrauma study, 1978-79, project coordinator Nat. Traumatic Coma Data Bank, 1979-88, project mgr. Comprehensive Cen. Nervous System Injury Ctr., 1979-86, mgr. neurotrauma research, 1984-91; asst. clin. prof. neurol. surg. U. Calif. San Diego Sch. Medicine, 1992—. Study dir. Internat. Tirilazad Study, 1991-95, Pfizer 606 Severe Head Trauma Study, 1997—. Author: Head Injury, 1981; Neuroscience Critical Care: Pathophysiology and Patient Management, 1990; contbr. articles to profl. jours. Mem. Internat. Soc. Study of Traumatic Brain Injury, Am. Assn. Neurosci. Nursing. Avocations: traveling, gardening. Office: 4130 La Jolla Village Dr La Jolla CA 92037-1480

MARSHALL, SHIRLEY ELIZABETH, elementary educator; b. Oneida, Ky., Feb. 10, 1948; d. Maynard Charles and Verne Imogene (Isaacs) Elza; m. Charles Byron Marshall, Jr., Feb. 21, 1970; 1 child, Juan Anthony. AA, Sue Bennett Jr. Coll., London, Ky., 1968; BS, Ea. Ky. U., 1977, MA, 1983. Lic. tchr., (Tex.), Ky. Tchr. Killeen (Tex.) Ind. Sch. Dist., 1977—. Student tchr. supr. U. Mary Hardin Baylor, Belton, Tex., 1980—. Recipient Herald award for excellence in edn. Killeen Daily Herald, 1989. Mem. Classroom Tchrs. Assn., Delta Kappa Gamma, Phi Delta Kappa. Republican. Baptist. Avocation: quilting. Home: 3106 Paintrock Dr Killeen TX 76549-3364 Office: Cedar Valley Elem Sch 4801 Chantz Dr Killeen TX 76542-3745

MARSHALL, THOMAS CARLISLE, applied physics educator; b. Cleveland, Ohio, Jan. 29, 1935; s. Stephen Irby and Bertha Marie (Bieger) M.; children— Julian, John B.Sc., Case Inst. Tech., 1957; M.Sc., U. Ill., 1958, PhD, 1960. Asst. prof. elec. engring. U. Ill., 1961-62; mem. faculty Columbia U., 1962—, asst. prof. elec. engring., 1962-65, assoc. prof., 1965-70, prof. engring. sci., 1970-78, prof. applied physics, 1978—. Author: Free Electron Lasers, 1985, Book of the Toade, 1992; contbr. articles to profl. jours. Research grantee Dept. Energy, Office Naval Research, NSF. Fellow: Am. Phys. Soc. (study group on directed energy weapons 1985—87); mem.: Free Election Lasers and Advanced Concepts in Accelerator Physics. Office: Columbia U 213 Mudd Bldg New York NY 10027 E-mail: tcm2@columbia.edu.

MARSHALL, VIRGINIA MARY, library media specialist, educator; b. Medford, Mass., Nov. 2, 1940; d. Frederick Edward and Louise Angela (Lombardi) Gordinier; m. Dana Philip Marshall, Apr. 18, 1970; children: Jennifer Susanne, Kristin Terese Justyne Marshall. BS in Secondary Edn. cum laude, Salem (Mass.) State Coll., 1962; MS in Secondary Edn., Boston State Coll., 1967; MS in Edn. Libr. Media, Bridgewater State Coll., Mass., 1992. Cert. secondary tchr. and libr. media specialsit, Mass. Tchr. English Somerville (Mass.) Sch. System, 1962-73; tchr. jr. high Blessed Sarament Sch., Walpole, Mass., 1983—, sch. libr. media sepcialist, 1991-97; sch. libr. media specialist North Attleboro Sch. Sys., 1997-99, Milford Sch. System, 1999—. Literary cons. Koller Enterprises, 1971; pres. Glass Castle, 1974-83, Ginny's Pincushion, 1983-87. Named Outstanding Young Educator, Somerville Jaycees, 1970, Am. Yearbook Outstanding Advisor, 1970, 71. Mem. NEA, Mass. Sch. Libr. Media Assn., Nat. Coun. English Tchrs. Avocations: reading, mountain climbing, sewing, bee keeping. Home: 17 Country Club Dr Walpole MA 02081-3417

MARSHALL, WALTER, special education educator; b. Wadesboro, N.C., Feb. 15, 1942; s. Andrew and Sarah (Lomax) M.; m. Paulette L. Gwyn, Feb. 12, 1966; children: Krista Colette, Malcolm Taussaint. BS in Health and Phys. Edn., Winston-Salem State U., 1965; MA in Intermediate Edn., Aant State U., 1976. Cert. special edn. tchr., N.C. Phys. edn. and social studies tchr. Lee County Schs., Sanford, N.C., 1965-69; spl. edn. tchr. High Point (N.C.) City Schs., 1969-92; case mgr. Guilford County Schs., High Point, 1993—. Mem. Winston-Salem Forsyth County Sch. Bd., 1992—; mem. ednl. legal adv. bd. NAACP, 1990-92; chmn. state edn. com. N.C. NAACP, 1988-91; bd. pres. Winston-Salem NAACP, 1986-92; exec. bd. N.C. Dem. Ctrl. Com., 1984-90, del. conv., San Francisco, 1984. Recipient Human Rel. award N.C. Assn. Educators, 1989, Disting. Alumni award Nat. Assn. for Equal Opportunity in Higher Edn., 1990. Mem. Assn. Classroom Tchrs. (pres. 1970-71), N.C. Assn. Classroom Tchrs. (dist. v.p. 1970-71), Coun. for Exceptional Children. Baptist. Home: 3246 Kittering Ln Winston Salem NC 27105-6923

MARSI, KENNETH LARUE, chemist, educator; b. Los Banos, Calif., Dec. 13, 1928; s. Sam and Wilma Evelyn (Soper) M.; m. Gertrude Irene Gutschenritter, Mar. 5, 1955; children: Marianne, Kenneth Scott, Brian Geoffrey, Teresa Jeanne. AB, San Jose State U., 1951; PhD, U. Kans., 1955. Sr. research chemist The Sherwin-Williams Co., Chgo., 1955-57; from asst. prof. to assoc. prof. chemistry Kans. State U., Ft. Hays, 1957-61; from asst. prof. to prof. Calif. State U., Long Beach, 1961-96, part time faculty, 1996—2002. Cons. chemist Douglas Aircraft, Santa Monica, Calif., 1964-67; cons. S-cubed, San Diego, 1983—. Author: Problems in Organic Chemistry, 1968; reviewer Prentice-Hall, Inc., Englewood Cliffs, N.J., 1961—; abstractor Chem. Abstracts, Columbus, Ohio, 1958-67; contbr. articles to profl. jours. Named Outstanding Prof. Calif. State U.,Long Beach, 1984, Trustees Outstanding Prof. Calif. State U. System, 1985. Mem. Am. Chem. Soc., Organic Sect. Am. Chem. Soc., Phi Beta Kappa, Sigma Xi (treas. Kans. chpt. 1954-55), Phi Lambda Upsilon (pres. 1954). Democrat. Episcopalian. Avocations: gardening, reading, biking, backpacking, genealogy. Home: 7 New York Ct Monarch Beach CA 92629-4524 E-mail: kmarsi@cox.net.

MARSICANO, HAZEL ELLIOTT, education educator; b. Wilkes-Barre, Pa., Sept. 1, 1932; d. Paul Good and Helen Grace (Buckalew) Elliott; m. Joseph R. Marsicano, Sept. 29, 1951; children: Joselle A., Elizabeth A. BS in Nursery-Elem. Edn., SUNY, Buffalo, 1966, MS in Elem. Sch. Prin. and Supr. Elem. S, 1970, EdD in Early Childhood Edn., 1977. Cert. kindergarten, elem. tchr., elem. prin. Tchr., prescb. dir. Niagara Falls (N.Y.) Pub. Schs., 1966-77; asst. prof. Ea. Mont. Coll., Billings, 1977-78, W.Va. U., Morgantown, 1978-83; prof. early childhood edn. Troy (Ala.) State U., dir. devel. reading program, 1983—; dir. Trojan Learning Ctr., Troy, Ala. Author numerous short stories and interactive video programs. Mem. Nat. Assn. Edn. Young Children, Ala. Assn. Tchr. Educators (Outstanding Tchr. Educator award 1990), Ea. Edn. Rsch. Assn., Ala. Assn. Young Children, So. Assn. for Children Under Six, Ala. Assn. Early Childhood Tchr. Educators (Outstanding Leadership award 1990), Post Secondary Reading Coun. Ala., Phi Delta Kappa, Delta Kappa Gamma (past pres.), Kappa Delta Pi. Avocations: leading workshops, cons. Home: 218 W Walnut St Troy AL 36081-2038

MARSON, STEPHEN MARK, social work educator; b. Columbus, Ohio, Mar. 2, 1951; s. Domenico Mark and Albina Clara (Spagnol) M.; m. Barbara Jean Miller, May 22, 1982; 1 child, Stephanie Grace. Student, Rio Grande Coll., 1970-71; BA, Ohio Dominican Coll., 1974; MSW, Ohio State U., 1976; PhD, N.C. State U., 1991. Cert. master social work. Intake worker Talbot Hall, St. Anthony Hosp., Columbus, 1974-76; case mgr. VITA Treatment Ctr., Columbus, 1976-77; prof., dir. Pembroke (N.C.) State U., 1977—; pres. Marson & Assocs., Lumberton, N.C., 1978—. Dir. U. N.C. at Pembroke, 1989—, coord. minor in applied gerontology, 1989—; dir. consortium Internet State Listservs for Social Work, 1994—; exams item writer Nat. Bds. Social Work. Author: 18 monographs; contbr. articles to profl. jours.; issues cons. Jour./Sex Rsch., 1980-88; book rev. editor and co-editor Jour. Law & Social Work, 1994-2001, sr.editor The Jour. of Social Work Values and Ethics. Sec. of bd. Rural Advancement Justice Project, Lumberton, 1983-90; bd. dirs. Robeson County Hospice, Lumberton, 1985—, Home Health Horizons, Lumberton, 1986—, Children's Transplant Assn., Larinburg, N.C., 1990-93. Recipient Adolf Dial award for scholarship and creative work, 2000-01; named Outstanding Young Man in Am., U.S. Jaycees, 1990. Mem. 10 profl. orgns., Loyal Order Moose. Unitarian Universalist. Home: 5203 McLeod Rd Lumberton NC 28358-8507 Office: U NC at Pembroke Social Work Program Pembroke NC 28372 E-mail: steve.marson@uncp.edu.

MARSTON-SCOTT, MARY VESTA, nurse, educator; b. St. Stephen, N.B., Can., Apr. 5, 1924; d. George Frank and Betsey Mildred (Babb) M.; m. John Paul Scott, June 30, 1979. BA, U. Maine, 1946; M.N., Yale U., 1951; M.P.H., Harvard U., 1957; MA, Boston U., 1964, PhD, 1969. Research asst. Roscoe B. Jackson Meml. Lab., Bar Harbor, Maine, 1946-48; nurse, 1952-54; instr. Yale U. Sch. Nursing, 1955-56; nurse cons. Div. Nursing, Washington, 1957-62; asso. prof. Frances Payne Bolton Sch. Nursing, Case-Western Res. U., Cleve., 1969-74; prof. grad. program community health nursing Boston U., 1974-86; assoc. prof. Coll. Nursing U. Ill., Chgo., 1986-94, assoc. prof. emerita, 1994—. Cons. in field. Contbr. articles to profl. jours. Served with USPHS, 1957-62. Fellow Am. Acad. Nursing; mem. Am. Psychol. Assn., Am. Public Health Assn., Am. Nurses Assn., Sigma Theta Tau. Home: Dirigo Pines 2 Hawthorn Ct Orono ME 04473

MARTAS, JULIA ANN, special education administrator; b. Bronx, N.Y., July 30, 1949; d. Julio and Emilia (Guerra) M. BS, CCNY, 1972, MS, 1975; postgrad., NYU. Cert. spl. edn. tchr., N.Y., sch. adminstrn. and supr. Tchr bilingual spl. edn. N.Y.C. Bd. Edn., 1972-82, regional coord. bilingual-spl. edn. div. spl. edn. Manhattan, 1982-86, profl. assocs., div. personnel, 1986-87, chancellor's monitor spl. edn. office of monitoring, 1987-88, dist. adminstr. spl. edn., 1988-95; dir. spl. edn. Instrl. Svcs., Rockford, Ill., 1995-99; asst. dir. spl. edn. tech. support svcs. D.C. Pub. Schs., Washington, 1999—2002, civil rights and non-traditional edn. specialist divsn. career and tech. edn., 2002—. Instr. grad. spl. edn. dept. Coll. of New Rochelle, L.I. U., Adelphi U., CCNY, 1984-95, U. Ill., Chgo., 1999; cons. sch. div. McGraw Hill Pub. Co., Globe Pub. Co., Bowmar Noble, Economy Pub. Co. Recipient Congl. Recognition USA, 1992, Cert. of Merit N.Y. State Senate, 1992. Mem. ASCD, Coun. for Exceptional Children, Ill. Coun. for Exceptional Children (regional dir., exec. bd. dirs. 1996-99), P.R. Educators Assn., N.Y.C. Assn. Dist. Adminstrs. Spl. Edn., Odd Fellows, House of Ruth. Office: DC Pub Schs 825 N Capitol St NE Washington DC 20002-4210

MARTENS, HELEN EILEEN, elementary school educator; b. Atkinson, Nebr., Jan. 13, 1926; d. Robert McKinley and Minnie Viola (Alfs) M. BS, Dana Coll., 1971; postgrad., U. Nebr., 1971-94, Wayne (Nebr.) U., 1971-94. Cert. tchr., Nebr. Rural sch. tchr. Dist. 231, Atkinson, Nebr., 1943-44, Dist. 77, Atkinson, Nebr., 1944-45, Dist. 119, Atkinson, Nebr., 1945-47; tchr. Emmet (Nebr.) Pub. Sch., 1947-59, O'Neill (Nebr.) Pub. Sch., 1959-99. Mgr. Saddle Horn Ranch for Youth. Mem. Holt County 4-H Coun., 1986-90, leader, 1946—; mem. youth edn. com. Holt County Cancer Soc., 1976-94; activity sec. Dr. Boots and Saddle Club, Holt County, 1969-95; demonstration tchr. Nebr. Tchrs. Help Mobile. Recipient Good Neighbor citation Knights of Aksarben, 1986, Amb. award O'Neill C. of C., 1986, Tchr. of Yr. World Herald Newspaper, 1986, Outstanding Elem. Tchr. Nebr. Rural Cmty. Schs., 1994; named Grand Marshall O'Neill St. Patrick's Parade, 1986. Mem. NEA, Nebr. Edn. Assn., O'Neill Edn. (sec., v.p., pres. 1960-94), Order Eastern Star, Alpha Delta Kappa, Delta Kappa Gamma (sec., v.p. 1959-94). Republican. Methodist. Avocation: ranching. Home: HC 69 Box 41 Atkinson NE 68713-9615

MARTENS BALKE, PATRICIA FRANCES, adult education educator; b. St. Louis, Nov. 27, 1943; d. John William and Mary Ruth (Bolds) Martens; m. George Joseph Miller, Aug. 7, 1965 (div.); children: Nicolette, George Jr., Jeffrey; m. Garrett Balke, Apr. 5, 2002. BS in Psychology, So. Ill. U., 1975; MA in Counseling, St. Louis U., 1990, PhD in Psychol. Founds., 1996. Cert. sexuality educator, hypnotherapist; lic. profl. counselor Nat. Bd. Cert. Counselors; cert. therapist and cons. Eye Movement Desensitization and Reprocessing. Primary, intermediate tchr. St. Hedwig Sch., St. Louis, 1961-66; tchr. jr. h.s. Assumption Sch., St. Louis, 1976-81; tchr. trainer grad. students Paul VI Cathechetical Inst., St. Louis, 1986-88; nat. tchr. trainer St. Louis, 1989—; pvt. practice psychotherapy, 1997—. Cons. Archdiocese L.A., Archdiocese St. Louis, Nat. Coun. Cath. Bishops, 1991; del. Nat. Cath. Ednl. Del. to Russia and Lithuania, 1993; frequent spkr. and presenter at schs., parishes ednl. confs., nat. and internat. religious edn. mtgs.; TV appearances on ABC and CTNA; nat. ednl. cons. Tabor Pub. Author: (videos) In God's Image: Male and Female, 1989, God Doesn't Make Junk, 1989 (Cath. Audio Visual Educators award 1991), (books) Parent to Parent, 1989, Sex Is Not A Four-Letter Word!, 1994. Recipient Award Cath. Press Assn., 1995. Mem. AACD, Nat. Cath. Educators Assn., Am. Assn. Sex Educators, Counselors, Therapists, Assn. for Religious Values in Counseling, Am. Sch. Counselor Assn., Am. Coll. Personnel Assn., Soc. for Sci. Study of Sex, Pi Lambda Theta. Avocations: travel, swimming, biking, movies, sharing youth activities. Office: 10411 Clayton Rd Ste 2 Saint Louis MO 63131

MARTH, ELMER HERMAN, bacteriologist, educator; b. Jackson, Wis., Sept. 11, 1927; s. William F. and Irma A. (Bublitz) M.; m. Phyllis E. Menge, Aug. 10, 1957. BS, U. Wis., 1950, MS, 1952, PhD, 1954. Registered sanitarian, Wis. Teaching asst. bacteriology U. Wis., Madison, 1949-51, research asst., 1951-54, project asso., 1954-55, instr. bacteriology, 1955-57, assoc. prof.food sci., bacteriology and food microbiology and toxicology, 1966-71, prof., 1971-90, prof. emeritus, 1990—. Vis. prof. Swiss Fed. Inst. Tech., Zurich, 1981; with Kraft Foods, Inc., Glenview, Ill., 1957-66, bacteriologist, 1957-59, rsch. bacteriologist, 1959-61, sr. rsch. bacteriologist, 1961-63; group leader microbiology, 1963-66; assoc. mgr. microbiology, 1966; mem. Intersoc. Coun. on Std. Methods for Exam. Dairy Products, 1968-84, chmn., 1972-78. Contbg. author books; editor: Jour. Milk and Food Tech, 1967-76, Jour. Food Protection, 1977-87; contbr. articles to profl. publs. Sec. Luth. Acad. Scholarship, 1961-71; WHO travel fellow, 1975 Recipient Nordica award for rsch. Am. Cultured Dairy Products Inst., 1979, Meritorious Svc. award APHA, 1977, 83, Sanitarian of Yr. award Wis. Assn. for food protection, 1983, Meritorious Svc. award Nat. Confectioners Assn., 1987, Joseph Mityas Meml. Laboratorian of Yr. award Wis. Lab. Assn., 1989, Quality of Comm. award Am. Agrl. Econs. Assn., 1992; named Highly Cited Rschr. Worldwide in Agrl. Scis., Inst. for Sci. Info., 1981-99. Fellow Inst. Food Technologists (Nicholas Appert award 1987, Babcock-Hart award 1989), Am. Dairy Sci. Assn. (Pfizer rsch. award 1975, Dairy Rsch. Found. award 1980, Borden award 1986, Kraft Inc. teaching award 1988), Am. Soc. Microbiology, Internat. Assn. Food Protection (charter fellow, hon. life, Educator award for rsch. and teaching food hygiene 1977, citation award 1984, NFPA Food Safety award 2000),

Coun. Sci. Editors, Inst. Food Technologists, Sigma Xi, Alpha Zeta, Kappa Eta Kappa, Phi Sigma, Phi Tau Sigma, Delta Theta Sigma, Gamma Sigma Delta, Gamma Alpha. Patentee in field. Office: U Wis Dept Food Sci 1605 Linden Dr Madison WI 53706-1519

MARTIN, BARBARA ANN, secondary education educator; b. Lexington, Ky., Apr. 11, 1946; d. Robert Newton and Juanita June (Karrick) M. AA, Beckley Coll., 1966; BS in Edn., Concord Coll., 1969; MA, Western Ky. U., 1974, rank I, 1982. Standard teaching cert., adminstrn., secondary edn., Ky. Tchr. Daviess County Mid. Sch., Owensboro, Ky., 1969—. Inservice speaker Daviess County Schs., Owensboro, 1969—; acad. writer Ky. Acad. Assn., Frankfort, 1992—. Author: Social Studies for Gifted Student, 1977; contbr.: (game) National Geographic Global Pursuit, 1988. Ky. rep. tchr. adv. coun. Nat. Rep. Party, Washington, 1993—; exec. com. Daviess County Rep. Party, 1987—. Named Outstanding Young Woman, 1978, Outstanding Social Studies Tchr., Ky. Coun. for Social Studies, 1978; recipient Outstanding Comty. Svc. award Owensboro (Ky.) City Commn. and Mayor, 1982. Mem. NEA (del., mid-atlantic coord. women's caucus 1969—), Ky. Edn. Assn. (del., legis. com. 1969—), 2d Dist. Assn. (del., pres. 1969—), Daviess County Edn. Assn. (del., pres. 1969—). Presbyterian. Avocations: writing, photography, gardening, family history, Ky. Wildcat basketball. Home: 4325 Fischer Rd Owensboro KY 42301-8109 Office: Daviess County Mid Sch 1415 E 4th St Owensboro KY 42303-0100

MARTIN, BARBARA JEAN, elementary school principal; b. Mt. Vernon, Tex., May 17, 1940; BA, Fisk U., Nashville, 1961; MEd, U. Ill., Chgo., 1979, PhD, 1992. Cert. tchr. kindergarten to 3rd grade, type 75 adminstr., Ill. Tchr. Chgo. Pub. Schs., 1969-93, prin., 1993—. Mem. Nat. Alliance Black Sch. Educators, Delta Kappa Gamma (sec. 1992—), Pi Lambda Theta, Alpha Kappa Alpha. Home: 825 E Drexel Sq Chicago IL 60615-3705 Office: O W Holmes Sch 955 W Garfield Blvd Chicago IL 60621-2240

MARTIN, BETTY J. speech, language pathologist; b. East St. Louis, Ill., Nov. 2, 1950; d. Nathaniel and Minnie Mae (Long) Gause; m. Leander Martin, Jr.; children: Leander III, Lavell, Kenneth. BS, So. Ill. Univ., 1978, MS, 1980; postgrad., So. Ill. U. Cert. speech-lang. pathologist, Ill., Mo., early intervention specialist, LD tchr.; lic., Ill. Bd. sec. State C.C., East St. Louis, 1970-75; speech-lang. pathologist East. St. Louis Sch. Dist. 189, 1980—. Site coord. Educom, St. Peter's, Mo., 1993. Tutor Project Love, East St. Louis, 1990; tchr. Vacation Bible Sch., East St. Louis, 1994, 95; sec. Steward BBd. #2, East St. Louis, 1994-96; staff mentor, cooperating clinician for student tchrs. in speech pathology. Mem. Am. Speech Hearing Lang. Assn. (cert.), Ill. Speech Hearing Assn., So. Ill. Speech Hearing Assn., Alliance for Mentally Ill, Natl. Alliance for Mentally Ill. Methodist. Home: 520 Green Haven Dr Swansea IL 62226-1801 Office: Mandela Elem Sch East Saint Louis IL 62201

MARTIN, CAROL JACQUELYN, literature educator, artist; b. Ft. Worth, Tex., Oct. 6, 1943; d. John Warren and Dorothy Lorene (Coffman) Edwards; m. Boe Willis Martin, Oct. 6, 1940; children: Stephanie Diane, Scott Andrew. BA summa cum laude, U. N. Tex., 1965; MA, U. Tex., El Paso, 1967. Tchr. Edgemere Elem. Sch., El Paso, Tex., 1965-66, Fulmore Jr. H.S., Austin, Tex., 1966-67, Monnig Jr. H.S., Ft. Worth, 1967-68, Paschal H.S., Ft. Worth, 1968-69; instr. Tarrant County Jr. Coll., Ft. Worth, 1968-69, 71-72; press sec. U.S. Sen. Gaylord Nelson, Washington, 1969-71; instr. Eastfield CC, Dallas, 1981, Richland CC Dist., 1982; instr. Meml. Student Ctr. UPlus Tex. A&M U., 2002—03. Artist Vt. Studio Ctr., 1998. Editor The Avesta Mag., 1964-65; exhibited in group shows at City of Richardson's Cottonwood Park, 1970-86, Students of Ann Cushing Gantz, 1973-85, Art About Town, 1979, 80, shows by Tarrant County and Dallas County art assns. Active Dallas Symphony Orch. League, Easter Seal Soc., Women's Auxiliary of Nexus, Dallas Hist. Soc., Women's Bd. of the Dallas Opera, Dallas Arboretum and Garden Club, Dallas County Heritage Soc., Nat. Mus. Women in Arts. Mem. Internat. Platform Assn., Mortar Bd., Alpha Chi, Sigma Tau Delta, Kappa Delta Pi, Delta Gamma. Democrat. Methodist. Avocations: travel, photography, snow skiing, oil painting. Address: 4055 Sweetwater Dr College Station TX 77845-9650

MARTIN, CAROLYN FRANCES, elementary education educator; b. Mt. Vernon, Ohio, Feb. 4, 1948; d. Charles Wayne and Blanche Evelyn (Rine) Mills; m. Terry E. Martin, Dec. 19, 1970. BS in Edn., Muskingum, 1970. Cert. tchr., Ohio. Tchr. Mt. Vernon (Ohio) City Schs., 1970—. Home: 344 Maple Ave Utica OH 43080-9756 Office: East Sch 714 E Vine St Mount Vernon OH 43050-3651

MARTIN, CATHERINE ELIZABETH, anthropology educator; b. N.Y.C., Feb. 14, 1943; d. Walter Charles and Ruth (Crucet) Strodt; children: Kai Stuart, Armin Wade. BA, Reed Coll., 1965; MA, UCLA, 1967, PhD, 1971. Cert. C.C. tchr., Ariz., Calif. From asst. to full prof. anthropology Calif. State U., L.A., 1970-96, prof. emeritus, 1996, coord. women's studies, 1979-88, acting dir. acad. advisement, 1992-93, dir. Can. studies, 1991, advisement coord., 1996, prof. emeritus, 1996; assoc. faculty Mohave C.C., Kingman, Ariz., 1996-99; adj. prof. No. Ariz. U., 1997-99, affiliate Women's Studies, 1998-99; adj. faculty anthropology Shasta Coll., 2001—. Contbr. chpts. to books and poetry to profl. publs. Cubmaster, den mother Boy Scouts Am., L.A. and Pasadena, 1982-85; leader Tiger Cubs, Boy Scouts Am., 1983. Recipient Outstanding Tiger Cub Leader award Boy Scouts Am., L.A., 1983, Cub Scout Growth award Boy Scouts Am., L.A., 1984. Fellow Soc. Applied Anthropology; mem. Am. Anthropol. Assn., Southwestern Anthropol. Assn. Avocations: reading, traveling, exploring cultural diversity.

MARTIN, CHARLES SEYMOUR, middle school educator; b. Lewiston, Maine, Dec. 26, 1961; s. Robert Charles and Annette Marion (Card) Martin; m. Margaret Ilene Davis, Aug. 20, 1988; 1 child, Danielle Elizabeth. BS in Health Edn., U. Maine, Farmington, 1984; MEd, Plymouth State Coll., 1988; cert. advanced studies, U. Maine, Orono, 1991. Cert. coach, health edn. tchr. K-12, life sci. tchr. 7-12. Health educator Stephens Meml. Hosp., Norway, Maine, 1984; health sci. tchr./coach Oxford Hills Jr. H.S., South Paris, Maine, 1984—. Contbr. articles to profl. jours. Dir. Paris Conservation Commission, 1990; asst. leader Boy Scouts Am. troop #130, South Paris, 1985. Named Blaines House Scholar State of Maine Dept. Edn., 1988; recipient metropolitan Life grant, 1988. Mem. Phi Delta Kappa, Phi Kappa Phi, Eta Sigma Gamma, Kappa Delta Pi. Republican. Avocations: fishing, camping, hiking, studying nature, athletics. Home: 67 E Oxford Rd South Paris ME 04281-6018 Office: Oxford Hills Mid Sch 100 Pine St South Paris ME 04281-1518

MARTIN, CLARA RITA, elementary school educator; b. Steubenville, Ohio, Oct. 14, 1953; d. Robert Emmett and Mary Agnes (Flynn) Joyce; m. Gary Dean Martin, July 8, 1978; children: Bradley A., Douglas A. BS in Elem. Edn., Coll. Steubenville, 1975; MS in Interdisciplinary Skillls, U. Dayton, 1984. Cert. tchr. Ohio. Reading specialist Steubenville City Sch. Dist., 1975; tchr. elem. schs. Harrison Hills City Sch. Dist., Jewett, Hopedale, Ohio, 1975—. Coord. spelling bee Harrison News Herald Spelling Bee, Cadiz, Ohio, 1984—2001. Asst. coord. Meml. Day Program, 1992; Jump Rope for Heart coord. Relay for Life, 2002. Mem.: Harrison Hills Tchrs. Assn. (grievance chair, chief negotiator 1980—, bldg. rep. 1985—, del. Ohio Edn. Assn. Conv. 1981—, co-pres. 1999—), Ladies Ancient Order Hibernians (sec. 1991—92, sec. Reach for Recovery 2000). Roman Catholic. Avocations: reading, travel. Home: 4059 State Hwy 43 Richmond OH 43944-7912

MARTIN, CONNIE RUTH, retired lawyer; b. Clovis, N.Mex., Sept. 9, 1955; d. Lynn Latimer and Marian Ruth (Pierce) M.; m. Daniel A. Patterson, Nov. 21, 1987; step-children: David Patterson, Dana Patterson. B in Univ. Studies, Ea. N.Mex. U., 1976, MEd, 1977; JD, U. Mo., Kansas City, 1981. Bar: N.Mex. 1981, U.S. Dist. Ct. N.Mex. 1981, Colo. 2002. Asst. dist. atty. State of N.Mex., Farmington, 1981-84; ptnr. Tansey, Rosebrough, Gerding & Strother, PC, Farmington, 1984-93; pvt. practice Connie R. Martin, P.C., Farmington, 1993-94; domestic violence commr. 11th Judicial Dist. Ct., State of N.Mex., 1993-94; with Jeffrey B. Diamond Law Firm, Carlsbad, N. Mex., 1994-96; assoc. Sager, Curran, Sturges and Tepper PC, Las Cruces, N. Mex., 1996-97, Holt & Babington PC, Las Cruces, 1997-2000; ret., 2000. Dep. med. investigator State of N.Mex., Farmington, 1981-84; instr. San Juan Coll., 1987, N.Mex. State U., 1995; spkr. N.Mex. Jud. Edn. Ctr., 1993-94; chair paralegal program adv. com., 1988, Adv Com., St Francis Clin., Presbyn. Med. Svs., 1994-96; bd. Bar Examiners State of N.Mex., 1989—, vice-chair, 1995-97, chair, 1997-99; asst. bar counsel Disciplinary Bd.; mem. profl. adv. com. Meml. Med. Ctr. Found., 1997-2000, trustee, 2000; mem. So. N.Mex. Estate Planning Coun., 1997-2000; mem. character and fitness com. Nat. Conf. Bar Examiners, 2002-03. Bd. dirs., exec. com. San Juan County Econ. Opportunity Coun., Farmington, 1982-83; bd. dirs. Four Corners Substance Abuse Coun., Farmington, 1984, N.Mex. Newspapers, Inc.; chmn. Cmty. Corrections-Intensive Supervision Panel, Farmington, 1987-88; jud. selection com. mem. San Juan County, 1991, Chavez County, 1995; nominating com. Supreme Ct./Ct of Appeals, 1991-96; treas. Ft. Morgan United Meth. Ch., 2001—, chmn. fin. com., 2002—. Recipient Distinguished Svcs. award for Outstanding Young Woman San Juan County Jaycees, 1984. Mem. N.Mex. Bar. Assn. (bd. dirs. elder law sect. 1993-96, peer rev. task force 1994-95, asst. to new lawyers com. 1986-87, local bar com. 1988, bd. dirs. young lawyers divsn. 1989-91, bd. dirs. real property probate and trust sect. 1994-97), San Juan County Bar Assn. (treas. 1985-87, v.p. 1987, pres. 1988), Farmington C. of C. (bd. dirs. 1991-93), Rocky Mountain Keeshond Club, Keeshond Club of Am. Methodist. Avocations: health, fitness, reading, dog show and therapy dog vol..

MARTIN, DAVID ALAN, law educator; b. Indpls., July 23, 1948; s. C. Wendell and Elizabeth Bowman (Meeker) M.; m. Cynthia Jo Lorman, June 13, 1970; children: Amy Lynn, Jeffrey David. BA, DePauw U., 1970; JD, Yale U., 1975. Bar: D.C. Law clk. to Hon. J. Skelly Wright U.S. Ct. Appeals (D.C. cir.), 1975-76; law clk. to Hon. Lewis F. Powell U.S. Supreme Ct., Washington, 1976-77; assoc. Rogovin, Stern & Huge, Washington, 1977-78; spl. asst. bur. human rights and humanitarian affairs U.S. State Dept., Washington, 1978-80; from asst. prof. to assoc. prof. U. Va. Sch. Law, Charlottesville, 1980-86, prof., 1986-91, Henry L. & Grace Doherty prof. law, 1991—2003, F. Palmer Weber Rsch. prof. civil liberties and human rights, 1992—95, 2000—03, Warner-Booker disting. prof. internat. law, 2003—. Cons. Adminstrv. Conf. U.S., Washington, 1988-89, 91-92, U.S. Dept. Justice, 1993-95, U.S. Dept. of State, 20033 gen. counsel U.S. Immigration and Naturalization Svc., 1995-98. Author: Immigration: Process and Policy, 1985, 5th edit., 2003, Asylum Case Law Sourcebook, 1994, 4th edit., 2003, The Endless Quest: Helping America's Farm Workers, 1994; editor: The New Asylum Seekers, 1988, Immigration Admissions, 1998, Immigration Controls, 1998, Rights and Duties of Dual Nationals: Evolution and Prospects, 2002; contbr. articles to profl. jours. Nat. governing bd. Common Cause, Washington, 1972-75; elder Westminster Presbyn. Ch., Charlottesville, 1982-84, 89-92; bd. dirs. Internat. Rescue Com., 2000—. German Marshall Fund Rsch. fellow, Geneva, 1984-85. Mem. Am. Soc. Internat. Law (v.p. 2003—, Book award 1986), Internat. Law Assn. Democrat. Office: U Va Sch Law 580 Massie Rd Charlottesville VA 22903-1738

MARTIN, DAVID JERNER, education educator; b. N.Y.C., Aug. 12, 1934; s. Henning J. and Ruth J. M.; m. Mary Lou Pierson, Sept. 13, 1958; children: David, Steven, Elizabeth. BA in Chemistry, Hope Coll., 1956; MS in Gen. Sci., Syracuse U., 1974; PhD in Sci. Edn., Ga. State U., 1991. Cert. mid. sch. and H.S. sci., math. tchr., Ga., N.Y. Sci. and math. tchr. Van Hornesville (N.Y.) Ctrl. Sch., 1958-60, Arabian Am. Oil Co., Dhahran, Saudi Arabia, 1960-71, sci. curriculum coord., 1971-75, profl. devel. coord., 1975-82; pres. Human Resources Devel. Internat., Marietta, Ga., 1982-86; sci. tchr. Marietta H.S., 1986-89; prof. sci. edn. Kennesaw State U., Marietta, 1990—, dir. Grad. Studies in Edn. and Tchr. Edn. Svcs., 1996—2000. Author: Elementary Science Methods: A Constructivist Approach, 1997, 3d edit., 2003, Constructing Early Childhood Education, 2000; editor, cons. The Weather Classroom, 1992. Exec. dir. Ga. Jr. Acad. Sci., 1994-2000; counselor Kappa Delta Pi, 1994—. Mem. Nat. Assn. for Rsch. in Sci. Tchg., Assn. for Edn. of Tchrs. in Sci., Southeastern Assn. for Edn. of Tchrs. in Sci., Ga. Acad. Sci., Nat. Sci. Tchrs. Assn., Ga. Sci. Tchrs. Assn. Avocations: classical violin, chamber music.

MARTIN, DAVID S. retired secondary school educator, administrator; b. N.Y.C., May 14, 1941; s. Perry Johnson and Polly Edith (Shedlov) M.; m. Florence E. Martin, Jan. 14, 1989; children: Drew Michael, Amy Davida. BA, Adelphi Coll., 1962, MA, 1966; profl. cert., Hofstra U., 1969. Cert. secondary tchr., sch. dist. adminstr., N.Y. Adj. assoc. prof. Pace U., White Plains, N.Y., 1978-92; tchr., computer coord. Jericho (N.Y.) Pub. Schs., 1962-99. Author: Teachers Manual for Introduction to Pascal; co-author: How To Prepare for SAT II: Physics, 6th edit.; also author other books; contbr. articles to profl. jours. Fulbright-Hays grantee, 1967-68; recipient Grand award L.I. Sci. Congress, 1958, Disting Achievement award Electronic Learning, 1983, Outstanding Accomplishment award RITEC, 1984. Mem. IEEE (sr.), Am. Assn. Physics Tchrs., Assn. Computing Machinery, Authors Guild, Jericho Tchrs. Assn., N.Y. State United Tchrs., Flambeau, Phi Delta Kappa, Sigma Pi Sigma. Home: 16 Elm Pl Sea Cliff NY 11579-1634

MARTIN, DAVID STANDISH, education educator; b. New Bedford, Mass., Aug. 24, 1937; s. Theodore Tripp and Elinor Louise (Raymond) M.; m. Susan Katherine Orowan, June 30, 1962. BA, Yale U., 1959; MEd, Harvard U., 1961, CAS, 1968; PhD, Boston Coll., 1971. Cert. tchr., prin. Tchr. Newton (Mass.) Pub. Schs., 1961-68, asst. prin., 1969-70; teaching asst. Boston Coll., Chestnut Hill, Mass., 1968-69; curriculum dir. Beverly (Mass.) Pub. Schs., 1970-73; prin. Mill Valley (Calif.) Pub. Schs., 1973-75, curriculum dir., 1975-80; chmn. dept. edn. Dominican Coll., San Rafael, Calif., 1978-80; coordinator undergrad. tchr. edn. Gallaudet U., Washington, 1980-85, dean sch. edn. and human svcs., 1985-95, prof. edn., 1995—2001, prof., dean emeritus, 2002—. Cons. Curriculum Devel. Assocs., Washington, 1975-2001; mem. bd. examiners Nat. Coun. Accreditation Tchr. Education; bd. dirs. USA-SINO Tchr. Education Consortium, Western Pa. Sch. for the Deaf; Fulbright fellow U. Witwatersrand, South Africa, 2003. Author: Case Studies in Curriculum, 1989; editor: Cognition, Education and Deafness, 1985, Advances in Cognition Education and Deafness, 1991; contbr. articles to profl. jours. Grantee Dept. Edn., 1970, 85, Knight Found., 1995-2001, Ford Found., 1998-2001. Mem. D.C. Assn. Colls. Tchr. Edn. (pres. 1989-92), Assn. for Supervision and Curricum Devel., Nat. Coun. for Social Studies, Am. Ednl. Rsch. Assn., Am. Assn. Colls. for Tchr. Edn. (bd. dirs.), Coun. for Exceptional Children, Phi Delta Kappa, Kappa Delta Pi (chair publ.), Ednl. Consulting Schs. and Univs. Democrat. Unitarian Universalist. Avocations: genealogy, sailing, classical organ, astronomy. Home and Office: 10 Colonial Farm Cir Marstons Mills MA 02648

MARTIN, DIANE CARAWAY, school librarian; b. Dallas, Nov. 2, 1956; d. Stone Walker and Eleanor Lynn (DeBray) C.; m. C.A. Martin III, July 30, 1977; children: C.Allan IV, Wesley Walker. BS magna cum laude, La. Tech. U., 1977; MLS, La. State U., 1978. Cert. English tchr., libr., La. Libr. Northwood Elem. Sch., Baton Rouge, 1978-80; reference libr. Ouachita Valley Pub. Libr., West Monroe, La., 1980-82; libr. River Oaks Elem. Sch., Monroe, La., 1988-90, River Oaks High Sch., Monroe, 1990-93; substitute tchr. Bd. dirs. Monroe YWCA, 1982-85, La. Tech. Alumni, Ruston, 1991-95, Teen Ct. Northeast La., Monroe, 1990-93, Children's Mus. N.E. La.; coord. Parents in Edn. Project Self Esteem, Monroe, 1992-94; coord. elem. dept. St. Paul's United Meth. Ch., Monroe, 1992—; rep. Ouachita Valley coun. Boy Scouts Am., 1991—, wolf den leader, 1993-94; mem., room mother PTO; exec. com. Parents' Adv. Com. for Gifted and Talented, Monroe City Schs.; youth coord. St. Paul's United Meth. Youth, 1995-97. Mem. ALA, Northeast La. Libr. Network, Monroe Jr. League (recording sec. 1992-93, chmn. social svcs. 1993—, corresponding sec. 1994), Monroe Racquet Club Tennis League, United Meth. Women (past pres.). Republican. Avocations: tennis, reading, singing, piano, cooking. Home: 3509 Lake Desiard Dr Monroe LA 71201-2078

MARTIN, DONNIS LYNN, adult education educator; b. Knox City, Tex., Sept. 7, 1948; s. Derrell Lee Martin and Audie Lee (Qualls) Kempe; m. Karen Marie Hanzevack, Dec. 24, 1988; children: Christina, Dustin, Shara. BA/BS, Met. State Coll. Denver, 1979; MA in Mgmt., U. Phoenix, 1990; EdD, N.C. State U., 1991. Cert. tchr. lang. arts. Program supr. wind energy sys. Rockwell Internat., Golden, Colo., 1980-83, mgr. plant tng., 1983-84, prin. orgn. devel. specialist, 1984-87; mgr. computer-based tng. courseware devel. No. Telecom, Inc., Raleigh, N.C., 1987-88, program mgr. documentation, 1988-89; edn. program specialist N.C. Dept. Cmty. Colls., 1991-92; pres. ERC Assocs., Cary, N.C., 1992-96; asst. prof. N.C. State U. Dept. Adult and C.C. Edn., Raleigh, 1996—. Contbr. articles to profl. jours. With USAF, 1973-80. Fellow Acad. Human Resource Devel.; mem. Am. Soc. for Tng. and Devel., Am. Ednl. Rsch. Assn., Am. Vocat. Edn. Rsch. Assn., Internat. Soc. Performance Improvement, Soc. Applied Learning Technologies, Soc. for Tech. Comm. (sr.), Omicron Tau Theta. Avocations: photography, boating, golf. Home: 5016 Sunset Fairways Dr Holly Springs NC 27540-7829 Office: N C State U PO Box 7801 Raleigh NC 27695-0001

MARTIN, DOROTHY SUE, secondary education educator, counselor; b. Hearne, Tex., Aug. 27, 1945; d. John Bud and Jimmie (Stroud) M. BS, Sam Houston State U., 1967; MEd, U. Alaska, 1988. Lic. tchr., counselor, Tex., Alaska. Tchr. Wharton (Tex.) Ind. Sch. Dist., 1967-69; tchr., coach Taylor Jr. High Sch., Fairbanks, Alaska, 1969-79; tchr., counselor Eielson High Sch. Fairbanks North Star Borough, 1980—, coach, 1980-85. Mem. com. on curriculum Fairbanks North Star Sch. Dist., 1969—, com. on phys. plant usage, com. student handbook, 1991—; Natural Helper coord. State of Alaska, Eielson High Sch., Fairbanks, 1988—, dist. coord. Sch. to Work, 1998-2000. Author: (pamphlet) Eielson Physical Education, 1980. Commr. Timberlane Rd. Svc. Area, North Pole, Alaska, 1988—. Grantee Fairbanks Sch. Dist., 1991. Mem. NEA, AAHPER, Phys. Edn. Assn. Tchrs. (v.p. 1990). Office: Eielson Jr/Sr High Sch Industrial Ave North Pole AK 99705

MARTIN, EDYTHE LOUVIERE, business educator; b. Breaux Bridge, La., Dec. 30, 1940; d. James Ivy and Volna Mary (Landry) L.; m. James Henry Martin, Aug. 23, 1969; 1 child, Lois Elizabeth. BS in Bus. Edn., U. Southwestern La., 1972; MEd in Supervision, La. State U., 1977, Specialist Degree in Ednl. Adminstrn., 1988, postgrad studies in Ednl. Adminstrn., 1989—. Geol. sec. Sohio Petroleum Co., Lafayette, La., 1960-67, Bintliff Oil & Gas Co., Lafayette, 1967-69; bus. tchr. Cottonport (La.) H.S., 1972-74; bus. instr. La. Tech. Coll., Crowley, La., 1975—. Team leader, mem. accrediting teams So. Assn. Colls. and Schs., 1978—, chmn. of steering com. for Acadian Tech. evaluation, 1991; speaker, presenter at meetings and seminars of educators. Publicity chairperson Miss Eunice (La.) Pageant, 1981-88; chairperson Eunice Lady of Yr. award, 1982; organizer chairperson, St. Jude Children's Hosp., Fund Raiser, Memphis, Eunice, 1985-91; PTC sec. St. Edmund Sch., Eunice, 1982-84; vol. March of Dimes, 1995—. Mem. Office Occupations Assn., La. Vocat. Assn. Inc., La. Vocat. Assn. (trade and indsl. divsn.). Democrat Roman Catholic. Avocations: collecting, travel. Home: 750 Viola St Eunice LA 70535-4340 Office: La Tech Coll 1933 W Hutchinson Ave Crowley LA 70526-3215

MARTIN, ERNEST LEE, academic administrator, historian, theologian, writer; b. Meeker, Okla., Apr. 20, 1932; s. Joel Chester and Lula Mae (Quinn) M.; m. Helen Rose Smith, Aug. 26, 1957 (div. 1980); children: Kathryn, Phyllis, Samuel; m. Ramona Jean Kinsey, June 27, 1987. BA, Ambassador U., 1958, MA, 1960, PhD, 1966. Dean faculty Ambassador U., St. Albans, Eng., 1965-72, chmn. dept. theology Pasadena, Calif., 1972-74; dir. Found. for Bibl. Rsch., Pasadena, 1974-84, Acad. for Scriptural Knowledge, Portland, from 1985. Dir. 450 coll. students with Prof. Benjamin Mazar Herodian Western Wall archaeol. excavations, Jerusalem, 1969-74. Author: Birth of Christ Recalculated, 1978, 2d edit., 1980, The Original Bible Restored, 1984, Secrets of Golgotha, 1987, 2d edit., 1996, The Star That Astonished the World, 1996, 101 Bible Secrets That Christians Do Not Know, 1993, The People That History Forgot, 1993, The Place of the New Third Temple, 1994, Restoring the Original Bible, 1994, The Biblical Manual, 1995, ABC's of the Gospel, 1997, The Essentials of New Testament Doctrine, 1999, The Temples that Jerusalem Forgot, 1999, Angels-The Fictions and the Facts, 2001. With USAFR, 1950, tech. sgt. USAF, 1950-54. Mem. Soc. Bibl. Lit. (advisor to Original Bible Project), Planetarium Soc. Home: Portland, Oreg. Died Jan. 16, 2002.

MARTIN, FREDERICK NOEL, audiology educator; b. N.Y.C., July 24, 1931; s. Philip and Mildred Ruth (Austin) M.; m. Mary Catherine Robinson, Apr. 4, 1954; children: David C., Leslie Anne. BA, Bklyn. Coll., 1957, MA, 1958; PhD, CUNY, 1968. Audiologist, Lenox Hill Hosp., N.Y.C., 1957-58; Audiologist Ark. Sch. for the Deaf, Little Rock, 1958-60; dir. audiology Bailey Ear Clinic, Little Rock, 1960-66; mem. faculty Bklyn. Coll., 1966-68, U. Tex., Austin, 1968—, endowed prof. audiology, 1982—. Author: Introduction to Audiology, 1975, 8th edit., 2003, interactive CD ROM, 2003, Pediatric Audiology, 1978, Medical Audiology, 1981, Basic Audiometry, 1986; editor: Remediation of Communication Disorders, Vol. 10, 1978, Hearing Disorders in Children, 1986, Effective Counseling in Audiology, 1994, Hearing Care for Children, 1996, Exercises in Audiometry, 1998; contbr. numerous articles to profl. jours. Served with USAF, 1951-55. Fellow Am. Speech-Language Hearing Assn., Am. Acad. Audiology; mem. Tex. Speech-Lang.-Hearing Assn., Am. Auditory Soc., Tex. Acad. Audiology. Home: 8613 Silver Ridge Dr Austin TX 78759-8144 Office: U Tex Austin TX 78712

MARTIN, GARY WILLIAM, computer and information science educator; b. Long Beach, Calif., Oct. 5, 1953; s. Joseph G. and Janet (Swanstrom) M. BA in Math., BS in Info. and Computer Sci., U. Calif., Irvine, 1975; MS in Math., U. Minn., Mpls., 1977. Tchg. asst. U. Minn., Mpls., 1975-77; instr. Yuba Coll., Woodland, Calif., 1977-78; learning skills specialist U. Calif., Davis, 1978-80; prof. computer and info. sci. Solano C.C., Fairfield, Calif., 1980—. Computer cons. Software Artistry, Davis, 1986—. Author: TURBO PASCAL: Theory and Practice of Good Programming, 1992, QBASIC: A Short Course in Structured Programming, 1994. Avocation: music. Office: Solano CC 4000 Suisun Valley Rd Fairfield CA 94534-3197 E-mail: gmartin@solano.cc.ca.us.

MARTIN, GEORGE M. pathologist, gerontologist, educator; b. N.Y.C., June 30, 1927; s. Barnett J. and Estelle (Weiss) M.; m. Julaine Ruth Miller, Dec. 2, 1952; children: Peter C., Kelsey C., Thomas M., Andrew C. BS, U. Wash., 1949, MD, 1953. Diplomate Am. Bd. Pathology, Am. Bd. Med. Genetics. Intern Montreal Gen. Hosp., Quebec, Can., 1953-54; resident-instr. U. Chgo., 1954-57; instr.-prof. U. Wash., Seattle, 1957—. Vis. scientist Dept. Genetics Albert Einstein Coll., N.Y.C., 1964, Rockefeller U., 1998-99; chmn. Gordon Confs. Molecular Pathology, Biology of Aging, 1974-79; chmn., nat. res. Plan on Aging Nat. Inst. on Aging, Bethesda, Md., 1985-89; dir. Alzheimer's Disease Rsch. Ctr. U. Wash., 1985—, assoc. dir., 1999—. Editor Werner's Syndrome and Human Aging, 1985, Molecular Aspects of Aging, 1995; contbr. articles in field to profl jours. Active Fedn. Am. Scientists. With USN, 1945-46. Recipient Allied Signal award in Aging, 1991, Rsch. medal Am. Agy. Assn., 1992, Kleemeier award, 1994, Paul Glenn award for aging rsch., 1998; named Disting. Alumnus, U. Wash.

Sch. Medicine, 1987; USPHS rsch. fellow dept. genetics, Glasgow U., 1961-62; Eleanor Roosevelt Inst. Cancer Rsch. fellow Inst. de Biologie, PHysiologie, Chimie, Paris, 1968-69; Josiah Macy faculty scholar Sir William Din Sch. Pathology, Oxford (Eng.) U., 1978-79, Humboldt Disting. scientist dept. genetics U. Wurzburg, Germany, 1991. Fellow: AAAS, Tissue Culture Assn. (pres. 1986—88), Gerontol. Soc. Am. (chmn. Biol. Sci. 1979, pres.-elect 2001, Brookdale award 1981, Lifetime Acheivement award for rsch. in alzheimer's disease World Alzheimer's Congress 2000); mem.: Am. Fedn. Aging Rsch. (pres. 1999—2001), Am. Soc. Investigative Pathology, Am. Soc. Human Genetics, Am. Assn. Univ. Pathologists (emeritus), Inst. Medicine. Democrat. Avocations: internat. travel, jazz music, biography. Home: 2223 E Howe St Seattle WA 98112-2931 Office: U Wash Sch Medicine Dept Pathology Rm K543 Seattle WA 98195 E-mail: gmmartin@u.washington.edu.

MARTIN, HELEN ELIZABETH, educational consultant; b. West Chester, Pa., Feb. 19, 1945; d. Thomas Edwin and Elizabeth Temple (Walker) M. BA, The King's Coll., N.Y.C., 1967; MEd, West Chester U., 1970; postgrad., Goethe Inst., Freiberg, Fed. Republic Germany, 1979, Oxford (Eng.) U., 1979. Nat. bd. cert. tchr. adolescent/young adult sci., 2000. Tchr. math. and sci. Unionville (Pa.) H.S., 1967-99; ret., 1999; ednl. cons. Adj. prof. West Chester U., 1989—; mem. Carnegie Forum on Edn. and the Economy. Mem. Pa. Rep. State Com., 1982-90, Rep. Com. of Chester County, 1984-94. Named Alumna of Yr., The King's Coll., 1987; recipient State Presdl. award, 1989, Frank G. Brewer Civil Air Patrol Meml. Aerospace award, 1989, Outstanding Achievement award U.S. Dept. Commerce, 1993; Bus. Week/Challenger Seven fellow, 1991. Fellow Am. Sci. Affiliation; mem. AAAS, Nat. Bd. Profl. Tchg. Stds. (founding dir., 1987-94), Satellite Educators Assn. (pres. 1990-2000), Nat. Sci. Tchrs. Assn., Nat. Coun. Tchrs. Math., Nat. Sci. Tchrs. Assn. (internat. lectr. 1987), Assn. for Sci. Edn. in U.K. (internat. lectr. 1987). Home: PO Box 605 Unionville PA 19375-0605 E-mail: SatTeacher@aol.com.

MARTIN, JACK, federal agency administrator; m. Bettye Martin; children: Randy, Ingrid. BS, MBA, Wayne State U.; postgrad., U. Minn. CPA. With Gen. Motors Corp., Detroit; various mgmt. positions Control Data; cons. acct. Touche Ross & Co. (now Deloitte and Touche); mng. dir., CEO, founder Jack Martin and Co. P.C., CPAs, 1975—; chmn., acting CEO Home Fed. Savings Bank, Detroit, 1995—; chmn. provider reimbursement rev. bd. U.S. Dept. Health and Human Svcs., 1991—94; CFO Dept. Edn., Washington, 2001—. Chmn. of bd. Health Alliance Plan; mem. investment com. Mercy Health Sys. (now Trinity Health); chair Mich. adv. com. U.S. Civil Rights Commn.; v.p. Merrill Palmer Inst. Wayne State U. Treas. Alzheimer's Assn. Mem.: AICPA (mem. practice stds. subcom.), Det. Athletic Club (bd. dirs.). Office: Dept Edn Office CFO 400 Maryland Ave SW Washington DC 20202-4110

MARTIN, JAMES HARBERT, school administrator, retired Air Force officer; b. Sparta, Tenn., Jan. 5, 1941; s. Harbert Rogers and Monia Gladys (Grissom) M.; m. Madoline Carter, Sept. 14, 1963; children: Erin Dawn, Ann Farley, John Harbert. MSBA, Tenn. Tech. U., 1963; MBA, Auburn U., 1975. CPA; cert. profl. logistician. Commd. USAF, 1963, advanced through ranks to col., 1983; dep. program mgr. B1B System Program Office, 1982-84; dir. logistics Aero. Systems Div., Wright-Patterson AFB, Ohio, 1984-86; dep. comdr. resources Incirlik Air Base, Adana, Turkey, 1986-88; comdr. Tyndall AFB, Panama City, Fla., 1988-90; vice comdr. Air Force Engring. and Svcs. Ctr., Tyndall AFB, 1990; ret., 1990; exec. dir. Lookout Mountain (Ga.) Golf Club, 1991-94; CFO Riverside Mil. Acad., Gainesville, Ga., 1994—. Mem. exec. bd. Gulf Coast coun. Boy Scouts Am., Pensacola, Fla., 1989-92; chmn. Bay County WalkAmerica (March of Dimes), Panama City, 1990. Decorated Legion of Merit (2). Mem. Air Force Assn., Masons. Republican. Methodist. Office: Riverside Mil Acad Box 565 2001 Riverside Dr Gainesville GA 30501-1227

MARTIN, JAMES KIRBY, historian, educator; b. Akron, Ohio, May 26, 1943; s. Paul Elmo and Dorothy Marie (Garrett) M.; m. Karen Wierwille, Aug. 7, 1965; children: Darcy Elizabeth, Sarah Marie, Joelle Kathryn Garrett. BA summa cum laude, Hiram Coll., 1965; MA, U. Wis., 1967, PhD, 1969. Asst. prof. history Rutgers U., New Brunswick, N.J., 1969-73, assoc. prof., 1973-79, prof., 1979-80, asst. provost, 1972-74, v.p. acad. affairs, 1977-79; vis. prof. Rutgers Ctr. of Alcohol Studies, 1978-88; prof. history U. Houston, 1980-97, disting. univ. prof., 1997—, chmn. dept., 1980-83; vis. prof. history Rice U., Houston, 1992. Chmn. bd. sponsors Papers of Thomas Edison Project, 1977-80; founding ptnr. PastQuest Rsch. Svcs., 1999. Author: Men in Rebellion, 1973, In the Course of Human Events, 1979, (with M.E. Lender) A Respectable Army: The Military Origins of the Republic, 1982 (contemporary mil. reading list), Drinking in America: A History, 1982, rev. edit. 1987, (with others) America and Its Peoples, 1989, concise edit. 1995, Benedict Arnold: Revolutionary Hero, 1997 (Homer D. Babbidge, Jr. award), audio edit., 2001; editor: Interpreting Colonial America, 1973, 2d edit. 1978, The Human Dimensions of Nation Making, 1976, (with K. Stubaus) The American Revolution, Whose Revolution?, 1977, 81, (with M.E. Lender) Citizen-Soldier: The Revolutionary War Journal of Joseph Bloomfield, 1982 (R.P. McCormick prize), Ordinary Courage: The Revolutionary War Adventures of Joseph Plumb Martin, 1993, 2d edit., 1999; mem. editl. bd. Papers of William Livingston Project, 1973-80, Houston Rev., 1981—, N.J. History, 1986—, Conversations with the Past Series, 1993-95; gen. editor Am. Social Experience Series, 1983-2002. Recipient N.J. Soc. of the Cin. prize for Disting. Achievement in Am. History, 1995, Hiram Coll. Alumni Achievement award, 1996. Mem. Tex. Assn. for Advancement History (bd. dirs. 1981-93, v.p. 1986-90), Inst. for Internat. Bus. Analysis (adv. coun. 1982-86), Am. Hist. Assn. (Beveridge-Dunning prize com. 1990-93), Orgn. Am. Historians, So. Hist. Assn., Soc. Historians Early Am. Republic (adv. coun. 1985-88), Soc. for Mil. History, Phi Beta Kappa, Phi Kappa Phi, Pi Gamma Mu, Omicron Delta Kappa, Phi Alpha Theta. Office: U Houston Dept History 4800 Calhoun Rd Houston TX 77204-3003

MARTIN, JANICE LYNN, special education educator; b. Louisville, Feb. 24, 1952; d. Thomas Joseph and Agnes Marie (Singhiser) Duddy; m. Reed Ammerman Martin Jr., Aug. 14, 1976; children: Susan, John. BS magna cum laude, U. Ga., 1974; MEd, U. Louisville, 1976, grad. dean's citation, 1984; cert., Western Ky. U., 1984. Tchr. Jefferson County Pub. Schs., Louisville, 1974—. Mem. curriculum coun. Jefferson County Pub. Schs., 1979-82. Mem. St. Joseph Cath. Orphan Soc., Louisville, 1981—; active Girl Scouts U.S., Louisville, 1988—. Recipient Grad. Dean's citation U. Louisville, 1976, Achievement in Edn. award Middletown Optimist Club, 1999, finalist Stella Edwards award for outstanding spl. edn. tchr. yr. Ky. Dept. Edn., 1998, 2000 Spirit award Middletown C. of C.; grantee Eisenhower Title II math. and sci., 1992, 93, Appalachian Ednl. Lab. Eisenhower Math. Grant Project, 1994. Mem. NEA, ASCD, Ky. Edn. Assn., Coun. for Exceptional Children (Outstanding Spl. Edn. Tchr. of Yr. 1990), Louisville Coun. Tchrs., Ky. Coun. Tchrs. of Math., Nat. Coun. Tchrs. Math., Jefferson County Tchrs. Assn., AAUW, Alpha Delta Kappa, Phi Kappa Phi, Phi Delta Kappa, Sigma Kappa. Democrat. Home: 2600 Hill Briar Ct Louisville KY 40241 Office: Jefferson County Pub Schs Middletown Elem 218 N Madison Ave Louisville KY 40243-1018

MARTIN, JEAN ANN, retired school system administrator, educator; b. Omaha, June 27, 1942; d. Clarid Fee and Frances Catherine (Dugan) McNeil; m. Robert William Martin, Dec. 28, 1968. BS, Pa. State U., 1963; MEd, U. Del., 1968; EdD, Wilmington Coll., 1997. Cert. English tchr., Pa., N.Y., Del., reading specialist, Va., N.Y., Del., secondary prin., reading supr., dir. of instrn., Del. Tchr. English Neshaminy Sch. Dist., Langhorn, Pa., 1963-65; tchr. English and reading Unionville (Pa.) Sch. Dist., 1965-68; tchr. reading Jamesville-DeWitt (N.Y.) Sch. Dist., 1968-69, South Colonie Sch. Dist., Albany, N.Y., 1969-70; tchr. English Bethlehem Ctrl. Sch. Dist., Delmar, N.Y., 1970-71, Smyrna (Del.) Sch. Dist., 1971-73; reading specialist, tchr. English Delmar (Del.) Sch. Dist., 1973-88; reading specialist Accomack (Va.) County Schs., 1988-93; sch. adminstr., ednl. diagnostician Del. Dept. Svc. for Children, Youth and Their Families, Middletown, 1994—2003. Adj. prof. Del. State U., 1997—99, Wilmington Coll., 2000—; chairperson H.S. Reading Task Force, Del. Commn. on Reading Success, 1999. Mem.: ASCD, Cedar Shores Condominium Assn. (sec.), Internat. Reading Assn. (ea. regional conf. gen. conf. chair 1997—99, regional conf. com. 1999—2001), Del. Assn. Sch. Adminstrs., Diamond State Reading Assn. (pres. 1985—86, editor DSRA Reader), Lions Club (New Castle, Del., pres. 2001), Alpha Delta Kappa (past pres. Theta chpt. and Del.). Home: 33 E 6th St New Castle DE 19720-5087 E-mail: jmart000@aol.com.

MARTIN, JOAN ELLEN, secondary education educator; b. Oak Park, Ill., Sept. 1, 1937; d. Emil and Jessie R. (Kotva) M. BS, North Cen. Coll., 1959; MA, Northwestern U., 1962; EdD, Okla. State U., 1983. Cert. tchr., phys. edn., adminstrn., driver edn. tchr., Ill. Tchr. Naperville (Ill.) Cen. High Sch., 1959-94, dept. chair, 1966-77. Instr. phys. edn. Triton Jr. Coll., Leyden, Ill., Naperville Pk. Dist., Girls Scouts, 1965-78; instr. Aurora U., 1997-2002, Chgo. State U., 1999-. Contbr. articles to profl. jours. Established tchr. stress/burnout Cons. Svc. Naperville Ctrl. H.S., 1983; chmn. health edn. com. North Ctrl. Evaluation team Thornton Twp. H.S., Harvey, Ill., 1984; rep. Naperville Tchrs. Assn. Bldg., 1985-94. Recipient NASPE Pres. Citation, 1990, YWCA Outstanding Woman Leader in DuPage County (Athletics) award, 1988, Ill. Assn. Health Phys. Edn. Recreation and Dance Honor award, 1981, Naperville Sch. Dist. (twenty five yeard award, 1984), Am. Red Cross (ten year svc.) award, 1980, Ill. Presdl. citation, 1999, Midwest Dist. Presdl. citation, 2000; Humble Oil scholar, 1965. Mem. ASCD, NEA, AAHPERD (meritorious svc. award 1987, honor award 1995), Midwest Assn. Health Phys. Edn. Recreation and Dance (v.p. phys. edn. divsn. 1980, 81, v.p. gen. divsn. 1994-96, bd. dirs., v.p. health divsn. 1999-02, honor award 1998), Ill. Assn. Health, Phys. Edn. Recreation and Dance (ad hoc com., long range planning com., exec. bd. and rep. assembly, rsch. com. chmn., jour. mng. editor, conv. program chmn., Pepi, honor fellow, quarter century award), Secondary Sch. Phys. Edn. Soc. (v.p., pres.), Ill. Edn. Assn., U.S. Orienteering Assn., Chgo. Area Orienteering Assn., Naperville Tchrs. Assn., Ill. H.S. Coll. Driver Edn. Assn., Women's Sports Found., Phi Epsilon Kappa. Home: 317 Elmwood Dr Naperville IL 60540-7206

MARTIN, JOANNE, educator; b. Salem, Mass., Sept. 25, 1946; d. Richard Drake and Nathalie (Ashton) M.; m. Beaumont A. Sheil, July 9, 1977; 1 child, Beaumont Martin Sheil. BA, Smith Coll., 1968; PhD in Social Psychology, Harvard U., 1977; PhD in Econs. and Bus. Adminstrn. (hon.), Copenhagen Bus. Sch., 2001. Assoc. cons. McBer & Co. (formerly Behavior Sci. Ctr. of Sterling Inst.), 1968-70, dir. govt. mktg., 1970-72; asst. prof. orgnl. behavior and sociology Grad. Sch. Bus., Stanford U., Calif., 1977-80; assoc. prof. grad. sch. bus. Stanford U., Calif., 1980-91, prof. grad. sch. bus., 1991—, dir. doctoral programs, grad. sch. bus., 1991-95, Fred H. Merrill prof. orgn. behavior and sociology, 1996—. Sec. Stanford U. Adv. Bd., 1995—96, vice chair, 1996—97; vis. scholar Australian Grad. Sch. Mgmt. U. N.S.W., 1989—90, Copenhagen Bus. Sch., 1998; vis. scholar dept. psychology Sydney (Australia) U., 1989—90; Ruffin fellow bus. ethics Darden Grad. Sch. Bus. Adminstrn. U. Va., 1990; mem. bd. advisors iMahal; bd. dirs. C.P.P., Inc.; mem. internat. adv. bd. Internat. Ctr. for Rsch. in Orgnl. Discourse, Strategy and Change; guest lectr. dept. psychology MIT, 1976—77; cons. in field. Mem. editl. bd. Adminstrv. Sci. Qtrly., 1984—88, Jour. Social Issues, 1981—83, Acad. Mgmt. Jour., 1984—85, Social Justice Rsch., 1985—90, Jour. Mgmt. Inquiry, 1991—, Orgn., 1994—, Jour. Mgmt. Studies, 1996—, Gender, Work and Organization, 1998—; co-author: five books; contbr. articles to profl. jours. Lena Lake Forrest Rsch. fellowship Bus. and Profl. Women's Found., 1978, James and Doris McNamara Faculty fellowship Grad. Sch. of Bus., Stanford U., 1990-91. Fellow: APA, Am. Psychol. Soc., Acad. Mgmt. (rep.-at-large 1983—85, divsn. program chair 1985—87, divsn. chair 1987—89, bd. govs. 1992—95, we. divsn. Promising Young Scholar award 1982, Disting. Educator award 2000, Sr. Scholar award 2003); mem.: Nat. Assn. Corp. Dirs. (adv. bd. 2000—). Office: Stanford U Grad Sch Bus Littlefield Ctr 353 Stanford CA 94305

MARTIN, JOHN DRISCOLL, school administrator; b. Chgo., July 28, 1954; s. Walter Roy and Constance Kathleen (Driscoll) M.; children: Patrick, Kelsey; m. Caroline J. Martin, Mar. 28, 1996. BA, Augustana Coll., 1976; MA, Northwestern U., 1982. Cert. tchr., Ill. Tchr. J.D. Darnall High Sch., Geneseo, Ill., 1976-77, St. Viator High Sch., Arlington Heights, Ill., 1977-79, Hoffman Estates (Ill.) High Sch., 1979-88, athletic dir., 1988-90, Adlai E. Stevenson High Sch., Lincolnshire, Ill., 1990—. Adv. com. Ill. High Sch. Assn., Bloomington, 1989-92; master tchr. Gov.'s Master Tchr. Program, 1984—. Mem. AAHPERD, Ill. Assn. Health, Phys. Edn., Recreation and Dance, Nat. Athletic Adminstrs. Assn., Ill. Athletic Dirs. Assn. (conf. chair 1995, cert. athletic adminstr.). Avocations: golf, reading. Office: 1 Stevenson Dr Lincolnshire IL 60069-2824 E-mail: jmartin@district125.k12.il.us.

MARTIN, JOHN SWANSON, retired education educator; b. Sulligent, Ala., May 7, 1939; s. Judson Roby and Frances Susan (Rutland) M.; m. Linda Ferrell Isaacs, June 3, 1978; 1 child, Belinda Frances. AA, Marion (Ala.) Mil. Inst., 1959; BA, Livingston U., 1961; MEd, Auburn U., 1965; EdS, U. Ala., 1975. Tchr., chmn. social studies dept. W.P. Davidson H.S., Mobile, Ala., 1961-92, dept. chmn., 1962-92; ret., 1992; instr. U. Ala., summers 1973-75; tchr. Internat. Lang. Sch./Mobile Bapt. Assn., Mobile, 1992—, Jesus Film Project, 1993, 1994, 1996, 1997, 1998, 1999, So. Bapt. M-Fuge Project, London, 2000, 2001, 2002, 2003, Dauphin Way Bapt. Ch., 1st Bapt. Snellville, India, 2001. Contbg. author publs. in field. Adv. com. sch. bd. race Mobile County Pub. Schs.; sponsor Fellowship of Christian Athletes Davidson H.S., Mobile; mem. adv. bd. Mobile Area Fellowship Christian Athletes; deacon, vice-chmn. deacon fellowship Dauphin Way Bapt. Ch., Mobile; mission trips Dauphin Way Bapt. Ch. to Nicaragua, 1994—96, Russia, Bulgaria, Republic of Macedonia, Brazil, others; mem. steering com. Cottage Hill Christian Acad. H.S. Recipient award for work with driver edn. Chrysler Corp., Outstanding Tchr. award Davidson Key Club, 1990, others; spl. recognition support Davidson NJROTC 1978-79 and 1980-81. Mem. NEA, Ala. Edn. Assn., Mobile County Edn. Assn. (past treas., exec. bd.), Retired Tchrs. of Ala., Retired Tchrs. of Mobile County, Nat. Coun. for Social Studies, Ala. Coun. for Social Studies, Mobile County Coun. for Social Studies (v.p. 1977-78), Ala. Hist. Assn., Capstone Coll. of Edn. Soc., Livingston Alumni Assn. (v.p. local chpt.), Phi Delta Kappa.

MARTIN, JOHN THOMAS, physician, author, educator; b. Cleve., June 8, 1924; s. Clarence Henry and Clara May (Feeney) M.; m. Marion Elizabeth George, Feb. 18, 1946; children: Thomas R., David B., Richard G., Janet E., Patricia L., Robert W. MD, U. Cin., 1948. Commd. 1st lt. USAF, 1949, advanced through grades to maj., 1953; resident in anesthesiology Lackland AFB Hosp., San Antonio, 1953-55; asst. chief USAF Sch. Anesthesiology, Lackland AFB, 1955-57; attending anesthesiologist Baylor U. Hosp., Dallas, 1957-58; cons. dept. anesthesiology Mayo Clinic, Rochester, Minn., 1958-72, head Meth sect. anesthesiology, 1966-72; assoc. clin. prof. anesthesiology, 1968-72; chmn. dept. anesthesiology Ochsner Med. Ctr., New Orleans, 1972-74; clin. assoc. prof. anesthesiology Tulane U. Sch. Medicine, New Orleans, 1972-74; prof. anesthesiology Med. Coll. Ohio, Toledo, 1974-90, chmn. dept. anesthesiology, 1980-89, emeritus prof. anesthesiology, 1990—. Editor, author: Positioning Patients Anesthesia/Surgery, 1978, 2d edit., 1987, 3d edit., 1997; editor ASA Handbook of Hosp. Facilities for Anesthesia, 1972, 2d edit., 1974; contbr. articles to profl. jours. Chmn. conductor selection com. Rochester Symphony Orch., 1963-66; pres. Rochester Civic Music, 1965. Mem. Internat. Anesthesia Rsch. Soc. (chmn. 1979-81, trustee 1965-90), Minn. Soc. Anesthesiologists (pres. 1966-67), Ohio Soc. Anesthesiologists (pres. 1988-89), Am. Med. Writers Assn. (pres. Minn. chpt. 1970-71), Assoc. Physicians Med. Coll. Ohio (bd. dirs. 1974-89), Am. Soc. Anesthesiology, Sigma Xi, Alpha Omega Alpha, Sigma Chi, Phi Chi. Republican. Avocations: medical writing, computers, music, fishing. Home: 4605 Woodland Ln Sylvania OH 43560-3221 Office: Med Coll of Ohio PO Box 10008 Toledo OH 43699-0008

MARTIN, JOSÉ GINORIS, education administrator; b. Feb. 4, 1941; married; two children. BS in Nuclear Engring. with honors, Miss. State U., 1964; MS in Nuclear Engring., U. Wis., 1966, PhD in Engring., 1970; MDP, Harvard U., 1997. Mem. faculty U. Mass., Lowell, 1975—96, grad. coord. for energy engring., 1984-90; chmn. chem. and nuclear engring. dept. Coll. of Engring., U. Mass., Lowell, 1990-96; dean Coll. Sci., Math and Tech. U. Tex., Brownsville, 1996—2000, provost and v.p. acad. affairs, 2000—, Houston Found. faculty chmn. sci. Bd. dirs. Enersol, Inc., Tech Prep of the Rio Grande Valley, Inc., Valley Regional Hosp.; Fulbright prof. Curso de Postgraduacão em Ecologia, U. Federale do Rio Crande do Sul, Porto Alegre, Brazil, 1995; vis. prof. Ariz. State U. Coll. of Architecture, 1983, U. Mex., 1976-77, I.M.E., Rio de Janeiro, 1973; dir. Mass. Photovoltaic Ctr., 1987-96; cons. Corp. for Energy Devel. of Andalucia, 1992-96, Corp. for the 1992 Universal Exposion in Seville, Spain, 1982-88; prin. gov.'s task force on energy Commonwealth of Mass., 1994. Contbr. numerous articles to profl. jours. Mem.: Sigma Xi. Home: RR 3 Box 12 Los Fresnos TX 78566-9710 E-mail: jmartin@utbl.utb.edu.

MARTIN, KATHRYN LINDA HAIN, middle school foreign language educator; b. Dayton, Ohio, Sept. 10, 1945; d. John Gordon and Alma Viola (Howe) Hain; m. Thomas Newton Martin, June 10, 1967 (div.); children: Christopher Thomas, Jennifer Kathryn. BA in French and Edn., Otterbein Coll., 1967; diplome d'Etude Francais, U. De Strasbourg, Strasbourg, France, 1966; MA in Tchg., Colo. Coll., 1996—98. Tchr. h.s. French & Eng. Jefferson H.S., Lakewood, Colo., 1967-68; tchr. h.s. French Cheyenne Mountain H.S., Colorado Springs, Colo., 1968-72; finance sec. First United Meth. Ch., Colorado Springs, Colo., 1982-90; lang. tchr. Canadian Govt. Lang. Program, Colorado Springs, Colo., 1980—89; French tchr. Timberview Mid. Sch. Dist. #20, Colorado Springs, Colo., 1999—2003, Mountain Ridge Middle Sch. Dist. #20, Colorado Springs, 1999—. Faculty adv. French club Cheyenne Mountain H.S., 1968-72; People to People tour leader People to People Tours Inc., Washington, 1971; vol. French for 1st grade, Steamboat Springs Elem. Sch., 1978-79; high sch. enrichment program Introductory French Grant Elem. Sch., 1980-81. Recipient Thomas S. Crawford Team award Acad. Sch. Dist. # 20, 1994. Mem. Colo. Congress Fgn. Lang. Tchrs. Avocations: travel, photography, tennis, hiking, reading. Home: 2909 San Luis Dr Colorado Springs CO 80909-1321 Office: Mountain Ridge Middle Sch 9150 Lexington Dr Colorado Springs CO 80920 E-mail: kathrynm@d20.co.edu.

MARTIN, LEO G. educational consultant; Commr. edn. dept. State of Maine, Augusta, 1992—96; founder Sch. Solutions, Inc., 1997—. Office: Edn Dept 25 Summer St Kennebunk ME 04043 Home: 10 Towne St Kennebunkport ME 04046*

MARTIN, LEONARD AUSTIN, II, music educator; b. McCook, Nebr., July 18, 1949; s. Austin Berwell and Marie Elizabeth (Kimbro) M. BA summa cum laude, Metro State Coll. Denver, 1971; MA, Denver U., 1972, PhD, 1984. Lic. tchr., adminstr., Colo. Music instr. Cross Exec. Sch. Music, Aurora, Colo., 1965—, Peetz (Colo.) elem. and secondary schs., 1972, 5 area sch. dists., Denver, 1973, Adams County Sch. Dist. 12, Denver, 1974-94. Past instr. U. Colo., Denver, U. No. Colo., Adams State Coll., U. Phoenix; faculty of tchr. edn. program U. Denver, 1994—; presenter in field. Author: High School Music Theory, 1978, Basic Music Theory, 1989, A Curriculum for Educational Licensure, 1994; contbr. articles to profl. jours. Youth choir dir. Faith Presbyn. Ch., Aurora, 1973-75, substitute dir. adult choir, 1987-90; mem. worship team, mem. choir Cornerstone Cmty. Ch., Glendale, Colo., 1991-93; substitute dir., Presbyn. Ch. Aurora, 1995-97; cornetist Aurora Summer Cmty. Band, 1965-71; mem. Colo. All-State Band, 1967; choir dir. Aurora First Presbyn. Ch., 1998—; lay preacher Presbyn. Ch. and Care Ctr., 2000—. Mem. NEA, ASCD, Colo. Edn. Assn., Music Educators Nat. Conf., Colo. Music Educators Assn., Denver Musicians Soc. (pres., recording sec.), Nat. Geog. Soc. Republican. Presbyterian. Avocations: collecting chime/strike clocks, elephants, silent 8 mm movies, swimming, bowling. E-mail: leomarti@du.edu.

MARTIN, LORRAINE B. humanities educator; b. Utica, N.Y., Aug. 18, 1940; d. Walter G. and Laura (Bochenek) Bolanowski; m. Charles A. Martin; children: Denise M. Stringer, Tracy M. Weinrich. Student, SUNY, Albany, 1958-60, postgrad., 1992—; BA in English and Edn. magna cum laude, Utica Coll. of Syracuse U., 1977; MS in Edn. and Reading, SUNY, Cortland, 1979, CAS in Edn. Adminstrn., 1984; postgrad., Syracuse U., 1990—. Cert. nursery, elem. tchr., secondary tchr., sch. adminstr. and supr., sch. dist. adminstr., reading specialist, N.Y. From tchr. to reading specialist, adminstrv. intern Poland (N.Y.) Cen. Sch., 1972-84; instr. reading Utica Coll. of Syracuse U., summer 1982-84; adminstr. spl. edn. and chpt. 1 remedial program Little Falls (N.Y.) City Sch. Dist., 1984-85; adminstr. adult and continuing edn. Madison-Oneida Bd. Coop. Ednl. Svcs., Verona, N.Y., 1985-86; dir. gen. programs Herkimer (N.Y.) Bd. Coop. Ednl. Svcs., 1986-88. Prof. English, SUNY SLN Internet English 1, children's lit., intro. edn., and honors program Herkimer County C.C. of SUNY, 1988—, participant brainstorming session on underprepared students SUNY, 1993, trainer tchr. performance evaluation program N.Y. State Dept. Edn., Herkimer, 1984, facilitator effective schs. program, 1986-88; co-developer edn. degree program; cons. Two-Yr. Coll. Devel. Ctr. SUNY, 1985-89, tchr. trainer for the Writing Process; developed summer reading, writing and study skills course for Bridge program; tchr. asst. cert. program; cons. in field. Author: The Bridge Program-Easing the Transition from High School to College, 1990; editorial bd. Research and Teaching in Developmental Education; contbr. to Teaching Writing to Adults Tips for Teachers: An Idea Swap, 1989; textbook reviewer for pubs., 1993—. Vol. arts and crafts fair HCCC Found.; advisor Network for Coll. Re-Entry Adults; mem. Coun. of Profs., Parents Weekend Com. Recipient Leader Silver award for volunteerism 4-H Coop. Extension, Utica, 1980; HCCC Found. grantee, Writing grantee Reader's Digest. Mem. Internat. Reading Assn., Assn. Supervision and Curriculum Devel., Nat. Coun. Tchrs. English, Conf. on Coll. Composition and Communication, Phi Kappa Phi, Alpha Lambda Sigma. Avocations: English, current events, travel, public and satellite television, computers. Home: 7099 Crooked Brook Rd Utica NY 13502-7203 Office: Herkimer County Comm Coll SUNY Reservoir Rd Herkimer NY 13350-1545

MARTIN, LOUIS FRANK, surgery and healthcare outcomes analyst; b. Troy, N.Y., Nov. 7, 1951; s. Eugene Lavern and Lois Jane (Perkins) Martin; m. Deborah Lynn Tjarnberg, Mar. 12, 1977; children: Jesse Tjarnberg, James Casey, Tyler Gene. BA, Brown U., 1973, MD, 1976; MS in Health Adminstrn., U. Louisville, 1993. Diplomate Am. Bd. Surgery, Am. Bd. Med. Mgmt. Resident in gen. surgery U. Wash. Affiliated Hosps., Seattle, 1977-78, U. Louisville, 1978-83, rsch. fellow trauma rsch. and health care ednl. adminstrn., 1980-82; asst. prof. surgery Pa. State U., Hershey, 1983-88, asst. prof. physiology, 1986-88, assoc. prof. surgery and cellular and molecular physiology, 1988-92; prof. surgery La. State U., New Orleans, 1992—, prof. preventative medicine and pub. health, 1994—; prof. neurosci., 1995—; med. dir. St. Charles Weight Mgmt. Ctr. La. State U., New Orleans, 1995—. Vis. scientist INSERM, Poste Orange, France, 1990-91; cons. TENET Health Care Corp. Med. Affairs Dept., 1995—, Ethicon Endo-Surgery, Inc., 2000—. Mem. editl. bd., Shock, 1994-97, Obesity Surgery, 1997—, Jour. Surgical Outcomes, 1997-99; author med.

books; contbr. articles to newspapers and profl. jours. Recipient Loyal Davis Traveling Surg. scholar ACS, 1990, Clin. Investigator award NIH, 1985-90. Mem.: ACS, Shape Up Am., New Orleans Surg. Soc. (pres. 1999), Soc. Univ. Surgeons, Soc. Internat. Chirurgie, Collegium Internat. Chirurgiae Digestivae, Assn. for Acad. Surgery (councilman 1988—90), Am. Physiol. Soc., Am. Coll. Critical Care Medicine, Am. Soc. Bariatric Surgery (program chmn. 1997, 1998, mem. exec. coun. 1997—2000). Home: 3005 Palm Vista Dr Kenner LA 70065-1560 Office: La State U Dept Surgery 1542 Tulane Ave New Orleans LA 70112-2825

MARTIN, MABEL JOYCE, early childhood educator; b. Arcadia, La. d. Charles Jr. and Poneva (Vernon) Williams; m. Horace Martin; children: John Christopher, Sherri Joyce. BS, U. Wis., Milw., 1965, MS, 1978. Head Start tchr. Northcott Neighborhood House, Milw., 1965; day care tchr. Day Care Svcs. for Children, Inc., Milw., 1965-66, adminstr., 1966-69; kindergarten tchr. Milw. Pub. Schs., 1969-75, elem. sch. supr., 1975-80, Head Start program dir., 1980—. Mem. early childhood planning coun. Milw. Pub. Schs. Bd. dirs. Wis. Child Care Improvement Project; active Wis. Com. Child Abuse. Mem. ASCD, Adminstrs. and Suprs. Coun., Nat. Head Start Assn., Wis. Head Start Dirs.' Assn., Metro Alliance of Black Sch. Educators, Milw. Kindergarten Assn., Delta Sigma Theta (corr. sec. alumni chpt.), Pi Lambda Theta. Democrat. African Methodist Episcopal. Avocation: music education. Office: Milw Pub Sch Head Start 5225 W Vliet St Milwaukee WI 53208-2627

MARTIN, MARGARET GATELY, elementary school educator; b. Teaneck, N.J., July 24, 1928; d. Martin F. and Grace (Hammell) Gately; m. Phillips H. Martin, June 27, 1953 (div. 1977); children: Paul H., Patrick W., Thomas P. BA, Hunter Coll., 1950, MA, 1953. Cert. elem. tchr. N.Y. Tchr. Pub. Sch. # 5, Queens, N.Y., 1950-53, Wappingers Cen. Sch., Wappingers Falls, N.Y., 1953-55, Jamestown Pub. Schs., 1968—95; ret., 1996. Tchr. Wenzler Day Care and Learning Ctr., 2000—03; tchr. religious edn. St. Francis of Assissi, Centerville, Ohio, 2001. Citizen amb. to Pargue and Russia People to People, 1995; tchr. Sunday sch. Sts. Peter and Paul Ch., Jamestown, 1977—95. Mem.: AAUW (pres. 1980—82, 1992—94, Edn. Found. Program award 1985), NEA, Jamestown Tchrs. Assn. (membership chair 1976—78, sec. 1982—84), Green Thumb Garden Club (pres. 1986—88, 1996—, v.p. 1991—93, 1995—96), Jamestown Inter Club Coun. (pres. 1984—86, v.p. 1995—96, Woman of the Yr. 1991), Delta Kappa Gamma (corr. sec. 1988—90, membership chair 1991—94, v.p. 1994—96, pres. 1998—2000). Republican. Roman Catholic. Avocations: gardening, needlepoint, travel, theater, genealogy. Home: 3708 Wenzler Dr Kettering OH 45429-3366 E-mail: peg3708@aol.com.

MARTIN, MARIE THERESA, school counselor; b. Perth Amboy, N.J., Oct. 10, 1943; d. Joseph and Clara (Belso) M. AB, Douglass Coll., 1965; EdM, Rutgers U., 1968; PhD, La Salle U., 1996. Tchr. Spanish, English, ESL New Brunswick (N.J.) H.S., 1965-85, sch. counselor, 1985-99; ret., 1999; pvt. practice profl. counselor, cons., tutor, 1999—. Urban rep. N.J. Fgn. Lang. Edn., 1975-85; bilingual counselor Perth Amboy (N.J.) Adult Edn., 1981; multicultural cons., 1986; exec. bd. dirs. Middlesex County Guidance Coun., 1987—; spkr. in field. Author: The ABC's of Self-Esteem: An Instructional Guide for Parents, 1996; editor Guide Lights newsletter, 1987-99; contbr. articles to profl. jours. Mem. NEA, Middlesex County Edn. Assn., N.J. Edn. Assn., Middlesex County Sch. Counselors Assn. (sec./pres. 1985—), Middlesex County Guidance Coun. (sec./pres. 1986—), N.J. Sch. Counselors Assn., N.J. Counseling Assn. Avocations: travel, reading, writing, crocheting, golf. Home and Office: 471A Delair Rd Monroe Township NJ 08831-4208 Fax: 609-395-1598.

MARTIN, MARTA, learning disability specialist, educator; b. Miami, Fla., Apr. 30, 1952; d. Martin Nemerof and Rita Auletta. BA in Psychology, Fla. Atlantic U., 1975; MAT, Nova U., Ft. Lauderdale, 1985; student, U. Tenn., 1970-73. Specific learning disability instr. Univ. Sch. of Nova U., 1980-85; dir. edn. Sylvan Learning Ctr., Palm Beach Gardens, Fla., 1987-89; specific learning disabilities tchr. Palm Beach Gardens Elem. Sch., 1989-92; owner, dir. Marta Martin Tutoring, Lake Park, Fla., 1990—; coord. learning resource labs. Progressive Sch., West Palm Beach, 1997-98; learning resource specialist Rosarian Acad., West Palm Beach, 1999—2001.

MARTIN, NATHANIEL FRIZZEL GRAFTON, mathematician, educator; b. Wichita Falls, Tex., Oct. 10, 1928; s. James Thelbert and Ethel Elizabeth (Nycum) M.; m. Joan Bowman, Apr. 10, 1954; children: Nathaniel Grafton, Jonathan Bowman. BS, North Tex. State U., 1949, MS, 1950; PhD, Iowa State U., 1959. Instr. Midwestern U., Wichita Falls, 1950-52; teaching asst. Iowa State U., Ames, 1955-59; from instr. to prof. math. U. Va., Charlottesville, 1959-96, prof. emeritus math., 1996, assoc. dean Grad. Sch. Arts and Scis., 1976-82; rsch. assoc. U. Calif., Berkeley, 1965-66. Guest lectr. U. Copenhagen, 1969-70; rsch. assoc. U. Warwick, Coventry, Eng., 1982; vis. mem. MSRI, Berkeley, 1992; vis. faculty Univ. Coll., London, 1992. Author: Mathematical Theory of Entropy, 1981; editor: McGraw-Hill Dictionary of Physics & Math, 1978, Sci. & Tech. Terms, 1974. Lt. USNR, 1952-55. Mem. Am. Math. Soc., Math. Assn. Am., Sigma Xi, Pi Mu Epsilon. Office: U Va Dept Math PO Box 400137 Kerchof Hall Charlottesville VA 22904-4137 E-mail: nfm@virginia.edu.

MARTIN, NORMAN FRANCIS, public relations executive; b. Half Moon Bay, Calif., July 8, 1914; s. Frank A. and Mary (Phillips) M. AB in Philosophy, Gonzaga U. Spokane, 1941; MA in Philosophy, 1942; STL in Theology, Colegio Maximo de San Miguel, Buenos Aires, 1948; MA in History magna cum laude, U. of Americas, Mexico City, 1950; D in History magna cum laude, Natl. U., Mexico City, 1957. Prof. English and History Colegio Centro America, Granada, Nicaragua, 1942-43; prof. English Colegio San Bartolome, Bogota, Columbia, 1944-45; prof. Latin American History Santa Clara (Calif.) U., 1958-80, dir. Grad. Fellowships, 1973-78, dir. Spl. Projects, 1978-89, prof. Emeritus History, 1980, asst. to pres. U. Rels., 1989—. Author: Vagabundos en la Nueva Espana, 1957; editor: Instruccion del Virrey Croix a Bucareli, 1960, Instruccion del Virrey Ortega, 1965; contbr. articles to profl. jours. Bd. trustees Santa Clara (Calif.) U., 1978-83, O'Connor Hosp. found., San Jose, 1989-95; bd. fellows Santa Clara (Calif.) U., 1983-93; juvenile adv. bd. Santa Clara (Calif.) City Police Dept., 1984-94. Recipient Guggenheim fellowship John Simon Guggenheim found., N.Y.C., 1961-62, rsch. award NEH, Washington, 1968-69. Mem. Jesuit Order in Cath. Ch., Am. Hist. Soc., Am. Cath. Hist. Soc., Latin Am. Studies Assn., Phi Alpha Theta. Republican. Roman Catholic. Avocations: classical music, swimming. Home: Nobili Hall Santa Clara University Santa Clara CA 95053-1600 Office: Varsi Hall Santa Clara University Santa Clara CA 95053-0001 E-mail: nmartin@scu.edu.

MARTIN, PAMELA AILEEN, special education educator; b. San Diego, Nov. 23, 1962; d. Harry Graham and Jessica Caroline Lois (Selby) M. BS in Social Work, Calif. U. Pa., 1984. From resident counselor I to counselor II Adelphoi Village, Inc., Latrobe, Pa., 1984-85; from residential instr. to on-duty residential instr. Grafton Sch., Inc., Winchester, Va., 1986—2001. Pvt. home care provider, 1987-92. Mem. NASW, Autism Soc. Am., Acad. Baccalaureate Social Workers, Jaycees. Methodist. Avocations: tap dancing, reading, sewing. Home: PO Box 1635 Winchester VA 22604-8135 E-mail: pang@visuallink.com.

MARTIN, PAUL CECIL, physicist, educator; b. Bklyn., Jan. 31, 1931; s. Harry and Helen (Salzberger) M.; m. Ann Wallace Bradley, Aug. 7, 1957; children: Peter, Stephanie Glennon, Daniel. AB, Harvard U., 1952, PhD, 1954. Mem. faculty Harvard U., Cambridge, Mass., 1957—, prof. physics, 1964-82, J. H. VanVleck prof. pure and applied physics, 1982—, chmn. dept. physics, 1972-75, dean divsn. engring. and applied scis., 1977-98, assoc. dean Faculty Arts and Scis., 1981-98, dean rsch. and info. tech., 1998—. Vis. prof. Ecole Normale Superieure, Paris, 1963, 66, U. Paris, Orsay, 1971; mem. materials rsch. adv. coun. NSF, 1986-89; bd. dirs. Mass. Tech. Pk. Corp., 1990—, exec. com., 1992—. Bd. editors: Jour. Math Physics, 1965-68, Annals of Physics, 1968-82, Jour. Statis. Physics, 1975-80, Proc. Nat. Acad. Scis., 2000—. Bd. dirs. Assoc. Univs. for Rsch. in Astronomy, 1979-85; bd. dirs. Assoc. Univs ., Inc., 1981—, exec. com., 1986-90, 92-94, chmn. bd. dirs., 1996-2000. NSF postdoctoral fellow, 1955; Sloan Found. fellow, 1959-62; Guggenheim fellow, 1966, 71 Fellow: AAAS (chair physics sect. 1986), Am. Phys. Soc. (councillor-at-large 1982—84, panel on pub. affairs 1983—86, chmn. nominating com. 1994), Am. Acad. Arts and Scis., NAS. Office: Harvard U Dept Physics Cambridge MA 02138 E-mail: martin@harvard.edu.

MARTIN, REBECCA J. elementary school educator; b. Perrysburg, Ohio, May 24, 1952; d. James Edward and Patty Joy (Sells) Daubenmire; m. Dale W. Martin, June 5, 1982; children: Amy Lynn, Emily Ann. BS in Elem. Edn., Ohio U., 1974; MS in Curriculum and Instrn., Ashland U., 1998. Cert. elem. tchr., Ohio; permanent cert., Ohio, 1998. Tchr. 2d grade Cedar Heights Elem. Sch., Lancaster, Ohio. Mem. Circleville YMCA. Mem. NEA, Ohio Edn. Assn., Lancaster Edn. Assn. Home: 229 Pontious Ln Circleville OH 43113-1552

MARTIN, RICHARD HOWARD, academic program director; b. Chgo., Nov. 4, 1939; s. Howard J. Martin and Lois H. (Heller) Martin Nasby; children from previous marriage, Scott, Todd; m. Joyce C. Davids, June 1, 1989; 1 child, Katie. BS, Lipscomb U., 1962; MS, Ind. U., 1967, EdD, 1981. Lic. tchr., Ind.; cert. police officer, Ind. Tchr., coach secondary Lake Ridge Schs., Gary, Ind., 1964-67; tchr. secondary Lake Station (Ind.) Schs., 1967-70; police officer Highland (Ind.) Police Dept., 1970-74; asst. prof. Ball State U., Muncie, Ind., 1974-81; dept. chair, assoc. prof. U. Nebr., Kearney, 1981-84; dep. dir. N.E. Multi-Regional Tng., North Aurora, Ill., 1984-85; prof., chair Aurora (Ill.) U., 1985-93; dir. criminal justice program Elgin (Ill.) C.C., 1993-2000; prof. criminal justice, dir. criminal justice program U. Findlay, Ohio, 2000—. Criminal justice curriculum devel. cons.; police accreditation cons.; conducted major criminal justice curriculum devel. at numerous instns. higher edn., 1976—; fitness instr. Author: Introduction to Criminal Justice, 2000; rev. editor Jour. Gang Crime, 1997—; contbr. numerous articles to profl. jours. Precinct committeeman Rep. Com., Calumet Twp., Ind., 1969; constable Law Enforcement Officer-Cts., Delaware County, Ind., 1978-81; mem. DuPage County State's Attys. Gang Commn., Wheaton, Ill., 1991—; sec. Woodstock (Ill.) Police and Fire Commn., 1994—, police commr., 1994-2000; commr. McHenry County Sheriff's Dept., 1995-2000. Curriculum Devel. award Ill. Bd. Edn., Ill. Acad. Criminology, Jour. Gang Crime & Rsch.; Ill. Bd. Higher Edn. grantee, 1993. Mem. Ill. Acad. Criminology (past bd. dirs., acting v.p. 1989-2000), Ill. Police and Fire Commrs. Assn., Acad. Criminal Justice Scis., M.W. Acad. Criminal Justice Scis., Chung Moo Quan Assn. Ill., Ill. Assn. Chiefs Police (cmty. policing com. 1998-200), Internat. Assn. Chiefs Police (PAC forum com. 2000—). Avocation: martial arts. Home: 15831 Oak Shade Ln Findlay OH 45840 Office: U Findlay 1000 N Main St Findlay OH 45840 E-mail: martin@findlay.edu., dmart@woh.rr.com.

MARTIN, RICHARD PETER, classics educator, consultant; b. Boston, May 19, 1954; s. Nicholas Richard and Marie Eileen (Daly) M.; children: Catherine, Thomas. AB, Harvard U., 1976, AM, 1978, PhD, 1981. Teaching fellow Harvard U., Cambridge, Mass., 1978-81; from asst. to assoc. prof. Princeton (N.J.) U., 1981-94, prof., 1994—99; Antony and Isabelle Raubitschek Prof. of Classics Stanford U., 2000—. Author: Healing, Sacrifice and Battle, 1983, The Language of Heroes, 1989, Myths of the Ancient Greeks, 2003; editor: Bulfinch, Mythology, 1991. Class of 1936 preceptor Princeton U., 1984-87. Devel. grantee Apple Computer Co., 1989. Fellow Onassis Found.; mem. Am. Philol. Assn., Celtic Studies Assn. of N.Am., Irish Texts Soc. Democrat. Roman Catholic. Office: Stanford Univ Bldg 20 Main Quad Stanford CA 94305-2080

MARTIN, ROGER HEMENWAY, artist, educator; b. Sept. 3, 1925; s. Roger Hemenway and Ellie Emelia (Oker) M.; m. Joan Catherine Fertig, June 19, 1954; children: Christopher, Rachel, Mari; m. Ann O'Grady, Sept. 23, 1990. Diploma with honors, Boston Mus. Sch., 1950; DFA (hon.), Montserrat Coll., 1998. Tchr. New Eng. Sch. Art, Boston, 1966-70; founding mem., assoc. prof. Montserrat Coll. Art, Beverly, Mass., 1970—91, prof. ameritus, 1991—; mem. faculty Gordon Coll., Wenham, Mass., 1976-84. One-man shows include Carl Siembab Gallery, Boston, 1969, Eugenics Gallery, Magnolia, Mass., 1969, Manchester (Mass.) Art Assn., 1970, 83, Marion (Mass.) Art Ctr., 1975, Galleria Roseanna, Boston, 1976, Stagecoach Ho. Gallery, Gloucester, Mass., 1977, Montserrat Sch. Visual Art Gallery, Beverly, 1979, Retrospective, 1990, Pingree Sch. Gallery, South Hamilton, Mass., 1980, Orphanos Gallery, Boston, 1987-88; exhibited in group shows at Rockport Art Assn., 1954-75, 80—, De Cordova and Dana Mus., 1965, Inst. Contemporary Art, Boston, 1964, Carl Siembab Gallery, Boston, 1968, 69, Eugenics Gallery, Magnolia, 1969, Phoenix Gallery, 1969, Montserrat Sch. Visual Art, 1970-83, Doll and Richards Gallery, Boston, 1973-75, Sch. St. Gallery, Rockport, 1983, 85, Orphanos Gallery, Boston, 1987-88, Judi Rotenberg Gallery, Boston, 1988-89; commns. includ Prose and Poetry, Child Life Mag.; contbr. articles to profl. jours.; illustrator Beacon Press, New Yorker Mag., N.Y. Times, Atlantic Monthly; woodcuts and paintings United Ch. Christ; case designer and carvings Fisk pipe organs Harvard U., Cambridge, Mass., Ho. Hope Presbyn. Ch., St. Paul, Pohick Ch., Lorton, Va., Stanford (Calif.) U., New Bern, N.C. Capt. Rockport Fire Dept., 1970-82; mem. Planning Bd. and Appeals Bd., Rockport. With USCG, 1942-46. Democrat. Home: PO Box 276 Rockport MA 01966-0376

MARTIN, RON, editor, superintendent of schools, consultant, minister; b. Rock Island, Tenn., Aug. 5, 1942; s. Houston and Bernie (Gribble) M.; m. Carolyn J. Odineal, Oct. 5, 1969. AA, Freed-Hardeman Coll., Henderson, Tenn., 1963; BA with honor, David Lipscomb Coll., 1973; MEd with highest honors, Mid. Tenn. State U., 1983; student, Leadership Inst., Harvard U. Grad. Sch. Edn., Oxford (England) U. Entered ministry Ch. of Christ 1963. Cons. Tenn. Dept. Edn., Nashville, 1977-82; tchr. remedial reading Warren County Schs., McMinnville, Tenn., 1972-74, elem. prin., 1974-77, tchr. Viola, Tenn., 1981-82, asst. prin. sr. high sch. McMinnville, 1982-85, supt. schs., 1987-92, editor newsletter, 1987—. Min., bible tchr. Warren County Chs. of Christ, McMinnville, Tenn., 1963—, Cumberland Valley Broadcasting, McMinnville, Tenn., 1963—90; bd. dirs. United Givers Fund. Vice chmn. Warren County Dem. Com., 1984-86; mem. bd. rev. Eagle Scouts, Boy Scouts Am., McMinnville, 1986—, chmn. 1999—; pres. Warren County Drug Task Force, 1987, 92; chmn. Leadership McMinnville, 1997; pres. Leadership Warren, 1998; chmn. cmty. svcs. K-T Dist. Com., 2001; chmn. Boy Scouts Am. Dist.; bd. dirs. United Givers Fund. Named Young Educator of Yr., Warren County Jaycees, 1976, Leader of Yr., 4-H Club, Warren County, 1974-76; recipient Leadership award Tenn. Acad. Sch. Leaders, 1983, Long Rifle award Disting. Dist. Boy Scouts Am. Svc., 2000, Vol. of Yr. award McMinnville-Warren County C. of C., 2001, Vol. of Yr. award RSVP, 2002; named Hometown Hero, So. Std., 2002. Mem. NEA, ASCD, Am. Adult Edn. Coun., Nat. Assn. Secondary Sch. Prins., Nat. Staff Devel. Coun., Am. Assn. Sch. Adminstrs., Coun. Adult Basic Edn., Tenn. Edn. Assn., Tenn. Adult Edn. Coun., Tenn. Literary Coun., Warren County Edn. Assn. (rep. assembly 1976, 83, Leadership award), Warren County Aviators and navigators (sec.), Commn. on Adult Basic Edn. (southeast regional rep. 1003-95), Commn. on Adult Basic Edn. (nat. sec. 1995, pres.-elect 1997, pres. 1998), Kiwanis (Warren County pres., disting. pres. 1995, disting. lt. gov. 1997—, cmty. svc. Ky.-Tenn. dist. chmn. 1999, dist. trainer 1997, new club builder 2000, edn. com. 2001, chmn. leadership edn. 2002-), Tenn. Assn. Adult and Cont. Edn. (pres. 2000, co-chair nat. conf. 2001). Avocations: reading, working on community projects, visiting outstanding school systems, teaching young people, developing educational ideas. Home: 4200 Crisp Springs Rd Mc Minnville TN 37110-5239 Office: Warren County Schs 2548 Morrison St Mc Minnville TN 37110-3617

MARTIN, TERESA ANN HILBERT, special education educator; b. Kingsport, Tenn., May 16, 1959; d. Bryan Hagan and Patsy Ruth (Owens) Hilbert; m. Harold Tony Martin, June 10, 1989. BS in Spl. Edn., Tenn. Tech. U., 1982, MA in Spl. Edn., 1983. Spl. edn. tchr. Gunnings Sch., Blountville, Tenn., 1984-85, S.E. H.S., Dalton, Ga., 1985-89, Murray County H.S., Chatsworth, Ga., 1989-94, N.W. H.S., Tunnel Hill, Ga., 1994—. Mem. Coun. for Exceptional Children, Delta Kappa Gamma (pres. 1994-96). Baptist. Avocations: reading, collecting norman rockwell memorabilia, needle work. Home: 140 Sharon Dr Gate City VA 24251-3328 Office: Northwest Whitfield HS 1651 Tunnel Hill Varnell Rd Tunnel Hill GA 30755-9247

MARTIN, TERRELL OWEN, retired university administrator; b. Florence, Ala., Mar. 25, 1937; s. Terrell Owen and Ruth Alice (Nowell) M. BS in Bus. Adminstrn., Erskine Coll., 1959; MS in Student Pers., Ind. U., 1964, D in Recreation, 1972. Dir. student activities Franklin Coll., Ind., 1964-66; acad. adv. U. Akron, Ohio, 1966-68; counselor, 1972-74; resident counselor Ind. U., Bloomington, 1968-72; dir. spl. programs and orgns. Indiana U. Pa., 1974-83; dean student devel. Tex. A&M U., Kingsville, 1983-87; dir. acad. counseling and advising So. Ill. U., Edwardsville, 1987-2003. 2d lt. U.S. Army, 1960. Mem. ACD, Am. Coll. Pers. Assn., Nat. Assn. Campus Activities, Nat. Assn. Student Pers. Adminstrs., Nat. Recreation and Park Assn., Phi Delta Kappa, Order of Omega. Democrat. Methodist. Avocations: travel, swimming, reading. Home: 901 Pine Cone Trail Anderson SC 29621

MARTIN, THOMAS SHERWOOD, history and political science educator; b. Athens, Ohio, May 18, 1938; s. William Oliver and Grace Dean M.; m. Nancy Joyce Coggeshall, Sept. 12, 1964 (div.). BA, Georgetown U., 1960; MA, Yale U., 1964, U. Chgo., 1965; PhD, U. Toronto, 1972. Lic. real estate profl., Fla. Prof. history and polit. sci. Champlain Coll., Lennoxville, Que., Can., 1972-93; edn. cons. Cape Coral, Fla., 1993—. Head dept. history and polit. sci. Champlain Coll., 1972-75; resp. Provincial History Curriculum Com., Que., Can., 1972-92, Provincial Polit. Sci. Curriculum Com., Que., 1980-92; mem. curriculua, hiring coms., Champlain, 1972-92. Editl. bd. The Canadian Forum mag., 1968-70; creator/cons. simulation games, 1972-92; contbr. articles to profl. jours. Mem. Rep. Nat. Com., Washington, 1995-96; candidate Cape Coral (Fla.) City Coun., 1997. Scholar French Govt., Aix-en-Provence, France, 1960-61; fellow Yale U., New Haven, Conn., 1962-64, Earhart fellow Relm Found., U. Chgo., 1964-65, Can. Coun. fellow Can. govt., London, Eng., 1969-71. Mem. Cape Coral Sailing Club (speaker's bur. 1993-96), Ft. Myers Sailing Club (bd. govs. 1993-95). Episcopalian. Avocations: sailing, writing, gardening, reading novels. Home and Office: 617 SE 47th St Apt 6 Cape Coral FL 33904-5507

MARTIN, TONY, humanities educator; b. Port of Spain, Trinidad, Feb. 21, 1942; arrived in U.S., 1969; s. Claude G. and Vida Beryl M. BSc in econ. with honors, U. Hull, England, 1968; MA, Mich. State U., 1970, PhD, 1973. Barrister-at-law Honorable Soc. Gray's Inn, London, 1965; asst. prof. of history, African-Afro Am. studies U. Mich., Flint, 1971-73; assoc. prof. history and Africana studies Wellesley (Mass.) Coll., 1973—75, assoc. prof. Africana studies, 1975—79, prof. Africana studies, 1979—. Vis. prof. of history U. Minn., 1975, The Colo. Coll., Colo. springs, 1985-86, vis. prof. of Afro-Am studies Brown U., Providence, R.I., 1991, Brandeis U., Waltham, Mass., 1974, 81; hon. rsch. fellow U. of the West Indies, Trinidad, 1986-87; lectr. DuBois-Padmore-Nkrumah, Ghana, 1990; cons. founds.; expert witness Congl. Hearings, 1987; guest lectr. numerous univs., U.S., Can., Caribbean, Australia, Africa, Eng. Author: Race First, 1976, Literary Garveyism, 1983, The Pan-African Connection, 1983, The Jewish Onslaught, 1993; reviewer articles for profl. jours.; contbr. articles to profl. jours., encys., and other ref. books; contbr. editor profl. jours. Pres. Union of West Indian Students in Gt. Britain and No. Ireland, 1966—68. Recipient Rsch. award Am. Philos. Soc., Phila., 1990, Cmty. award Emancipation Support Com. Mem. Assn. of Caribbean Historians, African Heritage Studies Assn., Assn. for the Study of Classical African Civilizations (John Henrik Clarke Living Legacy award), Nat. Coun. for Black Studies. Office: Wellesley Coll Africana Studies Dept Wellesley MA 02481 E-mail: amartin@wellesley.edu.

MARTIN, WILLIAM C. sociology educator, writer; b. San Antonio, Dec. 31, 1937; s. Lowell Curtis and Joe Bailey (Brite) M.; m. Patricia Dale Summerlin, Dec. 31, 1957; children: Rex Martin, Jeff Martin, Elisabeth Dale Martin Thomas. BA, Abilene Christian U., 1958, MA, 1960; BD, Harvard Divinity Sch., 1963; PhD, Harvard U., 1969. Instr. history Dana Hall Sch., Wellesley, Mass., 1965-68; instr. sociology Rice U., Houston, 1968-69, asst. prof. sociology, 1969-73, assoc. prof. sociology, 1973-79, prof. sociology, 1979—, Chavanne prof. religion and pub. policy, 1996—, master Sid W. Richardson Coll., 1976-81, chair dept. sociology, 1983—86, 1989—94, 2003—. Cons. films and TV documentaries; speaker in field. Author: These Were God's People, 1966, Christians in Conflict, 1972, A Prophet With Honor: Billy Graham Story, 1991 (Christianity Today's Critic's Choice award 1992), My Prostate and Me: Dealing With Prostate Cancer, 1994, With God on our Side: The Rise of the Religious Right in America, 1996; contbg. editor Tex. Monthly (Nat. Headliner award 1982); contbr. numerous articles to profl. jours. and pop mags.; numerous radio and TV appearances. Dir. House of the Carpenter, Inc., inner-city youth program, Boston, 1963-66, pres. and bd. dirs. non-profit housing corp.; bd. dirs. Fellowship Racial and Econ. Equality, 1970-71; mem. exec. com. Houston Coun. Human Rels. Recipient Nicholas Salgo Outstanding Tchr. award Rice U., 1971, 93, Brown Coll. award for Teaching in the Humanities Rice U., 1974, 76, George R. Brown Award for Superior Teaching, alumni Rice U., 1974, 76, 77, 84, for Excellence in Teaching, 1975, 82, Life Honor award, 1985, Sr. scholar James A. Baker III Inst. Pub. Policy; grantee Am. Coun. Learned Socs. and Am. Philos. Soc., 1974. Mem. Am. Sociol. Assn., Soc. Scientific Study Religion, Religious Rsch. Assn., Tex. Inst. Letters (J. Frank Dobie/Paisano fellowship 1980). Democrat. Protestant. Avocation: bicycling. Home: 2148 Addison Rd Houston TX 77030-1222 Office: Rice U Dept Sociology 6100 Main St Dept Houston TX 77005-1892 E-mail: wcm@rice.edu.

MARTIN, WILLIAM RUSSELL, nuclear engineering educator; b. Flint, Mich., June 2, 1945; s. Carl Marcus and Audrey Winifred (Rosene) M.; m. Patricia Ann Williams, Aug. 13, 1967; children: Amy Leigh, Jonathn William. BSE. in Engring. Physics, U. Mich., 1967; MS in Physics, U. Wis., 1968; MSE. in Nuclear Engring., U. Mich., 1975, PhD in Nuclear Engring., 1976. Prin. physicist Combustion Engring., Inc., Windsor, Conn., 1976-77; asst. prof. nuclear engring. U. Mich., Ann Arbor, 1977-81, assoc. prof. nuclear engring., 1981-88, prof. nuclear engring., 1988—, dir. lab. for sci. computation, 1986—2001, chmn. nuclear engring., 1990-94, assoc. dean for acad. affairs Coll. Engring., 1994-99, dir. Ctr. for Advanced Computing, 2002—. Cons. Lawrence Livermore Nat. Lab., Livermore, Calif., 1982—, Los Alamos (N.Mex.) Nat. Lab., 1980-89, 2001—, IBM, Inc., Kingston, N.Y., 1984, Rockwell Internat., Pitts., 1985. Author: Transport Theory, 1979; author tech. and conf. papers. Recipient Glenn Murphy award Am. Soc. for Engring. Edn., 1993; Disting. scholar U. Mich. Coll. Engring., 1967; vis. fellow Royal Soc., London, 1989. Fellow Am. Nuclear Soc.; mem. Am. Phys. Soc., Soc. for Indsl. and Applied Math., IEEE. Avocations: running, reading, skiing, sailing. Home: 420 Huntington Dr Ann Arbor MI 48104 Office: U Mich Dept Nuclear Engring Ann Arbor MI 48109 E-mail: wrm@umich.edu.

MARTIN, WILLIE PAULINE, retired elementary school educator, illustrator; b. Pendleton, Tex., May 27, 1920; d. Lester B. and Stella (Smith) M.; m. Charles M., June 23, 1946; 1 child, Charles Jr. BS, Middle Tenn. State U., Murfreesboro, 1944; MS, U. Tenn., 1965; postgrad., U. Ga., 1980. Cert. tchr., Tenn., Tex., Ga. Elem. tchr. Bd. Edn., Sparta, Tenn., 1940-44, home econs. tchr. Salado, Tex., 1944-46; rsch. technician Oak Ridge (Tenn.) Nat. Lab., 1946-50; art, gen. sci. tchr. Bd. Edn., State of Tenn., 1965-69, art, reading, elem. tchr., 1970-83, elem. tchr., 1984-86, ret., 1986; cons. Tex., 1990—. Tchr. aerospace edn. workshop Middle Tenn. State U., 1969; spkr. in field; cons. in field. Contbr. articles in field to profl. jours. Exhibitor Oak Ridge (Tenn.) Festival. Mem. Nat. Art Edn. Assn. (del. conv. Washington 1989, Balt. 1994), Ga. Art Edn. Assn. (del. state conv., dist. pres. 1974, del. conv. Savannah 1986, Augusta 1993, del. state conv. Athens 1994), Tenn. Edn. Assn. Methodist. Avocations: art, crafts, music, singing, reading. Home and Office: 1406 Flowing Wells Rd Augusta GA 30909-9767

MARTIN, WILMA IRISH, secondary education educator; b. Elmira, N.Y., Nov. 21, 1939; d. Philip Augustus and Hazel (Carr) Irish; m. Edward J. Lundy, June 30, 1961 (div. Mar. 1972); children: Edward P., Michelle L. McCafferty; m. Richard Martin, Oct. 29, 1972 (div. 1977). BA, Elmira Coll., 1961, MS, 1967. Cert. art tchr., Fla., N.Y., Ala. Art tchr. Horseheads (N.Y.) Sch. Dist., 1963-73; art tchr., dept. head Cypress Lake H.S., Ft. Myers, Fla., 1973-95. Art cons. Cape Coral (Fla.) Pks. and Recreation, summers 1980, 81; sch. steering com. and chair So. Assn. Schs. and Colls. Study, Ft. Myers, 1984, 89; cons., instr. Nova U., Labelle, Fla., summer 1988; chair H.S. art exhbn. Edison Festival Lights Com., Ft. Myers, 1990-94. Author, editor: (curriculum guide) Lee County High School Art Continuum, 1982. Named Lee County Tchr. of Yr., Rotary South, Ft. Myers, 1989, Lee County Art Educator of Yr., Lee Sch. Dist., Ft. Myers, 1993, Golden Apple finalist and grantee The Found. for Lee County Pub. Schs., Inc., 1993, 94; recipient Collegium for Advancement Tchg., The Found. for Lee County Pub. Schs., 1993. Mem. Nat. Art Edn. Assn., N.Y. State Art Edn. Assn. (area chair), Fla. Art Edn. Assn., Lee Art Educators Assn. (H.S. rep. 1991-95, Tchr. of Yr. 1993). Avocations: reading, travel, drawing, painting. Home: 60 County Road 521 Centre AL 35960-6167

MARTINES, EUGENIA BELLE, elementary school educator; b. Marion, Va., Feb. 28, 1939; d. Howard Kelly Gullion and Mary Enias Edwards-Gullion; m. Frank Fuentes Martines, May 23, 1959 (dec. Oct. 25, 1991). Student, Marion Jr. Coll., 1958; AA, Coll. of Sequoias, 1960; BEd, Calif. State U., Fresno, 1966; cert. in bilingual edn., Calif., 1996. Kindergarten tchr. Five Points (Calif.) Sch., 1962—63; 3d grade spl. edn. tchr., 6th grade and 1st grade tchr. Corcoran (Calif.) Joint Unified Schs., 1963—97. Mem. Kings County Citizens Adv. Bd. on Alcohol and Other Drugs, Hanford, Calif., 1986—2001, chmn., 1992; mem. Red Ribbon Com. on Kings County and Corcoran, 1989—2001, Kings County Health Adv. Bd., Hanford, 1997—2001, Kings County Master Plan on Alcohol and Other Drugs, Hanford, 1991—2001; tutoring students with dyslexia; credentials person region 6 Reform Party of Calif., 1997—. Recipient Poet Merit Silver Bowl award, Internat. Poet Soc., 2002. Mem.: NEA, Corcoran Faculty Assn., Calif. Tchrs. Assn., Internat. Soc. Poets, Soc. Children's WRiters, Romance Writers of Am., Valley Writer's Network (pres. 1991—92), Fiction Writers' Connection, Photographers Assn., Kings County Critiquing (cofounder), PTA (life), Nat. Writers' Club. Reform. Roman Catholic. Avocations: reading, writing, breeding chihuahuas, political activist. Address: PO Box 458 Corcoran CA 93212-0458 E-mail: eugenia@savy2k.net.

MARTINEZ, GUILLERMO BILL, administrator; b. Fort Worth, Oct. 22, 1944; s. Marion and Clara (Macias) M.; m. Olivia Villegas, Feb. 4, 1966; children: Elisa Ann, Leticia Marie. B of Music Edn., U. Tex., Arlington, 1972; M in Guidance Counseling, Tex. Christian U., 1975; postgrad., U. North Tex., 1980. Cert. adminstr., cert. supr., Novell adminstr. Tutoring supr. Tarrant County Jr. Coll., Fort Worth, 1972-75; prodn. supr. Bilingual Materials Devel. Ctr., Fort Worth, 1975-80; sr. programmer analyst Dallas Ind. Sch. Dist., 1980-82, assessment/evaluation specialist, 1982-84, tech. specialist, 1984-87, interim dir. instrnl. tech., 1987-89, dir. instrnl. tech., 1989-93; data processing supr. Bus. Magnet Ctr. Dallas Ind. Sch. Dist., 1993—. Adv. mem. Tex. Assessment of Acad. Skills, Austin, 1992-93, Technology Task Force, Dallas Sch. Dist., 1989-93; com. chair Electronic Sch. of the Future, Dallas Ind. Sch. Dist., 1989-93; adv. mem. Richland Jr. Coll., 1987, State Bd. of Edn. Tech. Stds., 1991. Evaluator (bilingual textbook) Estampas Historicas de los Estados Unidos, 1975-80. Pres. St. Andrew's Mex. Am. Coun., Fort Worth; v.p. St. Andrew's Sch. Bd., Fort Worth; bd. dirs., officer U. of Tex. Band Alumni, Arlington. With U.S. Army, 1966-69. Mem. Tex. Computer Edn. Assn. (pres. 1991, v.p. 1990, Plaque 1991, 92), Inst. for the Trans. Tech., Tex. Ctr. for Ednl. Tech. (bd. dirs., Plaque 1992), Nat. Assn. of Bilingual Edn. Roman Catholic. Avocations: photography, outside sports, fishing, camping, snorkeling. Office: Dallas Sch Dist 3700 Ross Ave Dallas TX 75204-5476

MARTINEZ, LUIS OSVALDO, radiologist, educator; b. Havana, Cuba, Nov. 27, 1927; came to U.S., 1962, naturalized, 1967; s. Osvaldo and Felicita (Farinas) M.; children Maria Elena, Luis Osvaldo, Alberto Luis; m. Nydia M. Ceballos. MD, U. Havana, 1954. Cert. in diagnostic radiology. Intern Calixto Garcia Hosp., Havana, 1954-55; resident in radiology Jackson Meml. Hosp., Miami, Fla., 1963-65, fellow in cardiovascular radiology, 1965-67; instr. radiology U. Miami, 1965-68, asst. prof., 1968, clin. asst. prof., 1968-70, assoc. prof., 1970-76, prof., 1976-91, clin. prof., 1991-94; chief radiol. svcs. VA Med. Ctr., 1991—. Assoc. dir. dept. radiology Mt. Sinai Med. Ctr., Miami Beach, Fla., 1969-91, chief divsn. diagnostic radiology, 1970-91, dir. residency program in diagnostic radiology, emeritus mem. med. staff, 1991; dir. Spanish Radiology Seminar. Reviewer Am. Jour. Radiology, Radium Therapy and Nuclear Medicine, 1978; contbr. articles to profl. jours. Former pres. League Against Cancer. Recipient Gold medal Interam. Coll. Radiology, 1975, Antoine Bèclere medal Internat. Congress Radiology, 1989, Carlos J. Finlay Gold medal Cuban Med. Convb., 1990, Honors Achievement award, Cert. of Merit Mallinckrodt Pharms., 1972-74; Luis O. Martinez M.D. Lecture named in his honor, Interam. Coll. Radiology. Mem. AMA (Physician's Recognition award 1971, 74-83), AAUP, Radiol. Soc. France (hon. 1991), Internat. Soc. Lymphology, Interam. Coll. Radiology (pres.), Internat. Coll. Surgeons, Internat. Coll. Angiology, Internat. Soc. Radiology, Cuban Med. Assn. in Exile, Am. Coll. Chest Physicians (assoc.), Radiol. Soc. N. Am., Am. Coll. Radiology, Am. Roentgen Ray Soc., Am. Assn. Fgn. Med. Grads., Am. Profl. Practice Assn., Am. Thoracic Soc., Pan Am. Med. Assn., Am. Assn. Univ. Radiologists, Brit. Inst. Radiology, Am. Heart Assn. (mem. council cardiovascular radiology), Faculty Radiologists, Soc. Gastrointestinal Radiologists, Am. Geriatrics Soc., Am. Coll. Angiology, Royal Coll. Radiologists, Am. Soic. Therapeutic Radiologists, Assn. Hosp. Med. Edn., Cuban Radiology Soc. in exile (founder, pres.), Cuban chpt. Inter Am. Coll. Radiology (founder, pres.), Am. Coll. Med. Imaging, Interasma, So. Med. Assn., N.Y. Acad. Scis., Fla. Thoracis Soc., Fla. Radiol. Soc., Dade County Med. Assn., Greater Miami Radiol. Soc., cuban Radiol. Soc. (sec.), Can. Assn. Radiologists, Soc. Thoracic Radiologists (founding mem.), Emeritus mem. Am. Coll. Angiology, 1989, Emeritus mem. Am. Heart Assn., 1992; hon. mem. numerous med. socs. of Mex., Cen. and S. Am. Roman Catholic. Office: 1201 NW 16th St Miami FL 33125-1624

MARTINEZ, MARCELLA, language educator; b. Durango, Colo., Sept. 25, 1958; d. Antonio José and Antonia Rosa (Montaño) Martinez; children: Jamie, Sean. BA, So. Oreg. State Coll., Ashland, 1990. Migrant bilingual resource tchr. Klamath Falls (Oreg.) City Schs., 1990-2000, Mills Elem., Ponderosa Jr. HS, Klamath Falls, 1990-93, Fairview Elem. Sch., Klamath Falls, 1993-94, Fairview Elem., Mills Elem., Klamath Falls, 1994-95, Mills Elem. Sch., Klamath Falls, 1994-2000; vol. Klamath Basin Sr. Citizen Svcs., 2000—01. Mem. 2d Lang. Com., 1994-2000. Troop leader Girl Scouts U.S., Klamath Falls, 1986—91; bilingual translator, 1996—99; vol. Casa San Martin, Gallup, N.Mex., 2002—; missionary Santa Maria Found., Mexico, 2003; mem. 2d Lang. Com., 1994—2000. Home: 910 N 1st St Apt C Gallup NM 87301-5275

MARTINEZ, NANCY MARIE, elementary education educator; b. Prescott, Ariz., Apr. 28, 1952; d. Gavino B. and Ruth Ann (Schoneberger) M. BA in Edn., U. Ariz., 1983; M in Spl. Edn., No. Ariz. U., 1988. Tchr. secondary spl. edn., K-12 Prescott Unified Sch. Dist., Ariz.; tchr.5th and 6th gradees Yarnell Sch. Dist., Ariz.; tchr. 5th grade Prescott Unified Sch. Dist., Ariz. Adj. faculty No. Ariz. U.; mentor in spl. edn. Prescott Coll. Mem. ASCD.

MARTINEZ, PATRICIA ANN, middle school educator, administrator; b. Phoenix, Oct. 12, 1963; d. Jack Leon and Eleanor Jean (Gripman) McMullen; m. Gerald Marc Martinez, Aug. 11, 1984. BA, Calif. State U., 1986, MA magna cum laude, 1994. Cert. tchr. Calif. Tchr. St. Athanasius Elem. Sch., Long Beach, Calif., 1987-93, vice prin., 1990-93; lang. arts specialist Washington Mid. Schs., Long Beach, 1993-96, spl. edn. tchr., 1996-97, U.S. history tchr., 1997—. Mentor tchr. St. Athanasius Elem. Sch., Long Beach, 1988-90, mem. restructuring team, family leader Site-Based Decision Making Com., new-tchr. coach. Mem. ACLU, Greenpeace, 1988—; mem. Focus on Youth. Mem. ASCD, NEA, AAUW, Nat. Cath. Edn. Assn., Internat. Reading Assn., Internat. Platform Assn., Tchrs. Assn. Long Beach, Calif. Tchrs. Assn., Christian Athletic Assn. (bd. dirs.), Kappa Delta Pi, Phi Kappa Phi. Democrat. Lutheran. Avocations: volleyball, weight-lifting, stephen king books, church choir, skiing. Home: 2901 1/3 E 4th St Long Beach CA 90814-1301 Office: Washington Mid Sch 1450 Cedar Ave Long Beach CA 90813-1705

MARTINEZ, VERA, academic administrator; b. San Bernardino, Calif., Nov. 12, 1939; d. Daniel Galvan and Adela (Machado) M.; 1 child, Stephanie Ann Murguia-Hammond. BA in Spanish, Calif. State U., 1962; MA in Sociology, U. Calif., Riverside, 1971, PhD in Ednl. Adminstrn., 1979. Spl. asst. to chancellor UCLA, 1979-81, dir., 1981-84; asst. dean Santa Monica (Calif.) College, 1984-85, dean, 1985-86, spl. assignment to pres., 1987-88, adminstrv. dean, 1990-92, 94-95, acting provost, 1992-94; pres. Fullerton (Calif.) Coll., 1995-98; vice chair instrnl. svcs. for dist. Fullerton, 1998-99; cons., 1999—. Presdl. appointee Nat. Institution Edn., Washington, 1971-75. Harvard fellow 1994. Mem. Cmty. Coll. League Calif., Calif. Assn. Cmty. Colls., Calif. Comm. Colls. (cons. chancellor's office 1992, bd. Latina Leadership 1988—), Nat. Network Hispanic Women (bd. dirs. 1980—). Home: 1041 Madison Pl Laguna Beach CA 92651-2805

MARTINEZ, WILLIAM, JR., Spanish language educator, multicultural issues consultant; b. National City, Calif., Feb. 6, 1961; s. William and Beatrice (Lara) M.; m. Eriko Ishikawa, Dec. 23, 1993. BA, San Diego State U., 1986, MA, 1988; PhD, U. Calif., Irvine, 1993. Tchg. asst. San Diego State U., 1986-88; tchg. assoc. U. Calif., Irvine, 1989-92, Pres.'s dissertation fellow, 1992-93; asst. prof. Spanish Calif. Poly. State U., San Luis Obispo, 1993-97, assoc. prof. Spanish, 1997—2002, prof. Spanish, 2002—, dept. chmn., 2000—. Chmn. student affairs com. Calif. State Internat. Programs, Long Beach, 1996-98, acad. coun. internat. programs, 1999-2001, humanities program, curriculum com., 2002-03; vice chmn. acad. senate Calif. Poly. State U., 1997-98; cons. Calif. State U. Task Force on Globalization, Long Beach, 1997. Co-author: Communicative Activities for the Foreign Language Classroom, 1999; editor (mag.) Cultures, 1996—; contbr. articles to profl. jours. Participant/cons. Mex. Coun. Gen. Task Force, Santa Maria, Calif., 1996-97; scholar-in-residence San Luis Arts Coun., 1999-2002. Mem. MLA, L.Am. Studies Assn., Assn. Calif. Lang. Profls., Ctrl. Coast Assn. Lang. Profls., Philol. Assn. Pacific, Phi Beta Kappa, Sigma Delta Phi, Golden Key. Avocations: photography, poetry writing.

MARTINEZ-PONS, MANUEL, psychologist, educator; b. Dominican Republic, Apr. 19, 1940; arrived in US, 1954; s. Manuel and Alsacia (Gorsd) Martinez. AA, U. State of N.Y., 1973, BS, 1975; BGS, U. Nebr., Omaha, 1973, MS, 1975; PhD, U. Nebr., Lincoln, 1977; MPh, CUNY, 1985, PhD, 1988. Lic. pilot. Rsch. assoc. CUNY, 1982-85, instr. computer programing, 1985-86, assoc. prof. Sch. Edn., Bklyn. Coll., 1986—. Adj. instr. U. Nebr., Lincoln, 1975—77, Omaha, 1978; adj. instr. City Coll. CUNY, 1980—81, adj. asst. prof. Medgar Evers Coll., 1985, adj. asst. prof. Queens Coll., 86. Author (with others): (book) Student Perceptions in the Classroom: Causes and Consequences, 1992; author: Research in the Social Sciences and Education: Principles and Process, 1997, Statistics in Modern Research: Applications in the Social Sciences and Education, 1999, The Psychology of Teaching and Learning: A Three-Step Guide, 2001, Le tranfert effectiv comme un processus d'auto-regulation, 2002, Continuum Guide to Successful Teaching in Higher Education, 2003; cons. editor: Jour. Exptl. Edn., 1997—; contbr. articles to profl. jours. Recipient numerous grants. Mem.: Am. Psychol. Soc., Am. Ednl. Rsch. Assn., Am. Mensa. Home: 453 Beach 138th St Rockaway Park NY 11694-1341 Office: Brooklyn Coll Sch of Edn Brooklyn NY 11210 E-mail: mpons@email.msn.com.

MARTINEZ-TABONE, RAQUEL, school psychologist supervisor; b. Santurce, P.R., Mar. 28, 1944; d. Santos and Amelia (Guzman) Gonzalez; m. Fernando Martinez, Oct. 13, 1962 (div. Mar. 1968); 1 child, Stuart Andrew; m. Francis J. Tabone, July 9, 1980; children: Francis N., Christopher M.; grandchildren (wards): Amanda Marie Martinez, Andrea Amelia Martinez. BA, Lehman Coll., 1973, MS, 1977; PD, Fordham U., 1985; MA, Yeshiva U., 1988; MEd, Bank Street Coll., 1990; PhD, Yeshiva U., 1994. Cert. elem. tchr., sch. psychologist, supr. and sch. adminstr., N.Y.; ordained interfaith minister, 1990. Elem. sch. tchr. N.Y.C. Bd. Edn., Bronx, 1973-84, sch. psychologist, com. on spl. edn., 1985-94, supr. sch. psychologists, 1994—. Adj. prof. NYU, 1992-94. Mem. Nat. Assn. Sch Psychologists (cert.), Coun. Exceptional Children, Orthopsychiat. Assn. Home: 17 Ritchie Dr Yonkers NY 10705-2543 Office: NYC Bd Edn 1887 Bathgate Ave # Edn Bronx NY 10457-6216

MARTINI, JOSEPH T(HOMAS), language educator, music educator, data processing executive; b. N.Y.C., Sept. 21, 1944; s. Joseph R. Martini; m. Sharon E. Schock, June 29, 1968; children: Maria T., Laura A., Joseph T. BA in French, Edn., Iona Coll., 1966; Cert. d'Etudes, U. Maine, Orono, 1967; MA in French, Edn., Lehman Coll., 1973. Cert. French tchr., N.Y. Chair fng. lang., data processing supr. Blessed Sacrament-St. Gabriel H.S., New Rochelle, N.Y., 1966-97; choirmaster Blessed Sacrament Ch., New Rochelle, N.Y., 1993—; fng. travel coord., dir. music and drama Blessed Sacrament-St. Gabriel H.S., 1971-97. Mem. Am. Assn. Tchrs. Italian, Am. Assn. Tchrs. French, Am. Coun. Tchg. Fgn. Lang., N.Y. State Fedn. Fgn. Lang. Tchrs. Roman Catholic. Avocations: theatre, music, directing, travel. Home: 143 Lawrence Pl New Rochelle NY 10801-1108 Office: Pleasantville HS 60 Romer Ave Pleasantville NY 10570

MARTINSON, JACOB CHRISTIAN, JR., academic administrator; b. Menomonie, Wis., Apr. 15, 1933; s. Jacob Christian and Matilda Kate (Wisner) M.; m. Elizabeth Smathers, Apr. 29, 1962; children— Elizabeth Anne, Kirsten Kate. BA, Huntingdon Coll., Ala., 1954, LLD (hon.), 1993; MDiv, Duke U., 1957; DDiv, Vanderbilt U., 1972; grad., Inst. Ednl. Mgmt., Harvard U., 1981. Ordained elder United Methodist Ch. Minister Trinity United Meth. Ch., Lighthouse Point, Fla., 1960-67; sr. minister First United Meth. Ch., Winter Park, Fla., 1967-71; supervising instr. Vanderbilt U. Div. Sch., Nashville, 1971-72; pres. Andrew Coll., Cuthbert, Ga., 1972-76, Brevard Coll., N.C., 1976-85, High Point (N.C.) U., 1985—. Bd. dirs. First Union Nat. Bank (now Wachovia), High Point, chmn. 1989; lectr. St. Mary's Theol. Soc., U. St. Andrews, Scotland; mem. exec. com. N.C. Ind. Colls. and Univs. Bd. advisors Uwharrie coun. Boy Scouts Am.; chmn. N.C. Friends of HIgher Edn., 1986. Recipient Hickman Preaching award Duke U. Div. Sch.; Glen Slough scholar Vanderbilt U., 1971; hon. fellow Westminster Coll., Oxford, Eng., 1994; Rotary Paul Harris fellow. Mem. Nat. Assn. Schs. and Colls. United Meth. Ch. (bd. dirs. 1982-85, 87-90, chmn. fin. com.), So. Assn. Colls. and Schs. (commn. on colls.), Ind. Coll. Fund. N.C. (trustee, exec. com.), Brevard C. of C. (pres. 1979), High Point C. of C. (chmn. 1992), Piedmont Ind. Coll. Assn. (chmn. 1991-93), Carolinas Intercollegiate Athletic Conf. (pres. 1991-93), Phi Theta Kappa. Methodist. Avocation: mountain hiking. Home: 1109 Rockford Rd High Point NC 27262-3607 Office: High Point U Office of Pres High Point NC 27262-3598

MARTIR, WILFREDO R. school counselor; b. Lares, P.R., Oct. 12, 1942; came to U.S., 1955; s. Ismael and Ramona (Rosado) M.; m. Merilyn A. Yeatts, Sept. 21, 1969 (div. Feb. 1984); m. Cathy J. Carle, July 15, 1991; chidren: Elana Eve, Travis A. BA, Andrews U., Berrien Springs, Mass., 1971, MA, 1974; EdD, Calif. Coast U., Santa Ana, 1984. Lic. tchr., counselor, adminstr., Wash. Tchr. Berrien Springs (Mich.) High Sch., 1971-73; counselor, tchr. Broadview Acad. High Sch., LaFox, Ill., 1973-74, Gem State Acad. High Sch., Caldwell, Idaho, 1974-76; bilingual edn. dir. Boise (Idaho) Dept. Edn., 1976-79; tchr., coach Cascade (Idaho) High Sch., 1979-80; prin. Rimrock High Sch., Grandview, Idaho, 1980-83; ESL dir. Office of Supt. of Edn., Olympia, Wash., 1983-85; counselor Zillan (Wash.) High Sch., 1985-88, Sunnyside (Wash.) High Sch., 1988—. Migrant tchr. Berrien County, Berrien Springs, summer 1972, 73; dir. migrant edn. Nampa (Idaho) Schs., summers 1976, 77, 78; camp dir. Boise Nat. Forest, Cascade, summer 1980; ESL instr. State Wash. Migrant Coun., Sunnyside, Wash., 1989—. With U.S. Army, 1966-68, Vietnam. Mem. Elks (inner guard 1988, 89), Lions (sec. 1991, 92). Democrat. Seventh Day Adventist. Avocations: writing, community instruction.

MARTOF, MARY TAYLOR, retired nursing educator; b. Charlotte County, Va., Feb. 8, 1935; d. James Russell and Ella (Lipscomb) Palmer; m. John Laning Taylor III, Oct. 3, 1959 (div. 1971); children: Tara, Laura; m. Steven Martof, Apr. 7, 1979. BSN, U. Md., Balt., 1973, MS in Nursing, 1976; EdD, N.C. State U., 1984. Clin. nurse Clin. Ctr., NIH, Bethesda, Md., 1969-73, nursing educator, 1973-79; instr. U. N.C., Chapel Hill, 1979-81; asst. prof. Tex. Christian U., Ft. Worth, 1984-88, U. Southwestern La., Lafayette, 1988-92; assoc. prof. nursing La. State U., New Orleans, 1992—2001, chmn. critical thinking Sch. Nursing, 1994-2000; mem. grad. coun. Sch. Nursing La. State U. Health Sci. Ctr., New Orleans, 2000—01, ret., 2001. Cons. nephrology nursing NIH, 1974-79; chmn. profl. edn. Am. Cancer Soc., New Orleans, 1990-96; chmn. rsch. com. Sch. Nursing, La. State U., 1995-98; reviewer/rschr. various pubs.; coord. oncology grand rounds La. State U. Med. Ctr., 1995-2001; judge for Rsch. Day, La. State U. Sch. Medicine, 1999-2001. Contbr. articles to profl. jours., rsch. publ., chpts. to books. Mem. faculty Am. Cancer Soc., Cancer Update, Ochsner Hosp., 1996-98. Recipient Merit award NIH, 1977, plaque Am. Cancer Soc., 1991-93. Mem. Sigma Theta Tau (Disting. Writer). Democrat. Episcopalian. Avocations: hiking, writing, cooking, gardening.

MARTON, LAURENCE JAY, researcher, educator, clinical pathologist; b. Bklyn., Jan. 14, 1944; s. Bernard Dov and Sylvia (Silberstein) M.; m. Marlene Lesser, June 27, 1967; 1 child, Eric Nolan BA, Yeshiva U., 1965, DSc (hon.), 1993; MD, Albert Einstein Coll. Medicine, 1969. Intern Los Angeles County-Harbor Gen. Hosp., 1969-70; resident in neurosurgery U. Calif.-San Francisco, 1970-71, resident in lab. medicine, 1973-75, asst. research biochemist, 1973-74, asst. clin. prof. depts. lab. medicine and neurosurgery, 1974-75, asst. prof., 1975-78, assoc. prof., 1978-79, prof., 1979-92, asst. dir. div. clin. chemistry, dept. lab. medicine, 1974-75, dir. divsn., 1975-79, acting chmn. dept., 1978-79, chmn. dept., 1979-92; dean med. sch. U. Wis., 1992-95, prof. pathology and lab. medicine and oncology, 1992-2000, prof. dept. human oncology, 1993-95. Interim vice chancellor Ctr. Health Scis., U. Wis., 1993-94; adj. prof. dept. lab medicine U. Calif., San Francisco, 1992—; pres., CEO SLIL Biomed. Corp., 1998-2000, chief sci. and med. officer, 2000—. Co-editor: Polyamines in Biology and Medicine, 1981; Liquid Chromatography in Clinical Analysis, 1981; Clinical Liquid Chromatography, vol. 1, 1984, vol. 2, 1984 Served with USPHS, NIH, 1971-73 Recipient Rsch. Career Devel. award Nat. Cancer Inst., Disting. Alumnus award Albert Einstein Coll. Medicine, 1992. Mem. Am. Assn. Cancer Rsch., AAAS, Acad. Clin. Lab. Physicians and Scientists, Am. Soc. Investigative Pathology, Alpha Omega Alpha. Jewish. Avocations: photography, art, music, travel. Home: 581 Military Way Palo Alto CA 94306 Office: SLIL Biomed Corp 1505 O'Brien Dr Ste B Menlo Park CA 94025

MARTORANA, BARBARA JOAN, secondary school educator; b. NYC, Oct. 18, 1942; d. Samuel and Joan Renee (Costello) M. BA, St. John's U., Jamaica, N.Y., 1970, MS in English Edn., 1972; advanced cert. computers in edn., L.I. U., 1988, profl. diploma in edn. adminstrn., 1990. Cert. sch. dist. adminstr., sch. adminstr. and supr., tchr. English grades 7-12, NY, Ed.D, Lit. Studies, Hofstra U., Hempstead, NY, 2003. Exec. sec. Am. Petroleum Inst., NYC, 1960-65; exec. asst. to v.p. Goldring, Inc., NYC, 1965-67; exec. asst. Rsch. Inst. for Cath. Edn., NYC, 1967-69; English tchr. St. Martin of Tours Sch., Amityville, NY, 1970-77, Oceanside Jr. HS, NY, 1977-78, Freeport HS, NY, 1979—. Rec. sec. Freeport (N.Y.) Tchr. Ctr. Policy Bd., 1986-89; co-chair Middle States Steering Com., Freeport, 1988-90; chair Freeport (N.Y.) H.S. Shared Decision Team, 1992-93; adv. bd. L.I. Writing Project, Garden City, N.Y., 1993—, co-leader Summer Insts.; adj. prof. literacy studies dept. Hofstra U., N.Y., 1999—. Co-author: (textbooks) Writing Competency Practice, 1980, Writing Competency Practice-Revised and Expanded, 1989. With Seaford (NY) Rep. Club, 1975—. Mem. ASCD, Nat. Coun. Tchrs. English (conf. on English edn.), N.Y. State English Coun., L.I. Writing Project. Avocations: reading, writing, traveling. Office: Freeport HS 50 S Brookside Ave Freeport NY 11520-3144 E-mail: engteech@aol.com.

MARTY, MARTIN EMIL, religion educator, editor; b. West Point, Nebr., Feb. 5, 1928; s. Emil A. and Anne Louise (Wuerdemann) Marty; m. Elsa Schumacher Marty, 1952 (dec. 1981); children: Frances, Joel, John, Peter, James, Micah, Ursula; m. Harriet Lindemann Marty, 1982. MDiv, Concordia Sem., 1952; STM, Luth. Sch. Theology, Chgo., 1954; PhD in Am. Religious and Intellectual History, U. Chgo., 1956; LittD (hon.), Thiel Coll., 1964; LHD (hon.), W.Va. Wesleyan Coll., 1967, Marian Coll., 1967, Providence Coll., 1967; DD (hon.), Muhlenberg Coll., 1967; LittD (hon.), Thomas More Coll., 1968; DD (hon.), Bethany Sem., 1969; LLD (hon.), Keuka Coll., 1972; LHD (hon.), Willamette U., 1974; DD (hon.), Wabash Coll., 1977; LLD (hon.), U. So. Calif., 1977, Valparaiso U., 1978; LHD (hon.), St. Olaf Coll., 1978, De Paul U., 1979; DD (hon.), Christ Sem.-Seminex, 1979, Capital U., 1980; LHD (hon.), Colo. Coll., 1980; DD (hon.), Maryville Coll., 1980, North Park Coll. Sem., 1982; LittD (hon.), Wittenberg U., 1983; LHD, Rosary Coll., 1984, Rockford Coll., 1984; DD (hon.), Va. Theol. Sem., 1984; LHD (hon.), Hamilton Coll., 1985, Loyola U., 1986; LLD (hon.), U. Notre Dame, 1987; LHD (hon.), Roanoke Coll., 1987, Mercer U., 1987, Ill. Wesleyan Coll., 1987, Roosevelt U., 1988, Aquinas Coll., 1988; LittD (hon.), Franklin Coll., 1988, U. Nebr., 1993; LHD (hon.), No. Mich. U., 1989, Muskingum Coll., Coe Coll., Lehigh U., 1989, Hebrew Union Coll. and Governors State U., 1990, Whittier Coll., 1991, Calif. Luth. U., 1993; DD (hon.), St. Xavier Coll. and Colgate U., 1990, Mt. Union Coll., 1991, Tex. Luth. Coll., 1991, Aurora U., 1991, Baker U., 1992; LHD (hon.), Luth. U., 1993, Calif. Luth. U., 1993, Midland Luth. Coll., 1995; DD, Hope Coll., 1993, Northwestern Coll., 1993; LHD (hon.), George Fox Coll., 1994, Drake U., 1994, Centre Coll., 1994, Fontbonne Coll., 1996; DD, Yale U., 1995; LHD (hon.), Otterbein Coll., 1996; ThD (hon.), Lycoming Coll., 1997; LHD, Dana Coll., 1998; LittD (hon.), Alma Coll., 1998, Concordia U. Portland, 1998, Niagara U., 1998; LHD (hon.),

Kalamazoo Coll., 1999, William Jewell Coll., 1999; LittD (hon.), U. Miami, 1999, Lynchburg Coll., 2003; DD (hon.), Trinity Coll., 2001, Wake Forest U., 2003; DHum (hon.), Westminster Choir Coll., 2001; LHD (hon.), U. Scranton, 2001; LittD (hon.), Lynchburg Coll., 2003; DD (hon.), Wake Forest U., 2003. Ordained to ministry Luth. Ch., 1952. Pastor, Washington, 1950—51; asst. pastor River Forest, Ill., 1952—56; pastor Elk Grove Village, Ill., 1956—63; prof. history of modern Christianity Div. Sch. U. Chgo., 1963—, Fairfax M. Cone Disting. Svc. prof., 1978—98, prof. emeritus, 1998—; assoc. editor Christian Century mag., Chgo., 1956—85, sr. editor, 1985—98; co-editor Ch. History mag., 1963—97. Pres. Park Ridge (Ill.) Ctr., 1989—, sr. scholar, 1989—; pres. Am. Inst. for Study of Health, Faith and Ethics, 1985—89; dir. fundamentalism project Am. Acad. Arts and Scis., 1988—; dir. The Pub. Religion Project, 1996—99; interim pres. St. Olaf Coll., 2000—01; sr. scholar Park Ridge Ctr., 1989—. Author: A Short History of Christianity, 1959, The New Shape of American Religion, 1959, The Improper Opinion, 1961, The Infidel, 1961, Baptism, 1962, The Hidden Discipline, 1963, Second Chance for American Protestants, 1963, Church Unity and Church Mission, 1964, Varieties of Unbelief, 1964, The Search for a Usable Future, 1969, The Modern Schism, 1969, Righteous Empire, 1970, Protestantism, 1972, You Are Promise, 1973, The Fire We Can Light, 1973, The Pro and Con Book of Religious America, 1975, A Nation of Behavers, 1976, Religion, Awakening and Revolution, 1978, Friendship, 1980, By Way of Response, 1981, The Public Church, 1981, A Cry of Absence, 1983, Health and Medicine in the Lutheran Tradition, 1983, Pilgrims in Their Own Land, 1984, Protestantism in the United States, 1985, Modern American Religion, The Irony of it All, Vol. 1, 1986, An Invitation to American Catholic History, 1986, Religion and Republic, 1987, Modern American Religion: The Noise of Conflict, Vol. 2, 1991; author: (with R. Scott Appleby) The Glory and the Power, 1992; editor (with Jerald C. Brauer): The Unrelieved Paradox: Studies in the Theology of Franz Bibfeldt, 1994; editor: (with Micah Marty) Places Along the Way, 1994; editor: Our Hope for Years to Come, 1995, Modern American Religion, Under God, Indivisible, Vol. 3, 1996, The One and the Many, 1997, The Promise of Winter, 1997, When True Simplicity is Gained, 1998, Politics, Religion, and the Common Good, 2000, Education, Religion, and the Common Good, 2001; editor: (jours.) Context, 1969—; editor: Second Opinion; sr. editor: The Christian Century, 1956—98; contbr. articles to religious publs. Chmn. bd. regents St. Olaf Coll., 1996—2001; dir. The Pub. Religion Project, 1996—2000; sr. regents St. Olaf Coll., 2002—. Recipient Nat. Medal Humanities, 1997, Alumni medal, U. Chgo., 1998; scholar Sr. scholar-in-residence, The Park Ridge Ctr., 1989—. Fellow: Soc. Am. Historians, Am. Acad. Arts and Scis. (dir. fundamentalism project 1988—94); mem.: Am. Antiquarian Soc., Am. Acad. Religion (pres. 1987—88), Am. Cath. Hist. Assn. (pres. 1981), Am. Soc. Ch. History (pres. 1971), Am. Philos. Soc. Lutheran. Office: 239 Scottswood Rd Riverside IL 60546-2223 E-mail: memarty@aol.com.

MARVIN, CHARLES ARTHUR, law educator; b. July 14, 1942; s. Burton Wright and Margaret Fiske (Medlar) M.; m. Elizabeth Maureen Woodrow, July 4, 1970 (div. July 1987); m. Elizabeth Dale Wilson, Mar. 20, 1999; children: Colin, Kristin. BA, U. Kans., 1964; postgrad., U. Toulouse, France, 1964-65; JD, U. Chgo., 1968, M of Comparative Law, 1970. Bar: Ill. 1969. Legal intern EEC, Brussels, 1970; lectr. law U. Kent, Canterbury, Eng., 1970-71; asst. prof. law Laval U., Quebec City, Que., Can., 1971-73; legal adv. constnl., internat. and adminstrv. law sect. Can. Dept. Justice, Ottawa, Ont., 1973-76; assoc. prof. law U. Man., Winnipeg, Can., 1976-77; dir. adminstrv. law project Law Reform Commn., Ottawa, 1977-80; prof. law Villanova (Pa.) U., 1980-83; dir. Adminstrv. Law Reform Project Can. Dept. Justice, 1983-85; prof. law Ga. State U., 1985—, assoc. dean, 1987-89. Legal advisor on adminstrv. code revision to Govt. of Kazakhstan, 1993; law faculty devel. adviser to Bulgaria, 1993; dir. internat. human rights law summer program Regent U. Sch. Law, 1998; lectr., Ivory Coast, 1998; Fulbright prof. Riga Grad. Sch. Law, Latvia, 2000-02, Fulbright sr. specialist, 2003—. Acad. mem. Ctr. Am. and Internat. Law. Fulbright scholar U. Toulouse, 1964-65, Summerfield scholar U. Kansas, 1961-64, U. Chgo. scholar, 1965-68; Ford Found. Comparative Law fellow, 1968-70. Mem. ABA, Ill. Bar Assn., Chgo. Bar Assn., Am. Soc. Internat. Law, Am. Fgn. Law Assn., Internat. Bar Assn., Internat. Law Assn., Can. Bar Assn., Can. Coun. on Internat. Law, Phi Beta Kappa, Omicron Delta Kappa, Phi Beta Delta, Phi Delta Phi. Office: Ga State U Coll Law PO Box 4037 Atlanta GA 30302-4037 E-mail: cmarvin@gsu.edu.

MARX, ANTHONY W. academic administrator; b. NYC, Feb. 28, 1959; s. Peter and Marion E. (Mankin) M.; m. Karen Barkey, Sept. 7, 1993; children: Joshua, Anna-Claire. Student, Wesleyan U., Middletown, Conn., 1977-79; BA, Yale U., 1981; MPA, Princeton U., 1986, MA, 1987, PhD, 1990. Adminstrv. aide to the pres. U. Pa., Phila., 1981-84; cons. SACHED Trust, Johannesburg, 1984, 86; vis. scholar Community Agy. for Social Enquiry, Johannesburg, 1988, 90; asst. prof. polit. sci. Columbia U., NYC, 1990—2003; pres. Amherst (Mass.) Coll., 2003—. Rsch. asst. Ctr. for Ednl. Rsch. and Devel., Santiago, Chile, 1985; cons. UNDP, N.Y.C., 1991; vis. scholar Ctr. for Afro-Asian Studies, Rio de Janeiro, Brazil, 1993. Author: Lessons of Struggle, 1992, Making Race and Nation: A Comparison of the United States, South Africa and Brazil, 1998 (Ralph J. Bunche award Am. Polit. Sci. Assn., 1999, Barrington Moore prize Am. Sociol. Assn., 2000); contbr. articles to profl. jours. Trustee, treas. Fund for Edn. in South Africa, N.Y.C., 1991—. Grantee J. D. & C.T. MacArthur Found., Chgo., 1989-90, Social Sci. Rsch. Coun., N.Y.C., 1992-93, U.S. Inst. Peace, Washington, 1992-93; named fellow H.F. Guggenheim Found., N.Y.C., 1994. Mem. Am. Polit. Sci. Assn., African Studies Assn., Coun. on Fgn. Rels. Office: Amherst Coll PO Box 5000 Amherst MA 01002-5000

MARZAN, SUZANNE M. foreign language educator; b. Chgo. BA, MA. Tchr. Spanish Lincoln-Way High Sch., New Lennox, Ill., 1981—, chair Spanish dept., 1999—. Office: Lincoln Way High sch 1801 E Lincoln Way New Lenox IL 60451

MARZOCCHI, JUDITH ANN, librarian; b. Lexington, Ky., Oct. 4, 1948; d. Charles B. and Jean Bennett (Hensley) Chidester; 1 child, Annette. BS, U. R.I., 1976; MS, Purdue U., Hammond, Ind., 1980; EdS, Purdue U., W. Lafayette, 1987. Libr. media specialist Sch. City of Hammond, 1978—. Co-author: Gifted/Talented Guidelines for Middle/High School and Computer Curriculum for K-5; contbr. articles to profl. jours. Recipient PTA Svc. award; Hammond Edn. Found. grantee; grantee Ind. Dept. Edn. Mem. ASCD, Nat. Coun. Tchrs. English, Assn. of Media Educators, Hammond Area Reading Coun., Ind. Assn. for Gifted and Talented, Kappa Delta Pi, Delta Kappa Gamma. Home: 6642 Monroe Ave Hammond IN 46324-1547

MASCETTA, JOSEPH ANTHONY, principal; b. Canonsburg, Pa., Sept. 2, 1931; s. Joseph Alphonso and Amalia (Ciavarra) M.; m. Jean Verrone, June 18, 1960; children: Lisa Marie, Linda Jo, Lori Jean. BS, U. Pitts., 1954; MS, U. Pa., 1963; cert. advanced study, Harvard U., 1970. Cert. tchr. math., phys. scis., adminstr. secondary sch., Pa. Tchr. chemistry Canonsburg High Sch., 1956-59, Mt. Lebanon High Sch., Pitts., 1959-75, chair sci. dept., 1967-75; coord. secondary curriculum Mt. Lebanon Sch. Dist., Pitts., 1975-81; prin. Mt. Lebanon Sr. High Sch., Pitts., 1981-91; ret., 1991; ednl. cons., 1991—. Vis. team Mid. States Assn. Colls. and Schs., Phila., 1967-78, chair vis. teams, 1981-96, Pa. state adv. com., 1988-91; sch. bd. and edn. commn. St. Patrick Sch., Canonsburg, 1972-85, 95-2002; regional dir. Pa. Jr. Acad. Sci., Pitts., 1976-82; ednl. cons. Pitts. area schs., 1992—; quality edn. com. Pitts. Diocese, 1995-97. Author: Modern Chemistry Review, 1968, Chemistry the Easy Way, 1989, rev. edit., 2003, Barron's SAT II, Chemistry, 1994, rev. edit., 2003; contbg. author: (ency.) Barron's Student Concise Ency., 1988, rev. 1994, Barron's New Student's Concise Ency., 1993, Perry Como Commemorative Booklet, 1998. Recipient Outstanding Tchr. award Spectroscopy Soc., 1973; grantee NSF, 1961, 62-63, 63, 67, 69-70, 73; sci. fellow GE, 1959. Mem. ASCD, Nat. Assn. Secondary Sch. Prins. (cert. recognition 1991), Pa. Assn. Curriculum & Supervision (exec. bd. dirs. 1985-87, regional pres. 1987), Western Pa. Assn. Curriculum & Supervision (v.p. 1983-85, pres. 1985-87, exec. bd. dirs. 1989-2001), Greater Canonsburg Heritage soc., Phi Delta Kappa. Roman Catholic. Avocations: painting, writing. Home: 451 McClelland Rd Canonsburg PA 15317-2258 E-mail: jmascett@bellatlantic.net.

MASCI, JOSEPH RICHARD, medical educator, physician; b. New Brunswick, N.J., Nov. 27, 1950; s. Joseph Nicholas and Delfina (Musa) M.; m. Elizabeth Bass, May 21, 1993; 1 child, Jonathan Samuel. BA, Cornell U., 1972; MD, NYU, 1976. Diplomate Am. Bd. Internal Medicine, Am. Bd. Infectious Diseases. Instr. medicine Boston U. Sch. Medicine, 1979—80, Mt. Sinai Sch. Medicine, N.Y.C., 1982—84, asst. prof. clin. medicine, 1984—88, asst. prof. medicine, 1988—90, assoc. prof. medicine, 1990—2003, prof. medicine, 2003—, chief infectious diseases, 1999—; assoc. dir. medicine Elmhurst Hosp. Ctr., NY, 1987—2002, dir. medicine, 2002—. Peer reviewer NIH, 1994—. Author: Primary and Ambulatory Care of the HIV-Infected Adult, 1992, Outpatient Management of HIV-Infection, 1996, 3d edit., 2001. Fellow Am. Coll. Chest Physicians; mem. ACP, Am. Soc. Microbiology, Assn. Program Dirs. Internal Medicine. Office: Elmhurst Hosp Ctr 79-01 Broadway Elmhurst NY 11373-1329

MASCIA-STRICKLER, MARTHA, special education educator; b. Detroit, Dec. 26, 1947; d. George Amedio and Evelyn Henrietta (Jacques) Mascia; m. Jerold Strickler, Sept. 17, 1988. BS, Wayne State U., 1971; MA, Oakland U., 1977. Cert. vocat. evaluator, tchr., guidance counselor, sex edn. educator, Mich. Para-profl. Oakland Intermediate Schs., Waterford, Mich., 1966-71, tchr. spl. edn., 1971-78; curriculum cons. Pontiac (Mich.) Schs., 1978-81, vocat. evaluator, 1981—. Curriculum sponsor Oakland Schs., Waterford, 1979. Author (handbook) Teacher Assistants Handbook, 1968; co-author (manual) Career Education Model, 1981. Program v.p. Oakland Audubon Soc., 1979-82, pres., editor, 1989; chpt. rep. Mich. Audubon Soc., 1990—, life mem. Recipient Cert. of Appreciation Vocat. Studies Ctr., U. Wis., 1986; scholar Alhambra Orgn., 1967-68. Mem. Mich. Assn. Vocat. Evaluation Specialists in Edn. (co-founder), Mich. Assn. Learning Disabilities Educators, Oakland County Assn. Spl. Svcs. Vocat. Cons. Avocations: reading, entertaining, world travel, cooking, birdwatching.

MASHAW, DAWN ELLA, elementary school educator, consultant; b. Oklahoma City, Jan. 26, 1962; d. Donald Hal and Betty Lou (Scott) Roddy; m. Anthony William Mashaw, June 4, 1988. BS, Ea. N.Mex. U., 1984, MEd, 1992. Spl. edn. tchr. various schs., Carlsbad, N.Mex., 1984-91; asst. prin. Edison Kindergarten Ctr., Carlsbad, N.Mex., 1990—96, tchr., 1991—96, spl. edn. tchr., 1998—. Mem.: AAUW, NEA, Phi Kappa Phi. Democrat. Baptist. Avocations: painting, quilting, reading. Home: PO Box 1424 Anadarko OK 73005-1424

MASHBURN, DONALD EUGENE, education educator; b. Johnson City, Tenn., June 10, 1944; s. Harvey and Martha (McNeese) M.; m. Mary Juanita McKee, May 30, 1970; 1 child, Donna Sue. BS, East Tenn. State U., 1965, MS, 1971. Tchr. Cocke County High Sch., Newport, Tenn., 1965-66, John S. Battle High Sch., Bristol, Va., 1966-94, Wallace Mid. Sch., Bristol, 1994-97; tech. support tchr. Meadowview (Va.) Elem. Sch., 1997-98, Rhea Valley Elem. Sch., Damascus, Va., 1997-98, Valley Inst. Elem. Sch., Bristol, Va., 1997-98, Watanga Elem. Sch., Abingdon, Va., 1997-98; with Info. Sys. and Media Prodn., Abingdon, 1998-99; tchr. Washington Coll. Acad., Limestone, Tenn., 2001; substitute tchr. Washington County (Tenn.) Schs., 2002—. Adj. faculty N.E. State Tech. C.C., Blountville, Tenn., 1984—. Mem. Ruritan (sec. Conklin club 1986-91, 98, 2001-03, pres. 1985, 92, 99, 2000, Davy Crockett dist. treas. 1993, zone gov. 2003). Republican. Methodist. Avocations: computers, farming. Home and Office: 195 Mashburn Rd Telford TN 37690-3132

MASI, JAMES VINCENT, electrical engineering educator; b. Norwalk, Conn., Sept. 21, 1938; s. James V. and Theresa G. (Nardi) M.; m. Sara C. Natale, Oct. 24, 1964 (dec. Feb. 1981); James V., Louis C., Edmund J., Terese L., Stephen F., Catherine M.; m. Patricia Begley, June 5, 1983. BS in Physics, Fairfield (Conn.) U., 1960; MS in Physics, L.I. U., 1970; PhD in Applied Sci., U. Del., 1980. Materials engr. Transitron Electronics Corp., Wakefield, Mass., 1960-62; sr. engr. Space Age Materials/Pfizer, Woodside, N.Y., 1962-65; sr. staff scientist Hartman Systems/ATO, Huntington, N.Y., 1965-69, Bunker Rame Corp., Trumbull, Conn., 1969-73; v.p. R&D U.C.E., Inc./Innotech, Norwalk, 1973-75; program devel. mgr. U. Del., Inst. of Energy Conversion, Newark, 1975-80; prof. elec. engring. Western New England Coll., Springfield, 1980-98; dir. of rsch. Shriners Hosp., Springfield, 1989-93; exec. dir. Northeast Ctr. Telecomm. Techs., Springfield, 1998—2001; prof. emeritus We. New Eng. Coll., 1998—. Author: Electrical Materials and Devices, 1995; co-author: Laboratory Book of Power, 1988; contbr. over 120 articles to profl. jours.; more than 70 patents in field. Planning bd. Town of Wilbraham, Mass., 1986-88, bd. appeals, 1988-91. Fellowship NSF, 1961-62; recipient Rsch. Teaching Excellence award AT&T, 1987. Fellow Am. Inst. Med. and Biol. Engrs.; mem. IEEE (pres. local chpt. 1984-86), ASM (sec., treas., v.p., pres. local chpt. 1985-89), N.Y. Acad. Scis., Electrochem. Soc., Am. Soc. Engring. Edn., Am. Assn. Physics Tchrs., Soc. Photographic Instrumentation engrs., Am. Vacuum Soc., Materials Rsch. Soc., Engring. Soc. Western Mass. (v.p., pres., bd. dirs. 1989-90, disting. engring. award, 1994), Engring. Soc. No. Mass. (disting. engring. award), Engring. in Medicine and Biology Soc., ASM Internat. (sec., pres. 1986-89). Achievements include over 70 patents and inventions. Home: 242 Spurwink Ave Cape Elizabeth ME 04107-9612 Office: WNEC 1215 Wilbraham Rd Springfield MA 01119

MASK-MONROE, ROSE MARIA, reading specialist, educator; b. Newport News, Va., Nov. 1, 1955; d. Curtis Van and Mary Ella (Pearson) Mask; m. Marke A. Monroe, Sept. 6, 1986 (div. May 1993); children: Monteece C., Jamila T. BA, Utica Coll. Syracuse U., 1976; MS, Morgan State U., 1984. Asst. Liberty Street Day Care, Newburgh, N.Y., 1969; jr. counselor Neighborhood Youth Corps, Newburgh, 1974; tutor, counselor Higher Edn. Opportunity Program, Utica, N.Y., 1976; tchr. English Balt. Pub. Schs., 1977-79; agt. Balt. Police Dept., 1979-88; instr. Bowie (Md.) State U., 1988-91; assoc. prof. Balt. City C.C., 1991—. Tutor reading Utica (N.Y.) Free Acad., 1975; tutor English, Utica Coll., 1976; reading clinician Towson (Md.) State U., 1984; instr. Reading Community Coll. Balt., 1987-91. Counselor Utica YWCA, 1974. Recipient Merit Sonitrol Security Systems award, 1983; grantee Ottawa Found., 1973, Utica Coll. Higher Edn. Opportunity Program, 1973. Mem. Vanguard Justice Soc. (sec. 1980-82), Alpha Kappa Alpha. Democrat. Baptist. Avocations: reading, singing, traveling. Office: 2901 Liberty Heights Ave Baltimore MD 21215-7807

MASLAND, LYNNE S. university official; b. Boston, Nov. 18, 1940; d. Keith Arnold and Camilla (Puleston) Shangraw; m. Edwin Grant Masland, Sept. 19, 1960 (div. 1975); children: Mary Conklin, Molly Allison; m. Steven Alan Mayo, July 1, 1995. Student, Mt. Holyoke Coll., South Hadley, Mass., 1958-60; BA, U. Calif., Riverside, 1970; MA, U. Calif., 1971; PhD, U. B.C., Vancouver, Can., 1994. Asst. pub. rels. dir. Inter-Am. U., San German, P.R., 1963-64; asst. to dir. elem. edn. Govt. of Am. Samoa, Pago Pago, 1966-68; project dir., cons. Wash. Commn. for Humanities, Seattle, 1976-80; exec. editor N.W. Happenings Mag., Greenbank, Wash., 1980-84; media specialist Western Wash. U., Bellingham, 1984-88, dir. pub. info., 1988—. Cons. William O. Douglas Inst., Seattle, 1978, Whatcom Mus. History and Art, Bellingham, 1977; instr. U. Nebr., Omaha, 1972-74, Western Wash. U., 1977-86; asst. adj. prof. Fairhaven Coll/. 1995—. Editor: The Human Touch: Folklore of the Northwest Corner, 1979, Proceedings: The Art in Living, 1980, Reports to the Mayor on the State of the Arts in Bellingham, 1980-81; contbr. numerous articles to profl. jours. Pres. LWV, Whatcom County, Bellingham, 1977-79; bd. dirs. N.W. Concert Assn., 1981-83, Wash. State Folklife Coun., 1985-90; docent Nat. Gallery, Washington, 1969; bd. dirs. Sta. KZAZ, nat. pub. radio, Bellingham, 1992-93. Univ. grad. fellow U. B.C., 1990-94. Mem. Coun. for Advancement and Support Edn. (Case Dist. VIII Gold award for Media Rels., dist. VIII bd. dirs. 2003—), Mount Baker Family Med. (bd. dirs.), Bellingham City Club, Rotary (bd. dirs. 1992-94, Paul Harris fellow 1999). Episcopalian. Avocations: boating, gardening, travel, piano. Office: Western Wash U High St Bellingham WA 98225

MASON, BARBARA E. SUGGS, educator; b. Champaign, Ill., July 9, 1952; d. Raymond Eugene and Hester Barbara (Nelson) Suggs; m. Frederick A. Mason, May 7, 1988. B of Music Edn., Northwestern U., 1974; MS in Music Edn., U. Ill., 1976, M of Music, 1985. Cert. music tchr. K-12, supervisory endorsement, voice performance and lit., Ill. Gen. music specialist Oak Park (Ill.) Sch. Dist. 97, 1976-82; tchr. for the gifted performing arts unit Champaign Community Schs., 1985-86; choral dir. Evanston (Ill.) Twp. H.S., 1986-87, dist. curriculum leader for gen. music, 1990-95; coord. for mid. level edn. Oak Park Sch. Dist. 97, 1995—. Adj. instr. Elmhurst Coll., 1990-95; curriculum cons. Office of Cath. Edn. Black History Com., Chgo., 1992—; acad. task team mem. Quigley Preparatory Sem., Chgo, 1993; curriculum cons., presenter Dept. of Mus. Edn., Art Inst. of Chgo., 1992; chmn. dist. comprehensive arts grant com. Dist. 97, Oak Park, 1992—. Bd. dirs. Oak Park and River Forest Children's Chorus, 1991-95; mem. arts fund com. Oak Park Area Arts Coun., 1993-95, bd. dirs., 1997. Grad. coll. fellowship U. Ill., 1984-85; recipient Award of Merit Those Who Excel Program Ill. State Bd. of Edn., 1993. Mem. NEA, ASCD, Nat. Middle Sch. Assn., Music Educators Nat. Conf., Ill. Alliance for Arts Edn. (svc. award selection com. 1993), In-and-About Chgo. Music Educators Club, Mu Phi Epsilon, Phi Delta Kappa. Roman Catholic. Office: Oak Park Sch Dist 97 970 Madison St Oak Park IL 60302-4430

MASON, BETTY G(WENDOLYN) HOPKINS, school system administrator; b. Tulsa, Mar. 3, 1928; d. Stacy Ervin and Carrie (McGlory) Hopkins; 1 child, Trena Janell Milliner Combs. BA, Bishop Coll., Marshall, Tex., 1949; MEd, Calif. State U., Haywood, 1974; EdD, U. Okla., 1986. Tchr. pub. schs., Kansas City, Mo., 1963-69; asst. Title I schs. Berkeley (Calif.) Unified Schs., 1970-71, asst. prin., 1971-72, dir. elem. edn., 1974-79; prin. Le Conte Elem. Sch., Berkeley, 1972-74; dir. high schs. Oklahoma City Pub. Schs., 1979-82, asst. supt., 1982-88; supt. of schs. Gary (Ind.) Pub. Schs., 1988-90; ednl. cons. Oklahoma City Pub. Schs., 1990-91, asst. supt., 1991-92, supt. of schs., 1992-95, ret., 1995. Mem. exec. bd. supt.'s initiative Nat. Urban League, N.Y.C., 1988-90. Author: Closed Chapter, 1999. Mem. exec. bd. YWCA, Gary, 1988-90, N.W. Ind. chpt. Urban League, Gary, 1988—; vol. supt. St. John Christian Heritage Acad., 1997. Named to, Okla. Educators Hall of Fame, 1999; recipient Citizen of Yr. award, Omega Phi Psi, 1985, Outstanding Woman in Edn. award, Okla. Commn. in Edn., 1987, Youth Svc. award, City and Mayor of Gary, 1988, Outstanding Educator award, Ind. U. Dons, 1989, Disting. Educator's award, 1993, Silver Beaver award, Boy Scouts Am., 1995, Woman of Yr. award, Girl Scouts, 1995, Best in Edn. Leadership award, Kappa Alpha Psi, 1998, Outstanding Sr. Soror award, Alpha Kappa Alpha, 1999. Mem. Am. Assn. Sch. Adminstrs., Nat. Assn. Black Educators, NW Ind. Supts. Coun., Phi Delta Kappa (Soror of yr. 1996), Alpha Kappa Alpha. Home: 2217 NW 119th St Oklahoma City OK 73120-7815

MASON, BETTY ROSE, elementary school educator; b. Emporia, Kans., Oct. 4, 1940; d. Virgil Roosevelt and Flora Rose (Leffler) Shellenberger; m. Donnie Lee Mason, Mar. 24, 1961; 1 child, Jeffry Lee. BS, Emporia State U., 1962, postgrad., 1978-79, Hays State U., 1967, Pittsburg (Kans.) State U., 1970, Wichita State U., 1971-72, 77-79, 82-83, 89-91, Holy Name Coll., 1974, Friends U., 1992-93. Cert. tchr. K-8 elem., K-9 reading specialist, 7-9 social studies and composition, 7-9 English, Kans. Tchr. 2d grade Kingman/Norwich Sch./Unified Sch. Dist. #331, Kingman, Kans., 1962—, profl. devel. chair, 1983—, profl. devel. records sec. for bd. edn., 1983—. Presenter numerous state devel. convs.; supr. student tchrs. state colls. Vol. Meals on Wheels Program, Kingman, 1973—; adminstr. Alice Ann Woodson Children's Fund, Unified Sch. Dist. # 331, Kingman, 1989—; mem. OES Dist. AIDS Assn. Kans., 1985—; sch. coord. learning for life program Boy Scouts Am. Unified Sch. Dist. # 331 Local Dist. Tech. grantee, 1983; recipient 25 Yr. Tchg. award U. Kans., 1987. Mem. Assn. Supervision and Curriculum Devel., Nat. Edn. Assn., Nat. Staff Devel. Coun., Kans. Staff Devel. Coun. (bd. dirs. 1992—), Kans. Edn. Assn., Ednl. Svcs. and Staff Devel. Assn. Ctrl. Kans. (mem. coun. 1987—), Order Ea. Star (Martha 1972-73, 79-92, assoc. conductress 1975, conductress 1976, Della chpt. assoc. matron 1977, Worthy Matron 1978), Mid Century Club (pres. 1989), Kans. Assn. Supervision and Curriculum Devel., Kans. Nat. Edn. Assn. Republican. Methodist. Avocations: collecting carved elephants, glass birds, raising birds, house and car restoration. Home: 120 W E Ave # F Kingman KS 67068-1120 Office: Unified Sch Dist #331 Kingman-Norwich 115 N Main St Kingman KS 67068-1333

MASON, ELLIOTT BERNARD, biologist, educator; b. Detroit, July 29, 1943; m. Marsha Lee Marquardt, April 17, 1971; children: Jennifer R., Julie A., Jessica M. BS, Loyola U., Chgo., 1965; MS, Wayne State U., Detroit, 1969, PhD, 1972. Asst. prof. biology George Mason U., Fairfax, Va., 1971-73; from asst. prof. to prof. biol. scis. SUNY, Cortland, 1973—, chmn. dept. biol. scis., 1994—. Co-author: Human Anatomy and Physiology, 4th edit., 1992; author: Human Physiology, 1983; contbr. articles to profl. jours. NSF grantee. Office: SUNY Dept Biol Scis Cortland NY 13045

MASON, GEORGE HENRY, business educator; b. Chgo., Sept. 11, 1929; s. Robert De Main and Dorothy Wills (Belden) M.; m. Constance Eleanor Wolcott, May 14, 1960. AB, Kenyon Coll., 1955; MBA, Cornell U., 1957; MF, Duke U., 1983. CFA. Investment officer Travelers Ins. Co., Hartford, Conn., 1957-88; exec.-in-residence U. Hartford, West Hartford, 1989-98, dir. Bus. Applications Ctr., 1998-2001. Vis. prof. Jagiellonian U., Cracow, Poland, spring 1996, Yang-En U., Quanzhou, Fujian, China, fall 1997; investment adv. coun. State of Conn., 1999-2003. Co-author: Timberland Investments, 1992. Mem.: Hartford Soc. Fin. Analysts, Assn. Investment Mgmt. and Rsch., Dataw Island Club, Mill Reef Club, Country Club of Farmington. Republican. Avocations: skiing, golf, writing.

MASON, GREGORY WESLEY, JR., secondary education educator; b. Chgo., Jan. 21, 1963; s. Gregory Wesley and Diana (Burton) M.; m. LaTanya Yvonne Brown, June 8, 1991; children: Gregory Arthur, Timothy Michael. BS, Ill. State U., 1986; MEd, U. Ill., Chgo., 1996. Cert. secondary tchr., gen. adminstr., Ill. Instr. City Coll. Chgo., 1986-89; instr. project alert Roosevelt U., Chgo., 1989-91, counselor project upward bound, 1991-93; tchr. math. Bowen High Sch., Chgo., 1993-95, chmn. profl. planning adv. com., 1994-95; tchr. math. Whitney M. Young Magnet H.S., Chgo., 1995-2000, chmn. dept. math., 1997-2000; adminstr. Chgo. Pub. Schs., 2000—. Instr. Ill. Math. and Sci. Acad., Aurora, summers 1993-96; lectr. Coll. Edn., Loyola U., Chgo., 1999-2001; tchr. coord. Golden Apple Found., 2000-01; mem. nat. adv. bd. Schs. and Scholars Program, Woodrow Wilson Nat. Fellowship Found. Mem. pres.'s coun. edn. com. Mus. Sci. and Industry; mem. Ill. Robotic Competition Adv. Bd. Named Outstanding Young Men of Am., 1985. Mem. ASCD, Nat. Coun. Tchrs. Math., Ill. Coun. Tchrs. Math., Ill. Coun. for Coll. Attendance (bd. dirs. 1993-97), Nat. Assn. Secondary Sch. Prins., Benjamin Banneker Assn., Masons, Phi Delta Kappa. Avocations: swimming, chess, reading, stock trading, computers. Home: 2729 W 84th St Chicago IL 60652-3909 Office: Chgo Pub Schs 1326 W 14th Pl Chicago IL 60608 E-mail: gmason@csc.cps.k12.il.us.

MASON, JOHANNA HENDRIKA ANNEKE, retired secondary education educator; b. Indramajoe, Indonesia, Feb. 17, 1932; came to U.S., 1957; d. Johannes Simon and Hendrika Jacoba (De Vroedt) Vermeulen; m. Alfred Bob Markholt, Feb., 1958 (div. Dec. 1966); children: Bob, Anneke, Joe Ralph, Lee Markholt; m. Rollin Mason, 1968 (div. 1978). French lang.

diploma with top honors, Paris Alliance Française, 1952; BA in Philosophy summa cum laude, U. Puget Sound, 1976, MA in Comparative Lit., 1979, BA in Edn., 1988. Cert. pub. sch. tchr. 4-12. Adminstrv. asst. to pres. N.V. Nutricia, Zoetermeer, The Netherlands, 1953-57; pvt. sec. Grad. Sch. Bus. Harvard U., Cambridge, Mass., 1957; adminstrv. asst., lectr. humanities divsn. U. Puget Sound, Tacoma, 1966-88; tchr. English and French h.s. and mid. sch. Tacoma, 1988-94. Mem. pres. staff orgn. U. Puget Sound, Tacoma, 1978-80, budget task force, 1981-86. Author: (poetry compilation) Journey, 1981, A Handfull of Bubbles, 1981, Echoes, Mirrors, Reflections, 1983; contbr. poetry to lit. mags. Mem. city's task force on hate crimes, Tacoma, 1992, translator, 1974-90; bd. dirs. Unitarian Universalist Assn. of Tacoma, 2003—. Selected to literary pub. art registry, City of Tacoma, 1999. Mem. So. Poverty Law Ctr., Amnesty Internat., Coun. Indian Nations, Phi Kappa Phi (nat. com. on comms. 1991-94, pres. chpt. 1973-77). Avocations: reading, hiking, theater, needlework, poetry. E-mail: anneke@mailbug.com.

MASON, LINDA, physical education educator, softball and basketball coach; b. Indpls., Jan. 29, 1946; d. Harrison Linn and Hazel Marie (Bledsoe) Crouch; divorced; children: Cassandra, Andrew. BS, Ind. U., 1968, MS, 1977. Cert. phys. edn. tchr., K-12, Ind. Tchr. phys. edn. Woodview Jr. H.S., Indpls., 1968-71; tchr. phys. edn., coach Ind. U.-Purdue U. of Indpls., 1972-76; basketball coach Butler U., Indpls., 1976-84; head softball coach, asst. basketball coach Westfield Washington High Sch., Westfield, Ind., 1985; tchr. phys. edn., basketball coach Orchard Park Elementary Sch., Carmel, Ind., 1985—; elem. physical edn. tchr. Carmel-Clay Schs., Carmel, 1985—; asst. varsity coach softball Carmel H.S., 1993-95, head varsity softball coach, 1996-99. Head coach Ind. Girls' H.S. All-Stars Basketball Team, Indpls., 1980. Named Coach of Yr. Dist. 4, Nat. Collegiate Athletic Assn., 1983, Coach of Yr. for softball ICGSA, 1997, coach ICGSA Girls All Stars, 1998. Mem. Delta Psi Kappa. E-mail: lmason@ccs.k12.in.us.

MASON, LORETTA YVONNE, elementary education educator; b. Phila., May 23, 1948; d. Junius Fletcher and Marie (Mann) Hicks; m. Chester Mason; children from previous marriage: Charles Taylor III, Malik Taylor, James II. BS, Cheyney U., 1969. Cert. tchr., Pa. Tchr. Phil. Sch. Dist., 1970—. Coord. Dept. of Recreation, Phila., summer, 1980; alem specialist Temple U., Phila., 1989—; fact coord. Nat. Football League, Phila., 1992—. Editor sch. newspaper, 1987-89, alem newsletter, 1992—. Vol. Am. Cancer Soc., 1989—, Sickle Cell Assn., 1989-90. Mem. NEA, Phila. Sch. Edn. Assn., Phila. Fedn. Tchrs., Cheyney Alumni Assn. Avocations: race car driving, movies, reading, listening to jazz, collecting crystals. Office: Leslie Pinckney Hill Sch 32nd Ridge Ave Philadelphia PA 19132

MASON, MARGARET CRATHER, elementary school educator; b. Wilmington, Del, Aug. 15, 1945; d. William F. and Regina (Mays) Crather; children: Donna Lynn, R. Brian. BA, U. Del., 1968; postgrad., Loyola Coll. Balt., Del. State Coll.; M in Ednl. Leadership, Wilmington Coll. Cert. English, secondary and elem. tchr., elem. prin., Del. Secondary tchr. English, Podua Acad., Wilmington; elem. tchr. St. John the Beloved Sch., Wilmington; elem. tchr. sci. Christina Sch. Dist., Wilmington, asst. prin. elem. sch. Active numerous community orgns. and local ch. Recipient Fire Safety Edn. award New Castle County Vol. Firefighters. Mem. Del. Assn. Sch. Adminstrs.

MASON, REBECCA SUSSA, retired secondary education educator; b. Knoxville, Tenn., Sept. 21, 1945; d. Max and Greta (Hans) M. BA, SUNY, Fredonia, 1967; MA, Columbia U., 1977. Cert. permanent tchr., N.Y. Tchr. music Kakiat Jr. High Sch., East Ramapo Ctrl. Sch. Dist., Spring Valley, N.Y., 1967-95, head dept., 1985—, condr. All Dist. Band, 1980, 97—, asst. condr., 1989-96; tchr. music Ramapo Sr. H.S., 1995-2001; ret., 2001. Bass clarinetist Rockland Suburban Symphony, Spring Valley, 1967-68; 1st clarinet Westchester Pops Band, White Plains, N.Y., 1967-68, South Orange (N.J.) Symphony, 1986-87, Rockland Community Band, Pearl River, N.Y., 1988—. Recipient various plaques, awards and letters of commendation East Ramapo Sch. Dist., 1968—, letter of commendation SUNY, 1990. Mem. Music Educators Nat. Conf., N.Y. State Sch. Music Assn., East Ramapo PTA (life). Avocations: travel, pottery, collecting autographs and baseball cards, quilting, counted cross-stitch. Home: 116 Hillcrest Ln Peekskill NY 10566

MASON, ROBERT MCSPADDEN, technology management educator, consultant; b. Sweetwater, Tenn., Jan. 16, 1941; s. Paul Rankin and Ruby May (McSpadden) M.; m. Betty Ann Durrence (div. 1980); children: Michael Dean, Donald Robert; m. Marilyn Killebrew Gell, July 17, 1981. SB, MIT, 1963, SM, 1965; PhD, Ga. Inst. Tech., 1973. Tech. staff mem. Sandia Labs., Livermore, Calif., 1965-68; rsch. scientist Ga. Inst. Tech., Atlanta, 1971-75, sr. rsch. scientist, 1975; prin. Metrics, Inc., Atlanta, 1975-80; pres. Metrics Rsch. Corp., Atlanta, 1980-86, Cleve., 1986-98, Tallahassee, 1998—; adj. prof. Weatherhead Sch. Mgmt. Case Western U., 1987-88, vis. prof., 1988-91, prof. for practice of tech. mgmt., 1991-98; dir. Ctr. Mgmt. Sci. and Tech., 1988-96; Sprint prof. mgmt. Coll. Bus. Fla. State U., Tallahassee, 1998—, chair mgmt. info. sys., 1998—2002. Co-author: Library Micro Consumer, 1986; co-editor: Information Services: Economics, Management, and Technology, 1981, Management of Technology V: Technology Management in a Changing World, 1996; co-author: The Impact of Office Automation on Clerical Employment, 1985-2000, 1985; Am. editor Technovation, 1994—; contbr. article series "Mason on Micros" to Libr. Jour., 1983-86, articles to various profl. publs. Mem. Internat. Assn. for Tech. Mgmt. (newsletter editor 1992-93, program chair internat. conf., 1996, pres. 1996-98, mem. exec. com. 1998—). Republican. Presbyterian. Avocations: flying, skiing, sailing, scuba diving, photography. Home: 811 Live Oak Plantation Rd Tallahassee FL 32312-2412 Office: Fla State U MIS Dept Coll of Bus Tallahassee FL 32306-1110 E-mail: rmmason@alum.mit.edu.

MASON, VIVIAN LEE CONWAY, elementary education educator; b. Richmond, Va., Jan. 16, 1942; d. Edward Gordon and Raconia (Boyd) Conway; m. Eugene Albertis Mason Jr., June 30, 1962; children; Eugene Albertis III, Yevette Matrease. BS, Va. Commonwealth U., 1976; postgrad., U. Richmond, 1979, Va. Union U., 1982, Hampton U., 1985. Cert. collegiate profl., Va. Tchr. Richmond (Va.) Pub. Schs., 1976—. Chairperson Am. Bus. Women's Assn., Richmond, 1990-91; trainer, cons. Project Head Start, 1987-89. Mem. Richmond Dem. Party, 1991-92, Alpha Kappa Alpha Sorority, Richmond, 1986-92. Mem. NEA, AAUP, Va. Edn. Assn., Richmond Edn. Assn. (bd. dirs. 1993, 95-97), NEA Women's Caucus, Am. Bus. Women's Assn. (Inner Circle award 1992, founder Edward Daniel McCreary Jr. Scholarship Fund 1994). Democrat. Avocations: writing children's literature, painting, jogging, working with youth and families. Home: 6319 Windcroft Rd Richmond VA 23225-6842 Office: Richmond Pub Schs 301 S 9th St Richmond VA 23219-3913

MASSA, CONRAD HARRY, religious studies educator; b. Bklyn., Oct. 27, 1927; s. Harry Frederick and Josephine W. (Lepold) M.; m. Anna W. Rossi, Aug. 19, 1951; children: Stephen Mark, Barbara Ann. AB with honors, Columbia U., 1951; M.Div., Princeton Theol. Sem., 1954, PhD, 1960; HHD, Lafayette Coll., 1987. Ordained to ministry Presbyn. Ch., 1954. Pastor Elmwood Presbyn. Ch., East Orange, N.J., 1954-57; asst. prof. homiletics Princeton Theol. Sem., 1957-61; sr. pastor Old First Ch., Newark, 1961-66, Third Presbyn. Ch., Rochester, N.Y., 1966-78; dean acad. affairs Princeton Theol. Sem., 1978-94, dean emeritus, 1994—, Charlotte W. Newcombe prof., 1978-95, Charlotte W. Newcombe prof. emeritus, 1995—. 1st moderator Synod of the Northeast, United Presbyn. Ch.; vis. prof. St. Bernard's Roman Cath. Sem., Rochester, 1968-70; keynote speaker 11th ann. conf. Inst. Theology, Yonsei U., Seoul, Republic of Korea, 1991. Author articles and book revs. Trustee Lafayette Coll., Easton, Pa., 1982-93. Served with U.S. Army, 1946-47. Mem. Acad. Homiletics, Am. Acad. Religion, Internat. John Bunyan Soc. Home: 14691 Blackbird Ln Fort Myers FL 33919-8346

MASSARE, JOHN STEVE, medical association administrator, educator; b. Rochester, N.Y., Feb. 16, 1949; s. Peter Anthony and Clara Marie (Skill) M.; 1 child, John Simon. BA, SUNY, Oswego, 1970; MS, SUNY, Brockport, 1973; postgrad., Ind. U., 1976-80; PhD, Columbia CommonwealthU., 2001. With Carnation Co., 1970-71; sales rep. Bausch and Lomb Co., Rochester, 1973-76; with CIBA Vision Corp., Atlanta, 1981-91; exec. dir. Contact Lens Assn. Ophthalmologists, New Orleans, 1992—. Adj. instr. Tulane U. Sch. Medicine, New Orleans, 1994—. Contbr. articles to profl. jours. Recipient Assoc. Inst. of Yr. award Ind. U., 1978, 79, Silver Javal Pin Internat. Contact Lens Coun., 1994; Robert C. Ezell fellow, 1979. Mem. Am. Assn. Soc. Execs., Contact Lens Soc. Am. (assoc., v.p. edn. fund com. 1990-92, bd. dirs. 1990-91). Avocations: reading, golf, personal fitness. Office: Contact Lens Assn (CLAO) 721 Papworth Ave Ste 206 Metairie LA 70005-4925

MASSARO, TRACI LYNN, special education educator; b. Gadsden, Ala., Jan. 16, 1969; d. James Michael Cushing and Sheltie Anna Griffin; m. Thomas Christopher Massaro, Aug. 18, 1992; children: Lorren Elizabeth, Ryan Thomas, Andrew Michael. BS in Spl. Edn., Jacksonville State U., 1992; M, Kennesaw State U., 2000. Tchr. Bartow County Schs., Cartersville, Ga., 1992-93, Douglas County Schs., Douglasville, Ga., 1993-99, Etowah County Schs., Gadsden, Ala., 1999—. Recipient Mamie Jo Jones scholarship, 1995, Hope Tchr. scholarship, 1996-98, Outstanding Grad. Student Special Edn. award, 1999, Pledge of Yr. award Gadsden City Coun., 2002. Mem. Coun. Exceptional Children (v.p. 1996-97, pres. 1997—), Kiwanis (Circle K, v.p. 1989-90. pres. 1990-91), Anchor Club (v.p. 1985-86, pres. 1986-87), Beta Sigma Phi (Gadsden City Coun. Pledge of Yr. 2002, Woman of Yr. 2003). Republican. Baptist. Avocations: crafting, sewing. Home: 505 Cosby St Gadsden AL 35903-6911

MASSE', DONALD DUANE, obstetrician, gynecologist, educator; b. Lafayette, Ind., Dec. 9, 1934; s. Otto A. and Frances Maxine (Johnson) M.; m. Mary Perkins, June 6, 1964; children: Stephanie Ann, Mark Christopher. BS, Purdue U., 1956; MD, Marquette U., 1964. Diplomate Am. Bd. Ob-Gyn. Resident in ob-gyn Wayne State U. Med. Sch., Detroit, 1964-69, clin. asst. prof. ob-gyn., 1969—; pvt. practice Detroit, 1969—99. With U.S. Army, 1957-60. Named to Jefferson H.S. Hall of Fame, Lafayette, Ind., 2003. Fellow Am. Coll. Ob-Gyn; mem. Nat. Med. Assn., Mich. Med. Soc., Wayne County Med. Soc., Detroit Med. Soc. (fin. sec. 1971-75), Alpha Phi Alpha. Avocations: golf, fishing. Office: St John Detroit Riverview Hosp Dept Ob-gyn 7733 E Jefferson Detroit MI 48214

MASSENGALE, MARTIN ANDREW, agronomist, university president; b. Monticello, Ky., Oct. 25, 1933; s. Elbert G. and Orpha (Conn) M.; m. Ruth Audrey Klingelhofer, July 11, 1959; children: Alan Ross, Jennifer Lynn. BS, Western Ky. U., 1952; MS, U. Wis., 1954, PhD, 1956; LHD (hon.), Nebr. Wesleyan U., 1987; DS (hon.), Senshu U., Tokyo, 1995. Cert. profl. agronomist, profl. crop scientist. Research asst. agronomy U. Wis., 1952-56; asst. prof., asst. agronomist U. Ariz., 1958-62, assoc. prof., assoc. agronomist, 1962-65, prof., agronomist, 1965-76, head dept., 1966-74, assoc. dean Coll. Agr. assoc. dir. Ariz. Agr. Expt. Sta., 1974-76; vice chancellor for agr. and natural resources U. Nebr., 1976-81; chancellor U. Nebr.-Lincoln, 1981-91, interim pres., 1989-91; pres. U. Nebr., 1991-94, pres. emeritus, 1994, found. disting. prof. and dir., 1994—. Chmn. pure seed adv. com. Ariz. Agrl. Expt. Sta.; past chmn. bd., pres. Mid-Am. Internat. Agrl. Consortium; coord. com. environ. quality EPA-Dept. Agrl. Land Grand U.; past chmn. bd. dirs. Am. Registry Cert. Profls. in Agronomy, Crops and Soils; bd. dirs. Ctr. for Human Nutrition; bd. dirs., trustee U. Nebr. Found.; chair bd. dirs. Agronomic Sci. Found., chmn. selection com; dir. devel. Secretariat, Filippo Maseri Florio World Prize for Disting. Rsch. in Agr.; exec. com. U. Nebr. Tech. Park, LLC; bd. dirs. Lincoln Ins. Group., Woodmen Accident & Life Co., LIG, Inc., Am. First, LLC; mem. adv. bd. Nat. Agrl. Rsch., Ext., Edn. and Econs., 1998—, vice chair secs. nat. adv. bd., mem. exec. com.; mem. nat. adv. bd. Trees Am., 1998—. Chmn. NCAA Pres.'s Commn., 1988-91; distbn. revenue com., standing com. on appointments North Ctrl. Assn. Commn. on Insts. Higher Edn., 1991; trustee Nebr. Hist. Soc. Found.; bd. dirs. Nebr. Hist. Soc.; bd. govs. Nebr. Sci. and Math. Initiative; mem. Knight Found. Commn. on Intercollegiate Athletics; bd. dirs. Great Plains Funds, IBP; hon. life trustee Nebr. Coun. on Econ. Edn.; hon. lifetime trustee Nebr. Coun. on Econ. Edn. With U.S. Army, 1956-58. Named Midlands Man of Yr., 1982, to We. Ky. U. Hall of Disting. Alumni, 1992, DeKalb Crop Sci. Disting. Career award, 1996, Outstanding Educator Am., 1970, Wayne County H.S., Monticello, Ky., Charter Hall of Fame, 2002; recipient faculty recognition award Tucson Trade Bur., 1971, Ak-Sar-Ben Agrl. Achievement award, 1986, Agrl. Builders Nebr. award, 1986, Walter K. Beggs award, 1986, Vol. of Yr. award for disting. svc. Nebr. Coun. on Econ. Edn., IANR Team Initiation award, Agri award Triumph of Agr. Expn., 1999, Exemplary Svc. to Agr. award Nebr. AgRels. Coun., 2000, Friend of LEAD award Nat. LEAD Alumni Assn., 2001, Outstanding Pres. award All-Am. Football Found., 2001; hon. state farmer degrees Ky., Ariz., Nebr. Future Farmers Am. Assns. Fellow AAAS (sect. chmn.), Crop Sci. Soc. Am. (past dir., pres. 1972-73, past assoc. editor, pres. western soc., disting. career award 1996), Am. Soc. Agronomy (past dir., vis. scientist program, past assoc. editor Agronomy Jour., Disting. Svc. award 1984); mem. Am. Grassland Coun., Ariz. Crop Improvement Assn. (bd. dirs.), Am. Soc. Plant Physiology, Nat. Assn. Colls. and Tchrs. Agr., Soil and Water Conservation Soc. Am., Ariz. Acad. Sci., Nebr. Acad. Sci., Agrl. Coun. Am. (bd. dirs., issues com.), Coun. Agrl. Sci. and Tech. (bd. dirs. budget and fin. 1979-82, 94—, treas., exec. com. 1997—), Nat. Assn. State Colls. and Land Grant Univs. (chmn. com. on info. tech. 1987-94, exec. com. 1990-92, bd. dirs. 1992-94), Edn. Engring. Professions (mem. commn.), Coll. Football Assn. (chmn., bd. dirs. 1986-88), Am. Assn. State Coll. and Univs. (task force instl. resource allocation), Assn. Am. Univs. Rsch. Librs. (steering com. 1992-94), Nebr. Crop Improvement Assn. (disting. svc. award), Grazing Lands Forum (pres.), Nebr. C. of C. and Industry, Nebr. Diplomats Inc. (hon. diplomate), Nebr. Vet. Med. Assn. (hon.), Sigma Xi, Phi Kappa Phi, Gamma Sigma Delta (Award of Merit), Alpha Zeta, Phi Sigma, Gamma Alpha, Alpha Gamma Rho, Phi Beta Delta, Golden Key Nat. Honor Soc., Innocents Soc. Office: U Nebr 220 Keim Hall Lincoln NE 68583-0953 E-mail: mmassengale1@unl.edu.

MASSEY, ELEANOR NELSON, school librarian, media specialist; b. Apr. 1, 1930; d. Walter K. and Jeanette (Perlman) Nelson; m. Marvin Donald Massey, June 29, 1952; children: Henry, David, Michael, Jonathan. BA, Douglass Coll., New Brunswick, N.J., 1952; postgrad., Rutgers U. Cert. ednl. media specialist. Children's librarian Westfield (N.J.) Pub. Library, 1952-55; librarian Franklin Jr. High Sch., Metuchen, N.J., 1959-61; media specialist Campbell Sch., Metuchen, 1962—; coordinator libraries Metuchen Pub. Schs., 1982—. Dir. Woodbridge-East Brunswick Area Coordination Council, 1982-85; mem. interim planning com. N.J. Library Network, 1984-85; cooperating tchr. Kean Coll. and Rutgers U., 1975—; speaker; bibliographer. V.p. Sisterhood Neve Shalom, Metuchen, 1960; dir. Neve Shalom, 1959-60; bd. dirs. Union-Middlesex Regional Library Cooperative, Region IV, Inc., 1985-89; active Metuchen Cable TV Adv. Commn., 1994—. Title II Demonstration Library grantee State of N.J., 1974-76, Sch.-Pub. Libr. Coop. grantee 1986, Metuchen Edn. Found grantee for AuthorsLive program, 1999. Recipient N.J. Gov.'s Tchr. Recognition award, 1991. Mem. Ednl. Media Assn. N.J. (exec. bd. 1976-78), ALA, N.J. Library Assn., Ednl. Media Assn. Middlesex County (treas. 1982-83). Office: Campbell Sch Talmadge Ave Metuchen NJ 08840 E-mail: tzimis@aol.com.

MASSEY, JAMES EARL, clergyman, educator; b. Ferndale, Mich., Jan. 4, 1930; s. George Wilson and Elizabeth (Shelton) M.; m. Gwendolyn Inez Kilpatrick, Aug. 4, 1951. Student, U. Detroit, 1949-50, 55-57; BTh, BRE, Detroit Bible Coll., 1961; AM, Oberlin Grad Sch. Theology, 1964; postgrad., U. Mich., 1967-69; DD, Asbury Theol. Sem., 1972, Ashland Theol. Sem., 1991, Huntington Coll., 1994; HumD, Tuskegee U., 1995; DD, Warner Pacific Coll., 1995; LittD, Anderson U., 1995; DD, Wash. and Jefferson Coll., 1997, North Park Theol. Sem., 1999. Ordained to ministry Ch. of God, 1951. Assoc. min. Ch. of God, Detroit, 1951-53; sr. pastor Met. Ch. of God, Detroit, 1954-76, pastor-at-large, 1976; spkr. Christian Brotherhood Hour, 1977-82; prin. Jamaica Sch. Theology, Kingston, 1963-66; campus min. Anderson Coll., Ind., 1969-77, asst. prof. religious studies, 1969-75, assoc. prof., 1975-80, prof. N.T. and homiletics, 1981-84; dean of chapel and univ., prof. religion and society Tuskegee U., Ala., 1984-89; dean, prof. preaching and bibl. studies Anderson Sch. Theology, 1989-95; dean emeritus and disting. prof.-at-large, 1995—. Chmn. Comm. on Higher Edn. in the Ch. of God, 1968-71; vice chmn. bd. publs. Ch. of God, 1968-78; dir. Warner Press, Inc.; rsch. scholar Christianity Today Inst. Author: When Thou Prayest, 1960, The Worshipping Church, 1961, Raymond S. Jackson, A Portrait, 1967, The Soul Under Seige, 1970, The Church of God and the Negro, 1971, The Hidden Disciplines, 1972, The Responsible Pulpit, 1973, Temples of the Spirit, 1974, The Sermon in Perspective, 1976, Concerning Christian Unity, 1979; gen. editor: Christian Brotherhood Hour Study Bible, 1979, Designing the Sermon, 1980; co-editor: Interpreting God's Word for Today, 1982; editor: Educating for Service, 1984, The Spiritual Disciplines, 1985, The Bridge Between, 1988, Preaching From Hebrews, 1992, The Burdensome Joy of Preaching, 1996, Sundays at The Tuskegee Chapel, 1999, Aspects of My Pilgrimage: An Autobiography, 2002, Remembering William L. Dawson, 2004; mem. editl. bd. The Christian Scholar's Rev. Leadership mag.; mem. editl. bd., contbg. editor Vol I New Interpreter's Bible,, 1990—; contbg. editor Preaching mag.; sr. editor Christianity Today mag. Mem. Corp. Inter-Vrsity Christian Fellowship; bd. dirs. World Vision. Served with AUS, 1951-53. Mem. Nat. Assn. Coll. and Univ. Chaplains, Nat. Com. Black Churchmen, Nat. Negro Evang. Assn. (bd. dirs. 1969-86). Office: 367 Beverly Rd Greensboro AL 36744-6034

MASSEY, PATTI CHRYL, elementary school educator; b. Electra, Tex., Nov. 18, 1952; d. Francis Leon and Violet V. (Inabinette) Perry; m. William S. Massey, July 18,1986. BS, Midwestern U., 1974; MEd, Southwest Tex. State U., 1979. Cert. elem. educator, reading specialist, coop. learning trainer, reading recovery tchr. Tchr. East Central Ind. Sch. Dist., San Antonio, 1975-89, San Antonio Ind. Sch. Dist., 1990—. Vol. Tex. Spl. Olympics, San Antonio, 1975—, Jimenez Thanksgiving Sr. Citizens Dinner, San Antonio, 1983—, Amateur Athletic Union Jr. Olympics, San Antonio, 1989, Amateur Athletic Union Nat. Basketball Tournament, San Antonio, 1990, U.S. Olympic Festival, San Antonio, 1993, Alzheimer's Memory Walk, 1992—. Named one of Outstanding Young Women in Am., 1983. Mem.: PTA (hon. life, sec. 1982—84), NEA, Tex. State Reading Assn., Alamo Reading Coun., Tex. State Tchrs. Assn., San Antonio Tchrs. Coun., Sigma Kappa (alumnae/collegiate rels. coord. 1998—, Outstanding Alumna 1988, 1991, Pearl Ct. award 1990, Outstanding Regional Alumna 1991), Alpha Delta Kappa, Kappa Delta Pi. Democrat. Methodist. Avocations: reading, volunteering, aerobic activities, baking. Home: 4527 Black Oak Woods San Antonio TX 78249-1478

MASSEY, THOMAS BENJAMIN, retired academic administrator, educator; b. Charlotte, N.C., Sept. 5, 1926; s. William Everard and Sarah (Corley) M.; m. Bylee Hunnicutt Massey, July 10, 1968; children: Pamela Ann, Caroline Forest. AB, Duke U., 1948; MS, N.C. State U., 1953; PhD, Cambridge U., 1968. Assoc. dean students Ga. Inst. Tech., Atlanta, 1950-58; lectr. U. Md. Univ. Coll., 1960-66, asst. dir. London, 1966-69, dir. Toyko, 1969-71, dir. Heidelberg (Fed. Republic of Germany), 1971-76, vice chancellor, 1976-78, chancellor, 1978-88, pres., 1988-98, pres. emeritus, 1998—. Served with USN, 1943-46. Mem. APA, Univ. Continuing Edn. Assn., Am. Assn. Higher Edn., Interernat. Confs. on Improving Learning and Tchg. at the Univ. (chair 1975—). E-mail: benm09056@aol.com.

MASSEY, WILLIAM S. mathematician, educator; b. Granville, Ill., Aug. 23, 1920; s. Robert R. and Alma (Schumacher) M.; m. Ethel Heap, Mar. 14, 1953; children— Eleanor, Alexander, Joan. Student, Bradley U., 1937-39; BS, U. Chgo., 1941, MS, 1942; PhD, Princeton, 1948. Mem. research dept. Princeton, 1948-50; from asst. prof. to prof. Brown U., 1950-60; prof. math. Yale, 1960—, Erastus L. Deforest prof. math, 1964-82, Eugene Higgins prof. math., 1983-91, Eugene Higgins prof. math. emeritus, 1991—, chmn. dept. math., 1968-71. Author: Algebraic Topology: An Introduction, 1967, Homology and Cohomology Theory, 1978, Singular Homology Theory, 1980, A Basic Course in Algebraic Topology, 1991; mem. editorial staff math. jours. Served as officer USNR, 1942-46. Fellow Am. Acad. Arts and Scis.; mem. Am. Math. Soc. Achievements include research in algebraic topology, differential topology, homotopy theory, fibre bundles. Home: 200 Leeder Hill Drive Hamden CT 06517-2729 Office: Yale U Math Dept PO Box 208283 New Haven CT 06520-8283

MASSOF, ROBERT WILLIAM, neuroscientist, educator; b. Minn., Jan. 2, 1948; m. Patricia Massof; children: Eric, Allison. BA, Hamline U., 1970; PhD, Ind. U., 1975. Postdoctoral fellow in ophthalmology Johns Hopkins U. Sch. Medicine, Balt., 1975-76, instr. ophthalmology, 1976-78, from asst. prof. to assoc. prof., 1978-91, prof. ophthalmology, 1991—, prof. neurosci., 1994—, prof. computer sci., 1994—, mem. staff applied physics lab., 2000—. Lectr. in field. Mem. editl. bd. Clin. Vision Scis., N.Y.C., 1986-94, Eye Care Technology/Computers in Eye Care, Folsom, Calif., 1992-96; patentee in field (5); contbr. articles to profl. jours. Recipient Manpower award, 1989, Tech. Transfer award NASA, 1993, Popular Mechanics Design and Engring. award, 1994, EyeCare Tech. Lifetime Achievement award, 1995, Richard E. Hoover Svc. award, 1995. Humanitarian award Lions, 2000, Disting. Svc. in Vision award Am. Pub. Health Assn., William Feinbloom award Am. Acad. of Optometry, 2000. Fellow Optical Soc. Am. (chmn. edn. coun. 1993-95, bd. dirs. 1993-95), Am. Acad. Optometry; mem. Assn. for Edn. and Rehab. of the Visually Impaired, Soc. for Info. Display, Am. Congress Rehab. Medicine, Assn. Rsch. in Vision and Ophthalmology. Office: Johns Hopkins Univ Lions Vision Ctr 550 N Broadway Fl 6 Baltimore MD 21205-2020

MASSY, WILLIAM FRANCIS, education educator, consultant; b. Milw., Mar. 26, 1934; s. Willard Francis and Ardys Dorothy (Digman) M.; m. Sally Vaughn Miller, July 21, 1984; children by previous marriage: Willard Francis, Elizabeth BS, Yale U., 1956; SM, MIT, 1958, PhD in Indsl. Econs., 1960. Asst. prof. indsl. mgmt. MIT, Cambridge, 1960-62; from asst. prof. to prof. edn. and bus. adminstrn. Stanford U., Calif., 1962-96, assoc. dean Grad. Sch. Bus., 1971, vice provost for rsch., 1971-77, v.p. for bus. and fin., 1977-88, v.p. fin., 1988-91, prof. emeritus, 1996—; prof. edn., dir. Stanford Inst. Higher Edn. Rsch., Calif., 1988-96; sr. v.p. P.R. Taylor Assocs., 1995-99; sr. rschr. Nat. Ctr. for Postsecondary Imrprovement, 1996—2002; pres. The Jackson Hole Higher Edn. Group, Inc., 1996—. Bd. dirs. Diebold, Inc., 1984—; mem. univ. grants com. Hong Kong, 1990-2003; mem. coun. Yale U., 1980-95; mgmt. cons. Stanford Mgmt. Co., 1991-93. Author: Stochastic Models of Buying Behavior, 1970, Marketing Management, 1972, Market Segmentation, 1972, Planning Models for Colleges and Universities, 1981, Endowment, 1991, Resource Allocation in Higher Education, 1996, Honoring The Trust, 2003; mem. editl. bd. Jour. Mktg. Rsch., 1964-70, Harcourt, Brace Jovanovich, 1965-71; contbr. articles to profl. jours. Bd. dirs. Palo Alto-Stanford chpt. United Way, 1978-80, Stanford U. Hosp., 1980-91, MAC, Inc., 1984-88, EDUCOM, 1983-86. Ford Found. faculty rsch. fellow, 1966-67 Mem. Am. Mktg. Assn. (bd. dirs. 1971-73, v.p. edn. 1976-77), Inst. Mgmt. Scis. Office: The Jackson Hole Higher Edn Group Inc PO Box 9849 Jackson WY 83002-9849

MASTEN, W. YONDELL, nursing educator; b. Alexandria, La., Sept. 7, 1940; d. Kelly and Alyne (Shankles) Bingham; m. Larry Burce Masten, May 27, 1960; children: Gordon, Larry Bryan, John, Lari. BS in Math., West Tex. State U., 1973, BSN, 1977; MS in Nursing, U. Tex., 1981; MS, Tex. Tech. U., 1978, PhD, 1985. Prof. Tex. Tech. U. Health Scis. Ctr. Sch. Nursing; women's health nurse practitioner, instr. Meth. Hosp. Sch. Nursing, Lubbock; head nurse Meth. Hosp., Lubbock; assoc. dean Tex. Tech. U. Health Scis. Ctr. Sch. Nursing. Faculty Tex. Tech. U., Lubbock. Contbr. articles to profl. jours. Mem. ANA, Assn. Women's Health Obstet. and Neonatal Nurses, Nat. League for Nursing, Human Factors Soc., Inst. Indsl. Engrs., Internat. Childbirth Edn. Assn., Sigma Theta Tau, Iota Mu.

MASTERS, BEDA M. elementary educator; b. McComb, Miss., Feb. 14, 1942; d. Robert C. and Selma Doris (Barksdale) Moak; m. Terry Labe Masters Sr., Oct. 12, 1940; children: Terry Labe Jr., Karen Denise Masters Ishee. AS, S.W. Miss. Jr. Coll., 1971; BS, U. So. Miss., 1975; M in Edn., William Carey Coll., 1981. Cert. elem. educator, Miss. Teller 1st Nat. Bank, McComb, 1971-72, Laurel, Miss., 1972-73; tchr. Jones County Schs., Laurel, 1975—. Presenter at reading confs. Mem. Internat. Reading Coun., Miss. Reading Coun., Laurel-Jones County Reading Coun. (pres. 1980-81, membership dir. 1988-89), Assn. for Excellence in Edn., PhiTheta Kappa, Phi Kappa Phi, Kappa Delta Pi, Delta Kappa Gamma (corr. sec. state Zeta Mu chpt. 1986-88, chmn. world fellowship 1990-92). Baptist. Avocations: swimming, sewing, cooking, travel, interior design. Home: 43 Jennings Masters Rd Laurel MS 39443-7728

MASTERS, JOHN CHRISTOPHER, psychologist, educator, writer; b. Terre Haute, Ind., Oct. 25, 1941; s. Robert William and Lillian Virginia (Decker) M.; m. Mary Jayne Capps, June 6, 1970; children— Blair Christopher, Kyle Alexander. AB, Harvard Coll., 1963; PhD, Stanford U., 1967. Asst. prof. Ariz. State U., Tempe, 1968-69; from asst. prof. to prof. U. Minn., Mpls., 1969-79; assoc. dir. Inst. Child Devel., 1974-79; Luce prof. pub. policy and the family, prof. psychology Vanderbilt U., Nashville, 1979-87, interim chair dept. psychology, 1986-88; pres. Profl. Mgmt. Group, Inc., 1991—; dir. Master Ventures, 1989—, Master Travel, 1989—. Assoc. editor: Child Development, 1973-76, Behavior Therapy: Techniques and Empirical Findings, 1974, 79, 88; editor: Psychol. Bull., 1987-89. Home: 4923 Old Oakleaf Dr Sarasota FL 34233-3947

MASTERS, JUDITH ANNE, elementary school educator; b. Fowler, Calif., Mar. 5, 1947; d. Thomas Clayton and Sarah Lois (Pearce) Hollingshead; m. Elmer Ray Masters, Aug. 5, 1966; children: Heather, Kimbereley, Paul, Aaron, Stacie. AA, Coll. of the Sequoias, Visalia, Calif., 1966; BA, So. Calif. Coll., 1975; MEd, Azusa Pacific U., 1987; M of Childhood Edn., Sch. of Bible Theology Sem., San Jacinto, Calif., 1988. Cert. elem. tchr., Calif. Dir. adult edn. Tranquility (Calif.) Sch. Dist., 1975-77; tchr. kindergarten Oliveview Christian Sch., Sylmar, Calif., 1977-79; tchr. kindergarten through 4th grades Hemet (Calif.) Unified Sch. Dist., 1979—; instr., cons./rschr. Sch. of Bible Theology Sem., 1979—. Cons. So. Calif. Theol. Sem., Stanton, 1992; mem. English textbook com. Hemet Unified Sch. Dist., 1983-84. Author: (children's books) Samson the Seasick Seagull, 1978, Elephant, Tiger, Kangaroo, 1980. Dir. Women's Missionary Coun., Riverside County, Calif., 1980-81; solicitor Am. Cancer Soc., Riverside County, 1984-85. Mem. NEA, Calif. Tchrs. Assn. (polit. action rep. 1992-93), Hemet Tchrs. Assn. (polit. action rep., sch. site rep. 1992-93). Republican. Mem. Assembly of God Ch. Avocations: knitting, reading, sewing, singing, travel. Home: 1400 E Menlo Ave Spc 36 Hemet CA 92544-3137 Office: Hemet Unified Sch 2350 W Latham Ave Hemet CA 92545-3637 also: Romana Elem Sch 41051 Whittier Ave Hemet CA 92544-6312

MASTERS, ROBERT EDWARD LEE, psychotherapist, neural researcher, human potential educator, philosopher; b. Jan. 4, 1927; s. Robert and Katherine (Leeper) Masters; m. Jean Houston, May 8, 1965. BA in Philosophy, U. Mo., 1951; PhD in Clin. Psychology, Humanistic Psychology Inst., 1974. Dir. Libr. of Sex Rsch., N.Y.C., 1962-66, Sensory Imagery Program, 1965-68; dir. rsch. Found. for Mind Rsch., N.Y.C. and Ashland, Oreg., 1965—. Dir. Zarathustra Project, Pomona, 1980—99; co-dir. Human Capacities Tng. Program, Ramapo, NJ, 1982—99; pvt. practice psychotherapy, neural re-edn., aging and geropsychology programs; prin. tchr. Hypnotherapist Tng., Pomona, 1982—99; pres. Human Capacities Corp., Ashland, 1982—. Author: Eros and Evil, 1962, Forbidden Sexual Behavior and Morality, 1964; co-author (with J. Houston): Varieties of Psychedelic Experience, 1966, Psychedelic Art, 1968; author: Mind Games, 1972, Listening to the Body, 1978, Psychophysical Method Exercises, vols. I-VI, 1983, The Goddess Sekhmet, 1987, The Masters Technique, 1987, Neurospeak, 1994, The Way to Awaken, 1997, Swimming Where Madmen Drown, 2002; contbr. articles to sci. publs., poetry, fiction and essays to profl. jours., lit. and art criticism and book revs.; author: Sekhmet-Images and Entrances, 2003. With USN, 1945—46, PTO. Grantee, Erickson Found., 1966, Kleiner Found., 1968, Babcock Found., 1970, Doris Duke Found., 1972. Fellow: Am. Acad. Clin. Sexologists (founder); mem.: AAAS, APA, N.Y. Acad. Scis., Am. Psychotherapy Assn. (diplomate), Assn. Humanistic Psychology, Am. Assn. Sex Educators, Counselors and Therapists, Am. Bd. Sexology (clin. supr.). Office: Found Mind Rsch PMB 501 2305 Ashland St Ste C Ashland OR 97520-3777

MASTERS, ROGER DAVIS, government and neurotoxicology educator; b. Boston, June 8, 1933; s. Maurice and S. Grace (Davis) M.; m. Judith Ann Rubin, June 6, 1956 (div. 1984); children— Seth J., William A., Katherine R.; m. Susanne R. Putnam, Aug. 25, 1984 BA, Harvard U., 1955; MA, U. Chgo., 1958, PhD, 1961; MA (hon.), Dartmouth Coll., 1974. Instr. dept. polit. sci. Yale U., 1961-62, asst. prof., 1962-67; assoc. prof. dept. govt. Dartmouth Coll., Hanover, N.H., 1967-73, prof., 1973-98, John Sloan Dickey Third Century prof., 1980-85, chmn. dept., 1986-89, Nelson A. Rockefeller prof., 1991-98, prof. emeritus, 1998—, rsch. prof., 1999—. Cultural attache Am. Embassy, Paris, 1969-71; chmn. France-Am. Commn. Edn. and Cultural Exch., 1969-71; vis. lectr. Yale U. Law Sch., 1988-89, Vt. Law Sch., 1993, 94; sect. editor Social Sci., Info., 1971—; chmn. exec. com. Gruter Inst. Law and Behavioral Rsch., 1995-98; pres. Found. for Neurosci. and Soc., 1998—. Author: The Nation Is Burdened, 1967, The Political Philosophy of Rousseau, 1968, The Nature of Politics, 1989, Beyond Relativism, 1993, Machiavelli, Leonardo, and the Science of Power, 1996, Fortune is a River, 1998; editor: Rousseau's Discourses, 1964, Rousseau's Social Contract, 1978; co-editor: Ostracism: A Social and Biological Phenomenon, 1986, Collected Writings of J.J. Rousseau, 1990—, Primate Politics, 1991, The Sense of Justice, 1992, The Neurotransmitter Revolution, 1994; editor Gruter Inst. Reader in Biology, Law, and Human Social Behavior, 1992. Served with AUS, 1955-57. Fulbright fellow Institut d'Etudes Politiques, Paris, 1958-59; joint Yale U.-Social Sci. Rsch. Coun. fellow, 1964-65; Guggenheim fellow, 1967-68; fellow Hastings Ctr. for Ethics and Life Scis., 1973-78. Mem. AAAS, Am. Polit. Sci. Assn., Assn. Polit. and Life Sci. (coun.), Am. Soc. for Legal and Polit. Philosophy, Internat. Soc. Human Ethology, Human Behavior Evolution Soc. Home: PO Box 113 South Woodstock VT 05071-0113 Office: Dartmouth Coll Dept Govt Silsby Hall HB6108 Hanover NH 03755 Business E-Mail: roger.d.masters@dartmouth.edu.

MASTRANGELO, BOBBI, artist, educator; b. Youngstown, Ohio, May 16, 1937; d. Herman Louis and Martha Bertha (Krause) Betschen; m. Alfred Anthony Mastrangelo, Dec. 20, 1958; children: Michael, Peter, Ann Marie. BS cum laude, SUNY, Buffalo, 1959. One-woman shows include Suffolk County Water Auth., Oakdale, N.Y., 1993—, N.Y. Hall of Sci., Corona, 1994, Mus. Pub. Works, Balt., 1996—, Islip (N.Y.) Mus., 1997, Toast Gallery, Port Jefferson, N.Y., 2003, Omni Gallery Invitational, Uniondale, N.Y., 2003; group shows include N.Y. Acad. Sci., N.Y.C., 1991, Staller Ctr. for Arts, Stony Brook, N.Y., 1992, Emerson Gallery, Hamilton Coll., Clinton, N.Y., 1995, Attleboro (Mass.) Mus., 2002; represented in permanent collections Balt. Pub. Works Mus., Heckscher Mus., Huntington, N.Y., Islip (N.Y.) Mus., N.Y.C. Fire Mus., Nat. Assn. Women Artists Permanent Collection, Jane Voorhees A. Zimmerli Art Mus., Rutgers U., others; recs. include Rejection, The Sound of Poetry, Nat. Libr. Poetry; poetry pub. in anthology From the Heart, 2003. Founder Com. for Litter Elimination and Neatness, 1986, chairperson, 1986-88. Grantee N.Y. Found. for Arts, 1992, 94; Paul Harris fellow Rotary Internat., 1996; recipient Disting. Alumni award Maryvale H.S., 1994, Aida Whedon Meml. award 1997. Mem. Nat. Assn. Women Artists (Eva Helman award 1992), Nat. Mus. Women in Arts, Art League L.I., Arts and Sci. Collaboration, N.Y. Soc. Women Artists, Smithtown Twp. Arts Coun. Avocations: sculptures, prints, hand paper making, poetry, creative writing. Home: 747 Coronado Dr Kissimmee FL 34759 E-mail: grateworks@aol.com.

MASTRO, VICTOR JOHN, mathematician, educator; b. N.Y.C., Sept. 15, 1948; s. Felix and Marie (Scardino) M.; m. Miriam Elena Bonano, Aug. 19, 1973; 1 child, Christopher. BS in Secondary Edn., Fordham U., 1970, MS in Secondary Edn., Math., 1973. Edn. cons., curriculum cons. Ind. Sch. 138-184, Bronx, N.Y., 1974-79; art sales cons. Intercraft Industries, Inc., Chgo., 1976-78; prof., coord. Hudson County C.C., Jersey City, N.J., 1979—; assoc. prof. math. Fordham U., Bronx, 1984—. Tutor vol. Hudson County C.C., 1979-92, faculty adviser, 1989-91; mentor, counselor Forum Italian Am. Educators, Bronx, 1982-87; speaker local radio programs; presenter workshops. Author multicultural and ethnomath. program, math. texts, videos and audio tapes, math. poem; contbr. articles to profl. publs. Mem. AAAS (text and video evaluator 1984-88), Am. Math. Assn., Nat. Coun. Tchrs. Math. (text evaluator). Roman Catholic. Achievements include development of multicultural mathematics programs for Afro-Americans, Native Americans, Hispanics, women, Italian, near- and far-East cultures. Home: 1907 Narragansett Ave Bronx NY 10461-1820 Office: Hudson County C C 168 Sip Ave Jersey City NJ 07306-3009

MATA, ELIZABETH ADAMS, English language educator, land investor; b. Raleigh, NC, Jan. 11, 1946; d. John Quincy Adams and Beulah Honeycutt; m. Juan Mata, June 21, 1968; children: Laura, Juan, Daniel. Student, Sweet Briar Coll., Paris, 1966-67; BA in French, Randolph-Macon Women's Coll., 1968; tchr. cert. in French and Spanish, N.C. State U., 1981; postgrad., U. Salamanca, Spain, 1983-86; MA in Spanish, NYU, 1986; cert. mentor tchr., N.C. State U., 1989; postgrad., Fordham U., 1994, U. N.C., 1995. Lic. real estate agt., NC; cert. ESL tchr. Tchr. ESL, Am. Inst., Madrid, 1968-69; tchr. English, Ay J Garriques, Madrid, 1968-74, pvt. classes, Madrid, 1975-78; tchr. French, Wake County Sch., Cary, NC, 1982—2003, tchr. Spanish, Apex, NC, 1982—; instr. ESL Wake Tech. Coll., Raleigh, NC, 1999—2003; Fulbright tchr. U. del Mar del Plata, Argentina, 2001—. Cons. ETS, 1999—2003. Named Tchr. of Yr., Apex HS, 1992-93. Mem. Am. Assn. Tchr. Spanish and Portuguese, Univ. Coun. on Edn., Alpha Kappa Delta (Beta Omicron chpt. hist. 1996-98, v.p. 1998-2000). Democrat. Avocations: sculpting, reading, gourmet cooking, restoring antiques, writing. Home: 643 Kings Fork Rd Cary NC 27511-5711

MATA, JOSEFINA, health education coordinator, educator; b. Juarez, Mex., Mar. 28, 1968; came to U.S., 1979; d. Angel and Irma Ulloa; m. Jesus Antonio Mata, Aug. 29, 1989; 1 child, Lizbeth Mata. BS, N.Mex. State U., 1991, MS, 1994, MPH, 1999. News translator Sta. RZOL Radio, El Paso, 1984-86; receptionist aid San Jacinto Sch., El Paso, Tex., 1985-86; nutritionist La Fe Clinic, El Paso, summer 1990; gang prevention and intervention counselor Families and Youth Inc., Las Cruces, N.Mex., 1992-93; health educator Adolescent Family Life, Las Cruces, 1993-95; health edn. and quality inspection coord. Ben Archer Health Ctr., Truth or Consequences, N.Mex., 1995-98; health edn. coord. La Clinica Familia, Las Cruces, 1998—. Mem. adv. bds. Corp. Extend in Svc., Las Cruces, 1993, Health Sci. Dept. N.Mex. State U., Las Cruces, 1995-98, Sierra County Adv. Sch., 1995-98, Am. Cancer Soc., Sierra County, N.Mex., 1995-98. Mem. cmty. involvement Kellog Found. N.Mex. state U., 1997; mem. Nat. Faculty Comenzando Bien March of Dimes Initiative. Grantee N.Mex. Dept. Health, 1994, 98, N.Mex. Teen Pregnancy Coalition peer edn. program, 1996-98; recipient Marathon Participation award Leukemia Soc. Am., 1996. Mem. MPH Assn., Am. Pub. Health Assn., USA Track & Field Assn., Mesilla Valley Track Club, Tobacco Free Coalition. Roman Catholic. Avocation: road racing. Office: La Clinica Familia 1100 S Main St Ste A Las Cruces NM 88005-2952

MATAN, LILLIAN KATHLEEN, educator, designer; b. Boston, Aug. 18, 1937; d. George Francis and Lillian May (Herbert) Archambault; m. Joseph A. Matan, Aug. 6, 1960; children: Maria, Meg, Tony, Elizabeth, Joan, Molly. BS, Seton Hall Coll., 1960; MA, San Francisco State U., 1984; EdD, U. San Francisco, 1999. Tchr. St. Jane de Chantal, Bethesda, Md., 1956-60; tchr. home econs. Surrottsville (Md.) H.S., 1960-61; tchr., head home econs. dept. Bruswick (Md.) H.S., 1972-73; designer Dudley Kelley and Assocs., San Francisco, Calif., 1976-84; designer (prin.) K. Matan Antiques and Interiors, Ross, Calif., 1985-87; designer Charles Lester Assocs., San Francisco, 1987-88; dean of students St. Rose Acad., San Francisco, 1988-90; dir., asst. devel. The Branson Sch., Ross, Calif., 1990-92; prin. St. Anselm Sch., San Anselmo, Calif., 1993-94; adminstrv. head Ring Mt. Day Sch., Tiburon, Calif., 1995-96; sabbatical, 1997-98. Ednl. cons. Head Start, Frederick County, Md., 1972-73. Pres. Cath. Charities, Marin County, Calif.; mem. Ecumenical Assn. for Housing, Marin County. Mem. KM (dame), Am. Soc. of Interior Designers, Am. Assn. Family and Consumer Scis., Serra Club, Phi Delta Kappa. Democrat. Home: PO Box 1140 Ross CA 94957-1140 E-mail: lmatan6561@aol.com.

MATARAZZO, RUTH GADBOIS, psychologist, educator; b. New London, Conn., Nov. 9, 1926; d. John Stuart and Elizabeth (Wood) Gadbois; m. Joseph D. Matarazzo, Mar. 26, 1949; children: Harris, Elizabeth, Sara. AB, Brown U., 1948; MA, Washington U., St. Louis, 1952, PhD, 1955. Diplomate in clin. psychology and clin. neuropsychology Am. Bd. Examiners Profl. Psychology. Rsch. fellow pediat. Washington U. Med. Sch., 1954-55; rsch. fellow psychology Harvard U. Med. Sch., 1955-57; asst. prof. med. psychology Oreg. Health Scis. U., Portland, 1957-63, assoc. prof., 1963-68, prof., 1968—, prof. emeritus, 1997—. Woman liaison officer Assn. Am. Med. Coll.s, 1979—90; cons. Tillamook Job Corps, Oreg. Bd. Med. Examiners, Social Security Adminstrn., Portland Ctr. Hearing and Speech. Author (E. Greif): (book) Behavioral Approaches to Rehabilitation: Coping with Change, 1982; contbr. chapters to books, articles to profl. jours. Fellow: Oreg. Psychol. Assn. (past pres.), Am. Psychol. Assn. (mem. policy and planning bd., mem. edn. and tng. bd., vice-chair accreditation bd., chair accreditation task force, accreditation bd.); mem.: AAAS, Portland Psychol. Assn. (past pres.), We. Psychol. Assn. (bd. dirs.), Sigma Xi. Home: 1934 SW Vista Ave Portland OR 97201-2455

MATEJKOVIC, EDWARD MICHAEL, athletic director, coach; b. Coatesville, Pa., July 19, 1947; s. Edward Michael and Helen Theresa (Kowalczyk) M.; m. Debra Lynne Wetherby, June 28, 1996; children: Jennifer Lynn, Leigh Allison, Jude Michael. BS, West Chester State U., 1969, MEd, 1975; EdD, Temple U., 1983. Tchr., coach Gt. Valley Sch. Dist., Malvern, Pa., 1970-82; asst. facilities dir. Temple U., Phila., 1982-83; athletic dir., football coach SUNY, Brockport, 1984-95; athletic dir. West Chester U., 1995—. Cons. Ednl. Cons., Inc., Brockport, 1985—; v.p. Ea. Collegiate Athletic Conf.; pres. Pa. State Athletic Conf. Contbr. articles to profl. jours. Mem. Games for the Physically Challenged, Brockport, 1986-90. Mem. AAHPERD, Am. Football Coaches Assn., Nat. Assn. Coll. Dirs. Athletes. Republican. Roman Catholic. Avocations: weight lifting, golfing, furniture refinishing, camping. Home: 529 E Saxony Dr Exton PA 19341-2066 Office: West Chester U Rm 220 Sturzebecker Health Sci Ctr West Chester PA 19383 E-mail: ematejkovi@wcupa.edu.

MATERA, CRISTINA, obstetrician-gynecologist, educator; b. Englewood, N.J., Sept. 29, 1960; MD, NYU, 1986. Cert. in ob-gyn. and reproductive endocrinology and infertility. Resident in ob-gyn. Columbia Presbyn. Med. Ctr./Presbyn. Hosp., N.Y.C., 1986-90, fellow, 1990-92; asst. prof. Columbia P&S, 1990—. Office: 50 E 77th St New York NY 10021-5856

MATERA, FRANCES LORINE, elementary school educator; b. Eustis, Nebr., June 28, 1926; d. Frank Daniel and Marie Mathilda (Hess) Daiss; m. Daniel Matera, Dec. 27, 1973. Luth. tchrs. diploma, Concordia U., Seward, Nebr., 1947, BS in Edn., 1956; MEd, U. Oreg., 1963. Elementary tchr. Our Savior's Luth. Ch., Colorado Springs, Colo., 1954-57; tchr. 5th grade Monterey (Calif.) Pub. Schs., 1957-59; tchr. 1st grade Roseburg (Oreg.) Schs., 1959-60; tchr. several schs. Palm Springs (Calif.) Unified Sch. Dist., 1960—93; tchr. 3rd grade Vista del Monte Sch., Palm Springs, Calif., 1973-93; ret., 1993. Named Tchr. of the Yr., Palm Springs Unified Schs. Mem. Kappa Kappa Iota (chpt. and state pres.). E-mail: Franmatera7@aol.com.

MATERO, JANET LOUISE, counselor, educator; b. Cadillac, Mich., Sept. 1, 1950; d. Leonard Egbert and Helen Marie (Peterson) Mattison; m. Michael Edgar Blanehard, Sept. 12, 1970 (div. Mar. 20, 1976); 1 child, Jennifer; Paul Able Matero, June 20, 1987; stepchildren: Michael, Timothy. AA, Northwestern Mich. Coll., Traverse City, 1970; BA, Ctrl. Mich. U., Mt. Pleasant, 1977, MA, 1980; PhD with high distinction, Trinity Coll. and Sem., Newburgh, Ind., 1996. Lic. profl. counselor, Mich. Sch. social worker Adams Ctrl. Schs., Monroe, Ind., 1973-75; career devel. counselor Region 7B Employment/Tng. Consortium, Harrison, Mich., 1977-78, dir. counseling programs, 1978-81; dir. counseling Gogebic C.C., Ironwood, Mich., 1981-84, dean student svcs., interim pres., 1984-89; pvt. counselor Christian Counseling Svcs., Negaunee, Mich., 1990—. Mem. Pvt. Industry Coun., Mich. Manpower, Ironwood, 1983-89; chair bd. trustees planning com. Gogebic C.C., Ironwood, 1985-89, ednl. cons., 1990-91; mem. faculty curriculum rev. com. Trinity Coll., Newburgh, Ind., 1996—; condr. workshops nd seminars. Vol. ARC, Decatur, Ind., 1970-75; vol. probation officer Isabella County Dist. Ct., Mt. Pleasant, Mich., 1975-80, Crisis Ctr., Ironwood, 1982-89; vol. counselor Women's Shelter, Marquette, Mich., 1993—. Mem. ACA, Am. Assn.. Christian Counselors, Mich. Counseling Assn., Mich. Assn. Marriage and Family Counselors, Internat. Assn. for Marriage and Family Counselors. Lutheran. Avocations: travel, cooking, sewing, gardening. Office: Christian Counseling & Cons Svcs Negaunee MI 49866 E-mail: jlmatero@portup.com.

MATHAY, JOHN PRESTON, elementary education educator; b. Youngstown, Ohio, Jan. 27, 1942; s. Howard Ellsworth and Mary Clara (Siple) M.; m. Sandra Elizabeth Rhoades, June 9, 1973 (div. Jan. 1986); children: Elizabeth Anne, Sarah Susannah; m. Judith Anne Matthy, June 19, 1988; 1 child, Andrew Micah. BA in History, Va. Mil. Inst., Lexington, 1964; Cert. Teaching, Cleve. State U., 1972; postgrad., Mich. State U., 1964-65; MEd, Westminster Coll., New Wilmington, 1986. Cert. asst. supt., elem. tchr., elem. prin., high sch. prin. Cabinet maker Artisian Cabinet, Orwig Cabinets, Cleve. and Howland, Ohio, 1970-72; tchr. Urban Community Sch., Cleve., 1972-73, Pymatuning Valley Schs., Andover, Ohio, 1973—. Cross country coach, 7th and 8th grade track coach, Andover. Bd. mem. Badger Sch. Bd., Kinsman, Ohio; trustee Kinsman Libr.; trustee, elder Kinsman Presbyn. Ch. Capt. U.S. Army Res., 1966-69. Martha Holden Jennings Found. scholar, Cleve., 1976. Mem. ASCD, Pymatuning Valley Edn. Assn. (pres. 1975-76, 91-92, 94-95), Ohio Edn. Assn., Am. Legion, Rotary (pres. 1991-92, sec. 1992-93, treas. 1995-98, Paul Harris fellow), Masons (jr. deacon 1984-85, 32d deg., York Rite commandery), Ashtabula County Antique Engine Club, Phi Delta Kappa. Republican. Presbyterian. Avocations: sailing, skating, ham radio, french and indian war reenacting, fishing, reading. Office: Pymatuning Valley Schs W Main St Andover OH 44003 Home: PO Box 418 Kinsman OH 44428-0228 E-mail: jamath@suite224.net.

MATHENY, ELIZABETH ANN, special education educator; b. South Bend, Ind., Jan. 31, 1954; d. Walter Lee and Josephine Mary (Hickey) M. BS in Spl. Edn., Tenn. Tech. U., 1978; MEd in Spl. Edn., West Ga. Coll., 1987; postgrad., Troy State U., 1991-92. Cert. spl. edn. tchr. Tchr. spl. edn. Hi-Hope Tng. Ctr., Lawrenceville, Ga., 1978; trainer Sunshine Sheltered workshop Assn. for Retarded Citizens, Knoxville, Tenn., 1979; tchr. spl. edn. Roopville (Ga.) Elem. Sch., 1979-83, Berkeley Lake Elem. Sch., Duluth, Ga., 1983-84, Baker H.S., Columbus, Ga., 1984-91, Spencer H.S., Columbus, 1991—. Mem.-at-large adv. bd. Muscogee County Spl. Olympics. Mem. NEA, Alpha Delta Kappa (Rho chpt. pres. 1994-96, pres.-elect 1992-94, rec. sec. 1990-92). Republican. Baptist. Avocations: arts and crafts, gardening, home renovating, walking, swimming. Home: 3615 Walton St Columbus GA 31907-2550 Office: Muscogee County Sch Dist Spencer H S Columbus GA 31903

MATHER, BETTY BANG, musician, educator; b. Emporia, Kans., Aug. 7, 1927; d. Read Robinson and Shirley (Smith) Bang; m. Roger Mather, Aug. 3, 1973. MusB, Oberlin Conservatory, 1949; MA, Columbia U., 1951. Instr. U. Iowa, Iowa City, 1953-58, asst. prof., 1959-65, assoc. prof., 1965-73, prof., 1973-96, prof. emeritus, 1996—. Editor Romney Press; vis. instr. U. Iowa, Iowa City, 1952-53. Rec. artist; author: Interpretation of French Music from 1675-1775, 1973, (with David Lasocki) Free Ornamentation for Woodwind Instruments from 1700-1775, 1976 (with Lasocki) The Classical Woodwind Cadenza, 1978, (with Lasocki) The Art of Preluding, 1984 (with Dean Karns) Dance Rhythms of the French Baroque, 1987, (with Gail Gavin) The French Noel, 1996. Mem. Nat. Flute Assn. (v.p. 1986-87, pres. 1987-88, chmn. bd. dirs. 1988-89). Home: 715 George St Iowa City IA 52246

MATHER, ELIZABETH G. TIFFANY, occupational therapist, educator; b. Phila., Oct. 21, 1928; d. Hans Cochrane and Sarah Elizabeth (Hall) Gordon; m. Phillip Miller Tiffany, Sept. 27, 1952 (dec. Dec. 1955); 1 child, Jennifer Sarah; m. Robert Worrell Mather, Jan. 11, 1986. BS, U. Pa., 1950, Cert. in Occupl. Therapy, 1951; MEd, Temple U., Phila., 1974. Occupl. therapist St. Christopher's Hosp. for Children, Phila., 1951-53; dir. occupl. therapy Retreat State Hosp., Hunlock Creek, Pa., 1953-58; dir. nursery sch. Summit Presbyn. Ch., Phila., 1958-60; occupl. therapist Soc. for crippled Children and Adults, Phila., 1960-62, Norristown (Pa.) State Hosp., 1962-64; dir. occupl. therapy Ea. Pa. Psychiat. Inst., Phila., 1964-71; assoc. prof. occupl. therapy Temple U., Phila., 1971-86, chmn. dept. occupl. therapy, 1986-90; ret. Book reviewer Readings of Am. Orthopsychiat. Assn.; contbr. chpts. to books. Mem. profl. adv. bd. Wissahickon Hospice, Phila., 1993-95; mem. Women's Bd., Burt-Melville Dept., Thomas Jefferson Hosp., Phila., 1992-95; bd. dirs. N.W. Interfaith Movement, Phila.; mem. com. on univ. access Temple U., Phila. Temple U. study leave, 1985. Fellow Am. Occupl. Therapy Assn. (state rep. 1972-74, Award of Recognition 1977); mem. Pa. Occupl. Therapy Assn., Am. Orthopsychiat. Assn., World fedn. Occupl. Therapy, Kendal-Crosslands (com. bd. 2001—). Mem. Soc. Of Friends. Avocations: hiking, travel, reading, sailing, music. Home: 122 Crosslands Dr Kennett Square PA 19348-2015

MATHER, IAN HEYWOOD, cell biologist, educator; b. Cheadle, Eng., June 24, 1945; came to US, 1973; naturalized, 1993; s. Eric Heywood and May (Chandley) M.; m. Frances Marie Twohig, May 25, 1974 (dec. Feb. 20, 2001); children: Stephen Eric, Elizabeth Heywood. BSc, U. Wales, 1966, PhD, 1971. Rsch. fellow U. Kent, Canterbury, England, 1970-72; rsch. assoc. Purdue U., West Lafayette, Ind., 1973-75; asst. prof. U. Md., College Park, 1975-80, assoc. prof., 1980-85, prof. animal scis., 1985—, disting. rsch. fellow, 2002—; Fogarty Found. sr. internat. fellow European Molecular Biology Lab., Heidelberg, Fed. Republic Germany, 1989-90. Mem. cell biology program NSF, Washington, 1978, 84-88; chmn. Gordon Conf. on Mammary Gland Biology, 1989. Contbr. articles to Jour. Biol. Chemistry,

Jour. Cell Biology, Biochem. Jour., Exptl. Cell Rsch., others; mem. editl. bd. Jour. Mammary Gland Biol. Neoplasia. Grantee NSF, 1978-89, 92-95, USDA, 1980, 85-89, 95—. Mem. AAAS, Biochem. Soc. (London), Am. Soc. Biochem. Molecular Biology, Am. Soc. Cell Biology, Am. Dairy Sci. Assn. (Am. Cyanamid, Dean Food awards), NY Acad. Sci., Sigma Xi (award). Achievements include research on epithelial cell polarity, cell biology of milk secretion. Office: U Md Dept Animal And Avian Scis College Park MD 20742-0001 E-mail: im2@umail.umd.edu.

MATHES, MARY LOUISE, state official, retired educator; b. Williamstown, Ky., July 26, 1919; d. Joseph Edward and Omega Mae (Rodgers) Myers; m. John Seldon Steers, Mar. 3, 1939 (div. 1945); 1 child, Linda Steers Dorn; m. Forest Andrew Mathes, Mar. 27, 1959; children: Forest Alva, Bette Josephine. AA, San Angelo Jr. Coll., 1958; BS in Edn., Tex. Wesleyan Coll., 1961; MA in Edn., Libr. Sci., Ariz. State U., 1969, MA in Edn., Audio Visual, 1972. Cert. tchr., Tex., N.Mex., sch. libr., Ariz., master tchr. libr. sci., Ariz. Tchr. Arlington (Tex.) Sch. Dist., 1961-64, Scottsdale (Ariz.) Sch. Dist., 1964-66, sch. libr., 1966-78; now ret.; apptd. by gov. of Ariz. to Coun. for State Art Facts & Dept. Pub. Recs. & Archives, 1994—. Sec. Scottsdale Edn. Assn., 1967-68, Scottsdale unit NEA, 1966-67; chmn. Elem. Sch. Librs., Scottsdale Sch. Dist., 1973; treas. Ariz. State Libr. Assn., 1973-74; past pres. Maricopa County Libr. Assn.; mem. Ariz. State Reading Coun., Kiva Elem. Sch. PTA, Scottsdale. Contbr. articles, columns to various publs. Vol. USO-ARC, 1941-45, Shadow Mountain Home Health Care, Ariz., 1986—; mem. ptnrs. program Ariz. State U., 1985; organizer, mgr. support group for ret. tchrs., Scottsdale, 1986—; docent Scottsdale Hist. Mus.; mem. Scottsdale Sr. Alliance, 1992-93, adv.; pres. Fun After Fifty, North Scottsdale United Meth. Ch., liturgist, active worship com., adminstrn. bd. Named Vol. of Yr., Beverly Enterprises, 1991-92. Mem. Scottsdale Boys and Girls Club (life, tutor latchkey kids 1993), Scottsdale Meml. Hosp. Aux. (life), Las Rancheras Rep. Women, Delta Kappa Gamm. Avocations: modeling, acting, volunteer work, public speaking. Home: 6263 E Marilyn Rd Scottsdale AZ 85254-2576

MATHEW, MARTHA SUE CRYDER, retired education educator; b. Hallsville, Ohio, Feb. 21, 1928; d. Earl and Minnie Ada (Hough) Cryder; m. Guy Wilbur Mathew, Mar. 25, 1949; children: John G., Jeffrey Bruce. BS, Ohio No. U., 1966. Cert. tchr., Ohio. Tchr. Immaculate Conception Sch., Celina, Ohio, 1961-64, Zane Trace Local Sch., Chillicothe, Ohio, 1964-93; ret., 1993. Mem. Juvenile Ct. Rev. Bd., Ross County, Chillicothe. Vol. ARC; band mem. Cicleville Pumpkin Show. Named Educator of Yr., Zane Trace Local, Ross County, 1993. Mem. Order Ea. Star (Worthy Matron 1976, 88, Evergreen chpt. 169, Adelphi), Ladies Oriental Shrine (treas., sec., v.p., pres.), Delta Kappa Gamma (com.). Republican. Methodist. Home: Kingston, Ohio. Died July 22, 2000.

MATHEWS, B. J. secondary education educator; b. Navasota, Tex., Nov. 27, 1948; s. Roy Lee Mathews and Clarissa Fuller-Mathews. BS, Jarvis Christian Coll., 1972; diploma in art, Stratford Career Inst., 2003; student, Art Ctr., Waco, TSTI, Southwest Sch. Art, San Antonio, TX, McLennan Community Coll., Waco. Cert. tchr., Tex., in specialized art, Art Instruction Sch., Minn. Tchr. Rochester (N.Y.) City Sch. Dist., 1972-75, Mexia (Tex.) Ind. Sch. Dist., 1977-92, Dallas Ind. Sch. Dist., 1992-93; prison tchr. Windham Sch. Dist., Hondo, Tex., 1993—2001; tchr. GED program Juvenile Detention Residential Ctr., Hondo, 1994-97. Publ. (songs) Ride the Tide, 1997, Desire Afire, 1998. Mem.: Broadcast Music Inc. Avocations: reading, writing, portrait painting, composing music, calligraphic lettering. Home: PO Box 971 Mexia TX 76667 Office: Texas Youth Commission 116 Burleson Rd Mart TX 76664

MATHEWS, BARBARA BAILEY, special education educator; b. Cambridge, Mass., Apr. 20, 1943; d. Herbert Sternbergh and Inez (Wells) Bailey; m. J.D. Mathews, Aug. 20, 1966 (div. 1987); children: David Herbert, Diana Grace. AB, Syracuse U., 1965, MS, 1992; postgrad., SUNY, Brockport, 1965-66, SUNY, Oswego, 1968-70. Cert. spl. edn. tchr., German tchr., sci. tchr., N.Y. Jr. high sch. German tchr., Phoenix, N.Y., 1965-68; high sch. German tchr. Parish, N.Y., 1968-71; sci. and German tchr. North Syracuse, N.Y., 1984-91; spl. educator resource room North Syracuse Cen. Schs., 1992-94; spl. educator Westmoreland Ctrl. Schs., N.Y., 1994-95. Steering com. ann. sci. fair North Syracuse Schs., 1985-87. Bd. mgrs. North Area YMCA, Liverpool, N.Y., 1982-84. Mem. Delta Phi Alpha, Chi Omega (past pres. alumnae, treas. 1966—). Home: 8100 Maple Rd Clay NY 13041-8908

MATHEWS, CHERI RENE, speech pathologist; b. Salmon, Idaho, Sept. 19, 1958; d. Howard Eugene and Ruth Ellen (Billings) Van Komen; m. James William Mathews, Sept. 10, 1983. BA in Speech and Hearing Pathology, Northwest Nazarene Coll.; MS in Speech Pathology, Idaho State U. Speech/lang. pathologist Humboldt County (Nev.) Sch. Dist., Winnemueca, 1982-83, Washoe County (Nev.) Sch. Dist., Reno, 1983—. Sec. Neighborhood Watch Program, Reno, 1984-86. Mem. Am. Speech Lang. and Hearing Assn. (cert. clin. competence). Avocations: stained glass, needlework, reading, gardening. Home: 9375 Pagoda Way Reno NV 89506-9638

MATHEWS, DONA JUNE, elementary educator; b. Shattuck, Okla., July 16, 1940; d. Cecil C. and Ferne T. (Wingo) m. BS in Edn., S.W. Okla. State U., Weatherford, 1962, M in Teaching, 1964, diploma reading specialist, 1967. Tchr. Pauls Elem. Sch., Attica, Kans., 1962-67; 2d grade tchr. and reading specialist Unified Sch. Dist. 210, Hugoton, Kans., 1967-91; pub. and pvt. tutor and reading asst. Vici (Okla.) Pub. Schs., 1991—. Mem. Internat. Reading Assn. Coun., High Plains Reading Coun. (pres.), Delta Kappa Gamma (pres.).

MATHEWS, E. ANNE JONES, library educator and administrator, consultant; b. Phila; d. Edmond Fulton and Anne Ruth (Reichner) Jones; m. Frank Samuel Mathews, June 16, 1951; children: Lisa Anne Mathews-Bingham, David Morgan, Lynne Elizabeth Bietenhader-Mathews, Alison Fulton Sawyer. AB, Wheaton Coll., 1949; MA, U. Denver, 1965, PhD, 1977. Field staff Intervarsity Christian Fellowship, Chgo., 1949-51; interviewer supr. Colo. Market Rsch. Svcs., Denver, 1952-64; reference libr. Oreg. State U., Corvallis, 1965-67; program dir. Ctrl. Colo. Libr. Sys., Denver, 1969-70; inst. dir. U.S. Office of Edn., Inst. Grant, 1979; dir. pub. rels., prof. Grad. Sch. Librarianship and Info. Mgmt. U. Denver, 1970-76, prof., dir. continuing edn., 1977-80; dir. office libr. programs, office ednl. rsch., improvement US Dept. Edn., Washington, 1986-91; dir. Nat. Libr. Edn., Washington, 1992-94; cons. Acad. Ednl. Devel., Washington, 1994—; cons. mil. installation vol. edn. rev. Am. Coun. on Edn., 1990—; from asst. prof. to prof., 1977—85. Mem. adv. com. Golden H.S., 1973—77; faculty assoc. Danforth Found., 1974—84; mem. secondary sch. curriculum com. Jefferson County Pub. Schs., Colo., 1976—78; vis. lectr. Simmons Coll. Sch. L.S., Boston, 1977; mem. book and libr. adv. com. USIA, 1981—91; spkr. in field; cons. USIA, 1984—85; del. Internat. Fedn. Libr. Assns., 1984—93; mem. adv. coun. White House Conf. on Librs. and Info. Svcs., 1991; cons. Walden U., Mpls., 2001. Author, editor 6 books; contbr. articles to profl. jours., numerous chpts. to books. Mem. rural librs. and humanities program Colo. planning and resource bd. NEH, 1982—83; bd. mgrs. Friends Found. of Denver Pub. Libr., 1976—82; pres. Faculty Women's Club, Colo. Sch. Mines, 1963—64; bd. dirs. Jefferson County Libr. Found., 1996—, v.p., 1997—2000. Mem.: ALA (visionary leaders com. 1987—89, mem. coun. 1979—83, com. on accreditation 1984—85, orientation com. 1974—77, 1983—84, pub. rels. com.), English Speaking Union, Assn. Libr. and Info. Sci. Edn. (comm. com. 1978—80, program com. 1977—78), Colo. Libr. Assn. (pres. 1974, bd. dirs. 1973—75, continuing edn. com. 1976—80), Mountain Plains Libr. Assn. (profl. devel. com. 1979—80, pub. rels. and publs. com. 1973—75, continuing edn. com. 1973—76), Am. Soc. Info. Sci. (chmn. pub. rels. 1971), Naples Philharm. League, Pelican Bay Women's League Fla., Mountain Rep. Women's Club (v.p. 1997—2000), Mt. Vernon (Colo.) Country Club, Cosmos Club (Washington). Avocations: travel, reading, museum and gallery activities, volunteer work. Home (Summer): 492 Mount Evans Rd Golden CO 80401-9626 E-mail: afmathews2@earthlink.net.

MATHEWS, MARSHA ANDERSON, English educator, poet, minister; b. St. Petersburg, FLa., Oct. 29, 1952; d. Allen Conrad and Doris Marsh A.; children: Gena Renee, Gretchen J. BA with high honors, Univ. Fla., 1974; MA, Fla. State Univ., 1980, PhD, 1987; MDiv, Asbury Theol. Sem., 1995. Tchg. asst. Fla. State Univ., Tallahassee, 1978-86; asst. prof. English Va. Intermont Coll., Bristol, 1987-91; adj. prof. Asbury Coll., Wilmore, Ky., 1991-95; pastor United Meth. Ch. Holston conf., 1995-2000; adj. prof. Univ. Va., Wise, 2000, Mountain Empire Cmty. Coll., Big Stone Gap, Ga., 2000; asst. prof. English Dalton (Ga.) State Coll., 2001—. Dir. Wesley Found. Campus Ministries, United Meth. Ch., 1996-2000. Contbr. articles to profl. jours. Clown, visits hosp. and nursing homes, 1996—; vol. Hospice of N.W. Ga. Mem. MLA, Nat. Coun. Tchrs. English, Assoc. Writing Program, Internat.Soc. Humor Studies, Phi Beta Kappa, Theta Phi, Lambda Iota Tau. Avocations: travel, water sports, Scrabble, reading. Home: 902 Cascade Dr #40 Dalton GA 30720 Office: Dalton State Coll 213 N College Dr Dalton GA 30720

MATHEWS, PAUL JOSEPH, health educator; b. Washington, Aug. 17, 1944; s. Paul Joseph and Ruth Irene (O'Malley) M.; m. Loretta Jeanne Calvo; children: Heather Marie, Amy Elizabeth, Timothy Hunter. AS, Quinnipiac Coll., 1971, BS, 1975; MPA, U. Hartford, 1978; EdS, U. Mo., Kansas City, 1989, PhD, 1998. Registered respiratory therapist; lic. respiratory therapist, Kans. Instr., clin. coord. New Britain (Conn.) Gen. Hosp., 1971-74; instr. Quinnipiac Coll., Hamden, Conn., 1974-76; chief respiratory therapy dept. Providence Hosp., Holyoke, Mass., 1974-80, dir. cardiology/neurology, 1977-80, asst. dir. planning, 1980-81; asst. prof. U. Kans. Sch. Allied Health, Kansas City, 1981-88, assoc. prof. respiratory care edn., 1988—, chmn. dept. respiratory care edn., 1981-93, assoc. prof. phys. therapy Grad. Sch., 1992—; U. Kans. Adj. assoc. prof. Ctr. on Aging U. Kans. Med. Ctr., 1987—; hon. prof. U. Costa Rica, San Jose, 1987—, U. Santa Paula, Costa Rica, 2000—; vis. prof. Nat. U. Medicine and Pharmacy, Ho Chi Mihn City, Vietnam, 2001—02; cons. FDA, 1988, NIH, 1988, 89, SUNY, Stony Brook, 1990, USPHS, 1994, 95, 1997-2001, Singapore Gen. Hosp., 1997-, Coll. Santa Paula, 1998- ; prin. Clin. Legal Cons., 1998—; hon. prof. Nat. U. of Medicine, Ho Chi Mihu City, Vietnam, 2001—02, cons., 2001. Mem. editl. bd. Nursing, 1989—, Neonatal Intensive Care, 1990—, Jour. Respiratory Care Edn., 1993—, Respiratory Therapy, 1988—, Respiratory Therapy Intern, 1991—, Respiratory Care Management, 1998—, RPN, 2002; sect. editor Focus, 1998—; author books, videotapes, and audiotapes in field; contbr. articles to profl. jours., chpts. in books; chair editl. bd. RPN Webzine, 2000. Recipient Creative Achievement award Puritan-Bennett Corp., 1984, 85, A. Gerald Shapiro award N.J. Soc. for Respiratory Care, 1990; internat. fellow Project HOPE, 1987, 92. Fellow: Am. Coll. Chest Physicians, Soc. Critical Care Medicine (chair respiratory care sect. 2001—02), Am. Assn. Respiratory Care (life; bd. dirs. 1984—87, v.p. 1987, pres.-elect 1988, pres. 1989), Coll. Critical Care Medicine; mem.: Midwest Bioethics Ctr., N.Y. Acad. Scis., Philippine Respiratory Care Soc. (hon.), Phi Lambda Theta, Lambda Beta, Sigma Xi. Avocations: scuba diving, reading, travel. Home: 8844 Hemlock Dr Overland Park KS 66212-2946 Office: U Kans Med Ctr 3901 Rainbow Blvd Kansas City KS 66160-0001

MATHEWS, WILLIAM EDWARD, neurological surgeon, educator; b. Indpls., July 12, 1934; s. Ples Leo and Roxie Elizabeth (Allen) M.; m. Eleanor Jayne Comer, Aug. 24, 1956 (div. 1976); children: Valerie, Clarissa, Marie, Blair; m. Carol Ann Koza, Sept. 12, 1987; 1 child, William Kyle. BS, Ball State U., 1958; DO, Kirksville Coll. Osteo. Med., 1961; MD, U. Calif., Irvine, 1962; fellow, Armed Forces Trauma Sch., Ft. Sam Houston, Tex., 1967-68. Diplomate Am. Bd. Neurol. and Orthopedic Surgery, Am. Bd. Pain Mgmt., Am. Bd. Indsl. Medicine, Am. Bd. Spinal Surgeons (v.p. 1990-92), Am. Bd. Forensic Medicine, Am. Bd. Traumatic Stress, Am. Bd. Clin. Neurosurgery, Am. Bd. Spinal Surgery. Intern Kirksville (Mo.) Osteo. Hosp., 1961-62; resident neurosurgery Los Angeles County Gen. Hosp., 1962-67; resident in neurosurgery Rancho Los Amigos Spinal Rehab. Ctr., 1964-65; with Brooke Army Hosp., Ft. Sam Houston, 1967-68; with 8th field hosp. U.S. Army Neurosurgeon C.O. & 933 Med. Corp, Vietnam, 1968-69; chief neurosurgery Kaiser Med. Group, Walnut Creek, Calif., 1969-77; staff neurosurgeon Mt. Diablo Med. Ctr., Concord, Calif., 1977—. Student rsch. fellow electromyography NIH, 1959—61; asst. prof. biochemistry Kirksville Coll. Osteo. Medicine, 1958—62; asst. prof. neuroanatomy U. Calif. Coll. Medicine, 1962—65; sec. Am. Fedn. Med. Edn., 1997—; chmn. Am. Bd. Spinal Surgery, 1998, Am. Bd. Med. Accreditation, 1999—; assoc. prof. dept. neurosci. Touro U. Coll. Osteo. Medicine. Author: Intracerebral Missile Injuries, 1972, Intrasellar Chordoma, 1976, Intraoperative Myelography, 1982, Thin Slice Computed Tomography of the Cervical Spine, 1985, Early Return to Work Following Cervical Disc Surgery, 1991, Iatrogenic Tethering of the Spinal Cord, 1998, Operative Treatment of Cervical Spondylotic Myelopathy, 2001, Surgical Treatment of Spondylotic Myelopathy, 2002; contbr. articles to profl. jours. Mem. adv. com. Rep. Presdl. Selection Com. Maj. U.S. Army, 1967-69, Vietnam. Recipient Disting. Svc. award Internat. Biography, 1987; scholar Psi Sigma Alpha, 1957. Fellow Congress Neurol. Surgeons (joint sect. on neurotrauma), Royal Coll. Medicine, Am. Acad. Neurologic and Orthopedic Surgeons (pres. 1981-82, bd. dirs. 1990—), Bay Area Spinal Surgery Soc., Internat. Coll. Surgeons; mem. AMA, Calif. Med. Assn., San Francisco Neurologic, Contra Costa County Med. Soc. Roman Catholic. Avocations: pen and ink art, golf, gardening. E-mail: bayareaneuro@aol.com.

MATHEWSON, HUGH SPALDING, anesthesiologist, educator; b. Washington, Sept. 20, 1921; s. Walter Eldridge and Jennie Lind (Jones) M.; m. Dorothy Ann Gordon, 1943 (div. 1952); 1 child, Jane Mathewson Holcombe; m. Hazel M. Jones, 1953 (div. 1978); children: Geoffrey K., Brian E., Catherine E. Brock, Jennifer A. Jehle; m. Judith Ann Mahoney, 1979 (div. 1990). Student, Washburn U., 1938-39; AB, U. Kans., 1942, MD, 1944. Intern Wesley Hosp., Wichita, Kans., 1944-45; resident anesthesiology U. Kans. Med. Ctr., Kansas City, 1946-48; pvt. practice specializing in anesthesiology Kansas City, Mo., 1948-69; chief anesthesiologist St. Luke's Hosp., Kansas City, 1953-69; med. dir., sect. respiratory therapy U. Kans. Med. Ctr., 1969-92, assoc. prof., 1969-75, prof., 1975-92, prof. anesthesiology emeritus, respiratory care edn., 1992—; examiner schs. respiratory therapy, 1975-95; oral examiner Nat. Bd. Respiratory Therapy; mem. Coun. Nurse Anesthesia Practice, 1974-78; prof. phys. therapy edn., 1993-98. Author: Structural Forms of Anesthetic Compounds, 1961, Respiratory Therapy in Critical Care, 1976, Pharmacology for Respiratory Therapists, 1977; contbr. articles to profl. publs.; mem. editorial bd. Anesthesia Staff News, 1975-84; assoc. editor: Respiratory Care, 1980-90, cons. editor, 1980—, editor-in-chief Respiratory Mgmt., 1989-92. Pres. Overland Park Civic Band, 1997, Overland Park Orch., 1998-2001; trustee Kansas City Mus., Kansas City Conservatory of Music, 1993—. Served to lt. comdr. USNR, 1956. Recipient Bird Lit. prize Am. Assn. Respiratory Therapists, 1976, Spl. Recognition award Am. Assn. Nurse Anesthetists, 1997. Mem. Mo. Soc. Anesthesiologists (pres. 1963), Kans. Soc. Anesthesiologists (pres. 1974-77), Kans. Med. Soc. (council), Phi Beta Kappa, Sigma Xi, Lambda Beta (hon.) Office: Kans Med Ctr 39th And Rainbow Blvd Kansas City KS 66160-0001 E-mail: hmathews@kumc.edu.

MATHEWSON, JUDITH JEANNE, special education educator; b. May 4, 1954; d. Robert Edward and Jeanne Eileen (Parcels) M. AA, Kansas City C.C., 1974; BS in Psychology (Secondary Edn.) and Journalism, Kans. State U., 1976; MS in Psychology and Spl. Edn., Emporia State U., 1979; MEd in Guidance and Counseling, U. Alaska, Anchorage, 2002. Cert. secondary tchr., Alaska; prof. recognized spl. educator. Spl. edn. tchr. grades 1-12 Wichita Pub. Schs., 1978-2001; mediation trainer Chugiak H.S., Anchorage, 1997-2001; bereavement facilitator Clark Jr. H.S., Anchorage, 1995—; tchr. grad. level classes U. Alaska, Anchorage, 2001. Adj. faculty Def. Equal Opportunity Mgmt. Inst., Patrick AFB, Fla., 1989-2002; lead instr. Youth Corps Challenge Program Alaska Nat. Guard, Ft. Richardson, 1993-95; staff trainer disability awareness, school to work. Contbr. articles to newspapers and newsletters. Mem. Nat. Hospice Assn. critical incident stress mgmt. team Alaska Police Chaplains, 1997—. Lt. col. Alaska Air N.G., 1986—. Decorated Air Force Commendation medal, Achievement medal, Cmty. Svc. medal, Jt. Svc. medal for Outstanding Achievement, Alaska Gov. Disting. Unit citation, Alaska Cmty. Svc. award, 1994. Mem. Coun. for Exceptional Children, Alaska N.G. Officers Assn. Roman Catholic. Avocations: computers, travel, teaching, bicycling. Home: 2104 F Scott Ct Montgomery AL 36106 E-mail: jjmathewson@att.net.

MATHIA, MARY LOYOLA, parochial school educator, nun; b. Hempstead, N.Y., Sept. 14, 1921; d. Paul John and Laura Marie (Linck) Mathia. BA, Coll. Mt. St. Joseph, 1953; M in Pastoral Studies, Loyola U.-Chgo., 1980. Joined Sisters of Charity of Cin., Roman Cath. Ch., 1941. Tchr. various schs. Ohio and Mich., 1943-62, St. John Bapt. Sch., Chillum, Md., 1962-63; social studies tchr. and dept. chmn. Holy Name High Sch., Cleve., 1963-69; ednl. cons. Diocese of Cleve., 1970-78; dir. edn. St. Benedict Ch., Crystal River, Fla., 1979-86; founding prin. Cen. Cath. Sch. of Citrus County, Lecanto, Fla., 1985-90, v.p. devel. and pub. rels., 1990-91; parish cons. and dir. adult edn., St. Scholastica, 1986—. Recipient Mother Seton award, 1998, St. Jude medal Award for Svc. to St. Scholastic Ch., presented by Rev. Robert Lynch, Bishop of the Diocese of St. Petersburg, 2002, St. Jude award. Republican. Office: St Scholastica Ch 4301 W Homosassa Trl Lecanto FL 34461-9106

MATHIEU, RICHARD GRABER, business educator; b. Bellefonte, Pa., July 1, 1960; s. Richard Detweiler and Doris (Graber) M.; m. Peggy Smith, Oct. 21, 1954; children: Pattie, Richard. BCE, U. Del., 1982; MS in Sys. Engring., U. Va., 1987, PhD in Sys. Engring., 1991. Asst. patent examiner U.S. Patent and Trademark Office, Washington, 1982-83; H.S. tchr., coach Severn Sch., Severna Park, Md., 1983-85; rsch. and tchg. asst. U. Va., Charlottesville, 1985-91; asst. prof. MIS, U. N.C., Wilmington, 1991-95, assoc. prof., 1995-99, Cameron fellow, 1994-95; assoc. prof. MIS, St. Louis U., 1999—, dept. chair, 2003—. Author: Manufacturing and the Internet, 1996; mem. editl. rev. bd. Jour. for Info. Sys. Edn., 1993—; assoc. editor IEEE Transactions on Systems, Man and Cybernetics; column editor IT Systems Column editor-computer; contbr. articles to profl. jours. Mem. IEEE (Computer Soc.), INFORMS. Home: 9301 Tea Rose Ln Saint Louis MO 63126-2611 E-mail: prmathieu@aol.com., Mathieur@slu.edu.

MATHIS, DAVID EDWIN, internist, educator; b. Quitman, Ga., Sept. 7, 1964; s. S. Edwin Mathis and Lyrice Emma (Shiver) McCranie; m. Allison Paige Scheetz, Feb. 13, 1993. BS, BA, Emory U., 1986; MD, Mercer U., 1990. Diplomate Am. Bd. Internal Medicine, Nat. Bd. Med. Examiners. Intern, then resident in internal medicine Mercer U. & Med. Ctr. Ctrl. Ga., Macon, 1990-93; dir. ambulatory resident medicine Med. Ctr. Ctrl. Ga., Macon, 1994—; instr. medicine Mercer U. Sch. Medicine, Macon, 1993-94, asst. prof. medicine, 1994-99, dir. ambulatory medicine, 1993—, assoc. prof. medicine, 1999—; med. dir. Anderson Health Ctrs., Macon, 2000—. Mem. attending staff Ctrl. Ga. Rehab. Hosp., Weeler County Hosp., Taylor Regional Hosp., 1993-95; prin. investigator ClinTrails/Merck, 1993-94; prin. investigator ALLHAT, Nat. Heart Lung Inst. of NIH. Contbr. articles to profl. jours. and chpt. to book. Fellow ACP; mem. AMA (physician's recognition award 1993, 96), ACP, Am. Geriatrics Soc., Am. Soc. Internal Medicine (med. edn. com. 1996-97, 97-98), So. Med. Assn., N.Y. Acad. Scis. Baptist. Office: Mercer U Sch Medicine Dept Internal Medicine 707 Pine St Ste 241 Macon GA 31201-2106

MATHIS, LOIS RENO, retired elementary education educator; b. Vinson, Okla., June 10, 1915; d. William Dodson and Trudie Frances (Brady) Reno; m. Harold Fletcher Mathis, June 6, 1942 (dec.); children: Robert F., Betty Mathis Sproule. BS, Southwestern Okla. U., 1939; MA, U. Pitts., 1945; PhD, Ohio State U., 1965. Cert. elem. tchr.; cert. elem. supr. Tchr. Okla. Pub. Schs., Tea Cross, 1936-39, Tipton, 1939-42, Ohio County Schs., Wheeling, W.Va., 1944-45, Norman (Okla.) Pub. Schs., 1951-52, Kent (Ohio) State U., 1954-60, Ohio State U., Columbus, 1961-62, Columbus (Ohio) Pub. Schs., 1967-80; ret., 1980. Ednl. cons. in field, 1965—. Mem. Women's Round Table, Columbus, 1986-88; mem. data collection com. 100 Good Schs., Columbus, 1982-84. Mem. AAUW (pres. 1986-88), Ohio State Univ. Women's Club, Phi Delta Gamma (pres. 1980-82), Pi Lambda Theta, Alpha Delta Kappa, Kappa Delta Pi (counselor 1976—, alumni counselor exec. coun. internat. 1990-92, Honor Key 1991). Democrat. Baptist. Avocations: reading, bell collecting and research, entertaining friends, church activities. Home: 4590 Knightsbridge Blvd Apt 242 Columbus OH 43214-4353

MATHISEN, HOWARD, psychologist, minister; b. Bklyn., June 3, 1938; s. Olaf and Hjordis K. (Skjaerum) M.; m. Kathleen Ann Poce, Sept. 20, 1980 (dec. Oct. 1987); children: Randi Sue, Lisa Jane; m. Carolynn Anne Burroughs, Aug. 22, 1992. BA, Taylor U., 1960; MDiv, Phila. Theol. Sem., 1963; postgrad., Luth. Theol. Sem., 1964—65; MA in Religion, Concordia Sem., 1967; postgrad., Rutgers U., 1975, Assumption Coll., 1971—76; DMin in Psychology, Andover Newton Theol. Sch., 1976. Lic. psychologist, Mass., marriage and family therapist, Mass.; cert. diplomate of sex therapy Am. Assn. Sex Educators, Counselors and Therapists; diplomate in marital and sex therapy Am. Bd. Family Psychology; diplomate Am. Bd. Sexology. Pastor Christ Meml. Ch., Phila., 1962-66, Zion Luth. Ch., Webster, Mass., 1967-73; dir. Human Svcs. Ctr. Hubbard Regional Hosp., Webster, 1973-81; pvt. practice psychology Boylston, Mass., 1976-81; co-dir. Counseling Affiliates, Worcester, Mass., 1981-97; dir. pastoral counseling Boston Road Clinic, Worcester, 1997—2001; dir. credentialing svcs. Capstan, Worcester, 1998-99; asst. pastor Concordia Luth. Ch., Worcester, 1976-98; dir. min. asst. program New Eng. Synod, Luth. Ch., 1991—; psychologist Prescott Health Care, 2002—. Adj. instr. psychology Nichols Coll., Dudley, Mass., 1981, Assumption Coll., Worcester, 1983-86. Dean ctrl. Mass. conf. New Eng. Synod, Luth. Ch., 1988-90; bd. dirs. Luth. Svc. Assn. New Eng., 1973-87, vice chmn., 1983-85, chmn., 1985-87; bd. dirs. Luth. Home of Worcester, 1987-92, chmn., 1987-89; chmn. bldg. com. Luth. Nursing Home, Worcester, 1977-79; chmn. Family Svcs. Com., 1981-83; mem. Mass. Adv. Com. Continuing Edn. for Nursing, 1979-81; bd. dirs. Family Planning Svcs. Ctrl. Mass., 1975-81; mem. tech. adv. subcom. substance abuse Ctrl. Mass. Health Sys. Agy., 1979-80. Fellow Acad. Family Psychology, Am. Acad. Clin. Sexologists; mem. APA, Am. Assn. Marriage and Family Therapy, Mass. Psychol. Assn., Mass. Assn. Marriage and Family Therapy, Acad. Managed Care Providers. Home: 6 Camelot Cir Dudley MA 01571-6110 Office: 130 Elm St Worcester MA 01609 E-mail: mathisen@charter.net.

MATHUR, IKE, finance educator; b. Jamshedpur, India, Nov. 22, 1943; came to U.S., 1961; s. Robert William and Ivy (Phillips) M.; children: Rebecca Lynn, Jason Gabriel. BS, Eastern Mich. U., 1965, MBA, 1968; PhD, U. Cin., 1974. Editor Am. Math. Soc., Providence, 1965-69; rsch. asst. U. Cin., 1969-72; instr. U. Dayton, Ohio, 1972-73; asst. prof. U. Pitts., 1973-77; assoc. prof. fin. So. Ill. U., Carbondale, 1977-81, prof., 1981—, chmn. fin., 1979-92, 94-95, dean Coll. Bus., 1992-94. Mgmt. trainer AID, Washington, 1978-81; Fulbright prof., Turku, Finland, 1983-84, Lisbon, Portugal, 1993. Author: Introduction to Financial Management, 1979, Cases in Managerial Finance, 1984, Personal Finance, 1989, Wealth Creation in Eastern Europe, 1992, Financial Management in Post Europe, 1992. Mem. Am. Fin. Assn., French Fin. Assn., Western Fin. Assn., Midwest Fin. Assn.,

Fin. Mgmt. Assn. Avocations: running, martial arts, travel. Home: 32 Apple Orchard Rd Carbondale IL 62903-7672 Office: So Ill U Coll Bus Carbondale IL 62901 E-mail: imathur@cba.siu.edu.

MATIAS, PATRICIA TREJO, secondary education educator; b. Havana, Cuba; came to U.S., 1967; d. Juan Mario and Maria (Rexach) Trejo; m. Miguel Matias, Mar. 20, 1972; children: Michael George, Mark Patrick. BA in French/Spanish, Ga. Coll., 1973; MAT in Spanish Edn., Ga. State U., 1985, EdS in Fgn. Lang. Edn., 1991, postgrad., 1998—. Cert. Spanish tchr., Ga. Spanish lead tchr. Wheeler High Sch., Marietta, Ga., 1980-2000; AP/gifted Spanish tchr. Walton High Sch., Marietta, Ga., 2000—. Part-time instr. Kennesaw State Coll., 1991-1998. VIP guest svc. goodwill amb. Olympics Games Com., Atlanta, 1995-96. Mem.: Fgn. Lang. Assn. Ga., Profl. Ga. Assn. Educators, Am. Assn. Tchrs. Spanish and Portuguese, Internat. Reading Assn., Sigma Delta Pi (hon.), Kappa Delta Pi. Avocations: golf, travel, gardening. Office: Walton High Sch 1590 Bill Murdock Rd Marietta GA 30062 E-mail: pmatias@aol.com.

MATICH, MATTHEW P. alternative secondary school English educator; b. San Pedro, Calif., June 30, 1962; B Fine and Comm. Arts, Loyola Marymount U., 1985; MEd, Nat. U., 1995. Cert. secondary sch. English tchr., Calif. Producer, newswriter KMET Radio, Hollywood, Calif., 1981-83, 85-86; news dir., broadcaster KXLU Radio, L.A., 1983-87; instr., counselor Columbia Sch. Broadcasting, Hollywood, 1985-88; radio reporter KRTH Radio, L.A., 1987-88; radio producer Transtar Radio Network, Hollywood, 1987-88; substitute tchr. L.A. Unified Sch. Dist., 1989-92; head coach freshman/sophomore football and varsity track coach San Pedro (Calif.) H.S., 1993—94; English tchr. Harbor Cmty. Adult Sch. AEWC (Alt. Edn. Work Ctr.) Drop-out Prevention Homestudy Program, 2001—. Founder, mem. adv. bd. Extracurricular Academics), San Pedro, 1994—97; founder local ethnic tribute/holiday Burrito Day in L.A., 1983—; instr. ESL San Pedro/Narbonne Adult Sch., 1996—, drop out prevention coord., 1998, assessment coord., 1999; adv. student paper Minor Chronicles, 1998—; organizer San Pedro Teen Summit, 1998-2001; adv. in field; disc jockey Spin Cycle, The Watt from Pedro Show on www.twfps.com, 2001-. Writer, prodr. radio program The Bluez Shift, 1983-87, poetry: It Can't Be, 1996. Mem. San Pedro Pirate Boosters, 1987. Mem. United Tchrs. L.A., Am. Fedn. Tchrs., Nat. Coun. Tchrs. English, Calif. Assn. Tchrs. English, Calif. Tchrs. Assn., Calif. Coun. Adult Educators, Dalmation Am. Club, Elks Club (scholarship com. 1990). Avocations: travel, music. Home: 457 W 40th Street F San Pedro CA 90731-7165 Office: 2731 S Averill Ave San Pedro CA 90731-5632 E-mail: imattamati@yahoo.com.

MATIN, A. microbiology educator, consultant; b. Delhi, India, May 8, 1941; came to U.S., 1964, naturalized, 1983; s. Mohd Said; m. Mimi Keyhan, June 21, 1968. BS, U. Karachi, Pakistan, 1960, MS, 1962; PhD, UCLA, 1969. Lectr. St. Joseph's Coll., Karachi, 1962-64; rsch. assoc. UCLA, 1964-71; sci. officer U. Groningen, Kerklaan, Netherlands, 1971-75; prof. microbiology and immunology Stanford U., Calif., 1975—, prof. Western Hazardous Substances Rsch. Ctr., 1981-98, faculty program in cellular and molecular genetics, 1985—, faculty cancer biology program, 1980—; cons. law offices Swidler Berlin Shereef Friedman, LLP, Washington, 1999—2001. Cons. Engenics, 1982-84, Monsanto, 1984-86, Chlorox, 1992-93; chmn. Stanford Recombinant DNA panel, mem. human subject panel, 2001--; mem. Accreditation Bd. for Engring. and Tech.; mem. internat. adv. com. Internat. Workshop on Molecular Biology of Stress Response: Meml. Found., Banaras U. and German Min. of Rsch., mem. panel Yucca Mountain Microbial Activity, Dept. of Energy, mem. study sect.; NASA study sect.; participant DOE, NABIR program draft panel; mem. study sect. NIH; convenor of microbiol. workshop and conf.; rev. panel DOE environ. mgmt. program; mem. rev. panels DOE NABIR program, TV panel GTL program, DOE, mem. Stanford Biosafety Panel; bd. dir. Chembiotek; keynote spkr., adv. bd. several internat. conf.; ASM Found. lectr. Mem. editl. bd. Jour. Bacteriology, Ann. Rev. Microbiol., Jour. Microbiology; reviewer NSF and other grants; contbr. numerous publ. to sci. jour. Fulbright fellow, 1964-71; recipient rsch. awards NSF, 1981-92, Ctr. for Biotech. Rsch., 1981-85, EPA, 1981—, NIH, 1989-92, UN Tokten, 1987, DOE, 1993—, Dept. Agrl., 1995-97, NASA, 1999—; recipient Star award EPA. Fellow Am. Acad. Microbiology; mem. AAAS, AAUP, Am Soc. for Microbiology (Found. lectr. 1991-93), Soc. Indsl. Microbiology, No. Soc. Indsl. Microbiology (bd. dirs.), Biophys. Soc., Am. Chem. Soc., Inst. Molecular Medicine (bd. dir.). Avocations: reading, music, hiking. Home: 690 Coronado Ave Stanford CA 94305-1039 Office: Stanford U Fairchild Sci Bldg Dept Microbiology & Immunology Stanford CA 94305-5124 E-mail: a.matin@Stanford.edu.

MATKOWSKY, BERNARD JUDAH, applied mathematician, educator; b. N.Y.C., Aug. 19, 1939; s. Morris N. and Ethel H. M.; m. Florence Knobel, Apr. 11, 1965; children: David, Daniel, Devorah. BS, CCNY, 1960; M.E.E., NYU, 1961, MS, 1963, PhD, 1966. Fellow Courant Inst. Math. Scis., NYU, 1961-66; mem. faculty dept. math. Rensselaer Poly. Inst., 1966-77; John Evans prof. applied math., mech. engring. & math. Northwestern U., Evanston, Ill., 1977—, chmn. engring. sci. and applied math. dept., 1993-99. Vis. prof. Tel Aviv U., 1972-73; vis. scientist Weizmann Inst. Sci., Israel, summer 1976, summer 1980, Tel Aviv U., summer 1980; cons. Argonne Nat. Lab., Sandia Labs., Lawrence Livermore Nat. Lab., Exxon Research and Engring. Co. Editor Wave Motion—An Internat. Jour., 1979-99, Applied Math. Letters, 1987—, SIAM Jour. Applied Math., 1976-95, European Jour. Applied Math., 1990-96, Random and Computational Dynamics, 1991-97, Internat. Jour. SHS, 1992—, Jour. Materials Synthesis and Processing, 1992—; mem. editl. adv. bd. Springer Verlag Applied Math. Scis. Series; contbr. chpts. to books, articles to profl. jours. Fulbright grantee, 1972-73; Guggenheim fellow, 1982-83 Fellow: AAAS, Am. Acad. Mechs.; mem.: Soc. Natural Philosophy, Com. Concerned Scientists, Conf. Bd. Math. Scis. (coun., com. human rights math. scientists), Am. Assn. Combustion Synthesis, Am. Physics Soc., Combustion Inst., Am. Math. Soc., Soc. Indsl. and Applied Math., Eta Kappa Nu, Sigma Xi. Home: 3704 Davis St Skokie IL 60076-1745 Office: Northwestern U Technological Institute Evanston IL 60208-0001 E-mail: b-matkowsky@northwestern.edu.

MATON, ANTHEA, education consultant; b. Burnley, Lancashire, England, Feb. 1, 1944; d. William Douglas Newton-Dawson and Beatrice Joan (Simpson) Bateman; m. K.F. Edward Asprey, Nov. 13, 1965 (div. 1978); children: George William Edward, Mariana Alexandra Beatrice; m. Paul Nicholas Maton, Mar. 23, 1978; 1 child, Petra Beatrice Suzanne. Tchg. cert., higher diploma, tchg. diploma; postgrad., U. Okla. Clin. instr. radiotherapy Hammersmith Hosp., London, 1970-75; prin. sch. radiotherapy Royal Free Hosp., London, 1977-80, acting supt., 1979-80; head of careers Putney High Sch. for Girls, London, 1981-83; head of physics St. Andrews Episc. High Sch., Bethesda, Md., 1984-88; vis. fellow Am. Assn. Physics Tchrs., 1988-89; nat. coord. project scope, sequence, and coordination Nat. Sci. Tchrs. Assn., 1989-91; exec. dir. ArtSci. Connections, Oklahoma City, 1991—; dir. exhbn. on art and physics Edn. Commections, Oklahoma City, 1994—. Vis. faculty physics Western Wash. U., 1995; vis. faculty Okla. Sch. Sci. and Math. 1995—; organizer U.S.-Soviet H.S. Physics Student Exch. and Visit, 1989; conducted numerous workshops on sci. curriculum reform and assessment reform, 1987—; faculty USA Physics Olympiad Team, 1986, 89; physics tchr. St. Andrews Episc. H.S., 1984-88, Putney H.S. for Girls, 1980-83, tchr. med. ethics, 1982-83; tchr. physics, anatomy and physiology, radiobiology Royal Free Hosp., 1977-80, contemporary physics edn. project, 1989—. Lead author Prentice Hall Sci., 1993; contbr. articles to profl. jours. Mem. Nat. Mus. Women Arts (charter), Women's Philharm. (charter); apptd. to scientific adv. bd. OMNIPLEX Sci. Mus., Okla. City; cons. Sta. WGBH, Boston, Smithsonian, Am. Mus. of Moving Image, UCLA, Del. Edn. Dept., Ark. Project Advise, Newcastle (Del.) Sch. Dist. Named one of Today's Leaders Okla. Edn. Equity Roundtable, 1992. Mem. NAFE, ASCD, AAUW (pub. policy chair 1995-96), NOW (coord. metro chpt. 1992-95, treas. Okla. state chpt. 1993-95, chair state membership 1997-98), Nat. Sci. Tchrs. Assn., Am. Assn. Physics Tchrs., N.Y. Acad. Scis., Soc. Radiographers U.K., Soc. Radiographers Radiotherapy. Avocations: gender and science, drawing, writing poetry, singing, making kaleidoscopes. Home and Office: 1303 NW 22d St Oklahoma City OK 73106-4058

MATORIN, SUSAN, social work administrator, educator; b. Boston, Jan. 9, 1943; d. Mervyn Donald and Eleanor (Marinoff) M.; m. Richard Charles Friedman, Nov. 24, 1978; 1 child, Jeremiah Simon. AB, Vassar Coll., 1964; postgrad., Columbia Sch. Social Work, 1966. Cert. social worker, N.Y. Chief social work Washington Heights Cmty. Svc., N.Y. State Psychiat. Inst., 1966-78; chief ambulatory social work in psychiatry Presbyn. Hosp., Columbia Med. Ctr., N.Y., 1978-81; dir. social work Payne Whitney Clinic of N.Y. Hosp., Cornell, 1981-97; program dir. Cornell Psychiatry IOP, 1997—. Mem. adv. coun., 2d vice chair Columbia U. Sch. of Social Work, 1994—; adj. assoc. prof. Columbia Sch. Social Work, 1977—; bd. trustees Selig Ednl. Inst. Jewish Bd. Family Svcs., N.Y.; spkr. in field. Contbr. articles to profl. jours. and books. Recipient Disting. Svc. award Columbia U., 1989, Centennial award, 1998. Fellow Am. Orthopsychiatry Assn.; mem. NASW (Met. chpt. licensing task force, bd. dirs.), Acad. Cert. Social Workers, Soc. for Social Work Adminstrs. in Health Care (N.Y. chpt. program co-chair 1994—, nominated Social Work Dir. of Yr. 1995). Democrat. Jewish. Avocations: family, playing piano, reading, walking, ballet and art. Home: 27 W 86th St Apt 9C New York NY 10024-3615 Office: Payne Whitney Clinic 525 E 68th St # 147 New York NY 10021-4870

MATSA, LOULA ZACHAROULA, social services administrator, educator; b. Piraeus, Greece, Apr. 16, 1935; came to U.S., 1952, naturalized 1962; d. Eleftherios Georgiou and Ourania E. (Fraguiskopoulou) Papoulias; m. Ilco S. Matsa, Nov. 27, 1953; 1 child, Aristotle Ricky. Student, Pierce Coll., Athens, 1948-52; BA, Rockford Coll., 1953; MA, U. Chgo., 1955. Diplomate clin. social worker; bd. cert. clin. social workers, N.Y. cert. social orkers, pub. employees fedn. Marital counselor Family Soc., Cambridge, Mass., 1955-56; chief unit II social svc. Queen's (N.Y.) Children's Psychiat. Ctr., 1961-74; dir. social svcs., supr.-coord. family care program Hudson River Psychiat. Ctr., Poughkeepsie, N.Y., 1974-91; supr. social work Harlem Valley Psychiat. Ctr., Wingdale, N.Y., 1991-93, Hudson River Psychiat. Ctr., 1993—. Field instr. Adelphi, Albany and Fordham univs., 1969—. Contbr. articles to profl. jours.; instrumental in state policy changes in treatment and court representation of emotionally disturbed and mentally ill. Fulbright Exch. student, 1952-53; Talcott scholar, 1953-55. Mem. NASW, Internat. Platform Assn., Internat. Coun. on Social Welfare, Acad. Cert. Social Workers, Assn. Cert. Social Workers, Pierce Coll. Alumni Assn. Democrat. Greek Orthodox. Home: 81-11 45th Ave Elmhurst NY 11373-3553

MATSON, VIRGINIA MAE FREEBERG (MRS. EDWARD J. MATSON), retired special education educator, author; b. Chgo., Aug. 25, 1914; d. Axel George and Mae (Dalrymple) Freeberg; m. Edward John Matson, Oct. 18, 1941; children: Karin (Mrs. Donald H. Skadden), Sara M. Drake, Edward Robert, Laurence D., David O. BA, U. Ky., 1934; MA, Northwestern U., 1941. Spl. edn. tchr. area high schs., Chgo., 1934-42, Ridge Farm, 1944-45; tchr. h.s. Pub. Schs. Lake County, Ill., 1956-59; founder Grove Sch., Lake Forest, Ill., 1958-87, ret., 1987. Instr. evening sch. Carthage Coll., 1965-66. Author: Shadow on the Lost Rock, 1958, Saul, the King, 1968, Abba Father, 1970 (Friends Lit. Fiction award 1972), Buried Alive, 1970, A School for Peter, 1974, A Home for Peter, 1983, Letters to Lauren, A History of the Methodist Campgrounds, Des Plaines, 1985; contbr. many articles to profl. publs. Mem. Friends of Lit. Dem. Recipient Humanitarian award Ill. Med. Soc. Aux. Dem. Home: 4133 Mockingbird Ln Suffolk VA 23434-7186

MATSUDA, FUJIO, retired university president; b. Honolulu, Oct. 18, 1924; s. Yoshio and Shimo (Iwasaki) M.; m. Amy M. Saiki, June 11, 1949; children: Bailey Koki, Thomas Junji, Sherry Noriko, Joan Yuuko, Ann Mitsuyo, Richard Hideo. BSCE, Rose Poly. Inst., 1949; DSc, MIT, 1952; DEng (hon.), Rose Hulman Inst. Tech., 1975. Rsch. engr. MIT, 1952-54; rsch. asst. prof. engring. U. Ill., Urbana, 1954-55; from asst. prof. engring. to prof. engring. U. Hawaii, Honolulu, 1955-66, chmn. dept. civil engring., 1962—63, v.p. bus. affairs, 1973-74, pres., 1974-84, exec. dir. Rsch. Corp., 1984-94; pres. Japan-Am. Inst. Mgmt. Sci., Honolulu, 1994-96. Dir. Hawaii Dept. Transp., Honolulu, 1963-73; v.p. Park & Yee, Ltd., Honolulu, 1956-58; pres. SMS & Assocs., Inc., 1960-63; pvt. practice structural engring., 1958-60; bd. dirs. C. Brewer & Co., Ltd., Buyco, Ltd., First Hawaiian Bank, BancWest Corp., Inc., Rehab. Hosp. of Pacific; CEO, chmn. bd. dirs. Pacific Internat. Ctr. High Tech. Rsch. With U.S. Army, 1943—45. Recipient Honor Alumnus award Rose Poly. Inst., 1971, Disting. Svc. award Airport Ops. Coun. Internat., 1973, Disting. Alumnus award U. Hawaii, 1974, 91; named Hawaii Engr. of Yr., 1972. Mem. NAE, NSPE, ASCE (Parcel-Sverdrup Engring. Mgmt. award 1986), Social Sci. Assn., Japan-Am. Soc. Honolulu (trustee 1976-84, adv. coun. 1984—), Japanese Hawaiian Econ. Coun., Sigma Xi, Tau Beta Pi. E-mail: fmatsuda@hawaii.rr.com.

MATSUDA, TAKAYOSHI, surgeon, educator, biomedical researcher; b. Tonan, Japan, 1937; came to U.S., 1965; MD, Keio Gijuku U., Tokyo, 1963. Diplomate Am. Bd. Surgery. Rotating intern Cook County Hosp., Chgo., 1965-66, resident in surgery, 1966-71, dir. burn ctr., 1975-93; asst. prof. surgery Kyorin U., Tokyo, 1971-75; asst. prof. U. Ill., Chgo., 1977—; pres. TM & Assocs., Oak Park, Ill., 1994—; CEO, Matsuda Clean Energy Co., Oak Park, 2001—. Cons. alternative medicine, cons. leadership devel., fin. freedom; investigator renewable energy; keynote spkr. at the 15th Ann Meeting of the Japanese Coll. of Surgeons, Fukora, Japan, 1990, 54th Ann. Meeting of the Japanese Soc. for Clincal Surgery, Tokyo, Japan, 1992; guest spkr. at the 18th Ann. Meeting of the Japanese Soc. Burn Assn., Tokyo, Japan, 1991. Editl. bd. Jour. Burn Care Rehab., 1987-93; contbr. numerous articles to profl. publ., chpt. to books, keynote spkr.: at the 15th annual meeting of the Japanese Coll. of Surgeons, Fukuoka, Japan, 1990, and the 54th annual meeting of the Japanese Soc. for Clinical Surgery, Tokyo, Japan, 1992; guest spkr. at the 18th annual meeting of the Japanese Burn Assn., Tokyo, Japan, 1991 Recipient Jerry and Thelma Stergios award for Excellence in Basic Rsch., U. Ill. at Chgo., 1979, The Superior Pub. Serv. award, County of Cook, State of Ill., 1993, featured in, "40 of the Very Best", mag., Doctor's Doctors, 1983. Fellow ACS; mem. Internat. Soc. Surgery, Internat. Soc. Burn Injuries, Am. Burn Assn., Am. Assn. Surgery Trauma, Soc. Critical Care Medicine, Chgo. Surg. Soc. Achievements include research in and devel. of a novel approach for the production of electricity without pollution; established the first human skin bank in the State of Illinois at the Burn unit of Cook County Hospital, 1977. Office: TM & Assocs Alternative Medicine Cons 103 Bishop Quarter Ln Oak Park IL 60302-2672 E-mail: takimatsuda@hotmail.com.

MATSUI, DOROTHY NOBUKO, elementary education educator; b. Honolulu, Jan. 9, 1954; d. Katsura and Tamiko (Sakai) M. Student, U. Hawaii, Honolulu, 1972-76, postgrad., 1982; BEd, U. Alaska, Anchorage, 1979, MEd in Spl. Edn., 1986. Clerical asst. U. Hawaii Manoa Disbursing Office, Anchorage, 1974-76; passenger service agt. Japan Air Lines, Anchorage, 1980; bilingual tutor Anchorage Sch. Dist., 1980, elem. sch. tchr., 1980—. Facilitator for juvenile justice courses Anchorage Sch. Dist., Anchorage Police Dept., Alaska Pacific U., 1992-93; mem. adv. bd. Anchorage Law-Related Edn. Advancement Project. Vol. Providence Hosp., Anchorage, 1986, Humana Hosp., Anchorage, 1984, Spl. Olympics, Anchorage, 1981, Municipality Anchorage, 1978, Easter Seal Soc. Hawaii, 1975. Mem. NAFE, NEA, Alaska Edn. Assn., Smithsonian Nat. Assoc. Program, Nat. Space Soc., Smithsonian Air and Space Assn., World Aerospace Edn. Orgn., Internat. Platform Assn., Nat. Trust for Hist. Preservation, Nat. Audubon Soc., Planetary Soc., Cousteau Soc., Alaska Coun. for the Social Studies, Alaska Coun. Tchrs. Math., World Inst. Achievment, U.S. Olympic Soc., Women's Inner Circle Achievement, U. Alaska Alumni Assn., World Wildlife Fund, Japanese-Am. Nat. Mus., Alpha Delta Kappa (treas. Alpha chpt. 1988-92, corr. sec. 1993-96, sgt. at arms 1996-98). Avocations: reading, sports, learning. Office: Anchorage Sch Dist 7001 Cranberry St Anchorage AK 99502-7145

MATSUMOTO, SHIGEMI, opera soprano, voice educator; b. Denver; d. Moriichi and Suki Matsumoto; m. Martin J. Stark. BA in Mus. Performance, Calif. State U., Northridge. Voice faculty music dept. Calif. State U., Long Beach, 1988—, U. So. Calif., 1997—; pvt. vocal instr., 1984—. Performances with over 40 opera cos. including opera cos. in Brussels, San Francisco, Phila., Portland, Oreg., Wolf Trap, Va., Kansas City, Mo., Tucson, San Antonio, Toledo/Dayton, Ohio, Augusta, Ga., Little Rock, Lake George, N.Y., also Spring Opera Theatre, and others; with over 50 symphonies including symphonies in Belgium, Lourdes, France, San Francisco, L.A., Phila., Mpls., Pitts., St. Louis, Houston, Denver, New Orleans, Memphis and Wichita, other cities; over 300 internat. recitals including Tokyo, N.Y.C., Washington, Chgo., L.A., San Francisco, Dallas, Houston, Vancouver, B.C., Kansas City, San Antonio, Milw.; lectr. demonstrations, master classes coll. campuses; adjudicator numerous vocal competitions; guest artist, lectr. Can. Fedn. Music Tchrs.; guest soloist 25th Anniversary Celebration Founding UN, 1970. Bd. dirs. So. Calif. Opera Guild, 1986-92, Guild Opera, 1987-92; founder The Jr. Guild, 1987; mem. cmty. outreach com. L.A. Music Ctr. Opera Cmty. Outreach Com. adv. Guild Opera Co., Inc., Riverside Opera; mem. The Classical Singers Assn. (founder, pres. 1992—), Japanese-Am. Citizen's League, 1989. Recipient 1st prize Western Regional Met. Opera Auditions; grand-prize winner San Francisco Nat. Opera Auditions; award winner Geneva Internat. Music Competitions; grantee Nat. Opera Inst., Classical Singers Inst. (pres. 1992—), Internat. Inst. Edn., Los Angeles Bur. Music; named Japanese Woman of Year in So. Calif., Japanese-Am. Soc. Mem. Am. Guild Mus. Artists, Nat. Assn. of Tchrs. of Singing. Home: Northridge View Estates 18342 Chatham Ln Northridge CA 91326-3603

MATSUMURA, DONNA SHIGEKO, secondary education English educator; b. Cleve., Oct. 24, 1950; d. Isamu J. and Alice Kiyoko (Okamura) M. BS in Edn., Ohio State U., 1972. Tchr., coach Columbus (Ohio) Pub. Schs., 1972-78; coach jr. varsity women's volleyball Ohio State U., Columbus, 1977-78, athletic tutor, 1974-78; dir. ice skating Nat. Youth Sports Program, Columbus, 1974-78; tchr. Dallas Pub. Schs., 1978—, coach, 1982-83, dir. drill team, 1989-97, staff devel. assoc., 1993-95, football and track coach, 1997-2000. English co-chair textbook com. Dallas Pub. Schs., 1991-92; McDougal Littel panel mem., 1992; offcl. USA Track and Field, Tex., 1992—; participant Tech. Immersion Project, 1998, Tech. Immersion Project-Advanced Placement, 1999; Tech. Immersion Project trainer, 1999. Jordan Fund grantee, 1999. Mem. Nat. Staff Devel. Coun. (tchr. technologist 1998-2001). Presbyterian. Avocations: dancing, reading, working out, sewing. Office: WH Adamson H S 201 E 9th St Dallas TX 75203-5213 Home: 9607 Summerhill Ln Dallas TX 75238-1041 E-mail: cmats@swbell.net.

MATSUOKA, YOSHIYUKI, science educator, researcher; b. Shimonoseki, Yamaguchi, Japan, June 2, 1955; arrived in U.S., 2002; s. Isamu and Sumie Matsuoka; m. Naoko Matsuoka, June 30, 1985; 1 child, Kei. BA, Waseda U., Tokyo, 1979; MA, Chiba (Japan) U., 1982, PhD, 1997. Planner & designer (mgr.) Nissan Motor Co. Ltd., Atsugi, Japan, 1982—96; asst. prof. Keio U., Yokohama, Japan, 1996—98, assoc. prof., 1998—2002, prof., 2003—. Vis. rschr. Tsukuba (Japan) U., 2001—02; vis. rsch. fellow Ill. Inst. Tech., Chgo., 2002; part-time lectr. Chiba U., 1993—, Tokyo Inst. Tech., 2001—. Design of automobile, Cetiro, 1988, Laurel, 1988, Skyline, 1989; editor: Kansei Engring. Internat. Editl. Bd., 2000—; contbr. papers to profl. jours. and confs. Mem.: IEEE, ASME, Assn. for Computing Machinery, Design Rsch. Soc., Japan Ergonomics Soc. (councilor 2001—), Japanese Soc. for Sci. of Design (dir., councilor 2002—, Prize for Paper 2001, Prize for Encouragement 1995). Achievements include design of automobiles, chairs, protectors; patents for automobiles, chairs, protectors. Avocations: travel, painting, piano, fishing, walking. Office: Keio Univ 3-14-1 Hiyoshi Kohoku-ku Yokohama 223-8522 Japan E-mail: matsuoka@mech.keio.ac.jp.

MATTAR, PHILIP, writer; b. Haifa, Palestine, Jan. 21, 1944; came to U.S. 1961; m. Evelyn Ann Keith, June 20, 1971; 1 child, Christina. MPhil, Columbia U., 1977, PhD, 1981. Exec. dir. Inst. for Palestine Studies, Washington, 1984-2001; assoc. editor Jour. Palestine Studies, Washington, 1985-2001; fellow Woodrow Wilson Ctr., 2001—02; sr. fellow U.S. Inst. Peace, 2002—03; guest scholar U.S. Inst. of Peace, 2003—. Adj. lectr. history Yale U., 1981; adj. prof. history Georgetown U., 1990, 91, 94. Author: Mufti of Jerusalem, 1988, 2d edit., 1991; co-editor: Encyclopedia of the Modern Middle East, 1996; editor: Encyclopedia of the Palentinians, 2000; contbr. articles to profl. jours., including Fgn. Policy, Middle East Jour., Middle Ea. Studies. Mem. adv. com. Human Rights Watch/Middle East. Vis. scholar Columbia U., 1984; Fulbright-Hays Rsch. fellow, 1978. Mem. Middle East Studies Assn., Middle East Inst. Avocations: jogging, chess, reading, travel. E-mail: pjmattar@aol.com.

MATTERN, DAVID BRUCE, elementary education educator; b. Harrisburg, Pa., Sept. 3, 1952; s. Kenneth Gordon and Betty Jane (Fisher) M.; m. Sheryl Lynn Young, Nov. 30, 1974; children: Melissa Ann, Marcia Lynn. BA in Elem. Edn., Cen. Coll., 1974; MS in Edn. Adminstrn., Iowa State U., 1982. Cert. elem. educator, edn. adminstr. Elem. tchr. Ringrose Elem. Sch., Wentworthville, N.S.W., Australia, 1975-77; tchr. 3rd-6th grade Lovejoy Elem. Sch., Des Moines, 1977-82, tchr. fifth grade, 1983—2003, asst. prin., 1991—; tchr. fifth grade Greenwood Elem. Sch., Des Moines, 2003—. Coord. gifted and talented program Des Moines Pub. Schs., 1979-88, curriculum specialist, 1988—; mem. Des Moines Math. Adv. Bd., 1983-84. Diaconate mem. Park Ave Christian Ch., Des Moines, 1979-96, chmn., 1988-90, 94-95, elder, 1998—. Mem. Iowa Coun. Tchrs. Math., Nat. Coun. Tchrs. Math., ASCD. Republican. Avocations: softball, basketball, swimming, travel, videography. Home: 4309 Beaver Hills Dr Des Moines IA 50310-6300

MATTESON, BARBARA ANN VANCE, secondary education educator; b. Ft. Collins, Colo., Mar. 1, 1940; d. Wilford Walton and Louise (Hinchliffe) Vance; m. David Russell Matteson, Apr. 9, 1961 (dec. Oct. 12, 1988); 1 child, Deborah Jean. BA, U. No. Colo., 1965; postgrad., U. Colo., 1967-78, Colo. State U., 1967-78, U. Wyo., 1978—. Tchr. reading and lang. arts Westminster (Colo.) H.S., 1968-78, Natrona County H.S., Casper, Wyo., 1978—, chmn. dept. lang. arts, 1981-87; tchr. Natrona Acad., 1994—. Coord. secondary lang. arts Natrona County Sch. Dist. 1, 1992-95, writing assessment facilitator, 1992-93. Named Outstanding Educator, Natrona County Sch. Dist. 1, 1990. Mem. ASCD, Nat. Coun. Tchrs. English, Wyo. ASCD, Delta Kappa Gamma. Avocations: reading, travel, dollhouses. Home: 2700 Belmont Rd Casper WY 82604-4644 Office: Natrona County HS 930 S Elm St Casper WY 82601-3603

MATTESON, CLARICE CHRIS, artist, educator; b. Winnipeg, Man., Can., Sept. 2, 1918; came to U.S., 1922; d. Sergis and Nina (Balter) Alberts; m. D.C. Matteson, 1956 (dec. 1976); children: Kemmer, Gretchen. BA, Met. State U., 1976; MA in Liberal Studies, Hamline U., 1986; PhD in Humanities, LaSalle U., 1995. Mem. Orson Welles' staff, Hollywood, Calif., 1945-46; owner Hilde-Gardes Co., L.A., 1952—56; instr. art North Hennepin C.C., Brooklyn Park, Minn., 1975-81; instr. continuing edn. for women U. Minn., 1980. Prodr., host TV program Accent on Art, St. Paul,

1979—; instr. art Lakewood C.C., 1979, U. Minn., Bloomington (Minn.) Sch. Dist., 1980-2003, Mpls. Sch. Dist., St. Paul Sch. Dist., 1981-2002, 03-04; guest artist Montserrat Gallery, Soho, N.Y.C., 1999; appeared as guest artist WCCO-TV, 1998; spkr. on TV, Nat. Am. Pen Women Spirituality and Creativity in Art, 2003. (one-woman shows) Decathlon Club, 1998, State Capital Rotunda, 1986, Lindbergh Home, 1988, Hamline U., 2002, exhibited (group shows) Mpls. Inst. Art, 1994—98, Art in Bloom, 1999—2002, St. Paul, 2000, Landmark Ctr., Hamline U., St. Paul, 2002, U. Minn. Womens Club, 2002, U. Minn. Womens Club Art Show, 2003, Fairmount Hotel, 2002; Exhibited in group shows at Art in Bloom, 1999—2003; (represented by) Gov. Ventura's Ofcl. Residence and now by Gov. Jim Pawlenty, 2003—04, Montserrat Art Gallery, N.Y.C., Gallery 416, Mpls., Jean Stephen Art Gallery, 1999—2002, Premier Gallery, 2001—02, (corr.) Schaumburg (Ill) Newspapers, 1962—68; prodr.: (TV series, host) Kids Art, 1995—, (series program) Internat. Cafe Internet Arts, 1996—; patentee plastic products; prodr.: Men Aware TV, 2001—02, Punt, Pass, or Pie TV, 2001—02; composer: I Want You Near; Exhibited in group shows at Women's Club, 2002—03, exhibited in group shows, Gov. Ventura's and Gov. Tim Pawlenty's, 2001—05. Active Minn. Orch. (WAMSO), Mpls., 1972—, vol. Recipient award for creative leadership Minn. Assn. for Continuing Adult Edn., 1977, Gold Cup award Bloomington Cable, 1989, Gov.'s Letter of Commendation, 1994; named Outstanding Grad. for past 25 yrs. Met. State U., 1997, Disting. Alumna John Marshall H.S., L.A., 2002, Outstanding Nominee of Grad. Students Met. State U., 2002; Park Cable TV grantee, 1982, Minn. Humanities Commn. grantee, 1985. Qem. ASCAP (award 1997-2003, award for popular music, 2003-04), AAUW (dir. arts com. 1989-90, bd. dirs. 1990-92), Am. Pen Women (Minn. chpt. 1994—, v.p. 1998), Internat. Biog. Assn. (dep. dir. Cambridge, Eng. 2001, participate art and comm. congress, 2001), Am. Composers Forum, Minn. Artists Assn., Minn. Territorial Pioneers (bd. dirs. 1995—, v.p. 1997-99, 1st v.p. 1999-2003, elected Minnesotan of Yr., 1999-2002, elected 1st v.p. 2003-04), Internat. Alliance for Women in Music, St. Paul Neighborhood Network (elected bd. dirs. TV station SPNN, 2002-04), N.Y. Neighborhood Network, Internat. Platform Speakers (award 1998), Mpls. Telecom. Network, Metro Cable Network, Adelphi Cable, DuLuth-Superior Cable, NDT, Eagan. Avocations: tennis, dancing, writing children's books, composing liturgical music. Home and Office: 2119 Sargent Ave Saint Paul MN 55105-1126

MATTHEWS, BARBARA LEE, teacher, consultant; b. Columbus, Colo., Oct. 28, 1940; d. Walden M. and Ruth May (Williams) W.; m. Ron D. Gary, June 18, 1966 (div. Dec. 1977); 1 child, Dean; m. Cecil A. Matthews, July 2, 1981; stepchildren: David, Bruce. BS in Edn., Ohio State U., 1962; MA in Reading, U. Northern Colo., 1969. Cert. tchr., Colo. Tchr. English and Bus. Olentangy High Sch., Delaware, Ohio, 1962-64, Aurora (Colo.) Cen. High Sch., 1964-66; tchr. English Adams City High Sch., Commerce City, Colo., 1966-68; tchr. Reading Isaac Newton Jr. High Sch., Littleton, Colo., 1968-69; tchr. Reading Campus Mid. Unit Cherry Creek Schs., Englewood, Colo., 1972-75, reading specialist Laredo Mid. Sch., 1975—. Instr. U. No. Colo., Greeley; conductor workshops bus. and reading edn., U. No. Colo., Aurora Pub. Schs., presentations Cherry Creek Council on Learning Disabilities. Mem. north central evaluation team Colo. mid. sch. programs. Recipient various teaching grants, awards, 1975—. Mem. Internat. Reading Assn. (pres. Arapahoe County coun. 1979-80, 89-90, regional conf. com. Colo. coun. 1976, numerous offices, editor newsletter, Outstanding Secondary Reading Tchr. Continuing Edn. award 1976), Nat. Mid. Sch. Assn. (planning com., registration chmn.), Colo. Assn. Mid. Level Edn. (session presenter, registration chmn.), Phi Delta Kappa. Democrat. Presbyterian. Avocations: reading, running, weight training, vocal music. Office: Laredo Mid Sch 5000 S Laredo St Aurora CO 80015-1749 E-mail: cecmatthew@aol.com.

MATTHEWS, BETTY PARKER, special education educator; b. Port Arthur, Tex., Dec. 9, 1929; d. Clarence G. and Florence (Sudduth) Parker; m. Paul A. Matthews, Mar. 25, 1955; children: Michael A., Scott P., Lisa M. Alexander. BS, La. Coll., 1975; MEd, Northwestern U., 1981. Specialist in edn. La., 1984; cert. elem. tchr., mentally retarded, learning disabled, ednl. cons., generic mild/moderate, assessment tchr., ednl. diagnostician, child search coord., La. 3d grade tchr. Rapides Parish Sch. Bd., Alexandria, La., 1975-76, tchr. spl. edn., 1976-81, assessment tchr., 1981-93, ednl. diagnostician, 1993—99; ednl. cons. Briarwood Psychiatric Hosp., Alexandria, La., 1986-93, Crossroads Psychiat. Hosp., Alexandria, 1993-96. Adj. prof. La. State U., Alexandria, 1990-98, La. Coll., Pineville; dir. Program to Assist Student Success. Dir. children's Bible study 1st Bapt. Ch., Pineville, La., 1985—. Mem. La. Ednl. Diagnosticians Assn. (regional rep. 1987-88, treas. 1988-90, Pres.'s Svc. award 1990-91, La. Assessment Tchr. of Yr. 1993), Coun. Exceptional Children, Reading Coun., Alpha Delta Kappa, Phi Delta Kappa, Epsilon Sigma Alpha (state pres., regional sec.). Home: 3050 Rigolette Rd Pineville LA 71360-7219

MATTHEWS, DIANNE FERNE, mathematics educator; b. New Hyde Park, N.Y., Nov. 30, 1966; d. Robert and Gloria (Hall) M.; m. Michael Leibowitz, Feb. 14, 1992. BS, SUNY, Stonybrook, 1987, MA in Math., 1989. Cert. tchr. math. Tchr. math., sci. Three Village Sch. Dist., Setauket, N.Y., 1989-91, advisor, coord. cheerleading and pep squad, 1989-92; coord., tchr. remedial math. Mid. County Sch. Dist., Centereach, N.Y., 1992—, advisor, coord. cheerleading and pep squad, 1992—. Adj. instr. coll. math. Suffolk C.C., Selden, N.Y., 1991—; judge L.I. Math. Fair., Selden, 1989—. Avocations: exercise, dancing, swimming, reading, crafts. Home: 57 Longstreet Dr Lake Grove NY 11755-2344

MATTHEWS, ELIZABETH WOODFIN, law librarian, law educator; b. Ashland, Va., July 30, 1927; d. Edwin Clifton and Elizabeth Frances (Luck) Woodfin; m. Sidney E. Matthews, Dec. 20, 1947; 1 child, Sarah Elizabeth Matthews Wiley. BA, Randolph-Macon Coll., 1948, LLD (hon.), 1989; MS in Libr. Sci., U. Ill., 1952; PhD, So. Ill. U., 1972; LLD, Randolph-Macon Coll., 1989. Cert. law libr., med. libr., med. libr. III. Libr. Ohio State U., Columbus, 1952-59; libr., instr. U. Ill., Urbana, 1962-63; lectr. U. Ill. Grad. Sch. Libr. Sci., Urbana, 1964; libr., instr. Morris Libr. So. Ill. U., Carbondale, 1964-67; classroom instr. So. Ill. U. Coll Edn., Carbondale, 1967-70; med. libr., asst. prof. Morris Libr. So. Ill. U., Carbondale, 1972-74, law libr., asst. prof., 1974-79, law libr., assoc. prof., 1979-85, law libr., prof., 1985-92, prof. emerita, 1993—. Author: Access Points to Law Libraries, 1984, 17th Century English Law Reports, 1986, Law Library Reference Shelf, 1988, 5th edit., 2003, Pages and Missing Pages, 1983, 2d edit., 1989, Lincoln as a Lawyer: An Annotated Bibliography, 1991. Mem. AAUW (pres. 1976-78, corp. rep. 1978-88), Am. Assn. Law Librs., Postdoctoral Acad. Higher Edn., Beta Phi Mu, Phi Kappa Phi. Methodist. Home: 811 S Skyline Dr Carbondale IL 62901-2405 Office: So Ill U Law Libr Carbondale IL 62901

MATTHEWS, ESTHER ELIZABETH, education educator, consultant; b. Princeton, Mass., June 20, 1918; d. Ralph Edgar and Julia Ellen (Cronin) M. BS in Edn., Worcester State Coll., 1940; EdM, Harvard U., 1943, EdD, 1960. Tchr. various Mass. schs., 1942-47; guidance dir. Holden (Mass.) Pub. Schs., 1947-53, Wareham (Mass.) Pub. Schs., 1954-57; counselor Newton (Mass.) High Sch., 1957-60, head counselor, 1960-66; assoc. prof. edn. U. Oreg., 1966-70, prof. edn., 1970-80, prof. emerita, 1980—. Vis. prof. U. Toronto, Ont., Can., summer 1971; lectr. on edn. Harvard U., 1963-66; cons. in field; lectr. various colls. and univs. Author book chpts.; contbr. numerous articles to profl. jours. and papers to conf. proc.; featured in spl. issue of Oreg. Counseling Assn. Jour., 1998. Recipient ACD award for contbn. to promote human rights, 1987. Mem. Nat. Vocat. Guidance Assn. (pres. 1974-75, chair nat. com. 1966-67, sec. 1967-68, bd. trustees 1968-71, editl. bd. Vocat. Guidance Quar. 1966-68), Oreg. Pers. and Guidance Assn. (Leona Tyler award 1973, Disting. Svc. award 1979), Oreg. Career Devel. Assn. (Disting. Svc. award 1987, Esther E. Matthews Ann. award established in her honor 1993). Home: 832 Lariat Dr Eugene OR 97401-6438

MATTHEWS, HEWITT WILLIAM, science educator; b. Pensacola, Fla., Dec. 1, 1944; s. Hewitt W. and Jestine Texas (Lowe) M.; m. Marlene Angela Mouzon, June 21, 1969; children: Derrick Hewitt, David Paul. BS in Chemistry, Clark Coll., 1966; BS in Pharmacy, Mercer U., 1968; MS in Pharm. Biochemistry, U. Wis., 1971, PhD in Pharm. Biochemistry, 1973. From asst. to assoc. prof. medicinal chemistry so. sch. pharmacy Mercer U., Atlanta, 1973-81, prof. pharm. scis., 1981—, Hood-Myer Alumni Chair prof., 1982—, dir. rsch., 1975-79, asst. to dean, 1979-80, asst. dean svcs., 1980-83, asst. provost, 1983-85, assoc. dean, 1985-89, acting dean, 1989-90, dean, 1990—. Rsch. chemist Ctr. Disease Control, Atlanta, 1976, vis. scientist hosp. infectious disease program, 1987, 88; pharmacist Dr.'s Meml. Hosp., Atlanta, 1978-80; vis. assoc. prof. Tex. So. U., Houston, 1979; lectr. pharmacology sch. anesthesia Ga. Bapt. Med. Ctr., 1979-85; lectr. advanced nutrition dept. allied healths Clark Coll., 1980-82, mem. adv. bd. sci. enrichment and rsch. program, 1986—; item writer Nat. Assn. Bds. Pharmacy Licensure Examinations, 1981, 83-87; mem. Ga. State Bd. Pharmacy Continuing Edn. Tripartite Com., 1986-89, Gov.'s Adv. Coun. Sci. and Tech. Devel., 1992-93; mem. various coms., advisor various univ. orgns. Mercer U.; presenter in field. Mem. editorial adv. bd. Jour. Nat. Pharm. Assn., 1981-83, reviewer, 1989, U.S. Pharmacist, 1982-83; mem. editl. bd. Pharmacy Today, Am. Pharm. Assn., 1995—; contbr. articles to profl. jours. Assoc. pastor Fellowship Faith Ch., Internat.; coach Little League Baseball, Fayette County 10 & Under Basketball; score keeper Fayette County Athletic Assn.; mem. Fayette C. of C. Project Fayette Housing and Labor Task Force; bd. dirs. met. Atlanta chpt. ARC, 1986—. Recipient Friend of Acad. Student Pharmacists award, 1991-92; named Outstanding Citizen of State of Ga., Ga. Ho. of Reps., 1992; grantee Bristol Labs., 1974, Pfeiffer Found., 1976-80, Hoechst-Roussel, 1982-91, Smith Kline Beckman Corp., 1986, Am. Cyanamid Co., 1987, Glaxo, Inc., 1988, Sandoz Pharm. Co., 1988, 89; fellow Am. Found. Pharm. Edn., 1968, pre-doctoral fellow NIH, 1970-73. Mem. Am. Soc. Hosp. Pharmacists, Am. Pharm. Assn., Am. Assn. Hosp. Pharmacists, Am. Assn. Colls. Pharmacy (chmn. profl. affairs com. 1984-85, rsch. and grad. affairs com. 1986-87, GAPS grant reviewer 1987, reviewer mgmt. systems manuel minorities 1988-89, coun. deans nominating com. 1990-91), Nat. Pharm. Assn. (v.p. 1994—, Recognition award 1990), Ga. Soc. Hosp. Pharmacists (continuing edn. com. 1986-87, strategic planning com. 1991), Ga. Pharm. Assn. (com. colls. 1984-85, continuing edn. com. 1986-87, commn. pharm. care 1991—), Tenn. Pharmacists Assn., Atlanta Acad. Instl. Pharmacists, Beta Kappa Chi, Kappa Epsilon (assoc.), Phi Kappa Phi, Phi Lambda Sigma, Rho Chi, Sigma Xi. Avocations: basketball, ping pong, reading, music. Home: 120 Hanover Cir Fayetteville GA 30214-1233 Office: Mercer U So Sch Pharmacy 3001 Mercer University Dr Atlanta GA 30341-4155

MATTHEWS, KATHERINE JEAN, principal; b. Kansas City, Mo., July 20, 1948; d. Carl Martin and Virginia Mae (Carlson) Olson; m. Stephen Henry Matthews, June 2, 1973; 1 child, Karen Elizabeth. BS, North Park Coll., 1970; MA, No. Ill. U., 1973; Cert. Advanced Study, Nat.-Lewis U., 1989. Tchr. elem. Meml. Sch., Houston, 1970-71; learning disablities specialsit Hononegah High Sch., Rocton, Ill., 1973; tchr. elem. Spl. Edn. Dist. McHenry County, Crystal Lake, Ill., 1973-74; tchr. learning disabilities Rockford (Ill.) Pub. Schs., 1974-77, diagnostic specialist, 1976-78, supr. spl. edn., 1978-90, asst. dir. student svcs., 1990-93; prin. John Nelson Elem. Sch., Rockford, 1993—. Asst. prof. Rockford Coll., 1988-92; cons. Child and Family Guidance Clinic, Rockford, 1988-92, Ill. State Bd. Edn., Springfield, 1988-90. Mem. Jr. League Rockford, 1985-88. Mem. Coun. of Exceptional Children (pres. 1970-71), Phi Delta Kappa. Avocations: traveling, reading, music, boating. Home: 4610 Sunderman Rd Rockford IL 61114-6270

MATTHEWS, KATHLEEN SHIVE, biochemistry educator; b. Austin, Tex., Aug. 30, 1945; d. William and Gwyn Shive; m. Randall Matthews. BS in Chemistry, U. Tex., 1966; PhD in Biochemistry, U. Calif., Berkeley, 1970. Post doctoral fellow Stanford (Calif.) U., 1970-72; mem. faculty Rice U., Houston, 1972—, chair dept., 1987-95, Wiess prof., 1989-96, Stewart Meml. chair, 1996—, dean natural scis., 1998—. Mem. BBCB study sect. NIH, Bethesda, Md., 1980-84, 86-88, BRSG adv. com., 1992-94; mem. adv. com. on rsch. programs Tex. Higher Edn. Coord. Bd., Austin, 1987-92; mem. undergrad. edn. initiative rev. panel Howard Hughes Rsch. Inst., Bethesda, 1991, mem. rsch. resources rev. panel, 1995, mem. predoctoral fellowships rev. panel, 2001, Trustee S.W. Rsch. Inst., Steering Com. Vinson & Elkins Women's Initiative Adv. Bd., 2001. Mem. editl. bd. Jour. Biol. Chemistry, 1988-93, assoc. editor, 1994-99; contbr. 140 reviewed papers. Fellow AAAS; mem. Am. Soc. Biochemistry and Molecular Biology (nominating com. 1993-94, 96-97, fin. com. 2001-2002), Protein Soc., Biophys. Soc. (pub. affairs com.), Am. Chem. Soc., Phi Beta Kappa. Office: Rice Univ PO Box 1892 6100 Main St MS102 Houston TX 77005-1892 E-mail: ksm@rice.edu.

MATTHEWS, KEVIN MICHAEL, architecture educator, researcher; b. Eugene, Oreg., Jan. 5, 1959; s. Herbert Maurice and Jennifer (Saunders) M.; m. Donna Marie Meredith. BA, U.Calif., 1982; MArch, U. Calif., 1988. Intern Esherick, Homsey, Dodge, Davis, San Francisco, 1987; lectr. U. Calif., Berkeley, 1988-89; prin. Matthews Assoc., Berkeley, 1985-90; CAD coord. Superconducting Super Collider, Dallas, 1989; asst. prof. dept. arch. U. Oreg., Eugene, Oreg., 1990—; dir. Design Integration Lab., Eugene, Oreg., 1992—; pres. Artifice, Inc., Eugene, Oreg., 1993—. CAD cons. SSC Central Design Group, Berkeley, 1987-88. Author: The Great Buildings Collection, 1994, DesignWorkshop, 1993. Recipient Rsch. grant Apple Computer Inc., 1991, 92, Curriculum Devel. grant., 1992. Mem. Am. Inst. Arch. (assoc.), Assn. Computing Machinery, Soc. Arch. Historians, Assn. Collegiate Schs. Arch. Avocations: sailing, backpacking, traditional blacksmithing. Office: Artifice Inc PO Box 1588 Eugene OR 97440-1588

MATTHEWS, LOIS MARR, musician, music educator; b. Washington, July 10, 1928; d. Ralph Dorian and Ruth Hayes Marr; m. Richard Matthews, June 23, 1956; children: Julia Louise Pagio, Christine Dorian Trout, Melanie Marr Doss. BA, Wilson Tchrs. Coll., 1950; MA in Music, Columbia U., 1953. Organist Calvary Meth. Ch., Arlington, Va., Cmty. Meth. Ch., Meml. Bapt. Ch. Mem.: DAR, Am. Guild Organists. Methodist. Avocations: piano, organ, painting. Home: 6329 Arbor Way Elkridge MD 21075

MATTHEWS, STEVEN RICHARD, culinary instructor, chef, consultant; b. Lowell, Mass., Mar. 31, 1962; s. Edward Joseph and Elizabeth Anne (Howcroft) M.; m. Carmen DeJesus Orellana, June 28, 1985; children: Christine, Adrian, Tania. Student, U. Lowell, 1981, Santa Monica (Calif.) Coll., 1982-83. Banquet sous chef Windsor, Dracut, Mass., 1976-80; head chef Charmer's Market, Santa Monica, 1981-83; exec. chef Rose Cafe, Venice, Calif., 1984-92; instr. culinary arts U. Calif.-L.A., Westwood, Calif., 1987-91; exec. chef Hennessey's Tavern Inc., 1992—. Cons. co-owner So. Calif. Chef, L.A., 1986; cons. Chatter's Restaurant, Sherman Oaks, Calif., 1988. Mem. Am. Culinary Fedn., Chef's De Cuisine Assn. Calif., The Wine Soc. of Am. Roman Catholic. Avocations: art, literature, photography. Office: 1845 S Elena Ave Redondo Beach CA 90277-5707

MATTHEWS, WYHOMME S. retired music educator, academic administrator; b. Battle Creek, Mich., July 22, 1948; d. Woodrow R. and LouLease (Graham) Sellers; m. Edward L. Matthews, Apr. 29, 1972; children: Channing DuVall, Triston Curran, Landon Edward, Brandon Graham. AA, Kellogg C.C., 1968; MusB, Mich. State U., 1970, MA, MusM, Mich. State U., 1972. Cert. elem. and secondary tchr., Mich. Tchr., vocal music dir. Benton Harbor (Mich.) Pub. Schs., 1971-72, dir. vocal music, 1972; dir. edn. head start program Burlington (N.J.) County, 1972-73; pvt. music tchr., 1973-89; tchr. Southeastern Jr. H.S., 1986-87, W.K. Kellogg Jr. H.S., 1987-89; chair visual and performing arts dept. Kellogg C.C., Battle Creek, Mich., 1989-99, dir. Eastern acad. Ctr., 1999—2003, ret., 2003. Part-time instr. Kellogg C.C., 1973—, dir. Eclectic Chorale, 1973—, dir., organizer Kellogg C.C. Eclectic Chorale Sacred Cultural Festival, 1979—, judge various contests; artistic dir. Battle Creek Sojourner Truth Monument Presentation Day, 1999; presenter in field. Pres. Dudley Elem. Sch., 1981-85; active Battle Creek Pub. Schs. PTA, Pennfield Pub. Schs. PTA, Mt. Zion African Meth. Episc. Ch.; v.p. Life Care Amb. Bd., 1990-2003; bd. dirs. Leila Aboretum Soc.; mem. Battle Creek Cmty. Found., Glen Cross Arts and Infrasture Fund. Mich. State U. fellow, 1971; recipient Outstanding Cmty. Svc. award, 1975, Sojourner Truth award, 2000, George award City of Battle Creek, 2000. Mem. Mich. Music Tchr. Assn., Nat. Music Tchrs. Assn., Battle Creek Music Tchrs. Assn., Battle Creek Morning Music Club (bd. dirs.), Nat. Leadership Acad., Battle Creek Cmty. Concert Assn. Home: 466 Alton Ave Battle Creek MI 49017-3212 E-mail: wmatth5278@aol.com.

MATTHEWS-BURWELL, VICKI, elementary education educator; Elem. tchr. New Plymouth Elem. Sch. Named State Tchr. of Yr. Elem., Idaho, 1993. Office: New Plymouth Elem Sch 704 S Plymouth Ave New Plymouth ID 83655-3062

MATTHIAS, JOHN EDWARD, English literature educator; b. Columbus, Ohio, Sept. 5, 1941; s. John Marshall and Lois (Kirkpatrick) M.; m. Diana Clare Jocelyn, Dec. 27, 1967; children— Cynouai, Laura. BA, Ohio State U., 1963; MA, Stanford U., 1966; postgrad., U. London, 1967. Asst. prof. dept. English U. Notre Dame, Ind., 1966-73, assoc. prof., 1973-80, prof., 1980—. Vis. fellow Clare Hall, Cambridge U., 1966-77, assoc., 1977— ; vis. prof. dept. English, Skidmore Coll., Saratoga Springs, N.Y., 1975, U. Chgo., 1980. Author: Bucyrus, 1971, Turns, 1975, Crossing, 1979, Five American Poets, 1980, Introducing David Jones, 1980, Contemporary Swedish Poetry, 1980, Bathory and Lermontov, 1980, Northern Summer, New and Selected Poems, 1984, The Battle of Kosovo, 1987, David Jones: Man and Poet: A Gathering of Ways, 1991, Reading Old Friends, 1991, Swimming at Midnight, 1995, Beltane at Aphelion, 1995, Pages: New Poems and Cuttings, 2000. Recipient Columbia U. Transl. award, 1978, Swedish Inst. award, 1981, Poetry award Soc. Midland Authors, 1984, Ingram Merrill Found. award, 1984, 90; Woodrow Wilson fellow, 1963, Lily Endowment fellow, 1993; Fulbright grantee, 1966. Mem. AAUP, PEN, Poets and Writers, Poetry Soc. Am. (George Bogin Meml. award 1990). Office: U Notre Dame Dept English Notre Dame IN 46556

MATTHIS, EVA MILDRED BONEY, retired academic administrator; b. Magnolia (Waycross), N.C., Aug. 18, 1927; d. James Horace and Eva Alice (Merritt) Boney; m. George Clifton Matthis, Aug. 31, 1949; 1 child, George Clifton Jr. AA, Louisburg Coll., 1946; BS, East Carolina U., 1969, MLS, 1971. Advt. mgr. Efirds, Wilmington, N.C., 1946-49; advt. acct. Lenoir Co. News, 1950; syn. aviation instrument instr. Serv-Air Aviation, Kinston, N.C., 1951-57; advt. account exec. Kinston Free Press, 1959-64; libr. Caswell Ctr., 1965-66; history tchr. North Lenoir High Sch., 1969-70; libr. Sampson Elem. Sch., 1970-72; head libr. media program Lenoir C.C., Kinston, 1972-76, dean, learning resources, 1976-89, dean, mktg. instl. devel., learning resources, 1989-91, dean, instl. advancement, 1991, v.p. instrnl. svcs. Alumni rep. East Carolina U. LS SACS Self-study, Greenville, 1987-89. Family editor: Heritage of Lenoir County, 1981. Developer Heritage Place, local history mus., 1988; pres. Jr. Women's Club, Kinston, 1960; dist. dir. N.C. Jr. Women's Club, 1961; mem. Kinston Mayor's All-Am. City Com., 1988, co-chair, 1996-97 ; rep. Lenoir County Bicentennial Com., Kinston, 1987; staff-parish chmn. Queen Street United Meth. Ch., 1988-90, mem. bishop's coun., 1988-90, com. chmn., 1988-90, chmn. fin. com., 1992—, bldg. com., 1992-94, Sunday Sch. tchr., mem. adminstrv. bd., 1984—; mem. Kinston Mus. com., 1990-92, Fireman Mus. com., 1992-93; chair archtl. survey, Lenoir county, 1993. Named Scouting Family of Yr., 1970; recipient merit award N.C. Hist. Soc., 1989, Excellence award Kinston C. of C., 1985, Educators Office Pers. Lenoir C.C., Adminstr. of Yr. award, 1990. Mem. N.C. C.C. Learning Resources Assn. (life, pub. info. officer 1989-92, exec. bd., dir. dist. II 1986-89, Achievement award 1992, Hon. Mention Libr. Jour. LIbr. of Yr. 1991), Librs. of Lenoir County (pres. 1985, 92), Lenoir County Hist. Assn. (v.p., exec. bd.), Coun. on Resource Devel., Hist. Lenoir County-Kinston Celebration, East Carolina U. Alumni Assn., Phi Beta Kappa, Delta Kappa Gamma (yearbook editor). Avocations: basketmaking, reading, gardening, grandmothering. Home: PO Box 6340 Kinston NC 28501-0340 also: 6532 English Oak Dr Raleigh NC 27615

MATTICE, HOWARD LEROY, retired education educator; b. Roxbury, N.Y., Sept. 23, 1935; s. Charles Pierce and Loretta Jane (Ellis) M.; m. Elaine Grace Potts, Feb. 4, 1956 (dec. Jan. 2002); children: Kevin, Stephen. BA, King's Coll., 1960; MA, L.I. U., 1965, NYU, 1969; cert., CUNY, 1972; EdD, NYU, 1978. Cert. tchr. N.Y., clin. educators trainer, Fla. Dept. Edn. Social studies tchr. N.Y.C. Bd. Edn., 1961-90, mid. and jr. H.S. asst. prin., 1970-72, 73-75; assoc. prof. edn. and history Clearwater (Fla.) Christian Coll., 1990-92, chmn. divsn. of edn., prof. edn. and history, 1992-99, ret., 1999; prof. of edn. and history Clearwater Christian Coll., 2002—; social studies curriculum writer Accelerated Christian Edn., 2003. Adj. lectr. history S.I. C.C., CUNY, 1969-75; curriculum writer N.Y.C. Bd. Edn., 1985, Accelerated Christian Edn., Largo, Fla., 2003—; program reviewer Fla. Dept. Edn., Tallahassee, 1994—; item writer GED Testing Svc., Washington, 1988-92; mem. So. Assn. Colls. and Schs. Accreditation Team H.S., 1995—. Chmn. bd. New Dorp Christian Acad., S.I., 1973-90; chmn. bd. deacons New Dorp. Bapt. Ch., S.I., 1981-90. Mem. ASCD, Assn. Tchr. Educators, Nat. Coun. Social Studies, So. Assn. Colls. and Schs. (h.s. accreditation review team 1995—). Avocations: reading, traveling, gardening.

MATTILA, MARY JO KALSEM, elementary and art educator; b. Canton, Ill., Oct. 26, 1944; d. Joseph Nelson and Bernice Nora (Milbauer) Kalsem; m. John Peter Mattila, Jan. 27, 1968. BS in Art, U. Wis., 1966; student, Ohio State U., 1972, Drake U., 1981; MS in Ednl. Adminstrn., Iowa State U., 1988. Cert. tchr., prin., supr., adminstr., art tchr., secondary tchr., Iowa. Tchr. 2d grade McHenry (Ill.) Pub. Schs., 1966-67, Wisconsin Hts. Schs., Black Earth, Wis., 1967-69; substitute tchr. Columbus (Ohio) City Schs., 1969-70; elem. art tchr. Southwestern City Schs., Columbus, 1972-73; adminstrv. intern Ames, Iowa, 1984-86; lead tchr. at Roosevelt Sch. Ames Cmty. Schs., 1986-87, art vertical curriculum chair, 1983-89, art educator, elem. and spl. edn., 1973—. Author articles. Active LWV, Ames, 1982—; fundraiser Altrusa, Ames, 1992—. Recipient Very Spl. Svc. award for Disting. Svc. in Very Spl. Arts, Gov. of Iowa, 1984. Mem. ASCD, NEA, Nat. Assn. Elem. Sch. Prins., Nat. Art Edn. Assn. Avocations: collecting old stoneware jugs, growing orchids, reading. Home: 2822 Duff Ave Ames IA 50010-4710 Office: Ames Cmty Schs 120 S Kellogg Ave Ames IA 50010-6719

MATTOON, SARA HALSEY (SALLY MATTOON), consultant, director; b. Bronxville, N.Y., July 8, 1947; d. Henry Amasa Jr. and Dorothy Ann (Teeter) M. AAS in Edn., Bennett Coll., 1967; BS in Edn., Pre-Medicine, So. Conn. State U., 1969; MA in Edn., Psychology, Social Welfare and Corrections, Calif. State U., Chico, 1976. Cert. tchr., Calif. Tchr. San Diego Unified Sch. Dist., 1969-72, Montgomery Creek Sch. Dist., Round Mountain, Calif., 1972-73; founder, tchr., dir. Chico Youth Devel. Ctr., Inc., 1973-80; pres. Exec. Excellence, San Diego and Weston, Conn., 1973-90; dir. EarthStar Alliance, San Diego, 1989—, Tucson, 1989—. Chmn. bd. dirs. Chico Youth Devel. Ctr., Inc., 1980—. Mem. Am. Assn. Profls.

Practicing Transcendental Mediation Program (pres. San Diego chpt. 1985-89), World Plan Exec. Coun. (bd. govs. 1978—, Info. and Inspiration award 1985). Office: 1163 N Thunder Ridge Dr Tucson AZ 85745-3378

MATTSON, BEVERLY LOUISE, special education educator; b. Little Rock, Aug. 26, 1946; d. Marvin George and Dorothy L. (Young) M. BS in Edn., U. Cen. Ark., 1968; MA, George Washington U., 1976; EdS, George Peabody Coll., 1980; PhD in Edn., George Mason U., 1994. Ednl. coord. Children's Hosp., Washington, 1976-78, 80-83, project adminstrn. med. ednl. tng. program, 1980-81, neuropsychol. assessor, 1979-80; cons. D.C. Assn. for Retarded Citizens, Washington, 1983-84; rsch. asst. Inst. for Study of Exceptional Children, U. Md., College Park, 1984-85; rsch. assoc. St. John's Child Devel. Ctr., Washington, 1985-87; rsch. cons. Calif. Rsch. Inst., San Francisco, 1988-89, SRI Internat., Menlo Park, Calif., 1990-91; no. regional coord. Va. Statewide Systems Change Project, George Mason U., Fairfax, 1990-91; adj. prof. George Mason U., Fairfax, 1982-87, 91-93; integration facilitator spl. edn. Arlington (Va.) Pub. Schs., 1991-93; asst. prof. divsn. continuing edn. U. Va., 1993—2000; coord. Nat. Assn. State Dirs. Spl. Edn., 1994-95; sr. program officer Acad. Edn. Devel., Washington, 1995-98; sr. rsch. assoc. RMC Rsch. Corp., 1998—; faculty assoc. Johns Hopkins U., Balt., 1998—2000. Pvt. cons., Arlington, 1978—; field reader grants U.S. Dept. Edn., Washington, 1990-92, 98. Editl. reviewer Teacher Education and Special Educator; contbr. articles to profl. publs., chpt. to book. Vol., v.p., treas. Devotion to Children; rec. sec. Alexandria Bus. and Profl. Women's Club. Recipient program devel. award dept. edn. George Mason U., 1983, Tech. Achievement award Acad. Edn. Devel., 1995, Svc. award Am. Occupl. Therapy Assn., 1996. Mem. ASCD, Nat. Staff Devel. Coun., Coun. for Exceptional Children, Am. Evaluation Assn., Am. Ednl. Rsch. Assn., D.C. Concerned Citizens for Spl. Edn. (sec.-treas. 1986-90), Alexandria Bus. and Profl. Women's Club (sec.). Avocations: chinese cooking, theater, symphony. Office: RMC Rsch Corp 1815 Fort Myer Dr Ste 800 Arlington VA 22209-1811 Home: Apt T2 1134 S Washington St Falls Church VA 22046-4026

MATTSON, RICHARD HENRY, neurologist, educator; b. Waterbury, Conn., May 9, 1931; s. George F. and Edith O. (Curtiss) Mattson; m. Elena Mary Hill, June 13, 1954; children: Richard Jr., Gail Mattson-Gates, Catherine Mattson-Fimmers; m. Martha Ann Crosier, Feb. 14, 2001; 1 child, Madelaine. BS, Yale U., 1953, MA (hon.), 1967; MD, Boston U., 1957; MS, U. Minn., 1962. Intern Wilford Hall USAF Hosp., San Antonio, 1957-58, chief neurology, cons. to surgeon gen., 1962-67; resident in neurology Mayo Clinic., Rochester, Minn., 1958-62; asst. clin. prof. neurology U. Tex. Med. Br., Galveston, 1964-67; asst. chief and chief of neurology VA Med. Ctr., West Haven, Conn., 1967-92; from asst. prof. to prof. neurology Yale U. Sch. Medicine, New Haven, 1967—, dir. med. studies dept. neurology, 1985—2002, dir. residency tng. program dept. neurology, 1985-96, dir. clin. neurosci. curriculum, 1990—2002, vice-chmn. for acad. affairs, 1995-99, admissions com., faculty promotions com., 1996-98. Dir. NIH Yale Epilepsy Program Project, 1985-2003; cons. VA Ctrl. Office, 1967-92, NIH, 1974-78, 97—, various pharm. cos.; chmn. Therapeutic Strategies Commn., 1997—, Internat. League Against Epilepsy. Author: Antipileptic Drugs, 2002, other related books; contbr. articles to profl. jours. Named Amb. for Epilepsy, Internat. League Against Epilepsy, 1989, Hans Berger Disting. scholar, 2001; recipient H.V. Jones award, Mayo Found., 1962, Best Clin. Trial award, Internat. League Against Epilepsy, 1988. Fellow: Am. EEG Soc., Am. Acad. Neurology; mem.: So. Clin. Neurol. Soc. (pres.), Am. Epilepsy Soc. (pres. 1986—87, William G. Lennox award 1994, Hans Berger Lecture award 1997, Novartis/ILAE Epileptology prize 1997, AES.Milken Clin. Investigator award 1997), Am. Neurol. Assn., Begg Honor Soc. Avocations: sailing, gardening.

MATULICH, SERGE, accounting educator, author; b. Split, Croatia, June 8, 1933; came to U.S., 1946; s. Daniel M. and Josephine (Schuster) Raseta; m. Margarete Manderscheid, Dec. 7, 1957; children: Alexander Matulich, Erika Matulich. BS in Acctg. with honors, Calif. State U., Sacramento, 1964; PhD in Bus., U. Calif., Berkeley, 1971. CPA, Fla.; cert. cost analyst. Grad. asst. U. Calif., Davis, 1964-65; asst. prof. Calif. State U., Hayward, 1966-67; assoc. in acctg. U. Calif., Berkeley, 1968-71, vis. asst. prof., 1974-75; asst. prof. Sch. Bus. Ind. U., 1971-76; assoc. prof. acctg. Sch. Bus. Tex. Christian U., 1976-84; vis. prof. U. North Tex., spring 1983; prof. Crummer Grad. Sch. Bus. Rollins Coll., Winter Park, Fla., 1984—2001, prof. emeritus, 2002—. Bd. dirs. Marconi Med. Ctr., Inc., Sacramento, 1967-71, Bazeghi Corp., Oakland, Calif., 1968-71, Crescent Gen. Corp., 1969-71 (also v.p.), Fin. Floorplans, Inc., Ft. Worth, 1980-2003, Way To Go, Inc., Orlando, Fla., 1988-2000, Unicorn Rsch. Corp., Orlando, 1989—, Global Ptnrs. Corp., Orlando, 1994-2000 (also sec.). Author number of fin. acctg., mgmt. acct., cost acctg. textbooks, study guides; contbr. many articles to profl. jours. With U.S. Army, 1956-58. Recipient U. Pitts. BEFEE grant, 1993, 94, Ernst & Ernst Acctg. Achievement award, 1967, EMBA Outstanding Prof. award Class of 1986, 88, Delta Sigma Pi Scholarship key, 1964; Fulbright fellowship, 1999; Fulbright Alumni Initiatives Awards program grant, 2000-02. Mem. AICPA, Am. Acctg. Assn., World Future Soc., Fulbright Assn. (founding mem., treas. mid-Fla. chpt. 2002--), Beta Alpha Psi, Beta Gamma Sigma. Avocations: classical music, travel. Home: 4621 N Landmark Dr Orlando FL 32817-1235 Office: Crummer Grad Sch Bus Rollins Coll 1000 Holt Ave Winter Park FL 32789-4499 E-mail: serge@rollins.edu., serge@unicorn.us.com.

MATURA, RAYMOND CARL, gerontologist, sociologist, educator; b. Phila., Jan. 8, 1948; s. William and Nell Sophia (Pincurek) M.; m. Pamela Kay (Black), June 7, 1975; children: Meagan Elise, Ryan Matthew. BA, Rio Grande Coll., Bidwell, Ohio, 1970; MA, Ohio U., 1973; PhD, U. Fla., 1982. Instr., asst. prof., then assoc. prof. Rio Grande Coll., Bidwell, Ohio, 1972-87, prof. sociology & gerontology Rio Grande, Ohio, 1987—. Vis. prof. U. Fla., Gainesville, 1981; ednl. cons. Agy. on Aging, Rio Grande, Ohio 1975—; pres. Ohio Network of Ednl. Cons.,in the Field of Aging, 1989—; pres. bd. dirs. Gailia County Sheltered Workshop, Cheshire, Ohio, 1981-85. Author: Elderly Issues, 1981; contbr. articles, book revs. to various publ. V.p. Ohio Assn. of Gerontology and Edn.; county coord., Ohio gubernatorial campaign, 1978, 82, 86, 90; exec. com. Gallia County Dem. party, 1982-03, vice-chmn., 1988-90; steering com. Gallipolis (Ohio) City Schs., 1985-87; lay minister Scared Heart Ch., 1982-03, v.p. ch. coun., 1984-90; pres. Rio Grande Baseball Assn.; coach children's basketball, soccer, baseball. Recipient Sears Outstanding Tchr. Award, 1990, Jones Tchr. Award, 1993. Mem. K.C. (Grand Knight), Lions, Alpha Kappa Delta. Roman Catholic. Home: 70 Kristi Dr Rio Grande OH 45674 Office: U Rio Grande PO Box 847 Bidwell OH 45614-9998

MATYJASZEWSKI, KRZYSZTOF, chemist, educator; b. Konstantynow, Poland, Apr. 8, 1950; came to U.S., 1985; s. Henryk and Antonina (Styss) M.; m. Malgorzata Kowalska, July 15, 1972; children: Antoni, Maria. BS, MS, Tech. U., Moscow, 1972; PhD, Polish Acad. Scis., Lodz, 1976; DSc, Lodz Poly., 1985. Postdoctoral fellow U. Fla., 1977-78; rsch. assoc. Polish Acad. Scis., 1978-84, CNRS, France, 1984-85; asst. prof. chemistry Carnegie Mellon U., Pitts., 1985-89, assoc. prof., 1989-93, prof., 1993—, head dept. chemistry, 1994-98, J.C. Warner prof., 1998—. Invited prof. U. Paris, 1985; vis. prof. U. Freiburg, 1988, U. Paris, 1990, 97, 98, U. Bayreuth, 1991, U. Strasbourg, 1992, U. Bordeaux, 1996, Univ. Ulm, 1999, U. Pisa, 2000; adj. prof., U. Pitts., 2000-, Polish Acad. Sci., 2000-; cons. Dow Corning, Midland, Mich., 1988-89, Arco, Phila., 1990-92, GE, Schenectady, 1992—, Amoco, Naperville, Ill., 1994-97, Reilly Ind., Indpls., 1994—, Air Products, Allentown, Pa., 1994-97. Author 7 books; mem. editorial bd. Macromolecules, Macromolecular Synthesis, Jour. Polymer Sci., Jour. Macromolecular Sci.-Pure and Applied Chemistry, Jour. Inorganic and Organometallic Polymers, Polymer, others; editor Progress Polymer Sci.; contbr. chpts. to books, more than 600 articles to profl. jours.; 27 patents in field. Recipient award Polish Acad. Sci., 1981, Presdl. Young Investigator award NSF, 1989, Humboldt award for Sr. U.S. Scientists, 1999, Pitts. award, 2001. Fellow: ACS (Carl S. Marvel award 1995, Polymer Chemistry award 2002), Internat. Union Pure and Applied Chemistry (corr. mem. polymer nomenclature), Polymer Materials Sci. Engring.; mem.: French Acad. Sci. (Elf chair 1998). Achievements include research in synthesis of well defined macromolecules via living and controlled polymerizations; organometallic polymers. Home: 9 Queens Ct Pittsburgh PA 15238-1519 Office: Carnegie Mellon U 4400 5th Ave Pittsburgh PA 15213-2617

MAUBERT, JACQUES CLAUDE, retired school superintendent; b. Provins, France, May 19, 1932; s. Jean Pierre and Simone Jeanne (Bocqueho) M.; m. Micheline Josephine Lathuille, June 16, 1956; children: Eric, Sandrine. MA, Dakar U., Senegal, 1969; CAPES, U. Bordeaux (France), 1971. Tchr. French Ministry Edn., Morocco, 1952-62, 1962—73, councellor and tchr., 1973-75, Lome, Togo, 1975-77, headmaster LeMans, France, 1977-79, headmaster Lycee Francais of San Francisco, 1979-85, headmaster, 1985-86, headmaster Lyceum Kennedy N.Y.C., 1986-2000; ret., 2000. Mem., pres. Commn. Reform for Tchg. French in Africa, Dakar, 1973—75; pedagogic councellor U. Benin, Togo, 1975—77. Author: French Literature for 11th Grade, 1975. Pres. Union des Francais de l' Etranger, San Francisco, 1983-85. Decorated officer The Acad. Palms (France). Roman Catholic. Avocations: swimming, tennis, classical music, jazz, opera. Home: 80 Longfellow Rd Mill Valley CA 94941-1591 E-mail: jacqmichmaub@comcast.net.

MAUCH, JEANNINE ANN, elementary education educator; b. Scribner, Nebr., Apr. 17, 1944; d. Oscar Herman Frederick and Viola Fredricka (Backhus) M. BS in Luth. Teaching, Concordia Coll., 1966, MEd, 1988. Cert. tchr., Nebr. Tchr. 1st, 2d, 3d and 4th grades St. Paul Luth. Ch., Perham, Minn., 1966-68; tchr. 3d and 4th grades Wheat Ridge (Colo.) Luth. Ch., 1968-70; tchr., prin. St. Mark Luth. Ch., Yonkers, N.Y., 1970-86; tchr. 3d, 4th and 5th grades Zion Luth. Ch., Plainview, Nebr., 1987—, prin., 1999-2000. Recipient 25-Yr. Svc. plaque Zion Luth. Ch., Plainview, 1992, 30-Yr. Svc. Plaque, 1997, others. Mem. Luth. Edn. Assn. Avocations: travel, craft shows, punch embroidery. Home: PO Box 218 Plainview NE 68769-0218

MAUCK, ELAINE CAROLE, retired secondary education educator; b. Martinsburg, W.Va., Dec. 25, 1946; d. Ace William and June Elaine (Burch) Gray; m. Jess Willard Mauck Jr., May 26, 1972. BA in Secondary Edn., Shepherd Coll., 1968; MS in Phys. Edn., W.Va. U., 1977. Cert. tchr., W.Va. Libr. asst. Shepherd (W.Va.) Coll., 1964-68; libr., rschr. King Daus. Nursing Sch., Martinsburg, W.Va., 1967-68; tchr. Washington Co. Schs., Hagerstown, Md., 1968-69, Berkele County Schs., Martinsburg, 1969-99; ret., 1999; owner E&J Enterprises, 1985—, Silver Age Svcs., 1996—, Crim de la Crim, 2000—. Mem. phys. edn. Mountain Top Summit W.Va. Bd. Edn., Charleston, 1993-95, Health Schs. com., 1990-93, Nutrition Cadre com., 1987-99; spkr. U. N.C., 1990. Mem. Calvary Meth. Ch., Martinsburg. Recipient Excellence award Berkeley County Sch. Bus., 1987-94, W.Va. Fitness award Pres.'s Challenge, 1992; grantee Women's Found., 1992. Mem. W.Va. Edn. Assn. (polit. action com. 1983-92), AAHPERD (Secondary Tchr. award 1993), W.Va. Alliance Health, Phys. Edn., Recreation, and Dance (Secondary Tchr. award 1992). Avocations: researcher, collecting first edition books. Home: 263 Nameless Way Martinsburg WV 25401-9803

MAUER, RICHARD I. educational association administrator; BBA, Campbell U., 1980, M in Edn. Guidance and Counseling, 1983; MPA, U. LaVerne, 1988. Edn. svcs. officer, specialist, Ft. Greely, Alaska; edn. svcs. officer Ft. Wainwright, Alaska, 1999—. Chair Alaska State Bd. Edn. and Early Devel., 2003—. Elected mem. Delta/Greely Sch. Bd.; dir., past pres. Assn. Alaska Sch. Bds. Office: PO Box 1302 Delta Junction AK 99737*

MAUGHMER, MARK DAVID, aerospace engineering educator; b. Columbus, Ohio, Jan. 18, 1950; s. Ernest C. and Shirley Ann (Frey) M.; m. Joan M. Yanusas, Aug. 5, 1972; children: Mark D., Kori Marie, Dylan N. BS, U. Ill., 1972, PhD, 1983; MS in Engring., Princeton U., 1975. Rsch. engr. dept. aerospace and mech. scis. Princeton (N.J.) U., 1974-77; prof. aerospace engring. Pa. State U., University Park, 1984—. Mem.Assoc. Fellow, AIAA, Internat. Orgn. for Sci. Tech. Soaring, Soaring. Soc. Am. Avocations: soaring, woodworking, squash. Home: RR 1 Box 965 Petersburg PA 16669-9415 Office: Pa State U Dept Aerospace Engring 229 Hammond Bldg University Park PA 16802-1401

MAULTSBY, MARILYN D. health science association administrator; b. Balt., 1953; BA, Case Western Res. U., 1975; MS, U. Cin., 1976. Dir. planning Md. Health Planning Commn., 1977—86; dir. regional policy Greater Balt. Com., 1986—88; dir. pub. policy BlueCross BlueShield Md., 1988—93, v.p. strategic planning and adminstrn., 1993—95; dir. devel. and mgmt. svcs. Fidelity Health Sys. Inc., 1996—98; exec. dir. Md. Health Care Found., 1998—. Chair Role Network 2000, Inc., 1995—; mem. Balt. City Bd. Fin., 1997—; mem., pres. Md. State Bd. Edn., 2002—; bd. mem. Md. Assn. Health Underwriters, N.W. Hosp. Ctr. Vice chair Bd. Associated Black Charities, 1996—98; chair nominating com. Md. Com. for Children, 1997—99; mem. Govs. Task Force on Charitable Giving, 1997—; chair, bd. mem. Associated Black Charities, 1998—; mem. audit and compliance com. LifeBridge Health, 1999—. Recipient Md. Top 100 Women award, Daily Record, 1998, 2000, 2002. Mem.: Omega Psi, Delta Sigma Theta. Office: Md State Bd Edn 200 W Baltimore St Baltimore MD 21201 also: Md Health Care Found 6470-C Dobbin Rd Columbia MD 21045*

MAURER, BARBARA GLEE, educational administrator; b. Coopeville, Wash., May 21, 1945; d. James Clifton and Roberta Margaret (Torrison) Lawrence; m. Paul Gerry Maurer, June 3, 1984; children: Karl Norsen, Curtis Norsen. BS in Edn., U. Idaho, 1967; MA in Edn. Adminstrn., U. Wash., 1982. Cert. tchr. K-12, Wash. Tchr. Seattle Pub. Schs., 1968-70, 76-78, 85-86, program mgr., 1978-83, curriculum specialist, 1983-85, Highline Sch. Dist., Seattle, 1986-87, curriculum coord., 1988—. Curriculum cons. Sch. Dists., Seattle, 1980—; bd. dirs., sec. Wash. Coun. Honors and Advanced Placement, 1990—; cons. MacMillan McGraw Hill, N.Y.C., 1992-93; editor newsletter Gifted Unltd., 1985-88; cert. trainer Lead Devel. Project; liaison adminstr. Project Leadership; adj. prof. Seattle Pacific U. Contbr. articles to profl. jours. Precinct com. chmn. Rep. Party, 1980-85. Recipient Outstanding Project award Nat. Diffusion Network, 1981, Project Leadership award Wash. Assn. Sch. Adminstrs., 1992, Leadership in Profl. Devel. Award Wash. State ASCD, 1992. Mem. ASCD, Nat. Assn. Social Studies, Nat. Assn. for Gifted, Nat. Coun. Tchrs. English, Wash. Assn. Edn. Talented and Gifted (award 1990, Outstanding Leader award 1995), Wash. Coalition for Gifted and Talented (sec. 1991-92), Rotary (bd. dirs., pres. 1996). Avocations: sailing, skiing, gardening, cooking. Office: Highline Sch Dist 15675 Ambaum Blvd SW Seattle WA 98166-2523

MAURER, BEVERLY BENNETT, school administrator; b. Bklyn., Aug. 23, 1940; d. David and Minnie (Dolen) Bennett; m. Harold M. Maurer, June 12, 1960; children: Ann Maurer Rosenbach, Wendy Maurer Rausch. BA, Bklyn. Coll., 1960, postgrad., 1961, U. Richmond, 1980-90, Va. Commonwealth U., 1980-90. Cert. tchr., N.Y., Va. Math. tchr. Col. David Marcus Jr. High Sch., Bklyn., 1960-61, Pomona (N.Y.) Jr. High Sch., 1967-68; math. tchr. Hebrew day sch. Rudlin Torah Acad., Richmond, Va., 1969-80, asst. prin., 1980-86, prin., 1986-89; dir. edn. Jewish Community Day Sch. Ctrl. Va., Richmond, 1990-93; ednl. cons., 1993—; owner East Coast Antiques. Propr. East Coast Antiques. Developed talented and gifted program, pre-admission program for children at Med. Coll. Va., 1982. Bd. dirs. Jewish Cmty. Ctr., Richmond, 1980s, Aux. to Med. Coll. Va., Richmond, 1980s, Aux. to U. Nebr. Med. Ctr., 1994—, Uta Hallee, 1994-97, Met. Omaha Med. Soc. Alliance, 1997—; bd. govs. Joslyn Fine Art Mus., 2000—; founder, exec. bd. dirs. Nebraskans For Rsch., 2001—; mem. adv. bd. Ronald McDonald House Charities, 2002. Recipient Master Tchr. award Rudlin Torah Acad., 1983. Mem. Jewish Cmty. Day Sch. Network, Anti-Defamation League, Jewish Women's Club, U. Nebr. Med. Ctr. Faculty Women's Club (adv. bd. Ronald McDonald House Charities 2002--). Avocations: collecting contemporary and art nouveau glass, world travel.

MAURER, KAREN ANN, special education educator; b. New Kensington, Pa., Apr. 5, 1954; d. James Clair and Carrie Carmella (Siciliano) Blissell; m. Kevin Michael Maurer, June 25, 1983; children: Kevin Shawn, Kari Ann, Katelyn Elisabeth. BS in Elem. Edn./Spl. Edn., Edinboro U. of Pa., 1976, MEd in Mental Retardation, behavior mgmt. specialist cert., Edinboro U. of Pa., 1979. Cert. Pa. Instructional II; cert. emotional support tchr. Tchr. of mental/phys. handicapped preschs. Dr. Gertrude A Barber Ctr., Erie, Pa., 1976-80; tchr. of primary socially/emotionally disturbed students N.W. Tri County Intermediate Unit, Edinboro, Pa., 1980-83; tchr. h.s. emotionally disturbed students Allegheny Intermediate Unit, Pitts., 1983-91, South Fayette Twp. Sch. Dist., McDonald, Pa., 1991—. Lead tchr. elem. spl. edn. dept. South Fayette Elem. Sch., McDonald, 1992-93; master tchr. elem spl. edn. dept. N.W. Tri-County Intermediate Unit, Edinboro, 1981-83; presenter staff devel. South Fayette Twp. Schs., McDonald, 1993. Life mem. Girl Scouts of Am., N.Y.C., 1998—; sponsor Multicultural Club of South Fayette H.S., McDonald, 1995—. Mem. Coun. for Exceptional Children, Pa. State Edn. Assn. (rep.), Pa. Assn. of Supervision and Curriculum Devel. (western region), Pa. Middle Sch. Assn. Democrat. Roman Catholic. Avocations: singing, sewing, church work. Home: 42 W Manilla Ave Pittsburgh PA 15220-2838 Office: South Fayette Twp Sch Dist 2250 Old Oakdale Rd Mc Donald PA 15057-2580

MAURER, LAWRENCE MICHAEL, acting school administrator, educator; b. Bklyn., Oct. 2, 1935; s. Charles and Ethel (Ryan) M.; married Mar. 20, 1970 (div. 1971); 1 child, Lalaine; m. Carol Schneider, July 27, 1971. B of Vocat. Edn., San Diego State U., 1976; MS in Sch. Adminstrn., Nat. U., 1981. Cert. sch. adminstr., tchr., c.c. educator, Calif. Commd. ensign USN, 1953; advanced through grades to chief, 1969; ret., 1972; tchr. San Diego County Office Edn., 1972—, acting vice prin., 1989—. Bd. dirs. Multi-cultural Affairs Com., San Diego, 1991—, Self Esteem Devel. C.C., San Diego, 1990—, Sch. to Career Commn., San Diego, 1986—; cons. Vocat. Edn. in Ct. Schs., San Diego, 1986—; adj. prof. U. Calif., San Diego, Nat. U.-Violence Prevention in Sch.; mentor tchrs. in tech. San Diego Office Edn., 1996—. Contbr. articles to profl. jours. Organizer Dem. party. Named Excellent Tchr. of Yr. Corp. for Excellence in Pub. Edn., 1992, mentor Tchr.-Tech., 1996; vocat. grantee, 1988. Mem. ASCD (bd. dirs.), Nat. Vocat. Educators, Calif. Reading Assn., Calif. Ct. Sch. Adminstrs. Avocation: civil rights activist. Home: 98-80 Magnolia Ave Santee CA 92071 Office: San Diego County Office Edn 6401 Linda Vista Rd San Diego CA 92111-7319

MAUZY, (MARTHA) ANNE, retired deaf educator, audiologist; b. Birmingham, Ala., June 1, 1929; d. Huell Olon and Verna Eleanor (Evans) Rogers; m. Billy Burton Rister, Mar. 30, 1951 (div. 1973); children: Melanie Kofnovec, Jennifer Tyson, Randy Rister; m. Oscar Holcombe Mauzy, Feb. 14, 1976 (dec. Oct. 2000); stepchildren: Catherine, Charles, James. BA, U. Tex., 1948; MEd, U. Houston, 1954. Cert. elem. tchr., tchr. of deaf, Tex.; lic. audiologist, Tex. Tchr. Aldine Schs., Houston, 1948-49, Spring Br. Schs., Houston, 1949-50, Victoria (Tex.) Schs., 1950-51, Pasadena (Tex.) Schs., 1951-55, Corpus Christie (Tex.) Schs., 1955-58; supr., dir. children's programs Speech and Hearing Inst., Houston, 1958-73; asst. prof. Speech and Hearing Inst. U. Tex., Houston, 1973-76, ret. Co-author (2 chpts. in book) Language and Learning of the Preacademic Child, 1985. Mem. Gov.'s Commn. for Women, Austin, 1983-86; mem. adv. coun. Coll. Edn., U. Tex., 1988—, chmn. centennial celebration, 1991; treas. Tex. Dem. Women (Outstanding Mem. 1992, chair fedn. conv. nat. Fedn. Dem. Women 1993); mem. U. Tex. Nursing Sch. Coun., 1999—, U. Tex. Adv. Coun. Athletics Found., 2002—. Recipient Disting. Alumni award Coll. of Edn. Univ. Tex., 1991. Mem. AAUW, Am. Speech and Hearing Assn., Tex. Speech and Hearing Assn. (sec. 1955-56, hon. award 1985), Tex. Speech-Lang.-Hearing Found. (pres. 1992-94), Senate Ladies Club (pres. 1983). Unitarian Universalist. Avocations: politics, educational opportunities through travel. Home: Apt 125 4100 Jackson Ave Austin TX 78731-6033

MAWDSLEY, JACK KINRADE, retired education program administrator; b. Granite City, Ill., Oct. 8, 1928; s. Daniel Edwin and Wella Elizabeth (Mueller) M.; m. Norma Jean Mosby, Aug., 16, 1952; children: Kim Ellyn, Beth Elaine. BE, So. Ill. U., 1950, MEd, 1954; EdD, Mich. State U., 1968. Tchr. Granite City (Ill.) Pub. Schs., 1950-51, 52-53, Fair Plain Schs., Benton Harbor, Mich., 1954-55; counselor Battle Creek (Mich.) Pub. Schs., 1955-58, prin., 1958-61, dir. secondary edn., 1961-69, asst. supt. instrn., 1969-71, assoc. supt., 1971-73, supt. schs., 1973-86; dir. edn. program W. K. Kellogg Found., Battle Creek, 1986-88, coord. edn. programs, 1988—; interim v.p. programs in youth, edn. and families W.K. Kellogg Found., Battle Creek, 1995-98. Adj. prof. edn. adminstrn. Mich. State U., East Lansing, 1975-86; dean selection com. Coll. Edn. Western Mich. U., Kalamazoo. Elder, trustee 1st Presbyn. Ch.; bd. dirs. Battle Creek Health System. Recipient Disting. Alumni award Dept. Ednl. Adminstrn., Mich. State U., 1982, Outstanding Alumni award So. Ill. U. Coll. Edn., 1994; named Educator of Yr., Mich. Congress PTA, 1977, Educator of Yr. Delta Sigma Theta, 1986. Mem. Am. Assn. Sch. Adminstrs. Found. (bd. dirs.), Mid-Am. Assn. Sch. Supts. (past pres.), Horace Mann League U.S. (past pres.), Mich. Assn. Sch. Adminstrn. Edn. Leadership com. (past chmn.), Mich. Mid. Cities Assn. (past pres.), Phi Delta Kappa, Phi Kapp Phi. Avocations: tennis, reading. Office: W K Kellogg Found 1 Michigan Ave E Battle Creek MI 49017-4005*

MAXCY, SPENCER JOHN, education educator; b. Chgo., June 22, 1939; s. Spencer Thomas and Marian Adele (Davis) M.; m. Doreen Kay Oliver, Sept. 6, 1970; children: Colleen Shivaun, Spencer Oliver. BA in History, Blackburn Coll., 1961; MA in History, Loyola U., 1965; PhD in Philosophy of Edn., Ind. U., 1972. Cert. tchr. social studies, Ill. Substitute tchr. Chgo. Pub. Schs., 1962-63; social studies tchr. Dist. 218, Blue Island, Ill., 1963-67; assoc. instr. Ind. U., Bloomington, 1969-72; asst. prof. La. State U., Baton Rouge, 1972-76, assoc. prof., 1976-85, full prof., 1985—. Author: Educational Leadership, 1991, Democracy, Chaos, and the New School Order, 1995, Ethical School Leadership, 2002; editor: (book) Postmodern School Leadership, 1994, (3 vols.) John Dewey and American Education, 2002; mem. editorial bd. Record in Ednl. Adminstrn. and Supervision, 1981-91, Internat. Jour. of Ednl. Reform, 1992—. Basketball coach YMCA, Baton Rouge, 1993, 94, 95. NDEA fellow U. Chgo., 1966-67, Ind. U. fellow, 1967-68. Fellow Philosophy of Edn. Soc.; mem. Am. Ednl. Rsch. Assn., S.W. Philosophy of Edn. Soc. (pres. 1974-93). Avocations: weightlifting, fishing. Home: 251 E Woodgate Ct Baton Rouge LA 70808-5408 Office: La State U Peabody Hall 111 Baton Rouge LA 70803-0001

MAXFIELD, GUY BUDD, lawyer, educator; b. Galesburg, Ill., May 4, 1933; s. Guy W. and Isabelle B. Maxfield; m. Carol Tunick, Dec. 27, 1970; children: Susan, Stephen, Karen. AB summa cum laude, Augustana Coll., 1955; JD, U. Mich., 1958. Bar: N.Y. 1959. Assoc. White & Case, N.Y.C., 1958-63; prof. law NYU, N.Y.C., 1963—; of counsel August & Kulunas, P.A. Author: Tennessee Will and Trust Manual, 1982, Federal Estate and Gift Taxation, 8th edit., 2002, Florida Will and Trust Manual, 1984, Tax Planning for Professionals, 1986; contbr. articles to law jours. Trustee Acomb Found., Newark, 1974—. With U.S. Army, 1958-64. Fellow Am. Coll. Tax Counsel; mem. ABA, Am. Law Inst., N.Y. State Bar Assn., Order of Coif, Phi Beta Kappa. Office: NYU Sch Law 40 Washington Sq S New York NY 10012-1099

MAXIN, ALICE J. educator, labor relations specialist, presenter, facilitator; b. Pitts., May 29, 1946; d. Albert L. and Erna (Bergquist) Hartman; m. Thomas M. Maxin Sr., June 17, 2000; children: Kimberly S., Stephen L. BS, Clarion (Pa.) State Coll., 1968, MEd, 1972; diploma, Inst. of Children's Lit., Conn., 1988, 94. Kindergarten tchr. Union Sch. Dist., Rimersburg, Pa., 1968-71, Leechburg (Pa.) Area Sch. Dist., 1972-95; intern Uniserv rep. Pa. State Edn. Assn., 1992, Uniserv rep., labor rels. specialist, 1995—, staff liaison Women's Leadership Tng. Cadre, 1996—2003, coord. leadership instrs. Alt. region rep. Pa. Bargaining Com., 1989-90; region rep. Pa. Coun. on Instrnl. and Profl. Devel., 1990-92; mem. lead tchr. steering com. ARIN Intermediate Unit, 1990-91; mem. Pa. Staff Devel. Coun. Author: From the Desk of the LEA-Leechburg Advance, 1989-92; guest columnist Valley News Dispatch, 1990-94. Mem. edn. study group Ptnrs. for Armstrong County's Econ., Kittaning, Pa., 1989; co-chmn. Armstrong-Ind.-Jefferson Tri-County Coord. Bargaining Coun., 1989-95; co-chair Act 178 for Profl. staff devel. Leechburg Area Sch. Dist., 1988-92; co-founder Allekiski Valley Coalition Concerned Tchrs.; mem. Westmoreland County Area Labor Mgmt. Coun. Mem. NEA, Pa. State Edn. Assn. (ret., Pa. staff orgn.-nat. staff orgn.), Leechburg Edn. Assn. (pres. 1987-95, head negotiations com. 1987-95), Armstrong County Pres. Coun. Methodist. Avocations: grandchild, interior decorating, writing, reading, travel. Home: RR 1 Box 1382 Leechburg PA 15656-9717 Office: Pa State Edn Assn Old Route 119 New Stanton PA 15672

MAXWELL, ARTHUR EUGENE, oceanographer, marine geophysicist, educator; b. Maywood, Calif., Apr. 11, 1925; s. John Henry and Nelle Irene M.; m. Colleen O'Leary, July 1, 1988; children: Delle, Eric, Lynn, Brett, Gregory, Sam Wade, Henry Wade. BS in Physics with honors, N.Mex. State U., 1949; MS in Oceanography, Scripps Instn. Oceanography, 1952, PhD in Oceanography, 1959. Jr. rsch. geophysicist Scripps Instn. Oceanography, La Jolla, Calif., 1950-55; head oceanographer Office Naval Rsch., Washington, 1955-59, head br. geophysics, 1959-65; assoc. dir. Woods Hole (Mass.) Oceanographic Instn., 1965-69, dir. rsch., 1969-71, provost, 1971-81; prof. dept. geol. scis., dir. Inst. Geophysics U. Tex., Austin, 1982-94, prof. emeritus dept. geol. sci., 1994—. Chmn. bd. govs. planning com. deep earth sampling, 1968-70, chmn. exec. com. deep earth sampling, 1971-72, 78-79, 91-92; mem. joint U.S./USSR com. for coop. studies of the world ocean NAS/NRC, 1973-80, chmn. U.S. nat. com. to Internat. Union Geodesy and Geophysics, 1976-80, vice chmn. outer continental shelf/environ. studies rev. com., 1986-93; chmn. U.S. nat. com. on geology NAS, 1979-83, chmn. geophysics rsch. bd. geophysics study com., 1982-87; nat. sea grant rev. panel NOAA, 1982-85, 90-2000, sci. adv. bd., 1998—; mem. vis. com. Rosensteil Sch. Marine and Atmospheric Studies U. Miami, 1982-86, dept. physics N.Mex. State U., 1986-94; acad. adv. com. Com. Exch. CIA, 1983-96; mem. Gulf of Mexico Regional Marine Rsch. Bd., 1992-96. Editor: The Sea, Vol. 4, Parts I and II, 1970; editorial adv. bd. Oceanus, 1981-92; contbr. articles to profl. jours. Chmn. tech. adv. com. Navy Thresher Search, 1963; mem. Mass. Gov's. Adv. Com. on Sci. and Tech., 1965-71. With USN, 1942-46, PTO. Recipient Meritorious Civilian Svc. award Chief Naval Rsch., 1958, Albatross award AMSOC, 1959, Superior Civilian Svc. award Assn. Sec. of Navy, 1963, Disting. Civilian Svc. award Sec. of Navy, 1964, Disting. Alumni award N.Mex. State U., 1965, Bruun Meml. Lecture award Intergovtl. Oceanographic Commn., 1969, Outstanding Centennial Alumnus award N. Mex. State U., 1988. Fellow Am. Geophys. Union (pres. 1976-78, pres. oceanography sect. 1970-72); mem. Marine Tech. Soc. (charter, pres. 1981-82), Cosmos Club. Achievements include research in heat flow through the ocean floor, in structure and tectonics of the sea floor. Home: 8115 Two Coves Dr Austin TX 78730-3122 Office: Univ Tex Inst Geophysics Bldg 600 4412 Spicewood Springs Rd Austin TX 78759 E-mail: art@utig.ig.utexas.edu.

MAXWELL, DAVID E. academic executive, educator; b. N.Y.C., Dec. 2, 1944; s. James Kendrick and Gertrude Sarah (Bernstein) M.; children: Justin Kendrick, Stephen Edward. BA, Grinnell Coll., 1966; MA, Brown U., 1968, PhD, 1974. Instr. Tufts U., Medford, Mass., 1971-74, asst. prof., 1974-78, assoc. prof. Russian lang. and lit., 1978-89, dean undergrad. studies, 1981-89; pres. Whitman Coll., Walla Walla, Wash., 1989-93; dir. Nat. Fgn. Lang. Ctr., Washington, 1993-99; pres. Drake U., Des Moines, 1999—. Chmn. steering com. Coop. Russian Lang. Program, Leningrad, USSR, 1981-86, chmn. 1986-90; cons. Coun. Internat. Ednl. Exch., 1974-94, bd. dirs., 1988-92, 93-94, vice chair, 1991-92, cons. Internat. Rsch. Exchs., 1976-83; mem. adv. bd. Israeli Lang. Policy Inst. Contbr. articles to scholarly jours. Bd. dirs. Iowa Rsch. Coun.; cmty. bd. dirs. Wells Fargo; bd. dirs. Iowa Wellness Coun.; mem. exec. com. Greater Des Moines Partnership; pres. Des Moines Higher Edn. Collaborative, 2000—. Fulbright fellow, 1970-71, Brown U., 1966-67, NDEA Title IV, 1967-70; recipient Lillian Leibner award Tufts U., 1970; citation Grad. Sch. Arts and Scis., Brown U., 1991. Mem. MLA, Am. Coun. Edn. (commn. on internat. edn., pres.'s coun. on internat. edn.), Am. Assn. Advancement of Slavic Studies, Am. Assn. Tchrs. Slavic and E. European Langs., Assn. Am. Colls., Am. Assn. Higher Edn., Am. Coun. Tchg. Fgn. Langs., Brown U. Alumni Assn., Phi Beta Kappa. Democrat. Avocations: tennis, running, music. Office: Drake Univ Office of the Pres 2507 University Ave Des Moines IA 50311-4505

MAXWELL, DELORES YOUNG, elementary school principal; b. Kansas City, Kans., Dec. 8, 1948; d. Edward and Zelma (Starks) Young; m. Donald L. Maxwell, Sept. 26, 1969; children: Dominique N., Donald E. BA in Elem. Edn., Cen. Mo. State U., 1971; MA in Elem. Edn., Webster Coll., 1977; Edn. Spec. in Elem. Adminstrn., Cen. Mo. State U., 1987. Cert. reading, adult basic edn., Mo. Tchr. Kansas City (Mo.) Sch. Dist., 1972-81, lang. specialist, chpt. I liaision, 1981-83, instrnl. asst., 1983-86, elem. prin., 1986—. Bd. dirs. Nat. Coun. Youth Leadership; presenter Nat. Assn. of Partners in Edn., Washington, 1988. Active NAACP, Kansas City, Mo., 1970-73, Peple United to Serve Humanity, Kansas City, 1985-88, v.p. women's com., chmn. aucion com.; attendance, code conduct com. Grandview (Mo.) Sch. Dist., 1986; chmn. fund raising com. Kans. City Chpt. Jack n' Jill Assn., 1988-92; chmn. svcs. to youth, co-chmn. project lead chaplain, com. mem. by laws com. Jackson County Mo. Chpt. Links Inc., 1988—, fundraising com. Elect Emanuel Cleaver Mayor Kansas City, Mo., 1991; active Palestine Missionary Bapt. Ch., 1973 Sch. Recipient Small Grant Partnership award Kansas City Sch. Dist., 1990-91, 91-92, 92-93. Mem. ASCD, Am. Fedn. Tchrs. (chmn. grievance com., mem. exec. bd. 1972-86), Internat. Reading Assn., Kansas City Adminstrs. Assn. (chmn. legis. com. 1987—), Mo. Assn. Elem. Sch. Prins. (Mo. dist. rep. legis. com. 1986—), Kans. City Assn. Elem. Sch. Prins. (pres. elect 1988, pres. 1989-90, bd. mem. 1990), Greater Kansas City Leadership Acad. U. Mo. (bd. mem.), Phi Delta Kappa. Democrat. Avocations: reading, sewing, traveling, visiting museums. Office: Kansas City Sch Dist 1211 Mcgee St Kansas City MO 64106-2416

MAXWELL, DIANA KATHLEEN, early childhood education educator; b. Seminole, Okla., Dec. 16, 1949; d. William Hunter and ImoJean (Mahurin) Rivers; m. Clarence Estel Maxwell, Jly 3, 1969; children: Amanda Hunter, Alexandra Jane. BS, U. Md., 1972; M of Secondary Edn., Boston U., 1974; PhD, U. Md., 1980. Cert. tchr., counselor, Tex. Tchr. Child Garden Presch., Adelphi, Md., 1969-71; tchr., dir. PREP Edn. Ctr., Heidelberg, Germany, 1972-74; tchr. N.E. Ind. Schs. Larkspur, San Antonio, 1974-77, 89-90, Headstart, Boyds, Md., 1978; dir., founder First Bapt. Child Devel. Ctr., Bryan, Tex., 1982-84; instr. English lang. Yonsei Med. Ctr., Seoul, Republic of Korea, 1985-87; asst. prof. Incarnate Word Coll., San Antonio, 1987-89; tchr. kindergarten Fairfax County Pub. Schs., Kings Park, Va., 1990-94; tchr. Encino Park, San Antonio, Tex., 1994-95; lectr. U. Tex., San Antonio, 1995-96; multi-age tchr., theater arts tchr. Ft. Sam Houston Elem. Sch., San Antonio, 1996—. Cons. Sugar N'Spice Child Devel. Ctr., Kilgore, Tex., 1980-90; bd. dirs. Metro Area Assn. for Childhood Edn. Internat., 1991-93. Author: (book revs.) Childhood Education, 1979, 80, 92. Block chairperson March of Dimes, 1991, 92, 93,, 2000-, 01, 02, Am. Heart Assn., Fairfax, Fa., 1991, 92, San Antonio, 2000, 01, 02, Am. Diabetes Assn., Fairfax, 1992; judge speaking com. Burke Optomists, 1992, 93, judge writing competition N.E. Ind. Sch. Dist., 1996; sec. Cole H.S. Cougar Club, Ft. Sam Houston, San Antonio, 1996-97, v.p., 1997-2002, chair project graduation, 2002—; Bible tchr. 1st Bapt. Ch., Alexandria, Va., 1993-95; tchr. kindergarten Trinity Bapt. Ch., San Antonio, 1995-99, tchr. 1st grade, 2001—. Named one of Outstanding Young Women of Am., 1983; Md. fellow State of Md., 1978, 79; Tech. grantee Tex. Edn. Agy., San Antonio, 1990, State of Va. and Fairfax County, Springfield, 1991; recipient Yellow Rose of Tex. vol. award Gov. of Tex., 1996, Dean's Outstanding Tchg. award U. Tex., San Antonio, 1995-96, Ft. Sam Houston Hero award, 2001, 02. Mem. ASCD, Internat. Reading Assn., Assn. Profl. Tchr. Educators, Edn. Internat., Assn. for Childhood Edn. Internat. (v.p., pres.-elect), Tex. Assn. Childhood Edn., Bexar County and Surrounding Areas Assn. Childhood Edn. Avocations: oriental brush painting, singing, collecting butterflies, children/teacher advocate. Home: 2602 Country Square St San Antonio TX 78209-2235 Office: Ft Sam Houston Elem Sch 3370 Nursery Rd San Antonio TX 78234-1479

MAXWELL, MARILYN JULIA, retired elementary education educator; b. Flint, Mich., Apr. 3, 1933; d. Clement Daniel and Gwendoline Mae (Evans) Rushlow; m. Dewey Theodore Maxwell, Apr. 22, 1965; 1 child, Bruce Dewey. Student, Baldwin-Wallace Coll., 1951-53; BS, U. Tenn., 1954-56, MEd, 1962. Cert. elem. edn. tchr.; lang. devel. specialist. Elem. tchr. Guy Selby Sch., Flint, Mich., 1956-58, Henry L. Barger Sch., Chattanooga, 1958-63, Dept. of Def. Sch., Seville, Spain, 1963-65, Loma Vista Elem. Sch., Lompoc, Calif., 1965-66, Crestview Elem. Sch., Lompoc, 1966-68, LaHonda Elem. Sch., Lompoc, 1969—2000, tchr.-in-charge, acting prin., 1997—2000; ret., 2000. Lang. arts mentor tchr. Lompoc Unified Schs., 1985-86. Mem. Calif. Hist. Soc. Mem. Internat. Reading Assn., Assoc. Mems. Libr. of Congress, Nat. Trust for Hist. Preservation, Am. Fedn. Tchrs., Computer Using Educators, Nat. Coun. Tchrs. Math., Calif. Ret. Tchrs. Assn. Home: 4219 Centaur St Lompoc CA 93436-1229 E-mail: dmaxwell@impulse.net.

MAXWELL, MARY ELLEN, school system administrator; Grad., St. Mary's Acad., 1961, N.C. Sch. Bds. Assn. Acad. Ret. child devel. adminstr. U.S. Naval Security Group Activity N.W., Chesapeake, Va.; chmn., mem. at large Currick County Bd. Edn., 1982—. Chairperson Currituck County Alcohol and Drug Task Force; bd. dirs. Colonial Coast Girl Scouts Coun.; mem. Edn. and Tng. Voluntary Partnership; active Albemarle Hopeline, Currituck County Relay for Life. Mem.: Nat. Coun. for the Accreditation of Tchr. Edn. (mem. exec. com.), Nat. Sch. Bds. Assn. (former pres. bd. dirs.), N.C. Sch. Bds. Assn. (bd. dirs.), Nat. Bd. for Profl. Tchg. Stds. (bd. mem.), Moyock Woman's Club, Currituck Christian Women's Club.*

MAXWELL, SANDRA ELAINE, guidance counselor; b. Memphis, Jan. 8, 1959; d. Nathaniel and Corine (Sims) Stevenson; m. Clyde Maxwell, Dec. 19, 1981; 1 child, Ryan. BS, Memphis State U., 1980, MS, 1985, postgrad., 1992. Cert. sch. counselor, spl. edn. tchr., cert. in adminstrn. and supervision, Tenn. Guidance counselor Memphis City Schs., 1981—. Mem. NEA, West Tenn. Counselor's Assn., Assn. Am. Sch. Counselors, Memphis Edn. Assn., Tenn. Edn. Assn. Home: 4552 Melwood St Memphis TN 38109-5253

MAXWELL, SARA ELIZABETH, psychologist, educator, speech pathologist, director; b. DuQuoin, Ill., Jan. 23; d. Jean A. (Patterson) Green; m. David Lowell Maxwell, Dec. 27, 1960 (div. Mar. 1990); children: Lisa Marina, David Scott; m. James F. Manning, July 19, 1997 (div. Aug. 1998). BS, So. Ill. U., 1963, MS, 1964, MSEd, 1965; MEd, Boston Coll., 1982; attended, Harvard U., 1983; PhD, Boston Coll., 1992. Cert. and lic. speech.-lang. pathologist, early childhood specialist, guidance counselor, sch. adjustment counselor, behavior specialist, EMT. Clin. supr. Clin. Ctr. So. Ill. U., Carbondale, 1964-65, grad. clin. instr., 1965-66; speech/lang. pathologist, sch. adjustment counselor Westwood (Mass.) Pub. Schs., 1967-93; grad. faculty Emerson Coll., Boston, 1979-81; cons. Mass. Dept. Mental Health, Boston, 1979-82; grad. clin. supr. Robbins Speech/Hearing Ctr., Emerson Coll., Boston, 1979-82; predoctoral intern in clin. psychology South Shore Mental Health Ctr., Quincy, 1985-86, devel. and clin. staff psychologist Hingham and Quincy, Mass., 1989-93, emergency svcs. team and respite house manager Quincy, Mass., 1990-93; cons. Westwood Nursery Preschs., 1986-93; pvt. practice Twin Oaks Clin. Assocs., Westwood, Mass, 1986-88, South Coast Counseling Assocs., Quincy, 1989-93. Cons. local collaboratives and preschs., Westwood, 1980-83; prof. workshops presenter Head Start, 1980; program specialist speech, lang., learning Broward County (Fla.) Schs., 1993-96, exceptional student edn. specialist, 1996-98; behavior specialist, 1999—; adj. prof. grad. sch. of psychology Nova Southeastern U., 1995—; chmn Broward County Action Rsch. Grant Project 2002-03; presenter Head Start, ASHA, CEC, APSC, IALP and other profl., nat. and state confs., 1980-99; invited del. to Sino-Am. Conf. on Exceptionality, Beijing Normal U., People's Republic of China, 1995. Contbr. articles to profl. jours., chpts. to textbooks. Mem. adv. coun. Westwood (Mass.) Bd. Health, 1977-80; emergency med. technician Westwood Pub. Schs. Athletic Dept., 1981. Vocat. Rehab. fellow So. Ill. U., 1964; Merit scholar Perry County, Ill., 1959-64, Credi meml. scholar So. Ill. U., 1964. Mem. Am. Speech & Hearing Assn. (nat. schs. com., nat. chairperson Pub. Sch. Caucus 1985-87), Am. Psychol. Assn., Assn. Psychiat. Svcs. for Children, Coun. Exceptional Children, Internat. Assn. of Logopedics, Rio Vista Civic Assn., Boston Coll. Alumni Assn., Harvard Club. Episcopalian. Avocations: squash, sailing, skiing. Office: Nova Southeastern U Ctr Psychol Studies Maxwell Maltz Psych Bldg 3301 College Ave Fort Lauderdale FL 33314-7796

MAXWELL, WILLIAM HALL CHRISTIE, civil engineering educator; b. Coleraine, No. Ireland, Jan. 25, 1936; came to U.S., 1958, naturalized, 1967; s. William Robert and Catherine Dempsey (Christie) M.; m. Mary Carolyn McLaughlin, Sept. 28, 1960; children: Katrina, Kevin, Wendy, Liam. BSc, Queen's U., Belfast, No. Ireland, 1956; MSc, Queen's U., Kingston, Ont., Can., 1958; PhD, U. Minn., 1964. Registered profl. engr., Ill. Site engr. Motor Columbus AG, Baden, Switzerland, 1956; tchg. asst. Queen's U., Kingston, 1956-58; from rsch. asst. to instr. U. Minn., Mpls., 1959-64; asst. prof. civil engring. U. Ill., Urbana, 1964-70, assoc. prof., 1970-82, prof., 1982-96, prof. emeritus, 1997—. Chmn. program com. 1st Internat. Conf. on New/Emerging Concepts for Rivers, Chgo., 1996. Editor: Water Resources Management in Industrial Areas, 1982, Water for Human Consumption, Man and His Environment, 1983, Frontiers in Hydrology, 1984, New/Emerging Concepts for Rivers, 1996. Vestryman Emmanuel Meml. Episcopal Ch., Champaign, Ill., 1977-80; state exhibitor Ministry Edn., Stormont, No. Ireland, 1953-56. Queen's U. Found. scholar, Belfast, 1954-56, R.S. McLaughlin travel fellow Queen's U., Kingston, 1958-59. Fellow ASCE (com. chmn. 1982-83), Internat. Water Resources Assn. (editor-in-chief Water Internat. 1986-93, sr. editor 1994-98, mem. publs. com. 1980-98, v.p. U.S. geog. com. 1986-91, chmn. awards com. 1995-97, bd. dirs. 1995-97, Editl. award 1994); mem. Am. Geophys. Union, Internat. Assn. for Hydraulic Rsch. Avocations: home construction, oil painting. Home: 1210 Devonshire Dr Champaign IL 61821-6527 Office: U Ill Dept Civil and Environ Engring Urbana IL 61801-2350 Business E-Mail: wmaxwell@uiuc.edu.

MAXWELL, WILLIAM LAUGHLIN, retired industrial engineering educator; b. Phila., July 11, 1934; s. William Henry and Elizabeth (Laughlin) M.; m. Judith Behrens, July 5, 1969; children: Deborah, William, Judith, Keely BMechE, Cornell U., 1957, PhD, 1961. Andrew Schultz Jr. prof. dept. indsl. engring. Cornell U., Ithaca, N.Y., 1961-98. Author: Theory of Scheduling, 1967. Recipient Disting. Teaching award Cornell Soc. Engrs., 1968, Ralph S. Watts Tchg. award, 1997. Fellow Informs, Inst. Indsl. Engrs.; mem. Nat. Acad. Engring. Home: 106 Lake Ave Ithaca NY 14850-3537

MAXWELL-BROGDON, FLORENCE MORENCY, school administrator, educational adviser; b. Spring Park, Minn., Nov. 11, 1929; d. William Frederick and Florence Ruth (LaBrie) Maxwell; m. John Carl Brogdon, Mar. 13, 1957; children: Carole Alexandra, Cecily Ann, Daphne Diana. BA, Calif. State U., L.A., 1955; MS, U. So. Calif., 1957; postgrad., Columbia Pacific U., San Rafael, Calif., 1982-86. Cert. tchr., Calif. Dir. Rodeo Sch., L.A., 1961-64; lectr. Media Features, Culver City, Calif., 1964—; dir. La Playa Sch., Culver City, Calif., 1968-75; founding dir. Venture Sch., Culver City, Calif., 1974—, also chmn. bd. dirs. Bd. dirs., v.p. Parent Coop. Preschools, Baie d'Urfe Que., Can., 1964—; del. to Ednl. Symposium, Moscow-St. Petersburg, 1992, U.S./China Joint Conf. on Edn., Beijing, 1992, Internat. Confedn. of Prins., Geneva, 1993, Internat. Conf., Berlin, 1994, Internat. Confedn. of Sch. Prins., Helsinki, Finland, 2000, Edinburgh, Scotland, 2003. Author: Let Me Tell You, 1973, Wet'n Squishy, 1973, Balancing Act, 1977, (as Morency Maxwell) Framed in Silver, 1985; (column) What Parents Want to Know, 1961—; editor: Calif. Preschooler, 1961-74; contbr. articles to profl. jours. Treas. Dem. Congl. Primary, Culver City, 1972. Mem. NASSP, Calif. Coun. Parent Schs. (bd. dirs. 1961-74), Parent Coop. Preschs. Internat. (advisor 1975—), Pen Ctr. USA West, Mystery Writers of Am. (affiliate), Internat. Platform Assn. Liberatarian. Home: 10814 Molony Rd Culver City CA 90230-5451 Office: Venture Sch 11477 Jefferson Blvd Culver City CA 90230-6115 E-mail: morencee@aol.com.

MAXWORTHY, TONY, mechanical and aerospace engineering educator; b. London, May 21, 1933; came to U.S., 1954, naturalized, 1961; s. Ernest Charles and Gladys May (Butson) M.; m. Emily Jean Parkinson, June 20, 1956 (div. 1974); children: Kirsten, Kara; m. Anna Barbara Parks, May 21, 1979 BS in Engring. with honors, U. London, 1954; MSE, Princeton U., 1955; PhD, Harvard U., 1959. Rsch. asst. Harvard U., Cambridge, Mass., 1955-59; sr. scientist, group supr. Jet Propulsion Lab., Pasadena, Calif., 1960-67, cons., 1968—; assoc. prof. U. So. Calif., L.A., 1967-70, prof., 1970—, Smith Internat. prof. mech. and aero. engring., 1988—, chmn. dept. mech. engring., 1979-89; cons. BBC Rsch. Ctr., Baden, Switzerland, 1972-82, J.P.L., Pasadena, Calif., 1968-80; lectr. Woods Hole Oceanographic Inst., Mass., summers 1965, 70, 72, 83. Forman vis. prof. aeronautics Technion Haifa, 1986; vis. prof. U. Poly.. Madrid, 1988, Inst. Soperiore Tech., Lisbon, 1988, Swiss Fed. Inst. Tech., Lausanne, 1989; assoc. prof. IMG, U. Joseph Fourier, Grenoble, 1980—, Ecole Superieure Physics and Indsl. Chemistry, Paris, 1995—; Shimizu vis. prof. Stanford U., 1996—. Mem. editorial bd. Geophys. Fluid Dynamics, 1973-79, 88-96, Dynamic Atmospheric Oceans, 1976-83, Phys. Fluids. 1978-81, Zeitschrift fuer Angewandte Mathematik und Physik, 1987-96; contbr. articles to profl. jours. Recipient Humboldt Sr. Scientist award, 1981-93, G.I. Taylor medal Soc. Engring. Sci., 2003; fellow Cambridge U., 1974, 93—, Australian Nat. U., 1978, Nat. Ctr. Atmospheric Rsch., 1976, Glennon fellow U. Western Australia, 1990, F.W. Mosey fellow, 1993, Sr. Queen's fellow in marine scis. Commonwealth of Australia, 1984. Fellow: Am. Phys. Soc. (chmn. exec. com. fluid dynamics divsn. 1974—79, Otto Laporte award 1990), Am. Acad. Arts and Scis.; mem.: NAE, European Geophys. Soc., Am. Geophys. Union. Office: U So Calif Dept Aerospace & Mech Engr Exposition Park Los Angeles CA 90089-1191 E-mail: maxworth@usc.edu.

MAY, AVIVA RABINOWITZ, music educator, linguist, musician; b. Tel Aviv; naturalized, 1958; d. Samuel and Paula Pessia (Gordon) Rabinowitz (div.); children: Chelley Mosoff, Alan May, Risa McPherson, Ellanna May/Gassman. AA, Oakton C.C., 1977; BA in Piano Pedagogy, Northeastern Ill. U., 1978. Folksinger, educator, musican Aviva May Studio/Piano and Guitar, 1948—; Sunday sch. dir. Canton (Ohio) Synagogue, 1952-54; nursery sch. tchr. Allentown (Pa.) Jewish Cmty. Ctr., 1954-56; Hebrew music tchr. Brith Shalom Cmty. Ctr., Bethlehem, Pa., 1954-62; Hebrew tchr. Beth Hillel Congregation, Wilmette, Ill., 1964-83; tchr. B'nai Mitzva, 1978; music dir. McCormick Health Ctrs., Chgo., 1978-79. Cove Sch. Perceptually Handicapped Children, Evanston, 1978-79; prof. Hebrew and Yiddish, Spertus Coll. Judaica, Chgo., 1980-89; Hebrew tchr. Anshe Emet Day Sch., 1989—, West Suburban Temple Har Zion, Oak Park, Ill., 1993—; music studio tchr. Cosmopolitan Sch., Chgo., 1992—. Tchr. continuing edn. Northeastern Ill. U., 1978-80, Niles Twp. Jewish Congregation, 1993—, also Jewish Cmty. Ctrs.; with Office Spl. Investigations, Dept. Justice, Washington; music dir. Temple Emanuel Rosenwald Sch. Composer classical music for piano, choral work, folk songs; developer 8-hour system for learning piano or guitar; contbr. articles to profl. jours. Recipient Magen David Adom Pub. Svc. award 1973; grantee Ill. State, 1975-79, Ill. Congressman Woody Bowman, 1978-79. Mem. Music Tchrs. Nat. Assn., Ill. Music Tchrs. Assn., Organ and Piano Tchrs. Assn., Am. Coll. Musicians, Ill. Assn. Learning Disabilities, North Shore Music Tchrs. Assn. (charter mem., co-founder), Sherwood Sch. Music, Friends of Holocaust Survivers, Nat. Yiddish Book Exch., Nat. Ctr. for Jewish Films, Chgo. Jewish Hist. Soc., Oakton C.C. Alumni Assn., Northeastern Ill. U. Alumni Assn. Democrat. Office: Aviva May Studio 410 S Michigan Ave Ste 920 Chicago IL 60605-1471 E-mail: arm801@aol.com.

MAY, BEVERLY, elementary school educator; m. William Raymond May; children: William Jr., Karri, David. BS in Elem. Edn., U. Houston, 1969, MEd, 1978. Cert. elem. tchr., profl. reading specialist, profl. supr., Tex. Clerical, secretarial Houston Ind. Sch. Dist., 1957-64, tchr. grades 2, 3, 7, elem. reading ctr., 1969-90, ret., 1990; ednl. materials rep. World Book/Childcraft, Houston, 1975-90; reading cons. Region IV Edn. Svc. Ctr., Houston, 1977-83; supr. reading lab. downtown campus U. Houston, 1985; clk. sec. Houston Ind. Sch. Dist., 1957-64, tchr. grades two, three, seven Elem. Reading Ctr., 1969-90. Pvt. reading skills and study skills specialist, 1975—; cons., presenter workshops in field. clerical/secretarial (1957-64). gr 2,3,7, elem. reading center, 1969-90. Participant TV-Radio broadcast ministries workshop 1st Bapt. Ch., Houston, 1988. Mem. Tex. State Reading Assn., Tex. Retired Tchrs. Assn., Inspirational Writers Alive, Soc. Children's Book Writers and Illustrators, Internat. Reading Assn., Greater Houston Area Reading Coun.

MAY, CHERYL ELAINE, university official; b. Kansas City, Mo., Feb. 22, 1949; d. Kenneth William and Norma Yvonne (Lithgow) Baker; m. Gary Dale May, Oct. 13, 1972; 1 child, Jared BA, U. Mo., 1974; MS, Kans. State U., 1985. Reporter Oceanside (Calif.) Blade Tribune Newspaper, 1969-70; writer photographer Kansas City (Mo.) Life Ins. Co., 1970-71; writer Milling & Baking News Mag., Kansas City, 1971-74; communications dir. Am. Maine Anjou Assn., Kansas City, 1975; engring. news editor Kans. State U., Manhattan, 1979-80, sci. writer, biology, 1981-84, editor rsch. mag., 1984-87, actg. dir., news svcs., 1988-89; dir. news svcs. Kansas State U., Manhattan, 1989-99; asst. editor Agr. Expt. Sta. Kans. State U., Manhattan, 1982-84, co-chmn. Native Am. Heritage Month, 1991, dir. media rels. and mktg., 2000—, faculty senate, 1991—97, 2002—. Author: Cattle Management, 1981, Legacy, 1983; contbr. articles to profl. jour. Vol. 4-H; vol. project dir. Riley County Hist. Soc., Manhattan, 1983; mem. Heart of Am. Indian Ctr., Kansas City, 1970-74, co-organizer child care program, Manhattan, 1975-76; publicity chmn. for Kans. State U., United Way, 1985-90; mem. Kans. steering com. 1992 White House Conf. on Indian Edn. Mem. Nat. Assn. Sci. Writers, Coun. for Advancement and Support Edn., Phi Kappa Phi. Avocations: photography, native american history and medicine. Office: Kans State U 9 Anderson Hall Manhattan KS 66506-0117 E-mail: may@ksu.edu.

MAY, DAVID A. retired dean; b. Buffalo, N.Y., May 23, 1947; children: Jordan D., Jared R. AAS in Bus. Adminstrn., Niagara County C.C., Sanborn, N.Y., 1983; BS in Pub. Adminstrn., Empire State Coll., 1988; MA in Orgn. Mgmt., U. Phoenix, 1996; PhD in Mgmt., LaSalle U., 1997. V.p. Simpson Security, Inc., Niagara Falls, NY, 1973—78; lt. Niagara Falls (N.Y.) Police Dept., 1986—98; dean N.Y. Paralegal Sch.; ret., 2002. Bd. mem. Nat. Conf. Christians and Jews, 1984-90, ARC, 1986-89, Music Sch. of Niagara, 1987-90, Niagara Falls Little Theatre, chmn., 1994; pres. Niagara Cmty. Ctr., Niagara Falls, 1987, Niagara Falls (N.Y.) Sch. Bd., 1988, Niagara Falls (N.Y.) Meml. Day Assn., 1990, 91, 93; lt. gov. N.Y. State Kiwanis, 1989; mem. Niagara Co. Lrgis., 1994. Recipient Svc. award Fellowship House Found., Niagara Falls, 1986; named Civic Leader of Yr., Niagara Cmty. Ctr., Niagara Falls, 1990. Mem. Kiwanis Club North Niagara Falls (pres. 1987, Kiwanian of the Yr. 1991), Lasalle Am. Legion (vice commdr. 1975), Lasalle Sportsmens Club (fin. sec. 1989). Avocations: playing tennis, golfing, amateur historian. Home: 2573 E 18th St 1st Fl Brooklyn NY 11235

MAY, EILEEN MARIE, elementary education educator; b. Bklyn., Aug. 10, 1945; d. Leo John and Helen Agnes (McGowan) Kelly; m. Albert William May, Aug. 16, 1975; children: Michael Raymond, James Leo. BA in Econs., Coll. of St. Elizabeth, 1967; cert. elem. edn., William Paterson Coll. N.J., 1983. Various retail mgmt. positions, N.J., 1967-77; tchr. St. Joseph's Sch., Maplewood, N.J., 1977-79, Sacred Heart Sch., Dover, N.J., 1979-82; tchr. compensatory edn. Lenape Valley H.S., Stanhope, N.J., 1987-90; tchr. Rev. George Brown Sch., Sparta, N.J., 1990—. Grantee A Plus for Kids, 1992. Mem. Nat. Cath. Edn. Assn., Nat. Coun. Tchrs. Math., Assn. of Math. Tchrs. N.J., N.J. Math. Coalition. Home: 127 Marne Rd Hopatcong NJ 07843-1843

MAY, GITA, language educator, literature educator; b. Brussels, Sept. 16, 1929; came to U.S., 1947, naturalized, 1950; d. Albert and Blima (Sieradska) Jochimek; m. Irving May, Dec. 21, 1947. BA magna cum laude, CUNY-Hunter Coll., 1953; MA, Columbia U., 1954, PhD, 1957. Lectr. French CUNY-Hunter Coll., 1953-56; from instr. to assoc. prof. Columbia U., N.Y.C., 1956—68, prof., 1968—, chmn., 1983-93, mem. senate, 1979-83, 86-88, chmn. Seminar on 18th Century Culture, 1986-89. Lecture tour English univs., 1965 Author: Diderot et Baudelaire, critiques d'art, 1957, De Jean-Jacques Rousseau à Madame Roland: essai sur la sensibilité préromantique et révolutionnaire, 1964, Madame Roland and the Age of Revolution, 1970 (Van Amringe Disting. Book award), Stendhal and the Age of Napoleon, 1977, Encyclopedia of Aesthetics, 1998, Dictionnaire de Diderot, 1999, French Women Writers, 1991, The Feminist Encyclopedia of French Literature, 1999; co-editor: Diderot Studies III, 1961; mem. editl. bd. 18th Century Studies, 1975-78, French Rev., 1975-86, 98—, Romanic Rev., 1959—, Women in French Studies, 2000—; contbg. editor: Oeuvres complètes de Diderot, 1984, 95; gen. editor: The Age of Revolution and Romanticism: Interdisciplinary Studies, 1990—. extensive essays on Diderot and George Sand in European Writers, 1984, 85, and on Rebecca West, Anita Brookner and Graham Swift in British Writers, 1996, 97, 99, Bayle, Fontenelle and Fénelon in Dictionary of Literary Biography, 2003, Voltaire's Candide (in Barnes and Noble Classics), 2003; contbr. articles and revs. to profl. jours. Decorated chevalier and officier Ordre des Palmes Acad.; recipient award Am. Coun. Learned Socs., 1961, award for outstanding achievement CUNY-Hunter Coll., 1963; Fulbright rsch. grantee, 1964-65; Guggenheim fellow, 1964-65, NEH fellow, 1971-72. Mem. AAUP, MLA (del. assembly 1973-75, mem. com. rsch. activities 1975-78, mem. exec. coun. 1980-83), Am. Assn. Tchrs. of French, Am. Soc. 18th Century Studies (pres. 1985-86, 2nd v.p. 1983-84, 1st v.p. 1984-85, One of Gt. Tchrs. award 1999), Soc. Française d'Etude du Dix-Huitième Siècle, Soc. Diderot, Am. Soc. French Acad. Palms, Soc. des Etudes Staëliennes, N.Am. Soc. for the Study of Jean-Jacques Rousseau, Soc. des Professeurs Français et Francophones d'Amérique, Phi Beta Kappa. Office: Columbia U Dept French/Romance Philol 516 Philosophy Hall MC4918 New York NY 10027 E-mail: gm9@columbia.edu.

MAY, JOHN RAYMOND, clinical psychologist; b. Rahway, NJ, Jan. 31, 1943; s. John Y. and Aline (Eichorn) M.; m. Brenda Lee Berg, June 17, 1967; children: Stacey Anne, John Jeffrey. BA in Psychology, Colgate U., 1965; PhD in Clin. Psychology, U. N.C., 1970. Clin. intern U. Wis. Med. Ctr., 1967-68; staff psychologist to chief, clin. svcs. divsn. Nat. Security Agy., Ft. Meade, Md., 1969-72; pvt. practice Columbia, Md., 1972—; cons., 1972—92, 2003—. Exec. dir. Psychol. Health Svcs., Inc., Columbia, 1976—84, 1993—2001, Columbia Psychol. Svcs., 1984—91, Cmty. Counseling Assocs., 1991—; co-dir. Columbia Addictions Ctr., 1994—98; adj. prof. Loyola Coll., 1970—72; cons. in field. Co-author films on mental health tng., articles in profl. jours. and manuals. Recipient Wallach award U. N.C., 1969, Humanitarian award Citizens Against Spousal Assault, 1989; USPHS fellow, 1966-69; VA fellow, 1965-66. Mem. APA, Md. Psychol. Assn. (exec. coun., various coms. 1977-91, treas. 1985-88, pres.-elect 1988, pres. 1989-90, past pres. 1990-91, Outstanding Profl. Contbn. to Psychology award 1993), Am. Bd. Sexology (diplomate), Assn. Advancement of Psychology, Am. Soc. Clin. Hypnosis, Am. Assn. Sex Educators, Counselors, and Therapists (cert. sex. therapist), Anxiety Disorders Assn. Am., Howard County Psychol. Soc. (pres. 1975-76). Home: 6264 Cardinal Ln Columbia MD 21044-3802 Office: 10774 Hickory Ridge Rd Columbia MD 21044-3646 E-mail: cca21044@msn.com.

MAY, KATRINA FORREST, elementary educator; b. Waverly, Tenn., Aug. 7, 1956; d. James Robert and Shirley Erline (McCaleb) Forrest; m. Jamie Wade May, May 19, 1978; 1 child, Robert Kyle. B Music Edn., Okla. Christian Coll., 1978; MA in Elem. Edn., Austin Peay State U., 1982. Tchr. Waverly (Tenn.) Elem. Sch., 1979-84, 1st Presbyn. Pre-Sch., Tuscaloosa, Ala., 1988-89, Walker Elem. Sch., Northport, Ala., 1989-93; tchr.-in-residence U. Ala., Tuscaloosa, 1993—. Rep. Humphreys County Edn. Assn., Waverly, 1981-82. Mem. Theatre Tuscaloosa, 1987-92, Children's Hands-On Mus., Tuscaloosa, 1991—, Tuscaloosa Community Singers, 1991—; pres. Tuscaloosa Civic Chorus, 1989-90. Mem. NEA, ASCD, Internat. Reading Assn., Ala. Reading Assn., Ala. Edn. Assn., Tuscaloosa County Edn. Assn. (rep. 1991—), Tuscaloosa Reading Coun. (treas. 1992—), Life After Basals, Delta Kappa Gamma. Avocations: piano, guitar, reading, cooking, scuba diving. Office: U Ala PO Box 870231 Tuscaloosa AL 35487-0154

MAY, MARY LOUISE, elementary education educator; b. Highland, Ill., Nov. 9, 1946; d. Cecil S. and Marie (Papp) Harmon; 1 child, Alesia Lovellette. BS, So. Ill. U., Edwardsville, 1973. Elem. tchr. Edwardsville Sch. Dist. 7, 1974—. Presenter math. confs., 1990—. Mem. Ill. Edn. Assn., Edwardsville Edn. Assn. (v.p. 1990-95, 2003—, pres. 1995-2002), Illini Tchrs. Whole Lang., Delta Kappa Gamma, Beta Sigma Phi (pres. laureate chpt.). Avocations: reading, writing, golf, counted cross-stitch, walking. Home: 16 Dorset Ct Edwardsville IL 62025-3920 Office: Woodland Sch 59 S State Route 157 Edwardsville IL 62025-3870

MAY, NORMA BUTLER, reading educator; b. Cairo, Ill., Sept. 6, 1940; d. John William and Irene Virginia (Cartwright) Butler; m. Willie L. May, July 4, 1964; children: Kristian, Karen. AS, Vincennes U., 1960; BS, Ind. State U., 1961, MS, 1966. Kindergarten tchr. Sch. Dist. 130, Blue Island, Ill., 1961-70; subs. tchr. Chgo. Bd. Edn., 1974-76; reading specialist Evanston Twp. H.S., Ill., 1976—. Recipient internat. teaching award Delores Kohl Found., 1994. Mem. NEA, ASCD, Nat. Coun. Tchrs. English, AAUW (presenter Title I IASA statewide conf. 1995), NAACP, Internat. Reading Assn., Ill. Edn. Assn., Jack & Jill of Am., U. Ill. Mothers Assn. (2d v.p. 1992-93, pres. 1993-94). Methodist. Avocations: reading, walking, theater, spectator sports, music. Home: 8333 S Dorchester Ave Chicago IL 60619-6401 Office: Evanston Twp HS 1600 Dodge Ave Evanston IL 60201-3494

MAY, PHILIP ALAN, sociology educator; b. Bethesda, Md., Nov. 6, 1947; s. Everette Lee and Marie (Lee) M.; m. Doreen Ann Garcia, Sept. 5, 1972; children: Katrina Ruth, Marie Ann. BA in Sociology, Catawba Coll., 1969; MA in Sociology, Wake Forest U., 1971; PhD in Sociology, U. Mont., 1976. NIMH predoctoral fellow U. Mont., Missoula, 1973-76; dir. health stats. and rsch. Navajo Health Authority, Window Rock, Ariz., 1976-78; asst. prof. U. N.Mex., Albuquerque, 1978-82, assoc. prof., 1982-89, prof., 1989—; dir. Ctr. on Alcoholism, Substance abuse and Addictions, U. N.Mex., Albuquerque, 1990-99, co-dir., 2000—02, sr. rsch. scientist, 2000—, assoc. dir., 2002—. Fetal alcohol syndrome study com. Inst. of Medicine/NAS, 1994-96; dir. Nat. Indian Fetal Alcohol Syndrome Prevention Program, Albuquerque, 1979-85; adv. bd. Nat. Orgn. on Fetal Alcohol Syndrome, Washington, 1990—; rsch. assoc. Nat. Ctr. for Am. Indian and Alaska Native Mental Health Rsch., 1986—; mem. U.S. Surgeon Gens. Task Force on Drunk Driving, 1988-89; prin. investigator fetal alcohol syndrome epidemiology rsch. in South Africa, 1997—; com. on pathophysiology and prevention of adolescent and adult suicide Inst. Medicine/NRC/NAS, 2000-02; cons. in field. Contbr. chpts. to books and articles to profl. jours. V.p. Bd. Edn., Laguna Pueblo, N.Mex., 1998—2002, pres., 2002—. Lt. (s.g.) USPHS, 1970—73. Recipient Spl. Recognition award U.S. Indian Health Svc., 1992, award Navajo Tribe and U.S. Indian Health Svc., 1992, Human Rights Promotion award UN Assn., 1994, Program award for Contbns. to Mental Health of Am. Indians, U.S. Indian Health Svc., 1996, O.B. Michael Outstanding Alumnus award Catawba Coll., 2000, Student Svc. award U. N.Mex., 2002. Mem. APHA, Am. Sociol. Assn., Population Ref. Bur., Coll. on Problems of Drug Dependence, Rsch. Soc. Alcoholism. Methodist. Home: 4610 Idlewilde Ln SE Albuquerque NM 87108-3422 Office: U NMex CASAA 2650 Yale Blvd Albuquerque NM 87106-3202 E-mail: pmay@unm.edu.

MAY, SCOTT C. special education educator; b. Seattle, Mar. 21, 1964; s. Kenneth Gordon and Susan Catherine (Carter) M. BS, Syracuse U., 1986, MS in Emotional Disturbance and Autism, 1989; postgrad., U. Melbourne, Australia, 1995—. Cert. spl. edn. tchr., N.Y., Hawaii, Alaska, Pa. Resident advisor Syracuse (N.Y.) U.; dir. after sch. program, lead tchr. Jowonio Sch., Syracuse, 1986-90; spl. edn. tchr. Lanai High and Elem., Lanai City, Hawaii, 1990-92; rschr. in tchr. tng., 1992-95; resource tchr. Mendenhall River Elem. and Dzantik'i Heeni Middle Sch., Juneau, Alaska, 1996-97; tchr. spl. edn. Floyd Dryden Mid. Sch., Juneau, 1997—, multidisciplinary team leader, 1998—. Instr. U. Alaska S.E., 1997—; mem. U.S. Spl. Edn. Delegation to Russia and the Czechoslovakia Republic. Advocate inclusive environments disabled students' programs. Mem. ASCD, Assn. for Persons With Severe Handicaps, Coun. for Exceptional Children. Home: PO Box 33802 Juneau AK 99803-3802 Office: 10014 Crazy Horse Dr Juneau AK 99801-8529

MAYBURY, GREG J. academic administrator; b. Hamilton, Ohio, July 23, 1951; s. Edward Charles and Betty Jeanne (Eicher) M.; m. Kathryn Ann Maybury, June 21, 1980; children: Christopher James, Kyle Edward, Kevin Greg. AB, Dartmouth Coll., 1973; MS, U. Ill., 1979. Instr. math. Choate Sch., Wallingford, Conn., 1973-77; mem. math. and computer faculty Parkland Coll., Champaign, Ill., 1980-88, v.p., 1988-90; dir. computing and info. tech. Hope Coll., Holland, Mich., 1990-92, dir. info. systems and adminstrv. svcs., 1992—. Mem. Am. Assn. Computing Machinery, Math. Assn. Am., Educom, Cause. E-mail: maybury@hope.edu.

MAYE-BRYAN, MAMIE ELLENE, elementary education educator; b. Greenville, N.C., July 29, 1954; d. John Walter Sr. and Beatrice Carr (Jones) Maye; children: Janielle Betrice, William Harrison IV, John Robert Bryan. BS, Va. State U., 1976; MA, U. Minn., 1977; degree in edn. specialist, U. Mo., Kansas City, 1984; degree in adminstrv. endorsement, U. Nebr., Omaha, 1996. Cert. tchr., Va., N.C., Kans., Nebr. Instr. music St. Paul's Coll., Lawrenceville, Va., 1977-79; teaching asst. U. Mo., Kansas City, 1979-82; instr. music St. Joseph Sch., Kansas City, 1979-83; vocal instr. Bishop Hogan High Sch., Kansas City, 1995; minister of music St. Paul's Presbyn. Ch., Kansas City, 1982-85; evaluator North Ctrl. Visiting Team, Kansas City, 1983-84; personal banker Corp. Woods Bank, Overland Park, Kans., 1983-85; instr. music Birchcrest Sch., Bellevue, Nebr., 1985-89; minister of music Mt. Carmel Baptist Ch., Bellevue, 1986—92; instr. vocal music Fort Crook Sch., Bellevue, 1989—; church pianist/accompanist Offutt AFB Chapel, Bellevue, 1993—; vocal music instr. LeMay Sch., Bellevue, Nebr., 1995—97. Music cons. Bellevue Pub. Schs., 1989—. Parliamentarian Omaha chpt. The Links, Inc., 1992—; sec. Nebr. PTA; v.p. Bellevue PTA, PTSA Coun., Bellevue Edn. Assn., life mem., PTA, Two Springs Elem. Sch., Nebr. State EDn. Assn., pres. Bellevue East PTSA. Named one of Outstanding Young Women in Am., 1976, 82, 83, 84, 91, 92, 93, 94. Mem. AAUP, Music Educators Nat. Confs., Nebr. Choral Dirs., Nebr. Arts Coun., Nebr. Choral Arts Soc., Bellevue Piano Fedn., Delta Sigma Theta, Phi Delta Kappa. Democrat. Baptist. Avocations: reading, Bible study, volleyball, walking. Home: 3431 Faye Dr Bellevue NE 68123-2616 Office: Fort Crook Sch 12501 S 25th St Bellevue NE 68123-5526

MAYEKAWA, MARY MARGARET, education counselor; b. Neptune, N.J., Nov. 13, 1941; d. Willis Gilbert and Thelma Anita Virginia (Anderson) Bills; m. Jackie Toshio Mayekawa, Nov. 28, 1970; 1 child, Leland Willis Magokichi. BA, Western Ky. U., 1965; postgrad., U. Va., 1966-68; MEd in Counseling, Coll. of William and Mary, 1971. Educator Fairfax County Schs., Annandale, Va., 1965-68; project transition counselor U.S. Army, Ft. Hood, Tex., 1971-73; student officer wives liason U.S. Army Transp. Sch., Ft. Eustis, Va., 1980-83; guidance counselor U.S. Army Japan IX Corp, Japan, 1983-87, 2d Infantry Divsn., Korea, 1987-89, USAF, Reese AFB, Tex., 1989—. Vol. Edn. Divsn. Tex. Tech. Mus., Lubbock, 1990—, mem. women's coun., 1990—; vestry Episcopal Ch., Okinawa and Sagamihara City, Japan, 1974, 76, 84-86; counselor Camp Blue Yonder, Reese AFB, Tex., 1989—. Capt. U.S. Army, 1968-71. Mem. Am. Counselor Assn., Mil. Educator Counselor Assn., Tex. Assn. for Counseling and Devel., Tex. Career Guidance Assn. Avocations: japanese flower arranging, japanese dollmaking, church activities, reading. Home: PO Box 16233 Lubbock TX 79490-6233

MAYER, DAN MICHAEL, emergency medicine educator; b. N.Y.C., Sept. 14, 1946; s. Harvey and Nana (Vogel) M.; m. Julia Eddy, Aug. 24, 1975; children: Memphis, Gilah, Noah. BSCE, The Cooper Union, N.Y.C., 1967; MD, Albert Einstein Coll. Medicine, 1973. Diplomate Am. Bd. Emergency Medicine. Intern Carney Hosp., Boston, 1973-74; med. dir. Burlington (Vt.) Peoples Free clinic, 1974-75; resident family practice Ea. Maine Med. Ctr., Bangor, 1976-77; pvt. practice Bangor, Maine, 1977-79; asst. dir. Phoenix Bapt. Family Practice, 1979-81; attending physician John C. Lincoln Hosp., Phoenix, 1981-84, Bronx (N.Y.) Mcpl. Hosp., 1984-85; dir. Inst. of Emergency medicine Albert Einstein Coll. Medicine, Bronx, 1984-85; asst. prof., then prof. emergency medicine Albany Med. Coll., 1987—; attending physician Albany Med. Ctr., 1987—. Course dir. evidence based health care studies Albany Med. Coll. Author: Case Studies in Emergency Medicine, 1991, Essential Evidence Based Medicine, 2004. Mem. Assn. Am. Med. Colls., Soc. Acad. Emergency Medicine. Office: Albany Med Coll 47 New Scotland Ave Albany NY 12208-3412

MAYER, DENNIS MARLYN, academic administrator, consultant; b. Bismarck, N.D., Mar. 11, 1928; s. Emil William and Hulda Esther (Becker) M.; m. Jo Anne Coffman, July 7, 1972; children: Jana, David, Kim. BS, U. N.D., 1950; MS, U. So. Calif., 1951, EdD, 1971. Tchr., coach John Park Sch., Las Vegas, Nev., 1951-53; counselor, tchr. Chino (Calif.) High Sch., 1953-57, Mt. San Antonio Coll., Walnut, Calif., 1957-58, dean of men, 1958-63, dir. student svcs., 1963-70, v.p., 1971-81; pres. Mt. San Jacinto (Calif.) Coll., 1981-87, Colo. Mountain Coll., Glenwood Springs, 1987—. Cons. Mira Costa Coll., Vista, Calif., 1985, Palos Verde Coll., Blythe, Calif., 1986, Cypress (Calif.) Coll., 1990—.; bd. dirs. Strategic Options Inst., Carbondale, Calif. Co-author: Excellence in Education, 1978; contbr. articles to profl. jours. Bd. dirs. United Way, Hemet, Calif., 1982-85, Double Check Retreat, Hemet, 1986-87, United Way, Glenwood Springs, Colo., 1988-90. Recipient United Way Leadership award, 1990. Mem. Calif. Student Svcs. Adminstrs. (pres. 1980-81, Educator of Yr. 1985), Calif. Higher Edn. Coun. (chmn. student svcs. 1982-83), Calif. Chief Exec. Officers (exec. bd. dirs. 1983-86), Inland Empire Edn. Assn. (chmn. 1985-86), Colo. Adminstrs. Assn. (pres. 1991—), Colo. Adult Literacy Commn. (bd. dirs.). Avocations: music, trombone, piano, tennis. Home: 457 High Tiara Ct Grand Junction CO 81503-8746 Office: Colo Mountain Coll 215 9th St Glenwood Springs CO 81601-3307

MAYER, ELIZABETH BILLMIRE, educational administrator; B.Ed., Nat. Coll. Edn., Evanston, Ill., 1953; M.A. in Liberal Studies, Wesleyan U., 1979. Teaching asst. Hull House, Chgo., 1950-51; teaching scholar Nat. Coll. Edn. Demonstration Sch., 1952-53; pre-sch. tchr. St. Matthew's Sch., Pacific Palisades, Calif., 1959-63, tchr. 2d grade, 1963-67; librarian Chandler Sch., Pasadena, Calif., 1971-72, tchr. 4th grade, 1972-80, curriculum coordinator 1st-8th grades, 1979-80; tchr. 4th-6th grades Inst. for Experimentation in Tchr. Edn., SUNY-Cortland, 1980; asst. prof. edn. SUNY-Cortland, 1980-82; founder, headmistress The Mayer Sch., Ithaca, N.Y., 1982-92, Ariz. State U., Tempe, 1992—, Coll. Edn., 1992-94, faculty liaison Acad. Affairs, 1994—. Mem. Nat. Council Tchrs. Math., Nat. Council Tchrs. English, Nat. Sci. Tchrs. Assn., Rotary Internat. (mem. bd. dirs. 1994-96), Phi Delta Kappa (officer 1980-81, 92-96), Mem. Leadership America, class of 1995. Office: Ariz State U PO Box 870101 Tempe AZ 85287-0101

MAYER, GEORGE MERTON, retired elementary education educator; b. Ellisburg, N.Y., July 11, 1936; s. Carlton Scott and Florence Geraldine (Allen) M.; m. Charlotte Ann Dawley, Aug. 31, 1963; children: Linda Sue Mayer Randall, Brian Keith, Amanda Leanne Hawkins. AA, Erie County Tech. Inst., 1957; BA in Edn., SUNY, Buffalo, 1966, MEd, 1973. Cert. tchr., N.Y. Lab. tech. Sylvania Electric Co., Buffalo, 1957-58; sch. driver, mechanic Ransomville (N.Y.) Bus Lines, 1959-66; coach driver Lockport (N.Y.) and Grand Island Transit Bus Lines, 1966-87; tchr. Thomas Marks Sch., Wilson, N.Y., 1965-82; tchr. remedial math. Wilson Sch. Dist., 1982-96; ret., 1996. Coach wrestling Wilson High Sch., 1977-88, coach jr. varsity football, 1972. Lay leader, mem. choir Ransomville United Meth. Ch., 1960-90; co-chmn. Niagara County Foster Parents, 1980—; bd. dirs. Town of Porter Recreation Commn. With N.Y. N.G., 1955-58, USAR, 1958-62. Mem. Wilson Tchrs. Assn., N.Y. State United Tchrs. Assn., N.Y. State Foster and Adoptive Assn. Republican. Avocations: music, electronics, sports, woodworking. Home: 2470 Youngstown Lockport Rd Ransomville NY 14131-9644 E-mail: geochar63@adelphia.net.

MAYER, GEORGE ROY, education educator; b. National City, Calif, Aug. 28, 1940; s. George Eberly and Helen Janet (Knight) M.; m. Barbara Ann Fife, Sept. 9, 1964 (div. June 1986); children: Kevin Roy, Debbie Rae Ann; m. Jocelyn Volk Finn, Aug. 3, 1986 (div. July 2003). BA, San Diego State U., 1962; MA, Ind. U., 1965, EdD, 1966. Cert. sch. psychologist; bd. cert. behavior analyst. Sch. counselor, psychologist Ind. U., Bloomington, 1964-66; asst. prof. guidance and ednl. psychology So. Ill. U., Carbondale, 1966-69; profl. edn. Calif. State U., L.A., 1966—. Cons. in field; adv. bd. Dept. Spl. Edn., L.A., 1986—, Alamansor Edn. Ctr., Alhambra, Calif., 1986-90, Jay Nolan Ctr. for Autism, Newhall, Calif., 1975-86; lectr. in field; study group on youth violence prevention Nat. Ctr. for Injury Prevention and Control, Divsn. Violence Prevention of the Ctrs. for Disease Control and Prevention, 1998. Author: Classroom Mgmt.: A Calif. Resource Guide, 2000, Tchng. Alternative Behavior-A schoolwide Calif. Resource Guide for Preventing Schoolwide Behavior Problems, 2003; co-author: Behavior Analysis for Lasting Change, 1991; contbr. articles to profl. jour. Recipient Outstanding Prof. award Calif. State U.-L.A., 1988; U.S. Dept. Edn. grantee, 1996—. Mem. Assn. for Behavior Analysis, Nat. Assn. Sch. Psychologists, Calif. Assn. Behavior Analysis (hon. life, pres., conf. chmn., Outstanding Contbr. to Behavior Analysis award 1997), Cambridge Ctr. for Behavioral Studies (adv. bd.), Calif. Assn. Sch. Psychologists (chmn. practitioners conf. 1994—). Avocations: horseback riding, fishing, swimming. Home: 10735 Frank Daniels Way San Diego CA 92131- E-mail: grmayer@aol.com.

MAYER, KATHERINE GENTZ, elementary education educator; b. Oceanside, N.Y., July 6, 1946; d. Howard A. and Ida M. (Hartz) Gentz; m. Daniel S. Mayer, Jr.; 1 child, Thaddeus D. Agar (from previous marriage). BS, U. Rochester, 1968; MEd, U. N.C., 1972. Cert. tchr. support specialist, Ga. Tchr. 5th grade Chapel Hill (N.C.)-Carrboro City Schs., 1968-73; tchr. grades 4, 5 Valdosta (Ga.) City Schs., 1978—. Vol. Am. Cancer Soc., Am. Heart Assn., March of Dimes, Valdosta; co-chair book fair AAUW, Valdosta, 1975. Mem. NEA, Ga. Assn. Edn., Valdosta Assn. Edn. (legis., membership coms., building rep.), Valdosta Recorder Consort. Avocations: playing recorder, bicycling, motorcycling. Office: West Gordon Sch 813 W Gordon St Valdosta GA 31601-3736

MAYER, PATRICIA LYNN SORCI, mental health nurse, educator; b. Chgo., July 22, 1942; d. Ben and Adonia (Grenier) Sorci; 1 child, Christopher David Mayer. AGS with high honors, Pima Community Coll., Tucson, 1983; BSN with honors, U. Ariz., 1986, MS in Nursing, 1987. RN, Ariz.; cert. addictions counselor, chem. dependency therapist; lic. pvt. pilot. Nurse educator, dir. CQI risk mgmt. U. Ariz., Tucson. Adj. clin. assoc. prof. U. Ariz. Coll. Nursing; field instr. U. Ariz. Coll. Bus. and Publ. Adminstr., Ariz. State U.; mem. Tucson Crisis Consortium Guilding Team; mem. team to implement crisis intervention tng. Tucson Law Enforcement. Contbr. articles to profl. jours. Recipient TMC Recognition award, 1998. Mem. Internat. Nurses Soc. on Addictions, Women in Healthcare, Phi Kappa Phi, Sigma Theta Tau, Pi Lambda Theta. Achievements include research in effectiveness of crisis stabilization in reducing syptoms of depression; effectiveness of inpatient treatment on functioning and symptomatology of psychiatric patients; ECT efficacy; effects of PYXIS in reducing medication trascription errors; factors that influence mothers to teach their adolescent daughters breast self-examination.

MAYER, RICHARD EDWIN, psychology educator; b. Chgo., Feb. 8, 1947; s. James S. and Bernis (Lowy) M.; m. Beverly Linn Pastor, Dec. 19, 1971; children: Kenneth Michael, David Mark, Sarah Ann. BA with honors, Miami U., Oxford, Ohio, 1969; MS in Psychology, U. Mich., 1971, PhD in Psychology, 1973. Vis. asst. prof. Ind. U., Bloomington, 1973-75; asst. prof. psychology U. Calif., Santa Barbara, 1975-80, assoc. prof., 1980-85, prof., 1985—, pres., chmn. dept., 1987-90. Vis. scholar Learning Rsch. and Devel. Ctr., U. Pitts., 1979, Ctr. for Study of Reading, U. Ill., 1984. Author: Foundations of Learning and Memory, 1979, The Promise of Cognitive Psychology, 1981, Thinking, Problem Solving, Cognition, 1983, 2d edit., 1992, BASIC: A Short Course, 1985, Educational Psychology, 1987, The Critical Thinker, 1990, 2d edit., 1995, The Promise of Educational Psychology, 1999; editor: Human Reasoning, 1980, Teaching and Learning Computer Programming, 1988; editor jours. Instructional Sci., 1983-87, Educational Psychologist, 1983-89. Sch. bd. officer Goleta (Calif.) Union Sch. Dist., 1981—. NSF grantee, 1975-88. Fellow APA (divsn. 15 officer 1987—, G. Stanley Hall lectr. 1988), Am. Psychol. Soc.; mem. Am. Ednl. Rsch. Assn. (divsn. C officer 1986-88), Psychonomic Soc. Democrat. Jewish. Avocations: computers, hiking, bicycling, reading, dogs. Office: U Calif Dept Of Psychology Santa Barbara CA 93016

MAYER, ROBERT ANTHONY, retired college president; b. N.Y.C., Oct. 30, 1933; s. Ernest John and Theresa Margaret (Mazura) M.; m. Laura Wiley Christ, Apr. 30, 1960. BA magna cum laude, Fairleigh Dickinson U., 1955; MA, NYU, 1967. With N.J. Bank and Trust Co., Paterson, 1955-61, mgr. advt. dept., 1959-61; program supr. advt. dept. Mobil Oil Co., N.Y.C., 1961-62; asst. to dir. Latin Am. program Ford Found., N.Y.C., 1963-65, asst. rep., 1965-67; asst. to v.p. adminstrn., 1967-73; officer in charge logistical services Ford Found., 1968-73; asst. dir. programs N.Y. Community Trust, N.Y.C., 1973-76; exec. dir. N.Y. State Council on the Arts, N.Y.C., 1976-79; mgmt. cons. N.Y.C., 1979-80; dir. Internat. Mus. Photography, George Eastman House, Rochester, N.Y., 1980-89, mgmt. cons., 1989-90; pres. Cleve. Inst. of Art, 1990-97; ret., 1997. Author: (plays) La Borgia, 1971, Alijandru, 1971, They'll Grow No Roses, 1975; mem. editl. adv. bd. Grants mag., 1978—80, exhibited profl. photography, 1993—. Mem. state program adv. panel NEA, 1977—80; mem. Mayor's Com. on Cultural Policy, N.Y.C., 1974—75; mem. pres.'s adv. com. Bklyn. campus L.I. U., 1978—79; bd. dirs. Fedn. Protestant Welfare Agys., N.Y.C., 1977—79, Arts for Greater Rochester, 1981—83, Garth Fagan's Dance Theatre, 1982—86; trustee Internat. Mus. Photography, 1981—89, Lacoste Sch. Arts, France, 1991—96, sec., 1994—96; mem. dean's adv. com. Grad. Sch. Social Welfare, Fordham U., 1976; mem. N.Y. State Motion Picture and TV Devel. Adv. Bd., 1984—87, N.Y. State Martin Luther King Jr. Commn., 1985—90, Cleve. Coun. Cultural Affairs, 1992—94; chmn. Greater Cleve. Regional Transit Authority Arts in Transit Com., 1992—95; bd. dirs. Friends of Ariz. State U. Ctr. for Latin Am. Studies, 1997—99, Villa Solana Townhouse Assn., 2001—, pres., 2000. Recipient Nat. award on advocacy for girls Girls Clubs Am., 1976 Mem. Nat. Assembly State Art Agys. (bd. dirs. 1977-79, 1st vice chmn. 1978-79), Alliance Ind. Colls. Art (bd. dirs. 1983-91, vice chmn. 1986-87, sec. 1987-89), N.Y. State Assn. Museums (bd. councilors 1983-86, pres. 1986-89), Assn. Ind. Colls. Art and Design (bd. dirs. 1991-97, exec. com. 1991-93, 96-97). Home: 2704 N 60th St Scottsdale AZ 85257-1012

MAYER, SUSAN LEE, nurse, educator; b. N.Y.C., Feb. 10, 1946; d. Hans and Frieda (Schein) Abramson; m. Steven Mayer, June 24, 1973; children: Jason, Stuart, Richard, Deborah. BSN, Hunter Coll., 1968; MA, NYU, 1974; EdD, Columbia U., 1996; postgrad., Yeshiva U., 1986, Adelphi U., 1987. RN, N.Y.; cert. in gerontology; cert. tchr., N.Y. Staff nurse ICU-CCU Montefiore Hosp., Bronx, N.Y., 1968; organizer CCU Jewish Meml. Hosp., N.Y.C., 1968; supr., adminstr. Morrisania City Hosp., N.Y.C., 1969-76; instr. Adelphi U., Garden City, N.Y., 1977-78; substitute nurse Great Neck (N.Y.) Pub. Schs., 1980-90; rsch. asst. to dean Adelphi U. Sch. Nursing, 1987-88; dir. ambulatory edn. North Bronx Healthcare Network, 2001—. Staff nurse Winthrop U. Hosp., Mineola, NY, 1987—90, per diem nurse, 1987—90; instr. dept. nursing edn. Bronx Mcpl. Hosp. Ctr. (now Jacobi Med. Ctr.), 1990—96; asst. prof. Helene Fuld Coll. Nursing, 1996—2001; adj. instr. Bronx C.C., 1992, Queensborough C.C., 1987—89; adj. asst. prof. Iona Coll. Sch. Nursing; adj. assoc. prof. Tchrs. Coll./Columbia U., 1997—; field nurse coord. RN Home Care Winthrop U. Hosp., Mineola, 1996—2001; dir. ambulatory edn. N. Bronx Healthcare Network, 2001—; lectr. and presenter in field. Contbr. articles to profl. jours. including Nursing and Health Care. Bd. dirs. Great Neck Synagogue, 1981-91, v.p. Sisterhood, 1978-79, pres., 1979-81; former bd. dirs. Russell Gardens Assn.; founder Work for Share Zedek Hosp., 1977—; past pres., fin. sec. L'Chaim chpt. Hadassah Nurse Coun. N.Y. State Regents scholar, 1963. Mem. ANA, Assn. Orthodox Jewish Scientists, Nat. League for Nursing, N.Y. Counties Registered Nurses Assn., N.Y. State Nurses Assn. (dist. 13 bd. dirs., past chmn. nurse practice com., past treas., past chair coun. ethical practice), Am. Assn. for History of Nursing, Nurses Edn. Alumni Assn. (historian), Sigma Theta Tau, Kappa Delta Pi. Democrat. Home: 28 Laurel Dr Great Neck NY 11021-2827 E-mail: sm192@columbia.edu.

MAYER, SUSAN MARTIN, art educator; b. Atlanta, Oct. 25, 1931; d. Paul McKeen and Ione (Garrett) Martin; m. Arthur James Mayer, Aug. 9, 1953; 1 child, Melinda Marilyn. Student, Am. U., 1949-50; BA, U. N.C., Greensboro, 1953; postgrad., U. Del., 1956-58; MA, Ariz. State U., 1966. Artist-in-residence Armed Forces Staff Coll., Norfolk, Va., 1968-69; mem. art faculty U. Tex., Austin, 1971—. Co-editor: Museum Education: History, Theory and Practice, 1989; author various mus. publs.; contbr. articles to profl. jours. Recipient award Austin Ind. Sch. Bd., 1985. Mem. Nat. Art Edn. Assn. (bd. dirs. 1983-87, award 1987, 91), Tex. Art Edn. Assn. (mus. edn. chair 1982-83, Mus. Educator of Yr. 1986), Tex. Assn. Mus. (mus. edn. chair), Austin Visual Arts Assn., Am. Assn. Mus. Office: U Tex Dept Art History Austin TX 78712

MAYER, VICTOR JAMES, geologist, educator; b. Mayville, Wis., Mar. 25, 1933; s. Victor Charles and Phyllis (Bachhuber) M.; m. Mary Jo Anne White, Nov. 25, 1965; children: Gregory, Maribeth. BS in Geology, U. Wis., 1956; MS in Geology, U. Colo., 1960, PhD in Sci. Edn., 1966. Tchr. Colo. Pub. Schs., 1961-65; asst. prof. SUNY Coll., Oneonta, 1965-67, Ohio State U., Columbus, 1967-70, assoc. prof., 1970-75, prof. ednl. studies, geol. scis. and natural resources, 1975-95, prof. emeritus, 1995—. Co-organizer symposa at 29th and 31st Internat. Geol. Congresses; internat. sci. edn. assistance to individuals and orgns. in Japan, Korea, Taiwan, Russia, and Venezuela; dir. NSF Insts., program for leadership Earth Sys. Edn., 1990-95; dir. Korean Sci. Tchrs. Insts., 1986-88, 95; keynote spkr. U.S.A. rep. Internat. Conf. on Geoscis. Edn., Southampton, Eng., 1993; co-convenor Second Internat. conf. on Geosci. Edn., Hilo, Hawaii, 1997; disting. vis. prof. SUNY, Plattsburg, 1994; vis. rsch. scholar Hyogo U., Japan, 1996; sr. Fulbright rschr. Shizuoka U., Japan, 1998; vis. prof. Korea Nat. U. of Edn., 2000. Contbr. articles to profl. jours. Served with USAR. Recipient Lifetime Disting. Svc. award to the Internat. Earth Sci. Edn. Cmty., 1997; named Disting. Investigator, Ohio Sea Grant Program, 1983. Fellow AAAS (chmn. edn. 1988-89), Ohio Acad. Sci. (v.p. 1978-79, exec. com. 1993-94, outstanding univ. educator 1995); mem. Nat. Sci. Tchrs. Assn. (bd. dirs. 1984-86), Sci. Edn. Coun. Ohio (pres. 1987-88), Sigma Xi, Phi Delta Kappa. Roman Catholic. Avocation: photography. Home: 111 W Dominion Blvd Columbus OH 43214-2607 Office: Ohio State U Dept Geol Scis 125 S Oval Mall Columbus OH 43210-1308 E-mail: mayer.4@osu.edu.

MAYER, WENDY WIVIOTT, special education educator; b. Madison, Wis., Aug. 25, 1962; dd. Wilbert W. and Matilda (Silbar) W. BS in Edn., Drake U., 1984; MS in Spl. Edn., U. Wis., Milw., 1990. Tchr. exceptional ednl. needs-emotionally disturbed and learning disabilities Mequon (Wis.)-Thiensville Sch. Dist., 1985—. Mem. Coun. for Exceptional Children.

MAYERS, JEAN, aerospace engineering educator; b. N.Y.C., June 8, 1920; s. Lou and Ida M.; m. Reva Lee Bookbinder, May 20, 1945; children: Eileen, Laurence. B.Aero. Engring., Poly. Inst. Bklyn., 1942, M.Aero. Engring., 1948. Research asst. aero. engring. Poly. Inst. Bklyn., 1946-48; aero. research scientist, structures research div. NACA, Langley Field, Va., 1948-56; successively prin. engr., engring. sec. head, engring. dept. head Sperry Utah Co. div. Sperry Rand Corp., 1956-61; vis. asso. prof. Stanford U., 1961-63, mem. faculty, 1963—, prof. aero. engring., 1967-83, prof. emeritus, 1984—, vice chmn. dept. aero. and astronautics, 1966-71. Vis. prof. Technion-Israel Inst. Tech., Haifa, 1970; Naval Air Systems Command Research prof. U.S. Naval Acad., 1978-79; Sci. adviser U.S. Army, 1963-72; cons. to govt. and industry, 1962-84 ; mem. ad hoc vis. com. on aero. engring. curricula Engrs. Council for Profl. Devel., 1969-70 Author articles, reports in field. ARC vol. USN Hosp., Bethesda, Md., 1992-97. Lt. comdr. USNR, 1942-46. Recipient U.S. Army Outstanding Civilian Service medal, 1973. Fellow AIAA (assoc., editor jour. 1967-70); mem. Naval Res. Assn., Mil. Officers of Am., Am. Soc. Engring. Edn., Aircraft Owners and Pilots Assn., Sigma Xi. Home: 1307 Estates Dr Fairfield CA 94533-9716

MAYFIELD, BLAYNE EUGENE, computer science educator; b. Cabool, Mo., Sept. 4, 1957; s. Billy E. and Eva O. (Mathis) M.; m. Annetta F. Barnett, June 30, 1979; children: Marcus, Brandon. BS in Computer Sci., U. Mo., Rolla, 1979, MS in Computer Sci., 1982, PhD in Computer Sci., 1988. Programmer, analyst Monsanto Co., St. Louis, 1979-81; analyst Southwestern Bell Tel., St. Louis, 1981-84; asst. prof. computer sci. Okla. State U., Stillwater, 1988-93, head dept. computer sci., 1993-2000, assoc. prof. computer sci., 1993—. Instr. televised course Nat. Tech. U., Ft. Collins, Colo., 1992—; mem. steering com. Mid-Am. Symposium on Emerging Techs., Talequah, Okla., 1995. Elder Sunnybrook Christian Ch., Stillwater, 1997—. Recipient G. Shake award Sigma Pi Fraternity Internat., 1988; summer faculty fellow NASA/Am. Soc. for Engring. Edn., 1991, 92; invited spkr. 16th symposium on Computer Systems, Monterrey, Mex., 1991. Mem. Assn. for Computing Machinery, Am. Assn. for Artificial Intelligence, Sigma Pi Fraternity Internat. (chpt. dir. 1983-87, province archon 1986-90). Avocations: jogging, model railroading, hammered dulcimer. Office: 218 Math Scis Dept Computer Sci Okla State U Stillwater OK 74078-1053 E-mail: bem@a.cs.okstate.edu.

MAYFIELD, WILLIAM STEPHEN, law educator; b. Gary, Indiana, Mar. 2, 1919; s. William Henry and Elnora Elizabeth (Williams) M.; m. Octavia Smith, Feb. 6, 1949 (dec.); children: Pamela L., William E., Stephanie K. Stokes; m. Mildred G. Harris, May 25, 1991. BA, Detroit Inst. Tech., 1946; JD, Detroit Coll. Law, 1949. Bar: Mich. 1949, U.S. Supreme Ct. 1996. Mem. firm Lewis, Rowlette, Brown, Wanzo and Bell, Detroit, 1949-51; atty. U.S. Office Price Stblzn., Detroit, 1951-53; referee Friend of the Court, Detroit, 1953-72; vis. prof. Law Center, La. State Univ., Baton Rouge, summer, 1979; prof. law So. U., Baton Rouge, 1972—. Mem. com. sci. and tech. in cts. La. Supreme Ct., 1978 Mem. regional bd. Boy Scouts Am., Detroit, 1961-63; Served with U.S. Army, 1942-46. Mem. Am. Bar Assn., Nat. Bar Assn., Wolverine Bar Assn., World Assn. Law Profs., Detroit Coll. Law Alumni Assn., Assn. Henri Capitanti, Comml. Law League Am., Ret. Officers Assn. (pres. Greater Baton Rouge 1985), Am. Legion, Mil. Order of the World Wars, Delta Theta Phi (Outstanding Prof. of Yr. award 1983) Office: 5909 Marina View Ct Prospect KY 40059-8865

MAYHEW, DAVID RAYMOND, political science educator; b. Putnam, Conn., May 18, 1937; s. Raymond William and Jeanie (Nicholson) M. BA, Amherst Coll., 1958; PhD, Harvard U., 1964. Tchg. fellow Harvard U., 1961-63; from instr. to asst. prof. polit. sci. U. Mass., Amherst, 1963-67; vis. asst. prof. Amherst Coll., 1965-66; faculty Yale U., 1966-77, prof. polit. sci., 1977—, chmn. dept., 1979-82, Alfred Cowles prof. govt., 1982-98, Sterling prof. polit. sci., 1998—. Olin vis. prof. Am. govt. Nuffield Coll., Oxford (Eng.) U., 2000-01. Author: Party Loyalty Among Congressmen, 1966, Congress: The Electoral Connection, 1974 (Washington Monthly ann. polit. book award 1974), Placing Parties in American Politics, 1986, Divided We Govern, 1991, America's Congress, 2000, Electoral Realignments, 2002. Recipient Richard E. Neustadt prize 1992, James Madison award, 2002, Yale Grad. Student Mentor award, 2002; Woodrow Wilson fellow, 1958-59, vis. fellow Nuffield Coll., Oxford, 1978, Guggenheim fellow, 1978-79, Hoover Nat. fellow, 1978-79, Sherman Fairchild fellow, 1990-91, fellow Ctr. for Advanced Study in Behavioral Scis., 1995-96. Fellow Am. Acad. Arts and Scis.; mem. Am. Polit. Sci. Assn. (nat. council 1976-78, Congl. fellow 1967-68), So. Polit. Sci. Assn., New Eng. Polit. Sci. Assn. Home: 100 York St Apt 5C New Haven CT 06511-5611 Office: Yale U Polit Sci Dept Box 208301 New Haven CT 06520-8301 E-mail: david.mayhew@yale.edu.

MAYHEW, ERIC GEORGE, medical researcher, educator; b. London, Eng., June 22, 1938; came to U.S., 1964; s. George James and Doris Ivy (Tipping) M.; m. Barbara Doe, Sept. 28, 1966 (div. 1976); 1 child, Miles; m. Karen Caruana, Apr. 1, 1978 (div. 1994); children: Ian, Andrea: m. Ludmila Khatchatrian, June 29, 1995. BS, U. London, 1960, MS, 1963; PhD, 1967; DSc, U. London, 1993. Rsch. asst. Chester Beatty Rsch. Inst., London, 1960-64; cancer rsch. scientist Roswell Pk. Meml. Inst., Buffalo, 1964-68, sr. cancer rsch. scientist, 1968-72, assoc. cancer rsch. scientist, 1979-93, dep. dir. exptl. pathology, 1988-93; prin. scientist The Liposome Co., Princeton, N.J., 1993-99, May Pharm Consulting, 2000—. Assoc. rsch. prof. SUNY, Buffalo, 1979-93; ad-hoc mem. NIH study sects., 1982-94; cons. to industry, 2000—. Editor jour. Selective Cancer Therapeutics, 1989-91; contbr. articles to Jour. Nat. Cancer Inst., Cancer Rsch. and many other profl. jours. Grantee NIH, Am. Heart Assn., and pvt. industry, 1972-93. Mem. Am. Assn. Cancer Rsch., N.Y. Acad. Sci. Achievements include development of liposomes for drug delivery and patents for new chemical entities and liposome delivery. Office: May Pharm Consulting 1782 S Seaview Ave Coupeville WA 98239 E-mail: eailkmay@aol.com.

MAYHUE, RICHARD LEE, provost, dean, pastor, writer; b. Takoma Park, Md., Aug. 31, 1944; s. J. Richard Mayhue and Myrtle Lorraine (Hartsell) Lee; m. Lois Elaine Nettleingham, June 18, 1966; children: Lee, Wade. BS, Ohio State U., 1966; MDiv, Grace Theol. Seminary, Winona Lake, Ind., 1974, ThM, 1977, ThD, 1981. Ordained pastor. Asst. pastor Grace Brethren Ch. of Columbus (Ohio), 1975-77; asst. prof. New Testament and Greek, Grace Theol. Seminary, Winona Lake, 1977-80; assoc. pastor Grace Cmty. Ch., Sun Valley, Calif., 1980-84, 89—; sr. pastor Grace Brethren Ch., Long Beach, Calif., 1984-89; sr. v.p., dean, prof. systematic theology and pastoral mins. The Master's Seminary, Sun Valley, 1989—; sr. v.p., provost The Master's Coll., Santa Clarita, Calif., 2000—. Bd. dirs. Grace Theol. Sem., 1987-89. Author: (booklets) The Biblical Pattern for Divine Healing, 1979, 2002, Snatched Before the Storm, 1980, 2002, (books) Divine Healing Today, 1983, How to Interpret the Bible for Yourself, 1986, A Christian's Survival Guide, 1987, Unmasking Satan, 1988, (2d edit., 2001), Spiritual Intimacy, 1990, Spiritual Maturity, 1992, The Healing Promise, 1994, What Would Jesus Say About Your Church?, 1995, 2d edit., 2001, Fight the Good Fight, 1999, 1 and 2 Thessalonians, 1999, Seeking God, 2000Practicing Proverbs, 2003; contbr., co-editor: Rediscovering Expository Preaching, 1992, Rediscovering Pastoral Ministry, 1994; contbr. A Festschrift In Honor of Homer A. Kent, 1991; contbr., assoc. editor MacArthur Study Bible, 1997; contbr.: The Master's Perspective on Difficult Texts, 1998, The Master's Perspective on Contemporary Issues, 1998, Tim LaHaye Prophecy Study Bible, 2000; contbr., co-editor: The Master's Perspective on Pastoral Ministry, 2002, The Master's Perspective on Biblical Prophecy, 2002; contbr., assoc. editor Think Biblically!, 2003; contbr. articles to profl. jours. Bd. dirs. Capitol Ministries, 1996—, Slavic Gospel Assn, 1993-2002; bd. elders Grace Cmty. Ch., 1989—; mem. bd. of ref. Coun. on Bibl. Manhood and Womanhood, 1991—. Recipient Bronze Star with Combat V USN, 1969. Mem. Evang. Theol. Soc., Nat. Fellowship Grace Brethren Ministers (pres. 1988), Far West Region Evang. Theol. Soc. (pres. 1995), Evang. Homiletics Soc. Avocation: n-gauge model railroading. Office: The Master's Seminary 13248 Roscoe Blvd Sun Valley CA 91352-3739 also: The Master's Coll 21726 Placerita Canyon Rd Santa Clarita CA 91321-1200

MAYNARD, JOAN, education educator; b. Louisa, Ky., Oct. 18, 1932; d. Macon Scott and Jeanette (Thompson) Chambers; m. Frank Maynard Jr., June 15, 1951 (dec. Oct. 1988); children: Mark Steven, Julia Beth Maynard McFann, Robert Blake. BA, Wittenberg U., 1977; MEd, Wright State U., 1980, MEd, 1984. Tchr., reading specialist Mechanicsburg (Ohio) Exempted Village Schs., 1976—; pres. TOTT Publs. Inc., Bellbrook, Ohio, 1988—99; ret., 1999. Rep. Career Edn., Mechanicsburg, 1981-88, mem. Thompson Grant Com., Mechanicsburg, 1987-88. Author: Mud Puddles, 1988, Mud Pies, 1989. Vol. Mechanicsburg Schs. Levy, 1980, 82, 88, Congl. Race, Campaign County, Ohio, 1982, 84, 86; cons. Urbana U., Ohio, 1988-90, 91, 92, 93; tutor Laubach Lit. Action, Urbana, 1989-90, 91-93, 94. Recipient Thompson grant, 1982, 88, 92. Mem. AAUW (edn. chmn. Champaign County chpt. 1988-89, treas. 1989-90), Internat. Reading Assn., Champaign County Reading Coun. (treas. 1990-91), Midwestern Assembly Lit. Young People (treas. 1989-93), Kappa Delta Pi. Avocations: collecting children's lit. books, travel, reading. Home: 1546 Parkview Rd Mechanicsburg OH 43044-9779 Office: Exempted Village Schs 60 High St Mechanicsburg OH 43044-1071

MAYO, CLYDE CALVIN, organizational psychologist, educator; b. Robstown, Tex., Feb. 2, 1940; s. Clyde Culberson and Velma (Oxford) M.; m. Jeanne Lynn McCain, Aug. 24, 1963; children: Brady Scott, Amber Camille. BA, Rice U., 1961; BS, U. Houston, 1964, PhD, 1972; MS, Trinity U., 1966. Lic. psychologist, Tex., La. Mgmt. engr. LWFW, Inc., Houston, 1966-72, sr. cons., 1972-78, prin., 1978-81; ptnr. Mayo, Thompson, Bigby, Houston, 1981-83; founder Mgmt. and Pers. Systems, Houston, 1983—. Counselor Interface Counseling Ctr., Houston, 1976-79; dir. Mental Health HMO Group, 1985-87; instr. St. Thomas U., Houston, 1979—, U. Houston Downtown Sch., 1972, 2002—, U. Houston, Clear Lake, 1983-88, U. Houston-Central Campus, 1984—; dir. mgmt. devel. insts. U. Houston Woodlands and West Houston, 1986-1991, adj. prof. U. Houston, 1991—, U. Houston, Clear Lake, 1998. Author: Bi/Polar Inventory of Strengths, 1978, LWFW Annual Survey of Manufacturers, 1966-81. Coach, mgr. Meyerland Little League, 1974-78, So. Belles Softball, 1979-80, S.W. Colt Baseball, 1982-83, Friends of Fondren Libr. of Rice U., 1988—; charter mem. Holocaust Mus. Mem. APA, Soc. Indsl. Orgn. Psychologists, Tex. Indsl. Orgnl. Psychologists (founder, bd. dirs. 1995—, pres. 1999-2002), Houston Psychol. Assn. (membership dir. 1978, sec. 1984), Tex. Psychol. Assn., Am. Psychol. Soc., Houston Area Indsl. Orgnl. Psychologists (bd. dirs. 1989-92), Found. Contemporary Theology, Forum Club, Meyerland Club (bd. dirs. 1988-92, pres. 1991). Home: 8723 Ferris Dr Houston TX 77096-1409 Office: Mgmt and Personnel Systems 4545 Bissonnet St Bellaire TX 77401-3121

MAYORA-ALVARADO, EDUARDO RENE, lawyer, law educator; b. Guatemala, Guatemala, Apr. 20, 1957; s. Eduardo Alfredo Mayora-Dawe and Adelaida (Alvarado) De Mayora; m. Alicia Bascunana, June 18, 1983; children: Javier Eduardo, Santiago, Jose Andres, Sebastian. JD, U. Rafael Landivar, Guatemala, 1980; LLM, Georgetown U., U.S.A., 1982; Diploma (2) in Principles Econ. Sci., U. Francisco Marroquin, Guatemala, 1991, LLD, 1997. Bar: Guatemala, 1980; cert. notary. Assoc. Mayora & Mayora, Guatemala, 1980-81, ptnr., 1982—, mem. tax adminstrn. bd., 1998-2000; prof. bus. law and principles of law U. Francisco Marroquin, Guatemala, 1984-87, prof. bus. law and principles of law Sch. of Econs., 1986-88, prof. constitutional law, dean Sch. of Law, 1989-2000, prof. principles of pvt. and pub. law, 1993; bd. dirs. Financiera de Inversion, S.A., Guatemala, 1988-96. Alt. dir. Seguros Alianza S.A., Guatemala, 1988-94; trustee U. Francisco Marroquin, 1989—; vis. prof. Pontificia U. Catolica, Porto Alegre, Brazil, 1994, Montpellier U. Sch. Law, France, 1995. Co-author: El Desafio Neoliberal, 1992; author: Teoría Constitucional para una sociedad libre Fundación República para una nueva generación, 1997; (essay) El Drama De La Arena Movedisa, 1993 (Charles Stillman award 1993); contbr. to profl. jours. Mem. Guatemala Bar Assn. (author articles Bar Law Jour. 1990—m v.p. ethics bd. 1985-86), Assn. De Amigos Del Pais, Fundacion Para La Cultura (v.p. 1994), Inst. Guatemalteco De Derecho Notarial, Phi Delta Phi, Guatemala Country Club. Roman Catholic. Avocations: reading, sailing, golf. Office: Mayora & Mayora15 Calle 1-04 Plz Centrica 3er Nivel #301 Zona 10 Guatemala City Guatemala also: PO Box 661447 Miami FL 33266-1447 E-mail: mayorae@intelnet.net.gt.

MAYS, DAVID ARTHUR, agronomy educator; b. Waynesburg, Pa., Apr. 17, 1929; s. Arthur Lynn and Edith N. (Breakey) M.; m. Betty Ann Sellers, Aug. 7, 1954; children: Gregory D., Laurie Ann. MS in Agronomy, Pa. State U., 1959, PhD in Agronomy, 1961. Cert. profl. agronomist. Asst. county agrl. agt. Pa. State, Washington, Pa., 1954-57; grad. rsch. asst. Pa. State U., University Park, Pa., 1957-61; asst. agronomist Va. Polytech. Inst. & State U., Middleburg, 1961-63; rsch. agronomist TVA, Muscle Shoals, Ala., 1963-88; prof. agronomy Ala. A&M Univ., Normal, Ala., 1989—. Editor: Forage Fertilization, 1974; contbr. articles to profl. jours. and chpts. to books, 1959—. 1st lt. U.S. Army, 1951-54, Korea. Mem. Am. Soc. Agronomy, Am. Forage and Grassland Coun. (Merit Cert. award 1976), Ala. Turfgrass Assn. Presbyterian. Home: 114 Kathy St Florence AL 35633-1428 Office: Ala A&M U Dept Plant and Soil Sci PO Box 1208 Normal AL 35762-1208

MAYS, GEORGE WALTER, JR., educational technology educator, consultant, tutor; b. Decatur, Ill., July 1, 1926; s. George Walter Sr. and Ida May (Lookabaugh) M.; children: Richard, Steven, John, James. BS in Edn., U. Ill., Champaign, 1950, MS in Edn., 1952; BSEE, U. md., 1960; cert., Calif. State U., Carson, 1987. Tchr. math. and physics Mahomet (Ill.) High Sch., 1950-52, prin., 1952-55; br. chief engring studies Nat. Security Agy., Ft. Meade, Md., 1955-62; sr. engr. Jet Propulsion Lab., Pasadena, Calif., 1962-71; tchr. math.-sci., chair Aviation High Sch., Redondo Beach, Calif., 1971-82; tchr. math. and physics, dept. chair Redondo Union High Sch., 1982-89; cons. ednl. tech. Apple Valley, Calif., 1989—; math. coord. Sci. and Tech. Ctr., Apple Valley, Calif., 1990—. Part-time instr. electronics Pasadena City Coll., 1963-72, Pepperdine U., 1975-76, math. Victor Valley Coll., 1991-97; instr. math. Acad. for Acad. Excellence, Apply Valley, 1998—. Author: Educational Technology Application Notes, 1989-90. With USN, 1944-46. Recipient Appollo Achievement award NASA, 1969. Mem. IEEE (life), Calif. Tchrs. Assn. (WHO award 1988-89), Nat. Coun. Tchrs. of Math., Computer Using Educators, Apple Valley Country Club, Victor Valley Aero Club. Avocations: reading, sports, computer usage, flying. Home and Office: 13458 Sunset Dr PO Box 745 Apple Valley CA 92307-0013

MAYS, GLENDA SUE, retired education educator; b. Freer, Tex., July 18, 1938; d. Archie Richard and Helen Hildred (Morgan) Cox; m. Dewey William Mays, Sept. 7, 1963; children: Rose Marie, Teresa Sue, Frank Dewey. BS, Tex. Tech. U., 1959, MA, 1961; PhD, North Tex. State U., 1969. Cert. tchr., supr., prin. Tchr. Lubbock (Tex.) Pub. Schs., 1959-61, Amarillo (Tex.) Pub. Schs., 1961-62, Austin (Tex.) Pub. Schs., 1962-63; curriculum intern/rsch. asst., elem. coord. U. Tex. at Austin, Hurst, Tex., 1963-65; asst. prof. McMurry U., Abilene, Tex., 1965-67; assoc. prof. Dallas Bapt. U., 1968-71; reading resource tchr., dept. chair Ft. Worth (Tex.) Ind. Sch. Dist., 1971-74, reading specialist, 1974-82, instructional specialist, 1982-95, ret., 1995; owner Cornucopia Antiques, Jewelry and Collectibles, Ft. Worth, 1969—, Cornucopia Estate and Appraisal Svcs., Ft. Worth, 1998—. Spkr. lang. acquisition and reading 7th World Congress in Reading, Hamburg, Germany, 1978. Advisor/writer (English textbook): McDouglas Littel Language, 1985-86; writer: Bilingual Stories for Ft. Worth Ind. Sch. Dist., 1979-80; contbr. poems to anthologies. Patron Kimbell Mus. Art, Ft. Worth, 1994—; mem. Nat. Cancer Soc., Ft. Worth, 1980—. Fulbright-Hays scholar, Kenya, Africa, 1970; grantee in fgn. langs. Nat. Endowment Arts U. Ark., 1987, Ft. Worth Ind. Sch. Dist. Study grantee U. London, 1978. Fellow ASCD, NEA, Tex. State Tchrs. Assn., Ft. Worth Edn. Assn., Internat. Reading Assn. (hostess 1st Tex. breakfast 1969), Nat. Geog. Soc., Smithsonian Instn., Libr. of Congress, Ft. Worth Reading Assn., Nat. Coun. for Social Studies spkr. social studies symposium N.Y.C. 1970, Tex. Elem. Prins. and Suprs. Assn. (sec. 1971-72). Avocations: travel, reading, music, writing, antique collecting. Home: 1225 Clara St Fort Worth TX 76110-1009

MAYSILLES, ELIZABETH, speech communication professional, educator; b. Sleepy Creek, W.Va. d. Evers and Rose (Scott) M. AB, W.Va. U.; MA, Hunter Coll., 1963; PhD, NYU, 1980. Announcer Radio Sta. WAJR, Morgantown, W.Va.; broadcaster Radio Sta. WGHF-FM, Rural Radio Network, N.Y.C.; group leader GMAC, N.Y.C.; instr. NYU, N.Y.C.; adj. prof. speech comm. Pace U., N.Y.C., 1978—2002; exec. adminstr. Am.-Scottish Found., N.Y.C., 1980-90; adminstrv. asst. Brit. Schs. and Univs. Found., Inc.; numerous radio and television appearances. Cons., lectr. in field. Vol. counselor Help Line, N.Y.C., 1971-75. Recipient Disting. Svc. award NYU Grad. Orgn., 1970-71. Mem. Internat. Platform Assn. (bd.

govs. 1980—), N.Y. Acad. Scis., English-Speaking Union, Caledonian Club N.Y. (bd. dirs. 1994-96, chieftain 2001-02). Avocations: reading, swimming, gardening, travel in England and Scotland. Home: 155 E 77th St Apt 6F New York NY 10021-1955

MAZE, THOMAS H. engineering educator; b. St. Paul, June 1, 1952; s. Robert O. and Viola A.E. (Schultz) M.; m. Leslie Foster Smith, Aug. 2, 1979; children: Lauren L. Simonds, Julie W. Simonds. BS in Civil Engring., Iowa State U., 1975; M of Engring., Urban and Pub. Systems, U. Calif., Berkeley, 1977; PhD in Civil Engring., Mich. State U., 1982. Asst. prof. dept. civil engring. Wayne State U., 1979-82; assoc. prof. sch. civil engring. and environ. sci. U. Okla., Norman, 1982-87; prof. dept. civil and construction engring. Iowa State U., Ames, 1988—, prof. in-charge transp. planning program, 1987—, dir. ctr. for transp. rsch. and edn., ext. and applied rsch., 1988-99; v.p. H.R. Green Corp., St. Paul, 1999—. Assoc. dir. inst. urban transp., transp. rsch. ctr. Ind. U., Bloomington, 1987—; dir. Midwest Transp. Ctr., U.S. Dept. Transp.'s Univ. Transp. Ctr. Fed. Region VII, 1990-96. Mem. ASCE, Am. Pub. Transit Assn., Its Am. (founding, instl. issues com., CVO com.), Am. Pub. Works Assn. (adj. workshop faculty mem. 1986-91, exec. coun. inst. equipment svcs. 1991—), Coun. Univ. Transp., Transp. Rsch. Bd. (mem. various coms., chair 8th equipment mgmt. conf. 1990), Inst. Transp. Engrs. (assoc. mem. dept. 6 standing com., chmn. various coms., pres. U. Fla. student chpt. 1976-79), Chi Epsilon (faculty advisor U. Okla. 1985-87), Sigma Xi. Office: HR Green Co 1326 Energy Park Dr Saint Paul MN 55108-5202

MAZLISH, BRUCE, historian, educator; b. NYC, Sept. 15, 1923; s. Louis and Lee (Reuben) M.; m. Neva Goodwin, Nov. 22, 1988; children from previous marriage: Cordelia, Peter, Anthony, Jared. BA, Columbia U., 1944, MA, 1947, PhD, 1955. Instr. history U. Maine, 1946-48, Columbia U., 1949- 50, Mass. Inst. Tech., 1950-53; dir. Am. Sch. in Madrid, Spain, 1953-55; mem. faculty Mass. Inst. Tech., 1955—, prof. history, 1965—, chmn. history sect., 1965-70, head dept. humanities, 1974-79. Vis. prof. Harvard U., Cambridge, Mass., 2001—02; scholars coun. Libr. of Congress, 2001—. Author: (with J. Bronowski) The Western Intellectual Tradition, 1960, The Riddle of History, 1966, In Search of Nixon, 1972, James and John Stuart Mill: Father and Son in the 19th Century, 1975, 2d edition, 1988, The Revolutionary Ascetic, 1976, Kissinger, The European Mind in American Policy, 1976, The Meaning of Karl Marx, 1984, A New Science: The Breakdown of Connections and the Birth of Sociology, 1989, The Leader, the Led and the Psyche, 1990, The Fourth Discontinuity: The Co-Evolution of Humans and Machines, 1993, The Uncertain Sciences, 1998; Editor: Psychoanalysis and History, 1963, rev. edit., 1971, The Railroad and the Space Program: An Exploration in Historical Analogy, 1965, (with Ralph Buultjens) Conceptualizing Global History, 1993, (with Leo Marx) Progress: Fact or Illusion, 1996; contbr. articles to profl. jours. Bd. dirs. Rockefeller Family Fund, 1987-97; v.p. Mount Desert Festival of Chamber Music, 1985—; bd. dirs. Toynbee Prize Found., 1992—, pres., 1997—. Served with inf. and OSS, AUS, 1943-45. Recipient Toynbee prize, 1986-87. Fellow Am. Acad. Arts and Scis. Clubs: Cambridge Tennis, Badminton and Tennis; Harbor (Seal Harbor, Maine). Home: 11 Lowell St Cambridge MA 02138-4725 Office: MIT 77 Massachusetts Ave Cambridge MA 02139-4307

MAZUMDER, JYOTIRMOY, mechanical and materials engineering educator; b. Calcutta, India, July 9, 1951; came to U.S., 1978; s. Jitendra Mohan and Gouri (Sen) M.; m. Aparajita, June 17, 1982; children: Debashis, Debayan. B in Engring., Calcutta U., 1973; diploma, PhD, Imperial Coll., London U., 1978. Rsch. scientist U. So. Calif., L.A., 1978-80; asst. prof. mechanical and indsl. engring. U. Ill., Urbana, 1980-84, assoc. prof., 1984-88, prof., 1988-96, co-dir. ctr. laser aided materials processing, 1990-96; Robert H. Lurie Prof. Engring. U. Mich., Ann Arbor, 1996—, dir. ctr. laser aided intelligent mfg., 1996—. Co-dir. ctr. laser aided material processing U. Ill., 1990-96; dir. Quantum Laser Corp., Edison, N.J., 1982-89; pres. Laser Scis., Inc., Urbana, 1988—; dir., CEO POM Inc., Plymouth, Mich.; vis. scholar physics dept. Stanford (Calif.) U., 1990. Author: (with others) Laser Welding; editor and co-editor more than 9 books including co-editor: Laser Materials Processing, 1984, 88; more than 250 technical papers; contbr. numerous articles to profl. jours. Fellow Am. Soc. of Metals and Laser Inst. of Am. (life, pres. 2000, editor-in-chief Jour. Laser Application); mem. Am. Inst. Metallurgical Engrs. (phys. mets. com. 1980—), Optical Soc. Am. Achievements include patent: weld pool visualization system for measurement of free surface deformation, apparatus and method for monitoring and controlling multi-layer cladding. Office: U Mich Dept Mech Engring & Mechs 2041 GG Brown Ann Arbor MI 48109-2125 E-mail: mazumder@umich.edu

MAZUR, DEBORAH JOAN, assistant principal; b. Highland Park, Mich., Apr. 22, 1958; d. Frank J. and Joan A. (Cader) M.; m. Michael J. Baker, Sept. 20, 1986 (div. Apr. 1997); children: Adam Joseph, John Michael, Ryan Francis. BS, Western Mich. U., 1981; MA, Oakland U., 1989, EdS, 2002. Spl. edn. resources room tchr. Capac Cmty. Schs., Mich., 1981-82; supr. group home Blue Water Developmental Housing, Port Huron, Mich., 1982-83; unit adminstr. group home Luth. Social Svcs. Mich., Detroit, 1983-85; mgr. sales Fin. Svcs. Am., Inc., Madison Heights, Mich., 1985-86; clinician, case mgr. Ditty, Lynch and Assocs., Birmingham, Mich., 1986-87; spl. edn. tchr. Pontiac (Mich.) Sch. Dist., 1987-96; counselor Warren (Mich.) Consol. Schs., 1996—2002; asst. prin. Warren Consol Schs., 2002—. Mem.: ASCD, ACA, Mich. Assn. Sec. Sch. Prins., Nat. Assn. Sec. Sch. Prins., Mich. Counseling Assn., Warren YMCA (bd. dirs.), Western Mich. U. Alumni Assn.

MAZZARELLA, JAMES KEVIN, business administration educator; b. Phila., Sept. 22, 1955; s. Samuel Charles and Rosemary C. (Queenan) M. BA, St. Joseph's U., 1977; MBA, La Salle U., 1981, cert., 2001; MA, Temple U., 1987; PhD, Columbia-Pacific U., 1987; DBA, Pacific-Western U., 1988; cert. in acctg., Thomas Edison State Coll., 1994; BS, SUNY, 1996; cert. in e-Bus. & e-Commerce, U. Ill., 2003. Cert. mgmt. acct.; cert. in fin. mgmt. Asst. mgr. Olney Oil & Burner Co., Phila., 1977-80; data processing Craig Fuel Co., Phila., 1980-84; supr. M. Kelley Son's Inc., Phila., 1984-86; adj. instr. Holy Family Coll., Phila., 1987-88, instr., 1989, asst. prof., 1989—. Adj. instr. Phila. (Pa.) Coll. Textiles, 1984-86, La Salle U., Phila., 1985—, Rosemont (Pa.) Coll., 1988-91. Mem. Acad. Fin. Svcs., Am. Econs. Assn., Am. Fin. Assn., Am. Statis. Assn., Nat. Assn. Bus. Econs., Am. Risk and Ins. Assn., Inst. Mgmt. Accts., Math. Assn. Am., Fin. Mgmt. Assn., Prodn. and Ops. Mgmt. Soc., Midwest Fin. Assn., Western Econs. Assn. Internat., Ea. Econ. Assn., Ea. Fin. Assn., Am. Mgmt. Assn., So. Fin. Assn., Multinat. Fin. Soc., Am. Math. Soc., Am. Law and Econs. Assn., Nat. Coun. Tchrs. Math. Roman Catholic. Home: 5101 N Fairhill St Philadelphia PA 19120-3126 Office: Holy Family College Grant & Frankford Ave Philadelphia PA 19114

MAZZIO-MOORE, JOAN L. radiology educator, physician; b. Belmont, Mass., Oct. 26, 1935; d. Frank Joseph and Maria L. Mazzio; children: James Thomas, Edwin Stuart. BA in Chemistry and Theology, Emmanuel Coll., 1957; MA in Genetics and Physiology, Mass. Wellesley Coll., 1961; PhD in Genetics, Bryn Mawr (Pa.) Coll., 1964; MD, Phila. Coll. of Medicine, 1977, MSc in Radiology, 1981. Instr. in biochemistry Gwynedd Mercy Coll., Springhouse, Pa., 1963—65; instr. in genetics Holy Family Coll., Phila., 1965—66; instr. in anatomy Phila. Coll. of Medicine, 1971—77, instr., 1973—77, asst. prof., 1977—84; prof. W.Va. Sch. of Medicine, 1984—2003; rotating intern Phila. Coll. of Medicine Hosp., 1977—78, resident in radiology and radiation therapy, 1978—81; advanced through grades to lt. col. USAR, 1984—2002; med. dir. 91W transition program U.S. Army Med. Corps Reserves, divsn. surgeon, 80th divsn. (IT). Author: (with Dr. DiVirgilito) Essentials of Neuropathology, 1974. Lector St. Ann's Cath. Ch., Phoenixville, Pa., 1981-84; treas. Hist. Soc. of Frankford, Phila., 1968-75, Sch. Mother's Assn., Devon (Pa.) Prep., 1980-81; organist St. Charles Catholic Ch., White Sulphur Spgs., 2001-. Col. med. corps U.S. Army, 1992—2003, ret. med. corps. U.S. Army, 2003. Mem. AAUP, Am. Acad. Family Physicians, Am. Assn. Women Radiologists, Am. Med. Women's Assn., Am. Osteo. Coll. of Radiology, Am. Soc. Clin. Oncology, Am. Soc. Therapeutic Readiologists, Hist. Soc. of Lewisburg (life), Pa. Osteo. Med. Assn., Pa. Osteo. Gen. Practitioner's Soc., Radiol. Soc. N.Am., Radiation Rsch. Soc., Res. Officers Assn. (life), W.Va. Soc. Osteo. Medicine, Greenbrier River Hike and Bike Trail. Home: RR 1 Box 179 Frankford WV 24938 Office: WVa Sch of Medicine 400 N Lee St Lewisburg WV 24901-1128 Fax: 304-497-2752. E-mail: drjmoore@mail.wvnet.edu.

MAZZOCCO, ANGELO, language educator, cultural historian, linguist; b. Cerreto di Vastogirardi, Isernia, Italy, May 13, 1936; came to U.S., 1954, naturalized, 1957; s. Giuseppe and Ida (Rotolo) M.; m. Elizabeth Hunt Davis, Oct. 7, 1990; children: Michael Ray, Marco Angelo. BS, BA, Ohio State U., 1959, MA, 1963; PhD in Romance Langs. and Lits., U. Calif., Berkeley, 1973. Instr. Spanish John Carroll U., Cleve., 1962-65; teaching asst. Italian U. Calif., Berkeley, 1966-69; asst. prof. Italian No. Ill. U., DeKalb, 1970-75; asst. prof. Spanish and Italian Mt. Holyoke Coll., South Hadley, Mass., 1975-78, assoc. prof., 1978-83, prof., 1983—, chair dept., 1981-84, 1993—96, chair Romance langs. and lits., 1989-93, 1999—2002. Assoc. Columbia U. Renaissance Seminar, 1981-90; fellow-in-residence Inst. for Advanced Study, Ind. U., Bloomington, 1998; mem. editl. adv. bd. Renaissance Quart.; interview NPR, 2000. Author: Linguistic Theories in Dante/Humanists, 1993; contbr. numerous chpts. to books, articles and revs. to profl. jours. Travel grantee Am. Coun. Learned Socs., 1985, Gladys Krieble Delmas Found. Rsch. grantee, 1993-94, 96-97; Italian-Am. traveling fellow U. Calif., 1969-70, NEH Italian Humanism summer sem. fellow, 1981, NEH/NSF award, 1995-98. Mem. MLA (exec. com. Medieval and Renaissance Italian Lit. 1981-85, assembly del. 1985-87), Am. Assn. Tchrs. Italian, Dante Soc. Am. (coun. assoc. 1985-90, coun. 1994-97), Medieval Acad., Renaissance Soc. Am. (discipline rep. Italian lit., 2000—, chmn. Nelson Prize com. 2003), Internat. Assn. Neo-Latin Studies, N.Am. Assn. History Lang. Soc., Assn. Internat. Studi di Lingua e Letteratura Italiana, Internat. Soc. Classical Tradition, Am. Boccaccio Assn. (v.p. 1982-83), Am. Assn. Italian Studies, Nat. Assn. Scholars, Nat. Ital. Am. Found. Office: Mt Holyoke Coll Dept Spanish and Italian South Hadley MA 01075 E-mail: amazzocc@mtholyoke.edu.

MAZZONI, KERRY, state agency administrator; b. 1951; children: Casey, Peter. BS in Child Devel., U. Calif., Davis. Mem. Calif. State Assembly, 1994—2000, mem. various coms. including edn., sch. facilities fin., banking and fin., utilities and commerce, and housing and cmty. devel.; sec. of edn. State of Calif., Sacramento, 2000—. Trustee Novato Unified Sch. Dist. Bd., 1987—, pres., 1990, 1993. Named Marin County Sch. Trustee of Yr., 1992. Office: Office of Sec for Edn Ste 600 1121 L St Sacramento CA 95814*

MAZZOTTA, GIUSEPPE FRANCESCO, Italian language and literature educator; b. Curinga, Calabria, Italy, Jan. 1, 1942; s. Pasquale and Rosa (Anania) M.; m. Carol Carlson, Mar. 2, 1972; children: Rosanna, Antony, Paula. BA, U. Toronto, Can., 1965, MA, 1966; PhD, Cornell U., 1969. Asst. prof. dept. romance studies Cornell U., Ithaca, N.Y., 1969-70, assoc. prof. dept. romance studies, 1973-78, prof. romance langs., 1978-83; asst. prof. dept. romance studies Yale U., New Haven, 1970-72, prof. Italian lang. and lit., 1983—; assoc. prof. Medieval Inst. U. Toronto, 1972-73. Author: Dante, Poet of the Desert: History and Allegory in the Divine Comedy, 1979, 2d edit., 1987, The World of Play: A Study of Boccaccio's Decameron, 1986, Dante's Vision and the Circle of Knowledge, 1993, The Worlds of Petrarch, 1993, The New Map of the World: The Poetic Philosophy of G.B. Vico, 1999, Cosmopoiesis: The Renaissance Experiment, 2001; mem. editl. bd. Yale Italian Studies, Dante Studies, Yale Jour. Criticism, Yale Jour. Law and Humanities. NEH fellow Cornell U., 1977, Guggenheim Found. fellow Yale U., 1986-87. Fellow Am. Coun. Learned Socs., Soc. for the Humanities; mem. Dante Soc. Am. (assoc.). Roman Catholic. Avocation: basketball. Office: Yale U 82-90 Wall St Fl 4 New Haven CT 06520 Home: 148 Peck Hill Rd Woodbridge CT 06525-1009

MAZZUCELLI, COLETTE GRACE CELIA, author, multimedia educator; b. Bklyn., Nov. 26, 1962; d. Silvio Anthony and Adeline Marie (De Ponte) M. BA, U. Scranton, 1983; MALD in Law and Diplomacy, Fletcher Sch., Tufts U., 1987; PhD, Georgetown U., 1996. Instr. Georgetown U., Washington, 1990, 1996; rsch. fellow Inst. fuer Europaeische Politik, Deutsche Gesellschaft fuer Auswaertige Politik, Bonn, Deutsch-Franzoesisches Inst., Ludwigsburg; asst. ratification process Treaty European Union, German Fgn. Minstry; cons. Jean Monnet Coun., Washington, 1994-98; dir. internat. programs Budapest Inst. Grad. Internat. and Diplomatic Studies, 1995-97; dir., founder Partnership Initiatives, 1997—; founding dir. internat. peace and conflict resolution grad. program Arcadia U., 1998-99; dir. fiscal affairs and strategic devel. Transatlantic Info. Exch. Svc., 1998-99; chair transatlantic internet multimedia seminar Southea. Europe (TIMSSE) Rotary Ctr., ScPo, Paris, 2000—03; sr. rsch. fellow East West Inst., 2001. Program officer, edn. NGO rep. UN Carnegie Coun. Ethics and Internat. Affairs, 2001—02; program devel. assoc. ctr. for Ednl. Outreach and Innovation Tchrs. Coll. Columbia U., 2002—; lectr. U.S. Info. Svc. Spkrs. Program in Europe, 1994; active IPSA Rsch. Com. on European Unification; instr. in-house tng. in negotiations Hungarian Fgn. Ministry, 1996—97; Hungarian Ministry Def. del. to NATO Accession Talks, 1997; advisor to bd. dirs. Transatlantic Info. Exch. Svc., 1997—98; dep. dir. Gen. Am.'s Regional Divsn. Internat. Biog. Ctr., Cambridge, England, 2003—; multi-media prof. German Fed. Armed Forces, Koblenz, Germany, 2003—. Commentator: Transatlantic Visions Column, TIESWeb.org, Salt&Pepper Column, EUObserver.com, 2003-; author: France and Germany at Maastricht Politics and Negotiations to Create the European Union, 1997, paperback 2d edit., 1999; asst. editor: The Evolution of an International Actor: Western Europe's New Assertiveness, 1990; author: Monnet Case Studies in European Affairs, 1995; contbr.: Dimensions of German Unification, 1994, Redefining European Security, 1999, United Nations Chronicle, 2001; also articles to profl. publs. Mem. founding cabinet World Peace and Diplomacy Forum, 2003—. Swiss U. grantee, 1984-85; Pi Gamma Mu scholar, 1985, Rotary grad. scholar, 1987-88, Fulbright scholar, 1991; Jean Monnet Coun. dissertation fellow, 1991, European Commn. fellow, 1992, Robert Bosch Found. fellow, 1992-93, Salzburg Seminar fellow, 1997, 21st Century Trust fellow Merton Coll., Oxford (Eng.) U., 2001, Bosch Pub. Policy fellow Am. Acad., Berlin, Aspen Inst., Berlin, 2001. Mem. Am. Polit. Sci. Assn., Deutsche Atlantische Gesellschaft, European Union Studies Assn., Robert Bosch Found. Alumni Assn. (mem. exec. com. 1994-96, 97-98, co-pres. 1999-2000), The Fletcher Club of N.Y. (v.p. 1998), Alpha Sigma Nu (student pres. 1984), Pi Gamma Mu (chpt. sec. 1982-84, Frank C. Brown scholarship medal 1984), Phi Sigma Tau (founder Scranton chpt.), Phi Alpha Theta, Pi Sigma Alpha, Alpha Mu Gamma, Delta Tau Kappa. Avocations: chess, swimming, poetry writing, astrology, karate. Home: 1864 74th St Brooklyn NY 11204-5752 Office: Tchrs Coll Columbia U 525 W 120th St New York NY 10027-6696 Business E-Mail: mazzucelli@tc.columbia.edu. E-mail: colettegrace@optonline.net.

MCABEER, SARA CARITA, school administrator; b. Logan, Utah, Aug. 19, 1906; d. Edward Thomas and Carrie Estelle (Martin) Harris; m. Frederick Alexander McAbeer, Dec. 24, 1929 (div. 1971); 1 child, Winifred. BA, Iowa State Tchr., Cedar Falls, 1929; postgrad., Sacramento (Calif.) Coll., 1956. Cert. high sch. adminstr. Clk., bookkeeper Curtis Jewelry, Kemmerer, Wyo., 1923-24; tchr. Miles High Sch., Miles, Iowa, 1929-30, Salinas (Calif.) High Sch., 1930-32; sec. supervised teaching U. Calif., Berkeley., 1934-41; tchr. Vallejo (Calif.) Jr. High Sch., 1947-50, Napa (Calif.) Jr. High Sch., 1950-52; dean of girls Napa High Sch., 1952-72. Active mem. Napa County Dem. Party, 1950-52, St. Thomas Altar Guild, Napa, 1973-99, Cmty. Projects, Inc., Napa, 1966-67, 77-94; mem., vol. tchr., bd. dirs. North Bay Suicide Prevention, Inc., Napa, 1972-91; leader Vallejo Girl Scouts, 1947-49; tchr. St. John's Cath. Ch., Napa, 1960-62. Recipient Vol. of Yr. North Bay Suicide Prevention Napa, 1986, Finalist continuing Svc. Vol. Ctr. Napa, 1988; Top Ten Ia. State Tchr. Cedar Falls scholar, 1929. Mem. Delta Kappa Gamma. Democrat. Roman Catholic. Avocations: needlepointing, bridge, dancing.

MCADAM, PAUL EDWARD, retired library administrator; b. Balt., Jan. 30, 1934; s. Joseph Francis Jr. and Irene Cecile (Heineck) McA. BA in Romance Langs., Johns Hopkins U., 1955, MA, 1956; MLS, Drexel U., 1970. Libr. Free Libr. Phila., 1969-81; br. mgr. Phila. City. Inst. Libr., 1974-81; dir. Am. Libr., Paris, 1981-85; libr. collection devel., libr. tech. svcs. Catonsville (Md.) C.C., 1986-89; assoc. v.p. learning resources Carroll C.C., Westminster, Md., 1989-99, assoc. v.p. emeritus, 1999—; adj. libr. C.C. of Baltimore County, Catonsville, Md., 1999—2002, instr. continuing edn., 2003—; adj. libr. Balt. Internat. Coll., 2000—; rschr. Transform, Inc., Columbia, Md., 2003—. Mem. adv. bd. Coop. Librs. Ctrl. Md., Annapolis, 1992-96, State Libr. Resource Ctr., Balt., 1994-95; bd. dirs. Renew, 1995—; del. Internat. Fedn. Libr. Assn, 1993, 95. Vol. MPT, 1989-2000, Walters Art Mus., 1991—, Md. Fine Arts Festival, 1991-97 AIRS, 1999—, Drexel U., 2002—. 1st lt. U.S. Army, 1956-58. Mem. ALA (membership com. 1996-98), Coll. Air Consortium, Congress Acad. Libr. Dirs. (treas. 1998-2000), Md. Libr. Assn. (hon.; membership chair 1993-96, awards chair 1996-97, 1999-2000, treas. 1997-99, chair fundraising task force 2001-02), Consortium Md. C.C. Libr. Dirs. (treas. 1998-2000), Beta Phi Mu. Democrat. Home: 524 Academy Rd Baltimore MD 21228-1814 Personal E-mail: PaulMcAd@aol.com.

MCADAMS, CHARLES ALAN, music educator; b. Memphis, June 3, 1958; s. Ernest Clinton and Jimmie Dee (Watson) McA.; m. Rebecca Carol Taylor, Aug. 9, 1980; children: James Alan, Kathryn Lynne. BS in Music Edn., Tenn. Technol. U., Cookeville, 1980; MS, U. Ill., 1981, EdD, 1988. Cert. tchr. K-12 instrumental music, Mo., Tenn. Dir. bands York Inst. H.S., Jamestown, Tenn., 1981-82, South Side H.S., Jackson, Tenn., 1982-83; assoc. prof. music (tuba/euphonium) Ctrl. Mo. State U., Warrensburg, 1983—. Freelance music contest adjudicator, 1983—; curriculum cons. to various pub. schs.; presenter in field. Asst. editor/author: (reference) The Tuba Source Book, 1995; active recitalist in solo recitals and as soloist with bands througout the Midwest; contbr. articles to profl. jours. Mem. Tubists Universal Brotherhood Assn. (regional chpt. coord. 1988-93, pub. rels. coord. 1994-95), Mo. Soc. for Music Tchr. Edn. (state chair 1994), Music Educators Nat. Conf., Pi Kappa Lambda, Phi Kappa Phi. Home: 305 Birch St Warrensburg MO 64093-1988 Office: Ctrl Mo State U Dept Music Warrensburg MO 64093

MCADAMS, FRANK JOSEPH, III, communications educator; b. Chgo., Nov. 18, 1940; s. Frank Joseph Jr. and Mary Irene (Geary) McA.; m. Patty Ann Rafferty, Dec. 27, 1966. BS, Loyola U., Chgo., 1967; MFA, UCLA, 1979. Instr. UCLA, 1981—, U. Calif., Irvine, 1989—. Adj. prof. Sch. of Cinema, U. So. Calif., L.A., 1991—; mem. judging panel Diane Thomas Awards, UCLA, 1986—; vis. lectr. screenplay structure U. Navarra, Pamplona, Spain, 1990; vis. lectr. Southampton Coll., L.I. U., 1997; mem. screenwriting adv. bd. U. Calif.-Irvine Extension, 1995—. Screenwriter: California Rain, 1978, Stagecoach Bravo, 1979; author: The American War Film: History and Hollywood, 2002; co-author: Final Affair, 2002. Precinct capt. Clinton-Gore, Orange County, Calif., 1992. Capt. USMC, 1966-72. Decorated Armed Forces Expeditionary medal (Laos), Vietnam Svc. medal, Rep. of Vietnam Campaign medal, Navy-Marine Corps medal, Navy Comm. medal with combat V; recipient award for best newspaper col. Orange County Press Club, 1974, HM for Best Series, 1974, Sam Goldwyn Screenwriting award Sam Goldwyn Found., 1978, 79. Mem. Writers Guild of Am. W., UCLA Theater Arts Alumni Assn., PEN Ctr. USA West. Democrat. Roman Catholic. Office: MAGLA PO Box 1511 Hollywood CA 90078-1511

MCADOO, CAROLYN, secondary school business educator; b. Athens, Tex., Mar. 19, 1943; d. Willie S. and Grace Lee (Dawson) Smith; m. Patrick Lee McAdoo, Sept. 9, 1962; children: Monica Lynn, Patrick Lee Jr. AA, Tex. Christian U., 1962; Coll. of SW, Coll. of S.W., 1970; MEd, Tex. Tech U., 1987. Cert. elem. and secondary tchr., Tex. Elem. tchr., adminstrv. sec. Seagraves (Tex.) Elem. Sch., 1972-80; tchr. bus. edn. Seagraves High Sch., 1980—. Cons. gifted and talented, 1989—. Officer local ch. Named Tex. Dist. 17 Bus. Tchr. of Yr., 1990. Mem. ASCD, Nat. Bus. Edn. Assn., Tex. Assn. Gifted and Talented, Assn. Tex. Profl. Educators, Tex. Bus. Edn. Assn. (pres. dist. 17 1991), Tex. Edn. Assn. (curriculum com.), Delta Kappa Gamma (v.p.). Home: PO Box 824 Seagraves TX 79359-0824

MCAFEE, JILL RANDOLPH, secondary education educator; b. Port Arthur, Tex., Jan. 6, 1953; d. Harvey Henry Sr. and Romaine (Robson) R.; 1 child, Heidi Ann. MEdin Supervision, Lamar U., 1990. Exec. asst. FISHCO, Inc., Houston; tchr. Cypress Fairbanks Ind. Sch. Dist., Houston. Curriculum coord. Lamar Challenge Creativity Camp, Single's Seminars and Edn.; dir. edn. Armand Bayour Nature Ctr. Mem. ASCD, Assn. Tex. Profl. Educators, Bluebonnet Coun., Nat. Sci. Tchrs. Assn., Tex. State Tchrs. Assn. (hospitality chair), Tex. Coun. for the Social Studies, Beta Beta Beta. Home: 3903 Park Wood Dr Denton TX 76208-5376

MCAFEE, JOHN WILSON, SR., retired principal; b. Hallsville, Tex., May 17, 1942; s. Howard Lawrence Sr. and Julia (Hart) McA.; m. Ruby Lee Runnels, May 31, 1966 (div.); children: Veronica Michelle, Charlotte Nichelle, John Wilson Jr.; m. Karen Walker, Nov. 23, 1993; children: Christopher Walker, Derrick Walker. BS, Bishop Coll., 1963; MEd, East Tex. State U., 1970, EdD, 1977. Tchr. Terrell (Tex.) Ind. Sch. Dist., 1963-79, prin., 1979-83, head start dir., 1979-83, Midland (Tex.) Ind. Sch. Dist., 1983-86, prin., 1986-98; now ret. Author and presenter video Coun. Minority Students, 1988; spkr. in field. Election judge City of Terrell, 1980-82; co-chairperson Census Redistricting Com., Terrell, 1981; bd. dirs. YMCA, Midland, 1983-90; rep. Dist. Tchr. Com., Midland, 1988-93; mem. distbn. panel United Way, Midland, 1990-93; speaker Achievement Day Wiley Coll., 1994, Baylor U., 1998, Multicultural Achievement Day, 1998. Recipient Helping Hands award Midland Reporter-Telegram, 1995; named Man of Distinction, Austin, Tex., 1990. Mem. NAACP (edn. chmn., chmn. dropout prevention program 1986-89), Tex. Elem. Prins. Assn. (dist. officer), Midland Prins. Assn., Renaissance Club (v.p., Achievement award 1980), Kappa Alpha Psi, Pi Lambda Theta, Phi Delta Kappa (historian 1980-81), Kappa Psi (Achievement award 1978). Mem. Ch. of Christ. Avocations: jazz music, accapella singing. Home: PO Box 9052 Midland TX 79708-9052 Office: Midland Ind Sch Dist 615 W Missouri Ave Midland TX 79701-5017

MCALEER, KATHY M. secondary school educator, language educator; b. L.I., Apr. 3, 1962; d. Eileen McAleer; m. Andy W. Heuser, Sept. 10, 1989; children: Brianna Heuser, Marissa Heuser. AA, Nassau C.C., 1984; BA, Adelphi U., 1988, MSW, 1992; grad. interpreter tng. program, Gallaudet U. LCSW; cert. tchr. Am. Sign Lang. NY, registered interpreter, transliterator for the deaf. Tchr. Am. Sign Lang. Bi Cultural Exch., Hempstead, NY, 1988—99, East Meadow Pub. Schs., NY, 1993—97, Great Neck Pub. Schs., NY, 1996—; coord. deaf studies program Hofstra U., Hempstead, 1996—. Mem.: LI Registry Interpreters for Deaf (pres. 1988—94). Office: Great Neck S HS 341 Lakeville Rd Great Neck NY 11020

MCALISTER, JANICE MARIE, elementary educator, radio announcer; b. Texarkana, Ark., Nov. 29, 1950; d. Frank James and Mary Melissa (Hopkins) Scott; m. Lonnie McAlister, June 16, 1980 (div. Oct. 1988); children: Miko LaShawn Matthews, Lionel Eugene. BS, Tex. Coll., 1973.

Intern Southwest Ednl. Devel. Lab., Austin, Tex., 1974; tchr. Brownsboro (Tex.) Ind. Sch. Dist., 1974-75; spl. edn. tchr. Jefferson (Tex.) Sch. Dist., 1976-78; math. tchr. Texarkana ISD, 1978-80; radio announcer Sta. KCMC, Texarkana, 1980-81; headstart tchr. Hudco Sch., Marshall, Tex., 1981-82; math. tchr. Jefferson Indep. Sch. Dist., 1982-90; elem. tchr. Texarkana Sch. Dist. #7, 1990-92; life sci. tchr. Denton Ind. Sch. Dist., 1992—. Avocations: reading, counseling, public speaking. Home: 2712 Golfing Green Dr Dallas TX 75234-4902 Office: Denton Ind Sch Dist 1307 Locust Denton TX 76201

MCALLISTER, ANN MARIE, social worker, educator; b. Birmingham, Ala., Sept. 5, 1938; d. Ernest and Clara (Graham) Motte; m. Aaron McAllister, Sept. 1, 1962; children: Adrienne, Annette. BA, Birmingham-So. Coll., 1959; MSW, Tulane U., 1961; PhD Tulane U., 2001. LCSW. Clin. social worker S.E. La. State Hosp., Mandeville, 1961-63, Ctrl. La. State Hosp., Pineville, 1963-76; prof. La. Coll., Pineville, 1976—. Mem. NASW, Alpha Kappa Delta, Phi Alpha, Omicron Delta Kappa. Baptist. Avocation: travel. Home: 105 Iris Cir Pineville LA 71360-4422 E-mail: mcallister@lacollege.edu.

MCALLISTER, DAVID FRANKLIN, publishing executive; b. Richmond, Va., July 2, 1941; s. John Thompson and Dorothy (Waits) McA.; m. Nancy Cooke; 1 child, Timothy Walt. BS, U. N.C., 1963; MS, Purdue U., 1967; PhD, U. N.C., 1972. Instr. computer sci. U. N.C., Greensboro, 1967-72; asst. prof. N.C. State U., Raleigh, 1972-76, assoc. prof., 1976-83, prof., 1983—. Grad. adminstr. dept. computer sci. N.C. State U., 1984-86., v.p. operations, CEM online Media Inc.1994—. Author: Discrete Mathematics in Computer Science, 1977; editor: Stereo Computer Graphics, 1993. Lt. (j.g.) USNR, 1963-65. Mem. IEEE, AAUP, Assn. for Computing Machinery, Soc. Photgrammetric Instrumentation Engring., Soc. for Info. Displays. Avocation: piano playing. Home: 3905 Meadow Field Ln Raleigh NC 27606-4470 Office: NC State U Computer Sci Dept Raleigh NC 27695-8206

MCALLISTER, RENA FARRELL, elementary educator; b. Chatham County, N.C., May 9, 1943; d. Clyde W. and Fallie (Johnson) Farrell; m. William H. McAllister III, June 13, 1965; children: William IV, Christopher, Jonathan, Benjamin. BA in Edn., U. N.C., Greensboro, 1965; MA in Edn., Va. Polytechnic Inst./State U., 1997. Cert. primary tchr., Va., reading specialist. Tchr. 2d grade Lansdale Elem. Sch., Norfolk, Va., 1965-66; instructional asst. Oakton (Va.) Elem. Sch., 1984-85; tchr. 1st grade Herndon (Va.) Elem. Sch., 1985—88, Fairhill Elem. Sch., Fairfax, Va., 1988—. Mem. Fairfax County Supt. Adv. Coun., 1989-90. Author: Jennifer's Journey, 1997. Washington Post mini-grantee Fairfax County, Fairhill Elem. Sch., 1989, 90, 91.. Mem.: Va. State Reading Assn., Greater Washington Reading Coun., Fairfax County Reading Tchrs. Assn., Phi Delta Kappa, Alpha Delta Kappa. Home: 10121 Ratcliffe Manor Dr Fairfax VA 22030-2427 Office: Fairhill Elem Sch 3001 Chichester Ln Fairfax VA 22031-2113 E-mail: Polly.McAllister@fcps.edu.

MCANDREW, FRANCIS THOMAS, psychology educator; b. Augsburg, Germany, Jan. 27, 1953; came to U.S., 1953; s. John Francis Paul and Jane Ann (Tuman) McA.; m. Maryjo Ann McCarthy, July 29, 1978; children: Timothy Ned, Maura Jill. BS in Psychology, King's Coll., 1974; PhD in Exptl. Psychology, U. Maine, Orono, 1981. Cornelia H. Dudley prof. psychology Knox Coll., Galesburg, Ill., 1979—2002, chair dept. psychology, 1993—2002. Head wrestling coach Knox Coll., Galesburg, 1985-89, 92-2000, program chair environ. studies, 1993-2001; vis. prof. U. Pretoria, South Africa, 1996; cons. C.E., U.S. Army. Author: Environmental Psychology, 1993; reviewer NSF, profl. jours.; contbr. articles to prol. jours. Fellow U. Maine, Orono, 1974-75. Mem. Am. Psychol. Soc., Animal Behavior Soc., Midwestern Psychol. Assn., Internat. Soc. for Human Ethology, Soc. for Personality and Social Psychology, Coun. Undergrad. Tchrs. of Psychology. Avocations: softball, raising tropical fish. Home: 733 Bateman St Galesburg IL 61401-2822 Office: Dept Psychology Knox Coll Galesburg IL 61401-4999 E-mail: fmcandre@knox.edu.

MCARDLE, BARBARA VIRGINIA, elementary school educator; b. Worcester, Mass., Sept. 4, 1925; d. Patrick Michael Brosnan and Nora Catherine Ferriter; m. William Henry McARdle, June 20, 1956. BS in Edn., Worcester State Tchrs. Coll., 1947, MEd, 1953. Elem. grade tchr. Grove St. Sch., Spencer, Mass., 1947—48, Allen L. Joslin Sch., Oxford, Mass., 1948—56, Euclid Sch., St. Petersburg, Fla., 1957—63, Wood Lawn Sch., St. Petersburg, 1963—91. Sch. rep. Pinellas County Tchrs. Assn., St. Petersburg, 1957—91; active Boys and Girls Club of Am.; vol. Dem. Orgn., St. Petersburg. Named to Kindergarten Playground at Wood Lawn Sch. Mem.: St. Jude's Guild, St. Anthony's Guild. Roman Catholic. Home: 5266 26th Ave N Saint Petersburg FL 33710

MCARTHUR, W(ILLIAM) FRANK, JR., academic administrator; b. Greenville, Ala., June 16, 1935; s. William Frank and Ollie (Majors) McA.; m. Jane Elizabeth Allen, Aug. 22, 1959; children: Elizabeth M. Tibbs, William Frank III. BS, U. Ala., 1957, MA, 1960, PhD, 1969. Band dir. Tuscaloosa Jr. H.S., 1956-60, Oneonta (Ala.) H.S., 1960-62, Tuscaloosa H.S., 1962-65; supr. music Tuscaloosa City Schs., 1965-67; asst. band dir. U. Ala., Tuscaloosa, 1967-69; band dir. McEachern H.S., Powder Springs, Ga., 1969-70, U. North Ala., Florence, 1970-75, dean sch. arts and sci., 1973-81; v.p. acad. affairs Delta State U., Cleveland, Miss., 1981—. Mem. Rotary Club of Cleveland (pres. 1992), Rotary Internat. (dist. 6800 gov. nominee 1993), Phi Delta Kappa, Kappa Delta Pi, Phi Mu Alpha, Phi Kappa Phi, Omicron Delta Kappa, Alpha Epsilon Delta. Methodist. Office: Delta State U 375 Ewing Cleveland MS 38733

MCAULAY, DIANNE LUCY, gifted education educator; b. Brockton, Mass., Aug. 5, 1940; d. Ernest Francis and Clarissa May (Atwood) Marcotte; m. William Alexander McAulay, Apr. 22, 1960; children: Laurie Mae McAulay Cambrola, W. Scott, Lisa Dianne. BA, U. R.I., 1972; MEd, R.I. Coll., 1974, cert. Adv. Grad. Studies, 1982; PhD, U. Conn., 1987. Cert. elem. tchr., secondary English tchr., educator of gifted, R.I. Sec. Met. Life Ins., Union Mut. Ins., Providence and Barrington, R.I., 1957-62; resource tchr. gifted and talented Cranston (R.I.) Pub. Sch.s, 1972—. Ednl. cons., South Kingstown, R.I., 1975—; discussion leader Great Books Found., 1976—; ednl. svcs. cons. New Eng. Power Svc., Westborough, Mass., 1978—; adj. prof. edn. and curriculum U. R.I., Kingston, 1979—, R.I. Coll., Providence, 1979—, dir. educator of gifted cert. program, 1981—; coach The Future Problem Solving Program, Ann Arbor, Mich., 1988—; adv. R.I. State Project Dirs. Gifted and Talented Programs, Providence, 1990—; lectr. Jason project, South Kingstown, 1991—; trainer Talents Unltd., 1991, ASCD's Tactics for Thinking, 1992; chairperson adv. bd. R.I. State Commr. of Edn. on Gifted and Talented, 1994—. Author: (film guides) Donald in Mathmagic Land, 1983, Powers of Ten, 1984, Current Events, 1985, Why Man Creates, 1986, (book) Type II Enrichment by Gifted/Talented Teachers, 1987. Adv. Save the Bay, Providence, 1981—; field tester, promoter R.I. Naturally Audubon Soc., Smithfield, 1978—; supporter U. R.I. Sch. Oceanography, Naragansett, 1989—; data collector, evaluator, R.I. Watershed Watch, Kingston, 1989—. Recipient 1st place R.I. Film, Video Competition Brown U., Providence, 1983; grantee Montclair (N.J.) State Coll. 1985, NSF Washington, 1993; named R.I. Tchr. of Yr. R.I. Farmers Bur., Warwick, 1992-93; Fulbright Mem. Fund awardee to live/study in Japan, 2003. Mem. ASCD, Nat. Sci. Tchrs. Assn., Ctr. Econ. Edn., Law Related Edn., S.E. New Eng. Marine Educators (exec. bd. 1987-91), R.I. State Advocates of Gifted Edn. (pres., v.p. 1982—), R.I. Agr. in Classroom (advocate), Phi Kappa Phi (highest distinction 1972). Avocations: expedition travel, wild plant propagation, jazz, sailing, fitness. Home: 150 Half Moon Trl Wakefield RI 02879-7706 Office: Glen Hills Sch Glen Hills Dr Cranston RI 02920 E-mail: DianneEdu@aol.com., rid21534@ride.ri.net.

MCAULIFFE, CATHERINE A. counselor, psychology educator, psychotherapist; b. Northampton, Mass., July 31, 1952; d. Francis G. and Emliy R. (Hanley) Ciarfella; m. Francis J. McAuliffe, Aug. 14, 1999; children: Richard Jr. DiPersio, Edward DiPersio, Mary Catherine DiPersio. BS in Elem. Edn., U. Conn., 1974; MS in Counseling, So. Conn. State U., 1988; postmaster's sch. counseling cert., Cen. Conn. State U., 1992. Cert. K-12 counselor, K-8 tchr. Conn., adult edn. tchr. 1st grade tchr. Granby (Conn.) Pub. Schs., 1974-75; pvt. psychotherapist Meriden, Conn., 1988—97; dir. counseling Paier Coll. Art, Hamden, Conn., 1988—91; h.s. counselor Sacred Heart H.S., Waterbury, Conn., 1990-91; sch. counselor Meriden Pub. Schs., Cheshire (Conn.) Pub. Schs., 1997—2000, Bridgeport (Conn.) Pub. Schs., 2001—. Pers. devel. counselor U. Conn., Waterbury, 1991—97; psychology instr. Paier Coll. Art, 1991—97. Scout leader Cub Scouts Am., Meriden, 1984-86, Girl Scouts Am., 1986-87; hospitality chairperson PTA, Meriden, 1984-85; vol. Rep. Party, Meriden, 1988. Mem.: Am. Assn. Christian Counselors, Conn. Sch. Counseling Assn., Conn. Sch. Counseling Assn., ACA, Phi Kappa Phi. Roman Catholic. Avocations: singing, directing choirs, playing keyboard, guitar, composing lyrics and music. Home: 15 Spring Glen Dr Meriden CT 06451-2720 Office: 265 George St Bridgeport CT 06604-3320

MCAVOY, ROGERS, educational psychology educator, consultant; b. Webster Springs, W.Va., Dec. 28, 1927; s. Ellis McLaughlin and Carolyn (McIntosh) McA.; m. Anne T. Limpe, Dec. 19, 1956 (div.); children: Carol Ann, Philip Ellis, Karen Lynelle; m. Irma Jean Tingler, July 7, 1973. BA, Fairmont State Coll., 1951; MA, W.Va. U., 1954; PhD, Ind. U., 1966. Tchr. biology Petersburg (W.Va.) High Sch., 1951-53; asst. dir. admissions Marshall U., Huntington, W.Va., 1953-55; registrar Glenville (W.Va.) State Coll., 1955-56; rsch. asst., asst. to dean Ind. U., Bloomington, 1956-61; asst. prof. ednl. psychology W.Va. U., Morgantown, 1961-65, assoc. prof., 1967-72, prof., 1973-97, prof. emeritus, 1997—. Cons. state and county ednl. systems, W.Va., others, 1965-89; cons. follow through program Stanford Rsch. Inst., 1969-72. Contbr. articles to profl. jours. Mem. Phi Delta Kappa (Disting. Svc. award 1982, 25-yr. svc. award 1990). Avocations: writing, book collecting, restoring houses, photography, reading. Office: WVa U 608 Allen Ave Morgantown WV 26505-5618

MCBEATH, GERALD ALAN, political science educator, researcher; b. Mpls., Sept. 13, 1942; s. Gordon Stanley and Astrid Elvira (Hjelmeir) McB.; m. Jenifer Huang, June 7, 1970; children: Bowen, Rowena. BA, U. Chgo., 1963, MA, 1964; PhD, U. Calif., Berkeley, 1970. Vis. asst. prof. polit. sci. Rutgers Coll., New Brunswick, N.J., 1970-72; asst. prof. John Jay Coll., CUNY, N.Y.C., 1972-74, 75-76; assoc. prof. Nat. Chengchi U., Mucha, Taipei, Taiwan, 1974-75; prof. polit. sci. U. Alaska, Fairbanks, 1976—, dept. chair, 1980—85, 1997—2002, dir. faculty devel., 1990-92, acting dean coll. liberal arts, 1991-93, dir. faculty devel., 1990-92. Cons. Inst. Social and Econ. Rsch., Anchorage, 1976-77; contract rschr. Alaska Dept. Natural Resources, Alaska Dept. Edn., Nat. Inst. Edn., others; staff dir. task force on internat. trade policy Rep. Conf., U.S. Senate. Sr. author: Dynamics of Alaska Native Self-Government, 1980; author monograph: North Slope Borough Government and Policymaking, 1981; jr. author: Alaska's Urban and Rural Governments, 1984; sr. editor: Alaska State Government and Politics, 1987; co-author: Alaska Politics and Government, 1994 (Am. Assn. State & Local History Commendation cert. 1995); author: The Alaska State Constitution, 1997, Wealth and Freedom: Taiwan's New Political Economy, 1998; editor: Alaska's Rural Development, 1982. Mem. bd. edn. Fairbanks North Star Borough, 1986-95, pres. 1989-90, 93-94, treas. 1991-93. Recipient Emil Usibelli Disting. Svc. award 1993; Chiang Ching-Kuo Found. fellow, 1995-97; named Outstanding Faculty Mem., Assn. Students U. Alaska, Fairbanks, 1979, Alumni Assn. U. Alaska, Fairbanks, 1981; grantee Nat. Inst. Edn., 1980-83, Alaska Coun. on Sci and Tech., 1982-84, Spencer Found., 1987-88, Chiang Ching-Kuo Found., 1995-97, NSF, 2000-03, EPA, 2002—. Mem. Am. Assn. Chinese Studies (bd. dir., 1999—, program chmn. 2003), Asian Studies on Pacific Coast (program chmn. 1983, bd. dirs. 1982-83); Assn. Asian Studies, Western Polit. Sci. Assn. (mem. editl. bd. Western Govtl. Rschr.), Am. Polit. Sci. Assn., Fairbanks N. Star Borough Bd. Edn. Home: 1777 Red Fox Dr Fairbanks AK 99709-6625 Office: U Alaska Dept Polit Sci Fairbanks AK 99775 E-mail: ffjam@uaf.edu.

MCBEE, LUCY ARMIJO, retired elementary education educator, administrator, singer, actress, writer; b. Santa Fe, Feb. 26, 1931; d. Jose Alfonso and Celine (Chaves) Armijo; m. Robert Levi McBee, June 13, 1959; children: Martin Christopher, Mark Antony, Mathieu A.C. Music cert., Kansas City Conservatory Music, 1952; BA in Econs., Avila Coll., 1952; postgrad. in theater, U. Mo., Kansas City, 1962; MA in Tchg., Webster Coll., 1974. Cert. Montessori tchr. Sec., translator fgn. dept. Commerce Bank Kansas City, Mo., 1952-53; sec., with econ. rsch. dept. Farmland Industries, Kansas City, 1953-59; sec. Western Electric, Kansas City, 1961-62; drama resident theatre tchr. Jewish Cmty. Ctr., Kansas City, 1962-63; Montessori tchr. Wee Wisdom Sch., Unity Village, Mo., 1964-67; Montessori/Spanish tchr. Montessori Sch., Blue Springs, Mo., 1967-68; tchr., dir. St. Peter's Day Sch., Kansas City, 1968-71; tchr., prin./adminstr. Loretto Sch., Kansas City, 1974-83; writer plays San Antonio, 1985—87; comptroller Charles Feldstein Co., Chgo., 1990-94. Drama/voice tchr. Backstage Workshop for profl. actors and singers, 1979-84; theatre tchr. Visitation Sch. Kans. City, 1983. Co-editor: The Clan MacBean Register, 2001—02. Mem., cantor Visitation Cath. Ch. Choir, Kansas City, 1948-85; computer consultation, data processing VA, Marion, Ind., 1988; fundraising, data processing, trainer Dukakis/Bentsen Presdl. Campaign, Chgo., 1987-88; fundraising office mgr. Simon for Senate Campaign, Chgo., 1988-89; comptroller Pres. Cook County Bd. Fundraising office, 1989-90; mem. Early Childhood Edn. Com., 1973-78, Holy Name Cathedral Choir, Chgo., 1988-94. Recipient Best Actress award U. Kans. City Theatre, 1958, Silver Tray award, Notre Dame de Sion Montessori Sch., Kans. City, 1971, St. Peter's Annual medal St. Peter's Episcopal Ch., Kansas City, 1974, VA award for svc. during Golden Age Games, Marion, Ind., 1988, 1st place award Irish Cultural Soc. Poetry Awards; named Miss Congeniality Dukakis-Bentsen Presdl. Campaign, Chgo., 1988. Mem.: Scottish Soc., The Clan McBean, San Antonio Poets Assn. Roman Catholic. Avocations: acting, singing, writing poetry, plays and music. Home: 7118 Walnut Trace San Antonio TX 78239-3058

MCBOYLE, GEOFFREY R. geography educator; BSin Geography, Aberdeen U., Scotland, 1964, PhD in Geography, 1969. Chair. dept. geography U. Waterloo, Waterloo, Canada, 1975-78, assoc. dean undergrad. studies, ednl. liaison, 1985-92, prof. geography, dean, office of environmental studies. Mem. com. Ont. univs. coun. on admissions, 1986-90, vice-chair, 1990-91; researcher in field. Mem. editl. bd. Climatological Bulletin, 1983-87; reviewer numerous profl. jours. Mem. ecol. and environ. adv. com. Regioanl Municipality of Waterloo, Ont., Can., 1986-87, environ. studies liaison com. Waterloo Adv. Com., 1987-92. Disting. Teacher Award, U. Waterloo, 1989; Univ. Disting. Teaching Award, Nat. Council for Geograhic Edn., 1994. Mem. Canadian Assn. Geographers (chair 1978-79, Ont. divsn. Service to Geography award 1993), North Am. Interstate Weather Modification Coun. (pubs. com. 1980), Canadian Assn. Co-operative Edn. (rsch. com. 1990—). Office: Univ Waterloo Faculty of Environmental Studies ES1 324 Waterloo ON Canada N2L 3G1*

MCBRAYER, LAURA JEAN H. school media specialist; b. Bremen, Ga., July 11, 1944; d. Robert Byron Holloman and Ruth Mildred (McGukin) McLaughlin; m. Dennis Durrett McBrayer; children: Keith, Dana, Scott, Leah. BA in English, West Ga. Coll., 1966, MEd, 1977, M in Media, 1982. Cert. media tchr., secondary English tchr., Ga. English tchr. Bremen (Ga.) H.S., 1966-72, Villa Rica (Ga.) H.S., 1974-75, Ctrl. H.S., Carrollton, Ga., 1975-78; libr., English tchr. Mt. Zion (Ga.) H.S., 1979-80; media specialist West Haralson Jr. H.S., Tallapoosa, Ga., 1980-86, Bremen H.S./Sewell Mid. Sch., Bremen, 1986—99. Mem., past sec. West Ga. Regional Libr. Bd., 1988—; sec. Warren P. Sewell LIbr. Bd., Bremen, 1989—, Haralson County Libr. Bd., 1988—; mem. choir First Bapt. Ch., Bremen, 1987-92; mem. centennial com. Dem. Party, Haralson County, 1989—. Mem. ALA, Ga. Libr. Media Assn., Ga. Libr. Assn., Ga. Assn. for Instrnl. Tech., Phi Delta Kappa (Tchr. of Yr. 1977). Avocations: photography, reading, walking, movies, music. Office: Sewell Mid-Bremen HS Media Ctr 504 Laurel St Bremen GA 30110-2128 Home: 308 Stonebridge Blvd Bremen GA 30110-2353

MCBRAYER, SANDRA L. educational director, homeless outreach educator; AA, San Diego Mesa Coll., 1981; BA in Applied Arts and Scis., San Diego State U., 1986, MA in Edn., 1990. Cert. presch.-kindergarten, grs. 1-12, adult edn., Calif. Tchr. asst. group homes Oz, The Bridge, Gatehouse, 1984-87; tchr. Hillcrest Receiving Home, 1987-88, Juvenile Hall, 1987-88, Comprehensive Adolescent Treatment Ctr., 1987-88; head tchr. the Monarch HS, 1988-96; CEO The Children's Initiative, San Diego. Lectr., cons. Ctrs. Careers Edn., Sch. Tchr. Edn. San Diego State U., 1990—; collaborator sch. dists. State Dept. Edn., Equity/Homeless Office, 1992—; staff devel. tng.; adj. prof. Coll. Edn., San Diego (Calif.) State U. Recipient award Exceptional Vols. Svc. Family Care Ctr., 1988, San Diego's 10 Leadership award Sta. KGTV, 1991, Celebrate Literacy award Internat. Reading Assn., 1992, Women of Vision in Edn. award LWV San Diego, 1992, Disting. Alumna of Yr.-Edn. award San Diego State U., 1992, Golden Bell award Calif. Sch. Bds. Found., 1992, Coun. of State Sch. Officers Nat. Tchr. of Yr. award 1994; named San Diego County Tchr. of Yr. by San Diego County Office of Edn., 1993, Calif. Tchr. of Yr. by State Dept. Edn., 1993, Nat. Tchr. of Yr., Pres. Clinton, 1994, Tech. Tchr. of Yr., Coun. on Tech. Tchr. Edn., 1994, Exceptional Svc. award Calif. State PTA, Humanitarian award Youth Advocacy Assn., Living Legacy award Internat. Women's Ctr.; recognized by local and nat. news media. Mem. NEA, Calif. Tchrs. Assn., Assn. Educators, Nat. Dropout Prevention Network, Calif. Homeless Coalition, Phi Kappa Phi. Office: The Childrens Initiative 4438 Ingraham St San Diego CA 92109*

MCBRIDE, DAVID FRANCIS, special education educator; b. Phila., July 12, 1951; s. Harry James and Etta May (Labor) McB. BA, LaSalle U., 1976; MEd, Temple U., 1979, EdD in Edn. Admin., 1993; C.A.S., Beaver Coll., 1984. Cert. spl. edn. tchr., Pa., N.J., prin., Pa., N.J., D.C. Spl. edn. tchr. Phila. Sch. Dist., 1980-82, resource rm. tchr., 1982-88, bilingual spl. edn. tchr., 1988-91; bilingual spl. edn. specialist, tchr. trainer D.C. Schs., 1991—. Adj. prof. spl. edn. George Mason U., Fairfax, Va., 1991—; instr. ESL Trinity Coll., Washington, 1991—; cons. Arriba, Inc., Washington, 1992—, Hispanic Mental Health Svcs., Phila., 1990—; cons. assessment of lang. minority students; curricula devel. bilingual, ESL spl. edn. programs. Contbr. rsch. articles to profl. jours. Community mem. D.C. Adv. Coun., 1991—. Mem. Coun. Exceptional Children, Nat. Assn. for Bilingual Edn. (capital affiliate). Avocations: linguistics, languages, creative writing (poetry). Home: 920 T St NW # 2 Washington DC 20001-4120 Office: DC Pub Schs W Wilson H S Nebraska & Chesapeake Aves Washington DC 20001

MCBRIDE, JUDITH, elementary education educator; BFA in Interior Design, Utah State U., 1963; MFA, U. Wyo., 1980. Art tchr. Beitel Elem. Sch., Laramie, Wyo., Spring Creek Elem. Sch., Laramie, Centennial Valley Elem. Sch., Laramie. Named Wyo. State Tchr. of Yr., 1993. Office: Spring Creek Elem Sch 1203 Russell St Laramie WY 82070-4682

MCBRIDE, KAREN SUE, school guidance counselor; b. Hinton, W.Va., Dec. 31, 1953; d. Ira and Betty Ann (Simmons) Patrick; m. Charles Lynn Jones, Jul. 3, 1976 (div. June 1985); m. Arnett Dean McBride, Oct. 18, 1986. BS, Concord Coll., 1975; M, W.Va., 1987. Cert. early childhood edn., elem. edn. tchr. Learning disabilites tchr. Riverview Sch., Hinton, W.Va., 1975, first, second grade tchr., 1975-80; first grade tchr. Hinton Area Elem., Hinton, W.Va., 1980-89; sch. counselor Summers Co. Schs., 1989-92, Hinton Area Elem., Hinton, W.Va., 1992—. Cons. W.Va. Dept. Edn., 1984—, coord. Summers County Drug Free Schs., Hinton, 1990-94; adv. bd. mem. Concord Coll. Head Start, Hinton, 1992—. Author: Let's Party, 1994, Developmental Guidance, 1994, Let's Celebrate, 1996, Team Up With Nutrition, 1998; co-creator Day Camp, 1991. Coach girls elem. basketball, Hinton, 1986-91; elem. cheerleader sponsor, Hinton, 1987, 88, 90, 91. Recipient Golden Apple award W.Va. Edn. Funds, 1983, Min-grant for classroom, 1983. Mem. W.Va. Edn. Assn. (chpt. pres., sec. 1975—), W.Va. Sch. Counselors Assn., Delta Kappa Gamma (chtp. treas. 1991—). Avocations: cross-stitch, quilting, reading science fiction. Home: HC 85 Box 322 Jumping Branch WV 25969-9500 Office: Summers County Bd Edn 116 Main St Hinton WV 25951-2439

MCBRIDE, MICHAEL JOSEPH, psychology educator, administrator; b. Eureka, Calif., Feb. 5, 1945; s. Mark and Anne Josephine (Relgi) McB.; m. Pamela Carol Behring, June 2, 1973; children: Mary Stasha Behring, William Mark Behring. AB in Classical Studies, St. Louis U., 1969, MS, 1975, PhD, 1980. Instr. Jesuit H.S., Sacramento, 1969-71, S.E. Mo. State U., Cape Girardeau, 1977, Gonzaga U., Spokane, Wash., 1978-96, chair dept. psychology, 1984—88, 1996—98, 2003—. Exch. prof. Chongqing (China) U., 1988-89. Mem. APA, Soc. for Personality and Social Psychology, Psi Chi. Democrat. Roman Catholic. Home: 1112 E 20th Ave Spokane WA 99203-3434 Office: Psychology Dept Gonzaga U 502 E Boone Ave Spokane WA 99258-1774

MCBRIDE, SHARON LOUISE, counselor, technical communication educator; b. Peoria, Ill., Dec. 5, 1939; d. Ralph Cannon and Joyce Eliz (Shoff) McB.; m. Armond B. Ciota, Jr., Apr. 23, 1960 (div.); children: Matthew Ciota, Eliz Faron, Thomas Ciota, Nathan Ciota. BA, Bradley U., 1960, MA, 1987. Various positions to undergrad. student adviser Bradley U., Peoria, 1972—; instr. Ill. Ctrl. Coll., East Peoria, 1987—. Chmn. bd. trustees Greater Peoria Mass Transit. Trustee West Peoria Twp., 1984-96; sec.-treas. Ill. Twp. Trustees, 1993-96; chairperson West Peoria Zoning Bd. Appeals; mem. policy com. Peoria Pekin Urbanized Area Transp. Study. Mem.: Am. Assn. Women in C.C., Am. Pub. Transit Assn. (transit bd., Region IV rep.), Am. Soc. Engring. Edn., Rotary Club (Peoria North), Lions (bd. dirs. West Peoria chpt. 1984—97, precinct com.). Republican. Avocations: travel, community volunteer. Home: 2413 W Kellogg Ave West Peoria IL 61604-5011

MC CABE, GERARD BENEDICT, retired library administrator; b. N.Y.C., Jan. 22, 1930; s. Patrick Joseph and Margaret Irene (McDonald) McC.; m. Jacqueline L. Maloney, Aug. 3, 1963 (dec. 1987); children: Theresa Marie, Rebecca Mary. BA in English, Manhattan Coll., 1952; A.M. in Library Sci. (scholar), U. Mich., 1954; MA in English, Mich. State U., 1959. Asst. acquisitions dept. U. Nebr. Library, Lincoln, 1954-56; chief bibliog. acquisitions dept. Mich. State U. Library, East Lansing, 1956-58; librarian Inst. Community Devel. and Service, Mich. State U., 1958-59; acquisitions librarian U. S. Fla., Tampa, 1959-66, asst. dir. planning and devel., 1967-70; assoc. dir. U. Ark. Library, Fayetteville, 1966-67; dir. univ. libraries Va. Commonwealth U., Richmond, 1970-82; dir. libraries Clarion U. of Pa., 1982-95; ret., 1995; libr. cons., 1995—. Editor: The Smaller Academic Library: A Management Handbook, 1988, Operations Handbook for Small Academic Library, 1989, Academic Libraries in Urban and Metropolitan Areas, 1992; co-editor ann. pub. Advances in Libr. Adminstrn. and Orgn., vols. 1-12, Insider's Guide to Libr. Automation: Essays of Practical Experience, 1993, Acad. Librs.: Their Rationale and Role in Am. Higher Edn., 1995, Introducing and Managing Academic Library Automation Projects, 1996, Leadership for Academic Librarians, 1998, Planning for a New Generation of Public Library Buildings, 2000, Planning the Modern Public Library Building, 2003; contbr. articles to profl. jours. Mem. ALA, Southeastern Libr. Assn. Home and Office: 2 Stayman Ct Apt J Baltimore MD 21228-6034 E-mail: bldlib@comcast.net.

MCCABE, SHARON, humanities educator, art educator; b. Flint, Mich., Sept. 6, 1947; AA, Pasco Hernando C.C., New Port Richey, Fla., 1988; BA in Art, U. South Fla., 1990, MA in Art, gifted endorsement, 1992, MLA in Humanities, 1996. Cert. gifted edn. tchr., Fla. Tchr. art Hernando County Schs., Spring Hill, Fla., 1990—; prof. humanities and art Pasco Hernando C.C., 1992—. Recipient numerous art awards, 1982—. Office: PHCC Humanities Dept 10230 Ridge Rd New Port Richey FL 34654-5199

MCCAFFERTY, EILEEN PATRICIA, elementary school educator; b. Phila., June 9, 1953; d. Thomas Patrick and Frances Catherine (Friel) McC. BS in Elem. Edn., St. Joseph's U., 1990; cert. religious studies, St. Charles Sem., Phila., 1978. Cert. tchr., Pa. Tchr. 2d grade Our Lady of Loreto, Phila., 1972—2000, St. Barnabas Sch., Phila., 2000—. Fellow Nat. Cath. Edn. Assn. Avocations: bicycling, gardening, ceramics. Office: St Barnabas Sch 64th & Buist Ave Philadelphia PA 19142

MCCAFFERY, MARGO, pain consultant, lecturer, author; b. Corsicana, Tex., Sept. 29, 1938; d. Marley William and Mary Katharine (Adams) Smith; m. John Richard Brewer, July 19, 1986; 1 child, Melissa Ruth. BSN, Baylor U., 1959; MS in Nursing, Vanderbilt U., 1961. RN, Calif., Tex. Asst. prof. pediatric nursing UCLA, 1962-70; pain mgmt. cons., lectr., L.A., 1970—; clinician, mgr. pain mgmt. unit Centinela Hosp. Med. Ctr., Inglewood, Calif., 1983-84. Mem. adv. bd. Jour. Pain and Sympton Mgmt.; mem. expert adv. com. on cancer pain relief WHO, 1989—. Author numerous books, including Nursing Management of the Patient with Pain, 1972, Pain: A Nursing Approach to Assessment and Analysis, 1983, (with C. Pasero) Pain: Clinical Manual, 1989, 2d edit., 1999; producer-writer audio and video tapes. Recipient Linda Richards award Nat. League for Nursing, Disting. Svc. award UCLA, Book of Yr. award Am. Jour. Nursing, Nursing 86 award; scholar Am. Nurses Found.; rsch. grantee NIH, Am. Nurses Found. Mem. ANA, Am. Acad. Nursing, Am Pain Soc., Internat. Assn. for Study Pain (founding), Onoclogy Nursing Soc., Sigma Theta Tau (rsch. grantee). Home and Office: 8347 Kenyon Ave Los Angeles CA 90045-2740

MCCALL, CHARLES BARNARD, health facility administrator, educator; b. Memphis, Nov. 2, 1928; s. John W. and Lizette (Kimbrough) McCall; m. Carolyn Jean Rosselot, June 9, 1951; children: Linda, Kim, Betsy, Cathy. BA, Vanderbilt U., 1950, MD, 1953. Diplomate Am. Bd. Internal Medicine, Am. Bd. Pulmonary Diseases. Intern Vanderbilt U. Hosp., Nashville, 1953-54; clin. assoc., sr. asst. surgeon USPHS, Nat. Cancer Inst., NIH, 1954-56; sr. asst. resident in medicine U. Ala. Hosp., 1956-57, chief resident, 1958-59; fellow chest diseases Nat. Acad. Scis.-NRC, 1957-58; instr. U. Ala. Med. Sch., 1958-59; from asst. prof. to assoc. prof. medicine U. Tenn. Med. Sch., 1959-69, chief pulmonary diseases, 1964-69; mem. faculty U. Tex. Sys., Galveston, 1969-75, prof. med. br., 1971-73; assoc. prof. medicine Health Sci. Ctr., Southwestern Med. Sch., Dallas, 1973-75, also assoc. dean clin. programs, 1973-75; dir. Office Grants Mgmt. and Devel., 1973-75; dean, prof. medicine U. Tenn. Coll. Medicine, 1975-77, Oral Roberts U. Sch. Medicine, Tulsa, 1977-78; interim assoc. dean U. Okla. Tulsa Med. Coll., 1978-79; clin. prof. medicine U. Colo. Med. Sch., Denver, 1979-80; prof. medicine, assoc. dean U. Okla. Med. Sch., 1980-82; exec. dean and dean U. Okla. Coll. Medicine, 1982-85; v.p. patient affairs, prof. medicine U. Tex. M. D. Anderson Cancer Ctr., 1985-94; chief of staff VA Med. Ctr., Oklahoma City, 1980-82. Exec. dir. Worldwide Healthcare Svcs., Inc., Waco, Tex., 1998—2002; clinic dir. Claremore Family Medicine, 2002, cons., 02; bd. dirs. Amigos Internacionales, Inc. Contbr. articles to med. jours. Fellow: ACP, Am. Coll. Chest Physicians; mem.: AMA, Am. Fedn. Clin. Rsch., So. Thoracic Soc. (pres. 1968—69), Am. Thoracic Soc., Sigma Xi, Alpha Omega Alpha. Baptist. Home: 10 1 Douglas Dr Claremore OK 74017-6626 Office: 1402 N Florence Claremore OK 74017 E-mail: cbmroadski1@aol.com., mccallcharles@sbcglobal.net.

MCCALL, LINDA AGNES, assistant principal; b. Altoona, Pa., Mar. 5, 1953; d. Lester Claude and Florence Agnes (Diehl) McC. BS, Juniata Coll., 1973; MEd, Pa. State U., 1976. Cert. instrnl. II in biology, social studies, program specialist, Pa.; cert. adminstrv. I and II, letter of eligibility, Pa. Tchr. Hollidaysburg (Pa.) Area Sch. Dist., 1974-91, chair sci. dept., 1985-91, asst. prin., 1991—. Instr. Pa. State U., Altoona, 1983—86; adv. bd. Peer Jury, Blair County, Pa., 1992—, Learning Through Svc., Hollidaysburg, 1992—. Mem. ASCD, Pa. Assn. Suprs. Curriculum Devel., Nat. Assn. Secondary Sch. Prins., Phi Delta Kappa, Rotary Internat. Avocations: bridge, travel. Home: 148 Elm St Hollidaysburg PA 16648-2929 Office: Hollidaysburg Area Sr H S 1510 N Montgomery St Hollidaysburg PA 16648-1909 E-mail: lindamcc@charter.net.

MCCALL, PATRICIA ALENE, secondary music education educator; b. Cleve., June 17, 1957; d. James Henry and Ada (Johnson) McC. BM, U. Wis., 1979; MM, U. Miami, 1982. Cert. tchr., Ga. Music tchr. Bibb County Pub. Schs., Macon, Dade County Pub. Schs., Miami, Fla., 1981-85; violinist Macon (Ga.) Symphony and String Quartet, 1985-95, Chromatic Duo, 1986—, Baronyx Trio, 1986-90; string coach Macon (Ga.) Symphony Youth Symphony, 1990-96; dir. Mid. Ga. String Orch., Macon, 1996-97; dir. youth philharm. Bibb County Pub. Schs., 1997—; dir., conductor Bibb County Pub. Schs. Youth Philharmonic, 1998—. Freelance violinist, Ga.; part-time prof. Mercer U., Macon, Ga., 1979-85, 86-94; pvt. instr., 1985—. Recipient Superior and Excellent medals Dist. II Ensemble Festival, 1986-2002. Mem.: NEA, Nat. Sch. Orch. Assn., Ga. Music Educators Assn., Ga. Edn. Assn., Am. String Tchrs. Assn., Music Educators Nat. Conf., Am. Viola Soc., Musicians Union. E-mail: lasido57@aol.com.

MCCALLA, SANDRA ANN, educational administrator; b. Shreveport, La., Nov. 6, 1939; d. Earl Gray and Dorothy Edna (Adams) McC. BS, Northwestern La. State U., 1960; MA, U. No. Colo., 1968; EdD, Tex. A&M U., 1987. With Caddo Parish Sch. Bd., Shreveport, 1960-88; asst. prin. Capt. Shreve H.S., 1977-79, prin., 1979-88, 94—; dir., dean divsn. edn. Northwestern State U., Natchitoches, La., 1988-94; instr. math. La. State U., 1979-81. Mem. adv. bd. Sta. KDAQ Pub. Radio, 1985-89, Shreveport Women's Commn., 1983-89. Named Educator of Yr. Shreveport Times-Caddo Tchrs. Assn., 1966, La H.S. Prin. of Yr., 1985, 87; recipient Excellence in Edn. award Capt. Shreve H.S., 1982-83; Danforth fellow, 1982-83. Mem. nat. Assn. Secondary Sch. prins., La. Assn. Prins. (Prin. of Yr. 1985), La. Assn. Sch. Execs. (Disting. Svc. award 1983), Times-Caddo Educators Assn. (Educator of Yr. 1984), Phi Delta Kappa, Kappa Delta Pi. Republican.

MCCALL-SMITH, CATHERINE ANN, elementary school educator; b. Inglewood, Calif., Nov. 28, 1967; d. Roger Eugene Mason and Mary Helen Maston; m. Charles Scott Smith; 1 child, Cauley Noel. B Music in Edn., Susquehanna U., Selinsgrove, Pa., 1990; BA Anthropology, Ohio U., 1996. Cert. music edn. grades K-12 tchr. 1990. Dir. mid. sch. bands Wellston City (Ohio) Schs., 1996—. Mem. Athens Brass Quintet. Mem.: Ohio Music Educators Assn., Athens Music Club. Avocations: exercising, photography. Office: Wellston City Schs 416 N Pennsylvania Ave Wellston OH 45692 Personal E-mail: mccall-smith@myexcel.com.

MCCALLUM, BENNETT TARLTON, economist, educator; b. Poteet, Tex., July 27, 1935; s. Henry DeRosset and Frances (Tartlon) McCallum; m. Sally Jo Hart, June 3, 1961. BA, Rice U., 1957, BSChemE, 1958, PhD, 1969; MBA, Harvard U., 1963. Chem. engr. Petro-Tex Chem. Corp., Houston, 1958-61; lectr. U. Sussex, England, 1965-66; asst. prof. to prof. U. Va., Charlottesville, 1967-80; prof. econs. Carnegie-Mellon U., Pitts., 1981-86, H. J. Heinz prof. econs., 1986—. Cons. Fec. Res. Bd., Washington, 1974—75; adviser Fed. Res. Bank, Richmond, Va., 1981—; rsch. assoc. Nat. Bur. Econ. Rsch., Cambridge, Mass., 1979—; mem. Shadow Open Market Com., 2000—; hon. advisor Inst. Monetary Econ. Studies, Bank Japan. Author: (book) Monetary Economics, 1989, International Monetary Economics, 1996; co-editor: Am. Econ. Rev., 1988—91, Carnegie-Rochester Conf. series pub. policy, 1995—; contbr. articles to profl. jours. Vis. scholar, IMF, Washington, 1989—90, Bank Japan, 1993, Victoria U. Wellington and Res. Bank New Zealand, 1995; NSF grantee, 1977—86. Fellow: Econometric Soc.; mem.: Am. Econ. Assn. Home: 219 Gladstone Rd Pittsburgh PA 15217-1111 Office: Carnegie-Mellon U Grad Sch Indsl Adminstrn 206 Pittsburgh PA 15213

MCCAMLY, JERRY ALLEN, secondary education educator; b. Battle Creek, Mich., Mar. 15, 1940; s. Derrol John and Adelee (Harding) McC.; m. Janet Aileen Pulatie, Aug. 25, 1962; children: Ty A., Jodi. BS in Edn., Ariz. State Coll., 1963; MA in Edn., Azusa Pacific Coll., 1978. Tchr. Casa Grande (Ariz.) High Sch., 1963-64, Whittier (Calif.) High Sch., 1964-65, Norwalk (Calif.)-LaMirada Unified Sch. Dist., 1965—. Cons. WASC Accrediting Assn., Burlingame, Calif., 1978—. Contbr. articles to profl. publs. Recipient Hon. Svc. award Norwalk Sch. PTA, 1986, Tchr.'s Medal Freedoms Found., 1977. Mem. L.A. Continuation Assn. (pres. 1980-81), Calf. Continuation Assn. (pres. 1981-82), World Future Soc. Republican. Methodist. Avocations: restoring classic corvettes, bowling, golf, travel, reading. Home: 25630 Sierra Calmo Ct Moreno Valley CA 92551-2162 Office: John Glenn High Sch 13520 Shoemaker Ave Norwalk CA 90650-4598

MCCAN, JAMES LAWTON, education educator; b. Plymouth, Ind., Aug. 10, 1952; s.Jean F. and Mildred P. (Hayn) McC.; m. Carolyn G. Splain, Jan. 16, 1971; children: Kendra, Brittany. B of Phys. Edn., Purdue U., 1974; MS in Edn., 1981, PhD, 1983. Tchr. reading and English Waynetown (Ind.) Mid. Sch., 1974-75, Yorkville (Ill.) H.S., 1979-80; reading specialist Purdue U., West Lafayette, Ind., 1983-89; program chair Basic Skills Advancement Ind. Voc-Tech. Coll., Lafayette, 1989-91; asst. prof., coord. student teaching Hillsdale (Mich.) Coll., 1991-95; dir. Student Achievement Zone, South Bend, Ind., 1995-96; assoc. prof. Nova Southeastern U., Ft. Lauderdale, Fla., 1996—. Contbr. articles and poetry to jours. Mem. Internat. Reading Assn., Fla. Reading Assn. Avocations: reading, music. Home: 1024 St Croix Ave Apopka FL 32703 Office: Nova Southeastern U Dept Edn Fort Lauderdale FL 33314

MCCANN, DIANA RAE, elementary education educator; b. Huron, S.D., Nov. 16, 1948; d. Ralph Henry and Rosina Agnes (Rowen) Yager; m. Gregory Charles McCann (dec. 1974); children: Grant Christopher, Holly Ann. BS, S.D. State U., 1972. Tchr. Bon Homme 4-2, Tyndall, S.D., 1972-74, Avon (S.D.) Sch., 1975-76, Bon Homme 4-2, Tyndall, 1976—. Rep. NCTM, SDCTM, 1989-90, pres-elect, 1990-92, pres., 1992-94, past pres. 1994-96, treas., 1999-; math. adv. bd. S.D. State, 1992—; coord. Presdl. awards in math. for SD, 1998—. 4-H leader, 1986—, sec.-treas. 4-H Club, 1992—; tournament coord. Bon Homme Youth Wrestling Club, 1986—93. Recipient Elem. Math. Presdl. award Nat. Sci. Found., 1993, Disting. Svc. award for Math. in SD, 2003. Avocation: gardening.

MCCANN, JOYCE JEANNINE, retired elementary education educator; b. Council Bluffs, Iowa, Dec. 15, 1926; d. Clyde Oliver and Reva Arleta (Myers) Tisher; m. Daniel Steven McCann, Aug. 14, 1960 (div. 1968); children: Marianne Rose, Daniel Patrick. BA, UCLA, 1955. Elem. tchr. L.A. Unified Sch. Dist., 1968-92. Recipient grant L.A. Bd. Edn., 1986-87. Mem.: Profl. Educators L.A., PEO Sisterhood, Delta Kappa Gamma (pres. Zeta Xi chpt. 2000—01). Republican. Avocation: violinist.

MCCANN, MARTHA SUE POWERS, reading and language arts educator; b. Imlay City, Mich., Sept. 28, 1935; d. Donald Franklin and Virginia (Matthews) Bade; m. Russell L. Powers, Dec. 21, 1957 (div. Apr. 1983); children: Jeffrey, Michael; m. Lyle J. McCann, Aug. 3, 1992. BS, Ea. Mich. U., 1960, MA, 1966; EdS, Oakland U., Rochester, Mich., 1983. Tchr. Imlay City Schs., 1956-60, pub. schs., Niles, Ill., 1960-61, Lakeville Sch., Battle Creek, Mich., 1961-63, Davison (Mich.) Cmty. Sch., 1963-91, elem. chmn., 1973-79, coord. Chpt. I reading and math., 1979-91; ret., 1991; instr. Ea. Mich. U. Ext., Ypsilanti, 1984—. Cons. on reading and lang. arts, tutor, Davison, 1965-91; instr. U. Mich., Flint, 1992; presenter lang. and reading workshops to various Mich. sch. dists., 1982—. Mem. various coms. Davison United Meth. Ch., 1965—; bd. dirs. Davison br. Genesee County Libr., 1993—. Recipient 1st Ann. Outstanding Tchr. award Davison Edn. Assn., 1986. Mem. Nat. Coun. Tchrs. English, Internat. Reading Assn., Mich. Reading Conf. (speaker 1984-86), Mich. Assn. Ret. Pers., Flint Area Reading Coun. (past pres.), Davison Schs. Ret. Tchrs. Club, Beta Sigma Phi (various offices 1975—). Home: 334 Rosemore Dr Davison MI 48423-1616

MCCANN, PATRICK JOHN, electrical engineering educator, researcher; b. Sacramento, July 31, 1958; s. John Paul and Marjorie Evelyn (Rundquist) McC.; m. Florence Anne Fusco, Oct. 20, 1990. BS, U. Calif., Berkeley, 1981; PhD, MIT, 1990. Machinist, toolmaker Lindsey Mfg., Azusa, Calif., 1977-78; machinist Coll. Chemistry U. Calif., Berkeley, 1980-81; process devel. engr. IBM, Burlington, Vt., 1981-84, device design engr., 1985, 88; prof. U. Okla., Norman, 1990—. Contbr. articles to profl. jours. including Jour. Applied Physics, Applied Physics Letters, Thin Solid Films, Jour. Crystal Growth. Lab. for Electronic Properties of Materials grantee NSF, 1992, Infrared Laser Devel. grantee NSF, 1995, 98, 2002. Mem. Materials Rsch. Soc. Achievements include patents for a chemical method for modification of a substrate surface to accomplish heteroepitaxial crystal growth and fabrication of high temperature semiconductor lasers and devel. of laser-based breath analysis tech. Office: U Okla 202 W Boyd St Rm 219 Norman OK 73019-1027

MCCANN, PETER PAUL, biology researcher, educator; s. Peter F. and Kathleen (Burnett) McC.; m. Danielle Soury, July 31, 1971. AB in Zoology, Columbia U., 1965; PhD, Syracuse U., 1970. Fellow NIH, Bethesda, Md., 1970-73; sr. scientist Ctr. of Rsch. Merrell Internat., Strasbourg, France, 1973-79; sr. biochemist Merrell Dow Rsch. Ctr., Cin., 1979-82; rsch. assoc. scientist Merrell Dow Rsch. Inst., Cin., 1982-84, dir. scientific and acad. liaison, 1984-90, dir. sci. adminstrn., 1988-90; prof. U. Cin. Coll. Medicine, 1981—; sr. dir., ctr. dir. Marion Merrell Dow Inc., Indpls., 1990-93; pres. Brit. Biotech Inc., Annapolis, Md., 1993-98; interim pres. U. Md. Biotech. Inst., College Park, Md., 1998-99; pres., CEO Oncostasis, Inc., 1999—2001, Mymetics Corp., 2001—03; GG. Co-vice chmn. Gordon Rsch. Conf. on Polyamines, 1987, co-chmn., 1989. Chief editor, co-author Inhibition of Polyamine Metabolism, 1987; co-editor, co-author: Enzymes as Targets for Drug Design, 1989; contbr. articles to profl. jours. Mem. Am. Soc. Cell Biology, Am. Soc. Tropical Medicine and Hygiene, Am. Soc. Biochemistry and Molecular Biology, Biochem. Soc. (editl. adv. bd. 1986-92, editor 1992-99), Soc. Protozoologists (editl. bd. reviewers 1989-95), Am. Philat. Congress, Inc. (pres. 1990-95), Am. Philat. Soc. (v.p. 1995-99, pres. 1999-2003). Achievements include patents for method of inhibiting the growth of protozoa, method of controlling phytopathogenic fungus. E-mail: 103226.706@compuserve.com.

MCCANN, SUSAN LYNN, elementary education educator; b. Forest Hills, N.Y., Feb. 11, 1947; d. Henry August and Frances Susan (Kleist) Kupsch; m. Kevin Daniel McCann, June 28, 1970; children: Christopher, Megan. BS in Edn., St. John's U., 1968, MS in Edn., 1971. Elem. tchr. Bellmore (N.Y.) Schs., 1968-76, Massapequa (N.Y.) Schs., 1987—. Pvt. tutor, Massapequa, 1968—; mem., chair N.Y. State Sch. Com., Massapequa, 1990—; chair Shared-Decision-Making, Massapequa, 1994-96, Ptnrs. in Reading, Massapequa, 1992-93. Chmn. cultural arts Birch Lane PTA, Massapequa, 1986-90; chmn. Earthday com. Unqua Sch., Massapequa, 1991—; vol. Am. Heart Assn., Bohemia, N.Y., 1991—, Nancy Waters Meml. Run, Seaford, N.Y., 1982-92; cmty. outreach chmn. Massapequa Fedn. Tchrs., 1995—; chmn. Sch. Pantry Donations, 1998—; coord. Pub. Assistance, 1991—. Recipient Cmty. Svc. Merit cert. Massapequa Bd. Edn., 1995, Nat. Lifetime award PTA, 1995, Disting. Svc. award Unqua PTA, 1997. Mem. Am. Fedn. Tchrs., N.Y. State United Tchrs. (gifts of the heart award 1994, cmty. svc. award 1995), Massapequa Fedn. Tchrs. (chair sch. holiday fundraisers 1993—, coord. pub. rels. 1996-98, outreach chmn. 1995-97). Avocations: cooking, baking, cross-country skiing, reading. Office: Massapequa Schs Merrick Rd Massapequa NY 11758 E-mail: skmteach@aol.com.

MCCARDELL, JOHN MALCOLM, JR., academic administrator; b. Frederick, Md., June 17, 1949; s. John Malcolm and Susan (Lane) McCardell; m. Bonnie Greenwald, Dec. 30, 1976; children: John Malcolm III, James Benjamin Lee. AB, Washington and Lee U., 1971; postgrad., John Hopkins U., 1972-73; PhD, Harvard U., 1976; Litt.D., Washington and Lee U., 1997. Asst. prof. history Middlebury (Vt.) Coll., 1976-80, assoc. prof. history, 1982-87, dean for academic devel., 1985-88, prof. history, 1987—, dean facuty, 1988-89, provost, v.p for academic affairs, 1989-91, acting pres., 1991-92, pres., 1992—; sr. rsch fellow U. S.C., Columbia, 1980-81, 96. Bd. dirs. Nat. Bank Middlebury. Author: The Idea of a Southern Nation, 1979 (Allan Nevins award, 1977); editor: A Master's Due, 1985. Sgt. USAR, 1971—77. Recipient Algernon Sydney Sullivan prize, Washington and Lee U., 1971, Charles Eliot medal, Eliot House Harvard U., 1976; fellow, NEH, 1980, Am. Philosophical Soc., 1979. Mem.: Vt. Hist. Soc., Am. Studies Assn., So. Hist. Assn., Orgn. Am. Historians, Am. Hist. Assn., Lambda Chi Alpha, Phi Beta Kappa, Omicron Delta Kappa. Office: Middlebury Coll Old Chapel Bldg Middlebury VT 05753

MCCARROLL, KATHLEEN ANN, radiologist, educator; b. Lincoln, Nebr., July 7, 1948; d. James Richard and Ruth B. (Wagenknecht) McC.; m. Steven Mark Beerbohm, July 10, 1977 (div. 1991); 1 child, Palmer Brooke. BS, Wayne State U., 1974; MD, Mich. State U., 1978. Diplomate Am. Bd. Radiology. Intern/resident in diagnostic radiology William Beaumont Hosp., Royal Oak, Mich., 1978-82, fellow in computed tomography and ultrasound, 1983, dir. divsn. emergency radiology, 2001—; radiologist, dir. radiologic edn. Detroit Receiving Hosp., 1984-2001, vice-chief dept. radiology, 1988-96, chief dept. radiology, 1996-2001. Pres.-elect med. staff Detroit Receiving Hosp., 1992-94, pres., 1994-96; mem. admissions com. Wayne State U. Coll. Medicine, Detroit, 1991-2001; trustee Detroit Med. Ctr., 1996-2001, dir. med. staff consolidation, 1996-97, mem. consol. med. exec. com., 1998-2001, chmn. credentials com., 1998-99, joint conf. com., 1998-99; officer bd. dirs. Dr. L. Reynolds Assoc., P.C., Detroit, 1991-94, 96-2001; presenter profl. confs.; assoc. prof. radiology Wayne State U. Sch. Medicine, Detroit, 1995—; health care cons./med. staff affairs, 1998—. Editor: Critical Care Clinics, 1992; mem. editorial bd. Emergency Radiology; contbr. articles to profl. publs. Named to Crain's Bus. Detroit, Detroit's 100 Most Influential Women, 1997. Mem.: AMA, Wayne/Oakland County Med. Soc., Mich. State Med. . Soc., Am. Soc. Emergency Radiologists (bd. dirs. 1996—2001, mem. exec. com. 1998—2001, bylaws com. 2001—), Am. Roentgen Ray Soc., Radio. Soc. N.Am., Am. Coll. Radiology (Mich. chpt. sec. 1995—98, alt. councilor 1999—2002, councilor 2002—, plain film and fluoroscopy accreditation com. 2003—), Phi Beta Kappa. Avocations: travelling, skiing, reading. Office: Wm Beaumont Hosp Dept Diag Radiology 3601 W 13 Mile Rd Royal Oak MI 48073

MCCARTHY, CATHERINE THERESE, elementary educator; b. Escanaba, Mich., Apr. 22, 1950; d. Robert Francis and Mary Frances (Koebel) Groos; m. J. Michael McCarthy III, Apr. 25, 1970; children: John Kevin, Sean Michael, Ryan Patrick. BS, Nazareth Coll., Kalamazoo, 1972; MA, Western Mich. U., 1981. Cert. continuing edn. tchr., Mich. Substitute presch. and kindergarten tchr. Am. Nursery Sch. and Kindergarten in Japan, Naka Meguro, Japan, 1972-73; tchr. ESL English Lang. Edn. Coun., Kanda, Japan, 1972-73; substitute tchr. Kalamazoo County Schs., Kalamazoo, 1973-74, 85-86; elem. tchr. St. Monica Sch., Kalamazoo, 1974-82; owner, mgr. Yarn Mcht., Kalamazoo, 1985-86; elem. tchr. Parchment Sch. Dist., Kalamazoo, 1986—. Edn. adv. bd. Nazareth Coll., 1976-82. Edn. commn., Sunday sch. tchr. St. Ambrose Ch., Parchment, Mich., 1976-84; asst. coach Am. Yough Soccer Orgn., Kalamazoo, 1982-84, 86-87; mem. Kalamazoo Women's Network, 1982-86. Excellence in Edn. incentive grantee, 1992; recipient Parchment Educator of Yr. award, 1992-93. Mem. NEA, Mich. Edn. Assn. (rep. bargainers coun. 1989-91, coordinating coun. 1990, baraginers assembly 1990—), Parchment Edn. Assn. (pres., bargainer 1988—, sec. 1997-98, v.p. 1998-99), Kalamazoo Weavers Guild (edn. chmn. 1984-89, newsletter editor 1993-95, sec. 1995-98, pres. 1996-97, WAFA sale chair 1998, conf. steering com. 1997—, chairperson weavers and fiber artists sale 1998). Home: 6886 Springbrook Ln Kalamazoo MI 49004-9665 Office: Northwood Elem Sch 5535 Keyes Dr Kalamazoo MI 49004-1581

MCCARTHY, HELEN H. civic worker, retired educator; b. Fresno, Calif. d. Frederick Henry and Louise A. (Scharenberg) Hacke; m. J. Thornton McCarthy, Mar. 2, 1946; children: Thornton Randall, Deborah McCarthy Edwards. BA with honors, U. Calif., Berkeley, 1943. Cert. tchr., Calif. Pres. Pasadena (Calif.) chpt. Nat. Assistance League, 1963-64, mem. admissions and inspection com.; active Nat. Charity League, 1966-72; mem. Pasadena philharm. com. Hollywood Bowl Assn., 1965-68; active Children's Hosp. Inc., Oakland, Calif., 1989-90, br. chmn., bd. dirs., 1993-96; pres. Cascade Guild, John Muir Hosp., Walnut Creek, Calif., 1990-91, Kiwanis Club of Rossmoor; pres.-elect Republican Club of Rossmoor. Republican. Presbyterian. Avocations: golf, swimming. Home: 5545 Terra Granada Dr Walnut Creek CA 94595-4054

MCCARTHY, JOANNE MARY, reading specialist; AB in Hist., Emmanuel Coll., 1967; MEd in Elem. Edn., Boston State Coll., 1969; EdD in Reading, Boston U., 1990. Cert. elem. tchr., sch. psychologist, hist. tchr., guidance counsleor, cons. tchr. reading, supr. reading, elem. prin., social studies tchr., English tchr., supr., dir., Mass. With dept. of def. Nat. Security Agy., 1967-68; tchr. St. Gregory's Sch., Dorchester, Mass., 1969-74; ednl. coord., tchr. Boston Children's Svcs., 1974-75; testing diagnostician Duxbury (Mass.) Pub. Schs., 1975-76; reading tchr. Duxbury High Sch., 1975-81; reading specialist Chandler Sch. and Duxbury Elem. Sch., 1981-97, Duxbury Middle Sch. and Alden Sch., 1997—99; adj. prof. Fisher Coll., Boston, 1999—2000; adj. prof., advisor Northeastern U., Boston, 2000—01; reading specialist Sacred Heart Sch., North Quincy, Mass., 2001—. Adult literacy program vol. Odwin Learning Ctr., Dorchester, 1990-92, reading specialist at Kennedy Day Sch., Franciscan Children's Hosp., 1999-2000 Presenter in field. Exec. bd. mem. Boston U. Sch. Edn. Alumni Assn. Mem.: Internat. Reading Assn., Boston (Mass.) U. Sch. Edn. Alumni Assn., Pi Lambda Theta.

MCCARTHY, JOHN, computer scientist, educator; b. Boston, Sept. 4, 1927; s. Patrick Joseph and Ida McCarthy; children: Susan Joanne, Sarah Kathleen, Timothy Talcott. BS, Calif. Inst. Tech., 1948; PhD, Princeton U., 1951. Instr. Princeton U., 1951—53; acting asst. prof. math. Stanford U., 1953—55; asst. prof. Dartmouth Coll., 1955—58; asst. and assoc. prof. communications scis. M.I.T., Cambridge, 1958—62; prof. computer sci. Stanford U., 1962—, Charles M. Pigott prof. Sch. Engring., 1987—94. Served with AUS, 1945-46. Recipient Kyoto prize, 1988, Nat. Medal of Sci., NSF, 1990. Mem.: NAE, NAS, Am. Assn. Artificial Intelligence (pres. 1983—84), Am. Math. Soc., Assn. for Computing Machinery (A.M. Turing award 1971), Am. Acad. Arts and Scis. Home: 885 Allardice Way Stanford CA 94305-1050 Office: Stanford U Dept Computer Sci Stanford CA 94305 E-mail: mccarthy@stanford.edu.

MCCARTHY, MARIE GERALDINE, program director, coordinator, educator; b. San Francisco, Nov. 7, 1940; d. Emmett Francis and Marie Delores (Costello) McC.; children: Peter, Robert, Todd Brockman. BA, Lone Mountain Coll., 1962; MA, Dominican Coll., San Rafael, Calif., 1972. Gen. secondary credential; cert. cmty. coll. chief adminstrv. officer, supr., history, basic edn., spl. edn., profl. edn. educator, counselor. Coord., counselor Work Incentive Program, Employment Devel. Dept., Marin County, Calif., 1970-72; coord., instr. Neighborhood Youth Corps Program, Marin County, Calif., 1972-74; coord. Marin City Project Area Com., Marin County, Calif., 1978-79; coord. basic skills program Coll. of Marin, Kentfield, Calif., 1973-79, edn. cons., 1980-83, pres. acad. senate, 1993—, coord. Disabled Students Program, 1984—. Faculty advisor Challenged Students Club, Coll. of Marin, Kentfield, 1983—, exec. coun. United Profs. of Marin, Local 1610, 1984-92, mem. staff devel. com., 1986-88, event coord. ann. student fundraiser for students with disabilities, 1985—, dist. psychol. disabilities task force, 1994—, dist. councilmem. Faculty Assn. Calif. C.C.s, 1994—, dist. budget com., 1994—, dist. master planning com., 1994—, mem. crisis intervention team, 1990—, editor DSPS Forum, 1995—; exec. com. Statewide Acad. Senate, 1995-96. Author: How To Learn To Study: Bridging the Study Skills Gap, 1982, The Faculty Handbook on Disabilities, 1993. Bd. dirs., v.p. CENTERFORCE, 1992—; bd. dirs. Marin Coalition, Marin Athletic Found., 1992—, Marin Ctr. for Ind. Living, 1994—, EXODUS, 1992—, sec.; past v.p. Bay Faculty Assn.; founder Youth Helping Homeless, 1990—; mem. Alliance for the Mentally Ill., 1994—, JERICHO, 1994—; founding bd. dirs. INSPIRIT, 1984—. Recipient Spl. Achievement award Calif. Youth Soccer Assn., 1980, Marin County Mother of Yr. award, 1984, Spl. Recognition awards The Indoor Sports Club for Physically Handicapped, 1984, 88-90, 92-93, Mom Makes the Difference honoree Carter Hawley Hale Stores, Inc., 1994, Cert. of Recognition, Marin Human Rights Commn., 1994, Hayward award, 1995, Buckelew Partnership award, 1995, Disting. Faculty award Com. Alumni Assn., 1995. Mem. AAUW, Calif. Assn. Postsecondary Educators for the Disabled, Faculty Assn. Calif. C.C.'s, Amnesty Internat. Platform Assoc.,, AHEAD, Commonwealth Club Calif., U.S. Soccer Fedn. Avocations: piano, singing, hiking, aerobics, meditation. Home: 6004 Shelter Bay Ave Mill Valley CA 94941-3040 Office: Coll of Marin College Ave Kentfield CA 94904

MCCARTHY, MARY ELEANOR, elementary physical education educator; b. Easton, Pa., Apr. 23, 1956; d. Thomas James and Eleanor Ann (Brewton) McC. BS, Edinboro U., 1978; MEd, East Stroudsberg, Pa., 1988. Elem. phys. edn. tchr. Phillipsburg (N.J.) Sch., 1978-80; head field hockey coach Sucon Valley High Sch., Hellertown, Pa., 1978-79; asst. basketball coach Phillipsburg High Sch., 1978-80; head field hockey coach Newton (N.J.) High Sch., 1980-85, head basketball coach, 1980-83; asst. basketball coach Sparta (N.J.) High Sch., 1983-86; ast. field hockey coach East Stroudsburg (Pa.) U., 1987-91, asst. lacrosse coach, 1987-90; elem. phys. edn. tchr. Merriam Ave. Sch., Newton, N.J., 1980—. Asst. coach Spl. Olympics, Newton, 1980—. Named N.J. Field Hockey Coach of Yr., Newark Star Ledger, 1984, Merriam Ave Sch. Tchr. of Yr., Newton Bd. Edn., 1991. Mem. AAHPERD, NEA, N.J. Alliance Health Phys. Edn., Recreation and Dance, Women's Internat. Bowling Congress, North Jersey Field Hockey Assn. (Sussex County rep. 1982-86), U.S. Field Hockey Assn. Avocations: bowling, photography. Home: 614 Barrymore St Phillipsburg NJ 08865-1664 Office: Merriam Ave Sch 81 Merriam Ave Newton NJ 07860-2423

MCCARTHY, MARY ELIZABETH (BETH) CONSTANCE, conductor, educator, music educator; b. Chgo., Apr. 8, 1961; d. Thomas Joseph and Loretta Ann McCarthy. BA, North Ctrl. Coll., 1983; postgrad., Goethe Inst., 1991, Ea. Ill. U., 1993; MusM in Choral and Instrumental Edn. and Cognition and Vocal Performance, Northwestern U., 1999. Profl. cantor Joliet/Rockford Dioceses, Ill., 1979—; assoc. condr. Chorus Orch. Band Ill. Math. and Sci. Acad., Aurora, 1989—2000; site coord. gifted program Ill. Math. and Sci. Acad. at Ea. Ill. U., Charleston, 1990—95; soloist Lincoln Opera Co., Chgo., 1991—94; chmn. Dept. Fine Arts Rosary H.S., Aurora, 1993—; dept. chair music Aurora U., 1995—; condr., artistic dir. Fox Valley Festival Chorus, Aurora, 1999—. Profl. role coach pvt. students, Ill., 1989—; condr., music dir. dinner theatres, summer stock, Ill., 1990—; artistic cons. oratory and recitals, Ill., 1993—; adjudicator orchs., chorus, bands, Ill., 1993—; cons. to critique Nat. Stds. for the Arts, Ill., 1994; master class clinician various choral orgns., Ill., 1995—; guest condr. fine arts festivals, Ill., 2001—; host Cath. Conf. Fine Arts Festival Rosary H.S., Aurora, 2002. Sec. The Beta Fin. Group, Sycamore, Ill., 1995—2002; conservation mem. Salmon Unlimited-Ill. chpt., 1997; religious edn. tchr. St. Peter and Paul Ch., Naperville, Ill., 1980—, cantor, 1976—, Rite of Christian Initiation for Adults sponsor, 1995. Recipient Internat. Bel-Canto Vocal Competition Opera award, Bel-Canto Found., 1995; fellow Richter fellow for internat. rsch./study, North Ctrl. Coll., 1982. Mem.: AAUW, Lyric Opera Chgo., Ill. Music Educators' Assn., Music Educators' Nat. Conf., Fox Valley Music Educators' Assn., North Ctrl. Coll. Alumni Assn., Northwestern U. Music Sch. Alumni Assn. (bd. dirs. 1998—2001), Northwestern Club Chgo., Alpha Psi Omega, Beta Beta Beta, Phi Alpha Theta. Avocations: art, travel, running, boating, reading. Office: Aurora Univ Music Dept 347 S Gladstone Aurora IL 60506

MCCARTHY, PATRICIA SUE, retired special education educator; b. Indpls., Jan. 20, 1949; d. Joseph John and Joan Rita (Hart) McC. BA, Purdue U., 1971; MS, Ind. State U., 1975. Cert. elem. tchr., in mental retardation, learning disabilities, emotionally handicapped, Ind. Tchr. educable mentally retarded Wabash (Ind.) City Schs., 1971—73; resource tchr. for mentally retarded, learning disabled, emotionally handicapped Indpls. Pub. Schs., 1973—2000, chairperson spl. svcs. team, 1984—2000; ret., 2000. Cons., tester pvt. and parochial schs., Indpls., 1982-1991. Ind. Dept. Pub. Instrn. and fed. govt. grantee, 1977-78. Mem. Purdue U. Alumni Assn., Ind. State U. Alumni Assn. Republican. Roman Catholic. Avocations: sports, travel, reading. Home: 595 Burr Oak Dr Carmel IN 46032-4575

MCCARTHY, ROBERT LANE, physics educator; b. Berwyn, Ill., Jan. 14, 1943; s. Samuel Lane and Mary Elizabeth (Carpenter) McC.; m. Betty Lee Minson, Sept. 11, 1965 (div. Apr. 1994); children: Michael, Daniel. BA in Physics summa cum laude, Harvard U., 1965; PhD in Physics, U. Calif., Berkeley, 1971. Enrico Fermi fellow U. Chgo., 1971-72; asst. prof. physics SUNY, Stony Brook, 1972-78, assoc. prof., 1978-86, prof. physics, 1986—, dir. undergrad. studies in physics, 1989-96. Chmn. Fermilab Users Exec. Com., Batavia, Ill., 1984-85; vis. scientist Fermilab, Batavia, 1988-89. Contbr. articles to profl. jours. Grantee NSF, 1972—. Fellow Am. Phys. Soc.; mem. AAAS. Achievements include development of first wide-aperture ring-imaging Cherenkov counter; first to calculate charge asymmetry in particles energy loss in matter; discovery of evidence for partons in production of hadrons by hadrons, discovery of the top quark. Office: State Univ NY Dept Physics Stony Brook NY 11794-3800

MCCARTOR, SHEILA SMITH, secondary school educator; b. Raymondville, Tex., May 4, 1941; d. M.D. Smith and Mae (Sansom) Jessie; m. Gary Don McCartor, July 20, 1999; m. Ira Yale Levanthal, Aug. 5, 1966; 1 child, Adam Yale. BS, N. Tex. State U., 1963, MEd, 1965; postgrad., Nova U., 1972, MIT, 1979. Elem. tchr. Grapevine (Tex.) Pub. Schs., 1963—65; tchr., team leader Lamplighter Sch., Dallas, 1965—. Task force for diversity Lamplighter Sch., 2002, mem. steering com., computer staff, 1979—84, sci. com., 1990—, chair, sci. com., 1993—94; presenter Internat. Conf. Tech. in Edn., U. London, 1994; pub. Internat. Conf. Tech. in Edn., 1993—94; staff Ind. Sch. Assn. of S.W. Beginning Tchr. Inst., 1993—94; presenter Internat. Coop. Learning Conf., Columbus, Ohio, 1996; pub. Dallas Opera Instrl. Series. Staff mem. Episc. Sch. Spirituality, Dallas, 1983, dir., 1989—. Mem.: Women of St. Francis (v.p. Dallas 1983, mem. task force diversity 2002). Office: Lamplighter Sch 11611 Inwood Rd Dallas TX 75229-3098

MCCARTY, PERRY LEE, civil and environmental engineering educator; b. Grosse Pointe, Mich., Oct. 29, 1931; s. James C. and Alice C. (Marsom) McC.; m. Martha Davis Collins, Sept. 5, 1953; children: Perry Lee, Cara L., Susan A., Kathleen R. BSCE, Wayne State U., 1953; MS in Sanitary Engring., MIT, 1957, ScD, 1959; DEng (hon.), Colo. Sch. Mines, 1992. Field engr. Edwin Orr Co., Dearborn, Mich., 1951-52; engr. Pate & Hirn, Detroit, 1952-53; field engr. Hubbell, Roth & Clark, Detroit, 1953; instr. civil engring. Wayne State U., 1953-54; field engr. George Jerome & Co., Detroit, 1954; engr. Civil Engrs., Inc., Detroit, 1956; assoc. Rolf Eliassen Assocs., Winchester, Mass., 1958-61; asst. prof. sanitary engring. MIT, 1958-62; faculty Stanford U., 1962—, prof. civil engring., 1967-75, Silas H. Palmer prof., 1975-99, Silas H. Palmer prof. emeritus, 1999—, chmn. dept. civil engring., 1980-85. Chmn. Gordon Rsch. Conf. Environ. Scis., 1972; vice chmn. environ. studies bd. NRC-NAS, 1976-80, mem. com. on phys. scis., math. and resources, 1985-88, bd. on radioactive waste mgmt., 1989-96, mem. com. geoscis., environment, resources, 1994-97. Co-author: Chemistry for Environmental Engineering and Science, 5th edit., 2003, Environmental Biotechnology Principles and Applications, 2001. Served with AUS, 1954-56. Recipient Tyler Prize for Environ. Achievement, 1992, Clarke Prize Outstanding Achievement Water Sci. and Tech., 1997; NSF faculty fellow, 1968-69. Fellow AAAS, Am. Acad. Microbiology, Am. Acad. Arts and Scis.; mem. ASCE (Walter L. Huber Rsch. prize 1964, Simon W. Freese Environ. Engring. award 1979, James R. Croes medal 1995), NAE, Am. Water Works Assn. (hon., life, chmn. water quality divsn. 1972-73, trustee rsch. divsn. 1980-85, Best Paper award 1985, A.P. Black Rsch. award 1989), Am. Soc. for Microbiology, Water Environment Fedn. (hon. 1989, Harrison P. Eddy award 1962, 77, Thomas Camp award 1975), Assn. Environ. Engring. Sci. Profs. (Disting. Faculty award 1966, Outstanding Publ. award 1985, 88, 98, Founders award 1992), Am. Soc. Engring. Edn.(vice-chmn. environ. engring. divsn. 1968-69), Internat. Assn. on Water Quality, Sigma Xi, Tau Beta Pi (fellow 1957-58). Home: 823 Sonoma Ter Stanford CA 94305-1024 Office: Stanford U Civil Environ Engring Dept Stanford CA 94305-4020 Business E-Mail: pmccarty@stanford.edu.

MCCARTY, RICHARD CHARLES, psychology educator, university dean; b. Portsmouth, Va., July 12, 1947; s. Constantine Ambrose and Helen Marie (Householder) McC.; m. Sheila Adair Miltier, July 15, 1965; children: Christopher Charles, Lorraine Marie, Ryan Lester, Patrick James. BS in Biology, Old Dominion U., 1970, MS in Zoology, 1972; PhD in Pathobiology, Johns Hopkins U., 1976. Rsch. assoc. NIMH, Bethesda, Md., 1976-78; asst. prof. U. Va., Charlottesville, 1978-84, assoc. prof., 1984-88, prof., 1988-2001, chair psychology, 1990-98, chair Coun. of Grad. Depts. Psychology, 1996-97; exec. dir. sci. directorate APA, Washington, 1998-2001; dean arts and sci. Vanderbilt U., Nashville, 2001—. Co-editor: Development of the Hypertensive Phenotype, vol. 19, Handbook of Hypertension, 1999; editor: Am. Psychologist, 2000—01. Lt. comdr. USPHS, 1976-78. Recipient Rsch. Scientist Devel. award NIMH, 1985-90; sr. fellow Nat. Heart Lung Blood Inst., NIH, 1984-85. Fellow AAAS, APA, Soc. Behavioral Medicine, Acad. Behavioral Med. Rsch., Am. Psychol. Soc., Am. Inst. Stress, Coun. for High Blood Pressure Rsch., AHA; mem. Internat. Soc. for Investigation of Stress (exec. bd. 1996-2001). Roman Catholic. Avocations: sports, gardening. Office: Office of the Dean Vanderbilt U Coll Arts and Sci 301 Kirkland Hall Nashville TN 37240

MCCARTY, RICHARD JOSEPH, consulting engineer; b. Warren, Ohio, Apr. 15, 1948; s. Ralph Edward and Ann Katheerine (Nelms) McC.; m. Cathy Rae Reid, May 12, 1970 (div.); children: Michelle Rae, Erica Ann; m. Nora Elaine Jennings, Dec. 5, 1981; 1 child, Trillion Nora. BA, Hiram Coll., 1991; MBA, Baldwin-Wallace Coll., 1993; postgrad., Nova U., 1993—; PhD, Am. Coll. Metaphys. Theology, 1995-96; postgrad., Am. Inst. Hypnosis, 1997—. Cert. K-12 tchr., adult tchr., spl. edn. tchr., Ohio. Engr. United Telephone Co., Warren, Ohio, 1969-70; cons. engr. Henkels & McCoy, Inc., Blue Bell, Pa., 1970-78, Lambic Telecom, Inc., N.Y.C., 1978-83, regional mgr. Warren, Ohio, 1985-88; v.p. McAreg Enterprises, Inc., Pocono Lakes, Pa., 1983-84; computer instr. Trumbull County Joint Vocat. Sch., Warren, 1988-90; pres., adminstr. Trillion Inst., Warren, 1990-91; cons. engr E.G. Keller and Assocs., Elkhart, Ind., 1991-97, Harris-McBurney Co., Jackson, Mich., 1997-2000, TCS, Bergen, N.Y., 2000—. Spkr. Steelworkers Reemployment Challenger, Youngstown, Ohio, 1990-92; edn. cons. to GM Corp. for Warren City Schs. state and fed. programs, 1994-95. Contbr. articles to profl. publs. Democrat. Avocations: coin collecting, art. Home: 305 Bank St Batavia NY 14020-1615 Office: TCS 7640 Creamery Rd Bergen NY 14416-9342

MCCARUS, ERNEST NASSEPH, retired language educator; b. Charleston, W.Va., Sept. 10, 1922; s. Nasseph Mitchell and Della (Saad) McC.; m. Adele Najib Haddad, Sept. 10, 1955; children: Peter Kevin, Carol Ann. Student, Morris Harvey Coll., 1939-40; AB, U. Mich., 1945, MA, 1949, PhD, 1956. Translation team capt. Allied Translators and Interpreters' Service, Allied Hqrs., Tokyo, Japan, 1946-47; mem. English Lang. Inst. staff U. Mich., 1948-52, mem. univ. expdn. to Near East, 1951, instr. univ., 1952-56, asst. prof. Arabic, 1956-61; dir. Fgn. Service Inst., Field Sch. Arabic Lang. and Area Study, U.S. Dept. State, Beirut, 1958-60; assoc. prof. dept. Near Ea. studies U. Mich., 1961-67, prof., 1967-95, chmn. dept., 1969-77, dir. Ctr. for Arabic Study Abroad, 1974-83, dir. U. Mich. Center for Near Eastern and North African Studies, 1983-92, assoc. dir. Ctr for Mid. Ea. and North African Studies, 1995-97, prof. emeritus, 1995—. Author: Grammar of Kurdish of Sulaimania, Iraq, 1958, (with H. Hoenigswald, R. Noss, J. Yamagiwa) A Survey of Intensive Programs in the Uncommon Languages, 1962, (with A. Yacoub) Elements of Contemporary Arabic, 1962, 3d edn., 1966, (with Raji Rammuny) First Level Arabic: Elementary Literary Arabic for Secondary Schools, 1964, Teacher's Manual to Accompany First Level Arabic, 1964, (with Jamal J. Abdullah) Kurdish Basic Course - Dialect of Sulaimania, Iraq, 1967, Kurdish Readers, Vol. I Newspaper Kurdish, Vol. II. Kurdish Essays, Vol. III Kurdish Short Stories, 1967, A Kurdish-English Dictionary, 1967, (with P. Abboud) Elementary Modern Standard Arabic, 1983, (with R. Rammuny) Word Count of Elementary Modern Literary Arabic Textbooks, 1969, (with P. Abboud, E.T. Abdel-Massih, S. Altoma, W. Erwin, R. Rammuny) Modern Standard Arabic Intermediate Level, 1971, (with R. Rammuny) A Programmed Course in Modern Literary Arabic Phonology and Script, 1974; editor: Language Learning, Vol. VII, 1956-57, Language Learning, Vol. XIII, 1963, An-Nashra, 1967-74, Contemporary Arabic Readers, Vols. I-V, 1962-66, The Development of Arab-American Identity, 1994; contbr. articles to scholastic jours. Served with AUS, 1942-46. Rockefeller fellow, 1951 Mem. Mich. Linguistic Soc. (pres. 1962-63), Am. Assn. Tchrs. Arabic (pres. 1973, exec. coun. 1979-81, 89-92), Middle East Studies Assn. (bd. dirs. 1973-75), Linguistic Soc. Am., Am. Oriental Soc., Linguistic Circle N.Y., Arabic Linguistic Soc. (pres. 1992). Home: 1400 Beechwood Dr Ann Arbor MI 48103-2940 E-mail: enm@umich.edu.

MCCASLIN, KATHLEEN DENISE, child abuse educator; b. Poughkeepsie, N.Y., Aug. 4, 1962; d. Nancy Ann Gosselin; m. David Wayne McCaslin, Sept. 27, 1986 (dec. Oct. 1990); 1 child, LeAnn; m. Larry Thomas Ward, July 14, 1998. BA, Adelphi Coll., 1984. Pub. speaker Impact Seminars, Littlestown, Pa., 1987-96; exec. dir. McCaslin Internat., Guffey, Colo., 1994—; pub. speaker The Family Advocate, Guffey, Colo., 1997—. Founder We the People, Colorado Springs, Colo., 1982; vol. counselor/facilitator Beginning Experience, Harrisburg, Pa., 1991-94. Author: (books) Trusting in God, 1993, Respecting Yourself, 1993, Loss and Recovery, 1992, (cd audio) One Child's Journey to Freedom, 1998. Troop leader Girl Scouts U.S., Guffey, Colo., 1998-2000. Recipient Outstanding Grad. award Adelphi Coll., Colorado Springs, 1984. Mem. ASCPA, World Wildlife Fedn., Arbor Day Found., S.W. Indian Found. Avocations: reading, hiking, needlework, gourmet cooking, gardening. Office: McCaslin Internat PO Box 100 Guffey CO 80820

MCCAULEY, ALFREDA ELLIS, elementary school principal; b. Greensboro, N.C., Sept. 24, 1942; d. David and Elizabeth (Stout) Ellis; m. John McCauley, June 6, 1964; children: Karen Alicia, Sue Lynn. BA, N.C. Cen. U., 1964; MS, N.C. A&T State U., 1976, 82; Dr., U. N.C., Greensboro, 1991. Cert. tchr., counselor, adminstr., N.C.; cert. principal exec. program. Music tchr. Durham (N.C.) County Schs., 1964-66, Greensboro Pub. Schs., 1968-76, counselor, 1976-88, prin., 1991—. Active Black Child Devel. Inst., Greensboro, 1988—. Mem. ASCD, NEA, Nat. Assn. Elem. Sch. Prins., N.C. Assn. Educators, N.C. Assn. Cupr. and Curriculum Devel., Greensboro Prin.'s Assn., Phi Delta Kappa, Alpha Kappa Alpha. Avocations: playing piano, singing, reading, cooking. Home: 5303 Stonehaven Dr Greensboro NC 27406-5830

MCCAULEY, BARBARA LYNNE, language educator; b. Kans. City, Mo., Mar. 2, 1951; d. J. C. and Rebecca Ernestine (Alley) McCauley. BSE, Ctrl. Mo. State U., 1973, MA, 1976; PhD, Fla. State U., 1993. Instr. Macon (Ga.) Coll., 1979-83; asst. prof. Gainesville (Ga.) CC, 1987-88; English instr. North Fla. CC, Madison, 1993—, divsn. chmn. humanities divsn., 2001—. Adj. prof. Fla. State U., Tallahassee, 1983—86, Tallahassee, 1989—93, vis. prof., 1988—89; adj. prof. Tallahassee CC, 1989—93. Contbr. articles to profl. jours. Bd. dirs. Northland Symphony, Kansas City, 1978—79, Macon Balllet, 1980—83. Mem.: Medival Soc. Am., Fla. Coll. English Assn., Internat. Assn. Found. Arts, Mythopoeic Soc., Internat. Arthurian Soc., Internat. Assn. Fantastic Arts, Alpha Pi Omega, Kappa Delta Pi, Sigma Tau Delta, Phi Kappa Phi. Avocations: art, music, dancing, poetry, fiction. Office: North Fla CC 1000 Turner Davis Dr Madison FL 32340 E-mail: mccauleyb@nfcc.edu.

MCCAUSLAND, CATHERINE LAIRD, nursing educator; b. Honolulu, Mar. 7, 1948; d. Francis H. Jr. and Laird M. (Sullivan) Forbes; m. Warren H. McCausland, June 20, 1987. AA, DeAnza Coll., 1968; BSN, Regents Coll., 1984; MSN, San Francisco State U., 1987. RN, Calif.; cert. critical care nurse. Staff nurse ICU Middlesex Hosp., London; critical care instr. St. Mary's Med. Ctr., San Francisco, dir. nursing edn., chair, nursing quality; assoc. faculty Profl. Growth Facilitators, San Clemente, Calif., 1990-92. Mem. AACN.

MCCAWLEY, AUSTIN, psychiatrist, educator; b. Greenock, Scotland, Jan. 17, 1925; arrived in U.S., 1954; s. Austin and Anna Theresa (McBride) McC.; m. Gloria Klein, Feb. 15, 1958; children: Joseph, Tessa. MBCHB, U. Glasgow, 1948. Diplomate Am. Bd. Psychiatry and Neurology; DPM Royal Coll. London. Intern Glasgow Royal Infirmary, Scotland, 1948; resident Inst. Living, Harford, Conn., 1954-57, clin. dir., 1960-66; med. dir. Westchestor br. St. Vincent's Hosp., N.Y.C., 1966-72; dir. psychiatry St. Francis Hosp., Hartford, 1972-88; prof. psychiatry U. Conn. Med. Sch., Farmington, 1983-93; pvt. practice, West Hartford, Conn., 1988—. Dir. psychiatry Kaiser Permanente of Conn., 1996-99. Co-author: The Physician, 1983; contbr. articles to profl. jours. Chmn. Bd. Mental Health, State of Conn., 1981-84, Search Com. for Commr. Mental Health, Conn., 1981; mem. Gov.'s Spl. Task Force on Mental health Policy, Conn., 1982. With RAF, 1948-50. Fellow: Am. Coll. Psychiatry (charter fellow, founder), Am. Psychiat. Assn.; mem.: Conn. Psychiat. Soc. (pres. 1978—79). Democrat. Roman Catholic. Avocation: music. Home and Office: 20 Worthington Dr Farmington CT 06032

MCCHESNEY, ROBERT MICHAEL, SR., political science educator; b. Effingham, Ill., Oct. 5, 1942; s. J.D. and Helen Grace (Russell) McC.; m. Laraine Freeman, Aug. 28, 1965; children: Robert M. Jr., Todd Patrick, Jennifer Laraine, Grant Russell, Brent Steven. BA, U. La., Lafayette, 1964; MA, U. Va., 1967, PhD, 1969. Asst. instr. U. Va., Charlottesville, 1967-68; chmn. dept. polit. sci. U. Ctrl. Ark., Conway, 1971-75, dean coll. scis. and humanities, 1976-82, v.p. for acad. affairs, 1982-89, disting. prof., 1989-90; provost U. Montevallo, Ala., 1990-92, pres., 1992—. V.p. Survey Rsch., Inc., Conway, 1989-92; spl. cons. U. Ark. System, Little Rock, 1989. Mem. Carmichael Found., Conway, 1975-79; exec. bd. Quapaw coun. Boy Scouts Am., Little Rock, 1982-88; Greater Ala. Area Coun., 1995—; chair Ala. Higher Edn. Partnership, Pres. Adv. Coun., 1999-2001. Capt. Med. Svc. Corps U.S. Army, 1968-71. Grantee State Justice Inst./Adminstrv. Office of Cts., Ark., 1989. Mem. Ala. Coun. Univ. and Coll. Pres. (chmn. 1993-95), So. Com. Colls. and Schs. (exec. coun. 1996-99), Birmingham C. of C., Montevall C. of C., Rotary (pres. Conway Club 1987-88, Paul Harris fellow 1986), Phi Beta Kappa, Phi Kappa Phi, Alpha Chi, Golden Key, Phi Alpha Theta, Phi Eta Sigma, Blue Key. Mem. Lds Ch. Avocations: hunting, fishing, golfing. Office: U Montevallo Station 6001 Montevallo AL 35115

MCCLAIN, ANGELA MARY, special education educator; b. Malone, NY, Aug. 3, 1967; d. William E. and Eleanor (Raville) McC.; m. Christopher Premo; children: Alexander Premo, Jenna Premo, Angela Mary Premo. AAS in Nursery Edn., Mater Dei Coll., Ogdensburg, NY, 1987; BS in Spl. Edn., SUNY, Plattsburgh, 1989, M in Spl. Edn., 1994. Spl. edn. tchr. preschool Franklin-Essex-Hamilton BOCES, Malone, 1989-96, Chateaugay Ctrl. Sch., NY, 1996—. Mem. Kappa Delta Pi. Office: Chateaugay Ctrl Sch River St Malone NY 12953 Home: 15569 State Route 30 Constable NY 12926-3707

MCCLAIN, CHARLES JAMES, educator; b. Ironton, Mo., Sept. 1, 1931; s. John F. and Hazel (Pierce) McC.; children: Anita, Melanie. BEd, S.W. Mo. State U., 1954; MEd, U. Mo., 1957, EdD, 1961; hon. degree, Busan Nat. U., Mo. Western State Coll., Kirksville Coll. Osteo. Medicine, Cen. Meth. Coll. Pres. Jefferson Coll., Hillsboro, Mo., 1963-70, N.E. Mo. State U., Kirksville, 1970-89; commr. higher edn. State of Mo., Jefferson City, 1989—95; monitor U.S. Dist. Ct. (we. dist.) Mo., 1997—; cons. U. SD. Panelist, presenter nat. and internat. edn. confs. Contbr. articles to profl. jours. Bd. dirs. United Meth. Found., Mo. Higher Edn. Loan Authority. Recipient Disting. Alumnus award S.W. Mo. State U., 1977, Disting. Svc. award U. Mo. Coll. Edn., G. Theodore Mitau award, 1983, Alumni award U. Mo.-Columbia, 1989; named Pub. Administr. of Yr. Mo. Inst. Pub. Adminstrn., 1986. Mem. Internat. Assn. Univ. Pres., Am. Assn. State Colls. and Univs., Am. Assn. Higher Edn. (bd. dirs.), Midwestern Higher Edn. Commn., Mo. Coun. Econ. Edn. (exec. com.), Mo. Acad. Sci. Home: 1201 Torrey Pines Dr Columbia MO 65203-4825

MCCLAIN, MARILYN RUSSELL, counselor; b. Laurelton, N.Y., Aug. 18, 1956; d. Russell H. and Lillian A. (Yarbrough) McClain; 1 child, Amy Lynne Roberts White. BS in Social Work, Harding U., 1977; MA in Adult Edn., Okla. State U., 1997. Career counselor Foothills Vo-Tech Sch., Searcy, Ark., 1977-78; social worker Dept. Social Svcs., Tulsa, 1978-79; owner, operator, instr. Spl. Deliveries Childbirth Preparation Ctr., Tulsa, 1980-85; mgr. One Hour Moto Photo, Tulsa, 1986-89; area mgr. Mervyn's, Tulsa, 1989-92; admissions counselor Rogers State U., Claremore, Okla., 1992-96, student counselor for health scis., 1996—. Primary advisor Adult Students Aspiring Prosper, Claremore, 1993—; pres. Rogers U. Staff Assn., 1995—97, mem. staff senate, 1995—, CASA adv., 1997—; parent educator Parenting Ptnrs., Claremore, 1994—95. Mem. Oologah PTA, 1990—97; sec. Oologah-Talala Sch. Found., 1994—95, pres., 1995—99, trustee, 1994—2001; mem. statue and hotel com. Rogers County Hist. Soc., Claremore, 1994—2002. Mem.: Am. Assn. Adult and Continuing Edn., Okla. Acad. Advising Assn., Sertoma. Republican. Baptist. Avocations: needlepoint, reading, piano. Home: 18021 Oaklawn Dr Claremore OK 74017-3681 Office: Rogers State Univ 1701 W Will Rogers Blvd Claremore OK 74017-3259 E-mail: mmcclain@rsu.edu.

MCCLAIN, PAULA DENICE, political scientist, educator; b. Louisville, Jan. 3, 1950; d. Robert Landis and Mabel (Molock) McC.; stepdau. of Annette Williams McClain; m. Paul C. Jacobson, Jan. 30, 1988; children: Kristina L., Jessica A. BA, Howard U., Washington, 1972; MA, Howard U., 1974, PhD, 1977; postgrad., U. Pa., 1981-82. Asst. prof. dept. polit. sci. U. Wis., Milw., 1977-82; assoc. prof. and prof. pub. affairs Ariz. State U., Tempe, 1982-91; prof. govt. and fgn. affairs U. Va., Charlottesville, 1991-2000, chair govt. and fgn. affairs, 1994-97; prof. dept. polit. sci. Duke

U., Durham, N.C., 2000—. Co-author: Can We All Get Along? Racial and Ethnic Minorities in American Politics, 1995, 3d edit. 2001, Race, Place and Risk: Black Homicide in Urban America, 1990; editor: Minority Group Influence, 1993; co-editor: Urban Minority Administrators, 1988. Mem. Nat. Conf. Black Polit. Scientists (pres. 1989-90), Am. Polit. Sci. Assn. (exec. coun. 1985-87, v.p. 1993-94), So. Polit. Sci. Assn. (exec. coun. 1992-95, v.p.-elect 2000-01), Internat. Polit. Sci. Assn. (exec. com. 1997-2003, v.p. 1997-2003), Midwest Polit. Sci. Assn. (v.p. 2002—). Office: Duke U Dept Polit Sci Perkins Libr PO Box 90204 Durham NC 27708-0204 E-mail: pmcclain@duke.edu.

MCCLAIN, SYLVIA NANCY (NANCY JO GRIMM), voice educator, vocalist; b. Worthington, Minn., July 16, 1943; d. Walter Deming and Naomi Leona (Deters) Grimm.; m. Joseph T. McClain (div. Feb. 1994); children: Raimund, Hermine. MusB with honors, Ind. U., 1966, MusM with honors, 1969; D of Musical Arts with commendation, U. Tex., Austin, 1989. Apprentice artist Santa Fe (N.Mex.) Opera, 1968-69; performing singer various concert and opera venues, Germany, 1970-78; asst. prof. dept. music Howard Payne U., Brownwood, Tex., 1980-82; asst. prof. voice dept. fine arts Southwestern U., Georgetown, Tex., 1986-91; assoc prof., chair voice dept. sch. music Hardin-Simmons U., Abilene, Tex., 1992-98; assoc. prof. music, coord. voice and opera U. Conn., Storrs, 1998—. Performer: (recital) Portraits of Women in Songs of Hugo Wolf. Vol. cons. Leadership of Edn. in Arts Professions, Austin, 1990-92, Austin Lyric Opera, 1983-92. Fulbright scholar, Stadtliche Hochschule für Musik, Stuttgart, Germany, 1969-70. Mem. Nat. Assn. Tchrs. of Singing, Phi Kappa Lambda, Mu Phi Epsilon. Avocations: exercise, reading, travel.

MCCLAIN, VEDA, education educator, department chairman; BA in English, Wesleyan U., 1979; MS in Edn., U. Ctrl. Ark., 1992; PhD in Reading Edn., U. Ga., 1997. Elem. sch. tchr., Little Rock; reading instr. Upward Bound Project U. Ga., Philander Smith Coll., Little Rock; tchg. asst., rsch. asst. Nat. Reading Rsch. Ctr. U. Ga., Athens; instr. dept. reading edn. Ark. State U., State University, asst. prof. reading, assoc. prof. reading edn., dir. Minority Tchr. Scholars Program, chair dept. edn., 2001—. Reviewer Reading Excellence Grants Ark. Dept. Edn. Mem.: Ark. Literacy Tchr. Educators, Ark. Reading Assn. (chair student membership com.), S.E. Literacy Consortium, Nat. Coun. Tchrs. English, Nat. Reading Conf., Internat. Reading Assn., S.W. Ednl. Lab. (bd. mem. 2003—). Office: Ark State Univ PO Box 2350 State University AR 72467*

MCCLANAHAN, LELAND, university director; b. Hammond, Ind., Mar. 14, 1931; s. Alonzo Leland and Eva (Hermanson) McC.; m. Lavaughn Adell Meyrer, June 5, 1954; children: Lindel, Loren. Diploma, Ctrl. Bible Coll., 1954; PhBB, Nat. Postgrad. Bible Acad., 1969; BA, Southwestern Coll., 1973; MA, Fla. State Christian Coll., 1964, ThD, 1970; PhD, Faith Bible Coll. and Sem., Ft. Lauderdale, Fla. and Marina, Lagos, Nigeria, 1969; MA, Bapt. Christian U., 1988; PhD, Freedom U., 1989; ThD, Bapt. Christian U., 1989, DLitt, 1990, PsyD, 1991; PhD, Hawaii U., 1995; DEd, Bapt. Christian U., 1992, D in Bus. Adminstrn., 1993; DD (hon.), Internat. Evangelism Crusades, 1969, Trinity Union Coll., 1991; LLD, La. Bapt. U., 1994; StD, PhD, Trinity Internat. U., 1994; HHD (hon.), La. Bapt. U., 1995; LittD (hon.), Cambridge Theol. Sem., 1995; PhD, LittD, PsyD, DBA, LLD, EdD, U. Hawaii, 1995; LittD(hon.), The Messianic Coll. of Rabbinical Studies; MA, Am. Bible Coll. & Sem., 1998; MDiv, Chapel Christian U., 1991; PhD, Midwestern U., 1998; D in Min., Am. Bible Coll. and Sem., 1999. Diplomate Nat. Bd. Christian Clin. Therapists; ordained pastor, Christian Ch., 1950; archbishop Hierarchical Christian Ch., 2000. Founder, pastor Evangel Temple, Griffith, Ind., 1954-73, Abundant Life Temple, Cocoa, Fla., 1974-77; mgr. ins. divsn. United Agys., Cocoa, Fla., 1979-81; assoc. pastor Merritt Assembly of God, Merritt Island, Fla., 1982-85, Palm Chapel, Merritt Island, 1987-89, 1990-93; founder Hawaii U., Merritt Island Offices, Merritt Island, Fla., 1990-97; chancellor Hawaii U. Merritt Island Offices, 1995-97; dir. Fla. Hawaii U. Schs., 1994-97; dir., founder Chapel Christian U., Merritt Island, Fla., 1990—; founder People's Ch. Internat., Inc., 2000—. Founder, dir. Griffith Youth Ctr., 1960-70, Todd Nursery Sch., Griffith, 1971-73; founder, chancellor Ind. Bible Coll., Griffith, 1971-73; dir. Chapel Counseling Ctr., Merritt Island, 1990-94; mem. national accreditation com. Hawaii U.; founder, pres. Brevard Humanity Ctr., Inc., 2002; founder Mini Job Link, 2002, Adult Edn., 2003. Author: Is Divine Healing For Today?, 1989, Truths From the Gospel of St. John, 1991, An Outline of the Revelation, 1993, Numbers in the Bible, 1994, An Outline of the Acts of the Apostle, 1995, An Outline of the Book of Proverbs, 2000; author 142 coll. courses and books. Recipient Disting. Svc. award U.S. Jaycees, 1966; named Hon. Lt. Col., Gov. Guy Hunt, 1988, Archbishop, Hierarchical Christ Ch., 2000. Fellow Am. Biog. Inst. (life); mem. Internat. Platform Assn., Order of Internat. Fellowship (life), Am. Inst. Clin. Psychotherapists, Am. Assn. christian Counselors, Nat. Christian Counseling Assn. (assoc., lic.), Internat. Assn. Pastoral Psychologists (lic.), Order of St. John, Knight of Malta (comdr. 1990). Republican. Avocations: reading, walking, watching sports, watching television adventures, weight lifting. Office: Chapel Christian Univ 870 Australian St Merritt Island FL 32953-4676 Office Fax: 321-453-0013.

MCCLARON, LOUISIANNA CLARDY, retired secondary school educator; b. Clarksville, Tenn., Dec. 12, 1929; d. Abe and Chinaster (Simpson) Clardy; m. Joe Thomas McClaron, July 17, 1965. BS, Tenn. State U., 1952; MA, Ohio State U., 1956; EdS, Tenn. State U., 1977; PhD, Vanderbilt U., 1981. Cert. secondary tchr., sch. adminstr., supr., Tenn. Tchr. Madison County Bd. Edn., Normal, Ala., 1952-58, Metro Nashville Bd. Edn., 1958-94; ret., 1994. Presenter workshops in field. Treas. Patterson Meml. United Meth. Ch., 1980. Mem.: NEA (ret.), Metro Nashville Ret. Tchrs. Assn., Tenn. Ret. Tchrs. Assn., Woodbine Cmty. Orgn. (sec.), Hadley Park Duplicate Bridge Club (past pres.), Les Nevvettes Social Club (past pres.), Alpha Delta Omega (housing treas. chpt. found.), Alpha Kappa Alpha, Delta Pi Epsilon (past pres.).

MCCLELLAN, EDWIN, Japanese literature educator; b. Kobe, Japan, Oct. 24, 1925; came to U.S., 1952; s. Andrew and Teru (Yokobori) McC.; m. Rachel Elizabeth Pott, May 28, 1955; children: Andrew Lockwood, Sarah Rose. MA, U. St. Andrews, Scotland, 1952; PhD, U. Chgo., 1957. Instr. English, U. Chgo., 1957-59, asst. prof. Japanese lang. and lit., 1959-63, assoc. prof., 1963-65, prof., 1965-70, Carl Darling Buck prof., 1970-72, chmn. dept. Far Eastern langs. and civilizations, 1966-72; prof. Japanese lit. Yale U., New Haven, 1972-79, Sumitomo prof. Japanese studies, 1979-98, Sterling prof. Japanese lit., 1998-2000, Sterling prof. emeritus Japanese lit., 2000—, chmn. dept. East Asian langs. and lits., 1973-82, 88-91, chmn. council humanities, 1975-77, chmn. council East Asian studies, 1979-82. Vis. lectr. Far Eastern langs. Harvard U., spring 1965; mem. adv. coun. dept. Oriental studies Princeton U., 1966-71; mem. Com. to Visit East Asian Studies, Harvard U., 1982-88; mem. Am. adv. com. Japan Found., 1985-95; mem. bd. Coun. for Internat. Exch. Scholars, 1981-84. Translator: Kokoro (Natsume Soseki), 1957, Grass on the Wayside (Soseki), 1969, A Dark Night's Passing (Naoya Shiga), 1976, Fragments of a Past (Eiji Yoshikawa), 1992; author: Two Japanese Novelists: Soseki and Toson, 1969, Woman in the Crested Kimono, 1985; mem. bd. editors Jour. Japanese Studies, 1986-99; contbr. articles to profl. jours. Liason intelligence officer Royal Air Force, Washington, 1945-47; bd. trustees Society Japanese Studies U. Wash., 1992-99. Served with Royal Air Force, 1944—48. Recipient Kikuchi Kan prize for contbn. to study of Japanese lit., Tokyo, 1994, Noma Lit. Translation prize, 1995, Order of the Rising Sun, Gold Rays with Neck Ribbon, Japanese Govt., 1998. Fellow Am. Acad. Arts and Scis. Home: 641 Ridge Rd Hamden CT 06517-2516

MCCLELLAN, THOMAS JAMES, math and science educator; b. Edsville, Miss., Mar. 14, 1944; s. Albert Lee and Jannie (Pempleton) McC.; m. Glorya Jean Cotten, May 3, 1975 (div. Apr. 1976); children: Kelly Tremayne, Terrie Lynn.; m. Joann Evelyn, June 11, 1978. BS in Biology, Chemistry, Miss. Valley State U., 1969; M of Math., Wayne State U., 1990; postgrad., Garrett Theol. Sem., 1991—. Tchr. Highland Park (Mich.) Pub. Schs., 1979-87; tchr. math., sci. Pontiac (Mich.) Pub. Sch. System, 1988—. Contbr. articles to profl. jours. Democrat. Baptist. Avocations: health, gourmet cooking, reading, tennis, basketball. Home: 26800 Shiawassee Rd Southfield MI 48034-3651 Office: Pontiac Ctrl High Sch 300 W Huron St Pontiac MI 48341-1420

MCCLELLAND, CRAIG ALEXANDER, architect, educator, business owner; b. Renton, Wash., Nov. 3, 1962; s. James Richard and Carol Anne (Hawkins) McC.; m. Kamilla Kuroda, June 25, 1989. BArch, U. Wash.; MArch, U. Ill. Lic. architect. Technician III, Wash. State Dept. Transportation, Seattle, 1985; project mgr. Van Horne and Van Horne, Seattle, 1986-87, Alexander Sasonoff, Seattle, 1989-91; arch. James and Scherer, Olympia, Wash., 1991-96; owner, arch. Alexander Archs., Olympia, 1996—2001; lectr., instr. South Sound C.C., Olympia, 1998—. Project arch. BJSS, Olympia, 1997—. Amb. Olympia C. of C., 1997, Shelton C. of C., 1997. Mem. AIA. Avocations: mountaineering, construction, reading, writing. Home and Office: 110 SE Eagles Nest Dr Shelton WA 98584-9261

MCCLELLAND, HELEN, music educator; b. Chgo., Dec. 5, 1951; d. Leon Leroy and Willie Jo (Darnell) McC.; (div. Sept. 1981); 1 child, Tasha Renee. Diploma in arts, Kennedy-King Coll., 1971; cert. in voice, Sherwood Music Coll., 1971-73; BS, Chgo. State U., 1975, MA in Adminstrn., 1983; D in Adminstrn. and Supervision, U. Calif., 1993. Tchr. Faulkner Sch., Chgo., 1975-78; tchr. music Harvey (Ill.) Pub. Sch. Dist. 152, 1978—. Dir. music Pleasant Green Missionary Bapt. Ch., Chgo., 1971—; mem. sch. bd. New World Christian Acad., Chgo., 1988—; bd. dirs. South Shore Drill Team, Chgo. Author: operetta So You Want to Be a Star, 1987. Cmty. worker People United to Save Humanity, Chgo., 1973, Harold Washington Orgn., Chgo., 1987; cmty. educator Chgo. Planned Parenthood, 1988; cmty. counselor Lincoln Cmty. Ctr., Chgo., 1975; mem. sch. bd. Dist. 160, 1994, now v.p.; mem. Ill. State Sch. Bd., 1997-98; bd. dirs. Operation P.U.S.H.; vice chmn. Ill. Assn. Sch. Bds., Ill. State Assn. Bd.; v.p. Sch. Dist. #160; ; mem. Grace M.B. Ch. Named Tchr. of the Yr., Faulkner Sch., 1976. Mem. Ill. Edn. Assn., NEA, Harvey Edn. Assn., Tennis Club, Traveling Club, Phi Delta Kappa, Pi Lambda Theta. Democrat. Baptist. Avocations: singing, bowling, piano. Home: 18029 Ravisloe Ter Country Club Hills IL 60478-5169

MCCLOSKEY, ANN FRANCES, elementary and secondary music educator; b. Jacksonville, Ill. d. Peter and frances Adorno Bonansinga; widowed; 1 child, William Peter. MusB, MacMurray Coll., 1930; MusM, Chgo. Mus. Coll., 1942. Music tchr. Pittsfield (Ill.) Pub. Schs., 1930-34, San Marino (Calif.) Schs., 1938; mem. voice tchg. faculty MacMurray Coll., Jacksonville, 1942-48, Thornton Jr. Coll., Harvey, Ill., 1965-73, Everett Dirksen Jr. H.S., Calumet City, Ill., 1965-73; pvt. voice and piano tchr. Lyon & Healy, Chgo., 1974-82. Concert mezzo soprano. Named Disting. Alumna, MacMurray Coll., 1995. Mem. Irving Music Tchrs., Nat. Music Tchrs. Home: 4137 Portland St Irving TX 75062-2953

MCCLOUD, ANECE FAISON, academic administrator; b. Dudley, N.C., May 29, 1937; d. J.D. Faison and Nancy Jane (Simmons) Faison-Cole; m. Verable Lancaster McCloud, June 1, 1959; children: Aja Siobhan, Carla Danette. BS, Bennette Coll., Greensboro, N.C., 1959; MA, U. Nebr., Omaha, 1989; Basic Mediations Skills, Ea. Mennonite Coll., 1994. Tchr. Lincoln Jr. High Sch., Greensboro, N.C., 1959-60, Woodbridge Airforce Base (Eng.), 1961-62; resident advisor and ednl. coord. Child Saving Inst., Omaha, 1967-71; asst. registrar for acad. records U. Nebr. Med. Ctr., Omaha, 1972-76, first dir. minority student affairs, 1976-85; assoc. dean of students Washington and Lee U., Lexington, Va., 1985—. Cons. Deans Forum on Revitalizing Health Profl. Edn., Dept. of Health and Human Svcs., 1985, Campus Alcohol Initiative, N.C. Gov.'s Inst. Alcohol and Substance Abuse, 1999—, Peer Rev., Health Careet Opportunity Program, 1982, 1984; cons. on simulated minority admissions Assn. Am. Med. Colls., Washington, 1979. Bd. mem., v.p. Rockbridge Area Housing Corp., Lexington, 1988-95; mem. Va. adv. com. U.S. Commn. on Civil Rights, 1995—; mem. Va. Identification Program for Advancement of Women in Higher Edn., 1995-96; treas. Mayor's Commn. on Status of Women, Omaha, 1977-78. Recipient Plaque for Outstanding Svc. to Washington and Lee Cmty., 1994, Cert. Acknowledgement of Contbn. to Edn., Omaha Pub. Schs., 1984, Cert. Black History Month Spkr., VA Hosp., Omaha, 1983, Vol. Program award Girls Club of Omaha, 1977; grantee Health Career Opportunity, Disadvantaged Assistance Office, Dept. Health and Human Svcs., 1976, 80, 83. Mem. Am. Assn. for Higher Edn., Nat. Assn. For Women in Edn., Am. Coll. Personnel Assn., Assn. of Am. Med. Colls., Am. Assn. of Counseling and Devel., Nebr. Assn. for Non-White Concerns (past sec.), Nebr. Assn. of Collegiate Registrars and Admissions Officers (chairperson sub.-com. on minority affairs 1978-89), Nat. Assn. of Med. Minority Educators (vice coord. 1982-83). Democrat. Avocations: social research, writing, interior decorating. Office: Washington & Lee U Payne Hall 3 Lexington VA 24450

MCCLUNG, KENNETH AUSTIN, JR., training executive, performance consultant; b. Decatur, Ga., Apr. 11, 1947; s. Kenneth Austin Sr. and Marianne (Conklin) McC.; m. Christina June Palensar, Mar. 21, 1975. BA, North Ga. Coll., 1969; MS, EdD, U. So. Calif., 1976. Commd. 2d lt. U.S. Army, 1969, advanced through grades to maj., 1980; col. USAR; sr. ptnr. Instrl. Design Group, Inc., Morristown, N.J., 1981-99; v.p., nat. learning dir. Jack Morton Worldwide, 1999-2000, nat. learning dir., 2000—02; ptnr. McClung, McClung & Assoc., Hertford, NC, 2002—. Bd. dirs. Nat. Productivity Ctr., Boulder, Colo., Price Waterhouse Learning Bd.; author/mgr. over 150 mgmt., sales, and tech. tng. programs; cons. in field. Author: Microcomputers for Medical Professionals, 1984, Microcomputers for Legal Professionals, 1984, Microcomputers for Investment Professionals, 1984, Microcomputers for Insurance Professionals, 1984, Personal Computers for Executives, 1984, French edit. 1985; co-author: Sales Training Handbook, 1989. Mem. ASTD, Internat. Soc. for Performance Improvement (pres. N.J. chpt. 1986-88, N.E. regional cons. 1989-90, nat. nomination chmn. 1990-91, nat. emerging tech. chmn. 1991-92). Avocations: sailing, tennis, bicycling, running, skiing. Home: 128 Back Creek Dr Hertford NC 27944 Office: McClung McClung & Assoc 128 Back Creek Dr Hertford NC 27944

MCCLURE, JULIE ANNE, literature educator; b. Naperville, Ill., Mar. 9, 1967; d. Paul Robert and Linda Kay (Schlytter) McClure. BS in English, No. Ariz. U., 1989; AA in Paralegal Studies, Am. Inst., Phoenix, Ariz., 1991. Cert. tchr. Ill., Ariz. Paralegal/payroll profl. Corp. Personnel Svcs., Phoenix, 1992—92; paralegal Robert A. Kelley Jr. & Assocs., Scottsdale, Ariz., 1993—94; English educator Long Wood Acad., Chgo., 1998—99; corp. sec. MacWilliams Corp., Benton Harbor, Mich., 1993—; English educator Maria H.S., Chgo., 1999—. Office: Regina Dominican High Sch 701 Locust Rd Wilmette IL 60091-2298

MCCLURE, MICHAEL CRAIG, secondary education administrator; b. Rosebud, Tex., Aug. 27, 1955; s. Charles Edison and Eunice (Mock) McC. BA in Biology, Tex. A&M U., 1977; MEd in Secondary Edn., Sam Houston State U., Huntsville, Tex., 1983; postgrad., U. Houston, 1993. Tchr. sci. Spring (Tex.) H.S., 1978—2002, chmn. dept. sci., 1982—2003. Workshop cons. Spring Ind. Sch. Dist., 1989—. Author curriculum guides. Named Tchr. of Yr., Spring H.S., 1983, 92; Tandy Tech. scholar, 1993. Mem. Nat. Sci. Tchrs. Assn., Assoc. Chemistry Tchrs. of Tex., Sci. Tchrs. Assn. Tex., Tex. Tchrs. Phys. Sci., Met. Houston Chemistry Tchrs. Assn., Century Club of Tex. A&M Former Students Assn., 12th Man Found. of Tex. A&M. Avocations: golf, music. Home: 22547 August Leaf Dr Tomball TX 77375-5440 Office: Spring HS 19428 I H 45 Spring TX 77373-2910 E-mail: mcmcclure@aol.com., craigm@springisd.org.

MCCLURE, MICHAEL JAY, secondary education educator; b. Van Wert, Ohio, Nov. 29, 1960; s. Roger Dean and Rosalie Ann (Elston) McC.; m. Heidi Ruth Field, July 16, 1983; children: Brian Michael, Rachel Elise. BS in Edn./Journalism, Bowling Green State U., 1983; MA in Ednl. Tech., Kent State U., 1988. Cert. tchr., Ohio. Tchr. journalism Roosevelt High Sch., Kent, Ohio, 1983—. Asst. to drama dir. Theodore Roosevelt High Sch., 1985-87; continuity writer TV Channel 57, Bowling Green, Ohio, 1982-83; presenter and cons. in field. Recipient First Pl. Yearbook awards Nat. Scholastic Press Assn., 1988—. Mem. Josten's Nat. Yearbook Adv. Bd. (charter). Republican. Avocations: desktop publishing, photography. Home: 600 Woodside Dr Kent OH 44240-2664 Office: Roosevelt High Sch 1400 N Mantua St Kent OH 44240-2380

MCCLURE, VERONICA ANN, elementary education educator; b. Muskogee, Okla., Mar. 3, 1952; d. Raymond Frederick and Veronica Alexina (Gillis) McGee; m. Gary Jerome McClure Sr., Dec. 26, 1971; children: Gary J., Bruce, Jeremy. BS in Edn., Northeastern State U., 1976, MEd in Counseling, 1978. Sch. counselor Cherokee Elem., Tahlequah, Okla., 1978-82; tchr. Greenwood Elem., Tahlequah, 1982-92; tchr., chairperson lang. arts dept. Ctrl. Elem., Tahlequah, 1993—; SOS sch. counselor Tahlequah Jr. H.S., 1996—; counselor Henderson (Tex.) H.S. Gesell test adminstr. Tahlequah (Okla.) Pub. Schs., 1980-94; educator Indian edn. J.O.M. Summer Sch., Tahlequah, 1987-94. Aide to Edn. grantee Elks Lodge, Tahlequah, 1991-94. Mem. NEA, Okla. Edn. Assn. Home: 1 Plz S PMB 175 Tahlequah OK 74465-0432 E-mail: mcclurer@tahlequah.k12.ok.us.

MCCOLLUM, SUSAN, elementary school educator; Grad., Butler County C.C.; BA in Edn., Emporia State U., 1974, MA in Edn., 1979. Nat. bd. cert. tchr. 1998. Tchr. Santa Fe Trail Sch. Dist., Carbondale (Kans.) Sch. Named Disting. Alumni, Emporia State U., 2002. Mem.: NEA, Nat. Bd. for Cert. Tchrs. in Kans. (state chair 2003—), Nat. Bd. for Profl. Tchg. Stds. (bd. mem. 2002—). Office: Carbondale Attendance Ctr 315 N 4th Carbondale KS 66414*

MCCOMAS, MARCELLA LAIGNE, marketing educator; b. Reno, Nev., Dec. 29, 1942; d. Quincy Alfred and Hazel Mae (Durham) McC.; m. Danny Paul Norwood, Nov. 24, 1990. BS in Mktg., San Jose (Calif.) State U., 1964, MA, 1966; MEd, Colo. State U., 1971; EdD, Auburn (Ala.) U., 1978. Chpt. advisor Earl Wooster Sr. HIgh Sch., 1966-75; dir. mass merchandising ctr. Auburn U., 1976-78; state advisor Ala. State Dept. of Edn., 1978-84, dist. specialist, 1981-84; collegiate advisor U. Houston, 1984—, state collegiate advisor, 1985—, assoc. prof. consumer sci. mdsg., 1988—. Contbr. articles to profl. jours. Mem. ASCD, DECA, Assn. Career & Tech. Edn. (pres. mktg. edn. divsn., 2002—), Mktg. Educators Tex., Nat. Bus. Edn. Assn. Baptist. Avocations: computer technology, reading, gardening, pets. Home: 1901 Coronado St Friendswood TX 77546-5906 Office: U Houston Coll of Technology Hdcs Houston TX 77204-6020

MCCONNELL, HARDEN MARSDEN, biophysical chemistry researcher, chemistry educator; b. Richmond, Va., July 18, 1927; s. Harry Raymond and Frances (Coffee) McConnell; m. Sophia Milo Glogovac, Oct. 6, 1956; children: Hunter, Trevor, Jane. BS, George Washington U., 1947; PhD, Calif. Inst. Tech., 1951; DSc (hon.) (hon.), U. Chgo., 1991, George Washington U., 1993. NRC fellow dept. physics U. Chgo., 1950—52; research chemist Shell Devel. Co., Emeryville, Calif., 1952—56; asst. prof. chemistry Calif. Inst. Tech., 1956—58, prof. chemistry and physics, 1963—64; prof. chemistry Stanford U., Calif., 1964—79, Robert Eckles prof. chemistry, 1979—, chmn. dept., 1989—2000, chmn. emeritus, 2000; founder Molecular Devices Corp., 1983—. Cons. in field. Contbr. Pres. Found. for Basic Rsch. in Chemistry, 1990—96; hon. assoc. Neurosci. Rsch. Program. Named Sherman Fairchild Disting. scholar, 1988; recipient Calif. sect. award, Am. Chem. Soc., 1961, award in pure chemistry, 1962, Harrison Howe award, 1968, Irving Langmuir award in chem. physics, 1971, Pauling medal, Puget Sound and Oreg. sects., 1987, Peter Debye award in phys. chemistry, 1990, Am. Achievement award, George Washington U., 1971, Disting. Alumni award, Calif. Inst. Tech., 1982, Dickson prize for sci., Carnegie-Mellon U., 1982, Wolf prize in chemistry, 1984, ISCO award, 1984, Wheland medal, U. Chgo., 1988, Nat. Medal Sci., 1989, Brucker prize, 1995, Gold medal, Internat. ESR Soc., Zavoisky award, 2000. Fellow: AAAS, Biophys. Soc.; mem.: NAS ((award in chem. scis. 1988), Serbian Acad. Scis. and Arts (fgn. mem.), Am. Chem. Soc (award in Surface Chemistry 1997, Welch award in Chemistry 2002), Am. Soc. Biol. Chemists, Am. Acad. Arts and Scis., Am. Phys. Soc., Internat. Acad. Quantum Molecular Scis. Achievements include patents in field. Office: Stanford U Dept Chemistry Stanford CA 94305

MCCONNELL, JEFFREY JOSEPH, computer science educator, researcher; b. Buffalo, Jan. 7, 1960; BA, Canisius Coll., 1981; MS, SUNY, Buffalo, 1986; PhD, WPI, 1989. Software engr. SCIPAR, Inc., Williamsville, N.Y., 1981-83; asst. prof. Canisius Coll., Buffalo, 1983-91, assoc. prof., 1991-96, dept. chair, 1990—, prof., 1996—. Program evaluator Computing Scis. Accreditation Commn./Computer Sci. Accreditation Bd., Stamford, Conn., 1992—; women's studies com. Canisius Coll., Buffalo, 1992—, co-chair Mid. States Accreditation Self-Study Programs, 1993-94; featured spkr. George Washington U. Tchg. Ctr., 1997; luncheon spkr. Rochester Inst. Tech. Insights, 1998. Robert H. Goddard fellow Worcester (Mass.) Poly. Inst., 1987; recipient award Computer Sci. Instrumentation Program, NSF, 1986, Dr. I. Joan Lorch Women's Studies award, 1993. Mem. Assn. Computing Machinery, Spl. Interest Group on Computer Sci. Edn., Eurographics. Office: Canisius Coll 2001 Main St Buffalo NY 14208-1035

MCCONNER, STANLEY JAY, SR., school system administrator; b. Detroit, Dec. 7, 1929; s. Walter Richard and Norma Louise (Hafford) McC.; m. Peggy Miller, June 1951(div.); children: Michele Jay, Stanley Jay; m. Dorothy Hamilton, Apr. 5, 1974. BS in Spl. Edn., Ea. Mich. U., 1953; MS in Reading, U. Conn., 1956; MS in Psychology, Cen. Conn. State U., 1967; PhD in Adminstrn., U. Sarasota, 1973; PhD in Adminstrn. and Policy Studies, Northwestern U., 1986. Tchr. Hartford (Conn.) Pub. Schs., 1953-67; asst. prof., asst. dir. U. Conn., Storrs, 1967-70; exec. dir. Balt. Pub. Schs., 1970-74; dean arts and scis. Kennedy, King Coll., Chgo., 1974-76; dean continuing edn. Chgo. State U., 1976-77, exec. dir. found., 1977-85; asst. prin. Pritzker-Grinker Sch., Chgo., 1985-86; coord. Body Awareness Resource Network Chgo. Health Info. Ctr., 1986-91; staff devel.-reading specialist African Am. studies dept. African Am. Studies Dept. Tucson Unified Sch. Dist., 1991—. Author: Famous Black Americans, 1972, Senate Bill 730: A Report Card, 1985, Techniques for Improving Performance in School. Bd. dirs. Girl Scouts U.S., Chgo., 1983, Roseland Community Hosp., Chgo., 1986; mem. Chgo. Urban League, Operation People United to Save Humanity, Chgo., Planned Giving Roundtable, Chgo., 1982-86. Named Community Ambassador-Norway Hartford Conn. Bus. Group, 1958; fellow Nat. Counselor Educator, Washington 1976; recipient achievement award, Nat. Assn. Pub. Continuing Adult Edn., Washington 1978; named to Hall of Fame Ea. Mich. U.,1988. Mem. Nat. Soc. Fundraising Execs., Chgo., 1982-86, Chgo. Urban League, 1988—, Operation PUSH, Chgo. 1988—, Phi Delta Kappa, Storrs, Conn., Am. Ednl. Research Assoc., Kiwanis of Chgo. Democrat. Episcopalian. Avocations: running, reading, cooking.

MCCORD, GLORIA DAWN HARMON, music educator, choral director, organist; b. Jacksonville, Fla., June 14, 1949; d. Earl H. and C. Grace (Lupo) Harmon; m. Mark L. McCord, Sr., Aug. 7, 1971; children: M. Lance, Ian H. BMus in Edn., Fla. State U.; MMus in Choral Conducting, La. State U.; DMA in Music Edn., U. Ga. Cert. tchr., Ga. Classroom music tchr. Nassau County (Fla.) Bd. Edn., 1971, Orange County (Fla.) Bd. Edn., 1971-74; choral dir., gen. music tchr. Fulton County (Ga.) Bd. Edn., 1974-75; dir. music Aldersgate United Meth. Ch., Slidell, La., 1978-86; tchr. for gifted and talented in music St. Tammany Parish Schs., La., 1988-91; asst. prof. arts and scis. Brenau U., Gainesville, Ga., 1991—99; registrar, pub. rels. dir., choral dir. Firespark Summer Sch. for Students Gifted in Arts, 1992—99; organist Riverside Mil. Acad., 1994—97; choral conductor, asst. dir. Kaleidoscope Sch. for Students Gifted in the Arts, 2002—. Presenter, adjudicator North Gwinnett Piano club, 1992, North Gwinnett Federated Festival, 1993, 95-2003, Ga. Music Educators Edn. Piano Festival, 1993; adjucator SC State Piano Concerto Competition, 2000, Ala. State Piano Competition, 2003; choir dir. Ga. Music Educators Dist. IX Honor Choir, 1993, others; series dir. radio broacast Panorama; adjudicator West Gwinnett Fed. Piano, 1995. Interim organist 1st United Meth. Chancel Choir, 1993, other positions; evaluator United Meth. Ch.; sec. Gainesville H.S. Band Boosters, Gainesville H.S. PTA, 1992-94. Recipient Lake Como (Orange county, Fla.) NEA Tchr. of the Yr., 1973, MENC Collegiate Chpt. Growth award, 1991-96, Gene M. Simons Meml. Fellowship award for Excellence in Music Edn., Choral, 2003. Mem. Am. Choral Dirs. Assn. (repertoire and standards chair), Pres. Assn. of Musicians, Coll. Music Soc., Am. Guild of Organists (chpt. sec. 2001-02, editor 2001—), Music Educators Nat. Assn (seminar facilitator 1993), Music Tchrs. Nat. Assn., Ga. Music Tchrs. Assn. (piano coord. of in-state spring auditions, 2002-), Ga. Music Educators (piano coord. in-state spring auditions 2002—), Sigma Alpha Iota, Pi Kappa Lambda (Beta Tau, 2002), Phi Kappa Phi. Office: Brenau Univ 1 Centennial Cir Gainesville GA 30501-3697

MCCORD, JEAN ELLEN, secondary art educator, coach; b. Ilion, NY, Oct. 20, 1952; d. Harold Shepard and Marian Alice (Bernier) Shepard; m. Colin McCord, May 10, 1977 (div. Sept. 1993). AA, Mohawk Valley C.C., Utica, N.Y., 1972; BA, SUNY, New Paltz, 1975, postgrad., 1976-77; student, Coll. Santa Reparata Sch. Art, Florence, Italy, 2001. Cert. art educator, N.Y. Jr. kindergarten tchr. Norfolk (Va.) Naval Base, 1978-79; jr. kindergarten and art tchr. Sunnybrook Day Sch., Virginia Beach, Va., 1979-81; tchr. art Fisher Elem. Sch., Mohawk, N.y., 1982-84, Mechanicstown Sch., Middletown, N.Y., 1984-88, Middletown (N.Y.) Start Ctr., 1986-87, tchr. synergetic edn., Middletown Tchr. Ctr., 1986-87; pvt. portfolio tutor Middletown, 1989-91; tchr. art Middletown Elem. Summer Sch., 1989—, Middletown H.S., 1987-97; tchr. Maple Hill Elem., 1997—. Sec. of policy and exec. bds. Middletown Tchr. Ctr., 1988-91, chmn. policy and exec. bds., 1991-92; com. mem. Bicentennial of Edn.; advisor Nat. Art Honor Soc., 1989-97; coord. After Sch. Program for Youth at Risk, 1995—, tchr., 1992-94; internat. com. for comm. Cambridge U., 2001. Actress, vocalist, designer in regional theatre, 1970—; artistic designer sch. plays and Creative Theatre Group; writer, dir. for local cabarets and charities; local muralist and portraitist, 1990—; set designer (off broadway) in N.Y.C. incl. Mother Posture, Seedless Grapes, The Pelican, New Village Prodns. benefit for AIDS, marquee 1st Theatre Mus. Village, Monroe, N.Y.; performer for Cancer Soc. fundraiser, 1997; producer, dir. Follies/Toys for Tots Campaign, 1997; performer for John Brigham Meml. Scholarship fundraiser, Ruthie Dino Marshall fundraiser, others; exhibited in shows in Lisbon, Portugal, 2001, Paramount Theatre, Middletown, N.Y., Cambridge, Eng., 2001, Vancouver, B.C., Can., 2002; executed mural M.H.S., Middletown, NY, 2001; set designer, Dracula, 2003. County svc. coord. Orange County Youth-In-Govt. (adv. 1988-91), Goshen, NY, 1991-93; Odyssey of the Mind Coach, 1984-92; chair edn. and cultural sem., Lisbon, Portugal, 1999; chair edn. and culture comm., Vancouver, Can.; art and music comm., Vancouver, Can.; chmn., internat. comms. com. Internat. Edn. Culture Com.; mem. Internat. Art and Music Com., Vancouver, 2002. Named for outstanding set design Times Herald Record, 1994; honored by Bd. Edn. Outstanding Educator, 1992, Apple award, 1999; named in S.W. Arts Mag., 2001, named Educator Yr. Am. Biog.Inst., 2003. Mem. Marine Corps League (hon.), NJROTC (hon. cadet 1997, Outstanding Contbn. to Arts award, Millenium Medal of Honor, 2000), Am. Biographical Inst. (chmn. ednl. culture com., 1999, mem. comms. com., chmn. edn. and culture com., 2002, mem. art and music com., 2002, mem. multicultural com., 2002), World Peace Diplomacy Forum. Episcopalian. Avocations: theatrical design, singing, calligraphy. Home: PO Box 4429 Middletown NY 10941-8429 Office: Middletown City Schs Wisner Ave Middletown NY 10940

MCCORD, SCOTT ANTHONY, chemistry educator; b. Orlando, Fla., Sept. 15, 1956; s. Randolph John and Genevieve (Sbordone) M. BA in Limnology and Music Edn., U. Ctrl. Fla., 1980; MME, Ind. U., 1982; EdD in Sci. Edn., U. Ctrl. Fla., 1995. Cert. tchr., Fla. Lab./field chemist U. Ctrl. Fla., Orlando, 1977-79; instr. chemistry Titusville (Fla.) High Sch., 1983—. Mem. lab. safety com. Brevard County (Fla.) Schs., 1989, chmn., 1991; cons. Space Port Fla. Authority, Cocoa, 1992, co-prin. investigator, 1992; sci. rsch. supr. Bionetics Corp., Kennedy Space Ctr., Fla., 1992; chemistry specialist Lockheed Space Ops., Kennedy Space Ctr., 1993; chmn. Brevard County Clash of Titans Sci. Acad. Competition, 1994, master of ceremonies, 1995; sci. and music adjudicator Nat. Excellence in Acads. Competition, Orlando, 1994. Co-author, editor: Brevard County Laboratory Safety Manual, 1991. Honorary liaison officer USAF Acad., Colorado Springs, 1986—. Named Outstanding Chemistry Tchr. Am. Chem. Soc., 1986-94; recipient various outstanding sci. rsch. teaching awards from industry and cmty. including NASA, Harris and Lockheed Martin Corps. Achievements include development of computer model program which simulates thermodynamic changes in neurons which undergo plasticity changes during learning. Home: 1720 Yorktown Ave Titusville FL 32796-4204 Office: Titusville High Sch 150 Terrier Trl Titusville FL 32780

MCCORMACK, GRACE, retired microbiology educator; b. Rochester, N.Y., Feb. 16, 1908; d. Walter and Maud (Brimacomb) McC. AB, U. Rochester, 1941; MS, U. Md., 1951. Technician U. Rochester Sch. Medicine and Dentistry and Atomic Energy, 1942-48; bacteriologist Dept. Interior U.S. Fish and Wildlife Svc., Coll. Park, East Boston, 1948-53, Md. State Dept. Health, Balt., 1953-55, VA Hosp., Canandaigua, N.Y., 1955-66; asst. to assoc. to microbiology prof. Monroe Community Coll., Rochester, N.Y., 1966-77; prof. Community Coll. of the Finger Lakes, Canandaigua, 1982-86, 88. Fellow Am. Inst. of Chems., Am. Biog. Inst. (hon. mem. rsch. bd. of advisors 1987—, Outstanding Educator of Yr. 1987), Royal Soc. of Health (Eng.), Intercontinental Biog. Assn. (Eng.); mem. Am. Soc. Microbiologists, N.Y. State Pub. Health Assn., Am. Inst. of Food Technologists, Nat. Found. of Infectious Diseases. Avocations: travel, reading. Home: 2001 Clinton Ave S Apt D101 Rochester NY 14618-5707

MCCORMACK, MARJORIE GUTH, psychology educator, career counselor, communications educator, public relations consultant; b. Jersey City; d. Joseph and Vera Guth; m. Kevin T. McCormack, 1961. BA, St. Peter's Coll., 1974; MA, Jersey City State Coll., 1990. Editor AT&T, N.Y.C., 1952-60, libr., 1960-67, St. Peter's Coll., 1967-71; pub. rels. mgr. Blue Cross of N.J., Newark, 1971-81; instr. history, econs. St. Aloysius H.S., Jersey City, 1981-82; pub. rels. cons. Creative Pub. Rels. Assocs., Queensbury, N.Y., 1981—; prof. psychology Hudson County C.C., 1995-97. Adj. instr. comm. St. Peter's Coll., 1982-88; copy editor Glens Falls, (N.Y.) Post-Star, 1986; dir. career placement Hudson County C.C., 1988-91. Bd. mgrs. Am. Cancer Soc., Jersey City, 1978-79; mem., sec. parish coun. St. Aloysius Ch., 1981-85; mem. Jersey City Tenants Orgn., 1981-98, Rent Leveling Bd. Jersey City, 1983-86, St. Peter's Coll. Cmty. Chorus, 1988-94; 2d v.p., pub. rels. chair Sodality of the Children of Mary of St. Teresa, 1993-95. Mem. AAUP, AAUW, NAFE (pub. rels. chmn. 1980-82), Mid Atlantic Career Counselors Assn., N.J. Assn. Counseling and Devel., N.J. Edn. Assn., Jersey City Bus. and Profl. Women's Assn. (legis. chmn. 1975-77, Nat. program award 1976, State Press award 1982), Hudson County Women's Network. Avocations: music, theatre, gourmet cooking.

MCCORMICK, DAVID JAMES, English language educator; b. Johnstown, Pa., Mar. 16, 1931; s. Clarence T. and Helen Marie (James) McC.; m. Darlene Louise Hengstenberg, Apr. 16, 1957; children: Jonathan, Jill, Christopher. BA, Alfred (N.Y.) U., 1953, MA, 1954. Cert. in secondary English, history and supervision, Pa. Prof. English Anatolia Coll., Salonika, Greece, 1957-58; tchr. secondary English Westmont Hilltop Sr. H.S., Johnstown, Pa., 1954-57, 58-62; assoc. prof. U. Pitts. at Johnstown, 1962-63; tchr. secondary English Franklin Regional Schs., Murrysville, Pa., 1963-92; supr. student tchrs. U. Pitts. and Chatham Coll., Pitts., 1992—. Chair Pub. Libr. Bd., Murrysville, 1969; pres. Franklin Regional PTA, Murrysville, 1966. NEH grantee, 1985, 86, 87, 88, 89, 90. Mem. NEA, Nat. Coun. Tchrs. English, Pa. State Edn. Assn., Franklin Regional Edn. Assn. Republican. Christian. Avocations: reading, football officiating, gardening, woodworking, family activities. Home: 3664 Hills Church Rd Export PA 15632-9371 Office: U Pitts Sch Edn Dept Instrn/Lng 4K25 Forbes Quadrangle Pittsburgh PA 15260

MCCORMICK, JAMES HAROLD, academic administrator; b. Indiana, Pa., Nov. 11, 1938; s. Harold Clark and Mary Blanche (Truby) McCormick; m. Maryan Kough Garner, June 7, 1963; children: David Harold, Douglas Paul. BS, Indiana U. of Pa., 1959; MEd, U. Pitts., 1961, EdD, 1963, postdoctoral, 1966, Columbia U., U. Mich., 1966-67, Harvard U., 1982. Tchr. Punxsutawney (Pa.) Area Joint Sch. Dist., 1959-61; adminstr. Baldwin-Whitehall Schs., Pitts., 1961-64; grad. asst. U. Pitts., 1962-63; asst. supt. instrn. Washington (Pa.) City Schs., 1964-65; prof. dept. edn. and psychology, asst. dean acad. affairs, acting dean acad. affairs, acting dean tchr. edn., asst. to pres., v.p. adminstrn. and fin. Shippensburg (Pa.) U., 1965-73; pres. Bloomsburg (Pa.) U., 1973-83, pres. emeritus, 1983—; chancellor Pa. State System Higher Edn., Harrisburg, 1983—2001, Minn. State Colls. and Univs., 2001—. Falk intern in politics, 1959; mem. adv. bd. Pa. Ednl. Policy Seminar; mem. Gov.'s Econ. Devel. Partnership Bd.; mem. higher edn. adv. coun. pa. State Bd. Edn.; past commr. Edn. Commn. of the States. Contbr. articles profl. jours. Named One of 10 Outstanding Young Men of Yr., Pa. Jr. C. of C.; recipient Young Leader in Edn. award Phi Delta Kappa, 1981, Disting. Alumnus award Indiana U. Pa., 1981, Outstanding Alumni award Bloomsburg U., 1984, Outstanding Alumnus award U. Pitts., 1985, Adler award Pa. Edn. assn., 1992; selected CIVITAS Prague mission, 1995, Presdl. Lectures, Kuwait U., 1993, Svc. Awd., Coll. and Univ. Pub. Rels., Assn. of PA (CUPRAP), 1999, Distig. Svc. Awd., PA Assn. of Councs. of Trustees (PACT), 1998, Alumni Assn. Leadership Awd., Bloomsburg Univ. PA, 1999.; McCormick Human Svcs. Ctr. named in his honor Bloomberg U., 1983; McCormick Ho. named in his honor Dixon U., 1994. Mem. Am. Assn. State Colls. and Univs. (Pa. state rep. 1988-93, former chmn. acad. and student pers. com., mem. com. on state rels. and task force on ednl. equity, chmn. policies and purposes com. 1996), Am. Coun. on Edn. (commn. on women in higher edn.), Nat. Assn. Sys. Heads, (exec. com., past pres.), Commn. State Colls. and Univs. (mem. and past chmn. govt. rels. and student rels. coms.), Assn. Governing Bds. (adv. coun.), Am. Assn. for Affirmative Action, Am. Assn. Higher Edn., Am. Assn. Sch. Adminstrs., Am. Assn. Univ. Adminstrs. (Tosney Leadership award 1993), Pa. Assn. Colls. and Univs. (bd. dirs., chair 1982), Natl. Ctr. for the Study of Sport in Soc., Pa. Black Conf. on Higher Edn., State Higher Edn. Ofcrs. (SHEEO), exec. com., fed. rels. liaison, Pers. Assn., Bloomsburg Area C. of C. (pres. 1983), Rotary (bd. dirs. through 1992), Phi Delta Kappa. Office: 500 Wells Fargo Pl 30 East 7th St Saint Paul MN 55101 Home: 2817 Oakwood Dr Harrisburg PA 17110-3903*

MCCORMICK, LINDA YANCEY, elementary education educator; b. Harrisonburg, Va., Sept. 7, 1965; d. Edward Custer and Margaret Joan (Caldwell) Yancey; m. James Coelman McCormick, Jr., Mar. 2, 1991; 1 child, Sarah Grace. BA in Polit. Sci., Hollins Coll., 1987; MEd, James Madison Univ., 1992. Tchr. Rockingham County Schs., Harrisonburg, 1987-88; tchr., instrnl. team leader Harrisonburg City Pub. Schs., 1988—, mem. early childhood adv. com., 1994. Adv. com. early childhood adv. com. Harrisonburg City Pub. Schs., 1994. Exec. bd. dirs. Big Bros./Big Sisters, Harrisonburg, 1991—; mem. Harrisonburg Rockingham Hist. Soc., 1994; exec. bd. dirs. Spotswood Elem. PTA, 1994-95, tchr. liason. Mem. DAR. Baptist. Avocation: geneological research. Home: 37 Paul St Harrisonburg VA 22801-4032

MCCORMICK, MICHAEL, history educator; b. Tonawanda, N.Y., Nov. 7, 1951; s. Jerome Anthony and Barbara Ann (Bowman) Mc.; m. Magda Jabbour, May 21, 1988; children: Thomas Kennedy III, Elena Sylvie. Grad., Cath. U. Louvain, Belgium, 1971, diploma in Medieval History, 1972, PhD, 1979. Rsch. assoc. Dictionary Medieval Latin Belgian Nat. Com., Louvain, 1976-79; rsch. assoc. Byzantine studies Dumbarton Oaks, Washington, 1979-87; from asst. prof. to prof. dept. history Johns Hopkins U., Balt., 1979-91; Goelet prof. medieval history Harvard U., Cambridge, Mass., 1991—. Author: Les Annales du haut Moyen âge, 1975, Index Scriptorum Operumque Latino-Belgicorum Medii aevi, XIIe siecle, 1977, vol. 2, 1979, Eternal Victory, Triumphal Rulership in Late Antiquity Byzantium and the Early Medieval West, 1986, 500 Unknown Glosses from the Palatine Virgil, 1992, Origins of the European Economy, 2001; edit. bd. Bulletin Codicologique, 1978-91, Am. Jour. Philology, 1982-88; bd. editors Speculum Anniversary Monographs, 1989-91. Recipient Mellow Disting. Achievement award, 2003; Guggenheim Meml. Found. fellow, 1985-86; Am. Coun. Learned Socs. grantee, 1987. Fellow Medieval Acad. Am. Roman Catholic. Office: Harvard U Dept History Robinson Hall Cambridge MA 02138

MCCORMICK, NORMAN JOSEPH, mechanical engineer, nuclear engineer, educator; b. Hays, Kans., Dec. 9, 1938; s. Clyde Truman and Vera Mae (Miller) McC.; m. Mildred Mirring, Aug. 20, 1961; children: Kenneth John, Nancy Lynn. BSME, U. Ill., 1960, MS in Nuclear Engring., 1961; PhD in Nuclear Engring., U. Mich., 1965. Postdoctoral researcher NSF, Ljubljana, Yugoslavia, 1965-66; asst. prof. Univ. Wash., Seattle, 1966-70, assoc. prof., 1970-75, prof., 1975—2003, prof. emeritus, 2003—. Scientist Sci. Applications, Inc., Palo Alto, Calif., 1974-75; mem. editorial bd. Transport Theory and Statis. Physics, 1982—. Author: Reliability and Risk Analysis, 1981; editor Jour. Progress in Nuclear Energy, 1980-85; contbr. more than 150 articles to profl. jours. Named Outstanding Alumnus in Nuclear Engring., Univ. Mich., Ann Arbor, 1986, Disting. Alumnus in Mech. Engring., Univ. Ill., Urbana, 1991. Fellow Am. Nuclear Soc.; mem. Biomed. Optics Soc., Am. Nuclear Soc., Optical Soc. Am. Achievements include patent in field, Method of Preparing Gas Tags for Identification of Single and Multiple Failures of Nuclear Reactor Fuel Assemblies. Office: U Washington Mech Engring PO Box 352600 Seattle WA 98195-2600

MCCORMICK, RICHARD LEVIS, academic administrator; b. New Brunswick, N.J., Dec. 26, 1947; s. Richard Patrick and Katheryne Crook (Levis) McCormick; m. Suzanne Dee Lebsock, Aug. 30, 1984; children: Elizabeth, Michael. BA in Am. Studies, Amherst Coll., 1969; PhD in History, Yale U., 1976. From asst. prof. to prof. Rutgers U., New Brunswick, NJ, 1976—92, dean Faculty Arts and Scis., 1989—92; exec. vice chancellor, provost, vice chancellor acad. affair U. N.C., Chapel Hill, 1992—95; pres. U. Wash., Seattle, 1995—2002, Rutgers U., New Brunswick, NJ, 2002—. Author: From Realignment to Reform: Political Change in New York State 1893-1910, 1981, The Party Period and Public Policy: American Politics from the Age of Jackson to the Progressive Era, 1986. Fellow, Am. Coun. Learned Socs., 1978—79, John Simon Guggenheim Meml. Found., 1985. Mem.: Phi Beta Kappa. Home: 1245 River Rd Piscataway NJ 08854 Office: Rutgers Univ New Brunswick NJ 08901

MCCOWN, GLORIA BOOHER, school system administrator; b. Dallas, Apr. 5, 1945; d. George T. and Lillian (Martine) Booher; m. James R. McCown, July 22, 1962 (dec. May 1994); children: Kelley Lynn, William Scott. BS, Houston Bapt. U., 1976; MEd, U. North Tex., 1983, EdD, 1992. Tchr. Fort Bend Ind. Sch. Dist., Stafford, Tex., 1976-78, Lancaster (Tex.) Ind. Sch. Dist., 1978-83, prin., 1983-87, dir. curriculum, 1987-88, asst. supt. instrn., 1988-91; dir. elem. edn. Keller (Tex.) Ind. Sch. Dist., 1992—. Author: Site Based Management The Role Of The Central Office, 1992. Life mem. Lancaster Coun. PTA, 1987—. Named Prin. of Yr., U. North Tex., 1987. Mem. ASCD, Tex. ASCD, Tex. Elem. Sch. Prins., Tex. Assn. Sch. Adminstrs., Internat. Reading Assn., Phi Delta Kappa. Office: Keller Ind Sch Dist 304 Lorine St Keller TX 76248-3435

MCCOWN, LINDA JEAN, medical technology educator; d. William Ernest and Mary Elizabeth McC. BS, Pa. State U., 1975; MS, U. Pitts., 1979. Cert. med. technologist, clin. lab. scientist. Microbiology aide Pa. State U., University Park, 1973-74; med. technologist, asst. supr., rsch. technologist Children's Hosp. of Pitts., 1975-80; asst. prof. med. tech., assoc. program dir. Ctrl. Wash. U., Ellensburg, 1980-99; asst. prof. clinilab. sci. Jewish Hosp. Coll. of Nursing and Allied Health at Wash. Univ. Med. Ctr., 1999—; affiliate asst. prof. U. Mo., St. Louis, 2000—. Critiquer, insp. Nat. Accreditation Agy. for Clin. Lab. Scis., Chgo., 1984—; test item writer Nat. Cert. Agy., Lenexa, Kans., 1989—; recruiter Am. Soc. Clin. Pathologists, Chgo., 1988-98; guest lectr. physician asst. program U. Wash., Seattle, 1996-99. Contbr. articles to profl. jours. Stephen ministry, deacon First Presbyn. Ch., Yakima, Wash., 1992-98; bd. dirs. The Campbell Farm, Wapato, Wash., 1990-95; rally chmn. Heifer Project Internat., Wapato, 1991-94; profl. affairs com. chairperson Mo. Orgn. for Clin. Lab. Sci., 1999-01; host com. Clin. Lab. Educators' Conf., 2001; identity com. Second Bapt. Ch., St. Louis, 2001—. Recipient Key to the Future award Mo. Orgn. Clin. Lab. Sci., 2000. Mem. Am. Soc. for Med. Tech. (mem. commn. on accreditation 1988-91), Wash. State Soc. for Clin. Lab. Sci. (conv. chair 1992, edn. chair 1986-94, 95-96, Pres.'s award 1992, convention hospitality chair and cons. 1998), Mo. orgn. for Clin. Lab Sci. (chmn. hematology sci. assembly 2001-2003), Columbia Basin Soc. Clin. Lab. Sci. (pres.-elect 1993, pres. 1994-95), Am. Assn. for Adult and Continuing Edn. (spkr., presenter internat. unit), Omicron Sigma, Phi Kappa Phi. Avocations: photography, tennis, travel, music. Office: Jewish Hosp Coll Mail Stop 90-30-625 306 S Kingshighway Blvd Saint Louis MO 63110-1028 E-mail: lmccown@bjc.org.

MCCOY, CAROLYN SMITH, middle school educator; b. DeWitt, Ark., Sept. 7, 1952; d. Cleo and Willie B. (Mosby) Smith; m. A.C. McCoy, Dec. 24, 1977; 1 child, Carla ShaNai. BS, U. Ark., 1974; MS in Edn., So. Ark. U., 1978. Cert. sci. tchr., Ark. Tchr. sci. DeWitt Pub. Schs., 1974—, tchr. sci. to gifted and talented, 1986-87. Tchr. adult edn. sci. Rice Belt Vocat.-Tech. Sch., DeWitt, 1975-77; mem. Project ADVISE (Alliance for Devel. Vision and Initiative for Sci. Edn. in Ark., 1991-92; chmn. textbook adoption com. for elem. schs. Ark. Dept. Edn., Little Rock, 1991-92; mem. NASA-Newest Honor Tchrs. Program, 1989-92, expert review team Southwest Edn. Devel. Labs, 1993, trainer to trainer program tech. coun. Ark. River Ednl. Svc. Coop.; mem. New Standards Project, 1993, U. Ark. Med. Scis. Sci. Enrichment Program. 1993; mem. steering com. dept. higher edn. Ark. Science Crusade 93-94, curriculum devel. team, 1993-94; mem. pilot project DeWitt Pub. Schs., State of Ark. Science Frameworks Devel., 1993-94; mem. frameworks team Hendrix Coll., 1993-94; regional coord. math and sci. Ark. Systematic Initiative. Author: Jammer's Right about Drug Abuse, 1988, A Family Raps about Drug Abuse, 1989. Bd. dirs. Literacy Coun. for Ark. County, Stuttgart, 1990-93; del. Ark. Dem. Conv., 1992; troop leader Girl Scouts U.S.A., Almyra, Ark., 1992; leader 4-H, Almyra, 1992. Named Tchr. of Yr., Oldsmobile Dealers Assn., 1989, Ark. Power & Light, 1990; recipient Young Alumni award So. Ark. U., 1992, Vol. of Yr. award Girl Scouts Am., 1993. Mem. NEA, NSTA, Ark. Sci. Tchrs. Assn., (Elem. Sci. Tchr. Spl. award 1989), Ark. Edn. Assn. (alt. bd. dirs. for bd. dirs.-at-large position 3, bd. dirs. 1985-86, task force on ednl. excellence 1990-92), Delta Sigma Theta. Democrat. Baptist. Avocation: reading. Office: DeWitt Mid Sch 301 N Jackson St De Witt AR 72042-1827

MCCOY, DAVID BRION, middle school educator; b. Elyria, Ohio, Sept. 8, 1954; BS in Edn., Ashland U., 1977; M Liberal Studies, Kent State U., 1990. Cert. tchr., Ohio. Tchr. Jackson Local Schs., Massillon, Ohio, 1978—. Pub. Spare Change Press, Massillon, 1979—. Author: (poems) The Geometry of Blue, 1995, Ohio Wineries Guidebook, 2002. Mem. local profl. devel. com. Jackson Local Schs. Mem. Jackson Meml. Tchr.'s Assn., Carson Long Mil. Alumni Assn. Office: Jackson Middle Sch 7355 Mudbrook Rd NW Massillon OH 44646-1103

MCCOY, DOROTHY ELOISE, writer, educator; b. Houston, Sept. 4, 1916; d. Robert Major and Evie Letha (Grimes) Morgan; m. Roy McCoy, May 22, 1942; children: Roy Jr., Robert Nicholas (dec.). BA, Rice U., 1938; MA, Tex. A&I U., 1968; postgrad., Ind. U., 1971, U. Calif., Berkeley, 1972, U. Calif., Santa Cruz, 1977. Cert. secondary tchr. BA Corpus Christi (Tex.) Independent Schs., 1958-84, MA, 1985; freelance writer Corpus Christi, 1987—; co-owner United Iron and Machine Works, Corpus Christi, 1946-82. Freelance lectr.; master tchr. Nat. Coun. Tchrs. English, 1971, Nat. Humanities Faculty, Concord Mass., 1977-78; mem. steering com. Edn. Summit, Corpus Christi, 1990-91, mem. summit update, 1991. Author: A Teacher Talks Back, 1990, Let's Restructure the Schools, 1992; contbr. articles and columns to profl. jours. Sr. advisor to U.S. Congress, Washington, 1982-85; trustee Corpus Christi Librs., 1987-90; mem. Corpus Christi Mus.; mem. Friends Corpus Christi Librs., chmn. publicity com., 1988; participant Walk to Emmaus Group, 1990, UPDATE, U. Tex., 1978-92; cons. Libr. Bd. Democracy competition Am. 2000; sec. adminstrv. bd. First United Meth. Ch., 1992-93. Recipient Teacher of Yr. Paul Caplan Humanitarian award, 1981, Advanced Senior Option Program award, 1968. Mem. AAUW, LWV, Phi Beta Kappa. Avocations: gardening, writing, lecturing, teaching. Home and Office: 612 Chamberlain St Corpus Christi TX 78404-2605

MCCOY, EILEEN CAREY, academic dean; b. Jersey City; d. James Bernard and Nan (Dalton) Carey; m. Thomas James McCoy (dec.); children: Thomas James III, Mary Eileen McCoy Whang. BA, Coll. St. Elizabeth, Convent Station, N.J., 1954; MA, Fairleigh Dickinson U., 1969, EdD, 1983; postgrad., Harvard U., 1985. Mem. faculty County Coll. Morris, Dover, N.J., 1970-75; dir. cmty. rels. Raritan Valley Community Coll., Somerville, N.J., 1977-79, dean continuing, community edn. and svcs., 1979-95; dean Evening Coll. and Extension Site, 1995-2000. Author: The Community Education Component of the Community College: New Jersey in Comparative Perspective, 1983. Mem. Morris County Bd. Freeholders, 1975-77, Branchburg Twp. Rep. Mcpl. Com., 1996—; founding chmn. Somerset County Commn. on Women, 1985-88; mem. adv. coun. Somerset County Office on Aging, 1987—; bd. dirs. Rolling Hills Girl Scout Coun., 1991-93, Irish Am. Pub. Action Com., 1993-, pres., 1994—; bd. advisors Somerset County United Way; mem. twp. com. Montgomery Twp., 1993-96, dep. mayor, 1994-95; bd. dirs. Edn. Found. Bridgewater-Raritan, 1993-2000; mem. Elizabeth Ministry Immaculate Conception Ch., Somerville, N.J., 1997-2001; bd. dirs. Montgomery Arts Coun., 1998-2000, pres., 1998, chmn. lecture com. 2000-2002. Recipient Righteous Gentile award Jewish Fedn. Somerset, Hunterdon and Warren Counties, 1989, Somerset County Tercentennial award, 1989, Woman of Achievement award Rolling Hills Girl Scout Coun., 1991, Irish Person of Yr., 2002, Fedn. Rep. Women Millicent Fenwick Outstanding Pub. Svc. award, 2002. Mem. Nat. Coun. Continuing Edn. and Community Svc. (bd. dirs. and region rep. 1987-90, Person of Yr. region 2 1989), Greater Somerset County C. of C. (v.p. and bd. dirs. 1988-92, Outstanding Woman in Business and Industry 1982), Rotary (pres. Branchburg, N.J., club 1989-90), Raritan Valley Art Assn., N.J. Watercolor Soc., Inc., Garden State Watercolor Soc. (Juror's

Merit award Third Annual Assoc. Member Juried Exhibn. 1999), Somerset Art Assn. (Art collector show 1999—), Montgomery Ctr. Arts, 1860 House (chmn. lecture com.). Republican. Roman Catholic.

MCCOY, ELIZABETH MILLS, French educator; b. Leesburg, Va., Nov. 4, 1942; d. Esker and Oma Mae (Herrell) Mills; m. Marshall P. Howard Griffith, June 20, 1964 (div. 1985); children: Mark Stephen, Laura Michelle, Seth Julian, Karen Elizabeth; m. Francis Maurice McCoy Jr., Nov. 8, 1986; children: Elizabeth Frazier, James Ramsey. BA, U. Md., 1964; postgrad., Old Dominion U. Cert. secondary French tchr., Md., Va. French tchr. Montgomery County Pub. Schs., Rockville, Md., 1964-69, Norfolk (Va.) City Pub. Schs., 1990—. Mem. mentor team Norfolk Pub. Schs., 1993—, SMART team, 1993—. Vol., project coord. Operation Smile Internat., Norfolk, 1993—, team mem., 1994—. Scholar-in-resident U. Va., 1992. Mem. Edn. Assn. Norfolk (legis. chair 1992—), Va. Edn. Assn. (resolutions com. 1994), NEA. Home: 720 Reasor Dr Virginia Beach VA 23464-2426 Office: Norfolk Pub Schs 1111 Park Ave Norfolk VA 23504-3619

MCCOY, GERALD LEO, superintendent of schools; b. Worthington, Minn., Dec. 4, 1936; s. Lawrence Joseph and Mildred Alice (Burns) McC.; m. Louise Marie Budde, Oct. 17, 1959; children: Susan, Peggy, Mary, Paul. BS, Mankato State U., 1960; MEd, U. Ill., 1963; EdD, U. Minn., 1978. Cert. English and speech tchr., prin., supt., Minn. Tchr. English, Springfield (Ill.) Schs., 1960-63; from tchr. English to prin. Burnsville (Minn.) Schs., 1964-73, asst. supt., 1974-80; supt. Eden Prairie (Minn.) Schs., 1980—. Policy bd. Ctr. for Applied Rsch. and Edn. Improvement, Mpls., 1990-92; bd. dirs. Minn. Coun. for Quality, Mpls. Mem. Fairview Ridges Planning Bd., Burnsville, 1977-80; bd. dirs. Eden Prairie Found., 1980-88; trustee Fairview Southdale Hosp., Edina, Minn., 1987—. Recipient Outstanding Svc. award Eden Prairie Found., 1988, Cmty. Contbns. award Minn. Cmty. Edn. Assn., 1990, Disting. Alumnus award Mankato State U., 1996; fellow Bush Exec. Fellows Program, 1983-84. Mem. ASCD, Am. Assn. Sch. Adminstrs., Minn. Assn. Sch. Adminstrs. (Minn. Supt. of Yr. award 1989), West Metro Assn. Sch. Adminstrs. (past pres.), Eden Prairie C. of C. (pres. 1980-88, Outstanding Svc. award 1987), Rotary, Lions, Optimists (Optimist of Yr. award Eden Prairie 1986), Phi Kappa Phi, Phi Delta Kappa. Avocations: fishing, hunting. Office: Eden Prairie Schs 8100 School Rd Eden Prairie MN 55344-2233

MCCOY, JOHN ELBERT, education educator; b. Morton, Miss., June 26, 1933; s. Kent McKinley and Katie (Dishman) McC.; m. Judy M. Lindsey, June 26, 1984; children: Gregory, Marcus, Jarrett, Katie. BS, Tougaloo (Miss.) Coll., 1955; MEd, DePaul U., Chgo., 1977; MA, Northeastern Ill. U., 1974; postgrad., So. Ill. U., summer 1964, 65, No. Ill. U., 1973. Lic. tchr., adminstr., supr. Ill. Tchr. McComb (Miss.) Pub. Sch., 1959-63, Manley Upper Grade Ctr., Chgo., 1963-75, Frederick Douglas Math. and Sci. Specialty Sch., Chgo., 1975—, U. Ill., Chgo., 1985-86. Part-time asst. credit mgr. Sears, Roebuck and Co., Chgo., 1965-77; mem. profl. pers. adv. com. Frederick Douglass Math. and Sci. Sch., Chgo., 1989-93, profl. pers. advisor, 1990-94, treas. social com., 1988-94, profl. problem com. Mem. adminstrv. bd. Gammon United Meth. Ch., Chgo., 1977-93, trustee, 1979-87. With USN, 1955-57. Mem. Chgo. Tchrs. Union, Am. Fedn. of Tchrs., Omega Psi Phi. Avocations: reading, collecting african american books, swimming. Home: Apt 2310 3950 N Lake Shore Dr Chicago IL 60613-3472

MCCOY, LINDA KORTEWEG, library director; b. Passaic, N.J., Oct. 12, 1948; d. Christian Adrian and Irene (Morse) Korteweg; m. Rudolph William, Aug. 1, 1970; children: Jill Ann, Lori Lynn. BA in Math. Edn., William Paterson, 1970, BA in Acctg., 1987, MA in Ednl. Media, 1993. Cert. math. tchr. grades 7-12, media specialist grades K-12, supr., N.J. Math. tchr. Woodrow Wilson Middle Sch., Clifton, N.J., 1970-71; media specialist Schs. 5, 11, 13, Clifton, 1971-78, Schs. 2, 5, Clifton, 1984-93, Clifton H.S., 1993-2000, network coord., 2000—01; dist. supt. media svcs. K-12 Clifton Pub. Schs., 2002—. Webmaster, Clifton Pub. Sch. Dist., 1998-02; adj. math. tchr. Tombrock Coll., West Paterson, N.J., 1970-72; adv. bd. Grove Hill Nursery Sch., Clifton, 1984-86; tchr's adv. bd. Clifton Bd. Edn., 1992-93. Treas. Advs. for Quality Edn., Clifton, 1990-93; exec. bd. Clifton (N.J.) Concert Choir Parents, 1992-96; mem. Middlestates Evaluation Com., 1995; chair Task Force for Coll. Preparation, 1996-97, tech. com. dist., 1995—, youth week advisor, 1996-2001; tchr. internet training Passaic County Ednl. Tech. Tng. Ctr., 1998-99; trustee Clifton Pub. Libr., 2000—. Recipient NSF computer study grant St. Peter's Coll., 1970-71, tel cable grant for tech. study at Sparkman Ctr., Colo., Internet Access for H.S. Media Ctrs. grant, 1995, N.J. Gov.'s Tchr. Recognition award N.J. State Bd. Edn., Trenton, 1992, Project NEAT (Internet) grant, 1998. Mem. Nat. Assn. Ednl. Tech. Specialists, Clifton Suprs.' Assn., N.J. Prins. and Suprs. Assn., N.J. Libr. Assn., Ednl. Media Assn. N.J., Assn. for Ednl. Comm. and Tech., N.J. Assn. Ednl. Technology, Internat. Soc. for Tech. in Edn., N.J. Libr. Trustee Assn., Pi Lambda Theta, Kappa Delta Pi. Avocations: computers, sewing. Home: 82 Mountainside Ter Clifton NJ 07013-1177 Office: Clifton High Sch 333 Colfax Ave Clifton NJ 07013-1701 E-mail: lmccoy@cliftonschools.org., llmccoy@cybernex.net.

MCCOY, MAUREEN, novelist, writing educator; b. Des Moines, Dec. 18, 1949; d. John Robert and Frances Ellen (Sullivan) McC. BA, U. Denver, 1972; MFA, U. Iowa, 1983. Writing fellow Fine Arts Work Ctr., Provincetown, Mass., 1983-85; freelance writer Provincetown, 1985-87; Albert Schweitzer fellow in humanities SUNY, Albany, 1987; assoc. prof. English Cornell U., Ithaca, N.Y., 1989—, dir. creative writing program, 1994-97. Author: Walking After Midnight, 1985, Summertime, 1987, Divining Blood, 1992; contbr. 2 entries to The Elvis Monologues, 1998. Recipient James Michener award Copernicus Found., 1984; Albert Schweitzer fellow, 1987-89, APPEL fellow, 1995; Hawthornden residency Hawthornden Castle Internat. Writer's Retreat, Scotland, 1996, Helene Wurlitzer Found. Taos, N.Mex., residency, 1996. Mem. Assoc. Writers Program, Am. Conf. Irish Studies. Office: Cornell U English Dept GS 250 Ithaca NY 14853

MCCOY, MILDRED BROOKMAN, retired elementary education educator; b. Princeton, W.Va., Nov. 23, 1924; d. Ralph William and Nannie Mae (Tabor) Brookman; m. Julius Rossey McCoy, Apr. 12, 1945 (dec. 1980); children: Michael David, Alan Dale. BA, Shepherd Coll., 1976. Elem. tchr. Baltimore County Bd. Edn., Balt., 1957-67, Washington County Bd. Edn., Md., 1967-86, ret., 1986. Docent Washington County Hist. Soc., Hagerstown, Md., 1990—, Washington County Art Mus., 1997—. AAUW grantee, 1993. Mem. Md. Ret. Tchrs. Assn., Hagerstown Women's Club, PEO. Episcopalian. Avocations: antiquing, hiking, traveling, reading. Home: 18824 Preston Rd Hagerstown MD 21742-2716

MCCOY, PATRICIA A. clinical special educator, writer, art and culture critic; b. Seattle, Wash., Dec. 20, 1951; d. Robert Wilson and Barbara (Foss) McC. BS, U. Nev., 1974; MA, NYU, 1983; postgrad. in psychoanalysis, Ctr. for Modern Psychoanalytic, Studies, N.Y.; postgrad. in applied linguistics, NYU. Lectr. in English CUNY, N.Y.C., 1984-88, John Jay Coll. of Criminal Justice, N.Y.C., 1988-91; clin. educator August Aichhorn Resdl. Treatment Ctr., N.Y.C., 1991-93, St. Vincent's Hosp. Psychiatry Inpatient, N.Y.C., 1993-95; with spl. edn. dist. 75 N.Y.C. Bd. Edn., 1995—2002. Lectr. contemporary art New Arts Program and others, east coast, 1991—; ind. curator, 1987—; instr. NYU. Editor: N.A.P. Texts jour., 1993—; contbr. articles to profl. jours., including Modern Psychoanalysis, Orthopsychiatry's Readings. Grantee N.Y. State Found. for the Arts, 1987, Pa. Coun. for the Arts, 1991, Mid-Atlantic, 1991, Nat. Endowment for the Arts for Texts, 1992, Pew Charitable Trust, 1993. Mem. Nat. Soc. Modern Psychoanalysts, Assn. Internat. des Critiques d'Art, Am. Orthopsychiatric Assn., N.Y. State Coun. Humanities Scholars Directory.

MCCOY, RHONDA LUANN, daycare administrator; b. Muncy, Pa., Apr. 22, 1968; d. Gary Edward Sr. and Twila Marie (Koch) McC. BS in Edn., Millersville (Pa.) U., 1990. Cert. in elem./early childhood edn., Pa. Substitute pre-sch. tchr. Magic Years, Williamsport, Pa., 1991-92, pre-kindergarten tchr., 1991-92; asst. dir. Angel Sta., Hughesville, Pa., 1992-93; dir., adminstr. Westfield (Pa.) Child Devel. Ctr., 1993—; adminstr. R.B. Walter Sch. Age, Lawrenceville, Pa., 1994—, Westfield Sch. Age, 1993—, Millerton (Pa.) Sch. Age, 1994-95. Home: 122 N Main St Hughesville PA 17737-1508

MCCOY, WESLEY LAWRENCE, musician, conductor, educator; b. Memphis, Jan. 27, 1935; s. Harlan Eftin and Gladys (Coggin) McC.; m. Carolyn June Noble, Aug. 26, 1960; children: Jill Laurene McCoy Kurtz, Scott Edward. B.Music Edn., La. State U., 1957, PhD, 1970; M of Music Edn, U. Louisville, 1958; M Sacred Music, So. Bapt. Theol. Sem., 1960. Minister of music Beechmont Bapt. Ch., Louisville, 1959-62; also instr. music So. Bapt. Theol. Sem., Louisville; asst. prof. music, dir. bands Carson Newman Coll., Jefferson City, Tenn., 1962-67; asst. prof. music U. S.C., Columbia, 1969-72; asso. prof. music U. Ark., Little Rock, 1972-77, prof., 1977-80, asst. dean for public service Coll. Fine Arts, 1978-79; condr. Wind Ensemble, River City Community Band, 1972-80, Oklahoma City Youth Symphony, 1985-89; chmn. dept. music Phillips U., Enid, Okla., 1980-82, chmn. fine arts div., 1982-84; music tchr. Bishop Sullivan H.S., 2003—. Minister music 1st United Meth. Ch., Edmond, Okla., 1983-2000; owner WJ Travel, Oklahoma City, 1985-2002; music dir. Bishop Sullivan H.S., 2003—. French horn player, Knoxville (Tenn.) Symphony Orch., 1962-67, Columbia Philharm. Orch., 1969-72, Ark. Symphony Orch., 1972-80, Enid-Phillips Symphony, 1980-84; contbr. to Ch. Musician, 1974-76, 85-86 Co-chmn. Jefferson County (Tenn.) Com. for Goldwater for Pres., 1962; mem. Pulaski County (Ark.) Republican Com., 1977-81; mem. Oklahoma County Rep. xec. Com., 1995-97; pres. Ctrl. Okla. LSU Alumni, 1997-98. Mem. S.C. Music Educators Assn. (pres. coll. div. 1971-73), Ark. Music Edn. Assn. (chmn. rsch. 1975-80), Phi Mu Alpha, Pi Kappa Lambda, Phi Delta Kappa, Alpha Tau Omega. Republican. Baptist. Home and Office: 8548 Kaylynn Ave Baton Rouge LA 70810 E-mail: wesleymccoy@yahoo.com.

MCCRADY, BARBARA SACHS, psychologist, educator; b. Evanston, Ill., May 7, 1949; d. James Frederick and Margaret Maxine (Miller) Sachs; m. Dennis D. McCrady, June 13, 1969; 1 child, Eric Paul. BS, Purdue U., 1969; PhD, U. R.I., 1975. Lic. clin. psychologist. Clin. project evaluator Butler Hosp., Providence, 1974-75, chief psychol. assessment program, 1975-76, chief problem drinkers' project, 1976-83; assoc. prof. psychology Rutgers U., Piscataway, N.J., 1983-89, prof. psychology, 1989-2000, prof. II, 2000—. From instr. to assoc. prof. psychiatry Brown U., Providence, 1975-83; acting dir. Rutgers Ctr. Alcohol Studies, Piscataway, 1990-92; reviewer Nat. Inst. on Alcohol Abuse and Alcholism, Washington, 1979-82, extramural scientific adv. bd., 1989-93; cons. Inst. Medicine, Washington, 1988-89. Author: The Alcoholic Marriage, 1977; editor: Marriage and Marital Therapy, 1978, Directions in Alcohol Aubse Treatment Research, 1985, Research on Alcoholics Anonymous: Opportunities and Alternatives, 1993, Addictions: A Comprehensive Guidebook, 1999. Grantee Nat. Inst. on Alcohol Abuse and Alcoholism, 1979-83, 1988—. Fellow Am. Psychol. Assn. (past pres. divsn. addictions); mem. Assn. for Advancement Behavior Therapy, Rsch. Soc. on Alcoholism (bd. dirs., 1999-2003). Avocations: horseback riding, skiing, piano. Office: Rutgers U Ctr Alcohol Studies 607 Allison Rd Piscataway NJ 08854-8001 E-mail: bmccrady@rci.rutgers.edu.

MCCRAE, LINDA REED, secondary education educator; b. Reading, Pa., May 27, 1945; d. Charles Abner and Marian Elizabeth (Stauffer) Reed; m. Richard Dean McCrae, June 28, 1970; children: Sean Christoph, Patrick Michael Richard Reed. BA cum laude, Albright Coll., 1967; MED in German, Kutztown U., 1969. Permanent tchr. cert., Pa. Tchr. German, Latin and English Muhlenberg Sch. Dist., Laureldale, Pa., 1967—2002. Instr. German, Reading Area C.C., 1971-72; instr. edn. methodology Albright Coll., Reading, 1975-76; mem. adj. faculty dept. German, Alvernia Coll., Reading, 1995; co-advisor Acad. Challenge, Laureldale, 1986—; mem. Wyomissing (Pa.) Sch. Dist. Strategic Planning. Author: Latina Vivit: A Guide to Lively Latin Classes, 1986, 95. Mem. Phi Delta Sigma, Delta Phi Alpha. Avocations: reading, writing, needlework, travel, gourmet dining.

MCCRARY, JUDY HALE, education educator; b. Tuscaloosa, Ala., Oct. 16, 1955; d. Rogene Bae and Berta Inez (Smelley) Hale. BA, David Lipscomb U., 1978; MEd, Ala. A&M U., 1989; PhD, Miss. State U., 1994. Art tchr. grades 7-8 Scottsboro (Ala.) Jr. High, 1978-81; headstart tchr. Bridgeport (Ala.) Elem. Sch., 1983-84, tchr. grade 1, 1984-87; migrant tchr. grades K-6 Stevenson (Ala.) Elem. Sch., 1987-89, kindergarten tchr., 1989-91; tchg. asst. Miss. State U., Starkville, 1991-94; asst. prof. Jacksonville (Ala.) State U., 1994—2000, assoc. prof., 2000—. Owner, operator The Art Studio, Scottsboro, 1981-83; presenter in field. Mem. beautification coun. C. of C., Scottsboro, 1983; mem., v.p. Doctoral Student's Assn., Starkville, 1991-94. Faculty Rsch. grantee Jacksonville State U., 1994-96. Mem. AAUW (sec. 1987-89, pres. 1989-91), DAR, Am. Assn. for Edn. Young Children, Mid South Ednl. Rsch. Assn., Ala. Assn. for Young Children, Beta Phi, Delta Kappa Gamma, Phi Delta Kappa (historian 1993-94). Avocations: traveling, home decorating, gardening, creative arts, racquetball. Office: Jacksonville State Univ Ramona Wood Bldg 700 Pelham Rd N Jacksonville AL 36265-1623 E-mail: jhale@jsucc.jsu.edu.

MCCRAW, JOHN RANDOLPH, JR., assistant principal; b. Lynchburg, Va., Nov. 23, 1942; s. John Randolph and Mabel L. (Bethel) McC.; m. Carolyn Lynn Mason, Aug. 3, 1968. BA, Emory and Henry Coll., 1965; MEd, U. Va., 1971; LLB, LaSalle Extension U., 1977; EdD, Va. Poly. Inst. and State U., 1987; cert., Oxford U., 1992. Cert. tchr., adminstr., Va. Tchr. govt. Martinsville (Va.) City Schs., 1965-89; asst. prin. Martinsville Jr. High Sch., 1989-90, Albert Harris Elem. Sch., Martinsville, 1990-93, Martinsville High Sch., 1993—. Dir. Martinsville City Schs. Self Studies, Va. Dept. Edn./So. Assn. Colls. and Schs., 1988-90. Author: The Legal History of Teacher Certification in the Commonwealth of Virginia, 1987, Hands-On Learning, 1993. Chmn. Martinsville Henry County Rep. party, state senate Rep. dist.; candidate for Martinsville City Coun. Mem. ASCD, Nat. Assn. Elem. Sch. Prins., Va. Assn. Elem. Sch. Prins., Va. Coaches Assn., Mid-Atlantic Notary Assn., Phi Delta Kappa. Baptist. Avocations: politics, law, current events, reading. Home: 1724 Meadowview Ln Martinsville VA 24112-5708 Office: Martinsville City Schs 710 Smith Rd Martinsville VA 24112-2531

MCCRAY, DOROTHY WESTABY, artist, printmaker, educator; b. Madison, S.D., Oct. 13, 1915; d. Robert Spencer and Annie Mary (Otter) Westaby; m. Francis F. McCray, Aug. 6, 1938 (dec. Jan. 1960); 1 child, Peter Michael. BA, State U. Iowa, 1937, MA in Painting, 1939; MFA in Printmaking, Calif. Coll. Arts and Crafts, Oakland, 1955; DHL (hon.), We. N.Mex. U., 2001. Prof. art Western N.Mex. U., Silver City, 1948-81, prof. emeritus, 1981—; profl. painter/printmaker McCray Studios, Silver City. Solo exhbns. include Mezzanine Gallery, Oakland, Calif., Art Directions Gallery, N.Y.C., Lebanon Valley Coll., Pa., Coralles Art Assn., N.Mex., Richard Levy Gallery, Albuquerque, numerous others; group exhbns. include Art Inst. Chgo., 1940-41, Phila. Acad., 1941, Kansas City Art Inst., 1941, 42, Smithsonian Inst., Washington, 1941, 58, Am. Fine Arts Gallery, N.Y.C., 1943, Joslyn Meml. Art Mus., Omaha, 1947, Mus. Fine Arts, Santa Fe, 1950, 51, 52, 53, 54, 56, 57, 58, 59, 63, 66, Oakland (Calif.) Art Mus., 1955, Cin. Art Mus., 1956, 58, NAD, Newton, Kans., 1956, Dallas Mus. Fine Arts, 1956, 58, Roswell (N.Mex.) Art Mus., 1958, Bradley U., Peoria, Ill., 1960, Highlands U., Las Vegas, 1960, Bklyn. Mus., 1961, Pa. Acad. Art, Phila., 1965, Museo de Arte Historia, Juarez, Mexico, 1978, The Shellfish Collection, Silver City, N.Mex., 1990, 91, Deming (N.Mex.) Ctr. for Arts, 1991, Grant County Art Guild, Pinos Altos, N.Mex., 1991, 92, Carlsbad (N.Mex.) Mus. and Art Ctr., 1992, Richard Levy Gallery, Albuquerque, 1992, Jonathon Green Gallery, Naples, Fla., numerous others; represented in pvt. and mus. collections throughout the United States. Named Hon. Citizen of S.D., 1983; Western N.Mex. U. Art Building named Dorothy McCray Art Building, 1982; recipient N.Mex. Gov.'s Award for Excellence and Contbns. to the Arts, 1992, numerous art awards in exhbns. Office: PO Box 322 Silver City NM 88062-0322

MCCRONE, ALISTAIR WILLIAM, retired academic administrator; b. Regina, Can., Oct. 7, 1931; BA, U. Sask., 1953; MSc, U. Nebr., 1955; PhD, U. Kans., 1961. Instr. geology NYU, 1959-61, asst. prof., 1961-64, assoc. prof., 1964-69, prof., 1969-70, supr. Rsch. Ship Sea Owl on L.I. Sound, 1959-64, asst. dir. univ. program at Sterling Forest, 1965-66, resident master Rubin Internat. Residence Hall, 1966-69, chmn. dept. geology, 1966-69, assoc. dean Grad. Sch. Arts and Scis., 1969-70; prof. geology, acad. v.p. U. Pacific, 1970-74, acting pres., 1971; prof. geology, pres. Calif. State U. Sys. Humboldt State U., Arcata, 1974—2002. Exec. coun. Calif. State U. Sys., 1974-2002, acad. senate Humboldt State U., 1974-2002, mem. chancellor's com. on innovative programs, 1974-76, trustees' task force on off-campus instrn., 1975-76, exec. com. Chancellor's Coun. of Pres., 1976-79, Calif. state del. Am. Assn. State Coll. and Univ., 1977-80; mem. Commn. on Ednl. Telecomm., 1983-86; chair Calif. State U. Statewide Task Force on Earthquake and Emergency preparedness, 1985-88, 95; chmn., mem. accreditation teams Western Assn. Sch. and Coll.; chair com. on energy and environ. Am. Assn. State Coll. and Univ., 1980-84; chair program com. Western Coll.Assn., 1983-84, panelist, 1983; chair. bd. dir. Assn. Am. Coll., 1992-93. Contbr. articles to profl. jour.; lectr. on geology Sunrise Semester program CBS Nat. Network, 1969-70; various appearances on local TV stas. Bd. trustees Presbyn. Hosp.-Pacific Med. Ctr., San Francisco, 1971-74; mem. Calif. Coun. for Humanities, 1977-82; mem. local campaign bd. United Way, 1977-83; mem. Am. Friends Wilton Park, 1980—; bd. dirs. Humboldt Convention and Visitors Bur., 1980-87, Redwood Empire Assn., 1983-87; bd. dirs. Calif. State Automobile Assn., 1988—, Am. Automobile Assn., 1990-93; bd. trustees Calif. State Parks Found., 1994-2000. Recipient Erasmus Haworth Disting. Alumnus award U. Kans., 2000; Shell fellow in geology U. Nebr., 1954-55; Danforth assoc. NYU, 1964. Fellow Calif. Acad. Sci.; mem. AAAS, Geol. Soc. Am., Am. Assn. U. Adminstrs. (nat. bd. 1986-89, 96-99, 2001-2002), St. Andrews Soc. NY (life), Rotary, Sigma Xi (pres. NYU chpt. 1967-69), Phi Kappa Phi. Avocation: golf. Office: Humboldt State U Univ Campus Arcata CA 95521

MCCRORY, ROBERT LEE, physicist, mechanical engineering educator; b. Lawton, Okla., Apr. 30, 1946; s. Robert Lee Sr. and Marjorie Marie (Garrett) McC.; m. Betsey Christine Wahl, June 14, 1969; children: Katherine Anne, John Damon, George Garrett. BSc, MIT, 1968, PhD, 1973. Physicist Los Alamos Nat. Lab., Albuquerque, 1973-76; scientist, coleader Lab. for Laser Energetics, U. Rochester, N.Y., 1976-77, sr. scientist, 1977—, dir. theoretical dir., 1979-90, dir., 1983—; assoc. prof. of physics and astronomy U. Rochester, 1980, prof. of mech. engring., 1983—, exec. dir. of govtl. rels. pres.'s office, 1997—. Author: Laser Plasma Interactions, 1989, Computer Applications in Plasma Science and Engineering, 1991; contbr. articles to profl. publs. Alfred P. Simon scholar, 1964-67; AEC fellow, 1985; recipient Edward Teller medal, 1994. Fellow Am. Phys. Soc. (mem. fellowship com., mem. exec. com. div. plasma physics, Excellence in Plasma Physics award). Office: U Rochester Lab Laser Energetics 250 E River Rd Rochester NY 14623-1212

MCCUBBIN, SHARON ANGLIN, elementary school educator; b. Fullerton, Calif., Nov. 20, 1948; d. Floyd Calvin and Grace Ann Anglin; m. David Paul White (div. 1990); children: Julie, Adrian, Matthew; m. Robert Patrick McCubbin, July 13, 1991. BA, U. Calif., 1973; MEd, Cleve. State U., 1993. Cert. clear multiple subject profl. pre-K, Calif., elem. Montessori tchr., early childhood edn.; cert. mid. childhood generalist, early childhood generalist Nat. Bd. Cert. Tchrs.; cert. Clear Crosscultural, Lang. and Acad. Devel. Tchr. Primanti Montessori, Orange, Calif., 1977-81; tchr., adminstr. Montessori of Orange, 1981-83, Tustin Hills Montessori, Santa Ana, Calif., 1983-89; tchr., cons. for Montessori programs Irvine (Calif.) Unified Sch. Dist., 1990—; Montessori elem. mentor tchr., 1990—. Cons. title VII programs Irvine Unified Sch. Dist., 1990—, GATE adv. bd. mem.; cons. for early childhood programs to local corps. Asst. Jr. Disabled Programs, Orange, 1988—. SBD fellow Johns Hopkins U., 1999. Mem. ASCD, AAUW, Assn. Montessori Internat., Assn. Montessori Internat./U.S.A., Assn. Montessori Internat. Elem. Alumni Assn. (regional rep. 1984), Am. Montessori Soc., N.Am. Montessori Tchrs. Assn., Pvt. Sch. Adminstrs., U. Calif.-Irvine Alumni Assn., Calif. Tchrs. Assn., Irvine Tchrs. Assn., Nat. Coun. Tchrs. Math., Nat. Coun. for Social Studies, Nat. Assn. for Edn. of Young Children. Home: PO Box 616 Tustin CA 92781-0616 Office: Irvine Unified Sch Dist 5050 Barranca Pkwy Irvine CA 92604-4698 also: Santiago Hills Elem 29 Christamon W Irvine CA 92620-1836 E-mail: smccubbi@iusd.k12.ca.us., smccubbi@aol.com.

MCCUE, ARTHUR HARRY, artist, educator; b. N.Y.C., Sept. 27, 1944; s. Raymond Noel and Alice (Cassidy) McC.; m. Lorraine Havel Bingham, Nov. 18, 1989. BFA, Pratt Inst., N.Y.C., 1967; MFA, U. Colo., 1969. Instr. art SUNY, Geneseo, 1969-72; instr. printmaking and drawing Ithaca (N.Y.) Coll., 1973-77, assoc. prof., 1987-2001, chmn. dept. art, 1977—, prof., 2001—. Guest speaker sch. supt.'s seminar Ithaca Coll., 1990; guest artist N.Y. State Pastel Artists Assn., Cooperstown, 1990, 92, Schweinfurth Meml. Art Ctr., 1990; cons., interpreter on wheelwrighting Onondaga County Parks, Salt Mus., Liverpool, N.Y., 1989-90; guest lectr. dept. art Tompkins Cortland Community Coll., 1987. One-man shows include Univ. Club, Boulder, Colo., 1968, David Gallery, Rochester, N.Y., 1973, Ithaca Coll., 1977, 79, 97, Art Gallery Adelphi U., Garden City, N.Y., 1980, Wagner Gallery, Lodi, N.Y., 1983, Ithaca House Gallery, 1984, 85, Schwein Furth Meml. Mus., Auburn, N.Y., 1986, Johnson Mus. Art, Ithaca, 1987, Upstairs Gallery, Ithaca, 1992, Lamoreaux Landing Wine Cellars Gallery, Lodi, N.Y., 1993, 97, 99, Trumanburg Conservatory Fine Arts, 1993, Wells Coll., Aurora, N.Y., 1995; exhibited in two-person shows at Harry McCue/David Smyth, Ithaca House, 1980, Hackworth/McCue, U. Pa., Edinboro, Grippi/McCue, Handwerker Gallery, Ithaca, McCue/Licht, Upstairs Gallery, Ithaca; exhibited in group shows at Internat. Gallery, Denver, 1969, Double U. Gallery, N.Y.C., 1977, Handwerker Gallery, 1980, 82, 84, 85, 86, 87, 89, 90, 91, 92, 93, 94, 95, 97, 98, 99, 00, Upstairs Gallery, 1993—, Everson Mus., Syracuse (2d prize printmaking 1987), New Visions Gallery, Ithaca, 1987-90, Elmira Coll., 1991, Cazenovia Coll., 1993, Cooperstown Nat., 1993, 96, 97, 01, Old Forge Art Assn., 1992, West End Gallery, Corning, N.Y., 1996, 97, 2001—, Galeria Mesa, Ariz., 1998, Wright State U., Dayton, Ohio, 2000, Wichita (Kans.) Ctr. for Arts, 2001, Purdue U., Lafayette, Ind., 2002, U. Wise, Parkside, Wis., 2003; nat. exhbns.: Fall River Art Show, Mass., 1973, 74, 76, Marietta (Ohio) Coll., 1974, 76, Arnot Mus., Elmira, N.Y., 1977, 96, 2001, Ft. Hays State U., 1984, 2003, U. Maine, 1985, 92, 93, 96-99, Everson Mus., 1985; included in book The American History Supply Catalogue, 1983, N.Y. Art Rev., 3d edit.; invited spl. guest at spl. showing Christie's Auction House, N.Y.C., 1984, Roch Meml. Art Gallery, 1991; commd. by Cornell U./Statler Hotel to design art work for hotel, 1988. Lodestar grantee, 1984. Home: 2423 Skinner Rd Lodi NY 14860-9739 Office: Ithaca Coll Dept Art Danby Rd Ithaca NY 14850-5736

MCCUE, EDMUND BRADLEY, mathematics educator; b. Worcester, Mass., Mar. 8, 1929; s. Felix Frederick and Frances (Bradley) McC. AB, Union Coll., 1950; MS, U. Mich., 1951; PhD, Carnegie-Mellon U., 1960. Asst. prof. Ohio U., Athens, 1958-63; prof. Inter-Am. Statis. Tng. Ctr. (CIENES), Santiago, Chile, 1963-64; assoc. prof. Am. U., Washington, 1964-87, prof. emeritus, 1987—. Mem. Inst. Math. Stats., Am. Statis. Assn., Math. Assn. Am. Home: 3040 Idaho Ave NW Apt 724 Washington DC 20016-5421 Office: Dept Math and Stats Am U Washington DC 20016

MCCULLOCH, ANNE MERLINE JACOBS, college dean; b. L.A., Mar. 20, 1948; d. Merlin Lee and Edna (Rammell) J.; m. Arlyn Cecil McCulloch, Sept. 17, 1977 (div. Mar. 1993); children: Justin Jacobs, Caroline Ranawn. BA, Coll. of Charleston, 1971; D of Arts, Idaho State U., 1975. Cert. secondary tchr., Idaho; cmty. coll. cert., Calif. Caseworker Dept. Social Svcs., Newport News, Va., 1970-71; asst. prof., then assoc. prof. polit. sci. Idaho State U., Pocatello, 1975-86, prof., 1986-89, grad. dir. polit. sci. dept., 1977-87; prof. Columbia (S.C.) Coll., 1989—, chmn. dept. history and polit. sci., 1991-98, interim dir. Leadership Inst., 1990-91, dean evening coll. and external programs, 1998—. Cons. Shoshone/Bannock Tribes, Ft. Hall, Idaho, 1986-87, 97; cons. S.C. ednl. TV film Snowbird Cherokee, 1993-95. Contbg. author: Native Americans and Public Policy, 1992; editor Native Am. Policy Network Newsletter, 1995—; assoc. editor Ency. Minorities in American Politics, 1999; contbr. articles to profl. jours. Mem. Idaho Gov.'s Blue Ribbon Econ. Commn., 1982-83; co-program chmn. Elizabeth Cady Stanton Conf., Columbia, 1995. Mem. Am. Polit. Sci. Assn. (coord. Native Am. studies 1995-96), So. Polit. Sci. Assn., So. Polit. Sci. Assn., Phi Kappa Phi, Pi Sigma Alpha, Phi Alpha Theta. Democrat. Mem. Lds Ch. Avocations: gardening, running, home remodeling. Home: 437 Southlake Rd Columbia SC 29223-6601 Office: Columbia Coll Evening Coll Columbia SC 29203 E-mail: amcculloch@colacoll.edu.

MCCULLOCH, LINDA, state official; b. Mont., Dec. 21, 1954; m. Bill McCulloch, 1978. BA in Elem. Edn., MA in Elem. Edn., U. Mont. Tchr. Pub. Schs, Mont., Ashland, Missoula, Bonner, 1978—95; rep. Mont. Ho. of Reps., Boise, 1995—2001; supt. pub. instrn. Mont., 2002—. Mem. juvenile justice, mental health, judiciary, Indian Affairs coms. Mont. Ho. Reps., 1997; minority caucus leader Ho. Reps., Helena, Mont., 1999; vice chair edn. com. Mont. Ho. Reps., 1999. Mem., officer PTA Assn., Helena, 1985—; bd. dirs. Missoula Developmental Svcs. Corp.; mem. adv. com. Missoula Youth Homes Foster Care. Recipient Mike and Maureen Mansfield Libr. scholaship, 1995, J.C. Penny Vol. Program award, 1998. Mem.: AAUW, LWV, Five Valleys Reading Assn., Mont. State Reading Coun., Mont. Fedn. Tchrs., Mont. Ednl. Assn., Mont. Libr. Assn. (Legislator of Yr. award 1997), Mont. Family Union, Montana Dem. Womens Club. Office: Mont Office Pub Instruction 1227 11th Ave Helena MT 59620-2501 Office Fax: 406-444-5658.

MCCULLOUGH, BENJAMIN FRANKLIN, transportation researcher, educator; b. Austin, Mar. 25, 1934; s. Benjamin Franklin and Mabel Cornelia (Kitteridge) McC.; m. Norma Jean Walsh, Sept. 1, 1956; children: Michael Wayne, Bryan Scott, Steven Todd, Franklin Norman, Melanie Jean. MSCE, U. Tex., 1962; PhD of Civil Engring., U. Calif., Berkeley, 1969. Registered profl. engr., Tex. Testing engr. Covair Aircraft Co., Ft. Worth, 1957; design and rsch. engr. Tex. Hwy. Dept., Austin, 1957-66; rsch. engr. Materials R&D, Inc., Oakland, Calif., 1966-68; from asst. to prof. U. Tex., Austin, 1969—, dir. transp. rsch., 1980-99. Contbr. articles to profl. jours. Mem. ASCE (Outstanding Paper award 1987), Transp. Rsch. Bd., Coun. Univ. Transp. Ctrs., Univ. Transp. Ctrs. Program, Am. Concrete Inst. Mem. Lds Ch. Avocations: coaching, sports, golfing, U.S. and Tex. history. Office: U Tex Transp Rsch Ctr 3208 Red River St Ste 200 Austin TX 78705-2650

MCCULLOUGH, DAVID, writer, educator; b. Pitts., July 7, 1933; s. Christian Hax and Ruth (Rankin) McC.; m. Rosalee Ingram Barnes, Dec. 18, 1954; children: Melissa (Mrs. John E. McDonald, Jr.), David, William Barnes, Geoffrey Barnes, Doreen Kane (Mrs. Timothy Lawson). BA, Yale U., 1955; HLD, Skidmore Coll., 1983, Rensselaer Poly. Inst., 1983; D of Engring. (hon.), Villanova U., 1984; hon. doctorate, Worcester Poly. Inst., 1984; LittD (hon.), Allegheny Coll., 1984; LHD (hon.), Wesleyan U., Middletown, Conn., 1984, Colo. Coll., 1985; LittD (hon.), Middlebury Coll., 1986, U. Indiana at Pa., 1991, U. S.C., 1993; HLD (hon.), U. N.H., 1991; LittD (hon.), U. Pitts., 1994, Union Coll., 1994, Washington Coll., 1994; LHD (hon.), Chatham Coll., 1994. Writer, editor Time, Inc., N.Y.C., 1956-61, USIA, Washington, 1961-64, Am. Heritage Pub. Co., N.Y.C., 1964-70; sr. contbg. editor Am. Heritage mag.; free-lance author, 1970—. Newman vis. prof. American civilization, Cornell U., fall 1989; mem. Bennington (Vt.) Coll. Writers Workshop, 1978-79; scholar-in-residence U. N. Mex., 1979, Wesleyan U. Writers Conf., 1982, 83; mem. adv. bd. Ctr. for the Book, Libr. of Congress; past vis. prof. Dartmouth Coll., Wesleyan U.; spkr. and lectr. in field. Author: The Great Bridge, 1972, The Path Between the Seas, 1977, The Johnstown Flood, 1968, Mornings on Horseback, 1981, Brave Companions, 1992, Truman, 1992 (Pulitzer Prize for biography 1993), John Adams, 2001 (Pulitzer prize for biography 2002); host TV series: Smithsonian World, 1984-88, The American Experience, 1988—; narrator numerous TV documentaries including The Civil War, Napoleon, 2000, Abraham & Mary Lincoln: A House Divided, 2001. Mem. Harry S. Truman Centennial Commn.; trustee Nat. Trust Hist. Preservation, Harry S. Truman Libr. Inst., Hist. Soc. Western Pa., Jefferson Meml. Found., Boston Pub. Libr.; hon. trustee Carnegie Inst.; founding mem. Protect Hist. Am. Guggenheim fellow; recipient N.Y. Diamond Jubilee award, 1973, cert. of merit Mcpl. Art Soc. N.Y., 1973, Nat. Book award for history, 1978, Francis Parkman prize, 1978, 93, Samuel Eliot Morison award, 1978, Cornelius Ryan award, 1978, Civil Engring. History and Heritage award, 1978, L.A. Times prize for biography, 1981, Am. Book award for biography, 1982, Harry S. Truman Pub. Svc. award, 1993, St. Louis Lit. award, 1993, Pa. Gov.'s award for excellence, 1993, Pa. Soc. Gold Medal award, 1994, Charles Frankel prize contributions to humanities Endowment Humanities and U.S. Govt., 1995, Disting. Contbns. to Am. Letters award. Nat. Book Found., Lit. Lion award N.Y. Pub. Libr., Emmy award for work in pub. TV, Gold medal Pa. Soc. Fellow Soc. Am. Historians (pres.); mem. ASCE (hon.), Am. Acad. Arts and Scis., Soc. Am. Historians (pres. 1991—). Avocations: travel, reader, landscape painter, sunday night spaghetti chef. Office: Janklow & Nesbit Associates 445 Park Ave # 13th New York NY 10022-2606

MCCULLOUGH, DEANNA CAROLYN, elementary education educator; b. Seymour, Ind., Dec. 21, 1956; d. Clifford Duncan and Zelpha Carolyn (Weekly) Bryant; m. Royce Dale McCullough, July 12, 1975; children: Jennifer, Bryan. BS in Elem. Edn., Ind. U., 1979, MS in Elem. Edn., 1981. Cert. tchr., Ind. Tchr. South Decatur Elem. Sch., Greensburg, Ind., 1979—. Choir dir. Westport (Ind.) Bapt. Ch., 1992—. Mem. NEA, Ind. State Tchrs. Assn., Decatur County Edn. Assn. Avocations: piano, reading, sewing.

MCCULLOUGH, EILEEN (EILEEN MCCULLOUGH LEPAGE, ELLI MCCULLOUGH), financial consultant, writer, editor, educator; b. Phila., Oct. 16, 1946; d. Charles Norman and Marie Teresa (Inglesby) McCullough; m. Clifford Bennett LePage Jr., Mar. 6, 1970; children: Clifford Bennett III, Alexander Pierce. BA in English and Secondary Edn., George Washington U., 1969; MEd in Gifted Edn., Temple U., 1972. Cert. secondary sch. tchr.; registered securities rep. Record-keeper child growth and devel. program Children's Hosp. of Phila., 1965; with advt. dept. Phila. Inquirer, 1966-67; with ops. control U.S. Civil Svc. Commn., Washington, 1967-69; mgr. N.J. Bell Telephone, Trenton, 1969; researcher Temple U., Phila., 1969-71; tchr. Wyomissing (Pa.), 1972-77; fin. cons. various orgns., 1984-93; cons. EMLCommunications Cons. Co., Reading, 1994—. Adj. instr. Reading (Pa.) Area C.C., 1978-81; lectr. English Albright Coll., Reading, 1981-84; founding mem. Common Cents Investment Club, 1983-93; founding and mng. ptnr. Klein LePage McCullough Partnership, Ocean City, N.J., 1982-96; presenter in field. Author: The Clue in the Snow, 1959; editor: 1st Complete Pocket Guide to Atlantic City Casinos, 1984, The Autobiography of Capt. Michael Kevolic, 1986; photographer Cherry Hill Mtg. Bd. dirs. Nat. Found. March of Dimes, Reading, 1969-75, chmn., 1974-75; bd. sch. dirs. Wyomissing Area Sch. Dist., 1984-92; bd. dirs. Wyomissing Pub. Libr., Reading, 1980-85; asst. chmn Region 8 Pa. Sch. Bds. Assn., 1989-91; dir. Saturday Morning Sch., Assn. for Children with Learning Disabilities, Reading, 1970; acting sec. Berks County Commn. for Women, Reading, 1993; active Reading Community Players, 1980; past bd. mem. Berks Ballet Theatre; past vol. Berks C. of C.; vol. mus. guide Reading Pub. Mus. and Art Gallery, 1999-2002, Berks County Chpt Am. Red Cross, 1997; presenter Green Circle, Reading Berks Human Rels. coun., Reading Pub. Schs., 1998-99. Fellow Pa. writing project; mem. AAUW (life; topic chmn.), Am. Assn. Individual Investors (life), Internat. Platform Soc., Women's Internat. Fedn. for World Peace. Avocations: dancing, singing. Home and Office: EMLCommunications Cons Co 10 Phoebe Dr Reading PA 19610-2857 Office: NJ Br PO Box 65 Somers Point NJ 08244 E-mail: akaellimay@aol.com.

MCCULLOUGH, HUBERT L., JR., educational association administrator; m. Dene McCullough. BS in Math., Mid. Tenn. State U., 1951. Chmn. McCullough Industries, bd. dirs.; chmn. Tenn. State Bd. Edn., 2000—. Office: Tenn State Bd Edn 9th Fl AndrewJohnson Tower 710 James Robertson Pkwy Nashville TN 37243-1050*

MCCULLOUGH, JOHN PHILLIP, management consultant, educator; b. Lincoln, Ill., Feb. 2, 1945; s. Phillip and Lucile Ethel (Ornellas) McC.; m. Barbara Elaine Carley, Nov. 29, 1968; children: Carley Jo, Ryan Phillip. BS, Ill. State U., 1967, MS, 1968; PhD, U. N.D., 1971. Adminstrv. mgr. McCullough Ins. Agy., Atlanta, Ill., 1963-68; ops. supr. Stetson China Co., Lincoln, 1967; asst. mgr. Brandtville Svc., Inc., Bloomington, Ill., 1968; instr. in bus. Ill. Ctrl. Coll., 1968-69; rsch. asst. U. N.D., Grand Forks, 1969-71; assoc. prof. mgmt. West Liberty State Coll., 1971-74, prof., 1974—. Chmn. dept. mgmt., West Liberty State Coll., 1974-82, dir. Sch. Bus., 1982-86, dean, 1986—, provost, 1998—, interim pres., 2001, dir. Small Bus. Inst., 1978—; mgmt. cons., Triadelphia, W.Va., 1971—; instr. Am. Inst. Banking, 1971—; lectr. W.Va. U., 1971—; adj. prof. MBA program Wheeling Coll., 1972—, U. Steubenville, 1982—; lectr. Ohio U., 1982—; profl. assoc. Inst. Mgmt. and Human Behavior, 1975—; v.p. West Liberty State Coll. Fed. Credit Union, 1976—; rep. W.Va. Bd. Regents Adv. Coun. of Faculty. Author: (with Howard Fryette) Primer in Supervisory Management, 1973; contbr. articles to profl. jours. Team leader Wheeling divsn. Am. Cancer Soc.; coord. Upper Ohio Valley United Fund, 1972-74; instr. AFL-CIO Cmty. Svcs. Program, Wheeling; project dir. Ctr. for Edn. and Rsch. with Industry; bd. dirs. Family Svc.-Upper Ohio Valley, Ohio Valley Indsl. and Bus. Devel. Corp., Inc., Labor Mgmt. Inst. Wheeling Salvation Army, Progress, Inc., Ohio Valley Health Svcs. and Edn. Corp. Recipient Svc. award Bank Adminstrn. Inst., 1974, United Fund, 1973, Acad. Achievement award Harris-Casals Found., 1971. Mem. Soc. Humanistic Mgmt. (nat. chmn.), ORgn. Planning Mgmt. Assn. (exec. com.), Spl. Interest Group for Cert. Bus. Educators (nat. dir.), Soc. Advancement Mgmt. (chpt. advisor), Acad. Mgmt., Adminstrv. Mgmt. Soc. (cert.), Am. Soc. Pers. Adminstrn. (cert.), Nat. Bus. Honor Soc. (Excellence in Tchg. award 1976, dir. 1974—), Alpha Kappa Psi (Dist. Svc. award 1973, Civic award 1977, chpt. advisor 1971—), Merit Found. W.Va. (Ednl. Excellence award), Delta Mu Delta, Delta Pi Epsilon, Delta Tau Kappa, Phi Gamma Nu, Phi Theta Pi, Pi Gamma Mu, Pi Omega Pi, Omicron Delta Epsilon. Home: 68 Elm Dr Triadelphia WV 26059-9620

MCCULLOUGH, RALPH CLAYTON, II, lawyer, educator; b. Daytona Beach, Fla., Mar. 28, 1941; s. Ralph C. and Doris (Johnson) McC.; m. Elizabeth Grier Henderson, Apr. 5, 1986; children from previous marriage: Melissa Wells, Clayton Baldwin. BA, Erskine Coll., 1962; JD, Tulane U., 1965. Bar: La. 1965, S.C. 1974. Assoc. Baldwin, Haspel, Maloney, Rainold and Meyer, New Orleans, 1965-68; asst. prof. law U. S.C., 1968-71, asso. prof., 1971-75, prof., 1975—, chair prof. of advocacy, 1982—, asst. dean Sch. Law, 1970-75, instr. Med. Sch., 1970-79, adj. prof. law and medicine Med. Sch., 1979—; adj. prof. medicine Med. U. S.C., 1984—; of counsel Finkel & Altman, 1978—. Adj. prof. pathology Med. U. S.C., 1985—; asst. dean U. S.C. Sch. Law 1970-75, Disting. prof. law, 2001, Disting. prof. law emeritus, 2003—; mem. fourth cir. adv. com. on rules and procedures U.S. Ct. Appeals, 2001—. Author: (with J.L. Underwood) The Civil Trial Manual, 1974, 7th supplement, 1987, The Civil Trial Manual II, 1984, 87, (with Myers and Felix) New Directions in Legal Education, 1970, (with Finkel) S.C. Torts II, 1986, III, 1990, IV, 1995; co-reporter S.C. Criminal Code, 1977, S.C. Study Sentencing, 1977. Trustee S.C. dist. U.S. Bankruptcy Ct., 1979— ; exec. dir. S.C. Continuing Legal Edn. Program.; bd. visitors Erskine Coll.; reporter S.C. Jury Charge Commn., 1991-95. Mem. ATLA, ABA, La. Bar Assn., S.C. Bar (sec. 1975-76, exec. dir. 1972-76, award of service 1978), New Orleans Bar Assn., Am. Law Inst., Am. Coll. Trial Lawyers, Southeastern Assn. Am. Law Schs. (pres.), S.C. Trial Lawyers Assn. (bd. govs. 1984-88), Forest Lake Club, Phi Alpha Delta. Republican. Episcopalian. Home: PO Box 1799 Columbia SC 29202-1799 Office: 1201 Main St Ste 1800 Columbia SC 29201-3294

MCCULLOUGH, V. BETH, pharmacist, educator; b. Harrison, Ark., May 15, 1953; d. A. G. and Willene L. (McLain) McC.; m. David Mark Pearson, Oct. 25, 1980; children: Colin McCullough-Pearson, Emily McCullough-Pearson. BS in Edn. cum laude, S.W. Mo. State U., 1976; BS in Pharmacy, U. Mo., 1981. Registered Pharmacist, Mo. Chief pharmacist Mt. Vernon Park Pharmacy, Springfield, Mo., 1981-89; dir. pharmacy Foster Health Care Group, Springfield, 1989-96; chief pharmacy ops. Balanced Care Corp./Foster Health Care Group, Springfield, 1996-97; cons. pharmacist Managed Healthcare Pharmacy divsn. Omnicare Corp., Springfield, 1997-2001; owner Med. Park Pharmacy, Eureka Springs, Ark., 2001—. Long term care pharmacy cons. Foster Health Care Group, Springfield, 1981-83, Managed Healthcare Pharmacy, Springfield, 1997-2001. Mem. NOW, Springfield, 1982—, assoc. mem. Animal Shelter League of the Ozarks, Nixa, Mo. Mem. Am. Soc. Cons. Pharmacists, Southwest Mo. Humane Soc., Mo. Equine Coun., Mo. Pharmacy Assn., Long Term Care Acad., Biokinetics (instnl. rev. bd. 1999-2001). Avocations: watercolor painting, jewelry making, horse breeding and showing. Office: 146 Passion Play Rd Eureka Springs AR 72632-9495 Home: 146 CR 238 Berryville AR 72616

MCCULLY, RUTH ALIDA, elementary education educator; b. Port Huron, Mich., Feb. 13, 1933; d. Leon Eugene Lounsberry and Rachel Elizabeth (DeSerano) Lounsberry-Maser; m. Donald Cecil McCully, Feb. 8, 1952 (dec. Nov. 1996); children: Stephen Donald, Robert Leon, Julie Ann. BS, Ea. Mich. U., 1976, MA, 1980. Asst. children's librarian Monroe County Library, Mich., 1962-64; dir. Weekday Nursery Sch., Youngstown, Ohio, 1964-71; dir. children's programs Lake-in-the-Woods, Ypsilanti, Mich., 1974-76; tchr. 1st grade Dundee Community Schs., Mich., 1976-88; tchr. young fives Dundee Community Schs., 1988-90; tchr. 1st grade, 1990-98, ret., 1998. Lay speaker Ann Arbor Dist., United Meth. Ch., 1979-98, dir., 1990-92; pastor Samaria Grace and Lulu United Meth. Chs., 1998; chmn. Dundee Community Caring and Sharing, 1982—; sec. Monroe County Food Bank, 1983—, Dundee Interfaith Coun., 1984—, Dundee Area Against Substance Abuse, 1984-88; bd. dirs. Habitat for Humanity, Monroe County, 1995—. Named Woman of Yr., United Meth. Women, Dundee United Meth. Ch., 1983, United Meth. Ann Arbor Dist. Coun. on Ministries; recipient cert. of Commendation Village of Dundee, 1993, State of Mich., 1994, J.C. Penney Gold Rule award for outstanding vol. svc., 1995. Mem. Phi Delta Kappa. Avocations: playing piano/guitar, needlework, sketching/painting, gardening, reading. Home: 510 E Monroe St Dundee MI 48131-1310 Office: Lulu United Meth Ch 12810 Lulu Rd Ida MI 48140-9718

MCCURRY, STEPHANIE, historian, educator; BA, U. Western Ont., 1981; MA, U. Rochester, 1983; PhD, SUNY, Binghamton, 1988. Asst. prof. U. Calif., San Diego, 1988—94, assoc. prof., 1994—98, Northwestern U., Evanston, Ill., 1998—. Mem. grad. student award com. CCHWP-CGWH/Berkshire Conf. Women Historians, 1993, 94; mem. award selection com. NEH, 1995; dir. Calif. History Project U. Calif., San Diego, 1996—98; dir. Alice Berline Kaplan Ctr. for the Humanities Northwestern U., Evanston, 2002—03; reviewer Oxford U. Press, U. N.C. Press, Harvard U. Press, U. Ill. Press, Johns Hopkins U. Press, U. Ga. Press; referee Am. Hist. Rev., Jour. Am. History, Gender and History, Jour. So. History, Ark. Hist. Quarterly; lectr. in field. Author: Masters of Small Worlds: Yeoman Households, Gender Relations and the Political Culture of the Antebellum South Carolina Low Country, 1995 (nominated for Pulitzer prize in history, 1995); contbr. articles to profl. jours. Recipient Frances Weir prize for history and lit., U. Western Ont., 1981, John Hope Franklin prize, Am. Studies Assn., 1996; fellow, John Simon Guggenheim Meml. Found., 2003; grantee, Am. Coun. Learned Socs., 1990; Rush Rhees and History Dept. fellow, U. Rochester, 1981—83, Doctoral fellow, Social Scis. and Rsch. Coun. Can., 1983—85, Smithsonian Instn., 1985—86, AAUW, 1986—87, Vis. scholar, Inst. for Rsch. on Women and Gender, Stanford U., 1994—95. Mem.: Am. Hist. Assn. (mem. Joan Kelly prize com. 1997—99), So. Assn. Women Historians (chair Willie Lee Rose prize 1999, mem. A. Elizabeth Taylor prize com. 1996, Willie Lee Rose prize 1997), So. Hist. Assn. (chair Francis B. Simkins award com. 1999—2001, mem. program com. ann. meeting 1997, Charles Sydnor prize 1996, Francis Butler Simkins prize 1997), Orgn. Am. Historians (co-chair program com. 2003). Office: Northwestern Univ Dept History Harris Hall #202 1881 Sheridan Rd Evanston IL 60208*

MCCUSKER, SISTER JOAN, music educator; b. Bklyn., Dec. 11, 1957; d. James Francis and Edna Joan (deNicola) McC. BM in Mus. Edn., Marywood Coll., 1979; MM in Mus. Edn., Ithaca Coll., 1990; PhD in Music Edn., Eastman Sch. Music, 2001. Cert. tchr., Pa., N.Y. Organist, choir dir. Holy Trinity Parish, Glen Burnie, Md., 1979-80; music tchr. St. Charles Borromeo, Arlington, Va., 1979-80, Most Precious Blood Sch., Balt., 1979-80, Nativity Sch., Scranton, Pa., 1980-81, St. Ephrem Sch., Bklyn., 1983-89, Notre Dame Elem. Sch., East Stroudsburg, Pa., 1989-90, St. Rose Elem. Sch./Sacred Heart H.S., Carbondale, Pa., 1990-93; music edn. instr. Marywood Coll., Scranton, 1992-93; music tchr. St. Joseph-by-the-Sea H.S., S.I., 1993-95; music edn. instr. Eastman Sch. Music, Rochester, N.Y., 1995-2000; asst. prof. Marywood U., Scranton, 2000—. Mem. Music Edn. Nat. Conf., 1983. Composer (sacred/vocal) Mass in D, 1980, Let Me Be Your Reed, 1983, The Word of Life, 1983, With One Voice, 1994. Mem. Nat. Cath. Educators Assn., Nat. Pastoral Musicians Assn., Pa. Music Edn. Assn., Kappa Gamma Pi (St. Catherine medal for Nat. Achievement 1978). Avocations: reading, composing music, crossword/cryto puzzles, travel. Home: Marywood U 2300 Adams Ave Scranton PA 18509 E-mail: mccusker@es.marywood.edu.

MCCUTCHAN, JUDITH KATHERINE, special education educator; b. Evansville, Ind., Oct. 12, 1941; d. Herbert Adelbert and Frances (Neblung) Grunow; m. Neil Jason McCutchan, Feb. 17, 1962; 1 child, Allen Neil. BS, U. N.D., 1979, MEd, 1986, PhD, 1992. Cert. spl. edn. tchr., elem. tchr. Tchr. substitute Grand Forks (N.D.) Pub. Schs., 1979-85, 95-96; grad. tchg. asst. U. N.D., Grand Forks, 1985-88; lectr. Mayville (N.D.) State U., 1988-89; tchr. spl. edn. Minot (N.D.) Pub. Schs., 1989-90, Upper Valley Spl. Edn. Unit, Grafton, N.D., 1991-95, Polk County Pub. Schs., Winter Haven, Fla., 1996-97, substitute tchr., 1998—. Rsch. asst. Bur. Ednl. Rsch. U. N.D., Grand Forks, 1986-87. Bd. dirs., sec./treas. Greater Grand Forks Emergency Food Cupboard, 1978-85; vol. chair memls. Am. Cancer Soc. East Polk County. Mem.: Order Ea. Star (Worthy Matron 1992—93, 1999—2000). Methodist. Avocations: bells, crafts, reading, gardening, travel. Home: 1740 Terry Cir NE Winter Haven FL 33881-2722

MCCUTCHEON, RANDALL JAMES, secondary school educator; b. Salem, Oreg., Mar. 4, 1949; s. James Vale and Delores (Bertholsen) McC. BS in Secondary Edn., U. Nebr., 1971. Announcer KRFS Radio, Superior, Nebr., 1966-67, KFMQ Radio, Lincoln, Nebr., 1968-75; grad. teaching asst. U. Nebr., Lincoln, 1971-73; tchr. East High Sch., Lincoln, 1975-85, Milton (Mass.) Acad., 1985-88, Valley High Sch., West Des Moines, Iowa, 1988-89, Albuquerque Acad., 1989—. Author: Get Off My Brain, 1985 (Best Books for Teenagers award NY Pub. Libr. 1998), Can You Find It?, 1989 (Ben Franklin Book of Yr. 1990); co-author: Communication Matters, 1993, Journalism Matters, 1997, Communication Applications, 2001. Named Dale E. Black Outstanding Young Speech Tchr. of Yr. Nebr. Speech Communication Assn., 1979, Nebr. Tchr. of Yr. Dept. Edn., 1985. Mem. Speech Communication Assn., Nat. Forensic League (Nat. Coach of Yr. 1987, Martin Luther King Jr. Svc. award 1999, Hall of Fame 2001. Avocations: travel, theatre, reading, writing, golf. Office: Albuquerque Acad 6400 Wyoming Blvd NE Albuquerque NM 87109-3899

MCCUTCHEON, RONALD EUGENE, social studies educator; b. Zanesville, Ohio, July 31, 1940; s. Ralph Dale and Helen Irene McC.; m. Catherine Marie Jorgensen; Apr. 2, 1966; children: Lois Sevim, Karin Elizabeth. BS in soc. studies edn., Ohio State U., 1965; MS, U. Oreg., 1971. Houseparent, cmty. devel. U.S. Peace Corps, Istanbul, Turkey, 1965-67; soc. studies tchr. Clev. Pub. Schs., 1967-68, Lakewood (Ohio) Pub. Schs., 1968-75, 76-94; geography and English tchr. Fulbright Exch. Program, Newton Aycliff, Eng., 1975-76; owner, oper. McCutcheon Info. Svcs., 1990—. Co-creator: (ednl. game) Industrialization, 1968. Mem. N.E. Ohio Returned Vols. Assn. (Beyond War award, 1987, Outstanding Svc. award, 1992), Turkish Am. Soc. No. Ohio, West Side Irish Am. Club, Ohio Norsemen (initiator, facilitator, 1993, membership chairperson, 1993-95, 99-2000). Avocations: bicycling, computers, gardening, genealogical and historical rsch.

MCDANIEL, BRIAN EDWIN, elementary school educator; b. Phoenixville, Pa., Nov. 10, 1950; s. Harold L. and Jean D. (Baird) McD.; m. Barbara A. Hagerman; 1 child, Craig Alastair. BS in Elem. Edn., Kutztown State U., 1972; perm. cert., Pa. State U., King of Prussia, 1974. Cert. tchr., Pa. Tchr. 6th grade Norristown (Pa.) Area Sch. Dist., 1972—. Mem. Motivation Task Force, Norristown Sch. Dist., 1991-92; team leader 6th grade, Stewart Middle Sch., Norristown, 1989—. Mem. CAP Ranger Squad 9010, Norristown, 1962-68; coach soccer Norristown Area Sch. Dist., 1990—, baseball coach, 1989, 90, 91, 94—; baseball coach Coventry (Pa.) Little League, 1992-94. Mem. NEA, Pa. State Edn. Assn., Edn. Assn. Norristown Area, Nat. Coun. Social Studies. Republican. Lutheran. Avocations: hiking, antiques, baseball, soccer. Home: 522 Upland St Pottstown PA 19464-5197 Office: Selma And Marshall St Norristown PA 19401

MCDANIEL, KAREN JEAN, university library administrator, educator; b. Newark, Nov. 16, 1950; d. Alphonso Cornell Cotton Jr. and Maude Jean (Smoot) Cotton Bledsoe; m. Rodney McDaniel Sr., Aug. 25, 1971; children: Rodney Jr., Kimberly Renee, Jason Bradley. BSBA, Berea Coll., 1973; MS in Libr. Sci., U. Ky., 1975, postgrad., 1977-78, 96—, Ky. State U., 1979-83, Ea. Ky. U., 1983. Asst. libr., instr. reference studies Paul G. Blazer Libr.-Ky. State U., Frankfort, 1975-79, asst. libr., instr. cataloging, 1980-83, head cataloging and classification, 1983; program coord. libr. svcs. Ky. Dept. Pub. Advocacy, Frankfort, 1983-85, libr. sr., 1985-87, program coord. state publs., 1987-89; dir. libr. svcs. Paul G. Blazer Libr.-Ky. State U., Frankfort, 1989—. Mem. adv. bd. African Am. Ednl. Archives Initiative, Wayne State U.; mem. subcom. on target groups Ky./White House Conf. on Libr. and Info. Svcs. II, chair, 1990-91. Contbg. author: Powerful Black Women, 1996, Notable Black American Women, Book II, 1996, Notable Black American Men, 1999, Kentucky Women, 1997, Encyclopedia of Louisville, 2000. Mem. State of Ky. Textbook Commn., 1993—; mem. Nat. Coun. Negro Women; adult membership Girl Scouts Am., 1987-94, asst. troop leader, 1991-93; active Frankfort H.S. PTA, 1994-96, Hearn Elem. Sch. PTA, 1983-94, Elkhorn Mid. Sch. PTA, 1991-97, Friends of Paul Sawyer Libr.; active St. John AME Ch.; mem. bd. Frankfort YMCA, 1995-97. Named Outstanding Alumnus, U. Ky. Sch. Libr. and Info. Sci., 1999. Mem. ALA, AAUP, NAACP, Assn. Coll. and Rsch. Librs., Black Caucus of ALA, Southeastern Libr. Assn., Land Grant and Tuskegee Libr. Dir.'s Assn. (vice-chair, chair 1994-98), State Assisted Acad. Libr. Coun. Ky. (sec. 1991-92, chair 1992-93), Ky. Libr. Assn. (sec. acad. sect. 1990-91), Ky.

Coun. Archives, Ky. Assn. Blacks in Higher Edn., Alpha Delta Kappa, Delta Sigma Theta. Democrat. African Methodist Episcopalian. Avocations: genealogical research, reading, needlework. Home: 147 Northwood Rd Frankfort KY 40601-1477 Office: Ky State U Paul G Blazer Libr Frankfort KY 40601

MCDANIEL, OLA JO PETERSON, retired social worker, educator; b. Hot Springs, Ark., Sept. 17, 1951; d. Milton Paul and Ella Floyd (Dickerson) Peterson; m. Daniel Tillman McDaniel, June 11, 1994; 1 child, Cadra Peterson. B Music Edn., Henderson State Coll., Arkadelphia, Ark., 1973; MA in Edn., Lindenwood Colls., St. Charles, Mo., 1983, cert. in social studies, 1977. Cert. tchr., Mo., Ark. Faculty Sch. Dist. St. Charles, 1974-84; adj. faculty Garland County C.C., Hot Springs, 1988-90; social worker Ark. Dept. Human Svcs., Hot Springs, 1990-94; substitute tchr. Hot Springs Sch. Dist., 1994-95; tutor St. Michael's Sch., Hot Springs, 1995—96; substitute tchr. Mt. Pine (Ark.) Sch. Dist., 1997-98. Substitute tchr. Mt. Pine Sch. Dist., 1997-98; soloist Congr. House of Israel, Hot Springs, 1965-73; cons. scholarships Hot Springs Music Club, 1988; const. student performance Garland County C.C., Hot Springs, 1988. Author, contbr. (learning activities) 3 R's for the Gifted: Reading, Writing, Research, 1982. Active Hot Springs Mid. Sch. PTO, 1996—98; vol. Hot Springs H.S.; founding mem. Friends of the Clinton Presdl. Libr., Nt. Campaign for Tolerance, 2003; hon. mem. Nat. Steering Com. to Reelect the Pres., Washington, 1995; mem. Dem. Nat. Com., Washington, 1994—, Pres.'s 2d Term Com., Washington, 1997; vol. Hot Springs Mayoral Campaign, 1993, Dem. Gubernatorial campaign, Hot Springs, 1990, Dem. campaign U.S. Congress Dist. 4, 2000; historian Virginia Clinton Kelley Dem. Women's Club of Garland County; mem. Dem. Ctrl. Com. of Garland County; vol. Garland County Dem. Hdqs., 2002. Recipient certs. of appreciation, St. Chrysostom's Am. Episcopal Ch., Hot Springs, 1990, Nat. Mus. Am. Indian, Washington, 1995, Alpha Chi, 1997, Hot Springs Mid. Sch., 1998, Parent Vol. award, 1998, Gov.'s Vol. Excellence award, 1997, 1998, cert. of recognition, Dem. Nat. Com., 2002. Mem.: AAUW, Nat. Campaign for Tolerance. A project of the Southern Poverty Law Center, Clinton Birthplace Foundation, Lindenwood Alumni, Henderson Alumni, Nat. Mus. Women in Arts (cert. appreciation 1997). Democrat. Roman Catholic. Avocations: advocate of welfare reform, reading, music. Home: 102 Woodberry St Hot Springs National Park AR 71913-2806

MCDANIEL, RICHARD W. artist, art educator; b. Berkeley, Calif., Aug. 31, 1948; BA, Calif. State U., San Diego, 1971; MFA, U. Notre Dame, (Ind.), 1984. Instr. drawing Ctrl. Conn. State U., New Britain, 1985-87; painting and drawing instr. Woodstock (N.Y.) Sch. Art, 1984-98; instr. Pacific Acad. Fine Arts, Santa Rosa, Calif., 1998—2001. Vis. artist Post Coll., Waterbury, Conn., 1987-88; condr. nationwide art workshops, 1991—; bd. advisors Woodstock Sch. Art, 1986-89, bd. dirs., 1989-98; bd. dirs. Pacific Acad. Fine Arts, Santa Rosa, Calif., 1998-2001. Author, illustrator: Catskill Mountain Drawings, 1990, Hudson River Drawings, 1994, The Drawing Book, 1995, Landscape, 1997; contbr. features in profl. art jours.; one-man shows include Lyman-Allyn Mus., Conn., 1983, U. Conn., 1990, Schenectady (N.Y.) Mus., 1991, Fairfield (Conn.) U., 1993, Hudson River Maritime Mus., N.Y., 1994, Redding (Calif.) Mus. Art and History, 1997, Sacramento Fine Arts Ctr., 1998; represented in permanent collections at New Britain (Conn.) Mus. Am. Art, Newport (R.I.) Art Mus., Redding Mus. Art and History, Hudson River Maritime Mus., Northwestern U. Hosp., Ill. McConnell Found., Calif., St. John's Med. Ctr., Wash., Fairfield (Conn.) U. Recipient residency fellowship Vt. Studio Colony, Johnson, Vt., 1990, Millay Colony, Austerlitz, N.Y., 1996. Mem. Pastel Soc. Am. (signature mem.), Pastel Soc. West Coast (signature mem.), Oil Painters Am. (signature mem.).

MCDANIEL, TIMOTHY ELTON, mathematics, statistics and business educator; b. Excelsior Springs, Missouri, Sept. 21, 1961; s. Everett Duncan and Leila Lynette (McDaniel); m. Kathleen Marie (Armato), June 23, 1984; children: Molly Lyn, Megan Marie, Anna Armato. BS math., polit. and computer sci., Rockhurst Coll., 1983; MS math. stats., Northwestern U., 1985; MA polit. sci., U. Mich., 1993. Asst. prof. math., stats. Buena Vista U., Storm Lake, Iowa, 1993—2001. Instr., cons. in social sci. methodology U. Mich., Ann Arbor, summers 1987—. Home: 515 Larchwood Dr Storm Lake IA 50588-3011 Office: Buena Vista U 610 W 4th St Storm Lake IA 50588-1713 E-mail: mcdaniel@bvu.edu.

MCDANIELS, PEGGY ELLEN, special education educator, consultant; b. Pulaski, Va., Jan. 4, 1945; d. James H. and Gladys M. (Hurd) Fisher; m. Robert A. McDaniels, Feb. 17, 1973; children: Dawn Marie, Robert C. A Gen Studies, Schoolcraft Coll., 1976; BA, Ea. Mich. U., 1980, MA, 1985. Cert. adminstr. Woodcock Johnson Psychoednl. Battery Orton-Gillingham Tng., learning disabilities educator. Payroll sec. Otto's Painting and Drywall, West Bloomfield, Mich., 1964-75; office mgr., closing sec. Bing Constrn. Co., West Bloomfield, 1964-75; substitute tchr. Wayne-Westland Schs., Westland, Mich., 1980-83, Farmington (Mich.) Schs., 1980-83; tchr. spl. edn. Romulus (Mich.) Community Schs., 1983-85, Cros-Lex Schs., Croswell, Mich., 1985-87, Pointe Tremble Elem. Sch., Algonac, Mich., 1987—. Organizer, recorder Tchr. Assistance Team, Algonac, 1991—. Mem. Coun. Exceptional Children (Golden Nugget award), Learning Disability Assn. (treas. 1988-90), Mich. Assn. Learning Disability Edn., ASCD. Avocations: camping, bicycling, reading. Home: 302 N Merritt Dr Midland MI 48640-7821

MCDERMITT, EDWARD VINCENT, lawyer, educator, writer; b. Hagerstown, Md., Nov. 29, 1953; s. Edward Bernard and Genevieve Natalie (Gallo) McD.; m. Jane Langmead Springmann, June 28, 1986; children: Edward S., Maureen K. BA, Georgetown U., 1975, MA, 1978; JD, U. Santa Clara, 1980; LLM, U. Pa., 1984. Bar: D.C. 1981, U.S. Dist. Ct. D.C. 1981. Rsch. asst. U. Santa Clara, Calif., 1980; pvt. practice Washington, 1981—; assoc. Law Offices of Miller & Loewinger, Washington, 1982; rsch. asst. U. Pa., Phila., 1983-84. Adj. asst. prof. Yale Gordon Coll. Liberal Arts, U. Balt., 1991—, vis. asst. prof., 1996; adj. assoc. prof. U. Md. Univ. Coll., 1998-2003, adj. prof., 2003—. Collegiatte prof., 2003—; lectr. law Columbus Sch. Law, Cath. U. Am., 1999—; mng. ptnr. J-L-S Svcs., Washington, 1985—, Early and Valuable Memorabilia, Md., 1985—; congl. intern to rep. Pat Schroeder, Washington, 1975; vol. atty. ACLU Nat. Capital area, Washington, 1982—; lectr. writing The Writer's Ctr., 1987—; participant program instrn. lawyers Harvard Law Sch., 1989—. Author: Overruled, Mr./Ms. Writer: An Argument in Favor of Accuracy in Depiction, How to Write an Uncommonly Good Novel, 1990, Return to Berlin, 1996, Toward a New Social (Democratic) Contract, 2000, John Marshall: Farmer Extraordinaire and the Seeds of Corporate Capitalism, 2001; author of works delivered at various confs. Is it Ethical to Teach Ethics on teh Web, 2000, International Human Rights: Final Bulwarks Against the War on Terrorism's Imperial Overreach at Home and Abroad, or, For What the Hell are We Fighting??!!, 2003, The Good and the Bad News on Enlightenment Thought in Modern Euro-Social Theory: More Than Good Works-Human Subjectivity in the Era of Exploitative Corporate Objectification, 2003, Huma Rights, Humiliation, Externalization/Objectification, and Guilt: More Than Good Works-Human Subjectivity in the Era of Exploitative Corporate Externalization, 2003, Gender, Social Identity, and the GLBT Community in a Globalised World: Do We Still Live in a Bi-Gendered World? Did We Ever??, 2003; contbr. articles to profl. jours. Vol. McGovern for Pres. campaign, Washington and Md., 1972, United Farmworkers Union, Washington, 1973-77, Urban Coalition Basketball League, Washington, 1977-78, Sarbanes re-election campaign, Md., 1982. Mem. D.C. Bar (cons., mem. lawyer/tchr. partnership program 1987—), Superior Ct. Trial Lawyers Assn., Washington Writers Group, Internat. Platform Assn., Assn. for Practical & Profl. Ethics, Pi Sigma Alpha. Roman Catholic. Avocations: photography, poetry, fiction writing, military history, bridge. Home and Office: 8000 Wildwood Dr Silver Spring MD 20912-7425

MCDERMON, LINDA GARRETT, elementary school educator; b. Nov. 29, 1949; d. Jack Sellars and Ruby (Varner) Garrett; m. John Nathan McDermon, Mar. 6, 1971; children: Jonathan, Daniel. BS in Child Devel., U. N.C., 1981, MS in Early Childhood, 1986. Cert. tchr., mentor, N.C. Tchr. Winston-Salem (N.C.)/Forsyth County Schs., 1982—. Coord./coach Odyssey of the Mind program Rural Hall (N.C.) Elem. Sch., 1992-93; participant N.C. Ctr. for Advancement of Teaching, Cullowhee, spring 1993. Past den leader, Tiger Cub coord., pack sec. Cub Scouts/Boy Scouts Am., Rural Hall, 1980-87; sec., active publicity, cultural arts and book fair events Rural Hall Sch. PTA, 1980-82; mem. Frields of Libr. Bd., Rural Hall, 1992-94. Named Dist. Cub Scouter of Yr., Piedmont dist. Boy Scouts Am., 1986, Tchr. of Yr. Rural Hall Sch., 1996, 97. Mem. ASCD, Nat. Coun. Tchrs. English, Nat. Coun. Tchrs. Math., Internat. Reading Assn. (membership chmn. local unit 1987), Nat. Sci. Tchrs. Assn., N.C. Assn. Educators (faculty rep. 1985, 92). Democrat. Avocations: reading, sewing, swimming, sailing, scuba diving. Home: PO Box 250 Rural Hall NC 27045-0250 Office: Rural Hall Elem Sch 275 College St Rural Hall NC 27045-9703

MCDERMOTT, CECIL WADE, mathematics educator, educational program director; b. Parkin, Ark., Aug. 19, 1935; s. Joe E. and Myrtle L. (Davis) McD.; m. Nelda Grace Lyons, June 4, 1961; children: Kevin Scott, Stephen Kyle. BS in Math., U. Ark., 1957; MS in Stats., Purdue U., 1962; EdD in Math. Edn., Auburn (Ala.) U., 1967. Cert. tchr. math., gen. sci., phys. sci., curriculum specialist supr. Instr. math. Sikeston (Mo.) H.S., 1957-59; state math. supr. Ark. Dept. Edn., Little Rock, 1959-65; ednl. cons. Auburn U., 1965-67; chmn., prof. math. Hendrix Coll., Conway, Ark., 1967-83; program dir. IMPAC Learning Sys., Inc., Little Rock, 1983—2002. Co-dir. NSF Inst. Tulane U., New Orleans, 1967-71; residential appraiser Morrilton (Ark.) Savs. & Loan, 1977-82; cons. Okla. Legis. Coun., Oklahoma City, 1987, Am. 2000 Project, Dallas, 1991; tchr. tng. panel Office Tech. Assessment, 1994; pres. Ark. Intercoll. Conf. Faculty Rep., 1974-84; study coord. Ark. Sci. and Tech. Authority, 2003—; cons. Ark. Sci. and Tech. Authority. Author: (audio-tutorial film) Primary School Mathematics, 1975; co-author: Modern Elementary Mathematics, 1978, Landmarks, Rudders and Crossroads, 1993, Modern Job, 1999, Essay on Jesus, 1999, Discourse on Educaton, 1999, Inner Thoughts and Outer Reflections, 2000, Riding the Waves of Change the Impac Story, 2000; designer (software) Mathematics/Basic Skills, 1989, 93; author numerous poems. Plan coord. Gov.'s Task Force on Telecomm. Planning, 1991-95; mem. Murphy Commn. Tech. Panel, 1997; bd. dirs. Hendrix Coll. Hall of Honor, 1993—. Rsch. grantee U.S. Office Edn., Washington, 1972-73, Rockefeller Found., Little Rock, 1983-85, Ross Found., 1997; Endowment scholar Hendrix Coll., Conway, Ark., 1987; recipient Cert. of Merit, Electronic Learning, 1987, Disting. Svc. award Nat. Tech. Leadership Coun., 2000, Excellence award Ark. Boys State, 2003, Leadership award Ark. Tech. in Edn., 2003; state honoree Nat. Gov.'s Assn., 1997; named to Hendrix Coll. Sports Hall of Honor, 2000, Ark. Boys State Hall of Fame, 2003. Mem. Ark. Amateur Union (chmn. state long distance running program 1969-72), Ark. Coun. Tchrs. Math. (chmn. regional conf. 1970), Am. Math. Soc., Math. Assn. Am. (pres. Okla./Ark. 1976-77), Phi Delta Kappa, Phi Kappa Phi, Pi Mu Epsilon. Episcopalian. Avocations: running, creative writing, farming, poetry. Home: 1204 Hunter St Conway AR 72032-2716

MCDERMOTT, KEVIN J. engineering educator, consultant; b. Teaneck, N.J., Nov. 21, 1935; s. Francis X. and Elizabeth (Casey) McD.; m. Ann McDermott, Aug. 3, 1959; children: Kathleen, Kevin, Donna, Michael. BSEE, N.J. Inst. Tech., 1965; MS Indsl. Engring., Columbia U., 1970; EdD, Fairleigh Dickinson U., 1975. Registered profl. engr., N.J. With Bell Telephone Labs., Murray Hill, N.J., 1960-65, Westinghouse Electic, Newark, 1965-67, Columbia U., NASA, N.Y.C., 1967-70, RCA Corp., N.Y.C., 1970-76, Ramapo (N.J.) Coll., 1976-80; prof. N.J. Inst. Tech., Newark, 1980—, chmn. engring. dept., 1983—. Dir. Computer Aided Design/Computer Aided Manufacture Robotics Consortium. Contbr. more than 50 articles to tech. jours. IBM fellow, 1987. Fellow IEEE, Soc. Mech. Engrs.; mem. Inst. Indsl. Engrs. Achievements include research in industrial robot work cells, manufacturing systems, expert systems, analysis of industrial robotics, flexible manufacturing systems, expert and vision systems in computer aided design and manufacturing.

MCDEVITT, HUGH O'NEILL, immunologist, educator; b. Cin., Aug. 26, 1930; MD, Harvard U., 1955. Diplomate: Am. Bd. Internal Medicine. Intern Peter Bent Brigham Hosp., Boston, 1955-56, sr. asst. resident in medicine, 1961-62; asst. resident Bell Hosp., 1956-57; research fellow dept. bacteriology and immunology Harvard U., 1959-61; USPHS spl. fellow Nat. Inst. Med. Research, Mill Hill, London, 1962-64; physician Stanford U. Hosp., Calif., 1966—; assoc. prof. Stanford U. Sch. Medicine, Calif., 1969-72, prof. med. immunology, 1972—, prof. med. microbiology, 1980—2001, Burt and Marian Avery Prof. Immunology, 1988—2001. Cons. physician VA Hosp., Palo Alto, Calif., 1968— Served as capt. M.C., AUS, 1957-59. Mem. NAS, AAAS, Am. Fedn. Clin. Rsch., Am. Soc. Clin. Investigation, Am. Assn. Immunologists, Transplantation Soc., Inst. Medicine, Royal Soc. (fgn.). Office: Sherman Fairchild Bldg Stanford U Sch of Medicine 299 Campus Dr MC5124 Stanford CA 94305-5124 E-mail: hughmcd@stanford.edu.

MCDIARMID, LUCY, English educator, author; b. Louisville, Mar. 29, 1947; m. Harris B. Savin, Oct. 13, 1984; children: Emily Clare, Katharine Eliza. BA, Swarthmore (Pa.) Coll., 1968; MA, Harvard U., 1969, PhD, 1972. Asst. prof. Boston U., 1972-74; from asst. prof. to assoc. prof. Swarthmore Coll., 1974-81; asst. prof. U. Md. Balt. County, Catonsville, 1982-84; prof. Villanova (Pa.) U., 1984—. Vis. prof. English Princeton U., 1995; mem. exec. com. Am. Conf. for Irish Studies, 1987-91, v.p., 1995-97, pres., 1997-99, past pres., internat. rep., 1999—. Author: Saving Civilization: Yeats, Eliot and Auden Between the Wars, 1984, Auden's Apologies for Poetry, 1990; co-editor: Selected Writings of Lady Gregory, 1995, High and Low Moderns: Literature and Culture, 1889-1939, 1996, The Irish Art of Controversy, 2003; contbr. articles to profl. jours. NEH fellow, 1981-82; ACLS grantee, 1976, Bunting Inst. fellow, 1981-82, Guggenheim fellow, 1993-94; vis. fellow N.Y. Inst. Humanities, 1993-95. Mem. MLA (exec. com. Twentieth Century Lit. divsn.), Internat. Assn. for Study Anglo-Irish Lit. (Am. sec.-treas. 1994-96), Phi Beta Kappa. Home: 1931 Panama St Philadelphia PA 19103-6609 Office: Villanova U Dept Of English Villanova PA 19085

MCDONALD, CHRISTIE ANNE, Romance languages and literature educator, writer; b. N.Y.C., May 4, 1942; d. John Denis and Dorothy (Eisner) McD.; m. Eugene Augustus Vance, June 11, 1965 (div. June 1986); children: Adam Vance, Jacob Vance; m. Michael David Rosengarten, Dec. 4, 1987. AB, Mt. Holyoke Coll., 1964; PhD, Yale U., 1969; MA (hon.), Harvard Coll., 1994. Acting instr. Yale U., New Haven, 1968-69; asst. prof. French U. Montreal, Que., Can., 1969-77, assoc. prof. French, 1977-83, prof., 1983, 86-93; prof. modern langs. Emory U., Atlanta, 1984-86; prof. romance langs. and. lits. Harvard U., Cambridge, Mass., 1994—, chmn. romance langs. and lits., 2000—. Author: The Dialogue of Writing, 1985, Dispositions, 1986, The Proustian Fabric, 1991; editor: The Ear of the Other, 1988, Transpositions, 1994. Recipient Clifford prize Am. Assn. 18th-Century Studies, 1994-95. Mem. Royal Soc. Can., Chevalier Palmes Académiques. Office: Harvard U 431 Boylston Hall Cambridge MA 02138

MC DONALD, GAIL FABER, musician, educator; b. Jersey City, Oct. 24, 1917; d. Samuel and Jennie (Weiss) Faber; m. George Walther, Nov. 17, 2000; children from previous marriage: Lora McDonald Ferguson, Charles McDonald, Henry McDonald. Diploma, Mannes Music Sch., N.Y.C., 1938; BA, U. Md., 1962; MusM, Cath. U., 1968; DMus Arts, U. Md., 1977. Legis. asst. Capitol Hill, 1943-46; pvt. tchr. piano and music theory Washington and Md., 1950—. Piano soloist Nat. Gallery Art, 1977; rec. artist Educo Records; lectr., performer Bach Sinfonias and Mendelssohn's Complete Songs Without Words; recorded complete solo piano works of Daniel Gregory Mason. Author: Muzio Clementi and the Gradus Ad Parnassum, 1968. Mem. D.C. Music Tchrs. Assn., Md. Music Tchrs. Assn. (pres. 1977—), D.C. Fedn. Music Clubs, Nat. Guild Piano Tchrs. (adjudicator 1972-2003), Friday Morning Music Club (performing mem.). Address: 801 N Monroe St Apt 602 Arlington VA 22201-2372

MCDONALD, JACQUELYN MILLIGAN, parent and family studies educator; b. New Brunswick, N.J., July 28, 1935; d. John P. and Emma (Mark) Milligan; m. Neil Vanden Dorpel; five children. BA, Cornell U., 1957; MA, NYU, 1971; MEd, Columbia U., 1992, EdD, 1993. Cert. in behavior modification, N.J.; cert. tchr. grades K-8, N.J.; cert. family life educator. Adj. instr. Montclair State U., 1982-93; instr. Edison C.C., Naples, Fla., 1994-96, Fla. Gulf Coast U., 1996—; family and comty. liason Family Resource Ctr., Fla. Gulf Coast U., 1996—. Parent vol. tng. project coord. Montclair Pub. Schs., 1984-86; coord. Collier County IDEAS for Parenting, Inc., Naples, 1993-97; tchr. parenting for teen mothers, adv. com. Crisis Parenting Women's Abuse Shelter, mem. adv. com.; co-chair Teenage Pregnancy Prevention Com. Welfare (WAGES) Coalition Region 24. Chairperson Interfaith Neighbors Juvenile Delinquency Prevention, N.Y.C., 1960-68; support family Healing the Children, 1970-90; founder The Parent Ctr., Montclair, 1983, Essex County N.J. Fair Housing Coun., 1990. Mem. Pre-Sch. Interagy. Couns., Raven and Serpent Hon. Soc. (pres. 1956). Psi Chi, Kappa Delta Pi. Avocations: swimming, tennis, golf, boating, hiking. Home: 27075 Kindlewood Ln Bonita Springs FL 34134-4370 Office: Fla Gulf Coast U Family Resource Ctr 10501 Fgcu Blvd S Fort Myers FL 33965-0001

MCDONALD, JACQUIE GAY, secondary school educator; b. Billings, Mont., Feb. 21, 1956; d. Richard G. and Margaret M. (Anderson) Rom; m. Alan James McDonald, Apr. 11, 1975; children: Kristina A., Caitlyn B., Megan M. BS in Edn., Eastern Mont. Coll., 1978; MS in Edn., Eastern Mont Coll., 2003. Lab. asst., math., fgn. lang. Billings (Mont.) Sr. High Sch., 1978-79, tchr., math, french, 1979—. Speaker in field. Editl. panel (online jour.) On-Math, 2003—. Mem. NEA, Nat. Coun. Tchrs. Math., Mont. Edn. Assn., Mont. Coun. Tchrs. Math., Billings Edn. Assn. Congregationalist. Avocations: jogging, aerobics, reading, hiking. Office: Billings Sr High Sch 425 Grand Ave Billings MT 59101-5999

MCDONALD, JOHN FRANCIS PATRICK, electrical engineering educator; b. Narberth, Pa., Jan. 14, 1942; s. Frank Patrick and Lulu Ann (Hegedus) McD.; m. Karen Marie Knapp, May 26, 1979. BSEE, MIT, 1963; MS in Engring., Yale U., 1965, PhD, 1969. Instr. Yale U., New Haven, 1968-69, asst. prof., 1969-74; assoc. prof. Rensselaer Poly. Inst., Troy, N.Y., 1974-86, prof., 1986—. Founder Rensselaer Ctr. for Integrated Electronics, 1980—. Contbr. more than 245 articles to profl. publs.; patentee in field. Recipient numerous grants, 1974—. Mem. ACM, IEEE (sr., assoc. editor Transactions on VSLI Design 1995—), Optical Soc., Acoustical Soc., Vacuum Soc., Materials Rsch. Soc. Office: Rensselaer Poly Inst Ctr for Integrated Electronics Troy NY 12181

MCDONALD, JOHN GREGORY, financial investment educator; b. Stockton, Calif., 1937; m. Melody McDonald. BS, Stanford U., 1960, MBA, 1962, PhD, 1967. Mem. faculty Grad. Sch. Bus. Stanford U., Calif., 1968—, now The IBJ prof. fin. Grad. Sch. Bus. Vis. prof. U. Paris, 1972, Columbia Bus. Sch., 1975, Harvard Bus. Sch. 1986; gov., vice chmn., bd. govs. NASD/NASDAQ Stock Market, 1987-90; mem. adv. bd. InterWest Venture Capital; dir. Investment Co. of Am., New Perspective Fund, Inc., Scholastic Corp., Varian Inc., EuroPacific Growth Fund. Contbr. articles to profl. jours. Bd. overseers vis. com. Harvard U. Bus. Sch., Cambridge, Mass., 1994-2000. Fulbright scholar, Paris, 1967—68. Office: Stanford U Grad Sch Bus 518 Memorial Way Stanford CA 94305

MCDONALD, LINDA WIRKLER, special education educator; b. Postville, Iowa, Dec. 15, 1953; d. Harvey Robert and Shirley Naomi (Jacobs) Wirkler; m. Paul Ray McDonald, Feb. 14, 1981; children: Jacob, Stephanie, Matthew, Lauren. BA in Elem. Edn., U. No. Iowa, 1976, MA in Spl. Edn., 1980. Cert. permanent profl. tchr., Iowa. Tchr. St. Mary's Sch., Waterloo, Iowa, 1976-77; tchr. spl. edn. Area Edn. Agy., Cedar Falls, Iowa, 1977—, union coun. rep., 1992—. Active Big Bros. and Big Sisters, 1978-93; bd. dirs. PTO, mem. publicity com., 1991-95; leader, sch. organizer, mem. pub. rels. com. Girl Scouts U.S.A., 1989-95. Mem. Phi Delta Kappa. Republican. Avocation: travel. Home: 895 Prospect Blvd Waterloo IA 50701-3954 Office: Area Edn Agy 2700 Grand Blvd Cedar Falls IA 50613-4720

MCDONALD, LOIS ALICE, elementary school educator; b. Grand Rapids, Mich., Feb. 19, 1930; d. Embert and Ruth Alfareta (Priest) Grooters; m. Ronald Gerard McDonald, July 17, 1954; children: Rodney Mark, Wendy Louise. BS, Western Mich. U., 1952, MA, 1974. Cert. elem. permanent tchr., Mich. Kindergarten and elem. tchr. Chalmers Sch., Algoma Twp., Sparta, Mich., 1952-54; elem. tchr. Loucks Sch., Peoria, Ill., 1955-56, Lakeside Sch., East Grand Rapids, Mich., 1957-58, Clyde Park Sch., Wyoming, Mich., 1958-63, 64-76; tchr. kindergarten Gladiola Sch., Wyoming, 1963-64; elem. tchr. Pinery Park Elem. Sch., Wyoming, 1976-85, Rogers Lane Sch., Wyoming, 1985-91; ret., 1991. Dir. John Knox Food Pantry, 1991—96; vol. Red Cross & West Mich. Trails of Girl Scouts, 1998—2002; ch. sch. supt. John Knox Presbyn. Ch., 1968—73; mem. Chancel Choir, 1977—98; bd. of dir. Second Harvest Gleaners of West Mich., 1993—2001. Mem.: MEA-NEA (life). Home: 33 13 Mile Rd NE Sparta MI 49345-9342

MCDONALD, PATRICIA LESLIE, education educator; b. Detroit, Apr. 5, 1945; d. Joseph Aloysious and Ethel Irene (Reynolds) McD. BA, Siena Heights Coll., 1969, MA, 1976; EdD, Western Mich. U., 1983. Elem. tchr. St. Anthony, St. Patrick, Ft. Lauderdale, Fla., 1969-75; coll. counselor Siena Hts. Coll., Adrian, Mich., 1975-76; faculty Siena Heights Coll., 1992—; therapist Macomb County Com. Mental Health, Mt. Clemens, Mich., 1976-83; adminstr. Human Devel. Program, Detroit, 1983-85; v.p., therapist Macomb Family Svcs., Mt. Clemens, 1985-92; assoc. dir. Archdiocese of Detroit, 1992-95; faculty Assumption Univ., Windsor, Ont., Can., 1995—, Univ. Detroit, 1994—; asst. dean met. Detroit program Siena Heights Coll., 1995—. Cons. IBM, various colls. and univs., Mich., Calif., 1980—. Adv. bd. Dominican Consultation Ctr., Detroit, 1983-91; bd. dirs. Macomb County Child Abuse and Neglect Coun., Mt. Clemens, 1985-92, bd. dirs. ARC, Detroit, 1994. Mem. Mich. Counselors Personal Assn. Roman Catholic. Home: 22727 Corteville St Saint Clair Shores MI 48081-2563

MCDONALD, W. WESLEY, political science educator; b. Balt., June 11, 1946; s. William E. and Marie C. (Hopkins) McD.; m. Alice Jean Baumgart, Aug. 3, 1996. BA, Towson State U., 1968; MA, Bowling Green (Ohio) State U., 1969; PhD, Cath. U. Am., 1982. Resident lectr. U. Md., College Park, 1973; rsch. asst. Russell Kirk, Mecosta, Mich., 1980; asst. prof. polit. sci. Elizabethtown (Pa.) Coll., 1980-86, assoc. prof. polit. sci., 1986—, chmn. dept. polit. sci., 1997-2000. Researcher Heritage Found., Washington, 1977; rsch. proposal reader U.S. Dept. Edn., Washington, 1989-91. Collaborator Viking Portable Conservative Reader, 1982; editor Helderberg Rev., 1970-7l, Towson State Jour. Internat. Affairs, 1967-68; contbr. articles to profl. jours. Mem. Howard County Councilmatic Districting Commn., Ellicott City, Md., 1976. Eisenhower Meml. fellow, 1978, Marguerite Eyer Wilbur fellow, 1980; Earhart Found. fellow, 2000-01; Russel Kirk Ctr. for Cultural Renewal fellow, 2001; recipient Alumni award Towson U., 1998. Mem. Am. Polit. Sci. Assn., Pa. Polit. Sci. Assn. (exec. bd. 1984-90, sec. 1999—), U. Profs. for Acad. Order (v.p. 1989-90, exec. com. 1990-93), Facquier County Va. Hist. Soc., Clan Donald USM, Soc. Gaelic-Am. Soc.,

The John Singleton Mosby Mus. Found. Republican. Home: 223 E Plum St Elizabethtown PA 17022-2743 Office: Elizabethtown Coll 1 Alpha Dr Elizabethtown PA 17022-2298 E-mail: mcdonaldw@etown.edu.

MCDONALD-WEST, SANDI MACLEAN, headmaster, consultant; b. Lowell, Mass., May 8, 1930; d. Walter Allan and Celina Louise (Lalime) MacLean; m. Thomas D. McDonald, Sept. 8, 1951 (div.); children: Todd F., Brooke Goodfriend, Ned M., Reid A., Heather McDonald McLean. BA, DePauw U., 1951; MA, Fairleigh Dickinson U., 1966; MEd, North Tex. State U., 1980. Cert. in Montessori teaching. Tchr., adminstr. Hudson (Ohio) Montessori Sch., 1966-68, Berea (Ohio) Montessori Sch., 1968-70, Creative Learning Ctr., Dallas, 1970-71; tchr., head of lower sch. The Selwyn Sch., Denton, Tex., 1971-83; tchr., headmaster Cimarron Sch., Enid, Okla., 1983-87; cons. Corpus Christi (Tex.) Montessori Sch., 1987-89, Azlann-Eren Horn Montessori Sch., Denton, 1989-95, Highland Meadow Montessori Acad., Southlake, Tex., 1994-2001. Ednl. dir., pres. Southwestern Montessori Tchg. Ctr., Inc., Denton, 1974—; adj. prof. North Tex. State U., Denton, 1979-80; cons., lectr. Am. Montessori Soc., N.Y.C., 1970—, Japanese Montessori Soc., 1978—, also pub. and pvt. schs., 1972—; chair commn. for accreditation Montessori Accreditation Coun. Tchr. Edn., 1991-97, chair emerita, 1997—. Developer various Montessori materials; contbr. articles to profl. jours. Mem. Am. Montessori Soc. (life), No. Ohio Montessori Assn. (pres. 1968-70), Assn. Montessori Internat., N.Am. Montessori Tchrs. Assn., LWV, Concerned Scientists. Avocations: ecology, golf, reading, travel. Home: 2005 Marshall Rd Denton TX 76207-3316 E-mail: swest4smtc@aol.com.

MCDONNELL, G. DARLENE, retired business educator; b. South Bend, Ind., Mar. 3, 1939; d. Roy Edward and Gizella Elizabeth Stroup; m. Dennis Eugene McDonnell, June 22, 1968; children: Lori, Jamie. BS, MA, Ball State U., 1962. Lic. real estate broker. Tchr. bus. edn. South Bend Cmty. Sch. Corp., 1962—2002, ret., 2002. Chmn. dept. bus. edn. LaSalle H.S., South Bend Cmty. Sch. Corp., 1972—95, BOA adv. bd., 1973—93. Co-editor (bus. edn. practice set simulation): Aaron's Insurance Agency, 1981. Mem.: Ind. Bus. Edn. Assn. (membership chmn.), Ind. State Tchrs. Assn., Bus. Office Assn. (intracurricular student sponsorship 1972—95), Delta Kappa Gamma, Kappa Delt Pi, Delta Pi Epsilon. Avocations: reading, golf. Home: 20440 Miller Rd South Bend IN 46614

MCDONOUGH-TREICHLER, JUDITH DIANNE, medical educator, consultant; b. L.A., Aug. 15, 1938; d. William Charles and Eleanor (Lewis) Anderson; m. Raymond Milan McDonough, Mar. 2, 1957 (div. Oct. 2, 1974); children: Joyce Churchill, Steven McDonough, Jill Cannon; m. John Rex Treichler, June 2, 1985. BS in Health Edn., Calif. State U., Long Beach, 1978; MS in Health Care Adminstrn., U. LaVerne, Calif., 1981; PhD in Pub. Health, Loma Linda U., Calif., 1991. Cert. registered nurse, Calif., health edn. specialist nat. Commn. for Health Edn. Credentialing. Dir. health edn. Nat. Med. Enterprises, Lakewood, Calif., 1972-80, Taif, Saudi Arabia, 1980-82, health educator Manila, Philippines, 1983; dir. health promotion and edn. Med. Ptnrs. US Family Care, Montclair, Calif., 1992-97; adj. faculty prof. U. LaVerne, Calif., 1986—, U. Phoenix, Ontario, Calif., 1996—, Crafton Hills Coll., Yucaipa, Calif., 1997—; owner, exec. v.p. JJS Health Edn. Cons., Rancho Cucamonga, Calif., 1996—. Rsch. asst. Loma Linda (Calif.) U., 1995-97; adv. bd. mem. Cerritos (Calif.) Coll., 1975-80, U. LaVerne, Calif., 1996—. Contbr. articles to profl. jours. Contbg. mem. La Liga Flying Samaritans, Rosario Mex., 1978-80, Friendship For Animals, Rancho Cucamong, Calif., 1995—. Recipient Dean's fellowship Loma Linda (Calif.) U., 1988. Mem. APHA, Calif. Scholarship Fedn., Nat. Coun. Against Health Fraud, World Clowns Assn., Clowns of Am. Internat., Calif. State U. Alumni Assn., Alpha Gamma Sigma. Avocation: clowning. Office: U LaVerne Dept Health Svcs Mgmt 1950 3d St La Verne CA 91750

MCDOUGAL, MARIE PATRICIA, retired educator, freelance writer and editor; b. Mt. Clemens, Michigan, Apr. 10, 1946; d. Allan Charles and Dorothy Nadine (Berger), Ling; m. Douglas Stevens McDougal, Aug. 23, 1969. BA, Central Mich. U., 1968; MA, Antioch U., Mich., 1997. Lic. tchr., Mich., 1968. Tchr. L'Anse Creuse High Sch., Harrison Twp., Mich., 1969-97; retired, 1997. Mem. L'Anse Creuse High Crisis Team, 1988-93, S.A.F.E. Task Force, Harrison Twp., 1986-98; spkr. in field. Author: Mount Clemens: Bath City U.S.A. in Vintage Post Cards, 2000; columnist: The Jour. Newspaper, 1983—90, writer: Introspective Mag., 1996—98, writer, editor: Antiquities Guide, 1997—98; author: Harrison Township, Michigan, 2002. Mem., L'Anse Creuse Athletic Boosters; chair Harrison Twp. Hist. Commn., 1993-2002; historian Harrison Twp.; founder, dir. Tranquil Life Fibromyalgic Support Group. Recipient Appreciation Award Macomb County Hist. Soc., 1989, Pres. Award for Lit. Excellence The Nat. Authors Registry, 1994. Mem. Soc. Children's Book Writers and Illustrators, Romance Writers Am., Venice Shores Property Owners (bd. dirs. 1994-2000, corr. sec. 1994-98), Detroit Working Writers, Red Hat Soc., L'Anse Creuse Public Sch. Alumni Assn. (steering com. 1996-98), Am. Auto Immune-Related Diseases Assn. Lutheran. Avocations: boating, crafts, reading. E-mail: ratisboat@wideopenwest.com.

MCDOWELL, ANNIE R. retired counselor; b. Lawtey, Fla., Sept. 12, 1934; d. Elbe and Rebecca (Strong) Hamilton; m. John D. Buckhanon, July 12, 1953 (div. June 1962); 1 child, Levon Buckhanon. BA, Fla. A&M U., Tallahassee, 1967; MEd, U. Ctrl. Fla., 1972; M in Guidance Counseling, Rollins Coll., 1975. Tchr. Orange County Pub. Schs., Orlando, Fla., 1967-73; equal opportunity counselor, coord. Valencia C.C., Orlando, 1973-97; ret., 1997. Mem. Valencia Black Adv. Bd., Orlando, Fla., 1973—, President's Status of Women, 1989—, Sisters Alive, Orlando, 1993—, Orlando Partnership, 1994—. Recipient Appreciation award African-Am. Cultural Soc./Valencia Coll., 1995. Mem. Mem. Nat. Hook-Up of Black Women (Honors ward 1988, pres. 1989), Friendship Club, Negro Coun. Women, Gamma Delta Pi. Democrat. Baptist. Home: 1549 Lawndale Cir Winter Park FL 32792-6160

MCDOWELL, DAVID LYNN, mechanical engineering educator; b. Red Oak, Iowa, Dec. 20, 1956; s. Leland Lee and Wilma McD.; m. Kathryn M. McDowell, May 26, 1979; children: Matthew Todd, Andrew Joel, James Neal. BSME, U. Nebr., 1979; PhDME, U. Ill., 1983. Asst. prof. mech. engrng. Ga. Inst. Tech., Atlanta, 1983-87, assoc. prof., 1987-92, prof., 1992—, regents prof., 1996—, Carter N. Paden Jr. Disting. chair in metals processing, 1998—. Dir. Mech. Properties Rsch. Lab., 1992—; presenter in field. Mem. editl. bd. Internat. Jour. Plasticity, Fatigue and Fracture of Engrng. Material Structure, Internat. Jour. Damage Mechs., (regional edit.) Internat. Jour. Fracture; contbr. over 200 articles to profl. jours. Recipient Alfred Noble prize ASCE, 1986, Ralph R. Teetor award Soc. Automotive Engrs., Outstanding Young Faculty award Dow Chem. Soc., 1990, Presdl. Young Investigator award NSF, 1986. Fellow ASME (Henry Hess award 1988, Nadai award 1997, editor Jour. Engrng. Material Tech. 1997-2002); mem. ASTM, Am. Soc. Metals Internat., Materials Rsch. Soc., Am. Acad. Mechanics, Am. Soc. for Engrng. Edn., Soc. Engrng. Sci. (v.p. 2001, pres. 2002), Pi Tau Sigma (Gold medal 1987). Home: 4275 Cedar Bluff Way SW Lilburn GA 30047-3185 Office: Ga Inst Tech GWW Sch Mech Engring Atlanta GA 30332-0405

MCDOWELL, DONNA SCHULTZ, lawyer, educator; b. Cin., Apr. 23, 1946; d. Robert Joseph and Harriet (Parronchi) Schultz; m. Dennis Lon McDowell, June 20, 1970; children: Dawn Megan, Donnelly Lon. BA in English with honors, Brandeis U., 1968; MEd, Am. U., 1972; C.A.S. with honors in Reading, Johns Hopkins U., 1979; JD with honors, U. Md., 1982; MS, Hood Coll., 1995; postgrad., U. Md. Bar: Md. 1982; cert. tchr. reading K-12, D.C.; advanced profl. cert. in English, Biology and Reading, Md. Instr. Anne Arundel & Prince George's C.C., Severna Park and Largo, Md., 1977-78; coll. adminstr. Bowie State Coll. (Md.), 1978-79; assoc. Miller & Bortner, Lanham, Md., 1982-83; sole practice Lanham, 1983-87, Gaithersburg, Md., 1987—; sci. tchr. D.C. Pub. Schs., 1999-2000; chair dept. English Montgomery County Pub. Schs., 2000—, English lit. tchr., 2002—03. Ednl. cons.; presenter in field. Chmn. Housing Hearing Com., Bowie, 1981-83; trustee Unitarian-Universalist Ch., Silver Spring, Md., 1979-83; bd. dirs. New Ventures, Bowie, 1983, Second Mile (Runaway House), Hyattsville, Md., 1983; officer Greater Laytonsville Civic Assn., 1989; founding mem. People to Preserve, Laytonsville; mem. Solid Waste Adv. Com., Montgomery County, Md.; election judge; presenter NCTE, SOMIRA, NCPS. Recipient Am. Jurisprudence award U. Md., 1981; Michael Jordan grantee, 2000, D.C. Pub. Schs. grantee. Mem. Phi Kappa Phi. Democrat. Avocations: gardening, reading, bluebirds, movies. Home: 24308 Hipsley Mill Rd Gaithersburg MD 20882-3132 E-mail: DonnaSMcD@aol.com.

MCDOWELL, ORLANDO, secondary education educator; b. Chgo., Sept. 4, 1963; s. Willis and Attie (McDowell) Newsome. AA, Olive-Harvey Coll., 1985; BA, Chgo. State U., 1992. Cert. tchr., Ill. Tchr. math. Chgo. Bd. Edn., 1992—; exec. mgr. Mid-West Mktg., Chgo., 1995-96. Spkr. in field. Mem., leader Nat. Rep. Com., Washington, 1995—; mem. Dem. Senate Com., Washington; candidate for U.S. Congress, 1996. Recipient Black Achievement award Harold Washington Jr. Coll., 1994. Mem. AAAS, ACLU (hon.), Internat. Coun. Fgn. Relationships, Acad. Sci., Chgo. Archtl. Found., Chgo. Hist. Soc., Chgo. State U. Alumni Bd., Chicagoland C. of C., Hon. Profs. Soc., Phi Theta Kappa. Home: 9034 S Essex Ave Chicago IL 60617-4051

MCDUNN, KATHLEEN EVELYN, nurse, nursing educator; B.S., DePaul U., 1976; M.S., No. Ill. U., 1985. Staff nurse U. Ill. Hosp., Chgo., 1976-78, asst. head nurse, 1978-80, acting head nurse, 1980; instr. nursing Little Co. of Mary Hosp. Sch. Nursing, Evergreen Park, Ill., 1980-84, acad. advisor, 1980-84; hosp.-home care coordinator Health Care at Home, Hinsdale, Ill., 1985-86; maternal child health nurse cons. Ill. Infant Mortality Reduction Initiative, Cook County Dept. Pub. Health, 1986-88, pub. health nursing supr., 1988-95, med. case mgmt. coord., 1995-97, asst. dir. nursing, Cook Co. Health Dept., 1997—. Mem. ANA, Am. Pub. Health Assn., Am. Nurses Found., Assn. for Care of Children's Health, Ill. Nurses Assn., DePaul U. Dept. Nursing Alumni Assn., Sigma Theta Tau.

MCDYER, SUSAN SPEAR, academic administrator; b. Bridgeton, N.J., July 18, 1948; d. Wallace H. and Oleta (Craddock) Spear; 1 child, Kristine Beth. AS, Widener U., 1968. Dir. fin. & personnel U. Pitts., 1986-87, dir. major gifts, assoc. dir. campaign for 3d century, 1987-89, exec. dir. univ. resources devel., dir. campaign 3d century, 1989-91; v.p. univ. rels., dir. campaign Gannon U., Erie, Pa., 1991—. Presenter in field. Bd. dirs. Discovery Sq., First Night Erie. Mem. AAUW, NAFE, Nat. Soc. Fundraising Exec., Am. Med. Colls. (pub. affairs com. 1989-91), Assn. Am. Med. Colls. (pub. affairs com. 1989-91), Coun. Advancement & Support Edn., St. Vincent Health System (bd. corps.), Erie Club, The Newcomen Soc. U.S., Presque Isle Partnership (dir.), C. of C. (dir.).

MCEACHERN, WILLIAM ARCHIBALD, economics educator; b. Portsmouth, N.H., Jan. 4, 1945; s. Archibald Duncan and Ann Teresa (Regan) McE.; m. Patricia Leonardo, Aug. 18, 1973. AB in Econs., Holy Cross Coll., 1967; MA in Econs., U. Va., 1969, PhD in Econs., 1975. Asst. prof. U. Conn., Storrs, 1973-78, assoc. prof., 1978-84, prof. econs., 1984—, dir. grad. studies, 1981-87. Econ. cons. U.S. Dept. Labor, 1977-79, FTC, 1979-82, Conn. Conf. on Municipalities, New Haven, 1975-76, 87-88; dir. Bipartisan Commn. on Conn. Finances, Hartford, 1982-83. Author: Managerial Control and Performance, 1975, Economics: A Contemporary Introduction, 6th edit., 2002; founding editor Quarterly Rev. on Conn. Economy, The Teaching Economist; contbr. articles to profl. jours. 1st lt. U.S. Army, 1969-71. Nat. Def. fellow U. Va., 1967-69, 72-73. Mem. Nat. Tax Assn., Am. Econ. Assn., Northeast Bus. and Econs. Assn. (founder, assoc. editor 1978-81), So. Econ. Assn., Western Econ. Assn. Office: U Conn Dept Econs U-63 341 Mansfield Rd Dept Econsu63 Storrs Mansfield CT 06269-9015

MCELDOWNEY, RENE, healthcare educator, consultant; b. Denver, Mar. 31, 1956; d. Raymond James and Barbara Louise (McNeal) Polanis; m. George Adams McEldowney Jr., June 1, 1984. AB, Morris Harvey Coll., Charleston, W.Va., 1977; BS, W.Va. State Coll., 1983; MBA, Marshall U., 1987; PhD, Va. Tech. U., 1994. X-ray technologist Charleston Area Med. Ctr., 1977-79, nuc. medicine technologist, 1979-84; asst. to v.p. acad. affairs Marshall U., Huntington, W.Va., 1984-87, mgmt. instr., 1987-89; asst. prof. Auburn (Ala.) U., 1992—. Rsch. cons. Netherland Sch. Govt., Das Hagg, Holland, 1990—; physics cons. Health Physics & Assocs., Roanoke, Va., 1991-92. Founder Food Search, Charleston, 1987-89; mem. Score, Huntington, 1988-89; literacy vol. Ala. Literacy Coun., Montgomery, Ala., 1993—; mem. Montgomery Jr. League, 1992—. Recipient scholarship Oxford U., 1991. Mem. ASPA, Am. Acad. Mgmt., Mortar Bd., Kappa Kappa Gamma. Avocations: book collecting, tennis, jogging, classical music. Office: Auburn U 1224 Haley Ctr Auburn AL 36849

MCELHINNEY, JAMES LANCEL, artist, educator; b. Abington, Pa., Feb. 3, 1952; s. James and Joan Howland (Carpenter) McE.; m. Victoria Maria Dávila, Sept. 12, 1981 (div.), m. M.L. Burnell Shively, May 14, 2003. Scholarship student, Skowhegan (Maine) Sch. of Art, 1973; BFA, Temple U., 1974; MFA, Yale U., 1976. Asst. prof. Moore Coll. Art, Phila., 1977-78, Skidmore Coll., Saratoga Springs, N.Y., 1979-87; adj. instr. UCLA, 1983, Moore Coll. Art, 1983, Tyler Sch. Art, Phila., 1983-86, U. of Arts, Phila., 1985-89; instr. Milw. Inst. Art and Design, 1991-93; vis. artist East Carolina U., Greenville, N.C., 1994-98; head painting and drawing program visual arts dept. U. Colo., Denver, 1998—; dir. study abroad program Feltre, Veneto, Italy, 2000—. Artist in residence Harper's Ferry Nat. Hist. Park, 1999; lectr. USAF Acad., 2001. One-man shows include Peninsula Ctr. for the Fine Arts, Newport News, Va., 1993, Danville (Va.) Mus., 1993, Second Street Gallery, Charlottesville, Va., 1995, F.A.N. Gallery, Phila., 1995, 1998, Greenville (N.C.) Mus. Art, 1996, Lee Hansley Gallery, Raleigh, N.C., 1996, 1998, 1999, Asheville (N.C.) Art Mus., 1996, William Havu Gallery, Denver, 2001—02, Mus. of the S.W., Midland, Tex., 2003, Letterkenny Arts Ctr., Donegal, Ireland, 2003, William Havu Gallery, 2001, Mus of Southwest, Midland, Tex., 2003, Letterkenny Arts Ctr., Donegal, Ireland, 2003, exhibited in group shows at Chrysler Mus., Norfolk, Va., 1999, Allen Sheppard Gallery, N.Y.C., 1999, Ucross Found., 2000, Nicolayseu Mus., 2000, Represented in permanent collections Chrysler Mus. Art, Denver Art Mus., Asheville Art Mus.; contbr. articles to various profl. mag., to profl. jours.; prin. works include multiple venues, 2003. Vol. Richmond (Va.) Nat. Battlefield Park, 1991—, Frontier Army Living History Corps of Discovery, U.S. Army C.E. Lewis and Clark Bicentennial, Topog. eng. 1st Divsn. Staff, Hdqs. Nat. Reft. (U.S.C.W.). Grantee painting, NEA, 1987—88, Ptnrs. in Arts, Richmond Arts Coun., 1995; rsch. grant, U. Colo., 2000, Faculty Devel. grant, 2003. Mem. Coll. Art Assn., SAR, Civil War Preservation Trust, Frontier Army L.H. Assoc.,Foote Family Assoc. Office: U Colo Coll Arts Media Box 177 PO Box 173364 Denver CO 80217-3364

MCELROY, ANNIE LAURIE, nursing educator, administrator; b. Quitman, Ga., Dec. 30, 1945; d. Frank H. Sr. and Ina Mae (Carpenter) McElroy; children: Laurie, Matt. Grad., Ga. Bapt. Sch Nursing, 1966; BS, Valdosta State U., 1988, MEd, 1989, postgrad., 1991; PhD, Ga. State U., 1994. Health aid, then head nurse Presbyn. Home, Quitman, 1966-68, 68-70; owner, bookkeeper Maddox Drugstore, Quitman, 1970-80; instr. health occupations Brooks County High Sch., Quitman, 1981-88, instr. nurses aides, 1983; instr. health occupations Lowndes High Sch., Valdosta, Ga., 1988-89; instr. dept. vocat. edn. Valdosta State U., 1989-92; dir. practical nursing program S.W. Ga. Tech. Coll., Thomasville, 1992—, coord. Allied Health diploma program, 1992—, dean Allied Health, 2002—. Recipient Most Disting. Alumna Ga. Bapt. Coll. Nursing, 2000. Mem. ASCD, NEA, AAUW, Ga. Edn. Assn., Nat. Assn. Educators, Ga. Assn. Educators, Assn. for Career and Tech. Edn., Assn. Indsl. and Tech. Tchr. Educators, Internat. Tech. Edn. Assn., Ga. Nurses Assn., Phi Delta Kappa, Phi Kappa Phi. Avocations: piano, saxophone, bassoon, walking. Home: 607 N Laurel St Quitman GA 31643-1221 E-mail: amcelroy@swgtc.net.

MCELROY, CHARLOTTE ANN, principal; b. Dimmitt, Tex., Oct. 24, 1939; d. William Robert and Mary Ilene (Cooper) McE. BA, West Tex. State U., 1962, MEd, 1964; postgrad., Calif. State U., Santa Barbara, 1966-68. Tchr. Amarillo (Tex.) Schs., 1962-65; 1st and 2d grade tchr. Ventura (Calif.) Schs., 1965-66, 4th, 5th and 6th grade tchr., 1966-74, elem. counselor, 1974-76, spl. edn. tchr., 1976-77, counselor, phys. edn. tchr., 1977-78; asst. prin. Cabrillo Jr. High Sch., Ventura Unified Schs., 1978-80; prin. E. P. Foster Elem. Sch., Ventura Unified Schs., 1980-84, Anacapa Middle Sch., Ventura Unified Schs., 1984—. Presenter in field. Recipient Nat. Blue Ribbon Sch. award Nat. Edn. Dept., 1990-91, Calif. Disting. Sch. award, 1989-90; named one of Outstanding Principals, State Calif., 1992-93. Mem. Ventura Adminstrs. Assn., Calif. League Middle Schs., Assn. Calif. Sch. Adminstrs., Kappa Kappa Gamma. Democrat. Avocations: skiing, reading, music, gardening. Home: 2250 Los Encinos Rd Ojai CA 93023-9709 Office: Anacapa Middle Sch 100 S Mills Rd Ventura CA 93003-3434

MCELROY, MAURINE DAVENPORT, financier, educator; b. Eastland, Tex., Sept. 28, 1913; d. William Fred and Mary Ewell (Johnson) Davenport; m. Kennedy King McElroy, Aug. 9, 1937 (dec. Mar. 1996); children: Mary M., Kennedy King Jr. BA, Tex. Tech U., 1937; MA, Hardin-Simmons U., 1941; PhD, U. Tex., 1964. Tchr. Eastland West Ward Elem. Sch., 1933-39, Eastland H.S., 1939-41, Miller H.S., Corpus Christi, Tex., 1951-54, Ray H.S., Corpus Christi, 1954-57; instr. Del Mar Coll., Corpus Christi, 1957-59; prin. Birdville H.S., Ft. Worth, 1942-43; feature writer Ark. Dem.-Gazette, Little Rock, 1948-51; assoc. prof. emeritus dept. English U. Tex., Austin, 1964—. Cons. in field. Contbr. articles to profl. publs. Patron art museums, theatrical orgns., hist. preservation; sponsor Shelter for Abused Women and Children; fin. mgr. trusts. Mem. AAUW, Am. Assn. Colls. Tchg. English, Coll. English Assn. (life), Renaissance Soc. Am. Avocations: travel, reading, theatre, horticulture. Home: 3215 Gilbert St Austin TX 78703-2221 Office: U Tex Austin Dept English Parlin Hall 108 Austin TX 78712

MCELROY, PATRICIA ANN, special education educator; b. Norman, Okla., Aug. 11, 1950; BS in Mental Retardation, Okla. State U., 1973; MEd in Learning Disabilities, La. State U., 1985, EdS in Curriculum & Instrn., 1999. Cert. mental retardation, mild/moderate-generic, learning disabilities, assessment tchr. Tchr. educable mentally retarded St. Michael's Spl. Sch., New Orleans, 1973-74, Blvd. Spl. Sch., Jefferson Parish, La., 1974-77; spl. edn. tchr., liturgist St. Rose of Lima Elem., New Orleans, 1977-78; singing tchr., liturgist Corpus Christi Elem. Sch., New Orleans, 1978-79; tchr. learning disabled Cath. High of Point Coupee Elem., New Roads, La., 1980; spl. edn. math. tchr. Sacred Heart Elem. Sch., Morgan City, La., 1980-81; regional coord. non-pub. schs. Spl. Ednl. Svcs. Corp., Baton Rouge, 1982-83; assessment tchr. Livingston (La.) Parish Sch. Bd., 1983—2000; state supr. ednl. diagnostic svcs. La. Dept. Edn., 2000—. Conductor workshops for faculties and parent groups; founding ptnr., bd. dirs., treas. Counseling and Diagnostic Assocs., Inc., 1989. Co-author: Celebrate Cycles B & C, A Creative Resource for Children's Sunday Liturgies. Chmn. fund-raising project La. Epilepsy Assn. Mem. La. Ednl. Assessment Tchrs. Assn. (state pres. 1990, past state pres. 1991, lobbyist), La. Assn. Sch. Execs., Pupil Appraisal Alliance La., Coun. for Exceptional Children, Coun. Ednl. Diagnostic Svcs., Coun. Adminstrs. Spl. Edn., Assn. for Prevention Child Abuse (bd. dirs. Livingston chpt.), La. Ednl. Diagnostic Assn. (state pres. 1994, state pres. 1999). Home: 12069 E Glenhaven Dr Baton Rouge LA 70815-6522 Office: La Dept Edn PO Box 94064 Baton Rouge LA 70804-9064

MCELWAIN, EDWINA JAY, retired elementary school educator; b. Wheeling, W.Va., Dec. 23, 1936; d. Edgar F. and Myrtle L. Buchanan; m. David Ray McElwain, Nov. 22, 1956; children: Diana Louise, David Alan. BS, Steubenville U., 1973. Cert. tchr. Ohio. Tchr. Springfield Local Sch. Dist., Amsterdam, Ohio, 1956-61; substitute tchr. Edison Local Sch. Dist., Bergholz, Ohio, 1973-77; tchr. Gregg Elem. Sch., Bergholz, 1977-97; ret., 1997. Tutor, Hammondsville, Ohio. Adult adviser 4-H Club, Jefferson County, 1970—81. Martha Holden Jennings Found. scholar, 1981—82. Mem.: Ohio Ret. Tchrs. Assn., Jefferson County Ret. Tchrs. Assn., Amsterdam Women's Club (v.p. 1999—2000, pres. 2002—), Delta Kappa Gamma (corr. sec. 1986—90, v.p. 1994—96, chmn. rsch. com. 1992—94, pres. 1996—2000, parliamentarian 2000—). Avocations: reading, stamp collecting, horses. Home: 1899 County Highway 59 Bergholz OH 43908-7928

MCELWAIN, FRANKLIN ROY, educational administrator; b. Caribou, Maine, Oct. 22, 1954; s. Ralph Bearce and Adrina (Roy) McE.; m. Joan Aucoin, June 17, 1978; children: Diana, Lauren, Spencer. BS in Agrl. Mechanization, U. Maine, 1977, MPA, 1988. Farmer Red Wagon Farms, Caribou, 1973-75; tchr. Cen. Aroostook High Sch., Mars Hill, Maine, 1977-85; rsch. asst. U. Maine Agrl. Experiment Sta., Presque Isle, summers 1982-85; tchr. Limestone (Maine) Jr./Sr. High Sch., 1985-93; asst. prin. Caribou (Maine) High Sch., 1993—96; curriculum dir. Caribou Bd. Edn., 1996—2002; supt. Caribou Sch. Bd., 2002—. Advisor Future Farmers Am., Limestone High Sch., 1985-93; text reviewer Delmar Pubs., Albany, N.Y., 1990-92; academic team leader Limestone High Sch., 1991-92. Sec. Caribou PTA, 1982; mem. Caribou Bd. of Edn. review com., 1991-92; mem. Parish Coun., Caribou, 1988-90; advisor Cath. Youth Orgn., Caribou, 1979-81. Named Maine Tchr. Yr., 1992, Agriscience Tchr. Yr., 1986; recipient Excellence in Edn. award U. Maine, 1992. Mem. Nat. Tchrs. Assn., Nat. Vocat. Agr. Tchrs. Assn., Maine Assn. Agr. Tchrs., Maine Resource Bank, Maine Edn. Talent Pool, Limestone Future Farmers Am. Alumni Assn. (sec. 1986—), Maine Dirigo Found., Maine Plant Food Ednl. Soc. Republican. Roman Catholic. Avocations: running, basketball, cross-country skiing, woodworking. Home: PO Box 551 Caribou ME 04736-0551 Office: 628 Main St Caribou ME 04736*

MCELWAINE, THERESA WEEDY, academic administrator, artist; b. Culver City, Calif., Nov. 15, 1950; d. Victor Louis and Doris Yvonne Weedy; m. James William McElwaine, Jan. 1, 1989. BA, Calif. State U., Fullerton, 1972, cert. secondary tchr., 1974; MFA in Photography, San Francisco Art Inst., 1981. Bookstore mgr., 1978-81; asst. dir. San Francisco Camerawork, 1981-83; exec. dir. Collective for Living Cinema, N.Y.C., 1984-85; dir. mktg. Am. Internat. Artists Mgmt., N.Y.C., 1986-87; asst. dean cont. edn. SUNY, Purchase, 1987-97, dir. comm., 1997—. Cons. Parabola Arts Foun., N.Y.C., 1985-86, Clarity Ednl. Productions, San Francisco, 1983, N.Y. State Coun. on Arts, 1986-91. Exhibited in group and solo shows at San Francisco Camerawork, Inc., Foto Gallery, N.Y.C., U. Calif., Berkeley, San Francisco Mus. Modern Art, Plymouth (England) Arts Ctr., Ariz. State U., Tempe, Vanderbilt U., Nashville, Floating Found. Photography, N.Y.C. Bd. dirs. San Francisco Camerawork, 1977-81; bd. advisors Collective of Living Cinema, 1985-87, Parabola Arts Found., 1986-92. Recipient Excellence awards Am. Inst. Graphic Arts, 1982-83. Home: 64A Valley Rd Cos Cob CT 06807-2533

MCELYEA, BARBARA JEANETTE, special education educator; b. Kingsport, Tenn., Mar. 29, 1952; d. Denver Nathaneil and Margaret Lee (Bilheimer) McE. BS in Human Rels., Milligan Coll., 1976. Cert. spl. educator K-12, psychology 8-12; cert. tchr. of visually impaired. Aide Johnson City (Tenn.) Pub. Schs., 1975-78; devel. technician Dawn of Hope Devel Ctr., Johnson City, 1978-83; tchr. Bristol (Tenn.) Regional Rehab. Ctr., 1983-84; technician, hometrainer Dawn of Hope Devel. Ctr., Johnson City, 1984-86; tchr. of the visually impaired Carter County Pub. Schs.,

Elizabethton, Tenn., 1986—, Keenburg Elem. Sch., Elizabethton, 1993—. Author: (poetry) Who Shall I Ever Be, 1973, Cam Carmel Peace, 1973 (3rd Pl. award 1971). Named to Dean's List Milligan Coll., 1975, 85, 86. Mem. NEA, Assn. for the Edn. and Rehab. of the Blind and Visually Impaired, Tenn. Edn. Assn., Carter County Edn. Assn. (bldg. rep. 1986-90, pres.), Coun. for Exceptional Children. Avocations: reading, writing, knitting.

MCEVOY, SHARLENE ANN, law educator; b. Derby, Conn., July 6, 1950; d. Peter Henry Jr. and Madaline Elizabeth (McCabe) McE. BA magna cum laude, Albertus Magnus Coll., 1972; JD, U. Conn., West Hartford, 1975; MA, Trinity Coll., Hartford, 1980, UCLA, 1982, PhD, 1985. Bar: Conn., 1975. Pvt. practice, Derby, 1984—; asst. prof. bus. law Fairfield (Conn.) U. Sch. Bus., 1986—92; adj. prof. bus. law, polit. sci. Albertus Magnus Coll., New Haven, 1978-80, U. Conn., Stamford, 1984-86; acting chmn. polit. sci. dept. Albertus Magnus Coll., 1980; assoc. prof. law Fairfield U., 1992-98, prof. bus. law, 1998—. Chmn. Women's Resource Ctr., Fairfield U., 1989-91. Staff editor Jour. Legal Studies Edn., 1989-94; reviewer Am. Bus. Law Assn. jour., 1988—, staff editor, 1995—; sr. articles editor N.E. Jour. Legal Studies in Bus., 1995-96; editor-in-chief N.E. Jour. Legal Studies, 2003—. Mem. Derby Tercentennial Commn., 1973—74; justice of the peace City of Derby, 1975—83; alt. mem. Parks and Recreation Commn., Woodbury, 1995—99; v.p. N.E. Acad. Legal Studies in Bus., 2001—02, 2001—02, pres-elect., program chair, 2003, pres., 2003—; editor-in-chief N.E. Jour. of Legal Studies, 2003—04; mem., treas. Woodbury Dem. Town Com., 1995—96, corr. sec., 1996—98; bd. dirs. Valley Transit Dist., Derby, 1975—77. Recipient Best Paper award N.E. Regional Bus. Law Assn., 1990, Best Paper award Tri-State Regional Bus. Law Assn., 1991; Fairfield U. Sch. Bus. rsch. grantee 1989, 91, 92, Fairfield U. rsch. grantee, 1994. Mem. ABA, Conn. Bar Assn., Acad. Legal Studies in Bus., Mensa (coord. SINISTRAL spl. interest group 1977—). Democrat. Roman Catholic. Avocations: running, sailing, tennis, swimming. Office: 198 Emmett Ave Derby CT 06418-1258 E-mail: samcevoy@mail.fairfield.edu.

MCEVOY-JAMIL, PATRICIA ANN, English language educator; b. Butler, Pa, June 26, 1955; d. Joseph Lawrence McEvoy and Janet Ann (McConnell) Beier; m. M. Jamal Jamil, Nov. 23, 1977; 1 child, Amirah M. MA in TESOL, Monterey Inst. Internat. Studies, 1984; MA in English, U. Notre Dame de Namur, 1995; EdD, U. San Francisco, 1996. Calif. C.C. credential for life. Instr. ESL City Coll. San Francisco, 1989-98, Can. Coll., Redwood City, Calif., 1989-98; lectr. ESL Stanford U., 1989—97, U. Notre Dame de Namur, 1991—98; co-owner, v.p. bd. MPA Co. Investments, Inc., Houston, 1998—. Presenter in field; vis. prof. EFL, Georgetown U., Washington, summer 1999; adj. ESL instr. U. Houston-Downtown, 2000-02, Mus. Fine Arts, Houston. Mem. leadership coun. So. Poverty Law Ctr.-contributed to Jimmy Carter Ctr.; ptnr. mem. Habitat for Humanity Internat.; team leader Rep. Party. Recipient ELITE Patron of Honor award, ELITE Stanford (Calif.) Hosp., 1989, 1990, Wall of Tolerance Award; faculty rsch. grant, U. Notre Dame de Namur, 1984, doctoral rsch. grant, U. San Francisco, 1992—93. Mem. AAUW, NAFE, Nat. Coun. Tchr. English, Tchr. English to Speakers Other Lang., Jimmy Carter Ctr. Team Leader for Rep. Party, Nat. Mus. Women Arts, Nat. Trust Historic Preservation, Phi Delta Kappa. Avocations: tennis, swimming, bicycling. Office: 5850 San Felipe Ste 500 No 117 Houston TX 77057 E-mail: docpamjam@hotmail.com.

MCEWEN, INGER THEORIN, retired secondary education educator, consultant; b. Goteborg, Sweden, July 22, 1935; came to U.S., 1955; m. William C. McEwen; children: Karin, Erik. BA, Peabody at Vanderbilt U., 1973, MLS, 1976. Cert. tchr. ESL, N.H. Libr. Scales Elem. Sch., Brentwood, Tenn., 1977-82; reference libr. Dartmouth Coll., Hanover, N.H., 1982-85; media supr. Hartford (Vt.) Sch. Dist., 1988-89; edn. asst. Supervisory Adminstrv. Union 22, Hanover, 1985-86, ESL tutor, 1992-97; tchr. ESL Hanover H.S. Dresden Sch. Dist., 1998-99; ret., 1999. Cons. White River Elem. Sch., White River Junction, Vt. Mem. No. New Eng. TESOL, Beta Phi Mu.

MCEWEN, IRENE RUBLE, physical therapy educator; b. Columbus, Ohio, May 19, 1943; d. John Mitchell and Isabel (Ruble) McE. BS in Phys. Therapy, U. Wash., 1965, MEd in Ednl. Psychology, 1973; PhD in Spl. Edn., Purdue U., 1989. Cert. pediatric clin. specialist Am. Bd. Phys. Therapy Spltys. (pediatric splty. coun.); lic. phys. therapist, Okla., Wash. Phys. therapist St. Vincent Hosp., Portland, Oreg., 1965-69; head phys. therapist Lowell Sch., Seattle, 1970-76; physiotherapist Spastic Centre of New South Wales, Mosman, Australia, 1976-77; head phys. therapist Seattle Sch. Dist., 1977-84; phys. therapist Mesa Pub. Sch., Ariz., 1984, Roosevelt Sch. Dist., Phoenix, 1984-86; rsch. fellow Purdue U., West Lafayette, Ind., 1986-89; tech. specialist Ind. Augmentative and Alternative Communication Tech. Team, West Lafayette, 1988-89; assoc. prof. phys. therapy U. Okla. Health Sci. Ctr., Oklahoma City, 1989-97, prof. phys. therapy, 1997—, Presbyn. Health Found. Presdl. prof., 1998, George Lynn Cross rsch. prof., 2003. Rschr., presenter in field. Mem. editl. bd., dep. editor, editor: Case Reports Phys. Therapy; co-editor: Physical and Occupational Therapy in Pediatrics; contbr. Mem.: Rehab. Engring. and Assistive Tech. Soc. N.Am., Internat. Soc. Augmentative and Alternative Comm., Coun. Exceptional Children, Assn. for Persons with Severe Handicaps, Am. Phys. Therapy Assn. (Margaret L. Moore Outstanding New Acad. Faculty mem. award 1992, Dorothy Briggs Sci. Inquiry award 1993, sect. on pediat. rsch. award 1998, sect. on pediat. Bud DeHaven Svc. award 2001), Am. Assn. Mental Retardation, Am. Acad. Cerebral Palsy and Devel. Medicine, Alpha Eta, Sigma Xi, Phi Kappa Phi. Office: U Okla Dept Rehab Sci PO Box 26901 Oklahoma City OK 73190-1090 E-mail: irene-mcewen@ouhsc.edu.

MCEWEN, LARRY BURDETTE, retired English and theater arts educator, author; b. Clay Center, Nebr., Aug. 4, 1934; s. Gerald E. and Marie L. (Pennington) McE.; m. Charlotte E. Alloway, Feb. 14, 1978; children: Diana J., Sheila J., Jennifer J. AB, Augustana Coll., Rock Island, Ill., 1962; MS, Ill. State U., 1968. Cert. tchr., Nebr., Ill. Prof. theatre arts Blackburn Coll., Carlinville, Ill., 1969-75; counselor divsn. vocat. rehab. Nebr. Dept. Edn., Lincoln, 1976-82; tchr. English Hastings (Nebr.) Sr. High Sch., 1983-92; tch. English, theatre arts J.D. Darnall Sr. H.S., Geneseo, Ill., 1962-68. Vis. lectr. Mt. Senario Coll., Ladysmith, Wis., 1971, Knox Coll., Galesburg, Ill., 1974, Hastings (Nebr.) Coll., 1976. Author: Much Ado About Shakespeare, 1992, Goose and Fables, 1994, To Honor Our Fathers and Mothers, 1997; author Apple Software; dir. 63 theatrical prodns.; author of 7 one-act plays; contbr. numerous articles to profl. publs. With USAF, 1951-52. Grad. fellow Ind. U., 1968-69; Quad-City Music Guild scholar, 1961-62. Mem. NEA, Neb. State Edn. Assn., Acad. Computers in Eng., Nat. Coun. Tchrs. English, Alpha Psi Omega, Alpha Phi Omega. Home and Office: 603 E 5th St Hastings NE 68901-5336 E-mail: lm11316@alltel.net.

MCFADDEN, BARBARA, secondary education educator; b. N.Y.C., Nov. 3, 1951; d. William Anthony and Matilda (Fuzia) McF. BA, Queens Coll., 1976; MS, St. John's U., 1980; profl. diploma in adminstrn., L.I. U., 1990. Cert. English tchr., adminstr. and supr., N.Y. Acting asst. prin., tchr. English Joseph Pulitzer Intermediate Sch., N.Y.C. Bd. Edn., Jackson Heights, N.Y., 1977—. Curriculum coord. interdisciplinary programs, coord. accelerated English program, participant curriculum developer Nat. Javits Project for Lang. Arts-U.S. Dept. Edn.; curriculum staff devel. presenter; coord sr. awards; advisor Nat. Honor Soc.; coord. carnival; pub. English Jour. In the News, Collaborative Grouping in the Classroom, Music in Lang. Arts. Named Tchr. of Month, 1990. Mem. ASCE (curriculum exhibitor 1993, 95), NASSP, Nat. Coun. Tchrs. English (drama/media minicourse, Ctr. of Excellence award 1989), N.Y. State English Coun. (Educator of Excellence in English 1994), N.Y. State English Coun. (presenter 1995), Phi Delta Kappa. Home: 22-56 80th St Apt 2A Flushing NY 11370-1339 Office: Joseph Pulitzer Intermediate Sch 33-34 80th St Jackson Heights NY 11372

MCFADDEN, DANIEL LITTLE, economist, educator; b. Raleigh, N.C., July 29, 1937; s. Robert S. and Alice (Little) McFadden; m. Beverlee Tito Simboli, Dec. 15, 1962; children: Nina, Robert, Raymond. BS, U. Minn., 1957, PhD, 1962; LLD, U. Chgo., 1992. Mellon fellow U. Pitts., 1962-63; from asst. prof. to assoc. prof. U. Calif., Berkeley, 1963—67, prof., 1967-77, E. Morris Cox Chair, prof. econ. Coll. Letters & Sci., 1990—, dir. Econometrics Lab., 1991—95, 1996—, chmn. dept. of econ., 1995—96; research prof. Yale U., New Haven, 1977-78; prof. MIT, Cambridge, Mass. Mem. econs. adv. panel NSF, 1969—71, Univs. Nat. Bur., 1974—77; chmn. NSF-NBER Conf. Econs. of Uncertainty, 1970—; bd. dirs. Nat. Bur. Econ. Rsch., 1976—77, 1980—83; mem. book com. Sloan Found., 1977—79; mem. rev. com. Calif. Energy Com. Forecasts, 1979; chmn. awards com. AEA, 1981—84. Editor: Jour. Statis. Physics, 1968—70, Econometric Soc. monographs, 1980—83; mem. bd. editors Am. Econ. Rev., 1971—74, Jour. Math. Econs., 1973—77, Transp. Rsch., 1978—80; assoc. editor: Jour. Econometrics, 1977—78. Mem. adv. com. Transp. Models Project, Met. Transp. Commn., 1975, City of Berkeley Coordinated Transit Project, 1975—76. Recipient John Bates Clark medal, 1975, Frisch medal, 1986, Nobel prize in Econs., 2000, Nemmers prize in Econs., Northwestern U., 2000, Richard Stone prize in Applied Econs., Jour. Econmetrics, 2000—01. Mem.: NAS (mem. com. basic rsch. social scis. 1982—87, mem. com. energy demand modelling 1983—84, mem. commn. behavioral and social scis. and edn. 1989—94), Transp. Rsch. Bd. (mem. exec. com. 1975—78), Math. Assn. Am., Am. Statis. Assn., Econometric Soc. (mem. exec. com. 1983—86, v.p. 1984, pres. 1985, Fisher-Schultz lectr. 1979, fellow 1969), Am. Econ. Assn. (mem. exec. com. 1985—87, v.p. 1994, pres.-elect), Am. Acad. Arts and Scis. Democrat. Avocations: bicycling, tennis, squash, sailing, skiing. Home: 1370 Trancas St # 152 Napa CA 94558-2912 Office: U Calif Berkeley Dept Econs 549 Evans Hall # 3880 Berkeley CA 94720-3880

MC FADDEN, JOSEPH MICHAEL, history educator; b. Joliet, Ill., Feb. 12, 1932; s. Francis Joseph and Lucille (Adler) McF.; m. Norma Cardwell, Oct. 10, 1958; children: Timothy Joseph, Mary Colleen, Jonathan Andrew. BA, Lewis Coll., 1954; MA, U. Chgo., 1961; PhD, No. Ill. U., 1968. Tchr. history Joliet Cath. High Sch., 1957-60; mem. faculty history dept. Lewis Coll., Lockport, Ill., 1960-70, asso. prof., 1967-70, v.p. acad. affairs, 1968-70; prof. history, dean sch. Nat. and Social Sci., Kearney (Nebr.) State Coll., 1970-74; prof. history, dean Sch. Social and Behavioral Scis., Slippery Rock (Pa.) State Coll., 1974-77; pres. No. State Coll., Aberdeen, S.D., 1977-82, U. S.D., Vermillion, 1982-88, U. St. Thomas, Houston, 1988-97, pres. emeritus, prof. history, 1997—. Served with USNR, 1954-56. Roman Catholic. Office: U St Thomas Office of Pres 3812 Montrose Blvd Houston TX 77006-4626 E-mail: mcfadden@stthom.edu.

MCFADDEN, NADINE LYNN, secondary education Spanish educator; b. Cleve., May 13, 1947; d. Frank and Helen (Senich) Mancini; m. Francis Joseph McFadden, Aug. 22, 1970; children: Ian Mancini, Kevin Mancini. BS in Edn., Ohio U., 1969; MA in Edn., Kent State U., 1990. Lic. tchr., Ohio. Dept. chair Spanish Parma (Ohio) City Schs., 1969—; ESL instr., pres. Jonah-Kater Distance Learning Inc., 1995—. Chaperone European cultural trips Parma City Schs., 1973-76, 80, 92, 95-97, strategic planning com., 1991-92; chmn. textbook com. Strongsville (Ohio) City Schs., 1990-92; program presenter in-svc. fgn. lang. tchrs., Coalition of Essential Schs., Parma; adj. prof. Fresno Pacific Coll. Mem. NEA, Am. Assn. Tchrs. Spanish and Portuguese, Ohio Modern Lang. Tchrs. Assn., Ohio Edn. Assn., Parma Edn. Assn. Avocations: travel, reading, quilting, gardening. Home: 17536 Brandywine Dr Strongsville OH 44136-7034 Office: Parma City Schs Ridge Rd Parma OH 44129

MCFADIN, HELEN LOZETTA, retired elementary education educator; b. Tucumcari, N.Mex., Sept. 7, 1923; d. Henry J. and LaRue Altha (Ford) Stockton; m. John Reece McFadin, July 3, 1946; 1 child, Janice Lynn McFadin Koenig. AB in Edn./Psychology, Highlands U., Las Vegas, N.Mex., 1956; MA in Teaching, N.Mex. State U., 1968; postgrad., U. N.D., 1965, St. Leo's Coll., St. Leo, Fla., 1970. Cert. tchr., K-12 reading/psychology specialist, N.Mex. Tchr. 1st and 2d grades Grant County Schs., Bayard, N.Mex., 1943-44; tchr. 4th grade Durango (Colo.) Pub. Schs., 1946-48; tchr. 2d grade Artesia Pub. Schs., Loco Hills, N.Mex., 1955; tchr. 3d grade Alamogordo (N.Mex.) Pub. Schs., 1957-66, h.s. reading specialist, 1966-72, elem. reading specialist, 1972-77, tchr. 4th grade, 1977-82, reading tchr. 7th grade, dept. chair, 1982-87; ret. N.Mex. State U., Alamogordo, 1987, instr. edn., 1987-90. Organizer reading labs. h.s., elem. schs., Alamogordo, 1966-77, designer programs and curriculum, 1957-89; presenter/cons. in field; cons. Mary Kay Cosmetics; rep. Excel Telecomms., Inc. Contbr. articles to profl. jours. Local and dist. judge spelling bees and sci. fairs Alamogordo Pub. Schs., 1987-98. Recipient Literacy award Otero County Reading Coun., 1986; inducted in Women's Hall of Fame, Alamogordo Women's Clubs, 1989. Mem. Am. Bus. Women's Assn. (pres. 1986-87, v.p. local chpt. 1999-00, named Woman of the Yr. 1988, 2003), NEA (del. 1957-87, Dedicated Svc. award 1987), N.Mex. Edn. Assn., Internat. Reading Assn. (mem. Spl. League of the Honored 1985, pres. 1975-76), N.Mex. Reading Assn. (bd. dirs. 1988-94, del. to 1st Russian reading conf. 1992, Dedicated Svc. award 1994), Tularosa Basin Hist. Soc., Beta Sigma Phi (pres. local chpt. 1998-99, formed new master chpt. 1999, Golden Cir. Anniversary award 2002), Kappa Kappa Iota (local pres. Kappa Conclave 1998-00, state officer, nat. com., co-chair nat. conv. 2000-02, Disting. Educator Emeritus Cert. of Merit 1988, VIP award 2000, 2002). Republican. Baptist. Avocations: reading, fashion modeling. Home: 2364 Union Ave Alamogordo NM 88310-3848

MCFARLAN, FRANKLIN WARREN, business administration educator; b. Boston, Oct. 18, 1937; s. Ronald Lyman and Ethel Warren (White) McF.; m. Margaret Karen Nelson, Dec. 17, 1971; children: Andrew, Clarissa, Elizabeth. AB, Harvard Coll., 1959, MBA, 1961, D.BA, 1965. Asst. prof. Harvard Bus. Sch., Boston, 1964-68, assoc. prof., 1968-73, prof. bus. adminstrn., 1973—, sr. assoc. dean, dir. rsch., 1991-95, sr. assoc. dean external rels., 1995-2000, sr. assoc. dean, dir. Asia Pacific, 2000—. Dir. Providian Fin. Corp., San Franciso, Li and Fung Corp., HOng Kong, Computer Sci. Corp., L.A. Author: (with Richard Nolan) Information Systems Administration, 1973; (with Linda Applegate and Robert Austin) Corporate Information Management, 6th edit., 2003, (with Linda Applegate and Robert Austin) Creating Business Advantages in Information Age, 2002, (with Cathleen Benko) Connecting the Dots, 2003; editor: (with Richard Nolan) Information Systems Handbook, 1973, Information Systems Research Challenge, 1984; sr. editor MIS Quar., 1986-88. Bd. dirs., pres. Belmont (Mass.) Day Sch., 1982-86; bd. dirs. Dana Hall Sch., Wellesley, Mass., 1982-94, chmn. bd., 1990-93; trustee Mt. Auburn Hosp., 1991-99, ch mn. bd., 1995-98, trustee care group, 1996—; trustee Winsor Sch., 1994-2000, Milton Acad., 2001--. 1st lt. U.S. Army, 1962-67. Mem.: The Country (Brookline, Mass.). Republican. Episcopalian. Home: 37 Beatrice Cir Belmont MA 02478-2657 Office: Harvard Bus Sch Soldiers Field Rd Boston MA 02163-1317 E-mail: fmcfarlan@hbs.edu.

MCFARLAND, CARMEN RENEA, elementary education educator, counselor, music educator; b. Tulsa, Jan. 2, 1957; d. Louis Thomas and Beverly Jack (Trail) M. BS in Edn., Northeastern State U., 1989, MS in Counseling, 1992. Cert. tchr., counselor. Accounts receivable staff Ramsays Dept. Store, Grove, Okla., 1974-76; sec.-pres., teller First State Bank, Tahlequah, Okla., 1978-79; counselor-in-residence Northeastern State Univ., Tahlequah, Okla., 1979-83; installment loan/proof operator Bank of Okla., Grove, 1983-84; asst. underwriter Aircraft Ins. Co., Richardson, Tex., 1984-86; adminstrv. asst. The Travelers Ins. Co., Dallas, 1986-89; music tchr., counselor Turkey Ford Sch., Wyandotte, Okla., 1990-94; h.s. vocat. tchr. Grove Pub Sch., Grove, Okla., 1995-96; tchr. 5th grade Grove Upper Elem. Sch., 1995—; sci. tchr. Grove Elem. Sch., 1995—2001; sch. counselor Grove Lower Elem. Sch., 2001—. Tutor, piano/voice tchr. pvt. practice, Grove, 1981—; ESL tchr. Am./Chinese Ctr., Dallas, 1987-88; activities dir. Honeycreek Retirement Village, Grove, 1988-90. Ch. pianist, ch. clk. Grand Lake Bapt. Ch., 1989—. Mem. ASCD, NEA, Okla. Edn. Assn. (local pres. 1992-93, 93-94), Am. Assn. for Counseling and Devel., Joplin Piano Tchrs. Assn., Delta Kappa Gamma (local pres. 2001-2002). Republican. Home: 34450 S 620 Rd Grove OK 74344-8141 Office: Grove Lower Elem Sch Grove OK 74344

MCFARLAND, DAVID E. university official; b. Enid, Okla., Sept. 25, 1938; s. Eugene James McF. and Lydia May (Catlin) Lawson; m. Marcia Ruth Lake, Nov. 27, 1958 (div. 1978); children: Jennifer, Jeffrey, Jon, Julie; m., Susan Kaye Siler, Mar. 3, 1979 (div. 1994); 1 child, Matthew Chapple; m. Barbara Ambrogio, Oct. 1994. BS, Wichita State U., 1961, MS, 1964; PhD, U. Kans., 1967. Stress analysis engr. Boeing Co., Wichita, Kans., 1957-64; instr. U. Kans., Lawrence, 1964-67; asst. v.p., dean Wichita State U., 1967-81; dean. sch. tech., Pittsburgh State U., Kans., 1981-85; provost, v.p. acad. affairs Cen. Mo. State U., 1985-88; pres. Kutztown U. of Pa., 1988—. Author: Mechanics of Materials, 1977; Analysis of Plates, 1972. Contbr. articles to tech. jours. Office: Kutztown U of Pa Office of Pres Kutztown PA 19530

MCFARLAND, ELLA MAE GAINES, secondary school educator, elementary school educator; b. Laneview, Va., July 27, 1938; s. Charles Brown and Estelle Grace Hundley, Preston Hundley (Stepfather); m. Alfred Jr., Feb. 9, 1957 (div. May 1974); children: Alfred III, Barrett, Jeffrey, Kyra, Forrest, Estelle, Carter, Robin. AA, Delaware County C.C., Media, Pa., 1971; BS Elem. Edn., West Chester State U., 1973; MEd, Widener U., 1983. Instrnl. II masters equivalent Pa. Dept. Edn. Elem. sci. tchr. Title 1 Chester-Upland Dist., Chester, Pa., 1973—76; elem. tchr. Chester Upland Sch. Dist., Chester, Pa., 1973—2001; coord. women's sch. Women's Sch., Phila., 1985—91; focus adult edn. Delaware County C.C., Chester, Pa., 1992—95, coord. GED grant, 1999—; dir. nursery sch. Mount Pleasant Bapt. Ch., Twin Oaks, Pa., 1982—83; tchr. pregnant teens GED Project Pride Girls Inc., Wilmington, Del., 2000—. Tng. for GED Pa. Dept. Edn. Active Women's Commn. Delaware County, Media, Pa., 1985—89, Friends to the Women's Commn., Media, Pa., 1994—2003; sec. Nova Vista Civic Assn., Chester, Pa., 1993—2003; active Bethany Bapt. Ch., Chester, Pa. Recipient Cmty. Svc. award, Fine Arts Ctr., Chester, Pa., 1998, Outstanding Cmty. Svc. award, Spencer A.M.E. Ch., Chester, Pa., 1999, Mother's Club Bethany. Mem.: NAACP (life; bd. mem.), Phi Delta Kappa (epistoles 1990—95). Avocations: workshops, seminars, religious learning, reading. Home: Box 248 215 Gingko Ln Chester PA 19016-0248 Office: Delaware County CC 2600 W 9th St Rm 200 Chester PA 19013 E-mail: emcfar38@aol.com.

MCFARLAND, LESLIE KING, special education educator; b. Canton, Ohio, July 13, 1954; d. John Edward and Nadine Mae (Phillips) King; m. James David McFarland, July 16, 1977. BS in Edn., Bowling Green State U., 1976. Cert. specific learning disabilities, spl. edn. tchr. K-12, developmentally handicapped spl. edn. tchr. K-12, elem. tchr. 1-8, Ohio. Tchr. developmentally handicapped Warren (Ohio) City Schs., 1976—. Bd. dirs. McFarland and Son Funeral Svcs., Inc., v.p., 1992—. Mem. Fine Arts Coun. Trumbull County, 1988-95; bd. dirs. Warren Dance Ctr., sec., 1988-90; bd. dirs. Warren Chamber Orch., 1986-92; mem. Trumbull County Women's History Com., 1993—; deacon 1st Presbyn. Ch., 1994. Mem. NEA, Ohio Edn. Assn., Warren Edn. Assn., AAUW (past sec.), Embroiderers' Guild Am. (Western Res. chpt.). Avocations: embroidery, needlepoint, camping, travel. Home: 619 Perkins Dr NW Warren OH 44483-4617

MCFARLAND, MARY A. elementary and secondary school educator, administrator, consultant; b. St. Louis, Nov. 12, 1937; d. Allen and Maryann (Crawford) Mabry; m. Gerald McFarland, May 30, 1959. BS in Elem. Edn., S.E. Mo. State U., 1959; MA in Secondary Edn., Washington U., St. Louis, 1965; PhD in Curriculum and Instrn., St. Louis U., 1977. Cert. tchr. elem., secondary, supt., Mo. Elem. tchr. Berkeley Sch. Dist., St. Louis, 1959-64; secondary tchr. Parkway Sch. Dist., St. Louis, 1965-75, social studies coord. K-12, 1975—2001, dir. staff devel., 1984—2000. Adj. prof. Maryville U., St. Louis, 1990—; cons. pvt. practice, Chesterfield, Mo; spkr. Internat. Social Studies, South Korea, 1998, cons., Latvia, 2001, 2003. Co-author: (text series) The World Around Us, 1990, 3d rev. edit., 1995, Adventures in Time and Place, 1998, Macmillian Social Studies series, 2003; contbr. articles to profl. jours. Nat. faculty Nat. Issues Forum, Dayton, Ohio. Mem. ASCD, Social Sci. Edn. Consortium, Nat. Coun. for Social Studies (pres. 1989-90), Mo. Coun. for Social Studies (pres. 1980-81). Democrat. Methodist. Avocations: music, sailing.

MCFARLAND, MICHAEL C. academic administrator; b. Boston, 1948; AB in Physics, Cornell U., 1969; M in Elec. Engring., Carnegie M in Elec. Engring., PhD in Elec. Engring., Carnegie Mellon U.; MDiv, ThM in Social Ethics, Weston Sch. Theology. Ordained to ministry Jesuits, 1984. Cons. AT&T Bell Labs., 1985—86; assoc. prof. computer sci. Boston Coll., 1986—96, dept. chair; prof. computer sci., dean Coll. Arts and Scis. Gonzaga U., Spokane, 1996—2000; pres. Coll. of the Holy Cross, Worcester, Mass., 2000—. Bd. dirs. U. Scranton. Avocation: running. Office: Coll of the Holy Cross 1 College St Worcester MA 01610-2395

MCFARLAND, PHILIP JAMES, educator, writer; b. Birmingham, Ala., June 20, 1930; s. Thomas Alfred McFarland and Alice Lucile Sylvester; m. Patricia Katherin Connors, July 23, 1960; children: Philip James Jr., Joseph Thomas. BA, Oberlin Coll., 1951; MA, Cambridge U., 1957. Textbook editor Houghton Mifflin Co., Boston, 1958-64; tchr. English Concord (Mass.) Acad., 1965-95. Author: A House Full of Women, 1960, Sojourners, 1979, Seasons of Fear, 1984, Sea Dangers, 1985, The Brave Bostonians, 1998; sr. editor: Houghton Mifflin Literature Series, 6 vols., 1972, Focus on Literature, 7 vols., 1978; editor: Composition: Models and Exercises, 5 vols., 2d edit., 1971. Lt. j.g. USN, 1951-55. Mem. Mass. Hist. Soc. Democrat. Avocations: bicycling, trekking. Home: 18 Independence Ave Lexington MA 02421-5939

MC FARLAND, ROBERT HAROLD, physicist, educator; b. Severy, Kans., Jan. 10, 1918; s. Robert Eugene and Georgia (Simpson) McF.; m. Twilah Mae Seefeld, Aug. 28, 1940; children: Robert Alan, Rodney Jon. BS and BA, Kans. State Tchrs. Coll., Emporia, 1940; Ph.M. (Mendenhall fellow), U. Wis., 1943, PhD, 1947. Sci. instr., coach high sch., Chase, Kans., 1940-41; instr. navy radio sch. U. Wis., Madison, 1943-44; sr. engr. Sylvania Elec. Corp., 1944-46; faculty Kans. State U., 1947-60, prof. physics, 1954-60, dir. nuclear lab., 1958-60; physicist Lawrence Livermore Radiation Lab. U. Calif., 1960—69; dean Grad. Sch., U. Mo., Rolla, 1969-79, dir. instnl. analysis and planning, 1979-82; prof. physics U. Mo., Rolla, 1969-84, prof. emeritus physics dept., 1985—; v.p. acad. affairs U. Mo. System, 1974-75; Intergovtl. Personnel Act appointee Dept. Energy, Washington, 1982-84; vis. prof. U. Calif., Berkeley, 1980-81. Mem. Grad. Record Exams. Bd., 1971-75, chmn. steering com., 1972-73; cons. Well Surveys, Inc., Tulsa, 1953-54, Argonne Nat. Lab., Chgo., 1955-59, Kans. Dept. Pub. Health, 1956-57, cons. in residence Lawrence Livermore Radiation Lab., U. Calif., 1957, 58, 59, med. physics U. Okla. Med. Sch., 1971, grad. schs., PhD physics program, Utah State U., 1972; physicist, regional counselor Office Ordnance Research, Durham, N.C., 1955. Contbr. over 110 articles to profl. jours.; patentee in field of light prodn., vacuum prodn., controlled thermonuclear reactions. Active Boy Scouts Am., 1952—, mem. exec. bd. San Francisco Bay Area council, 1964-68, Ozark Council, 1986—; chmn. Livermore (Calif.) Library Bond drive, 1964. Mem. Kans. N.G., 1936-40. Recipient Silver Beaver award Boy Scouts Am., 1968, Community Service award C. of C., 1965, Disting. Alumnus award Kans. State Tchrs. Coll., 1969. Fellow AAAS, Am. Phys. Soc., Kiwanis Internat.; mem. AAUP (chpt. pres. 1956-57), Am. Assn. Physics

Tchrs., Mo. Acad. Sci., Mo. Assn. Phys. Sci. Tchrs., Am. Soc. Engring. Edn., Kiwanis (lt. gov. Mo.-Ark. dist. 1984-85, internat. accredited rep. 1985-92, Disting. Lt. Gov. 1985, Tablet of honor award 1997), Sigma Xi, Lambda Delta Lambda, Xi Phi, Kappa Mu Epsilon, Kappa Delta Pi, Pi Mu Epsilon, Gamma Sigma Delta, Phi Kappa Phi. Home: 416 W Spring St Apt 3 Neosho MO 64850-1777 Office: U Mo Dept Physics Rolla MO 65401

MCFARLAND, WILLIAM JOSEPH (JOE MCFARLAND), academic administrator; b. Sterling, Kans., July 25, 1929; s. Armour James and Sylvia Jane Louise (Hutcheson) McF.; m. Mary Roberta Dill, Dec. 21, 1951; children: William Joseph, Kathryn Ann, Matthew Curtis. BA, Sterling Coll., 1951; MA, U. No. Colo., 1957; EdD, Ind. U., 1966; PhD (hon.), Sterling Coll., 1992, Geneva Coll., 2001. Cert. tchr. and adminstr., pilot. Elem. prin., coach, tchr., supt. schs. Turon Pub. Schs., Kans., 1953-59; assoc. prof. edn., dir. student teaching, head edn. dept. Emporia State U., Kans., 1959-68; assoc. exec. sec. Kans. NEA, Topeka, 1968-71; dir. acad. affairs Kans. Bd. Regents, Topeka, 1971-84; pres. Geneva Coll., Beaver Falls, Pa., 1984-92; cons., scholar in residence Christs Coll., Taipei, Taiwan, 1992—2002; headmaster Am. Acad. Nicosia, Cyprus, 2002—. Chmn. scholarship selection com. Beech Aircraft Co., Wichita, Kans., 1979-84; pres. coun. Nat. Assn. Intercollegiate Athletics, Kansas City, Kans., 1984-92. Contbr. articles to profl. jours. Pres. Topeka Fellowship, Inc., 1977-84; mem. exec. coun., v.p. Boy Scouts Am., Emporia and Topeka, 1963-83; legis. liason person NEA, Topeka, 1968-71; chmn. Kans. Commn. on Aerospace Edn., 1971-83, Gov's. Commn. on Sch. to Work, 1995—; trustee Sterling Coll., Kans., 1971-84, Geneva Coll., 1973-84; sec. Pa. Found. Ind. Colls.; bd. dirs. United Way, Beaver County, Pa., 1985-92, ARC of Beaver County, 1985-92, Beaver Valley C. of C., 1985-88; mem. Christian Coll. Coalition, 1984-92. With U.S. Army, 1951-53, Korea. Recipient Lieber Meml. Teaching award Ind. U., Bloomington, 1966; Disting. Service award Sterling Coll., 1983; VIP award Sta. WREN, Topeka, 1971. Mem. Assn. Governing Bds. (exec. com.), Pa. Assn. Colls. and Univs., Nat. Assn. Ind. Colls. and Univs., Beaver Valley C. of C., ARC (pres. local chpt.), Knife and Fork Club (bd. dirs. 1979-84, Rotary (life, pres. 1986-87, Paul Harris fellow 1988, chmn. scholarship selection com. Rotary Found.), Phi Delta Kappa (v.p. 1969-73) Republican. Presbyterian. Avocations: flying, football officiating, golf, hunting. Home and Office: 2709 SW Boswell Ave Topeka KS 66611-1604

MCFARLANE, WALTER ALEXANDER, lawyer, educator; b. Richlands, Va., May 4, 1940; s. James Albert and Frances Mae (Padbury) McF.; m. Judith Louise Copenhaver, Aug. 31, 1962. BA, Emory and Henry Coll., 1962; JD, U. Richmond, 1966. Bar: Ba. 1966, U.S. Supreme Ct. 1970, U.S. Ct. Appeals (4th cir.) 1973, U.S. Ct. Appeals (D.C. cir.) 1977, U.S. Dist. ct. (ea. dist.) Va. 1973. Asst. atty. gen. Office Va. Atty. Gen., Richmond, 1969-73, dep. atty. gen., 1973-90; exec. asst., chief counsel, dir. policy Gov.'s Office Commonwealth of Va., 1990-94, supt. Dept. Correctional Edn., 1994—. Acting dir. Dept. Juvenile Justice, 1997, State Bd. Dept. Criminal Justice Svcs., 1994-; prof. adj. staff U. Richmond, 1978-2003, A.L.Philpott disting. prof. T.C. Williams Sch. Law, 2003; chmn. transp. law com. Transp. Rsch. Bd., Nat. Rsch. Bd. Nat. Acads. Sci. and Engring., Washington, 1977-85, 88-94, chmn. legal affairs com., 1978-85, chmn. environ., archeol. and hist. com., 1985-90; mem. State Water Commn., 1994-96, mem., Coun. of State Govts. Henry Toll Fell., 1988, Legal Task Force, 1988-2002. Contbr. articles to profl. jours. Mem. exec. com., bd. govs. Emory and Henry Coll., 1985-98; pres. Windsor Forest Civic Assn., Midlothian, Va., 1975-76; bd. dirs. Greater Midlothian Civic League, 1980-86, v.p., 1980; instr. water safety ARC, 1962-87; chmn. bldg. com. Mt. Pisgah United Meth. Ch., 1980-85, pres. men's club, 1980-81; bd. dirs. cen. Va. chpt. Epilepsy Assn. Va., 1988-91. Capt. JAGC, USAF, 1966-69. Recipient J.D. Buscher Disting. Atty. award Am. Assn. State Hwy. and Transp. Ofcls., 1983, John C. Vance legal writing award Nat. Acads. Sci. and Engring., 4th ann. outstanding evening lectr. award Student Body, U. Richmond, 1980. Mem. Chesterfield Bar Assn., Richmond Bar Assn. (bd. dirs. 1989-93), Richmond Scottish Soc. (bd. dirs. 1980-82), Emory and Henry Coll. Alumni Assn. (chpt. pres. 1971-73, regional v.p. 1974-77, pres. 1981-83), Meadowbrook Country Club (bd. dir. 2001-). Home: 9001 Widgeon Way Chesterfield VA 23838-5274 Office: 101 N 14th St Richmond VA 23219-3684

MC FERON, DEAN EARL, mechanical engineer, educator; b. Portland, Oreg., Dec. 24, 1923; s. Wallace Suitor and Ruth Carolyn (Fessler) McF.; m. Phyllis Grace Ehlers, Nov. 10, 1945; children: David Alan, Phyllis Ann, Douglas Dean, Donald Brooks. Student, Oreg. State Coll., 1942-43; BSME with spl. honors, U. Colo., 1945, MSME, 1948; PhD, U. Ill., 1956. Instr. U. Colo., Boulder, 1946-48; assoc. prof. U. Ill., 1948-58; rsch. assoc. Argonne (Ill.) Nat. Lab., 1957-58; prof. mech. engring., assoc. dean U. Wash., Seattle, 1958-82, prof. emeritus, 1983—. Cons. to industry, 1959-80 Served with USNR, 1942-46, to comdr. Res., 1946-72. Co-recipient Outstanding Tech. Applications Paper award ASHRAE, 1974; Ednl. Achievement award Soc. Mfg. Engrs., 1970; NSF faculty fellow, 1967-68 Mem. ASME, Am. Soc. Engring. Edn., U.S. Naval Inst. (life), Sigma Xi (nat. dir. 1972-80, nat. pres. 1978), Tau Beta Pi, Sigma Tau, Pi Tau Sigma. Home: 4008 NE 40th St Seattle WA 98105-5422 Office: U Wash Dept Mech Engring Seattle WA 98195-0001

MCGANN, JEROME JOHN, English language educator; b. N.Y.C., July 22, 1937; s. John Joseph and Marie Violet (Lecouffe) McG.; m. Anne Patricia Lanni, July 26, 1938; children: Geoffrey, Christopher, Jennifer. BS, Le Moyne Coll., 1959; MA, Syracuse U., 1962; PhD, Yale U., 1966; LHD (hon.), U. Chgo., 1996. From asst. prof. to prof. U. Chgo., 1966-75; prof. Johns Hopkins U., Balt., 1975-80; Dreyfuss prof. humanities Calif. Inst. Tech., Pasadena, 1980-86; John Stewart Bryan univ. prof. U. Va., Charlottesville, 1987—. Author: Swinburne: An Experiment in Criticism, 1972 (Melville Cane award 1972), The Romantic Ideology, 1983, The Beauty of Inflections, 1985, Social Values and Poetic Acts, 1987, Towards a Literature of Knowledge, 1989, The Textual Condition, 1991, Black Riders: The Visible Language of Modernism, 1993; editor: The New Oxford Book of Romantic Period Verse, 1993, Poetics of Sensibility: A Revolution in Literary Style, 1996, Byron: Complete Poetical Works, 7 vols., 1980-93, Dante Gabriel Rossetti and the Game That Must Be Lost, 2000, The Complete Writings and Pictures of Dante Gabriel Rosetti: A Hypermedia Research Archive, 2000—, Radiant Textuality, Literature after the World Wide Web, 2001, Byron and Romanticism, 2002, D.G. Rosetti. Collected Poetry and Prose, 2003; author, editor 24 scholarly books and 4 poetry books. Recipient Mellon Achievement award, 2003, Richard Lyman award, 2002; Fulbright fellow, Fels Found. fellow, Eng., 1965-66; Guggenheim fellow, Eng., 1970-71, 74-75; NEH fellow, Eng. and Europe, 1975-76, 87-88, 2003—. Fellow Am. Acad. Arts and Scis.; mem. MLA. Address: English Department Bryan Hall U VA Charlottesville VA 22903

MCGANN, LISA B. NAPOLI, language educator; b. West Hartford, Conn., Sept. 07; d. James Napoli; m. Edward Harrison McGann, Jr. BA, Vassar Coll., 1980; MA, Columbia U., 1983, postgrad., 1991-95; MA, Middlebury Coll., 1987. Cert. tchr. French, ESL and Italian, Conn. Cmty. English program coord. Tchrs. Coll. Columbia U., N.Y.C., 1982-83; mgr. English tchg. com. Jr. League N.Y., N.Y.C., 1983-84; asst. dir. ESL Fordham U., N.Y.C., 1988-89; ESL instr. Laguardia C.C., CUNY, Long Island City, N.Y., 1983—, Columbia U., 1983-96. ESL instr. Yale U., 1988, 89; ESL specialist, tchr. UN, N.Y.C., 1990. Big sister Highland Hts., New Haven, 1976-77; ESL tchr. Boys and Girls Club, Astoria, N.Y., 1992. Recipient awards and scholarships. Mem. Nat. TESOL Soc., Am. Assn. Tchrs. Italian, Italian-Am. Hist. Soc., Nat. Italian Am. Found. (coun.), The Statue of Liberty-Ellis Island Found., Inc. Roman Catholic. Avocations: ballet, reading, travel, real estate, tennis.

MCGARRY, FREDERICK JEROME, civil engineering educator; b. Rutland, Vt., Aug. 22, 1927; s. William John and Ellen (Dunn) McG.; m. Alice M. Reilly, Oct. 7, 1950 (dec. Jan. 1971); children: Martha Ellen, Alice Catherine, Joan Louise, Carol Elizabeth, Susan Elizabeth, Janet Marian. AB, Middlebury (Vt.) Coll., 1950; S.B., MIT, 1950, S.M., 1953. Faculty MIT, 1950—2002, prof. civil engring., 1965—2002, prof. materials sci. and engring., 1974—2002, head materials divsn., 1964—2002, dir. materials rsch. lab., 1964—2002, assoc. dir. inter-Am. program civil engring., 1961—2002, dir. summer session, 1983—2002; ret., 2002. Contbr. numerous articles to profl. jours. Recipient Best Paper award Soc. Plastics Industry, 1968, 91. Mem. AAAS, ASTM, Soc. Rheology, Soc. Plastics Engrs., Am. Soc. Metals, Sigma Xi. Home: 90 Bakers Hill Rd Weston MA 02493-1774 Office: Mass Inst Tech 77 Massachusetts Ave Cambridge MA 02139-4301

MCGEE, HAROLD JOHNSTON, former academic administrator; b. Portsmouth, Va., Apr. 13, 1937; s. Harold Valentine McGee and Clara Mae (Johnston) Webber; m. Mary Frances Eure, Mar. 22, 1959; children: Harold Johnston, Mary Margaret, Matthew Hayden; m. Linda Gayle Stevens, Apr. 3, 1976; 1 child, Andrew Meade. BS, Old Dominion U., 1959; MEd, U. Va., 1962, EdD, 1968. Tchr. Falls Church (Va.) City Schs., 1959-62; asst. dean, then dean of admissions Old Dominion U., Norfolk, Va., 1962-65; field rep., program officer, sr. program officer U.S. Office Edn. Bur. Higher Edn., Charlottesville, 1965-70; provost Tidewater Community Coll., Portsmouth, 1970-71; founding pres. Piedmont Va. Community Coll., Charlottesville, 1971-75; various offices including dean grad. sch., asst. to pres., v.p. student affairs, v.p. adminstrv. affairs, sec. bd. visitors James Madison U., Harrisonburg, Va., 1975-86; pres. Jacksonville (Ala.) State U., 1986-99, pres. emeritus, 1999—. Bd. dirs. Marine Environ. Scis. Consortium, Dauphin Island, Ala., Gulf South Conf., chmn., 1990—92, Ala. Coun. Univ. Pres., 1991—92; bd. dirs. Trans America Athletic Conf., chmn., 1998—99. Author: Impact of Federal Support, 1968, The Virginia Project, 1976. Mem. United Way Calhoun County Ala., 1986—92, Knox Concert Series Adv. Bd., Anniston, Ala., Leadership Ala., Anniston Mus. Natural History Found.; bd. dirs. Southland Athletic League. Mem. NCAA (coun. 1991-95), ACA, Soc. Coll. and Univ. Planning Am. Assn. Higher Edn., Capital City Club (Montgomery, Ala.), Rotary, Phi Delta Kappa. Episcopalian.

MCGEE, JANE MARIE, retired elementary school educator; b. Paducah, Ky., Nov. 3, 1926; d. William Penn and Mary Virginia (Martin) Roberts; m. Hugh Donald McGee, Oct. 11, 1946; children: Catherine Jane McGee Bacon, Nancy Ann McGee McManus, Darby Alia McManus, Delaney Alyssa McManus. BS in Elem. Edn., Murray State U., 1948; cert. in gifted edn., Nat. Coll. Edn., 1976. Tchr. Hazel (Ky.) Pub. Schs., 1948-49, Pittsford (Mich.) Pub. Schs., 1949-50, Leal Elem. Sch., Urbana, Ill., 1950-53, Cleveland Elem. Sch., Skokie, Ill., 1953-57; pvt. tutor, pre-sch. tchr., 1953-61; tchr. Woodland Park Elem. Sch., Deerfield, Ill., 1968-83; ret., 1983; beauty and skin care cons. Mary Kay Cosmetics, Gunnison, Colo., 1984—; co-owner Eagles Nest B&B, 1996—2002. Soprano Western State Coll. and Cmty. Chorus, Gunnison, 1986-97, European concert tour, 1990. Mem. AAUW, Top o' the World Garden Club (sec. 1984—2002, winner first place at numerous garden club shows). Republican. Baptist. Avocations: flower arranging, crafts, knitting, bird watching, rock collecting. Home: 109 San Juan Dr Sequim WA 98382-9326

MCGEE, LYNDA PLANT, guidance counselor; b. L.A., Nov. 22, 1960; d. Larry Earle and Dolores (Balin) Plant; m. William Granville McGee, Dec. 21, 1996; 1 child, Roman Earle. BA in English Edn. cum laude, Xavier U., 1984; MEd in Counseling Psychology, U. Ill., 1986; cert. in coll. counseling, UCLA, 1997. Pupil pers. svcs. credential in counseling. English tchr., decathalon coach Dorsey H.S., L.A., 1986-94; English tchr. St. Monica Cath. H.S., Santa Monica, Calif., 1994-98, Downtown Magnets H.S., LA, 1998—2000, guidance counselor, 2000—; faculty advisor Teach for Am., 2003. Instr. Crenshaw-Dorsey Adult Sch., 1988-89; ind. coll. counselor, L.A., 1999—. Author: Active Learning Through Teacher Research, 1997. Mem. sch. decision making coun. Downtown Magnets H.S., L.A., 1998-99; bd. dirs. urban schs. com. UCLA, mem. h.s. initiative com., 2000. Fellow Nat. Endowment, 1994, 2000, UCLA, 1996, 97. Mem. Nat. Assn. Coll. Admission Counselors, Calif. Assn. Sch. Counselors, West of Westwood Homeowners Assn. (bd. mem.), Multiracial Americans of So. Calif. (bd. mem.), Western Assn. Coll. & Admission Counselors, Order Ea. Star, Zeta Phi Beta. Democrat. Avocations: reading, traveling, acting. Office: Downtown Magnets HS 1081 W Temple St Los Angeles CA 90012-1513 E-mail: sisofe@aol.com.

MCGEE, LYNNE KALAVSKY, principal; b. Jersey City, N.J., July 25, 1949; d. Michael V. and Ann (Fedowitz) Kalavsky; m. Thomas Robert McGee, Aug. 12, 1972; children: Todd Michael, Ryan Thomas. BS, St. Francis Coll., Loretto, Pa., 1971; MEd, Seton Hall U., 1972; EDS, Fla. Atlantic U., 1978, EdD, 1986. Cert. tchr., Fla., N.J., prin., Fla. Asst. prin. for curriculum Palm Beach County (Fla.) Bd. Edn., 1980-82, asst. prin. for student svcs., 1982-86, asst. prin. for adminstrn., 1986-91; prin. Belle Glade (Fla.) Elem. Sch., 1991-94, New Horizons Elem. Sch., Wellington, Fla., 1994-99, Binks Forest Elem. Sch., Wellington, Fla., 1999—2002, Jupiter (Fla.) H.S., 2002—. Adj. prof. grad. Nova U., 1991—. Office: Jupiter HS 500 N Military Tr Jupiter FL 33458-

MCGEE, MICHAEL JAY, protective services official, educator; b. Ft. Worth, June 9, 1952; s. Cecil Carl McGee and Helen Ruth (Peeples) McGee-Furrh; m. Carol Lee Garbarino, Sept. 18, 1982; children: Megan Rose, John Michael, Molly Caitlin. Student, U. Tex., 1970-73, Western Oreg. State U., 1983; AAS in Fire Protection Tech., Colo. Mountain Coll., 1990. Lic. fire suppression systems insp., Colo., vocat. educator, Colo.; cert. hazardous materials technician, Colo., 1992, EMT, Colo.; cert. fire investigator, 2002, fire safety hazardous materials instr., evaluator. Driver Massengale Co., Austin, Tex., 1970-73; gen. mgr. Sundae Palace, Austin, 1973-74; staff mem. Young Life, Colorado Springs, Colo., 1970-75; mgr. Broadmoor Mgmt. Co., Vail, Colo., 1974-76; technician Vail Cable Communications, 1976-77; dep. chief, fire marshal Vail Fire Dept., 1977—, fire sci. coord., 1995—, emergency med. program coord., 1996—2002; 2000v.p. HAZPRO (Hazardous Materials and Fire Safety Consulting Firm), 1996; pres. Fire Protection Tng. & Consulting, Inc., 1999; v.p. OTB, LLC, 2002—. Dist. rep. Joint Coun. Fire Dist. Colo., 1983-85; co-chmn. Eagle County Hazardous Materials, 1984-85, mem. planning com., 1987-90; mem. accountability com. Eagle County Sch. Dist., 1991-96, mem. budget rev. com., 1991-93, vice chair accountability com. 1992-93, chmn. accountability com., 1993-96; mem. policy rev. com., 1993-96, bldg. coord., team coach Odyssey of the Mind at Eaglevale Elem. Sch., 1995; invited dir. workshops Colo. Dept. Edn. Dist. Accountability Convention, Colo. Springs, 1995; pres. Fire Protection Tng. and Cons., Inc.; instr., trainer EMP Am. Inc. Chmn. Eagle County chpt. ARC, 1980-83, disaster chmn., 1977-80; tng. officer Eagle Vol. Fire Dept., 1988-90; mem. parish coun. St. Mary's Parish, Eagle County, 1989-90; mem. citizen's adv. com. Colo. Mountain Coll., 1990-91, bd. dirs. 1990; bldg. coord., team coach Odessey of the Mind, Eagle Valley Elem. Sch., 1994-95, 97-98, 98-99, coach Destination Imagination, 1999-2000; mem. facilities master planning com. Engle County Sch. Dist., 1996-97; mem. planning com. 1999 World Alpine Ski Championships; program coord. Eagle County Driver's Edn. Named Alumnus of the year, Co. Mountain Coll., 2001. Mem.: KC (charter Grand Knight, Eagle Count chpt.), Colo. State Fire Chiefs Assn., Colo. State Fire Marshals Assn., Nat. Fire Protection Assn., Internat. Assn. Arson Investigators (Colo. chpt.), Internat. Platform Assn. Office: Vail Fire Dept 42 W Meadow Dr Vail CO 81657-5000 E-mail: mmcgee@vailgov.com.

MCGEE, REECE JEROME, sociology educator emeritus; b. St. Paul, Oct. 19, 1929; s. Reece John and Vivian Jeanette (McFarland) McG.; m. Betty Ann Enns, June 10, 1950 (div. 1978); children: Kaelin Christine, Reece Jon, Shanna Beth; m. Sharron Ann Onken, Dec. 2, 1978. BA, U. Minn., 1952, MA, 1953, PhD, 1956. Asst. prof. Humboldt State Coll., Arcata, Calif., 1956; rsch. assoc. U. Minn., Mpls., 1957; asst. prof. U. Tex., Austin, 1957-61, assoc. prof., 1961-64; vis. assoc. prof. Macalester Coll., St. Paul, 1964-65, prof., 1965-67; prof., master tchr. Purdue U., West Lafayette, Ind., 1967—95, head. dept. sociology and anthropology, 1987-92, prof. emeritus, 1995—. Co-author: The Academic Marketplace, 1958; author: Academic Janus, 1971; co-editor: Teaching Sociology: The Quest for Excellence, 1984; editor: Teaching the Mass Class, 1986, 2nd edit., 1991. Sgt. U.S. Army, 1950-51. Reece McGee Disting. professorship named in honor by bd. trustees of Purdue U., 1995. Mem. Am. Sociol. Assn. (Teaching award sect. on undergrad. edn. 1982, Teaching award 1994), North Cen. Sociol. Assn. (Teaching award 1987), AAUP, Phi Beta Kappa. Democrat. Episcopalian. Avocations: sailing, motorcycles. Office: Purdue U Stone Hall 1365 Dept Sociology & Anthropol West Lafayette IN 47907-1365*

MCGEE, SUE, pediatrics nurse, educator, administrator; BSN, West Tex. State U., 1977; MSN, U. Tex., 1979; postgrad., Tex. Tech. U., 1982—. Staff nurse pediat., newborn nursery High Plains Bapt. Hosp., Amarillo, Tex., 1974-78; instr. pediat. Amarillo Coll., 1978-82; missionary Fgn. Mission Bd. So. Bapt. Conv., Mauritius, 1982-87; staff educator pediat. N.W. Tex. Hosp., Amarillo, 1987-88; dir. nursing resource ctr. Amarillo Coll., 1987-94, divsn. chmn. nursing, 1994—2003. Cons. Buckner Children's Home, Amarillo, 1992. Bd. dirs. Amarillo Pregnancy Crisis Intervention Ctr., 1991-2003. Helene Fuld, 1992, Telecom. Infrastructure Fund grant, 2002.

MCGEE, THOMAS DONALD, materials engineer, educator; b. Tripoli, Iowa, June 9, 1925; s. Nacy Waters and Maude Sophia (Ridenour) M.; m. Avis Morse, Dec. 28, 1948 (div. 1976); children: Evelyn, Timothy, James, Matthew; m. Clara Thomas McGee, July 5, 1981 (dec. 1994); m. Dorothy Leone Tschopp, March 15, 2003. BS in Mech. Engring., BS in Ceramic Engring., Iowa State U., 1948; MS, Iowa State U, 1958; PhD, Iowa State U., 1961. Rsch. engr. A. P. Green Industries, Mexico, Mo., 1948-54; rsch. engr. supr. A.P. Green Industries, Mexico, 1954-56; asst. prof. Iowa State U., Ames, Iowa, 1956-61, assoc. prof., 1961-65, prof., 1965—. Author: Principles and Methods of Temperature Measurement, 1988; contbr. articles to profl. jours. Lt. US Navy, 1946-56. Mem. Nat. Inst. Ceramic Engrs. (pres. 1985-86), Am. Soc. Engring. Edn., Soc. for Glass Tech., Am. Ceramic Soc., Am. Assn. Engr. Soc. (bd. govs. 1985-91), Accred. Bd. Engring. Tech. (dir. 1979-86), Keramos Frat. (gen. sec. 1986-91), Kiwanis. Achievements include patents for biomedical engineering. Office: Iowa State U 3053 Gilman Ames IA 50011-0001 E-mail: tmcgee@iastate.edu.

MCGEE, WILLIAM TOBIN, intensive care physician; b. Port Chester, NY, May 23, 1957; s. James R. and Mary (Delzotto) McG.; m. Sarah McGrath; children: Erin, Kelly, Mary, Kate. BA in Physics, Dartmouth Coll., 1979; MD, N.Y. Med. Coll., 1983; M in Health Adminstrn., Clark U., 1997. Diplomate Am. Bd. Internal Medicine with spl. qualifications in Critical Care. Resident in internal medicine Baystate Med. Ctr., Springfield, Mass., 1983-86, intensivist, acting dir. surg. ICU, 1990-95; fellow in critical care St. Louis U./St. John's Mercy Med. Ctr., St. Louis, 1986-88; intensivist critical care divsn. Baystate Med. Ctr., Springfield, MA, 1990-98, dir. ICU quality improvement, 1998—. DeWitt Wallace fellow rehab. medicine Rusk Inst. NYU Med. Ctr. Fellow Coll. Chest Physicians (Cecile Lehman Mayer award 1993); mem. AMA, Soc. Critical Care Medicine (presdl. citation 2000, internal medicine specialty award 2000), Am. Soc. Parenteral and Enteral Nutrition. Roman Catholic. Avocations: skiing, biking, hiking, sailing, windsurfing. Office: Baystate Med Ctr 759 Chestnut St Springfield MA 01199-1001 E-mail: william.t.mcgee@bhs.org.

MCGHEE, ELAINE SIMMONS, school director, consultant; b. Newark, Nov. 13, 1937; d. Joseph Dalise and Lula (Roberts) Simmons; divorced; children: Darren Fitzgerald, Elissa Anyika. BA, Rider Coll., 1959; MA, Jersey City State Coll., 1971; adminstrv. cert., Montclair State Coll., 1972; postgrad., Nova U., 1993—. Tchr. Jersey City (N.J.) Pub. Schs., 1961-68, counselor, 1968-71, PPS supr., dir. programs and svcs., 1990—; guidance counselor Hillside (N.J.) Pub. Schs., 1972-73, East Orange (N.J.) Pub. Schs., 1973-84; supr. guidance Plainfield (N.J.) Pub. Schs., 1984-90. Cons. Petra Group, Chantilly, Va., 1991—; counselor/instr. Seton Hall Upward Bound, S. Orange, N.J., 1977—. Mem. N.J. State Dept. Voc. Panel, 1986. Baptist. Avocations: modeling, interior decorating. Office: Jersey City Pub Schs 346 Claremont Ave Jersey City NJ 07305-1634

MCGHEE, KATHERINE ELAINE, art education educator; b. Derry, Pa., May 1, 1952; d. George and Margaret Scolastica (Mlinarchek) Danko; m. Jimmy Scott McGhee, July 31, 1977; children: Windsor Castille, Caribbea Laise. BS, W.Va. Wesleyan Coll., 1974; MA, Ind. State U., 1979; PhD, Ohio State U., 1988. Cert. tchr., W.Va. Elem. tchr. art Upshur County sch. System, Buckhannon, W.Va., 1974-82; instr. art W.Va. Wesleyan Coll., Buckhannon, 1980-89; asst. prof. art edn., cons. U. Ctrl. Fla., Orlando, 1989—, dir. very spl. arts festival, 1991—; dir. art edn. Tenn. Tech. U., Cookeville, 1995-96. Co-author: After School Arts Program, 1990, First Start in the Arts, 1990, video, 1990; contbr. articles to profl. jours. Mem. adv. bd. Orlando Mus. of Art, 1990-91; coord. start with arts Very Spl. Arts, Tallahassee, Fla., 1993— Mem. NEA, U.S. Soc. Edn. Through Art, Nat. Art Edn. Assn., Internat. Soc. Edn. Through Art. Unitarian Universalist. Avocations: sculpture, interior design, illustrating children's books, jewelry making, fabric design. Office: Tenn Tech U Dept Music and Art Box 5045 Cookeville TN 35801

MCGIFFORD, DIANA, legislator, writer, elementary school educator; PhD in English, U. Manitoba. Tchr. Manitoba Pub. Schs.; editor Contemporary Verse 2; critic New Democrat; elected minister legis. assembly Province of Manitoba, Winnipeg, 1995, appointed minister of advanced edn. and tng., 2002—. Mem. Urban Safety Com. for Women and Children, Winnipeg, Canada; founding mem. Dec. 6th Women's Meml. Com.; vol. Klinic, YWCA, Planned Parenthood.; chair Fort Garry Women's Resource Ctr.; bd, dirs. Carter Daycare. Office: Legis Bldg 450 Broadway Winnipeg MA RC3 0Y8 Canada

MCGILL, CATHY BROOME, gifted and talented education educator; b. Gastonia, N.C., Sept. 26, 1945; d. Harold Beeler and Christine (Hicks) Broome; m. Paul Furman McGill, July 5, 1969; children: Paul Bryan, Harold Marcus. BA, Mars Hill Coll., 1967; MA, Appalachian State U., 1968. Tchr. 6th grade Victory Elem. Sch., Gastonia, N.C., 1968-69; lang. arts, social studies and music tchr. Northside Mid. Sch., West Columbia, S.C., 1969-71, Fulmer Mid. Sch., West Columbia, 1972-76; tchr. Pine View Elem. Sch., West Columbia, 1978-81; tchr. sci. and lang. arts Heiskell Sch., Atlanta, 1981-82; tchr. lang. arts and gifted Fulmer Mid. Sch., 1982-85; itinerant gifted tchr. Lex II, West Columbia, 1985—. In-svc. presenter Lex II, 1992-95. Pianist Holland Ave. Bapt. Ch., Cayce, S.C., 1970—2000, Lexington Presbyn. Ch., 2001-03; pianist Saxe Gotha Presbyn. Ch., 2003—, vacation Bible sch. dir., 1982-93, youth choir dir., 1982-85; neighborhood solicitor Arthritis Found., Columbia, S.C., 1993-95. Mem. Nat. Assn. for Gifted Children, Palmetto State Tchrs. Assn., Alpha Delta Kappa (chaplain 1993—). Republican. Avocations: music, reading. Home: 1404 Martins Crossing Ct Gilbert SC 29054-8672

MCGILL, CLYDE WOODROW, principal; b. Wood River, Ill., Nov. 1, 1954; s. Clyde W. Sr. and Macel M. (Maulding) McG.; m. Tamera Lynn Willis, July 21, 1979; children: Joseph D., Kristi L. BS in Edn., So. Ill. U., 1979, MS in Ednl. Adminstrn., 1988. Tchr. sci. Beltline Christian Sch., 1980-81; tchr. Southwestern Sch. Dist., Piasa, Ill., 1981-82; tchr. sci. East Alton (Ill.) Jr. High, 1989—, prin., 1991—. Mem. choir 1st Bapt. Ch. Rosewood Heights, Ill., 1970—, trustee, 1974-77, 89—, pres. camp bd.,

1989—, dir. sr. high summer camp, 1989—; vol. Rosewood Heights Fire Dept., 1974—, sec., 1974-76, dist. trustee, 1975-80, pres., 1983-85; mem. citizens adv. coun. Roxana Sch. Dist., 1987-89, pres. coun., 1989. Avocations: baseball, softball, hunting. Home: 60 Dugger St East Alton IL 62024-1741

MCGILL, JUDY ANNELL MCGEE, early childhood and elementary educator; b. Kosciusko, Miss., Oct. 16, 1949; d. Reeves and Martha Lee (Thompson) McGee; m. Ronald Eugene McGill, June 5, 1971; 1 child, Thomas Eugene. Student, U. Colo., 1979, James Madison U., 1974; BS, Miss. State U., 1971; MEd, Northeast La. U., 1984. 4th grade tchr. Harrison County Schs., Gulfport, Miss., 1971; 1st and 2d grade tchr. Oktibbeha County Schs., Starkville, Miss., 1971-72; 4th grade tchr. Natchez-Adams (Miss.) County Schs., 1972-74; 2d and 3d grade tchr. Shenandoah County Schs., Woodstock, Va., 1974-78; elem. tchr. Jefferson County Schs., Lakewood, Colo., 1980-81; 7th and 8th grade tchr. Ouachita Parish Schs., Monroe, La., 1982; elem. sch. tchr. Union Parish Schs., Farmerville, La., 1982-85; early childhood and elem. tchr. Ouachita Parish Schs., Monroe, La., 1985-95; master tchr., intern assessor Quachita Parish Schs., Monroe, La., 1993-95; elem. tchr. Scottsboro (Ala.) City Schs., 1995—, Hands-On Activity Sci. Program lead tchr. and insvc. instr., 1998—. In-svc. instr. Natchez-Adams County Schs., 1972-74, Shenandoah County Schs., 1974-78; trainer Sci. Rsch. Assocs., Woodstock, 1978; chairperson curriculum revision Ouachita Parish Schs., 1986-92, staff devel. trainer, 1990-92. Den leader Boy Scouts Am., West Monroe, La., 1986-88; sponsor Young Astronauts Coun., 1995--. Grantee La. Quality in Sci. and Math., 1994-95, Jr. League Monroe, 1994-95, MEAD, 1997-98. Mem. NEA, ASCD, La. Assn. on Children Under Six (Jane Herrin grantee 1987, v.p., program chair 1988-94), N.E. La. Reading Coun. (chair grants 1987-88, Reading Tchr. of Yr. 1987-88). Methodist. Avocations: downhill skiing, target shooting, sourdough baking. Home: 2185 July Mountain Blvd Scottsboro AL 35768-7502 E-mail: jamcgill@scottsboro.org.

MCGILLIVRAY, KAREN, retired elementary school educator; b. Richland, Oreg., Aug. 24, 1936; d. Kenneth Melton and Catharina (Sass) McG. BS in Edn. cum laude, Ea. Oreg. State U., 1958; MRE, Pacific Sch. Religion, 1963. Cert. tchr., Oreg. 4th grade tchr. Salem (Oreg.)-Keizer Pub. Schs.; ret., 1995. Contbr. articles to profl. jours. U.S. Govt. grantee. Mem.: NEA (rep. assembly), Salem Edn. Assn. (officer), Oreg. Ret. Educators Assn. (officer), Oreg. Edn. Assn. (rep. assembly), NEA-Ret. Oreg. (state officer), Wash. State Scottish Terrier Club, Cascade Scottish Terrier Club, Scottish Terrier Club Am., Phi Delta Kappa (officer), Delta Kappa Gamma (officer). United Methodist. Home: PO Box 1262 Mcminnville OR 97128-1262 E-mail: karen@mcgillivray.org.

MCGINN, BERNARD JOHN, religious educator; b. Yonkers, N.Y., Aug. 19, 1937; s. Bernard John and Catherine Ann (Faulds) McG.; m. Patricia Ann Ferris, July 10, 1971; children: Daniel, John. BA, St. Joseph's Sem., Yonkers, N.Y., 1959; Licentiate in Sacred Theology, Gregorian U., Rome, 1963; PhD, Brandeis U., 1970. Diocesan priest Archdiocese N.Y., N.Y.C., 1963-71; prof. U. Chgo., 1969—, Naomi Shenstone Donnelly prof., 1992—2003, emeritus, 2003—. Program coord. Inst. for Advanced Study of Religion, Divinity Sch., U. Chgo., 1980-92. Author: The Calabrian Abbot, 1985, Meister Eckhart, 1986, Foundations of Mysticism, 1991, Growth of Mysticism, 1994, Antichrist, 1994, Flowering of Mysticism, 1998; editor: (series) Classics of Western Spirituality, 1978, (book) God and Creation, 1990. Fellow Medieval Acad. Am., Am. Acad. Arts and Scis. Home: 5701 S Kenwood Ave Chicago IL 60637-1718 Office: U Chgo Divinity Sch 1025 E 58th St Chicago IL 60637-1509 E-mail: bmcginn@uchicago.edu.

MCGINN, CHERIE M. secondary education educator; b. Oil City, Pa., Feb. 5, 1949; d. Rendall Baxter amd Helen Joyce (Kunselman) Agnew; 1 child from previous marriage, Joshua Edward; m. Stephen James McGinn, Jan. 1, 1983; 1 child, Kathleen Erin. BS, Clarion (Pa.) U., 1971. Cert. secondary tchr., Md. Grad. asst. Clarion U., 1971—72; tchr. Montgomery County Pub. Schs., 1972—. Chmn. Montgomery Blair H.S., Silver Spring, Md., 1994—; program dir. G.B.T.L.A., Inc., 2002—; cons. curriculum, Upper Marlboro, Md.; panelist Odyssey 1984, Excellence in Edn., Md. Humanities Coun., Balt., 1984; vol. reader grant proposal Coun. for Basic Edn., fellow, 1983, 91, NEH, Washington, 1984—. Fellow NEH, 1989, 92, 95, 2000. Mem.: NEA, ASCD, Montgomery County Educators Assn., Md. Tchrs. Assn., Montgomery County Social Studies Coun., Md. Social Studies Assn., Nat. Coun. for Social Studies, U.S. Capitol Hist. Soc. Democrat. Unitarian Universalist. Home: 14228 Rutherford Rd Upper Marlboro MD 20774-8564 Office: Montgomery Blair HS 51 University Blvd E Silver Spring MD 20901-2451 E-mail: Cherie_McGinn@fc.mcps.k12.md.us.

MCGINN, JILL MARIE, special education educator, speech pathologist; b. Newton, Kans., Sept. 23, 1962; d. Duane Francis McGinn and Nancy Ann (Hall) Steffen. MA in Communicative Disorders and Sci., Speech, Lang. Pathology, Wichita State U., 1991. Lic. tchr. spl. edn., Kans. Dental hygienist Dr. Frederick Carlton, Wichita, 1980-88; speech pathologist Spl. Edn. Interlocal # 618, Goddard, Kans., 1991—. Mem. Am. Speech and Hearing Assn., Kans. Speech and Hearing Assn. Avocations: softball, landscaping, gardening, woodwork, swimming. Home: 221 E 5th St Halstead KS 67056

MCGINNIS, HARRILL COLEMAN, humanities educator; b. Richmond, Va., Aug. 11, 1943; s. Harrill and Elizabeth Coleman McGinnis. BA, U. of the South, Sewanee, Tenn., 1965; MA, Tulane U., 1967; PhD, U. Va., 1971. Instr. U. of the South, Sewanee, Tenn., 1967—68; asst. prof. Ga. State U., Atlanta, 1970—72; asst. then assoc. prof. U. Tenn., Nashville, 1972—79; prof. Tenn. State U., Nashville, 1979—. Dir. Atlanta Urban Obs., 1971. Contbr. articles to profl. jours. State bd. dirs. Tenn. Common Cause, Nashville, 1974—75, ACLU Tenn., Nashville, 1974—78; pres. dist. 10 Am. Contract Bridge League, 1998—2002. Mem.: Tenn. Polit. Sci. Assn. (exec. com. 1994—2003, pres. 2001—02). Home: 21 Vaughns Gap Rd A18 Nashville TN 37205-4321 Office: Tenn State U 3500 John Merritt Blvd Nashville TN 37209 Office Fax: 615-963-5497. Business E-Mail: cmcginnis@tnstate.edu.

MCGINNIS, JOAN ADELL, retired secondary school educator; b. Erie, Pa., Jan. 20, 1932; d. Roy Hamilton and Sara Zelma (Gorman) Sjöberg; m. Richard H. Edwards, Aug. 6, 1954 (div. 1965); m. George William McGinnis, Dec. 29, 1966 (dec. Apr. 1994). BA, St. Lawrence U., Canton, N.Y., 1953. Cert. tchr., Calif. Spl. proxies Sun Life Assurance Co., Montreal, 1952-53; pvt. sec. Detroit Trust, 1953-54; tchr. Sunny Hills H.S., Fullerton, Calif., 1966—95; ret., 1995. Contr. Mission Viejo (Calif.) Sheet Metal, 1980-81; dept. sec. fgn. lang. dept. Sunny Hills HS, 1966-80, dept. chair, 1987-89; internat. baccalaureate examiner in Spanish, 1991-2001, French, 1992-2001; advanced placement examiner in Spanish, 1990-2002, Internet tutorer, 1998—; pharmacy clk., 2000—. Sec. Meth. Ch., Lancaster, Calif., 1964—96. Mem. Am. Assn. Tchrs. Spanish and Portuguese, Modern Classical Lang. Assn. Calif., Fgn. Lang. Assn. Orange County (Exptl. Tchr. of Orange County award 1994), Am. Women's Orgn. Republican. Avocations: languages, music, drama. Home: 26382 Estanciero Dr Mission Viejo CA 92691-5401

MCGINNIS, TINA MARIE, art educator; b. Flint, Mich., July 26, 1954; d. Keith Raymond and Katherine Ann (Luce) McG.; children: Katrina Marie, Robert Raymon. A of Liberal Arts, Mott. C.C., 1990, A in Gen. Studies, 1992; BS, U. Mich., 1993; M in Art of Teaching, Marygrove Coll., 1999. Tchr. art Valley Sch., Flint, Mich., 1991-92; substitute tchr. Swartz Creek (Mich.) Schs., 1993-94, Flint Cmty. Schs., 1993-94; tchr. Mott Adult High Sch., Flint, 1986-94; tchr. art Flint Inst. Art, 1991-94, Grand Blanc (Mich.) Parks & Recreation, FLint, 1993-96, Lapeer (Mich.) Cmty. Schs., 1994-96, Carman-Ainsworth Cmty. Schs., Flint, Mich., 1996—. Author of poems. Mem. ASCD, NEA, Nat. Art Edn. Assn., Mich. Edn. Assn., Mich. Art Edn. Assn. (conf. demonstrator 1993), Greater Flint Arts Coun., U. Mich. Alumni Assn., Kappa Delta Pi. Avocations: making jewelry, painting, metal smithing, reading, floral design. Office: Dye Elem Sch 1174 S Graham Rd Flint MI 48532-3562

MCGLOHON, REEVES, education administrator; b. Charlotte, N.C., July 2, 1947; s. Loonis R. and Nan (Lovelace) McG.; m. Peggy Martin; children: Max, Allan, Brooke. AB in Econs., Lenoir Rhyne Coll., 1969; MEd, U. N.C., 1972. Cert. tchr., adminstr., N.C. Tchr. Charlotte (N.C.)/Mecklenburg Schs., 1969-71; cons. N.C. Dept. Pub. Instrn., Raleigh, 1972-75; exec. asst. Am. Assn. Sch. Adminstrs., Washington, 1975-76; dir. fed. programs N.C. Dept. Pub. Instrn., Raleigh, 1977-82, dep. state supt., 1982-90; asst. supt. Gaston County Schs., Gastonia, N.C., 1991-94, dept. supt., 1995—. Bd. dirs. S.E. Regional Edn. Lab., Rsch. Triangle Park, N.C., 1985-90; dir. N.C. Leadership Inst. for Principals, Raleigh, 1979-82. Bd. dirs. Holy Angels, Inc., 1997—, United Way of Gaston Co., 1997. With U.S. Army, 1970-72. Named Top Pub. Mgr. in N.C., Duke U., 1986. Mem. AASPA, Am. Assn. Sch. Adminstrs., Pers. Adminstrs. of N.C., Mt. Holly Rotary Club (pres. 1997), Phi Delta Kappa. Democrat. Baptist. Avocations: golf, gardening. Home: 124 Fites Creek Rd Mount Holly NC 28120-1148 Office: Gaston County Schs 943 Osceola St Gastonia NC 28054-5482

MCGLONE, MARY ELLEN, marketing and fashion consultant, writer; b. Cin., Jan. 2, 1943; d. Morris S. and Rose Caroline (Fremmel) Hermann; m. Samuel D. McGlone, Nov. 4, 1967; children: Michael, Molly, Michelle. BA, Barat Coll., 1964; postgrad. U. Minn., Mankato State U., Troy State U., Northeastern Ill. State U. Freelance fashion coord., cons., model, 1967— ; asst. dir. fashion merchandising and self-improvement Lowthian Coll. (formerly Patricia Stevens Sch.), Mpls., 1968-70; mgr. Patricia Stevens Modeling Agy., Mpls., 1970; instr., dir. fashion merchandising ITT-Minn. Sch. Bus., Mpls., 1971-81, asst. dir. placement, 1981-82, student services coord., 1982-87; mktg. dir. the Marsh, Minnetonka, 1989-92; owner, dir. Plaza 3 Models & Talent; mktg. dir. Jeanne Piaubert Cosmetics/PariSpa; columnist Skyway News, Mpls., 1978-87, freelance writer, 1987—, former fashion editor; originator Reach Out & Touch Me, ann. fashion for blind and handicapped. Bd. dirs. Minn. Heart Assn., 1970-71, 91-92, Minn. Lupus, 1991-93, Combined Health Appeal, 1992; publicity chmn. cookie drive Girl Scouts U.S.A., 1983. Barat scholar, 1960-64; Ill. State scholar, 1960-64; NDEA fellow, 1965. Mem. Minn. Press Club (bd. dirs. 1991-92), Fashion Group (dir., program chmn. 1982-83, past treas.), Sales and Mktg. Execs. Club: N.W. Pilots Wives (past pres.). Author: (with others) The Person You Are, 1978, 2d edit., 1985; (with Mayer) Kids' Chic, 1984; columnist Entourage, Rapport; editor The Marsh Monthly, MSB News, Minn. Fashion Group News, Placement World; contbr. articles to Woman's World, Minn. Monthly, Creative Service, WITT's. Home: 8712 Sandro Rd Bloomington MN 55438-1229

MCGLOWN, BRENDA PRYOR, special education educator; b. Memphis, Tenn., Oct. 31, 1946; d. George and John Ella (Hobbs) Pryor; m. Andrew McGlown III, Dec. 29, 1979; 1 child, Toya Angeliqué. BA, LeMoyne-Owen, 1970; MEd, Memphis State U., 1977. Cert. tchr., Tenn. Tchr. Memphis (Tenn.) City Schs., 1970—. Mem. Inservice Com. Spl. Edn., Memphis, 1990-91, Adminstrv. Adv. Com., Memphis, 1992-93. Author: (test) Adaptive Reading Special Needs, 1986-87, (curriculum) Adaptive Social Studies, 1991-92. Mem. Dist. 33 Adv. Bd., Memphis, 1990-92; officer Shelby County Election Commn., Memphis, 1991-92, election official, 1996-97; mem. People's Rescue Mission, South Memphis, 1989-90; vol. Spl. Olympics, 1990. Recipient Tchr. Excellence award Memphis Rotary Club, 1993; named Tchr. of Yr., Coun. of Exceptional Children, 1988; grantee Memphis Rotary Club, 1988-89, 91-92, 96-97, 97-98. Mem. NEA, Tenn. Edn. Assn., Memphis Edn. Assn., Tenn. Assn. for Children with Learning Disabilities, Zeta Phi Beta Sorority. Avocations: reading, cooking. Home: 5819 W Fox Bend Cv Memphis TN 38115-3804 Office: Grahamwood Elem Sch 3950 Summer Ave Memphis TN 38122-5210

MC GLYNN, SEAN PATRICK, physical chemist, educator; b. Dungloe, Ireland, Mar. 8, 1931; arrived in U.S., 1952, naturalized, 1957; s. Daniel and Catherine (Brennan) Mc Glynn; m. Helen Magdalena Salacz-von Dohnanyi, Apr. 11, 1955 (div.); children: Sean Ernst, Daniel Julian, Brian Charles, Sheila Ann, Alan Patrick; m. Maureen G. Potts, Oct. 23, 1985; children: Shane Joseph, Brennan John, Colin Patrick. BS, Nat. U. Ireland, 1951, MS, 1952; PhD, Fla. State U., 1956. Fellow Fla. State U., 1956, U. Wash., 1956-57; mem. faculty La. State U., 1957—, prof. chemistry, 1964—, Boyd prof. chemistry, 1967—, dean Grad. Sch., 1981-82, vice chancellor rsch., 1981-91. Assoc. prof. biophysics Yale U., 1961; Humboldt prof. physics U. Bonn, Germany, 1979—80; cons. to pvt. cos. Author (with others): (book) Molecular Spectroscopy of the Triplet State, 1969, Introduction to Applied Quantum Chemistry, 1971, Photophysics and Photochemistry in the Vacuum Ultraviolet, 1985, The Geometry of Genetics, 1988; editor: Wiley-Interscience Monographs in Chem. Physics; contbr. articles to profl. jours., chapters to books. Recipient award, Baton Rouge Coun. Engring. and Sci. Socs., 1962—63, Sr. Scientist award, Alexander von Humboldt Found., 1979, Disting. Rsch. medal, U. Bologna, Italy, 1979; fellow, Rsch. Corp., 1960—63; Sloan fellow, 1964—68. Mem.: AAAS, Am. Phys. Soc., Am. Chem. Soc. (S.W. Regional award 1967, Fla. sect. award 1970, Coates award 1977). Achievements include research in molecular electronic spectroscopy; electronic structure; energy transfer; molecular genetics; bioenergetics; mathematical biology; optoaccoustics; optogalvanics. Home: 12048 Pecan Grove Ct Baton Rouge LA 70810-4835 E-mail: chspm@lsu.edu., maureen.potts@worldnet.att.net.

MCGOLDRICK, KATHRYN ELIZABETH, anesthesiologist, educator, writer; b. Worcester, Mass., 1946; MD, Cornell U., 1970. Diplomate Am. Bd. Anesthesiology. Intern N.Y. Hosp.-Cornell Med. Ctr., 1970—71; resident anesthesiology Peter Bent Brigham Hosp., Boston, 1971—73; fellow pediat. anesthesiology Children's Hosp. Med. Ctr., Boston, 1973—74; prof. anesthesiology Yale U., New Haven, 1992—2001; prof., chmn. dept. anesthesiology N.Y. Med. Coll., Valhalla, 2001—. Med. dir. ambulatory surgery Yale-New Haven Hosp., 1991—2001. Editor-in-chief Survey of Anesthesiology, 1995—; mem. editl. bd. Anesthesia Web, 1999—. V.p., trustee Wood Libr.-Mus. Anesthesiology, 1998—2001, pres., 2001—. Fellow Am. Coll. Anesthesiology; mem. AMA, Am. Soc. Anesthesiologists, Conn. State Soc. Anesthesiologists (pres. 1998-2000), Assn. Univ. Anesthesiologists, Acad. Anesthesiology, Soc. Ambulatory Anesthesia (pres-elect 2003). Office: Dept Anesthesiology NY Med Coll Valhalla NY 10595

MCGOLDRICK, WILLIAM PATRICK, educational consultant; b. N.Y.C., Nov. 17, 1946; s. William Patrick and Mary Margaret (Flanagan) McG.; m. Elizabeth Margaret Coyne, July 5, 1969; 1 child, Margaret. BA, Siena Coll., Loudonville, N.Y., 1968; MA, Syracuse U., 1973. Dir. pub. rels. Harrisburg (Pa.) Area Community Coll., 1971-74; asst. to pres. for pub. rels. SUNY, Oswego, 1974-77; dir. of major gifts Coll. of William and Mary, Williamsburg, Va., 1977-80; dir. of devel. Rensselaer Poly. Inst., Troy., N.Y., 1980-85, v.p. inst. rels., 1985-95; ptnr. Washburn & McGoldrick, Inc., Latham, N.Y., 1995—. Trustee Coun. Advancement and Support Edn., Washington, 1993-95. Bd. dirs. Big Bros., Albany, N.Y., 1980-83, Harrisburg Boy's Club, 1971-74, Oswego C. of C., 1974-77, Samaritan Hosp., Troy, N.Y., 1989-96, St. Anne Inst., Albany, N.Y., 1993-96, Unity House, Troy, 1993-99, pres., 1996-98; mem. Siena Coll. Bd. Assoc. Trustees, 1999—; trustee Cath. Charities of The Diocese of Albany, N.Y., 2001—. Mem. Siena Coll. Alumni Assn. (bd. dirs. 1983-85). Roman Catholic. Home: 16 Carriage Hill Dr Latham NY 12110-4947 Office: Washburn & McGoldrick 8 Century Hill Dr Ste 1 Latham NY 12110-2116 E-mail: mcgold@wash-mcg.com.

MCGONIGAL, SHIRLEY JOAN O'HEY, secondary education educator; b. Phila., Aug. 13, 1920; d. Joseph Matthew and Alice Agnes (Smith) O'Hey; m. Edward Stephen McGonigal, Oct. 30, 1948; children: Alice, Stephen, Richard, Nancy Lynn, Michelle, Barry Joseph. BA, Coll. of Chestnut Hill, 1942, postgrad., 1943-44, Community Coll. Mays Landing, N.J., 1955-56, postgrad., 1983-84. Libr. Pa. Dept. of Agr., Wynnemore, 1943-45; tchr. grade sch. Barren Hill, Pa., 1945-46, Mays Landing, 1962-83; tchr. English Oakcrest High Sch., Mays Landing, 1984—. Tchr. Literacy Vols. of Am., Atlantic County, N.J., 1983—. Mem. exec. com. Betty Bacharach Rehab. Ctr., Ventnor, N.J.; sec. adv. bd. Children's Seashore Hosp., Ventnor, N.J.; chairperson Atlantic Cultural and Hist. Com., Northfield, N.J. Recipient Cert. of Appreciation, Family Svc. Assn., Svc. award Oakcrest High Bd. of Edn., 1967-82, Cert. of Appreciation, Rutgers U., Svc. Plaque, County Cultural and Hist. Com., 1988-90. Mem. AAUW, Nat. Edn. Soc. (life), Navy League of U.S., Delta Kappa Gamma (fellow, scholarship com. 1979). Republican. Roman Catholic. Avocations: writing, reading, gardening, swimming, scuba diving. Home and Office: Box 539 221 Lenape Ave Mays Landing NJ 08330-1843

MCGOVERN, BARBARA ELIZABETH ANN, elementary education educator; b. Newton, Mass., July 24, 1936; d. Joseph and Katherine Frances (Broderick) McG. BS in Edn., Lowell State Tchrs. Coll., 1957; postgrad., Salem State Coll., 1959-64, Andover-Newton Theol. Sem., 1965-68. Cert. tchr., Mass. 2d grade tchr. Thomson Sch., North Andover, Mass., 1957-58; 1st, 4th and 5th grade tchr. Franklin Sch., North Andover, 1958-95, coord. various intergenerational programs, 1970—2003, ret., 1995; owner B.E.A.M.S Dreams, North Andover, 2000—03. Cons. City of Lawrence Youth Commn., 1993—; panelist Holy Cross Coll., 1993. Camp counselor, 1952-70; tchr. arts and crafts Lawrence Jewish Comty. Ctr., 1954-55; asst. coach 6th-8th grade Girl's Basketball and Softball and Jr. Varsity Softball, 1958-67; sec. Kings Daus., 1958-65; leader Girl Scouts Am., 1960-63; vol. Civil Def., 1965-68; coord. holiday programs Franklin Sch., 1970-93, 95-96, Spl. Friends Program, 1989-95, 96, Hobby Show, 1982-2003, Audio Visual com., Pen Pals with City of Lawrence Sch., 1989-95; sec. North Andover PTO, 1970-74, v.p., 1974-79, rep., 1979-84, chair social com., 1972-90; day capt. Ground Observer Corp., Methuen, Mass., 1958-65; softball umpire ASA, 1974-76; coach Bantam Group Pro Bowl, North Reading, Mass., 1990-95; coun. mem. Sch. Improvement, 1985-90; active Matching Families with Shut Ins in Chs., 1994—; vol. cons. North Andover Sch. Sys., 1995; mem. 350th Anniversary North Andover commn., 1995-96; coord. Carvell chpt. Blind in Merrimack Valley, 1995-96; bd. dirs. Partners in Edn. of Lawrence, 2000-03; active in choirs and coms. in various chs. Recipient citation of recognition Mass. Ho. of Reps., 1988, Congressman Chet Akins, 1988, award Nevins Home, 1988, Point of Light award Eagle Tribine, 1990, Those Who Care award Elder Svcs. of Merrimack Valley, 1990, Living Tribute award Acad. Manor Nursing Home, 1990, plaque Prescott Nursing Home, 1992, Sportsmanship award Lawrence Recreation Women's Softball League, 1989, 90. Mem. AARP, Mass. Intergenerational Network (sec. 1991—), North Andover Tchrs. Assn., Andover (Mass.) Assn. of U.C.C. (ch. and min. commn., 1998-2003), Meerimac Valley Choral Arts Soc., N. Andover (Mass.) Rotary (charter, cmty. svc. com., 2002-03, co-coord. HS interact club, 2002-03, bd. dir., 2002-03, chess club coord., 2002-03, counselor, 2002-03), Lawrence Rod and Gun Club (life, bd. dirs. 1972-73, v.p. 1973-75, pres. 1975-84). Republican. Avocations: softball, ten pin bowling, mickey mouse, drawing, painting. Home: 42 York St Andover MA 01810-2601 Office: Franklin Sch Cypress Ter North Andover MA 01845

MCGOWAN, SISTER MARY KENAN, retired alumni affairs director; b. Albany, N.Y., Sept. 2, 1933; d. Francis Joseph and Irene Helen (Moreau) McG. BA in math., Coll. St. Rose, 1968; MA in theology, St. Michael's Coll., 1976. Joined Sisters of Mercy, Roman Cath. Ch., 1951. Elem. sch. tchr. Albany Diocese, Albany, Troy, Ilion, Waterford, N.Y., 1954-63; math. tchr. Cath. Cen. H.S., Troy, N.Y., 1963-96, alumni dir., 1979-96; pastoral adminstr. St. John Francis Regis Ch., Grafton, NY, 1993—, Sacred Heart Ch., Berlin, NY, 1997—. Democrat. Roman Catholic. Avocations: walking, touring new eng. Home: PO Box 234 Grafton NY 12082-0234 Office: St John Francis Church Owen Rd Grafton NY 12082

MCGOWAN, THOMAS, education educator, dean; Prof. Coll. Edn. Ariz. State U.; prof., dean Ctr. for Curriculum and Instrn. U. Nebr., Lincoln. Mem.: Ind. Coun. for the Social Studies (bd. dirs.), Ariz. Coun. for the Social Studies (past-pres.), Nat. Coun. for the Social Studies, Nat. Bd. for Profl. Tchg. Stds. (bd. mem., bd. dirs., mem. exec. com). Office: Univ Nebr Lincoln Ctr for Curriculum and Instrn 118 Henzik Hall Lincoln NE 68588-0355*

MCGRADY, DONALD LEE, retired Spanish language educator; b. Greenhurst, Md., Jan. 17, 1935; s. Francis Guy and Lida Amelia (Ewing) McG.; m. Marina Ignacia Pedroza, Sept. 6, 1958; children: Martha, Sandra, Daniel, Arthur. BA, Swarthmore Coll., 1957; AM, Harvard, 1958; PhD, Indiana Univ., 1961. Instr. U. Tex., Austin, 1961-63, asst. prof., 1963-64, U. Calif., Santa Barbara, 1964-67, assoc. prof., 1967-69, U. Va., Charlottesville, 1969-71, prof., 1971-94; prof. emeritus, 1994—. Vis. assoc. prof. U. Calif., Berkeley, 1969. Author: La Novela Histórica en Colombia, 1877-1959, 1962, Mateo Alemán, 1968, Critical edition of Jorge Isaacs María, 1970, Bibliografía sobre Jorge Isaacs, 1971, Jorge Isaacs, 1972, Critical edition of Cristóbal de Tamariz Novelas en verso, 1974, Critical edition of Lope de Vega's La francesilla, 1981, Critical edition of Lope de Vega's La bella malmaridada, 1986, Critical edition of Lope de Vega, Fuente Ovejuna, 1993, Critical Edition of Lope de Vega, Peribañez, 2 vols., 1997-98. Guggenheim fellow Guggenheim Found., N.Y., 1972-73, NEH fellow NEH, Washington, 1976-77. Mem. Comediantes. Home: 530 N 1st St Charlottesville VA 22902-4613

MCGRADY, STEPHANIE JILL, speech communications educator; b. Enid, Okla., May 25, 1950; d. James Monroe and Evelyn Fern (Pursell) Payne; m. Charles Radford, May 10, 1969 (div. 1976); children: Stacy, Steven; m. Ron L. McGrady, Nov. 28, 1992. BA, No. Okla. State U., 1978; MA, Okla. State U., 1979; postgrad., UCLA, Ctrl. State U., Okla. State U., U. LaVerne, U. Calif. Riverside. Lic. tchr., Okla., Calif.; C.C. credential, Calif. Tchr. English, drama, speech, music Crescent (Okla.) Pub. Schs., 1980-86; tchr. English and drama Palmdale (Calif.) H.S., 1986-89, Desert Winds H.S., Lancaster, Calif., 1988-91; tchr. English Highland H.S., Palmdale, 1991-92; instr. speech comm. Antelope Valley Coll., Lancaster, Calif., 1988—; edn. program advisor, Antelope Valley Acad. Ctr. Chapman Univ., Palmdale; tchr. English and speech Lancaster H.S., 1997-98, tchr. English and drama, 1998—. Tchr. power cons. Antelope Valley Union H.S., Palmdale, 1987-88, reader's theatre cons., Lancaster and Palmdale, 1987-92, mentor tchr., Lancaster, 1991-92, curriculum writer, Lancaster, 1989-92; owner, mgr. Golden Goose, Palmdale; tchr. ceramics, porcelain dolls. Author: (screenplays) Color Blind, 1988, Forever Yours, 1992; performed stage, TV, movies; directed more than 25 prodns. Bd. dirs. Cedar St. Theatre, Lancaster, 1987-89, mem. adv. bd., 1988-89; bd. dirs. Palmdale Repertory Theatre, 1992, mem. adv. bd., 1994—, v.p., 1997-98. Mem. SAG, Am. Fedn. TV Actors. Republican. Avocations: theatre, piano, writing, painting, ceramics.

MCGRATH, ANNA FIELDS, retired librarian; b. Westfield, Maine, July 4, 1932; d. Fred Elber and Nancy Phyllis (Tarbell) Fields; m. Bernard McGrath (div.); children: Timothy, Maureen, Patricia, Colleen, Rebecca. BA, U. Maine, Presque Isle, 1976; MEd, U. So. Maine, 1979; MLS, U. R.I., 1982. Libr. U. Maine, Presque Isle, 1976-86, assoc. libr. dir., 1986-89, interim libr. dir., 1989-92, dir., 1992-94, spl. collection libr., 1994-97, ret.,

1997. Editor: County: Land of Promise, 1989. Mem. Friends of Aroostook County Hist. Ctr. at Libr., U. Maine-Presque Isle; mem. Plymouth (Mass.) Spiritualist Ch. Mem. Inst. Noetic Scis., Am. Mensa, Sierra Club. E-mail: amcgrath@maine.edu.

MCGRATH, CHERYL JULIA, elementary education educator; b. Milw., Feb. 17, 1947; d. Elmer William and Marjorie (Bleiler) Scherkenbach; m. Robert Edward McGrath, July 25, 1970; children: Edward, Erin, Molly. BA in Edn., Alverno Coll., Milw., 1969. Cert. tchr., Wis. Tchr. grade 1 Greenfield (Wis.) Pub. Schs., 1969-72, St. Lawrence Sch., Wisconsin Rapids, Wis., 1972-80; tchr. grades 7-8 Our Lady Queen of Heaven, Wisconsin Rapids, Wis., 1980-85; substitute work Wisconsin Rapids (Wis.) Pub. Schs., 1987-88, tchr. grade 2, 1988—. Bd. mem. Girl Scouts Samoset Coun., Stevens Point, Wis., 1979-84; com. Math Their Way, 1992-94, Report Card, 1990-93, Able Learner, 1990-92, Peer Tutoring, 1989-91, Wisconsin Rapids Pub. Schs. Recipient Advance Religious Cert. award Diocese of Lacrosse, Wis., 1978. Mem. NEA, Wis. Rapids Edn. Assn., Wis. Edn. Assn., Alverno Coll. Alumnae Assn. Republican. Roman Catholic. Avocations: reading, boating, early childhood development, travel, computer programming. Home: 294 15th Ave Nekoosa WI 54457-8063 Office: Wisconsin Rapids Pub Schs 510 Peach St Wisconsin Rapids WI 54494-4663

MCGRATH, JANE LEE, education educator, writer; b. Evansville, Ind., Oct. 4, 1945; d. Alva and Mildred (Hutson) Williams; m. Larry W. McGrath, Dec. 22, 1969. BA, Ariz. State U., Tempe, 1967, MA, 1969, EdD, 1972. Reading specialist K-12 Wilson Elem. Dist., Phoenix, 1967-69; mem. fculty Maricopa Colls., Phoenix, 1970—. Author: Building Strategies for College Reading, 1995, Understanding Diverse Viewpoints, 1999, Basic Skills and Strategies for College, 2002. Chair Mayor's Com. on Employment of Handicapped, Tempe, 1980-83; mem. Gov.'s Com. on Employmnet of Handicapped, State of Ariz., 1980-87. Named Outstanding Citizen, City of Phoenix, 1981, City of Tempe, 1982; named Innovator of Yr., League for Innovation/Maricopa Colls., 1991. Mem. Nat. Assn. for Devel. Educators, Coll. Reading and Learning Assn. Office: Paradise Valley CC 18401 N 32nd St Phoenix AZ 85032-1210

MCGRATH, MARY ANN PAULINE, consumer researcher, marketing educator; b. Chgo., June 17, 1946; d. Walter Edwin and Jeanette Magdalene (Zielinski) Ostrenga; m. William Joseph McGrath, July 6, 1968; children: William, Geoffrey, Megan. BS in Math., Loyola U., 1968; MBA, Northwestern U., 1973, PhD, 1988. Prof. mktg. Loyola U., Chgo., 1986—. Dir. MS in integrated mktg. comm. program Loyola U., Chgo. Home: 943 Edgemere Ct Evanston IL 60202-1428 Office: Loyola Univ Chgo 820 N Michigan Ave Chicago IL 60611-2147

MCGREEVY, MARY SHARRON, former psychology educator; b. Kansas City, Kans., Nov. 10, 1935; d. Donald and Emmy Lou (Neubert) McG.; m. Phillip Rosenbaum (dec.); children: David, Steve, Mariya, Chay, Allyn, Jacob, Dora. BA in English with honors, Vassar Coll., 1957; postgrad., New Sch. for Social Rsch., NYU, 1958-59, Columbia U., 1959-60, U. P.R., 1963-65, U. Mo., 1965-68, U. Kans.; PhD with distinction, U. Calif., Berkeley, 1969. Exec. Doubleday & Co., N.Y.C., 1957—60; chief libr. San Juan Sch., PR, 1962—63; NIMH drug rschr. Russell Sage Found., Clinico de los Addictos, Rio Piedras, PR, 1963—65; psychiat. rschr. U. PR Med. Sch., PR, 1963—65; psychiat. researcher U. Kans. Med. Ctr., Kansas City, 1966—68; rsch. assoc. Ednl. Rsch., 1965—69; from assoc. prof. to disting. prof. U. Calif., Berkeley, 1968—69, ret., 1969. Yacht owner Encore; lectr. in philosophy; founder Simone de Beauvoir Cir., Inc. Author: (poetry) To a Sailor, 1989, Dreams and Illusions, 1993, Wedding: A Celebration, 1998, The Red Hibiscus, 2000, Irish Poems, 2000, The Swan, 2001, Sea Poems, 2002, Memoir of Annette Van Howe, 2002; contbr. articles to profl. jours. Mem. U.S. Holocaust Meml. Mus., Women in the Arts. Nat. Gallery, Jewish World Congress, 2000—, Friends Everglades, Nat. Wildlife Assn., Nat. Coun. Jewish Women (photographer 2000-), 1999—; publicity chair Nat. Coun. Jewish Women, 2000—02; vol. Broward County Hist. Commn., Friends of the Libr., Ft. Lauderdale Libr., 1969—, Broward County Libr. Found., FAU Wimberly Libr. Found.; mem. Naval Air Sta. Ft. Lauderdale Hist. Assn., 1994—, Am. Friends of Bodleian Libr., Oxford, England, Irish Cultural Inst., Ft. Lauderdale, Ft. Lauderdale Hist. Soc., Nat. Trust Hist. Preservation, Frances Loeb Lehman Art Gallery, Vassar Col., Ctr. de las Artes, Miami, Friends of Modern Mus. Art, Friends of the Guggenheim, Friends of Met. Mus. Art, Nelson-Atkins Mus. Art, Nat. Gallery of Art of Ireland, Norton Mus. Art, Palm Beach, Friends of Mus. of Art, Ft. Lauderdale, Friends of U. Mo. Libr., Johnson County Mental Health Assn., Pine Crest Columns Soc., Ft. Lauderdale Philharm. Soc., Menninger Found., 1997—, Navy League Broward County; founder Dora Achenbach McGreevy Poetry and Philosophy Found., Inc., 1989—, exec. dir., 1989—, Plus X Cath. Women's Club; active Fla. Atlantic U. Found., 1993—. Recipient Cert. for Svc. Broward County Hist. Commn., 1994, Nat. Women's History Project award, 1995; honored by Broward County Women's Hist. Coalition, 1996; Sproul fellow, Bancroft Libr. fellow, Russell Sage Found. fellow; postdoctoral grant U. Calif. Mem.: NOW, AAUW (corr. sec. 1991—95, bd. dirs. 1991—2001, Jeanne Faiks meml. scholarship fund com. 1992—98, Nat. Ednl. Found. book brunch com. 1994—98, chair cultural events 1995—, chair 1998, rec. sec. 1998—2002, book brunch com. 2000—01, photographer, honoree Ednl. Found. Fund 1993, cert. appreciation 2000), Fla. Women's Consortium, Southwestern Philosophy Assn., Soc. Phenomenology and Existentialism, Nietzsche Soc., Fla. Philosophy Assn. (spkr. 1991, 1993, chair self in philosophy 1994), Mo. Sociol. Assn., Poets of the Palm Beaches (yearly poetry anthology 1992—, 1st prize free verse ann. contest 1996), South Fla. Poetry Inst. (yearly poetry anthology 1991—98), Union of Concerned Scientists, Women in Psychology, Nat. Acad. Poets, Nat. Women's History Project Orgn., Internat. Soc. Universal Dialogue, Am. Philos. Assn., Nat. Women's Political Caucus, Pem-Hill Alumni Assn., Vassar Alumni Assn., Secular Humanists (bd. dirs. 1992—98, program chair 1995—98, publicity chair 1998—99), Oxfam Am., Smithsonian Instn., Fla. State Poets Assn., Inc., Broward Women's Hist Coalition (bd. dirs. 1991—98, archivist 1991—98, ad hoc com., Hall of Fame Women's History awards 1989—98), Fla. Atlantic U. Chamber Music Soc., Libr. Congress, Sierra (conservation com. 1979—, co-chair beach clean-up 1993, archivist 1993—95, Redwoods chpt. 1997, newspaper reporter, environ. com.), Vassar Club (N.Y., Kansas City, South Fla. and Palm Beach chpts.). Democrat. Roman Catholic. Achievements include first to use methodone treatment and rehabilitation at drug clinic in Puerto Rico. Avocations: poetry, painting, sailing, tennis, the beach.

MCGREGOR, F. DANIEL, education educator; b. Indiana, Pa., Aug. 8, 1946; s. Ralph Murray and Elaine (Kennedy) McG.; m. Bonnie J. Corridoni. BS in Edn., Ind. U., 1972, MEd, 1977; cert. prin., U. Pitts., 1979; cert. supt., Indiana U., 1988. Prin. Blairsville (Pa.) Saltsburg Sch. Dist., 1970-83, Kiski Area Sch. Dist., Vandergrift, Pa., 1984-87; regional coord. Dept. of Edn., Harrisburg, Pa., 1987; dir. edn. Pa. Dept. Corrections, 1987-91; prof. Elem. Edn. Indiana (Pa.) U., 1991-93; prin. Duquesne Sch. Dist., 1993—. Dir. edn. Pa. Dept. Corrections; prof. Westmoreland C.C. Chmn. Ind. County Housing Authority, 1976-98. Staff sgt. USAF, 1969-70, Vietnam. Recipient Jefferson Freedom award Gov. Pa., 1983. Mem. Pa. Congress of Parents and Tchrs. (life).

MCGREGOR, JAMES HARVEY SPENCE, comparative literature educator; b. Frostburg, Md., Oct. 1, 1946; s. James Harvey and Mary (Twigg) McG.; 1 child, Raphael Harvey Gais; m. Sarah Spence, May 25, 1985; 1 child, Edward Isham Spence. BA, Princeton U., 1968, PhD, 1975. Prof. dept. comparative lit. U. Ga., Athens, 1980—, assoc. head, 2002—. Vis. prof. dept. English Colgate U., Hamilton, N.Y., 1979-80; vis. prof. dept. Italian U. Calif., Berkeley, 1984-85. Author: Image of Antiquity, 1991, Shades of Aeneas, 1991; editor, translator: Sack of Rome, 1993; editor: Approaches to Teaching Boccaccio's Decameron, 2000. Rome Prize fellow in post-classical humanistic studies Am. Acad. in Rome, 1981-82. Mem. MLA, Am. Assn. Italian Studies, Internat. Assn. for Study of Italian Lang. and Lit., Am. Boccaccio Assn. (past pres.). Office: U Ga 232 J Brown Hall Athens GA 30606-6204

MCGREGOR, JANET EILEEN, elementary school educator; b. Pittsfield, Mass., Jan. 6, 1949; d. Joseph Patrick and Edith Cecilia (Wendell) Feeley; m. Ronald Lee McGregor, Jan. 21, 1972; children: Joshua, Jason. BS in Elem./Early Childhood Edn., Fla. State U., 1971; MEd, U. South Fla., 1996. Tchr. 4th grade South Lake Elem. Sch., Titusville, Fla., 1971-74; tchr. 1st and 2d grades Peace River Elem. Sch., Port Charlotte, Fla., 1974-90; tchr. 1st grade Deep Creek Elem. Sch., Punta Gorda, Fla., 1990—. Workshop presenter Charlotte County Schs., Port Charlotte, 1989—; cons. Lee County Schs., Ft. Myers, Fla., 1993; seminar presenter (level 3 interns) U. South Fla., Ft. Myers, 1992-94; presenter in field. Co-author: Charlotte's Arithmetic Basic Skills, 1980. Religious edn. tchr. Sacred Heart Ch., Punta Gorda, 1988—, lector, 1994—; Brownie leader Girl Scouts U.S., Port Charlotte, 1976; bd. dirs. Swim Team, Lane 4, Punta Gorda, 1991-93, cert. stroke and turn official, 1995—. Recipient Nat. Presdl. award for excellence in teaching math. NSF/Nat. Coun. Tchrs. Math., 1994, State Presdl. award for excellence in teaching math., 1993; named Charlotte County Tchr. of the Yr., Charlotte County Schs., 1993; profiled on Disney Presents the Am. Teacher, 1994; Disney/Am. Tchr. Honoree in Maths., Disney Corp. along with Campbells Soup Co., 1994. Mem. Nat. Coun. Tchrs. Math., Fla. Coun. Tchrs. Math., Coun. of Presdl. Awardees in Math., Fla. League Tchrs., Phi Delta Kappa, Alpha Delta Kappa. Democrat. Roman Catholic. Avocations: reading, sailing, camping, cross-stitch. Home: 3114 Newbury St Port Charlotte FL 33952-7100 Office: Deep Creek Elem Sch 26900 Harbor View Rd Punta Gorda FL 33983-3604

MCGREGOR, RALPH, textile chemistry educator, consultant, researcher, author; b. Leeds, Eng., Feb. 11, 1932; s. Robert and Evelyn (Hutchison) McG.; m. Maureen Mabel McGaul, Aug. 8, 1959; children— Alasdair, Ralph, Francine. B.Sc with 1st class honors, Leeds U. (Eng.), 1953, Ph.D. in Applied Chemistry, 1957, D.Sc., 1979. Chemistry tchr. Roundhay Sch., Leeds, 1956-58; Courtauld research fellow U. Manchester, 1958-59, lectr. in polymer and fiber sci., 1959-68; vis. sr. researcher Ciba A.G., Basel, Switzerland, 1965-66; sr. scientist Fibers div. Allied Corp., Petersburg, Va., 1968-70; from assoc. prof. to prof., Cone Mills Disting. prof. textile chemistry N.C. State U., Raleigh, 1970—; spl. invited prof. Tokyo Inst. Tech., 1986; vis. sr. rsch. Tech. Chem. Lab Swiss Fedn. Inst. Tech., 1993. Recipient LeBlanc medal Leeds U., 1953; research medal Dyers Co., 1976; Perkin travel fellow, 1962; U.S.-Japan NSF Coop. Sci. Program grantee, 1981; N.C. Japan Ctr. fellow. Mem. Am. Chem. Soc., Am. Assn. Textile Chemists and Colorists (Olney medal 1984), Soc. Dyers and Colorists, Fiber Soc., AAUP, Sigma Xi, Phi Kappa Phi, Phi Sigma Iota. Author: Diffusion and Sorption in Fibres and Films, 1974. Contbr. articles to profl. jours. Home: 8276 Hillside Dr Raleigh NC 27612-7221 Office: NC State Univ PO Box 8301 Raleigh NC 27695-0001

MCGREGOR, SCOTT DUNCAN, optometrist, educator; b. Berkeley, Calif., Sept. 5, 1953; s. Duncan Charles and Catherine Wala (Guthrie) McG.; m. Michele Rae Gates, Mar. 7, 1981; children: Brittany Erin, Brent Duncan, Shane Donovan. AS magna cum laude, Reynolds Coll., Richmond, Va., 1976; BS, Coll. William and Mary, 1980; OD, So. Coll. Optometry, Memphis, 1986. Lic. optometrist, Tex., Va., Tenn.; cert. Nat. Contact Lens Examiners. Paramedic, EMT-A, City of Newport News, 1974-76; instr. nursing CNC-Riverside Sch. Nursing, Newport News, 1976-80; optician White Med. Ctr., Newport News, 1976-80; pvt. practice, Dallas, 1986—; founder, dir. ophthalmic technician program Dallas and Collin County C.C., 2002—. Adj. prof. So. Coll. Optometry, 1987—; dir. optometric svcs. Optometric Eye Assn., Dallas, 1989—. Inventor ocular cancer detector. Team physician Tex. Spl. Olympics, Dallas, 1991—. Fellow Nat. Acad.; mem. Am. Optometric Assn., Tex. Optometric Assn. (legis. cons. 1987, legis. advisor 1987—), Am. Acad. Optometric Physicians, North Tex. Optometric Assn. Avocations: filmmaking, camping. Office: Preston Doctors Ctr 8215 Westchester Dr Dallas TX 75225-6103

MCGRORY, MARY KATHLEEN, retired college president; b. N.Y.C., Mar. 22, 1933; d. Patrick Joseph and Mary Kate (Gilvary) McG. BA, Pace U., 1957; MA, U. Notre Dame, 1962; PhD, Columbia U., 1969; DHL, Albertus Magnus Coll., 1984; LLD, Briarwood Coll., 1990; DHL, Trinity Coll., 1991. Prof. English Western Conn. State U., Danbury, 1969-78; dean arts and scis. Ea. Conn. State U., Willimantic, 1978-80, v.p. for acad. affairs, 1981-85; pres. Hartford (Conn.) Coll. for Women, 1985-91; sr. fellow U. Va. Commonwealth Ctr., Charlottesville, 1991-92; exec. dir. Soc. Values in Higher Edn./Georgetown U., Washington, 1992-96; ret., 1996. Pres. MKM Assocs., Holland, Mass., 1983—. Author: Yeats, Joyce & Beckett, 1975. Bd. dirs. Hartford Hosp., 1985-93; chmn. bd. govs. Greater Hartford Consortium Higher Edn., 1989-90. Fels Found. fellow, 1966-67, NEH summer fellow, 1975; Ludwig Vogelstein Found. travel grantee, 1973. Mem. New Eng. Jr. Community and Tech. Coll. Coun. (v.p. 1988-91), Am. Assn. Higher Edn., Med. Acad. of Am., Greater Hartford C. of C. (bd. dirs. 1989-91), Hartford Club (bd. dirs. 1988-91). Avocations: writing, swimming, piano. Address: 44 Forest Dr Holland MA 01521-9702

MCGRUDER-HOULIHAN, RUBY LEE, special education educator; b. Clarksdale, Miss., Sept. 9, 1950; d. Saul and Irene (Radiford) McGruder; m. Robert A. Houlihan, July 27, 1974; 1 child, Coleen Tess. BS, U. Mass., 1975; M, So. Conn. State U., New Haven, 1983; 6th Yr. Cert. in Adminstrn./Supervision, 1992; postgrad., Century U., Mex., 1993—. Cert. tchr., Conn., Mass., N.H. Tchr. spl. edn. Bridgeport (Conn.) Schs. System, 1980-90; tchr. spl. edn., cons. Conn. Correctional Dept., Cheshire, 1990-93; owner North Country Alternative Sch., Littleton, N.H., 1993—. Tchr. social studies and reading Hill House High, New Haven, Conn., 1988-89. Contbr. articles to profl. jours. Mem. Aging Com., Cheshire, Conn., 1991-92; bd. dirs. Lafayette Arts Coun., 1992. Mem. Soc. for Protection of Forests, Preservation Soc., Hist. Soc. (bd. dirs. 1980-92), Audubon Soc., Women's Pistol Club. Republican. Roman Catholic. Avocations: horseback riding, roller skating, classical music. Office: North Country Alternative Sch PO Box 805 Main St Littleton NH 03561

MCGUIRE, CAMILLE HALL, elementary education educator; b. Wayne County, Miss., Mar. 2, 1949; d. Howard Edward Sr. and Margaret Louise (Cochran) Hall; m. Richard Jay McGuire Sr., Mar. 17, 1972; 1 child, Richard Jay Jr. BS, U. Mobile, 1971; MEd, U. South Ala., 1978. Cert. early childhood edn. 1st grade tchr. Holloway Elem. Sch., Mobile, Ala., 1971-75, Orchard Elem. Sch., Mobile, 1976-87; v.p., buyer Pestop Exterminator Inc., Mobile, 1987-91; 2nd grade tchr. O'Rourke Elem. Sch., Mobile, 1991—. Pvt. tutor, Mobile, 1978—; 1st and 2nd grade chairperson Orchard and O'Rourke Schs., mobile, 1978—; supr. tchr.-trainer coll. students, 1973-86; chairperson So. Accreditation for Pub. Schs., 1979, 94; leader constant profl. growth through workshops, 1971-94. Mem. Mobile Opera Guild, 1986-91; mem. adult choir Hilcrest Bapt.Ch., 1971—, dir. children's choir, 1983—. Named Outstanding Reading Tchr. Metro Mobile Reading Coun., 1985-86. Mem. ASCD, Ashley Estates Garden Club (achievement task force 1995), Assn. Univ. Women. Avocations: reading, water sports, snow skiing in montana and new mexico. Office: Pauline O'Rourke Elem 1975 Leroy Stevens Rd Mobile AL 36695-4145

MCGUIRE, JOANN MICHELE, elementary education educator; b. Oxnard, Calif., July 2, 1950; d. Albert James and Letha Elizabeth (Harrison) McGuire. BS, Phillips U., 1972, MEd, 1990. Tchr. phys. edn. Glenwood Elem. Sch., Enid (Okla.) Pub. Schs., 1973—. Basketball coach Waller Jr. High Sch., Enid, 1975-88, 92—. Mem. Okla. Jr. Olympic Commn. Elected to Okla. Hall of Fame as umpire Okla. Amateur Softball Assn., 1989; named Indicator Fat, Nat. Amateur Softball Assn., Okla. City, 1991. Mem. AAHPERD, Okla. Assn. Health, Physical Edn., Recreation and Dance, Enid Edn. Assn. (sec.), N.W. Dist. Amateur Softball Assn. (life, pres. 1986—), Okla. Amateur Softball Assn. (mem. state jr. olympic commn. 1990—). Democrat. Lutheran. Avocations: stamp collecting, baseball autograph collection, softball. Home: 201 Rosanne St Enid OK 73703-3519 Office: Glenwood Elem Sch 824 N Oakwood Rd Enid OK 73703-3782

MC GUIRE, JOSEPH WILLIAM, business educator; b. Milw., Mar. 14, 1925; s. William B. and Marion (Dunn) McG.; m. Margaret Drewek, Aug. 20, 1946; children: Laurence, Karen, Eileen, Kevin. Ph.B., Marquette U., 1948, D.BA (hon.), 1981; MBA, Columbia U., 1950, PhD, 1956; LL.D. (hon.), St. Benedict's Coll., 1968. Asst. prof. U. Wash. Coll. Bus. Adminstrn., Seattle, 1954-56, assoc. prof., 1956-61, prof., 1961-63; prof., dean U. Kans. Sch. Bus., 1963-68; dean Coll. Commerce and Bus. Adminstrn., prof. U. Ill., Urbana, 1968-71; v.p. planning U. Calif., Berkeley, 1971-74, prof. adminstrn. Irvine, 1973-95, assoc. dean exec. degree programs, 1990-94, prof. emeritus, 1995—. Vis. prof. Netherlands Coll. Econs., Rotterdam, 1957-58, dept. econs. U. Hawaii, 1962-63, Michael Smurfit Grad. Sch. of Bus. Univ. Coll., Dublin, Ireland, 1993, Am. U. of Armenia, 1993, Henley Mgmt. Coll., Eng., 1999; Ford. vi. rsch. prof. Carnegie-Mellon U. Grad. Sch. Indsl. adminstrn., 1987-88; cons. editor Wadsworth Pub. Co., 1964-70, Goodyear Pub. Co., 1973-81, Scott Foresman & Co., 1981-90. Author: Business and Society, 1963, Theories of Business Behavior, 1964, Factors Affecting the Growth of Manufacturing Firms, 1963, Inequality; The Poor and the Rich in America, 1968; Editor, contbr.: Interdisciplinary Studies in Business Behavior, 1962, Contemporary Management: Issues and Viewpoints, 1973. Served with USAAF, 1943-45. Recipient McKenzie awards, 1963, 65 Fellow Am. Acad. Mgmt. (bd. govs. 1967-70), Internat. Acad. Mgmt.; mem. Am. Assn. Collegiate Schs. Bus. (dir. 1970-71), Am. Econ. Assn., AAUP, Am. Inst. Decision Scis., Western Econs. Assn., Western Tax Assn. (dir. 1977-80), Assn. Social Econs. (exec. council 1970-75, pres. 1973-74), Western Acad. Mgmt. (dir. 1975-81, pres. 1980-81), Phi Beta Kappa, Beta Gamma Sigma. Home: 54 Lessay Newport Coast CA 92657-1060

MCGUIRE, PATRICK PEARSE, academic administrator; b. Flushing, N.Y., May 3, 1962; s. Michael Anthony McGuire and Sheila (Burkel) Gentner. BA, St. John's U., 1984; MA, Fordham U., 1986; EdD, Columbia U., 1994; postgrad., Harvard U., 1995. Educator Monsignor Scanlan High Sch., Bronx, 1985-90; educator St. John's Prep. Sch., Astoria, N.Y., 1990-92; asst. dean grad. sch. arts & scis. St. John's U., N.Y.C., 1992—, asst. prof. theology, 1988—. Mem. Am. Assn. Higher Edn., Assn. Cath. Colls. and Univs., Coun. of Graduate Schs., Nat. Acad. Advising Assn. (grad. students commn. chair-elect 1997—), Am. Counseling Assn., Am. Coll. Personnel Assn., Coll. Theology Soc., Religious Edn. Assn., Am. Conf. Acad. Deans. Home: 13-05 135th St College Point NY 11356-2035 Office: Saint John's U Saint John Hl Rm 135 Jamaica NY 11439-0001

MCGUIRE, SANDRA LYNN, nursing educator; b. Jan. 28, 1947; d. Donald Armstrong and Mary Lue (Harvey) Johnson; m. Joseph L. McGuire, Mar. 6, 1976; children: Matthew, Kelly, Kerry. BSN, U. Mich., 1969, MPH, 1973, EdD, 1988, MSN, 1997. Staff nurse Univ. Hosp., Ann Arbor, Mich., 1969; pub. health nurse Wayne County Health Dept., Eloise, Mich., 1969-72; instr. Madonna Coll., Livonia, Mich., 1973; pub. health coord. Plymouth Ctr. for Human devel., Northville, Mich., 1974-75; asst. prof. cmty. health nursing U. Mich., Ann Arbor, 1975-83; asst. prof. U. Tenn., Knoxville, 1983-88, assoc. prof., 1990—, gerontol. nurse practitioners program coord., 1998—, chair MSN program Coll. Nursing. Dir. Kids Are Tomorrow's Srs. Program, 1988—; resource person Gov.'s Com. Unification of Mental Health Svcs. in Mich.; spkr. profl. assns. and workshops. Author (with S. Clemen-Stone and D. Eigsti)): Comprehensive Community Health Nursing, 1981, Comprehensive Community Health Nursing, 5th edit., 1998, Comprehensive Community Health Nursing, 6th edit., 2002. Bd. dirs. Ctr. Understanding Aging, 1987-93, v.p., 1995; bd. dirs. Mich. chpt. ARC, 1980-83, Knoxville chpt., 1984-85; founder Knoxville Intergenerational Network, 1989. Recipient John W. Runyan, Jr. Cmty. Health Nursing award U. Tenn. Memphis, 2002; USPHS fellow, 1972-73, Robert Woodruff fellow Emory U., 1996-97, Hewlett Innovative Tech. fellow U. Tenn., Knoxville, 1999-00, Profl. Devel. awardee U. Tenn. Knoxville, 1996-97, 99-2000. Mem. ANA, Tenn. Nurses Assn., Nat. Conf. Gerontol. Nurse Practitioners, Nat. Gerontol. Nursing Assn., Mich. Pub. Health Assn. (chmn. mental health sect. 1976, dir., co-chmn. residential svcs. com. 1976-79, chmn. health svcs. 1979-82), Nat. Assn. Retarded Citizens, Mich. Assn. Retarded Citizens, Nat. Coun. on Aging, Ctr. for Understanding Aging (v.p. 1994-95), Plymouth (chmn. residential svcs. com. 1975-77), Tenn. Assn. Retarded Citizens, So. Nursing Rsch. Soc., Sigma Theta Tau, Pi Lambda Theta, Phi Kappa Phi. Home: 11008 Crosswind Dr Knoxville TN 37922-4011 Office: 1200 Volunteer Blvd Knoxville TN 37996 E-mail: smcguire@utk.edu.

MCGUIRE, TIMOTHY WILLIAM, economics and management educator; b. Englewood, N.J., Nov. 30, 1938; s. Charles James and Marie (McCarthy) McG.; children: Timothy William Jr., Gretchen Elizabeth, Michael Joseph; m. Nancy Paule Melone, 1991. BS in Indsl. Mgmt., Carnegie Inst. Tech., 1960, MS in Econs., 1961; PhD in Econs., Stanford U., 1968. Staff mem. Coun. Econ. Advisors, 1963-64; rsch. assoc. in econs. Grad. Sch. Indsl. Adminstrn., Carnegie Mellon U., Pitts., 1964-66, asst. prof. econs., 1966-69, assoc. prof., 1969-75, prof., 1975-79, prof. mgmt. and econs., 1982—, dep. dean, 1983-90; prof. social scis. and econs. Dept. Social Scis. Carnegie Mellon U., Pitts., 1981-82; prof. econs., chmn. dept. U. Iowa, Iowa City, 1979-80; dean, Harry B. Miller prof. bus. Charles H. Lundquist Coll. Bus., U. Oreg., Eugene, 1994-98; sr. exec. v.p., chief operating officer Mgmt. Sci. Assocs., Inc., Pitts., 1998—. Sr. visitor U. Cambridge, Eng., summer, 1970; bd. dirs. Mgmt. Sci. Assocs., Inc., Pitts.; bd. visitors Joseph M. Katz Grad. Sch. Bus., U. Pitts. Contbr. articles to profl. jours. Bd. trustees, mem. bus. adv. coun. Point Park Coll.; chmn. corp. adv. bd. Point Park Coll./Pitts. Ctr. Sports, Arts and Entertainment Mgmt. Woodrow Wilson Nat. Hon. fellow Carnegie Inst. Tech., 1960-61; Stanford U. fellow, 1961-62; fellow Ford Found., 1962-63, 70-71. Mem.: Soc. Judgment and Decision Making, Internat. Soc. Bayesian Analysis, Omicron Delta Kappa, Tau Beta Pi. Home: 118 Lakeland Dr Mars PA 16046-2114 Office: Mgmt Sci Assocs Inc RockPointe Bus Airpark 400 MSA Dr Tarentum PA 15084-2808 E-mail: tmcguire@msa.com.

MCGUIRE, WILLIAM JAMES, social psychology educator; b. N.Y.C., Feb. 17, 1925; s. James William and Anne M. (Mitchell) McG.; m. Claire Vernick, Dec. 29, 1954; children— James William, Anne Maureen, Steven Thomas. BA, Fordham U., 1949, MA, 1950; PhD, Yale U., 1954; PhD (hon.), Eötvös U., Budapest, Hungary, 1990. Postdoctoral fellow U. Minn., 1954-55; assoc. prof. psychology U. Ill., 1958-61; prof. Columbia U., 1961-67, U. Calif., San Diego, 1967-70; vis. prof. London Sch. Econs., 1970-71; asst. prof. Yale U., New Haven, 1955-58, prof., 1970—, chmn. dept. psychology, 1971-73. Mem. adv. panel for sociology and social psychology NSF, 1963-65; mem. review panel for social scis. NIMH, 1968-72, cons., 1974-95. Author: Content and Processes in the Experience of Self, 1988, A Perspectivist Approach to Strategic Planning, 1989, Structure of Attitudes and Attitude Systems, 1989, The Content, Structure, and Operation of Thought Systems, 1991, Explorations in Political Psychology, 1993, Creative Hypothesis Generating in Psychology, 1997, Constructing Social Psychology: Creative and Critical Processes, 1999, After a Half Century of Election Studies: Whence, Where and Whither, 2001; contbr. to Ency. Brit.; editor Jour. Personality and Social Psychology, 1967-70; cons. editor European Jour. Social Psychology, 1978—, Jour. Applied Social Psychology, 1983—, Jour. Exptl. Social Psychology, 1994—, Comm. Rsch., 1988—, Human Comm. Rsch., 2001—, Jour.

Commn., 2002—, Applied Psychology in Hungary, 2002; contbr. Ency. Psychology. With AUS, 1943-46. Recipient Ann. Social Psychology award AAAS, 1964, Gen. Electric Found. awards, 1963, 64, 66, Disting. Scientist award Soc. Exptl. Social Psychology, 1992, Disting. Sci. award Internat. Soc. Political Psychology, 1999; grantee NSF, 1960-79, NIH, 1979-99; Fulbright fellow Louvain (Belgium) U., 1950-51, Ctr. for Advanced Study in Behavioral Scis. fellow, 1965-66, Guggenheim fellow, 1970-71, William James fellow Am. Psychol. Soc., 1989—. Fellow APA (pres. divsn. personality and social psychology 1973-74, Disting. Sci. Contbn. award 1988), Am. Acad. Arts and Scis.; mem. Am. Sociol. Assn., Am. Assn. Pub. Opinion Rsch., Sigma Xi; Am. Acad. Arts Sci. Home: 225 St Ronan St New Haven CT 06511-2313 Office: Yale U Dept Psychology PO Box 208205 New Haven CT 06520-8205 E-mail: william.mcguire@yale.edu.

MCGUIRL, MARLENE DANA CALLIS, law librarian, educator; b. Hammond, Ind., Mar. 22, 1938; d. Daniel David and Helen Elizabeth (Baludis) Callis; m. James Franklin McGuirl, Apr. 24, 1965. AB, Ind. U., 1959; JD, DePaul U., 1963; MALS, Rosary Coll., 1965; LLM, George Washington U., 1978; postgrad., Harvard U., 1985. Bar: Ill. 1963, Ind. 1964, D.C. 1972. Asst. DePaul Coll. of Law Libr., 1961-62, asst. law libr., 1962-65; ref. law librarian Boston Coll. Sch. Law, 1965-66; libr. dir. D.C. Bar Libr., 1966-70; asst. chief Am.-Brit. Law Divsn. Libr. of Congress, Washington, 1970, chief, 1970-90, environ. cons., 1990—; counsel Cooter & Gell, 1992-93; adminstr. Washington Met. Transit Authority, 1994—. Libr. cons. Nat. Clearinghouse on Proverty Law, OEO, Washington, 1967-69, Northwestern U. Nat. Inst. Edn. in Law and Poverty, 1969, D.C. Office of Corp. Counsel, 1969-70; instr. law librarianship Grad. Sch. of U.S. Dept. of Agr., 1968-72; lectr. legal lit. Cath. U., 1972; adj. assoc. prof., 1973-91; lectr. environ. law George Washington U., 1979—; judge Nat. and Internat. Law Moot Ct. Competition, 1976-78, 90—; pres. Hamburger Heaven, Inc., Palm Beach, Fla., 1981-91, L'Image de Marlene Ltd., 1986-92, Clinique de Beauté Inc., 1987-92, Heads & Hands Inc., 1987-92, Horizon Design & Mfg. Co., Inc., 1987—; dir. Stoneridge Farm Inc., Gt. Falls, Va., 1984—. Contbr. articles to profl. jours. Mem. Georgetown Citizens Assn.; trustee D.C. Law Students in Ct.; del. Ind. Democratic Conv., 1964. Recipient Meritorious Svc. award Libr. on Congress, 1974, letter of commendation Dirs. of Pers., 1976, cert. of appreciation, 1981-84. Mem. ABA (facilities law libr. Congress com. 1976-89), Fed. Bar Assn. (chpt. council 1972-76), Ill. Bar Assn., Women's Bar Assn. (pres. 1972-73, exec. bd. 1973-77, Outstanding Contbn. to Human Rights award 1975), D.C. Bar Assn., Am. Bar Found., Nat. Assn. Women Lawyers, Am. Assn. Law Libraries (exec. bd. 1973-77), Law Librarians Soc. of Washington (pres. 1971-73), Exec. Women in Govt. Home: 3416 P St NW Washington DC 20007-2705 E-mail: mmcguirl@wmata.com.

MCHALE, CAROL ANN, secondary education educator; b. Detroit, Feb. 19, 1944; d. Joseph Frank and Stella Julia (Duch) Gasperut; m. Dennis Paul McHale, Nov. 29, 1974; children: Robert, Matthew. AB, U. Detroit, 1966; M in Gen. Secondary Edn., Wayne State U., 1969. Cert. specialist in gen. secondary edn., Mich. Tchr. English Shrine High Sch., Royal Oak, Mich., 1966-86, Birmingham (Mich.) Bro. Rice High Sch., 1986-88, Shrine Acad., Royal Oak, Mich., 1988—. Roman Catholic. Avocations: golf, tennis, reading. E-mail: cam244@aol.com.

MCHENRY, LOUISA BETH, special education educator; b. Malvern, Ark., Jan. 14, 1961; d. John Robert and Lou Vena (Weller) McH. BS, Henderson State U., Arkadelphia, Ark., 1983; MEd, East Tex. State U., 1987. Cert. tchr., Ark., Tex.; cert. ednl. examiner, speech therapist; cert. in spl. edn., elem. edn.; lic. speech therapy asst., Tex. Speech therapist Texarkana (Ark.) Pub. Sch., 1983-85, tchr. self-contained spl. edn., 1985-92, tchr. community based instrn. for moderately to severely retarded students, 1992-94; ednl. specialist Temple Meml. Rehab. Ctr., Texarkana, 1995—. Area dir. Spl. Olympics, 1987-92, cert. coach, 1983—. Mem. Coun. for Exceptional Children (pres. Texarkana chpt. 1989, divsn. v.p.), Jr. League Texarkana, Alpha Sigma Alpha (rush com.). Democrat. Presbyterian. Avocations: swimming, reading, golf, camping. Office: 1315 Walnut St Texarkana TX 75501-4446

MCHENRY, TIMOTHY HOWARD, elementary education educator; b. Colunbus, Ohio, Dec. 19, 1945; s. Howard Almond and Bettie Marie (Summers) McH.; m. Marianne L. Moehle, April 26, 1980 (div.). BS in Education, Miami U., Ohio, 1967; MA in Education, Kent State U., 1970. Cert. elem. tchr., prin., Ohio. Tchr. grade 4 Lorain City Schs., Ohio, 1967-68, Clearview Local Schs., Lorain, Ohio, 1968-70; tchr. grade 5 Grandview Heights City Schs., Ohio, 1970-73; tchr. grade 6 Madison Local Schs., Groveport, Ohio, 1973-75; head tchr., grade 6 tchr. Midview Local Schs., Grafton, Ohio, 1975-76; elem. substitute tchr. Elyria City Schs., Ohio, 1976-81; agent Banker's Life Ins. Co., Avon Lake, Ohio, 1977; hourly employee, inspector metall. dept. U.S. Steel Co., Lorain, Ohio, 1977-82; tchr. grade 1 Cleveland Pub. Schs., Ohio, 1982-85, tchr. grade 3, 1985—. Scoutmaster Boy Scouts Am., Avon Lake, 1967-70, 76-88, Columbus, 1970-76, Sheffield Lake, 1988-90, asst. scoutmaster, 1988—; mem. Church Choir, Lorain, 1980—; tchr. grade 1-3, Church Sch., Lorain, 1984—. Recipient Commendation cert. Ohio House Rep., Columbus, 1988, Scouter's key Boy Scouts Am., 1970, 93, God and Svc. Adult Religious award Boy Scouts Am., 1992, Dist. award of Merit Boy Scouts Am., 1992. Mem. Internat. Reading Assn., Ohio Council I.R.A., Assn. Supervision and Curriculum Devel., Lillian Hinds Reading Assn. (sec. 1985-88, v.p. 1988-90, pres. 1990-92, program com. 1993—). Avocations: swimming, music listening, stamp collecting, sports watching. Home: 4880 Greenwood Dr Sheffield Lake OH 44054-1517

MCHOES, ANN MCIVER, academic administrator, computer systems consultant; b. San Diego, June 17, 1950; d. Donald Anthony and Ann Mae McIver; children: A. Genevieve, Katherine Marie. BS in Math., U. Pitts., 1973, MS in Info. Sci., 1986. Tech. writer Westinghouse Electric Corp., Pitts., 1973—79; pres. McHoes & Assocs., Pitts., 1981—; dir. enrollment svcs. Chatham Coll., Pitts., 2002—. Mem. adj. faculty computer sci., Carlow Coll., Pitts., 1992—, Duquesne U., 1997-99; cons. Westinghouse Electric Corp., 1988-99, PNC Bank, Pitts., 1988—, CBS Corp., 1996-99, Intel, 1998—, McDonalds Corp., 1998-2001, commonwealth of Pa. Healthy Women Project, 1998—; vis. lectr. Pa. State U., State College, 1990-91; judge Pa. Jr. Acad. Sci., Pitts., 1993—; vol. tutor Greater Pitts. Literacy Coun., 1996-98; webmaster NVR Mortgage, 1998-2000; bd. dirs. Pitts. Playback Theatre, 2000-2001. Co-author: Understanding Operating Systems, 1991, 2d edit., 1997, 3d edit., 2000 (used in colleges and univs., North Am., Europe, Africa, Asia and Australia); assoc. editor: (4-vol. ency.) Computer Science for Students, 2002. Recipient 2001 Texty Excellence award Text and Academic Authors Assn., 2001. Mem. IEEE Computer Soc., Assn. Computing Machinery, Info. Sys. Security Assn. (chpt. sec. 1991-94, v.p. 1995-96, membership chair 1994—), Pa. Mid. Sch. Assn. (conf. exhibit chair 1996-97). Avocations: travel, tennis, golf. Office: Chatham Coll Braun Hall Woodland Rd Pittsburgh PA 15232

MCHUGH, BETSY BALDWIN, sociologist, educator, journalist, business owner; b. Concord, N.H., 1928; d. Walter Killenbeck and Eliza Alice (Hunt) Slater; m. Michael Joseph McHugh, Dec. 19, 1954; children: Betsy, Michael. MusB in Vocal Music, Syracuse (N.Y.) U., 1954; grad. student, Cornell U. Tchr. pub. schs., Juneau, Alaska, 1966-85. Owner, founder Cashè Pub. Co., Tampa, Fla., and Juneau, 1986—, Nikish Ki Lodges and Youth Camps subsidiaries Baldwin Enterprises. Named one of Alaska's Outstanding Educators, Gov. Alaska Woman's Commn., 1985, Uno of Yr., 1993, 94, Internat. Una of Yr., 1993, 94, one of 2000 Most Notable Women, 1994, Better Profl. WOmen, 1993, 94. Mem. Can. Nat. Libr., Nat. Press Club, Bus. Assn. N.Y. State, Libr. of Congress, Can. Bus., D.C. C. of C., Mex. C. of C., Sigma Delta Chi. Avocations: snorkeling, writing, sociology, dancing, music.

MCILVAINE, WILLIAM L. secondary school educator; b. Knoxville, Tenn., Apr. 24, 1935; s. Victor Caryl and Eleanor (Dickinson) McI.; m. Ruby Christine Smith, June 11, 1960; children: Ruby Celeste McIlvaine Davis, Joanna Noelle McIlvaine. Student, Mars Hill Coll., 1957-59; B Music Edn., N.E. La. State U., 1962; MCM in Conducting, New Orleans Bapt. Theol. Sem., 1968; M in Microcomputers with high honors, Nat. Radio Inst., 1987; MS in Edn. Adminstrn., N.C. Agrl. and Tech. State U., 1991. Cert. tchr., La., Ala., N.C.; cert. ednl. adminstr., supervision in curriculum, computers on grad. level, 1987. Band dir. Jefferson County Schs., Birmingham, Ala., 1962-63; dir. music, edn. and youth programs Front St. Bapt. Ch., Statesville, N.C., 1963-66; assoc. pastor, dir. music and youth programs Sugar Creek Bapt. Ch., Charlotte, N.C., 1968-70; band dir. Charlotte Mecklenburg Schs., 1970-73, Randolph County Schs., Asheboro, N.C., 1973-90; tchr. East Montgomery H.S., Biscoe, N.C., 1990-96; ret., 1996. Chmn. computer curriculum devel. com., Troy, N.C., 1991-92. Music dir. Calvary United Meth., Asheboro, 1989-92, West Bend United Meth., Asheboro, 1992-94; dir. adult divsn. Sunday Sch., outreach leader 1st Bapt. Ch., 1995—, deacon, 1997—, instrumental ensemble dir., 1997—. Mem. ASCD, NEA, N.C. Assn. Educators. Republican. Avocations: research, woodwork. Home: 3234 Meredith Country Rd Asheboro NC 27205-1232 Office: East Montgomery H S PO Box 768 Biscoe NC 27209-0768

MCILWAIN-MASSEY, NADINE, foundation administrator; b. Canton, Ohio, July 29, 1943; d. Willie J. and Mabel W. (White) Williams; m. Albert H. McIlwain, Aug. 20, 1966 (dec. June 1989); children: Jeaneen J., Floyd R.; m. William P. Massey, July 4, 2002. BA, Malone Coll., 1970; MA, U. Akron, 1978; MEd, Ashland U., 1990. Cert. tchr. social studies, sociology. Lab. asst. Canton City Health Dept., 1962-65; telephone operator Ohio Bell Telephone Co., 1965-71, svc. cons., 1970-71; tchr. Canton City Schs., 1971-90, curriculum specialist, 1985-90; prin. Alliance (Ohio) City Schs., 1990—2002; program officer Sisters of Chairty Found., Canton, 2002—. Chair Stark Met. Housing Authority, Canton, 1992—; v.p. Alliance Symphony Assn., 1991—; mem. Canton City Coun., 1985-86; bd. dirs. Canton Players Guild; mem. minority outreach com. Canton Cultural Ctr.; v.p. Canton City Bd. Edn.; life mem. Alliance br. NAACP; active Canton Urban League, Alliance Area Farmworkers Housing Assn., Alliance Project Hope. Recipient Black History award Stark County African-Am. History Month Com., 1975, Polit. award Nat. Black Women's Leadership Caucus, 1981, Liberty Bell award Stark County chpt. ABA, 1989, Achievement award Alliance br. NAACP, 1993, Nat. Educator award Milken Family Found., 1993, Ohio Humanitarian award for Edn. State of Ohio of Adminstrv. Svcs. Civil Rights Divsn. and Martin Luther King Jr. Holiday Commn., 1994, Golden Dove award Multi-Development Assn.; named Woman of Yr., Canton Negro Oldtimers Athletic Assn., 1982, Woman of Yr., Am. Bus. Women's Assn., 1983, Woman of Yr., Aphesis Deliverence Christian Ch.. Mem. NEA, Nat. Alliance of Black Sch. Educators, Nat. Sociol. Hon. Soc., Ohio Mid. Sch. Assn., Ohio Coun. for Social Studies (exec. bd. dirs.), Ohio Edn. Assn. (Doris L. Allen minority caucus), Canton Profl. Educators Assn., Leila Green Alliance of Black Sch. Educators, Stark County African-Am. Fedn., Delta Sigma Theta. Home: 3409 Tradewinds Cove NW Canton OH 44708 Office: Sisters of Charity Found 200 Market Ave S Canton OH 44702 E-mail: jagging0533@sbcglobal.net.

MCINERNY, RALPH MATTHEW, philosophy educator, writer; b. Mpls., Feb. 24, 1929; s. Austin Clifford and Vivian Gertrude (Rush) McI.; m. Constance Terrill Kunert, Jan. 3, 1953; children: Cathleen, Mary, Anne, David, Elizabeth, Daniel. BA, St. Paul Sem., 1951; MA, U. Minn., 1952; PhD summa cum laude, Laval U., 1954; LittD (hon.), St. Benedict Coll., 1978, U. Steubenville, 1984; DHL (hon.), St. Francis Coll., Joliet, Ill., 1986; DHL, St. John Fisher Coll., 1994, St. Anselm Coll., 1995, Holy Cross Coll., New Orleans, 2001. Instr. Creighton U., 1954-55; prof. U. Notre Dame, Ind., 1955—, Michael P. Grace prof. medieval studies, 1988—, dir. dept., 1978-85. Vis. prof. Cornell U., 1988, Cath. U., 1971, Louvain, 1983, 95; founder Internat. Catholic Univ.; disting. vis. prof. Truman State U., Mo., 1999; Joseph lectr., Rome, 2003. Author: (philos. works) The Logic of Analogy, 1961, History of Western Philosophy, vol. 1, 1963, vol. 2, 1968, Thomism in an Age of Renewal, 1966, Studies in Analogy, 1967, New Themes in Christian Philosophy, 1967, St. Thomas Aquinas, 1976, Ethica Thomistica, 1982, History of the Ambrosiana, 1983, Being and Predication, 1986, Miracles, 1986, Art and Prudence, 1988, A First Glance at St. Thomas: Handbook for Peeping Thomists, 1989, Boethius and Aquinas, 1989, Aquinas on Human Action, 1991, The Question of Christian Ethics, 1993, Aquinas Against the Averroists, 1993, The God of Philosophers, 1994, Aquinas and Analogy, 1996, Ethica Thomistica, 1997, Student Guide to Philosophy, 1999, Vernunftgemässes Leben, 2000, Characters in Search of Their Authors, 2001, Conversion of Edith Stein, 2001, John of St. Thomas, Summa Theologiae, 2001, Defamation of Pius XII, 2001, Very Rich Hours of Jacques Maritain, 2003; (novels) Jolly Rogerson, 1967, A Narrow Time, 1969, The Priest, 1973, Gate of Heaven, 1975, Rogerson at Bay, 1976, Her Death of Cold, 1977, The Seventh Station, 1977, Romanesque, 1977, Spinnaker, 1977, Quick as a Dodo, 1978, Bishop as Pawn, 1978, La Cavalcade Romaine, 1979, Lying Three, 1979, Abecedary, 1979, Second Vespers, 1980, Rhyme and Reason, 1981, Thicker than Water, 1981, A Loss of Patients, 1982, The Grass Widow, 1983, Connolly's Life, 1983, Getting Away with Murder, 1984, And Then There Were Nun, 1984, The Noonday Devil, 1985, Sine Qua Nun, 1986, Leave of Absence, 1986, Rest in Pieces, 1985, Cause and Effect, 1987, The Basket Case, 1987, Veil of Ignorance, 1988, Abracadaver, 1989, Body and Soil, 1989, Four on the Floor, 1989, Frigor Mortis, 1989, Savings and Loan, 1990, The Search Committee, 1991, The Nominative Case, 1991, Sister Hood, 1991, Judas Priest, 1991, Easeful Death, 1991, Infra Dig, 1992, Desert Sinner, 1992, Seed of Doubt, 1993, The Basket Case, 1993, Nun Plussed, 1993, Mom and Dead, 1994, The Cardinal Offense, Law and Ardor, 1995, Let's Read Latin, 1995, Aguinas and Analogy, 1996, The Tears of Things, 1995, Half Past Nun, 1997, On This Rockne, 1997, Penguin Classic Aquinas, 1997, The Red Hat, 1998, What Went Wrong With Vatican II, 1998, Lack of the Irish, 1998, Irish Tenure, 1999, Grave Undertakings, 1999, Heirs and Parents, 2000, Shakespearean Variations, 2000, Book of Kills, 2001, Triple Pursuit, 2001, Still Life, 2001, Sub Rosa, 2001, Emerald Aisle, 2001, John of St. Thomas, Summa Theologiae, 2001, Law and Ardor, 2001, As Good as Dead, 2002, Celt and Pepper, 2002, Prodigal Father, 2002, Last Things, 2002, Ablative Case, 2003; editor The New Scholasticism, 1967-89; editor, pub. Crisis, 1982-96; pub. Catholic Dossier, 1995—, Fellowship of Cath. Scholars Quar., 2003—. Exec. dir. Wethersfield Inst., 1989-92; bd. govs. Thomas Aquinas Coll., Santa Paula, Calif., 1993-2001; bd. dirs. Southern Cross Found., 1999—. With USMC, 1946-47. Fulbright rsch. fellow, Belgium, 1959-60, NEH fellow, 1977-78, NEA fellow, 1983, Catholic Scholars fellow; Fulbright scholar, Argentina, 1986, 87, Outstanding Philosophical scholar Delta Epsilon Sigma, 1990; recipient Thomas Aquinas medal U. Dallas, 1990, Thomas Aquinas Coll., 1991, Maritain medal Am. Maritain Assn., 1994, P.G. Wodehouse award CRISIS Mag., 1995; Gifford lectr. Glasgow U., Scotland, 1999-2000, Joseph lectr. Pontifical Gregorian Inst., Rome, 2003. Fellow Pontifical Roman Acad. St. Thomas Aquinas; mem. Am. Philos. Assn., Am. Cath. Philos. Assn. (past pres., St. Thomas Aquinas medal 1993), Cath. Acad. Scis., Am. Metaphys. Soc. (pres. 1992), Internat. Soc. for Study Medieval Philosophy, Medieval Acad., Mystery Writers Am. (Lifetime Achievement award 1993), Authors Guild, Fellowship Cath. Scholars (pres. 1992-95, pres.'s com. arts and humanities 2002--, Cardinal Wright award 1996, Premio Roncevalles de Narvrre 2002). Home: 51236 Golfview Ct Granger IN 46530-6500 Office: U of Notre Dame Jacques Maritain Ctr 714 Hesburgh Notre Dame IN 46556-5677

MCINTIRE, LARRY VERN, biomedical engineering educator; b. St. Paul, June 28, 1943; s. James Lawrence and Lenore Vineal (Converse) McI.; m. Suzanne G. Eskin, June 27, 1997. BChemE, MS, Cornell U., 1966; MA, Princeton U., 1968, PhD, 1970. Registered profl. engr., Tex. Asst. prof. Rice U., Houston, 1970-74, assoc. prof., 1974-78, prof. chem. engring., 1978—, E.D. Butcher prof., 1983—, chmn. dept., 1981-91, chmn. Bioscis. and Bioengring. Inst., 1991—, chmn. rsch. coun., 1988-91, dir. Biomed. Engring. Lab., 1980—, chmn. dept. biomed. engring., 1997—; spke faculty coun., 1994-95. Adj. prof. medicine Baylor Coll. Medicine, Houston, 1982—, U. Tex. Med. Sch., Houston, 1982—, M.D. Anderson Cancer Ctr., 2001—; chmn. blood/materials working group NIH, Bethesda, Md., 1982-85; mem. surgery and bioengring. study sect. NIH, 1984-88, 99—; mem. com. on bioprocessing NRC, 1991-94; chmn. rheology subcom. Internat. Coun. on Thrombosis and Hemostasis, 1985-89. Contbr. over 250 articles to profl. jours. Recipient Merit award NIH, 1989; NSF fellow Cornell U., Princeton U., 1965-69, NATO-NSF postdoctoral fellow Imperial Coll., London, 1976-77. Fellow Am. Inst. Med. Biol. Engring. (sec., treas. 1993-96, pres. 1997-98), AICHE (officer local sect. 1980-81, 86, Food Pharm. and Bioengring. divsn. award 1992, divsn. chair 1998), AAAS; mem. Biomed. Engring. Soc. (bd. dirs. 1992-97, pres. 1995-96, Disting. lectr. 1992), N.Am. Soc. Biorheology (v.p. 1992-94, pres. 1994-96), N.Y. Acad. Scis., Am. Heart Assn. (coun. on thrombosis, exec. com. 1994—), Faculty Club Rice U. (bd. dirs., chmn. 1982-84), Sigma Xi (nat. lectr. 1993-96), Nat. Acad. Engring. Presbyterian. Avocations: tennis, squash, classical music, hiking. Office: Rice U Inst Bioscis and Bioengring John W Cox Lab Biomed Engring Houston TX 77251-1892

MCINTOSH, CAROLYN MEADE, retired educational administrator; b. Waynesburg, Ky., Oct. 21, 1928; d. Clarence Hobert and Sarah Letitia (Bentley) Meade; m. Edgar G. McIntosh, Aug. 21, 1948; children: Wayne, Jeanne, Penny, Jimmi, Carol. BS, Miami U., Oxford, Ohio, 1962; MEd, Xavier U., Cin., 1966. Elem. tchr., Ohio, 1961-79; prin. New Richmond (Ohio) Sch. Dist., 1980-91, ret., 1991. Tchr. Clermont County Adult Edn. Program, 1970-95, Clermont County dir.of Headstrart 1971-72, Clearmont County Rep. to Ohio elem. adminstr., 1985-87, Pres. Clermont and Brown County adminstr., 1988-89; apptd. student achievement liaison team, New Richmond Bd. Edn. Editor Ret. Tchrs. Newsletter. Pres. New Richmond Bd. Edn.; v.p. U.S. Grant Vocat. Sch. Bd. Edn.; mem. Clermont County Excellence in Edn. Com.; mem. edn. adv. com. Clermont Coll., mem. long range planning com., 1999; ; mem. adv. bd. Bethany Children's Home; mem. Clermont 2001 Com.; mem. Rep. Ctrl. Com. of Clermont County; mem. New Richmond Continuous Improvement Com., 1999; mem. Clermont County Kids Voting Com.; mem. com. Renaissance New Richmond; judge Claremong/Brown County Lit. Coun. Ann. Spelling Bee. Recipient New Richmond Adminstr. of the Yr. award City of New Richmond, 1989; named citizen of yr. Monroe Twp., 1996; selected for sr. leadership charter class, Clermont 2000—. Mem. AAUW, ASCD, NAESP, Nat. Sch. Bd. Assn., Ohio Sch. Bd. Assn., Ohio Assn. Elem. Sch. Adminstrs. (all county legis. liaison), Ohio County Ret. Tchrs. Assn., Clermont County Ret. Tchrs. Assn. (pres.), Order Eastern Star, Clermont County Comm. Svcs. Bd. (apptd. 1998), Phi Delta Kappa, Delta Kappa Gamma (pres. chpt.). Baptist.

MCINTOSH, CECILIA ANN, biochemist, educator; b. Dayton, Ohio, Apr. 30, 1956; d. Russell Edward McIntosh and Geraldine Rita (Cochran) Slemp; m. Kevin Smith Schweiker, May 28, 1978 (div. Mar. 1989); children: Katrina Lynn McIntosh Schweiker, Rebecca Sue McIntosh Schweiker. BA in Biology cum laude, U. South Fla., 1977, MA in Botany, 1981, PhD in Biology, 1990. Rsch. assoc. U. South Fla., Tampa, 1981-86; sci. mentor Ctr. for Excellence, U. So. Fla., Tampa, 1984-90; tchg. and rsch. asst. dept. biology U. South Fla., Tampa, 1986-90; postdoctoral fellow dept. biochemistry U. Idaho, Moscow, 1990-93; asst. prof. dept. biol. scis. East Tenn. State U., Johnson City, 1993-98, assoc. prof., 1998—, grad. student coord., 1997—2003; adj. assoc. prof. dept. biochemistry Quillen Coll. Medicine East Tenn. State U., Johnson City, 1995—; metabolic biochemistry program dir. NSF DMCB, 2003—04. Sci. mentor U. So. Fla. Ctr. for Excellence, Tampa, 1984-90; rsch. forum judge Coll. Medicine Rsch. Forum, East Tenn. State U., Johnson City, 1994—; program dir. biomolecular sys. NSF, 2003—. Contbr. articles to sci. jours. including Plant Sci., Plant Physiology, Archives Biochemistry and Biophysics. Sci. fair judge East Tenn. Regional Sci. Fair, Johnson City, 1994—. Strenghthening program grantee USDA, 1994-95, 97-98, Seed grantee, 1995-97, plant genetic mechanisms grantee, 1998-2001; rsch. devel. grantee East Tenn. State U. Rsch. Devel. Coun., 1994-96, 97-98, 2001-2002; grantee USDA NRI, 1998-2001; co-grantee Howard Hughes Med. Inst., 2000-2004. Mem. Am. Assn. Women in Sci., Am. Soc. Plant Biologists, Phytochem. Soc. N.Am. (treas. 1998-2002), Sigma Xi (sci. fair workshop coord. Appalachian chpt. 1995, Dissertation award 1991). Achievements include characterization of new enzyme in plant flavonoid biosynthesis; biochemical characterization of plant mitochondrial membrane tricarboxylate and phosphate transporters and TCA cycle enzymes. Office: East Tenn State U Dept Biol Scis Box 70 703 Johnson City TN 37614-0703 E-mail: mcintosc@mail.etsu.edu.

MCINTOSH, JOYCE EUBANKS, special education educator, educator; b. Miami, Fla., July 5, 1947; d. Harvey and Lillie Mae (Jones) Eubanks; m. Willie E. McIntosh, Feb. 12, 1968 (dec. Feb. 1987); 1 child, Weldon R. McIntosh. AA, Miami Dade C.C., 1969-71; EdB, U. Miami, 1971-73; MS, Nova U., 1977-86. Asst. classroom spl. edn. resource tchr. Dade County Sch. Dist., Miami, 1969-73, edn. resource tchr., 1973-92, asst. prin., 1992—. Class rep. at large U. Alumni Sch. Edn., Coral Gables, Fla., 1989-92; dir. at large U. Miami, Gen. Alumni Bd., 1992. Mem. Missionary Soc., Miami, 1991, The Family Christian Soc., Local/Nat. Alliance of Black Sch. Educators. Cert. Accomplishment Metro Dade County, Miami, Fla., 1974, U. Miami, Coral Gables, Fla., 1990, Miami Dade C.C., Fla., 1969; Cert. Appreciation Kappa Delta Pi, Miami, Fla., 1988. Mem. ASCD, Coun. for Exceptional Tchr. Edn., Miami Mus. Sci. Democrat. Methodist. Avocations: interior decorating, orchid grower, community volunteer.

MCINTYRE, ELIZABETH JONES, multi-media specialist, educator; b. Teaneck, N.J., July 17, 1939; d. Paul J. Jones and Ann Cecilia O'Leary; m. John Peter McIntyre, Jan. 30, 1960; children: John P. III, Paul M., Patricia M., Maura M. Student, Rosemont Coll., 1957—59; BS in Edn., Seton Hall U., 1961; degree, Caldwell Coll., 1976. Cert. Tchr. N.J., 1976, Libr. N.J., 1976. Tchr. 4th grade Corpus Christi Sch., Hasbrouck Heights, NJ, 1960—61; media specialist Gould & Grandview Sch., North Caldwell, NJ, 1961—63, Parsippany Twp. Sch., Parsippany, NJ, 1974—2000. Grantee, Parsippany Bd. Edn., 1981, 1989. Mem.: AAUW, Women of Irish Heritage. Republican. Roman Catholic. Avocations: gardening, reading. Home: 12 South Tamarack Drive Brielle NJ 08730

MCINTYRE, HUGH BAXTER, neurology educator; b. Jacksonville, Fla., June 26, 1935; s. Hugh Baxter and Helen (Watson) McI.; m. Patricia Ann Bowne, July 11, 1959; children: Anne Louise, Hugh Cameron. BS, U. Fla., 1957, MD, 1962; PhD, UCLA, 1972. Diplomate Am. Bd. Psychiatry and Neurology, Am. Bd. Qualification in Electroencephalography; lic. med. examiner, Calif., Fla. Intern straight medicine UCLA Med. Ctr., 1962-63, resident I medicine, 1963-64, resident I neurology, 1964-65, resident II neurology, 1965-66, sr. resident neurology, 1966-67; spl. rsch. fellow Nat. Inst. Nervous Disorders Harbor-UCLA Med. Ctr., 1969-72, staff physician, chief div. neurophysiology, 1972—; asst. prof. neurology in residence UCLA Sch. Medicine, 1972-74, adj. assoc. prof. neurology, adj. prof. neurology, 1972—; adj. prof. biomed. scis. U. Calif., Riverside, 1983—99; assoc. chair dept. neurology Harbor-UCLA Med. Ctr., 1990—. Bd. dirs. Harbor/UCLA Med. Found., Inc., 1986-2001; assoc. examiner Am. Bd. Psychiatry and Neurology, 1974-84, Am. Bd. Clin. Neuophysiology, 1975—; civilian cons., lectr. neurology U.S. Naval Hosp., Long Beach, Calif., 1970-85; acad. cons. St. Mary Med. Ctr., Long Beach, 1982—, Long Beach Meml. Hosp., 1973—; chmn. Orange Coast Coll. Electro-Diagnostic Technician Adv. Com., 1973—; site visit team mem. Joint Rev. Com. on Edn. in EEG Tech. and Divsn. Allied Health and Accreditaiton of AMA, 1976—. Editor-in-chief Bull. Clin. Neuroscis., 1976-92; author: The Primary Care of Seizure Disorders, 1982, Primary Care: Symposium on Clinical Neurology, Vol. II, 1984; contbr. articles to profl. jours. Lt. comdr., M.C., USNR, 1967-69. Recipient Certs. of Appreciation, San Deigo County Epilepsy Soc., 1968, Orange Coast Coll., 1989. Fellow ACP, Am Acad. Neurology, Am. EEG Soc. (com. on guidelines in EEG, mem. edn. com.); mem. Am. Acad. Neurology, L.A. Soc. Neurology and Psychiatry (pres. 1979), Fedn. Western Soc. Neurol. Sci., L.A. County Med. Assn., Western Electroencephalographic Soc. (pres. 1994), Internat. Soc. Neuroendocrinology, Am. Epilepsy Soc., Calif. Epilepsy Soc. (bd. dirs., 2nd v.p. 1982-86, svc. award 1985). Republican. Presbyterian. Avocations: sailing, backpacking, skiing, music. Office: Harbor UCLA Med Ctr 1000 W Carson St Torrance CA 90502-2004

MCINTYRE, JOHN ANDREW, environmental and economic planner, geography educator; b. Chgo., Mar. 4, 1958; s. Donald Merrill McIntyre and Rosemary Martha (Windgassen) Peters; m. Nancy Lynn Curtis, Sept. 17, 1983. Ba in Geog. Studies, So. Ill. U., 1988, MS in Geography, 1993; diploma in econ. devel., U. Okla., 1993; grad. cert. in pub. adminstrn., Ind. State U. Cert econ. developer; cert. planner. Sales mgr. Bally Mfg. Inc., Chgo., 1981-87; dir. econ. devel. Riverbend Growth Assn., Godfrey, Ill., 1987-91; dir. Argonne Regional Consortium, Palos Hills, Ill., 1991-93; cmty. devel. dir. Homer Twp., Lockport, Ill., 1993—. Adj. faculty dept. natural scis. Joliet (Ill.) Jr. Coll., 1994—; mem. mktg. com. I&M Canal Nat. Heritage Corridor, Lockport, 1993—; bd. dirs. Applied Geography Conf., Denton, Tex., 1993—. Contbr. articles to profl. jours. Trustee Village Orland Hills, Ill., 1992-94; instr. Jr. Achievement, Orland Park, 1993; facilitator Riverbend in 90's, Alton, Ill., 1989-91. Sgt. USAF, 1977-81. Recipient Superior Lit. award Mid-Am. Econ. Devel. Coun., Deerfield, Ill., 1993. Mem. Assn. Am. Geographers (meteorology splty. group), Am. Econ. Devel. Coun. (Howard Roepke award 1994), Am. Planning Assn. (environ. splty. group), Am. Inst. Cert. Planners. Libertarian. Achievements include research on geographic information systems as applied to economic development, on economic impacts of federal research laboratories at local and regional levels; research on environmental and geological aspects of the Illinois and Michigan canal national heritage corridor. Home: 9212 Quail Ct Orland Hills IL 60477-5916 Office: Homer Twp 14350 W 151st St Lockport IL 60441-6776 E-mail: rogueplanner@chicago.usa.com.

MCINTYRE, LOLA MAZZA, music educator; b. Hammond, Ind., Sept. 23, 1955; d. Tony and Isabell Emma Mazza, Wanda Marie Mazza (Stepmother); m. William Russell McIntyre; children: William, Alexander. BMus, Hope Coll., Holland, Michigan, 1978; MMus, U. Tenn., 1989. Cert. nat. cert. piano 1991, Mich. Music Tchg. K-12 1978, Ind. applied music tchg. 2002. Music tchr. Saugatuck (Mich.) Pub. Schs., 1978—79; owner, tchr. The Studio of Holland, Holland, Mich., 1979—81; parish dir. music ministries Lafayette Diocese of Ind., Carmel, Ind., 1991—97; pvt. piano tchr. Carmel, Ind., 1976—; assoc. adj. prof. piano U. Indpls., 2001—. Prodr.: (Audio Recording) Alleluia!, 1996; author: (Multi-media Instructional CD-ROM) Bach's Musette, 2000. Friend Mus. Miniature Enthusiasts, Carmel, 2001—; docent Indpls. Symphony Orch., 1999. Recipient Concerto Competition award, Hope Coll., 1977. Mem.: Ind. Piano Tchrs. Guild (web designer, webmaster 2001—), Gtr. Indpls. Piano Tchrs. Assn. (v.p., theory chmn. 2000—02), Ind. Music Tchrs. Assn. (state advisor, music tech. 2001—02), Music Tchrs. Nat. Assn., Delta Omicron (life; chpt. pres. 1977—78, Star of Delta Omicron 1978). Roman Catholic. Avocations: miniatures, golf, quilting, travel, concerts. Office: U Indpls Music Dept 1400 E Hanna Ave Indianapolis IN Personal E-mail: lmcintyre@indy.rr.com. Business E-Mail: lmcintyre@uindy.edu.

MCINTYRE, PETER MASTIN, physicist, educator; b. Clewiston, Fla., Sept. 26, 1947; s. Peter Mastin and Ruby Eugenia (Richaud) McI.; m. Rebecca Biek, June 29, 1968; children: Peter B., Colin H., Jana M., Robert J. AB with honors, U. Chgo., 1967, MS, 1968, PhD, 1973. Asst. prof. Harvard U., Cambridge, Mass., 1975-80; group leader Fermilab, Batavia, Ill., 1978-80; assoc. prof. Tex. A&M U., College Station, 1980-84, prof. physics, 1985—, assoc. dean Coll. of Sci., 1990-92; pres. Accelerator Tech. Corp., Bryan, Tex., 1988—. Dir. Tex. Accelerator Ctr., The Woodlands, 1991—93. Recipient IR-100 award, Indsl. Rch. Mag., 1980; fellow, Sloan Found., 1976—78. Fellow: Am. Phys. Soc. (pres. Tex. sect. 1990—91); mem.: AAAS. Achievements include Proton-Antiproton Colliding Beams; patents for Continuous Unitized Tunneling System, Gigatron High Power Microwave Amplifier, Microstrip Chamber for Medical Imaging; E-beam assisted removal of mercury and sub-micron carbon particles from power plant exhausts; Electronic Pasteurization Sys. for killing bacteria in food and removing organic contaminants in water; 16 Tesla Superconducting magnets for future hadron colliders; silicon microdevices for DNA sequencing; structured cable using high-temperature superconductors for practical coils, proton-driven thorium fission for electric power production; flux-coupled isochonous cyclotron driver for thorium-cycle nuclear fission power; creation of new laboratory/problem solving curriculum for first-year college physics. Home: 611 Montclair Ave College Station TX 77840-2868 Office: Tex A&M U Dept Physics College Station TX 77843-0001

MCINTYRE, RICHARD RAWLINGS, II, elementary school educator; b. Houston, Nov. 20, 1946; s. Richard Rawlings and Emma Ruth (Blossom) McI.; m. Bonnie Antoinette Kimball, Dec. 23, 1973; 1 child, Richard Rawlings III. BA in History, Trinity U., San Antonio, 1969; MEd, Columbus (Ga.) Coll., 1983. Cert. tchr., phys. edn. coach, tech. specialist. Mgmt. trainee Deering Miliken, Manchester, Ga., 1972; tchr. Meriwether County Pub. Schs., Manchester, 1972—. Instr. adult edn., Greenville, Ga., 1985-89; coach Manchester Elem. Acad. Team, 1995-99, Mountain View Elem. Acad. Team, 1999—. Editor newsletter Per Ardua, 1985-91. Coord. Jump Rope for Heart, Am. Heart Assn., Manchester Elem. Sch., 1985—; del. State Dem. Convs.; mem. State Dem. Com., 1990-96; coach West Ga. Wolverines Wheelchair Sports Team, 2001—; pres. Meriwether County Heart Assn, 1991-92. Capt. U.S. Army, 1969-72, Vietnam. Decorated Bronze Star; Nat. Presbyn. scholar, 1965-67. Mem. Meriwether Assn. Educators (past pres., treas., pres. 1996-98), Ga. Assn. Educators (chmn. state spelling bee com. 1987—, legis. contact team and polit. action com.), NEA, Ga. Supporters of Gifted, Warm Springs Merchants Assn. (pres. 1993-95), Jaycees, Clan MacIntyre Assn. (treas. 1994-96), Scottish Am. Mil. Soc. Avocations: scottish heritage, genealogy, stamps, chess, computers. Home: 3950 Chalybeate Springs Rd Woodland GA 31836 Office: Mountain View Elem Sch 2600 Judson Bulloch Rd Manchester GA 31816

MCIVER, ANNE POOSER, school system administrator; b. Orangeburg, S.C. d. William Madison and Cornelia (Brown) Pooser; m. Earl Edward McIver, Apr. 17, 1960; children: Catherine, Earl Edward Jr. BA, Hunter Coll., 1959; MS, L.I. U., 1966; postgrad., Fordham U., 1972; B in Religious Edn., United Christian Coll., N.Y.C., 1980. Cert. counselor, sch. adminstr.-supr., elem. sch. prin., N.Y. Ast. prin., elem. guidance counselor N.Y.C. Bd. Edn., edn. adminstr. Mem. Am. Assn. for Counseling Devel., Assn. for Multicultural Counseling, Internat. Roundtable for Advancement of Counseling. Home: 668 Hawthorne St Brooklyn NY 11203-1804

MCKAY, DIANNE ADELE MILLS, humanities educator, educator; b. New Brunswick, N.J., Mar. 23, 1947; d. George M. and Dorothy Allen Mills; m. Thomas McKay III; children: Robert Allen, Heather Anne. BA in Am. Studies, Douglass Coll., 1969; MA, U. Pa., 1970, postgrad. Cert. substitute tchr., N.J. Mgr., trainer Fidelity Mut. Life Ins. Co., 1977-80; instr. humanities U. So. Colo., 1991—, Burlington County Coll., 1990—, Fairleigh Dickinson U., 2000—. Trustee New Covenant Presbyn. Ch., 1988—; mem. Hainesport Twp. Bd. Edn., 1983-90, 93-96, v.p., 1985-90; mem. Hainesport Twp. Zoning Bd. Adjustment, 1983-94, chair, 1985-89; bd. dirs. Burlington County Girl Scout Coun., 1993-95, Girl Scouts of the South Jersey Pines, 1995-96, Burlington County Red Cross, 1994—; Burlington County Com. on Women, 1993-98, chair, 1994; adv. com. mem. N.J. Coalition for Battered Women, 1993-97; gender equity task force N.J. State Employment and Tng. Commn., 1993-95; equity adv. com. N.J. Dept. Edn., 1993--, chair, 1998; chair N.J. Coun. on Gender Parity in Labor and Edn.; chair N.J. Adv. Commn. on the Status of Women, 1998--. Mem. LWV, AAUW (pres. N.J. 1995-98, bd. dirs., exec. com, v.p. N.J. membership 1989—, br. pres. 1985-87), Assoc. Alumnae of Douglass Coll. (bd. dirs. 1989—, alumnae class pres. 1985-89, 94—), Douglass Soc., Delta Kappa Gamma. Home: 12 Whittier Dr Hainesport NJ 08036-4812

MCKAY, JOHN PATRICK, history educator; b. St. Louis, Aug. 27, 1938; s. John Price and Eleanor Jeffrey McKay; m. JoAnn Ott, Apr. 21, 1961; children: John Philip, Thomas Jeffrey. BA, Wesleyan U., Middletown, Conn., 1961; MA, Tufts U., 1962; PhD, U. Calif., Berkeley, 1968. From instr. to assoc. prof. history U. Ill., Urbana, 1966-76, prof., 1976-99, prof. emeritus, adj. tchg. prof., 1999—. Mem. author's adv. bd. Houghton Mifflin Co., Boston, 1992-94. Author: Pioneers for Profit: Foreign Entrepreneurship and Russian Industrialization, 1885-1913, 1970 (Herbert Baxter Adams prize Am. Hist. Assn. 1970), Tramways and Trolleys: The Rise of Urban Mass Transit in Europe, 1976; co-author: (with B. Hill and J. Buckler) A History of Western Society, 1979, 7th edit., 2003, (with B. Hill, J. Buckler and P. Ebrey) A History of World Societies, 1983, 6th edit., 2001; mem. editl. bd. Bus. History Rev., 1980—. Fellow for western Europe, Fgn. Area Program, 1964-66, John Simon Guggenheim fellow, 1970, Internat. Rsch. Exch. fellow, USSR, 1970, fellow NEH, 1984. Mem. Am. Hist. Assn., Econ. History Assn., Bus. History Conf., World History Assn., French Hist. Soc. Avocations: hiking, travel, gardening, cooking. Office: U Ill Dept History 810 S Wright St Urbana IL 61801

MCKAY, LAURIE MARIE, special education educator; b. Cadillac, Mich., Sept. 10, 1960; d. Leonard Max and Mary Ann (Pierzina) Tykwinski; m. John William McKay, June 27, 1992; 1 child, Abbe Rose; stepchildren: David John, Chad Richard. BA in Psychology, Mich. State U., 1983; cert., Ctrl. Mich. U., 1990; postgrad., Grand Valley State U., 1992—. Cert. tchr. elem. edn., emotionally impaired, Mich. Tchr. spl. edn. Reed City (Mich.) Pub. Schs., 1990-91; instrl. aide Wexford-Missaukee Intermediate Sch., Cadillac, Mich., 1983-89, tchr. spl. edn., 1991—. Rep., mem. student assistance program com., CCD instr. grade 4 Wexford-Missaukee Profl. Assn.; water safety instr. ARC, 1995. Cookie mgr. Crooked Tree Girl Scout Coun., Cadillac, 1989. Mem. Mich. Assn. of Tchrs. of Emotionally Disturbed Children, Coun. for Exceptional Children, Wexaucola Reading Coun. Democrat. Roman Catholic. Avocations: cross-country skiing, skating, baking, gardening, swimming. Home: 710 E Garfield St Cadillac MI 49601-2022 Office: Wexford Missaukee Sch Dist 9905 S 13 Rd Cadillac MI 49601-9352

MCKEAN, DAVID JESSE, medical science researcher; b. Indiana, Pa., Jan. 21, 1946; BS, Juniata Coll., 1967; PhD, Johns Hopkins, 1972. Dean Mayo Clinic, Rochester, Minn., 1987-91, prof. immunology, 1987—, chair dept. immunology, 1991-2000. Recipient Rsch. Career Devel. award, Nat. Cancer Inst., 1979—84. Office: Mayo Clinic 1st St SW Rochester MN 55905-0001 E-mail: mckean.david@mayo.edu.

MCKECHNIE, JOHN CHARLES, gastroenterologist, educator; b. Louisville, Feb. 1, 1935; s. Albert Hay and Edna Scott (Johnson) M.; children: Steven Keith, Kevin Stuart. BA, U. Louisville, 1955; MD, Baylor Coll. Medicine, 1959. Diplomate Am. Bd. Internal Medicine, Am. Bd. Gastroenterology. Intern Jefferson Davis Hosp., Houston, 1959-60; resident in internal medicine Baylor Affiliated Program, Houston, 1960-61, 65-66; gen. practice medicine, Benham, Ky., 1964; practice medicine specializing in gastroenterology, Houston, 1966— ; clin. instr. Baylor Coll. Medicine, Houston, 1966-69, asst. prof., 1969-72, assoc. prof., 1972-77, prof., 1977— ; mem. staff Methodist Hosp.; cons. Ben Taub Hosp., St. Luke's Episcopal Hosp. Served to capt. USMC, 1962-64. Fellow Am. Coll. Gastroenterology (gov. Tex. 1979-80, trustee 1981-84), ACP; mem. AMA, So. Med. Assn., Tex. Med. Assn., Am. Gastroent. Assn., Digestive Disease Found., Am. Soc. Gastrointestinal Endoscopy, Tex. Soc. Gastrointestinal Endoscopy, Houston Gastroent. Soc. (pres. 1983), Alpha Omega Alpha. Republican. Presbyterian. Contbr. numerous articles to profl. jours. Office: 6560 Fannin St Ste 1630 Houston TX 77030-2734

MCKEE, CATHERINE LYNCH, law educator, lawyer; b. Boston, June 7, 1962; d. Robert Emmett and Anne Gayle (Tanner) Lynch; m. Bert K. McKee Jr., Dec. 25, 1990; children: Timothy Kingston, Shannon Lancaster. BA in Biol. Sci., U. Calif. Berkeley, 1984; JD, U. San Diego, 1988. Bar: Calif. 1988, U.S. Dist. Ct. (cen., so. and ea. dists.) Calif. 1989, U.S. Ct. Appeals (9th cir.) 1989. Assoc. Parkinson, Wolf, Lazar & Leo, L.A., 1988-89, McCormick & Mitchell, San Diego, 1989-91; prof. Mt. San Antonio Coll., Walnut, Calif., 1994—, mock trial coach, 1994—2000, dir. paralegal program, 1999—2003. Cert. rev. hearing officer, Orange County, 1994—; legal counsel Imperial Valley Lumber Co., Valley Lumber and Truss Co., 1998—; coach nat. champion C.C. mock trial team, 2000; mem. acad. senate exec. coun. Mt. San Antonio Coll., 1996-2000, chmn. campus equivalency com., 1999, chair paralegal program adv. com., 1999—; mem. East San Gabriel Valley regional occupl. program adv. com., 2003—. Contbr. weekly newspaper column, 1993-99; prodr., star videos An Attorney's Guide to Legal Research on the Internet, 1998, 99; co-author: Jeff and Catherine's World's Best List of Legal (and Law-related) Internet Sites. Chair scholarship com. U. Calif. Alumni Assn., Berkeley, 1995—; capt. auction team SCATS Gymnastics, 2000—02. Named Cmty. Person of Yr. Diamond Bar C. of C., 1995. Mem. NEA, State Bar Calif. (probation monitor 1993—), Ea. Bar Assn. L.A. (trustee 2000—), Calif. Tchrs. Assn., Am. Inns of Ct., Calif. Assn. Lanterman-Petris-Short Hearing Officers. Avocations: weight lifting, photography, reading. Office: Mount San Antonio Coll 1100 N Grand Ave Walnut CA 91789-1341 E-mail: cmckee@mtsac.edu.

MCKEE, CHRISTOPHER FULTON, physicist, educator, astronomer, educator; b. Washington, Sept. 6, 1942; m. Suzanne P. McKee; 3 children. AB in Physics summa cum laude, Harvard U., 1963; PhD in Physics, U. Calif., Berkeley, 1970. Physicist Lawrence Livermore (Calif.) Labs., 1969-70, cons., 1970—; rsch. fellow in astrophysics Calif. Inst. Tech., Pasadena, 1970-71; asst. prof. astronomy Harvard U., Cambridge, 1971-74; asst. prof. physics and astronomy U. Calif., Berkeley, 1974-77, assoc. prof., 1977-78, prof., 1978—, Miller Rsch. prof., 1984-85, 99; chair dept. physics, 2000—; assoc. dir. Space Scis. Lab., Berkeley, 1978-83, acting dir., 1983-84, dir., 1985-98, Theoretical Astrophysics Ctr., Berkeley, 1985. Co-chair Astronomy and Astrophysics Survey com., NRC, 1998-2001. Fannie and John Hertz Found. fellow, 1963-69, Guggenheim fellow, 1998; Sherman Fairchild Disting. scholar, 1981, Nat. Acad. Scis., 1992. Fellow AAAS, Am. Phys. Soc. (exec. com. astrophysics div. 1986-88); mem. Am. Astron. Soc. (councillor 1981-84), Am. Acad. Arts and Scis., Internat. Astron. Union, Phi Beta Kappa. Office: U Calif Dept Physics Berkeley CA 94720-0001

MCKEE, DAVID LANNEN, economics educator; b. St. John, N.B., Can., Apr. 18, 1936; arrived in U.S., 1961; s. Horace George and Mary K. (Lannen) McK.; m. Yosra A. Amara, Dec. 23, 1995. BA magna cum laude, St. Francis Xavier, 1958; MA, U. N.B., Fredericton, 1959; PhD, U. Notre Dame, 1966. Lectr. Ind. U., Ft. Wayne, 1965-66, asst. prof., 1966-67, Kent (Ohio) State U., 1967-69, assoc. prof., 1969-74, prof. econs., 1974—. Author: Growth, Development, and the Service Economy in the Third World, 1988, Schumpeter and the Political Economy of Change, 1991, Urban Environments in Emerging Economies, 1994; editor: Canadian American Economic Relations: Conflict and Cooperation on a Continental Scale, 1988, Hostile Takeovers: Issues in Public and Corporate Policy, 1989, Energy, the Environment and Public Policy, 1991, External Linkages and Growth in Small Economies, 1993; co-author: Developmental Issues in Small Island Economics, 1990, Accounting Services, the International Economy and Third World Development, 1992, Accounting Services, Growth, And Change in the Pacific Basin, 1996, Accounting Services and Growth in Small Economies, Evidence from the Caribbean Basin, 1998, Accounting Services, the Islamic Middle East and the Global Economy, 1999, Offshore Financial Centers, Accounting Serivces and the Global Economy, 2000, Crisis, Recovery, and the Role of Accounting Firms in the Pacific Basin, 2002, others; co-editor: Regional Economics: Theory and Practice, 1970, Spatial Economic Theory, 1970, Urban Economics: Theory Development and Planning, 1970, Structural Change in an Urban Industrial Region, 1987; contbr. articles to profl. jours. Mem. Internat. Acad. of Bus. Disciplines (pres. 2003—), Am. Soc. for Competitiveness (adv. bd.), Am. Econ. Assn. Roman Catholic. Home: 616 Yacavona Dr Kent OH 44240-3318 Office: Kent State U Dept Econs Kent OH 44242-0001 Fax: 330-672-9808. E-mail: dmckee@bsa3.kent.edu.

MCKEE, JUDITH NELSON, elementary school educator; b. Iowa Falls, Iowa, Nov. 8, 1939; d. Herbert and Emma (Czako) Nelson; m. Bernard B. McKee, Oct. 20, 1962; children: Susan Jennifer Ziegler, Blair David. BA, U. No. Iowa, 1961; MA, Roosevelt U., 1967; postgrad., Ill. State U. Cert. tchr. K-9, learning disabilities K-12. Tchr. 2d grade Dist. 25 Pub. Schs., Arlington Heights, Ill., 1961-67; itinerant tchr. learning disabilities N.W. Suburban Spl. Edn. Dist., Palatine, Ill., 1968-72; tchr. Winnetka (Ill.) Pub. Sch. Nursery, 1974-75; tchr. spl. edn. North Suburban Spl. Edn. Dist., Glenview, Ill., 1975-76; tchr. gifted Worlds of Wisdom and Wonder, Evanston, Ill., 1985-87; instr. astronomy North Cook County Ednl. Svc. Ctr., Glenview, 1987; mem. faculty Nat. Louis U., Evanston, Ill., 1991—2003, DePaul U., Chgo., 2000—01, U. No. Iowa, Cedar Falls, 2002—03; tchr. primary grades dist. 39 Wilmette, Ill., 1976—99. Cons. various internat., nat., state, and local sch. dists. and edn. svc. ctrs., 1991-2003. Author: (with others) Physical Science Activities for Elementary and Middle School, 1987, Fact, Fiction, and Fantasy, 1995; contbr. articles to profl. jours. Named Ill. Honors Sci. Tchr. NSF, Ill. State. U., 1989-91. Mem. Internat. Reading Assn. (internat., state, local presenter), Nat. Sci. Tchrs. Assn. (internat., nat., state, and local workshop presenter 1985-91, ret. adv. bd., 2000-03), Coun. Elem. Sci. Internat., Ill. Sci. Tchrs. Assn. (presenter, finalist Golden Apple award, Presdl. Award), Phi Delta Kappa. Presbyterian. Avocation: naturalist activities. Home: 315 Fairview Ave Winnetka IL 60093-4210

MCKEE, RICHARD MILES, animal studies educator; b. Cottonwood Falls, Kans., Oct. 8, 1929; m. Marjorie Fisk, June 22, 1952; children: Dave, Richard, Annell, John. BS in Agriculture, Kans. State Coll. Agriculture and Applied Sci., 1951; MS in Animal Husbandry, Kans. State U., 1963; PhD in Animal Science, U. Ky., 1968. Herdsman Moxley Hall Hereford Ranch, Coun. Grove, Kans., 1951-52, 54-55, Luckhardt Farms, Tarkio, Mo., 1955-58; asst. mgr. L&J Crusoe Ranch, Cheboygan, Mich., 1958-59; asst. instr., cattle herdsman Kans. State U., Manhattan, 1959-65, from asst. prof. to assoc. prof., 1959-65, prof., departmental teaching coord., 1976-99. Program participant and/or official judge numerous shows, field days including Kans. Jr. Hereford Field Day, Kans. Jr. Shorthorn Field Day, Better Livestock Day, Kans. Jr. Livestock Assn., Am. Jr. Hereford Assn. Field Day, Cheyenne, Wyo., 1973, Kans. Jr. Polled Hereford Field Day, Am. Jr. Shorthorn Assn., Kans. City, Mo., 1965, Am. Internat. Jr. Charolais Assn. Show, Lincoln, Nebr., 1976, Am. Royal 4-H Livestock Judging Contest, Kans. City, 1975, Jr. Livestock Activities various cattle breed assns. nationwide, 1977-81; served on numerous breed assn. coms.; judge County Fairs; official judge 14 different Nat. Beef Breed Shows U.S. and Can.; conducted 60 livestock judging and showmanship schs. at county level. Contbr. articles to profl. jours. Deacon 1st Presbyn. Ch., Manhattan, 1969-75, Sunday Sch. tchr., Chancel choir, elder; project leader com. mem. 4-H; foster parent Kans. State U. Football Program. Lt. USMC, 1952-54, Korea. Named Hon. State Farmer of Kans.; Hall of Merit Honoree for Edn. by Am. Polled Hereford Assn., 1985; NDEA scholar U. Ky., 1966-67; Miles McKee Student Enrichment Fund established at Kans. State U. Mem. Am. Soc. Animal Sci., Kans. Livestock Assn. (beef cattle improvement com. 1970-78, cow-calf clinic com. 1973, 74, 75, 76, 77, 78), Nat. Assn. Colls. and Tchrs. Agriculture, Block and Bridle Club, Am. Jr. Hereford Assn. (hon.), FarmHouse, Sigma Xi, Phi Kappa Phi, Alpha Zeta, Gamma Sigma Delta, Alpha Tau Alpha (hon.). Home: 901 Juniper Dr Manhattan KS 66502-3148 Office: Dept of Animal Scis & Industry Kansas State U Manhattan KS 66506

MCKEE, RONALD GENE, vocational education educator; b. Williamsville, Mo., May 5, 1947; s. Enos Elmer and Elsie Mae (Chiles) McK.; m. Sondra Mae Malone, Dec. 1, 1968; 1 child, David. Student, Pearl River C.C., 1992-94; BS in Geol. Engring., U. Miss., 1999. Cert. tchr., Miss. Enlisted man, electronics warfare repairman USAF, 1966-73; enlisted man USCG, 1973, advanced through grades to electronics technician 1st class, 1973-87; ret., 1987; tchr. electronics Picayune (Miss.) Vocat.-Tech. Ctr., 1988-95, Pascagoula (Miss.) P.S.D. Applied Tech. Ctr., 1995—. Mem. Vocat. Indsl. Clubs. Am. Avocations: radio-controlled airplanes, oil painting, infrared target shooting, amateur radio. Home: 2205 Dolphin Rd Gautier MS 39553-7080 Office: Pascagoula Sch Dist Applied Tech Ctr 2602 Market St Pascagoula MS 39567-5158 E-mail: ronmckee@hotmail.com.

MCKEE, TIMOTHY CARLTON, taxation educator; b. South Bend, Ind., Mar. 9, 1944; s. Glenn Richard and Laura Louise (Niven) McK.; m. Linda Sykes Mizelle, Oct. 13, 1984; children: Brandon Richard. BS in Bus. Econs., Ind. U., 1970, MBA in Fin., 1973, JD, 1979; LLM in Taxation, DePaul U., 1980. Bar: Ill. 1980, U.S. Dist. Ct. (no. dist.) Ill. 1980; CPA,, Va.; cert. govt. fin. mgr. Procedures analyst Assocs. Corp., South Bend, Ind., 1969-71; asst. dir. fin. Ind. U., Bloomington, Ind., 1971-79; sr. tax mgr. Peat Marwick Mitchell & Co., Chgo., Norfolk, Va., 1979-84; corp. counsel K & K Toys, Norfolk, 1984; assoc. prof. acctg. Old Dominion U., Norfolk, 1985-98, chmn. dept., 1994-95, chmn. acctg., fin. and law dept., 1995, univ. prof. dept. acctg., 1998—. Computer coord. Peat, Marwick, Mitchell & Co., 1982-84; micro computer cons. Old Dominion U., 1985-91. Contbr. articles to profl. jours. Mem. Friends of Music, Bloomington, 1978, Art Inst., Chgo., 1981; loaned exec. United Way, Chgo., 1981; telethon chmn. Va. Orch. Group, Norfolk, 1983. Mem. Assn. Govt. Accts., Am. Acctg. Assn., Am. Assn. Atty. CPAs, Inc., Am. Tax Assn., Fin. Execs. Inst. (pres. 1995-96), Hampton Rds. Tax Forum, Inst. Internal Auditors, Beta Alpha Psi, Beta Gamma Sigma. Home: 412 Rio Dr Chesapeake VA 23322-7144 Office: Old Dominion U Constant Hall Rm 2153 Norfolk VA 23529

MCKEEL, LILLIAN PHILLIPS, retired education educator; b. Rocky Mount, N.C., Aug. 23, 1932; d. Ellis Elma and Lillian Bonner (Archbell) Phillips; m. James Thomas McKeel Jr., July 23, 1955; children: Sarah Lillian McKeel Youngblood, Mary Kathleen McKeel Welch. BA, U. N.C., 1954; MEd, Pa. State U., 1977, DEd, 1993. Tchr. State Coll. (Pa.) Area Schs., 1964-90; instr. Pa. State U., University Park, 1990-93; asst. prof. Shippensburg (Pa.) U., 1993—2001; ret., 2001. Mem. of panel NSTA Book Rev. Panel/Outstanding Sci. Tradebooks for Children, Washington, 1992; faculty sponsor Shippensburg U. Sch. Study Coun., 1993-95. Contbr. articles to profl. jours. Recipient Presdl. award for Excellence in Sci. and Math. Tchng., NSF, Washington, 1990; finalist Tchr. of Yr. program Pa. Dept. Edn., Harrisburg, 1992, cert. Recognition, Hon. Robert Casey/Gov., Harrisburg, Pa., 1991; named Achieving Women of Penn State, Pa. State U., 1993. Mem. Nat. Sci. Tchrs. Assn., Soc. Presdl. Awardees, Assn. Edn. Tchrs. in Sci., Coun. Elem. Sci. Internat., Phi Delta Kappa (Disting. Svc. award 1992), Pi Lambda Theta, Phi Kappa Phi. Avocations: photography, collecting antique toys. Home: 637 Wiltshire Rd State College PA 16803 E-mail: lmcke637@aol.com.

MCKELLIPS, TERRAL LANE, mathematics educator, university administrator; b. Terlton, Okla., Dec. 2, 1938; s. Raymond Orlando and Patrice Lillian (Fuller) McK.; m. Karen Kay Sweeney, Sept. 7, 1958; children: Marty Suzanne, Kyle Bret. BS in Edn., S.W. Okla. State U., 1961; MS, Okla. State U., 1963, EdD, 1968. Asst. prof. S.W. Okla. State U., Weatherford, 1962-66; prof., dept. chmn. Cameron U., Lawton, Okla., 1968-72, 73-83, prof., dean Sch. Math. Applied Scis., 1983-89, provost, 1989—2001. Vis. prof. Okla. State U., Stillwater, 1972-73. Contbr. articles to profl. jours. State coord. Dept. Leadership Inst., Am. Coun. Edn., 1982-83; chair Okla. State Regents for Higher Edn. Coun. on Instrn., 1997-98. NSF Sci. Faculty fellow, 1966-68. Mem. Math. Assn. Am. (cons. bur. 1975—), Nat. Coun. Tchrs. Math., Lawton Country Club (dir. 1982-89, pres. 1986-89), Pi Mu Epsilon, Phi Kappa Phi. Democrat. Avocations: golf, genealogy. E-mail: terralm@cameron.edu.

MCKELLOP, HARRY ALDEN, biomechanical engineering educator; b. LA, Nov. 7, 1945; s. Thomas and Opal McK.; m. Tovya Wager, Nov. 5, 1989; 1 child, Rachelle Tashi. BS in Mech. Engring., UCLA, 1970, MS in Mech. Engring., 1972; PhD in Mech. Engring., U. So. Calif., 1988. Adj. asst. prof. surgery U. Calif., 1979-80; instr. rsch. orthopaedics U. So. Calif., L.A., 1980-89, asst. prof. orthopaedics, 1989-95, asst. prof. biomed. engring., 1993-95, assoc. prof. orthopaedics and biomed., 1995-98, dir. rsch., 1994-98; dir. J. Vernon Luck Orthopaedic Rsch. Ctr., L.A., 1993—; v.p. rsch. Orthopaedic Hosp., L.A., 1996—; prof. in residence Dept. Orthop. Surgery U. Calif., 2001—. Contbr. over 75 articles to profl. jours. Recipient John Charnley award, 1994, 2000; NIH grantee, 1994-97; awardee Kappa Delta, 1998. Fellow Am. Inst. Med. and Biol. Engring.; mem. Orthopaedic Rsch. Soc., Am. Acad. Orthopaedic Surgeons, Hip Soc. Achievements include development of wear resistant Polythylene for Joint Replacements; developed total system for fixing complex femur fractures. Office: Orthopaedic Hospital 2400 S Flower St Los Angeles CA 90007-2629 E-mail: hmckellop@laoh.ucla.edu.

MCKENDALL, ROBERT ROLAND, neurologist, virologist, educator; b. Providence, Feb. 18, 1944; s. Benjamin Salvatore and Pauline McK.; m. Joyce Marie Podlesak, Oct. 12, 1973; children: Lauren Patricia, Alexis Victoria. BA, Columbia Coll., N.Y.C., 1965; MD, Tufts U., 1969. Diplomate Am. Bd. Neurology & Psychiatry. Resident in neurology Rush-Presbyn.-St. Lukes Hosp., Chgo., 1970-74; neurovirology fellow U. Calif., San Francisco, 1974-78, asst. prof. neurology, 1981-84, U. Tex. Med. Br., Galveston, 1984-88, assoc. prof. neurology, microbiology, immunology, 1988—. Mem. neurology core com. AIDS Clin. Trials Group of NIH; mem. toxicity related clin. diagnotis com. Adult Clin. Trials Group of NIH. Editor: (textbook) Viral Diseases-Handbood of Clinical Neurology, 1989, Handbook of Neurovirology, 1994; contbr. over 40 articles to profl. jours.; editl. reviewer Neurology, 1990, Annals of Neurology, 1990-96, Jour. Neurol. Scis., 1997—. Mem. Sch. Dist. Parent Adv. Bd., Dickinson, Tex., 1992—94. Recipient Young Investigator award NIH, 1978-81, Career Devel. award VA Rsch. Svc., 1981-84, Herpes Simplex Infection grant, 1984-86, AIDS Clin. Trials grant NIH, 1992—. Mem. Am. Soc. Microbiology, Am. Fedn. Clin. Rsch., Am. Assn. Immunologists, Soc. for Neurosci. Office: U Tex Med Br Dept Neurology E-39 301 University Blvd Galveston TX 77555-0539

MCKENNA, JAMES RICHARD, agronomy educator; b. Orange, N.J., Feb. 27, 1942; s. John Frances and Esther Hope (Rice) McK.; m. Judith Ann Morse, June 21, 1969 (div. Nov. 1979); children: Catherine Jean, Jennifer Lynn; m. Debra Lynn Morris, Mar. 22, 1980. BS, U. R.I., 1964; MS, U. Maine, 1970; PhD, Va. Poly. Inst. and State U., 1988. Tchr. sci. Patton Acad., Sch. Dist. 25, Patten, Maine, 1964-68; rsch. asst. Dept. Plant and Soil Sci., Orono, Maine, 1968-70; tchr. biology Houlton (Maine) High Sch., Sch. Dist. 29, 1970-78; extension agt. Maine Coop. Extension Svc., Houlton, 1978-79, Va. Coop. Extension Svc., Harrisonburg, 1979-84; instr. dept. crop and soil environ. sci. Va. Poly. Inst. and State U., Blacksburg, 1984-88, prof., 1988—. Ind. farmer, Houlton and Patten, 1964-78; cons. Mali (W. Africa) Farming Systems Rsch/Extension Project, U.S. AID, 1988-91. Assoc. editor: Jour. Natural Resources and Life Scis. Edn.; contbr. articles to profl. jours. Chmn. Town Planning Bd., Houlton, 1977; master of ceremonies Mountain Acad. Coun., Blacksburg, 1989. Recipient Young Scientist award Am. Forage and Grassland, Springfield, Ill., 1987, Excellence in Acad. Advising award Alumni Assn. of Va. Poly. Inst. and State U., 1991; Nat. Assn. of Coll. & Teachers of Agrl. Fellow, 1993, Diggs Tchg. scholar 1996. Fellow Am. Soc. Agronomy (chair crops com. 1991, Agronomic Resident Edn. award 1997); mem. Crop Sci. Soc. Am. (vice chair collegiate crops judging 1990), Nat. Assn. Colls. and Tchrs. of Agr. (ea. regional dir., 2000, v.p. 2002, presdl. nominee 2003), Va. Poly. Inst. and State U. Faculty Assn. (sec. faculty affairs com. 1991), Gamma Sigma Delta (teaching award of merit 1990). Mem. Ch. of Brethren. Achievements include development of global orientations for course and curriculum in deptartments of crops and soil environmental science, of undergraduate BS degree in Environmental Science, of practice of using prolific (multiple ear) corn as part of sustainable production, of recommendations for rock phosphate use on sorghum/cowpea association in Mali of system for establishment of warm-season grasses no-till in Virginia. Home: 404 Dunton Dr Blacksburg VA 24060-5130 Office: Va Poly Inst and State Univ 235 Smyth Hall Blacksburg VA 24061*

MCKENNA, MALCOLM CARNEGIE, vertebrate paleontologist, curator, educator; b. Pomona, Calif., July 21, 1930; s. Donald Carnegie and Bernice Caroline (Waller) McK.; m. Priscilla Coffey, June 17, 1952; children: Douglas M., Katharine L., Andrew M., Bruce C. BA, U. Calif., Berkeley, 1954, PhD, 1958. Instr. dept. paleontology U. Calif., Berkeley, 1958-59; asst. curator dept. vertebrate paleontology Am. Mus. Natural History, N.Y.C., 1960-64, assoc. curator, 1964-65; Frick assoc. curator, chmn. Frick Lab., 1965-68, Frick curator, 1968; Frick curator dept. vertebrate paleontology Am. Mus. Nat. History, N.Y.C., 1968-01. Asst. prof. geology Columbia U., N.Y.C., 1960-64, assoc. prof., 1964-72, prof. geol. scis., 1972-01; research assoc. U. Colo. Mus., Boulder, 1962—; adj. prof.geology U Wyoming, 2000— Contbr. articles on fossil mammals and their evolution, the dating of Mesozoic and Tertiary sedimentary rocks, and paleogeography and plate tectonics to profl. jours. Bd. dirs. Bergen Community (N.J.) Mus., 1964-67, pres., 1965-66; trustee Flat Rock Brook Nature Assn., N.J., 1979-93, Raymond Alf Mus., Webb Sch. of Calif., 1980—, Dwight-Englewood Sch., Englewood, N.J., 1968-80; bd. dirs. Flat Rock Brook Nature Assn., N.J., 1979-84; trustee Claremont McKenna Coll., Calif., 1983-91; Planned Parenthood Bergen County, N.J., 1979-88, Mus. No. Ariz., 1978-85, 87-93. Nat. Acad. Scis. exchange fellow USSR, 1965 Fellow AAAS, Explorers Club, Geol. Soc. Am.; mem. Grand Canyon Natural History Assn. (bd. dirs. 1972-76), Soc. Systematic Zoology (coun. 1974-77), Soc. Vertebrate Paleontology (v.p. 1975, pres. 1976), Am. Geophys. Union, Am. Soc. Mammalogists, Paleontol. Soc. (award 1992), Soc. for Study Evolution, Polish Acad. Scis. (fgn.), Sigma Xi, Am. Acad. of Arts and Scis. E-mail: m4pmckenna@indra.com.

MCKENNA, RICHARD HENRY, consultant; b. Covington, Ky., Dec. 19, 1927; s. Charles Joseph and Mary Florence (Wieck) McK.; m. Patricia M. Macdonald, Jan. 6, 1979; children: Linda Ann, Theresa K., Joan Marie; stepchildren: Stuart J. Goodman, Ann Elizabeth Goodman. BS in Commerce, U. Cin., 1959; MBA, Xavier U., Cin., 1963. Acct. Andrew Jergens Co., Cin., 1947-55; treas., dir. Ramsey Bus. Equipment, Inc., Cin., 1955-59; asst. to pres. Oakley Die and Mfg. Co., Cin., 1959-60, Electro-Jet Tool Co., Inc., Cin., 1959-60; pvt. practice acctg., Cin. and, No. Ky., 1960=62; bus. mgr. St. Joseph Hosp., Lexington, Ky., 1962-66; asst. adminstr. fin. U. Ky. Hosp., Lexington, 1966-70; v.p., CFO, St. Lawrence Hosp., Lansing, Mich., 1970-87; v.p., CFO, asst. sec.-treas. St. Joseph's Hosp., Inc., Savannah, Ga., 1987-95, St. Joseph's Health Ctr., Inc., Savannah, 1987-90; chmn. bd. McKenna & McKenna Assocs., Inc., Savannah, 1983—. Adj. faculty Aquinas Coll., Grand Rapids, Mich., 1980-89, asst. prof.; chmn. bd. North Grand River Coop. Laundry, 1986-87; former mem. adv. com. to commr. of fin. State of Ky. Chmn. Cath. divsn. Oak Hills Bus. Com.; mem. spkrs. com. Oak Hill Sch. Dist.; bd. dirs. Savannah YMCA, 1992-94, mem. exec. com., 1994-96; bd. dirs. Habersham br. YMCA, 1992-96, chmn. bd., 1994-96. With U.S. Mcht. Marine, 1945-47, U.S. Army, 1948-51. Mem. AICPA (ret.), Healthcare Fin. Mgmt. Assn. (past dir. Ky. chpt. Follmer award), Am. Mgmt. Assn., Ky. Soc. CPAs, Mich. Hosp. Assn. (former mem. com. on reimbursement), Ga. Hosp. Assn. (com. on fin. and mgmt.), Delta Mu Delta, Alpha Sigma Lambda.

MCKENNEE, ARDEN NORMA, art educator, retired, consultant; b. N.Y.C. d. Archibald McKennee and Norma (Bischof) Kirkley. BA, U. Minn., 1953. Exec. sec. John & Mable Ringling Mus. of Art, Sarasota, Fla., 1964-79, mus. edn. programmer, 1980-94; ret., 1994. Mem. Very Spl. Arts Adv. Bd. for Sarasota County, 1988-94. Mem. Nat. Art Edn. Assn., Delta Gamma Alumni Assn.

MCKENNEY, MURIEL ANITA, art educator, engineer; b. Chgo., Ill., Aug. 26, 1923; d. Myron Bedrose and Salome Mary (Attarian) Donchian; m. William James McKenney, Feb. 21, 1949; children: Mary Dierker, William James III, Christine, James, Audrey, Bruce. BFA U. Colo., 1983. Editor, writer Aurora (Colo.) Advocate Newspaper, 1965—70; engr. drafting, writer, editor AT&T, Englewood, Colo., 1970—90; art tchr. City of Aurora, Colo., 1991—. Recipient 1st pl., U. Colo., 1982, City of Aurora, 1995. Mem.: Denver Art Mus., Aurora Artist Guild (adv. bd. 1995, 1st pl. award 1996), Denver Botanic Gardens (advisory, program chair 1996, spl. events 1992—, SCFD award 1996). Avocations: marionettes, dancing, painting, gardening, ballet. Home: 408 S Xanadu St Aurora CO 80012

MCKENZIE, ANDRÉ, academic administrator, educator; b. Chgo., May 4, 1955; s. Alberta Chisholm. BS, Ill. State U., 1977, MS, 1979; MEd, Columbia U., 1985, EdD, 1986. Assoc. residence hall dir. No. Ill. U., DeKalb, 1979-82; asst. dir. student activities Northeastern Ill. U., Chgo., 1982-84; assoc. dean of students St. John's U., Jamaica, N.Y., 1986-89, dir. opportunity programs, 1989-91, asst. v.p., 1991-93; acting dean St. Vincent's Coll., 1993-94, assoc. v.p., 1994—, adj. asst. prof. Sch. Edn. Tng. specialist Anti-Defamation League, N.Y.C., 1989—; cons. coll. Greek letter orgns., 1988—; mem. N.Y State policy bd. Higher Edn. Opportunity Program, 1990-92, v.p., 1992—; facilitator leadership skills workshops, 1986—. Contbr. articles to profl. jours. Mem. N.Y. Urban League, N.Y.C., 1994—, 100 Black Men, N.Y.C. Edn. Policy fellow Inst. for Ednl. Leadership, 1990-91. Mem. Assn. for Humanistic Edn. and Devel. (pres. area II 1992—), Nat. Assn. Student Pers. Adminstrs. (mem. adv. bd. region II 1988-91), Am. Coll. Pers. Assn., Nat. Coun. African-Am. Men, Alpha Phi Alpha (Bro. of Yr. Eta Tau chpt. 1976). Avocations: racquetball, drawing, reading. Office: St Johns U Newman Hall 149 Jamaica NY 11439-0001

MCKENZIE, STANLEY DON, academic administrator, English educator; b. Yakima, Wash., July 10, 1942; s. Don Guy and Jean Elizabeth McKenzie; m. Michal A. Koehler, Sept. 21, 1968 (div. Sept. 1974); 1 child, Thomas Charles. BS, MIT, 1964; MA, U. Rochester, 1967, PhD, 1971. Prof. lit. Rochester (N.Y.) Inst. Tech., 1967--, asst. to v.p. student affairs/judicial affairs, 1972-87, 92-94, acting dean, Coll. Liberal Arts, 1987-88, provost, v.p. acad. affairs, 1994--. Vice-chair bd. dirs. RIT Rsch. Corp., Rochester, 1994-2001; bd. dirs. CIMS Print, Rochester, Am. Coll. Mgmt. & Tech., Dubrovnik, Croatia. Author: Shakespeare Studies, 1987; (with others) The Practice of Theory, 1992, Other Voices, Other Views, 1999. Mem.: MLA, AAUP, ACLU. Democrat. Avocations: hiking, reading. Office: Rochester Inst Tech 6 Lomb Memorial Dr Rochester NY 14623-5604 E-mail: SDMPRO@RIT.edu.

MCKEOWN, LAURIE ANNE, elementary school educator; b. Batavia, NY, Feb. 17, 1964; d. Karl and Gloria Anne (Jackson) Grohs; m. Donald Michael McKeown, May 25, 1991; children: Monika Anne, Karla Marie, Charles Michael. BS in Edn., BA in Psychology, SUNY, Geneseo, 1986, MS in Edn., 1987. Cert. elem., spl. edn. and reading tchr. NY. Tchrs. asst. Warsaw (N.Y.) Ctrl. Sch., 1986-87, spl. edn. tchr. elem., 1987-97, dept. head, 1989-94, tchr. elem., 1997—. Mem. Delta Kappa Gamma. Republican. Methodist. Office: Warsaw Ctrl Sch W Court St Warsaw NY 14569 Business E-Mail: l.mckeown@warsawk-12.ny.us.

MCKEOWN, MARY ELIZABETH, educational administrator; d. Raymond Edmund and Alice (Fitzgerald) McNamara; m. James Edward McKeown, Aug. 6, 1955. BS, U. Chgo., 1946; MS, DePaul U., 1953. Supr. h.s. dept. Am. Sch., 1948-68, prin., 1968-99, trustee, 1975—2002, v.p., 1979, ednl. dir., 1979—2002, exec. v.p., 1992—2002; cons. and trustee, 2002—. Author study guides for algebra, geometry, and calculus. Mem.: Distance Edn. and Tng. Coun. (chair person rsch. and edn. com. 1988—93), N. Ctrl. Assn. Colls. and Schs. (exec. bd. 1990—93), NASSP, LWV. Office: 2200 E 170th St Lansing IL 60438-1002

MCKEOWN, REBECCA J. principal; b. Wayne, Okla., Apr. 4, 1937; d. William S. and Ila Rebekah (Mitchell) Lackey; m. Loren Ferris, Apr. 5, 1958; children: Michael, Thomas, Nancy, David. BS, Okla. State U., 1966; MEd, U. Okla., 1976. Cert. elem. tchr., elem. prin. 6th grade tchr. Ponca City (Okla.) Pub. Schs., 1966-67; 1st and 6th grade tchr. Peru Elem. Sch., Auburn, Nebr., 1967-69; 4th grade tchr. Woodland Hills Sch., Lawton, Okla., 1971-76; asst. prin. Douglass Learning Ctr., Lawton, Okla., 1976-78; prin. Lincoln Elem. Sch., Lawton, Okla., 1978-84, Hugh Bish Elem., Lawton, Okla., 1984—. Recipient Disting. Achievement award Lawton Bd. Edn., 1992, Adminstr. of Yr. award Lawton Area Reading Coun., 1993, Arts Adminstr. of Yr. award Okla. Alliance for Arts, 1993, Nat. Blue Ribbon Sch. Recognition award 1993-94, D.A.R.E. Adminstrn. award Lawton Police Dept., 1993. Mem. ASCD, Okla. Reading Coun., Okla. ASCD, Lawton Area Reading Coun., Elem. Prins. Assn. (pres. 1986-87), PEO Sisterhood. Democrat. Methodist. Avocations: reading, walking, music, cooking. Home: 3122 NW Denver Ave Lawton OK 73505-3864 Office: Lawton Pub Schs 751 NW Fort Sill Blvd Lawton OK 73507-5421

MC KETTA, JOHN J., JR., chemical engineering educator; b. Wyano, Pa., Oct. 17, 1915; s. John J. and Mary (Gelet) McK.; m. Helen Elisabeth Smith, Oct. 17, 1943; children: Charles William, John J. III, Robert Andrew, Mary Anne. BS, Tri-State Coll., Angola, Ind., 1937; BSE., U. Mich., 1943, MS, 1944, PhD, 1946; D.Eng. (hon.), Tri-State Coll., 1965, Drexel U., 1977; Sc.D., U. Toledo, 1973. Diplomate: registered profl. engr., Tex., Mich. Group leader tech. dept. Wyandotte Chem. Corp., Mich., 1937-40, asst. supt. caustic soda div., 1940-41; teaching fellow U. Mich., 1942-44, instr. chem. engring., 1944-45; faculty U. Tex., Austin, 1946—, successively asst. prof. chem. engring., assoc. prof., then prof. chem. engring., 1951-52, 54—, E.P. Schoch prof. chem. engring., 1970-81, Joe C. Walter chair, 1981-94, prof. emeritus, 1994—. Asst. dir. Tex. petroleum research com., 1951-52, 54-56, chmn. chem. engring. dept., mem. bd. regents, Tri State Univ, 56-, disting. service in truteeship, 2002, 1950-52, 55-63, dean Coll. Engring., 1963-69; exec. vice chancellor acad. affairs U. Tex. System, 1969-70; editorial dir. Petroleum Refiner, 1952-54; pres. Chemoil Cons., Inc., 1957-73; chmn. Tex. AEC, So. Interstate Nuclear Bd., 1963-70; mem. Tex. Radiation Adv. Bd., 1978-84; chmn. Nat. Energy Policy Com., 1970-72, Nat. Air Quality Control Com., 1972-85; mem. adv. bd. Carnegie-Mellon Inst. Research, 1978-84; pres. Reagans's rep. on U.S. Acid Precipitation Task Force, 1982-88; apptd. mem. Nuclear Waste Tech. Rev. Bd., 1992-97. Author: series Advances in Petroleum Chemistry and Refining (10 vols.); Chmn. editorial com.: series Petroleum Refiner; mem. adv. bd.: series Internat. Chem. Engring. mag; exec. editor: series Ency. of Chem. Processing and Design (68 vols.). Bd. regents Tri-State U., 1957—. Recipient Bronze plaque Am. Inst. Chem. Engrs., 1952, Charles Schwab award Am. Steel Inst., 1973, Lamme award as outstanding U.S. educator, 1976, Joe J. King Profl. Engring. Achievement award U. Tex., 1976, Gen. Dynamics Teaching Excellence award, 1979, Triple E award for contbns. to nat. issues on energy, environment and econs. Nat. Environ. Devel. Assn., 1976, Boris Pregal Sci. and Tech. award NAS, 1978, Internat. Chem. Engring. award, Italy, 1984, Pres. Herbert Hoover award for advancing well-being of humanity and developing richer and more enduring civilization Joint Engring. Socs., 1989, Centennial award exceptional contbn. Am. Soc. Engring. Edn., 1993; named Disting. Alumnus U. Mich Coll. Engring., 1953, Tri-State Coll., 1956; fellow Allied Chem. & Dye, 1945-46; named Disting. fellow Carnegie-Mellon U., 1978; Chem. Engring. Dept. at U. Tex. named The John J. McKetta Ctr. for Excellence in Chem. Engring. Edn. in his honor, 1995, Chem. Engring. Dept. at Tri State U. named The Dr. John J. McKetta Chem. Engring. Dept. in his honor, 1998. Mem. Am. Chem. Soc. (chmn. Central Tex. sect. 1950), Am. Inst. Chem. Engrs. (chmn. nat. membership com. 1955, regional exec. com., nat. dir., nat. v.p. 1961, pres. 1962, service to soc. award 1975), Am. Soc. Engring. Edn., Chem. Markets Research Assn., Am. Gas Assn. (adv. bd. chems. from gas 1954), Houston C. of C. (chmn. refining div. 1954, vice chmn. research and statistics com. 1954), Engrs. Joint Council (dir.), Engrs. Joint Council Profl. Devel. (dir. 1963-85), Nat. Acad. Engring., Sigma Xi, Chi Epsilon, Alpha Psi Omega, Tau Omega, Phi Lambda Upsilon, Phi Kappa Phi, Iota Alpha, Omega Chi Epsilon, Tau Beta Pi, Omicron Delta Kappa. Home: 5227 Tortuga Trl Austin TX 78731-4501 E-mail: mcketta@mail.utexas.edu., mcketta@che.utexas.edu.

MCKHANN, GUY MEAD, physician, educator; b. Boston, Mar. 20, 1932; s. Charles Fremont and Emily (Priest) McKhann; m. Katherine E. Henderson, Nov. 30, 1957 (div. 1983); children: Ian, James, Emily, Guy, Charles; m. Marilyn S. Albert, Sept. 27, 1997; children: Joshua, Katie. Student, Harvard U., 1948—51; MD, Yale U., 1955. Intern N.Y. Hosp., 1955—56; asst. resident pediat. Johns Hopkins Hosp., Balt., 1956—57; clin. assoc. NIH, Bethesda, Md., 1957—60; resident neurology Mass. Gen. Hosp., Boston, 1960—63; asst. and assoc. prof. pediat. and neurology Stanford (Calif.) U., 1963—69; prof. neurology Johns Hopkins, Balt., 1969—, Kennedy prof. neurology, head neurology dept., 1969—88, prof. neurology, dir. Zanvyl Krieger Mind Brain Inst., 1988—2000; acting dir. for clin. activities Nat. Inst. Neurol. Diseases and Stroke NIH, 2000—01. Served with USPHS, 1957—60. Scholar, Markle, 1964—69, Joseph P. Kennedy Jr., 1963—69. Fellow: AAAS; mem.: Inst. Medicine, Soc. Neurosci., Am. Neurochem. Soc., Am. Neurol. Assn., Alpha Omega Alpha. Achievements include research in on normal and abnormal human nervous system. Home: 6526 Montrose Ave Baltimore MD 21212-1023 Office: Zanvyl Krieger Mind/Brain Inst Johns Hopkins U 338 Krieger Hall Baltimore MD 21218 E-mail: guy.mckhann@jhu.edu.

MCKILLOP, KEVIN JAMES, JR., psychology educator; b. Hicksville, N.Y., Oct. 5, 1962; s. Kevin James Sr. and Helen Elaine (Grau) McK. BA in Psychology and English, Flagler Coll., 1984; MS in Psychology, U. Fla., 1986, PhD in Psychology, 1990. Vis. instr. Franklin and Marshall Coll., Lancaster, Pa., 1989-90; vis. asst. prof. Bowdoin Coll., Brunswick, Maine, 1990-91, Iowa State U., Ames, 1991-92; assoc. prof. psychology Washington Coll., Chestertown, Md., 1992—. Contbr. articles to profl. jours. Mem. APA, AAUP, Am. Psychol. Soc., Ea. Psychol. Soc. Avocations: cycling, tennis, basketball. Office: Washington Coll 300 Washington Ave Chestertown MD 21620-1438

MCKIMMEY, MARTHA ANNE, writer; b. Uvalde, Tex., Apr. 9, 1943; d. Aubrey Allan and Nellie Grey (Roberts) Stovall; m. Vernon Hobart McKimmey Jr., July 3, 1965; children: Annette Gay, Patrick Allan. BS, Howard Payne Coll., Brownwood, Tex., 1964; MEd, Tex. Christian U., 1969; PhD, Tex. Women's U., 1995. Cert. elem. tchr., Tex. Tchr. Ft. Worth Ind. Sch. Dist., 1964-66, White Lake Sch., Ft. Worth, 1979-80, Meadowbrook Christian Sch., Ft. Worth, 1983-87. Contbr. articles to mags. Mem. Am. Christian Writers. Home: 140 Gene Lee Rd Mineral Wells TX 76067-1738

MCKINLEY, NORMA ELIZABETH, education educator; b. N.Y.C., Jan. 26, 1939; d. Mongor Nobel and Florence Emma (Werner) Anderson; m. Michael Robert McKinley, June 8, 1959; 1 child, Scott Alan. BS in Edn., Ohio U., 1960; MEd, Ashland U., 1978. Cert. elem. educator, Ohio, N.J.; supr., Ohio. Tchr. Johnstown (Ohio)-Monroe Local Schs., 1960-61, Whitehall (Ohio) City Schs., 1961-62, Ashland (Ohio) City Schs., 1962-91; adj. prof. U. Cin., 1978-81; instr. Ashland U., 1987-91, adj. prof., 1991—. Cons. law-related edn. Ashland County, chem. awareness. Mem. Athena Study Club, Ashland, Rep. Women's Club, Ashland. Recipient ABA First Pl. Pub. Svc. award for Law Day/Citizenship Project of Ashland City Sch. Dist., 1986, First Pl. award of Ohio Coun. of Econ. Edn., 1985-86, 80-81, Exemplary Juvenile Justice Program award of Ohio Assn. Juvenile Ct. Judges for Ashland City Sch. Dist. Law-Related Edn. Project, 1985, Award of Merit, Ohio State Bar Assn., 1978-79, Am. Lawyers Cert. of Appreciation, 1989; named Jennings scholar, 1974-75. Mem. NEA, AAUP, Ohio Edn. Assn., Ohio Coun. Social Studies, Alpha Delta Kappa. Avocations: golf, travel, boating, swimming, reading, gardening. Home: 404 Lakeshore Rd # 4 Ashland OH 44805-8612 Office: Ashland U 101 Kates Ctr Ashland OH 44805

MCKINLEY-PAYTON, LINDA JO, educator; b. Franklin, Tenn., June 9, 1958; d. George Allen Sr. and Betty Jo (Martin) McKinley; divorced; 1 child, Ashley. BA in Edn., U. South Fla., 1980; M in Edn. Curriculum, Nat. Louis U., 1996. Cert. tchr. gifted students; cert. ESOL. Asst. dir. Palnez Sch., Tampa, Fla., 1981-83; tchr. English Hillsborough County Pub. Schs., Tampa, 1983—, mem. sch. improvement team; tchr. Bloomingdale Sr. H.S., Valrico, Fla., 1998—. Tchr. Dowdell Jr. H.S., 1983-96; county demonstration tchr. English, Instrl. Resource Classroom, 1985-89; active Tchrs. as Advisor program, 1988-96; advisor student coun. Dowdell Jr. High, 1985-95. Judge acad. awards competition Hillsborough County, 1989, 90; tutor Tampa Urban League; chair Socibulls; tchr. FUSE; adult after sch. tchr. Named Tchr. of Yr., Dowdell Jr. High Sch., 1990. Mem. Nat. Assn. Tchrs. English, Fla. Assn. Tchrs. English, Hillsborough County Assn. Tchrs. English, Kappa Delta Pi. Democrat. Mem. Ch. of Christ. Avocations: arts, crafts, gardening, carpentry, reading. Home: 1530 Thistledown Dr Brandon FL 33510-2068 Office: Bloomingdale Sr H S 1700 Bloomingdale Ave Valrico FL 33594-6220

MCKINNELL, ROBERT GILMORE, retired zoology, genetics and cell biology educator; b. Springfield, Mo., Aug. 9, 1926; s. William Parks and Mary Catherine (Gilmore) McK.; m. Beverly Walton Kerr, Jan. 24, 1964; children: Nancy Elizabeth, Robert Gilmore, Susan Kerr. AB, U. Mo., 1948; BS, Drury Coll., 1949, DSc (hon.), 1993; PhD, U. Minn., 1959. Rsch. assoc. Fox Chase Cancer Ctr., Phila., 1958-61; asst. prof. biology Tulane U., New Orleans, 1961-65, assoc. prof., 1965-69, prof., 1969-70; prof. zoology U. Minn., Mpls., 1970—76, prof. genetics and cell biology St. Paul, 1976—99, prof. emeritus, 1999—. Vis. scientist Dow Chem. Co., Freeport, Tex., 1976; guest dept. zoology U. Calif., Berkeley, 1979; Royal Soc. guest rsch. fellow Nuffield dept. pathology John Radcliffe Hosp., Oxford U., 1981-82; NATO vis. scientist Akademisch Ziekenhuis, Ghent, Belgium, 1984; faculty rsch. assoc. Naval Med. Rsch. Inst., Bethesda, Md., 1988; secretariat Third Internat. Conf. Differentiation, 1978; organizer, secretariat 6th Internat. Conf. on Pathology of Reptiles and Amphibians, 2001; mem. amphibian com. Inst. Lab. Animal Resources, NRC, 1970-73, mem. adv. coun., 1974; mem. panel genetic and cellular resources program NIH, 1981-82, spl. study sect., Bethesda, 1990. Author: Cloning: Amphibian Nuclear Transplantation, 1978, Cloning, A Biologist Reports, 1979; sr. editor: Differentiation and Neoplasia, 1980, Cloning: Leben aus der Retorte, 1981, Cloning, of Frogs, Mice, and other Animals, 1985, (with others) The Biological Basis of Cancer, 1998, (with D.L. Carlson) Pathology of Reptiles and Amphibians, 2002, also symposium procs. in field; mem. editl. bd. Differentiation, 1973—; mem. bd. advisors Marquis Who's Who; contbr. articles to profl. jours. Served to lt. USNR, 1944-47, 51-53. Recipient Outstanding Teaching award Newcomb Coll., Tulane U., 1970; Disting. Alumni award Drury Coll., 1979, Morse Alumni Tchg. award U. Minn., 1992; Rsch. fellow Nat. Cancer Inst., 1956-58, Prince Hitachi award Japanese Found. Cancer Rsch., 1998; Sr. Sci. fellow NATO, 1974. Fellow AAAS, Linnean Soc. (London); mem. Am. Assn. Cancer Rsch. (emeritus), Am. Assn. Cancer Edn. (sr.), Am. Assn. History of Medicine, Am. Inst. Biol. Scis., Indian Soc. Devel. Biology (lifetime emeritus), Internat. Soc. Differentiation (pres. 1994-96), Minn. Acad. Medicine, Gown-in-Town Club, Sigma Xi. Office: 140 Gortner Lab Biochemistry 1479 Gortner Ave Saint Paul MN 55108 E-mail: mckin002@umn.edu.

MCKINNEY, BRENDA JANE, mathematics educator; b. Longview, Tex., Sept. 15, 1948; d. Billy Joe and Betty Jane (Smith) Cabbiness; m. Ronald Lester McKinney, Sept. 10, 1966; children: Kit, Jeff. BS in Math., MS in Math., Stephen F. Austin U. Tchr. math. Forest Park Jr. High Sch., Longview, Tex., 1973-76, Longview High Sch., 1976—79, 1985—2001, Spring Hill High Sch., Longview, 1979-85, Kilgore Jr. Coll., 2003. Named Longview News Jour. Reader's Choice Best Tchr. East Tex., 2000. Mem.: Gregg County Ret. Tchrs. Assn., Tex. Ret. Tchrs. Assn., Good Shepherd Med. Ctr. Aux. Avocations: reading, raising angus cattle. Home: 289 Mackey Rd Longview TX 75605-9637

MCKINNEY, JANE-ALLEN, artist and educator; b. Owensboro, Ky., Jan. 8, 1952; d. William Holland and Jane Wilhoit (Moore) McK. BA, Scarritt Coll., Nashville, 1974; MA, Vanderbilt U., 1977; MFA, Memphis Coll. of Art, 1993. Grad. asst. dept. art Peabody Coll. for Tchrs., Vanderbilt U., Nashville, 1975-76; tchr. Smyrna (Tenn.) Comprehensive Vocat. Ctr., 1977-78; pres., bd. dirs. Jane Allen Flighton Artworks Inc., Nashville, 1978—; jeweler Wright's Jewelry Store, Clarksville, Tenn., 1982; tchr. art Belmont U., Nashville, 1984-88, Met. Centennial Park Art Ctr., Nashville, 1988-91, Cheekwood Mus. of Art, Nashville, 1990-94, Nossi Coll. of Art, Nashville, 1991-94, Western Ky. U., Bowling Green, 1991-94. Ednl. cons. fine art Nossi Coll. Art, Nashville, 1993—; artist for Women of Achievement awards, sculptures and jewelry YWCA, Nashville, 1992—; artist for Bus. Award Sculpture, C. of C., Nashville, 1990. One and two person shows include Cheekwood Mus. Art, 1981, 93, Owensboro Mus. Fine Art, 1992, Western Ky. U., 1992-94, Belmont U., 1984, others; exhibited in group shows, including Watkins Art Inst., Nashville, 1991, Western Ky. U., 1992, Parthenon, Nashville, 1992, Owensboro Mus. Art, 1993, Tenn. Performing Arts Ctr., 1995; invitational and juried exhibits include Sculptors of Mid. Tenn. Arts in the Airport, Nashville, 1996, Nat. Coun. on the Edn. of Ceramics Arts, Rochester, N.Y., 1996, Ceramic Exhibn. Tenn. State U., 1996, and numerous others; represented in permanent collections including Chattanooga's Visitors Ctr., IBM, Bapt. Hosp., Nations Bank of Tenn., Mass. Pub. Libr., First Am. Bank Corp., Andrew Jackson Hermitage Mus., Tenn. State U., also numerous pvt. collections. Adv. bd. Belmont U., Nashville, 1984—, Nossi Coll. Art, 1993—; mem edn. com. Nat. Mus. of Women in the Arts, Tenn., 1992—; artist for fundraising sculpture Arthritis Found., Nashville, 1989-90; vol. singer VA Hosp., Nashville, 1989—; bd. dirs. Visual Arts Alliance Nashville, 1996; vol. soloist Vet.'s Hosp., 1991-96; artist for ann. fundraiser YWCA, 1993-96; mem. So. Regional Honors Coun. Recipient Best Tchr. award Nossi Coll. Art, 1992-93; grantee City of Chattanooga Welcome Ctr., 1993, Memphis Arts Festival Spl. Projects, 1994, 96. Mem. AAUW, Assn. of Visual Artists, Soc. of N.Am. Goldsmiths, Visual Artists Alliance of Nashville, Nat. Art Edn. Assn., Internat. Sculpture Ctr., Nat. Coun. on Edn. of the Ceramic Arts, Tenn. Assn. of Craft Artists, Coll. Art Assn. Avocations: boating, running, singing, dancing, hiking. Home: PO Box 120454 Nashville TN 37212-0454

MCKINNEY, OWEN MICHAEL, retired security executive, consultant; b. Jeffersonville, Ind., Mar. 9, 1950; s. Owen Howard and Frances Marie (Hall) McK.; m. Janice Elaine Wilson, Sept. 2, 1972; 1 child, Sean Michael. BS in Police Adminstrn., U. Louisville, 1976; AA, SUNY, Albany, 1978; MS in Adminstrn. of Justice, U. Louisville, 1978; diploma in pastoral ministries, So. Bapt. Conv., 1980; MAT in Secondary Edn., U. Louisville, 1987; cert., Ctr. Ednl. Leadership, 1995, Leadership Ky., 1996; MEd in Instrnl. Tech., U. Louisville, 2002. Cert. 5-12 tchr., learning disabilities, behavior disorders, physically handicapped, community-based edn., learning strategies, social skills, history, geography, polit. sci., sociology, Ky. Probation and parole officer Commonwealth of Ky., Louisville, 1978; security mgr. First Nat. Tower John W. Galbreath & Co., Louisville, 1981-82; v.p. Safety Arms Security & Police Equipment Co., Portsmouth, Va., 1980; area mgr. CPP Security Svc., Norfolk, Va., 1979-80, Louisville, 1982-83; tchr. Jefferson County Pub. Schs., Louisville, 1985-88, spl. edn. tchr., 1988—98; pres. Cambridge Cons Inc, Louisville, 1995—2002. Owner Owen McKinney Detective Agency, Louisville, 1973-79, The McKinney Agency, Louisville, 1983-87; commr. City of Richlawn, Ky., 1990-92; presenter in field. Editor, writer, publisher The Renaissance Magazine, 1979-81; editor, publisher: Security Gazette, 1982, The Private Investigator, 1983-84, Private Security Report, 1983; editor, writer: (newspaper) Richlawn Gazette, 1990, 91; contbr. articles to profl. jours. Mem. George Bush for Pres., Jefferson County, 1988, Rebecca Jackson for Jefferson County Clerk, 1989, Owen M. McKinney for City Comsnr., Richlawn, 1989, Al Brown for U.S. Congress, 3d congl. dist., Louisville, 1990, Vote for the Library Tax campaign, Jefferson County, 1992; Rep. del. 3d congl. dist. meeting 32d Legis. Dist., 1990, del. Rep. State Conv. 32nd legis. dist. chmn. 1993-94; hon. amb. labor Sec. Labor, Ky. Staff sgt. U.S. Army, 1969-73, Vietnam, mem. USAR, 1977-85, hon. air assault soldier. Recipient Commendation medal U.S. Army, 1971, cert. of appreciation Pres. of U.S., 1973, Outstanding Staff award JCPS, 1991, 92, 93, 94, 95, 96, 97, 98, Minerva award U. Louisville, 1993, Disting. Citizen award Mayor City Louisville, Cold War Cert. of Recognition Sec. of Def., U.S., 2000; named to Hon. Order Ky. Cols., sr. fellow U. Louisville Soc., numerous others; named Duke of Paducah Mayor City of Paducah, Ky.; named hon. citizen and given key to City of Mayfield, Ky. Mem. VFW (life), Internat. Assn. Profl. Security Cons., Assn. U.S. Army (life), Am. Soc. Indsl. Security (cert. protection profl. 1985-, chmn. seminar com. Louisville chpt. 1983-84, cert. appreciation Louisville chpt. 1984, Quarter Century Club award 2001), Coun. Exceptional Children (chpt. gen. bd. 1988-89, v.p. 1989-90, pres. elect 1990-91, chpt. pres. 1991-92, 97-98, state gen. bd. 1991-92, chpt. past pres. 1992-93, 98—, state v.p. 1993-94, state pres.-elect 1994-95, state pres. 1995-96, 96-97, state past pres. 1997-98, Svc. award 1990, cert. merit Ky. Fedn. 1990, 98, cert. Outstanding Svc. 1991-92, outstanding mem. of yr. award 1993, 98, awarded profl. recognized spl. educator), Acad. Security Educators and Trainers, Nat. Crime Prevention Alumni Assn., Internat. Crime Prevention Through Environ. Design, Commonwealth Atty.'s Citizen Adv. Coun., DeMolay Alumni Assn. (life, Rep. DeMolay award 1976, 25 Yr. mem. award 1991), U. Louisville Alumni Assn. (exec. com. 1976—), Am. Mensa Soc., elected to chap. exec. com., 1998-99, Am. Legion, York Rite, Scottish Rite, USCG Aux., The Wild Geese (hon.), Masons (past master, grand lodge com.), Order of Eastern Star, Grotto, KP (chancellor comdr. 1994, Internat. Svc. award 1993), Rosicrucian Order, Royal Order Scotland (life), Societas Rosicruciana in Civitatibus Foederatis VII (life), Shrine, Golden Key Hon. Soc. (life), Internat. High 12 (Internat. Svc. award 1994, chpt. 1st v.p. 1996, chpt. pres. 1997), Alpha Phi Sigma (nat. criminal justice hon. soc. (life), Phi Delta Kappa (chpt. sec. 1992-93, v.p. 1993-94, Mem. Recognition Cert. 1995). Avocations: reading, tennis, weight lifting, photography, master scuba diver. Home: 7400 Moredale Rd Louisville KY 40222-4139

MCKINNEY, SHANNON J. retired secondary school educator; b. Huntingburg, Ind., Sept. 12, 1942; d. Lester Maxey and Clarice V. Corn; m. David E. McKinney, May 18, 1963; children: David E. Jr., Karla K. BS, Oakland City U., 1965; MA, U. Evansville, 1971. Tchr. Plainville (Ind.) H.S., 1965—66, Barr-Reeve H.S., Montgomery, Ind., 1966—67, Dale (Ind.) H.S., 1967—69, East Gibson Sch. Corp., Oakland City, Ind., 1969—2001; ret., 2001. Author: (poetry) Apple Skins, 2001, (novels) Fences, 2002; contbr. articles, short story to profl. pubIs. Sec., bldg. rep., v.p. East Gibson Classroom Tchr.'s Assn., Oakland City. Recipient Hon. Mention, Rising Sun Fund Poetry Competition, 2002. Mem.: NEA, Ind. State Tchr.'s Assn. Avocations: gardening, writing, camping, travel, photography. Home: 1542 E Arthur Church Rd Winslow IN 47598

MCKINNEY-KELLER, MARGARET FRANCES, retired special education educator; b. Houston, Mo., Nov. 25, 1929; d. George Weimer and Thelma May (Davis) Van Pelt; m. Roy Calvin McKinney Sr., Nov. 11, 1947 (dec. Feb. 1990); children: Deanna Kay Little, Roy Calvin Jr.; m. Clarence Elmore Keller, June 8, 1991; 1 stepchild, Dennis Lee Keller (dec.). BS with honors, Bradley U., 1963, MA in Counselor Edn., 1968, postgrad., 1992, U. Ill., 1993—, Aurora Coll., Ill. Ctrl. Coll. In real estate, Peoria, Ill., 1951-57; tchr. Oak Ridge Sch., Willow Springs, Mo., 1947-48, pvt. kindergarten, Washington, Ill., 1957-59, Dist. 50 Schs., Washington, Ill., 1959-67; tchr. socially maladjusted Washington Twp. Spl. Edn. Coop., 1967-70; tchr. behavior disordered Tazewell-Mason Counties Spl. Edn., Washington, Ill., 1970-78; resource tchr. Dist. 50 Schs., Washington, 1978-94; ret., 1994. Cons. moderator Active Parenting Group, Washington, 1972—; adv. bd. to establish Tazewell County Health Dept., 1960s; pres. gov. bd. Faith Luth. Day Care Ctr., Washington, 1970—, Washington Sr. Citizens, 1982-91; coach Spl. Olympics, Washington, 1979—; pres. Faith Luth. Ch. Coun., Washington, 1985-86; laity v.p. No. Conf. Evang. Luth. Ch. Am., Ctrl. Ill., 1986-92; vol. Proctor Hosp., 1994—. Mem. AAUW, Washington Bus. and Profl. Women (pres. 1979-80, 88-89, dist. 9 dir. 1995-96), Am. Legion Aux., German-Am. Soc., Alpha Delta Kappa (state office, ctrl. region). Avocations: travel, cooking, oil painting, crocheting. Home: 603 Sherwood Park Rd Washington IL 61571-1828

MCKINNEY-LUDD, SARAH LYDELLE, middle school education, librarian; b. Feb. 29, 1948; BA, U. Md., 1973; MA, Cen. Mich. U., 1975; MA in Legal Studies, Antioch Sch. Law, Washington, 1982; postgrad., Sch. Edn. George Washington U., 1989—; PhD in Christian Edn., Family Bible Coll. and Seminary. Cert. advanced profl. tchr. grades 5 through 12, Md., cert. adminstr. Tchr. of learning disabled Azores (Portugal) Elem. Sch., 1974-76; tchr. English Spaulding Jr. High Sch., Forestville, Md., 1976-82, Prince George's Cmty. Coll., 1982-84, Benjamin Tasker Sch., Bowie, Md., 1982-85, Crossland Night Sch., Temple Hills, Md., 1984-85, Thomas Pullen Mid. Sch., Landover, Md., 1985-87, Kettering (Md.) Mid. Sch., 1985-88, Kenmoor Mid. Sch., Landover, 1988-91; tchr. English, libr. Drew Freeman Mid. Sch.(formerly Francis Scott Key Mid. Sch.), District Heights, Md., 1991—. Chair multicultural com., chair sch. based mgmt. Francis Scott Key Mid. Sch., 1992—; reader Jarvis Grants, U.S. Dept. Edn., 1990—; acad. coord. Prince George's County Steel Band-Positive Vibrations. Contbr. articles to various publs. Mem. Md. State Tchr.'s Legis. Com., 1987-90; chairperson Profl. Rights and Responsibility, 1978-81; active Prince George's Com. on Acad. Achievement, Prince George's Com. Women's Fair Steering Com., Md. State Hosp. Bd., Prince George's County affiliate United Black Fund, area speakers bur.; programs chairperson, sec. Project Safe Sts.-2000, 1989; pres. Bowie Therapeutic Nursery; judge ACT-SO NAACP, Washington, 1989—; mem. exec. bd. Prince George's County chpt., 1984-89; active polit. campaigns; bd. dirs. Landover Ednl. Athletic Recreational Non-Profit Found. of Washington Redskins. Recipient Dorothy Wyod award for women's rights, 1998, Agnes Meyer Outstanding Educator award Wash. Post, 2000. Mem. Md. State Tchrs. Assn. (editor Women's Caucus, Dorothy Lloyd award for Women's Rights 1998), Sigma Gamma Rho (Community Activist award 1992), Delta Kappa Gamma. Office: Walker Mill Middle Sch 800 Karen Blvd Capitol Heights MD 20743-3314

MCKINSEY, ELIZABETH, humanities educator, consultant; b. Columbia, Mo., Aug. 10, 1947; d. J. Wendell and A. Ruhamah (Peret) McK.; m. Thomas N. Clough, June 18, 1977; children: Emily, Peter. BA, Radcliffe Coll., 1970; PhD, Harvard U., 1976. From instr. to asst. prof. English Bryn Mawr (Pa.) Coll., 1975-77; from asst. to assoc. prof. English Harvard U., Cambridge, Mass., 1977-85; dir. Bunting Inst. Radcliffe Coll., Cambridge, 1985-89; dean Carleton Coll., Northfield, Minn., 1989—2002, prof., 2002—. Author: Niagara Falls: Icon of the American Sublime, 1985; contbr. articles and revs. to profl. jours. and lit. mags. NEH fellow, 1980; Carnegie Found. for the Advancement of Tchg. vis. scholar, 2003. Mem. MLA, Am. Conf. Acad. Deans, Nat. Coun. for Rsch. on Women (assoc.), Am. Studies Assn., Nat. Assn. Women in Edn., Phi Beta Kappa (pres. Iota of Mass. chpt. 1986-89). Home: 815 2nd St E Northfield MN 55057-2308 Office: Carleton Coll 1 N College St Northfield MN 55057-4001 E-mail: emckinse@carleton.edu.

MCKINSEY, LYNN, elementary education educator; b. Evansville, Ind., May 29, 1945; d. Claud and Janice Elizabeth (Clements) McK. BA, Purdue U., 1967; MA, Ball State U., 1978; gifted and talented cert., Purdue U., 1984; adminstrv. cert., Butler U., 1993. Cert. elem. tchr. NSW, Australia, Ind. 5th grade tchr., Eielson AFB, Alaska, 1967-70; 3d and 4th grade tchr. Moree and Narellan, Australia, 1971-72; 5th grade tchr. U.S. Dept. Def., West Germany, 1974-76, Decatur Twp. Schs., Indpls., 1977-83, dist. gifted/talented coord., 1985-86; tchr.-in-residence Butler U., Indpls., 1986-88; tchr. gifted and talented Decatur Twp. Schs., 1983-94, Wayne Twp. Schs., Indpls., 1994—. Methods instr. math., U. Indpls., 1994-96; methods instr. math, sci. and social studies, Butler U., 1983-87; math. facilitator Ind. Dept. Edn., 1986—, intern, ednl. cons., 1994; mem. bd. Ind. Math. adv. com., 1994—. Contbr. State Math Proficiency Guide, 1989—, Technology Utilization in Math, 1994-95; contbr. State Acad. Math Bowl, 1998, 99; reviewer math materials, U.S. Dept. Edn., 1998. Bd. mem. Ind. Repertory Theater, Indpls., 1982-97. Recipient Ind. Presdl. award for math., NSF, 1996; Ind. Tchr. of Yr. finalist, Ind. Dept. Edn., 1999. Mem. Nat. Coun. Tchrs. Math. (chair coms. 1986—), Coun. Presdl. Awardees of Math., Ind. Assn. Gifted, Ind. Coun. Tchrs. of Math. (bd. mem. 1984—), Ctrl. Ind. Coun. Tchrs. Math. (past pres., bd. mem., v.p./pres. 1992—), state bd. mem. NCREL, 1996-, reviewer test items, Ind. Dept. Edn., 1997-, Tri Kappa (past pres.). Avocations: bridge, skiing, reading, travel, crafts.

MCKISSICK-MELTON, S. CHARMAINE, mass communications educator; b. Durham, N.C., July 31, 1955; d. Floyd Bixler Sr. and Evelyn C. (Williams) McKissick; div. 1990; children: Maceo Christopher Kemp Jr., Daniel Ernest Kemp. BA, U. N.C., 1977; MA, No. Ill. U., 1978; PhD, U. Ky., 1993-96. Sales mgr. WDUR-AM Radio, Durham, 1979-83; account exec. WTVD-TV 11, Durham, 1983, WKFT-TV 40, Fayetteville, N.C., 1984-85; office mgr. Atty. M. Christopher Kemp, Sr., Lumberton, N.C., 1985-88; learning disabled/extremely mentally handicapped tchr. Lumberton Jr. High Sch., 1988; account exec. WQOK-FM Radio, Raleigh, N.C., 1989; instr. Fayetteville State U., 1989, A&T State U., Greensboro, N.C., 1988-93; assoc. prof. Bennett Coll., Greensboro, 1989—, chair dept. mass comm., 1991-93. Vis. prof. U. Notre Dame, Ind., 1992. Bd. dirs. N.C. Ctr. for Study of Black History, Durham, 1989-96, Durham Bus. and Profl. Chain, 1990-91, Women's Shelter for hope, Durham, 1989-91, Southeastern Family Violence Ctr., Lumberton, 1985-89; faculty adv. Lmbda Phi Eta.. Coca Cola Faculty fellow U. Notre Dame, 1992, Lyman T. Johnson Rsch./Tchg. fellow, 1993-96. Mem. AAUP (Bennett Coll. chpt. founding mem, pres. N.C. chpt. 2002-03), Bennett Coll. Faculty Senate (exec. com. 1991-93), Women in Comm. (faculty advisor 1989-93), Am. Women in Radio and TV (N.C. chpt. pres. 1985-86). Avocations: swimming, aerobics, reading, public speaking. Home: 705 Reynolds Ave Durham NC 27707-4641 Office: Bennett Coll PO Box 25 Greensboro NC 27402-0025

MCKNIGHT, JOYCE SHELDON, adult educator, community organizer, mediator; b. Meadville, Pa., Oct. 12, 1949; d. Seth Carlyle and Juanita Bessie (Sheets) Sheldon; m. Hugh Frank McKnight, Aug. 22, 1970; children: Frank Nathan, Joanna Michelle. BA in Psychology and Sociology, Allegheny Coll., 1971; MEd in Counseling, Gannon Coll., 1977; EdD, Pa. State U., 1995. Cert. nat. counselor. Asst. met. dir. Ecumenical Inst., Chgo. and Tulsa, 1970-73; health planner East Okla. Devel. Dist., Muskogee, 1973; juvenile counselor Tulsa County Aftercare Program, 1973; program specialist psycho-social rehab. Counseling Svcs. Ctr., Corry, Pa., 1975-77; counselor Adult Diploma Program, Corry, Pa., 1974-79; dir. Anchor House Agy., Corry, Pa., 1977-78; community programs dir. Warren-Forest Counties Econ. Opportunity Coun., Warren, Pa., 1979-80; dir. Corry Ctr. Mercyhurst Coll., Corry, Pa., 1981-87; cons. Pulaski, Pa., 1987-89. Adj. faculty Mercyhurst, 1981-87, program devel. cons., 1987-89, program devel. cons. for new ch. Heritage Hills Ch., 1988-89; adj. faculty Allegheny Coll., 1984, Jamestown C.C., 1991-93; planner Pa. State U., Shenango Valley, 1989; mentor Empire State Coll. SUNY, 1989-93; coord. adult svcs. Alfred State Coll., 1992-95, adj. faculty mem., 1994-95, distance edn. team, 1994-95; dir. Inst. for Support of Cmty. Initiative, 1995-97; dir. McKnight Mediation, 1997-2002; mem. faculty Cambria County Area C.C., 1998-2002, adj. grad. faculty Pa. State U., 2000, dept. chair, Ctr. Distance Learning, Empire State Coll., SUNY; cons. higher edn., cmty. svc., ch. growth. Contbr. articles to profl. jours; co-author: Doing Doing Democracy Workbook, 2003 Pres., Corry Concerned for Youth, Inc., 1975-77; pres. Community Care Coun. of Agys., Corry, 1976-79, sec., 1975; mem. steering com. Vol. Action Ctr., Corry, 1977, bd. dirs. Erie County Citizens Coalition for Human Svcs., Erie, 1979-80, Horizon House for Women, 1981-87; mem. coordinating bd. Corry Reindustrialization Coun. 1983-87; mem. Allegany County N.Y Gateway Project, 1993-95. Mem. NAACP (Johnstown chpt., adv. com. family ctr.), Pa. Assn. Pub. Continuing Adult Edn. (dir. 1977-78), Pa. Assn. for Adult Continuing Edn. (bd. dirs. 1985-90) Cambria County Comty. Action (bd. dirs.), Coalition of the So. Alleghenies, SEAD, Saratoga Springs Women in Leadership, Saratoga Springs. Mennonite. Home: 20 Pine Rd Box 321 Lake Luzerne NY 12846 Office: Ctr Distance Learning Empire State Coll Saratoga Springs NY 12866 Business E-Mail: joyce.mcknight@esc.edu. E-mail: jmedcon@aol.com.

MCKNIGHT, LENORE RAVIN, child psychiatrist, educator; b. Denver, May 15, 1943; d. Abe and Rose (Steed) Ravin; m. Robert lee McKNight, July 22, 1967; children: Richard Rex, Janet Rose. Student, Occidental Coll., 1961-63; BA, postgrad., U. Colo., 1965-67; MD, U. Calif., San Francisco, 111969. Diplomate in adult and child psychiatry Am. Bd. Psychiatry and Neurology. Intern in pediat. Children's Hosp., San Francisco, 1969-70; resident in gen. psychiatry Langley Porter Neuropsychiat. Inst., 1970-73, fellow in child psychiatry, 1972-74, asst. clin. prof., 1974—; pvt. practice child psychiatry, Walnut Creek, Calif., 1974-93; child psychiatrist Kaiser Permanente Med. Group, 1993—. Child psychiatrist Youth Guidance Center, San Francisco, 1974-74; asst. clin. prof. psychiatry U. Calif. San Francisco Med. Ctr. Internat.; med. dir. CPC Walnut Creek (Calif.) Hosp., 1990-93. Insts. Edn. fellow U. Edinburgh, 1964; grantee to study childhood nutrition NIH, 1966. Fellow Am. Acad. Child and Adolescent Psychiatry, Internat. Arabian Horse Assn. Office: Kaiser Martinez Inpat Psych 200 Muir Rd Martinez CA 94553-4672

MCKONE, MARY KATHERINE, elementary school educator; b. Hartford, Conn., Dec. 19, 1946; d. Thomas Christopher and Mary (Sullivan) McK. AA, Elizabeth Seton Coll., 1966; BA, Coll. of St. Elizabeth, 1968; MEd, U. Hartford, 1976. Cert. tchr., Conn. Tchr. St. Brigid Sch., West Hartford, Conn., 1969-83; substitute tchr. West Hartford, 1983-86; tchr. Mark Twain Sch., West Hartford, 1986—. Vol. Emergency Room, St. Francis Hosp., Hartford; sec. Parish Coun., Ch. of St. Timothy, West Hartford; v.p., com. chmn. Jr. League, Hartford, 1980-93; mem. Democrat. Town Com., 1991-93. Mem. ASCD, Conn. Coun. for Social Studies (bd. dirs. 1983-88, sec. 1985-87, v.p. 1987-88), Jr. League of Hartford (sustainer chmn. bd. dirs. 1995-97). Roman Catholic. Avocations: reading, travel, needlepoint. Home: 13 Maple Ln Avon CT 06001-4523 Office: Mark Twain Sch 395 Lyme St Hartford CT 06112-1026

MCKOWEN, DOROTHY KEETON, librarian, educator, consultant; b. Bonne Terre, Mo., Oct. 5, 1948; d. John Richard and Dorothy (Spoonhour) Keeton; m. Paul Edwin McKowen, Dec. 19, 1970; children: Richard James, Mark David. BS, Pacific Christian Coll., 1970; MLS, U. So. Calif., 1973; MA in English, Purdue U., 1985, PhD, 2003. Libr.-specialist Doheny Libr., U. So. Calif., L.A., 1973-74; asst. libr. Pacific Christian Coll., 1974-78; serials cataloger Purdue U. Librs., 1978-88; head children's and young adult svcs. Kokomo-Howard County Pub. Libr., Ind., 1988-89, coord. children's and tech. svcs., 1989-91; cataloger, network libr. Ind. Coop. Libr. Svcs. Authority, 1991-2001; libr. cons. and contractor, 2001—. Mem. adj. faculty.C.C. of Ind., 2001—, Purdue U., 2003—; lectr. Purdue U., 2003—. Mem. ALA, MLA, Soc. Early Americanists, Assn. for Libr. Collections and Tech. Svcs. (bd. dirs. 1986-90, 95-96, vice chair, chair-elect coun. of regional groups 1986-88, chair 1988-90, conf. program com. 1986-88, internat. rels. com. 1986-88, micropub. com. 1986-87, subject analysis com., membership com. 1988-90, planning and rsch. com. 1988-90, chair program initiatives com. 1991-93, orgn. and bylaws com. 1991-92, 99-2001), Network OCLC Svc. Mgrs. (MARC Task Force 2000-01), Ind. Coun. Libr. Automation (bibliog. stds. task force), Ind. Libr. Fedn. (chair tech. svcs. divsn. 1984-85), Ohio Valley Group Tech. Svcs. Libr. (chmn. 1985-86). Republican. Home: 7625 Summit Ln Lafayette IN 47905-9729 E-mail: mckowen@remconline.net.

MCKOWN, MELISSA ANNE, elementary school educator; b. Huntsville, Ala., Oct. 14, 1959; d. Leonard Bancroft and Helen (Carter) Murray; 1 child, Erin. BS cum laude, U. Tenn., 1981; MSEd in Early Childhood magna cum laude, U. West Ga., 1997. Cert. elem. and early childhood tchr., Tenn., Ga. 5th grade tchr. Our Lady of Perpetual Help Sch., Chattanooga, 1981-83; 2d grade tchr. Ringgold (Ga.) Elem. Sch., 1985-93, 2d-3d grade tchr., 1993—96, 4th-5th grade tchr., 1996—. Summer sch. tchr. McCallie Sch., Chattanooga, 1989, 90, 91, Girls Prep. Sch., Chattanooga, 1989, 90; chair Student Support Team, 2000—; mentor tchr. Galaxy Sci. Program, 2002—; program instr. Galaxy Sci. program State of Ga., 2003—. Chmn. children's activities Ronald McDonald House Fair of Chattanooga, 1991; vol. firefighter Ringgold-Catoosa County Fire Dept., 1988-97; mem. Houston Antique Glass Mus., Chattanooga, 1987—. Mem. Nat. Coun. Tchrs. of Math. (presider, speaker S.E. conf. 1990, speaker Ga. conf. tchrs. of math. 1990), Am. Heart Assn. (logistics com. 1998—), Pi Lambda Theta. Avocations: backpacking, crafts, reading, science. Office: Ringgold Elem Sch 322 Evitt Ln Ringgold GA 30736-2820

MCKOY, PHYLLIS COFIELD, elementary school educator; b. Newport News, Va., June 13, 1959; d. Ralph and Leila (Scott) C.; m. Carl Zarankarvich McKoy, Mar. 26, 1983. BS, U. Va., 1981; MEd, George Mason U., 1993. Cert. elem. tchr., administr., supr., Va. Classroom tchr. Fairfax County (Va.) Pub. Schs., 1981-90, consulting tchr., peer observer, 1990-93, asst. prin., 1993—. Mem. ASCD, Nat. Coun of Negro Women (recording sec. 1991-92), Fairfax Assn. Elem. Sch. Prins., Alpha Kappa Alpha, Phi Delta Kappa. Democrat. Baptist. Avocations: reading, theater. Home: 10597 Winfield Loop Manassas VA 20109-8227

MCLAIN, SANDRA BRIGNOLE, art educator; b. N.Y.C., Mar. 4, 1936; d. Raymond and Frances (Pace) Brignole; m. Lyn Gerald, Aug. 18, 1959 (div. Sept. 1978); 1 child, Kevin Brian. BS in Dance, Juilliard Sch., 1959; student, Md. Coll. Art and Design, 1974-75, 84, Norwich U., 1986-89; MA in Art Edn., Vt. Coll., 1989. Cert. tchr art, art specialist, Vt. Dancer Ericka Thimey's Dance Theatre, Washington, 1959-64; tchr. dance various schs., Washington, Md., Va., 1959-72; dir., choreographer Washington Contemporary Dance Ensemble, 1964-70; adminstr. Washington Ethical Soc.,

1986-88; art specialist Montgomery County Pub. Schs., Rockville, Md., 1989—. Dir. summer arts program Montgomery County Schs., Silver Spring, Md., 1989—. Exhibited in group shows in Washington met. area, 1980—, Chesapeake Bay area, 1986. Asst. to dir., cons. Washington Youth Orch. Program, Calvin Coolidge High Sch., 1960-74; vol., fundraiser crafts for the homeless program Washington Ethical Soc., 1989—. Mem. NEA, Md. Art Edn. Assn. Home: 7511 Jackson Ave Takoma Park MD 20912-5706

MCLAIN, WILLIAM TOME, principal, educator; b. Washington, July 10, 1935; s. Ronald Alpha and Dorothy Smithson (Tome) McL.; m. Meurial Claire Webb, Nov. 20, 1977; 1 child, Laura Louisa McLain. BA, U. Del., 1957, MEd, 1966. Secondary Prin. Cert., Del. Math. tchr. Newark Sch. Dist., 1957-69, high sch. adminstrv. asst., 1969-78; high sch. assoc. prin. New Castle County Sch. Dist., Newark, 1978-81; high sch. asst. prin. Christina Sch. Dist., Newark, 1981-84, middle sch. asst. prin., 1984-87, prin. adult edn. program, 1987—. Treas., past chmn. Del. Coalition for Literacy; past pres. Del. Assn. for Adult and Cmty. Edn. Recipient Tchrs. medal, Freedoms Found., 1968, Silver Beaver award, Boy Scouts Am., 1967, Walace Johnson Cmty. Svc. award, New Castle County C. of C., 1979, Adult and Family Lit. Outstanding Svc. award, State of Del., 1992, Pres.'s award, Del. Assn. for Adult and Cmty. Edn., 2001, Cross and Flame award for svc. to children and youth, United Meth. Men, 2003. Mem. Interagency Coun. on Adult Lit. United Methodist. Avocations: travel, history. Home: 95 Dallas Ave Newark DE 19711-5123 Office: Christina School District 925 Bear Corbitt Rd Bear DE 19701-1323

MCLANE, HENRY EARL, JR., philosophy educator; b. Statesboro, Ga., Aug. 18, 1932; s. Henry Earl and Lillie Ora (Beasley) McL.; m. Barbara Helen Gardner, Nov. 7, 1934; children— Debra Lynn, Shawn Creg BA, George Washington U., 1955; postgrad., Johns Hopkins U., 1955-56; MA, Yale U., 1958, PhD, 1961. Instr. philosophy Washburn U. of Topeka, Kans., 1960-61, asst. prof., 1961-64, assoc. prof., 1964-65; vis. assoc. prof. philosophy Coll. of William and Mary, Williamsburg, Va., 1965-66, assoc. prof., 1967-77, prof., 1978-96, prof. emeritus, 1996—. Diving coach Coll. of William and Mary, 1976-87. Contbr. articles to profl. publs. Danforth Found. fellow, 1955-60 Mem. Am. Philos. Assn. Democrat. Baptist. Avocations: playing violin; music. Home: 116 Dogwood Dr Williamsburg VA 23185-3743

MCLAREN, KARLENE MARIE, special education educator; b. Pontiac, Mich., Nov. 20, 1942; d. James Joseph and Ethel Margaret (Mertens) Lamberton; m. Malcolm Bruce McLaren, Jan. 29, 1965; children: Cameron Bruce, Kathleen Marie, Sean Matthew. BS in Edn., Cen. Mich. U., 1965; postgrad., Wayne State U., 1965, Mich. State U., 1965-68; MEd, Ea. N.Mex. U., 1982; postgrad., N.Mex. State U., 1981; Non-Profit Mgmt. cert., Angelo State U., 2003. Cert. spl. edn. preK-12, learning disabled K-12, N.Mex. Spl. edn. tchr. Waterford (Mich.) Twp. Schs., 1965-68, Bd. of Co-op Edn. Svcs., Huntington, N.Y., 1969; home ctr. tchr. Sch. and Parents Assisting with Readiness of Kids in Early Years Program Wayne-Westland Sch., Wayne, Mich., 1973-74, music coord., 1974-75; spl. edn. tchr. Villa Solano Program State of N. Mex., Roswell, 1978-81; K-6 resource tchr. Roswell (N. Mex.) Ind. Sch. Dist., 1981-87, early childhood spl. edn. tchr., 1987—2000; dept. chair Devel. Delay Presch., 1992—2000; mid. sch. resource room tchr. Dexter (N.Mex.) Consol. Schs., 2000—02; dir. children's ministries First United Meth. Ch., San Angelo, Tex., 2001—02; child devel. specialist Tex. Workforce Ctr. Child Care Svcs., San Angelo, 2002—. Cons. Chaves County Cmty. Action Program, Roswell, N. Mex., 1978; mem. Presch. Planning Com., Individualized Edn. Program Com., Roswell Schs., 1986, transition process com., 1987-88, Edn. of the Handicapped-B Adv. Com., Roswell Schs., 1988-2000, N.Mex. Region 14 Adv. Coun., 1989-98, Devel. Disabled Definition Task Force, State of N. Mex., Santa Fe, 1990; parent advisor STEP HI Program Sch. for the Deaf, Albuquerque, N. Mex., 1989-92, INSITE - Multiple Handicapped Sensory Im-paired Infants, Albuquerque, 1990-92; workshop presenter N. Mex. Sch. for the Visually Handicapped; presenter Magic Yrs. Conf., Albuquerque, 1992—. Dir. St Mark Luth. Ch. Choir, Roswell, 1980-90; mem. 1st Presbyn. Ch. Choir, Roswell, 1989-2000; mem. Cmty. Chorus, Roswell, 1984-92. Recipient Recognition certs., Waterford Orgn. for Retarded Children, 1968, Roswell Spl. Olympics, 1979, '86, Very Spl. Arts, Santa Fe, 1990, Cert. Appreciation, Sch. and Parents Assisting with Readiness of Kids in Early Years Program, Wayne, Mich., 1974. Mem. Waterford Orgn. for Retarded Citizens, Coun. for Exceptional Children (visually handicapped, early childhood divs.), N. Mex. Coun. for Exceptional Children (treas. 1984-87, fin. chair 1986-87, conf. planning com. 1979, 1989), ARC N.Mex., Parents Reaching Out, Roswell Council for Exceptional Children (newsletter editor, 1978-80. pres. 1986, 1991) Avocations: barbershop singing, bicycling, sewing. Office: Tex Workforce Ctr Child Care Svc 202 Henry O Flipper St San Angelo TX 76903 Home: 3214 Timber Ridge Dr San Angelo TX 76904-6906

MCLAUGHLIN, ANNE ELIZABETH, secondary education educator; b. Springfield, Mass., Sept. 16, 1942; d. Terrence John and Sara Anne (Hartford) McTiernan. BA, Elms Coll., 1966; MEd, U. Lowell, 1976; M in Edn. Adminstrn., Salem State U., 1988; postgrad., Harvard U., 1995. Cert. reading specialist Mass., N.H.; cert. adminstr. Mass., N.H. Tchr. reading John Duggan Middle Sch., Springfield, Mass., 1967-72, Andover (Mass.) High Sch., 1972-74; with Middlesex Ho. Corrections, Bellrica, Mass., 1974-76; clinician, cons. Northeastern U., Boston, 1976-77; reading specialist Coop. Mid. Sch., N.H., 1977—. Evaluator New England Assn. Schs. and Colls., 1987; instr. Elms Coll., Chicopee, Mass., 1991—; chairperson Sch. Adminstr. Unit # 16 staff devel. com., Exeter Area Jr. High. Sch. improvement com.; co-pres. Seacoast Reading Coun.; founder Libr. Card Program for Am. Libr. Week; evaluator New Eng. Assn. Schs. & Colls. Fellow Nat. Endowment for Arts, 1979; recipient commendation Internat. Reading Assn., 1992. Mem. NEA (legis. com.), Exeter Edn. Assn. (rep. to Congress), Peace and Justice for Children Caucus, Granite State Reading Coun., Assn. for Supervision and Curriculum Devel., Nat. Coun. Tchrs of English. Avocations: skiing, boating, world traveling. Home: 2 Elbow Ln # B Newburyport MA 01950-2725 Office: Sch Adminstr Unit # 16 Front St Exeter NH 03833

MCLAUGHLIN, CAROLYN LUCILE, elementary school educator; b. Pensacola, Fla., June 16, 1947; d. John Franklin and Mamie Lou (Rayburn) Wells; m. Richard Allen McLaughlin, Sept. 5, 1969; children: Allen Wayne, Kristen Lynn. BA, U. West Fla., 1970. Cert. early childhood, elem. edn. tchr., ESOL. Elem. tchr. Santa Rosa Sch. Bd., Milton, Fla., 1970—2003, reading specialist tchr., 2002—03. Lobbyist for edn. State Fla. Legis. Com., 2001—03. Mem. County Tchr. Edn. Coun., Santa Rosa, v.p., 1995—97, pres., 1998—2000, 2001—03; youth ch. tng. tchr., music and youth dir., Sunday sch. youth tchr. Billory Bapt. Ch., East Bay Bapt. Ch., Midway Bapt. Ch., 1970—95, Navarre Bapt. Ch.; dir. Bible Sch. Holley Assembly God, 2001. Grantee Jr. League 1986, 91-99, Chpt. II Fed. grantee Elem. and Secondary Edn. Act, 1992. Mem.: Santa Rosa Reading Assn. (treas. 2001—03), Santa Rosa Profl. Educators (dist VII rep., negotiations team com., county calendar com., sec. county restructuring steering com., county curriculum com., tchr. of yr. com.), Fla. Reading Assn., Internat. Reading Assn. (v.p. Santa Rosa chpt. 1998—99, pres.-elect 1999—2000, pres. 2001—03), Navarre C. of C. (edn. com. 1998—2001, 2001—03), Kiwanis (children priority one com. 1998—2001). Home: 3586 Ginger Ln Navarre FL 32566-9616 E-mail: richcarol@cs.com, mclaughlincl@mail.santarosa.klz-fl.us.

MCLAUGHLIN, CONSTANCE NETHKEN, middle school science educator; b. Elkins, W.Va., Feb. 3, 1949; d. Ralph David and Helen Irene (Shreve) Nethken; m. Terry Walthall McLaughlin, May 23, 1970; 1 child, Veronica McLaughlin Mercure. BS in Chemistry, W.Va. U., 1971; MA in Sci. Edn., U. No. Colo., 1980; cert. in Ednl. Adminstrn., U. Denver, 1988. Cert. tchr., Colo. Tchr. Jefferson County Schs., Golden, Colo., 1982—. Participant Process Consultation Cadre Jefferson County Schs., Jefferson County Life Sci. Cadre. Recipient Outstanding Tchr. award Colo. Awards Com. Mem. Colo. Biology Tchrs. Assn., NEA, Colo. Assn. Sch. Execs., Alpha Delta Kappa. Methodist. Avocations: woodworking, cross-stitch.

MCLAUGHLIN, JACK M. superintendent; m. Sheryl McLaughlin; 4 children. BEd, U. Calif., Santa Barbara; MEd, DED, USC. From tchr. to asst. supt. Calif. Pub. Schs., 1963—74; supt. Sunnyvale City schs., Calif., 1974—87, Hemet Unified Sch. Dist., Calif., 1987—94, Berkeley Unified Sch. Dist., Calif., 1994—2001; supt. of pub, instrn, State of Nev., Carson City, 2001—. Pres. Calif. Urban Sch. Dists.; founding mem. Minority Student Achievement Network; mem. Calif. State Budget Rev. Com., Calif. Spl. Edn. Task Force, Coun. Chief State Sch. Officials; charter mem. Calif. Edn. Rsch. Coun.; commr Edn. Commn. of the States; bd. dirs. WestEd. Mem adv. com. Spl. Olympics; mem Nev. Hospitality Found. Mem.: Urban Supts. Assn., Am. Assn. Sch. Adminstrs., Screenwriters Guild Am. Office: Nev Dept Edn 700 E Fifith St Carson City NV 89701-5096 Office Fax: 775-687-9101. E-mail: ack@nsn.k12.nv.us.

MCLAUGHLIN, LISA MARIE, educational administrator; b. Sioux City, Iowa, Dec. 27, 1957; d. Donald James and Shirley Jean (Bartlett) Warden; m. Steven A. McLaughlin, Apr. 22, 1978; children: Mark Alan, Catherine Lynn. BS, Ctrl. State U., Edmond, Okla., 1978, MEd, 1982; EdD, Okla. State U., 2000. Cert. tchr., Okla. Tchr. learning disabilities Putnam City Schs., Oklahoma City, 1979—80, tchr. visually impaired, 1980—81; devel. therapist Child Study Ctr., Okla. Teaching Hosps., Oklahoma City, 1981—83; ednl. cons. Oklahoma City, 1983—85; regional program specialist Okla. State Dept. Edn., Oklahoma City, 1985—87, spl. edn. data cons., 1987—90, tech. assistance officer, 1990—91, asst. state dir. spl. edn., 1991—92; ednl. cons., vision specialist, special edn. adminstr. Edmond, 1992—95; asst. elem. prin., 1995—96; elem. prin., 1996—98; dir. spl. svcs. Western Hts. Publ Schs., Oklahoma City, 1998—99, asst. supt., 1999—. Contbr. chpt. to book. Mem. coun. on adminstrn. Ione br. YWCA, Oklahoma City, 1985-88, 92-94; mem.-at-large bd. dirs. Met. br. YWCA, Oklahoma City, 1989-91; mem. adv. com. Okla. Sch. for Blind, 1992—; chmn. Parkview Sch. for Blind Ednl. Found., 1994-96; legis. liaison Olka. Dirs. of Spl. Svcs., 1994—; bd. dirs. Prevent Blindness Okla., 1998—, pres., 2001—, bd. dirs. Prevent Blindness Am., 2002—. Mem. Coun. Exceptional Children (v.p. Oklahoma City chpt. 1988-89, Spl. Educator of Yr. 1991), Learning Disabilities Assn., Assn. for Edn. and Rehab. of Blind and Visually Impaired (state pres. Okla. chpt. 1989-90), Advocates and Parents of Okla. Sight Impaired (treas. 1984-87), Okla. Women in Edn. Adminstrn., Delta Kappa Gamma (2d v.p. 1990-92), Kappa Delta Pi. Avocations: handmade bobbin lacemaking, reading, piano, walking. Office: 8401 SW 44th St Oklahoma City OK 73179-4010

MCLAUGHLIN, MARGARET BROWN, educator, writer; b. Miami Beach, Fla., Aug. 24, 1926; d. J. Clifford and Grace Lindsey (DuPre) Brown; m. Francis Edward McLaughlin, Oct. 30, 1982 (dec.). BA cum laude, U. Miami, 1946; MA, Duke U., 1949; PhD, Tulane U., 1976. Instr., lectr. in English U. Miami, Coral Gables, Fla., 1946-47, 56-61, 73-91, 2000; English tchr. Narimasu Am. Sch., Tokyo, 1963-65; asst. prof. Manchester Coll., North Manchester, Ind., 1965-67; instr. Miami-Dade C.C., 1977, 81; dir. writing workshop for fgn. students U. Miami Sch. Medicine, 1991-92; adj. prof. English, Asian and Liberal studies Fla. Internat. U., Miami, 1997—. Prodr. Dade County Cable TV series Caribbean Writers and Their Art, 1991; prodr., host cable tv series Haiti Cherie, 1993-94. Contbr. articles to popular mags. and newspapers; contbr. play reviews to Internet pub. Trustee Mus. Sci., Miami, 1977-78. Mem. Am. Lit. Assn. (Henry Adams Soc.), Egyptology and Asian Civilizations Soc. Miami (bd. dirs., pres. 1976-78, 83-85), Miami Internat. Press Club (scholarship chmn. 2002—), South Fla. Writers' Assn. Avocations: travel, editing, writing, civic speaking. Home and Office: 1621 S Bayshore Dr Miami FL 33133-4201 Office Fax: 305-858-7224. E-mail: mjmbjb711@aol.com.

MCLAUGHLIN, PHILIP VANDOREN, JR., mechanical engineering educator, researcher, consultant; b. Elizabeth, N.J., Nov. 10, 1939; s. Philip VanDoren and Ruth Evans (Landis) McL.; m. Phoebe Ann Feeney, Aug. 19, 1961; children: Philip VanDoren III, Patrick Evans, Christi M. Barton. BSCE, U. Pa., 1961, MS in Engring. Mechanics, 1964, PhD in Engring. Mechanics, 1969. Assoc. engr. Boeing-Vertol, Morton, Pa., 1962-63, engr. II, 1963; rsch. engr. Scott Paper Co., Phila., 1963-65, rsch. project engr., 1965-69, sr. rsch. project engr., 1969; asst. prof. theoretical and applied mechanics U. Ill., Urbana, 1969-73, asst. dean engring., 1971-72; project mgr. Materials Scis. Corp., Blue Bell, Pa., 1973-76; assoc. prof. mech. engring. Villanova (Pa.) U., 1976-81, prof., 1981—2003, prof. emeritus, 2003—. Cons. Naval Air Engring. Ctr., Lakehurst, N.J., 1977-79, U.S. Steel Corp., Trenton, 1980-82, RCA Corp., Moorestown, N.J., 1986, Coal Tech Corp., Merion Station, Pa., Air Products and Chems., Inc., Allentown, Pa., 1988, Aircraft divsn. Naval Air Warfare Ctr., Patuxent River, Md., 1995-96, Christini Technologies, Phila., 1999—, Alpha Sci. Corp., Southeastern, Pa., 2000-01, Materials Rsch. & Design, Inc., Rosemont, Pa., 2002-, DETechs., King of Prussia, Pa., 2002—; vis. prof. dept. engring. U. Cambridge, Eng., 1990-91. Reviewer: for sci. and tech. jours.; contbr. numerous articles to profl. jours. Rsch. grantee NSF, 1970-72, Naval Air Engring. Ctr., 1978-84, Lawrence Livermore Nat. Lab., 1979-81, Naval Air Devel. Ctr., 1985-86, RCA Corp., 1986-87; sr. rsch. assoc. NRC, Washington, 1983-84; USN-Am. Soc. for Engring. Edn. sr. faculty fellow, 1995. Mem.: ASME (life; chmn. applied mechanics divsn. Phila. sect. 1981—83, mem. materials divsn. com. on composites 1992—), ASCE (life; chmn. engring. mechanics divsn. com. on inelastic behavior 1977—79, assoc. editor Jour. Engring. Mechanics Divsn. 1977—79, mem. aerospace divsn. com. on structures and materials 1986—95), Am. Soc. Composites, Am. Soc. Engring. Edn., Am. Acad. Mechanics, Sigma Xi. Achievements include research and consulting on composite materials and structures, structural analysis and design and inelastic behavior. Office: Villanova U Dept Mech Engring 800 Lancaster Ave Villanova PA 19085-1681 E-mail: philip.mclaughlin@villanova.edu.

MCLAUGHLIN, VIRGINIA BARLOW, elementary educator, reading specialist; b. Pitts., May 31, 1953; d. Robert Allen and Eleanor (Hay) McL. AA, Centenary Coll., 1973; BEd, U. Pitts., 1986, reading specialist cert., 1988. Cert. elem. tchr., reading specialist, Pa. Substitute tchr. Pitts. Pub. Schs., 1986-89, chpt. 1 reading specialist, 1989-92, reading recovery, elem., 1992—. Tchr. Read Aloud, Pitts., 1991-92; mem. design team for restructured sch., 1992; recording sec. Pitts. Assn. Kindergarten Tchrs., 1997—. Mem. Highland Park Community Club, Carnegie Inst., Pitts., 1990—. Mem. ASCD, NCTE, Assn. for Childhood Edn., Internat. Reading Assn., 3 Rivers Reading Coun. (v.p. elect 1993—, pres. 1995-96). Avocations: skiing, swimming, reading, cooking, furniture refinishing. Office: Pitts Pub Schs Sheredan Elem Pittsburgh PA 15212

MCLEAN, GLORIA DAWN, elementary education educator; b. Philippi, W.Va., May 7, 1952; d. Vernon Bliss and Edythe Grace (Holmes) Howdershelt; m. Elbert Ray McLean, June 6, 1971; children: Adam Scott, Anastasia Grace. Student, W.Va. U., 1970-72, Alderson-Broadus Coll., 1972-75. Tchr. music Belington (W.Va.) Jr. High, Kasson (W.Va.) Jr. High, 1975-77, Belington Elem. Sch., 1977—. Pvt. lessons to 13 students; dir. elem. sch. chorus. Pianist Nestorville United Meth., Ch., 1963—, dir. youth and adult choir, 1970—, ch. bell choir; vol. Ladies Aid, Nestorville, 1962—. Mem. Delta Kappa Gamma (music com. 1990), Order of Eastern Star. Avocations: sewing, spending time with family. Home and Office: Belington Elem Sch RR 2 Box 624 Philippi WV 26416-9208

MCLEAN, IAN SMALL, astronomer, physics educator; b. Johnstone, Scotland, Aug. 21, 1949; s. Ian and Mary (Small) McL.; (div.); 1 child, Jennifer Ann; m. Janet Wheelans Yourston, Mar. 4, 1983; children: Joanna, David Richard, Graham Robert. BS with hons., U. Glasgow, Scotland, 1971, PhD, 1974. Rsch. fellow dept. astronomy U. Glasgow, 1974-78; rsch. assoc. Steward Obs. U. Ariz., Tucson, 1978-80; sr. rsch. fellow Royal Obs. U. Edinburgh, Scotland, 1980-81, sr. sci. officer Royal Obs., 1981-86; prin. sci. officer Joint Astronomy Ctr., Hilo, Hawaii, 1986-89; prof. dept. physics and astronomy UCLA, 1989—, dir. Infrared Imaging Detector Lab., 1989—; assoc. dir. UC Observatories, 2001—. Author: Electronic and Computer-Aided Astronomy: From Eyes To Electronic Sensors, 1989, Infrared Astronomy with Arrays: The Next Generation, 1994, Electronic Imaging in Astronomy: Detectors and Instrumentation, 1997; contbr. articles to profl. jours. Recipient Exceptional Merit award U.K. Serc, Edinburgh, 1989; NSF grantee, 1991, 93. Fellow Royal Astron. Soc.; mem. Internat. Astron. Union (pres. com. Paris chpt. 1988-91, v.p. 1985-88), Inst. Physics, Am. Astron. Soc. Achievements include discovery of relationship between polarization of light and orbital inclination of close binary stars; development of first CCD spectropolarimeter, first fully automated infrared camera for astronomy used to achieve images of faintest high redshift galaxies, first twin-channel infrared camera; first high resolution infrared spectrograph for studies of brown dwarfs, galactic center and high redshift galaxies; research in optical and infrared astronomy, use of CCDs and infrared array detectors. Office: UCLA Dept Physics and Astronomy 405 Hilgard Ave Los Angeles CA 90095-9000

MCLEAN, JAMES ALBERT, artist, educator; b. Gibsland, La., Nov. 25, 1928; s. Charles Edward and Lucille (Bowdon) McL.; m. Ocelia Jo Perkins, Nov. 27, 1954; 1 child: Gregory Scott. BA, Southwestern La. Inst., 1950; BD, So. Meth. U., 1953; MFA, Tulane U., 1961. Meth. student dir. Centenary Coll., Shreveport, La., 1957-59; head art dept. LaGrange (Ga.) Coll., 1964-66; assoc. prof. art Ga. State U., Atlanta, 1967-68, prof. art, 1968-95; ret., 1995. Exhibited in numerous group shows including Brooklyn Mus., 1976-77, Positive/Negative Exhbn., 1988, Siggraph Exhbn. 1988, 89, Clemson U. Nat. Print and Drawing Exhbn., 1989, Purdue U. Small Print Exhbn., 1990. Mem. Siggraph. Avocations: animation, puppetry. Home: 1256 Dunwoody Knoll Dr Atlanta GA 30338-3219 E-mail: jmc545694@aol.com., mcle231@bellsouth.net.

MCLEAN, JULIANNE DREW, concert pianist, educator; b. Stoneham, Mass., Sept. 12, 1928; d. Benjamin Drew and Elizabeth Anna McLean; m. Carmelo Addario, Oct. 18, 1958 (dec.); 1 child, Angela Elizabeth Addario. BMusic, Conservatory of Music, Kansas City, Mo., 1949, MMusic, 1950. Concert pianist NAC, U.S., Europe, Near and Far East, 1956—; tchr. pvt. classes, Kans., Hawaii, Va., 1956—; rec. artist Wichita State U., 1987—; lectr. in field. Musician: appearances on TV; musician: (invited pianist) Survivors of Andrea Doria Reunion; musician: live on Vatican Radio. Bd. dirs. Maud Powell Found., Falls Church, Va., 1995—. Recipient scholarships. Mem. Mu Phi Epsilon. Roman Catholic. Avocation: cooking.

MCLEAN-WAINWRIGHT, PAMELA LYNNE, educational consultant, college educator, counselor, program developer, clinical therapist; b. Rockville Centre, N.Y., Oct. 25, 1948; d. George Clifford Sr. and Violet Maude (Jones) McLean; m. Joseph Charles Everest Wainwright Jr., Jan. 20, 1982; children: Joseph Charles Everest III, Evan Clifford Jerome. BS, NYU, 1973; MEd, Fordham U., 1974; MSW, Adelphi U., 1986. Qualified clin. social worker. Tchr. Martin Deporres Day Care Ctr., Bklyn., 1973-77; dir. student pers. svcs. Ujamaa Acad., Hempstead, N.Y., 1977-78; coord. Hempstead, 1978; ednl. opportunity counselor SUNY, Farmingdale, 1978-79; assoc. prof. student pers. svcs. Nassau C.C., Garden City, N.Y., 1979-93; with counseling/advisement for health occupations program Ctrl. Fla. C.C., Ocala, N.Y., 1991-95; social work assoc. dept. home care U. Fla./Shands Hosp., Gainesville, 1995—. Founder, program dir. Adult Individualized Multi-Svc. Program, Garden City, 1985—. Mem. L.I. Coalition for Full Employment; mem. citizens adv. coun. Nassau Tech. Ctr., Women-on-Job Task Force, Port Washington, N.Y.; mem. adv. bd. Region 2 Displaced Homemakers Network; bd. dirs. Children's Greenhouse Inc., 1987-89, mem. founding com., 1980-81; civil rights adv., 1963—; mem. adv. bd. L.I. Cares, Hempstead, 1986-90; pres., CEO Faith-Builders Ministries; coord. Black male coll. explorers program Inverness/Fla. A&M U. Recipient Women's History Month citation Nassau County, N.Y., 1988, honoree in edn. Women-on-Job Task Force, 1989, Alumni Achievement award Fordham U. Grad. Sch. Edn., 1994. Mem. Assn. Black Psychologists, Assn. Black Women in Higher Edn. (bd. dirs.), Nat. Assn. Black Coll. Alumni, Nat. Assn. Female Execs., Women's Faculty Assn. Nassau Community Coll. (pres. 1986-88), L.I. Women's Council for Equal Edn. Employment and Tng. Avocations: music collecting, writing poetry, travel, photography, sewing.

MCLELLAN, LAURA JOHN, biology educator; b. Trenton, N.J., Feb. 7, 1956; d. Donald Lyle and Ethle May (John) M. BS, Mich. State U., 1979, MS, 1983; PhD, Kans. State U., 1988. Postdoctoral fellow Smithsonian Instn., Washington, 1989-90; lectr. in sci. Marymount U., Arlington, Va., 1989-90; vis. asst. prof. Coastal Carolina U., Conway, S.C., 1990-91; asst. prof. biology Ctrl. Mo. State U., Warrensburg, 1991-97; adj. asst. prof. Ocean County Coll.; tchr. natural and environ. study Pineland Inst.; tchr. LBI Arts and Sci. Found., 2000—03. Contbr. articles to profl. jours.; reviewer Jour. Mammalogy, Prarie Naturalist/NSF. Mem. AAAS, Am. Soc. Mammalogists, East African Natural History Soc., Soc. for Study of Evolution, Soc. Systematic Zoology, S.W. Assn. Naturalists, Sigma Xi, Phi Beta Delta. Home: PO Box 1009 Beach Haven NJ 08008-0001

MCLEOD, MARILYNN HAYES, retired educational administrator, farmer; b. Lake View, S.C., Jan. 2, 1924; d. Cary Victor and Benna (Price) Hayes; m. Charles Edward McLeod, Aug. 24, 1947; children: Cary Franklin, Mary Marilynn. BA, Furman U.; MEd, U. S.C., 1952, EdD, 1986. Tchr. Hamer-Kentyre Sch., Hamer, SC, 1944-45, Bennettsville (S.C.) City Schs., 1946-59, Clio (S.C.) Elem. Sch., 1960-63; asst. prof. elem. edn. St. Andrews Presbyn. Coll., Laurinburg, NC, 1964-67; instr. U. S.C., Florence, 1971; reading supr., coord. instrn. Marlboro County Sch. Dist., Bennettsville, SC, 1967-86; prin. Marlboro County Child Devel. Ctr., 1986-87; asst. prin. Bennettsville High Sch., 1987-89, Marlboro County High Sch., 1989-92; farmer, 1960—; ret. Mem. Marlboro County Sch. Dist. Bd., 1992-96. Author: The History of Education in Marlboro County, South Carolina, 1737-1895, 1988. Adminstrv. bd. Trinity United Meth. Ch., 1982—, chmn. pastor-parish relations com., 1979-98; trustee Trinity United Meth. Ch., 2000-; pianist Men's Bible Class Trinity; trustee Epworth Children's Home, chmn. personnel com., Columbia, S.C., 1982-94, bd. mem. Hospice of Marlboro County, 1992-97. Mem. NEA (life), Internat. Reading Assn., S.C. Edn. Assn. (life), S.C. Reading Assn., Assn. Secondary Prins., S.C. Internat. Reading Assn., Marlboro County Edn. Assn., Pee Dee Internat. Reading Assn., Marlborough Hist. Soc., Marlboro Arts Coun., Marlboro County Assn. for Mental Retardation, Dillon County Farm Bur., Clio Federated Women's Club, Palmetto Book Club, Soc. Internat. outstanding women educators, Delta Kappa Gamma. Home: PO Box 38 127 S Main St Clio SC 29525-3004

MCLEOD, STEPHEN GLENN, education educator, language educator; b. Pensacola, Fla., Mar. 30, 1949; AA, Pensacola Jr. Coll., 1969; BA, U. West Fla., 1971; MA, Vanderbilt U., 1973; EdD, Nova Southeastern U., 1992. Commd. 2d lt. U.S. Army, 1978, advanced through grades to capt., 1981, resigned, 1984; sr. assoc. prof. mil. edn. program St. Leo Coll., Hurlburt Field, Fla., 1984-92; adj. instr. Pensacola Jr. Coll., 1984—86, 1991—2003; West Fla. cluster adminstr. programs for higher edn. Nova Southeastern U., Pensacola/Ft. Lauderdale, Fla., 1994—2003; asst. prof. English Jackson State U., Miss., 2003—. Contbr. articles to profl. jours. Capt. U.S. Army, 1975-84. Recipient Rsch. award Phi Delta Kappa, 1989.

Mem. Internat. Fellowship of Christians and Jews, Two-Year Coll. English Assn. Southeast, Nat. Coun. Tchrs. English. Avocations: golf, travel, Israeli dance. Home: 1400 JR Lynch St PO Box 190411 Jackson MS 39217 E-mail: mcleods@bellsouth.net.

MCLIN, HATTIE ROGERS, school system administrator; b. Prentiss, Miss., Dec. 8, 1946; d. Javan Wilson Sr. and Alberta (Davis) Rogers; m. Prentiss McLin, June 29, 1968; children: Albert Marie, Prentiss II, Javan Wilson. BS, Jackson State U., 1968, MA, 1972, EdS, 1981, EdD, 1987. Tchr. Hinds County Pub. Schs., Clinton, Miss.; assoc. prof. edn. Paul Quinn Coll., Waco, Tex.; asst. prin. Jackson (Miss.) Mcpl. Separate Sch. Dist., 1992; prin. Johnson Elem. Sch., Jackson, Miss. Adj. prof. Jackson State U., Hinds Community Coll., Jackson. Sec. Jackson City Planning Bd.; bd. dirs. Nurture for Bapt. Chs., Greater Fairview Bapt. Ch.; mem. PTA., Youth Leadership Jackson C. of C., C. of C. Youth Devel. Name Outstanding Elem. Prin., Miss. Educator or the Yr.; Levi Strauss grantee, 1985, 86. Mem. ASCD, Miss. ASCD, NEA, Miss. Assn. Educators, Nat. Assn. Young Children, Bus. Profl. Women Orgn., Kappan Honors Orgn., Kappa Pi Honor Soc., Zeta Phi Beta. Office: Johnson Elem Sch 3319 Oak Park Dr Jackson MS 39212-4124

MCLOONE, EUGENE P. education educator; b. Phila., Nov. 11, 1929; married. BA, LaSalle Coll., 1951; MS in Govt. Mgmt., U. Denver, 1952; PhD, U. Ill., 1961. Carnegie fellow U. Denver, 1951-52; staff Ark. Legis. Rsch. Coun. Study on Sch. of Fin., 1952; rsch. asst. Bur. of Edni. Rsch. U. Ill., 1952-55; Fed. Exec. fellow The Brookings Instn., 1961; specialist Sch. of Fin. U.S. Office of Edn., 1958-65; postdoctoral rsch. fellow Stanford U., 1966-67; rsch. dir. Nat. Ctr. for Edn. Stats./U.S. Dept. Edn., Washington, 1979-81; assoc. prof. U. Md. Coll. Edn., College Park, 1967-75, prof. edn. dept. edn. policy, planning and adminstrn., 1975-96, assoc. prof. dept. econs., 1967-94; sr. staff scientist George Washington U., 1966-67; post-doct. fellow Stanford U., 1967-68; assoc. dir. rsch. divsn. NEA, Washington, 1968-69, staff contact, com. for sch. fin., 1968-70; atty. gen. State of N.J., 1981-83, State of W.Va., 1981; prof. emeritus U. Md., College Park, 1996—. Cons. Addison-Wesleyan Pubs., 1992-93, Bur. of Spl. Edn., Dept. Edn., 1992, Jour. Econs. and Edn., 1989-95, Jour. Edn. Fin., 1989—, Nat. Tax Assn., 1989, Office Edn. Rsch. and Improvement, 1989, others; lectr. in field; panel mem. Statis. for Supply and Demand of Pre-Collegiate Sci. and Math. Tchrs., Nat. Rsch. Coun., NAS, 1986-90; with Heald Commn. Higher Edn. N.Y., 1960; treas. Brightright of Johnstown, 2000. Author: Pre-College Science and Mathematics Teachers: Monitoring Supply, Demand, and Quality, 1990, Report of Panel, Toward Understanding Teacher Supply and Demand: Priorities for Research and Development Interim Report, Profiles in School Support, 1969-70; co-author: Public School Finance: Profiles of the State, 1979, Documentation and Analysis of Maryland Special Services Information System, 1977; contbr. articles to profl. jours.; editor books in field. Treas. Birthright of Johnstown, 2000-02. Grantee Ford Found., 1966-68, Bur. of the Handicapped, U.S.O.E., 1977, Nat. Ctr. for Edn. Stats., 1971, 73; recipient awards in field. Mem. NEA, Am. Econ. Assn., Am. Assn. Sch. Adminstrs., Am. Edn. Fin. Assn. (pres.-elect 1995-96, pres. 1996-97, immediate past pres. 1997-98, Outstanding Svc. awsard for Contbns. to Field 2000), Phi Delta Kappa.

MCLURKIN-HARRIS, KIMBERLY ELANA, secondary education educator; b. Washington, Mar. 09; d. Samuel Louis and Wheatley McLurkin; m. David Harris, Oct. 11, 1986; children: David Jr., Elana. BA, Clark Atlanta U., 1982; MA, U. Ky., 1985. Tchr. U.S. history, dept. chmn. world studies Montgomery County Pub. Schs., Rockville, Md., 1985—. Mem. editorial bd. Montgomery Times, Silver Spring, Md., 1992-93. Pres. Friends of Olney Theatre. Mem. Theta Omega Omega (v.p. 1990-92, pres. 1993-95), Alpha Kappa Alpha (Pres. of Yr. for North Atlantic Region 1994). Office: 2400 Bel Pre Rd Silver Spring MD 20906-2308

MCMAHAN, GALE ANN SCIVALLY, education educator; b. Anna, Ill., Oct. 19, 1946; d. George Oliver and Jessie Lee (Johnson) Scivally; m. Joe Henry McMahan, Dec. 14, 1963; children: Randy Scott, Joseph Paul. BS, So. Ill. U., 1971, MS, 1974, PhD, 1994. Cert. tchr., supr., adminstr., Ill. Resource tchr. Jonesboro (Ill.) Sch. Dist. 43, 1971-73, dir. early intervention, 1991-94; resource tchr. Anna Sch. Dist. 37, 1973-94; supt. Lick Creek Sch. Dist. 16, Buncombe, Ill., 1994-95, Vienna (Ill.) Pub. Sch. Dist. 55, 1995-97; assoc. prof. S.E. Mo. State U., Cape Girardeau, 1997—. Lectr. Shawnee C.C., Ullin, Ill., 1986-88, So. Ill. U., Carbondale, 1990, 92, 93; reader U. Ill. Bd. Edn., Springfield, 1989, 92; mem. adv. bd. for early intervention Anna Interagy. Coun., 1991—, Ill. Interagy. Coun., Springfield, 1991—; mem. peer monitor spl. edn. dept. Ill. Bd. Edn., 1993—, mem. monitoring team for tchr. preparation programs; mem. content adv. com. Ill. Cert. Testing Sys., 1994—. Co-author: (video) Jenny...Our Child of Today!, 1991; editor: Churches in Clear Creek Association, 1988. Recipient Those Who Excel in Edn. award of recognition Ill. Bd. Edn., 1992, grantee, 1990—. Mem. Coun. Exceptional Children (presenter 1991, tchr. edn. divsn. 1998-2003, tech. and media divsn. 1998-2002), Internat. Coun. for Exceptional Children, Assn. Childhood Edn. Internat. (program reviewer for nat. accreditation of tchr. edn.), Ill. Supt. Assn., Ill. Prin. Assn., Ill. Women Adminstrs., Anna Elem. Edn. Assn. (pres. 1992-94), DAR, Delta Kappa Gamma (scholar 1989-90, co-contbr. article to Bull. 1993), Phi Kappa Phi, Kappa Delta Phi, Phi Delta Kappa. Baptist. Avocations: genealogy, reading, painting, walking, swimming. Home: 4890 State Route 146 E Anna IL 62906-3530 Office: 1 University Plz Cape Girardeau MO 63701-4710

MCMAHON, JOHN JOSEPH, college official; b. Elizabeth, NJ, Mar. 3, 1946; s. John J. and Bertha L. (Walton) McM.; m. Barbara A. McMahon, Aug. 14, 1970. BS, Providence Coll., 1968; MS, U. Hawaii, 1975; PhD, Oreg. State U., 1985. Dir. marine option program U. Hawaii, Honolulu, 1975-79; edn. specialist Oreg. State U., Newport, Oreg., 1980; coord. edn. programs Wash. Dept. Wildlife, Olympia, Wash., 1984-86; mgr. programs and exhibits Seattle Aquarium, Seattle, 1986-90; divsn. chmn. Maritime Tng. Ctr. Inst. Tng. & Devel., Wood Constrn. Program, Seattle C.C., 1990-92; dean Sea Edn. Assn., Inc., Woods Hole, Mass., 1992-94; dean comm. and design Seattle Ctrl. C.C., 1994—. Cons. John McMahon & Assocs., Bainbridge Island, Wash., 1990. Contbr. articles to profl. jours. Mem. Nat. Marine Educators Assn. (founding, pres.), Nat. Coun. Instructional Adminstrs., Nat. Coun. Occupl. Educators, Wash. Environ. Edn. Task Force, N.Y. Acad. Scis. Office: Seattle Ctrl CC 1701 Broadway #2BE3176 Seattle WA 98122-2413

MCMAHON, MAEVE, middle school administrator; Pres. Marian Ctrl. Mid. Sch., New Orleans, 1996—. Recipient DOE Elem. Sch. Recognition Program award, 1989-90. Office: Marian Ctrl Mid Sch 2221 Mendez St New Orleans LA 70122-5276

MC MAHON, MARGARET GARVEY, nursing educator; b. N.Y., Apr. 12, 1951; d. John J. and Anne (Merone) Garvey; m. James McMahon, Mar. 19, 1994. BSN, Molloy Coll., 1973; MPS, C.W. Post Coll., 1978; MSN, Adelphi U., 1981. Cert. diabetes educator, health edn. specialist. Staff RN telemetry St. Francis Hosp., Roslyn, N.Y., 1973-81; staff devel. instr. Boswell Hosp., Sun City, Ariz., 1982; med.-surg. edn. specialist Phoenix Bapt. Hosp., 1983; health edn. mgr., 1985-91; adminstr. employee devel. CIGNA Healthcare, 1991—. Mem. ASTD, Nat. League for Nursing, Assn. Diabetes Educators, Sigma Theta Tau. Office: 8826 N 23rd Ave Phoenix AZ 85021-4154

MCMAHON, PAMELA SUE, dietitian, educator; b. Jersey City, N.J., Apr. 29, 1948; d. William Louis and Pauline Lucille (Oldenberg) Zogbaum; m. Martin James McMahon, June 26, 1971; children: Conor Martin, Timothy James. BS, Douglass Coll., 1970; MS, Framingham State Coll., 1975; PhD, U. Md., 1992. Registered dietitian. Home economist Thomas J. Lipton, Englewood, N.J., 1970-71; dietitian Waltham (Mass.) Hosp., 1971-72, Boston U., 1972; cons. Arthur D. Little, Cambridge, Mass., 1972-79; assoc. prof. nutrition and food sci. U. Ky., Lexington, 1979—97; dir. didactic program in dietetics U. Fla., 1998—. Dir., coord. dietetics program U. Ky., Lexington, 1992-97. Contbr. articles to profl. jours. Mem. Am. Dietetic Assn., Food Svc. Sys. Mgmt. Edn. Coun. (bd. dirs., regional del. 1986-88), Ky. Dietetic Assn. (bd. dirs. 1996-97). Home: 2814 NW 58th Blvd Gainesville FL 32606-6400 Office: Univ Fla Food Sci and Human Nutrition Dept 359 FSHN Gainesville FL 32611-0360 E-mail: psmcmahon@mail.ifas.ufl.edu.

MCMAHON-DUMAS, CARMEN ELETHEA, education educator; b. St. Elizabeth, Jamaica, Aug. 25; came to U.S., 1974; d. John O. and Hepzibah B. (Cooper) Robertson; m. L.C. McMahon (dec. 1988); children: Carol McLeod, Lance McMahon, Cheryl McMahon Lee, Michele McMahon. Diploma, Bethelehem Tchrs. Coll., Malvern, Jamaica, 1956; BA with honors, U. W.I., Kingston, 1969; MEd, Howard U., 1972; EdD, George Washington U., 1981. Cert. ednl. adminstr., supr. teaching English. Tchr. Dept. Edn., Jamaica; head. English dept. Caenwood Tchrs. Coll., Jamaica, 1969-70; prin. Haile Selassie Secondary Sch., Jamaica, 1970-76; supr. instrn. Washington D.C. Pub. Sch., 1978-79; dir. profl. devel. acad. Md. State Dept. Edn., 1980-82; dir. practicums, prof. edn. Nova U., Ft. Lauderdale, Fla., 1983-93. Co-editor jour. Geographica Literaria, 1968. Leader 4-H Clubs, St. Ann, Jamaica, 1965-70; singer St. Andrew Singers, Kingston, Jamaica, 1970-74; mem. Multi-Cultural Orgn., Broward County, Fla., 1989—; chair edn. Sister Cities Orgn., Dade County, 1991-92. Named Outstanding Educator Mico Coll. Alumni Assn., 1992; recipient Gov. Gen.'s Leadership award 4-H Clubs; Jamaica Independence scholar 1970. Mem. ASCD (bd. dirs. 1992-96), Fla. Assn. for Supervision and Curriculum Devel. (bd. dirs. 1987—, chief editor jour. 1991-92, Participation and Svc. cert. 1989), George Washington U. Assn. Sch. Adminstrs., St. Andrews Assn. Tchrs. and Sch. Adminstrs. (pres. 1974-76). Home: PO Box 1105 Roswell GA 30077-1105 Office: Nova U 3301 College Ave Fort Lauderdale FL 33314-7721

MCMAHON MASTRODDI, MARCIA A. secondary education educator, artist; b. Akron, Ohio, Dec. 26, 1953; d. James R. and Marla June McMahon; m. Dennis W. Mastroddi, Aug. 22, 1987. BA in Art, Ursuline Coll., Cleve., 1978; MA in Art, Western Res. U., 1980. Cert. K-12 art tchr., Ill. Instr. art Cuyahoga C.C., Warrensville Heights, Ohio, 1978-87; lectr. art Spoon River Coll., Canton, Ill., 1989, Ill. Ctrl. Coll., Peoria, 1990; tchr. art CBS Alternative H.S., Beardstown, Ill., 1993-95, Ursuline Acad., Springfield, Ill., 1996-97, Dist. 186, Springfield, 1997-98; tchr. art, chmn. dept. Tower Hill (Ill) Consol. Unified Sch. Dist. 66, 1999—. Lectr. art for gifted Lincoln Land C.C., Springfield, part-time 1995-98, Case Western Res. U., Cleve., 1980, Shard Hill Art Gallery, Farmington, Ill., 1989, Bot. Garden, 1998, Ursuline Coll., Cleve., 1979, Peoria Art Guild, 1990—, Ill. State Mus., Springfield, 1995—, Unity Gallery, 1999—, Rushville (Ill.) Arts Coun., 1999, Taste of Champaign (Ill.) Art Ctr. Sq. Show, 1999, Lincoln Prairie Trail Art Show, 2001; author: (wiht Marcia Mcmahon) Diana Speaks to the World, 2002. Houseparent Am. Youth Hostels, 1988-89. Recipient svc. award for tchr. Cuyahoga C.C., 1989, Rosie Richmond award Springfield Area Arts Coun., 1998. Mem. Prairie State Orchid Soc., Ill. tate Mus. Soc., Washington Park Bot. Gardens, Tower Hill Art Club. Mem. Unity Ch. Avocations: designing jewelry, hiking, sketching, portraiture, collecting antiques.

MCMANIGAL, SHIRLEY ANN, university educator, dean emerita; b. Deering, Mo., May 4, 1938; d. Jadie C. and Willie B. (Groves) Naile. BS, Ark. State U., 1971; MS, U. Okla., 1976, PhD, 1979. Med. technologist, 1958-75; chair dept. med. tech. U. So. Miss., Hattiesburg, 1979-83, Tex. Tech U. Health Scis. Ctr., Lubbock, 1983-87, dean Sch. Allied Health, 1987-97. Gov.'s appointee to statewide health coord. coun., 1994-97. Leadership Tex., 1992; Lt. Alumnae Regl. dir., 1994-97. Recipient Citation, State of Tex., 1988; named Woman of Yr., AAUW, Tex. div., 1990, Woman of Excellence in Edn. YWCA, Lubbock, 1990. Mem.: AAUW (Tex. bd. dirs. 1990—94, mem. ednl. found. internat. fellows panel 1994—98, chair 1998—2001), Tex. Soc. Med. Tech. (Educator of Yr. 1990), Tex. Soc. Allied Health Professions (pres. 1990—91), So. Assn. Allied Health Deans at Acad. Health Ctrs., Nat. Assn. Women in Edn., Am. Soc. Med. Tech., Clin. Lab. Mgmt. Assn. (chair edn. com. 1989, 1991), Phi Beta Delta, Alpha Eta. Home: 24633 Ivory Cane Dr 103 Bonita Springs FL 34134

MCMANNESS, LINDA MARIE, language educator; b. St. Louis, Mo., June 11, 1955; d. Donald R. and Gloria Jean McManness. BA, S.W. Baptist U., 1977; MA, U. Wash., 1987, PhD, 1990. Tchr. Spanish & Eng. Lamar H.S., Lamar, Mo., 1977—81; mgr. Lerner NY, Joplin and Springfield, Mo., 1981—85, Tulsa, 1981—85; acct. U. Wash., Seattle, 1985—86, grad. tchg. asst., 1986—90; assoc. prof. Spanish & Portuguese Baylor U., Waco, Tex., 1990—. Dir. Spanish grad. studies Baylor U., 1996—99. Author: Lexical Categories in Spanish: The Determiner, 1996, book reviews to profl. jours. Co-pres. Cen-Tex Foreign Lang. Collaborative, Waco, 1994—96; cook Meals on Wheels, Waco, 1997—; dir. global Christian ventures Baylor U., 1999—. Mem.: AAUP, Linguistic Assn. of S.W., South Ctrl. Modern Lang. Assn. Office: Baylor Univ PO Box 97393 Waco TX 76798

MCMANUS, MARY HAIRSTON, academic administrator; b. Danville, Va., Nov. 23; d. Benjamin and Essie (Walton) Hairston; m. Booker Taliaferro McManus, June 27; children: Philip, Kenneth. BA, MA, Va. State U., Petersburg; PhD, U. Md. Cert. in English lang. and lit. edn. Instr. English Va. State U., Petersburg; lectr. English European div. U. Md., Berlin; instr. English Fayetteville (N.C.) State U.; instr. ESOL Venice (Ill.)-Lincoln Tech. Ctr.; lectr. English Anne Arundel C.C., Arnold, Md.; asst. prof. English Bowie (Md.) State U., 1984—, dir. honors program, 1993-2000, dean honors coll., 2000—. Cons. Anne Arundel County Govt., Glen Burnie, Md., Prince George's County Govt., Upper Marlboro, Md.; mem. adv. bd. Collegiate Press, Alta Loma, Calif. Recipient Outstanding Educator award Prince George's County Fire Dept., Women of Achievement BSU, 2000, 2001. Mem. MLA, Nat. Coun. Tchrs. English, Coll. Lang. Assn., Chums Inc. (pres. 1995-98), Middle Atlantic Writers Assn., Kiwanis, Alpha Kappa Alpha, Sigma Tau Delta. Democrat. Avocations: reading, travel. Home: 432 Lakeland Rd N Severna Park MD 21146-2420 Office: Bowie State U 14000 Jericho Park Rd Bowie MD 20715-3319 E-mail: mmcmanus@bowiestate.edu., mephm@hotmail.com.

MCMASTER, JULIET SYLVIA, English language educator; b. Kisumu, Kenya, Aug. 2, 1937; emigrated to Can., 1961, naturalized, 1976; d. Sydney Herbert and Sylvia (Hook) Fazan; m. Rowland McMaster, May 10, 1968; children: Rawdon, Lindsey. BA with honors, Oxford U., 1959; MA, U. Alta., 1963, PhD, 1965. Asst. prof. English U. Alta., Edmonton, Can., 1965-70, assoc. prof., 1970-76, prof. English, 1976-86, Univ. prof., 1986—2000, prof. emeritus, 2000—. Author: Thackeray: The Major Novels, 1971, Jane Austen on Love, 1978, Trollope's Palliser Novels, 1978, (with R.D. McMaster) The Novel from Sterne to James, 1981, Dickens the Designer, 1987, Jane Austen the Novelist, 1995; co-editor: Jane Austen's Business, 1996, Cambridge Companion to Jane Austen, 1997; gen. editor Juvenilia Press, 1993-2002; illustrator/editor children's picture book: (by Jane Austen) The Beautifull Cassandra, 1993; contbr. articles to profl. jours. Fellow Can. Coun., 1969-70, Guggenheim Found., 1976-77, Killam Found., 1987-89; recipient Molson prize in Humanities for Outstanding Contbn. to Canadian Culture, 1994. Fellow Royal Soc. Can.; mem. Victorian Studies Assn. Western Can. (founding pres. 1972), Assn. Can. Univ. Tchrs. English (pres. 1976-78), MLA, Jane Austen Soc. N.Am. (dir. 1980-91). Office: U Alta Dept English Edmonton AB Canada T6G 2E5 E-mail: juliet.mcmaster@ualberta.ca.

MCMEEKING, ROBERT MAXWELL, mechanical engineer, educator; b. Glasgow, Scotland, May 22, 1950; came to U.S., 1972; s. Robert Maxwell and Elizabeth Higginson (Craighead) McM.; m. Norah Anne Madigan, Sept. 4, 1976; children: Gavin Robert, Anne Catherine. BSc with 1st class honors, U. Glasgow, 1972; MS, Brown U., 1974, PhD, 1977. Acting asst. prof. Stanford (Calif.) U., 1976-78; asst. prof. U. Ill., Urbana, 1978-82, assoc. prof., 1982-85; prof. U. Calif., Santa Barbara, 1985—, chmn. mech. and environ. engring. Santa Barabara, 1992—95, 1999—2003. Cons. in field. Co-editor Intermetallic Matrix Composites, 1990; assoc. editor Jour. Applied Mechanics, 1987-93; editor Jour. Applied Mechanics, 2002—; contbr. articles to profl. jours.. Vis. fellow Cambridge U., 1983, 95-96. Fellow ASME, Am. Acad. Mechanics; mem. AAAS, Sigma Xi. Office: U Calif Materials Dept Mech Engring Dept Santa Barbara CA 93106

MC MENIMEN, KATHLEEN BRENNAN, secondary education educator; b. June 15, 1944; d. John Joseph and Catherine (Healy) Brennan; m. Joseph Paul McMenimen, Aug. 22, 1970; children: Meghan, Joseph Paul. BS in Edn., Boston Coll., 1966, MEd, 1974. Tchr. Boston pub. schs., 1966—2002; pvt. ednl. cons. McMenimen Assocs., 2002—. Tchr. Operation Head Start, Charlestown, Mass., summers 1966-68; ednl. dir. John F. Kennedy Family Service Center, Charlestown, 1969; seminar leader Worcester (Mass.) State Coll., 1974. Author: A Curriculum Guide for Operation Head Start, 1970; prodr.: (cable) Tick-Talk. Bd. dirs. John F. Kennedy Family Svc. Ctr., 1970-71; mem. Waltham Dem. City Com., 1975—; commr. Waltham Housing Authority, 1982-86; mem. Waltham City Coun., 1986—; elected to Waltham City Coun., 1986-87, re-elected, 1988—, v.p., 1988, chair fin. com., 1990; ward councillor City of Waltham, 1976-78, councillor-at-large, 1986-99, 2002-04; candidate for mayor City of Waltham, Mass., 1999. Recipient Commendation for cmty. svc. Waltham City Coun., 1978, Disting. Svc. award Waltham Jaycees, 1978, Disting. Dem. award, 1996. Mem. Boston Coll. Alumni Assn. (bd. dirs. 1972-74, sec. 1987, treas. 1988, v.p. 1989, pres. 1990), Boston Tchrs. Union. Home: 147 Trapelo Rd Waltham MA 02452-6305

MCMICHAEL, JEANE CASEY, real estate company executive, educator; b. Clarksville, Ind., May 7, 1938; d. Emmett Ward and Carrie Evelyn (Leonard) Casey; m. Norman Kenneth Wenzler, Sept. 12, 1956 (div. 1968); m. Wilburn Arnold McMichael, June 20, 1978. Student Ind. U. Extension Ctr., Bellermine Coll., 1972-73; student, Ind. U. S.E., 1973—, Kentuckiana Metroversity, 1981—; grad. Realtors Inst., Ind. U., 1982. Grad. Leadership Tng., Clark County, Ind.; lic. real estate broker, Ind., Ky.; master Grad. Realtors Inst., Cert. Residential Splst., Cert. Real Estate Broker. Owner, pres., mgr. McMichael Real Estate, Inc., Jeffersonville, 1979-88, 91-98; mgr., owner Buzz Bauer, 1979-88, 88-91; mng. broker Parks & Weisberg Realtors, Jeffersonville, Ind., 1989-96; instr. pre-license real estate Ivy Tech. State Coll., 1995-96, ISTR Real Estate Tng. Concepts, Inc. Pres. congregation St. Mark's United Ch. of Christ, 1996, mem. long range plan and property acquisition, 1996-98; pres. Mr. and Mrs. Class, chmn., fin. trustee, bus. adv., chmn. devel. com., 1993, 94, chmn. com. long range planning, 1997; chmn. bd. trustees Brooklawn Youth Svcs., 1988-95, chmn., 1994-96; bd. dirs. Noah's Ark, Inc., 1998-99, sec./treas., 1999—; chmn. social com. Rep. party Clark County (Ind.); v.p. Floyd County Habitat for Humanity, 1991, 94-95. Recipient cert. of appreciation Nat. Ctr. Citizen Involvement, 1983; award Contact Kentuckiana Teleministries, 1978. Mem. Nat. Assn. Realtors (nat. dir. 1989—), Ind. Assn. Realtors (state dir. 1987—, quick start spkr. 1989-91), Nat. Women's Coun. Realtors (state pres., chmn. coms., state rec. sec. 1984, state prs. 1985-86, Nat. Achievement award 1982, 83, 84, 85, 86, 87, 88, 89, 90, nat. gov. Ind. 1987, v.p. region III 1988, Ind. Honor Realtor award 1982—), Women's Coun. of Realtors (spkr. 1990-94, Mem. of Yr. 1988), Ky. Real Estate Exch., So. Ind. Bd. Realtors (program chmn. 1986-87, bd. dirs., pres. 1988—, Realtor of Yr. 1985, instr. success series 1989-92, Snyder Svc. award 1987, Omega Tau Rho award 1988, excellence in Edn. award 1989), Ind. Assn. Realtors (state dir. 1985—, bd. govs. instr./trainer, spkr. 1989-94, chair bd. govs. 1991), Toastmasters (pres. Steamboat chpt.), Psi Iota Xi. Office: McMichael Properties Inc 23 Arctic Springs Jeffersonville IN 47130-4701

MCMILLAN, ADELL, retired educational administrator; b. Portland, Oreg., June 22, 1933; d. John and Eunice A. (Hoyt) McM. AB in Social Sci., Whitman Coll., 1955; MS in Recreation Mgmt., U. Oreg., 1963. Program dir. Erb Meml. Union, U. Oreg., Eugen, 1955-68; program cons. Willard Straight Hall, Cornell U., Ithaca, N.Y., 1966-67; assoc. dir. Erb Meml. Union, U. Oreg., Eugene, 1968-75, dir., 1975-91, dir. emeritus, 1992—. Editor, co-author: College Unions: Seventy-Five Years, 1989; interviewer, editor oral history interviews, 1978, 92-94, 96; author: A Common Ground--Erb Memorial Union 1950-2000. Bd. dirs. United Way, Lane County, Oreg., 1976-83, 87-97, 98—,pres., 1982-83, 88-90; commr. Eugene City Planning Commn., 1992—; mem. Hist. Rev. Bd., 1992—; mem. Tree Commn., 1992-93; bd. dirs., treas., 1994-95, Eugene Opera Co., 1992-2000; bd. dirs. Eugene Pub. Libr. Found., 2002—; pres.-elect City Club of Eugene, 2003—. Named Woman of Yr. Lane County Coun. Orgns., Eugene, Oreg., 1985; re-named Erb Meml. Union Art Gallery, U. Oreg. as Adell McMillan Art Gallery, 1998. Mem. Assn. Coll. Unions-Internat. (v.p. 1977-80, pres. 1981-82, Butts-Whiting award 1987, hon. 1992, editor Vets. newsletter, 1993-2000), Zonta Club of Eugene, Zonta Internat. (pres. 1984-86, dist. treas. 1990-92, 92-94), Emerald Valley Women's Golf Club (pres. 1995). Democrat. Episcopalian. Avocations: golf, reading. Office: 55 W 39th Ave Eugene OR 97405-3344 E-mail: adellmcm@oregon.uoregon.edu.

MCMILLAN, BETTIE BARNEY, English language educator; b. Fayetteville, N.C., Mar. 14, 1941; d. Booker T. and Sarah Estelle (Barney) McM.; children: Gregory L., Kenneth A., Ronald D., Pamela M., Deirdre Y., Michael A. BA in Psychology/Sociology, Meth. Coll., 1978. Program supr. Adminstrv. Office of the Cts.-Guardian Ad Litem Program, Raleigh, N.C.; English instr. Cmty. Coll., Fayetteville, N.C.; info. specialist, case mgr. Big Bros./Big Sisters, Fayetteville. Author: A Plea For Love, 1995, The Language of Love (award of merit 2002), Fires of Passion (Pres. award for literary excellence, Nat. Authors Registry, 2003), (song) Love Is Waiting, 2003, (poems) I Am Love, Language of Love, 2002; contbr. Celebrations of Honor: a collection of poems and essays from around the world, 2003. Leader, nat. officer United Order of Tents, Norfolk, Va., 1982-92; vol. N.C. Guardian Ad Litem, Raleigh, 1992—; mem. Atlanta Com. for Olympic Games, 1996. Recipient Copyright award plaque Copywright award, 1996, Poet Merit award Nat. Libr. Congress, 1995, Shakespeare Trophy of Excellence, 2002, Poet of Yr. Medallion, 2002, Pres. award for Lit. Excellence, 2003. Mem. Internat. Soc. of Poets (Disting. mem., 1995-96, Poets Choice award 1995), Sigma Omega Chi. Baptist. Avocations: reading, writing, literary works, community volunteer, gardening, travel. Home: 5509 Ramshorn Dr Fayetteville NC 28303-2736

MCMILLEN, JULIE LYNN, English, speech educator; b. Olney, Ill., Dec. 19, 1954; d. Glenn Everett and Carol Marie (Blood) Bowen; m. Robert Nelson McMillen, June 5, 1976. BA, Ea. Ill. U., 1976, MA, 1980. Tchr. English, speech Cmty. Unit Sch. Dist. # 10, Bridgeport, Ill., 1976—. Recipient Isabella Coleman award, 1976. Mem. DAR (regent 1984-86, treas. 1990—), Order Ea. Star (Worthy Matron 1982, 85, 89, 92, 97, 2002, 03, grand rep. N.D. 1986-88, grand lectr. 1986—, grand rep. R.I. 1997-98, grand martha 2001), Delta Kappa Gamma (pres. 1996-98, v.p. 1994-96, state music com. 1995-97, 99—). Republican. Avocations: reading, singing, piano, collecting dolls and music boxes. Home: 1106 Willow Dr Lawrenceville IL 62450-2481 Office: Red Hill High Sch 908 Church St Bridgeport IL 62417-1845

MCMILLIAN, MARILYN LINDSEY, elementary educator, health, home economics; b. San Antonio, Feb. 23, 1952; d. Jesse Monroe Jr. and Louise (Ottenhouse) Lindsey; m. Joe Curtis McMillian, Dec. 16, 1978; children: Thomas Lindsey, Tyler Remington. BS in Edn. with Kindergarten Edn., Southwest Tex. State U., 1975. Kindergarten tchr. North Forrest Indep. Sch. Dist., Houston, 1976-78, Pearsall (Tex.) Indep. Sch. Dist., 1978-79, Dilley (Tex.) Indep. Sch. Dist., 1979—. Mem. Greater Houston Area Reading Coun., Houston, 1977-78, Gifted and Talented Com., Dilley, 1988-92. Mem. Delta Kappa Gamma (vice pres. 1990-92) Methodist. Avocations: interior decorating, antique collecting, travel. Home and Office: PO Box 192 Dilley TX 78017-0192

MCMORROW, MARGARET MARY (PEG MCMORROW), retired secondary school educator; b. N.Y.C., Dec. 18, 1924; d. Patrick Joseph and Ellen Veronica (Quinn) McIntyre; m. Joseph Patrick McMorrow, Oct. 12, 1948; children: Linda Karen, Robert Michael (dec.), Patrice Ann, Jane Ellen. BS, Queens Coll., 1946; MS in Edn., Hofstra U., 1959. Space controller Am. Airlines Co., N.Y.C., 1946-48; bus. rep. N.Y. Telephone Co., N.Y.C., 1948-52; tchr. Elwood Sch. Dist, Huntington, N.Y., 1965-89, ret., 1989. Fellow Elwood Tchrs. Assn., L.I. Scribes, N.Y. State United Tchrs., Mensa; mem. Elwood Ret. Tchrs. Assn., Alpha Lambda Omicron. Roman Catholic. Avocation: calligraphy.

MCMULLEN, DAVID WAYNE, education educator; b. Canton, Ill., Apr. 6, 1957; s. Earl Eugene and Juanita Elaine (Estep) McM.; m. Faye Anne Whitaker, Mar. 28, 1981; 1 child, James Earl. BS, Bradley U., 1980, MS, 1984; PhD, U. Ill., 1989. Cert. sec. tchr., Ill. Tchr. 7th and 8th grade sci. Bartonville (Ill.) Grade Sch., 1980-83; grad. asst., instr. U. Ill., Urbana, 1985-89; instr. Bradley U., Peoria, Ill., 1987-89, assoc. prof. edn., 1989—, dir. Ctr. Rsch. and Svc. Coll. Edn. and Health Scis., 1995-98. Instr. gifted program Bradley U. Inst. for Gifted and Talented Youth, Peoria, 1984-85, 88-2000; computer cons. MicroComputer Cons., Morton, Ill., 1984-85; instr. Computer Terminal, Peoria, 1984; system operator Free Ednl. Electronic Mail, Peoria, 1991-96. Author: (software) Science Fair Success, 1984. Sec. bd. Common Place, Peoria, 1992. Mem. ASCD, NSTA, Internat. Soc. for Tech. in Edn., Phi Delta Kappa, Phi Kappa Phi, Phi Alpha Theta. Mem. Christian Ch. (Disciples Of Christ). Avocations: computers, amateur radio, woodworking. Office: Bradley Univ 1501 W Bradley Ave Peoria IL 61625

MCMULLEN, JENNIFER ANNE, secondary school educator; b. Abilene, Tex., May 16, 1970; d. Robert Milton McMullen, Sr. and Ouida Anne (Mitchell) McMullen. BA cum laude, Harding U., 1992, MEd, 1994. Tchr. Ctrl. Ark. Christian Sch., North Little Rock, 1994—95; instr. First Class Driving Sch., Bossier City, La., 1995—; tchr. for homebound, hospitalized teenagers Caddo Parish Sch. Bd., Shreveport, La., 2001—; tchr. BASE Ctr., Bossier Parish Sch. Bd., La., 2002—. Mem.: ASCAP, Southern Songwriters Guild (sec.). Avocations: singer, songwriter, musician, youth group support team mem.. Personal E-mail: dixiegarden@aol.com.

MCMULLEN, JOHN HENRY, JR., manufacturing company executive, educator; b. Phila., Sept. 9, 1944; s. John Henry and Clara (Johnson) McM.; m. Evelyn Corrine Lawson, July 19, 1964; children: Yolanda, John III, Yvette, Yvonne. BS, Tuskegee U., Ala., 1969; MBA, Anna Maria Coll., 1984; postgrad., New Enb. Sch. Law. Cert. purchasing mgr. Asst. program planner Ingall's Shipbldg., Pascagoula, Miss., 1969-71; indsl. engr. supr. Luken's, Coatesville, Pa., 1971-76; mgr. mfg. engring. Newport News (Va.) Shipbldg., 1976-78; gen. supr. Polaroid Corp., Cambridge, Mass., 1978-85; mfg. mgr. Keene Corp., East Providence, Mass., 1985-86; master scheduler Prime Computer, Natick, Mass., 1987-89; small bus. and small disadvantaged bus. liaison officer GTE Govt. Systems Corp. (now Gen. Dynamics), Needham Heights, Mass., 1989—; mng. small bus. programs Gen. Dynamics, CA Sys., Taunton, Mass., 1999—. Instr. Anna Maria Coll., Paxton, Mass., 1983-86; adv. bd. Purchasing Ctr. Ct.-apptd. spl. advocate Suffolk County Juvenile Ct., Boston, 1983; bd. dirs. Mattapan (Mass.) Cmty. Health Ctr., 1983-93, treas. 1984-86, pres. 1987-91; treas. ADAPT, Inc., Roxbury, Mass., 1986-88, v.p., 1988-89; active Urban League Ea. Mass., 1987-91; pres., founder Alpha Phi Alpha Edn. Found, 1983-87; bd. dirs. Dr. William Price unit Am. Cancer Soc. Mem. Nat. Assn. Purchasing Mgmt. (minority bus. devel. group 1991—, contbr. Purchasing Today mag., Charles J. McDonald Minority Bus. Advocacy of Yr. award 1997), Purchasing Mgmt. Assn. Boston (treas. 1996-97), Inst. Indsl. Engrs., Exec. MBA Assn. Anna Maria Coll. (bd. dirs. 1983-86), Nat. Black MBA Assn. (co-founder, treas. Boston chpt. 1985-87), Afro-Am. Cultural Assn. Sharon (founder), Polaroid Found., Tuskegee Alumni Club (chpt. fin. sec. 1985-96, pres. 1992-93, asst. reginal fin. sec. 1988-90, asst. regional dir. 1985-91, regional dir. 1993-97, Outstanding Alumni award 1988), Tuskegee Nat. Alumni Assn. (bd. dirs.), Elks, Shriners, Alpha Phi Alpha (chpt. pres. 1981-86, Alpha Man of Yr. 1986). Avocations: bowling, racquetball, jogging, chess, motorcycling. Home: 8 Pine St Sharon MA 02067-1616 Office: 400 John Quincy Adams Rd Taunton MA 02780-1069 E-mail: tuskegee@alumnidirector.com., john.mcmullen@gdcas.com.

MCMULLEN, KRISTI KAY, elementary school educator; b. Greenfield, Iowa, July 9, 1962; d. Dennis Ray and Eleanor Kay (Bissell) Tietz; m. Myron Leroy McMullen Jr., June 22, 1985; children: Michael Ryan, Kira Marie. BA in Elem. Edn. and Spl. Edn., U. No. Iowa, 1984; MS in Learning Disabilities, Creighton U., 1992. Jr. high sch. resource tchr. Clarinda (Iowa) Community Sch. Dist., 1984-85; elem. spl. edn. tchr. Lewis Ctrl. Sch. Dist., Council Bluffs, Iowa, 1985-97, 4th grade tchr., 1997—. Mem. social studies dist. com. Lewis Ctrl. Sch. Dist. V.p. Jr. Treynor Women; bd. dirs., bible sch. tchr. United Ch. of Christ. Mem. NEA, Iowa Edn. Assn., Lewis Ctrl. Edn. Assn., Cognitive Coaching, Sat-Ra Temple # 59 Daus. of Nile. Mem. United Ch. of Christ. Avocations: golf, family, children. Home: PO Box 128 Treynor IA 51575-0128 Office: Kreft Elem Sch 3206 Renner Dr Council Bluffs IA 51501-7954

MCMULLIN, ERNAN VINCENT, philosophy educator; b. Donegal, Ireland, Oct. 13, 1924; came to U.S., 1954; s. Vincent Paul and Carmel (Farrell) McM. BSc, Maynooth (Ireland) Coll., 1945, BD, 1948; postgrad. theoretical physics, Dublin Inst. Advanced Studies, 1949-50; BPh, U. Louvain, Belgium, 1951, LPh, 1953, PhD, 1954; DLitt (hon.), Loyola U., Chgo., 1969, Nat. U. Ireland, 1990; PhD (hon.), Maynooth Coll., Ireland, 1995; D Lang. Arts (hon.), Stonehill Coll., 2000; DLaws (hon.), U. Notre Dame, 2002. Ordained priest Roman Catholic Ch., 1949; faculty U. Notre Dame, 1954-57, 59—, assoc. prof. philosophy, 1964, prof. philosophy, 1966-94, prof. emeritus, 1994—, chmn. dept., 1965-72, O'Hara prof. philosophy, 1984-94. Postdoctoral fellow Yale U., 1957-59; vis. prof. U. Minn., 1964-65, U. Cape Town, summers 1972-73, UCLA, 1977, Princeton U., 1991, Yale U., 1992; Cardinal Mercier lectr. U. Louvain, Belgium, 1995, U. Oslo, 1997; mem. exec. bd. Coun. Philos. Studies, 1970-75; chmn. philosophy of sci. div. Internat. Congress Philosophy, 1968, 73; chmn. U.S. Nat. Com. for History and Philosophy of Sci., 1982-84, 86-87. Author: Newton on Matter and Activity, 1978, The Inference That Makes Science, 1992; editor: The Concept of Matter, 1963, Galileo, Man of Science, 1967, The Concept of Matter in Modern Philosophy, 1978, Death and Decision, 1978, Issues in Computer Diagnosis, 1983, Evolution and Creation, 1985, Construction and Constraint: The Shaping of Scientific Rationality; co-editor: (with J.T. Cushing) The Philosophical Consequences of Quantum Theory, 1989, The Social Dimensions of Science, 1992; cons. editor Studies History and Philosophy of Science, 1970-75, 1983—, Brit. Jour. Philos. Sci., 1988—, Perspectives on Science, 1992—, Ency. of the Scientific Revolution, 1994—, Oxford Companion to the History of Science and its Uses, 1998—. Romanell-Phi Beta Kappa Prof. of Philosophy, 1993-94; NSF rsch. grantee Yale U., 1957-59, Cambridge U., 1968-69; vis. rsch. fellow Cambridge U., 1973-74, 83, 87, U. Pitts., 1979; Hon. fellow St. Edmund's Coll., Cambridge. Fellow Am. Acad. Arts and Scis., Internat. Acad. History Sci.; mem. AAAS (chmn. sect. L 1977-78), Am. Cath. Philos. Assn. (pres. 1966-67, Aquinas medal 1981), Philosophy of Sci. Assn. (governing bd. 1969-73, pres. 1980-82), Metaphys. Assn. Am. (exec. coun. 1968-72, pres. 1973-74, Founder's medal 1997), Am. Philos. Assn. (exec. coun. 1977-81, pres. western divsn. 1983-84), History of Sci. Soc. (exec. coun. 1988-92). Address: PO Box 1066 Notre Dame IN 46556-1066

MCMURRY, JOHN EDWARD, chemistry educator; b. N.Y.C., July 27, 1942; s. Edward and Marguerite Ann McMurry; m. Susan Elizabeth Sobuta, Sept. 4, 1964; children: Peter Michael, David Andrew, Paul Matthew. BA, Harvard U., 1964; MA, Columbia U., 1965, PhD, 1967. Prof. chemistry U. Calif., Santa Cruz, 1967-80, Cornell U., Ithaca, N.Y., 1980—. Author: textbooks; assoc. editor: Accounts of Chem. Rsch., 1975—95. Recipient Humboldt Sr. Sci. award, 1987; Sloan Found. fellow, 1969-71; Career awardee NIH, 1975-80. Fellow AAAS; mem. Am. Chem. Soc. Home: 625 Highland Rd Ithaca NY 14850-1411 Office: Cornell Univ Dept Chemistry Baker Lab Ithaca NY 14853 E-mail: jem24@cornell.edu.

MCNAIR, GLORIDINE DELORIS, counseling administrator; b. Climax, Ga., Mar. 9, 1941; d. Love and Fannie McNair. BA, Fla. A&M U., 1962, MA, 1966. Guidance counselor Hillsborough County Bd. of Pub. Instrn., Tampa, Fla., 1963—; social studies tchr. Hills County Bd. of Pub. Instruction, 1963—69. Mem. Carver City Lincoln Gardens Civic Orgn., Tampa, Fla., 1988—96; v.p. Tampa Hills Urban League, 1998—99, pres., Friends of Libr., Tampa, 1996—. Recipient Vol. of Yr. award, Tampa Hills Urban League, 1981, Philantrophic award, 1987. Mem.: NAACP, Hills Counseling Assn. (sec./treas. 1986—89, chmn. awards 1998—99, bd. mem.), Delta Sigma Theta (pres. 1984—88). Democrat. Baptist. Avocations: piano, garage sales, refinishing furniture. Home: 4321 Green Street Tampa FL 33607 Office: 9401 N Blvd Tampa FL 33612

MCNAIRN, PEGGI JEAN, speech pathologist, educator; b. Dallas, Sept. 22, 1954; d. Glenn Alton Harmon and Anna Eugenia (McVay) Hicks; m. Kerry Glen McNairn, Jan. 27, 1979; children: Micah Jay, Nathan Corey. BS in Speech Pathology, Tex. Christian U., 1977, MS in Communications Pathology, 1978; PhD in Edn., Kennedy Western U., 1991. Cert. speech pathologist, mid mgmt., asst. tech. practitioner. Staff speech pathologist, asst. dir. infant program Easter Seal Soc. for Crippled Children and Adults Tarrant County, Ft. Worth, 1978-80; staff speech pathologist, spl. edn. lead tchr. Sherrod Elem. Sch. Arlington (Tex.) Ind. Sch. Dist., 1981-84, secondary speech/lang. specialist, early childhood assessment staff, 1984-89, mem. state forms com., 1985-86, chairperson assessment com., 1986-87; owner, dir. Speech Assocs., 1989—92; cons. augmentative communication Prentke Romich Co., 1992-97; distance learning coord. Edn. Svc. Ctr., Tex. Womens U., 1998—2001; asst. tech. specialist, ednl. cons. Edn. Svc. Ctr., Ft. Worth, 2001—. Adj. prof., clin. supr. Tex. Christian U., Ft. Worth, 1978-79; clin. speech pathologist North Tex. Home Health Assn., Ft. Worth, 1980-92; adj. prof. Tex. Women's Univ., 1997—. Author: Quick Tech Activities for Literacy, 1993, Readable, Repeatable Stories and Activities, 1994, Quick Tech Magic: Music-Based Literacy Activities, 1996, AAC Feature Match Software, 1996, A First Course in Dysphagia, 2001. Chair United Cerebral Palsy Toy Lending Libr., 1989-90; dir. comms. & tech. Easter Seal Soc. for Children & Adults; sunday sch. tchr. 1st United Meth. Ch., Arlington, 1982-87; active South Arlington Homeowners Assn., Arlington, 1985-87; 3rd v.p. Bebensee Elem. PTA. Recipient Outstanding Svc. to Handicapped Am. Biog. Inst., 1989; Cert. of Achievement John Hopkins U. for computing to assist persons with disabilities, 1991. Mem. Internat. U.S. Tex. Socs. for Augmentative and Alternate Comm. (sec. Tex. branch, exec. bd. mem. 1996-98), Neurodevelopmental Assn., Assn. for Curriculum and Supervision, Am. Speech and Hearing Assn., Tex. Speech-Lang.-Hearing Assn., Tex. Speech and Hearing Assn. (task force mem for augmentative comm.) Teaching Tex. Tots Consortium, Tex. Christian U. Speech and Hearing Alumni Assn., Kappa Delta Pi, Alpha Lambda Delta. Democrat. Avocations: doll making, sewing. Home: 4924 Brazoswood Cir Arlington TX 76017-1094 Office: Edn Svc Ctr Region XI 3001 N Fwy Fort Worth TX 76106

MC NALLEN, JAMES BERL, marketing executive; b. Heber Springs, Ark., Feb. 17, 1930; s. George Berl and Sally Lou (Brown) McN.; AB, Columbia, 1951; MBA, N.Y.U., 1960, PhD, 1975; m. Marianne Patricia Kakos, Mar. 4, 1952 (dec. Sept. 1990); children: James Lawrence, Marianne Victoria, Thomas Berl (dec.), John Kennedy. Mktg. asst. Am. Petroleum Inst., N.Y.C., 1954-67, coor. products mktg. 1967-69, asst. dir., div. fin. and acctg., 1969-70; corp. mgr. mktg. research Atlantic Richfield Co., N.Y.C., 1970-71; lectr. bus. adminstrn. Sch. Bus. Adminstrn. U. Conn., Storrs, 1972-75, asst. prof., 1975-76; mktg. research specialist, market research and mktg. div. Office Customer Service Support, Fed. Supply Service, GSA, Washington, 1976-78, mgr. mktg. research Office of Requirements, 1978-82, mgr. forecasting and bus. analysis Office of Mgmt., 1982-84; Mem. U.S. del. U.S.-Saudi Arabian Joint Econ. Commn., Riyadh, 1984-88, mktg. specialist, tng. officer Cen. Supply Mgmt. Devel. Project, 1984-88; spl. asst. commr. Office of Customer Service and Mktg., 1991; chief Program Devel. and Support, Office Transp. Audits, 1992-93, dep. dir. regulations & program developing, 1993—; GSA Fed. Supply Svc., Washingon, 1988—; pres. McNallen Investment Co., Arlington, Va.; ptnr. McNallen Enterprise, Big Spring, Tex.; lectr. mktg. Va. Poly. Inst., Reston, 1976-77, George Mason U., 1977-84, Georgetown U., 1978-80; adj. prof. mgmt. Univ. District Columbia, 1980-84. Mem. planning bd. Twp. of South Brunswick (N.J.), 1966-67; bd. dirs., sec., vice chmn. South Brunswick Mcpl. Utilities Authority, 1966-68; pres. South Brunswick Library Assn., 1965-69; comdg. officer Naval Air Intelligence Res. Unit, Lakehurst, N.J., 1970-71, commdg. officer Naval Investigative Svc. HQ Res. Unit, Washington, 1978-79, inspector gen. Naval Res. Intelligence Area 19, Washington, 1981, dep. area comdr. Co. IVTU, Dist. 19, Washington, 1982. Lt. (jr. gr.) USN, 1951-54, capt. USNR, 1976-87; ret. 1987. Mem. Naval Res. Assn., (pres. Washington chpt. 1978-79, pres. 5th dist. 1979-81, mem. nat. exec. com. 1979-81), Ret. Officers Assn., Naval Order U.S., Mil. Order World Wars, Res. Officers Assn. (exec. v.p. Washington D.C. Nat. Navy chpt. 1982-84), U.S. Naval Inst., Smithsonian Assocs., S. Brunswick Jaycees (pres. 1964-65, state v.p. N.J. State Jaycees 1965-66, named Jr. Chamber Internat. Senator), Ancient Order Hibernians (Chevy Chase, Md.), KC, Wolf Trap Friends, Kennedy Ctr. Friends. Recipient Gold medal Am. Mktg. Assn., 1960. Roman Catholic. Contbr. articles in field to profl. jours. Home: 2 Park Pl Apt 21W Hartford CT 06106-5007 Office: GSA - FSS Office Trans Audits 18th & F St NW Rm G35ffwpa Washington DC 20405-0001

MCNAMARA, BRENDA NORMA, secondary school educator; b. Blackpool, Lancashire, Eng., Aug. 8, 1945; arrived in U.S., 1946; d. Michael James and Nola (Welsby) Jones; m. Michael James McNamara, July 19, 1969. BA in History, Calif. State U., Long Beach, 1967; postgrad., Calif. State U., various campuses, 1967—. Cert. secondary tchr. and lang. devel. specialist Calif. Tchr. history West HS, Torrance, Calif., 1968—, dept. chair, 1989-99, 2000—. Cons. Golden State Exam. in History Calif. State Dept. Edn., 1998; state del. NEA Annual Meeting, 2000, 02, local del., 03; cons. in field. Co-author: (book) World History, 1988. Western Internat. Studies Consortium grantee, 1988. Mem.: Am. Hist. Assn., Nat. Coun. Social Studies, Nat. Tchrs. Assn., So. Calif. Coun. Social Studies, Torrance Tchrs. Assn. (bd. dirs. 1992—), Calif. Coun. Social Studies, Calif. Tchrs. Assn. Avocations: travel, theater, mystery reading, gourmet cooking. Office: West H S 20401 Victor St Torrance CA 90503-2255

MCNAMARA, TIMOTHY JAMES, mathematics educator; b. Buffalo, June 24, 1952; s. Vincent Michael and Peggy Jo (Matthews) McN.; m. Julie Ann McCready, Aug. 25, 1979; children: James Vincent, Lucille Ann. BA in Math., Niagara U., 1975; EdM, SUNY, Buffalo, 1979, MBA, 1984; cert., Sch. Adminstrv. & Supr., 1997; PhD in Math., Pacific Western U., 1998. Tchr. Williamsville East High Sch., East Amherst, N.Y., 1975-84, Maryvale Sr. High Sch., Cheektowaga, N.Y., 1984-86; tchr. gifted math. program SUNY, 1987-90; coord. math. The Nichols Sch ., Buffalo, 1991-93; K-12 math. supr. West Irondequoit Schs., Rochester, 1993-2000; asst. prof. math. Monroe C.C., Rochester, 2000—. Lectr. in field. Author: Italics, 1997, Key Concepts in Mathematics, 2003; faculty editor student math. jour. The Nth Degree; contbr. articles to profl. jours. Recipient N.Y. State Presdl. award for Excellence in Secondary Math. Teaching, 1993, finalist, 1990, 91. Mem. Nat. Coun. Tchrs. Math., Assn. Math. Tchrs. N.Y. State (exec. bd. dirs. 1992-94), N.Y. State Assn. Math. Suprs., Assn. Math Tchrs. Rochester Area (exec. bd. dirs. 1993—, v.p. 1998-99, pres. 1999-2001), Phi Delta Kappa. Avocations: gardening, travel, running. Home: 1093 Marigold Dr Webster NY 14580-8765 Office: Monroe CC 228 E Main St Rochester NY 14604 E-mail: tmcnamara@monroecc.edu.

MCNAMARA-NEEDLER, TAMARA SUE, elementary education educator; b. Marion, Ind., Apr. 30, 1959; d. Thomas H. and Margaret L. (Huber) McNamara; m. Douglas Gilbert, Aug. 27, 1977 (div. Jan. 1992); children: Ike, Dominice; m. Brian Needler, July 31, 1993. BS, Ball State U., 1989, MA in Edn., 1992. Cert. tchr., Ind. 2d grade tchr. Columbian Elem. Sch., Bluffton, Ind., 1989-91, East Side Elem. Sch., Bluffton, 1991-93, Bluffton Harrison Mid. Sch., 1993-94; prin. Pennville Elem., Portland, Ind., 1994-95, Gen. Shanks Elem. Sch., Portland, 1995—. Author: First Grade in Review: Getting a Head Start on Second Grade, 1993. Bd. dirs. Jr. Achievement of Wells County, Bluffton. Recipient Sallie Mae Outstanding First Yr. Tchr. award Student Loan Mktg. Assn., 1989-90. Fellow Optimist Internat., Pi Lambda Theta, Phi Delta Kappa; mem. Golden Key Nat. Honor Soc. Avocations: writing, gardening, painting, hiking, fishing. Home: 2613 W 900 S Poneto IN 46781-9709

MCNAMARA-RINGEWALD, MARY ANN THÉRÈSE, artist, educator; b. Hempstead, N.Y., Apr. 11, 1935; d. William George Schlichtig and Alice Agnes Rakeman; m. Raymond Anthony McNamara, Apr. 22, 1957 (div. Sept. 1975); children: Thomas William, Raymond Gerard, William Daniel, Peter Joseph, James Francis Jude; m. John Drew Ringewald, Feb. 17, 1984. BS, Fordham U., 1957, Barbizon Sch., NYC, 1953; M in Studio Arts, Adelphi U., 1972; postgrad., Parsons Sch. Design, 1973-75; student, Art Students League, N.Y.C., 1973-74; postgrad., Goddard Coll., Calif., 1986-87; student, Progoff Intensive Jour. Program, N.Y.C., 1999—, Cape Cod Sch., 1993. Cert. elem. edn. and art N.Y. Elem. sch. art tchr. Dept. Edn., Freeport, N.Y., 1957-58, Farmingdale, NY, 1967; jr. and h.s. art tchr. Massapequa (N.Y.) Sch. Dist., 1970-90; owner, pres. South Shore Creative Arts Ctr., Massapequa, 1975; pvt. art tchr. various locations, 1970-90. Illustrator Doubleday, Inc., N.Y.C.; art advisory bd. Chesapeake Coll, Wye Mills, Md., 1995— (lectr., 1998, 99, 2000), Snow Princess, Fordham U., 1954; symposium coord. Hofstra U., N.Y.; lectr. Naples Philharm., 1992; judge, lectr. in field; architectural designer, M.E, 1977, M.D., 1988-, F.L., 1990. One-woman shows include Fordham U., 1954, Andonia Gallery, Massepequa, N.Y., 1974, Isis Gallery, Islip, N.Y., 1974, For the Birds, Salisbury, Conn., 1978, Harguen Gallery, Pt. Jefferson, N.Y., 1979, Adelphi U., Garden City, N.Y., 1992, Wohlfarth Gallery, Washington, 1994-95, SpanBauer Gallery Naples, Fla., 1996, Naples Philharmonic, Naples, Fla., 1992, Gallery 44, Millbrook, N.Y., 1997-98; groups shows: Acad. of Arts, Easton, Md., 1993. works exhibited at Kennedy Gallery, Key West, Fla., 1997-99, Chesapeake Coll., Md., 1998-99; represented in pvt. collections General Motors, The Benedictines, Prudential Life, St. Michael's Maritime Mus., Yupo Corp., Japan; illustrator: From a Lighthouse Window, Chesapeake Bay Maritime Mus., 1992 (Best of Balt. Book award 1993, Book award Tabasco N.Y.C. 1994); original poetry published. Pres. AAUW, L.I., 1969-71; bd. dirs. L.I. (N.Y.) Art Tchrs. Assn., 1973-76; docent U.S. Fish and Wildlife Svc., Washington, 1994-95; mem. Am. Farmland Trust; vol. Delmarva Chpt., ARC, 2001-. Recipient Nat. Middle Sch. Art Tchrs. award, Nassau County Middle Sch. Art Tchrs. Assn., 1988, Very Spl. Arts Festival for Handicapped, 1977, Festival of Creation, Diocese of RVC, 1975, Catalyst, 1975; named to Outstanding Young Women of Am., 1969; works featured in Nat. Anthology of Poetry, 1953. Mem. Internat. Welcome Fla. Assn. Series (lectr. 1994—), Nat. League Am. Pen Women (founder, pres. Naples, Fla. br. 1995—), Nat. Gallery Art (copyist 1993—), Order of the Benedictines (oblate 1990—), Working Artists Forum (Easton, Md.), NY State Art Tchrs. Assn. (bd. mem. 1972-80). Roman Catholic. Avocations: horticulture, travel, illuminations, poetry. Address: Marafour 5493 Anderby Dr Royal Oak MD 21662 Office: Marafour Studio 27098 Del Ln Bonita Springs FL 34135-4409

MCNEIL, BARBARA JOYCE, radiologist, educator; b. Cambridge, Mass., Feb. 11, 1941; d. Archibald Pius and Katherine (Joyce) McNeil. AB, Emmanuel Coll., 1962; MD, Harvard U., 1966, PhD, 1972. Diplomate Am. Bd. Nuc. Medicine. Intern Mass. Gen. Hosp., Boston, 1966—67, resident in nuclear medicine, 1971—73; prof. radiology and clin. epidemiology Harvard Med. Sch. and Brigham & Women's Hosp., Boston, 1983—, dir. ctr. for cost effective care, 1980—93; chmn. dept., Ridley Watts prof. health care policy Harvard Med. Sch., 1988—. Chmn. Blue Cross-Mass. Hosp. Assn. Fund for Coop. Innovation, 1981—87; mem. Prospective Payment Assessment Commn., 1983—91; mem. nat. adv. coun. Agy. for Health Care Policy, Rsch. and Evaluation, 1991—96. Editor: Critical Issues in Medical Technology, 1982; contbr. articles to profl. jours. Fellow: AAAS, Am. Coll. Nuc. Physicians (Presdl. award 1995); mem.: Soc. Nuc. Medicine, Am. Coll. Radiology, Inst. Medicine (coun. 1991—), Am. Acad. Arts and Scis. Office: Harvard Med Sch Dept Health Care Policy 180 Longwood AveRm 202-A Boston MA 02115-5821

MCNEIL, HELEN JO CONNOLLY, nursing educator, public health administrator; b. Olympia, Wash., June 15, 1925; d. James Ambrose and Corinne Marie (Bordeaux) Connolly; m. Robert Phillip McNeil, Aug. 16, 1947; children: Sheryl Ann Andrews, Robert John, Maureen Connolly McNeil, Kevin Charles. BSN, Seattle Coll., 1947; MSN, U. Wash., 1961, postgrad., 1974-80. RN Wash., S.C., Tex., Va., cert. pub. health nurse, 1962. Clinic nurse Schutt Clinic, Bremerton, Wash., 1947-49; staff nurse Providence Hosp., Seattle, 1950-60, Overlake Hosp., Bellevue, Wash., 1961-62; pub. health nurse Seattle King County Health Dept. and Vis. Nurse Svc., 1962-64, pub. health nurse supr., 1964-65, assoc. dir. pub. health nursing and vis. nurse svc., 1965-70, health planning and evaluation specialist, 1970-73, adminstr. S.E. dist., 1973-78, adminstr. Ctrl. dist., 1979-81, adminstr. N. dist., 1981-84, dir. nursing rsch., 1984-85; lectr. Sch. Nursing U. Wash., Seattle, 1985-87; mem. faculty S. Puget Sound C.C., Olympia, 1987-88; vis. faculty Sch. Nursing Clemson (S.C.) U., 1988; instr. coll. nursing allied health U. Tex., El Paso, 1988-90; dir. pub. health nursing Commonwealth Va., Richmond, 1990-93; lectr. Sch. Nursing Seattle U., 1995; cons. Seattle, Seaview, Wash., 1995—. Mem. panel in nursing edn. Am. Assn. Colls. of Nursing, 1985—87; adj. assoc. prof. Sch. Pub. Health U. N.C., Chapel Hill, 1980—92; adj. asst. prof. U. Wash. Sch. Nursing, 1965—85; rev. com. nursing census USPHS, 1970—72; health care cons., 1976; lectr. Congress on Nutrition, Rio de Janeiro, 1978. Author: Feasting on a Moveable Island, 1980, Reaching Out, 1998; contbr. articles to profl. jours., chpts. to books. Mem. task force Seattle Health Policy, 1981, Seattle 2000 Commn., 1973; lectr. Internat. Congress Social Psychiatry, Athens, 1974; with Project Hope Internat. Approaches in Health Care of Elderly, Milwood, Va., 1983, 84; co-project dir. occupl. health con. edn. for cmty. nurses divsn. nursing U. Wash., 1983-86; mem. ARC Disater Team, Seattle, 1995-97, Parent and Home Health Bd., Richmond, Va., 1990-93. With U.S. cadet nursing corps USPHS, 1943-47. Stress Rsch. grantee Heath Resources Adminstrn., 1974; W. K. Kellog Found. grantee U. Tex., El Paso, 1990, grantee U. Wash., 1983-86; recipient Nursing Adminstrn. recognition award Jour. Nursing Adminstrn., 1993. Fellow: APHA (nursing sect. pres. 1992—93, Ruth B. Freeman Disting. Career award 1998); mem.: Assn. State and Territorial Dirs. Nursing (emeritus 1990—), Seattle Mgmt. Assn. (pres. 1976, Disting. Adminstrv. Svc. award City of Seattle 1976), Wash.

State Pub. Health Assn. (pres. 1976—77, Adminstrv. Svc. award 1975), Assn. Cmty. Health Nurse Educators (founder, pres. 1985), Seattle U. Alumni (mem. nursing adv. bd. 1993—96, Cmty. Svc. Alumni award 1992), Alpha Tau Delta, Sigma Theta Tau (internat. rsch. conf. Seoul, South Korea 1984). Avocations: gardening, travel, writing, cooking, paddocks for six hourses. Home and Office: PO Box 173 Seaview WA 98644-0173

MCNEMAR, DONALD WILLIAM, academic administrator; b. Wilmington, Ohio, June 1, 1943; s. Robert Arthur and Kathryn (Hunt) McN.; m. Britta Schein, Aug. 18, 1968; children— Heather Osborn, Galen Rebecca. BA, Earlham Coll., Richmond, Ind., 1965; PhD, Princeton U., 1971. Asst. prof., then asso. prof. govt. Dartmouth Coll., 1970-81, assoc. dean faculty social scis., 1978-81; headmaster Phillips Acad., Andover, Mass., 1981-94; cons. Conflict Mgmt. Group, Cambridge, Mass., 1994-96; pres. Guilford Coll., Greensboro, N.C., 1996—. Regional adv. bd. BayBank, 1981-94. Mem. exec. com. N.H. Coun. World Affairs, 1975-81; com. mem. Quaker office UN, 1978-82; trustee Sch. Yr. Abroad, 1981-94, Prep for Prep, 1988-94, Earlham Coll., 1989-95, Northfield Mount Hermon Sch., 1994—. Danforth fellow, 1965-69 Office: Guilford Coll 5800 W Friendly Ave Greensboro NC 27410-4108

MCNIEL, NORBERT ARTHUR, retired educator; b. Moody, Tex., Dec. 22, 1914; s. Arthur A. and Gertrude (Burt) McN.; B.S., Tex. A. and M. Coll., 1935, M.Ed., 1952, Ph.D., 1955; m. Jane Edith Richter, Aug. 13, 1939; children— Rebecca McNiel McAulay, Ruth McNiel Garner, Fred, Larkin. Tchr. high sch., Alvin, Tex., 1935-41; supr. McLennan County Vocat. Sch., Waco, Tex., 1946-51; adviser fgn. programs Tex. A. and M. Coll. System, Pakistan, 1955-56; mem. faculty Tex. A. and M. U., 1957-79, prof. genetics, 1972-79, prof. emeritus, 1979— . Served to lt. col. AUS, 1941-46. Decorated Bronze Star; recipient Disting. Faculty award Assn. Former Students Tex. A. and M. U., 1964. Mem. Am. Legion (post comdr. 1946-50), China-Burma-India Vets. Assn. (basha comdr. 1982-83, state dept. chaplain 1986—). Mem. Ch. of Christ. Club: Kiwanis (lt. gov. div. 9 T-0 dist. 1977-78). Home: 12068 Spring Valley Rd Moody TX 76557-4006

MCNULLY, LYNNETTE LARKIN, elementary education educator; b. Iowa City, Iowa, Jan. 22, 1966; d. Ernest F. and Karen (Schaeferle) Larkin; m. William S. McNully, May 14, 1988; children: Bronwyn, Rachel. BA in English, U. Okla., 1987; MEd in Early Childhood Edn., East Tex. State U., 1994. Cert. tchr., Tex. Pre-kindergarten, kindergarten and 1st grade tchr. Dallas Pub. Schs., 1989—98; 1st grade and reading recovery tchr. Lancaster (Tex.) Pub. Schs., 1998—. Founding mem. site-based mgmt. coun. Arlington Park Sch., 1994-96. Vol. North Texas Irish Festival, Dallas, 1992, On the Wing Again, Ferris, Tex., 1993-97. Named Tchr. of Yr., Arlington Park Sch., Dallas, 1992. Elem. Tchr. of Yr., Lancaster Ind. Sch. Dist., 2002; Write, Right! grantee Dallas Jr. League, 1993. Mem. Nat. Assn. for Edn. of Young Children, Reading Recovery Coun. N.Am., PTA (exec. bd. 1993-96), Phi Beta Kappa. Avocations: needlecrafts, hiking, genealogy, hammered dulcimer.

MCNULTY, CAROL JEANNE, elementary education educator; b. Alton, Ill., July 12, 1936; d. Robert Waldemore and Jessie Adele (Scheldt) Fensterman; m. Thomas Wayne McNulty, June 9, 1957; children: Brian Munro, Timothy Robert, Kevin Wayne. BS in Edn., Ill. State U., 1957, MS in Edn., 1967. Cert. tchr., Ill. 1st grade tchr. Bloomington (Ill.) Pub. Schs., 1957-67, remedial reading tchr., 1968-73; instr. reading practicum Ill. State U., Normal, 1972-73, instr. children's lit., 1973-78; 2d grade tchr. Epiphany Sch., Normal, 1978—. Summer sch. tchr. grades 1 and 2 Bloomington Pub. Schs., 1985-88, mem. adv. coun., 1973-76, mem. curriculum coun., 1975-78; part-time assoc. Gingerbread House Ednl. Toystore, Bloomington, 1989—. Leader Cub Scouts, Bloomington, 1972-74; tchr. Wesley Meth. Ch., Bloomington, 1972-77, substitute tchr., 1989-92. Golden Jubilee scholar PTA, 1953-57. Mem. Ill. Reading Coun., Tri County Reading Assn., Delta Kappa Gamma (com. chair, recording sec. 1960—). Avocations: reading, travel, crafts, antiquing. Home: 7 Charles Pl Bloomington IL 61701-1803

MCNULTY, JOHN KENT, lawyer, educator; b. Buffalo, Oct. 13, 1934; s. Robert William and Margaret Ellen (Duthie) McN.; m. Linda Conner, Aug. 20, 1955 (div. Feb. 1977); children: Martha Jane, Jennifer, John K. Jr.; m. Babette B. Barton, Mar. 23, 1978 (div. May 1988). AB with high honors, Swarthmore Coll., 1956; LL.B., Yale U., 1959. Bar: Ohio 1961, U.S. Supreme Ct. 1964. Law clk. Justice Hugo L. Black, U.S. Supreme Ct., Washington, 1959-60; vis. prof. Sch. Law U. Tex., summer 1960; assoc. Jones, Day, Cockley & Reavis, Cleve., 1960-64; prof. law U. Calif., Berkeley, 1964-91, Roger J. Traynor prof. law, 1991—2002, Roger J. Traynor prof. emeritus, 2002—. Of counsel Baker and McKenzie, San Francisco, 1974-75; acad. visitor London Sch. Econs., 1985, Cambridge U., 1994, U. Edinburgh, 1994; vis. fellow Wolfson Coll., Cambridge, 1994, U. Innsbruck, 1996, Trinity Coll., Dublin, 1997; vis. prof. Yale U., U. Tex., U. Leiden, U. Tilburg, U. Tokyo, U. San Diego, others; lectr. univs. Cologne, Hamburg, Hitotsubashi, Kansei, Keio, Kyoto, London, Munich, Seoul, Tokyo, Tilburg, Amsterdam, Rotterdam, Vienna Econ., Tohoku, Tübingen, Waseda, Toronto, Queens, Jefferson, Leuven; mem. adv. bd. Tax Mgmt. Author: Federal Income Taxation of Individuals, 6th edit., 1999, Federal Estate and Gift Taxation, (with McCouch)6th edit., 2003, Federal Income Taxation of S Corporations, 1992; (with Westin & Beck) Federal Income Taxation of Business Enterprises, 1995, 2d edit., 1999; mem. bd. overseers Berkeley Jour. Internat. Law. Guggenheim fellow, 1977 Mem. ABA, Am. Law Inst. (life), Internat. Fiscal Assn. (coun. U.S. br.), Order of Coif, Phi Beta Kappa. Home: 1176 Grizzly Peak Blvd Berkeley CA 94708-1741 Office: U Calif Sch Law 422 Boalt Hl Berkeley CA 94720-7200 E-mail: mcnultyj@law.berkeley.edu.

MCNULTY, ROBERTA JO, educational administrator; b. Cin., July 17, 1945; d. Edward Norman and Ruth Marcella (Glass) Stuebing; children: Meredith Corinne, Brian Edward, Stephen Barrett. BS in Edn., U. Cin., 1967; MA in Edn., Coll. of Mount St. Joseph, 1989; PhD in Ednl. Adminstrn. and Supervision, Bowling Green State U., 1993. Cert. Pathwise trainer, profl. devel. coord. Elem. tchr. St. Mary Sch., Urbana, Ohio, 1968, Urbana (Ohio) City Schs., 1968-70, middle sch. tchr., 1970-71; off-campus liaison Mt. St. Joseph Coll., 1987-89; adj. faculty Bowling Green State U., 1990—; gen. edn. supr., testing coord. curriculum devel. Northwest Ohio Ednl. Svc. Ctr., Wauseon, Ohio, 1992—; tech. cons. Regional Profl. Devel. Ctr., 1995—. Lamaze instr. Scioto Meml. Illustrated Lamaze Edn., Portsmouth, Ohio, 1983-84, Tiffin (Ohio) Childbirth Edn. Assn., 1984-87; edn. symposium com. chair Project Discovery, 1995-96; proficiency test rev. com. Ohio Dept. Edn., 1993—. Grad. editor Am. Secondary Edn., 1989-92. Mem. sch. bd. St. Mary Sch., Urbana, 1971-75; mem. parent adv. com. Wheelersburg (Ohio) Local Schs., 1978-84; mem. parents coun. U. Evansville, 1990-93; exec. dir. Am. Cancer Soc., Tiffin, Ohio, 1985; treas. Parents' Boosters Club, Portsmouth YMCA, 1979-84; chmn. Y-Wives com. Tiffin-Cmty. YMCA, 1984-87; mem. Archbold (Ohio) Teen Issues Adv. Com., 1995-96. Recipient Doctoral fellowship Bowling Green State U., 1989-92, Svc. Appreciation award Cub Scouts, 1990-92. Mem. ASCD, Ednl. Leadership Assn., N.W. Ohio Assn. for Supervision and Curriculum Devel., Ohio Sch. Suprs. Assn., Ohio Coun. Tchrs. English Language Arts, Assn. Tchr. Educators, Ohio Assn. Tchr. Educators (nat. del.), Phi Delta Kappa. Office: Northwest Ohio Ednl Svc Ctr 602 S Shoop Ave Wauseon OH 43567-1712

MCNULTY-MAJORS, SUSAN ROSE, special education administrator; b. Fargo, N.D., Oct. 5, 1944; d. Leo G. McNulty and Jane Lyon (McDonald) McNulty-Schmallen; d. Herbert G. Schmallen (stepfather); m. B. Joseph Majors II. BS, N.D. State U., 1966; MA, U. Mich., 1969. Lic. tchr., Mass., Minn.; lic. ind. clin. social worker, alcohol and drug counselor. Tchr. sci. Incarnation Sch., Mpls., 1966-67; tchr. English George Daly Jr. High Sch., Flint, Mich., 1967-68; tchr. New Boston (Mich.) Elem. Sch., 1969-70; tchr. home econs. Newton (Mass.) Jr. High Sch., 1970-73; program adminstr. Bell Hill Recovery Ctr., Wadena, Minn., 1973-80, exec. dir., 1980-85; coord. emotionally and behavior disordered edn. Wadena Pub. Schs. TOW Spl. Edn. Coop., 1985-94; dir. spl. edn. PAWN Spl. Edn. Coop., Park Rapids, Minn., 1994-95; educator, cons. emotional/behavioral disorders Northland High, Remer, Minn., 1995—; therapist Neighborhood Counseling, Wadena, Minn., 1995—; emotional/behavioral disorders educator, dir. spl. edn. Remer-Longville Dist. 118, Remer, Minn., 1996—. Mem. Wadena Tech. Adv. Bd., 1978-2000. Mem. adv. bd. Todd-Wadena Cmty. Corrections, Long Prairie, Minn., 1975-2003, chair, 1997; mem. Woodview adv. bd., 1990—; mem. fund adminstrn. bd. Ctrl. Minn. Initiative, 1996-99; mem. diversity adv. coun. Minn. Dept. Children Families and Learning, 2002-03. Fresh Air Camp fellow U. Mich., 1968; recipient Ashland Oil Golden Apple Achievement award. Roman Catholic. Avocations: sailing, biking, reading. Home: 843 7th St SW Wadena MN 56482-1934 Office: Northland High Remer MN 56672

MCNUTT, MARGARET H. HONAKER, secondary school educator; b. W.Va., July 7, 1935; d. Vanus Jerome and M. Montague (Humphrey) Honaker; m. Alfred Dudley McNutt; children: Mary Margaret McNutt Sirchia, Marilyn Diane McNutt Furubotten. BS, Concord Coll., 1957; MS, Va. Poly. Inst. and State U., 1965. Tchr. Mercer County Schs., Bluefield, W.Va., 1957-63; tchr., chair dept. L.A. Unified Sch. Dist., 1964-99; ret., 1999. Supr. student tchg. secondary edn. Calif. State U., Northridge. Advisor Future Bus. Leaders Am., 1981-91. Grantee State of Calif., 1975; named Faculty Role Model, Calif. Assn. CPAs, 1988, L.A. chpg., 1988. Mem. NEA, DAR, United Tchrs. L.A., Calif. Tchrs. Assn., United Daus. of Confederacy, Order Ea. Star, Sigma Sigma Sigma. Presbyterian. Avocations: writing, reading, tennis, dancing, painting. Home: 8032 Sale Ave West Hills CA 91304-3719 E-mail: NHMcNutt@aol.com.

MCPARTLAND, JAMES MICHAEL, university official; b. N.Y.C., Sept. 26, 1939; s. James J. and Helen M. (Leddy) McP. BS, Cornell U., 1961, MS, 1963; PhD, Johns Hopkins U., 1968. Rschr. U.S. Office Edn., Washington, 1965-67, U.S. Commn. Civil Rights, Washington, 1967-68; asst. dir. Ctr. Social Orgn. Schs., Johns Hopkins U., Balt., 1968-75, co-dir., 1976-94; dir., 1994—. Co-author: Equality of Educational Opportunity, 1966, Encyclopedia of Educational Research, 1992, Review of Research in Education, 1993; co-editor: Violence in Schools, 1977, Comprehensive Urban School Reform, 2002. Mem. Am. Ednl. Rsch. Assn., Am. Sociol. Assn., Am. Statis. Assn. Democrat. Roman Catholic. Avocation: music. Home: 1102 S Streeper St Baltimore MD 21224-4873 Office: Johns Hopkins U CSOS 3003 N Charles St Ste 200 Baltimore MD 21218-3888 E-mail: jmcpartland@csos.jhu.edu.

MCPARTLAND, PATRICIA ANN, health educator and administrator; b. Passaic, N.J. d. Daniel and Josephine McP. BA, U. Mo., 1971; MCRP, MS in Preventive Medicine, Ohio State U., 1975; EdD in Higher and Adult Edn., Columbia U., 1988; cert. distance edn., Tex. A&M U., 2000, cert. distance edn. web pub. cert., 2001. Cert. health edn. specialist, distance edn. web pub., grants specialist; workforce devel. profl. Sr. health planner Merrimack Valley HSA, Lawrence, Mass., 1977—79; planning cons./adminstr. Children's Hosp., Boston, 1979—80; exec. dir. Nat. Assn. for Alternatives in Workforce Devel., Inc., Marion, Mass., 1980—. V.p., cons. New Bedford (Mass.) Cmty. Health Ctr, 1993—94; chmn. edn. and tng. com. Health and Human Svc. Coalition, 1988—89; mem. project expert panel Office of Minority Health, 1997—2003; mem. New Eng. Regional Minority Health Conf. Com., 1997—99; vis. lectr. Bridgewater State Coll.; lectr. in field; project expert panel Office Minority Health's Culturally and Linguistically Appropriate Svcs.; mem. New Eng. Regional Minority Health Conf. Com., 2001—03. Mem. editl. bd. Jour. Healthcare Edn. and Tng., 1989-93; author: Promoting Health in the Workplace, 1991; reviewer Qualitative Health Rsch. Jour.; contbr. articles to profl. jours. Vol. spkr. March of Dimes Found., Wareham, Mass., 1992-93; coll.-wide vocat. Cape Cod C.C., Hyannis, Mass., 1989—; planning adv. 2nd Internat. Symposium, Pasco, Wash., 1992; v.p. New Bedford chpt. Am. Cancer Soc., 1985-90. Recipient award Excellence in Continuing Edn. Nat. AHEC Ctr. Dirs. Assn., 1994, 95, 96, 97, Sec.'s awards for Outstanding Progam in Community Health, Nat. Cancer Inst., Washington, 1990. Mem.: APHA, Nat. Assn. Workforce Devel. Profls. (bd. dirs.), Nat. Planning Conf. (mem. com. 1984—87), Southeastern Mass. Health Planning (bd. dirs., sec. 1982—87), Inst. for Disease Prevention (steering com. 1982—). Avocations: writing, acting, dance, theatre, travel, hiking. Home: PO Box 1116 Marion MA 02738-0020 Office: Southeastern Mass AHEC PO Box 69 2 Spring St Marion MA 02738-1519 E-mail: pmcpartland@comcast.net., smahec@tiac.net.

MCPEAK, ALLAN, career services director, educator, lawyer, consultant; b. Hot Springs, Ark., Oct. 1, 1938; s. Kenneth L. and Dorothy (Whiteman) McPeak; m. Judith L. Mathison, Oct. 26, 1973. BA, U. Fla., 1960, JD, 1965; MS, Nova U., 1984; PhD, Fla. State U., 1987, MS in Instrnl. Sys., 1994. Bar: Fla. 1965, U.S. Supreme Ct. 1980. Sole practice, Naples, Fla., 1965—85; asst. dir. The Career Ctr. Fla. State U., 1987, assoc. dir. The Career Ctr., 1989; dir. career svcs. U. South Ala., Mobile, 1994—. Cons. in human rels., orgnl. devel. and career devel., Tallahassee, 1984—94, Mobile, 1994—; pres. Lawyers Abstract Svc., Naples, 1978—80; organizer Marine Savs. and Loan, Naples, 1980—81. Contbr. articles to profl. jours. With U.S. Army, 1960—63. Mem.: Fla. Bar Assn., Ala. Assn. Colls. and Employers, So. Assn. Colls. and Employers, Nat. Assn. Colls. and Employers, Blue Key, Pi Sigma Alpha.

MCPHAIL, JOANN WINSTEAD, writer, publisher, art dealer; b. Trenton, Fla., Feb. 17, 1941; d. William Emerson and Donna Mae (Crawford) Winstead; m. James Michael McPhail, June 15, 1963; children: Angela C. McPhail Morris, Dana Denise McPhail Gaizutis, Whitney Gold McPhail Casso. Student, Fla. So. Coll., 1959-60, St. John's River Jr. Coll., Palatka, Fla., 1960-61, Houston (Tex.) C.C. With Jim Walter Corp., Houston, 1961-62; receptionist, land lease sec. Oil and Gas Property Mgmt. Inc., Houston, 1962-63; sec. to mng. atty. State Farm Ins. Co., Houston, 1963-64; saleswoman, decorator Oneil-Anderson, Houston, 1973; sec. Law Offices of Ed Christensen, Houston, 1980-82; advt. mgr. Egalitarian Houston (Tex.) C.C. Systems, 1981; fashion display artist, 1985-86; entrepreneur, writer, art agt. Golden Galleries and Antiques, Houston, 1990-95; owner, property mgr. APT Investments, 1994-98; lyricist, publisher Anna Gold Classics, 1995—, writer song lyrics, 1996—. Freelance writer, photographer: Elegance of Needlepoint, 1970, S.W. Art Mag., A Touch of Greatness, 1973, Sweet 70's Anthology, The Budding of Tomorrow, 1974 (award); columnist, photographer: Egalitarian: Names Can be Symbols, Design Your Wall Covering, Student Profile, 1981, National Library of Poetry, Fireworks (award), 1995; contbr. poetry various publs.; playwright, 1993—; screenwriter, 1996—; writer, pub. The Missing Crown, religious drama World Wide Christian Radio, Sta. KCBI-FM, KYND-AM, and other radio stas., 1996—, baby publ. Hello...World...Hello, 1997; author: (poetry) The Budding of Tomorrow, 1997; music pub., 1999—. Vol. PTO bd. Sharptown Middle Sch. Mem. ASCAP, Manuscriptors Guild. Methodist. Home: 361 N Post Oak Ln Apt 333 Houston TX 77024-5950

MCPHAIL-GEIST, KARIN RUTH, secondary school educator, real estate agent, musician; b. Urbana, Ill., Nov. 23, 1938; d. Wilber Harold and Bertha Amanda Sofia (Helander) Tammeus; m. David Pendleton McPhail, Sept. 7, 1958 (div. 1972); children: Julia Elizabeth, Mark Andrew; m. John Charles Geist, June 4, 1989 (div. 1995). BS, Juilliard Sch. Music, 1962; postgrad., Stanford U., 1983-84, L'Academia, Florence and Pistoia, Italy, 1984-85, Calif. State U., 1986-87, U. Calif., Berkeley, 1991, 92. Cert. tchr., Calif.; lic. real estate agt., Calif. Tchr. Woodstock Sch., Musoorie, India, 1957, Canadian, Tex., 1962-66, Head Royce Sch., Oakland, Calif., 1975-79, 87—, Sleepy Hollow Sch., Orinda, Calif., 1985-2001; realtor Freeholders, Berkeley, Calif., 1971-85, Northbrae, Berkeley, Calif., 1985-92, Templeton Co., Berkeley, 1992—99. Organist Kellogg Meml., Musoorie, 1956-57, Mills Coll. Chapel, Oakland, 1972—; cashier Trinity U., San Antonio, 1957-58; cen. records sec. Riverside Ch., N.Y.C., 1958-60; sec. Dr. Rollo May, N.Y.C., 1959-62, United Presbyn. Nat. Missions, N.Y.C., 1960, United Presbyn. Ecumenical Mission, N.Y.C., 1961, Nat. Coun. Chs., N.Y.C., 1962; choral dir. First Presbyn. Ch., Canadian, Tex., 1962-66; assoc. in music Montclair Presbyn. Ch., Oakland, 1972-88; site coord., artist, collaborator Calif. Arts Coun. Artist; cons. music edn. videos and CD Roms Clearvue EAV, Chgo., 1993—. Artist: produced and performed major choral and orchestral works, 1972-88; prodr. Paradiso, Kronos Quartet, 1985, Magdalena, 1991, 92, Children's Quest, 1993—. Grantee Orinda Union Sch. Dist., 1988. Mem. Berkeley Bd. Realtors, East Bay Regional Multiple Listing Svc., Calif. Tchrs. Assn., Commonwealth Club (San Francisco). Democrat. Home: 7360 Claremont Ave Berkeley CA 94705-1429

MCPHEE, MARTHA, literature educator; BA magna cum laude, Bowdoin Coll., 1987; MFA, Columbia U., 1994. Fiction tchr. Gotham Writer's Workshop, N.Y.C., 1993—97; adj. prof. creative writing Columbia U., 1997—99; writer, asst. prof. creative writing Hofstra U., 2002—. Author: (novels) Bright Angel Time, 1998, Gorgeous Lies, 2002, (nonfiction) Girls: Ordinary Girls and Their Extraordinary Pursuits, 2000; translator: Crossing the Threshold of Hope, 1994, author short stories; contbr. articles to publs. Fellow, John Simon Guggenheim Meml. Found., 2003. Office: Hofstra Univ Hempstead NY 11549-1000*

MCPHERON, JOANN MARIE, music educator, poet; b. Racine, Wis., Feb. 19, 1938; d. Joseph Eugene-Reath and Ann Bernadette (Mostek) Stetka; m. Lamont Preston McPheron II, Oct. 14, 1961; children Dawn Marie and Lamont P. III (twins). Student, U. Wis., Parkside, 1958-60. Adminstrv. asst. Racine County Social Svc. Dept., Wis., 1958-63; pvt. piano, music theory tchr. Racine, 1970—. Contbr. poems to anthologies and mags.; performer Racine Summer Theater, 1957. Asst. programs Children's Theatre, Racine, 1975; chmn. Minority Scholarship Program, 1970; active Roosevelt Sch. PTA, 1968—74; vol. All Saints Hosp., 2002—, Performing Arts Ctr., Milw., 1994—97; mem. Milw. Zoo, Art Inst. Chgo., United Performing Arts, Milw., Milw. Art Mus.; vol. fundraiser Miller Ride for the Arts, 1994—2000, AIDS March, Milw.; contbr. Racine Arts Coun.; bd. dirs. St. Luke's Hosp. Aux., Racine, Wis., 1992—98. Recipient award for poetry Racine Art Coun., 1990; nominated Graduates of Distinction William Horlick H.S., Racine, 1992. Fellow Wis. Fellowship of Poets; mem. Racine Music Tchrs. Assn., Wis. Music Tchrs. Assn., Music Tchrs. Nat. Assn., Root River Poets. Mem. Unitarian Universalist Ch. Avocations: grandchildren, poetry, walking, gardening, painting. Home: 516 Augusta St Racine WI 53402-4408

MCPHERSON, DONALD SCOTT, employment relations educator, arbitrator/mediator; b. Sharon, Pa., June 11, 1947; s. Donald McMillan and Lily (Smith) McP.; m. Linda Jo Leighty, Aug. 16, 1969; 1 child, Kimra Leigh. BA, Indiana U. of Pa., 1969, MA, 1971; PhD, U. Pitts., 1977. Dir. residence life Indiana U. of Pa., 1969-77, prof. employment rels., 1977-93, chmn. dept., 1977-87, disting. univ. prof., 1993—. Pres. Assn. Pa. State Coll. and Univ. Faculty, Indiana U. Pa. chpt., 1980. Author: Resolving Grievances, 1983; contbr. articles to profl. jours. Elder Calvary Presbyn. Ch., 1983—; sec. St. Andrew's Soc. of Indiana, 1991-94. Recipient disting. faculty award for svc., Commonwealth of Pa., 1983, Outstanding Alumni award, Indiana U. of Pa., 1983. Mem. Nat. Acad. Arbitrators, Am. Arbitration Assn., Assn. for Conflict Resolution, Indsl. Rels. Rsch. Assn. (exec. dir. Western Pa. chpt. 1982-89), Found. for Indiana U. of Pa. (bd. dir. 1977-82), Indiana Coun. on the Arts, Indiana U. of Pa. Alumni Assn. (pres. 1975-79), Clan MacPherson Assn. (life), Phi Kappa Phi. Democrat. Presbyterian. Home: 240 Oriole Ave Indiana PA 15701-1419 Office: Indiana U of Pa Dept Indsl Rels Indiana PA 15705-0001

MCPHERSON, FRANCES ANNE, university special education educator; b. Hopkinsville, Ky., Feb. 22, 1950; d. John William and Frances (McCoogh) McP; m. James D. Brackett, June 9, 1991; children: Anda, Eli. BA in English, Vanderbilt U., 1971; MEd in Emotionally Disturbed, U Ga., 1981, MEd in Learning Disabilities, 1987, PhD, 1991. Cert. tchr., Tenn., Ga. Ednl. therapist Rutland Ctr. Psychoeducational Ctr., Athens, Ga., 1972-75; tchr. spl. edn., head dept. learning disabilities Oglethorpe County High Sch., Lexington, Ga., 1985-88; grad. asst. U. Ga., Athens, 1988-91, student clinician, 1990-91, asst. to evaluation coord. Learning Disabilties Clin., 1990-91, asst. prof. exceptional children, 1991; asst. prof. spl. edn. dept. edn. No. Mich. U., Marquette, 1991-94; asst. prof. spl. edn. U. S.C., Spartenburg, 1994—. Faculty sponsor, advisor The Continuum, Marquette, 1991-94; mem. staff No. Mich. Ctr. for Rsch. for Social and Ednl. Programs, Marquette, 1991-94; supr. asst. Mich. Sci. Olympiad, Marquette, 1991-94; univ. trainer. Outcomes Tng. Project, Office Spl. Edn., Mich. Dept. Edn., East Lansing, 1992-94, faculty sponsor, advisor Kappa Delta Pi. Co-author: (chpt.) Adults with Learning Disabilities, 1996. Active PTO, Athens, 1987-91, Marquette, 1991-94. Recipient Excellence Teaching award, 1993; named NAtions Bank Tchr. of Yr., 1995-96. Mem. ASCD, Am. Ednl. Rsch. Assn., S.C. Edn. Assn. (faculty advisor-student chpt.), Coun. for Learning Disabilities, Coun. for Exceptional Children, Learning Disabilities Assn., Mensa, Phi Delta Kappa. Avocations: ceramics, gardening. Address: 1016 Textile Rd Spartanburg SC 29301-1748

MC PHERSON, JAMES MUNRO, history educator; b. Valley City, N.D., Oct. 11, 1936; s. James Munro and Miriam (Osborn) McPherson; m. Patricia Rasche, Dec. 28, 1957; 1 child, Joanna Erika. BA, Gustavus Adolphus Coll., 1958; PhD, Johns Hopkins U., 1963. From mem. faculty to prof. Princeton U., 1962—91, George Henry Davis '86 prof. Am. history, 1991—. Jefferson lectr., 2000. Author: Struggle for Equality, 1964 (Ainsfield-Wolf award race rels., 1965), The Negro's Civil War, 1965, Marching Toward Freedom: The Negro in the Civil War, 1968, Blacks in America: Bibliographical Essays, 1971, The Abolitionist Legacy: From Reconstruction to the NAACP, 1975, Ordeal by Fire: The Civil War and Reconstruction, 1981, 1992, Battle Cry of Freedom: The Civil War Era, 1988 (Pulitzer prize for history, 1989), Abraham Lincoln and the Second American Revolution, 1991, Images of the Civil War, 1992, What They Fought For 1861-1865, 1994, The Atlas of the Civil War, 1994, Drawn With the Sword: Reflections on the American Civil War, 1996, For Cause and Comrades: Why Men Fought in the Civil War, 1997 (Lincoln prize, 1998), Lamson of the Gettysburg: The Civil War Letters of Lt. Roswell H. Lamson, U.S. Navy, 1997 (Theodore and Franklin D. Roosevelt prize in naval history, 1998), Is Blood Thicker than Water? Crisis of Nationalism in the Modern World, 1998, Writing the Civil War: The Quest to Understand, 1998, To the Best of My Ability, 2000, The American Presidents, 2000, Days of Destiny, 2001, Crossroads of Freedom: Antietam, 2002, Hallowed Ground: A Walk at Gettysburg, 2003. Fellow Danforth fellow, 1958—62, Guggenheim fellow, 1967—68, Huntington-Nat. Endowment for Humanities, 1977—78, Behavioral Scis. Ctr., Stanford U., 1982—83, Huntington-Seaver Inst., 1987—88. Mem.: Orgn. Am. Historians, So. Hist. Assn., Am. Hist. Assn. (pres. 2003—), Am. Philos. Soc., Phi Beta Kappa (Jefferson lectr. 2000). Home: 15 Randall Rd Princeton NJ 08540-3609

MCPHERSON, LARRY E(UGENE), photographer, educator; b. Newark, Ohio, May 1, 1943; s. Eugene Edward and Ethel Grace (Lehman) McP. BA, Columbia Coll., Chgo., 1976; MA, No. Ill. U., 1978. Instr. Columbia Coll., 1971-76; assoc. prof. photography U. Memphis, 1978—. Instr. Sch. of Art Inst. Chgo., spring 1972; workshop instr. Ohio State U., Columbus, summer 1980, VSW Summer Inst., Rochester, N.Y., summer 1988. One-man shows include Art Inst. Chgo., 1969, 78, 81, Dayton Art Inst., 1992; exhibited in group shows at Mus. Modern Art, N.Y.C., 1978, Corcoran Gallery Art, Washington, 1982, George Eastman House, Rochester, N.Y., 1982, New

Orleans Mus. Art, 1992, Milw. Art Mus., 1996, Birmingham Mus. Art, 1996, Art Inst. Chgo., 1997; represented in permanent collections Mus. Modern Art, Art Inst. Chgo., George Eastman House, New Orleans Mus. Art, Mus. Fine Arts, Houston, Memphis Brooks Mus. Art, The Dayton Art Inst., Birmingham Mus. Art, Milw. Mus. Art, Ogden Mus. So. Art; author: "Memphis", Santa Fe, NM: Center for American Places, 2002. Faculty Devel. grantee U. Memphis, 1983, 92, 99; grantee-fellow Nat. Endowment for Arts, 1975, 79; Guggenheim fellow, 1980. Mem. Soc. Photog. Edn. Home: 7725 Shadow Bend Ln Arlington TN 38002-8051 Office: U Memphis Dept Art Memphis TN 38152-0001 E-mail: lmcphrsn@memphis.edu.

MCPHERSON, MARY PATTERSON, charitable foundation executive; b. Abington, Pa., May 14, 1935; d. John B. and Marjorie Hoffman (Higgins) McP. AB, Smith Coll., 1957, LL.D., 1981; MA, U. Del., 1960; PhD, Bryn Mawr Coll., 1969; LLD (hon.), Juniata Coll., 1975, Smith Coll., 1981, Princeton U., 1984, U. Rochester, 1984, U. Pa., 1985; LittD (hon.), Haverford Coll., 1980; L.H.D. (hon.), Lafayette Coll., 1982; LHD (hon.), U. Pa., 1985, Med. Coll. Pa., 1985. Instr. philosophy U. Del., 1959-61; asst., fellow and lectr. dept. philosophy Bryn Mawr Coll., 1961-63, asst. dean, 1964-69, assoc. dean, 1969-70; dean Bryn Mawr Coll. (Undergrad. Coll.), 1970-78, assoc. prof., from 1970; acting pres. Bryn Mawr Coll., 1976-77, pres., 1978-97, pres. emeritus, 1997—; v.p. The Andrew W. Mellon Found., 1997—. Bd. dirs. Agnes Irwin Sch., 1972-90, Shipley Sch., 1972-90, Phillips Exeter Acad., 1973-76, Wilson Coll., 1976-79, Greater Phila. Movement, 1973-77, Internat. House of Phila., 1974-76, Josiah Macy, Jr. Found., 1977—, Carnegie Found. for Advancement Teaching, 1978-86, Univ. Mus., Phila., 1977-79, University City Sci. Center, 1979-85, Brookings Inst., 1984-90, Phila. Contributionship, 1985—, Carnegie Corp. N.Y., 1985-94, Nat. Humanities Ctr., 1986-91, Amherst Coll., 1986-98, Humanity in Action, Inc., 1997—, Goldman Sachs Asset Mgmt., 1997—, The Spencer Found., 1993—, Am. Sch. Classical Studies, 1996—, Bank St. Coll., 1998—, Smith Coll., 1998—. Mem. Am. Philos. Soc., Am. Acad. of Arts and Scis., Cosmopolitan Club. Office: The Andrew W Mellon Found 140 E 62nd St New York NY 10021-8124*

MCPHERSON, MELVILLE PETER, academic administrator, former government official; b. Grand Rapids, Mich., Oct. 27, 1940; s. Donald and Ellura E. (Frost) McP.; m. Joanne McPherson; 4 children. JD, Am. U., 1969; MBA, Western Mich. U., 1967; BA, Mich. State U., 1963. Peace Corps vol., Peru, 1965-66; with IRS, Washington, 1969-75; spl. asst. to pres. and dep. dir. Presdl. Pers. White Ho., Washington, 1975-77; mng. ptnr. Washington office Vorys, Sater, Seymour & Pease, 1977-81; adminstr. AID, Washington, 1981-87; dep. sec. Dept. Treasury, Washington, 1987-89; group exec. v.p. Bank of Am., San Francisco, 1989-93; pres. Mich. State U., East Lansing, 1993—. Mem. D.C. Bar Assn., Mich. Bar Assn. Republican. Methodist. Office: Office of the Pres Mich State U 450 Administration East Lansing MI 48824-1046

MCPHERSON, MICHAEL STEVEN, former academic administrator, economist; b. June 6, 1947; married; 2 children. BA Math., U. Chgo., 1967, MA Econs., 1970, PhD Econs., 1974. Instr. econs. dept. U. Ill., Chgo., 1971—74; asst. prof. econs. Williams Coll., 1974—81, assoc. prof. econs., 1981—84, prof. econs., 1984—96, chmn. econs. dept., then dean of faculty, 1986—91; pres. Macalester Coll., St. Paul, 1996—2003, Spencer Found., Chgo., 2003—. Cons. Data Resources, Inc., 1979, Nat. Rsch. Coun. Commn. Human Resources, 1979, Modern Lang. Assn., 1980, Nat. Acad. Edn., 1980, Smith Coll., 1982, The Coll. Bd., 1983, Rand Corp., 1985—86, U.S. Dept. Edn. Ctr. Statis., 1986. Co-author (with M.O. Shapiro): Keeping College Affordable: Government and Educational Opportunity, 1991, The Student Aid Game: Meeting Need and Rewarding Talent in American Higher Education, 1998; co-author: (with D. Hausman) Economic Analysis and Moral Philosophy, 1996; editor: The Demand for the New Faculty in Science and Engineering, 1980, Democract Development and the Art of Trespassing: Essays in Honor of Albert O. Hirschman, 1986; contbr. articles to profl. jours. Trustee Coll. Bd., 1997—. Fellow Study fellow, Am. Coun. Learned Socs., 1977—78, vis. fellow, Princeton U., 1977—78, sr. fellow, Brookings Inst., 1984—86; grantee, Ford Found., 1981—83, Mellon Found., 1984—86. Home: 1750 Summit Ave Saint Paul MN 55105-1834 Office: Office of the Pres 875 N Michigan Ave Ste 3930 Chicago IL 60611-1803

MCPHERSON, MILTON MONROE, history educator; b. Beatrice, Ala., Oct. 19, 1928; s. Laurence Milton and Annie Mae (Bell) McP.; m. Carolyn Elizabeth Coley, Dec. 16, 1955; children: Milton Jr., Herbert L., Gretchen M. BA, U. Ala., 1950, MA, 1959, PhD in Am. History, 1970. Asst. prof. history Miss. Coll., Clinton, 1959-60, Mercer U., Macon, Ga., 1960-61, Ala. Coll., Montevallo, 1961-62, Pensacola (Fla.) Jr. Coll., 1962-68; assoc. prof. history Troy (Ala.) State U., 1968-87, prof. history, 1987-89; prof. history emeritus, 1989—. Author: The Ninety-Day Wonders: OCS and the Modern American Army, 2001; editor: Memories That Lingered: The Life and Times of Laurence Milton McPherson, 1993, Timeless Moments: Essays in American History, 1995. 1st lt. U.S. Army, 1950-53. Mem. NEA, Ala. Hist. Assn., So. Hist. Assn. Avocations: writing, reading, photography, walking, traveling. Home: 206 Sherwood Ave Troy AL 36081-4534

MCQUEEN, PAMELA, principal; BA in English, MA in Secondary Edn. and English, No. Ky. U. Cert. rank I in secondary adminstrn. Xavier U. Tchr., prin.; prin. Villa Madonna Acad. H.S., Villa Hills, Ky., 1996—. Office: Villa Madonna Acad HS 2500 Amsterdam Rd Fort Mitchell KY 41017-5316

MCQUEEN, SANDRA MARILYN, educator, consultant; b. Greenville, SC, Nov. 30, 1948; d. Clement Edgar and Sarah Elizabeth (Gentry) McQ. BA, Presbyn. Coll., 1970; MA, Presbyn. Sch. Christian Edn., 1972; PhD, Ga. State U., 1987. Cert. early childhood, spl. edn., ESL gifted tchr., spl. edn. supr., Ga. Dir. christian edn. com. Rock Spring Presbyn. Ch., Atlanta, 1972-74; early childhood educator Atlanta Bd. Edn., 1974-80, educator gifted children, 1980—; educator ESL, 2001—. Curriculum developer, in-svc. educator Atlanta Bd. Edn., 1989—; tchr., cons. Ga. Geographic Alliance. Mem. Justice for Women, Atlanta, 1980—, chair, 1985-86, co-chair, 1989-91; mem. Rock Spring Chancel Choir, Atlanta, 1978—, sec., 1987-89; active Rock Spring Presbyn. Ch., Atlanta, 1972—, elder, 1986-88, 91-93; active Refugee Resettlement, Greater Atlanta Presbytery, 1989—; coun. mem. Crossties Network, 1991—; suburban art com. High Mus. Young Careers; active Alliance Theatre Angel, Metro Atlanta Gifted Consortium, Suburban Arts Com.; troop com. chair Boy Scouts Am., 1992—; del. leader People to People Friendship Caravan, 1992-93, 95; assoc. envoy for Latvia, 1996 Olympics; del. Saxony Exch., 2001; coord. coun. Atlanta Interfaith Sisterhood, 1996—; active Cobb County Blue Ribbon Edn. Com., 1999-2002, Buckhead Bus. Assn. Leadership Class 2000, Six Star Refugee Partnership, 2000—. Named Tchr. of Yr. Sutton Middle Sch., 1985; Apple Corp. grantee, 1986; Fulbright scholar, 1990. Mem. NEA, ASCD, Ga. Edn. Assn., Ga. Assn. for Gifted Children, Atlanta Assn. Educators, Metro Consortium Gifted Educators, Ga. Supporters of Gifted, Nat. Assn. for Gifted Edn., Fulbright Assn., Coun. Evang. Chs. in Nicaragua, Crossties Network of Foxfire, Kappa Delta PI. Office: 4360 Powers Ferry Rd NW Atlanta GA 30327-3417 E-mail: challenge@mindspring.com.

MCRAE, JOHN HENRY, educational administrator; b. N.Y.C., Jan. 3, 1948; s. Elliott Hampton and Grace (Williams) McR.; m. Marcia Owens, Dec. 19, 1990; 1 child, John Ashton. AA, Mid. Ga. Coll., 1968; MS, Valdosta State Coll., 1971, MEd, 1975, EdS, 1983. Cert. adminstr., supr., Ga. Tchr. Sallas Mahone Sch., 1970-79; prin. S.L. Mason Sch., Valdosta, Ga., 1979-86; headmaster Valwood Sch., Valdosta, 1986-88; prin. Bullock County Sch., Statesboro, Ga., 1988-90; asst. prof. Ga. So. U., Statesboro, Ga., 1990-92; dir. student asst. program Mental Health for South Ga. Dist., Valdosta, 1992-94, dir., edn. adminstr., 1994—. Recipient Disting. Alumni award Valdosta State Coll., 1978, Hayes-Fulbright scholarship, 1977; named Tchr. of Yr., State of Ga., 1978, one of Outstanding Young Men of Am., 1978, 79, 81. Mem. Ga. Tchrs. of Yr. (founder, charter, pres. 1992—), Nat./State Tchrs. of Yr. Assn., Kappa Delta Pi, Phi Delta Kappa, Omicron Delta Kappa, Sigma Phi Epsilon. Republican. Episcopalian. Home: 2210 Twin Lakes Dr NE Bainbridge GA 31717-5278

MCRANEY, JAMES THOMAS, choral music educator; s. James Howard and Thyrza Maude (Gardner) McR.; m. Willie Ruth Blailock, Aug. 18, 1960; children: Laura Elise, James Thomas Jr., Jeffrey Alan. MB, BS in Edn., Miss. Coll., 1960; MA, George Peabody Coll. Tchrs., 1961; EdD, U. Ga., 1993. Choral mus. dir. Bass High Sch., Atlanta, 1962-67, Cross Keys High Sch., Atlanta, 1967—92, Dunwoody High Sch., Dunwoody, Ga., 1986—88, Sequoyah Jr. High Sch., Doraville, Ga., 1989—92; exec. dir. Ga. Mus. Educators Assn., 1992—94; adj. prof. music Reinhardt Coll., Waleska, Ga., 1998—. Music minister various chs., Ga., 1962—; tchg. asst. U. Ga., 1980-81; choral dir. European concert tours Ga. Youth Chorale, Atlanta, 1974, Partners-of the-Americas exch. concert, Recife, Brazil, 1977, European tour Am. Youth Symphony and Chorus, Pitts., 1978, European tour U.S. Youth in Concert, Atlanta, 1979; cons. State Dept. Edn.; mem. music faculty Ga. Governor's Honors Program (gifted), 1973, 74. Editor/compiler (music materials) Ga. Sight Reading Book, 1984-87; contbr. articles in field; choral conductor albums, 1968, 72, 78, 79. Active Boy Scouts Am. (scoutmaster, mem. exec. com. Cub Scout Pack 534, merit badge counselor Troop 534, Atlanta); pres., mem. exec. com. Henderson High Sch. Soccer Booster Club, Chamblee, Ga. 1982-85; mem. Ga. Adv. Coun. Edn. 1983-87; rep. Ga. Dept. Edn. at White House Conf. Edn. Luncheon, 1983 (tchrs. of yr.); exec. dir. Ga. Tchs. of Year Assn., 1992-99. Recipient Citations of Commendation Ga. House Reps., 1976, 83, Ga. Senate, 1983, Ga. Gov. Joe Frank Harris, 1983; named Ga. Tchr. of Yr. State Dept. Edn., Atlanta, 1983, DeKalb County Tchr. of Yr. DeKalb Bd. Edn., 1983; Ga. Mus. Educators' Assn. Distinguished Service award, 1998, Distinguished Career award, 2002. Mem. Am. Choral Dirs. Assn. (bd. dirs. Ga. chpt.), Ga. Mus. Educators Assn. (state choral chmn. l965-67, lst v.p. l973-75, 83-85, 2d v.p. l975-77, 89—, pres. 1987-89), Music Educators Nat. Conf. (bd. dirs. so. div. l987-89, pres. so. div. 1994-96, nat. chair-elect MENC Hist. Special Rsch. Interest Group, 2002-), Kappa Delta Pi, Phi Mu Alpha Siinfonia, Pi Kappa Lambda. Democrat. Baptist. Avocations: travel, photography. Home: 2636 Whiteleigh Ct NE Atlanta GA 30345-1437

MC ROSTIE, CLAIR NEIL, economics educator; b. Owatonna, Minn., Dec. 16, 1930; s. Neil Hale and Myrtle Julia (Peterson) McR.; m. Ursula Anne Schwieger, Aug. 29, 1968. BSBA cum laude, Gustavus Adolphus Coll., 1952; MA in Mktg., Mich. State U., 1953; PhD in Fin., U. Wis., 1963; postgrad., U. Minn., 1971-72, Am. Grad. Sch. Internat. Mgmt., 1980-81; cert., Coll. for Fin. Planning, 1990. Cert. fin. planner. Faculty Gustavus Adolphus Coll., St. Peter, Minn., 1958-96; emeritus prof., 1996—; chmn. dept. econs. and bus. Gustavus Adolphus Coll., 1967-83, chmn., mem. various coms., 1971-96; teaching asst. Sch. Commerce, U. Wis., 1960-62. Lectr. European div. U. Md., 1966-67; vis. prof. Am. Grad. Sch. Internat. Mgmt., 1980-81; pres. Minn. World Trade Week, Inc., 1987; bd. arbitrators NASD Regulations Inc. Editor: Global Resources: Perspectives and Alternatives, 1978, The Future of the Market Ecomomy, 1979. Congregation pres. First Luth. Ch., St. Peter, Minn., 1972-73, 93, chmn. pastoral call com., 1968-69, chmn. staffing com., 1975, mem. ch. council, 1968-74, 89-93; chmn. social ministry com. Minn. Synod, Luth. Ch. Am., 1975, mem. long range planning com. Southwestern Minn. Synod; chmn. Rep. council arts professions, scis., Minn., 1968-70, co-chmn. state task force on Vietnam, 1968; mem. adv. commn. Minn. Dept. Manpower Services, 1967-71; mem. North Central Regional Manpower Adv. Com.; bd. dirs. Midwest China Resource Study Center; del. White House Conf. Aging, 1971. Served with U.S. Army, 1954-56. Recipient Leavey Found. award Freedoms Found., Valley Forge, Pa.; Research fellow Fed. Res. Bank of Chgo., 1962-63 Mem. Nat. Assn. Securities Dealers (bd. arbitration), Fin. Execs. Inst., Fin. Planners Assn., Minn. Econs. Assn. (bd. dirs. 1974-75, 79-80), Masons (master, Royal Arch chpt., Zuhrah Shrine Temple, Scottish Rite), Royal Order Scotland, Alpha Kappa Psi, Iota Delta Gamma, Sigma Epsilon. Lutheran. Avocations: bird watching, backpacking, fitness and health. Home: 1208 Pine Pointe Curv Saint Peter MN 56082-1344

MCROY, WILLIE CLIFFORD, information systems educator; b. West Frankfort, Ill., Feb. 1, 1940; s. Willie and Samantha Odell (Sims) McR.; m. Janice Frances Moore, June 22, 1974; children: Lara Frances, Willie Clifford Jr. BA in Zoology, So. Ill. U., 1962; MS in Computer Sys. Mgmt., Naval Postgrad. Sch., Monterey, Calif., 1975. Commd. ensign USN, 1962, advanced through grades to lt. comdr.; ret., 1983; mgr. learning ctr. Valcom Computer Ctr., Springfield, Ill., 1984-85; vocat. instr. MacMurray Coll., Jacksonville, Ill., 1985-90, coll. coord. Jacksonville Correctional Ctr., 1990-2000; info. sys. instr. Wake Tech. C.C., Raleigh, N.C., 2001—. Instr. Lincoln Land C.C., Springfield, 1983-86, John Wood C.C., Quincy, Ill., 1986-90. Scoutmaster Boy Scouts Am., Norfolk, Va., 1969-70; youth soccer coach Kings Grant Soccer Assn., Virginia Beach, Va., 1978-83, Farmersville (Ill.)-Waggoner Assn., 1983-85, Jacksonville Soccer Assn., 1985-88. Republican. Baptist. Avocations: gardening, reading, computers. Office: Wake Tech CC 9101 Fayetteville Rd Raleigh NC 27603-5696 Home: 8105 Robincrest Ct Fuquay Varina NC 27526-9582 E-mail: wcmcroy@waketech.edu.

MCSORLEY, RITA ELIZABETH, adult education educator; b. Baraboo, Wis., Feb. 13, 1947; d. Charles Gervase and Bertie Ellen (Baker) Collins; m. William David McSorley III, June 6, 1967; children: William David IV, Kathryn Rita, Stephen Charles, Matthew Thomas. B Liberal Studies, Mary Washington Coll., Fredericksburg, Va., 1988; MEd, U. Va., Charlottesville, 1994. Adult edn. instr. Waipahu (Hawaii) Cmty. Sch. for Adults, 1989-91, literacy coord., 1990-91; dir. religious edn. Marine Meml. Chapel, Quantico, Va., 1992-94; adult edn. instr. Prince William County Schs., Quantico, 1992-93; coord. computer assisted lang. learning project Literacy Coun. No. Va., Falls Church, 1995-96; ednl. cons. Fairfield Lang. Techs., Harrisonburg, Va., 1996-97; adult edn. coord. N.E. Ind. Sch. Sys., San Antonio, 2000—. Mem. sch. bd. Quantico Dependent Schs., 1980-82; vol. Boy Scouts Am., Quantico and Pearl City, Hawaii, 1985-97. Mem. TESOL, U. Va. Alumni Assn. Roman Catholic. Avocations: quilting, genealogical research, travel. Office: NEISD 10333 Broadway San Antonio TX 78217 E-mail: rmcsor@neisd.net.

MCTAGGART, PATRICK WILLIAM, principal; b. East Chicago, Ind., Dec. 3, 1950; s. Frederick M. and Dolores R. (Gourley) McT. BS, Ball State U., 1972; MS, Purdue U., 1977, EdS, 1985. Cert. secondary adminstrn. and supervision. Tchr. Griffith (Ind.) Jr. H.S., 1973-82, asst. prin., 1982-88; prin. Roosevelt Mid. Sch., Monticello, Ind., 1988—. Elder First Presbyn. Ch. Monticello, Ind., 1997—. Mem. ASCD, Nat. Mid. Sch. Assn., Ind. Prin. Leadership Acad. (grad. 1992-93), Ind. Assn. Sch Prins., Sportsmen Acting for the Environ, Ducks Unltd. Avocations: fishing, hunting, golf, tennis, wildlife art collecting. Home: 3608 E Bailey Rd Monticello IN 47960-7041 Office: Roosevelt Mid Sch 721 W Broadway St Monticello IN 47960-2010

MCTAGGART, TIMOTHY THOMAS, secondary education educator; b. Danville, Pa., Dec. 8, 1949; s. Thomas Francis and Mary Elizabeth (Russial) McT. BS, Bloomsburg (Pa.) U., 1971; MDiv, St. Vincent Coll., Latrobe, Pa., 1974; MEd, Millersville (Pa.) U., 1980; EdD, Pacific Western U., Honolulu, 1991. Cert. in secondary edn., Pa. Math. tchr. Lancaster (Pa.) Cath. High Sch., 1978-85; math. and computer sci. tchr. Columbia (Pa.) Sr. High Sch., 1985—. Head track coach Columbia High Sch., 1986—. Mem. Pa. Athletic Assn. (football ofcl.), K.C. (knight 4th deg.). Home: 728 Sharon Dr Mount Joy PA 17552-9711 Office: Columbia H S 901 Ironville Pike Columbia PA 17512-9513

MCVAY, BARBARA CHAVES, secondary education mathematics educator; b. Dallas, July 6, 1950; d. Joe M. and Dorothy May (Nock) Chaves; m. David Clyde McVay, Dec. 23, 1968; 1 child, Kathryn McVay Hearn. BS in Math., U. Tex., Arlington, 1971, MS in Math., 1999. Cert. secondary tchr. math., English, Tex. Tchr. math. C.W. Nimitz High Sch. Irving (Tex.) Ind. Sch. Dist., 1972—. Bldg. rep. Dallas Tchrs. Credit Union, 1982—; part time lab. instr. North Lake/Dallas County Community Coll., Irving, 1988—. Tchr. Sunday sch. North Dallas Bapt. Ch., 1971-80; ch. tng. leader 1st Bapt. Ch., Irving, 1981-85. Mem. NEA, Tex. State Tchrs. Assn., Irving Edn. Assn. (rep. 1980—), Nat. Coun. Tchrs. Math., Tex. Coun. Tchrs. Math., Greater Dallas Coun. Tchrs. Math., Math. Assn. Am., Delta Kappa Gamma. Republican. Avocations: crafts, sewing, needlework. Office: CW Nimitz High Sch 100 W Oakdale Rd Irving TX 75060-6833 Personal E-mail: bjcmcvay@yahoo.com. Business E-Mail: bmcvay@irvingisd.net.

MCVICKER, JESSE JAY, artist, educator; b. Vici, Okla., Oct. 18, 1911; s. Jesse Allen and Clara Mae (Hendrick) McV.; m. Laura Beth Paul, Aug. 20, 1938. BA, Okla. State U., 1940, MA, 1941. Faculty Okla. State U., Stillwater, 1941—, prof. art, 1959-77, prof. emeritus, 1977—, head dept., 1959-77. Exhbns. include Med. Mus. Art, Mus. Non-Objective Painting, Chgo, Art Inst., N.A.D., Library of Congress, San Francisco Mus. Art, Denver Art Mus., Pa. Acad. Fine Arts, Carnegie Inst., Print Club Phila., Salon Des Realities Nouvelles, Paris, France, Dallas, Mus. Fine Arts, Galleria Origine, Rome, Italy, Whitney Mus. Am. Art; represented in permanent collections Library of Congress, Seattle Art Mus., Dallas Mus. Fine Arts, Met. Mus. Art, Joslyn Meml. Art Mus.; bibliography Graphic Works by J. Jay McVicker, 1986. Served with USNR, 1943-46. Mem. Soc. Am. Graphic Artists, Audubon Artists (John Taylor Arms award 1990), Print Club Phila., Pi Kappa Alpha.

MCVICKER, MARY ELLEN HARSHBARGER, museum director, art history educator; b. Mexico, Mo., May 5, 1951; d. Don Milton and Harriet Pauline (Mossholder) Harshbarger; m. Wiley Ray McVicker, June 2, 1973; children: Laura Elizabeth, Todd Michael. BA with honors, U. Mo., 1973, MA, 1975, PhD, 1989. Instr. Ctrl. Meth. Coll., Fayette, Mo., 1978-85, mus. dir., 1980-85; project dir. Mo. Com. Humanities, Fayette, 1981-85, Mo. Dept. Natural Resources Office Hist. Preservation, 1978-85; owner Memories of Mo. and Tour Tyme, Inc., 1986-96; prof. history Kemper Mil. Coll., 1993-2000; dir. devel. The Salvation Army, Columbia, Mo., 2000-01; exec. dir. Friends of Historic Boonville, 2001—. Author: History Book, 1984. V.p. Friends Hist. Boonville, Mo., 1982-87, pres., 1989-90; bd. dors. Mus. Assocs. Mo. U., Columbia, 1981-83, Mo. Meth. Soc., Fayette, 1981-84; chmn. Bicentennial Celebration Methodism, Boonville, Mo., 1984; pres. Arts and Sci. Alumni, U. Mo., 1992-94; bd. dirs. Mo. Humanities Coun., 1993-97. Recipient Gov.'s award Excellence in Coll. Teaching, 1998. Mem. Mo. Alliance Hist. Preservation (charter), AAUW (treas. 1977-79), Am. Assn. Mus., Centralia Hist. Soc. (project dir. 1978), Mus. Assocs. United Meth. Ch. (charter, bd. dir. 1981-83), Mortar Bd., Women's Club (treas. 1977-79), United Meth. Women's Group (charter), Phi Beta Kappa. Democrat. Avocations: collecting antiques, gardening, family farming, singing, travel. Home: 22151 Highway 98 Boonville MO 65233-3022 Office: Friends of Historic Boonville PO Box 1776 Boonville MO 65233 E-mail: mcvicker@undata.com.

MCWALTERS, PETER, school system administrator; b. Oct. 8, 1946; m. Alice Bond McWalters; children: Jennifer, Molly, Katherine. BA in History and Philosophy, Boston Coll., 1968; MS in Pub. Adminstrn., SUNY Brockport, 1979, cert. advanced study ednl. adminstrn., 1981. Permanent N.Y. State Teaching Cert social studies 7-12, Sch. Adminstrn., Sch. Dist. Adminstrn. Tchr.-trainer Eng. for speakers other langs. U.S. Peace Corps., Rep. Philippines; tchr. Eng. for speakers other langs. City Sch. Dist., Rochester, N.Y., 1970-71; tchr. social studies Interim Jr. High Sch., Rochester, 1971-78; Magnet Sch. planning specialist City Sch. Dist., Rochester, 1978-81, coord. Mgmt. Inst., 1980-81, supervising dir. planning and budgeting, 1981-85, supt. schs., 1985-91; commr. elem. and secondary edn. State of R.I., 1992—. Bd. dirs. Nat. Ctr. Edn. and Economy, mem. new standards project; bd. dirs. Ctr. Ednl. Devel., Rochester; mem. Edn. Commn. of States, Coun. Chief State Schs. Officers, Coun. Great Cities Schs., 21st Century Edn. Commn. Bd. dirs. Urban League, Rochester; mem. United Way Task Force, Rochester; gov. bd., exec. com. Rochester New Futures Initiative, Inc.; mem. Goals for Greater Rochester, Inc. Mem. Am. Assn. Sch. Adminstrs., Assn. Supervision and Curriculum Devel., Phi Delta Kappa. Office: Elem and Sec Office Shepard Bldg 255 Westminster St Providence RI 02903-3414*

MCWETHY, PATRICIA JOAN, educational association administrator; b. Chgo., Feb. 27, 1946; d. Frank E. and Emma (Kuehne) McW.; m. H. Frank Eden; children: Kristin Beth, Justin Nicholas. BA, Northwestern U., 1968; MA, U. Minn., 1970; MBA, George Washington U., 1981. Geog. analyst CIA, McLean, Va., 1970-71; rsch. asst. NSF, Washington, 1972-74, spl. asst. to dir., 1975, assoc. program dir. human geography and regional sci. program, 1976-79; exec. dir. Assn. Am. Geographers, Washington., 1979-84, Nat. Assn. Biology Tchrs., Reston, Va., 1984-95, Nat. Sci. Edn. Leadership Assn., Arlington, Va., 1995-97; edn. dir. Nat. Alliance for Mentally Ill, Arlington, 1998-99. Prin. investigator grant on biotech. equipment ednl. resource partnership NSF, 1989-93, NSF funder internat. symposium on Basic Biol. Concepts: What Should the World's Children Know?, 1992-94; co-prin. investigator NSF grant, 1995-97; mem. chmn.'s adv. com. Nat. Com. Sci. Stds. and Assessment, 1992-95; mem. Commn. for Biology Edn., Internat. Union Biol.. Sci., 1988-97; mem. exec. com. Alliance for Environ. Edn., 1987-90, chmn. program com., 1990; condr. seminars in field; lectr. in field. Author monograph and papers in field; editor handbook. NSF grantee, 1989-93, 95-97; NSF fellow, 1968-69; recipient Outstanding Performance award, NSF, 1973. Mem. Phi Beta Kappa.

MCWILLIAM, JOANNE ELIZABETH, retired religion educator; b. Toronto, Ont., Can., Dec. 10, 1928; d. Cecil Edward and Edna Viola (Archer) McW.; children, Leslie Mary Giroday, Elizabeth Dewart, Sean Dewart, Colin Dewart; m. C. Peter Slater, June 6, 1987. BA, U. Toronto, 1951, MA, 1953, U. St. Michael's, Toronto, 1966, PhD, 1968; DD honoris causa, Queen's U., Kingston, Ont., 2003. Asst. prof. religious studies U. Toronto, 1968-74, assoc. prof., 1974-87, prof., 1987, chairperson dept. religious studies, 1990-92, 93-94; Mary Crooke Hoffman prof. of Dogmatic Theology The Gen. Theol. Sem., N.Y.C, 1994-99; ret., 1999. Author: The Theology of Grace of Theodore of Mopsuestia, 1971, Death and Resurrection in the Fathers, 1986; editor: Augustine: Rhetor to Theologian, 1991, Toronto Jour. Theology. Mem. Can. Soc. for Patristic Studies (pres. 1987-90), Conf. Anglican Theologians (pres. 1990-91), Can. Soc. for the Study of Religion, Can. Theol. Soc., Am. Theol. Soc., Am. Acad. Religion. Anglican. Home: 59 Duggan Ave Toronto ON Canada M4V 1Y1 E-mail: joanne.mcwilliam@utoronto.ca.

MCWILLIAMS, CHRIS PATER ELISSA, elementary school educator; b. Cin., Oct. 23, 1937; d. Ray C. and Mary Loretta (Collins) Pater; m. Nabeel David Elissa, Aug. 15, 1964 (dec. Aug. 1975); children: Sue Renee Caplan, Ramsey Nabeel; m. Jim Bill McWilliams, Apr. 14, 1977 (dec. Sept. 1993). BA, Our Lady of Cin. Coll., 1959; MEd, Xavier U., 1965. Cert. tchr. elem., social studies, environ. edn., Tex. Elem. tchr. Cin. Parochial Schs., 1960-64, Champaign County Schs., Urbana, Ohio, 1968; tchr. social studies St. Mary's Elem. Sch., Urbana, 1968-73; tchr. Granbury (Tex.) Ind. Sch. Dist., 1981—2002, All Saints Cath. Sch., Dallas, 2002—. Instr. Tarleton

State U., Stephenville, Tex., 1989-90. Contbr. (text) Texas: Yesterday, Today and Tomorrow, 1988; music editor (newspaper) Jerusalem Star, 1966. Me. Hood Gen. Hosp. Aux., 1978—2002; chmn. Hood County Blood Drive, Granbury, 1978-82. Recipient scholarship Our Lady of Cin. Coll., 1955, Betty Crocker Homemaker award, Gen. Mills, 1955. Mem. Tex. Alliance for Geog. Edn., Phi Delta Kappa. Roman Catholic. Avocations: piano, reading, needlework, cooking, walking. Home: 3801 E 14th St #204 Plano TX 75074

MCWILLIAMS, ELIZABETH ANN, elementary school educator; b. Sheffield, Ala., Sept. 12, 1950; d. Johnny Clarence and Flora (Despigno) Brumley; m. Andy Christopher McWilliams, July 4, 1974; 1 child, Amanda Elizabeth. BS in Edn., U. North Ala., 1973, MA in Edn., 1976, AA cert. in edn., 1986. Residence hall asst. U. North Ala., Florence, 1973-74; tchr. Colbert County Bd. Edn., Tuscumbia, Ala., 1974—. Tchr. Growing Health Program, Tuscumbia, 1989—; presenter to tchrs. U.S. Space Camp, Huntsville, Ala., 1990—. Rep. campaign worker, Tuscumbia, 1988; Dem. campaign worker, 1990. Chpt. II grantee Ala. Dept. Edn., 1987. Fellow NEA; mem. Ala Edn. Assn. (faculty rep. 1990—, del. assembly 1993, 2003, treas. dist. 4 uniserv), Colbert County Edn. Assn. (sch. rep. to exec. bd., faculty rep. 1990—, sec. 1997-2003), Phi Delta Kappa, Alpha Delta Kappa (rec. sec. 1992-94, corr. sec. 1994—. Baptist. Avocations: reading, swimming, jogging. Home: 2120 Red Rock Rd Tuscumbia AL 35674-7021 Office: Cherokee Mid Sch 4595 Old Lee Hwy Cherokee AL 35616-5515

MCWILLIAMS, MARGARET ANN, home economics educator, author; b. Osage, Iowa, May 26, 1929; d. Alvin Randall and Mildred Irene (Lane) Edgar; children: Roger, Kathleen. BS, Iowa State U., 1951, MS, 1953; PhD, Oreg. State U., 1968. Registered dietitian. Asst. prof. home econs. Calif. State U., L.A., 1961-66, assoc. prof., 1966-68, prof., 1968-92, prof. emeritus, 1992—, chmn. dept., 1968-76; pres. Plycon Press, 1978—. Author: Food Fundamentals, 1966, 7th edit., 1998, Nutrition for the Growing Years, 1967, 6th edit., 1999, Experimental Foods Laboratory Manual, 1977, 4th edit., 1994, 5th edit., 2000, Lifelong Nutrition, 2001, (with L. Kotschevar) Understanding Food, 1969, Illustrated Guide to Food Preparation, 1970, 8th edit., 1998, (with L. Davis) Food for You, 1971, 2d edit., 1976, The Meatless Cookbook, 1973, (with F. Stare) Living Nutrition, 1973, 4th edit., 1984, Nutrition for Good Health, 1974, 2d edit., 1982, (with H. Paine) Modern Food Preservation, Fundamentals of Meal Management, 1978, 2d edit., 1993, 3d edit., 1997, (with H. Heller) Food Around The World, 1984, Foods: Experimental Perspectives, 1989, 4th edit., 2000, Food Around the World: A Cultural Perspective, 2003. Chmn. bd. Beach Cities Symphony, 1991-94. Recipient Alumni Centennial award Iowa State U., 1971, Profl. Achievement award, 1977; Phi Upsilon Omicron Nat. Founders fellow, 1964; Home Economist in Bus. Nat. Found. fellow, 1967; Outstanding Prof. award Calif. State U., 1976. Mem. Am. Dietetic Assn., Inst. Food Technologists, Phi Kappa Phi, Phi Upsilon Omicron, Omicron Nu, Iota Sigma Pi, Sigma Delta Epsilon, Sigma Alpha Iota. Home: PO Box 220 Redondo Beach CA 90277-0220 Fax: 310-798-2834.

MCWILLIAMS, MARY ANN, school administrator; b. Shreveport, La., July 5, 1944; d. Joseph Vivian and Helen Claire (McKinney) McW. BS, Northwestern State U., 1966; MEd, U. North Tex., 1989. Cert. composite sci., Tex., adminstrn. cert. Tchr. biology Willapa Valley Schs., Menlo, Wash., 1966-67; med. technologist Meth. Hosp., Houston, 1967-68; tchr. biology Caddo Parish Schs., Shreveport, 1968-74, 77-79; advt. account exec. Sta. KCOZ Radio, Shreveport, 1979-80; coord. tng./documentation Tri-State Computer Svcs., Shreveport, 1980-83; tchr. biology, team leader Plano (Tex.) Ind. Sch. Dist., 1983-94, environ. studies coord., coord. for environ. outdoor sch. camp program, 1994—, coord. for environ. outdoor sch. camp program, 1994—; dir. Holifield Sci. Learning Ctr., Plano, 1994—. Chmn. ednl. improvement coun. Plano Ind. Sch. Dist., 1990-94; tchr. trainer Jason V Project, Dallas, 1993-94; dir. Environ. Studies Camp, Plano, 1994—; cons. to Campis Outdoor Learning Ctr. project Tex. Tech U., Junction, 2003—. Mem. Dallas Mus. of Art, 1987—; bd. mgrs. Camp Classen, Oklahoma City YMCA, 1996—; creator students as scientists water quality testing program City of Plano, 1997; mem. Collin County Commrs. Planning Com.; mem. adv. bd. Collin County Parks Found., 2001—; mem. adv. bd. Collin County Residential Outdoor Edn. Camp, 2002—, chmn. facilities, infrastructure, programming and environ. subcom., 2002—. Named Jane Goodall Environ. Educator of Yr., Jane Goodall Inst. and Boreal Labs., Dallas, 1993, one of Outstanding Young Women of Am., 1980. Mem. NEA, Nat. Sci. Tchrs. Assn., Sci. Tchrs. of Tex. Roman Catholic. Avocations: travel, water sports, walking/hiking, birding, reading. Office: Plano Ind Sch Sys 2700 W 15th St Plano TX 75075-7524

MEAD, IRENE MARIE, lawyer, engineer, educator; b. Gary, Ind., Aug. 3, 1952; d. Robert R. and Marian F. Mead; m. Thomas R. Broadbent, Sept. 5, 1981. BSCE, Mich. State U., 1975; JD cum laude, T.M. Cooley Law Sch., 1980. Bar: Mich. 1980, U.S. Dist. Ct. (we. dist.) Mich. 1980, U.S. Dist. Ct. (ea. dist. Mich. 1986, U.S. Ct. Appeals (6th cir.) 1985, U.S. Ct. Appeals (4th cir.) 2002; registered profl. engr., 1980. Transp. engr. Mich. Dept. Transp., Lansing., 1975-80, litigation coord., 1981-83; rsch. atty. Mich. Ct. Appeals, Lansing, 1980; sole practice Haslett, Mich., 1981-83; asst. atty. gen. Office Mich. Atty. Gen., Lansing, 1983-88, asst. dep. atty. gen. legal ops., 1988-97, asst. in charge Liquor Control Divsn., 1997—2002; ptnr. Honigman Miller Schwartz & Cohn, Lansing, 2002—. Adj. prof. civil engring. Mich. State U., East Lansing, 1980-83; cons. engring., spl. project, Hwy. Safety Office, Mich. State U., East Lansing. Mem. ABA, Soc. for Women in Transp. (founding pres. 1977-78), Women in State Govt., Ingham County Bar Assn. (exec. council young lawyers sect. 1980-81). Office: Honigman Miller Schwartz and Cohn LLP 222 N Washington Sq Ste 400 Lansing MI 48933- E-mail: imm@honigman.com.

MEAD, KATHRYN NADIA, astrophysicist, educator; b. Jacksonville, Fla., Aug. 6, 1959; d. Charles A. Mead and Nadia L. Mead. BS in Physics, Rensselaer Poly. Inst., 1981, MS in Physics, 1983, PhD in Physics, 1986. Cooperative rsch. assoc. Naval Rsch. Lab., Washington, 1986-88; adj. asst. prof. Union Coll., Schenectady, N.Y., 1988-90, vis. asst. prof., 1990-93. Vis. sci. Nat. Radio Astronomy Obs., 1994-975 Mem. bd. visitors Bolles Sch., Jacksonville Fla. Recipient Career Devel. award Dudley Observatory, 1990, Faculty Rsch. Fund award Union Coll., 1990, 92, award Fund for Astrophysical Rsch., 1992. Mem. AAUW, Am. Astron. Soc. (editor Status 1995-98, Gaposchkins Rsch. Fund award 1991), Assn. for Women in Sci. (pres. So. Ariz. chpt. 1997), Sigma Xi, Sigma Pi Sigma. Achievements include discovery of the existence of molecular clouds and star formation much farther from the center of the Milky Way than previously known; research on molecular clouds and star formations outside the solar circle in our Galaxy, broad CO line wings near T-Tauri stars, the origin and structure of isolated dark globules, high resolution studies of the HII region/molecular cloud interface in NGC1977.

MEAD, PHILIP BARTLETT, healthcare administrator, obstetrician, educator; b. Poughkeepsie, N.Y., June 23, 1937; s. Ralph Allen and Altina (Gervin) Mead; m. Ann Elaine Smith, June 27, 1964; children: Ralph Allen II, David Smith. BA, Hamilton Coll., 1959; MD, Cornell U., 1963. Diplomate Nat. Bd. Med. Examiners, Am. Bd. Ob-gyn. Intern in medicine Bellevue Hosp., N.Y.C., 1963-64; resident in ob-gyn. N.Y. Hosp./Cornell Med. Ctr., N.Y.C., 1964-69; asst. prof. U. Vt. Coll. Medicine, Burlington, 1971-76, assoc. prof., 1976-81, prof., 1981—2001, prof. emeritus, 2001—; hosp. epidemiologist Med. Ctr. Hosp. of Vt., Burlington, 1984-93; dir. clin. sys. Vt. Acad. Med. Ctr., Burlington, 1993-95; sr. v.p., med. dir. Fletcher Allen Health Care, Burlington, 1995-97; prof., chmn. ob-gyn. U. Vt. Coll. Medicine, 1997—2001, prof. and chmn. emeritus, 2001—; physician leader women's health care svcs. Fletcher Allen Health Care, Burlington, 1997—2001. Lt. comdr. M.C. USN, 1969—71. Fellow: ACOG, Infectious Disease Soc. Am.; mem.: Soc. Hosp. Epidemiologists, Infectious Disease Soc. Ob-Gyn. (pres. 1987—88), Phi Beta Kappa, Alpha Omega Alpha. Home: 203 Pinehurst Dr Shelburne VT 05482-6882 Office: Fletcher Allen Health Care 111 Colchester Ave Burlington VT 05401-1416 E-mail: PBMeadMD@aol.com.

MEADE, ANGELA KAYE, special education educator; b. Bryon, Ohio, Mar. 14, 1969; d. Douglas MacAuther and Thelma Judy (Williams) Smith; m. Steven Andrew Meade, June 1, 1991; 1 child, Alexander Jefferson. AA in Edn. summa cum laude, AA in Gen. Studies, S.W. Va. C.C., 1989; BA in English with distinction, M Tchg. in Spl. Edn., U. Va., 1992. Cert. K-12 tchr. learning disabilities and mental retardation, Va. Tchr. spl. edn. Newport News (Va.) Pub. Schs., 1992—. Yearbook sponsor Newport News (Va.) Pub. Schs., 1992—, implemented collaborative tchg. program, 1994—, writing lead tchr., 1998—; counselor Summer Youth Program, Lebanon and Richmond, Va., 1993-94. Organizer Spl. Olympics Va., Newport News, 1993-94. Mem. ASCD, Internat. Reading Coun., Newport News Reading Coun. (co-chmn. banquet 1993-95).. Avocations: reading, writing. Office: Woodside HS 13456 Woodside Ln Newport News VA 23608-1809 E-mail: akm69@aol.com.

MEADE, DOROTHY WINIFRED, retired educational administrator; b. N.Y.C., Jan. 26, 1935; d. Percival and Fraulien Franklin; m. Gerald H. Meade (div. 1987); 1 child, Myrla E. BA in Am. History, Queens Coll., Flushing, N.Y., 1970; MA in Corrective Reading, Bklyn. Coll., 1975; BA in Religious Edn., United Christian Coll., Bklyn., 1980; postgrad., Bklyn. Coll., 1984. Tchr. social studies cluster Pub. Sch. 137, Bklyn., 1979-83, curriculum coord. Follow Through Program, 1984-88, adminstrv. intern, 1983-84; staff developer social studies Cen. Sch. Dist. 23, Bklyn., 1988-89, dist. coord. Project Child, 1989-91. Mem. faculty Coll. of New Rochelle, Bklyn., 1994-97. Participant Crossroads Africa, 1958; active Agape Tabernack Internat. Fellowship, 2000; former mem. Ch. of the Master; theol. intern Mt. Lebanon Bapt. Ch., 2001. Mem. African Christian Tchrs., N.Y. Pub. Sch. Early Childhood Edn., N.Y. Geography Inst., Women Organizing, Mobilizing, Bldg. Pentecostal. Avocations: bicycling, swimming, roller skating, singing, traveling. Home: 538 E 86th St Brooklyn NY 11236

MEADOR, DANIEL JOHN, law educator; b. Selma, Ala., Dec. 7, 1926; s. Daniel John and Mabel (Kirkpatrick) M.; m. Janet Caroline Heilmann, Nov. 19, 1955; children: Janet Barrie, Anna Kirkpatrick, Daniel John. BS, Auburn U., 1949; JD, U. Ala., 1951; LLM, Harvard U., 1954; LLD (hon.), U. S.C., 1998. Bar: Ala. 1951, Va. 1961. Law clk. to Justice Hugo L. Black U.S. Supreme Ct., 1954-55; assoc. firm Lange, Simpson, Robinson & Somerville, Birmingham, Ala., 1955-57; faculty U. Va. Law Sch., Charlottesville, 1957-66, prof. law, 1961-66; prof., dean U. Ala. Law Sch., 1966-70; James Monroe prof. law U. Va., Charlottesville, 1970-94, prof. emeritus, 1994—; asst. atty. gen. U.S., 1977-79; dir. grad. program for judges, 1979-95. Fulbright lectr., U.K., 1965-66; vis. prof. U.S. Mil. Acad., 1984; chmn. Southeastern Conf. Assn. Am. Law Schs., 1964-65; chmn. Cts. Task Force Nat. Adv. Commn. on Criminal Justice, 1971-72; dir. appellate justice project Nat. Ctr. for State Cts., 1972-74; mem. Adv. Coun. on Appellate Justice, 1971-75, Coun. on Role of Cts., 1978-84; bd. dirs. State Justice Inst., 1986-92; exec. dir. commn. on structural alternatives Fed. Ct. Appeals, 1998-99. Author: Preludes to Gideon, 1967, Criminal Appeals-English Practices and American Reforms, 1973, Mr. Justice Black and His Books, 1974, Appellate Courts: Staff and Process in the Crisis of Volume, 1974, (with Carrington and Rosenberg) Justice on Appeal, 1976, Impressions of Law in East Germany, 1986, American Courts, 1991, 2000 (with J. Bernstein) Appellate Courts in the United States, 1994, His Father's House, 1994, Unforgotten, 1999, (with Rosenberg and Carrington) Appellate Courts: Structures, Functions, Processes, and Personnel, 1994; editor: Hardy Cross Dillard: Writings and Speeches, 1995; editor Va. Bar News, 1962-65; contbr. articles to profl. jours. 1st lt. U.S. Army, 1951-53; col. JAGC, USAR ret. Decorated Bronze Star.; IREX fellow German Dem. Republic, 1983 Mem. ABA (chmn. standing com. on fed. jud. improvements 1987-90), Ala. Bar Assn., Va. Bar Assn. (exec. com. 1983-86), Am. Law Inst., Am. Judicature Soc. (bd. dirs. 1975-77, 80-83), Soc. Pub. Tchrs. Law, Am. Soc. Legal History (bd. dirs. 1968-71), Order of Coif, Raven Soc., Phi Delta Phi, Omicron Delta Kappa, Kappa Alpha. Presbyterian. Office: U Va Sch Law 580 Massie Rd Charlottesville VA 22903-1738

MEADOR, JOHN MILWARD, JR., university dean; b. Louisville, Nov. 4, 1946; s. John Milward and Ruth Inez (Miller) M.; m. Judith Ann Hay, Dec. 22, 1969; children: John Milward III, Elise Kathleen. BA, U. Louisville, 1968; MA, U. Tex., 1972, MLS, 1973; cert. in pub. adminstrn., U. Utah, 1982. Cert. tchr., Ky., Tex. Stacks supr. U. Louisville Librs., 1965-68; English bibliographer M.D. Anderson Libr. U. Houston, 1973-74, head reference dept. social scis. and humanities, 1974-77, head gen. reference dept., 1977-80; asst. dir. pub. svcs. Marriott Libr. U. Utah, Salt Lake City, 1980-84; dean libr. svcs. S.W. Mo. State U., Springfield, 1984-93; dean librs. U. Miss., Univeristy, 1993—2003; dir. librs. SUNY, Binghamton, 2003—. Bd. dirs. Mo. Libr. Network Corp., 1984-90, St. Louis, S.W. Mo. Libr. Network, Springfield; cons. Dayco Corp., Springfield, 1984-86; chmn. Mo. Northwestern Online Total Integrated Systems (NOTIS) Users Group, 1988-89. Co-author: The Robinson Jeffers Collection at the University of Houston, 1975; contbr. articles to profl. jours. Sponsor Community Alternative Svc. Program, Springfield and St. Louis, 1985-93; mem. governing bd. Mo. Rsch. and Edn. Network, MOREnet, 1991-93; With U.S. Army, 1969-71, Vietnam. Recipient Nat. Essay award Propeller Club of U.S., 1964; named to Honorable Order of Ky. Colonels, Gov. Ky., 1978; summer scholar English-Speaking Union, Edinburgh, Scotland, 1968; Apple Computer's Higher Edn. Acad. Devel. Donation Program grantee, 1990. Mem. ALA, Am. Assn. for Higher Edn., Assn. Coll. Rsch. Librs., Bibliog. Soc. Am., Libr. Adminstrn. and Mgmt. Assn., other profl. orgns., English-Speaking Union Club, Rotary (chmn. students guests com. Springfield chpt. 1986-89, chmn. scholarships com. 1989-90, bd. dirs. 1990-91, bd. dirs. Oxford chpt. 1995-96), Phi Kappa Phi. Avocations: raising pure bred airedale terriers, fishing, book collecting. Home: PO Box 223 Binghamton NY 13902-0223 Office: Binghamton Univ SUNY Bartle Library Binghamton NY 13902-6012 Fax: 607-777-4848. E-mail: jmeador@binghamton.edu.

MEADORS, ALLEN COATS, health administrator, educator; b. Van Buren, Ark., May 17, 1947; s. Hal Barron and Allene Coats (Means) M. AA, Saddleback Coll., 1981; BBA, U. Ctrl. Arki., 1969; MBA, U. No. Colo., 1974; MPA, U. Kans., 1975; MA in Psychology, Webster U., 1979, MA in Health Svcs. Mgmt., 1980; PhD in Adminstrn., So. Ill. U., 1981. Assoc. adminstr. Forbes Hosp., Topeka, 1971-73; asst. dir. health svcs. devel. Blue Cross Blue Shield of Kans., Topeka, 1973-76; asst. dir. Kansas City Health Dept. (Mo.), 1976-77; program dir., asst. prof. So. Ill. U., Carbondale, 1978-82, Webster U., St. Louis, 1978-82; assoc. prof., dir. divsn. health adminstrn. U. Tex., Galveston, 1982-84; exec. dir. N.W. Ark. Radiation Therapy Inst., Springdale, Ark., 1984-87; prof., chmn. dept. health adminstrn. U. Okla., Oklahoma City, 1989-90, dean Coll. Pub. Health, 1989-90; mem. faculty Calif. State U., Long Beach, 1977-81; mem. grad. faculty Sch. Bus. Adminstrn. U. Ark., Fayetteville, 1984-87; prof., chmn. dept. health adminstrn. U. Okla., 1987-90; dean Coll. Health, Social and Pub. Svcs. Ea. Wash. U., Cheney, 1990-94; CEO, dean Pa. State U., Altoona, 1994-99; chancellor U. N.C., Pembroke, 1999—. Cons. Surgeon Gen. Office and Air Force Sys. Contbr. articles to profl. jours. Command bd. dirs. Blair County Hall of Fame, Blair County Hist. Soc., Martin Luther King Hosp., Health Care Svcs. Adv. Bd.; bd. dirs., mem. exec. com. Altoona Symphony Orch.; bd. dirs. Southwestern Regional Med. Ctr., Home Health Agy. With Med. Svc. Corps, USAF, 1969-73. Fellow Am. Coll. Healthcare Execs.; mem. Am. Hosp. Assn., C. of C. (v.p.). Home: Chancellors Residence Pembroke NC 28372 Office: U NC at Pembroke Chancellors Office PO Box 1510 Pembroke NC 28372-1510 E-mail: acm@uncp.edu.

MEADOWS, LOIS ANNETTE, elementary education educator; b. Harrisville, W.Va., Jan. 12, 1948; d. Orvle Adam and Una Pauline (Slocum) Ingram; m. David Alan Meadows, June 15, 1969; children: Lynecia Ann, Eric Justin. BA, Glenville State Coll., 1969; MA, W.Va. U., 1980. Cert. music, elem. edn., reading, computer tech. edn., W.Va.; nat. cert. elem. tchr. Tchr. grade six Acad. Park-Portsmouth (Va.) City Schs., 1969-73; elem. substitute Wood County Schs., Parkersburg, W.Va., 1973-77; real estate agt. Nestor Realty, Parkersburg, 1974-77; tchr. grade five/music Emerson Elem. Wood County Schs., Parkersburg, W.Va., 1977-78, tchr. grade three, 1978—; edn. cons. World Book, Parkersburg, 1986—. Mentor tchr.-trainer Wood County Schs., parkersburg, 1990—; W.Va. S.T.E.P. Test com./trainer W.Va. Dept. Edn., Charleston, 1994—, mem. pool of talented educators, presenter sessions goals and objectives Ctr. Profl. Devel. Gov.'s Inst.; grant writer and spkr. in field; mem. W.Va. Dept. Edn. State Writing Manual Com., 1996-2001; coord. W.Va.-Ohio-Ky. Nat. Read-In.; presenter Gov's Summer Insts. for Ctr. for Profl. Devel., 1994—; mem. standards com. 4th grade writing assessment W.Va. Dept. Edn., 1994—. Author: (reading projects) Operation Blackout, 1986-94 (grant 1994), The Reading Room, 1988 (grant 1990), Storytime at the Mall, 1986— (grant 1994, 95); contbg. author W.V. Math Workbook, 1998, 99. Life mem. Emerson PTA, Parkersburg, 1977—; Sunday Sch. tchr. North Parkersburg Bapt. Ch., 1976-98, children's choir dir., 1976-88; fund raiser local charities, Parkersburg. Women of Excellence and Leadership Timely Honored award, W. Va. State Reading Tchr. of Yr., 1988, Finalist W. Va. State Tchr. of Yr., W.Va. Dept. Edn., 1993, Wood County Tchr. of Yr., 1993, Ashland Oil Golden Apple Achiever award, 1995, Ashland Oil Tchr. Achievement Award Winner (1 0f 10 for WV), 1998, Wood Co. PTA Outstanding Educator of Yr. award, 1995-96, award for ann. contbrs. and project work Emerson PTA, Wealth award Women of Excellence and Leadership Timely Honored, 1993, 2001; Nat. writing fellow W.Va. Writing Project, 1999. Mem. W.Va. Reading Assn. (pres. 1993-94, mem. chmn. 1994—, Spl. Svc. award 1997), Internat. Reading Assn., Wood County Reading Coun. (past pres. 1986-88, 90-92), Am. Fedn. Tchrs., Delta Kappa Gamma. Republican. Avocations: children's literature, collecting autographed books, bridge, basket weaving, family times. Home: 142 Jomar Dr Parkersburg WV 26104-9169 Office: Wood County Schs Emerson Elem 1605 36th St Parkersburg WV 26104-1939

MEAGHER, JOAN CECELIA, elementary education educator; b. Balt., June 6, 1948; d. Joseph Alfred Morris and Florence Cecelia (Geyton) Treece; m. Bernard Francis Meagher, Sept. 6, 1969; 1 child, Thomas Francis. BS, Towson U., 1970, MEd, 1974; MS, Johns Hopkins U., 1983. Cert. elem. tchr., reading specialist, Md. Classroom tchr. Baltimore County Pub. Schs., Balt., 1970-92, reading specialist, 1992—. Mem. State of Md. Internat. Reading Assn. Coun. (pres. 1997-98), Balt. County Coun. Internat. Reading Assn. (pres. 1989-91).

MEAL, LARIE, chemistry educator, researcher, consultant; b. Cin., June 15, 1939; d. George Lawrence Meal and Dorothy Louise (Heileman) Fitzpatrick. BS in Chemistry, U. Cin., 1961, PhD in Chemistry, 1966. Rsch. chemist U.S. Indsl. Chems., Cin., 1966-67; instr. chemistry U. Cin., 1968-69, asst. prof., 1969-75, assoc. prof., 1975-90, prof., 1990—, rschr., 1980—. Cons. in field. Contbr. articles to profl. jours. Mem. AAAS, N.Y. Acad. Scis., Am. Chem. Soc., NOW, Planned Parenthood, Iota Sigma Pi. Democrat. Avocations: gardening, yard work. Home: 2231 Slane Ave Norwood OH 45212-3615 Office: U Cin 2220 Victory Pky Cincinnati OH 45206-2822

MEALER, LYNDA REAM, physical education educator; b. Lima, Ohio, Sept. 19, 1946; d. Don A. and Sue (Pringle) Duncan; m. Ben T. Mealer, Aug. 29, 1970; children: Thomas Lee, Theresa Lynn. AA, LaSalle U., Chgo., 1976; BS, La. State U., 1983,, 1992. Office mgr. M. Quick Ins., Glenmora, La., 1975-77; ind. bus. owner Glenmora (La.) Exxon, 1977-82; kindergarten tchr. Glenmora (La.) Elem. Sch., 1986-87; 4th grade tchr., 1983-86, 92-94; 6th grade tchr. Forest Hill (La.) Acad., 1989-90; 4th grade tchr. Glenmora (La.) Elem. Sch., 1992-94; phys. edn. tchr., 1994—. Intervention strategist Drug Free Schs., Rapides Parish, La., 1994-95; crisis intervention Team Glenmora (La.) Elem. Sch., 1994-95. Author: (poem) Who's Who in Poetry, 1993, Vengeance is Mine, 1988. Sec., pres. Glenmora (La.) Garden Club, 1974-87; sec., pres., legis. chair Bus. and Profl. Women, Glenmora, La., 1981-91. Recipient Student Svc. award Student Govt. Assn., La. State U. 1983, Lifetime mem. Gamma Beta Phi, La. State U., 1983, Scholarship award Sm. Assn. Women, Alexandria, La., 1992, Lifetime/charter mem. Golden Key Hon. Soc., Baton Rouge, La., 1992. Mem. NEA, La. Assn. Educators, Rapides Fedn. Tchrs. Avocations: reading, sewing, arts and crafts, home decorating, writing. Home: 1512 Billings Rd Glenmora LA 71433-4318 Office: Glenmora Elementary School PO Box 1188 Glenmora LA 71433-1188

MEANS, DWIGHT BARDEEN, JR., financial consultant, educator; b. Pitts., July 21, 1943; s. Dwight B. Sr. and Betty (Feick) M.; div.; children: Melissa Means Morris, Blake Elizabeth. BSEE, Carnegie-Mellon U., 1965; MBA, U. Pitts., 1969, PhD, 1984. Various positions Bell Telephone Co. Pa., Pitts., 1965-70; asst. prof., dept. chair C.C. Allegheny County, Pitts., 1970-78; from asst. to assoc. prof. Saginaw (Mich.) Valley State U., 1978-86; prof., dept. chair Clarion (Pa.) U. Pa., 1986-88; asst. prof. U. Memphis, 1988-95; adj. prof. numerous univs., 1996—; cons., 1995—. Presenter in field. Reviewer Fin. Practice and Edn., Jour. Econs. and Fin., Jour. Real Estate Rsch., Jour. Applied Bus. Rsch; contbr. articles to profl. jours. Mem. Acad. Fin. Svcs. (program com. 1990-95), Am. Econ. Assn., Midsouth Acad. Econs. and Fin. (dir. 1993-95), Fin. Mgmt. Assn. (program com. 1989), Midwest Fin. Assn. (program com. 1995-96), S.W. Fin. Assn. (program com. 1994-95), So. Fin. Assn. (program com. 1992-95). Avocations: hunting, fishing, camping, reading. Home: 138 Owendale Ave Pittsburgh PA 15227-1951 E-mail: meansdb@aol.com.

MEANS, JOHN BARKLEY, foreign language educator, association executive; b. Cin., Jan. 2, 1939; s. Walker Wilson and Rosetta M. Means. BA, U. Ill., 1960, MA, 1963, PhD, 1968. U.S. govt. intelligence rsch. analyst on Brazil CIA, Washington, 1962-64; assoc. prof. Spanish and Portugese Temple U., Phila., 1972-82, prof. Portuguese and critical langs., 1982—2003, prof. emeritus, 2003—, co-chmn. dept. Spanish and Portuguese, 1971-75, dir. Center for Critical Langs., 1975—2003, dir. Inst. for Langs. and Internat. Studies, 1987—2003, chmn. dept. Germanic and Slavic Langs. and lit., 1992-94, chair univ. core programs, 1995-97. Cons. on Brazilian-Portuguese and second lang. acquisition and self instrnl. programs for less commonly taught langs., 1968—2003; cons. editor for langs. Norton Pubs., 1979—95; cons. in field. Editor: Essays on Brazilian Literature, 1971; author (with others): Language in Education: Theory and Practice, 1988—; co-dir. CD-ROM Critical Language Series, 1999—; contbr. articles to profl. jours. Trustee Bristol Riverside Theatre, Pa., 1990—2002; mng. trustee Means Charitable Trust, 1993—. 1st lt. U.S. Army, 1960—62. Fellow, U. Ill., 1967; grantee, U.S. Dept. Edn., 1979—83, Japan Found., 1980, 1982, 1989—91, ARCO Chem. Found., 1991, 1993; NDEA fellow, 1962, 1964. Mem.: MLA, Joint Nat. Com. for Langs. (bd. dirs.), Nat. Assn. state Univs. and Lang Grant Colls. (commn. on internat. affairs), Nat. Coun. Orgns. Less Commonly Taught Langs. (exec. sec.-treas. 1990—2001), Am. Coun. on Tchg. Fgn. Lang., Nat. assn. Self-Instrnl. Lang. Programs (exec. dir. 1977—98, editor jour. 1978—94, exec. dir. emeritus 1999—), Nat. Coun. on Langs. and Internat. Studies (bd. dirs.), Sigma Delta Pi, Phi Lambda Beta, Pi Kappa Phi. Home: PO Box 829 Washington Crossing PA 18977-0829 Office: Temple U Ctr for Critical Langs Anderson Hall 1114 W Berks St Philadelphia PA 19122-6090 E-mail: means@temple.edu.

MEARDY, WILLIAM HERMAN, retired educational association administrator; b. Peoria, Ill., Feb. 28, 1925; s. Herman and Madeleine (McReynolds) Meardy; m. Joyce Dorothy Horn, Mar. 28, 1946; children: William

Wesley, Karen Lynn. Student, Bradley U., 1948—51; BA, Calif. State U., LA, 1952, MA, 1958; postgrad., UCLA, 1964. Tchr. La Puente (Calif.) Union HS, 1953-56; acad., personal and job placement counselor Mt. San Antonio Coll., Walnut, Calif., 1956-63; dean student pers. svcs. Rio Hondo Coll., Whittier, Calif., 1963-67; dean student services and activities Shasta Coll., Redding, Calif., 1967-70; exec. sec. Coun. Cmty. Coll. Bds., Evanston, Ill., 1970-72; founding exec. dir. Assn. Cmty. Coll. Trustees, Washington, 1972-88, ret. Contbr. articles to profl. jours. Chmn. West Covina (Calif.) coun. Boy Scouts Am., 1960—61; vol. driver Presbyn. Hosp., Whittier, Calif.; bd. dirs. Nat. Coun. Responsible Pub. Interest Groups. With USN, 1943—46, 1st lt. USAFR, 1952. Mem.: Shriners, Masons. Home and Office: 13675 Sycamore Dr Whittier CA 90601-3848 E-mail: wmeardy2001@yahoo.com.

MECHLEM, DAPHNE JO, vocational school educator; b. Cin., Oct. 20, 1946; d. Louis Edward Griffith and Esther Eileen (Calvert) Griffith-Schultz; m. James T. Mechlem, Nov. 18, 1967 (div. June 1983); 1 chld, Louis Henry. BS summa cum laude, U. Cin., 1982, MS, 1983, MEd, 1984. Cert. vocat. and adult dir., supr., cosmetology instr. Stylist, mgr. Fashion Flair Styling, Cin., 1965-70, Ann Wolfe Coiffures, Cin., 1970-71; salon owner Curls by Daphne, Cin., 1971-77; tchr. Gt. Oaks Joint Vocat. Sch. Dist., Cin., 1976-83, adminstrv. intern, 1983; probation officer Hamilton County Juvenile Ct., Cin., 1983-96; tchr. Gt. Oaks Joint Vocat. Sch. Dist., Cin., 1983—. Facilitator High Schools That Work Design team, 1999—; spkr., presenter workshops in field. Author: Critical Issues in Campus Policing, 1983; lectr: workshops, seminars and classes. Sec.-treas. Cin. Fashion Guild; mem. Great Oaks local profl. devel. com., 1999—. Mem. ASCD, Nat. Cosmetology Assn., Criminal Justice Assn., Am. Vocat. Assn., Ohio Vocat. Assn., Ohio Vocat. Cosmetology Tchrs. Assn. (2d v.p., continuing edn. adminstr.). Avocations: flying, travel, counseling. Home: 5776 Pleasant Hill Rd Milford OH 45150-2301

MEDALIE, MARJORIE LYNN, educational administrator, consultant; b. Bklyn., June 25, 1947; d. Charles and Bette P. (Feldman) Drucker; m. Randolph Medalie, Mar. 26, 1970; children: Jeremy Chad, Daniel Bradley. BA, Ithaca Coll., 1969; MA, Adelphi U., 1973, spl. edn. cert., 1985; profl. diploma, C. W. Post Coll., 1991. Cert. spl. educator, sch. dist. adminstr. Tchr. English, Island Trees (N.Y.) Sch. Dist., 1970-73, West Hempstead (N.Y.) Sch. Dist., 1973-76; tchr. spl. edn. Summit Sch., Forrest Hills, N.Y., 1976-77; coord. alternative class program Huntington (N.Y.) U.F.S.D. # 3, 1982-86; tchr. spl. edn. self-contained classroom Center Moriches (N.Y.) Sch. Dist., Riverhead, N.Y., 1986-88; lead tchr. for alternative high schs. Bd. Coop. Scnl. Svcs. 1, Riverhead, N.Y., 1988—. Presenter in field. V.p. Am. Cancer Soc., Melville, N.Y., 1974-81; mgr. Tri-Village Little League, Greenlawn, N.Y., 1986-90; active edn. com. Temple Chaverim. Mem. ASCD, Nat. Coun. Tchrs. English, United Fedn. Tchrs., East End Counselors Assn., Western Suffolk Counselors, Kappa Delta Pi, Epsilon Nu Gamma. Jewish. Avocations: skiing, reading, travel, boating, cooking.

MEDDLES, SHARON DIANE GUNSTREAM, school counselor; b. Pasadena, Calif., Feb. 9, 1947; d. Jarrell William and Vivian Irene (Heffner) Gunstream; m. Larry Wayne Meddles, June 16, 1973; children: Brittany Dawn, Brooke Reneé. BA in English, Pasadena Coll., 1968; MEd in Counseling, U. Phoenix, 1996. Cert. tchr., Ariz. English and music tchr. Coronado Hills Jr. H.S. Adams County Dist. 12, Thornton, Colo., 1969-72; 8th grade lang. arts tchr. Ocotillo Sch. Washington Elem. Sch. Dist. 6, Phoenix, 1972-76, homebound tchr., 1985-86, 88-90; sr. high tchr. N.W. Christian Acad., Glendale, Ariz., 1986-87; 7th and 8th grade English and reading tchr. Cholla Mid. Sch. Washington Sch. Dist., Phoenix, 1990-96, sch. counselor Lakeview and Sunburst Elem. Schs., 1996-2000; adminstrv. asst. Sunburst Elem. Sch., Glendale, 2000—02, student svcs. specialist, 2002—. Adj. faculty mem. Southwestern Coll., 2000—01. Core group leader Cmty. Bible Study, Phoenix, 1988-90; bd. dirs. Orangewood Ch. of the Nazarene, Phoenix, 1982-84, 93, 2003-; local pres. Nazarene World Missionary Soc., 1982-84; dist. dir. Point Loma Alumni Bd., San Diego, 1990-93, sec., 1993-96; mem. Orangewood Ch. of the Nazarene. Republican. Avocation: singing. Home: 1115 W Le Marche Ave Phoenix AZ 85023-4429

MEDEIROS, M. JOYCE, community health educator; b. Boston, Feb. 17, 1954; d. Raymond A. and D. Jean (Russell) Harrington; m. Joseph A. Medeiros, July 26, 1977; children: Jessica A., Jo Ellen. Grad., Youville Hosp. Sch. Practical Nursing, 1973; BS in Cmty. Health Edn., U. Maine, Farmington, 1992. Lic. social worker. Staff nurse Goddard Meml. Hosp., Stoughton, Mass., 1973-87; dist. dir. Somerset Family YMCA, 1988-90; ITV aide Skowhegan (Maine) H.S., 1990-91; intern Somerset Residential Care Ctr., 1991-92, WARNACO, 1992; dir. edn. Sebasticook Valley Hosp., 1992-96; spl. needs edn. tech. transition III MSAD # 59 Madison (Maine) H.S., 1996-99; children's case mgr. Youth & Family Svcs., 1999—2003. Camp nurse, dir. 4-H Camp Farley, 1982-87, Camp at Eastward Starks, Maine, 1990. Selectman Town of Starks, 1995. Completed 2000 Honolulu Marathon, Leukemia, Lymphoma Soc. Mem.: Phi Sigma Pi, Eta Sigma Gamma. Avocations: camping, bowling, photography, ceramics, collecting music boxes. Home: 241 Dill Rd Starks ME 04911

MEDICUS, HILDEGARD JULIE, retired dentist, orthodontist, educator; b. Frankfurt, Germany, July 25, 1928; came to U.S., 1961, naturalized, 1995; d. Gustav and Elizabeth Berta (Neunhoeffer) Schmelz; m. Heinrich Adolf Medicus, June 15, 1961. DMD, U. Marburg, W. Germany, 1953; orthodontics diploma, U. Düsseldorf, W. Germany, 1957. lic. dentist, N.Y. Postdoctoral fellow dental sch. U. Zürich, Switzerland, 1957; postdoctoral fellow U. Liège, Belgium, 1958, Forsyth Dental Ctr., Boston, 1959, orthodontic rsch. affiliate, 1963—74; sch. dentist Pub. Sch. Sys., Zürich, 1975—76; dental hygiene instr. Hudson Valley C.C., Troy, NY, 1976—77; pvt. practice Troy, NY, 1977—89. Active Hudson Mohawk Swiss Soc. Mem. AAUW, ADA, European Orthodontic Soc., German Orthodontic Soc. Presbyterian. Achievements include study of functional orthodontic appliances and growth and development. Home: 1 The Knoll Troy NY 12180-7284

MEDIN, JULIA ADELE, mathematics educator, researcher; b. Dayton, Ohio, Jan. 16, 1929; d. Caroline (Feinberg) Levitt; m. A. Louis Medin, Dec. 24, 1950; children: Douglas, David, Thomas, Linda. BS in Maths. Edn., Ohio State U., 1951; MA in Higher Edn., George Washington U., 1977; PhD in Counseling and Edn., Am. U., 1985. Cert. tchr., Fla., Md. Rsch. engr. Sun Oil Co., Marcus Hook, Pa., 1951-53; tchr. maths. Montgomery County Pub. Schs., Rockville, Md., 1973-88; asst. prof. maths. U. Ctrl. Fla., Orlando, 1988-90, sr. ednl. technologist Inst. for Simulation and Tng., 1990-99; sr. assoc. Mgmt. and Ednl. Tech. Assocs., 1999—. Adv. steering com. U.S. Dept. Edn. Title II, Washington, 1985-89; sr. math. educator, rschr. Inst. for Simulation and Tng., Orlando, 1988-90; judge, co-chair GII Nar. Awards; co-acad. advisor I/ITSEC Conf.; condr. nationwide rsch. project on effective use of technology in the classroom; spkr. in field. Author: Loc. of Cont. and Test Anxiety of Mar. Math. Studies, 1985; contbg. author: Math for 14 & 17 Yr. Olds, 1987; editor: Simulation and Computer-Based Technology for Education; contbr. articles to profl. jours. Dem. committeewoman Town of Monroeville, Pa., 1962; religious sch. dir. Beth Tikva Religious Sch., Rockville, 1971; cons. Monroeville Mental Health, 1960. Mem. Nat. Coun. Tchrs. Math., Math. Assn. Am. (task force on minorities in math.), Women in Math. in Edn., Nat. Coalition for Tech. in Edn. and Tng., Phi Delta Kappa, Kappa Delta Pi. Home and Office: 11401 Ridge Mist Ter Potomac MD 20854-7002 E-mail: jmedin@comcast.net.

MEDINA-DIAZ, MARIA DEL ROSARIO, education educator; b. N.Y.C. BA in Edn., U. P.R., Rio Piedras, 1980, MS in Edn., 1986; PhD in Ednl. Psychology, U. Wis., 1991. Lic. secondary sch. math. tchr. Math. tchr. Dept. Pub. Instrn., San Juan, P.R., 1981-86; project asst. U. Wis., Madison, 1989-91; asst. prof. U. P.R., Rio Piedras, 1992—. Advance opportunity fellow U. Wis., Madison, 1986-89; Nat. Hispanis Scholarship Fund scholar, 1988. Mem. APA, Assn. Math. Tchrs. P.R. (v.p. 1993-94, 96-97, pres. 1997-98), Psychometric Soc., Am. Ednl. Rsch. Assn., Nat. Coun. Ednl. Measurement, Nat. Coun. Tchrs. Math., Am. Evaluation Assn. Office: U PR Faculty Edn Rio Piedras PR 00931

MEDVED, SANDRA LOUISE, elementary education educator; b. Moscow, Idaho, May 26, 1953; d. Donald James and Pearl Helen (Brown) Jensen; m. Jeffrey Alan Medved, Aug. 6, 1977. BS in Edn., U. Idaho, 1975; postgrad., Boise State U., 1976, U. Idaho, 1977—. Tchr. St. Mary's Elem. Sch., Boise, Idaho, 1975-78, Coeur d'Alene (Idaho) Sch. Dist., 1978—. Tchr. edn. U. Idaho, 1987-88; instr. Lewis and Clark State Coll., 1994-98; lead tchr. Coeur d'Alene Sch. Dist., 1997-2000, assessment literacy facilitator, 2001—, decade of change com./leadership, 1997—2002, supervision and evaluation com., 1998—2001, puppeteer, 1985-91, tchr. edn. instr., 1986-88, 92-94, lang. arts com., 1988—, dist. coord. handicap awareness program, 1989-91, staff devel. curriclum adv. com., 1990-95, mentor tchr., 1990-93, 99-2000, mem. phonics spelling com., 1996-98, mem. Educator of the Yr. com., 1997—, mem. staff devel. com., 1997—, mem. leadership team, 2002—; active Idaho State Sch. Reform Com., 1994-95; rep. Goals 2000 Tchr. Forum, 1995. Vol. Kootenai County Diversion Program, Coeur d'Alene, 1980's. Recipient grants EXCEL, Coeur d'Alene, 1991-92. Mem. ASCD, NEA, Idaho Edn. Assn., Coeur d'Alene Edn. Assn., Internat. Reading Assn., Panhandle Reading Assn., Phi Delta Kappa. Avocations: reading, swimming, walking, kayaking. Office: Sorensen Elem Coeur D Alene Sch Dist 9th and Coeur d'Alene Ave Coeur D Alene ID 83814

MEEGAN, BROTHER GARY VINCENT, school administrator, music educator; b. Syracuse, N.Y., Oct. 29, 1952; s. Vincent John and Kathryn Joan (Gettino) M. AAS in Music, Onondaga C.C., 1975; B Music Edn., Syracuse U., 1978; MS in Ednl. Leadership, Calif. State U., Hayward, 1990; postgrad., U. So. Calif., 1991-92, Washington Theol. Union, 1993, U. Tex., 1997. Cert. music educator, adminstr., Calif. Tchr. music West Genesee Cen. Schs., Camillus, N.Y., 1979-80, Modesto (Calif.) City Sch. Dist., 1983-87, Shiloh Sch. Dist., Modesto, 1987-90; asst. prin. Sylvan Union Sch. Dist., Modesto, 1990-93; mem. faculty, dir. studies Holy Cross H.S., San Antonio, Tex., 1995-97; prin. Five Wounds Cath. Sch., San Jose, Calif., 1997—. Bd. dirs. Modesto Performing Arts, 1984-89; prin. conductor Stanislaus Youth Symphony, Modesto, 1985-89. Bd. dirs. Townsend Opera Players, Modesto, 1985-87, Modesto Arts Coun., 1986. Mem. ASCD, Nat. Acad. Tel. Arts and Scis., Am. Ednl. Rsch. Assn., Music Educators Nat. Conf., Calif. Music Educators Assn. (task force 1989-90), Stanislaus County Music Educators Assn. (pres. 1989-90), Phi Delta Kappa. Roman Catholic. Avocations: writing, performing, marching band, santa clara vanguard drum and bugle corps. Office: Five Wounds Sch 1390 Five Wounds Ln San Jose CA 95116-1127

MEEHAN, ROBERT HENRY, human resources executive, electronics company executive, business educator; b. Hackensack, N.J., June 19, 1946; s. Horace Miles and Pauline Jeannette (Pente) M.; m. Ruth Ann Auletta, Sept. 28, 1969; children: Robert Michael, Brian John. BA, Montclair State U., 1968; MA magna cum laude, Fairleigh Dickinson U., 1972; D in Profl. Studies, Pace U., 1997. Cert. secondary sch. tchr. of social studies, N.J., compensation and benefits profl. Job analyst Citicorp, N.Y.C., 1969-70, sr. job analyst, 1970-72, ofcl. asst., 1972, project specialist human resources practices/policy rev., 1973, project specialist attitude surveys, 1973-75, human resources officer nat. banking group, 1975-76; asst. dir. human resources N.Y. Power Authority, White Plains, 1976-84, dir. compensation, 1984-93, dir. compensation and human resources info. sys., 1993-94, dir. compensation and benefits strategy and devel., 1994-95, dir. compensation and benefits, 1995-98; dir. compensation Philips Electronics N.Am., 1998-2000; mng. dir. R.H. Meehan Assocs., Human Capital Cons., Maywood, NJ, 2000—01; dir. compensation, benefits and HRIS, ASML, Tempe, Ariz., 2001—. Instr. World at Work, Scottsdale, Ariz., 1986—, course coord., 1992-94, mem. cert. and currency com., 1988-89, direct compensation com. 1990-91, chmn. 1992-93, bd. dirs. 1993; adj. assoc. prof. Lubin Grad. Sch. Bus., Pace U., 1995-2001; mem. N.Y. Power Pool Salary com., 1990-98, chair, 1998; spkr. at profl. confs. Sr. author: Managing a Direct Pay Program, Cert. Course 4A, 1991, Determining Compensation Costs: An Approach to Estimating and Analyzing Expense, 1991; editor books; mem. exec. adv. panel Acad. Mgmt. Exec., 1993—; contbr. articles to profl. jours. Scoutmaster, Boy Scouts Am., Ridgefield Park, N.J., 1968; also scouting coord., Maywood, N.J., 1982-83; vestryman, sr. warden St. Martin's Episcopal Ch., Maywood, 1977-84. Mem. Soc. for Human Resource Mgmt. (mem. compensation and benefits com. 1998-2001), Metro Phoenix Human Resource Assocs., 2002—, Human Resources Assn. N.Y. (compensation com. 1998-2001), Acad. Mgmt. (exec. adv. panel jour. The Exec.), N.Y. Compensation Assn., 2000-01, Order DeMolay (master councilor 1963, 65, scribe, adv. bd. 1965-68, Meritorious Svcs. award 1965), Psi, Delta Mu Delta, Beta Gamma Sigma. Episcopalian. Avocations: golf, sailing, furniture making. Office: ASML 8555 S River Pkwy Tempe AZ 85284 Business E-Mail: Robert.Meehan@asml.com.

MEEK, AMY GERTRUDE, retired elementary education educator; b. Frostburg, Md., Jan. 3, 1928; d. Arthur Stewart and Amy Laura (Brain) M. BS, Frostburg State U., 1950; MEd, U. Md., 1956; postgrad., Columbia U., 1964, Am. U., 1968-70. Cert. tchr., Md. Tchr. elem. sch. Prince Georges County Schs., Bradbury Heights, Md., 1950-51, Allegany County Schs., Cumberland, Md., 1951-60, Frostburg, 1960-84; now ret. Author (with others): Stir Into Flame, 1991; contbr. articles to profl. jours. Mem. Frostburg Hosp. Aux., 1987-91; bd. dirs. Frostburg Hist. Mus., 1989—, Coun. of Alleghenies, 1991, sec., 1991-2003; sec. Braddock Estates Civic Assn., Frostburg, 1988; mem. com. Frostburg Libr., 1989; tchr. Ch. Conf. Schs. Missions, 1970; vol. tutor, 1986-92; pres. Ch. Women United, Frostburg, 1989-95; trustee Frostburg United Meth. Ch., 1992—; pres. Cumberland-Hagerstown dist. United Meth. Women, 1985-89, chmn. fin. interpretation Balt. Conf., 1990-94; lay spkr. United Meth. Ch., 1975—, endowment fund com. Balt. conf., 1992-2003, bd. ordained ministry Cumberland-Hagerstown dist., 2000—; pres. bd. dirs. Frostburg Mus., 2000—. Mem. AAUW (pres. 1993-95, treas. Md. divsn. 1974-76, Woman of Yr. award Frostburg br. 1980, New Frostburg Libr. Bldg. Com. 1994-98, chair pub. policy com. Frostburg br. 2001—, treas. libr. fund 2002—). Republican. Avocations: travel, reading, gardening, genealogy, historical research.

MEEK, BARBARA SUSAN, elementary education educator; b. Monaca, Pa., Feb. 8, 1951; d. Michael Frederick and Sarah Ellen (Hall) Fronko; m. Joseph William Meek Jr., Nov. 25, 1977. BS in Edn., Ohio U., 1973; MA in Edn., Marietta Coll., 1999. Cert. elem. tchr., Ohio. 3d grade tchr. Warren Local Schs., Vincent, Ohio. Martha Holden Jennings scholar, 1976-77. Mem. NEA, Ohio coun. Tchrs. Math., Ohio Coun. Internat. Reading Assn., Ohio Edn. Assn., Warren Local Edn. Assn. Home: 5371 Veto Road Vincent OH 45784-5118

MEEK, FORREST BURNS, retired trading company executive; b. Tustin, Mich., June 11, 1928; s. Robert B. and Electa I. (Gallup) M.; m. Jean R. Grimes, June 26, 1953; children: Sally, Thomas, Nancy, Charles. AA, Spring Arbor Coll., 1950; AB, Mich. State U., 1953; postgrad., U. Ga., 1965; MA, Cen. Mich. U., 1967. Exec. sec., chmn. bd. Edgewood Press, Clare, 1971—; gen. mgr. Blue Water Imports, 1985; dir. Ctr. for Chinese-Am. Scholarly Exchs., Inc., 1989-97; gen. mgr. Blue-Water Internat. Trading Co., Inc.; retired, 1998. Vis. prof. Wuhan U., China, 1986—87; dist. office mgr. Fed. Decennial Census, 1990; instr. phys. geology and astronomy Mid Mich. C.C., 2002, instr. astronomy, 2001—03; mem., chmn. Red team East Ctrl. Mich. Planning and Devel. Regional Commn. Author: Michigan Timber Battleground, 1976, Michigan Heartland, 1979, One Year in China, 1988, Michigan Logging Railroad Era, 1850-1963, 1989, Railways and Tramways, 1990, Lumbering in Eastern Canada, 1991, Pearl Harbor Remembered, 1991, Heroes of The Twentieth Century, 2000. Coordinator Clare County Bicentennial Com., 1975-76; Rep. fin. chmn., Clare County, 1966-71, asst. treas. 10th dist. Mich, 1967-69; trustee local sch. bd., 1992-96; chmn. local county jury bd., 1991-98; mem. bd. commrs. Clare County (Mich.) Dist. 4 Commn., 1998-2000, 2003—. Mem. Am. Entrepreneur Assn., Mich. Sci. Tchrs. Assn., Mich. Hist. Soc., Heartland Mich. Geneal. Soc., White Pine Hist. Soc. (exec. sec.). Republican. Avocations: astronomy, silviculture. Fax: 989-386-4511. E-mail: Edgewoodpreas@usa.com.

MEEK, VIOLET IMHOF, retired dean; b. Geneva, Ill., June 12, 1939; d. John and Violet (Krepel) Imhof; m. Devon W. Meek, Aug. 21, 1965 (dec. 1988); children: Brian, Karen; m. Don M. Dell, Jan. 4, 1992. BA summa cum laude, St. Olaf Coll., 1960; MS, U. Ill., 1962, PhD in Chemistry, 1964. Instr. chemistry Mount Holyoke Coll., South Hadley, Mass., 1964-65; asst. prof. to prof. Ohio Wesleyan U., Delaware, Ohio, 1965-84, dean for ednl. svcs., 1980-84; dir. annual programs Coun. Ind. Colls., Washington, 1984-86; assoc. dir. sponsored programs devel. Rsch. Found. Ohio State U., Columbus, 1986-91, dean, dir. Lima, 1992—2003; ret., 2003. Vis. dean U. Calif., Berkeley, 1982, Stanford U., Palo Alto, Calif., 1982, reviewer GTE Sci. and Tech. Program, Princeton, N.J., 1986-92, Goldwater Nat. Fellowships, Princeton, 1990-98. Co-author: Experimental General Chemistry, 1984; contbr. articles to profl. jours. Bd. dirs. Luth. Campus Ministries, Columbus, 1988-91, Luth. Social Svcs., 1988-91, Americom Bank, Lima, 1992-98, Art Space, Lima, 1993—, Allen Lima Leadership, 1993—, Am. House, 1992—, Lima Vets. Meml. Civic Ctr. Found., 1992—; chmn. synodical coms. Evang. Luth. Ch. Am., Columbus, 1982; bd. trustees Trinity Luth. Sem., Columbus, 1996—; chmn. Allen County C. of C., 1995—, chair bd. dirs., 1999; bd. dirs. Lima Syphomy Orch., 1993—, pres. bd. dirs., 1997— Recipient Woodrow Wilson Fellowship, 1960. Mem. Nat. Coun. Rsch. Adminstrs. (named Outstanding New Profl. midwest region 1990), Am. Assn. Higher Edn., Phi Beta Kappa. Avocations: music, skiing, woodworking, civil war history, travel. Home: 209 W Beechwold Blvd Columbus OH 43214-2012 Office: Ohio State U 4240 Campus Dr Lima OH 45804-3576

MEEKS, HERBERT LESSIG, III, pastor, former school system administrator; b. National City, Calif., May 12, 1946; s. Herbert Lessig Jr. and Hazel Evelyn (Howard) M.; m. Ardena Lorraine Bice, June 30, 1971; children: Herbert Lessig IV, Laura Dawn, Misty Danae. Grad. in Theology, Bapt. Bible Coll., 1972; BS in Interdisciplinary Studies, Liberty U., Lynchburg, Va., 1989; MS in Edn., Tenn. Temple U., 1989; MA in Religion, Liberty U., 1990. Tchr. Mt. Vernon Christian Sch., Stockbridge, Ga., 1975-82; prin. Mt. Zion Christian Acad., Jonesboro, Ga., 1982-90; elem. prin. Des Moines Christian Sch., 1990-93; prin. N.W. Acad., Houston, 1993-94; sr. pastor 1st Bapt. Ch. Genoa, Houston, 1994—. Instr. ARC, Atlanta; candidate Ga. Ho. of Reps., Atlanta, 1980; bd. dirs. Concerned Christian for Good Govt., Atlanta, 1980-82; notary pub., Clayton County, Ga., 1983-90. Served to sgt. USAF, 1966-69. Mem. Assn. Christian Schs. Internat. (conv. planning com. 1985-90, accreditation/cons. chmn., Behind the Scenes award 1986), Nat. Rifle Assn. (life), Am. Pistol and Rifle Assn. Republican. Avocations: flying, hunting, politics, econs. Home: 12102 Palmcroft St Houston TX 77034-3721 Office: 1st Bapt Ch Genoa 12717 Almeda Genoa Rd Houston TX 77034-4639

MEEKS, LINDA MAE, women's health nurse, educator; b. Elkhart, Ind., Aug. 11, 1952; d. Alfred G. and Marie E. (Woodward) Moses; m. Gary F. Meeks, Aug. 11, 1973; children: Michael, Daniel, Kelcie. Diploma, Meml. Hosp. Sch. Nursing, South Bend, Ind., 1973. Cert. childbirth educator; cert. parent as tchrs. parent educator. Labor and delivery staff nurse Meml. Hosp., South Bend, 1973-83, childbirth educator, 1980-87; staff nurse Genesis Alternative Birth Ctr., Mishawaka, Ind., 1983; staff nurse family-centered maternity care, obstetrics Meml. Hosp., South Bend, 1987—; home visit nurse Meml. Home Care, South Bend, 1995—98; coord. Mother Matters Program Meml. Hosp., South Bend, 1998—. Pres. Pregnancy and Childbirth Edn. Svcs. Inc., 1988-98. Mem. Assn. Women's Health, Obstetrics and Neonatal Nurses, Childbirth Educators Tng. Assn. (bd. dirs.), Internat. Childbirth Edn. Assn., Am. Soc. Psychoprophylaxis in Obstetrics.

MEEKS, PATRICIA LOWE, language educator; b. Enid, Okla., Oct. 21, 1928; d. Henry Preston and Veda Gay (Combs) Lowe; m. James Donald Meeks, Feb. 28, 1953 (div. Aug. 1975); children: Mary Gay, Ann Lowe, James Robert David. BA, Phillips U., 1951; MA in English, U. Colo., 1973. Cert. tchr., Colo., Okla. Tchr. English Garber (Okla.) High Sch., 1952-53; tchr. English and journalism Hillcrest High Sch., Dallas, 1955-57; teaching asst. U. Colo., Boulder, 1965-66; tchr. English Cherry Creek High Sch., Englewood, Colo., 1966-91; supr. grades K-12 reading and lang. arts Oklahoma City Pub. Schs., 1991-98; English cons., 1998—. Adj. prof. English, Oklahoma City C.C., 2002—; cons. Coll. Bd. Rocky Mt. Region, Denver, 1973-91; advanced placement reader, table leader Coll. Bd. and Ednl. Testing Svc., Princeton, N.J., 1970-90, SAT reader, 1989-94, table leader, 1994-98, reader, 1999—. Grantee Fulbright Found., 1980-81; grantee NEH, 1986, English-Speaking Union, 1987; IDEA fellow. Mem. English-Speaking Union (pres. Oklahoma City chpt. 1998-), Nature Conservancy, Audubon Soc. Republican. Episcopalian. Avocations: art history, bird watching, jazz, reading. Home: 2700 NW 68th St Oklahoma City OK 73116-4712 E-mail: PLMEEKS@aol.com.

MEEKS, WAYNE A. religious studies educator; b. Aliceville, Ala., Jan. 8, 1932; s. Benjamin L. and Winnie (Gavin) M.; m. Martha Evelina Fowler, June 10, 1954 (dec. May 29, 1996); children: Suzanne, Edith, Ellen; m. Judith Colton, Mar. 18, 2000. BS, U. Ala.-Tuscaloosa, 1953; BD, Austin Presbyn. Theol. Sem., 1956; MA, Yale U., 1964, PhD, 1965; Doctor Theologiae honoris causa, U. Uppsala, Sweden, 1990. Instr. religion Dartmouth Coll., Hanover, N.H., 1964-65; asst. prof. religious studies Ind. U., Bloomington, 1966-68, assoc. prof., 1968-69; assoc. prof. religious studies Yale U., New Haven, 1969-73, prof. religious studies, 1973-84, Woolsey prof. Bibl. studies, 1984—, emeritus, 1999—, dir. divsn. Humanities, 1988-91. Author: Go From Your Father's House, 1964, The Prophet-King, 1967, Moral World of the First Christians, 1986, First Urban Christians, 1983, Origins of Christian Morality, 1993, In Search of the Early Christians, 2002; contbr. articles to profl. jours. Fulbright fellow, 1956-57; Kent fellow, 1962-64; NEH fellow, 1975-76; Guggenheim fellow, 1979-80. Fellow Brit. Acad.; mem. Soc. Bibl. Lit. (pres. 1985), Am. Acad. Religion (bd. dirs. 1974-77), Studiorum Novi Testamenti Societas (editl. bd. 1979-82). Democrat. Presbyterian. Avocations: cabinet-making, hiking. Office: Yale U Dept Religious Studies PO Box 208287 New Haven CT 06520-8287 E-mail: wayne.meeks@yale.edu.

MEEPAGALA, GAMINIE, economics educator; b. Talangama, Sri Lanka, Sept. 27, 1955; s. Carnelis Meepagala and Alice Nona (Ponsuge) Tissera. BS with honors, U. Sri Lanka, 1978; MA in Econs., PhD in Econs., SUNY, Albany, 1986. Asst. lectr. U. Sri Lanka, Jaffna, 1978-79; asst. dir. Cen. Bank Ceylon, Colombo, Sri Lanka, 1979-81; lectr., teaching asst. SUNY, Albany, 1981-86; vis. asst. prof. Ind. U., Bloomington, 1986-87, Tex. Tech U., Lubbock, 1987-88; assoc. prof. econs. Howard U., Washington, 1988—. Contbr. articles to profl. jours. Mem. Am. Econ. Assn., Econometric Soc. Buddhist. Home: 8516 60th Ave College Park MD 20740-2652 Office: Howard U Dept Econs Washington DC 20059-0001 E-mail: gmeepagala@fac.howard.edu.

MEEZAN, ELIAS, pharmacologist, educator; b. N.Y.C., Mar. 5, 1942; s. Maurice and Rachel (Epstein) M.; m. Elisabeth Gascard, May 14, 1967;

children: David, Nathan, Joshua. BS in Chemistry, CCNY, 1962; PhD in Biochemistry, Duke U., 1966. Asst. prof. physiology and pharmacology Duke U., Durham, N.C., 1969-70; asst. prof. pharmacology U. Ariz., Tucson, 1970-75, assoc. prof., 1975-79; prof., chmn. dept. pharmacology U. Ala., Birmingham, 1979-89, prof., dir. Metabolic Diseases Rsch. Lab., 1989-93, prof. dept. pharmacology, 1993—. Asso. editor: Life Sci, 1973-79. Helen Hay Whitney postdoctoral fellow, 1966-69; recipient NIH Research Career Devel. award, 1977-79 Mem. Am. Soc. Pharmacology and Exptl. Therapeutics, Am. Soc. Biol. Chemistry, AAUP, AAAS, N.Y. Acad. Sci., Assn. Med. Sch.Pharmacology. Democrat. Jewish. Achievements include isolation of retinal microvasculature; development of method for isolating ultrastructurally and chemically intact basement membranes. Home: 1202 Cheval Ln Birmingham AL 35216-2037 Office: U Ala Dept Pharmacology Birmingham AL 35294-0001 E-mail: Elias.Meezan@ccc.uab.edu.

MEFFORD, NAOMI RUTH DOLBEARE, secondary education and elementary education educator; b. Pittsfield, Ill., Feb. 10, 1944; d. Donald Pryor and Ruth Allyne (Utter) Dolbeare; m. Clark L. Mefford, Feb. 8, 1964; children: Joseph Clark, Christopher Lee. BA, William Penn Coll., 1977; MA, N.E. Mo. State U., 1986, EdS, 1991. Cert. profl. tchr., adminstr., Iowa. Undergrad. instr. Buena Vista, Ottumwa, Iowa, 1984-87; grad. instr. So. Prairie AEA and Marycrest Coll., Ottumwa, 1988-92; tchr. Ottumwa Schs., 1985—; adj. inst. in English Indian Hills Cmty. Coll., 1998, 2000. Dir. summer sch. Ottumwa, 1991-93, Organizer Outdoor Edn. Camp. 2002. Chmn. Hosp. Major Fund Raiser, Ottumwa, 1995. Mem. AAUW (pres. Iowa chpt. 1996—1998), Delta Kappa Gamma. Home: 8 Country Club Pl Ottumwa IA 52501-1417 Office: Eisenhower School 2624 Marihon Rd Ottumwa IA 52501-1400

MEGANATHAN, RANGASWAMY, microbiologist, educator; b. Coimbatore, Tamilnadu, India, Jan. 15, 1942; s. Pannaikinar N. and Savithiri Rangaswamy; m. Ami Damodaran, Jan. 20, 1969; 1 child, Indirajith Meganathan. BS in Agr., U. Madras (India), 1963; MS in Microbiology, Okla. State U., 1968, PhD in Microbiology, 1970. Postdoctoral fellow U. Wis., Madison, 1970-72, U. Rochester (N.Y.), 1972-73; rsch. assoc. U. Pitts., 1976-82; asst. prof. microbiology No. Ill. U., Dekalb, 1982-85, assoc. prof. microbiology, 1985-91, prof. microbiology, 1991—, presdl. rsch. prof., 2002—. Author (book chpt.) Escherichia coli and Salmonella, 1996; contbr. articles to profl. jours. NIH grantee, 1989-93, 94—. Fellow Am. Acad. Microbiology; mem. AAAS, Am. Soc. Microbiology, Am. Soc. Biochemistry and Molecular Biology. Achievements include discovery of most of the intermediates, enzymes and genes in the vitamin-K biosynthetic pathway. Office: Biol Sci Dept No Ill U Dekalb IL 60115

MEGAY-NESPOLI, KAREN PATRICIA, elementary school educator; b. N.Y.C., May 4, 1954; d. Charles A. and Audrey J. (Duddy) Megay; m. Michael A. Nespoli, Oct. 13, 1979; children: Lauren Brynn, Caitlin Bree. BA, CUNY, 1976, MS, 1978; profl. diploma in adminstrn. & supr., St. John's U., 1986; EdD, Columbia U., 1998. Tchr. 3d grade Our Lady of the Miraculous Medal Sch., Queens, N.Y., 1977-84, adminstrv. asst. to prin., 1980-84, primary coord., 1981-84; tchr. 4th grade P.S. 87, Queens, 1984—86. Adj. asst. prof. CW Post campus L.I. U. Author: The First Year for Elementary School Teachers, 1983; contbr. articles to profl. jours. Mem. AAUW, ASCD, Internat. Reading Coun., Nat. Assn. Gifted Children, Nat. Coun. Math. Tchrs., Nassau Reading Coun., Phi Delta Kappa, Kappa Delta Pi. Office: LI U CW Post Campus Dept Curriculum and Instrn 720 Northern Blvd Greenvale NY 11548

MEGILL, ALLAN D. historian; b. Regina, Sask., Can., Apr. 20, 1947; came to U.S., 1980; s. Ralph Peter and Jean Tudhope (Dickson) M.; divorced; children: Jason Robert, Jessica Susan, Jonathan David; life ptnr. Rita Felski; 1 child, Maria Megill Felski. BA, U. Sask., 1969; MA, U. Toronto, 1970; PhD, Columbia U., 1975. From instr. to prof. history U. Iowa, Iowa City, 1974-90; prof. history U. Va., Charlottesville, 1990—. Rsch. fellow in history of ideas Australian Nat. U., Canberra, 1977—79, temp. lectr. modern European studies, 1979; dir. d'études invité École des Hautes Études en Scis. Sociales, Paris, 1997. Author: Prophets of Extremity, 1985, Karl Marx: The Burden of Reason, 2002; editor: Rethinking Objectivity, 1994; co-editor: The Rhetoric of the Human Sciences, 1987; cons. editor: Jour. of History of Ideas, 1986—89, mem. editl. bd.:, 1990—, Rethinking History, 1996—, U. Press of Va., 1991—94; contbr. articles to profl. jours. Chmn. Page-Barbour and Richard Lectures com. U. Va., 1994-96. Mem. Am. Hist. Assn. Office: U Va Corcoran Dept of History PO Box 400180 Charlottesville VA 22904 E-mail: megill@virginia.edu.

MEGILL, DAVID WAYNE, music educator, author; b. Independence, Kans., Mar. 4, 1947; s. Mervin Ralph and Alma Marie (Fields) M.; m. Janet Rose Holmes, June 26, 1971; children: Kristin Rose, Holly Elizabeth. BA, U. Calif., Berkeley, 1969, MA, 1971; PhD., U. Calif., San Diego, 1991. Tchr. El Camino High Sch., Carmichael, Calif., 1971-75; prof. music Mira Costa Coll., Oceanside, Calif., 1975—, pres. acad. senate, 1982-84, 95-96. Lectr. U. Calif., Davis, 1973-75; cons. legal firm Slaff, Mosk & Rudman, Los Angeles, 1987—; vis. prof. U. Calif., San Diego, 1997. Author: Jazz, 1987, 6th edit., 1991, 8th edit., 1992, 9th edit., 2000, Fundamentals of Music Online, 2003, Music Appreciation Online, 2003; composer jazz chorale Monday's Child Blues, 1975, Jazz Issues, 1995; computer programmer Music designer II, 1983, exptl. music lab. MOGO 1991; contbr. articles to profl. jours. Recipient Gerald Hay award for tchg. excellence Acad. Senate of Calif. C.C., 1996. Democrat. Avocations: computer sound synthesis, music performance. Bus. Home: 4174 Bryan St Oceanside CA 92056-3437 Office: Mira Costa Coll 1 Barnard Dr Oceanside CA 92056-3820 E-mail: dwmegill@miracosta.edu., dave@emegill.com.

MEGNA, STEVE ALLAN, secondary school educator; Secondary tchr. Vernon (NJ) H.S. Recipient Tech. Excellence award Internat. Tech. Edn. Assn. and Tech. Edn. Assn. N.J., 1992, Tech. Program of Yr. award Tech. Edn. Assn. N.J., 1989. Office: Vernon HS Rte 565 Vernon NJ 07462

MEHAFFEY, MARK EDWARD, retired art educator, artist; b. Ann Arbor, Mich., Dec. 25, 1950; s. Howard Henry and Maxine Delores M.; m. Rose Marie Kain, Nov. 6, 1971. BFA with honors, Mich. State U., 1973. Arts educator Lansing (Mich.) Pub. Schs., 1974—2002; ret., 2002—. Work featured in (books) Best of Watercolor, 1995, Places in Watercolor, 1996, Creative Watercolor, 1996, Splash 5 - The Glory of Color, 1998. Recipient Patron award Mich. Watercolor Soc. Mem. Am. Watercolor Soc. (signature), Nat. Watercolor Soc. (signature, Beverly Geen Meml. Purchase award), La. Watercolor Soc., Midwest Watercolor Soc. (signature, Skyledge - Top award 1999), Watercolor West Soc. (signature, 3rd award 1997), Rocky Mountain Watermedia Soc. (signature). Avocation: salt water fly fishing. Home: 5440 Zimmer Rd Williamston MI 48895-9181 E-mail: markmaws@aol.com.

MEHLER, BARRY ALAN, humanities educator, journalist, consultant; b. Bklyn., Mar. 18, 1947; s. Harry and Esther Mehler; m. Jennifer Sue Leghorn, June 2, 1982; 1 child, Isaac Alan. BA, Yeshiva U., 1970; MA, CCNY, 1972; PhD, U. Ill., 1988. Rsch. assoc. Washington U., St. Louis, 1976-80, instr. history, 1977; NIMH trainee racism program U. Ill., Champaign, 1981-85, rsch. asst. IBM EXCEL project, 1986-88; asst. prof. humanities Ferris State U., Big Rapids, Mich., 1988-93, assoc. prof., 1993-99, prof., 1999—. Media cons. Scientist's Inst. for Pub. Info., N.Y.C., 1980-98; cons. Calif. Humanities Coun., 1995, ZDF/arte (Zweite Deutsches Fernshen--German pub. TV), 1995, House Subcom. on Consumer Protection, 1994, McIntosh Commn. for Fair Play in Student-Athlete Admissions, 1994, Can. Broadcast Svc., Toronto, Ont., 1985-92, Am. Civil Liberties Union, Nat. Human Genome Rsch. Inst.; judge Women's Caucus Awards for Excellence, St. Louis, 1989-91, 93; dir. Inst. for Study of Acad. Racism, 1993—; mem. Pres.'s. Initiative on Race, 1998, One Am. initiative, named Promising Practices; presenter Performance Art in the Classroom, Minority Equity Conf. XI, 2001. Contbg. editor: Encyclopedia of Genocide, 1997; contbr. more than 100 articles and revs. to profl. jours. Mem. vol. com. parents A Different Look at DARE, 1995; mem. adv. bd. Homes for the Homeless, Austin, Tex., 2000-01, Internat. Inst. for Study of Psychiatry and Psychology Washington, 1999—; founder, sec.-treas. Internat. Com. to Free Russell Smith, 1977-79; co-founder Gay Peoples Alliance, St. Louis, 1978; mem. adv. bd. Stop Prison Rape, 2001. Recipient cert. of recognition Ferris State Bd. of Control, 1994, Hesburgh award for excellence in undergrad. edn., TIAA-CREFF and Am. Coun. on Edn., 2000; NSF rsch. fellow, 1976-80, Babcock fellow U. Ill., 1985-86; grantee Rockefeller Found., 1977; structured learning assistance program grantee Office of Minority Affairs, Lansing, Mich., 1994-97. Mem. Am. Hist. Soc., Behavior-Genetics Assn., NAACP, Ctr. for Dem. Renewal, History of Sci. Soc., Internat. Behavioral and Neural Geneteics Soc., Orgn. Am. Historians, B'nai B'rith (Anti-Defamation League), Coalition for Human Dignity, Facing History. Jewish. Avocations: hiking, camping. Home: 216 Rust Ave Big Rapids MI 49307-1726 Office: Ferris State U 901 S State St Big Rapids MI 49307-2295 E-mail: bmehler@netonecom.net.

MEHLINGER, HOWARD DEAN, education educator; b. Hillsboro, Kans., Aug. 22, 1931; s. Alex and Alice Hilda (Skibbee) M.; m. Carolee Ann Case, Dec. 28, 1952; children: Bradley Case, Barbara Ann, Susan Kay. BA, McPherson (Kans.) Coll., 1953; MS in Edn, U. Kans., 1959, PhD, 1964. Co-dir. social studies project Pitts. pub. schs., 1963-64; asst. dir. fgn. relations project North Central Assn. Schs. and Colls., Chgo., 1964-65; mem. faculty Ind. U., Bloomington, 1965-97, prof. history and edn., 1974-97, dean Sch. Edn., 1981-90, dir. Ctr. for Excellence in Edn., 1990-99. Social studies adviser Houghton Mifflin Pub. Co.; cons. U.S. Office Edn. Co-author: American Political Behavior, 2d edit., 1977, Count Witte and the Tsarist Government in the 1905 Revolution, 1972, Toward Effective Instruction in the Social Studies, 1974, School Reform in the Information Age, 1995, Technology and Teacher Education: A Guide for Educators and Policymakers, 2002; editl. bd. Education and Society, history tchr.; editor: UNESCO Handbook on the Teaching of Social Studies, 1981; co-editor: Yearbook on the Social Studies, 1981. STAG grantee Dept. State, 1975 Mem. NEA, Nat. Council Social Studies, Am. Edn. Research Assn., Am. Hist. Assn., Am. Assn. for Advancement Slavic Studies, Phi Beta Kappa, Phi Alpha Theta, Pi Sigma Alpha, Phi Delta Kappa. Home: 3271 N Ramble Rd E Bloomington IN 47408-1094

MEHLMAN, MAXWELL JONATHAN, law educator; b. Washington, Nov. 4, 1948; s. Jacob and Betty (Hoffman) M.; m. Cheryl A. Stone, Sept. 15, 1979; children: Aurora, Gabriel. BA, Reed Coll., 1970, Oxford U., England, 1972; JD, Yale U., 1975. Bar: D.C. 1976, Ohio 1988. Assoc. Arnold & Porter, Washington, 1975-84; asst. prof. Case Western Res. U., Cleve., 1984-87, assoc. prof., 1987-90, prof. law, 1990-96, Arthur E. Petersilge prof., 1996—, prof. biomed. ethics, 1998—. Spl. counsel N.Y. State Bar, N.Y.C., 1988-94, Nat. Kidney Found., 1991; cons. Am. Assn. Ret. Persons, Washington, 1992. Editor: High Tech Home Care, 1991, (with T. Murray) Encyclopedia of Ethical, Legal and Policy Issues in Biotechnology; author: (with J. Botkin) Access to the Genome: The Challenge to Equality, 1998, (with Andrews and Rothstein) Genetics: Ethics, Law and Policy, 2002; contbr. articles to profl. jours. Active steering com. AIDS Commn. Greater Cleve., 1986-90. Rhodes scholar, 1970; Rsch. grantee NIH, 1992-94, 97—. Mem. Am. Assn. Law Schs. (chmn. sect. on law, medicine and health care 1990), Phi Beta Kappa. Avocations: skiing, choral music, sea kayaking. Office: Case Western Reserve U Sch Law-Law Medicine Ctr Gund Hall 11075 E Blvd Cleveland OH 44106

MEHNE, PAUL RANDOLPH, associate dean, medical educator; b. Wilmington, Del., May 27, 1948; s. Paul Herbert and Doris Ruth (Longfritz) M.; m. Carol Ann Starner, June 12, 1971; children: Meredith Lynn, Amy Elizabeth. BS in Environ. Sci., SUNY, Syracuse, 1970; PhD, SUNY, 1976, Syracuse U., 1976. Asst. prof. Sch. Allied Health East Carolina U., Greenville, N.C., 1975-76, assoc. dir. Ctr. Edn. Devel. and Evaluation Sch. Medicine, 1976-79, coord. of curriculum Sch. Medicine, 1979-81, asst. dean, 1981-85, assoc. dean, 1985-89, assoc. prof., 1988-89, dir. Ctr. Health Scis. Edn. and Info., 1988-89; assoc. dean U. Pa., Phila., 1989—91; assoc. dean acad. and student affairs, assoc. prof. environ. and community medicine, family medicine Robert Wood Johnson Med. Sch., Piscataway, N.J., 1992—; chair u.-wide telemedicine videocom distance learning com. U. Medicine and Dentistry N.J., 1995-2000, chmn. acad. info. tech. adv. com., 1996-98. Chmn. exec. bd. dirs. MEDCOMP Supercomputer Consortium, Athens, Ga., 1986—89; vis. prof. U. N.C., Chapel Hill, 1986, Tulane U., New Orleans, 1988. Contbr. articles to profl. jours. Chmn. Cmty. Appearance Commn., Greenville, 1980—85; ex officio trustee Cooper Hosp. Univ. Med. Ctr., 2001—. Recipient Interactive Video Instrn. award Digital Equipment Corp., 1985, Med. Edn. Cost Containment award Kate B. Reynolds Health Care Trust, 1985-88, Telemedicine and Med. Informatics award, 1996-99, U.S. Dept. Commerce NTIA/TIIAP award for telemedicine, 1996-98. Mem. IEEE, APHA, Am. Med. Informatics Assn., Am. Edn. Rsch. Assn., Assn. Am. Med. Colls. (chair consortium on student and profl. well-being 1993-94, steering com. Clin. Campus Deans 2000—, sec.-treas. Orgn. of Regional Med. Campuses, 2003—), Soc. for Med. Decision Making, Am. Telemedicine Assn., Soc. of Tchrs. of Family Medicine. E-mail: mehne@umdnj.edu.

MEHR, VERN CONRAD, minister, educator; b. San Francisco, Oct. 23, 1949; m. Vina D. Tull, Oct. 12, 1968; children: Christopher, Jonathan, Vern Adrian, Benjamin. BA, Union U., Jackson, Tenn., 1975; student, Lambuth Coll., 1983; MEd, Memphis State U., 1984, postgrad., 1984-88, Trevecca Nazarene Coll., 1987-89. Lic. to ministry So. Bapt. Conv., 1967, ordained, 1983. Youth dir. Mt. Zion Bapt. Ch., McNairy, Tenn., 1968-75; Sunday sch. tchr. Piney Grove Bapt. Ch., Silerton, Tenn., 1975-82; pastor Forty Forks Bapt. Ch., Bethel Springs, Tenn., 1983—; chaplain Jackson-Madison County Gen. Hosp., 1996—. Tchr. Whiteville (Tenn.) Elem. Sch., 1981-93, Grand Junction (Tenn.) Elem. Sch., 1993-99, Bolivar Ctrl. High Sch., 1999-, Jackson State C.C., 1987-2000, S.W. Tenn. Cmty. Coll., 2001-. Contbr. articles to profl. jours. Chaplain, capt. CAP. 1989-2003, Savannah, Tenn., 1989-2003; cubmaster, asst. scoutmaster, asst. dist. chmn., trainer Boy Scouts Am., 1977-83, 91-95; mem. aux. Tenn. Performing Arts Coun. Adv. Com. Mem. Tenn. Bapt. Chaplains Assn., Shiloh Bapt. Assn (mem. exec. com. 1983—), Tchr. Study Coun., Aviation's Creative Educators Sci., Kappa Delta Pi. Home: 178 Tull Garner Rd Bethel Springs TN 38315-4216

MEHRABIAN, ROBERT, aerospace engineer, academic administrator; b. Tehran, Iran; BS, PhD, MIT. Former prof. MIT, U. Ill., Urbana; dean U. Calif. Coll. of Engring., Santa Barbara, until 1990; past dir. Ctr. Materials Sci. Nat. Bur. of Standards; pres. Carnegie-Mellon U., Pitts., 1990—97; sr. v.p. & segment exec. aerospace and electronics Teledyne Technologies, 1997—98, exec. v.p. & segment exec., aerospace and electronics, 1998—99, pres., CEO, and chmn. aerospace and electronics segment, 1999—. Mem.: NAE. Office: Teledyne Technologies 12333 West Olympic Blvd Los Angeles CA 90064*

MEIBAUER, AMERY FILIPPONE, special education educator; b. Newark, Mar. 4, 1955; d. Frederick J. and Gloria J. (Ricciardi) Filippone; m. Karl D. Meibauer, Sept. 4, 1981; children: Karlee Constance, Lea Agnes, Madeline Kelly. BA, Marymount Coll., 1973; MS in Spl. Edn., Monmouth Coll., West Long Branch, N.J., 1985. Cert. elem. tchr., tchr. of handicapped, N.J. Counselor Rehab. Ctr. Monmouth Ctr. for Vocat. Rehab., Tinton Falls, N.J.; tchr. neurologically impaired Harbor Sch., Eatontown, N.J., Oceanport (N.J.) Bd. Edn.; basic skills instr. Red Bank (N.J.) Bd. Edn. Supplemental instr. West Long Branch (N.J.) Bd. Edn.; transitional neurologically impaired tchr. Lenna Conrow Sch., Long Branch, N.J.; spl. edn. tchr. Long Branch Middle Sch., Long Br. Bd. Edn.; resource specialist Audrey W. Clark Elem. Sch. Named one of Outstanding Young Women of Am. Gen. Fedn. Women's Clubs, 1987. Mem. NEA, ASCD, N.J. Edn. Assn. Home: 67 Werah Pl Oceanport NJ 07757-1538 E-mail: harborshuttle@comcast.net.

MEIER, DEBORAH, principal; M in History, U. Chgo.; degree (hon.), Harvard U., Yale U., Brown U., Columbia Tchrs. Coll. Co-founder, prin. N.Y. Ctrl. Park East Elem. and Secondary Sch.; co-prin. Mission Hill Elem. Sch., Roxbury, 1997—. Bd. mem. Nat. Acad. Edn., Ctr. for Collaborative Edn., Boston, Panasonic Found., Fairtest. Author: The Power of Their Ideas: Lessons to America from a Small School in Harlem, 1995, Will Standards Save Public Education, 2000, In Schools We Trust, 2002, Creating Communities of Learning in an Era of Testing and Standardization; mem. editl. bd.: The Nation, Dissent and the Harvard Education Letter; contbr. articles to profl. jours. Trustee Ednl. Alliance and Educators for Social Responsiblity. Recipient MacArthur award; Sr. Annenberg fellow, 1994—97. Mem.: Coalition of Essential Scis., Nat. Bd. for Profl. Tchg. Stds. (founding mem.), Carnegie Found. for Advancement in Edn. (bd. mem., vice chair). Office: Mission Hill Elem Sch 67 Alleghany St Boston MA 02120*

MEIER, ENGE, pre-school educator; b. N.Y.C., Jan. 17; d. Rudolf and Kate (Furstenow) Pietschyck; children: Kenneth Randolph, Philip Alan. BBA, Western States U., 1987, MBA, 1989. Tchr. nursery sch., Neu Ulm, Fed. Republic Germany, 1963-64; sec. Brewster (N.Y.) Mid. Sch., 1969-72; teaching asst. Brewster Elem. Sch., 1972-73; office asst. Bd. Coop. Edn., Yorktown Heights, N.Y., 1973-76; sec. Am. Can. Co., Greenwich, Conn., 1976-77, adminstrv. sec., 1977-79, exec. sec., 1979-84; adminstrv. asst. U. Tex., Austin, 1984-85, 88-90, adminstrv. assoc., 1985-86, sr. adminstrv. assoc., 1986-88; exec. asst. DTM Corp., Austin, 1990; funds asst. mgr. Tex. Assn. Sch. Bds., Austin, 1991-92; nursery sch. tchr. Westlake Presbyn. Sch., Austin, 1992-95; tchr. Grace Covenant Christian Sch., 1995-96; office mgr. Dr. G. Roebuck, Austin, 1996—. Docent LBJ Libr. and Mus., Austin, 1984—; mem. Women's Polit. Caucus, 1988—; bd. dirs. Leadership, Edn. and Devel., 1991. Mem. Women in Mgmt., Bus. and Profl. Women (pres. 1989, bd. dirs. Austin chpt. 1987—), Women's C. of C. Presbyterian. Avocations: golf, swimming. E-mail: enge@rr.austin.com.

MEIER, SHEILA ROSALIND, secondary school educator; b. Hammond, Ind., Oct. 20, 1948; d. Victor Throne and Virginia Rosalind (Kleen) Oberg; m. Ronald Thomas Meier, Sept. 14, 1968; children: Kevin Christopher, David Joshua, Erin Ronnell. AAS in Computer Sci., Alvin (Tex.) Community Coll., 1968; BS in Math., U. Houston, 1986. Cert. tchr., Tex. Asst. programmer Amoco Chems., Texas City, Tex., 1967-71; tchr. math. and computer sci. Sante Fe (Tex.) Ind. Sch. Dist., 1986—. Adj. math instr. Coll. Mainland Tex. City., Tex., 2000—. Vol. Hitchcock (Tex.) Ind. Sch. Dist., 1979-81; cub scout den leader Boy Scouts Am., Hitchcock, 1982-84; sponsor Santa Fe Jr. Engring. Tech. Soc. and Math Club. Memm. NEA, Nat. Coun. Tchrs. Math., Tex. Coun. Tchrs. Math., Tex. Tchrs. Assn., Calculus and Elem. Analysis Tchrs. Houston, Alpha Chi. Lutheran. Avocations: camping, hiking, refinishing antiques. Home: PO Box 12 Hitchcock TX 77563-0012 Office: Santa Fe Ind Sch Dist PO Box 370 Santa Fe TX 77510-0370

MEIER, WILBUR LEROY, JR., industrial engineer, educator, former university chancellor; b. Elgin, Tex., Jan. 3, 1939; s. Wilbur Leroy and Ruby (Hall) M.; m. Judy Lee Longbotham, Aug. 30, 1958; children: Melynn, Marla, Melissa. BS, U. Tex., 1962, MS, 1964, PhD, 1967. Planning engr. Tex. Water Devel. Bd., Austin, 1962-66, cons., 1967-72; research engr. U. Tex., Austin, 1966; asst. prof. indsl. engring. Tex. A&M U., College Station, 1967-68, assoc prof., 1968-70, prof., 1970-73, asst. head dept. indsl. engring., 1972-73; prof., chmn. dept. indsl. engring. Iowa State U., Ames, 1973-74; prof., head sch. of indsl. engring. Purdue U., West Lafayette, Ind., 1974-81; dean Coll. Engring., Pa. State U., University Park, 1981-87; chancellor U. Houston System, 1987-89; prof. indsl. engring. Pa. State U., University Park, 1989-91; dir. div. engring. infrastructure devel. NSF, Washington, 1989-91; dean Coll. Engring. N.C. State U., 1991-93, prof. indsl. engring., 1991—; program mgr. ABB Electric Systems Tech. Inst., Raleigh, N.C., 2000—. Mem. bd. visitors Air Force Inst. Technology; cons. Ohio Bd. Regents, 1990, U. Arizona, 1989, Indsl. Rsch. Inst., St. Louis, 1979, Environments for Tomorrow, Inc., Washington, 1970-81, Water Resources Engrs., Inc., Walnut Creek, Calif., 1969-70, Computer Graphics, Inc., Bryan, Tex., 1969-70, Kaiser Engrs., Oakland, Calif., 1971, Tracor, Inc., Austin, 1966-68, div. planning coordination Tex. Gov.'s Office, 1969, Office of Tech. Assessment, 1982-86, Southeast Ctr. for Elec. Engring. Edn., 1978— ; mem. rev. team Naval Rsch. Adv. Com. Editor: Marcel Dekker Pub. Co., 1978—; Contbr. articles to profl. jours. Recipient Bliss medal Soc. Am. Mil. Engrs., 1986, Am. Spirit award USAF, 1984; named Outstanding Young Engr. of Yr. Tex. Soc. Profl. Engrs., 1966, Disting. Grad. Coll. Engring., U. Tex. at Austin, 1987; USPHS fellow, 1966. Fellow AAAS, Am. Soc. Engring. Edn. (chmn. indsl. engring. divsn. 1978-83), Inst. Indsl. Engrs. (dir. ops. rsch. div. 1975, pres. Ind. chpt. 1976, program chmn. 1973-75, editorial bd. Trans., publ. chmn., newsletter editor engring. economy div. 1972-73, v.p. region VIII 1977-79, exec. v.p. chpt. ops. 1981-83, pres. 1985-86), Soc. Mfg. Engrs. (Internat. Edn. award 2000), World Acad. Productivity Sci.; mem. ASCE (sec.-treas. Austin br. 1965-66, chmn. rsch. com., tech. coun. water resources planning and mgmt. 1972-74), Am. Assn. Engring. Socs. (bd. govs. 1984-86), Nat. Assn. State Univ. and Land Grant Colls. (mem. engring. legis. task force 1983-87), Assn. Engring. Colls. Pa. (pres. 1985-86, treas. 1981-87), Air Force Assn. (advisor sci. and tech. com. 1984-87), Nat. Soc. Profl. Engrs., Profl. Engrs. in Edn. (vice chmn. N.E. region 1985-87, bd. govs. 1983-85), Sigma Xi, Tau Beta Pi, Alpha Pi Mu (asso. editor Cogwheel 1970-75, regional dir. 1976-77, exec. v.p. 1977-80, pres. 1980-82), Phi Kappa Phi, Chi Epsilon. Lodges: Rotary. Home: 7504 Grist Mill Rd Raleigh NC 27615-5411

MEIKSIN, ZVI H. electrical engineering educator; b. 1926; BSEE, Israel Inst. Tech., Haifa, 1950, Dipl. Ing., 1951; MSEE, Carnegie Mellon U., 1953; PhDEE, U. Pitts., 1959. Registered profl. engr., Pa. Design engr. McGraw Edison, Cannonsburg, Pa., 1953-54; sr. project engr. Westinghouse Electric Corp., Pitts., 1956-59; prof. dept. elec. engring. U. Pitts., 1959-91, prof. emeritus, 1995—; pres. Transtek, Inc., Pitts., 1995—. Cons. entr. 33 orgns. in U.S., Europe, 1959—. Author: Thin & Thick Films, 1976, Active Filter Design, 1990; co-author: Electronic Design, 1980, 84, Microprocessor Based Design, 1986; jour. referee profl. publs., 1970—; contbr. articles to profl. jours.; inventor, holder 7 patents in field.. Fellow IEEE (award coms.); mem. Eta Kappa Nu, Sigma Xi. Office: Transtek Inc 35 Wilson St Ste 103 Pittsburgh PA 15223-1719 E-mail: meiksin@transtekcorp.com.

MEINDL, ROBERT JAMES, English language educator; b. Wausau, Wis., Sept. 17, 1936; s. George Martin and Adeline Emilie (Goetsch) M.; m. Victoria Lynn Chavez; children: Karin Rose, George Andrew, Damian Kurt, Erika Wittmer, Christopher Smith, Gabrielle Remelia. BS, U. Wis., 1958; MA, U. Conn., 1960; PhD, Tulane U., 1965; postdoctoral studies, U. Calif., Berkeley, 1967—68, Goethe Inst., Liblar, Germany, 1970, U. Cologne, Germany, 1970. Teaching asst. U. Conn., Storrs, 1958-60; teaching fellow Tulane U., 1960-62; lectr. U. Wis., Green Bay, 1963-65; asst. prof. English Calif. State U., Sacramento, 1965—2002, prof. emeritus English, 2002—. Translator: Studies in John Gower, 1981; book rev. editor Studia Mystica Jour., 1984-89; contbr. numerous articles to profl. jours. With USNR, 1953-61, 79-96. Nat. Endowment for the Humanities fellow Stanford U., 1982. Mem. MLA (life), Medieval Acad. Am. (life), Medieval Assn. of Pacific, Early English Text Soc., John Gower Soc., New Chaucer Soc. Home: 2301 Pennland Dr Sacramento CA 95825-0329 Office: Calif State U 6000 J St Sacramento CA 95819-2605

MEINEL, DIANE HARTWIG, music educator; m. Fredrick Alan Meinel; 1 child, Seth Andrew. Student, Lawrence Univ.; BS, MacMurray Coll.; postgrad. in spl. edn., Nat. Coll. of Edn. Cert. tchr., Wis., Ill.; registered recreation therapist. Tchr., head organist Our Saviors Luth. Ch., Zion, Ill.; remedial & music tchr., head organist, sr. choir accompanist St. John's Evang. Luth. Sch., Libertyville, Ill.; intern Jacksonville (Ill.) State Hosp.; tchr. Valley View Elem. Sch., Ashwaubenon, Wis. Guest carilloneur Internat. Carillon Festival, Springfield, Ill.; head organist, sr. choir accompanist Atonement Luth. Ch., Green Bay; Destination Imagination Coach, Children's choir; dir. Tone Chime Choir, dir. at Valley View Elementary; dir. music Bethel Lutheran Ch., Green Bay. Future Medics scholar, Knapp scholar; Nat. Def. edn. grantee. Mem. Guild of Carillonneurs N.Am. (cert.), Am. Guild Organists, Music Educators Nat. Conf., Am. Guild English Handbell Ringers, Am. Assn. Lutheran Musicians, Wis. Choral Dirs. Assn., Am. Choral Dirs. Assn. Home: 2583 Cherrywood Ln Green Bay WI 54304-1951

MEINER, SUE ELLEN THOMPSON, gerontologist, nurse practitioner, nursing educator and researcher, legal nurse consultant; b. Ironton, Mo., Oct. 24, 1943; d. Louis Raymond and Verna Mae Thompson; m. Robert Edward Meiner, Mar. 5, 1971; children: Diane Romeril, Suzanne. AAS, Meramec C.C., 1970; BSN, St. Louis U., 1978, MSN, 1983; EdD, So. Ill. U., Edwardsville, 1991. RN, Mo., Nev.; cert. gerontol. nurse practitioner; cert. clin. specialist in gerontol. nursing. Staff RN St. Joseph's Hosp., St. Charles, Mo., 1976-78; nursing supr. Bethesda Gen. Hosp., St. Louis, 1975-76, 71-74; adult med. dir. Family Care Ctr.-Carondelet, St. Louis, 1978-79; program dir., lectr. Webster Coll./Bethesda Hosp., Webster Groves, Mo., 1979-82; diabetes clin. specialist Washington U. Sch. Medicine, St. Louis, 1982; chmn. dept. nursing, asst. prof. St. Louis C.C., 1983-88; vis. nurse assoc. St. Louis, 1970—71; chmn. dept. nursing, asst. prof. Barnes Hosp. Sch. Nursing, 1988-89; instr. U. Mo., St. Louis, 1989; assoc. prof. St. Charles County C.C., St. Peters, Mo., 1990-92, Deaconess Coll. of Nursing, 1991-93; patient care mgr. Deaconess Hosp., St. Louis, 1993-94; assoc. prof. Jewish Hosp. Coll. of Nursing and Allied Health, 1994-99; gerontol. nurse, rschr. Wash. U. Sch. Med., St. Louis, 1996-2000; asst. prof. nursing U. Nev. Coll. Health Scis., Las Vegas, 2000—. Nat. dir. edn. Nat. Assn. Practical Nurse Edn. and Svc., Inc., St. Louis, 1984-86; mem. task force St. Louis Met. Hosp. Assn., 1987-88; mem. adv. com. Bd. Edn. Sch. Nursing, St. Louis, 1986-90; grant coord. Kellogg Found. Gerontology and Nursing, 1991-92; project dir. NIH Grant Washington U. Sch. Medicine, St. Louis, 1996—2000; mem. editorial bd. Geriatric Nursing Journ., 1999-2002; legal nurse cons. Author and editor profl. books; contbr. articles to profl. jours. Chmn. bd. dirs. Creve Coeur Fire Protection Dist. Mo., 1984-89; vice chmn. Bd. Cen. St. Louis County Emergency Dispatch Svc., 1985-87; asst. leader Girl Scouts U.S., St. Louis, 1975; treas. Older Women's League, St. Louis, 1992-93. Recipient Woman of Worth award Gateway chpt. Older Women's League, 1993. Mem.: ANA, Am. Soc. of Aging, Nat. League for Nursing, Am. Nurses Found., Am. Coll. Nurse Practitioners, Am. Acad. Nurse Practitioners, Job's Daus. (guardian 1979—80), Order Ea. Star (chaplain 1970), Creve Coeur C. of C., Sigma Theta Tau (fin. chmn. 1984, archivist 1985—87, Zeta Kappa chpt. v.p. 2001—03), Kappa Delta Pi, Sigma Phi Omega (Iota chpt. pres. 1990—91). Avocations: travel, reading. Home and Office: 3722 Violet Rose Ct Las Vegas NV 89147-7400 E-mail: sue.meiner@ccmail.nevada.edu., agingwell2002@msn.com.

MEINTS, CLIFFORD L. chemistry educator; b. Kansas City, Mo., May 23, 1930; s. John Albert and Amelia Johanna (Meyer) M.; m. Lita Joyce Klein, June 13, 1953; children: Linda C. Meyer, Glen Alan, Myra L. Coger, Kirk L. BS, Purdue U., 1953; MS, Ohio U., 1954; PhD, U. Okla., 1957. G.W. Carver prof. chemistry Simpson Coll., Indianola, Iowa, 1957—. Owner tutoring svc. Expand Your Expertise, Indianola, 1978—; pub.'s reviewer lab. manuals, 1995—. Mem. Am. Chem. Soc., Midwestern Assn. Chemistry Tchrs. Liberal Arts Colls., Gt. Plains Assn. Chemistry Tchrs. Liberal Arts Colls., Phi Lambda Upsilon. Office: Simpson Coll 701 N C St Indianola IA 50125-1264

MEISEL, MARTIN, English and comparative literature educator; b. N.Y.C., Mar. 22, 1931; s. Joseph and Sally (Rössler) Mörsel; m. Martha Sarah Winkley, Dec. 22, 1957; children— Maude Frances, Andrew Avram, Joseph Stoddard AB, Queens Coll., 1952; MA, Princeton U., 1957, PhD, 1960; postgrad., U. Rome, 1959. Instr. English Rutgers U., New Brunswick, N.J., 1957-58; instr., asst. prof., assoc. prof. Dartmouth Coll., Hanover, N.H., 1959-65; prof. English U. Wis., Madison, 1965-68; prof. English and comparative lit. Columbia U., N.Y.C., 1968—, Brander Matthews prof. dramatic lit., 1987—, chmn. dept., 1980-83, 99-01, acting v.p. arts and scis., 1986-87, v.p. arts and scis., 1989-93. Trustee Columbia U. Press, 1990-94. Author: Shaw and the 19th Century Theater, 1963, Realizations: Narrative, Pictorial, and Theatrical Arts in 19th Century England (George Freedley Meml. award Theater Libr. Assn. 1984, Barnard Hewitt award Am. Theatre Assn. 1984), 1983; mem. editorial and adv. bds. Jour. Victorian Studies, PMLA, Jour. Contemporary Lit., Bull. Rsch. in the Humanities, 19th Century Contexts. Served with U.S. Army, 1954-56 Fellow Guggenheim Found., 1963-64, 1987-88, Am. Council of Learned Socs., 1970-71, Inst. for Advanced Studies in the Humanities, Edinburgh, 1977, Huntington Library and Art Gallery, 1978, 80, 83, Nat. Humanities Ctr., 1983-84, Wilson Ctr., Smithsonian Instn., 1987-88. Mem. MLA, Am. Soc. Theatre Rsch., North Am. Victorian Studies Assn., Assn. of Historians of 19 Century Art, Century Assn. Home: 18 Bacon Hill Rd Pleasantville NY 10570-3502 Office: Columbia U 611 Philosophy Hall New York NY 10027 E-mail: mm28@columbia.edu.

MEISSNER, ANN LORING, psychologist, educator; b. Richland Center, Wis., Nov. 26, 1924; d. Frank Gilson Woodworth and Leona Bergman; m. Hans Meissner, July 4, 1946 (div. 1953); children: Edie, John Arthur; m. Corbin Sherwood Kidder, Oct. 28,1979. BS, U. Mich., 1953; MS, U. Wis., 1960, PhD, 1965; MPH, U. Calif., Berkeley, 1969; diploma, Gestalt Inst., Cleve., 1974, U. Minn., 1993; D for Life Long Learning (hon.), St. Mary's U., Winona, Minn., 2001. Lic. psychologist, Minn. Assoc. dir. Coop. Sch. Rehab. Ctr., Mpls., 1965-72; assoc. prof. W.Va. U., 1972-74; psychologist Alternative Behavior Assn., Mpls., 1974-79, Judson Family Ctr., Mpls., 1979-84; pvt. practice St. Paul, 1984—. Dir. nursing Augsburg U., Mpls., 1974-76; adj. prof. St. Mary's Coll., Mpls., 1979—; mem. staff Gestalt Inst. Twin Cities, Mpls., 1978-88; dir. Today Per., Mpls., 1980-91; mem. State Bd. Psychology, Mpls., 1982-86; adv. bd. doctoral program U. St. Thomas, St. Paul, adj. faculty, 1993. Recipient Disting. Human Svc. Profl. award N. Hennepin C.C., Mpls., 1981. Mem. APA, Minn. Women Psychologists, Elder Zest (pres. 2002). Episcopalian. Avocation: swimming. Home: 111 Kellogg Blvd E Apt 1501 Saint Paul MN 55101-1214 Office: 332 Minnesota St # 1255 Saint Paul MN 55101-1314 E-mail: croneann@mac.com.

MEISSNER, DOROTHY THERESA, reading specialist; b. Jersey City, N.J., Apr. 20, 1932; d. John and Mary (Garofalo) Biondo; m. Carl Frederick Meissner; children: Kathleen Ann, Mary Gretl. BA summa cum laude, Jersey City State Coll., 1970, MA summa cum laude, 1974. Cert. tchr. of reading, reading specialist, supr. and adminstr.; cert. guidance counselor. Metallographer Engelhard Industries, Newark, N.J., 1953-61; 2nd grade tchr. Rutherford (N.J.) Bd. Edn., 1970-74, 4th grade tchr., 1974, reading specialist, 1974-94, 94—; instr. Fairleigh Dickinson U., Rutherford, 1977. Spl. edn. steering com. Kearny (N.J.) Pub. Schs., 1968-69; G&T adv. coun. Rutherford Pub. Schs., 1978-79; v.p. Union Fin. Chain, Rutherford, 1985-89, pres., 1989-92; adj. prof. reading dept. Jersey City State Coll. Contbr. articles to profl. jours.; designer sculpture; artist charcoal drawing (hon. mention 1987). Lector Roman Cath. Ch., Kearny, 1988—; coord. William Carlos Williams Project, Rutherford, 1984. Recipient Gov.'s Tchr.'s Recognition State of N.J., 1987, Mary G. Filosa reading tchr. of yr. award N.J. Reading Tchrs. Assn., 1996-97; seminar grantee N.J. Coun. for Humanities, 1995. Mem. Internat. Reading Assn. (program chair 1992-93, v.p. 1994-95, pres. 1995—, rec. sec. North Jersey coun. 1996—, svc. project chair 2000-2002, Celebrate Literacy award 2002), N.J. Reading Assn. (tchr. of yr. 1996-97, hospitality chair for conf., bd. dirs., awards com. chairperson 2000-2002), Women's Coll. Club, Phi Delta Kappa, Kappa Delta Pi. Avocations: reading, tennis, gardening, art, music. Home: PO Box 355 Kearny NJ 07032-0355

MEISTER, ELYSE S. reading specialist; b. Bklyn., May 23, 1944; d. Irving and Syd (Kushner) Spitz; m. Myron S. Meister, Aug. 15, 1965; children: Lynn Mueller, Jill Kimmel, Adrienne. BA, Bklyn. Coll., 1966; MA, Montclair State Coll., 1986. Cert. adminstr., supr., reading specialist. Elem. tchr. East Orange (N.J.) Sch. Dist., 1979-85; reading tchr. West Orange (N.J.) Sch. Dist., 1985-94; instr. reading Kean Coll., Union, N.J., 1994—. Cons. Estelle Finkel Assocs., Livingston, N.J., 1994—. Mem. LWV (bd. dirs.), ASCD, Phi Kappa Phi. Avocations: tennis, golf, reading.

MEISTER, KAREN OLIVIA, educator; b. Newark, May 19, 1944; d. Bernice Hendricks Huebner; children: Christin, Brian, Erin. BA, Kean Coll., 1966, MA, 1987. Tchr. Union (N.J.) Bd. Edn., 1970-74; instr. Roselle (N.J.) Bd. Edn., 1982—; adj. prof. Union County Coll., 1987—92, Raritan Valley Cmty. Coll., Somerset, 1992—; Ind. Cons. Mary Kay Inc. Trainer Lit. Vol. Am., 1989-91. Mem. NEA, N.J. Edn. Assn., Internat. Reading Assn., N.J. Reading Assn., Suburban Reading Coun. Avocation: antiques. Office: Harrison Sch 310 Harrison Ave Roselle NJ 07203-1495

MELADY, THOMAS PATRICK, academic administrator, ambassador, author, public policy expert, educator; b. Norwich, Conn., Mar. 4, 1927; m. Margaret Judith Badum; children: Christina, Monica. BA, Duquesne U., 1950; MA, Cath. U. Am., 1952, PhD, 1954. Former mem. faculties Fordham and St. John's Univs.; founder Inst. African Affairs Duquesne U., 1957; cons. to founds., govts., corps., 1959-67; hon. doctorates from 28 univs. Africa Service Inst.; prof. Afro-Asian affairs, chmn. dept. Asian studies and NonWestern civilization Seton Hall U., South Orange, N.J., 1967-69, regent, 1987-90; prof. Afro-Asian affairs, dir. Office of Internat. Studies, 1973-74; exec. v.p., prof. politics St. Joseph's U., Phila., 1974-76; pres. Sacred Heart U., Fairfield, Conn., 1976-86, prof. polit. sci., 1976-86, pres. emeritus, 1986—; asst. sec. for postsecondary edn. U.S. Dept. Edn., Washington, 1981-82; amb. to Burundi, 1969-72; amb. to Uganda, 1972-73; sr. adviser to U.S. del. to 25 UN Gen. Assembly, 1970; chmn. Conn. Conf. Ind. Colls., 1979-81; pres., chief exec. officer Conn. Pub. Expenditures Coun., 1986-89; U.S. amb. to The Holy See, Vatican City, 1989-93, 94-95; exec. dir. Cath. Network of Vol. Svc., 1993-94; v.p. Capital Formation Counselors, 1993—. Disting. vis. prof. George Washington U. and St. John's U., 1993—94; vis. prof. Rome Grad. Ctr., 1998—99, Pontifical Gregorian U., 2001; chmn. nat. com. Cath. Campaign for Am., 1994—99; counsel to govts. and bus.; prof., sr. diplomat in residence Inst. of World Politics, 2001—. Author: Ambassadors Story: The United States and The Vatican in World Affairs, 1994, and 16 other books. Knighted by Pope Paul VI, 1968 and by Pope John Paul II, 1983, 91; honored by 6 countries; recipient Native Son award, Grand Cross, Order of Malta, 1993. Mem.: Soc. of The Cincinnati, The Sacred Mil. Constantinian Order of St. George, Order of Malta. E-mail: ambmelady@aol.com.

MELDONIAN, SUSAN LUCY, elementary education educator; b. N.Y.C., Apr. 21, 1955; d. John Sarkis and Margaret (Avdoyan) M. BA in Elem. Edn., William Paterson Coll., Wayne, N.J., 1977, MEd in Reading, 1993. Cert. tchr. K-8, reading specialist, K-12, N.J. Basic skills tchr. K-4 Walter O. Krumbiegel Sch., Hillside, N.J., 1979; tchr. 1st grade Margaret L. Vetter Sch., Eatontown, N.J., 1979-88, Cherry Hill Sch., River Edge, N.J., 1988-94, tchr. 3d grade, 1994—. Contbg. author: Moving Forward with Literature: Basals, Books and Beyond, 1993; contbr. articles to profl. jours. Mem. NEA, N.J. Edn. Assn., Internat. Reading Assn., Pi Lambda Theta. Mem. Armenian Apostolic Ch. Avocations: piano, singing, travel, bowling. Office: Cherry Hill Sch 410 Bogert Rd River Edge NJ 07661-1899

MELDRUM, DEIRDRE RUTH, electrical engineering educator; b. Loma Linda, Calif., Mar. 14, 1961; d. Ronald Murray and Barbara Ruth (Howard) M.; m. Peter Jan Wiktor; children: Thaddeus Meldrum Wiktor, Genevieve Meldrum Wiktor. BSCE, U. Wash., 1983; MSEE, Rensselaer Polytech. Inst., 1985; PhDEE, Stanford (Calif.) U., 1993. Design engr. Wash. State Dept. of Transp., Seattle, 1982-83; mem. tech. staff Jet Propulsion Lab., Pasadena, Calif., 1985-87; NASA fellow, Amelia Earhart fellow Stanford U., Palo Alto, 1989-92; asst. prof. elec. engring. U. Wash., Seattle, 1992-98, assoc. prof. elec. engring., 1998—2001, prof., 2001—. Mem. adv. panel for ILI Program NSF, Washington, 1993, mem. spl. emphasis panels NIH on genome automation. Contbr. articles to profl. jours. Recipient Spl. Emphasis Rsch. Career award NIH, 1993—, Ralph R. Teetor Edn. award Soc. of Automotive Engrs., 1993, Presdl. Early Career award for Scientists and Engrs., 1996. Mem. IEEE, AIAA, AAAS, Soc. of Women Engrs., Sigma Xi. Avocations: bicycling, back country skiing, rowing, traveling, photography.

MELÉNDEZ, ZULMA CECILIA, bilingual/bicultural education evaluator; b. Santurce, P.R. d. Miguel Antonio and Consuelo (Torres) Carrio. AA in Psychology, Bronx C.C., 1976; BA in Psychology, Columbia U., 1981; MS in Edn., CUNY, 1990. Lic. tchr., N.Y.C., bilingual spl. edn. tchr. (Spanish), N.Y. Project coord., tchr. The Ednl. Alliance, N.Y.C., 1975-79; cons. to pres. Strategic Learning Systems Inst., Bayside, N.Y., 1982-92; asst. dir. Ednl. and Vocat. Rehab. Svcs., Samaritan Village Inc., Forest Hills, N.Y., 1983-84; rsch. assoc. Columbia U. Sch. Social Work, N.Y.C., 1985-86; tchr./trainer, asst. to Bronx coord. The Inst. of Tng. for Future Careers, N.Y., 1985-86; bilingual spl. edn. tchr. The Bilingual Sch. P25, N.Y.C., 1987-89, P17 at 89, N.Y., 1989-90, Multi-lingual/Multi-cultural Sch. P53, N.Y.C., 1990-91, N.Y.C. Dist. 3 Com. on Spl. Edn., 1991—; bilingual/bicultural edn. evaluator, diagnostician, cons. PS 165, N.Y.C., 1991—. Cons. in field for numerous orgns. Mem. Nat. Assn. for Bilingual Edn., N.Y. State Assn. for Bilingual Edn., Coun. for Exceptional Children, Coun. for Ednl. Diagnostic Svcs., Puerto Rican Educators Assn. Office: Pub Sch 165 Rm 406 Sch Based Support Team 234 W 109th St New York NY 10025-2228

MELHISER, MYRNA RUTH, secondary education educator; b. Owensboro, Ky., Mar. 20, 1937; d. John Robert and Annie Laurie (Nicholson) Gregory; m. Robert Harold Melhiser, July 17, 1964 (wid.); 1 child, Amy Ruth. BA English, Ky. Wesleyan Coll., 1958; MA English, Western Ky. U., 1971. Cert. tchr. English, Ky. Tchr. of English Owensboro High Sch., 1958-59; tchr. music and English Daviess County Jr. High, Owensboro, 1959-62; tchr. of English Daviess County High Sch., Owensboro, 1962-96, head English dept., 1983-93; tchr. English Ky. Wesleyan, 1998—. Organist, dir. of choirs, various chs. in Owensboro, 1954-88; interim organist First Bapt. Ch., Owensboro, 1994-95; cluster leader under KERA, Daviess County High. Pres. Owensboro Concert Assn., 1984-89, 95-96. Mem.: Nat. Fedn. of Music Club (pres. Saturday musicals 2000—), Delta Kappa Gamma. Republican. Baptist. Avocations: reading, music, golf, travel. Home: 1921 Mayfair Avenue Owensboro KY 42301-4672

MELICHAR, BARBARA EHRLICH, educational administrator; b. Butte, Mont., Oct. 12, 1949; d. Louis Earl and Jennie Muriel (Friberg) Ehrlich; m. Kenneth Edward Melichar, Mar. 21, 1972; 1 child, Leah Jane. BA, U. Mont., 1972; MEd, U. Ga., 1988, EdD, 1993. Adminstr. North Ga. Tech. Inst., Clarkesville, Ga., 1986—. Editorial assoc.: Adult Basic Edn. jour. Mem. Am. Assn. Adult and Continuing Edn., Phi Kappa Phi, Kappa Delta Phi. Avocations: knitting, walking, hockey fan. Office: North Ga Tech Inst PO Box 65 Clarkesville GA 30523-0065

MELICHER, RONALD WILLIAM, finance educator; b. St. Louis, July 4, 1941; s. William and Lorraine Norma (Mohart) M.; m. Sharon Ann Schlarmann, Aug. 19, 1967; children: Michelle Joy, Thor William, Sean Richard. BSBA, Washington U., St. Louis, 1963, MBA, 1965, DBA, 1968. Asst. prof. fin. U. Colo., Boulder, 1969-71, assoc. prof., 1971-76, prof. fin., 1976—, chmn. fin. divsn., 1978-86, 90, chmn. fin. and econ. divsn., 1993-2000, MBA/MS programs dir., 1990-93, chmn. fin. divsn., 2003—. Assoc. dir. space law bus. and policy ctr. U. Colo., 1986-87; rsch. cons. FPC, Washington, 1975-76, GAO, Washington, 1981, RCG/Hagler, Bailly, Inc., 1985—, Ariz. Corp. Commn., 1986-87, Conn. Dept. Pub. Utility Control, 1989, U.S. SEC, 1992-95; cons. tech. edn. IBM Corp., 1985-91; dir. ann. Exch. Program for Gas Industry, 1975-94; instr. ann. program Nat. Assn. Regulatory Utility Commrs., Mich. State U., 1981-94. Co-author: Real Estate Finance, 1978, 3d edit., 1989, Financial Management, 5th edit., 1982; Finance: Introduction to Markets, Institutions and Management, 1980, 84, 88, 92, Finance: Introduction to Institutions, Investments, and Management, 9th edit., 1997, 11th edit., 2003, Entrepreneurial Finance, 2003; assoc. editor Fin. Mgmt. Jour., 1975-80, The Fin. Rev., 1988-91. Recipient News Ctr. 4 TV Teaching award, 1987, MBA/MS Assn. Teaching award, 1988, Boulder Faculty Assembly Teaching award, 1988, Grad. Bus. Students Teaching award, 1995, 98; grantee NSF, 1974, NASA, 1986, 87; scholar W.H. Baughn Disting., 1989-2000, U. Colo. Pres.'s Teaching, 1989—. Mem. Fin. Mgmt. Assn. (mem. com. 1974-76, regional dir. 1975-77, v.p. ann. mtg. 1985, v.p. program 1987, pres. 1991-92, exec. com. 1991-93, bd. trustees 1992-99, chmn. 25th Anniversary com. 1994-95, mem. search. com. for editor of Financial Mgmt. Jour., 1995-96, chmn. search com. editor of Fin. Practice and Edn. Jour. 1996, mem. search com. for sec./treas. 1999, 2001), Am. Fin. Assn. Western Fin. Assn. (bd. dirs. 1974-76), Fin. Execs. Inst. (acad. mem. 1975—), Ea. Fin. Assn., Southwestern Fin. Assn., Midwest Fin. Assn. (bd. dirs. 1978-80), Alpha Kappa Psi, Beta Gamma Sigma. Presbyterian. Home: 6348 Swallow Ln Boulder CO 80303-1456 Office: U Colo Coll Bus PO Box 419 Boulder CO 80303 E-mail: Ronald.Melicher@colorado.edu.

MELICK, GEORGE FLEURY, mechanical engineer, educator; b. Morristown, N.J., Sept. 7, 1924; s. George Fleury and Esther Purdy (Udall) M.; m. Florence Miriam Bevins, Dec. 28, 1946; children: Robert A., Linda S., Judith E., Karen L. BSE, Princeton U., 1944; MS, Stevens Inst. Tech., 1955; ME, Columbia U., 1963; MA, NYU, 1970. Registered profl. engr., N.J. Asst. chief engr. Worthington Corp., Harrison, N.J., 1946-55; asst. prof. Stevens Inst. Tech., Hoboken, N.J., 1955-58; assoc. in mech. engring. Columbia U., N.Y.C., 1958-61; assoc. prof. mech. engring., dean Rutgers U., New Brunswick, N.J., 1961-77; cons. engr. Stone & Webster Engring. Corp., Cherry Hill, N.J., 1977-87; dir. engring. mgmt. program Drexel U., Phila., 1987-91; chmn. bd. Anastasio & Melick Assocs., Cherry Hill, N.J., 1987—. Cons. Worthington Corp., Harrison, 1956-65, Pub. Svc. Elec. & Gas, Newark, 1966-76. Author: John Mark and the Origin of the Gospels, 1979. Mem. countycom. Dem. Party, Franklin Twp., N.J., 1976. 1st lt. U.S. Army, 1945-52. Decorated Bronze Star medal. Mem. ASME (life), Am. Soc. Engring. Mgmt. (life), Am. Soc. Engring. Edn. (life), Soc. Bibl. Lit., Am. Acad. Religion (charter), Sigma Xi, Pi Tau Sigma, Tau Beta Pi. Presbyterian. Home: 9 Attleboro Ct Red Bank NJ 07701-5410 Office: Anastasio & Melick Assocs 30 Crofton Commons Cherry Hill NJ 08034-1142

MELIUS, PAUL, biochemist, educator; b. Livingston, Ill., Nov. 21, 1927; s. Louis and Tina (Contoyanis) M.; m. Vaya Gourbis, Sept. 10, 1976; children: Randall Scott, Paul Mark, Alan Lane, Lisa Buffet. BS, Bradley U., 1950; MS, U. Chgo., 1952; PhD, Loyola U., Chgo., 1956. Prof. chemistry Auburn U., Ala., 1957—91, Disting. lectr., 1982-83, ret., 1991. Co-author: Problem Workbook Biochemistry, 1973; contbr. 75 articles to Biochem. Jour., Biochemica, Biophysica Acta, Jour. Am. Chem. Soc., Jour. CancerRsch., Jour. Medicinal Chemistry, others. Bd. dirs. United Way, Auburn, 1987-89. Cpl. U.S. Army, 1946-47. NIH spl. fellow, 1968-69, 1962; recipient NATO award for rsch., 1976; rsch. grantee NSF, NIH, EPA, DuPont, 1964-84. Mem. Am. Chem. Soc. (chairman local sect. 1982, nat. councillor 1984-90), Am. Soc. Biol. Chemistry, English Biochem. Soc. Achievements include research on the structure of thermal polymers of amino acids; role of vitamin B6 homolog in growth and reproduction of rats; metabolism of benz(a)pyrene in fish; purification and characterization of kidney leucine aminopeptidase and pancreatic lipase. Home: 336 Bowden Dr Auburn AL 36830-5654

MELLISH, GORDON HARTLEY, economist, educator; b. Toronto, May 3, 1940; came to U.S., 1958; s. Gordon Day and Catherine (Hartley) M.; m. Nancy Bernice Newell (div. Nov. 1972); m. Diane Evelyn Bostow, Jan. 1, 1978 (div. 1999); children: Jennie Bostow, Luke Bostow. BA, Rockford (Ill.) Coll., 1962; PhD, U. Va., 1965. Econs. educator U. South Fla., Tampa, 1965-89; pvt. practice Tampa, Fla., 1966—. Vis. prof. U. Va., 1969, Hillsborough Jr. Coll., 1968; vis. lectr. U. Tampa, 1965, 74. Contbr. articles to profl. jours. Mem. Tampa Yacht and Country Club, Tampa Club, Leadership Tampa Alumni. Democrat. Avocations: sailing, skiing. Home: 2510 W Shell Point Pl Tampa FL 33611-5033 E-mail: gmellish@tampabay.rr.com.

MELLO, MICHAEL WILLIAM, educational administrator; b. Waterbury, Conn., Apr. 8, 1941; s. Manuel Sousa and Mary Doris (Araujo) M.; m. Elizabeth Ann Ambaragocy, Feb. 11, 1973; children— William Michael, David Michael. B.Ed., R.I. Coll., 1962, M.Ed., 1965. With Portsmouth Sch. Dept. (R.I.), 1962—, dir. instructional tech., 1968-81, dir. grant programs, 1975-81, dir. instrn., 1981-89, asst. supt., 1989—; instr. R.I. Coll. Pres. Citizens Scholarship Found. of Bristol, R.I., Inc., 1963-66; bd. trustees Portsmouth Free Library, 1981—, v.p. 1981-82, pres., 1982-84, 85—, treas., 1984-85. Served with U.S. Army, 1966-68. Mem. NEA, Assn. Ednl. Communication and Tech., R.I. Audiovisual Edn. Assn. (pres. 1969-71), Assn. Supervision and Curriculum Devel., R.I. Ednl. Media Assn. (pres. 1984-85, bd. dirs. 1980—, recipient Man of the Yr. award 1974, Linda Aldrich Leadership award 1992), R.I. Assn. Sch. Supts. (position paper chairperson, 1987-88), Portsmouth Sch. Adminstrs. Assn. (pres. 1978-80). Home: 486 Water St Portsmouth RI 02871-4229 Office: 29 Middle Rd Portsmouth RI 02871-1250

MELLORS, ROBERT CHARLES, physician, scientist, educator; b. Dayton, Ohio, 1916; s. Bert S. and Clementine (Steinmetz) M.; m. Jane K. Winternitz, Mar. 25, 1944; children: Alice J., Robert C., William K., John W. PhD, Western Res. U., 1940; MD, Johns Hopkins, 1944. Diplomate Am. Bd. Pathology. Intern Nat. Naval Med. Ctr., Bethesda, Md., 1944-45; rsch. fellow medicine Meml. Center Cancer and Allied Diseases, N.Y.C., 1946-50; rsch. fellow pathology Meml. Ctr. Cancer and Allied Diseases, 1950-53, asst. attending pathologist, 1953-57, assoc. attending pathologist, 1957-58. Sr. fellow Am. Cancer Soc., 1947-50; sr. clin. rsch. fellow Damon Runyon Meml. Fund, 1950-53; asst. attending pathologist Meml. Hosp., N.Y.C., 1953-57, assoc. attending pathologist, 1957-58; asst. attending pathologist Ewing Hosp., N.Y.C., 1953-57, assoc. attending pathologist, 1957-58; instr. biochemistry Western Res. U., 1940-42; rsch. assoc. Poliomyelitis Rsch. Ctr. and Dept. Epidemiology Johns Hopkins U. Sch. Hygiene, 1942-44; asst. prof. biology Meml. Ctr. Cancer and Allied Diseases, N.Y.C., 1952-53; asst. prof. pathology Sloan Kettering div. Cornell U., 1953-57, assoc. prof., 1957-58; prof. pathology Cornell U. Med. Coll., 1961-90, prof. emeritus, 1990—; adj. prof. pathology N.Y. Med. Coll., 1997—; assoc. attending pathologist N.Y. Hosp., 1961-72, attending pathologist, 1972-86; pathologist-in-chief, dir. labs., 1958-84, emeritus, 1984-85, hon. staff, 1986—; assoc. dir. rsch. Hosp. for Spl. Surgery, N.Y.C., 1958-69, dir. rsch., 1969-84, emeritus, 1984-85, scientist emeritus, 1986—; mem. rsch. adv. com. NIH, 1962-66; adv. com. Nat. Inst. Environ. Health Sci., 1966-69; com. nomenclature and classification of disease Coll. Am. Pathologists, 1960-64. Author: Analytical Cytology, 1955, 2d edit., 1959,

Analytical Pathology, 1957, also 5 med. sch. tchg. documents online. Served as lt. (j.g.), M.C. USNR, 1944-46. Recipient Kappa Delta award Am. Acad. of Orthopedic Surgeons, 1962 Fellow Royal Coll. Pathologists, Molecular Medicine Soc., Am. Soc. Clin. Pathology; mem. Internat. Soc. for Optical Engring., Am. Assn. Pathologists, Am. Assn. Immunologists, Am. Soc. Biochemistry and Molecular Biology, Am. Coll. Rheumatology, Am. Orthopedic Assn. (hon.). Home: 3 Hardscrabble Cir Armonk NY 10504-2222

MELMAN, CYNTHIA SUE, special education educator; b. Pottsville, Pa., Nov. 13, 1946; d. Earl J. and Lillian (Zubroff) M. BA in English, Lebanon Valley Coll., 1969; MEd, Western Md. Coll., 1978. Advanced profl. cert. Md. State Dept. Edn. English tchr. Susquehanna Twp. Sch. Dist., Harrisburg, Pa., 1969-70; tchr. of the deaf Am. Sch. for the Deaf, West Hartford, Conn., 1978-80; sign lang. interpreter for the deaf Montgomery County Pub. Schs., Rockville, Md., 1980-81, tchr. of the deaf/hard of hearing, 1981—. In-svc. program masters plus 30, Montgomery County Pub. Schs., Rockville, 1982-96, base sch. rep. for energy saving and recycling program, 1994-95. Co-author: (one workbook in a series) Writing Sentences, 1981. Mem.: NEA, Montgomery County Assn. for Hearing Impaired Children. Avocations: theater, movies, music, reading, walking.

MELMER, RICK, state agency administrator; BA, Dakota Wesleyan U.; MA, SD State U.; EdD, U. Wyo. Supt. schs. Sioux Ctr. Cmty. Sch. Dist., Iowa, 1991—95, Watertown (SD) Sch. Dist., 1995—2003; sec. edn. SD Dept. Edn., Pierre, 2003—. Office: SD Dept Edn 700 Governors Dr Pierre SD 57501*

MELNICK, JANE FISHER, journalism, creative writing and literature educator; b. Boston, Sept. 26, 1939; d. Richard T. and Mary (Holcombe) Fisher; m. Burton A. Melnick, Dec. 1962 (div. 1969); 1 child, Benjamin A. BA cum laude, Radcliffe Coll., 1962; MA, NYU, 1985, PhD in Am. Studies, 1991. News writer, photographer, freelance editor, 1962—75; editor/writer In These Times, Chgo., 1976-78, Seven Days, N.Y.C., 1978-81; instr. writing, Am. lit. NYU, 1981-86, Loyola U., Chgo., 1988-91; asst. prof. Elmhurst (Ill.) Coll., 1991-96; writer, coll. prep. tutor, 1997—2002. Contbr. revs., articles on culture and news to various publs. Recipient Mademoiselle mag. fiction contest award, 1962, Phi Beta Kappa award for best creative work by an undergrad. Radcliffe Coll., 1959; NEA grantee, 1973, dean's dissertation fellow NYU, 1987. Mem. MLA, Mid-Am. Am. Studies Assn. (exec. bd., chair essay judging com. 1995-96). Avocations: home renovation, travel. Home: 5000 N Marine Dr Apt 15A Chicago IL 60640-3226

MELNICK, MICHAEL, geneticist, educator; b. N.Y.C., Sept. 24, 1944; s. Lester and Evelyn (Rosenberg) M.; m. Anita Goldberger, June 19, 1966; children: Cliff, Lynn. BA in Biology, NYU, 1966, DDS, 1970; PhD in Genetics, Ind. U., 1978. Instr. oral medicine Ind. U., Indpls., 1973-74, fellow in med. genetics, 1974-77, asst. prof. med. genetics, 1977-78; rsch. assoc. prof. U. So. Calif., L.A., 1978-85, assoc. prof., 1985-89, prof. genetics, 1989—. Cons. in human genetics NIH, Bethesda, Md., 1977-88, grant reviewer, 1978—; manuscript referee Am. Jour. Human Genetics, Chgo., 1980—, Am. Jour. Med. Genetics, Helena, Mont., 1980—; MRC vis. prof. McGill U., Montreal, que., 1990. Author, editor 5 books on human genetics; editor-in-chief Jour. Craniofacial Genetics, 1980-2000; contbr. more than 100 articles to profl. jours. Mem. nat. bd. Com. of Concerned Scientists, N.Y.C., 1983—; vice chmn. Youth Towns of Israel, L.A., 1986—. Capt. M.C. U.S. Army, 1970-73. Recipient Ind. U. Disting. Alumnus award, 1984; Warwick James fellow U. London/Guy's Hosp., 1992. Fellow AAAS; mem. Soc. Craniofacial Genetics (pres. 1978-79), Soc. for Developmental Biology, Am. Soc. Human Genetics, Sigma Xi. Achievements include research in delineated major gene causation of cleft lip and palate; delineated insulin-like growth factor, type 2, receptor control of fetal lung, salvary gland and palate development; application of probability neural networks to multi-gene analysis. Avocations: art, philosophy, chess. Office: Univ of Southern California Den 4266 Mc 0641 Los Angeles CA 90089-0641 E-mail: mmelnick@usc.edu.

MELNICK, RALPH, library director, secondary school educator; b. N.Y.C., Sept. 14, 1946; s. Lester and Evelyn Melnick; m. Rachel Shana Levy, June 1, 1969; children: Joshua Jacob, Ross David. BA, NYU, 1968; MS in LS, Columbia U., 1970, MA, 1974, MPhil, 1975, PhD, 1977. Libr., archivist Am. Jewish Hist. Soc., Waltham, Mass., 1971-72, freelance archivist, 1985-89; libr., archivist Zionist Archives and Libr., N.Y.C., 1975-77; head spl. collections Coll. of Charleston, S.C., 1977-84; libr., dir. tchr. religion Williston Northampton Sch., Easthampton, Mass., 1984—. Vis. prof. Judaic studies U. Mass., Amherst, 2002—03. Author: From Polemics to Apologetics, 1981, The Stolen Legacy of Anne Frank, 1997, Life and Work of Ludwig Lewisohn, Vol. I, 1998, Vol. II, 1998, Justice Betrayed, 2002. Founding mem., archivist Avery Inst. for Afro-Am. History and Culture, Charleston, 1980-84. Rsch. fellow Am. Philos. Soc., 1980, Loewenstein fellow Am. Jewish Archives, 1981, fellow NEH, 1984. Mem. ALA, Assn. for Jewish Studies, Authors Guild, Phi Beta Kappa. Avocations: book collecting, antiques, travel. Office: Convent of the Sacred Heart 1 E 91st St New York NY 10128-0689 E-mail: ralphmelnick@hotmail.com.

MELNYK, STEVEN ALEXANDER, business management educator; b. Hamilton, Ont., Can., Apr. 12, 1953; came to U.S., 1980; s. Stephen and Mary (Sahan) M.; m. Christine Ann Halstead, July 10, 1976; children: Charles Edward Phillip, Elizabeth Victoria Michaela. BA in Econs., U. Windsor, Ont., 1975; MA in Econs., U. We. Ont., London, 1976, PhD in Ops. Mgmt., 1981. Asst. prof. ops. mgmt. Mich. State U., East Lansing, 1980-85, assoc. prof., 1985-90, prof., 1990—. Author: Shop Floor Control, 1985, 87, Production Activity Control, 1987, Computer Integrated Manual, 1992-96, Operations Management A Valve Driven Approach, others. Recipient Tchr.-Scholar award Mich. State U., 1985, other awards. Mem. Am. Prodn. and Inventory Control Soc. (software editor 1991—, cons. 1980—, Paul Berkobile award 1992), Nat. Assn. Purchasing Mgrs., Decision Sci. Inst. (editor procs. 1991, Outstanding Theoretical Paper award 1982), Soc. Mfg. Engrs., Inst. Mgmt. Sci. Episcopalian. Avocations: civil war history, baseball history, bicycling. Office: Mich State U N327 NBC East Lansing MI 48824-1122

MELONAKOS, CHRISTINE MARIE, educational administrator; b. Shelby, Mich., Apr. 29, 1960; d. L.V. Charles and Dorothy June (Arman) Besemer; m. Paul W. Melonakos, May 31, 1983; children: Christian, Timothy, Kandice, Emerson. BS in Psychology, Brigham Young U., 1989. Presch. tchr. Minnieland, Manassas, Va., 1989-90; kindergarten tchr. Manassas Christian Sch., 1990-91; presch. owner Appleseed Presch., Manassas, 1991-92; pres., founder Applebrook Family Enrichment Network, Fremont, Mich., 1992-95, Applebrook Inst., Newaygo, Mich., 1994—. Pub. spkr. various orgns., 1990-95; parent educator various orgns., Va. and Mich., 1989-95; creator (tchg. method) Interactive Assistance, 1992. Author: Starting Right, 1993, Cooperation Kit, 1993, Parenting Success Program, 1995; editor Motivated Mother Newsletter, 1990-91. Sec. PTA, Manassas, 1991-92; children's program dir. Parents Anonymous, Manassas, 1991. Recipient Va. Mother of Yr. award Am. Mothers Assn., 1992. Mem. ASCD, Interactive Parents Assn. (founder, pres. 1993—). Republican. Avocations: sewing, antiques, country line dancing, victorian postcards. Address: 16414 Palomino Pl Apt 102 Santa Clarita CA 91387-4614

MELROY, JANE RUTH, business educator; b. Columbus, Nebr., Apr. 5, 1957; d. David Morris Sr. and Catherine Hanna (Carson) Hamilton; m. Dennis Lee Melroy, Feb. 28, 1976; children: Tobin Ray, Brent Carson, Erin Jane. BA in Edn., Kearney (Nebr.) State Coll., 1980; MS in Edn., U. Nebr., Kearney, 1990. Cert. tchr., Nebr., Kans. Tchr. bus. York (Nebr.) High Sch., 1980-84, Broken Bow (Nebr.) High Sch., 1984-88, Skyline High Sch., Pratt, Kans., 1989—. Adj. faculty Pratt Community Coll., 1988-90. Contbg. author: Computers in Business Education, 1986, Computer Enrichment Handbook, 1990. Cubmaster Boy Scouts Am., Pratt, 1988-89, com. chmn., 1990-92, bd. mem.-at-large Kanza coun., 1991-94. Mem. NEA, Nat. Bus. Edn. Assn., Kans. Bus. Edn. Assn., Mountain-Plains Bus. Edn. Assn., Nebr. State Bus. Edn. Assn. (rep. Sandhill dist. 1986-88), Skyline Edn. Assn. (pres. 1992-93, 97-98, treas. 1990-91, chief negotiator 1998—, named Tchr. of Yr. 1998-99), Kans. Nat. Edn. Assn. (bd. dirs. Ark Valley Dist. 1990-91, sec. 1995-99, comm. commr. 1996-2002, chmn. 2000-01, RA cluster del. 1993—, v.p. 2001—), Nebr. Future Bus. Leaders Am. (bd. dirs. 1986-88), Delta Kappa Gamma (treas. 1994-2002). Republican. Episcopalian. Avocations: reading, travel, cooking, quilting. E-mail: jmelroy@usd438.k12.ks.us.

MELSON, RENÉ HARBER, elementary school educator; b. Atlanta, Dec. 4, 1954; d. Talmon Eugene and June (Slaton) Harber; children: Presley, Cameron. BS in Elem. Edn., Ga. State U., 1977. Cert. tchr., Ga. Tchr. Greater Atlanta Christian Schs., Norcross, Ga., 1977-82, 88—. Republican. Ch. of Christ. Avocations: reading, quilting, cross stitch. Home: 445 Cambria Ln SW Lilburn GA 30047-3076 Office: Greater Atlanta Christian PO Box 277 Norcross GA 30091-0277

MELTEBEKE, RENETTE, career counselor; b. Portland, Oreg., Apr. 20, 1948; d. Rene and Gretchen (Hartwig) M. BS in Sociology, Portland State U., 1970; MA in Counseling Psychology, Lewis and Clark Coll., 1985. Lic. profl. counselor, Oreg.; nat. cert. counselor; Veriditas trained labyrinth facilitator. Secondary tchr. Portland Pub. Schs., 1970-80; project coord. Multi-Wash CETA, Hillsboro, Oreg., 1980-81; coop. edn. specialist Portland C.C., 1981-91; pvt. practice career counseling, owner Career Guidance Specialists, Lake Oswego, Oreg., 1988—. Mem. adj. faculty Marylhurst (Oreg.) Coll., 1989-93, Portland State U., 1994—, Lewis and Clark Coll., 2001—; assoc. Drake Beam Morin Inc., Portland, 1993-96; career cons. Managed Health Network, 1994—, Career Devel. Svcs., 1990—, Life Dimensions, Inc., 1994; presenter Internat. Conf., St. Petersburg, Russia, 1995. Rotating columnist Lake Oswego Rev., 1995-99; creator video presentation on work in Am. in 5 langs., 1981. Pres. Citizens for Quality Living, Sherwood, Oreg., 1989; mem. Leadership Roundtable on Sustainability for Sherwood, 1994-95; bd. dirs. Bus. for Social Responsibility for Oreg. and Southwestern Wash., 1999, 2000. Recipient Esther Matthews award for outstanding contbn. to field of career devel., 1998. Mem.: Assn. for Humanistic Psychology (presenter nat. conf. Tacoma 1996), Oreg. Career Devel. Assn. (pres. 1990), Nat. Career Devel. Assn., Willamette Writers. Avocations: walking, swimming, bicycling, cross-country skiing, photography. Home: 890 SE Merryman St Sherwood OR 97140-9746 Office: Career Guidance Specialists 15800 Boones Ferry Rd Ste C104 Lake Oswego OR 97035-3492

MELTON, JUNE MARIE, nursing educator; b. St. Louis, Oct. 16, 1927; d. Thomas Jasper and Alice Marie (Sloas) Hayes; m. Malcolm Adrian Essen, July 12, 1947 (dec. July 1978); children: Alison, William, Terrence, Mark, Cathleen, Melodie; m. Denver A. Melton, Sept. 6, 1989 (dec.). Grad., Jewish Hosp. Sch. Nursing, 1948; student, U. Mo., Lincoln U., U. Colo., Stephens Coll., U. S.W. RN, Mo.; nurse ARC. Instr. home nursing U. Mo., Columbia, 1948-49; acting dir. nurses, 1957-68; supr. instr., obstet. supr. Charles E. Still Hosp., Jefferson City, Mo.; supr. nurse ICU, primary nurse St. Mary's Health Ctr., Jefferson City; health dir. Algoa Correctional Instn., Jefferson City, 1979-83; home health vis. nurse A&M Home Health, Jefferson City, 1983-96, parish nurse, 1998—. Mem. adv. bd. A&M Home Nursing, Jefferson City; instr. GED Lincoln U., Jefferson City; participant study of premature baby nursing U. Colo., 1964. Vol. ARC, Belle-Rolla, Mo., instr. home nursing; missionary to Togo, West Africa Mo. Synod. Luth. Ch., 1996—97, parish nurse, 1998—, harvester for Christ, 1999—; parish nurse Ysleta Luth. Mission, 2002. Mem. U.S. Nurse Corps. Democrat. Lutheran. Avocations: fishing, sewing, reading, traveling. Home: Winterwood Estates 15 B St Holts Summit MO 65043

MELTZER, BERNARD DAVID, law educator; b. Phila., Nov. 21, 1914; s. Julius and Rose (Welkov) M.; m. Jean Sulzberger, Jan. 17, 1947; children: Joan, Daniel, Susan. AB, U. Chgo., 1935, JD, 1937; LL.M., Harvard U., 1938. Bar: Ill. 1938. Atty., spl. asst. to chmn. SEC, 1938-40; assoc. firm Mayer, Meyer, Austrian & Platt, Chgo., 1940; spl. asst. to asst. sec. state, also acting chief fgn. funds control div. State, 1941—43; asst. trial counsel U.S. prosecution Internat. Nuremberg War Trials, 1945-46; from professorial lectr. to disting. svc. prof. law emeritus U. Chgo. Law Sch., 1946—; counsel Vedder, Price, Kaufman & Kammholz, Chgo., 1954-55, Sidley and Austin, Chgo., 1987-89. Hearing commr. NPA, 1952-53; labor arbitrator; spl. master U.S. Ct. Appeals for D.C., 1963-64; bd. publs. U. Chgo., 1965-67, chmn., 1967-68; mem. Gov. Ill. Adv. Commn. Labor-Mgmt. Policy for Pub. Employees in Ill., 1966-67, Ill. Civil Service Commn., 1968-69; cons. U.S. Dept. Labor, 1969-70 Author: Supplementary Materials on International Organizations, 1948, (with W.G. Katz) Cases and Materials on Business Corporations, 1949, Labor Law Cases, Materials and Problems, 1970, supplement, 1972, 75, 2d edit., 1977, supplements, 1980, 82 (with S. Henderson), 3d edit. (with S. Henderson), 1985, supplement, 1988; also articles. Bd. dirs. Hyde Park Community Conf., 1954-56, S.E. Chgo. Commn., 1956-57. Served to lt. (j.g.) USNR, 1943-46. Mem. ABA (co-chmn. com. devel. law under NLRA 1959-60, mem. spl. com. transp. strikes), Ill. Bar Assn., Chgo. Bar Assn. (bd. mgrs. 1972-73), Am. Law Inst., Coll. Labor and Employment Lawyers, Am. Acad. Arts and Scis., Order of Coif, Phi Beta Kappa Home: 1219 E 50th St Chicago IL 60615-2908 Office: U Chgo Law Sch 1111 E 60th St Chicago IL 60637-2776

MELTZER, E. ALYNE, elementary school educator, social worker, volunteer; b. Jersey City, May 16, 1934; d. Abraham Samuel and Fannie Ruth (Nydick) Meltzer. BA, Mich. State U., 1956. Acctg. clk. Louis Marx Co. Inc., N.Y.C., 1957-60; tchr. social studies Haverstraw HS, NY, 1960-61; tchr. Sachem Ctrl. Sch. Dist., Farmingville, NY, 1961-63, East Paterson Sch. Dist., NJ, 1964-65; case worker dept. social svc. Human Resource Adminstrn., N.Y.C., 1966-89. Mem. Yorkville Civic Coun., 1988—93; policy advisor Senator Roy Goodman Adv. Com., Albany, 1987—90; mem. Temple Shaaray Tefila. Recipient Sabra Soc. Plaque award, State of Israel New Leadership Divsn., N.Y.C., 1979, Prime Min. Club Plaque award, State of Israel Bonds, 1986—87, 1996, Pin award, 1986—87, 1990, 1994—96, others. Mem.: AAUW, Jewish Genealogy Soc., Assn. Ref. Zionists Am., Am. Jewish Com., Internat. Coun. Jewish Women (participant Jerusalem seminar 1991), Nat. Coun. Jewish Women (life; participant nat. conv. 1987, Albany Inst. 1987, Washington Inst. 1987, N.E. dist. conv. 1988, Albany Inst. 1988, Israel Summit V 1988, Washington Inst. 1989, sec. sect. pub. affairs com. 1990—93, mem. state and sec. pub. affairs com. 1990—, Albany Inst. 1991, Washington Mission 1991, co-chair Hunger Program Sunday Family Soup Kitchen 1991—93, nat. Israel affairs com. 1991—96, bd. dirs. N.Y. sect. 1991—, Jewish/Israel affairs com. sect. 1991—, Washington Inst. 1992, participant nat. conv. 1993, Albany Inst. 1993, chair Roosevelt Island Svcs. 1993—2003, participant nat. conv. 1996, Israel Roundtable 1996—99, co-chair fundraising jour. 1998—2000, co-chair sec. Yad B'Yad (Hand in Hand with Israel) cmty. svc. project 1999—, film festival com. Eleanor Leff Jewish Women's Resource Ctr. 2001—02, co-chair sec. Jewish/Israel Affairs com. 2001—, life mem. N.Y. and Rockland County sects., Outstanding Vol. award 1973—74, 1990—91, Donor award 1987—93, 1996), Jewish Hist. Soc. N.Y., Mich. State U. Alumni Orgn. (life; sec. N.Y. chpt. 1959—60), Mothers and Others, Rockland County Jewish Home for the Aged (life), Women's League for Israel (life), Hadassah (life), Sierra Club.

MELTZER, ROBERT CRAIG, lawyer, educator; b. Chgo., July 31, 1958; s. Franklyn Richard and Zelma (Cohen) M. BA, U. Colo., 1980; cert., Inst. de Internat., Strasbourg, France, 1984; JD, No. Ill. U., DeKalb, 1985; postgrad., U. Salzburg, Austria, 1985. Bar: Ill. 1985, U.S. Dist. Ct. (no. dist.) Ill. 1985, U.S. Ct. Appeals (7th cir.) 1988, U.S. Supreme Ct. 1989. Law clk. Hurwitz & Abramson, Washington, 1980, Mayer, Brown & Platt, Chgo., 1983; lawyer UN WHO, Geneva, Switzerland, 1985; assoc. Robert C. Meltzer & Assocs., Chgo., 1986-91, Katz, Randall & Weinberg, Chgo., 1991-93, Arnstein & Lehr, Chgo., 1993-98, Grotefeld & Denenberg, Chgo., 1998-99; pres. Visanow.com., Inc., Chgo., 1999—. Adj. prof. internat. law Ill. Inst. Tech/Chgo.-Kent Coll. Law, 1994-98; creator online immigration processing. Contbr. articles to profl. jours.; editor The Globe, Springfield, Ill., 1984-99. Pro bono lawyer Fed. Bar Assn., Chgo., 1985-98. Recipient Medal of Appreciation, Ministry of Justice, Beijing, 1996. Mem. Ill. State Bar Assn. (internat. and immigration law sect. 1985—99, chair internat. law sect. 1990-91, Editor's award 1989, 94, 99), Am. Immigration Law Assn. Avocations: history, bread baking, golf, arts, music. Home: 71 E Division St Chicago IL 60610 Office: Visanow com Inc 350 N La Salle St 1400 Chicago IL 60610 E-mail: meltzer@visanow.com.

MELTZER, YALE LEON, economist, educator; b. N.Y.C., Nov. 3, 1931; s. Benjamin and Ada (Luria) M.; m. Annette Schoenberg, Aug. 7, 1960; children: Benjamin Robert, Philippe David. BA, Columbia U., 1954, postgrad. Sch. Law, 1954-55; MBA, NYU, 1966. Asst. to chief patent atty., prodn. mgr. Beaunit Mills, Inc., Elizabethton, Tenn., 1955—58, prodn. mgr., 1956—58; rsch. chemist N.Y. Med. Coll., N.Y.C., 1958-59, H. Kohnstamm & Co., Inc., N.Y.C., 1959-66, mgr. comml. devel., market rsch., patents and trademarks, 1966-68; sr. security analyst Harris, Upham & Co., Inc., 1968-70; instr. dept. econs. NYU, N.Y.C., 1972-79; adj. prof. dept. acctg., fin. and mgmt. Pace U., N.Y.C., 1974-80, adj. assoc. prof., 1980-84; lectr. dept. polit. sci., econs. and philosophy Coll. S.I., CUNY, N.Y.C., 1977-82, asst. prof. dept. polit. sci., econs. and philosophy, 1983—. Lectr. bus., fin., econs., sci. and tech.; presenter papers confs. Author: Soviet Chemical Industry, 1966; Chemical Trade with the Soviet Union and Eastern European Countries, 1967; Chemical Guide to GATT, The Kennedy Round and International Trade, 1968; Phthalocyanine Technology, 1970; Hormonal and Attractant Pesticide Technology, 1971; Urethane Foams: Technology and Applications, 1971; Water-Soluble Polymers: Technology and Applications, 1972; Encyclopedia of Enzyme Technology, 1973; Economics, 1974; Foamed Plastics: Recent Developments, 1976; Water-Soluble Resins and Polymers: Technology and Applications, 1976; Putting Money to Work: An Investment Primer, 1976; (with W.C.F. Hartley) Cash Management: Planning, Forecasting, and Control, 1979; Water-Soluble Polymers: Recent Developments, 1979; Putting Money to Work: An Investment Primer for the '80s, 1981, updated edit., 1984; Water-Soluble Polymers: Developments since 1978, 1981; Expanded Plastics and Related Products: Developments Since 1978, 1983; contbr. articles to profl. publs.; translator Russian, French and German tech. lit. Mem. AAAS, Am. Econ. Assn. Home: 14110 82nd Dr Apt 537 Jamaica NY 11435-1106 Office: Coll Staten Island 2800 Victory Blvd Staten Island NY 10314-6609

MELZER, BARBARA EVELYN, minister; b. Queens, N.Y., July 1, 1946; d. Anthony A. Jr. and Irene C. Melzer BS in Elem. Edn., SUNY, Geneseo, 1967; AA in Acting, Am. Acad. Dramatic Arts, 1971; MA in Edn., Adelphi U., 1971; diploma in adminstrn. and supervision, L.I. U., 1977, MA in Theater, 1981; MDiv, N.Y. Theol. Sem., 1992. Cert. minister of youth; ordained to ministry United Methodist Ch., 1997, ordained elder, 2000. Tchr. Unified Sch. Dist. #30, Valley Stream, N.Y., 1967-96; pastor Beach and East Quogue United Meth. Chs., 1996-2000, Woodbury (N.Y.) United Meth. Ch., 2000—; pastoral gestalt therapist. Cons. workshops in Christian edn., youth and children's ministries. Formerly active Christian edn. and youth ministry Grace United Meth. Ch., Valley Stream; mem. Syosset-Woodbury Interfaith Clergy Group. Mem. Internat. Assn. Women Mins., PEO. E-mail: WUMC11797@aol.com.

MENARD, ALBERT ROBERT, III, physics educator; b. Boston, July 17, 1943; s. Albert Robert Jr. and Laura Eunice (McManus) M.; m. Anne Elaine Dozer, Aug. 29, 1970; children: Laura Elizabeth, Andrew Russell. BA, Amherst Coll., 1965; MS, U. Minn., 1969; PhD, U. Fla., 1974. Asst. prof. W.Va. State Coll., Institute, 1974-75, Bloomsburg (Pa.) State Coll., 1975-76, Washington Coll., Chestertown, Md., 1976-77; asst. prof. physics Washington and Jefferson Coll., Washington, Pa., 1977-80, Saginaw Valley State U., University Center, Mich., 1980-88, assoc. prof. physics, 1988-96, prof. physics, 1996—. Cons. USAF, Dayton, Ohio, 1981-83, Fulbright lectr., Ankara, Turkey, 1991-92. Troop com. chair Saginaw area Boy Scouts Am., 1986-89. Grantee USAF, 1981, 82. Mem. Am. Phys. Soc., Am. Assn. Physics Tchrs, Rotary. Republican. Presbyterian. Home: 2790 Clairmount Saginaw MI 48603 Office: Saginaw Valley State Univ Dept Physics University Center MI 48710-0001

MENCEY, HELEN VERONICA LOUISE, special education educator; b. Anahuac, Tex., Oct. 19, 1960; d. Milton M. and Narvis C. (Malone) M. BFA, Sam Houston State U., 1983; tchr. cert., Lamar U., 1985; MEd, Prairie View Coll., 1989; postgrad., Tex. Woman's U., 1990, U. Houston, 1990. Dyslexia spec. Service. ctr., 1995. Tutor in field. Mem. NEA, ACLD, Tex. State Tchrs. Assn., NAFE, Tex. Reading Assn., Internat. Reading Assn., Platform Soc., Pi Lambda Theta. National Education Assn., 1998-. Natural Assoc. Female EXC Assoc. Children Learning Disabilites. Avocations: writing poetry, weight lifting.

MENCHACA, ROBERT, elementary education educator; b. Del Rio, Tex., Jan. 24, 1952; s. Antonio and Alicia (Espinoza) M.; m. Estella Calzada; children: Roberto Jr., Antonio, Rosalva, Mariza, Daniel. BS in Edn., Sul Ross State U., 1973; MEd, East Tex. State U., 1980. Bilingual kindergarten tchr. San Felipe-Del Rio I.S.D., 1974-77, Dallas I.S.D., 1978-84, Seguin I.S.D., 1984-90, North East I.S.D., 1990-92, tchr. 4th grade, 1992-2000, tchr. kindergarten, 2000—. Speaker, presenter in field. Author: Fue David, 1992, Una noche inolvidable, 1992, Daniel y el dia de la pesca, 1992, (with E. Menchaca) Daniel Goes Fishing, 1992. Nominated Tchr. of Yr. Tex. Assn. Bilingual Edn., 1992. Mem. Tex. State Reading Assn. (v.p.-elect Tex. coun. reading and bilingual child group, Tchr. Excellence award 1991), Internat. Reading Assn., Nat. Assn. Bilingual Edn., Tex. Assn. Bilingual Edn. (Bilingual Tchr. of Yr. award 1992), San Antonio Area Assn. Bilingual Edn. (recognized for teaching excellence 1992, Tchr. of Yr. award 1992), Alamo Reading Coun. (bd. dirs., co-chair San Antonio libr. found., treas. 1992-93, Tex. State Tchrs. Assn. Indiv. award for Human and Civil Rights 1995, Excellence in Teaching award 1991). Office: Olmos Elementary School 1103 Allena Dr San Antonio TX 78213-4199

MENDEL, LISA LUCKS, audiologist, educator; b. Wilmington, Del., Dec. 26, 1961; d. George Harold and Louise Irene (Silva) L.; m. Maurice I. Mendel, Mar. 18, 1990. BS in Edn., U. Ga., 1983, M in Edn., 1984; PhD in Speech & Hearing Scis., U. Calif., Santa Barbara, 1988. cert. audiologist. Ednl. audiologist N.E. Ga. Coop. Edn., Athens, Ga., 1984; clin. rsch. fellow House Ear Inst., L.A., 1985-87, auditory rsch. cons., 1987-88; asst. prof. audiology Pa. State U., University Park, 1988-89; assoc. prof. U. Miss., University, 1989—. Cons. Clarksdale (Miss.) City Schs., 1990-92, Applied Physics Lab., Johns Hopkins U. Contbr. articles to profl. jours. Recipient awardee, U. Miss., 1990; fellow, Am. Speech Lang. Hearing Assn., 1998; grantee, U. Calif., 1985—87, U. Miss., 1989—95. Mem. Am. Speech-Language-Hearing Assn., Am. Auditory Soc., Acoustical Soc. Am., Am. Acad. Audiology.

MENDELSON, EDWARD JAMES, English literature educator; b. N.Y.C., Mar. 15, 1946; s. Ralph and Grace Bernice (Stein) M.; m. Cheryl Neel Noble, 1990; 1 child, James. BA, U. Rochester, 1966; PhD, Johns Hopkins U., 1969. Instr. English Yale U., New Haven, 1969-70, asst. prof., 1970-76, assoc. prof., 1976-79; vis. assoc. prof. Columbia U., N.Y.C., 1979-80, assoc. prof. English, 1981-83, prof., 1983—; vis. assoc. prof. English Harvard U., Cambridge, Mass., 1977-78; lit. executor Estate of

W.H. Auden. Author: Early Auden, 1981; editor: Homer to Brecht, 1977, Pynchon: A Collection of Critical Essays, 1978, The English Auden, 1978, Later Auden, 2000; editor: Complete Works of W.H. Auden, 1988—; contbg. editor PC Mag. Fellow Am. Council Learned Socs., 1974-75, NEH, 1980-81, Guggenheim Found., 1986-87 Mem. Acad. Lit. Studies, Societe Européne de Culture Office: Columbia U Dept English 602 Philosophy Hall New York NY 10027

MENDELSON, SOL, physical science educator, consultant; b. Checonovska, Poland, Oct. 10, 1926; came to U.S., 1927; s. David C. and Frieda (Cohen) M. BME, CCNY, 1955; MS, Columbia U., 1957, PhD, 1961. Prof. engring. CCNY, 1955-58; sr. scientist Sprague Electric Co., North Adams, Mass., 1962-64, Airborne Instruments Lab., Melville, N.Y., 1964-65; phys. metallurgist Bendix Rsch. Lab., Southfield, Mich., 1966-67; cons., rschr., writer, N.Y.C. and Troy, Mich., 1968-72; adj. prof. phys. sci. CUNY, 1972-87. Contbr. numerous articles to sci. jours. Mem. Am. Phys. Soc., Fedn. Am. Scientists, Sigma Xi, Tau Beta Pi, Pi Tau Sigma. Achievements include rsch. on theory and mechanisms of Martensitic transformations; rsch. on degeneracy in phase transitions and its universal nature which shows that revolutions in sci. are still possible.

MENDENHALL, GORDON LEE, education educator; b. Winchester, Ind., Sept. 8, 1947; s. Paul G. and Evelyn N. (Pursley) M.; m. Susan Matchett, June 23, 1973; children: Tyler G., Erin E. BA in Zoology, Chemistry, Taylor U., 1969; MA in Secondary Edn., Ball State U., 1972, EdD in Sci. Edn., 1995. Tchr. Union City (Ind.) H.S., 1969-70, Craig Middle Sch., Indpls., 1970-75, Lawrence Ctrl. H.S., Indpls., 1975-90; teaching asst. Ball State U., Muncie, 1990-92; tchr. biology, human genetics Lawrence North H.S., Indpls., 1992—2003; asst. prof. MA in tchg. program U. Indpls., 2003—. Instr. U. Indpls., summer, 1985-95, U. St. Thomas, Houston, summer 1987-90; cons. NSF, Washington, 1984—; cons. Videodiscovery, Inc., Seattle, 1994—; edn. com. Great Lakes Regional Genetics Group, Madison, Wis., 1989-98. Co-editor Genetic Messenger newsletter, 1993-94; contbr. articles to profl. jours. Recipient Ind. Presdl. Award in Sci., NSF, 1986, Golden Apple Ind. U., 1995; fellow Lilly Open, 1982, Access Excellence Genentech Inc., 1994, Bill and Lea Armstrong, 1996; Tandy Tech. scholar, 1990; Lilly Creativity grantee. Mem. Nat. Sci. Tchrs. Assn., Nat. Assn. Biology Tchrs. (Ind. Outstanding Biology Tchr. 1989), Hoosier Assn. Sci. Tchrs. Methodist. Home: 8741 Ginnylock Dr Indianapolis IN 46256-1161 also: 6465 Harrison Ridge Blvd Indianapolis IN 46223

MENDENHALL, ROBERT W. educational executive; b. Pasadena, Calif., 1954; BS in Univ. Studies, Brigham Young Univ., 1977; PhD in Instrnl. Psychology and Tech., Brigham Young U., 2003. Gen. mgr. Wicat Inst., Orem, Utah, 1977-80; pres., dir. Wicat Systems Inc., Orem, Utah, 1980—92; exec. v.p., dir. Jostens Learning Corp., San Diego, 1992—94; gen. mgr. IBM K-12 Edn., Atlanta, 1994—96, exec. cons., 1997—98; pres. Western Govs. U., Salt Lake City, 1999—. Mem. bd. for bus. and econ. devel. State of Utah, 1997—2001; mem. Commn. Tech. and Adult Learning, 1999—2000; adv. bd. Partnership for 21st Century Skills, 2003—. Office: Western Gov U 2040 E Murray Holladay Rd Salt Lake City UT 84117 E-mail: rwm@wgu.edu.

MENDER, MONA SIEGLER, writer, music educator; b. May 24, 1926; d. George and Freda (Steierman) Siegler; m. Irving M. Mender, Aug. 25, 1946; children: Donald Matthew, Judith Jill. BA, Mt. Holyoke Coll., 1947. Instr. piano and music theory, Fair Lawn, N.J., 1947-75. State edn. chmn. N.J. Symphony Orch., Newark, 1980-82, state chmn. bd. regents, 1983-84, bd. dirs., 1983-91. Author: Music Manuscript Preparation: A Concise Guide, 1991, Extraordinary Women in Support of Music, 1997, The Cock Crows No More, 2000. Recipient Women's Network commendation Sen. Bill Bradley, 1984. Mem. Mountain Ridge Country Club (West Caldwell, N.J.), Plantation Golf and Country Club (Venice, Fla.).

MENDEZ, ANGELA M. small business owner; b. Elmhurst, N.Y., Apr. 27, 1972; d. Paulina Magdalena Mendez, Rodolfo Alfonso Mendez; life ptnr. Marlene T. Monday. BA, So. Conn. State U., 1999. Co-author: Essential Love: poems about mothers and fathers, daughters and sons, 1999; contbr. articles to poetry jours. Mem.: Conn. Poetry Soc. (v.p. 1998—99, Joseph Brodine Nat. Poetry award 1997). Roman Catholic. Avocations: reading, painting, travel, poetry. Home: PO Box 26401 West Haven CT 06516 Personal E-mail: poetryang@hotmail.com. Business E-Mail: poemlovr@yahoo.com.

MENDEZ, C. BEATRIZ, obstetrician, gynecologist, educator, gynecologist, consultant; b. Guatemala, Apr. 21, 1952; d. Jose and Olga (Sobalvarro) M.; m. Mark Parshall, Dec. 12, 1986. BS in Biology and Psychology, Pa. State U., 1974; MD, Milton Hershey Coll. Medicine, 1979. Diplomate Am. Bd. Ob-gyn.; cert. in advanced operative laparoscopy and hysteroscopy Accreditation Coun. for Gynecologic Endoscopy, Inc. Resident in ob-gyn. George Washington U., Washington, 1979-83; pvt. practice Santa Fe, 1985-95, Locum Tenens, 1996; contract physician Lovelace Health Sys., Albuquerque, 1996-98; clin. instr. dept. ob-gyn. U. N.Mex. Sch. Medicine, Albuquerque, 1983—85, 1996—98; pvt. practice anti-aging medicine, 2001—02; cons. to med. facilities; med. dir. The Sterling Inst., 2001—02, Med. Spa Profl. Alliance, 2002—; med. cons. Med. Spa Conf., 2001—. Bd. dirs. Hershey (Pa.) Coll. Medicine, 1977—82; chair perinatal com. St Vincent's Hosp., Santa Fe, 1986—89, mem. quality assurance com., 1986—95, chief ob-gyn., 1992—94; Vol. physician Women's Health Svcs., Santa Fe, 1995—96; clin. instr. dept. ob-gyn. U. N. Mex. Sch. Medicine, Albuquerque, 1997—; med. dir. The Sterling Inst., Santa Fe; med. advisor Med. Spas Conf., 2001—. Med. advisor: MedicalSpa Mag., 2001—. Vol. Women's Health Svcs., Santa Fe, 1985-95. With USPHS, 1983-85. Mosby scholar Mosby-Hersey Med. Sch., Hershey, 1979. Fellow: ACOG (Continuing Edn. award 1986—); mem.: AMA (Physician Recognition award 1986—), Residents Assn. George Washington U. (co-founder 1981—83), Am. Soc. Coloscopy and Cervical Pathology, Am. Fertility Soc., Internat. Soc. Endoscopy, Am. Assn. Gynecol. Laparascopists, Am. Acad. Anti-aging Medicine. Democrat.

MENDEZ, CELESTINO GALO, mathematics educator; b. Havana, Cuba, Oct. 16, 1944; came to the U.S., 1962; naturalized, 1970. s. Celestino Andres and Georgina (Fernandez) M.; m. Mary Ann Koplau, Aug. 21, 1971; children: Mark Michael, Matthew Maximilian. BA, Benedictine Coll., 1965; MA, U. Colo., 1968, PhD, 1974, MBA, 1979. Asst. prof. maths. scis. Met. State Coll., Denver, 1971-77, assoc. prof., 1977-82, prof., 1982—2002, chmn. dept. math. scis., 1980-82, adminstrv. intern office v.p. for acad. affairs, 1989-90; vis. assoc. prof. of math. U. Mich., Ann Arbor, 2002—. Assoc. editor Denver Met. Jour. Math. and Computer Sci., 1993—; contbr. articles to profl. jours. including Am. Math. Monthly, Procs. Am. Math. Soc., Jour. Personalized Instrn., Denver Met. Jour. Math. and Computer Sci. and newspapers. Mem. advt. rev. bd. Met. Denver, 1973-79; parish outreach rep. S.E. deanery, Denver Cath. Cmty. Svcs., 1976-78; mem. social ministries com. St. Thomas More Cath. Ch., Denver, 1976-78, vice-chmn., 1977-78, mem. parish coun., 1977-78; del. Adams County Rep. Conv., 1972, 74, 94, Colo. 4th Congl. Dist. Conv., 1974, Colo. Rep. Conv., 1982, 88, 90, 92, 96, 98, 2000, Douglas County Rep. Conv., 1980, 82, 84, 88, 90, 92, 94, 96, 98, 2000; alt. del. Colo. Rep. Conv., 1974, 76, 84, 2000, 5th Congl. dist. conv., 1976, mem. rules com., 1978, 80, precinct committeeman Douglas County Rep. Com., 1976-78, 89-92, mem. ctrl. com., 1976-78, 89-92; dist. 29 Rep. party candidate Colo. State Senate, 1990; mem. Colo. Rep. Leadership Program, 1989-90, bd. dirs., 1990-98; Douglas county chmn. Rep. Nat. Hispanic Assembly, 1989—; bd. dirs. Rocky Mountain Better Bus. Bur., 1975-79, Rowley Downs Homeowners Assn., 1976-78; trustee Hispanic U. Am., 1975-78; councilman Town of Parker, Colo., 1981-84, chmn. budget and fin. com., 1981-84; chmn. joint budget com. Town of Parker-Parker Water and Sanitation Dist. Bds., 1982-84; commr. Douglas County Planning Commn., 1993-97; dir. Mile High Young Scholars Program, 1995-98. Recipient Excellence in Tchg. award U. Colo. Grad. Sch., 1965-67; grantee Benedictine Coll., 1964-65, Math. Assn. Am. SUMMA grantee Carnegie Found. N.Y., 1994; program dir., grantee NSF, 1995-98; nominated candidate for first v.p Math. Assn. Am., 1999, for 2d v.p., 2001. Mem. Math. Assn. Am. (referee rsch. notes sect. Am. Math. Monthly 1981-82, gov. Rocky Mountain sect. 1993-96, investment com. 1996-02, devel. com. 1995-01, task force on reps. 1994-96, sci. policy com. 2000—, bd. govs. 1993-96, 2002—), Am. Math. Soc., Nat. Coun. Tchrs. Math., Colo. Coun. Tchrs. Math. (bd. dirs. 1994-96), Colo. Internat. Edn. Assn., Assoc. Faculties of State Insts. Higher Edn. in Colo. (v.p. 1971-73). Republican. Roman Catholic. Home: 39 Hummingbird Dr Castle Rock CO 80104-9047 Office: PO Box 173362 Denver CO 80217-3362

MENDIOLA, ANNA MARIA G. mathematics educator; b. Laredo, Tex., Dec. 21, 1948; d. Alberto and Aurora (Benavides) Gonzalez; m. Alfonso Mendiola Jr., Aug. 11, 1973; children: Alfonso, Alberto. AA, Laredo C.C., Tex., 1967; BA, Tex. Woman's U., 1969, MS, 1974. Tchr. math. Laredo Ind. Sch. Dist., 1969-81; instr. math. Laredo C.C., 1981—, organizer Jaime Escalante program, 1991-92; tech. prep. com. mem., 1991-92; ednl. coun., sec. Christen Mid. Campus, 1992-94; mem. site based campus com. Martin H.S., 1994-2000. Vis. instr. St. Augustine Sch., Laredo. 1987-88; evaluator So. Assn., Corpus Christi, 1981, So. Assn. Colls. and Schs., United H.S., 1991; mem. quality improvement coun. Laredo C.C., 1993-94; mem. instrn. coun. Laredo C.C., 1995-96; participant SC3 Calculus Reform Inst., NSF, 1996; mem. adv. com. on core curriculum Tex. Higher Edn. Coord. Bd., 1997-99, mem. adv. com. on transfer issues and field of study, 2000—; mem. Laredo C.C. self-study steering com. So. Assn. Colls. and Schs. Reaffirmation, 1997-99, coord. honors program, 1999—; math. dept. chair 2002—; faculty assoc. NSF-LCC Rio Grande River Project, 1998-2000. V.p., bd. dirs. Our Lady of Guadalupe Sch., Laredo, 1988-91; sec. Laredo C.C. Faculty Senate, 1986-87, v.p., 1995-96, pres., 1996-97; rep. Laredo Ind. Sch. Dist. Parent Adv. Coun., 1997-98. Recipient Teaching Excellence award NISOD, 1993; named LCC Innovator of the Month, 1998. Mem. AAUW (pres. 1979-81, v.p. 1987-89, scholarship chair 1993-94, membership chair 1994-95, bylaws chair 1996-97, pub. policy chair 1997-99), Am. Math. Assn. Two-Yr. Colls., Tex. State Tchrs. Assn., Tex. C.C. Tchrs. Assn. (campus rep., sec. math. sect. 1997-98, vice chair math. sect. 1998-99, chair math. sect. 1999-2000, chair audit com. 1999-2000, co-chair membership com. 2001-02, mem. profl. devel. com., 2003—), Tex. Woman's U. Alumnae Assn., Blessed Sacrament Altar Soc., Delta Kappa Gamma (membership chair 1993-96, v.p. 2000-02). Democrat. Roman Catholic. Office: Laredo CC West End Washington St Laredo TX 78040 E-mail: amendiola@laredo.edu.

MENDIUS, PATRICIA DODD WINTER, editor, educator, writer; b. Davenport, Iowa, July 9, 1924; d. Otho Edward and Helen Rose (Dodd) Winter; m. John Richard Mendius, June 19, 1947; children: Richard, Catherine M. Graber, Louise, Karen M. Chooljian. BA cum laude, UCLA, 1946; MA cum laude, U. N.Mex., 1966. Cert. secondary edn. tchr., Calif., N.Mex. English teaching asst. UCLA, 1946-47; English tchr. Marlborough Sch. for Girls, L.A., 1947-50, Aztec (N.Mex.) High Sch., 1953-55, Farmington (N.Mex.) High Sch., 1955-63; chair English dept. Los Alamos (N.Mex.) High Sch., 1963-86; sr. technical writer, editor Los Alamos Nat. Lab., 1987—. Adj. prof. English, U. N.Mex., Los Alamos, 1970-72, Albuquerque, 1982-85; English cons. S.W. Regional Coll. Bd., Austin, Tex., 1975—; writer, editor, cons. advanced placement English test devel. com. Nat. Coll. Bd., 1982-86, reader, 1982-86, project equality cons., 1985-88; book selection cons. Scholastic mag., 1980-82. Author: Preparing for the Advanced Placement English Exams, 1975; editor Los Alamos Arts Coun. bull., 1986-91. Chair Los Alamos Art in Pub. Places Bd., 1987-92; chair adv. bd. trustees U. N.Mex., Los Alamos, 1987-93; pres. Los Alamos Concert Assn., 1972-73, 95-98; chair Los Alamos Mesa Pub. Libr. Bd., 1990-94, chair endowment com., 1995-99. Mem. Soc. Tech. Communicators, AAUW (pres. 1961-63, state bd. dirs. 1959-63, Los Alamos coordinating coun. 1992-93, pres. 1993-94), DAR, Order Ea. Star, Mortar Bd., Phi Beta Kappa (pres. Los Alamos chpt. 1969-72, 99, v.p. 1996-99, pres. 2000-01), Phi Kappa Phi, Delta Kappa Gamma, Gamma Phi Beta. Avocations: swimming, reading, hiking, astronomy, singing. Home: 124 Rover Blvd Los Alamos NM 87544-3634 Office: Los Alamos Nat Lab Diamond Dr Los Alamos NM 87544 E-mail: mendius@qwest.net., pmendius@lanl.gov.

MENDON, KAREN JEANETTE, middle school education educator; b. Oct. 22, 1949; AA, Mt. San Antonio Jr. Coll., 1969; BA, Calif. State U., Long Beach, 1972; std. elem. credential, U. Calif., Irvine, 1976; MA in Curriculum and Devel., Coll. St. Thomas, 1984; Lang Devel. Specialist cert., UCLA, 1993. Phys. edn. tchr. Montebello Intermediate Montebello Unified Sch. Dist., 1972—. Phys. edn. mentor tchr. Montebello Unified Sch. Dist., 1990-93, site adminstrv. internship, 1989-90, demonstration sch. coord., 1991—; mem. Healthy Kids Healthy Calif. ad hoc com., health cirruculum ad hoc com., mentor tchr., earthquake com., planning com., faculty club, recreation adv. com., coord. personal best program, leadership team, disaster search and rescue team; chair discipline com.; presenter in field. Author: Ideas, Activities and Games to Expend, Enrich and Enhance Your Physical Education Program (grades 3-8). Recipient L.A. County Healthy Fitness Leader award, 1994, Am. Tchr. Honoree award Walt Disney, 1995. Mem. ASCD, NEA, AAHPERD, PTA (Sch. Svc. award 1977), Calif. Assn. Health, Phys. Edn., Recreation & Dance (Unit 413 Outstanding Mid. Sch. Phys. Educator award 1993, Southern Dist. Outstanding Mid. Sch. Phys. Educator award 1993, Calif. Outstanding Mid. Sch. Phys. Educator award 1994).*

MENDOZA, PEGGY ANN GILBERT, elementary education educator, writer; b. L.A. d. James and Dorothy Elizabeth (Backus) Gilbert; m. Tommy Bravo Mendoza, July 10, 1982; 1 child, Caitlin Elizabeth. Assocs., Long Beach City Coll., 1982; BA, Calif. State U., Long Beach, 1985. Cert. tchr., Calif. Elem. tchr. Mark Keppel Sch., Paramount, Calif., 1987-89, Hamilton Sch., Anza, Calif., 1989-92, Hemet (Calif.) Elem. Sch., 1992-93; mid. sch. tchr. Cottonwood Sch., Aguanga, Calif., 1993-96, independent study program tchr., coord., 1996-98, K-1 instr., 1998-99. Creative mag. advisor Cottonwood Sch., 1993-94, yearbook advisor, 1993-94, 94-95, 95-96, acad. decatholon coach, 1995, 96; program quality review Hemet Unified Sch. Dist., 1996. Author: White Dove Remembers, 1996. Mem. Calif. Tchr.'s Assn., Hemet Tchr.'s Assn. Democrat. Roman Catholic. Avocations: writing, doll collecting, home improvements. Home: 49780 Kiowa Dr Aguanga CA 92536-9741

MENDYK, SANDRA L. English educator; b. Derby, Conn., Dec. 30, 1943; d. Andrew John and Michalina (Gagliardi) Mendyk. BS, So. Conn. State U., New Haven, 1983; MS in English, So. Conn. State U., 1991. Copy editor Valley Pub. Co., Derby, Conn.; tchr. 7th grade Saint Mary-Saint Michael Sch., Derby, head English Dept. With U.S. Army, 1976-80. Mem. Nat. Coun. Tchrs. English, Conn. Coun. Tchrs. English. Home: 33 Ells St Ansonia CT 06401-3010

MENEFEE, SAMUEL PYEATT, lawyer, anthropologist; b. Denver, June 8, 1950; s. George Hardiman and Martha Elizabeth (Pyeatt) M. BA in Anthropology and Scholar of Ho. summa cum laude, Yale U., 1972; diploma in Social Anthropology, Oxford (Eng.) U., 1973, BLitt, 1975; JD, Harvard U., 1981; LLM in Oceans, U. Va., 1982, SJD, 1993; MPhil in Internat. Rels., U. Cambridge, Eng., 1995. Bar: Ga. 1981, U.S. Ct. Appeals (11th cir.) 1982, Va. 1983, La. 1983, U.S. Ct. Mil. Appeals 1983, U.S. Ct. Internat. Trade 1983, U.S. Ct. Claims 1983, U.S. Ct. Appeals (10th cir.) 1983, U.S. Ct. Appeals (fed., 1st, 3d, 4th, 5th, 6th, 7th, 8th and 9th cirs.) 1984, D.C. 1985, Nebr. 1985, Fla. 1985, U.S. Supreme Ct. 1985, U.S. Ct. Appeals (D.C. cir.) 1986, Maine 1986, Pa. 1986. Assoc. Phelps, Dunbar, Marks, Claverie & Sims, New Orleans, 1983-85; of counsel Barham & Churchill PC, New Orleans, 1985-88; sr. assoc. Ctr. for Nat. Security Law U. Va. Sch. Law, 1985—, fellow Ctr. for Oceans Law and Policy, 1982-83, sr. fellow, 1985-89, Maury fellow, 1989—, adv. bd., 1997—. Vis. lectr. U. Cape Town, 1987; vis. asst. prof. U. Mo.-Kansas City, 1990; law clk. Hon. Pasco M. Bowman, U.S. Ct. Appeals (8th cir.), 1994-95; vis. prof. Regent U., 1996-97, scholar-at-large, 1997—, prof., 1998—; adv. The Am. Maritime Forum/The Mariners' Mus., 1997-98; lectr. various nat. and internat. orgns.; mem. ICC Consultative Task Force on Comml. Crime, 1996—. Author: Wives for Sale: An Ethnographic Study of British Popular Divorce, 1981, Contemporary Piracy and International Law, 1995, Trends in Maritime Violence, 1996; co-editor: Materials on Ocean Law, 1982; contbr. numerous articles to profl. jours. Recipient Katharine Briggs prize Folklore Soc., 1992; Bates traveling fellow Yale U., 1971, Rhodes scholar, 1972; Cosmos fellow Sch. Scottish Studies U. Edinburgh, 1991-92, IMB fellow, ICC Internat. Maritime Bur., 1991—, Piracy Reporting Ctr. fellow, Kuala Lampur, 1993—, Huntington fellow The Mariners Mus., 1997. Fellow Royal Anthrop. Inst., Am. Anthrop. Assn., Royal Asiatic Soc., Royal Soc. Antiquaries of Ireland, Soc. Antiquaries (Scotland), Royal Geog. Soc., Soc. Antiquaries; mem. ABA (vice-chmn. marine resources com. 1987-90, chmn. law of the sea com. subcom. naval warfare, maritime terrorism and piracy 1989—, mem. law of the sea com. steering com. 1996—, mem. working group on terrorism), Southeastern Admiralty Law Inst. (com. mem.), Maritime Law Assn. (proctor, com. mem., chmn. subcom. law of the sea 1988-91, vice chmn. com. internat. law of the sea 1991—, chair working group piracy 1992—, UNESCO study group, 1998—), Marine Tech. Soc. (co-chmn. marine security com. 1991—), Selden Soc., Am. Soc. Internat. Law, Internat. Law Assn. (com. mem., rapporteur Am. br. com. EEZ 1988-90, rapporteur Am. br. com. Maritime Neutrality 1992, observer UN conv. on Law of the Sea meeting of States Parties 1996, chmn. Am. br. com. on Law of the Sea 1996—), rapporteur joint internat. working group on uniformity of the law of piracy 1998—, (Com. Maritime Internat.), Am. Soc. Indsl. Security (com. mem.), U.S. Naval Inst., USN League, Folklore Soc., Royal Celtic Soc., Internat. Studies Assn., Royal Scottish Geog. Soc., Royal African Soc., Egypt Exploration Soc., Arctic Inst. N.Am., Internat. Studies Assn., Am. Hist. Soc., Internat. Assn. Rsch. on Peasant Diaries (nat. editor 1996—), Nat. Eagle Scout Assn., Raven Soc., Jefferson Soc., Fence Club, Mory's Assn., Elizabethan Club, Yale Polit. Union, Leander Club, Cambridge Union, United Oxford and Cambridge Univ. Club, Yale Club (N.Y.C.), Paul Morphy Chess Club, Pendennis Club, Round Table Club (New Orleans), Phi Beta Kappa, Omicron Delta Kappa. Republican. Episcopalian. Avocations: anthropology, archaeology, social history, crew, hill walking. Office: U Va Ctr Nat Sec Law 580 Massie Rd Charlottesville VA 22903-1738

MENESTRINA, ANGEL, elementary school educator; b. Ft. Wayne, Ind., Oct. 16, 1957; d. Richard DeWayne and Katherine Suzanne (Rehnen) Brown; m. Ricky Dean Menestrina, June 27, 1981; children: Anthony Richard, Alexander Joseph. BA, St. Mary-of-the-Woods Coll., 1980; MS, Ind. State U., 1986. Cert. elem. tchr., Ind. 4th grade tchr. Queen of Angels Sch., Ft. Wayne, 1980-84, Davis Park Sch., Terre Haute, Ind., 1985—99, Rio Grande Sch., 1999—. Mem. Ind. Textbook Adoption Com., Terre Haute, 1988-92. Mem. Internat. Reading Assn., Kappa Gamma Pi, Phi Kappa Phi. Roman Catholic. Avocations: walking, reading, water skiing.

MENEVEAU, CHARLES VIVANT, mechanical engineering and applied sciences educator, researcher; b. Paris, Dec. 4, 1960; came to U.S., 1985; s. Louis Henry and Patricia (Mendez) M.; m. Brigitte Renate Werkmeister, May 17, 1986; children: Max Oliver, Nicole Beatrice. BSME, U. Tech. Santa Maria, Valparaiso, Chile, 1985; MS, Yale U., 1987, MPhil, 1988, PhD, 1989. Registered profl. engr., Chile. Teaching asst. Yale U., New Haven, Conn., 1986-87, rsch. asst., 1987-89, postdoctoral fellow, 1989; postdoctoral assoc. Stanford (Calif.) U. and NASA Ames, 1989-90; asst. prof. mech. engring. Johns Hopkins U., Balt., 1990-94, assoc. prof., 1994-96, prof., 1996—. Mem. rev. com. The Physics of Fluids Jour., N.Y.C., 1989—, NSF, Washington, 1990—, Am. Soc. for Engring. Edn., Washington, 1990, Comptes Rendus de L'Acad. Scis., Paris, 1991, Phys. Rev. Letters, N.Y.C., Phys. Rev. A, N.Y.C., Jour. Fluid Mechanics, Cambridge, Eng. Contbr. articles to Jour. Fluid Mechanics, Phys. Rev. Letters, Jour. Atmospheric Sci., Physics of Fluids, Jour. Computational Physics, Nuc. Physics B, Physica A, Proceedings Royal Soc. of London, Phys. Rev. A, Combustion and Flame Pure & Applied Geophysics. Recipient Henry Prentiss Becton Prize for Excellence in Rsch. award Yale U., 1989, Frenkiel award, 2001. Fellow Am. Phys. Soc.; mem. ASME, Am. Acad. Mechanics, Sigma Xi. Achievements include discoveries related to the fractal geometry of turbulent flows; first to use three-dimensional wavelet transform and to find turbulent energy backscatter in wavelet space; prediction made about experimental verification in turbulence of multifractal two-point statistics, and experimental studies of subgrid modeling of turbulent flows, using thermal anemiometry, particle-image-velocimetry and field measurements in the atmospheric boundary layer. Office: Johns Hopkins U Dept Mech Engring Baltimore MD 21218

MENG, GUANG JUN, librarian, educator; b. Beijing, Feb. 2, 1934; s. Shao Meng and Lian Sun; m. Yu Wang, Nov. 25, 1962; two children. Grad., Inst. Fgn. Langs., China, 1954, Info. Sci. Dept. U. Su-Tech, 1960. From asst. libr. to prof., instr. PhD students Documentation and Info. Ctr. Chinese Acad. Scis., Beijing, 1958—. Author: An Introduction to Library and Information Science, 1982, 2d edit., 1991, Selected Works of Meng Guangjun, 1988, An Introduction to Information Resources Management, 1998, Advance in Library and Information Science Research in Foreign Countries, 1999; editor-in-chief Libr. and Info. Svc.; contbr. articles to profl. jours.

MENG, HEINZ KARL, biology educator; b. Baden, Republic of Germany, Feb. 25, 1924; arrived in U.S., 1929; s. Richard Ludwig and Elise (Merkel) M.; m. Elizabeth Agnes (Metz), June 20, 1953; children: Robin Elizabeth, Peter Paul. BS, Cornell U., 1947, PhD, 1951. Cert. tchr. ornithology, entomology, and vertebrate zoology. Biology prof. State Univ. of N.Y., New Paltz, NY, 1951—2002, prof. emeritus, 2003—. Dir. No. Am. Falconer's Assn., 1967-76. Author: Falcons Return, 1975; revised edit., 1992; pioneer in field of incaptivity breeding of Peregrine falcons. Named one of 100 champions of conservation of the 20th century Nat. Audubon Soc., 1998; grantee State Univ. of N.Y., 1957, 58, 61, NSF, 1967; IBM, 1980, 82, 83, 85, 86, 87, 88, 91, 93; Eppley Found. Rsch., 1993. Fellow Explorers Club; mem.: Am. Ornithologists Union, Wilson Ornithological Soc., Cooper Ornithological Soc., New Paltz Peregrine Falcon Found. (pres. 1977—), Wildlife Soc. Avocations: falconry, fly fishing, painting. Home: 10 Joalyn Rd New Paltz NY 12561-2115 Office: State Univ NY Dept Biology New Paltz NY 12561

MENGEL, CHRISTOPHER EMILE, lawyer, educator; b. Holyoke, Mass., Sept. 11, 1952; s. Emile Oscar and Rose Ann (O'Donnell) M.; m. Ellen Christine Creager, Dec. 6, 1991; children: Meredith Anne, Celia Claire; step-children: Cara Elizabeth Creager, Kristen Michele Creager. Student, U. Notre Dame, 1970-71; BA, Holy Cross Coll., 1974; JD, Detroit Coll. Law, 1979. Bar: Mich. 1979, U.S. Dist. Ct. (ea. dist.) Mich. 1989, U.S. Ct. Appeals (6th cir.) 1990. Tchr. Holyoke Pub. Schs., 1974-76; assoc. Fried & Sniokaitis P.C., Detroit, 1980-82; prof. Detroit Coll. Law, 1982-85; pvt. practice Detroit, 1982-91; mng. ptnr. Berkley, Mengel & Vining, PC, 1992—. Mem. coun. St. Ambrose Parish, Grosse Pointe Park, Mich., 1985-88, pres. 1986-87. Matthew J. Ryan scholar, 1970; recipient Disting. Brief award Thomas M. Cooley Law Rev., 1996. Mem. ABA, Mich. Bar Assn., Detroit Bar Assn. Democrat. Roman Catholic. Avocations: baseball, sailing, photography. Home: 1281 N Oxford Rd Grosse Pointe MI 48236-1857 Office: Berkley Mengel & Vining PC 3100 Penobscot Bldg Detroit MI 48226 E-mail: cmengel@flash.net.

MENHENNETT, VICTORIA ANN, special education educator; b. Pueblo, Colo., Jan. 2, 1953; d. Sosten Rivale and Virginia (Maes) Rivales; m. Thomas Barry Menhennett, July 20, 1990; 1 child, Tabor Ann. AA, Trinidad State Coll., 1973; BA, Adams State Coll., 1975, MA, 1987. Cert. tchr., Colo. Tchr. Kim (Colo.) Sch. Dist., 1975-76, Pritchett (Colo.) Sch. Dist., 1976-85, Lamar (Colo.) Sch. Dist., 1985—. Chair accreditation com. Pritchett Schs.; curriculum specialist Lamar Schs., counseling com. Washington Elem. Sch. Mem. Colo. Coun. Learning Disabled, Phi Delta Kappa.

MENNING, BARBARA SUSAN, elementary school educator, language educator; b. Jersey City, Nov. 22, 1954; d. Walter Thomas and Marian Matilda (Lange) Fritz; m. Gerald Douglas Menning, Jan. 7, 1982; children: Melanie and Aleisha (twins). Student, U. Nat. Autonoma Mex., Mexico City, 1975-76; BA in Spanish Edn. cum laude, Glassboro (N.J.) State Coll., 1977; MS in Edn. cum laude, Wayne (Nebr.) State Coll., 1984. Cert. elem. tchr., Spanish tchr., Nebr. Tchr. English, U. Nac. Autonoma Mex., 1975-76; tchr. Spanish, Cinnaminson (N.J.) Mid. and High Sch., 1977-81; tchr. ESL, Glassboro Adult Edn., 1977-78, A.B.E. tchr. math., 1978-79; Chpt. I remedial tchr. Orchard (Nebr.) Pub. Schs., 1984-87, elem. tchr., 1987—2000, mem. student assistance team, 1990—; tchr. Spanish Hastings (Nebr.) SR. H.S., 2000—. Mem. A+ Sch. Improvement Team, 1991-99. Mem. Orchard Tchrs. Assn. (Tchr. of Yr. award 1987), Hastings Edn. Assn. Avocations: travel, softball, camping, rubber stamping. Home: 1213 Hillcrest Dr Juniata NE 68955-3124 Office: Hastings Sr HS 1100 14th St Hastings NE 68901 E-mail: bmenning@esu9.org.

MENNINGER, ROSEMARY JEANETTA, art educator, writer; b. N.Y.C., Feb. 2, 1948; d. Karl Augustus and Jeanetta (Lyle) M. BA, Washburn U., 1983, BFA, 1984. Cert. tchr., Kans. Rsch. specialist, grant writer Navajo Tribe Navajo Community Coll., Many Farms, Ariz., 1969, 71; adminstrv. asst., counselor San Francisco Drug Treatment Program, 1972-73; exec. dir. Inst. Applied Ecology, San Francisco, 1973-80; coord. Calif. Community Gardening program Gov.'s Office State of Calif., Sacramento, 1976-80; editor Whole Earth Catalogs and CoEvolution Quar., Sausilito, Calif., 1973-80; editor, rsch. specialist Dept. Agr. Scis. Colo. State U., Ft. Collins, 1981-82; instr. Mulvane Art Ctr., Topeka, 1982-86, 90—; art tchr. Topeka Pub. Schs., 1985—. Author: Community Gardening in California, 1977; editor: (newspaper) California Green, 1977-80; contbr. articles to profl. jours. Mem. San Francisco Parks and Recreation Open Space Commn., 1975-78; mem. master plan task force Calif. State Fair, Sacramento, 1978-80; commr. Gov.'s Commn. on Children and Families, Topeka, 1988-89; bd. dirs. The Villages, Inc., 1989—. Democrat. Presbyterian. Avocations: painting, gardening, swimming. Home: 4152 SW 6th Ave Apt 115 Topeka KS 66606-2157 E-mail: rmenning@networksplus.net.

MENO, LIONEL R. academic administrator; Commr. edn. Tex. Edn Agy., Austin; dist. supt. Board of Coop. Education Services, Angola, NY, 1995—99; dean Coll. Edn. San Diego State U., 1999—. Office: 5500 Cempanile Dr San Diego CA 92182*

MENZ, PAMELA, adult and vocational education educator; b. Union City, Okla., Aug. 22, 1953; d. Lawrence B. and Viola M. (Hagemier) Menz; m. David Wyrick, Aug. 16, 1975 (div. Oct. 1988); 1 child, Adam. MS in Edn., Okla. State U., 1975; MEd, U. Ky., 1992. Cert. tchr., Okla., Ky. Instr. in jobs program Fayette County Adult Edn., Lexington, Ky., 1990—; head tchr. after sch. program James Lane Allen Elem., Lexington, Ky., 1991; head tchr. Creative Activities Program Cardinal Valley Elem. Sch., Lexington, 1992-93; dir., instr. pre-vocational program Francis Tuttle Vo-Tech, Oklahoma City, 1993—. Mem. NEA, Learning Disabilities Assn., Am. Home Econs. Assn., Home Economists in Edn., Am. Vocat. Assn., Ky. Home Econs. Assn., Phi Upsilon Omicron (sec. alumni chpt. 1992—). Democrat. Avocations: quilting, reading, tennis, travel, skiing. Home: 2573 Crescent Park Dr Chetek WI 54728-9311 Office: Francis Tuttle Vo-Tech 12777 N Rockwell Ave Oklahoma City OK 73142-2789

MERAT, FRANCIS LAWRENCE, engineering educator; b. Frenchville, Pa, Aug. 22, 1949; s. Lawrence Clarence and Lucille Magdalen (DeMange) M. BSEE, Case Western Res. U., 1972, MSEE, 1975, PhD, 1978. Rsch. engr. Case Western Res. U., Cleve., 1978-79, asst. prof. engring., 1979-85, assoc. prof., 1985—, exec. officer dept. elec. engring. and applied physics, 1994-98, with elec. engring. and computer sci., 1998-99, interim chair dept. elec. engring. and computer sci., 1999-2000, assoc. chair dept. elec. engring. and computer sci., 2001—02, assoc. chair divsn. elec. and computer engring., 2003—; co-founder, sec./treas. PGM Diversified Industries, Inc., Parma Heights, Ohio, 1986—. Fellow summer faculty program USAF, Griffiss AFB, NY, 1980, US Army, Ft. Belvoir, Va., 1987; cons. various law firms (expert forensic engr., patent infringement), NASA Glenn Rsch. Ctr. Contbr. articles to tech. jour. Named Disting. Advisor, Nat. Assn. Acad. Counseling and Advising, 1985. Mem. IEEE (sect. chmn. 1983-84, reviewer IEEE Robotics and Automation), Soc. Mfg. Engr., Assn. Computing Machinery, Soc. Photo-optical Instrumentation Engr., Sigma Xi. Roman Catholic. Avocations: photography, science fiction, movies. Home: 4398 Groveland Rd University Heights OH 44118-3958 Office: Case Western Res Univ 10900 Euclid Ave Cleveland OH 44106-7071 E-mail: flm@po.cwru.edu.

MERCADANTE, ANTHONY JOSEPH, special education educator; b. Newark, Mar. 10, 1951; s. Anthony Joseph Jr. and Anna Rose (Cocuzzo) Mercadante; m. Barbara Ferrarri, May 27, 1979; children: Anthony, Lisa, David. BS in Edn., Seton Hall U., 1973; MA in Audiology and Communication Sci., Kean Coll., 1978; cert. in adminstrn. and supervision, U. S. Fla., 1987. Cert. audiologist, adminstr./supr., tchr. bus. edn., tchr. hearing impaired. Acctg. clk. supply divsn. U.S. Steel Corp., Newark, 1973-75; acctg. and bookkeeping instr. Sch. Data Programming, Union, NJ, 1976-78; bus. adminstrn. instr., curriculum coord. Roberts-Walsh Bus. Sch., Union, 1978-83; clin. audiologist Eastern Speech, Lang. and Hearing Ctr., Woodbridge, NJ, 1980-83; ednl. audiologist exceptional student edn. dept. Polk County Pub. Schs., Bartow, Fla., 1983—. Advisor Fla. Audiologists Edn., Orlando, 1987—; mem. multidisciplinary team Polk County Pub. Schs., Bartow, 1983—, mem. planning com. Project Healthy Start, 1994—96. Coach S. Lakeland (Fla.) Babe Ruth Baseball League, 1993, 1995, mgr., 1994. Mem.: AARP, Fla. Speech, Lang. and Hearing Assn., Am. Speech Lang. and Hearing Assn. Avocations: tennis, golf, bowling, swimming, coaching. Home: 6122 Donegal E Lakeland FL 33813-3713 Office: Polk Life and Learning Ctr 1310 S Floral Ave Bartow FL 33830-6399

MERCALDO, DAVID, elementary school educator, writer; b. Bklyn., Nov. 12, 1946; s. Isaac and Rose Mercaldo; m. Linda Ann Ciaravino, Dec. 16, 1995. BA in Edn., Ctrl. Bible Coll., 1967; MS in Edn., Richmond Coll., 1970; PhD in Humanities, Columbia Pacific Coll., 1996. Cert. learning disabilities tchr. N.Y., elem. tchr. N.Y. Tchr. N.Y. Pub. Sch., Staten Island, NY, 1968—73, Bd. Coop. Ednl. Svcs., L.I., 1973—78, asst. prin., 1978—81; prin. City of Tulsa, Tulsa, Okla., 1981—88; assoc. dir. The Summit Sch., Forest Hills, NY, 1988—89; tchr. City of N.Y., Staten Island, 1989—. Prof. Columbia Commonwealth U., Missoula, Mont., 2001; pres. Skyline Theater, Staten Island, 1992—. Author: (plays) Apartment to Let, 1979, FERRY, 2002. Named one of Outstanding Young Men of Am., Fuller Dees Inst., 1995; recipient Westinghouse award, S.I. Tech. Inst., 1997. Mem.: United Fedn. Tchr., Beaux Arts Soc., Sons of Italy. Conservative. Moravian. Avocations: writing, composing, keyboard, model building, architecture. Home: 414 Pendale St Staten Island NY 10306

MERCER, CHET ATOM, retired elementary educator; b. Missoula, Mont., June 3, 1946; s. J. William and Genevieve E. (Gruly) M.; m. Linda K. Adams, Sept. 8, 1973; children: Chet W., Daniel T., Rheanna M. BA in Edn., U. Mont., 1971, MEd, 1976. Tchr. Lolo (Mont.) Sch. Dist. 7, 1971-74; tchr. Browning (Mont.) Sch. Dist. 9, 1974-78; prin. elem. sch. Heart Butte (Mont.) Sch. Dist. 1, 1978-79, supt., 1979-80; tchr. Frenchtown (Mont.) Sch. Dist. 40, 1980-96; ret., 1996. Medic fire fighter Frenchtown Vol. Fire Dept., 1982—. With USMC, 1965-71, Vietnam. Avocations: hunting, fishing, sports, reading. Home: 6050 Mercer Ln Missoula MT 59808-8941

MERCER, EVELYN LOIS, retired guidance counselor; b. Ellensboro, N.C., Apr. 25, 1934; d. Milton Bernadine Robinson Sr. and Lois Lenora Robinson; m. Theodore Roosevelt Mercer Sr. (div. June 1978); children: Theodore Roosevelt Jr., Brian Vincent, David Lemuel. BS in Math., Livingstone Coll., 1957; MEd in Guidance and Counseling, U. Cin., 1972; student, U. Akron, 1973, Miami U., Ohio, 1973—75, U. Akron, 1974. Cert. math tchr. Ohio, 1963, guidance counselor Ohio, 1972, lic. profl. counselor Ohio Counselor & Social Worker Bd., 1984. Math tchr. Jackson County Pub. Schs., Gumberry, NC, 1957—60, Cin. Pub. Schs., Cin., 1963—72, guidance counselor, 1972—73, Winton Woods City Sch. Dist., Cin., 1973—94, ret., 1994. Mem. adv. com. conselor edn. U. Cin., Cin., 1975—76; admissions adv. bd. Cin. Tech. Coll., Cin., 1975—81, The Ohio State U., Columbus, Ohio, 1982—85; nursing sch. adv. bd. Deaconess Hosp. Sch. Nursing, Cin., 1983—88; dir. Sch. Counseling Cons. Svc., Cin., 1994—, Charlotte, NC, 1994—. Docent Mint Mus., Charlotte; mem. housing commn. City of Forest Park, Cin., 1974—76; Dem. precinct exec. Hamilton County Bd. Elections, Cin., 1974—96. Named Outstanding Counselor of Yr., Inroads of Cin., 1984. Mem.: NEA, AAUW (pres. Charlotte br. 2001—03), Am. Assn Coll. Admissions Counselors, Ohio Assn. Coll. Admissions Counselors, Ohio Sch. Counselors Assn., Ohio Edn. Assn., Livingstone Coll. Alumni Assn., U. Cin. Alumni Assn., Nat. Assn. Advancement for Colored People, Les Birdies Golf Club Charlotte (founder 1999, pres. 1999—2001), Order of Eastern Star, Zeta Phi Beta. Democrat. Methodist. Avocations: golf, travel, bridge, volunteering, gardening. Home and Office: 4101 Rye Mill Ct Charlotte NC 28277

MERCER, FRANCES DECOURCY, artist, educator; b. Centreville, Miss., June 14, 1944; d. John Homer Jr. and Patricia Powers (Given) Mercer. BA in English Lit., U. Miami, 1969, MA in History of Art, 1971; MFA in Painting, San Francisco Art Inst., 1974. Cert. tchr. Fla. Instr. South Fla. Art Inst., Hollywood, Fla., 1979—81; tchg. asst. San Francisco Art Inst., 1974; instr. Broward C.C., Ft. Lauderdale, Fla., 1979—83; owner 17th St. Galleries, Ft. Lauderdale, 1984—91; tchr. Broward County Sch. Bd., 1980—82; adj. prof. Fla. Atlantic U., 1979—80. Exhibited in group shows at Grove Art Gallery, Coconut Grove, Fla., 1973, Emanuel Walter Gallery, San Francisco, 1975, The Lucian LaBandt Gallery, 1976, The Both Up Gallery, Berkeley, Calif., 1976, Discover Ctr., Ft. Lauderdale, 1980, Nova U. Artoberfest, Art and Culture Ctr. Hollywood, 1981, Indian Hammock Hunt and Riding Club, Okeechobee, Fla., 1998, A.E. Backus Gallery and Mus., Ft. Pierce, Fla., 2000, pvt. collections. Scholar Tuition scholar, San Francisco Art Inst., 1972, 1973, 1974. Avocations: photography, trail hiking, kayaking, golf, sailing. Home: #200 Blue Heron Ln 32801 Hwy 441 Okeechobee FL 34972 E-mail: fmercer@floridawatercolors.com.

MERCHANT, ROLAND SAMUEL, SR., hospital administrator, educator; b. N.Y.C., Apr. 18, 1929; s. Samuel and Eleta (McLymont) M.; m. Audrey Bartley, June 6, 1970; children: Orelia Eleta, Roland Samuel, Huey Bartley. BA, NYU, 1957, MA, 1960; MS, Columbia U., 1963, MSHA, 1974. Asst. statistician N.Y.C. Dept. Health, 1957-60, statistician, 1960-63, N.Y. Tb and Health Assn., N.Y.C., 1963-65; biostatistician, adminstrv. coord. Inst. Surg. Studies, Montefiore Hosp., Bronx, N.Y., 1965-72; resident in adminstrn. Roosevelt Hosp., N.Y.C., 1973-74; dir. health and hosp. mgmt. Dept. Health, City of N.Y., 1974-76; from asst. adminstr. to adminstr. West Adams Cmty. Hosp., L.A., 1976; spl. asst. to assoc. v.p. for med. affairs Stanford U. Hosp., Calif., 1977-82, dir. office mgmt. and strategic planning, 1982-85, dir. mgmt. planning, 1986-90; v.p. strategic planning Cedars-Sinai Med. Ctr., L.A., 1990-94; cons. Roland Merchant & Assocs., L.A., 1994—. Clin. assoc. prof. dept. family, cmty. and preventive medicine Stanford U., 1986—88; dept. health rsch. and policy Stanford U. Med. Sch., 1988—90. With U.S. Army, 1951—53. Fellow, USPHS. Fellow: APHA, Am. Coll. Healthcare Execs.; mem.: N.Y. Acad. Scis. Home: 27335 Park Vista Rd Agoura Hills CA 91301-3639

MERCURIO, EDWARD PETER, natural science educator; b. Orange, Calif., Dec. 28, 1944; s. Peter Amadeo and Jeanne (Monteleone) M.; m. Jeanne Roussel Gable, Oct. 18, 1980 (div. Dec. 1984); 1 child, Katherine Roussel; m. Patricia Ann Kahler, Apr. 12, 1987; children: Peter Edward, Rose Sierra. BA, UCLA, 1967, MA, 1970, CPhil, 1978. Research asst. UCLA, 1971, teaching asst., 1968-71; instructional assoc. Golden West Coll., Huntington Beach, Calif., 1972-73; cons. Monterey County Planning Dept., Salinas, Calif., 1980; prof. Hartnell Coll., Salinas, Calif., 1973—. Photographer in field, Calif., 1961—; lectr. in field, Calif., 1970—; cons. in field, 1980—; rschr. in field, 1994—. Fellow Woodrow Wilson Nat. Fellowship Found., 1967. Mem. AAAS, Sierra Club. Democrat. Avocations: writing and performing original songs, hiking, backpacking, plant and animal breeding, mountain bicycle riding. Home: 647 Wilson St Salinas CA 93901-1346 Office: Hartnell Coll 156 Homestead Ave Salinas CA 93901-1628 E-mail: mercurio@jafar.hartnell.edu.

MEREDITH, CATHY, education educator; b. Memphis, Mar. 20, 1957; d. Wilson Euril S. and Tommie Jean (Smith) Meredith; children: Curtis Michael, Meredith Lee Anne. BS in Home Econs., U. Tenn., Martin, 1979; MS in Counseling & Student Pers., Memphis State U., 1981; EdD in Instrn. and Curriculum, U. Memphis, 1996. Cert. tchr. pre K-8, adminstrn. and supr. Grad. asst. U. Memphis, 1994-96; tchr. Memphis City Schs., 1979-96, asst. prin., 1996—98; asst. prof., dir. undergrad tchr. edn. program Christian Bros. U., 1998—. Tenn. state math. specialist team Memphis City Schs., 1992-94, math. tchr. trainer, 991-94; grad. student rep. dean's adv. com. U. Memphis, 1994-95; team mem. Tchrs. Acad. Math. and Sci., U. Tenn., 1991-95; author, presenter various workshops Nat. Coun. Tchrs. Math., 1991—. Tchr. self-help Arthritis Found., West Tenn. chpt., 1985, mem. telephone com., 1982-85; mem. Memphis 2000 com., 1992-94. Grantee South Ctrl. Bell, Tenn., 1991, Memphis Rotary Found. grantee, 1992. Mem. ASCD, Nat. Coun. Tchrs. Math., Assn. Childhood Edn. Internat. (treas. 1987-89, state v.p. for membership 2002—), Tex. Assn. Mid. Schs. (West Tenn. bd. dirs. 2000-03), Alpha Omicron Pi (regional dir. 1982-83, fin. adv. 1980-85,, alumnae chpt. pres. 1992, award 1983), Phi Delta Kappa, Kappa Delta Pi, Delta Kappa Gamma (v.p. 2001-02, rec. sec. 2002—). Roman Catholic. Avocations: antiques, crafts, reading, historical houses. Home: 4349 Sequoia Rd Memphis TN 38117-1640 Office: Christian Bros U 650 East Parkway South Memphis TN 38104

MEREDITH, THOMAS C. academic administrator; Vice chancellor exec. affairs U. Miss., until 1988; pres. Western Ky. U., Bowling Green, 1988-97; chancellor U. Ala. Sys., Tuscaloosa, 1997—2002. Office: Chancellor Univ Sys Ga 270 Washington St SW Atlanta GA 30334-9007 E-mail: chancellor@usg.edu.

MEREDITH, TIA KATHRYN JOHNSON, elementary school educator; b. Pa., Apr. 2, 1966; d. William T. and Joann K. (Pierce) J. BS in Edn., Indiana U. of Pa. 5th and 6th grade social studies tchr. Cameron County Sch. Dist., Emporium, Pa., 1988-89; 6th through 8th grade tchr. St. Mary's (Pa.) Parochial Sch., 1989; tchr. grades 4-8 St. Leo's Sch., Ridgway, Pa., 1991-95; grades 6 to grade 8 sci. and math. tchr. Sacred Heart Sch., 1995—2002; tchr. St. Marys Cath. M.S., 2002—. Democrat. Methodist. Avocations: showing horses, training horses. Home: 136 Green Rd Kersey PA 15846

MERENDINO, K. ALVIN, surgical educator; b. Clarksburg, W.Va., Dec. 3, 1914; s. Biagio and Cira (Bivona) M.; m. Shirley Emma Jane Hill, July 6, 1943; children: Cira Anne Watts, Nancy Jane Napuunoa, Susan Hill Mitchell, Nina Merendino-Sarich, Maria King Merendino-Stillwell. BA, Ohio U., 1936, LLD (hon.), 1967; MD, Yale U., 1940; PhD, U. Minn., 1946. Diplomate Am. Bd. Surgery, Am. Bd. Thoracic Surgery. Intern Cin. Gen. Hosp., 1940-41; resident U. Minn. Hosp., Mpls., 1941-45; rsch. asst. Dr. Owen H. Wangensteen, 1942-43; trainee Nat. Cancer Inst., 1943-45; dir. program in postgrad. med. edn. in surgery Ancker Hosp., St. Paul, 1946-48; instr. dept. surgery U. Minn., Mpls., 1944-45, asst. prof. dept. surgery, 1945-48; assoc. prof. dept. surgery U. Wash., Seattle, 1949-55, dir. exptl. surgery labs., dept. surgery, 1950-72, prof. dept. surgery, 1955-81, prof. emeritus, 1981—, prof. and adminstrv. officer dept. surgery, 1957-64, prof., chmn., 1964-72; chmn. dept. surgery King Faisal Specialist and Rsch. Ctgr., Riyadh, Saudi Arabia, 1976, dir. med. affairs, 1976-79, dir. Cancer Therapy Inst., spl. cons. to Coun., supr. for exec. mgmt., assoc. dir. med. affairs, 1981-82; dir. ops. King Faisal Med. City, Riyadh, 1981-85. Mem. adv. com. for med. rsch., Boeing Airplane Co., 1959-67, chmn., 19621 cons. Children's Orthopedic Hosp., Seattle, 1972-82; mem. adv. com. on heart disease and surgery for crippled children's svc., Wash. State Dept. Health and Div. Vocational Rehab., 1961; mem. surgery study sect. NIH, 1958-62, subcom. on prosthetic valves for cardiac surgery, chm. 1st Nat. Conf., 1960, mem. adv. com. 2d Nat. Conf. on Prosthetic Heart Valves, 1969, Surgery A study sect. chmn., 1970-72, Nat. Heart and Lung Inst. Tng. Com., 1965-69; cons. VA, Seattle, 1949-59, 65-81; mem. adv. com. on hosps and clinics, USPHS, 1963-66; mem. surgery test com. Nat. Bd. Med. Examiners, 1963-67; mem. surgery resident rev. com., Conf. Com. on Grad. Edn. in Surgery, 1963-73, vice-chmn., 1972-73; chmn. 2d Saudi Arabian Med. Conf., Riyadh, 1978; mem. com. on postgrad. med. edn., Kingdom of Saudi Arabia Ministry of Health, 1978-79. Editor in chief: Prosthetic Valves for Cardiac Surgery, 1961; assoc. editor: Prosthetic Heart Valves, 1969; mem. editorial bd. Am. Jour. Surgery,. 1958-83, Jour. Surg. Rsch., 1961-69, Pacific Medicine and Surgery, 1964-68, King Faisal Hosp. Medicine Jour. (renamed Annals of Saudi Medicine), 1981-85; contbr. articles to profl. jours., chpts. to books; producer movies on surgery. Recipient cert. of merit Ohio U. Alumni Assn., 1957, Outstanding W.Va. Italian-Am. award W.Va. Italian Heritage Festival Inc., Clarksburg, W.Va., 1984, Spirit of Freedom award A. James Mancin, Sec. State W.Va., 1984, Disting. W. Virginian award State of W.Va., 1984, John Baird Thomas Meml. award Ohio U.; named Surgery Alumnus of Yr., U. Minn., 1981, Disting. Citizen Wash. State, Lt. Gov. John Cherberg, 1981; NIH grantee, 1951-76; Verdi scholar Yale U. Fellow ACS (numerous coms., bds.), Soc. of Univ. Surgeons (councilman at large 3 yrs.), Internat. Soc. Surgery; mem. Am. Surg. Assn. (adv. mem. com. 1959-64, v.p. 1972-73), Am. Assn. for Thoracic Surgery, Halsted Soc., Henry N. Harkins Surg. Soc., N. Pacific Coast Surg. Assn., Seattle Surg. Soc. (honored special tribute annual meeting 1997), So. Surg. Soc. (Arthur H. Shipley award 1972), Am. Bd. Surgery 1958-64 (vice chmn. 1962-63, chmn. 1963-64, emeritus 1964—); University Club, Seattle Golf Club, Phi Beta Kappa, Sigma Xi, Beta Theta Pi (sec., pres.), Phi Beta Pi (hon.). Republican. Episcopalian. Avocations: golf, fly fishing, bird hunting, gardening. Home: The Highlands Shoreline WA 98177

MERICLE, ROBERT BRUCE, mathematics educator; b. Omaha, June 4, 1938; s. Robert Bruce and Olga Lorrayne (Dyba) M.; m. Gael Tonia Sylce, Aug. 24, 1963; children: Erik Bruce, Andrea Lyn, Melanie Anne. BS in Math., Iowa State U., 1960; MS, U. Md., 1964; PhD, Wash. St. U., 1970. Instr. U. Maine, Orono, 1964-66, Wash. State U., Pullman, 1966-70; asst., assoc. prof. Mankato (Minn.) State U., 1970-74; dir., acad. computer svc. Mich. Tech. U., Houghton, 1974-77; prof. math. Mankato State U., 1977—. Mem. Am. Math. Soc., Math. Assn. Am. Office: Minn State Univ Mankato Dept Math 273 Wissink Hall Mankato MN 56002-8400

MERIDETH, SUSAN CAROL, healthcare educator; b. St. Louis, May 25, 1956; d. George Getzel Brody and Jacquie Jean Lammers; m. John Wolf Merideth, July 28, 1979; children: Laura, Michelle. AAS, St. Louis C.C., 1977; BS, Fontbonne U., 1979; Master of Bus. Adminstrn., Maryville U., 1994. Presch. tchr. various instns., San Diego, 1979—82, Greater San Diego Health Plan, San Diego, 1985—87; supr. Cmty. Care Network, San Diego, 1987—90; mgr. St. John's Mercy Med. Ctr., St. Louis, 1990—95; contracts mgr. Nashua Eye Assocs., Nashua, 1996—98; practice mgr. Found. Med. Ptnrs., Nashua, 1998—99; assoc. prof. Hesser Coll., Manchester, NH, 2000—. Mem.: AAUP, Nat. Bus. Edn. Assn., Phi Theta Kappa (faculty advisor Alpha Nu Upsilon chpt. 2002—, mem. Pi Kappa chpt.). Office: Hesser Coll 3 Sundial Ave Manchester NH 03103

MERILAN, JEAN ELIZABETH, statistics educator; b. Columbia, Mo., Sept. 18, 1962; d. Charles Preston and Phyllis Pauline (Laughlin) M. PhD in Statistics, U. Ariz., 1996; AB summa cum laude, U. Mo., 1985, MA in Math., MA in Stats., 1987; PhD in Stats., U. Ariz., 1996. Grad. teaching asst. U. Mo., Columbia, 1985-87; grad. rsch. asst. U. Ariz., Tucson, 1988-89, grad. tchg. asst., 1989-93. Nat. Merit scholar, Univ. Curators scholar U. Mo., 1981-85, Grad. Acad. scholar U. Ariz., 1990-91, Arts and Sci. Grad. scholar U. Mo., 1985-87; Gregory fellow U. Mo., 1985-87, Faculty of Sci. fellow U. Ariz., 1987-88. Mem. Am. Statis. Assn., Inst. Math. Stats., Soc. for Indsl. and Applied Math., Biometric Soc., Am. Math. Soc., Math. Assn. Am., Golden Key Nat. Honor Soc., Sigma Xi, Phi Beta Kappa, Phi Kappa Phi, Phi Eta Sigma, Pi Mu Epsilon.

MERILAN, MICHAEL PRESTON, astrophysicist, educator, dean; b. Columbia, Mo., Jan. 5, 1956; s. Charles Preston and Phyllis Pauline (Laughlin) M.; m. Karene Anne Yanuklis, Sept. 2, 1995. BS summa cum laude in Physics, U. Mo., Columbia, 1978, MS, 1980; PhD in Astronomy, Ohio State U., 1985. Grad. tchg. asst. U. Mo., Columbia, 1978-80; grad. tchg. assoc., instr. dept. astronomy Ohio State U., Columbus, 1980-85; asst. prof. dept. physics and astronomy SUNY, Oneonta, 1985-91, assoc. prof., 1991—, chmn. dept. physics and astronomy, 1990-93, acting dean divsn. sci. and social sci., 1993-96, dean, 1996—. Astron. cons. Ohio Dept. Natural Resources, 1982-83; Oneonta smart node advisor Cornell Nat. Supercomputer Facility, Oneonta, 1987-92. Contbr. articles to profl. jours. O.M. Stewart fellow U. Mo., 1979; U. Mo. Curators scholar, 1974-78; Mahan Writing award U. Mo., 1975. Mem. AAAS, Am. Astron. Soc., Astron. Soc. Pacific, Internat. Amateur Profl. Photoelectric Photometry Assn., Sigma Xi, Phi Eta Sigma, Phi Kappa Phi, Phi Beta Kappa, Pi Mu Epsilon, Sigma Pi Sigma, Omicron Delta Kappa. Achievements include analytic and numeric investigation of protostellar hydrodynamics; determination of the properties of static and slowly rotating partially degenerate semirelativistic stellar structures. Office: Dean Sci and Social Sci SUNY-Oneonta 336 Netzer Bldg Oneonta NY 13820 E-mail: merilamp@oneonta.edu.

MERINI, RAFIKA, foreign language, cultures and literatures educator; b. Morocco; d. Mohamed M. and Fatima Merini. BA in English cum laude, U. Utah, 1978, MA in Romance Langs. and Lits., 1981; postgrad., U. Wash., 1980-82; cert. in translation, SUNY, Binghamton, 1988, PhD in Comparative Lit., 1992. Tchg. asst. U. Utah, Salt Lake City, 1978-80, U. Wash., Seattle, 1980-82; adminstrv. asst., tchr. French, interpreter The Lang. Sch., Seattle, 1982-83; lectr. Pacific Luth. U., Tacoma, spring 1983; instr. French and Spanish Ft. Steilacoom C.C. (now Pierce C.C.), 1983—85; tchg. asst. dept. romance langs. SUNY, Binghamton, 1985-87, tchg. asst. women's studies dept., summer 1988, tchg. asst. comparative lit. dept., 1986-88; vis. instr. Union Coll., Schenectady, N.Y., 1988-89; vis. instr. dept. fgn. langs. and lits. Skidmore Coll., Saratoga Springs, N.Y., 1989-90; asst. prof. dept. modern and classical langs. State U. Coll., Buffalo, 1990—96, assoc. prof. dept. modern and classical langs., 1996—. Coord. BSC women's studies interdiscipinary unit State U. Coll., Buffalo, 1993-99, adviser French Club, 1990-93; founder, dir. Trois-Pistoles French Immersion Program, U. Western Ont., 1994, 95; presenter, spkr. in field. Author: Two Major Francophone Women Writers, Assia Djébar and Leïla Sebbar: A Thematic Study of Their Works, 1999, 2d printing, 2001; mem. editl. bd. Jour. Middle Eastern and North African Intellectual and Cultural Studies; contbr. articles to profl. jours. Grantee Nat. Defense Student award U. Utah, 1974; also numerous other grants and awards. Mem. MLA, Am. Assn. Tchrs. French, Women in French, Conseil Internat. d'Etudes Francophones, Pi Delta Phi, Soc. Hon. Française, Kappa Theta (hon.). Home: PO Box 1063 Buffalo NY 14213-1063 Office: State Univ Coll-Buffalo Modern & Classical Langs 1300 Elmwood Ave Buffalo NY 14222-1095

MERK, FREDERICK BANNISTER, biomedical educator, medical researcher; b. Cambridge, Mass., Feb. 21, 1936; s. Frederick and Lois Alberta (Bannister) M.; m. Linda Jean Poole, Oct. 22, 1966 (dec. Dec. 1994); children: John F., R. Daniel; m. Laura Ann Bradford, July 11, 1998; 1 stepchild, Letty A. Bradford. AB, Harvard Coll., 1958; PhD, Boston U., 1971. Asst. prof. pathology Boston U. Sch. Medicine, 1972-73; assoc. prof. dept. pathology Tufts U. Sch. Medicine, Boston, 1973—2002, assoc. prof. dept. anatomy, 1973—2002, emeritus prof. pathology and anatomy, 2002—, part time tchr. anatomy, 2002—, dir. electron microscopy facility, 1975-85. Cons. electron microscopy Mass. Gen. Hosp., Boston, 1964-85; cons. toxicol. testing Transgenic Scis., Worcester, Mass., 1988-91, U.S. Army, 1998-2001. Contbr. more than 60 articles to profl. jours. Trustee Broadway United Meth. Ch., Lynn, Mass., chmn. 1994-2000; lay rep. of Ch. to ann. New Eng. Conf., 2000—. Recipient Disting. Career in Tchr. award, 2002; grantee, NIH, 1994—98. Mem. Am. Soc. Cell Biology, Fedn. Am. Soc. Exptl. Biology, Am. Assn. Anatomists, Microscopy Soc. Am., Boston Cancer Rsch. Assn., Sigma Xi. Achievements include research on biology of cells in target organs responding to hormones with emphasis on benign prostatic hypertrophy (enlargement) and prostate cancer. Home: 17 Jefferson Rd Winchester MA 01890-3116 Office: Tufts Univ Sch Medicine Dept Anatomy 136 Harrison Ave Boston MA 02111-1800 E-mail: fmerk@hotmail.com.

MERLING, STEPHANIE CAROLINE, speech and language pathologist; b. Whiteville, N.C., June 2, 1948; d. Ellis Garland and Lois Jayne (Rice) Osborne; m. Paul David Merling, Oct. 18, 1969; children: Paul David, Jr., Jeremy Daniel. BS Speech-Lang. Pathology/Audiology, Andrews U., 1988; MA in Speech-Lang. Pathology, We. Mich. U., 1989. Adminstrv. sec. Andrews U., Berrien Springs, Mich., 1982-89; speech-lang. pathologist Dowagiac (Mich.) Union Schs., 1989-92, South Bend (Ind.) Comm. Sch. Corp., 1993-99; speech-lang. pathologist hearing impaired program Berrien Springs (Mich). Pub. Schs., Mich., 1999—. Pottery registrar and vol. Madaba Plains Archaeol. Inst., Andrews U., excavations in Amman, Jordan, 1984, 91, 93, 96, 99. Recipient Nat. AMBUCS scholarship Am. Businessmen's Assn., 1988, 89, Nat. Collegiate Speech and Hearing Pathology award U.S. Achievement Acad., 1988, Computer-based Telecom. in Elem. Classroom grant Ind. Dept. Edn., 1995. Mem. Am. Speech-Lang.-Hearing Assn. (cert.), Ind. Speech-Lang.-Hearing Assn. Avocations: archaeology, music, horses, oil painting, travel. Home: 5225 Park Rd Eau Claire MI 49111-9426 Office: Berrien Springs Pub Schs 1 Sylvester Ave Berrien Springs MI 49103 E-mail: merling@andrews.edu.

MERLINO, DANI MICHELLE, physical education educator; b. Phila., Dec. 17, 1954; d. Alan Abraham and Sallie Harriet (Nozick) Paris; m. John Joseph Merlino, Sept. 16, 1987; children: Rian Ashlee, Roy Vincent, Rain Brittney, Taylor Paige, Jonathan. BA in health, Phys. Edn., Rowan Coll., Glassboro, N.J., 1993. Asst. mgr. First Peoples Bank, Westmont, N.J., 1972-80; lighting asst. Billows Elec. Co., Phila., 1978-80; substitute tchr. Stratford (N.J.) Sch. System, 1987—, Haddon Twp. High Sch., Westmont, 1987—. Adj. faculty Camden County Coll., Blackwood, N.J., 1992—. Author poetry. Softball coach Stratford, 1990—; phys. edn. camp counselor Camp Hilltop, Medford, N.J., 1971-73; faculty Wellness Ctr., Camden County Coll., 1992—. Mem. AAHPERD. Jewish. Avocations: writing, weight-lifting, swimming, running. Office: Camden County Coll Blackwood St Blackwood NJ 08021

MEROLA, JOSEPHINE, elementary education educator; b. Bklyn., July 9, 1949; d. Patsy A. Merola Salvato; 1 child, Vincent Patsy. BS in Edn., St. Joseph's Coll., 1970; MS in Elem. Edn., L.I. U., 1975. Cert. elem. tchr., N.Y. 1st grade tchr. Our Lady of Perpetual Help Sch., Bklyn.; 2d grade tchr. Our Lady of Guadalupe Sch., Bklyn. Leader workshops in field. Recipient St. Elizabeth Ann Seton award for Outstanding Teaching in Diocese of Bklyn., 1992. Mem. ACEI. Home: 1244 73rd St Brooklyn NY 11228-2015

MERRELL, JO ANN, secondary education educator, writer; b. New London, Conn., Feb. 16, 1945; d. George Francis and Marie Rose (Blaine) Melnechuk; m. Thomas Garner Merrell, Nov. 20, 1965; children: Cathy, David, John. BS in Physics, Calif. State U., Long Beach, 1967; tchg. credential, U. Calif., Irvine, 1988; MAST, Calif. State U., Fullerton, 1997; grad. diploma in Astronomy, U. We. Sydney, Australia, 2002. Supt. Sunday Sch. Grace Cmty. Ch., El Toro, 1978-82; tchr. Capistrano Valley Christian Sch., San Juan Capistrano, Calif., 1983-90, El Toro (Calif.) High Sch., 1990-91; edn. coord. San Juan Capistrano Rsch. Inst., 1991-94; author, editor Tchr. Created Materials Pub. Co., 1992—; tchr. sci. and math. Santa Margarita H.S., 1994—2001, Tarbut V'Torah H.S., Irvine, Calif., 2001—. Math. mentor and tchr., U. Irvine (Calif.), 1987; speaker math. conventions, So. Calif., 1987—. Author: Stories for Family Devotions, 1994, Simple Machines, 1994, Calculators, 1992, Base 10 Blocks, 1992, Hands-On Math, 1993, Connecting Math and Science, 1993; editor: Electricity and Magnetism, 1994. Recipient Presdl. award for Excellence in Math Teaching Orange County Math Coun., 1988, 96, 99; named Outstanding Math./Sci. Tchr. TANDY Corp., 1990. Mem. Nat. Sci. Tchrs. Assn., Nat. Coun. Tchrs. of Math., Nat. Space Soc., Calif. Math. Coun., Am. Nuclear Sci. Tchrs. Assn., San Jose Hist. Soc., Orange County Math. Coun., Am. Assn. Physics Tchrs.

MERRIAM, JANET PAMELA, special education educator; b. L.A., Jan. 11, 1958; d. Allen Hugo and Linda (Teagle) Warren; m. Marshal Lockhart Merriam, Aug. 4, 1984 (div. June 1991); 1 child, Jennifer Elizabeth. BA, San Jose State U., 1981. Cert. tchr. learning handicapped, lang. devel. specialist, Calif. Asst. youth edn. dir. Christ Ch. Unity, San Jose, 1988-90; substitute tchr. Santa Clara (Calif.) Unified Sch. Dist., 1990; spl. day class tchr. Oak Grove Sch. Dist., San Jose, 1990—. Sunday sch. tchr. Christ Ch. Unity, San Jose, 1980-92. Mem. Coun. for Exceptional Children, Learning Disabilities Assn. Calif., Calif. Assn. Resource Specialists Plus. Republican. Avocations: reading, star trek, old movies. Home: 1657 Glenville Dr San Jose CA 95124-3808 Office: 530 Gettysburg Dr San Jose CA 95123-3234

MERRICK, BARBARA BARNHART, school administrator; b. Hagerstown, Md., Aug. 24, 1939; d. C. Paul and Henrietta (Wagner) B.; m. Roger B. Merrick, Dec. 29, 1964; children: Daniel, Elizabeth. BA, Coll. William and Mary, 1961. Cert. tchr., Md. Tchr. Lock Raven Elem. Sch., Towson, Md., 1961-64, Am. Sch. Beirut, 1967-68, Parents Coop. Sch., Jeddah, Saudi Arabia, 1969-70, Cairo (Egypt) Am. Coll., 1974, Khartoum (Sudan) Am. Sch., 1976-78, Charles County Alternative Sch., La Plata, Md., 1979-80, Saudi Arabian Internat. Sch., Riyadh, 1982-84; prin. Christ Ch. Day Sch., La Plata, 1991—. Bd. dirs. Children's Aid Soc., Mattowoman Creek Arts Ctr.; sec. Charles County Scholarship Fund Bd., 1990—. Mem. AAUW (pres. 1990—), Nat. Coun. Tchrs. Math., Nat. Assn. Elem. Sch. Prins., Women's Club So. Md. (treas.), Phi Delat Kappa, Delta Kappa Gamma. Democrat. Methodist. Avocations: travel, sports. Home: 8220 Fairground Rd La Plata MD 20646-4710 Office: Christ Church Day Sch Charles St La Plata MD 20646

MERRICK, BEVERLY GEORGIANNE, journalism, communications educator; b. Troy, Kans., Nov. 20, 1944; d. Horace Buchanan Merrick and Vola Yolantha (Clausen) Maul; m. John Douglas Childers, July 10, 1963 (div. 1998); children: John Kevin, Pamela Christine, Jessica Faye. BA in Journalism with honors, BA in English with honors, Marshall U., 1980, M Journalism, 1982; M Creative Writing, Ohio U., 1986, cert. in Women's Studies, 1984, PhD in Mass Comm. with honors, 1989. Reporter, photographer Ashland (Ky.) Daily Ind., 1981; tchr., instr. Albuquerque Pub. Schs., 1986—89; gen. assignment reporter, photographer Rio Rancho (N.Mex.) Observer, 1986; editor, rsch. cons. Ins. Pub. Law, Sch. of Law U. N.Mex., Albuquerque, 1990; asst. prof. Ga. So. U., Statesboro, 1991—94; assoc. prof. dept. mass comm. U. S.D., Vermillion, 1994; from asst. to assoc. prof. dept. journalism and mass comm. N. Mex. State U., Las Cruces, 1995—; faculty, photographer the Washington Ctr., 1999; sabbatical N.Mex. State U., 2002—03; mng. editor, features and photo editor, newspaper exec., Custer County chief Cmty. Newspapers Holdings Inc., 2002—03. Part-time tchr., tchg. assoc. Ohio U. Athens, 1981—84; part-time copy editor Albuquerque Tribune, 1991; vis. prof. East Carolina U., Greenville, NC, 1989—90; adj. prof. Embry-Riddle U., Kirtland AFB, N.Mex., 1989, Kirtland AFB, 91; organizer diversity conf., 1st amendment conf. Ga. So. U.; mem. session MIT, 1989; chair campus com. N. Mex. State U.; faculty Wash. Ctr. Nat. Women in Leadership Interns Program, 1999; leadership trainer N.M. No. U., Abiquiu, 1999; photographer/journalist Comstock Windmill Festival, Comstock Rock Festival, Comstock Godstode, 2003; presenter in field. Author: (poetry) Navigating the Platte, 1996, Pearls for the Casting, 1987, Closing the Gate, 1993, (monograph) Jane Grant, The New Yorker and Ross, 1999; photographer, documentary reporter : (TV films) Windmill Festival; Comstock Rocks; Godstock, 2003; contbr. poems to profl. pubs., jours., chapters to books. Pub. rels. liaison Nat. Convention Bus. and Profl. Women, Albuquerque, 1988; pres. Albuquerque Bus. and Profl. Women, 1986-87, Rio Rancho Civic Assn., 1987-89, So. Ohio Improvement League, 1973-76; pres. bd. dirs. Pine Creek Conservancy Dist., 1976-83; chair Ted Turner and Jane Fonda Com., 1996, Sam Donaldson Native Sun Benefit Com., 1999; gov., girls State counselor, N.M., 2000; chair poster contest on media literacy Las Cruces Pub. Schs., So. N.Mex. Literacy Coun. Named Truly Fine Citizen of Ohio, Ohio Gen. Assembly, 1973, Outstanding Homemaker of Ohio, Gov. of Ohio, 1974, Outstanding Citizen, N.Mex. Legislature, 1988; grantee Reader's Digest, 1980, 83; John Houk Meml. grantee W.Va. Women's Conf., 1982; fellow Nat. Women's Studies Inst., Lilly Found., 1983, Freedom Forum Ethics, 1995, Am. Newspaper Inst., 1995; Newsday fellow Am. Soc. Newspaper Editors, 1998; E.W. Scripps scholar, 1984; recipient Silver Clover award 4-H, Writing award Aviation/Space Writers Assn., 1981, 1st place open rsch competition Nat. Assn. Women's Deans, Adminstrs. and Counselors, 1990 award 16th Ann. Gov.'s Awards for Outstanding N.Mex. Women, 2001; rsch. grantee N.Mex. State U., 1996. Mem. Soc. Profl. Journalists, Assn. for Edn. in Journalism and Mass Comm. (mem. nat. conv. com. 1993-94, vice head mag. divsn. 1995-96, head mag. divsn., 1996-97, chair southwest colloquium 1998), S.W. Edn. Coun. for Journalism and Mass Comm. (conf. chair 1998, bd. dirs. 1999-2002), Western Journalism Historians Assn. (conf. chair Berkeley Sch. Journalism 1999), N.Mex. State Poetry Soc. (pres. 1987-89), Sigma Tau Delta. Home: 985 Ivydale Dr Las Cruces NM 88005-0927

MERRICK, ROSWELL DAVENPORT, educational association administrator; b. Kings County, NY, July 20, 1922; s. George Roswell and Marguerite Regina M.; m. Gladys K. Kinley, June 26, 1948; children—Gregory, Susan, Peter. BS, Springfield Coll., 1944; MA, N.Y. U., 1947; Ed.D., Boston U., 1953. Assoc. prof., head basketball coach Ctl. Conn. U., New Britain, 1946-53; asst. dean (Coll. Edn.); dir. div. health, phys. edn., recreation and athletics So. Ill. U., Carbondale, 1953-58; exec. dir. Nat. Assn. Sport and Phys. Edn., Reston, Va., 1958-91, US Fitness and Sport Coun., 1991—. Contbr. articles to profl. jour. Mem. US Olympic Com. Served with USAAF, 1944-46. Mem. AAHPERD, Mt. Vernon Yacht Club. Methodist. Address: 167 Redwood La Weems VA 22526

MERRILL, ARTHUR LEWIS, retired theology educator; b. Tura, Assam, India, Sept. 14, 1930; s. Alfred Francis and Ida (Walker) M.; m. Barbara Jean Mayer, Aug. 18, 1951 (dec. June 1978); children: Margaret Jean, Katherine Merrill Nelson, Robert L.; m. Margaret Z. Morris, Sept. 11, 1985. BA, Coll. of Wooster, 1951; BD with distinction, Berkeley Bapt. Div. Sch., 1954; PhD, U. Chgo., 1962. Ordained to ministry United Ch. of Christ, 1954. Asst. prof. Bapt. Missionary Tng. Sch., Chgo., 1957-58; assoc. prof. Mission House Theol. Sem., Plymouth, Wis., 1958-62, United Theol. Sem. Twin Cities, New Brighton, Minn., 1962-67, prof., 1967-95, prof. emeritus, 1995—. Author: United Theological Seminary of the Twin Cities: An Ecumenical Venture, 1993; co-author: Biblical Witness and the World, 1967; co-editor: Scripture in History and Theology, 1977; contbr. articles to profl. publs. ATS-Lilly postdoctoral fellow, 1966-67. Mem. Soc. Bibl. Lit., Am. Schs. Oriental Rsch., Israel Exploration Soc., Minn. Theol. Libr. Assn. (pres. 1994-95). Home: 36177 Wabana Rd Grand Rapids MN 55744-6446 E-mail: artgaro@paulbunyan.net.

MERRILL, EDWARD WILSON, chemical engineering educator; b. New Bedford, Mass., Aug. 31, 1923; s. Edward Clifton and Gertrude (Wilson) M.; m. Genevieve de Bidart, Aug. 19, 1948; children: Anne de Bidart, Francis de Bidart. AB, Harvard U., 1945; DSc, MIT, 1947. Research engr. Dewey & Almy div. W.R. Grace & Co., 1947-50; mem. faculty MIT, 1950-98, prof. chem. engring., 1964-98, Carbon P. Dubbs prof., 1973-96, emeritus, 1998—. Cons. in biochem. engring. Harvard U. Health Svcs., 1982-94; cons. in field. Contbr. articles to profl. jours. on polymers, rheology, med. engring.; patentee chem. and rheological instruments. Pres. bd. trustees Buckingham Sch., Cambridge, 1969-74; trustee Browne and Nichols Sch., Cambridge, 1972-74, hon. trustee, 1974—. Fellow Am. Inst. for Med. and Biol. Engring., Am. Acad. Arts and Scis.; mem. AIChE (Alpha Chi Sigma award 1984, Charles M.A. Stine award 1993, Founders award 2000), Am. Chem. Soc., Soc. for Biomaterials (Clemson U. Award 1990, Founders award 2003). Home: 90 Somerset St Belmont MA 02478-2010 Fax: 617-489-2165. E-mail: emerrill@mit.edu.

MERRILL, THOMAS WENDELL, lawyer, educator; b. Bartlesville, Okla., May 3, 1949; s. William McGill and Dorothy (Glasener) Merrill; m. Kimberly Ann Evans, Sept. 18, 1973; children: Jessica, Margaret, Elizabeth. BA, Grinnell Coll., 1971, Oxford U., 1973; JD, U. Chgo., 1977. Bar: Ill. 1980, U.S. Dist. Ct. (no. dist.) Ill. 1980, U.S. Ct. Appeals (5th cir.) 1982, U.S. Ct. Appeals (7th cir.) 1983, U.S. Ct. Appeals (9th and DC cirs.) 1984, U.S. Supreme Ct. 1985. Clk. U.S. Ct. Appeals (DC cir.), Washington, 1977-78, U.S. Supreme Ct., Washington, 1978-79; assoc. Sidley & Austin, Chgo., 1979-81, counsel, 1981-87, 90—; dep. solicitor gen. U.S. Dept. Justice, 1987-90; prof. law Northwestern U., Chgo., 1981—2003, John Paul Stevens prof., 1993—2003; prof. law Columbia U., 2003—. Co-author: (book) Property: Takings, 2002; contbr. articles to profl. jours. Rhodes scholar, Oxford U., 1971, Danforth fellow, 1971. Home: 2828 Broadway Apt 7C New York NY 10025 Address: 435 W 116th St New York NY 10027

MERRION, ARTHUR BENJAMIN, mathematics educator, tree farmer; b. Williamstown, N.J., Oct. 25, 1938; s. Anthony Robert and Eva May Merrion; m. Martha Jane Banse, Dec. 26, 1965 (div. May 1977); children: Benjamin Thomas, Elizabeth Jane. AB in Math., Pfeiffer Coll. (now Univ.), 1965; MS in Numerical Sci., Johns Hopkins U., 1976. Navigations scientist Def. Mapping Agy. Hydrographic Ctr., Suitland, Md., 1966-78; fellow ops. rsch. analysis Sec. Army Pentagon, Washington, 1978-80; ops. rsch. analyst Asst. Sec. Army, Washington, 1980-86; tree farmer Huntingtown, Md., 1986-98. Instr. math. and stats. Embry-Riddle Aeronautical U., 1993-94; math. instr. Charles County C.C., 1990-91; tutor Literary Coun. Author: A Short Story By Edgar Allen Pooh. With U.S. Army, 1957-58. Mem. Md. Soc. SAR. Achievements include successful experimentation in applying mathematical chaos theory to weather modification. Avocations: chess, violin, Judo, wrestling, ice skating. Home: PO Box 1639 West Jefferson NC 28694-1639

MERRITT, CAROL RUTH, middle school educator; b. Des Moines, Nov. 5, 1944; d. Herbert Wesley and Anna Gelene (Satre) M. BS in Edn., Huntington (Ind.) Coll., 1962; MS in Psychology, Goddard Coll., Plainfield, Vt., 1982. Cert. tchr., Kans., Mo. Counselor, tchr. YMCA, Wichita, 1962-68; tchr. 5th grade Riverside Elem. Sch., Ft. Wayne, Ind., 1969-70, Lincoln Elem. Sch., Huntington, 1971-74; substitute tchr. St. Louis area, 1974-75; kindergarten tchr. Raymore, Mo., 1975-76; tchr. 7th grade St. Joseph Parochial Sch., Kansas City, Mo., 1978-79; tchr. 6th and 7th grades Rosedale Mid. Sch., Kansas City, Kans., 1979-84; tchr. 7th grade Coronado Mid. Sch., Kansas City, 1984-85; tchr. 6th, 7th and 8th grades Argentine Mid. Sch., Kansas City, 1986-93. Treas., Squire Pk. Neighborhood Assn., Kansas City, Mo., 1989-91; seminar leader Colonial Presbyn. Ch., Kansas City, Mo., 1980-90. Mem. NEA, Calif. Trails Assn. Avocations: painting, playing violin, swimming. Office: Argentine Mid Sch 22D And Ruby Kansas City KS 66106

MERRITT, CAROLE ANNE, secondary school educator; b. Trenton, N.J., Oct. 30, 1943; d. Angelo Joseph and Katherin Paulline (Petruccio) Tramontana; 1 child, Stephen;m. John Howard Merritt, June 10, 1992. BA, Glassboro State U., 1965; MA, Salisbury State U., 1992. Tchr. Steinert H.S., Hamilton, N.J., 1965-70, Bode Sch., St. Joseph, Mo., 1971-84, Parkside H.S., Salisbury, Md., 1985—. Contbr. articles to profl. jours., including Tchr., Sch. & Cmty. Vol. Crisis Ctr., Joseph House, Peninsular Med. Ctr., Salisbury Zoo, Salisbury Arts Coun. Mem. Delta Kappa Gamma, Kappa Delta Pi, Phi Delta Kappa. Avocations: swimming, exercise, reading, ceramics, travel. Office: Parkside HS 1015 Beaglin Park Dr Salisbury MD 21804-9311 Home: 27140 Scotland Pkwy Salisbury MD 21801-2437

MERRITT, LORETTA GAETANA, principal, primary education educator; b. Passaic, N.J., Dec. 21, 1944; d. James A. and Rosalia (Ricci) Domino; m. Robert V. Merritt, Apr. 29, 1973. BA in Elem. Edn., William Paterson, 1966; MA in Edn. Adminstrn., Kean Coll. N.J., 1987; postgrad., various colls., 1984-90. Cert. early childhood/nursery sch. tchr., prin., supr. First grade, kindergarten and pre-kindergarten tchr. Roosevelt Sch. #10, Passaic, N.J., 1966-97, acting asst. prin., 1993; tchr. elem. math, reading Martin Luther King Sch. #6, Passaic, 1997-2000; prin. early childhood Passaic Pub Sch. #16, Passaic, 2000—. Adv. mem. pupil assistance coun. #10 Sch., Passaic, 1986—, chairperson site-based coun., 1992-94, mem.-advisor devel. kindergarten full-day curriculum com., 1992, mem.-advisor for devel. basic skills checklist test com., 1992, mem. dist. steering com., 1993-94. Recipient Gov.'s Convocation on Excellence in Tchg., N.J. State Dept. Edn., Trenton, 1987, Passaic County Tchr. of the Year, 1987-88. Mem. NEA, Nat. Assn. Edn. Young Children, N.J. Edn. Assn., Edn. Assn. Passaic (rep. 1993-95), N.J. Assn. Elem. Sch. Prins., N.J. Prins. and Suprs. Assn., Passaic Assn. Suprs. and Prins., Kindergarten Tchrs. Assn., PTO Dist. #10 (cons. 1994), Kappa Delta Phi. Avocations: arts and crafts, gardening, traveling. E-mail: loleka21@aol.com.

MERTE, HERMAN, JR., education educator, mechanical engineer; b. Detroit, Apr. 3, 1929; s. Herman and Anna Marie (Mitterer) M.; m. Bernice Marie Brant, Sept. 17, 1952; children— Kenneth Edward, James Dennis, Lawrence Carleton, Richard Brant, Robert Paul. BS in Marine Engring, U. Mich., Ann Arbor, 1950, BS in Mech. Engring, 1951, MS, 1956, PhD, 1960. Faculty U. Mich., 1959—67, prof. mech. engring., 1967—2000, prof. emeritus, 2000—. Vis. prof. Tech. U. Munich, Germany, 1974-75 Served to lt. (j.g.) USNR, 1952-55. NSF sr. postdoctoral fellow, 1967-68 Mem. ASME, Am. Soc. Engring. Edn., Am. Assn. U. Profs. Home: 3480 Cottontail Ln Ann Arbor MI 48103-1706 Office: U Mich Heat Transfer Lab 2026 G G Brown Lab Ann Arbor MI 48109-2125

MERTEN, ALAN GILBERT, academic administrator; b. Milw., Dec. 27, 1941; s. Gilbert Ervin and Ruth Anna (Ristow) M.; m. Sally Louise Otto; children: Eric, Melissa. BS, U. Wis., 1963; MS, Stanford U., 1964; PhD, U. Wis., 1970. Asst. prof. U. Mich., Ann Arbor, 1970-74, assoc. prof., 1974-81, prof., 1981-86, assoc. dean, 1983-86; dean U. Fla., Gainesville, 1986-89; dean Johnson Grad. Sch. of Mgmt. Cornell U., Ithaca, N.Y., 1989-96; pres. George Mason U., Fairfax, Va., 1996—. Bd. dirs. Comshare, Inc., Ann Arbor, Citigroup Mut. Funds, Digital Net, Brainbench; mem. Fla. Gov.'s Select Com. on Workforce 2000, 1988-89. Author: Internal Control in U.S. Corporations, 1980, Senior Management Control of Computer-Based Information Systems, 1983. Mem. Airport Authority, Gainesville, Fla., 1986-89. Served to capt. USAF, 1963-67. Lutheran. Home: 11020 Popes Head Rd Fairfax VA 22030-4608 Office: George Mason U Office of Pres Fairfax VA 22030-4444 E-mail: amerten@gmu.edu.

MERTINS, DETLEFF, architect, educator, architect, department chairman; BArch, U. Toronto, Can.; PhD in Arch., Princeton U. Instr. U. Toronto, 1991—2003, Can. Rsch. chair in arch., 2001—03; prof., chair dept. arch. U. Pa. Sch. Design, 2003—. Vis. prof. Columbia U., Harvard U., Princeton U., Rice U. Recipient Konrad Adenauer Rsch. prize, Alexander von Humboldt Found. and Royal Can. Soc., 2003; vis. scholar fellow, Can. Ctr. for Arch., 1998. Office: Univ Pa 207 Meyerson Hall Philadelphia PA 19104-6311*

MERTZ, FRANCIS JAMES, university president; b. Newark, Sept. 24, 1937; s. Frank E. and Marian E. (Brady) M.; m. Gail Williams, Apr. 11, 1964; children: Lynn, Christopher, Suzanne, David, Amy, Jonathan. BA, St. Peter's Coll., 1958; JD, NYU, 1961; LLD (hon.), Felician Coll., 1984, Stevens Inst. Tech., Hoboken, N.J., 1988, Fairleigh Dickinson U., 1999, Kunghnam Univ., 1999, Coll. St. Elizabeth, 2002. Bar: N.J. 1967. Exec. v.p. St. Peter's Coll., Jersey City, 1972-78; v.p., CFO N.Y. Med. Coll., Valhalla, 1978-79; dir. adminstrn. Sage Gray Todd and Sims, N.Y.C., 1979-81; pres. Ind. Coll. Fund N.J., Summit, 1981-90, Assn. Ind. Colls. and Univs. N.J., Summit, 1982-90, Fairleigh Dickinson U., Teaneck, N.J., 1990-99, pres. emeritus. Bd. dirs., chmn. Ready Found., St. Joseph's Home for the Blind, 1998—; chmn. bd. regents Seton Hall U., 2002—. Home: 167 Stanie Brae Dr Watchung NJ 07069-6233 Office: Fairleigh Dickinson U 285 Madison Ave Madison NJ 07940-1099 E-mail: mertz@fdu.edu.

MERVILLE, LAWRENCE JOSEPH, finance educator; b. Nashville, Apr. 7, 1943; s. Lawrence Augustus Merville and Emma June (Collier) Park; m. Sheryl Wolff, Aug. 9, 1968; 1 child, Lauren Anne. BA, Vanderbilt U., 1965; MBA, U. Tex., 1968, PhD, 1971. Fin. analyst Tex. Instruments, Dallas, 1968-70; asst. prof. fin. Ind. U., Bloomington, 1971-73; prof. fin. U. Tex., Dallas, 1973—. Pres. Merville & Assocs., Dallas; cons. Tex. Pub. Utility Com., Austin, 1983-85. Author: Economics and Finance, 1990; contbr. articles to profl. jours. Dir. Pub. Utility Programs, Dallas, 1978-82, Pub. Utility Ctr., Dallas, 1981-87. NSF fellow U. Tex., Austin, 1965. Mem. Am. Fin. Assn., Fin. Mgmt. Assn. (program com.), Western Fin. Assn. (program com.), Soc. for China Studies, Dallas Economist Club (membership com.), Phi Beta Kappa. Republican. Avocations: travel, jogging, fishing, theatre. Office: Univ Tex Dallas 2601 N Floyd Rd Richardson TX 75080-1407

MERWIN, DEBRA LEE, university counseling director; b. Amarillo, Tex. d. Robert Wayne and Hallie Mae (Hammond) Davis; m. William Charles Merwin. BA in Psychology, West Tex. State U., 1975; MEd in Counseling and Career Guidance, No. Mont. Coll., Havre, 1983; EdD in Adult and Higher Edn. Counseling, Mont. State U., 1990. speaker Am. Assn. State Colls. and Univs., Whistler, B.C., Can., summer 1992, spkr. Student Leadership Conf., St. Lawrence U., 1995, AASCU spkr. Tuscon, 1995; spkr. pres. and spouses Am. State Colls. and Univs., Blain, Wash., 1996; cons. Peninsula Regional Med. Ctr., 1997-98; cons., presenter workshops in field;

mem. Women's Symposium Com., 1997-98. Social worker dept. child protection Social and Rehab. Svcs., Havre, 1976-79; youth counselor Human Resource Devel. Coun., Havre, 1979-80; counselor, instr. No. Mont. Coll., Havre, 1980-87; mem. faculty Stone Child Coll., Box Elder, Mont., 1987-89; dir. counseling svcs. St. Lawrence U., Canton, N.Y., 1989—; presdl. assoc. SUNY, 1991—. Cons., presenter workshops in field. Career edn. grantee State of Mont, 1979, Spl. Svcs. grantee U.S. Govt. No. Mont. Coll., 1987, Supplemental Instrn. grantee 1st Bank System No. Mont. Coll., 1986, Unsung Hero award Potsdam Coll. Found., 1992, Diversity Leadership award U. Md. Ea. Shore, 1997. Mem. ACA, Am. Coll. Pers. Assn., Coll. Student Pers. N.Y., North Country Coun. on Alcoholism, Counselors for Admission and Advising Com. St. Lawrence U., N.Y. Fedn. Alcoholism Counselors, Omicron Delta Kappa. Avocations: skiing, golfing, hiking, canoeing, traveling. Home: 20226 Country Club Dr Estero FL 33928-2001 Office: University Maryland Eastern Shore Student Development Center Princess Anne MD 21853

MERWIN, EDWIN PRESTON, healthcare educator, consultant; b. Revere, Mass., Oct. 13, 1927; s. George Preston and Edith Charlotte (Miller) Merwin; m. Marylynn Joy Bicknell, Nov. 3, 1979; stepchildren: Charles John Burns, Patrick Edward Burns, Stephen Allen Burns, John David Light, Robert Allen Light, Frederick John Light;1 child from previous marriage, Ralph Edwin. BS, U. So. Calif., 1955, postgrad., 1957, San Fernando Valley State Coll, 1965—66; MPH (USPHS fellow), U. Calif., Berkeley, 1970; PhD, Brantridge Forest, Eng., 1971. Tng. office Camarillo (Calif.) State Hosp., 1961—66; asst. coord. mental retardation programs State of Calif., Sacramento, 1966—67; project dir. Calif. Coun. Retarded Children, Sacramento, 1967—69; asst. dir. Golden Empire Comprehensive Health Coun., Sacramento, 1970—76, health care cons., 1976—77; gen. ptnr. EDRA Assocs., 1976—. Tchr. Ventura (Calif.) Coll., 1962—66, Merritt Coll., Oakland, Calif., 1969; cons. Calif. Dept. Health, 1977—78, Calif. Office Statewide Health Planning and Devel., 1978—79, chief health pers. info. and analysis sect., 1981—82, asst. chief divsn. health professions devel., 1981—84, asst. dep. dir., 1984—85; chief health professions career opportunity program State of Calif., Sacramento, 1979—81; project dir. Alzheimer Disease Insts., Calif., 1986—87; chief demonstration project sect. divsn. Health Projects and Analysis, 1987—89, chief policy analysis and professions devel. sect., 1989—93; sr. adj. prof. Golden Gate U., 1976, mem. adv. com. health faculty, 1995—; lectr. continuing edn. program U. Calif., Berkeley; instr. Los Rios CC Dist., 1982—; mem. Task Force New Health Care Sys. Macedonia; cons. NIMH, HEW, Calif. Assn. Health Facilities; founder, cons. Internat. U. Am., 1995—. Author (with Fred Heck): (book) Written Case Analysis, 1982; author: (with Carl Brooks) Health Algorythm - circa 2030, 1999; editor: T. patrick Heck Meml. Case Series, 1982; contbr. articles to profl. jours. Mem. health adv. coun. San Juan Sch. Dist., 1972—73; treas. Calif. Camping and Recreation Coun., 1972—73; bd. dirs. Sacramento Rehab. Facility, 1970—86, v.p., 1973—76; bd. dirs. Sacramento Vocat. Svcs., 1986—93; founder, life mem. S.O.T.S., 1989—. Recipient Pres.'s award, Golden Gate U., 1982. Mem.: AAAS, DAV (life), Calif. State Sheriffs Assn., Nat. Assn. Retarded Children (dir., Svc. award 1984), Sacramento Mental Health Assn., Calif. Pub. Health Assn., Am. Assn. Mental Deficiency, Sacramento Assn. Retarded (life), Miles Merwin Assn., SCAPA Praetors U. So. Calif., Marines Meml. Assn. (life), Am. Legion, Phi Kappa Tau. Home: 8008 Archer Ave Fair Oaks CA 95628-5907 Office: Golden Gate U 3620 Northgate Blvd Ste 100 Sacramento CA 95834-1619

MERZBACHER, EUGEN, physicist, educator; b. Berlin, Apr. 9, 1921; came to U.S., 1947, naturalized, 1953; s. Siegfried and Lilli (Wilmersdoerffer) M.; m. Ann Townsend Reid, July 11, 1952; children: Celia, Charles, Matthew, Mary. Licentiate, U. Istanbul, 1943; AM, Harvard U., 1948, PhD, 1950; DSc (hon.), U. N.C., Chapel Hill, 1993. High sch. tchr., Ankara, Turkey, 1943—47; mem. Inst. Advanced Study, Princeton, NJ, 1950—51; vis. asst. prof. Duke U., Durham, NC, 1951—52; from mem. faculty to Kenan prof. physics U. N.C., Chapel Hill, 1952—91, Kenan prof. emeritus, 1991—. Vis. prof. U. Wash., 1967-68, U. Edinburgh, Scotland, 1986; Arnold Bernhard vis. prof. physics Williams Coll., 1993; chair Internat. Conf. on Physics of Electronic and Atomic Collisions, 1987-89; sr. advisor APS, 1998-99. Author: Quantum Mechanics, 3d edit., 1998; also articles. NSF Sci. Faculty fellow U. Copenhagen, Denmark, 1959-60; recipient Thomas Jefferson award U. N.C., 1972; Humboldt sr. scientist award U. Frankfurt, Germany, 1976-77. Fellow AAAS, Am. Phys. Soc. (pres. 1990); mem. Am. Assn. Physics Tchrs. (Oersted medal 1992), Sigma Xi. Achievements include research on applications of quantum mechanics to study atoms and nuclei. Home: 1396 Halifax Rd Chapel Hill NC 27514-2724 E-mail: merzbach@physics.unc.edu.

MESELSON, MATTHEW STANLEY, biochemist, educator; b. Denver, Col., May 24, 1930; s. Hymen Avram and Ann (Swedlow) M.; m. Jeanne Guillemin, 1986; children: Zoe, Amy Valor. Ph.B., U. Chgo., 1951, D.Sc. (hon.), 1975; PhD, Calif. Inst. Tech., 1957; Sc.D. (hon.), Oakland Coll., 1964, Columbia, 1971, Yale U., 1987, Princeton U., 1988. From research fellow to sr. research fellow Calif. Inst. Tech., 1957-60; asso. prof. biology Harvard U., 1960—, prof. biology, 1964-76, Thomas Dudley Cabot prof. natural scis., 1976—. Recipient Eli Lilly award microbiology and immunology, 1964, Alumni medal U. Chgo., 1971; Lehman award 1975, Presidential award 1983, N.Y. Acad. Scis., 1975; Alumni Disting. Svc. award Calif. Inst. Tech., 1975; Leo Szilard award Am. Phys. Soc., 1978; MacArthur fellow, 1984-89. Fellow AAAS (Sci. Freedom and Responsibility award, 1990); mem. NAS (Molecular Biology prize 1963), Inst. Medicine, Am. Acad. Arts and Scis., Fedn. Am. Scientists (chmn. 1986-88, Pub. Svc. award 1972), Coun. Fgn. Rels., Accademia Santa Chiara, Am. Philos. Soc., Royal Society (London), Académie des Sciences (Paris), Genetics Soc. Am. (Thomas Hunt Morgan medal 1995). Office: Harvard U Fairchild Biochem Bldg 7 Divinity Ave Cambridge MA 02138-2019

MESHKE, GEORGE LEWIS, drama and humanities educator; b. Yakima, Wash., Oct. 7, 1930; s. George Joseph and Marye Elizabeth (Lopas) M. BA, U. Wash., 1953, MA, 1959, PhD in Drama, 1972. Cert. tchr., Wash. Tchr. English and drama Zillah High Sch., Wash., 1955-58, high sch., Bellevue, Wash., 1958-60, Federal Way, Wash., 1960-70; dir., actor Old Brewery Theatre, Helena, Mont., 1962-66; prof. drama Yakima Valley C.C., Yakima, 1970-2000, part-time instr., 2001—. Casting dir., dir. summer seminar Laughing Horse Summer Theatre, Ellensburg, Wash., 1989-96, Children's Lit. Inst., 2000; adj. prof. grad. studies Ctrl. Wash. U., Tchr. Exch., London, 1995, People-to-People Exch., China, 2000, Mongolia, Manchuria, 2001; lectr. Inquiring Mind series Wash. State Humanities, 1989-91; regional dir. Am. Coll. Theatre Festival, Washington, 1980-86; arts dialogue J.F. Kennedy Ctr., Washington, 1987—; casting dir., actor Hollywood Ind. Prodns.; adv. coun. Kennedy Ctr. Author, producer Towers of Tomorrow, 1985, The Halls of Yesterday-Yakima Hist. drama; appeared in Yakima, Washington, 1998. Regional bd. dirs. Common Cause, Yakima, 1971-73; active Nat. Hist. Soc., Nat. Wilderness Soc., Roosevelt Meml. Found., Wash. State Commn. Humanities, Drama League. With U.S. Army, 1953-55, Austria. Recipient Gold medal Kennedy Ctr., 1985, Wash. State Humanities medal, 1983, NISAD medal, 1989, Wash. State Drama award, 1999. Mem. ACLU, VFW, Wash. Edn. Assn., N.W. Drama Assn., Am. Edn. Theatre Assn., Am. Fedn. Tchrs., Kennedy Libr., Amnesty Internat. Carter Libr., Libr. Congress (assoc.), Phi Delta Kappa. Democrat. Avocations: travel, mountain climbing, skiing, reading. Home: 5 N 42nd Ave Yakima WA 98908-3214 Office: Yakima Valley CC 16th And Nob Hill Blvd Yakima WA 98907

MESKILL, VICTOR P. academic administrator, educator; b. Albertson, N.Y., May 9, 1935; s. James Joseph and Ida May (Pfalzer) M.; m. Gail King Heidinger, 1986; children by previous marriage— Susan Ann, Janet Louise, Gary James, Glenn Thomas, Kenneth John, Matthew Adam. BA, Hofstra U., 1961, MA (grad. scholar), 1962; PhD, St. John's U., 1967; postgrad. insts., Ohio State U., 1968; postgrad., Harvard U., 1972, NYU, 1973; DSc (hon.), Samara State Aerospace U., Russia, 1993; LHD (hon.), St. John's U., 1995; DCL (hon.), Moscow Internat. U., Russia, 1996; DCL (hon.), D Ecology/Biosphere (hon.), Coll. Puschino State U., Moscow, 1996; D of Pedagogy (PdD) (hon.), Dowling Coll., 1997; D of Econs. (hon.), U. Istanbul, Turkey, 1997; D of Sci., Yanshan U., Peoples' Republic of China, 1998. Lab. asst., instr. biology Hofstra U., 1960-62; N.Y. State teaching fellow St. John's U., 1962-63; instr. biology Nassau (N.Y.) C.C., 1963-64; tchr. sci. Central H.S. Dist. 2, Floral Park, N.Y., 1963-64; lectr. biology C.W. Post Coll., Greenvale, N.Y., 1963-64, instr. biology, 1964-67, asst. prof., 1967-68, assoc. prof., 1968-74, assoc. dir. Inst. for Student Problems, supr. student tchrs., 1967-68, asst. dean Coll., dean summer sch., coordinator Admissions Office, coordinator adult and continuing edn. programs, 1968-69; dean adminstrn. C.W. Post Ctr. of L.I. U., 1969-70, v.p. adminstrn., 1970-77, prof. biology, 1975-77; pres. Dowling Coll., Oakdale, L.I., 1977-2000, pres. emeritus, 2000—. Cons. in edn. and biology; chem. technician, detective Tech. Rsch. Bur., Nassau County Police Dept., 1958-63, mem. sci. adv. com., 1970; mem. adv. coun. Aerospace Edn. Coun. Inc., 1968; trustee, mem. state legis. com. Commn. Ind. Colls. and Univs.; mem. evaluation teams Mid. States Assn., 1971—; mem. higher edn. adv. com. N.Y. State Senate; mem. Nassau-Suffolk Comprehensive Health Planning Coun.; chmn. Internat. and Mediterranean Studies Group Conf. Contbr. articles to profl. jours. Founding mem., vice-chmn. bd. trustees Nassau Higher Edn. Consortium; bd. dirs. Suffolk County coun. Boy Scouts Am.; mem. N.Y. State Energy Rsch. and Devel. Authority, Town of Islip Devel. Commn.; chmn. bd. trustees L.I. Regional Adv. Coun. Higher Edn.; chmn. L.I. Mid Suffolk Bus. Action; bd. dirs. Southside Hosp., N.Y.; v.p. L.I. Forum for Tech.; former commr. Suffolk County Vanderbilt Mus.; mem. Bus. Coun. N.Y.; hon. mem. U. Pau and Pays de l'Adour, Pau, France, 1994; hon. prof. Minjiang U., Fuzhou, Peoples Republic of China, 1994; active mem. Universal Life Keeping Problems Acad., Dept. Justice Russian Fedn., Moscow. Decorated commendatore dell'Ordine al Merito (Italy); NSF rsch. grantee, 1967-69; Named Tchr. of Year, Aesculapius Med. Arts Soc., C.W. Post Coll. of L.I. U., 1967; Disting. Faculty Mem. of Year, C.W. Post Ctr. L.I. U., 1977, Educator of Yr. WLIW Channel 21, 1996, Officier dans l'ordre des Palmes Académiques, 2001; recipient George M. Estabrook award Hofstra U., 1978, Higher Edn. Leadership award Corning Glass Works, 1987, Disting. Leadership award L.I., 1989, Diploma Merito Garibaldi Inst., Rome, Diploma of Honor, Rsch. Ctr. for Islamic History, Art and Culture, Istanbul, Turkey, Advancement for Commerce and Industry Disting. Svc. award in field of edn., 1997. Mem. AAAS, Coun. Advancement and Support of Edn., Am. Assn. Collegiate Registrars and Admissions Officers, Am. Assn. Higher Edn., Am. Inst. Biol. Scis., Am. Soc. Zoologists, Am. Assn. U. Adminstrs., Commn. on Ind. Colls. and Univs. (trustee), Nat. Assn. Biology Tchrs., Nat. Sci. Tchrs. Assn., Soc. Protozoologists, N.Y. Acad. Scis., Camilo Josè Cela Found. (hon.), Met. Assn. Coll. and Univ. Biologists (founder, mem. steering com.), Bus. Coun. N.Y., Oakdale C. of C. (founding mem., dir.), Russian Soc. Plant Physiologists (corr.), Universal Life Keeping Problems Acad. Moscow, Tsiolkovski Space Acad. Moscow (fgn.), Univ. Club (N.Y.C.), Wings Club (N.Y.C.), Nat. Arts Club (N.Y.C.), L.I. Coun. Fgn. Rels., L.I. Assn. Commerce and Industry (v.p. edn., dir.), Alpha Chi, Kappa Delta Pi, Phi Delta Kappa, Sigma Xi, Beta Beta Beta, Alpha Eta Rho, Delta Mu Delta, Kappa Delta Rho. E-mail: vpmphd@aol.com.

MESLANG, SUSAN WALKER, educational administrator; b. Norfolk, Va., Sept. 15, 1947; d. Stanley Clay and Sybil Bruce (Moore) Walker. BS in Edn., Old Dominion U., 1973, MS in Spl. Edn., 1986. Cert. tchr., Va.; cert. grants specialist Nat. Grant Writers Assn. Child devel. specialist Norfolk Pub. Sch., 1973-77, tchr. spl. edn., 1979-82, San Diego Pub. Schs., 1977-79; ednl. evaluator Va. Ctr. Psychiatry, Portsmouth, 1983-84; instr. child study, spl. edn. Norfolk, 1990—; dir. CHANCE Program, Norfolk, 1983—; dir. rsch. & grants devel. Darden Coll. Edn. Old Dominion U., 1989—. Cons. Eastern Va. Ctr. Children & Youths, Norfolk, 1993—, Cmty. Mental Health Ctr., Portsmouth, Va., 1993—. Bd. dirs. Va. Zool. Soc., Norfolk, 1990—, Va. Opera Assn., Norfolk, 1995—; mem. Norfolk Democratic com., 1995—, Children's Hosp. King's Downtown Cir., 1994—; dir. Va. Assistive Tech. Southeast Va. Dept. Rhabilitative Svcs., Norfolk, 1992—. Recipient Honor award Norfolk Commn. Persons with Disabilities, 1993, Commendation Va. House, 1994. Mem. Assn. Persons Supported Employment, Regional Grants Collaboration Group, Norfolk Pub. Schs. Spl. Edn. Adv. Com., Hampton Rds. Coalition Persons with Phys. & Sensory Disabilities. Democrat. Methodist. Avocations: tennis, sailing, walking. Office: Old Dominion U Coll Edn 4607 Hampton Blvd Norfolk VA 23508

MESSBARGER, EDWARD JOSEPH, physical education educator, university coach; b. Parnell, Mo., July 26, 1932; s. Fred A. and Anna (O'Day) M.; m. Jane Schneider, June 17, 1961; children: Edward, Letitia, Monica. BS in Secondary Edn., Northwest Mo. State, 1956; MA in Health and Phys. Edn., No. Colo. State, 1958. Coach, tchr. Fillmore (Mo.) High Sch., 1956-57; coach AD, dept. chair, tchr. Benedictine Heights Coll., Tulsa, 1957-60, U. Dallas, 1960-63; coach, dept. chmn. St. Mary's U., San Antonio, 1963-78; assoc. prof., basketball coach Angelo State U., San Angelo, Tex., 1978—. Banquet speaker, Tex., Mo., Ill., Kans., Okla, 1957—. Contbr. articles to profl. jours. Active basketball clinics, Tex., 1957-90; mem. Mayor's Coun. for Handicapped, San Angelo, 1978—. With USN, 1952-54, Korea. Named Conf. Coach of Yr. Big State Conf., Tex., Lone Star Conf., Nat. Coach of Yr. Nat. Assn. Intercollegiate Athletics, 1974, Tex. Major Coll. Coach of Yr., State of Tex., 1974, to Hall of Fame Nat. Assn. Intercollegiate Athletics, 1990, to Northwest Mo. Athletic Hall of Fame, 1990, to St. Mary's Athletic Hall of Fame, 1991. Mem. Am. Alliance for Health, Phys. Edn., Recreation and Dance, Tex. Assn. Basketball Coaches, Tex. Assn. Coll. Tchrs., Coaches Assn., Nat. Assn. Intercollegiate Athletics Coaches Assn., Nat. Assn. Basketball Coaches (publs. com.), KC. Roman Catholic. Avocations: golf, water sports. Home: 5218 N Bentwood Dr San Angelo TX 76904-8701 Office: Angelo State U Ave N At Jefferson San Angelo TX 76909-0001

MESSERSCHMIDT, JOYCE IRENE, retired elementary school educator; b. LaGrange Twp., Wis. Teaching cert., Racine Kenosha Norman Sch., 1948; BEd, Wis. State Coll., Whitewater, 1957; MS, U. Wis., Whitewater, 1973. Cert. elem. tchr., Wis. 2d grade tchr. Elkhorn (Wis.) Area Schs.; kindergarten and 1st grade tchr. Sharon (Wis.) Community Schs.; rural sch. tchr. Walworth County, Elkhorn; 1st grade tchr. Elkhorn (Wis.) Area Schs.; ret., 1993. Cooperating tchr. for student tchrs. and interns, mentor for 1st yr. tchrs., chmn. kindergarten-3d grade level Elkhorn Area Schs. Commendation cert. Kenosha, Racine and Walworth Counties, 1993. Mem. NEA, Wis. Edn. Assn., Elkhorn Edn. Assn. (mem. coms.), So. Wis. Edn. Assn., Kiwanis (Tchr. of Yr. 1991), Alpha Delta Kappa (past pres., v.p., sec., mem. coms., chair local chpt., state corr. sec.).

MESSICK, RICHARD DOUGLAS, educational administrator; b. Andalusia, Ala., Feb. 15, 1931; s. Verbia Travis and Mary Lizzie (Carter) M.; m. Sara Alice Murphy, June 23, 1957; 1 child, Sarah Cordelia Messick Champion. BS in Sci., Troy State U., 1956; MA in Trade and Indsl. Edn., U. Ala., 1968; postgrad., Troy State U., 1974. Farmer Abbeville (Ala.) Farm, 1949-52, 62-64; phys. lab. tester Gulf Oil Corp., Mobile, Ala., 1956; mathematician Vitro Corp., Eglin AFB, Fla., 1958-62; computer programmer Lytle Corp., Eglin AFB, 1958-62; tchr. math. Abbeville High Sch., 1964-65, coord. trade and industry, 1965—. Author: (poetry) The Teachers Verse, 1985, Red Neck Country Humor, 1993. Mem. Ala. Vocat. Assn. (plaque 1986, T & I Vocat. Tchr. of Yr. award 1992), Ala. Vocat. Indsl. Clubs Am. Assn. (Advisor of Yr. award 1985), Henry County Vocat. Edn. Assn. (voting del. 1983, treas. 1983-84, pres. 1985, 91-92), Kiwanis (pres. Abbeville 1970-71, treas. 1975), Abbeville High Sch. Vocat. Indsl. Club Am. (sponsor 1968-92), Abbeville High Sch. Key Club (sponsor 1988-92). Democrat. Baptist. Avocations: farming, gardening, serving as santa claus in christmas parades. Home: PO Box 191 Abbeville AL 36310-0191 Office: Abbeville High Sch PO Box 519 300 S Trawick St Abbeville AL 36310-2433

MESSINA, PAUL FRANCIS, education consultant; b. Newport, R.I., Aug. 31, 1962; s. Nunzio Francis and Ilse Ingeborg (Maibaum) M. BS, SUNY, Albany, 1988; MS, Tex. A&M, Texarkana, 1992. Cert. tchr., Tex., La. Instr. math and physics St. Mary's High Sch., Natcitoches, La., 1989-91, Liberty-Eylau High Sch., Texarkana, Tex., 1991-93, chm. dept. sci., 1992-93; preventive medicine officer U.S. Army, 1993-98; edn. cons. Hewlett-Packard Co., Irving, Tex., 1998—. Adj. instr. physics Northwestern State U., Natchitoches, 1989-91; adj. instr. math. Texarkana Coll., 1991-93; mem. Merrill Pub. Physics Adv. Coun., 1990-93; adj. instr. physics Ga. Mil. Coll., 1993-95. With U.S. Army, 1988-89, USAR. Tandy Tech. scholar Tandy Corp., 1992; grantee Eisenhower mini-grant, Liberty-Eylau Ind. Sch. Dist., Texarkana, 1992. Mem. NEA, Tex. State Tchrs. Assn. (bldg. rep.), Am. Assn. Physics Tchrs., Tex. Acad. Sci., Sci. Tchrs. Assn. Tex., Cen. La. Astronomy Soc., U.S. Profl. Tennis Registry, Nat. Tennis Acad. Roman Catholic. Avocations: tennis, computing, music. Office: U Tex San Antonio 6900 N Loop 1604 W San Antonio TX 78249 Home: 117 1st St Boerne TX 78006-2910

MESSING, CAROL SUE, communications educator; b. Bronx, N.Y. d. Isidore and Esther Florence (Burtoff) Weinberg; m. Sheldon H. Messing; children: Lauren, Robyn. BA, Bklyn. Coll., 1967, MS, 1970. Tchr. N.Y.C. Bd. Edn., 1967-72; prof. lang. arts Northwood U., Midland, Mich., 1973-93, prof., 1993—. Owner Job Match, Midland, 1983-85; cons. Mich. Credit Union League, Saginaw, 1984-87, Nat. Hotel & Restaurant, Midland, 1985-89, Univ. Coll. program, Continuing Edn. program, Northwood U., 1986—, Dow Chem. Employee's Credit Union, 1988—. Author: (anthology) Symbiosis, 1985, rev. edit., 1987, Controlling Communication, 1987, rev. edit., 1993, Creating Effective Team Presentations, 1995; co-author: PRIMIS, 1993. Mem. LWV, Nat Coun. Tchrs. English, Kappa Delta Pi, Delta Mu Delta (advisor). Avocations: reading, sewing. Office: Northwood U 4000 Whiting Dr Midland MI 48640-2311

MESSNER, RICHARD STEPHEN, school system administrator; b. N.Y.C., Nov. 8, 1939; s. Blasius and Anna (Kuti) M.; m. Eugenia Mancuso, Oct. 22, 1968 (div. 1974); 1 child, Stephanie; m. Mary Theodorakis, May 28, 1976' stepchildren: Paul, Nicole. BS, Alderson-Broaddus Coll., 1961; MBA, Fairleigh Dickinson U., 1972; MEd, Rutgers U., 1980. Acctg. mgr. McGraw-Hill, Hightstown, N.J., 1968-71; bus. coord. Fairleigh Dickinson U., Rutherford, N.J., 1971-73; dep. treas. County of Somerset, Somerville, N.J., 1973-78; asst. dir. of adminstrv. svcs. Somerset County Vo-Tech, Bridgewater, N.J., 1978-82; dir. adminstrv. svcs. Somerset County Vocat. Tech., Bridgewater, 1982-85, asst. supt. for bus., 1985—, acting supt., 1987-88, supt. of schs., 1992—. Bd. dirs. Edn. Svcs. Commn., Somerset County. Dep. mayor Franklin Twp., N.J., 1975, mayor, 1975-76; commr. Urban Enterprize Zone Authority, N.J., 1984—; treas. Somerset County Reps., 1985-91; bd. dirs. Somerset Alliance Future, 1992—, Greater Raritan Pvt. Industry Coun., 1992—; mem. Middlesex, Hunterdon, Somerset Pvt. Industry Coun., 1992—; co-chair Somerset ITV Consortium Inc.; bd. dirs. Greater Raritan Valley Workforce Investment Bd, Somerset County Workforce Investment Bd., 1992—; trustee Somerset/Hunterdon Bus.- Edn. Partnership, 1992—. With U.S. Army, 1962-64. Recipient Outstanding Bus. Person of the Yr., Somerset County C. of C., 1995. Mem. Am. Soc. Bus. Officers Internat. (chmn. purchasing com. Reston, Va. chpt. 1986-88, legis. com. 1988—), N.J. Assn. Bus. Ofcls. (chmn. legis. com. Bordentown, N.J. chpt. 1985—), N.J. Assn. Sch. Adminstrs., Somerset County Adminstrs., Somerset County Bus. Ofcls. (v.p. Somerville chpt. 1991—), N.J. Edn. Assn. (adv. com. 1984—), VFW, Masons, Phi Delta Kappa. Baptist. Avocations: sports, world war ii history, golf. Home: 32 Pin Oak Rd Skillman NJ 08558-1320

MESTAD, GARY ALLEN, education educator; b. Mason City, Iowa, Feb. 14, 1946; s. Orval Alden and Trina W. (Linne) M.; m. Merikay Linda Marth, Aug. 15, 1970. BS, Mankato State U., 1970; MS, Drake U., 1997. Cert. tchr., Iowa. Tchr. social studies Garner-Hayfield Schs., Garner, Iowa, 1970—; head coach high sch. varsity girls' softball Garner Hayfield Schs., Iowa; head coach jr. high girls' softball. Sports writer Garner Leader and Signal, 1971—; contbr. articles on basketball instruction to profl. publs. Mem. NEA, Iowa State Edn. Assn., Iowa Mid. Sch. Assn., Garner-Hayfield Tchrs. Assn., Iowa Athletic Coaches Assn. Avocations: collecting baseball cards, phonograph records and compact discs. Home: 520 Grove Ave Garner IA 50438-1452 Office: Garner Hayfield Sch 1080 Division St Garner IA 50438-1740

METALLO, FRANCES ROSEBELL, mathematics educator; b. Jersey City, N.J. d. Vincenzo James and Lucille (Frank) M. BA in Math., Jersey City State Coll., 1985, MA in Math. Edn., 1987. Math. tchr. Emerson High Sch., Union City, N.J., 1990-92; math tchr. gifted/talented program Jefferson Annex Woodrow Wilson Sch. Dist. Union City, 1992-95; math tchr. Woodrow Wilson Sch., Dist. Union City, 1995—. Adj. tchr. math. Hudson County C.C., 1987—, Jersey City State Coll., 1986—, tutor, 1983-86; reviewer for Nat. Coun. Tchrs. Math mag., A Plus for Kids Tchr. Network, 1994, grantee 1993, 96 Contbr. articles to profl. publs.; author, History of the Abacus and Study of Sorubah, The Abaacus: It's History and Application Module 17, A concise Dictionary of Math and Symbols, Smile, Basic Algebra is Fun. Nominee Pres. award for sci. and math tchg. Mem. Nat. Coun. Tchrs. Math., Assn. Math. Tchrs. of N.J., Alumni Assn. Jersey City State Coll., Math. Assn. Am., Am. Soc. Prevention of Cruelty to Animals, Assn. of Women in Math., Am. Math. Soc., Dozenal Soc., Kappa Delta Pi, Phi Delta Kappa. Avocations: developing classroom math. materials, crochet, embroidery, piano. Office: 80 Hauxhurst Ave Weehawken NJ 07086-6837

METCALF, ETHEL EDGERTON, retired elementary school educator; b. Rutherfordton, N.C. d. John Harris and Estelle Caroline (Weeks) Edgerton; m. John Samuel Metcalf, June 3, 1954; children: Anne, Caroline. AA, Gardner-Webb Coll., 1951; BS, Limestone Coll., 1953. Cert. secondary and elem. tchr. Tchr. Harris (N.C.) High Sch., 1953-57, Glenwood (N.C.) High Sch., 1958-59, Paris High Sch., Greenville, S.C., 1959-60, Nebo (N.C.) High Sch., 1961-62; tchr. spl. edn. Forest City (N.C.) Elem. Sch., 1962-64; tchr. Mt. Vernon Elem. Sch., Forest City, 1965-68, North Belmont (N.C.) Elem. Sch., 1969-70, Ruth Elem. Sch., Rutherfordton, N.C., 1970-92. Cheerleader advisor, Ruth Sch., 1975-80, chair sci. fair, 1980-88, organizer, advisor Just Say No club, 1985-92. Mem. NEA, N.C. Assn. Educators (sch. rep. 1980-85). Democrat. Baptist. Avocations: writing, drawing/painting, swimming, crafts, walking. Home: 3635 Hudlow Rd Rutherfordton NC 28139-8063

METCALF, PHILIP LESLIE, mathematics educator, career/technical coordinator; b. North Webster, Ind., Aug. 28, 1948; s. William Edwin and Edna Lunetta (Lentz) M.; m. Karilyn Sue Fetterhoff, Aug. 9, 1970. BS, Ball State U., 1970; MS, St. Francis Coll., 1975. Tchr. math. Wawasee Cmty. Schs., Syracuse, Ind., 1971-97, career and tech. coord., 1999—. Vis. prof. Ball State U., Muncie, Ind., 1997-99. Mem. study commn. Ind. State Govt., Indpls., 1989-91, mem. profl. stas. bd., 1992-98, chairperson, 1994-98; bd. visitors Butler U.; Tchrs. Coll. alumni bd. Ball State U. Sgt. U.S. Army NG, 1970-76. Awarded Sagamore of the Wabash, Gov. of Ind., 1999. Mem. NEA, Assn. Tchr. Educators, Nat. Coun. Accreditation of Tchrs. Edn. (bd. examiners 1993-98), Ind. State Tchrs. Assn. (bd. dirs. 1991-98), Wawasee Cmty. Educators Assn. (pres. 1981), Am. Assn. Career and Tech. Educators, Ind. ASsn. Area Vocat. Dists., North Ctrl. Assn. (amb. 2002—), Sigma Alpha Epsilon. Democrat. Baptist. Avocations: gardening, body-building, movies, reading, piano. Home: 624 S Dixie Dr North Webster IN 46555-9404 Office: Wawasee High Sch 1 Warrior Path Bldg 1 Syracuse IN 46567-9170 E-mail: metp@wawasee.k12.in.us.

METCALF, VIRGIL ALONZO, economics educator; b. Branch, Ark., Jan. 4, 1936; s. Wallace Lance and Luella J. (Yancey) M.; m. Janice Ann Maples, July 2, 1958; children: Deborah Ann, Robert Alan. BS in Gen. Agr., U. Ark., 1958, MS in Agrl. Econs., 1960; Diploma in Econs., U. Copenhagen, 1960; PhD in Agrl. Econs., U. Mo., 1964. Asst. prof. U. Mo., Columbia, 1964-65, asst. to chancellor, 1964-69, assoc. prof., 1965-69, prof., exec. asst. to the chancellor, 1969-71; prof. econs., v.p. administrn. Ariz. State U., Tempe, 1971-81, prof. Sch. Agribus. and Natural Resources, 1981-88, prof. internat. bus. Coll. of Bus., 1988—99, prof. emeritus, 2000—. Asst. to the chancellor U. Mo., 1964-69, coord. internat. programs and studies, 1965-69, mem. budget com., 1965-71, chmn., co-chmn. several task forces; cons. Ford Found., Bogota, Colombia, 1966-67; mem. negotiating team U.S. Agy. for Internat. Devel., Mauritania, 1982, cons., Cameroon, 1983, agrl. rsch. specialist, India, 1984, agribus. cons., Guatemala, 1987, 88, asst. dir. Reform Coops. Credit Project, El Salvador, 1987-90; co-dir. USIA univ. linkage grant Cath. U., Bolivia, 1984-89; cons. World Vision Internat., Mozambique, 1989. Contbr. numerous articles to profl. jours. Mem. City of Tempe U. Hayden Butte Project Area Com., 1979; bd. commrs. Columbia Redevel. Authority; mem. workable project com. City of Columbia Housing Authority. Econs. officer USAR, 1963, econ. analyst, 1964-66. Fulbright grantee U. Copenhagen, 1959-60, U. Kiril Metodij, Yugoslavia, 1973. Mem. Am. Assn. Agrl. Economists, Soc. for Internat. Devel., Samaritans (chmn. 1976, bd. dirs. 1976, mem. task force of health svc. bd. trustees 1974, health svc. 1974-78, chmn. program subcom. 1975), Kiwanis, Blue Key, Gamma Sigma Delta, Alpha Zeta, Alpha Tau Alpha. Democrat. Home: 1357 W Crystal Springs Dr Gilbert AZ 85233-6606

METIU, HORIA ION, chemistry educator; b. Cluj, Romania, Mar. 7, 1940; s. Ion and Erna (Weisser) M.; m. Jane Farrell, Oct. 8, 1971; children: Michael, Ion. BSChemE, Politechnic Inst., Bucharest, 1961; PhD in Theoretical Chemistry, MIT, 1974. Postdoctoral fellow MIT, Cambridge, Mass., 1974-75, U. Chgo., 1975-76; prof. U. Calif., Santa Barbara, 1976—. Mem. exec. com. phys. chemistry div. Am. Chem. Soc., 1992. Assoc. editor, mem. editl. bd. Jour. Chem. Physics; mem. editl. bd. Jour. Phys. Chemistry; contbr. over 300 articles to profl. jours. Named Sloan fellow, 1978, Dreyfus Tchr.-scholar, 1978, Solid State Chemistry Exxon fellow, 1979, Fellow of Japan Soc. for the Promotion of Sci., 1992. Fellow Am. Phys. Soc.; mem. Am. Chem. Soc. Achievements include devel. of Metastable Quenching Spectroscopy; devel. of theory of rate constants for chem. reactions; theory of photodissociation with short pulses; theory of crystal surface growth; theory of surface enhanced spectroscopy. Home: 1482 Crestline Dr Santa Barbara CA 93105-4635 Office: U Calif Santa Barbara CA 93106

METRAS, GARY (LEO), English educator; b. Holyoke, Mass., Apr. 1, 1947; s. Albert Herve and Doris Rita (Suprenant) M.; m. Natalie Lukiwsky, Oct. 19, 1968; children: Jason Gary, Nadia Mary. BA in English magna cum laude, U. Mass., 1972; MA in Creative Writing, Goddard Coll., Plainfield, Vt., 1981. Lic. secondary English tchr., Mass. Tchr. Hampshire Regional High Sch., Westhampton, Mass., 1972—2003, coord. Eng. dept., 1997—2003. Editor, pub. Adastra Press, Easthampton, 1979—. Author: The Night Watches, 1981, Destiny's Calendar, 1985, Seven Stones for Seven Poems, 1990, Seagull Beach, 1995, Today's Lesson, 1997, Until There is Nothing Left, 2003; editor: The Adastra Reader, 1987; contbg. editor Rag Mag. Lit. Jour., Goodhue, Minn., 1984-85. Sgt. USAF, 1966—70. Mass. fellow in poetry Mass. Found. for Arts, 1984. Home: 16 Reservation Rd Easthampton MA 01027-1227

METREY, GEORGE DAVID, social work educator, academic administrator; b. Milw., July 23, 1939; s. Richard Joseph and Catherine (Evans) M.; m. Cheryl Ann Mosca, June 21, 1969 (dec. May 7, 2000); 1 child, Mary Beth. AB, Marquette U., 1961; MSW, Fordham U., 1963; PhD, NYU, 1970. Lic. ind. clin. social worker, R.I., N.J. Social worker N.J. Diagnostic Ctr., Edison, 1963-64, asst. social work supr., 1964-66, dir. psychiat. social work, 1966-70; coordinator undergrad. social work program Kean Coll., N.J., 1970-73, assoc. prof. social work, 1970-74, prof., 1974-79, chmn. dept. sociology, anthropology and social work, 1973-77, dir. social work program, acting assoc. dean Sch. Arts and Sci., 1977-79; dean Sch. Social Work, prof. R.I. Coll., Providence, 1979—, ast. v.p. acad. affairs, 2000—02. Field instr. Fordham U. Sch. Social Service, 1966-70, adj. prof., 1969-77; adj. assoc. prof. Rutgers U. Grad. Sch. Social Work, 1972-73 Mem. program com. R.I. affiliate Am. Heart Assn., 1980-90, bd. dirs., 1983-89, chmn. program com., 1985-87, exec. com., 1985-87; sec. bd. dirs. Adoption R.I., 1987-89, pres. bd. dirs., 1989-92. Recipient Fordham U. Grad. Sch. Social Svc. Outstanding Alumni, 1984, Spl. Disting. Svc. award R.I. Coll. Alumni Assn., 1996. Mem. NASW (N.J. Social Worker of Yr. 1977, pres. 1978-80, parliamentarian R.I. 1981—, treas. R.I. chpt. 1986-87, mem. nat. competence cert. commn. 1989-91, nat. 2d v.p. 1978-80, chair nat. program com. 1981-83), Coun. on Social Work Edn. (bd. dirs. 1979-82, mem. commn. on accreditation 1996-2002, mem. commn. on ednl. policy, 2002—), Acad. Cert. Social Workers, Nat. Assn. Deans and Dirs. Schs. Social Work (nominating com. 1993-96, program com. 1993-96), Alpha Phi Omega, Gamma Pi Mu, Alpha Delta Mu (regional v.p.). Roman Catholic. Home: PO Box 206 Wyckoff NJ 07481-0206 Office: RI Coll Sch Social Work Providence RI 02908 E-mail: gmctrey@ric.edu.

METZ, DONALD JOSEPH, retired science educator; b. Bklyn., May 18, 1924; s. Emil Arthur and Madeline Margaret (Maas) M.; m. Dorothy Gorman, Aug. 30, 1947. BS, St. Francis Coll., Bklyn., 1947; DSc (hon.), St. Francis Coll., 1984; MS, N.Y. Poly. U., 1949, PhD, 1955. From lectr. to prof. St. Francis Coll., 1947-76; from assoc. to sr. scientist sci. edn. Brookhaven Nat. Lab., Upton, N.Y., 1954-93, ret., 1993. Ednl. cons. Brookhaven Nat. Lab., Upton, N.Y., 1993-95. With U.S. Army, 1943-46, ETO. Roman Catholic. Home: 147 Southern Blvd East Patchogue NY 11772-5810

METZ, HELEN CHAPIN, retired Middle East analyst; b. Beijing, Apr. 13, 1928; d. Selden and Mary Paul (Noyes) Chapin; m. Ronald Irwin Metz, July 14, 1951; children: Mary Selden Metz Evans, Helen Winchester Metz Ketchum, Grace Chapin Metz. AB, Vassar Coll., 1949; MA, Am. U., Beirut, 1954; postgrad., Berkeley Div. Sch. of Yale U., 1966-69. Hostess to The Honorable Selden Chapin, U.S. Amb. to the Netherlands, The Hague, 1950; instr. Beirut Coll. for Women (now Beirut Univ. Coll.), 1954-55, Madeira Sch., Greenway, Va., 1959-60; rsch. analyst Arabian Am. Oil Co., Dhahran, Saudi Arabia, 1956-58, 63-66; administrv. asst. Office Anglican Archbishop, Jerusalem, 1969-75; instr. Mercyhurst Coll., Erie, Pa., 1977-79; exec. dir. Internat. Inst., Erie, 1978-81; dep. head, devel. officer Brent Internat. Sch., Baguio, Philippines, 1981-82; analyst, sr. analyst Fed. Rsch. div. Libr. of Congress, Washington, 1983-87, supr. Middle East, North Africa, 1987-90, supr. Middle East, Africa, Latin Am., 1990-99. Editor: Libya: A Country Study, 1989, Iran: A Country Study, 1989, Iraq: A Country Study, 1990, Israel: A Country Study, 1990, Jordan: A Country Study, 1991, Egypt: A Country Study, 1992, Nigeria: A Country Study, 1992, Sudan: A Country Study, 1992, Somalia: A Country Study, 1993, Saudi Arabia: A Country Study, 1993, Persian Gulf States: Country Studies, 1994, Algeria: A Country Study, 1995, Indian Ocean: Five Island Countries, 1995, Turkey: A Country Study, 1996, Dominican Republic and Haiti: Country Studies, 2002. Mentor Edn. for Ministry St. Margaret's Ch., Washington, 1984-92, 99—; mem. mission devel. adv. com. Diocese Washington, 1987-90, mem. evangelism com., 1990-93. Vassar Coll. fellow, 1954-55. Mem. Middle East Studies Assn., Middle East Inst., Phi Beta Kappa (prize, 1949). Democrat. Episcopalian. Avocations: reading, double-crostics. Home: 3001 Veazey Ter NW Apt 334 Washington DC 20008-5455 E-mail: hchapinmetz@aol.com.

METZ, PHILIP JOHN, mathematics educator; b. Paterson, N.J., Aug. 22, 1939; s. Peter William and Clara (Ferraro) M.; m. Dorothy C. Miller, Aug. 1, 1970; children: Christine, Philip Jr. BA, St. Francis U., Bklyn., 1970; MEd, William Paterson U., 1980. Cert. elem. social studies, math. tchr., N.J. 6th grade tchr. Notre Dame Sch., New Hyde Park, N.Y., 1960-62; 7th and 8th grade tchr. St. Brigid's Sch., Bklyn., 1963-69; 6th and 7th grade tchr. St. Brendan's Sch., Clifton, N.J., 1970-72; 8th grade tchr. Holy Name Sch., Garfield, N.J., 1972-74; spl. edn. math. tchr. Passaic County Vocat. Tech. High Sch., Wayne, N.J., 1974-76; adj. instr. Passaic County C.C., Paterson, N.J., 1976-78, assoc. prof. math., 1978—. Textbook reviewer Harper Collins Pub., Chgo., 1991-92, Scott Foresman, N.Y.C., 1989-90; cons. math. grants; active weekend programs for gifted and talented, Passaic County Community Coll., Paterson, 1988-90; presenter workshops in field. Recipient plaque for Outstanding Svc. Passaic County Community Coll. Faculty Assn. Mem. Math. Assn. Am., N.J. Edn. Assn. (local treas. 1978—), Math. Assn Two Yr. Colls. N.J., William Paterson Alumni Assn., St. Francis Alumni Assn. Democrat. Roman Catholic. Avocations: fishing, coins, sports. Home: 45 Garden Ave # 2 West Paterson NJ 07424-3337

METZ, ROXIE ANNE, art educator; b. New Rochelle, N.Y., July 2, 1955; d. Calvin Leon and Dorothy Mary (Belton) Metz. B.F.A., Coll. New Rochelle, 1978, M.A. in Art/Psychology, 1984. Asst. residence supr. Westchester Assn. for Retarded Citizens, White Plains, N.Y., 1978-79; art tchr. New Rochelle City Sch. Dist., 1979— . Vol. New Rochelle Hosp. Med. Ctr., 1977— ; active New Rochelle Community Action Agy., 1973-74; art tchr. Hawthorne (N.Y.) Cedar Knolls Union Free Sch. Dist. Mem. N.Y. State United Tchrs., Am. Fedn. Tchrs. Democrat. Christian. Address: 80 Guion Pl Apt 8T New Rochelle NY 10801-3837

METZGER, BRUCE MANNING, clergyman, educator; b. Middletown, Pa., Feb. 9, 1914; s. Maurice Rutt and Anna Mary (Manning) M.; m. Isobel E. Mackay, July 7, 1944; children— John Mackay, James Bruce. AB, Lebanon Valley Coll., 1935, DD, 1951; ThB, Princeton Theol. Sem., 1938, ThM, 1939; AM, Princeton U., 1940, PhD, 1942; LHD (hon.), Findlay U., 1962; DD (hon.), St. Andrews U., Scotland, 1964; DTheol (hon.), Münster U., Fed. Republic Germany, 1970; DLitt (hon.), Potchefstroom U., South Africa, 1985. Ordained to ministry Presbyn. Ch. USA, 1939. Teaching fellow N.T. Princeton Theol. Sem., 1938-40, mem. faculty, 1940—, prof. N.T. lang. and lit., 1954-64, George L. Collord prof. N.T. lang. and lit., 1964-84, emeritus, 1984—. Vis. lectr. Presbyn. Theol. Sem. South, Campinas, Brazil, 1952, Presbyn. Theol. Sem. North, Recife, Brazil, 1952; mem. Inst. for Advanced Study, Princeton, 1964-65, 73-74; scholar-in-residence Tyndale House, Cambridge, 1969; vis. fellow Clare Hall, Cambridge, 1974, Wolfson Coll., Oxford U., 1979, Macquarie U., Sydney, Australia, 1982, Caribbean Grad. Sch. of Theology, Jamaica, 1990, Seminario Internacional Teológico Bautista, Buenos Aires, 1991, Griffith Thomas Lectrs., Dallas Theol. Sem., 1992; mem. mng. com. Am. Sch. Classical Studies, Athens, Greece; mem. Standard Bible com. Nat. Coun. Chs., 1952—, chmn., 1975—; mem. seminar N.T. studies Columbia U., 1959-80; mem. Kuratorium of Vetus-Latina Inst., Beuron, Germany, 1959—; adv. com. Inst. N.T. Text Rsch., U. Münster, 1961—, Thesaurus Linguae Graecae, 1972-80; Collected Works of Erasmus, 1977—; chmn. Am. com. versions Internat. Greek N.T., 1950-88; participant internat. congresses scholars, Aarhus, Aberdeen, Bangor, Basel, Bonn, Brussels, Budapest, Cairo, Cambridge, Copenhagen, Dublin, Exeter, Frankfurt, Heidelberg, London, Louvain, Manchester, Milan, Munich, Münster, Newcastle, Nottingham, Oxford, Prague, Rome, St. Andrews, Stockholm, Strasbourg, Toronto, Trondheim, Tübingen; mem. Presbytery, N.B. Author: The Saturday and Sunday Lessons from Luke in the Greek Gospel Lectionary, 1944, Lexical Aids for Students of New Testament Greek, 1946, enlarged edit., 1955, A Guide to the Preparation of a Thesis, 1950, An Introduction to the Apocrypha, 1957, Chapters in the History of New Testament Textual Criticism, 1963, The Text of the New Testament, Its Transmission, Corruption, and Restoration, 1964, 3d enlarged edit., 1992, (with H.G. May) The Oxford Annotated Bible with the Apocrypha, 1965, The New Testament, Its Background, Growth, and Content, 1965, 3d edit., 2003, Index to Periodical Literature on Christ and the Gospels, 1966, Historical and Literary Studies, Pagan, Jewish, and Christian, 1968, Index to Periodical Literature on the Apostle Paul, 1960, 2nd edit., 1970, A Textual Commentary on the Greek New Testament, 1971, 2d edit., 1994, The Early Versions of the New Testament, 1977, New Testament Studies, 1980, Manuscripts of the Greek Bible, 1981, The Canon of the New Testament, 1987, (with Roland Murphy) The New Oxford Annotated Bible with the Apocrypha, 1991, (with M.D. Coogan) The Oxford Companion to the Bible, 1993, Breaking the Code-Understanding the Book of Revelation, 1993, Reminiscences of an Octogenarian, 1997, (with Coogan) The Oxford Guide to People & Places of the Bible, 2001, (with Coogan) The Oxford Guide to Ideas and Issues of the Bible, 2001, The Bible in Translation, Ancient and English Versions, 2001; mem. editorial com.: Critical Greek New Testament, 1956-84; chmn. Am. com., Internat. Greek New Testament Project, 1970-88; sec. com. translators: Apocrypha (rev. standard version); editor: New Testament Tools and Studies, 30 vols, 1960-2000, Oxford Annotated Apocrypha, 1965, enlarged edit., 1977; Reader's Digest Condensed Bible, 1982; co-editor: United Bible Societies Greek New Testament, 1966, 4th edit., 1993; compiler: Index of Articles on the New Testament and the Early Church Published in Festschriften, 1951, supplement, 1955, Lists of Words Occurring Frequently in the Coptic New Testament (Sahidic Dialect), 1961, Annotated Bibliography of the Textual Criticism of the New Testament, 1955, (with Isobel M. Metzger) Oxford Concise Concordance to the Holy Bible, 1962, (with R.C. Dentan and W. Harrelson), The Making of the New Revised Standard Version of the Bible, 1991; contbr. articles to jours. Chmn. standard bible com. Nat. Coun. Chs., 1977-2000. Recipient cert. Disting. Svc. Nat. Coun. Chs., 1957, Disting. Alumnus award Lebanon Valley Coll. Alumni Assn., 1961, citation of appreciation Laymen's Nat. Bible Assn., 1986, Disting. Alumnus award Princeton Theol. Sem., 1989, lit. competition prize Christian Rsch. Found., 1955, 62, 63, E.T. Thompson award, 1991. Mem. Am. Philos. Soc., Soc. Bibl. Lit. (pres. 1970-71, past del. Am. Coun. Learned Socs.), Am. Bible Soc. (bd. mgrs. 1948—, chmn. com. transls. 1964-70), Am. Philol. Assn., Studiorum Novi Testamenti Societas (pres. 1971-72), Cath. Bibl. Assn., N.Am. Patristic Soc. (pres. 1972), Soc. Textual Scholarship (pres. 1995), Am. Soc. Papyrologists; hon. fellow, corr. mem. Higher Inst. Coptic Studies, Cairo; corr. fellow Brit. Acad. (Burkitt medal in Bibl. studies 1994). Republican. Home: 20 Cleveland Ln Princeton NJ 08540-3050 Office: Princeton Theol Sem 64 Mercer St Princeton NJ 08542-0803 E-mail: denise.schwalb@ptsem.edu.

METZGER, CAROLYN DIBBLE, accountant, educator; b. South Bend, Ind., May 27, 1924; d. Harry Hurlburt and Mae Floretta (Parker) Dibble; m. Franklin Dale Metzger, Aug. 17, 1946; children: Lawrence, Bruce, Douglas. BS in Acctg. with honors, Ind. U., South Bend, 1972, MS in Bus. Adminstrn., 1975. CPA, Ind. Ptnr. Metzger and Co. CPAs, South Bend, 1972-84; mng. ptnr. Metzger and Mancini CPAs, South Bend, 1984-93. Adj. prof. Ind. U., South Bend, 1975-90. Treas. St. Joseph County Rep. Party, 1973-79, co-auditor candidate, 1973, 77; mem. exec. coun. audit com. Ind. U., Bloomington, 1978-88; mem. alumni bd. dirs. Ind. U., South Bend, 1974-81, orgn. com., 1973, founding pres., 1974, rep. to alumni assn., exec. coun., 1975-81, chancellor's com. on curriculum priorities, 1975; bd. dirs., sec., vice chmn. Michiana Community Hosp., 1977-80, 90-93; vol. speaker Women in Bus., 1975-91; guest tour guide Spl. Olympics, Chgo., 1987, numerous others; mem. Hoosiers for Higher Edn., 1992—. Recipient Athena award South Bend C. of C., 1992, Alumni award Ind. U., 1993. Mem. AICPA (mem. exam, tax forms and sml. bus. coms., Pub. Svc. award 1989), Ind. CPA Soc. (mem. ethics com., bd. dirs., Pub. Svc. award 1989), Am. Women's Soc. CPAs (nat. bd. dirs. 1979-81, charter pres. local chpt. 1982), Nat. Assn. Accts. (pres. 1978-79, bd. dirs.), Order of the Eastern Star. Presbyterian. Avocations: pilot, volunteering, reading, swimming, travel. Home and Office: Metzger and Mancini CPAs PO Box 4143 South Bend IN 46634-4143

METZGER, VERNON ARTHUR, management educator, consultant; b. Baldwin Park, Calif., Aug. 13, 1918; s. Vernon and Nellie C. (Ross) Metzger; m. Beth Alrene Metzger, Feb. 19, 1955; children: Susan, Linda, David. BS, U. Calif., Berkeley, 1947, MBA, 1948. Estimating engr. C.F. Braun & Co., 1949; prof. mgmt. Calif. State U., Long Beach, 1949-89, prof. emeritus, 1989—, founder Sch. of Bus. Mgmt. cons. Mem. Fire Commn., Fountain Valley, Calif., 1959—60; mem. mgmt. task force to promote modern mgmt. in Yugoslavia, U.S. State Dept., 1977; mem. State of Calif. Fair Polit. Practices Commn., Orange County Transit Com.; pres. Orange County Dem. League, 1967—68. With USNR, 1942—45. Recipient Outstanding Svc. award, Orange County. Fellow: Soc. Advancement Mgmt. (life; dir.); mem.: Orange County Indsl. Rels. Rsch. Assn. (v.p.), Acad. Mgmt., Tau Kappa Upsilon, Alpha Kappa Psi, Beta gamma Sigma. Home: 1938 Balearic Dr Costa Mesa CA 92626-3513

METZLER, MARY FINK, elementary education educator; b. Washington, Feb. 14, 1931; d. Mathias Boger and Lucy Mae (Black) Fink; m. Irvin C. Smith, Jr., June 19, 1954 (div. June 1979); children: Cathy Ann, Irvin C. III, David Mathias, John Wesley; m. James Robert Metzler, Dec. 20, 1986; children: Kimberly, Michelle, James. BEd, U. Miami, 1955. Cert. tchr., Fla. Tchr. Duval County Sch. Bd., Jacksonville, Fla., 1955—. Instr. Dale Carnegie Courses, Jacksonville, 1979-89; storyteller Storytellers League of Jacksonville. Author: Sparkling Speech, 1982. Republican. Baptist-Methodist. Avocations: painting, community theatre, singing, public speaking, storytelling. Home: 2735 Safeshelter Dr W Jacksonville FL 32225-4740

METZLER, RUTH HORTON, genealogical educator; b. Eden, New York, Aug. 4, 1927; d. John Morris and Bernice Louise (Horton); m. Henry George Metzler, Sept. 4, 1948; children: Kathleen, Ronald, Janice, Margaret. Attended, Wheaton Coll., 1945-48; BA (hon.), Wilmington Coll., 1956; MLS, State Univ. of N.Y., Geneseo, 1962. Cert. tchr., libr. media splty., N.Y. Cataloging typist Peoria Pub. Libr., Ill., 1949-52; cataloging asst. Wilmington Coll. Libr., Ohio, 1953-56; sch. libr. K-12 Nunda Ctrl. Sch., NY, 1956-65; head libr. media ctr. Irondequoit H.S., Rochester, NY, 1965-84; pres. Rochester Geneal. Soc., NY, 1989-93; instr., lectr. Rochester Mus. and Sci. Ctr., NY, 1990—. Author of several family histories. Organizing instr. Genealogy workshops, Rochester Mus. and Sci. Ctr; contbg. lectr. Nat. Geneal. Conf., Rochester, 1990; others. Mem. N.Y. Libr. Assn.,;N.Y. State Tchr. Retirement Sys.; New Eng. Hist. and Geneal. Soc.; Kodak Geneal. Soc., N.Y.; State Coun. of Geneal.; Genealogy Round Table of Monroe County (del. 1996—); Rochester Geneal. Soc.; Geneal. Educators (organizing mem. 1996). Republican. Baptist. Avocations: family history photography, genealogy, writing.

METZNER, BARBARA STONE, university counselor; b. St. Louis, June 9, 1940; d. Wendell Phillips and Lois Custer (Rake) Metzner. AB, Ind. U., 1962, MS, 1964, EdD, 1983; BA, Purdue U., 1979. Asst. dean students U. Ill., Urbana, 1964-68; undergrad. advisor UCLA, 1966-69; asst. dean students Ohio State U., 1969-72; student affairs officer San Diego State U., 1972-76; sr. counselor Ind. U. - Purdue U., Indpls., 1976—. Supr. Ednl. Testing Svc., Indpls., 1980-90; cons. editl. bd. Nat. Acad. Advising Assn., Manhattan, Kans., 1987-93; adj. prof. Ind. U., 1987—; mgr. Info. Svcs. Univ. divsn. Ind. U.-Purdue U., Indpls., Ind., 1989-91. Contbr. articles to profl. jours., chpts. to books. Mem. Marion County Precinct Election Bd., 1980-92; mem. exec. com. Ind. Allied Health Assn., 1983-84; VIP escort Pan Am. Games, 1987. Spencer Found. grantee, 1985. Mem. AAAS, APA, Am. Edn. Rsch. Assn., Assn. Instl. Rsch., Kappa Alpha Theta (vol. charity benefits 1980-90), Phi Beta Kappa. Avocations: tennis, chinese cooking, fine arts. Office: IUPUI 815 W Michigan St Indianapolis IN 46202-5199

MEY, JACOB LOUIS, linguistics educator; b. Amsterdam, The Netherlands, Oct. 30, 1926; arrived in Denmark, 1952; s. Jacob Louis and Wynanda (Meyer) M.; m. Kari Lothe, July 15, 1957 (div. 1964); m. Inger Hansen, Sept. 18, 1965; children: Kari Anne, Sara Katrine, Jacob Louis IV, Inger Elise, Alexandra Rebecca, Kristianna Henrikke. Lic. in philosophy, U. Nijmegen, The Netherlands, 1951; PhD, U. Copenhagen, 1960; PhD (hon.), U. Zaragoza, Spain, 1993. Lectr. linguistics Oslo U., 1960-66; assoc. prof. U. Tex., Austin, 1966-72; prof. Odense (Denmark) U., 1972-96, J.W. Goethe U., Frankfurt, Germany, 1996-97, U. Campinas, Brazil, 1997, U. Haifa and Haifa Technion, Israel, 1998—99, Södertörns U. Coll., Stockholm, 1999, U. Brasília, 2000, 2002. Vis. assoc. prof. Georgetown U., Washington, 1967; rsch. fellow Rand Corp., Santa Monica, Calif., 1963; rsch. scientist Charles U., Prague, Czechoslovakia, 1965; vis. fellow Yale U., New Haven, 1979, Northwestern U., Evanston, Ill., 1989, 94-95, Warwick (Eng.) U., 1991; vis. scientist City U., Hong Kong, 1993-94; sr. rsch. assoc. Ctr. for Advanced Interdisciplinary Studies, Brasilia, Brazil, 2002-03. Author: La Catégorie du Nombre en Finnois Moderne, 1961, On the notion 'To Be' in Eskimo, 1969, Whose Language: A Study in Linguistic Pragmatics, 1985, Pragmatics: An Introduction, 1993, 2d edit., 2001, When Voices Clash: A Study in Literary Pragmatics, 2000, As Vozes da Sociedade, 2001; editor: Pragmalinguistics: Theory and Practice, 1979, Concise Ency. of Pragmatics, 1998; co-editor: Encyclopedia of Language and Linguistics, 1995, 2d edit., 2005; editor-in-chief Jour. Pragmatics, Oxford, Eng., 1977—, RASK Internat. Jour. Lang. and Comm., Odense, 1996—, assoc. editor-in-chief Internat. Jour. Cognition and Tech., 2001—03, mem. adv. bd. Pragmatics, 1988—, Discourse and Soc., 1990—, Psyke & Logos, 1988—, Revue de Sémantique et Pragmatique, 1997—, Text, 1998—, Miscellanea (Zaragoza), 1997—. Japan Found. scholar Tsukuba U., Ibaraki, Japan, 1983; fellow Sloane Found., 1979, Sasakawa Found., 1985, Andersen Cons., 1993. Mem. Linguistic Cir. Copenhagen, Linguistic Soc. Am., Internat. Pragmatics Assn. (mem. cons. bd. 1987—), Cognitive Technology Soc. (v.p. 2000—). Roman Catholic. Avocations: outdoor activities, water sports, bicycling, music, Japanese calligraphy. Address: 1100 W 29th St Austin TX 78703-1915 Office: U of So Denmark Inst Lang & Comm Campusvej 55 DK-5230 Odense Denmark E-mail: jam@language.sdu.dk.

MEYER, ANDREW U(LRICH), electrical engineer, educator, consultant; b. Berlin, Apr. 21, 1927; came to U.S., 1949; s. Edmund and Elsbeth (Stelzer) M.; m. Elisabeth Voigts, Dec. 26, 1964; children: Michele C., Lydia N. MS, Northwestern U., 1958, PhD, 1961. Devel. engr. Associated Rsch., Inc., Chgo., 1950, 53; project engr. Sun Electric Corp., Chgo., 1953-55; assoc. elec. engr. Armour Rsch. Found., Ill. Inst. Tech., Chgo., 1956-57; mem. tech. staff Bell Labs., Whippany, N.J., 1961-65; assoc. prof. elec. engring. NJ Inst. Tech., Newark, 1965—68, prof. elec. engring., 1968—2002, prof. emeritus, 2002—. Vis. prof. Middle East Tech. U., Ankara, Turkey, 1969-70. Author: (with J.C. Hsu) Modern Control Principles and Applications, 1968. With U.S. Army, 1951-52. Mem. IEEE (sec. new tech. and sci. activities com. 1967-68), IEEE Control Systems Soc. (chpt. chmn. 1964-65), AAAS, AAUP, Am. Automatic Control Coun. (biomed. systems com. 1975-84), Internat. Fedn. Automatic Control (biomed. systems com. 1975-84), Soc. Indsl. and Applied Math., Am. Soc. Engring. Edn., Internat. Assn. Math. and Computers in Simulation, N.Y. Acad. Sci., Assn. for Rsch. in Vision and Ophthalmology, Sigma Xi (pres. NJ chpt.), Eta Kappa Nu. Achievements include development of system analysis with application to biomedical engineering problems including modelling and clinical use of computers. Home: 746 Ridgewood Rd Millburn NJ 07041-1823 Office: NJ Inst Tech Elec/Computer Engring Dept University Heights Newark NJ 07102 E-mail: meyer@njit.edu.

MEYER, BETTY JANE, former librarian; b. Indpls., July 20, 1918; d. Herbert and Gertrude (Sanders) M.; B.A., Ball State Tchrs. Coll., 1940; B.S. in L.S., Western Res. U., 1945. Student asst. Muncie Public Library (Ind.), 1936-40; library asst. Ohio State U. Library, Columbus, 1940-42, cataloger, 1945-46, asst. circulation librarian, 1946-51, acting circulation librarian, 1951-52, adminstrv. asst. to dir. libraries, 1952-57, acting asso. reference librarian, 1957-58, cataloger in charge serials, 1958-65, head serial div. catalog dept., 1965-68, head acquisition dept., 1968-71, asst. dir. libraries, tech. services, 1971-76, acting dir. libraries, 1976-77, asst. dir. libraries, tech. services, 1977-83, instr. library adminstrn., 1958-63, asst. prof., 1963-67, asso. prof., 1967-75, prof., 1975-83, prof. emeritus, 1983—; library asst. Grandview Heights Public Library, Columbus, 1942-44; student asst. Case Inst. Tech., Cleve., 1944-45; mem. Ohio Coll. Library Center Adv. Com. on Cataloging, 1971-76, mem. adv. com. on serials, 1971-76, mem. adv. com. on tech. processes, 1971-76; mem. Inter-Univ. Library Council, Tech. Services Group, 1971-83; mem. bd. trustees Columbus Area Library and Info. Council Ohio, 1980-83. Ohio State U. grantee, 1975-76. Mem. ALA, Assn. Coll. and Research Libraries, AAUP, Ohio Library Assn. (nominating com. 1978-81), Ohioana Library Assn., Ohio Valley Group Tech. Services Librarians, No. Ohio Tech. Services Librarians, Franklin County Library Assn., Acad. Library Assn. Ohio, PEO, Beta Phi Mu, Delta Kappa Gamma. Club: Assn. Faculty and Profl. Women Ohio State U. Home: Apt B138 6000 Riverside Dr Dublin OH 43017

MEYER, BETTY JEAN, physical education educator; b. Hudson, S.D., Oct. 23, 1943; d. Thomas G. and Hazel Jeanette (Lundstrom) Eidsness; m. Edwin T. Meyer, Aug. 8, 1970. BS in Edn., So. State Coll., Springfield, S.D., 1967. Cert. tchr., Nebr. Tchr. instrumental and vocal music Geddes (S.D.) Pub. Sch., 1965-66; physical edn. tchr. Harmony (Minn.) Area Schs., 1967-70; physical edn., music tchr. Holy Trinity Grade Sch., Hartington, Nebr., 1970-71, instrumental, vocal music tchr., 1979-80, physical edn. tchr., jr. high sch. coach, 1981-93; instrumental, vocal music tchr., asst. coach Wynot (Nebr.) Pub. Schs., 1971-75. Mem. AAHPERD, Nebr. Assn. for Health, Physical Edn., Recreation and Dance, Nat. Fedn. Interscholastic Coaches, Nebr. Coaches Assn. Roman Catholic. Avocations: softball, bowling, cross word puzzles. Home: 411 S Madison St Hartington NE 68739-2000 Office: Holy Trinity Grade Sch 502 N Broadway St Hartington NE 68739-5108

MEYER, BILLIE JEAN, special education educator; b. Kansas City, Mo., July 27, 1943; d. Charles William and Dorothy Ellen (Alt) Emerson; m. Kenneth Lee Morris, Aug. 24, 1963 (div. Oct. 1985); 1 child, Darla Michele Morris Stewart; m. Gordon Frederick Meyer, June 1, 1986 (dec. May 1994); stepchildren: Ardith Helmer, Susan Stanford, Gary, Geneace, Patti Draughon, Shari Mohr. BS in Edn., Northeastern State U., 1965, M in Tchg., 1968. Cert. tchr., Okla.; cert. visually impaired, Braille. Substitute tchr. Muskogee (Okla.) Pub. Schs., 1965; elem. tchr. Okla. Sch. for the Blind, Muskogee, 1965-67, elem. tchr., computer tchr., 1969-98, visually impaired cons., 1998—. Adj. lectr. Northeastern State U., Tahlequah, summers 1990-92, 94-2002; on-site team mem. Nat. Accreditation Coun., 1987; mem. com. revision cert. stds., State of Okla., 1982, adj. lectr., 1998, Braille taks force mem. 1996-98; adv. com. mem. nat. evaluation systems Inc. Okla. Educators Cert. Exams Author: A Sequential Math Program for Beginning Abacus Students, 1979. Mem. Assn. of Edn. and Rehab. of the Blind and Visually Impaired, Okla. Assn. of Ednl. Rehab. of the Blind and Visually Impaired (pres.-elect 1985-86, pres. 1986-87, sec. 1993-97), Computer Using Educators, Epsilon Sigma Alpha (state pres. 1981-82, Girl of Yr. 1971, 98.). Avocations: stained glass, photo preservation, gardening, traveling, bird watching. Office: 814 N F St Muskogee OK 74403-2611 E-mail: jmijer@yahoo.com.

MEYER, ELLEN L. academic administrator; Pres. Atlanta Coll. Art, 1992—. Office: Atlanta Coll Art President 1280 Peachtree St NE Atlanta GA 30309-3502

MEYER, ERIC KENT, jouralist, educator, consultant; b. Marion, Kans., Aug. 23, 1953; s. Otto William Jr. and Joan Aileen (Wight) M.; divorced; 1 child, Nathaniel Jeremy Meyer-Gleason. BS, U. Kans., 1975; MA, Marquette U., 1997. Sunday editor, reporter, copy editor The Daily Pantagraph, Bloomington, Ill., 1975-77; news photo and graphics editor, asst. news editor, copy editor, reporter Milw. Jour., 1977-94; instr. Marquette U., Milw., 1993-96; assoc. prof. U. Ill., Urbana, 1996—; mng. ptnr. Newslink Assocs., 1995—; rsch. scientist Nat. Ctr. Supercomputing Applications, 1996—2000. Co-owner Marion County Record, Kans., Hillsboro Star-Jour. and Peabody Gazette-Bulletin, Kans. Author: Tomorrow's News Today: Strategic Guide to Online Publishing, 1995, 8th edit., 2000, Designing Information Graphics, 1997; online pub. Newslink.org. Pres. Spring Terrace Homeowners, Milw., 1981-83. Recipient awards UPI, 1983-85, photography award, reporting award AP, Ill., 1976-77, photo award Kans. Press Assn., 1998, design award, 1999. Mem. Soc. Profl. Journalists (bd. dirs. Milw. chpt. 1995-96, treas.), Soc. News Design, Assn. for Edn. in Journalism and Mass Communications (mem. exec. com. newspapers divsn. 1997-2000), Am. Copy Editing Soc. Republican. Methodist. Avocations: photography, bicycling, amateur computer programming. Home: 1508 Devonshire Dr Champaign IL 61821-5905 Office: U of Ill 025 Gregory Hall Urbana IL 61801

MEYER, FRANCES MARGARET ANTHONY, elementary and secondary school educator, health education specialist; b. Stella, Va., Nov. 15, 1947; d. Arthur Abner Jr. and Emmie Adeline (Murray) Anthony; m. Stephen Leroy Meyer, Aug. 2, 1975. BS, Longwood Coll., 1970; MS, Va. Commonwealth U., 1982, PhD, 1996. Cert. tchr., Va. Health, phys. edn., and dance tchr. Fredericksburg (Va.) City Pub. Schs., 1970-89; AIDS edn. coord. Va. Dept. Edn., Richmond, 1989-90, health edn. specialist, 1990-94, comprehensive sch. health program specialist, 1994—2003; ednl. cons. Fredericksburg, Va., 2003—. Mem. rev. bd. Nat. Commn. for Health Edn. and Credentialing, Inc., conf. and profl. devel. rev., 1996-2000. Author (with others): Elementary Physical Education: Growing through Movement-A Curriculum Guide, 1982; contbr. articles to profl. jours. Dir. Va. Children's Dance Festival, 1981—96, 1997—; vol. ARC, Fredericksburg, 1976—84, 1997—2001, Va. affiliate AHA, 1982—93, 1999—2001; mem. ctrl. steering com. Health, Mental Health and Safety in Schs. Nat. Guidelines Project, Am. Acad. Pediat., 2000—02; Va. Affiliate Am. Cancer Soc. Richmond, Va.; bd. dirs. Va. HIV/AIDS Network ARC, 1997—2001. Recipient gov.'s medal for substance abuse and prevention edn. State of Va., 1997, Alumni Cmty. Svc. award Va. Commonwealth U., 1998, Youth Edn. award for Leadership in the healthy devel. of children Am. Cancer Soc., 2002. Mem.: AAPHERD (chmn. divsn. 1970—, So. dist. applied strategic planning com. chair 2002—, past v.p., nominating com., strategic planning com., social justice com., So. Dist. honor award 1995, pres.'s recognition award 1997, svc. award 1997, So. Dist. honor award 1999, nat. honor award 1999), NEA, ASCD, AAUW (com. 1989—90, 1995—), Dance Edn. Orgn. (charter mem.), Va. Assn. for Health, Phys. Edn., Recreation and Dance (various coms. 1970—, health edn. editor Va. Jour. 1994—, past pres., Tchr. of Yr. 1983, Va. Honor award 1988), Va. Alliance for Arts Edn. (adv. bd. 1980—83, 1989—90, 1994—96), Am. Coll. Health Assn. (curriculum and tng. rev. panel 1992—94), Soc. State Dirs. Health, Phys. Edn. and Recreation (legis. affairs com. 1994—98, mem. applied strategic planning com. 1994—2001, pres.-elect 1997, pres. 1998, past pres. 1999, think tank chair 2000—02, applied policy & legis. com. 2002—, Healthis acad. rev. com. 2003—, Presdl. award 1996, Presdl. Recognition award 1997, 2000, Simon A. McNeely Honor award 2000), Va. Health Promotion and Edn. Coun. (bd. dirs. 1990—96), Internat. Coun. for Health, Phys. Edn., Recreation, Sport and Dance (internat. commns. for health edn. and commn. for dance and dance edn., mem. jour. articles rev. com.), Va. Alliance for Arts Edn., Va. Mid. Sch. Assn., Va. Edn. Assn., Nat. Mid. Sch. Assn., Nat. Dance Assn. (bd. dirs. 1996—, pres. 2001—03, Presdl. citation 1998, svc. award 1998, 2000, Pres.'s Merit award 2001), Nat. Network for Youth Svcs. (adv. bd. 1994—98, rev. panel), Longwood Coll. Alumni Coun. (bd. dirs. 1987—90), Delta Kappa Gamma (pres. Beta Eta chpt. 1988—90). Baptist. Avocations: travel, dancing, swimming, reading, theatrical performances.

MEYER, FRED ALBERT, JR., political science educator; b. Milw., Oct. 7, 1942; s. Fred Albert and Rose Henrietta (Hafemann) M. BA, U. Wis., 1964; MA, U. Wis., Milw., 1966; PhD, Wayne State U., 1974. Instr. Carroll Coll., Waukesha, Wis., 1970-71; prof. Polit. Sci. Ball State U., Muncie, Ind., 1971—. Editor Ind. Jour. Polit. Sci. Co-editor: Determinants of Law Enforcement Policies, 1979, Evaluating Alternative Law Enforcement Policies, 1979; co-author: The Criminal Justice Game, 1980; co-editor: State Policy Problems, 1993. Chair adv. com. on sex discrimination Ind. Civil Rights Commn., 1983-84; chair Ind. Sexual Harassment Task Force, 1989-92; chair Gender Fairness Coalition of Ind., Indpls., 1988-93, sec., 1994-97, chair 1998—; chair Ind. Found. on Gender-Based Edn., Indpls., 1988-93, 1998-2001, Gender Fairness Found. Ind., 2002—; chmn., Perham com. task force on women coll. scis. and humanities Ball State U., 1998-; sec. Healthy Mothers Healthy Babies of Delaware County, 1995-96, vice chair, 1996—; mem. coun. Policy Studies Orgn., 1994-98; bd. dirs. LWV Ind., 1998-2000, Ind. Pro-Choice Action League, 1984-90; chair Perham com. task force status of woman Coll. Scis. & Humanities, 1997—. Recipient grant to produce videotape on access to prenatal care in Delaware County, Ind. Hoosier Heartland chpt. March of Dimes, Muncie, 1990; Ford Found. Legis. fellow Mich. Senate, 1965-66. Mem. Am. Polit. Sci. Assn., Policy Studies Orgn., Midwest Polit. Sci. Assn., Western Polit. Sci. Assn., So. Polit. Sci. Assn., Audubon Soc., Sierra Club. Avocations: reading, art history, listening to music, animal welfare. Office: Polit Sci Dept Ball State U Muncie IN 47306-0001

MEYER, GOLDYE W. psychologist, educator; b. Wilkes Barre, Pa., Feb. 6, 1927; d. Harry Samuel Weisberger and Jennie Iskowitz; div.; children: Jodie, Howard, Natlee. BS, Wilkes U., Wilkes Barre, 1962; MS, Temple U., Phila., 1964; PhD, U. Conn., Storrs, 1975. Day camp dir. JCC, Wilkes Barre, 1962-64; chemistry instr. Wilkes U., Wilkes Barre, 1962-64, U. Bridgeport, Conn., 1964-65, prof. sec. edn., 1966-74, assoc. prof. counseling and human resources, 1974-78, prof. counseling and human resources, 1978-91; owner pvt. cons. firm, Bridgeport, 1977-90; pvt. psychotherapy practice Fairfield, Conn., 1975—; internat. bioenergetic analysis trainer, 1981—; trainer bioenergetic analysis Conn. Bioenergetic Soc., Conn., 1980-83; adj. prof. Nova U., Ft. Lauderdale, Fla., 1991-93; doctoral adv., acad. supr. Columbia-Pacific U., San Rafael, Calif., 1992—; adj. prof., doctoral adv. The Union Inst., Cin., 1994—. Dir. Fairfield (Conn.) Orgnl. Cons., 1977-90, Brooklawn Family Ctr., Fairfield, 1985—; mem. human resources adv. bd. U. Bridgeport, 1986-90; mem. bd. edn. adv. bd. Bridgeport Schs., 1984-87; leader AIDS caregiver support group The Yale New Haven Hosp., 1992—. Contbr. articles to jours, chpts. to books. Co-chair Fairfield Citizens for Edn. Recipient Doctoral Rsch. Grant U. Conn., 1974, Multicultural Rsch. Grant U. Bridgeport, 1980. Mem. ACLU, NOW, APA, Internat. Inst. for Bioenergetic Analyses (internat. ethics com.), Am. Acad. Psychotherapists, Nat. Substance Abuse Counselors, Conn. Coun. for Substance Abuse Counselors, Mass. Soc. for Bioenergetic Analysis (chair ethics com. 1993-97), E.M.D.R. Internat. Assn., Sierra Club, Appalachian Club. Jewish. Avocations: photography, tennis, biking, traveling, music. Home: 615 Brooklawn Ave Fairfield CT 06432-1807

MEYER, JAMES PHILIP, secondary school educator, social studies educator; b. Berwyn, Ill., May 2, 1946; s. Albert Fred and Eleanore Ann (Szydlowski) M.; m. Candice Marie Richter, Dec. 19, 1970; children: Teri Lynn, David Philip. Student, Athenaeum of Ohio, 1964-66, Maryknoll Coll., 1966-67; BA in Classics, Loyola U., Chgo., 1969; postgrad., Roosevelt U., 1972-76, U. Ill., 1990, Bradley U., 1994. Cert. tchr. 6-12, Ill. Tchr. Cass Sch. Dist. # 63, Darien, Ill., 1969—. Football coach Cass Sch. Dist. #63, Darien, Ill. 1969-84, basketball and softball coach, 1969-87; official scorekeeper and statistician at Downers Grove N. Girls Basketball, 1988—. Campaign mgr. Citizens for Donohue 13th dist. U.S. Congress, Naperville, Ill., 1984; campaign. coord. County Bd. candidate, Lombard, Ill., 1986, sec. DuPage County Dems., Lombard, 1986-90; bd. dirs., program com. Jr. Achievement, Chgo., 1987—. Recipient Excellence in Teaching award Ill. Math. and Sci. Acad., Aurora, Ill., 1991, Bus.-Edn. Partnership award Ill. State Bd. Edn., 1994. Mem. Ill. Norsk Rosemalers Assn. (computer records com., Swedish days com.). Roman Catholic. Avocation: computers. Home: 4216 Elm St Downers Grove IL 60515-2115 Office: Cass Sch Dist # 63 8502 Bailey Rd Darien IL 60561-5333

MEYER, JOHN EDWARD, nuclear engineering educator; b. Pitts., Dec. 17, 1931; s. Albert Edward and Thelma Elizabeth (Brethauer) M.; m. Gracyann Lenz, June 13, 1953; children: Susan Meyer Heydon, Karl, Karen Meyer Gleasman, Thomas. BS, MS, Carnegie Inst. Tech., 1953, PhD (ASME Student award 1955), 1955. Engring. and mgmt. positions Westinghouse Bettis Atomic Power Lab., West Mifflin, Pa., 1955-75; vis. lectr. U. Calif., Berkeley, 1968-69; prof. nuclear engring. MIT, 1975-98, ret., 1998. Cons. in field. Author papers in field. Recipient Bettis Disting. Service award, 1962, Outstanding Tchr. award nuclear engring. M.I.T., 1979, Alumni Merit award Carnegie Mellon U., 1987. Fellow Am. Nuclear Soc.; mem. ASME, Sigma Xi.

MEYER, JUDITH CHANDLER PUGH, history educator; b. Detroit, Oct. 22, 1948; d. Howard Chandler and Margaret Elizabeth (Bentley) Pugh; m. Paul Rudolph Meyer Jr., Aug. 17, 1974; children: Matthew Paul, Timothy Chandler. BA, Lawrence U., 1970; MA, U. Iowa, 1972, PhD, 1977. Tchg. asst. U. Iowa, Iowa City, 1974-76; instr. Ind. Cen. U., Indpls., 1977-78; asst. prof. history Smith Coll., Northampton, Mass., 1978-79; lectr. Fairfield (Conn.) U., 1985, 87, 89; lectr. in history U. Conn., Stamford, 1981-89, asst. prof. history Waterbury, 1989-95, assoc. prof. history, 1995—. Author: (monograph) Reformation in La Rochelle: Tradition and Change in Early Modern Europe, 1500-1568, 1996; contbr. articles to profl. jours. NDEA fellow U. Iowa, 1970-73, Fulbright fellow, Paris and La Rochelle, France, 1973-74, jr. faculty summer fellow and rsch. grantee The Rsch. Found., U. Conn., 1991-92. Mem. Am. Hist. Assn., Soc. for Reformation Rsch., 16th Century Studies Conf. Methodist. Avocations: reading, music, travel, hiking. Home: 184 College Park Dr Fairfield CT 06824 Office: U Conn-Waterbury 32 Hillside Ave Waterbury CT 06710-2217

MEYER, KATHLEEN MARIE, gifted education educator, writer; b. St. Louis, Oct. 29, 1944; d. Richard Henry and Leonora (Moser) Bailey; children: Richard, Amy, Mindy, Heidi. BA, Webster Coll., Webster Groves, Mo., 1966; MA, Fla. Atlantic U., 1981; postgrad., No. Ill. U., 1982—. Cert. secondary tchr., tchr. of gifted, Mo., Ill. Tchr. English Notre Dame High Sch., St. Louis, 1966-67; tchr. English, chmn. dept. Rosary High Sch., Aurora, Ill., 1981-91; instr. English DeKalb Coll. (now Ga. Perimeter Coll.), Decatur, Ga., 1992—2001; tchr. gifted program Fulton County, Ga., 1999—; instr. English North Metro Tech., 2001, Kennesaw State U., 2002—. Editor, writer; mem. adv. bd Univ. High Sch.; mem. joint enrollment coun. DeKalb Coll. Freelance editor, writer, consultant. Mem. ASCD, Nat. Coun. Tchrs. English. E-mail: kmeyer1029@yahoo.com.

MEYER, LISA MARIE, elementary school educator; b. Livonia, Mich., Nov. 15, 1961; d. James Theo and Dolores Lola Bishop; m. John Melville Meyer, May 22, 1982; children: Jessica Ellen, Brittany Allyssa. AA, Henry Ford C.C., Dearborn, Mich., 1981; B in Music Edn., Ea. Mich. U., 1987; M in Elem. Edn., Wayne State U., 1991. Cert. tchr. music edn., elem. edn. Mich. Elem. music tchr. Detroit Pub. Schs., 1987—89; music tchr. Dearborn Pub. Schs., 1989—95, music resource tchr., 1995—. Adj. instr. William Tyndale Coll., Farmington Hills, Mich., 1986—; cons. Ideas, LLC, West Norwalk, Conn., 2000—; mem. adv. bd. Ward Pre-Sch., Northville, Mich., 1987—90. Named one of Best 100 for Music Edn. in Am., Music Tchr. Nat. Assn., 2001; recipient Named one of Best of 100 for Music Edn. in Am., 2002. Mem.: Mich. Music Educator Assn. (Outstanding Adminstr. award 2001, 2002), Am. Orff Schulwerk Assn., Nat. Assn. Music Edn. Avocations: singing, camping, hiking. Home: 43069 Devon Ln Canton MI 48187 Office: Dearborn Pub Schs 18700 Audette Dearborn MI 48124 Fax: 313-730-3021. E-mail: meyerl@dearborn.k12.mi.us.

MEYER, MARA ELLICE, special education consultant, principal; b. Chgo., Oct. 28, 1952; d. David and Harriett (Lazar) Einhorn; m. Leonard X. Meyer, July 20, 1986; children: Hayley Rebecca, David Joseph. BS in Speech and Hearing Sci., U. Ill., 1974, MS in Speech and Lang. Pathology, 1975, postgrad. in pub. policy PhD program, 1990—. Cert. speech and lang. pathologist, spl. edn. tchr., reading tchr. Speech and lang. pathologist Macon-Piatt Spl. Edn. Dist., Decatur, Ill., 1975-76; speech and lang. pathologist, reading specialist, learning disabilities coord. Community Consolidated Sch. Dist. # 59, Arlington Heights, Ill., 1976-87; test cons. Psychol. Corp., San Antonio, 1987-89; adj. prof. Nat.-Louis U., Evanston, Ill., 1985-87, 2003—; ednl. cons. The Psychol. Corp., 1987-89, Am. Guidance Svc., Circle Pines, Minn., 1989-94; pvt. practice ednl. cons. Deerfield, Ill., 1994—. Project dir. Riverside Pub. Co., Chgo., 1993-94; mem. adv. coun. to Headstart, Dept. Human Svsc., City of Chgo., 1990-99; cons. Spl. Edn. Dist. of Lake County, 1995—, Waukegan (Ill.) Pub. Schs., 1997; cons. Lake Zurich Pub. Schs., 1996-98; asst. prin., inclusion coord. Mundelein (Ill.) Sch. Dist., 1999-2001; spl. edn. adminstr. Wilmette Schs., 2001-2003. Area coord. Dem. Party, Lake County, Ill., 1978—; pres. Park West Condo Assn., Lake County, 1983-88. Mem. NEA, ASCD, Nat. Assn. Elem. Prins., Nat. Family Partnership Network, Am. Speech-Lang. and Hearing Assn., Ill. Speech-Lang. and Hearing Assn., Ill. Prins. Assn., Internat. Reading Assn., Coun. on Exceptional Children. Avocations: swimming official, leisure reading, technical reading. Home: 1540 Central Ave Deerfield IL 60015-3963 E-mail: einhorn1@earthlink.net., mara52_1999@yahoo.com.

MEYER, MARGARET VAUGHAN, librarian, educator; b. Phila., Mar. 13, 1919; d. Clifford and Fannie (Lehman) Vaughan; m. Donald Robert Meyer, Sept. 3, 1949 (dec. Mar. 2002); children: Karen, Frederick E., Julie Meyer Ramos. BEd, UCLA, 1942; MLS, U. So. Calif., 1967. Elem. tchr. Indio Sch. Dist., Indio, Calif., 1942-43, Lawndale Sch. Dist., Lawndale, Calif., 1943-44, L.A. Unified Schs., 1946-53; program libr. City of Pasadena Libr., Pasadena, Calif., 1965-85. Co-author (Spanish-English): Centeno Collection-Annotated, 1977; author (biog. and notes, 2 CDs): Clifford Vaughan classical music. Organizer, chmn. libr. com. PTA, L.A., 1961—64, hon. life mem., 1964; vol. Com. Solidarity People of El Salvadore, L.A., 1985—97; mem. Citizens Com. Save Elysian Park, L.A., 1987—, L.A. County Mus. Art, 1986—, Friends of Pasadena Pub. Libr., 1986—. Mem.: ALA (del. 1967—80), L.A. Pub. Libr., Libr. Found. (charter mem.), Calif. Libr. Assn., Am. Fedn. Tchrs. (exec. bd. L.A. chpt.), Denishawn Repertory Dancers (hon. bd. dirs.), Sierra Club. Avocations: music, reading, swimming, gardening, games. Home: 1525 Upshur-NW Washington DC 20011

MEYER, PAULINE MARIE, retired special education educator; b. Gilead, Nebr., Dec. 15, 1928; d. Bernhard Martin and Helena Sophia (Vorderstrasse) Hellbusch; m. Calvin John, June 8, 1951 (dec. Nov. 1973); 1 child, Phyllis; m. Tim Gaspar. BA, U. Nebr., 1968, MA, 1972. Tchr. rural schs., Thayer County, Nebr., 1946-66, Fairbury (Nebr.) Pub. Sch., 1966-91, ret., 1991. Mem. Bus. and Profl. Women's Club (pres. 1987-90), Delta Kappa Gamma (pres.). Democrat. Lutheran. Avocations: refinishing furniture, quilting, reading.

MEYER, PRISCILLA ANN, Russian language and literature educator; b. Aug. 26, 1942; d. Herbert Edward and Marjorie Rose (Wolff) M.; m. William L. Trousdale, Sept. 15, 1974; 1 dau., Rachel V. BA, U. Calif., Berkeley, 1964; MA, Princeton U., 1966; PhD, 1971. Lectr. in Russian lang. and lit. Wesleyan U., Middletown, Conn., 1968-71; asst. prof., 1971-75; assoc. prof., 1975-88; prof., 1988—. Vis. asst. prof. Yale U., 1973, adv. coun. dept. Slavic lang. and lit. Princeton U., 1998-2002. Co-editor: Dostoevsky and Gogol, 1979; editor: Life in Windy Weather (by Andrei Bitov), 1986, author: Find What the Sailor Has Hidden: Vladimir Nabokov's Pale Fire, 1988; co-editor: Essays on Gogol: Logos and the Russian Word, 1992; co-editor: Nabokov's World, 2001; translator stories; mem. editl. bd. Slavic and East European Jour., 1999—; contbr. articles to profl. jours. Scholar Internat. Rsch. and Exch. Bd., 1973; grantee Ford Found., 1964-68, 70; hon. vis. fellow Sch. Slavonic and East European Studies London U., 1997, 2001. Mem. Am. Coun. Tchrs. Russian (dir. 1983-86), Am. Assn. Tchrs. Slavic and East European Studies, Internat. Vladimir Nabokov Soc. (v.p. 1983-85, 2002—), Tolstoi Soc., Dostoevsky Soc., Conn. Acad. Arts and Scis. Office: Russian Dept Wesleyan U Middletown CT 06459-0001 E-mail: pmeyer@wesleyan.edu.

MEYER, ROBERT LEE, secondary education educator; b. St. Joseph, Mo., July 9, 1952; s. Robert James and Jerry Lee (Patterson) M.; m. Barbara Anita Stickles, Aug. 2, 1986. BS in Edn., Mo. Western State Coll., 1974; MA in Edn., U.S. Internat. U., 1988. Cert. tchr., Calif., Mo.; cert. specialist learning handicapped, resource specialist cert., adminstr., Calif. Spl. edn. tchr., learning handicapped Mann Jr. High Sch., San Diego, 1978-80, Serra High Sch., San Diego, 1980-84, Morse High Sch., San Diego, 1984-85; magnet seminar tchr. Bell Jr. High Sch., San Diego, 1985-91; project resource tchr., dir. student activities Serra High Sch., San Diego, 1991-94, resource specialist, 1994-95; magnet coord. Ctr. for Sci., Math. and Computer Tech. Samuel Gompers Secondary Sch., San Diego, 1995-97; dean of students, attendance coord. Scripps Ranch H.S., non-athletic event coord., 1997-98; asst. prin. Mountain Empire Jr./Sr. H.S., 1998—2001; dean of students Gompers Secondary Sch., 2001—. Chmn. resource com. Western Assn. Schs. & Colls. accreditation Serra High Sch., San Diego, 1995, chmn. process com. Western Assn. Schs. and Colls. accreditation Gompers Secondary Sch., San Diego, 1996-97, sch. site coun., 1992-97, gov. team mem., 1992-95, chair spl. edn. dept., 1983, mem. sch. leadership team, 1992-95, sr. class advisor, 1994-95, liaison Partnerships in Edn., 1996-97; monitor City Schs. Race Human Rels. Monitoring Team, 1991-92, African Am. students pupil advocate program adv. coun., 1995-97; restructuring coord. Senate Bill 1274 Grant, 1993-95, resource specialist, 1994-95; chmn. process com. Western Assn. Schs. and Colls. accreditation Gompers Sec. Sch., adv. com. mem. African Am. students program; co-chmn. race/human rels. com. Scripps Ranch H.S., 1997-98. Contbr.: (book) History of Andrew Meyer Family, 1989. Alternate del. Dem. Party 6th Dist. and State Conventions, Holt County, Mo., 1976; mem. Nat. Conf. Minitown Race/Human Rels. Camp Coord., Scripps Ranch H.S. Recipient star adminstr. award Calif. FFA, 2000. Mem. Assn. Calif. Sch. Adminstrs., Optimist Club, Delta Chi. Democrat. Roman Catholic. Avocations: collecting political buttons, antiques, travel. E-mail: rmeyer@mail.sandi.net.

MEYER, RUTH ANN, retired physical education and dance educator; b. St. Louis, Oct. 24, 1944; d. Oliver Richard and Ruth Katherine (Popp) M. BS in Phys. Edn., Lindewood Coll., 1967; MS in Phys Edn., Western Ill. U., 1973; MA in Dance Edn., Lindewood Coll., 1977. Cert. tchr. Mo. Tchr. Normandy (Mo.) Sch. Dist. Garfield Elem., 1967—97; speaker seminar U. Mo., St. Louis, 1974-75; tchr. Lindenwood Coll., St. Charles, Mo., 1977, Florissant (Mo.) Valley Community Coll., 1980; ret., 1997. Co-founder Mo. Dance Edn. Workshops, Mo., 1978-80; pres. St. Louis Women's Phys. Edn. Club, 1985, St. Louis Suburban Phys. Edn., 1975-76. Contbr. articles to profl. jours. Mem. Ch. of the Master United Ch. Christ Outreach Com. (sec.), Florissant, 1990—. Tucson Creative Dance scholar, 1967. Mem. AAHPERD, Mo. Assn. Health Phys. Edn. Recreation and Dance (dance div. chair 1979-80, Helen Manley award 1984, Robert M. Taylor Svc. award 1998), Normandy Tchrs. Assn., Mo. Nat. Edn. Assn., Nat. Edn. Assn., Nat.

Dance Assn. (children's dance commn. 1985), Assn. Profl. Chaplains. Democrat. Avocations: volleyball, stained glass, bowling, playing cards, church volunteering. Home: 1205 Hudson Rd Ferguson MO 63135-1443 Office: Normandy Sch Dist 3855 Lucas And Hunt Rd Saint Louis MO 63121-2919

MEYER, SUSAN MOON, speech language pathologist, educator; b. Hazleton, Pa., Mar. 8, 1949; d. Robert A. and Jane W. (Walters) Moon; m. John C. Meyer Jr., Feb. 16, 1989; children: Chris, Scott. BS, Pa. State U., 1971, MS, 1972; PhD, Temple U., 1983. Cert. tchr., Pa. Speech-lang. pathologist, instr. Elmira (N.Y.) Coll., 1973-74; speech-lang. pathologist Arnot-Ogden Hosp., Elmira, 1973-74; supr. Sacred Heart Hosp. Speech and Hearing Ctr., Allentown, Pa., 1974-75; speech-lang. pathology instr. Kutztown (Pa.) U., 1975-78, asst. prof., 1978-82, assoc. prof., 1982-85, prof., 1985—. Owner Speech and Lang. Svcs., Allentown, 1975-87; cons. Vis. Nurses Assn., Allentown, 1975-85, Home Care, Allentown, 1975-85. Author: Survival Guide for the Beginning Speech-Language Clinician, 1998. Mem. Am. Speech-Lang.-Hearing Assn. (cert., councilor 1986-89, numerous Continuing Edn. awards), Pa. Speech-Lang.-Hearing Assn. (cert., v.p. profl. preparation 1985-89, Appreciation award 1987-89, 2001), Northea. Speech and Hearing Assn. Pa. (pres. 1984-86, Outstanding Dedication award 1985, Honors of the Assn. award 1999), Coun. Suprs. Speech-Lang. Pathology and Audiology. Avocations: family activities, cross-country skiing, British sports cars, reading. Bus. Office: Kutztown U Dept Speech-Lang Kutztown PA 19530 E-mail: smeyer@kutztown.edu.

MEYER, TODD KENT, secondary school educator; b. Spencer, Iowa, Sept. 3, 1964; s. Cleber Daniel and Marlys Elaine (Fie) M.; m. Lynette Elizabeth Frohrip, Jan. 1, 1994. BA in Comm./Theater Arts, U. No. Iowa, 1987, BA in Social Sci. Edn., 1990; MA in History, U. S.D., 1995. Tchr. Am. history Waterloo East (Iowa) H.S., 1990; tchr. Am. studies, Am. history Watertown (S.D.) H.S., 1990—, tchr. Advanced Placement history, 1997—. Drama dept. dir. Watertown H.S., 1993-95; adv. WHS Travel Club, 1992—; treas. Social Sci. Consortium S.D., 1996-98; state contact person Nat. Coun. History Edn., 1996-98; adj. prof. Am. history Mt. Marty Coll., 1996—; mem. NICEL seminar on U.S. Supreme Ct., 1995, Stratford Hall Slavery Seminar, 1997. Contbr. articles to local newspapers. Vol. ARC, Cedar Falls, Iowa, 1985-90, Spl. Olympics, Cedar Falls, 1985-90; bd. dirs. Watertown Town Players Cmty. Theater, 1992-95, 97—; mem. ch. coun. First Congl. Ch., 1996-98. NEH Thomas Jeffer Seminar fellow, 1992, Monticello-Stratford Hall Summer Seminar, Thomas Jefferson Meml. Found., 1993, James Madison Meml. Found. fellow, 1993-95. Mem. S.D. Social Studies Coun. (pres. 1993-94, treas. 1996-98), Nat. Coun. Social Studies, Nat. Coun. History Edn., S.D. State Hist. Soc., Nat. Trust for Hist. Preservation, Robert E. Lee Meml. Assn., Codington County Hist. Soc. Home: 17059 Firestone Cir Farmington MN 55024-9397 Office: Watertown High Sch 200 9th St NE Watertown SD 57201-2863

MEYER, WARREN GEORGE, vocational educator; b. Plymouth, Wis., May 12, 1910; s. charles Martin and Lillie Margaret (Liese) M.; m. Marion Magdaline Lehmann, June 19, 1939; children: Karen Rhem, Stephen George. BA, U. Wis., 1932; MS, NYU, 1933. Asst. buyer Mandel bros., Chgo., 1933-34, The Davis Store, Chgo., 1934-35; divsn. head Sears Roebuck & Co., Lansing, Mich., 1935-36, Detroit, 1936-37; mktg. instr. Vocat. Adult Sch., West Allis, Wis., 1937-38; adult field instr. Wis. Vocat. Schs., 1938-41; state supr. Dept. Vocat. Edn., Topeka, Kans., 1941-46; prof. vocat. edn. U. Minn., Mpls., 1946-76, vocat. prof. emeritus, 1976—. Vocat. edn. cons. U.S. Dept. State, Frankfurt, Germany, 1951; mktg. edn. cons. Va. Poly. Inst. and State U., Blacksburg, 1960-70, U. Mass., Amherst, 1966; adv. coun. mem. Nat. Ctr. for Vocat. Edn., Columbus, Ohio, 1965-75. Lead author: Retail Marketing Principles and Practices, 1964-82 edits.; co-author: Coordination in Cooperative Vocational Education, 1975; lead author: Retail Marketing, 1988; editor: Vocational Education and Nations Economy, 1977. Lt. (s.g.) USNR, 1944-46. Recipient Tchr. Edn. Acad. award Coun. for Distributive Tchr. Edn., 1969, Horace Morse Standard Oil award U. Minn., 1972, John Robert Gregg award Nat. Bus. Edn. Assn., 1973. Mem. Am. Vocat. Assn. (hon. life), Lions (sec. 1980-98), Men of Yorke, Delta Pi Epsilon. Home: 7500 York Ave S Edina MN 55435-5633 E-mail: warmeyer@aol.com.

MEYEROWITZ, ELLIOT MARTIN, biologist, educator; b. Washington, May 22, 1951; s. Irving and Freda (Goldberg) M.; m. Joan Agnes Kobori, June 17, 1984; 2 children. AB, Columbia U., 1973; MPhil, Yale U., 1975, PhD, 1977. Rsch. fellow Stanford U., Calif., 1977-79; asst. prof. biology Calif. Inst. Tech., Pasadena, 1980-85, assoc. prof., 1985-89, prof., 1989—, George W. Beadle prof. biology, 2002—, chair, 2000—. Mem. editl. bd. Trends in Genetics, Current Biology, Cell, Devel., Genome Biology; contbr. articles to profl. jours. Recipient LVMH Sci. pour l'Art Sci. prize, 1996, Internat. prize for biology, Japan, 1997, Mendel medal, U.K., 1997, Wilbur Cross medal Yale U., 2001; Jane Coffin Childs Meml. fund fellow, 1977-79, Sloan Found. fellow, 1980-82. Fellow: AAAS; mem.: NAS (Lounsbery award 1999), Academie des Scis. (fgn. mem./France), Internat. Soc. for Plant Molecular Biology (pres. 1995—97), Genetics Soc. Am. (pres. 1999, medal 1996), Bot. Soc. Am. (Pelton award 1994), Am. Soc. Plant Biologists (Gibbs medal 1995), Am. Acad. Arts and Scis., Am. Philos. Soc. Office: Calif Inst Tech Divsn Biology Pasadena CA 91125-0001 E-mail: meyerow@caltech.edu.

MEYERS, BEATRICE NURMI, retired primary school educator, director; b. Paynesville, Mich., Sept. 14, 1929; d. Charles Victor Nurmi and Elizabeth (Sillanpaa)Nurmi-Rengo; m. David C. Meyers, July 18, 1953; children: D. Keith, Kirsten, Kimberly Jan. BA, Mich. State U., 1952, MA, 1957. Tchr. Ferndale (Mich.) Pub. Schs., 1952-53, Houghton (Mich.) Pub. Schs., 1953-55, Holt (Mich.) Pub. Schs., 1955-57, Indpls. Pub. Schs., 1957-58, Billings (Mont.) Pub. Schs., 1958-59; dir., operator Tiny Tots Kindergarten, Downers Grove, Ill., 1964-70; tchr. Sch. Dist. 68, Woodridge, Ill., 1970-88; with Finnish Folk Dancers of Chgo., 1982-88. Recipient Disting. Service award, Suomi Coll., Hancock, Mich., 1985-86, 90. Mem. NEA, AAUW, LWV (Fla. chpt., mem. sec. 1990-93, pres. 1997), Ill. Edn. Assn. Retirees, Finnish Coun. Am. (sec.), Finnish-Am. Club (pres. Chgo. chpt. 1981-84, bd. dirs. 1988-89, mem. sec. 1994-95), League of Finnish Am. Soc. (pres. Chgo. chpt. 1981-84), Finn Ladies Chgo. (treas. 1984-86, pres. 1986-88), Salolampi (nat. Finnish lang. camp bd. dirs. Concordia Coll., Moorhead, Minn. 1991—), Scandinavian Club Pasco County (pres. 1995-2001), Sun Coast Finnish Am. Club (membership chair 1995—, chorus dir. 1994—, social chair 1988—), Vasa Club of Suncoast. Avocations: tennis, golf, photography, sewing, knitting, reading. Home: 3634 Nettle Creek Ct Holiday FL 34691-2504

MEYERS, DOROTHY, education consultant, writer; b. Chgo, Jan. 9, 1927; d. Gilbert and Harriet (Levitt) King; m. William J. Meyer, Oct. 9, 1947; children: Lynn Meyer, Jeanne Meyer. BA, U. Chgo., 1945, MA, 1961; postgrad., Columbia U., Northwestern U. Instr. sr. adults Chgo. Bd. and/City Coll., Chgo., 1961-78; coord. pub. affairs forum and health maintenance program City Coll. Chgo.-Jewish Cmty. Ctrs., Chgo., 1975-78; lectr. adult program City Coll. Chgo., 1984. Tchr. Dade County Adult edn. Program, Miami, Fla., 1985—86; cons., lectr. in field. Contbr. Chmn. legis. PTA; discussion leader Great Decisions, 1984—86; chmn. civic assembly Citizens Sch. Com.; v.p. cmty. rels. Womens Fedn. and Jewish United Fund; discussion leader LWV, Fgn. Policy Assn.; program chmn. Jewish Cmty. Ctrs., 1966—67, sr. adult com.; art and edn. com. mem. Chgo. Mayor's Com. for Sr. Citizens and Handicapped; com. on media Met. Coun. on Aging; active Bon Secour's Villa Maria Hosp.; founder Mt. Sinai Hosp., Miami Beach; sponsor Miami Heart Inst.; com. mem. March of Dimes; amb. Project Newborn U. Miami Prenatal Unit; bd. dirs. Coun. Jewish Elderly Open U.; bd. mem. Royal Notable Alzheimer Care Unit-Douglas Home Miami; bd. dirs. Alzheimer Day Care Ctr. Douglas Garden Home; bd. dirs. Villa Maria Found. Archdiocese Miami; bd. dirs. Angels Villa Maria, 1999—2001; bd. dirs. Villa Maria Rehab. and Skilled Nursing Hosp. Archdiocese Miami, 1999—2002. Recipient Prima Donna award, Men's Opera Guild, 1995, 1999, Honor award, Miami Children's Hosp., 1996. Mem.: ASA, Gastrointestinal Rsch. Found., Women in Comm., Chgo. Met. Sr. Forum (media com.), Nat. Coun. Aging, Gerontol. Assn., Brandeis Women's Aux., Mus. Art Ft. Lauderdale, Nat. Assn. Real Estate Bds., Nat. Coun. Jewish Women, Women's Aux. Jewish Cmty. Ctr., Coun. Women Chgo. Real Estate Bd., Chgo. Real Estate Bd., Cultural Ctr., Miami Internat. Press Club, Mus. Art boca Raton, Mus. Contemporary Art (life), Brandeis U., Art Inst. Chgo., Circumnavigator Club (Chgo. and Fla. chpts.).

MEYERS, ERIC MARK, religion educator; b. Norwich, Conn., June 5, 1940; s. Karl D. and Shirlee M. (Meyer) M.; m. Carol Lyons, June 25, 1964; children: Julie Kaete, Dina Elisa. AB, Dartmouth Coll., 1962; MA, Brandeis U., 1964; PhD, Harvard U., 1969. Lerner prof. religion, archeol., bibl. study, ancient hist. Duke U., Durham, N.C., 1969—, dir. grad. program in religion, 1979-86, 2001—; dir. Annenberg Inst., Phila., 1991-92. Pres. Am. Schs. of Oriental Rsch., Balt., 1990—96; commentator on biblical archaeology; dir. 8 digs Israel, Italy, 1970—2000. Author: 10 books; co-author: The Cambridge Companiion to the Bible, 1997; editor (in chief): The Oxford Encyclopedia of Archaeology in the Near East, 5 vols., 1997; contbr. articles more than 350 to profl. jours.; frequent guest (TV series) A&E channel, Discovery channel; frequent guest : History Channel. Jewish. Avocations: singing (baritone), golf, the arts, travel. Home: 3202 Waterbury Dr Durham NC 27707-2416 Office: Duke U 118 Gray Bldg PO Box 90964 Bldg Durham NC 27708-0964 E-mail: emc@duke.edu.

MEYERS, JAMES B. secondary education educator; Social studies tchr. Farmington (N.H.) High Sch. Named N.H. State Social Studies Tchr. of Yr., 1993. Office: Farmington High Sch 1 Thayer Dr Farmington NH 03835

MEYERS, KAREN DIANE, lawyer, educator, corporate officer; b. Cin., July 8, 1950; d. Willard Paul and Camille Jeannette (Schutte) M.; m. William J. Jones, Mar. 27, 1978. BA summa cum laude, Thomas More Coll., 1974; MBA, MEd, Xavier U., 1978; JD, U. Ky., Covington, 1978. Bar: Ohio 1978, Ky. 1978; CLU; CPCU; cert. structured settlement cons. Clk. to mgr. Baldwin Co., Cin., 1970-78; adj. prof. bus. Thomas More Coll., Crestview Hill, Ky., 1978—. CSSC-U. Notre Dame, 1994, CSSC, 1994; asst. sec., asst. v.p., sr. counsel The Ohio Life Ins. Co., Hamilton, 1978-91; prin. KD Meyers & Assocs., 1991; v.p. Benefit Designs, Inc., 1991-96, Little, Meyers, Garretson & Assocs., Ltd., Cin., 1996—; adj. prof. Miami U., 1998—. Bd. dirs. ARC, Hamilton, 1978-83, vol., 1978—; bd. dirs. YWCA, Hamilton, 1985-91. Gardner Found. fellow, 1968-71; recipient Ind. Progress award Bus. & Profl. Women, 1990. Fellow Life Mgmt. Inst. Atlanta; mem. ABA, Soc. Chartered Property Casualty Underwriters (instr. 1987—), Cin. Bar Assn., Butler County Bar Assn., Ohio Bar Assn., Ky. Bar Assn. Roman Catholic. Avocations: aerobics, jogging, crafts. Home: 7903 Hickory Hill Ln Cincinnati OH 45241-1363

MEYERS, WILLIAM VINCENT, lawyer; b. Washington, Jan. 14, 1940; s. Theodore Albert and Alice Mae (Vincent) M.; m. Karen Anne, June 10, 1961; children: Michelle, William Vincent, Jason, Michael. BA, U. Md., 1961; JD, Georgetown U., 1964. Bar: Md. 1964, D.C. 1965, U.S. Supreme Ct. 1978. Assoc. Nylen & Gilmore, Hyattsville, Md., 1964-68, ptnr., 1968-75; pres., mng. officer Meyers, Rodbell and Rosenbaum P.A., Riverdale, Md., 1975—. Atty. Bd. Suprs. of Elections for Prince George's County (Md.), 1969-78; gen. counsel Bank Md., 1978-84, bd. dirs., 1978-84; chmn. County Exec.'s Task Force on Alternative Funding Sources, 1982; co-founding dir., vice-chmn., gen. counsel Cmty. Bank Md., 1988-96, chmn. 1996-2001; bd. dirs., gen. counsel, vice-chmn. Cmty Bankshare Md., Inc., 1988-96, chmn. bd., CEO, 1996-2001; lectr. on alcoholic beverage law, estate planning and legis. lobbying to civic groups; trustee Md. Client Security Trust Fund, 1993—; mem. Gov.'s Task Force on Jud. Nominating Commns., 1995, Md. Econ. Devel. Commn., 1995—; bd. dirs. F&M Bank, Md., 2001—. Edtl. bd. Georgetown Law Jour., 1963-64. Bd. dirs. Greater Laurel Area C. of C.; chmn. bus. polit. action com. Prince George's County, 1982-87; bd. dirs. Prince George's Hosp. Ctr. Found. Inc., 1992—, vice-chmn., 1993-99, chmn., 1999—; mem. Md. Port Commn., 2000—; chmn., pres. Govt. House Found. Inc., 1996— Mem. ABA, D.C. Bar Assn., Prince Georges County Bar Assn., Md. State Bar Assn., Am. Judicature Soc., Md. Bar Found., Prince George's C. of C. (life; pres. 1980-81, award of Excellence 1980, Outstanding Svc. award 1982, 83, Pres.'s award 1983), Balt. Corridor C. of C. (bd. dirs. 1979-84), Congressional Country Club, U. Md. Prince George's County Alumni Assn. (former pres.). Home: 12211 Drews Ct Rockville MD 20854-1135 Office: 6801 Kenilworth Ave Ste 400 Riverdale MD 20737-1331

MEYERSON, BARBARA TOBIAS, elementary school educator; b. Rockville Centre, N.Y., May 17, 1928; d. Sol and Hermine (Sternberg) Tobias; m. Daniel Meyerson, Sept. 4, 1962 (dec. Apr. 1989); children: George D., Barbara Meyerson Ayers. BEd, SUNY, New Paltz, 1948; postgrad., NYU, Hofstra U. Tchr. kindergarten Dix Hills (N.Y.) pub. schs., Hicksville (N.Y.) pub. schs., Valley Stream (N.Y.) pub. schs.; tchr. 6th grade Flushing (N.Y.) Bd. Edn. Dist. commr. Boy Scouts Am., mem. tng. staff, organizer new units; founder, sec. Repertory Theatre, Rio Rancho, N.Mex.; bd. dirs. Italian Am. Assn., Rio Rancho; vol. Rio Rancho City Hall Pub. Offices; vol. reading and spl. edn. classes Rio Rancho Pub. Schs; mem. Park and Recreation Bd. Commrs., Rio Rancho. Mem. ACE, VFW Aux. (jr. v.p. 1999—), United Fedn. Tchrs. Home: 6127 Cottontail Rd NE Rio Rancho NM 87124-1545 E-mail: barbtobias@aol.com.

MEYERSTEIN, DAN, college president, chemistry educator; b. Jerusalem, Oct. 7, 1938; s. Rolf and Hermine (Fried) M.; m. Naomi Rishpon, June 24, 1962; children: Michal, Ronit, Ruth, Gil. MS, Hebrew U., 1961, PhD, 1965. Rschr. Soreq Nuc. Rsch. Ctr., Rehovoth, Israel, 1961-65; postdoctoral fellow Argonne (Ill.) Nat. Lab., 1965-67; mem. faculty Ben Gurion U. Negev, Beer Sheva, Israel, 1968—, prof. chemistry, 1979—, dir. libr., 1979-89, dir. Coal Rsch. Ctr., 1986-90; pres. Coll. Judea and Samaria, 1995—. Mem. editl. bd. Israel Jour. Chemistry, 1982-90. Fellow Royal Soc. Chemistry (assoc.); mem. Israel Chem. Soc. (pres. 1988-91), Am. Chem. Soc. Home: 10 Hinanit St Omer 84965 Israel Office: Ben Gurion U Chemistry Dept The Coll Judea and Samaria Ariel Israel E-mail: pres@ycariel.yosh.ac.il., danmeyer@bgumail.bgu.ac.il.

MEYSENBURG, MARY ANN, principal; b. L.A., Sept. 16, 1939; d. Clarence Henry and Mildred Ethel (McGee) Augustine; m. John Harold Meysenburg, June 17, 1967; children: Peter Augustine, Amy Bernadette. BA magna cum laude, U. So. Calif., 1960; MA Pvt. Sch. Adminstrn. magna cum laude, U. San Francisco, 1995. Cert. elem. tchr., Calif. Auditor, escrow officer Union Bank, L.A., 1962-64; v.p., escrow mgr. Bank of Downey, Calif., 1964-66; cons., tchr. Santa Ana (Calif.) Coll. Bus., 1964-66; elem. tchr. St. Bruno's Sch., Whittier, Calif., 1966-70, Pasadena (Calif.) Unified Sch. Dist., 1971-84, Holy Angels Sch., Arcadia, Calif., 1985-89; vice prin., computer coord. Our Mother of Good Counsel, L.A., 1989-93; prin. St. Stephen Martyr, Monterey Park, Calif., 1993-2000, Holy Trinity Sch., L.A., 2000—. Mem. Writing to Read Bd.; trainer Riordan Found., 1998—; master catechist religious edn. L.A. Archdiocese, 1988—. Author: History of the Arms Control and Disarmament Organization, 1976; organizer, editor newsletter Cath. Com. for Girl Scouts and Campfire. Counselor Boy Scouts Am., 1985—; eucharistic min. Our Mother of Good Counsel, 1985—95, Holy Angels Ch., Arcadia; sec. of senatus Legion of Mary, 1980—85; mem. Cath. com.Girls Scouts U.S.A. and Campfire; vice chmn. acad. affairs L.A. Archdiocese, 1985—90, deanery chairperson Dept. of Edn.; bd. dirs. Alumni Assn. Sacred Heart H.S., 1999—. Recipient Pius X medal L.A. Archdiocese, 1979, St. Elizabeth Ann Seton award Cath. Com. for Girl Scouts, 1988, St. Anne medal Cath. Com. for Girl Scouts, 1989, Bronze Pelican award Cath. Com. for Boy Scouts, 1989; grantee Milken Family Found., 1989, 92. Mem.: Western Assn. Schs. and Colls. (team chairperson), Phi Kappa Phi, Phi Delta Kappa (historian 1991—92, founds. rep. 1992—93, treas. 1993—94, 1st v.p. 1994—95, pres. 1995—96, advisor 2001—02, Svc. award 1999), Phi Beta Kappa, Chi Lambda Theta, Phi Lambda Theta. Avocations: tennis, walking, swimming, reading. Home: 6725 Brentmead Ave Arcadia CA 91007-7708

MEZACAPA, EDNA S. music educator, elementary school educator; b. Flint, MI, Jan. 23, 1948; d. Jack E. and Vlasta A. Tremayne; m. Nicklas A. Mezacapa, July 25, 1970; children: Amy Anne, Sara Marie. MusB, Heidelberg Coll., Tiffin, Ohio, 1970. Gen. music tchr. Bellevue (Ohio) City Schs., 1969—73; youth choir dir. Findlay Episc. Ch., Findlay, Ohio, 1975—78; subs. tchr. Rochester (N.Y.) Schs., 1979—81; youth choir dir. Ch. of the Epiphany, Rochester, 1979—81; music tchr., K-8 St. Mary's Cath. Sch., Kalamazoo, 1981—82, St. Ludmila Cath. Sch., Cedar Rapids, Iowa, 1984—86; tchr. Christian edn. Calvary Episc. Ch., Rochester, Minn., 1986—87; subs. music tchr., 1-6 Rochester City Schs., Rochester, Minn., 1988—90, music tchr., 1-6, 1990—. Dir. Calvary Episc. Youth Choir, 1995—96, Suzuki Orch., 2001—03. Dir. youth choir Calvary Episcopal Ch., 1996—97; dir. Suzuki Orch., 2001—03.

MIAO, SHILI, plant biology and wetland ecology researcher; came to US, 1986; d. Ji Ming and Shenyun (Mao) M.; 1 child, Sonia. BS, S.W. China Normal U., 1982, MS, 1984; PhD, Boston U., 1990. Tchr. Sixtieth Primary Sch., Chonging, 1972-78; teaching asst., biology dept. S.W. China Normal Univ., Chonging, 1984-86, lectr., biology dept., 1987—; postdoctoral fellow Harvard Univ., Cambridge, Mass., 1990-94; sr. environ. scientist South Fla. Water Mgmt. Dist., 1994—. Vis. scholar Harvard U., 1986-87. Contbr. chpt. to Ecological Studies on Evergreen Broadleaved Forests, 1988, Modern Ecology of Am., articles to Ecology and Oecologia. Recipient Presdl. fellowship Boston Univ., 1987-90. Mem. Ecol. Soc. Am., Ecol. Soc. China, Internat. Biologists Assn. Office: Water Mgmt Dist South Fla ESRO-7140 3301 Gun Club Rd # Esro-714 West Palm Beach FL 33406-3007

MIASKIEWICZ, THERESA ELIZABETH, secondary education educator; b. Salem, Mass., Aug. 29, 1933; d. Chester and Anastasia (Zmijewski) M. BA, Emmanuel Coll., Boston, 1954. Cert. tchr., Mass.; lic. real estate broker, Mass. Tchr. fgn. lang. dept. Salem Sch. Dept., 1954-94; head tchr. Salem High Sch., 1954-94; ret., 1994. Playground instr. City of Salem summers, 1951-54; mem. vis. com. New Eng. Assn. Secondary Schs. and Colls., Salem Sch. Com., 1996—; mem. Salem Sch. Com., 1996-99, vice chair, 1999; sch. com. rep. Coun. on Aging, 1998. Vol. Salem Hosp., 1979-88, Salem Hosp. Aux., 1980-98, House of Seven Gables, Salem, summers, 1987-89; Eucharistic min., North Shore Med. Ctr. Aux.; mem. com. Salem Sch., 1996-99. Mem. Am. Assn. Ret. Persons (NRTA divsn.), Ret. State, County and Mcpl. Employees Assn., Nat. Ret. Tchrs. Assn., Mass. Ret. Tchrs. Assn., Mass. Fedn. Polish Women's Clubs (v.p. 1988-89, pres. 2003—, regional chmn. Presentation Ball), Mass. Assn. Sch. Coms. (chmn. bldgs. and grounds 1998, curriculum health adv. 1996-97, assessment com. 1997, chair pers. com. 1998, fin. com. 1998, chair sch. bldg. com. 1998, 99, prins. search com. 1998-99), Essex County Retired Tchrs. Assn. (rec. sec. 2001), Polish Bus. and Profl. Women's Club Greater Boston (past corr. sec., chmn. scholarship com.,pres. 1988-89). Avocations: travel, floral design, cooking, reading, arts and crafts.

MICCO, TAMMY LYNN, elementary education educator; b. New Castle, Pa., Sept. 14, 1970; d. Harry Anthony and Georgia Ann (Padula) M. BS in Psychology, U. Pitts., 1992, MA in Elem. Edn., 1993, cert. in children's lit. Tutor student athletes U. Pitts., 1991-95; intern Falk Lab. Sch., U. Pitts., 1992-93; technology facilitator Seneca Valley Sch. Dist./Evans City (Pa.) Sch., 1993—. Mem. tech. adv. bd. Seneca Valley Sch. Dist., Harmony, Pa., 1993—; in-svc. dir. Evans City Sch., 1994—. Vol. Office of Disabled Student Svcs., U. Pitts., 1989-93; tchr.'s asst. Frick Internat. Acad., Pitts., 1991-92, girls' softball coach, 1995-96; Sunday sch. tchr. St. Vitus Parish, 1997-2000. Mem. Pa. State Edn. Assn., Pa. Sci. Tchrs. Assn., Kappa Delta Pi, Psi Chi. Democrat. Roman Catholic. Avocations: sports, travel, children's activities. Office: Evans City Sch 345 W Main St Evans City PA 16033-1235

MICH, CONNIE RITA, mental health nurse, educator; b. Nebr., Feb. 5, 1926; d. Henry B. and Anna (Stratman) Redel; m. Richard Mich. BSN, Alverno Coll.; postgrad., Marquette U.; MSN, Cath. U. Am. Asst. clin. dir. in-patient svcs. Fond du Lac (Wis.) County Health Ctr., 1974-78; head nurse, program coord. acute psychiat. unit St. Agnes Hosp., Fond du Lac, 1979-83; mental health clinician Immanuel Med. Ctr., Omaha, 1984-89; instr., clin. supr., asst. prof. psychiat. mental health Coll. St. Mary, Omaha, 1989-93; med. programs dir. Inst. Computer Sci. Ltd., 1989—. Program dir. med. programs Gateway Coll., Omaha, 1995; chairperson Examining Coun. on RNs; writer items State Bd. Test Pool Exam.; pres. Milw. Coun. Cath. Nurses; vice chairperson Wis. Conf. Group Psychiat. Nursing Practice. Mem. Sigma Theta Tau, Pi Gamma Mu.

MICHAEL, ALFRED FREDERICK, JR., physician, medical educator; b. Phila. s. Alfred Frederick and Emma Maude (Peters) M.; m. Jeanne Jones; children: Mary, Susan, Carol. MD, Temple U., 1953. Diplomate: Am. Bd. Pediatrics (founding mem. sub-bd. pediatric nephrology, pres. 1977-80). Diagnostic lab. immunology and pediatric nephrology intern Phila. Gen. Hosp., 1953-54; resident Children's Hosp. and U. Cin. Coll. Medicine, 1957-60; postdoctoral fellow dept. pediatrics and biochemistry Med. Sch., U. Minn., Mpls., 1960-63, assoc. prof., 1965-68, prof. pediatrics, lab. medicine and pathology, 1968-88, dir. pediatric nephrology, 1968—97, Regents' prof., 1986—, head dept. pediatrics, 1986-97, interim dean, 1996-97, dean, 1997—2002. Established investigator Am. Heart Assn., 1963-68. Past mem. editl. bd. Internat. Yr. Book of Nephrology, Am. Jour. Nephrology, Kidney Internat., Clin. Nephrology, Am. Jour. Pathology; contbr. articles to profl. jours. Served with USAF, 1955-57. Recipient Alumni Achievement award Temple U. Sch. Medicine, 1988; NIH fellow, 1960-63, 92-2002, Guggenheim fellow, 1966-67. Fellow AAAS; mem. AMA, Am. Soc. Clin. Investigation, Assn. Am. Physicians, Am. Pediat. Soc., Soc. for Pediat. Rsch., Am. Assn. Investigative Pathology, Am. Soc. Cell Biology, Am. Soc. Nephrology (coun., pres.-elect 1992—, pres. 1993, John Peters award), Internat. Soc. Nephrology, Soc. for Exptl. Biology and Medicine, Minn. Med. Assn. Home: 1986 Lower Saint Dennis Rd Saint Paul MN 55116-2820

MICHAEL, COLETTE VERGER, language educator, writer; b. Marseille, France, Mar. 3, 1937; arrived in US, 1954; d. Raymond Marc and Fanny (Kindler) Verger; children: Barbara, Peggy, Monique, Alan, David, Gerard. PhB, U. Wash., 1969, MA in Roman Langs., 1970; MS in History of Sci., U. Wis., 1975, PhD in French, 1973. Tchr. French U. Wis., 1973—75, Shimer Coll., Mt. Carroll, Ill., 1976; prof. French No. Ill. U., DeKalb, 1977. Author: Choderlos de Laclos: The Man, His Work and His Critics, 1982, (poetry) Intemperies, 1982, Sens Dessus Dessous, 1984, Choderlos de Laclos, Les Millieux Philosophiques et le Mal, 1984, The Marquis de Sade: The Man, His Works, and His Critics, 1986, Les tracts féministes, 1986, Essai sur le caractere, les moeurs et l'esprit des femmes, 1987, Negritude: An Annotated Bibliography, 1988, Le Divorce en France, 1988, Sade: His Ethics and Rhetoric, 1989, Chemistry, 1991, Grounds of Natural Philosophy, 1998, Sur les Femmes, 2003. Fellow, Ford Found., 1970—73, NEH, 1977. Mem.: 18th Century Studies Assn., Am. Philos. Assn., Fedn. Internat. Prof. Francais, Am. Assn. Tchrs. French, Aircraft Owners and Pilot Assn. Home: 635 Joanne Ln Dekalb IL 60115-1862 Office: No Ill U 315 Weston Hall Dekalb IL 60115 E-mail: cmichael@niu.edu.

MICHAEL, GARY G. retired retail supermarket and drug chain executive, university administrator; b. 1940; m. Meryle Kay Michael; 3 children. BS in Bus., U. Idaho, 1962. Staff acct. Ernst & Ernst, CPA's, 1964-66; with Albertson's, Inc., Boise, Idaho, 1966—2001, acct., 1966-68, asst. controller, 1968-71, controller, 1971-72, v.p., controller, 1972-74, sr. v.p. fin., treas., 1974-76, exec. v.p., 1976-84, vice chmn., CFO, corp. devel. officer, 1984-91, chmn., CEO, 1991—2001; interim pres. U. Idaho, Moscow, Idaho, 2003—. Bd. dirs. Questar Inc., Boise Cascade, Food Mktg. Inst., Clorox, Harrah's Entertainment, Highway 12 Ventures. Served to 1st lt. U.S. Army, 1962-64. Office: Clorox 1221 Broadway Oakland CA 94612 also: U Idaho Admin Bldg, Room 105 Moscow ID 83844-3151 Business E-Mail: gmichael@uidaho.edu.*

MICHAEL, JERROLD MARK, public health specialist, former university dean, educator; b. Richmond, Va., Aug. 3, 1927; s. Joseph Leon and Esther Leah M.; m. Lynn Y. Simon, Mar. 17, 1951; children: Scott J., Nelson L. BCE, George Washington U., 1949; MSE, Johns Hopkins U., 1950; MPH, U. Calif., Berkeley, 1957; DrPH (hon.), Mahidol U., 1983; ScD (hon.), Tulane U., 1984. Commd. ensign USPHS, 1950, advanced through grades to rear adm., asst. surgeon gen., 1966; ret., 1970; dean Sch. Pub. Health, U. Hawaii, Honolulu, 1971-92, prof. pub. health, 1971-95; emeritus prof. pub. health U. Hawaii, Honolulu, 1995—; adj. prof. global health George Washington U., 1997—. Bd. dirs. Nat. Health Coun., 1967-78, Nat. Ctr. for Health Edn., 1977-90; mem. nat. adv. coun. on health professions edn., 1978-81; chmn. bd. dirs. Kuakini Med. Ctr., Honolulu; sec., treas. Asia-Pacific Acad. Consortium Pub. Health; vis. prof. U. Adelaide, 1993, George Washington, 1994; hon. prof. Beijing Med. U., 1994; adj. prof. internat. pub. health Goerge Washington U., 1997—. Contbr. articles to profl. jours.; assoc. editor Jour. Environ. Health, 1958-80, Asia-Pacific Jour. of Pub. Health, 1986-95. Pres. Commd. Officers Found., 2000—. Served with USNR, 1944-47. Decorated Meritorious Svc. medal, comdr. Royal Order of Elephant (Thailand); recipient Walter Mangold award, 1961, J.S. Billings award for mil. medicine, 1964, Gold medal Hebrew U., Jerusalem, 1982, San Karcil Gold medal, Malaysia, 1989, Disting. Svc. award Pacific Island Health Officers Assn., 1992, USPHS awards, Commd. Officers Assn. Brutsche award, 1999, others. Fellow Am. Public Health Assn.; mem. Am. Acad. Health Adminstrn., Am. Soc. Cert. Sanitarians, Nat. Environ. Health Assn., Am. Acad. Environ. Engrs. Clubs: Masons. Democrat. Jewish. Home: 16736 Gooseneck Ter Olney MD 20832-2456

MICHAEL, MARY AMELIA FURTADO, freelance writer, retired educator; b. Portugal; m. Eugene G. Michael; children: David, Douglas, Gregory. BA, Albertus Magnus Coll.; MS, U. Bridgeport, 1975; CAS, Fairfield U., 1982. Cert. secondary sch. sci. tchr., ednl. adminstr. Housemaster, sci. tchr. Fairfield (Conn.) Pub. Schs., adminstrv. housemaster, sci. tchr., sci. dept. coord., 1992, retired, 1992; freelance fin. rsch. and investment writer and cons., 1994—. Author: The Art and Science of Cooking, 1996; contbr. articles to profl. jours. Mem. Discovery Mus., Conn. Arts & Sci. Mus. Mem. AAUW (bd. dirs. 1998-2000), LWV, Conn. Assn. Suprs. and Curriculum, Fairfield Sch. Adminstrs. Assn., Retired Educators of Fairfield, Fairfield Hist. Soc., Alpha ONE Antitrypsin Assn. Avocations: collecting antiques, gourmet cooking, collecting old cookbooks and recipes, photography, writing. Home: 942 Valley Rd Fairfield CT 06432-1671

MICHAEL, NOREEN, commissioner, educator; Commr. of edn. Virgin Islands Dept. Edn., Charlotte, 2002—. Office: Commr of Education 44-46 Kongena Gade St Thomas VI 00802

MICHAEL, SUZANNE, sociologist, educator; b. Ft. Bragg, N.C., Feb. 21, 1951; d. Walter Otto and Carola (Nussbaum) M. BA, SUNY, Binghamton, 1973; MS, Columbia U., 1976; PhD in Sociology, CUNY, 1998. With Downstate Med. Ctr., Bkyn., 1976-84, dir. treatment, 1981-83, chief social worker, 1981-84; dir. interagy. affairs Bur. Sch. Children & Adolescent N.Y.C. Dept. Health, 1984-89; dir. program devel. and community affairs Family Health Svcs., N.Y.C. Dept. Health, 1989-92; acad. internship program dir. Hunter Coll. Ctr. for Study of Family Policy, N.Y.C., 1992—2002; asst. prof. Adelphi U. Sch. Social Work, Garden City, NY, 2002—. Co-founder, co-chmn. N.Y.C. Social Workers Coop., 1976-82; cons. People Against Sexual Abuse, Bklyn., 1985-87; N.Y.C. Bd. Edn., 1988-89; mem. N.Y.C. HIV Rev. Panel, 1985-90; coord. N.Y.C. Pediatric HIV Adv. Unit, 1987, 92-2000; adj. prof. sociology Hunter Coll. (CUNY), cons. immigrant health. Mem. editl. bd. Jour. Immigrant Health, 1998—. Mem. social svc. bd. N.Y. Soc. for Ethical Culture, N.Y.C., 1982-88; v.p. for progs. N.Y. Soc. for Ethical Culture, N.Y.C., 1984-88; mem. exec. adv. com. N.Y. Ctr. for Immigrant Health, 1990—; mem. exec. com. Caucus on Refugee and Immigrant Health, 1995-2001. NIMH grantee, 1977, U.S. Dept. Edn. grantee, 1993-95, 99-2001. Mem. NASW, APHA, Phi Beta Kappa. Avocations: hiking, cross-country skiing, photography, traveling. Home: 160 W 71st St New York NY 10023-3901 Office: Adephi U Sch Social Work Garden City NY 11530 E-mail: michael@adelphi.edu.

MICHAELIDES, DOROS NIKITA, internist, medical educator; b. Nicosia, Cyprus, Jan. 7, 1936; came to U.S., 1969; s. Nikita P. and Elpinike (Taliadorou) M.; m. Eutychia J. Loizides, Feb. 27, 1965; children: Nike-Elsie, Joanna-Doris. MD magna cum laude (Royal Greek Govt., Scholar) U. Athens, 1962; DTM and H (Greek State Scholarship, Found. Scholar) U. Liverpool, Eng., 1967; MSc in Clin. Biochemistry (Greek State, Scholarship Found. Scholar), U. Newcastle-upon-Tyne (Eng.), 1969. Diplomate Am. Bd. Family Practice, Am. Bd. Allergy and Immunology; qualified Am. Bd. Internal Medicine; cert. in infectious diseases and immunochemistry, Eng. Clk., intern U. Uppsala, Sweden, 1962; resident Nicosia Gen. Hosp., 1963-66; fellow U. Liverpool Hosps., 1967; fellow internal and clin. medicine Royal Infirmary, U. Edinburgh, 1967-68; rsch. fellow Royal Victoria Infirmary, U. Newcastle-upon-Tyne, 1968-69; resident internal medicine Bapt. Meml. Hosp., Memphis, 1969-72; fellow in chest diseases Western Okla. Chest Disease Hosp., 1970-71; chief clin. immunology/respiratory care ctr. Erie, Pa.; chief respiratory care ctr. VA Med. Ctr., Erie, 1972-84, acting chief dept. medicine, 1980-81; asst. clin. prof. medicine Hahnemann U. Sch. Medicine, Phila., 1977—, Gannon U., Erie, 1977—. Mem. staff internal medicine Hamot Med. Ctr., immunology and chest diseases Metro Health Ctr., Erie; preceptor medicine St. Vincent's Health Ctr.; affiliate staff Cleveland Clinic Found.; vol. physician Greek Nat. Guard, Cyprus, 1964. Author: The Occurrence of Proteolytic Inhibitors in Heart and Skeletal Muscle, 1969; Blood Gases, Acid-Base and Electrolytes Disturbances, 1980; Immediate Hypersensitivity: The Immunochemistry and Therapeutics of Reversible Airway Obstruction, 1980; The Equivalent Potency of Corticosteroid Preparations used in Reversible Airway Obstruction, 1981; contbr. articles to med. jours. Recipient citation for outstanding svcs. to vets. DAV, 1975, citation Adminstr. U.S. Vets. Affairs, 1978. Fellow ACP (life), Am. Assn. Cert. Allergists, Am. Coll. Allergy and Immunology (com. autoimmune diseases), Am. Assn. Clin. Immunology and Allergy (pulmonary com.), Am. Coll. Chest Physicians (life; critical care com.), Royal Soc. Medicine, Am. Coll. Angiology, N.Y. Acad. Scis., Am. Coll. Clin. Pharmacology, Am. Assn. Cert. Allergists. Greek Orthodox. Home: 4107 State St Erie PA 16508-3129 Office: Allergy Immunology & Chest Diseases 1611 Peach St Ste 220 Erie PA 16501-2121 E-mail: dnm777@pol.net.

MICHAELIS, KAREN LAUREE, law educator; b. Milw., Mar. 30, 1950; d. Donald Lee and Ethel Catherine (Stevens) Michaelis; m. Larry Severtson, Aug. 2, 1980 (div. Aug. 1982); 1 child, Quinn Alexandra Michaelis Severtson. BA, U. Wis., 1972, BS, 1974, MS, 1985, PhD, 1988, JD, 1989; MA, Calif. State U., L.A., 1979. Bar: Wis., U.S. Dist. Ct. (we. dist.) Wis. Asst. prof. law Hofstra U., Hempstead, N.Y., 1990-93; assoc. prof. Ill. State U., Normal, 1993-95, Wash. State U., Pullman, 1995—2002; pvt. practice Madison, Wis., 2002—. Author: (book) Reporting Child Abuse: A Guide to Mandatory Requirements for School Personnel, 1993, Theories of Liability for Teacher Sexual Misconduct, 1996, Postmodern Perspectives and Shifting Legal Paradigms: Searching for a Critical Theory of Juvenile Justice, 1998, Student As Enemy: A Legal Construct of the Other, 1999; editor: Ill. Sch. Law Quar., 1993—95; mem. editl. bd. Jour. Sch. Leadership, 1991—99, People & Education: The Human Side of Edn., 1991—96, Planning and Changing, 1993—95. Mem.: ABA, Edn. Law Assn. (bd. dirs. 1998—2000, co-chair publs. com. 1998—), Nat. Orgn. Legal Problems Edn. (mem. publs. com. 1993—2001, mem. program com. 1995, exec. bd.), Nat. Coun. Profs. Ednl. Adminstrn. (mem. Morphet Fund com. 1993—2000, mem. program com., mem. editl. bd. 1994—95), State Bar Wis. Office: 437 S Yellowstone Dr Ste 105 Madison WI 53719

MICHAELS, CINDY WHITFILL (CYNTHIA G. MICHAELS), educational consultant; b. Plainview, Tex., Aug. 31, 1951; d. Glenn Tierce and Ruby Jewell (Nichols) Whitfill; m. Terre Joe Michaels, July 16, 1977. BS, W. Tex. State U., 1972; MS, U. Tex., Dallas, 1976; postgrad. cert., E. Tex. State U., 1982; grad., Garland Citizens Police Acad., 2000. Registered profl. ednl. diagnostician Tex., cert. supr. gen. and spl. edn., elem. edn. tchr., K-8 English tchr., spl. edn. tchr. generic and mental retardation Tex. Gen. and spl. edn. tchr. Plano (Tex.) Ind. Sch. Dist., 1972-76; dependents' sch. tchr. U.S. Dept. Def., Office of Overseas Edn., Schweinfurt, Germany, 1976-77; asst. dir. edn. dept. spl. edn. Univ. Affiliated Ctr., U. Tex., Dallas, 1977-80; asst. to acting dir. edn., dept. pediat., Southwestern Med. Sch. Univ. Affiliated Ctr., U. Tex. Health Sci. Ctr., Dallas, 1980-82; dir. Collin County Spl. Edn. Coop., Wylie, Tex., 1982-89; dir. spl. svcs. Terrell (Tex.) Ind. Sch. Dist., 1989-92; cons. for at-risk svcs. instrnl. svcs. dept. Region 10 Edn. Svc. Ctr., Richardson, Tex., 1992-93, cons. for staff devel., 1993-95; cons. Title I Svcs., 1995-96; ind. rep. Am. Comm. Network, 1995—; owner Strategic Out-Source Svcs., Garland, Tex., 1996—. Regional cons., presenter, spkr. Region 10 Adminstrs. Spl. Edn., Dallas, 1982—92; grant reviewer Tex. Edn. Agy., Austin, 1984, state conf. presenter, spkr., 92, Tex. Assn. Bus. Sch. Bds., Houston, 1991; cons. S.W. regional tng. program educators U. So. Miss., 1992—93; regional coord. HS mock trial competition State Bar Tex., 1993; regional liaison Tex. Elem. Mentor Network, 1993—96; state presenter Tex. Vocat. Educators Conf., 1994; ednl. cons. Strategic Outsource Svcs., 1996—. Active Dance-A-Thon United Cerebral Palsy, Dallas, 1986; area marcher March of Dimes, Dallas, 1990, Park Cities Walkathon Multiple Sclerosis, 1994, 1995; bd. dirs. New Beginnings Ctr. Domestic Violence Agy., 2001—. Named Outstanding Young Women in Am., 1981; grantee, Tex. Edn. Agy., 1990—92, Job Tng. & Partnership Act, 1991, Carl Perkins Vocat. Program, 1991. Mem.: Tex. Coun. Adminstrs. Spl. Edn. (region 10 chairperson 1985—87, state conf. presenter 1989, 1992), Garland Citizens Police Acad. Alumnae, Alpha Delta Pi (Richardson alumnae, philanthropy chair 1988, v.p. 1989—91, 1994—2000, v.p., sec. 1993—94). Avocations: aerobics, skiing, travel, dancing. Home: 2613 Oak Point Dr Garland TX 75044-7809 also: 232 Broadmoor Alto NM 88312

MICHAELS, JENNIFER TONKS, foreign language educator; b. Sedgley, England, May 19, 1945; d. Frank Gordon and Dorothy (Compston) Tonks; m. Eric Michaels, 1973; children: Joseph, David, Ellen. MA, U. Edinburgh, 1967, McGill U., 1971, PhD, 1974. Teaching asst. German dept. Wesleyan U., 1967-68; instr. German dept. Bucknell (Pa.) U., 1968-69; teaching asst. German dept. McGill U., Can., 1969-72; prodn. asst. Pub. TV News and Polit. program, Schenectady, N.Y., 1974-75; from asst. prof. to assoc. prof. Grinnell (Iowa) Coll., 1975-87, prof., 1987—. Vis. cons. German dept. Hamilton Coll., 1981; cons. Modern Lang. dept. Colby Coll.; panelist NEH, 1985; spkr. in field. Author: D.H. Lawrence, The Polarity of North and South, 1976, Anarchy and Eros: Otto Gross' Impact on German Expressionist Writers, 1983, Franz Jung: Expressionist, Dadaist, Revolutionary and Outsider, 1989, Franz Werfel and the Critics, 1994; contbr. numerous articles, revs. to profl. jours. Mem. MLA, Am. Assn. Tchrs. of German, Soc. Exile Studies, German Studies Assn. (sec. treas. 1991-92, v.p. 1992-94, pres. 1995-96, numerous coms.). Democrat. Avocations: music, travel, reading. Office: Grinnell Coll German Dept PO Box 805 Grinnell IA 50112-0805 E-mail: michaels@grinnell.edu.

MICHAELS, JOHN G. mathematics educator; b. Rochester, N.Y., Jan. 31, 1942; BA, Fordham U., 1963; MA, U. Rochester, 1966, PhD, 1968. Postdoctoral fellow and rsch. assoc. Carnegie-Mellon U., Pitts., 1968-70; asst. prof. of math. SUNY, Brockport, 1970-73, assoc. prof. math., 1973-80, prof. math., 1980—, chmn., dept. math., 1995-97. Co-editor: (book) Applications of Discrete Mathematics, 1991; co-author: (books) Intermediate Algebra, 1982, Linear Algebra, 1977; author: (videotape series) Calculus, 1984-85; project editor: Handbook of Discrete and Combinatorial Mathematics, 2000; co-author (website) Discrete Math. and Its Applications, 5th edit., 2003. Mem. Math. Assn. Am., Phi Beta Kappa, Sigma Xi. Office: SUNY Brockport Dept Math 350 New Campus Dr Brockport NY 14420-2914 E-mail: jmichael@brockport.edu.

MICHALAK, JANET CAROL, reading education educator; b. Buffalo, Mar. 22, 1949; d. Theodore and Thelma Ruth (Roesch) Vukovic; m. Gerald Paul Michalak, June 19, 1971; children: Nathan, Justin. BS in Edn., SUNY Coll. at Buffalo, Buffalo, 1970; MS in Edn., SUNY, Buffalo, 1971, EdD, 1981. Cert. tchr. nursery, kindergarten, grades 1-6, reading tchr., English tchr. grades 7-12, N.Y. Reading tchr. Tonawanda (N.Y.) Sch. System, 1971-80; instr. Niagara County C.C., Sanborn, N.Y., 1980-82, asst. prof., 1982-85, assoc. prof., 1985-91, prof., 1991—; adj. lectr. SUNY, Buffalo, 1990-91. Recipient Pres.'s award for Excellence in Teaching, Niagara County C.C., 1990, Nat. Inst. for Staff & Orgnl. Devel. Excellence award, 1991, SUNY Chancellor's award for Excellence in Teaching, 1991. Mem. Coll. Reading Assn., Internat. Reading Assn., N.Y. Coll. Learning Skills Assn., Niagara Frontier Reading Coun. (bd. dirs. 1986-88, 97—). Republican. Avocation: reading. Home: 184 Montbleu Dr Getzville NY 14068-1329 Office: Niagara County CC 3111 Saunders Settlement Rd Sanborn NY 14132-9487

MICHALIK, JOHN JAMES, legal educational association executive; b. Bemidji, Minn., Aug. 1, 1945; m. Diane Marie Olson, Dec. 21, 1968; children: Matthew John, Nicole, Shane. BA, U. Minn., 1967, JD, 1970. Legal editor Lawyers Coop. Pub. Co., Rochester, NY, 1970—75; dir. continuing legal edn. Wash. State Bar Assn., Seattle, 1975—81, exec. dir., 1981—91; asst. dean devel. and cmty. rels. Sch. Law U. Wash., 1991—95; dir., CEO Assn. Legal Adminstrs., Vernon Hills, Ill., 1995—. Fellow: Coll. Law Practice Mgmt.; mem.: Nat. Trust Hist. Preservation, Am. Mgmt. Assn., Am. Soc. Assn. Execs. Lutheran. Office: Assn Legal Adminstrs #325 175 E Hawthorn Pkwy Ste 325 Vernon Hills IL 60061-1460 E-mail: jmichalik@alanet.org.

MICHALOWICZ, KAREN DEE, secondary education educator; b. Garrett, Ind., Nov. 7, 1942; d. Perry Linsey and Irene Veronica (Viers) Shuman; children: Joleen, Michael. AB, Cath. U., 1964; MA in Ednl. Psychology, U. Va., 1990. Tchr. St. Anthony Sch., Falls Church, Va.; math. coord., tchr. Queen of Apostles Sch., Alexandria, Va.; chair math. dept., tchr. Langley Upper Sch., McLean, Va. Adj. prof. George Mason U.; leader, spkr. numerous workshops; VQUEST lead tchr./trainer. Contbr. articles to profl. jours. Named AAUW Tchr. of the Yr., 1994, Presdl. Award in Math., 1994; Woodrow Wilson fellow, 1991, SCIMAT/NSF, 1992; Yale U. scholar, summer 1987. Mem.: Women and Math. Edn. (past pres.), Va. Assn. Ind. Schs., Va. Mid. Sch. Assn., Va. Assn. for Supervision and Curriculum Devel., Math. Assn. Am., Va. Coun. Tchrs. math. (Va. Outstanding Math. Tchr. 1992), Nat. Coun. Tchrs. Math., ASCD. Office: The Langley Sch 1411 Balls Hill Rd Mc Lean VA 22101-3415

MICHALSKI, WACŁAW (ŻUR-ŻUROWSKI WACŁ MICHALSKI), adult education educator; b. Pierzchnica, Poland, Sept. 14, 1913; came to the U.S., 1951; s. Antoni and Józefa (Skrybuś) M.; m. Urszula Lewandowska, Nov. 12, 1959 (dec. 1986); 1 child, Anthony Richard. MA, Tchr.'s Coll., Poland, 1934; grad., Officer's Mil. Sch., Poland, 1934-35; postgrad., U. Wis. M.A.T.C., 1951-55. Lic. real estate broker, Wis. Tchr. jr. high sch., Poland, 1936-39; mgr. acctg. Ampco Metal Co., Milw., 1951-84; tchr., educator Marquette U., U. Wis. Ext., Milw., 1962-90, Milw. Area Tech. Coll., 1963—. Real estate agt. ShoreWest Realtors, Milw., 1955—. Contbr. articles to profl. jours. Archivist Holy Cross Brigade and Nat. Armed Forces of Poland, 1991-96. With underground resistance, Poland, 1939-45; officer Holy Cross Brigade, Poland, 1944-55, which joined U.S. 3rd Army, Czechoslovakia, 1945; Polish guard U.S. Army, Germany, 1945-47; officer Internat. Refugee Orgn., Germany, 1947-51. Recipient Polish Heritage award Pulaski Coun. Milw., 1992, Cert. of Appreciation State Hist. Soc. Wis., 1987, Vol. Svc. award Inner Agy. Coun. Volunteerism, 1986, Cert. of Commendation for Exemplary Work as an Older Worker in Our Community Milw. Com. for Nat. Older Work Week, 1995. Mem. Polish Am. Congress, N.Am. Polish Ctr. Study, Polish Western Assn. Am. (Diploma of Merit 1988), Vets. Orgns. WWI, WWII. Roman Catholic. Avocations: chess, bridge. Home: 5505 Bentwood Ln Greendale WI 53129-1314 Office: Shorewest Realtors 5300 S 108th St Hales Corners WI 53130-1368 E-mail: wmichalski@shorewest.com.

MICHAUD, GEORGES JOSEPH, astrophysics educator; b. Que., Can., Apr. 30, 1940; s. Marie-Louis and Isabelle (St. Laurent) M.; m. Denise Lemieux, June 25, 1966. BA, U. Laval, Que., 1961, BSc, 1965; PhD, Calif. Tech. Inst., Pasadena, 1970. Prof. U. Montreal, Can., 1969—; dir. Ctr. Rsch. en Calcul Appliqué, 1992-96, assoc. dean of grad. studies, 1997-2000. Recipient Steacie prize NRC, 1980, Medaille Janssen, Acad. Scis., Paris, 1982, Prix Vincent, ACFAS, 1979; Killam fellow Conseil des Arts, 1987-89. Office: Universite de Montreal Dept de Physique Montreal QC Canada H3C 3J7 E-mail: georges.michaud@umontreal.ca.

MICHEL, DANIEL JOHN, broadcast educator, writer, photographer, artist; b. New Orleans, June 18, 1949; s. Nolan Joseph and Evelyn Marie (Breaux) M. Diploma, Sta. WKG-TV, 1986; BA in Mktg. Mgmt., Kensington U., 1989; cert. diploma photography, Media West, 1990; cert., Art Instrn. Schs. Inc., 1991, Brit.-Am. Sch. of Writing, 1991. Instr. English East Baton Rouge Sch. Bd., 1982-84; instr. broadcast prodn. Sta. WKG-TV, Baton Rouge, 1986—; freelance writer Baton Rouge, 1987—; technician, photographer Evangeline Downs Race Track. Announcer Nat. Sports Festival, Baton Rouge, 1985. Writer song lyrics including I've Sat So Long, Now I Became Lonely, stage plays, works in Libr. of Congress, 1982—. Camera dir. La. Pub. Broadcasting Fund Raising, Baton Rouge, 1986—; instr. TV broadcasting Boy Scouts Am., Baton Rouge, 1986—. Mem. Lafayette Art Assn. (2d v.p. 1994). Roman Catholic.

MICHELS, ROBERT, psychiatrist, educator; b. Chgo., Jan. 21, 1936; s. Samuel and Ann (Cooper) M.; m. Verena Sterba, Dec. 23, 1962; children—Katherine, James. BA, U. Chgo., 1953; MD, Northwestern U., 1958. Intern Mt. Sinai Hosp., N.Y.C., 1958-59; resident in psychiatry Columbia Presbyn.-N.Y. State Psychiat. Inst., N.Y.C., 1959-62; mem. faculty Coll. Physicians and Surgeons, Columbia U., N.Y.C., 1964-74, assoc. prof., 1971-74; psychiatrist student health service Columbia U., 1966-74; supervising and tng. analyst Columbia U. Center for Psychoanalytic Tng. and Research, 1972—; attending psychiatrist Vanderbilt Clinic, Presbyn. Hosp., N.Y.C., 1964-74; Barklie McKee Henry prof. psychiatry Cornell U. Med. Coll., N.Y.C., 1974-93, chmn. dept. psychiatry, 1974-91, Stephen and Suzanne Weiss dean, 1991-96; provost for med. affairs Cornell U., 1991-96, Walsh McDermott U. prof. of medicine, 1996—, univ. prof. psychiatry, 1996—; psychiatrist-in-chief N.Y. Hosp., 1974-91, attending psychiatrist, 1991—. Attending psychiatrist St. Luke's Hosp. Ctr., N.Y.C., 1966—. Co-author: The Psychiatric Interview in Clinical Practice, 1971; contbr. articles to profl. jours. Served with USPHS, 1962-64. Mem. Am. Psychiat. Assn., Am. Coll. Psychiatrists, N.Y. Psychiat. Soc., Royal Medico-Psychol. Assn., Psychiat. Rsch. Soc., Assn. Rsch. in Nervous and Mental Diseases, Assn. Acad. Psychiatry, Am. Psychoanalytic Assn., Internat. Psychoanalytic Assn., Ctr. Advanced Psychoanalytic Studies, N.Y. Acad. Scis., Alpha Omega Alpha. Office: Cornell U Med Coll 418 E 71st St New York NY 10021-4894

MICHELSEN, W(OLFGANG) JOST, neurosurgeon, educator, retired; b. Amsterdam, Holland, Aug. 20, 1935; came to U.S., 1936; s. Jost Joseph and Ingeborg Mathilde (Dilthey) M.; m. Constance Richards, Sept. 21, 1963 (div. 1987); children: Kristina, Elizabeth, Ingrid; m. Claude Claire Grenier, Mar. 30, 1988 (div. Oct. 1992); m. Martha Reed, Sept. 21, 1996. AB magna cum laude, Harvard U., 1959; MD, Columbia U., 1963. Diplomate Am. Bd. Neurol. Surgery. Intern in surgery Case Wester Res. U. Hosps., Cleve., 1963-64; asst. resident in neurology Mass. Gen. Hosp., Boston, 1964-65; asst. resident, then chief resident neurol. surgery Columbia-Presbyn. Med. Ctr., N.Y.C., 1965-69; from instr. to assoc. prof. neurosurgery Columbia U. Coll. Physicians and Surgeons, N.Y.C., 1969-89, prof. clin. surgery, 1990—; fellow in neurosurgery Presbyn. Hosp., N.Y.C., 1969-71, dir. neuro vascular surgery, 1989-90; dir. neurosurgery St. Luke's Roosevelt Hosp. Ctr., N.Y.C., 1990—; prof. and chmn. dept. neurological surgery Albert Einstein Coll. Medicine, Bronx, N.Y., 1992-97; dir. neurosurgery Montefiore Med Ctr, Bronx, 1992-97; ret., 1997. Asst. attending in neurosurgery, St. Luke's Hosp. Ctr., 1970—; cons. neurosurgeon Nyack (N.Y.) Hosp., 1972—, Englewood (N.J.) Hosp., 1972—; vis. prof. neurosurgery Tufts U., 1975, Emery U., 1977, Presbyn.-St. Luke's Hosp. Ctr., Chgo., 1978, Yale U., 1980; guest faculty Northwestern U., 1977, 78, U. Chgo., 1977, Colby Coll., 1980; mem. numerous panels on neurosurgery. Contbr. articles to profl. publs. 1st lt. U.S. Army, 1954-57. Grantee NIH, USPHS. Fellow ACS, Am. Heart Assn.; Mem. AMA, Am. Assn. Neurol. Surgeons (mem. sect. pediatric neurosurger), Neurosurg. Soc. Am. (v.p. 1984-85, pres. 1987-88), Congress Neurol. Surgeons, N.Y. Neurosurg. Soc., Neurosurg. Soc. State N.Y., N.Y. Acad. Scis., Assn. Rsch. in Nervous and Mental Diseases, Internat. Neurosurg. Soc., Internat. Pediatric Neurosurg. Soc., N.Y. State Med. Soc., N.Y. County Med. Soc. Office: 330 Borthwick Ave Ste 108 Portsmouth NH 03801

MICHELSOHN, MARIE-LOUISE, mathematician, educator; b. N.Y.C., Oct. 8, 1941; d. Marcel and Lucy Friedmann; children: Didi, Michelle. BS, U. Chgo., 1962, MS, 1963, PhD, 1974. Asst. prof. U. Calif. San Diego, La Jolla, 1974-75; lectr. U. Calif., Berkeley, 1975-77; mem. Inst. des Hautes Études Scientifiques, Bures sur Yvette, France, 1977-78; asst. prof. SUNY, Stony Brook, 1978-82, assoc. prof., 1982-88, prof., 1988—. Visitor Inst. Matematica Pura e Aplicada, Rio de Janeiro, 1980, Rsch. Inst. for Math. Scis., Kyoto, Japan, 1986, Tata Inst., Bombay, 1986-87; vis. mem. Inst. des Hautes Études Scientifiques, Bures-sur-Yvette, 1983-84, 93, 99-2000; dir. grad. program Dept. of Math SUNY, Stony Brook; rsch. prof. Math. Scis. Rsch. Inst., 1993-94. Author: Spin Geometry, 1989; contbr. articles to Am. Jour. Math., Acta Mathematica, Inventiones Mathematicae, Procs. London Math. Soc., Jour. Algebraic Geometry. Grantee NSF. Mem. Am. Math. Soc. Achievements include research in complex geometry, characterization of balanced spaces, Clifford and spinor cohomology, the geometry of spin manifolds and the Dirac operator, riemannian manifolds of positive curvature, the theory of algebraic cycles. Office: SUNY Dept Math Stony Brook NY 11794-0001

MICHENER, CHARLES DUNCAN, entomologist, educator, researcher; b. Pasadena, Calif., Sept. 22, 1918; s. Harold and Josephine (Rigden) Michener; m. Mary Hastings, Jan. 1, 1941; children: David, Daniel, Barbara, Walter. BS, U. Calif., Berkeley, 1939, PhD, 1941. Tech. asst. U. Calif., Berkeley, 1939-42; asst. curator Am. Mus. Natural History, NYC, 1942-46, assoc. curator, 1946-48, rsch. assoc., 1949—; assoc. prof. U. Kans., 1948-49, prof., 1949-89, prof. emeritus, 1989—, chmn. dept. entomology, 1949-61, 72-75, Watkins Disting. prof. entomology, 1959-89, acting chmn. dept. systematics, ecology, 1968-69, Watkins Disting. prof. systematics and ecology, 1969-89; dir. Snow Entomol. Museum, 1974-83, state entomologist, 1949-61. Vis. rsch. prof. U. Paraná, Curitiba, Brazil, 1955—56. Author (with Mary H. Michener): (book) American Social Insects, 1951; Am. editor: Insectes Sociaux, 1954—55; editor: (jour.) Evolution, 1962—64; Am. editor: Insectes Sociaux, 1962—90; author (with S. F. Sakagami): (book) Nest Architecture of the Sweat Bees, 1962; assoc. editor: Ann. Rev. Ecology and Systematics, 1970—90; author (with S. F. Sakagami): (book) The Social Behavior of the Bees, 1974; author: (with M. D. Breed and H. E. Evans) The Biology of Social Insects, 1982; author: (with D. Fletcher) Kin Recognition in Animals, 1987; author: (with R. McGinley and B. Danforth) The Bee Genera of North and Central America, 1994; contbr. articles to profl. jours.; author (with R. McGinley and B. Danforth): (book) The Bees of the World, 2000. Served to capt. San Corps AUS, 1943—46. Recipient Disting. Rsch. medal, Internat. Soc. Hymenopterists, 2002; fellow Guggenheim, U. Paraná, 1955—56, Africa, 1966—67, Fulbright, U. Queensland, 1958—59; scholar Rsch., U. Costa Rica, 1963. Fellow: AAAS, Royal Entomol. Soc. London, Am. Acad. Arts and Sci., Am. Entomol. Soc., Entomol. Soc. Am. (C. V. Riley award 1999); mem.: NAS, Kans. Entomol. Soc. (pres. 1950), Linnean Soc. London (corr.), Soc. Systematic Zoologists (hon.; pres. 1969), Russian Entomol. Soc. (hon.), Brazilian Acad. Sci. (corr.), Internat. Union Study Social Insects (pres. 1977—82), Am. Soc. Naturalists (pres. 1978), Soc. Study Evolution (pres. 1967). Home: 1706 W 2nd St Lawrence KS 66044-1016 Office: U Kans Snow Hall 1460 Jayhawk Blvd Lawrence KS 66045-7523 E-mail: michener@ku.edu.

MICHTA, ANDREW ALEXANDER, educator, researcher; b. Poland, Apr. 4, 1956; s. Józef and Adela (Stokowiec) M.; m. Cristina Brescia Michta; 1 child, Chelsea. BAiin English and Philosophy, St. Mary's Coll., 1980; MA in Am. Studies, Mich. State U., 1982; PhD in Internat. Rels., Johns Hopkins U., 1987. Vis. scholar Hoover Institution, Stanford, Ct., 1987-88; asst. prof. internat. studies Rhodes Coll., Memphis, 1988-92, assoc. prof. internat. studies, 1992-98, prof. internat. studies, 1998—. Author: Red Eagle: The Army in Polish Politics, 1990, East Central Europe After the Warsaw Pact Security Dilemma, 1992, The Government and Politics of Post-Communist Europe, 1994, Post-Communist Eastern Europe Crisis and Reform, 1994, Polish Foreign Policy Reconsidered: Challenges of Independence, 1995, The Soldier Citizen: The Politics of the Polish Army after Communism, 1997, America's New Allies: Poland, Hungary and the Czech Republic in NATO, 1999; contbr. numerous articles to profl. jours. Fulbright rsch. scholar, Warsaw, 1995, rsch. scholar Woodrow Wilson Ctr., Washington, 1995, Pub. Policy scholar Woodrow Wilson Ctr., 2000; Title VIII grantee U.S. State Dept., 1988-92, NEH grantee, 1989. Mem. Interant. Inst. for Strategic Studies (London), Am. Polit. Sci. Assn., Am. Assn. Advancement Slavic Studies, Internat. Studies Assn. Episcopalian. Avocations: sports, music, reading. Office: Internat Studies Dept Rhodes Coll 2000 N Parkway Memphis TN 38112-5414

MICK, DEBORAH WEST FAIRCHILD, elementary education educator; b. Lorain, Ohio, Feb. 3, 1952; d. Harold Cole and Carolyn Elaine (Fordyce) West; m. Bruce Allen Fairchild, June 22, 1974 (div. 1986); children: Stephanie, Jared, Elizabeth; m. Alvin R. Mick, Oct. 12, 2001. BA in Music and Sociology, Houghton Coll., N.Y., 1974; student, U. N. Ala., Florence, 1984-85; BS in Elem. Edn., Ashland Coll., Ohio, 1987; MEd in Curriculum and Instrn., Ashland U., 1991. Cert. tchr., Ohio, adminstr. Music tchr. Yamaha Sch. Music, Newbury, N.Y., 1975-76; pvt. piano tchr. Petersburg, Va., 1976-79; jr. high reading tchr. Clearview Schs., Lorain, Ohio, 1987—; tchr. Durling Elem. Clearview, Lorain, Ohio, Vincent Elem./Kindergarten, 1989-90; kindergarten tchr. Erieview Elem. Sch., Avon Lake, Ohio, 1990-91; 3rd grade tchr. Westview Elem. Sch., Avon Lake, 1991-92, tchr. primary, 1992—. Games club advisor Clearview Jr. High, Lorain Ohio 1987--; spelling bee advisor Clearview jr. high, Lorain Ohio 1987—; student coun. advisor Westview Elem., 1998-2001, choir pianist, 1998—. FLOWC Advt. Com. Fort Lee Officer's Wives Club, Va. 1978-79; OWC Sec. Finger Lakes Officer's Wives Club, Seneca N.Y. 1981-82; OWC V.P. Fla. Officers Wives Club, Seneca Army N.Y., 1982-83; Choir Pianist Faith Baptist Ch., Amherst Ohio 1986--. Mem. NEA, Ohio Edn. Assn., Kappa Delta Pi. Democrat. Baptist. Avocations: music, reading, water sports, swimming, boating, water skiing. Home: 2633 Vassar Ave Lorain OH 44053-2359 Office: Westview Elem Sch 155 Moore Rd Avon Lake OH 44012-1127

MICKENS, ADELINE, elementary education educator; b. Macon, Miss., Mar. 9, 1953; d. Matthew Thomas Draper and Nalvina Harlen Mickens; children: Frederick Mosley, Stephen Mosley. BA, Columbia (Mo.) Coll., 1990; student, U. Mo., Kansas City. Cert. elem. tchr., tchr. lang. arts K-8, tchr. reading, Mo. Reading paraprofl. East St. Louis (Ill.) Sch. Dist. 69, 1979-85; paraprofl. Columbia Pub. Schs., 1986-90; tchr. Lincoln (Nebr.) Pub. Schs., 1990-91, tchr. reading, oral comm. Park Mid. Sch., 1996—; tchr. sci., math. and reading Kansas City (Mo.) Magnet Schs., 1991-96. Sec. to bd. dirs. Anderson-Hayes Day Care, Columbia, 1990; collaborating tchr. Teaching Excellence Teams Project, Kansas City, Mo., 1994—; mem. adj. faculty Met. C.C. Campaign coord. Twp. Supr., East St. Louis, 1978; pres. bd. trustees Christ Unity Ch., 2000-02. Mem. NEA (co-chmn. minority affairs com.). Mem. Unity Ch. Home: 2200 N 52nd St Lincoln NE 68504-2910 Office: Park Mid Sch 855 South 8th St Lincoln NE 64114-1821

MIDDEN, WILLIAM ROBERT, chemist, educator; b. Wood River, Ill., May 19, 1952; BS, St. Johns U., 1974; PhD in Biochemistry, The Ohio State U., 1978. Postdoctoral fellow The Ohio State U., 1978-79, The Johns Hopkins U., Balt., 1980-81, rsch. assoc. dept. environ. health scis., 1981-83, asst. prof. dept. environ. health scis., 1983-87; adj. asst. prof. dept. pathology Med. Coll. of Ohio, Toledo, 1988-97; asst. prof. dept. chemistry Ctr. for Photochemical Scis., Bowling Green (Ohio) State U., 1987-95, assoc. prof., 1995—. Vis. scientist Laboratoire Acide Nucleique, Departement de Recherche Fondamentale sur La Matiére Condensée, Service D'études des Systémes et Archit ctures Moléculaires, Centre D'Etudes Nucléaires, Grenoble, France, 1989; lectr. and seminar presenter in field; cons. Synergistic Lab., Libby, Mont., 1988, Fresh Products, Inc., Toledo, 1989, Calderon Automation, Inc., Bowling Green, 1989, Ricerca, Inc., Painesville, Ohio, 1988-91. Contbr. numerous articles to profl. jours. and monographs/ Recipient Master Tchr. award Bowling Green State U., 1993, Grad. Rsch. Asst. award, 1992-93; grantee: NIH, 1986, 87, Bowling Green State U., 1988, 1992-93, NSF, 1989, 2003—, U.S. Dept. Edn., 2001—. Mem. AAAS, Am. Chem. Soc., Omicron Delta Kappa. Office: Bowling Green State U Dept Chemistry Bowling Green OH 43402

MIDDLEBROOK, DIANE WOOD, English language educator, writer; b. Pocatello, Idaho, Apr. 16, 1939; d. Thomas Isaac and Helen Loretta (Downey) Wood; m. Jonathan Middlebrook, June 15, 1963 (annulled 1976); 1 child, Leah Wood; m. Carl Djerassi, June 21, 1985. BA, U. Wash., 1961; MA, Yale U., 1962, PhD, 1968; LittD (hon.), Kenyon Coll., 1999. Asst. prof. Stanford (Calif.) U., 1966-73, assoc. prof., 1973-83, prof., 1983-2001, dir. Ctr. for Rsch. on Women, 1977-79, prof. emerita, 2002—. Author: Walt Whitman and Wallace Stevens, 1974, Worlds into Words: Understanding Modern Poems, 1980, Anne Sexton, A Biography, 1991, Suits Me: The Double Life of Billy Tipton, 1998, Her Husband: Hughes and Plath, a Marriage, 2003; editor: Coming to Light: American Women Poets in the Twentieth Century, 1985; author: (poetry) Gin Considered as a Demon, 1983. Founding trustee Djerassi Resident Artists Program, Woodside, Calif., 1980—83, chair, 1994; trustee San Francisco Art Inst, 1993. Finalist Nat Book Award, 1991; recipient Yale Prize for Poetry; fellow Independent Study, NEH, 1982—83, Bunting Inst, Radcliffe Col, 1982—83, Guggenheim Found, 1988—89, Rockefeller Study Ctr, 1990. Mem.: MLA, Authors Guild, Internat. Assn. U. Profs. English, Biographers Club. Avocations: collecting art, theater. Home: 1101 Green St Apt 1501 San Francisco CA 94109-2012 Office: Agent Georges Borchardt 136 E 57th St New York NY 10022 E-mail: dwm@stanford.edu.

MIDDLETON, ANTHONY WAYNE, JR., urologist, educator; b. May 6, 1939; s. Anthony Wayne and Dolores Caravena (Lowry) M.; m. Carol Samuelson, Oct. 23, 1970; children: Anthony Wayne, Suzanne, Kathryn, Jane, Michelle. BS, U. Utah, 1963; MD, Cornell U., 1966. Intern U. Utah Hosps., Salt Lake City, 1966-67; resident in urology Mass. Gen. Hosp., Boston, 1970-74; practice urology Middleton Urol. Assocs., Salt Lake City, 1974—. Mem. staff LDS Hosp., chmn. divsn. urology, 1995—, Salt Lake Regional Med. Ctr., 1977—79, 1984—86; assoc. clin. prof. surgery U. Utah Med. Coll., 1977—; vice-chmn. bd. govs. Utah Med. Self-Ins. Assn., 1980—81, 1996—, chmn., 1985—87; chmn. med. adv. bd. Uroquest Co., 1996—99; med. dir. Uromed, prostate microwave co., 1999—2000, Utah divsn. Rocky Mountain Prostate, 2001—, Utah-Idaho Lithotripsy, 2001—. Editor: AACU-FAX, 1992—; assoc. editor Millenial Star Brit. LDS mag., 1960-61; contbr. articles to profl. jours. Mem. U. Utah Coll. Medicine Dean's Search Com., 1983—84; bd. dirs. Utah Symphony, 1985—2002, Primary Children's Found., 1989—96; mem. Utah Crime Reparations Bd., 2000—, chmn., 2002—; vice chmn. Utah Med. Polit. Action Com., 1978—81, chmn., 1981—83, Utah Physicians for Reagan, 1983—84; del. Utah State Rep. Conv., 2000—01; chmn. Utah Med. Polit. Action Com., 1981—83; bishop, later stake presidency Ch. Jesus Christ Latter-day Saints; bd. dirs. Utah chpt. Am. Cancer Soc., 1978—86, Utah Symphony and Opera, 2002—, Timpanogos Club, 1978—, 2d asst. to pres., 2002—03, 1st asst. to pres., 2003—. Capt. USAF, 1968—70. Mem.: AMA (del. to Ho. of Dels. 1998—, chmn. ref. com. I 2001, mem. governing coun. SSS 2002—, alt. del. to Ho. of Dels., 1987-88, 89-92, 94, 96-98), ACS, Am. Assn. Clin. Urologists (bd. dirs. 1989—90, nat. pres.-elect 1990—91, pres. 1991—92, nat. bd. chmn. urologic polit. action com. UROPAC 1992—98, Disting. Svc. award 2000), Salt Lake Surg. Soc. (treas. 1977—78), Utah Urol. Assn. (treas. 1977—78, pres. 1978—79), Salt Lake County Med. Assn. (sec. 1965—67, pres. liaison com. 1980—81, pres.-elect 1981—83, pres. 1984), Am. Urologic Assn. (socioecons. com. 1987—90, chmn. western sect. socioecons. com. 1989—90, chmn. western sect. health policy com. 1990—2002, pres.-elect western sect. 1999—2000, pres. 2000—01), Utah Med. Assn. (pres. 1987—88, Disting. Svc. award 1993), Beta Theta Pi (chpt. pres. Gamma Beta 1962), Alpha Omega Alpha, Phi Beta Kappa. Republican. Home: 2798 Chancellor Pl Salt Lake City UT 84108-2835 Office: 1060 East 1st South Salt Lake City UT 84102-1520 E-mail: awmiddleton@msn.com.

MIDDLETON, CHARLENE, retired medical and surgical nurse, educator; b. Ennis, Tex., Sept. 13, 1922; d. Charles Silvester and Harriet Eugenia (Ford) M. Diploma, Scott and White Hosp., Temple, Tex., 1945; AA, Temple Jr. Coll., 1947; BA, U. Tex., Austin, 1956. Nurse coord., ambulatory care svcs. Naval Regional Med. Ctr., Long Beach, Calif.; instr. nursing arts Scott and White Hosp., evening supr.; now ret. Lt. comdr. U.S. Navy, 1957-77. Mem. Scott and White Alumni Assn. (past pres. Dist. 7).

MIDDLETON, DAVID, physicist, applied mathematician, educator; b. N.Y.C., Apr. 19, 1920; s. Charles Davies Scudder and Lucile (Davidson) M.; m. Nadea Butler, May 26, 1945 (div. 1971); children: Susan Terry, Leslie Butler, David Scudder Blakeslee, George Davidson Powell; m. Joan Bartlett Reed, 1971; children: Christopher Hope, Andrew Bartlett, Henry H. Reed. Grad., Deerfield Acad., 1938; AB summa cum laude, Harvard U., 1942, AM, 1945, PhD in Physics, 1947. Tchg. fellow electronics Harvard U., Cambridge, Mass., 1942, spl. rsch. assoc. radio rsch. lab., 1942-45, NSF predoctoral fellow physics, 1945-47, rsch. fellow electronics, 1947-49, asst. prof. applied physics, 1949-54; cons. physicist Cambridge, 1954—, Concord, Mass., 1957-71, N.Y.C., 1971—; adj. prof. elec. engring. Columbia U., 1960-61; adj. prof. applied physics and comm. theory Rensselaer Poly. Inst., Hartford Grad. Ctr., 1961-70; adj. prof. communication theory U. R.I., 1966—; adj. prof. math. scis. Rice U., 1979-89. U.S. del. internat. conf. Internat. Radio Union, Lima, Peru, 1975; lectr. NATO Advanced Study Inst., Grenoble, France, 1964, Copenhagen, 1980, Luneburg, Germany, 1984; mem. Naval Rsch. Adv. Com., 1970-77; mem., cons. Inst. Def. Analyses; mem. sci. adv. bd. Supercomputing Rsch. Ctr., 1987-91; cons. physicist since 1946, orgns. including Johns Hopkins U., SRI Internat., Rand Corp., USAF, Cambridge Rsch. Ctr., Comm. Satellite Corp., Lincoln Lab., NASA, Raytheon, Sylvania, Sperry-Rand, Office Naval Rsch., Applied Rsch. Labs., U. Tex., GE, Honeywell Transp. Sys. Ctr. of Dept. Transp., Dept. Commerce Office of Telecom., NOAA, Office Telecom. Policy of Exec. Office Pres., Nat. Telecom. and Info. Adminstrn., Sci. Applications Inc. (SAIC), Naval Undersea Warfare Ctr., Lawrence Livermore Nat. Labs., Planning Rsch. Corp., Applied Physics Labs. U. Wash., 1992—, Kildare Corp., 1995—, Karmanos Cancer Inst., 1997-2001, others. Author: Introduction to Statistical Communication Theory, 1960, 3d edit., 1996, Russian edit. Soviet Radio Moscow, 2 vols., 1961, 62, Topics in Communication Theory, 1965, 87, Russian edit., 1966; sci. editor English edit. Statistical Methods in Sonar (V.V. Ol'shevskii), 1978; mem. editl. bd. Info. and Control, Advanced Serials in Electronics and Cybernetics, 1972-82; contbr. articles to tech. jours. Recipient award (with W.H. Huggins) Nat. Electronics Conf., 1956; Wisdom award of honor, 1970; First prize 3d Internat. Symposium on Electromagnetic Compatibility Rotterdam, Holland, 1979; awards U.S. Dept. Commerce, 1978 Fellow AAAS, IEEE (life, awards 1977, 79), Am. Phys. Soc., Explorers Club, Acoustical Soc. Am., N.Y. Acad. Scis., Electromagnetics Acad. MIT; mem. Am. Math. Soc., NAE, Author's Guild Am., Harvard Club (N.Y.C.), Cosmos Club (Washington), Dutch Treat (N.Y.C.), Phi Beta Kappa, Sigma Xi. Achievements include research in radar, telecommunications, underwater acoustics, oceanography, seismology, systems analysis, electromagnetic compatibility, communication theory; pioneering research in statistical communication theory. Home and Office: 127 E 91st St New York NY 10128-1601 Address: MIND 48 Garden St Cambridge MA 02138-1561 Home (Summer): 13 Harbor Rd Harwich Port MA 02646

MIDDLETON, DAWN E. education educator; b. Pottstown, Pa. d. William H. and Sara G. Bowman; m. Stephen R. Mourar, June 1983; children: William Middleton, Shelly Mourar. AA in Early Childhood Edn., Montgomery Community Coll., 1972; BS in Elem. Edn., West Chester State Coll., 1974; MA in Edn. Curriculum and Instrn. Edn., Pa. State U., 1982, DEd, 1984. Instr. Continuing Edn. Pa. State U., University Park; dir. specialized early childhood programs and svcs. Wiley House, Bethlehem, Pa.; dir. Children's Sch. of Cabrini Coll., Radnor, Pa.; dept. chmn., prof. edn. Cabrini Coll., Radnor. Home: 208 Bethel Rd Spring City PA 19475-3200

MIDDLETON, DEBORAH O, secondary educator, reading specialist; b. St. Louis, Apr. 9, 1956; d. Charles Harold and Bobbie Lee (Coburn) Downs; m. Kent Douglas Middleton, Mar. 29, 1980; children: Michael Scott, Samantha Lee. BA summa cum laude, U. Denver, 1978; MEd, U. Ill., Chgo., 1983; cert. advanced studies, Nat.-Louis U., Evanston, Ill., 1992. Cert. tchr., reading specialist, adminstr., Ill. Tchr. Lafayette High Sch., Ballwin, Mo., 1978-80; tchr., debate coach Glenbrook South High Sch., Glenview, Ill., 1980-81; tchr., speech coach, reading specialist Glenbrook North High Sch., Northbrook, Ill., 1981—, coord. Chpt. I, 1989—. Editor: Public Speaking Today, 1992. Mem. ASCD, Nat. Forensic League (dist. chmn. Chgo. 1987-89), Nat. Coun. Tchrs. English, Ill. Speech and Theatre Assn. (workshop leader 1987—), Phi Beta Kappa. Avocations: reading, softball, bicycling. Home: 4021 Bordeaux Dr Northbrook IL 60062-2139 Office: Glenbrook North High Sch 2300 Shermer Rd Northbrook IL 60062-6700

MIDDLETON, GEORGE, JR., clinical child psychologist; b. Houston, Feb. 26, 1923; s. George and Bettie (McCrary) M.; m. Margaret MacLean, Nov. 17, 1953. BA in Psychology, Birmingham-Southern Coll., 1948; MA in Psychology, U. Ala., Tuscaloosa, 1951; PhD in Clin. Psychology, Pa. State U., 1958. Lic. psychologist, La.; diplomate Am. Coll. Forensic Examiners, Am. Bd. Psychol. Specialities. Asst. clin. psychology Med. Coll. Ala., Birmingham, 1950-52; dir. dept. psychology Bryce Hosp., Tuscaloosa, 1952-54; instr. counseling Coll. Bus. Adminstrn. Pa. State U., 1956-58; asst. prof. spl. edn. McNeese State U., 1962-65, assoc. prof. spl. edn., 1962-65; dir. La. Gov.'s Program for Gifted Children, 1963—; prof. spl. edn. McNeese State U., 1965-73, prof. psychology, 1973-74; pvt. practice clin. psychology and neuropsychology, 1974—; cons. psychologist Calcasieu Parish Sch. Bd., 1975—. Vis. scholar U. Victoria, BC, Can., 1970-71. Mem. Am. Psychol. Assn., Nat. Acad. Neuropsychology, Internat. Neuropsychol. Soc., La. Psychol. Assn. (pres. 1973-74), La. Sch. Psychol. Assn., S.W. La. Psychol. Assn. (pres. 1965, 73, 84), La. State Bd. Examiners Psychologists (chmn. 1977-78), Coun. for Exceptional Children, Am. Coll. Forensic Examiners, 1996. Assn. for the Gifted. Episcopalian. Home and Office: 2001 Southwood Dr Ste A Lake Charles LA 70605-4139

MIDDLETON, GREGORY ALFONSO, elementary school educator; b. N.Y.C., Feb. 12, 1967; s. James Raymond and Florence Marie (Ashe) M. BA in Urban Studies, Fordham U., 1991, MS in Elem. Edn., 1992; PD in Sch. Dist. Adminstrn., Coll. of New Rochelle, N.Y., 2001. Cert. tchr., N.Y. Family asst. N.Y.C. Bd. Edn., 1989-91; tchr. Archdiocese of N.Y., N.Y.C., 1991-92, N.Y.C. Bd. Edn., 1992-93, New Rochelle City Sch. Dist., 1993—2001; asst. prin. The Murray Ave. Sch. Mamaroneck (N.Y.) Union Free Sch. Dist., 2001—03; asst. prin. The Mamaroneck Ave. Sch., White Plains Cmty. Sch. Dist., 2003—. Mem. adv. bd., youth min. Pierre Toussaint Inst., N.Y.C., 1984-99. Assoc. dir. The N.Y. Boy's Choir, N.Y.C., 1983-97; mem. Ctrl. Harlem Vicariate Coun., N.Y.C., 1993-96. Fellow Fordham U., 1991. Democrat. Roman Catholic. E-mail: eachone@aol.com.

MIDDLETON, HERMAN DAVID, SR., theater educator; b. Sanford, Fla., Mar. 24, 1925; s. Arthur Herman and Ruby Elmerry (Hart) M.; m. Amelia Mary Eggart, Dec. 1, 1945; children— Herman David, Kathleen Hart. BS, Columbia U., 1948, MA, 1949; PhD, U. Fla., 1964; postgrad., N.Y. U., 1950, Northwestern U., 1951. Instr., dir. drama and speech Maryville (Tenn.) Coll., 1949-50; instr., designer, tech. dir. theatre U. Del., 1951-55; asst. prof., head dept. drama U. N.C., Greensboro, 1956-59, assoc. prof., head dept. drama and speech, 1959-65, prof., head dept., 1965-74, prof., 1974-79, Excellence Fund prof. dept. communication and theatre, 1979-90, prof. emeritus, 1990. Designer Chucky Jack, Great Smokey Mountains Hist. Soc., Gatlinburg, Tenn., 1956, designer, dir., 1957; communications cons. N.C. Nat. Bank, 1968, Jefferson Standard Life Ins. Co., Greensboro, N.C., 1969, Gilbarco, Inc., Greensboro, 1969-70, 73 Drama critic, columnist: Sunday Star, Wilmington, Del., 1952; theatre editor: Players Mag, 1959-61; theatre columnist: Sunday editions Greensboro Daily News, 1959-62; contbr. articles to profl. jours. Mem. N.C. Arts Council Commn., 1964-66, Guilford County Bi-Centennial Celebration Commn., 1969-70; pres. Shanks Village Players, Orangeburg, N.Y.C., 1947-48, Univ. Drama Group, Newark, Del., 1954-55; bd. dirs. Broadway Theatre League Greensboro, 1958-60, Greensboro Community Arts Council, 1964-67, 69-72, Greensboro Community Theatre, 1983-86, Carolina Theatre Commn., 1990—; organizer-cons. The Market Players, West Market St. United Meth. Ch., 1979-82. Served with USN, 1943-46. Recipient O. Henry award Greensboro C. of C., 1966, Gold medallion Amoco Oil Co., 1973, Suzanne M. Davis award Southeastern Theatre Conf., 1975, Marian A. Smith Disting. Career award N.C. Theatre Conf., 1990. Mem. Am. Nat. Theatre and Acad. (organizer, exec. v.p. Piedmont chpt. 1957-60), Am. Theatre Assn. (chmn. bd. nominations 1971-72), Am. Coll. Theatre Festival (regional festival dir. 1973, 80, regional dir., mem. nat. com. 1978-80), Assn. for Theatre in Higher Edn. (founding mem. 1986-87), Speech Communication Assn. Am., Nat. Collegiate Players, Southeastern Theatre Conf. (bd. dirs. 1963-68, 87-92, pres. 1965, pres. pro-tem 1966), Carolina Dramatic Assn. (bd. dirs. 1958-59), N.C. Drama and Speech Assn. (pres. 1966-67), N.C. Theatre Conf. (co-organizer 1971, bd. dirs. 1984-92, pres. 1987-88), Assn. for Theater in Higher Edn., Phi Delta Kappa, Phi Kappa Phi, Theta Alpha Phi, Alpha Psi Omega. Democrat. Methodist. Home: 203 Village Ln Unit A Greensboro NC 27409-2517

MIDDLETON, MARY, secondary education educator; b. Lackawana, N.Y., Nov. 13, 1942; d. Arthur Jordan and Kathryn (Sternburg) M. BS in Edn., Ohio State U., 1965; postgrad., Akron U., 1970, Cleve. State U., 1981-84. Profl. cert. in edn. Tchr. Columbus (Ohio) Schs., 1966-68, Brooklyn (Ohio) Schs., 1968-98. Co-dir. C.A.R.E. (Chem. Abuse Reduced through Edn.), Brooklyn (Ohio) City, 1986-95, Englist dept. chair, acad. team advisor Brooklyn (Ohio) Schs., 1987-98; mem. dimensions of learning task force Bklyn. Schs., 1997; core team mem. Comprehensive Mgmt., 1996-98. Contbr. articles to profl. jours. Campaign worker North Olmsted (Ohio) Dem. club, 1988, 92, 96; recreation dir. Country Club Condominiums, 1992-2000. Recipient N.E. Ohio Writing Project fellowship Martha Holden Jennings, Cleve. State U., 1985. Mem. Cinnamon Woods Condominiums Assn. (bd. dirs., pres.), Re-elect the Pres. Com., Ohio State U. Alumni Assn. Pres.'s Club, Neighbors Who Care (pub. rels. com., editor), Phi Mu. Methodist. Avocations: swimming, reading, travel, tennis. Home: 24026 S Sunny Side Dr Sun Lakes AZ 85248

MIDDLETON, RICHARD A. school system administrator; Bachelors Degree, Trinity U.; Masters Degree, U. Tex., San Antonio; PHD, U. Tex. Tchr. history and govt. Roosevelt H.S. N.E. Ind. Sch. Dist., San Antonio, 1972, supt., 1990—. Mem.: Carnegie Found. for Advancement Tchg. (bd. mem.). Office: Cmty Rels Office Ste 602 8961 Tesoro Dr San Antonio TX 78217*

MIDELFORT, HANS CHRISTIAN ERIK, history educator; b. Eau Claire, Wis., Apr. 17, 1942; s. Peter Albert and Gerd (Gjems) M.; m. Corelyn Forsyth Senn, June 16, 1965 (div. Dec. 1981); children: Katarina, Kristian; m. Cassandra Clemons Hughes, May 25, 1985 (div. April 1996); 1 child, Lucy; m. Anne L. McKeithen, June 22, 1996. BA, Yale U., 1964, MPhil, 1967, PhD, 1970. Instr. Stanford (Calif.) U., 1968-70; asst. prof. U. Va., Charlottesville, 1970-72, assoc. prof., 1972-87, prof., 1987—, Charles Julian Bishko prof. history, 1996—. Vis. prof. Harvard U., Cambridge, Mass., 1985, U. Stuttgart, Germany, 1988, U. Bern, Switzerland, 1988, Wolfson Coll., Oxford U., 2002, Yale U., 2003; prin. Brown Coll., U. Va., 1996-2001; Dwight Terry lectr. Yale U., 2003. Author: Witch Hunting in Southwestern Germany, 1972 (Gustave Arlt prize 1972), Mad Princes of Renaissance Germany, 1994 (Roland H. Bainton prize 16th Century Studies Conf. 1995), A History of Madness in 16th Century Germany, 1999 (Ralph Waldo Emerson prize, Phi Beta Kappa, 1999, Roland H. Bainton prize 16th Century Studies Conf. 2000); editor: Johann Weyer, On Witchcraft, 1998; translator: Imperial Cities and the Reformation (Bernd Moeller), 1972, Revolution of 1525 (Peter Bickle), 1981, Shaman of Oberstdorf (Wolfgang Behringer), 1998. Mem. Soc. Reformation Rsch. (pres. 1992-93). Office: U Va Dept History Charlottesville VA 22903 E-mail: hem7e@virginia.edu.

MIELKE, JON ALAN, elementary school administrator; b. Racine, Wis., Mar. 29, 1954; s. Paul Gilbert and Gloria Ester (Bronson) M.; m. Judy Mae Pelz, June 16, 1979; children: Jeremy, Justin, Jonathan. BA, Concordia Coll., 1979, MA, 1986. Lic. elementary administrator, Wis. Tchr. Grace Luth. Sch., St. Petersburg, Fla., 1979-84; adminstr. First Immanuel Luth. Sch., Cedarburg, Wis., 1986—. Mem. Ea. Ofcls. Assn., Luth. Educators Assn., Assn. for Supervision and Curriculum Devel. Republican. Avocations: officiating high school and college basketball, golf, softball, water skiing. Home: N76w7182 Linden St Cedarburg WI 53012-1116 Office: First Immanuel Lutheran Sch W67n622 Evergreen Blvd Cedarburg WI 53012-1848

MIEROW, SHARON ANN, special education educator; b. Milw., Aug. 9, 1950; d. Leonard Norbert and Esther Marie (Kramer) Banaszynski; children: Natalie Ann, Noelle Marie. MusB, St. Norbert Coll., 1972. Educator music Alverno Coll. Young Peoples Arts, Milw., 1980-85, Cullins Lake-Pointe Elem. Sch., Rowlett, Tex., 1988-90, Naamen Forest High Sch.,

Garland, Tex., 1990-92; educator spl. edn. Dobbs Elem. Sch., Rockwall, Tex., 1992-96, Nebbie Williams Elem. Sch., Rockwall, Tex., 1996—; educator music pvt. practice, Rockwall, Tex., 1992—. In-home instr. for families with children who have autism. Cantor O.L.O.L. Cath. Ch., Rockwall, 1996, 97. Named Tchr. of Yr., 1989-90, 97-98. Mem. Nat. Music Tchrs. Assn., Tex. Music Tchrs. Assn., Garland Music Tchrs. Assn., Mu Phi Epsilon. Democrat. Avocations: family, reading, travel, musicals, theater. Home: 1009 Signal Ridge Pl Rockwall TX 75032-5414 Office: Nebbie William Elem Sch 350 Dalton Rd Rockwall TX 75087-7061

MIEUX, DONNA MARIE, special education educator; b. L.A., Feb. 10, 1949; d. Donald Lee and Alma Olivia (Johnson) Troy; m. Isom (Ike) Mieux, June 9, 1972; children: Kendra Desiree, Andre Donald. BA in Sociology, U. Calif., Santa Barbara, 1971; MA in Spl. Edn., U. Akron, 1976; EdD, Nova Southeastern U., 1993. Cert. spl. edn.; cert. tchr. Lang. enrichment tchr. L.A. Unified Sch. Dist., 1972-74; resource specialist Whittier (Calif.) City Sch. Dist., 1976-79, Hacienda La Puente (Calif.) Unified Sch. Dist., 1979—, mentor. tchr., 1993—, tchr. severely handicapped, 1989-92, artist-of-the-month developer, stamp club sponsor, 1988-90. Developer, coord. before sch. tutorial program for at-risk students, 1990—; adj. faculty psychology The Union Inst., L.A., 1994—; instr. writing Mt. San Antonio Coll., Walnut, Calif., 1994—. Sunday sch. tchr. United Ch. of Christ, Claremont, Calif., 1989-93; mem. PTA, La Puente, 1972—; vol. Rancho Los Amigos Hosp., Brownies, Girl Scouts USA, various sports activities, 1969—. Recipient scholarship Compton Tchrs. Assn., 1967, Martin Luther King scholarship Calif. Tchrs. Assn., 1990; fellow Occidental Coll., 1971. Mem. Nat. Tchrs. Assn., Calif. Tchrs. Assn. Democrat. Avocations: sculpturing, writing, viewing high quality foreign movies, tennis. Office: Palm Elem Sch 14740 Palm Ave Hacienda Heights CA 91745

MIGIMOTO, FUMIYO KODANI, retired secondary education educator; b. Oxnard, Calif, Jan. 2, 1918; d. Katsutaro and Yoshio Kodani; m. Tadao Migimoto, June 1956. BA, UCLA, 1939, cert. teaching, 1940; MA, Oberlin Coll., 1953; cert. in teaching, U. Hawaii, 1956. Cert. secondary tchr., Calif., Hawaii. Asst. to dean of coll. Oberlin Coll., Ohio; English tchr. Jackson Coll., Honolulu, Hawaii State Dept. Edn., Honolulu; retired. Mem. textbook evaluation com. Hawaii. Author many poems, editor, military newsletters 1993-1999. Hawaii State Dept. Edn. grantee. Mem ASCD, Internat. Soc. Poets, Pan-Pacific S.E. Asia Women's Assn. Hawaii (past exec. v.p.), Hawaii Edn. Assn., Hawaii State Retired Tchr. Assn., Oahu Retired Tchr. Assn., Alliance for Drama Edn., UCLA Alumni Assn., Oberlin Alumni Assn., Poetry Acad., Alpha Delta Kappa (past chpt. exec. pres., chmn. frat. edn.). Home: 999 Wilder Ave Apt 303 Honolulu HI 96822-2628

MIGUEL, LINDA J. critical care nurse, nursing educator; b. Honolulu, Dec. 6, 1946; d. Gregory and Irene N. (Calasa) Furtado; children: Joseph H. Miguel Jr., Brett A. Miguel. ADN, Maui Community Coll., Kahului, Hawaii, 1980; BSN, U. Hawaii, 1987, MS, 1990. RN, Hawaii. Charge nurse ICU-CCU Maui Meml. Hosp., Wailuku, 1980-88; nursing instr. Maui Community Coll., Kahului, 1988; unit supr.-coronary care Straub Clinic and Hosp., Honolulu, 1988-90; nursing instr. Kapiolani Community Coll., Honolulu, 1990-92; edn. dir. Waianae Health Acad., 1992-96; nursing svcs. mgr. Kula Hosp., Maui, 1997-98; edn. dir. Waianae (Hawaii) Health Acad., 1992-97, 98—. Researcher in field. Contbr. articles to profl. jours. Outer Island Students Spl. Nursing scholar, 1989, Rsch. scholarship, 1989. Mem. AACN, Hawaii Nurses Assn., Hawaii Soc. for Cardiovascular and Pulmonary Rehab., Assn. Am. Women in C. C.s, Sigma Theta Tau. Home: 98-402 Koauka Loop Apt 1202 Aiea HI 96701-4572 Office: Waianae Health Acad 86-088 Farrington Hwy Ste 202 Waianae HI 96792-3042 E-mail: miguell001@hawaii.rr.com.

MIHAL, SANDRA POWELL, systems analyst; b. Balt., Dec. 15, 1941; d. Sanford William and Mary Louise (Barry) Powell; m. James George Anderson, June 15, 1963; children: Robin Marie, James Brian, Melissa Lee, Derek Clair; m. Charles Turner Barber, Apr. 18, 1978; stepchildren: Gretchen Jayco, Katrina Hope; m. Ladislaw Paul Mihal, May 25, 1991; stepchildren: Alexander Paul, Suzie May, Natasha Elizabeth, Rudy Darius. BA, Mt. St. Agnes Coll., 1963; MA, N.Mex. State U., 1970, Purdue U., 1975; EdD, Vanderbilt U., 1990. Cert. tchr., Md. Tchr. Ridgely-Dulaney Jr. H.S., Towson, Md., 1964; grad. asst. N.Mex. State U., Las Cruces, 1967—69; acad. advisor, instr. polit. sci. Purdue U., West Lafayette, Ind., 1974—78; prof., acad. sys. analyst U. So. Ind., Evansville, 1978—82; assoc. prof., chair dept. computer info. sys. Henderson (Ky.) C.C., 1982—88; prof. computer tech., divsn. chair Anne Arundel C.C., Arnold, Md., 1988—91; computer sys. analyst immigration and naturalization svc. Dept. of Justice, Washington, 1991—92, Glynco, Ga., 1995—; dep. program mgr. distributed learning Fed. Law Enforcement Training Ctr., Homeland Security, Glynco, Ga., 2002—. Bd. dirs. Ind. Polit. Sci. Assn., Muncie, 1984-88, Internat. Studies Assn.-Midwest, Chgo., 86-88; pres. Ky. Acad. Computer Users' Group, Lexington, 1985-86; mem. telecom. adv. bd. C.C. Sys., Annapolis, Md., 1990-91; computer sys. network analyst CLARC Svcs., Pt. Charlotte, Fla., 92-95; adj. prof. history and polit. sci. Edison C.C., Punta Gorda, Fla., 1993-95. Author: Learning By Doing BASIC, 1983, Computers Learning By Doing, 1984; contbr. to several profl jours. 1980-90; author, spkr. series Faculty/Staff Edison CC 94, Ednl. Tech. Nova U., 1995. Block coord. several neighborhood assns.; computer adv. bd. Henderson County Sch., 1982-88; chmn. Newburgh (Ind.) Youth Orgn., 78-86; judge Sci. Fair, Annapolis, 1988-90; nomination bd. Ky. Higher Edn. Assn., 1989-91; mem. Charlotte Chorale, Port Charlotte, 1992-94, Peace River Power Squadron, Port Charlotte, 1994-96. Coast Guard Aux., 1995-97. Md. State Tchr. Bd. Edn. scholar, 1960-63; fellow Sloan Found., 1973-75, U. Ky., 1984. Mem, Soc. Applied Learning Tech., Assn. Computing Machinery (v.p. 85—), Am. Legion, Pi Gamma Mu. Democrat. Mem. Ch. Of Christ. Avocations: sailing, singing, swimming, cooking, playing the dulcimer. Home: 112 Oak Ridge Rd Brunswick GA 31523-9741

MIKA, JOSEPH JOHN, library school director, educator, consultant; b. McKees Rocks, Pa., Mar. 1, 1948; s. George Joseph and Sophie Ann (Stec) M.; m. Marianne Hartzell; children: Jason-Paul Joseph, Matthew Douglas, Meghan Leigh. BA in English, U. Pitts., 1969, MLS, 1971, PhD in Libr. Sci., 1980. Asst. libr., instr. Ohio State U., Mansfield, 1971-73; asst. libr., asst. prof. Johnson State Coll., Vt., 1973-75; grad. asst., tchg. fellow Sch. Libr. and Info. Sci., U. Pitts., 1975-77; asst. dean, assoc. prof. libr. svc. U. So. Miss., Hattiesburg, 1977-86; dir. libr. and info. sci. program Wayne State U., 1986—95, 2002—, prof., 1994—2001. Cons. to libraries; co-owner Libr. Jobs Network, Libr. Tng. Network. Editor Jour. of Edn. for Libr. and Info. Sci., 1995—. Col. USAR. Decorated DSM. Mem. ALA (councilor 1983-86, 98-2001, chmn. constn. and bylaws com. 1985-86), Assn. Libr. and Info. Sci. Edn. (chmn. membership com. 1982-83, chmn. nominating com. 1982, exec. bd. 1986), Miss. Libr. Assn. (pres.-elect 1985), Mich. Libr. Assn. (chair libr. edn. com. 1989), Leadership Acad. (oversight com. 1989-95), Assn. Coll. and Rsch. Librs. (chmn. 1982-83, chmn. budget com. 1982-83), Soc. Miss. Archivists (treas., exec. bd. 1981-83), Mich. Ctr. for the Book (chair 1994-2001), Kiwanis (Hattiesburg), Beta Phi Mu (pres.-elect 1987-89, pres. 1989-91), Phi Delta Kappa. Home: 222 Abbott Woods Dr East Lansing MI 48823-1995 Office: Wayne State U Libr and Info Sci Program 106 Kresge Library Detroit MI 48202 E-mail: aa2500@wayne.edu.

MIKISKA, JENIFER ANN, public relations executive; b. Moline, Ill., Oct. 16, 1959; d. Murle J. and Annabelle (Blackman) K.; 1 child from previous marriage, Nathaniel Glen Kell Hardy; m. Edward S. Sutton, Oct. 18, 1991. Student, Monmouth Coll., 1977-78, Carl Sandburg Jr. Coll., 1978-79; cert. in landscape design cons., Lifetime Career Sch., 1982. Farmer, Carthage, Ill., 1978-88; staff writer, photographer Hancock County Jour. Pilot, Carthage, 1978-79; bookkeeper, receptionist Hancock Svc. Co., Carthage, 1979; spl. programs dir. WCAZ Radio, Carthage, 1981-82; legis. asst. Ill. State Rep. Kent Slater, 1987-88; pub. rels. dir. Meml. Hosp. and Hancock County Nursing Home, Carthage, 1988-91; mktg. mgr., govt. rels. specialist, co-owner Sutton & Sons Refuse Disposal Svc., Inc., St. Louis, 1991—2002; landscape designer, mgr. field oper. landscape divsn. Frisella Nursery, Inc., Florissant, Mo., 2003—. Speaker in field. Editor, writer newsletter STAT. Cem. Nat. Women's Polit. Caucus, 1983—; campaign coord. Kent Slater for State Rep., Hancock County, 1983-88; mem. Hancock County Rep. Women, 1984—; bd. dirs. Quad City Coalition Against Domestic Violence, 1985-88, v.p. 1987-88, co-chair fundraising 1986-87; mem. home econs. program coun. Hancock County Coop. Extension Svc. 1984-88, sec., 1985-86, chair, 1986-88, sec.-treas. exec. coun., 1985-86, chair, 1986-88; sec. young farmer com. Hancock County Farm Bur., 1985-88. Recipient award Young Farmers Dist. award Ill. Farm Bur., 1987. Mem. Ill. Healthcare Pub. Rels. Soc., Am. Soc. for Hosp. Mktg. and Pub. Rels., Am. Hosp. Assn. (mem. spl. pub. rels. subcom. task force 1988-89), Carthage Bus. and Profl. Women (fin. com. 1985, legis. com. 1986-91, mem. young careerist com. 1988-89), Future Farmers Am. Alumni (life), Hancock County Econ. Devel. Assn. (sec. 1988-89, 1st v.p. 1990-91, chair healthcare subcom. 1989-91, mem. transp. com. 1988-89). Republican. Avocations: politics, painting, reading, horseback riding.

MIKOLYZK, THOMAS ANDREW, librarian; b. Kenosha, Wis., Sept. 9, 1953; s. Andrew John and Charlotte Elaine (McIver) M.; m. Ann J. Moyer, May 26, 1973 (div. June 1981); children: Kari, Emily; m. Amy L. Kessel, Sept. 4, 1982; 1 child, Alice; 1 stepchild, David. BA in English and Elem. Edn., Beloit (Wis.) Coll., 1982; MA in Libr. Sci., U. Chgo., 1986; cert. in advanced study, Concordia U., 1995. Libr. asst. Beloit Coll., 1980-82; sports writer Beloit Daily News, 1981-83; tchr. Turner Mid. Sch., Beloit, 1983; tchr., libr. Horizon's Edge Sch., Canterbury, N.H., 1983-85; libr. U. Ill., Chgo., 1985-86, Lake Forest (Ill.) Coll., 1986-89, Dist 62, Des Plaines, Ill., 1989-93; libr., dir. summer program Avery Coonley Sch., Downers Grove, Ill., 1993-97; libr. Prevention First, Inc., Chgo., 1999—. Dir. edn. cons., 1993—. Author: Langston Hughes-A Bio-Bibliography, 1990, Oscar Wilde: An Annotated Bibliography, 1993. Campaign mgr. United Way, Delavan, Wis., 1978-79; deacon 1st Congregation Ch., Des Plaines, 1990. Mem. Ill. Sch. Libr. Assn., Ind. Sch. Assn. Ctrl. States, U.S. Chess Fedn. Avocations: chess, bibliography, book collecting, sailing. Home: 7361 Prescott Ln La Grange IL 60525-5037 Office: 720 N Franklin St Chicago IL 60610-7214

MIKULAS, JOSEPH FRANK, graphic designer, educator, painter; b. Jacksonville, Fla., Sept. 15, 1926; s. Joseph and Marina (Zeman) M.; m. Joyce Gregory Haddock, Sept. 29, 1946; children: Joyce Marina Mikulas Abney, Juliana Claire Mikulas Catlin. Student, Harold Hilton Studios, 1942-540. Art dir. Peeples Displays, Inc., 1945-50, 53-56, Douglas Printing Co., Inc., 1950-53, 56-59; ptnr., graphic design exec. Benton & Mikulas Assocs., Inc., Jacksonville, 1960-67; pres. Mikulas Assocs., Inc., Jacksonville, 1968-92. Exec. graphic designer, retired dir. communications, adj. prof. advt. design Jacksonville U.; mem. adv. bd. Pub. TV. Chmn. Youth Resources Bur.; chmn. Mayor's Medal Com. Creator over 40 trademarks for local, regional, nat. and internat. use by corps. based in Jacksonville. Sr. Warden, St. John's Cathedral. Served with USAAF, 1945. Recipient Gold medal Am. Advt. Fedn., 4th dist., 1971; numerous other awards, 1960-81. Mem. Advt. Fedn. Jacksonville (past pres. 1970), Jacksonville Watercolor Soc. (past pres.), San Jose Country Club, River Club, Art Dirs. of Jacksonville (past pres.), Masons, Rotary (past pres. S. Jacksonville 1970, Paul Harris fellow), Torch of Jacksonville (past pres. 1977). Home: 2014 River Rd Jacksonville FL 32207-3906

MIKURIYA, MARY JANE, retired educational agency administrator; b. Pitts., Oct. 8, 1934; d. Tadafumi and Anna (Schwenk) M.; m. J. Anton Jungherr, June 8, 1977 (div. Dec. 1992); children: Anna Schwenk Mikuriya Jungherr, Anton Jungherr Jr. BA, Brown U., 1956; MA, San Francisco State U., 1970. Cert. tchr. and adminstr., Calif. Tchr. Castilleja Sch. for Girls, Palo Alto, Calif., 1958-60, Mpls. Pub. Schs., 1961-62; tchr., evaluator, adminstr. San Francisco Unified Sch. Dist., 1963-73; HEW fellow U.S. Dept. of Edn., Washington, 1973-74, edn. program specialist, 1974-76; with adminstrv. staff San Francisco Unified Sch. Dist., 1976-98, ret., 1998. Interviewer, bd. dirs. U.S. Servas, 1978—; active Unitarian Ch., 1978—; host Internat. Diplomacy Coun., 1985—. Mem. Japanese-Am. Citizens League. Avocation: international travel. Home: 361 Mississippi St San Francisco CA 94107-2925

MILAN, MARJORIE LUCILLE, early childhood education educator; b. Ludlow, Colo., June 24, 1926; d. John B. and Barbara (Zenonian) Pinamont; m. John Francis Milan, June 18, 1949; children: Barbara, J. Mark, Kevin. BA, U. Colo., 1947, MA, 1978; PhD, U. Denver, 1983. Cert. tchr., adminstr., supt., Colo. Tchr. Boulder (Colo.) Pub. Schs., 1947-49, Denver Pub. Schs., 1949-51, 67—; adminstr. T. Tot Kindergarten, Denver, 1951-55; tchr. Colo. Women's Coll., Denver, 1956-57; adminstr. Associated Schs., Denver, 1956-67. Adv. bd. George Washington Carver Nursery, Denver, 1960-85. Mem. Assn. Childhood Edn. (state bd. 1960—, Hall of Excellence 1991), Rotary (pres. chpt. 1994-95), Philanthropic Ednl. Orgn., Phi Delta Kappa, Delta Kappa Gamma. Avocations: swimming, music. Home: 1775 Lee St Lakewood CO 80215-2855

MILANDER, HENRY MARTIN, educational consultant; b. Northampton, Pa., Apr. 17, 1939; s. Martin Edward and Margaret Catherine (Makovetz) M.; children: Martin Henry, Beth Ann. BS summa cum laude, Lock Haven U., Pa., 1961; MA, Bowling Green (Ohio) State U., 1962; EdS (Future Faculty fellow 1964), U. No. Iowa, 1965; EdD, Ill. State U., Normal, 1967. Instr. Wartburg Coll., Waverly, Iowa, 1962-64; asst. prof. Ill. State U., 1966-67; dean instrn. Belleville (Ill.) Area Coll., 1967-69; v.p. acad. affairs Lorain County Community Coll., Elyria, Ohio, 1969-72; pres. Olympic Coll., Bremerton, Wash., 1972-87, Northeastern Jr. Coll., Sterling, Colo., 1988-95; ednl. cons., 1995—. Pres. Bremers, Inc., 1986-87. Contbr. articles to profl. jours. Pres. Kitsap County Comprehensive Health Planning Council, 1975-76; pres. Logan County Colo. United Way, 1992-93. Recipient Faculty Growth award Wartburg Coll., 1963, Community Service award, 1975, Chief Thunderbird award, 1985. Mem. Am. Assn. C.C., Am. Assn. Sch. Adminstrs., N.W. Assn. Cmty. and Jr. Colls., Wash. Assn. C.C. (pres. 1984-85), Wash. C.C. Computing Consortium (chmn. bd. dirs. 1985-87), Puget Sound Naval Bases Assn. (pres. 1982-86), Wash. Assn. C.C. Pres. (pres. 1984-85), Bremerton Area C. of C. (pres. 1977-78), Colo. Assn. C.C. Pres. (pres. 1993-94), Rotary (pres. Sterling Club 1992-93), Kappa Delta Pi, Phi Delta Kappa. Lutheran. Home: 1290 Raven Creek Dr NW Bremerton WA 98311-9042

MILANO, HEATHER CASEY, retired secondary education educator; b. St. John, N.B., Can., Mar. 2, 1934; B.A. in L.S., St. Francis Xavier U., Antigonish, N.S., Can., 1956; M.Sc. in Audiovisual Edn., Western Conn. State Coll., Danbury, 1976; married, 2 children. Librarian various schs., 1957-59; library media specialist Putnam Valley (N.Y.) Central Sch. Dist. 2, 1972— . Mem. cultural com. Putnam Valley Pub. Library, 1972-74; media council rep. to Bd. Coop. Ednl. Services, Yorktown Heights, N.Y., 1973— . Mem. N.Y. State United Tchrs., Sch. Librarians of Southeastern N.Y. Pi Lambda Theta. Certified library media specialist, N.Y. State. Home: 132 Wauquanesit Dr Brewster MA 02631-1215

MILANO, MARYANN T. elementary school educator; b. N.Y.C., Oct. 13, 1950; d. Salvatore Joseph and Angela Lee (Nardone) M. BA, Marymount Manhattan Coll., 1972; MA, Columbia U., N.Y.C., 1973. Cert. tchr., N.Y. Tchr. Our Lady of Perpetual Help, Pelham Manor, N.Y., 1973-74, Our Lady of Grace Sch., N.Y.C., 1974-79, Pub. Sch. 103, N.Y.C. Bd. Edn., Bronx, 1979—. Mem. Pub. Sch. 103 PTA, 1979—. Recipient Educator of Yr. awrd Dist. 11, Bronx, 1991. Democrat. Roman Catholic. Avocations: travel, reading, embroidery and crewel, theater. Home: 178 Garth Rd Apt 2I Scarsdale NY 10583-3835 Office: Pub Sch 103 4125 Carpenter Ave Bronx NY 10466-2601

MILANOVICH, NORMA JOANNE, training and development company executive; b. Littlefork, Minn., June 4, 1945; d. Lyle Albert and Loretta (Leona) Drake; m. Rudolph William Milanovich, Mar. 18, 1943 (dec.); 1 child, Rudolph William Jr. BS in Home Econs., U. Wis., Stout, 1968; MA in Curriculum and Instrn., U. Houston, 1973, EdD in Curriculum and Program Devel., 1982. Instr. human svcs. dept. U. Houston, 1971-75; dir. videos project U. N.Mex., Albuquerque, 1976-78, dir. vocat. edn. equity ctr., 1978-88, asst. prof. occupational edn., 1982-88, coord. occupational vocat. edn. programs, 1983-88, dir. consortium rsch. and devel. in occupational edn., 1984-88; pres. Alpha Connection Tng. Corp., Albuquerque, 1988—; exec. dir. Trinity Found., 1991—; pres. Athena Leadership Ctr., 1999—. Adj. instr. Cen. Tng. Acad., Dept. Energy, Wackenhut; mem. faculty U. Phoenix; adj. faculty So. Ill. U., Lesley Coll., Boston; lectr. in field. Author: Model Equitable Behavior in the Classroom, 1983, Handbook for Vocational-Technical Certification in New Mexico, 1985, A Vision for Kansas: Systems of Measures and Standards of Performance, 1992, Workplace Skills: The Employability Factor, 1993; editor: Choosing What's Best for You, 1982, A Handbook for Handling Conflict in the Classroom, 1983, Starting Out...A Job Finding Handbook for Teen Parents, Going to Work...Job Rights for Teens; author: JTPA Strategic Marketing Plan, 1990, We, The Arcturians, 1990, Sacred Journey to Atlantis, 1991, The Light Shall Set You Free, 1996; editor: Majestic Raise newsletter, 1996—, Celestial Voices newsletter, 1991—. Del. Youth for Understanding Internat. Program, 1985—90; mem. adv. bd. Southwestern Indian Poly. Inst., 1984—88; com. mem. Region VI Consumer Exch. Com., 1982—84; coord. various countries Worldwide Conf. for Peace on Earth, Italy, Jordan, Azaru, Africa, India, 1999—2004; coord. Customized Leadership Programs, 2004; bd. dirs. Albuquerque Single Parent Occupational Scholarship Program, 1984—86. Grantee N.Mex. Dept. Edn., 1976-78, 78-86, 83-86, HEW, 1979, 80, 81, 83, 84, 85, 86, 87. Mem. ASTD, Am. Vocat. Assn., Vocat. Edn. Equity Coun., Nat. Coalition for Sex Equity Edn., Am. Home Econs. Assn., Inst. Noetic Scis., N.Mex. Home Econs. Assn., N.Mex. Vocat. Edn. Assn., N.Mex. Adv. Coun. on Vocat. Edn., Greater Albuquerque C. of C., NAFE, Phi Delta Kappa, Phi Upsilon Omicron, Phi Theta Kappa. Democrat. Roman Catholic. Office: Athena Leadership Ctr Scottsdale AZ 85259 E-mail: info@athenalctr.com.

MILES, DONNA REGINA, educator, researcher; b. Albuquerque, Dec. 17, 1969; d. John Herman Gieske, Helen Edith Gieske; m. Thomas Raymond Miles; children: Ashleigh, Brittany, Madeline. BS, U. N.Mex., 1991; PhD, U. Colo., 1997. Postdoctoral fellow Nat. Inst. on Drug Abuse, Balt., 1997—98, Inst. for Drug and Alcohol Studies, Va. Commonwealth U., Richmond, 1998—2001; asst. prof. dept. human genetics Va. Commonwealth U., Richmond, 2001—. Fellow, U. Colo., Boulder, 1992—93; scholar Bldg. Interdisciplinary Rsch. Careers in Women's Health award scholar, 2001. Mem.: Behavioral Genetics Assn., Phi Beta Kappa. Achievements include research in in substance abuse. Office: Va Commonwealth Univ PO Box 980003 Richmond VA 23298 Business E-Mail: dmiles@hsc.vcu.edu.

MILES, EILEEN FITZ, private school educator; b. Balt., Mar. 1, 1940; d. Mark and Marion (Kramer) Fitz; m. Clarence Pierce Miles, June 29, 1963; children: Melissa, Melanie, Meredith, Mark. BA in Secondary Edn., U. Md., 1962, MA in Am. Studies, 1966; postgrad., Trinity Coll., 1989, 90. Cer. advanced profl. tchr., Md. Social studies and English tchr. Lackey Sr. H.S., Indian Head, Md., 1963; social studies tchr. Bladensburg (Md.) Sr. H.S., 1965-69; substitute tchr. Montgomery County (Md.) Pub. Sch., 1979-83; social sci. tchr. Holy Cross Acad., Kensington, Md., 1983—, dept. chmn., 1990—. Sponsor student page program Md. Gen. Assembly, Annapolis, 1987—; moderator Georgetown U. Invitational Model UN, Washington, 1987—; mem. Md. student assistance program team Drug Free Schs., 1992—, KAIROS team leader, 1989—. Recipient Cert. of Recognition, Nat. Bicentennial Competition on the Constn. and Bill of Rights, 1987-88. Mem. NEA, ASCD, Nat. Coun. Social Studies, Assn. Ind. Schs. of Greater Washington, Gamma Phi Beta. Avocations: swimming, stock and option investing and trading, soccer, travel. Home: 8626 Wild Olive Dr Potomac MD 20854-3438 Office: Acad of the Holy Cross 4920 Strathmore Ave Kensington MD 20895-1299

MILES, KENNETH ONTARIO, academic program director; b. Washington; s. Lessie Olivia Walker. BA, U. Va., 1992, MEd, 1998. Tchr., coach Gonzaga Coll. High Sch., Washington, 1993-95; acad. lifeskills coord. U. Va., Charlottesville, 1995-97; coord. acad. support football Syracuse (N.Y.) U. Athletic Dept., 1997—2002; dir. student svcs. Sch. Info. Studies Syracuse (N.Y.) U., 2002—. Mem. Nat. Assn. of Student Personnel Adminstrs., Nat. Assn. of Grad. Admissions Profls.. Black Coaches Assn., Nat. Assn. Advisors Athletics (chmn. ethnic concerns com. 1999-2000). Democrat. Baptist. Avocation: weight training. Office: Syracuse U Sch Info Studies 4-206 Ctr for Sci and Tech Syracuse NY 13244-4100 Fax: 315-443-5673. E-mail: komiles@syr.edu.

MILES, LEON F. (LEE MILES), marketing educator; b. Pitts., July 18, 1954; m. Nancy E. Dodson, May 14, 1976; 1 child, Brian C. AA, Point Park Coll., 1976, BA in Psychology, 1983; MEd in Instrn. and Learning, U. Pitts., 1988. Cert. mktg. edn. and coop. work experience tchr., Pa.; cert. entrepreneurship instr. Instr. fashion merchandising program Art Inst. Pitts., 1985-87; tchr. diversified occupations North Area Alternative High Sch., Allison Park, Pa., 1987; tchr., coord. mktg. edn. Taylor Allderdice High Sch., Pitts., 1988—. Mktg. edn. tchr. cert. exam validator Ednl. Testing Svc., 1990, PSAT essay evaluator, 1994; mem. Blue Ribbon Sch. Self-Evaluation Com., 1995. Author curriculum materials. Adult leader Pitts. area Boy Scouts Am., 1985-96, exploring advisor. Recipient Excellence in Tchg. award U. of Pitts. Sch. of Edn. and Pitts. Post Gazette, 1994. Mem. (DECA) Distbv. Edn. Clubs Am. (chpt. advisor, state officer advisor, state collegiate pres. 1987-88), Nat. Mktg. Edn. Assn., Pa. Mktg. Edn. Assn. (Western region v.p. 1990-91, Tchr. of Yr. 1990). Home: 1521 Beechview Ave Pittsburgh PA 15216-3335 Office: Taylor Allerdice High Sch 2409 Shady Ave Pittsburgh PA 15217-2409

MILES, RAYMOND EDWARD, former university dean, organizational behavior and industrial relations educator; b. Cleburne, Tex., Nov. 2, 1932; s. Willard Francis and Wilma Nell (Owen) M.; m. Lucile Dustin, Dec. 27, 1952; children: Laura, Grant, Kenneth. BA with highest honors, U. North Tex., 1954, MBA, 1958; PhD, Stanford U., 1963. Clk. Santa Fe R.R., Gainesville, Tex., 1950-55; instr. mgmt. Sch. Bus. U. North Tex., Denton, 1958-60; asst. prof. organizational behavior and indsl. relations Sch. Bus. Adminstrn. U. Calif.-Berkeley, 1963-68, assoc. prof., 1968-71, prof., 1971—, assoc. dean Haas Sch. of Bus., 1978-81, dean, 1983-90; dir. Inst. Indsl. Relations, 1982-83; cons. various pvt., pub. orgns. Author: Theories of Management, 1975, (with Charles C. Snow) Organization Strategy, Structure and Process, 1978, (with Charles C. Snow) Fit, Failure, and the Hall of Fame, 1994; co-author: Organizational Behavior: Research and Issues, 1976; co-editor, contbg. author: Organization by Design: Theory and Practice, 1981. Served to 1st. lt. USAF, 1955-58. Mem. Acad. Mgmt. Democrat. Unitarian Universalist. Home: 8640 Don Carol Dr El Cerrito CA 94530-2733 Office: U Calif Walter A Haas Sch Bus Berkeley CA 94720-0001 E-mail: miles@haas.berkeley.edu.

MILES, RICHARD BRYANT, mechanical and aerospace engineering educator; b. Washington, July 10, 1943; s. Thomas Kirk and Elizabeth (Bryant) M.; m. Susan McCoy, May 14, 1983; children: Thomas, Julia. BSEE, Stanford U., 1966, MSEE, 1967, PhD in Elec. Engring., 1972. Rsch.

assoc. elec. engring. dept. Stanford (Calif.) U., summer 1972; asst. prof. mech. and aerospace engring. dept. Princeton (N.J.) U., 1972-78, assoc. prof., 1978-82, prof., 1982—, chmn. engring. physics program, 1980-96, acting chmn. dept. mech. and aero. engring., 2002. Lectr. Northwestern Poly. U., Xian, China, 1987; rsch. scientist CNRS; vis. prof. U. Marseilles, France, 1995. Contbr. articles to profl. publs., chpt. to book and conf. procs.; patentee in field. Bd. dirs. Fannie and John Hertz Found., Livermore, Calif., 1989—. Fannie and John Hertz Found. fellow, 1969-72. Fellow AIAA (Aerodynamic Measurement Tech. TC award 2000) Optical Soc. Am.; mem. IEEE (sr.), Am. Phys. Soc. Office: Princeton U Mech & Aerospace Engring D-414 Eng Quad Olden St Princeton NJ 08544-0001

MILES, RUBY WILLIAMS, secondary education educator; b. Petersburg, Va., Jan. 19, 1929; d. Richard Allen and Elizabeth (Penny) Williams; m. John Oscar Miles, Jan. 7, 1950 (div. 1966); children: Karen Jonnia Miles George, Steven Ricardo. BA, Va. State Coll., Petersburg, 1971, MA, 1977. Cert. high sch. tchr., Va. Tchr. English Dinwiddie (Va.) Sch., 1971-78, Clarksville (Tenn.) Sch., 1978-80, Petersburg Pub. Schs., 1982—, head English dept., 1991-96, ret., 1996; instr. St. Paul's Coll., Lawrenceville, Va., 1981-82; asst. prof. St. Leo Coll., Ft. Lee, Va., 1988; instr. english/speech Bethany Baptist Church, Petersburg, VA, 1998—. Tchr., counselor Upward Bound project Va. State U., summer, 1974; tchr. Hopewell Pub. Schs., Va. summer 1983—; instr. John Tyler C.C., Fort Lee, Va., 1992—; adj. prof. Richard Bland Coll., Coll. William and Mary, 2001-02. Songwriter: A Day in September; author: Deal With the Downs, 2003. Bd. dirs. Playmaker Fellows Ltd., Petersburg, 1983; co-dir. Exclusively Youth Models, 1984-85. Recipient Leadership award Va. Edn. Assn., 1985. Mem. Petersburg Edn. Assn. (past pres.), Am. Bus. Women's Assn., Nat. Orgn. for Women, Nat. Assn. Female Execs., NEA, Nat. Coun. Tchrs. English, Jr. Civic League, Delta Sigma Theta. Avocations: writing, travel. Home: 2733 Rollingwood Rd Petersburg VA 23805-2317 E-mail: rubymiles@adelphia.net.

MILES, SUZANNE LAURA, dean; b. Omaha, Nebr., Feb. 17, 1953; d. Ronald Ray Miles and Marian Genene (Ganaros) Pflasterer; m. Robert Hill Mason, July 7, 1975; children: Miles, Maraka. BS, Northwestern U., 1975; MA, Ariz. State U., 1978; PhD, U. Ariz., 1992. Cert. coll. tchr., Ariz. Admissions advisor Oakland U., Rochester, Mich., 1979-83; faculty U. Phoenix, Tucson, 1984—; ednl. program planner Pima Cmty. Coll., Tucson, 1991-92, assoc. dean of instrn., 1992-97, dean math. and comms. arts, 1997—. Co-chair instnl. climate task force Pima C.C., 1995—, EC project adminstr., 1995-97; adj. lectr. U. Ariz., 1997—; presenter in field. Vice chair U. High Parent Bd., Tucson, 1996—; moderator Rincon Congrl. Ch., Tucson, 1997-98; hospice vol. Tucson Med. Ctr., 1994—. Kellogg fellowship League for Innovation, U. Tex., 1997—; recipient Omaha North High Outstanding Alumni award, 1995. Mem. AAUW (Tucson chpt. corp. rep. 1996—), Am. Assn. of Women in C.C. (PCC chpt. pres. 1996-97), Way Up Women's Orgn. (Ariz. chpt. conf. com. 1995-97). Republican. United Ch. of Christ. Avocations: theatre, dance, travel, camping. Home: 6492 E Sun Cir Tucson AZ 85750-1932 Office: Pima Cmty Coll Downtown 1255 N Stone Ave Tucson AZ 85709-3002

MILEWSKI, STANISLAW ANTONI, ophthalmologist, educator; b. Bagrowo, Poland, June 16, 1930; s. Alfred and Sabina (Sicinska) M.; came to U.S., 1959, naturalized, 1967; BA, Trinity Coll., U. Dublin (Ireland), 1954, MA, 1959, B. Chir., M.B., B.A.O., 1956; m. Anita Dobiecka, July 11, 1959; children: Andrew, Teresa, Mark. House surgeon Hammersmith Hosp. Postgrad. Sch. London, 1958; intern St. Raffael Hosp., New Haven, 1960-61; resident in ophthalmology Gill Meml. Hosp., Roanoke, Va., 1961-64; practice medicine specializing in surgery and diseases of the retina and vitreous; mem. staff Manchester (Conn.) Meml. Hosp., 1964-71, chief of ophthalmology, sr. attending physician St. Francis Hosp., Hartford, Conn., 1971—; asst. clin. prof. ophthalmology U. Conn., 1972— . Clin. fellow Montreal (Que., Can.) Gen Hosp., McGill U., 1971-72, Mass. Eye and Ear Infirmary, Harvard Med. Sch., Boston, 1974; diplomate Am. Bd. Ophthalmology. Fellow ACS; mem. AMA, New England Ophthal. Soc., Conn. Soc. Eye Physicians, Vitreous Soc. Republican. Roman Catholic. Home: 127 Lakewood Cir S Manchester CT 06040-7086 Office: 191 Main St Manchester CT 06040-3556 also: 43 Woodland St Ste 100 Hartford CT 06105-2370

MILEY, GEORGE HUNTER, nuclear and electrical engineering educator; b. Shreveport, La., Aug. 6, 1933; s. George Hunter and Norma Angeline (Dowling) M.; m. Elizabeth Burroughs, Nov. 22, 1958; children: Susan Miley Hibbs, Hunter Robert. BS in Chem. Engring., Carnegie-Mellon U., 1955; MS, U. Mich., 1956, PhD in Chem.-Nuclear Engring., 1959. Nuclear engr. Knolls Atomic Power Lab., Gen. Electric Co., Schenectady, 1959-61; mem. faculty U. Ill., Urbana, 1961—, prof., 1967—, chmn. nuclear engring. program, 1975-86, dir. Fusion Studies Lab., 1976—, fellow Ctr. for Advanced Study, 1985-86; dir. rsch. Rockford Tech. Assocs. Inc., 1990-94; pres., dir. rsch. NPL Assocs. Inc., 1994—; chief scientist Lattice Energy, LLC, 2001—. Vis. prof. U. Colo., 1967, Cornell U., 1969-70, U. New South Wales, 1986, Imperial Coll. of London, 1987; mem. Ill. Radiation Protection Bd., 1988—; mem. Air Force Studies Bd., 1990-94; chmn. tech. adv. com. Ill. Low Level Radioactive Waste Site, 1990-96; chmn. com. on indsl. uses of radiation Ill. Dept. Nuclear Safety, 1989-2000. Author: Direct Conversion of Nuclear Radiation Energy, 1971, Fusion Energy Conversion, 1976; editor Jour. Fusion Tech., 1980-2001; U.S. assoc. editor Laser and Particle Beams, 1982-86, mng. editor, 1987-91, editor-in-chief, 1991-2002; U.S. editor Jour. Plasma Physics, 1995-2003. Served with C.E. AUS, 1960. Recipient Western Electric Tchg.-Rsch. award, 1977, Halliburton Engring. Edn. Leadership award, 1990, Edward Teller medal, 1995, Scientist of Yr. award Jour. New Energy, 1996, Scientist of the Yr. award Inst. for New Energy 1996, Cert. Recognition award NASA, 2003; NATO sr. sci. fellow, 1975-76, Guggenheim fellow, 1985-86, Japanese Soc. Promotion of Sci. fellow, 1994. Fellow IEEE, Am. Nuclear Soc. (dir. 1980-83, Disting. Svc. award 1980, Outstanding Achievement award Fusion Energy divsn. 1992), Am. Phys. Soc.; mem. Am. Soc. Engring. Edn. (chmn. energy conversion com. 1967-70, pres. U. Ill. chpt. 1973-74, chmn. nuclear divsn. 1975-76, Outstanding Tchr. award 1973), Sigma Xi, Tau Beta Pi. Presbyterian. Achievements include research on fusion, energy conversion, reactor kinetics. Office: U Ill 214 Nuclear Engring Lab 103 S Goodwin Ave Urbana IL 61801-2901 E-mail: georgehm@aol.com.

MILFORD, NANCY WINSTON, writer, English educator; b. Dearborn, Mich. d. Joseph Leo and Vivienne Winston; m. Kenneth Hans Milford, Mar. 24, 1962 (div. 1985); children: Matthew, Kate, Nell. BA, U. Mich.; MA, Columbia U., N.Y.C., 1964, PhD, 1972. Prof. English and writing Bard Coll., Annandale-on-Hudson, N.Y., 1983-90; vis. prof. English Vassar Coll., Poughkeepsie, N.Y., 1984; adj. prof. English grad. program in creative writing NYU, N.Y.C., 1991-94; vis. prof. English U. Mich., Ann Arbor, 1993, 94; Annenberg fellow Brown U., Providence, 1995—; vis. prof. Hunter Coll., CUNY, 2002—03, distinguished lectr. English, 2003—. Founder, mem. Writers Room, Inc., 1978—, bd. dirs., past pres. Author: Zelda, A Biography, 1970, Savage Beauty, The Life of Edna St. Vincent Millay, 2001; contbr. revs., essays and articles to various publs. Lit. panelist N.Y. State Coun. on Arts, N.Y.C., 1976-79. Guggenheim fellow, 1978, Lila Wallace-Reader's Digest writing fellow, 1992-95, Woodrow Wilson vis. fellow U.S. Govt./USIA, S.C., 1995, Fulbright fellow, 1996-97, 1999—; recipient Lit. Lion award N.Y. Pub. Libr., 1984. Mem. PEN, Author's Guild (mem. exec. coun. 1971-89), Soc. Am. Historians (exec. bd. dirs. 1971-88). Avocations: fencing, sailing. Office: Janklow & Nesbit Assocs Lit Agts 445 Park Ave New York NY 10022

MILGRAM, JEROME H. marine and ocean engineer, educator; b. Phila., Sept. 23, 1938; s. Samuel J. and Fannie M. BSEE, BS in Naval Architecture and Marine Engring., MIT, 1961, MS, 1962, PhD in Hydrodynamics, 1965. Registered profl. engr., Mass. With Scripps Inst. Oceanography, San Diego, summer 1961; project engr. Block Assocs., Cambridge, Mass., 1961-67; asst. prof. MIT, Cambridge, 1967-70, assoc. prof., 1970-77, prof. ocean engring., 1977-89, William I. Koch prof. marine tech., 1989—. Rsch. assoc. in biophysics Harvard U. Med. Sch., 1974-76; vis. prof. in naval architecture and marine engring. U. Mich., 1988-89; design dir. Am. 3 Found., 1991-95; guest investigator Woods Hole Oceanog. Instn., 1996—; vis. prof. Johns Hopkins U., 1996-97. Contbr. articles to profl. jours.; patentee in field. Recipient Am. Bur. Shipping award, 1961, Alan Berman Outstanding Rsch. Publ. award U.S. Naval Rsch. Lab., 1990, AT&T Design Innovation award, 1992. Fellow Soc. Naval Archs. and Marine Engrs. (life); mem. NAE (life), Nat. Rsch. Coun. (marine bd. 1998-2001). Home: 20 Blossom Hill Rd Winchester MA 01890-3455 Office: MIT 77 Massachusetts Ave Rm 5-318 Cambridge MA 02139-4307 E-mail: jmilgram@mit.edu.

MILGRAM, RICHARD MYRON, music school administrator; b. Moultrie, Ga. s. Bernard Byron and Libbie Elaine M.; m. Judith Lee Milgram; children: Rhonda Beth, Gary David. MusB, Berklee Coll. Music, Boston; MusM, Boston U. Cert. tchr. Mass., Conn. Tchr. Norwood (Mass.) Pub. Schs., 1969-72; asst. prof. Merrimack Coll., North Andover, Mass., 1972-75; tchr. Guilford (Conn.) Pub. Schs., 1975-77; pres., co-founder Shoreline Sch. Art and Music, Branford, Conn., 1978—. Mem. music edn. coun./student tchr. practicum com. Westfield (Mass.) State Coll., 1978-81, New Haven Arts Coun.; judge various music competitions; performance Carnegie Hall, 1997, Quick Ctr. for the Arts/Fairfield U., 1998; guest condr. Conn. Symphonic Band, 1997. Contbr. revs. to music jours. Mem. Phi Mu Alpha Sinfonia. Office: Shoreline Sch Art and Music Inc 482 E Main St Branford CT 06405-2919

MILGROM, FELIX, immunologist, educator; b. Rohatyn, Poland, Oct. 12, 1919; came to U.S., 1958; naturalized, 1963; s. Henryk and Ernestina (Cyryl) M.; m. Halina Miszel, Oct. 15, 1941; children: Henry, Martin Louis. Student, U. Lwow, Poland, 1937-41, U. Lublin, 1945; MD, U. Wroclaw, Poland, 1947; MD (hon.), U. Vienna, Austria, 1976, U. Lund, Sweden, 1979, U. Heidelberg, Fed. Republic Germany, 1979, U. Bergen, Norway, 1980; DSc (hon.), U. Med. Dent., N.J., 1991. Rsch. assoc., prof. dept. microbiology Sch. Medicine U. Wroclaw, 1946-54, chmn. dept., 1954; prof., head dept. microbiology Sch. Medicine, Silesian U., Zabrze, Poland, 1954-57; rsch. assoc. Svc. de Chime Microbienne, Pasteur Inst., Paris, 1957; rsch. assoc. prof. dept. bacteriology and immunology U. Buffalo Sch. Medicine, 1958-62; assoc. prof., then prof. and disting. prof. microbiology Sch. Medicine, SUNY, Buffalo, 1962—, chmn. dept., 1967-85. Author: Studies on the Structure of Antibodies, 1950; co-editor: International Convocations on Immunology, 1969, 75, 79, 85, Principles of Immunology, 1973, 2d edit., 1979, Principles of Immunological Diagnosis in Medicine, 1981, Medical Microbiology, 1982; editor in chief Internat. Archives of Allergy and Applied Immunology, 1965-91; contbg. editor Vox Sanguinis, 1965-76, Transfusion, 1966-73, Cellular Immunology, 1970-83, Transplantation, 1975-78; contbr. numerous articles to profl. jours. Recipient Alfred Jurzykowski Found. prize, 1986, Paul Ehrlich and Ludwig Darmstaedter prize, 1987. Mem. Am. Assn. Immunologists, Transplantation Soc. (v.p. 1976-78), Am. Acad. Microbiology, Coll. Internat. Allergologicum (v.p. 1970-78, pres. 1978-82, hon. mem. 1990—), Polish Acad. Arts and Scis., Sigma Xi. Achievements include research on the serology of syphillis, Tb, rheumatoid arthritis, organ and tissue specificity including blood groups, transplantation and autoimmunity. Home: 474 Getzville Rd Buffalo NY 14226-2555

MILLARD, ESTHER LOUND, foundation administrator, educator; b. Metaline, Wash., June 10, 1909; d. Peter S. and Emily Christine (Dahlgren) Lound; m. Homer Behne Millard, Apr. 25, 1951 (dec. May 1962). BA, U. Wis., 1933, MA, 1935. Cert. tchr., Oreg., Wis. Instr. U. Hawaii, Honolulu, 1938-43; joined USN, 1943, advanced through ranks to lt. commdr., resigned, 1952; dir. Millard Sch., Bandon, Oreg., 1954-81; pres. Millard Found., Bandon, 1984—. Trustee Falcon Found., Colorado Springs, Colo., 1986—; established scholarship fund for med. sch. students, U. Wis, Millard honors program benefitting cadets at USAF Acad. Recipient Bardeen Fellow, U. Wis. Med. Sch. Mem. Bascom Hill Soc. (U. Wis.), Women's Meml. Found. (charter), Phi Beta Kappa. Republican. Avocations: reading, music, gardening. Home: 56557 Tom Smith Rd Bandon OR 97411-6309

MILLER, ADELE ENGELBRECHT, educational administrator; b. Jersey City, July 31, 1946; d. John Fred and Dorathea Kathryn (Kamm) Engelbrecht; m. William A. Miller, Jr., Dec. 21, 1981. BS in Bus. Edn., Fairleigh Dickinson U., 1968, MBA magna cum laude, 1974; cert. in pub. sch. adminstrn. and supervision, Jersey City State Coll., 1976. Bus. tchr. Jersey City Bd. Edn., 1967-99, coord. coop. bus. edn. programs, 1973-99, acting v.p., 1985-86, prin. of summer sch., 1986, chmn. dept., 1996-99. Adj. instr. St. Peter's Coll., 1974-75; curriculum cons. Cittone Bus. Sch., 1981-82; mem. adv. coun. Dickinson H.S., 1973-99, chmn., 1978-80; organizer, bd. dirs. Frances Nadel and Cooke-Connolly-Coffey-Witt Faculty Meml. Scholarships, 1978-99; trustee Dickinson H.S. Parents Coun., 1985-88. Co-author: New Jersey Cooperative Business Education Coordinators Resource Manual, 1984; author coop. bus. edn. study course Jersey City Pub. Schs., 1980, 84. Mem. Citizens Adv. Coun. to Mayor of Jersey City, 1968—71; organizer, dir. Jersey City Youth Week, 1970—72; chmn. juv. conf. com. Hudson County Juv. Ct., 1978—; v.p., sec., trustee, chmn. dinner-musicale Jersey City Coll.-Comty. Orch., 1979—88; explorer scouting adv. bd. Hudson-Hamilton coun. bd. Scouts Am., 1985—88; trustee YWCA of Hudson County, 1988—99; dir. CREATE Charter High Sch., 2001—. Recipient Dickinson H.S. Key Club Tchr. of Yr. award 1971, Merrill-Lynch Outstanding Performance in Edn. award, 1995; named Educator of Yr. Dickinson H.S. Parents Coun., 1987-88. Mem.: AAUW (edn. chmn., sec. N.J. divsn., del. to White House briefing on edn., women's issues, arms control, dist. coord., chmn. nominations, historian), NEA, Vocat. Edn. Assn. N.J., N.J. Bus. Edn. Assn., N.J. Coop. Bus. Edn. Coords. Assn. (pres., v.p., sec., treas., Coop. Edn. Coord. of Yr.), Jersey City Edn. Assn. (bldg. dir.), N.J. Edn. Assn., Lake Hopatcong Yacht Club, Coll. Club Jersey City (pres., v.p., sec.), Jersey City Woman's Club (scholarship chmn., adviser Jr. Woman's Club), NJ Fedn. Women's Clubs, Internat. Rotary (nominating com. 2002, asst. gov. 2003, Vocational Svc. award 2001), Rotary (asst. gov. dist. 7490 2001, nominations com. 2001, Paul Harris Fellow, Walter Head Fellow, Vocat. Svc. award 2001), Phi Delta Kappa. Home: PO Box 8004 13 King Rd Jersey City NJ 07307 E-mail: millerassoc@nac.net.

MILLER, ALWIN VERMAR, educational advisor, consultant; b. Dardanelle, Ark., Oct. 12, 1922; s. William Marshall and Ollie Vernice (Green) M.; m. Patricia Jane Knox, Dec. 31, 1945; children: Carol, Alwin, William, Nitiya, Thomas. AA, Ark. Poly. Inst., 1939; BS, BA with honors, UCLA, 1947, MEd, 1948, EdD, 1956; cert., Internat. Inst. Ednl. Planning, (UNESCO), 1967-68. Instr. Chico (Calif.) State Coll., 1948-49; assoc. prof. So. Oreg. Coll., Ashland, 1949-57; edn. advisor AID, Washington, 1957-75; cons. on internat. devel. Upper Marlboro, Md., 1975—. Lt. col. USAF, 1942-46. Mem. ASTD, Soc. Internat. Devel., Internat. Soc. Ednl. Planning, Res. Officers Assn. (v.p. D.C. dept. 1986-87, treas. 1991-97, pres.-elect 1997, pres. 1998-99, Reilly Meml. Scholarship com. 1999-2002, retirement com. 2002-), Am. Legion (post comdr. 1995-96, 99-2000, dept. vice comdr. 1996-97, dept. comdr. 1997-98, vice chmn. nat. security 1999-), Mil. Order World Wars (chpt. pres. 1999-2002, nat. security com. 2002-, nat. legis. com. 2002-, sr. vice comdr. Dept. of Md., 2003-), Nat. Sojourners, Mil. Order of Temple of Jerusalem, Forty and Eight (grand conducteur 2000-2001), Lions, Masons, Shriners, K.T., Phi Delta Kappa. Democrat. Office: 8107 Bird Ln Greenbelt MD 20770-2104 E-mail: avmiller46@cs.com.

MILLER, ANA MARIE, elementary education educator; b. Ft. Davis, Tex., July 22, 1956; d. Catarino and Candida Eva (Granado) Talavera; m. Tommy Camacho Sr., Mar. 30, 1975; children: Thomas Jr., Cecilia; m. Don Miller, Jan. 27, 2001. BA in Lit., U. Tex., Odessa, 1989. Cert. elem. tchr., English tchr. Tchr. Lyndon Baines Johnson Elem. Sch., Odessa, 1989—99, Noel Elem. Sch., 1999—2000, Nimitz Jr. HS, 2000—02, Noel Elem. Sch., 2002—. Mem. Assn. Tex. Profl. Educators, Permian Basin Reading Coun., Phi Delta Kappa. Avocations: reading, cake decorating, traveling. Home: 1417 Cimarron Ave Odessa TX 79761-4220

MILLER, ANGELA PEREZ, bilingual and special education educator; b. Chgo., 1936; d. Jesse and Emily (Ibarra) P.; m. John F. Miller, May 6, 1961 (div.); 1 son, Dion. BA, U. Ill., 1958; MA, Northeastern Ill. U., 1975; MEd, DePaul U., 1984; PhD, U. Ill.-Chgo., 1990. Cert. elem. tchr., spl. edn., bilingual edn., adminstrn. Ill. Tchr. Chgo. pub. schs., 1962-70, field adminstr., 1985-88; exch. tchr. Mex. City schs., 1970-71; asst. prin. Burns Elem. Sch., Chgo., 1972-77, Benito Juarez H.S, Chgo., 1977-85; prin. Blaine Elem., 1989; from field adminstr. to dir. staff tng. and devel. Office of Reform Implementation, 1985—94; asst. prof. DePaul U., Chgo., 1994—2002; adj. asst. prof. U. Ill., Chgo., 2002—03. Vis. asst. prof. U. Ill., Chgo., 1992—93. Pres., bd. dirs. Latino Inst., 1993-99; active Consortium Chgo. Sch. Rsch., 1995—, co-chair, 1996-98; active Ill. Adv. Coun. on the Edn. Children with Disabilities, 1996-2002, Fulbright to Brazil, 2000. Recipient Outstanding Contbn. to Edn. award, PUSH/Excel, 1997, Sor Juana Lifetime Achievement award, Mexican Fine Arts Ctr. Mus., 2002. Mem. ASCD, Nat. Staff Devel. Coun., Am. Ednl. Rsch. Assn., Nat. Assn. Bilingual Edn. Office: Univ Illinois 1040 W Harrison St MC 147 Chicago IL 60607-7133 E-mail: apmiller@uic.edu.

MILLER, ANNETTA, university administrator; b. Ft. Wayne, Ind., Sept. 8, 1921; m. Sidney Miller; children: Ronald, Frederick, Mark. RN, Jewish Hosp., Phila., 1943; BA in Art History, Wayne State U., 1995. Nurse U.S. Army Nurse Corps, Europe, 1944-45; mem. Wayne State U. Bd. Govs., 1997—. Mem. Mich. State Bd. Edn., 1970-95, treas., 1975-76, v.p., 1977-78, 89-90, sec., 1983-84, co-pres., 1993-94. Alt. del. Dem. Nat. Conv., 1980, del., 1972. Recipient Silver Scroll award UN; Healthy Children award Comprehensive Sch. Health Coords. Assn., 1993, Spl. Recognition award Mich. Edn. Assn., 1994, Outstanding Achievement award Mich. Coun. for Maternal and Child Health, 1993, Wonder Woman award Women's Survival Ctr., 1999; numerous others. Mem. Anthony Wayne Soc., Ams. for Dem. Action, Gray Panthers, Sierra Club, People for the Am. Way. Office: Wayne State U Bd Govs 4165 Faculty/Adminstrn Bldg Detroit MI 48202

MILLER, APRIL D. special education educator; b. McKeesport, Pa., Apr. 11, 1961; d. Albert L. and Mary M. Roney. BS, Ohio State U., 1983, MA, 1988, PhD, 1992. Cert. tchr. K-12 reading, K-12 spl. edn., supervision, Ohio. Mem. adj. faculty Ashland U., Columbus, Ohio, 1989-92, Wright State U., Dayton, Ohio, 1991-92, Ohio Dominican Coll., Columbus, 1991-92; asst. prof. U. So. Miss., Hattiesburg, 1992-96, assoc. prof., chair dept. spl. edn., 1996—2000, prof., spl. edn., 2000—03, assoc. dean Coll. Edn. and Psychology, 2000—03; prof., dean Tex. Woman's U. Coll. Prof. Edn., 2003—. Presenter convs. various nat. profl. orgns.; ednl. cons. local edn. agys., 1992—. Contbr. articles to profl. jours. Faculty senator U. So. Miss., 1995-96; mem. coun. U. So. Miss. Tchr. Edn. Coun., 1994-2003; vol. Assn. for Retarded Citizens, Very Spl. Arts Festival, Spl. Olympics, 1992-2003. Mem. Coun. for Exceptional Children (nominee Susan Phillips Gorin award 1996, faculty advisor 1992-98), Assn. for Behavioral Analysis (Outstanding Svcs. award 1994, com. chair profl. devel. 1995-97, coord. internat. sci. and engring. fair initiative 1993-97), Phi Delta Kappa (conf. planner U. So. Miss. 1996, v.p. programs chpt. 75 1994-95, pres. 1995-96). Home: 3109 Union Lake Dr Denton TX 76210 Office: TWU PO Box 425769 Denton TX 76204

MILLER, ARJAY, retired university dean; b. Shelby, Nebr., Mar. 4, 1916; s. Rawley John and Mary Gertrude (Schade) M.; m. Frances Marion Fearing, Aug. 18, 1940; children: Kenneth Fearing, Ann Elizabeth (Mrs. James Olstad). BS with highest honors, UCLA, 1937; LL.D. (hon.), 1964; postgrad., U. Calif.-Berkeley, 1938-40; LL.D. (hon.), Washington U., St. Louis; LL.D., Whitman Coll., 1965, U. Nebr., 1965, Ripon Coll., 1980. Teaching asst. U. Calif. at Berkeley, 1938-40; research technician Calif. State Planning Bd., 1941; economist Fed. Res. Bank San Francisco, 1941-43; asst. treas. Ford Motor Co., 1946-53, controller, 1953-57, v.p., controller, 1957-61, v.p. finance, 1961-62, v.p. of staff group, 1962-63, pres., 1963-68, vice chmn., 1968-69; dean Grad. Sch. Bus., Stanford U., 1969-79, emeritus, 1979—. Former chmn. Automobile Mfrs. Assn., Econ. Devel. Corp. Greater Detroit; councillor The Conf. Bd.; past chmn., life trustee Urban Inst.; mem. Public Adv. Commn. on U.S. Trade Policy, 1968-69, Pres.'s Nat. Commn. on Productivity, 1970-74. Trustee Internat. Exec. Svc. Coirps.; hon. trustee The Brookings Instn.; dir. emeritus S.R.I. Internat.; dir. Pub. Policy Inst. Calif.; former pres. Detroit Press Club Found.; former chmn. Boy Area Coun. Capt. USAAF, 1943-46. Recipient Alumnus of Year Achievement award UCLA, 1964; Distinguished Nebraskan award, 1968; Nat. Industry Leader award B'nai B'rith, 1968 Fellow Am. Acad. Arts and Scis. Clubs: Pacific Union, Bohemian. Presbyterian.

MILLER, ARTHUR HAWKS, JR., librarian, archivist, educator; b. Kalamazoo, Mar. 15, 1943; s. Arthur Hawks and Eleanor (Johnson) M.; m. Janet Carol Schroeder, June 11, 1967; children: Janelle Miller Moravek, Andrew Hawks. Student, U. Caen, Calvados, France, 1963-64; AB, Kalamazoo Coll., 1965; AM in English, U. Chgo., 1966, AM in Librarianship, 1968; PhD, Northwestern U., 1973; postgrad., Lake Forest Grad. Sch. Mgmt., 1990—91. Reference libr. Newberry Libr., Chgo., 1966-69, asst. libr. pub. svcs., 1969-72; coll. libr. Lake Forest (Ill.) Coll., 1972-94, archivist and libr. for spl. collections, 1994—. Co-author: 30 Miles North: A History of Lake Forest College, Its Town, and Its City of Chicago, 2000, Lake Forest Estates, People, and Culture, 2000, Classic Country Estates Lake Forest, 2003. Pres. Lake Forest/Lake Bluff Hist. Soc., 1982-85, bd. dirs., 2003—; pres. Ill. Ctr. for Book Bd., 1992-93; mem. Ragdale Found., 1992-96, Lake Forest Found. for Hist. Preservation, 1997—, v.p., 2000-02. Mem. Caxton Club. Presbyterian. Home: 169 Wildwood Rd Lake Forest IL 60045-2462 Office: Lake Forest Coll Donnelley Libr/LIT 555 N Sheridan Rd Lake Forest IL 60045-2399 Fax: 847-735-6296. E-mail: amiller@lakeforest.edu.

MILLER, ARTHUR RAPHAEL, law educator; b. N.Y.C., June 22, 1934; s. Murray and Mary (Schapin) Miller; m. Ellen Monica Joachim, June 8, 1958 (div. 1978); 1 child, Matthew Richard; m. Marilyn Tarmy, 1982 (div. 1988); m. Sandra L. Young, 1992 (div. 2001). AB, U. Rochester, 1955; LLB, Harvard U., 1958; student, Bklyn. Coll., 1952, 55, CCNY, 1955. Bar: N.Y. 1959, U.S. Supreme Ct. 1959, Mass. 1983. With Cleary, Gottlieb, Steen & Hamilton, N.Y.C., 1958-61; assoc. dir. Columbia Law Sch. Project Internat. Procedure, N.Y.C., 1961-62; instr. Columbia U. Law Sch., 1961-62; asso. prof. U. Minn. Law Sch., 1962-65; prof. law U. Mich. Law Sch., 1965-72; vis. prof. Harvard U. Law Sch., 1971-72, prof., 1972-86, Bruce Bromley prof., 1986—. Rsch. assoc. Mental Health Rsch. Inst., 1966-68; dir. project computer assisted instn. Am. Assn. Law Schs., 1968-75; spl. rapporteur State Dept. concerning chpt. II of Hague Conv., 1967; del. U.S.-Italian Conf. Internat. Jud. Assistance, 1961, 62; chmn. task force external affairs Interuniv. Communications Council, 1966-70; mem. law panel, com. sci. and tech. info. Fed. Council Sci. and Tech., Pres.'s Office Sci. and Tech., 1969-72; mem. adv. group Nat. Acad. Sci. Project on Computer Data Banks, 1970-78; mem. spl. adv. group to chief justice Supreme Ct. on Fed. Civil Litigation; mem. com. on automated personal data systems HEW, 1972-73; chmn. Mass. Security and Privacy Council, Mass. Commn. on Privacy; mem. U.S. Commn. New Technol. Uses Copyrighted Works, 1975-79; reporter U.S. Supreme Ct.'s Adv. Com. on

Civil Rules, 1978-86, mem. 1986-91; faculty Fed. Jud. Ctr.; reporter study on complex litigation Am. Law Inst.; bd. dirs. Research Found. on Complex Litigations, 1975-80; bd. overseers Rand Inst. on Civil Justice, 1998-2002. Author: The Assault on Privacy: Computers, Data Banks, and Dossiers, 1971, Miller's Court, 1982; (with others) New York Civil Practice, 8 vols., Civil Procedure Cases and Materials, 7th edit., 1997, Federal Practice and Procedure: Civil, 34 vols., 1969—, CPLR Manual, 1967; host syndicated TV shows in Context, Miller's Law, Miller's Court, Headlines on Trial; legal expert Good Morning America. Served with AUS, 1958-59. Recipient Nat. Emmy award for The Constitution, That Delicate Balance. Mem. Am. Law Inst. Office: Harvard U Harvard Law Sch Cambridge MA 02138

MILLER, BERNICE DEARING, funeral director, member school board; b. Altavista, Va. d. Joseph B. and Thelma B. (Younger) Dearing; m. Jack Miller; 1 child, Tscharner Jaenese. BA in Bus. Adminstrn., Howard U., 1965. Tchr. Pittsylvania County Sch. System, Gretna, Va., 1965-78; dir. Miller Funeral Home, Inc., Gretna, 1978—. Treas. Callands-Gretna Voters League, 1985—; mem. coop. office edn. adv. bd. Gretna High Sch., 1980—; vice chmn. Pittsylvania County Sch. Bd., 1989—; mem. president's adv. panel for minority concerns Danville C.C., 1990—. Recipient outstanding svc. to community plaque Callands-Gretna Voters League, 1988. Mem. Va. Morticians Assn., Western Dist. Funeral Dirs. Assn. (Woman Mortician of Yr. 1992), Va. Funeral Dirs. Assn., Gretna Mchts. Assn. (bd. dirs.), NAACP. Avocations: travel, listening to music, walking, shopping. Home: RR 2 Gretna VA 24557-9802

MILLER, BETTIE GENE, librarian, educator; b. nr. Clovis, N.Mex., June 21, 1926; d. Nephi D. and Sadie Elizabeth K. (Elliott) Gerber; m. Edwin Lee Baldridge, Jan. 14, 1945 (div. 1962); children: K. Dianne, Richard D., Debra Sue; m. W.F., Miller, Jr., Nov. 7, 1969; stepchildren: Margaret, Bud. BS in Edn. with honors, Eastern N.Mex. U., 1966, also postgrad.; MSLS, Wayne State U., 1968. Cert. tchr., libr., N.Mex. Soc. editor State Line Tribune, Farwell, Tex., 1960-61; clk. typist Agriculture Stblzn. and Conservation, Farwell, 1961-62; Farmers Home Adminstrn., Portales, N.Mex., 1962-63; libr., tchr. Portales Sr. HS, 1965-88, ret., 1988. Past 4-H group leader; active Campfire Girls; sponsor La Cima Libr. Club, 1965-88; mem. Rep. Presdl. Task Force, 1984. Ea. N.Mex. U. scholar, 1944, 63-66; NDEA fellow, 1966-67. Mem. NEA (N.Mex.), Family Motor Coach Assn., Family Cmty. Edn., Friends of Portales Libr. (charter, life, chpt. sec. 1978-79), N.Mex. Edn. Assn., Portales Edn. Assn. (sec. 1969-70, bldg. rep. 1976-78, 85-87, v.p. 1978-79, 87-88, pres. 1979-80, supt.'s adv. com. 1978-80), N.Mex. Libr. Assn. (sec. childrens and young adult sect. 1973-74), N.Mex. Media Assn. (v.p. 1984—), Delta Kappa Gamma (2d v.p. 1984-85, sec. 1988-90), Alpha Delta Kappa. (charter, sec. 1984-85). Mem. Ch. of Christ. Lodges: Good Sam Internat. (life, crimson circle, local chpt. charter mem., sec. and newsletter editor 1983-84, 92, treas. 1999-2001, pres. 2002), Overland Trailblazers West. Home: PO Box 510 Portales NM 88130-0510

MILLER, BEVERLY WHITE, former college president, educational consultant, consultant; b. Willoughby, Ohio; d. Joseph Martin and Marguerite Sarah (Storer) White; m. Lynn Martin Miller, Oct. 11, 1945 (dec. 1986); children: Michaela Ann, Craig Martin, Todd Daniel, Cass Timothy, Simone Agnes. AB, Western Res. U., 1945; MA, Mich. State U., 1957; PhD, U. Toledo, 1967; LHD (hon.), Coll. St. Benedict, St. Joseph, Minn., 1979; LLD (hon.), U. Toledo, 1988. Chem. and biol. researcher, 1945-57; tchr. schs. in Mich., also Mercy Sch. Nursing, St. Lawrence Hosp., Lansing, Mich., 1957-58; mem. chemistry and biology faculty Mary Manse Coll., Toledo, 1958-71, dean grad. div., 1968-71, exec. v.p., 1968-71; acad. dean Salve Regina Coll., Newport, R.I., 1971-74; pres. Coll. St. Benedict, St. Joseph, Minn., 1974-79, Western New Eng. Coll., Springfield, Mass., 1980-96, pres. emerita, 1996—. Higher edn. cons., 1996—; cons. U.S. Office Edn., 1980; mem. Springfield Pvt. Industry Coun./Regional Employment Bd., exec. com., 1982-94; mem. Minn. Pvt. Coll. Coun., 1974-79, sec., 1974-75, vice chmn., 1975-76, chmn., 1976-77; cons. in field. Author papers and books in field. Corporator Mercy Hosp., Springfield, Mass. Recipient President's citation St. John's U., Minn., 1979; also various service awards; named disting. alumna of yr. U. Toledo, 1998. Mem. AAAS, Am. Assn. Higher Edn., Assn. Cath. Colls. and Univs. (exec. bd.), Internat. Assn. Sci. Edn., Nat. Assn. Ind. Colls. and Univs. (govt. rels. adv. com., bd. dirs. 1990-93, exec. com. 1991-93, treas. 1992-93), Nat. Assn. Biology Tchrs., Assn. Ind. Colls. and Univs. of Mass. (exec. com. 1981-96, vice chmn. 1985-86, chmn. 1986-87), Nat. Assn. Rsch. Sci. Tchg., Springfield C. of C. (bd. dirs.), Am. Assn. Univ. Adminstrs. (bd. dirs. 1989-92), Delta Kappa Gamma, Sigma Delta Epsilon. Office: 6713 County Road M Delta OH 43515-9778

MILLER, CARL CHET, business educator; b. Richmond, Va., June 23, 1961; s. Carl Chester and Nancy Ellis (Peters) M.; m. Laura Bridget Cardinal, Dec. 28, 1982. BA summa cum laude, U. Tex., 1982, PhD, 1990. Shift mgr. Frontier Enterprises, Austin, Tex., 1983; instr. Ind. U., Bloomington, 1983—84; tchg. asst. U. Tex., Austin, 1984—85, instr., 1985, rsch. assoc., 1985—89; asst. prof. bus. Baylor U., Waco, Tex., 1989—95, assoc. prof. bus., 1995—97; vis. assoc. prof. bus. Cornell U., Ithaca, NY, 1997—98; assoc. prof. bus., dir. ctr. exec. edn. Baylor U., 1998—2000; assoc. prof. bus., area coord. acctg. and mgmt., faculty dir. exec. MBA program Wake Forest U., Winston-Salem, NC, 2000—. Vis. prof., rschr. bus. Duke U., Durham, N.C., 1998-1999; reviewer Acad. of Mgmt. Jour., Briarcliff Manor, N.Y., 1991—, Orgn. Sci., Providence, 1990, 94—. Contbr. articles to profl. jours., chpts. to books; author numerous conf. papers; liaison Tex. Conf. on Orgns., Austin, 1989-97, treas., 1998-2000. Bd. dirs. Windridge Home Owners Assn., Dallas, 1993—97; bd. advs. Cin. Glory Drum and Bugle Corps, 1995—2000; pres. Assn. Mgmt., Austin, 1985—87. Recipient Young Rschr. award, Hankamer Sch. Bus., 1992, Outstanding Tchr. award, FuQua Sch. Bus., 1999, Outstanding Educator Award, Babcock Grad. Sch., 2002, rsch. fellow, Babcock Grad. Sch. Mgmt., 2000—03; grantee, Hankamer Sch. Bus., 1990, 1991, 1992, 1994—97, Grad. Sch. Bus., U. Tex. Bonham Meml. Rsch. Fund, 1985, 1989, rsch. fellow, Babcock Grad. Sch., 2002. Mem. Acad. Mgmt. (divsnl. regional liaison 1994-96, reviewer ann. meeting 1987, 88, 93—), Inst. Mgmt. Scis., Strategic Mgmt. Soc.,(McKinsey Best Paper Panel, 2002, 2003); Phi Beta Kappa (chpt. scholarship chair 1992-94), Phi Kappa Phi. Avocations: sailing, reading, golf.

MILLER, CARL F. secondary school educator; b. Pitts., Mar. 25, 1967; s. Robert A. and Joanne N. Miller; m. Rachel A. Perry, June 14, 2003; children: Caroline, Emily. BS in Music Edn., Indiana U. Pa., 1989. Dir. of bands Crawford Ctrl. Sch. Dist.-Cochranton (Pa.) H.S., 1990—. Music/visual adjudicator Pa. Fedn. Contest Judges, Pitts., 1993—, Allegheny Judges Assn., Erie, Pa., 1994—. Deacon First Presbyn. Ch., Meadville, Pa., 2000—01. Mem.: NEA, Pa. Interscholastic Marching Band Assn., Crawford County Music Educators Assn., Lakeshore Marching Band Assn. (pres.), Crawford Ctrl. Edn. Assn., Pa. State Edn. Assn., Pa. Music Educators Assn., Music Educators Nat. Conf. Republican. Avocations: golf, computers, music. Office: Cochranton HS 127 Second St Cochranton PA 16314

MILLER, CATE, psychologist, educator; b. Baton Rouge, Apr. 1, 1964; d. Benjamin Robertson and Mertie Cate (Barnes) Miller, Jr. BA, Cath. U., 1985; MEd, Harvard U., 1986; MPhil, Columbia U., 1989, PhD, 1991. Lic. psychologist, N.Y. Psychology intern NYU Med. Ctr., Rusk Inst., N.Y.C., 1988-89, rsch. scientist, 1990—; pvt. practice specializing in psychotherapy N.Y.C., 1991—. Adj. asst. prof. Columbia U., N.Y.C., 1991—. Columbia U. Merit scholar, 1987-88. Mem. APA, Nat. Trust for Hist. Preservation, Phi Beta Kappa, Sigma Xi, Phi Delta Kappa. Democrat. Avocations: tennis, theatre, cycling. Office: NYU Med Ctr Rusk Inst 400 E 34th St New York NY 10016-4901

MILLER, CHRISTINE TALLEY, physical education educator; b. Wilmington, Del., Sept. 11, 1959; d. Willard Radley and Anna Rose (Oddo) Talley; m. Jeffrey Lynch Miller, Nov. 14, 1987; children: Radley Edward, Rebecca Anna. BS in Phys. Edn., U. Del., 1981, MS in Phys. Edn., 1984. Cert. phys. edn. tchr., Del. Phys. edn. tchr. Pilot Sch. Inc., Wilmington, 1981-85; EKG technician Christiana Care Health Sys., Newark, 1978—; phys. edn. tchr. Red Clay Consol. Sch. Dist., Wilmington, 1985—. Mem. stds. revision com. Del. Dept. Pub. Instrn., 1991; mem. stds. rev. com. Red Clay Consol. Sch. Dist., 1993-94, curriculum revision com., 1988-92; coach spl. olympics, 1985-88. Contbg. author: A Legacy of Delaware Women, 1987. Jump Rope for Heart coord. Am. Heart Assn., Newark, 1994—; mem. Gov.'s Coun. for Lifestyles and Fitness, State of Del., 1991-93. Recipient Gov.'s Cup award for outstanding phys. edn. program Gov. Mike Castle, Del., 1991, Gov.'s award for health and fitness, 1999. Mem. AAHPERD, Del. Assn. for Health, Phys. Edn., Recreation and Dance (sec. 1981-86, v.p. health, treas. 1999-2001, Outstanding Phys. Edn. Tchr. of Yr. 1986, 99). Home: 1206 Arundel Dr Wilmington DE 19808-2137

MILLER, CHRISTOPHER L, education educator; PhD, Yale U., 1983. Frederick Clifford Ford prof. Yale U., Dept. of French and African Am. Studies, 1982—. Fellowship, John Simon Guggenheim Meml. Found., 2003. Office: Yale U PO Box 208251 New Haven CT 06520-8251

MILLER, COLLEEN, vocational rehabilitation specialist, career counselor; BS in Elem. Edn., Villa Maria Coll., 1973; MEd in Guidance and Counseling, Gannon U., 1975; cert. mktg., U. Pitts., 1981, cert. indsl. rels. and pers., 1982; MBA, Robert Morris U., 1985. Cert. rehab. counselor; commn. on rehab. counselor cert.; cert. case mgr. Ins. Rehab. Specialist Commn.; cert. sr. disability analyst, Am. Bd. Disability Analysts; cert. youth ministry tng. program for adult vol. Diocese Pitts.; lic. edn. specialist II elem. and secondary guidance; lic. instrnl. I elem. edn., lic. profl. counselor, Penn. Elem. tchr., guidance counselor Turtle Creek Area Sch. Dist., Pa., 1974-76, 78-79; elem. guidance counselor North West Tri County Intermediate Unit, North East Dist., Edinboro, Pa., 1976-78; career counselor Westinghouse Electric Corp., East Pitts., Pa., 1979-83; vocat. rehab. specialist Intracorp, Forest Hills, Pa., 1984-89; referral devel. specialist Greater Pitts. Rehab. Hosp., Monroeville, Pa., 1989-90; vocat. rehab. specialist, career counselor Consulting Svc., Inc., East Pitts., 1989—. Mem.: ACA, AAUW, NAFE, Robert Morris U. Alumnae Assn., Villa Maria Coll. Alumnae Assn., Gannon U. Alumnae Assn., Pitts. Claims Assn., Pa. Counseling Assn., Nat. Assn. Rehab. Profls. in the Pvt. Sector, Am. Rehab. Counseling Assn., Am. Rehab. Counseling Assn. Pa., Am. Assn. Christian Counselors. Office: PO Box 159 East Pittsburgh PA 15112-0159

MILLER, CONSTANCE JOHNSON, educator; b. Jacksonville, Fla., Mar. 16, 1948; d. Shepheard and Victoria (Fisher) Johnson; children: Rodney Johnson, Larry Miller. BS, Fla. Meml. Coll., 1972. Tchr., family planning educator Urban League of Greater Miami, Fla., 1972-73; recreation leader YMCA of Greater Miami, 1973-74; recreation therapist Dade County Corrections and Rehab., 1974-76; tchr. Broward County Sch. Bd., Ft. Lauderdale, Fla., 1976—, Hollywood Hills H.S., Hollywood, Fla., 1986—. Coach McNicol and Hallandale Middle Sch., Hollywood, Fla., 1976-87, Hollywood Hills Sr. H.S., 1992-97; asst. athletic dir. Hollywood Hills H.S., 1998—. Assoc. min. New Birth Bapt. Ch., Miami; mem. NAACP. Democrat. Avocations: cooking, collecting oldies, decorating, golfing, traveling. Home: 20680 NE 4th Ct Apt 202 Miami FL 33179-1880

MILLER, DAVID EMANUEL, physics educator, researcher; b. Bethel, Vt., Aug. 30, 1943; s. Manuel Southworth and Lucille (Shurtleff) M. BA, U. Vt., 1965; MA, SUNY, Stony Brook, 1967, PhD, 1971; Habilitation in Theoretical Physics, U. Bielefeld, Germany, 1978. Instr. physics SUNY, Stony Brook, 1970-71; Wissenschaftlicher asst. Freie U., Berlin, 1972-75; scientist U. Bielefeld, 1975-78, Heinrich-Hertz Stipendium, 1977-78; privat dozent U. Bielefeld, 1978-83, univ. prof., 1987—; asst. prof. of physics Pa. State U., Hazleton, 1983-86, assoc. prof., 1986-92, prof., 1992—. Recipient Heinrich-Hertz stipendium, 1977-78, Fulbright award U. Wroclaw, Poland, 1997. Mem. Am. Phys. Soc., Am. Assn. Physics Tchrs., Fulbright Assn., Deutsche Physikalische Gesellschaft, Deutscher Hochschulverband, N.Y. Acad. Sci., Am. Math. Soc., Phi Beta Kappa, Sigma Xi. Home: PO Box 611 Conyngham PA 18219-0611 Office: Pa State U High Acres Hazleton PA 18201 E-mail: om0@psu.edu., dmiller@physik.uni-bielefeld.de.

MILLER, DAVID JULIAN, psychologist, educator; b. Berkeley, Calif., Mar. 9, 1952; s. Shully Leon and Anna Elizabeth Miller. Cert., U. Paris, 1972; BA in Psychology, U. Calif., Berkeley, 1974; MS in Psychology, U. Wis., 1976; EdD in Ednl. Psychology, U.S. Internat. U., 1989. Instr. psychology, counselor Imperial Valley Coll., Imperial, Calif., 1976-79; instr. psychology San Diego State U., 1979; dean students Grossmont Coll., San Diego, 1979-80; corp. tng. mgr. Gt. Am. Bank, San Diego, 1981-90; prof. psychology, chair counseling dept. Victor Valley Coll., Victorville, Calif., 1990—. Adj. prof. psychology Nat. U., San Diego, 1981-97; cons. to govt. and pvt. orgns., Calif., Ariz., 1979—; speaker in field. HEW grantee, 1979. Mem. APA, Am. Soc. for Tng. and Devel., Orgn. Devel. Network, San Diego Pers. and Guidance Assn. (bd. dirs. 1981-84), Greater San Diego Bus. Assn. (bd. dirs. 1984-87). Office: Victor Valley Coll 18422 Bear Valley Rd Victorville CA 92392-5850 Home: 4620 Adams Ave San Diego CA 92116 E-mail: millerd@vvc.edu.

MILLER, DENNIS DIXON, economics educator; b. Chillicothe, Ohio, May 1, 1950; s. Kermit Baker and Martha (Ralston) M. BA, Heidelberg Coll., 1972; MA, U. Colo., 1979, PhD, 1985; D (hon.), Ternopil Acad. Nat. Economy, Ukraine, 2000. Instr. in econs. Am. U., Cairo, Egypt, 1982-84; internat. economist USDA, Washington, 1985-86; prof. Baldwin-Wallace Coll., Berea, Ohio, 1987—. Rsch. assoc. Internat. Ctr. Energy and Econ. Devel., Boulder, 1979—82, Inst. Behavorial Sci., Boulder, 1979—82, Boulder, 1984—85; vis. scholar Hoover Instn., Stanford U., Palo Alto, 1986; acad. advisor Heartland Inst., Chgo., 1988—, Buckeye Ctr; book reviewer Choice mag., 1984—; manuscript reviewer Dryden Press, 1994—96; pub. policy advisor Heritage Found.'s Listing, Washington, 1991—; econ. cons. gen., 1991—; vis. prof. Mithibai Coll., U. Bombay, 1991; coord. agy. Air Quality Pub. Adv. Task Force, 1993; v.p. Adam Ferguson Inst., 1996—97; vis. prof. The U. of the Autonomous Regions of the Caribbean Coast of Nicaragua, Bluefields, 1996, The Ternopil Acad. of Nat. Economy Ukraine, 1997; Fulbright sr. specialist Discipline Peer Rev. Com., 2001. Recipient Earhart Found. fellow, 1977—78; grantee Sr. fellow, Found. for the Def. of Democracies, 2003—; scholar Fulbright scholar, 1999—2000. Fellow Found. Def. Democracies (sr.); mem. AAAS, Am. Econs. Assn., Cleve. Coun. on World Afairs, Assn. Pvt. Enterprise Edn., Ohio Assn. Economists and Polit. Scientists (v.p. 2000-01, pres. 2001-02), Intertel, Middle East Inst., Sierra Club, Nature Conservancy, Mensa, Eagle Scout. Avocations: running, tennis, reading, travel. Home: 12 Adelbert St Apt 2 Berea OH 44017-1753 Office: Baldwin Wallace Coll Dept Of Econs Berea OH 44017 E-mail: dmiller@bw.edu.

MILLER, DIANE MOON, data processing educator; b. Montgomery, Ala., Feb. 22, 1942; d. Benjamin Alfred and Georgia Elizabeth (Godwin) Moon; m. James Edward Miller, June 6, 1964; children: Deborah Elaine, Michael Edward. BA, Auburn U., 1964; BS, U. West Fla., 1981, MA, 1970, MBA, 1988; PhD, U. Ala., 1992. Cert. systems profl., data processor. Systems analyst Dept. Navy, Pensacola, Fla., 1980-86; asst. prof. U. So. Miss., 1986—. Author: (hist. novel) Onesie Delilah, 2002. Fellow Faculty fellow, NASA, Stennis Space Ctr., Miss., 1993—. Mem. Decision Scis. Inst., Inst. for Mgmt. Sci., Data Processing Mgmt. Assn. (bd. dirs. 1992-93, chair edn. com.), Internat. Assn. for Computer Info. Systems, Assn. for Bus. Simulation and Experiential Learning; Phi Kappa Phi, Beta Gamma Sigma, Sigma Iota Epsilon. Democrat. Methodist. Avocation: visual and performing arts. Office: U So Miss 730 E Beach Blvd Long Beach MS 39560-6259

MILLER, DIXIE DAVIS, elementary school educator; b. Lubbock, Tex., June 3, 1940; d. Leroy and Sara Edna (Lightfoot) Davis; m. Greg Miller, Aug. 10, 1968; 1 child, Jason Davis. BS in Edn., Tex. Christian U., 1961, MEd, 1967; postgrad., Tex. Wesleyan U. Cert. elem., early childhood, secondary English tchr., Tex. Elem. tchr. Denver Pub. Schs., Ft. Worth Pub. Schs., Albuquerque Pub. Schs., Birmingham (Mich.) Pub. Schs., Aledo (Tex.) Ind. Sch. Dist., Gwinnett County Pub. Schs., Lawrenceville, Ga. Group leader Young Author's Conf.; insvc. leader creative writing; presenter in field. Active PTA, PTO. Named Tchr. of Yr., Dyer Elem. Sch., Lawrenceville, 1979, 82, Grayson Elem. Sch., 1986, Educator of Yr. award Lawrenceville Jaycees, 1981, Les Evans Chpt. award Tex. Assn. for Supervision and Curriculum Devel., 1989, Excellence in Tchg. award Tex. State Reading Assn., 1998. Mem. NEA, Internat. Reading Assn., Assn. Childhood Edn. Internat., Ga. Assn. Educators, Mich. Edn. Assn., Tex. Tchrs. Assn. Home: 113 Squaw Creek Rd Weatherford TX 76087-8240

MILLER, DONNA PAT, library administrator, consultant; b. Lindale, Tex., Dec. 13, 1948; d. Donald Edward and Patsy Ruth (Dykes) Pool; m. James D. Miller, Aug. 17, 1991; children: James Jr., John, Julie, Jaynie. BS in Music, Tex. Woman's U., 1971, MA in Music, 1976; MLS, U. North Tex., 1987. Cert. music and learning resources tchr. Band dir. Grapevine (Tex.) Mid. Sch., 1971-77; pvt. music tchr. Mesquite, Tex., 1978-79; band dir. T.W. Browne Mid. Sch., Dallas, 1979-84, Vanston Mid. Sch., Mesquite, 1984-86; elem. libr. McKenzie Elem. Sch., Mesquite, 1986-90, Reinhardt Elem. Sch., Dallas, 1990-91, Range Elem. Sch., Mesquite, 1991-92; dir. libr. svcs. Mesquite Ind. Sch. Dist., 1992-95; libr. dir. Craig-Moffat County Pub. Libr., Craig, Colo., 1995—; adj. prof. Tex. Woman's U., Denton, 1993—. Mem. sci. adv. bd. Gale Rsch., Inc., Detroit, 1993—; cons. Region V Edn. Svc. Ctr., Beaumont, Tex., 1994—. Author: Developing an Integrated Libr. Program Reviewer Booklist Mag., 1986—, The Book Report Mag., 1992—; contbr. articles to mags. Mem. ALA, ASCD, Tex. Libr. Assn., Phi Delta Kappa, Beta Phi Mu. Avocations: running, reading, writing, music. Office: Craig-Moffat County Libr 570 Green St Craig CO 81625-3028

MILLER, DOROTHEA HELEN, librarian, educator; b. Macedonia, Iowa, Mar. 10, 1925; d. Carl Hamilton and Dorothy Marie (Wilson) Stempel; m. Ruben Roy Miller, Sept. 30, 1945 (dec. May 1987); children: Cecilia Rogge, Catherine Miller-King, Constance Miller. Student, U. Denver, 1942-45, State U. Iowa, 1960; BA with honors, Kearney (Nebr.) State Coll., 1966; ME, U. Nebr., 1970. Cert. media specialist Nebr. Libr. Oakland (Iowa) Pub. Libr., 1956-61; elem. libr. Grand Island (Nebr.) Pub. Schs., 1962-65, elem. libr. supr., 1965-78, media specialist, 1978-86; ret., 1986. Cons. Nat. Def. Edn. Act Inst. for Advanced Study in Ednl. Media Concordia Coll., 1967. Vol. Denver Mus. of Natural History, 1994-96, Nat. Def. Edn. Act Inst. Libr. Materials for Minority Students, Queens Coll., N.Y. Named Outstanding Educator in Am. Acad. of Am. Educators, 1973-74; rsch. grantee Howard Sch., 1966. Mem. AAUW, Cherry Creek Woman's Club, Nebr. Congress Parents and Tchrs. (hon. life), Order Ea. Star (assoc. matron). Democrat. Methodist. Avocations: genealogy, watercolors, calligraphy, poetry. Home: 13991 E Marina Dr Apt 303 Aurora CO 80014-3788 E-mail: TheaMil03@aol.com.

MILLER, DOROTHY ELOISE, education educator; b. Ft. Pierce, Fla., Apr. 13, 1944; d. Robert Foy and Aline (Mahon) Wilkes. BS in Edn., Bloomsburg U., 1966, MEd, 1969; MLA, Johns Hopkins U., 1978; EdD, Columbia U., 1991. Tchr. Cen. Dauphin East H.S., Harrisburg, Pa., 1966-68, Aberdeen (Md.) H.S., 1968-69; asst. dean of coll., prof. Harford C.C., Bel Air, Md., 1969—. Owner Ideas by Design, 1995—; mem. accreditation team Mid. States Commn., 1995— ; statewide writing skills assessment com., statewide English stds. com. Md. Higher Edn. Commn. 1997-2001, English composition com., 1997—, English alignment com., 2002—; adj. prof. U. Balt., 2001. Editor: Renewing the American Community Colleges, 1984; contbr. articles to profl. jours. Pres. Harlan Sq. Condominium Assn., Bel Air, 1982, 90-96, Md. internat. divsn. St. Petersburg Sister State Com., 1993-2001; edn. liaison AAUW, Harford County, Md., 1982-92; cen. com. mem. Rep. Party, Harford County, 1974-78; crusade co-chair Am. Cancer Soc., Harford County, 1976-78; mem. faculty adv. com. Md. Higher Edn. Commn., 1993-96; people's adv. coun. Harford County Coun., 1994-2003. Recipient Nat. Tchg. Excellence award Nat. Inst. for Staff and Orgn. Devel., U. Tex.-Austin, 1992. Mem. Nat. Mus. Women in the Arts (charter). Republican. Methodist. Avocations: skiing, swimming, golf, reading, image consulting. Office: Harford Community Coll 401 Thomas Run Rd Bel Air MD 21015-1627 E-mail: demiller@harford.cc.md.us.

MILLER, EDNA RAE ATKINS, secondary school educator; b. Clarksville, Ark., Dec. 28, 1915; d. Sammie Lawrence and Dora May (Turner) Atkins; m. Oscar E. Miller, Feb. 27, 1936; children: Myrna Sue Miller Hanses, William Samuel. BE, Sacramento State Coll., 1966. Tchr. one rm. sch., Johnson County, Ark., 1933-35; tchr. elem. Placerville, Calif., 1953-61; tchr. spl. edn. and mentally retarded County of El Dorado, Placerville, Calif., 1961-74; ret. El Dorado (Calif.) County, 1974. Author: Mother Lode of Learning: One Room Schools of El Dorado County, 1990. Mem. Friends of the Libr. of El Dorado County, Placerville, 1974—; historian People-to-People Internat., 1975-90, Sister City Program, 1975-90. Recipient Cert. of Appreciation, Lung Assn. Sacramento and Emmagrant Trails, 1978, Cert. of Appreciation, Ret. Tchrs. of El Dorado County, 1984, 86, 88. Mem. El Dorado County Hist. Soc., Children's Home Soc. (assoc.), Epsilon Chi chpt. Delta Kappa Gamma (pres. Placerville chpt. 1966-68). Democrat. Baptist. Avocations: research, gardening, painting, cake decorating, quilting. Home: 6061 Golden Center Ct Apt 304 Placerville CA 95667-6234

MILLER, ELEANOR, English language and literature educator; b. Mill Valley, Calif. BA with honors, U. Nev., 1966, PhD in English with honors, 1970. Instr. English Valley Coll., San Bernardino, Calif., 1983-84, Crafton Hills Coll., Redlands, Calif., 1984-86, Coll. of the Desert, Palm Springs, Calif., 1986-90; prof. English Composition & Literature So. Nev. C.C., Las Vegas, 1990—. Chair teaching-learning excellence com. So. Nev. C.C., Las Vegas, 1991-94, new faculty mentor, 1995—. Author: English Placement Grading, 1991, CCSN Writing Across the Curriculum, 1994, New Faculty Mentoring, 1997, Teaching Excellence, 1998. Advisor/participant Women's Re-entry Ctr., Palm Springs/Las Vegas, 1989-94; vol. Womyn's Festival Com., U. Nev., Las Vegas, 1994—; mem. adv. bd. Collegiate Press, 1998—. Mem. AAUW, Nat. Coun. Tchrs. English, Nev. State Tchrs. English, Nev. Adult Edn. Assn., Nev. Humanities Com., Mountain Plains Adult Edn. Assn., U. Nev. Alumni Assn., Women in Comm., Phi Kappa Phi. Avocations: reading, travel. Office: So Nev CC 3200 E Cheyenne Ave North Las Vegas NV 89030-4228

MILLER, ELMER SCHAFFNER, anthropologist, educator; b. Elizabethtown, Pa., Apr. 26, 1931; s. Raymond K. and Sarah (Schaffner) M.; m. Anna Lois Longenecker, June 13, 1953; children: Rosina Sue, Lisa Lynn. BA in Bible and Philosophy, Eastern Mennonite Coll., 1954, ThB, 1956; MA in Anthropology, Hartford Seminary Found., 1964; PhD, U. Pitts., 1967. Instr. Temple U., Phila., 1966-67, asst. prof., 1967-71, assoc. prof., 1971-80, prof., 1980-96, emeritus prof., 1996—. Chmn. dept. anthropology Temple U., 1970-77, 80-82; dir. Temple U. Abroad, Rome, 1982-85, assoc. dean arts and scis., Phila., 1986-89; mem. Univ. Sci. Ctr., Phila., 1973—; interviewer Latin Am. Scholarship Program, Boston, 1985—; mem. field faculty Goddard Coll., 1975-82. Author: Introduction to Cultural Anthropology, 1979, A Critically Annotated Bibliography, 2 vols., 1980, Harmony and Dissonance in Argentine Toba Society, 1980, Nurturing Doubt: From Mennonite Missionary to Anthropologist in the Argentine Chaco, 1995; editor: Peoples of the Gran Chaco, 1999. Mem. Mayor's Sci. and Tech. Adv. Coun., Phila., 1972-75. Mem. Am. Anthrop. Assn., Germantown Cricket Club (admissions com. 1991-94). Democrat. E-mail: esmiller@temple.edu.

MILLER, ELOUISE DARLENE, primary education educator; b. Alton, Kans., Nov. 24, 1930; d. Clarence Sylvester and Laura Areta (Sparks) M. BS, Ft. Hays State U., 1956, MS, 1961, EdS, 1970; postgrad., Temple U., 1966. Cert. tchr., Kans. Tchr. Liberty Sch., Alton, 1948—49, Mt. Hope Sch., Osborne, Kans., 1949—50, Woodston (Kans.) Grade Sch., 1950-55; tchr. 1st grade Unitied Sch. Dist. 489, Hays, Kans., 1956-65, tchr. kindergarten, 1965—, chmn. kindergarten, 1983—. Tchr. remedial reading, fed. program, Hays, summers, 1970—. Primary supt. Sunday sch. Hays Meth. Ch., 1976—. Named to Kans. Tchrs. Hall of Fame Inc., 1989. Mem. NEA (pres. Hays 1962-63, del. Kans. 1980—), AAUW, Internat. Reading Assn. (charter pres. 1965-67), Meth. Ch. Women, Kans. Hist. Soc., Hays Arts Coun., Delta Tau (pres. Hays 1959-61), Delta Kappa Gamma, Phi Delta Kappa (Cunningham award 1989), Phi Kappa Phi. Avocations: travel, reading, jogging, bicycling. Home: 2729 Hickory St Hays KS 67601-1610 Office: Lincoln Sch 1906 Ash St Hays KS 67601-3297

MILLER, FRANCES ELIZABETH, assistant superintendent; b. Chestertown, Md., May 23, 1939; d. Edward Rood Sr. and Mary Margaret (Durham) Walls; m. Albert Russell Miller, Dec. 17, 1961 (div.); 1 child, Tracey Lynne. BS, West Chester (Pa.) State U., 1961; MEd in Adminstrn., Kent (Ohio) State U., 1970; postgrad., Towson (Md.) Coll., Loyola Coll., 1981—. Cert. phys. edn. tchr., secondary prin., supr., supt. Tchr. Kent County Pub. Schs., Chestertown, 1961-69, coord. fed. programs, 1972-82, supr. bus. affairs, 1982-86, dir. adminstrv. svcs., 1987-89, asst. supt. adminstrv. svcs., 1989—; specialist in health edn. Eastern Shore Md. Consortium, Centreville, 1970-71; tchr. Kent County High Sch., Chestertown, 1971-72. Dir. Md. Legal Svcs. Trust, Annapolis, 1991—. Mem. Am. Assn. Sch. Adminstrs., Internat. Assn. Sch. Bus. Ofcls. (rsch. and fin. coms. Reston, Va. chpt. 1989—, chmn. registration St. Michael's, Md./D.C. chpt. 1988—). Democrat. Methodist. Avocations: camping, reading, yard work, youth sports. Office: Kent County Pub Schs 215 Washington Ave Chestertown MD 21620-1654

MILLER, FRANCIE LORADITCH, counseling administrator; b. Avilton, Md., Apr. 18, 1937; d. John William and Agnes Wilda (Broadwater) Loraditch; m. George Aloys Miller, Feb. 27, 1965; children: Peter Raymond, Sandra Patricia. Student, Kent State U., 1955-57; BA in English, Calif. State U., Dominguez Hills, 1978, Ma in English, 1980. Flight attendant Western Airlines, L.A., 1957-65; lectr. English Calif. State U., Carson, 1980—82, 1998—2002, asst. coord. learning assistance ctr., 1979-84, asst. dir. univ. outreach svcs., 1984-96, lectr., 1997—, asst. dean acad. affairs, 2001—. Dir. advisement & transfer svcs. Marymount Coll., Palos Verdes, Calif., 1996—2001; mem. L.A. Regional Intersegmental Adv. Bd., 1996. Editor: Campus Staff Newsletter, 1992—96. Vol. Olympic Games, L.A., 1984; participant Civic Chorale, Torrance, 1993—; campus rep. Statewide Alumni Coun., Sacramento, 1982—84; apptd. statewide campus adv. com. Project Assist, 1996. Scholar Acad., Kent State U., 1955. Mem.: Western Assn. Coll. Admission Counselors, Nat. Acad. Advising Assn., Calif. Intersegmental Articulation Coun. (newsleter editor 1993—96, vice chair 1995—96), Palos Verdes C. of C. (bd. dirs. 1998), Phi Kappa Phi (chpt. pres. 1992—98, mem. comm. com. 1996). Republican. Roman Catholic. Avocations: singing, dancing, golf. Office: Marymount Coll 30800 Palos Verdes Dr E Palos Verdes Peninsula CA 90275-6273 E-mail: fmiller@marymountpv.edu.

MILLER, GAIL ANN, elementary school educator; b. Buffalo, Apr. 10, 1955; d. John F. and Joan M. (Simon) Holtz; m. Robert G. Miller Jr., Aug. 25, 1979; children: John Robert, Brianna Lynne. BS in Edn., St. Bonaventure U., Olean, N.Y., 1977; MS in Reading, SUNY, Fredonia, 1979. Faculty reading SUNY, Fredonia, 1992; title I reading tchr. Dunkirk (N.Y.) Pub. Sch. #3, 1979—, team tchr. pilot multi-age grades 2-3, 1994—. Co-dir. Sch. # variety show; presenter/lectr. various confs. Co-editor Celebrations newsletter. Coord. Vacation Bible Sch., First United Presbyn. Ch., Silver Creek, N.Y., 1985-91, Sunday sch. tchr., elder, clk of session and mem. edn. com. Named Tchr. of Month, Dunkirk Rotary, 1993. Mem. Internat. Reading Assn. (Chautauqua coun.). Republican. Avocations: writing, reading, golf. Home: 1845 Lake Rd Silver Creek NY 14136-9725 Office: Dunkirk Public School #3 Lamphere St Dunkirk NY 14048

MILLER, GERALDINE (TINCY), real estate company executive, educational association administrator; m. Vance Miller; 4 children. BS, So. Meth. U.; MS in Reading, Tex. A&M U. Vice chmn. Henry S. Miller Cos., 1994—. Tchr. reading lab. Tex. Scottish Rite HOsp. for Crippled Children, Highland Park Presbyn. Hillier Sch. for Dyslexia; bd. mem. Literacy Instrn. for Tex. Mem. Tex. State Bd. Edn., 1988—, pres., 2003—; chair fundraising events United Cerebral Palsy Assn., Dallas Opera, Dallas Symphony Orch., TACA, Crystal Charity Ball; active I Have A Dream Found., Nat. Orton-Dyslexia Soc., Boy's and Girl's Club Greater Dallas, Dallas County Heritage Soc. Recipient Hall of State award for civic involvement, Dallas Hist. Soc., 1995, Tom Landry award of excellence in volunteerism, 1999. Mem.: Acad. Lang. Therapist Assn., Internat. Reading Assn., Kappa Delta Pi, Phi Delta Kappa. Republican. Address: 1100 Providence Tower West 5001 Spring Valley Rd Dallas TX 75244-3910*

MILLER, HARVEY ALFRED, botanist, educator; b. Sturgis, Mich., Oct. 19, 1928; s. Harry Clifton and Carmen (Sager) M.; m. Donna K. Hall, May 9, 1992; children: Valerie Yvonne, Harry Alfred, Timothy Merk, Tanya Merk, Jasper Adam. BS, U. Mich., 1950; MS, U. Hawaii, 1952; PhD, Stanford U., 1957. Instr. botany U. Mass., 1955-56, Miami U., Oxford, Ohio, 1956-57, asst. prof., 1957-61, assoc. prof., curator herbarium, 1961-67, adj. prof. botany, 1985—, vis. prof., 1994—; prof., chmn. program in biology Wash. State U., 1967-69; vis. prof. botany U. Ill., 1969-70; prof., chmn. dept. biol. scis. U. Cen. Fla., 1970-75, prof., 1975-94; v.p. Marine Research Assocs. Ltd., Nassau, 1962-65; assoc. Lotspeich & Assocs., natural systems analysts, Winter Park, Fla., 1979-94; v.p. D.H. Miller and Assocs., Oxford, 1994-97. Adj. prof. environ. mental sci. Seminole Cmty. Coll., 2002—; botanist U. Mich. Expdn. to Aleutian Islands, 1949-50; prin. investigator Systematic and Phytogeographical Studies Bryophytes of Pacific Islands, NSF, 1959, Miami U. Expdn. to Micronesia, 1960; dir. NSF-Miami U. Expdn. to Micronesia and Philippines, 1965; prin. investigator NSF bryophytes of So. Melanesia, 1983-86; research assoc. Orlando Sci. Ctr., Orlando; vis. prof. U. Guam, 1965; cons. tropical botany, foliage plant patents, also designs for sci. bldgs.; field researcher on Alpine meadows in Irian Jaya, 1991, 1992; adj. prof. U. W. Ala., 1997-2000. Author: (with H.O. Whittier and B.A. Whittier) Prodromus Florae Muscorum Polynesiae, 1978, Prodromus Florae Hepaticarum Polynesiae, 1983; Field Guide to Florida Mosses and Liverworts, 1990; editor: Florida Scientist, 1973-78; contbr. articles to sci. jours. Bd. dirs. Astronauts Scholarship Found. (formerly Mercury Seven Found.), 1975—, chmn. scholarship and grant selection com., 1985—. Recipient Acacia Order of Pythagoras; recipient Acacia Nat. award of Merit; Guggenheim fellow, 1958 Fellow AAAS, Linnean Soc. London; mem. Pacific Sci. Assn. (chmn. sci. com. for botany 1975-83), Assn. Tropical Biology, Am. Inst. Biol. Scis., Am. Bryol. Soc. (v.p. 1962-63, pres. 1964-65), Brit. Bryol. Soc., Bot. Soc. Am., Internat. Assn. Plant Taxonomists, Internat. Assn. Bryologists, Mich. Acad. Sci. Arts and Letters, Am. Soc. Plant Taxonomists, Fla. Acad. Sci. (exec. sec. 1976-83, pres. 1980), Nordic Bryol. Soc., Acacia, Explorers Club, Sigma Xi, Phi Sigma, Beta Beta Beta Home: PO Box 390457 Deltona FL 32739-0457 Office: Miami U Dept Botany Oxford OH 45056 E-mail: bryolaladonna@aol.com.

MILLER, IRIS ANN, landscape architect, urban designer, educator; b. Pitts., Jan. 6, 1938; d. Bernard and Sadye (Topel) Ress; m. Lawrence Alan Miller, Jan. 24, 1959; children: Bradley Stuart, Richard Lyle, Stefan Ress. BS cum laude, U. Pitts., 1959, MEd in Secondary Edn., 1961; postgrad. in psychology and counseling, U. Md., 1962-68; MArch, Cath. U. Am., 1979. Tchr. various pub. and pvt. schs., Pitts., Monroeville, Pa., Montgomery County, Md., 1959-61, 63-64; free lance landscape design Washington, 1965-81; architecture design and research O'Neil and Manion Architects, Bethesda, Md., 1979, 81; architecture design and drawing Frank Schlesinger Architects/Planners, Washington, 1979-80; prin. Iris Miller Urbanism and Landscape Design, 1982—; cons. architecture design Washington, 1982—. Vis. lectr. Cath. U. Am., Washington, 1983-86, vis. asst. prof., 1987-93, adj. asst. prof., 1993-96, adj. assoc. prof., 1997—, dir. landscape, arch. studies, 1986-89, dir. landscape studies, 1990—; urban design cons. Techworld, Washington, 1984-86; devel. dir. Tech. 2000 Mus., 1985-86; dir., presenter lectr. series resident assoc. program Smithsonian Instn., Washington, 1982, 83, 85, 87, 89, 98; dir., founder 7th, 8th and 9th Sts. Group Streetscape project, Washington, 1986-89, others; founder Charrette urban design seminar, Washington, Dallas, Alexandria, Va., St. Louis and Cleve., 1982-89; initiator, participant Sarasota (Fla.) Regional Urban Design Assistance R/UDAT Team, 1983, seminar Nat. Gallery Art, Washington, 1984, Nat. Arboretum, 1988, symposia Cath. U. Am., 1987—; invited jury panel, Fulbright Travel Awards, 1997-99; Lambda Alpha Internat. Hon. Soc., 1998—;facilitator/panel North Capital St./Fruxton Circle Charette, 2001; invited panel Japan Triennial Echigo-Tsumari, 1999, 2000; spkr., team leader McMillan Reservoir Charrette, Washington, 1999; apptd. mem. D.C. Downtown Partnership Streetscape subcom., 1989-91, D.C. Interactive Downtown Task Force Streetscape and Traffic subcom., 1996; D.C. Stakeholder Signage Subcommittee, 1997—, D.C. Stakeholder Traffic Subcommittee, 1998, D.C. Stakeholder Streetscape Subcom., 1999; co-founder, co-chmn. Brookland/CUA Neighborhood Improvement Partnership, 1999—; founder, co-dir. symposium. Libr. of Congress, 1995; dir. symposium D.C. Interagy. Task Force Seminar on Streetscape and Signage, 1995; dir., mem. steering com. numerous confs. in field; invited participant Congress for New Urbanism, 1994—; program spkr. U.S. Embassy Amman, Jordan, 1992, ICOMOS, 1992, 93, U. Va., 1993, Ecole Nationale Superieure du Paysage/Versailles, France, 1993, U. Osaka, Japan, 1993, 95, 96, 97 Tokyo Inst. Tech. U., 1993, Chiba Inst. Tech., Japan, 1998, SUNY, Buffalo, 1994, U. Colo., Denver, 1994, Mayors Inst. on City Design, St. Louis, 1994, Tongji U., Shanghai, China, 1995, 97, Tsinghua U., China, 1995, 98; jury critic Cath. U. Am., 1980-99, U. Puerto Rico, U. Va., 1993, Tsinghua U., China, 1998; instr. ceramics, Bethesda, Md., 1975-76. Author, co-editor: (book) Urban Design: Visions and Reflections, 1991, Capital Visions: Reflections on a Decade of Urban Design Charrettes and a Look Ahead, 1995, (map and text) Visions of Washington: Composite Plan of Urban Interventions, 1991; author: D.C. Streetscape & Signage Resource Manual, 1996; co-author: Retrospective Catalogue: Collegiate Exhibition for Excellence in Urban Design, 1997, Washington In Maps, 2002; contbr. articles to profl. jours.; landscape design featured in major landscape archtl. jours. in US and Japan, 1998, 2000; featured nationally in Assoc. Press articles on fragrant landscapes, 1999; curator, author exhbn. and catalogue on Washington Maps Sumner Sch. Mus., 1987, 92, U. Md., 1993, Embassy of France, 1993, SUNY Buffalo, 1994, U. Calif., Berkeley, 1994, U. Toronto, Can., 1995; curator, author exhbn. ACSA Ann. Meeting, Montreal, 1994; co-curator, author exhbn. and catalogue Octagon Mus., 1987; project dir., curator Paris-Washington Exhbn., 1987—; exhibitor, installation, Tokyo, Japan, 1997; recent residential and other landscape projects include Univ. Club. Wash., 1997-98, Salle de Fete Site Plan, Francheville, France, 1993, Kahn Residence, Arlington, Va., 1993-94, Marks Residence, Silver Spring, Md., 1993, Nesse, Lewis Residence, Silver Spring, 1992, Friedman Residence, Washington, 1992, Drysdale Hershon Residence, Washington, 1991, Miller Residence, Washington, 1990—, Sexton Residence, Kenwood, Chevy Chase, Md., 1990, 95, Romano Residence, Fairfax Station, Va., 1989, Mushinski Residence, Bethesda, Md., 1989, 8th St. Mall Washington, 1987-88, Mishkin, Jennis Residence, Bethesda, 1988, Cramer Residence, Bethesda, 1988; recent home design and renovations include Sexton Residence, Chevy Chase, 1994, Miller Jayapal Residence, San Francisco, 1993, Marks Residence, Silver Spring, 1993, Miller Residence, 1991, Washington, Mishkin Jennis Residence, Bethesda, 1988. Co-chmn. stamp com. Bicentennial Washington, 1987-90; founding mem. Washington Network, 1986-89; mem. adv. panel L'Enfant Forum, Washington, 1987-90, Hist. Georgetown Found., 1989-90; trustee John J. Sexton Fund for Local Govt. Studies, Sch. Pub. Affairs, U. Md., College Park, 1983-93; dir., founder Pub.-Pvt. Partnership and Univ. Scholarship Outreach Inner-City H.S. Program, Cath. U. Am., Washington Pub. Schs., 1985—; dir., founder Intern Exch. Program Landscape Architecture France-U.S.A., Cath. U. Am., U. Va., Friends of Vieilles Maisons Francaises, 1991-98, study-travel Asia Arch./Landscape Scholarship Fund, 1998—; dir., co-founder Intern Exch. Program Landscape Architecture China-U.S.A., Cath. U. Am., Tongji U., Shanghai, 1995—, Osaka U., Japan, 1996—, Chiba Inst. Tech., Japan, 1998-99; historic landscape com. U.S./Internat. Coun. on Monuments and Sites, 1990—; active Cultural Alliance Greater Washington, Nat. Trust Historic Preservation, Ikebana Internat., His. Soc. Washington, Nat. Mus. for Bldg. Arts; alumni coun. Sch. Architecture and Planning, Cath. U. Am., 1986—; mem. com. on environment Congress for New Urbanism, 1994—. Travel rsch. grantee Cath. U. Am., 1978, 79; grantee Govt. France, 1985, NEA (2), 1982, 92; recipient Program Devel. award Cath. U. Am., 1978. Mem. AIA (assoc., nat., regional and urban design exhbn. and panel, chmn. edn. subcom. 1987-96, sec. edn. subcom. 1997—, chmn., founder data base on design edn. and urban design, chmn. edn. conf. 1983, chmn. newsletter 1993, edn. com. D.C. chpt. 1981-83, Charrette co-chmn., program devel. award 1982), Assn. Collegiate Schs. Architecture (spkr. N.E. region conf. 1989, spkr. ann. meeting 1991-92, chmn. panel 1989—, chair Collegiate Exhbn. for Excellence in Urban Design 1990—, author conf. procs. 1991-93, Citation for Urban Design 1993, 95), Am. Soc. Landscape Architects (Potomac chpt. strategic planning com. 1994-95), Am. Planning Assn., U.S.-Internat. Coun. on Monuments and Sites (program spkr. 1987, 92, 93, hist. landscapes com.), Friends Vieilles Maisons Francaises (program spkr. 1987, 92), Friends of Vieilles Maisons Francaises, Congress for New Urbanism (com. on environment 1994—), Alpha Epsilon Phi (pres. D.C. alumni 1965-67). Avocations: photography, japanese flower arranging, tennis, jogging. Home: 3820 52nd St NW Washington DC 20016-1924

MILLER, JAMES EDWARD, computer scientist, educator; b. Lafayette, La., Mar. 21, 1940; s. Edward Gustave and Orpha Marie (DeVilbiss) M.; m. Diane Moon, June 6, 1964; children: Deborah Elaine, Michael Edward. BS, U. La., Lafayette, 1961, PhD, 1972; MS, Auburn U., 1964. Systems engr. IBM, Birmingham, Ala., 1965-68; asst. prof. U. West Fla., Pensacola, 1968-70, chmn. systems sci., 1972-86; grad. rschr. U. La., Lafayette, 1970-72; computer systems analyst EPA, Washington, 1979; prof., chmn. computer sci. and stats. U. So. Miss., Hattiesburg, 1986-92, prof., 1992—2003; program evaluator Computer Sci. Accreditation Commn., 1986-92; prof. computer sci. and stats. U. So. Miss. Gulf Coast, Long Beach, 2003—. Cons., lectr. in field; co-dir. NASA/Am. Soc. Engring. Edn. Faculty Fellowship Program-Stennis Space Flight Ctr., 1990—. Author numerous articles for tech. publs. Mem. Assn. Computing Machinery (editor Computer Sci. Edn. spl. interest group bull. 1982-97), Data Processing Mgmt. Assn. (dir. edn. spl. interest group 1985-86), Am. Soc. for Engring. Edn. Democrat. Methodist. Office: U So Miss Computer Sci 730 E Beach Blvd Long Beach MS 39560-1000 E-mail: jim.miller@usm.edu.

MILLER, JAN DEAN, metallurgy educator; b. Dubois, Pa., Apr. 7, 1942; s. Harry Moyer and Mary Virginia (McQuown) M.; m. Patricia Ann Rossman, Sept. 14, 1963; children: Pamela Ann, Jeanette Marie, Virginia Christine. BS, Pa. State U., 1964; MS, Colo. Sch. of Mines, 1966, PhD, 1969. Rsch. engr. Anaconda Co., Mont., 1966; asst. prof. metallurgy U. Utah, Salt Lake City, 1968-72; rsch. engr. Lawrence Livermore Lab., Calif., 1972; assoc. prof. U. Utah, 1972-78, prof., 1978-2000, Ivor D. Thomas prof., 2000—, dept. chmn., 2002—. Cons. on processing of mineral resources to various cos. and govt. agys. Editor: Hydrometallurgy, Research, Development, and Plant Practice, 1983, others; contbr. over 300 articles to profl. jours.; 25 patents in field. Recipient Marcus A. Grossman award Am. Soc. Metals, 1974, Van Diest gold medal Colo. Sch. Mines, 1977, Extractive and Processing Lectr. award The Minerals, Metals and Materials Soc., 1992, Disting. Achievement medal Colo. Sch. of Mines, 1994; Centennial fellow Coll. of Earth and Mineral Scis., Pa. State U., 1996, Best Paper award for fundamental rsch. 2000 TAPPI Recycling Symposium, 2000. Mem. NAE, AIME (Henry Krumb lectr. 1987, Richards award 1991, Mineral Industry Edn. award 1997, Aplan award 2003), Soc. Mining, Metallurgy and Exploration (chmn. mineral processing divsn. 1980-81, Disting. Mem. award 1992, Antoine M. Gaudin award 1992), Fine Particle Soc., Am. Chem. Soc., Soc. Mining Engrs. (bd. dirs. 1980-83, program chmn. 1982-83, Taggart award 1986, Stefanko award 1988, 2002), Metall. Soc. (Extractive Metallurgy Tech. award 1988); clubs: Salt Lake Swim and Tennis; U. Utah Faculty. Baptist. Office: U Utah Metall Engring 135 S 1460 E Rm 412 Salt Lake City UT 84112-0114 E-mail: jdmiller@mines.utah.edu.

MILLER, JANE CUTTING, elementary education educator; Tchr. Lawrence Barnes Sch., Burlington, Vt., 1972—. Recipient State Tchr. of Yr. Elem. award Vt., 1992. Office: Lawrence Barnes Sch 123 North St Burlington VT 05401-5126

MILLER, JEAN ELLEN, academic development director; b. Brockton, Mass., Mar. 10, 1928; d. John Wright and Dorothy (Dean) M. AB, Brown U., 1949; ME an dMA, Middlebury Coll., 1949—56. Tchr. pub. high schs., 1949-50; tchr., counselor Mt. Vernon Sem., Washington, 1956-58; asst. head, tchr. Masters Sch., Dobbs Ferry, N.Y., 1958-63; dir. student pers. Bennington (Vt.) Coll., 1963-64; head mistress St. Timothy's Sch., Stevenson, Md., 1964-77; regional dir. AFS Internat., N.Y.C., 1978-84; head mistress Vivian Webb Sch., Claremont, Calif., 1984-87; head Palmer Sch., Miami, Fla., 1988-90; dir. devel. Poly Prep Country Day Sch., Bklyn., 1991-96, Stratton Mountain Sch., Vt., 1996—98. Cons. Md. State Edn. Com., Balt., 1960's. Fundraiser Brown U., Providence, 1992-94; pres. Women of Brown of So. Calif., 1986-88; chair Pembroke Ctr. Tchg. and Rsch. on Women, Providence, 1994—, Vt. Women's Fund, 2002—, Vt. Humanities Coun., 2002—; bd. dirs. Dorset Theatre Festival, 1998—, Martha Canfield Libr. Mem. NOW, Nat. Assn. Ind. Schs. (bd. dirs. 1968-78, chmn. 1976-78), Nat. Mus. for Women in the Arts (charter), Dorset Field Club, Sierra Club. Avocations: golf, gardening, travel, reading. Home: PO Box 349 Arlington VT 05250-0349

MILLER, JEAN PATRICIA SALMON, art educator; b. Little Falls, Minn., Sept. 28, 1920; d. Albert Michael and Wilma (Kaestner) Salmon; m. George Fricke Miller, Sept. 8, 1951 (dec. Apr. 1991); children: Victoria Jean, George Laurids. BS, St. Cloud State Tchrs. Coll., 1942; MS, U. Wis., Whitewater, 1976. Lic. cert. secondary English, art, Wis. Tchr. elem. and secondary art Pub. Schs. Sauk Center, Minn., 1943; tchr. secondary art Bd. Edn., Idaho, 1945; tchr. elem. and secondary art Elkhorn (Wis.) Area Schs., 1950-78; tchr. art adult edn. Kenosha Tech. Coll., Elkhorn, Wis., 1969; cooperating tchr., supr. art majors in edn. U. Wis., Whitewater, 1970-77. Coord. Art Train Project, Walworth County. Represented in permanent collections Irwin L. Young Auditorium, U. Wis., Whitewater. Sec. Walworth County Needs of Children and Youth, Williams Bay, Wis., 1956-57; co-chair, sponsor Senate Bill 161-art requirement for h.s. grad., 1988-89. Recipient Grand award painting Walworth County Fair, 1970, 3rd award painting Geneva Lake Art Assn., Lake Geneva, Wis., Acrylic Painting First award Badlants Art Assn., 1994. Mem. Nat. Art Edn. Assn., Wis. Women in Arts, Wis. Art Edn. Assn., Wis. Regional Artists Assn. (co-chmn. Wis. regional art program 1992, 93, corr. sec. 1992—), Walworth County Art Assn. (bd. dirs. 1979-94, pres. 1986-87), Badlands Art Assn., Kiwanis, Elks, Alpha Delta Kappa (pres. Theta chpt. Wis. 1968-70), Delta Kappa Gamma (Iota chpt.). Home and Office: 215 5th St N Richardton ND 58652-7107

MILLER, JEANNE-MARIE ANDERSON (MRS. NATHAN J. MILLER), English language educator, academic administrator; b. Washington, Feb. 18, 1937; d. William and Agnes Catherine (Johns) Anderson m. Nathan John Miller, Oct. 2, 1960. BA, Howard U., 1959, MA, 1963, PhD, 1976. Instr. dept. English Howard U., Washington, 1963-76, asst. prof., 1976-79, assoc. prof., 1979-92, prof., 1992-97, prof. emeritus, 1997—, asst. dir. Inst. Arts and Humanities, 1973-75, asst. acad. planning, office v.p. for acad. affairs, 1976-90. Cons. Am. Studies Assn., 1972-75, Silver Burdett Pub. Co., NEH, 1978—; mem. adv. bd. D.C. Libr. for Arts, 1973—. Editor, Black Theatre Bull., 1977-86; Realism to Ritual: Form and Style in Black Theatre, 1983; assoc. editor Theatre Jour., 1980-81; contbr. articles to profl. jours. Mem. Washington Performing Arts Soc., 1971—, Friends of Sta. WETA-TV, 1971—, Mus. African Art, 1971—, Arena Stage Assocs., 1972—, Washington Opera Guild, 1982—, Wolf Trap Assocs., 1982—, Drama League N.Y., 1995, Shakespeare Theatre, 2001—, Met. Opera Guild, 2002—. Ford Found. fellow, 1970-72, So. Fellowships Fund fellow, 1973-74; Howard U. rsch. grant, 1975-76, 94-97, ACLS grant, 1978-79, NEH grant, 1981-84. Mem.: LWV (D.C. chpt.), MLA, ACLU, AAUP, Folger Shakespeare Libr., Acad. Am. Poets, Am. Theatre and Drama Soc., Studio Mus. Harlem, Nat. Mus. Women in Arts, Nat. Bldg. Mus., Winterthur Guild, Hist. Soc. Washington, D.C. Preservation League, Nat. Trust Historic Preservation, Zora Neale Hurston Soc., Langston Hughes Soc., Ibsen Soc., Friends of Kennedy Ctr. for Performing Arts, Am. Assn. Higher Edn., Coll. Lang. Assn., Common Cause, Am. Assn. Higher Edn., Am. Studies Assn., Coll. English Assn., Nat. Coun. Tchrs. English, Sierra Club, Pi Lambda Theta. Democrat. Episcopalian. Home: 504 24th St NE Washington DC 20002-4818

MILLER, JO ANN, education educator, college official; b. Shelbyville, Mo., June 13, 1940; d. Carl Edward and Mary Lillian (Wood) Willey; m. Robert William Miller, Mar. 1, 1961; children: David William, Mariann Denise. BA in English, Mo. Bapt. Coll., St. Louis, 1979; MEd, U. Mo., St. Louis, 1981; PhD in Higher Edn. Adminstrn., St. Louis U., 1992. Cert. English, libr. sci. and adult edn. tchr., Mo. Instr. adult edn. Jefferson Coll., Hillsboro, Mo., 1976-82; tchr. English, De Soto (Mo.) Sch. Dist., 1981-84; dean students Mo. Bapt. Coll., 1984-88, assoc. prof. edn., chmn. div. edn., asst. acad. dean, 1988-95, dean student info., 1996—, seminar presenter and facilitator, 1993—, dean student life, 1996—. Adj. prof. S.W. Bapt. U., Bolivar, Mo., 1994—; mem. Mo. Task Force for Tchr. Edn. Stds., 1993. Contbr. articles to profl. jours. Mem. resolutions com. So. Bapt. Conv., Nashville, 1989; mem. program com. Jefferson Bapt. Assn., 1992—. Named Parkway Outstanding Educator of Yr., 1992; ednl. policy fellow Mo. Fellows, 1993. Mem. ASCD, AAUW, Mo. Bapt. Coll. Alumni Assn., Phi Lambda Theta, Sigma Tau Delta. Avocations: needlepoint, travel, collecting antiques. Home: PO Box 411642 Saint Louis MO 63141-1642 Office: Mo Bapt Coll One College Park Dr Saint Louis MO 63141-8613

MILLER, JOANNE LOUISE, middle school educator; b. Milton, Mass., Apr. 4, 1944; d. Joseph Louis and Marion Theresa (Saulnier) Fasci; m. William Frederick Miller, Dec. 4, 1962; 1 child, Robert Joseph. BS, U. Oreg., 1972, MS in Curriculum and Instrn., 1973; EdD, Brigham Young U., 1980; postgrad., Oreg. State U., 1995. Lic. counselor, tchr., adminstr., Oreg. Tchr. South Lane Sch. Dist., Cottage Grove, Oreg., 1973—, lang. arts div. chairperson, 1975-78, 89-90, reading coord., 1978-79, 7th grade block chairperson, 1982-92, mid. sch. talented and gifted coord., 1992-93, counselor, 1991-93. Mem. Oreg. State Assessment Content Panel Reading, Salem, 1987-88, 97—; mem. Oreg. Lang Arts Curriculum Devel. Com., Salem, 1985-87; del. to Citizen Amb. Program of People to People Internat. 1st U.S.-Russia Joint Conf. on Edn., Moscow, 1994. Vol. Am. Cancer Soc., Am. Diabetes Assn., 1990—; aux.- charter mem. Assistance League of Eugene. Mem. ACA, NEA, Internat. Reading Assn., Am. Sch. Counselor Assn., Oreg. Counseling Assn., Oreg. Edn. Assn., South Lane Edn. Assn., Oreg. Reading Assn., Oreg. Mid. Level Assn., Delta Kappa Gamma, Alpha

Rho State (v.p. 1995-97, pres. 1997—). Democrat. Roman Catholic. Avocations: travel, reading. Home: 85515 Appletree Dr Eugene OR 97405-9738 Office: Lincoln Mid Sch 1565 S 4th St Cottage Grove OR 97424-2955

MILLER, JOHN EDWARD, army officer, technology executive, educational administrator; b. Paragould, Ark., May 8, 1941; s. Wardlow Knox and Anna Mae (Danford) M.; m. Joan Carolyn Capano, Oct. 5, 1968; children: C. Claire, J. Andrew, JoAnna M., Mary Ellen. BS in Math., S.W. Mo. State U., 1963; MS in Ops. Rsch., Ga. Inst. Tech., 1971; postgrad., Yale U., 1991. Commd. 2d lt. U.S. Army, 1963, advanced through grades to lt. gen., 1993; student, then author, instr., grad. studies faculty mem. U.S. Army Command and Gen. Staff Coll., Ft. Leavenworth, Kans., 1974—77; bn. comdr. 4th Brigade, 4th Inf. Divsn., Wiesbaden, Germany, 1977—79; ops. and tng. officer 8th Inf. Div., Badkreuznach, Germany, 1979—81; student U.S. Army War Coll., Carlisle, Pa., 1982; divsn. chief Office Dep. Chief of Staff for Rsch. Devel. and Acquisition, Dept. Army, Washington, 1982—84; brigade comdr., chief of staff 9th Inf. Divsn., Ft. Lewis, Wash., 1984—87; asst. for combat devels. U.S. Army Tng. and Doctrine Command, Ft. Monroe, Va., 1987—88; asst. divsn. comdr. for ops. and tng. 8th Inf. Divsn., Baumholder, Germany, 1988—89; dep. comdt. U.S. Army Command and Gen. Staff Coll., Ft. Leavenworth, 1989—91; comdr. 101st Airborne Divsn., Ft. Campbell, Ky., 1991—93; comdt. U.S. army command, gen. staff coll. U.S. Army, Ft. Leavenworth, 1993—95; dep. comdg. gen. U.S. Army Tng. and Doctrine Command, Ft. Monroe, Va., 1995—97; exec. dir. learning solutions Oracle Corp., Reston, Va., 1997—2000, v.p. bus. develop, 2000—02, exec. dir. def. bus. ops., 2000—03, v.p. govt. ops., 2003—. Apptd. mem. Am. U. MBA adv. bd., 1999; apptd. chair exec. bd. Nat. Academies, Army Sci. and Tech., 2001, Army Sci. Bd., 1999, Def. Sci. Bd., 2003; selected guest lectr. Def. Experts Exch., JFK Sch. Govt., Harvard U. and Peoples Liberation Army, China. Vice chmn. Distaff Found., 2003—. Decorated Disting. Svc. medal U.S. Army; recipient Outstanding Alumni award, S.W. Mo. State U., 1993. Mem. Assn. U.S. Army, Disabled Am. Vets Assn., 101st Airborne Divsn.Assn. Republican. Avocations: tennis, skiing, sailing. Office: 1910 Oracle Way Reston VA 20190-4733

MILLER, JOHN NELSON, banker, educator; b. Youngstown, Ohio, Sept. 15, 1948; s. W. Frederic and Julia Elizabeth (Lohman) M. MusB in Cello, Westminster Coll., 1970; MBA in Fin., U. Pa., 1974. Asst. br. mgr. Mahoning Nat. Bank, Youngstown, 1970-72; asst. dir. fin. svcs. dept. Mellon Bank N.Am., Pitts., 1974-76; v.p., head cash mgmt. divsn. Md. Nat. Bank, Balt., 1976-78; v.p., mgr. corp. cash mgmt. divsn. N.Y. Bank of Am., N.Y.C., 1978-80; dir. cash mgmt., strategic planning, product mgmt. and tng. Bank of Am. S.F., 1980-81; v.p., global account officer for utilities/telecomm. Bank of Am., N.Y.C., 1981-84, team leader, CFO, corp. payment divsn. large corp. sales, 1984-87, mgr. credit preparation and analysis unit N.Am. divsn., 1987-88; v.p.,eastern region mgr. cash mgmt. divsn. Wells Fargo Bank of N.Y., 1988-90, v.p., mgr. Eastern, Midwestern, Rocky Mt., Pacific & nat., 1990-93; v.p. and group sales mgr. Bank of Am., NT and SA Fgn. Currency Svcs., San Francisco, 1993-94; v.p., regional sales mgr. Bank of Am. Global Payment Svcs., Bank of Am., 1994-99, sr. v.p., 1999—. Lectr. Wharton Grad. Sch., U. Pa., Am. Mgmt. Assn. cash mgmt. seminars, Bank Adminstrn. Inst.; speaker Payment Sys. Inc., Corp. EFT Seminar, Atlanta, Nat. Conf. Treasury Mgmt. Assn.; mem. Corp. Payment Task Force, N.Y.C., Corp. EFT Cost-Benefit Task Force. Chmn. ann. giving program Wharton Grad. Sch., 1977-79; trustee San Francisco Performances, 1993-99; bd. trustees Westminster Coll., New Wilmington, Pa., 2003—. Mem. Wharton Grad. Sch. Alumni Assn., (pres. local club, rep., nat. dir., mem. exec. com.), Bank Adminstrn. Inst. (mem. subcom. interindustry commn.), Am. Nat. Standards Inst. (subcom. interindustry optical scan standards) Cash Mgmt. Inst. (dir.), Omicron Delta Kappa, Mchts. Club Balt., Univ. Club Pitts., Rotary. Office: CA4-706-06-01 1850 Gateway Blvd Concord CA 94520-3282

MILLER, JOHN PATRICK, secondary education educator; b. Lebanon, Pa., June 10, 1947; s. Victor W. and Florence A. (Coleman) M.; m. Linda L. Loose, Aug. 26, 1967; children: Suzanne L., Kelly E., Ryan P., John B., Steven K. BS, Millersville U., 1969, MA, 1974. Cert. secondary education social sci. H.S. instr., social studies dept. chmn. Palmyra (Pa.) Area Sch. Dist., 1969—92, 1998—2003. Baseball coach Palmyra (Pa.) Area Sch. Dist., 1969-74, football announcer, 1971-91; football announcer state playoffs Pa. State Interscholastic Athletic Assn., Harrisburg, 1991. Author: Immigration in Lebanon County, 1974. Dir. Annville (Pa.)-Cleona Recreation Assn., 1976-94. Named Outstanding Educator, Lebanon County Ednl. Soc., Lebanon, 1979, Rotary Club Palmyra, Pa., 1994, Outstanding Educator in Lebanon County, Lebanon Valley C. of C., 1999. Mem. NEA, Pa. State Edn. Assn., Palmyra Edn. Assn. (pres. 1971, 80, 84, 93, 94, 95, 96), Pa. State Sports Hall of Fame. Republican. Roman Catholic. Avocations: softball, volleyball, studying history, baseball, travel. Home: 720 Pearl St Annville PA 17003-2223 Office: Palmyra Area Sch Dist 1125 Park Dr Palmyra PA 17078-3447

MILLER, JOHN T., JR., lawyer, educator; b. Waterbury, Conn., Aug. 10, 1922; s. John T. and Anna (Purdy) M.; children: Kent, Lauren, Clare, Miriam, Michael, Sheila, Lisa, Colin, Margaret. AB with high honors, Clark U., 1944; JD, Georgetown U., 1948; Docteur en Droit, U. Geneva, 1951; postgrad., U. Paris, 1951. Bar: Conn. 1949 (inactive), D.C. 1950, U.S. Ct. Appeals (2d, 3d, 5th, 10th, 11th and D.C. cirs.), U.S. Supreme Ct. 1952. With Econ. Cooperation Adminstn. Am. Embassy, London, 1950-51; assoc. Covington & Burling, 1952-53, Gallagher, Connor & Boland, 1953-62; pvt. practice Washington, 1962—. Adj. prof. law Georgetown U. Law Ctr., Washington, 1959—; mem. Panel on Future of Internat. Ct. Justice. Co-author: Regulation of Trade, 1953, Modern American Antitrust Law, 1958, Major American Antitrust Laws, 1965; author: Foreign Trade in Gas and Electricity in North America: A Legal and Historical Study, 1970, Energy Problems and the Federal Government: Cases and Material, 8th edit., 1996; contbr. articles, book revs. to legal publs. Trustee Clark U., 1970-76, De Sales Sch. of Theology, 1993-97; mem. bd. advisors Georgetown Visitation Prep. Sch., 1978-94, trustee, 1994-96, emeritus trustee, 1996—; former fin. chmn. troop 46 Nat. Capital Area coun. Boy Scouts Am.; pres. Thomas More Soc. Am., 1996-97. 1st lt. U.S. Army, 1943-46, 48-49. Decorated Bronze Star; recipient 10 yr. teaching award Nat. Jud. Coll., 1983. Mem. ABA (coun., chmn. adminstrv. law sect. 1972-73, ho. dels. 1991-93), AAUP, D.C. Bar Assn., Energy Bar Assn. (pres. 1990-91), Congl. Country Club, Army and Navy Club (bd. govs. 2000—), DACOR, Prettyman-Leventhal Am. Inn of Ct. (master 1988-99, pres. 1995-96), Sovereign Mil. Order of Malta (knight). Republican. Roman Catholic. Home: 4721 Rodman St NW Washington DC 20016-3234 Office: 1001 Connecticut Ave NW Washington DC 20036-5504 E-mail: jtmillerjr@erols.com.

MILLER, JOSEF M. otolaryngologist, educator; b. Phila., Nov. 29, 1937; married, 1960; 3 children. BA in Psychology, U. Calif., Berkeley, 1961; PhD in Physiology and Psychology, U. Wash., 1965; MD (hon.), U. Göteborg, Sweden, 1987; MD (h.c.), U. Turku, Finland, 1995. USPHS fellow U. Mich., 1965-67, rsch. assoc., asst. prof. dept. Psychology, 1967-68, prof., dir. rsch. dept. Otolaryngology, dir. Kresge Hearing Rsch. Inst., 1984—; asst. prof. depts. Otolaryngology, Physiology and Biophysics U. Wash., Seattle, 1968-72, rsch. affiliate Regional Primate Rsch. Ctr, 1968-84, assoc. prof., 1972-76, acting chmn. dept. Otolaryngology, 1975-76, prof., 1976-84; Lunn and Ruth Townsend prof. comm., 1996—. Mem. study sect. Nat. Inst. Neurol. and Communicative Disorders and Stroke, NIH, 1978-84, ad hoc bd. dirs. sci. counselors, 1988; sci. rev. com. Deafness Rsch. Found., 1978-83, chair, 1983—; mem. faculty Nat. Conf. Rsch. Goals and Methods in Otolaryngology, 1982; adv. com. hearing, bio-acoustics and biomechanics Commn. Behavioral and Social Scis. and Edn., Nat. Rsch. Coun., 1983—; hon. com. Orgn. Nobel Symposium 63, Cellular Mechanisms in Hearing, Karlskoga, Sweden, 1985; cons. Otitis Media Rsch. Ctr., 1985-89, Pfizer Corp., 1988; faculty opponent U. Göteborg, Sweden, 1987; rsch. adv. com. Galludet Coll., 1987; chair external sci. adv. com. House Ear Inst., 1988-91; author authorizing legis. Nat. Inst. Deafness and Other Comm. Disorders, NIH, 1988, co-chair adv. bd. rsch. priorities com., bd. dirs. Friends adv. coun., 1989—, chair rsch. subcom., 1990-93, treas., bd. dirs., 1996—; grant reviewer Mich. State Rsch. Fund, NSF, VA; reviewer numerous jours. including Acta Otolaryngologica, Jour. Otology, Physiology and Behavior, Science. Mem. editorial bd. Am. Jour. Otolaryngology, 1981—, AMA, Am. Physiology Soc., Annals of Otology, Rhinology and Laryngology, 1980—, Archives of Oto-Rhino-Laryngology, 1985-93, Hearing Rsch., Jour. Am. Acad. Otolaryngology-Head and Neck Surgery, 1990—. Bd. dirs. Internat. Hearing Found., 1985—. Fellow U. Wash., 1962-65, Kresge Hearing Rsch. Inst., U. Mich., 1965-67; recipient award Am. Acad. Otolaryngology; grantee Deafness Rsch. Found., U. Wash., 1969-71; rsch. grantee NIH, 1969-73. Mem. AAAS, Am. Acad. Otolaryngology and Head and Neck Surgery (com. rsch. in otolaryngology 1971-82, continuing edn. com. 1975-79, NIH liaison com. 1988—, program steering com. jour. 1990, Pres. Citation 1997), Am. Auditory Soc., Am. Otological Soc., Am. Neurotological Soc., Am. Otologic Honor Soc., Acoustical Soc. Am. (com. rsch. psychol., physiol. acoustics 1969-78), Fedn. Am. Physiol. Soc., Fedn. Am. Socs. Exptl. Biology, Soc. Neurosci., Assn. Rsch. Otolaryngology (sec.-treas. 1979-80, pres. elect 1981, pres. 1982. program dir. mtg. 1983, award of merit com. 1985, 95-96, chair 1988, program dir., pres. symposium homeostatic mech. of inner ear 1993), Finnish Acad. Otolaryngology (hon.), Sigma Xi. Office: U Mich Kresge Hearing Rsch Inst 1301 E Ann St Rm R5032 Ann Arbor MI 48109-0506

MILLER, JUDITH ANN, elementary education educator; b. Chgo., Dec. 16, 1956; d. Clarence William and Jean E. Miller; children: Carey Michael, Rachael Marie. BA, Nat. Coll. Edn., 1978. Cert. tchr., Ill. Buyer, mgr. Learning Village Store, Chgo., 1977-80; adminstrv. and tech. cons. Chatham Bus. Assn., Chgo., 1980-81; adminstrv. asst. Chatham-Avalon Local Devel. Corp., Chgo., 1981-82; dir. Devel. Inst., Chgo., 1983-85; sub-tchr. Chgo. Bd. Edn., 1985-87; cadre tchr. John J. Pershing Magnet Sch., Chgo., 1987-88; tchr. Charles N. Holden Sch., Chgo., 1988—. Master tchr. Columbia Coll. Sci. Inst., Chgo., 1992—. V.p. parent aux. bd. Link Unltd., Chgo., 1992-94. Mem. Chgo. Tchrs. Union, Ill. Fedn. Tchrs., Alpha Kappa Alpha. Roman Catholic. Office: Charles N Holden Sch 1104 W 31st St Chicago IL 60608-5602

MILLER, KEN LEROY, religious studies educator, consultant, writer; b. San Antonio, July 29, 1933; s. Eldridge and Paskel Dovie (Vick) M.; m. Eddie Juanell Crawford, June 14, 1953 (dec. Apr. 1981); children: Kimberly Miller Stern, Kerry, Karen Miller Davis; m. Carolyn Gayle Conatser, May 4, 1982; children: Sheila Stanley, Keith Conatser. BA, Abilene Christian U., 1958; MEd, Trinity U., 1965; EdD, Ariz. State U., 1975. Cert. tchr., Tex. Tchr. SAn Antonio Ind. Sch. Dist., 1957-58; tchr., adminstr. N.E. Ind. Sch. Dist., San Antonio, 1958-69; min. edn. MacArthur Park Ch. of Christ, San Antonio, 1960-69; prin. Ralls (Tex.) Ind. Sch. Dist., 1969-70; minister of edn. S.W. Ch. of Christ, Phoenix, 1970-74; adminstr., tchr. Lubbock (Tex.) Christian Sch./U., 1974-77; minister of edn. Sunset Ch. of Christ, Lubbock, 1977-87; prof. religious edn. Harding U., Searcy, Ark., 1987-98; tchr. ESL, Pitman Creek Ch. of Christ, Plano, Tex., 2002—03. Curriculum cons. Sweet Pub. Co., Ft. Worth, 1988-98; leader internat. and nat. religious edn. workshops and seminars. Author: Moral and Religious Stages of Development, 1975, (curriculum) Old Testament Personalities, 1980, Organization, Administration, Supervision of the Bible School, 1993, Recruiting, Training, Retaining Teachers in the Bible School, 1993, Curriculum for the Bible School, 1993; editor: Recipes for Living and Teaching, 1982, (curriculum) Growing in Knowledge, 1977-90, The MINNITH series, 1991-2003; guest editor, contbr. Christian Family 1984. With U.S. Army, 1954-56. Mem. Christian Educators, Christian Edn. Assn., Religious Edn. Assn., Assn. Secondary Schs. and Colls., Alpha Psi Omega, Sigma Tau Delta. Republican. Mem. Ch. of Christ. Avocations: fishing, hunting, reading, travel, writing, poetry readings. Home: 1417 Thames Dr Plano TX 75075-2734 E-mail: cmillerway@yahoo.com.

MILLER, KIM ZANESKI, elementary education educator; b. Riverhead, N.Y., July 2, 1965; d. Martin G. and Barbara A. Zaneski. BA in Psychology, Allegheny Coll., 1987, MA in Edn., 1989. Tchr. 5th grade St. Felicitas Sch., Euclid, Ohio, 1987-88; substitute tchr. Riverhead (N.Y.) Sch. Dist., 1989-91; asst. tchr. The Waterfront Sch., Sag Harbor, N.Y., 1991-92; tchr. Center Moriches (N.Y.) Head Start, 1992—; early childhood devel. specialist Long Island Head Start, 1993—. Mem. Riverhead Polish Town Civic Assn., 1989-90; dir. Riverhead Town Rep. Club, 1984-85. Mem. ASCD, Nat. Assn. for Edn. of Young Children, Ea. Suffolk Reading Coun. Avocations: computers, travel, children's lit.

MILLER, LAURA ANN, linguistic anthropologist, educator; b. L.A., Dec. 15, 1953; d. Walter Eugene Carlos Valdez-Miller; m. Roland John Erwin, 1988. BA, U. Calif., Santa Barbara, 1977; MA, UCLA, 1983, PhD, 1988. Cert. (life) community coll. instr., Calif. Sr. English instr. Teijin Ednl. Sys. Co., Osaka, Japan, 1978-81; tchg. asst. UCLA, 1983-84, tchg. fellow, 1986-87; asst. prof. Phila. Coll. Textiles and Sci., 1990-93; vis. asst. prof. U. Pa., Phila., 1993-95; asst. prof. Loyola U., Chgo., 1995-2000, assoc. prof., 2000—. Lectr. Calif. State U., Dominiquez Hills, 1983-85, El Camino Community Coll., Torrance, Calif., 1986, U. Pa., Phila., summers 1989, 90, 91, 92; vis. asst. prof. Temple U., Phila., 1990; project coord. Nat. Fgn. Lang. Ctr., Johns Hopkins U., Washington, 1989-92; Japanese instr. GE Aerospace, Moorestown, N.J., 1989, 91; Japan program cons. West Chester (Pa.) U., 1989; rsch. analyst ZEMI Corp., L.A., 1986; lang. analyst Japan Conv. Svcs., Tokyo, 1985; vis. faculty U. Pa., 1993-94; exec. com. Midwest Japan Seminar, 1997-02. Editor: Jour. Asian Culture, 1984, assoc. editor, 1987; asst. editor: The American Asian Review, 1992-93, assoc. editor, 1993—; contbr. articles to profl. jours. Chair Act 101 Acad. Achievement Program, Phila., 1990-92; mem. Greater Phila. Internat. Network, 1990. Grantee Dept. Edn., 1972-73, UCLA, 1985; Nat. Resource fellow Dept. Edn., 1982-83, UCLA-Japan Exch. Program fellow, 1986-87. Fellow: Soc. for Applied Anthropology, Am. Anthrop. Assn. (pres.-elect 2001—); mem.: Am. Anthropological Assn., Soc. for Linguistic Anthropology, Soc. for Applied Anthropology, Assn. for Japanese Bus. Studies, Assn. for Asian Studies, Internat. Pragmatics Assn. Home: 2653 Hillside Ln Evanston IL 60201-4933 Office: Loyola U Chgo Dept Sociology/Anthropology 6525 N Sheridan Rd Chicago IL 60626-5344

MILLER, LAWRENCE DONALD, retired middle school educator; b. Council Bluffs, Iowa, Nov. 18, 1947; s. Donald George and Frances Ellen (McNish) M.; m. Teresa Marie Largent, Oct. 13, 1984; 1 child, David Aaron. BS, Northwest Mo. State Coll., 1969; MA, U. Mo., Kansas City, 1972. Cert. reading tchr., lang. arts tchr. Tchr. reading Hickman Mills C-1 Sch. Dist., Kansas City, Mo., 1969-96; ret., 1996; facilitator staff devel. Hickman Mills C-1 Sch. Dist., Kansas City, 1994—. Instr. U. Mo. Kansas City, 1971-80, Avila Coll., Kansas City, 1974-79, Kans. U., Lawrence, 1971, 72, Northwest Mo. State U., Maryville, 1993—, Baker U., Overland Park, Kans., 1995—; cons. Ft. Osage (Mo.) Sch. Dist., 1993-94; spkr./presenter Mo. Spkrs. Bur., Columbia, 1991—; cons., spkr. over 200 sch. dists. Contbr. articles to profl. jours. With USAR, 1970-78. Recipient "For Kids Sake" Caring award KCTV-5, 1990. Mem. ASCD, Mo. ASCD (state bd., rewards and incentive com.), Nat. Staff Devel. Coun., Mo. Mid. Sch. Assn. (Tchr. of Yr. 1991), Phi Delta Kappa. Avocations: custom furniture building, reading. Home: 7906 Spring Valley Rd Belton MO 64012-5353 Office: Hickman Mills C-1 Sch Dist 10530 Greenwood Rd Kansas City MO 64134-3049 E-mail: lmiller45@kc.rr.com.

MILLER, LEROY PAUL, JR., secondary English educator; b. Holyoke, Mass., Feb. 21, 1949; s. Leroy Paul Sr. and Rose Marie (Danehey) M. AA, Northampton (Mass.) Jr. Coll., 1972; BA, U. New. Eng., Biddeford, Maine, 1974; MEd, Springfield (Mass.) Coll., 1977; postgrad., Am. Internat. Coll., Springfield. Cert. elem. tchr., English tchr., history tchr., guidance counselor Mass. Sch. adjustment counselor Holyoke Pub. Schs., 1978-79, ednl. programmer, 1979-80, tutor Chpt. I, 1980-81; tutor Amherst (Mass.) Pub. Schs., 1982-84; tchr. West Springfield (Mass.) Pub. Schs., 1985-86; tchr. English Springfield Pub. Schs., 1986—. Fundraiser M. Marcus Kiley Mid. Sch.; alumni counselor U. New Eng., 1977—. Mem. NEA, ASCD, Nat. Coun. Tchrs. English, Mass. Tchrs. Assn., Springfield Edn. Assn. (faculty rep. 1986—), U. New Eng. Alumni Assn. (v.p. 1990—), Elks, Psi Chi. Democrat. Roman Catholic. Avocations: reading, bowling. Home: 2 Gerard Way Holyoke MA 01040-1204 Office: M Marcus Kiley Mid Sch 180 Cooley St Springfield MA 01128-1108 E-mail: lmill55169@aol.com.

MILLER, LILLIE M. nursing educator; b. Atlanta, Nov. 16, 1937; d. George W. and Lillie M. (Reese) McDaniel; m. Harold G. Miller, June 30, 1962; children: Daren K., Lisa K. Diploma in nursing, Jewish Hosp. of Cin., 1959; BSN, U. Cin., 1961; MEd, Temple U., 1970; MSN, Villanova U., 1987. RN, Pa.; cert. sch. nurse, cert. clin. specialist in med.-surg. nursing ANCC. Instr. sch. nursing Jewish Hosp. Cin., 1959-62; instr. Phila. Gen. Hosp. Sch. Nursing, 1962-67; sch. nurse Norristown (Pa.) Area Sch. Dist., 1967-70; nursing instr. Villanova U., Villanova, Pa., 1988; asst. prof. Montgomery County C.C., Blue Bell, Pa., 1983-93, assoc. prof, 1993-98, prof., 1998—. Advisor Student Nurses Assn. Pa. Pi Tau Delta scholar, Chapel of Four Chaplains. Mem.: ANA, Pa. Med. Soc. (patient adv. bd. 2001—), Villanova U. Alumni Assn., Temple U. Alumni Assn., Jewish Hosp. Alumni Assn., Pa. League for Nursing, Nat. League for Nursing, Phi Theta Kappa, Sigma Theta Tau. E-mail: lmiller@mc3.edu.

MILLER, LINDA KAREN, retired secondary school educator, social studies educator, law educator; b. Kansas City, Jan. 22, 1948; d. Bennie Chris and Thelma Jane (Richey) M. B of Secondary Edn., U. Kans., 1970; M of Secondary Edn., U. Va., 1978, EdD, 1991. Tchr. social studies Pierson Jr. High Sch., Kansas City, 1970-72; substitute tchr. Fairfax (Va.) Pub. Schs., 1972-73; reading aide Lake Braddock Secondary Sch., Burke, Va., 1973-74; tchr. social studies Mark Twain Intermediate Sch., Alexandria, Va., 1974-75, Herndon (Va.) Intermediate Sch., 1975-78, Fairfax High Sch., 1978—86, 1987—2002; ret., 2002. Cons. in field; instr. Sch. Law Cmty. Coll. So. Nev., Las Vegas, 2003. Named Pre-Collegiate Tchr. of Yr., Orgn. Am. Historians, 1996, Secondary Tchr. of Yr., Nat. Coun. for Social Studies, 1996, U. Va., 1997, Outstanding Secondary Tchr., Va. Hist. Soc., 1998, Va. Geography Tchr. of Yr., 1999, Global Technet Tchr. of Yr., Nat. Peace Corps Assn., 1999, Nat. Peace Educator, 2002; recipient George Washington medal, Valley Forge Freedom Found., 1988, Excellence in Tchg. award, U. Kans. Sch. Edn., 1999, Celebrating Tchg. Excellence award, Am. Coun. Tchrs. Russian, 1998, World History Tchg. prize, World History Assn., 2002, Humanities Leadership award, Nat. Endowment Humanities, 2003; fellow, Korean Soc., 2000, Am. Revolution fellow, N.Y. Hist. Soc., 2001. Mem. Nat. Coun. Social Studies (curriculum com. 1991-94), Am. Legal History Soc., Orgn. Am. Historians, Nev. Coun. Social Studies, U. Va. Alumni Assn. Republican. Episcopalian. Avocation: doll collecting.

MILLER, LINDA KAY, reading specialist; b. Wheeling, W.Va., Jan. 27, 1953; d. Ernest F. and Hilda M. (Fletcher) Luscher; m. David L. Miller, Feb. 2, 1974. AB in Edn., Fairmont State Coll., 1973; MA in Reading, cert. reading specialist, W.Va. U., 1976; paralegal degree, Am. Inst. Paralegals, 1980; reading recovery cert., Marshall U., 1998. Cert. elem. edn. Elem. classroom tchr. Brooke County Schs., Wellsburg, W.Va., 1975-90, Title 1 reading specialist, 1990—, reading recovery tchr., 1997—. Recipient cert. for profl. devel. The Office of the Gov. of W.Va., 1993. Mem. ASCD, Internat. Reading Assn., Reading Recovery N.Am. Coun., W.Va. State Reading Assn., Keystone State Reading Assn., Ohio County Lang. Arts Coun., Brooke County Reading Coun. Avocations: reading, walking, cooking. Home: 2225 Marianna St Wellsburg WV 26070-1045

MILLER, LYNN BRECKENFELDER, health and physical education educator; b. Milw., Dec. 2, 1964; d. Roy Arthur and Nancy Lee (Sobocinski) B.; m. Brian L. Miller. BS, Winona State U., 1987; MPH, Ill. Benedictine Coll., Lisle, 1992; postgrad., No. Ill. U. Tchr. health and phys. edn. Newark (N.Y.) Cen. Sch. Dist., 1987-88, Wheaton (Ill.) Warrenville Dist. 200, 1988—; coach track and volleyball Wheaton Warrenville South High Sch., 1989-94. Coach track West Chicago H.S., 1997-2000, Hubble Mid. Sch., 1999—; coach volleyball, Hubble Mid. Sch., 1995—. Vol. Wheaton Recycling Ctr., 1990-94. Named Acad. All Am. U.S. Achievement Acad., 1987, outstanding student major, Nat. Assn. Sport and Phys. Edn., 1987; recipient traineeship USPHS, 1989. Mem. NEA, AAHPERD, Ill. Edn. Assn., Ill. Assn. Health, Phys. Edn., Recreation and Dance, Warrenville Lions club, Kappa Delta Pi. Democrat. Avocations: softball, volleyball, crafts, floral arranging, golf. E-mails. Home: 2 S 573 Continental Dr Warrenville IL 60555 Office: Hubble Mid Sch 603 S Main St Wheaton IL 60187-5240 E-mail: coachmller@aol.com., blmiller@aol.com.

MILLER, MARGARET ALISON, education educator; b. L.A., Dec. 17, 1944; d. Richard Crump and Virginia Margaret (Dudley) M.; m. Spencer Hall, Aug. 21, 1967 (div. 1977); 1 child, Justin Robinson; m. Alan Blair Howard, Oct. 7, 1990. BA in English summa cum laude, UCLA, 1966; postgrad., Stanford U., 1966-67; PhD in English, U. Va., 1971. Instr. English U. Va., Charlottesville, 1971-72; from asst. prof. to assoc. prof. U. Mass., Dartmouth, 1972-83, prof. English, 1983-86, co-dir. women's studies program, 1981-83, asst. to dean arts and scis., 1983-85, asst. to pres., 1985-86; acad. affairs coord. State Coun. Higher Edn. for Va., Richmond, 1986-87, assoc. dir. for acad. affairs, 1987-97; pres. Am. Assn. for Higher Edn., Washington, 1997-2000; pres. emerita Am. Assn. Higher Edn., Washington, 2000—; prof. higher edn. policy U. Va., Charlottesville, 2001—. Head English sect. transitional summer program Brown U., 1976; instr. honors program Va. Commonwealth U., 1991-93; cons. Coun. Rectors, Budapest, 1993, Minn. State U. System, Mpls., 1992, U.S. Dept. Edn., Washington, 1990—, S.C. Higher Edn. Commn., 1989-90, Edn. Commn. States, Denver, 1994-2000; presenter in field; participant UNESCO World Conf. on Higher Edn., 1998; adv. commr. Edn. Commn. of the States, 1998-2000; chair steering com. Washington Higher Edn. Secretariat, 1997-2000; mem. Nat. Postsecondary Edn. Cooperative, 1997-2000; cons. Nat. Ctr. for Pub. Policy and Higher Edn., 1998—; bd. dirs. Nat. Ctr. for Edn. Mgmt. Sys., 2001—, Edn. Direct; participant Aspen Inst., 1998; exec. editor Change mag., 2000—; judge Tchrs. Ins. Annuity Assn./Coll. Retirement Equity Fund Hesburgh awards, 1999—. Contbr. articles to profl. jours. Mem. Am. Assn. Higher Edn. (leadership coun.), Am. Coun. on Edn. (exec. com. identification program in Va. 1988-97, participant nat. identification program's 41st nat. forum for women leaders in higher edn. 1989, adv. bd. Policy Inst.), Phi Beta Kappa. Avocations: reading, gardening, travel. Home: 2176 Lindsay Rd Gordonsville VA 22942-1620 Office: Curry Sch Edn U Va 405 Emmett St S Charlottesville VA 22903 E-mail: pmiller@virginia.edu.

MILLER, MARGERY SILBERMAN, psychologist, speech pathologist, medical educator and administrator; b. May 7, 1951; d. Bernard and Charlotte Silberman; m. Donald F. Moores; children: Kip Lee, Tige Justice. BA, Elmira Coll., 1971; MA, NYU, 1972; EdS, MS, SUNY-Albany, 1975; MA, Towson State U., 1987; PhD, Georgetown U., 1991. Lic. speech pathologist Md., lic. psychologist Md., cert. tchr. nursery-6th grades, spl. edn. N.Y., nationally cert. sch. psychologist. Speech and lang. pathologist Mental Retardation Inst. Flower and Fifth Ave. Hosp., N.Y.C., 1971—72; cmty. speech/lang. pathologist, dir. speech and hearing svc. N.Y. State Dept. Mental Hygiene, Troy, 1972—74; instr. comm. disorders dept. Coll. St. Rose, Albany, NY, 1975—77; clin. supr. U. Md., College Park, 1978;

speech/lang. pathologist Md. Sch. for Deaf, Frederick, 1978—84; auditory devel. specialist Montgomery County Pub. Schs., Rockville, Md., 1984—87; coord. Family Life program Nat. Acad. Gallaudet U., Washington, 1987—88, interim dir., 1988—89; dir. Counseling & Devel. Ctr. N.W. Campus, Washington, 1989—93; prof. psychology, coord. psychology internship program Gallaudet U., Washington, 1993—; lic. practicing psychologist Bethesda, Md., 1998—. Instr. sign lang. program Frederick C.C.; dance instr. for deaf adolescents; diagnostic cons. on speech pathology. Author: It's O.K. To Be Angry, 1976; contbr. chpt. to Cognition, Education, and Deafness: Directions for Research and Instruction, 1985; mem. editl. rev. com. Gov.'s Devel. Disabilities Coun. Md., 1984; presenter at confs.; contbr. articles to profl. jours. Vol., choreographer Miss Deaf Am. Pageant, 1984. Office of Edn. Children's Bur. fellow, 1971. Mem.: Am. Assn. of Higher Edn., Am. Psychol. Assn., Nat. Assn. Sch. Psychologists, Nat. Assn. of Deaf, Am. Speech, Lang. and Hearing Assn. (cert. clin. competence in speech/lang. pathology). Office: Gallaudet U 800 Florida Ave NE Washington DC 20002-3660 E-mail: margery.miller@gallaudet.edu.

MILLER, MARIAN ROBERTA, elementary education educator; b. St. Joseph, Mo., Sept. 28, 1939; d. Robert Woodrow and Willa (Payne) Thomas; m. John Raymond Miller, Dec. 3, 1960; children: Sean, Shannon, Stacy. BS in Edn., N.W. Mo. State U., 1961, MS in Edn., 1981. Tchr. Ft. Osage Sch. ., Independence, Mo., 1962-65, 70-77, St. Joseph (Mo.) Bd. Edn., 1962-65, Brookfield (Conn.) Bd. Edn., 1977-92. Recipient Conn. Environ. award, 2000. Mem. ASCD, NEA, Conn. Edn. Assn., Broofield Edn. Assn. (rep. sec.), Nat. Assn. of Gifted, Phi Delta Kappa.

MILLER, MARILYN LEA, library science educator; AA, Graceland Coll., 1950; BS in English, U. Kans., 1952; AMLS, U. Mich., 1959, PhD of Librarianship and Higher Edn., 1976. Bldg.-level sch. libr. Wellsville HS, Kans., 1952-54; tchr.-libr. Arthur Capper Jr. HS, Topeka, 1954-56; head libr. Topeka HS, Topeka, 1956-62; sch. libr. cons. State of Kans. Dept. of Pub. Instrn., 1962-67; from asst. to assoc. prof. Sch. Librarianship Western Mich. U., Kalamazoo, 1967-77; assoc. prof. libr. sci. U. NC, Chapel Hill, 1977-87, prof., chair dept. libr. and info. studies Greensboro, 1987-95, prof. emeritus, 1996—. Vis. faculty Kans. State Tchrs., Emporia, 1960, 63, 64, 66, U. Minn., Mpls., 1971, U. Manitoba, Winnipeg, Can., 1971; vis. prof. Appalachian State U., Boone, NC, 1987; adv. bd. sch. libr. media program Nat. Ctr. for Ednl. Stats., 1989, user rev. panel, 1990; chair assoc. dean search com. Sch. Edn., 1988, coord. Piedmont young writers conf., 1989-94, 97-99, chair race and gender com., 1990-93, SACS planning and evaluation com., 1990-91, learning resources ctr. adv. com., 1991-93; hearing panel for honor code U. NC Greensboro, 1988-91, assn. women faculty and administrv. staff, 1987-95, faculty coun., 1987-95, chair, 1994-95, univ. libr. com., 1987-88, com. faculty devel. in race and gender scholarship, 1990-92; lectr. and cons. in field. Mem. editl. bd. The Emergency Librarian, 1981-97, Collection Building: Studies in the Development and Effective Use of Library Resources, 1978-96; contbr. chpt. to books, articles to profl. jour. Children's libr. specialists to visit Russian sch. and pub. libr., book publs., Moscow, Leningrad, Tashkent, 1979; hon. del. White House Conf. on Libr. and Info. Svcs., Washington, 1991; head del. Romanian Summer Inst. on Librarianship in U.S., 1991; citizen amb. People to People Internat. Program, People's Republic of China, 1992, Russian and Poland, 1992, Russia, 1994, Barcelona, 1995; exec. bd. dirs. Friends of Greensboro Pub. Libr., 1996-99, chair gift shop and coffee shop adv. com., 1996-2002; chair Citizens Materials Adv. com., 1999—, Citizens Strategic Long Range Planning com., 1994-95, 2001-02, chair, 2002—, Sch. Pub. Libr. com., 2002-. Recipient Freedom Found. medal, 1962, Disting. Svc. to Sch. Librs. award Kans. Assn. Sch. Librs., 1982, Disting. Svc. award Graceland Coll., 1992, Disting. Alumnus award Sch. Libr. and Info. Studies, U. Mich., 1988, Contribution to Libr. Info. Sci. award Assn. Libr. Info. Sci., 1999; Delta Kappa Gamma scholar, 1972. Mem.: ALA (awards com. 1971—72, chair Chgo. conf. resolutions 1972, chair 1973—75, resolutions com. 1976—78, adv. com. Nat. Ctr. Ednl. Stats. 1984, standing com. libr. edn. 1987—91, yearbook adv. com. 1988—90, chair 1989—90, pres. 1992—93, exec. dir. 1994, chair rsch. com., chiar search com., Disting. Svc. award Am. Assn. Sch. Librs. 1993), Friends of N.C. Pub. Librs. (bd. dirs. 2000—), So. Assn. Colls. and Schs. (accreditation team 1988), Southeastern Libr. Assn. (chair libr. educators sect. 1990—92), N.C. Assn. Sch. Librs., Assn. Libr Svc. to Children (bd. dirs. 1976—81, pres. 1979—80, rsch. com. 1982—85, chair 1984—85), Assn. Ednl. Comms. and Tech., Am. Assn. Sch. Librs. (nominating com. 1980, pub. com. 1981—82, chair search com. exec. dir. 1985, v.p., pres.-elect 1985—86, pres. 1986—87, coord. coms. nat. stds. vision and implementation 1995—98), N.C. Libr. Assn. (life; edn. libr. com. 1978—80, 1982—86, bd. dirs. 1987—99, exec. bd. status women roundtable 1989—, chmn.-elect 1995—97, chmn. 1997—99, commn. on status of sch. librs. 1999—2000).

MILLER, MARTIN EUGENE, school system consultant, negotiator, lobbyist; b. Decatur, Ill., May 14, 1945; s. Floyd Homer and Vivian LaVerne (Gould) M.; m. Sherry Kay Bandy, May 25, 1968; children: Liane, Laura. BS, U. Ill., 1968; MEd, U. North Fla., 1974. Cert. math. tchr.; cert. ednl. adminstrn. and supervision. Tchr. Decatur (Ill.) Pub. Schs., 1968, Clay County Sch. Bd., Green Cove Springs, Fla., 1970-74, coord. cert. pers., 1974-77, dir. instructional pers., 1977-78, dir. pers. svcs., 1978-81, asst. supt. for human resources and labor rels., 1981-93, dir. cmty. and govtl. rels., 1993-97; gen. dir. govtl. rels. Duval County Pub. Schs., Jacksonville, Fla., 1997—2001; pres. Miller Consulting Group, Inc.; v.p. Sch. Dist. Mgmt. Svcs., Inc. Past mem. Edn. Stds. Commn., Tallahassee, 1985-93, vice chmn., 1988-92; past mem. Blue Cross-Blue Shield Adv. Coun., Jacksonville, Fla.; past mem. Fla. Ednl. Leaders Forum. Served as staff sgt. USAF, 1968-70. Mem.: Fla. Ednl. Legis. Liaisons (past pres.), Fla. Edn. Negotiators (past pres.), Fla. Assn. Sch. Adminstrs., Am. Assn. Sch. Adminstrs., Phi Delta Kappa. Republican. Presbyterian. Avocations: home computers, music, swimming. Home: 1612 Bay Cir W Orange Park FL 32073-4746 Office: 1612 Bay Circle West Orange Park FL 32073 E-mail: martinmiller@MillerConsultingGroup.com.

MILLER, MARY KATHLEEN, secondary education educator; b. Mishawaka, Ind., Nov. 24, 1943; d. John Edward and Carolyn M.; m. Robert Alan Miller, Jan. 1, 1971; children: Brendan Alexander, Stacey Ann. BA, U. Ill., 1965, MA, 1968. Cert. secondary education tchr., N.J. Tchr. French, English, Beaumont H.S., St. Louis, 1965-66; tchr. English as a Fgn. Lang., Raghunath H.S., Meerut, India, 1968-69; tchr. English as a 2d Lang., Milw. Area Tech. Coll., 1969-71, Coll. William and Mary, Williamsburg, Va., 1971-73; tchr. English, French, religion St. Pius H.S., Piscataway, N.J., 1973-74; tchr. English as a 2d Lang., East Windsor Cmty. Edn., Hightstown, N.J., 1977-82; tchr. English as a 2d Lang. grades 7-12 East Windsor Bd. Edn., Hightstown, 1982—. State secondary rep. N.J. TESOL/BE, 1992-96; mem. bilingual adv. bd. N.J. Office Bilingual Edn., 1996-98; mem. Mercer County Profl. Devel. Bd., 1998-2002. Gov.'s tchr.'s grant Commr. of Edn., N.J., 1986, India tchr.'s grant Fulbright Edn. Found., 1968-69. Mem. TESOL, N.J. Edn. Assn. (bldg. rep. 1992-98), East Windsor Edn. Assn., Cranbury Hist. Soc., Kappa Delta Pi. Avocations: tennis, biking, travel, swimming, writing. Office: Hightstown HS 25 Leshin Ln Hightstown NJ 08520-4001

MILLER, MARY MARGARET, elementary education educator; b. Youngstown, Ohio; d. James Williard and Lyda Mae (Swift) Cox; m. William Roger Miller; children: Daphne, William Jr., Laurel, Jason. BS in Edn., Northwestern U., Evanston, Ill., 1959; MS in Spl. Edn., William Paterson Coll., 1995. Lic. tchr., primary, kindergarten, Ohio, elem. edn., handicapped, N.J. Tchr. 2nd grade Woodside Sch., Austintow, Ohio, 1959-60; tchr. 1st grade McKinley Sch., Elyria, Ohio, 1960-61; tchr. spl. edn. Brookside Sch., Allendale, N.J., 1988-95; 2nd grade tchr. Hillside Sch., Allendale, 1995—. Mem. Dist. Math. Curriculum Com., Allendale, Allendale Edn. Found. Mem. ASCD, Pi Lambda Theta, Kappa Delta Pi. Office: Hillside Sch Hillside Ave Allendale NJ 07401

MILLER, MARY RITA, former college educator; b. Williamsburg, Iowa, Mar. 4, 1920; d. James Carl and Bernadette (O'Meara) Rush; m. Clarence Glenn Miller, June 2, 1947 (dec. Aug. 1987); 1 child, Ronald Rush; m. William J. Gibbons, July 14, 1992 (dec. June 2001). BA, U. Iowa, 1941; MA, Denver U., 1959; PhD, Georgetown U., 1969. From instr. to asst. prof. Regis Coll., Denver, 1962-65; from asst. prof. to prof. U. Md., College Park, 1968-91, prof. emeritus, 1991—. Author: Children of the Salt River, 1977, Place—Names of the Northern Neck of Virginia, 1983; contbr. numerous articles and revs. Avocations: research, travel, reading, farming. Home: 2825 29th Pl NW Washington DC 20008-3501

MILLER, MAVIS MOSS, school administrator, social worker; b. Irwin County, Ga., June 4, 1953; d. Jimmie Lee and Ruthie Mae (Stephenson) Moss; children: Denitra Michell, LaTravia Lemar, Samantha Levette. BS, Albany State Coll., 1975; MEd, Ga. State U., 1980, M in Adminstrn., 1996. Cert. tchr., Ga. Tchr. Irwin County Bd. Edn., Ocilla, Ga., 1975-91, coord. drug edn., 1991—. Coord. Youth Alliance Project, Ocilla, 1991—; chair Ocilla Drug Adv. Bd., 1991—, Irwin County Action Team, Ocilla, 1992—; evaluator Ga. Tchr. Evaluation Instrument; implementer Good Touch Bad Touch. Former Adult leader Ocilla area Boy Scouts Am.; mem. Irwin County Arts Coun., Ocilla Civic Club; chair com. Community Svc. Ctr. Named Tchr. of Yr. 1983-84. Mem. NEA, Ga. Edn. Assn., Ga. Assn. Educators (pres.), Irwin County Child Abuse Coun., Irwin County Heart Assn., Troubled Children Com., Delta Sigma Theta. Democrat. Baptist. Avocation: reading. Office: Irwin County Bd Edn 210 Apple St Ocilla GA 31774

MILLER, MAYNARD MALCOLM, geologist, educator, research institute director, explorer, legislator; b. Seattle, Jan. 23, 1921; s. Joseph Anthony and Juanita Queena (Davison) M.; m. Joan Walsh, Sept. 15, 1951; children: Ross McCord, Lance Davison. BS magna cum laude, Harvard U., 1943; MA, Columbia U., 1948; PhD (Fulbright scholar), St. John's Coll., Cambridge U., Eng., 1957; student, Naval War Coll., Air War Coll., Nat. Def. U., Oak Ridge Inst. Nuclear Sci.; D of Sci. (hon.), U. Alaska, 1990. Registered profl. geologist, Idaho. Asst. prof. naval sci. Princeton (N.J.) U., 1946; geologist Gulf Oil Co., Cuba, 1947; rsch. assoc., coord., dir. Office Naval Rsch. Juneau Icefield Rsch. Project, Am. Geog. Soc., N.Y.C., 1948-53; staff scientist Swiss Fed. Inst. for Snow and Avalanche Rsch., Davos, 1952-53; instr. dept. geography Cambridge U., 1953-54, 56; assoc. producer, field unit dir. film Seven Wonders of the World Cinerama Corp., Europe, Asia, Africa, Middle East, 1954-55; rsch. assoc. Lamont Geol. Obs., N.Y.C., 1955-59; sr. scientist dept. geology Columbia U., N.Y.C., 1957-59; asst. prof. geology Mich. State U., East Lansing, 1959-61, assoc. prof., 1961-63, prof., 1963-75; dean Coll. Mines and Earth Resources U. Idaho, Moscow, 1975-88, prof. geology, dir. Glaciological and Arctic Scis. Inst., 1975—; dir., state geologist Idaho Geol. Survey, 1975-88; rep. Legislature of State of Idaho, Boise, 1992-2000. Prin. investigator, geol. sci. contracts and projects for govt. agys., univs., pvt. corps., geographic socs., 1946—; geophys. cons. Nat. Park Svc., NASA, USAF, Nat. Acad. Sci.; organizer, leader USAF-Harvard Mt. St. Elias Expdn., 1946; chief geologist Am. Mt. Everest Expdn., Nepal, 1963; dir. Nat. Geographic Soc. Alaskan Glacier Commemorative Project, 1964—; organizer, field leader Nat. Geographic Soc. Joint U.S.-Can. Mt. Kennedy Yukon Meml. Mapping Expdn., 1965, Muséo Argentino de Ciencias Naturales, Patagonian expdn. and glacier study for Inst. Geologico del Peru & Am. Geog. Soc., 1949-50, adv. missions People's Republic of China, 1981, 86, 88, 98, geol. expdns. Himalaya, Nepal, 1963, 84, 87, USAF ice survey mission to Ellesmere Land, North Pole and Polar Sea, 1951; organizer, ops. officer pioneering USN-LTA blimp geophysics flight to Ice Island T-3 and North Pole area for Office Naval Rsch., 58; prin. investigator U.S. Naval Oceanographic Office sea and pack ice Rsch. Ice Island T-3 Polar Sea, 1967-68, 70-73; dir. lunar field sta. simulation USAF-Boeing Co., 1959-60; prin. investigator Nat. Geographic Soc. 30 Yr. Remap of Lemon, Taku and Cathedral Massif Glaciers, Juneau Icefield, 1989-2002; exec. dir. Found. for Glacier and Environ. Rsch., Pacific Sci. Ctr., Seattle, 1955-95, 1997—, chmn., 1992—, pres., 1955-85, trustee, 1960—, organizer, dir. Juneau Icefield Rsch. Program (JIRP), 1946—; cons. Dept. Hwys. State of Alaska, 1965; chmn., exec. dir. World Ctr. for Exploration Found., N.Y.C., 1968-71; dir., mem. adv. bd. Idaho Geol. Survey, 1975-88; chmn. nat. coun. JSHS program U.S. Army Rsch. Office and Acad. Applied Sci., 1982-90; sci. dir. U.S. Army Rsch. Office and DOD Nat. Sci. and Humanities Symposia program, 1991—; disting. guest prof. China U. Geoscis., Wuhan, 1981—, Changchun U. Earth Scis., People's Republic of China, 1988—; adj. prof. U. Alaska, 1986—. Author: Field Manual of Glaciological and Arctic Sciences; co-author books on Alaskan glaciers and Nepal geology; contbr. over 200 reports, sci. papers to profl. jours., ency. articles, chpts. to books, monographs; prodr., nat. lectr. films and videos. Past mem. nat. exploring com., nat. sea exploring com. Boy Scouts Am.; past mem. nat. adv. bd. Embry Riddle Aero. U.; bd. dirs. Idaho Rsch. Found.; pres. state divsn. Mich. UN Assn., 1970-73; mem. Centennial and Health Environ. Commns., Moscow, Idaho, 1987—. With USN, 1943-46, PTO. Decorated 11 campaign and battle stars; named Leader of Tomorrow Seattle C. of C. and Time mag., 1953, one of Ten Outstanding Young Men U.S. Jaycees, 1954; recipient commendation for lunar environ. study USAF, 1960, Hubbard medal (co-recipient with Mt. Everest expdn. team) Nat. Geog. Soc., 1963, Elisha Kent Kane Gold medal Geog. Soc. Phila., 1964, Karo award Soc. Mil. Engrs., 1966, Franklin L. Burr award Nat. Geog. Soc., 1967, Nat. Commendation Boy Scouts Am., 1970, Disting. Svc. commendation plaque UN Assn. U.S., Disting. Svc. commendation State of Mich. Legis., 1975, Outstanding Civilian Svc. medal U.S. Army Rsch. Office, 1977, Outstanding Leadership in Minerals Edn. commendations Idaho Mining Assn., 1985, 87, Nat. Disting. Tchg. award Assn. Am. Geographers, 1996; recipient numerous grants NSF, Nat. Geog. Soc., NASA, ARO, M.J. Murdock Trust, Dept. of Interior, others, 1948—. Fellow Geol. Soc. Am., Arctic Inst. N.Am., Explorers Club; mem. AAAS (councillor, Pacific divsn. 1978-88), AIME, ASME (hon. nat. lectr.), Am. Geophys. Union, Internat. Glaciological Soc. (past councilor), Assn. Am. State Geologists (hon.), Am. Legis. Exch. Coun., Am. Assn. Amateur Oarsmen (life), Am. Alpine Club (past councilor, life), Fulbright Assn., Alpine Club (London), Appalachian Club (hon. corr.), Brit. Mountaineering Assn. (hon., past v.p.), The Mountaineers (hon.), Cambridge U. Mountaineering Club (hon.), Himalyan Club (Calcutta), English Speaking Union (nat. lectr.), Naval Res. Assn. (life), Dutch Treat Club, Circumnavigators Club (life), Adventurers Club N.Y. (medalist), Am. Legion, VFW, Harvard Club (N.Y.C. and Seattle), Sigma Xi, Phi Beta Kappa (past pres. Epsilon chpt.), Phi Kappa Phi. Republican. Methodist. Avocations: skiing, mountaineering, photography. Home: 514 E 1st St Moscow ID 83843-2814 Office: U Idaho Coll Sci and Earth Resources Moscow ID 83844-3022 also: Found Glacier & Environ Rsch 4470 N Douglas Hwy Juneau AK 99801-9403 E-mail: jirp@uidaho.edu.

MILLER, MICKEY LESTER, retired school administrator; b. Albuquerque, July 26, 1920; s. Chester Lester and Myra Easter (Cassidy) M.; m. Louise Dean Miller, Aug. 30, 1946; children: Linda Miller Kelly, Lee Miller Parks, Lynne Miller Carson. BS, U. N.Mex., 1944; MS, Columbia U., 1949. Coach, tchr. math. Jefferson Jr. H.S., Albuquerque, 1946-49; coach, dept. chair, athletic dir. Highland H.S., Albuquerque, 1949-64, asst. prin., 1964-70; dist. program coord. Albuquerque Pub. Schs., 1970-90; ret., 1990. Author: Guide to Administration of Secondary Athletics, 1990; author brochures, handbooks, articles. Pub. mem. N.Mex. Bd. Dentistry, 1992—. With USN, 1942-46. Recipient Honor award S.W. Dist. Am. Alliance Health, Phys. Edn., Recreation and Dance, 1971, N.Mex. Coaches Assn., 1981, Hall of Fame award N.Mex. Activities Assn., 1985; named Retiree of Yr., S.W. Dist. Am. Alliance Health, Phys. Edn., Recreation and Dance, 1994; named to U. N.Mex. Alumni Lettermen Hall of Honor, 1994; named to Albuquerque Sports Hall of Fame, 1995. Mem. AAHPERD (life, budget/nominating rep. 1985, honor award 1999), U. N.Mex. Alumni Assn., U. N.Mex. LOBO Lettermen Club (pres., treas. 1972). Democrat. Methodist. Avocations: golf, travel, baseball scouting. Home: Albuquerque, N.Mex. Died Apr. 27, 2003.

MILLER, NANCY ELLEN, health facility administrator, educator; b. Aug. 20, 1947; d. Jerome H. and Kathy P. Miller. BA, NYU, 1969; MA, Harvard U., 1970; PhD, U. Chgo., 1978; cert., Washington Sch. Psychiatry, 1981; postgrad., Washington Psychoanalytic Inst, 1981. Clin. psychologist City of Chgo. Dept. Mental Health, 1971-77; rsch. asst. dept. psychiatry U. Chgo., 1972-75, rsch. assoc., 1975-77; exec. sec. Sci. Rev. Group NIMH, 1977-79, chief clin. rsch. program Ctr. Studies Mental Health Aging, 1977-86, chief clin. rsch. program Mental Disorders Aging Rsch. Br., 1986-93; chief clin. and exptl. rsch. program schizophrenia rsch. divsn. clin and treatment rsch. NIMH, NIH, 1993-96; sr. sci. policy analyst Office of Sci. Policy, Office of Dir. NIH, 1996—. Instr. clin. geriatric psychiatry Georgetown U. Sch. Medicine; clin. faculty psychiatry dept. Navy Med. Command, Nat. Capital Region; clin. prof. dept. psychiatry Uniformed Svcs. U. Health Scis.; clin. faculty dept. psychology George Washington U.; del. White Ho. Conf. Aging, 1981. Author (with Gene Cohen): (book) Clinical Aspects of Alzheimer's Disease and Senile Dementia, 1981, Schizophrenia and Aging: Schizophrenia, Paranoia and Schizophreniform Disorders in Late Life, 1988; author: (with E. Erlenmeyer-Kimling) Life-Span Research on the Prediction of Psychopathology, 1986; author: (with Lester Luborsky, Jacques Barber and John Doherty) Psychodynamic Research, 1993; author: (with Katherine Magruder) Cost-Effectiveness of Psychotherapy, 1999; mem. editl. bd. Jour. Ednl. Gerontology, 1976—80, Neurobiology of Aging, 1980—86, Profl. Psychology, 1980—85, Psychoanalytic Psychology, 1983—88, Clin. Gerontologist, 1983—, Am. Jour. Orthopsychiatry, 1985—90; mem. editl. bd.: Internat. Psychogeriatrics, 1989—, Am. Jour. Geriatric Psychiatry, 1992—96; contbr. articles to profl. jours. Recipient Recognition award, Dept. HHS. Mem.: APA, AAAS, Soc. Psychotherapy Rsch., Soc. Neurosci., Internat. Psychogeriatric Assn., Internat. Neuropsychol. Soc., Internat. Brain Rsch. Orgn., Internat. Assn. Gerontology, Gerontol. Soc. Am., Washington Psychoanalytic Soc., DC Psychol. Assn., Boston Soc. Gerontologic Psychiatry, Am. Psychoanalytic Assn., Am. Orthopsychiat. Assn., Pi Lambda Theta, Phi Delta Kappa. Home: 3617 Newark St NW Washington DC 20016-3179 Office: NIH Office Sci Policy Office of the Dir Bldg 1 9000 Rockville Pike Rm 218 Bethesda MD 20892-0003 E-mail: nm68k@nih.gov.

MILLER, NEWTON EDD, JR., communications educator; b. Houston, Mar. 13, 1920; s. Newton Edd and Anastasia (Johnston) M.; m. Edwina Whitaker, Aug. 30, 1942; children: Cathy Edwina, Kenneth Edd. BS, U. Tex., 1939, MA, 1940; PhD, U. Mich., 1952; LL.D., U. Nev., Reno., 1974. Tutor U. Tex., Austin, 1940-41, instr., 1941-45, asst. prof. speech, 1945-47; research asst. Navy Conf. Research, 1947-52; mem. faculty U. Mich., Ann Arbor, 1947-65, successively lectr., instr., asst. prof. speech, 1947-55, assoc. prof., 1955-59, prof., 1959-65, asst. dir. summer session, 1953-57, assoc. dir., 1957-63, asst. to v.p. acad. affairs, 1963-65; chancellor U. Nev., Reno, 1965-68, pres., 1968-73, U. Maine, Portland-Gorham, 1973-78; chmn. communications dept. No. Ky. U., 1978-87, emeritus, 1987—, interim gen. mgr. Sta. WNKU, 1985-86. Mem. adv. com. to commr. of edn. U.S. Office of Edn., Accreditation and Instl. Eligibility, 1976-79, acting chmn., 1977-78; mem. Judicial Edn. Study Group Am. Univ. Law Inst., 1977-78; mem. Nat. Accreditation Commn. for Agys. Serving Blind and Physically Handicapped, 1988-97, pres., 1991-92, bd. dirs., 1999—. Author: Post War World Organization, Background Studies, 1942, (with J.J. Villareal) First Course in Speech, 1945, (with W.M. Sattler) Discussion and Debate, 1951, Discussion and Conference, 2d edit., 1968, (with Stephen D. Boyd) Public Speaking: A Practical Handbook, 1985, 2d edit., 1989; co-editor: Required Arbitration of Labor Disputes, 1947. Pres. bd. dirs. Perry Nursery Sch., 1956-57, Sierra Cmty. Orch., 1989-94; mem. Ann Arbor Bd. Edn., 1959-65, Washtenaw County Bd. Edn.; sec. bd. dirs. Behringer Crawford Mus.; bd. dirs. Siera Arts Found., 1992—; pres. Reno/Sparks Theater Cmty. Coalition, 1994-96; mem. Nev. Humanities Com., 1994-2001. Recipient Gov.'s Disting. Svc. to Arts award, 2003. Mem. Mich. Assn. Sch. Bds. (dir.), N.W. Assn. Colls. and Secondary Schs. (chmn. higher commn. 1971-73), Am. Forensic Assn. (pres. Midwest sect. 1950-53), Central States Speech Assn. (pres. 1958-59), Mich. Speech Assn. (exec. sec. 1950-55), Speech Communication Assn. (chmn. fin. bd.), Assn. Western Us. (chmn. 1971-72), Coun. on Naturopathic Med. Edn., Delta Sigma Rho (nat. v.p. 1948-52), Phi Kappa Phi. Address: 1480 Ayershire Ct Reno NV 89509-5248

MILLER, NORMAN CHARLES, JR., editor, reporter; b. Pitts., Oct. 2, 1934; s. Norman Charles and Elizabeth (Burns) M.; m. Mollie Rudy, June 15, 1957; children— Norman III, Mary Ellen, Teri, Scott. BA, Pa. State U., 1956. Reporter Wall Street Jour., San Francisco, 1960-63, reporter N.Y.C., 1963-64, bur. chief Detroit, 1964-66, Washington corr., 1966-72, Washington bur. chief, 1973-83; nat. editor Los Angeles Times, 1983-97; lectr. journalism U. So. Calif., 1997—2001; ret., 2001. Author: The Great Salad Oil Swindle, 1965 Served to lt. (j.g.) USN, 1956-60. Recipient Disting. Alumnus award Pa. State U., 1978; George Polk Meml. award L.I. U., 1963; Pulitzer Prize, 1964 Mem.: Gridiron (Washington). Roman Catholic. Avocation: tennis.

MILLER, PATRICIA ANN, adult education educator; b. Mich., Dec. 19, 1933; d. Bernard James and Veronica Loretta (Hominga) M.; m. Mar. 2, 1957 (div. 1981); children: Sharon, Paula, Philip Jr., Douglas. BA, Mich. State U., 1955. Tchr. Perry (Mich.) Pub. Schs., 1955-56, Glen Lake (Mich.) Cmty. Schs., 1956-57, various pub. schs., Mich., 1957-61, Traverse City (Mich.) Pub. Schs., 1963; salesperson Theta's Real Estate, Traverse City, 1977-88, 93—, Century 21 Real Estate, Traverse City, 1988-90; tchr. Montessori Children's Ctr., Traverse City, 1984; instr./facilitator adult edn. Enterprise Learning Lab., Kingsley/Traverse City, 1986-94, Traverse Bay area, 1994; instr. Mich. Works Learning Lab., 1998—. Instr./facilitator Pvt. Ind. Coun., summer 1991-94, 95—; pvt. tutor Grand Traverse, 1986-94; bus. ptnr. FitzMiller Learning Ctr., 1992; mem. learning ctr. task force Northwestern (Mich.) Coll., Traverse City, 1994, 95; lectr., condr. workshops in field. Contbr. articles to profl. jours. Mem. League of Women Voters, Traverse City, 1984; vol. Women's Resource Ctr., Traverse, 1983; ambassador Nat. Cherry Festival, Traverse City, 1984. Recipient Cert. of Appreciation, Traverse Bay Intermediate Schs., 1985, award for work in field of improving adult literacy Traverse City Area Pub. Schs. Bd. End., 1991-92; named Region 7 Tchr. of Yr., Mich. Dept. Edn., 1990. Mem. Mich. Reading Assn. (named Mich. Adult Edn. Tchr. of Yr. 1991), Mich. Lit. Coun., Northwestern Mich. Reading Assn. (hon.), Alpha Xi Delta. Avocations: travel, reading, golf, walking. Office: MIch Works Learning Lab 1209 S Garfield Ave Ste C Traverse City MI 49686 also: PO Box 4231 Traverse City MI 49685-4231

MILLER, PATRICK WILLIAM, research administrator, educator; b. Toledo, Sept. 1, 1947; s. Richard William and Mary Olivia (Rinna) M.; m. Jean Ellen Thomas, Apr. 5, 1974; children: Joy, Tatum, Alex. BS in Indstrl. Edn., Bowling Green State U., 1971, MEd in Career Edn. and Tech., 1973; PhD in Indstrl. Tech. Edn., Ohio State U., 1977; Master's cert. Govt. Contract Adminstrn., George Washington U., 1995. Tchr. Montgomery Hills Jr. High Sch., Silver Spring, Md., 1971-72, Rockville (Md.) High Sch., 1973-74; asst. prof. Wayne State U., Detroit, 1977-79; assoc. prof., grad. coord. indstrl. edn. and tech. Western Carolina U., Cullowhee, N.C., 1979-81; assoc prof. U. No. Iowa, Cedar Falls, 1981-86; dir. grad. studies practical arts and vocat.-tech. edn. U. Mo., Columbia, 1986-89; devel. editor Am. Tech. Pubs., Homewood, Ill., 1989-90; proposal mgr. Nat. Opinion Rsch. Ctr. U. Chgo., 1990-96; dir. grants & contracts City Colls. Chgo., 1996-99; assoc. v.p. acad. affairs Prairie State Coll., 1999—2001, also dean workforce devel. and career edn., 1999—2001; ret., 2001. Pres. Patrick W. Miller and Assocs., Munster, Ind., 1981—; presenter, advisor and cons. in field. Author: Nonverbal Communication: Its Impact on Teaching and Learning, 1983, Teacher Written Tests: A Guide for Planning, Creating, Administering and Assessing, 1985, Nonverbal Communication: What Resarch Says to the Teacher, 1988, How To Write Tests for Students, 1990, Nonverbal Communication in the Classroom, 2000, Nonverbal Communication in the Workplace, 2000, Grant Writing: Strategies for Developing Winning Proposals, 2d edit., 2002, Test Development: Guidelines, Practical Suggestions and Examples, 2001; mem. editl. bd. Jour. Indsl. Tchr. Edn., 1981-88, Am. Vocat. Edn. Rsch. Jour., 1981-85, 94—, Tech. Tchr., 1982-84, Jour. Indsl. Tech., 1984—, Jour. Vocat. and Tech. Edn., 1987-90, Human Resource Devel. Quar., 1989—; also articles. Sec. U. No. Iowa United Faculty, Cedar Falls, 1983-84, pres., 1984-86. Lance cpl. USMC, 1966-68, Vietnam. Recipient editl. recognition award Jour. Indsl. Tchr. Edn., 1984, 86, 88; named One of Accomplished Grads. of Coll. Tech., Bowling Green State U., 1995. Mem. ASTD, Am. Ednl. Rsch. Assn., Assn. for Career and Tech. Edn., Am. Vocat. Edn. Rsch. Assn., Nat. Assn. Indsl. Tech. (chmn. rsch. grants 1982-87, pres. industry divsn. 1991-92, chmn. exec. bd. 1992-93, past pres. 1993-94, Leadership award 1992, 93), Nat. Assn. Indsl. and Tech. Tchr. Educators (pres. 1988-89, past pres. 1989-90, trustee 1990-93, Outstanding Svc. award 1988, 90), Internat. Tech. Edn. Assn., Coun. Tech. Tchr. Edn., Epsilon Pi Tau, Phi Delta Kappa. E-mail: miller9147@aol.com.

MILLER, PEGGY GORDON ELLIOTT, university president; b. Matewan, W.Va., May 27, 1937; d. Herbert Hunt and Mary Ann (Renfro) Gordon; m. Robert Lawrence Miller, Nov. 23, 2001; children from previous marriage: Scott Vandling Elliott III, Anne Gordon Elliott. BA, Transylvania Coll., 1959; MA, Northwestern U., 1964; EdD, Ind. U., 1975. Tchr. Horace Mann H.S., Gary, Ind., 1959-64; instr. English Am. Inst. Banking, Gary, 1969-70, Ind. U. N.W., Gary, 1965-69, lectr. Edn., 1973-74, asst. prof. edn., 1975-78, assoc. prof., 1978-80, supr. secondary student tchg., 1973-74, dir. student tchg., 1975-77, dir. Office Field Experiences, 1977-78, dir. profl. devel., 1978-80, spl. asst. to chancellor, 1981-83, asst. to chancellor, 1983-84, acting chancellor, 1983-84, chancellor, 1984-92; pres. U. Akron, Ohio, 1992-96, S.D. State U., 1998—. Sr. fellow Nat. Ctr. for Higher Edn., 1996-97; vis. prof. U. Ark., 1979-80, U. Alaska, 1982; bd. dirs. Lubrizol Corp., A. Schulman Corp., First Nat. Bank Brookings, Commn. on Women in Higher Edn., Akron Tomorrow, Ohio Aerospace Consortium, Ohio Super Computer Com.; holder VA Harrington disting. chair in edn., 1994-96, Charles G. Herbrich chair in leadership mgmt., 1996— Author: (with C. Smith) Reading Activities for Middle and Secondary Schools: A Handbook for Teachers, 1979, Reading Instruction for Secondary Schools, 1986, How to Improve Your Scores on Reading Competency Tests, 1981, (with C. Smith and G. Ingersoll) Trends in Educational Materials: Traditionals and the New Technologies, 1983, The Urban Campus: Educating a New Majority for a New Century, 1994, also numerous articles. Bd. dirs. Meth. Hosp., N.W. Ind. Forum, N.W. Ind. Symphony, S.D. Art Mus., Boys Club N.W. Ind., Akron Symphony, NBD Bank, John S. Knight Conv. Ctr., Inventure Pl., Akron Roundtable, Cleve. Com. Higher Edn. Recipient Disting. Alumni award Northwestern U., UA Disting. Alumni award, 1994, numerous grants; Am. Council on Edn. fellow in acad. adminstrn. Ind. U., Bloomington, 1980-81. Mem. Assn. Tchr. Educators (nat. pres. 1984-85, Disting. Mem. 1990), Nat. Acad. Tchrs. Edn. (bd. dirs. 1983—), Ind. Assn. Tchr. Educators (past pres.), North Ctrl. Assn. (mem. commn. at large), Am. Assn. State Colls. and Univs. (sr. fellow 1996-98, acting v.p. divsn. acad. and internat. programs 1997, bd. dirs.), Am. Coun. Edn. (bd. dirs., exec. com.), Leadership Devel. Coun. ACE, Ohio Inter Univ. Coun. (chairperson), Internat. Reading Assn., Akron Urban League (bd. dirs.), P.E.O., Cosmos Club, Phi Delta Kappa (Outstanding Young Educator award), Delta Kappa Gamma (Leadership/Mgmt. fellow 1980), Pi Lambda Theta, Pi Kappa Phi, Chi Omega. Episcopalian. Avocation: music. Home: 929 Harvey Dunn St Brookings SD 57006-1347 Office: South Dakota State Univ Office of the Pres Adminstrn Bldg 201 Brookings SD 57007-0001 E-mail: Peggy_Miller@sdstate.edu.

MILLER, PEGGY MCLAREN, retired management educator; b. Tomahawk, Wis., Jan. 12, 1931; d. Cecil Glenn and Gladys Lucille (Bame) McLaren; m. Richard Irwin Miller, June 25, 1955; children: Joan Marie, Diane Lee, Janine Louise. BS, Iowa State U., 1953; MA, Am. U., 1959; MBA, Rochester Inst. Tech., 1979; PhD, Ohio U., 1987. Instr. Beirut Coll. for Women, 1953-55, U. Ky., Lexington, 1964-66, S.W. Tex. State U., San Marcos, 1981-84; home economist Borden Co., N.Y.C., 1955-58; cons. Consumer Cons., Chgo., Springfield, Ill., 1972-77; sr. mktg. rep. N.Y. State Dept. Agr., Rochester, 1978-79; asst. prof., coord. bus. and mgmt. Keuka Coll., Keuka Park, N.Y., 1979-81; lectr. mgmt. Ohio U., Athens, 1984-2000; ret., 2000. Home: 17 Briarwood Dr Athens OH 45701-1302 E-mail: pmmiller@aol.com.

MILLER, PETER N. historian, educator; BA, Harvard Coll.; MA, Harvard U.; PhD, U. Cambridge. Asst. prof. U. Md.; rsch. fellow U. Cambridge, 1990—93; Mellon instr. in social scis. U. Chgo., 1993—96; prof. cultural history Bard Coll., NY, 2001—. Author: Defining the Common Good: Empire, Religion and Philosophy in Eighteenth-Century Britain, 1994, Peiresc's Europe: Learning and Virtue in the Seventeenth-Century, 2000; co-author: The Song of the Soul: Understanding Poppea, 1992; contbr. articles to profl. jours. Fellow, NEH, John D. and Catherine T. MacArthur Found., Wissenschaftskolleg zu Berlin, Warburg Inst., John Simon Guggenheim Meml. Found., 2003. Office: Bard Grad Ctr 18 W 86th St New York NY 10024*

MILLER, ROBERT FRANK, retired electronics engineer, educator; b. Milw., Mar. 30, 1925; s. Frank Joseph and Evangeline Elizabeth (Hamann) M.; m. La Verne Boyle, Jan. 10, 1948 (dec. 1978); children: Patricia Ann, Susan Barbara, Nancy Lynn; m. Ruth Winifred Drobnic, July 26, 1980. BSEE, U. Wis., 1947, MSEE, 1954, PhD in Elec. Engring., 1957. Profl. engr., Wis. Instr. physics Milw. Sch. Engring., 1949-53; sr. engr. semicondr. Delco Electronics/GMC, Kokomo, Ind., 1957-67, asst. chief engr., 1967-70, mgr. product assurance, 1970-73, dir. quality control, 1973-85; asst. prof. elec. engring. tech. Purdue U., Kokomo, 1986-90; ret., 1990. Ind. cons., Kokomo, 1990—; mem. Ind. Microelectronics Commn., Indpls., 1987—. Author tech. papers; co-author lab. manuals. Bd. dirs. Howard Community Hosp. Found., Kokomo, 1974—; trustee YMCA, Kokomo, 1990—, bd. dirs., 1967-90. Named Disting. Alumnus U. Wis., Madison, 1980, 90. Mem. IEEE (life), Am. Soc. Quality Control (bd. dirs. sect. 0918, advisor Cen. Ind. sect. bd. 1988—), Sigma Xi, Tau Beta Pi, Phi Kappa Phi, Eta Kappa Nu. Presbyterian. Home: 3201 Susan Dr Kokomo IN 46902-7506

MILLER, ROBERT MICHAEL, publishing executive; children: Jeremy Richard, Eric Robert. AAS in Graphic Design Tech., Invor Hills C.C., 1994. Account mgr. Webb Pub. Co., Maxwell Group, St. Paul, 1977-88; account exec. Russ Moore Assocs., Eagn, Minn., 1988-89; pres. Jeric Pubs., Inc., Inver Grove Heights, Minn., 1989-91; pub., owner Jeric Pub. Group, Inc., South Saint Paul, Minn., 1992-95. Cons., bd. dirs. Auto Ctr. St. Paul, 1990-91, J&E Constrn., Inver Grove Heights, 1990-92. Pub., account mgr. Explore Minn. Calendar, 1988; pub., account exec. Sr's. Choice Mag., 1989; pub. There is No November, 1991.

MILLER, ROBERT STEVEN, secondary school educator; b. Van Nuys, Calif., Aug. 9, 1963; s. Frederick Earl and Mary (Brash) M. AA, L.A. Valley Coll., 1984; BSBA, Calif. State U., 1987, MA in History, 1990. Cert. substitute tchr., 1993-96. Study group leader, study skills researcher Ednl. Opportunity Program Calif. State U., L.A., 1989-93, faculty mem. History Dept., lectr., 1990-92; sec., treas. Agate/Amethyst World, Inc., Van Nuys, Calif., 1986-91, v.p., 1992-96; with Summer Bridge Program Calif. State U., L.A., 1994-96; tchr. history Chatsworth (Calif.) H.S., 1996—. Mng. editor jour. Perspectives, 1990, editor-in-chief, 1991. Jake Gimbel scholar, 1989. Mem. Am. Historians Assn., The Soc. for Historians of Am. Fgn. Rels., Phi Alpha Theta (v.p. 1990, pres. 1991, Eta Xi chpt., Ledeboer Family scholar 1989), Pi Sigma Epsilon (v.p. 1986-87, pres. 1988 Phi chpt.), Mu Kappa Tau (pres. and founder 1989, Calif State U. LA chpt.). Democrat. Roman Catholic. Home: 13750 Runnymede St Van Nuys CA 91405-1515 Office: Chatsworth HS 10027 Lurline Ave Chatsworth CA 91311-3153

MILLER, ROBERTA DORIS, elementary school educator; b. Lynn, Mass., May 14, 1940; d. Morris and Lorraine Miller. BS in Edn. cum laude, Lesley Coll., Cambridge, Mass., 1961; M in Edn., Salem (Mass.) State Coll., 1964; postgrad., Boston U. Tchr. Brookline (Mass.) Pub. Schs., 1968—. Pilot math. programs Ednl. Devel. Corp., Newton, Mass., 1988-89; pilot sci. programs TV series 3! 2! 1! Contact!, 1991; developer curriculum materials in math. and lang. arts Brookline Pub. Schs., 1969—, presenter workshops math. for new tchrs., 1984—; faculty mem. Suffolk U., Boston, 2000—. Coord. presentation of programs to nursing homes and vets. hosps.; coord. fundraising victims and schs. of Hurricane Andrew, 1992; chair, coord. fundraising for victims of the Midwest floods, 1993. Mem. NEA, Mass. Tchrs. Assn. Avocations: travel, reading, music. E-mail: bobdorrob@yahoo.com.

MILLER, RONALD BAXTER, English language educator, writer; b. Rocky Mount, NC, Oct. 11, 1948; s. Marcellus Cornelius and Elsie (Bryant) M.; m. Jessica Garris, June 5, 1971 (div. 1998); 1 child, Akin Dasan; m. Diana L. Ranson, Sept. 3, 2000. BA magna cum laude, N.C. Ctrl. U., 1970; AM, Brown U., 1972, PhD, 1974. Asst. prof. English Haverford Coll., Haverford, Pa., 1974-76; assoc. prof. English, dir. Black lit. program U. Tenn., Knoxville, Tenn., 1977-81, prof. English, dir. Black lit. program, 1982-92, Lindsay Young prof. liberal arts and English, 1986-87; prof. English, dir. Inst. for African Am. Studies U. Ga., Athens, 1992—. Instr. summer sch. Roger Williams Coll., Bristol, R.I., 1973; lectr. SUNY, 1974; Mellon prof. Xavier Univ., New Orleans, 1988; Irvine Found. visiting scholar Univ. San Francisco, 1991. Author: (reference guide) Langston Hughes and Gwendolyn Brooks, 1978, The Art and Imagination of Langston Hughes, 1989 (Am. Book award, 1991), (monograph) Southern Trace in Black Critical Theory: Redemption of Time, 1991; editor, contbr.: Black American Literature and Humanism, 1981, Black American Poets Between Worlds, 1940-60, 1986; co-author and co-editor: Call and Response The Riverside Anthology of African American Literary Tradition, 1998, ed., "The Short Stories", Collected Works of Langston Hughes 15, 2002; mem. editl. bd. Tenn. Studies in Lit., 1991-93, Black Fiction Project (Yale-Cornell-Duke-Harvard), 1985—, U. Ga. Press, 1994-97; contbr. numerous articles and revs. to profl. jour. Recipient award Am. Coun. of Learned Soc., 1978, Golden Key Faculty award Nat. Golden Key, 1990, 95, Alpha award for disting. svc. U. Ga. Athens, 1993, Am. Book award, 1991; Lilly Sr. Tchg. fellow U. Ga. Athens, 1994, Lanston Hughes prize, 2001; Nat. Rsch. Coun. sr. fellow, 1986-87, NDEA fellow, 1970-72, Ford Found. fellow, 1972-73, NEH fellow, 1975; Nat. Fellowships Fund dissertation grant, 1973-74, others. Mem. MLA (exec. com. Afro-Am. Lit. Discussion Group 1980-83, chair 1982-83, mem. del. assembly 1984-86, 97-99, com. on langs. and lits. of Am. 1993-97, chair 1996), Langston Hughes Soc. (pres. 1984-90, exec. editor Langston Hughes Review 1993—). Office: U Ga Inst African Am Studies Athens GA 30602 E-mail: rbmiller@uga.edu., rbmiller6@charter.net.

MILLER, SALLY LIPLES, English language teacher; b. Scranton, Pa., July 24, 1954; d. Paul J. and G. Leila (Harris) Liples; m. Walter J. Miller, Jr., Nov. 12, 1976; children: Kathleen, Suzanne. BA in Psychology/Comm. Arts, Marywood Coll., 1976; MEd Curriculum and Instrn., U. Va., 1994. Cert. tchr., Va. Substitute tchr. Scranton (Pa.) Sch. Dist., 1978; grade 7-8 English/U.S. history Holy Cross Regional Sch., Lynchburg, Va., 1979-81; tchr. English Roanoke (Va.) Cath. Sch., 1987—2002; tchr. English and theatre arts Roanoke Co. Sch. Sys., 2002—. Drama dir. Roanoke Cath. Sch., 1988-02; sch. newspaper adviser, 1991-02; webmaster RCS site, 2000—. Leader Girl Scouts U.S., Roanoke, 1987—; Sunday Sch. tchr. St. Andrew's Ch., Roanoke, 1982-92, vacat. Bible sch. tchr., 1984-88, 2002—, bd. dirs. Christian Formation com., 1983-87. Edn. grantee Dow Jones Newspaper Inst., Va. Commonwealth U., 1990; recipient Outstanding OMer, Odyssey of the Mind, Vinton, Va., 1994, Tchr. Achievement award Diocese of Richmond, 2000; Kathryn Ann Rattenbury Meml. scholarship, 2000. Mem. Jour. Edn. Assn., Va. Assn. Journalism (bd. dirs. 1991-96), Diocesan Master Curriculum Coun., Roanoke Co. Ednl. Assn., Va. Ednl. Assn., NEA, Kappa Gamma Pi. Republican. Roman Catholic. Avocations: book collector, softball coach, volleyball coach. Home: 8311 Willow Ridge Rd Roanoke VA 24019-1814 Office: Hidden Valley HS 5000 Titan Trl Roanoke VA 24018 E-mail: smiller@rcs.k12.va.us.

MILLER, SANDRA PERRY, middle school educator; b. Nashville, Aug. 3, 1951; d. James Ralph and Pauline (Williams) Perry; m. William Kerley Miller, June 22, 1974. BS, David Lipscomb U., 1973; MEd, Tenn. State U., 1983, cert. in spl. edn., reading splty., 1986. Cert. tchr., Tenn. Tchr. Clyde Riggs Elem. Sch., Portland, Tenn., 1973-86; tchr. social studies Portland Mid. Sch., 1986—. Adv. bd. tech. and comm. in edn. Sumner County Sch. Bd., Gallatin, Tenn., 1990—; co-dir., cons. Tenn. Students-at-Risk, Nashville, 1991—; assoc. edn. cons. Edn. Fgn. Inst. Cultural Exch., 1991-92; fellow World History Inst., Princeton (N.J.) U., 1992—; awards com. Tenn. Dept. Edn., Nashville, 1992; U.S. edn. amb. E.F. Ednl. Tours, Eng., France, Germany, Belgium, Holland, 1991; ednl. cons. HoughtonMifflin Co., Boston; apptd. Tenn. Mini-Grants award com., Tenn. 21st Century Tech. Com.; mem. Tenn. Textbook Com., 1995, Think-Tank on 21st Century Edn., Tenn. and Milliken Nat. Educator Found.; apptd. to Gov.'s Task Force Commn. on 21st Schs., Gov.'s Task Force for Anti-Drug and Alcohol Abuse Among Teens; mem. nat. com. for instnl. tech. devel. Milken Family Found. Nat. Edn. Conf., 1996; apptd. to Instrnl. Tech. Devel.-Project Strand, 1996 Milken Family Found., Nat. Edn. Conf.; appointed curriculum com. Bicentennial WW II Meml., 1996-97; developed State Model Drop-Out Prevent Program, 1996-97; U.S. tchr. amb. to Ukraine, Am. Coun. for Internat. Edn.; Sumner County music dir. Sumner Enrichment Program, 2001-02; mem. awards com. for U.S., Am. Couns. for Internat. Edn., Washington, 2002. Author curriculum materials; presenter creative crafts segment local TV sta., 1990-93; producer, dir. documentary on edn. PBS, Corona, Calif., 1990. Mem. nat. com. instnl. tech. devel. project Strand of the 1996 Milken Family Found. Nat. Edn. Conf., L.A., 1996; performer Nashville Symphony Orch., 1970—73; leader Sumner County 4-H Club, 1976—86; mem. Woodrow Wilson Nat. Fellowship Found. on Am. History, Princeton U., 1994; co-chair Inter Media Cable Commn.; apptd. tchr. mentoring program Midd Tenn. State U. and Tenn. State U. Dept. Edn.; chmn. Comcast Cable TV Commn., 2003—. Recipient Excellence in Tchg. award U. Tenn., 1992, 93, award for Outstanding Teaching in Humanities Tenn. Humanities Coun., 1994; named Tchr. of Yr. Upper Cumberland dist. Tenn. Dept. Edn., 1991-92, 92-93, Mid. Tenn. Educator of Yr. Tenn. Assn. Mid. Schs., 1991, Tenn. Tchr. of Yr. Tenn. Dept. Edn., 1992, Nat. Educator of Yr. Milken Family Found., 1992, U.S. Tchr. Ambassador to Ukraine, Am. Coun. Internat. Edn., Washington; grantee Tenn. Dept. Edn. for Devel. of Model Drop Out Prevention Program, 1996. Mem. NEA, ASCD, Sumner County Edn. Assn. (sch. rep. 1973—, Disting. Tchr. of Yr. 1992), Tenn. Edn. Assn. (rep. 1973—), Nat. Geographic Tenn. Alliance (rep. 1990—, grantee 1990), Tenn. Humanities Coun. (rep. 1990—), Nat. Coun. Social Studies, Internat. Platform Assn. Baptist. Avocations: crafts, doll collecting, reading, music, fashion modeling. Office: Portland Mid Sch 604 S Broadway Portland TN 37148-1624

MILLER, SARABETH, secondary education educator; b. Apr. 6, 1927; d. Clayton Everett and Margaret (Noland) Reif; m. Lloyd Melvin Miller, Dec. 2, 1944; children: Virginia, Shirley, Judith, John, Nola, Steven. BA, Valparaiso U., 1972, MA in L.S., 1977; postgrad., Purdue U., 1983, Ind. U., 1986, postgrad., 1991, Art Inst. Ft. Lauderdale, Fla., 1992, Ind. State U., 1996, postgrad., 1997, St. Joseph U., 1998. Lic. tchr. Ind., cert. data processing. Office employee Porter County Herald, Hebron, Ind., 1954—55, Little Co. of Mary Hosp. and Home, San Pierre, Ind., 1960—65, Jasper County Co-op, Tefft, Ind., 1965—69, Hannon's, Valparaiso, 1969—72; tchr. art DeMotte (Ind.) elem. sch., 1972—76, Kankakee Valley High Sch., Wheatfield, Ind., 1976—. Participant Lilly Creative Tchr.'s Workshop. Participant (art and lit. mag.) Mirage; contbr. articles. Leader 4-H Club, Kouts; participant North Ctrl. Regional Forum, 1991, 1992, 1993; mem., elder Kouts Presbyn. Ch.; mem. adv. com. secondary sch. showcase Valparaiso U. Recipient various prizes, Lake Ctrl. (Ind.) Fair, 1975, 1980, photography award, Ind. Dept. Tourism, 1976, Porter County Fair, 1989, 1996, 1998, 2000, 2001, Gainer Bank Calendar award, 4-H Alumni award, 2002, 4-H 45 yr. leader tenure award, 1994; grantee, Nat. Gallery of Art, 1993; Lilly Endowment fellow, Lilly Extending Tchr. Creativity Inst., 1987, 1994, 1995, 1996, 2002, 2003. Mem.: NEA, North Ctrl. Assn. Secondary Schs. (mem. evaln. team), Kankakee Valley Tchrs. Assn., Ind. Art Edn. Assn., Ind. Tchrs. Assn., Nat. Art Edn. Assn. Presbyterian. Home: 1056 S Baums Bridge Rd Kouts IN 46347-9712 E-mail: smiller@kv.k12.in.us.

MILLER, SHELBY ALEXANDER, chemical engineer, educator; b. Louisville, July 9, 1914; s. George Walter and Stella Katherine (Cralle) M.; m. Jean Adele Danielson, Dec. 26, 1939 (div. May 1948); 1 son, Shelby Carlton; m. Doreen Adare Kennedy, May 29, 1952 (dec. Feb. 1971). BS, U. Louisville, 1935; PhD, U. Minn., 1943. Registered profl. engr., Del., Kans., N.Y. Asst. chemist Corhart Refractories Co., Louisville, 1935-36; teaching, rsch. asst. chem. engring. U. Minn., Mpls., 1935-39; devel. engr., rsch. chem. engr. E.I. duPont de Nemours & Co., Inc., Wilmington, Del., 1940-46; assoc. prof. chem. engring. U. Kan., Lawrence, 1946-50, prof., 1950-55; Fulbright prof. chem. engring. King's Coll. Durham U., Newcastle-upon-Tyne, Eng., 1952-53; prof., chem. engring. U. Rochester, 1955-69, chmn., 1955-68; assoc. lab. dir. Argonne (Ill.) Nat. Lab., 1969-74; dir. Ctr. Ednl. Affairs, 1969-79, sr. chem. engr., 1969-84, ret., cons., 1984—. Vis. prof. chem. engring. U. Calif., Berkeley, 1967-68; vis. prof. U. of Philippines, Quezon City, 1986; cons. in field. Editor: Chem. Engring. Edn. Quar, 1965-67; sect. editor: Perry's Chem. Engrs.' Handbook, 5th edit., 1973, 6th edit., 1984, 7th edit. 1997; contbr. to McGraw-Hill Ency. Sci. and Tech., 5th edit., 1982, 6th edit., 1987, 7th edit., 1992; contbr. articles to profl. jours. Sec. Kans. Bd. Engring. Examiners, 1954-55; mem. adv. com. on tng. Internat. Atomic Energy Agy., 1975-79; treas. Lawrence (Kans.) League for Practice Democracy, 1950-52; sec. Argonne Credit Union, 1994-97. Fellow AAAS, Am. Inst. Chemists, Am. Inst. Chem. Engrs. (past chmn. Kansas City sect.); mem. Am. Chem. Soc. (past chmn. Rochester sect.), Soc. Chem. Industry, Am. Soc. Engring. Edn. (past chmn. grad. studies div.), Am. Nuclear Soc., Filtration Soc., Triangle, Sigma Xi, Sigma Tau, Phi Lambda Upsilon, Tau Beta Pi, Alpha Chi Sigma. Presbyterian. Home: 825 63rd St Downers Grove IL 60516-1962 Office: Argonne Nat Lab Chem Tech Divsn Argonne IL 60439-4837 E-mail: millers@cmt.anl.gov.

MILLER, STANLEY ODELL, educational diagnostician; b. Alexandria, La., Dec. 1, 1956; s. Stanley Odell and Elma Bell (Cannon) M.; m. Betty Louise Bridges, June 30, 1978; children: Laurie Elizabeth, Michael Treyson. BA, La. Coll., 1982; MEd, Northwestern State U., 1987, M, 1989. Cert. tchr., La. Spl. edn. tchr. Rapides Parish Sch. Bd., Alexandria, 1984-89, assessment tchr., ednl. diagnostician, 1989—. Trustee La. Coll., Pineville, 1992—. Co-chair La. Rep. Tchr. Adv. Coun., Baton Rouge, 1990-92; mem. Nat. Rep. Senatorial Com., Washington, 1992-93. Mem. NEA, La. Assn. Educators, Internat. Assn. Childhood Educators (local pres. 1991-92), Rapides Assn. Educators (pres. 1988-90). Republican. Baptist. Avocations: camping, softball. Home: 92 Er Slay Rd Deville LA 71328-9212 Office: Rapides Parish Sch Bd J B Lafarque Spl Edn Ctr 4515 New York Ave Alexandria LA 71302-3628

MILLER, STEVEN MAX, humanities educator; b. Portland, Ind., Feb. 9, 1950; s. J. Max and Belva Kathryn (Kitty Booher) M.; m. Fran Felice Koski, May 30, 1985 (div. 1992). BA in English with high honors, Coll. of William and Mary, 1972; MA in English Lang. and Lit., Ind. U., 1975, PhD in English Lang. and Lit., 1985. Sr. libr. asst. cataloger rare books and spl. collections Lilly Libr., Bloomington, Ind., 1972-76; prof. English Millersville (Pa.) U., 1985—; dir. univ. honors program Millersville (Pa.) U., 1999-2001, dir. Honors Coll., 2001—. Cons. women writers project Brown U., Providence, 1990-95. Contbr. articles to profl. jours. Grantee NEH, 1991, 92. Mem. MLA, John Donne Soc. Am., Spenser Soc. Episcopalian. Avocation: gardening. Office: Millersville U Honors Coll PO Box 1002 Millersville PA 17551-0302

MILLER, SUZANNE MARIE, state librarian; b. Feb. 25, 1954; d. John Gordon and Dorothy Margaret (Sabatka) M.; 1 child, Altinay Marie. BA in English, U. S.D., 1975; MA in Library Sci., U. Denver, 1976, postgrad. in law, 1984. Librarian II U. S.D. Sch. of Law, Vermillion, 1977-78; law libr. U. LaVerne, Calif., 1978-85, instr. in law, 1980-85; asst. libr. tech. svcs. McGeorge Sch. Law, Calif., 1985-99, prof. advanced legal rsch., 1994-99; state librarian S.D. State Library, Pierre, S.D., 1999—. Co-author (with Elizabeth J. Pokorny) U.S. Government Documents: A Practical Guide for Library Assistants in Academic and Public Libraries, 1988; contbr. chpt. to book, articles to profl. jours. Pres. Short Grass Arts Coun., 2001—03; bd. dirs. Black Hills Playhouse Bd., 1999—, S.D. Ctr. for the Book Bd., 2002—. Recipient A. Jurisprudence award Bancroft Whitney Pub. Co., 1983. Mem.: ALA, Western Coun. State Librs. (sec. 2001—02), Chief Officers of State Libr. Agys. (sec. 2002—), Western Pacific Assn. Law Librs. (sec. 1990—94, pres. elect 1994—95, pres. 1995—96, local arrangements chair 1997), No. Calif. Assn. Law Librs. (mem. program com., inst. 1988), Mt. Plains Libr. Assn. (S.D. rep. to exec. bd. 2001—), So. Calif. Assn. Law Librs. (arrangements com. 1981—82), Am. Assn. Law Librs., S.D. Libr. Assn. Roman Catholic. Home: 505 N Grand Ave Pierre SD 57501-2014 Office: SD State Library 800 Governors Dr Pierre SD 57501-2235 E-mail: suzanne.miller@state.sd.us.

MILLER, WALTER LUTHER, pediatrician, educator; b. Alexandria, Va., Feb. 21, 1944; s. Luther Samuel and Beryl (Rinderle) M. SB, MIT, 1965; MD, Duke U., 1970. Diplomate Am. Bd. Pediatrics. Intern, then resident Mass. Gen. Hosp., Boston, 1970-72; staff assoc. NIH, Bethesda, Md., 1972-74; sr. resident U. Calif., San Francisco, 1974-75, rsch. fellow, 1975-78, asst. prof. pediatrics, 1978-83, assoc. prof., 1983-87, prof., 1987—, dir. Child Health Rsch. Ctr., 1992—, faculty biomed. scis. grad. program, 1982—, faculty genetics grad. program, 1998—, assoc. prof. metabolic rsch. unit, 1983-87, dir. peidat. endocrinology tng. program, 1994—, chief divsn. endocrinology, 2000—. Editor DNA and Cell Biology Jour., 1983—; mem. editl. bds. numerous sci. jours.; contbr. articles to profl. jours., chpts. to books. Del. Dem. Nat. Conv., N.Y.C., 1976. Served with USPHS, 1972-74. Recipient Nat. Rsch. Svc. award NIH, 1975, Clin. Investigator award, 1978, Albion O Bernstein award N.Y. Med. Soc., 1993, Clin. Endocrinology Trust medal Brit. Endocrine Soc., 1993, Henning Andersen prize European Soc. Pediatric Endocrinology, 1993, Samuel Rosenthal Found. prize for excellence in acad. pediatrics, 1999. Fellow: AAAS, Molecular Medicine Soc.; mem.: Androgen Excess Soc. (founding mem., bd. dirs. 2002—), Am. Soc. Biochem. Molecular Biology, Lawson Wilkins Pediat. Endocrine Soc. (edn. com. 1992—96, coun. 1995—96, corp. adv. bd. 1998—2002), Am. Soc. Clin. Investigation, Am. Soc. Human Genetics, Endocrine Soc. (fin. com. 1999—2002, Edwin B. Astwood lecture award 1988), European Soc. for Paediatric Endocrinology (hon.), Japanese Soc. for Pediat. Endocrinology (hon.), We. Soc. Pediat. Rsch. (Ross Rsch. award 1982), Soc. Pediat. Rsch., Am. Pediat. Soc., Am. Acad. Pediats.,

Assn. Am. Physicians, Am. Soc. for Microbiology, Theta Delta Chi. Achievements include patents in field. Office: U Calif Med Ctr Dept Pediat 1466 4th Ave San Francisco CA 94143-0978

MILLER, WAYNE CLAYTON, student services administrator, notary public; b. Columbus, Ohio, Feb. 23, 1949; s. Eugene H. and Beulah M. (Stoll) M. BA, Owosso Coll., 1971; MA, Mich. State U., 1979. Mgr. adminstrv. svcs. John Wesley Coll., Owosso, Mich., 1972-75, instr., social sci., 1975-78, dir., career planning, 1978-79; acad. advisor Spring Arbor (Mich.) Coll., 1979-81, instr., history, 1979-81; acad. counselor Franklin U., Columbus, 1981-83, asst. dir. acad. advising, 1983-85, dir., acad. advising, 1985-92, instr. Film Appreciation, 1985—, asst. dir., student svcs., 1992-97, dir., student svcs., 1997-2000, asst. v.p. student svcs., 2000—. Advisor Franklin U. Student Senate, Columbus, 1982-84; inst. creative activities program Ohio State U., Columbus, 1990-98; discussion panelist Educable TV-25 Worl d Film Classics series, 1990-2002; juror social issues category The Columbus Internat. Film and Video Festival, 1994, chair edn. category, 1995—; mem. spkrs. bur. Franklin U. Editor: (newsletter) New Directions, 1985-91; assoc. editor: Movies on Media Handbook. Co-host Columbus Mus. Art Film Series, 1996; scholar, rschr. Westerville Civic Symphony, 1997; judge Miss East-Ctrl. Ohio Scholarship program, 2000, Bus. and Profl. Women of Ohio State Speakoff Competition, 2001; mem. nat. nominating com. 1997 Outstanding Young Women am. and Young Men Am.; bd. trustees Film Coun. Gtr. Columbus. Named one of Outstanding Young Men in Am., 1982, 85. Mem.: Future Bus. Leaders Am. (competition judge state conf. 1997—), Ohio Coll. Pers. Assn., Am. Film Inst., Nat. Acad. Advising Assn. (Cert. of Merit award 1986, Outstanding Instnl. Advising award 1994), Nat. Film Soc. (life), Nat. Euchre Players Assn. (dir. adminstrn.), Columbus Kiwanis (chair career guidance com. 1993—2002), Phi Beta Lambda. Avocations: film studies, history, sherlock holmes memorabilia, charitable activities, playing cards. Home: 2729 Brittany Oaks Blvd Hilliard OH 43026-8575 Office: Franklin U 201 S Grant Ave Columbus OH 43215-5399

MILLER, WEBSTER THEODIS, retired secondary education educator; b. Texarkana, Tex., Aug. 11, 1923; s. York and Daisy (Wilson) M. BS, Prairie View A&M U., 1950, MS, 1951; M in Teaching Sci., U. Ariz., 1971; EdD, U. San Francisco, 1987. Cert. tchr. Calif. Tchr. sci. Edna (Tex.) Ind. Sch. Dist., 1951-62, Plain View (Tex.) Ind. Sch. Dist., 1962-66, Phoenix Ind. Sch. Dist., 1968-71, Pomona (Calif.) Unified Sch.Dist., 1971—, ret., 1992. Voter registration vol. Dem. Conv., Pomona, 1992. With U.S. Army, 1943-46. Recipient Vol. award L.A. Organizing Com., 1984; named Tchr. of Yr., 1990; NSF fellow, 1983, 92, L.A. Ednl. Partnership fellow, 1986. Mem. Nat. Sci. Tchrs. Assn. Democrat. Avocations: tennis, choral singing, reading. Home: 9627 Hickory St Los Angeles CA 90002-2546

MILLER, WILLIAM CHARLES, architect, educator; b. San Francisco, May 11, 1945; s. Francis Leland and Ethel Lorene (Britt) M.; m. Beverly Jean McConnell, Dec. 22, 1968; children: Britt A., David A. BArch, U. Oreg., 1968; MArch, U. Ill., 1970. Registered architect, Ariz., Kans., Utah. Asst. prof. Coll. Architecture U. Ariz., Tucson, 1970—77; assoc. prof. dept. architecture Kans. State U., Manhattan, 1977-86, prof., 1986-92, head dept., 1990-92; prof. Coll. of Architecture and Planning U. Utah, Salt Lake City, 1992—, dean, 1992—2002; architect various firms; disting. vis. prof. of architecture U. Ill., Urbana/Champaign, 2003. Guest lectr. in field; presenter numerous profl. socs. and orgns.; dir. west ctrl. region Assn. Collegiate Schs. Architecture, 1988-91, chair theme paper sessions ann. meeting, San Francisco, 1990, chair regional paper sessions ann. meeting, Washington, 1991, co-chair adminstrv. conf., Milw., 1995; bd. dirs. Nat. Archtl. Accrediting Bd., 1996-99; mem. Utah Architects Lic. Bd., 2000—; vis. prof. U. Ill., Urbana Champlain, Ill., 2003. Author: Alvar Aalto: An Annotated Bibliography, 1984; co-editor: The Architecture of the In-Between, 1990, Architecture: Back to Life, 1991; contbr. over 60 articles to profl. jours., chpts. to books. Bd. dirs. Assist, Inc., 1992-2002, Artspace, Inc., 1997-2002, Contemporary Arts Group, 1992-96, Salt Lake City Art Design Bd., 1995-2003. Recipient Svc. awards Assn. Collegiate Schs. Architecture, Nat. Coun. Archtl. Registration Bds., Nat. Archtl. Accrediting Bd. Fellow AIA (pres-elect Flint Hills, treas. Utah, exec. com., treas., exec. com. Western Mountain region, elected coll. of fellows 1997); mem. Am.-Scandinavian Found., Soc. for Advancement Scandinavian Studies, Tau Sigma Delta. Office: U Utah Coll Architecture & Planning Salt Lake City UT 84112 E-mail: miller@arch.utah.edu.

MILLER, WILLIAM FREDERICK, research company executive, educator, business consultant; b. Vincennes, Ind., Nov. 19, 1925; s. William and Elsie M. (Everts) M.; m. Patty J. Smith, June 19, 1949; 1 son, Rodney Wayne. Student, Vincennes U., 1946-47; BS, Purdue U., 1949, MS, 1951, PhD, 1956; DSc (hon.), 1972. Mem. staff Argonne Nat. Lab., 1955-64, assoc. physicist, 1956-59, dir. applied math. div., 1959-64; prof. computer sci. Stanford U., Palo Alto, Calif., 1965-97, Herbert Hoover prof. pub. and pvt. mgmt. emeritus, 1997—, assoc. provost for computing, 1968-70, v.p. for rsch., 1970-71, v.p., provost, 1971-78; mem. Stanford Assocs., 1972—; pres emeritus., CEO SRI Internat., Menlo Park, Calif., 1979-90; chmn. bd., CEO SRI Devel. Co., Menlo Park, David Sarnoff Rsch. Ctr., Inc., Princeton, N.J. Chmn. bd. dirs. Borland Software; chmn. bd. dirs. Sentius Corp.; professorial lectr. applied math. U. Chgo., 1962-64; vis. prof. math. Purdue U., 1962-63; vis. scholar Ctr. for Advanced Study in Behavioral Scis., 1976; mem. adv. coun. BHP Internat., 1990-97; computer sci. and engring bd. NAS, 1968-71; mem. Nat. Sci. Bd., 1982-88; corp. com. computers in edn. Brown UU., 1971-79; mem. policy bd. EDUCOM Planning Coun. on Computing in Edn., 1974-79, chmn., 1974-76; mem. ednl. adv. bd. Guggenheim Meml. Found., 1976-80; com. postdoctoral and doctoral rsch. staff NRC, 1977-80, computer sci. and telecom.; dir. Fund Am., 1977-91, Fireman's Fund Ins., 1977-91, Wells Fargo Bank and Co., 1996-97, Varian Assocs. Inc., 1973-96. Mem. editl. bd. Pattern Recognition Jour, 1968-72, Jour. Computational Physics, 1970-74. Served to 2d lt. F.A. AUS, 1943-46. Recipient Frederic B. Whitman award United Way Bay Area, 1982, Sarnoff Founders medal, 1997, David Packard Civic Entrepreneurship Team award, 1998, Robert K. Jaedicke Silver Apple award Stanford U. Bus. Sch. Alumni, 1998, The Dongbaeg medal Order of Civil Merit, The Rep. of Korea, 2000, The Okawa prize, The Okawa Found. for Info. and Telecoms., 2000, Most Mentor awa4rd Internat. Angel Investors, 2002; named to Silicon Valley Engring. Hall of Fame, 2001, Jr. Achievement Bus. Hall of Fame, 2002. Fellow IEEE (life), Am. Acad. Arts and Scis., AAAS; mem. Soc. Indsl. and Applied Math., Assn. Computing Machinery, Nat. Acad. Engring., Sigma Xi, Tau Beta Pi (Eminent Engr. 1989). Office: Stanford U Grad Sch Bus Stanford CA 94305

MILLER, WILLIAM HUGHES, theoretical chemist, educator; b. Kosciusko, Miss., Mar. 16, 1941; s. Weldon Howard and Jewel Irene (Hughes) M.; m. Margaret Ann Westbrook, June 4, 1966; children: Alison Leslie, Emily Sinclaire. BS, Ga. Inst. Tech., 1963; AM, Harvard U., 1964, PhD, 1967. Jr. fellow Harvard U., 1967-69; NATO postdoctoral fellow Freiburg (Germany) U., 1967-68; asst. prof. chemistry U. Calif., Berkeley, 1969-72, assoc. prof., 1972-74, prof., 1974—, dept. chmn., 1989-93, chancellor's prof., 1998—, Kenneth S. Pitzer disting. prof., 1999—. Fellow Churchill Coll., Cambridge (Eng.) U., 1975-76; hon. prof. Shandong U., People's Republic of China, 1994. Alfred P. Sloan fellow, 1970-72; Camille and Henry Dreyfus fellow, 1973-78; Guggenheim fellow, 1975-76, Christensen fellow St. Catherine's Coll., Oxford, 1993; recipient Alexander von Humboldt-Stiftung U.S. Sr. Scientist award, 1981-82, Ernest Orlando Lawrence Meml. award, 1985, Hirschfelder prize in theoretical chemistry, U. Wis., 1996, Alumni Achievement award Ga. Inst. Tech., 1997, Spiers medal Faraday divsn. Royal Soc. Chemistry, London, 1998. Fellow AAAS, Am. Acad. Arts and Scis., Am. Phys. Soc. (Irving Langmuir award 1990); mem. NAS, Am. Chem. Soc. (Theoretical Chemistry award 1994, Ira Remsen award 1997, Peter Debye award 2003), Internat. Acad. Quantum Molecular Sci. (Ann. prize 1974). Office: U Calif Dept Chemistry Berkeley CA 94720-0001

MILLER-LANE, BARBARA See LANE, BARBARA

MILLERO, FRANK JOSEPH, JR., marine and physical chemistry educator; b. Mar. 16, 1939; s. Frank Joseph and Jennie Elizabeth (Marta) M.; m. Judith Ann Busang, Oct. 2, 1965; children: Marta, Frank, Anthony. BS, Ohio State U., 1961; MS, Carnegie-Mellon U., 1964, PhD, 1965. Chemist Nat. Bur. Standards, 1961; tchg. adn rsch. asst. Carnegie-Tech., 1961-65; rsch. chemist ESSO Rsch. and Engring. Co., Linden, N.J., 1965-66; chemist of rsch. and sci. U. Miami, 1966-68, asst. prof., 1968-69, prof. marine and phys. chemistry, 1969—. Assoc. dean grad. studies, Rosenstiel Sch. Marine and Atmospheric Studies, 1987—, assoc. dean rsch., 1995—; vis. prof. U. Kiel, W.Ger., 1975, Water Research Inst., Rome, 1979-80, U. Goteborg, Sweden, 1986; mem. UNESCO Panel for Ocean Standards, 1976—, NSF Panel, 1973-75, 82, Ocean Sci. Bd., 1981-83; chmn. Gordon Conf., 1983; cons. in field. Contbr. numerous articles to profl. jours. Coach Little League, Miami, Fla. Recipient Gold medal for Contbns. to Marine Chemistry U. Zagreb, Croatia, 1990, Gold medal award for Sci. Achievements Fla. Acad. Sci., 1992, Disting. Faculty Scholar award U. Miami, 1996. Fellow Geochem. Soc. and European Assn. for Geochemistry, Am. Chem. Soc. Geochemistry (divsn. medal), Am. Geophysical Union; mem. AAAS, N.Y. Acad. Sci., Omicron Delta Kappa, Sigma Xi (Prof. Yr. 1989). Democrat. Roman Catholic. Home: 7720 SW 90th Ave Miami FL 33173-3482 Office: Rosenstiel Sch Marine and Atmospheric Studies U Miami Miami FL 33149

MILLER-YOUNG, CORRIENE CALHOUN, nursing educator; b. N.Y.C., Oct. 22, 1959; d. Timothy E. Calhoun and Suzetta Franklin; children: Christopher, Jeremy, James, Aja. BSN, Rutgers U., Newark, 1982; postgrad., Memphis State U., 1992—. RN, N.J., Tenn.; cert. wound ostomy nurse; cert. wound and ostomy specialist. Staff nurse Muhlenberg Hosp., Plainfield, N.J., 1981-86, Kimberly Nurses, Union, N.J., 1986-89; health coord. Neighborhood House, Plainfield, 1989-91; staff nurse/nurse clinician Bapt. Meml. Hosp., Memphis, 1991-2000; LPN instr. Tenn. Tech. Ctr., Memphis, 1994—. Named Nurse of Month, Kimberly Nurses, 1987. Mem. ANA, Kappa Delta Pi.

MILLETT, MICHAEL FREDRIC, education educator; b. Portland, Maine, Jan. 19, 1955; s. Myron Anson and Shirley Louise (Cline) M.; m. Elaine Louise Morin, Feb. 18, 1978; children: Andrea, Brandon. BS in Elem. Edn., U. Maine, 1977. Tchr. Ashland (Maine) Cen. Sch., 1977—, elem. basketball coach, baseball coach, 1977-84, head tchr., computer coord., 1985—. Girls' jr. varsity basketball coach Ashland Community High Sch., 1978-84; sch. coord. New Eng. Math. League Contest, 1983—. Bd. dirs. Aroostook Valley Health Ctr., Ashland, 1986-93; sec. Ashland Dem. Party, 1986—. Mem. NEA, Maine Tchrs. Assn., Ashland Area Tchrs. Assn. (pres. 1979-80), Nat. Coun. Tchrs. Math., Assn. Tchrs. Math. in Maine, Maine Sci. Tchrs. Assn., Ashland Rotary Club (pres. 1989-90). Roman Catholic. Avocations: reading, outdoor activities, travel. Home: PO Box 364 Ashland ME 04732-0364 Office: Ashland Ctrl Sch PO Box Q Ashland ME 04732-0556

MILLETTE, ROBERT JOSEPH, elementary education educator; b. St. Paul, Sept. 2, 1951; s. Gordon Pierre and Mary Anna (Thuening) M.; m. Eileen Mary Harber-Schreiber, June 28, 1975; children: Amy Marie, Kimberly Jo. AA, Anoka-Ramsey Jr. Coll., Coon Rapids, Minn., 1971; BS in Elem. Edn., Moorhead State Coll., 1973; MS in Elem. Edn., Mankato State Coll., 1979. Cert. K-6 tchr., driver edn., coach, Minn. 5th grade tchr. Fairmont (Minn.) Pub. Schs., 1973-81; 2nd grade tchr. William Budd Elem. Sch., Fairmont, 1981—2002, 2d grade tchr., 2003—, 5th grade tchr., 2002—03. Driver edn. instr. Cmty. Edn. and Recreation, Fairmont, 1982-2002, Granada Huntley East Chain Schs., 2002—; 5th grade level coord. Fairmont Pub. Schs., 1975-81, 2nd grade level coord., 1983-92, dist. 454 tech. com., 1993-94. Trustee pastoral coun. St. John Vianney Ch., Fairmont, 1986-88, September Fest Chmn., 1987; pres. PTA St. John Vianney Sch., Fairmont, 1984-85; diocesan rep. Diocese of Winona, Minn., 1984-86. Mem. NEA, Minn. Edn. Assn. (bd. dirs. 1995-98), Edn. Minn., AFL-CIO Am. Fedn. Tchrs., Fairmont Edn. Assn. (sec.-treas. 1981—), Minn. Driver and Traffic Safety Edn. Assn., Gt. Plains UniServ (comm. chmn. 1993, sec.-treas. 1996-2002), Great S.W. United (sec.-treas. 2002—), KC (Grand Knight 1994). Roman Catholic. Avocations: golf, antiques, flea markets, travel. Home: 811 Albion Ave Fairmont MN 56031-3002 Office: Wm Budd Sch 1001 Albion Ave Fairmont MN 56031-3010

MILLIES, PALMA SUZANNE, school system administrator; b. N.Y.C., Apr. 30, 1943; d. Arpad Geza and Palma Regina (Franko) George; m. Robert John Millies; 1 child, Jennifer. BA in English and French magna cum laude, Elmhurst (Ill.) Coll., 1965; MA with honors, No. Ill. U., 1969; cert. advanced study, U. Ill., 1984; PhD in Curriculum Instrn. and Evaluation, U. Ill., Chgo., 1989. Cert. gen. adminstrn., spl. K-12 teaching and supervising, secondary sch. teaching, Ill. Lang. arts and French instr. Albright Middle Sch., Villa Park, Ill., 1965-70; English instr. Willowbrook High Sch., Villa Park, 1970-87, asst. prin. for instrn., 1988-91; dist. coord. gifted program High Sch. Dist. 88, Villa Park, 1982-86; asst. to dir. Chgo. Area Sch. Effectiveness Coun. Coll. Edn., U. Ill., 1986-87; asst. supt. for instrn. Maine Twsp. High Sch. Dist. # 207, Park Ridge, Ill., 1991—. Instr. Nat.-Louis U., 1991, Roosevelt U., 1991; presenter in field; co-founder West Suburban Dirs. Curriculum, 1989; adj. prof. Nat. Coll. Edn., Lombard, Ill., 1988; chairperson AFT Supt.'s Search Com., Villa Park, 1988; mem. task force on gifted edn. State BD. Edn., Springfield, Ill., 1988; adj. prof. U. Ill., Chgo., 1988, 87. Contbr. articles to profl. jours. Mem. Am. Ednl. Rsch. Assn., ASCD, Nat. Coun. Tchrs. English, Ill. Coun. for Gifted (corr. sec.), West Suburban Dirs. Instrn., Villa Park C. of C. (sec.), Phi Delta Kappa. Home: 611 Heritage Ct Naperville IL 60565-3393 Office: 1131 S Dee Rd Park Ridge IL 60068-4379

MILLMAN, MARILYN ESTELLE, elementary school educator; b. Lynn, MA, Nov. 28, 1936; d. Benjamin and Dora (Goldman) Millman. BS, Boston U., 1958. Elem. tchr. Beverly (Mass.) Sch. Dist., 1958—64, Lagunitas (Calif.) Sch. Dist., 1964—65, San Rafael (Calif.) City Schs., 1965—97; founder, pres. Marilyn Millman Scholarship Found., 1997—. Vol. chair and bd. dirs. Susan G. Komen Breast Cancer Found.

MILLON-WISNESKI, SHARON MARIE, critical care nurse, educator; b. Phila., June 22, 1952; d. Charles Edward and Hilda Marie (Riley) Ashley. Degree in Nursing, Wesley Coll., 1979, BSN, 1985; MSN, Widener U., 1991, D in Nursing Sci., 2003. ACLS. Charge nurse, med.-surg. ICU Milford (Del.) Meml. Hosp.; clin. instr. Wesley Coll., Dover, Del., Del. Tech. and CC, Dover; critical care per-diem nurse Med. Ctr. Del., Newark; instr. nursing Del. State U., Dover, 1991-95, asst. prof., 1995—. Part-time staff nurse med. ICU Med. Ctr. of Del., Newark; apptd. rev. bd. Del. Medicaid Drug Utilization Rev. Bd., 1993—; mem. Del. Bd. Nursing Practice Adv. Com., 1994—; co-chair nurse practice com., Del. Nurses Asn., 2003. Contbr. chapters to books. Recipient Young Publisher of Yr. award Assn. of Black Nursing Faculty, Inc., 1999, Dissertation award Assoc. of Black Nursing Faculty, Inc., 2001; named Faculty Mem. of Yr., Del. Student Nurse Assn., 1999, Young Pub. of Yr., Assn. Black Nursing Faculty, 1999. Mem.: AAUW, AACCN, ANA (mem. nurse strategic action team 1993—, rev. panelist ANA continuing edn. ind. study 1995—97), Am. Lung Assn. (bd. dirs. Del. chpt. 2003—), Nat. Assn. Black Nurses Inc., Inst. Constituent Mems. in Nursing Practice, Ea. Nurses Rsch. Soc., Del. Nurses Assn. (chmn. nursing practice com. 1992, editor The Reporter 2003—, Del. Nurse of Yr. 1993), Assn. Black Nursing Faculty, Inc. (bd. dirs., state coord., Young Pub. of Yr. 1999, Pres. award 2000, Dissertation award), Wesley Coll. Hon. Soc. Nursing (treas.), Chi Eta Phi, Sigme Theta Tau. Home: 336 Pine Valley Rd Dover DE 19904-7113 E-mail: pinevalley@earthlink.net.

MILLS, BARRY, academic administrator, lawyer; b. Providence, Sept. 8, 1950; m. Karen Gorden Mills. BA in Biochemistry and Govt. cum laude, Bowdoin, 1972; PhD, Syracuse U., 1976; JD, Columbia U., 1979. Bar: N.Y. 1980. Mem. Debevoise & Plimpton, NYC, 1979—86, ptnr., 1986—; pres. Boudoin Coll., Brunswick, Maine, 2001—. Acad. affairs com. Bowdoin Coll., Brunswick, Maine, bd. trustees, 1994—2000, chmn. bd. student affairs com. Harlan Fiske Stone scholar, Columbia Law Sch., 1979. Mem. Assn. of Bar of City of N.Y. Office: Debevoise & Plimpton 875 3rd Ave Fl 23 New York NY 10022-6225 also: Boudoin Coll Hawthorne-Longfellow Hall 5700 College Station Brunswick ME 04011-8448

MILLS, BELEN COLLANTES, early childhood education educator; b. Philippines; s. Ricardo and Epifania (Tomines) C.; m. Ralph A. Mills; children: Belinda Mills Keiser, Roger A. BSE, Leyte Normal Coll., Tacloban, Leyte, Philippines, 1954; MS in Edn., Ind. U., 1955, EdD, 1967. Prof. emeritus early childhood edn. Fla. State U., Tallahassee, 2002. Early childhood cons. to ednl. agys. and orgns. Author books on early childhood edn., phonics-based children's books and acad. readiness computer programs; contbr. articles to profl.jours. Smith-Mundt Fulbright scholar. Mem. Nat. Assn. for Edn. of Young Children, Nat. Assn. Early Childhood Tchr. Edn., World Coun. for Curriculum and Instrn., Assn. Childhood Edn. Internat. Home: PO Box 20023 Tallahassee FL 32316-0023 E-mail: raintown@polaris.net.

MILLS, CAROL JANE, secondary education educator; b. Yakima, Wash., Feb. 23, 1946; d. Stanley Lionel and Mildred Davis (Shaw) Quinn; m. Donald Dwane Mills, July 12, 1969; children: Michael Robert, Jason Tyler. BA in History/Edn., Wash. State U., 1968; postgrad., schs. in Oreg. and Wash., 1980-92; MEd, Heritage Coll., Toppenish, Wash., 1995. Cert. tchr. K-12, Wash. Tchr. Northshore Sch. Dist., Bothell, Wash., 1968-69; substitute tchr. various locations, 1970-78; tchr. Volusia County Schs., DeLand, Fla., 1978-79; tchr. social studies Yakima Sch. Dist., 1979—. Mem. h.s. standards com. Yakima Sch. Dist., 1985—; participant Wash. State-Hyogo (Japan) Social Studies Tchr. Exch., Kobe, 1992. Mem. stewardship/fin. com. Westpark United Meth. Ch., Yakima, 1991—. Grantee Tchr. Leadership Travel grant, Freeman Found., 1999, Tech. Grant, Bill & Melinda Gates, 2002, Bill & Melinda Gates Tchr. Leadership Project, 2002. Mem. Nat. Coun. for Social Studies, Journalism Edn. Assn., Wash. State Coun. for Social Studies (secondary rep. 1994—, Secondary Social Studies Tchr. of Yr. 2000), Delta Delta Delta (dist. pres. 1978-81). Avocations: sewing, travel, boating. Office: Eisenhower HS 702 S 40th Ave Yakima WA 98908-3331

MILLS, DON HARPER, pathology and psychiatry educator, lawyer; b. Peking, China, July 29, 1927; came to U.S., 1928; s. Clarence Alonzo and Edith Clarissa (Parrett) M.; m. Lillian Frances Snyder, June 11, 1949; children: Frances Jo, Jon Snyder. BS, U. Cin., 1950, MD, 1953; JD, U. So. Calif., 1958. Diplomate Am. Bd. Law in Medicine. Intern L.A. County Gen. Hosp., 1953-54, admitting physician, 1954-57, attending staff pathologist, 1959—; pathology fellow U. So. Calif., L.A., 1954-55, instr. pathology, 1958-62, asst. clin. prof., 1962-65, assoc. clin. prof., 1965-69, clin. prof., 1969—, clin. prof. psychiatry and behavioral sci., 1986—. Asst. in pathology Hosp. Good Samaritan, LA, 1956-65, cons. staff, 1962-72, affiliating staff, 1972-91; dep. med. examiner Office of LA County Med. Examiner, 1957-61; instr. legal medicine Loma Linda (Calif.) U. Sch. Medicine, 1960-66, assoc. clin. prof. humanities, 1966-95; cons. HEW, 1972-73, 75-76, Dept. of Def., 1975-80; bd. dirs. Am. Bd. Legal Medicine, Inc., Chgo.; med. dir. Profl. Risk Mgmt. Group, 1989-2001; med. dir., Octagon Risk Svcs., Inc., 2001—. Column editor Newsletter of the Long Beach Med. Assn., 1960-75, Jour. Am. Osteopathic Assn., 1965-77, Ortho Panel, 1970-78; exec. editor Trauma, 1964-88, mem. editl. bd., 1988—; mem. editl. bd. Legal Aspects of Med. Practice, 1972-90, Med. Alert Comms., 1973-75, Am. Jour. Forensic Medicine and Pathology, 1979-87, Hosp. Risk Control, 1981-96; contbr. numerous articles to profl. jours. Bd. dirs. Inst. for Med. Risk Studies, 1988—; mem. adv. bd. Pacific Ctr. for Health Policy and Ethics, 1997—, chmn., 1999—. Recipient Ritz Heerman award Calif. Hosp. Assn., 1986, Disting. fellow Am. Acad. Forensic Scis., 1993, Genesis award Pacific Ctr. for Health Policy and Ethics, 1993, Founder's award Am. Coll. Med. Quality, 1994. Fellow Am. Coll. Legal Medicine (pres. 1974-76, bd. govs. 1970-78, v.p. 1972-74, chmn. malpractice com. 1973-74, jour. editl. bd. 1984—, gold medal 1999), Am. Acad. Forensic Sci. (gen. program chmn. 1966-67, chmn. jurisprudence sect. 1966-67, 73-74, exec. com. 1971-74, 84-88, v.p. 1984-85, pres. 1986-87, ethics com. 1976-86, 91-2001, chmn. ethics com. 1994-2001, long-term planning com. 1990—, jour. editl. bd. 1965-79); mem. AMA (jour. editl. bd. 1973-77), AAAS, ABA, Am. Coll. Med. Quality (hon. life), Calif. Med. Assn., L.A. County Med. Assn., L.A. County Bar Assn., Am. Health Lawyers Assn., Calif. Soc. Hosp. Attys. Home: 700 E Ocean Blvd Unit 2606 Long Beach CA 90802-5039 Office: 5000 Airport Plaza Dr Ste 250 Long Beach CA 90815-4959 Office Fax: 562-420-5999. E-mail: Don.Mills@octagonrs.com.

MILLS, EDWIN SMITH, economics educator; b. Collingswood, N.J., June 25, 1928; s. Edwin Smith and Roberta (Haywood) M.; m. Barbara Jean Dressner, Sept. 2, 1950; children: Alan Stuart, Susan Dorinda; m. Margaret M. Hutchinson, Jan. 22, 1977. BA, Brown U., 1951; PhD, U. Birmingham, Eng., 1956. Asst. lectr. Univ. Coll. North Staffordshire, Eng., 1953-55; instr. MIT, 1955-57; mem. faculty Johns Hopkins, Balt., 1957-70, prof. econs., 1963-70, chmn. dept. econs., 1966-69; prof. econs. and pub. affairs, Gerald L. Phillippe prof. urban studies Princeton U., 1970-75, prof. econs., 1975-87, chmn. dept., 1975-77; Gary Rosenberg prof. real estate and fin. Kellog Sch. Mgmt. Northwestern U., Evanston, Ill., 1987—96, emeritus prof., 1996—. Vis. research fellow Cowles Found., Yale, 1961; sr. profl. staff Council Econ. Advisers, 1964-65 Author: The Burden of Government, 1986. 2d lt. U.S. Army, 1946—48. Recipient numerous rsch. grants and contracts, 1960—95. Mem. Am. Econ. Assn., Phi Beta Kappa. Home: 1 Calvin Cir Apt B105 Evanston IL 60201-1953 Office: Northwestern U Ctr Real Estate Rsch Kellogg Graduate School 2001 Sheridan Rd Evanston IL 60208-2001

MILLS, ELIZABETH ANN, retired librarian; b. Cambridge, Mass., Apr. 1, 1934; d. Ralph Edwin and Sylvia Elizabeth (Meehan) McCurdy; m. Albert Ernest Mills, July 6, 1957; 1 child, Karen Elizabeth. BA, Duke U., 1956; MS, Simmons Coll., 1973; postgrad., Boston Coll., Framingham State U., Bridgewater State U. Sec. Lowell House, Harvard U., Cambridge, Mass., 1956-57; substitute libr., tchr. Wellesley (Mass.) H.S., 1972-73, Needham (Mass.) H.S., 1972-73; libr. Tucker Sch. Media Ctr., Milton (Mass.) Pub. Schs., 1973-94, chmn. computer curriculum com., 1982, mem. computer study com., 1988-91, bldg. coord. gifted program, 1981-94; libr. Milton (Mass.) H.S., 1994-98; ret., 1998. Contbr. articles to profl. jours. Active Girl Scouts U.S.A., U.S. Power Squadron, Gt. Blue Hill, Mass., 1974-94. Mem. ALA, Am. Assn. Sch. Librs., Assn. Libr. Svc. Children, Mas. Assn. Ednl. Media, Mass. Sch. Libr. Assn., Beta Phi Mu, Kappa Delta, Delta Kappa Gamma. Republican. Episcopalian. Home: 177 Jarvis Cir Needham MA 02492-2034

MILLS, KATHLEEN CLAIRE, anthropology and mathematics educator; b. Pitts., Dec. 27, 1948; d. Clair I. and Ruth (McDowell) Wilson; m. William G. Mills, May 27, 1978; 1 child, David Lee. AS, Kilgore Coll., 1968; BS, Met. State Coll., Denver, 1982; MA in Secondary Edn., U. Colo., 1987, MA in Anthropology, 1989. Staff U.S. Geol. Survey, Denver,

1980-82; computer application specialist Petroleum Info., Englewood, Colo., 1982-83; entry level geologist La. Land and Exploration, Denver, 1983-86; prof. anthropology and math. C.C. of Aurora, 1987-96, GED coord., 1996; prof. anthropology Red Rocks C.C., 1994-98; supr. Janus Mutual Funds, Denver, 1998—2001; trainer Anthem Blue Cross Blue Shiedl, Denver, 2001—. Excavation supr. Caesarea Maritima, Israel, 1989-96 Drafter U.S. Oil and Gas Map, 1981. Mem. Am. Schs. Oriental Rsch., Denver Natural History Mus., Archaeol. Inst. Am. Colo. Archaeol. Soc., Nat. Geog. Soc. Avocations: bicycling, reading, hiking, travel. Home: 7946 E Mexico Ave Denver CO 80231-5687 Office: Anthem BCBS 700 Braodway Denver CO 80273-0001

MILLS, LETHA ELAINE, physician, educator; b. Norwalk, Conn., Nov. 14, 1952; d. Clifford Wheeler and Letha Lucille (Jones) M.; m. Lloyd Herbert Maurer, Sept. 1, 1984; children: Adam, Jason, Stephen. BA, U. Pa., 1974; MD, Dartmouth U., 1977. Diplomate Am. Bd. Internal Medicine, Am. Bd. Hematology, Am. Bd. Oncology. Internal medicine intern Dartmouth-Hitchcock Med. Ctr., Hanover, N.H., 1977-78, internal medicine resident, 1978-80, hematology fellow, 1981-83, U. Wash., 1980-81; with Lawy-Hitchcock Clinic, Lebanon, N.H., 1986—; asst. prof. medicine Dartmouth Med. Sch., Hanover, N.H., 1983-91, assoc. prof. medicine, 1991—. Med. advisor N.H. Breast Cancer Coalition, 1994—; mem. Gov.'s Adv. Panel on Cancer and Chronic Diseases, Concord, N.H., 1996—. Contbr. articles to profl. jours. Mem. Am. Soc. Hematology, Am. Soc. Clin. Oncology, Am. Fedn. Clin. Rsch. (mem. bone marrow transplant com. cancer and leukemia group B), Phi Beta Kappa, Alpha Omega Alpha. Democrat. Avocation: family. Home: 286 Maple Hill Rd Norwich VT 05055-9623

MILLS, NANCY ANNE, elementary education educator; b. Madisonville, Ky., Oct. 2, 1937; d. Leslie Owen and Ruby A. (Baker) Hawkins; m. Orton Leroy Mills, May 11, 1957; children: Charles Leroy, Roy Leslie. BS in Edn., Ind. U., South Bend, 1970, MS in Edn., 1972; Ednl. Specialist dergree, Ind. U., 1978. Cert. elem. tchr., Ind. Tchr. elem. South Bend Schs., 1972-97. Gifted cadre' Purdue U-For Ind., Lafayette, 1988—; presenter workshops; cons. econ. edn.; started gifted program South Bend Schs.; adj. prof. St. Mary's Coll., Notre Dame, Ind., 1999. Chmn. new ch. com. Nazarene Ch., South Bend, 1990; supr. students with Student Exch., France, 1991-96. Recipient Olan Davis award Econs. of Am. Purdue U., 1997; named Woman of Yr., Profl. and Bus. Womans Club, 1989; Inst. for Chem. Edn. grantee, 1989. Mem. Ind. Coun. Econ. Edn. (cons. 1987—, Tchr. of Yr. for State of Ind. 1992), Delta Kappa Gamma. Avocations: sewing, travel. Home: 16320 Wellington Pky Granger IN 46530-8309 Office: Muessel Sch 1213 California Ave South Bend IN 46628-2701

MILLS, PATRICIA JAGENTOWICZ, political philosophy educator, writer; b. Newark, Mar. 18, 1944; d. Alexander A. and Louise A. (Breunig) Jagentowicz; 1 child, Holland. BA, Rutgers U., 1973; MA, SUNY, Stony Brook, 1975; PhD, York U., Toronto, Ont., Can., 1984. Lectr. U. Toronto, 1984—85, vis. scholar, 1985—86, asst. prof. philosophy, 1986—88; asst. prof. polit. theory U. Mass., Amherst, 1988—91, assoc. prof. polit. theory, 1991—. Vis. scholar Pembroke Ctr. for Tchg. and Rsch. on Women, Brown U., 1999-2000; lectr. philosophy dept. Smith Coll., spring 1992; manuscript referee Social Scis. and Humanities Rsch. Coun. Can., 1985-86, 87-88, 91-92, Polity: Jour. of Northeastern Polit. Sci. Assn., 1990, 91; invited spkr. New Sch. for Social Rsch., 1990, Coll. Holy Cross, 1991, NEH seminar, Mt. Holyoke Coll., 1992, U. Pitts., 1993, Antigone Conf., SUNY Buffalo, 1997; presenter paper 20th World Congress Philosophy, 1998. Author: Woman, Nature, and Psyche, 1987; editor: Feminist Interpretations of G.W.F. Hegel, 1996; author, contbr.: (book chpts.) The Sexism of Social and Political Theory: Women and Reproduction from Plato to Nietzsche, 1979, Ethnicity in a Technological Age, 1988, Taking Our Time: Feminist Perspectives on Temporality, 1989, Renewing the Earth: The Promise of Social Ecology, 1990, The Future of Continental Philosophy and the Politics of Difference, 1991, Ecological Feminist Philosophies, 1996, The Phenomenology of Spirit Reader, 1998, Hegel and Law, 2002; contbr. articles to profl. jours. Dir. Drop-In Ctr., Newark, 1972-73; mem. N.J. Abortion Project, 1971-73; mem. Fortune Soc., N.J., 1972; grassroots organizer against the war in Vietnam, N.J., 1970-71; grassroots organizer women's movement, N.J. and N.Y., 1971-73. Recipient Disting. Tchg. award Delta Lambda chpt. Pi Sigma Alpha Honor Soc., U. Mass., 1997; postdoctoral fellow Social Scis. and Humanities Rsch. Coun. Can., 1983-85; scholar York U., 1975; faculty grantee for tchg. U. Mass., 1991-92. Mem. Am. Philos. Assn. (conf. presenter 1995 meeting), Soc. for Phenomenology and Existential Philosophy (presenter conf. papers 1988, 91, 92), Hegel Soc., Ancient Philosophy Soc., Soc. for the Study of Women Philosophers. Office: U Mass Thompson Hall Dept Polit Sci Amherst MA 01003 E-mail: pjmills@polsci.umass.edu.

MILLS, RICHARD P. school system administrator; BA with honors, Middlebury Coll., 1966; MA in Am. History, Columbia U., 1967, MBA, 1975, EdD, 1977. Tchr. history Dalton Sch., N.Y.C., 1967—71; creator with others Elizabeth Seeger Sch., N.Y.C., 1971—73; planning assoc. N.J. Dept. of Edn., 1975-78, dir. policy analysis, 1978-80, dep. asst. commr., 1980-82, spl. asst. to the commr., 1982-84; spl. asst. to Gov. Thomas H. Kean of N.J., 1984-88; commr. of edn. State of Vt., 1988-95, State of N.Y., 1995—; pres. Univ. of the State of N.Y., 1995—. Adj. asst. prof. Columbia Univ. Tchrs. Coll., 1977; adj. assoc. prof. Rider Coll., N.J., 1979; cons. task force to oversee fiscal reform in Newark, 1975; tchr. The Dalton Sch., N.Y.C., 1967-71, Elizabeth Seeger Sch., N.Y.C., 1971-73; mem. Carnegie Task Force on Learning in the Primary Grades; chair mgmt. group Nat. Alliance for Restructuring Edn.; bd. New Stds. Project; mem. bd. Nat. Ctr. on Edn. and the Economy. Contbr. articles to profl. jours. U.S. rep. to standing com. European Ministers of Edn., 1987. Office: NY State Edn Dept 111 Edn Bldg 89 Washington Ave Albany NY 12234-4909*

MILLS, SYLVIA JANET, secondary education educator; b. Chgo., Oct. 5, 1954; d. Clarence Thomas and Janet Lucille (Curry) Mills; children: Ean O'Harrel Gay Mills, Raymond Ear Echols II. BA in Journalism, Columbia Coll., Chgo., 1979; MA in Instructional Design, U. Iowa, 1993, secondary tchg. cert. in journalism, 1996. Edn. Beat reporter Chgo. Daily Defender Newspapers, 1979-80; tech. writer/editor, data mgmt. supr., ops./planning analyst Sonicraft, Inc., Chgo., 1983-88; sec. and pub. rels. officer Female Entrepreneurs of Chgo., 1988-89; adminstrv. asst./editor Student Devel. Office, City Colls. of Chgo., 1989-91; rsch. intern Am. Coll. Testing, Inc., Iowa City, Iowa, 1991-93; grad. asst. U. Iowa Grad. Coll., Iowa City, 1993-95. Rsch. asst. Ctr. for Evaluation and Assessment, U. Iowa, 1995-96. Bd. dirs. All in a Kid's Day Summer Immersion Program, Iowa City, 1994; mem. PTA Beasley Acad. Ctr., Chgo., 1988-90, PTO, Iowa City, 1992-93. Mem. ASCD, Alpha Kappa Alpha (treas., dean of pledges 1973-74). Avocations: reading, writing. Home: PO Box 742 Keokuk IA 52632-0742

MILLSAPS, ELLEN MCNUTT, English language educator; b. Sheffield, Ala., Feb. 10, 1947; d. Ershell Jerome and Annie Inez (Quillen) McNutt; m. Douglas Edward Millsaps, Nov. 27, 1971; 1 child, Stephen Edward. BA, Miss. Coll., 1969; MA, U. Tenn., 1972, PhD, 1976. Tchg. asst. U. Tenn., Knoxville, 1970—71; assoc. prof. English, dept. head Walters State C.C., Morristown, Tenn., 1971—79; prof. English, dir. writing across curriculum, dir. composition Carson-Newman Coll., Jefferson City, Tenn., 1979—; tchg. asst. U. Tenn., Knoxville, 1975—76. Cons. on writing Omicron Nu, 1989, Tenn. Network Foxfire Tchrs., 1992. Editor: Writing at Carson-Newman Coll., 1996, 98, 2002; contbr. essays to profl. jours. Recipient Disting. Faculty award Carson-Newman Coll., 1997; NDEA fellow, 1969-72, John C. Hodges fellow U. Tenn., 1975; rsch. grantee Appalachian Coll. Mellon Found., 1993, Appalachian Coll. Assn., 1995, 99. Mem.: Soc. for Study So. Lit., Conf. on Coll. Composition and Comm., Nat. Coun. Tchrs. English, South Atlantic MLA, Alpha Lambda Delta, Delta Omicron, Kappa Delta Pi, Sigma Tau Delta, Alpha Chi (region v.p. 1992-94, region pres. 1994-96, nat. coun. rep. 1997—., nat. v.p. 2003—). Baptist. Avocations: needlework, music, reading. Home: 7604 Sagefield Dr Knoxville TN 37920-9223 Office: Carson-Newman Coll PO Box 71957 Jefferson City TN 37760-7001 E-mail: emillsaps@cn.edu.

MILLSAPS, RITA RAE, elementary school educator; b. Magdalena, N.Mex., Jan. 14, 1937; d. Samuel Thomas Martin and Geneva Opal (Nicholson) Martin Freeman; m. Daryl Ray Millsaps, June 26, 1955; children: Michael (dec.), Kathleen, Marian, Larry. Student, Delta C.C., 1981-82; BA, Calif. State U., Sacramento, 1986, MEd in Curriculum and Instrn., 1993. Cert. elem. educator, Calif. Tchr. Mokelumne Hill Elem. Sch., Calaveras County, Calif. Mem. ASCD, Internat. Reading Assn., Calif. Elem. Edn. Assn. Home: PO Box 1413 San Andreas CA 95249-1413

MILO, ELIZABETH, special education educator; b. Voitsberg, Steiermark, Austria, Sept. 22, 1949; arrived in U.S., 1952; d. Adam Puhl and Maria Grosseibl; m. Kerry Richard Milo, June 24, 1972; children: Kristal, John, Jessica. BA in German, BS in Edn., Youngstown State U., 1998. Cert. tchr. certification Pa., Ohio. Fin. sec./bookkeeper St. John's Episc. Ch., Sharon, Pa., 1993—99; tchr., coord. of after sch. program, ESL support tchr. Sharon Sch. Dist., Sharon, Pa., 1999—. Recipient Vindicator award in Humanities, Youngstown (Ohio) Vindicator, 1999. Mem.: Clarence P. Gould Soc., Delta Phi Alpha, Phi Kappa Phi. Avocations: reading, tole painting. Home: PO Box 478 West Middlesex PA 16159 Office: Sharon Middle-High Sch 1129 E State St Sharon PA 16146

MILOY, LEATHA FAYE, university program director; b. Marlin, Tex., Mar. 12, 1936; d. J. D. and Leola Hazel (Rhudy) Hill; m. John Miloy, June 20, 1960; children: Tyler Hill, David Reed, Nancy Lee. BA, Sam Houston State U., 1957; MS, Tex. A&M U., 1967, PhD, 1978. Dir. pub. affairs Gulf Univs. Rsch. Corp., College Station, Tex., 1966-69; asst. dir. Ctr. for Marine Resources Tex. A&M U., College Station, 1974-76, dir. edn. svcs., 1974-78; dir. info. and spl. svcs. Tex. Woman's U., Denton, 1978-79; asst. v.p. univ. advancement S.W. Tex. State U., San Marcos, 1979-83, asst. to pres., 1983-84, v.p. student and instl. rels., 1984-90, v.p. univ. advancement, 1990-93, dir. capital campaign, 1993-98. Vis. lectr. humanities and sea U. Va., 1972-73; cons. Office Tech. Assessment, Washington, 1976-86, Tex. A&M U., Galveston, 1979-82, Bemidji State U., Glassboro State Coll., 1984; mem. Task Force on Edn. and Pub. Interest, 1987-88. Editor: The Ocean From Space, 1969; author, editor Sea Grant 70's, 1970-79 (Sea Grant award 1973-74); contbr. articles to profl. jours. Ad hoc mem. Marine Resources Coun. Tex., Austin, 1971-72, Tex. Energy Adv. Coun., 1974-75; chmn. United Way, Bryan, Tex., 1976; com. mem. various local elections, 1974-78. NSF grantee, 1970-78; recipient Marine Resources Info. award NSF, 1969-71, Tex. Energy Info. award Gov.'s Office, 1974-75, Tex. Water Info. award Dept. Interior, 1977-79. Mem. Nat. Soc. Fundraising Execs., Coun. for the Advancement and Support Edn. (bd. dirs. 1979-81, Disting. Achievement award 1998), Coun. Student Svcs. (v.p. Tex. 1988-90). Avocations: reading, painting, fishing. Home: PO Box 752 Buchanan Dam TX 78609-0752 E-mail: lmiloy@tstar.net.

MILTON, CORINNE HOLM, art history educator; b. Nogales, Ariz., Oct. 16, 1928; d. Walter and Louise (Oates) Holm; m. Lee B. Milton, July 17, 1950 (dec. Oct. 1986); children: Bruce, Marina, Alan, Stuart. BA in Polit. Sci., U. Ariz., 1951, MLS, 1982; tchg. cert., U. N.Mex., 1973. Cert. secondary sch. tchr., Ariz., C.C. tchr., Ariz., Calif. Real estate sales agt. Walter Holm & Co., 1951-67; French and history tchr. Dept. State Overseas Schs., Washington, 1968-76; Sci. Tran Sci. Translating Co., Santa Barbara, Calif., 1976-78; libr. City of Nogales, 1982-83, City of Tucson, 1990-93; lectr. U. Ariz. Extension, Tucson, 1984—; Spanish instr. Pima Coll., Tucson, 1990-93. Mem. Ariz.-Sonora Gov.'s Commn., Phoenix, 1993—; evaluator Ariz. Coun. for Humanities. Author, abstracter ABC Clio Press, 1976-78. Mem. Ariz. Opera Guild, 1989-96; bd. dirs. Hilltop Gallery, Nogales, 1989—; hostess, translator Tuscon Internat. Vis. Coun., 1994-96; lectr. on art history to cmty. schs. and retirement homes, Tucson, 1989—. Mem. UN Coun., Tucson Mus. Art (docent 1989—), Sunbelt World Trade Assn., Pimeria Alta Hist. Soc., Sierra Club. Democrat. Episcopalian. Avocations: hiking, raising greyhounds. Home: 6981 E Jagged Canyon Pl Tucson AZ 85750-6196

MILTON, LEONHARDA LYNN, elementary and secondary school educator; b. Minneota, Minn., Apr. 7, 1924; d. John and Mathilde (Bockman) Hinderlie; m. John Ronald Milton, Aug. 3, 1946; 1 child, Nanci. BA, U. Minn., 1949. Cert. tchr., Minn., Colo., S.D. Visual art tchr. Humboldt High Sch., St. Paul, 1949-57, Vermillion (S.D.) Middle Sch., 1972—; tchr. Kuns Miller Jr. High Sch., Denver, 1960-61. Occupational therapist N.D. State Hosp., Jamestown, 1959-60. Exhibited prin. works in numerous shows in Minn., N.D., S.D. Active local arts coun. and arts ctr. Recipient S.D. Gov.'s award Arts for Outstanding Svc. in Arts Edn., 1999. Mem. Nat. Art Edn. Assn. (State Art Educator award 1983), S.D. Art Educators (pres. 1980-83), S.D. Alliance for Art Edn. (pres. 1985-88). Democrat. Lutheran. Avocations: reading, visual artwork, travel. Home: 630 Thomas St Vermillion SD 57069-3631 Office: Vermillion Mid Sch Princeton St Vermillion SD 57069

MIMS, ALBERT DURANT, physician, educator; b. Kingstree, S.C., Sept. 27, 1952; s. John Durant and Edna Lorraine (Scott) M.; m. Julia Ann Guerry; children: Alice Scott, Anna Catherine, Susan Rivers. BS, U. S.C., 1973; MD, Med. U. S.C., 1978. Diplomate Am. Bd. Family Practice. Intern, then resident, 1978-81; practice medicine Lake City (S.C.) Pee Dee Family Practice, 1981—; sr. ptnr. Lake City (S.C.) Family Practice, 1982—. Assoc. prof. Med. U. S.C., Charleston, 1984—; mem. med. adv. bd. Companion Health-Coastal, Columbia, S.C., 1985—; chmn. family practice rev. S.C. Med. Coll. Forum, Columbia, 1985-86; chief of staff Lower Florence County Hosp., Lake City, 1986-87, bd. dirs., 1988—. Chmn. Lake City Pub. Health Bd., 1986—. Fellow Am. Acad. Family Practice; mem. Florence County Med. Soc., S.C. Med. Assn., AMA, Am. Acad. Family Physicians, Med. U. S.C. Alumni Assn. (life), U. S.C. Alumni Assn. Lodges: Rotary. Republican. Presbyterian. Avocations: golf, tennis, hunting. Office: Lake City Family Practice Mercy St Lake City SC 29560

MIMS, FRANCES LARKIN FLYNN, retired English language educator; b. Union, S.C., Sept. 24, 1921; d. Philip Dunne and Edith Kennedy (Smith) Flynn; m. Paul S. Mims Jr., Aug. 25, 1948; children: P. Larkin, P. Linda, Paul S. III. BA, Converse Coll., 1942; MA, Wofford Coll., 1947; PhD, U. S.C., 1972. Lang. tchr. Aiken (S.C.) High Sch., 1943-47; supervisory tchr. dept. edn. U. S.C., Columbia, 1947-50; chmn. dept. sociology Anderson (S.C.) Coll., 1956-67; asst. prof. Erskine Coll., Due West, S.C., 1967-72; freelance writer, researcher Anderson, 1972-75; mem. faculty, dir. writers' confs. Anderson Coll., 1976-84, prof., chmn. dept. English, 1985-92. Author: Buy Hyacinths (poetry), 1971, Jeannie (novel), 1972; contbr. essays, articles to lit. and gen. interest mags. Pres. Anderson County Arts Coun., 1975, Anderson County Writers' Guild, 1976. Mem. S.C. Acad. Authors (life, bd. govs.). Episcopalian. Home and Office: 1212 Rutledge Way Anderson SC 29621-4057

MIMS, PAULA CAIN, secondary education educator; b. Dothan, Ala., Dec. 5, 1954; d. Bennie E. and Bobbie (Casey) Cain; m. Tom Wesley Mims Jr., Sept. 20, 1975; children: Casey Leigh, Ashley Elizabeth. AA in Bus. Adminstrn., Wallace State C.C., Dothan, 1975; BS in Bus. Edn., Troy State U., 1981; tech. cert., MEd, Auburn U., 1997; adminstrv. cert., Troy State U., 1998. Vocat. cert. Auburn U., 1982. Instr. bus. edn. Eufaula (Ala.) H.S., 1981—. Mem. supt. adv. com. Eufaula City Schs., 1993-94. Advisor, sponsor Future Bus. Leaders of Am., Eufaula, 1981—; active Sunday Sch. First Bapt. Ch. of Abbeville; active women's com. ALFA Ins. Co., Henry County, Ala., 1984—. Scholar tech. program for Ala. tchrs. State Dept. of Edn., 1995-97. Mem. NEA, Nat. and Ala. Career Tech. Edn. Assn., Eufaula Tchrs. Assn., Delta Kappa Gamma (v.p.). Avocations: drawing, painting, decorating, reading. Home: 804 County Rd 74 Abbeville AL 36310-9509 Office: Eufaula HS 530 Lake Dr Eufaula AL 36027-9564

MIN, HOKEY, business educator; b. Seoul, South Korea, June 28, 1954; s. Byungjoo and Hangwon (Seo) M. BA, Hankuk U. of Fgn. Studies, Seoul, South Korea, 1978; MBA, Yonsei U., Seoul, South Korea, 1980, U. S.C., 1982; PhD, Ohio State U., 1987. Freelance writer Chas. E. Merrill Pub. Co., Columbus, Ohio, 1983; teaching assoc. Ohio State U., Columbus, 1983-87; asst. prof. U. New Orleans, 1987-89, Northeastern U., Boston, 1989-92, Auburn U., 1992-98; exec. dir. Logistics and Distbn. Inst./U. Louisville, 1998—; prof. supply, chair mgmt. U. Louisville, disting. univ. scholar, 2002—. Cons. Shoe Corp. Am., Columbus, 1983-84, Nationwide Ins. Co., 1984, Russell Athletic Wear, Master Lock, Westpoint Stevens, 1997, Briggs and Stratten, 1998. Contbr. articles to profl. jours. Recipient Most Outstanding Rsch. award Coll. Bus. at Auburn U., 1993, 98, Citation of Excellence award, 1997. Mem. Decision Scis. Inst., Inst. Mgmt. Scis., Ops. Rsch. Soc. Am., Am. Prodn. and Inventory Soc., Coun. of Logistics Mgmt., Southeastern Decision Scis. Inst. (Hon. Mention 1986), Southeastern TIMS (Best Student Paper 1986). Republican. Avocations: portrait painting, ice skating, golf, science fiction. Office: Univ Louisville Louisville KY 40292-0001

MINAULT, GAIL, history educator; b. Mpls., Mar. 25, 1939; d. Paul Adrien and Martha (McKim) M.; m. Thomas Graham, May 13, 1967 (div. 1973); 1 child, Mark Emlen (dec.); m. Leon W. Ellsworth, Apr. 11, 1992; children; Laila Minault, Alex Ellsworth. BA, Smith Coll., Northampton, Mass., 1961; MA, U. Pa., 1966, PhD, 1972. Trainee U.S. Info. Agy., Washington, 1961-62; jr. officer U.S. Info. Svc., Beirut, Lebanon, 1962-63, asst. cultural affairs officer Dacca, East Pakistan, 1963-64; asst. prof. U. Tex., Austin, 1972-79, assoc. prof., 1980-95, prof., 1996—. Author: The Khilafat Movement: Religious Symbolism and Plitical Mobilization Among Indian Muslims, 1982; editor: The Extended Family: Women's Political Participation in India and Pakistan, 1981, Abul Kalam Azad: An Intellectual and Religious Biography, 1988, Secluded Scholars: Women's Education and Muslim Social Reform in Colonial India, 1998; translator: Voices of Silence, 1986. Nat. Humanities Ctr. fellow, 1987-88, Social Sci. Rsch. Coun. fellow, 1993, NEH, 1994-95. Mem. Assn. for Asian Studies, Berkshire Conf. Women Historians, Am. Inst. Pakistan Studies (sec. 1994-96). Democrat. Avocations: swimming, singing, traveling, photography. Office: U Tex Dept History Austin TX 78712

MINDES, GAYLE DEAN, education educator; b. Kansas City, Mo., Feb. 11, 1942; d. Elton Burnett and Juanita Maxine (Mangold) Taylor; m. Marvin William Mindes, June 20, 1969 (dec.); 1 child, Jonathan Seth. BS, U. Kans., 1964; MS, U. Wis., 1965; EdD, Loyola U., Chgo., 1979. Tchr. pub. schs., Newburgh, N.Y., 1965-67; spl. educator Ill. Dept. Mental Health, Chgo., 1967-69; spl. edn. supr. Evanston (Ill.) Dist. 65 Schs., 1969-74; lectr. Loyola U., Chgo., 1974-76, Coll. St. Francis, Joliet, Ill., 1976-79; asst. prof. edn. Oklahoma City U., 1979-80; prof. sch. edn. DePaul U., 1993-99, acting dean, 1998-99, prof. edn., 1999—, dir. EdD program, 2000—02, chair tchr. edn., 2003—. Lectr. Northeastern Ill., U. Chgo, 1974, North Park Coll., Chgo., 1978; vis. asst. prof., rsch. assoc. Roosevelt U. Coll. Edn., Chgo, 1983-87, Albert A. Robin campus prof., dir. R&D dir. tchr. edn., dir. early childhood, dir. grad. edn. ctr., 1993; search com. multicultural student affairs, v.p. advancement, DePaul U.; chair Roosevelt U. Senate, 1986-89; trustee Roosevelt U., 1987-93; co-chair ILAEYC Bldg. Bridges; alt. rep. faculty coun. DePaul U. Sch. Edn., faculty adv. com. to univ. plan. and info. tech., panel on grievances, 1995-99, comprehensive pers. devel. com., 1995-99; tng. sub-com. adv. Ill. Dept. Children & Family Svcs., 1993-95; panel of advisers comprehensive pers. devel. sys. Ill. State Bd. Edn., 1995-99; mentor, cons. to partnerships project tng. early intervention svcs. U. Ill., Champaign; panelist Ill. Initiative for Articulation between Ill. Bd. Higher Edn. and Ill. Cmty. Coll. Bd., Early Childhood Assessment Sys.; co-chair, panelist Bansenville Pub. Schs.; cons. in field; project evaluator Chgo. Tchr. Collaborative, Dept. Edn., 1999—; chair U. Tchg. Learning Tech. com., 2001—; mem. ISBE/NCATE Partnership Com., 2002. Author: Assessing Young Children, 2d edit., 2003; (with Marie Donovan) Building Character: Five Enduring Themes for a Stronger Early Childhood Curriculum PK-3, 2000; editor: DePaul U. Sch. Edn. Newsletter; co-author: Planning a Theme Based Curriculum for 4's or 5's, 1993, Assessing Young Children: 1996, Encyclopedia of Children's Play, 1997; mem. editl. bd. Ill. Sch. R&D, Ill. Divsn. Early Childhood Edn. Adv. Com. to Ill. Bd. Edn.; contbr. articles to profl. jours. Bd. dirs. North Side Family Day Care, 1981; northside affiliate Mus. Contemporary Art, 1991-96; active Gov's Task Force on Alternative Rts. to Cert., 1999; edn. adv. com. Okla. Dept. Edn., 1979-80; adv. bd. bilingual early childhood program Oakton C.C.; adv. bd. early childood tech. assistance project Chgo. Pub. Schs., Lake View Mental Health, 1986-90; planning com. Lake View Citizens Coun. Day Care Ctr., 1978-79; local planning coun. Ill. Dept. Child and Family Svcs.; childcare block grant tng. sub. com.; chair teen com. Florence G. Heller JCC, membership com.; adv. bd. Harold Washington Coll. Child Devel., regional tech. assistance grant LICA; mem. parents. com. Francis W. Parker Sch.; mem. assessment task force Dept. Human Svcs., City of Chgo., 2001-02; trustee Congregation Kol Ami., 2000-03. U. Kans. scholar, 1960, Cerebral Palsy Assn. scholar, 1965; U. Wis. fellow in mental retardation, 1964-65. Fellow: Am. Orthopsychiat. Assn.; mem.: ASCD, Found. for Excellence in Tchg. (selection com. Golden Apple 1989—94), Ill. Assn. for Edn. Young Children (co-chair bldg. bridges project), Ill. Coun. for Exceptional Children, Coun. for Exceptional Children, Am. Ednl. Rsch. Assn., Nat. Assn. for Edn. Young Children (tchr. edn. bd. 1990—94, editl. rev. bd.), Pi Lambda Theta, Phi Delta Kappa, Alpha Sigma Nu. Office: DePaul Univ Sch Of Edn Chicago IL 60614 E-mail: gmindes@depaul.edu.

MINDIN, VLADIMIR YUDOVICH, information systems specialist, chemist, educator; b. Tbilisi, Georgia, USSR, June 6, 1939; came to U.S., 1992; naturalized U.S. citizen, 1997; s. Yuda Isaakovich and Sofia Markovna (Ioffe) M.; m. Irina Alexandrovna Pleshivaia, July 1, 1964; children: Liya, Yakov. MS, Georgian Tech. U., Tbilisi, 1961, PhD, 1969. Sr. rsch. scientist Georgian Tech. U., 1970-80, assoc. prof. phys. chemistry, 1980-92; founder, head computational chemistry lab. Georgian Acad. Sci., Tbilisi, 1980-92; investigator Beltran Inc., Bklyn., 1993-94, prin. investigator, 1994-95; statistician AFP, Inc., Manhasset, N.Y., 1995-98, info. systems dir., 1998-2001; prof. dept. computer sys. and math. Globe Inst. Tech., N.Y.C., 2001—. Cons. DNS Sci., Inc., Bklyn., 1992-97; chief scientific officer, BioNova, Inc., Forest Hills, N.Y., 1997-2001, v.p. info. sys., 2001—. Author: (with A.G. Morachevskii and A.S. Avaliany) Liquid Cathodes, 1978, (with A.V. Sarukhanishvily and J.S. Galuashvily) Inorganic Substances Thermodynamic Parameters Calculation on Computers by Landia Method, 1987; (with S.M. Mazmishvily and D.V. Eristavy) Album of Compositions of Condensed and Gaseous Phase of Silica-Carbon System, 1988 (Georgian Chem. soc. award 1989), (with A.V. Sarukhanshvily) Chemical Thermodynamics, 1990; (with D.V. Eristavy) Investigation on Thermodynamics of Interaction in Boron and Silicon Containing Systems By Means of Digital Chemistry Methods, 1994; contbr. articles to profl. jours. Grantee Dept. Def., 1994-95. Mem. Am. Statis. Assn., Minerals, Metals, Materials Soc., Assn. Engrs. and Scientists for New Ams. (assoc. exec. dir. 1993-94). Achievements include co-development of the first complete phase diagram of the silica-carbon system; patents (with others): method of manganese salt solutions obtaining, method of manufacturing of porous electrodes, method of manganese obtaining, device for electrochemical measurement during electrolysis of melted media, working of sulphur ores, nonferrous metals aulphate ores roasting process, unhydrous manganese chloride producing process, a way of working sulphide ores containing nonferrous metals, furnace charge for silicomanganese obtaining, the batch for the medium carbonic ferromanganese smelting. Home: 70

Dahill Rd Apt 5A Brooklyn NY 11218-2232 Office: BioNova Inc 102-05 63 Rd Ste #1 Forest Hills NY 11375 also: Globe Inst Tech 291 Broadway 2d Fl New York NY 10007 E-mail: mindin@globe.edu.

MINDLIN, PAULA ROSALIE, retired reading educator; b. N.Y.C., Nov. 27, 1944; d. Simon S. and Sylvia (Naroff) Bernstein; m. Alfred Carl Mindlin, Aug. 14, 1965; 1 child, Spencer Douglas. BA in Edn., Bklyn. Coll., 1965; MS in Edn., Queens Coll., 1970, Specialist Sch. Adminstrn, 1973. Tchr. Dist. 16 Pub. Sch., Bklyn., 1965-68; reading tchr. Dist. 29 Pub. Sch. and Dist. 16, Bklyn., 1968-85; instr. insvc. courses Cmty. Sch. Dist. 29, Queens Village, NY, 1984-93, reading coord. Reading/Comm. Arts Program, 1985-90, dir. reading, 1990-94. Adj. lectr. York Coll., 1989; dir. Chpt. 1 Program (Nat. Recognition 1994, U.S. Sec. of Edn.); curriculum cons., 1997—98. Recipient svc. award N.Y. State Reading Assn. Coun., 1996. Mem. Internat. Reading Assn., Queensboro Reading Coun. (pres. 1994-96, Educator of Yr. award 1994), Nassau Reading Coun. Avocations: reading, gardening.

MINEKA, SUSAN, psychology educator; b. Ithaca, N.Y., June 2, 1948; d. Francis Edward and Muriel Leota (McGregor) M. BA in Psychology magna cum laude, Cornell U., 1970; PhD, U. Pa., 1974. Lic. psychologist, Ill. Prof. psychology U. Wis., Madison, 1974-85, U. Tex., Austin, 1986-87; prof. Northwestern U., Evanston, Ill., 1987—. Co-dir. Panic Treatment Ctr., EvanstonHosp., 1988-99; mem. NIH Panic Consensus Panel, 1991. Editor Jour. Abnormal Psychology, 1990-94; contbr. articles to profl. jours. Grantee NSF and NIMH, 1988-97; fellow Ctr. for Advanced Study in the Behavioral Scis., Stanford, Calif., 1997-98. Fellow APA (bd. sci. affairs 1992-94, chair 1994, pres. divsn. 12, sect. 3 1995), Am. Psychol. Soc., Psychonomic Soc. (bd. dirs. 2001, 04); mem. Assn. for Advancement Behavior Therapy, Midwestern Psychol. Assn. (pres.-elect 1995-96, pres. 1996-97), Internat. Primatol. Soc., Internat. Soc. for Rsch. on Emotion, Soc. for Rsch. in Psychopathology (mem. exec. bd. 1992-94, 2000-03), Phi Beta Kappa, Sigma Xi. Democrat. Office: Northwestern U Psychology Dept Evanston IL 60208-0001

MINER, MARY ELIZABETH HUBERT, retired secondary school educator; b. Provident City, Tex., Mar. 25, 1921; d. Fred Edward and Charlotte Alice (Haynes) Hubert; m. Daniel Bowen Miner, Jan. 29, 1945 (dec. Aug. 1979); children: Charlotte Martelia Miner Williams, Daniel Bowen Jr., Mary Elizabeth Miner Martinez, Joseph Frederick, William McKinley (dec.). BA, Rice U., 1942; postgrad., U. Houston, East Tenn. State U., 1959, U. Tenn., 1961. Cert. tchr. math., English, French, history, Tex., 8th grade, math., English, French, Am. history grades 9-12. Math. tchr. Crosby (Tex.) H.S., 1942-43; office mgr. Uvalde Rock Asphalt, Houston, 1943-44; tchr. math., English, health Rogersville (Tenn.) H.S., 1947-49, 55-78; tchr. math., English, French Ch. Hill. (Tenn.) H.S., 1949-51, 53-55; tchr. 8th grade Rogersville (Tenn.) City Schs., 1951-53; tchr. math. Cherokee Comprehensive H.S., Rogersville, 1978-84. Chmn. math. and sci. planning com., Hawkins County, Tenn., 1977-79; pvt. tutor, Rogersville. Tchr. ladies Bible class Rogersville United Meth. Ch., 1952—, mem. choir, 1979—, sec., 1967-96, sec. adminstr. bd. dirs.; blood donor ARC, Rogersville, 1974-75; leader Girl Scouts Am., 1956-58, 65-72, Cub Scout den mother Boy Scouts Am., 1951-53, 66-68, 68-70. Lt. Women's Corps USNR, 1944-47. Recipient Apple award Sta. WKGB, 1956. Mem. NEA (life), Tenn. Edn. Assn. (life), Rogersville Bus. and Profl. Women (pres. 1953-55, treas. 1948-53), Am. Legion Aux. (pres.), Delta Kappa Gamma (Alpha Iota chpt. pres.), Hawkins Ret. Tchrs. Assn. (pres. 1984-85). Republican. Avocations: bridge playing, playing piano, teaching, sewing, visiting children. Home: Rogersville, Tenn. Died Aug. 7, 2000.

MINETREE, JAMES LAWRENCE, III, retired military officer, educator; b. Balt., Feb. 21, 1937; s. James Lawrence and Rhoda (Blossom) M.; m. Martha Milling, Apr. 9, 1983; children: James Lawrence IV, Peter Milling, Jennifer Grace, Margaret Warner; stepchildren: Rachael, Aubrilyn. B, U. Nebr., Omaha, 1971; MA, U. So. Calif., L.A., 1973. Commd. 2d lt. U.S. Army, 1964, advanced through grades to lt. col., 1979; mem. Nat. Intelligence Coun. CIA, Langley, Va., 1979-82; ret. U.S. Army, 1982; with GE Aerospace Sys., Reston, Va., 1982-85; dir. Crisis Mgmt. Info. Sys. BDM, Tysons Corner, Va., 1985-86; pres. Analytical Scis. Inc., Vienna, Va., 1986-90; founder Nat. Inst. for Urban Search and Rescue, Santa Barbara, Calif., 1982—; adj. prof. U. Md. U. Coll., College Park, 1992—; founder, pres. Wilson Inst. for Humanitarian Assistance, Springfield, Va., 1998—. Trustee Nat. Assn. for Search and Rescue, Fairfax, Va., 1984-88; mem. nat. adv. bd. Congl. Fire Svcs. Inst., Washington, 1990-96. Author: Disaster mgmt. officer Fed. Emergency Mgmt. Agy., Washington, 1993-2000; U.S. Govt. rep. European Coun., Athens, Greece, 1990; conceived U.S. Nat. and Internat. Urban Search and Rescue Teams, 1987; bd. dirs. Downtown Benefits Dist., Balt., 1993; tchr. disadvantaged inner-city youth. Decorated Legion of Merit (2), Bronze Star (2), Air medal, Meritorious Svc. medal, Army Commendation medal (3), Vietnam Cross of Gallantry, Civic Action medal, others, Dominican Republic and Republic of Vietnam; recipient Presdl. citation Pub. Svc. The White House, Washington, 1995. Mem. VFW, Nat. Def. Exec. Res., Assn. U.S. Army, Am. Legion. Republican. Episcopalian. Avocations: humanitarian assistance, education, sailing, skiing, pastoral ministry. Home: RR 1 Box 52-1 Mill Creek Rd Millboro VA 24460 E-mail: peteminetree@mqwnet.com.

MINEY, MAUREEN ELIZABETH, middle school educator; b. Bklyn., Nov. 12, 1946; d. Patrick F. and Grace A. (Dillon) M. BS, St. Thomas Aquinas Coll., 1968; MA, Manhattan Coll., 1973; postgrad., N.Y.U., Montclair State Coll. Tchr. Nanuet (N.Y.) Pub. Schs., 1968—, acad. team leader, 1985—. Supt. tchr. coun. Nanuet Pub. Schs., 1973-75, camp instr. 6th grade, 1975—; mem. middle sch. curriculum com., 1987—, computer adv. com., 1987—, middle sch. improvement com., 1988—, dist. writing com., 1989—, middle sch. adv. com.; dist. lang. arts com., 1994—, dist. math. task force, dist. leadership team, 2000—; dist. mentor, 2001-; presenter NCTE nat. conv. N.J. Sci. Tchrs. Assn., N.Y. State Mid. Sch. Assn. Active Nanuet PTA. Mem. ASCD, Nat. Mid. Sch. Assn., N.J. Assn. for Middle Level Edn., N.Y. State Middle Sch. Assn., Nat. Coun. Tchrs. Math., Am. Fedn. Tchrs., Nat. Coun. Tchrs. English, Am. Mus. Natural History, Met. Mus. Art, N.Y. State United Tchrs., N.Y. Zool. Soc., N.Y. Bot. Garden, N.J. Coun. Tchrs. English, N.J. Sci. Tchrs. Assn., N.Y. Outdoor Edn. Assn., Hudson Valley Orienteering, U.S. Orienteering Fedn., Liberty Sci. Ctr., Nanuet Tchrs. Assn., Internat. Reading Assn. (presenter), Delta Kappa Gamma. Avocations: walking, reading, bicycling, arts and crafts. Office: A MacArthur Barr Mid Sch 143 Church St Nanuet NY 10954-3030

MINGO, JOE LOUIS, elementary school educator; b. Kershaw, S.C., Nov. 14; s. John L. and Ella (Wilson) M. BA in Elem. Edn., U. S.C., 1980, MEd, 1982, postgrad., 1994—. Cert. tchr. elem. edn., early childhood edn. Singer operator Springs Industries, Lancaster, S.C., 1972-79; with BJH Realty, Columbia, S.C., 1980-81, Carabo Inc., Columbia, 1980-85; tchr. 3d grade Sumter County (S.C.) Sch. Dist. #2, 1982-86, tchr. 4th grade, 1986-94, tchr. math, 1994—; lead tchr. math Shaw Heights Elem. Sch., Shaw AFB, S.C., 1993—; asst. principal Sumter Co. Sch. Dist. #2, 2000-01. Author poetry in New Voices in Am. Poetry, 1986, 88. With USAF, 1984—, Desert Storm. Avocation: writing. Office: 5355 Cane Savannah Rd Wedgefield SC 29168 E-mail: jmingo@scsd2.k12.sc.us., joemingo@aol.com.

MINI, ANNE ALEXANDRA APOSTOLIDES, writer, educator; b. Oakland, Calif., Sept. 30, 1966; d. Norman and Kleo Varvara (Apostolides) M. AB, Harvard U., 1988; MA, U. Chgo., 1991; PhD, U. Wash., 1995. Freelance writer, Seattle, 1995—; pres. Thesisadvisor.com, 2000—; owner First Reader Editing, Seattle, 2002—. Lectr., tchg. asst. U. Wash., Seattle, 1991-95, Nancy Hartsock Rotating Chair, 1995. Author: The General Strike of 1934, 1988, Alexis de Tocqueville in Historical Context, 1991, An Expressive Revolution, 1995, Security Issues, 1996, Favorite Son, 1999, Background Noise, 2001, The Buddha in the Hot Tub, 2003. Precinct com. officer Seattle Dem. Com., 1996—; del. King County Dem. Ctrl. Com., Seattle, 1996—, mem. bylaws com., 1999; polit. campaign cons., 1998—; mem. Wash. State Dem. Platform Com., 1998, 2000; Wash. state del. Dem. Nat. Conv., 2000. Radcliffe scholar, 1984-88; grantee U. Wash., 1995, 90, U. Chgo., 1989-91, Norcroft Writing Fellowship, 2002. Avocations: 18th and 19th century french liberalism, gourmandry, viticulture. Office: PO Box 27242 Seattle WA 98125-1742 E-mail: authoress1@foxinternet.com.

MINNERLY, ROBERT WARD, retired headmaster; b. Yonkers, N.Y., Mar. 21, 1935; s. Richard Warren and Margaret Marion (DeBrocky) M.; m. Sandra Overmire, June 12, 1957; children: Scott Ward, John Robert, Sydney Sue. AB, Brown U., 1957; MAT, U. Tex., Arlington, 1980. Tchr., coach Rumsey Hall Sch., Washington, Conn., 1962-64, Berkshire Sch., Sheffield, Mass., 1964-70, asst. head, 1969-70, headmaster, 1970-76; dir. Salisbury (Conn.) Summer Sch. Reading and English, 1970; prin. upper sch. Ft. Worth Country Day Sch., 1976-86; headmaster Charles Wright Acad., Tacoma, 1986-96; ednl. cons. The Edn. Group, 1996-2000; interim dir. Harold E. LeMay Mus., 2001—02. Cons. Tarrant County Coalition on Substance Abuse, 1982-84; mem. mayor's task force Tacoma Edn. Summit, 1991-92; bd. dirs. World Cultural Interaction, Gig Harbor, Wash. Contbr. articles to profl. jours. Bd. dirs. Tacoma/Pierce County Good Will Games Art Coun., 1989, Multicare Found., Tacoma, 2002, Tacoma Baseball Found., 2003—; mem. exec. com. Am. Leadership Forum, 1991-95; bd. dirs. Broadway Ctr. for Performing Arts, Tacoma, 1988-94, 96-98, mem. exec. com., 1990-93; elected Wash. State Bd. Edn., 1996-2001; bd. dirs. Tacoma Youth Choir, 2000-03. Named Adminstr. of Yr. Wash. Journalism Edn. Assn., 1991; recipient Columbia award, Wash. Fedn. Ind. Schs., 2000. Mem. Pacific N.W. Assn. Ind. Schs. (chmn. long-range planning com. 1989-92, exec. com. 1990-92, 91, v.p. 1994). Republican. Presbyterian. Home and Office: 4214 39th Avenue Ct NW Gig Harbor WA 98335-8029

MINNEY, BARBARA ANN, elementary educator and administrator; b. Lancaster, Pa., Oct. 5, 1948; d. Jack K. and Amy Teresa (Luttenberger) Dunlap; m. Michael Jay Minney, June 28, 1975; 1 child, Michael Jayson. BS in Edn., West Chester (Pa.) U., 1969; MEd, Millersville (Pa.) U., 1971, postgrad., 1989, Temple U., 1991. Cert. tchr., supr., prin., Pa. Elem. tchr. Sch. Dist. of Lancaster, 1970-91, adminstrv. asst., 1991-93, elem. prin., 1993—2000, elem. tchr., 2001—. Jury commr. County of Lancaster, 1978-86. Named Outstanding Young Women Am., 1980, Dist. Alumnus, McCaskey High Sch., 2001. Lutheran. Home: 1011 Woods Ave Lancaster PA 17603-3126

MINOR, MARIAN THOMAS, elementary and secondary school educational consultant; b. Richmond, Va., Apr. 16, 1933; d. James Madison and Florence Elwood (Edwards) M. BS, U. Va., 1955; MEd, William and Mary Coll., 1968; postgrad., Va. Commonwealth U., 1987-88. Cert. guidance, health and phys. edn. Educator Richmond (Va.) Pub. Schs., 1955-90, ednl. cons., 1990—. Educator Sch. Nursing Med. Coll. Va., Richmond, 1958-68; camp dir. Manakin, Va., 1956-68; nat. basketball ofcl. Richmond (Va.) Bd. Ofcls., 1952-77; mem. faculty adv. com. Albert Hill Middle Sch., Richmond, 1965-90, dept. chmn., 1960-90, Tchr. of Yr., 1980; textbook adoption Richmond (Va.) Pub. Sch., 1975, 85, curriculum planner, 1978-79, 82-83, 84-85; PTA coord. Albert Hill Middle Sch., Richmond, 1985-89, chmn. self-study and accreditation team, 1987-88. Mem. Sherwood Park Civic Assn., Richmond, 1960-98; v.p. alumni weekend Mary Washington Alumni Assn., Fredericksburg, Va., 1965, 66, v.p. annual giving, 1967; chmn. basketball ofcl. examiners Richmond Bd. Women Ofcls., 1966-76; bd. dirs., homeowner adv., constrn. crewman, family svcs. com. Habitat for Humanity, 1994-2002, Blitz Build 2000 adv. chmn.; mem. exec. com. Northminster Bapt. Ch., 1991-94, 99-2002, deacon, clk., 97-99, worship team, 1999—, premises chair, 1991-94, mem. by-laws revision com., 1986, 98, 99, srs. task force chmn., v.p., sr. fellowship, regional Befriender Ministry adv. coun. Recipient J.C. Penney Golden Rule award, 1996, Outstanding Vol. award Habitat for Humanity, 1998, Outstanding Svc. award Albert Hill PTA, 1988. Mem. AAUW, AAHPERD, Va. Health Phys. Edn. Assn., Va. Ret. Tchrs. Assn., Train Collectors Assn., King and Queen Hist. Soc., Mortar Bd., Alpha Phi Sigma, Kappa Delta Pi. Republican. Avocations: gardening, genealogy, local history, antiques. Home and Office: 1507 Brookland Pky Richmond VA 23227-4707

MINOW, NEWTON NORMAN, lawyer, educator; b. Milw., Jan. 17, 1926; s. Jay A. and Doris (Stein) M.; m. Josephine Baskin, May 29, 1949; children: Nell, Martha, Mary. BS, Northwestern U., 1949, JD, 1950, LLD (hon.), 1965, U. Wis., Brandeis U., 1963, Columbia Coll., 1972, Govs. State U., 1984, De Paul U., 1989, RAND Grad. Sch., 1993, U. Notre Dame, 1994, Roosevelt U., 1996, Barat Coll., 1996, Santa Clara U. Sch. Law, 1998. Bar: Wis. 1950, Ill. 1950. With firm Mayer, Brown & Platt, Chgo., 1950-51, 53-55; law clk. to chief justice Fred. M. Vinson, 1951-52; adminstrv. asst. to Ill. Gov. Stevenson, 1952-53; spl. asst. to Adlai E. Stevenson in presdl. campaign, 1952, 56; ptnr. firm Stevenson, Rifkind & Wirtz, Chgo., N.Y.C. and Washington, 1955-61; chmn. FCC, Wash., 1961-63; exec. v.p., gen. counsel, dir. Ency. Brit., Chgo., 1963-65; ptnr. Sidley Austin Brown & Wood, Chgo., 1965-91, sr. counsel, 1991—. Former trustee, past chmn. bd., adv. trustee Rand Corp.; past chmn. Chgo. Ednl. TV; chmn. pub. rev. bd. Arthur Andersen & Co., 1974-83; chmn. bd. trustees Carnegie Corp. of N.Y., 1993-97, trustee, 1987-97; Annenberg U. prof. com. policy and law Northwestern U., 1987-2003; dir. Annenberg Washington Program, 1987-96. Author: Equal Time: The Private Broadcasters and the Public Interest, 1964; co-author: Presidential Television, 1973, Electronics and the Future, 1977, For Great Debates, 1987, Abandoned in the Wasteland: Children, Television, and the First Amendment, 1995; contbr.: As We Knew Adlai. Trustee Notre Dame U., 1964-77, 83-96, life trustee, 1996, Mayo Found., 1973-81; trustee Northwestern U., 1975-87, life trustee, 1987—; co-chmn. presdl. debates LWV, 1976, 80, presdl. debate commn., 1993—; bd. govs. Pub. Broadcasting Svc., 1973-80, chmn. bd., 1978-80; chmn. bd. overseers Jewish Theol. Sem., 1974-77; trustee Chgo. Orchestral Assn., 1975-87, life trustee, 1987—. With AUS, 1944-46. Named 1 of Am.'s 10 Outstanding Young Men 1961; recipient George Foster Peabody Broadcasting award, 1961; Ralph Lowell award, 1982 Fellow Am. Bar Found., Am. Acad. Arts and Scis.; mem. Northwestern U. Alumni Assn. (medal 1978), Comml. Club (pres. 1987-88), Chgo. Club, Century Club (N.Y.C.). Democrat. Office: Sidley Austin Brown & Wood Ste 4800 10 S Dearborn St Chicago IL 60603 E-mail: nminow@sidley.com.

MINTON, DENISE DAWSON, special education educator; b. Argentia, Nfld., Can., Nov. 29, 1956; d. Clifford Bernard and Marguerite (Hines) Dawson; m. Donald E. Minton Jr., Feb. 8, 1975; children: Misty, Erica, Donald, Kevin. BA, Lynchburg Coll., 1978. Cert. tchr., Va., N.C. Tchr. spl. edn. Lynchburg Tng. Sch., Madison Heights, Va., 1977-83, edn. supr., 1979-80; tchr. spl. edn. Horry County Schs., Conway, S.C., 1983-85, Brunswick County Schs., Ash, N.C., 1987—. Counselor Hope Harbor Home, Brunswick County, 1989-91. Recipient Spl. Olympics Coaches award Ash Parks and Recreation, 1989, 90. Mem. Profl. Book Club. Episcopalian. Avocations: comping, hiking, swimming, water skiing, cooking. Office: Waccamaw Elem Sch RR 1 Ash NC 28420-9801

MINTON, JOHN DEAN, historian, educator; b. Cadiz, Ky., July 29, 1921; s. John Ernest and Daisy Dean (Wilson) M.; m. Betty Jo Redick, June 8, 1947; children— John Dean, James Ernest. AB in Edn, U. Ky., 1943, MA in History, 1947; PhD, Vanderbilt U., 1959. Instr. history U. Miami, Fla., 1951; tchr. Broward County Pub. Sch. Sys., U. Miami evening divsn., 1951-53; prin. Trigg County (Ky.) H.S., 1953-58; prof. history We. Ky. U., Bowling Green, 1958-86, ret., dean Grad. Coll., 1964-71, v.p. for adminstrv. affairs, 1970-79, interim pres., 1979, v.p. for student affairs, 1981-86, part-time prof., 1986-96. Author: The New Deal in Tennessee, 1932-1938, 1979; contbr. articles to profl. jours. Former mem. Gen. Bd. Discipleship, United Meth. Ch.; with Louisville Bd. Discipleship; lay spkr. Louisville Conf. Meth. Ch.; bd. dirs. Higher Edn. Found., Meth. Ch., Jesse Stuart Found. Served with USNR, 1943-46. Mem. NEA, Ky. Edn. Assn., So. Hist. Assn., Ky. Hist. Soc., Bowling Green C. of C. (bd. dirs.), Civitan Club (pres. Cadiz 1956), Phi Alpha Theta, Phi Eta Sigma, Kappa Delta Pi Home: 645 Ridgecrest Way Bowling Green KY 42104-3818

MINTY, JUDITH MAKINEN, poet, literature and creative writing educator; b. Detroit, Aug. 5, 1937; d. Karl Jalmer and Margaret (Hunt) Makinen; m. Edgar Sheldon Minty (dec. July 2002); children: Lora Ann, John Reed, Ann Sheldon. BS, Ithaca Coll., 1957; MA, Western Mich. U., 1973; PhD (hon.), Mich. Technol. U., 1997. Asst. prof., vis. poet-in-residence Ctrl. Mich. U., Mount Pleasant, Mich., 1977-78; assoc. prof., vis. poet-in-residence Syracuse U., N.Y., 1979; prof., poet-in-residence Humboldt State U., Arcata, Calif., 1982-93, prof. emerita English, 1993—. Guest lectr. English Grand Valley State U., Allendale, Mich., 1974-77; poet-in-prison pilot project Muskegon Correctional Facility, Mich., 1977; vis. poet-in-residence Interlochen Ctr. for Arts, Mich., 1980, U. Oreg., Eugene, 1983, U. Nebr., Lincoln, 1994, U. Alaska, Anchorage, 1999-2000; vis. lectr. English U. Calif., Santa Cruz, 1981-82. Author: (books of poetry) Lake Songs and Other Fears, 1974 (U.S. award 1973), Yellow Dog Journal, 1979, reprinted 1992, Letters to My Daughters, 1980, In the Presence of Mothers, 1981, Counting the Losses, 1986, Dancing the Fault, 1991, The Mad Painter Poems, 1996, 2d edit., 2003, Walking With the Bear: Selected and New Poems, 2000. John Atherton fellow in poetry Breadloaf Writers Conf., 1974, Yaddo fellow, 1978, 79, 82; recipient Eunice Tietjens award Poetry mag., 1974, Montalvo award for Excellence in Poetry, 1989, Mark Twain award Soc. for Study of Midwestern Lit., Mich. State U., 1998; Creative Artists grantee Mich. Coun. for Arts, 1981, 83, Found. for Women Residency grantee Hopscotch House, 1994; Charles H. Hackley Disting. lectr., Hackley Libr., Muskegon, Mich., 1996. Mem. PEN (syndicated fiction awards 1985, 86, Calif. fiction award 1987), Poetry Soc. Am., Acad. Am. Poets, Associated Writing Programs, Nat. Audubon Soc., Wilderness Soc., Sierra Club, Nature Conservancy. Avocations: birding, hiking, environmentalist. Home: 7113 S Scenic Dr New Era MI 49446-8005 E-mail: judminty@aol.com.

MINTZ, JOEL ALAN, law educator; b. N.Y.C., July 24, 1949; s. Samuel Isaiah and Eleanor (Streichler) M.; m. Meri-Jane Rochelson, Aug. 25, 1975; children: Daniel Rochelson, Robert Eli. BA, Columbia U., 1970, LLM, 1982, JSD, 1989; JD, NYU, 1974. Bar: N.Y. 1975, U.S. Dist. Ct. (so. and ea. dists.) N.Y. 1982, U.S. Ct. Appeals (2d cir.) 1982. Atty. enforcement div. EPA, Chgo., 1975-76, chief atty. case devel. unit, 1977-78, policy advisor to regional adminstr., 1979; sr. litigation atty. Office Enforcement, EPA, Washington, 1980-81; asst. prof. environ. law Nova U. Law Ctr., Ft. Lauderdale, Fla., 1982-85, assoc. prof., 1985-87, prof., 1987—. Author: State and Local Government Environmental Liability, 1994, Enforcement At the EPA: High Stakes, 1995; author: (with others) Environmental Law, 4th edit., 2000, State and Local Taxation and Finance In A Nutshell, 2nd edit., 2000; contbr. articles to legal jours. and treatises. Mem. ABA, Environ. Law Inst. Assocs., Fla. Bar (assoc.), Internat. Coun. Environ. Law, Internat. Union for Conservation of Nature (commn. on environ. law), Assn. Am. Law Schs. (exec. com., state and local govt. law sect.), Ctr. for Progressive Regulation (scholar), Phi Alpha Delta. Avocations: reading, fitness walking, canoeing. Home: 2060 NE 209th St Miami FL 33179-1628 Office: Nova Southeastern U Law Ctr 3305 College Ave Fort Lauderdale FL 33314-7721 E-mail: mintzj@nsu.law.nova.edu.

MINTZ, NORMAN NELSON, investment banker, educator; b. N.Y.C., Sept. 18, 1934; s. Alexander and Rebecca (Nelson) M.; m. Marcia Lynn Belford, Aug. 27, 1960; children: Geoffrey Belford, Douglas Nelson. AB, Bucknell U., 1955; PhD, NYU, 1966. Asst. gen. mgr. Ross Products Inc., N.Y.C., 1957-59; media analyst Benton & Bowles Inc., N.Y.C., 1960; asst. prof. fin. Syracuse U., 1965-69; asst. prof. econs. Columbia U., N.Y.C., 1968-72, assoc. dean Grad. Sch. Arts and Scis., 1972-77, dep. provost, 1977-80, acting provost, 1978-79, sr. v.p., 1980-82, exec. v.p. for acad. affairs, 1982-89, exec. v.p., ret., 1990—; mng. dir. Loeb Ptnrs. Corp., 1990—. Economist U.S.-P.R. Commn. on Status of P.R., 1965-66; bd. dirs. Loeb Holding Corp., Loeb Ptnrs. Corp., Sr. Network, Inc., Comm. Mgmt. Sys., Inc., Exxel/Atmos, Inc., Evare, L.L.C., Intersections, Inc., Loeb Arbitrage Fund. Author: Monetary Union and Economic Integration, 1970; contbr. articles to profl. jours. Dir. Citizens Budget Commn., Conf. on Jewish Social Studies, 1975—94, N.Y.C. Coun. on Econ. Edn., 1993—. 1st lt. Signal Corps. U.S. Army, 1955—57. Earhart Found. fellow, 1963-65 Mem. Am. Econ. Assn., Am. Fin. Assn., Royal Econ. Soc., India House Club, Phi Beta Kappa, Omicron Delta Epsilon. Office: care Loeb Ptnrs 61 Broadway New York NY 10006-2701 E-mail: nmintz@loebpartners.com.

MINTZ, PATRICIA POMBOY, secondary education educator; b. N.Y.C., Sept. 1, 1934; d. Emil and Bertha (Armel) Pomboy; m. Edward A. LeVay Jr.; 1 child from previous marriage, Peter Graham Mintz. AB in History with honors, Barnard Coll., 1956; AM in English, Tchrs. Coll., N.Y.C., 1967, EdD, 1980. Cert. English tchr., adminstr. and supr. dist. level. English, history tech. Fieldston Sch., N.Y.C., 1960-67; English chmn. Byram Hills Schs., Armonk, N.Y., 1967-72; supr. dist. English/lang. arts North Shore Schs., Glen Head, N.Y., 1972—. Instr. English Columbia U., 1966; dir. Upward Bound English Program, Fieldston Sch., 1967; program chmn. L.I. Writing Conf., 1984-90; program chair N.Y. State English Coun. Conf., 1993. Editor: America, The Melting Pot Anthology, 1969; author: Film Guides for Educational Films, 1972-73. N.Y. Found. for Arts grantee, 1988—, Title III Matching Grant, Writing Program for North Shore Schs., 1977-78. Mem. ASCD, Nat. Coun. Tchrs. English, N.Y. State English Coun., L.I. Lang. Arts Coun., Coun. Adminstrs. and Suprs.

MINTZ, SIDNEY WILFRED, anthropologist; b. Dover, N.J., Nov. 16, 1922; s. Solomon and Fromme Leah (Tulchin) M.; m. June Mirken, May 1952 (div. Dec. 1962); children: Eric Daniel, Elizabeth Rachel; m. Jacqueline Wei, June 6, 1964. BA, Bklyn. Coll., 1943; PhD, Columbia U., 1951; MA, Yale U., 1963. Mem. faculty dept. anthropology Yale U., New Haven, 1951-74, prof., 1963-74; prof. anthropology Johns Hopkins U., Balt., 1974-97, prof. emeritus, 1997—. Vis. prof. anthropology MIT, 1964-65, Princeton U., 1975-76; directeur d'études associé E.P.H.E., Paris, 1970-71; professeur associé. Coll. de France, Paris, 1988; editor Yale U. Press Caribbean Series, 1957-74; Lewis Henry Morgan lectr. U. Rochester, 1972; Christian Gauss lectr. Princeton U., 1979; Harry Hoijer lectr. UCLA, 1981; Duijker Found. lectr., Amsterdam, 1988; Rodney lectr. U. Warwick, 1993; W.E.B. DuBois lectr. Howard U., 2003; Goveia lect. U. W.I., 2003. Author: (with others) People of Puerto Rico, 1956, Worker in the Cane, The Life History of a Puerto Rican Sugar Cane Worker, 1960, Caribbean Transformations, 1974, Sweetness and Power, 1985, (with Richard Price) The Birth of African-American Culture, 1992, Tasting Food, Tasting Freedom, 1996. Served with USAAF, 1943-46. Recipient William Clyde DeVane medal Yale U., 1972, Huxley medalist Royal Anthrop. Inst., 1994, disting. lectr. award Am. Anthrop. Assn., 1996; named Social Sci. Rsch. Coun. Faculty Rsch. fellow, 1958-59, Guggenheim fellow, 1957, Fulbright fellow, 1966-67, 70-71, NEH fellow, 1978-79, Smithsonian Inst. Regents' fellow, 1986-87. Fellow Am. Anthrop. Assn.; mem. Am. Ethnol. Soc. (v.p., pres.-elect 1967-68), Royal Anthrop. Soc. Gt. Britain and Ireland, Am. Acad. Arts and Scis., Sigma Xi. Home: 111 Hamlet Hill Rd #107 Baltimore MD 21210 E-mail: mintzsw@jhu.edu.

MIRABAL, ANGELA PRINCE, special education educator; b. Tuscaloosa, Ala., Jan. 25, 1967; d. Bennie Andrew and Mary Clara (McCollum) Prince; m. Daniel Mirabal, Feb. 9, 1996. BS in Specific Learning Disabilities, U. Ala., 1991; MA in Reading, Nova Southeastern U., Ft. Lauderdale, Fla., 1994; postgrad., Nova U., Ft. Lauderdale. Tchr. Coral Springs (Fla.) Mid. Sch., 1991-95; ESE specialist Ft. Lauderdale H.S., 1995—. Trainer

N.J. Writing Project of Tex., Ft. Lauderdale, 1994—; dept. head exceptional student edn. Coral Springs Mid. Sch., 1994-95. Mem. ASCD, Nat. Reading Assn., Fla. Reading Assn., Coalition of Essential Schs., South Fla. Cr. Ednl. Leaders. Democrat. Baptist. Avocations: reading, listening to music, travel. Home: 6811 Bayfront Cir Margate FL 33063-7031 Office: Fort Lauderdale HS 1600 NE 4th Ave Fort Lauderdale FL 33305-3002

MIRACLE, DONALD EUGENE, elementary school educator; b. Pineville, Ky., Jan. 4, 1952; s. Oliver Eugene and Ruth Edna (Borah) M.; m. Peggy Sifton; children: Mark Buis, David Buis. BS in Edn., Cumberland Coll., 1975; cert., Ea. Ky. U., 1984. Cert. tchr. Ky. Tchr. Bell County Bd. Edn., Pineville, 1975—. Ky. Ednl. Reform Act Fellows Cohort II, Frankfort, Ky., 1993—. Mem. adminstrv. coun. Covenant United Meth. Ch., Middlesboro, Ky., 1994-96, mem. choir, 1992—, dir. hand bell choir, 1997-98; tchr. leader Ky. Mid. Grades Math. Tchr. Network. Mem. NEA, Nat. Coun. Tchrs. Math., Ky. Edn. Assn., Cumberland Coun. of Tchrs. of Math. (exec. coun., advisor 1993-94, pres.-elect 1995-96). Avocations: gemology, fishing, motorcycling, bowling. Home: PO Box 222 Middlesboro KY 40965-0222 Office: Yellow Creek Elem 4840 Cumberland Ave Middlesboro KY 40965-2704

MIRCHANDANEY, ARJAN SOBHRAJ, mathematics educator; b. Hydrabad, Sind, India, Aug. 13, 1923; s. Sobhraj Gurmukhdas and Jamuna Mohanlal (Advani) M.; m. Padma Kalachand Lalwani, Oct. 20, 1958; 1 child, Haresh. BS, U. Bombay, India, 1943; MS, U. Bombay, 1946; PhD, U. Conn., 1984. Asst. prof. math. D.G. Nat. Coll., U. Bombay, 1943-47; lectr. Jai Hind Coll. U. Bombay, 1949-60, lectr. postgrad. classes, 1953-78, prof. math. Jai Hind Coll., 1960-69, prof., head dept. math. Jai Hind Coll., 1969-78; asst. prof. math. No. Ill. U., DeKalb, 1979-80, Knox Coll., Galesburg, Ill., 1982-85; prof. math. Defiance (Ohio) Coll., 1986—. Coord. math. coll. sci. improvement program for Bombay colls., 1971-74; vis. prof. math. St. Lawrence U., Canton, N.Y., 1978; vis. asst. prof. Cornell U., Ithaca, N.Y., 1985-86; postgrad. lectr. U. Bombay, 1953-78; external examiner Shivaji U., Kolhapur, India, 1972-74; presenter Internat. Congress on Relativity and Gravitation, Munich, 1988, Internat. Congress History of Sci., Munich, 1989, Internat. Conf. on Space, Time, Gravitation, St. Petersburg, Russia, 1996. Author: A Course in Elementary Trigonometry, 1954, 3d edit., 1965; contbr. articles, papers to profl. jour., chpt. to book. Mem. Nat. Ctr. for Performing Arts, Bombay, 1969-78. Grantee Defiance Coll., 1989. Mem. Am. Math. Soc., Math. Assn. Am. Achievements include research in field theory of electromagnetics and photic field theory. Home: 112 Ivy Brook Ln Chapel Hill NC 27516-8083 Office: Defiance Coll 701 N Clinton St Defiance OH 43512-1610

MIRCOVICH, KAREN S. principal; b. Corpus Christi, Tex., Apr. 2, 1957; d. Richard Dix and Dolores Marie (Griffith) M. BA in Edn. Curriculum-Instrn. cum laude, Tex. A&M U., 1979; MS in Edn. Curriculum-Instrn., Corpus Christi State U., 1992. Cert. elem. tchr., Tex., ednl. diagnostician, mid-mgr. Elem. tchr. Gregory-Portland (Tex.) Ind. Sch. Dist., 1980-89, Elizabeth Cook Primary Sch., Ingleside, Tex., 1989—, Gilbert J. Mircovich Elem., Ingleside, Tex., 1998—2000, prin., 2000—. Mem. Tex. Tchrs. Assn. (treas. 1988-89), Tex. Elem. Prin. Suprs. Assn., Phi Theta Kappa, Delta Kappa Gamma. Home: 1404 Austin St Portland TX 78374-2405

MIRENBURG, BARRY LEONARD, publishing executive, educator; b. N.Y.C., Feb. 16, 1952; s. Fred and Mildred (Solomon) M. BS, Mercy Coll., 1979; BFA, Cooper Union, 1980; MBA, N.Y. Inst. of Tech., 1983; MA, Columbia U., 1983, postgrad., 1983—; MFA, Syracuse U., 1990; postgrad., Columbia U. Tchrs. Coll., 1997. Pres., pub. Barlenmir House, N.Y.C., 1972—; pres., owner Barlenmir House Theatres, Inc., N.Y.C., 1978—; head Design Graphics N.Y. Inst. of Tech., N.Y.C., 1979—; pres., creative dir. The Corp. Communications Group, N.Y.C., 1985—, Mirenburg & Co., N.Y.C., 1985—. Instr. unranked Parsons Sch. of Design, N.Y.C., 1979—, coord. computer graphics, 1990-91; asst. prof. Fashion Inst. of Tech., N.Y.C., 1979-81; corp. art dir. Music Sales/Quick Fox, N.Y.C., 1982-85; adj. assoc. prof. Grad.. Sch. Coll. of New Rochelle, N.Y., 1985—; founder, exec. dir. Am. Health and Fitness Alliance, 1998—. Recipient more than 125 awards and honors for art and design; Fulbright scholar, 1991. Mem. AAUP, Nat. Coun. Art Adminstrs., Am. Inst. Graphic Arts, Soc. Publ. Designers, Am. Ctr. for Design, Art Dirs. Club, Soc. Indsl. Designers, Coll. Art Assn., Mensa. Home and Office: 301 E 38th St New York NY 10016-2750

MIRICH, DAVID GAGE, secondary education language educator; b. Rock Springs, Wyo., June 17, 1956; s. John Jack and Kay Marie (Garvin) M. Student, U. de Filologia, Sevilla, Spain, 1981-82; BA in Psychology, Dakota Western U., 1981; teaching cert., U. Colo., 1989; postgrad., U. de Complutense, Madrid, 1991, Universidad de Salamanca, Spain, 1993; MA in Bilingual/Spl. Edn., U. Colo., 1995; postgrad., 1994—. Pvt. practice tchr., interpreter, Sevilla, 1981-83; tchr. bilingual Horace Mann Middle Sch., Denver (Colo.) Pub. Schs., 1989-92; tchr. bilingual/ESOL coord. North High Sch., Denver (Colo.) Pub. Schs., 1992—. Tchr. on spl. assignment, secondary bilingual and ESOL edn. Denver Pub. Schs., 1994-95. Founder, chmn. Boulderiety Conv., Boulder, Colo., 1989-92; candidate Boulder Valley Sch. Bd., 1989; founder, pres. Front Range Children's Orthodontic Fund, Denver, 1991-92. With USN, 1974-75. Named Vol. of Week., Vol. Boulder (Colo.) County, 1987, Hero of the Week, Rocky Mountain News, 1994. Mem. Nat. Assn. Bilingual Edn. (Nat. Bilingual Tchr. of Yr. 1994), Colo. Assn. Bilingual Edn. (v.p. 1993-95, Colo. Bilingual Tchr. of Yr., 1994). Avocations: horses, breeding dogs, languages, travel, real estate restoration. Home: 2224 Hooker St Denver CO 80211-5043 Office: West HS 9th and Elati Sts Denver CO 80203

MIRK, JUDY ANN, retired elementary educator; b. Victorville, Calif., June 10, 1944; d. Richard Nesbit and Corrine (Berghoefer). BA in Social Sci., San Jose (Calif.) State U., 1966, cert. in teaching, 1967; MA in Edn., Calif. State U., Chico, 1980. Cert. elem. edn. tchr., Calif. Profl. psychology trainee John F. Kennedy U., Orinda, Calif., 1997—99; tchr. Cupertino (Calif.) Union Sch. Dist., 1967-95; lead tchr. lang. arts Dilworth Sch., San Jose, 1988-90, mem. supt.'s adv. team, 1986-90, mem. student study team, 1987-95; ret. Mem. student study team, 1987-95; mem. Dilworth Sch. Site Coun., 1981-95. Mem. The Commonwealth Club of Calif, Phi Mu. Green Party. Avocations: photography, natural history, watercolors. Home: 2075 Redwood Dr Santa Cruz CA 95060-1238

MIRKIN, GABE BARON, allergist, pediatrician, medical writer, educator, radio personality, talk show host; b. Brookline, Mass., June 18, 1935; s. Mitchell and Vera (Baron) M.; children: Gene, Jan, Jill, Geoffrey, Kenny; m. Diana Purdie Rich, 1998. BA, Harvard U., 1957; MD, Baylor U., 1961. Diplomate Am. Bd. Pediatrics, Sub Bd. Allergy, Am. Bd. Allergy and Immunology, Am. Bd. Sports Medicine. Resident in pediatrics Mass. Gen. Hosp., Boston, 1961-63; fellow allergy, immunology, dermatology Johns Hopkins Hosp., Balt., 1963-65; allergy, immunology, dermatology, sports medicine pvt. practice, Silver Spring, Md., 1966—. Tchg. fellow pediat. Harvard Med. Sch., 1962-63; tchg. fellow allergy and immunology Johns Hopkins Med. Sch., 1963-65; asst. prof. dept. phys. edn. U. Md., College Park, 1976-83; assoc. clin. prof. dept. pediat. Georgetown U. Sch. of Medicine, 1984—. Author: The Sportsmedicine Book, 1978, Getting Thin, 1983, Dr. Gabe Mirkin's Fitness Clinic, 1986, The Complete Sportsmedicine Book for Women, 1985, 2d rev. edit. 1991; (with Shangold) Women and Exercise, 1988, Dr. Gabe Mirkin's Fatfree, Flavorfull Book, 1995; (with Diana Mirkin) The 20 Gram Diet, 1995, The 20/30 Fat and Fiber Diet Plan, Dr. Gabe Mirkins Pocket Guide to Fitness & Sports; (with Rich) The Whole Grains Cookbook, 1997, The Good Food Book, 2001, Healthy Heart Miracle, 2004; author (newsletter) The Mirkin Report, 1990—; columnist: N.Y. Times, 1978-89, United Features, 1989-94, Washington Post, 1976, Singer Media Corp., 1994-99; appearances on P.M. Mag. WDVM-TV, Washington, 1979, House Party, NBC TV, 1990, The Learning Channel; host internationally syndicated radio talk show, 1996—; daily radio spots on fitness and nutrition, CBS Radio Stations News Svc., 1979—; host talk show on health fitness and nutrition, KMOX Radio, St. Louis, 1982-98; nightly talk show host NBC Washington, WRC, 1982-84, 87—, WNTR, 1984-86; weekly spots for Physicians Radio Network, 1984-85; daily talk show syndicated by Sun Radio Network, 1992; weekly talk show WEEI, Boston, 1993-94, others; columnist and contbg. editor to health and fitness mags.; contbr. articles to profl. jours., chpts. to books. Major USAF, 1968-70. Fellow Am. Coll. Allergists, Am. Assn. Cert. Allergists, Am. Assn. for Clin. Immunology and Allergy, Am. Acad. Pediatrics, Am. Acad. Allergy and Immunology. Avocation: bicycle tandem riding. Office: 10901 Connecticut Ave Kensington MD 20895-1645 E-mail: gabe@drmirkin.com.

MIRONE-BARTZ, DAWN, secondary school and community college educator; b. Mt. Vernon, N.Y., Sept. 21, 1963; d. Robert and Joann Mirone (Perrotta) M.; m. Greg Bartz; 1 child, Katherine. BA in Journalism and Speech Comm., U. R.I., 1985; MA in Social Sci. Edn., Columbia U., 1987; cert. in social scis. and English, Calif. State U., Long Beach, 1991; postgrad., U. Mass., 1995, Calif. State U., Fullerton, 1996—. Cert. tchr., Calif, N.Y. Reporter Std. Times, North Kingstown, R.I., 1984-85; tchg. asst. Greenwich (Conn.) H.S., 1985-86; journalism and English tchr. Evander Childs H.S., Bronx, 1986-88; dir. edn. Bellwood Med. Health Ctr., Bellflower, Calif., 1988-89; social sci. and English tchr. Regency H.S., Long Beach, 1989-90; social sci., English, speech, and journalism tchr. Laguna Beach (Calif.) H.S., 1990—, activities dir., 1992-95, mem. scholarship com., 1991, 94; journalism instr. Saddleback Coll., Mission Viejo, Calif., 1994-97; cultural diversity coord. Laguna Beach (Calif.) H.S., 1993-96. Mem. citywide youth violence commn. City of Laguna Beach/Sch. Dist., 1992-94; sch. coord. Close Up Washington, Laguna Beach, 1991—. Recipient Nat. Svc. award PTA, 1993; grantee Laguna Beach City Coun., 1992, Recognition award for Journalism, 1994. Mem. Am. Polit. Sci. Assn., Am. Scholastic Press Assn. (1st pl. award 1994, 95, 96, 97), Journalism Education Assn., Quill & Scroll Soc. (Internat. 1st pl. award 1994, 2d place 1996), Columbia U. Press Assn. (2d pl. award 1997). Avocations: motor cross racing, skiing, rollerblading. Office: Laguna Beach HS 625 Park Ave Laguna Beach CA 92651-2340

MIRUCKI, MAUREEN ANN, retired academic administrator; b. Lima, NY, May 23, 1937; d. Loring Francis and Margaret M. (Keough) Donegan; m. Charles J. Mirucki, May 27, 1967; children: Molly, Marc. BS, Nazareth Coll., 1958; MS, Syracuse (N.Y.) U., 1966. Cert. bus. edn. tchr., N.Y. Tchr. East Bloomfield (N.Y.) Schs., 1958-59, North Syracuse (N.Y.) Schs., 1959—97. Mem. bus. staff Syracuse U., 1967-69; chairperson bus. dept. Cicero (N.Y.) North Syracuse High Sch., 1986-97. Mem. Bus. Tchrs. Assn. N.Y. State, Delta Phi Epsilon. Avocations: piano, golf, skiing, travel. Home: 5732 Pierson Rd Fayetteville NY 13066-9640

MIRVIS, DAVID MARC, health administrator, cardiologist, educator; b. Hampton, Va., Dec. 20, 1945; s. Allan and Lena (Sear) M.; m. Arlynn Shara Katz, June 30, 1968; children: Simcha Zev, Tova Aliza, Shoshana Fruma. Student, Yeshiva Coll., N.Y.C., 1966, MD, 1970. Diplomate Am. Bd. Internal Medicine. Intern U. Tenn., Memphis, 1970-71, fellow, resident, 1973-75, asst., assoc. prof., 1973-83, prof., 1983—, assoc. dean, 1987-97, dir. divsn. health svcs. and policy rsch., 1997-99, dir. Ctr. for Health Svcs. Rsch., 2000—; fellow, cardiovascular physiology NIH, Bethesda, Md., 1971-73. Chief of cardiology Memphis VA Med. Ctr., 1983-87, chief of staff, 1987-97; pres. Rsch., Inc., 1990-94. Author, editor: Body Surface Electrocardiographic Mapping, 1988; author: Electrocardiography: A Physiologic Approach; contbg. editor Jour. Electrocardiology, 1984—, Am. Jour. Noninvasive Cardiology, 1986—, Am. Jour. Cardiology, 1999—. Grantee NIH, 1975-89. Fellow Am. Heart Assn. (coun. on circulation), Am. Coll. Cardiology; mem. Am. Soc. Clin. Investigation., So. Soc. Clin. Rsch. Democrat. Home: 5676 Redding Ave Memphis TN 38120-1848 Office: U Tenn 66 N Pauline St Ste 463 Memphis TN 38105-5126

MISAWA, MITSURU, finance educator; b. Ina-shi, Japan, Sept. 18, 1936; came to U.S., 1996; s. Fukuji and Kaneyo (Haba) M.; m. Kuniko Ishii, Mar. 6, 1965; children: Anne Megumi, Marie Lei. LLB, Tokyo U., 1960; LLM, Harvard U., 1964; MBA, U. Hawaii, 1965; PhD, U. Mich., 1967. Officer Indsl. Bank Japan, Tokyo, 1960-89; dir. IBJ Lease, Tokyo, 1989, pres. N.Y.C., 1989—; prof. fin. U. Hawaii, Honolulu, 1996—, dir. ctr. Japanese global investment fin., 1998—. Mem. Waialae Country Club, Tokyo Am. Club. Avocation: golfing. Home: Imperial Plaza 725 Kapiolani Blvd Apt 811 Honolulu HI 96813 Office: Univ Hawaii Dept fin Econs Instn 2404 Maile Way Honolulu HI 96822-2223 E-mail: misawa@busadm.cba.hawaii.edu.

MISCELLA, MARIA DIANA, humanities educator; b. N.Y.C., July 11, 1929; d. Nicola and Giovanna (Tangorra) Torelli; m. Emilio Miscella, Feb. 27, 1954 (dec. Sept. 30, 1996); children: Delia, Marisa, Giuliana. Tchr. Degree, Istituto Magistrale, Lecce, Italy, 1946; postgrad., U. Naples, 1946-48; BA, Hunter Coll., 1954, MA, 1972. Cert. secondary educator, N.Y. state, N.Y.C. English corr. GE Co., Rome, 1950-51; corr. Spanish & French Pettinos Import & Export Co., N.Y.C., 1952-53; tchr. Italian Harrison (N.Y.) H.S., 1967-87, St. John's U., Queens, N.Y., 1987-89; lectr. Italian various orgsn., N.Y. State, 1987—; lectr. Italian lit. and history various colls. and univs., N.Y., 1987—. Moderator of club Harrison (N.Y.) H.S., 1967-87. Mem. Little Neck (N.Y.) Civic Assn., 1970-95, Am. Assn. Ret. People, Douglaston, N.Y., 1994—; founder, treas. Italian Am. Women's Ctr., 1997—. Recipient scholarship Columbia U., 1954, Letter of Commendation, Bd. Regents, Albany, N.Y., 1980; named Woman of Yr., Consortium of L.I. Italian Am. Orgns., 1992. Mem. AAUW (hostess, v.p. 1990-93, cert. of commendation 1996), Am. Assn. Tchrs. of Italian (sec. Societa Onoraria Italica 1979-91), Ams. of Italian Heritage (bd. mem. 1982—), Sons of Italy (John Marino Lodge cultural com. mem 1994—, Merit award 1995), Assn. Italian Am. Educators (dir./historian by-laws com. 2000), N.Y. State United Tchrs., Am. Fedn. Tchrs., Nat. Italian Am. Found., Douglaston Women Club, Retirees Club. Roman Catholic. Avocations: reading, writing, travel, going to theatre, playing bridge.

MISENER, ALAN FRANCIS, science educator; b. Montague, Mass., Mar. 4, 1944; s. Alan Miller and Mary Lillian (Roache) M.; m. Christine Ann Camandona; children: Eric, Craig, Darren. BS, U. Mass., 1967; MS, Wesleyan U., 1973; MA, SUNY, Stonybrook, 1971. Cert. tchr., N.Y. Tchr. Three Village Schs., Setauket, N.Y., 1967—. Avocations: golf, vocal music. Office: Three Village Schs Nichols Rd Setauket NY 11733

MISHKIN, PAUL J. lawyer, educator; b. Trenton, N.J., Jan. 1, 1927; s. Mark Mordecai and Bella (Dworetsky) M.; m. Mildred Brofman Westover; 1 child, Jonathan Mills Westover. AB, Columbia U., 1947, JD, 1950; MA (hon.), U. Pa., 1971. Bar: N.Y. State bar 1950, U.S. Supreme Ct. bar 1958. Mem. faculty Law Sch. U. Pa., Phila., 1950-72; prof. law U. Calif., Berkeley, 1972-75, Emanuel S. Heller prof., 1975—2000, Emanuel S. Heller prof. emeritus, 2000—. Cons. City of Phila., 1953; reporter study div. jurisdiction between state and fed. cts. Am. Law Inst., 1960-65; mem. faculty Salzburg Seminar in Am. Studies, 1974; Charles Inglis Thompson guest prof. U. Colo., 1975; John Randolph Tucker lectr., 1978, Owen J. Roberts Meml. lectr., 1982; vis. fellow Wolfson Coll., Cambridge U., 1984; vis. prof. Duke U. Law Sch., 1989. Author: (with Morris) On Law in Courts, 1965, (with others) Federal Courts and the Federal System, 2d edit, 1973, 3d edit, 1988; contbr. articles to profl. jours. Trustee Jewish Publ. Soc. Am., 1966-75, Ctr. for Law in the Pub. Interest, 2001–; mem. permanent com. Oliver Wendell Holmes Devise, 1979-87. With USNR 1945-46. Rockefeller Found. rsch. grantee, 1956; Center for Advanced Study in Behavioral Scis. fellow, 1964-65; recipient Russell Prize for Excellence in Teaching, 1996. Fellow Am. Acad. Arts Scis., Am. Bar Found.; mem. Am. Law Inst., Order of Coif, Phi Beta Kappa. Home: 91 Stonewall Rd Berkeley CA 94705-1414 Office: U Calif Sch Law Boalt Hall Berkeley CA 94720

MISHNE, JUDITH MARKS, social work educator, psychotherapist; b. Cleve., Feb. 21, 1932; d. Moses Isaac and Lillian (Kemelman) Marks; (div.); 1 child, Jonathan. BS, U. Wis., 1953; MSW, Case Western Res. U., 1955; cert., Inst. of Psychoanalysis, Chgo., 1974; DSW, CUNY, 1981. Caseworker Akron (Ohio) Child Guidance Ctr., 1955—56, Cleve. Child Guidance Ctr., 1956-58, Jewish Family Svc., Cleveland Heights, 1959-62; sch. social worker Orange Bd. Edn., Pepper Pike, Ohio, 1962-66; unit supr. Bellefaire of Jewish Children's Bur., Cleve., 1964-66; assoc. prof. sch. of social svcs. adminstrn. U. Chgo., 1966-76; assoc. prof. sch. social work Columbia U., N.Y.C., 1977-79; from assoc. prof. to prof. sch. social work NYU, 1979—. Summer faculty mem. sch. social work Smith Coll., Northampton, Mass., 1975-82; cons. Pritzker Children's Hosp., Chgo., 1968-74, Madden Hosp., Chgo., 1973-75, Queens Child Guidance Clinic, Jamaica, N.Y., 1979-80, Roosevelt Hosp., N.Y.C., 1983, Jewish Family Svc., Hackensack, N.Y., 1986-87; vis. lectr. U. Haifa (Israel) Sch. Social Work, 1994. Author: Clinical Work With Children, 1983, Clinical Work With Adolescents, 1986, Evolution and Application of Clinical Theory: Perspectives From Four Psychologies, 1993, The Learning Curve: Elevating Children's Academic and Social Competence, 1996, Multiculturalism and the Therapeutic Process, 2002; editor: Psychotherapy and Training in Clinical Social Work, 1980; co-editor: (with others) Ego and Self Psychology: Group Intervention With Children and Adolescents, 1983. Named Disting. Practitioner in Social Work Nat. Academics of Practice, 1983; recipient Spencer Found. award NYU, 1987, Spl. Achievement award PhD Alumni Assn. CUNY, 1996; Vis. scholar Bar Ilan U. Sch. of Social Work, Israel, 1993, 94. Mem. Assn. of Child and Adolescent Therapists, Nat. Fedn. Socs. for Social Work, Coun. on Social Work Edn., Nat. Acad. of Practice in Social Work, Assn. for Psychoanalytic Self Psychology. Democrat. Home: 225 W 88th St # 4E New York NY 10024-2303 Office: NYU Sch of Social Work 2 Washington Sq N New York NY 10003-6669

MISKIEWICZ, SUSANNE PIATEK, educational administrator; d. Edward Walter and Charlotte Teresa (Kardel) Piatek; m. Randall Lee Grover; 1 child, Michelle Lee Grover Domenico; m. Raymond Richard Miskiewicz; children: Lisa Marie, Raymond Edward. BA, Newark State Coll., 1972; MA, Kean Coll., 1976. Cert. prin./supr., supr., reading specialist, elem. edn., nursery sch., N.J. Tchr. Linden (N.J.) Bd. Edn., 1973-79, 87-90, Linden Adult Sch., 1981-88, dir., 1986—88; tchr. Roselle (N.J.) Bd. Edn., 1991, New Providence (N.J.) Bd. Edn., 1991—2001, dept. head lang. arts K-12, coord. mid. coll., 1996-99, asst. adminstr., 1999—2001; edn. program devel. specialist N.J. Dept. Edn., 2002—. Cons., trainer N.J. Dept. Edn., Trenton, 1987-90; cons. Am. Guidance Svc., Minn., 1979—; mem. bd. edn. Linden, 1991-94, v.p., 1993-94; presenter NJEA Conv., 1976, Edn. Fair, Washington, 1973. Reviewer: Prep, Keymath, You and Your Small Wonder, Books 1 and 2, 1979-88. Treas. Kean U. Diversity Coun., Union, NJ, 2000—; sec., treas., v.p. PTA, Linden, 1984—92; mem., v.p. Gen. Pulaski Com., Linden, 1985—; mem., sec., v.p., treas. Linden Summer Theatre, 1978—85; leader Girl Scouts Am., Linden, 1987—91; trustee Linden Free Pub. Libr., 1999—; mem. Middlesex County Chamber of Commerce, 2002—, Middlesex County Work Investment Bd., 2002—; chair Middlesex County Curriculum Coun., 2002—; trustee St. Teresa' Ch., Linden, 1970—73; advisor St. Elizabeth's Ch. Altar Server Soc., 1994—98, lector, 1998—2002, eucharistic min., 2000—02. Scholar Holocaust Ctr. Kean U.; Jewish Labor Com. fellow. Mem. NEA, ASCD, Nat. Coun. Tchrs. English (state leader 1999-2002), Lang. and Literacy Assn., N.J. ASCD, Internat. Reading Assn., N.J. Reading Assn., N.J. Edn. Assn., N.J. Coun. Tchrs. English (bd. dirs. 1998—, treas. 2000), New Providence Edn. Assn. (pres. 1995-2001), Middlesex County C. of C., NJ Juvenile Justice Officers, Diversity Coun. 2000 (treas. 1998-2002), Phi Delta Kappa. Roman Catholic. Avocations: reading, crafts, golf. Home: 43 Palisade Rd Linden NJ 07036-3828 Office: NJ Dept Edn 1501 Livingston Ave N New Brunswick NJ 08902 E-mail: suem908@aol.com.

MISRA, RAGHUNATH PRASAD, physician, educator; b. Calcutta, W. Bengal, India, Feb. 1, 1928; came to U.S., 1964; s. Guru Prasad and Anandi M.; m. Therese Rettenmund, Sept. 13, 1963; children: Sima, Joya, Maya, Tara. BSc with honors, Calcutta U., 1948; MBBS, Med. Coll., Calcutta, 1953; PhD, McGill U., Montreal, Que., 1965. Diplomate Am. Bd. Anatomical and Clin. Pathology. Asst. prof., dir. kidney lab. U. Louisville Sch. Medicine, 1964-68; asso. investigator and dir. kidney lab Mt. Sinai Hosp., Cleve., 1968-73; asst. prof. Case Western Reserve Med. Sch., Cleve., 1973-76; asst. prof., dir. kidney lab. La. State U., Sch. Medicine, Shreveport, 1976-80, assoc. prof., 1980-86; prof. La. State U., Sch. of Medicine, Shreveport, 1986—98, emeritus prof., 1998—, dir. Ocular Pathology Lab., 1988—. Cons. VA Med. Ctr., Shreveport, 1977-98, EA Conway Meml. Hosp., Monroe, La., 1980-98. Author: Atlas of Skin Biopsy, 1983. Pres. India Assn. of Shreveport, 1979, 81. Recipient Tallisman Fellowship, Mt. Sinai Hosp., 1970-73. Fellow Am. Coll. Pathologists, Am. Soc. Clin. Pathologists, Am. Coll. of Internat. Physicians, U. Calcutta Med. Alumni Assn. Am. (pres. 1992-93), Sigma Xi (pres. 1987-89). Democrat. Hindu. Avocations: photography, travel. Office: La State U Sch Medicine 1501 Kings Hwy Shreveport LA 71103-4228 E-mail: rmisra@lsuhsc.edu.

MISSAL, JOSEPH BANNAN, mathematics and business educator; b. Waltham, Mass., Nov. 6, 1941; s. Joseph Benedict Jr. and Mary Alice (Bannan) M.; m. Anita Elizabeth Wiggs, July 24, 1965 (div. Mar. 1995); children: Amy Leeanne Shy, Daniel Casey, Bradley Benedict, John Wayland; m. JoAnne Murrah Smith, Oct. 31, 1995. BS, U.S. Mil. Acad., 1964; MS, U.S. Naval Postgrad. Sch., 1969; MSEd, James Madison U., 1993. Cert. Nat. Bd. Profl. Tchg. Stds., 02. Commd. 2d lt. U.S. Army, 1964, advanced through grades to col., 1987, ret., 1992; instr. Dominion Bus. Sch., Harrisonburg, Va., 1994; tchr. Teenage Parenting Programs Arlington (Va.) County Pub. Schs., 1994—. Dist. commr. Boy Scouts of Am., 1994—; info. specialist Smithsonian Mus., Washington, 1992—. Mem. Ops. Rsch. Soc. of Am., Nat. Bus. Edn. Assn., Nat. Coun Tchrs. of Math., Ind. Telephone Pioneers of Am., Assn. of U.S. Army, Armed Forces Comm. and Electronics Assn. Roman Catholic. Avocations: woodworking, scouting, dancing. Home: 306 N Lincoln St Arlington VA 22201-1730 E-mail: missalj@aol.com.

MISSAL, STEPHEN JOSEPH, art educator, portraitist; b. Albuquerque, Apr. 23, 1948; s. Joshua Morton and Pegge Lenore (McComb) M.; m. Elizabeth (Sperry); children: David J., Kele M. BFA, Wichita State U., Kans., 1970, MFA, 1972. Head art dept. White Mountain Sch., Littleton, NH, 1972-74; mem. art faculty N.E. Mo. State U., Kirksville, Mo., 1974-77; free-lance artist Denver, 1977-79; mem. art faculty Scottsdale C. C., Scottsdale, Ariz., 1979-84, Phoenix Coll., Mesa C.C., 1984—; mem. faculty, head of drawing Art Inst., Phoenix, 1996—. interim graphic design chmn., 1998—. Art adjudicator, 1974— ; staff artist Scottsdale Daily Progress, 1979-85; stage set designer Phoenix Little Theatre, 1978; Scottsdale Stagebrush Theatre, 1981. Co-author: Exploring Drawing for Animation, 2003; illustrator: The Field Guide to Rock Climbing and Mountaineering, 1974—, Wizards of the Coast role playing game; exhibited in group shows Tulsa Midwest Competition, 1972 (purchase award), 1973, 14th Midwest Exhbn., Joslyn Art Mus., Omaha (purchase award), 1976, Festival VIII (Scottsdale Ctr. for Arts Award), 1977; Springfield Mus. of Art Nat. Competition, 1987; Nat Forest Svc. Competition, 1991; Wyo. Stamp Competition top 40 exhibition, 1994; Sternberg Mus. Nat. Competition, 1999; LePreCon Regional Art Show Best Exhibit, 2001 Violinist Dartmouth Coll. Civic Symphony, 1972-74, Scottsdale Civic Orch., 1979—. Mem., Nat. Coll. Art Assn., Midwest Coll. Art Assn. Office: Art Inst Phoenix 2233 W Dunlap Phoenix AZ 85021 E-mail: flyingduckstudio@hotmail.com.

MISSAN, RICHARD SHERMAN, lawyer, educator; b. Oct. 5, 1933; s. Albert and Hannah (Hochberg) Missan; m. Aileen Louise Missan; children: Hliary, Andrew, Wendy. BA, Yale U., 1955, JD, 1958. Bar: NY 59, U.S. Dist. Ct. (so. and ea. dists.) NY 79, U.S. Ct. Appeals (2d cir.) 93. Assoc. Kaye, Scholer, Fierman, Hays & Handler, N.Y.C., 1962—67; ptnr. Schoenfeld & Jacobs, N.Y.C., 1968—78, Walsh & Frisch, N.Y.C., 1979—80, Gersten, Savage & Kaplowitz, N.Y.C., 1980—87; v.p., gen. counsel Avis, Inc., 1987—88; pvt. practice N.Y.C., 1988—. Spl. prof. law Hofstra U., 1988—; mem. panel of mediators U.S. Dist. Ct. (ea. dist.) NY. Revision author: Corporations, New York Practice Guide (Business and Commercial). Mem.: ABA, Assn. Bar City NY (mem. com. on corrections, chmn. subcom. on legis., chmn. subcom. on juvenile facilities, mem. com. on atomic energy, mem. com. on mcpl. affairs, mem. com. on housing and urban devel.), Fed. Bar Coun., NY State Bar Assn., Yale Club.

MISTACCO, VICKI E. foreign language educator; b. Bklyn., Nov. 18, 1942; d. Anthony Sebastian and Lucia (Lalli) M. BA, NYU, 1963; MA, Middlebury Coll., 1964; M of Philosophy, Yale U., 1968, PhD, 1972. Instr. French Wellesley Coll., Mass., 1968-72, asst. prof. French, 1972-78, assoc. prof. French, 1978-84, prof. French, 1984—, chmn., 1978-81. Nat. adv. bd. Sweet Briar Jr. Yr. in France, Va., 1978—. Contbr. articles to profl. jours. Fulbright fellow, 1963-64, Woodrow Wilson fellow, 1964-67; NEH fellow, 1983-84, 94-95. Mem.: SIEFAR, N.E. MLA, MLA, Soc. Internat. pour l'Etude des Femmes de l'Ancien Regime, Women in French, Am. Assn. Tchrs. French, Phi Beta Kappa. Democrat. Roman Catholic. Avocations: photography, travel. Office: Wellesley Coll Dept French 106 Central St Wellesley MA 02481-8268

MITCHAM, PATRICIA ANN HAMILTON, educator; b. El Paso, Tex., Sept. 8, 1942; d. Leverett Chandler and Annabelle Hamilton; m. Eugene Louis Mitcham III, Apr. 20, 1968; children: Shirley Dianne, Steven Craig. BA, Tex. Western U., 1964; postgrad., U. Ala., Huntsville, 1993—, U. Calif., Irvine, 1983-85; MA in English, U. Ala., 1997. Educator U. Tex., El Paso, 1964-66; instr. Hardin Simmons U., Abilene, Tex., 1966-67; tchr. El Paso Pub. Schs., 1968—70, 1974—79; English instr. Los Angeles Unified Sch. Dist., 1979-87; instr. English and social studies Huntsville (Ala.) City Schs., 1988—2003; ret., 2003. Tng. supr. of vols. Army Community Service, Ft. Bliss, Tex., 1971-73, asst. supr., 1973-74. Aerospace edn. officer CAP, 1987, dep. comdr., testing and pub. affairs officer; mem. Decatur Composite, Huntsville Composite. Mem. DAR, ASCD, Internat. Platform Assn., Nat. Coun. Tchrs. English, Calif. Soc. Mayflower Descs., Huntsville Gem and Mineral Soc. (rec. sec. 1988-89, pres. 1990-92), Kappa Delta Epsilon, Phi Delta Kappa. Independent. Episcopalian. Avocations: lapidary, painting, writing. Home: 1919 McDowling Dr SE Huntsville AL 35803-1221

MITCHELL, ANN MARGARET, nursing educator, psychiatric nurse practitioner; b. Pitts. d. John G. and Joan M. RN diploma, Pa. State U., 1974, BS, 1976, MS, 1979; PhD, U. Pitts., 1987. Clin. nurse specialist Western Psychiat. Inst. and Clinic, Pitts., 1985-89; pvt. practice, traveling nurse, cons. Pa., Calif, 1989-91; rsch. asst. prof. U. Pitts. Sch. Nursing, Pitts., 1991-95, asst. prof. nursing & psychiatry, 1995—. Bd. trustees Mayview State Hosp., 2001—. Collaborator: Interpersonal Relationship Skills Tng. Program, 1978, Rels. Tng., 1984. Mem. Exec. Women's Coun., Greater Pitts., Inc., 1992. Recipient traineeship Pa. State U., University Park, 1976-78, scholarship U. Pit ts., Pa., 1980-82; grantee faculty scholar Uppsala (Sweden) U., 1996, Keio (Japan) U., Tokyo, 1998. Mem. ANA, Am. Assn. Suicidology, Am. Found. Suicide Prevention (bd. dirs. Pitts. chpt.), Psychiat. Nurse Mgrs. Pa., Inc. (hon.), Assn. Clin. Nurse Specialists, Sigma Theta Tau, Kappa Delta Pi. Home: 5826 Nicholson St Pittsburgh PA 15217-2341 Office: Univ Pitts Sch Nursing # 415 Victoria Bldg 3500 Victoria St Pittsburgh PA 15213-2543

MITCHELL, BRENDA JOYCE, special education educator, consultant; b. Vidalia, Ga., Feb. 12, 1960; d. James Rayburn and Melva Joyce (Handley) M. AA in Liberal Arts, Brewton Parker Coll., 1979; BS in Spl. Edn., Augusta Coll., 1986, MEd, 1990, EdS, 2003. Interrelated resource tchr. Saluda (S.C.) Elem., 1986-89; self-contained spl. edn. tchr. Riverside Mid. Sch., Saluda, 1989-90; interrelated resource tchr. Levi White Elem., Augusta, Ga., 1990—96; spl. edn. cons. Richmond County Spl. Edn. Dept., 1996—. Vol. coord. Spl. Olympics, Augusta, 1990—; steering com. Learning/Intellectually Disabled Consortium, Augusta, 1990-92, chairperson, 1992-93. Mem. Coun. Exceptional Children (hospitality com. 1990-91, v.p. 1992-93, pres.-elect 1993-94, pres. 1994-95). Avocations: traveling, snow skiing, photography, reading. Home: 4750 Brookgreen Rd Augusta GA 30907

MITCHELL, BRIAN CHRISTOPHER, college president; b. Lowell, Mass., Feb. 23, 1953; s. Christopher Joseph and Doris Katherine (McEvoy) M.; m. Maryjane Murphy, June 28, 1975; children: Jeffrey Ryan, Patrick Joseph. BA, Merrimack Coll., 1974; MA, U. Rochester, 1976, PhD, 1981. Chair history dept. Anna Maria Coll., Paxton, Mass., 1982-85; program officer Nat. Endowment Humanities, Washington, 1985-91; pres. Commn. Ind. Colls. and Univs. Pa., Harrisburg, 1991-98, Washington and Jefferson Coll., Washington, Pa., 1998—. Instr. U. Mass., Lowell, 1977-85; adj. prof. George Mason U., Fairfax, Va., 1988-91; cons. Lowell Nat. Hist. Park, 1977-81, Lowell Heritage State Park, 1977-78. Author: The Paddy Camps: The Irish of Lowell, 1821-1861, 1988, On The North Bank, 1984; editor: Building the American Catholic City, 1986; contbg. author: From Paddy to Stud, 1986. Mem. Pa. Humanities Coun.; mem. Pa. Hist. and Mus. Commn.; chair Pa. selection com. Rhodes Scholarship Trust. Grantee Am. Coun. Learned Socs., 1985, NEH. Mem. Am. Hist. Assn. (Albert J. Beveridge award), Orgn. Am. Historians, Nat. Assn. Ind. Colls. and Univs. Roman Catholic. Office: Washington and Jefferson Coll Pres Office Washington PA 15301

MITCHELL, CAROL ELAINE, publishing executive, writer, educator; b. Columbus, Aug. 11, 1949; d. William Earl and Betty Jane (Tyson) Johnson; m. Larry Lindsay Mitchell, Mar. 3, 1973; 1 child, Mark Lindsay. BS, Ohio State U., 1971. Cert. English tchr. 7-12. Pres. Sparrow House Pub., Columbus, 1990—; instr. adult edn. Columbus Pub. Schs., 1992—. Judge Excellence in Writing Columbus Pub. Schs., 1992. Author: Paths of Blessings, 1991; editor, writer, prodr.: Columbus pub. schs. adult and juvenile literacy ednl. t.v., 1993. Mem. NAFE, NEA, Ohio Edn. Assn., Internat. Platform Assn. Home: 228 Sherbourne Dr Columbus OH 43219-2972 Office: 342 Sherbourne Dr Columbus OH 43219-2942

MITCHELL, CAROLYN COCHRAN, foundation administrator's executive assistant; b. Atlanta, Dec. 27, 1943; d. Clemern Covell and Agnes Emily (Veal) Cochran; m. W. Alan Mitchell, Aug. 30, 1964; 1 child, Teri Marie. AB magna cum laude, Mercer U., 1965, M in Svc. Mgmt., 1989. Caseworker Ga. Dept. Family & Children Svc., Macon, 1965-67, Covington, 1967-69; presch. dir. Southwestern Theol. Sem., Ft. Worth, 1969-70; presch. tchr., dir. Noah's Ark Day Care, Bowden, Ga., 1970-72, First Bapt. Ch., Bremen, Ga., 1972-75; preschool tchr., dir. Roebuck Pk. Bapt. Ch., Birmingham, Ala., 1975-79; freelance office mgr. and bookkeeper Macon, 1979-84; asst. to pres. Ga. Wesleyan Coll., Macon, 1984-98; asst. to pres., CEO Medcen Cmty. Health Found., Macon, 1998—. Exec. dir. Ga. Women of Achievement, 1991-95; dir. Macon Arts Alliance, 1987-91; mem. Cultural Plan Oversight Com., 1989-90. Active Get Out the Vote Task Force, Macon, 1981-95, Macon Symphony Guild, 1986-91; dep. registrar Bibb County Bd. Elections, Macon, 1981-95; asst. sec. Ronald McDonald House Ctrl. Ga., 1999-2000. Mem. AAUW (bd. dirs. Ga. chpt., v.p. 1991-93, chair coll.-univ. rels. com. 1993-94, bylaws com. 1991-92, v.p., sec., treas., historian, newsletter editor, Macon chpt., Named Gift Honoree 1988, 2000), NAFE, NOW, Women's Network for Change, Am. Mgmt. Assn., Presdl. Assts. in Higher Edn., Religious Coalition for Reproductive Choice, The Interfaith Alliance, Women's Polit. Orgn. Macon, Sigma Mu. Democrat. Baptist. E-mail: mitchell.carolyn@mccg.org.

MITCHELL, CONNIE, director; m. George Mitchell, Sr.; children: Carlata, George Jr. Tchr. adv. Office Adminstrv./Instrnl. Pers. Detroit Pub. Schs. Dir. Ednll. Enrichment Acad. Active Meth. Children's Home Soc. Named Middle Sch. Tchr. of Yr., Newsweek Mag./WDIV-TV, 1994, Tchr. of Yr., Detroit Pub. Schs., 1994; recipient Golden Apple Tchr. award, Wayne County Regional Edn. Svc. Agy. Mem.: Nat. Bd. for Profl. Tchg. Stds. (bd. mem.), Alpha Kappa Alpha. Office: Detroit Pub Schs Schs Ctr Bldg 3031 W Grand Blvd Detroit MI 48202*

MITCHELL, GLENN M. chemistry researcher, educator; b. Phila., Jan. 20, 1972; s. Charles F. and Marie Mitchell. BS in Chemistry, Drexel U., 1994, MS in analytical/Phys. Chemistry, 1996. Student tutor, supr., lab. technician Bucks County C.C., Newtown, Pa., 1990-92; undergrad. rschr. Drexel U., Phila., 1992-94, grad. chemistry instr., mass spectrometry rschr., 1994—. Recipient Alexander V. Kornilew award Drexel U., 1994. Mem. Am. Chem. Soc., Am. Inst. of Chemists (Outstanding Achievement award 1994), Am. Soc. for Mass Spectrometry. Office: Drexel U Dept Chemistry 32nd & Chestnut Sts Philadelphia PA 19104

MITCHELL, GLORIA JEAN, principal, educator; b. Plant City, Fla., Oct. 14, 1945; d. Jessie Mae (Anderson) Smith; m. Thero Mitchell, Sept. 19, 1969; children: Tarra Shariss Patrick, Thero Jr. BS, Bethune-Cookman Coll., 1967; MA, U. Detroit, 1974; postgrad., U. Wash., 1990. Cert. tchr., adminstr. Wash. Tchr. Dade County Schs., Miami, Fla., 1967-71, Agana (Guam) Presch., 1971-72, Detroit Pub. Schs., 1973-76, Prince Williams Schs., Dale City, Va., 1976-81; counselor/tchr. State of Alaska, Ketchikan, 1981-85; tchr. Bellevue (Wash.) Schs., 1985—2000, prin., 1992—96, Seattle Sch. Dist., 1996—. Bd. dirs. YMCA Bothell, Wash., chair sustaining drive, 1994-95; bd. dirs. Cascadia C.C., Bothell, 1996—; mem. Profl. Educators Stds. Bd. Recipient Golden Acorn award PTA-Lake Hills Schs., 1986, Golden Apple award KCTS TV, Seattle, 1994-95; named West Field Vol. of Yr., YMCA, Bothell, Wash., 1987, Woman of Yr., Woodinville (Wash.) Region II Prin. of Yr., Bellevue, 1994 Mem. ASCD, Nat. Alliance Black Sch. Educators, Wash. Alliance Black Sch. Educators (pres.). Avocations: golf, community volunteerism. Office: 1700 E Union Seattle WA 98122

MITCHELL, JAMES KENNETH, civil engineer, educator; b. Manchester, N.H., Apr. 19, 1930; s. Richard N. and Henrietta (Moench) M.; m. Virginia D. Williams, Nov. 24, 1951; children: Richard A., Laura K., James W., Donald M., David L. BBCE, Rensselaer Poly. Inst., 1951; MS, MIT, 1953, DSc, 1956. Mem. faculty U. Calif., Berkeley, 1958-93, prof. civil engring., 1968-89, chmn. dept., 1979-84, Edward G. and John R. Cahill prof. civil engring., 1989-92, Edward G. and John R. Cahill prof. civil engring. emeritus, 1993—; Via prof. civil engring. Va. Poly. Inst. and State U., Blacksburg, 1994-99, Univ. Disting. prof., 1996-99, Univ. Disting. prof. emeritus, 1999—. Geotech. cons., 1960—. Author: Fundamentals of Soil Behavior, 1976, 2d edit., 1993; contbr. articles to profl. jours. Asst. scoutmaster Boy Scouts Am., 1975-82; mem. Moraga (Calif.) Environ. Rev. Com., 1978-80. Served to 1st lt. AUS, 1956-58. Recipient Exceptional Sci. Achievement medal NASA, 1973, Berkeley citation, 1993, Chief of Engrs. Outstanding Svc. award U.S. Army Corps Engrs., 1999. Mem. ASCE (hon., Huber prize 1965, Middlebrooks award 1962, 70, 73, 2001, Norman medal 1972, 95, Terzaghi lectr. 1984, Terzaghi award 1985, pres. San Francisco sect. 1986-87), NAS, Nat. Acad. Engring. (vice chair civil engring. sect. 2001-03, chair 2003-05), Am. Soc. Engring. Edn. (We. Electric Fund award 1979), NRC (geotech. bd. chmn. 1990-94, bd. on infrastructure and constrn. environ. 1994-96, transp. rsch. bd. exec. com. 1983-87), Internat. Soc. Soil Mechanics and Geotech. Engring. (v.p. N.Am. 1989-94, Kevin Nash Gold medal 2001), Earthquake Engring. Rsch. Inst., Japanese Geotech. Soc. (internat. hon. mem.), Brit. Geotech. Soc. (Rankine lectr. 1991), Sigma Xi, Tau Beta Pi. Office: Va Tech Dept Civil Engring Blacksburg VA 24061-0105 E-mail: jkm@vt.edu.

MITCHELL, JOHN DIETRICH, theatre arts institute executive; b. Rockford, Ill., Nov. 3, 1917; s. John Dennis Royce and Dora Marie (Schroeder) M.; m. Miriam Pitcairn, Aug. 25, 1956; children: John Daniel, Lorenzo Theodore, Barbarina Mitchell Heyerdahl. BSS, Northwestern U., 1939, MA, 1941; EdD, Columbia U., 1956; HHD (hon.), Northwood U., 1986. Dir., producer Am. Broadcasting Co., N.Y.C., 1942-46; assoc. editor Samuel French, Publ., N.Y.C., 1946-48; assoc. prof. Manhattan Coll., N.Y.C., 1948-58; pres. Inst. for Advanced Studies in the Theatre Arts, N.Y.C., 1958-97. Founder, pres. Eaton St. Press, Key West, Fla., 1994, Mitchell Performing Arts Ctr., Campus Acad., Pa., 2001; bd. dirs. Beneficia Found., Jenkintown, Pa. Author: Staging Chekhov, 1990, Actors Talk, 1991, Gift of Apollo, 1992, Staging Japanese Theatre: Noh and Kabuki, 1995, Men Stand on Shoulders, 1996; author: (aka Jack Royce) The Train Stopped at Domodossola, 1993, Murder at the Kabuki, 1994, Dressed to Murder, 1997, Way to the Towers of Silence, 1997, Bewitched by the Stage, 1997, Troubled Paradise, 1998, The Wallpaper Murder, 1998, Death in the Suit of Lights, 1999, Too Beautiful to Live, 2002. Trustee emeritus Northwood U., Midland, Mich., 1972-91; patron Met. Opera, N.Y.C.; golden donor Am. Ballet Theatre. Named hon. conch Key West (Fla.) Commrs., 1994; dedication of Mitchell Performing Arts Ctr., Bryn Athyn, Pa., 2001. Mem. Met. Mus., Key West Arts and Hist. Soc., Spencer Family Assn. Mayflower Soc., Key West Literary Seminar (emeritus), Nippon Club N.Y.C. Mem. Community Ch. Avocations: tai chi chuan, swimming, collecting musical recordings, books. Home and Office: Apts 105-106 W La Brisa 1901 Roosevelt Blvd Key West FL 33040 Fax: 305-296-5827. E-mail: jdm@keysdigital.com.

MITCHELL, LOUISE TYNDALL, special education educator; b. St. Louis, Oct. 25; d. Walter Eugene and Nellie May (Otey) Tyndall; m. Felix Mitchell Sr., Sept. 30, 1958; children: Felix Jr., Jeane Mitchell-Carr. AA, Stowe Tchrs. Coll., St. Louis, 1947; BA, Harris Tchrs. Coll., St. Louis, 1958; MA, St. Louis U., 1965. Cert. elem. tchr., secondary English and math., reading clinician. Tchr. math. Hadley High Sch., St. Louis, 1958-59; tchr. Emerson Elem. Sch., St. Louis, 1969-67; head dept. spl. edn. Laclede Elem. Sch., St. Louis, 1967-68, coord. curriculum, 1968-70; adminstrv. asst. Delmar High Sch., St. Louis, 1970-72; assoc. prof., reading clinician, mgr. apprentice tchrs. Harris Tchrs. Coll., 1972-78; chair dept. spl. edn. Cleveland High Sch., St. Louis, 1978-84, chmn. faculty, 1982-84; head dept. spl. edn. S.W. High Sch., St. Louis, 1984-87, tchr., mentor, 1987—. Mentor St. Louis Pub. Schs., 1988-89. Author: (handbook) Teachers Aide, 1987, curriculum guides, 1974, 78; co-author (curriculum guide) Fundamental Curriculum, 1990. Chair Rsch. and Status Black Women, St. Louis, 1974; charter mem. Triagle Club YWCA, 1970. Recipient Community Svc. award Top Ladies Distinction, St. Louis, 1981, 50 Yrs. Outstanding Svc. award A.M.E. Ch., St. Louis, 1987, Salute to Excellence in Edn. recognition St. Louis Am. Newspaper, 1991. Mem. NAACP, Am. Fedn. Tchrs., Nat. Coun. Negro Women, Colored Womens' Fed. Clubs, Women Achievement (coord. youth 1989), St. Louis U. Alumni Assn., (Svc. award 1986), Ch. Women United, Order Ea. Star (past Worthy Matron 1978), Sigma Gamma Rho (chaplain 1988-90), Phi Delta Kappa. Avocations: reading, writing, pub. speaking, drama, singing. Home: 4537 Fair Ave # A Saint Louis MO 63115-3054

MITCHELL, LUCILLE ANNE, retired elementary school educator; b. Dayton Corners, Ill., Oct. 19, 1928; d. Roy Rollin and Edna May (Whitehouse) Sheppard; m. Donald L. Mitchell; children: David, Diane, Barbara Rock, Patricia Reaves. BS in Edn., Augustana Coll., 1966; MS in Edn., Western Ill. U., 1972, Edn. Specialist, 1974. Tchr. Carbon Cliff (Ill.) Elem. Sch., 1962-65, Moline (Ill.) Bd. Edn., 1967-92. Mem. textbook selection com. Moline Bd. Edn., 1967-84; tchr. of gifted Moline Bd. Edn., 1985-87. Contbr. (poetry) Footprints Through the Forest, 2000, Best Poems and Poets of 2001, 2001. Counselor to pastor Cmty. of Christ, 2001—02, elder in priesthood. Named Ill. Master Tchr., State of Ill., 1984. Mem. Ill. Edn. Assn. (various coms.), Moline Edn. Assn. (various coms.), Delta Kappa Gamma (program chmn. 1978-79, recording sec. 1980-81). Avocations: organ, piano, oil and water color painting, writing poetry, teaching Bible study classes. Home: 3214 55th Street Ct Moline IL 61265-5740 E-mail: donnlucy@aol.com.

MITCHELL, MICHAEL KIEHL, elementary and secondary education educator, minister; b. Phila., Oct. 27, 1932; s. Robert Bartow and Louise Room (Keyser) M.; m. Gloria (Nell) Wilburn, Nov. 12, 1960; children: Donald Kiehl, Robert Alan. B in Edn., U. Miami, 1955; MEd, Tex. A&M U., 1975, PhD, 1978; grad., Internat. Sch. Christian Comm., Front Sight Handgun Tng. Acad., 2000. Cert. elem. and secondary edn., Fla., Tex., Alaska; lic. comml. pilot; ordained priest Contemporary Cath. Ch., 2002. Tchr. math. Dade County Pub. Schs., Miami Springs, Fla., 1955-60; tchr. elem. Greenwood Sch. Dist., Midland, Tex., 1961-63; from tchr. social studies, English to tng. coord. Midland (Tex.) Sch. Dist., 1963-75; prin. rsch. investigator Tex. A&M U., College Station, 1977-78; project dir. Edn. Profl. Devel. Consortium, Richardson, Tex., 1978-79; sr. rsch. scientist Am. Airlines, Dallas, 1979-83; pres. North Rsch. Inc., Anchorage, Alaska, 1983-84; vocat. edn. curriculum specialist Anchorage Sch. Dist., 1984-87; sci. tchr., dept. head McLaughlin Youth Ctr. Anchorage (Alaska) Sch. Dist., 1987-2001; ret., 2001. Adj. prof. U. Alaska, Anchorage, 1987-89; evaluation team N.W. Accreditation Assn., Anchorage, 1985; asst. min. United Meth. ch., 1990-94; min. Christian Cmty. Fellowship, 1994—; deacon 1st Congl. Ch., Anchorage; instr. Flight and Ground Sch.; online counselor New Hope Online Svcs. of Crystal Cathedral Ch. of Rev. Robert H. Schuller; minister Sunday ch. svcs. McLaughlin Youth Ctr., AK State Reform Sch., 1999-2001; security officer Guardian Security, 2003—. Dir., v.p. Anchorage Comty. Theater, 1984-89; marriage commr. 3d Jud. Dist. Alaska, Anchorage, 1989-93; vol. United Way, Anchorage, 1984-90, Tony Knowles for Gov. Campaign, Anchorage, 1990, 94, Mark Begich for Mcpl. Assembly Campaign, 1991, Cheryl Clementson for Mcpl. Assembly Campaign, 1993; drum maj. Alaska Highlanders Scottish Bagpipers. With U.S. Army, 1946-47. Tex. Edn. Agy. fellow, Austin, 1975, Ednl. Profl. Devel. fellow, 1975-78. Mem. NEA, NSTA, SAG, NRA (life), Alliance for Separation of School and State, Anchorage Edn. Assn., Am. Correctional Edn. Assn., Alaska Airmans Assn. (life, bd. dirs. 1983-89), Mensa (life), Am. Legion (life), Clowns of Am., Alaska Sci. Tchrs. Assn. (life), Alaskan Aviation Safety Found., Tex. Assn. Aerospace Tchrs. (life), Former Students Assn. Tex. A&M U., Vets. Underaged Mil. Svc. (life), Am. Legion (life), Guns Am. (life), Phi Delta Kappa, Phi Kappa Phi. Libertarian. Avocations: commercial pilot, professional acting, faa accident prevention counselor. Home: 6626 Foothill Dr Anchorage AK 99504-2620 Office: Christian Cmty Fellowship 6626 Foothill Dr Anchorage AK 99504 E-mail: michaelmitchell@gci.net.

MITCHELL, MOZELLA GORDON, English language educator, minister; b. Starkville, Miss., Aug. 14, 1936; d. John Thomas and Odena Mae (Graham) Gordon; m. Edrick R. Woodson, Mar. 20, 1951 (div. 1974); children: Cynthia LaVern, Marcia Delores Woodson Miller. AB, LeMoyne Coll., 1959; MA in English, U. Mich., 1963; MA in Religious Studies, Colgate-Rochester Divinity Sch., 1973; PhD, Emory U., 1980. Instr. in English and Speech Alcorn A&M Coll., Lorman, Miss., 1960-61; instr. English, chmn. dept. Owen Jr. Coll., Memphis, 1961-65; asst. prof. English and religion Norfolk State Coll., U. Norfolk, Va., 1965-81; assoc. prof. U. South Fla., Tampa, 1981-93, prof., 1993—; pastor Mount Sinai AME Zion Ch., Tampa, 1982-89; presiding elder Tampa dist. AME Zion Ch., 1988—; pastor, founder Love of Christ AME Zion Tabernacle, Branden, Fla., 1993—; candidate for bishop AME Zion Ch., 2003—. Vis. assoc. prof. Hood Theol. Sem., Salisbury, N.C., 1979-80, St. Louis U., 1992-93; vis. asst. lectr. U. Rochester, N.Y., 1972-73; co-dir. Ghent VISTA Project, Norfolk, 1969-71; cons. Black Women and Ministry Interdenominational Theol. Ctr; lectr. Fla. Humanities Coun., 1994-95; Meml. lectr. Mordecai Johnson Inst., Colgate Rochester Div. Sch., 1997. Author: Spiritual Dynamics of Howard Thurman's Theology, 1985, Howard Thurman and the Quest for Freedom, Proc. 2d Ann. Howard Thurman Convocation (Peter Lang), 1992, African American Religious History in Tampa Bay, 1992;, New Africa in America: The Blending of African and American Religious and Social Traditions Among Black People in Meridian, Mississippi and Surrounding Counties (Peter Lang), 1994, also articles, essays in field; editor: Martin Luther King Meml. Series in Religion, Culture and Social Devel.; editorial bd. Cornucipia Reprint Series. Mem. Tampa-Hillsborough County Human Rels. Coun., 1987—; founder Women at the Well, Inc.; del. 7th assembly World Coun. Chs., Canberra, Australia, 1991, 17th World Meth. Coun., Rio de Janiero, 1996; del. 18th World Meth. Coun., Brighton, England, 2001; mem. connectional coun. A.M.E. Zion Ch., Charlotte, 1984—, staff writer Sunday sch. lit., 1981—, mem. jud. coun.; pres. Fla. Coun. Chs., Orlando, Fla., 1988—90, pres.-elect, 1998—, pres. exec. bd., 2000. Recipient ecumenical leadership citation Fla. Coun. Chs., 1990, Inaugural lectr. award Geddes Hanson Black Cultural Ctr. Princeton Theol. Sem., 1993; fellow Nat. Doctoral Fund, 1978-80; grantee NEH, 1981, Fla. Endowment for Humanities, 1990—, U. South Fla. Rsch. Coun., 1990—. Mem. Coll. Theology Soc., Am. Acad. Religion, Soc. for the Study of Black Religion (pres. 1992-96), Joint Ctr. for Polit. Studies, Black Women in Ch. and Soc., Alpha Kappa Alpha. Phi Kappa Phi. Democrat. Methodist. Avocations: piano, poetry, tennis, bicycling, Scrabble. Office: U South Fla 301 CPR Religious Studies Dept Tampa FL 33620 E-mail: mozellam@aol.com.

MITCHELL, PAULA KAY, elementary education educator; b. Houston, May 26, 1966; d. Carl Kenneth and Sandra Jean (O'Gilvie) Blacksher; m. John Eugene Mitchell, July 15, 1989. BS in Curriculum and Instrn. cum laude, Tex. A&M U., 1989; M in Lang. Literacy, Tex. Tech U., 1996. Cert. classroom edn. 1st and 4th grade tchr., sci. coord. Babenhausen (German) Elem., Dept. Def. Dept. Schs., 1990-91; 6th grade math and sci. tchr. Spangdahlem (German) Middle Sch., Dept. Def. Dept. Schs., 1991-92; 5th grade lang. arts tchr. St. Mary's Hall, San Antonio, 1992-93; 4th grade lang. arts and 6th grade sci. tchr. All Saints Episcopal Sch., Lubbock, Tex., 1993—. Young astronauts co-dir. All Saints Episcopal Sch., Lubbock, 1993—, coord. campus literary mag., 1994—. Campaign vol. San Antonio (Tex.) Rep. Party, 1991-92; reading instr. vol. San Antonio Literacy Coun., 1992. Mem. Nat. Coun. Tchrs. English, Internat. Reading Assn., Caprock Area Writing Project (presenter), Kappa Delta Pi, Phi Kappa Phi. Episcopalian. Office: All Saints Episcopal Sch 3222 103rd St Lubbock TX 79423-5200

MITCHELL, PAULA LEVIN, biology educator, editor; b. N.Y.C., Nov. 2, 1951; d. Louis X. and Jane (Schanfeld) Levin; m. Forrest Lee Mitchell, July 28, 1979 (div. 1993); children: Robert, Evelyn; m. Edward S. Haynes, June 6, 1994. BA in Biology, U. Pa., 1973; PhD in Zoology, U. Tex., 1980. Rsch. assoc. dept. entomology La. State U., Baton Rouge, 1981-84; vis. prof. dept. biol. scis Tarleton State U., Stephenville, Tex., 1984-93; asst. prof. dept biology Winthrop U., Rock Hill, SC, 1993—99, assoc. prof., 1999—; adj. asst. prof. dept. entomology Clemson Univ., Clemson, SC, 1996—. Adj. asst. prof. dept. biology Tex. Christian U., Fort Worth, 1985-88; editor Entomol. Soc. Am., Lanham, Md., 1986-93. Subject editor Jour. Agrl. Entomology, 1994-98; contbr. articles to profl. jours. Branch sec. AAUW, Stephenville, 1986-87. U. fellow U. Tex., Austin, 1973—76, Fulbright Sr. Rsch. Scholar, New Delhi, India, 2001—02. Mem. Entomol. Soc. Am., Ga. Entomol. Soc., Southwestern Entomol. Soc., S.C. Entomol. Soc. Office: Winthrop U 202 Life Sci Bldg Rock Hill SC 29733-0001

MITCHELL, PAULA RAE, nursing educator, college dean; b. Independence, Mo., Jan. 10, 1951; d. Millard Henry and E. Lorene (Denton) Gates; m. Ralph William Mitchell, May 24, 1975. BS in Nursing, Graceland Coll., 1973; MS in Nursing, U. Tex., 1976; EdD in ednl. Adminstrn., N.Mex. State U., 1996. RN, Tex., Mo.; cert. childbirth educator. Instr. nursing El Paso (Tex.) C.C., 1979-85, dir. nursing, 1985—, acting divsn. chmn. health occupations, 1985-86, divsn. dean, 1998-99, dean health occupations, 1999-2000, curriculum facilitator, 1984-86, dean health occupations, math and sci., campus dean, 2000—. Ob-gyn. nurse practitioner Planned Parenthood, El Paso, 1981-86, med. com., 1986-98; cons. in field. Author: (with Grippando) Nursing Perspectives and Issues, 1989, 93; contbr. articles to profl. jours. Founder, bd. dirs. Health-CREST, El Paso, 1981—85; mem. pub. edn. com. Am. Cancer Soc., El Paso, 1983—84, mem. profl. activities com., 1992—93; mem. El-Paso City-County Bd. Health, 1989—91; mem. Govt. Applications Rev. Com. Rio Grande Coun. Govts., 1989—91; mem. collaborative coun. El Paso Magnet H.S. for Health Care Professions, 1992—94; co-chair health and human svcs. task force Unite El Paso Health, 1996—98, mem. steering com., 1999—2000; co-chair health taskforce El Paso Cmty. Legis. Agenda, 1997—99; mem. adv. com. Ctr. for Border Health Rsch., Paso del Norte Health Found., 1998—; mem. Leadership El Paso, 1999; mem. health profl. shortage task force Greater El Paso C. of C., 2001—, mem. health care coun., 2002—; bd. dirs. Border Health Inst., El Paso, 2001—. Capt. U.S. Army, 1972—78. Decorated Army Commendation medal, Meritorious Svc. medal. Named to Women's Hall of Fame, El Paso Commn., 1999, named Outstanding Alumni, N.Mex. State U., 2002-03. Mem. Nat. League Nursing (resolutions com. Assocs. Degree coun. 1987-89, accreditation site visitor, AD coun. 1990—, Tex. edn. com. 1991-92, Tex. 3d v.p. 1992-93, Tex. 1st v.p. 1997-99, nominating com. 1999-2000), Am. Soc. Psychoprophylaxis Obstetrics, Nurses Assn. Am. Coll. Ob-Gyn. (cert. in ambulatory women's healthcare, chpt. coord. 1979-83, nat. program rev. com. 1984-86, corr. 1987-89), Advanced Nurse Practitioner Group El Paso (coord. 1980-83, legis. com. 1984), Am. Phys. Therapist Assn. (commn. on accreditation, site visitor for phys. therapist asst. programs 1991—), Orgn. Assoc. Degree Nursing (Tex. membership chmn. 1985-89, chmn. goals com. 1989—, nat. bylaws com. 1990-95), Am. Vocat. Assn., Am. Assn. Women Cmty. and Jr. Colls., Tex. Orgn. Nurse Execs., Nat. Coun. Workforce Edn. (articulation task force 1986-89, program standards task force 1991-93), Nat. Coun. Instrnl. Adminstrs., Tex. Soc. Allied Health Profls., Tex. Nurses Assn. (pres.-elect dist. one 2002-2003, pres. 2003—2004), Nat. Soc. Allied Health Profls. (edn. com. 1993-96), El Paso C. of C. (healthcare coun. 2001—), Sigma Theta Tau, Phi Kappa Phi. Mem. Christian Ch. (Disciples Of Christ). Home: 4616 Cupid Dr El Paso TX 79924-1726 Office: El Paso C C PO Box 20500 El Paso TX 79998-0500 E-mail: paulam@epcc.edu.

MITCHELL, PENNY, school counselor; b. Grenada, Miss., July 18, 1964; d. James Edward and Ola Mae (McAnally) M. BS in Edn., Blue Mountain Coll., 1986; MEd in Psychology, U. Miss., 1992. Cert. counselor, tchr., coach, Miss. Tchr., coach Calhoun Acad., Calhoun City, Miss., 1987-89; sr. sec. U. Miss., University, 1990-93; counselor Brookhaven (Miss.) Acad., 1993—. Youth and activities dir. Duck Hill (Miss.) Bapt. Ch., summer 1984, Pope (Miss.) Bapt. Ch., summer 1986, First Bapt. Ch. Bruce, Miss., 1986-90; recreation dir. Camp Garaywa, Jackson, Miss., summer 1985. Organizer Rep. Senator Race, Oxford, Miss., 1992. Mem. ASCD, Miss. Counseling Assn. Republican. Avocations: reading, jogging, cross-stitching. Office: Brookhaven Acad PO Box 3339 Brookhaven MS 39603-7339

MITCHELL, PETER KENNETH, JR., educational consultant; b. Bklyn., June 12, 1949; s. Peter Kenneth and Joan Marie (Hayes) Mitchell; 1 child, Elyse Alexandra. Cert. in French lang. proficiency, U. de Neuchatel, Switzerland, 1969; BA, SUNY, Geneseo, 1970; MS in French, L.I. U., 1975. Tchr. French, Spanish and English Mid. Country Sch. Dist., Selden, NY, 1972-81; tech. asst. to dir. internat. affairs dept. Am. Fedn. Tchrs., Washington, 1981—90; asst. to gen. sec. Internat. Fedn. Free Tchrs. Unions, Amsterdam, Netherlands, 1986—91; exec. dir. Internat. Reading Assn., Newark, Del., 1990-91; owner Insights Out Assocs., Newark, Del., 1992—97. Dir. mktg. Jr. Achievement Del., 1994—99. Contbr. articles to profl. jours. Recipient Father of the Yr. award, Nat. Multiple Sclerosis Soc., 1998. Mem.: Amnesty Internat., Washington U. Club, Blue and Gold Club. Avocations: reading, music.

MITCHELL, PHILIP MICHAEL, aerospace engineer, consultant, educator; b. Mobile, Ala., Feb. 12, 1953; s. Philip Augustus and Betty J. (Hardy) M. BS in Aeros. magna cum laude, Embry-Riddle Aero. U., Daytona Beach, Fla., 1980, MS in Aeros., 1987; MBA in Ops. and Project Mgmt., Wright State U., 1997. Radar systems engr. ITT, Van Nuys, Calif., 1980-82; commd. 2d lt. USAF, 1982, advanced through grades to maj., 1994; grad. rsch. asst. Wright State U., 1995-97; instr. Air Force Inst. Tech., Wright-Patterson AFB, 1997—. Adj. prof. European div. Embry-Riddle Aero. U., 1988-90; aerospace cons., 1987—. Recipient Meritorious Svc. medal with cluster, Commendation medal with one oak leaf cluster, Air Force Achievement medal. Fellow Brit. Interplanetary Soc.; mem. AIAA (sr.), Soc. Logistics Engrs., Am. Prodn. and Inventory Control Soc., Air Force Assn., Royal Scottish County Dance Soc., Masons (32 deg.), Scottish Rite, Sigma Iota Epsilon. Episcopal. Avocations: flying, skiing, scottish country dancing. Home: 1385 Wayne St B Troy OH 45373 Office: Air Force Inst Tech/LSM Twining Hall Bldg 641 Wright Patterson AFB OH 45433-7765 E-mail: philip.mitchell@afit.edu.

MITCHELL, RIE ROGERS, psychologist, counselor, educator; b. Tucson, Feb. 1, 1940; d. Martin Smith and Lavaun (Peterson) Rogers; m. Rex C. Mitchell, Mar. 16, 1961; 1 child, Scott Rogers. Student, Mills Coll., 1958-59; BS, U. Utah, 1962, MS, 1963; postgrad., San Diego State U., 1965-66; MA, PhD, UCLA, 1969. Diplomate Am. Bd. Psychology; registered play therapist, supr.; cert. sandplay therapist. Tchr. Coronado (Calif.) Unified Sch. Dist., 1964-65; sch. psychologist Glendale (Calif.) Unified Sch. Dist., 1968-70; psychologist Glendale Guidance Clinic, 1970-77; asst. prof. ednl. psychology Calif. State U., Northridge, 1970-74, assoc. prof., 1974-78, prof., 1978—. Chmn. dept. ednl. psychology, 1976-80, 2000—, acting exec. asst. to pres. Calif. State U., Dominguez Hills, 1978-79; cons. to various Calif. sch. dists.; pvt. practice psychology, Calabasas, Calif. Author: Sandplay: Past Present & Future, 1994; contbr. numerous articles to profl. jours. Recipient Outstanding Educator award Maharishi Soc., 1978, Woman of Yr. award U. Utah, 1962, Profl. Leadership award Western Assn. Counselor Edn., 1990, Disting. Tchg. award Calif. U. Northridge, 1994. Mem. APA, Calif. Assn. Counselor Edn., Supervision and Adminstrn. (dir. 1976-77), Western Assn. Counselor Edn. and Supervision (officer 1978-82, pres. 1980-81), Assn. Counselor Edn. and Supervision (dir. 1980-81, program chmn. 1981-82, treas. 1983-86, Presdl. award 1986, Leadership award 1987), UCLA Doctoral Alumni Assn. (pres. 1974-76), Am. Ednl. Rsch. Assn., Calif. Women in Higher Edn. (pres. chpt. 1977-78), Calif. Concerns (treas. 1984-86), Sandplay Therpists of Am. (fin. officer 1996-2000, bd. mem. 1993—, media chair, 1995, bylaws chair, 1994-96, exceptions com. chair, 1995-96), Pi Lambda Theta (pres. chpt. 1970-71, chairwoman nat. resolutions 1971-73). Home: 4503 Alta Tupelo Dr Calabasas CA 91302-2516 Office: Calif State U Counselor Edn Dept Northridge CA 91330-0001

MITCHELL, ROBERT CURTIS, physicist, educator; b. Ft. Dodge, Iowa, Mar. 29, 1928; s. Curtis Bradshaw and Mabel Cecilia (Higgins) M.; m. Mary Jo Bennett, Aug. 30, 1949; children: Drake Curtis, John Douglas, Mari Cecilia. BS, N.Mex. State U., 1949; MS, U. Wash., 1952; PhD, N.Mex. State U., 1966. Researcher Anderson Labs., West Hartford, Conn., 1952-53; rsch. asst. U. Conn., Sunspot, N.Mex., 1953; solar observer Harvard Coll. Observatory, Sunspot, 1953-54; tchr. Colo. Rocky Mt. Sch., Carbondale, 1954-56, Gadsden High Sch., Anthony, N.Mex., 1956-62; assoc. prof. Cen. Wash. U., Ellensburg, 1966-71, prof. physics, 1971-93, dept. chair, 1990-93. Photographer: (slide set of stars) The Night Sky, 1981. Mem. Habitat for Humanity. Mem. Am. Assn. Physics Tchrs. (chair com. on astronomy edn. 1990-92), Astron. Soc. of Pacific. Democrat. Presbyterian. Home: 1061 Lyons Rd Ellensburg WA 98926-7225

MITCHELL, RONNIE MONROE, lawyer, educator; b. Clinton, N.C., Nov. 10, 1952; s. Ondus Corneilius and Margaret Ronie (Johnson) M.; m. Martha Cheryl Coble, May 25, 1975; children: Grant Stephen, Mitchell, Meredith Elizabeth Mitchell. BA, Wake Forest U., 1975, JD, 1978. Bar: N.C. 1978, U.S. Dist. Ct. (ea. dist.) N.C. 1978, U.S. Ct. Appeals (4th cir.) 1983, U.S. Supreme Ct. 1984. Assoc. atty. Brown, Fox & Deaver, Fayetteville, N.C., 1978-81; ptnr. Harris, Sweeny & Mitchell, Fayetteville, 1981-91, Harris, Mitchell & Hancox, 1991-96, Harris & Mitchell, 1997-98, Harris, Mitchell, Burns & Brewer, 1998-2000, Mithchell, Brewer, Richardson, Adams, Burns and Boughman, 2000—. Adj. prof. law Norman Adrian Wiggins Sch. of Law, Campbell U; bd. dirs. Mace, Inc. Contbr. chpts. to books. Chmn. Cumberland County Bd. Adjustment, 1985-92, Cumberland County Rescue Squad, 1986-93; bd. dirs. Cumberland County Rescue Squad, Fayetteville, 1983-91. Recipient U.S. Law Week award Bur. Nat. Affairs, 1978. Mem. ABA, ATLA, Twelfth Judicial Dist. Bar Assn. (pres. 1988-89), N.C. Bar Assn. (councillor Young Lawyers divsn. 1982-85), N.C. Legis. Rsch. Commn. (family law com. 1994), Cumberland County Bar Assn. (mem. family law com., N.C. State Bar Bd. legal specialization), N.C. Acad. Trial Lawyers, Fayetteville Ind. Light Infantry Club, Dem. Men's Club (pres. 1993-94), Moose, Masons. Home: RR 1901 Water Oaks Dr Fayetteville NC 28301-9125 Office: Mitchell Brewer Richardson Adams Burns and Boughman 308 Person St Fayetteville NC 28301-5736

MITCHELL, THEODORE REED, academic administrator; b. San Rafael, Calif., Jan. 29, 1956; s. Theodore Robert and Genevieve Dolores (Doose) Mitchell; m. Christine M. Beckman, July 8, 1995; children: Caroline Mitchell Beckman, Theo Beckman. BA, Stanford U., 1978, MA, 1980, PhD, 1983. Asst. prof. Dartmouth Coll., Hanover, NH, 1981—86, assoc. prof., 1986—87, chair dept. edn., 1987—91; dep. to pres. and provost Stanford U., Calif., 1991—92; dean Sch. Edn. and Info. Studies UCLA, 1992—96, vice chancellor, 1996—98; v.p. for edn. and strategic initiatives The J. Paul Getty Trust, 1998—99; pres. Occidental Coll., 1999—. Trustee Stanford U., 1985—90, Thetford Acad., Vt., 1989—91; bd. dirs. L.A. Edn. Partnership, L.E.A.R.N. Author: Political Education, 1985, Sociology of Education, 1998. Bd. dirs. Children Now, Oakland, Calif., 1994—, Gateway Learning Corp., 1996—. Office: Occidental Coll Office of Pres 1600 Campus Rd Los Angeles CA 90041

MITCHELL, WAYNE LEE, health care administrator; b. Mar. 25, 1937; s. Albert C. and Elizabeth Isabelle (Nagel) M.; m. Marie Galletti. BA, U. Redlands, Calif., 1959; MSW, Ariz. State U., 1970, EdD, 1979. Social worker various county, state, and fed. agys., 1962-70; social worker Bur. Indian Affairs, Phoenix, Ariz., 1970-77, USPHS, 1977-79; asst. prof. Ariz. State U., 1979-84; with USPHS, Phoenix, 1984—. Lectr. in field. Contbr. articles to profl. jours. Bd. dirs. Phoenix Indian Comty. Sch., 1973-75, ATLATL, 1994-98, Partnership for Comty. Devel. Ariz. State U.-West, 1996-99, Cen. Ariz. Health Sys. Agy., 1982-85; mem. Phoenix Area Health Adv. Bd., 1975, Comty. Behavioral Mental Health Bd., 1976-80, Fgn. Rels. Com., Phoenix; trustee Heard Mus. Anthropology, Phoenix, 1996; apptd. Ariz. State Bd. Behavioral Health Examiners, 2000-2002. With USCG, 1960-62. Recipient Comty. Svc. award Ariz. Temple of Islam, 1980, Ariz. State U., 1996, Dir. Excellence award Phoenix Area IHS Dir., 1992, 93, Nat. IHS Dir.'s award for outstanding svc., 2000l; named in Voices and Faces, 2003. Mem. NASW (Lifetime Achievement award 2003), Fgn. Rels. Coun., Am. Hosp. Assn., U.S.-China Assn., Kappa Delta Pi, Phi Delta Kappa, Chi Sigma Chi. Democrat. Congregationalist. Home: PO Box 9592 Phoenix AZ 85068-9592 E-mail: drwlmitch@msn.com.

MITCHELL, WILLIAM DEWEY, JR., educational consultant; b. Greenville, S.C., June 15, 1933; s. William Dewey and Victoria Louise (Rickenbacker) M.; m. Peggy P. Atkins, Feb. 13, 1954; children: Vicki Mitchell Smith, Lisa Mitchell Cheek. BS in Indsl. Edn., Clemson U., 1955; MAT, Converse Coll., 1970. Cert. tchr., S.C., Tchr. Beaufort High Sch., S.C., 1957-61, Jenkins Jr. High Sch., Spartanburg, S.C., 1961-67; dean evening svcs. Spartanburg Tech. Coll., 1967-88; self employed cons., 1989—. Pres. Beaufort Civitan Club, S.C., 1960, Sunrise Civitan Club, 1968; sec. Beaufort County Fair Assn., 1960; lt. gov. zone B, S.C. Dist. Civitan Internat., Spartanburg, 1969; adv. com. Anderson Vocat. Ctr. Served with U.S. Army, 1955-57. Republican. Baptist. Club: Shirts and Skirts (pres. 1983-84) (Boiling Springs, S.C.). Avocation: western style square dancing. Home: PO Box 53 Liberty SC 29657-0053 also: PO Box 53 Liberty SC 29657-0053

MITCHELL-DONAR, SUSAN NANCY, school system administrator; b. Augusta, Maine, May 4, 1953; d. Gates William Walter Mitchell and Jeannette Rose Cyr Sylvester; m. Robert Anthony Donar, Aug. 4, 1979; children: Mitchell Adrien, Matthew John. BS, U. Maine, 1978; MBA, Thomas Coll., 1990; postgrad., Nova U., 1993—. Bus. instr. dept. head Medomak Valley High Sch., Waldoboro, Maine, 1979-81, bus. instr., 1986-87; sec. Kennebec Valley Med. Ctr., Augusta, Maine, 1981-83, Lisbon (Maine) High Sch., 1985-86; dir. Vocat. Curriculum Resource Ctr. of Maine Kennebec Valley Tech. Coll., Fairfield, Maine, 1987—. Adv. bd. Thomas Coll., Waterville, 1990-92, Kennebec Valley Tech. Coll., Fairfield, 1991—; pres. St. Mary's Home & Sch. Assn., Augusta, 1990-92; sec. Augusta West Little League, 1991—. Recipient Appreciation award Maine Vocat. Guidance Assn., 1992, Recognition award Legal Secs. Assn., 1988. Mem. ASCD, Bus. Edn. Assn. of Maine (Appreciation award 1990), Maine Vocat. Assn., Maine Tchrs. Assn., Am. Vocat. Assn. Home: 38 Wildwood Rd Augusta ME 04330-4939 Office: Kennebec Valley Tech Coll 92 Western Ave Fairfield ME 04937-1337

MITCHUM, MARGARET ELAINE, secondary educator; b. Kingstree, S.C., Apr. 10, 1945; d. Walter Barlow and Lilas Mae (Boyd) M. BA, Limstone Coll., 1967; MEd, U. S.C., 1979. Tchr. Georgetwon County Dept.Edn., Hemingway, S.C., 1967—. Contact person United Way, Georgetown, S.C., 1990. Grantee Freedoms Found., 1982; recipient History Tchr. of Yr. award DAR, 1990, 92. Baptist. Office: Pleasant Hill High PO Box 181A Hemingway SC 29554-0181

MITSAKOS, CHARLES LEONIDAS, education educator, consultant; b. Lowell, Mass., Oct. 17, 1939; s. Leonidas A. and Vasiliki (Sampatakakis) M.; m. Stella Martakos, June 23, 1963; children: Charles L. Jr., Andria Estelle. BS in Edn., Lowell State Coll., 1961; EdM, Boston U., 1963, EdD, 1977. Tchr., team leader, social studies curriculum specialist Lexington (Mass.) Pub. Schs., 1961-67; social studies coord., cons. Chelmsford (Mass.) Pub. Schs., 1967-78; asst. supt. of schs. Andover (Mass.) Pub. Schs., 1978-83; supt. of schs. Winchester (Mass.) Pub. Schs., 1984-92; clin. faculty supr. Sch. Edn., Boston Coll., Chestnut Hill, Mass., 1992-93; prof. edn., chair dept. edn. Rivier Coll., Nashua, N.H., 1993—. Ednl. cons. to schs. and sch. dists. in 15 states, U.S. V.I., U.S. Dept. Def. Dep. Schs. and Ministries of Edn., 1970—; facilitator Sch. Adminstrs. Leading with Tech. (SALT), Bill and Melinda Gates Found. funded project, 2002—; dir. Mid. Sch. Staff Devel. Inst. for Social Desegregation Program, Fairfield County, S.C., 1972; mem. staff, lectr. in team tchg. and social studies edn. NSF Insts., Stanford U., Ind. U., SUNY, Geneseo, Xavier U., U. N.C., Boston U., 1968-75; sr. lectr. sch. adminstrn. and curriculum devel. Sch. Grad. Studies, Rivier Coll., 1977-93, numerous others. Author, gen. editor: (multimedia program for elem. sch.) The Family of Man Social Studies Program, 1971-77; co-author: (textbooks) America! America!, 1977, revised 2d edit., 1987, Ginn Social Studies, 1987; author: (workbook) America! America! Workbook, 1982, (textbook) Earth's Geography and Environment, 1991; others. Mem. Coun. Tchr. Edn. N.H. Dept. Edn., Fin. Com. and Steering Com. So. N.H. Sch. to Careers Partnership; mem., bd. dirs., past pres. Social Sci. Edn. Consortium; past chmn. task force on teenagers and religious edn. Greek Orthodox Archdiocese of North and South Am.; former trustee U. Lowell; chairperson affirmative action com., chairperson com. to oversee U. Lowell Rsch. Found.; former mem. ad hoc budget com. Town of Winchester; former mem. bd. dirs., chairperson nominating com. and search com. for resident dirs. Andover Com. for A Better Chance; fund-raising chairperson, mem. edn. com., former trustee, newsletter editor local ch. Recipient Disting. Alumni award U. Lowell, Coll. of Edn., 1987. Democrat. Greek Orthodox. Avocations: writing travel articles, mosaic iconography, travel, reading. Office: Rivier Coll 420 Main St Nashua NH 03060-5086 E-mail: cmitsakos@rivier.edu.

MITSTIFER, DOROTHY IRWIN, honor society administrator; b. Gaines, Pa., Aug. 17, 1932; d. Leonard Robert and Laura Dorothy (Crane) Irwin; m. Robert Mitchell Mitsifer, June 17, 1956 (dec. Aug. 1984); children: Kurt Michael, Brett Robert. BS, Mansfield U., 1954; MEd, Pa. State U., 1972, PhD, 1976. Cert. home economist. Tchr. Tri-County High Sch., Canton, Pa., 1954-56, Loyalsock Twp. Sch. Dist., Williamsport, Pa., 1956-63; exec. dir. Kappa Omicron Phi, Williamsport, Pa., 1964-86, Kappa Omicron Phi, Omicron Nu, Haslett, Mich., 1986-90, Kappa Omicron Nu, East Lansing, Mich., 1990—. Prof. continuing edn. Pa. State U., University Park, 1976-80; prof. Mansfield (Pa.) U., 1980-86, pres.'s intern, 1984-86. Editor Kappa Omicron Nu Forum, 1986—; contbr. articles to profl. jours. Pres., bd. dirs. Profl. Devel. Ctr. Adv. Bd., Vocat. Edn., Pa. State U., 1980-86. Mem. ASCD, Am. Home Econs. Assn., Mich. Home Econs. Assn. (exec. dir. 1986-96), Am. Vocat. Assn., Am. Soc. Assn. Execs., Assn. Coll. Honor Socs. (sec.-treas. 1976—), Coll. Edn. Alumni Soc. Pa. State U. (pres. 1986-88, bd. dirs. 1980-90), Kappa Delta Pi. Avocations: sewing, camping, fishing. Home: 1425 Somerset Close St East Lansing MI 48823-2435 Office: Kappa Omicron Nu 4990 Northwind Dr Ste 140 East Lansing MI 48823-5031 E-mail: dmitstifer@kon.org.*

MITTEN, DAVID GORDON, classical archaeologist; b. Youngstown, Ohio, Oct. 26, 1935; s. Joe Atlee and Helen Louise (Boyd) M.; children: Claudia Antonia Sabina, Eleanor Elizabeth. BA, Oberlin Coll., 1957; MA in Classical Archaeology, Harvard U., 1958, PhD in Classical Archaeology, 1962. From instr. dept. fine arts to assoc. prof. Harvard U., Cambridge, Mass., 1962-69, James Loeb prof. classical art and archaeology, 1969—; curator ancient art Harvard U. Art Mus., Cambridge, Mass., 1976-96, George M.A. Hanfmann curator ancient art, 1996—. Assoc. dir. Harvard-Cornell Sardis Expdn., 1976—; Whitehead vis. prof. archaeology Am. Study of Classical Studies, Athens, Greece, 1990-91. Author: (with S.F. Doeringer) Master Bronzes from the Classical World, 1967, Classical Bronzes: Mus. Art, RISD, 1975, (with Arielle P. Kozloff) The Gods Delight: The Human Figure in Classical Bronze, Cleve. Mus. Art, 1988. Woodrow Wilson fellow Harvard U., 1958; Fulbright fellow Am. Sch. Classical Studies at Athens, 1959-60; Archaeol. Inst. Am. Olivia James fellow, 1969-70; John Simon Guggenheim Found. fellow, 1976-77. Mem. Archaeol. Inst. Am., Assn. Field Archaeology (co-founder), Am. Schs. Oriental Rsch., Brit. Sch. Archaeology (Athens, Greece), Am. Numismatic Soc. Office: Sackler Mus 316 Harvard Univ 485 Broadway Cambridge MA 02138-3845 E-mail: mitten@fas.harvard.edu.

MITTLER, GENE ALLEN, art educator; b. Elyria, Ohio, Sept. 7, 1934; s. Gene and Marion (Szabo) M.; m. Maria Luisa Azparren, July 26, 1960; children: Carmen, Teresa, Pilar. BS, Bowling Green State U., 1957, MFA, 1963; postgrad., Case Western Res. U., 1966-67; PhD, Ohio State U., 1971. Cert. art tchr., Ohio. Art instr. Ely Jr. High Sch., Elyria, Ohio, 1959-61; teaching asst. Bowling Green (Ohio) State U., 1961-63; art instr. Oberlin (Ohio) Coll., 1964; supr. art Lorain (Ohio) Pub. Schs., 1963-68; rsch. assoc. Ohio State U., Columbus, 1968-71; assoc. prof. art edn. Ind. U., Bloomington, 1971-82; prof. art edn. Tex. Tech. U., Lubbock, Tex., 1982—. Editorial adv. bd. Studies in Art Edn., 1975-79; curriculum cons. J. Paul Getty Ctr. for Edn. in the Arts, L.A., 1984-87; manuscript cons. Holt, Rinehart and Winston, N.Y.C., 1989-90, Harcourt, Brace, Jovanovich, N.Y.C., 1975-76; adv. com. art Lorain Community Coll., 1966-67. Author: Art in Focus, 1986, 89, 92; co-author: Creating and Understanding Drawing, 1988, 94, Exploring Art, 1992, Understanding Art, 1992; contbr. articles to profl. jours. Art cons. City of Lorain, 1967-68. With U.S. Army, 1957-59. Named Outstanding Grad. Fine and Performing Arts, Bowling Green State U., 1992, Eminent scholar Va. State U., 1990, Outstanding Faculty Mem. Arts and Scis., Mortarboard Tex. Tech U., 1984; recipient Maris and Mary H. Proffitt grant Ind. U., 1980, NEA grant Nat. Inst. Edn., 1974. Mem. Nat. Art Edn. Assn., Tex. Art Edn. Assn. Roman Catholic. Avocations: reading, travel, collecting art. Home: 2700 Chinquapin Oak Ln Arlington TX 76012-2842 Office: Dept of Art Tex Tech U Lubbock TX 79409

MITTMAN, NEAL, nephrologist, medical educator; b. NYC, Jan. 24, 1953; s. Arnold Mittman and Tess Blumenthal; m. Candace Clark Martin, Sept. 21, 1980; children: Alexander Clark, Zachary Wade. BA, CUNY-Queen's Coll., 1973; MD, N.Y. Med. Coll., 1977. Diplomate Am. Bd. Internal Medicine, Am. Bd. Nephrology. Intern N.Y. Med. Coll./Met. Hosp. Ctr., N.Y.C., 1977-78, resident, 1978-80; resident in nephrology Albert Einstein Coll. Medicine, Bronx, N.Y., 1980-82; asst. prof. medicine Mt. Sinai Sch. Medicine, 1982-86; assoc. chief divsn. nephrology Beth Israel Med. Ctr., N.Y.C., 1982-86, L.I. Coll. Hosp., Bklyn., 1986—; assoc. prof. clin. medicine SUNY Health Sci. Ctr., Bklyn., 1993—. Med. adv. bd. Nat. Kidney Found. NY/NJ, NYC, 1994-2002, grants and fellowship rev. com., 1995-2002; sec. med. adv. bd., chmn. corp. partnerships com. Kidney and Urology Found. Am., 2002--. Co-editor: Ambulatory Peritoneal Dialysis, 1990; contbr. articles to med. jours. Recipient Clin. Rsch. award NIH, 1980-82; named one of N.Y. Met. Best Drs., Castle, Connolly Med., Ltd., 1997, 98, 99, 2000, 01, 02. Fellow ACP; mem. Am. Soc. Nephrology, Am. Soc. Artificial Internal Organs, Am. Soc. Hypertension, Internat. Soc. Nephrology, N.Y. Soc. Nephrology (sec.-treas. 1996-97, v.p. 1997-98, pres. 1998-99), Met. Renal Care Network (bd. dirs., sec.). Avocations: country living, opera, gourmet cooking. Office: L I Coll Hosp 339 Hicks St Brooklyn NY 11201-5509

MIXON, DEBORAH LYNN BURTON, elementary school educator; b. Charleston, S.C., Mar. 26, 1956; d. Harold Boyd and Peggy Wynell (Seagraves) Burton; m. Steven Douglas Schmidt (div. Mar. 1982); 1 child, Julie Ann Schmidt; m. Timothy Lamar Mixon, Oct. 11, 1982; children: Phillip Lamar, Catherine Elizabeth. BS in Edn., U. Ga., 1994. Cert. early childhood and gifted in-field educator, Ga. Office coord. Morrison's Cafeteria, Athens, Ga., 1974-76; cashier Winn-Dixie, Athens, 1976-78; data entry clk. Athens Tech. Data Ctr., 1978-79; adminstrv. sec. U. Ga., Athens, 1980-86; sec. to plant mgr. Certain Teed Corp., Athens, 1986-87; s. adminstrv. sec. U. Ga., Athens, 1987-93; tchr. 4th grade Hall County Sch. Sys., Gainesville, Ga., 1994-2000, tchr. kindergarten, 2000—. Leader Cub Scouts den Boy Scouts Am., 1993-94; troop vol. Girl Scouts U.S., 1992—; vol. leader 4-H Clarke County, Athens, 1992-94. Presdl. scholar U. Ga., 1993-94. Mem.: Ga. Assn. for Gifted Children, Ga. Assn. Educators, Kappa Delta Epsilon (perfect scholar 1994), Golden Key, Delta Kappa Gamma. Avocations: hiking, camping, swimming, canoeing, reading. Home: 171 Scottwood Dr Athens GA 30607-1338 E-mail: debbie.mixon@hallco.org., dmixon@hotmail.com.

MIYAMOTO, CURTIS TRENT, medical educator; b. Bristol, Pa., Nov. 26, 1957; s. Sadao and Amy E. Miyamoto; m. Maria Amparo Gomez, Sept. 24, 1983; children: Maria Victoria, David James, Robert Paul. BS, Muhlenberg Coll., 1979; MD, U. Navarra, Pamplona, Spain, 1986. Lic. physician, Pa.; cert. radiation oncologist; bd. cert. radiation oncology Am. Bd. Radiology. Co-founder Brain Tumor Ctr. Med. Coll. Pa. Hahnemann U., Phila., 1994-99; assoc. med. dir. Gynecologic Oncology Ctr., Phila.,

1996-99; assoc. prof., chief clin. svc. Med. Coll. Pa. Hahnemann U., Phila., 1999-2001, vice chmn., 2001; med. educator West Mich. Cancer Ctr., Kalamazoo, 1999; prof., chmn. dept. radiation oncology Temple U. Hosp., Phila., 2001—. Bd. dir. Richard Zaloga Found., Old Forge, Pa.; former mem. risk mgmt., quality improvement com., former instnl. rev. bd. Med. Coll. Pa. Hahnemann U.; former mem. faculty Radiatin Oncology Self Assessment Program. Author: (with others) Management of Salivary Gland Lesions, 1992, Radioimmunoglobulins in Cancer Therapy, Principles and Practice of Radiation Oncology, 1996, (book chpt.) Combined Modality Therapy of Central Nervous System Tumors, 2001, radiation Therapy Principles for High Grade Gliomas, Quarterly Update: Principles and Practice of Radiation Oncology, 2001; co-author: (with others) Radiobiology in Radiotherapy, 1988, Recent Results in Cancer Research-Systemic Radiotherapy with Monoclonal Antibodies, 1996, Radioimmunoglobulins in Cancer Therapy, Principles and Practice of Radiation Oncology, 1996; contbr. articles to profl. jours. including Am. Jour. Clin. Oncology, Internat. Jour. Radiation Oncology; mem. editl. bd. Radiation Oncology Investigations; article reviewer Am. Jour. Clin. Oncology. Mem. worship com. First Presbyn. Ch., Morristown, N.J., 1996; v.p. PTA, Glenolden, Pa., 1993. Outstanding scholar Hahnemann U., 1991. Fellow AMA (Physician's Recognition award 1994), Am. Cancer Soc.; mem. Interat. Coll. Physicians & Surgeons, Coll. Physicians Phila., Am. Soc. for Therapeutic Radiology and Oncology, Alpha Phi Omega (life), Sigma Xi. Republican. Presbyterian. Achievements include extensive work with biologic response modifiers. Home: 101 Pheasant Fields Ln Moorestown NJ 08057 Office: Temple Univ Hosp Dept Radiation Oncology 3401 North Broad St Philadelphia PA 19140 E-mail: miyamoc@tuhs.temple.edu.

MIYAMOTO, MICHAEL DWIGHT, neuroscience educator, researcher; b. Honolulu, Apr. 22, 1945; s. Donald Masanobu and Chisako (Moriwaki) M.; m. Janis Ways Chin, June 16, 1973; children: Julie Lynn, Scott Michael. BA, Northwestern U., 1966, PhD, 1971. Instr. Rutgers Med. Sch., Piscataway, N.J., 1970-72; asst. prof. U. Conn. Health Ctr., Farmington, 1972-78; assoc. prof. East Tenn. State U., Johnson City, 1978-87, prof., 1987—. Contbr. articles to Jour. Theoretical Biology, Jour. Physiology, Pharmacol. Revs. Grantee Pharm. Mfg. Assn. Found., 1975, Epilepsy Found. Am., 1976, NIH, 1975, 78, 88, 92, 94. Mem.: AAUP, Soc. Neurosci. (Appalachian chpt.), Am. Soc. for Pharmacology and Exptl. Therapeutics. Presbyterian. Home: 318 Baron Dr Johnson City TN 37601-3934 Office: East Tenn State U Dept Pharmacology PO Box 70577 Johnson City TN 37614-1708

MIYOSHI, MASAO, literature educator, writer; b. Tokyo, May 14, 1928; came to U.S., 1952; s. Katsunai Miyoshi and Hisae Takahama; m. Elizabeth Ann Lester, July 27, 1953 (div. 1977); m. Martha L. Archibald, Apr. 8, 1977; children: Kathy Michele, Owen Malcolm, Melina Cybele. BA, U. Tokyo, 1951; MA, NYU, 1955, PhD, 1963. Instr., lectr. Gakushin U., Tokyo, 1951-52, 54-55; from asst. prof. to assoc. prof. to prof. English U. Calif., Berkeley, 1963-87; Edwin O. Reischauer prof. Japanese studies Harvard U., Cambridge, Mass., 1984-85; Hajime Mori prof. lit. U. Calif., San Diego, 1986—. Vis. prof. U. Chgo., 1978-81; dir. regional seminar, Japanese studies U. Calif., Berkeley, 1980-86, dir. Japanese studies, San Diego, 1989-95; dir. council on East Asian studies, 1997-2000. Author: The Divided Self, 1969, Accomplices of Silence, 1975, As We Saw Them, 1979, Off Center, 1991; editor: Postmodernism and Japan, 1989, Japan in the World, 1993, The Cultures of Globalization, 1998, Learning Places, 2002, (book series) Asia-Pacific: Culture, Politics, and Society. Guggenheim fellow, 1971-72, 75-76. Mem. MLA, Assn. for Asian Studies, Internat. Comparative Lit. Assn. Office: U Calif 9500 Gilman Dr La Jolla CA 92093-5004

MIZELL, JILL ANGELIQUE, education educator, consultant; b. Mpls., Mar. 22, 1968; d. Bernard Dwight Mizell and Ruth Ann Mizell-Jiles. D in Edn., U. Ga., 1999. Cert. guidance counselor. Daycare dir. Kids Stay and Play, Roswell, Ga., 1995—2001; asst. prof. State U. W. Ga., Carrollton, 1999—. Edn. cons. W. Ga. Regional Ednl. Svc. Agy., Griffin, 2001—. Contbr. articles to profl. jours. Recipient Title II Impacting Student Learning grant, State of Ga., 1999, 2000. Mem.: Nat. Coun. Tchrs. Math., Am. Edn. Rsch. Assn., Ga. Assn. Profl. Educators, Carrollton C. of C., Phi Delta Kappa (treas. 2001—02). Avocation: Dancing, Swimming, Traveling, Reading. Home: 490 Tall Deer Dr Fairburn GA 30213 Office: State U W Ga 240 Edn Annex Carrollton GA 30118 Office Fax: 770 836-4612. E-mail: jmizell@westga.edu.

MIZELLE, TERESA KAY, secondary education educator; b. N.C., June 3, 1956; d. Edward D. and Clara Margaret (Jackson) M. BA, Va. Wesleyan Coll., Norfolk, 1978; MA, Old Dominion U., Norfolk, 1981, CAS, 1987, PhD, 1995. Tchr. English Chesapeake (Va.) Pub. Schs., 1978-91, staff asst. to dep. supt., 1991-95, staff asst. to supt., 1995—2000, dir. staff devel., asst. to supt., 2000—. Asst. chairperson English dept. Deep Creek High Sch., 1978-91. Recipient Acad. award AAUW. Mem. ASCD, VSRA, Nat. Coun. Tchrs. English, Va., Assn. Supervision and Curriculum Devel., Va. Assn. Tchrs. English, Tidewater Assn. Tchrs. English. Home: 1119 Hazel Ave Chesapeake VA 23325-2901

MIZRUCHI, MARK SHELDON, sociology and business administration educator; b. New Haven, Dec. 10, 1953; s. Ephraim Harold and Ruth (Trachtenberg) M.; m. Katherine Teves, June 1981 (div. June 1995); 1 child, Joshua. BA, Washington U., 1975; MA, SUNY, Stony Brook, 1977, PhD, 1980. Statis. analyst Albert Einstein Coll. of Medicine, Bronx, N.Y., 1980-83, asst. prof. psychiatry, 1981-87, supr. statis. svcs., 1983-87; asst. prof. sociology Columbia U., N.Y.C., 1987-89, assoc. prof. sociology, 1989-91; prof. sociology and bus. adminstrn. U. Mich., Ann Arbor, 1991—. Author: The American Corporate Network, 1904-1974, 1982, The Structure of Corporate Political Action, 1992; editor (with M. Schwartz) Intercorporate Relations, 1987. Recipient Presdl. Young Investigator award NSF, 1988-93; grantee NSF, 1987-88, 93-95, 99-2000, 2002-03; invited fellow Ctr. for Advanced Study in the Behavioral Scis., 1989. Mem. Am. Sociol. Assn., Acad. Mgmt., Internat. Network for Social Network Analysis, Sociol. Rsch. Assn. Office: Dept Sociology Univ Mich Ann Arbor MI 48104-2590

MLYNIEC, WALLACE JOHN, law educator, lawyer, consultant; b. Berwyn, Ill., July 10, 1945; s. Casimir Adele and Adeline Mary Mlyniec; m. Abby L. Yochelson, 1985. BS, Northwestern U., 1967; JD, Georgetown U., 1970. Bar: D.C. 1971, Alaska 1971, U.S. Dist. Ct. D.C. 1971, U.S. Ct. Appeals (D.C. cir.) 1971, U.S. Supreme Ct. 1974. Exec. dir. ABA stds. U.S. Cir. Jud. Conf. on ABA Stds., Washington, 1971-73; dir. Juvenile Justice Clinic Georgetown U., Washington, 1973—, prof. law, 1973—. Lupo-Rico prof. clin. legal studies, 1998—; coord. clin. edn, 1986-89, assoc. dean, 1989—; cons. Nat. Adv. Com. on Juvenile Justice, Washington, 1979-80; cons. pvt. and pub. agys. on juvenile and criminal justice, 1974—; chmn. Juvenile Justice Adv. Group, D.C., 1980-82; mem. Nat. Resource Ctr. on Child Abuse and Neglect. Recipient Stuart Stillar Found. award, 1994; Meyer Found. grantee, 1980-82; Swedish Bicentennial fellow, 1985; disting. vis. scholar in pediat. law, Loyola U. Law Sch., Feb. 2001. Mem. ABA (mem. adv. com. on family ct. rules 1984, chair com. on juvenile justice 1998—), Am. Assn. Law Schs. (mem. com. on polit. interference 1983-84, chair 1991, standing com. on clin. edn., William Pincus award 1996), D.C. Bar Assn. (chmn. juvenile justice sect. 1973).

MO, YI-LUNG, structural engineering educator; b. Taichung, Taiwan, Aug. 28, 1955; s. Tzai-Nan and In-Fang (Teng) M.; m. Grace H.C. Wu, Sept. 26, 1985; children: Steven, Sophia. BS, Nat. Cheng Kung U., 1977; MS, Nat. Taiwan U., 1979; PhD, U. Hannover, Germany, 1982; MS, DePaul U., 1989. Assoc. prof. Nat. Cheng Kung U., Tainan, 1991-94, prof., 1994-2000; rsch. asst. Nat. Taiwan U., Taipei, 1977-79, U. Hannover, 1979-82; postdoctoral rsch. assoc. U. Houston, 1982-84; structural engrng. designer Sargent & Lundy Engrs., Chgo., 1984-89, engrng. analyst, 1989-91; rsch. prof. U. Houston, 1999-2000, prof. dept. civil and environ. engrng., 2000—. Alexander von Humboldt vis. prof. U. Hannover, 1995; vis. engr. Korean Power Engrng. Co., Seoul, 1990; vis. scholar Stanford U., 1998. Author: Dynamic Behavior of Concrete Structures, 1994. Recipient Disting. Rsch. award Nat. Sci. Coun., Taiwan, 1999, Rsch. Creativity award, 2000; scholar Friedrich Ebert Stiftung, 1982, Prestressed System Inc., 1982-84; Alexander von Humboldt Rsch. fellow, Germany, 1995. Fellow Alexander von Humboldt Stiftung, Germany; mem. ASCE, Am. Concrete Inst., Am. Biog. Inst. Rsch. Assn., Internat. Assn. for Bridge and Structural Engrng., Internat. Biog. Assn. England, N.Y. Acad. Sci. Office: Dept Civil Environ Engrng U Houston Houston TX 77204-4003 E-mail: yilungmo@egr.uh.edu.

MOAK, MARY JANE, secondary education art educator; b. West Point, Miss., July 8, 1949; m. David Moak, July 15, 1978. BFA, Miss. U. for Women, 1971; MEd, Miss. Coll., 1976. Cert. tchr., La. Tchr. art Pearl (Miss.) High Sch., 1972-78, Archbishop Chapelle High Sch., Metairie, La., 1978—, chmn. dept. fine arts, 1991—, chmn. gifted and talented program, 1989—. Calligrapher State Bd. Dentistry, 1984-93; artist Rhino Contemporary Craft Co., 1990-2000. Creator gourd and pine needle baskets Miss. Craftsman Guild, 1990-2000. Mem. Nat. Cath. Edn. Assn., Nat. Art Edn. Assn., La. Art Edn. Assn., New Orleans Mus. Art. Avocations: photography, cooking, pine needle basketry, art history, photography. Office: Archbishop Chapelle High Sch 8800 Veterans Memorial Blvd Metairie LA 70003-5235

MOAZZAMI, SARA, civil engineering educator; b. Tehran, July 24, 1960; d. Morteza Moazzami and Ezzat Akbari. BS, George Washington U., 1981; MS, U. Calif., Berkeley, 1982, PhD, 1987. Rsch. asst. George Washington U., Washington, 1980-81; teaching asst. U. Calif., Berkeley, 1982-83, rsch. asst., 1983-87; prof. Univ. Conn., Stamford, 1987-91, Calif. Polytechnic State U., San Luis Obispo, 1991—. Mem. 1989 Santa Cruz Earthquake Reconnaissance Team, Earthquake Engrng. Rsch. Inst., Oakland, Calif., 1989; speaker internat. confs. in field. Author: (book) 3-D Inelastic Analysis of Reinforced Concrete Frame-Wall Structures, 1987. Recipient Genevieve McEnerney fellowship U. Calif., Berkeley, 1981-82, Martin Mahler prize in Materials Testing, George Washington U., 1981, Columbian Women Soc. scholarship, Washington, 1979-80. Mem. Am. Soc. Civil Engrng. (scholarship 1980), Earthquake Engrng. Rsch. Inst., Soc. Women Engrs. Avocations: biking, swimming, sewing, travel. Office: Calif Polytechnic State Univ Sch Engrng San Luis Obispo CA 93407

MOBERG, VERNE, Swedish language educator, translator; b. East Moline, Ill., July 6, 1938; d. Vernon O. and Anne E. Moberg. BA, U. Ill., 1960; MA, SUNY, Stony Brook, 1976; PhD, U. Wis., 1984. Assoc. editor Harper's mag., N.Y.C., 1961-65; book editor Pantheon Books, N.Y.C., 1968-71; v.p. The Feminist Press, Old Westbury, N.Y., 1972-74; lectr. Scandinavian langs. Columbia U., NYC, 1988—. Vis. asst. prof. U. Va., Charlottesville, 1981-82; vis. asst. prof. Swedish, Gustavus Adolphus Coll., St. Peter, Minn., 1984-85, UCLA, 1991-92; adj. assoc. prof. Swedish, NYU, 1982-94; translator in field. Recipient numerous grants, including grants from govts. of Sweden and Norway. Office: Columbia Univ Swedish PRogram Dept Germanic Langs New York NY 10027-3847

MOBERLY, LINDEN EMERY, educational administrator; b. Laramie, Wyo., Jan. 4, 1923; s. Linden E. and Ruth (Gathercole) M. BS, Coll. Emporia, 1952; MS, Kans. State Tchrs. Coll., 1954; m. Viola F. Mosher, Apr. 29, 1949. Tchr. sci., Florence, Kans., 1952-54, Concordia, Kans., 1954-56, Grand Junction, Colo., 1957-60; asst. prin. Orchard Mesa Jr. High Sch., Grand Junction, 1960-66, prin., 1967-84; field cons. Nat. Assn. Secondary Sch. Prins., 1985—. Sgt. USMC, 1941-46. Recipient Outstanding Secondary Prin. award Colo. Assn. Sch. Execs., 1978. Mem. NEA, VFW, Nat. Assn. Secondary Prins. (bd. dir. 1979-83), Colo. Edn. Assn. (bd.dir. 1968-71), Colo. North Central Assn. Colls. and Secondary Schs., Colo. Assn. Secondary Sch. Prins. (bd. dir. 1974-77), Lions, Sons of the Revolution, Marine Corps League (life), VFW (life), Masons (award of Excellence 1990). Home: 2256 Kingston Rd Grand Junction CO 81503-1221

MOBLEY, EMILY RUTH, library dean, educator; b. Valdosta, Ga., Oct. 1, 1942; d. Emmett and Ruth (Johnson) M. AB in Edn., U. Mich., 1964, AM in Libr. Sci., 1967, postgrad., 1973-76. Tchr. Ecorse (Mich.) Pub. Schs., 1964-65; adminstrv. trainee Chrysler Corp., Highland Park, Mich., 1965-66, engrng. libr., 1966-69; libr. II Wayne State U., Detroit, 1969-72, libr. III, 1972-75; staff asst. GM Rsch. Labs. Libr., Warren, Mich., 1976-78, supr. reader svcs., 1978-81; libr. dir. GMI Engrng. & Mgmt. Inst., Flint, Mich., 1982-86; assoc. dir. for pub. svcs. & collection devel., assoc. prof. libr. sci. Purdue U. Librs., West Lafayette, Ind., 1986-89, acting dir. librs., assoc. prof. libr. sci., 1989, dean librs., prof. libr. sci., 1989—; Esther Ellis Norton Disting. Prof. Libr. Sci. Purdue U., West Lafayette, Ind., 1997—. Adj. lectr. U. Mich. Sch. Libr. Sci., Ann Arbor, 1974-75, 83-86; grants reader Libr. of Mich., 1980-81; project dir. Mideastern Mich. Region Libr. Cooperation, 1984-86; cons. Libr. Coop. of Macomb, 1985-86, Clark-Atlanta U., 1990-91; search com. for new dir. of libr. Smithsonian Instn., 1988; mem. GM Pub. Affairs Subcom. on Introducing Minorities to Engrng.; presenter in field. Author: Special Libraries at Work, 1984, numerous other publs.; mem. editl. bd. Reference Svcs. Rev., 1989—, Infomanage, 1993-97. Mem. corp. vis. com. for librs. MIT, 1990—, Carnegie-Mellon U., 1998—; mem. Ind. Statewide Libr. Automation Task Force, 1989-90; mem. state tech. strategy subcom. on info. tech. and telecomms. Ind. Corp. for Sci. & Tech., 1989; mem. nat. adv. com. Libr. of Congress, 1988; trustee Libr. of Mich., 1983-86, v.p., 1986, long range plan com., 1979-82, task force on document access and delivery, 1977-79; info. project mem. Rep. Nat. Conv., 1980; bd. dirs. Small Farms Assn., Southfield, Mich., Lafayette Symphony Orch., YWCA. Recipient Bausch & Lomb award for sci. achievement, 1960, Cert. for Outstanding Performance in Acad. Achievement State of Mich. Ho. of Reps., 1976, Spl. Tribute for Outstanding Contbns. Libr. of Mich. Bd. Trustees, 1986, Disting. Alumnus award U. Mich. Sch. Info. & Libr. Studies, 1989; U. Mich. Regents Alumni scholar, 1960-64; CIC doctoral fellow in libr. sci., 1973-76. Mem. ALA (com. on accreditation, subcom. to rev. 1972, standards for accreditation 1988-89, OLOS minority internship com. 1988-89, nominating com. 1992-93, mem. coun. resolutions com. 1993-97), Assn. Coll. & Rsch. Librs. (task force on libr. sch. curriculum 1988-89, com. on profl. edn. 1990-92), Libr. Adminstrn. & Mgmt. Assn., Assn. Rsch. Librs. (bd. dirs. 1990-93), Spl. Librs. Assn. (pres. 1987-88, fellow 1991, com. mem.), Alpha Kappa Alpha, Phi Kappa Phi, Sigma Xi, Iron Key. Office: Purdue U Librs Stewart Ctr Lafayette IN 47907

MOBLEY, WILLIAM HODGES, management educator, researcher, author, executive; b. Akron, Ohio, Nov. 15, 1941; BA, Denison U., 1963; PhD, U. Md., 1971. Registered psychologist, Hong Kong. Mgr. employee rels. rsch. PPG Industries, Pitts., 1971-73; prof. U. S.C., Columbia, 1973-80; head dept. of mgmt. Tex. A&M U., College Station, 1980-83, dean. Coll. of Bus. Adminstrn., 1983-86, exec. dep. chancellor, 1986-88, pres., 1988-93; chancellor Tex. A&M U. Sys., College Station, 1993-94; prof. mgmt. Tex. A&M U., College Station, 1980-96; pres. PDI Global Rsch. Consortium, Ltd., Hong Kong, Dallas, London, 1996—2002; prof. mgmt. China Europe Internat. Bus. Sch., Shanghai, 2002—; pres. Legend Global Pacific Ltd., Hong Kong, 2003—. Vis. fellow Cornell U., 1994, vis. prof. Hong Kong U. Sci. and Tech., 1995-97, U. Hong Kong, 1998. Author: Employee Turnover, 1982, Advances in Global Leadership, vol. I, 1999, vol. II, 2001. Bd. dirs. Internat. Food and Agrl. Devel. and Econ. Coop., U.S. AID, 1992-94; mem. tri-lateral task force on N.Am. Higher Edn. Coop., USIA, 1993-95; trustee SIOP Found., 1998-2001, AMMA Found., Denison U.; mem. Pres. Bush's Commn. on Minority Bus. Devel., 1990-92, U.S. Com. of the Pacific Econ. Coop. Coun., 1995—; bd. dirs. Medici Med. Corp., 1992—, Concept Tech. Ltd., 1999—. Sr. Fulbright scholar Found. for Scholarly Exchange, Republic China, 1978-79; recipient DAAD, Rep. Germany, 1984; Fellow NDEA U.S. Dept. of Edn., 1968-71. Fellow APA, Am. Psychol. Soc.

MOCIVNIK, PATRICIA ANN, physical education educator; b. Chgo., Apr. 17, 1965; Student, Mid-Am. Nazarene Coll., 1983-85; BS in Biology, John Brown U., 1988; MS in Exercise Sci., U. Ark., Fayetteville, 1991. Wellness evaluator Corp. Wellness Program John Brown U., Siloam Springs, Ark., 1986-88; substitute tchr., head tennis coach Rogers (Ark.) Sr. High Sch., 1989-90; instr. sci. NorthWest Ark. C.C., Rogers, 1989-90; instr. human performance and wellness Trinity Coll., Deerfield, Ill., 1991—, head tennis coach, 1991—, asst. coach women's basketball, 1991—. Cons. Deerfield Parks and Recreation Dept., New Hope Christian Acad., Rogers Pub. Schs., Rogers C. of C.; speaker, coach various summer sports camps. Mem. AAHPERD, NAFE, AAAS, Nat. Assn. Intercollegiate Athletics (chair spl. projects com. 1991—, profl. growth and devel. com. 1991—), Nat. Assn. Girls and Women in Sport, Nat. Assn. Sport and Phys. Edn. (Elite Corps, Outstanding Phys. Edn. Major 1988), Altrusa Internat., Alpha Chi, Gamma Epsilon. Avocations: music, computers. Home: 15863 Kedzie Cir Rogers AR 72758-9646 Office: Trinity Coll 2077 Half Day Rd Deerfield IL 60015-1241

MOCK, LARRY JOHN, elementary education educator; b. Quincy, Ill., Jan. 13, 1950; s. Frank Paul and Elizabeth Katherine (Hugenberg) M. BS, Quincy U., 1972; MEd, Ga. State U., 1985, specialist in edn., 1989, postgrad., 1993—. Cert. tchr. grades 1-8, Ga. Tchr. grade 4 Cmty. Dist. #3, Clayton, Ill., 1972-74; tchr. adult edn. Atlanta (Ga.) Pub. Schs., 1975-91, tchr. grade 5, 1991-94, tchr. grade 3, 1994-95; asst. prin. Atlanta Pub. Schs. Author: Daily Living Lab Manual, 1978. Chairperson Ho. Dist. 68 Dekalb County Dem. Party, Atlanta, 1993-94. Mem. NEA (Atlanta chpt.), ASCD, Am. Parkinson Disease Assn., East Atlanta Cmty. Assn. (treas., sec., v.p. 1980-93), Parkside PTA. Avocations: traveling, gardening, family geneology, local history, scotty terrier dog shows. Home: 1213 Gracewood Ave SE Atlanta GA 30316-2665

MODER, JOHN JOSEPH, non-profit administrator; b. St. Louis, Apr. 9, 1948; s. Helen (Freihaut) Moder. BA in English and Philosophy, St. Mary's U., San Antonio, 1970; MA in Philosophy, Fordham U., 1972, PhD in Philosophy, 1977; M Div, U. St. Michael's, 1979. Mem. faculty Assumption High Sch., East St. Louis, Ill., 1973—74, Vianney High Sch., St. Louis, 1975—76; faculty mem. Irish Christian Bros. Sch., Mono Mills, Canada, 1977—79; asst. prof. philosophy St. Mary's U., San Antonio, 1979—86, assoc. prof. philosophy, trustee, co-chmn. peace commn., 1986—88, pres., 1988—2000, Jr. Achievement South Tex., 2000—01; tchr. Alamo Heights H.S., 2001—02; v.p., COO Hispanic Assn. Colls and Univs., 2002—. Bd. advisors Communities-in-Schs., San Antonio, 1988-2000. Avocations: hiking, reading, travel, running. Office: 8415 Datapoint Drive Ste 400 San Antonio TX 78229

MODERACKI, EDMUND ANTHONY, music educator, conductor; b. Hackensack, N.J., July 18, 1946; s. Edmund Joseph and Helen Theresa (Fisher) Moderacki; m. Brenda Wing Moderacki. BA, Montclair State Coll., 1968, postgrad., 1970-71; MA, Hunter Coll., 1970, postgrad., 1970-72, Newark State Coll., 1969-70, Seton Hall U., 1970, Rutgers U., 1976-78, Ctr. for Understanding Media, 1973. Tchr. music pub. schs., River Vale, N.J., 1968—; asst. condr. Ridgewood (N.J.) Symphony Orch., 1969—, trustee, pres., 1986-87, 94-95; artistic dir. Ridgewood (N.J.) Symphony, 2001—; asst. condr. Adelphi Chamber Orch., 1994-95; condr. Project Symphony, 2003. Tuba soloist Rutherford Cmty. Band, Ridgewood Village Band, Waldwick Band, Ridgewood Concert Band, 1978—, trustee, 1985—, guest condr., 1985, 86, 88, 93; mgr. All Bergen High Sch. Band, 1994; condr. All Bergen County High Sch. Band, 2001. Author: Images of America: River Vale. Town historian River Vale; mem. steering com. Bergen County Teen Arts, 1991—. Recipient County Exec. Vol. award, 1991, Tchr. Recognition award Gov. of State of N.J., 1990; Bergen County PTA fellow, 1976. Mem. NEA, Music Educators Nat. Conf., N.J. Orch. Assn. (trustee 1981-85), N.J. Edn. Assn. (alt. del. assembly 1983-93, mem. state membership com. 1986—), Music Educators Bergen County (bd. mem. at-large 1995-97, treas. 1997-2000, pres.-elect 2000-2002, pres. 2002—), River Vale Edn. Assn. (pres. 1981-83, 88-91, 2000-03), Brigade Am. Revolution (bd. dirs. at large 1991-95, info. officer 1989-95, adj. 1996-2000, editor Brigade Press 2002-), Phi Mu Alpha Sinfonia, Kappa Delta Pi. Home: 740 White Birch Rd Township Of Washington NJ 07676 Office: Woodside Sch Rivervale NJ 07675

MODESTINO, JAMES WILLIAM, electrical engineering educator; b. Boston, Apr. 27, 1940; s. William and Mary Elizabeth (Dooley) M.; m. Leone Marie MacDougall, Aug. 25, 1962; children: Michele Marie, Lee Ann. BS, Northeastern U., 1962; MS, U. Pa., 1966; MA, Princeton U., 1968, PhD, 1969. Mem. tech. staff Gen. Telephone Electronics Labs., Waltham, Mass., 1969-70; asst. prof. Northeastern U., Boston, 1970-72; prof. Rensselaer Poly. Inst., Troy, NY, 1972-93, inst. prof., 1993—2001, dir. Ctr. for Image Processing Rsch., co-dir. Internat. Ctr. for Multimedia Edn.; prof., chmn. dept. elec. and computer engrng., U. Miami. Vis. prof. U. Calif., San Diego, 1981-82; vis. faculty fellow GE Corp. R&D Ctr., 1988-89; vis. prof. MIT, Cambridge, Mass., 1995-96; pres. Modcom Inc., Ballston Lake, N.Y., 1981—; v.p. ICUCOM Inc., Troy, N.Y., 1986-2001. Recipient Sperry Faculty award Sperry Corp., 1986. Fellow IEEE (S.O. Rice Prize Paper award 1984, mem. bd. of govs. Info. Theory Soc. 1988-92) Avocations: sailing, jogging, tennis, skiing. Office: 1251 Memorial Dr PO Box 248294 Coral Gables FL 33124 E-mail: modestino@ipl.rpi.edu.

MODZELESKI, WILLIAM, government agency administrator; BA in Polit. Sci., U. Bridgeport; MPA, C.W. Post Coll. Juvenile justice and corrections specialist U.S. Dept. Justice, staff dir. coordinating coun. on juvenile justice and delinquency prevention, dir. family violence programs, fed. coord. High Impact Cities Program; exec. dir. Nat. Commn. on Drug-Free Schs. U.S. Dept. Edn., Washington, assoc. dep. under sec. Office of Safe and Drug-Free Schs. Contbr. articles to profl. jours. With U.S. Army, Vietnam. Office: US Dept Edn FOB-6 Rm 3E314 400 Maryland Ave SW Washington DC 20202*

MOE, JANET ANNE, elementary school educator, church organist; b. Sacramento, May 24, 1946; d. Joseph Robert and Virginia Lou (Jones) Mangan; m. Edward Earl Moe, Aug. 23, 1969 (dec. Aug. 2002); children: Erik John, Erin Jean Moe Mitchell. BA, Calif. Luth. U., 1968; std. secondary tchg. credential, Calif. State U., Sacramento, 1969, crosscultural, lang. and acad. devel. cert. (CLAD), 1996; cert. in Orff Schulwerk Levels I, II and III, U. Calif. Santa Cruz, 1987; MS, preliminary adminstrv. credential, Nat. U., Sacramento, 2001. Elem. tchr. Gloria Dei Luth. Sch., Sacramento, 1969—73; elem. music specialist Sacramento City Unified Sch. Dist., 1982—. All-city elem. choir coord. Sacramento City Unified Sch. Dist., 1999—2001; chorus dir. Sierra Mountain Music Camp, Sacramento, 2001. Touring choir Sacramento City Coll., Italy, 1998, 1998, 2002, 2002; touring choir So. Calif. and Hawaii Calif. Luth. U., 1967—68; task force to restore music and the fine arts Sacramento City Unified Sch. Dist., 1999—2000; organist Gloria Dei Luth. Ch., 1970—2002, Luth. Ch. of Good Shepherd, 2003—. Recipient Hon. Svc. award, PTA Bear Flag Sch., Sacramento, 1992; Save the Music grantee, VH1, 2002. Mem.: NEA, Calif. Music Educators Assn. (elem. rep., mem. bd. Capitol Sect., Outstanding Music Educator award 1996, Save the Music grant 2002, Outstanding Music Educator award 2003), Nat. Audubon Soc. Republican. Lutheran. Avocations: birdwatching, travel, yoga, reading, hiking. Home: PO Box 109 Elk Grove CA 95759-0109

MOE-FISHBACK, BARBARA ANN, counseling administrator; b. Grand Forks, N.D., June 24, 1955; d. Robert Alan and Ruth Ann (Wang) Moe; m. William Martin Fishback; children: Kristen Ann, William Robert. BS in Psychology, U. N.D., 1977, MA in Counseling and Guidance, 1979, BS in Elem. Edn., 1984. Cert. elem. counselor, Ill. Tchr. United Day Nursery, Grand Forks, 1977-78; social worker Cavalier County Social Svcs., Langdon, N.D., 1979-83; elem. sch. counselor Douglas Sch. Sys., Ellsworth AFB, S.D., 1984-87, Jacksonville (Ill.) Sch. Sys., 1987—. Vol. Big Sister Program, Grand Forks, 1978-84; leader Pine to Prairie coun. Girl Scouts U.S., 1980-82; tchrs. asst. Head Start Program, Grand Forks, 1979. Mem. AACD, NEA, AAUW (local br. newsletter editor 1980-81, br. sec. 1981-83), Ill. Assn. Counseling and Devel., Ill. Sch. Counselor Assn., Ill. Edn. Assn., Am. Sch. Counselor Assn., Kappa Alpha Theta (newsletter, mag. article editor 1976-77), Jaycettes (dir. 1982-83). Avocations: cooking, camping, curling, ceramics, creative writing. Home: 291 Sandusky St Jacksonville IL 62650-1844 Office: 310 N Clay Ct Jacksonville IL 62650

MOELLER, DADE WILLIAM, environmental engineer, educator; b. Grant, Fla., Feb. 27, 1927; s. Robert A. and Victoria (Bolton) M.; m. Betty Jean Radford, Oct. 7, 1949 (dec. Oct. 1998); children: Garland Radford, Mark Bolton, William Kehne, Matthew Palmer, Elisabeth Anne. BSCE, Ga. Inst. Tech., 1947, MS in Environ. Engring., 1948; PhD in Nuclear Engring., N.C. State U., 1957. Commd. jr. asst. san. engr. USPHS, 1948, advanced through grades to san. engr. dir., 1961; rsch. engr. Los Alamos Sci. Lab., 1949-52; staff asst. Radiol. Health Program, Washington, 1952-54; rsch. assoc. Oak Ridge Nat. Lab., 1956-57; chief radiol. health tng. Taft San. Engring. Ctr., Cin., 1957-61; officer charge Northeastern Radiol. Health Lab., Winchester, Mass., 1961-66; assoc. dir. Kresge Center Environ. Health, Harvard Sch. Pub. Health, 1966-83, prof. engring. in environmental health, head dept. environmental health scis., 1968-83, dir. Office of Continuing Edn., 1982-84, assoc. dean continuing edn., 1985-93; environ. cons., 1993—; pres. Dade Moeller & Assocs., Inc., 1993—. Cons. radiol. health. Author: (textbook) Environmental Health, 2d edit., 1997; contbr. articles to profl. jours. Chmn. Am. Bd. Health Physics, 1967-70; mem. com. 4 Internat. Commn. on Radiol. Protection, 1978-85; chmn. nat. air pollution manpower devel. adv. com. U.S. EPA, 1972-75; mem. adv. com. reactor safeguards U.S. NRC, 1973-88, chmn., 1976, chmn. adv. com. nuclear waste, 1988-93. Named to Ga. Inst. Tech. Engring. Hall of Fame, 1999; recipient Disting. Engring. Alumnus award, N.C. State U., 2001. Fellow Am. Pub. Health Assn., Am. Nuclear Soc.; mem. AAAS, Am. Acad. Environ. Engrs., Nat. Coun. Radiation Protection and Measurements (hon.), NAE, Health Physics Soc. (pres. 1971-72, Robley D. Evans Commemorative medal 2003). Home and Office: 257 River Island Rd New Bern NC 28562-3669

MOERDYK, CHARLES CONRAD, school system administrator; b. Kalamazoo, Sept. 4, 1948; s. Vernon Frank and Eileen Marie (Riverside) M.; m. Cheryl Ann Rudge, July 29, 1967 (div. 1984); children: Paulette Ann, Carie Ann; m. Cynthia Marie Peters, Sept. 1, 1984. BBA, Western Mich. U., 1970; M of Edn. Adminstrn., Northern Mich. U., 1990. CPA Mich. 1974. Acct. J.R. Rugg & Co., Grand Rapids, Mich., 1970-71; controller Newman Visual Edn. Inc., Grand Rapids, Mich., 1971-73; asst. auditor gen. State of Mich., Lansing, 1973-74; ptnr. Goodman deMink & Cerutti, Kalamazoo, 1974-79; cons. pvt. practice, Kalamazoo & Crystal Falls, Mich., 1980-85; interim dir. support svcs. Planned PArenthood Assn., Chgo., 1981-82; bus. mgr. Breitung Twp. Schs., Kingsford, Mich., 1985-89, Alma (Mich.) Pub. Schs., 1989-96. Adj. prof. Davenport Coll., Alma, 1991—; dir., treas. Gra Co Fed. Union, Alma, 1991-94; pres. Anselara, Ltd., 1996—. Mem. World Future Soc. Avocations: singing, aviation. Home: PO Box 305 Alma MI 48801-0305 Office: Anselara Ltd 230 Fleming Dr Alma MI 48801-2178

MOESER, JAMES CHARLES, university chancellor, musician; b. Colorado City, Tex., Apr. 3, 1939; s. Charles Victor and Virginia (James) M.; m. Jesse Kaye Edwards, Jan. 26, 1963 (div. July 1984); children: James Christopher, Kathryn Carter; m. Susan Kay Smith Dickerson, June 21, 1987. B.Mus., U. Tex., 1961, M.M., 1964; postgrad. (Fulbright grantee), Hochschule fur Musik, Berlin, 1961-62; D.MA (Univ. fellow), U. Mich., 1966. Chmn. dept. organ, asst. prof. organ U. Kans., 1966-69, assoc. prof., 1969-74, prof., 1974-86, dean Sch. Fine Arts, 1975-86, Carl and Ruth Althaus disting. prof. organ, 1985-86; organist, choirmaster Plymouth Congl. Ch., Lawrence, Kans., 1967-86; organist nat. conf. Music Tchrs. Nat. Assn., Portland, Oreg., 1972, L.A., 1974; dean Coll. Arts and Architecture, Pa. State U., State College, 1986-96; chancellor U. Nebr., Lincoln, Nebr., 1996—2000, U.N.C. - Chapel Hill, Chapel Hill, NC, 2000—. Concert organist, on tour, W. Ger., 1977, Lisbon (Portugal) Festival, 1978, 81, recitals for, Musica Festiva da Costa Verde, Portugal, 1981; organist concerts, W. Ger., 1982, 86, 87; world premier Paul Creston's 3d Symphony for Organ and Orchestra, Kennedy Ctr., Washington, 1982. Bd. govs. Josephson Inst. Ethics, 1998-2002; trustee N.C. Symphony Soc., Inc., 2001—; mem. vis. com. Meml. Ch., Harvard U. Recipient Palmer Christian award U. Mich., 1981, Disting. Alumnus awrd Grad. Sch. U. Tex., 2001; Kent fellow Danforth Found.; Danforth Assoc. Mem. Am. Guild Organists (past dean chpt., nat. dir. student groups 1973-75, nat. chmn. com. on profl. edn. 1983—, chmn. 2d nat. conf. on organ pedagogy 1984, 3d nat. conf. 1986, v.p. 1986—). Episcopalian. Home: 1000 Raleigh Rd Chapel Hill NC 27517-4415 Office: UNC Office of the Chancellor PO Box 9100 Chapel Hill NC 27599-0001 E-mail: james_moeser@unc.edu.

MOFFATT, MINDY ANN, elementary school educator, educational training specialist; b. Mpls., Aug. 3, 1951; d. Ralph Theron and La Vone Muriel (Bergstrom) M. Student, UCLA, 1972-73; BA, Calif. State U., Fullerton, 1975, MS in Edn., 1991. Cert. elem. tchr., Calif. Tchr. early childhood edn. program Meadows Elem. Sch., Valencia, Calif., 1977—78; tchr. United Parents Against Forced Busing, Chatsworth, Calif., 1978—80; founding tchr. Gazebo Two Sch. for Young Gifted and Creative Children, Summerville, SC, 1980—81; tchr. Anaheim (Calif.) Union H.S. Dist., 1981—89, mentor, tchr., 1985—88; tchr. Greentree Elem. Sch., Irvine, Calif., 1989—90; with Thurston Mid. Sch., Laguna Beach, Calif., 1990—92; tng. specialist Scripps Clinics and Rsch. Found., LaJolla, Calif., 1993—94; tchr. White Hill Mid. Sch., Ross Valley Sch. Dist., San Anselmo, Calif., 1994—95, J.B. Davidson Mid. Sch., San Rafael, Calif., 1996—2000; asst. prin. Ventura (Calif.) H.S., 2000—01; lang. arts specialist in writing Ventura Unified Sch. Dist., 2001—. Cons. writing project U. Calif., Irvine, 1982—; textbook cons. McDougal, Littell & Co., Evanston, Ill., 1984-86; facilitator Summer Tech. Tng. Inst., Irvine, 1987. Co-author: Practical Ideas for Teaching Writing as a Process, 1986, 4th edit., 1997, Thinking/Writing: Fostering Critical Thinking Through Writing, 1991, Reading, Thinking, and Writing About Culturally Diverse Literature, 1995; contbr. articles to profl. jours. Mem. Our Ultimate Recreation (Orange County, Calif., chairperson social com. 1983, chairperson backpacking 1983, v.p. 1993-94). Avocations: whitewater rafting, canoeing, bicycling, skiing, backpacking. Office: Ventura Unified Sch Dist 120 E Santa Clara Ventura CA 93001 E-mail: mmoffatt@vtusd.k12.ca.us.edu.

MOFFETT, DAWN SCHULTEN, retired elementary education educator; b. Phila., Nov. 22, 1946; d. Emil Ferdinand and Helen Marie (McPhee) Schulten; m. Thomas Lee Moffett, July 25, 1970; children: Carolyn Dawn, Deborah Leanne, William Lee. BS, Bloomsburg U., 1968; postgrad., Temple U., 1969-71. Cert. tchr., Pa. Tchr. 4th grade Hatboro-Horsham Sch. Dist., Horsham, Pa., 1968-69, tchr. 1st grade, 1969-72; kindergarten tchr.'s aide Quantico (Va.) Sch. Dist., 1972-73; kindergarten tchr. U-Gro Learning Centres, Palmyra, Pa., 1986-87; subs. tchr. Ctrl. Dauphin Sch. Dist., Harrisburg, Pa., 1989-90, Lower Dauphin Sch. Dist., Hummelstown, Pa., 1989-90, Milton Hershey Sch., Hershey, Pa., 1987-90; tchr., grade 2 S.E. Elem. Sch., Lebanon, Pa., 1990-91, tchr. continuous progress program, grades 1-3, 1991—95, tchr. 1st grade, 1995—2002. Sch. dir. Derry Twp. Sch. Dist., Hershey, 1983-87, 96-97, Dauphin County Vo-Tech Sch., Harrisburg, 1984-87; trustee First United Meth. Ch., 1988-90, mem. coun. of ministries, 1988-90, 95-2002, dir. higher edn., 1995-2002; sec. Derry Twp. Libr. Bd., 1987-93, 2003—; mem. Hershey Libr. Endowment Bd., 1986-2002, chmn., 2000-02; pres. Friends of Hershey Pub. Libr., 1986-88; active PTO. Recipient Svc. award Pa. Sch. Bds. Assn., 1987, Dauphin County Tech. Sch., 1987, Derry Twp. Sch. Dist., 1987, Award of Excellence in Edn., Lebanon Valley C. of C., 2000; inductee Lebanon County Ednl. Honor Soc., 2002. Mem. AAUW (pres. Hershey 1978-80, Outstanding Woman of Yr. 1982), NEA, Pa. State Edn. Assn., Pa. Libr. Assn., Internat. Reading Assn., Nat. Tchrs. English. Republican. Avocations: snow skiing, swimming, crocheting, counted cross-stitch, quilting. Home: 357 Laurie Ave Hummelstown PA 17036-9720 E-mail: dsmoff@aol.com.

MOFFETT, KAREN ELIZABETH, physical education educator, guidance counselor; b. Indpls., June 29, 1958; d. Charles Richard and Julie V. (Godo) Tiede; m. Monte Joe Moffett, June 25, 1988. BS, Ind. U., 1981, MS, 1987; MA, Ball State U., 1995. Tchr., coach Delphi (Ind.) Cmty. Schs., 1981-87, Whitko Cmty. Schs., South Whitley, Ind., 1987-95; guidance counselor New Prairie H.S., New Carlisle, Ind., 1995-96, Chesterton (Ind.) H.S., 1996—. Mem. AAHPERD, Ind. Assn. Health, Phys. Edn., Recreation and Dance, Ind. Assn. Track and Cross-Country Coaches, Ind. Coaches of Girl's and Women's Sports, Ind. Counselor's Assn., Phi Delta Kappa. Avocations: travel, reading, needlecrafts, aerobic dancing, walking. E-mail. Home: 1556 Admiral Dr Porter IN 46304-9106 E-mail: karen13m@yahoo.com., karen.moffett@duneland.k12.in.us.

MOFFETT, KENNETH LEE, superintendent schools; b. Mt. Vernon, Wash., May 6, 1935; s. Charles R. and Edith May Moffett; m. Diane Muriel Buckley, July 30, 1966; children: Kendis Charlene, Patrick Charles. BA, Western Wash. State U., 1957; MA, Calif. State U., LA, 1958—60; EdD, U. So. Calif., 1972. Tchr. pub. schs., Inglewood, Calif., 1957—61, 1963—65; asst. prin., 1965—69; prin., 1969—73; tchr. U.S. Dependent Sch., Pirmasens, Fed. Republic Germany, 1961—62; asst. prin. Erlangen, Fed. Republic Germany, 1962—63; asst. supt. Inglewood Sch. Dist., Calif., 1973—76; supt. Lennox Sch. Dist., Calif., 1976—86, ABC Unified Sch. Dist., Cerritos, Calif., 1986—96; interim supt. Oak Pk. Unified Sch. Dist., Calif., 2003—. Mem. adv. bd. Ad Hoc Com. on Mental Health for Tchrs., LA, 1980—81; chmn. scholarship com. Bank of Am., 1979—84; educator in residence Pepperdine U., 1994—2001. Mem. adv. com. LA Area coun. Boy Scouts Am., 1981—83; mem. support group for U. So. Calif., 1978—84; bd. dirs. Centinela Valley Guidance Clinic, Inglewood, 1978—82. Named Am. Assn. of Sch. Adminstrs. Nat. Supt. of the Yr., 1994; recipient Svc. awards, PTA, Inglewood, 1973, Lennox, 1982. Mem.: Centinela Valley Trustees and Adminstrs. Assn. (sec.-treas. 1977—78), Centinela Valley Supts. Group (chmn. 1980—84), Assn. Calif. Sch. Adminstrs. (region chmn. 1980—82, Svc. award 1982), Centinela Valley Adminstrs. Assn. (charter pres. 1979—80). Republican. Methodist.*

MOFFETT, THOMAS DELANO, music educator; b. Smiths, Ala., Sept. 19, 1942; s. Early Moffett and Estella Sparks; m. Gloria Jean Marshall, Dec. 22, 1968; children: Stephanie Viloria, Marlon Delano. BS, Fla. A&M U., 1963; MEd, Auburn U., 1972, EdD, 1981. Cert. tchr., Ga. Band dir. Drake High Sch., Auburn, Ala., 1963-66, Talbotton Rd. Jr. High Sch., Columbus, Ga., 1966-78; asst. prin. Waddell Elem. Sch., Columbus, Ga., 1978-81; prin. St. Mary's Elem. Sch., Columbus, Ga., 1981-90, Dimon Elem. Sch., Columbus, Ga., 1990; music supr. Muscogee County Sch. Dist., Columbus, Ga., 1990-93; assoc. prof. music Troy (Ala.) State U., 1993—. Freelance musician. Active membership drive YMCA, Columbus, 1991; mem. adv. bd. Boy Scouts Am. Pack 120, Columbus, 1981-89; mem. bd. dirs. Southeastern U.S. Band Clinic, Youth Orch. Greater Columbus. Recipient citation Achievement in Edn., Omega Psi Phi, 1981, Past President's award Muscogee Elem. Prins. Assn., 1989, Outstanding Alumni award Fla. A&M, 1987; named Boss of Yr., Muscogee Assn. Edn. Office Personnel, 1989. Mem. NEA, Music Educators Nat. Conf., Ala. Music Educators Assn., Troy State Educators Assn., Phi Delta Kappa, Phi Mu Alpha. Democrat. Methodist. Avocations: golf, bowling, singing, saxophone. Home: PO Box 5501 Columbus GA 31906-0501 Office: Troy State U Smith Hall Troy AL 36082 E-mail: tmoffett@troyst.edu.

MOGGE, HARRIET MORGAN, educational association executive; b. Cleve. d. Russell VanDyke and Grace (Wells) Morgan; m. Robert Arthur Mogge (div. 1977); 1 child, Linda Jean. BME, Northwestern U.; postgrad., Ill. State U. Instr. piano, Evanston, Ill., 1954-58; instr. elem. music pub. schs., Evanston, 1959; editl. asst. archivist Summy-Birchard Co., Evanston, 1964-66, asst. to editor-in-chief, 1966-67, cons., 1968-69, ednl. dir., 1969-74, also historian, 1973-74; supr. vocal music jr. high sch., Watseka, Ill., 1967-68; asst. dir. profl. programs Music Educators Nat. Conf., Reston, Va., 1974-84, dir. meetings and convs., 1984-94, mgr. direct mktg. svc., 1981-89; sr. cons. Conv. Cons. Svc., 1993—2003, ret., 2003—. Mng. editor Am. Suzuki Jour., 1972-74, Gen. Music Today, 1987-91; mgr. display advt. Model T Times, 1971—; vice chair editl. bd. Exposition Mgmt., 1991-93. Active various cmty. drives. Mem. Music Educators Nat. Conf., Am. Choral Dirs. Assn., In and About Chgo., Music Educators Assn. (bd. dirs.), Suzuki Assn. Ams. (exec. sec. 1972-74, Disting. Svc. award 1996), Internat. Assn. Exposition Mgmt. (cert.; mem. edn. com. 1979-88, chmn. edn. com. 1985-87, bd. liaison edn. com. 1987-88, bd. dirs. Washington chpt. 1983-85, nat. bd. dirs. 1986-91, nat. v.p. 1989, nat. pres. 1990, Disting. Svc. award 1996), Bus. and Profl. Women's Club Watseka (bd. dirs. 1968-70), Antique Automobile club (registrar ann. meeting 1961-86), Model T Ford Club Internat. (v.p. 1971-72, 76-77, pres. 1981, treas. 1983-87, bd. dirs. 1971-87), Mu Phi Epsilon, Kappa Delta (province pres. 1960-66, 72-76, regional chpts. dir. 1976-78, nat. dir. scholarship 1981-84). Republican. Presbyterian. Home and Office: 1919A Villaridge Dr Reston VA 20191-4824

MOGHADAM, AMIR, consultant, educational administrator; BSME, U. London, 1983; PhD in Aeronautical Engring., U. Cambridge, 1987. Postdoctoral rschr. U. Calif., Santa Barbara, 1987-88; asst. prof. Northrop U., L.A., 1988-91, v.p. faculty senate, 1990-91; acad. and ednl. adminstrv. positions Northrop-Rice Inst. of Tech., Inglewood, Calif., 1991-96, dean/campus dir., 1996-98, pres., 1999—2002; pres., CEO Aeronautics Innovation Inc., Irvine, Calif., 1993—; dir. student affairs, info. and computer sci. U. Calif., Irvine, 1998-99; pres., CEO Aerolearn.com, Irvine, 1999—2002; CEO MaxKnowledge, Inc., Santa Ana, Calif., 2002—. Contbr. articles to profl. jours. Mem. AIAA,ASTD, Am. Soc. Engring. Edn., Tau Alpha Pi, Tau Beta Pi, Sigma Gamma Tau. Office: Maxknowledge Inc 601 N Parkcenter Dr Ste 208 Santa Ana CA 92705

MOGHISSI, KAMRAN S. obstetrician, retired gynecologist; b. Tehran, Iran, Sept. 11, 1925; arrived in U.S., 1959, naturalized, 1965; s. Ahmad and Monireh (Rohani) Moghissi; m. Ida Laura Tedeschi, Jan. 2, 1952; children: Diana J., Soraya R. ChB, MB, U. Geneva, 1951, MD, 1952. Diplomate Am. Bd. Ob-Gyn., Am. Bd. Reproductive Endocrinology. Intern U. Hosp., Geneva, 1951-52, Horton Gen. Hosp., United Oxford Hosps., Banbury, England, 1952-53; resident in ob-gyn. Gloucestershire Royal Hosp., England, 1953-54, St. Helier Hosp., London, 1954-55, Leeds Regional Hosp. Bd., Yorkshire, England, 1955-56, Detroit Receiving Hosp., 1961, attending gynecologist, 1962; assoc. prof. ob-gyn. U. Shiraz Med. Sch., Iran, 1957-59; rsch. assoc. ob-gyn. and physiol. chemistry Wayne State U., Detroit, 1959-61, from asst. prof. to prof., 1962-2000, prof. emeritus, 2001—, dir. divsn. reproductive endocrinology and infertility, 1970-94, vice chmn., 1983-88, chmn. dept. ob-gyn., 1988-91; sr. attending physician ob-gyn. Hutzel Hosp., Detroit, 1963, vice chief, 1978-82, 83-89, chief, 1982-83, 88-91, chief staff, 1991-93; attending surgeon, chief ob-gyn. Harper-Grace Hosp., 1983-84; obstetrician, gynecologist, chief Detroit Med. Ctr., 1988-91. Developer exhibits in medicine, movies and tchg. prodns.; lectr. in field. Mem. editl. bds.; contbr. chapters to books, articles to profl. jours. Fellow: ACOG, ACS, Am. Gynecol. and Obestetric Soc.; mem.: AMA (mem. ho. dels. 1992—), European Soc. Human Reproduction and Embryology, Soc. Gynecologic Investigation, Soc. Assisted Reproductive Tech., Soc. Reproductive Surgeons, Soc. Reproductive Endocrinology and Infertility (pres. 1990), Ctrl. Assn. Ob-Gyn., Mich. Soc. Ob-Gyn., Wayne County Med. Soc., Am. Soc. Andrology, Soc. Study Reproduction, Am. Soc. Reproduction Medicine (formerly Am. Fertility Soc.) (pres. 1990—91), Club Pelican Bay. Home: 12733 Sycamore Pte Plainwell MI 49080 Office: Hutzel Hosp 4707 Saint Antoine St Detroit MI 48201-1498 E-mail: kmoghiss@med.wayne.edu.

MOGIL, H(ARVEY) MICHAEL, meteorologist, educator; b. N.Y.C., July 9, 1945; s. Nathan and Linda (Balansky) M.; m. Sheila Rose Schleiderer, Mar. 13, 1965 (div. 1987); children: Fredrika Sharon, Allyn Keith; m. Barbara G. Levine, Feb. 6, 1988. BS in Meteorology, Fla. State U., 1967, MS in Meteorology, 1969. Cert. cons. meteorologist. Cons. How the Weatherworks, Rockville, Md., 1979—; trainer NOAA, Washington, 1985-95; instr. U. Mo., Columbia, 1989-92, Loyola Coll., Balt., 1992-96; tchr. 5th grade math. and sci. Sandy Spring Friends Sch., 1995-96; instr. Ramapo Coll., 1998—. Co-chair Project "Sky Awareness Week", Rockville, 1991—; adv. bd. Rockville Consortium for Sci., 1990—; dir. edn. Storm Ctr. Comms., Elliott City, Md. Co-author: Weather Study Under a Newspaper Umbrella, 1989, The Amateur Meteorologist, 1993, Anytime Weather Everywhere, 1996, Tornadoes, 2001; creator video tape tchr. guide Our Sea of Clouds, 1992, A Hurricane: Through the Eyes of Children, 1993; contbr. numerous articles to profl. jours. Mem. Nat. Sci. Tchrs. Assn. (reviewer 1983—), Nat. Earth Sci. Tchrs. Assn., Nat. Weather Assn. (chmn. tng. com. 1986-89, Mem. of the Yr. 1988), Am. Meteorol. Soc. Avocations: biking, reading, gardening, travel.

MOHANTY, SUNIL K. finance educator, researcher; b. Cuttack, Orissa, India, Oct. 28, 1958; arrived in came to U.S., 1985; s. Biswanath and Khyana Prava Mohanty; m. Tamera Lyn Bach; children: Rani, Raj. B of Tech., Indian Inst. Tech., Kharagpur, India, 1981; MBA, Minn. State U., 1989; D of Bus. Adminstrn., Cleve. State U., 1995. Jr. engr. Engrs. India Ltd., New Delhi, 1981—83, asst. engr., 1983—85; bus. cons. Small Bus. Devel. Ctr., Mankato, Minn., 1986—87; instr. dept. of mktg. Minn. State U., Mankato, 1988—89; asst. prof. U. St. Thomas, Mpls., 2001—; vis. asst. prof. of fin. Hofstra U., Hempstead, NY, 1994—95, assitant prof. of fin., 1995—2001; asst. prof. of fin. U. of St. Thomas, Minneapolis, Minn., 2001—. Mem. editl. bd.: Acad. Fin. Studies, 2000—, Acad. Comml. Banking and Fin., 2001—; contbr. articles to profl. jours. (ANBAR Citation of Highest Quality Rating, 1997). Recipient Outstanding Rsch. award, Acad. of Acctg. and Fin. Studies, 2002. Mem.: Allied Acads. Inc. (Outstanding Rsch. award 2002), Fin. Mgmt. Assn. Internat. (assoc.), Ea. Fin. Assn. (assoc.), Am. Fin. Assn. (assoc.), Beta Gamma Sigma, Phi Kappa Phi. Avocations: tennis, swimming, travel. Office: U St Thomas 1000 Lasalle Ave Minneapolis MN 55403 Office Fax: 651-962-4710. Business E-Mail: skmohanty@stthomas.edu.

MOHIUDDIN, YASMEEN NIAZ, economics educator; b. Aligarh, India, Feb. 25, 1948; came to U.S., 1974, naturalized, 1994. d. Niaz Ahmed Siddiqui and Bismillah Niaz Ahmed; m. Muhammad Mohiuddin Siddiqi, July 29, 1972; children: Umar Mohiuddin Siddiqi, Nazia Mohiuddin Siddiqi. BA, U. Karachi, Pakistan, 1965, MA, 1967, Vanderbilt U., Nashville, 1978, PhD, 1983. Staff economist Inst. Devel. Econs., Karachi, Pakistan, 1967-69; from asst. prof. to assoc. prof. U. Karachi, Pakistan, 1969-74, 78-81, 83-85, prof., 1991; tchr. asst. Vanderbilt U., Nashville, Tenn., 1977-78; instr., asst. prof. U. of the South, Sewanee, Tenn., 1981-83, 85-90, assoc. prof., 1990-96, prof., 1996—; chair dept. econs., 1997—; cons. World Bank, Washington, D.C., 1988—, World Food Program, Rome, Italy, 1989—, chair dept. econs., 1997—. Vis. prof. Vanderbilt Univ., summer, 1988, 97, 99; cons. Internat. Fund for Agrl. Devel., Rome, Italy, 1991—, Food and Agrl. Orgn., 1996—, UN Development Program, 1996—, U.S. Agy. Internat. Devel., 1999—; assoc. exec. editor Jour. Asian Econs., N.J., 1989—; keynote speaker Soc. for Internat. Devel., Bangladesh, 1990; apptd. by gov. to Tenn. Econ. Coun. on Women; lecturer in the field. Contbr. articles to profl. jours. Adv. bd. mem. Tenn. Network for Cmty. Econ. Devel.; bd. dirs. Appalachian Women's Guild, 1994-96, Cumberland Ctr. for Justice and Peace, 1994—; panelist AAUW. Internat. Labor Orgn. travel grantee, 1985, Soc. Internat. Devel. travel grantee, 1985, 91, Can. Internat. Devel. Agy. travel grantee, 1985, U. of South Rsch. grantee, 1986-89, 90—, U. Ky. travel grantee, 1987, 90, 95, Ford Found. fellow, 1974-78, 81, Ford Found. travel grantee, 1992, U Wis. Women's Studies fellow, 1983, fellow Transfer of Knowledge Through Expatriate Nat. UNDP programme. Mem. LWV, NOW (co-pres. Sewanee chpt. 1988-89), Nat. Social Sci. Assn., Ea. Econ. Assn., Soc. for Internat. Devel., Pakistan Fedn. of U. Women, Am. Com. on Asian Econ. Studies, Toastmasters Internat. Club, Bread for the World, Pakistan Women's Assns. Moslem. Avocations: community development work, clogging, travel, chess, reading. Home: 735 University Ave Sewanee TN 37383-1000 Office: U of the South Dept Econs Sewanee TN 37383-0001

MOHLER, MARIE ELAINE, nurse educator; b. Kenmare, N.D., Mar. 2, 1946; d. Ervin and Katie M. (Nichol) Hansen; children: Zane, Tracy, KyLynn, Todd, Lynnette. Diploma in nursing, Trinity Hosp. Sch. Nursing, Minot, 1967; BSN, Mont. State U., 1969, M in Nursing, 1970; diploma nurse midwifery, SUNY, Bklyn., 1973. RN, N.D.; cert. nurse midwife Am. Coll. Nurse Midwifes. Staff nurse pediatrics Trinity Hosp., Minot, 1967; resident nurse girl's dormitory Mont. State U., Bozeman, 1967-68; staff nurse med.-surg. wards Bozeman (Mont.) Deaconess Hosp., 1969; relief nurse Student Health Ctr. Mont. State U., Bozeman, 1970; camp nurse Camp Pinemore Minoqua, Wis., 1971; part-time staff nurse labor & delivery-maternity-newborn Bannock Meml. Hosp., Pocatello, Idaho, 1972-75, cons. maternal-newborn, pediatric wards, 1972-75; staff nuse maternity-newborn ward John Moses Hosp., Minot, 1977; part time staff nurse maternal-newborn ward St. Joseph's Hosp., Minot, 1978-81; nurse assessor Luth. Social Svc. N.D. and Family Care Network, 1991-93. Instr. Ariz. State U., Tempe, 1971-72, No. Ariz. U., Flagstaff, 1972, Idaho State U., Pocatello, 1972-75; asst. prof. Minot (N.D.) State Coll. divsn. Allied Health, 1975-76; instr. medicine U. Miss. Med. Ctr., Jackson, 1976-77; assoc. prof. Minot (N.D.) State U. Coll. Nursing, 1977—; senate pres. Minot State U. faculty, 1991-92; pres. coun. coll. faculties N.D. U. Sys., 1993-94, chair faculty compensation com., 1993-94, 96-97, others; mem. budget and salary com., constl. rev. com. Minot State U., 1993-94, others. Author of various videotapes and slide series. Recipient Minot C. of C. Disting. Prof. award, 1986; Burlington No. Found. Faculty Achievement award, 1987; grantee in field. Mem. Assn. Women's Health, Obstetric and Neonatal Nurses (chair legis. chpt., sect. sec.-treas. 1999-2001), Mabel Meug Honor Soc., Alpha Tau Delta, Sigma Theta Tau. Office: Minot State Univ Coll Nursing 500 University Ave W Minot ND 58707-0002

MOHR, BARBARA JEANNE, secondary school educator; b. Santa Monica, Calif., Jan. 26, 1953; d. Edgar Kirchner and Beatrice Jeanne (Anderson) M. BA, Calif. State U., Fullerton, 1976; MS, Calif. State U., 1982. Multiple Subject Teaching Credential, 1977, Single Subject Tchr. Credential, 1977. Substitute tchr. Fullerton (Calif.) Sch. Dist., 1977-78, tchr., 1978—, mentor, 1984-96. Tchr. calligraphy Laguna Rd. Sch., 1985-92, student coun. advisor, 1988-92, advisor Just Say No Club, 1986-94. Named Tchr. of Yr. Fullerton Sch. Dist., 1989; recipient Hon. Svc. award Laguna Rd. Sch. PTA, 1989; Weingart fellow Nat. Gallery of Art Tchr. Inst., 1996. Mem. NEA, Calif. Tchrs. Assn., Fullerton Elem. Tchrs. Assn., Calif. State U. Alumni Assn., Phi Kappa Phi. Avocations: calligraphy, gardening, travel.

MOHRDIECK, WILLIAM ALLEN, mathematician, educator; b. Chgo., Jan. 7, 1938; s. Ralph Frederick and Marion Veronica (Rogers) M.; m. Katherine Stumpf, Apr. 25, 1964; children: Thomas Ralph, Gregory Adam, Bertrand Michael. BA in Medieval and Modern European History, U. Chgo., 1962; MS in Math., Ill. Inst. Tech., 1975; EdD, Vanderbilt U., 1992. Head math. dept. St. Philip High Sch., Chgo., 1964-69; tchr. math. and philosophy Dist. 24, Ill. High Schs., Mt. Prospect, 1969-85; dir. R&D programs Ednl. Svc. Region Cook County, Chgo., 1983-87; head. sci., math. and tech. dept. Notre Dame High Sch., Niles, Ill., 1987—. Contbr. articles to profl. jours. Coach students advanced placement calculus, sponsor Youth Action Club, Prospect High Sch., 1974; commr. Youth Commn. Niles Twp., Morton Grove, Ill., 1976-80; sec. computer programmer Morton Grove Blood Donor Progra, 1980—. With USAR, 1960-66. Hewlett Packard grantee, 1993. Mem. ASCD, Nat. Coun. Tchrs. Math., Am. Assn. Philosophy Instrs., New Vistas Ednl. Assn. (founder). Avocations: traveling, fine music, dining, good conversation, exercising. Home and Office: 5 Smithwood Dr Morton Grove IL 60053-2926

MOHRING, HERBERT, economics educator; b. Buffalo, N.Y., Sept. 8, 1928; m. June 12, 1953. AB in Econs. and Maths. with honors, Williams Coll., 1950; PhD in Econs., MIT, 1959. Rsch. assoc. Willow Run Rsch. Ctr., U. Mich., Ann Arbor, 1951-52; teaching fellow dept. econs. MIT, Cambridge, 1952, 53-54; asst. study dir., study dir. Survey Rsch. Ctr. U. Mich., Ann Arbor, 1954-57; rsch. assoc. Resources for Future, 1957-58; rsch. economist Transp. Ctr., Northwestern U., Evanston, Ill., 1958-61; assoc. prof. U. Minn., Mpls., 1961-67, prof., 1967—95, prof. emeritus, 1995—. Cons. econ. survey Liberia Northwestern U., Evanston, Ill., 1961; adj. prof. law U. Minn., 1969—71; vis. prof. econ. York U., 1971—73, U. Toronto, 1972—73, U. B.C., 1983, U. Calif., Irvine, 1990, Irvine, 1996—; vis. prof. polit. economy Johns Hopkins U., 1974; vis. prof. dept. econs. and stats. Nat. U., Singapore, 1982—83; dir. grad. studies dept. econs. U. Minn., 1977—81. Author: (with Mitchell Hartwitz) Highway Benefits: An Analytical Framework, 1962 (trans. into Japanese), Transportation Economics, 1976; (trans. into Japanese and Korean) The Economics of Transport, 1993; bd. editors Am. Econ. Rev., 1971-73, Jour. Urban Econs., 1979-90; contbr. articles to profl. jours., chpts. to books. 2d lt. USAF, 1953. Mem. Am. Econ. Assn., Royal Econ. Soc., Econometric Soc. Office: U Minn Dept Econs Minneapolis MN 55455-0430 Home (Winter): 9 Rustling Wind Irvine CA 92612-3210 E-mail: mohring@econ.umn.edu., mohring@uci.edu.

MOHRMAN, KATHRYN J, academic administrator; B.A., Grinnell College, 1967; M.A., Univ. of Wisconsin, Madison, 1969; Ph.D., George Washington Univ., 1982. Dean of undergrad. studies Univ. of Maryland, College Park, 1988—93; pres. The Colo. Coll., Colo. Springs, 1993—2002; exec. dir. Hopkins-Nanjing Center for Chinese & Amer. Studies, Johns Hopkins Univ., 2003—. Office: 1740 Washington Ave NW 638 Washington DC 20036*

MOHRMANN, RAE JEANNE, retired elementary school educator; b. St. Louis, Feb. 8, 1948; d. Gilbert H. and Virginia R. (Miller) Schenkel; 1 child, Gregory G. BS in Elem. Edn., S.E. Mo. State U., Cape Giradeau, 1970; M Elem. Edn., Cert. Reading, U. Mo., St. Louis, 1976; Cert. Elem. Adminstrn., N.E. Mo. State U., Kirksville, 1980. Cert. elem. edn., kindergarten, English 7-9, reading K-12, elem. adminstrn. Tchr. Ritenour Sch. Dist., St. Louis, 1970-72, Dallas Ind. Sch. Dist., 1972-73; reading specialist Normandy Sch. Dist., St. Louis, 1974—2000, asst. prin., 1991-94, ret., 2000; tchr. recreational sports dept. U. Mo., St. Louis, 1996—. Summer coord. Normandy Reading Clinic, St. Louis, 1977-81; tchr. summer program Hazelwood Sch. Dist., St. Louis, 1989-94; adj. prof. U. Mo., St. Louis, 1987-96; tutor St. Vincent's Children's Home, St. Louis, 1978-2000; acting prin. McKinley Sch., Normandy Dist., St. Louis, 1991-92, student assistance team, 1985-2000, mem. Mo. Sch. Improvement Program, 1993-96, chmn. sch. improvement com., 1984-2000, bldg. resource team, 1993-2000; presenter Coun. on Child Abuse and Neglect Conf., 1981. Active Unity Luth. Ch., St. Louis, 1954—, bd. mem. 1990-92, pres.-elect, 2000, pres. 2000-01; mem. Pasadena Players, 1986-94; mem. Normandy Cmty. Adv. Coun., St. Louis, 1990-98; with Habitat for Humanity, 1996—. Mem. St. Louis Suburban Internat. Reading Assn. (bd. dirs. 1993-2002, vice pres. elect 1995, pres. 1995-96), U. Mo. St. Louis Alumni Assn. (chpt. sec. 1992-94, pres. 1994-96, main bd. mem. 1992—), Alpha Delta Kappa, Tri Delta Alumni (v.p. philanthropy 2001—). Avocations: running, volleyball, aerobics. Home: 115 Georgia Ave Saint Louis MO 63135-2606 E-mail: raeruns@aol.com.

MOISTNER, MONA SUE, adult education educator; b. New Castle, Ind., Jan. 11, 1955; d. Kenneth Orlando Jr. and Mary Belle (Williams) M. AA in Liberal Studies/English, Ind. U. East, Richmond, 1997, BA in English, 1999; polstgrd., Ind. U. Cert. substitute tchr., Ind. Disability accomodations asst. Ind. U. East, Richmond, 1999—. Part-time faculty humanities dept. Ivy Tech. State Coll., Richmond, 2000—; staff photographer Huddleston Farmhouse Inn Mus., Hist. Landmarks Found. Ind., Cambridge City, 1998-99, time-period poetry reading, 2000. Dick and Joanne Reynolds scholar Ind. U. East, 1997-2000, Ruth Brown scholar, 1996, Judith Roman scholar, 1994. Mem. Ind. U. Alumni Assn., Hist. Landmarks Found. Ind., Am. Legion Aux. Methodist. Avocations: composing and performing poetry, writing short stories, studying the romantic poets and writers, traveling. E-mail: mmoistne@indiana.edu.

MOJICA, AGNES, academic administrator; Chancellor Inter Am. U. of PR, San German, P.R. Chair governing bd. Hispanic Assn. Colls. and Univs., 1995-96, co-chair leadership group; chair governing bd. Intercollegiate Athletic League, 2001-02. Pres., Consortium of Presidents and Chancellors for the Prevention of the Use and Abuse of Drugs and Alcohol, 1998-2002. Mem., Assn. Industrialists of P.R., Western C. of C., Am. Assn. Higher Edn., Assn. Profl. Women, Altrusa, Rotary (hon.), Alpha Delta Kappa, Phi Delta Kappa. Office: Inter Am U PO Box 5100 San German PR 00683-9801 E-mail: amojica@sg.inter.edu.

MOKULEHUA, JOCELYN KOJIMA, elementary school educator; b. Ewa Oahu, Hawaii, Sept. 13, 1947; d. Hiroshi and Kume (Sato) Kojima; m. Leslie Y.L. Mokulehua, Dec. 13, 1969; 1 child, Thomas Masaru. BEd, U. Hawaii, 1969, MEd, 1971. Cert. elem. tchr., Hawaii. Tchr., 1969; resource tchr. Cen. Oahu Dist., Wahiawa, 1991—. Cons. Hawaii Writing Project, co-dir. lit. inst., 1998-2003. Named Tchr. of Yr., Cen. Oahu Dist., 1991. Mem. Internat. Reading Assn. (hawaii state coord., Eleanor M. Johnson award 1991), Nat. Coun. Tchrs. English, Ka Hui Heluhelu (local reading coun., v.p., pres.), Pi Lambda Theta. Home: 156 Iliwai Dr Wahiawa HI 96786-2305 Office: Waiau Elem Sch 98-450 Hookanike St Pearl City HI 96782-2399

MOLDENHAUER, NANCY A. social worker, educator; BSEd, Valparaiso U., 1976; MSW, cert. specialist in aging, U. Mich., 1984. Instr. Meiji Gakuin and Tokyo Med. and Dental U., 1977-81; corp. communication trainer Saito Internat., Inc., Tokyo, 1981-82; conf. coord. Ctr. for Japanese Studies U. Mich., Ann Arbor, 1982-84; gerontol. social worker Turner Geriatric Clinic U. Mich. Hosps., Ann Arbor, 1983-84; med. social worker Mo. Bapt. Med. Ctr., St. Louis, 1985-88; geriatric social work specialist Program on Aging Jewish Hosp. Wash. U. Med. Ctr., St. Louis, 1988-92; dir. case mgmt. and corp. svcs. Aging Consult, St. Louis, 1993-95; libr. media specialist, elem. tchr. Michigan City Area Schs., Ind., 1999—. Adj. prof. Washington U., St. Louis, 1991-95; trainee in aging NIH, 1983-84; dir. Nat. Adult Day Svc. Assn., Nat. Coun. Aging, Washington, 1995-96; registration mgr. Landmark Edn. Corp., Alexandria, Va., 1997-98. Co-author: Positive Attitudes, Positive Aging: A Guide for Positive Actions in Later Life, NASDA Curriculum for Directors and Administrators, Adult Day Services - The Next Frontier, Handbook of Home Health Care Administration. Del. White House Conf. Aging, 1995. Named OWL Woman of Worth, 1993. Mem. NEA, ASCD, NASW, Acad. Cert. Social Workers, Gerontol. Soc. Am., Am. Soc. Aging, Nat. Coun. on Aging, Alzheimer's Assn., Older Women's League (local bd. dirs., pres. 1991-95, nat. bd. dirs., v.p. 1993-96), Challenge Metro (bd. dirs., pres. 1986-90). Avocations: gourmet cooking, restaurants, wine, movies, travel. Office: 107 Kaye Ln Michigan City IN 46360-1730

MOLINA, MARIO JOSE, physical chemist, educator; b. Mexico City, Mar. 19, 1943; arrived in U.S., 1968; s. Roberto Molina-Pasquel and Leonor Henríquez; m. Luisa Y. Tan, July 12, 1973; 1 child, Felipe. Bachillerato, Acad. Hispano Mexicana, Mexico City, 1959; Ingeniero Químico, U. Nacional Autónoma de México, 1965; postgrad., U. Freiburg, Fed. Republic Germany, 1966—67; PhD, U. Calif., Berkeley, 1972. Asst. prof. U. Nacional Autónoma de México, 1967—68; research assoc. U. Calif.-Berkeley, 1972—73, U. Calif.-Irvine, 1973—75, asst. prof. phys. chemistry, 1975—79, assoc. prof., 1979—82; sr. rsch. scientist Jet Propulsion Lab., 1983—89; prof. dept. earth, atom and planet sci., dept. chemistry MIT, Cambridge, 1989—96, Martin prof. atmospheric chemistry, 1997—. Inst. prof., 1997—. Recipient Tyler Ecology award, 1983, Esselen award for chemistry in pub. interest, 1987, Max-Planck-Forschungs-Preis, Alexander von Humboldt-Stiftung, 1994, Nobel Prize in Chemistry, 1995, Sasakawa prize, UNEP, 1999. Mem.: NAS, Inst. of Medicine, Am. Geophys. Union (Pres.'s Com. on Advisors on Sci. and Tech. 1994—2000), Am. Phys. Soc., Am. Chem. Soc. Achievements include discovery of the theory that fluorocarbons deplete ozone layer of stratosphere. Home: 8 Clematis Rd Lexington MA 02421-7117 Office: MIT Dept of EAPS 77 Mass Ave # 54-1814 Cambridge MA 02139-4307 E-mail: mmolina@mit.edu.*

MOLINDER, JOHN IRVING, engineering educator, consultant; b. Erie, Pa., June 14, 1941; s. Karl Oskar and Carin (Ecklund) M.; m. Janet Marie Ahlquist, June 16, 1962; children: Tim, Karen. BSEE, U. Nebr., 1963; MSEE, Air Force Inst. Tech., 1964; PhD EE, Calif. Inst. Tech., 1969. Registered profl. engr., Calif. Project officer Ballistic Systems Div., Norton AFB, Calif., 1964-67; sr. engr. Jet Propulsion Lab., Pasadena, Calif., 1969-70; prof. engring. Harvey Mudd Coll., Claremont, Calif., 1970—; prin. engr. Qualcomm Inc., 1996-97, part-time, 1997—; contractor Boeing Satellite Systems, 2000—02. Part-time lectr. Calif. State U., L.A., 1970-74; mem. tech. adv. panel Kinemetrics, Pasadena, 1985-86; part-time mem. tech. staff Jet Propulsion Lab., Pasadena, 1974-97, rep. NASA Hdqrs., Washington, 1979-80; vis. prof. elec. engring. Calif. Inst. Tech., 1982-83. Contbr. articles to profl. jours. Served to capt. USAF, 1963-67. Mem.: IEEE (sr.). Avocations: bicycling, reading, computers. Office: Harvey Mudd Coll Dept Engring 301 E 12th St Dept Of Claremont CA 91711-5901

MOLITORIS, BRUCE ALBERT, nephrologist, educator; b. Springfield, Ill., June 26, 1951; s. Edward and Joyce (Tomasko) M.; m. Karen Lynn Wichterman, June 16, 1973; children: Jason, Jared, Julie. BS, U. Ill., 1973, MS in Nutrition, 1975; MD, Wash. U., 1979. Resident Sch. Medicine U. Colo., Denver, 1979-81, nephrology fellow, 1981-84, asst. prof. medicine, 1984-88, assoc. prof. medicine, 1988-93, prof., 1993; dir. nephrology Ind. U. Med. Sch., Indpls., 1993—; vis. scientist U. Colo., MCDB, Boulder, 1989-90, Max Planck Inst., Federal Republic of Germany, 1984-85. NIH reviewer, 1991-94; dir. home dialysis Denver VA Ctr., 1984-93; vis. scientist dept. molecular biology Colo. State U., Ft. Collins, 1998. Mem. editl. bd. Am. Jour. Physiology, 1989-2000, Am. Jour. Kidney Diseases, 1991--; assoc. editor Jour. Investigative Medicine, 1994-99; contbr. articles to profl. jours. Pres. Cherry Creek Village South Homeowners Assn., 1989-90, Pickwick Commons Home Owners Assn., 1999; v.p. Our Father Luth. Ch., Denver, 1989-90; coun. mem. King of Glory Luth. Ch., Indpls., 1999-2002; coach Cherry Creek Soccer Assn., Greenwood Village, 1988-91, Centennial Little League Titans Basketball; bd. dirs. CSSA, 1993. Recipient Upjohn Achievement award, 1979, Liberty Hyde Bailey award, 1973. Mem. Am. Assn. Physicians, Am. Soc. Nephrology (program chmn. 2002-03), Internat. Soc. Nephrology, N.Y. Acad. Sci., Am. Soc. Clin. Investigation, Am. Fedn. for Clin. Rsch. (nat. counselor 1991-94), Western Assn. Physicians. Avocations: bridge, fishing, antiques, hiking. Office: Indiana Univ Med Ctr Fesler Hall 115 1120 South Dr Indianapolis IN 46202-5135 E-mail: bmolitor@iupui.edu.

MOLLER, JACQUELINE LOUISE, elementary education educator; b. Oneida, N.Y., June 21, 1942; d. Charles and Mary Louise (Dunne) M. BS, SUNY, Oswego, 1964. Cert. tchr., N.Y. Tchr. Oneida Sch. Dist., 1964—. Recipient 1st Pl. award WCNY TV, 1993, Outstanding award, 1995, Case award for innovative teaching with telecomm. N.Y. State Pub. TV, 1992, 94; Mid. State Tchrs. Ctr. grantee, 1992, 94, 95. Mem. Oneida Tchrs. Assn. (former sec. 1966-70), Parent-Tchr-Student Assn. (life, sec.), Delta Kappa Gamma (former pres., treas.). Avocations: golf, computers, public acess television participant, reading. Home: 588 Stoneleigh Rd Oneida NY 13421-1814 Office: Willard Prior Elem Sch East Ave Oneida NY 13421

MOLLO, JOSEPH ANTHONY, university administrator; b. Binghamton, N.Y., Oct. 7, 1954; s. Joseph Anthony and Nena Lucy Mollo; m. Judith Moyer, May, 1995 (div. July 1998). BS, SUC, Buffalo, 1976, MSEd, 1977. Mgr. recreational svcs. SUC, Buffalo, 1978—83; dir. fin. aid, recruiting St. Joseph's Sch. Nursing, Elmira, NY, 1984—86; residence dir. SUNY, Morrisville, 1986—88, assoc. dir. campus life Purchase, 1988—91; dir. student activities Ferrum Coll., Va., 1991—2000; dir. campus activities and events U. Maine, Orono, 2000—. Coord. blood drive ARC, SUNY, Purchase, 1988-91, vol., Roanoke, Va., 1991-2000; vol. Project Safe Kids, Roanoke, 1995-99; fund raising coord., We. Va. AIDS Coun., Roanoke, 1997, St. James Cmty. Ctr., Ferrum, Va., ARC, Roanoke, 1998, Franklin County Schs., Rocky Mountain, Va., 1999; vol. Toys for Tots, Roanoke, 1997-99 . With USNR, 1986. Recipient Hudson Valley Blood Bank, 1991, Meritorious Svc. award Area Eight Spl. Olympics, 1992. Mem. Nat. Assn. Campus Activities (unit regional leadership team 1992-2000, unit coord. Va. 1994-97, regional coop. buyer 1997-99, vol. devel. coord. 1999-2000, Outstanding Campus Activities Profls., 1999). E-mail: joe.mollo@umit.maine.edu.

MOLLOFF, FLORENCE JEANINE, speech and language therapist; b. St. Louis, Aug. 28, 1959; d. Lawrence Allan and Rietta Gertrude (Fiegenbaum) M. BS, Fontbonne Coll., St. Louis, 1983; MEd summa cum laude, Nat. Louis U., St. Louis, 1989; student, Project ACCESS Inst., 1992, Judevine Ctr. Autistic Children Tng., 1992. Cert. speech correctionist, Mo. Intern St. Louis State Sch. for Profoundly Retarded, 1983-84; speech therapist St. Louis Pub. Schs., 1984—; Judvine Ctr. for Autistic Children Tng., 1992; speech/lang. therapist St. Louis Pub. Schs./Autism Program, 1992-93, 97—; speech/lang. therapist Michael Sch. Medically Fragile and Multiply Handicapped Michael Sch. Medically Fragile and Multiply Handicapped, 1993-96; speech and lang. pathologist autism program Buder, 1996—, Buder and Fanning, 1997—2000. Speech, lang. therapist St. Louis Pub. Schs./Michael Sch. for Medically Fragile and Multiply Handicapped, 1993—; ednl. cons. program devel. Mo. Coalition for Environ., St. Louis, Columbia, Kansas City, 1990—; cons., trainer in puppetry Kids on the Block, St. Louis Pub. Schs., 1988—; vol. grant writer West End Restoration Corp.; speech/lang. therapist Mid. Sch. for Medically Fragile and Multiply Handicapped, 1993-96. Author: (pseudonym F.J. Molotschnikov) 91 Seconds to Armageddon, 1999; author, creator transition curriculum: Consultative Resource Program, 1989; creator puppet program: Save Our Astonishing Planet, 1990; ednl. cons. program devel. young St. Louis audiences (adapted program for severe to profoundly handicapped children "Arabian Nights", 1994; editor: Strides Newsletter, St. Louis, 1996-98; contbr. artist St. Louis Internat. Jazz Mus.; vol. grant writer West End Restoration Corp. Educator, lobbyist Coalition for the Environ., St. Louis, 1990, newsletter editor, 2000-01; activist, lobbyist Housing Now, St. Louis, 1989; foster parent Christian Children's Fund, 1986—; activist Habitat for Humanity Internat., 1994—; mem., fundraiser Gateway I Have a Dream Found., 1995—; mem. nat. steering com. (hon.) Pres. Clinton's Re-election, 1995; contbg. mem. Dem. Nat. Com., 1995—; vol. grant writer West End Restoration Corp.; mem. Emily's List; participant Cross-Cultural Solutions Project, New Delhi, India, 1998; mem. World Affairs Coun., St. Louis, Mo., 2002. Mem. AAUW, ASCD, Coun. Exceptional Children (state rep. Mo. divsn. for children with communicative disorders 1988-89, presenter nat. conv. 1989), Internat. Platform Assn., Am. Fedn. Tchrs. (bldg. rep. 1992), Nat. Arbor Day Found., Nat. Parks and Conservation Assn., Nat. Women's Polit. Caucus, Mo. Assn. for Augmentative Comm. Systems, Met. St. Louis Women's Polit. Caucus, Emily's List, Am. Med. Writers Assn., Soc. for Tech. Com., NEA (editor Strides newsletter 1996-97, grantee Internet project, sec. St. Louis 1997-99), Mo. NEA, Amnesty Internat., World Affairs Coun. St. Louis. Democrat. Avocations: puppetry, international affairs, running track, film, debate. Home: 9823 Lullaby Ln Saint Louis MO 63114-2510

MOLLOY, MARGOT KATHERINE, secondary physical education educator; b. Haverhill, Mass., Apr. 20, 1940; d. James J. Sr. and Katherine E. (Ryan) M. BS, Russell Sage Coll., Troy, N.Y., 1962, MA, 1964. Cert. tchr., N.Y. Phys. edn. tchr. Middle Country Sch. Dist., Centereach, N.Y., 1963-67, East Islip (N.Y.) Sch. Dist., 1967-95. Mgr. Nantucket (Mass.) Tennis Club, 1985; active Sect. XI Suffolk County, L.I., N.Y., 1967-95. Recipient award for outstanding contbns. to girls' and women's sports Stony Brook U., 1993. Mem. AAHPERD, N.Y. Assn. Health, Phys. Edn., Recreation and Dance, Assn. of Women Phys. Educators of N.Y. State. Avocations: tennis, golf, skiing, bridge, reading.

MOLLOY, SYLVIA, Latin American literature educator, writer; b. Buenos Aires, Aug. 29, 1938; came to U.S. 1967; d. Herbert Edward and Margarita Berta (Chasseing) M. Licence es Lettres, U. Paris, 1960, Diplome D'Etudes Superieures, 1961, Doctorat de U. Paris, 1967. Asst. prof. Spanish SUNY, Buffalo, 1967-69; asst. prof. Spanish Vassar Coll., Poughkeepsie, N.Y., 1969-70, Princeton U., Princeton, N.J., 1970-73, assoc. prof., 1973-81, Emory L. Ford prof., 1981-86; prof. Spanish Yale U., New Haven, 1986-90; Albert Schweitzer prof. of Humanities NYU, 1990—. Author: La Diffusion de la Litterature Hispanoamericaine en France, 1972, Las Letras de Borges, 1979, En Breve Carcel, 1981, At Face Value: Autobiographical Writing in Spanish America, 1991; co-author Women's Writing in Latin America, 1991, Hispanisms and Homosexualities, 1998, El Comun Olvido, 2002; author short stories and contbr. articles to profl. jours.; cons., editorial bd. Revista Iberoamericana, 1979-81, 1985-89, Latin Am. Literary Rev., 1985—, Revista de Filología, Buenos Aires, 1985— Fellow Am. Philos. Soc., 1970, NEH, 1976; Social Sci. Research Council grantee, 1983; Guggenheim Found. fellow, 1986-87 Mem. MLA (pres.), Asociacion Internacional de Hispanistas, Instituto Internacional de Literatura Iberoamericana

MOLNAR, THOMAS, philosophy and religion educator, writer; b. Budapest, Hungary, June 26, 1921; s. Alexander and Aurelie (Blon) M. MA in French Lit., MA in Philosophy, Université de Bruxelles, 1948; PhD, Columbia U., 1952; PhD honoris causa, U. Mendoza (Argentina), 1986. Prof. French and world lit. Bklyn. Coll., 1957—. Adj. prof. European intellectual history L.I. U., 1967—; guest prof. polit. philosophy Potchefstroom U., South Africa, 1969; guest prof. philosophy Hillsdale Coll., Mich., 1973-74; vis. prof. Yale U., 1983; vis. prof. philosophy U. Dijon, France, 199p; prof. philosophy of religion U. Budapest, 1991—, permanent vis. prof. philosophy of religion dept. philosophy, 1991—; prof. philosophy Pázmány Péter Cath. U., Budapest, 1997—. Author: Bernanos, His Political Thought and Prophecy, 1960, The Future of Education, 1961, The Decline of the Intellectual, 1962, The Two Faces of American Foreign Policy, 1962, Africa, A Political Travelogue, 1965, Utopia, The Pernennial Heresy, 1967, Sartre, Ideologue of Our Time, 1968, Ecumenism or New Reformation?, 1968, The Counter-Revolution, 1969, La Gauche vue d'en face 1970, L'Animal politique, 1974, The European Dilemma, 1974, God and the Knowledge of Reality, 1974, Le Socialisme sans visage, 1976, Authority and Its Enemies, 1976, Christian Humanism, A Critique of the Secular City and Its Ideology, 1978, Le Modèle dèfigurè, l'Amerique de Tocqueville à Carter, 1978, Theists and Atheists, A Typology of Non-Belief, 1980, Politics and the State: A Catholic View, 1982, Le Dieu Immanent, 1982, Tiers-Monde, Idèologie Rèalitè, 1982, L'Eclipse du Sacré, 1986, The Pagan Temptation, 1987, Twin Power: Politics and the Sacred, 1988, L'Europe entre Parenthèses, 1990, Philosophical Grounds, 1991, The Church, Pilgrim of Centuries, 1991, L'Amèicanologie, Le triomphe du modèle planètaire?, 1991, Az Ideális èllam kritikája, 1991, L'Hègèmonie libèrale, 1992, The Emerging Atlantic Culture, 1994, Archetypes of Thought, 1995, Return to Philosophy, 1996, La modernite et ses antidotes, 1996, A Modernseg Politikai Elvei, 1998, Moi, Symmague, 1999, A beszelo Isten, 2003; contbr. articles to profl. jours. Grantee Relm Found. grantee, 1963-64, 66-67, Earhart Found., 1992; recipient Silver medal City of Nice, 1987, Silver Cross Hungarian Republic, 1998, Szechenyi prize Hungarian Republic, 2000, Stephanus prize Hungarian Cath. Publ., 2002. Home: 238 Heights Rd Ridgewood NJ 07450-2414

MOLONEY, WILLIAM J. school system administrator; BA in History and Polit. Sci., MA in History and Polit. Sci., Harvard U.; PhD in ednl. mgmt., Harvard U., Cambridge, Mass.; postgrad, studies in Slavic History, Oxford and U. of London. Supt. Calvert county pub. schools, Prince Frederick, Md., 1993—97; commr. edn. Colo. Dept. Edn., Denver, 1997—; sec. Colo. bd. edn., 1997—. Chmn. Edn. Leaders Coun., Washington; adj prof. Various Univs.; bd, dirs. Bds. of the Ctr. for Workforce Preparation, Ednl. Excellence Network. Co-author: (Books) The Content of America's Character, Education Innovation: An Agenda to Frame the Future; newspaper columnist:. Office: Colo Dept Education 201 E Colfax Ave Rm 500 Denver CO 80203 E-mail: moloney_w@cde.state.co.us.*

MOLZ, FRED JOHN, III, hydrologist, educator; b. Mays Landing, N.J., Aug. 13, 1943; s. Fred John Jr. and Viola Violet (MacDonald) M.; m. Mary Lee Clark, Dec. 17, 1966; children: Fred John IV, Stephen Joseph. BS in Physics, Drexel U., 1966, MCE, 1968; PhD in Hydrology, Stanford U., 1970. Hydraulic engr. U.S. Geol. Survey, Menlo Park, Calif., 1970; asst. prof. Auburn (Ala.) U., 1970-74, alumni asst. prof., 1974-76, alumni assoc. prof., 1976-80, asst. dean research, 1979-84, dir. Eng. exptl. sta., 1981-84, prof., 1980-84, Feagin prof., 1984-89, Huff eminent scholar, 1990-95; SCUREF disting. scientist Clemson U., 1995—. Cons. Battelle N.W., Richland, Wash., 1982-83, 84-85, Argonne (Ill.) Nat. Labs., 1983-85, Electric Power Rsch. Inst., Menlo Park, Calif., 1984-85, U.S. NRC, 1991-97. Author: (with others) Numerical Methods in Hydrology, 1971, Modeling Wastewater Renovation, 1981; contbr. articles to profl. jours. Recipient Disting. Faculty award Auburn U. Alumni Assn., 1987; grantee EPA, 1986, 90, 97, DOE, 1980, 83, 98, U.S. Dept. Edn., 1991, NSF, 1992, 94, 97. Fellow Am. Geophys. Union (Horton award 1992); mem. Am. Soc. Agronomy, Nat. Ground Water Assn., Geol. Soc. Am., Internat. Assn. Hydrogeologists, Internat. Assn. for Mathematical Geology. Avocations: reading, travel, investing. Home: 213 Amethyst Way Seneca SC 29672-6851 Office: Clemson U Dept Environ Engring & Sci 342 Computer Ct Anderson SC 29625-6510 E-mail: fredi@clemson.edu.

MONAGHAN, M. PATRICIA, education educator, writer, poet; b. Bklyn., Feb. 15, 1946; d. Edward Joseph and Mary Margaret (Gordon) M. BA in English, U. Minn., 1967, MA in English, 1971; MFA, U. Alaska, 1981; PhD, The Union Inst., 1995. News editor U. Alaska, Fairbanks, 1970-71; pub. rels. dir. Walker Art Ctr., Mpls., 1972; editor Minn. Monthly Minn. Pub. Radio, St. Paul, 1973-74; women's editor Daily News miner, Fairbanks, 1975; lectr., head English dept. Tanana Valley C.C., Fairbanks, 1976-87; instr. writing The Neighborhood Inst., Chgo., 1987-89; dir. cont. edn. St. Xavier U., Chgo., 1990—; assoc. prof. DePaul U. Sch. for New Learning, Chgo. Booklist reviewer ALA, Chgo., 1987—. Author: Book of

Goddesses and Heroines, 1981, 90, Working Wisdom, 1994, O Mother Sun New View of Feminine, 1994, (poetry) Seasons of the Witch, 1992 (Friends of Lit. award 1992), (poems) Dancing with Chaos, 2002, The Red Haired Girl from the Bog, 2003, Meditation: The Complete Guide, 1999. Mem. South Shore Cultural Ctr., Chgo., 1989-92; bd. dirs. Athena Ctr. Recipient Rsch. award NUCEA, 1993, Univ. Alaska, 1987. Mem. Am. Conf. on Irish Studies, Soc. Midland Authors, Authors Guild. Democrat. Mem. Soc. Of Friends. Office: DePaul Univ Sch for New Learning 243 S Wabash Ave Fl 7 Chicago IL 60604-2302 E-mail: pmonagha@depaul.edu.

MONAGHAN, W(ILLIAM) PATRICK, immunohematologist, retired naval officer, health educator, consultant; b. Ashtabula, Ohio, June 24, 1944; s. Paul E. and June E. (Sober) M. m. Mary Lou Gustafson, Mar. 15, 1976; children: Ian Patrick, Erin Kelly. BS, Old Dominion U., Va., 1968; MS in Biology, Bowling Green State U., 1972, PhD, 1975. Enlisted U.S. Navy, 1961, commd. ensign Med. Service Corps, 1969, advanced through grades to comdr., 1983; staff med. technologist officer Nat. Naval Med. Ctr., Bethesda, Md., 1969; clin. lab. and blood bank officer USS Sanctuary (AH-17), S. Vietnam, 1969-70; clin. lab. officer Naval Med. Ctr., Charleston, S.C., 1970-72; blood bank fellow U.S. Army Med. Rsch. Lab., Ft. Knox, Ky., 1972-73; head blood bank Nat. Naval Med. Ctr., 1975-85, faculty and course dir. for immunohematology med. tech., 1976-84, dir. blood bank, 1976-84; asst. prof. pathology George Washington U. Sch. Medicine, Washington, 1976-83, assoc. prof., 1983-88; mem. faculty Walter Reed Army Med. Ctr., Washington, 1976-88; asst. dean grad. and continuing edn. Uniformed Svcs. U. of Health Sci., Washington, 1984-88, ret., 1988; prof. Grad. Sch. Nursing Uniformed Svcs. U. of Health Sci., 1994-2000; prof. Coll. Health, Fla. Internat. U., North Miami, Fla. V.p. Met. Washington Blood Banks, 1976-81, ex officio mem. bd. dirs. 1981-87; cons. D.C. chpt. Hemophiliac Found., 1977-78; spl. USN rep. Am. Soc. Med. Tech., 1976-88; dir. N.E. area blood system Navy Blood Program, 1978-88; mem. tri-service blood bank com. Dept. Def. Blood Program, 1978-88; faculty and program adv. com. ARC, Washington, 1978-84, Johns Hopkins Med. Sch., Balt., 1978-85; faculty U. Tenn. Center for Health Scis., Memphis, 1978, U. Ill. Sch. Medicine, Peoria, 1978-79, Grad. Sch. Nursing Uniformed Svcs. U. of Health Scis., Bethesda, Md.; guest lectr. NIH Blood Bank, 1978-90; adj. assoc. prof. Bowling Green State U., Ohio, 1981-89; bd. dirs. Exam, Inc., Rockville, Md. Navy editor Procs. Armed Forces Med. Lab. Scientists, 1976, 79. 80, editor-in-chief, 1982-85; assoc. editor Am. Jour. Med. Tech., 1978-88, Jour. Allied Health; Navy editor History of the Blood Program of the U.S. Mil. Svcs. in Vietnam and S.E. Asisa, 1976; contbr. articles to profl. jours.. Decorated numerous combat and svc. medals; USN grantee, 1977-89. Mem. Am. Soc. Med. Technologists (chmn. immunohematology task group 1976), Am. Blood Commn. (task force 1976, regionalization), Am. Assn. Blood Banks (sci. assembly 1976—, adminstrv. sect. 1976—, blood component therapy com. 1977-79, edn. com. 1976-83), AAAS, Am. Soc. Clin. Pathologists, Soc. Mil. Surgeons, Naval Inst., Sigma Xi, others Home: 534 NE Olive Way Boca Raton FL 33432-4152 Business E-Mail: monaghan@fiu.edu. E-mail: wpatrickmonaghan@aol.com.

MONAHAN, JOHN T. law educator, psychologist; b. N.Y.C., Nov. 1, 1946; s. John Joseph and Dorothy (King) M.; m. Linda Costa, Aug. 24, 1969; children: Katherine, John. BA, SUNY, 1968; PhD, Ind. U., 1972. Asst. prof. U. Calif., Irvine, 1972-80; prof. U. Va., Charlottesville, 1980-84, Doherty prof., 1985—. Dir. mental health law MacArthur Found., Chgo., 1988-98. Author: Predicting Violent Behavior, 1981 (Guttmacher award 1981), Social Science in Law, 1998. Recipient Disting. Contbn. Pub. Policy award APA, Washington, 1990, Isaac Ray award, APA, N.Y., 1996. Mem. APA, Inst. of Medicine Office: U Va Sch Law 580 Massie Rd Charlottesville VA 22903-1738 E-mail: jmonahan@virginia.edu.

MONCRIEF, JAMES LORING, educational administrator; b. Limestone County, Ala., Sept. 19, 1935; m. Sue Evans; 4 children. BS, Samford U., 1958; MS, U. So. Miss., 1959; postgrad., Fla. State U., 1961, Ga. So. U., 1979-82, U. S.C., 1984—. Instr. dept. social scis. U. So. Miss., Hattiesburg, 1958-59; chmn. dept. social scis. North Fla. Jr. Coll., Madison, 1959-62; asst. prof. social scis. Jacksonville (Ala.) State U., 1962-64; exec. dean Jefferson State Coll., Birmingham, Ala., 1964-68; dir. community coll. mental health workers project So. Regional Edn. Bd., Atlanta, 1968-70; dir. career edn. and tng. N.C. Dept. Mental Health, Raleigh, 1970-71; asst. prof., coord. dir. health related professions U. Tex./Pan Am., Edinburg, 1971-74; tchr., asst. prin., prin. Chatham-Savannah (Ga.) Bd. Edn., 1974-78; prin. Williamsburg-Blakeley High Sch., Kingstree, S.C., 1978-86, Gaffney (S.C.) Sr. High Sch., 1986-92, Laurens (S.C.) Dist. 55 H.S., 1992-94; dist. office adminstr., exec. dir. secondary programs Sch. Dist. Pickens County, Easley, S.C., 1994—. Past adj. assoc. prof. div. allied health East Carolina U., Greenville, N.C.; past asst. prof., coord. div. health related professions, U. Tex./Pan Am. Contbr. to profl. publs. Bd. dirs., exec. com., project rev. com. Pee Dee Health Systems Agy.; deacon West End Bapt. Ch., Gaffney, S.C.; mem. blue ribbon com. Williamsburg County Civic Auditorium; bd. dirs. Boys Club Am., Cherokee County Suicide Intervention Ctr., Inc.; pres. Cherokee County div. Am. Heart Assn.; past pres. S.C. High Sch. League; bd. advisers Cherokee Pastoral Counseling Ctr., Gaffney; active S.C. Bus. Edn Partnership for Excellence Edn. With U.S. Marines, Korea, Vietnam. Fullbright scholar Brazil, 1962. Mem. Cherokee C. of C., Lions, Christian Businessmen's Com., Laurens C. of C., Rotary. Office: Sch Dist Pickens County 1348 Griffin Mill Rd Easley SC 29640-8885

MONDRY, DIANE, secondary school educator; b. Reginas, Sask., Can. 3 children. Career and tech. edn. tchr. Cmty. H.S., Grand Forks, ND. Part-time instr. dept. info. sys. and bus. edn. U. N.D. Recipient Outstanding Tchr. award, Nat. Assn. Vocat. Edn. Spl. Needs Pers. Mem.: NEA, Assn. for Career and Tech. Edn. (immediate past pres. 2001—02), Nat. Bd. for Profl. Tchg. Stds. (bd. mem.). Office: Cmty High Sch 500 Stanford Rd Grand Forks ND 58203-2748*

MONEGRO, FRANCISCO, psychology educator, alternative medicine consultant; b. La Vega, Dominican Republic, Apr. 20, 1949; s. Francisco Monegro-Fdez and Ana A. (Pena) Monegro. Grad. cum laude, Pontifical U., Santiago, Dominican Republic, 1973; grad. psychology, Autonomous U. Santo Domingo, 1978, MD, 1986; MA in Ednl. Psychology, Tech. Inst. Santo Domingo, 1981; PhD in Nutrition, LaSalle U., Mandeville, La., 1993. Cert. natural health profl., hypnotherapist, profl. biofeedback profl.; diplomate in behavioral medicine, diplomate in pain mgmt.; lic. in psychology Autonomous U. Santo Domingo, 1978. Tchr. Peace H.S., Santo Domingo, Dominican Republic, 1975-76; dir. dept. psychology Holy Trinity Ednl. Ctr., Santo Domingo, 1978-80; prof. Sch. Medicine Tech. Inst. Santo Domingo, 1986-87; dir. dept. psychology Interam. U., Santo Domingo, 1988-89; prof. psychology and medicine Autonomous U. Santo Domingo, 1978-89, psychologist, counseling dept., 1979-84; staff mem. spl. edn. Bd. Edn. Dist. X, Bronx, N.Y., 1991-93; founder, chmn. N.Y. Inst. for Holistic Life, N.Y.C., 1991—; prof. psychology CUNY at HCC, Bronx, 1990—. Founder, pioneer in behavioral medicine Behavioral Medicine Clinic, Santo Domingo, 1987-94. Author: Biofeedback-Bio-retroalimentacion, 1988, Holistic Behavioral Medicine, 1993, Biomagnetic Medicine: Secrets and Power of Magnetic Energy, 1996, Psychology and Life Mind, Body and Society, 1997, (interactive CD-ROMs) Psychology and Life, 2000, Developmental Aphasia, 2002; editor, pub.: BOEST, 1978, Dominican Bull. Behavioral Medicine, 1987, Holistic Life/Vida Holistica, 1991, others. Mem. Dominican Psychol. Assn. (treas. 1978-79), Soc. Behavioral Medicine, Assn. for Advancement of Behavior Therapy, Am. Acad. Pain Mgmt., Assn. for Applied Psychophysiology and Biofeedback. Democrat. Roman Catholic. Avocations: computers, golf, basketball, swimming, travel. Home: PO Box 302 Bronx NY 10458-0302 Office: NY Inst for Holistic Life 976 Mclean Ave Ste 370 Yonkers NY 10704-4105

MONETA, GIOVANNI BATTISTA, research educator; b. Genoa, Italy, Oct. 4, 1958; s. Umberto and Agnese Moneta; m. Satu Synnöve Kekkonen-Moneta. Degree, U. Padua, 1983; MA, PhD, U. Chgo., 1990. Assoc. rschr. Northwestern U., Chgo., 1987-88; rsch. fellow U. Helsinki, 1989; rschr. Finnish Inst. Occupational Health, Helsinki, 1989-93, INSERM, Paris, 1993-94, EHESS, Paris, 1994-96; assoc. prof. U. Padua, Italy, 1996-97, Chinese U. Hong Kong, 1997-2001; rsch. fellow Harvard Bus. Sch., Boston, 2001—. Cons. in edn. and tng. NIVA, Helsinki, 1989-93. Recipient Volvo award in clin. scis. ISSLS, 1991, Vice-Chancellor's Exemplary Tchg. award Chinese U. Hong Kong, 1999. Avocations: chess, cooking, anthropology, fine arts. Home: via della Rotonda 9 16011 Arenzano Italy Office: Harvard Bus Sch Soldiers Field Boston MA 02163 E-mail: gbmoneta@hotmail.com.

MONEY, JOHN WILLIAM, psychologist, educator; b. Morrinsville, New Zealand, July 8, 1921; came to U.S., 1947, naturalized, 1962; s. Frank and Ruth (Read) M. MA with honors, Victoria U. Coll., New Zealand, 1943; postgrad., U. Pitts., 1947; PhD, Harvard U., 1952; DHL (hon.), Hofstra U., 1992. Jr. lectr. philosophy and psychology U. Otago, New Zealand, 1945-47; part-time vis. lectr. Bryn Mawr Coll., Pa., 1952-53; mem. faculty Johns Hopkins U., Balt., 1951—, prof. med. psychology, 1972-86, assoc. prof. pediatrics, 1959-86, prof. emeritus med. psychology and pediatrics, 1986—; psychologist Johns Hopkins Hosp., 1955—, founder psychohormonal research unit, 1951, founding mem. gender identity com., 1966. Vis. prof. pediats. Albert Einstein Coll. Medicine, 1969, U. Nebr. Coll. Medicine, 1972; vis. prof. endocrinology Harvard U., 1970; vis. prof. ob-gyn. U. Conn., 1975; Rachford lectr. Children's Hosp., Cin., 1969; bd. dirs. Sex Info. and Edn. Coun. U.S., 1965-68, Neighborhood Family Planning Ctr., 1970-82; mem. task force homosexuality NIMH, 1967-69; mem. study sect. devel. and behavioral scis. NIH, 1970-74; mem. task force on nomenclature Am. Psychiat. Assn., 1977-79, 85-87; pres. Am. Found. Gender and Genital Medicine and Sci., 1978—; bd. advisors Elysium Inst., 1980-2000; mem. external com. for rev. of Inst. for Sex Rsch., Ind. U., 1980; mem. sci. adv. bd. Kinsey Inst. for Rsch. in Sex, Gender and Reprodn., 1982-97; hon. chmn. internat. adv. bd. Nat. Inst. Rsch. in Sex Edn., Counseling and Therapy, 1991; Kan Tongpo vis. prof. dept. psychiatry U. Hong Kong, 1994. Mem. editl. bd. numerous jours.; field editor Medicine and Law: an Internat. Jour., 1982-95; subject of TV documentary Coming Home, 1999. Recipient Hofheimer prize Am. Psychiat. Assn., 1956, Gold medal Children's Hosp., Phila., 1966, citation Am. Urol. Assn., 1975, Harry Benjamin medal of honor Erickson Ednl. Found., 1976, Outstanding Contbn. award Md. Psychol. Assn., 1976, Lindemann lectr. pediatrics Cornell U., 1983, Bernadine Disting. lectr. U. Mo., 1985, Maurice W. Laufer Meml. lectr. Bradley Hosp. and Brown U., 1986, Disting. Scholar award Harry Benjamin Internat. Gender Dysphoria Assn., 1987, Outstanding Rsch. Accomplishments award Nat. Inst. Child Health and Human Devel., 1987, Gloria Scientae Polish award, 1991, Lifetime Outstanding award for Treatment of Sex Offenders, 1991, Richard J. Cross award Robert Wood Johnson Med. Sch., 1992, Career Achievement award N.Y. Soc. Forensic Scis., 1994, Coun. of Sex Edn. and Parenthood Internat. award, 1994, gold medal for lifetime achievement World Assn. Sexology, 1995, sexology medal Am. Acad. Clin. Sexology, 1996, Magnus Hirschfeld medal for sexual scis., 2002; named Sexologist of Yr. Polish Acad. Sex. Sci., 1988; James McKeen Cattell fellow Am. Psychol. Soc., 1993; subject of book John Money: A Tribute (E. Coleman, editor), 1991. Fellow: AAAS (life), Soc. Sci. Study Sex (charter, pres. 1974—76, award 1976, Past Pres. award 1987, Kinsey award western regional chpt. 1996, John Money award named in his honor 2003), Nat. Inst. Rsch. Sex Edn., Counseling and Therapy (hon.), Harriet Lane Alumni Soc.; mem.: APA (master lectr. 1975, Disting. Sci. award 1985), Nat. Assn. Sexology (chief patron), Internat. Coll. Pediats., Md. Soc. Med. Rsch., N.Y. Acad. Scis., Internat. Soc. Psychoneuroendocrinology, European Soc. Pediat. Endocrinology (corr.), Asian Fedn. for Sexology (hon.), Soc. Andaluza de Sexologia (hon.), Assn. Sexologists (life), Am. Assn. Sex Educators, Counselors and Therapists (hon. awards 1976, 1985), Columbian Sexol. Soc. (hon.), Czechoslovak Sexology Soc. (hon.; internat. adv. bd. 1995), New Zealand Soc. on Sexology (hon.; life), Soc. Brasileira de Sexologia (hon.), Can. Sex Rsch. Forum (hon.), Assn. Especialistas en Sexologia (hon.), Internat. Acad. Sex Rsch. (charter, award 1991), Lawson Wilkins Pediat. Endocrine Soc. (founder), Soc. Pediat. Psychology, Internat. Orgn. Study Human Devel., Deutsche Gesellschaft fur Sexualforschung. Home: 2104 E Madison St Baltimore MD 21205-2337 Office: Johns Hopkins Hosp Baltimore MD 21205 E-mail: jmoney@mail.jhmi.edu.

MONEY, MAX LEE, family nurse practitioner; b. Pineville, Ky., Apr. 17, 1949; s. Arthur Lee and Laura (Hendrickson) M. ASN, Lincoln Meml. U., 1991, BSN, 1993; MSN, U. Ky., 1997. RN, Ky., Tenn.; cert. family nurse practitioner. Staff nurse ICU Pineville Cmty. Hosp., 1991-93, med.-surg. flr. supr., 1993-94, med. surg. staff nurse, 1994-97; asst. prof. Sch. Nursing Lincoln Meml. U., Harrogate, Tenn., 1994—2001; dir. emergency dept., family nurse practitioner Middlesboro Appalachian Regional Hosp., 1997—2003; family nurse practitioner Med. Ctr. Clinic, New Tazewell, Tenn., 2003—. Mem. profl. adv. bd. Comprehensive Home Health, Middlesboro, Ky., 1994; in-svc. educator Pineville Cmty. Hosp., 1994. Agent coll. fair Lincoln Meml. U., 1994, organizer breast cancer awareness seminar Schenck ctr., 1994, coord. Operation HealthCheck, 2001, MARH Free Clinic; tchr. Sunday sch. Harmony Bapt. Ch., Pineville, 1994. Recipient Bronze Good Citizenship award Nat. Soc. of Sons of Am. Revolution, 1991, Nursing Leadership award Tenn. Nurses Assn., 1991. Mem. ANA, AANP, Nat. League Nursing (adv. 1992—), Ky. Nurses Assn., Ky. Coalition Nurse Practitioners/Nurse Midwives, Sigma Theta Tau. Avocations: tea rose gardening, swimming, gospel music. Home: RR 1 Box 53 Pineville KY 40977-9706 Office: Med Ctr Clinic New Tazewell TN 37825 Office Fax: 423-526-5624. E-mail: maxmoney@tcnet.net.

MONEY, RUTH ROWNTREE, infant development and care specialist, consultant; b. Brownwood, Tex. m. Lloyd Jean Money; children: Jeffrey, Meredith, Jeannette. BA in Biology, Rice U., 1944; MA in Devel. Psychology, Calif. State U., Long Beach, 1971; BA in Early Childhood Edn., U. D.C., 1979. Rsch. psychologist Early Edn. Project, Capitol Heights, Md., 1971-73; lectr. No. Va. C.C., Anandale, 1973-74; tchr. preschs. Calif. and Va., 1979-81; dir. various preschs., Washington and Va., 1981-85; instr. guided studies Pacific Oaks Coll., Pasadena, Calif., 1986-88; cons. parent/infant programs Resources for Infant Educarers, L.A., 1986—; founder, dir. South Bay Infant Ctr., Redondo Beach, Calif., 1988-92; instr. child devel. Harbor Coll., L.A., 1992-93. Bd. dirs. Resources for Infant Educarers, 1986—; pres. bd. dirs. South Bay Infant Ctr., Redondo Beach, 1988-94, treas., 1994-98. Producer (ednl. videos) Caring for Infants, 1988—. Mem. League of Women Voters, 1956—, v.p., 1972-76. Mem. Nat. Assn. for Edn. of Young Children, Assn. for Childhood Edn. Internat., Infant Devel. Assn. Calif. Avocations: traveling, hiking. Home: 904 21st St Hermosa Beach CA 90254-3105 Office: Resources for Infant Educarers 1550 Murray Cir Los Angeles CA 90026-1644 E-mail: ruthmoney@earthlink.net.

MONISMITH, CARL LEROY, civil engineering educator; b. Harrisburg, Pa., Oct. 23, 1926; s. Carl Samuel and Camilla Frances (Geidt) M. BSCE, U. Calif., Berkeley, 1950, MSCE, 1954. Registered civil engr., Calif. From instr. to prof. civil engring. U. Calif., Berkeley, 1951—, chmn. dept. civil engring., 1974-79, Robert Horonjeff prof. civil engring., 1986—, prof. emeritus, 1996. Cons. Chevron Rsch. Co., Richmond, Calif., 1957-93, U.S. Army CE Waterways Expt. Sta., Vicksburg, Miss., 1968—, B.A. Vallerga, Inc., Oakland, Calif., 1980-98, ARE, Austin, Tex. and Scotts Valley, Calif., 1978-92; cons. Bechtel Corp., San Francisco, 1982-86. Contbr. numerous articles to profl. jours. Served to 2d lt. C.E., U.S. Army, 1945-47. Recipient Rupert Myers medal U. NSW, 1976; named Henry M. Shaw Lectr. in Civil Engring., N.C. State U., 1993; sr. scholar Fulbright Found., U. NSW, 1971, Nat. Asphalt Pavelent Assn. R.D. Kenyon Rsch. and Edn. award for Outstanding Contbns. for Hot Mix Asphalt Tech., 2002; named Disting. Engring. Alumnus, Coll. Engring., U. Calif., Berkeley, 1996. Fellow: AAAS; mem.: ASTM, NAE, NRC (assoc.), NAS (assoc.), ASCE (hon.; pres. San Francisco sect. 1979—80, ednl. activities com. 1989—91, State of Art award 1977, James Laurie prize 1988), Nat. Assn. of the Nat. Acads., Asphalt Inst. (Roll of Honor 1990), Calif. Asphalt Pavement Alliance, Am. Soc. Engring. Edn., Internat. Soc. Asphalt Pavements (hon.; chmn. bd. dirs. 1988—90), Assn. Asphalt Paving Technologists (hon. W.J. Emmons award 1961, 1965, 1985), Transp. Rsch. Bd. (assoc.; chmn. pavement design sect. 1973—79, K.B. Woods award 1972, 1st disting. lectureship 1992, Roy W. Crum award 1995). Avocations: swimming, stamp collecting. Office: U Calif Dept Civil Engring 215 Mclaughlin Hall Berkeley CA 94720-1720 E-mail: clm@maxwell.berkeley.edu.

MONIZ, ERNEST JEFFREY, government official, former physics educator; b. Fall River, Mass., Dec. 22, 1944; s. Ernest Perry and Georgina (Pavao) M.; m. Naomi Hoki, June 9, 1973; 1 child, Katya BS, Boston Coll., 1966; PhD, Stanford U., 1971. Prof. physics MIT, Cambridge, 1973-97, dir. Bates Linear Accelerator Ctr. Middleton, 1983-91, head physics dept., 1991-95, 97; under sec. U.S. Dept. Energy, Washington, 1997—. Cons. Los Alamos Nat. Lab., 1975-95; assoc. dir. for sci. Office of Sci. and Tech. Policy, Exec. Office of the Pres., 1996-97. Contbr. articles to profl. jours. Office: Office of UnderSecretary US Dept Energy 1000 Independence Ave SW Washington DC 20585-0001

MONKS, LINDA ANN, art educator; b. Montclair, N.J., Aug. 28, 1949; d. Charles and Lillian Bieksha; m. Robert Norman Monks, Apr. 17, 1971; children: Alyson, Shelly, Clayton. BFA, Montclair State Coll., 1972; MAT, Montclair State U., 1996. Subsitute tchr. Byram Bd. of Edn., 1980; driver Frank L. Black, Inc., Andover, N.J., 1985-90; tech. asst. Montclair State Coll., Upper Montclair, N.J., 1993-94; substitute tchr. Hopatcong (N.J.) Bd. Edn., 1995, Lenape Valley Regional H.S., Stanhope, N.J., 1990-95; art instr. Lakeview Learning Ctr., Wayne, N.J., 1995-96, Future Kids, Cresskill, NJ, 1996—97, State of N.J., 1998—99, Lacordaire Acad., Upper Montclair, NJ, 1999—. Steering com. Crayola Dream-Makers, Upper Montclair, N.J., 1993; treas. Montclair State Art Educators, Upper Montclair, 1993; pub. rels. rep. Children With Attention Deficit Disorders, Newton, N.J., 1988. Mem., pres., treas. Cranberry Lake Fire Dept. Women's Aux., Byram, 1987-94. Recipient Merit scholarship State of N.J., 1967. Mem. Nat. Art Edn. Assn., Phi Kappa Phi, Kappa Delta Pi. Avocations: flying airplanes, motorcycling, weaving, crafts, reading. Office: Lacordaire Acadamy 155 Lorraine Ave Verona NJ 07044

MONKS, REGINA See WATKISS, REGINA

MONMONIER, MARK, geographer, graphics educator, essayist; b. Balt., Feb. 2, 1943; s. John Carroll and Martha Elizabeth (Mason) M.; m. Margaret Janet Kollner, Sept. 4, 1965; 1 child, Jo Kerry. BA, Johns Hopkins U., 1964; MS, Pa. State U., 1967, PhD, 1969. Asst. prof. U. Rhode Island, Kingston, 1969-70, SUNY, Albany, 1970-73; assoc. prof Syracuse U., N.Y., 1973-79, prof., 1979-98, Disting. prof. geography, 1998—. Cons. N.Y. State, Albany, 1974-93, Nat. Geog. Soc., 1987, Microsoft Corp., 1993-99, Belmont Rsch., 1995, AT&T Rsch., 1996-97, George Philip Ltd., England, 1996-97; rsch. geographer U.S. Geol. Survey, Reston, Va., 1979-84; dep. dir. N.Y. Ctr. for Geographic Info. and Analysis, 1989-90; Robinson vis. fellow George Mason U., 1985; Ida Beam Disting. vis. prof. U. Iowa, 1985; mem. adv. bd. GIS Law and Policy Inst., 1994-98; adv. bd. Philip Lee Philips Soc.; cons. and expert witness various law firms, 1995—; co-dir. History of Cartography in the Twentieth Century project, 1999--; mem. mapping sci. com. NRC, 2000—. Author: Maps. Distortion and Meaning, 1977, Computer-assisted Cartography, 1982, Technological Transition in Cartography, 1985, Maps with the News, 1989, How to Lie with Maps, 1991, French edit., 1993, 2nd edit., 1996, Japanese edit., 1995, German edit., 1996, Korean edit., 1998, Czech edit., 2000, Mapping it Out, 1993, Cartographies of Danger, 1997, Air Apparent, 1999, Bushmanders and Bullwinkles, 2001; : Spying with Maps, 2002; ; co-author: The Study of Population: Elements, Patterns, Processes, 1982, Map Appreciation, 1988; author: Drawing the Line, 1995; co-editor: History of Cartography Project, 1997—; assoc. editor The American Cartographer, Falls Church, Va., 1977—82; editor: The American Cartographer, 1982—84; assoc. editor Mapping Scis. and Remote Sensing, 1987—97. contbg. editor Cartographica, 1984—, mem. editl. adv. bd. Mercator's World, 1997—. Statistician, Police Dept. Syracuse, 1978-80. Fellow John Simon Guggenheim Meml. Found., 1984, centennial fellow Pa. State U. Coll. Earth & Mineral Scis., 1996; recipient Chancellor's citation for Disting. Acad. Achievement, 1993, Disting. Geographer award Pa. Geog. Soc., 2000, O.M. Miller Cartographic medal, Am. Geog. Soc., 2001. Mem.: Soc. History Tech., Philip Lee Phillips Soc., Pa. Acad. Sci. (editl. bd. 1989—2000), N.Am. Cartographic Info. Soc. (editl. bd. 1998—2001), Can. Cartographic Assn. (Award of Distinction 2002), Authors Guild, Am. Cartographic Assn. (pres. 1983—84), Assn. Am. Geographers (Media Achievement award 2000), Tau Beta Pi, Pi Tau Sigma, Sigma Xi (pres. Syracuse chpt. 2001—02). Roman Catholic. Home: 302 Waldorf Pky Syracuse NY 13224-2240 Office: Syracuse U Dept Of Geography Syracuse NY 13244-1020 E-mail: mon2ier@syr.edu.

MONROE, EDWIN WALL, physician, former university dean; b. Laurinburg, N.C., Mar. 10, 1927; s. Robert Andrew and Berrie (Bryant) M.; m. Nancy Laura Gaquerel, Mar. 14, 1953; 1 dau., Martha Lynn. Student, U. Louisville, 1945-46; BS, Davidson Coll., 1947; post grad., U. N.C. Sch. Medicine, 1947-49; MD, U. Pa., 1951. Intern Med. Coll. Va. Hosp., Richmond, 1951-52; resident internal medicine N.C. Meml. Hosp., U. N.C., 1952-56, chief resident, asst. in medicine, 1955-56, instr. medicine, 1956-57; pvt. practice specializing in internal medicine Greenville, N.C., 1956-68; dean Sch. Allied Health and Social Professions, 1968-71; dir. health affairs East Carolina U., 1968-71, vice-chancellor health affairs, 1971-79; assoc. dean East Carolina U. (Sch. Medicine), 1979-86; mem. staff Pitt County Meml. Hosp.; exec. dean East Carolina U. Sch. of Medicine, 1986-90. Mem. regional adv. group N.C. Regional Med. Program, 1970-76; mem. facilities adv. com. N.C. Div. Vocat. Rehab., 1969-74; mem. N.C. Gov.'s Adv. Coun. Comprehensive Health Planning, 1974, Coastal Plains Mental Health Authority, 1969-74; pres. Ea. Area Health Edn. Ctr., 1974-82, exec. dir., 1982-90. Del. White House Conf. on Aging, 1981; mem. N.C. Commn. on Jobs and Econ. Growth, 1986-88, N.C. Health Coordinating Coun., Raleigh, 1977-86, Nat. Adv. Environ. Health Scis. Coun., Washington, 1980-84; exec. dir. Kate B. Reynolds Charitable Trust, 1990-93. Recipient Priestly prize U. Pa. Sch. Medicine, 1951, John G. Walsh award Am. Acad. Family Physicians, 1988. Fellow ACP; mem. AMA, Assn. Am. Med. Colls., Pitt County Med. Soc. (pres. 1968), N.C. Med. Soc. (pres. 1990-91), Greenville (N.C.) Country Club, Sigma Xi. Democrat. Avocation: golf. Home: 104 Longmeadow Rd Greenville NC 27858-3714

MONROE, KATHERINE DIANE OSBORNE, secondary education educator; b. Williamson, W.Va., July 2, 1947; d. Bill and Carrie Lorraine (Adkins) Osborne; m. B. Ed Monroe Jr. BS in Edn., Concord Coll., 1969; MEd in Guidance/Counseling, U. Del., 1976; MEd in Adminstrn., Old Dominion U., 1992. Cert. social sci. tchr., guidance counselor and adminstr. Tchr. Ctrl. Mid. Sch., Dover, Del., 1969-78, Princess Ann H.S., Virginia Beach, Va., 1978-81, First Colonial H.S., Virginia Beach, Va., 1981-82, Green Run H.S., Virginia Beach, Va., 1982-89, Salem H.S., Virginia Beach, Va., 1989—. Recipient Excellence in Tchg. Constition, John Marshall Found., Richmond, Va., 1991. Mem. NEA, Va. Edn. Assn., Virginia Beach Edn. Assn., Nat. Coun. Social Studies, Va. Coun. Social Studies (Tidwater region coord. 1979-80). Avocations: reading, cooking, crafts. Home: 1400 Franklin Dr Virginia Beach VA 23454-1532 Office: Salem High Sch 1993 Sun Devil Dr Virginia Beach VA 23464-8905 E-mail: dmonroe@exis.net.

MONROE, SIDNI MCCLUER, special education educator; b. Alexandria, Minn., Mar. 11, 1949; d. Frank and Catharine (Peterson) Shapiro; m. Larry K. Monroe, July 21, 1973; 1 child, Colin Yung Hwan. BA in Math., SUNY, Buffalo, 1971; postgrad., Pitts. State U., 1976-78; MA in Spl. Edn., Marshall U., 1984; postgrad., Columbia U., 1984-85. Cert. secondary math., learning and severely handicapped, gifted tchr., Calif. Insvc. tchr. trainer math. U.S. Peace Corps, 1971-75; tchr. spl. edn. Unified Sch. Dist. # 250, 1976-78, Joplin (Mo.) Regional Ctr., 1978-80; grad. teaching asst., cons. asst. Marshall U., Huntington, W.Va., 1982; program dir. Ohio Ctr. for Youth and Family Devel., Ironton, Ohio, 1982-84; office mgr. Ctr. for Study and Edn. of Gifted Columbia U., N.Y., 1984-85; dir. residential assessment, diagnostic edn. specialist State. Dept. Edn. Diagnostic Ctr., L.A., 1986-92. Del. Citizen Amb. Program Early Childhood Spl. Edn. to Russia and Ea. Europe, 1992; cons. in field. Mem. Coun. Exceptional Children.

MONROE, WILLIAM SCOTT, librarian; b. Pottstown, Pa., Mar. 15, 1952; s. Ivan Bernard Monroe and Flora E. (Moses) Olinger; m. Rebecca Leuchak, June 2,. 1978. BA in History, Temple U., 1979; MS in Libr. Sci., Drexel U., 1984; MA in History, Columbia U., 1988, MPhil in History, 1991. Libr., cataloger Tchrs. Coll. Columbia U., N.Y.C., 1984-86; humanities bibliographer NYU, 1986-91; head collection devel. Brown U., Providence, 1993—. Contbr. articles to profl. jours. U.S. Dept. Edn. fgn. lang. and area studies fellow, 1990-91. Mem. ALA, Am. Hist. Assn., Medieval Acad. of Am. Mem. Soc. Of Friends. Avocation: singing and playing music. Office: Brown U Box A Providence RI 02912 E-mail: william_monroe@brown.edu.

MONSON, DIANNE LYNN, literacy educator; b. Minot, N.D., Nov. 24, 1934; d. Albert Rachie and Iona Cordelia (Kirk) M. BS, U. Minn., 1956, MA, 1962, PhD, 1966. Tchr. Rochester (Minn.) Pub. Schs., 1956-59, U.S. Dept. Def., Schweinfurt, West Germany, 1959-61, St. Louis Park (Minn.) Schs., 1961-62; instr. U. Minn., Mpls., 1962-66; prof. U. Wash., Seattle, 1966-82; prof. literacy edn. U. Minn., Mpls., 1982-97, prof. emeritus, 1997—. Chmn. curriculum and instrn. U. Minn., 1986—89. Co-author: Scott Foresman Reading, 2000, New Horizons in the Language Arts, 1972, Children and Books, 6th edit., 1981, Experiencing Children's Literature, 1984, (monograph) Research in Children's Literature, 1976, Language Arts: Teaching and Learning Effective Use of Language, 1988, Reading Together: Helping Children Get A Good Start With Reading, 1991; assoc. editor: Dictionary of Literacy, 1995. Recipient Outstanding Educator award U. Minn. Alumni Assn., 1983, Alumni Faculty award U. Minn. Alumni Assn., 1991. Fellow Nat. Conf. Rsch. in English (pres. 1990-91); mem. ALA, Nat. Coun. Tchrs. English (exec. com. 1979-81), Internat. Reading Assn. (dir. 1980-83, Arbuthnot award 1993, Reading Hall of Fame 1997), U.S. Bd. Books for Young People (pres. 1988-90). Lutheran. Home: 515 S Lexington Pkwy # 604 Saint Paul MN 55116 E-mail: monso001@tc.umn.edu.

MONSON, JAMES EDWARD, electrical engineer, educator; b. Oakland, Calif., June 20, 1932; s. George Edward and Frances Eleanor (Fouche) M.; m. Julie Elizabeth Conzelman, June 25, 1954; children— John, Jamie, Jennifer. BSEE, Stanford U., 1954, MSEE, 1955, PhD in Elec. Engring., 1961. Mem. tech. staff Bell Telephone Labs., Murray Hill, N.J., 1955-56; devel. engr. Hewlett-Packard Co., Palo Alto, Calif., 1956-61; Robert C. Sabini prof. engring. emeritus Harvey Mudd Coll., 1961—. Mem. governing bd. Claremont Unified Sch. Dist., 1966-71, pres., 1969-70; pres. Claremont Civic Assn., 1974-75; bd. dirs. Claremont YMCA, 1978-82, Coastal Health Alliance, 1999-. Fellow NSF, 1954-55, Japan Soc. Promotion Sci., 1984; Fulbright Rsch. grantee, 1975-76; Fulbright sr. lectr., 1980. Fellow IEEE; mem. Phi Beta Kappa, Sigma Xi. Home: PO Box 1029 Point Reyes Station CA 94956-1029 Office: Harvey Mudd Coll 301 E 12th St Claremont CA 91711-5901 E-mail: james_monson@hmc.edu., j.monson@ieee.org.

MONSON, ROBERT JOSEPH, education educator; b. St. Paul, July 2, 1947; s. Robert Joseph and Lorraine (Pieruccioni) M.; m. Tracey Monson, Dec. 18, 1970 (dec. 1986); 1 child, Ashley Taylor. BA, St. Thomas Coll., St. Paul, 1969, MA, 1971; PhD, St. Louis U., 1975. Tchr. St. Bernards Schs., St. Paul, 1969-71; asst. prin. Mamaroneck (N.Y.) High Sch., 1975-78; prin. Chapel Hill (N.C.) High Sch., 1978-81; asst. sch. supt. Sch. Dist. South Orange-Maplewood (N.J.), 1981-85; supt. schs. Beachwood (Ohio) pub. schs., 1985-87, Westwood (Mass.) pub. schs., 1987-94, Mendota Heights, Minn., 1994-99; sr. lectr. Lesley Coll., 1990-2000; assoc. prof. Tchrs. Coll. Columbia U., N.Y.C., 1999—. Rsch. cons. NSF, 1975. Contbr. articles to profl. jours. Named Educator of Yr., AGPA, 1981; postdoctoral fellow Harvard U., 1977. Mem. Prins Ctr. Harvard U. (bd. dirs. 1989-91). Roman Catholic. Home: 957 Lake Ave Greenwich CT 06831 Office: 525 W 120th St Box 67 New York NY 10027

MONTAGNA, BERNICE DONNA, education educator; b. Bridgeport, Conn., Mar. 31, 1953; d. Philip Romano and Catherine (MacDaniel) Echinger; m. Robert John Montagna, June 9, 1979; children: Cariann, Robert. AA, Broward Community Coll., 1974; BS, Southern Conn. State U., 1977, degree in ednl. leadership, 1996; MAT, Sacred Heart U., 1992. Cert. tchr. Conn. Substitute tchr. East Haven (Conn.) Bd. Edn., 1981-82, instructional aide, 1985-92; tchr. North Haven (Conn.) Bd. Edn., 1992—. Leader Girl Scouts Am., North Haven, 1989-91. Mem. NEA, Conn. Reading Assn., Conn. Edn. Assn., Kindergarten Assn. Conn., North Haven Edn. Assn., Assn. Supervision & Curriculum Devel. Avocations: reading, cooking, arts/crafts. Home: 10 Rance Ct North Haven CT 06473-3454

MONTAGUE, MARY ELLEN, retired secondary school educator, small business owner; b. Georgetown, Ohio, Aug. 12, 1933; d. Carroll Russel and Martha Gail (Lucas) Martin; m. Patrick E. Montague, Feb. 14, 1958; children: Catherine, Michael. BS, Fla. State U., 1955; MS, West Ga. Coll., 1989. Cert. tchr., Ga., Fla., N.C. Tchr. Duval County Schs., Jacksonville, Fla., 1955-59, InterLangue, Paris, 1971-74, Jackson County Schs., Sylva, NC, 1976-79, Fulton County Schs., Atlanta, 1959-71, 80-95, Creekside H.S., Fairburn, Ga., until 1995; ret., 1995; writer, compiler family histories, short stories and poems; owner-operator The Freeze Ho. Bed & Breakfast, Sylva, NC, 2003—. Author various curriculum guides, 1964—. Hostess Tour of Homes, Fairburn, Ga., 1989, 90, 91; vestry person St. Andrews Ch., Peachtree City, Ga., 1989-92. Fellow Smithsonian Instn.; mem. Nat. Coun. Social Studies, Delta Kappa Gamma (1st v.p. 1990-91, pres. 1991-94, dist. treas. 1994—). Home and Office: 71 Sylvan Hts Sylva NC 28779-2523

MONTANO, ROBERT ALLEN, elementary education educator; b. L.A., Oct. 28, 1950; s. Alfonso and Blanca (Lara) M.; m. Ruth Arcela Escamilla, Sept. 10, 1972. AA, East L.A. Coll., 1972; BA, Calif. State U., Long Beach, 1974. Cert. bilingual educator, Calif. Instrnl. asst. Long Beach Unified Sch. Dist., 1972-76; elem. tchr. grades 2-6 bilingual Lucia Mar Unified Sch. Dist., Arroyo Grande, Calif., 1976—. Adj. prof. dept. edn. Calif. Poly. U., San Luis Obispo, 1988—; mem. bilingual com. Lucia Mar United Sch. Dist., 1976—92. Recipient Pionero award Vision Unida, 2000, Outstanding Cmty. Svc. award Calif. Assn. of Bilingual Educators, 2002. Mem. Calif. Tchrs. Assn., NEA, AFT, Assn. Mex.-Am. Educators (region v.p., chpt. pres., v.p., treas., Outstanding Educator award 1993). Avocations: music, poetry, writing songs and lyrics, volleyball. Office: Oceano Elem Sch 1551 17th St Oceano CA 93445-9303 E-mail: randblues2@aol.com.

MONTE, WILLIAM DAVID, education educator, educator; b. San Diego, Aug. 17, 1958; s. Thomas Gilbert Monte and Lisa Ruth Veale; m. Amy Lisa Schuenemann, Jan. 9, 1982; children: Sarah Nicole, William David. BS in Ministry, Bethany Coll., Santa Cruz, Calif., 1981; MA in Theology, Fuller Theol. Sem., Pasadena, Calif., 1987; MA in Edn., Claremont (Calif.) Grad. Sch., 1991, postgrad., 1992—. Cert. multiple subjects, Calif. Tchr. Mira Mesa Christian Sch., San Deigo, 1982-83; tchr. ESL Armenean Social Svc. Ctr., L.A., 1988-89; substitute tchr. Baldwin Park (Calif.) Unified Sch. Dist., 1988-89; tchr. Upland (Calif.) Unified Sch. Dist., 1989-94; faculty assoc. office tchr. edn. Claremont Grad. Sch., 1994—. Adj. faculty dept. edn. Whittier Coll., 1995—; founder, pres. ednl. cons. firm DIDASKEIN, San Dimas, Calif., 1986—. Contbr. articles to profl. jours. AB 1470 Tech. grantee State of Calif., 1990-91; Minority Student fellow Claremont Grad. Sch., 1992-93. Mem. Religious Edn. Assn., Computer Using Eductors, Assn. for Moral Edn., Assn. for Religion and Intellectual Life, Pi Lambda Theta. Avocations: computers/multimedia, tennis, photography, creative writing, model building. Home: 538 Andover Ave San Dimas CA 91773-3201 Office: Claremont Grad Sch 121 E 10th St Claremont CA 91711-3911

MONTEIRO, GEORGE, English educator, writer; b. Cumberland, R.I., May 23, 1932; s. Francisco José and Augusta (Temudo) M.; m. Lois Ann Hodgins, Aug. 14, 1958 (div. 1992); children: Katherine, Stephen, Emily; m. Brenda Murphy, Mar. 25, 1995. AB, Brown U., 1954; AM, Columbia U., 1956; PhD, Brown U., 1964; DHL (hon.), U. Mass., Dartmouth, 1993. From instr. to assoc. prof. Brown U., Providence, 1961-72, prof. English, 1972-99, prof. Portuguese, 1984-99, adj. prof., 1999—. Vis. prof. Providence Coll., 1967-68; Fulbright prof. Am. lit. U. Sao Paulo, 1969-71. Author: Henry James and John Hay: The Record of a Friendship, 1965, The Coffee Exchange: Poems, 1982, Robert Frost and the New England Renaissance, 1988, Double Weaver's Knot: Selected Poems, 1989, The Presence of Camões, 1996, The Presence of Pessoa, 1998, Stephen Crane's Blue Badge of Courage, 2000, Fernando Pessoa and Nineteenth-Century Anglo-American Literature, 2000; editor: The Man Who Never Was: Essays on Fernando Pessoa, 1982, The Correspondence of Henry James and Henry Adams, 1877-1941, 1992, Conversations with Elizabeth Bishop, 1996; translator: In Crete with the Minotaur and Other Poems, 1980, Fernando Pessoa: Self Awareness and Thirty Other Poems, 1988, A Man Smiles at Death with Half a Face, 1991. Decorated Order of Prince Henry the Navigator (Portugal). Office: Brown U Portuguese & Brazil Studies Providence RI 02912-0001 E-mail: georgemonteiro@prodigy.net.

MONTEITH, LARRY KING, chancellor emeritus; b. Bryson City, N.C., Aug. 17, 1933; s. Earl and Essie (King) M.; m. Nancy Alexander, Apr. 19, 1952; children: Larry, Carol, Steve. BSEE, N.C. State U., 1960; MSEE, Duke U., 1962, PhDEE, 1965. Registered profl. engr., N.C. Mem. tech. staff Bell Telephone Labs., Burlington, N.C., 1960-62, Resch. Triangle Inst., Raleigh, 1962-66, group leader rsch. sect., 1966-68; adj. asst. prof. elec. engring. N.C. State U., Raleigh, 1965-68, assoc. prof., 1968-72, prof., 1972—, head dept. elec. engring., 1974-78, dean of engring., 1978-89, interim chancellor, 1989-90, chancellor, 1990-98, chancellor emeritus, 1998—. Contbr. articles to profl. jours. With USN, 1952-56. Recipient Disting. Engring. Alumnus award Duke U., 1984, Outstanding Engring. Achievement award N.C. Soc. Engrs., 1990, Disting. Engring. Alumnus award N.C. State, 1999. Fellow IEEE, Am. Soc. for Engring. Edn.; mem. NSPE (edn. adv. group), Raleigh C. of C. (bd. dirs.), Rotary Internat. (Paul Harris fellow Rotary Found. 1991), Phi Beta Kappa, Sigma Xi, Sigma Iota Rho, Phi Kappa Phi, Eta Kappa Nu, Tau Beta Pi, Sigma Beta Delta.

MONTENEGRO, JEAN BAKER, English language educator; b. Syracuse, N.Y. d. Ernest Monroe and Lucy Maebelle (Atkins) Baker; 1 child, Al H. Johnson Fr. BA, U. Ky., 1955; MA, No. Ariz. U., 1975, Azusa Pacific U., 1982. Cert. adminstr., supr.; cert. tchr. lang. arts, phys. edn., health edn., journalism. Sr. high sch. phys. edn. instr. San Francisco Unified, 1964, Grossmont Unified, San Diego, 1964-66; prof. phys. edn., recreation, health edn. Imperial (Calif.) Valley Coll., 1966-81, prof. journalism, 1981-88, prof. English, 1981—. Staff devel. coord. Imperial Valley Coll., 1988-94, gender equity coord., 1990-91; coord. Am. Assn. Women in Cmty. and Jr. Colls., San Diego and Imperial County, 1988-90; elected to serve 3 yr. term on Acad. Senate, Imperial Valley Coll., 1994-96. City editor Imperial Valley Press, summer 1989, copy editor, summers 1989, 91; editor Downtown El Centro Assn. newsletter, ARCHES editor Calif. Women for Agriculture Imperial Valley chpt. newsletter Food for Thought; editor Pvt. Industry Coun. newsletter Ptnrs. Pres. Substance Abuse Adv. Bd. Imperial County, 1976-78; v.p. Imperial Valley Methodone Bd. Dirs., 1974-80; v.p. Imperial County Alcohol Adv. Bd., 1978-80; recreation commr. City of Brawley, 1976-78; auditor Rep. Women, 1990-96; sec. S.W. Rep. Women, 1997; head judge Literacy Vols. Am. Spelling Bee; elected sec. Imperial County Rep. Ctrl. Commn., 1997. Recipient Arab award Imperial Valley Coll. Student Body, 1989; named Vol. of Yr., Imperial Juvenile Justice Commn., 1982, Woman of Yr., Imperial County, 1995; apptd. to commn. State of Calif. C.C. League, 1990. Mem. Journalism Assn. So. Calif. (sec. 1988), Pvt. Industry Coun.-Imperial Valley Downtown El Centro Assn., Sunrise Optimists Club (dir. pub. rels.). Presbyterian. Avocations: jogging, walking, reading. Office: Imperial Valley Coll PO Box 158 Imperial CA 92251-0158

MONTERO, DARREL MARTIN, social worker, sociologist, educator; b. Sacramento, Mar. 4, 1946; s. Frank and Ann Naake; divorced; children: David Paul, Lynn Elizabeth, Laura Ann, Emily Kathryn. AB, Calif. State U., 1970; MA, UCLA, 1972, PhD, 1974. Postgrad. researcher Japanese-Am. Research Project UCLA, 1971-73, dir. research, 1973-75; assoc. head Program on Comparative Ethnic Studies, Survey Research Ctr. UCLA, 1973-75; asst. prof. sociology Case Western Res. U., Cleve., 1975-76; asst. prof. urban studies, research sociologist Pub. Opinion Survey, dir. urban ethnic research program U. Md., College Park, 1976-79; assoc. prof. Ariz. State U., Tempe, 1979—. Cons. rsch. sect. Viewer Sponsored TV Found., Los Angeles, Berrien E. Moore Law Office, Inc., Gardena, Calif., 1973, Bur. for Social Sci. Research, Inc., Washington, Friends of the Family, Ltd., Nat. Sci. Found. Author: Japanese Americans: Changing Patterns of Ethnic Affiliation Over Three Generations, 1980, Urban Studies, 1978, Vietnamese Americans: Patterns of Resettlement and Socioeconomic Adaptation in the United States, 1979, Social Problems, 1988; mem. editorial bd. Humanity and Society, 1978-80; contbr. articles to profl. jours. Served with U.S. Army, 1966-72. Mem. Am. Sociol. Assn., Am. Assn. Pub. Opinion Research (exec. council, standards com.), Am. Ednl. Research Assn., Council on Social Work Edn., Soc. Study of Social Problems, D.C. Sociol. Soc., Am. Soc. Pub. Adminstrn., Nat. Assn. Social Workers, Pacific Sociol. Assn. Office: Ariz State Univ Sch Social Work Tempe AZ 85281

MONTES, FELIX MANUEL, educational researcher, technological consultant; b. Caripito, Monagas, Venezuela, Oct. 20, 1953; came to U.S., 1981; s. Henry Victor Adams and Elia Margarita Montes. Systems analyst, Ctrl. Occidental U., Barquisimeto, Venezuela, 1976; BS, U. Ariz., 1983, MS in Mgmt. Info., 1985; PhD in Ednl. Psychology, U. Ariz., 1990. Systems analyst Regional Computer Co., Barquisimeto, 1976-81; assoc. faculty Ctrl. Occidental Univ., Barquisimeto, 1977-81; grad. rsch. asst. U. Ariz., Tucson, 1988-89; immersion lang. tchr. U.S. State Dept., Marana, Ariz., 1989-90; project dir. U. Ariz., Tucson, 1990-91; ednl. rsch. in teaching Intercultural Devel. Rsch. Assn., San Antonio, Tex., 1991—. Tech. cons. Tex. Assn. Bilingual Edn., San Antonio, 1993-94. Developer (software) Classroom Support System, 1984-90, Automatic Generation of Rsch. Info., 1991-94; contbr. articles to Newsletter Interculture Devel. Rsch. Assn., 1992—. Adv. Children Intercultural Devel. Rsch. Program, 1991—; spkr. to edn. profls. at univs. and confs. Recipient scholarship Univ. Ariz., 1984-90, fellowship Charles Stewart Mott Found., San Antonio, 1994-95, Recognition award City Commn. on Literacy, San Antonio, 1994. Mem. Internat. Soc. for Tech. in Edn., Am. Ednl. Rsch. Assn., Hispanic Assn. Colls. and Univs., S.W. Ednl. Rsch. Assn., Nat. Coun. on Measurement in Edn., La. Soc. Nat. Hispanica, Sigma Delta Pi, Phi Kappa Phi. Avocations: universal edn., space exploration, universal literacy, planet earth. Office: Intercultural Devel Rsch Assn 5835 Callaghan Rd Ste 350 San Antonio TX 78228-1125

MONTESI, ALBERT JOSEPH, retired English educator; b. Memphis, Jan. 10, 1921; s. Alexander and Amelia (Boldreghini) M. BS, Northwestern U., 1949; MA, U. Mich., 1950; PhD, Pa. State U., 1955. Grad. asst. Pa. State U., State College, 1951-52, instr., 1952-55; asst. prof. The Citadel, Charleston, SC, 1955-57; from asst. prof. to prof. English St. Louis U., 1957-90. Vis. prof. Wesleyan U., Middleton, Conn, 1964, SUNY, Buffalo, 1968, U. of the Ruhr, Bochum, Germany, 1974-75; spkr. in field; mem. panel James Joyce Festival, Frankfurt, Germany, 1984. Author: (poetry) Windows and Mirrors, 1984, Robots and Gardens, 1989, Peter Bentley: The Detective Cat, 1990, Drowned Titanic Passenger, 1991, LaFayette Square, 1999, Hist. Survey of the Southern Review (1935-1942), 1999, Old Souland, Union Sta. St. Louis, 2000, Quit Poems, St. Louis; assoc. editor St. Louis Lit. pub., 1981, West End, 2000; also books: Union Sta., Hist. No. St. Louis, Downtown St. Louis. Mem. rsch. coun. Pa. State U., 1954-55. Grantee St. Louis U., 1985-89. Mem. MLA. Democrat. Roman Catholic. Avocations: bridge, writing, cooking. Home: 22 Benton Pl Saint Louis MO 63104-2411

MONTFORD, CLAUDIAN HAMMOND, retired gifted and talented education educator; b. Bainbridge, Ga., Jan. 31, 1947; d. Eugene and Ruth Lee (Clark) Hammond; m. Redolphus Montford, Dec. 21, 1968; children: Randolph Eugene, Rudolph Levell. BA in Early Childhood and Elem. Edn., Newark State-Kean Coll., Union, N.J., 1969; MA in Scis. Edn., Fairleigh Dickinson U., 1996. Cert. tchr., N.J. Cashier Sears, Roebuck and Co., Watchung, N.J., 1965-68; tchr. sci. Camp Crusades, Plainfield, N.J., 1969; tchr. cons. Bank Street Coll., N.Y.C., 1973; tchr. gifted and talented edn. Plainfield Bd. Edn., 1969—72, 1974—2002, tchr. dir. Title I compensatory reading program, 1970-72, tchr. advisor instrnl. coun., 1981-83. Playground dir. Plainfield Recreation Dept., 1967-68. Fundraiser Black United Fund N.J., 1990, chmn., 1991-93; elem. coord. Sci. Fair, Plainfield, 1991-98; design-coach Am.'s Choice Sch. Design Reform, 1999-2002. Recipient 1st gov.'s tchr. recognition N.J. Dept. Edn., 1986, Excellence in Edn. award Frontiers Internat., 1988; grantee N.J. Dept. Edn., 1983, Tech. grantee AT&T, 1996, Union Carbide Corp., 1997-99, Evergreen Schs. N.J. Parent Participation Program grant, 2001; New Zealand Study Tour scholar Plainfield Bd. Edn., 1993. Mem. NEA, N.J. Edn. Assn., Union County Edn. Assn., Plainfield Edn. Assn., Evergreen Edn. Assn. Seeking Ednl. Equity and Diversity Project, Assn. Math. Tchrs. N.J. (exec. coun.), N.J. Systemic Sci. Initiative (adv. bd.). Democrat. Baptist. Avocations: reading, sewing and dress designing, macrame, horticulture, computer programming. Office: Evergreen Sch 1033 Evergreen Ave Plainfield NJ 07060-2698

MONTGOMERY, ANNA FRANCES, elementary school educator; b. Spokane, Wash., Nov. 5, 1945; d. Carl Jacob and Edna Frances (Evans) Kuipers; m. William Lee Montgomery Jr., Oct. 7, 1989. AA, Mid. Ga. Coll., 1965; BS in Elem. Edn., Woman's Coll. of Ga., 1966; MEd, Ga. Coll., 1969, specialist in edn., 1973; studied Brit. ednl. sys., London, 1978. Cert. elem. tchr., Ga. Classroom tchr. Muscogee County Sch. Dist., Columbus, Ga., 1966—2002, reading tchr. Title 1 tutorial program, summer 1975, instr. staff devel. program, 1977-80; social sci. lead tchr. Wesley Heights Elem. Sch., Columbus, 1992—2002, chmn. mgmt. team, 1997-98. Tennis and athletic instr. Camp Tegawitha, Tobyhanna, Pa., 1970; social studies textbook adoption com. Muscogee County Sch. Dist., 1977-78, 82-83, 98-99, sick leave com., 1993-95; judge Columbus Regional Social Sci. Fair, 1977, 93-96; basic skills program comprehensive planning task force Muscogee County Sch. Dist., 1995-96, com. to revise the basic skills program in social studies, 1980; presenter in field. Editor: Muscogee County School District's Handbook for Beginning Teachers, 1979. Treas. Wesley Heights PTA, 1983-86; vol. Med. Ctr. Aux., Columbus, 1975-79; pres. pastor's Bible study class St. Luke United Meth. Ch., 1993-94, 96, 97, 98, mem. Sarah Cir. 11, sec., 1969-71, 78-80, co-chmn., 1974-76, chmn., 1976-78; mem. Bessie Howard Ward Handbells Choir; devel. chmn. Ga. state divsn. Centennial/fellowships com. AAUW, 1974-76. Recipient Valley Forge Tchrs. medal Freedoms Found. at Valley Forge, 1975, Outstanding Tchr. of Yr. award Wesley Hts. Elem. Sch., 1975, Muscogee County Sch. Dist., 1979; named Very Important Lady award Girl Scouts Am., Columbus, 1976, Outstanding Young Woman Am., 1982. Mem. AAUW (chmn. centennial fellowship com. Columbus br. 1973-75), Ga. PTA (hon. life), Profl. Assn. Ga. Educators (bldg. rep. Muscogee County chpt. 1983-2002, sec. 1992-94, treas. 1994-98, pres.-elect 1998-2000, Muscogee County's sys. rep. to the state 2000-02, social chmn. 2002-03), Nat. Coun. Social Studies (hostess and registration coms. ann. meeting 1975), Ga. Coun. for Social Studies, Ga. Sci. Tchrs. Assn., Atlanta Alumni Club, Valley Area Sci. Tchrs. (corr. sec. 1996-98), Ga. Coll. Alumni Assn., Mid. Ga. Coll. Alumni Assn., Order of Amaranth (charity 1991-93, 95, truth 1994, assoc. conductress 1996, conductress 1997, assoc. matron 1998, royal matron 1999), Scottish Rite Ladies Aux., Ga. Ret. Educators Assn., Muscogee Ret. Educators Assn., Alpha Delta Kappa (Rho chpt., sec. 1975-76, pres.-elect 1976-78, pres. 1978-80, chaplain, 1996-98), Delta Kappa Gamma (Beta Xi chpt., pres. 1980-82, chmn. pubs. and publicity 1976-78, chmn. profl. affairs 1978-80, nominations com. chair 1980-82, chmn. world fellowship and fund raising 1984-86, 96—, chmn. fin. 1990-92, chmn. membership 1994-96, 2000—), Order Internat. Fellowship in Edn., Wesley Heights Elem. Sch. PTA, Phi Delta Kappa (Chattahoochee Valley Ga. chpt.), Phi Theta Kappa. Avocations: reading, organic gardening, travel, fishing, playing clarinet and handbells. Home: 5134 Stone Gate Dr Columbus GA 31909-5573

MONTGOMERY, DILLARD BREWSTER, musician, educator; b. Memphis, Jan. 1, 1936; s. Mary Joyce Montgomery; m. Joyce Helena Beale, Dec. 9, 1965; 1 child, Lisa Jenean. BS, Tenn. State U., 1962, MA, 1968. Profl. musician Nashville Assn. Musicians, 1958—; band dir., keyboardist The New Imperials, Nashville, 1962—; tchr. Met. Nashville Schs., 1962-94, ret., 1994; asst. prin. W.A. Bass Middle Sch., 1984-93, prin., 1993-94. Choir dir. John Wesley United Meth. Ch., Nashville, 1958—, Dixon United Meth. Ch., 1970-71, Braden United Meth. Ch., 1985-2002; profl. model Terrance Hunt Agy., 1999—. Served with USAF, 1955-58. Mem. NEA, Tenn. Edn. Assn., Met. Nashville Edn. Assn., Nat. Musicians Union, Tenn. State U. Alumni Assn. (life), Alpha Phi Alpha (life). Democrat. Methodist. Avocations: electronics, photography, traveling. Home: 638 W Nocturne Dr Nashville TN 37207 E-mail: dmontgo1@bellsouth.net.

MONTGOMERY, DORIS STROUSTRUP HENRIKSEN, primary school educator; b. Grinsted, Denmark, May 13, 1951; came to U.S., 1967; d. Jens Stroustrup and Edith (Johansen) Henriksen. AA, Gaston Coll., 1971; BS in Edn., Western Carolina U., 1973. Tchr. 2d grade McDowell County Schs., Marion, N.C., 1973-74, Gaston County Schs., Gastonia, N.C., 1974-81; kindergarten tchr. Dallas (Tex.) Ind. Sch. Dist., 1988—. Mem. Kindergarten Tchrs. Tex., Sci. Tchrs. Tex., Kappa Delta Pi (Mu Eta chpt.). Lutheran. Avocations: crafts, bicycling, camping, traveling. Office: Dallas Ind Sch Dist John F Peeler Sch 810 S Llewellyn Ave Dallas TX 75208-6312

MONTGOMERY, ELIZABETH ANNE, English language educator; b. Santa Monica, Calif., Nov. 5, 1965; d. William Fairbairn and Janice Lynn (Winkler) M. BA in Lit., Claremont McKenna Coll., 1987, MA in Edn., 1995. Cert. tchr., Calif. Tchr. English Berlitz Internat., Beverly Hills, Calif., 1990; tchr. ESL Canoga Park (Calif.) H.S., 1990-91; tchr. English Inlingua Lang. Sch., Fribourg, Switzerland, 1991, Berlitz Internat., Berne, Switzerland, 1991; tchr. English-ESL Internat. Sch. Berne, 1991-92; writer Flintridge Cons., Pasadena, Calif., 1992-93; tchr. English Pomona (Calif.) H.S., 1993—. Mem. Task Force on Proficiency Testing, Pomona, 1994-95. Watson fellow Thomas J. Watson Found., 1987-88. Mem. ASCD, NEA, Calif. Tchrs. Assn., Calif. Assn. for Bilingual Edn., Nat. Coun. Tchrs. English, Associated Pomona Tchrs. Home: # 184 1781 Appleton Way Pomona CA 91767-3519 Office: Pomona H S 475 Bangor St Pomona CA 91767-2443

MONTGOMERY, GILLESPIE V. (SONNY MONTGOMERY), former congressman; b. Meridian, Miss., Aug. 5, 1920; s. Gillespie M. and Emily (Jones) M. BS, Miss. State U. Mem. Miss. Senate, 1956-66, 90th-104th Congresses from 3rd Miss. Dist., 1967-96; chmn. vets. affairs com., 1981-94; mem. vets. affairs com., chmn. spl. com. on S.E. Asia 90th-102d Congresses, 1978-96; ranking minority mem., 1994-96; mem. armed services. com. 90th-103d Congresses, chmn. select com. on missing persons in southeast Asia, 1975-96; mem. vets. affairs com.; mem. Woodcock Commn., 1977; CEO, pres. The Montgomery Group, Alexandria, Va., 1997—. Pres. Miss. N.G. Assn., 1959; pres. Miss. Heart Assn., 1967-68. Served with AUS, World War II, Korea, ret. maj. gen. Miss N.G. Decorated Bronze Star medal, Combat Inf. Badge; recipient Miss. Magnolia award, 1966, Lifetime Achievement award Mil. Educators & Counselors Assn., 1992. Mem. VFW, Am. Legion 40 and 8, Congl. Prayer Breakfast Group (pres. 1970) Lodges: Masons; Shriners; Scottish Rite. Democrat. Episcopalian. Office: The Montgomery Group 11 Canal Center Plz Ste 104 Alexandria VA 22314-1595*

MONTGOMERY, GRETCHEN GOLZÉ, secondary education educator; b. Washington, Sept. 16, 1941; d. Alfred Rudolph and Marjorie (Lodge) Golzé; m. Charles Williams, Jan. 25, 1963 (div. Oct. 1975); children: Rebecca, Matthew; m. Jerry L. Montgomery, May 14, 1977. BA, Marietta Coll., 1963. Cert. tchr., Ohio. Tchr. Warren Local Sch. Dist., Vincent, Ohio, 1963-67; dir. Betsey Mills Club, Marietta, Ohio, 1975-80; tchr. Wolf Creek Sch. Dist., Waterford, Ohio, 1980—. Mem. lang. arts course of study com. Washington County, Marietta, 1985—, mem. competency based edn. testing com., 1985—; mem. ednl. planning com. Wolf Creek Edn., Waterford, 1988-91, mem. testing com., 1988—, mem. textbook com., 1989-90; mentor tchr. Washington County, 1991—, mentor tchr. trainer, 1994—, local and regional profl. devel. coms., 1997—. Jennings scholar Martha Holden Jennings Found., 1982. Mem. NEA, Nat. Coun. Tchrs. English, Ohio Coun. Tchrs. English Lang. Arts, Wolf Creek Local Tchrs. Assn. (sec. 1985—), Ohio Edn. Assn., Ohio Tchr. Leader Network. Avocations: reading, gardening, spectator sports, theater. Home: 105 Rathbone Ter Marietta OH 45750-1443 Office: Wolf Creek Schs PO Box 45 Waterford OH 45786-0045

MONTGOMERY, JERRY LYNN, retired education educator; b. Owensville, Ind., Apr. 21, 1935; s. Philip Matthew and Lois Caroline (Anderson) M.; m. Murelyn Ann Rogers, Sept. 21, 1957 (div. Apr. 1976); stepchildren: Rebecca Williams Slominski, Matthew Williams; m. Gretchen Wendelroth Golzè, May 14, 1977; children: Robin Schneider, Lori Abbott, Vicki Randolph. BS, Purdue U., 1957; MA, Ball State U., 1964, EdD, 1969. Vocat. agrl. Milton (Ind.) Pub. Schs., 1957-58, Carthage (Ind.) Pub. Schs., 1958-61; sci. tchr. Angola (Ind.) City Schs., 1961-66; grad. asst. Ball State U., 1966-69, asst. prof. biology, 1969; edn. prof. Marietta (Ohio) Coll., 1969—2001; sci. educator Project Discovery, Athens, Ohio, 1994-99; Discovery dir. Dist. #11, 1997-98. Goal #4 com. Marietta (Ohio) City Schs., 1993-96, grade 4 profiency test content rev. and rangefinder coms. Ohio Dept. of Edn., Columbus, Ohio, 1994-2002; mem. young engrs. and scientists Marietta Telesis Group, Marietta, 1992-96; vis. prof. physics Ohio State U., 1994; grant evaluator Wash. State Cmty. Coll. and Regional Profl. Devel. Ctr., 1999—; Praxis III evaluator State of Ohio, 1997—; mem. exec. bd. Ohio Math. and Sci. Coalition, 2001—. Recipient Outstanding Educator Martha Holden Jennings Found., 1989. Mem. Assn. of Tchr. Educators (credentials com. 1991-2000), Nat. Sci. Tchrs. Assn., Sci. Edn. Coun. Ohio, Ohio Acad. of Sci., Phi Delta Kappa. Avocations: reading, canoeing, traveling, fishing, golf. Home: 105 Rathbone Ter Marietta OH 45750-1443 Office: Marietta Coll 215 5th St Marietta OH 45750-4033 E-mail: montgomj@marietta.edu.

MONTGOMERY, JOHN RICHARD, pediatrician, educator; b. Burnsville, Miss., Oct. 24, 1934; s. Guy Austin and Harriet Pauline (Owens) M.; m. Dottye Ann Newell, June 26, 1965; children: John Newell, Michelle Elizabeth. BS, U. Ala., 1955, MD, 1958. Intern U. Miss., Jackson, 1958-59, resident in pediat., 1959-60, Baylor Coll. Medicine, Houston, 1960-61, fellow in pediat. infectious diseases and immunoloty, 1964-66, asst. prof. pediat., 1966-70, assoc. prof., 1970-75; chief pediat. programs U. Ala. Sch. Medicine, Huntsville, 1975-95, prof., 1975-97, prof. emeritus, 1997—. Bd. dirs. State Bd. Health, Ala. Bd. Med. Examiners; adv. com. Ala. EMS for Children. Contbr. articles to books and profl. jours. Served with AUS, 1961—62, Korea, ret. col. USAR, 1999. Mem. Soc. Pediat. Rsch., Am. Assn. Immunologists, Infectious Diseases Soc., N.Y. Acad. Scis., Am. Acad. Pediats. (pres. Ala. chpt. 1991-93), Sigma Xi, Phi Beta Kappa. Achievements include assisting in development of germ-free invironmental bubble to protect patient with no natural immunity (patient later subject of movie The Boy in the Plastic Bubble, 1976). Personal E-mail: dnjrmont@bellsouth.net.

MONTGOMERY, REX, biochemist, educator; b. Halesowen, Eng., Sept. 4, 1923; came to U.S., 1948, naturalized, 1963; s. Fred and Jane (Holloway) M.; m. Barbara Winifred Price, Aug. 9, 1948 (dec.); children: Ian, David, Jennifer, Christopher. BSc, U. Birmingham, Eng., 1943, PhD, 1946, DSc, 1963. Rsch. assoc. U. Minn., 1951-55; mem. faculty U. Iowa, Iowa City, 1955—, prof. biochemistry, 1963—, assoc. dean U. Iowa Coll. Medicine, 1974-95, v.p. rsch., 1989-90. Vis. prof. Nat. Australian U., 1969-70; mem. physiol. chemistry study sect. NIH, 1968-72; mem. drug devel. contract rev. com., 1975-87; chmn. com. biol. chemistry NAS, 1961-64; pesticide and fertilizer adv. bd. Iowa Dept. Agr., 1990-91; bd. dirs. Wallace Tech. Transfer Found., 1989-93; chmn. bd. dirs. Neurotron Inc., 1990-95; mem. rsch. com. Iowa Corn Promotion Bd., 1995-2001; rsch. dir. Biotech. Byproducts Consortium, 1989—; cons. in field. Author: Chemical Production of Lactic Acid, 1949, Chemistry of Plant Gums and Mucilages, 1959, Quantitative Problems in Biochemical Sciences, 2d edit., 1976, Biochemistry: A Case-Orientated Approach, 6th edit., 1996; mem. editl. adv. bd. Carbohydrate Rsch., 1968-80; mem. editl. bd. Molecular Biotherapy, 1988-92; contbr. articles to profl. jours. Postdoctoral fellow Ohio State U., 1948-49; fellow Sugar Research Found., Dept. Agr., 1949-51 Fellow: Royal Soc. Chemistry. Home: 701 Oaknoll Dr Iowa City IA 52246-5168 Office: U Iowa Coll Medicine Dept Biochemistry Iowa City IA 52242 E-mail: rex-montgomery@uiowa.edu.

MONTGOMERY, ROSE ELLEN GIBSON, secondary education educator, organist; b. Barbourville, Ky. d. Charles Butler and Mattie Cecilia (Corey) Gibson; m. William Goebel Montgomery; children: Pamela Janeese, Leilani Rose, William Goebel Jr. (dec.). BS, Hawaii Pacific U., 1965; MEd, Bowie (Md.) State U., 1970; postgrad., U. Philippines, 1970-73, U. Md., 1980-82; PhD, Am. Internat. U., 1995. Cert. tchr., Md. Tchr. Pearl Harbor Luth. Elem. Sch., Honolulu, 1965-67, Dept. Def. Schs., Luzon, The Philippines, 1973-92, Prince George's County Schs., Bowie, 1967-70, 73-92, Laurel, Md., 1992-96. Ch. organist Pearl Harbor Meml. Ch., 1963-67, Clark Air Base Chapel, Luzon, 1970-73. Co-author: (handbook) World of Work, 1972; inventor 6-string guitar chord stamp for tchg. guitar. Active Girl Scouts U.S. and Boy Scouts Am., Honolulu; developer Meml. Garden, Bowie, 1973-74. Named Outstanding Organist, Pearl Harbor Christian Ch., 1966; recipient base comdr.'s award Clark Air Base, 1970-73, Outstanding Tchr. of Yr. award City of New Carrollton, Md., 1987, Md. Tchr. of Yr. for Prince George's County, 1993. Mem. NEA (life), Prince George's County Edn. Assn. (del.). Republican. Roman Catholic. Avocations: organ, guitar, story telling. Home: 2802 Stonybrook Dr Bowie MD 20715-2157 Office: Dwight David Eisenhower Mid Sch 13725 Briarwood Dr Laurel MD 20708-1301

MONTGOMERY, TOMMIE SUE, political scientist, educator; b. Miami, Fla., Mar. 25, 1942; d. Clyde Waldron and Edith Elaine (Felton) M.; M. Carlos Francisco Gamba, July 11, 1987 (div. 1993); m. A. David Abrahams, June 23, 2001. AB, Wesleyan Coll., 1963; MA, Vanderbilt U., 1969; PhD, NYU, 1977. Instr. CUNY, 1973-75; asst. prof. Richmond Coll., S.I., N.Y., 1975-76, Bklyn. Coll., 1976-78, Ithaca (N.Y.) Coll., 1983-84; vis. asst. prof. Dickinson Coll., Carlisle, Pa., 1984-86; assoc. prof. Agnes Scott Coll., Decatur, Ga., 1986-93; vis. assoc. prof. Emory U, 1993; sr. rsch. fellow So. Ctr. for Internat. Studies, Atlanta, 1993-94; sr. rsch. assoc. North-South Ctr. U. Miami, Fla., 1994-96; rsch. cons. dept. telemedicine Ptnrs. Health Care Sys., 1998; grants mgr. telemedicine dept. Partners Healthcare Sys., Boston, 1998-99; contract sr. assoc. Abt Assocs., Inc., Cambridge, Mass., 1999-2000; contract assoc. Isaacson, Miller, Boston, 2000—02. Cons. Calif. State U., Chico, 1986, Camino Film Projects, L.A., 1988—89, Ctrl. Am. Task Force Presbyn. Ch., 1982, 88, UN Higher Commr. for Refugees, Belize, 1991, UN Observer Mission, El Salvador, 1993—94; sr. scholar UN Inst. Disarmament Rsch. Project on Disarmament and Conflict Resolution, Geneva, 1994—95, U.S. Agy. Internat. Devel., El Salvador, 1996; vis. lectr. Tufts U., Medford, Mass., 1997; vis. prof. Trent U., Peterborough, Ont., 2002—03. Author: Revolution in El Salvador: Origins and Evolution, 1982, Revolution in El Salvador: From Civil Strife to Civil Peace, 1994; editor: Mexico Today, 1982, Peacemaking and Democratization in the Western Hemisphere, 2000; contbr. articles to books and profl. jours. Deacon Old South Ch., Boston, 1998-2001; mem. coun. St. Paul's Anglican Ch., Lindsay, Ont., 2002-03. Recipient grants CUNY, 1978, Fulbright Found., 1986, 91, 2004, North-South Ctr., 1993-94, U.S. Inst. Peace and Ford Found., 1995-96. Mem.: Latin Am. Studies Assn., Fulbrights Assn. Avocations: photography, travel. Home: RR 6 19 Blue Water Ave Lindsay ON Canada K9V 4R6 E-mail: tsmada@allstream.net.

MOODY, CHERYL ANNE, social services administrator, social worker, educator; b. Winston-Salem, N.C., July 31, 1953; d. Fred Bertram and Mary Edna (Weekley) M. BSW with honors, Va. Commonwealth U., 1975; MSW, U. Mich., 1979. Social worker Family Svcs., Inc., Winston-Salem, 1974-77; sch. social work intern Huron Valley Jr. H.S., Milford, Mich., 1977-78; children's social work intern Downriver Child Guidance Clinic, Allen Park, Mich., 1978-79; children's svcs. specialist Calhoun County Dept. Social Svcs., Battle Creek, Mich., 1979-81; children's psychiat. social worker Eastern Maine Med. Ctr., Bangor, 1981-82, sr. med. social worker, 1982-85; clin. social worker Ctr. for Family Svcs. in Palm Beach County, Inc., West Palm Beach, Fla., 1988-89, Jupiter, Fla., 1989-91; dir. children's programs Children's Home Soc. of Fla., West Palm Beach, 1985—. Asst. prof. social work Fla. Atlantic U., Boca Raton, 1993—. Vol. group leader Lupus Found., Boca Raton, 1994—. Mem. NASW, Acad. Cert. Social Workers. Democrat. Methodist. Avocations: reading, knitting, drawing. Home: 6212 62nd Way West Palm Beach FL 33409-7130 Office: Children's Home Soc of Fla 2045 Broward Ave West Palm Beach FL 33407-6101

MOON, CATHERINE HYLAND, art therapist, art therapy educator; b. Ashtabula, Ohio, Dec. 10, 1955; d. Eugene Arthur and Marjorie Jeanette (Dippel) Hyland; m. Bruce Lee Moon, Aug. 20, 1977; children: Jesse Logan, Brea Hyland. BFA, Columbus Coll. Art and Design, 1978; MA in Alcohol & Drug Abuse Ministry, Meth. Theol. Sch. Ohio, 1993. Registered art therapist. Art therapist, co-dir., clin. internship in art therapy Harding Psychiat. Hosp., Worthington, Ohio, 1980-96; instr. art therapy Columbus (Ohio) Coll. Art and Design, 1987-89; mem. faculty grad. art therapy program Marywood U., Scranton, Pa., 1997—2001; asst. prof. grad. art therapy program Sch. Art Inst. Chgo., 2001—. Mem. adj. faculty expressive therapies Lesley Coll. Grad. Sch., Cambridge, Mass. Author: Studio Art Therapy: Coltivating the Artist Identity in the Art Therapist, 2002. Mem. Am. Art Therapy Assn. (program chair 1992-93, conf. chair 1994-97), Ill. Art Therapy Assn. Democrat. Avocations: oil and acrylic painting, mixed media art, camping, hiking, running. Home: 305 Dunbar Rd Mundelein IL 60060-1166 Office: Sch Art Inst Chgo Art Therapy Dept 37 S Wabash Chicago IL 60603-3103

MOON, JAMES RUSSELL, technology education educator; b. St. Cloud, Minn., Apr. 12, 1950; s. Glenn Howard and Audrey Katherine (Berg) M.; m. Corrine Mae St. Aubin, July 14, 1978; children: Sheri Ann, Brian Michael. BS, St. Cloud State U., 1972; MS, Bemidji State U., 1975. Tech. edn. tchr. Minnetonka (Minn.) Pub. Schs., 1972—2003, dist. dept. chmn. tech. edn., 1993-95. Voc. standards com. Minn. Dept. Edn., 1995; mem. State Planning Com., 1989-2003. Designer/engr.: Row Crop Tractor, 1975; contbr. articles to profl. jours. Recipient Anchor award Minn. Pub. Schs., 1991, Tchr. Excellence award Internat. Tech. Edn. Assn., 1994, Disting. Tech. Educator Citation, 2002, Minnetonka Co-curricular Advisor of Yr., 2001; named Disting. Tech. Educator, Internat. Tech. Edn. Assn. Mem. Minn. Valley Tech. Edn. Assn. (sec. 1974), Minn. Tech. Edn. Assn. (mem. supermileage state competition com. 1989-2003), Tech. Edn. Tchr. of Yr. 1993, Disting. Svc. award 1991, 92, 94. Joyce Gustafson Meml. award, 2003). Presbyterian. Avocations: antique car restoration, reading technology related, outdoorsman. Home: 2037 20th St SE Buffalo MN 55313-4813 Office: Minn H S 18301 Highway 7 Minnetonka MN 55345-4114

MOON, SPENCER, author, program consultant, educator; b. Talladega, Ala., May 11, 1948; s. Glascoe McCann and Florence Edna (Moon) Jackson; m. Lisa Grant, Sept. 2002. Baccalaureate in Filmmaking, Antioch Coll., 1977; MA in Film and Video Prodn., Columbia Pacific U., 1989. Film editor Sta. KPIX-TV, San Francisco, 1977-79, stage mgr., technician, 1979-91; prof. African-Am. studies dept. City Coll., San Francisco, 1995-2000, also cons.; office mgr. Nat. Writers Union/West, 2000—02; bank officer Wells Fargo Bank. Cons. Black Filmmakers Hall of Fame, Oakland, Calif., 1985-91, San Francisco Internat. Film Festival, 1986-90; cons. Castro-Valencia, Evans, S.E., and Phelan campuses City Coll., 1996-2000; artist in residence Calif. Arts Coun., San Bruno, 1986-89; program cons. KMTP-TV, 1991. Author: Reel Black Talk: A Sourcebook of 50 American Filmmakers, 1997; co-author: Blacks in Hollywood: Five Favorable Years, 1987-1991, 1992; producer, dir.: (film) Strivin' and Survivin', 1977, (videos) Interracialism: The National Denial, 1981, 5 Days In July, 1986, Art From Jail, 1989; contbr. articles to profl. jours. Mem. Nat. Writers Union, Bay Area Black Media Coalition (life, svc. award 1984, media award 1997), Internat. Alliance Theatrical Stage Employees (journeyman local 16). E-mail: moonrye@aol.com.

MOONEY, BURTON LEE, secondary school educator, editor; b. Greenfield, Mass., Dec. 30, 1945; s. James Joseph Mooney and Dorthea Wilberta Atkins; m. Barbara Louise Vosburgh, Apr. 4, 1977 (div. Aug. 4, 1991); m. Lois Ann Hallet, May 30, 1997. BA in English, U. Calif., Chico, 1973; MA in Edn., Rollins Coll., 1981. Tchr. Polk County Sch. Bd., Lakeland, Fla., 1974—. Head tchr. Elem. Polk Opportunity Ctr., Lakeland, 1987—94; adj. tchr. Polk C.., Winter Haven, Fla., 1983—96; owner, pub. Writer's Helper, Lakeland, 1985—; editor-in-chief The Pride of Polk City newspaper, Auburndale Sun newspaper. Author: People, Places, Pets and Animals, 1989, Dreative Writing Workbook, 2003; freelance writer. With USAF, 1963-68. Decorated Bronze Star. Mem. VFW (life post 8002-Lakeland), Disabled Am. Vets. (life), Kung Fu Karate Assn. (black belt). Republican. Mem. Lds Ch. Avocations: coaching, music, swimming. Home: 1422 Creekwood Run Lakeland FL 33809 Office: PO Box 8172 Lakeland FL 33809 E-mail: bmoonwrite@aol.com.

MOONEY, MICHAEL C. athletic administrator, soccer coach; b. College Park, Md., Nov. 14, 1961; s. James J. and Beverly K. (Lauer) M.; m. Jean W. Barnett, Aug. 2, 1986; children: Trevor, Allison. BS, U. Buffalo, 1983; MS, Canisius Coll., 1985. Residence hall dir. SUNY, Geneseo, 1985-86, dir. intramurals and recreation, 1986-91, facility mgr. sports and recreation, 1991-99, men's varsity soccer coach, 1985—, asst. dir. athletics, 1999—2003, assoc. dir. athletics and recreation, 2003—. Chair all-conf. com. SUNY Athletic Conf., Fredonia, N.Y., 1987—, soccer guide editor, 1989—; mem. men's divsn. III soccer com. NCAA, 1999—, nat. com. chair, 2001-03; mem. scheduling com. SUNYAC Conf., 2002, mem. fin. com., eligibility com., 2002—; mem. soccer All-Am. com. NSCAA, 1992—; referee USSF, 1983—. Mem. Am. Alliance Health and Phys. Edn., Nat. Soccer Coaches Assn. Am. (all-Am. com. 2001, divsn. IIi nat. chair all-am. com.), Nat. Intramurals/Recreation Sports Assn., Nat. Ski Patrol (patroller 1978—), U.S. Tennis Assn. Avocations: golf, tennis, skiing. Office: SUNY Geneseo 1 College Cir Geneseo NY 14454-1401 E-mail: monney@geneseo.edu.

MOONEY, PATRICIA ANNE, sales executive, educator; b. Bronx, N.Y., June 6, 1948; d. Peter Joseph and Helen (Houlihan) M.; m. Anthony John Grasso, Nov. 21, 1970 (div. 1977); 1 child, A. Benjamin. BA, Coll. New Rochelle, N.Y., 1970, MS, 1975. Tchr. Archdiocese of N.Y., Harrison, 1970-78; salesperson N.Y. Telephone, N.Y.C., 1978-82; sales instr. AT&T, Aurora, Colo., 1983, sales mgr. N.Y.C., 1984, mgr. sales support dept., 1985, mgr. pricing and contract support dept. Morristown, N.J., 1986, mgr. new bus. support dept. Bridgewater, N.J., 1987, sales br. mgr. Englewood, Colo., 1988-92, sales change mgmt. orgn. Bridgewater, N.J., 1993, data networking customer svc. process mgmt. Bedminster, N.J., 1994, large bus. customer svc. strategy, 1995-97; bus. process improvement Nextel, McLean, Va., 1997-98; operational process improvement, retention, after-market sales and ordering exec. Aerial (nowVoicestream), Tampa, Fla., 1998-2000; operational process improvement Intermedia (now Worldcom), Tampa, 2000—01; tchr. Belleville (NJ) Sch. Dist., 2002—. Bd. dirs. Camp Rising Sun. Mem.: Coll. New Rochelle Alumni. Roman Catholic. Avocations: performing arts, travel, skiing. Home: 3 Tulip Ln Morristown NJ 07960-6768 E-mail: pamooney@att.net.

MOONEY, PATRICIA EILEEN, elementary school educator, coach; b. Chgo., Mar. 17, 1941; d. William Patrick and Catherine Helen (Schultz) Connors; m. George William Mooney, Oct. 13, 1973; children: Elizabeth Ann, Geoffrey George. BS, Ball State U., 1962; MS, Ind. U., 1967; cert., Mankato U., 1991. Cert. tchr. Health and phys. edn. tchr., coach Griffith (Ind.) Sch., 1962-68; elem. phys. edn. tchr. Manitowoc (Wis.) Schs., 1968-69; health, phys. edn. tchr., coach Spring Lake (Minn.) Park Schs., 1969-74; coach, substitute tchr. Roseville (Minn.) Schs., 1975-89, spl. edn. program asst., 1989-92; elementary phys. edn. specialist South Washington County, Cottage Grove, Minn., 1992-93; devel. adaptive phys. edn. specialist Burnsville (Minn.) Schs., 1993-94, North St. Paul, Maplewood and Stillwater Schs., 1994-96, Roseville Area Schs., 1996—. Ofcl. Minn. State high sch. ofcl., St. Paul, 1980—; pres. Ctrl. Park PTA, Roseville, 1985—86; leader Girl Scouts USA, Hammond, Ind., 1963—68, Roseville, 1981—94, vol. coord., 1986, sr. advisor, 1965, mem. planning bd.; youth coach Roseville Recreation Dept., 1983—88; instr. Twin Cities Ski Club, St. Paul. Mem. Minn. Assn. Health, Phys. Edn., Recreation and Dance, Apostle Islands Yacht Charter Assn. Avocations: walking, sailing, skiing, gardening, reading. Home: 445 Minnesota Ave Roseville MN 55113-4665

MOONEY, ROBERT THURSTON, health care educator; b. Bryan, Tex., Jan. 5, 1935; s. Archie T. and Eda Belle (Arrington) M.; m. Jean Russell, June 24, 1955; children: Cynthia Mooney Conyers, Sandra Mooney Cook. BS, Tex. A&M U., College Station, 1958, MEd, 1963. Cert. trainer. Tchr. Navasota (Tex.) Ind. Sch. Dist., 1958-61, Bay City (Tex.) Ind. Sch. Dist., 1961-65, dir. audio-visual instrn., 1965-66; ednl. media specialist Ednl. Media Labs., Austin, Tex., 1967-68; dir. edn. and tng. Bexar County Hosp. Dist., San Antonio, 1968-75; asst. prof. Southwest Tex. State U., San Marcos, 1974-80, assoc. prof., 1980—, chmn. allied health scis., 1976-81, dir. health svcs. mgmt., 1988-90, dir. Health Resource Ctr., 1981-82; mayor pro tem City of San Marcos, 1995-96. Dir. Sch. Paramed. Tng., Bexar County Hosp. Dist., San Antonio, 1970-72; cons. pvt. contractor, San Marcos, 1975—; mem. community/environ. task force Cen. Tex. Health Systems Agy., 1977; mem. health occupations edn. adv. com. Tex. Edn. Agy., 1989-91; mem. summer games organizing com. Tex. Spl. Olympics, 1990-91, security chmn., 1990; mem. health occupations projects adv. com. U. Tex., Austin, 1990-91. Author: Overhead Projection, 1968; (with Sister Rene Fisher and Beth Knox) Guidelines for the Development of a Hospital-Wide Education Service, 1979; contbr. articles to profl. jours. Chmn. disaster svc. Hays County Red Cross, San Marcos, 1988-89, bd. dirs., 1986-89; res. comdr. San Marcos Police Res., 1984-85; treas. Hays/Caldwell Counties Alcohol and Drug Abuse Coun., 1984-85, exec. bd. mem., 1984-85; res. dep. Hays County Sheriffs Dept., 1985-86, San Marcos Police Dept., 1986-87; zoning commr. City of San Marcos, 1991-93, city councilman, 1993-96; bd. dirs. Hays County Ctrl. Appraiser Dist., 1994-97; bd. pres. San Marcos/Hays County EMS; planning and zoning commr. City of San Marcos, 1997-2001; v.p. Hays County Appraisal Dist. Bd., 1996-98; chair Planning and Zoning Commn., City San Marcos, 1998-2000; pres. San Marcos Coun. Neighborhood Assns., 2001-02; pres.-elect Heritage Assn. San Marcos, 2002—. Mem. ASTD, Am. Coll. Healthcare Execs., Soc. Human Resource Mgmt., Am. Soc. Healthcare Edn. and Tng. (bd. mem. 1971-72), Am. Hosp. Assn., Tex. Soc. Healthcare Educators (pres. 1971-72, pres. 1991-92, disting. svc. and achievement award 1989), Bay City Classroom Tchrs. Assn. (pres.), Navasota Classroom Tchrs. Assn. (pres.), Alamo Tng. and Insvc. Coun. Hosp. and Allied Health Educators (pres. 1969-71), Internat. Personnel Mgmt. Assn. (publs. adv. bd. 1988), Tex. Hosp. Assn., Assn. of Univ. Programs in Health Adminstrn., Soc. for Human Resource Mgmt. (reviewer HR magazine 1990-96), Heritage Assn. San Marcos (pres.-elect 2002-03, pres 2003—), Kiwanis, Hays County A&M Club (pres. 2002-03). Avocations: hunting, fishing. Home: 133 E Sierra Cir San Marcos TX 78666-2533 E-mail: rm02@swt.edu.

MOONEY, VITA MARIA ELENA, social studies educator, tax examiner; b. Riverdale, N.Y., Aug. 29, 1941; d. Giovanni Carmen and Carmela Helen (Salvatore) Mariella; m. James Vincent Mooney, Aug. 18, 1962 (div. Aug. 1972); children: Lisa C. Finnegan, Paul F., Timothy J. BA Social Scis., BA Psychology, Nazareth Coll., 1977; MA in Liberal Studies, SUNY, Stony Brook, 1991. Cert. social studies tchr., spl. edn. tchr. Caseworker Dept. Social Svcs., Rochester, 1979-80; substitute tchr. 6 sch. dists., Rochester and L.I., N.Y., 1980—; tax examiner IRS, Holtsville, N.Y., 1988—; tutor BOCES, Nassau, NY. Tutor N.Y. State Rsch., 1988-92, at risk students, 1999-; now substitute tchr. 3V Schs., Setauket, N.Y., 1989—. Insp. Bd. Elections, Suffolk County, 1986—; vol. geriatric unit Brookhaven Meml. Hosp., 1979, consumer com. U. Rochester Community Outreach, 1973-79, Mather Hosp., 1993; tutor disabled students Brentwood Schs., Brent, L.I. Mem. Overeaters Anonymous (pres. St. Charles-Port Jefferson, N.Y. chpt.), Nat. Treasury Employees Union, N.Y. State Tchr.'s Union. Avocations: reading, music, dancing, swimming, art. Home: PO Box 681 Ridge NY 11961 also: PO Box 1495 Miller Place NY 11764-8274

MOOR, ANNE DELL, education director; b. Atlanta, Mar. 29, 1947; d. Kenneth Orman and Lida Louise (Springer) Dupree; m. Philip Ellsworth Moor, June 6, 1970; children: Andrew, Laura. BA, La Grange Coll., 1968. Cert. elem. edn. tchr., Tenn. Tchr. DeKalb County Bd. Edn., Atlanta, 1968-71, Briarcliff Bapt. Presch., Atlanta, 1972-73, Tates Sch., Knoxville, 1973-76; dir. after sch. care Cedar Springs Presbyn., Knoxville, 1993—. Discussion leader Bible Study Fellowship, Knoxville, 1980-93. Mem. Assn. for Childhood Edn. Internat., Nat. Sch. Age Care Assn., Tenn. Assn. for Young Children, Tenn. Sch. Age Care Assn., Knoxville Area Assn. for Young Children. Presbyterian. Avocations: watercolor, hiking, needlework, vocal soloist. Office: Cedar Springs Presbyn Ch 9132 Kingston Pike Knoxville TN 37923-5227

MOORE, ALICE CRAVENS, retired secondary school educator; b. Ridgely, Tenn., Dec. 14, 1947; d. Ezell and Rosa May (Stem) Ivy; m. Robert J. Cravens (dec. 1987); children: Christina Gann, Robert J. Cravens II, Casey Vandiver; m. Mark Allen Moore, 1991; stepchildren: Kristina, Hailey. BS in Edn., U. Tenn., Martin, 1968; MEd, U. Memphis, 1976; postgrad., Freed-Hardemann U., 1988-91, Cumberland U., 1990-91. Cert. tchr., Tenn. Classroom tchr. Lake County Schs., Ridgely, 1968-69; Humboldt (Tenn.) City Schs., 1969—. Motivational and inspirational speaker to ladies' groups and religious groups; interactive video tchr. Gibson County Schs., Humboldt, 1990—. Author: A New Song, 1988, Ways Which Be in Christ, 1990, Comforted of God, 1990; contbr. articles to profl. jours. Bd. dirs. Humboldt Pub. Libr., 1994—. Named Outstanding Young Educator Humboldt Exch. Club, 1976, Tchr. of Yr. Humboldt C. of C., 1994, Outstanding Tchr. Using Emerging Technologies South Ctrl. Bell, 1994, 95. Avocations: bible study, reading, walking. Home: 228 Humboldt Gibson Rd Humboldt TN 38343-6006 Office: Humboldt Jr High Sch 1811 Ferrell St Humboldt TN 38343-2599

MOORE, BENJAMIN, educational administrator; b. Phenix City, Ala., May 30, 1948; s. James and Katie Bertha (Perry) M.; m. Gwendolyn Yvonne Langston, July 3, 1971; children: Keesha Rushelle, Benjamin Keith II. BS, Ala. State U., 1971; MS, Southern Ill. U., 1974. Cert. tchr., adminstr. Mo. Tchr. Phenix City (Ala.) Pub. Sch., 1971-72; physical dir. YMCA Greater St. Louis, 1972-73; tchr. Providence Edn. Ctr., St. Louis, 1973-74, St. Louis Pub. Schs., 1974-78; sales rep. N.Y. Life Ins. Co., St. Louis, 1978-80; agy. mgr. N.C. Mut. Ins. Co., Black Jack, Mo., 1980-86; tchr. Sch. Dist. Riverview Gardens, St. Louis, 1980-86; adminstr. Sch. Dist. University City (Mo.), 1986-88, Parkway Sch. Dist., Chesterfield, Mo., 1988—. Pres. Riverview Garden NEA, St. Louis, 1983-85. Life mem. Urban League Met. St. Louis; organizer St. Louis Nat. Black Leadership-Initiative on Cancer, 1988; phone coord. Clk. of Circuit Cts., St. Louis, 1981. Mem. Nat. Alliance Black Sch. Educators, St. Louis Assn. Secondary Sch. Prins., Parkway Adminstrn. Assn., St. Louis Alliance Black Sch. Educators (charter), Polemarch, Kappa Alpha Psi. Methodist. Avocations: swimming, fishing, reading. Office: Parkway West High Sch 14653 Clayton Rd Chesterfield MO 63017 Address: 1308 Popular Dr Atlanta GA 30349

MOORE, BETTY JEAN, retired education educator; b. L.A., Apr. 4, 1927; d. Ralph Gard and Dora Mae (Shinn) Bowman; m. James H. Moore, Nov. 25, 1944 (div. 1968); children: Barbara, Suzanne, Sandra; m. George W. Nichols, Oct. 15, 1983. BA, Pasadena Coll., 1957; MA, U. Nev., 1963; PhD, U. Ill., 1973. Tchr. Calif. Elem. Schs., 1953-63; sec. tchr. Calif. pub. schs., 1963-68; asst. prof. Ea. Ill. U., Charleston, 1968-71; grad. teaching asst. U. Ill., Champaign, 1971-73; asst. prof. to assoc. prof. S.W. Tex. State U., San Marcos, 1973-83, prof. edn., 1983-89, ret., 1989, prof. emeritus, 1995—. Sch. evaluator; cons. in field; reading clinic dir. S.W. Tex. State U., 1974-85; cons. Min. Edn., Rep. of Singapore, 1980, 97; citizen ambassador People to People, China, 1998. Contbr. articles to profl. jours.; author: Teaching Reading, 1984; producer/dir. 5 ednl. videos. Active fund raising various charitable orgns.; vol. reading cons., Ariz. pub. schs., 2000-03. Mem. Internat. Reading Assn. (chpt. pres. 1964-65), Nat. Coun. Tchrs. English, AAUP. Presbyterian. Avocations: reading, writing, swimming, cooking. Office: Southwest Tex State U C & I Dept San Marcos TX 78666

MOORE, CALVIN C. mathematics educator, administrator; b. N.Y.C., Nov. 2, 1936; s. Robert A. and Ruth (Miller) M.; m. Doris Lienhard, Sept. 14, 1974. AB summa cum laude, Harvard U., 1958, MA, 1959, PhD in Math., 1960. Research instr. U. Chgo., 1960-61; asst. prof. U. Calif. at Berkeley, 1961-65, assoc. prof., 1965-66, prof. math., 1966—, dean phys. scis., 1971-76, chair dept. math., 1996—2002; dir. Center Pure and Applied Math, 1977-80; dep. dir. Math. Scis. Research Inst., 1981-85; asst. v.p. acad. planning and personnel U. Calif. Systemwide Adminstrn., 1985-86, assoc. v.p. acad. affairs, 1986-94. Mem. Inst. for Advanced Study, 1964-65; mem. at large NRC, 1971-73; mem. Math. Sci. Edn. Bd., 1991-93, mem. exec. com.; mem. Pres.'s Com. on Nat. Medal Sci., 1979-81; chair task force on rewards and recognition in math. scis. Joint Policy Bd. for Math., 1993-95. Chmn. bd. govs.: Pacific Jour. Math., 1972-76; editor: Mathematische Zeitschrift, Ill. Jour. Math, Pacific Jour. Math.; exec. editor research announcements; mng. editor: Bull. Am. Math. Soc.; contbg. editor: Advances in Mathematics; contbr. articles to profl. jours. Fellow Am. Acad. Arts and Scis., Am. Assn for Advancement Sci.; mem. Am. Math. Soc. (exec. com., council mem. at large, v.p., chmn. bd. trustees, com. on sci. policy). Home: 1408 Eagle Point Ct Lafayette CA 94549-2328 Office: U Calif at Berkeley Dept Math Evans Hall Berkeley CA 94720

MOORE, CARL GORDON, chemist, educator; b. Zanesville, Ohio, Feb. 7, 1922; s. Henry Carl and Hilda Marie (Oberfield) M.; m. Sheila Marie O'Toole, Nov. 2, 1951; children: Carl, Patrick, Martina, Michael, Maureen, Regina, Madeleine, Terence. BS in Chem. Engring., Ga. Inst. Tech., 1947; MS in Chem. Engring., Carnegie Mellon U., 1948, postgrad., 1948-51, U. Newark, Del., 1973-74. Cert. tchr., Pa., Del. Chemist Manhattan Project, Oak Ridge, Tenn., 1944-46; chem. engr. Koppers Co., Pitts., 1946-47; rsch. chemist E.I. DuPont de Nemours & Co., Wilmington, Del., 1951-73; tchr. Chester (Pa.)-Upland Sch., 1974-78; tutor Del. Tutoring, Wilmington, 1981-88; instr. Del. Tech. and C.C., Wilmington, 1982-90, U. Del., Newark, 1984—. Author tech. reports on hydrogen over voltage of titanium and zirconium. Adult leader Wilmington area Boy Scouts Am., 1953-73; tchr. Sunday sch., Wilmington, 1962-67; group leader U.S. Census Bur., 1980. Sgt. U.S. Army, 1943-46. Mem. Am. Chem. Soc., Sigma Xi. Achievements include 13 patents, production of TiO_2 Rutile by chloride process, 100% oxygen oxidation of $TiCl_4$, 100% anatase by chloride process; research on turbulence and structure of water. Home and Office: 1913 Oak Lane Rd Wilmington DE 19803-5237 E-mail: cgsmmoore@aol.com.

MOORE, CHARLES GERALD, educational administrator; b. Spartanburg, S.C., Oct. 29, 1949; s. Charles Edward and Betty Louise (Jarrett) M.; m. Carolyn Lancaster, June 15, 1977. BS, Clemson U., 1971, MA in Edn., 1983, postgrad., 1987—. Cert. vocat. dir., secondary supr., supt., prin. Agriculture tchr. Dorman High Sch., Spartanburg, 1977-87, asst. prin., 9th grade prin., 1987-90, asst. prin. 11th grade, 1990, vice prin. adminstrn., 1990-93; dir. technology edn. Spartanburg County Sch. Dist. 6, 1990-93; prin. Boiling Springs H.S., Spartanburg Dist. 2, 1993-96, Dorman H.S., Spartanburg, 1996-97; dir. secondary edn. Spartanburg Dist. 2 Schs., 1997—2000; prin. Boiling Springs H.S., 2000—. Mem. steering com. Upstate Tech. Prep. Consortium, 1990-93. Maj. USAFR, 1971-95.. Named S.C. Honor Roll Tchr., Dist. Tchr. of Yr., SCASC Administr. Yr. S.C., 2003. Mem. ASCD, Am. Assn. Sch. Adminstrs., Nat. Assn. Secondary Sch. Prins., Am. Vocat. Assn., S.C. Assn. Sch. Adminstrs., S.C. Assn. Secondary Sch. Prins., (life) Air Force Assn. Home: 141 Waite Ave Spartanburg SC 29302-3089 E-mail: geraldmoore@charter.net.

MOORE, CHARLOTTE CHANDLER, educational association administrator; b. Fairview Park, Ohio, Feb. 18, 1960; d. Wilbur Sweetser and Electa Louise (Waterman) Bailey; m. George Louis Moore, Feb. 11, 1984; children: Andrew Wayne, Amy Charlot, Katherine Elizabeth. Student, Wilson Coll., 1979-80; sec. cert., Katherine Gibbs Sch., 1980-81. Sec. to computer ops. officer Fifth Third Bank, Cin., 1981-83; adminstrv. asst. to sr. v.p. Bradford Adjustment Svcs., Inc., Cin., 1983-84; cultural arts chair Taylor Mill (Ky.) Elem. PTA Bd. Dirs., 1985-93, Sixth Dist. Ky. Congress of Parents & Tchrs. Bd. Dirs., Covington, Ky., 1989-91, Ky. Congress of Parents & Tchrs., Inc., Frankfort, Ky., 1991-93. Reflections art program Taylor Mill Elem. PTA, 1985-92; chair Sixth Dist. KCPT, Covington, 1989-91, Ky. Congress of Parents & Tchrs., Frankfort, 1991-93; picture person program chair Taylor Mill PTA, 1986-98; rschr., grant coord. Ky. History Elem. Sch. Program, 1991. Grantee Ky. Arts Coun., 1990, 91, Ky. Humanities Coun., 1991. Mem. Nat. Art Edn. Assn., Ky. Art Edn. Assn., Ky. Alliance for Arts Edn. Bd. Dirs., Behringer Crawford Mus., Greater Cin. YMCA, Cin. Zool. Soc. Avocations: reading, swimming, camping, snowmobiling, collecting art. Home: 729 Mill Valley Dr Covington KY 41015-2281

MOORE, DAN STERLING, insurance executive, sales trainer; b. Lincoln, Nebr., June 27, 1956; s. Jack Leroy and Carolyn Marie (Bachman) M.; m. Marla Janine Collister, June 2, 1979; children: Tyler David, Anna Rose. Student, Red Rocks Coll., 1977. Lic. ins. exec. Asst. mgr. European Health Spa, Englewood, Colo., 1975-78; sales mgr. Colo. Nat. Homes, Westminster, 1979-80; sales assoc. Dale Carnegie, Denver, 1981; sales mgr. Paramount Fabrics, Denver, 1981-84; sales assoc. Mighty Distbg., Arvada, Colo., 1984-87; divsn. mgr. Nat. Assn. for Self Employed/United Group Assn., Englewood, Colo., 1987—. Divsn. mgr. Communicating for Agr. Assn., 1993-98, Am. Bus. Coalition, 1997-2000, Am. for Financial Security, 1999—. Leader, trainer Alpine Rescue Team, Evergreen, Colo., 1971-74; minister Jehovah's Witnesses, 1972—. Avocations: golf, skiing, backpacking, scuba diving, tennis. Home: 892 Nob Hill Trl Franktown CO 80116-7917 Office: Nat Assn Self Employed/United Group 10579 W Bradford Rd Ste 100 Littleton CO 80127-4247 E-mail: sterlingmoore@att.net.

MOORE, DANIEL EDMUND, psychologist, educator, retired educational administrator; b. Pitts., Dec. 31, 1926; s. John Daniel and Alma Helen (Goehring) M.; m. Rose Marie Blunkosky, Nov. 11, 1949; children: Catherine Chiodo, Claire Marie Moore Caveney, Mary Moore Brilmyer, Suzanne Moore Gray, Elizabeth Moore Sullivan. BSEd, Duquesne U., 1949, MEd, 1952; postgrad., California (Pa.) State Coll., 1954-56, U. Pitts., 1958-59, Mt. Mercy Coll., 1959-60, Cath. U. Am., 1966, W.Va. U., 1970-72. Lic. psychologist; cert. sch. psychologist. Tchr. math. Cecil Twp. Sch. Dist., McDonald, Pa., 1949-52, Pitts. Public Schs., 1952-53; with Mt. Lebanon Twp. (Pa.) Sch. Dist., 1953-88, psychologist, 1954-71, dir. pupil personnel svcs., 1988; psychol cons. Peters Twp. Sch. Dist., McMurray, Pa., 1961-88; psychol. cons. Blackhawk Sch. Dist., Beaver, Pa., 1989—98; psychol cons. Quaker Valley Sch. Dist., Sewickley, Pa., 1989-90; lectr., supr. Grad. and Undergrad. Sch. Edn. Duquesne U.; psychologist DePaul Inst., Pitts., 1992—98. Lectr. ednl. psychology Grad. Sch. Edn., Duquesne U., 1957-92, supr. student tchrs., 1989-92; ednl. cons. St. Francis Schs. Nursing, New Castle and Pitts., 1959-91; mem. test adv. bd. Ednl. Records Bur., 1976-86; hearing officer Right to Edn. Office, Dept. Edn., Harrisburg, Pa., 1975—; in-svc. adv. bd. Pa. Dept. Edn. Hearing Officers. Mem. Chartiers Valley Sch. Dist. Bd., 1963-94, pres., 1971, v.p., 1991; mem. Pkwy. West Tech. Sch. Bd. 1965-67; bd. dirs. secondary sch. rsch. program Ednl. Testing Svc., Princeton, 1971-85; bd. dirs. Robert E. Ward Home for Children, 1975-87, St. Agatha Parish Coun., 1988—, Pathfinder Sch., 1989, v.p., 1990-94, pres. sch. bd., 1991-92; vol. Bridgeville Area Food Bank, 1988—; chairperson Parish 100 Jubilee Ceremony, Goodwill Villa Bd., Goodwill Plaza, Inc., Goodwill Villa Bd. of Incorporators, 1992—; pres. bd. dirs. Goodwill Plaza, 1992—; jubilee chairperson St. Agatha's, Bridgeville, Pa. With USNR, 1945-48. Henry C. Frick grantee, 1970, 73; named Jaycee Educator of Yr. for South Hills Area, Ward Home Outstanding Community Leader, 1984, Outstanding Cmty. Leader, Chartiers Valley Human Rels. Coun., 1998; recipient Human Rels. award Chartiers Valley Interrelationships Soc., 1998. Mem. Am., Pa. psychol. assns., Coun. Exceptional Children (pres. 1957), Phi Delta Kappa (pres. chpt. 1974-75, chmn. lay awards com. 1979-2001, Svc. Key award 1985). Roman Catholic. Home: 213 Station St Bridgeville PA 15017-1806

MOORE, DAVID SHELDON, statistics educator, researcher; b. Plattsburg, N.Y., Jan. 28, 1940; s. Donald Sheldon and Mildred (Roberts) M.; m. Nancy Kie Bok Hahn, June 20, 1964; children: Matthew, Deborah. AB, Princeton U., 1962; PhD, Cornell U., 1967. Asst., assoc. then prof. profl. stats. Purdue U., West Lafayette, Ind., 1967—96, Shanti S. Gupta disting. prof. stats., 1996—, asst. dean Grad. Sch., 1977—80, dir. Stats. and Nat. Sci., 1980—81. Program dir. NSF, Washington, 1980-82, cons. 1981— ; cons. NRC, Washington, 1982-85, content expert Annenberg/CPB project TV series, 1987, 89, 92; mem. U.S. Nat. Commn. Math. Instrn., 1999-2001. Author: Statistics Concepts and Controversies, 1978, 5th edit. 2001, Introduction to the Practice of Statistics, 1989, 3d edit., 1999, Basic Practice of Statistics, 1995, 2d edit., 2000; assoc. editor Internat. Stat. Rev., 1992-95, Jour. Stat. Edn., 1993-96; contbr. articles to profl. jours. Danforth Found. Grad. fellow, 1962-67. Fellow Am. Statis. Assn. (pres. 1998, Founders award 2001), Inst. Math. Statis. (governing coun. 1984-88); mem. Internat. Stat. Inc. (mem. coun. 1993-95), Math. Assn. Am. (Haimo award for Disting. Coll. and Univ. tchg. of Math, Ind. sect., 1994). Home: 4840 Jackson Hwy West Lafayette IN 47906-9209 Office: Purdue U Dept Stats West Lafayette IN 47907-1399*

MOORE, DONALD WALTER, academic administrator, school librarian; b. Culver City, Calif., June 9, 1942; s. Raymond Owen and Jewel Elizabeth (Young) M.; m. Dagmar Ulbrich, Mar. 28, 1968; 1 child, Michael. AA, L.A. Valley Coll., 1967; BA in History, Calif. State U., Northridge, 1970; MA in Learning Disability, Calif. State U., 1973; MLS, U. So. Calif., 1974. Part time librarian L.A. Pierce Coll., Woodland Hills, Calif., 1974—; instr. reading L.A. Trade Tech. Coll., 1978-80, pres.'s staff asst., 1983-87; instr. learning skills L.A. City Coll., 1987-88, dir. amnesty edn., 1988-92, dir. English and citizenship program, 1992—. Adj. instr. computer sci. L.A. Trade-Tech. Coll., 1983—. Author: A Guidebook to U.S. Army Dress Helmets, 2000; contbr. fiction, articles, revs. to various publs. Mem. Ednl. Writers Am., Little Big Horn Assn. Republican. Roman Catholic. Avocations: writing, collecting U.S. frontier military memorabilia, computing. Office: LA City Coll Citizenship Program 855 N Vermont Ave Los Angeles CA 90029-3516

MOORE, DUNCAN THOMAS, optics educator; b. Biddeford, Maine, Dec. 7, 1946; s. Thomas Fogg Moore and Virginia Robinson Wing; m. Gunta Liders, July 1995. BA in Physics, U. Maine, 1969, DSc (hon.), 1995; MS in Optics, U. Rochester, 1970, PhD in Optics, 1974. Asst. prof. U. Rochester, N.Y., 1974-78, assoc. prof., 1978-86, prof., 1986—, Kingslake prof., 1993—, dean engring. and applied sci., 1995-97, prof. biomed. engring., 2001—, exec. dir. Univ., Industry and Govt. Partnership for Advanced Photonics, 2001—02; pres., founder Gradient Lens Corp., Rochester, 1980; dir. N.Y. State Ctr. Advanced Optical Tech., Rochester, 1987-94; assoc. dir. technology White House Office Sci. & Technology Policy, Washington, 1997-2000; CEO, Infotonics Tech. Ctr. Inc., 2002—. Vis. scientist Nippon Schlumberger, Tokyo, 1983; Congl. fellow Am. Phys. Soc., Washington, 1993—94; sci. advisor to Sen. John D. Rockefeller IV, W.Va., 1993—94; exec. dir. U. Rochester Industry and Govt. Partnership for Advanced Photonics, 2001—02; mem. environ. and energy svc. rev. com. Idaho Nat. Engring. and Environ. Lab., 2001—02; mem. vis. com. NASA-Goddard Space Flight Ctr., 2002; mem. applied engring. and tech. directorate vis. com. Goddard Space Flight Ctr., 2002. Contbr. numerous articles to profl. jours.; patentee in field. Chmn. Hubble Indpendent Rev. Panel, 1990-91; mem. adv. bd. high tech. Rochester C. of C., 1988-93. Recipient Disting. Inventor of Yr. award Rochester Intellectural Property Law Assn., 1993, Grin Optics award Japanese Applied Physics Soc., 1993, Sci. and Tech. award Greater Rochester C. of C., 1992; named Engr. of Yr., Rochester Engring. Soc., 1999. Mem.: NRC, NAE, Am. Inst. Physics (state dept. fellowship selection com. 2001—), Coalition for Photonics and Optics (chair 1996—97), Forum on Physics and Soc. (exec. com. 1996—97), Coun. Sci. Soc. (co-chair govt. affairs com. 1996—97), Materials Rsch. Soc., Am. Assn. Engring. Soc. (bd. govs. 1995—97, Nat. Engring. award 1999), Optical Soc. Am. (bd. dirs. 1987—89, editor Applied Optics 1990—92, bd. dirs. 1992—97, v.p. 1994, pres. 1996, Leadership award 2001), Am. Soc. Precision Engring., Am. Ceramic Soc. (Edward Orton, Jr. Meml. lectr 2002), Lasers and Electro-Optics Soc. IEEE. Home: 4 Claret Dr Fairport NY 14450-4610 Office: U Rochester Inst Optics PO Box 270186 Rochester NY 14627-0186 E-mail: moore@optics.rochester.edu.

MOORE, FRANK JAMES, artist, educator; b. Columbus, Ohio, June 25, 1946; s. James F. and Constance (Chidester) M.; 1 child, Koala Bear. BA, Univ. N.M., 1972; MA in Psychology, Univ. Without Walls, Berkeley, Calif., 1976; MFA in Performanc, Video, San Francisco Art Inst., 1983. Tchr. univ. possibilities Inter-Rels., Inc., Berkeley, 1988—. Dir. Theater Human Melting, Berkeley, 1975-82; mgr. Blind Lemon Theatre, Berkeley, 1977-81; founder, dir. Internet News Svc. LUVer Alternative News, 2000—. Author: Cherotic Magic, 1990, rev. edit., 2003, Art of a Shaman, 1991, (poetry) Chapped Lap, 2000; co-author: Vision Theater, 1994; editor (mags.) The Cherotic (r)Evolutionary, 1991-1999; pub., editor Inter-Rels., Inc., Berkeley, 1993—; contbr. (anthologies) Range of Motion, 1993, Consider the Alternatives, 1996, Male Lust, 2000, Disability Culture Rap (video documentary), 2000, Beneath the Surface, 2000; contbr. articles to jours., periodicals, mags., newspapers; host of live weekly internet show, 1998—; creator of 3 large websites on the internet; founder, dir. award winning internet radio sta. Love Underground Vision Radio (Luver), 1999—, Frank Moore's Unlimited Possibilities, Pub. Access TV, Berkeley, Calif., 2001—, Deep Core Magic, Pub. Access TV, Berkeley, Calif., 2003—; prodr., writer, dir.: Feisto, 2001. Performance Art fellow NEA, 1985; recipient Showcase award Cleve. Pub. Theatre Performance Art Festival, 1990, Hon. Mention, East Bay Video Festival, 1991, Second place, 1992, Best of Bay Performance Artist, Bay Guardian, San Francisco, 1992, Hon. Recognition Berkeley Video Festival, 1997, Best Feature Film, Berkeley Video & Film Festival, 2002. Avocations: computers, music, pop culture. Office: Inter Rels Inc PO Box 11445 Berkeley CA 94712-2445 E-mail: fmoore@eroplay.com.

MOORE, GEORGE BARNARD, poet, educator; b. Pasadena, Calif., July 12, 1950; s. George Crosby and Jessica Francis (Barnard) Moore. BS, Lewis and Clark Coll., 1975; MA, U. Colo., 1981, PhD, 1990. Instr. dept. English U. Colo., Boulder, 1980-90, instr. dept. continuing edn., 1983—, instr. Sewall acad. program, 1987, 88, 91—. Judge, panelist Arts and Humanities Assembly of Boulder, 1995-99; judge Colo. Coun. on Arts, Boulder, 1994. Author: Long Way Around, 1992, Petroglyphs at Wedding Rocks, 1997, Gertrude Stein's The Making of Americans, 1998, Headhunting: Poems, 2002. Recipient Creative Work award Arts and Scis. U. Colo., 1986, Covisions Recognition award Colo. Coun. on Arts, 1996. Mem. MLA, Am. Culture Assn. (area chair politics and lit. 1996—), Am. Soc. for Aesthetics (v.p. Rocky Mountain divsn. 1996-99, pres. 2000-02), Western Lit. Assn., Rocky Mountain Modern Lang. Assn. Office: U Colo Sewall Acad Program Boulder CO 80309-0001

MOORE, HAROLD BLAINE, middle school educator; b. Cleveland, Tenn., Sept. 29, 1955; s. Harry Lee and Glenna Jacqueline (Hawkins) M.; m. Sandra Lee Wyatt, Dec. 15, 1978. BA, Tenn. Tech. U., 1979. Tchr., coach Glenn L. Martin Jr. High Sch., Crossville, Tenn., 1979—. Mem. Cumberland County Edn. Assn. (assn. rep. 1989—, chief negotiator 1990-92). Avocations: puzzle-solving, reading novels, sports. Office: Glenn L Martin Jr High Sch 314 Miller Ave Crossville TN 38555-4037

MOORE, HERFF LEO, JR., management educator; b. San Antonio, Jan. 24, 1937; s. Herff Leo Moore Sr. and Constance (Benesh) Wold; m. Helen Lucille Weidert, Nov. 1991; children by previous marriage: Terri Lynne, Christopher Scott, Kimberly Anne. BSBA, The Ohio State U., 1964; MBA, U. Tex., 1968; MS in Community Svcs., U. Rochester, 1976; PhD, U. Tex. at Arlington, 1980. Cert. sr. profl. in human resources (life). Prodn. mgmt., quality assurance officer Sacramento (Calif.) Air Logistics Ctr. USAF, 1964-67; personnel mgmt., adminstrv. cons. Aero. Systems Div. Wright-Patterson AFB, Dayton, Ohio, 1968-73; pers. mgmt. and quality assurance cons. Defense Contract Adminstrv. Svcs. Dist. Hdqrs., Rochester, N.Y., 1973-76; lectr. in mgmt. and doctoral student The Univ. of Tex. at Arlington, 1976-79; asst. prof. bus. adminstrn. Ea. Ky. U., Richmond, 1979-81; assoc. prof. mgmt. East Tex. State U. at Texarkana, 1981-83, Saint John Fisher Coll., Rochester, 1983-85, U. Cen. Ark., Conway, 1985-99, ret., 1999. Pres. H.M.C.C. Mgmt. Group, Conway, 1988—; participant Leadership Texarkana Leadership Tng., 1981-82; mgmt. cons., devel. trainer, Calif., N.Y., Ark., Ohio, N.J., Fla., Ga., Tex., 1964—. Author: (with others) Language, Customs and Protocol: A Guidebook for International Students and Employees, 1992; contbr. numerous articles to profl. jours. Capt. USAF, 1964—76. Recipient Significant Performance Contbr. award Def. Supply Agy., 1975; Nat. scholar Phi Kappa Phi, 1968; named Honor Grad. USAF Officers Tng. Sch., 1964. Mem. Soc. for Human Resource Mgmt. (tng. and devel. com. 1989-94, select panel on edn. 1989-91, coll. rels. com. 1989-92, bd. dirs. area IV 1987-91, sec., treas. Ark. coun. 1986-87), Ark. Human Resources Assn. (pres. 1991-92, bd. dirs. 1991-93), Acad. Mgmt., Soc. Human Resource Mgmt. (superior merit awards student chpt. U. Ctrl. Ark. 1985-90, 93), Alpha Kappa Psi, Phi Kappa Phi, Sigma Iota Epsilon. Mem. Assembly Of God Ch. Avocations: golf, chess, political buttons. Home: 1910 Amelia Dr Conway AR 72034-3315

MOORE, JANET RUTH, nurse, educator; b. Bridgeport, Conn., Sept. 19, 1949; d. Robert Hartland and Florence (Merritt) Bessom; m. William James Moore, Sept. 5, 1971; children: Jeffrey, Gregory. AA, Green Mountain Coll., 1969; diploma, Mass. Gen. Hosp., 1974; BSN, Am. Internat. Coll., 1980; MSN, U. Mass., 1993. RN, Mass.; cert. gerontol. clin. nurse specialist ANCC. Nurse's aide Lynn (Mass.) Hosp., 1967-69, staff nurse, 1972-73; nursing asst. U.S. Army Hosp., Ft. Polk, La., 1971-72; staff nurse Ludlow (Mass.) Hosp., 1980-85; staff edn. instr. Springfield (Mass.) Mcpl. Hosp., 1985-88; dir. staff edn. Jewish Nursing Home, Longmeadow, Mass., 1988-93; instr. Baystate Med. Ctr. Sch. Nursing, Springfield, Mass., 1993-99. Nurse Camp Wilder, Springfield, 1981-84; clin. instr. Holyoke (Mass.) C.C., 1990, Elms Coll., 1999—; co-dir. Robin Read Adult Day Health, 1999—. Contbr. articles to jour., chpts. to books. Mem. Jr. League of Springfield, 1981-88, Cmty. Health Edn. Coun. for Children and Adolescents; bd. dirs. Mass. Soc. for Prevention of Cruelty to Children, Springfield, 1985-90; bd. dirs. Coun. of Chs., chair divsn. on aging, 1989-90; mem. respite com. Alzheimer's Assn. Western Mass., 2000—; mem. human rights com. Berkshire Hill Music Acad., 2003—. Mem. Sigma Theta Tau, Alpha Chi. Avocations: walking, swimming, rollerblading. Home: 104 Burleigh Rd Wilbraham MA 01095-2620 Office: Robin Read Adult Day Health West Springfield MA 01089 E-mail: jrbmoore@hotmail.com.

MOORE, JEAN MOORE, secondary education educator; b. Selma, Ala., Oct. 30, 1945; d. James Freeman and Millie Jane (Bean) Moore; m. Herman Moore, Jr., June 27, 1975; stepchildren: Kevin, Kelvin. Diploma, Selma U., 1965; BS in English and History, Ala. State U., 1967, MEd in Secondary Edn., 1973. Cert. secondary tchr., Ala. Tchr. Keith High Sch., Orrville, Ala., 1967-75, 95—. Asst. sec. matron's div. Ala. Women's Bapt. State Conv., 1985—. Named Tchr. of Yr., Dallas County High Sch., 1983, 85; Selma U. Bus. and Profl. Womens scholar, 1964. Mem. NEA, Nat. Council Tchrs. English, Ala. Edn. Assn., Academic and Curriculum Devel. Assn., Dallas County Profl. Tchrs. (sec. 1984-85), Elks (Elk of Yr. award, Selma 1983), Order Eastern Star. Democrat. Home: 2712 Prospect Ln Selma AL 36703-1432

MOORE, JEANNE, retired art educator and administrator; b. LA, Aug. 28, 1932; d. George E. and Ellen Kearny (Patrick) Moore. AA, Pasadena (Calif.) City Coll., 1952; BA with honors, UCLA, 1954; MM, U. So. Calif., 1965, DMA, 1970. Music tchr. Arvin (Calif.) H.S., 1955-60, Santa Maria (Calif.) H.S., 1960-65, Arroyo H.S., El Monte, Calif., 1965-66; asst. prof. edn. U. Victoria, B.C., Can., 1968-70; asst. prof. music edn. Bowling Green (Ohio) State Coll., 1970-71; prof. music West Chester (Pa.) State Coll., 1971-72; lectr. music San Jose (Calif.) State U., 1972-73; asst. prof. music Madison Coll., Harrisonburg, Va., 1974-76; coord. fine arts W.Va. Dept. Edn., Charleston, 1977-98, ret., 1998. Choral dir. Santa Maria Choral Soc., 1963—64, Silver Lake Presbyn. Ch., L.A., 1966—67, Wesley United Meth. Ch., San Jose, 1972—74; cons./contbr. Nat. Study of Sch. Evaluation, Falls Church, Va., 1983—85, 1989; ednl. cons. W.Va. Symphony Orch., 2002—03. Co-author: Beyond the Classroom: Informing Others, 1987; editor: W.Va. Symphony League, 2003—. Staff mem. Gov's Task Force on Arts Edn., W.Va., 1990—94, Grantee, Nat. Endowment for Arts, 1989—92. Mem.: W.Va. Art Edn. Assn. (bd. dirs., Outstanding Adminstr. award 1991, 1993, 1997, 1998), W.Va. Music Educators Assn. (bd. dirs., Presdl. award

1990, Disting. Svc. award 1998), Music Educators Nat. Conf., Nat. Coun. State Suprs. Music (pres. 1984—86), Nat. Art Edn. Assn., Mu Phi Epsilon, Pi Kappa Lambda, Phi Delta Kappa. Home: 102 Brammer Dr Charleston WV 25311-1738

MOORE, JERRY SCOTT, lawyer, law educator; b. Little Rock, Nov. 17, 1960; s. Bobby Gene and Linda Sue (Scott) M.; children: Nicole Marie Been, Keeton Scott, Stephen Matthew, Jesse Thomas. Assoc., Rogers State Coll., 1986; Bachelors, Bartlesville Wesleyan Coll., 1988; JD, U. Okla., 1991. Bar: Okla. 1991, U.S. Dist. Ct. (ea. dist.) Okla. 1991, U.S. Dist. Ct. (we. and no. dists.) Okla. 1992, U.S. Ct. Appeals (10th cir.) 1992, Cherokee Nation Tribal Ct. Okla. 1994, Muscogee (Creek) Nation Tribal Ct. Okla. 1993. Apprentice welder Ramco Pipeline, Inc., Chickasha, Okla., 1979-81; welder CYLX Engring. Inc., Bartlesville, Okla., 1981-84; clk. Legal Aid of Western Okla., Norman, 1989; legal intern Edmonds, Cole & Hargrave, Oklahoma City, 1990; atty. Baker & Baker, Tahlequah, Okla., 1991-95; asst. dist. atty. Dist. 27 State of Okla., Tahlequah, 1995—. Adj. prof. Northeastern State U., Tahlequah, 1995—. Recipient Cleveland County Legal Aid scholarship U. Okla., 1990-91, Am. Jurisprudence award U. Okla., 1991, Scholastic Progress award Bur. Nat. Affairs, 1991; named to All Dist. 6 Team Nat. Christian Coll. Athletic Assn., 1986-87, 87-88, Acad. All Dist. 9 team Nat. Assn. Intercollegiate Athletics, 1987-88; named Acad. All-Am., Nat. Assn. Intercollegiate Athletics, 1987-88. Mem. Okla. Bar Assn., Tulsa County Bar Assn., Creek Nation Bar Assn., Cherokee County Bar Assn. (del. 1993, 95, 96, 98, 200, 2001, 2002, v.p. 1993-94, pres. 1994-95). Democrat. Methodist. Avocations: basketball, fishing, golf, boating, skiing. Home: PO Box 1541 Tahlequah OK 74465-1541 Office: Dist Attys Office 27th Dist 213 W Delaware St Tahlequah OK 74464-3641

MOORE, JOHN WARD, chemistry educator; b. Lancaster, Pa., July 17, 1939; s. Joseph D. and Lillian B. M.; m. Elizabeth Augustin, Aug. 26, 1961. AB, Franklin & Marshall Coll., 1961; PhD, Northwestern U., 1965. Asst. prof. Ind. U., Bloomington, 1965-71; assoc. prof. Eastern Mich. U., Ypsilanti, 1971-76, prof., 1976-89, U. Wis., Madison, 1989—, W.T. Lippincott prof., 2000—. Cos. Ecology Ctr. of Ann Arbor, 1979-81; vis. prof. U. Wis., Madison, 1981-82; vis. assoc. prof. U. Nice, France, 1987—; dir. Project SERAPHIM, 1982—, Inst. for Chem. Edn., 1989—. Editor Jour. Chem. Edn.: Software, 1988-96, Jour. Chem. Edn., 1996—; contbr. articles to profl. jours. Recipient Disting. Faculty award for rsch., publ. and svc. Ea. Mich. U., 1977, sci. faculty profl. devel. award NSF, 1979, Disting. Faculty award Mich. Assn. Governing Bds., 1982, Catalyst award Chem. Mfg. Assn., 1982, silver medal CASE Prof. Yr., 1986, George C. Pimentel award in chem. edn. Am. Chem. Soc., 1991, James Flack Norris award in chem. edn., 1991, Upjohn award for excellence in tchg., 1993, Underkofler award for excellence in tchg. Wis. Power & Light Co., 1995, Talbot prize for visual excellence, 2003, Benjamin Smith Reynolds award for excellence in tchg. engrs., 2003. Home: 3995 Shawn Trl Middleton WI 53562-3521 Office: U Wis Dept Chemistry Dept Chemistry 1101 University Ave Madison WI 53706-1322 E-mail: jwmoore@chem.wisc.edu.

MOORE, JOHN WILLIAM, former university president; b. Bayonne, N.J., Aug. 1, 1939; s. Frederick A. and Marian R. (Faser) M.; m. Nancy Baumann, Aug. 10, 1968; children: Matthew, Sarah, David. BS in Social Sci. and Edn., Rutgers U., 1961; MS in Counseling and Student Pers. Svcs., Ind. U., 1963; EdD, Pa. State U., 1970. Asst. to dean Coll. Edn. Pa. State U., University Park, 1968-70; asst. to dean students U. Vt., Burlington, 1970-71, asst. prof. edn. adminstrn., 1973-76, asst. v.p. acad. affairs, 1973-76, assoc. v.p. acad. affairs, 1976-77; v.p. policy and planning Old Dominion U., Norfolk, Va., 1977-78, exec. v.p., 1982-85; pres. Calif. State U., Stanislaus, Turlock, 1985-92, Ind. State U., 1992-2000. Author: (with others) The Changing Composition of the Work Force: Implications for Future Research and Its Application, 1982, also articles, papers presented at profl. meetings Pres. United Way, Modesto Calif., 1989; campaign chair United Way Wabash Valley, Terre Haute, Ind.; bd. dirs. Pvt. Industry Coun., Modesto, 1989, Union Hosp., Swope Mus., Am. Assn. Colls. and Univs.; bd. dirs., exec. com. Alliance for Growth and Progress, Terre Haute, Ind., 1992—, Terre Haute C. of C., Wabash Valley United Way, Bus. and Modernization Tech. Corp., Ind. Econ. Devel. Commn., PSI Energy. Recipient Disting. Svc. award Old Dominion U. Alumni Assn., 1985, Hispanic C. of C., 1982; recipient Community Svc. award Norfolk Commn. Edn., 1985, Leadership award United Way,1 986, Svc. award Pvt. Industry Coun., 1989; Alumni fellow Pa. State U., 1990. Mem. Am. Assn. State Colls. and Univs. (rep. Calif. chpt. 1988-92, bd. dirs. 1994—), Gould Med. Found. (bd. dirs. 1988-92, trustee 1988-92), Modesto Symphony Orch. Assn. (bd. dirs. 1990-92), Am. Coun. Edn., Commn. on Women in Higher Edn., Turlock C. of C. (bd. dirs. 1988-92), Rotary. Methodist. Avocations: fitness training, skiing, coaching youth sports, golf. Office: Ind State U Condit House Terre Haute IN 47809-0001

MOORE, JULIE KAY, middle school educator; b. Ann Arbor, Mich., June 15, 1959; d. Robert Walter and Carol Kay (Hutchison) Koch; m. Charles Donald Moore, Aug. 15, 1981. BS, No. Mich. U., 1981; MS in Spl. Edn., Nat. U., 1990. Tchr. Upward Bound U. of Guam, Agana, 1984, Bishop Baumgartner Jr. High Sch., Agana, 1983-86, St. Rita's Sch., San Diego, 1987-89; edn. coord. San Diego Union/Tribune, 1989-90; tchr. Ctrl. Kitsap Jr. High Sch., Silverdale, Wash., 1990—. Newspaper in edn. cons., bd. mem. Pacific Northwest Newspaper Assn., Tacoma, 1990—; bd. dirs. Wash. Orgn. for Reading Devel., 1992—; coop. facilitator vocat./tech. edn., spl. edn. Ctrl. Kitsap Sch. Dist. Author: (mag.) Newspaper in Education Information Service, 1992, Northwest Reading Jour., 1993. Recipient 2020 grant Ctrl. Kitsap Sch. Dist., 1991. Mem. NEA, Internat. Reading Assn., State of Wash. Collaboration for Integration (steering com.), Wash. Orgn. for Reading Devel. (bd. newspaper in edn. com. 1992—). Home: 3969 Greenbriar Pl SE Port Orchard WA 98366 Office: Ctrl Kitsap Sch Dist 9210 Silverdale Way NW Silverdale WA 98383-9197

MOORE, KENNETH JAMES, agronomy educator, scientist; b. Phoenix, June 6, 1957; s. George Taylor and Barbara Joyce (Amy) M.; m. Gina Marie McCarthy Aug. 11, 1979; children: Ellyn Elizabeth, David Taylor, Mark Daniel. BS in Agr., Ariz. State U., 1979; MS in Agronomy, Purdue U., 1981, PhD in Agronomy, 1983. Asst. prof. agronomy U. Ill., Urbana, 1983-87; assoc. prof. N.Mex. State U., Las Cruces, 1988-89; rsch. agronomist Agrl. Rsch. Svc., USDA, Lincoln, Nebr., 1989-93; prof. Iowa State U., Ames, 1993—. Adj. assoc. prof. U. Nebr. Lincoln, 1989-93, prof., 1993-96; sr. rsch. fellow Ag Rsch. Grasslands, New Zealand, 1998; dir. MS in Agronomy Distance Edn. program Iowa State U., 1995—. Founding editor Crop Mgmt., 2002--; assoc. editor Agronomy Jour., 1989-93, tech. editor, 1994-97; assoc. editor Crop Sci., 1994; contbr. chpts. to books. Bd. dirs. Lincoln Children's Mus., 1991-93, Children's Svcs. of Ctrl. Iowa, 1996-97; bd. dirs. Children's Mus. Ctrl. Iowa, 1997-2002, pres., 2000-01; mem. mgmt. com. N.E. YMCA, Lincoln, 1991-93; mem. youth policy forum Lincoln YMCA, 1991-92. Recipient Point of Light award USDA, 1991. Fellow Am. Soc. Agronomy (bd. dirs. 2002—), Crop Sci. Soc. Am. (divsn. chmn. 1990-92, pres. 2003-, exec. com. and bd. dirs. 2002—, Young Crop Scientist award 1993); mem. Am. Forage and Grassland Coun. (Outstanding Young Scientist award 1982, merit award 1991). Republican. Presbyterian. Avocations: swimming, fishing, music. Office: Iowa State U Agronomy Dept 1567 Agronomy Hl Ames IA 50011-0001

MOORE, LARRY GLENN, school system administrator; b. Indpls., July 27, 1950; s. William R. and E. LaVon (Slinker) Birge; m. Doris J. Vaught; children: Ronin G., Clayton R., Jacob Y. BA, Hanover (Ind.) Coll., 1972; MA, Ball State U., 1976; EdS, Ind. U., 1979; EdD, U. Sarasota, 1996. Cert. secondary tchr. and adminstr., Ind. Tchr. math. Madison (Ind.) Consolidated Schs., 1972-79; asst. prin. Southwestern Schs., Hanover, Ind., 1979-81; prin. Trimble County High Sch., Bedford, Ky., 1981-83, Crothersville (Ind.) Jr.-Sr. High Sch., 1984-86, South Spencer (Ind.) H.S., 1986-90; supt. Connelton (Ind.) City Schs., 1993—. Edn. chmn. Perry County Substance Abuse Com., Tell City, 1994—; bd. dirs. Perry County Health Dept., 1994—; mem. cmty. ctr. facility com. City of Cannelton, Ind., 1994—. With USMC, 1969-72. Mem. Ind. Assn. Pub. Sch. Supts., Ind. High Sch. Athletic Assn., Nat. Assn. Secondary Sch. Prins., Nat. Fedn. Interscholastic Officals Assn., North Ctrl. Assn. vis. com. chmn.), Am. Legion, Kiwanis (treas. Cannelton club 1993—), Mensa, Phi Delta Kappa. Avocations: travling, racquetball, reading. Office: Cannelton City Schs 109 S 3rd St Cannelton IN 47520-1504

MOORE, MARGARET BEAR, American literature educator; b. Zhenjiang, China, Mar. 14, 1925; came to U.S., 1929; d. James Edwin Jr. and Margaret Irvine (White) Bear; m. Rayburn S. Moore, Aug. 30, 1947; children: Margaret Elizabeth Moore Kopcinski, Robert Rayburn. BA, Agnes Scott Coll., 1946; MA, U. Ga., 1973. Book rev. editor East Ark. Record, Helena, Ark., 1948-50; bibliographer Perkins Libr. Duke U., Durham, N.C., 1950-52; instr. in English Hendrix Coll., Conway, Ark., 1955-56, U. Ctrl. Ark., Conway, 1958-59; editor Inst. Cmty. & Area Devel. U. Ga., Athens, 1974-79; tchr. Latin Athens Acad., 1980-81; ind. scholar Athens, 1981—. Author (book revs.) Am. Lit., 1989, 94, 2000, Nathaniel Hawthorne Rev., 1992, The Salem World of Nathaniel Hawthorne, 1998; contbr. articles to profl. jours. Tchr. Presbyn. Ch., Va., Ark., N.C. and Ga., 1945—; deacon, elder First Presbyn. Ch., Athens, 1974—. Mem.: MLA, Nathaniel Hawthorne Soc. (exec. com. 1987—90, sec. 1997—2000), South Atlantic MLA, Soc. for Study of So. Lit., Philol. Assn. Carolinas, Am. Lit. Assn., Va. Hist. Soc., House of Seven Gables, Peabody Essex Mus., Phi Beta Kappa, Mortar Board, Phi Kappa Phi. Avocations: reading, walking, travel. Home: 106 Saint James Dr Athens GA 30606-3926

MOORE, MARILYN PATRICIA, community counselor; b. Nashville, Jan. 16, 1950; m. Roy Allen Moore; children: Christopher Manuel, Christina Marilyn, Catrina Marilyn. Merchandising cert., Bauder Coll., 1969; BS, Tenn. Wesleyan Coll., 1975; MEd., Tenn. Tech., 1979, EdS, 1981. Lic. profl. adminstr. and tchr., Tenn. Head resident/counselor Tenn. Wesleyan Coll., Athens, 1974-75; tchr. Rhea County Dept. Edn., Dayton, Tenn., 1975-81, prin., 1981, 84-86; adj. coll. instr. Tenn. Tech. U., Cookeville, 1981—, coord. off campus program, 1981-86; tchr. Rhea County Dept. Edn., Dayton, 1982-83, prin., 1983-86, supt. schs., 1986-90; evaluator, community intervention counselor Behavioral Health Svcs., Kingsport, Tenn., 1992-94, cmty. intervention counselor, 1994—. Voting mem. Rhea County Purchase and Fin., Dayton, 1986—; adj. faculty East Tenn. State U., 1991, Holston Svcs., 1991. Chairperson Polit. Action Com. for Edn., Dayton, 1978-81; bd. dirs. Battered Women, Inc., Crossville, Tenn., 1987—; chairperson allocations United Way, Dayton, 1987-88; mem. Tenn. Sheriff's Assn., Nashville, 1988—; aide-de-camp Rep. Shirley Duer, Nashville, 1987; life mem. Presdl. Task Force, 1991—. Recipient Cert. Appreciation, Am. Legion, 1988, Cert. Participation, Very Spl. Arts, 1989, Am. Fedn. of Police Edgar Hoover award, 1991, John Edgar Hoover Meml. Gold medal, 1991; named Hon. Mem. Staff, Senator Anna Belle O'Brien, Nashville, 1987. Mem. NEA (past del.), Tenn. Edn. Assn., Tenn. Orgn. Sch. Supts., Alliance for a Drug Free Tenn. (chairperson 1987-91), Women Hwy. Safety Leaders Tenn. (county leader 1989—), USAF Aux. Aerospace (capt. 1987—), Tenn. Assn. Sch. Bus. Officials, Dayton C. of C., Nat. Police Assn. (Am. Patriotism award 1993). Republican. Methodist. Avocations: workshops, classes, readings on law and the Am. legal system. Home: 205 Santa Fe Dr Bristol TN 37620-6441 Office: AKard Sch 224 Mount Area Dr Bristol TN 37620-7116

MOORE, MARK TOBIN, art educator, artist, retired museum curator; b. Washington, Jan. 19, 1954; s. Selden George and Dorothy May (Tobin) M.; m. Denise Annette Poole, Oct. 20, 1987 (div. Jan. 1995); 1 child, James Tobin. BA in Art, U. Charleston, 1983; MA in Art, Marshall U., 1985; MFA in Painting, W.Va. U., 2000. Art instr. Ohio U., Ironton, Ohio, 1985-87, Ashland (Ky.) C.C., 1985-87, U. Charleston, W.Va., 1985-87; art specialist U.S. Army Europe/Giessen Arts and Crafts, 1987-91; exhibits coord. W.Va. State Mus., Charleston, 1992-93, exhibits dir., 1993-98; grad. tchg. asst. art dept. W.Va. U., Morgantown, 1999-2000, vis. adj. prof., 2001; asst. prof. art W. Va. State Coll., Institute, 2001—. Art instr. U. Charleston, 1995-98, W.Va. State Coll. Inst., 1995-98; adj. instr. art dept. Marshall U., Huntington, W.Va., 1998; gallery adv. bd. U. Charleston, 1997. One-person shows include Sunrise Art Mus., 1996, Sleeth Gallery, W.Va. Wesleyan Coll., 1995, Perspective Galerie, Giessen, 1990, Alderson-Broadus Coll., Phillipi, W.Va., 2001, Cultural Ctr. of Fine Arts, Parkersburg, W.Va., 2002, Hurricane, W.Va., 2002; group shows include Salon of French and Allied Forces, The Palace of Luxemburg, Paris, Ariel Gallery, N.Y.C., 1989, Huntington (W.Va.) Mus. Art, 1992, 94, 97, Gov.'s Mansion W.Va., 1997, Omaha Ctr. for Contemporary Art, 1999, The Dairy Barn Cultural Arts Ctr., Athens, Ohio, 2000, Paul Mesaros Gallery, W.Va. U., Morgantown, 2000, OCAF, Athens, Ga., 2002, 03, W.Va. State Mus., 2002, 03, Beckley, W.Va., 2002, Avampeto Discovery Mus., Clay Ctr., Charleston, W.Va., 2003, Fayetteville (N.C.) State U., 2003, Rosenthal Art Gallery, Fayetteville, N.C., 2003. With USN, 1972-83. Recipient Arthur Carpenter award for excellence in art, 1985, Merit award Nat. Collage Soc. Juried Exhbn., Cleve., 1998, award of excellence Allied Artists W.Va. Juried Exhbn., Sunrise Mus., Charleston, 1998, 2d place merit award, OCAF, Athens, Ga., 2002; WVa./NEA profl. devel. grantee, 2003—. Office: WVa State Coll Dept Art Institute WV 25112 Home: 1210 Dudley Rd Charleston WV 25314 Studio: Blue Door Studios 223 1/2 Hale St Charleston WV 25314 E-mail: mooremt@mail.wvsc.edu.

MOORE, MARSHA LYNN, elementary school educator, counseling administrator; b. Washington, May 19, 1946; d. Marshall Alexander and Doris Virginia (Diggs) Moore. BA, Howard U., 1967; MEd, U. Md., 1973. Sch. counseling K-12, cert. tchr. grades 1-6, sci. resource tchr. grades 1-6. 1st grade demonstration tchr. Anne M. Goding Sch. D.C. Pub. Schs., 1967—72; counselor Balt. County Schs., Towson, Md., 1972—77; fashion coord., mgr. Wallach's Ladies' Store, Nanuet, NY and Livingston, NJ, 1977—80; adult edn. cons., counselor East Orange (N.J.) Adult High Sch., 1980—83; coord. lang. arts Faith Hope Christian Sch., 1983—84; minority counselor Essex County C.C., Newark, 1984—85; equal opportunity fund counselor, instr. Kean Coll., Union, NJ, 1985—87; tchr. 6th grade Randle Highlands Elem. Sch., 1987—90; tchr. 5th and 6th grade Brookland Sch., Washington, 1990—98; 5th grade tchr., math. and sci. resource tchr. Shepherd Elem. Sch., Washington, 1998—2000; tchr. 6th grade math and sci. Bertie Backus Mid. Sch., Washington, 2002—03; ret., 2003. Coord. counselor Summer Youth Program, East Orange, 1982; career fair coord. East Orange Adult H.S., 1981, Essex County C.C., 1985; mem. discipline com. PTA Shepherd Sch., Washington, 1998—2002; liaison, exec. bd., hospitality com., multicultural com. PTA, 2000—02; math.-a-thon coord. St. Jude's, 2000, coord. parent math. workshop, 2000—02, sci. resource tchr., United States, 2000—02; coord. Sci. Careers Expo and 1st Sci. Bee, 2001; co-sponsor Student Coun., 2001—02; facilitator DCACTS, 2001—02; math. tutor, 2000—01; sgt.-at-arms WT Union Sch. Orgn., 2002—03. Editor: Sci. newsletter. Chmn. Teen Lift, NJ, Delteens, Washington; 2d v.p. Washington Pan-Hellenic Coun., 1994—96, fin. sec., 1996—98, co-chair Greek Forum, 1996—98; mentor Best Friends, Inc. Mem.: NAACP, AFT, Nat. Mid. Sch. Assn., Nat. Sci. Tchrs. Assn., Washington Tchrs. Union, U.S. Tennis Assn., Howard U. Alumni Assn. (reunion planning com. 1967, N.J. coord. 1980—87, v.p. Washington 1989—91, pres. 1991—93, parliamentarian Washington chpt. 1999—2001, chairperson membership com. Wash. chpt. 2003—, life mem. Washington chpt.), Schomburg Rsch. Ctr. (N.Y.C.), Kennedy Ctr. for Performing Arts, Friends of Andrew Rankin Chapel (adj. sec. 1994—97, newsletter co-chair, fundraising and archives coms.), Delta Sigma Theta (Diamond Life mem.). Episcopalian. Avocations: tennis, gardening, landscape designing, swimming, travel.

MOORE, SISTER MARY FRANCIS, parochial school educator; b. Bklyn., Aug. 17, 1928; d. Daniel and Mary Frances (Downing) M. B in Social Studies, St. Francis Coll., Bklyn., 1971; M in Elem. Edn., L.I. U., Bklyn., 1976; cert. in adminstrn. and supervision, Manhattan Coll., Riverdale, N.Y., 1988. Joined Sisters of Mercy, Roman Cath. Ch., 1957. Acct. N.Y. Tel. Co., Bklyn., 1945-57; tchr. 2nd grade St. Mary's Sch., Roslyn Heights, N.Y., 1960-62; tchr. 1st grade St. Brigid's Sch., Bklyn., 1962-68; tchr. 2nd and 6th grades St. Jerome's Sch., Bklyn., 1968-74; tchr. 3rd grade St. Bernard's Sch., Bklyn., 1974-81, tchr., prin., 1981-82, prin., 1982-85; tchr. 1st grade Maria Regina Sch., Seaford, 1985—2002. Cooperating tchr. for tchr. tng. program St. Joseph's Coll., Brentwood, L.I., N.Y., 1968-70. Recipient Appreciation award Bergen Beach Civic Assn., Bklyn., 1985, The Thomas Cuite Meml. award Ancient Order of Hibernians, 1993. Mem. Nat. Cath. Edn. Assn. (tchr. assoc.). Roman Catholic. Avocations: reading, walking, baseball, movies, enjoying friends. Office: Maria Regina Sch 4045 Jerusalem Ave Seaford NY 11783-1627

MOORE, MARY JULIA, special education educator; b. Pitts., Oct. 10, 1949; d. Edward Henry and Julia Ann (Polkabla) Sauer; 1 child, Jason Michael Sauer; m. John Harold Moore, Oct. 27, 1990; 1 adopted child, Jocelyn Quan. BS in Art Edn., Edinboro State Coll., 1971; MS in Spl. Edn., Clarion State Coll., 1980; postgrad. U. Pitts., 1988—. Cert. art tchr., spl. edn. tchr. for mentally retarded. Tchr. Polk (Pa.) State Sch. & Hosp., 1971-72; vol. VISTA, Bath, N.Y., 1972-73; tchr. Polk Ctr., 1973-80, program specialist, 1980-92; residential svc. supr., qualified mental retardation profl. Polk (Pa.) Ctr., 1992—. Lectr., speaker, video on local TV on history of Polk Ctr., 1987. Patentee beer bottle shaped cake pan; cakes displayed in TV videos and in various mags.; creator history video Polk Ctr., Some Leaky Boot Statues, Polk Center--100 Years; creator video A Century of Care-The History of the Evolution of Institional Care of the Devlopment Disabled. Past vol. Big Bros./Big Sisters. Democrat. Roman Catholic. Avocations: cake decorating, reading. Home: PO Box 97 Franklin PA 16323

MOORE, MELVIN G. school system administrator; b. Snow, Okla., Jan. 14, 1944; s. Manuel G. and Millie K. (Crownover) M.; m. Merlene S. Klinge, Feb. 24, 1962; (div. Dec. 1979); children: Torri Lynn Moore Wilson, Michael Trevor; m. Christine B. Levak, June 21, 1982; 1 child, Lyndsey Laura Victoria. BS, Oreg. Coll of Edn., Monmouth, 1967, MS, 1971; PhD, U. N.C., Chapel Hill, 1977. Cert. tchr., adminstr. Tchr. Dallas Pub. Schs., Dallas, Oreg., 1968-70; instr., teaching research div. OSSHE, Monmouth, 1971-72; asst. to dir., tech. assistance devel. systems U. N.C., Chapel Hill, 1972-74; adminstrv. intern, bur. of edn. for handicapped U.S. Office of Edn., Washington, 1974-75; research asst. U. N.C., Chapel Hill, 1975-76; asst. research prof. to assoc. research prof. OSSHE, Monmouth, 1976-79; dir. clin. svcs. Ea. Oreg. Hosp. & Tng. Ctr., Pendleton, 1980; dir. special edn. Hillsboro Union High Sch. Dist., 1980-92, Washington County Edn. Svc. Dist., Portland, Oreg., 1992—. Mem. Oreg. Early Childhood Spl. Edn. Interagy. Adv. Com., 1993—; program dir. Marion County Mental Health Divsn., Salem, Oreg., 1977-79; asst. dir. WESTAR U. Wash., Seattle, 1977-78, dir., 1979-80. Contbr. articles to profl. jours. Bd. dirs. Coalition in Oreg. for Parent Edn., Salem, 1986—; legis. com. Confederation of Oreg. Sch. Adminstrs., Salem, 1987—; adv. bd. Oreg. Adv. Coun. for Handicapped Children, Salem, 1988—, Tualatin Valley Mental Health Dept., Portland, 1984—, Oreg. Early Childhood Spl. Edn. Interagency Adv. Com., 1993—. Recipient Exemplary Service award, Coalition in Oreg. for Parent Edn., Salem, 1988, Recognition of Service award, Portland Tech. Edn. Consortium, 1988. Mem. Coun. of Exceptional Children (gov. 1970-71), Assn. for Retarded Citizens, Confederation of Oreg. Sch. Adminstrs. (pres. 1986-87), Assn. for Supervision and Curriculum Devel. Democrat. Avocations: sailing, fly fishing, reading. Home: 5205 SW 49th Dr Portland OR 97221-1803 Office: Washington County ESD 5825 NE Ray Cir Hillsboro OR 97124-6436

MOORE, MITCHELL JAY, lawyer, law educator; b. Lincoln, Nebr., Aug. 29, 1954; s. Earl J. and Betty Marie (Zimmerlin) M.; m. Sharon Lea Campbell, Sept. 5, 1987. BS in Edn., U. Mo., Columbia, 1977, JD, 1981. Bar: Mo. 1981, U.S. Dist. Ct. (we. dist.) Mo. 1981, Tex. 1982, U.S. Ct. Appeals (8th cir.) 1998. Tchr. Clinton Mid. Sch., 1978; sole practice Columbia, Mo., 1981—. Coordinating atty. student legal svcs. ctr. U. Mo., Columbia, 1983-89. Mem. Columbia Substance Abuse Adv. Commn., 1989—; bd. dirs. Planned Parenthood of Ctrl. Mo., Columbia, 1984-86, Opportunities Unltd., Columbia, 1984-86, ACLU of Mid-Mo., 1991-98; Libertarian candidate for Atty. Gen. of Mo., 1992, 2000, for 9th congl. dist. U.S. Ho. of Reps., 1994, 96, for Mo. State Rep. 23d dist., 1998, mem. Probation and Parole Citizens Adv. Bd., 1997-99. Mem. Boone County Bar Assn., Assn. Trial Lawyers Am., Phi Delta Phi. Libertarian. Unitarian Universalist. Avocations: softball, camping, Tae Kwon Do. Office: 1210 W Broadway Columbia MO 65203-2126 E-mail: mmoore259@mchsi.com.

MOORE, MYRNA M. elementary school educator; b. Howard County, Iowa, Dec. 23, 1934; d. Paul J. and Ethel (Stevenson) Laue; m. Robert E. Moore, Aug. 5, 1956; children: Alan P., Nancy S. Profl. Tchrs. Cert., Iowa State Tchrs. Coll., 1954; BA, Upper Iowa Coll., Fayette, 1965; MS, U. Iowa, 1988. Tchr. remedial reading jr. high Valley Community Sch. Dist., Elgin, Iowa, tchr. grade 5, tchr. grade 6. Mem. Chickasaw County Conservation Bd., Iowa Assn. County Conservation Bds. Recipient cert. of appreciation Fayette County Conservation Bd. Mem. Nat. Sci. Tchr. Assn., Iowa Acad. Sci., Iowa Reading Coun., Iowa Tchr. Assn., N.E. Iowa Lang. Arts Tchrs. (exec. bd.). Home: 105 Drewelow Ave Fredericksburg IA 50630

MOORE, NANCY NEWELL, English language educator; b. Deadwood, S.D., Apr. 11, 1939; d. Harold Richard and Laura Mae (Howe) Newell; m. John Howard Moore, Feb. 23, 1962 (div. Oct. 1980). BA, Lake Forest Coll., 1961; MA, Northwestern U., 1963; PhD, U. Ill., 1968. Instr. of English U. Ill., Champaign-Urbana, 1967-68; asst. prof. of English U. Wis., Stevens Point, 1968-72, assoc. prof., 1972-76, prof., 1976—, asst. to chancellor for women, 1972-74, dept. chmn., 1974-77, chmn. faculty senate, 1981-84. Contbr. articles to profl. jours. Recipient grant for Canadian Studies, Can. Govt., 1986. Mem. AAUW, NOW, Midwest MLA, Assn. for Can. Studies in U.S., Shakespeare Assn. Am., Women in Higher Edn., Phi Eta Sigma. Unitarian Universalist.

MOORE, PAMELA RAE, elementary school educator; b. Paulding, Ohio, Feb. 22, 1959; d. Loren J. and Louella I. Thomas; m. Chet Moore, Dec. 10, 1977; children: Amy Renae, Cheryl Kae. BS, Defiance Coll., 1990; MS, St. Francis U., 1995. H.s. learning disabilities tchr., Paulding, 1991—99; mid. sch. reading tchr., 1999—. Home: 819 E Wayne St Paulding OH 45879

MOORE, PENELOPE, retired school librarian; b. Sylacauga, Ala., Apr. 16, 1937; d. Frank Durward and Dorothy (Roberts) M. BA, Birmingham-So., 1959; MA, U. Miss., Oxford, 1960; MLS, U. Ala., Tuscaloosa, 1973. English tchr. Sylacauga (Ala.) High Sch., 1960-62, Lee High Sch., Huntsville, Ala., 1962-68; office mgr. Bell and Lang Law Firm, Sylacauga, 1969-72; libr. Mountainview Elem. Sch., Sylacauga, 1973-96. Bd. dirs. Sylacauga Arts Coun., 1980—, Isabel A. Comer Mus. and Arts Ctr., Aylacauga, 1982-88, A Plus, Montgomery, Ala., 1992—; founder Sylacauga Community Chorus, 1976; active Ala. Libr. Media Leadership Group. Recipient Outstanding Achievement award Sylacauga Arts Coun., 1989; named Sylacauga Woman of the Yr. by Sylacauga Exchange Club, 1983, Ala. State Tchr. of Yr., 1992, Outstanding Vol. by United Way of Sylacauga, 1993. Mem. Ala. Libr. Assn., Ala. Instrl. Media Assn., Libr. and Media Profl. Orgn. (Outstanding Svc. to Ala. Librs. 1992), S.E. Regional Vision for Edn., Alpha Delta Kappa. Republican. United Methodist.

MOORE, PETER BARTLETT, biochemist, educator; b. Boston, Oct. 15, 1939; s. Francis Daniels and Laura Benton (Bartlett) M.; m. Margaret Sue Murphy, Jan. 30, 1966; children: Catherine, Philip. BS, Yale U., 1961, MA (hon.); PhD, Harvard U., 1966. Postdoctoral fellow U. Geneva, 1966-67, MRC Lab. of Molecular Biology, Cambridge, Eng., 1967-69; asst. prof., then assoc. prof. dept. molecular biophysics Yale U., New Haven, 1969-76, assoc. prof. dept. of chemistry, 1976-79, prof., 1979—2002, Sterling prof., 2002—, chmn. dept. chemistry, 1987-90. Contbr. articles to profl. jours. Guggenheim Found. fellow, 1979-80. Fellow AAAS; mem. Am. Chem. Soc., Am. Soc. Biol. Chemists and Molecular Biologists, Nat. Acad. Scis., Am. Acad. Arts and Scis., Biophys. Soc. (editor Biophys. Jour. 1997-2002) Office: Yale U Dept of Chemistry 225 Prospect Ave New Haven CT 06512-1958

MOORE, PRIMUS MONROE, JR., elementary educator, counselor, administrator; b. McAlester, Okla., Sept. 30, 1947; s. Primus M. and Mamie Artie Mae (Collins) M.; m. Veronica Marie Davis, Feb. 14, 1979; children: Lee Charles, Tamarah Michelle. BS in Edn., Langston U., Okla., 1969; postgrad., Purdue U., Ind.; MS in Edn., Ind. U., 1979; postgrad., East Cen. U., Okla. Ind. life teaching cert., Okla. K-8 teaching, computer repair. Tchr. John Vohr Elem. Sch., Gary, Ind., 1970, Jefferson Elem. Sc., Gary, Ind., 1971-76; media technician Pulsaki Middle Sch., Gary, Ind., 1976-77, Gary Tchr. Ctr., Gary, Ind., 1977-80; libr.,media technician Martin Luther King Acad., Gary, Ind., 1980-82; tchr. Will Rogers Elem.,Puterbaugh Middle, McAlester, Okla., 1982-90; counselor Jefferson, Eugene Field & Wm. Gay, McAlester, Okla., 1990-91; vice prin. Puterbaugh Middle Sch, McAlester, 1991-94; prin. Eugene Field Elem. Sch., McAlester, 1994—2002; dir. McAlester Profl. Devel. Ctr., 2002—. Cons. Gary Model Cities Community Ctr., Gary, Ind., 1971-73; reporter, photographer McAlester News Capital & Democrat, McAlester, Okla., 1983-89. Co-author: McAlester Computer Curriculum Guide, 1986, Crossroads Descipline, 1988, Leading Learning Communities: Standard for What Principals Should Know and Be Able To Do, 2001. Mem. McAlester Planning Commn., Okla., 1990, Pitts. County Fair Trust Authority, 1988-93, Pitts. County Sheriff Res., 1989—, McAlester Singers, 1988-99; mem. southeast regional adv. bd. Dept. Mental Health & Substance Abuse Svc. Recipient I Dare You Leadership, L'Ouverture Alumni Assn., McAlester, Okla., 1965, military leadership award, Assn. U.S. Army, Ft. Leonard Wood, Mo., 1979. Mem. Nat. Assn. Elem. Sch. Prins., Okla Edn. Assn., Okla. Assn. Elem. Sch. Prins. (past pres.), Assn. Supervision Curriculum Devel., Nat. Staff Devel. Coun., Kappa Alpha Psi, Kappa Kappa Psi, Phi Delta Kappa. Democrat. Lutheran. Avocations: tennis, cycling, gardening, woodcarving, golf. Home: 417 N 10th St Mcalester OK 74501-4816 Office: McAlester Public Schools PO Box 1027 Mcalester OK 74502-1027

MOORE, RAYBURN SABATZKY, American literature educator; b. Helena, Ark., May 26, 1920; s. Max Sabatzky and Sammie Lou (Rayburn) M.; m. Margaret Elizabeth Bear, Aug. 30, 1947; children: Margaret Elizabeth Moore Kopcinski, Robert Rayburn. AB, Vanderbilt U., 1942, MA, 1947; PhD, Duke U., 1956. Script writer King Biscuit Time, Interstate Grocer Co., KFFA, 1947-50; Vice pres. Interstate Grocer Co., Helena, 1947-50; research and grad. asst. Duke U., 1952-54; asst. prof. English, Hendrix Coll., Conway, Ark., 1954-55, asso. prof., 1955-58, prof., 1958-59; asso. prof. U. Ga., Athens, 1959-65, prof., 1965-90, prof. emeritus, 1990—, chmn. Am. studies program, 1968-90, chmn. div. lang and lit., 1975-90. Vis. scholar Duke U., 1958, 64 Author: Constance Fenimore Woolson, 1963, For the Major and Selected Short Stories of Constance Fenimore Woolson, 1967, Paul Hamilton Hayne, 1972, A Man of Letters in the Nineteenth-Century South: Selected Letters of Paul Hamilton Hayne, 1982; sr. editor: History of Southern Literature, 1985, Selected Letters of Henry James to Edmund Gosse (1882-1915): A Literary Friendship, 1988, The Correspondence of Henry James and the House of Macmillan, 1877-1914: All the Links in the Chain, 1993, The Letters of Alice James to Anne Ashburner, 1873-1878, Resources for American Literary Study, vol. 27 numbers 1 and 2, 2001; mem. editorial bd. U. Ga. Press, 1972-74, Ga. Rev., 1974-82, chmn., 1980-82; contbr. articles, revs. to profl. jours. Adv. bd. Letters of Henry James complete edit., 1995—, editl. bd., 1997—; troop com. Boy Scouts Am., Athens, 1973-75; deacon, elder Presbyterian Ch., 1962—; Lamar Meml. Lectures com. Mercer U., 1984-91. Capt. US Army, 1942-46, PTO. Recipient John Hurt Fisher award South Atlantic Assn. Depts. English, 2000, honoree English Language and Lit., Philoological Assn. of Carolinas, 1990. Mem. MLA (exec. com. Gen. Topics VI 1972-75), Soc. Study So. Lit. (exec. com. 1968-69, 74-79, 85-88, 91-94, v.p. 1981-82, pres. 1983-84), South Atlantic Grad. English Coop. Group (exec. com. 1969-79, chmn. 1971-72), South Atlantic MLA (exec. com. 1975-77, nominating com. 1985-87), Am. Lit. Assn. (chair Simms Soc. Sessions 1993-2003), Va. Hist. Soc., Philological Assn. Carolinas, Edgar Allan Poe Soc., William Gilmore Simms Soc. (exec. com. 1993-94, pres.-elect 1993-95, chmn. Simms sessions Am. Lit. Assn. 1993—), Constance Fenimore Woolson Soc., Blue Key, Phi Beta Kappa, Sigma Chi. Office: U Ga Dept English Park Hall Athens GA 30602-6205

MOORE, REGINA DENISE, healthcare facility educator, therapist; b. Franklin, Ind., May 8, 1962; d. Johnny Cilous and Virginia Flake (Knight) M.; m. James Leonard Born II, Dec. 23, 1989. BA, Franklin Coll., 1984. Lic. tchr., Ind., Mich. Recreation dir. Franklin Pks. and Recreation, 1984-85; tchr./counselor VisionQuest, Tucson, 1985-87; tchr. Charter Hosp., Ft. Wayne, Ind., 1987-89; program specialist Ind. U., Martinsville, 1989-90; activity therapist Charter Hosp., Indpls., 1989—. Ropes course cons. Charter Outpatient Svc., Indpls., 1992—. Vol. Wheeler Mission, Indpls., 1991, Hoosier Environ. Coun., Indpls., 1991-92. Mem. Assn. for Childhood Edn. Internat., Coun. for Exceptional Children. Avocations: backpacking, skiing, rock climbing, organic gardening, bicycling. Office: Charter Counseling Ctr 5660 Caito Dr Bldg 3 Indianapolis IN 46226-1372

MOORE, RICHARD KERR, electrical engineering educator; b. St. Louis, Nov. 13, 1923; s. Louis D. and Nina (Megown) M.; m. Wilma Lois Schallau, Dec. 10, 1944; children: John Richard, Daniel Charles. BS, Washington U. at St. Louis, 1943; PhD, Cornell U., 1951. Test equipment engr. RCA, Camden, N.J., 1943-44; instr. and rsch. engr. Washington U., St. Louis, 1947-49; rsch. assoc. Cornell U., 1949-51; rsch. engr., sect. supr. Sandia Corp., Albuquerque, 1951-55; prof., chmn. elec. engring. U. N.Mex., 1955-62; Black and Veatch prof. U. Kans., Lawrence, 1962-94; prof. emeritus, 1994—; dir. remote sensing lab. U. Kans., 1964-74, 84-93. Pres. Cadre Corp., Lawrence, 1968-87; cons. cos., govt. agys. Author: Traveling Wave Engineering, 1960; co-author: (with Ulaby and Fung) Microwave Remote Sensing, Vol. I, 1981, Vol. II, 1982, Vol. III, 1986; contbr. to profl. jours. and handbooks. Lt. (j.g.) USNR, 1944-46. Recipient Achievement award Washington U. Engring. Alumni Assn., 1978, Outstanding Tech. Achievement award IEEE Geosci. and Remote Sensing Soc., 1982, Louise E. Byrd Grad. Educator award U. Kans., 1984, Irving Youngberg Rsch. award U. Kans., 1989, Australia prize, 1995. Fellow AAAS, IEEE (sect. chmn. 1960-61, Outstanding Tech. Achievement award coun. oceanic engring. 1978); mem., NAE, AAUP, Am. Soc. Engring. Edn., Am. Geophys. Union, Internat. Sci. Radio Union (chmn. U.S. commn. F 1984-87, internat. vice chmn. commn. F 1990-93, chmn. 1993-96), Kiwanis, Sigma Xi, Tau Beta Pi. Presbyterian (past elder). Achievements include research in submarine communications, radar altimetry, radar as a remote sensor, radar oceanography; patent for polypanchromatic radar. Home: 1712 Carmel Dr Lawrence KS 66047-1840 Office: U Kans R S & Remote Sensing Lab 2335 Irving Hill Rd Lawrence KS 66045-7612 E-mail: rmoore@sunflower.com.

MOORE, ROBERT PAUL, elementary school educator; b. Houston, July 1, 1968; s. Robert Vance and Joyce Mae (Mikulenka) M. A in Behavioral Scis., San Jacinto Jr. Coll., Pasadena, Tex., 1988; BS in Edn. cum laude, U. Houston, 1991, M in Mid-Mgmt., 1996. Cert. tchr., Tex. Tchr. 5th grade math., sci., social studies and lang. arts W.A. Carpenter Elem. Sch., J.P. Dabbs Elem. Sch., Deer Park, Tex., 1992—; adv. com. campus improvement com. W.A. Carpenter Elem. Sch., Deer Park, 1992-94, rep. dist. improvement com., 1996-97, campus tech. support leader, 1996-97; campus lightspan coord. J.P. Dabbs Elem. Sch., Deer Park, 1997-98. Chmn. yearbook com., 1992-95, sponsor student coun., 1992-94, 97-98, mem. inclusion com., 1993-94, portfolio assessment com., 1993-94, hall monitor supr., 1995—; mem. social studies essential elements clarification team, 1995-97. Mem. ASCD, NEA, Nat. Coun. Tchrs. Math., Assn. Tex. Profl. Educators, Tomorrow's Tchrs. Club, Phi Delta Kappa, Kappa Delta Pi. Roman Catholic. Avocations: hunting, fishing, reading, running, history.

MOORE, ROSEMARY KUULEI, art gallery administrator; b. San Diego, Apr. 16, 1955; d. Edward James and Rina Larn (Young) M.; m. Lance Wesley Holter, June 16, 1994; children: Ian Everest Yannell, Jade River Holter, Sean Maru Yannell, Michael McKinley Yannell, Sarah Lehua Hotter. Student, U. So. Calif., L.A., 1975, U. Hawaii, Kahului, 1980. Project coord. Hawaiian Sea Village, Amfac Property Corp., Kaanapali, 1979-80; shopping ctr. mgr. Whalers Village, Amfac Property Corp., Kaanapali, 1980-83; comm. mgr., adminstrv. dir. Amfac Property Corp., Kaanapali, 1983, property mgr., 1983-85; v.p. Kahikinui (Hawaii) Homes Project, 1990-93; chair, com. rels. dir. Haleakala Waldorf Sch., Kula, Hawaii, 1991-92, headmaster, 1992-95; mgr. Viewpoints Gallery, Mokawao, Hawaii, 1999—; dir. Viewpoints Galleries, Maui, Hawaii, 1999—; pres. Merchants Assocs., 2000—. Author: Lightworker, 1990, Mikey & Cocoa are Friends, 1992; contbr. articles to profl. jours. Coord. hwy. beautification Dept. Transp., Maui, 1992—; mem. steering com. Valley Isle Voters Assn., Maui, 1994. Mem. Nat. Wildlife Soc., Cousteau Soc. Avocations: writing, surfing, skin diving, hiking, camping. Office: Viewpoints Gallery 3620 Baldwin Ave Ste 101 Makawao HI 96768-9500

MOORE, SALLY FALK, anthropology educator; b. N.Y.C., Jan. 18, 1924; d. Henry Charles and Mildred (Hymanson) Falk; m. Cresap Moore, July 14, 1951; children: Penelope, Nicola. BA, Barnard Coll., 1943; LL.B., Columbia U., 1945, PhD, 1957. Asst. prof. U. So. Calif., Los Angeles, 1963-65, assoc. prof., 1965-70, prof., 1970-77, UCLA, 1977-81; prof. anthropology Harvard U., Cambridge, Mass., 1981—, Victor Thomas prof. anthropology, 1991—, dean Grad. Sch. Arts and Scis., 1985-89. Author: Power and Property in Inca Peru, (Ansley Prize 1957), 1958, Law as Process, 1978, Social Facts and Fabrications, 1986, Moralizing States, 1993, Anthropology and Africa, 1994, Law and Anthropology, 2004. Trustee Barnard Coll., Columbia U., 1991-92; master Dunster House, 1984-89. Rsch. grantee Social Sci. Rsch. Coun., 1968-69, NSF, 1972-75, 79-80, Wenner Gren Found., 1983; Guggenheim fellow, 1995-96. Fellow Am. Acad. Arts & Scis., Am. Anthrop. Assn., Royal Anthrop. Inst. (Huxley medallist, lectr. for 1999); mem. Assn. Polit. and Legal Anthropology (pres. 1983), Am. Ethnological Soc. (pres. 1987-88), Assn. Africanist Anthropologists (pres.-elect 1995, pres. 1996-98). Democrat. Office: Harvard U 348 William James Hall Cambridge MA 02138

MOORE, SANDRA BUCHER, mathematics educator; b. Norfolk, Va., Jan. 5, 1946; d. Clayton Merrill and Helen (Wilson) Bucher; m. Robert Curtis Moore, Aug. 1, 1970; children: Kimberley Anne, Tara Elayne. BS, Radford Coll., 1968; MS, Old Dominion U., 1988. Cert. profl. tchr., Va. Elem. tchr. Hampton (Va.) City Schs., 1968-89, Title I math. specialist, 1989—. Math. text reviewer McGraw-Hill Pubs., N.Y., 1985; reader of Eisenhower Proposals, U.S. Dept. of Edn., Washington, 1991; curriculum writer CII WHRO-TV, Hampton Rds., 1987-90. Author: (lesson plan) Computer Teacher Contest, 1987 (1st Pl. award 1987). Mem. Hampton Fedn. Tchrs., AFT, 1981-94, Womans Club, 1969-91; officer Poquoson H.S. Band Boosters, 1990-94. Recipient Tech. Educator of Yr. award CII-WHRO-TV, 1989. Mem. AFT (treas. 1988-92, 3d v.p. 1992-94), Va. Ednl. Computer Assn., Va. Coun. Tchrs. Math., Peninsula Coun. Tchrs. of Math. Democrat. Methodist. Avocations: crafts, sewing, gardening, spectator sports. Home: 9 Far St Poquoson VA 23662-2115

MOORE, SANDRA KAY, counselor, administrator; b. Sellersville, Pa., June 28, 1943; d. Sheldon Ellsworth and Olive (Moyer) McElroy; m. Thomas Van Moore, June 8, 1963; children: Thomas Shawn, Tara Quinn, Tammy Colleen, Thador Shelby. Student, East Stroudsburg (Pa.) U., 1961-63; BA, Gwynedd-Mercy Coll., 1986; MS, Chestnut Hill Coll., 1990. Cert. in student assistance program. Crisis counselor Archbishop Ryan H.S., Phila., 1989-90; guidance counselor Mt. St. Joseph Acad., Flourtown, Pa., 1990-93, dir. guidance, 1993—. Lectr. Gwynedd-Mercy Coll., Gwynedd, Pa., 1995—; lectr. in field. Author: So You Want to Go to College, 1994. Bd. dirs. Today, Inc., Hilltown, Pa., 1976-80; mem. Hilltown (Pa.) Civic Assn., 1975-85; pres. Bux-Mont Neighbors, Souderton, Pa., 1985, John M. Grasse Home and Sch. Assn., Perkasie, Pa., 1981; chairwoman Christian Edn. Com., Perkasie, 1994. Mem. APA, Ind. Counselors Assn., Nat. Assn. for Coll. Admissions Counselors, Specialists in Schs., Pa. Assn. Secondary Sch. and Coll. Admission Counselors. Democrat. Lutheran. Avocations: horseback riding, reading, writing, travel, collecting antique santa claus'. Office: Mount Saint Joseph Academy 120 W Wissahickon Ave Flourtown PA 19031-1802

MOORE, TARA SUE, special education educator; b. Jacksonville, Ill., July 4, 1958; d. James Edward and Barbara Ann (Sadler) Cockerill; m. Danny Ray Moore, July 23, 1977; children: Jessica Ann, Gerald James. BS in Elem. Edn., Spl. Edn., MacMurray Coll., 1980. Cert. tchr. elem. and spl. edn., Ill. Tchr. 3rd grade North Greene Unit Dist. # 3, Roodhouse, Ill., 1985—. Mem. Sci. Lit. Com., Roodhouse, 1989-91, Staff Devel. Com., Roodhouse, 1992—. Tchr. catechism St. Marks, Wincester, Ill., 1977-92, 94-95; sec. St. Marks Altar and Rosary Soc., 1987-88, mem., 1976—; active Winchester Elem. PTA, 1986—, Scott County Band Boosters, 1990—. Mem. Am. Fedn. Tchrs., Ill. Fedn. Tchrs., North Greene Edn. Assn. Roman Catholic. Avocations: sewing, cooking, hiking. Office: 250 E Sherman St White Hall IL 62092-1359

MOORE, TIMOTHY JOEL, health and fitness consultant; b. Washington, Feb. 2, 1959; s. Durrell Daniel and Betty Jane (Middlesworth) M. BA, U. Md., 1981, MA, 1984, PhD, 1994. Track/strength coach U. Md., College Park, 1982-88; program dir. Inst. Human Performance, Langley Park, Md., 1984-85; pres. Exercise Sci., Inc., Greenbelt, Md., 1985-95; dir. Prince George's C.C., Largo, Md., 1989-93, Nat. Hosp. Orthopaedics and Rehab., Landover, Md., 1993-95; fitness editor Shape & Living Fit Mag., Woodland Hills, Calif., 1996-98; pvt. cons., 1998—. Presenter in field; TV and internet contbr. Contbr. articles to profl. publs., books. Mem. Am. Coun. Exercise (cert.), Nat. Commn. Health Edn., Am. Coll. Sports Medicine, Nat. Strength and Conditioning Assn., Omicron Delta Kappa. Avocations: art, music. Home: 913 Euclid St Apt 6 Santa Monica CA 90403-3090

MOORE, VIRGINIA BRADLEY, librarian; b. Laurens, S.C., May 13, 1932; d. Robert Otis Brown and Queen Esther (Smith) Bradley; m. David Lee Moore, Dec. 27, 1957 (div. 1973). BS, Winston-Salem State U., 1954; MLS, U. Md., 1970. Cert. in libr. sci. edn. Tchr. John R. Hawkins H.S., Warrenton, N.C., 1954-55, Happy Plains H.S., Taylorsville, N.C., 1955-58, Young and Carver elem. schs., Washington, 1958-65; libr. Davis and Minor elem. schs., Washington, 1965-72, Ballou Sr. H.S., Kramer Jr. H.S., Washington, 1972-75, 78-80, Anacostia Sr. H.S., Washington, 1975-77, 80-95; libr. I, adult svcs. Greenbelt (Md.) Br. Libr., 1997—. Dir. ch. libr. workshops Asbury United Meth. Ch., Washington, 1972—74, 1976; spkr., presenter Ch. and Synagogue Libr. Assn., 1975, 80, 83, spkr. spring workshop, 99, presenter, 2000; mem. serials com. Prince George's County Meml. Libr. Sys., 2000—; chair-competency based curriculum D.C. pub. schs., 1978—93; chair local arrangements launching Nat. Sch. Libr. Media Month U.S. Capitol, 1985; mem. 1st libr. and info. sci. del. to People's Republic China, 1985; mem. faculty 1st established pub. svc. acad. in nation Anacostia Sr. H.S., 1990—95; coord. Nat. Libr. Week workshop Greenbelt Libr. Prince George's County Meml. Libr. Sys., 2002; presenter in field. Author: (bibliography) The Negro in American History, 1619-1968, 1968; (with Helen E. Williams) Books By African-American Authors and Illustrators for Children and Young Adults, 1991; TV script for vacation reading program, 1971, sound/slide presentation D.C. Church Librs.' Bicentennial Celebration, 1976; video script and tchr.'s guide for Nat. Libr. Week Balloon Launch Day, 1983; bibliography Black Literature/Materials, 1987; contbr. articles to profl. jours. Co-chmn. nat. libr. involvement com. Martin Luther King, Jr. Fed. Holiday Commn., 1990—99, chmn., 1996—99; trustee LeRoy C. Merritt Humanitarian Fund, 2002; libr. Mt. Carmel Bapt. Ch., Washington, 1984, chair ch. libr. com., 2000—, ad hoc com. for churchwide programs, 2001—, libr. Sunday Sch. Mother's Day coord., 1990—94, jr. ch. pianist, 1994—97, Sunday Sch. adult dept. pianist, 1984—, co-chmn. African-Am. History Mo. commn., 1996—, chmn. publicity com., 1996—99, com. renovation of Rev. Arthur H. Pace Libr. Multipurpose Rm., vice-chair publicity liaison com., 1999—, soprano sanctuary choir, 1995—, soprano soloist women's day and tribute commemoration, 1998, music com., 1998—; chmn. social responsibilities roundtable Martin Luther King Jr. holiday task force Am. Libr. Assn., 1999—; rec. sec. Washington Pan-Hellenic Coun., 1975. Named outstanding educator, Mt. Carmel Bapt. Ch., 1984; recipient Outstanding Congl. Libr., Ch. and Synagogue Libr. Assn., 2001, certs. of award, D.C. Pub. Libr., 1980, D.C. Pub. Schs., 1983; fellow Grad. fellow, U. Md., 1969; scholar NDEA scholar, Central State Coll., Edmond, Okla., 1969, U. Ky., 1969, Ball State U., 1969. Mem. ALA (councilor-at-large 1983-91, 96—, Freedom to Read Honor Roll, 1999, chmn.), LWV (sec. Prince George's County, Md. 1997-99, v.p. 1999-2000, pres. 2000—), AARP, Internat. Assn. Sch. Librs., NEA (life), Am. Assn. Sch. Librs. (coms. 1973-83, 1987—), D.C. Assn. Sch. Librs. (pres. 1971-73, citation 1973, newsletter editor 1971-75, 83), Intellectual Freedom Com. (chmn. 1983-99), Freedom to Read Found., Soc. Sch. Librs. Internat. (charter), Intellectual Freedom Roundtable (bd. dirs. exec. com. 1989-91), D.C. Libr. Assn., Md. Libr. Assn., Md. Ednl. Media Orgn., Internat. Platform Assn., S.E. Neighbors Club, Am. First Day Cover Soc., Nat. Coun. of Negro Women, Zeta Phi Beta (v.p. chpt. 1972-74), Delta Kappa Gamma (v.p. Alpha chpt. 1990-92, pres. 1992-95, Nu State D.C. membership chmn. 1991-92, rec. sec. 1994-95, v.p. 1995-97, liaison U.S. Forum 1995-97, 99—, spkr., state pres. 1997-99, steering com. speaker Soc. Internat. Legislative seminar 1998). Democrat. Achievements include being First Lady Laura Bush's guest at White House to launch Nat. Libr. Week, 2003. Home: 2100 Brooks Dr Apt 721 Forestville MD 20747-1016 Office: Prince Georges County Meml Libr Sys Greenbelt Br Libr 11 Crescent Rd Greenbelt MD 20770-1891

MOORE, VIRGINIA LEE SMITH, elementary education educator; b. Middletown, N.Y., May 13, 1943; d. James William and Anna Van Alst (Suydam) Smith; m. Thomas J. Moore, Oct. 16, 1965 (div. Apr. 1980); 1 child, Christian Thomas. AA in Liberal Arts, Orange County C.C., 1963; BA in Sociology magna cum laude, SUNY, Buffalo, 1965; MS in Edn., SUNY, New Paltz, 1980; MS in Edn. of Gifted, Coll. New Rochelle, 1990, cert. elem. edn., staff devel., 1994; cert. sch. adminstrn., 1994. Cert. elem. tchr., N.Y. Spl. edn. tchr. The Devereux Found., Glen Loch, Pa., 1965-66; elem. tchr. Harris Sch., Coatesville, Pa., 1967, Pine Bush (N.Y.) Cen. Schs., 1967-70, 78-00, substitute tchr., 1970-71; nursery sch. tchr. Olivet Meth. Nursery Sch., Coatesville, Pa., 1976-78; profl. devel. coord. Pine Bush Sch. Dsit., 1998. Presenter ednl. workshops Pine Bus Sch. Dist., Haldane Sch. Dist., Cold Spring, NY, Eldred Sch. Dist., Marlboro, NY, Middletown (N.Y.) Tchr. Ctr., N.Y. State Tech. Edn. Assn., Brookhaven Nat. Lab., NY, 1994, Nevele Conference Ctr., Ellenville, NY, 1995, Rochester (N.Y.) Inst. Tech., 1996, SUNY, Oswego, 1996, Rennselaer Poly. Inst., Troy, NY, 1997, Marriot Conf. Ctr., Syracuse, NY, 1999, Sci. Tchrs. Assn. N.Y. State, Nevele Conf. Ctr., Ellenville,, 1995, Internat. Tech. Edn. Assn., Indpls., 1999; participant math., sci. and tech. on elem. level program NSF, 1997—2000. Contbr. articles to profl. jours., sci. and tech. articles to profl. publs. Pres. Redtown Residents' Assn., Middletown, 1988—; sec. Orange County C.C. Alumni Bd. Dirs. Recipient Dean's Acad. Excellence award Coll. of New Rochelle, 1991, Orange County Conservation Tchr. of Yr., 1993, N.Y.S. Conservation Tchr. of Yr., 1993, Presdl. award for excellence in math. and sci. tchg. N.Y. State, 1997; Partnership in Edn. grantee Area Fund Orange County, N.Y., 1991, Energy grantee Orange and Rockland Utilities, 1995, Tech. grantee Mid-Hudson Tchr. Ctr., 1997, 98, Energy grantee N.Y. State Electric and Gas, 1998. Mem. NSTA, Internat. Tech. Edn. Assn. (N.Y. State Elem. Sch. Tchr. Excellence award 1998-99), N.Y. State United Tchrs., Sci. Tchrs. Assn. N.Y. State (Outstanding Sci. Tchr. award 1992, Excellence in Sci. Tchg. award 1995), N.Y. State Tech. Edn. Assn. (Tech. grantee 1999), Phi Beta Kappa. Baptist. Avocations: piano, reading, local environmental issues, development of interactive science museum exhibits. Home: 1672 Route 211 E Middletown NY 10941-3718

MOORE, WANDA JOHNSON, elementary education educator; b. Wilmington, N.C., June 18, 1951; d. Melvin Monroe and Mary Lee (Thomas) Johnson; m. Alexander Moore, Jan. 27, 1979; children: Eric N. Johnson, Gina Monique. BS, N.C. Ctrl. U., 1973; postgrad., U. N.C., Wilmington, 1982. Cert. tchr., N.C. Tchr Rocky Point Elem. Sch., Rocky Point, N.C., 1973—. Treas. Girls, Inc., Wilmington, 1989—. Active Talent Teen, Inc., Wilmington, 1991, WBMS Radio Scholarship Drive, Wilmington, 1991, Project First N.C. State Dept. Pub. Instrn., Raleigh, N.C., 1992. Mem. N.C. AE. Home: 1308 S 7th St Wilmington NC 28401-6324 Office: Rocky Point Elem School Rocky Point School Rd Rocky Point NC 28457

MOORE, WAYNE ANDREW, information specialist, educator; b. Roanoke, Va., July 9, 1958; s. William D. and Mildred B. (Blasko) M.; m. Frances Marie Lesko, July 12, 1980; children: Bryan Wayne, Allison Marie. BS in Mktg. Edn., Rider Coll., 1980, MA in Bus. Edn. and Office Adminstrn., 1983; EdD, Temple U., 1993. Cert. tchr., N.J., office automation profl. Tchr., job coord. Cranford (N.J.) High Sch., 1980-81; adminstrv. asst. Rider Coll., Lawrenceville, N.J., 1981-82; instr. Middlesex County Vocat. and Tech. Sch., Piscataway, N.J., 1982-84, Rider Coll., Lawrenceville, 1983-88; asst. prof. Ind. (Pa.) U., 1988—. Dir. N.J. Health Occupations Students Am., 1983-87; coord. Vocat. Indsl. Clubs Am., 1984-86. Co-author: Advertising - A Course of Study, 1979; editor: Handbook for DECA Chapters, 1981. Recipient Leadership award Phi Delta Kappa 1983, Robert D. Joy award for Excellence in Distributive Edn. 1980. Mem. Future Bus. Leaders Am., Nat. Bus. Edn. Assn., Office Systems Rsch. Assn., Eastern Bus. Edn. Assn., N.J. Bus. Edn. Assn., Pa. Bus. Edn. Assn., Delta Pi Epsilon, Phi Beta Lambda, Omicron Delta Kappa, Pi Omega Pi. Office: Indiana U of Pa 9 Mcelhaney Hl Indiana PA 15705-0001

MOORE, WILLIAM PAUL, educational psychologist, researcher; b. Kansas City, Mo., Jan. 5, 1958; s. William Stone and Lola (Kester) M.; m. Kelly Rae Howlett, Aug. 1, 1987; 1 child, William Samuel. BS in Secondary Edn., U. Kans., 1981, MA in Curriculum and Instrn., 1984, PhD in Ednl. Psychology, 1991. Cert. tchr., Kans., Mo. Social scis. instr. Parsons (Kans.) Unified Sch. Dist., 1981-82; social scis. instr., dept. chair Turner Unified Sch. Dist., Kansas City, 1984-86; asst. testing coord. U. Kans., Lawrence, 1988-89; program evaluation, ednl. rschr. Kansas City Pub. Schs., 1989-92; sr. rsch. coord. U. Kans., 1992-93, asst. prof., dir. rsch., 1993-95. Mem. adv. bd. U. Kans. Med. Ctr., 1994; sr. mng. cons. Great Plains Rsch. and Evaluation, 1995—. Mem. editl. bd. Occupational Therapy Jour. Rsch., 1994—; contbr. articles to profl. jours. Bd. dirs. Child Abuse Prevention Coalition, Mission, Kans., 1994—, Lighthouse Pre-Sch., Kansas City, Mo., 1996—. Recipient faculty rsch. award U. Kans., 1994. Mem. ASCD, APA, Am. Psychol. Soc., Nat. Coun. on Measurement in Edn., Am. Ednl. Rsch. Assn. Democrat. Avocations: sailing, golfing, tennis. Home and Office: 1032 N Sumac Dr Olathe KS 66061-9227

MOORE, WILLIAM VINCENT, political science educator; b. Columbia, Mo., Apr. 13, 1944; s. Willis and Mabelle (Rogers) M.; m. Suzanne Shelton, July 14, 1967 (div. Feb. 1984); children: Mark, Laura. BA, So. Ill. U., 1966, MA, 1968; PhD, Tulane U., 1975. Instr. Fla. Meml. Coll., Miami, 1968-69, Xavier U., New Orleans, 1970-72; asst. prof. to assoc. prof. polit. sci. Coll. of Charleston, S.C., 1972-83, prof., 1983-99, disting. prof., 1999—, scholar-in-residence, 1976, dir. summer sessions, 1984-87, chmn. dept., 1987-93, dir., masters in pub. adminstrn. dept., 1993-99. Chmn. S.C. Interagy. Merit Coun., Columbia, 1987-99; instr. jr. statesmen program Northwestern U., Evanston, Ill., 1996. Author: Political Extremism in the U.S.A., 1983; co-author: Politics and Government in South Carolina, 1994; contbr. articles to profl. jours. Grantee U. N.C., 1980; rsch. fellow U. S.C., 1983; named Prof. of Yr., S.C. Gov., 1997. Mem. Am. Polit. Sci. Assn., So. Polit. Sci. Assn., S.C. Polit. Sci. Assn. (pres. 1983-84), Phi Kappa Phi (chpt. pres. 1982-84), Pi Sigma Alpha (chpt. pres. 1987-93), Pi Alpha Alpha. Avocations: tennis, racquetball. Home: 378 Cross St Charleston SC 29407-6977 Office: Coll of Charleston Polit Sci Dept Charleston SC 29424

MOORE-BERRY, NORMA JEAN, secondary school educator; b. Hampton, Ark., Jan. 7, 1949; d. James E. and Alma Lee (McRae) Moore, Sr.; children: Rhemona Moore, Nerissa Moore. BA in English Edn., U. Ark., Pine Bluff, 1971; MA in Reading Edn., So. Ark. U., 1985; postgrad., Henderson State U., 1986, U. Ark., 1989-90. Cert. mid. and secondary English tchr., adult edn., all levels reading. Tchr. English Chidester (Ark.) Sch. Dist., 1971-73; tchr. English, adult edn. instr. Lewisville (Ark.) Sch. Dist., 1973-92, secondary tchr., 1973-93, reading tutor, 1991—; instr. adult edn. Texarkana (Ark.) Pub. Sch. Dist., 1984-91; tchr. English Ctrl. High Sch., 1984-93, Hall Sr. High Sch., Little Rock, 1987-90. Chmn. English dept. Lewisville Sch. Dist.; instr. English Ctrl. High Sch., summer 1992; tchr. Ctrl. High Sch. Summer Sch., Little Rock Sch. Dist., summer 1994; English and reading secondary instr., 1994-95; reading tchr. Southeast Tech. Coll., Pine Bluff, Ark., 1996. Sponsor sr. class; active sch. charity fund-raising; organizer, sponsor Lewisville Reading Club, Lewisville English Club; bible study group Bethel CME Ch., Stamps, Ark., adult class Sunday sch. tchr.; sponsor, sec. ceo com. Ethnic Club Lewisville High Sch.; v.p. Women's Missionary Soc. Bethel AME Ch., Stamp, Ark., stewardess, sec., 2001-03. Named Tchr. Yr., 1984, Lewisville Mid. Sch. Reading/English Tchr., Woman of Yr. ABI, 1993-94. Mem. ASCD, Nat. Coun. Tchrs. English, Ark. Edn. Assn., Ark. Tchr. Retirement Assn., Ark. Reading Coun. Assn. (lit. coun.), Lewisville Edn. Assn. (treas. 1993-94), Phi Delta Kappa. Home: 1221 Hope Rd Stamps AR 71860-4807 Office: 424 Magnolia Street Stamps AR 71860

MOORER, ANNETTE JOHNSON See WYNDEWICKE, KIONNE ANNETTE

MOORER, FRANCES EARLINE GREEN, vocational educator; b. Aliceville, Ala., Oct. 4, 1929; d. Elbert Pierce and Frances Earline (McKee) Green; m. Melvin M. Moorer Sr., June 1, 1957; children: Barbara, Melvin Jr., Marguerite, Franklin. BS, U. Ala., 1952; MS, Auburn U., 1960. Cert. home econs. tchr. Vocat. home econs. tchr. Meringo County High Sch., Thomaston, Ala., 1950; home demonstration agt. Ala. Ext. Svc., Weedowee, Ala., 1951, Prattville, Ala., 1952, Jasper, Ala., 1953; home econ. instr. Auburn (Ala.) U.; home econ. tchr. Autaupa County, Prattville, 1977—. Recipient Horace A. Moses scholarship Ala. Ext. coop., 1954. Mem. Ala. Home Econs. Assn., Ala. Assn. Ret. Persons, Ala. Edn. Assn., Ala. Vocat. Assn., Delta Kappa Gamma, Order Eastern Star. Democrat. Avocation: stamps. Home: 103 Lynn Dr Prattville AL 36066-5015 Office: Vocat Home Econs Upper Kingdom Prattville AL 36067

MOORHEAD, PAUL SIDNEY, geneticist; b. El Dorado, Ark., Apr. 18, 1924; s. Earle William and Ethel (Martin) M.; m. Betty Blanton Belk, June 8, 1949 (dec. 1989); children: Ann, Emily, Mary; m. Rebecca Otter, 1992. AB, U. N.C., 1948, MA in Zoology, 1950; PhD, U. Tex., 1954. Research assoc. U. Tex. Med. Sch., Galveston, 1954-56, U. Pitts. Med. Sch., 1956-58; assoc. mem. Wistar Inst. Anatomy and Biology, Phila., 1959-69; assoc. prof. genetics and pediatrics U. Pa. Sch. Medicine, 1969-85, emeritus, 1985—; mem. rsch. staff Children's Hosp., Phila., 1974-85, mem. rsch. staff emeritus, 1985—. Contbr. numerous articles on genetics and cytology to sci. jours. Served to ensign USNR, 1942-46. Fellow AAAS; mem. Am. Soc. Human Genetics, AAUP, Environ. Mutagenesis Soc., Tissue Culture Assn. (pres. 1980-82), N.Y. Acad. Scis., Sigma Xi. Home and Office: PO Box 4 Claiborne MD 21624-0004

MOORHEAD, ROLANDE ANNETTE REVERDY, artist, educator; b. Périgueux, France; d. RémyJean and Andrée Marcelle (Lavollée) Reverdy; m. Elliott Swift Moorhead, III, Sept. 30, 1960; children: Edward Marc, Roland Elliott, Rémy Bruce. Degree in liberal arts, Coll. Technique, Nice, France, 1954. Bi-lingual sec., France, 1957-58, French Embassy, Washington, 1959-60, 68-70; chmn. exhibit com. Lauderdale-By-The-Sea Art Guild, Ft. Lauderdale, Fla., 1972-75, v.p., 1972-74, founder group 5 Women Artists; exhibit com. Broward Art Guild, Ft. Lauderdale, Fla., 1976; treas., dir. Alliance Francaise, Miami, Fla., 1973-75. Juror, lectr. in field; invited guest artist Franco-Am. Art Show, Curemonte, France, 1996-97. One-woman shows include numerous galleries, Ft. Lauderdale area, 1971—, Ocean Club Art Gallery, Ft. Lauderdale, 1971-74, Pier 66 Gallery, Ft. Lauderdale, 1973, 75, 76, Ft. Lauderdale City Hall, 1974, 77-78, 81-88, 91-94, 95-2000, St. Basil Orthodox Ch., North Miami Beach, 1977, Galerie Vallombreuse, Biarritz, France, 1977, Gallerie Mooffe, Paris, 1978, Galerie du Palais des Fêtes, Périgueux, 1978, 88, Le Club Internat., Ft. Lauderdale, 1979, Leonard Gallery, Ft. Lauderdale, 1990-92, Tallahassee (Fla.) Capitol Bldg., 1990, Lighthouse Pt. (Fla.) Gallery, 1990, Hollywood (Fla.) Art and Cultural Ctr., 1987, 89, 90, 91, 93, 95, Ft. Lauderdale Arts Inst., 1991, 93-95, Dover Gallery, Boca Raton, Fla., 1992; Galerie Mouffe, Paris, 1978, Glass Gallery, Pembroke Pines, Fla., 2001; exhibited in group shows Gallery YES, Wilton Manors, Fla., 2001, Wave Gallery, Key west, Fla., Webber Art Center, Ocala, Fla., 2003; Broward Art Guild, 1971, 73, 74, Point of Am. Gallery, Ft. Lauderdale, 1971, 73, Internat. Festival, Miami, 1976, Internat. Salon, Biarritz, 1977, Internat. Summer Salon, Paris, 1977, Fine Art Gallery Show and Competition, Long Galleries, Ft. Lauderdale, 1979, Pembroke Pines (Fla.) City Hall, 1982, Hollywood City Libr., 1982, also area banks, ch. and libr., numerous local art festivals, Schacknow Mus. Plantation, Fla., 2000, Ft. Lauderdale Mus. Art, 2000; represented in permanent collections: Fr. Lauderdale City Hall, DAV Hdqrs., Washington, Associated Aircraft Co., March of Dimes Bldg. (both Ft. Lauderdale), Oakland Pk. Libr., Fla., St. Josephs Convent, St. Augustine, Fla., US Air Force Mus., Ohio, Main Line Fleets, Inc., Palm Beach, Fla., Creditreform, Dusseldorf, Germany, St. Front Cathedral, Périgueux, St. Sacerdoce Cathedral, Sarlat, France, Club Med, Fla. and Caribbean, also numerous pvt. collections US and Europe; author art manual for Broward Arts Coun., Fla., 1986. Recipient Best in Show award Internat. Salon, Biarritz, 1977; named artist in residence Broward County Sch., 1985. Mem. Am. Soc. Portrait Artists, Nat. Assn. Women Artists, Fla. Watercolor Soc., Palm Beach Watercolor Soc., Nat. League Am. Penwomen, Art 24, Périgueux, Internat. Soc. Marine Painters, Am. Watercolor Soc., Cathedral St. Sacerdoce, Nat. Mus. Women in Arts, Nat. Mus. Am. Indian, Gold Coast Water Color Soc. (pres. 1984-87), 2+3 The Artist Orgn., Union des Francais de l'Etranger. Office: PO Box 8692 Fort Lauderdale FL 33310-8692

MOORMANN, VIKKI PATRICIA, secondary education educator; b. Spokane, Wash., Oct. 1, 1946; d. Victor Charles and Patricia E. (Billberg) Lamb; m. Donald B. Moormann, May 29, 1976. BA, Gonzaga U., 1968; postgrad., U. Idaho, 1995—. Tchr. secondary English Coeur d' Alene (Idaho) Sch. Dist., 1969—2002; supr. student interns U. Nev., 2002—03; with Idaho State U., 2003. Cons. Dept. Edn. Nat. Diffusion Network, Washington, 1983—, Tchr.'s Inc. Author: Save Our Sanity, 1994. Idaho Humanities grantee. Mem. ASCD, NEA, Idaho Edn. Assn., Coeur d' Alene Edn. Assn. (chair various coms. 1976—), Delta Kappa Gamma. Democrat. Avocations: reading, travel.

MOOS, DANIEL JAMES, retired surgeon, educator; b. Fargo, N.D., 1915; BS, MB, MD, U. Minn., 1938. Diplomate Am. Bd. Surgery. Intern Mpls. Gen. Hosp., 1937-39, fellow in surgery, 1940-42; prof. emeritus U. Minn. Fellow ACS; mem. AMA, Am. Assn. Surgery of Trauma.

MOOS, PAMELA SUE, family development specialist; b. Des Moines, May 26, 1970; d. Burle Ralph and Alice Louise (Corey) Carrigan; m. James Moos, July 11, 1998. BA in Social Sci. cum laude, U. No. Iowa, Cedar Falls, 1992. Tchr. social studies and English, 7th, 8th, and 9th grades Twin Wells Indian Sch., Sun Valley, Ariz., 1992-93; tchr. history 9th-11th grades Des Moines Christian Sch., 1993-94; eligibility specialist Systemed Pharmacy, Inc., Des Moines, 1994-96; family devel. specialist Good Samaritan Urban Ministries, Des Moines, 1996—. Vol., Campus Crusade for Christ, L.A., 1992. Mem. Kappa Delta Pi, Phi Alpha Theta, Psi Chi. Republican. Methodist. Avocations: chess, reading, playing the flute, needlework. Office: Good Samaritan Urban Ministries Des Moines IA 50314

MOOS, VERNA VIVIAN, special education educator; b. Jamestown, N.D., July 1, 1951; d. Philip and Violena (Schweitzer) M. BS in Edn., Valley City State U., 1973; MEd, U. So. Miss., 1983, EdS, 1988; AA, Minot State U., 1987; postgrad., East Tex. State U., U. Tex., N.D. State U., U. N.D., Kans. State U., McGill U. Supr. recreation Valley City (N.D.) Recreation Dept., 1969-73; tchr. Harvey (N.D.) Pub. Schs., 1973-75; tchr. spl. edn. Belfield (N.D.) Pub. Schs., 1975-77; edn. therapist N.D. Elks Assn., Dawson, 1976-77; tchr. spl. edn. Dickinson (N.D.) pub. Schs., 1977-87; ednl. technician ABLE, Inc., Dickinson, 1984-87; tchr. spl. edn. Pewitt Ind. Sch. Dist., Omaha and Naples, Tex., 1987—; tchr. adult edn. N.E. Tex. C.C., Mt. Pleasant, 1989—. Local and area dir. Tex. Spl. Olympics, Austin, 1988—; local, regional and state dir. N.D. Spl. Olympics, 1972-87; local coord. Very Spl. Arts Festival; mem. Am. Heart Assn., 1979-87, N.D. Heart Assn., 1979-87; mem. adminstrv. bd. First United Meth. Ch., Naples, Tex., 1994—; active Communities-In-Sch. program for at-risk students, 1995—. Named Dickinson Jaycees Outstanding Young Educator, 1979, Dickinson C. of C. Tchr. of Yr., 1985, Dallas area Coach of Yr., Tex. Spl. Olympics, 1993, Dir. of Yr., N.D. Spl. Olympics, 1985. Mem. NEA, Coun. Exceptional Children, Naples C. of C., Delta Kappa Gamma (scholar), Phi Delta Kappa, Kappa Delta Pi. Avocations: travel, reading, working, sports. Home: PO Box 788 Omaha TX 75571-0788 Office: Pewitt CISD PO Box 1106 Omaha TX 75571-1106

MORA, BENEDETTO P. elementary school administrator; b. Bklyn., Dec. 19, 1946; s. Louis and Beatrice Mora; m. Kathleen R. Gribbin, June 28, 1969; children: Michael, Brian. BS, U. Bridgeport, 1968; MA, Glassboro (N.J.) Coll., 1978. Cert. tchr., supr., prin., chief sch. adminstr. Elem. tchr. Mullica Twp. (N.J.) Sch., 1968-70, Pleasantvile (N.J.) Schs., 1970-78, coord. of math., 1978-82, supr. of math., 1982-89, supr. of curriculum, instr., 1989-91, dir. curriculum, instr., 1991—. Adj. prof. Jersey City State Coll., 1982; per diem cons. for K-8 math. Holt/Reinhart & Winston, 1981-87; workshop presenter Atl. County Dept. of Edn. Mem. Pleasantville/Absecon Coordination Team, 1988—; Pleasantville Edn. Found., 1987-92. Grantee N.J. Dept. Edn., 1980, 81, 87. Mem. ASCD, Pleasantville Adminstrn. Assn. (treas. 1989, pres. 1985-89), N.J. Prin. and Supr. Assn. (del. 1989), Nat. Assn. Elem. Sch. Prin., New Jersey Prins. and Suprs. Assn., Assn. Math. Tchrs. N.J. Office: Pleasantville Pub Schs 115 W Decatur Ave Pleasantville NJ 08232-3121

MORA, GABRIELA, language educator, researcher; b. Santiago, Chile; d. Carlos Mora and Rosario Cruz; m. Harold Fruchtbaum, June 20, 1972. PhD in Hispanic Lit., Smith Coll., 1971. Prof. de Castellano Santiago Coll., 1957—60; asst. prof. Spanish CUNY, N.Y.C., 1971—76; instr. Spanish U. Mass., Amherst, Mass., 1963—69; asst. prof. Spanish Columbia U., N.Y.C., 1977—80; assoc. prof. Spanish Rutgers U., New Brunswick, NJ, 1989—98, prof. II of Spanish, 1998—. Book evaluator U. Tex., Austin, Duke U., Durham, NC, 1996; cons. reader PMLA. Author: Hostos intimista: Introduccion a su Diario, 1976, Theory and Practice of Feminist Literary Criticism, 1982, Diario de Hostos Introduction, 1990, En Torno al Cuento, 1994, El Cuento Modernista, 1996, Clemente Palma: El Modernismo Decadente y Gótico, 2000. Mem.: MLA (chair divsn. L.Am. 1995—96), L.Am. Studies Assn. (Juror prize 1998). Home: 560 Riverside Dr 7K New York NY 10027 Office: Rutgers U 105 George St New Brunswick NJ 08901-1414

MORAH, FRANK NWOKEDI IGBEKWE, adult education educator, researcher; b. Umudioka, Anambra, Nigeria, Mar. 23, 1951; s. Julius Onuora and Alice Okoye; m. Chinwe Clementina Okafor, Feb. 8, 1986; children: Nnamdi, Chioma, Chukwuka, Obianuju, Ogochukwu. BSc in Chemistry, U. Ibadan, Nigeria, 1976, MSc in Chemistry, 1978, PhD in Organic Chemistry, 1982. Med. rep. Biode Pharm Ind. Ltd., Lagos, Nigeria, 1977; lectr. U. Ibadan, Ibadan, Nigeria, 1978-82, Coll. Edn., Nsugbe, Nigeria, 1982-86, Bendel State U., Ekpoma, Nigeria, 1986-88; prof. U. Calabar, Nigeria, 1989—, head dept. chem., 2002—. Author: Calculations in Modern Chemistry, 1986; Advanced Organic Chemistry, 1999; editor: Jour. Science Edn., 1985-86; contbr. articles to profl. jours. Mem. Sci. Assn. Nigeria, Sci. Tchrs. Assn. Nigeria, Chem. Soc. Nigeria (life). Avocations: hunting, football, table tennis, lawn tennis, driving. Office: Dept Chem U Calabar PMB 1115 Calabar Nigeria

MORAHAN-MARTIN, JANET MAY, psychologist, educator; b. N.Y.C., Jan. 13, 1944; d. William Timothy and May Rosalind (Tarangelo) Morahan; m. Curtis Harmon Martin, June 2, 1979; 1 child, Gwendolyn May. AB, Rosemont (Pa.) Coll., 1965; MEd, Tufts U., 1968; PhD, Boston Coll., 1978. Asst. mkt. rsch. analyst Compton Advt. Co., N.Y.C., 1965-67; mkt. rsch. analyst Ogilvy & Mather Advt., N.Y.C., 1967; ednl. rsch. asst. Tufts U., Medford, Mass., 1968-69; counselor Psychol. Inst. Bentley Coll., Waltham, Mass., 1971-72; dir. counseling svcs. Bryant Coll., Smithfield, R.I., 1972-75, psychology instr., 1972-76, asst. prof. psychology, 1976-81, assoc. prof. psychology, 1981-91, prof. psychology, 1991—. Bd. dirs. Multi-Svc. Ctr., Newton, Mass., 1980-82. Contbr. articles to profl. jours., chpts. to books; reviewer APA Conv., 1985—, Teaching of Psychology Jour., 1988—, Collegiate Micro-Computer Jour., 1991, 93, Nat. Soc. Sci. Jour., 1991; mem. editl. bd., spl. edit. editor Cyber Psychology and Behavior. Bd. dirs. Wellesley (Mass.) Community Children's Ctr., 1986-90, Coun. for Children, Newton, Mass., 1984-86. NIMH fellow, 1967-68; NSF grantee, 1974-76, U.S. Office Edn. grantee, 1980. Mem. APA, Mass. Audubon Soc., Internat. Soc. for Online Mental Health (founding mem.), Soc. for Tchg. of Psychology, Soc. Computers in Psychology. Avocations: photography, antiques, gardening, literature. Home: 17 Fuller Brook Rd Wellesley MA 02482-7108 Office: Bryant Coll 1150 Douglas Pike Smithfield RI 02917-1291 E-mail: jmorahan@bryant.edu.

MORALES, MARCIA PAULETTE MERRY, language educator, archaeologist; b. Denver, Dec. 10, 1946; d. Paul Robert Merry and Berneice Roberta Lyddon; m. Jorge Bernardo Morales, Dec. 28, 1977; children: Marcia Paloma, Elisa Berenice, Andrea Paul-Etta. BA, U. Denver, 1969; MA cum laude, U. Am., 1975. Rsch. asst. dept. anthropology U. Ill., Puebla, Mexico, 1972—75; tchr. Eng., art history Escuela Preparatoria, Cuautla, Mexico, 1975—76; tchr., coord. Eng. Colegio Oquetza, Cuautla, 1982—91; tchr. anthropology, Eng. Centro Cultural Iberoamericano, Cuernavaca, Mexico, 1992—95; tchr. Spanish Aztec (N.Mex.) HS, 1996—. Instr. Spanish Fort Lewis Coll., Durango, Colo., 1997—. Contbr. chapters to books Ancient Chalcatzingo, 1987. Fellow: Durango Heartbeat (pres. 1997—), San Juan Audubon Soc. (treas. 1996—). Methodist. Avocations: hiking, birdwatching, travel.

MORALES, SANDRA LEE, secondary school educator; b. Sunnyside, N.Y., Oct. 15, 1934; d. John Joseph and Mabel Marnes (O'Brien) Lee; m. Hernan Morales, July 19, 1958; children: Martita Morales Sageser, Anita Morales Frost, Michael, Kathryn, Christina. BA in Chemistry, St. John's U., 1955; MS in Sci. Edn., U. Colo., 1972. Tchr. sci. St. Joseph's High Sch., Bklyn., 1955-56; tchr. algebra, biology All Saints High Sch., Bklyn., 1956; tchr. physics, gen. sci., math. Adelphi Acad., Bklyn., 1956-58; tchr. A.P. chemistry, gen. sci., sr. sci. Antilles H.S., San Juan, P.R., 1958-64, head dept. chemistry, 1962-64; sci. dept. head, tchr. life scis., earth scis. Pauline Meml. Sch., Colorado Springs, Colo., 1981-95; tutor pvt. practice, Colorado Springs, Colo., 1995—. Mem. Pauline Meml. PTO, 1973-95, 98—, pres., 1977-79; bd. dirs. Pointe Sublime Water Bd., Colorado Springs, 1980-92; pres. Colorado Springs Intercity Tennis, 1977-79; vol. Humane Soc., Colorado Springs, 1996—, Outdoor Colo., 1996—. Mem. AAUW, Colo. Tennis Assn., Am. Audubon Soc. Republican. Roman Catholic. Avocations: hiking, photography, tennis, astronomy, bird watching.

MORAN, BARBARA BURNS, librarian, educator; b. Columbus, Miss., July 8, 1944; d. Robert Theron and Joan (Brown) Burns; m. Joseph J. Moran, Sept. 4, 1965; children: Joseph Michael, Brian Matthew. AB, Mount Holyoke Coll., S. Hadley, Mass., 1966; M in Librarianship, Emory U., Atlanta, 1973; PhD, SUNY, Buffalo, 1982. Head libr. The Park Sch. of Buffalo, Snyder, NY, 1974-78; prof. Sch. Info. and Libr. Sci. U. N.C., Chapel Hill, 1981—, asst. dean, 1987-90, dean, 1990-98, prof. and dir. internat. programs, 1999—. Participant various seminars; evaluator various edn. progs.; cons. in field; bd. govs. UNC Press, 1998—. Author: Academic Libraries, 1984; co-author: (with Robert D. Stueart) Library and Information Center Management, 6th edit., 2002; contbr. articles to profl. jours., chpts. to books; mem. editl. bd. Jour. Acad. Librarianship, 1992-94, Coll. and Rsch. Libraries, 1996-2002. Coun. Libr. Resources grantee, 1985, Univ. Rsch. Coun. grantee, 1983, 89, others. Mem. ALA, Assn. for Libr. and Info. Sci. Edn., Popular Culture Assn., N.C. Libr. Assn., Beta Phi Mu. Home: 1307 Leclair St Chapel Hill NC 27517-3034 Office: Univ NC Sch Info & Libr Sci Chapel Hill NC 27599-0001 E-mail: moran@ils.unc.edu.

MORAN, DORIS ANN, educational consultant, mathematics educator; b. English, W.Va., Oct. 19, 1944; d. William and Margaret (Pruitt) Vinson; m. John L. Moran, Mar. 17, 1973; children: Geoffrey Patrick, Lauren Kathleen, Randy Allen. BS in Edn., Southwestern U., Georgetown, Tex., 1986. Cert. Elem. Edn., Math. Social worker W.Va. Dept. Welfare, Beckley, 1963-68; dir. pub. rels. Meml. Med. Ctr., Corpus Christi, Tex., 1969-75; exec. dir. Kidney Found. Tex. Coastal Bend, Corpus Christi, Tex., 1975-76; tchr. math. Killeen (Tex.) Ind. Sch. Dist., 1986-94; ednl. cons. Creative Edn. Inst., Waco, Tex., 1994—. Curriculum writer, 1989— Killeen Ind. Sch. Dist., mem. dist. testbook adoption task force, 1990-91, pre-algebra math module trainer, 1991—, mentor, 1991-94, dept. chmn., 1991-94; sponsor Yearbook Smith MS, Fort Hood, Tex., 1987-93; trainer Reaching the Hard to Teach, 1993—. Bd. mem., chmn. pub. rels. United Way Coastal Bend, Corpus Christi, Tex., 1976, Mental Health Assn., Corpus Christi, Tex., 1972-75; pub. rels. chmn. City of Corpus Christi Ambulance Steering Com., 1972; conf. chmn. Tex. Hosp. Pub. Rels. Assn., Corpus Christi, Tex., 1972. Named fellow Tex. Alternative Blueprint for Curriculum Devel., 1992; recipient Outstanding Tchr. award Killeen (Tex.) Jr. League, 1994. Mem. ASCD, Tex. ASCD, Tex. Computer Educators Assn., Nat. Coun. Tchrs. Math., St. Peter's Episcopal Ch., Tex. Coun. Tchrs. Math. Episcopalian. Avocations: sewing, gardening, reading, computers, travel. Home: PO Box 12 Rockport TX 78381-0012 Office: Creative Edn Inst 5000 Lakewood Dr Waco TX 76710-2921

MORAN, EMILIO FEDERICO, anthropology and ecology educator; b. Habana, Cuba, July 21, 1946; s. Emilio F. Sr. and Caridad B. (Corrales) M.; m. Maria del Carmen Mendez, (div. 1970); m. Millicent Fleming, Dec. 15, 1972 (div. 2003); 1 child, Emily Victoria (div. 2003). BA, Springhill Coll., 1968; MA, U. Fla., 1969, PhD, 1975. Asst. prof. Ind. U., Bloomington, 1975-79, assoc. prof., 1979-84, chmn. dept. anthropology, 1980-87, prof. dept. anthropology, 1984—, Rudy prof. anthropology, 1996—, dir. Anthrop. Ctr. Tng. and Rsch. on Global Environ. Change, 1992—. Co-dir. Ctr. for Study of Instns., Population and Environ. Change, 1996—; leader Focus 1, Land-Use/Cover Change Program, 1999—; vis. prof. soil sci. N.C. State U., Raleigh, 1984; adv. panelist NSF, Washington, 1987-88, 90. Author: Developing the Amazon, 1981, Human Adaptability, 1982, The Human Ecology of Amazonian Populations, 1993; editor: The Dilemma of Amazonian Development, 1983, The Ecosystem Concept in Anthropology, 1984, The Ecosystem Approach in Anthropology, 1990, The Comparative Study of Human Societies, 1995, Transforming Societies, Transforming Anthropology, 1996; mem. editl. bd. Jour. Latin Am. Studies (Japan), 1992—, Jour. Forest and Conservation History, 1986-95, Anthropol. Linguistics, 1982-87, World Cultures, 1987-97, Human Ecology, 1993—. Grantee Fulbright Found., 1973, 1976, 1989, NIMH, 1974, NSF, 1991-93, 93—, Dept. of Energy, 1991-95, Wenner-Gren, 1989, NICHD, 1997-2001, NASA, 1998—, NOAA, 2000—; recipient A.J. Hanna Disting. Lectr. Rollins Coll., 1985, ERDAS award for best sci. paper, 2000, Robert McNetting award Assn. Am. Geographers, 2002; postdoctoral fellow Tinker Found., 1983-84; Guggenheim Meml. Found. fellow, 1989; named Disting. Ecologist Colo. State U., 1987. Fellow AAAS (nominations com. 1987—, coun. rep. to bd., chmn., 2003—), Am. Anthrop. Assn. (chmn. panel on devel., chmn. task force on environment, pres. anthropology and environ. sect. 1995-98), Linnean Soc. London. Home: 915 S Baldwin Dr Bloomington IN 47401 Office: Ind U Student Bldg 240 Bloomington IN 47405

MORAN, JOAN JENSEN, physical education and health educator; b. Chgo., Sept. 25, 1952; d. Axel Fred and Mary J. (Maes) J.; m. Gregory Keith Moran. BS in Edn., Western Ill. U., 1974; MS in Edn., No. Ill. U., 1978. Cert. tchr., Ill. Tchr., coach East Coloma Sch., Rock Falls, Ill., 1974—. Part-time recreation specialist Woodhaven Lakes, Sublette, Ill., 1975-79; cons. Ill. State Bd. Edn., Springfield, 1984—; instr. NDEITA, Ill., 1988—; facilitator Project Wild, Ill., 1990—. Instr. ARC, Rock Falls, 1978—, Am. Heart Assn., Rock Falls, 1978—; exec. bd. East Coloma Cmty. Club; fitness del. to Russia and Hungary, 1992; cons. Alcohol Awareness & Occupant Restraint Ill. State Bd. Edn., Substance Abuse Guidance Edn. Com., Rock Falls Drug Free Cmty. Grant com., Whiteside County CPR Coord. com. Recipient Western Ill. U. Alumni Achievement award, 1993, Western Ill. Master Tchr. award, 1993, Svc. award Ill. Assn. Health, Phys. Edn., Recreation and Dance, 1991, 92, Outstanding Young Woman award, 1986, Phys. Educator of Yr. award, 1988; named Mid. Sch. Phys. Edn. Tchr. of Yr. Midwest AAHPERD, 1993, Ill. Assn. Health, Phys. Edn., Recreation and Dance, 1992, Gov.'s Coun. Health and Phys. Edn. award, 1991, Am. Tchr. of Yr. award Walt Disney Co., 1993, Excel award Ill. State Bd. Edn., 1995, finalist Ill. Tchr. of Yr., 1996, Milkin Nat. Educator award, 1997, Health Edn. award and Quarter Century award Ill. Assn. Health, Phys. Edn., Recreation and Dance, 1999, Presidential citation, 1998; named to USA Today Tchr. Team, 2000. Mem.: AAHPERD (Health Tchr. of Yr. midwest chpt. 2001), Environ. Edn. Assn. Ill., East Coloma Edn. Assn. (pres., pub. rels., v.p. 1993—94), Ill. Edn. Assn., No. Dist. Ill. Assn. Health, Phys. Edn., Recreation and Dance (newsletter editor 1984—85, exec. bd. 1985—90, treas. 1985—90), Ill. Assn. Health, Phys. Edn., Recreation and Dance (v.p. teenage youth 1988—90, pres. 1994, past pres., conv. coord. 1995, Honor Fellow award 1996). Democrat. Lutheran. Avocations: skiing, hiking, biking, reading, traveling. Home: 1903 E 41st St Sterling IL 61081-9449

MORAN, PATRICIA EILEEN, special education educator; b. Abington, Pa., May 31, 1960; d. Francis Joseph Moran, Jr. and Kathryn Sydney Burness. BS, West Chester State U., 1983; MA in Reading, Calif. State U., San Bernardino, 1990; reading specialist credential, Calif. State U., 1992. Cert. spl. edn. tchr., Pa., Ca.; cert. reading specialist, Calif. Devel. specialist mentally handicapped Community Found., Perkasie, Pa., 1980-83, group home supr., 1983-84; tchr., seriously emotionally disturbed children Martin Luther King Sch., Plymouth Meeting, Pa., 1984-85; tchr. learning handicapped children Ramona Elem. Sch., Moreno Valley Unified Sch. Dist., Calif., 1985—, Seneca Elem. Sch., Moreno Valley, Calif., 1993-96, 1st grade tchr., 1996—. Mem. adv. bd. Pub. Edn. for Everyone in Regular Schs., Moreno Valley, 1990—, pilot adv. bd. Moreno Valley Unified Sch. Dist., 1992—; advisor, cons. Inclusion Model Pilot Program, Moreno Valley, 1991—. Choir mem. Newman Ctr., Riverside, Calif., 1990—. Mem. Inland Empire Coun. Internat. Reading Assn. (Reading award Teaching 1992), Internat. Reading Assn., Kappa Delta Pi. Democrat. Avocations: reading, travel, singing, horseback riding, photography. Office: Seneca Elem Sch 11615 Wordsworth Rd Moreno Valley CA 92557-8451

MORAN, RACHEL, lawyer, educator; b. Kansas City, Mo., June 27, 1956; d. Thomas Albert and Josephine (Portillo) Moran. AB, Stanford U., 1978; JD, Yale U., 1981. Bar: Calif. 1984. Assoc Heller, Ehrman, White & McAuliffe, San Francisco, 1982-83; prof. law U. Calif., Berkeley, 1984—, Robert D. and Leslie-Kay Raven prof. law, 1998—. Vis. prof. UCLA Sch. Law, 1988, 2002Stanford (Calif.) U. Law Sch., 1989, NYU Sch. Law, 1996, U. Miami Sch. Law, 1997, U. Tex. Law Sch., 2000; chair Chicano/Latino Policy Project, 1993-96; dir. Inst. for Study Social Change, 2003—. Contbr. articles to profl. jours. Recipient Disting. Tchg. award, U. Calif. Mem.: ABA, Calif. Bar Assn., Am. Law Inst., Phi Beta Kappa. Democrat. Unitarian Universalist. Avocations: jogging, aerobics, reading, listening to music. Office: U Calif Sch Law Boalt Hall Berkeley CA 94720

MORAN, WILLIAM EDWARD, academic administrator; b. White Plains, N.Y., May 28, 1932; s. Frank Joseph and Margaret Mary (Farrell) M.; m. Barbara Carol Baillet, Apr. 20, 1963; children: Kathryn, Kevin, Colin, Christian. AB, Princeton U., 1954; MBA, Harvard U., 1959; PhD, U. Mich., 1967. Mgmt. cons. Booz, Allen & Hamilton, N.Y.C., 1959-61; mem. adminstrv. staff Harvard U., Boston, 1961-63; asst. exec. v.p. SUNY-Stony Brook, 1966-71; chancellor Flint Campus U. Mich., 1971-79, U. N.C., Greensboro, 1979-94; sr. v.p. Connors Investor Svcs., Inc., 1994—. Bd. dirs. Greensboro, N.C. Connors Investor Services, Reading, Pa., Cross Engring. & Sales Co., 2001—, Piedmont Land Conservancy, 2001—, U. N.C. at Greensboro Investment Fund, 2001—. Contbr. articles to profl. jours. Pres. So. Univ. Conf., 1987. Served with USN, 1954-57. Mem. N.C. Assn. Colls. and Univs. (pres. 1992), Princeton Club (N.Y.), Rotary. Home: 5206 Barnfield Rd Greensboro NC 27455-2136

MORDINI, MARILYN HEUER, physical education educator; b. Waukegan, Ill., Aug. 23, 1936; d. Lester and Evelyn (Scott) Heuer; m. Robert D. Mordini, Feb. 24, 1962; children: Robert Jr., Bruce, Beth. BS in Phys. Edn., Ill. State U., 1958; MS in Phys. Edn., Chgo. State U., 1984; MS in Adminstrn., Northeastern Ill. U., 1994. Tchr. phys. edn. Libertyville (Ill.) Pub. Schs., 1958-63, Highland Park (Ill.) Pub. Schs., 1978-81, North Chicago (Ill.) Sch. Dist. 187, 1981—. dir. intramural sports, 1985-92. Tchr. phys. edn. Highland Park Summer Migrant Program, 1981-90; adv. bd. Park Dist. Highland Park, 1982-84. Rep. United Way, North Chicago, 1990-92; bd. dirs. Lake County divsn. Am. Heart Assn., 1992-96, chmn. Highland Park/Highwood br. Lake County divsn., 1995-96. Mem. AAHPERD, Ill. Assn. Health, Phys. Edn., Recreation and Dance (exec. bd. v.p. children 1997, pres. N.E. dist. 1995-96, Elem. Phys. Educator of Yr. 1991), Am. Fedn. Tchrs., Delta Kappa Gamma. Home: 2035 Grange Ave Highland Park IL 60035-1719

MORDUKHOVICH, BORIS SHOLIMOVICH, mathematician, educator, researcher; b. Moscow, Apr. 8, 1948; came to U.S., 1988; s. Sholim T. and Rosa Z. (Lyubarsky) M.; m. Margaret A. Gankin, Apr. 29, 1969; children: Yelena, Irina. MS in Applied Math., Byelorussian State U., Minsk, USSR, 1971, PhD in Math., 1973. Rsch. engr. Sci. Rsch. Inst. Automation, Minsk, 1971-73; sr. scientist Byelorussian Sci. Rsch. Inst. Land Reclamation Water Mgmt., Minsk, 1973-88; prof. math. Byelorussian State U., 1973-88, Wayne State U., Detroit, 1989—. Vis. scientist Ctr. Math. Rsch., U. Montreal, 1989, U. Pau, France, 1990, Inst. Nat. Rsch. Info. Autom. (INRIA), Rocquecourt, France, 1990; vis. prof. Inst. for Math. and Its Applications, Mpls., 1993, U. NSW, Sydney, Australia, 1993, Banach Intern. Math. Ctr., Warsaw, 1993; intern Inst. Applications Systems Analysis, Laxenburg, Austria, 1994, 95; U. Uppsala, Sweden, 1995, U. Porto, Portugal, 1995, U. Limoges, France, 1996, Technoin, Haifa, Israel, 1997, Peking U., Beijing, China, 1998, U. Bourgogne, Dijou, France, 1999, U. Chile, Santiago, 2000, U. Paul Sabatier, Toulouse, France, 2000. Author rsch. monographs; contbr. over 180 articles to profl. jours.; patentee in field. Mem. Am. Math. Soc., Soc. Indsl. and Applied Math. Avocations: lit., history, tourism. Office: Wayne State U 1150 FAB Dept Math Detroit MI 48202 E-mail: boris@math.wayne.edu.

MOREAU, CINDY LYNN, elementary education educator; b. Eunice, La., Mar. 14, 1964; d. Eldon Joseph and Elaine Marie (Oliver) Naquin; m. Andrew Moreau Jr., Nov. 21, 1981; children: Brookes Landon, Logan Chance. BA magna cum laude, McNeese State U., Lake Charles, La., 1994. Cert. early childhood edn. tchr., La. Early childhood tchr. St. Edmund Elem. Sch., Eunice, 1994—. Democrat. Roman Catholic. Avocations: flower gardening, needlepoint, wood painting. Office: St Edmund Elem Sch 331 N 3rd St Eunice LA 70535-3394

MOREHOUSE, LAWRENCE GLEN, veterinarian, educator; b. Manchester, Kans., July 21, 1925; s. Edwy Owen and Ethel Merle (Glenn) M.; m. Georgia Ann Lewis, Oct. 6, 1956; children: Timothy Lawrence, Glenn Ellen. BS in Biol. Sci., DVM, Kans. State U., 1952; MS in Animal Pathology, Purdue U., 1956, PhD, 1960. Lic. vet. medicine. Veterinarian County Animal Hosp., Des Peres, Mo., 1952-53; supr. Brucellosis labs. Purdue U., West Lafayette, Ind., 1953-60; staff veterinarian lab. svcs. USDA, Washington, 1960-61; discipline leader in pathology and toxicology, animal health divsn. USDA Nat. Animal Disease Lab., Ames, Iowa, 1961-64; prof., chmn. dept. veterinary pathology U. Mo. Coll. Vet. Medicine, Columbia, 1964-69, 84-86, dir. Vet. Med. Diagnostic Labr., 1968-88, prof. emeritus, 1986—. Cons. USDA, to comdg. gen. U.S. Army R&D Command, Am. Inst. Biol. Scis., NAS, to Surg. Gen., Miss. State U., St. Louis Zoo Residency Tng. Program, Miss. Vet. Med. Assn., Okla. State U., Pa. Dept. Agr., Ohio Dept. Agr. Co-editor: Mycotoxic Fungi, Mycotoxins, Mycotoxicoses: An International Encyclopedic Handbook, 3 vols., 1977; contbr. articles on diseases of animals to profl. jours. Active Trinity Presbyn. Ch., Columbia, 1964-2002; bd. dirs. Mo. Symphony Soc., Columbia, 1989-92. Pharmacists mate second class USNR, 1943-46, PTO; 2d. lt. U.S. Army, 1952-56. Recipient Outstanding Svc. award USDA, 1959, merit cert., 1963, 64, Disting. Svc. award U. Mo. Coll. Vet. Medicine, 1987, Dean's Impact award, 1996. Fellow Royal Soc. Health London; mem. AAAS, Am. Assn. Vet. Lab. Diagnosticians (E.P. Pope award 1976, chmn. lab. accreditation bd. 1972-79, 87-90, pres. 1979-80, sec.-treas. 1983-87), World Assn. Vet. Lab. Diagnosticians (bd. dirs. 1984-94, dir. emeritus 1994—), N.Y. Acad. Sci., U. S. Animal Health Assn., Am. Assn. Lab. Animal Sci., Mo. Soc. Microbiology, Am. Assn. Avian Pathologists, N.Am. Conf. Rsch. Workers in Animal Diseases, Mo. Univ. Retirees Assn. (v.p. 1996-98, pres. 1998-99). Presbyterian. Avocations: classic cars, boating, genealogy. Home: 916 Danforth Dr Columbia MO 65201-6164 Office: U Mo Vet Med Diagnostic Lab PO Box 6023 Columbia MO 65205-6023

MOREHOUSE, RICHARD EDWARD, psychology educator; b. LaCrosse, Wis., May 21, 1941; s. Ervin Lenard and Anna Martha (Weiland) Morehouse; m. Rita Spangler, Aug. 20, 1966; 1 child, Lyda Ann. BS, U. Wis., 1971, MST, 1973; PhD, The Union Inst., 1979. Teaching asst. U. Wis., LaCrosse, 1971-72; ednl. cons. Coop. Ednl. Svcs. Agy., LaCrosse, 1972-80; dir. coop. edn. Viterbo U., LaCrosse, 1980-85; from asst. to prof. psychology Viterbo Coll., LaCrosse, 1985—. Dept. chmn. Viterbo U., LaCrosse, 1986—93, chair, 1995—; vis. scholar Tex. Wesleyan U., Ft. Worth, 1993—94. Co-author: Student Study Guide for Human Development Across the Lifespan, 1991, 1994, Beginning Qualitative Research, 1994; co-editor: Analytic Teaching, 1991—96; editor, 1996—; author: Five Year Longitudinal Study of Healthy Families, 2001. Grantee Gifted Edn., Elem. and Secondary Edn. Act, 1976—79, Tchr. Tng., Cmty. Awareness, Wis. Humanities, 1982, Coll., Cmty. Symposium, 1983. Mem.: Am. Psychol. soc. (charter), N.Am. Assn. for Cmty. Inquiry (founder, 1st pres. 1994). Democrat. Unitarian Universalist. Home: 1131 Charles St La Crosse WI 54603-2508 Office: Viterbo Coll 815 9th St S La Crosse WI 54601-4777 E-mail: remorehouse@viterbo.edu.

MORENO, ROSA-MARIA, modern languages educator; b. Guatemala City, Guatemala, Sept. 4, 1946; d. Armando and Lily (Cordon) Moreno; children: Liza Maria, Angie Michele, David William. Diploma, Liceo Bilingue, Guatemala, 1964; BA, Ohio State U., 1982, MA in Policy and Leadership, 1995; MA in Spanish Lit., Ohio U., 2000. Fgn. dept. asst. Banco del Agro, Guatemala, 1964-66; regional mgr. asst. gen. food div. Incasa, Guatemala, 1966-68; translator/asst. human rsch. ctr. Ohio State U., Columbus, 1968-69, dirs. asst. internat. program, 1969-71, acad. program coord. dept. Slavic and East European langs., 1971-97, mem. adminstrv. resources mgmt. sys. liaison team, 1996-97; asst. chmn. modern langs. Ohio U., Athens, Lancaster and Ea. campuses, 1997-99, grad. tchr. assoc. Spanish Athens, 1998-2000, instr. modern langs., 2000—. V.p./treas. St. Anthony Sch. Bd., Columbus, 1982-86; bd. dirs. St. Francis DeSales Sch., Columbus, 1991-95; liaison on the comms. and edn. team Adminstrv. Resource Mgmt. Sys. Project, 1996-97. Mem. Dobro Slovo Slavic Honor Soc., Phi Kappa Phi, Sigma Delta Pi. Avocations: reading, traveling. Office: Ohio U Dept Modern Langs Gordy Hall 259 Athens OH 45701 E-mail: moreno@ohio.edu.

MORENO, ZERKA TOEMAN, psychodrama educator; b. Amsterdam, The Netherlands, June 13, 1917; d. Joseph and Rosalia (Gutwirth) Toeman; m. Jacob L. Moreno, 1949; 1 child, Jonathan D.; 1 stepchild, Regina. Student, Willesden Tech. Coll., 1937-38, NYU, 1948-49. Cert. trainer, educator, practitioner of psychodrama and group psychotherapy Am. Bd. Examiners. Rsch. asst. Psychodramatic and Sociometric Insts., N.Y.C., 1942-51; pres. Moreno Inst., N.Y.C. and Beacon, N.Y., 1951-82; trainer in psychodrama Studiefrämjandet, Stockholm, 1976-83, Finnish Psychodrama Assn., Lahti, Finland, 1976-83. Lectr., trainer, Gt. Britain, Australia, New Zealand, Norway, Sweden, Italy, Germany, Japan, 1976-96, Argentina, Brazil, Greece, The Netherlands, Denmark, Belgium, Spain, Israel, Korea and Taiwan, 1977—; hon. pres. Chinese Zerka Moreno Inst., Nanjing, China; acad. advisor mental health Nanjing Brain Hosp., China, 1997. Co-author: Psychodrama, Surplus Reality, and the Art of Healing, (book of poetry) Love Songs to Life, 1971, 93; co-author: Psychodrama, Vol. II, 1967, Vol. III, 1969, The First Psychodramatic Family, 1964. Named hon. citizen Comune di Roma, Assessorato Alla Cultura, 1983, Municipalidad de la Ciudad de Buenos Aires, 1984, Hon. Mem. Federacao Brasiliero de Psicodrama, Sao Paulo, 1996; first recipient of prize from Astrid Badina Stiftung (Baden-Baden), 1999; nominated for Sigmund Freud award psychotherapy City of Vienna, 1999. Fellow Am. Soc. Group Psychotherapy and Psychodrama (pres. 1967-69, hon. pres. 1988—, sec.-treas. 1955-66); hon. mem. Internat. Assn. Group Psychotherapy (treas. 1974-76, bd. dirs. 1976-80), Soc. Psicodrama Sao Paulo (hon.), Sociedad Argentina Psicodrama (hon.). Home: The Colonnades C24 2600 Barracks Rd Charlottesville VA 22901-2198 Fax: 434-245-4007.

MOREST, DONALD KENT, neuroscientist, educator; b. Kansas City, Mo., Oct. 4, 1934; s. F. Stanley and Clara Josephine (Riley) M.; m. Rosemary Richtmyer, July 13, 1963 (dec. 2002); children: Lydia, Claude. BA, U. Chgo., 1955; MD, Yale U., 1960. Sr. asst. surgeon USPHS, Bethesda, Md., 1960-63; asst. prof. U. Chgo., 1963-65; asst. to assoc. prof. Harvard Med. Sch., Boston, 1965-77; prof., dir. Ctr. for Neurol. Scis. U. Conn. Health Ctr., Farmington, 1977—; prof. commn. scis. U. Conn., Storrs, 2002—. Cons. NIH, Bethesda, 1975—, European Commn. Contbr. articles to profl. jours. and books. Recipient Loeser award U. Conn. Health Ctr., Farmington, 1982; Career Devel. awardee NIH, 1971; named Javits neurosci. investigator NIH, 1984, Claude Pepper awardee, 1990. Mem. Am. Assn. Anatomists (C. Judson Herrick award 1966), Soc. for Neurosci., Assn. for Rsch. in Otolaryngology, Conn. Acad. Sci. and Engring. (elected), Cajal Club (pres. 1980). Avocations: flute, badminton. Home: 18 Shady Ln West Simsbury CT 06092-2232 E-mail: kent@neuron.uchc.edu.

MORETTI, ROBERT JAMES, psychologist, educator; b. Chgo., Aug. 28, 1949; s. James John and Elva Eve (Bonini) M.; m. Carol L. Curt, Dec. 6, 1986. BS in Psychology, Loyola U., Chgo., 1971, PhD in Clin. Psychology, 1982; MA in Behavioral Sci., U. Chgo., 1976; diploma in analytical psychology, Jung Inst., Chgo., 1997. Lic. clin. psychologist, Ill. Rsch. fellow Ill. State Psychiat. Inst., Chgo., 1974-76; clin. asst. prof. Loyola U. Sch. Dentistry, Chgo., 1976-81; asst. prof. behavioral scis. Northwestern U. Dental Sch., Chgo., 1981-91, assoc. prof., 1991—2000. Asst. dir. clin. tng., dir. health psychology Northwestern U. Med. Sch., 1988-93; asst. prof. Grad. Sch., Northwestern U., 1986-91, assoc. prof., 1991—; faculty mem. C.G. Jung Inst., Chgo., 1993—, mem. tng. com., 1999-2000; staff Northwestern Meml. Hosp.; sr. faculty AIDS Mental Health Edn. and Evaluation Project, 1986-89, dir. relaxation and epilepsy project, 1991—; pvt. practice clin. psychology, 1983—;Jungian analysis, 1997—. Mem. editl. bd. Jour. of Am. Analgesia Soc., 1987-93; contbr. articles to profl. jours., chpts. to books. Served with Ill. Army Nat. Guard, 1971-77. Kellogg fellow Am. Fund Dental Health, 1981. Mem. APA, Ill. Psychol. Assn., Assn. Applied Psychophysiology and Biofeedback, Soc. Personality Assessment, Internat. Stress Mgmt. Assn., Chgo. Soc. Jungian Analysts (sec. 1999-2001, v.p. 2002—), Internat. Assn. for Analytical Psychology, Inst. Noetic Scis., Assn. for Study of Dreams. Home: 3458 N Normandy Ave Chicago IL 60634-3717 Office: 151 N Michigan Ave Apt 801 Chicago IL 60601-7543 E-mail: r-moretti@northwestern.edu.

MOREWITZ, STEPHEN JOHN, behavioral scientist, consultant, educator; b. Newport News, Va., May 14, 1954; s. Burt M. and Ruth (August) M., Lora Friedman (stepmother). BA, Coll. William and Mary, 1975, MA, 1978; PhD, U. Chgo., 1983. Rsch. asst. Michael Reese Hosp., Chgo., 1979-84; asst. social scientist Argonne (Ill.) Nat. Lab., 1984-85; asst. to dean, asst. prof. U. Ill., Chgo., 1988-92, sr. rsch. splst., 1991-92; vol. rsch. staff San Francisco Gen. Hosp., 1993-97; pres. S. Morewitz, PhD & Assocs., Chgo. and Buffalo Grove, Ill., 1988—, San Francisco, 1992—. Part-time sociology faculty DePaul U., Chgo., 1985—; mem. faculty St. Elizabeth's Hosp., 1987—88; assoc. prof. Calif. Coll. Podiatric Medicine, 1997—2000, prof., rsch. dean, 2000—02; adj. prof. Calif. Sch. Podiatric Medicine, 2003—; cons. in field. Co-author: Medical Malpractice, 1996; contbr. articles to profl. jours., chapters to books. Vol. docent Garfield Farm Mus., LaFox, Ill., 1979—; curator Saving of S.S. Quanza, Chgo., 1991—. Mem. Am. Pub. Health Assn. (Top 10 Injury Poster award 2000), Am. Diabetes Assn. (profl. sect.), Assn. for Behavioral Scis. and Med. Edn., Am. Sociol. Assn. (cert., nat. finalist med. sociology), Soc. Behavioral Medicine, Generalist in Med. Edn., Sociol. Practice Assn., Soc. Study Social Problems (divsn. chmn., Outstanding Scholar award 2003). Avocations: theater, museum design, swimming, environmental preservation, farming. Office: S Morewitz PhD & Assocs PMB M858 28 E Jackson Blvd 10 Fl Chicago IL 60604

MOREY, CHARLOTTE ANN, elementary school educator, music educator; b. Dickinson, N.D., Dec. 1, 1949; d. Clarence William Hartman and Catherine Sills; m. Michael Scott Morey, June 19, 1971; children: Christopher Michael, Melissa Kay. BS, Dickinson State Coll., 1971. Elem. music specialist Slope County Schs., Amidon, ND, 1971—72, New England Pub. Schs., 1972—75, 1980—80; jr. high sch. music specialist McKenzie County Pub. Schs., Watford City, 1976—78; elem. music specialist Hettinger Pub. Sch., 1985—2000, Lincoln Elem. Sch., Fargo, 2000—. Contbr. articles to profl. jours. Flutist cmty. bands, Hettinger, Bismark, Fargo, 1981—; organist Luth. Ch., Regent, New England, Watford City, Hettinger, 1965—2000. Recipient Disting. Svc. award, Internat. Misic Camp, 1999. Mem.: Music Educators Assn. N.D. (clinician & adjudicator 1971—), Orgn. Am. Kodaly Educators (clinician 1995—), N.D. Music Educators Assn. (state chair, bd. dirs., exec. bd., Music Educator of Yr. 2001), N.D. Am. Choral Dirs. Assn. (state pres. 2001—, past repertoire & stds. chair). Avocations: cross stitch, gardening, cooking, reading. Office: Lincoln Elem Sch 2120 9th St S Fargo ND 58103

MOREY, PHILIP STOCKTON, JR., mathematics educator; b. Houston, July 11, 1937; s. Philip Stockton and Helen Holmes (Wolcott) M.; m. Jeri Lynn Snyder, Sept. 5, 1964; children: William Philip, Christopher Jerome. BA, U. Tex., 1959, Ma, 1961, PhD, 1967. Asst. prof. math. U. Nebr., Omaha, 1967-68; assoc. prof. Tex. A&I U., Kingsville, 1968-76; prof. Tex. A&M U., Kingsville, 1976—. Lectr. U. Tokyo, 1976, U. Hokkaido, 1977, 88. Contbr. articles to Tensor N.S., Internat. Jour. Engring. Sci, Tex. Jour. Sci. Recipient Researcher of Yr. awrd Tex. A&I Alumni Assn., 1985. Mem. Tex. Acad. Sci. (chmn. math. sect. 1982, 85, 99), Am. Math. Soc., Tensor Soc., (Japan). Achievements include research in extensor analysis, tensor analysis, differential geometry, mathematical physics. Home: 1514 Lackey St Kingsville TX 78363-3199 Office: Tex A&M Univ Dept Math Kingsville TX 78362 E-mail: kfpsm00@tamuk.edu.

MORGAN, ALAN DOUGLAS, state education official; m. Harriet Morgan; 4 children. B in Elem. Edn., N.Mex. Highlands U., 1969, MA in Guidance and Counseling, 1971; D in Edn. Leadership, U. Nev., 1995. State supt. education State of N.Mex., 1985—97; pres. High Desert Govt. Rels. Inc., Albuquerque; interim state edn. sec. N.Mex., 2003. Bd. dirs. Agy. Instrnl. Tech.*

MORGAN, ANDREW LANE, urologist, educator; b. May 13, 1920; s. James Albert and Elsie Edna (Johnson) M.; m. Miriam Cleary, June 9, 1951; children: Andrew Lane, Christine, Martha, James. Exch. fellowship, St. John's U., Shanghai, China, 1939—40; BA, Dartmouth Coll., 1942; MD, Cornell U., 1945. Diplomate Am. Bd. Urology. Intern Lenox Hill Hosp., N.Y.C., 1945-46; resident Queen's Med. Ctr., Honolulu, 1948-50, Yale U., 1950-52; practice medicine, specializing in urology Honolulu, 1952-87; ret., 1987. Chmn. dept. surgery Queen's Med. Ctr., 1979; clin. prof. urology John Burns Sch. Medicine, U. Hawaii; mem. renal transplant team St. Francis Med. Ctr. Past pres. Hawaii Med. Libr., 1957-58. Served to capt., AUS, 1946-48. Fellow ACS; mem. AMA, AM. Urol. Assn. (past pres. Western sect.), Hawaii Med. Assn., Societe Internationale d'Urologie, Honolulu County Med. Soc. (bd. govs. 1970-76, treas. 1978-79), Pacific Club (Honolulu). Episcopalian. Home: 44 Puako Beach Dr Kamuela HI 96743-9707

MORGAN, ANNE MARIE G. broadcast journalist, educator; b. Paducah, Ky., Apr. 23, 1955; d. Ralph Edward and Vera Christine Gill; m. Michael William Morgan, Nov. 19, 1977; children: Deborah, Jon, James. BA in Govt. and Psychology, Coll. William and Mary, 1976; MA in Polit. Sci., U. Richmond, 1997; postgrad. in Pub. Policy, Va. Commonwealth U., 1998. HS tchr. James-City County Sch., Williamsburg, Va., 1977, Colonial Hts. Sch., Va., 1977-79; TV and radio journalist Capitol News, Richmond, Va., 1984—, Va. Pub. Broadcasting, Richmond, Va., 1984—, WRIC-TV and WTVR-TV, Richmond, 1984—2000; broadcast news anchor Va. News Network, Richmond, Va., 2000—02; journalist WVTF Radio, Roanoke, 2002—. Asst. prof. polit. sci. U. Richmond, Va., 1998—. Author: (with others) Controversies in American Public Polity, 1999, Opposing Viewpoints Series, 1991. Sec. Parents' Guidance/Pupil Pers. Guidance Com., Powhatan, Va., 1996—98; bd. dirs. Va. Pub. Broadcasting, Richmond, 2000—02, Va. Adv. Coun. Adult Edn. and Literacy, Richmond, 1999—2002, Coun. Child Care and Early Childhood Devel., Richmond, 1995—96; chair bd. dirs. State Bd. for Cmty. Colls., Richmond, 1997—2002; chair Va. Coun. Status of Women, Richmond, 1994—2002. Recipient Gov. proclamation Anne Marie Morgan Day in Commonwealth Va., Gov. Va., 1997; Meritorious award Va. Assoc. Press Broadcasters, 2002; Univ. of richmond Faculty Svc. Award, 2003. Mem.: Soc. Profl. Journalists, Soc. Profl. Journalists (Va. profl. chpt.), Nat. Fedn. Press Women, Va. Press Women, Capitol Corrs. Assn., Am. Polit. Sci. Assn., Pi Sigma Alpha. Avocations: music, singing, mentoring.

MORGAN, BETTY MITCHELL, artist, educator; b. Raleigh, N.C., Apr. 17, 1948; d. Carlton Turner and Miriam Grace (Sexton) M.; m. Thomas Vance Morgan, June 24, 1972; children: David Vance, Thomas Mitchell. BS, Appalachian State U., 1970; MA in Art Edn., U. Ga., 1972; postgrad., Calif. State U., Northridge, 1983. Cert. tchr., Calif., Ga., N.J., N.C., Mass. Tchr. art Randolph Jr. High Sch., Charlotte, N.C., 1971-72, Oconee County Intermediate Sch., Watkinsville, Ga., 1972-77; tchr. English 1st Bapt. Day Sch., Van Nuys, Calif., 1982-83; freelance artist, tchr. Hillsborough, N.J., 1984-86; instr. Torrance Ctr. Creative Studies U. Ga., Athens, 1987-93; tchr. Benton Elem. Sch., Nicholson, Ga., 1988-89; tchr. art Jackson County Sch. System, Jefferson, Ga., 1989-93; instr. Danforth Mus. Sch., 1995—, DeCordova Mus. Sch., 1995—; art tchr. Eliot Sch., Needham, Mass. Lectr. art and civic assns., Ga., 1987-93, 95—; tchr. art Needham Pub. Schs., 1995—; freelance artist, 1976—; exhibiting mem. Loef Gallery, Athens, 1986-93; art editor Appalachian State U. Yearbook, Boone, N.C., 1970; coord. Japanese and Australian Children's Art Exch., 1992-93; presenter Mass. Music Tchrs. Assn. Conf. Cover illustrator Philanthropic Ednl. Orgn., 1991; exhibitor group and solo shows in N.J., Calif., N.C., Ga., and Mass., 1976—; works displayed in pvt. and pub. collections in U.S., Australia, Europe, corp. collections including AT&T Comm., Thomas Cook Travel Agy., Nat. Utilities, Inc., Trust Co. Bank N.E. Ga. Docent Art Appreciation in Schs., Hillsborough, N.J., 1984-86; cub den leader Athens and Hillsborough area Boy Scouts Am., 1985-88; mem. Am. Cancer Soc., Athens, 1987-89; vol. Am. Lung Assn., 1988. Selected for Tchr. to Japan program Japanese C. of C., 1992; winner 1st pl. award for artwork San Fernando Valley Artist Assn., Northridge, 1983; recipient Supt.'s Excellence in Tchg. award Needham (Mass.) Pub. Schs., 1997; named Tchr. of Yr. by Benton Elem. Sch., 1992-93. Mem. Profl. Assn. Ga. Educators, Philanthropic Ednl. Orgn., Ga. Art Edn. Assn., Nat. Art Edn. Assn., Athens Art Assn., Mass. Art Edn. Assn. Avocations: painting, tennis, reading, hiking. Home: 14 Valley Rd Natick MA 01760-3415

MORGAN, BEVERLY HAMMERSLEY, middle school educator, artist; b. Wichita Falls, Tex. d. Vernon C. and Melba Marie (Whited) Hammersley; m. Robert Lewis Morgan, Sept. 21, 1957 (div. 1972); children: Janet Claire, Robert David. BA, So. Meth. U.; MA, U. Ala., 1980, AA certification, 1982; postgrad., U. Tex., 1991—. Cert. art tchr., Tex., Ala.; cert. elem. tchr., Ala. Tchr. art Ft. Worth Pub. Schs., 1955-60; tchr. English, Lincoln County Schs., Fayetteville, Tenn., 1961-62; elem. tchr. Huntsville (Ala.) Pub. Schs., 1960-61, 62-68, tchr. art, 1972-92, 93-94. One-woman shows include U. Ala., 1980, Huntsville Art League, 1981, and various other art gallerys, art shows and exhbns. Mem. HAL Gallery, Huntsville, Madison County Sr. Art Gallery. Mem. Huntsville Mus. Art, Am. Contract Bridge League. Republican. Avocations: bridge, travel, collecting Hammersley English bone china. Home: 12027 Chicamauga Trl SE Huntsville AL 35803-1544

MORGAN, FRANK, mathematics educator; BS, MIT, 1974; MA, Princeton U., 1976, PhD, 1977; ScD (hon.), Cedar Crest Coll., 1995. Moore instr. to assoc. prof., Green prof. MIT, Cambridge, 1977-87; chmn. Dept. Math. Williams Coll., 1988—94, Meenan 3d Century prof., chmn. dept. math., 1997—2003. Vis. prof. Rice U., Houston, 1982-83, Stanford U., 1986-87; mem. Inst. Advanced Study, Princeton, N.J., 1990-91; vis. prof. disting. tchg. Princeton U., 1997—; adj. prof. U. Mass., 1992—. Author: Geometric Measure Theory, 1988, 3d edit., 2000, Riemannian Geometry, 1993, revised edit., 2001, Calculus Lite, 1995, 2d edit., 1997, The Math Chat Book, 2000; contbr. over 100 articles to profl. jours. Recipient Haimo award for disting. coll. or univ. tchg. of math. Math. Assn. Am., 1993; grantee NSF, 1977—. Mem.: Math. Assn. Am. (2d v.p. 2000—02). Office: Williams College Dept of Mathematics Williamstown MA 01267*

MORGAN, GEORGE EMIR, III, financial economics educator; b. Carmel, Calif., Jan. 2, 1953; s. George Emir Jr. and Dolores (Przydzial) M.; m. Donna Batts Vail, Dec. 31, 1977; 1 child, Abbie Vail. BS in Math., Georgetown U., 1973; MS in Stats., U. N.C., 1975, PhD in Fin., 1977. Sr. fin. economist Office of the Compt. of the Currency, Washington, 1978-79; asst. prof. U. Tex., Austin, 1979-84; assoc. prof. Va. Poly. Inst., Blacksburg, 1984-89, dir. PhD program, 1985-89, prof., 1989—, Suntrust prof. fin., 1995—, head dept. fin., 1995-96, acting head dept. fin., 1999-2000; assoc. dir. bus. rsch. Ctr. Comml. Space Comms., 1990-92; assoc. dir. Ctr. for Wireless Telecomms., 1992-94; exec. dir. Ctr. for Wireless Telecom., 2001—, Space and Wireless Bus. Ctr., 1994-2001. Editor (newsletter) 90 Day Notes, 1986-90. Mem. Am. Econ. Assn., Am. Fin. Assn., Am. Statis. Assn., So. Fin. Assn., Fin. Mgmt. Assn., Macintosh Blacksburg Users Group (faculty advisor 1989-92), Beta Gamma Sigma. Avocation: macintosh personal computers. Office: Va Poly Inst Dept Fin 1016 Pamplin Hall Blacksburg VA 24061

MORGAN, HARRY NEW, education educator; b. Blenheim, Va., June 6, 1926; s. John Alexander and Cheyney (Lewis) M.; children: Parris Mitchell, Lawrence Milan. BS, NYU, 1949; MSW, U. Wis., 1969; EdD, U. Mass., 1970. Cert. social worker, N.Y. Dir. N.E. region Head Start, N.Y.C., 1965-67; program coord. Bank St. Coll., N.Y.C., 1967-70; prof. and chmn. African-Am. Studies Ohio U., Athens, 1970-72, Syracuse (N.Y.) U., 1972-84; prof. and chmn. earl chldhood edn. West Ga. Coll., Carrollton, 1984—. Conducted rsch. studies on cmty. and classroom issues, 1984-95. Author: Affective Education for Cognitive Development, 1967, The Learning Community, 1970, Historical Perspectives on the Education of Black Children, 1995, Cognitive Styles and Classroom Learning, 1997, The Imagination of Early Childhood Education, 1999, Real Learning: A Bridge to Neuroscience, 2003. Bd. dirs. Marcy Settlement House, Bklyn., 1962-65; pres., co-founder bd. Met. Sch. for Arts, Syracuse, 1975; founder housing cooperative, Syracuse, trustee Davis-Putter Scholarship Fund. Mem. APA, Am. Ednl. Rsch. Assn., Assn. Study of African Am. Life and History. Avocation: antiques. Home: 2284 Lakeview Pky Villa Rica GA 30180-8082 Office: State U West Ga Maple St Carrollton GA 30118-0001 E-mail: hmorgan@westga.edu.

MORGAN, JACQUI, illustrator, painter, educator, writer; b. N.Y.C., Feb. 22, 1939; d. Henry and Emily (Cook) Morganstern; m. Onnig Kalfayan, Apr. 23, 1967 (div. 1972); m. Tomás Gonda, Jan. 1983 (dec. 1988). BFA with honors, Pratt Inst., Bklyn., 1960; MA, CCNY, 1978. Textile designer M. Lowenstein & Sons, N.Y.C., 1961-62, Fruit of the Loom, N.Y.C., 1962; stylist-design dir. Au Courant, Inc., N.Y.C., 1966—; assoc. prof. Pratt Inst., Bklyn., 1977—. Guest lectr. U. Que., Syracuse U., Warsaw TV & Radio, Poland, NYU, Parsons Sch. Design, N.Y.C., Sch. Visual Arts, N.Y.C., Va. Commonwealth U., Fashion Inst. of Tech., others; mem. profl. juries; curator Tomás Gonda retrospective exhbn.; condr. workshops. One-person shows include Soc. Illustrators, N.Y.C., 1977, Art Dirs. Club, N.Y.C., 1978, Gallerie Nowe Miasto, Warsaw, 1978, Gallerie Baumeister, Munich, W.Ger., 1978, Hansen-Feuerman Gallery, N.Y.C., 1980, Krannert Mus./U. Ill., 1998, Art Gallery at Marywood U., Scranton, Pa., 1998; group shows include Mus. Contemporary Crafts, N.Y.C., 1975, Smithsonian Instn., Washington, 1976, Mus. Warsaw, 1976, 78, Mus. Tokyo, 1979, Nat. Watercolor Soc., 1989, Salmagundi Club, 1990, New Eng. Watercolor Soc. Open, 1990, Miss. Watercolor Grand Nat., 1990, Illustration West 29, 1990, Adirondack Nat., 1990, Die Verlassenen Schuhe, 1993, N.Y. restaurant Sch., 1994, Lizan-Tops Gallery, 1996, The Art Club, 2000; represented in permanent collections: Smithsonian Instn., Mus. Warsaw; author, illustrator: Watercolor for Illustration; produced 3 instrnl. watercolor videos; series of prints pub., 1995; series of plates publ., 1995; co-curator Tomas Gonda Retrospective, Va. Commonwealth U., Rutgers U., Carnegie Mellon U., others in U.S., Museo Del Arte Moderno, Buenos Aires, Ulmer Mus., Ulm, Germany; illustrator Lights Along the Path, 1999, The Healing Garden, 1999; contbr. articles to profl. jours. Recipient more than 200 awards from various orgns. including Soc. Illustrators, Fed. Design Coun., Comm. Arts Mag., Am. Inst. Graphic Arts, N.Y. Art Dirs. Club, Print Design Ann. Mem. Graphic Artists Guild (dir. 1975-79), Soc. Illustrators, Women Artists of the West, Pa. Watercolor Soc. Studio: 176 E 77th St Apt 11C New York NY 10021-1910

MORGAN, JAMES JOHN, environmental engineering educator; b. N.Y.C., June 23, 1932; s. James and Anna (Treanor) M.; m. Jean Laurie McIntosh, June 15, 1957; children— Jenny, Johanna, Eve, Michael, Martha, Sarah BCE, Manhattan Coll., 1954; MSCE, U. Mich., 1956; postgrad., U. Ill., 1956-60; PhD, Harvard U., 1964; ScD (hon.), Manhattan Coll., 1989. Instr. civil engring. U. Ill., Urbana, 1956-60; assoc. prof. U. Fla., Gainesville, 1963-65, Calif. Inst. Tech., Pasadena, 1965-69, prof. environ. engring., 1969-87, Marvin L. Goldberger prof. environ. engring. sci., 1987—, dean of students, 1972-75, dean grad. studies, 1981-84, v.p. student affairs, 1980-89; exec. officer environ. engring. sci., 1993-96. Mem. environ. studies bd., NRC, 1974-80; chmn. Acid Deposition Sci. Adv. Com., Calif., 1983-98; chmn. Gordon Rsch. Conf. on Environ. Sci.; Water, 1970. Author: (with Werner Stumm) Aquatic Chemistry, 1970, 2d edit., 1981, 3rd edit. 1996; editor Environ. Sci. and Tech., 1966-74; contbr. articles to profl. jours. Recipient Stockholm Water prize, 1999, Clarke Water prize, 1999. Mem. ASCE (award 1997), Am. Chem. Soc. (award 1980), AAAS, Am. Soc. Limnology and Oceanography (editorial bd. 1977-80), Nat. Acad. Engring., Assn. Environ. Engring. Profs. (award 1981, 83, 94), Am. Water Works Assn. (award 1963), Sigma Xi, Chi Epsilon. Democrat. Roman Catholic. Avocations: tennis; folk music. E-mail: morgan. E-mail: morgan_j@caltech.edu.

MORGAN, JAMES PHILIP, pharmacologist, cardiologist, educator; b. Cin., Jan. 13, 1948; s. James Weldon and Dorcas Adele (Meyer) M.; m. Kathleen Greive, Dec. 22, 1973; children: James Patrick, Jonathan Michael. BS, U. Cin., 1970, PhD, 1974, MD, 1976. Diplomate Am. Bd. Internal Medicine, Am. Bd. Cardiovascular Disease. Fellow in internal medicine Mayo Clinic, Rochester, Minn., 1976-79, fellow in cardiovascular disease, 1979-83; asst. in medicine Beth Israel Hosp., Boston, 1983—. Instr. pharmacology U. Cin., 1975—76; asst. prof. pharmacology, instr. medicine Mayo Clinic, 1981—83; asst. prof. medicine Harvard U., Boston, 1983, assoc. prof., 1988—96, Herman Dana prof. medicine, 1996—; affiliate faculty, dept. pharmacology Harvard Med. Sch., 1986—; chief and prgram dir. cardiovascular divsn. Beth Israel Hosp., 1994—2001, vice chmn. medicine, 2000—. Contbr. articles to profl. jours. Recipient Young Investigators award Am. Coll. Cardiology, 1982, Balfour award Mayo Clinic, 1983, Advanced Cardiac Life Support Spl. Recogition award Mayo Clinic, 1983, Rsch. Career Devel. award NIH, 1985-90. Mem. AMA, Am. Heart Assn., Biophys. Soc. Am. Soc. Pharmacology and Exptl. Therapeutics, Masons. Avocation: philatelics. Office: Beth Israel Deaconess Med Ctr 330 Brookline Ave Boston MA 02215-5400 E-mail: jmorgan@caregroup.harvard.edu., jmorgan@biomc.harvard.edu.

MORGAN, JOHN AUGUSTINE, university executive, consultant; b. Medford, Mass., Feb. 4, 1936; s. John Augustine and Mary Frances (Maley) M.; m. Jean Marie Doyle, Jan. 8, 1959 (div. 1980); 1 child, John Patrick. BS, Boston U., 1956; MS, U. Colo., 1963; diploma, War Coll., 1967; EdD, Nova U., 1980. Commd. 2d lt. USAF, 1956, advanced through grades to col., 1978, served various Air Force ops., combat, 1954-72; dir. planning Def. Indsl. Ctr., Phila., 1970-73, dir. ops., 1973-74; dir. weapon sys. USAF, Belleville, Ill., 1974-76; v.p. Piedmont Tech. Coll., Greenwood, S.C., 1978-84, exec. v.p., 1984-94; pvt. practice as cons. Greenwood, S.C., 1978—. Doctoral adv. Nova U., Ft. Lauderdale, Fla., 1983—, dir. team, 1988-90; S.C. lectr.; exec. bd. Internat. Alumni Assn., 1990-92; adv. bd. County Bank, 189-91; bd. regents U. S.C. Leadership Program; security cons. Centennial Olympic Games, 1996, Winter Games, 2002. Author: Retrenchment in the 80s, 1981 (Nat. Practicum of Yr. award 1981); contbr. articles to profl. jours. Chmn. Piedmont Found. Fund Dr., Greenwood, 1985; regional dir. Leadership S.C., 1989—; mem. PTO; state bd. ETV, 2000—; bd. dirs. Piedmont Coll. Found. Named Educator of Yr. S.C. Tech. Assn., 1981, 86, 87, Leadership S.C., 1989-92 (state bd. regents 1992—, Presdl. medallion for Outstanding Svc. 1994); recipient Alumni award Nova Southeastern U., 1996. Mem. Am. Assn. Community Jr. Colls., S.C. Assn. Govt. Purchasing Ofcls. (bd. dirs. 1989-92), S.C. Assn. State Planning Ofcls., C. of C. (chmn. govt. affairs), Star Fort Officers Assn. (v.p. 1990-92), Greenwood Running Club, Greenwood Riding Hunt Club, Am. Legion, Kiwanis (local bd. dirs. 1989-92, chmn. fin. com. 1992-93), Elks. Home: Gatewood 101 Hawthorne Ct Greenwood SC 29646-9264 E-mail: morganj@nova.edu.

MORGAN, JOHN DAVID, middle school educator; b. Wilmington, Del., June 7, 1937; s. Eberlin Starr and Elizabeth M. (McKelvie) M. BS, West Chester U., 1960, MEd, 1966. Tchr. Chichester Jr. High Sch., Boothwyn, Pa., 1960-71, Beverly Hills Jr. High Sch., Upper Darby, Pa., 1971-80, Beverly Hills Mid. Sch., Upper Darby, 1980-92; sec. membership First Presbyn.Ch., West Chester, Pa., 1997—. Vol. AARP, Meals on Wheals, 1992-, Habitat for Humanity of Chester County, 1999-. Presbyterian. Avocations: collectibles, stamps, travel. Home: 9 S Brandywine St West Chester PA 19382-2826

MORGAN, JOYCE ELIZABETH, elementary school educator; b. Pitts., June 8, 1940; d. Richard Gailbreth and Pauline (Wasil) Cunningham; m. John R. Morgan; children: Janet Lynn, Jennifer Ann, Joy Ellyn, Jamie Elizabeth. BS, Calif. State U., 1962. Elem. tchr. Chartiers Valley Sch. Dist., Pitts., 1971—. Mem. Tchrs. & Adminstrs. for Better Schs. Com., 1993-94. Facilitator Our Lady of Grace Bible Sch., Scott Twp., 1975-78, CCD tchr., 1978-82, mem. choir, 1982-85, mem. folk group choir, 1990-93, tchr. children's liturgy, 1993-94. Republican. Roman Catholic. Avocations: reading, landcaping, plants, travel.

MORGAN, JUNE SMITH, elementary education director; b. Highpoint, N.C., Aug. 19, 1949; d. Junie and O'Neale (Theo) Smith; m. William Madison Morgan, Dec. 23, 1972; children: Timothy Madison, Katherine Marie. BA, Furman U., 1971; MEd, U. S.C., 1975, cert. edn. specialist, 1988. Elem. sch. tchr. Spartanburg (S.C.) Sch. Dist. #7, 1971-80, Spartanburg Sch. Dist. #3, Glendale, 1980-88; asst. prin. Union (S.C.) County Schs., 1988-89, dir. elem. curriculum, 1989-90, dir. elem. edn., 1990—. Pres. Gaffney (S.C.) Bus. and Profl. Women's Club, 1981-83, Gaffney Little Theatre, 1988-90, S.C. Fedn. of Bus. and Profl. Women's Clubs, Inc., 1990-91; mem. Goucher Dem. precinct exec. com., Gaffney, 1980—. Named Career Woman of Yr., Gaffney Bus. and Profl. Women's Club, 1985; nominee Nat. Edn. Goals Assessment Coun., U.S. Dept. Edn., Washington. Mem. ASCD (S.C. bd. dis., program award chmn.), Nat. Staff Devel. Coun., Internat. Reading Assn., Phi Delta Kappa. Lutheran. Avocations: reading, music, handwork, crafts. Home: 2812 Bancroff Rd Columbia SC 29223-2102 Office: Union County Schs PO Box 907 Union SC 29379-0907

MORGAN, LONA SCAGGS, speech professional educator; b. Chillicothe, Ohio, Oct. 2, 1949; d. Drewey P. and Ruth A. (McCloskey) Scaggs; m. Terry A. Morgan, Dec. 23, 1972; 1 child, Zachary Drew Morgan. BS in Hearing and Speech Sci., Ohio U., 1971; MEd in Adminstrn., Supervision, U. South Fla., 1983. Cert. speech and hearing sci., ednl. adminstrn. Speech pathologist Ross County Soc. for Crippled Children and Adults, Chillicothe, 1971; speech pathologist Zanesville (Ohio) City Schs., 1971-72, Hernando County Schs., Brooksville, Fla., 1973-74, Pasco County Sch. Dist., New Port Richey, Fla., 1974—, speech pathologist, speech mentor, 1994—. Recipient Pasco Pub. Schs. Found. grant, 1993. Mem. Fla. Speech and Hearing Assn., West Paco Jr. Woman's Club, Phi Delta Kappa. Methodist. Avocations: reading, travel, country-western line dancing. Home: 7011 Tanglewood Dr New Port Richey FL 34654-5721 Office: Pasco County School Board Calusa Elem School 5720 Orchid Lake Dr New Port Richey FL 34654

MORGAN, LOU ANN, physical education educator; b. Andrews, N.C., Apr. 26, 1949; d. Jerry Myditt and Alice Josephine (O'Dell) Long; m. Frederick Wayne Morgan, July 9, 1972; children: Mandi Marie, Chad William. BS, Mars Hill Coll., 1971. Tchr. Farmer (N.C.) Elem. Sch., 1971-74, Flat Rock (N.C.) Jr. High Sch., 1974-81; craft dir. Camp Windy Wood, Tuxedo, N.C., 1981-84; tchr. weekday early edn. 1st Bapt. Ch., Hendersonville, N.C., 1983-84; phys. edn. specialist Dana (N.C.) Elem. Sch., 1984—. Co-author: (video) Outdoor Education ... Success for Everyon, 1993. Mem. scholarship com. 1st Bapt. Ch., Hendersonville, 1993—, mem. weekday early edn. com., 1985-86, mem. recreation/activities com., 1993-94. Named Outstanding Spring Vol. Henderson County Parks and Recreation, 1992; recipient Gov.'s Award for Fitness N.C. Gov.'s Coun. on Phys. Fitness and Health, 1994. Mem. AAHPERD, N.C. Assn. Health, Phys. Edn., Recreation and Dance (phys. edn. Western regional rep. 1994-95, Phys. Edn. Leadership Tng. steering com. 1989, 93, presider, presenter 1991, 94, Norm Leafe State Phys. Edn. Tchr. of Yr. 1990). Republican. Baptist. Avocations: painting, gardening, biking, fitness. Home: 447 Sunset Dr Hendersonville NC 28791-1617 Office: Dana Elem Sch PO Box 37 Dana NC 28724-0037

MORGAN, MARY ANNE, secondary education educator; b. Camden, N.J., Sept. 15, 1943; children: Elizabeth Anne, James Frederick. Student, Moore Coll. Art, Phila., 1961; BFA, Temple U., 1965; MEd, Rutgers U., 1984. Cert. elem. and secondary tchr., N.J., cert. prin. Tchr. art Sterling High Sch., Somerdale, N.J., 1965-68, head fine arts dept., advisor, coach, 1976—. Advisor Teen Inst. of the Garden State, N.J., 1991-92. Recipient N.J. Arts Achievement award Very Spl. Arts, 1998, N.J. Gov. award, 1998, Alfred Dimartini Exceptional Tchr. award, 1999, Equity Leader Achievement award NJ Dept. Edn. Mem. NEA, N.J. Edn. Assn., Art Educators N.J. (cons., resources speaker 1982—), Nat. Art Edn. Assn., Citizens Community Bd., Mcpl. Alliance, Order Ea. Star, Delta Kappa Pi, Delta Kappa Gamma. Home: 535 Beech Ave Laurel Springs NJ 08021-3003 Office: Warwick Rd Somerdale NJ 08083

MORGAN, MARY LOU, retired education educator, civic worker; b. Chgo., Mar. 5, 1938; d. William Nicholas and Esther Lucille (Galbraith) Wanmer; m. James Edward Morgan, May 30, 1963. BA in Bus. Edn. and Econs., Wichita State U., 1971, MEd in Student Pers. and Guidance, 1974; postgrad., Kans. State U., 1986. Cert. bus. tchr., Kans. Reservationist Braniff, Wichita, Kans., 1961-62; stenographer, fin. analyst, clk.-typist Boeing Co., Wichita, 1962-68, tng., pers. and records positions, 1979-93; pers. cons. Rita Pers. Svc., Wichita, 1974-75; adminstrv. aide, manpower specialist, job developer City of Wichita, 1975-76; account exec., employment counselor Mgmt. Recruiters, 1976-77; pers. mgr., patient cons. Women's Clinic, 1977; vocat. rehab. counselor State of Kans., Parsons, 1977-79; pvt. detective Investigation Svcs., Wichita, 1981-84; instr. career devel. Wichita State U., 1988-90. Paralegal asst. Turner & Hensley, Wichita, 1975. Coord. funding Women's Crisis Ctr., Wichita, 1975; docent Carver Mus., Hoover Mus.; vice chmn. Hist. Preservation Commn.; founder, coord. Ann. Women's Chautauqua; Precinct committeewoman Wichita Dem. Com., 1992—94; pres. Jasper County-Newton County Dems., 1998; mem. Grover Beach Dems., 2001—; bd. dirs. City of Wichita, Wichita Commn. on Status of Women, 1988—91. Mem.: NOW (founder, 1st pres., v.p. program chmn. Wichita chpt. 1969—93, asst. state coord. polit. action com. Wichita chpt. 1993—95, at-large state bd. Joplin com. 1994—95, 1997—98, 1999—2000, at-large state mem. Grover Beach chpt. 2001—), AARP, LWV (v.p. issues study Joplin area league 1998—2000, Grover Beach league 2001—, off board dir. 2002—03, bd. dirs. 2003—), AAUW (bd. dirs. edn., equity, women's issues Joplin br. 1999—2000, Grover Beach br. 2001—, pres. Grover Beach br. 2002—, mem. state pub. policy com.), State Pub. Policy Com. Avocations: water skiing, boating, collecting victorian clothing, travel.

MORGAN, RAYMOND VICTOR, JR., university administrator, mathematics educator; b. Brownwood, Tex., May 10, 1942; s. Raymond Victor and Lovey Lucile (Tate) M.; m. Mary Jane Folks, Aug. 13, 1967; children: Jason Wesley (dec.), Jeremy Victor. BA, Howard Payne U., 1965; MA, Vanderbilt U., 1966; PhD, U. Mo., 1969. Asst. prof. So. Meth. U., Dallas, 1969-75; assoc. prof. Sul Ross State U., Alpine, Tex., 1975-82, math. dept. chmn., 1976-85, prof., 1982—, dean of scis., 1979-86, exec. asst. pres., 1985-90, pres., 1990—. Bd. dirs. Tex. Internat. Edn. Consortium. Author textbook: Agricultural Mathematics, 1978; author articles. Bd. dirs. Texas Rural Communities, 1998—; founder regional commr. Alpine Soccer League, 1984; v.p. coach Alpine Baseball League, 1983; pres. Alpine PTA, 1982-83; founder, pres. So. Meth. U. Faculty Club, 1973-75; mem. exec. com. Tex. Assn. Coll. and Univ. Student Personnel Adminstrs., 1990-92; mem. commn. on colls. class of 2003 So. Assn. of Colls. and Schs. NSF grantee, 1979. Mem. Am. Assn. Higher Edn., Tex. Assn. Coll. Tchrs. (chpt. v.p. 1978-79), Math. Assn. Am. (chmn. Tex. sect. 1985-86), So. Assn. Colls. and Schs. (mem. commn. on colls. 1999—), Lions Club (pres. 1979-80, Lion of Yr. 1980, 83), Alpine Country Club. Republican. Mem. Ch. of Christ. Avocations: motocycling, golf, shooting. Home: PO Box 1341 Alpine TX 79831-1341 Office: Sul Ross State U E Highway 90 PO Box C114 Alpine TX 79831-0114 E-mail: rvmorgan@sulross.edu.

MORGAN, RHELDA ELNOLA, secondary school educator; b. St. Louis, June 10, 1947; d. Harry and Lillie Bertha (Citizen) Marbry; m. Edward Lee Morgan; 1 child, Tawanna Ka-Rhelda. BA in Edn., Harris-Stowe Coll., 1968; MA in Teaching, Webster U., 1981; postgrad., St. Louis U., 1989—. Primary tchr. Brunswick Elem. Sch., Gary, Ind., 1969-72, Walbridge Sch., St. Louis, 1972-84; lang. arts tchr. Ford Mid. Sch., St. Louis, 1984-87; lang. arts tchr., lang. dept. chairperson Marquette Visual & Performing Arts Mid. Sch., St. Louis, 1987-88; English tchr. Cen. Visual & Performing Arts High Sch., St. Louis, 1988-89, social studies tchr., 1989-90, English/fgn. lang. dept. chairperson, 1989-93; counselor Hugh O'Brian Youth Seminar, St. Louis, 1992, 93; English tchr. Soldan Internat. High Sch., St. Louis, 1993—. Cons. for scholarship pageant edn. dept. Ch. of God in Christ, Jurisdiction 1, St. Louis, 1988-89; mem. adj. faculty Harris-Stowe State Coll., 1994—; mem. edn. adv. com. Principia Coll., 1993—; supervising tchr. for apprentices and practice tchrs. Recipient Trophy for 14 Yrs. as Aux. Treas. Mem. Nat. Coun. Tchrs. English, Popular Culture/Am. Culture, Ladies Aux. VFW (treas. 2910, 1972-86). Pentecostal. Avocations: reading, crocheting.

MORGAN, ROBERT GEORGE, accounting educator, researcher; b. Sanford, Maine., Feb. 20, 1941; s. George Andrew and Katherine (Gray) M.; children: Robert George, Katherine Neva. BA, Piedmont Coll., Demorest, Ga., 1969; MAcctg., U. Ga., 1971, PhD, 1974. CPA, N.C.; cert. mgmt. acct. Asst. prof. acctg. U. Wyo., Laramie, 1974-76, Drexel U., Phila., 1976-80; assoc. prof. acctg. U. N.C., Greensboro, 1980-83; prof. acctg. Loyola Coll., Balt., 1983-85; chmn. dept. acctg. East Tenn. State U., Johnson City, 1985-92, prof. acctg., 1985—. Editor jour. The Mgmt. Rev., 1983-85; contbr. articles to profl. jours. Treas. Running Brook PTA, Columbia, Md., 1984-85. Mem. AICPA, Inst. Mgmt. Accts. (pres. East Tenn. chpt. 1995-96), Am. Acctg. Assn., Acad. Acctg. Historians, Tenn. Soc. Acctg. Educators (pres. 1986-87), Beta Gamma Sigma, Beta Alpha Psi. Methodist. Avocation: golf. Office: E Tenn State U Dept Acctg PO Box 70710 Johnson City TN 37614-0710 Home: 401 Belleair Ln Bristol VA 24201-1508 E-mail: morgan@etsu.edu., morganjewellry@msn.com.

MORGAN, ROSETTA RICHARDSON, elementary education educator; b. Orange, Tex., Mar. 25, 1954; d. Frank Allen and Janice Marie (Masters) Richardson; m. Alton Wayne Morgan, Aug. 10, 1974; 1 child, Brandon Malachi. BA, McNeese State U., 1977, MEd, 1983, cert. adminstrn., 1988, 92; cert. tchr. appraiser, Tex. Edn. Agy., 1989. Cert. elem. tchr., Tex., computer literacy tchr., mid mgmt. administr. Elem. edn. tchr. Buna (Tex.) Ind. Sch. Dist., 1977-81; elem. edn. tchr., grade dept. chmn., substitute asst. prin. Vidor (Tex.) Ind. Sch. Dist., 1984—. Rep. faculty coun. Vicor Ind. Sch. Dist., 1986-88, chmn. instrnl. leadership com. Oak Forest Elem., 1992. Team mother Little League of Vidor, Tex., 1992. Baptist. Avocations: painting, reading, cooking, travel, gardening. Home: 704 Lynne Cir Orange TX 77630-8847 Office: Oak Forest Elem 2400 Highway 12 Vidor TX 77662-3497

MORGAN, RUTH PROUSE, academic administrator, educator; b. Berkeley, Calif., Mar. 30, 1934; d. Ervin Joseph and Thelma Ruth (Prcesang) Prouse; m. Vernon Edward Morgan, June 3, 1956; children: Glenn Edward, Renée Ruth. BA summa cum laude, U. Tex., 1956; MA, La. State U., 1961, PhD, 1966. Asst. prof. Am. govt., politics and theory So. Meth. U., Dallas, 1966-70, assoc. prof., 1970-74, prof., 1974-95; prof. emeritus, 1995—; asst. provost So. Meth. U., Dallas, 1978-82, assoc. provost, 1982-86, provost ad interim, 1986-87, provost, 1987-93, provost emerita, 1993—; pres. RPM Assocs., 1993—; v.p. Chem. Abatement Tech., Inc., 1995—. Tex. state polit. analyst ABC, N.Y.C., 1972-84. Author: The President and Civil Rights, 1970; mem. editorial bd. Jour. of Politics, 1975-82, Presdl. Studies Quar., 1980—; contbr. articles to profl. jours. Active Internat. Women's Forum, 1987—, City of Dallas Redistricting Commn., 2001; trustee Hockaday Sch., 1988-94, The Kilby Awards Found., 1993-95; bd. dirs. United Way, Met. Dallas, 1993-99; adv. com. U.S. Army Command and Gen. Staff. Coll., 1994-97; founder Archives of Women of the Southwest, 1992, chmn. adv. com. 1995-99; charter mem. Girls, Inc. Aux; mem. Women's Ctr. Dallas, Dallas Women's Found. Mem. Am. Polit. Sci. Assn., So. Polit. Sci. Assn. (mem. exec. coun. 1979-84), Southwestern Polit. Sci. Assn. (pres. 1982-83, mem. exec. coun. 1981-84), The Dallas Assembly, The Dallas Forum of Internat. Women's Forum (pres. 1996-97), Charter 100 Club (pres. 1991-92), Nat. Mus. for Women in the Arts (charter), The Women's Mus. (charter), Ctr. for the Study of the Presidency, Dallas Summit Club (pres. 1992-93), Phi Beta Kappa, Pi Sigma Alpha, Phi Kappa Phi, Theta Sigma Phi. Avocations: photography, travel.

MORGAN, SHERRY RITA GUY, school system administrator; b. Knoxville, Tenn., Sept. 4, 1949; d. O.D. Warner and Virginia Rita (Kuster) Guy; m. Charles W. Morgan, June 19, 1971. BS, U. Tenn., 1971, MS, 1978, EdD, 1985. Lic. tchr. and prin. Sales mgr. Miller's Inc., Knoxville, Tenn., 1971-74; tchr. Knoxville/Knox County Schs., 1976-85; prin. Knox County Schs., Knoxville, 1985—, Knoxville City Schs., Anderson Elem. Sch., 1985-89, Knox County Schs., Lincoln Park Elem. Sch., 1989-93, Sterchi Elem. Sch., 1993—2003; supt. Roman Cath. Diocese, Knoxville, 2003—. Grad. asst., field experience coord. U. Tenn., 1983-85; mem. admissions bd. U. Tenn. Coll. Edn., 1984-85, 85—; faculty assoc. Coll. Edn. U. Tenn; adj. faculty U. Tenn., Knoxville, 1992-93. Mem. Lady Vols. Boost Her Club, Knoxville, 1987—, Leadership Edn., Diocese of Knoxville Evangelization Coun.; parish coun. stewardship commr., Holy Ghost Ch., 2001—, eucharistic min. 1999-, lector 1997-; lifetime mem., Ladies of Charity; hosp. chair

NCAA Women's Final Four; chair art activities Kids on the Town Arts Coun., Knoxville, 1989; mem. RCIA team Holy Ghost Ch., also Re-Membering Ch. dir.; v.p. Boys and Girls Club Christenberry Heights, 1992-93, pres., 1993-94, mem. managerial bd., 1990—; mem. Leadership Knoxville '95; adv. bd. Knox County Adopt-A-School, 1994-95; bd. visitors, steering com. Coll. Edn., U. Tenn., pres.'s trust; mem., parliamentarian PTA, 1993-2001; parish rep. Diocese Knoxville Evangelization Coun.; Powell adv. bd., bd. dirs. Boys and Girls Club Halls. Named one of Outstanding Young Women Am., 1984, Women of Achievement U. of Tenn. Commn. on Women, 1983; recipient award Gov.'s Acad. Tchrs. of Writing, 1989, Leadership Educator award C. of C., 1990; Learning Disabilities Assn. Conf. scholar, 1991, Gabbard scholar, 1995, Gerald Read scholar, 1996, 2000, rsch. scholar, 2000; grantee Prins. For 21st Century. Mem. AAUW (coord. sec. 1990-92), Tenn. ASCD, Tenn. Assn. Sch. Supervision and Adminstrn. (jour. rev. bd. publ. Tenn. Edn. Leadership), Internat. Reading Assn., Knox County Elem. Prins. Assn. (rsch. chmn. 1989—, nominating chmn. 1991-92, equity com. 1992—), U. Tenn. Pres.'s Club, Phi Delta Kappa (v.p. Alpha Kappa chpt. 1990-91, pres. 1992-93, advisor 1993-94, 94-95, del. 1994-95, internat. area coord. 1994—, editor newsletter 1988-89, sec. 1989-90, 21st century leadership initiative com., dist. VIII rep., bd. dirs. 1998-2001, internat. pres. 2003—). Roman Catholic. Avocations: walking, reading, golf, photography. Office: PO Box 11127 Knoxville TN 37939

MORGAN, STEPHAN SHANE, ophthalmologist, educator; b. Webb City, Mo., Nov. 30, 1938; s. James Laroy and Ferne (Gladden) M.; m. Jill Holtgrieve, June 17, 1961; children: Stephan S. Jr., Amy Susanne. BA, DePauw U., 1960; MD, St. Louis U., 1964; MS, U. Minn., 1968. Diplomate Am. Bd. Ophthalmology. Intern Vanderbilt U., Nashville, 1964-65; fellow in ophthalmology Mayo Clinic, Rochester, Minn., 1965-68; staff ophthalmologist Naval Hosp., Portsmouth, Va., 1968-70; pvt. practice, St. Louis, 1970—. Assoc. clin. prof. ophthalmology med. sch. St. Louis U., 1982—; pres. staff Forest Park Hosp., St. Louis, 1984, bd. dirs., 1985-87. Lt. comdr. USN, 1968-70. Fellow Am. Acad. Ophthalmology, ACS; mem. St. Louis Ophthalmological Soc. (pres. 1983), Mayo Clinic Assn. of Fellows (pres. 1976), Firerock Country Club, Old Warson Country Club. Republican. Avocations: fly fishing, golf, gardening. Home: 2209 Croydon Walk Saint Louis MO 63131-3331 Office: Hampton Village Ophthalmology Inc 16 Hampton Village Plz Saint Louis MO 63109-2128

MORGAN, STEPHEN CHARLES, academic administrator; b. Upland, Calif., June 2, 1946; s. Thomas Andrew and Ruth Elizabeth (Miller) M.; m. Ann Marie McMurray, Sept. 6, 1969; 1 child, Kesley Suzanne. BA, U. La Verne, 1968; MS, U. So. Calif., 1971; EdD, U. No. Colo., 1979. Devel. officer U. La Verne, Calif., 1968-71, asst. to pres., 1971-73, dir. devel., 1973-75, v.p. devel., 1975-76, pres., 1985—; dir. devel. U. So. Calif., L.A., 1976-79; exec. dir. Ind. Colls. No. Calif., San Francisco, 1979-85. Dir. Ind. Colls. So. Calif., L.A., 1985—. Bd. dirs. Mt. Baldy United Way, Ontario, Calif., 1988-98, McKinley Children's Ctr., San Dimas, Calif., 1989-99, LeRoy Haynes Ctr. for Family and Children's Svcs., 2000—; chair nat. com. on higher edn. Ch. of Brethren, Elgin, Ill., 1988-90; dir. Pomona Valley Hosp. Med. Ctr., 1992-98, 99—, Inter Valley Health Plan, 1992-97, PFF Bank and Trust, 2001—. Mem. Assn. Ind. Calif. Colls. and Univs. (exec. com. 1989—, vice-chmn. 1996-2000, chmn. 2000-2002), L.A. County Fair Assn. (bd. dirs., chmn. 2002—), Western Coll. Assn. (exec. com. 1992-98, pres. 1996-98), Western Assn. Schs. and Colls. (sr. accrediting commn. 1996-2001), Pi Gamma Mu. Avocations: orchid culture, fly fishing, golf. Home: 2518 N Mountain Ave Claremont CA 91711-1579 Office: U LaVerne Office Pres 1950 3rd St La Verne CA 91750-4401 E-mail: morgans@ulv.edu.

MORGAN, SYLVIA DENISE (MRS. HAROLD MORGAN), school administrator, poet; b. Rome, Ga., Sept. 1, 1952; d. Herman Hamilton and Garnette Lucille (Strickland) Haynes; m. Harold Morgan, Feb. 22, 1980; 1 child, Amber. BS in English, Knoxville Coll., 1974; MEd, Ga. State U., 1977; EdS, Jacksonville State U., 1989. From tchr. to ednl. supr. Ga. Sch. for the Deaf, Cave Spring, 1974—96, ednl. supr., 1996—2002, coord. family and student svcs., 2002—. Co-owner Uncle John's BBQ. Grad. Ga. Leadership Program. Mem. NAACP, NEA, Ga. Assn. Educators, Ga. Educators for the Hearing Impaired, Am. Assn. Persons with Disabilities, Coun. Exceptional Children (recognized as preferred spl. edn. tchr.), Floyd County and Tng. Svc. Ctr., Ga. Sch. for Deaf Alumni Assn., Ga. Assn. of the Deaf, Caregivers Assn. Avocations: speaking, writing poetry. Home: 8 Tasso Cir Rome GA 30161-5776 E-mail: sylvia@bellsouth.net.

MORGAN, TIM DALE, physical education educator; b. Covington, Ky., Jan. 8, 1964; s. Thomas Benjamin and Audrey (Crider) M.; m. Shirley Mae Oliver, Nov. 9, 1992; children: Joshua David-Thomas, Andrew Jacob. BS in Phys. Edn., Ch. Recreation, Campbellsville Coll., 1991; MS in Phys. Edn., Ea. Ky. U., 1992, MS in Recreation and Park Adminstrn., 1993, MA in Allied Health, 1997; postgrad., U. Ky., 1997—; diploma in fitness and nutrition, Internat. Corr. Schs., 1992. Cert. in real estate, Ky. Asst. facility coord. Bapt. Student Union No. Ky. U., Highland Heights, 1986-88, supr. health ctr., 1986-87; dept. asst. Campbellsville (Ky.) Coll., 1988-91; mem. staff dept. phys. edn. Ea. Ky. U., Richmond, 1991-92, intramurals facility coord., 1992-93, phys. edn. instr., 1993—. Survey coord. Champions Against Drugs, Campbellsville, 1990-91; adminstr. phys. testing Ky. State Police, Ea. Ky. U., Richmond, 1992-96. Fellowship dir. Bapt. Student Union, 1987-88, commuter coord., 1989, dir., adminstr. recreation, 1992; summer missionary So. Bapt. Conv. Home Mission Bd., Atlanta, 1987-89; vol. Christian Life Ctr., Campbellsville Bapt. Ch., 1990-91; music dir., tchr. coll. Sunday sch. Acton (Ky.) Bapt. Ch., 1990. Lance Cpl. USMC, 1982-88. Mem. AAHPERD, Ky. Assn. Health, Phys. Edn., Recreation and Dance. Democrat. Avocations: outdoor recreation, photography, volleyball, fitness and recreational activities. Home and Office: Ea Ky U 1 University Dr # Cpo1259 Campbellsville KY 42718-2190

MORGAN-LAWLER, BARBARA, speech educator; b. Talladega, Ala., Sept. 29, 1949; d. Otherl James and Lizzie (Garrett) Morgan; m. James Lawler III, Dec. 13, 1969; 1 child, Erikka Janeen. BA, Talladega Coll., 1971; MS, Jacksonville State U., 1971; AA, U. Montevallo, 1984. Cert. tchr., Ala. Tchr. communications Gadsden (Ala.) State Community Coll.; tchr. speech/theater Talladega Coll.; broadcast journalist, disc jockey Sta. WEYY Radio, Talladega; tchr. English lit. advanced placement Talladega City Bd. Edn. Bd. advisers Talladega Coll. Contbr. articles to Curriculum Guide in Research and Writing. Recipient Chi Honors Se Miner, Outstanding Advanced Placement award, 1988, Super Tchr. cert. Ala. Humanities Found., 1995, 97. Mem. NEA, Ala. Edn. Assn., Ala. Speech and Theatre Assn., Nat. Coun. Tchrs. English, ACTE, Internat. Thespian Soc. (Outstanding Theatre Dir.), AASSP, Talladega Coll. Local Alumni Assn., Zeta Phi Beta. Home: 929 College St Talladega AL 35160-4801 Office: Talladega HS 1177 Mcmillan St E Talladega AL 35160-3128

MORI, ALLEN ANTHONY, academic administrator, consultant; b. Hazleton, Pa., Nov. 1, 1947; s. Primo Philip and Carmella (DeNoia) M.; m. Barbara Epoca, June 26, 1971; 1 child, Kirsten Lynn. BA, Franklin and Marshall Coll., Lancaster, Pa., 1969; MEd, Bloomsburg U. Pa., 1971; PhD, U. Pitts., 1975. Spl. edn. tchr. White Haven (Pa.) State Sch. and Hosp., 1969-70, Hazleton Area Sch. Dist., 1970-71, Pitts. Pub. Schs., 1971-74; supr. student tchrs. U. Pitts., 1974-75; prof. spl. edn. U. Nev., Las Vegas, 1975-84; dean coll edn. Marshall U., Huntington, W.Va., 1984-87; dean coll. edn. Calif. State U., L.A., 1987—2003, provost, v.p. acad. affairs Dominguez Hills, 2003—. Hearing officer pub. law 94-142 Nev. Dept. Edn., Carson City, 1978—; mem. Nev. Gov.'s Com. on Mental Health and Mental Retardation, 1983-84; cons. Ministry Edn., Manitoba, Can., 1980-82; pres. Tchr. Edn. Coun. State Colls. and Univs., 1993-94. Author: Families of Children with Special Needs, 1983; co-author: Teaching the Severely Retarded, 1980, Handbook of Preschool, Special Education, 1980, Adapted Physical Education, 1983, A Vocational Training Continuum for the Mentally and Physically Disabled, 1985, Teaching Secondary Students with Mild Learning and Behavior Problems, 1986, 93, 99; author numerous articles, book revs. and monographs. Bd. dirs. Assn. Retarded Citizens San Gabriel Valley, ElMonte, 1989-94. Recipient grants U.S. Dept. Edn., 1976-91, Nev. Dept. Edn., W.Va. Dept. Edn., Calif. State U. Chancellor's Office. Mem. Assn. Tchr. Educators, Coun. for Exceptional Children (div. on Career Devel. exec. com. 1981-83), Nat. Soc. for Study of Edn., Phi Beta Delta, Phi Delta Kappa, Pi Lambda Theta. Avocations: wine collecting, travel. Office: Calif State U Dominguez HIlls 1100 E Victoria Carson CA 90747

MORIARTY, J. JOSEPH, management and technology consultant; b. Seattle, Sept. 25, 1950; s. John Francis Crowley and Patricia Mae (McCarthy) M.; m. Cynthia Serna, June 15, 1975; children: Kerry Serna, Michael John. BA in Philosophy, St. John's Coll., Camarillo, Calif., 1972; MS in Ednl. Adminstrn., U. So. Calif., 1975, postgrad., 1977. K-12 teaching and adminstrn. credentials, Calif. Tchr., adminstr. Archdiocese of L.A., Santa Fe Springs, Calif., 1972-76; asst. prin. Temple City (Calif.) Unified Sch. Dist., 1976-77, Chico (Calif.) Unified Sch. Dist.., 1977-78; measurement cons. Westinghouse Info. Systems, Sunnyvale, Calif., 1978-79, region mktg. mgr., 1979-81; v.p. mktg. Creative Programming Inc. subs. R.V. Weatherford Co., Pasadena, Calif., 1981-83, v.p. mktg. parent co., 1981-84; pres., sr. cons. Kerry Cons. Group, Claremont, Calif., 1984—. Mem. adv. bd. Thomas Jefferson Ctr., Pasadena, 1989—, C.S. Lewis Found., Redlands, Calif., 1992—; keynote speaker state edn. assns., W.I., N.J., Ill., Calif., Colo., Hawaii, 1985—; cons. HP, IBM, Unisys, Wang, 1985—. Contbg. editor Ednl. IRM Quar., 1991—. Bd. dirs. Archdiocese of L.A. Sem. Alumni Assn., 1991—. Named Tchr. of Yr., St. Paul High Sch., 1974; Calif. State scholar, 1968-71, grad. fellow, 1973-76. Mem. Am. Asssn. Sch. Adminstrs., Assn. Sch. Bus. Ofcls., Phi Delta Kappa. Avocations: mountain biking, golf. Home: Kerry Cons Group 976 W Foothill Blvd Ste 392 Claremont CA 91711

MORICE, LINDA KAY, school system administrator; b. Detroit, Aug. 16, 1948; d. William and Dorthy Marie (Moyer) Cunningham; m. James Lee Morice, June 13, 1970; 1 child, Sarah Elizabeth. BA, Hanover Coll., 1970; MA, U. Mo., 1972; PhD, St. Louis U., 1992. Cert. secondary tchr., prin., supt., Mo. Social studies tchr. Hazelwood Sch. Dist., St. Louis, 1970-77; adult basic edn. tchr. Parkway Sch. Dist., St. Louis, 1978-81; cons., author pvt. practice, St. Louis, 1981-91; tchr. social studies Ladue Sch. Dist., St. Louis, 1986-91, asst. prin., 1991-93, asst. to sch. dist. supr., 1993—. Ednl. cons. St. Louis Post-Dispatch, 1978-81; reader AP exam. Ednl. Testing Svc., Princeton, N.J., 1989-91. Author: Skyjack, 1986, Trial of Joan of Arc, 1991, Trial of Socrates, 1991. Recipient Allan J. Ellender fellowship Close Up Found., Washington, 1977. Mem. ASCD, Nat. Assn. Secondary Sch. Prins., Mo. Assn. Secondary Sch. Prins., Phi Delta Kappa, Pi Lambda, Theta. Mem. United Ch. of Christ. Home: 208 N Warson Rd Saint Louis MO 63124-1329 Office: Ladue Sch Dist 9703 Conway Rd Saint Louis MO 63124-1698

MORITA, TOSHIYASU, technology professional; b. Tokyo, Feb. 8, 1967; s. Hiroshi and Fusako (Ishikawa) M. Grad. high sch., 1985. Programmer Origin Systems, Inc., Austin, Tex., 1987; engr. Cyclops Electronics, Boerne, 1988-90; programmer Taito R&D, Bothell, Wash., 1990; mgr. new tech. LucasArts Entertainment, San Rafael, Calif., 1990-93; tech. dir. Sega Tech. Inst., Redwood City, Calif., 1993-94, Sega of Am., Redwood City, 1994-96, SegaSoft, Redwood City, 1996-97; dir. tech. Sega Am., Redwood City, 1997—. Mem. IEEE Computer Soc. (affiliate), Mensa.

MORIUCHI, K. DEREK, secondary school educator; b. L.A., 1958; BA, UCLA, 1981; MA, Calif. State U., L.A., 1982. Cert. single subject tchg. credential in math., nat. bd. cert. tchr., cert. cross cultural lang. acquisition devel. Tchr. math. Marshall Mid. Sch., 1986—90, Ganesha H.S., 1991—93; tchr. history Stevenson Middle Sch., L.A., 1993—2003, chairdept. math. Mem.: Calif. Math. Coun. (spkr. 2000—03), Nat. Bd. for Profl. Tchg. Stds. (bd. mem. 2001—), Pi Lambda Theta. Office: Stevenson Middle Sch 725 S Indiana St Los Angeles CA 90023

MORK, GORDON ROBERT, historian, educator; b. St. Cloud, Minn., May 6, 1938; s. Gordon Matthew and Agnes (Gibb) Mork; m. Dianne Jeannette Muetzel, Aug. 11, 1963; children: Robert, Kristiana, Elizabeth. BA, Yale U., 1960; MA, U. Minn., 1963, PhD, 1966. Instr. history U. Minn., Mpls., 1966; lectr., asst. prof. U. Calif., Davis, 1966-70; mem. faculty Purdue U., West Lafayette, Ind., 1970—, assoc. prof., 1973-94, prof. history, 1994—, dir. honors program humanities, 1985-87, dir grad. studies history, Am. studies, 1987-93, mem. Jewish studies com., 1980—, head dept. history, 1998—2003; resident dir. Purdue U.-Ind. U. Program, Hamburg, Germany, 1975-76. Rsch. fellow in humanities U. Wis., Madison, 1969—70; mem. test devel. com. advanced placement European history Ednl. Testing Svc., 1993—99, chair, 1995—99; cons. Coll. Bd. and Ednl. Testing Svc., 1999—. Author: Modern Western Civilization: A Concise History, 3d edit., 1994; editor: The Homes of Ober-Ammergau, 2000; mem. adv. bd. Teaching History, 1983—, History Teacher, 1986—2002. Mem. citizens task force Lafayette Sch. Corp., 1978—79; bd. dirs. Ind. Humanities Coun., 1986—89; elder Ctrl. Presbyn. Ch., Lafayette, 1973—75, deacon, 1996—99, trustee, 2001—; bd. dirs., sec. Murdock-Sunnyside Bldg. Corp., 1980—. Mem.: Com. History in Classroom (treas. 1990—93), Soc. History Edn., German Studies Assn., Am. Hist. Assn., Internat. Soc. History Didactics (v.p. 1991—95, 1996—2000), Phi Beta Kappa. Home: 1521 Cason St Lafayette IN 47904-2642 Office: Purdue U Dept of History West Lafayette IN 47907-2087 E-mail: gmork@purdue.edu.

MORLEY, CONNIE ANN, elementary school educator; b. Blossburg, Pa., Aug. 13, 1948; d. Edward W. and Hazel Jean (Ogden) Skullney; m. Raymond E. Morley; children: Timothy Raymond, Heather Marie. BS, Mansfield (Pa.) State Coll., 1969; MS, Drake U., 1981, EdD, 1992. Cert. mid. child, generalist Nat. Bd. Cert. Tchr., 2001, nat. bd. cert. tchr. Tchr. self-contained 4th grade Des Moines pub. schs. Mem. ASCD. Home: 3706 SW Court Ave Ankeny IA 50021-9215

MORNES, AMBER J. BISHOP, consultant, computer software trainer, analyst; b. Ft. Rucker, Ala., Oct. 20, 1970; d. David Floyd and Holly Brooke (Decker) Bishop; m. David Michael Mornes, May 22, 1993. BA in Psychology, U. Colo., Boulder, 1992. Asst. dir. admissions Rocky Mountain Coll. Art and Design, Denver, 1992-94, placement and alumni svcs. coord., 1995-96; computer software instr. Knowledge Alliance, New Horizons Computer Learning Ctr., Aurora, Colo., 1996-97; analyst Andersen Cons., Denver, 1997—. Vol. Colo. Art Educator Assn., 1993—. Mem. APA (student affiliate), Nat. Art Edn. Assn., Colo. Art Edn. Assn. Office: Andersen Cons 1225 17th St Ste 3200 Denver CO 80202-5503

MORONEY, LINDA L.S. (MUFFIE), lawyer, educator; b. Washington, May 27, 1943; d. Robert Emmet and Jessie (Robinson) M.; m. Clarence Renshaw II, Mar. 28, 1967 (div. 1977); children: Robert Milnor, Justin W.R. BA, Randolph-Macon Woman's Coll., 1965; JD cum laude, U. Houston, 1982. Bar: Tex. 1982, U.S. Ct. Appeals (5th cir.) 1982, U.S. Dist. Ct. (so. dist.) Tex. 1982, U.S. Supreme Ct. 1988. Law clk. to assoc. justice 14th Ct. Appeals, Houston, 1982-83; assoc. Pannill and Reynolds, Houston, 1983-85, Gilpin, Pohl & Bennett, Houston, 1985-89, Vinson & Elkins, Houston, 1989-92. Adj. prof. law U. Houston, 1986-91, dir. legal rsch. and writing, 1992-96, civil trial and appellate litigation and mediation, 1996—. Mem. ABA, State Bar Tex., Houston Bar Assn., Assn. of Women Attys., Tex. Women Lawyers, Order of the Barons, Phi Delta Phi. Episcopalian. Home and Office: 4010 Whitman St Houston TX 77027-6334

MORONT-FIGUERO, PATRICIA, language educator; b. Sagua la Grande, Cuba, Sept. 10, 1956; came to U.S., 1961; d. Antonio and Melba Rosa (Quintero) Moran; m. Francisco P. Figuero; children: Kyle Miller, Tyler Miller; married, Mar. 14, 1998. AA, Palm Beach Jr. Coll., 1976; BA in Mass Comms., U. South Fla., 1980. Cert. tchr., Fla. Prodr. and hostess Spanish Pub. Affairs Talk Show, Sta. WTOG-TV, St. Petersburg, Fla.; pub. svc. dir. WTOG-TV, St. Petersburg, Fla., 1979-82; asst. promtions dir. Busch Gardens, Tampa, Fla., 1983; tchr. Spanish and English, Pinellas Sch. Bd., Largo, Fla., 1990-92, Palm Beach Sch. Bd., Boca Raton, Fla., 1990-92; high sch. tchr. and cmty. rels dir. New Eng. Inst. Tech. and Fla. Culinary Inst., West Palm Beach, Fla., 1992-98; comm., pub. rels. coord. Delray Med. Ctr., Delray Beach, Fla., 1998-99; ESOL/Spanish tchr. Polo Pk. Mid. Sch., Wellington, Fla., 2001—03; resource tchr. Sch. Bd. Palm Beach (Fla.) County, 2003—. ESOL instr. Adult Vocat. Edn., Lantana, Fla., 1991-92; resource tchr. secondary & career edn., Palm Beach County Sch. Bd., 2001-03 Mem. tech. prep. mktg. com. Palm Beach County Sch. Bd., also chairperson tech. prep. scholarship com. Mem. Women in Comm. (chmn. awards and recognition, bd. dirs., 1st v.p. 1998-99), Assn. for Women in Comm. (bd. dirs., chmn. awards and recognition com. 1997-98). Avocations: photography, tennis, dancing.

MOROWITZ, HAROLD JOSEPH, biophysicist, educator; b. Poughkeepsie, N.Y., Dec. 4, 1927; s. Philip Frank and Anna (Levine) M.; m. Lucille Rita Stein, Jan. 30, 1949; children: Joanna Lynn, Eli David, Joshua Alan, Zachary Adam, Noah Daniel. BS, Yale U., 1947, MS, 1950, PhD, 1951. Physicist Nat. Bur. Stds., 1951-53, Nat. Heart Inst., Bethesda, Md., 1953-55; mem. faculty Yale U., 1955-88, assoc. prof. biophysics, 1960-68, prof. molecular biophysics and biochemistry, 1968-88, master Pierson Coll., 1981-86; mem. faculty George Mason U., Fairfax, Va., 1988—, Robinson prof. biology and natural philosophy, 1988—; dir. Krasnow Inst. for Advanced Study, 1993-98. Chmn. com. on models for biomed. rsch. NRC, 1983-85, mem. bd. on basic biology, 1986-92. Author: Life and the Physical Sciences, 1964, (with Waterman) Theoretical and Mathematical Biology, 1965, Energy Flow in Biology, 1968, Entropy for Biologists, 1970, (with Lucille Morowitz) Life On The Planet Earth, 1974, Ego Niches, 1977, Foundations of Bioenergetics, 1978, The Wine of Life, 1979, Mayonnaise and the Origin of Life, 1985, Cosmic Joy and Local Pain, 1987, The Thermodynamics of Pizza, 1991, Beginnings of Cellular Life, 1992, (with James Trefil) The Facts of Life, 1992, Entropy and the Magic Flute, 1993, The Kindly Dr. Guillotin, 1997, The Emergence of Everything, 2002; editor Complexity, 1994-2002; contbr. articles to profl. jours. Mem. sci. adv. bd. Santa Fe Inst., 1991-97, co-chmn. sci. adv. bd., 2000—. Mem. Biophys. Soc. (exec. com. 1965), Nat. Ctr. for Rsch. Resources (coun. 1987-92). Office: George Mason U Mail Stop 2A1 Krasnow Inst Advanced Study Fairfax VA 22030

MORREALE, JOSEPH CONSTANTINO, higher education administrator, public administration educator, economic and financial consultant; b. Bronx, N.Y., Oct. 26, 1944; s. Joseph Vincent Morreale and Grace (Soricelli); m. Barbara McAdorey; children: Gwenn F., Margaret I., Adam J.; stepchildren: Neil J., Michael D., John D. BA, Queens Coll. CUNY, 1967; MA, SUNY, Buffalo, 1969, PhD in Econs., 1972; MS in Higher Ednl. Adminstrn., SUNY, Albany, 1989. Asst. prof. econs. Western Mich. U., Kalamazoo, 1970-74; rsch. assoc. U. Wis., Madison, 1974-75; asst. to assoc. prof. health svcs. adminstrn., econs. Grad. Sch. Pub. Health U. Pitts., 1975-79; assoc. to prof. econs., environ. studies Bard Coll., Annandale-On-Hudson, N.Y., 1979-88; vis. rsch. fellow Grad. Sch. Edn., H.E. Adminstrn. SUNY, Albany, 1988-89; prof., chmn. dept. pub. adminstrn. Grad. Sch. Pace U., White Plains, N.Y., 1989-96; vice provost for planning assessment and instnl. rsch. Pace U., N.Y.C., Westchester, 1996-98, v.p. planning, assessment, rsch. and acad. support, 1998—, sr. assoc. provost, v.p., 2001—. Health care and govt. fin. cons. to fed. agencies, state and local govts., pvt. firms, 1979—; adj. prof. law Pace U., 1990-96; adj. prof. pub. adminstrn. Grad. Sch. Pub. Affairs, SUNY-Albany, 1990-96; vis. prof. U. Lancaster, Eng., 1984-85; rsch. assoc., bd. dirs. Hudsonia Environ. Rsch., Annandale, 1985-95; fin. planner Prudential Fin. Svcs., Newburgh, N.Y., 1987-89. Author: Health Care Economics, 1977, Post Tenure Review and Renewal: Experienced Voices, 2002; editor: The U.S. Medical Care Industry, 1974, Post-tenure Review: Policies, Practices, Precautions, 1997; contbr. articles to profl. jours. Appoint pub. rep. Westchester County Deferred Compensation Bd., Mt. Kisco Planning Bd. Recipient NDEA fellowship, 1967-70, Pharm. Mfg. Assn. fellowship, 1969-70, post-doctoral fellowship Health Econ. Rsch. Ctr. U. Wis., 1974-75, rsch. fellowship Grad. Sch. Edn. SUNY-Albany, 1988-89, ACE fellowship UNC, Charlotte, 1995-96, sr. rsch. fellow Harvard IEM Inst., 2000. Mem. Am. Soc. for Pub. Adminstrn., Am. Econ. Assn., Am. Ednl. Fin. Assn., Assn. Instl. Rsch., Am. Assn. Higher Edn., Am. Coun. Edn. (fellow 1995-96), N.Y. State Govt. Fin. Officers Assn. (bd. dirs. 1990-95). Mem. Soc. Of Friends. Avocations: photography, tennis, music, environ. concerns. Office: Pace U VP 1 Pace Plz New York NY 10038-1598

MORRELL, JANINE MARJORIE DACUS, secondary education educator; b. San Antonio, Nov. 24, 1957; d. Dayle McClain and Marjorie Lucille (Voskuhl) Dacus; m. Dave Charles Morrell, Oct. 11, 1981; children: Morgan Marjorie, Alexandra Janine, Taylor Lynn. BS in Secondary Edn., U. Tex., 1980. Cert. social studies tchr., Tex. Tchr. world history Clear Creek H.S., League City, Tex., 1983-84, tchr. world geography, including honors class, 1984-90; tchr. U.S. history and world geography Clear View Alternative H.S., League City, 1991—. Mem. Houston 100 Club, 1994; participant Houston Rodeo Chili Cook-off, 1992—. Tchr. of Yr. finalist Clear Lake Rotary Club, Houston, 1994. Mem. Tex. Fedn. Tchrs. Avocations: country and western dancing, waterskiing, reading, gardening. Home: 15722 Blackhawk Blvd Friendswood TX 77546-2904 Office: Clear View Alternative HS 400 S Kansas Ave League City TX 77573-4070

MORRING, DOROTHY WILSON, elementary education educator; b. Colerain, NC, Dec. 5, 1952; d. Joseph Trannie and Maude (Roulhac) Wilson; m. Don Michael Morring, Oct. 31, 1975; children: Deanna, Don Jr., Dalan. BS in Elem. Edn., Elizabeth City State U., 1975; student, N.C. Ctr. Advancement Teaching, 1987; MA in Edn., East Carolina U., 1988. Cert. tchr., N.C. Tchr. 2d grade Perquimans Ctl. Sch., Winfall, N.C., 1975-76, tchr. 3rd grade, 1976-81; tchr. kindergarten Perquimans Ctl. Sch., Hertford (N.C.) Grammer Sch., 1981-92; tchr. 1st grade Hertford Grammer Sch., 1992—; tchr. kindergarten, grade level. chmn., 1994-95. Steering com. Perquimans 2000, Hertford, 1992-93. Active Hertford Grammar Sch. PTA, 1990-92, Cen. Elem. Sch. PTA, Perquimans Mid. Sch. PTA, Elizabeth City (N.C.) chpt. Jack and Jill Inc., 1990—; sec. Cornerstone Missionary Bapt. Ch. Trotman Troubadours Support Group, Elizabeth City, 1993—. Recipient Outstanding Young Educator award Perquimans County, 1984, Outstanding Elem. Math. Tchr. award, 1985, Tchr. of Yr., 1991. Mem. NEA, MADD, Internat. Reading Assn., NC Reading Assn., NC Assn. Educators (Perquimans County sec.), NC N.G. Assn. (life). Democrat. Baptist. Avocations: art, decorating, reading, movies. Home: 1508 Herrington Rd Elizabeth City NC 27909-5974

MORRIS, CINDRA ANN, librarian, educator; b. Gettysburg, Pa, Apr. 15, 1948; d. Merle Thomas and Gladys Mae (Dutterer) Sheely; m. Thomas Earl Morris Jr., Oct. 21, 1972; children: Ryan, Beth. BS, Lock Haven U., Pa., 1970; MEd, Bloomsburg U., Pa., 1990. Cert. Elem. Tchr., Libr., Pa. Elem. tchr. Pennsbury Sch. Dist., Fallingston, Pa., 1970-90, elem. sch. libr., 1990—97, ms libr., 1997—. Mem. NEA, Pa. State Edn. Assn., Pennsbury Edn. Assn., Bucks County Libr. Assn. Avocations: reading, knitting, exercise. Office: Charles H Boehm Middle Sch 866 Big Oak Rd Yardley PA 19067

MORRIS, DIANE MARIE, special education consultant, travel consultant; b. Joliet, Ill., June 17, 1953; d. Milton W. and Anna Mae (Jungles) M. Assoc., Joliet Jr. Coll., 1973; BS in Spl. Edn., Ill. State U., 1975, MS in Spl. Edn., 1980. Cert. in spl. edn., learning disabilities, behavior disorders, educable mentally handicapped, regular edn.; approval in spl. early childhood; cert. in travel cons.; supervisory endorsement for learning disabled, behavior disorders, educable mentally handicapped. Summer sch. aide Laraway Sch., Joliet, 1970, 71; bookstore employee Joliet Jr. Coll., 1972-73; spl. edn. aide Joliet Pub. Grade Schs., 1975-76, tchr. spl. edn., 1976-82, supportive learning specialist, 1982—; travel cons. Wanderlich Travel, Joliet, 1982—. Mem. inst. adv. com. Will County Regional Supt.'s Office, Joliet, 1983-89, master tchr. selection com., 1987; mem. adv. bd. Emily Howe Fisk Found.-Altrusa Club, Joliet, 1992—; participant learning disabled rsch. studies, 1980, 87. Mem., holder several offices Joliet Bus. and Profl. Women, 1982—; sec. Joliet Altrusa Club, 1991—; del. to China, Citizens Amb. Program, Spokane (Wash.) chpt., 1984. Recipient Disting. Svc. Scroll, Joliet PTA Coun., 1982. Mem. Coun. for Exceptional Children (cons. leadership tng. inst. 1994), Ill. Coun. for Exceptional Children (regional dir. 1989-96, asst. editor newsletter, Clarissa Hug Tchr. of Yr. 1994), Will County Coun. for Exceptional Children (pres. 1983, Program award 1993-94, Disting. Svc. award 1984), Delta Kappa Gamma, Alpha Delta Kappa, Kappa Delta Pi. Avocations: travel, biking, reading. Home: 16255 W Diane Way Manhattan IL 60442-9775 Office: Joliet Pub Grade Schs 420 N Raynor Ave Joliet IL 60435-6065

MORRIS, GEORGE L. neurologist, educator; b. Lincoln, Nebr., May 6, 1958; s. George L. and Berniece E. Morris; m. Nancy S. Morris, Nov. 25, 1983; children: Gillian L., Spencer S. BA in Chemistry and Life Sci., U. Nebr., Lincoln, 1979; MD, U. Nebr., Omaha, 1984. Cert. Am. Bd. Psychiatry and Neurology, Am. Bd. Clin. Neurophysiology. Instr. U. Cin., 1988—89, asst. prof. neurology, 1989—90, Med. Coll. Wis., Milw., 1990—95, assoc. prof. neurology, 1995—2001, prof. neurology, 2001; dir., regional epilepsy program St. Luke's Med. Ctr., Milw., 2001—. Editl. bd. Clin. Drug Investigation Drugs in R & D, London, 2000—. Contbr. articles to profl. jours., chapters to books. Semi-profl. worker Habitat for Humanity, Milw., 1991—95; Sunday Sch. tchr. Christ Episc. Ch., Milw., 1991—2000. Fellow Muscular Dystrophy Assn., 1988; grantee NIH, 1992, 1998. Mem.: AMA, Epilepsy Assn. S.E. Wis. (chmn. bd. dirs. 1992—95), Milw. Neuropsychiatric Soc. (pres. 1995—96), Ctrl. Epilepsy EEG Soc. (pres. 1997—), Am. Assn. Neurology (mem. com. 1998—), Am. EEG Soc., Am. Epilepsy Soc. (membership com. 1990—). Episcopalian. Avocations: bicycling, running, soccer, woodcarving, playing cello. Office: St Lukes Med Ctr 2801 W Kinnickinnic River Pkwy Milwaukee WI 53226

MORRIS, HENRY MADISON, JR., education educator; b. Dallas, Oct. 6, 1918; s. Henry Madison and Ida (Hunter) M.; m. Mary Louise Beach, Jan. 24, 1940; children: Henry Madison III, Kathleen Louise, John David, Andrew Hunter, Mary Ruth, Rebecca Jean. BS with distinction, Rice Inst., 1939; MS, U. Minn., 1948, PhD, 1950; LLD, Bob Jones U., 1966; LittD, Liberty U., 1989. Registered profl. engr., Tex. Jr. engr. Tex. Hwy. Dept., 1938-39; from jr. engr. to asst. engr. Internat. Boundary Commn., El Paso, 1939-42; instr. civil engring. Rice Inst., 1942-46; from instr. to asst. prof. U. Minn., Mpls., also research project leader St. Anthony Falls Hydraulics Lab., 1946-51; prof., head dept. civil engring. Southwestern La. Inst., Lafayette, 1951-57, Va. Poly. Inst., Blacksburg, 1957-70; v.p. acad. affairs Christian Heritage Coll., San Diego, 1970-78, pres., 1978-80; dir. Inst. for Creation Rsch., 1970-80, pres., 1980-96, pres. emeritus, 1996—. Author (with Richard Stephens): (report) Report on Rio Grande Cosnervation Investigation, 1942; author: 2d edit That You Might Believe, 1946; author: (with Curtis Larson) (book) Hydraulics of Flow in Culverts, 1948; author: The Bible and Modern Science, 1951, rev. edit, 1968; author: (with John C. Whitcomb) The Genesis Flood, 1961; author: Applied Hydraulics in Engineering, 1963, The Twilight of Evolution, 1964, Science, Scripture and Salvation, 1965, Studies in The Bible and Science, 1966, Evolution and the Modern Christian, 1967, Biblical Cosmology and Modern Science, 1970, The Bible has the Answer, 1971, Science and Creation: A Handbook for Teachers, 1971; author: (with J.M. Wiggert) Applied Hydraulics, 1972; author: A Biblical Manual on Science and Creation, 1972, The Remarkable Birth of Planet Earth, 1973, Many Infallible Proofs, 1974, Scientific Creationism, 1974; : 2d edit, 1985, Troubled Waters of Evolution, 1975, The Genesis Record, 1976, Education for the Real World, 1977, 1991, (book) The Scientific Case for Creation, 1977, The Beginning of the World, 1977, 2d edit, 1991, Sampling the Psalms, 1978, King of Creation, 1980, Men of Science, Men of God, 1982, 2d edit, 1988, Evolution in Turmoil, 1982, The Revelation Record, 1983, History of Modern Creationism, 1984, 2d edit, 1993, The Biblical Basis for Modern Science, 1984, 2002, Creation and the Modern Christian, 1985, Science and the Bible, 1986, Days of Praise, 1986, The God Who is Real, 1988, 2d edit., 2000, The Remarkable Record of Job, 1987; author: (with Martin Clark) The Bible Has the Answer; author: (with Gary E. Parker) What is Creation Science?, 1982; author: 2d edit., 1988, The Long War Against God, 1989; author: (with John D. Morris) Science, Scripture and the Young Earth, 1989; author: The Bible Science and Creation, 1991, Creation and the Second Coming, 1991, Biblical Creationism, 1993, The Defender's Bible, 1995, The Modern Creation Trilogy, 1996, The Heavens Declare the Glory of God, 1997, That Their Words May be Used Against Them, 1998, The Origin of Earth and its People, 1999, Defending the Faith, 1999, Treasures in the Psalms, 2000, Solomon and His Remarkable Wisdom, 2001, God and the Nations, 2002, The Incredible Journey of Jonah, 2003. Fellow AAAS, ASCE, Am. Sci. Affiliation; mem. Am. Soc. Engring. Edn. (sec.-editor civil engring. divsn. 1967-70), Trans-Nat. Assn. Christian Schs. (pres. 1983-95), Creation Rsch. Soc. (pres. 1967-73), Am. Geophys. Union, Geol. Soc. Am., Am. Assn. Petroleum Geologists, Geochem. Soc., Gideons (pres. La. 1954-56), Phi Beta Kappa, Sigma Xi, Chi Epsilon, Tau Beta Pi. Baptist. Home: 6733 El Banquero Pl San Diego CA 92119-1129 Office: Inst for Creation Rsch 10946 Woodside Ave N Santee CA 92071

MORRIS, JANE ELIZABETH, home economics educator; b. Marietta, Ohio, Nov. 28, 1940; d. Harold Watson and LaRue (Graham) M. Student, U. Ky., 1960; BS, Marietta Coll., 1962, postgrad., 1963; MA, Kent State U., 1970, postgrad., 1985-87, Coll. Mt. St. Joseph, 1984-86, John Carroll U., 1986, Ashland Coll., 1987. Cert. high sch. tchr., Ohio. Tchr. home econs. Chagrin Falls (Ohio) Mid. and High Sch., 1963-95; pres. JEM Creations, Inc., 1995—. Head cheerleading advisor Chagrin Falls H.S., 1970-80, freshman class advisor, 1981-82, head fine and practical arts dept., 1982-84, sophomore class advisor, 1982-85, 87-89, mem. prin.'s cabinet, 1987-88, tchr., adminstr. adv. coun., 1990-93. Vice chmn. The Elec. Women's Round Table, Inc., Cleve., 1968, chmn., 1969-71; treas. Trees Condominium Assn., 1981-83, pres., 1991-94; active Chagrin Falls chpt. Am. Heart Assn., Am. Cancer Soc., Geauga County Humane Soc., Valley Save a Pet; pres. Eagles Nest Condo Assn., 1999-2002. Mem. AAUW, NEA, PEO, Career Edn. Assn., Ohio Edn. Assn., Ohio Retired Tchrs. Assn., Chagrin Falls Edn. Assn. (bldg. rep. 1986-95, negotiating team 1990, negotiating com. 1993, commendation State of Ohio rep. assembly 1995), Nat. Soc. Arts and Letters (treas.), Marietta Coll. Alumni Assn. (mem. Mid Ohio Valley chpt.), Washington County Hist. Soc., Marietta Photographic Soc., Friends of the Mus. Campus Martius Mus., Order Ea. Star (mem. Marietta chpt. no. 59), Alpha Xi Delta (treas. alumni bd.). Methodist. Avocations: swimming, interior design, sewing, gourmet cooking.

MORRIS, JERRY DEAN, retired academic administrator; b. Gassville, Ark., May 11, 1935; s. James Henry and Maud Idella (Taylor) M.; m. Marilyn Jo Pitman, June 11, 1955; children: Joseph, Neil, Laura, Kara. BS, U. Ark., 1960, MEd, 1964, EdD, 1971. Cert. sch. adminstr., Ark. High sch. tchr. Cotter (Ark.) Pub. Schs., 1959-60, high sch. prin., 1960-63; jr. high prin. Mountain Home (Ark.) Pub. Schs., 1963-66, high sch. prin., 1966-67, asst. supt., 1967-69; editor Ark. Sch. Bds. Newsletter, U. Ark., Fayetteville, 1969-70; dir. placement services Tex. A&M U.-Commerce (formerly East Tex. State U.), 1970-71, dean admissions & records, 1971-73, dean grad. sch., 1973-81, v.p. acad. affairs, 1982-86, pres., 1987-97; retired, 1997. Cons. Ark. Basic Edn., 1970, U. Cen. Ark., Conway, 1972, coordinating bd. Tex. Colls. & Univs., Austin, 1981. Pres. Commerce C. of C., 1975; bd. dirs. Commerce Lions Club, 1977; chmn. Commerce United Way, 1978; mem. Commerce Indsl. Devel. Assn., 1974—. Named an Outstanding Young Man in Edn., Ark. Jaycees, 1966, Outstanding Young Man in Am., 1967, named pres. emeritus Tex. A&M Brd. of Regents. Mem. Tex. Assn. Coll. Tchrs., Assn. Tex. Grad. Schs. (pres. 1978-79), Coun. of So. Grad. Schs. (bd. dirs. 1976-79), Coun. of Grad. Schs. in U.S., Coun. of Pub. U. Pres. and Chancellors (exec. com. 1989-90, 1996-97), Assn. of Tex. Colls. and Univs. (exec. com. 1989-90), Tex. Internat. Edn. Consortium (exec. com. 1990—), Alliance for Higher Edn. (bd. dirs. 1986—), Phi Delta Kappa. Methodist. Avocations: jogging, gardening, reading, singing, travel. Home: ET Sta PO Box 3001 Commerce TX 75429-3001 Office: Tex A&M U-Commerce ET Station Commerce TX 75429

MORRIS, LOIS LAWSON, education educator; b. Antoine, Ark., Nov. 27, 1914; d. Oscar Moran and Dona Alice (Ward) Lawson; m. William D. Morris, July 2, 1932 (dec.); 1 child, Lavonne Morris Howell (dec.). BA, Henderson U., 1948; MS, U. Ark., 1951, MA, 1966; postgrad., U. Colo., 1954, Am. U., 1958, U. N.C., 1968. History tchr. Delight H.S., Ark., 1942-47; counselor Huntsville Vocat. Sch., 1947-48; guidance dir. Russellville Pub. Sch. Sys., Ark., 1948-55; asst. prof. edn. U. Ark., Fayetteville, 1955-82, prof. emeritus, 1982—. Ednl. cons. Ark. Pub. Schs., 1965-78. Author: Biographical Essays, 2000; contbr. articles to profl. jours. Mem. Hist. Preservation Alliance Ark.; pres. Washington County Hist. Soc., 1983-85, Pope County Hist. Assn.; mem. Ark. Symphony Guild; charter mem. Nat. Mus. in Arts; bd. dirs. Potts Inn Mus. Found. Named Ark. Coll. Tchr. of Yr., 1972; recipient Plaque for Outstanding Svcs. to Washington County Hist. Soc., 1984. Mem. LWV, AAUW, NEA, Washington County Hist., Soc. (exec. bd. 1977-80), Ark. Edn. Assn., Ark. Hist. Assn., Pope County Hist. Assn. (pres. 1991-92), The Ga. Hist. Soc., U. Ark. Alumni Assn., Sierra Club, Nature Conservancy, Ark. River Valley Arts Assn., Phi Delta Kappa, Kappa Delta Pi, Phi Alpha Theta. Democrat. Episcopalian. Address: 1601 W 3d St Russellville AR 72801-4725

MORRIS, MARJORIE LYNNE, language arts educator; b. Indpls., Sept. 25, 1947; d. Albert and Sylvia (Forman) M.; m. Bill J. Reister, Aug. 25, 1979; children: Jason, Matthew. BA in English, Ind. U., 1969, MA in English, 1972. Cert. English tchr. grades 7-12. Lang. arts tchr. Hughes H.S., Cin., 1970-72, Salem (Ind.) Mid. Sch., 1973—. Curriculum writer Hughes H.S., 1971; lang. arts. chmn. Salem Mid. Sch., 1984—; grant writer pub. rels., 1990-91; arts coord. Salem Coord. Schs., 1978-82, 90-91; freelance lang. arts cons., 1995—, leadership facilitator, 1998—. Chmn. bd. dirs. Awareness Washington County, Salem, 1993-95, co-dir., 2001—; leader, state horse and pony com. 4-H, Ind., 1984-88, area II horse and pony chmn., 1984-88; chmn. Smedley Scholarship Fund, 1986—. Mem. Ind. Mid. Level Edn. Assn. (regional bd. dirs., region 12 dir. 1992-98), Delta Kappa Gamma (chmn. profl. affairs 1992-2002). Avocations: horseback riding & showing, reading, photography. Home: 5105 W Arrow Rd Salem IN 47167-8937 Office: Salem Mid Sch 1001 N Harrison St Salem IN 47167-1687 E-mail: mmorris@salemschools.com.

MORRIS, MICHAEL DALE, athletic director, educator; b. Pocahontas, Ark., Aug. 8, 1952; s. Murl Daniel and Willa Dean (Hawkins) M.; children: Heather E., Holly A. BS/BSE, U. ctrl. Ark., 1975; MS, Kans. State U., 1977, U. Ill., 1980; EdS, Ball State U., 1985; PhD, U. Miss., 1991. Cert. phys. edn. tchr., mid-mgmt. adminstr., Tex.; cert. gen. sci. and phys. edn. tchr., Ark. Athletic dir., educator Ranger (Tex.) Coll. Adj. prof. Am. U. of Hawaii. Capt. U.S. Army, 1976-84. U. Ill. grad. assistantship, 1978-79; U. Miss. doctoral fellow, 1988-91. Mem. Am. Legion, Hon. Order Ky. Cols., Kappa Delta Pi, Phi Delta Kappa, Pi Kappa Alpha. Republican. Mem. Lds Ch. Avocations: camping, hiking, outdoor family-related activities. Home: PO Box 102 Ranger TX 76470

MORRIS, PATRICIA SMITH, media specialist, writer, educator; b. Franklin, N.J., Jan. 31, 1940; d. Joseph P. and Pauline C. Smith; m. Carl W. Morris; children: Margaret, Sarah, Maureen. BA, Paterson State Coll.; MLS, Rutgers U.; MEd, George Washington U. Media specialist Hanover Park (N.J.) Regional H.S. Bd. Edn. Author: Stepping into Research!, 1990; 6 Vols. of Young Adult Reading Activities Library, 1993. Exec. co-dir. N.J. Connection; mem. exec. bd. Highlands Regional Libr. Cooperative. Recipient N.J. Gov's. Tchr. Recognition award, 1989, Pres. award EMA, 1995, Dora Stolfi award MCSMA, 1997; named Outstanding Ednl. Media Specialist of N.J., 1990. Mem. ALA, NEA, Am. Assn. Sch. Librs., N.J. Edn. Assn., Morris County Sch. Media Assn. (past pres.), Ednl. Media Assn. N.J. (exec. bd.). Office: Whippany Park HS Whippany Rd Whippany NJ 07981

MORRIS, ROBERT DARRELL, reading education educator; b. Durham, N.C., Nov. 25, 1947; s. Robert James and Lily B. (O'Kelly) M.; m. Verda Wilson Ingle, July 20, 1978; children: Joseph, Katherine. BA in Psychology, Randolph-Macon Coll., 1972; MA in Psychology, U. Richmond, 1976; EdD in Reading Edn., U. Va., 1980. Spl. edn. tchr. Culpeper (Va.) County Schs., 1974-76; assoc. prof. edn. Nat. Coll. Edn., Evanston, Ill., 1979-89; prof. edn. Appalachian State U., Boone, N.C., 1989—. Dir. reading clinic Nat. Coll. Edn., 1981-87, Appalachian State U., 1989—; dir. Howard St. Tutoring Program, Chgo., 1979-85; creator, cons. Early Steps Reading Intervention Program, various cities, 1987—. Author: Howard Street Tutoring Manual, 1999; contbr. articles to profl. jours. Mem. Nat. Reading Conf., Internat. Reading Assn. (Exemplary Reading Program award 1987), Internat. Dyslexia Assn. Avocations: basketball, football, baseball, fishing, blues music. Office: Appalachian State U Reading Clinic Boone NC 28608-0001

MORRIS, ROBERT RENLY, minister, clinical pastoral education supervisor; b. Jacksonville, Fla., Feb. 15, 1938; s. Joseph Renly and Sybil (Stephens) M.; m. Lenda Smith, Dec. 7, 1963; children: Christopher Renly, Jennifer Kelly. BA, U. Fla., 1959; MDiv, Columbia Theol. Sem., Atlanta, 1962, ThM, 1967, D Ministry, 1990. Ordained to ministry Presbyn. Ch. (U.S.A.), 1962. Min. to students Ga. State Coll., Atlanta, 1959-60; asst. min. Trinity Presbyn. Ch., Atlanta, 1960-62; min. Clanton (Ala.) Presbyn. Ch., 1963-65, Kelly Presbyn. Ch., McDonough, Ga., 1965-67; pastoral counselor Ga. Assn. for Pastoral Care, Atlanta, 1966-68; coord. pastoral svcs. Winter Haven (Fla.) Hosp. and Community Health Ctr., 1969-79; min. Presbytery of Greater Atlanta, mem. div. pastoral care, 1984-86; dir. clin. pastoral edn. Emory Ct. for Pastoral Svcs., Atlanta, 1979-98; dir. pastoral svcs. Emory U. Hosp., Atlanta, 1998—2003, The Emory Clinic, Atlanta, 1998—2003, Crawford Long Hosp., 2000—03; interim exec. dir. Assn. for Clin. Pastoral Edn., 2003—. Adj. faculty Candler Sch. Theology, 1979-88. Contbr. book chpts., articles to profl. jours. Mem. AIDS Task Force, Atlanta, 1988-95, Task Force on Chem. Dependency, 1988; pres. bd. dirs. Atlanta Hosps. Hospitality Ho., 1998-2000. Mem. Am. Assn. Pastoral Counselors, Profl. Chaplains Assn., Am. Assn. Marriage and Family Therapists (clin.), Assn. for Clin. Pastoral Edn. (cert. supr., gen. assembly nominating com. 1984, chmn. 1985, coord. ann. conf. 1986, long range planning com. of C com., standards com. S.E. region 1990-93), Am. Assn. Adult and Continuing Edn., Beta Theta Pi. Democrat. Avocations: antique key collecting, canoeing, fishing, sailing. Home: 11 Westchester Sq Decatur GA 30030-2370 E-mail: rmorro2@emory.edu.

MORRIS, STEPHEN ALLEN, elementary school educator; b. Garden Grove, Calif., Mar. 2, 1957; s. Eddie Melvin and Lesta Joy (Birdsall) M.; m. MariLynn Edith; stepchildren: Tyler, Trevor. BS in Phys. Edn., Calif. State U., Fullerton, 1987. Cert. tchr., Calif. Elem. tchr. Riverside (Calif.) Unified Sch. Dist., 1990—. Lectr. Calif. Elem. Edn. Assn., Torrance, 1994—, The Edn. Ctr., Torrance, 1994—; cons. Inland Area Math. Project, Riverside, 1992—. Author: Everything You Wanted to Know About Division...In a Day!, 1993. Mem. Benjamin Franklin Elem. Sch. Site Coun., Riverside, 1992. Mem. ASCD, Nat. Coun. Tchrs. Math., Calif. Math. Coun. Baptist. Avocations: running, cycling, silkscreening. Home: 6823 Laurelbrook Dr Riverside CA 92506-6268 Office: Ben Franklin Elem Sch 19661 Orange Terrace Pky Riverside CA 92508-3256

MORRIS, SYLVIA MARIE, university official; b. Laurel, Miss., May 6, 1952; d. Earlene Virginia (Cameron) Hopkins Stewart; m. James D. Morris, Jan. 29, 1972; children: Cedric James, Taedra Janae. Student, U. Utah, 1970-71. From adminstrv. sec. to adminstrv. mgr. mech. engring. U. Utah, Salt Lake City, 1972—. Mem. Community Devel. Adv. Bd., Salt Lake City, Utah, 1984—; nom. chmn. and del. to Dem. Mass Meeting, 1988. Recipient Presdl. Staff award, 1994. Mem. NAACP, NAFE, Consortium Utah Women in Higher Edn. Baptist. Avocations: reading, travel, participant gospel music workshop. Home: 9696 Pine Brook Dr South Jordan UT 84095-2318 Office: U Utah 2202 MEB Mech Engr Dept Salt Lake City UT 84112

MORRIS, TAMA LYNN, nursing educator; b. Johnstown, Pa., June 24, 1960; m. Jeffrey J. Morris, June 2, 1984 BSN, Indiana U. Pa., 1982; MSN, Marquette U., 1989. RN, Wis., N.C. Staff nurse pediatrics Indiana (Pa.) Hosp.; staff nurse post partum, nursery St. Luke's Meml. Hosp., Racine, Wis., head nurse nursery, head nurse maternal-child. Lectr. U. Wis., Milw., U. N.C., Charlotte. Mem. AWHONN, Sigma Theta Tau. Home: 10225 Lampkin Way Charlotte NC 28269-8630

MORRISEY, MICHAEL A. health economics educator; b. Crookston, Minn., Mar. 20, 1952; s. Charles Arthur and Eleanor E. (LaFleur) M.; m. Elaine M. Mardian, Aug. 26, 1972; children: Michelle Ann, David Michael. BA, No. State U., Aberdeen, S.D., 1974; MA in Econs., U. Wash., 1975, PhD in Econs., 1979. Rsch. asst., specialist Battelle HARC, Seattle, 1976-79; sr. economist Am. Hosp. Assn., Chgo., 1979-85; sr. economist, asst. dir. Hosp. Rsch. & Ednl. Trust, Chgo., 1983-85; vis. scholar Northwestern U., Evanston, Ill., 1984-85; assoc. prof. U. Ala., Birmingham, 1985-88, prof., 1988—, disting. faculty investigator, 1999-2000; dir. Lister Hill Ctr. for Health Policy, Birmingham, 1990—. Dep. editor Med. Care, Cleve., 1987—96; mem. Pa. Mandates Benefits Rev. Panel, Harrisburg, 1987—, Ala. Task Force on Rural Health Care Crisis, 1989; mem. health svcs. devel. grants rev. com. Agy. for Health Care Rsch. and Quality, Rockville, Md., 1992—96; cons. in field. Author: Price Sensitivity in Health Care, 1992, Cost Shifting in Health Care, 1994, Managed Care and Changing Health Care Markets, 1998; mem. editl. bd. Health Svcs. Rsch., 1985-94, Health Affairs, 1998—, Jour. Gerontology, 1998-2001, Health Svcs. and Outcomes Rsch. Methodology, 1999—, Health Adminstrn. Press, 1999-2002, Med. Care Rsch. and Rev., 2000—; contbr. more than 115 articles to profl. jours. Recipient John D. Thompson prize in health svc. rsch., Assn. Univ. Programs in Health Adminstrn., 1991, UAB Pres. award for excellence in tchg., 2000—01; fellow, Employee Benefits Rsch. Inst.; grantee, Nat. Ctr. Health Svcs. Rsch., NIH, Agy. for Health Care Rsch. and Quality, Robert Wood Johnson Found.; Adj. scholar, Am. Enterprise Inst., 2002—. Mem.: Internat. Health Econs. Assn. (treas. 1994—2000, sec.-treas. 2000—), Acad. Health (chmn. com. 2000), Am. Econ. Assn. Republican. Roman Catholic. Office: UAB Sch Pub Health Birmingham AL 35294-0022 E-mail: morrisey@uab.edu.

MORRISON, BARBARA HANEY, educational administrator; b. Ft. Campbell, Ky., June 27, 1953; d. Charles L. and Rosemary (Blakeman) Haney; m. J.D. Morrison; 1 child, Carol Marie. BA, U. Ala., 1978; MS, Troy State U., 1985. Cert. profl. healthcare quality, healthcare quality and risk mgmt. cons. Dir. quality improvement and edn. Charter Med. Corp., Dothan, Ala., 1992-96, dir. edn., 1987-96, student assistance program dir.; classroom tchr. Ozark, Ala.; dir. Westgate Learning Ctr., Albany, Ga., 1993-96; chief ops. officer Pathway, Inc., Enterprise, Ala., 2002—. Mem. drug adv. bd. Houston County Schs. Mem. ASCD, NEA, Ala. Edn. Assn., Coun. for Children with Behaviour Disorders, Assn. for Healthcare Quality, Dothan-Houstan C. of C. (edn. com.), Alpha Delta Kappa.

MORRISON, CRAIG SOMERVILLE, physical education educator; b. Montreal, Que., Can., Sept. 14, 1946; came to U.S., 1982; s. Samuel and Olive Somerville (Cameron) M. BPE, U. N.B., 1970; MS, Springfield Coll., 1976; EdD, Brigham Young U., 1982. Tchr., high sch. Dept. Edn. Geelong, Victoria, Australia, 1971-72, Ea. Twps. Regional Sch. Bd., Que., Can., 1972-73, Gladstone, Queensland Dept. Edn., 1974; lectr. Charles Stuart U., 1974-79; grad. teaching asst. Brigham Young U., Provo, Utah, 1980-82; temporary asst. prof. U. Louisville, 1982-84; tchr., physical edn. Laurel Sch., Cleve., 1985-86; asst. prof. U. Tex., Div. Edn., San Antonio, 1987-89, Okla. State U., Stillwater, So. Utah U., chair dept. phys. edn., 2001—. Acting coord. phys. edn. U. Tex., 1988-89; lectr. Ballarat Coll. Advanced Edn., Ballarat Victoria, Australia, 1986-87, U. Wyo., Laramie, 1984-85, vis. lectr. U. Victoria, B.C., 1979-80; coord. sports medicine symposium Utah Summer Games, 1991-93. Mem. edit. rev. bd. The Physical Educator, 1992-95; (textbook) Qualities Analysis of Human Movement; contbr. articles to profl. jours. Mem. AAHPERD, Utah AHPERD, Nat. Assn. Phys. Edn. in Higher Edn., Triathlon Fedn. USA, Can. AHPERD, Tex. AHPERD, Phi Kappa Phi. Avocations: running, triathlon, duathlons, music, painting.

MORRISON, DONALD FRANKLIN, statistician, educator; b. Stoneham, Mass., Feb. 10, 1931; s. Daniel Norman and Agnes Beatrice (Packard) M.; m. Phyllis Ann Hazen, Aug. 19, 1967; children: Norman Hazen, Stephen Donald. BS in Bus. Adminstrn, Boston U., 1953, AM, 1954; MS, U. N.C., 1957; PhD, Va. Poly. Inst. and State U., 1960; MA (hon.), U. Pa., 1971. Mem. staff Lincoln Lab., M.I.T., 1956; cons. math. statistician NIMH, Bethesda, Md., 1956-63; mem. tech. staff Bell Labs., Holmdel, N.J., 1967; mem. faculty, dept. stats. Wharton Sch., U. Pa., 1963-99, prof. stats., 1973-99, chmn. dept., 1978-85, prof. emeritus, 2000—. Author: Multivariate Statistical Methods, 3d edit., 1990, Applied Linear Statistical Methods, 1983; editor: The American Statistician, 1972-75; assoc. editor: Biometrics, 1972-74; contbr. articles to profl. jours. Served with USPHS, 1956-58. NSF grantee, 1966 Fellow Am. Statis. Assn., Inst. Math. Stats.; mem. Internat. Statis. Inst., Royal Statis. Soc., B&M R.R. Hist. Soc., Nat. R.R. Hist. Soc., R.R. and Locomotive Hist. Soc., N&W Hist. Soc., Bridge Line Hist. Soc., N.E. Elec. Rwy. Hist. Soc. Democrat. Lutheran. Home: 118 E Brookhaven Rd Wallingford PA 19086-6327 E-mail: donaldm@wharton.upenn.edu.

MORRISON, FRED LAMONT, law educator; b. Salina, Kans., Dec. 12, 1939; s. Earl F. and Madge Louise (Glass) M.; m. Charlotte Foot, Dec. 27, 1971; children: Charles, Theodore, George, David. AB, U. Kans., 1961; BA, Oxford (Eng.) U., 1963, MA, 1968; PhD, Princeton U., 1966; JD, U. Chgo., 1967. Bar: Minn. 1973. Asst. prof. law U. Iowa, Iowa City, 1967-69; assoc. prof. law U. Minn., Mpls., 1969-73, prof. law, 1973-90, Oppenheimer Wolff and Donnelly prof., 1990-97, acting dean, 1994-95, Popham Haik/Lindquist & Vennum prof., 1998—; counselor on internat. law U.S. State Dept., Washington, 1982-83. Of counsel Popham, Haik, Schnobrich & Kaufman, Mpls., 1983-97. Mem. adv. com. on internat. law U.S. Dept. State, Washington, 1987-89; mem. internat. adv. bd. Inst. on Internat. Law, Kiel, Germany, 1989—. Home: 1412 W 47th St Minneapolis MN 55409-2204 Office: U Minn Law Sch 229 19th Ave S Minneapolis MN 55455-0400

MORRISON, GREGG SCOTT, theology educator, college administrator; b. Rome, Ga., Mar. 9, 1964; s. Glen Warren and Joyce (Lannom) M.; m. Laura Edge, Jan. 21, 1995. BS in Acctg., U. Ala., 1986; MDiv, Samford U., 1996; postgrad., Emory U., 1998-2000, Catholic U. Tax assoc. Coopers & Lybrand, Atlanta, 1986, tax specialist, 1987-88, tax supr. Birmingham, Ala., 1988-89, sr. tax assoc., 1990-91, tax mgr., 1991-93; min. outreach Shades

Mountain Bapt. Ch., 1993-96; dir. external rels. Beeson Div. Sch., Samford U., Birmingham, Ala., 1996—2001; interim pastor New Prospect Bapt. Ch., Jasper, Ala., 1998, Bluff Park Bapt. Ch., Birmingham, 1999. Adj. faculty Beeson Divinity Sch., Bethel Sem. of the East, John Leland Ctr. for Theol. Studies. Active United Way Ctrl. Ala., Inc., Birmingham, 1989; pres. student govt. assn. Beeson Div. Sch. of Samford U., 1995-96; bd. dirs. Ctr. for Urban Missions, Inc., Birmingham, chmn. fin. com., 1991-94, 96-2001; bd. dirs. Univ. Cmty. Coop., Inc., Tuscaloosa; sec.-treas., pres. ACCESS; treas. Martin Luther King Unity Breakfast Planning Com.; southside campaign capt. Boy Scouts Am.; mem. planned giving adv. group Bapt. Hosp. Found., Inc.; deacon Shades Mt. Bapt. Ch., 1992-94, 96-99, mem. strategic planning com. chmn. Innercity Ministry Partnership Task Force, 1996-2001; adv. bd. Baptist Ctr. Leadership Devel; mem. long range planning com. City of Vestavia Hills, Ala. Named one of Outstanding Young Men Am., 1996. Mem. Soc. Bibl. Lit., Evang. Theol. Soc., Inst. Bibl. Rsch., Tyndale Fellowship Biblical Theol. Rsch., Birmingham Hist. Soc. (planning com. 1990-91), PGA (fin. com.), Cath. Bibl. Assn., Vestavia Country Club, Theta Chi (treas. Alpha Phi house corp. 1992-94). Republican. Baptist. Avocations: golf, tennis, reading, politics. Home: 3004 Panorama Trl Birmingham AL 35216

MORRISON, HARRIET BARBARA, retired education educator; b. Boston, Feb. 23, 1934; d. Harry and Harriet (Hanrahan) M. BS, Mass. State Coll., 1956, MEd, 1958; EdD, Boston U., 1967. Elem. tchr. Arlington (Mass.) Pub. Schs., 1956-67; instr. U. Mass., 1967; asst. prof. edn. No. Ill. U., Dekalb, 1967-71, assoc. prof., 1971-85, prof., 1985-97; ret., 1997. Author: The Seven Gifts, 1988; editor Vitae Scholasticae. Mem. ASCD, Am. Ednl. Studies Assn., Philosophy of Edn. Soc., Midwest Philosophy Edn. Soc., Ill. ASCD, Pi Lambda Theta. Home: 834 S 8th St Dekalb IL 60115-4551

MORRISON, HELENA GRACE, guidance counselor; b. Neillsville, Wis., Aug. 20, 1957; d. Harold Allen and Nettie Stella (Schafer) Freedlund; m. William James Morrison, Sept. 11, 1981; 1 child, Meghan Marie. BS, U. Wis., Stevens Point, 1980; MEd, Nat. Louis U., Evanston, Ill., 1990; cert., Western Ky. U., 1994, postgrad. Cert. guidance counselor; cert. tchr. Tchr. grades 2 through 3 Pittsville (Wis.) Elem. Sch., 1980-82; tchr. grade 2 Vernon Parish Schs., Leesville, La., 1987-88; tchr. grade 3 Dept. Def. Dependant Schs., Vogelweh, Germany, 1989-92; student svcs. specialist, tchr. gifted edn. LaRue County Schs., Hodgenville, Ky., 1993—, gifted coord., 1995—. Leader grade 3 team Vogelweh Elem. Sch., 1990-92; editor Hodgenville Elem. Sch. Yearbook, editor HES News, 1993—. Statistician Kaiserslantern Softball, Vogelweh, 1991; coach girls softball LaRue County Softball, Hodgenville, 1994. Mem. ASCD, Nat. Geog. Soc., Ky. Assn. for Gifted Edn., Ky. Counseling Assn. Avocations: softball, bicycling, sewing, reading. Home: 3220 Dangerfield Rd Hodgenville KY 42748-9223 Office: Hodgenville Elem Sch 208 College St Hodgenville KY 42748-1400

MORRISON, JOHN HORTON, lawyer; b. Sept. 15, 1933; BBA, U. N.Mex., 1955; BA, U. Oxford, 1957; JD, Harvard U., 1962. Bar: Ill. 1962, U.S. Supreme Ct. 1966. Assoc. Kirkland & Ellis, Chgo., 1962-67, ptnr., 1968-99. Named Hon. Officer Most Excellent Order Brit. Empire, 1994; Rhodes scholar. Mem. ABA, Internat. Arbitration (arbitrator, mediator London Ct.), Internat. Bar Assn., Assn. Am. Rhodes Scholars (pres. 1998—), Chgo. Internat. Dispute Resolution Assn. (dir.). Home: 2717 Lincoln St Evanston IL 60201-2042 Business E-Mail: jmorrison@kirkland.com. E-mail: jhmobe@aol.com.

MORRISON, K. JAYDENE, education counseling firm executive; b. Cherokee, Okla., Aug. 22, 1933; d. Jay Frank and Kathryn D. (Johnson) Walker; m. Michael H. Morrison, July 11, 1955 (dec. 1991); children: Jay, Mac. BS, Okla. State U., 1955, MS, 1957; postgrad., U. Colo., 1965, Ctrl. State U., Okla., 1967—70, postgrad., 1984, U. Denver, 1981—82. Lic. coun. Okla., marriage and family therapist, cert. sch. psychologist, counselor. Psychologist Cushing Pub. Schs., Okla., 1955—57, Indpls. Pub. Schs., 1958—59; counselor, tchr. spl. edn. Helena-Goltry Pub. Schs., Okla., 1965—73; psychometrist Okla. State Title III Program, Alva; sch. psychologist Okla. State Dept. Edn., Enid, 1977—85; pres., dir. Ventures in Learning, Inc., Helena, 1984—. Career counselor, Oklahoma City, 1985—86; rural specialist Okla. Conf. Chs. AG LINK, 1986—88; v.p., sec./treas. Okla. Made, Inc., Oklahoma City, 1988—89; sch. psychologist Okla. City Pub. Schs., 1988—93; therapist and pub. sch. liason Chisholm Trail Counseling Svc., 1993—95; coord. Statewide Farm Stress Program, 1994—95; therapist Greenleaf Drug/Alcohol Rehab., 1988—89; sec., treas. Okla. Pure; part-time counselor Clayton Clinic, 1987—89; cons. Okla. Family Inst., 1990—93; with Dept. Edn. Behavior Mgmt. Ctrl. Dist., Hawaii, 1995—. Author: Coping with ADD/ADHD, 1995; co-author: Coping With a Learning Disability, 1992. Chmn. Alfalfa County Excise and Equalization Bd., Cherokee, 1979—83; asst. state coord. Okla. Am. Agr. Movement, Oklahoma City, 1982—83; co-chmn. Alfalfa County Dem. Party, Cherokee, 1976—83; sec.-treas. 6th Dist. Okla. Dem. State Exec. Bd., 1983—87; counselor United Meth. Counseling Ctr., 1987—88; mem. Elder Christian Ch. Named Citizen of Yr., Okla. chpt. Nat. Assn. Social Workers, 1988; recipient Tchr. of Yr. award, Helena Masonic Lodge, 1967, Spl. award, Okla. Women for Agr., 1979. Mem.: Okla. Assn. Learning Disabilities, Garfield County Interagy. Task Force, Okla. Sch. Psychologists Assn., Nat. Assn. Sch. Psychologists, Okla. Soc. Advancement Biofeedback, Biofeedback Soc. Am., Chi Omega Alumni, Delta Kappa Gamma. Office: PO Box 917 Nederland CO 80466-0917 Business E-Mail: JaydeneMor@aol.com.

MORRISON, MARGARET L. artist, educator, consultant; b. Atlanta, Oct. 06; d. Watson Russell Sr and Eva D. Morrison. BS in Edn., U. Ga., 1970. Cert. tchr., Ga. Supr. KPMG, Atlanta, 1971-97; art tchr. Decatur (Ga.) City Schs., Decatur, Ga., 1997-99; pvt. instr. in art and edn., 2000—. Pvt. practice cons. interior design, 1998—; consumer bd. AC Nielsen. Exhbns. include Coastal Ctr. for the Arts, St. Simons Island, Ga., Gallery One, St. Simons Island, Decatur Arts Alliance, Acad. Midi, Paris, The Glynn County Art Assn., Jekyll Island, Ga., L'Orangerie Mus., Paris. Royal patron Hutt River Province, Queensland, Australia, 1995; active High Mus. Art, Atlanta, 1989—; bd. govs. Internat. Biog. Ctr.; adv. bd. Am. Biog. Inst.; mem. consumer panel AC Nielsen. Fellow Acad. Midi (hon.); mem. DAR, NAFE, AAUW, Internat. Platform Assn., Nat. Mus. Women in Arts, Allied Artists of Ga., Pen and Ink, U. Ga. Alumni Soc., AC Nielsen Comsumer Bd. mem., Internat. Biographical Ctr., Bd. of Adv. Home and Office: PO Box 2590 Decatur GA 30031-2590

MORRISON, NANCY JANE, art educator; b. Hannibal, Mo., Oct. 29, 1953; d. Wiley Russell Morrison and Marguerite Grace Taylor; m. Stephen Mark Graboski. BFA, U. Kans., Lawrence, 1976; MFA, Md. Inst. Coll. Art, Balt., 1990. Art instr. Dundalk (Md.) C.C., 1990—91, Anne Arundel County Continuing Edn., Anne Arundel, Md., 1991; vis. artist St. Paul Sch. for Girls, Balt., 1991; art instr. Essex (Md.) C.C., 1991—94, Longview C.C., Lee's Summit, Mo., 1995—, Notre Dame de Sion, Kansas City, Mo., 1995—. Mem. Lee's Summit Arts Coun., 2002, 03; grad. student rep., Gallery Com. Md. Inst. Coll. Art, 1989—90; fine arts chair Student Union Activities Bd., Lawrence, 1974—75; grad. studies asst. to Dir. Mt. Royal Sch. Painting Maryland Inst. Coll. Art, 1989—90. Sitting In, 1973, exhibitions include Kans. Art Commn., Fox Gallery, MICA, Dundalk Gallery, New Eng. Fine Art Inst., Mulvane Art Mus., Spivia Art Ctr., Nelson-Atkins Mus. Art, Chatauqua Gallery Art, Bauhouse Gallery, Mus.. Contemporary Arts, Balt. Mem.: Mo. Art Edn. Assn.., Nat. Art Edn. Assn., Lee's Summit Garden Club (treas. 2002—). Avocations: drawing, painting, gardening, genealogy.

MORRISON, RAY LEON, library administrator, graduate education educator; b. Boise, Idaho, Sept. 17, 1952; s. Duane Alton and Wilma Lucille (Bybee) M.; m. Barbara Ann Derrenbacher, Apr. 2, 1977; children: Eric, Shawn. BJ, San Jose State U., 1974, MA in Library Sci., 1975; CAS in Library Sci., U. Ill., 1984; EdD, U. Ark., 1992. Reference librarian Olivet Nazarene Coll., Kankakee, Ill., 1975-80; Bibl. Inst. librarian Pittsburg (Kans.) State U., 1980-85; library dir. Mid-Am. Nazarene U., Olathe, Kans., 1986—. Adj. prof. edn. Mid Am. Nazarene U. Author: Library Skills Workbook, 1981, 2d rev. edit., 1983; contbr. articles to profl. jours., book revs. to pubs. Pres. bd. dirs. Olathe Libr.; dist. commr. Boy Scouts Am. Mem. ALA, Kans. Libr. Assn., Christian Librarians Fellowship, Nazarene Librarians Fellowship, Kans. Libr. Network Bd., Kansas City Met. Libr. Network. Republican. Mem. Ch. of Nazarene. Avocations: cross country skiing, NASCAR, olympic games, track and field, reading. Home: 1904 S Parkwood Dr Olathe KS 66062-2806 Office: Mid-Am Nazarene U PO Box 1776 Olathe KS 66051-1776

MORRISON, SAMUEL FERRIS, secondary school educator; b. Glasgow, Scotland, Oct. 7, 1941; came to U.S., 1949; s. Thomas Green and Susan (McCaskill) M.; m. Kathryn Emily Schnaible, Aug. 14, 1971; 1 child, Ian James. BA, U. Wyo., 1968, MEd, 1985. Tchr. social studies Platte County Sch. Dist. 1, Wheatland, Wyo., from 1968, athletic dir., from 1987. With U.S. Army, 1963-65. Mem. NEA, Wyo. Edn. Assn., Platte County Edn. Assn. (pres. 1972-73). Democrat. Presbyterian. Avocations: golf, woodworking, photography. Home: Wheatland, Wyo. Died Apr. 11, 2002.

MORRISON, SARAH LYDDON, author; b. Rochester, N.Y., May 19, 1939; d. Paul William and Winifred (Cowles) Lyddon. BA, U. Vt., 1961. Sec. asst. Glamour mag., N.Y.C., 1961-63, Vogue mag., N.Y.C., 1963-65; asst. editor Venture mag., N.Y.C., 1966-71; dir. pub. rels. for tourism Commonwealth of P.R., N.Y.C., 1971-75; asst. Am. Legion, Washington, 1988-98; owner Sarah Lyddon Morrison Pub. Rels., Washington, 1999—. Author: The Modern Witch's Spellbook, 1971, Book II, 1983, The Modern Witch's Dream Book, 1985, The Modern Witch's Book of Home Remedies, 1988, The Modern Witch's Book of Healing, 1991, The Modern Witch's Book of Symbols, 1997, Modern Witch's Guide to Magic and Spells, 1998. Mem. Washington Club, DAR (dir. pub. rels. Emily Nelson chpt. 1999, 2000), Colonial Dames XVII. Avocations: travel, reading, swimming, rock music, cooking. E-mail: sarahlyd@aol.com.

MORRISON, SHIRLEY MARIE, nursing educator; b. Stuttgart, Ark., June 13, 1927; d. Jack Vade Wimberly and Mabel Claire (Dennison) George; m. Dana Jennings, Mar. 12, 1951 (dec. Dec. 1995); children: Stephen Leslie, Dana Randall, William Lee, Martha Ann Morrison Comardo. Diploma, Bapt. Hosp. Sch. Nursing, Nashville, 1949; BSN, Calif. U., Fullerton, 1977; MSN, Calif. U., L.A., 1980; EdD, Nova Southeastern U., 1987. RN, Tex., Calif.; cert. pub. health nurse, Calif.; cert. secondary tchr., Calif. Staff nurse perinatal svcs. Martin Luther Hosp., Anaheim, Calif., 1960-77, relief 11-7 house supr., 1960-77; dir. vocat. nursing program Inst. Med. Studies, 1978-81; mem. faculty BSN program Abilene (Tex.) Intercollegiate Sch. Nursing, 1981-92, dir. ADN program, 1992-97; nursing educator Cisco Jr. Coll., Abilene, Tex., 1997—. Mem. profl. adv. bd. Nurse Care, Inc., Abilene, 1988-2003. Mem. adv. bd. parent edn. program Abilene Ind. Sch. Dist., 1985—; active Mar. Dimes, Abilene, 1990—, Ednl. Coalition for Bob Hunter, Abilene, 1994; bd. dirs. Hospice Big Country, Abilene, 1987—, The House That Kerry Built, 2000—. Grantee NIH, 1992; recipient Nat. Humor Project award Jour. Nursing Jocularity, 1996. Mem. Nat. Orgn. Assn. Degree Nurses (mem. program com. 10th anniversary nat. conv.), Tex. Orgn. Assoc. Degree Nurses, So. Nursing Rsch. Soc. (rsch. presenter), Health Edn. Resource Network Abilene (founding mem., pres. elect, pres. 1995-96), Sigma Theta Tau (bd. dirs. Internat. Omicron Zeta chpt. 1999—). Democrat. Methodist. Avocations: traveling, reading. Home: PO Box 2583 Abilene TX 79604-2583 Office: Cisco Jr Coll Dept Nursing PO Box 2583 Abilene TX 79604-2583 E-mail: shirleyfromtx@webtv.net.

MORRISON, WILLIAM FOSDICK, business educator, retired electrical company executive; b. Bridgeport, Conn., Mar. 14, 1935; s. Robert Louis and Helen Fosdick (Mulroney) M.; m. E. Drake Miller, Dec. 14, 1957 (div. Sept. 1972); children: Donna Drake, Deanne Fosdick, William Fosdick; m. Carol Ann Stover, Nov. 20, 1972. BA in Econs., Trinity Coll., 1957. Mgr. purchasing dept. Westinghouse Electric Co., Lima, Ohio, 1960-68, mgr. mfg. Upper Sandusky, Ohio, 1969, gen. mgr. Gurabo, P.R., 1970-71, mgr. tng. Pitts., 1972-84, program mgr. Sunnyvale, Calif., 1984-89, procurement project dir., 1990-94; prof. San Jose State U., Calif., 1993—, Golden Gate U., San Francisco, 1995—; lead negotiator Advanced Micro Devices, Santa Clara, Calif., 1995-97; prof. U. Calif., Berkeley, 1996—2002, Menlo Coll., 1998-2001. Negotiation cons. and trainer, 1969—; lead negotiator ReSound Corp., 1998-99; mgr. renovation project San Jose State U., 1999-2000. Author: The Pre-Negotiation Planning Book, 1985, The Human Side of Negotiations, 1994; contbr. articles to profl. jours. Bd. dirs. Valley Inst. of the Theatre Arts, Saratoga, Calif., 1986-90, Manhattan Playhouse, 1989-94; chmn. Sensory Access Found. Golf Tournament, 1995-96. Served to capt. USAFR, 1958-64; mem. protocol office World Cup USA, 1994. Named Man of the Yr. Midwest Lacrosse Coaches Assn., 1983, recipient Service award U.S. Lacrosse Assn., 1982. Mem. Nat. Assn. Purchasing Mgmt. (pres. Lima chpt. 1966-67, dir. nat. affairs 1967-68, dist. treas. 1968-70). Clubs: Sunnyvale Golf Assn. (vice-chmn. 1985, chmn. 1986, 93, handicap scorer 1992-93). Lodges: Elks. Avocation: golf. Home: 3902 Duncan Pl Palo Alto CA 94306-4550 Office: San Jose State U Coll of Bus 1 Washington Sq San Jose CA 95112-3613 E-mail: wfmorrison@earthlink.net.

MORROW, BRUCE WILLIAM, educational administrator, business executive, consultant, author; b. Rochester, Minn., May 20, 1946; s. J. Robert and Frances P. Morrow; m. Jenny Lea Morrow. BA, U. Notre Dame, 1968, MBA in Mgmt. with honors, 1974, MA in Comparative Lit., 1975; grad., U.S. Army Command and Gen. Staff Coll., 1979. Cert. project mgmt. profl. Project Mgmt. Inst., 2003. Chmn. elem. German U. Notre Dame, 1973-75; co-mgr. Wendy's Old Fashioned Hamburgers, South Bend, Ind., 1976-77; adminstrn. mgr. Eastern States Devel. Corp., Richmond, Va., 1977; v.p. JDB Assocs., Inc., Alexandria, Va., 1976-78; sr. cons. Data Base Mgmt., Inc., Springfield, Va., 1979-80; owner Aardvark Prodns., Alexandria, 1980-82; sys. analyst/staff officer Hdqrs., Dept. Army, Washington, 1980-84; chmn. bd. Commonwealth Dominion Corp., Sierra Vista, Ariz., 1982—. Strategic planner, dep. comdr. Fort Pickett, Blackstone, Va., 1986—89; dir. continuing edn. Southside Va. C.C., Alberta, 1989—91; co-founder S.W. Bus. Group, Tucson, 1995—99; pres. Sierra Vista Golf, Inc., Ariz., 1994—95; Cochise County team leader Ariz. Coun. Econ. Conversion, 1994—95; mem. com. Ariz. Small Bus. Initiative, 1994—99; internet webmaster, 1996—; exec. dir. Southea. Ariz. Contrs. Assn., 1997—98; corp. adminstr. Garcia Cos., Sierra Vista, Tucson, Phoenix, 1997—99; property adminstr. Brown & Root Svcs., Ft. Huachuca, Ariz., Land Between the Lakes, Ky., 1999—2000, logistics coord., 2001—02; dir. assessment ctr. TSA project NCS Pearson, Nashville, 2002—, Fresno, Calif., 2002—. Author (radio series) Survival in the Computer Jungle, 1986, (classroom text) Introduction to Computers, 1988, 2d edit., 1993, Defense Conversion Handbook, 1995, business Assessment Manual, 1996, Employee Manual Guide, 1996, Business Plan Guide, 1996, Marketing Plan Guide, 1996, (screenplay) Gray Rock, 2000; contbg. columnist Notre Dame mag., 1974-86; exec. prodr. (motion picture) Beneath the Law, 1995-96; composer songs. Active Boy Scouts Am., 1960-69; firefighter Roanoke Wildwood Vol. Fire Dept., 1991-93. Lt. col. USAR, ret. Decorated Bronze Star, Army commendation medals, Army Achievement medal, Meritorious Svc. medals, Parachutist's badge, Army Gen. Staff badge. Mem. VFW (life), Nat. Eagle Scout Assn., Lake Gaston C. of C. (bd. dirs.), Am. Legion, Sierra Vista Area C. of C., Lions (v.p. local club), Friends Internat. (Am. v.p. 1969-71, Boeblingen, Germany), Order of DeMolay, Beta Gamma Sigma, Delta Phi Alpha. Office: Commonwealth Dominion Corp 334 Landing Strip Rd Hardin KY 42048-9413 E-mail: cdc@theriver.com.

MORROW, DAVID ANDREW, secondary education educator; b. Van Buren, Maine, Dec. 5, 1950; s. Laurence and Anne Marie (Lavoie) M; m. Robertine Thibodeau, June 20, 1975. BS magna cum laude, U. So. Maine, 1981; student, U. Maine. Indsl. arts/tech. and vocat. tchr. Van Buren (Maine) Community High/Mid. Sch., 1971-87; tech. edn. tchr. Ashland (Maine) Community High/Mid. Sch., 1987—. With USN, 1969-71. Recipient Tchr. Excellence award Internat. Tech. Edn. Assn., Maine, 1992. Mem. NEA, Internat. Tech. Edn. Assn. (Tchr. Excellence award 1993), Tech. Edn. Assn. Maine (Tech. Tchr. of Yr. 1993), Maine Tchrs. Assn., Ashland Tchrs. Edn. Assn., Assn. Supervision and Curriculum Devel., Aroostook Tech. Edn. Assn. Maine. Roman Catholic. Avocations: photography, computers, canoeing, skiing, playing guitar. Home: 9 Skyview Dr Presque Isle ME 04769-2460 Office: Ashland Comty High Sch Hayward St Ashland ME 04732

MORROW, DENNIS ROBERT, school system administrator, consultant; b. Viroqua, Wis., July 9, 1951; s. Clayton Stuart and W. Elaine (Kegley) M.; m. Patricia Lee Bergren, Aug. 4, 1973; children: Sarah Elizabeth, Gretchen Elaine, David Robert. BA, U. Minn., 1975, PhD, 1984; MA, Coll. St. Thomas, 1976. Tchr., dean Blaine Sr. High Sch., Mpls., 1975-78; asst. prin. Mounds View Pub. Schs., St. Paul, 1978-81; prin. Batavia (N.Y.) High Sch., 1981-83, Bklyn. Ctr. High Sch., Mpls., 1983-88, Hong Kong Internat. Sch., Tai Tam, 1988-90, Roseville Area Schs., St. Paul, 1990-91; asst. supt. Bklyn. Ctr. Schs., 1991-93, supt., 1993—. Accreditation team leader North Cen. Assn. Schs. and Colls., Minn., 1986-88; forum lectr. Restructuring Edn., 1988-94. Contbr. articles to profl. jours. Bd. dirs. Hong Kong Community Drug Adv. Coun., 1988-90, North Hennepin Leadership Acad., 1992—, Leadership Mpls., 1987-88, Voyageur Outward Bound Sch., 1992—. LBJ fellow U.S. Ho. of Reps., 1977. Mem. Rotary Internat., Univ. Minn. Alumni Club. Republican. Avocations: mountaineering, sailing. Office: Bklyn Ctr Schs 6500 Humboldt Ave N Minneapolis MN 55430-1800

MORROW, LESLEY MANDEL, literacy and elementary education educator; BS, Syracuse U.; MA, N.J. City U.; PhD, Fordham U. Cert. early childhood tchr., elem. tchr., reading specialist K-12, supr., prin. Tchr. Bradford Elem. Sch., Montclair, NJ, 1964—68; demonstration tchr. Lab. Elem. Sch. William Paterson U., NJ, 1968—70; instr. edn. dept. Chapman Coll., Orange, Calif., 1970—71; instr. learning and tchg. dept. St. John's U., NY, 1971—74; instr. comm. scis. dept. and early childhood dept. Kean U., NJ, 1974—79; asst. prof. edn. dept. Douglas Coll. Rutgers U., New Brunswick, NJ, 1979—85, assoc. prof. Grad. Sch. Edn., 1986—91, chair dept. learning and tchg., 1991—93, 2000—02, prof. literacy and early childhood/elem. edn. Grad. Sch. Edn., 1991—. Coadjutant faculty N.J. City U., 1974—76, Fordham U., 1974—76, William Paterson U., 1974—76; cons. in field; author Scott Foresman Basal Reading Series, 1991—97; mem. adv. bd. Sesame Street PBS Children's TV Workshop, 1993—98; sr. author William H. Sadlier Reading Programs, 1998—; mem. adv. bd. Reading Rainbow PBS Program, 2002—. Recipient Disting. Achievement for Excellence in Ednl. Journalism award, Ednl. Press Assn. Am., 1989, Literacy award, N.J. Reading Assn., 1996, Spl. Svc. award, 2000, grants and scholarships in field. Fellow: Nat. Conf. on Rsch. in English; mem.: Nat. Assessment Ednl. Progress (adv. bd. 1992, 1994), Internat. Reading Assn. (pres. 2003—, Outstanding Tchr. Educator of Reading award 1995). Office: Rutgers The State U NJ Grad Sch Edn Rm 206A 10 Seminary Pl New Brunswick NJ 08901-1183*

MORROW, NANA KWASI SCOTT DOUGLAS, choreographer, writer, filmmaker, educator; b. NYC, Jan. 29, 1954; s. Alfred Lionel and Lorraine (Lopez) Morro. BFA in Dance, SUNY, Purchase, 1976; MA in Choreography, UCLA, 1986. Prin. instr. Phil Black Dance Studio, N.Y.C., 1969-77; dir. dance divsn. No. Ill. U., DeKalb, 1976-78; artistic dir., resident choreographer No. Ill. Repertory Dance Co., 1976-78; artistic dir. Scott Morrow Dance Theatre Co. and Sch., L.A., 1978-85; prin. instr. Mary Tyler Moore Los Angeles Dance Ctr., 1979-80; resident dance master South Coast Repertory Acting Conservatory, Calif., 1979-82; vis. prof. Wright State U., Ohio, 1981; ballet master, resident choreographer Empire State Ballet, Buffalo, 1984-85; asst. prof. U. Kans., Lawrence, 1985-88. Choreographer Morrow Dance Theatre-in-Residence, U. Kans., 1985-88, 92d St. Dancer Ctr., YMHA and YWHA, NYC, 1989; founder, dir. Jazz Dance Ministry for Racial Reconciliation, Peace and Healing, N.Y.C., 1988—; assoc. dir., dir. edn. pub. sch. dance programs K-12, Bronx Dance Theatre Performing Arts Ctr., NYC, 1990-93; faculty Internat. Summer Sch. Royal Acad. Dancing, NYC, 1991-92, Calif. State U. Sys. Summer Inst. for Tchg. and Learning, 1994; sr. faculty Lilly Conf. on Coll. Tchg., Miami U., Ohio, 1991—; dance specialist State Edn. Dept. Summer Inst. on Assessment in Arts, NY, 1992; founder, dir. in chief Inst. Advancement Edn. Dance, NYC, 1992-02; adv. bd. Internat. Found. for Performing Arts Medicine, 1992—; adv. Performing Arts Medicine Ctr., Kessler Inst. Rehab., NJ, 1995—; Walter H. Annenberg disting. vis. artist-scholar The Renaissance Sch., NYC, 1995-96; cons. presenting and commissioning program Nat. Endowment for Arts, 1993-95; peer rev. panel Fund for Innovation in Edn. US. Edn. Dept., 1993-94; co-chmn. dance edn. com. World Dance Allliance: Americas Ctr., 1993-97; internat. artistic advisor Noyam Exptl. Dance Co. and Rsch. Project, Ghana, 1998—; founder, min. in chief Embassy of Sekyere Kwamang Traditional Area, Asante Nation, Ghana, 1998—; internat. adv. bd. Ctr. for Nat. Culture, Kumasi, Astante Nation, Ghana, 2001—. Choreographer: (mus. theater) Broadway Musical Classics on International Tour, (musical stage rev) Bebop Hot, (film musicals) Chestnuts, Rainbows Edn., (documentary film) Broadway Babies, (teleseries) Adventures of Hans Christen Andersen, (telespecial) Rapsodia Afrikiko: A Celebration in Dance, (indsl. show) Le Parfum Salvador Dali, (nightclub) The African Room, N.Y.C.; choreographer, asst. Broadway musical Safari 300: A Musical Experience of 300 Years of Black Culture, Song & Dance; film dir., editor Of One Blood: Returning Home to Africa, 1999 (Best Documentary Film award Black Internat. Cinema Festival); co-author, dir., choreographer, co-star (nat. stage prodn.) Realizing the Dream! One Community at a Time; world premieres presented at festivals including Morningside Dance Festival, NYC, Mid Am. Dance Festival, L.A. Dance Kaleidoscope Festival, Middfest Internat., Ohio, Smithsonian Instn's Duke Ellington Festival, Washington, Marche Internat. de Disque et de l'Edition Musicale, Cannes, France, Anokyekrome Festival, Kumasi, Asante Nation, Ghana, Royal Performance King Nana Barimah Abeyie Ntori Nimpah II, Sekyere Kwamang, Asante Nation, Ghana, Black Internat. Cinema Festival, Berlin; creator over 40 ballets; contbr. to profl. publs. Nat. Festival for the Performing Arts Choreographers fellow, 1989; Josephine & Randolph Stewart African Heritage Fund Edn. and Rsch. grantee, 1997; named Master Educator and Disting. Fellow, Am. Bd. Master Educators, 1987; Alvin Ailey scholar, Sch. Am. Ballet scholar, Harkness House for Ballet Arts scholar; recipient Grand Prize for Choreography, Ann. Internat. Artistic Impression Competition, 1991, citation U.S. Edn. Dept., 1993, contbns. to growth and advancement of performing arts award, U.S. Arts Coun. Co-op, 1993, instrnl. approach recognized as an ednl. innovation Internat. Bur. Edn., UNESCO, 1996; named Traditional Chief and Spl. Advisor in Edn. and Human Devel. to King, Sekyere Kwamang, Asante Nation, Ghana, 1997, Pan-African and Humanitarian Vision award African Profiles USA mag., 2001. Office: Embassy Sekyere Kwamang Trad Area Asante Nation Rep Ghana 84-12 35th Ave Ste 3H Jackson Heights NY 11372 E-mail: nanasmorrow@hotmail.com.

MORROW, WALTER EDWIN, JR., electrical engineer, university laboratory administrator; b. Springfield, Mass., July 24, 1928; s. Walter Edwin and Mary Elizabeth (Ganley) M.; m. Janice Lila Lombard, Feb. 25, 1951; children: Clifford E., Gregory A., Carolyn F. S.B., M.I.T., 1949, S.M., 1951. Mem. staff Lincoln Lab., MIT, Lexington, Mass., 1951-55, group leader, 1956-65; head div. communications MIT Lincoln Lab., 1966-68, asst. dir., 1968-71, asso. dir., 1972-77, dir., 1977-98, dir. emeritus, 1998—. Contbr.

articles to profl. publs. Recipient award for outstanding achievement Pres. M.I.T., 1963, Edwin Howard Armstrong Achievement award IEEE Communications Soc., 1976 Fellow IEEE, Nat. Acad. Engring. Achievements include patent for synchronous satellite, electric power plant using electrolytic cell-fuel cell combination. Office: MIT Lincoln Lab PO Box 73 Lexington MA 02420-9108

MORROW, WINIFRED BRYANT, artist, educator; b. Duluth, Ga., Oct. 27, 1946; d. Frank Winfred and Lucy Virginia (Dillard) Bryant; m. James David Williams, July 24, 1966 (div. Dec. 1974); m. Richard Lewis Morrow, Aug. 10, 1991; 1 stepchild, Charles Richard. Student, Young Harris (Ga.) Coll., 1964-65; BFA, U. Ga., 1969, postgrad., 1977, 78; MEd, West Ga. Coll., Carrollton, 1976; edn. specialist degree, Berry Coll., 1999. Cert. tchr., Ga. Tchr. art Haralson County Bd. Edn., Buchanan, Ga., 1969-72; tchr. art, sci. and phys. edn. Floyd County Bd. Edn., Cave Spring, Ga., 1972-78, tchr. art Coosa, Ga., 1978-84, Lindale, Ga., 1984-89, Bartow County Bd. Edn., Cartersville, Ga., 1989-99; ret. Co-founder, trustee Alton Holman Heritage Arts, Inc., Cave Spring, 2000-, trustee, 2002; arts festival juror Cave Spring (Ga.) Hist. Soc., 1976-97, arts festival coord., 1987, 88, arts festival judges coord., 1985—. Watercolor artist. Trustee Cave Spring United Meth. Ch., 1993—, pianist, 1975-97, choir mem., 1997—; chair investigating com. State Sch. for the Arts, Cave Spring, 1987. Mem. NEA, Nat. Art Edn. Assn., Ga. Assn. Educators, Ga. Art Edn. Assn. (award of excellence 1986), Rome Area Coun. for the Arts, Cave Spring Hist. Soc. (bd. dirs. 1975-96, 2002—, chmn. 1975-85). Avocations: copper enameling, piano, poetry, dulcimer. Home: 7385 Rome Rd Cave Spring GA 30124 Office: Alton Holman Heritage Arts Inc 3 Georgia Ave PO Box 390 Cave Spring GA 30124

MORSE, JEAN AVNET, higher education administrator, lawyer; b. NYC, Jan. 2, 1947; d. Samuel and Helen Avnet; m. Stephen John Morse, Dec. 26, 1966; 1 child, Elisabeth Avnet Morse. BA in History with high honors, Wellesley Coll., 1968; JD cum laude, Harvard U., 1971. Bar: Mass. 1971, Calif. 1974. Law clk. Superior Ct. Commonwealth of Mass., Boston, 1971-72; atty. Palmer & Dodge, Boston, 1972-74; assoc. to ptnr. Kaplan, Livingston, Goodwin, Berkowitz & Selvin, Beverly Hills, Calif., 1974-81; ptnr. Hufstedler & Kaus, LA, 1981-87, of counsel, 1988; dep. assoc. dean, dir. coll. office, Sch. Arts and Sci. U. Pa., Phila., 1989-93; lectr. sociology, U. Pa. Sch. Arts and Sci., Phila., 1991; acting asst. provost U. Pa., Phila., 1991-92, dean's acad. planning cons., 1992-93; assoc. dean for admin. NYU Sch. Law, NYC, 1993—94; dep. to pres. U. Pa., 1994-95; exec. dir. Commn. on Higher Edn. Mid. States Assn. of Coll. and Sch., Phila., 1996—. Bd. dir. Women in Bus., 1985-88, The Women's Bldg., 1985-86; chair individual rights sect. LA County Bar Assn., 1985-86.

MORSE, KAREN WILLIAMS, academic administrator; b. Monroe, Mich., May 8, 1940; m. Joseph G. Morse; children: Robert G., Geoffrey E. BS, Denison U., 1962; MS, U. Mich., 1964, PhD, 1967; DSc (hon.), Denison U., 1990. Rsch. chemist Ballistic Rsch. Lab., Aberdeen Proving Ground, Md., 1966-68; lectr. chemistry dept. Utah State U., Logan, 1968-69, from asst. to assoc. prof. chemistry, 1969-83, prof. chemistry dept., 1983-93, dept. head Coll. Sci., 1981-88, dean Coll. Sci., 1988-89, univ. provost, 1989-93; pres. Western Wash. U., Bellingham, 1993—. Mem., chair Grad. Record Exam in chemistry com., Princeton, N.J., 1980-89, Gov.'s Sci. Coun., Salt Lake City, 1986-93, Gov.'s Coun. on Fusion, 1989-91, ACS Com. on Profl. Tng., 1984-92; cons. 1993; nat. ChemLinks adv. com. NSF, 1995; bd. advisor's orgn. com. 2008 summer Olympic Games, Seattle, 1995; faculty Am. Assn. State Colls. and Univs. Pres.'s Acad., 1995, 96; chair Wash. Coun. of Pres., 1995-96; bd. dirs. Whatcom State Bank; NCAA Divsn. II Pres.'s Coun., 1999—, CHEA bd., 2000—; Nat. Rsch. Coun. Chem. Svcs. Roundtable, 1999—. Contbr. articles to profl. jours. Mem. Cache County Sch. Dist. Found., Cache Valley, Logan, 1988-93; swim coach, soccer coach; trustee First United Presbyn. Ch., Logan, 1979-81, 82-85; adv. bd. Sci. Discovery Ctr., Logan, 1993, KCTS-TV, Bellingham, 1996—, Seattle Opera Bd., 1999—; mem. bd. dirs. United Way, Whatcom County, 1993—; exec. com. Bellingham-Whatcom Econ. Devel. Com., 1993—. Recipient Disting. Alumni in Residence award U. Mich., 1989, Francis P. Garvan and John M. Olin medal, 1997. Fellow AAAS; mem. Am. Chem. Soc. (Utah award Salt Lake City and Cen. dists. 1988, Garvan-Olin medal 1997), Am. Assn. State Colls. and Univs. (mem. policy and purposes com. 1995, chair 1996), Bus. and Profl. Women Club (pres. 1984-85), Philanthropic Edn. Orgn., Phi Beta Kappa, Sigma Xi, Phi Beta Kappa Assocs., Phi Kappa Phi, Beta Gamma Sigma. Avocations: skiing, biking, photography. Office: Western Washington U Office Pres 516 High St Bellingham WA 98225-5946

MORSE, STEPHEN SCOTT, virologist, immunologist, epidemiologist; b. N.Y.C., Nov. 22, 1951; s. Murray H. and Phyllis Morse; m. Marilyn Gewirtz, Feb. 1991. BS, CCNY, 1971; MS, U. Wis., 1974, PhD, 1977. NSF trainee dept. bacteriology U. Wis., Madison, 1971-72, rsch. asst., 1972-77; Nat. Cancer Inst. rsch. fellow Med. Coll. Va./Va. Commonwealth U., Richmond, 1977-80, instr. microbiology, 1980-81; asst. prof. microbiology Rutgers U., New Brunswick, N.J., 1981-85; rsch. assoc. Rockefeller U., N.Y.C., 1985-88, asst. prof., 1988-96, adj. faculty, 1996—; asst. prof. to assoc. prof. epidemiology, Mailman Sch. Pub. Health Columbia U., 1996—; program mgr. Def. Advanced Rsch. Projects Agy., 1996-2000; dir. Ctr. Pub. Health Preparedness, Mailman Sch. Pub. Health Columbia U., 2000—02. Cons. U.S. Congress Office Tech. Assessment, Washington, 1989; chair conf. on emerging viruses NIH, 1989; mem. com. microbial threats to health, chair subcom. on viruses Inst. Medicine-NAS, 1990—92, steering com. Forum on Emerging Infections; chair program for monitoring emerging diseases (ProMED) Fedn. Am. Scientists, 1993—. Author: Emerging Viruses, 1993, Evolutionary Biology of Viruses, 1994; sect. editor: Ctr. for Disease Control and Prevention Jour., Emerging Infectious Diseases, 1995—2002, mem. editl. bd.: Ctr. for Disease Control and Prevention Jour., 2003—, Biosecurity and Bioterrorism, 2003—. Fellow: N.Y. Acad. Scis. (vice chair microbiology sect. 1994—96, chair 1996—98); mem.: Marine Biology Lab., Am. Assn. Immunologists, Am. Soc. Microbiology, Sigma Xi. Office: Columbia U Mailman Sch Pub Health Ctr Pub Health Preparedness 722 W 168th St New York NY 10032-3722 E-mail: ssm20@columbia.edu.

MORSE-MCNEELY, PATRICIA, poet, writer, retired middle school educator; b. Galveston, Tex., Apr. 2, 1923; d. Bleecker Lansing Sr. and Annie Maud (Pillow) Morse; m. Chalmers Rankin McNeely, Mar. 22, 1949 (div. Aug. 1959); children: David Lansing McNeely, Timothy Ann McNeely Caldwell, Patricia Grace McNeely Dragon, Abigail Rankin McNeely. BS in Edn., U. Tex., 1972; MA in Ednl. Psychology, Spl. Edn. LLD, U. Tex., San Antonio, 1976, MA in Ednl. Psychology Counseling Spl. Edn., 1981. Cert. tchr. Tex., profl. counselor. Sec./adminstrv. sec. various cos., Galveston & Austin, Tex., 1945-49, 60-70; dep. clk. Ct. of Civil Appeals, Galveston, 1947-48; police stenographer Austin Police Dept., 1970-74; history and spl. edn. tchr. N.E. Ind. Sch. Dist., San Antonio, 1974-76; spl. edn. tchr. S.W. Ind. Sch. Dist., San Antonio, 1978-81; vocat. adjustment coord. East Ctrl. Ind. Sch. Dist., San Antonio, 1981-82; counselor, tchr. Stockdale (Tex.) Ind. Sch. Dist., 1982-84; clinic sec. Humana Hosp., Dallas, 1985-87; tchr. history and spl. edn. Dallas Ind. Sch. Dist., 1987-2000; ret., 2000. TSTA/NEA assn. rep. Hill Mid. Sch., Dallas, 1988—89, E.B. Comstock Mid. Sch., Dallas, 1991—2000. Author: (poetry) Texas City, 1947, A Gift of Love, 1978, The Key, 1991, The House, The Gull's Quill, 2001, Pat's Portfolio, 2002; contbr., articles to prof. newspapers and profl. jours. V.p. zone, sec., libr., com. mem. Parents Without Ptnrs., Inc., Austin, 1965—72, chmn. internat. ad hoc com. for writing leadership tng. program, 1968, newsletter editor, 1967—72. Mem.: AARP, NEA (life), San Gabriel Writers League, Soc. Children's Book Writers, Writers League Tex., Soc. Children's Book Writers and Illustrators, Nat. Trust for Edn. (trustee), Tex. Writers' League (San Gabriel chpt.), U. Tex. Austin Alumni Assn. (First Bernice Milburn Moore scholarship award 1972), U. Tex. San Antonio Alumni (del. to Tex. State Tchrs. Assn. Conf. 1978—81, 1991—97), Internat. Libr. Poetry (Hall of Fame 1997), Assn. Am. Poets, Nat. Edn. Assn. (life), Tex. State Tchrs. Assn. (life), Internat. Soc. Poets (life). Episcopalian. Avocations: writing, reading, music, sewing/handcrafts, book collecting. E-mail: pmmcneely@prodigy.net.

MORT, GARY STEVEN, physical education educator; b. San Francisco, Jan. 2, 1959; s. Robert Joseph and Antoinette Patricia (Dominguez) M.; m. Rochelle Ann Dias, Aug. 02, 1980; children: Aaron Nicholas, Courtney Faith. BS Phys. Edn., San Jose State, 1983; MS Ednl. Adminstrn., Nat. Univ., Fresno, Calif., 1989. Cert. tchr. phys. edn., Calif. Tchr. phys. edn. Alum Rock Unified, San Jose, Calif., 1984-85, Clovis (Calif.) Unified Schs., 1985—, 1993—. Found. grantee Clovis Found., 1993-94; named Coach of the Yr., North Yosemite League, Fresno area, 1990. Mem. AAHPERD (presenter nat. conv. 1992, 93, 95), Calif. Assn. Health, Phys. Edn., Recreation and Dance), U.S. Water Polo (dist. sec. 1974—), Calif. Consortium of Ind. Study. Avocations: golf, rock climbing, skiing, running and hiking. Home: 8564 Chickadee Ln Clovis CA 93611-9461 Office: Gateway High Sch Enterprise High Sch 1550 Herndon Ave Clovis CA 93611-0598

MORTENSEN-SAY, MARLYS, school system administrator; b. Yankton, S.D., Mar. 11, 1924; d. Melvin A. and Edith L. (Fargo) Mortensen; m. John Theodore Say, June 21, 1951; children: Mary Louise, James Kenneth, John Melvin, Margaret Ann. BA, U. Colo., 1949, MEd, 1953; Adminstrv. Specialist, U. Nebr., 1973. Tchr. Huron (S.D.) Jr. H.S., 1944-48, Lamar (Colo.) Jr. H.S., 1950-52, Norfolk Pub. Sch., 1962-63; sch. supr. Madison County, Madison, Nebr., 1963-79. Mem. ASCD, NEA (life) AAUW, Am. Assn. Sch. Adminstrs., Dept. Rural Edn., Nebr. Assn. County Supts., N.E. Nebr. County Supts. Assn. Assn. Sch. Bus. Ofcls., Nat. Orgn. Legal Problems in Edn., Nebr. Edn. Assn., Nebr. Sch. Adminstrs. Assn. Republican. Methodist. Home: 1222 W S Airport Rd Norfolk NE 68701-1349

MORTIMER, ARMINE KOTIN, literature educator; b. Detroit, May 13, 1943; d. Arra Steve and Georgia Victoria Avakian; m. Joel Tepper Kotin, Sept. 1, 1962 (div. Nov. 1969); children: Daniel, Ilana; m. Rudolf George Mortimer, Aug. 18, 1980. BA, Radcliffe Coll., 1964; MA, UCLA, 1970; PhD, Yale U., 1974. Prof. French lit. U. Ill., Urbana, 1974—. Author: The Narrative Imagination: Comic Tales by Philippe de Vigneulles, 1977, La clôture narrative, 1985, The Gentlest Law: Roland Barthes's The Pleasure of the Text, 1989, Plotting To Kill, 1991, Writing Realism: Representations in French Literature, 2000; co-editor: (with K. Kolb) Proust in Perspective: Visions and Revisions, 2002. Avocation: violin. Office: U Ill 707 S Mathews Ave Urbana IL 61801-3625 Fax: 217-384-5424. E-mail: armine@uiuc.edu.

MORTIMER, GARTH EUGENE, mathematics educator; b. South Williamsport, Pa., July 7, 1941; s. Eugene Lewellyn and Margaret Lucinda (Fisher) M.; m. Ann Charlotte Bensley, Nov. 27, 1965; children: Julianne, Timothy Scott, Melissa. BS in Edn., Mansfield U., 1963; MS in Edn., Elmira (N.Y.) Coll., 1970; postgrad., Alfred (N.Y.) U., 1964-65, U. Maine, summer 1966. Cert. tchr. N.Y. Tchr. Campbell (N.Y.) Cen. Sch., 1963-67; tchr. math. Horseheads (N.Y.) Cen. Sch., 1967—, chmn. dept. math., 1972-78. Chief negotiator Horseheads Tchrs. Assn., 1978-89. Contbg. editor: 11th Year Mathematics, 1984. Coach Cinderella Softball, Little League, Soccer, Horseheads, 1978-87. Named Female Team Coach of Year Elmira Kiwanis, 1991 for undefeated girl's basketball. Mem. Assn. Math. Tchrs. of N.Y. State, Elks. Methodist. Avocations: computers, baseball card collecting, coin collecting, sports. Office: Horseheads Cen Sch One Raider Ln Horseheads NY 14845

MORTIMER, RICHARD WALTER, mechanical engineer, educator; b. Phila., Dec. 7, 1936; s. Horace and Almira Duffield (Matthews) M.; m. Doris Claire Ridler, June 29, 1957; children: Patrick Lee, David Walter, James Matthew, Daniel Scott. BSME, Drexel U., 1962, MSME, 1964, PhD, 1967. Prof. Drexel U., Phila., 1967—, assoc. dean grad. sch., 1974-76, head dept. mech. engring., 1976-85, assoc. v.p. acad. affairs, 1985-89. Mem. exec. com. Engring. Accreditation Com., N.Y.C., 1986-91. Contbr. over 40 articles to profl. jours. Pres. Haverford (Pa.) Twp. Sch. Dist., 1980-83. With U.S. Army, 1958-60. With U.S. Army, 1958—60. Recipient Achievement award Am. Soc. Nondestructive Testing, 1973, Best Tech. Paper award, 1973; fellow NASA, 1967, 68; grantee numerous orgns. including NASA, USAF, NSF, 1967-87; Fellow Members awd., Am. Soc. for Engineering Education, 1992. Fellow Am. Soc. Engring. Educators; mem. ASME (mem. numerous coms., bds. and chairs 1976-92). Republican. Episcopalian. Achievements include research in fields of structural dynamics and composite materials.

MORTON, CLAUDETTE, education administrator; b. Billings, Mont., Jan. 21, 1940; d. Hugh Wesley and Timey Delacy (Hopper) M.; m. Larry Roy Johnson, July 5, 1959 (div. 1987); 1 child, Eric Roy Johnson; m. George Miller, Sept. 3, 1987. BA in Drama, U. Mont., 1963, MA in Drama, 1964, EdD in Edn., 1990. Cert. tchr., adminstrv., Mont. Tchr. English, supr. Moorhead (Minn.) State U., 1964-65; sub. tchr. Missoula and Glassgow (Mont.) Sch. Dists., 1965-70; English tchr., dir. speech, drama Glasgow H.S., 1970-78; English specialist, liaison to county supr. Office of Public Instrn., Helena, Mont., 1978-86; exec. sec. and state agy. dir. Bd. of Pub. Edn., Helena, 1986-90; dir. Mont. rural edn. ctr. and western Mont. coll. assoc. prof. edn. U. Mont., Dillon, 1990-96; exec. dir. Mont. Small Schs. Alliance, Helena, 1996—. Mem. rural edn. adv. com. Northwest Reginal Edn. Lab., Portland, 1991-96, adv. bd. Ctr. for Study of Small and Rural Schs. U. Okla., 1993—; mem. Blue Ribbon Schs. Panel, U.S. Dept. Edn., 1994, 96—. Editor: Visions: Healthy Living for the 21 Century, 1992; contbr. articles to profl. jours. Mem. Ch. Pub. Policy Mont. Arts Coun., 1978-86, chair Mont. Cult. Advocacy, 1982-86; state. pres. AAUW, Mont., 1988-90, theatre content ch. arts assessment planning com. Coun. of Chief State Sch. Officers. Mem. Nat. Assessment Ednl. Progress (arts assessment, oversight com.), Nat. Rural Edn. Assn. (Howard A. Dawson award for svc. 1995), Nat. Coun. of Tchrs. of English, Am. Assn. Colls. of Tchr. Educators, Am. Edn. Rsch. Assn., Mont. Alliance for Arts Edn., Delta Kappa Gamma, Phi Delta Kappa. Democrat. Congregationalist. Avocations: travel, hiking, cross country skiing, politics. the arts. Office: Ste 516 7 W 6th Ave Helena MT 59601-5036

MORTON, HAZEL CAUDLE, elementary education educator; b. Winston-Salem, N.C., Aug. 20, 1934; d. William Henry and Katie (Sullivan) Caudle; m. James H. Morton, July 23, 1966; 1 child, Kimberley Ann. BS, Winston-Salem State U., 1956; MA, U. Conn., 1961. Cert. elem. tchr., Del. Tchr. primary Fairview Elem. Sch., Charlotte, N.C., 1956-61, Evan G. Shortlidge Sch., Wilmington, Del., 1961-78, Joseph M. McVey Sch., Newark, Del., 1978—. Organist, directress Ctrl. Bapt. Ch. Choir, Wilmington, Del.; bd. dirs. Community Presbyn. Day NUrsery, Wilmingotn, 1974-76. Mem. NEA, NAACP, Del. Edn. Assn., Christina Edn. Assn., New Castle County Edn. Assn., Young Women's Christian Assn., Chapel of Four Chaplains (hon.), Winston-Salem State U. Alumni Assn., Eagle Glen Civic Assn., Phi Beta Kappa, Zeta Phi Beta. Baptist. Avocations: music, reading, drawing, oil painting, bowling, sports. Home: 4 Whitehaven Dr New Castle DE 19720-3720

MORTON, LAUREL ANNE, elementary education educator; b. Cin., July 27, 1954; d. James William and Rosemary (Danner) M. BA in Social Sci., Calif. State U.-Stanislaus, Turlock, 1978; teaching credential, Calif. State Polytech U., Pomona, 1986; MA in Edn., Calif. State Poly. U., Pomona, 1992. Cert. tchr., Calif., Colo. Sr. loan clk. Shearson Am. Express Mortgage Corp., Newport Beach, Calif., 1978-82; adminstrv. asst. Investco Corp., Santa Barbara, Calif., 1982-83; supr. loan servicing dept. County Savs. Bank, Santa Barbara, 1983-84; comm. asst. Fuller Theol. Sem., Pasadena, Calif., 1984-85; elem. tchr. Howard Sch., Ontario, Calif., 1986-91; tchr. Bon View Elem. Sch., Ontario, 1992-2000, 4th grade team leader, 1993-94, track leader, 1995-96, 99-2000; tchr. Longley Way Elem. Sch., Arcadia, Calif., 2000—. Tchr. sponsor Performing Arts Club, Bon View Elem. Sch., 1996-97, 97-98. Mem. Nat. Honor Soc., Phi Kappa Phi, Zeta Tau Alpha. Avocations: tennis, theater, dancing, travel, museums or venues of educational interest. Home: 1919 Stonehouse Rd Sierra Madre CA 91024-1409 Office: Longley Way Elem Sch 2601 S Longley Way Arcadia CA 91007

MORTON, MARILYN MILLER, retired genealogy and history educator, lecturer, researcher, travel executive, director; b. Water Valley, Miss, Dec. 2, 1929; d. Julius Brunner and Irma Faye (Magee) Miller; m. Perry Wilkes Morton Jr., July 2, 1958; children: Dent Miller Morton, Nancy Marilyn Morton Driggers, E. Perian Morton Dyar. BA in English, Miss. U. for Women, 1952; MS in History, Miss. State U., 1955. Cert. secondary tchr. Tchr. English, speech and history Starkville HS, Miss., 1952-58; part-time instr. Miss. State U., 1953-55; spl. collection staff Samford U. Libr., Birmingham, Ala., 1984-92; lectr. genealogy and history, instr. Inst. Genealogy & Hist. Rsch., Samford U., Birmingham, 1985-93, assoc. dir., 1985-88, exec. dir., 1988-93; founding dir. SU British and Irish Inst. Genealogy & Hist. Rsch. Samford U., Birmingham and British Isles, 1986-93; owner, dir. Marilyn Miller Morton Brit-Ire-U.S. Genealogy, Birmingham, 1994—95, 1994—95. Instr. genealogy classes Samford U. Metro Coll., 1986-94; lformer ectr. nat. conf. Fedn. of Geneal. Soc. Contbr. articles profl. jour. Miss. state pres. Future Homemakers Am., 1947-48; active Birmingham chpt. Salvation Army Aux., 1982-87. Named to Miss. U. for Women Hall of Fame, 1952. Fellow Irish Geneal. Rsch. Soc. London; mem. Nat. Geneal. Soc. (mem. nat. program com. 1988-92, lectr. nat. mtgs.), ex-mem., Assn. Profl. Genealogists, Soc. Genealogists London, mem., Antiquarian Soc. Birmingham (sec., 2d v.p. 1982-84), DAR (regent Cheaha chpt. 1977-78), Daus. Am. Colonists (regent Edward Waters chpt. 1978-79), Nat. League of Am. Penwomen, Phi Kappa Phi (charter mem. Samford U. chpt. 1972). Avocations: reading, research, travel, bridge, chess. Home: 3508 Clayton Pl Birmingham AL 35216-3810

MORTON, MICHAEL RADER, career and technology education director; b. W.Va., Feb. 27, 1942; s. Shirley and Ruth Morton; m. Kathleen Morton; children: Matthew, Mark; 1 stepchild, Kelly Wechsler. BS in Edn., W.Va. U., 1964, MEd, 1966. Tchr. Fairfax (Va.) County Pub. Schs., 1964-70, Va. State, Richmond and Hampton, Va., 1968-70; supr. Frederick (Md.) County Pub. Schs., 1970-73; exec. dir. Md. Coun. on Vocat.-Tech. Edn., Annapolis, 1973-93. Co-chair, founder Md. Ctr. Values Edn., Balt.; bd. advisors Md. Ctr. for Quality and Productivity, U. Md., College Park; mem. Nat. Assessment of Vocat. Edn., Md. Commn. on Funding of Pub. Edn.; mem. program improvement panel Nat. Ctr. for Rsch. in Vocat. Edn., U. Calif., Berkeley, 1993—; co-developer SETN Career Devel. Collaborative, 1995. Contbr. articles to profl. jours. Mem. Nat. Coun. Local Adminstrs., Nat. Assn. State Couns. on Vocat. Edn., Am. Vocat. Assn., Md. Soc. Assn. Execs.. Iota Lambda Sigma. Avocation: tennis. Home: 5072 37th St N Arlington VA 22207-1823 Office: Chattanooga Pub Schs 1161 W 40th St Chattanooga TN 37409-1317

MORTON, PATSY LOU, social worker; b. Columbia, Mo., Sept. 15, 1951; d. Delbert Alan and Patsy J. (Johnson) M.; 1 child, Mike A. Morton BSW, U. Mo., 1977; MSW, Washington U., 1979. Lic. clin. social worker. Recreation therapist St. Louis State Hosp., 1978-79; case mgr. Belleville (Ill.) Mental Health, 1979; social worker/dir. of social svc. St. Francis Hosp., Litchfield, Ill., 1979-81; social worker, supr. day treatment Macoupin County Mental Health, Carlinville, Ill., 1981-83; social worker II Dept. of Children and Family Svcs., Springfield, Ill., 1984-91; sch. social worker Southeastern Spl. Edn. Coop., St. Marie, Ill., 1991-92, West Ctrl. Ill. Spl. Edn. Coop., Macomb, Ill., 1992—; social work cons. McDonough Dist. Hosp., Macomb, Ill., 1996—2002, Carthage (Ill.) Meml. Hosp., 1999—2000. Field internship instr, sch. social worker U. Ill., 1996—97, St. Ambrose U., 2002—03; adv. bd. School Social Work Jour., 2003—. Advisor Explorer Post, St. Louis State Hosp., 1978—79; coord. Fulton County Next Steps Team, 1995—97; host family Youth for Understanding, 1995—98; mem. Cuba Ch. of Nazarene, 2000—, Sunday sch. tchr. pre-teens, 2001—02. Mem.: Ill. Assn. Sch. Social Worker (com. mem. 1991—92, conf. com. 1994—97, regional rep. 1994—98, sec. 1998—99, webmaster 1999—2001, pres.-elect 2001—02, pres. 2002—03), Phi Delta Kappa (membership com. 1994—95). Avocations: counted cross stitch-designing and stitching, computers, reading, rubber stamping, scrapbooks. Home: PO Box 895 Cuba IL 61427-0895 Office: WCISEC 130 S Lafayette St Macomb IL 61455-2231 E-mail: plmorton@winco.net.

MORTON, WILLIAM EDWARDS, environmental epidemiology educator, occupational medicine specialist; b. Boston, June 30, 1929; s. Arthur Snow and Irma Claire (Edwards) M.; m. Jean Carolee Staley, Aug. 11, 1956; children: Carol, Kristen, Thomas. B.S., U. Puget Sound, 1952; M.D., U. Wash., 1955; M.P.H., U. Mich., 1960, D.P.H., 1962. Diplomate Am. Bd. Preventive Medicine. Sr. asst. surgeon USPHS, Denver, 1956-58; resident Community Hosp., San Mateo, Calif., 1958-59; epidemiologist Colo. Heart Assn., Denver, 1962-67; assoc. prof. pub. health Oreg. Health Sci. U., Portland, 1967-70, prof., 1970-72, prof., head environ. medicine div., 1972-97, prof. emeritus pub. health, 1997—; cons. epidemiology Oreg. State U. Environ. Health Sci. Ctr., Corvallis, 1972-79, Oreg. Comprehensive Cancer Program, Portland, 1973-81; mem. grant rev. panel EPA, Washington, 1979-83; cons. Bonneville Power Adminstrn., Vancouver, Wash., 1980-82; lectr. in field. Contbr. articles to profl. jours. Mem. Physicians for Social Responsibility, Portland, 1980—. Fellow Am. Coll. Epidemiology, Am. Coll. Preventive Medicine, Am. Coll. Occupational Medicine; mem. Northwest Assn. Occupational Medicine (pres. 1974-75), AAUP (pres. chpt. 1982-83), Soc. for Epidemiologic Research. Office: Oreg Health Scis U 3181 SW Sam Jackson Park Rd Portland OR 97239

MOSBAUGH, GARY RAY, agriculturist, educator; b. Noblesville, Ind., Oct. 29, 1955; s. Leon Ray and Florence Elaine (McKinley) M.; m. Annette Jo LaVallee, June 2, 1979; children: Jeremy, Todd, Kimberly, Sue. BS, Purdue U., 1978, MS, 1979. Cert. tchr., Ind. Agrl. edn. tchr. Southmont High Sch., Crawfordsville, Ind., 1979—. Mem. NEA, Assn. Career Tech. Edn., Nat. Assn. Agrl. Educators, Ind. Ass. Agrl. Educators, Ind. Assn. Career Tech. Edn., Ind. State Tchrs. Assn. Home: RR 7 Box 108 Crawfordsville IN 47933-8814 Office: Southmont High Sch 6425 Us Highway 231 S Crawfordsville IN 47933-9400

MOSCA, CHRISTOPHER PATRICK, principal; b. Newton, Mass., July 2, 1957; s. Antonio and Nicoletta (Errico) M.; m. Gina Montini Mosca, July 20, 1991. BS, Trinity Coll., 1979; MEd, Plymouth State Coll., 1989; Cert. advanced grad. study, Castleton State Coll., 1993. Cert. tchr. and adminstr., Vt., N.H., Conn. Tchr., tutor Eagle Hill Sch., Hardwick, Mass., 1979-82; tchr., athletic coach Lalumiere Sch., LaPorte, Ind., 1982-85, Windsor (Vt.) High Sch., 1985-89; assoc. prin. Rutland (Vt.) High Sch., 1989-93; prin. Springfield (Vt.) High Sch., 1993-96, Goffstown (N.H.) Area H.S. Mem. Springfield Workforce Investment Bd. Mem. ASCD, NASSP, Phi Delta Kappa. Avocations: white water rafting, nordic and alpine skiing, travel, outdoor cooking.

MOSELEY, KAREN FRANCES FLANIGAN, educational consultant, retired school system administrator, educator; b. Oneonta, NY, Sept. 18, 1944; d. Albert Francis and Dorothy (Brown) Flanigan; m. David Michael McLaud, Sept. 8, 1962 (div. Dec. 1966); m. Harry R. Lasalle, Dec. 24, 1970 (dec. Feb. 1990); 1 child, Christopher Michael; m. Kel Moseley, Jan. 22, 1994. BA, SUNY, Oneonta, 1969; MS, SUNY and Hockerill Coll., Eng., 1970. Cert. secondary edn. tchr., Fla., Mass., N.Y. Tchr. Hanover (Mass.) Pub. Schs., 1970-80; lobbyist Mass. Fed. Nursing Homes, Boston, 1980-84; tchr., dept. chair Palm Beach County Schs., Jupiter, Fla., 1985-95; ret.,

1996; chair of accredidation Jupiter H.S., 1990-91. Fulbright tchr., Denmark, 1994-95. Author: How to Teach About King, 1978, 10 Year Study, 1991. Del. Dem. Conv., Mass., 1976-84; campaign mgr. Kennedy for Senate, N.Y., 1966, Tsongas for Senate, Boston, 1978; dir. Plymouth County Dems., Marshfield, Mass., 1978-84; Sch. Accountability Com., 1991-95; polit. cons. Paul Tsongas U.S. Senate, Boston, 1978-84, Michael Dukakis for Gov., Boston, 1978-84; mem., spkr. PBC chpt. ARC; disaster team vol. Palm Beach County Red Cross. Mem. AAUW (North Palm Beach County, officer), NEA (life), Nat. Honor Soc. Polit. Scientists, Classroom Tchrs. Assn., Palm Beach County Classroom Tchrs. Assn., Mass. Coun. Social Studies (bd. dirs. Boston chpt. 1970-80), Mass. Tchrs. Assn. (chair human rels. com. Boston chpt. 1976-80), Plymouth County Social Studies (bd. dirs. 1970-80), Mass. Hosp. Assn. (bd. dirs. Boston chpt. 1980-84), Nat. Coun. for Social Studies, Fulbright Alumni Assn., Prologue Soc., Forum Club of the Palm Beaches, Fla. History Ctr., Marine Life Ctr., Norton Mus. Art. Roman Catholic. Avocations: reading, fishing, traveling, art collector, snorkeling. Home: 369 River Edge Rd Jupiter FL 33477-9350

MOSELEY, THERESA A. guidance counselor, actress; b. Ft. Bragg, N.C., Feb. 27, 1958; d. Clarence B. and Hazel Mae (Stinney) M. BA, Ga. State U., 1988; MEd, Bowie State U., 1994; PhD, Am. U., Washington, 1998. Receptionist Brannell Coll., Atlanta, Ga., 1981-84; red coat Continental Airlines, Newark, N.J., 1988-93; counselor U. Md., College Park, 1994; counselor, tchr. Prince Georges County Sch., Upper Marlboro, 1995—. Mem. Assn. for Multi-cult. counseling and devel., 1993—, Md. Assn. for Counseling and Devel., 1993—, v.p. Montgomery County Parent Policy Coun., Rockville, Md., 1994-95; founder, pres. TereSerenity Place Inc., 1998—. Vol. Dem. Convention, Atlanta, 1988. With U.S. Army, 1976-80. Recipient Outstanding Educator Prince George's County C. of C. Mem. ACA, Am. Sch. Counseling Assn., Nat. Assn. for the Edn. of Young Children, Md. State Tchrs. Assn. (del. 1998), Md. Assn. for Counseling and Devel., Prince Georges County Edn. Assn., AFTRA, SAG, Chi Sigma Iota. Democrat. Baptist. Avocations: acting, singing, dancing, photography, travel. Home: 12223 Castlewall Ct Bowie MD 20720

MOSER, ROYCE, JR., physician, medical educator; b. Versailles, Mo., Aug. 21, 1935; s. Royce and Russie Frances (Stringer) M.; m. Lois Anne Hunter, June 14, 1958; children: Beth Anne Moser McLean, Donald Royce. BA, Harvard U., 1957, MD, 1961; MPH, Harvard Sch. Pub. Health, Boston, 1965. Diplomate Am. Bd. Preventive Medicine (trustee 1989-98). Commd. officer USAF, 1962, advanced through grades to col., 1974; resident in aerospace medicine USAF Sch. Aerospace Medicine, Brooks AFB, Tex., 1965-67; chief aerospace medicine Aerospace Def. Command, Colorado Springs, Colo., 1967-70; comdr. 35th USAF Dispensary Phan Rang, Vietnam, 1970-71; chief aerospace medicine br. USAF Sch. Aerospace Medicine, Brooks AFB, 1971-77; comdr. USAF Hosp., Tyndall AFB, Fla., 1977-79; chief clin. scis. div. USAF Sch. Aerospace Medicine, Brooks AFB, 1979-81, chief edn. div., 1981-83, sch. comdr., 1983-85, ret., 1985; prof. dept. family and preventive medicine U. Utah Sch. Medicine, Salt Lake City, 1985—, vice chmn. dept., 1985-95; dir. Rocky Mountain Ctr. for Occupl. and Environ. Health, Salt Lake City, 1987—2003. Cons. in occupl., environ. and aerospace medicine, Salt Lake City, 1985—; presenter in field. Author: Effective Management of Occupational and Environmental Health and Safety Programs, 1992, 2d edit. 1999; contbr. book chpts. and articles to profl. jours. Past pres. 1st Bapt. Ch. Found., Salt Lake City, 1987-89; chmn. numerous univ. coms., Salt Lake City, 1985—; bd. dirs. Hanford Environ. Health Found., 1990-92; preventive medicine residency rev. com. Accreditation Coun. Grad. Med. Edn., 1991-97; ednl. adv. bd. USAF Human Sys. Ctr., 1991-96; chmn. long-range planning com. Am. Bd. Preventive Medicine, 1992-95. Decorated Legion of Merit (2); recipient Harriet Hardy award New England Coll. Occupl. and Environ. Medicine, 1998, Rutherford T. Johnstone award Western Occupl. and Environ. Med. Assn., 2002. Fellow Aerospace Med. Assn. (pres. 1989-90, chair fellows group 1994-97, Harry G. Mosely award 1981, Theodore C. Lyster award 1988, Eric Liljencrantz award 2001), Am. Coll. Preventive Medicine (regent 1981-82), Am. Coll. Occupl. and Environ. Medicine (v.p. med. affairs 1995-97, Robert A. Kehoe award 1996); mem. Internat. Acad. Aviation and Space Medicine (selector 1989-94, chancellor 1994-98), Soc. of USAF Flight Surgeons (pres. 1978-79, George E. Schafer award 1982), Phi Beta Kappa. Avocations: photography, fishing. Home: 664 Aloha Rd Salt Lake City UT 84103-3329 Office: Rocky Mountain Ctr Occupl & Environ Health 75 S 2000 E Salt Lake City UT 84112-8930 E-mail: rmoser@rmcoeh.utah.edu.

MOSES, HAMILTON, III, medical educator, hospital executive, management consultant; s. Hamilton Jr. and Betty Anne (Theurer) M.; m. Elizabeth Lawrence Hormel, 1977 (dec. 1988); m. Alexandra McCullough Gibson, 1992. BA in Psychology, U. Pa., 1972; MD, Rush Med. Coll., Chgo., 1975. Clk. Nat. Hosp. for Nervous Diseases, London, 1974; intern in medicine Johns Hopkins Hosp., Balt., 1976-77, resident in neurology, 1977-79, chief resident, 1979-80, assoc. prof. neurology, 1986-94, vice chmn. neurology and neurosurgery, 1980-88, v.p., 1988-94, dir. Parkinson's Ctr., 1984-94; dir. neurol. inst., prof. neurology and neurosurgery and mgmt. U. Va., Charlottesville, 1994-97; sr. advisor Boston Cons. Group, 1995—; prof. Darden Sch. Bus. U. Va., Charlottesville, 1994-98; cons. neurologist Mass. Gen. Hosp., Boston, 1997—; vis. prof. neurology and psychiatry Harvard U. Sch. Medicine, Boston, 1997-99; chmn. The Alerion Inst., 2003—. Sr. advisor Ptnrs. Healthcare, Boston; spl. advisor Nat. Health Svc., Eng., 1988-91. Editor, major author: Principles of Medicine, 1985-96; editor newsletter Johns Hopkins Health, 1988-94; contbr. numerous articles to med. jours. Mem. com. on med. ministries Episcopal Diocese Md., Balt., 1987; bd. dirs. Valleys Planning Ct.; trustee McLean Hosp., Belmont, Mass., 1997—. Fellow Am. Acad. Neurology (sec. 1989-91), Royal Soc. Medicine (U.K.) (overseas fellow 2000—); mem. Am. Neurol. Assn., Md. Neurol. Soc. (pres. 1984-86), Movement Disorders Soc. Republican. Avocations: landscape photography, sailing. Office: PO Box 150 North Garden VA 22959-0150 also: 4800 Hampden Ln Bethesda MD 20814-2930

MOSES, JOEL, computer scientist, educator; b. Petach Tikvah, Israel, Nov. 25, 1941; came to U.S., 1954, naturalized, 1960; s. Bernhard and Golda (Losner) M.; m. Margaret A. Garvey, Dec. 27, 1970; children: Jesse, David. BA, Columbia U., 1962, MA, 1963; PhD, MIT, 1967. Asst. prof. dept. elec. engring. and computer sci. M.I.T., 1967-71, assoc. prof., 1971-77, prof., 1977—, assoc. dir. Lab for Computer Sci., 1974-78, assoc. head computer sci. and engring., dept. elec. engring. and computer sci., 1978-81, head dept., 1981-89, D.C. Jackson prof., 1989-99, dean Sch. Engring., 1991-95, provost, 1995-98, prof. engring. sys. divsn., 1999—, Inst. prof., 1999—. Vis. prof. Harvard Grad. Sch. Bus. Adminstrn., 1989-90; vis. adj. sr. rsch. scientist Columbia U. FU Found. Sch. Engring. and Applied Sci., 1998. Editor: The Computer Age: A Twenty Year View, 1979; co-originator Knowledge Based System Concept; developer MACSYMA system for formula manipulation. Recipient Achievement award MIT Lab. for Computer Sci., 1985. Fellow IEEE, AAAS, Am. Acad. Arts and Scis.; mem. Nat. Acad. Engring., Assn. for Computing Machinery, Am. Soc. Engring. Edn. (Centennial Cert.). Office: MIT Lab Computer Sci NE43-407 Cambridge MA 02139 E-mail: moses@mit.edu.

MOSES-FOLEY, JUDITH ANN, elementary school educator; b. Steubenville, Ohio, Sept. 1, 1936; d. Joseph and Katherine Ann (Pavich) Moses; m. John P. Foley, 1958 (div. 1986); children: Katherine Ann Foley, John Joseph Foley, Sean Michael Foley, Judith Kristina Foley; m. John H. Murphy, 1986 (dec. 1992). BS in Edn., Ohio U., 1958; MA in Ednl. Adminstrn., Fresno Pacific U., 1981; postgrad., Brigham Young U., 1982-84, U. San Francisco, 1985-86, U. N.Mex., 1993-98, Western N.Mex. U., 1997-98. Cert. in ednl. adminstrn., Calif.; tchr., N.Mex., Ohio; spl. edn., bilingual/TESOL, and as transition resource specialist, N.Mex.; notary pub., N.Mex. Adminstr., tchr. health and social sci., coach Madera (Calif.) Unified Schs., 1958-81; chair dept. phys. edn. Dos Palos (Calif.) H.S., 1963-64; prin. Chowchilla (Calif.) Elem. Schs., 1981-85; instr. phys. edn. Merced (Calif.) C.C., 1981-85; supt., prin. St. Luke's Sch., Merced, 1985-86; instr. polit. sci. and bus. adminstrn. West Hills C.C., Lemore, Calif., 1985-86; instr. phys. edn. Mohave C.C., Kingman, Ariz., 1989-90; transition resource specialist Silver Consol. Sch., Silver City, N.Mex., 1993—. Adj. prof. early childhood edn. Western N.Mex. U., Silver City; spl. edn. resource specialist Silver HS, Silver City, 1990—, coach U.S. acad. decathlon, 1991-99; grant writer Circle of Life, 1994-97; coord., grant writer R.E.: Learning; mem. North Ctrl. Accreditation Steering Com., 1992-95; v.p. divsn. transition and curriculum devel. State of N.Mex., sch. to work grant writer, 1997—; mem. N.Mex. State Bd. com. U.S. Acad. Decathlon, 1993—; developer lang. arts, social studies transition curriculum 9-12 Silver Consolidated Schs., N.Mex.; tchr. Acad. N.Mex. Goals 2000; coord. Southwest Regional Cooperative Ctr. Sch. to Work; profl. std. commn. N.Mex. State Licensure and Competencies, 1999-2000; mem. State N.M. Dept. Edn. State Licensing Competency Revision Com., 1999; instr. English 9-12, 2001-. Pres. Bobby Sox Softball League, Madera, 1975-78; head coach track and field Jr. Olympics, Madera County, 1970-81; coord. Gathering of War Birds Airshow, Madera, 1976-79; fundraiser Cliff Pop Warner Football, 2002-03, Cliff Cloverleaf 4-H, 2002-03 Recipient Master Tchr. award Calif. State U., Fresno, 1978-79; recipient scholarships and grants. Mem. AAHPER, AAUW, Nat. Notary Assn., Am. Assn. Ret. Persons, Coun. for Exceptional Children, Steubenville H.S. Alumni Assn., Toltec Property Owners. Mem. ASCD. Avocations: flying, jewelry design, painting, water skiing, fishing. Home: PO Box 2 Buckhorn NM 88025-0002 Office: Silver Consol Schs 3200 N Silver St Silver City NM 88061-7283 Fax: (505) 535-2929.

MOSHE, SOLOMON L. neurology and pediatrics educator; b. Athens, Greece, May 8, 1949; came to U.S., 1973; s. Leon and Sarina Moshe; m. Nancy Cornblath, June 26, 1977; 1 child, Jared. MD, Nat. U. Athens, 1972. Diplomate Am. Bd. Pediat., Am. Bd. Psychiatry and Neurology, Am. Bd. Clin. Neurophysiology. Inter, then resident in pediat. U. Md. Hosp., Balt., 1973-75; fellow in pediatric neurology Albert Einstein Coll. Medicine, Bronx, N.Y., 1975-78, rsch. fellow in neurology and neurosci., 1978-79, asst. prof. neurology, 1979-84, assoc. prof. neurology, 1984-89, prof. neurology, 1989—, asst. prof. pediat., 1979-85, assoc. prof. pediat., 1985-91, prof., 1991—, prof. neurosci., 1989—. Mem. sci. adv. bd. Charles U. 3d Sch. Medicine, Prague, Czechoslovakia, 1990—; chmn. profl. adv. bd. Epilepsy Soc., Inc., Pearl River, N.Y., 1991-97; Hans Berger lectr., 1995. Author: (with Pellock and Salon) The Parke-Davis Manual on Epilepsy, 1992, (with Schwartzkroin, Noebels and Swann) Brain Development and Epilepsy, 1995; co-editor: Childhood Epilepsies and Brain Development, 1989-98; co-inventor computer software Spike Simulator. Coach East Hudson Youth Soccer League, 1989—. Recipient Michael prize, 1984, rsch. recognition award Am. Epilepsy Soc., 1990, Amb. of Epilepsy award Internat. League Against Epilepsy, 1999; Jacob K. Javits neurosci. grantee, 1995—; Martin A. and Emily L. Fisher fellow in neurology and pediat., 1997. Mem. Am. Epilepsy Soc. (second v.p. 1998-99), Am. EEG Soc. (pres.-elect 1996-97), Ea. Assn. Electroencephalographers (pres. 1992-94). Office: Albert Einstein Coll Med Kennedy Bldg Rm 316 1410 Pelham Pkwy S Bronx NY 10461-1101

MOSHOYANNIS, PHILLIP DEMETRI ALEXANDER, educator; b. Manhattan, NY, Mar. 30, 1968; s. Demetri S. M. and Susan Elizabeth Perry. BS, Cornell U., 1990; MA, Columbia U., 1992, MPhil, 1999. Tchr. 4th grade A. Fantis Parochial Sch., Bklyn., 1990-91; substitute tchr. Oyster Bay, East Norwich, N.Y., 1992-93; social studies specialist Sch. of Transfiguration, Corona, N.Y., 1993-94; tchr. 5th grade Lee Ave. Sch., Hicksville, N.Y., 1995—. Adj. asst. prof. Nassau CC, Garden City, NY, 1994—. Capt. U.S. Army N.G., 1990—. Decorated Army Commendation medal, Army Achievement medal, Nat. Def. Svc. medal, Def. Liberty medal. Mem. NEA (N.Y. bd. dirs., N.Y. human rights com.), Am. Sociol. Assn., Hicksville Congress Tchrs. (1st v.p.), Am. Hellenic Ednl. Progressive Assn., Am. Legion, Kappa Delta Pi. Home: 1 Cortelyou St W Huntington Station NY 11746-3306 Office: Lee Ave Sch 1 7th St Hicksville NY 11801-5421

MOSIER, STEPHEN RUSSELL, college program director, physicist; b. San Rafael, Calif., Nov. 14, 1942; s. Russell Glenn and Marjorie Jean (Carhart) M.; m. Catherine Priscilla Spindle, June 14, 1964; children: Catherine Priscilla, Roger Carhart. BS, Coll. William & Mary, 1964; PhD, U. Iowa, 1970. Rsch. scientist NASA/Goddard Space Flight Ctr., Greenbelt, Md., 1971-78; dir. U.S.-Japan programs NSF, Washington, 1978-81, dir. U.S.-France program, 1981-83; assoc. v.p. internat. affairs U. Houston System, 1983-86; dir. rsch. svcs. U. N.C., Greensboro, 1986-98, assoc. provost rsch. and fed. rels. Charlotte, 1998—, interim chief info. officer, 2000—01. Adv. bd. Cameron Applied Rsch. Ctr., Charlotte, 1998—; chmn., bd. dirs. N.C. Assn. for Biomed. Rsch., Raleigh, 1989—; bd. dirs. Ctr. for Applied Tech., Houston, 1984-86; rsch. cons. various univs. Contbr. articles to Jour. Geophys. Rsch., Solar Physics, Nature, Transactions (IEEE). Mem. exec. bd. Old North State Coun. Boy Scouts Am., Greensboro, 1987-98; Scout leader, Washington, Houston, Greensboro. Mem. AAAS, Am. Geophys. Union, Soc. Rsch. Adminstrs., Sigma Xi. Methodist. Achievements include research in magnetospheric physics, solar physics, international science and technology policy. Office: Office Rsch U NC Charlotte NC 28223-0001

MOSKAL, ANTHONY JOHN, former dean, professor, management and education consultant; b. South Amboy, N.J., May 31, 1946; s. Anthony Joseph and Jennie (Salamon) M.; m. Kathryn Jean Coakley, July 8, 1978; 1 child, Nicole Elizabeth. AB, Villanova (Pa.) U., 1968, MA, 1972; MEd, Ga. State U., 1974; PhD, Columbia Pacific U., San Rafael, Calif., 1987. Prin. instr. U.S. Army, Ft. Benning, Ga., 1969-71; research mgr. Blue Cross and Blue Shield, Columbus, Ga., 1972-74; sales rep. J.C. Penney Co., Parlin, N.J., 1974-76; dean of students Alliance Coll., Cambridge Springs, Pa., 1976-77; tchr. Sayreville (N.J.) pub. schs., 1977-79; county 4-H agt. Rutgers U., New Brunswick, 1979-86; pres. Eagle Assocs., South Amboy, N.J., 1985—. Adj. faculty Georgian Ct. Coll., Lakewood, NJ, 1987—, U.S. Army Command and Gen. Staff Coll., Ft. Leavenworth, Kans., 1989—2000, Nat. Def. U., Washington, 1991—2000; cons. dir. Union County Ednl. Svcs. Commn., 2000—; cons. in mgmt., leadership, edn., volunteerism, youth programs, career planning; spl. liaison to Mcpl. Bd. Edn., Sayreville, 1991—95, Sayreville, 2000—; area admissions rep. U.S. Mil. Acad., 1984—91. Contbr. articles to profl. jours. Mem. Boy Scouts Am.; counselor, mem. dist. com. Ctrl. N.J. Coun. Boy Scouts Am., 1982—; pres., bd. dirs. Vol. Action Ctr., Middlesex County, NJ, 1979—87; pres. Sayreville War Meml. H.S. Band Parents Assn., 1994—96; county committeeman Middlesex County, 1990—94, 2000—; dir. religious edn. Sacred Heart Parish, South Amboy, NJ, 1988—91. With U.S. Army, 1969—71, with U.S. Army, 1990—92, lt. col. USAR. Decorated Meritorious Svc. medal, Army Commendation medal (2), Mil. Outstanding Vol. Svc. medal; recipient Order of the Arrow award Boy Scouts Am., 1960, 20th Century award of Achievement, Nat. Assn. Chiefs of Police, Desert Shield/Desert Storm medal State of N.J., Disting. Svc. medal State of N.J.; United Way of Ctrl. Jersey grantee, 1984, others. Mem.: ASCD, Holy Name Soc., U.S. Army Officer Candidate Alumni Assn., Am. Fedn. Police (award of merit 1989, legion of honor 1990, J. Edgar Hoover Meml. medal 1991, St. Michael the Archangel award 1992, patriotism award 1993), Nat. Assn. Ext. 4-H Agts. (regional contact 1981—83, cert. appreciation 1983), Res. Officers Assn., Mil. Police Regtl. Assn., N.J. Assn. 4-H Agts. (pres. 1985—86, outstanding svc. citation 1981, 1987), Vietnam Vets. of Am. (life; rec. sec., honor guard), Nat. Infantry Assn. (life), Nat. Eagle Scout Assn., Am. Legion, K. of C. (3d degree officer, ch. activities dir., degree team co-capt., 4th degree officer, vol. coord. fife and drums corps, color corps comdr., diocesan degree team, Family of Mo., 4th degree Family of Yr., Dist. Color Corps Man of Yr., Assembly Color Corps Man of Yr., Knight of Mo. (3), 3d degree Family of Yr.), Kiwanis, Pi Gamma Mu, Epsilon Sigma Phi, Alpha Phi Omega. Republican. Roman Catholic. Avocations: reading, music, recreational camping, travel, woodworking. Office: Eagle Assocs 166 Luke St South Amboy NJ 08879-2231

MOSKOS, CHARLES C. sociology educator; b. Chgo., May 20, 1934; s. Charles and Rita (Shukas) M.; m. Ilca Hohn, July 3, 1966; children—Andrew, Peter. BA cum laude, Princeton, 1956; MA, UCLA, 1961, PhD, 1963; LHD (hon.), Norwich U., 1992, Towson U., 2002. Asst. prof. U. Mich., Ann Arbor, 1964-66; assoc. prof. sociology Northwestern U., Evanston, Ill., 1966-70, prof., 1970—. Fellow Progressive Policy Inst., 1992—; mem. Presdl. Commn. on Women in the Mil., 1992. Author: The Sociology of Political Independence, 1967, The American Enlisted Man, 1970, Public Opinion and the Military Establishment, 1971, Peace Soldiers, 1976, Fuerzas Armadas y Societdad, 1984, The Military--More Than Just A Job?, 1988, A Call to Civic Service, 1988, Greek Americans, 1989, Soldiers and Sociology, 1989, New Directions in Greek American Studies, 1991, The New Conscientious Objection, 1993, All That We Can Be, 1996, Reporting War When There Is No War, 1996, The Media and the Military, 2000, The Postmodern Military, 2000. Chmn. Theodore Saloutos Meml. Fund; mem. Archdiocesean Commn. Third Millenium, 1982-88; mem adv. bd. Vets. for Am., 1997—; mem. Congl. Commn. on Mil. Tng. and Gender-Related Issues, 1998-99, Nat. Security Study Group, 1998-2001. Served with AUS, 1956-58. Decorated D.S.M., Fondation pour les Etudes de Def. Nat. (France), S.M.K. (The Netherlands); named to Marshall rsch. chair ARI, 1987-88, 95-96; Ford. Found. faculty fellow, 1969-70; fellow Wilson Ctr., 1980-81, guest scholar, 1991; fellow Rockefeller Found. Humanities, 1983-84, Guggenheim fellow, 1992-93, fellow Annenberg Washington Program, 1995; grantee 20th Century Fund, 1983-87, 92-94, Ford Found., 1989-90; recipient Nat. Educator Leadership award Todd Found., 1997, Book award Washington Monthly, 1997, Honored Patriot award Selective Svc. Sys., 1998; Pub. Policy fellow Wilson Ctr., 2002; Eisenhower chair Royal Mil. Acad. Netherlands, 2002. Mem. Am. Sociol. Assn., Internat. Sociol. Assn. (pres. rsch. com. on armed forces and conflict resolution 1982-86), Am. Polit. Sci. Assn., Inter-Univ. Seminar on Armed Forces and Soc. (chmn. 1987-99), Am. Acad. Arts and Scis. Greek Orthodox. Home: 2440 Asbury Ave Evanston IL 60201-2307

MOSKOWITZ, HERBERT, management educator; b. Paterson, NJ, May 26, 1935; s. David and Ruth (Abrams) Moskowitz; m. Heather Mary Lesgnier, Feb. 25, 1968; children: Tobias, Rebecca, Jonas. BS in Mech. Engring., Newark Coll. Engring., 1956; MBA, U.S. Internat. U., 1964; PhD, UCLA, 1970. Rsch. engr. GE, 1956-60; systems design engr. Gen. Dynamics Convair, San Diego, 1960-65; asst. prof. Purdue U., West Lafayette, Ind., 1970-75, assoc. prof., 1975-79, prof., 1979-85, Disting. prof., 1985-87, James B. Henderson Disting. prof., 1987-91, Lewis B. Cullman Disting. prof. mfg. mgmt., 1991—, dir. Dauch Ctr. Mgmt. Mfg. Enterprises. Cons. AT&T, Inland Steel Co.; adv. panelist NSF, 1990—. Author: Management Science and Statistics Texts, 1975—90; contbr. articles to jours. in field. Bd. dirs. Sons of Abraham Synagogue, Lafayette; mem. Lafayette Klezmorem, 1973—. Capt. USAF, 1956—60. Recipient Disting. Doctoral Student award, UCLA Alumni Assn., 1969—70; Fulbright Rsch. scholar, 1985—86. Fellow: Decision Scis. Inst. (sec. 1985—87, v.p. 1978—80); mem.: Ops. Rsch. Soc. Am./Inst. Mgmt. Sci. (liaison officer 1977—, panelist, advisor NSF and Fulbright Scholar program 1993—), Pi Tau Sigma, Tau Beta Pi. Jewish. Avocations: jewish music, tennis. Home: 1430 N Salisbury St West Lafayette IN 47906-2420 Office: Purdue U Krannert Grad Sch Mgmt Dauch Ctr Mgmt Mfg Enterprises West Lafayette IN 47907-2056

MOSKUS, JERRY RAY, academic administrator, educator; b. Springfield, Ill., Dec. 10, 1942; s. Raymond Charles and Jean (Riley) M.; children: Elizabeth, Jane, Jennifer, Julianne, Jonathan. BS in English, Ill. State U., 1965, MS in English, 1968, PhD in Edn. Adminstrn., 1983. Tchr. English Saybrook (Ill.) Arrowsmith High Sch., 1966-69; instr. Lincoln Land Community Coll., Springfield, 1969-71, asst. to pres., 1971-73, dir. rsch., 1973-75, dean, 1975-84, v.p. acad. svcs., 1984-85; exec. v.p. Des Moines Area Community Coll., Ankeny, Iowa, 1985-90; pres. Lane Community Coll., Eugene, Oreg., 1990—2001, Metro. Cmty. Coll., Omaha, 2001—. Bd. dirs. Iowa Children's & Family Svcs., Des Moines, 1986-90; bd. dirs. United Way of Lane County, 1990-94. Mem. League for Innovation in The Community Coll., Springfield Rotary, Phi Delta Kappa, Sigma Tau Delta. Office: Metro Cmty Coll 5730 N 30th St Omaha NE

MOSLAK, JUDITH, retired music educator; b. New Kensington, Pa., Sept. 16, 1942; d. Michael B. and Edith V. Moslak. MusB, Marygrove College, Detroit, Mich., 1964; MA, University of Detroit, 1967; student internat. piano workshops, France, 1998, Austria, 2000, Norway, 2002. Cert. Orff-Schulwerk Levels 1, 2, 3 1973. Assistant organist Archdiocese of Detroit, Mich., 1957—67; organist/choir director Immaculate Heart of Mary Ch., Detroit, 1964—65; elem. vocal music tchr. Detroit Pub. Schs., 1964—69; elem. vocal music cons. Farmington (Mich.) Pub. Schs., 1969—97; pvt. piano tchr. Piano Studio of Judith Moslak, West Bloomfield, Mich., 1997—; adj. asst. prof. music Madonna Univ., Livonia, Mich., 2003—. Adj. asst. prof. music Madonna U., Livonia, Mich., 2003—. Mem.: Oakland Piano Tchrs. Forum, Mich. Assn. Calligraphers, Livonia Area Piano Tchrs. Forum, Music Tchrs. Nat. Assn., Am. Guild Organists (Detroit chpt.), Am. Orff-Schulwerk Assn. (treas. 1973—75), Friends of Four Hands (charter bd. mem. 1981), Delta Kappa Gamma (treas. 1994—96). Roman Catholic. Avocations: calligraphy, travel, ensemble piano performance, digital photography. Personal E-mail: J88am@aol.com.

MOSLEY, ELAINE CHRISTIAN SAVAGE, principal, chief education officer, consultant; b. St. Louis, Mo., Mar. 4, 1941; d. John W. Savage and Mabel (Mahone) Christian; m. Melvin Ronell Mosley, Aug. 7, 1966; children: Dawn Edith, Melanie Denise, Dana Jean, John Melvin. BS, Lincoln U., 1964, MEd, 1973; EdD, Okla. State U., 1982. Tchr. St. Louis Pub. Sch. System, 1964-70, Immaculate Conception Sch., Jefferson City, 1970-73; counselor Bartlesville (Okla.) Sch. System, 1973-75, elem. prin., 1975-83, Bartlesville Pub. Sch. System, 1983-85, Oak Park (Ill.) Pub. Sch. System, 1985-87; founder, prin., chief edn. officer Corp. Community Schs. of Am., Chgo., 1987—. Adj. instr. Langston U. Urban Ctr., Tulsa, Okla., 1983; edn. cons. pub. speaking, workshops, seminars, nat., 1985—; bd. regents Rogers State Coll., Okla., 1978-85; adv. bd. First Nat. Bank, Okla., 1982-85; nat. edn. adv. bd. Channel One, Whittle Communications, 1989-91. Freelance writer in field. Active Westside Assn. Community Action, Chgo., mem. nat. adv. bd. Marwen Found., mem. early childhood adv. bd. North Ctrl. Regional Ednl. Lab. Named Citizen of the Day for contbns. to edn. Bartlesville Area C. of C., 1976; numerous other awards, citations. Mem. League of Black Women (Black Rose award for Edn. 1990), Assn. Supervision and Curriculum Devel., Nat. Assn. Edn. Young Children, Nat. Black Child Devel. Inst., Delta Sigma Theta (West Suburban chpt.), Jack & Jill of Am., Inc. (West Suburban chpt.). Democrat. Baptist. Avocations: writing, poetry reading (oral), singing, traveling, cooking. Home: 5666 Cascade Dr Lisle IL 60532-2047 Office: Corp Community Schs of Am 751 S Sacramento Blvd Chicago IL 60612-3365

MOSLEY, LINDA CAROL, elementary school educator; b. Waco, Tex., Jan. 26, 1954; d. Charlie Lester and Elenora Bertha (Jahnke) Noel; m. Wendell Guyton Mosley, Aug. 3, 1973; 1 child, Christopher Lee. BS, Baylor U., 1976, MS, 1980. Cert. tchr., kindergarten endorsement, reading specialist, Tex. Tchr. St. Mary's Parochial Sch., West, Tex., 1976-77, Troy (Tex.) Ind. Sch. Dist., 1977—. Treas. PTA, Troy, 1980-81. Mem. NEA, Tex. State Tchrs. Assn., Tex. Coun. Tchrs. Math., Tex. Assn. of Gifted/Talented, Troy Educators Assn. (sec.-treas. 1985-88, v.p. 1988-91, pres. 1993-94),

Order of Ea. Star, Daus. of the Nile. Baptist. Avocations: gardening, canning, camping, reading. Home: PO Box 116 Eddy TX 76524-0116 Office: Troy Ind Sch Dist Troy Mid Sch PO Box 409 Troy TX 76579-0409

MOSLEY-MATCHETT, JONETTA DELAINE, communications educator; b. Pitts., Jan. 13, 1955; d. Joseph and Auvelia Janet (Williams) Howell; m. Reginald Tederrell Mosley, July 27, 1973 (div. Aug. 1980); 1 child, Kelly Bree; m. Victor Matchett, July, 1, 1995. BSEET, Old Dominion U., 1980; JD, So. Meth. U., 1984; MBA, U. Tex., Arlington, 1986, PhD in Bus. Adminstrn., 1997. Assoc. elec. engr. Philip Morris, U.S.A., Richmond, Va., 1980-81, Vought Corp., Grand Prairie, Tex., 1981-82; intern patent asst. LTV Corp., Dallas, 1982; briefing asst. Office of Gen. Counsel, Dallas; regional editor EDN Mag., Newton, Mass., 1984-93; pres. Sterling Impression, Inc., Arlington, 1987—. Asst. prof. mktg. U. Tex., Arlington, 1994—. Editor newsletter Dataline, 1982-83. Earl Warren Legal Tng. scholar, 1981-84. Mem. Nat. Soc. Profl. Engrs., Nat. Tech. Assn., Profl. Assn. Diving Instrs., Phi Alpha Delta. Democrat. Roman Catholic. Avocations: scuba diving, motorcycling, pocket billiards, sewing, computers. Office: U Tex Box 19469 Arlington TX 76017-0469

MOSS, BEN FRANK, III, art educator, painter; b. Phila., Feb. 28, 1936; s. B. Frank Jr. and Helen Charlotte (Figge) M.; m. Jean Marilyn Russel, Aug. 26, 1960; children: Jennifer Kathleen, Benjamin Franklin IV. BA, Whitworth Coll., 1959; postgrad., Princeton Theol. Seminary, 1959-60; MFA, Boston U., 1963; MA (hon.), Dartmouth Coll., 1993; studied with Walter Murch, Karl Fortess and Herman Keys. Instr. Gonzaga U., Spokane, Wash., 1964-65; assoc. prof., dir. MFA and vis. artist program Fort Wright Coll., Spokane, 1965-72; acting dean, co-founder Spokane Studio Sch., 1972-74; prof. painting and drawing Sch. Art and Art History U. Iowa, Iowa City, 1975-88; George Frederick Jewett prof. art Dartmouth Coll., Hanover, N.H., 1993—. Chmn. studio art dept. Dartmouth Coll., Hanover, 1988-94, Vt. Studio Ctr., Johnson, 1990; area head painting U. Iowa, 1985; artist-in-residence Queens Coll., U. Melbourne, Australia, 1993-94; vis. artist, lectr. Northwest Mo. State U., Maryville, 1996, Houghton (N.Y.) Coll., 1996, Gordon Coll., Wenham, Mass., 1996, Northwestern U., Evanston, Ill., 1997, Colo. State U., Ft. Collins, 1997, Ravenscroft Sch., Raleigh, N.C., 1997, Coe Coll., Cedar Rapids, Iowa, 1998, Seattle Pacific U., 2002, Bowling Green U., Ohio, 2003, Williams Coll., Willamstown, Mass., 2003, numerous others. Represented by Pepper Gallery, Boston, Francine Seders Gallery, Ltd., Seattle, Susan Conway Galleries, Washington; one-man shows include Susan Conway Galleries, 1990, Dartmouth Coll., 1989, 94, Kraushaar Galleries, 1981, 83, 87, Swarthmore Coll., Pa., 1984, Stony Brook (N.Y.) Sch., 1982, Saint-Gaudens, Picture Gallery, Cornish, N.H., 1981, Kans. State U., 1980, Francine Seders Gallery, Seattle, 1979, 82, 99, Hudson D. Walker Gallery, Fine Arts Work Ctr., Provincetown, Mass., 1978, Arnot Art Mus., Elmira, N.Y., 1977, Kirkland Coll., Clinton, N.Y., 1977, Juniper Tree Gallery, Spokane, 1975, Middlebury (Vt.) Coll., 1971, Seligman Gallery, Seattle, 1967, 69, Cheney Cowels Meml. Mus., Spokane, 1967, Loomis Chaffee Sch., 1995, Tasis England Am. Sch., 1994, Queens Coll., U. Melbourne, 1994, Houghton Coll., 1996, Gordon Coll., 1996, N. W. Mo. State U., 1996, Princeton Theol. Sem., 2001, Taylor U., Upland, Ind., 2002, Bedford Art Mus., Mass., 2003, Brattleboro Mus. and Art Ctr., 1995, Nat. Acad. and Design, 1995, Messiah Coll., 1995, 97, 99, 2001, 2003, Phillips Exeter Acad., 1995, Susan Conway Galleries, 1993, 96, Chase Gallery City Hall, Spokane, 1993, Colby-Sawyer Coll., New London, N.H., 1992, Pepper Gallery, Boston, Mass., 1998, 2000, Idaho State U., Pocatello, 1972, Krcurs Gallery, N.Y.C., 2001, Augustana Coll., Rock Island, Ill., 2002, New England Coll., Henniker, N.H., 2003, others; exhibited in group shows at Blair Acad., Blairstown, N.J., 1996, Albright Knox Gallery, Buffalo, N.Y., 1995-96, Smith Coll., North Hampton, Mass., 1996, Nat. Acad. Design, N.Y.C., 1995, Boston U., 1995, Brattleboro (Vt.) Mus. and Art Ctr., 1995, Susan Conway Galleries, 1989—, Middlebury Coll. Mus. Art, Babcock Galleries, N.Y.C., Albany Inst. History and Art, Owensboro (Ky.) Mus. Fine Art, Westmoreland Mus. Art, Greenburg, Pa., Md. Inst. & Coll. Art, 1993-94, Gallery 68, 1992, Vt. Studio Ctr. Visiting Critics, Vergennes, 1992, 79th Ann. Maier Mus. Art, Randolph, Macon Women's Coll., Lynchburg, Va., 1990, Del. Ctr. Contemporary Arts, Wilmington, 1988, U. Iowa, 1976, 78, 80, 82, 84, 86, 88, Bladen Meml. Mus., Fort Dodge, Iowa, 1987, Phila. Mus. Art, 1986, Union League Club, N.Y.C., 1986, Blackfish Gallery, Portland, 1986, Columbia (S.C.) Mus. Art, 1985, Columbus Mus. Art, 1982-86, Paine Art Ctr., Oshkosh, Wis., 1985, Burpee Art Ctr., Rockford, Ill., 1985, Ill. State U., Normal, 1985, Wilkes Coll., Wilkes-Barre, Pa., 1985, Albright-Knox Mus., Buffalo, N.Y., 1984, Ark. Art Ctr., Little Rock, 1984, Millersville (Pa.) U., 1983, Fairfield (Conn.) U., 1983, Marion Koogler McKay Inst., San Antonio, 1983, Boston City Hall Gallery, 1983, Cedar Rapids (Iowa) Mus. Art, 1982, Montclair (N.J.) Jr. League, 1981, Iowa Arts Coun., Des Moines, 1980-81, Pepper Gallery, Boston, 1997-98, Spheris Gallery Fine Art, 1997, The Art Spirit Gallery of Fine Art, Walpole, N.H., 1997, Coeur d' Alene, Ind., 1998, numerous others. Sr. Faculty fellow Va. Ctr. for Creative Arts, 1996, Dartmouth Coll., 1993, MacDowell Colony, 1992, Devel. grant U. Iowa, 1980, 86; Summer fellowship U. Iowa, 1979, Rsch. and Travel grantee Ford Found., 1979-80, Yaddo Found., 1965, 72, Travel grantee U. Iowa Found., 1986,; recipient Disting. Alumni award Boston U., 1988 Mem. NAD (academician mem.), Coll. Art Assn. Independent. Presbyterian. Avocations: music, poetry, travel, tennis. Office: Dartmouth Coll Hb 6081 Studio Art Hanover NH 03755

MOSS, MELVIN LIONEL, anatomist, educator; b. N.Y.C., Jan. 3, 1923; s. Maurice and Ethel (Lander) M.; m. Letty Salentijn, Apr. 1970; children (by previous marriage)— Noel Morrow, James Andrew. AB, N.Y. U., 1942; D.D.S., Columbia, 1946, PhD, 1954. Mem. faculty Columbia, 1954—, prof., 1967-93; prof. emeritus, 1993; also dean Columbia (Sch. Dental and Oral Surgery.). Recipient Lederle Med. Faculty award, 1954-56 Fellow AAAS, Royal Anthrop. Soc. Gt. Britain; mem. Am. Assn. Anatomists, Am. Assn. Phys. Anthropologists, Internat. Assn. Dental Research (craniofacial biology award), Am. Soc. Zoologists, Sigma Xi, Omicron Kappa Upsilon. Achievements include research, numerous publs. on skeletal growth and application of computer-assisted methods of numerical and graphic analysis of growth. edu. Home: 560 Riverside Dr New York NY 10027-3202 E-mail: MLM7@columbia.

MOSS, MYRA ELLEN (MYRA MOSS ROLLE), philosophy educator; b. L.A., Mar. 22, 1937; m. Andrew Rolle, Nov. 5, 1983. BA, Pomona Coll., 1958; PhD, The Johns Hopkins U., 1965. Asst. prof. Santa Clara (Calif.) U., 1968-74; prof. Claremont McKenna Coll., 1975—, chmn. Dept. of Philosophy, 1992-95. Assoc. dir. Gould Ctr. for Humanities, Claremont, Calif., 1993-94; adv. coun. Milton S. Eisenhower Libr./Johns Hopkins U., 1994-96, 2001--. Author: Benedetto Croce Reconsidered, 1987; translator: Benedetto Croce's Essays on Literature & Literary Criticism, 1990; co-author: Values and Education, 1998; assoc. editor Special Issues; Journal of Value Inquiry, 1990-95 (Honorable Mention, Phoenix award); cons. editor Jour. Social Philosophy, 1988—; assoc. editor: Value Enquiry Book Series, 1990-95; editor: The Philosophy of José Gaos, by Pio Colonnello, Value Inquiry Book Series, 1997. Bogliasco fellow, Liguria, Italy, 2000. Mem. Am. Philos. Assn., Am. and Internat. Soc. for Value Inquiry, Soc. for Aesthetics, Collingwood Soc. (life), Phi Beta Kappa (hon.). Avocations: gardening, horseback riding. Office: Claremont McKenna Coll 850 Columbia Ave Claremont CA 91711-3901

MOSSBERG, BARBARA CLARKE, educational writer and speaker; b. Hollywood, Calif., Aug. 9, 1948; d. Gerard Theodore and Antonina Rose (Rumore) Clarke; m. Christer Lennart Mossberg, June 21, 1974; children: Nicolino Clarke Mossberg, Sophia Antonina Clarke Mossberg. BA, UCLA, 1970; MA, Ind. U., 1972, PhD, 1976. From asst. to assoc. prof. U. Oreg., Eugene, 1976-88, assoc. and acting dean Grad. Sch., 1984-85, dir. Am. studies, 1984-86; exec. dir. VIA Internat., Washington, 1988-93; assoc. provost and dir. external rels. Hobart and William Smith Colls., Geneva, N.Y., 1993-94; sr. fellow Am. Coun. Edn., Washington, 1993—; pres. Goddard Coll., Plainfield, Vt., 1997—. Prof., bicentennial chair U. Helsinki, Finland, 1982-83, sr. Fulbright Disting. lectr., 1990-91; Mellon fellow, moderator, resource fellow Aspen Inst., 1984, 88, 89; U.S. scholar in residence U.S. Info. Agy., Washington, 1986-88; dir. Am. studies summer inst. Swedish Ministry of Edn. and Culture, Uppsala U., 1986, 87, 88; dir. M. R. Smith coun. scholars Am. Coun. on Edn., Washington, 1994; spl. advisor to pres. and interim dean Coll. Arts and Scis., Nat. U., 1996. Author: Emily Dickinson, 1983 (Choice award 1983); contbr. articles to profl. jours. U.S. rep. The Lahti (Finland) Internat. Writer's Reunion, 1983, Can. Couchiching Conf., 1994; spkr. Oreg. Commn. for the Humanities, Oreg., 1983-86; adv. bd. mem., moderator The Next Stage, Washington, 1993. Rsch. grantee U. Oreg., 1979, Nat. Endowment for the Humanities, Sweden, 1980, Am. Coun. Learned Socs., U. Manchester, 1985; Disting. Inst. scholar Mt. Vernon Inst., Washington, 1994, others. Mem. Emily Dickinson Soc. (founding mem., bd. mem., v.p. and program chair 1988-90), Soc. for Values in Higher Edn., Soc. Women Geographers, Women's Fgn. Policy Group, The Writer's Ctr. Avocations: poetry, photography, architecture, art, travel. Office: Goddard Coll 123 Pitkin Rd Plainfield VT 05667-9432

MOSSINGHOFF, GERALD JOSEPH, lawyer; b. St. Louis, Sept. 30, 1935; m. Jeanne Carole Jack, Dec. 29, 1958; children: Pamela Ann Jennings, Gregory Joseph, Melissa M. Ronayne. BSEE, St. Louis U., 1957; JD with honors, George Washington U., 1961. Bar: Mo. 1961, D.C. 1965, Va. 1981. Project engr. Sachs Electric Corp., 1954-57; dir. congl. liaison NASA, Washington, 1967-73, dep. gen. counsel, 1976-81; asst. Sec. Commerce, commr. patents and trademarks U.S. Patent Office, 1981-85; pres. Pharm. Rsch. and Mfrs. Am., Washington, 1985-96; Cifelli prof. intellectual property law George Washington U., Washington, 1996—; sr. counsel Oblon, Spivak, McClelland, Maier & Neustadt, Arlington, Va., 1997—. Amb. Paris Conv. Diplomatic Conf.; adj. prof. George Mason U. Law Sch. Recipient Exceptional Svc. medal NASA, 1971, Disting. Svc. medal, 1980, Outstanding Leadership medal, 1981, Jefferson medal, 2000; Disting. Alumnus George Washington U., 1996; granted presdl. rank of meritorious exec., 1980; Disting. Pub. Svc. award Sec. of Commerce, 1983 Fellow Am. Acad. Pub. Adminstrn.; mem. Reagan Alumni Assn. (bd. dirs.), Cosmos Club, Knights of Malta, Order of Coif, Eta Kappa Nu, Pi Mu Epsilon. Home: 1530 Key Blvd Penthouse 28 Arlington VA 22209-1532 Office: Oblon Spivak McClelland Maier & Neustadt 1755 Jefferson Davis Hwy Fl 4 Arlington VA 22202-3509

MOSSMAN, KENNETH LESLIE, academic administrator, health physicist, radiobiologist; b. Windsor, Ont., Can., Apr. 14, 1946; came to U.S., 1968; s. Meyer David and Sarah (Kutchai) M.; m. Blaire Susan Volman, Aug. 30, 1970. BS, Wayne State U., 1968; MS, U. Tenn., 1970, PhD, 1973; MEd, U. Md., 1988. Asst. prof. Georgetown U., Washington, 1973-79, assoc. prof., 1979-85, chmn. dept. radiation sci., prof., 1985-90; asst. v.p. rsch., prof. Ariz. State U., Tempe, 1990—. Mem. Radiation Rsch. Soc., Health Physics Soc. (bd. dirs. 1988-90, Elda E. Anderson award 1984), Cosmos Club. Avocations: music, theater, jogging, travel.

MOSTERT, PAUL STALLINGS, mathematician, educator; b. Morrilton, Ark., Nov. 27, 1927; s. Johannes F.T. and Lucy (Stallings) M.; m. Barbara Bond; children: Paul Theodore, Richard Stallings, Kathleen, Kristina. AB, Rhodes Coll., 1950; MS, U. Chgo., 1951; PhD, Purdue U., 1953. Mem. faculty Tulane U., 1953-70, prof. math., 1962-70, chmn. dept., 1968-70; prof. math. U. Kans., 1970-91, prof. emeritus math., 1991—, chmn. dept., 1970-73. Vis. prof. U. Tubingen, Germany, 1962-63; vis. prof. math. U. Ky., 1984-85; mem. Inst. Advanced Study, Princeton, 1967-68; chmn. Rhodes Coll. Sci. Initiative Task Force, 1989-90; pres. Equix, Inc., 1984-85, Pennfield Biomechanics Corp., Inc., 1985-89, Equix Biomechanics, 1989-97; pres. Equix Rsch. Corp., 1989—; proprietor Mostert Group, 1997—, EquiMost. Co-author: Splitting in Topological Groups, 1963, 3d edit., 1993, Elements of Compact Semigroups, 1966, The Cohomology Ring of Finite and Compact Abelian Groups, 1974; editor: Proc. Conf. Transformation Groups at New Orleans, 1969, Questiones Mathematicae, 1973-95; co-founder, exec. editor: Semigroup Forum, 1970-85, mng. editor, 1967-85, editor, 1985-88; creator 9 software programs. Mem. Ky. Statewide Exptl. Program to Stimulate Competetive Rsch. Com., 1994-96. With USNR, 1945-46. Recipient Rsch. award Small Bus. Innovative Rsch., 2000, 03; Sr. postdoctoral fellow NSF, 1967-68. Mem. Am. Math. Soc. (mem. at large coun. 1972-75, chmn. com. on acad. freedom, tenure and employment security 1973-76), Assn. Mems. of Inst. for Advanced Studies, Thoroughbred Owners and Breeders Assn. Office: 3298 Roxburg Dr Lexington KY 40503-3432

MOTHERSHEAD, J. LELAND, III, dean; b. Boston, Jan. 10, 1939; s. John L. Jr. and Elizabeth Rankin (Crossett) M.; m. Therese Petkelis, June 23, 1963; 1 child, John Leland VI. BA, Carleton Coll., 1960; MA in Tchg., Brown U., 1963. Tchr. Tabor Acad., Marion, Mass., 1962-63, Chadwick Sch., Rolling Hills, Calif., 1963-66; tchr., adminstr. Flintridge (Calif.) Prep. Sch., 1966-75, head lower sch., 1972-74, dir. student affairs, 1974-75; tchr. Southwestern Acad., San Marino, Calif., 1979-83, dean, 1983—. Mem. Rotary (pres. San Marino Club 1994-95, gov. dist. 5300 1998-99). Avocation: building historic wooden ship models. Home: 1145 Oak Grove Ave San Marino CA 91108-1028 Office: Southwestern Acad 2800 Monterey Rd San Marino CA 91108-1798 E-mail: lmothers@pacbell.net.

MOTT, JUNE MARJORIE, school system administrator; b. Faribault, Minn., Mar. 8, 1920; d. David C. and Tillie W. (Nelson) Shifflett; m. Elwood Knight Mott, Oct. 18, 1958. BS, U. Minn., 1943, MA, 1948. Tchr. high schs. in Minn., 1943-46, 48-53, 54-57; script writer Hollywood, Calif., 1953-54; tchr. English, creative writing and journalism Mt. Miguel H.S., Spring Valley, Calif., 1957-86, chmn. English dept., 1964-71, chmn. dist. English coun., 1967-68; elected mem. Grossmont Union H.S. Governing Bd., from 1986, clk. sch. bd., 1989, v.p. governing bd., 1989-90, 93, pres. sch. bd., 1991-92, v.p., 1992-93, pres. governing bd., 1993-94, v.p., 1998. Mem. Press Bur., Grossmont (Calif.) H.S. Dist., 1958-86. Author, editor in field; scriptwriter TV prodn. Lamp Unto My Feet, Jam Dandy Corp.; free-lance writer, cons. travel writier, photographer; editor, publ. Listening Heart, 1989. Vice chmn. polit. action San Diego County Regional Resource Ctr., 1980-81; mem. S.D. Bd. of Alcohol and Drug Abuse Prevention, 1990—, Curriculum Com. Grossmont Dist., 1990—, Site Facilities Com., Master Planning Com., 1992—, East County Issues and Mgmt. Com., 1990—, East County Women in Edn.; apptd. del. Calif. Sch. Bds. Assn., 1992—, del. assembly, 1992—, apptd. to Race/Human Rels. Com., 1992—, elected to region 17 del. assembly, 1993—; v.p., pub. rels. chmn. Lemon Grove Luth. Ch., 1962-78, 89—, v.p., 1993, pres., 1994, chair concert series, 1997—. Writing project fellow U. Calif., San Diego, 1978; named Outstanding Journalism Tchr., State of Calif., Outstanding Humanities Tchr., San Diego County, Tchr. of Yr. for San Diego County, 1978, Woman of Yr., Lemon Grove Soroptimists, 1990; U. Cambridge scholar, 1982. Mem. ASCD, NEA, AAUW, Nat. Coun. Tchrs. English, Nat. Journalism Assn., Calif. Assn. Tchrs. English, Calif. Tchrs. Assn., So. Calif. Journalism Assn., Calif. Sch. Bds. Assn. (elected del. region 17, del. assembly 1993—), Calif. Elected Women's Assn. for Edn. Rsch. (ednl. cons. 1990), Lemon Grove C. of C., San Diego County Journalism Educators Assn. (pres. 1975-76), Grossmont Edn. Assn. (pres. 1978-80), Greater San Diego Coun. Tchrs. English, Nat. Writers Club, Am. Guild Theatre Organists, Am. Guild Organists (Palomar chpt.), Am. Poets, L.G. Friends of the Libr., Libr. Congress, Palomar chpt. Organ Soc., San Diego Mus. Art, Lemon Grove Hist. Soc., Lemon Grove Friends of Libr., Spreckels Organ Soc., Calif. Ret. Tchrs. Assn. (membeship chairwoman 1986-89, pres. chpt. #69 1989-94, parlimentarian 1992-93, chair bylaws 1996—), Lemon Grove C. of C. (mem. econ. devel. com. 1994—), Nat. Sch. Bds. Assn., Order Ea. Star, Kiwanis (pres. elect Lemon Grove chpt. 1992, program chmn., pres. 1993-94), Sigma Delta Chi, Delta Kappa Gamma (pres. Theta Gamma chpt. 1993—). Democrat. Died Aug. 25, 2002.

MOTT, MARY ELIZABETH, retired educational administrator; b. West Hartford, Conn., July 10, 1931; d. Marshall Amos and Mary Herman Mott. BA, Conn. Coll. for Women, 1953; MA, Western Res. U., 1963. Cert. tchr., Ohio; cert. computer tchr., Ohio. Mgr. sales promotion Cleve. Electric Illuminating Co., 1953-60; tchr. Newbury Bd. Edn., Ohio, 1960-67, West Geauga Bd. Edn., Chesterland, Ohio, 1967—97, ret., 1997. Chmn. state certification com. in computers ECCO, Mayfield, Ohio, 1983—, exec. bd., 1980—. Asst. dir. West Geauga Day Camp, Chesterland, 1968. Mem. Ednl. Computer Consortium Ohio, West Geauga Edn. Assn. (exec. bd. 1975-97), Delta Kappa Gamma. E-mail: pci238@aol.com.

MOTT, PEGGY LAVERNE, sociologist, educator; b. Stephenville, Tex., Mar. 23, 1930; d. Artemis Victor Dorris and Tempie Pearl (Price) Hickman; m. J.D. Mott, Sept. 11, 1947 (dec. Apr. 1988); children: Kelly A. Wilcoxson, Kimberly S. Mott. BA, Southwest Tex. State U., 1980, MA, 1982. Cert. instr. ceramic arts Nat. Ceramic Art Inst., 1972. Instr. ceramics Arts & Crafts Ctr. Lackland AFB, San Antonio, 1969-72, dir. sales Arts & Crafts Ctr., 1972-77; asst. instr. S.W. Tex. State U., San Marcos, 1980-82; instr. sociology Palo Alto Coll., San Antonio, 1991—. Author: Screaming Silences, 1994, (poem) Concho River Rev., 1993, Inkwell Echos, 1989-95, Lucidity, The T.O.P. Hwupp, 1994-95, Hwap, Patchwork Poems, 1995; co-author: Activities, Field Studies for Students. Vol. coord. Fisher Houses, Inc., Lackland AFB, 1992—; parliamentarian Artistic Expressions, 1996—. Named Vol. of Month, USAF, 1976, 77, 78, Vol. of Quarter, 1976, 77, 78, 84, Vol. of Yr., 1980. Mem. Internat. Soc. Poets, Clipper Ship Poets, San Antonio Poets Assn. (v.p. 1991-92, pres. 1992-93, Poet Laureate 1994-95), San Antonio Ethnic Arts Soc., San Antonio Poetry Festival. Avocations: reading, writing, needlework. Home: 1307 Canyon Ridge Dr San Antonio TX 78227-1727 E-mail: profpurple@msn.com.

MOTTLEY, MELINDA, secondary education educator; b. Richmond, Va., Mar. 11, 1948; d. Samuel Morton and Zoa (Robinson) M. BS, Longwood Coll., 1970; MA in Art Edn., Va. Commonwealth U., 1982; postgrad., Parsons Sch. Design, 1984. Tchr. art and jewelry Thomas Jefferson H.S., Richmond, 1972-83; art resource tchr. Arts and Humanities Ctr., Richmond, 1983-87; tchr. art and jewelry John Marshall H.S., Richmond, 1988—98; studio art, honors, AP studio instr. Richmond Cmty. H.S., 1998—. Yearbook advisor Richmond Cmty. H.S., 1999—2002; adj. instr. Va. Commonwealth U., Richmond, 1985—89; art cons. Richmond Pub. Schs., 1970—71; mem. tchrs. adv. bd. Va. Mus. Fine Arts, Richmond, 1993—2003. Exhibited jewelry in group shows at Hand Workshop, Richmond, 1985, 86, 87, Va. Craftsmen, 1989, Va. Mus. Fine Art, 1990, 91, 92, Arts on the Square Gallery, Richmond, 1993, 94, Women's Caucus, Logan Fine Arts Gallery, Midlothian, Va., 1996, Nations Bank Richmond, 1990, others. Bd. dirs. Cmty. Sch. for Arts, 1994—2000. Recipient Riches award of excellence, Taylor Pub. Co., 2002, Merit award for tchg. excellence, Scholastic, Inc., 2002; grantee, Va. Commn. for Arts, 1987, 1996, 1998, 2000, Ptnrs. in the Arts Richmond Arts Coun., 1995, 1996, 1997; Tchr. Incentive grantee, Richmond Pub. Schs., 1995, 1996, 1998. Mem. Va. Art Edn. Assn. (sec., pres. Ctrl. region 1990-95, state sec. 1993-95, Secondary Tchr. of Yr. award 1990), John Marshall H.S. Tchr. of the Yr. award 1994, Richmond Craftsmans Guild (v.p. 1988-90), Women's Caucus for Art, Va. Alliance for Arts, Soc. N. Am. Goldsmiths. Presbyterian. Avocations: singing, printmaking, painting, jewelry design, piano. Office: Richmond Community HS 5800 Patterson Ave Richmond VA 23226

MOTYKA, SUSANNE VICTORIA, music educator; b. Manhattan, N.Y., May 29, 1949; d. John Szenher and Anna Victoria Galluccio; m. William Joseph Motyka, Aug. 29, 1976; children: Matthew, Caroline, Eric. B in Music Edn., Coll. Misericordia, 1971. Cert. secondary tchg. Tchr., Tunkhannock, Pa., 1971—73, 1976—80; head music dept. Wyoming Sem., Kingston, Pa., 1973—76; choral dir. Dallas (Pa.) H.S., 1990; tchr. Gate of Heaven Sch., Dallas, 1991—2002. Orch. dir. Bishop O'Reilly, Kingston, 2000—02; choir dir., organist Gate of Heaven Ch., Dallas, 2000—02; counselor Jr. Mozart, Wilkes-Barre, Pa., 1976—2002. Recipient Padereski award, Nat. Coll. Musicians, Washington, 1997—2001. Mem.: NCTA, Music Educators Nat. Conf., Nat. Guild Piano Tchrs. Home: 3 Laselle Ave Shavertown PA 18708

MOUDON, ANNE VERNEZ, urban design educator; b. Yverdon, Vaud, Switzerland, Dec. 24, 1945; came to U.S., 1966; d. Ernest Edouard and Mauricette Lina (Duc) M.; m. Dimitrios Constantine Seferis, Dec. 30, 1982; children: Louisa Moudon, Constantine Thomas. BArch with honors, U. Calif., Berkeley, 1969; DSc, Ecole Poly. Fed., Lausanne, Switzerland, 1987. Fed. Register of Swiss Archs. Rsch. assoc. Bldg. Sys. Devel., Inc., San Francisco, 1969-70; sr. project planner J.C. Warnecke and Assocs., N.Y.C., 1973-74; archtl. cons. McCue, Boone & Tomsick, San Francisco, 1974-76; asst. to assoc. prof. architecture MIT, Cambridge, Mass., 1975-81, Ford internat. career chair, 1977-79; sec. Assn. Collegiate Schs. Arch., 1978-80; assoc. prof. urban design U. Wash., Seattle, 1981-87, prof. architecture, landscape architecture, urban design and planning, 1987—, dir. urban design program, 1987-93, assoc. dean acad. affairs Coll. Arch. and Urban Planning, 1992-95; dir. Cascadia Cmty. and Environ. Inst., Seattle, 1993-98. Lectr. architecture U. Calif., Berkeley, 1973-75; sr. rschr. Kungl Tekniska Hogskolan, Sch. Architecture, Stockholm, 1989; faculty assoc. Lincoln Inst. Land Policy, 1997—; mem. adv. com. Robert Wood Johnson Found., 2002—. Author: Built for Change, 1986; editor: Public Streets for Public Use, 1987, 91, (monograph) Master-Planned Communities, 1990, Urban Design: Reshaping Our Cities, 1995, Land Supply Monitoring with Geographic Information Systems, 2000; contbr. articles to profl. jours. Recipient Applied Rsch. award, Progressive Architecture, 1983; fellow Nat. Endowment for the Arts, 1986—87, Urban Land Inst., 1999—; grantee Nat. Endowment for the Arts, 1976—89, Wash. State Dept. Transp., 1991—2003, NIH, 1995—2000, CDC, 2001—. Fellow: Inst. for Urban Design. Avocations: walking, gardening, skiing. Home: 3310 E Laurelhurst Dr NE Seattle WA 98105-5336 Office: U Wash Box 355740 PO Box Jo-40 Goul Seattle WA 98195-5740

MOULTHROP, REBECCA LEE STILPHEN, elementary education educator; b. Lubbock, Tex., Mar. 5, 1944; d. Lee Edward and Geraldine (Lansford) Stilphen; m. John Stephen Martin Moulthrop, June 1967 (div. 1968); 1 child, Paul Martin. BS in edn., U. New Mex., 1966; MS in reading edn., Calif. State U., Fullerton, 1971; postgrad., U. LaVerne. Elem. tchr. Arnold Heights Elem. Sch., Moreno Valley, Calif., 1966-67, Hawthorn Elem. Sch., El Monte, Calif., 1968-69; chap. 1 reading specialist Posey Elem. Sch., Lubbock, 1971-72; elem. tchr. Arnold Heights Elem. Sch., Moreno Valley, 1972-74, Sunnymead Elem. Sch., Moreno Valley, 1974-80, Moreno Elem. Sch., Moreno Valley, 1980-88; chap. 1 program coord. Edgemont Elem. Sch., Moreno Valley, 1988-91; elem. tchr. Sunnymeadows Elem. Sch., Moreno Valley, 1991—. Assertive discipline cons. Moreno Valley (Calif.) Unified Sch. Dist., 1979-85, mentor/tchr., 1985-89, adminstrn. designee/trainee, 1988-95; effective tchg./supervision coach Riverside (Calif.) County Sch. Office, 1984-87. Mem. NEA, Calif. Reading Assn., Internat. Reading Assn., Reading Edn. Guild, Delta Kappa Gamma, Phi Delta Kappa. Avocations: traveling, dancing, painting. Home: 23820 Ironwood Ave Unit 56 Moreno Valley CA 92557-8109 Office: Moreno Valley Unif Sch Dist 13911 Perris Blvd Moreno Valley CA 92553-4306

MOUNTAIN, CLIFTON FLETCHER, surgeon, educator; b. Toledo, Apr. 15, 1924; s. Ira Fletcher and Mary (Stone) M.; m. Merel Ann Grey; children: Karen Lockerby, Clifton Fletcher, Jeffrey Richardson. AB, Harvard U., 1947; MD, Boston U., 1954. Diplomate Am. Bd. Surgery. Dir. dept. statis. rsch. Boston U., 1947-50; cons. rsch. analyst Mass. Dept. Pub.

Health, 1951-53; intern U. Chgo. Clinics, 1954, resident, 1955-58, instr. surgery, 1958-59; sr. fellow thoracic surgery Houston, 1959. Mem. staff U. Tex. Anderson Cancer Ctr.; asst. prof. thoracic surgery U. Tex., 1960-73, assoc. prof surgery, 1973-76, prof., 1976-94, prof. emeritus, 1995—, prof. surgery Sch. Medicine, 1987—, chief sect. thoracic surgery, 1970-79, chmn. thoracic oncology, 1979-84, chmn. dept. thoracic surgery, 1980-85, cons. dept. thoracic and cardiovascular surgery, 1996—, chmn. program in biomath. and computer sci., 1962-64, Mike Hogg vis. lectr. in S. Am., 1967; prof. surgery U. Calif., San Diego, 1996—; pres., chmn. Mountain Found. for Lung Cancer Rsch. and Edn., 1997—; mem. sci. mission on cancer USSR, 1970-78, and Japan, 1976-84; mem. com. health, rsch. and edn. facilities Houston Cmty. Coun., 1964-78; cons. Am. Joint Com. on Cancer Staging and End Result Reporting, 1964-74, Tex. Heart Inst., 1994-96; mem. Am. Joint Com. on Cancer, 1974-86, chmn. lung and esophagus task force; mem. working party on lung cancer and chmn. com. on surgery Nat. Clin. Trials Lung Cancer Study Group, NIH, 1971-76; mem. plans and scope com. cancer therapy Nat. Cancer Inst., 1972-75, mem. lung cancer study group, 1977-89, chmn. steering com., 1973-75, mem. bd. sci. counselors divsn. cancer treatment, 1972-75; hon. cons. Shanghai Chest Hosp. and Lung Cancer Ctr., Nat. Cancer Inst. of Brazil; sr. cons. Houston Thorax Inst., 1994-96. Editor The New Physician, 1955-59; mem. editl. bd. Yearbook of Cancer, 1960-88, Internat. Trends in Gen. Thoracic Surgery, 1984-91; contbr. articles to profl. jours., chpts. to textbooks. Chmn. profl. adv. com. Harris County Mental Health Assn.; bd. dirs. Harris County Chpt. Am. Cancer Soc. Lt. USNR, 1942-46. Recipient award Soviet Acad. Sci., 1977, Garcia Meml. medal Philippine Coll. Surgeons, 1982, Disting. Alumni award Boston U., 1988, Disting. Achievement U. Tex. M.D. Anderson Cancer Ctr., 1990, Disting. Svc. award Internat. Assn. for the Study of Lung Cancer, 1991, Disting. Alumnus award Boston U. Sch. of Medicine, 1992, ALCASE Internat. award for excellence, 1997, Rudolf Nissen medal German Soc. Cardiovascular and Thoracic Surgery, 1998, named hon. pres. First Internat. Congress on Thoracic Surgery, 1997; Fellow ACS Am. Coll. Chest Physicians (chmn. com. cancer 1967-75), Am. Assn. Thoracic Surgery, Inst. Environ. Scis., N.Y. Acad. Sci., Assn. Thoracic and Cardiovascular Surgeons of Asia (hon.), Hellenic Cancer Soc. (hon.), Chilean Soc. Respiratory Diseases (hon., hon. pres. 1982). Mem. AAAS, Am. Assn. Cancer Rsch., AMA, So. Med. Assn., Am. Thoracic Soc., Soc. Thoracic Surgeons, Soc. Biomed. Computing, Am. Fedn. Clin. Rsch., Internat. Assn. Study Lung Cancer (pres. 1976-78), Am. Radium Soc., European Soc. Thoracic Surgeons, Pan-Am Med. Assn., Houston Surg. Soc., Soc. Surg. Oncology, James Ewing Soc., Sigma Xi. Achievements include conception and development of program for application of mathematics and computers to the life sciences, of resource for experimental designs, applied statistics and computational support; concept and implementation of multidisciplinary, site specific cancer mgmt. clinics; first clinical use of physiological adhesives in thoracic surgery; demonstration of clinical behavior of undifferentiated small cell lung cancer; first laser resection of lung tissue at thoracotomy; development of international system for staging of lung cancer. E-mail: cmountain@ucsd.edu.

MOUNTJOY, HELEN W. educational association administrator; married; 3 children. Grad., Vanderbilt U. Mem. Ky. State Bd. Edn., 1991—, chairperson, 1998—. Mem. Ky. Literacy Partnership; mem. edn. adv. com. Coun. State Govts.; mem. Owensboro adv. bd. BB&T Bank. Chairwoman Daviess County Sch. Bd.; chair Owensboro Mercy Health Sys. Bd. Trustees, Leadership Owensboro Bd. Recipient Disting. Svc. award, Nat. Assn. State Bds. Edn., 2002. Mem.: Owensboro C. of C. (mem. edn. com., mem. citizens com. on edn.). Address: 449 Browns Valley Rd Utica KY 42376*

MOUNTS, NANCY, secondary education educator; Tchr. home econs. North High Sch., Sioux City, Iowa; tech. prep. specialist Cen. Campus, Sioux City, 1995—. Recipient State Tchr. of Yr. Home Econs. award Iowa, 1992. Office: Cen Campus 1121 Jackson St Sioux City IA 51105-1434

MOUSSEAU, DORIS NAOMI BARTON, retired elementary school principal; b. Alpena, Mich., May 6, 1934; d. Merritt Benjamin and Naomi Dora Josephine (Pieper) Barton; m. Bernard Joseph Mousseau, July 31, 1954. AA, Alpena Community Coll., 1954; BS, Wayne State U., 1959; MA, U. Mich., 1961, postgrad., 1972-75. Prof. cert. ednl. adminstr., tchr. Elem. tchr. Clarkston (Mich.) Community Schs., 1954-66; elem. sch. prin. Andersonville Sch., Clarkston, 1966-79, Bailey Lake Sch., Clarkston, 1979-94; ret., 1994. Oakland County rep. Mich. Elem. and Mid. Schs. Prins. Assn. Retirees Task Force, 1996. Cons., rsch. com. Youth Assistance Oakland County Ct. Svcs., 1968-88; leader Clarkston PTA, 1967-94; chair Clarkston Sch. Dist. campaign, United Way, 1985, 86; mem. allocations com. Oakland County United Way, 1987-88. Recipient Outstanding Svc. award Davisburg Jaycees, Springfield Twp., 1977, Vol. Recognition award Oakland County (Mich.) Cts., 1984, Heritage Chair for 40 yrs. svc. with Clarkston (Mich.) Cmty. Schs., 1994. Fellow ASCD, MACUL (State Assn. Ednl. Computer Users); mem. NEA (del. 1964), Mich. Elem. and Middle Sch. Prins. Assn. (treas., regional del. 1982—, pres.-elect Region 7 1988-89, program planner, pres. 1989-90, sr. advisor 1990-91, Honor award Region # 7 1991), Mich. Edn. Assn. (pres. 1960-66, del. 1966), Clarkston Edn. Assn. (author, editor 1st directory 1963), Women's Bowling Assn., Elks, Spring Meadows Country Club (Sr. Ladies Net Champion 1999), The Dream Golf Club, Phi Delta Kappa, Delta Kappa Gamma (pres. 1972-74, past state and nat. chmn., Woman of Distinction 1982). Republican. Avocations: golf, gardening, reading, cross country skiing, clarinet. Home: 6825 Rattalee Lake Rd Clarkston MI 48348-1955

MOUSSOUTTAS, MICHAEL M. medical educator; b. NYC, Sept. 7, 1968; s. Constantine and Christina Moussouttas; m. Maria Iuanow, Nov. 5, 2000. BA, NYU, 1990; MD, SUNY Syracuse, 1994. Lic. N.Y., 1995, diplomate Am. Bd. Neurology. Intern North Shore U. Hosp., Manhasset, NY, 1994—95; resident Mt. Sinai Hosp., NYC, 1995—98; neurovascular fellow Yale-New Haven Hosp., 1998—2000; asst. prof. N.Y. Med. Coll., Valhalla, 2000—03, Seton Hall U. Neuroscience Inst., 2003—. Neurovascular program dir. N.Y. Med. Ctr., 2000—03. Contbr. articles to profl. jours. Mem.: Am. Heart Assn., Am. Acad. Neurology. Greek Orthodox. Avocations: sports, chess, travel. Office: Dept Neurology Munger Pavillion 4th Fl Valhalla NY 10595

MOW, VAN C. engineering educator, researcher; b. Chengdu, China, Jan. 10, 1939; B. Aero. Engring., Rensselaer Poly. Inst., 1962, PhD, 1966. Mem. tech. staff Bell Telephone Labs., Whippany, N.J., 1968-69; assoc. prof. mechanics Rensselaer Poly. Inst., Troy, N.Y., 1969-76, prof. mechanics and biomed. engring., 1976-82, John A. Clark and Edward T. Crossan prof. engring., 1982-86; prof. mechanical engring. and orthopedic bioengring. Columbia U., N.Y.C., 1986—; dir. Orthopedic Research Lab., Columbia-Presbyn. Med. Ctr., N.Y.C., 1986—, Stanley Dicker prof. of biomed. engring., 1998—. Vis. mem. Courant Inst. Math. Sci., NYU, 1967-68; vis. prof. Harvard U., Boston, 1976-77; chmn. orthopaedics and musculoskeletal study sect. NIH, Bethesda, Md., 1982-84; hon. prof. Chengdu U. Sci. Tech., 1981, Shanghai Jiao Tong U., 1987; mem. grants rev. bd. Orthopaedic Rsch. Edn. Found., 1992-96; bd. dirs. Hoar Rsch. Found., 1993—; chmn. adv. com. divsn. Med. Engring. Rsch. Nat. Health Rsch. Inst., Taiwan, 1999—; cons. in field. Assoc. editor Jour. Biomechanics, 1981—, Jour. Biomech. Engring., 1979-86; chmn. editorial adv. bd. Jour. Orthopedic Rsch., 1983-90; adv. editor Clin. Orthopedic Rel. Rsch., 1993—; contbr. numerous articles to profl. jours. Founder Gordon Research Conf. on Bioengring. and Orthopedic Sci., 1980. NATO sr. fellow, 1978; recipient William H. Wiley Disting. Faculty award Rensselaer Poly. Inst., 1981; Japan Soc. for Promotion Sci. Fellow, 1986, Fogarty Sr. Internat. fellow, 1987; Alza disting. lectr. Biomed. Engring. Soc., 1987; H.R. Lissner award ASME, 1987, Kappa Delta award AAOS, 1980, Giovani Borelli award, 1991. Fellow ASME (chmn. biomechanics divsn. 1984-85, Melville medal 1982), Am. Inst. Med. Biol. Engring.; mem. NAE, Orthopaedic Rsch. Soc. (pres. 1982-83), Am. Soc. Biomechanics (founding), Internat. Soc. Biorheology, U.S. Nat. Com. on Biomechanics (sec.-treas. 1985-90, chmn. 1991-94), Inst. of Medicine, Nat. Acad. Sci. Office: Dept Biomed Engring Columbia U 351 Engring Terr MC 8904 1210 Amsterdam Ave New York NY 10027 E-mail: vcm1@columbia.edu.

MOWERY, J. RONALD, geologist, physicist, educator; b. Princeton, N.J., Nov. 2, 1939; s. J. Harry and Dorothy E. (Miller) M.; m. Nancy J. Bricker, Aug. 10, 1963 (div. Jan. 10, 1990); children: Stephen A., Karen L.; m. Judy A. Bauer, Dec. 27, 1992. BS, Shippensburg State U., 1964; MS, U. S.D., 1969. Tchr., dept. chmn. Pen Argyl (Pa.) Area H.S., 1964-68; prof. geology and physics Harrisburg (Pa.) Area C.C., 1969—; cons. Personal Profl. Svc., Harrisburg, 1980—. Cons. Dunn Geosci., Harrisburg, 1977, R.E. Wright & Assocs., Harrisburg, 1980-82. Author: Physical Science Laboratory Manual, 1973; editor: Geology & Hydrology of Delaware River Basin, 1982, (field guidebook) Susquehanna River Valley, 1983; developer/producer phys. sci. video course for coll. freshman, 1996. Cubmaster Boy Scouts Am., 1973-76; commr. Susquehanna Twp. Bd. Commn., 1984-89. With USN, 1958-63. NSF rsch. grantee, 1973, 92; recipient NISOD award 1996. Mem. AAAS, Harrisburg Area Geol. Soc. (pres. 1970), Nat. Assn. Geology Tchrs. Republican. Avocation: mineral and fossil collecting. Home: 273 W Main St Hummelstown PA 17036-1425 Office: Harrisburg Area CC 1 Hacc Dr Harrisburg PA 17110-2903 E-mail: jrmowery17036@yahoo.com.

MOWLANA, HAMID, international relations and communication educator; b. Tabriz, Iran, Feb. 25, 1937; came to U.S., 1958; s. Karim Seyyed Agha Mowlana and Robab Ibrahimi; m. Bonnie J. Byrnes. BA equivalent, U. Tehran and Northwestern U., 1959; MS, Northwestern U., 1960, PhD, 1963. Asst. prof. U. Tenn., Knoxville, 1965-68; assoc. prof. Am. U., Washington, 1968-71, prof., 1971—, dir. internat. comm. studies, 1968—. Vis. prof. various univs., 1968-2000. Author: Global Information and World Communication, 1986, 96, The Passing of Modernity, 1992, Global Communication in Transition, 1997, others. Mem. Internat. Assn. Media and Comm. Rsch. (pres. 1994-98). Avocations: walking, photography, gardening, tennis. Office: Am U Sch Internat Svc Washington DC 20016 E-mail: mowlana@american.edu.

MOWRER-REYNOLDS, ELIZABETH LOUISE, educational psychology educator; b. Camden, N.J., Jan. 5, 1955; d. Philip Aubrey and Louise Jamison (Koykka) M.; 1 child, Cali Jo., m. James O. Reynolds. BA, Trenton State U., 1977; MEd, Rutgers U., 1982, EdD, 1990. Rschr. assit. for dyslexia reading grant Rutgers U., New Brunswick, NJ, 1979-84; co-adj. prof. Rutgers Univ., New Brunswick, 1989—90; assoc. prof. U. Idaho, 1990—. Faculty in residence housemother for farmhouse Fraternity, Univ. of Idaho; progam coord. Univ. of Idaho Gifted & Talented. Author: (book) Study Guide for Good and Brophy, 1995, Contemporary Educational Psychology;Study Guides for Woolfolk, 1998, 2001; contbr. articles prof. jour. Recipient Evelyn Headley Award, Rutgers Univ., 1991, Coll. of End. tchg., public service, and advising award, Univ. of Idaho, 1993, Pi Beta Tchg. Excellance Award, 1995, Faculty Tchg. Excellance Award, Univ. of Idaho, 1994, 1995, 2001. Mem. Phi Delta Kappa (rsch. coord. 1991—, chmn. 1991—), Psi Chi, Am. edn. rsch. assoc., 1991—,Northwest Assoc. of Tchr. Educators, 1991—, (state rep., 1992), Am. Assoc. of Univ. Women, 1993, Acad. of Science, 1994—. Lutheran. Avocations: horseback riding, backpacking, camping, fishing, hunting.

MOWRY, ROBERT DEAN, art museum curator, educator; b. Quinter, Kans., Sept. 27, 1945; s. Eugene Adrian and Pearl Helen (Kreft) M. BA with honors, U. Kans., 1967, MA with honors, 1974, MPhil with honors, 1975. Curatorial asst., translator Nat. Palace Mus., Taipei, Taiwan, 1975-77; asst. curator Oriental art Fogg Art Mus., Harvard U., Cambridge, Mass., 1977-80; curator Mr. and Mrs. John D. Rockefeller 3d collections Asia Soc., N.Y.C., 1980-86; curator Asian art Harvard U. Art Mus., Cambridge, 1986-92, curator Chinese art, head dept. Asian art, 1992—2002, Alan J. Dworsky curator of Chinese Art, head dept. Asian art, 2000—. Lectr. dept. fine arts Harvard U., Cambridge, 1987-94, sr. lectr. Chinese and Korean art, 1994—; lectr. grad. program Cooper-Hewitt Mus., N.Y.C., 1983-86, Inst. Asian Studies, N.Y.C., 1982-97. Author: Handbook of the Mr. and Mrs. John D. Rockefeller 3d Collection, 1981, The Chinese Scholar's Studio: Artistic Life in the Late Ming Period, 1987, China's Renaissance in Bronze: The Robert H. Clague Collection of Later Chinese Bronzes 1100-1900, 1993, Ancient China, Modern Clay: Chinese Influences on Five Ceramic Artists, 1994, Hare's Fur, Tortoise Shell and Partridge Feathers: Chinese Brown and Black Glazed Ceramics, 400-1400, 1996, World within Worlds: The Richard Rosenblum Collection of Chinese Scholars' Rocks, 1996, Heaven and Earth Seen Within: Song Ceramics from the Robert Barron Collection, 2000, Weaving China's Past: The Amy S. Clague Collection of Chinese Textiles, 2000, From Court to Caravan: Chinese Tomb Sculptures from the Collection of Anthony M. Solomon, 2002; contbg. editor Art and Auction, N.Y.C., 1982-86; contbr. articles to profl. jours. Vol. U.S. Peace Corps, Seoul Nat. U., Republic of Korea, 1967-69. Hackney scholar Freer Gallery Art, Washington, 1975-76; fellow U. Kans., Lawrence, 1971-75, J.D. Rockefeller 3d Fund, N.Y.C., 1976-77, Samuel Kress Found., N.Y.C., 1975; grantee Nat. Endowment for the Arts, 1995, Asian Cultural Coun., 1999, Bressler Found., 2000, Ajax Found., 2002. Mem. Coll. Art Assn., Assn. for Asian Studies, Am. Com. for South Asian Art, Am. Assn. Mus., Nat. Trust for Hist. Preservation. Avocations: movies, reading, theatre, dance, opera, concerts. Office: Harvard U Art Mus Asian Dept 485 Broadway Cambridge MA 02138-3845 E-mail: mowry@fas.harvard.edu.

MOXLEY, JACQULYN CATHERINE, elementary education educator; b. Phila., Sept. 9, 1955; d. Paul Allen and Virginia Catherine (Carpenter) Killeen; m. Ronald Whelchel Moxley, May 29, 1976; children: Robert, Steven, Cathleen. BA, Glenville (W.Va.) State Coll., 1976; MA, W.Va. Coll. Grad. Studies, 1985; grad., W.Va. Tchrs. Acad., 1992. Tchr. Fair Haven Christian Sch., Charleston, W.Va., 1976-77, Mill Creek Elem. Sch., Pecks Mills, W.Va., 1977-79, Spruce Grade Sch., Sharples, W.Va., 1979-93, Sharples Elem.-Mid. Sch., 1993—. Cons. on social studies curriculum goals Logan County Bd. Edn., Logan, W.Va., 1993, mem. curriculum study group early childhood com., 1995; sec. faculty senate Spruce Grade Sch., 1990-93, mem. curriculum team, 1991-93, mem. sch. improvement coun., 1992-93; sec. faculty senate and curriculum team Sharples Elem. Sch., 1993-95, mem. sch. improvement coun., 1993-95. Advisor Washington Dist. Redskins Majorettes, Ramage, W.Va., 1993. Recipient Tchr. of Yr. award Spruce Grade Sch., 1992, Sharples Elem.-Mid. Sch., 1994. Democrat. Methodist. Avocations: sewing, crafts. Home: RR 2 Box 178C Danville WV 25053-9568 Office: Sharples Elem-Mid Sch Drawer B Sharples WV 25183

MOYA, OLGA LYDIA, law educator; b. Weslaco, Tex., Dec. 27, 1959; d. Leonel V. and Genoveva (Tamez) M.; children: Leanessa Geneva Byrd, Taylor Moya Byrd. BA, U. Tex., 1981, JD, 1984. Bar: Tex. 1984. Legis. atty. Tex. Ho. of Reps., Austin, 1985; atty. Tex. Dept. Agr., Austin, 1985-90; asst. regional counsel U.S. EPA, Dallas, 1990-91; from asst. prof. to assoc. prof. South Tex. Coll. of Law, Houston, 1992-97; prof. law South Tex. Coll. Law, Houston, 1997—. Author: (with Andrew L. Fono) Federal Environmental Law: The User's Guide, 1997, 2d edit., 2001. Bd. dirs. Hermann Children's Hosp., Houston, 1993-97; mem. Leadership Tex., Austin, 1991—; bd. trustees Meml. Hermann Healthcare Sys. Found., 1997-99; bd. dirs. Tex. Clean Water Coun., Austin, 1992, Met. Transit Authority of Harris County, 1999—; U.S. del. to UN Conf. on the Environ. for Latin Am. and the Caribbean, San Juan, P.R., 1995. Recipient Nat. Top 12 Hispanics in Law, Miller Brewing Co., 1996; Vol. of Yr. award George H. Hermann Soc., 1995, Hispanic Law Prof. of Yr. Hispanic Nat. Bar Assn., 1995. Mem. ABA (environ. law sect.), Hispanic Bar Assn. (bd. dirs. 1992—, Excellence award 1995, 96), Mex.-Am. Bar Assn. Office: South Tex Coll of Law 1303 San Jacinto St Houston TX 77002-7013

MOYA, SARA DREIER, educational association administrator; b. N.Y.C., June 9, 1945; d. Stuart Samuel and Hortense (Brill) Dreier; m. P. Robert Moya, May 30, 1966; children: J. Brill, Joshua D. BA, Wheaton Coll., Norton, Mass., 1967; postgrad., Mills Coll., Oakland, Calif., 1967-68; MPA, Ariz. State U., 1995, PhD, 2002. Mem. Paradise Valley (Ariz.) Town Coun., 1986-98, vice mayor, 1990-92; instr. advanced pub. exec. programs Ariz. State U. Chmn. Gov.'s Homeless Trust Fund Oversight Com., 1991—; pres. Ctr. for Acad. Precosity, Ariz. State U., Tempe, 1987-95; bd. dirs. Ariz. Assn. Gifted and Talented; participant 3d session Leadership Am., 1990; mem. steering com. Maricopa County Homeless Continuum of Care, 1999—, mem. planning subcom., 2000—; mem. planning com. N.E. Valley Family Advocacy Ctr., 2001—; adj. prof. planning and landscape arch. Ariz. State U. Mem. Citizens Adv. Bd. Paradise Valley Police Dept., 1984-86, Valley Citizens League Task Force on Edn., bd. trustees Paradise Valley Sch., 2002—, Socio-Economic Indications Group, 2002—, Pewate Sch. Found., 2002—; bd. dirs. Valley Leadership Inc., 1988-94; chair Maricopa Assn. Govts. Task Force on Homeless, 1989-92, 95-98; mem. Emergency Food and Shelter Program, FEMA bd. Maricopa County and Ariz., 1989—, chmn., 1996—; dir. Valley Youth Theater, 1990-93, Maricopa County Homeless Accomodation Sch., 1991—. Mem. ASPA (bd. dirs. 1996-98, pres. 1999-2000), Ariz. Women in Mcpl. Govt. (sec. 1988-89, bd. dirs. 1986—, pres. 1989-90), Western Social Sci. Assn., Ariz. State U. Students of Pub. Affairs Network (sec./treas. 1996-98), Data Network for Human Svcs. (bd. dirs. 1990-93), Maricopa Assn. Govts. (regional coun. 1988-98, vice-chmn. mag. regional devel. policy com. 1989-91, chair 1992-98, mag. joint econ. devel./human resources subcom. 1990-94, mag. youth policy adv. com. 1994-98, blue ribbon com. 1995-97, vision 2025 com. 1997-2000, chair urban features subcom. 1998-2000, valley vision 2025 steering com. 1999-2000), Maricopa Assn. Govts. (air quality policy com. 1994-96), Ariz. Acad., Ariz. Planning Assn. (bd. dirs., citizen planner, 1996-98), Paradise Valley Country Club, Phi Kappa Phi, Pi Alpha Alpha. Republican. Avocations: traveling, golfing, reading. Home: 5119 E Desert Park Ln Paradise Valley AZ 85253

MOYARS-JOHNSON, MARY ANNIS, university official; b. Lafayette, Ind., July 19, 1938; d. Edward Raymond and Veronica Marie (Quigg) Moyars; m. Raymond Leon Molter, Aug. 1, 1959 (div. 1970); children: Marilyn Eileen Molter Davis, William Raymond Molten Johnson, Ann Marie Molten Guentert; m. Thomas Elmer Johnson, May 25, 1973 (div. 1989); children: Thomas Edward, John Alan, Barbara Suzanne. BS, Purdue U., 1960; MA, Purdue U., West Lafayette, Ind., 1991, postgrad., 1985—. Grader great issues Purdue U., West Lafayette, 1960-63, writer ednl. films, 1962-65, publicity dir. convocations and lectures, 1969-74, devel. officer Sch. Humanities, 1979-88, asst. to dir. Optoelectronics Rsch. Ctr., 1989-90, mgr. indsl. rels. Sch. Elec. and Computer Engring., 1990—2002, assoc. v.p. for info. tech., for comm., 2002—; tchr. English and math. Benton Community Schs., Fowler, Ind., 1966-69; pub. rels. dir. Sycamore Girl Scout Coun., Lafayette, Ind., 1974-78; dir. pub. info. Ind. Senate, Majority Caucus, Indpls., 1977-78; sr. script writer Walters & Steinberg, Lafayette, 1988-89. Author: Colonial Potpourri, 1975, Ouiatanon--The French Post Among the Ouia, 2000; co-author: Historic Colonial French Dress, 1982, 2nd edit., 1998; contbr. articles to profl. jours. Bd. govs. Tippecanoe County Hist. Assn., Lafayette, 1981-97. Mem. Women in Comms., Inc. (v.p. program, Pres. award 1983), Ctr. for French Colonial Rsch. (dir. 1986-89, editor 1988-89), Palatines to Am., Ind. History Assn., Ind. Hist. Soc., French Colonial Hist. Soc. Roman Catholic. Avocations: history, genealogy, embroidery. Home: 924 Elm Dr West Lafayette IN 47906-2246 Office: Purdue Info Tech Young Hall West Lafayette IN 47906-3560 E-mail: moyars@purdue.edu.

MOYER, ANNA BLACKBURN, retired secondary and elementary school educator; b. Lock Haven, Pa., Nov. 27, 1938; d. Edwin Conley and Charlotte Catherine (Eisenhower) Blackburn; m. John C. Moyer, May 28, 1960; 1 child, Johanna Lee Moyer Michalik. BS in English cum laude, Lock Haven State Coll., 1962; MEd, Pa. State U., 1976; postgrad., Lock Haven U., 1996-97. Cert. tchr. Pa. English, journalism tchr. Lock Haven Area Sch. Dist., 1962-64; devel. reading tchr. Bellefonte (Pa.) Area Sch. Dist., Pa., 1970-73; devel., remedial reading tchr., student govt. adv. Williamsport (Pa.) Area Sch. Dist., Pa., 1975-95; title 1 reading tchr. Lose Elem. Sch., 1995—2000; title 1 tchr. Cochran Elem. Sch. and St. Boniface Elem. Sch., Williamsport, 1999—2000; ret., 2000. Speaker in field. Coord. Williamsport Students Engaged in Real Vol. Efforts, 1990-1995 Mem. Delta Kappa Gamma. Republican. Avocations: needlework, reading, cooking. Home: Dunrovin Lane 14707 Coudersport Pike Lock Haven PA 17745

MOYER, LINDA LEE, artist, educator, author; b. Niles, Mich, Feb. 11, 1942; d. Roy Delbert and Estelle Leona (Beaty) Moyer; m. Brock David Williams Dec. 3, 1994; 1 child from previous marriage, Metin Ata Gunsay. Student, Occidental Coll., 1959-61; BA, UCLA, 1964; MA, Calif. State U., Long Beach, 1977, MFA, 1980. Cert. tchr. secondary edn., cert. computer graphics, Calif. Instr. art. Huntington Beach Union HS, Calif., 1967-81, Calif. State U., Long Beach, 1981-85, Saddleback Coll., Mission Viejo, Calif., 1986-88, Fullerton Coll., Calif., 1990, 94, Goldenwest Coll., Huntington Beach, 1990. Artist-in-residence St. Margaret's Episc. Sch., San Juan Capistrano, 1993; lectr., workshop presenter Santa Barbara C.C., Calif., 1992; series lectr. Rancho Santiago Coll., 1985, 90; lectr. Cypress Coll., 1986, Watercolor West, 1987, others; methods and materials show instr. Am. Artist Mag., 1996, 97, 98, 99, 99, 2000, 01, 03; juror fine art exhbns; presenter workshops in field; website co-founder watercolor-online.com. Exhibited in group shows at Owensboro, Mus. Fine Arts, Ky., 1979, Newport Harbor Art Mus., Newport Beach, Calif., 1981, Burpee Art Mus., Rockford, Ill., 1981, one-woman shows include Orange County Ctr. Contemporary Art, 1982, 1985, exhibited in group shows at Nat. Acad. Galleries, NYC, 1982, one-woman shows include Laguna Beach Mus. Art, Calif., 1982, Orlando Gallery, Sherman Oaks, Calif., 1983, exhibited in group shows at Leslie Levy Gallery, Scottsdale, Ariz., 1983, Art Inst. So. Calif., 1984, one-woman shows include Orange County Ctr. Contemporary Art, 1985, Cerritos Coll., Norwalk, Calif., 1986, Louis Newman Galleries, Beverly Hills, 1986, exhibited in group shows at Saddleback Coll., Mission Viejo, Calif., 1988, one-woman shows include Louis Newman Galleries, Beverly Hills, 1988, exhibited in group shows at Ch. of Jesus Christ of LDS Mus. Art and History, Salt Lake City, 1988, Riverside (Calif.) Art Mus., 1989, one-woman shows include Louis Newman Galleries, Beverly Hills, 1990, exhibited in group shows at Ch. of Jesus Christ of LDS Mus. Art and History, Salt Lake City, 1991, one-woman shows include Westmont Coll., Santa Barbara, 1992, Maturango Mus., Ridgecrest, Calif., 1996, exhibited in group shows at Mt. San Antonio Coll., Calif., 1996, Springville Art Mus., Utah, 1999, Kimball Art Ctr., Park City, Utah, 2003, others, Represented in permanent collections Springville Mus. Art, Home Savs. Bank of Am., Nat. Bank of La Jolla, Greenburg Deposit Bank, Ashland, Ky., INMA Gallery, Saudi Arabia, exhibited in group shows at Springville Art Mus., Utah, 2000, Represented in permanent collections pvt. collectors; author: Light Up Your Watercolors Layer by Layer, 2003. Recipient Gold Medal of Honor, Am. Watercolor Soc., 1982, Walser S. Greathouse medal, 1988, Gold Medal of Honor for watercolor Allied Artists Am., 1982, cash merit award Ch. of Jesus Christ Latter Day Saints Mus. Art and History, 1991, Best of Show award Utah Watercolor Soc., 2000, 2d award, Religious and Spiritual Art of Utah Exhbn., 2d award, 1998, 3d award, 1999, Best of Show, Challenge of Champions, Watercolor Art Soc. Houston, 2003. Signature mem. Nat. Watercolor Soc., Watercolor West (1st award 1984, N.W.S. award 1999, pres. 1999-2001), Watercolor West (life), Utah Watercolor Soc. Mem. Lds Ch. Avocations: reading, playing piano, genealogy. Home and Office: 22 Lakeview Stansbury Park UT 84074 E-mail: lindamoyer@watercolor-online.com.

MOYER, RALPH OWEN, JR., chemist, educator; b. New Bedford, Mass., May 19, 1936; s. Ralph Owen and Annie (Brown) M. BS, U. Mass., Dartmouth, 1957; MS, U. Toledo, 1963; PhD, U. Conn., 1969. Devel. engr. Union Carbide Corp., Fostoria, Ohio, 1957-64; asst. prof. chemistry Trinity Coll., Hartford, Conn., 1969-76, assoc. prof., 1976-86, prof., 1986-91, Scovill prof. chemistry, 1991—; dept. chmn., 1983, 85-88. Vis. lectr. U. West Indies, Kingston, Jamaica, 1985; rsch. collaborator Brookhaven Nat. Lab., Upton, N.Y., 1977-78. Contbr. articles and chpt. to profl. pubs. With U.S. Army, 1959. Mem. Am. Chem. Soc. (chmn. Connecticut Valley sect. 1984), N.Y. Acad. Scis., Sigma Xi (pres. Hartford chpt. 1990-91). Achievements include two patents for carbon fibers. Home: 9 Grandview Ter Wethersfield CT 06109-3240 Office: Trinity Coll 300 Summit St Hartford CT 06106-3100

MOYLAN, JOHN L. secondary school principal; Prin. DeMatha Cath. High Sch., Hyattsville, Md., 1969-2000, asst. to rector for instnl. advancement, 2000—. Recipient Blue Ribbon Sch. award U.S. Dept. Edn., 1983-84, 90-91, Disting. Prin. award Archdiocese of Washington, 1991, Sch. Adminstr. award Md. Music Educators Assn., 1992, Disting. Ednl. Leadership award Washington Post, 1993. Office: DeMatha Cath High Sch 4313 Madison St Hyattsville MD 20781-1692

MOYNIHAN, GARY PETER, industrial engineering educator; b. Little Falls, N.Y., Mar. 5, 1956; s. Peter H. and Frances S. (Ferjanec) M.; m. Eleanor T. McCusker, Mar. 10, 1984; children: Andrew Ross, Keith Patrick. BS in Chemistry, Rensselaer Polytech. Inst., 1978, MBA in Opsl. Mgmt., 1980; PhD in Indsl. Engring., U. Ctrl. Fla., 1990. Prodn. supr. Am. Cyanamid, Bound Brook, N.J., 1978-79, Nat. Micronetics, Kingston, N.Y., 1980-81; assoc. mfg. engr. Martin Marietta Aerospace, Orlando, Fla., 1981-82, indsl. engr., 1982-85, sr. indsl. engr., 1985-87, group indsl. engr., 1987-90; asst. prof. indsl. engring. U. Ala., Tuscaloosa, 1990-96, assoc. prof., 1996—2001, prof., 2001—. Cons. in field. Contbr. articles to profl. jours. Regents scholar N.Y. State Bd. Regents, 1974-78; rsch. fellow NASA, 1992-93, 98-99; rsch. grant BellSouth Telecomm., 1994-96; recipient Outstanding Tchg. award AMOCO Found., 1993-94, Ralph R. Teetor Engring. Educator award Soc. Automotive Engrs, 2000. Mem. IEEE (sr.), Inst. Indsl. Engrs. (sr. mem., chpt. dir. 1991-95, chpt. pres. 1996-97), Aerospace & Def. Soc. (v.p. fin. and adminstrn. 1994-97). Achievements include design and development of information systems applications for the aerospace and foundry industries; 4 software copyrights. Office: U Ala Dept Indsl Engring Tuscaloosa AL 35487-0001

MPINGA, DEREK AMOS, mathematics educator; b. Kadoma, Zimbabwe, Aug. 8, 1943; married. AS, North Greenville Coll., 1970; BS in Math. and Physics, Carson Newman Coll., 1972; MA in Math., Tex. Christian U., 1975; MRE, Southwestern Theol. Seminary, 1976, EdD in Edn. Adminstrn., 1979. From instr. to asst. to prin. adminstrv. affairs Sanyati (Zimbabwe) High Sch., 1966-69; from field edn. adjunct to grad. teaching asst. Southwestern Theol. Seminary, Ft. Worth, 1976-79; prof. edn., adminstrn., acad. dean Bapt. Theol. Seminary Zimbabwe, Gweru, 1979-83; prof. edn., adminstrn., acad. dean, vice prin. Nairobi (Kenya) Grad. Sch. Theology, 1983-85; instr. math. and physics Americus (Ga.) High Sch., 1985-87; asst. prof. math. Tarrant County Jr. Coll. N.E., Ft. Worth, 1987-92; prof. math. North Lake Coll., Irving, Tex., 1992—; dir., Inst. of Science Technol. Engring. and Math., 1993—. Adj. tchr. math. Tarrant County Jr. Coll., Ft. Worth, 1977-79, Nashville High Sch., 1982-83; mem. accrediting coun. theol. edn. in Africa and Madagascar, 1982-89; exec. dir. Leadership Devel. Assocs., Arlington, Tex. Dir. youth ministries Calvary Bapt. Ch., 1962-66, Sanyati Bapt. Ch., 1966-69; founding mem. Bapt. Youth Ministry Zimbabwe, 1963-83; chmn. bd. dirs. Bapt. Book Stores, 1980-83; sec. gen. Bapt. Conv. Zimbabwe, 1980-83; mem. world hunger and relief com. Bapt. World Alliance, 1980-90, founding mem. Internat. Conf. Theol. Educators, 1982—, All Africa Bapt. Fellowship, v.p., 1982-86; Africa adv. bd. Living Bibles Internat., 1981-84; deacon First Bapt. Ch., Arlington, 1991-94. Mem. Math. Assn. Am., Am. Math. Assn. Two Year Colls. (devel. math. com. 1989—, equal opportunity in math. com. 1989—, nominating com. 1993—, student math. league 1993—, del. Tex.-N.Mex. region 1993—), So. Assn. Colls. and Schs. (reaffirmation team 1992-93), Tex. Math. Assn. Two Year Colls. (chair devel. math. com. 1989-92), Tex. Jr. Coll. Assn., Tex. Faculty Assn., Phi Theta Kappa, Sigma Pi Sigma, Kappa Mu Epsilon. Home: 655 Goodpasture Island Rd Eugene OR 97401-1522

MRAK, ROBERT EMIL, neuropathologist, educator, electron microscopist; b. Oakland, Calif., Dec. 18, 1948; s. Emil Marcel and Vera Dudley (Greaves) M.; m. Paula Elizabeth North, Oct. 18, 1980; children: Lara North, Eric North, Ian North. BS in Math., U. Calif., Davis, 1970, MD, 1975, PhD in Zoology, 1976. Diplomate Am. Bd. Pathology, Am. Bd. Neuropathology. Resident in pathology Vanderbilt U. Hosp., Nashville, 1976-78, fellow in molecular biology, 1978-80; asst. prof. pathology Vanderbilt U., 1980-84, U. Ark. for Med. Scis., Little Rock, 1984-87, assoc. prof. pathology and anatomy, 1987-93, prof. pathology and anatomy, 1993—98, chief neuropathology, 1999—, dir. neuropathology core, Alzheimer Disease Core Ctr., 2001—, prof. pathology, anatomy and neurobiology, 1998—. Chief electron microscopy VA Hosp., Little Rock, 1984-98; cons. in neuropathology Ark. Children's Hosp., Little Rock, 1984—. Editl. bd. mem. Jour. Neuropathy & Explt. Neurology, 1996-99, Human Pathology, 1996—; contbr. articles and abstracts to profl. jours. Rsch. grantee VA, 1980-83, 86-89, Muscular Dystrophy Assn., 1981-85, NIH, 1986-90, 95—. Mem. Am. Assn. Neuropathologists, Soc. for Neurosci., U.S. and Can. Acad. Pathology. Avocations: running, skiing. Office: U Ark for Med Scis #517 4301 W Markham St Little Rock AR 72205-7101 E-mail: mrakroberte@uams.edu.

MRUK, CHRISTOPHER J. psychologist, educator; b. Mt. Clemens, Mich., May 21, 1949; s. Joseph and Veronica (Harris) M; m. Marsha Jean Oliver, Dec. 24, 1983. BS, Mich. State U., 1971; MA, Duquesne U., 1974, PhD, 1981. Lic. clin. psychologist, Ohio, Pa. Staff psychologist Mon Valley Mental Health Ctr., Monessen, Pa., 1981-82; dir. counseling St. Francis Coll., Loretto, Pa., 1982-83; prof. Firelands Coll., Bowling Green State U., Huron, Ohio, 1984—. Cons. psychologist Firelands Cmty. Hosp., Sandusky, Ohio, 1988—. Author: Self-Esteem: Research, Theory and Practice, 1995, 2d edit., 1999; co-author: Zen and Psychotherapy: Integrating Traditional and Non-Traditional Approaches, 2003; contbr. chpts. in books and articles to profl. jours. Bd. dirs. Safe Harbour Domestic Violence Ctr., Sandusky, 1992. Mem. Am. Psychol. Assn. Avocations: computers, writing, working out.

MUCK, RUTH EVELYN SLACER (MRS. GORDON E. MUCK), education educator; b. Buffalo, July 17, 1910; d. Robert A. and Hattie E. (Sheridan) Slacer; B.S., State U. Coll. at Buffalo, 1938, M.S., 1952; Ed.D., State U. N.Y. at Buffalo, 1966; m. Gordon E. Muck, Dec. 27, 1934; 1 child, Linda Mae McGuire. Tchr. pub. schs., Lockport, N.Y., 1931-42; tchr. primary level campus sch. State U. Coll., Buffalo, 1942-66, prof. edn. div. elem., from 1966, now emeritus; cons. tchr. edn. workshops, Minn., Fla. Dir. youth edn. United Meth. Ch., 1960-69; pres. United Meth. Women, Grand Island, N.Y.; bd. dirs. United Meth. Found., West N.Y., 1986-92, N.Y. Dist. United Meth. Extension Soc., Buffalo, 1988-94; pres. Town of Lockport N.Y. Hist. Soc., 1987—; vol. community svc.; dir. children's used clothing shop. Recipient Mission Recognition award United Meth. Women, 1994, ecumenical cmty. svc. award, 1998. Mem. Assn. Tchr. Educators (state pres. 1972-73), Internat. Reading Assn. (chmn. 1969-71), Delta Kappa Gamma, Pi Lambda Theta. Home: 1091 Stony Point Rd Grand Island NY 14072-2712

MUDD, ANNE CHESTNEY, mediator, law educator, real estate broker; b. Macon, Ga., June 30, 1944; d. Bard Sherman Chestney and Betty (Bartow) Houston; children: Charles Lee Jr., Richard Chestney, Robert Jason. BA, U. Louisville, 1966, MA, 1976; JD, John Marshall Law Sch., 1998. Math statistican U.S. Bur. Census, Jeffersonville, Ind., 1966-70; instr. math. U. Louisville, 1975-77, Coll. DuPage, Glen Ellyn, Ill., 1978-85, 92; tchr. math and substitute tchr. Lyons Twp. High Sch., La Grange, Ill., 1986-91; realtor First United Realtors, Western Springs, Ill., 1989-92; owner, mgr. retail bus., 1992—2000; lawyer, 1998—. Adj. prof. law. Editor: Mathematics Textbook, 1991-92. Steering com. Village Western Springs, 1986-87; bd. dirs. Children's Theater, 1987-91; sec. Collaborative Law Inst. of Ill., Leave a Legacy N.E. Ill. Outreach Com.; major gift task force Am. Cancer Soc. DuPage County. Mem.: LWV (pres. 1983—85, bd. dirs.), Assn. for Conflict Resolution, Mediation Coun. Ill. Avocations: gardening, politics, local govt.. Home: 3958 Hampton Ave Western Springs IL 60558-1011

MUDD, SHERYL KAY, secondary school educator, guidance counselor; b. Ft. Thomas, Ky., July 14, 1960; d. Robert Leslie and Marvel Maxine (Youtsey) M.; m. Jackie Elaine Nichols, Lawrence Robert, Gerald Leslie, Randy Kent, Ronald Lee, Rhonda Dee, Michael Todd. BA, Transylvania U., 1982; MEd in Guidance Counseling, Xavier U., 1988; MEd in Instrnl. Supervision, No. Ky. U., 2001. Cert. elem. tchr., K-12 phys. edn. tchr., instrnl. leadership K-12, Ky. Substitute tchr. Pendleton County Schs., Falmouth, Ky., 1982-84, Campbell County Schs., Alexandria, Ky., 1982-84; tchr. No. Elem. Sch., Butler, Ky., 1984-86; tchr. math. Pendleton Mid. Sch., Falmouth, 1986-88, tchr. reading, 1988-89, tchr. health and phys. edn., 1989-92, 95—; tchr. 7th and 8th grades Risk Youth, 1992-95; tchr. health and phys. edn. 6th -8th grades Phillip A. Sharp Mid. Sch., Butler, 1995—. Named to Honorable Order of Ky. Colonels, Commonwealth of Ky., 1979, 96, Tchr. of Yr., Pendleton Mid. Sch., 1989, 93, 94, 95, 96. Mem. ASCD, AAHPERD, Assn. for Advancement Health and Phys. Edn., AACD, Ky. Assn. for Gifted Assn., Ky. Mid. Sch. Assn., No. Ky. Assn. Counseling and Devel. Democrat. Roman Catholic. Avocations: basketball, softball, volleyball, bowling, field hockey. Home: 50 Tammy Ln Butler KY 41006-9609 Office: Phillip A Sharp Mid Sch 35 Wright Rd Butler KY 41006

MUELLER, CHARLES BARBER, surgeon, educator; b. Carlinville, Illinois, Jan. 22, 1917; s. Gustav Henry and Myrtle May (Barber) M.; m. Jean (Mahaffey), Sept. 7, 1940; children: Frances Ann, John Barber, Richard Carl, William Gustav. BA, U. Ill., 1938; MD, Washington U., St. Louis, 1942; LHD (hon.), Blackburn Coll., 1987; DSC (hon.), State Univ. of N.Y., Syracuse, 2002; DSc (hon.), McMaster U., 2003. Intern, then resident in surgery Barnes Hosp., St. Louis, 1942-43, 46-51; asst. prof. Wash. U. Med. Sch., 1951-56; prof. surgery, chmn. dept. State Univ. of N.Y. Med. Sch., Syracuse, 1956-67; prof. surgery Mc Master U. Med. Sch., Hamilton, Canada, 1967—, chmn. dept., 1967-72. Contbr. articles to profl. journals. Served in USNR, 1943—46. Decorated Purple Heart with 2 oak leaf clusters, Bronze Star; recipient Favorite Son Award So. Ill. Med. Soc., 1996; Jackson Johnson fellow, 1938-42; Rockefeller post war asst., 1946-49; Markle scholar, 1949-54. Mem. ACS (v.p. 1987-88, Disting. Svc. Award 1984), Am. Surg. Assn., Ctrl. Surg. Assn., Soc. Univ. Surgeons, Assn. Acad. Surgery, Royal Coll. Physicians and Surgeons (Duncan Graham Disting. Svc. Award 1992), Phi Beta Kappa, Sigma Xi, Alpha Omega Alpha, Phi Kappa Phi.

MUELLER, DIANE, hotel executive; m. Tim Mueller; children: Ethan, Erica. V.p., co-owner Okemo Mountain Resort, Ludlow, Vt., 1982—. Mem. Vt. State Bd. Edn., 1998—, chmn., 2003—; past mem. Green Mountain Union H.S. Bd., Chester; founder Okemo Cmty. Challenge. Named Citizen of the Yr., Vt. C. of C., 2001. Office: Okemo Mountain Resort 77 Okemo Ridge Rd Ludlow VT 05149*

MUELLER, DON SHERIDAN, retired school administrator; b. Cleve., Nov. 4, 1927; s. Don P. and Selma Christina (Ungericht) M.; m. Vivian Jean Santrock, Aug. 27, 1947 (dec. 1993); chlidrne: Carl Frederick, Cathy Ann. BS, Mt. Union Coll., 1948; MA, U. Mich., 1952; EdS, Mich. State U., 1968; PhD, Clayton U., 1977. Tchr. Benton-Harbor Fair Plain (Mich.) Schs., 1947-52; dir. music edn. Okemos (Mich.) Pub. Schs., 1952-64; jr.-sr. high prin. Dansville (Mich.) Schs., 1964-68; prin. DeWitt (Mich.) H.S., 1968-73; supt. Carsonville (Mich.)-Port Sanilac Schs., 1973-94; ret., 1994. Recipient Cmty. Leader Am. award, 1968, 72, 73-74, Acad. Am. Educators award, 1973-74. Mem. NEA, ASCD, Am. Assn. Sch. Adminstrs., Mich. Assn. Sch. Adminstrs., Mich. Assn. Sch. Bds., Mich. Sch. Band/Orch. Assn. (pres. dist. 5 1958-60, sec. 1962-63), Clinton Prins. Assn. (pres. 1972-73), Ingham Prins. Assn. (pres. 1967-70), Okemos Edn. Assn. (pres. 1962-63), River Area Supts. Assn. (pres. 1979-80). Home: 4290 Guilford Ln Fort Gratiot MI 48059-4013

MUELLER, GERHARD G(OTTLOB), retired financial accounting standard setter, retired educator; b. Eineborn, Germany, Dec. 4, 1930; came to U.S., 1952, naturalized, 1957; s. Gottlob Karl and Elisabeth Charlotte (Hossack) M.; m. Coralie George, June 7, 1958; children: Kent, Elisabeth, Jeffrey. AA, Coll. of Sequoias, 1954; BS with honors, U. Calif.-Berkeley, 1956, MBA, 1957, PhD, 1962; D Econs. (hon.), Swedish Sch. Econs. and Bus. Adminstrn., 1994; D Laws (hon.), Kwansei Gakuin U., 2000. CPA (ret.), Wash. Staff accountant FMC Corp., San Jose, Calif., 1957-58; faculty dept. accounting U. Wash., Seattle, 1960-96, assoc. prof., 1963-67, prof., 1967-96, chmn. dept., 1969-78, dir. grad. profl. acctg. program, 1979-90, sr. assoc. dean, 1990-95, acting dean, 1994, Hughes M. Blake prof. internat. bus. mgmt., 1992-95, Julius A. Roller prof. acctg., 1995-96, mem. fin. acctg. stds. bd., 1996—2001; ret., 2001. Dir. U. Wash. Acctg. Devel. Fund, Overlake Hosp. Med. Ctr., Bellevue, 1984-96, chmn. bd. trustees, 1991-93; cons. internat. tax matters U.S. Treasury Dept., 1963-68; cons. Internat. Acctg. Rsch., 1964-96; vis. prof. Cranfield Sch. Mgmt., Eng., 1973-74, U. Zurich, Switzerland, 1973-74; lectr. in field. Author: International Accounting, 1967; co-author: Introductory Financial Accounting, 3d edit., 1991, A Brief Introduction to Managerial and Social Uses of Accounting, 1975, International Accounting, 1978, 2nd edit., 1992, Accounting: An International Perspective, 1987, 4th edit., 1997; editor: Readings in International Accounting, 1969, Accounting-A Book of Readings, 2d edit., 1976, A New Introduction to Accounting, 1971, A Bibliography of Internat. Accounting, 3d edit., 1973, Essentials of Multinational Accounting— An Anthology, 1979, Frontiers of International Accounting, 1986, AACSB Curriculum Internationalization Resource Guide, 1988; contbr. chpts. to books, numerous articles to profl. jours. Recipient U. wash. Disting. Tchg. award, 1983, Disting. Svc. award, U. Wash., 1984; fellow Price Waterhouse Internat. Acctg. Rsch. fellow, 1962—64, Ford Found. fellow, 1958—59. Fellow Acad. Internat. Bus.; mem. AICPA (internat. practice exec. com. 1972-75, exec. coun. 1987-89, Disting. Achievement in Acctg. Edn. award 2000), Am. Acctg. Assn. (pres. 1988-89, acad. v.p. 1970-71, chmn. adv. bd. internat. acctg. sect. 1977-79, Wildman medal 1986, Nat. Outstanding Educator 1981, Disting. Internat. Lectr. in Black Africa 1987, Outstanding Internat. Acctg. Educator 1991), Wash. Soc. CPAs (pres. 1988-89, Outstanding Educator award 1985, Pub. Svc. award 1995), Acctg. Edn. Change Commn. (chmn. 1994-96), Beta Alpha Psi (Acad. Acct. of Yr. 1987), Beta Gamma Sigma (Disting. scholar 1978-79), Alpha Gamma Sigma. Home: 15794 Dovewood Ct Poway CA 92064-2282 Business E-Mail: gmueller@u.washington.edu.

MUELLER, JOHN ERNEST, political science educator, dance critic and historian; b. St. Paul, June 21, 1937; s. Ernst A. and Elsie E. (Schleh) M.; m. Judy A. Reader, Sept. 6, 1960; children: Karl, Karen, Susan AB, U. Chgo., 1960; MA, UCLA, 1963, PhD, 1965. Asst. prof. polit. sci. U. Rochester, N.Y., 1965-69, assoc. prof., 1969-72, prof., 1972-2000, prof. film studies, 1983-2000, founder, dir. Dance Film Archive, 1973—; prof. polit. sci., Woody Hayes chair of nat. security studies Ohio State U., 2000—. Lectr. on dance in U.S., Europe, Australia, 1973—; OP-ED columnist Wall St. Jour., 1984—, L.A., Times, 1988—, N.Y. Times, 1990—; mem. dance panel NEA, 1983-85; columnist Dance Mag., 1974-82; dance critic Rochester Dem. and Chronicle, 1974-82; mem. adv. bd. Dance in Am., PBS, 1975. Author: War, Presidents and Public Opinion, 1973 (book selected as one of Fifty Books That Significantly Shaped Public Opinion Rsch. 1946-95 Am. Assn. Pub. Opinion Rsch. 1995), Dance Film Directory, 1979, Astaire Dancing: The Musical Films, 1985 (de la Torre Bueno prize 1983), Retreat From Doomsday: The Obsolescence of Major War, 1989, Policy and Opinion in the Gulf War, 1994, Quiet Cataclysm: Reflections on the Recent Transformation of World Politics, 1995, Capitalism, Democracy, and Ralph's Pretty Good Grocery, 1999; co-author: Trends in Public Opinion: A Compendium of Survey Data, 1989; editor: Approaches to Measurement, 1969, Peace, Prosperity, and Politics, 2000; co-editor Jour. Policy Analysis and Mgmt., 1985-89; mem. editl. bd. Pub. Opinion Quar., 1988-91, Jour. Cold War Studies, 1999—, Ohio State U. press, 2001—; prodr. 12 dance films/recorded commentator on 2nd soundtrack of laser disc edit. Swing Time, 1986; co-adapter (musical) A Foggy Day, 1998; prodr. Shaw Festival Niagara-on-the-Lake, Ont., 1998, 99. Grantee NSF, 1967-70, 74-75, NEH, 1972-73, 74-75, 77-78, 79-81; Guggenheim fellow, 1988. Mem. Am. Acad. Arts and Scis., Am. Polit. Sci. Assn., Dance Critics Assn. (bd. dirs. 1983-85). Home: 420 W 5th Ave Columbus OH 43201-3159 Office: Ohio State U Polit Sci Dept Columbus OH 43210-1373

MUELLER, ROSE ANNA MARIA, humanities educator; b. Dec. 24, 1948; arrived in U.S., 1954, naturalized, 1966; d. Vincenzo and Antonina (Adamo) Siino; m. Robert Raymond Mueller, June 21, 1971; children: Benjamin, Christopher. BA, Hunter Coll., 1971; MA, PhD, CCNY, 1977. Instr. lang arts Morton Coll., Cicero, 1982—90; prof. humanities Columbia Coll., Chgo., 1990—. Author: Introduction and Translation of Montemayor's Diana, 1988, poems; translator. Fellow, NEH, 1985, 1990, 1995, Fulbirght fellow, 2002—. Mem.: MLA, L.Am. Studies Assn., Renaissance Soc. Am. Home: 46108 Glenwood Ave New Buffalo MI 49117 Office: Columbia Coll Chgo Dept Liberal Edn 600 S Michigan Ave Chicago IL 60605

MUELLER, SUSAN GAHAGAN, secondary school educator; b. Chgo., Nov. 18, 1965; d. John Patrick and Janice Lynn (Dickert) Gahagan; m. Robert Charles Mueller, June 25, 1994. BA in Internat. Rels., U. Colo., Boulder, 1987; MEd in Curriculum Devel., DePaul U., 1993. Social studies educator Lake View H.S., Chgo., 1992-93, York Cmty. H.S., Elmhurst, Ill., 1993-99, Maine Twp. H.S. West, Des Plaines, Ill., 1999—. Sponsor Mid. Am. Model UN, 1993-99, multi-cultural program dir., 1994-99; mem. Chgo. Area Women's History Conf., 1994. Mem. dean's adv. bd. Coll. Edn., DePaul U., Chgo., 1993—. Mem. Chgo. Coun. Fgn. Rels., Profl. Edn. Club (DePaul U.), Kappa Delta Phi. Office: Maine Twp HS West 1855 S Wolf Rd Des Plaines IL 60018

MUFFOLETTO, MARY LU, retired school program director, consultant, editor; b. Chgo., May 25, 1932; d. Anthony Joseph and Lucile (Di Giacomo) M. PhB in Philosophy, DePaul U., 1959; ME. U. Ill., 1967. Tchr. elem. edn. Community Cons., Palatine, Ill., 1959-65; tchr. gifted children Sch. Dist. 15, Palatine, 1965-67, curriculum supr., 1967-75, dir. gifted edn. program, 1972-95, coord. state and fed. programs, 1975-95, asst. prin., 1975-95, retired, 1995; assoc. prof. Nat. Coll. Edn., Evanston, Ill., 1979-95; editor Tchg. Ink, Inc., 1995—. Chairperson State Bd. of Edn. Adv. Com. on Gifted Edn., Springfield, Ill., 1977-85; pres. No. Ill. Planning Commn. for Gifted, 1978-80. Editor: (tchr. activity books) Teaching Ink, 1995—. Mem. Nat. Coun. for Social Studies, Assn. for Curriculum and Supervision, Coun. for Exceptional Children, U. Ill. Alumni Assn. (pres. Champaign chpt. 1982-85, Loyalty award), Kiwanis, Phi Delta Kappa (sec. 1985-87). Home: 21302 W Brandon Rd Kildeer IL 60047-8618

MUIR, WILLIAM LLOYD, III, academic administrator; b. Norton, Kans., Mar. 20, 1948; s. John Thomas and Rosalie June (Benton) M. BBA, Kans. State U., 1977. Asst. sec. of state State of Kans., Topeka, 1971-72, fin. adminstr. atty. gen. office, 1972-79, comptr. Office of Gov., 1979-87, sec. of cabinet, 1979-87, asst. sec. adminstrn., 1986-87; dir. econ. devel. Kans. State U., Manhattan, 1987-91, asst. to v.p. for cmty. rels., 1991—2002, faculty rep., senator Student Governing Assn., 1992—, mem. union governing bd., 1997—, asst. v.p. for cmty. rels., 2002—. Chmn. housing appeals bd. City of Manhattan, 1996—; trustee Kans. State U. Found., 1993—; mem. Leadership Kans., 1989; state officer Native Sons and Daus., 1997—2002, pres., 2001; bd. dirs. United Way Riley County, 1989—99, chmn., 1992; treas. Flint Hills Regional Leadership Program, 2002—, trustee, 1992—. Mem.: Nat. Geog. Soc., Friends of Cedar Crest Assn., Sierra Club, Blue Key, Masons (Scottish Rite), Alpha Kappa Psi, Alpha Tau Omega (nat. officer, bd. govs. Alpha Tau Omega Found.). Episcopalian. Avocations: travel, volunteer work, advising. Home: 2040 Shirley Ln Manhattan KS 66502-2059 Office: Kansas State U 122 Anderson Hall Manhattan KS 66506-0100 E-mail: billmuir@ksu.edu.

MUIR-BROADDUS, JACQUELINE ELIZABETH, psychology educator; b. Brantford, Ontario, Canada, Dec. 14, 1961; came to U.S., 1986; d. Jack Edward and Ellen Joann (MacKinnon) M. BA, U. Guelph, Can., 1984, MA, 1986; PhD, Fla. Atlantic U., 1990. Teaching asst. U. Guelph, Guelph, Ontario, Canada, 1984-86; rsch. asst. Fla. Atlantic U., Boca Raton, 1986-90, instr., 1987, 89; assoc. prof. Southwestern U., Georgetown, Tex., 1990—2002, prof., 2002—. Intern psychometrist Hosp. for Sick Children, Toronto, 1985, Wellington County Sch. Bd., 1985; adj. instr. Broward Community Coll., Coconut Creek, Fla., 1987. Author: (with others) Annals of Child Development, 1988, Interactions Among Strategies, Knowledge, and Aptitude in Cognitive Performance, 1990, Children's Strategies: Contemporary Views of Cognitive Development, 1990, Gifted Underachievers: Insights from the Characteristics of Strategic Functioning Associated with Giftedness and Achievement, 1995, The Effects of a Knowledge Base manipulation on Individual Differences in Processing Speed V Recall, 1995, Name Seven Words, 1998, Conservation as a Predictor of Individual Differences in Children's Susceptibility to Leading Questions, 1998, Neuropsychological Test Performance of Children with ADHD Relative to Test Norms and Parent Behavioral Ratings, 2002. Recipient Alma Mater scholarship, Entrance scholarship, U. Guelph, 1980, Daniel Brown Meml. scholarship, Fla. Atlantic U., 1988, Dissertation award APA, 1990; finalist Thesis Contest Ontario Psychol. Assn., 1986. Mem.: Cognitive Devel. Soc., Southwestern Psychol. Assn., Soc. Rsch. in Child Devel. Avocation: tennis. Home: 5702 Greenledge Cv Austin TX 78759-6244 Office: Southwestern U Dept Of Psychology Georgetown TX 78626

MUJICA, BARBARA LOUISE, language educator, writer; d. Louis and Frieda (Kline) Kaminar; m. Mauro E. Mujica, Dec. 26, 1966; children: Lillian Louise, Mariana Ximena, Mauro Eduardo Ignacio. AB, UCLA, 1964; MA, Middlebury Coll., 1965; PhD, NYU, 1974. Instr. French UCLA, 1963-64; assoc. editor modern langs. Harcourt Brace Jovanovich, N.Y.C., 1966-73; instr., asst. prof. Romance langs. CUNY, 1973-74; prof. Spanish Georgetown U., Washington, 1974—. Mem. faculty NEH Summer Inst., 1980. Author: (book) A-LM Spanish, Levels I-IV, 1969—74, Readings in Spanish Literature, 1975, Calderon's Characters: An Existential Point of View, 1980, Pasaporte, 1980, rev. edit., 1984, Aqui y ahora, 1979, Entrevista, 1982, Iberian Pastoral Characters, 1986, Texto y Espectáculo, 1987, Et in Arcadia Ego, 1990, Texto y Vida: Introduccion a la Literature Española, 1990, Antología de la Literatura Española: La Edad Media, 1991, Renacimiento y Siglo de Oro, 1991, Siglos XVII y XIX, 1999, Texto y

Vida: Introduccion a la Literature Hispano-Americana, 1992, Looking at the Comedia in the Year of the Quincentennial, 1993, Premio Nobel, 1997, Books of the Americas, 1997, El Texto Puesto en Escena, 2000, (novels) Sanchez Across the Street, 1997, The Deaths of Don Bernardo, 1990, Far From My Mother's Home, 1999, Frida: A Novel, 2001; editor: (book) Milenio, 2002, Teresa de Jesus: Espiritualidad y feminismo, Comedia Performance Jour.; editor, pub. Verbena: Bilingual Rev. of Arts, 1979—85, sr. assoc. editor, bd. dirs. Washington Rev., mem. editl. bd. Bull. of Comediantes Hispana. Named winner, E.L. Doctorow Internat. Fiction Competition, 1992; named one of 50 Best Op Eds of Decade, N.Y. Times, 1990; recipient Pangolin prize best short story, 1998, Hoepner award for fiction; grantee, Spanish Govt., 1987, Poets and Writers of N.Y.; Penfield fellow, 1971. Mem.: MLA (pres. Golden Age sect.), Assn. Hispanic Classical Theater (bd. dirs.). Office: Georgetown U Dept Spanish Washington DC 20057-1039

MUKHERJEE, AMIYA K. metallurgy and materials science educator; PhD, Oxford (Eng.) U., 1962. Prof. U. Calif., Davis. Recipient Alexander von Humboldt award Fed. Republic Germany, 1988, Albert Easton White Disting. Tchr. award Am. Soc. Materials, 1992, Pfeil medal and prize Inst. Materials, 1993, U. Calif. prize and citation, 1993, Anatoly Bochvar medal U. Moscow, 1996, Inst. medal Max Planck Inst. for Metallforschung, 1997. Office: U Calif Davis Dept Chem Engring & Material Sci Davis CA 95616 E-mail: akmukherjee@ucdavis.edu.

MUKHERJEE, DEBI PRASAD, medical educator; b. Krishnanagar, India, Oct. 26, 1939; came to U.S., 1963; s. Prafulla Kumar and Gouri Bala (Ganguly) M.; m. Bandana, May 21, 1970; children: Avik, Shomik. Student, Jadavpur U., 1957-61; BS, MIT, 1965, MS, 1966, ScD, 1969; MBA, U. Conn., 1980. Sr. rsch. engr. Goodyear Tire & Rubber, Akron, Ohio, 1969-74; tech. specialist, group leader David & Geck, Danbury, Conn., 1974-87; rsch. program mgr. Dow Corning Wright, Arlington, Tenn., 1987-90; devel. scientist Union Carbide, Bound Brook, N.J., 1991-92; assoc. prof. orthopaedic biomechanics and biomaterials La. State U. Med. Ctr., Shreveport, 1992—, coord. bioengring., 1992—. Author: Biophysical Properties of Skin, 1971, Encyclopedia of Polymer Science and Engineering, 1989; patentee in field. Sec., program chair Akron Polymer Lectr. Group, 1972-74. Rsch. grantee Am. Heart Assn., Akron, 1974—, Sch. Dentistry La. State U., 1992-94. Mem. IEEE, Am. Soc. Composites, Orthopaedic Rsch. Soc., Soc. Biomaterials. Avocations: sports, reading, travel. Office: La State U Dept Orthopaedic Surgery 1501 Kings Hwy Shreveport LA 71103-4228 E-mail: dmukhe@isuhsc.edu.

MUKHOTI, BELA BANERJEE, economics educator; b. Vikrampur, Bengal, India, Mar. 1, 1932; came to U.S., 1965; d. Priyanath and Labanya (Ganguli) B.; m. Santi Ranjan Mukhoti, Dec. 14, 1957 (dec. 1988); children: Jayati, Mona. BA in Econs. with honors, Calcutta U., 1950, MA in Econs., 1953; PhD in Econs., London Sch. Econs., 1964. Rsch. specialist U. Ky., Lexington, 1965-66; assoc. prof. Memphis State U., 1966-68, U. No. Iowa, Cedar Falls, 1972-74; asst. prof. Lakehead U., Ont., Can., 1968-69; rsch. officer Planning Commn. Govt. of India, New Delhi, 1969-71; agrl. economist Econ. Rsch. Svc., USDA, Washington, 1979-86; prof. econs. Rowan U., Glassboro, N.J., 1987—. Author: Agriculture and Employment in Developing Countries--Strategy for Effective Rural Development, 1985; Measures of Development, 1986, International Monetary Fund and Low-Income Countries, 1986, Impact of Agricultural Growth Patterns on Import Demand for Food and Agricultural Commodities, 1983; contbr. articles to profl. jours. Recipient Rhoda Freeman recognition award N.J. Coll. and Univ. Coalition for Women's Edn., 1988, merit award Rowan U., 1989; Sr. Ernest Cassels Trust grantee, 1962-63, Brit. Univ. and Coll. Tchr.'s Assn. grantee, 1964, also various univs. and colls., 1965—. Mem. Am. Econ. Assn., Ea. Econ. Assn., Internat. Assn. Agrl. Econs., Assn. Indian Econ. Studies (exec. com. 1990—), Congress Econ. and Polit. Democracy Internat. (program com. 1990), Am. Friends London Sch. Econs., Assn. Indians in Am., Sanskriti (exec. com. 1985, pres. 1990). Hindu. Avocations: horticulture, cooking, photography, travel. Home: 49 E Holly Ave Sewell NJ 08080-2603 Office: Rowan U Dept Econs Bunce Hall Glassboro NJ 08028 E-mail: mukhoti@rowan.edu.

MULASE, MOTOHICO, mathematics educator; b. Kanazawa, Japan, Oct. 11, 1954; came to U.S., 1982; s. Ken-Ichi and Mieko (Yamamoto) M.; m. Sayuri Kamiya, Sept. 10, 1982; children: Kimihico Chris, Paul Norihico, Yurika. BS, U. Tokyo, 1978; MS, Kyoto U., 1980, DSc, 1985. Rsch. assoc. Nagoya (Japan) U., 1980-85; JMS fellow Harvard U., Cambridge, Mass., 1982-83; vis. asst. prof. SUNY, Stony Brook, 1984-85; Hedrick asst. prof. UCLA, 1985-88; asst. prof. Temple U., Phila., 1988-89; assoc. prof. U. Calif., Davis, 1989-91, prof., 1991—, vice chair dept. math., 1995-96, chair dept. math., 1998—2001. Mem. Math. Scis. Rsch. Inst., Berkeley, Calif., 1982-84, Inst. for Advanced Study, Princeton, N.J., 1988-89; vis. prof. Max-Planck Inst. for Math., Bonn, Germany, 1991-92, Kyoto U., 1993, 94, Humboldt U., Berlin, Germany, 1995, 1996, 2002. Contbr. articles to profl. jours. Treas. Port of Sacramento Japanese Sch., 1990-91. Mem. Am. Math. Soc. (com. on internat. affairs 1993-96). Avocation: music. Office: U Calif Dept Math Davis CA 95616 E-mail: mulase@math.ucdavis.edu.

MULCAHY, RICHARD PATRICK, history educator, consultant; b. Greensburg, Pa., Mar. 18, 1958; s. Patrick Francis and Frances Catherine (Bell) M. BA, St. Vincent Coll., 1980; MA, Duquesne U., 1982, U. Pitts., 1985; PhD, W.Va. U., 1988. Tchg. asst. Duquesne U., Pitts., 1980-82; instr. history La Roche Coll., Pitts., 1982-83; lectr. history W.Va. U., Morgantown, 1988-89; asst. prof. U. Pitts., Titusville, Pa., 1989-95, assoc. prof., 1995—, dir. social sci. divsn., 1997—. Reader, referee Okla. U. Press, Norman, 1990, U. Tenn. Press, Knoxville, 2000; archival cons. W.Va. U., Morgantown, 1992; summer faculty Chautauqua Inst. Spl. Schs., 1996-99. Mem. editl. adv. bd. Collegiate Press., 1993; author: A Social Contract for the Coal Fields: The Rise and Fall of the UMWA Welfare and Retirement Fund, 1946-78, 2000; author chpt. to book; co-editor: Health & Medicine-Encyclopedia of Appalachia; contbr. articles to profl. jours. Woods scholar W.Va. U., 1987; fellow Ctr. for No. Appalachian Studies, Saint Vincent Coll., Latrobe, Pa., 1996—. Mem. AAUP (mem. Pitt. exec. coun. 1991—, elected sec. Pa. conf.(2000), Chautaugua Lit. and Sci. Cir. (class of 1999), Soc. of the Hall in the Grove, Guild of the Seven Seals, Appalachian Studies Assn., Am. Fedn. Tchrs., Phi Alpha Theta. Democrat. Roman Catholic. Avocations: computer programming, ham radio. Office: U Pitts 504 E Main St Titusville PA 16354-2010

MULERT, LYNNE CAROL, school counselor; b. Dubuque, Iowa, Jan. 30, 1949; d. Robert and Donna Meyer; m. Robert Ken Mulert, June 28, 1969; children: Troy, Travis. BS, U. So. Fla., 1993, MA, 1997. Guidance counselor Collier County Schs., Naples, Fla., 1997—. Mem.: ACA. Home: 2719 Wind Feather Trl Reno NV 89511

MULHOLLAND, BARBARA ANN, school director; b. Pendleton, Oreg., Sept. 27, 1951; d. John Gordon Bensel and D. Lois (Carey) Bohlender; children: Sage, David; m. Harold Palmer Mulholland; stepchildren: Kelli, Hoag, Ryan. Cert., Fla. Inst. Tech., 1969; BA, Western Wash. U., 1974; cert. in manual interpretation, Blue Mountain Coll., 1987; MS in Edn., Lewis and Clark Coll., 1988. Cert. tchr., Wyo., interpretoe, domestic violence counselor, Oreg., fed. contract specialist, Wash. Housing and employment commr. City of Bellingham, Wash., 1970-74; contract specialist U.S. Forest Svc., Seattle, 1974-76; ind. contract cons. Seattle and Tacoma, 1976-78; loan specialist Island Savs. and Loan, Mt. Vernon, Wash., 1978-80; materials specialist Umatilla County Edn. Svc. Dist., Pendleton, Oreg., 1980-87; specialist for hearing impaired Fremont County Sch. Dist. 1, Lander, Wyo., 1988-91; instr. sign lang. and edn. Cen. Wyo. Coll., Riverton, 1988-97; dir. title VII and V programs and curriculum Wyo. Indian Schs., Ethete, 1991-96; ednl. cons., 1992—; spl. edn. instr., Summer Sch. Inst. dir. Poplar (Mont.) Pub. Schs., 1997-98. Spl. edn. instr., summer sch. dir. Poplar Pub. Schs., 1997-98; tchr. spl. edn. and forensics Midway High Sch., Hewitt, Tex., 1998-2001; tchr. Univ. Mid. Sch., Waco, Tex., 2001—; instr. McLennan Comm. Coll., Waco, Tex., 2000—; north ctrl. accreditation team Wyo. Indian Schs., 1991-96; English instr. Blue Mountain C.C.; forensics coach Vanguard Prep. Sch., 2000—; drama dir. Lander Dist. 1. Author, illustrator sign lang. edn. materials. Mem. Fairhaven com. Fairhaven Coll., Bellingham, 1970-71, advocate, 1970-72; mem. Bellingham Landlords' Assn., 1970-74; rep. Pioneer Sq. Assn., Seattle, 1976-78; vol. counselor Domestic Violence Svcs., Pendleton, Oreg., 1982-87; vol. sign lang. interpreter, Wyo., 1988-98. Named Outstanding Vol., Domestic Violence Svcs., Pendleton, 1986; recipient Exceptional Svc. award United Way Umatilla County, 1986, Outstanding Instr. award Ctrl. Wyo. Coll., 1990. Mem. ASCD, NEA, Nat. Indian Edn. Assn., Nat. Assn. Bilingual Edn., Wyo. Speech and Hearing Assn., Conv. Am. Instrs. of Deaf, Ethete Ednl. Assn., Wyo. Edn. Assn. Avocations: singing, guitar, needlework, drawing, cooking. Office: 9708 Brookwood Cir Woodway TX 76712-3217 E-mail: teaching2@earthlink.com.

MULHOLLEN, MICHAEL EDWARD, education director; b. Franfurt, Germany, May 22, 1960; came to U.S., 1966; s. James Lawrence and Margie Ruth (Joslin) M. AA, Ctrl. Tex. Coll., Killeen, 1985; BA, Columbia Pacific U., 1987, MA, 1988; PhD, La Salle Univ., 1993. Instr. foreign lang. Def. Lang. Inst., Monterey, Calif., 1979-81; prof. criminal justice Nat. Training Ctr., Ft. Irwin, Calif., 1982-84; tchr. Russian Def. lang. Inst., Monterey, 1984-86; edn. adminstr. Mil. Intelligence Acad., Augsburg, Germany, 1986-89; dir. edn. Computer Processing Institute, East Hartford, Conn., 1989-92; pres. M.E.M. & Assocs., Manchester, Conn., 1992—. Author: Criminal Justice, 1989, Criminal Law, 1989, Russian Review Grammar Text Book, 1993. With U.S. Army, 1978-89. Fellow Conn. Soc. CPAs; mem. ABA, Am. Trial Lawyers Assn. Avocations: foreign languages, financial planning, law. Home: 66 Cushman Dr Manchester CT 06040-2314

MULKERN-KOLOSEY, SANDY KATHLEEN, college counselor, educator, realtor; b. Needham, Mass., Apr. 09; d. Thomas Joseph and Elizabeth (Bjornson) Mulkern; m. Michael George Kolosey, July 15, 1972; 1 child, Michael Thomas Kolosey. AA, Coll. of Marin, Kentfield, Calif., 1989, AS/Dental Asst., 1990; BA in Clin. Psychology, San Francisco State U., 1991; MA in Counseling/Psychology, U. San Francisco, 1993, postgrad., doctoral student in organ. and leadership, U. San Francisco. Cert. in pupil pers. svcs., psychol. svcs. Acad. advisor, counselor Santa Rosa (Calif.) Jr. Coll., 1992—. Ednl. cons., San Francisco Bay area, 1994; career coach and workshop facilitator, Sonoma County. Mem. AAUW, APA, Alumni Assn. U. San Francisco and San Francisco State U., Golden Key Nat. Honor Soc., Psi Chi, Alpha Gamma Sigma, Phi Delta Kappa. Avocations: bicycling, reading, computers, travel, real estate investing. Home: PO Box 750401 Petaluma CA 94975-0401 Office: ReMax 775 Baywood Dr Petaluma CA 94954

MULL, JOCELYN BETHE, school administrator; b. Nassau, N.Y., Oct. 21, 1968; divorced; 1 child, Eron Michael. BA, SUNY, Buffalo, 1981, MA, 1989. Dir. edn. Ctr. for Positive Thought, Mus. African Am. Arts and Antiquities, Buffalo, 1978-83; tchr. English, Buffalo Bd. Edn., 1980—, cons. tchr. inclusion project, 1991-93, fed. magnet curriculum specialist Futures Acad., 1993—; case mgr. spl. edn., gifted and comprehensive programs Crenshaw H.S., L.A., 1995, case mgr., coord. spl. edn., GATE coord., peer tutoring coord., 1996—. Case mgr. spl. edn. and GATE coord. Crenshaw H.S. Author: (poetry) Goti, Paja, Mguu-The Knee, A Thigh and The Leg, 1980, Strength in the Water, 1995. Rec. coord., publicist Lighthouse Interdenominational Choir, 1988-94; project coord. Performing Artists Collective, Western N.Y. United Against Drugs, Buffalo, 1993—; mem. Mayor's Arts and Adv. Coun. Against Drugs and Violence, 1995. Recipient Educator of Excellence award PUSH Excel, Operation PUSH, 1981, N.Y. State English Coun., 1994, Creative Arts award, 1980, citation Martin Luther King Jr. Arts and Scis. award, 1986—, Outstanding Commemorative Youth award for performing arts and cmty. svc., 1980. Mem. ASCD, NEA (spl. edn. com.), Buffalo Tchrs. Fedn. (multicultural com.), AAUW, Phi Delta Kappa. Avocations: composing, singing, writing poetry. Office: Crenshaw High School 5010 11th Ave Los Angeles CA 90043-4896

MULLEEDY, JOYCE ELAINE, nursing service administrator, educator; b. Paterson, N.J., Aug. 30, 1948; d. Edward and Jane (Van De Weert) Schuurman; m. Philip Anthony Mulleedy, May 14, 1982. BS, Paterson State Coll., 1970. RN; cert. emergency nurse, emergency med. technician, paramedic; cert. lay spkr. United Meth. Ch. Pub. health nurse Vis. Nurse Assn. Bergen County, Ramsey, N.J., 1970-72; health dir. Camp Fowler Assn., Speculator, N.Y., 1973-76; exec. dir. Am. Cancer Soc., Speculator, 1976-77; pub. health nurse Hamilton County Nursing Svc., Lake Pleasant, N.Y., 1977-80, supervising pub.health nurse, 1980-82, dir. patient svcs., 1982-86; quality improvement coord. Susquehanna-Adirondack Regional Emergency Med. Svcs. Program, 1986-96; dir. ednl. svcs. Adirondack Applachian Regional Emergency Med. Svcs. Program, 1996—. Mem. Emergency Med. Svcs. regional faculty N.Y. State Dept. Health, 1988—; mem. profl. adv. com. Hamilton County Nursing Svc., Indian Lake, N.Y., 1992—. Author: Advanced Assessment and Treatment of Life Threatening Pediatric Emergencies, 1995, Orientation to EMS for Emergency Dept. Physicians and Nurses, 1996. Bd. dirs. Am. Cancer Soc.-Hamilton County Unit, Speculator, 1972-76, Speculator Vol. Ambulance Corps, Inc., 1974—, ARC-Hamilton County Chpt., Lake Pleasant, 1981-88; mem. adminstrv. bd. dirs. Grace United Meth. Ch., Speculator, 1982—, Rainbow Christian Children's Ctr., 1992-98. Recipient Svcs. award Am. Legion, 1977; Martha Hazen scholar Am. Legion, 1966. Mem. Adirondack-Appalachian Regional Emergency Med. Svcs. Coun. (chmn. 1982-87, chmn. tng. com. 1982—), Emergency Nurses Assn., Hamilton County Emergency Med. Svcs. Coun. (sec.-treas. 1974-90, instr. 1974—). Republican. Home: PO Box 203 Speculator NY 12164-0203 Office: Adirondack-Appalachian Regional Emergency Med Svcs Prog PO Box 212 Speculator NY 12164-0212

MULLEN, CHARLES FREDERICK, health educator; b. Washington, June 14, 1938; s. DeWitt Cliffton and Annabelle (Fischer) M.; m. Rita Mae Keintz, Oct. 23, 1996; children from a previous marriage: Henry John, Elizabeth Mary. BA, U. Va., 1962; BS, New England Coll. Optometry, 1969, OD, 1970; D of Ocular Sci., So. Coll. Optometry, 1994. Dir. clinics New Eng. Coll. Optometry, Boston, 1970-76; exec. dir. The Eye Inst., Pa. Coll. Optometry, Phila., 1976-90; dir. optometry svc. Dept. VA, Washington, 1990-96; pres. Ill. Coll. Optometry, Chgo., 1996—2002. Adj. clin. prof. SUNY, N.Y.C., 1990—; mem. Dept. VA Spl. Subcom. Eye Care, Washington, 1990-96; observer Eye Coun., Nat. Eye Inst., Bethesda, Md., 1990-96, del. Am. Nat. Stds. Inst., 1990-96. Contbr. articles to profl. jours. Host parent Overbrook Sch. Blind, Phila., 1985-86; vol. Big. Bros., West Chester, Pa., 1988-89; bd. dirs. Clavary Schlter, Washington, 1990-92; mem. gifts com. Mus. Sci. and Industry. Lt. (j.g.) USNR. Mem. Am. Acad. Optometry, Am. Pub. Health Assn., Am. Optometric Assn., Nat. Assn. VA Ops., Assn. Mil. Surgeons U.S. (chmn. optometric sect. 1991, 95), Assn. Schs. & Colls. Optometry, Ill. Optometric Assn. Democrat. Episcopalian. Home: 5504 Muustead Dr Alexandria VA 22311 E-mail: cfmlaex@aol.com.

MULLEN, FRANK ALBERT, former university official, clergyman; b. Lafayette, Ind., Apr. 7, 1931; s. Albert Edwin and Bernice Elizabeth (Weidlich) M.; m. Ruth Charlotte Ackerman, May 28, 1960 (dec. Oct. 1969). BA, Wabash Coll., Crawfordsville, Ind., 1953; MDiv, Yale U., 1956; DD (hon.), Yale U., New Haven, 1988. Ordained to ministry Christian Ch. (Disciples of Christ), 1956. Exec. dir. YMCA of Wilmington, Del., 1956-60, YMCA of Greater N.Y., N.Y.C., 1960-74; pastor St. Marks United Ch. of Christ, Ridgewood, N.Y., 1973-99; assoc. dir. Campaign for Yale, Yale U., N.Y.C., 1975-79; min. Cmty. Ch. of Elmhurst, N.Y., 1974-99; dir. devel. Bapt. Med. Ctr., N.Y.C., 1980-83; dir. devel. Div. Sch. Yale U., New Haven, 1984-97; dir. planned giving Guideposts, Inc., Carmel, N.Y., 1983-84. Life mem. bd. advisors Yale U. Divinity Sch., 1997—; trustee Park Avenue Christian Ch., N.Y.C., 1999—; dir. bd. ch. ext. Christian Ch., Disciples of Christ, 2000—. Recipient Liberty Bell award Queens County Bar Assn., 1969, Alumni award of merit Wabash Coll., 1970; Wright fellow Yale U., 1955, fellow Trumbull Coll., 1985—. Mem. Assn. Theol. Schs., Coun. for Advancement in Secondary Edn., Wellness Assn., Travelers' Century Club, Circumnavigators Club. Home and Office: 17833 Croydon Rd Jamaica NY 11432-2203

MULLEN, NANCY LEE, reading specialist, educator, travel consultant; b. Glendale, Calif., Oct. 18, 1940; d. Dale Winton and Ernestine (Welch) B.; m. Terrance J. Mullen, Dec. 27, 1965 (div. 1971); children: Patrick John (dec.), Lynda Michelle. BS in Mktg., U. Ariz., 1963; BS in Elem. Edn., SUNY, Buffalo, 1965; MA in Remedial Reading, U. N.M., 1984. Cert. K-12 reading specialist, K-6 elem. edn., N.M. Dept. mgr. Broadway So. Calif., L.A., 1963-65; tchr. grade 3 North Tonawanda (N.Y.) Pub. Schs., 1969-68; tchr. elem. grades Albuquerque Pub. Schs., 1971-80, chpt. I reading specialist, 1980—2003; ret., 2003. Cons. in field. Recipient Excellence in Edn. award Bd. Edn., Albuquerque, 1986. Mem. ASCD, Internat. Reading Assn., Santa Fe Opera Guild, Phi Delta Kappa. Democrat. Methodist. Home: 1710 Escalante Ave SW Albuquerque NM 87104-1011

MULLEN, ROBERT CHARLES, school system administrator; b. Muskogee, Okla., Nov. 13, 1944; s. Charles W. and Kathryn B. (Hunt) M.; m. Celesta Rose Schmidt, June 25, 1966; children: Charles, Robert, Michael, Kevin. BS, Minot (N.D.) State U., 1966, MS, 1967; EdD, U. No. Colo., Greeley, 1981. Speech pathologist Benton-Tama-Iowa-Poweshiek Dept. Spl. Edn., Toledo, Iowa, 1967-68, hearing clinician, 1968-69, coord. speech and hearing, 1969-73; dir. ACCA Speech and Hearing Ctr., Fairbanks, Alaska, 1973-75; asst. dir. Alaska Treatment Ctr., Anchorage, 1975-76, exec. dir., 1976-79; dir. Reno County Edn. Coop. USD #610, Hutchinson, Kans., 1981-85, Rio Blanco Bd. Endl. Svcs., Rangely, Colo., 1985-89; supt. Rangely Pub. Schs. RE-4, 1989—. V.p. bd. dirs. Horizon Inc., Steamboat, Colo.; pres. Vocat. Edn. Adv. Bd., Colo. No. Community Coll., Rangely, 1988. Co-author: Exceptional Individuals: An Introduction, 1993. Commr. Mayor's Health Commn., Anchorage, 1976-79; Alaska rep. Nat. Conf. on Aging, Washington; bd. mem. Spl. Edn. Adv. Bd., U. No. Colo., 1988; state com. mem. Colo. Parent/Profl. Partnership, Denver, 1988-90; mem. planning com. White house Conf. on Handicapped; mem. bd. govs. Colo. Alliance for Sci., 1996. U.s. Office Edn. grantee, Greeley, Colo., 1980, 81. Mem. Am. Assn. Sch. Adminstrs., Coun. Exceptional Children, Colo. Assn. Sch. Execs. Roman Catholic. Avocations: fishing, swimming, writing, geneology. Office: Rangely Pub Schs 402 W Main St Rangely CO 81648-9901

MULLEN, RUSSELL EDWARD, agricultural studies educator; b. Atlantic, Iowa, Sept. 4, 1949; AA, Southwestern C.C., Creton, Iowa, 1969; BS in Agriculture, N.W. Mo. State U., 1971, MS in Edn., 1972; PhD in Crop Physiology and Mgmt., Purdue U., 1975. Grad. asst. N.W. Mo. State U., Maryville, 1971-72; grad. teaching asst. Purdue U., West Lafayette, Ind., 1972-74, grad. instr., 1974-75, temporary asst. prof., 1975-76; asst. prof. U. Fla., Gainesville, 1976-78; from asst. prof. to prof. Iowa State U., Ames, 1978—86, prof., 1986—. Recipient Ensminger Interstate Disting. Tchr. award Nat. Assn. Colls. Tchrs. Agriculture, 1992, Am. Soc. Agronomy Resident Edn. award, 1999; Am. Soc. Agronomy fellow, 1998. Office: Iowa State U Dept Agronomy 1126 Agronomy Hl Ames IA 50011-0001*

MULLEN, TERRI ANN, retired special education educator; b. St. Louis, Apr. 01; d. William Earl and Sophia Kinniff; m. Thomas Patrick Mullen; children: David, Mark, Debi. BS in Edn., S.E. Mo. State U.; M in Sch. Adminstrn., Calif. State U., 1978, M in Spl. Edn., 1981; EdD in Institutional Mgmt., Pepperdine U., 1985. Cert. spl. edn., std. sec., std. elem., adminstrv. svc. K-12, cmty. coll. instr. Tchr. Irvine (Calif.) Unified Sch. Dist., 1972-84; lectr., spl. edn. Calif. State U., Fullerton, 1989-90; asst. prin. Moreno Valley (Calif.) Unified Sch. Dist., 1984-85; adminstr. of spl. svcs. Centralia Sch. Dist., Buena Park, Calif., 1984-89; elem. prin. Capistrano Unified Sch. Dist., San Juan Capistrano, 1989-93; spl. edn. tchr., dept. chair Moreno Valley (Calif.) Unified Sch. Dist., 1993—. Chair, cmty. staff ednl. planning com. Santiago Elem. Sch., Irvine Unified Sch. Dist., 1981; dir., staff devel. for spl. programs pers. Centralia Sch. Dist., Buena Park, 1984-89; workshop presenter Assn. of Calif. Sch. Adminstrs. Conf., San Francisco, 1983. Author: Resource Book of Classroom Interventions for the Collaborative Teaching Model, 1994, Tips of the Trade for the Classroom Aide, 1984; contbr. articles to profl. jours. Adv. bd. for sp. edn. Calif. State U. Fullerton, 1988-89. Recipient Cmty. Svc. award Disneyland, 1992, 93; named Outstanding Educator of Yr. Rotary Club, 1983. Mem. Coun. for Exceptional Children, Kappa Delta Pi, Phi Kappa Phi. Avocations: roller skating, fashion design, interior design, computer applications, writing. E-mail: tmullen@pacbell.net.

MULLENIX, LINDA SUSAN, lawyer, educator; b. N.Y.C., Oct. 16, 1950; d. Andrew Michael and Roslyn Marasco; children: Robert Bartholomew, John Theodore, William Joseph. BA, CCNY, 1971; M Philosophy, Columbia U., 1974; PhD Pres.'s fellow, 1977; JD, Georgetown U., 1980. Bar: D.C. 1981, U.S. Dist. Ct. D.C. 1981, U.S. Ct. Appeals (D.C. cir.) 1981, U.S. Supreme Ct. 1986, Tex. 1991, U.S. Ct. Appeals (5th cir.) 1995. U. Md. European divsn., Ramstein, Germany, 1974; instr. N.Y. Inst. Tech., N.Y.C., 1976; assoc. prof., lectr. George Washington U., Washington, 1977-80; asst. prof. Am. U., Washington, 1979; assoc. Pierson, Ball & Dowd, Washington, 1980-81; clin. prof. Loyola U. Law Sch., L.A., 1981-82; asst. prof. Cath. U. Law Sch., Washington, 1984-86; assoc. prof., 1986-90; prof., 1990; Reuschlein disting. vis. chair Villanova Law Sch., 2000. Vis. asst. prof. CCNY, 1977, Cooper Union Advancement Sci., Art, N.Y.C., 1977, Loyola U. Law Sch., L.A., 1982-83, Cath. U. Law Sch., Washington, 1983-84; jud. fellow U.S. Supreme ct. and fed. Jud. Ctr., 1989-90; Bernard J. Ward Centennial prof. U. Tex., 1991—; vis. prof. Harvard Law Sch., 1994-95, Mich. Law Sch., 1996; adj. instr. Fordham U., N.Y.C., 1975-76, adj. asst. prof., 1977. Author: ExamPro: Civil Procedure, 1998, Civil Procedure Roadmap, 1997, Casenotes: Federal Courts, 1997, Mass Tort Litigation: Cases and Materials, 1996; co-author: Understanding Fedeeral Courts, 1998, Federal Courts in the Twenty-First Century, 1996, 2d edit., 2002; Moore's Federal Practice and Procedure, 1991, 97; editor bibliographies Polit. Theory, A. Jour. Polit. Philosophy, 1972-74, The Tax Lawyer Jour., 1978-80; columnist The National Law Jour., 1998—; contbr. editor review of U.S. Supreme Ct. Cases; co-reporter Report and Plan of Civil Justice Reform Act Adv. Group, S.d., Tex., 1991; assoc. reporter ALI, Restatement of the Law Governing Lawyers; contbr. articles to profl. jours. Alt. del. Dem. State Conv., 1980. Fellow NDEA, 1971-74; N.Y. State Regents Scholar, 1967-71. Mem. ABA (reporter task force on class actions 1995-97), Am. Law Inst., D.C. Bar Assn. (com. on ethics, CLE and the Model Rules 1987), Am. Assn. Law Schs. (exec. com. sect. on civil proc. 1987-88, exec. com. sec. on conflicts of law 1991-92,chair prof. devel. com. 1991-93), Jour. Legal Edn. (editl. bd. 1997-1999), Phi Beta Kappa. Home: 722 Crystal Creek Dr Austin TX 78746-4730 Office: U Tex Sch Law 727 E Dean Keeton St Austin TX 78705-3224

MULLER, MERVIN EDGAR, computer scientist, statistician, educator; b. Hollywood, Calif., June 1, 1928; s. Emanuel and Bertha (Zimmerman) Muller; m. Barbara McAdam, July 13, 1963; children: Jeffrey McAdam, Stephen McAdam, Todd McAdam. AB, UCLA, 1949, MA, 1951, PhD, 1954. Instr. in math. Cornell U., 1954-56; rsch. assoc. in math. Princeton (N.J.) U., 1956-59, sr. scientist statis. and elec. engring., 1968-69; sr. statistician, dept. mgr. IBM, N.Y.C., White Plains, 1956-64; prof. computer sci. and stats. U. Wis., 1964-71; prof. computer sci. George Mason U., 1985; dept. dir. World Bank, Washington, 1971-81, sr. advisor, 1981-85; Robert M. Critchfield prof. computer info. sci. Ohio State U., 1985-98, prof.

emeritus, 1994-98, dept. chair, 1985-94. Chair sci. and tech. info. bd. NRC, NAS; bd. dirs. Advanced Info. Tech. Ctr., Columbus, Ohio. Mem. editl. bd. Computation and Stats., 1990, Jour. Computational and Graphical Stats., 1990; contbr. articles to profl. jours. Trustee First Unitarian Ch., Bethesda, Md., 1975—79. Rsch. grantee, AT&T, Columbus, 1987. Fellow: World Acad. Productivity Sci., Am. Statis. Assn.; mem.: Internat. Assn. Statis. Computing (sci. sec. 1979—83, pres. 1977—79), Internat. Statis. Inst. (mem. steering com. Internat. Rsch. Ctr. 1987—89). Avocations: reading, jogging, walking, bridge. Home: 4571 Clairmont Rd Upper Arlington OH 43220-4501 Office: Ohio State U Dept Computer Info Sci Rm 395 2015 Neil Ave Columbus OH 43210-1210 E-mail: mmuller@columbus.rr.com.

MULLER, PATRICIA ANN, nursing administrator, educator; b. N.Y.C., July 22, 1943; d. Joseph H. and Rosanne (Bautz) Felter; m. David G. Smith, Mar. 19, 1988; children: Frank M. Muller III, Kimberly M. Muller. BSN, Georgetown U., 1965; MA, U. Tulsa, 1978, EdD, 1983. RN. Staff devel. coord. St. Francis Hosp., Tulsa, 1978-79, asst. dir. for nursing svc., nursing edn., 1979-82, dir. dept. edn., 1982-98, St. Francis Health Sys., 1998—2002, cons., 2002—. Mem. faculty Okla. U., Northeastern U., Tulsa U.; presenter at confs. and convs. Contbg. editor JOPAN, 1992-2001; contbr. articles to profl. jours. Mem. Leadership Tulsa, 1991; bd. dirs. Am. Heart Assn., Ronald McDonald House. Mem. ANA, Nat. League for Nursing, Am. Soc. for Nursing Svc. Adminstrs., Am. Soc. for Health Manpower Edn. and Tng., Okla. Nurses Assn., Okla. Orgn. of Nurse Execs. (pres. 1992-93), Sigma Theta Tau. Address: 6203 W Utica Ct Broken Arrow OK 74011 E-mail: mullsmi@aol.com.

MULLER, PETER O. geographer, educator; b. Godalming, Surrey, U.K., May 10, 1942; came to U.S., 1950; s. Hans and Lilly (Frank) M.; m. Nancy L. Kohler, June 11, 1966; children: Elizabeth, Christa. BA, CCNY, 1963; MA, Rutgers U., 1966, PhD, 1971. Instr./asst. prof. Villanova (Pa.) U., 1966-70; asst./assoc. prof. Temple U., Phila., 1970-80; chair dept. geography U. Miami, Coral Gables, Fla., 1980-2000, prof., 1980—. Acad. advisor Annenberg/Corp. for Pub. Broadcasting, Washington, 1993-96; cons. Columbia U. Press, N.Y.C., 1990-98. Co-author: Geography: Realms, Regions and Concepts, 9 edits., 1985—, Physical Geography of Global Environment, 3 edits., 1993—, Contemporary Suburban America, 1981, Concepts and Regions in Geography, 2002; contbr. articles to profl. jours.; book rev. editor Urban Geography, 1986-2000, Annals Assn. Am. Geographers, 2000—, Profl. Geographer, 2000—; co-editor Urban Geography, 2003—. Fellow NSF, 1985, Econ. Devel. Adminstrn./U.S. Dept. Commerce, 1984-87, NEH, 1985. Mem. Assn. Am. Geographers (councillor 1978-79), Am. Geog. Soc., Nat. Coun. for Geographic Edn., Phi Beta Kappa. Office: Univ of Miami Dept Geography Ferré Bldg Rm 223 Coral Gables FL 33124 E-mail: pmuller@miami.edu.

MULLER, RICHARD STEPHEN, electrical engineer, educator; b. Weehawken, NJ, May 5, 1933; s. Irving Ernest and Marie Victoria Muller; m. Joyce E. Regal, June 29, 1957; children: Paul Stephen, Thomas Richard. ME, Stevens Inst. Tech., Hoboken, N.J., 1955; MSEE, Calif. Inst. Tech., 1957, PhD in Elect. Engring. and Physics, 1962. Test engr. Wright Aero/Curtiss Wright, Woodridge, N.J., 1953-54; mem. tech. staff Hughes Aircraft Co., Culver City, Calif., 1955-61; instr. U. So. Calif., L.A., 1960-61; asst. prof., then assoc. prof. U. Calif., Berkeley, 1962-72, prof., 1973—. Guest prof. Swiss Fed. Inst. Tech., 1993; founder, dir. Berkeley Sensor and Actuator Ctr., 1985—; chmn. sensors electron devices NRC Army Rsch. Lab., 2003—; chmn. steering com. Internat. Sensor and Actuator Meeting. Co-author: Device Electronics for Integrated Circuits, 1977, 3d, rev. edit., 2002, Microsensors, 1990; editor-in-chief IEEE/ASME Jour. Microelectromech. Sys., 1998—; contbr. over 200 articles to profl. jours. Pres. Kensington (Calif.) Mcpl. Adv. Coun., 1992-98; trustee Stevens Inst. Tech., 1996—. Fellow Hughes Aircraft Co., 1955-57, NSF, 1959-62, NATO postdoctoral fellow, 1968-69, Fulbright fellow, 1982-83, Alexander von Humboldt prize, 1993, Tech. U. Berlin, 1994; Berkeley citation, 1994, Stevens Renaissance award, 1995, Career Achievement award Internat. Conf. on Sensors and Actuators, 1997. Fellow IEEE (life, Cledo Brunetti award 1998, Millennium prize 2000); mem. IEEE Press Bd., NAE, NRC (chmn. sensors adv. bd. U.S. Army Rsch. Lab. 2003-, liaison between NAE and NRC 2003—), Nat. Materials (adv. bd. 1994-98), Electron Devices Soc. (adv. com. 1984-98). Achievements include 18 U.S. and foreign patents; construction of first operating micromotor. Office: U Calif Dept EECS 401 Cory Hl Berkeley CA 94720-1770 E-mail: rsmuller@pacbell.net.

MULLIGAN, LOUISE ELEANORE, retired English literature educator; b. Carson, N.D., July 2, 1910; d. Thomas Edwin and Bessie Pearl (Gutcher) Griffith; m. Patrick Joseph Mulligan, Nov. 18, 1930; children: Sheila, Patrick, James, Elizabeth, Mary. BA, Bridgewater State U., 1962; MA, Boston Coll., 1968; PhD, U. Mass., 1975. Tchr. Braintree (Mass.) High Sch., 1962-67; prof. North Adams (Mass.) State Coll., 1967-80. Adj. prof. Sacred Heart U., Bridgeport, Conn., 1981-82, Fla. So. Coll., Arcadia, Fla., 1990-93, Adult & Community Edn., Port Charlotte, Fla., 1993—; pres. Mass. League Sch. Publs., 1927-28, Mass. Speech League, 1966-67; bd. dirs. New England Assn. Tchrs. English, 1970-71. Author: America Sings, 1961. Recipient Citizenship award Charlotte Local Edn. Found., 1993. Mem. AAUW (program chair 1990-92, edn. chair 1989-90, pub. policy chair 1992-93, historian 1997—), Univ. Club Charlotte County (pres. 1990-91, program chair 1993). Democrat. Roman Catholic. Avocations: golf, bridge, travel. Home: 157 South St Apt 223 Plymouth MA 02360-1716 E-mail: loumpc59@aol.com.

MULLIN, MARY ANN, career counselor; b. Passaic, N.J., Feb. 9, 1943; d. M. Joseph and Rose M. (Rienzi) DeVita; m. John G. Mullin Jr.; children: Kathleen, John, Robert. BA in Comms., William Paterson Coll., 1991, MA in Urban Studies, 1994; postgrad., Jersey City State U., 1995—. Office mgr. Joseph DeVita, Inc., Paterson, N.J., 1978-94; grad. rsch. asst. William Paterson Coll., Wayne, N.J., 1992-94; ednl. broker/counselor Bergen County Tech. Inst., Hackensack, N.J., 1994-95; grad. admissions counselor Sch. Arch. N.J. Inst. Tech., Newark, 1995-98; sr. info. and referral specialist rsch. and eval. Girl Scouts Am., 1998—. Pres., bd. dirs. Lenni Lenape Girl Scout Coun., Bulter, N.J., 1989-96; pastoral care/eucharistic min. St. Anthony's Ch., Hawthorne, N.J., 1978—; eucharistic min. Wayne (N.J.) Gen. Hosp., 1978—. Recipient Thanks badge Girl Scouts Am., 1996, Honor pin Lenni Lenape Girl Scout Coun., 1991, Outstanding Vol. Svc. award Paterson Task Force, 1994; named Vol. of Week, The Record, 1993. Mem. Pi Lambda Theta (dir. rsch. projects Beta Chi chpt. 1994-96, Outstanding Svc. award 1995, regional chair N.E. conf. Beta Chi chpt. 1996). Democrat. Roman Catholic. Avocations: girl scout activities, travel. Home: 519 Goffle Hill Rd Hawthorne NJ 07506-3056 Office: Girl Scouts US Sch Arch 420 5th Ave Fl 9 New York NY 10018-2798

MULLINIX, BARBARA JEAN, special services director; b. Detroit, Nov. 1, 1949; d. John Chisholm and Elizabeth May (Nunneley) Bow; m. Barry Wayne Mullinix, Apr. 8, 1971; children: Erik, Kelley. BS in Spl. Edn., Ea. Mich. U., 1970, endorsement in emotionally impaired edn., 1984, MA, 1973, endorsement in learning disabilities, 1978, endorsement in spl. edn. adminstrn., 1987; EdD, Wayne State U., 1993. Cert. tchr., Mich. Tchr. self-contained spl. edn., mentally impaired Wayne-Westland (Mich.) Community Schs., 1970-73, tchr., cons. for emotionally impaired-learning disabilities, 1977-92, dept. head, 1986-92, program specialist pre-sch. level, 1992-94; dir. spl. edn. Wayne-Westland (Mich.) Cmty. Schs., 1994—. Deacon Kirk of Our Savior, Westland, 1986-89. Presbyterian. Avocations: reading, boating, genealogy. Home: 11970 Glenview Dr Plymouth MI 48170-3080 Office: Wayne Westland Schs 36745 Marquette St Westland MI 48185-3235

MULLINS, JACK ALLEN, cardiologist, educator; b. Oklahoma City, 1952; MD, U. Okla., 1982. Diplomate in internal medicine, cardiovasc. disease, interventional cardiology Am. Bd. Internal Medicine. Intern U. Tex., Houston, 1982-83, resident in internal medicine, 1983-85; fellow in cardiology U. Okla., Oklahoma City, 1985-88; dir. cardiac cath. lab. Columbia Bayshore Med. Ctr., Pasadena, Tex.; clin. instr. cardiology Baylor Coll. Medicine, 1988—, U. Tex. Med. Sch., Houston, 1988—. Mem. ACP, Am. Coll. Cardiology. Office: Cardiovasc Ctr PA 3337 Plainview St Ste 8 Pasadena TX 77504-1924

MULLINS, SHARON GOUDY, secondary education educator; b. Memphis, July 6, 1945; d. Lawrence Booth and Doris Eileen Goudy; children: Melissa Eileen, Thomas Lawrence. BBA, U. Memphis, 1967, MEd, 1969, postgrad., 1985. Chmn. bus. edn. dept. Germantown (Tenn.) H.S., 1970-95; tech. tchr., webmaster Olive Branch (Miss.) HS, 2002—. Online instr. SW Tenn. C.C., 2000—. Treas. Pleasant Hill United Meth. Ch., Olive Branch, 1988-90. Named Sunday Sch. Regional Dist. Tchr. of Yr. United Meth. Ch., 1980. Mem. NEA, West Tenn. Bus. Edn. Assn. (chmn. 1970-71), Miss. Assn. Educators, Delta Kappa Gamma. Home: 1496 Laughter Rd Nesbit MS 38651-9381 Office: Olive Branch HS 9366 E Sandidge Olive Branch MS 38654

MULLIS, LELIA CHRISTIE, retired secondary school educator; b. Ringgold, Ga., Dec. 7, 1949; d. LeLand Leonidas and Ruth (Dills) Christie; m. Olen D. Mullis, Feb. 2, 1991; children from previous marriage: Michael Farrell Ewton, Leland Clay Ewton, Justin Heath Ewton. AA in Edn., Dalton Jr. Coll., 1968; BS, U. Tenn., Chattanooga, 1971; MEd, Berry Coll., 1975; EdS, W. Ga. Coll., 1982; EdD in Curriculum and Instrn., U. Ga., 1991. Tchr. Whitfield County Pub. Schs., 1971—2003, ret., 2003. Adj. prof. U. Tenn., Chattanooga, 2003—. Mem.: Assn. Childhood Edn. Internat. Democrat. Episcopalian. Home: 106 Hickory Ridge Trl Ringgold GA 30736-7368 E-mail: lmullis607@aol.com.

MULVAGH, CHARLENE FRANCES, special education educator; b. Springfield, Mass., Nov. 16, 1949; d. Eugene Joseph and Frances Catherine McCarthy; m. Peter Joseph Mulvagh, Feb. 9, 1990; children: Aaron Joseph, Edward Daniel. BA, Cardinal Cushing Coll., 1972; MEd, Am. Internat. Coll., 1990. Tchr. spl. edn. Windsor (Conn.) Pub. Schs., 1972-76, Lower Merion (Pa.) Pub. Schs., 1977-83, Springfield (Mass.) Pub. Schs., 1984-87, Windsor Locks (Conn.) Pub. Schs., 1987-88, Windsor Pub. Schs., 1988—. Parent advocate South Windsor Pub. Schs., 1991-94, Chicopee Pub. Schs., Chico, Mass., 1993-94, South Hadley (Mass.) Pub. Schs., 1991-94. Mem. Kappa Gamma Pi. Democrat. Roman Catholic. Avocations: skiing, music. Home: 134 Pine Grove Dr South Hadley MA 01075-2199 Office: Windsor Bd Edn Windsor CT 06095

MULVANEY, MARY JEAN, physical education educator, department chairman; b. Omaha, Jan. 6, 1927; d. Marion Fowler and Blanche Gibons (McKee) M. BS, U. Nebr., 1948; MS, Wellesley Coll., 1951; LHD (hon.), U. Nebr., 1986. Instr. Kans. State U., Manhattan, 1948-50, U. Nebr., Lincoln, 1951-57, asst. prof., 1957-62, U. Kans., Lawrence, 1962-66; assoc. prof. U. Chgo., 1966-76, prof., 1976-90, prof. emeritus, 1990—, chmn. women's divsn., 1966-76, chmn. dept. phys. edn. and athletics, 1976-90; mem. vis. com. on athletics MIT, 1978-81, Wellesley Coll., 1978-79. Dir. athletics office U. Chgo., 2003—. Recipient Honor award Nebr. Assn. Health, Phys. Edn. and Recreation, 1962, U. Nebr. Alumni Achievement award, 1998; named to U. Chgo. Athletics Hall of Fame, 2003. Mem. AAHPERD, Nat. Collegiate Athletic Assn. (mem. coun. 1983-87), Collegiate Coun. Women Athletic Adminstrs., Midwest Assn. Intercollegiate Athletics for Women (chmn. 1979-81), Nat. Assn. Collegiate Dirs. of Athletics (mem. exec. com. 1976-80, Hall of Fame 1990), Ill. Assn. Intercollegiate Athletics for Women (chmn. 1978-80), Univ. Athletic Assn. (sec. 1986-90, mem. exec. com. 1986-90, mem. dels. com. 1986-90, chmn. athletic adminstr.'s com. 1986-88), Mortar Bd., Alpha Chi Omega. Home: 5821 Kennelley Ct Lincoln NE 68516-3799 E-mail: maryjeanmulvany@aol.com.

MULVEY, GERALD JOHN, meteorologist; b. Cambria Heights, N.Y., Dec. 20, 1949; s. George Patrick and Estelle Florence M.; m. Katherine Louise Strick, July 7, 1973. BS in Physics, York Coll., Jamaica, N.Y., 1971; MS in Atmospheric Sci., SUNY, Albany, 1973; PhD in Atmospheric Sci., Colo. State U., 1977. Cert. cons. meteorologist, CCM. Rsch. assoc. dept. atmospheric sci. Colo. State U., 1977—78; mgr. dept. atmospheric physics Meteorology Rsch., Inc., Altadena, Calif., 1978—80; sr. rsch. engr. Lockheed Martin Missiles and Space, Sunnyvale, Calif., 1980—97; advanced programs mgr. Lockheed Martin Western Devel. Labs., 1997—98; lectr. dept. geoscis. San Francisco State U., 1995—98; advanced programs mgr. Lockheed Martin Global Telecomm., Sunnyvale, Calif., 1998—99; prin. sys. engr. DIVA Sys. Corp., Redwood City, Calif., 1999—2002; sr. mgr. Northrop Grumman, 2002—. Co-author: Environmental Impacts of Artificial Ice Nucleating Agents, 1978; contbr. articles to profl. jours. including Analytical Chemistry and Jour. Applied Meteorology. Mem. Cupertino (Calif.) Libr. Commn., 1989—93; v.p. bd. dirs. Cupertino Libr. Found., 2000—01. Mem. AAAS, Am. Meteorological Soc., Internat. Soc. Measurement and Control (v.p. Santa Clara valley 1996-97), Sigma Xi. Roman Catholic. Achievements include verifying/documenting of long range transport of active cloud nucleating agents. Office: Nothrop Grumman Mission One Space Rsch Park R10/1791 Redondo Beach CA 90278 E-mail: gerrymulvey@att.net.

MULVEY, MARY CROWLEY, retired adult education director, gerontologist, senior citizen association administrator; b. Bangor, Maine, Aug. 17, 1909; d. Michael J. and Ann Loretta (Higgins) Crowley; m. Gordon F. Mulvey, Jan. 25, 1940. BA, U. Maine, 1930; MA, Brown U., 1953; EdD, Harvard U., 1961; LHD (hon.), U. Maine, 1991. Chair R.I. Com. on Aging, 1953-65; dir. adminstrn. on aging State of R.I., 1960-63; co-founder Nat. Coun. Sr. Citizens, 1961; pres. Nat. Sr. Citizens Edn. and Rsch. Ctr., Washington, 1963—; 1st v.p. Nat. Coun. Sr. Citizens, 1976-2001; guidance counselor Providence Sch. Dept., 1963-65; dir. adult edn. City of Providence Sch. Dept., 1965-79; reg. prog. rep. Title V, Older Ams. Act, Nat. Coun. Sr. Citizens, Washington, 1980-94. Major role in enactment of Medicare and Older Americans Act, 1950-65; del., adv. com. White House Conf. on Aging, 1961, 71, 81, 95; cons. Fed. Housing for the Aging, Washington, 1963-65, tech. rev. com. Older Ams. Act Title IV, 1966-70; instr. preparing for retirement, developer women's program U. R.I., 1963-80; appt. by Pres. Carter to Fed. Coun. Aging, 1979, pres. R.I. State Coun. Sr. Citizens, 1982-98; charter mem. adv. bd. Coll. Arts and Humanities, U. Maine, 1992-96. Contbr. articles to profl. jours. Charter mem. U. Maine Friends of Mus. Art, 1997—; chair sr. citizen's rally Nat. Coun. Sr. Citizens, Washington, 1998. Recipient Cert. of award as Project Dir. of Sr. AIDES Employment Program, 1968-79, Medicare award R.I. State Coun. Sr. Citizens and Nat. Coun. Sr. Citizens, 1985, Disting. Achievement award U. Maine, 1980, Disting. Achievement award Berwick Acad., 1981, Justice for All award R.I. Bar Assn., 1981, Woman of Yr. award Nat. Sr. Pageant, 1982, R.I. Women 1st R.I. Sec. of State, 1991, citation Syracuse U., 1991, R.I. Dept. Elderly Affairs, 1993, 10th, 25th and 30th Anniversaries Title V Sr. Employment award Nat. Coun. Sr. Citizens, 1978, 93, 98, Lifetime Achievement award, 1994, Co-Founder and Continuing Bd. Mem. award, 1995, Svcs. for Sr. Citizens award, 1995, 30-yr. Sr. Aides award Nat. Sr. Citizens Edn. and Rsch. Ctr., 1999; named to R.I. Heritage Hall of Fame, 1993; Citation by Gov. Lincoln Almond for contbns. to R.I., 1996; Humanitarian award U. Maine Reunion, 2000; Soroptomists fellow in rsch. in gerontology Harvard U., 1955, 57, 59. Fellow Gerontol. Soc. Am.; mem. ACA, AAUW, Am. Assn. Adult and Continuing Edn., Harvard U. Alumni Assn. (Alumni award R.I. chpt. 1986), U. Maine Alumni Assn., Brown U. Alumni Assn., Harvard 1920 Club, Charles William Elliot Soc. (charter), Charles F. Allen Soc., Stillwater Soc. U. Maine (charter, Presdl. award for achievement), Paul Hamus Soc. Harvard, Pi Lambda Theta, Delta Delta Delta. Achievements include development of adult literacy program; has had 5 books published for teaching adult basic education and English as a second language. Home: 118 Evergreen Ln Windham ME 04062-4713

MULVIHILL, MAUREEN ESTHER, writer, educator, scholar; b. Detroit; d. Charles James and Esther (Byrne) M.; m. Daniel R. Harris, June 18, 1983. PhD, U. Wis., 1983; postgrad., Columbia U., Yale U., Met. Mus. Art. Instr. U. Detroit, 1968-70, Wayne State U., Detroit, 1969-70, Penn Valley C.C., Kansas City, Mo., 1970-71; project writer Office of Gov., State of Wis., Madison, 1972-82; corp. comm. dir. Gruntal & Co., N.Y.C., 1983-85; vis. asst. prof. Hunter Coll. CUNY, 1984; assoc. fellow Inst. for Rsch. in History, N.Y.C., 1984-89; vis. asst. prof. Touro Coll., N.Y.C., 1985; mem. Princeton (N.J.) Rsch. Forum, 1991—; cons. writer-editor Securities Industry Automated Corp./NYSE, N.Y.C., 1986-94. Proposal evaluator NEH, Washington, 1989—; juror Clifford Com. Am. Soc. for 18th Century Studies, 1991; vis. faculty NYU, 1983-85, 93, Marymount Manhattan Coll., 1993-94; vis. assoc. prof. Fordham U.-Lincoln Ctr., 1994-96; vis. prof. English, St. Joseph Coll., Bklyn., 1997, Berkeley Coll., Manhattan, 2000-2001, Mercy Coll., Manhattan, 2002—; guest spkr. Bklyn. Mus., Bklyn. Pub. Libr., NYU, Princeton U., Utah State U., S.W. Tex. State U., Irish Hist. Soc., N.Y.C.; corp. liaison Irish Art Exhbn., U.S., U.K.; writer mktg. com. Saatchi & Saatchi, N.Y.C., 1998-99; cons. book devel., book proposal evaluator MLA, N.Y.C., 1998—; cons. writer Wall Street Office, Bank of N.Y., N.Y.C., 2000—. Contbr. to profl. publs.; editor: (book) Poems by Ephelia (ca. 1679), 1992, 1993, Ephelia, 2003. Recipient scholarships and awards Wayne State U., 1966, 67-68, U. Wis., 1971-81, Inst. Rsch. History, N.Y.C., 1984-89; NEH fellow, 1990-91, Princeton Rsch. Forum, N.J., 1992, 95, 97, Honors List of Scholars & Tchrs, Women's Caucus, Am. Soc. Eighteenbth-Century Stds, 2001. Democrat. Roman Catholic. Avocations: rare book collecting (17th and 18th century English, Irish and continental women writers). Home: One Plaza St W Brooklyn NY 11217-3748 E-mail: mulvihill@nyc.rr.com.

MUMFORD, DAVID BRYANT, mathematics educator; b. Worth, Sussex, Eng., June 11, 1937; came to U.S., 1940; s. William Bryant and Grace (Schiott) M.; m. Erika Jentsch, June 27, 1959 (dec. July 30, 1988); children: Stephen, Peter, Jeremy, Suchitra; m. Jenifer Moore, Dec. 29, 1989. BA, Harvard U., 1957, PhD, 1961; D.Sc. (hon.), U. Warwick, 1983, Norwegian U. Sci. Tech., 2000, Rockefeller U., 2001. Jr. fellow Harvard U., 1958-61, assoc. prof., 1962-66, prof. math., 1966-77, Higgins prof., 1977-97, chmn. dept. math, 1981-84; U. prof. Brown U., 1996—. V.p. Internat. Math. Union, 1991-94, pres., 1995-98. Author: Geometric Invariant Theory, 1965, Abelian Varieties, 1970, Introduction to Algebraic Geometry, 1976, 2 and 3 Dimensional Patterns of the Face, 1999, Indra's Pearls, 2002. Recipient Fields medal Internat. Congress Mathematicians, 1974; MacArthur Found. fellow, 1987-92. Fellow Tata Inst. (hon.); mem. Accad. Nazionale dei Lincei, Nat. Acad. Scis., Am. Acad. Arts and Scis., Am. Philosophical Soc. Home: 65 Milton St Milton MA 02186-2322 Office: Brown U 182 George St Providence RI 02912-9056

MUMMERT, JACK R. mathematics educator; b. Elmhurst, Ill., June 30, 1962; s. Roy Harold and Virginia Lee (McCullough) M. AS in Secondary Edn., Rend Lake Coll., 1985; BS in Math., So. Ill. U., 1987, MS in Math., 1989. Cert. secondary tchr., Ill. Teaching asst. Rend Lake Coll., Ina, Ill., 1984-85, instr., 1988-90; student tchr. Herrin (Ill.) High Sch., 1987; grad. asst. So. Ill. U., Carbondale, 1988-89; reviewer Ill. Coun. Tchrs. Math., 1989—; adminstrv. asst., cons. Sci. Literacy-ICTM, Carbondale, 1990-91; instr. John A. Logan Coll., Carterville, Ill., 1990-91, Southeastern Ill. Coll., Harrisburg, 1991—, chair math. and sci. divsn., 2001—. Co-chair Ill. Articulation Initiative Maths. Majors Panel, 1997—. Editor, co-author: Calculators in the Classroom, 1990, Calculator Activities for the 7-12 Classroom, 1991; editor: The Math ConneXion, 2002-03; author numerous poems. Recipient Excellence award, Nat. Inst. Staff and Orgnl. Devel., 2003. Mem. Nat. Coun. Tchrs. Math., Ill. Coun. Tchrs. Math., Am. Math. Assn. Two-Yr. Colls., Ill. Math. Assn. Community Colls., Pi Mu Epsilon, Gamma Beta Phi, Kappa Delta Pi. Avocations: environmental issues, sports photography, cooking, antiques. Office: Southeastern Ill Coll 3575 College Rd Rm B215 Harrisburg IL 62946-4925

MUNDHEIM, ROBERT HARRY, law educator; b. Hamburg, Germany, Feb. 24, 1933; m. Guna Smitchens; children: Susan, Peter. BA, Harvard U., 1954, LLB, 1957; MA (hon.), U. Pa., 1971. Bar: N.Y. 1958, Pa. 1979. Assoc. Shearman & Sterling, N.Y.C., 1958-61; spl. counsel to SEC Washington, 1962-63; vis. prof. Duke Law Sch., Durham, N.C., 1964; prof. law U. Pa., Phila., 1965—. Univ. prof. law and fin., 1980-93, dean, 1982-89, Bernard G. Segal prof. law, 1987-89; co-chmn. Fried, Frank, Harris, Shriver & Jacobson, N.Y.C., 1990-92; exec. v.p., gen. counsel Salomon Inc., 1992-97; sr. exec. v.p., gen. counsel Salomon Smith Barney Holdings, Inc., 1997-98; of counsel Shearman & Sterling, 1999—; gen. counsel U.S. Dept. Treasury, Washington, 1977-80, trustee and pres. Am. Acad. in Berlin, 2000—; chmn. legal adv. bd. NASDAQ, chmn. legal adv. bd. NASD; pres. Appleseed Found.; trustee New Sch. U.; bd. dirs. eCollege, Salzburg Seminar, The Kitchen; gen. counsel Chrysler Loan Guarantee Bd., 1980; mng. dir., mem. mgmt. bd. Salomon Bros. Inc., N.Y.C., 1992-97; overseer Curtis Inst. Fin., 2000—. Author: Outside Director of the Publicity Held Corporation, 1976; American Attitudes Toward Foreign Direct Investment in the United States, 1979; Conflict of Interest and the Former Government Employee: Re-thinking the Revolving Door, 1981; chmn. adv. bd. Jour. Internat. Econ. Law, 1996-97. Trustee SEC Hist. Soc. With USAF, 1961-62. Recipient Alexander Hamilton award U.S. Dept. Treasury, 1980, Harold P. Seligson award Practicing Law Inst., 1988, Francis J. Rawle award, ABA-ALI, 1992, Anti-Defamation League Human Rels. award, 1999. Mem. ABA (task force on corp. responsiblity), Am. Law Inst., San Diego Securities Regulation Inst. (exec. com.). Office: Shearman & Sterling 599 Lexington Ave Fl 16 New York NY 10022-6069

MUNDSCHENK, JANE MARIE, special education educator; b. Columbus, Nebr., Dec. 26, 1957; d. William Krohn and Iva Margaret (Haas) M. BS, Dana Coll., Blair, Nebr., 1980; Cert., Mayo Sch. Health Related Scis., Rochester, Minn., 1982; MA, U. No. Colo., 1984. Lic. spl. edn. tchr., S.D., Nebr., Colo. Orientation/mobility tchr. S.D. Sch. for Visually Handicapped, Aberdeen, 1985—, adv. bd., 1989—. Mem. Coun. for Exceptional Children, Am. Phys. Therapy Assn., Assn. for Edn. and Rehab. of Blind and Visually Impaired (pres. Dakotas chpt. 1993-95), Aberdeen Lioness Club (pres. 1991-92). Avocations: reading, counted cross-stitch, cooking. Office: SD Sch for Visually Handicapped 423 17th Ave SE Aberdeen SD 57401-7616

MUNGER, JANET ANNE, education administrator; b. N.J., Feb. 27, 1947; d. Victor J. and Ann L. Ferri Munger. BA, Fairleigh Dickinson U., 1968, MA, 1971; EdD, Seton Hall U., 1985. Cert. sch. adminstr., prin., supr. Tchr. Meml. Sch. No. 11, Passaic, N.J., 1968-70; dir., tchr. Morristown Head Start Program, N.J., 1970-71 (summers); curriculum devel. specialist N.J. State Coun. Arts Grant Program, 1973 (summer); tchr. Ctrl. Sch., Montville, N.J., 1970-73, William Mason Sch., Montville, 1973-81; tchr. gifted and talented William Mason, Valley View and Woodmont Schs., Montville, 1981-82; coord. of curriculum instr. South Plainfield (N.J.) Bd. Edn., 1986-91, supr. fed. and state projects, 1989-92, supr. ednl. programs, 1992-94, prin., 1994—2001, dir. curriculum and instrn., 2001—03; supt. of schs. Farmingdale, NJ, 2003—. Presenter in field profl. assns.; researcher, writer, cons., 1982—. Mem. ASCD, NEA, Am. Assn. Sch. Adminstrs., N.J. Assn. Sch. Adminstrs., N.J. Edn. Assn., Assn. Secondary Sch. Prins., Prins. and Suprs. Assn., New Eng. Coalition Ednl. Leaders, N.J. Assn. Fed. Program Adminstrs., Phi Delta Kappa, Kappa Delta Pi. Office: Farmingdale Bd Edn 49 Academy St Farmingdale NJ 07727

MUNGER, PAUL DAVID, company executive, educational administrator; b. Selma, Ala., Oct. 12, 1945; s. Paul Francis and Arlene Lorraine (McFillen) M.; m. Paula Jean Dominici, May 30, 1969; children: Kimberley Beth, Christopher David. AB in Philosophy, Kenyon Coll., 1967; MA in Govt., Ind. U., 1969. Commd. 2d lt. USAF, 1969, advanced through grades to capt., resigned, 1978; asst. dir. faculty devel. Ind. U., Bloomington, 1974-77; from asst. dean to dean continuing studies Am. U., Washington, 1980-83, asst. provost acad. devel., 1983-84; dir. Commn. on Future Acad. Leadership, Washington, 1984-86; v.p. Acad. Strategies, Washington, 1986-88; pres. Strategic Edn. Svcs. Inc., Sterling, Va., 1988—. Bd. dirs. Munger Acad., 1989—. Bd. advisors Madeira Sch., McLean, Va., 1993-96; treas. Bus.-Higher Edn. Fedn., Washington, 1992-2000; asst. scoutmaster Boy Scouts Am., 1991-93, scoutmaster, 1994-97; dir. Czech-Am. Lacrosse Found., 1996—; bd. dirs. Thomas Jefferson H.S. for Sci. and Tech. Found., 1999-2001, PTSA, 1996-98, chair bus. rels. com., 1996-98. Mem. Am. Soc. Tng. & Devel. (chmn. strategic planning com. 1993-95, continuing profl. edn. electronic forum coord. 1995-97), Assn. Continuing Higher Edn., Am. Soc. Curriculum Devel. Office: Strategic Education Services Inc 624 W Church Rd Sterling VA 20164-4608 E-mail: pdmunger@strategicedservices.com.

MUNGER, PAUL R. civil engineering educator; b. Hannibal, Mo, Jan. 14, 1932; s. Paul O and Anne M.; m. Frieda Anna Mette, Nov. 26, 1954; children: Amelia Ann Munger Fortmeyer, Paul David, Mark James, Martha Jane Munger Cox. BSCE, Mo. Sch. Mines and Metallurgy, 1958, MSCE, 1961; PhD in Engring. Sci., U. Ark., 1972. Registered profl. engr., Mo., Ill., Ark. Instr. civil engring Mo. Sch. Mines and Metallurgy, Rolla, 1958-61, asst. prof., 1961-65; assoc. prof. U. Mo., Rolla, 1965-73, prof., 1973-99; dir. Inst. River Studies, U. Mo., Rolla, 1976-93; exec. dir. Internat. Inst. River and Lake Systems, U. Mo., Rolla, 1984-93, interim chmn. CE dept., 1998-99. Mem. NSPE, Mo. Soc. Profl. Engr., Am. Soc. Engring. Edn., ASCE, Nat. Coun. Engring. Examiners (pres. 1983-84), Mo. Bd. Architects, Profl. Engr. and Land Surveyors (chmn. 1978-84, 95-2002).

MUNGUIA, GAY YAEGER, elementary school educator, secondary school educator; b. Tyler, Tex., Aug. 17, 1934; d. George Allen and Alice Rhoda (Sanders) Yeager; m. Douglas A. Thibodeaux, June 10, 1955 (div. Nov. 1979); children: Lane David, Lynn Alice, Lee Douglas; m. Jeffrey Joe Wheeler, Sept. 25, 1982 (div. June 1992); m. Michael Anthony Munguia, June, 1995. BA in History and English, Lamar U., 1955; MEd, Sam Houston State U., 1995. Cert. tchr., Tex. Tchr. Ball High Sch., Galveston, 1955-58; high schs. tutor Mich., La., Tex., 1958—88; coll. tutor Tex., 1971—77; receptionist Theatre Under the Stars, Houston, 1978; asst. mgr. Heavenly Body Health Spa, Houston, 1979-80; salesperson Carbondale, Colo., 1980-82; dept. supr. Glenwood Med. Assoc., Glenwood Springs, Colo., 1983-88; tutor Colo. Mt. Coll., Glenwood Springs, 1988—; ladies mgr., aerobics instr. Tex. Lady-Texan Spa, Houston, 1988-89; tchr., curriculum devel. Inter-Faith Child Devel. Ctr., The Woodlands, Tex., 1989—97; kindergarten tchr. Couroe Indept. Sch. System, 1997—. Curriculum devel. cons. St. Barnabas Ch., Glenwood Springs, 1983-85, St. Christopher's Pre-Sch., Houston, 1968-70; text book cons. Galveston schs., 1957. Author weekly coll. activity column, essays, poems, children's stories; acted, directed and produced local dramas including Truman Capote's A Christmas Memory; acted in sevaral movies and TV commls. Century Casting, 1978-81. Vol. St. Barnabas Ch. Thrift Gift Sale, 1983-85, St. Christopher's Thrift Shop, 1960-69; outreach chmn. St. Barnabas Ch. Vestry, 1983-86; active Walden Cmty. Ch., 1988—. Recipient Humanitarian of Yr., Conroe Ind. Sch. Dist., 2002, Tchr. of Yr., 2003. Mem. Alpha Chi Omega, Pi Kappa Phi. Episcopalian. Avocations: writing, drama, Bible, dancing, camping. Home: 13310 Northshore Dr Montgomery TX 77356-5329 Office: Anderson Elem 1414 E Dallas Conroe TX 77301-3626

MUNIR, YUSUF, vocational education administrator; b. Lumenburg County, Va., Mar. 16, 1934; s. Joseph Harrison and Ada (Stokes) Rather; m. Celia Albritton, Feb. 18, 1952; children: Elizabeth, Yusuf II, Daud, Ishmael, Saladin, Masha, Kenyetta, Ibn Yusuf, Mubarak Ibn Yusuf, Najib Hassim. BS, R.I. Coll., 1977, 88, MEd, 1983; doctoral fellow, Walden U., 1992; DD (hon.), U. Islam, Chgo., 1975. Minister Nation of Islam, Boston, 1952-75, World Commmunity of Islam, Providence, 1975-84; tchr. indsl. arts Nathanael Green Mic. Sch., 1984-86; tchr. tech. Mt. Pleasant High Sch., Providence, 1986-90; asst. prin. Hope Essential High Sch., Providence, 1990-92; coord. Hanley Vocat. Ctr., Providence, 1992—. Prin. summer sch. Providence Sch. Dept., 1982-84; bus. cons. Orgn. Industrialization Ctr., Providence, 1989. Pres. Community Planning Assn., Providence, 1973, Inter-Faith Ministers Assn., Providence, 1975, Mayors Task Force Community Devel., 1979; master troop # 85 Boy Scouts Am., Providence, 1978; spiritual advisor Adult Correctional Inst., Warwick, R.I., 1978-82; bd. dirs. Challenge House, Providence, 1980-83. Named Outstanding Coord. Occupational Indsl. Ctr., 1980, Outstanding Tchr. Resource Linker Providence Tchrs. Union, 1989; recipient Leadership award GE, 1985, Community Svc. award John Hope Settlement House, 1991. Mem. Am. Soc. Notaries, Nat. Inst. Occupational Health and Safety (cert. 1984), African Am. Educators Assn. (treas. 1992-93), Black Adminstrs. ORgn. (sec. 1991-92), Doctorate Assn. N.Y. Educators, MAsons (master, jr. warden 1994, Mayor's Key fo the City 1994). Avocations: woodcraft, art, cabinet making, model making. Office: James L Hanley Vocat Tech Ctr 91 Fricker St Providence RI 02903-4035

MUNITZ, BARRY, arts and foundation administrator; b. Bklyn., July 26, 1941; m. Anne Tomfohrde. BA, Bklyn. Coll., 1963; MA, Princeton U., 1965, PhD, 1968; cert., U. Leiden, Netherlands, 1962; hon. doctorate, Claremont U., Calif. State Univ. Sys., Whittier Coll., U. Notre Dame. Asst. prof. lit. and drama U. Calif., Berkeley, 1966-68; staff assoc. Carnegie Commn. Higher Edn., 1968-70; acad. v.p. U. Ill. System, 1971—76; v.p., dean faculties Central campus U. Houston, 1976-77, chancellor, 1977-82; pres., COO Federated Devel. Co., 1982-91; vice chmn. Maxxam Inc., L.A., 1982-91; chancellor Calif. State U. System, Long Beach, Calif., 1991-98; prof. English lit. Calif. State U., L.A., 1991—; pres., CEO, trustee J.Paul Getty Trust, L.A., 1998—. Bd. dirs. KCET-TV, SLM Holdings, KB Home; cons. in presdl. evaluation and univ. governance; trustee Princeton U. Author: The Assessment of Institutional Leadership, also articles, monographs. Mem. art mus. vis. com. Princeton and Harvard; former chair bd. dirs. ACE; former co-chair trustees planning com. Gardner Mus.; former chair Calif. Gov. Transition Team. Recipient Distng. Alumnus award Bklyn. Coll., 1979, U. Houston Alumni Pres.'s medal, 1981; Woodrow Wilson fellow. Fellow Am. Acad. Arts and Scis.; mem. Phi Beta Kappa. Office: J Paul Getty Trust 1200 Getty Center Dr Ste 400 Los Angeles CA 90049-1681 E-mail: bmunitz@getty.edu.

MUNLU, KAMIL CEMAL, finance educator; b. Istanbul, Turkey, July 14, 1954; came to U.S., 1981; s. Adnan and Jale Sidika (Konari) M. BA in Econs., Calif. State U., Long Beach, 1983; MBA in Bus. Adminstrn., Nat. U., San Diego, 1986, MS in Logistics, 1988; M in Internat. Bus. Adminstrn., U.S. Internat. U., San Diego, 1990; DPA, U. La Verne, Calif., 1995. Adj. prof. Woodbury U., Burbank, Calif., 1998—. Adj. prof. Nat. U., San Diego, 1999, U. La Verne, Calif., 2000. Mem. Turkish Army, 1984-85. Avocations: art, boating, golfing, reading, travel.

MUNN, EUFEMIA TOBIAS, elementary school principal; b. Malabang, Philippines, Nov. 23, 1937; came to U.S., 1967; d. Cayetano D. and Gabriela (Catulong) Tobias; m. Merton D. Munn, Aug. 21, 1966. BA in Bus. Adminstrn., Silliman U., 1960; Teaching Cert., Whitworth Coll., 1970, MEd, 1972. Cert. tchr., prin., Wash. Asst. to dean of women Silliman U., Dumaguete City, Philippines, 1960-63, asst. dean of women, 1963-66; sec. to rsch. dir. United Board for Christian Higher Edn. in Asia, N.Y.C., 1966-69; sec.-receptionist Whitworth Coll., Admissions Office, Spokane, 1971-72; spl. edn. tchr. Lakeland Village, Medical Lake, Wash., 1973-75; instr. Sheldon Jackson Coll., Sitka, Alaska, 1974-77; spl. edn. tchr., adminstr. Med. Lake Sch. Dist., 1977; prin. Blair Elem., Med. Lake, 1977—. Mem. Wash. State Safe Schs. Adv. Com., Olympia, Wash., 1992; trainer of trainers; presenter in field. Mem. NAESP, AAUP, AWSP, AAUW, N.E. Principals (sec. 1990-91), Wash. State Prin. Assn., Internat. Reading Assn., Phi Lambda Theta. Republican. Presbyterian. Avocations: writing, reading, cooking, walking, enabling people. Home: 10912 S Sunnyslope Rd Medical Lake WA 99022-9526 Office: Blair Elem Sch S 10912 Sunnyslope Rd Fairchild Air Force Base WA 99011

MUÑOZ, MARGARET ELLEN, reading specialist; b. Jacksonville, Ill., Jan. 30, 1947; d. George William and Lois Lottie (Ankrom) Greene; m. Juan James Muñoz, Mar. 31, 1972; children: Aaron Joseph, Lauri Elizabeth. BA, Culver-Stockton Coll., 1969; MA, Western Ill. U., 1971. Cert. tchr. reading K-12 and English 7-12, Mo. Tchr. lang. arts 10-12 Quincy (Ill.) Sr. H.S., 1970-72; tchr. lang. arts 7-12 Sch. Dist. R-S, New Raymer, Colo., 1972-73; tchr. lang. arts 9-12 Kansas City (Mo.) Sch. Dist., 1973-78; tchr. lang. arts 10-12 Ft. Osage Sch. Dist., Independence, Mo., 1978-80; Tchr. Title I Reading 7-8 Independence Pub. Schs., 1980-81, 89—, tchr. ESL and Am. Indian K-12, 1985-89; Title I reading tchr. middle campus Bingham 7th Grade Ctr., 1998—2001; lang. arts instructional specialist Pioneer Ridge Sch., 2001—03; Title I reading tchr. Santa Fe Trails Elem. Sch., 2003—. Chair Profl. Devel.-Palmer, Independence, 1993-97, Palmer-Bingham, 1998-99; sponsor Sharing Stories With Children, Independence, 1993—; sr. leader Mo. Assessment Program, 2001—; presenter reading strategies Ottawa U., Overland Park, Kans., 1994, Chpt. I State Conf., 1994, Ann. Assessment & Authentic Performance Conf., Olathe, Kans., 1996, Assessment Conf., Olathe, 1996; mem. Dist. Profl. Devel., Independence, 1994-98; mem. adv. bd. Kansas City Regional Profl. Devel. Ctr., 1995-98. Active Blue Ridge Blvd. United Meth. Ch., Kansas City, 1982—; officer Mothers' Coun., Boy Scouts Am., Kansas City, 1993—; mem. Kansas City Regional Profl. Devel. Coun.; co-chair Reading Strategies, 1997-99. Mem. ASCD, Mo. Nat. Edn. Assn., Independence/Ft. Osage Internat. Reading Assn. (com. chair 1984—), PTA (life). Avocations: reading, sewing, walking, time with family. Office: Santa Fe Trails Elem Sch 1301 S Windsor Independence MO 64055-1196

MUNOZ, RICARDO, JR., obstetrician-gynecologist, educator; b. Jacksonville, Fla., May 2, 1954; MD, Meharry Med. Coll., 1979. Cert. in ob-gyn., recert. Intern Brooke Army Med. Ctr., Ft. Sam Houston, Tex., 1979-80, resident in ob-gyn., 1981-84; with Nix Med. Ctr., San Antonio, Santa Rosa Med. Ctr., San Antonio, Bapt. Meml. Hosp. Sys., San Antonio, Meth. Health Care Sys. Clin. assoc. prof. dept. ob-gyn. U. Tex. Health Sci. Ctr., San Antonio. Mem. AMA, ACOG, Am. Coll. Physician Execs., Am. Assn. Gynecol. Laparoscopists, Am. Fertility Soc., Tex. Med. Assn., TMF, Bexar County Med. Soc. Office: Riverwalk Ob-Gyn PLLC 414 Navarro St Ste 1200 San Antonio TX 78205-2501 also: 525 Oak Centre Dr Ste 320 San Antonio TX 78258-3916

MUNRO, DONALD JACQUES, philosopher, educator; b. New Brunswick, N.J., Mar. 5, 1931; s. Thomas B. and Lucile (Nadler) M.; m. Ann Maples Patterson, Mar. 3, 1956; 1 child, Sarah de la Roche. AB, Harvard U., 1953; PhD (Ford Found. fellow), Columbia U., 1964. Asst. prof. philosophy U. Mich., 1964-68, assoc. prof., 1968-73, prof. philosophy, 1973-96, prof. philosophy and Asian langs., 1990-96; prof. emeritus philosophy and Chinese, 1996—; chmn. dept. Asian langs. and cultures U. Mich., 1993-95; vis. research philosopher Center for Chinese Studies, U. Calif., Berkeley, 1969-70; asso. Center for Chinese Studies, U. Mich., 1964—; chmn. com. on studies of Chinese civilization Am. Council Learned Socs., 1979-81. Mem. Com. on Scholarly Communication with People's Republic China, NAS, 1978-82, China Council of Asia Soc., 1977-80, Com. on Advanced Study in China, 1978-82, Nat. Com. on U.S.-China Rels., Nat. Faculty of Humanities, Arts and Scis., 1986—; Evans-Wentz lectr. Stanford U., 1970; Fritz lectr. U. Wash., 1980; Gilbert Ryle lectr. Trent U., Ont., 1983; John Dewey lectr. U. Vt., 1989; Ch'ien Mu lectr. Chinese U. Hong Kong, 2002-2003. Author: The Concept of Man in Early China, 1969, the Concept of Man in Contemporary China, 1977; editor: Individualism and Holism, 1985, Images of Human Nature: A Sung Portrait, 1988, The Imperial Style of Inquiry in Twentieth Century China, 1996. Mem. exec. com. Coll. Literature, Sci. and The Arts U. Mich., 1986-89. Served to lt. (j.g.) USNR, 1953-57. Recipient letter of commendation Chief Naval Ops.; Disting. Svc. award U. Mich., 1968, Excellence in Edn. award, 1992; Rice Humanities award, 1993-94; Nat. Humanities faculty fellow, 1971-72; John Simon Guggenheim Found. fellow, 1978-79; grantee Social Sci. Rsch. Coun., 1965-66, Am. Coun. Learned Socs., 1982-83, China com. grantee NAS, 1990; vis. rsch. scholar Chinese Acad. Social Scis. Inst. Philosophy, Beijing, 1983, dept. philosophy Beijing U., 1990. Mem. Assn. for Asian Studies (China and Inner Asia Council 1970-72), Soc. for Asian and Comparative Philosophy. Clubs: Ann Arbor Racquet. Home: 14 Ridgeway St Ann Arbor MI 48104-1739 Office: Dept Philosophy U Mich Ann Arbor MI 48104

MUNRO, RODERICK ANTHONY, business improvement coach; b. Toronto, Ont., Can., Jan. 16, 1955; came to U.S., 1956; s. William George and Georgina Antoinette M.; m. Elizabeth J. Rice, 1994. BA, Adrian Coll., 1979, secondary provisional cert., 1981; MS, Eastern Mich. U., 1984; ednl. specialist, Wayne State U., 1998; PhD, Cambridge State U., 1999. Cert. quality engr., quality auditor, hypnotherapist, cert. quality mgr. Tchr. Lincoln Park H.S., Mich., 1980-82; mgmt. trainee Fabricon Automotive, River Rouge, Mich., 1982-84; statis. process control coord. ASC, Inc., Southgate, Mich., 1984-86; quality engr. container divsn. Johnson Controls, Inc., Manchester, Mich., 1987-88; program dir. Ford Motor Co., Dearborn, Mich., 1988—2001; bus. improvement coach RAM Q Universe, Inc., Reno, 2001—. Cons. in field, 1986—. Served to sgt. USMCR, 1974-80. Fellow Am. Soc. for Quality (bd. dirs., past cert. com., past chmn. Greater Detroit sect., past chair human resources divsn. Testimonial award 1988, 2002, Disting. Svc. award 1989, 96); mem. ASTD, Internat. Assn. Counselors and Therapists (cert.), Aircraft Owners and Pilots Assn., Am. Statis. Assn. (past pres. Greater Detroit chpt.), Internat. Soc. for Performance Improvement, Assn. Quality and Participation. Office: RAM Q Universe Inc 1135 Terminal Way Ste 209 Reno NV 89502-2168 Office Fax: 231-386-9256. E-mail: doctormunro@yahoo.com.

MUNROE, DONNA SCOTT, marketing executive, healthcare and management consultant, educator; b. Cleve., Nov. 28, 1945; d. Glenn Everett and Louise Lennox (Parkhill) Scott; m. Melvin James Ricketts, Dec. 23, 1968 (div. Aug. 1979); 1 child, Suzanne Michelle; m. Peter Carlton Munroe, Feb. 14, 1981. BS in Sociology, Portland (Oreg.) State U., 1976, BS in Philosophy, 1978, MS in Sociology, 1983. Lectr. Portland State U., 1977-79; writing, editorial cons. Worth Pubs., N.Y.C., 1978-79; statis. cons. health scis. U. Oreg., Portland, 1979-82; statis. cons. Morrison Ctr. for Youth and Family Svcs., Portland, 1979-82; writer Equitable Savs. & Loan, Portland, 1981-82; mgr. acct. and projects. Electronic Data Systems, Portland, 1982-87; exec. dir. corp. mktg. and planning CMSI, Portland, 1987-95; prin. Certus Enterprises Inc., Portland, 1995—. Mem. Am. Mgmt. Assn., Am. Mktg. Assn., Am. Soc. for Quality Control, City Club of Portland, Sigma Xi. Democrat. Episcopalian. Home and Office: 536 SW Cheltenham St Portland OR 97201-2602

MUNSTERMAN, INGRID ANITA, assistant principal; b. The Hague, The Netherlands, Dec. 10, 1957; d. Theodorus and Hendrica Doesburg; m. Patrick Dean Munsterman. AA, Chaffey Coll., 1977; BA, Calif. State U., 1979; MA, Calif. State U., 1990. From elem. tchr. to asst. prin. Colton Joint Unified Sch. Dist., Calif., 1980—. Adj. faculty U. Redlands, Calif., 2000—, Nat. U., Calif., 2001—.

MUNUZ, FLORENCE BATT, education educator; b. Phila., Apr. 2, 1937; d. Charles Webster and Ida M. (Griffiths) Batt; 1 child, Erol. BA, Glassboro (N.J.) State Coll., 1972; MA, U. Chgo., 1978. Cert. tchr., N.J., Ill., Pa. Prof. Oakton Coll., Des Plaines, Ill.; tchr., dental hygienist Sch. Dist. of Phila.; cons. Child Care Ctr., Evanston, Ill. Fulbright scholar, Manchester, Eng., 1990. Mem. NEA, Nat. Assn. for Edn. Young Children, Am. Coun. Nanny Schs., Assn. for Childhood Edn. Internat., N.Am. Soc. for Serbian Studies, Nat. Assn. Certfied Nursery Nurses, Internat. Nanny Assn.

MURAD, SOHAIL, engineer educator; b. Rawalpindi, Panjab, Pakistan, May 4, 1953; came to U.S., 1975; s. Akram and Ruh Afza (Azim) M.; m. Penelope Ann Newland, Dec. 15, 1979; children: Adam, Anita. BSChE, U. Engring., Lahore, Pakistan, 1974; MSChE, U. Fla., 1976; PhD of Chem. Engr., Cornell U., 1979. Sr. engr. Exxon Rsch. and Engr. Co., Florham Park, N.J., 1981-82; asst. prof., assoc. prof. U. Ill., Chgo., 1979-91, prof., 1991—. Adv. bd. mem. Computer Applications in Engineering Education, N.Y.C., 1994—. Contbr. (ency.) Ency. of Fluid Mechanics, 1989, articles to profl. jours. Grantee Dept. Energy, 1987—, NSF, 1985—, NATO, 1985—; fellow Ballistic Rsch. lab., 1985. Mem. AIChE, Am. Chem. Soc. (grantee 1994—), Am. Philatelic Soc. Office: Univ Ill MC 110 810 S Clinton St Chicago IL 60607-4408 E-mail: murad@uic.edu.

MURAI, NORIMOTO, plant molecular biologist, educator; b. Sapporo, Japan, Mar. 4, 1944; came to U.S., 1968; s. Nobuo and Hideko (Odagiri) M.; m. Andreana Lisca, Nov. 14, 1977; 1 child, Naoki. BS, Hokkaido U., 1966, MS, 1968; PhD, U. Wis., 1973. Rsch. assoc. dept. botany U. Wis., Madison, 1974-78, project assoc. dept. bacteriology, 1979, postdoctoral fellow dept. plant pathology, 1980-82; lab. head dept. molecular biology Nat. Inst. Agrobiol. Resources, Tsukuba, Japan, 1983-84; assoc. prof. plant pathology and crop physiology La. State U., Baton Rouge, 1985-92, prof., 1992—. Adj. prof. biochemistry, full mem. grad. faculty and interdept. studies in plant physiology and genetics La. State U.; mem. study sect. on minority biomed. rsch. support program NIH, 1993; grant reviewer USDA, NSF, NIH. Reviewer manuscripts Genome, Protein Engring., Plant Cell, Plant Physiol., Planta, Plant Molecular Biology, Plant Cell Report, Australia Jour. Plant Physiol. Named Honors Rschr., Phi Delta Kappa, 1989; grantee Fulbright Found., 1968, Sci. and Tech. Agy., Tokyo, 1984, La. Edn. Quality Support Fund, 1988, 89, 91, 94, 95, 97, 98, Monsanto Co. Fund, 1992, 93, U.S. Dept. Agr., 1995, Rockefeller Found., 1995-96. Mem. AAAS, Am. Soc. Plant Physiologists, Internat. Soc. Plant Molecular Biology, Japan Molecular Biology Assn., Crop Sci. Soc. Am., Fulbright Assn., Sigma Xi, Gamma Sigma Delta, Phi Delta Kappa. Avocations: running, skiing, gardening, golf, tennis. Office: La State U Dept Plant Path Crop Baton Rouge LA 70803-0001

MURARKA, SHYAM PRASAD, science and engineering educator, administrator; b. Jaynagar, Bihar, India, Mar. 13, 1940; came to U.S., 1966; s. Bihari L. and Suti Murarka; m. Saroj Murarka, May 21, 1962; children: Sumeet, Amal. BS in Chemistry with honors, Bihar U., Muzaffarpur, 1958, MS in Chemistry, 1960; PhD in Chemistry, Agra (India) U., 1970; PhD in Materials Sci. and Metals, U. Minn., 1970. Lectr., rsch. assoc. Bihar U., 1960-61; trainee Atomic Energy Est., Trombay, Maharastra, 1961-62, sci. officer, 1962-66; rsch. asst. U. Minn., Mpls., 1966-70, rsch. assoc., 1970-72; mem. tech. staff, supr. Bell Labs., Murray Hill, NJ, 1972-84; prof. Rensselaer Poly. Inst., Troy, NY, 1984—2002, dir. Ctr. for Integrated Electronics and Electronics Mfg., 1994-96, dir. Ctr. for Advanced Interconnect Sci. and Tech., 1996-2000, dir. Sematech Ctr. of Excellence, 1989-96, Elaine S. & Jack S. Parker chair engring., 1997—2002, prof. emeritus, 2002—. Cons. Bell Labs., Murray Hill, N.J., 1984-89, Applied Materials, Santa Clara, Calif., 1997-99. Author: Silicides for VLSI Applications, 1983, Metallization Theory and Practice for VLSI and ULSI, 1993; (with others) Electronic Materials Science and Technology, 1989, Chemical Mechanical Planarization of Microelectronic Materials, 1997, Copper Fundamental Mechanisms for Micorelectronic Applications, 2000, Interlayer Dielectrics for Semiconductor Technologies, 2003; co-editor: Advanced Metallizations in Microelectronics, 1990, Advanced Metallization and Processing for Semiconductor Devices and Circuits II, 1992, Interface Control of Electrical, Chemical, and Mechanical Properties, 1994, Advaned Metallization for Devices and Circuits, 1994, Microelectronics Technology and Process Integration, 1994, Low Dielectric Constant Materials Synthesis in Microelectronics, 1995, Interlayer Dielectrics for Semiconductor Technologies, 2003; contbr. book chpt. Transition Metal Silicides, 1983. Mem. Tri-City India Assn.'s Indian Comty. Support Group, Albany, 1996. Recipient Gold medal Bihar U., 1960; Univ. Grants Commn. scholar, 1961. Fellow IEEE, Am. Vacuum Soc., Am. Soc. Metals and Electrochem. Soc. (Thomas Callinan award 1987, Electronics Divsn. award 2001); mem. Materials Rsch Soc., Bihar U. Chem. Soc. (hon. life). Achievements include 15 patents in field, over 560 rsch. papers and talks.

MURCHISON, MARGARET LYNNE, educator; b. Sikeston, Mo., July 11, 1946; d. Daniel Henry and Margaret Murchison. BA in English and History, Union U., 1968; MA in English, U. Miss., 1970, PhD of English, 1978. Cert. tchr. secondary English, Gifted/Talented. Tchg. asst. English U. Miss., University, 1969-75; tchr. English, dept. chair Oxford (Miss.) H.S., 1975-2000; assoc. dir. summer sch. U. Miss., University, 2000—02, dir. credit programs Office of Outreach, 2002—. Dir. program for gifted U. Miss., University, 1980—. Editl. asst. Nat. Food Svc. Mgmt. Inst., University, 1991—. Mem. Nat. Coun. Tchrs. English, Rotary (Paul Harris Fellow 1992). Home: 108 Douglas Dr Oxford MS 38655-2804 Office: Office of Summer Sch PO Box 9 University MS 38677-0009 E-mail: mmurchis@olemiss.edu.

MURCKO, ANITA CECILIA, medical consultant, educator; b. Tripoli, Libya, Nov. 8, 1959; d. Edward Bernard and Bernadette Valaria (Smetana) M.; m. Mark Randall Wallace, Dec. 30, 1989. BS in Chemistry magna cum laude, U. Pitts., 1981, MD, 1985; postgrad., Ariz. State U., 1995-96. Diplomate Nat. Bd. Med. Examiners, Am. Bd. Internal Medicine; cert. Internat. Soc. Bone Densitometry. Clin. chemistry lab. technician, phlebotomist, surg. pathology asst. St. Francis Med. Ctr., Pa., 1978-82; intern in categorical internal medicine Ind. U. Med. Ctr., 1985, resident in categorical internal medicine, 1986-88; evening physician coord. emergency dept. Wishard Meml. County Hosp., Ind., 1987-88; staff internist, patient edn. coord. Samaritan Physician Ctr., Ariz., 1988-90; advisor/educator utilization mgmt. Samaritan Health Syss., Ariz., 1988-96, clin. instr. dept. internal medicine, 1988—; ptnr. Internal Medicine Assocs., PC, Ariz., 1990-93; advisor/reviewer/vice chairperson Malpractice Ins. Co. Ariz., 2001; ptnr. Ptnrs. in Medicine PC, Ariz., 1993—; healthcare divsn. cons. Arthur Andersen LLP, 1994-96; cons./beta tester Medvoice, 1995—; clin. preceptor nurse practioner cert. program Ariz. State U., 1995—; health outcomes cons., assoc. clin. coord. Health Svcs. Adv. Group, Inc., Phoenix, 1996—, assoc. med. dir., 1998-2000, med. dir., 2000—02, chief med. officer, 2002—. Rsch. asst. dept. crystallography U. Pitts., 1979-81, teaching asst., tutor dept. chemistry, 1979-81; founding mem., bd. dirs. Primecare Med. Svc. Orgn., 1993-97; chmn. bd. dirs. Primecare Physicians, 1995-97; guest lectr. grad. sch. bus. Ariz. State U., 1996—; presenter in field. Contbr. articles to profl. jours. Recipient Svc. award Am. Cancer Soc., 1978; named one of Outstanding Young Women of Am., 1981. Mem. AMA (Young Physicians Outreach award 1990), ACP, Ariz. Soc. Internal Medicine (Young Internist of Yr. 1993, 97), Ariz. Med. Assn., Ariz. State Physician Assn. (contract rev. com. 1995-96, credentialing com. 1997—), Ariz. Osteoporosis Coalition, Maricopa County Med. Soc., Med. Leadership Coun., Med. Outcomes Trust, Ctr. Sci. in the Pub. Interest. Office: 1515 N 9th St Ste D Phoenix AZ 85006-2523 E-mail: azpro.amurcko@sdps.org.

MURDOCH, COLIN, cultural organization administrator; Pres. San Francisco Conservatory Music, Calif., 1992—. Office: San Francisco Conservatory Music Office Pres 1201 Ortega St San Francisco CA 94122-4411*

MURDOCK, CHARLES WILLIAM, lawyer, educator; b. Chgo., Feb. 10, 1935; s. Charles C. and Lucille Marie (Tracy) M.; m. Mary Margaret Hennessy, May 25, 1963; children: Kathleen, Michael, Kevin, Sean. BSChemE, Ill. Inst. Tech., 1956; JD cum laude, Loyola U., Chgo., 1963. Bar: Ill. 1963, Ind. 1971. Asst. prof. law DePaul U., 1968-69; assoc. prof. law U. Notre Dame, 1969-75; prof., dean Law Sch. Loyola U., Chgo., 1975-83, 86—; dep. atty. gen. State of Ill., Chgo., 1983-86; of counsel Chadwell & Kayser, Ltd., 1986-89. Vis. prof. U. Calif., 1974; cons. Pay Bd., summer 1972, SEC, summer 1973; co-founder Loyola U. Family Bus. Program; arbitrator Chgo. Bd. Options Exch., Nat. Assn. Securities Dealers, N.Y. Stock Exch., Am. Arbitration Assn.; co-founder, mem. exec. com. Loyola Family Bus. Ctr., 1990—; bd. dirs. Plymouth Tube Co., 1993—. Author: Business Organizations, 2 vols., 1996; editor: Illinois Business Corporation Act Annotated, 2 vols., 1975; tech. editor The Business Lawyer, 1989-90. Chmn. St. Joseph County (Ind.) Air Pollution Control Bd., 1971; bd. dirs. Nat. Center for Law and the Handicapped, 1973-75, Minority Venture Capital Inc., 1973-75. Capt. USMCR. Mem. ABA, Ill. Bar Assn. (cert. of award for continuing legal edn.), Chgo. Bar Assn. (cert. of award for continuing legal edn., bd. mgrs. 1976-78), Ill. Inst. Continuing Legal Edn. (adv. com) Roman Catholic. Home: 2126 Thornwood Ave Wilmette IL 60091-1452 Office: Loyola U Sch Law 1 E Pearson St Chicago IL 60611-2055 E-mail: cmurdoc@luc.edu.

MURDOCK, JOHN T., II, academic organization administrator, publishing company executive; b. Harrogate, Eng. arrived in U.S., 1987; s. John T. and Cynthia (Gell) M. Exec. dir. Nat. Valedictorian Soc., Louviers, Colo., 1996—; sr. editor Valedictorian Press, Louviers, 1997—; pres. NVS Acad. Resource Corp., Redmond, Wash., 2000—. Mem.: Am. Hort. Soc., Royal Anthrop. Soc., Soc. for Am. Archaeology. Avocations: ancient history, gardening, visiting university campuses. Office: Nat Valedictorian Soc PO Drawer 250 Louviers CO 80131

MURDOCK, WILLIAM JOHN, librarian; b. N.Y.C., Nov. 19, 1942; s. William and Catherine T. (Ryan) M.; m. Barbara Tyra, Nov. 24, 1968. BS, Manhattan Coll., 1964; MLS, Pratt Inst., 1966; MA, NYU, 1972. Librarian N.Y. Pub. Libr., N.Y.C., 1964-67; serials librarian Manhattan Coll., Riverdale, N.Y., 1967-70; asst. prof. CUNY-Lehman Coll., Bronx, 1970-77, chief circulation libr., 1970-77; univ. libr. Pace U., Pleasantville, N.Y., 1977—. Chmn. Coun. of Librarians, N.Y.C., 1988-89. Contbr. articles to profl. jours. Candidate for bd. trustees Mt. Kisco, N.Y., 1991; mem. Republican. Nat. Com., 1989—; mem. Cath. Big Bros., Westchester, 1983—. Mem. ALA, N.Y. Libr. Assn., Westchester Libr. Assn. (treas. 1981-83), Westchester Assn. Libr. Dirs. (sec. 1986-87), AAUP, Assn. Coll. and Rsch. Librarians, Am. Legion. Avocations: travel, baseball, skydiving, auto cross racing. Office: Pace U 861 Bedford Rd Pleasantville NY 10570-2799

MUREZ, MELANIE GOODMAN, linguist, language services company owner, former educator; b. L.A., May 11, 1954; d. Max A. and Marlyene (Monkarsh) Goodman; m. James Douglas Murez, Sept. 20, 1986. BA cum laude, UCLA, 1974, MA, 1977, postgrad., 1981. Tchr. Temple Emmanuel Sch., L.A., 1974-76; new accounts rep. 1st L.A. Bank, 1975-76; instr. in French UCLA, 1976-81; instr. Concorde Internat. High Sch., L.A., 1981-82; mgr. L.A. Olympic Orgn. Com., 1982-84; owner, pres. Lang. Svcs. Internat., L.A., 1984—. Customer svc. rep. TWA, L.A., 1981; tour guide JetAmerica, L.A., 1981. Mem. L.A.-Bordeaux Sister City Com., 1976. Mem. So. Calif. Translators and Interpreters Assn., Citroen Car Club Am. Democrat. Jewish. Avocations: sports, movies, reading. Home and Office: Lang Svcs Internat 804 Main St Venice CA 90291-3218 E-mail: info@language.net.

MURILLO, CAROL ANN, secondary school educator; b. Portland, Oreg., Mar. 1, 1948; d. Carl Harvey and Frances Berniece Bryan; children: Michelle Frances, Adam Carlos Bryan. BA, Seattle Pacific U., 1970. Multiple subjects tchg. credential Calif., reading specialist credential Calif., secondary tchg. credential Calif. Exec. sec. Sybron Corp. - Heritage Laboratories, Inc., Seattle, 1971—72; elem. tchr. Highlands Acad., Daly City, Calif., 1973—74; dir. of childrens' ministries Resurrection City Ch., Berkeley and Oakland, Calif., 1980—82; interim prin. and tchr. Hilltop Christian Sch., Vallejo, Calif., 1982—93; cfo, ceo asst., event planner Mario Murillo Ministries, Inc., San Ramon, Calif., 1993—98; elem. sch. tchr. Vallejo City Unified Sch. Dist., Calif., 1998—2002. Mem. Falconette Academic Honors Club, Seattle, 1968—70. Editor (contributor): (book) Religious - Inspirational, 2000; editor: I'm the Christian the Devil Warned You About, 1996, Love Letters to Dangerous Christians, 1996; contbr. articles to religious magazines. Spkr. Lay Leadership conf.; worship leader religious retreats; corp. sec., trustee bd. mem. First Assembly of God, Inc., Ch. on the Hill, Vallejo, Calif., 1998—2002; mem. bd. dirs. Hilltop Christian Sch., Vallejo, 1997—2002. Mem.: Delta Kappa Gamma (grantee 1999). Avocation: travel. Home: 3008 Georgia St Vallejo CA 94591 Personal E-mail: carolannmurillo@msn.com.

MURKISON, EUGENE COX, business educator; b. Donalsonville, Ga., July 2, 1936; s. Jeff and Ollie Mae (Shores) M.; m. Marilyn Louise Adams, July 3, 1965; children: James, David, Jennifer. Grad., U.S. Army JFK Spl. Warfare Sc., 1967, U.S. Naval War Coll., 1972, U.S. Army Command/Staff Coll., 1974; BSA, U. Ga., 1959; MBA, U. Rochester, 1970; PhD, U. Mo., 1986. Surveyor USDA, Donalsonville, Ga., 1956-59; commd. 2d lt. U.S. Army, 1959, advanced through grades to lt. col., 1974, inf. bn. leader, 1967-68; mechanized comdr. (G-3), ops. officer Brigade Exec. Officer, Korea, Europe and U.S., 1968-70; prof. leadership & psychology West Point, N.Y., 1970-73; ops. officer (J-3) Office of Chmn. Joint Chiefs of Staff, Washington, 1974-77; prof. mil. sci. and leadership Kemper Mil. Sch., 1977-81; ret. U.S. Army, 1981; instr. U. Mo., Columbia, 1981-84; asst. prof. Ga. So. U., Stateboro, 1984-89, assoc. prof., 1989-94, prof., 1995—, chair grad. curriculum & programs task force, 1996-99. Vis. prof. mgmt. and bus. U. Tirgoviste, Romania, 1994, 95, 96, 98, 99, 2000; vis. prof. human resource mgmt. Tech. U. Romania, Cluj-Napoca, 1998-99, 2000; chmn. grad. programs curriculum com. GSU, 1998-2002. Author: (with Gheorghe Ionescu) Human Behavior in Organizations, 2000; contbr. numerous articles to profl. jours. and chpts. to books. V.p. Optimist Club, 1993-94, dir., 1993, 96-97, v.p., 1994-95; trustee Pittman Pk. Meth. Ch., Statesboro, 1992-99, chmn., trustee, 1995-96, adminstrv. bd., 1986-2000, Staff-Parish com., 2002-2003. Decorated Bronze Star medal with oak leaf cluster; recipient Devel. award Ga. So. U., 1990, Tchg. award U. Mo., 1983, Albert Burke Rsch. award, 1992, Best Paper award 10th Ann. conv. of Internat. Acad. of Bus., Internat. Educator of Yr. award, others; grantee IREX, 1994, SOROS, 1995, 96. Mem. VFW, Inst. Mgmt. Sci., So. Mgmt. Assn., Inst. for Info. and Mgmt. Sci., Internat. Acad. Bus. (program chair 1994, 95), Acad. Mgmt., Bus. History Conf., Ga. Hist. Soc., Newcomen Soc., Blue Key, Scabbard & Blade, Beta Gamma Sigma, Alpha Zeta. Republican. Avocations: bus. history, mil history, tomato prodn., hiking, boating. Office: Ga So U Coll Bus Adminstrn Statesboro GA 30460-8154 E-mail: murkison@gasou.edu.

MUROFF, LAWRENCE ROSS, nuclear medicine physician, educator; b. Phila., Dec. 26, 1942; s. John M. and Carolyn (Kramer) M.; m. Carol R. Savoy, July 12, 1969; children: Michael Bruce, Julie Anne. AB cum laude, Dartmouth Coll., 1964, B of Med. Sci., 1965; MD cum laude, Harvard U., 1967. Diplomate Am. Bd. Radiology, Am. Bd. Nuclear Medicine. Intern Boston City Hosp., Harvard, 1968; resident in radiology Columbia-Presbyn. Med. Ctr., N.Y.C., 1970-73, chief resident, 1973; instr. dept. radiology, asst. radiologist Columbia U. Med. Ctr., N.Y.C., 1973-74; dir. dept. nuc. medicine, computed tomography and MRI Univ. Cmty. Hosp., Tampa, Fla., 1974-94, H. Lee Moffitt Cancer Hosp., Tampa, 1994—; pres. Edn. Symposia Inc., Tampa, 1975-2001; pres., CEO Imaging Cons. Inc., Tampa, 1994—; chmn. bd. Am. Phys. Ptnrs. Inc. (Radiologix), Dallas, 1996-98. Clin. asst. prof. radiology U. South Fla., 1974-78, clin. assoc. prof., 1978-82, clin. prof., 1982—; clin. prof. U. Fla., 1988-. Contbr. articles to profl. jours. Lt. comdr. USPHS, 1968-70. Fellow Am. Coll. Nuclear Medicine (disting. fellow., Fla. del.), Am. Coll. Nuclear Physicians (regents 1976-78, pres.-elect 1978, pres. 1979, fellow 1980), Am. Coll. Radiology (councilor 1979-80, 91-96, 2001—, chancellor 1981-87, chmn. commn. on nuclear medicine 1981-87, fellow 1981); mem. Am. Assn. Acad. Chief Residents Radiology (chmn. 1973), AMA, Boylston Soc., Fla. Assn. Nuclear Physician (pres. 1976), Fla. Med. Assn., Hillsborough County Med. Assn., Radiol. Soc. N.Am., Soc. Nuclear Medicine (coun. 1975-90, trustee 1980-84, 86-89, pres. Southeastern chpt. 1983, vice chmn. correlative imaging coun. 1983), Fla. Radiol. Soc. (exec. com. 1976-91, treas. 1984, sec. 1985, v.p. 1986, pres. elect 1987, pres. 1988, gold medal 1995), West Coast Radiol. Soc., Soc. Mag. resonance Imaging (bd. dirs. 1988-91, chmn. ednl. program 1989, chmn. membership com. 1989-93), Clinical Magnetic Resonance Soc. (pres. elect 1995-98, pres. 1998-2000), bd. dirs, 1995—). Office: 16804 Avila Blvd Tampa FL 33613-5220

MURPHEY, ARTHUR GAGE, JR., law educator; b. Macon, Miss., June 16, 1927; s. Arthur Gage and Elizabeth (Crutcher) Murphey; m. Linda Chaney, May 17, 1975; 1 stepchild, Leslie Jo Thomas;children from previous marriage: Mason Alexander, Arthur Nesbit. Student, Vanderbilt U., 1947-48; AB, U. N.C., 1951; JD, U. Miss., 1953; postgrad., London Sch. Econs., U. London, 1953-54; LLM, Yale U., 1962. Assoc. Satterfield, Ewing Williams and Shell, Jackson, Miss., 1953; asst. prof. U. Ga., Athens, 1956-58, Emory U., Atlanta, 1958-61, U. Akron, 1962-63, assoc. prof., 1963-67; prof. U. Ark., Little Rock, 1967-96, asst. dean Sch. Law, 1970-73, Ark. Bar Found. prof., 1996-97, Ark. Bar Found. prof. emeritus, 1997—. Vis. lectr. Case Western Res. U., Cleve., 1966; vis. prof. U. Miss., 1977. Faculty editor: Jour. Pub. Law, 1958—61; faculty advisor Ga. Bar Jour., 1958—61; contbr. articles to profl. jours. With USAAF, 1945—47. Fulbright scholar, 1953—54, Sterling fellow, 1961—62, Ford Found. grantee, 1964. Mem.: ABA, Phi Beta Kappa, Beta Theta Pi, Phi Delta Phi. Reformed Episcopal Ch. Home: 1918 Old Forge Dr Little Rock AR 72227-5515 Office: U Ark Sch Law 1201 McMath Ave Little Rock AR 72202-5142

MURPHEY, MURRAY GRIFFIN, history educator; b. Colorado Springs, Colo., Feb. 22, 1928; s. Bradford James and Margaret Winifred (Griffin) M.; children— Kathleen Rachel, Christopher Bradford, Jessica Lenoir. AB, Harvard U., 1949; PhD, Yale U., 1954. Asst. prof. U. Pa., Phila., 1956-61, assoc. prof., 1961-66, prof., 1966-2000, chmn. dept. Am. civilization, 1969-81, 87-94. Author: Development of Peirce's Philosophy, 1961, Our Knowledge of the Historical Past, 1973, (with E. Flower) A History of Philosophy in America, 1977, Philosophical Foundations of Historical Knowledge, 1994. Democrat. Home: 200 Rhyle Ln Bala Cynwyd PA 19004-2324

MURPHREE, JON TAL, clergyman, philosophy and theology educator, academic administrator; b. Wedowee, Ala., Dec. 17, 1936; s. Hobart and Winnie Mae (Crumpton) M.; m. Sheila Marie Black, June 12, 1971; children: Marisa, Mark. BA, Asbury Coll., Wilmore, Ky., 1959; MDiv, Asbury Theol. Sem., 1964; MA, U. Ky., 1975; LittD, Toccoa Falls Coll., 1997. Ordained to ministry Meth. Ch., 1964. Pastor Meth. Ch., Wedowee, 1953-56, Crandall, Ind., 1956-59, Clarkesville, Ind., 1959-60; gen. evangelist United Meth. Ch., 1965-80; adminstrv. dir. Servants in Faith and Tech., Lineville, Ala., 1980-81; prof. philosophy, theology and homiletics Toccoa Falls Coll., Toccoa, Ga., 1981—2002; acad. dean, v.p. acad. affairs Vennard Coll., University Park, Iowa, 2002—. Author: Adventure Not Alone, 1969, Giant of a Century Trail, 1969, The Incredible Discovery, 1972, When God Says You're Okay, 1975, A Loving God and a Suffering World, 1981, Made to be Mastered, 1984, Serving in Faith, 1990, The Love Motive, 1990, Responsible Evangelism, 1994, Miracles of Grace, 1996, Divine Paradoxes, 1998, Heritage of the Lord, 2001, Trinity and Human Personality, 2001, Security in Christ, 2002; editor Evangelade Echoes, 1965-80, The Provoker, 1980-81; contbr. articles to profl. jours. Avocations: sports, carpentry, reading. Home: 609 Fairview Dr Oskaloosa IA 52577 Office: Vennard Coll PO Box 29 University Park IA 52595

MURPHREE, KENNETH DEWEY, elementary school educator; b. Memphis, July 28, 1953; s. Dewey and Garneita (Bryant) M.; m. Beverly Ann Hurt, Sept. 7, 1974. AE, N.W. Miss. Jr. Coll., Senatobia, 1973; BSE, Delta State U., 1975, ME, 1976, Ednl. Specialist degree in adminstrn. and supervision, 1992. Grad. asst. dept. elem. edn. Delta State U., 1975—76; elem. tchr. Helena West - Helena Pub. Schs., Helena, 1976—81; prin. Woodruff Elem. Sch., West Helena, 1981—93, Westside Elem. Sch., 1993—97, Barton Elem. Sch., Barton, 1997—. Mem. NAESP, ASCD, Ark. Assn. Ednl. Adminstrs., Ark. Assn. Elem. Sch. Prins., East Ark. Schoolmasters Assn., Lions (pres., past pres., 1st v.p., bd. dirs. tail twister West Helena), Phi Theta Kappa (past pres. Theta Sigma chpt.), Kappa Delta Pi, Phi Delta Kappa. Office: Barton Elem Sch Hwy 85 S Barton AR 72312 E-mail: murphree@blsd.grsc.k12.ar.us.

MURPHY, AUSTIN DE LA SALLE, economist, educator, banker; b. NYC, Nov. 20, 1917; s. Daniel Joseph and Marie Cornelia (Austin) M.; m. Mary Patricia Halpin, June 12, 1948 (dec. May 1974); children: Austin Joseph, Owen Gerard; m. Lee Chilton Romero, Dec. 14, 1974; stepchildren: Thomas Romero, Robert Romero (dec.). AB, St. Francis Coll., Bklyn., NY, 1938; AM (Hayden fellow 1938-40), Fordham U., 1940, PhD, 1949, Canisius Coll., 1986. Instr. econ. Fordham U., 1938-41; Instr. econ. Georgetown U., 1941-42; asst. statistician, statis. controls Bd. Econ. Warfare, 1942; sr. econ. rsch. editor NY State Dept. Labor, NY, 1947-50; lectr. econ. Fordham U. Sch. Edn., 1946-55; instr. NYU Sch. Commerce, 1949-51; dean sch. bus. adminstrn. Seton Hall U., South Orange, NJ, 1950-55; Albert O'Neill prof. Am. enterprise, dean sch. bus. adminstrn. Canisius Coll., Buffalo, 1955-62; dir. edn. dept. NAM, 1962-63; exec. v.p. Savs. Banks Assn. NY State, 1963-70; chmn., pres. River Bank Am. (formerly East River Savs. Bank), 1970-89, vice chmn., dir., 1989-96, chmn. adv. bd., 1996-98. Charter trustee Savs. Bank Rockland County, 1965-70; dir. Bank of Charleston (SC), 1989-91; chmn. bd., trustee Savs. Bank Life Ins. Fund, 1983-87; chmn. dist. I, mem. adv. coun. Conf. State Bank Supr., 1986-93; bd. dir. MSB Fund, Inc. Author: (with Fleming Frasca, and Mannion) Social Studies Review Book, 1946, Leading Problems of New Jersey Manufacturing Industries, (with Bullock & Doerflinger), 1953, Reasons for Relocation, 1955, Forecast of Industrial Expansion in Buffalo and the Niagara Frontier, 1956, Metropolitan Buffalo Perspective, 1958; editor Handbook of New York Labor Statistics, 1950. Mem. Livingston (NJ) Charter Commn., 1954-55; mem. capital expenditures com., City of Buffalo, 1957-63; trustee Fordham U., 1973-79, NY Med. Coll., 1978-81; bd. dir. NY council Boy Scouts Am., 1974—, Jr. Achievement of Buffalo, 1958-63, Invest-in-Am. 1st lt. US Army, 1942-46. Named Knight of Malta, 1971. Mem. NAM (chmn. ednl. aids com. 1958-63), Am. Fin. Assn., Def. Transp. Assn. (life), Nat. Assn. Mut. Savs. Banks (bd. dir., treas. 1976-81), Friendly Sons. St. Patrick (1st v.p., 1976-77), DownTown Lower Manhattan Assn. (dir., vice chmn. 1982-93), Union League Club (pres. 1991-93), Larchmont Yacht Club, Carolina Yacht Club, KC, Alpha Kappa Psi, Pi Gamma Mu. Office: RB Asset Corp 645 5th Ave New York NY 10022-5910 Home: 2409 103 Theall Rd Rye NY 10580-1406

MURPHY, BIANCA CODY, psychology educator; b. N.Y.C., June 12, 1950; d. Joseph Thomas and Bianca (Rivoli) Cody. BA, Marymount Manhattan Coll., 1971; MEd, Northeastern U., 1974; EdD, Boston U., 1982; MPA, Harvard U., 1999. Diplomate Am. Bd. Sexology. Staff psychologist Mystic Valley Mental Health, Winchester, Mass., 1978-81; prof. psychology Wheaton Coll., Norton, Mass., 1987—. Adj. instr. psychology U. Mass., Boston, 1977—; psychologist Newton (Mass.) Psychotherapy Assocs., 1981—; mem. bd. for the Advancement of Psychology in the Pub. Interest, 1998—, chair, 2001. Contbr. articles to profl. jours. Fellow Am. Orthopsychiat. Assn. (chmn. nuclear issues study group 1987-90); mem. APA (com. on women and psychology 1993—, chair 1995), ACA, Assn. for Women in Psychology. Home: 10 Roberts Ave Newton MA 02460-1516

MURPHY, DAVID BRUCE, secondary education educator; b. Tacoma, Feb. 21, 1949; s. James Irvin Murphy and Barbara Mae (Mesaros) Stecker. BA in Edn., Western Wash. U., 1971, postgrad., 1974-92. Cert. K-12 edn. H.S. art tchr., yearbook advisor Bellingham (Wash.) Sch. Dist., 1971-84, Tacoma (Wash.) Sch. Dist., 1984—. Counselor Am. Inst. for Fgn. Study, Greenwich, Conn., 1975-83. Avocations: painting, stained glass works, gardening, traveling, music. Home: 15737 Wilaire Dr SE Lawrence Lk Yelm WA 98597-7447 Office: Lincoln High Sch 701 S 37th St Tacoma WA 98418-6799

MURPHY, DONN BRIAN, theater educator; b. San Antonio, July 21, 1930; s. Arthur Morton and Claire Frances (McCarthy) M. BA, Benedictine Coll., 1954; MFA, Catholic U., 1956; PhD, U. Wis., 1964. Prof. Georgetown U., Washington, 1954—2000, prof. emeritus, 2000—; pres., exec. dir. Nat. Theatre Corp., Washington, 1985—. Tech. theater liaison The White House, Washington, 1961-65; arts commr. Arlington County, Va., 1996—. Author: A Director's Guide to Good Theatre, 1968, Stage for a Nation, 1985, Helen Hayes: A Bio-Bibliography, 1993; (plays) Creation of the World, 1970, Something of a Sorceress, 1971, Tyger/Tyger, 1977; (with others) Eleanor: First Lady of the World, 1984. Cpl. U.S. Army, 1950-52. Recipient Outstanding Svc. award Am. Theatre Assn., 1984, Forrest Roberts award No. Mich. U., 1977 Georgetown U. award for Excellence in Tchg., 1997; Ford Found. fellow, 1963; inducted Coll. Fellows of Am. Theatre, 1994. Democrat. Roman Catholic. Avocations: travel, motorcycling. Home: 2636 Military Rd Arlington VA 22207-5118

MURPHY, JAMES LEE, college dean, economics educator; b. Detroit, Feb. 14, 1939; s. Philip E. and Julie T. M.; m. Linda J. Masson, July 31, 1965; children— Janel K., John R. BS, Spring Hill Coll., 1961; MS, Purdue U., 1963, PhD, 1964. Asst. prof. econs. U. N.C., Chapel Hill, 1964-67, assoc. prof., 1967-72, prof., 1972—, chmn. dept., 1975-85, dir. summer session, 1987-88, dean summer sch., 1988—. Vis. prof. Thammasat U., Bangkok, Thailand, 1968-69, Econs. Inst., U. Colo., Boulder, 1979, U. New South Wales, Sydney, Australia, 1980, overseas program U. Utah, 1974; cons. in field, 1968—. Author: Introductory Econometrics, 1973, Introductory Statistical Analysis, 1975, 2d edit., 1980, Spanish lang. edit., 1987, Statistical Analysis for Business and Economics, 1985, Statistical Analysis, 1993. NDEA fellow, 1961-64; NSF grantee, 1969-71 Mem. Assn. Univ. Summer Sessions (past pres.), N.Am. Assn. Summer Sessions (pres.). Republican. Roman Catholic. Office: U NC Dept Econs Gardner Hall PO Box 3305 Chapel Hill NC 27515-3305

MURPHY, JEANETTE CAROL, education educator; b. Hot Springs, S.D., June 6, 1931; d. George W. and Jessie S. (Whetstone) M.; A.B., U. S.D., 1960; M.S. in Edn. Adminstrn., Chadron State Coll., 1978, Ed.S. Ednl. Adminstrn., 1979, Ph.D in Ednl. Adminstrn., U. Mo., 1987. Mgr. cen. supply, operating rooms specialist Luth. Hosp., Hot Springs, 1957-58, 60-61; tchr. Spanish and French, Sidney (Nebr.) High Sch., 1962-64; reservations clk. Peninsula Hosp., Burlingame, Calif., 1964-65; tchr. San Lorenzo Valley Unified Schs., Felton, Calif., 1965-67; propr. Masters Career Inst., Salinas, Calif., 1969-70; tchr. English and Spanish Oglala Community High Sch., Pine Ridge, S.D., 1970-72; tchr. biology and substitute Hot Springs High Sch., 1971-73; clk. Fall River County (S.D.) Treas.'s Office, 1973-74; Title I adminstr. Loneman Day Sch., Ogala, S.D., 1974-75, adminstr., 1975-77; contract dir. and exec. officer bd. Unified Sch. Bd. Found., Inc., Pine Ridge, 1977-78; grad. asst. div. edn. and psychology Chadron (Nebr.) State Coll., 1978-79; supt. schs. Lyman (Nebr.) Pub. Schs., 1979-80, Kadoka (S.D.) Sch. Dist., 1981-83; registered rep. for IDS/Am. Express, 1983-84; grad. teaching asst. doctoral program in edn. adminstrn. with spl. emphasis in polit. sci. U. Mo., 1984-86 ; asst. state dir. for Mo. North Central Assn., 1984-86; assoc. prof. edn. U. Nebr. at Kearney, 1987—; rsch. assoc. joint effort U. Mo.-Columbia and Mo. House of Reps., 1985-86; pres. Faculty Senate U. Nebr., Kearney, 1994-95, bd. dirs. Kearney Fed. Credit Union, mem. grad. faculty. Author: The Missouri Career Development and Teacher Excellence Plan: An Initial Study of Missouri Career Ladder Program, 1987, My Plan Book: For The Student Teacher, 1990, Teaching Reflectively About Contemporary Issues in Education, 1993; contbr. articles to profl. publs. Chairperson Heart Fund Drive, Hot Springs, 1974-76; Bible sch. tchr. United Presbyn. Women, 1976-77; mem. choir Presbyn. Ch., 1970-76. Served with WAC, 1954-57. Rsch. grant for study of Brain Devel., 1990-92. Mem. Assn. Tchr. Educators, Nebr. Assn. Tchr. Educators, Mizzou Alumni Assn., Daus. of Nile, Internat. Order Job's Daus. of S.D. (past. grand guardian, grand sec.), Order Ea. Star (past matron), Phi Delta Kappa (historian, v.p. membership ctrl. Nebr. chpt.). Democrat.

MURPHY, JENNY LEWIS, special education educator; b. Trenton, Mo., Sept. 6, 1947; d. Homer Lewis and Betty Jo (Jennings) Kidd; mm. Larry D. Murphy, July 2, 1971; children: Daniel Joe, Jaclyn Kate. BS in Elem. Edn., Cen. Mo. State U., 1969. Cert. elem. tchr., severe devel. delayed edn., Mo. Tchr. severely handicapped Mo. State Sch., Chillicothe, 1981-84; dir., tchr. Grundy County Learning Ctr., Trenton, 1984-86; tchr., dir. spl. svcs. Livingston County R-III schs., Chula, Mo., 1986—. Curriculum developer for ind. living State Schs. Mo. Mem. com. Trenton Handicap Bd., 1984-86; v.p. adv. bd. Ret. Sr. Vol. Program, Trenton, 1984-86. Mem. Coun. for Exceptional Children (children-mental retardation divsn. 1986—, profl. devel. com. 1991-94, 98—), Mo. Tchrs. Assn., N.E. Mo. Local Adminstrs. Spl. Edn., Classroom Tchrs. Assn. (v.p. 1988-89, sec. 1994—). Democrat. Methodist. Home: 127 SE Olive Ln Trenton MO 64683-8324 Office: Livingston County R-III Sch PO Box 40 Chula MO 64635-0040

MURPHY, JOHN CARTER, economics educator; b. Ft. Worth, July 17, 1921; s. Joe Preston and Elsie (Carter) M.; m. Dorothy Elise Haldi, May 1, 1949 (dec. Jan. 1997); children: Douglas C., Barbara E.; m. Teiko Kanazawa, June 17, 2000. Student, Tex. Christian U., 1939-41; BA, North Tex. State U., 1943, BS, 1946; AM, U. Chgo., 1949, PhD, 1955; postgrad., U. Copenhagen, 1952-53. Instr. Ill. Inst. Tech., 1947-50; instr. to assoc. prof. Washington U., St. Louis, 1950-62; vis. prof. So. Meth. U., Dallas, 1961, prof., 1962-90, prof. emeritus, 1990—, dir. grad. studies in econs., 1963-68, chmn. dept., 1968-71, faculty summer program in Oxford, 1982-91, dir., 1991, pres. faculty senate, 1988-89, co-dir. Insts. on Internat. Fin., 1982-87. Vis. prof. Bologna (Italy) Ctr., Sch. Advanced Internat. Studies, Johns Hopkins U., 1961-62; UN tech. assistance expert, Egypt, 1964; vis. prof., spl. field staff Rockefeller Found., Thammasat U., Bangkok, 1966-67; sr. staff economist Coun. Econ. Advisers, 1971-72, U.S. dels. econ. policy com. and working party III OECD, 1971-72, U.S. del. 8th meeting Joint U.S.-Japan Econ. Com., 1971; cons. Washington U. Internat. Econs. Rsch. Project, 1950-53, U.S. Treasury, 1972, Fed. Res. Bank Dallas, 1994—; referee NSF; witness and referee congl. coms.; lectr. USIA Program, Germany, 1961-62, 84, Philippines, South Viet Nam, Thailand, 1972, France, Belgium, 1984; lectr. Southwestern and Midwestern Grad. Sch. Banking; adj. scholar Am. Enterprise Inst. for Pub. Policy Rsch., 1976—. Author: The International Monetary System: Beyond the First Stage of Reform, 1979; (with R.R. Rubottom) Spain and the U.S.: Since World War II, 1984; editor: Money in the International Order, 1964; contbr. articles to profl. books and jours. Chmn. rsch. com. on internat. conflict and peace Washington U., 1959-61; lectr. mgmt. tng. programs Southwestern Bell

Telephone Co., 1961-66, St. Louis Coun. on Econ. Edn., 1958-61; mem. regional selection com. H.S. Truman Fellowships, 1976-89; pres. Dallas Economists, 1981, Town and Gown of Dallas, 1980-81; mem. Dallas Com. on Fgn. Rels. Lt. USNR, 1943-46. Decorated Silver Star; Fulbright scholar to Denmark, 1952-53; Ford Found. Faculty Research fellow, 1957-58; U.S.-Spanish Joint Com. for Cultural Affairs fellow, 1981; Sr. Fulbright lectr. Italy, 1961-62 Mem. Am. Econ. Assn., So. Econ. Assn. (bd. editors Jour. 1969-71), Midwest Econ. Assn., Am. Fin. Assn., Soc. Internat. Devel., Peace Rsch. Soc., Southwestern Social Sci. Assn. (pres. econs. sect. 1971-72), AAUP (chpt. pres. 1964-65). Home: 7831 Park Ln Apt 266-D Dallas TX 75255 Office: So Meth Univ Dept Econs Dallas TX 75275-0001

MURPHY, MARGARET A. nursing educator, adult nurse practitioner; b. NYC, Apr. 4, 1934; d. William J. and Margaret (Burchill) Allen; m. Raymond L.H. Murphy, Jr., July 12, 1958; children: Raymond L.H. III, Michael W., Ann Murphy Postell, Maureen D: Murphy Olsen, Alice M., Matthew D. BSN, St. Joseph Coll., West Hartford, Conn., 1955; MS, NYU, 1957; PhD, Boston Coll., Chestnut Hill, Mass., 1987. RN Mass., cert. adult nurse practitioner. Instr. Boston U. Sch. Nursing, 1971-72; pulmonary clin. nurse specialist Pulmonary Assocs., Boston, 1972-73; pulmonary nurse clinician Tufts U., Medford, Mass., 1973-76; from instr. prof. nursing to assoc. prof. nursing Boston Coll., 1976—2001, assoc. prof. emeritus, 2001, chmn. adult health nursing, 1988-92, dir. adult nurse practitioner program, 1987—2001, dir. Kennedy Audio Visual Resource Ctr., 1991-95, coord. MBA-MSN program, 1993-99. Rschr. in lung sound patterns in health and disease, women's attitudes toward menopause. Co-editor: Pharmacotherapeutics and Advanced Nursing Practice, 1998; co-author: (CD-ROM) Learning Lung Sounds, 2002; contbr. articles to profl. jours. Fellow USPHS, 1957-58; grantee Uniformed Svcs. U. Health Scis., 1995-96. Fellow: Am. Coll. Nurse Practitioners; mem.: ANA, Mass. Thoracic Soc. (chmn. com. on nursing practice, counselor 1989—91), Am. Thoracic Soc., Mass. Nurses Assn. (co-chmn. cabinet on legis. 1985—88), Sigma Theta Tau (chmn. awards and scholarships com. Alpha Chi chpt. 1994—96, pres. 1996—98, newsletter editl. bd. 1998—2003, Alpha Chi chpt. Mentor award 2001). E-mail: murphy@bc.edu.

MURPHY, MARY PATRICIA, elementary education educator; b. Buffalo, Mar. 5, 1950; d. Anthony Ralph and Lena (Tirone) Scime; m. Dennis Patrick Murphy, May 4, 1973; children: Gregory Raymond, Daniel Anthony. BS, Damien Coll., 1972; MS in Elem. Edn., SUNY, Buffalo, 1975. Cert. elem. and secondary tchr., N.Y., Nat. Bd. Profl. Tchg. Stds. Tchr. grade 4 North Tonwanda (N.Y.) Sch. Dist., 1972-75; from tchr. grades 1 and 2 to staff devel. specialist Shenendehowa Ctrl. Sch. Dist., Clifton Park, NY, 1984—2002, staff devel. specialist, 2002—, instr., effective tchg. program, 2003—. Assistance tchr. mentor program Shenendehowa Sch. Dist., 1993—; presenter in field. Active PTA(life mem. award, 1998), Am. Diabetes Assn., Juvenile Diabetes Found., part. Mentor/Intern program. Shenendehowa Ctrl. Sch. Dist. grantee, 1988-90. Mem. ASCD, Am. Fedn. Tchrs., N.Y. United Tchrs., N.Y. Coun. Tchrs. English, Intergenerational Writers' Conf., Internat. Women's Writing Guild. Avocations: reading, cross-country skiing. Home: 120 East Ave Saratoga Springs NY 12866-8743 Office: Shenendehowa Ctrl Sch Dist Karigon Sch 970 Route 146 Clifton Park NY 12065-3643

MURPHY, PATRICIA HURLBURT, special education educator; b. Cin., Nov. 2, 1945; d. Allen Kellogg and Ruth Miriam (Hirsch) Hurlburt. BS, U. Cin., 1967, MEd, 1970. Cert. prin., Ohio. Tchr. Cin. Pub. Schs., 1967-71, tchr. handicapped, 1980-90, elem. tchr. severe behavior, 1990—; tchr. hearing impared Hamilton County Pub. Schs., Cin., 1971-73; pvt. tchr. Cin., 1978-80. Del. to China, Coun. Internat. Ednl. Exch., N.Y.C., 1992. Vol. Travelers Aid Soc., Cin., 1975-76, Cin. Zoo, 1976-79, Polit. Campaign for U.S. Rep., Cin., 1976, 78, 82, Mayor's Com. on Edn., 1990; sch. chairperson United Way Campaign, Cin., 1989-92; chair Sch. Tax Levy, Cin., 1990, 91; chosen to do demonstration on China, V.P. Quayle, 1991. Named Tchr. of Yr., Coun. Exceptional Children, 1986; Greater Cin. Edn. Found. grantee, 1985. Mem. Cin. Coun. of Educators, Cin. Fedn. Tchrs. (bldg. rep. 1989—), Westwood Civic Assn., Austistic Soc., U. Cin. Alumni Assn. (25th reunion com.). Avocations: antique hunting and auctions, swimming, reading mysteries. Home: 2876 Mckinley Ave Cincinnati OH 45211-7151

MURPHY, PAUL IRWIN, special education administrator; b. Chgo., Feb. 21, 1951; s. Paul I. and Rita (Palmer) M.; m. Margaret Geimer, Oct. 19, 1974; children: Paul Joseph, Anne Marie. BSEd, Ill. State U., 1974; MSEd in Adminstrn., No. Ill. U., 1983. Tchr. adaptive phys. edn. Philip Rock Ctr. for Deaf and Blind, Glen Ellyn, Ill., 1981-83; tchr. behavior disorder Sch. Assn. for Spl. Edn. in DuPage County, Downers Grove, Ill., 1983-85, prin., 1985—. Interpreter Police Dept. Oakbrook Terrace, Ill., 1976-78, police commr., 1993—; mem. youth comm. City of Oakbrook Terrace, 1983-87; asst. cub scout master Boy Scouts Am. Named Man. of Yr. City of Oakbrook Terr., 1986, Outstanding Alumni in Edn. No. Ill. U., DeKalb, Ill., 1989; recipient Outstanding Svc. award City of Oakbrook Terr., 1986, Those Who Excel award Ill. State Bd. Edn., Springfield, 1989. Mem. ASCD, Ill. Adminstrn. Spl. Edn., Ill. Coun. Exceptional Children, Nat. Staff Devel. Coun., Nat. Coun. Exceptional Children, Ill. Deaf/Blind Benevolent Assn. (v.p. 1981-84, bd. dirs. 1984-85), Lions (bd. dirs. Oakbrook Terr. chpt. 1987-91, founder, Gov. award Merit). Roman Catholic. Avocations: fishing, boating, duck decoy carving. Home: 17w283 16th St Villa Park IL 60181-4038 Office: Sch Assn for Spl Edn in DuPage County 6 S 331 Cornwall Naperville IL 60540

MURPHY, RANDALL DEE, middle school educator, administrator; b. Decatur, Ala., May 6, 1965; s. Dock Draper and Barbara Ann (Slayton) M.; m. Angela Migliaccio, May 16, 1987; 1 child, Ashley Nicole. BS, Athens (Ala.) State Coll., 1988; MS, Ala. A&M U., 1992. Cert. tchr., adminstr., Ala. Tchr. Hazel Green (Ala.) Sch., 1988-89, Madison (Ala.) Mid. Sch., 1989-90, Liberty Mid. Sch., Madison, 1990-92, adminstr., 1992—. Chair So. Assn. Accreditation, Ala., 1991-92. Mem. NEA, Ala. Edn. Assn., Madison County Edn. Assn., Ala. Sci. Tchrs. Assn. Democrat. Mem. Ch. of Christ. Avocations: tennis, swimming, singing, judging beauty pageants. Home: 297 Murphy Cir Madison AL 35756-8136 Office: Liberty Mid Sch 281 Dock Murphy Dr Madison AL 35758-7655

MURPHY, ROBERT FRANCIS, biology educator and researcher; b. Bklyn, NY, Aug. 25, 1953; s. Robert Francis and Marguerite Ann (McClean) M.; m. Vivian Mathilde Grosswald, Aug. 15, 1981 (div. May 1990); children: Robert Emile, Charles Francis; m. Cynthia Ann Miller, Nov. 23, 1991; 1 child, Michael James. BA, Columbia U., 1974; PhD, Calif. Inst. Tech., 1980. Rsch. assoc. Columbia U., NYC, 1979-83; from asst. prof. dept. biol. sci. to prof. Carnegie Mellon U., Pitts., 1983—2003, prof. biomed. engring., 2003—. Assoc. Pitts. Cancer Inst., 1986—; mem. Cell Biology study panel NSF, Washington, 1989-92, rsch. experiences for undergrads. study panel, 1997-99; Biol. Sci. study sect. NIH, 1993-97, SSS-I study sect., 1999-2000, Computational Biol. study sect., 2002-; co-chair. Cytometry Devel. workshop, 1999—; dir. Beckman scholars program, Carnegie Mellon, Pitts., Pa., 1998-99, Merck Computational Biology and Chemistry, 1999—. Co-editor: Applications of Fluorescence in the Biomedical Sci., 1986, Endosomes and Lysosomes: A Dynamic Relationship, 1993; contbr. over 90 articles to profl. jour. Recipient Presdl. Young Investigator award NSF, 1984; Damon Runyon-Walter Winchell Cancer Found. fellow, 1979; grantee NIH, NSF, Am. Cancer Soc., Am. Heart Assn. Mem. AAAS, Internat. Soc. Analytical Cytology, Internat. Soc. Computational Biology, Am. Soc. Cell Biology, Sigma Xi. Achievements include co-development of flow cytometry standard data file format; develop. of flow cytometric methods for the study of endocytosis, computational biology curriculum; rsch. in analysis of endosome acidification and lysosome biogenesis, pattern analysis applications to fluoresence microscope images. Home: 2537 Club House Dr Wexford PA 15090-7956 Office: Carnegie Mellon U 4400 5th Ave Pittsburgh PA 15213-2617 E-mail: murphy@cmu.edu.

MURPHY, ROBERT JAMES, language educator, consultant; b. Decatur, Ind., Aug. 31, 1941; s. James William and Catherine Agnes (Schumacker) Murphy; m. Linda L. Nolan, June 28, 1975; 1 child, Christina Lyn. BS in Edn., Ball State U., 1963; MS in Edn., St. Francis U., 1967; postgrad., U. Denver, 1986, Ball State U., 1972. Cert. English, speech, drama and journalism tchr. Ind. Speech and drama tchr. Rochester (Ind.) H.S., 1976—78; chair dept. English Lawrenceburg (Ind.) H.S., 1978—81, Holy Family H.S., Denver, 1981—86; prin. Randall-Moore Sch., Denver, 1986—87; dir. edn. Mansfield Bus. Sch., Denver, 1987—89; prin. St. John the Bapt. Cath. Sch., Ft. Wayne, Ind., 1989—94; pres., founder Murphy Ednl. Consulting, Ft. Wayne, Ind., 1995—, D/B/A Alternative Edn. Curriculum and The Learning Kaleidoscope, Pensacola, Fla., 1995—. Cons. Am. Printing House for Blind, Louisville, 1999—; cons., writer, spkr. homeschooling groups, 1995—; exec. dir., co-founder The Kaleidoscope Edn. Ctr., Ft. Wayne, Ind., 2003, co-founder, dir., 03; tchr., supr. Aurora (Colo.) Evening H.S., 1986—87; tchr. U. St. Francis, Ft. Wayne, 2003—; edn. coord., tchr. M.A.Y.A. Unity Ctr., Ft. Wayne, 2003. Author: All in One Big Book, 1998, The Pump Man, 1998; co-author: Teaching the Student with a Visual Impairment, 2000, author reading and writing curriculum. Bd. dirs. Ft. Wayne Pub. Transp. Co., 2000—, The League for Blind and Disabled, Ft. Wayne, 2000—; chmn. bd. dirs. The United Voice Coalition, Ft. Wayne, 2002—; chmn. bd. dirs. State Ind. Alliance Cmty. Inclusion, 2003—; site visitor U.S. Dept of Edn. Blue Ribbon Sch., 1991. Named Advocate of Yr., League for the Blind and Disabled, 2002; recipient Disting. Graduate award, Decatur (Ind.) Cath. Elem. and HS, 2003. Avocations: gardening, hiking, swimming.

MURPHY, ROBIN ROBERSON, computer science educator; b. Mobile, Ala., Aug. 25, 1957; d. Fred Blakely and Ada Lee (Wills) Roberson; m. Kevin Eddy Murphy, Aug., 27, 1982; children: Kathleen Freebern, Allan Roberson. B in Mech. Engring., Ga. Inst. Tech., 1980, MS in Computer Sci., 1989, PhD in Computer Sci., 1992. Project engr. Dow Chem. USA, Plaquemine, La., 1980-84; software project engr. Turbitrol Co., Atlanta, 1984-86; asst. prof. dept. math. and comp. sci. Colo. Sch. Mines, Golden, 1992—, assoc. dir. Ctr. Robotics and Intelligent Systems, 1994—, mem. DARPA/IDA Def. Study Group 6, 1998—. Mem. NSF vis. com. on computer sci. curriculum U. Va., Charlottesville, 1992-95. Author: (with others) The Handbook of Brain Theory and Neural Networks, 1995, Artificial Intelligence for Mobile Robots, 1997, AI for Mobile Robots, 1997; spl. column editor Robotics and Autonomous Systems, 1997—; contbr. articles to profl. jours. Rsch. grantee NSF, 1993—. Advanced Rsch. Projects Agy., 1994—, NASA, 1994—, Northrop Grumman, 1997—; Rockwell Internat. Doctoral fellow. Mem. AAAI, IEEE, AIAA, Assn. Computing Machinery.

MURPHY, SHIRLEY HUNTER, reading specialist; b. Atlanta, June 29, 1947; d. John Henry and Ruby Lee (Wilson) Hunter; m. Robert Leslie Murphy, July 10, 1979 (May 1979); children: Lisa Denise, Ricardo Leslie. BS in Elem. Edn., Morris Brown Coll., 1969; M in Reading, Atlanta U., 1978; Cert. in Adminstrn., West Ga. Coll., 1991; Edn. Specialist in Adminstrn., Jacksonville State U., 1994; postgrad., U. Sarasota, 1995—. Cert. tchr., Ga. Tchr. Social Circle (Ga.) City Schs., 1969-70, DeKalb County Sch. Sys., Decatur, Ga., 1970-80, reading specialist, 1980—. Fin. sec. Am. Bus. Women's Assn., Atlanta, 1989-94. Mem. NAACP, Internat. Reading Assn., Profl. Assn. Ga. Educators, DeKalb Assn. Educators. Baptist. Avocations: reading, traveling, baton twirling. Home: 3441 Columbia Ct Decatur GA 30032-7234

MURPHY, SUELLEN, home economics educator; b. High Point, N.C., July 22, 1955; d. Kenneth Shelley and Frances Rebecca (Moore) M. BS in Home Econs., U. N.C., Greensboro, 1977, MEd, 1981. Tchr. High Point (N.C.) City Schs., 1979-83; tchr. Greensboro City Schs., 1984-94, Ben L. Smith H.S., Greensboro, 1994—99, Lexington (N.C.) Sr. H.S., 1999—. Named Outstanding Tchr. Allen Mid. Sch., Greensboro, 1992. Mem.: NC Assn. Educators. Democrat. Methodist. Avocation: sewing. Home: 1309 National Hwy Thomasville NC 27360-2317 Office: Lexington Sr High Sch 26 Penry St Lexington NC 27292

MURPHY-LIND, KAREN MARIE, health educator, dermatology nurse; b. Boston, Oct. 7, 1953; d. William Joseph and Mary Catherine (Mulcahy) Murphy; m. Gary W. Lind, Feb. 28, 1976; 1 child, Nicholas. RN, AS, Laboure Coll., Dorchester, Mass., 1993. Health edn./cmty. outreach coord. Mass. Gen. Hosp., Charlestown Health Care Ctr., 1993-96, dermatology nurse, 1993—, Dept. Pub. Health breast cancer initiative outreach worker, 1992-96, advisor cmty. adv. bd., 1992—, substance abuse initiative dir. cmty. health, 1996—. Mem. Health Charlestown Coalition, 1993—; bd. dirs. Am. Cancer Soc. Cen. Boston Breast, 1995-96, co-chair cancer control core team, 1995-96. Recipient Lifesaver pub. edn. award Am. Cancer Soc., Metro North, Mass., 1994, Make A Difference award, 1995. Mem. Am. Cancer Soc. (Ctrl. Boston bd. dirs. 1995-96, co-chair Boston breast cancer control team 1995-96), Mass. Nurses Assn., Dermatology Nurses Assn., Soc. Pub. Health Edn. Home: 387 Central Ave Milton MA 02186-2803 Office: MGH Bunker Hill Health Ctr 73 High St Charlestown MA 02129-3037

MURRAY, ABBY DARLINGTON BOYD, psychiatric clinical specialist, educator; b. Johnstown, Pa., Mar. 1, 1928; d. Frank Reynolds Boyd and Marion Gasson Allen; m. Joseph Christopher Murray, Sept. 16, 1950; children: Anne, Joseph Jr., Mary, John, James. BSN, Georgetown U., 1950; MS Edn. in Guidance and Counseling, L.I. Univ., Brookville, N.Y., 1976; MEd Psychiat. Clin. Specialist, Columbia U., 1977; postgrad., Ctr. for Family Learning, New Rochelle, N.Y., 1981-82. Lic. marriage and family counselor; provisional cert. sch. counselor, N.Y. Sch. nurse Huntington (N.Y.) Pub. Schs.; with VA Med. Ctr., Northport, Va., 1973-76; prof. U. Md., Balt., 1978-79, L.I. Univ., Brookville, 1979-81; psychiat. clin. specialist VA Med. Ctr., Brooklyn, Va., 1984-87, East Orange, N.J., 1987-89; nurse educator Ft. Monmouth, N.J., 1989—; ret., 1996. Family therapist Family & Cmty. Counseling Agy., Red Bank, N.J., 1989—; program planner, Ft. Monmouth; adj. prof. Monmouth U., 1997-98; lic. profl. marriage and family counselor, N.J., 1996-99. Republican. Roman Catholic. Avocation: tennis. Address: 116 Manor Dr Red Bank NJ 07701-2462

MURRAY, ANDREW, peace studies educator; b. Roanoke, Va., June 25, 1942; s. Max Andrew and Dorothy (Garst) M.; m. Teresa Kathleen Robinson, June 22, 1963; children: Kristin Alease, Kimberly Garst. AB, Bridgewater (Va.) Coll., 1964; MDiv, Bethany Theol. Sem., Oak Brook, Ill., 1968, DMin, 1980. Ordained to ministry Ch. of Brethren, 1968. Pastor Peace Ch. of Brethren, Portland, Oreg., 1968-71; campus min. Juniata Coll., Huntingdon, Pa., 1971-85, asst. prof. religion, 1973-85, prof. peace and conflict studies, 1986—, dir. peace and conflict studies, 1975—, dir. Baker Inst., 1986—. Cons. to numerous colls. and univs. in U.S. and Can., 1975—; Staley disting. lectr. Staley Found., 1981, 88; vis. scholar Pa. State U., 1990; mem. Internat. Assn. Univ. Pres./UN Commn. on Arms Control, N.Y.C., 1991—; dir. UN Seminar on Arms Control and Disarmament, 1993—. Author: PACS as Applied Liberal Arts, 1984; writer, performer, producer rec. Just As I Am, 1991, also others. Mem. Pa. Commn. on Ministry in Higher Edn., 1979-86. Recipient Beechley award for disting. acad. svc. Juniata Coll., 1991. Mem. Nat. Peace Studies Assn. (charter, chmn. exec. com. 1988—), Nat. Pastors Assn. (pres. 1975). Democrat. Avocations: sailing, swimming, cooking, music, soaring. Home: 2110 Moore St Huntingdon PA 16652-2105 Office: Baker Inst Juniata Coll Huntingdon PA 16652

MURRAY, BARBARA ANN LIBS, elementary educator; b. Detroit, Apr. 29, 1941; d. Edward Joseph and Marie Eleanor (Marantette) Libs; m. Joseph Campbell Murray, Jr., Dec. 12, 1934 (dec. Nov. 1985); children: Elizabeth Marie, Mary Katherine. BA, U. Mich., 1963, MA, 1969. Cert. tchr., Mich., Pa. Elem. tchr. Ann Arbor (Mich.) Pub. Schs., 1963-72, 86—; elem. and middle sch. tchr. Perkiomen Valley Sch., Collegeville, Pa., 1982-86; supervising tchr. U. Mich., Ann Arbor, 1965-72, U. Mich. and Eastern Mich. U., 1987—. Mem. corp. bd. Mich. State U., 1992—96, corp. bd. pres., 1987—2002; mem. corp. bd. U. Mich., 1986—2001. Solicitor United Way, Ann Arbor, 1990. Mem.: Nat. Coun. Tchrs. Math., Mich. Reading Assn. (sch. improvement team 1989—2000, health com. 1991—, tech. com.), U. Mich. Alumni Club, Delta Kappa Gamma, Alpha Xi Delta. Roman Catholic. Avocations: gourmet cooking, designing, singing, walking, swimming. Home: 2611 Essex Rd Ann Arbor MI 48104-6553

MURRAY, DOROTHY SPEICHER, retired secondary school educator; b. Garrett, Pa., Oct. 27, 1913; d. Harry Blaine and Ada Chloe (Brumbaugh) Speicher; m. Ralph F. Murray, June 4, 1937. AB, Juniata Coll., 1934; MS, Queen's Coll., 1963. Cert. secondary tchr., Pa.; cert. tchr./ supr. secondary edn., N.Y. Tchr., librarian Boswell (Pa.) High Sch., 1934-37; sec. to pres. Cornell Iron Works, Inc., L.I., N.Y., 1939-52; instr. reading clinic NYU, 1953; instr. Poppenhusen Inst., College Point, N.Y., 1954-59; tchr. Union Free Sch. Dist. 15, Jericho, N.Y., 1958-62; supr. English dept. Jericho High Sch., 1962-65, coordinator reading, 1965-72; vol. tchr. Adams County Prison, Gettysburg, Pa., 1982-89. Author: Reading in the Content Area, 1968, The English Language, 1983, Crashing the Language Barrier, 1987, A Library For Adams Co., 1988, One Man's Shadow: The H.B. Speicher Story, 1997, An Open Invitation to Explore the Wily Ways of Words, 1997, Chronicles of a Word Watcher at Work, 1999, Word Work Ahead, 2001, Michael's World, 2002; contbr. articles to profl. jours. Bd. dirs. Office for the Aging, 1976-79, sec. Adams County Prison Task Force, 1986-91; sec. Friends of Library, Gettysburg, 1987-90. Linguistics grantee Inst. for Tchrs. English Columbia U., 1964-65, Adult Basic Edn. grantee Pa. Dept. Edn., 1989-90; recipient citation South Cen. Reading Coun. Internat. Reading Assn., 1989. Mem. Adams County Hist. Soc., N.Y. State Ret. Tchrs. Assn. Republican. Presbyterian. Avocations: writing, teaching, public speaking.

MURRAY, HAYDN HERBERT, geology educator; b. Kewanee, Ill., Aug. 31, 1924; s. Herbert A. and Ardis M. (Adams) M.; m. Juanita A. Appenheimer, Dec. 16, 1944; children: Steven, Marilyn, Lisa. BS, U. Ill., 1948, MS, 1950, PhD, 1951. Asst. prof. geology Ind. U., 1951-53, assoc. prof., 1953-57, prof., chmn. dept. geology, 1973-84, prof. geology, 1984-94, prof. emeritus, 1994—; dir. research Georgia Kaolin Co., Elizabeth, N.J., 1957-60, mgr. ops., 1960-62, v.p. ops., 1962-64, exec. v.p., 1964-73. Bd. dirs. Sabia Corp. Contbr. numerous articles to profl. jours.; patentee in field. Trustee Union Found., E.J. Grassmann Trust. Served with AUS, 1943-46. Recipient Disting. Svc. award Ind. U., 1993, Lifetime Achievement award Ind. Profl. Geologists. Fellow Geol. Soc. Am., Mineral Soc. Am., Am. Ceramic Soc. (v.p. 1974-75), Tech. Assn. Pulp and Paper Industry; mem. Clay Minerals Soc. (pres. 1965-66, Disting. mem. 1980), Soc. Mining Metallurgy and Exploration (dist. mem., pres. elect 1987, pres. 1988, Hal Williams Hardinge award 1976, found. bd. trustees 1993-96), Internat. Clay Minerals Soc. (pres. 1993-97), Am. Assn. Petroleum Geologists, Am. Inst. Profl. Geologists (pres.-elect 1990, pres. 1991), Am. Geol. Inst. Found. (dir. 1990-96), Geol. Soc. Am. Fdn. (trustee 1992-97), Nat. Acad. Engring. Home: 3790 S Inverness Farm Rd Bloomington IN 47401-9141

MURRAY, JAMES MICHAEL, librarian, law librarian, legal educator, lawyer; b. Seattle, Nov. 8, 1944; s. Clarence Nicholas and Della May (Snyder) M.; m. Linda Monthy Murray. MLaw Librarianship, U. Wash., 1978; JD, Gonzaga U., 1971. Bar: Wash. 1974, U.S. Dist. Ct. (we. dist.) Wash. 1975, U.S. Dist. Ct. (ea. dist.) Wash. 1985. Reference/reserve libr. U. Tex. Law Libr., Austin, 1978-81; assoc. law libr. Washington U. Law Libr., St. Louis, 1981-84; law libr., asst. prof. Gonzaga U. Sch. Law, Spokane, 1984-91; libr. East Bonner County Libr., 1991-97, U.S. Cts. Libr., Spokane, 1997—. Mem. state adv. bd. Nat. Reporter on Legal Ethics and Profl. Responsibility, 1982-91; cons. in field. Author: (with Reams and McDermott) American Legal Literature: Bibliography of Selected Legal Resources, 1985, (with Gasaway and Johnson) Law Library Administration During Fiscal Austerity, 1992; editor Tex. Bar Jour. (Books Appraisals Column), 1979-82; contbr. numerous articles and revs. to profl. jours., acknowledgements and bibliographies in field. Bd. dirs. ACLU, Spokane chpt., 1987-91, Wash. Vol. Lawyers for the Arts, 1976-78. Mem. ABA, Idaho Libr. Assn., Wash. State Bar Assn. (law sch. liaison com. 1986-88, civil rights com. 1996-97). Home: 921 W 29th Ave Spokane WA 99203-1318 Office: US Cts Libr 920 W Riverside Ave Ste 650 Spokane WA 99201-1008 Office Fax: 509-353-0540. E-mail: james_murray@lb9.uscourts.gov.

MURRAY, JOHN EDWARD, JR., lawyer, educator, university president; b. Phila., Dec. 20, 1932; s. John Edward and Mary Catherine (Small) M.; m. Isabelle A. Bogusevich, Apr. 11, 1955; children: Bruce, Susan, Timothy, Jacqueline. BS, LaSalle U., 1955; JD scholar, Cath. U., 1958; SJD fellow, U. Wis., 1959. Bar: Wis. 1959, Pa. 1986. Assoc. prof. Duquesne U. Sch. Law, Pitts., 1963-64, prof., 1965-67, Villanova U. Sch. Law, 1964-65, U. Pitts. Sch. Law, 1967-84, dean, 1977-84; dean Sch. Law Villanova U., 1984-86; disting. svc. prof. U. Pitts., 1986-88; pres. Duquesne U., Pitts., 1988—. Cons. to law firms; chmn. Pa. Chief Justice's com. on comprehensive jud. and lawyer edn. Author: Murray on Contracts, 1974, 90, Murray, Commercial Transactions, 1975, Murray, Cases & Materials on Contracts, 1969, 76, 83, 91, Purchasing and the Law, 1978, Problems & Materials on Sales, 1982, Murray, Problems & Materials on Secured Transactions, 1987, Sales & Leases: Problems and Materials in National/International Transactions, 1993. Mayor Borough of Pleasant Hills, Pa., 1970-74. Mem. Assn. Am. Law Schs. (life, editor Jour. Legal Edn.), mem. Am. Law Inst. Democrat. Roman Catholic. Office: Duquesne U Pres Office Adminstrn Bldg Ofc Pittsburgh PA 15282-0001

MURRAY, JOHN PATRICK, psychologist, educator, researcher; b. Cleve., Sept. 14, 1943; s. John Augustine and Helen Marie (Lynch) M.; m. Ann Coke Dennison, Apr. 17, 1971; children: Jonathan Coke, Ian Patrick. PhD, Cath. U. Am., 1970. Rsch. dir. Office U.S. Surgeon Gen. NIMH, Bethesda, Md., 1969-72; asst. to assoc. prof. psychology Macquarie U., Sydney, Australia, 1973-79; vis. assoc. prof. U. Mich., Ann Arbor, 1979-80; dir. youth and family policy Boys Town Ctr., Boys Town, Nebr., 1980-85; prof., dir. Sch. Family Studies and Human Svcs. Kans. State U., Manhattan, 1985-98, interim assoc. vice provost rsch., 1998—2000, disting. prof., 2003—. Scholar-in-residence Mind Sci. Found., San Antonio, 1996-97; mem. children's TV com. CBS, 1996-99. Author: Television and Youth: 25 Years of Research and Controversy, 1980, The Future of Children's TV, 1984, (with H.T. Rubin) Status Offenders: A Sourcebook, 1983, (with E.A. Rubenstein, G.A. Comstock) Television and Social Behavior, 3 vols., 1972, (with A. Huston and others) Big World, Small Screen: The Role of Television in American Society, 1992, (with C. Fisher and others) Applied Developmental Science, 1996; contbr. numerous articles to profl. jours. Mem. Nebr. Foster Care Rev. Bd., 1982-84; mem. Advocacy Office for Children and Youth, 1980-85; mem. Nat. Coun. Children and TV, 1982-87; trustee The Villages Children's Homes, 1986—, Menninger Found., 1996—; mem. children's TV adv. bd. CBS-TV, 1996-99. Fellow Am. Psychol. Assn. (pres. div. child youth and family svcs. 1990); mem. Internat. Comm. Assn., Soc. Rsch. in Child Devel., Royal Commonwealth Soc.

(London), Manhattan Country Club. Home: 1731 Humboldt St Manhattan KS 66502-4140 Office: Kans State U Office Vice Provost Rsch 101 Fairchild Hall Manhattan KS 66506-1100 E-mail: jpm@ksu.edu.

MURRAY, JOHN PATRICK, education educator; b. Watertown, N.Y., Mar. 7, 1947; s. Patrick and Madeline Irene (Palmer) M.; m. Judy Irene Farr, Aug. 31, 1968; children: Todd Michael, Tyson Patrick. BA, SUNY, 1969; MA, Ariz. State U., 1971; EdS, Wright State U., 1987; PhD, Ohio State U., 1990. Prof., adminstr. Clark State C.C., Springfield, Ohio, 1971-92; assoc. dean curriculum., instrn. Genesee C.C., Batavia, N.Y., 1992-96; asst. prof. SUNY, Brockport, N.Y., 1996-98; assoc. prof. higher edn. adminstrn. Tex. Tech. U., Lubbock, 1998—. Cons. Ministry of Edn., Yemen, 1986—2003; presenter in field. Contbr. articles to profl. jours. NEH grantee, 1978, 78-81, 79, 94, NSF grantee, 1982, Ohio Program Humanities grantee, 1988, Ohi Bd. Regents REACH grantee, 1990; Ohio Humanities scholar, 1987-92, scholar Am. Assn. C.C. Study Coun., 1998; recipient Disting. Svc. award Ohio Youth Commn., 1974, Disting. Rsch. award Tex. Tech. U., 2000. Mem. Lions. Avocations: scuba, photography. Office: Tex Tech U Coll Edn Mailstop 1071 Lubbock TX 79401-1071 E-mail: 030747@msn.com., John.Murray@TTU.edu.

MURRAY, KAREN LEE, special education educator; b. Connellsville, Pa., Nov. 22, 1947; d. Robert George and Dorothy Ann (Smorada) Kelly; m. Michael Andrew Murray, Nov. 25, 1967; children: Heather, Susan. BS summa cum laude, Trenton State Coll., 1983, MEd, 1988. Spl. edn. tchr. Bucks County Intermediate Unit # 22, Doylestown, Pa., 1983—. Mem. Coun. for Exceptional Children, Kappa Delta Pi, Phi Kappa Phi, Delta Zeta. Avocations: sewing, gardening, collecting victorian antiques. Home: 127 E Marshall Ave Langhorne PA 19047-2115 Office: Bucks County Intermediate Unit 22 Doylestown PA 18901

MURRAY, MARY, educational consultant; b. Beverly, Mass. d. Edward James and Anne (Dowd) Murray. AS in Nursing, Endicott Coll.; AB, Boston Coll., 1985; MSEd in Early Childhood and Elem. Edn., Wheelock Coll., 1993. Cert. tchr. Mass. Tchr. Glen Urquhart Sch., Beverly Farms, Mass., 1982-87, kindergarten asst., 1982-83, kindergarten tchr., 1983-85, first grade tchr., 1985-87, dir. extended day program, 1982-85, coord. summer camp program, 1984-86; lower sch. assoc. Shady Hill Sch., Cambridge, Mass., 1987-88; rsch. asst. Wheelock Coll., Boston, 1987-91; tchr. kindergarten, curriculum coord. Prospect Hill Parents' and Children's Ctr., Waltham, Mass., 1988-91; ednl. cons. Beverly Farms, Mass., 1992—; mentor, tchr., faculty summer compass program Lesley Coll. Grad. Sch. of Edn., Cambridge, Mass., 1994-96; tchr. 6th grade sci. tech. and engring. Briscoe Mid. Sch., Beverly, 1999—2002. Lifeguard supr. West Beach Corp., 1980—86; mem. cert. team Ind. Sch. Assn. Mass., 1983—88, Nat. Assn. Educators Young Children, 1989—91; cons. Activities Club, Inc., Waltham, 1986—91; founder, dir. Summer Enrichment, Lanesville, Mass., 1987—89; mem. adv. bd. Power Industries, Wellesley Hills, Mass., 1989—92; mem. Early Childhood Adv. Coun., Medford, Mass., 1990—93; buyer Cottage & Castle LLC, Pride's Crossing, Mass., 1997—98; presenter workshops. Author: curriculum materials, activity kits for children. Active Mass. Spl. Olympics; youth activities coord. Farms/Prides Cmty. Orgn., Feed the Hungry Project, Beverly, Good Friday Walk Orgnl. Com.; mem. Friends Beverly Farms Libr., Beverly Farms Improvement Soc.; water saftey instr. ARC; tchr. religious edn. program St. Margaret Parish, Beverly Farms, 1970—; synod group leader Archdiocese of Boston, 1987; dir., coord. St. Margaret Parish, Beverly Farms, 1989—, mem. parish visitation com., 1995, 2001, chmn. child abuse prevention team, 2002—, parish coun. mem., 2002—. Grad. grantee, Wheelock Coll., 1993. Mem.: ASCD, Assn. Childhood Edn. Internat., Nat. Sci. Tchrs. Assn., Boston Coll. Alumni Assn. (mem. B.C.-Young Alumni Club 1987—95, program coord./spl. event 1988—90). Democrat. Roman Catholic. Avocations: reading, gardening, photography, seasonal sports, travel. Home: 650 Hale St Beverly Farms Beverly MA 01915-2117

MURRAY, NEIL VINCENT, computer science educator; b. Schenectady, N.Y., July 14, 1948; s. Robert Emslie and Eileen Marie (Milano) M. BS in Engring. Physics, Cornell U., 1970; MS in Computer and Info. Sci., Syracuse U., 1974, PhD in Computer and Info. Sci., 1979. Rsch. asst. Syracuse (N.Y.) U., 1977-78; instr. computer sci. dept. LeMoyne Coll., Syracuse, 1978-79, asst. prof., 1979-82; asst. prof. computer sci. SUNY, Albany, 1982-87, assoc. prof., 1987-97, prof., 1997—, dept. chair, 1999—. Treas. CADE, Inc., Assn. Automated Reasoning; presenter in field. Contbr. articles to profl. jours. Mem. IEEE Computer Soc., Am. Assn. Artificial Intelligence, Assn. Automated Reasoning, Assn. Computing Machinery. Home: 1125 Glenmeadow Ct Niskayuna NY 12309-2511 Office: SUNY Dept Computer Sci L1 67A Albany NY 12222-0001 E-mail: nvm@cs.albany.edu .

MURRAY, PHYLLIS CYNTHIA, educator; b. Farmville, Va., Nov. 3, 1938; d. Claude and Frazure Young; m. Robert William Murray, Dec. 14, 1963; 1 child, Sidney Adolphus. BA, CUNY-Hunter Coll., 1960; MS, U. Pa., 1961; diploma, Cornell U., 1980; cert., Vassar Coll., 1991. Tchr. D.C. Bd. Edn., Washington, 1961-63, N.Y. Bd. Edn., 1963—. TV prodr. TCI, Mamaroneck, N.Y., 1990—; radio host Sta. WVOX Radio, New Rochelle, N.Y., 1994—; founder One Love Tennis, White Plains, 1994—. Author: Huggy Bean Visits Ethiopia, 1985, The Colorful World of Huggy Bear, 1985; co-author: UFT Martin Luther King Instructional Package, 1990, Encounters in Living History: Activity Based Lessons on the Enslaved Africans of the North, 1996; author: Oral History of James Austin; contbr. articles to profl. jours. Mem. Town and Village Civic Club, Scarsdale, N.Y., 1994—; mem. African adv. bd. Philipsburg Manor, 1999; alumna Women's Cmapaign Sch., Yale U., 1999; dir. First Vacation Bible Sch., Trinity Luth. ch., Scarsdale. Mem. NAACP (life), U.S. Tennis Assn.,, United Fedn. of Tchr. (del. unity 1993, mem. unity com. 1994—), Ea. Tennis Assn. (at-large), Alpha Kappa Alpha (Silver Star 1991). Home: 1181 Post Rd Scarsdale NY 10583-2023 Office: Bd of Edn PS75X 984 Faile St Bronx NY 10459-3703 E-mail: pmur75@aol.com.

MURRAY, ROBB, software educator, voiceover professional; b. Lima, Ohio, Sept. 12, 1953; s. Emmett Jr. and Pauline (List) M. Student, Kalamazoo Coll., 1971-72, Ohio State U., 1974; BA cum laude, Bob Jones U., 1975; MA, U. Chgo., 1977. Reference librarian Chgo. Pub. Library, 1977-80; computer programmer Sears Roebuck & Co., Chgo., 1980-83; software product cons. Davka Corp., Chgo., 1983-84; software tng. specialist Beatrice U.S. Foods, Chgo., 1984-86; comml. voiceover talent Chgo., 1986—; software tng. cons., 1986—; sr. exec. distbr. Nu Skin Internat., Provo, Utah, 1990—. Software instr., conf. presenter Project Micro Ideas, Glenview, Ill., 1982-84. Composer, producer (rec.) Classical Mosquito, 1982, Oh, Marsha!, 2001; editor, contbr.: Come Reminisce with Me, 2003; co-inventor (computer adventure game) The Lion's Share, 1983; producer, talent: (comml. voice tape) The Refreshing Voice, 1987, (indsl. voice tape) The Credible Voice, 1987, nat. TV comml. O'Boises are O'Boisterous Keebler Products, 1988-89, Brain Bash, Tiger Toy Products, 1992-93. Counselor Metrohelp Crisis Hotline, Chgo., 1979; adult edn. instr. Lincoln Park Cmty. Ctr., Chgo., 1989—; vol. Children's Meml. Hosp., 1994-96. Mem. Highlife Adventures, Chgo. Area Internet Soc., Chgo. OD Network, Lincoln Park Pacers, Am. Mensa, Goals Clubs Am., CODE. Avocations: internet surfing, running (Am.'s Marathon 1986, 88, 89), shopping, travel, writing. Home and Office: 444 W Saint James Pl Apt 1203 Chicago IL 60614-2767

MURRAY, TERESA MARIE, elementary education educator; b. Pottsville, Pa., July 7, 1950; d. Joseph John and Gloria Barbara (Mozloom) DeMarkis; m. William Bernard Murray, Sept. 21, 1974; children: Megan Gloria, William Gerard. BA in Elem. Edn., Kutztown U., 1990, postgrad. in Elem. Counseling, 1994—. 1st grade tchr. Holy Redeemer Sch., Minersville, Pa., 1990-92, 5th, 6th, 7th and 8th grade tchr., 1992—. Sci., reading coord. Holy Redeemer Sch., Minersville, 1992-94. Mem. St. Clair Women Club. Roman Catholic. Avocations: reading, crafts, painting, golf. Home: 128 N Morris St Saint Clair PA 17970-1061 Office: Holy Redeemer Sch 538 Sunbury St Minersville PA 17954-1016

MURRAY, THOMAS HENRY, bioethics educator, writer; b. Phila., July 30, 1946; s. Thomas Henry and Colombia Rita (Lucci) M.; m. Sharon Marie Engelkraut, Jan. 1968 (div. Sept. 1975); children: Kathleen Elizabeth, Dominique Maria, Peter Albert; m. Cynthia Sarah Aberle, Apr. 1, 1978; 1 child, Emily Sarah Aberle. BA in Psychology, Temple U., 1968; PhD in Social Psychology, Princeton, 1976. Instr. New Coll., Sarasota, Fla., 1971-75; asst. prof. Interdisciplinary Studies Miami U., Oxford, Ohio, 1975-80, assoc. prof., 1980; assoc. social behavioral studies The Hastings Ctr., Hastings-on Hudson, N.Y., 1980-84; assoc. prof. Inst. Med. Humanities U. Tex Med. Br., Galveston, Tex., 1984-86, prof., 1986-87; prof., dir. Ctr. Biomed. Ethics Case We. Reserve U., Cleve., 1987-99, Susan E. Watson prof. bioethics, 1998—99; pres. The Hastings Ctr., Garrison, N.Y., 1999—. Mem. Nat. Bioethics Adv. Commn., 1996-2001; mem. ethical, legal and social issues working group Human Genome Project NIH/Dept. Energy, 1989-95. Author: The Worth of a Child, 1996; founder, editor Med. Humanities Rev.; mem. editl. bd. Human Gene Therapy, Cloning, Politics and the Life Scis., Hastings Cetr. Report, Jour. of Law, Medicine and Ethics; editor: Encyclopedia of Ethical, Legal, and Policy Issues in Biotechnology. Fellow NEH, 1977-78, 1979-80, Aspen Inst., 1989. Fellow Hastings Ctr.; mem. APHA, Assn. Practical and Profl. Ethics, Am. Soc. Law Medicine and Ethics (bd. dirs. 1993-97), Assn. Integrative Studies (bd. dirs. 1980-87, pres. 1983), Soc. Health and Human Values (chair program dirs. sect. 1989-90, faculty assn. 1989-90, SHHV program com. 1990, pres.-elect 1992-93, pres. 1993-94), Am. Soc. Human Genetics (chair social issues com. 1998-99), Am. Coll. Ob-Gyn. (com. on ethics 1996-2001), Am. Soc. Bioethics and Humanities (pres.-elect 1998-99, pres. 1999-2000), Human Genome Orgn. (ethics com.), World Anti-Doping Agy. (ethics and edn. com.). Office: The Hastings Ctr 21 Malcolm Gordon Rd Garrison NY 10524-5555

MURRAY, TRACY, economics educator, consultant; b. Tonasket, Wash., Nov. 17, 1940; s. Robert Joseph and Ruth (Olson) M.; m. Katherine Ann Paton, Nov. 25, 1966; children: Elizabeth Lynn, Scott R. BA, Wash. State U., 1962; MA, Mich. State U., 1965, PhD, 1969. Asst. prof. econs. U. N.Mex., Albuquerque, 1966-68; asst. prof., assoc. prof. Ga. Inst. Tech., Atlanta, 1969-74; assoc. prof. NYU, N.Y.C., 1974-78; Phillips Petroleum Co. disting. prof. U. Ark., Fayetteville, 1978—; economist UN, Geneva, 1971-73, U.S. Internat. Trade Commn., Washington, 1987-89, UN, Geneva, 1992. Econ. cons. UN, N.Y.C., Geneva, Vienna, Austria, 1975—, OAS, Washington, 1977—, World Bank, Washington, 1985-93, govts. of U.S., Colombia, Argentina, Morocco, Uruguay, OECD, Paris, 2001-02; prof. Toulouse Bus. Sch., France, 2001—. Author: Trade Preferences for Developing Countries, 1977, Handbook of International Business, 1982, 2d edit., 1988, Handbook of International Management, 1988; contbr. articles to profl. jours. IBM fellow Europe, 1976, U.S. Dept. State lecture grantee, 1978, 80, 81. Mem. Am. Econ. Assn., Acad. Internat. Bus. Office: U Ark BA 402 Fayetteville AR 72701

MURRELL, DEBORAH ANNE, music educator, speaker, writer; b. Louisville, Ky., July 7, 1942; d. James Howard and Mayme Ruth (Manning) M. AB, Ea. Ky. U., 1964; MA, Western Ky. U., 1975; MACE, So. Bapt. Theol. Sem., Louisville, 1983; postgrad. in music, Ind. U. Band and choral dir. Hardin County Pub. Schs., Elizabethtown, Ky., 1964-66; dir. instrumental and vocal music Bullitt County Schs., Shepherdsville, Ky., 1966-74; band dir. Clark County Schs., Winchester, Ky., 1974-76; band and choral dir., head coach h.s. girls basketball Carroll County Schs., Carrollton, Ky., 1978-81; cons., speaker Nat. Single Adults, Louisville, 1981—; minister of single and sr. adults Temple Terr. First Bapt. Ch., Tampa, Fla., 1983-88; minister of adults First Bapt. Ch., Winston-Salem, N.C., 1988-91; minister of adults and evangelism Taylors (S.C.) First Bapt. Ch., 1991-93; music specialist Bullitt County Pub. Schs., Shepherdsville, Ky., 1993—2003; interim min. of music Bullitt Lick Bapt. Ch., Shepherdsville, Ky., 1999-2000; music specialist Pleasant Grove Elem. Sch., Mt. Washington, Ky., 2000—03, ret., 2003—; instrumental instr. Performing Arts Ctr., Mt. Washington, 2002—. Bd. dirs. Good News Clubs, Inc., Louisville, 1966-73; task force mem. single adults Bapt. Sunday Sch. Bd., Nashville, Tenn., 1991-93; Master's Men Orch., Inc., Louisville, 1993-99—; internat. spkr. to single adults, Eng. and Brazil, 1987-93, 2000; mentor Music Educators Nat. Conf., 2003—. Author: (with others) Single Adult Resource and Recipient, 1986, Single Adult Ministry, 1987; interviewee (video) Bapt. Sunday Sch. Bd., 1983-93; contbg. writer Christian Single Mag., 1980-93; prodr., dir.: PGE Sings the Music of America, 2002. Band hostess Ky. Derby Festival Commn., Louisville, 1980-83; internat. and nat. spkr. single adult ministries, 1981—; founder, organizer Bullitt County Music Festival, 1968—; mem. Louisville Bats Baseball Orgn., 2003-. Named Ky. Col. Commonwealth of Ky., Frankfort, 1978. Mem. NEA, Music Educators Nat. Conf., Ky. Edn. Assn., Ky. Music Educators Assn. (dist. officer 1964-81, 97-2001), Bullitt County Edn. Assn., Bullitt County Music Tchrs. Assn. (v.p. 1994-98, pres. 1998-99, sec. 2000-2001, v.p. 2002-2003), Religious Educators Assn., N.C. Religious Edn. Assn. (publicity, promotion com. 1990-91), Pilot Mt. Bapt. Assn. (mem. exec. com. N.C. 1989-91), Ea. Ky. U. Alumni Assn., Nat. Alumni Band (chmn. 1975-78), Tampa Bay Bapt. Assn. (con. 1983-88), Fern Creek High Sch. Alumni Assn., Phi Delta Kappa. Home and Office: 2805 Alice Ave Louisville KY 40220-1703 E-mail: dasailboat@msn.com.

MURRELL, ESTELLE C. elementary school educator; b. Warren County, Ky., Feb. 13, 1931; d. James B. and Mary Ellen (Johnson) Clark; m. Allen Leslie Murrell, Mar. 14, 1953; children: Leslie Allen, Lisa Ellen. BS, Western Ky. U., 1956. Cert. elem. tchr., Ky. 5th grade tchr. Bowling Green (Ky.) Ind. Bd. Edn.; 6th grade tchr. Warren County Bd. Edn., Bowling Green; 4th grade tchr. Hardin County Bd. Edn., Elizabethtown, Ky.; 4th, 6th and 7th grades tchr. lang. arts Bowling Green Bd. Edn.; tchr. Draughons Jr. Coll., Bowling Green, Ky. Named to Leader of Am. Elem. Edn., 1971, 73. Mem. NEA, Ky. Edn. Assn., Bowling Green Edn. Assn. (membership chair), Nat. Coun. Tchrs. English, Ky. Coun. Tchrs. English Lang. Arts, Ky. Retired Tchrs. Assn. Home: 1404 Woodhurst St Bowling Green KY 42104-3322

MURRI, LUELLA DAVIS, personnel and language professional; b. Boston, July 28, 1920; d. Arthur DeForest and Gertrude Davis; m. Albert Thomas Murri, Sept. 15, 1951 (dec. Nov. 1973); children: Thomas Allen, Daniel Glenn. Diploma Univ. Studies, U. Paris, 1939; BA in French summa cum laude, Wheaton Coll., Norton, Mass., 1940; MA in French, Radcliffe Coll., 1941. Position classifier Navy Dept., N.Y.C., 1944-45, VA, Boston, 1946, Navy Dept., Phila., 1946-51; chief classification sect. Office of Price Stablzn., Phila., 1951-53; survey leader, then tech. asst. to chief classification div. U.S. Civil Svc. Commn., Phila., 1953-55; pvt. tchr. French, Springfield, Va., 1975-81. Co-chmn. fgn. lang. subcom. citizens' curriculum adv. com. Sch. Bd., Fairfax County, Va., 1965-69; rep. Compagnons de la Parole Française, Vienna, Va. and Ceret, France, 1975, 76, mem. host com. bi-centennial visit of Ceretans to Vienna, Va., 1976. Editor: Magnetic Field Therapy Handbook, 1993; moderator (TV program) America's Best Kept Medical Secrets, 1994, photographer (exhibitions) in India Thru Your Lens, Smithsomian Inst., 2001, host (TV series) Photographers of Northern Virginia, 2001—. Parent rep. self-study com. North Springfield Elem. Sch., Springfield, Va., 1965-66, vol. tchr. French, 1967-68; vol. tutor Literacy Coun. No. Va., Fairfax County, Va., 1987-88. Recipient French and German prizes, Wheaton Coll., 1940, 1st Place wildlife category, Hon. Mention humor category photography competition Soc. Expeditions, 1990; grant to AAUW Ednl. Found. named in her honor by Springfield-Annandale (Va.) br., 1969. Mem. AAUW (pres. Springfield-Annandale br. 1964-66), No. Va. Photog. Soc. (Comml. Print Photographer of Yr. 1999, Nature's Best mag. award 2003, numerous awards), Antarctican Soc., Circumnavigators Club, Phi Beta Kappa. Democrat. Mem. Unitarian Ch. Avocations: photography, swimming, walking, dancing, exotic travel. Home: 5426 Lehigh Ln Springfield VA 22151-3423

MURRY, FRANCIE ROBERTA, special education educator; b. Waukegan, Ill. BA, Ctrl. Wash. U., 1980, MEd, 1988; PhD, U. Va., 1991. Cert. tchr., Wash. Spl. edn. tchr. Adna (Wash.) Sch. Dist., 1980-81; itinerant spl. edn. tchr. Ellensburg Sch. Dist., Kittitas, Wash., 1981-85; dist. cons., spl. edn. tchr. Ellensburg (Wash.) Sch. Dist., 1985-86, at-risk project cons./coord., 1987-88; dist. cons., spl. edn. tchr. Yelm (Wash.) Sch. Dist., 1986-87; grad. asst. Commonwealth Ctr. Edn. of Tchrs., Va. Behavior Disorders, Charlottesville, Va., 1988-89; grad. instr. U. Va., Charlottesville, 1990, grad. intern, 1990; asst. prof. U. Wyo., Laramie, 1991-93, U. No. Colo., Greeley, 1993-96, assoc. prof., 1996—. Adj. instr. Ctrl. Wash. U., Ellensburg, 1987-91; cons. Ellensburg Sch. Dist., 1987, Yelm Sch. Dist., 1989, Hampton (Va.) City Schs., 1989, U. Va., Behavior Disorders Project, 1990, Auburn (Ala.) U., 1991, Niobrara Sch. Dist., 1991, 92, 93; in-svc. presenter; nat. and internat. conf. speaker. Contbr. articles to profl. jours. Mem. North Ctrl. Evaluation Team, Wyoming Indian High Sch., 1992. Grantee N.W. Spl. Edn., 1980, Vocat. Edn. Spl. Project, 1982, Title VI-B, 1982, Wash. Edn. Rsch. Assn., 1988, Wash. Mental Health, 1988, Region 10, Va. Commonwealth Div., 1989; Dean's fellow, Curry Sch. Edn., U. Va., 1990, U. Va. Deptl. fellow, 1989; recipient Outstanding scholarship Assn. Colls. and Schs. Edn. in State Univs. and Land Grant Colls., 1992. Mem. ASCD, Am. Ednl. Rsch. Assn., Coun. for Exceptional Children (Va. chpt. v.p. 1990), Coun. for Exceptional Children with Behavior Disorders (pres., Wyo. rep. 1992, 93), Coun. for Exceptional Children with Devel. Delays, Tchr. Educators of Children with Behavior Disorders (pres. 1992, v.p. 1993), Colo. Fedn. for Exceptional Children (child advocacy networker 1996—), Ea. Ednl. Rsch. Assn., Phi Delta Kappa. Office: 310 McKee Hall U of No Colo Greeley CO 80639

MURTAGH, FREDERICK REED, neuroradiologist, educator; b. Phila., Nov. 20, 1944; s. Frederick and Mary (Shaner) M.; (div.); children: Ryan David, Kevin Reed; m. Dorothy Rossi. BA, William and Mary Coll., 1966; MD, Temple U., 1971. Prof., dir. neuroradiology U. S. Fla., Tampa, 1978—. Author: Imaging Anatomy of Head and Spine, 1991. Author: Imaging Anatomy of Head & Spine, 1991. Lt. USNR, 1972-74. Mem. Am. Coll. Radiology (cert. added qualification in neuroradiology 1995), Assn. Univ. Radiologists, Am. Soc. Neuroradiology (sr. mem.), Radiol. Soc. N.Am., Southeastern Neuroradiology Soc. Office: U South Fla 3301 Alumni Dr Tampa FL 33612-9413

MURTAUGH, MAUREEN ANN, nutrition educator; b. Lower Marion, Pa., July 26, 1961; d. James Leo Jr. and Margaret Anne Murtaugh. BS in Clin. Nutrition, Syracuse U., 1983; PhD in Nutritional Sci., U. Conn., 1991. Registered dietitian, Ill. Clin. dietitian Marriott Corp., Easton, Md., 1983-84, Arlington, Va., 1984-86; rsch. asst. U. Conn., Storrs, 1986-91; asst. prof. Rush U., Chgo., 1991-99, assoc. prof., 1999; postdoctoral fellow in epidemiology U. Minn., Mpls., 1999—2002; assoc. prof. nutrition epidemiology U. Utah, Salt Lake City, 2002—. Mem. Am. Inst. Nutrition, Am. Dietetic Assn. (chair perinatal nutrition practice group 1997-98), No. Ill. Diabetes Assn. (mem. nutrition com. 1992-99, bd. dirs. 1996-99). Roman Catholic. Office: U Utah Dept Family Preventive Medicine 375 Chiipeta Way Ste A Salt Lake City UT 84108

MUSACCHIO, MARILYN JEAN, nurse midwife, educator, administrator; b. Louisville, Dec. 7, 1938; d. Robert William and Loretta C. (Liebert) Poulter; m. David Edward Musacchio, May 13, 1961; children: Richard Peter, Michelle Marie. BSN cum laude, Spalding Coll., 1968; MSN, U. Ky., 1972, cert. in nurse-midwifery, 1976; PhD, Case Western Res U., 1993. RN; cert. nurse-midwife; advanced registered nurse practitioner; registered nurse-midwife. Staff nurse gynecol. unit St. Joseph Infirmary, Louisville, 1959-60, staff nurse male gen. surgery unit, 1960; instr. St. Joseph Infirmary Sch. Nursing, Louisville, 1960-71; from asst. prof. to assoc. prof., dir. dept. nursing edn. Ky. State U., Frankfort, 1972-75; asst. prof. U. Ky. Coll. Nursing, Lexington, 1976-79, assoc. prof., coord., 1979-92, acting coordinator nurse-midwifery, 1982-84, coordinator for nurse-midwifery, 1987-92; assoc. prof., dir. nurse-midwifery U. Ala., Birmingham, 1992-96, assoc. prof., 1997-98; dean, prof. Tenn. Technol. U., Cookeville, 1998—. Cons. in field. Mem. editorial bd. Jour. Obstet., Gynecol. and Neonatal Nursing, 1976-82; author pamphlet; contbr. articles to profl. jours. Mem.Louisville Safety Coun., 1973-80. Brig. Gen. Army Nurse Corps, USAR, 1992-95. Recipient Disting. Citizen award City of Louisville, 1977, Jefferson Cup award Jefferson County, Ky., 1991; named Outstanding Alumna, Mercy Acad., 1993; named to Hall of Disting. Alumni, U. Ky., 1995; recipient scholarships and fellowships, other awards. Fellow Am. Acad. Nursing; mem. AWHONN, NAFE, ANA, Nurse Assn. Am. Coll. Ob-Gyn. (charter; nat. sec. 1970-72, chmn. dist. V 1969), Am. Coll. Nurse-Midwives, Res. Officers Assn., Assn. Mil. Surgeons U.S., Sr. Army Res. Comdr. Assn., Assn. U.S. Army, Army Nurse Corps. Assn., Army War Coll. Alumni Assn. (life). Roman Catholic. Avocations: reading, candy making, cake decorating, cooking, sewing. Home: PO Box 5001 Cookeville TN 38505-0001 Fax: 931-372-6244. E-mail: mmusacchio@tntech.edu.

MUSCARELLA, CHRISTOPHER JAMES, finance educator; b. New Brunswick, N.J., Aug. 30, 1952; s. Mark Benjamin and Virginia (Pickert) M.; m. Bobbie Jean Weidner, June 1, 1985; children: Sarah Anne, Aaron Matthew BSEE, U. Notre Dame, 1974, MBA, 1976; PhD, Purdue U., 1983. Asst. prof. So. Meth. U., Dallas, 1984-90; sr. fin. economist U.S. Securities & Exch. Commn., Washington, 1990-91; prof., L.W. Roy and Mary Lois Clark tchg. fellow Pa. State U., University Park, 1991—. Vis. asst. prof. U. Notre Dame, Ind., 1979, U. Oreg., Eugene, 1980—82, U. Utah, Salt Lake City, 1982—84; Dale S. Coenen vis. prof. free enterprise Darden Grad. Sch. Bus. Adminstrn. U. Va., 2000; J. William Fulbright Disting. Chair Portugese Cath. U., Lisbon, 2001. Editor (assoc.): Jour. Fin. Rsch., 1993—99. Mem.: European Fin. Assn., Fin. Mgmt. Assn. (northeast regional dir. 1994—96, v.p. program 2002, assoc. editor Survey and Synthesis Soc. 2001—), Am. Fin. Assn. Avocation: genealogy. Office: Coll Bus Adminstrn 609 BAB University Park PA 16802 E-mail: cmuscarella@psu.edu.

MUSE, JAMES MICHAEL, bank executive, finance educator; b. Salem, Mass., June 22, 1960; s. James Joseph and Gertrude Marie (Coté) M.; m. Patricia Ann Tyrrell, May 30, 1986; children: Kristine Amy Kelleher, Michael Thomas Kmiec. BS in Bus. Adminstrn., Salem State Coll., 1983; CFP, Fairfield U., 1990, postgrad. Nat. Sch. Banking, 1995; postgrad. Sch. Bank Mktg., U. Colo., 1999; MBA, Fairfield U., 2003. Cert. Fin. Mktg. Profl., Inst. of Cert. Bankers; cert. employee plan specialist. Retail sales mgr. Salem (Mass.) 5 cents Saving Bank, 1982-84; retirement plans mgr. Andover (Mass.) Savings Bank, 1984-86; asst. treas. Bank 5 For Savings, Arlington, Mass., 1986-91; asst. v.p., trust officer Cambridge (Mass.) Savings Bank, 1991-97; v.p., dir. retail fin. svcs. Beverly (Mass.) Nat. Bank, 1997—2003; pres. Hannah Ins. Agy., 2000—03; v.p. regional strategic cons. Infinex Fin. Group, Farmington, Conn., 2003—. Chmn., treas. Mass. Retirement Plans Consortium, Boston, 1987; mem. faculty Endicott Coll., Beverly, Mass., New Eng. Coll. Fin., Boston, The Financial Planning Assn. Chair bd. dirs. ARC, Beverly, Mass.; bd. dirs. Beverly Teen YMCA, North Shore United Way; bd. dirs., vice chair North Shore Music Theatre Corp. Circle; former moderator, trustee First Federated Ch., Beverly, Mass., 1992—2002; treas. Babe Ruth Baseball, Beverly, 1992—94; pres. basketball booster club Beverly H.S., 1994, 1995, 1996; treas. Friends of Emma Found.; bd. dir. ABA Mktg. Network NE chpt.; mem. United Ch. of Christ. Mem.: Bank Mktg. Assn., Mass. Bankers Assn (bd. dir.s). Avocations: kayaking, skiing, golf, the ocean, community involvement. Home: 7 Cross St Beverly MA 01915-3808 Office: Infinex Financial Group 10 Waterside Dr Farmington CT 06032

MUSE, WILLIAM VAN, academic administrator; b. Marks, Miss., Apr. 7, 1939; s. Mose Lee and Mary Elizabeth (Hisaw) M.; m. Anna Marlene Munden, Aug. 22, 1964; children: Amy Marlene, Ellen Elizabeth, William Van. BS (T.H. Harris scholar), Northwestern La. State U., 1960; MBA (Nat. Def. Grad. fellow), U. Ark., 1961, PhD (Nat. Def. Grad. fellow), 1966. Instr. U. Ark., 1962-63; field supr. Tau Kappa Epsilon Fraternity, 1963-64; asst. prof. Ga. Tech., 1964-65; assoc. prof., chmn., dir. rsch. Ohio U., 1965-70; dean Coll. Bus. Appalachian State U., Boone, N.C., 1970-73; dean Coll. Bus. Adminstrn. U. Nebr., Omaha, 1973-79, Tex. A&M U., College Station, 1979-82, vice chancellor, 1983-84; pres. U. Akron, Ohio, 1984-92, Auburn U., Ala., 1992-2001; chancellor East Carolina U., 2001—. Author: Business and Economic Problems in Appalachia, 1969, Management Practices in Fraternities, 1965; Contbr. articles to profl. jours. Found. for Econ. Edn. fellow, 1967. Mem. Blue Key, Omicron Delta Kappa, Phi Kappa Phi, Delta Sigma Pi, Beta Gamma Sigma, Pi Omega Pi, Tau Kappa Epsilon, Phi Beta Kappa. Clubs: Rotarian. Office: Chancellors Office East Carolina Univ 103 Spilman Bldg Greenville NC 27858-4353 E-mail: musew@mail.ecu.edu.

MUSGROVE, DAVID RONALD, governor; b. Sardis, Miss., July 29, 1956; s. Henry and Nina (Rogers) M.; children: Jordan, Carmen, Rae. AA, Northwest Miss. C.C., 1976; BS, U. Miss., 1978, JD, 1981. Bar: Miss. Ptnr. Smith, Musgrove & McCord, Batesville, Miss., 1981—2000; lt. gov. State of Miss., 1996—2000, gov., 2000—. State sen. Miss. State, 1988-96; chair Nat. Conf. Lt. Govs., 1998-99. Pres. Batesville Jaycees, 1982-83; chair Panola County Heart Fund, 1985-86; deacon First Bapt. Ch., Batesville, 1983-2000. Fellow Miss. Bar Found; mem. Am. Inns Ct., Panola County Bar Assn., Tri-County Bar Assn., Miss. Young Lawyers Assn. Democrat. Office: Office of the Governor PO Box 139 Jackson MS 39205-0139*

MUSIALA, ROSALIE, principal, educator; b. Ventimiglia, Sicily, Italy, Aug. 16, 1947; came to U.S., 1954; d. Placido Bonadonne and Grazia Pollina; m. Robert A. Musiala, July 1, 1972; children: Grace, Robert, Paul. BS in Edn., DePaul U., 1969, MA, 1976; postgrad., Nat. Louis U., 1999—. First grade tchr. St. Jerome Sch., Chgo., 1969-76; preschool tchr. St. Edward Sch., Chgo., 1984-98; principal Pope John XXIII Sch., Evanston, Ill., 1998—. Treas. Ill. Language and Literacy Coun. Mem.: Nat. Coun. Tchrs. English, Ill. Reading Coun., Internat. Reading Assn. Roman Catholic. Office: Pope John XXIII Sch 1120 Washington St Evanston IL 60202-1620

MUSICK, PAT, artist, sculptor, art educator; b. L.A., Sept. 14, 1926; d. Mark Melvin and Emma Lucille (Ferguson) Tapscott; m. John Elmore Musick, Aug. 18, 1946 (dec. Nov. 1977); children: Cathleen M. Goebel, Melinda M. King, Laura M. Wright; m. Gerald Paul Carr, Sept. 14, 1979. MA, Cornell U., 1972, PhD, 1974. Rsch. asst. Cornell U., Ithaca, N.Y., 1971-73; prof. SUNY, Oswego, 1974-76, U. Houston, 1976-85; postdoct. fellow Med. Sch. U. Tex., Galveston, 1978. Adj. prof. Syracuse (N.Y.) U., 1974-76, U. Ark., Fayetteville, 1986—; mem. nat. adv. coun. Rocky Mountain Coll., Billings, Mont., 1996-97; mem. com. site integrated art planning, art selection com. Walton Arts Ctr., Fayetteville, Ark., 1988-90; pres. CAMUS, Inc., Huntsville, Ark., 1995—. One-woman exhibns. include Tulsa Ctr. Contemporary Arts, 1989, Huntsville (Ala.) Mus. Art, 1992, Springfield (Mo.) Mus. Art, 1992, Ark. Arts Ctr., Little Rock, 1992, Walton Arts Ctr., Fayetteville, Ark., 1992, 95, Amarillo (Tex.) Mus. Art, 1995, Goddard Gallery State Fair C.C., Sedalia, Mo., 1996, Charles B. Goddard Ctr., Ardmore, Okla., 1997, U. Ark., Little Rock, 1997, Albrecht Kemper Mus., 1998, tour of 7 Tex. museums, 1998—; group exhibns. include Senator David Pryor's Offices, Washington, 1991-93, Ark. Art Ctr., Little Rock, 1994, Walton Arts Ctr., 1994; permanent collections Jewish Theol. U., Ark. Aerospace Edn. ctr., Ark. Arts Ctr., Dartmouth Coll., Huntsville (Ala.) Mus. Art, Internat. Ctr. Transp. Studies, Promus Hotels, U. Houston, Springfield (Mo.) Art Mus., U. Ozarks, Walton Arts Ctr., U. Ark., Mirrilton, Washington Regional Hosp., Fayetteville, Ark., Cornell U. Fine Arts scholar U. So. Calif., 1944; Touring grantee Ark. Arts Coun., NEA, 1987-88, Assistance grantee Ark. Arts Coun., 1997; Connemara Found. fellow, 1998; recipient Gold Medal Pizzo Calabro (Italy) Internat. Invitational, 1983, Gold Medal Southeastern Mus. Conf., 1993, Richard A. Florsheim Art Fund award, 1997; winner 9th Ann. Outdoor Sculpture Competition, Miami U., Ohio, 1998, Tour of Six Tex. Mus., 1998-99, Irving (Tex.) Art Ctr., 2000, Ozarks Woodland Sculpture Garden, 2000, Monarch Sculpture Garden, 2001, Buffalo Bayou Artpark, Houston, 2002, Ark. ARt Ctr., 2003. Avocations: cooking, swimming, reading, writing poetry. Home: 1655 Madison 1200 Huntsville AR 72740 Office: CAMUS Inc PO Box 919 Huntsville AR 72740-0919

MUSKOPF, MARGARET ROSE, elementary school educator; b. Saint Louis, July 18, 1942; d. George Oliver and Providence Pearl Knittel; m. Donald R. Muskopf, Mar. 29, 1969. AA, Chaffey Jr. Coll., Alta Loma, Calif., 1962; BA, San Diego State U., 1964; Qigong cert., Xiyuan Hosp., Beijing, China, 1999; Reiki master, 1991; cert., Holos Inst., 1998. Cert. elem. tchr., remedial reading K-12. Elem. tchr. LaMesa-Spring Valley Sch., 1964-70; jr. h.s. tchr. state operated schs., Adak, Alaska, 1970-73; remedial reading tchr. Ritnour Dist., Overland, Mo., 1973-77; dir. Sch. Metaphysics, 1978-79; Tai Chi tchr. Rockhaven, House Springs, Mo., 1988—2000; energy tchr. Sisters of St. Benedict Kordes, Ferdinand, Ind., 1998-99. Co-owner Passport to Wellness, Webster Groves, Mo., 2001—. Foster parent Bur. Indian Affairs, Alaska, 1970-73; hospice vol. St. Anthony's Hosp., St. Louis, 1989-92; vol. tchr. Maria Ctr. Sch. Sisters Notre Dame, St. Louis, 1987-91; vol. Mercy Ctr., Sisters of Mercy, St. Louis. Mem. Greenpeace, Amnesty Internat., Children Internat., Women's Connection Network. Avocations: tai chi, qigong, volunteering, reading.

MUSTARD, JAMES FRASER, research institute executive; b. Toronto, Oct. 16, 1927; s. Allan Alexander and Jean Ann (Oldham) M.; m. Christine Elizabeth Sifton, June 4, 1952; children: Cameron, Ann, Jim, Duncan, John, Christine. MD, U. Toronto, 1953; PhD, Cambridge U., 1956. Asst., then assoc. prof pathology U. Toronto, 1963-66, asst. prof. medicine, 1965-66, hon. prof. pathology, 1990—; prof. pathology McMaster U., Hamilton, Ont., Can., 1966-88, prof. emeritus, 1988—, chmn. pathology, 1966-72, dean faculty health. scis., 1972-80, v.p. faculty health scis., 1980-82; bd. dirs., pres. Can. Inst. Advanced Rsch., Toronto, 1982-96, founding pres., 1996—. Mem. Ont. Coun. Health, 1966-72; chmn. Task Force Health Planning for Ont., Ministry Health and Govt. Ont., 1973-74; mem. Ont. Coun. Univ Affairs, 1975-81; chmn. Adv. Coun. Occupl. Health and Safety, 1977-83; mem. Royal Commn. Matters Health and Safety Arising Use of Asbestos in Ont., 1980-83; mem. Bovey Commn. Study Future Devel. Univ. in Ont., 1984-85; mem. Premier's Coun. Ont., 1986-95, Premier's Coun. Health Strategy, 1988-91; chmn. ctrs. excellence com. Govt. Ont., 1987-91; mem. Prime Minister's Nat. Adv. Bd. on Sci. and Tech., 1987-91, Ottawa, vice chmn., 1988-91; chmn. bd. dirs. Inst. Work and Health, 1990-2002; mem. adv. bd. Man. Ctr. for Health Policy and Evaluation, 1991—; vice chmn. Internat. Ctr. Health and Soc., 1994—; bd. dirs. Ballard Powers Sys., Inc.; chmn. Ballard Power, 1997—2001. Bd. dirs. Heart and Stroke Found. Can., 1971-82, Heart and Stroke Found. Ont., 1982-87; bd. govs. McMaster U., 1978-82; bd. dirs. McMaster U. Med. Centre, 1972-82; trustee Aga Khan U., Karachi, Pakistan, 1985—, mem. chancellor's commn., 1992-95. Decorated Order of Ont., companion Order of Can.; recipient Disting. Svc. award Can. Soc. Clin. Investigation, J. Allyn Taylor Internat. prize, 1988, Internat. award Gairdner Found., 1967, James F. Mitchell award, 1972, Izaak Walton Killam prize in health sci. Can. Coun., 1987; Robert P. Grant medal Internat. Soc. on Thrombosis and Haemostasis, 1987, Disting. Career award for contbns., 1989, F.N.G. Starr award Can. Med. Assn., 2001. Home: 422 Sumach St Toronto ON Canada M4X 1B5 Office: Founders' Network of CIAR 401 Richmond St W Ste 281 Toronto ON Canada M5V 3A8

MUSTO, DAVID FRANKLIN, physician, educator, historian, consultant; b. Tacoma, Jan. 8, 1936; s. Charles Hiram and Hilda Marie (Hanson) Mustoe; m. Emma Jean Baudendistel, June 2, 1961; children: Jeanne Marie, David Kyle, John Baird, Christopher Edward. BA, U. Wash., 1956, MD, 1963; MA, Yale U., 1961. Lic. physician, Conn., Pa. Clerk Nat. Hosp. for Nervous Disease, London, 1961; intern Pa. Hosp., Phila., 1963-64; resident Yale U. Med. Ctr., New Haven, 1964-67; spl. asst. to dir. NIMH, Bethesda, Md., 1967-69; vis. asst. prof. Johns Hopkins U., 1968-69; asst. prof. Yale U., 1969-73, assoc. prof., 1973-78, sr. rsch. scientist, 1978-81, prof., 1981—, exec. fellow Davenport Coll., 1983-88; mem. adv. editorial com. Yale Edits. Private Papers James Boswell, 1975—; cons. Exec. Office of Pres., 1973-75; mem. White House Strategy Coun., 1978-81; mem. panel on alcohol policy NAS, Washington, 1978-82; cons. White House Conf. on Families, 1979-80. Vis. fellow Clare Coll., Cambridge U., 1994; mem. alcohol adv. com. Nat. Assn. Broadcasters, 1994—; DuMez lectr. U. Md.; Walter Reed meml. lectr. Richmond Acad. Medicine; Galdston lectr. N.Y. Acad. Medicine; Sirridge lectr. U. Mo. Med. Sch.; Clendening lectr. U. Kans. Med. Sch. Author: The American Disease: Origins of Narcotic Control, 1973, expanded edit., 1987, 3rd edit., 1999; co-author: (with P. Korsmeyer) The Quest for Drug Control: Politics and Federal Policy in a Period of Increasing Drug Use, 1963-1981, 2002; editor: One Hundred Years of Heroin, 2002, Drugs in America: A Documentary History, 2002. Historian Pres.'s Commn. on Mental Health, 1977-78; adv. U.S. Del. to UN Commn. Narcotic Drugs, Geneva, 1978-79; mem. nat. coun. Smithsonian Instn., Washington, 1981-90, hon. mem., 1991—; hist. cons. Presdl. Commn. Human Immuno-deficiency Virus Epidemic, 1988; mem. nat. adv. com. on anti-drug program Robert Wood Johnson Found., 1989-2002; mem. nat. adv. com. on internat. narcotic policy UN Assn. of U.S.A., 1991; mem. adv. com. causes drug abuse Office Tech. Assessment, Congress U.S., 1992-94; commr. Conn. Alcohol and Drug Abuse Commn., 1992-93; bd. dirs. Coll. on Problems of Drug Dependence, 1990-94; trustee Assocs. of Cushing-Whitney Med. Libr., 1994—. With USPHS, 1967-69. Fellow: Coll. Problems of Drug Dependence, Am. Psychiat. Assn. (disting.); mem.: Soc. of Cin. in the State of Conn. (pres. 1998—2001), English-Speaking Union (pres. New Haven br. 1995—98), Am. Assn. History of Medicine (William Osler medal 1961), Am. Hist. Assn., Am. Inst. History of Pharmacy (Kraemers award 1974), New Haven County Med. Assn. (chmn. bicentennial com. 1983), Century Assn., Athenaeum Club (London), Cosmos Club. Office: Yale U PO Box 207900 New Haven CT 06520-7900

MUTALIPASSI, LOUIS RICHARD, psychologist, educator; b. Kansas City, Kans, Jan. 23, 1937; s. Louie R. Mutalipassi and Cleda E. (Miller) Wolverton; m. Edalee Kenworthy, July 14, 1962 (div. 1970); 1 child, Annemarie; m. Laura Ruth Posner, July 17, 1976; 2 children: Michael and Anthony. BA in Psychology, U. Calif., Santa Barbara, 1962; MA in Psychology, UCLA, 1965, PhD in Psychology, 1969. Lic. psychologist, Calif. Staff psychologist VA Med. Ctr., LA, 1969—76, chief psychology svc. Albany, NY, 1976—80; clin. assoc. prof. psychology UCLA, U. So. Calif., LA, 1980—; chief psychology svc. VA Med. Ctr., Long Beach, Calif., 1980—97, ret., 1997; clin. psychologist in pvt. practice Cypress, Calif., 1982—. Oral commr. State Bd. Med. Examiners, Calif., 1996—. Contbr. articles to profl. jour.; presenter in field. With USAF, 1954-58. Mem. APA. Avocations: golf, photography. E-mail: lrmteetime@aol.com.

MUTCHELKNAUS, AUDREY J. special education educator; b. Freeman, S.D., June 11, 1939; d. Paul Z. and Velissa M. (McCann) Wipf; m. Charles L. Mutchelknaus, Aug. 10, 1958; children: Robbie J., Teresa Gunderson, Kevin, Stacy Garrett(dec.). BS, U. S.D., 1972, MA, 1983. Tchr. jr. high lang. arts Freeman Pub. Sch., SD, 1972—81, spl. educator, 1981—2003. Oral interpretation coach Freeman High Sch., 1974—84, quiz bowl coach, 1976—2003. Study Skills grantee, S.D. Dept. Edn., 1984. Home: 316 E 3d Freeman SD 57029-2247

MUTISPAUGH, MARY JANE, principal; b. Lexington, Va., Dec. 2, 1956; d. Russell Everett and Mary Mowbray (Clemmer) Emore; m. John Stanley Mutispaugh, June 30, 1979; children: Meaghan Marie, Lauren Elizabeth. BA in Social Sci., James Madison U., 1979, MEd in Secondary Adminstrn., 1987. Cert. tchr., adminstr., Va. Tchr. Brownsburg (Va.) Middle Sch., 1979-81, Natural Bridge Hish Sch., Natural Bridge Sta., Va., 1981-85, Parry McCluer Middle Sch., Buena Vista, Va., 1985-88, Parry McCluer High Sch., Buena Vista, Va., 1988-94; prin. Lylburn Downing Mid. Sch., Lexington, Va., 1994—. Instr. Dabney S. Lancaster C.C., Clifton Forge, Va., 1989—; sponsor, advisor Nat. Honor Soc., Buena Vista, Va., 1992-93. Grade rep. Waddell PTA, Lexington, Va., 1989-92; troop leader Girl Scouts Am., Lexington, 1989—; pres. Lexington Fire Dept. Ladies Aux., 1990-93; active Rockbridge League of Women Voters, 1992-93, Lexington Dem. Com., 1992-93. Mem. Nat. Assn. Secondary Sch. Prins., Va. Assn. Secondary Sch. Prins., Va. Coun. for Social Studies (Western Va. Tchr. of Yr., 1987, regional rep. 1991-94, sec. 1995), Buena Vista Edn. Assn., Rockbridge Edn. Assn., Delta Kappa Gamma (Beta Epsilon chpt. pres. 1990-92), Phi Delta Kappa (U. Va. chpt.). Presbyterian. Avocations: reading, genealogical research, cross stitching. Home: 2555 Holly Ave Buena Vista VA 24416-1617 Office: Lylburn Downing Mid Sch 302 Diamond St Lexington VA 24450-2802

MUZEKARI, THOMASINE DABBS, adult education educator; b. Columbia, S.C., Dec. 4, 1941; d. Jesse Thomas and Margaret Salina (Scott) Dabbs; m. William Muzekari, May 7, 1966; children: Laura Farrar, William Theodore. Student, U. S.C., 1961-62, EdD, 1994; BA, Columbia Coll., 1983, MEd, 1987. Cert. tchr., S.C. Tchr. Richland Sch. Dist. One, Columbia, 1983-89, staff devel. cons., 1989-98, dir. adult and cmty. edn., 1998—; adjunct prof. U. S.C., 1995—. Pvt. cons. specializing in learning styles, integrated curriculum active learning brain rsch., 1993—; adj. prof. Columbia Coll., 1999—; presenter in field. Writer, producer, narrator televised recert. course for tchrs. Middle School Today, 1991. Named Wil Lou Gray Educator of Yr., Columbia Coll., 1999; S.C. Dept. Edn. grantee, 1992—. Mem. S.C. ASCD (assoc.), S.C. Adult Edn. Dirs. (bd. mem. 1999-2000), S.C. Network of Women Adminstrs. in Edn. (regional chairperson 1994-95, exec.. bd. 1995-96, pres. 1997-98), Nat. Staff Devel. Coun., affiliate rep., 1997-99, S.C. Devel. Coun. (governing com. 1994-95, bd. mem. 1995-96, pres.-elect 1997-98, pres. 1998—), Alpha Delta Kappa (sgt.-at-arms 1988-90), Phi Delta Kappa. Republican. Methodist. Avocations: gardening, aerobic exercise, reading. Office: Richland One 1616 Richland St Columbia SC 29201-2657 also: 2430 Atlas Rd Columbia SC 29209

MWENDA, KENNETH KAOMA, legal consultant, advisor, educator; LLB, U. Zambia, 1990; Gr.Dip, LCCI, U.K, 1991; DMS, IoC, U.K, 1992; BCL, U. Oxford, U.K., 1994; MBA, U. Hull, U.K, 1995; DBA, Pacific Western U., L.A., 1996, PhD in Publs., 1999; PhD, U. Warwick, U.K., 2000. Cert. Bar, Zambia, 1991; cert. cumpolsory edn., devels. in comml. securities, intellectual property law. Worked in trust funds and co-financing dept. Vice-Presidency of World Bank, Washington, 1998-99, worked in poverty reduction, mgmt. and pub. sector reform unit, 1999; worked as counsel in legal dept. World Bank, Washington, 1999-2000, projects officer, 2000—03, sr. projects officer, 2003—. Vis. prof. U. Miskolc Sch. Law, Hungary, 1996; lectr. U. Zambia Law Sch., 1991—95, vis. prof., 2001; lectr. Warwick U. Law Sch., 1995—98; spkr. and presenter in field. Author: Legal Aspects of Corporate Capital and Finance, 1999, Contemporary Issues In Corporate Finance and Investment Law, 2000, Banking Supervision and Systemic Bank Restructuring, 2000, Zambia's Stock Exchange and Privatization Programme, 2001, The Dynamics of Market Integration: African Stock Exchange's in the New Millennium, 2000, Banking Supervision and Microfinance Regulation: Lessons from Zambia, 2002, Principles of Arbitration Law, 2003, Frontiers of Legal Knowledge: Business and Economic Law in Context, 2003. Tutor U. Zambia Law Sch., 1991-95. Staff Devel. fellow in law U. Zambia, 1991, U. Yale Law Faculty fellow, 1998; Rhodes scholar U. Zambia, 1992, U. Oxford, 1992-94, U. Hull, 1994-95. Fellow Royal Soc. Arts. of England, Inst. Commerce of England; mem. Internat. Bar Assn., Law Assn. of Zambia, Brit. Assn. Lawyers for Def. of Unborn. Office: The World Bank 1818 H St NW Washington DC 20433-0001 E-mail: kmwenda@yahoo.com., kmwenda@worldbank.org.

MYCKANIUK, MARIA ANNA, elementary and special education educator; b. Denver, July 1, 1955; d. Mykola and Stafania (Iwachiw) M. BA, U. No. Colo., 1977; MEd, The Citadel, 1990. Cert. tchr., S.C., Fla. Tchr. kindergarten, 3rd grade St. Catherine's Sch., Denver, 1977-81; remedial tchr. St. Vincent's Home and Sch., Denver, 1978-80; tchr. kindergarten, coord. day camp La Petite Learning Ctr. and Little People's Landing Ctr., Littleton, Colo., 1982-83; tchr. exceptional children Randall-Moore Accelerated Sch., Denver, 1982-83; tchr. 1st grade Bonner Elem. Sch., Macedonia, S.C., 1983-84; tchr. 2nd grade Westview Elem. Sch. Berkeley County Sch. Dist., Goose Creek, S.C., 1984-90; tchr. primary edn. learning disabled Old Kings Elem. Sch. Flagler County Sch. Dist., Palm Coast, Fla., 1990—. Mem. adv. com. spl. edn. dept. The Citadel, Charleston, S.C., 1989-90; ednl. cons. Child Find Study Team, 1990—. Active Nat. Wildlife Fedn., 1980—, Gibbs Art Mus., Charleston, 1987-90; tutor Adult Literacy Program, Charleston, 1988-90; co-coord. children's program Piccolo/Spoleto Festival, Charleston, 1989; bd. dirs. Palm Coast Taxpayers Assn., 1991—; active Spl. Olympics, Odessey of the Mind. Recipient Critical Need Tchr. award State of Fla., 1990-91. Mem. Coun. for Exceptional Children, Alpha Delta Kappa, Phi Delta Kappa. Avocations: professional clown and storyteller, theater, travel, music, foreign languages. Home: 8 Prince Michael Ln Palm Coast FL 32164-7154

MYERS, ADELE ANNA, artist, educator, nun; b. Bklyn., Oct. 4, 1925; d. Everett Ecil and Anna Maria (Menig) M. Student, U. Notre Dame; BS in Edn., Fordham U., 1956; MA in Fine Arts, Villa Schifanoia, Florence, Italy, 1962; postgrad., NYU, Pratt Graphics Ctr., Columbia U. Cert. permanent tchr. art, grades K-12, N.Y.; joined Sparkill Dominican Sisters, Roman Cath. Ch., 1944. Tchr. art Monsignor Scanlon H.S., Bronx, N.Y., 1956-60, Albertus Magnus H.S., Bardonia, N.Y., 1961-62; founder, dir. Thorpe Intermedia Gallery, Sparkill, N.Y., 1976-91; prof., chairperson art dept. St. Thomas Aquinas Coll., Sparkill, 1962-78, adj. prof., 1978-99. Design cons. sr. housing devels. Thorpe Village and Dowling Gardens, Sparkill, N.Y., 1981—; mem. adv. bd. Bogliasco Found., N.Y.C. and Italy, 1997—; freelance curator contemporary art exhbns., 1986—. Commd. works include cross in fresco and cement St. Peter's Ch., Yonkers, N.Y., 1990, outdoor sidewalk mosaic Thorpe Village, 1997, stained glass windows for meditation rm. Dowling Gardens, 1996, outdoor mosaic, meditation garden Dominican Sisters, Sparkill, 2001, stained glass windows Our Lady of Rosary Chapel, Dominican Convent, 2001, Way of the Cross in fresco and cement, Chapel at St. Thomas Aquinas Coll., Sparkill, N.Y., 2002; exhibited sculpture in fresco and cement, most recently at ArtBldrs. Gallery, Jersey City, 1994-95, Rockland Ctr. for Arts, 1995, 96, 99, St. John's Chapel Gallery, Newark, 1996, Piermont Flywheel Gallery, N.Y., 2002, Azarian-McCullough Gallery, Sparkill, N.Y., 2001, 04, Visions Gallery, Albany, N.Y., 2001; one-woman shows include Hopper Ho. Art Ctr., Nyack, 1992, Piermont Flywheel Gallery, 1996, 98, 2000, 01, 02, ArtBuilders Gallery, 1996, 2003, Azarian-McCullough Gallery, 2003, Old Ch. Cultural Ctr. Gallery, Demarest, N.J., 1997; represented in pub. and pvt. collections; works and exhibits reviewed in various publs., including N.Y. Times, Star Ledger, Suburban People, Arts Happenings; featured on cable TV program, N.J., 1988. Apptd. art in pub. places com. Rockland County, 1987-92; founding bd. dirs. Arts Fund Rockland, 1989-91. Villa Schifanoia scholar, 1960; Sister Adele Myers Scholarship established in her name St. Thomas Aquinas Coll., 1986; recipient award for Outstanding Contbn. in Field of Art, Rockland County Women's Network, Rockland C.C., Suffern, N.Y., 1980, 1st Ann. Arts award Rockland County Execs., 1987. Mem. Nat. Mus. Women in Arts, Internat. Sculpture Ctr., Christians in Visual Arts. Democrat. Avocations: reading, travel, visiting places of historical interest. Home: Dominican Convent 175 Route 340 Sparkill NY 10976-1041

MYERS, ALFRED FRANTZ, retired state education official, educator; b. Crooked Creek State Park, Pa., Feb. 19, 1936; s. Jacob Alfred Jr. and Ida Gertrude (Schaeffer) M. BA, Lehigh U., 1958, MA, 1966; postgrad., George Peabody Coll., 1971-72. Instr. Grand River Acad., Austinburg, Ohio, 1966, Culver (Ind.) Mil. Acad., 1966-68, Kiskiminetas Springs Sch., Saltsburg, Pa., 1968-71; asst. prof. social studies Ind. State U., Terre Haute, 1972-73; divsn. trainer Ency. Britannica, Rochester, N.Y., 1973-75; mgr. Rupp's, Kittanning, Pa., 1976-77; criminal justice sys. planner Pa. Commn. on Crime and Delinquency, Harrisburg, 1977-80; rsch. assoc. Pa. Dept. Edn., Harrisburg, 1980-89, basic edn. assoc., 1989-98; assoc. EdVise, Harrisburg, 1998-2001; ret. Vol. tchr. Global Vols., Xi'an, China, 1999. Social work Dominican Rep., 1958. Served to 1st lt. USAF, 1958-63, capt. USAFR, 1963-71. Mem.: ACLU, Pa. Fedn. Tchrs., Pa. Coun. for Social Studies, Pa. Assn. Adult Continuing Edn., Nat. Coun. Social Studies, Mid. States Coun. for Social Studies (pres. 1987—88), Gay Lesbian and Straight Edn. Network, Conf. Latin Americanist Geographers, Am. Hist. Assn., Am. Fedn. Tchrs., Am. Acad. Polit. and Social Sci., Acad. Polit. Sci., People for Am. Way., Nat. Braille Assn., Orgn. Am. Historians, Pa. Hist. Assn., Phi Beta Kappa, Phi Delta Kappa. Home: 849 Melissa Ct Enola PA 17025-1551

MYERS, ALLEN RICHARD, rheumatologist; b. Balt., Jan. 14, 1935; s. Ellis Benjamin and Rosina (Blumberg) M.; m. Ellen Patz, Nov. 26, 1960; children: David Joseph, Robert Todd, Scott Patz. BA, U. Pa., 1956; MD, U. Md., 1960. Diplomate Am. Bd. Internal Medicine, Am. Bd. Rheumatology. Intern Univ. Hosp., Balt., 1960-61, resident in medicine Ann Arbor, Mich., 1961-64; fellow in rheumatology Mass. Gen. Hosp. and Harvard Med. Sch., Boston, 1966-69; dir. clin. tng. rheumatology U. Pa. Sch. Medicine, Phila., 1969-72, chief rheumatology sect., 1972-78; dep. chair medicine Temple U. Sch. Medicine, Phila., 1978-84, acting chmn. medicine, 1984-86, dean, 1991-95, prof. medicine, 1978—, assoc. v.p. Health Scis. Ctr., 1988-95. Vis. prof. Cardiothoracic Inst., U. London, 1988; mem. med. adv. bd. Scleroderma Rsch. Found., Santa Barbara, Calif., 1986. Mem. editl. bd. Arthritis & Rheumatism, 1985—90, Brit. Jour. Rheumatology, 1989—94; editor: Systemic Sclerosis, 1985, Medicine, 1986, 1993, 1996, 2000. Pres. Phila. Health Care Congress, 1994—; adv. com. Pa. Lupus Found., 1976—; bd. dirs. Phila. Conv. and Visitors Bur., 1994—. With USPHS, 1964-66. Recipient Margaret Whitaker prize U. Md. Sch. Medicine, 1960, Lindback Found. award Temple, 1981; named Physician of Yr. Temple U. Hosp., 1986. Master: Am. Coll. Rheumatology; fellow: ACP, Phila. Coll. Physicians (pres. 2000); mem.: Am. Fedn. Clin. Rsch. Avocations: walking, classical music, reading. Office: Temple U Sch Medicine 3400 N Broad St Philadelphia PA 19140-5104

MYERS, BETTY J. retired elementary music specialist; b. Kansas City, Mo., Feb. 24, 1935; d. Marion O. and Jennie Lillian (Dickinson) Williams; m. Alfred M. Myers, June 6, 1958; children: Sherylyn, Douglas, Carol. BS in Edn., Cen. Mo. State U., 1956; MS in Edn. Adminstrn., CMSU, 1976. Elem. tchr. Kansas City Pub. Schs., 1956—58, elem. classrm. tchr., 1962—80, elem. music tchr., 1980—94; elem. tchr. R5 Schs., Parkville, Mo., 1958—60. Leader adult Sunday sch., 1972- Mem. Am. Bus. Women's Assn. (v.p., sec., treas., chair com. 1980-2000, pres. pres. 1984-85, Woman of Yr. 1985), Internat. Order of King's, Daus. and Sons (pres. city Union 1983-85, v.p. Mo. br. 1987-90, pres. 1998-2002, Internat. Chautaugua dir. 1994-98), Delta Kappa Gamma (pres. 1984-86, pres. Kansas City area coun. 1985-87, pres. chpt. 2002-). Baptist. Avocation: church pianist. Home: 13407 E 51st St Kansas City MO 64133-2631

MYERS, CAROL ANN, elementary education educator; b. El Paso, Jan. 15, 1946; d. Ernest Weldon and Dorris Louise (Webster) Goans; m. Baxter Ellis Myers Jr., Oct. 20, 1973. BS in Edn., U. Tex., El Paso, 1968. Cert. elem. tchr., Tex. Tchr. El Paso Pub. Schs., 1968-76, 78-88; tchr. reading Summerville (S.C.) Ind. Sch. Dist., 1976-78; tchr. Ysleta Ind. Sch. Dist., El

Paso, 1988-95. Facilitator Region XIX Edn. Ctr., El Paso, 1990-92; presenter mini conf. El Paso IRA, 1993, 94. Treas. Trident Amateur Radio Club, Charleston, S.C., 1977-78; sec. West Tex. Repeater Assn., El Paso, 1980; mem. W.T. Cozby Libr. Bd., 1998—, chmn. 1998-2000; bd. dirs. Coppell Women's Club, 1996—, newsletter editor 1996—. Named outstanding tchr., Edgar Park Sch., 1970-71, Hughey Sch., 1986, Friend El Paso Children Assn. for Childhood Edn., 1994; recipient spl. award El Paso County Coun. Internat. Reading Assn., 1995. Mem. NEA, Assn. Childhood Edn. Internat. (pres. El Paso 1985-86), Tex. Assn. Childhood Edn. (sec. coun. 1992-93), Tex. State Reading Assn., Ysleta Tchr. Assn., Tex. State Tchr. Assn., Coppell Women's Club (pres.-elect 2002-03), Back Porch Lit. Gild (pres.-elect 2002-03), Delta Kappa Gamma (newsletter editor 1990-93, 98—, treas. 1994-96). Avocation: amateur radio. Home: 245 Plantation Dr Coppell TX 75019-3212 E-mail: carolann6313@verizon.net.

MYERS, CAROLE ANN, artist, educator; b. Shawnee, Okla., Dec. 28, 1934; d. Daniel and Ardith Irene (Dawkins) Ash; m. Roy William Myers, Mar. 2, 1952 (dec. Feb. 25, 2000); children: Randall Craig, Lisa Danelle. Tchr. watercolor and mixed media/collage workshops, Kanuga Watercolor Workshops, NC, 2000, Palm Beach Watercolor Soc., Fla., 2003. One-woman shows include Hawaii Watercolor Soc., Honolulu, Kapaa, Kaui, Hawaii, 1991, Webster's World, St. Antonin Noble Val, France, 1993, Maine Cost Art workshops, Port Clyde, Maine, 1994, Paint Yosemite Nat. Pk., Calif., 1994, Exp. Water Collage, Albuqureque, N. Mex., 1998, Coupeville Arts Ctr., Coupeville, Wash., 1998, Palm Springs Desert Mus., Palm Springs, Calif., 2000, Sedona Art Ctr., Ariz., 2000, Palm Beach Watercolor Soc., Fla., 2003, Mabee-Gerrer Mus. Art, Shawnee, Okla., 1992, exhibitions include Rocky Mt. Nat. Watermedia, Colo., exhibited in group shows at San Diego Watercolor Soc. Internat., 1983 (Arts n' Frame award, 1987, La Jolla Art Assn. & Poovey Purch award, 1991, Calhoun Gal. award, Nat. Watercolor Soc. 83rd Annual, Airfloat Strongbox award, 2003, many others), exhibitions include Watercolor Soc. 65th, 66th, 71st Ann, Calif., Am. Painters in Paris, France, Watercolor U.S.A. and Travel exhbn., Nat. Acad. Design 159th and 167th Anns., N.Y.C.; contbr. articles to profl. jours. Recipient 112th Exbhn. award, Am. Watercolor Soc., Young-Hunter Meml. award, High Winds Medal award, Nat. Soc. Painters Casein and Acrylic, 26th ann. award, Erlanger Meml. award, 29th ann. De Sola Mendes award, 33d ann. Peterson Meml. award, 40th ann. Kaplan award, N.Y.C., 1st prize, 23rd Internat. Exhbn. Watercolor Art Soc., Houston, 2000, Am. Watercolor Soc. 112th Annual, Young-Hunter Mem. award, Watercolor Art Soc., Houston, 124th Annual High Winds Medal award, Nat. Soc. Painters Casein & Acrylic Annual, N.Y.C., Erlanger Mem. award, de Sola Mendes award, Peterson Mem. award, Kapalan award; grantee Artist -in-Residence, Nat. Edowment for Arts, 1972. Mem.: Nat. Watercolor Soc. (signature mem.), Am. Watercolor Soc.

MYERS, CHARLOTTE WILL, biology educator; b. Harbor Beach, Mich., Jan. 5, 1930; d. Louis John and Ruth (Sageman) Wills; m. John Jay Myers, Dec. 27, 1958; children: Sandra, Andrew, Susan Ruth. BA in Biology, U. Mich., 1951, MS in Edn., 1952. Tchr. biology Birmingham (Mich.) Pub. Schs., 1952-59; tchr. art pvt. practice, Birmingham, 1962-78, Santa Fe, 1979—. Instr. Oakland U., Pontiac, Mich., 1975-77; demonstrator, coord. Internat. Porcelain Art Teaching, Birmingham and Santa Fe, 1972—. V.p. PTA, Birmingham, 1957; founder Future Tchrs., Birmingham, 1956; area chmn. Muscular Dystrophy, Birmingham, 1963-64; leader Girl Scouts Am., Birmingham, 1969-71. Mem. N.Mex. State Fedn. Porcelain Artists (sec. 1986—), Mich. China Painting Tchrs. Orgn. (pres. 1973-77), Rocky Mountain Outdoor Writers and Photographers (bd. dirs. 1995—), N.Mex. Outdoor Writers and Photographers (v.p. 2002-03), Internat. Porcelain Arts Tchrs., Artists Equity (treas. 1981-83), Porcelain Arts Club (pres. 1979-81, treas. 1987-89). Democrat. Presbyterian. Avocations: gardening, needlework, travel. Home and Office: 9 Cibola Cir Santa Fe NM 87505-9006

MYERS, DAVID ALAN, middle school music educator; b. Burlington, Vt., Apr. 24, 1956; s. Alan R. and Joanne F. (Beauchemin) M.; m. Shelle O'Lena, July 10, 1982; children: Lauren R., Carly E. BS in Music Edn., U. Vt., Burlington, 1978, MEd, 1992. Cert. tchr. music K-12, Vt. Counselor, instr. U. Vt. Summer Music Session, Burlington, 1975-81; music instr. band, chorus, gen. music Hazen Union Sch. Jr.-Sr. H.S., Hardwick, Vt., 1978-82; instr., condr., counselor Friends of Music Day Camp, Burlington, 1984-92; dir. instrumental music Shelburne (Vt.) Mid. Sch., 1982—; bandmaster, condr., percussionist, arranger 40th Army Band, Colchester, Vt., 1981—. Guest condr. music festivals, New Eng., 1980—. Composer: (band music) Windridge, 1988, La Menagerie des Jouets, 1991, Spartacus, 1995, For Praise and Honor, 1995, A Seafaring Rhapsody, 1995, Green Mountain Tapestry, 1995, Prelude and March Humoresque, 1996, When the Stars Begin to Fall, 1997, Changing of the Guard, 1997, With Silent Eyes, They Look to the Sea, 1998, Danza Barbarica, 1999, Satin and Brass, 1999, A Pastoral Suite, 2000, Battered Brass Blues, 2000, Snow Country, 2001, Regalia, 2001, Variations on a Boboobo Song, 2002, Bagatelle for Flutes, 2003, Saxcapade, 2003, Mansfield Fantasy, 2003; contbr. chpt. to books, article to profl. jours.; freelance composer and arranger, 1984—. Founder, dir. Shelburne (Vt.) Cmty. Band, 1990-93; coach Georgia (Vt.) Youth Soccer, 1992-95; choir dir. Ascension Ch., Georgia, Vt., 1994-99. Decorated Meritorious Svc. medal, Army Commendation medal, Army Achievement medal; recipient Gov.'s commendation for excellence in arts and cmty. svc. State of Vt., 1991; named Tchr. of Yr. Shelburne PTO, 1985-86. Mem. ASCAP, U.S. Army Warrant Officer Assn., Vt. Music Educators Assn., Am. Legion, Assn. for Concert Bands. Avocations: gardening, carpentry, bowling, running, music performance. Office: Shelburne Cmty Sch Harbor Rd Shelburne VT 05482 E-mail: Dmyers@scsvt.org.

MYERS, DEBRA TAYLOR, elementary school educator, writer; b. Balt., Feb. 5, 1953; d. James Zachary and Gene Elizabeth (Blubaugh) Taylor; m. Kenneth Lee Myers Jr., June 18, 1977; children: Kenneth Andrew, Katherine Elizabeth. BS in Elem. Edn., Towson State U., 1975, MEd, 1983. Cert. tchr., Md. 5th grade tchr. N.W. Mid. Sch., Taneytown, Md., 1975-80; home and hosp. sch. tchr. Balt. County Schs., 1992-93; tchr. educator in elem. edn. dept. Towson (Md.) State U., 1993—94; 2d grade tchr. Balt. County Pub. Schs., 1994—, mentor/trainer, gifted and talented resource tchr.; tchr. educator in elem. edn. dept. Towson (Md.) State U., 2003. Workshop leader, guest lectr. Harford (Md.) County Schs., Balt. County Schs., United Meth. Commn. on the Young Child, Balt.; primary talent devel. cadre mem., workshop dir., spkr. Contbr. articles to children's mags. and jours. Mem. Renew, A Randallstown Cmty. Group Assn., Balt., 1993—; bd. dirs. Child Devel. Ctr., Milford Mill United Meth. Ch., 1992—; coord. Jr. Fieldstone Garden Club. Recipient Outstanding Vol. award Balt. County PTA, 1992, 93, 94; named N.W. Area Educator of Yr., 1999. Mem. Kappa Delta Pi. Avocations: travel, reading, writing for children, volunteering, spending time with family. Home: 3607 Blackstone Rd Randallstown MD 21133-4213 Office: Office of Gifted and Talented Edn and Magnet Programs 6019 Charles St Towson MD 21204

MYERS, DONALD ALLEN, university dean; b. Nebraska City, Nebr., Dec. 17, 1932; s. Merle D. and Ruth Irene (Potter) M.; m. Dixie Lois Ashton, Aug. 10, 1957; 1 son, Eric; m. Lilian Rose Bautista, Apr. 18, 1966; children: Sherri, Johnny, David; m. Alice L. Twining, July 15. 1990; 1 child, Aaron. BA, Mcpl. U. Omaha, 1956; MA, U. Chgo., 1957, PhD, 1962. Asst. supt. Sch. Dist. Riverview Gardens, Mo., 1962-65; research assoc. NEA, Washington, 1965-66; curriculum and research specialist Inst. for Devel. of Ednl. Activities, Los Angeles, 1966-70; assoc. prof. SUNY, Albany, 1970-73; head dept. curriculum and instrn. Olka. State U., Stillwater, 1973-79; dean Coll. Edn., U. Nebr., Omaha, 1979-85; dean Sch. Edn. Old Dominion U., Norfolk, Va., 1985—. Author: Teacher Power, 1973, Open Education Reexamined, 1973; contbr. articles, chpts. to profl. jours., books. Washington intern in edn. Ford Found., 1965-66 Democrat. Home: 1272 Belvoir Ln Virginia Beach VA 23464-6746 Office: Coll Edn Old Dominion Univ Norfolk VA 23508-1506

MYERS, ELLEN HOWELL, historian, educator; b. Bryan, Tex., Feb. 16, 1941; d. Douglas Wister and Ann Olive (Emery) Howell; m. William Allen Myers, Dec. 23, 1967; 1 child, William Webb. Student, Mt. Vernon Jr. Coll., 1959—61, U. Madrid, 1961—62; BA, Sophie Newcomb Coll. of Tulane U., 1963; MA, U. Va., 1965, PhD, 1970. Lectr. U. Houston, 1966—67; instr. Okla. State U., Stillwater, 1967—70; asst. prof. San Antonio Coll., 1970—73, assoc. prof., 1973—77, prof. history, 1977—. Author: (student's rev. manuals, instrs. manuals) The American Nation, 1975, 1977, 1979, 1983, 1987, Test Bank for the West Transformed, 2000; contbr. articles to profl. jours. Mem. S.W. Conf. Commn. on Higher Edn. and Campus Ministry Meth. Ch., 1978—81; bd. dirs. Family Svc. Assn., 1978—85, pres., 1983—84; bd. dirs. San Antonio Area Red Cross, 1979—85, Laurel Heights Weekday Sch., 1980—83, chmn., 1982—83. Mem.: AAUP (exec. com. San Antonio Coll. 1973—74), Conf. on L.Am. History, S.W. Conf. on L.Am. Studies (exec. com. 1974—75), Tex. C.C. Tchrs. Assn., Tues. Musical Club, Jr. League of San Antonio (bd. dirs. 1977—79), Kappa Alpha Theta, Phi Alpha Theta. Democrat. Methodist. Home: 307 Arcadia Pl San Antonio TX 78209-5950 Office: 1300 San Pedro Ave San Antonio TX 78212-4201

MYERS, GERALDINE RUTH, special education educator, consultant; b. Massillon, Ohio, Apr. 22, 1924; d. Clinton Alvin and Edna Frances (Piper) Koontz; m. Ralph Richards; children: Beth (Richards) Herthel, Robyn; m. Gerald Thomas Myers. BA, Heidelberg Coll., 1946; MA, Wayne State U., 1962. Tchr. South Rockwood (Mich.) High Sch., 1946-48; secondary sch. tchr. Riverview (Mich.) Community Schs., 1953-59, secondary counselor, 1959-63; social worker Washoe County Welfare Dept., Reno, 1963-64; tchr. Washoe County Sch. Dist., Reno, 1964-66, s.e. transitional counselor, 1966-90; ednl. cons., 1990—. Summer relief case worker Washoe County Welfare Dept., 1964-66; guest lectr. U. Nev., Reno, 1967-75, supr. student tchrs., 1990—; lectr. Truckee Meadows C.C., Reno, 1979-88. Editor: (newsletter sch. dist. s.e.) Of Special Note, 1969-90. Mem. Nev. Gov.'s Com. on Employment of Handicapped, 1990. Nev. winner for School-Work Experience Program, Nat. Sch. Adminstrs., 1989; inducted in Lake Hall of Fame, Hartville, Ohio, 1996. Mem. Coun. for Exceptional Children (pres. 1986-87, newsletter editor 1983-89, Frank South award 1987), Washoe County Tchrs. Assn. (disting. svc. award 1977), Phi Delta Kappa (educator of yr. 1984). Republican. Home: 12160 Georgian Cir Reno NV 89511-9211

MYERS, GLORIA JEAN, elementary education educator; b. Atlantic, Iowa, Feb. 14, 1949; d. Louis E. Sr. and Jean M. (Horacek) M. BA in Elem. Edn., U. No. Iowa, 1971, MA in Spl. Edn., 1978. Cert. tchr., K-14 endorsements in behavioral disorders and mental disabilities, Iowa. Title I remedial reading tchr. Council Bluffs (Iowa) Pub. Schs., 1971-75; K-12 multicategorical resource tchr. Walnut (Iowa) Community Sch., 1975—. Mem. planning com. for annual transition fair for S.W. Iowa, Pottawattamie County, 1987-2002. Recipient Outstanding Achievement award Loess Hills Area Edn. Agy., 1989, Excellence in Edn. award, 1992, named Profl. Person of the Yr., 1997, Outstanding Tchr., Optimists, 1998. Mem. NEA, Iowa Edn. Assn. (local chpt. pres., v.p., sec., treas.), Walnut Edn. Assn. (pres. local chpt., co-chmn.), Delta Kappa Gamma Soc. Internat. (sec.). Home: PO Box 301 Walnut IA 51577-0301 Office: PO Box 528 Walnut IA 51577-0528

MYERS, HAROLD MATHEWS, academic administrator; b. Doylestown, Pa., Apr. 13, 1915; s. Carl and Alice W. Myers; m. Margaret F. Smith, July 19, 1946 (dec. Sept. 1963); children: Donald Smith, Dean Chappell, Deborah Kay; m. L. Marjorie Bellau, Nov. 28, 1964. BS in Commerce, Drexel Inst. Tech., 1938, DSc in Commerce (hon.), 1983; postgrad., Temple U., 1940-41, U. Omaha, summer 1957. Instr. coop. edn., dir. grad. placement Drexel U., Phila., 1938-46, asst. dean men, dir. student bldgs., adj. instr. labor econs., 1946-52, dean of men, 1952-55, treas., 1955-57, v.p., treas., 1957-80, sr. v.p., 1980-82, sr. v.p. emeritus, 1982-87, interim pres., 1987-88, pres. emeritus, 1988—, life trustee, 1986—. Regional dir. First Pa. Banking and Trust Co., 1959-76; dir. Sadtler Rsch. Labs., Inc., 1963-69, Almo Indsl. Elecs., Inc., 1966-68; dir., treas. Uni-Coll Corp., 1974-81; bd. dirs. Beulah Cemetary Assn., asst. treas., 1984-89, treas., 1989-90, v.p. and treas., 1980—; bd. dirs., mem. exec. com. Univ. City Sci. Ctr., 1974-90, dir. emeritus, 1991—, chmn. fin. com., 1976-88, vice chmn., 1988-90. Contbr. articles to profl. jours. Bd. dirs. Internat. House of Phila. Inc., 1954-81, exec. com., 1972-81; active Phila. coun. Boy Scouts Am., 1953—, hon. chmn., 1985-97, pres., 1982-83; citizens fire prevention com. Phila. Fire Dept., 1970-86; bd. dirs. United Fund Greater Phila., 1983-87, Luth. Ch. of Am. Common Investing Fund, 1976-82, NCCJ, Inc., Phila. and South Jersey region NCCJ, 1959-65; dir. Phila. Coun. of Chs., 1954-61, pres. jr. coun., 1950-51; bd. dirs., pres. Ea. Assn. Coll. and Univ. Bus. Officers, 1967-68; pres. Nat. Assn. Coll. and Univ. Bus. Officers, 1971-72; treas. Lambda Chi Alpha Found., 1970-84, dir. emeritus, 1984—; pres. Broadmoor Pines Home Owners Assn., 1993-94; dir. PalmAire Cmty., Inc., 1993-95, chmn. security com., 1995—. Comdr. USNR, ret. Recipient Silver Beaver award Boy Scouts Am., 1963, Mary M. Hart award Phila. coun. Boy Scouts Am., 1986, Drexel Alumni Varsity Club award, 1966, Drexel U. Evening Coll. Alumni Assn. award, 1973, Drexel U. Anthony J. Drexel Paul award, 1988, Dept. of Army Cert. of Appreciation for Patriotic Civilian Svc., 1979, Disting. Bus. Officer award Nat. Assn. Coll. and Bus. Officers, 1989, Disting. Svc. in Trusteeship award Assn. Governing Bd. Univs. and Colls., 1989; named Educator of Yr., Phila. coun. Boy Scouts Am., 1989; named to Legion of Honor, Chapel of Four Chaplins; Drexel U. student dormitory named Myers Hall in his honor, 1984; 1 of 100 alumni honored Centennial of Drexel U., 1992. Mem. AARP, Am. Legion (life), Mil. Order World Wars (perpetual, comdr. Phila. chpt. 1958-59), Ret. Officers Assn. (life), Swedish Colonial Soc. Phila. (sec. 1968), Welsh Soc. Phila. (life), Internat. Frat. Lambda Chi Alpha (pres. 1966-70), Vet. Corps 1st Regiment Infantry, N.G.P. (hon.), Penn Club, Union League Phila. (pres. 1980-81), Sarasota Yacht Club, Masons, Rotary (Paul Harris fellow), Gulf Coast Corvair Club.

MYERS, HELEN PRISCILLA, music educator; b. Palo Alto, Calif., June 5, 1946; d. Henry Alonzo Myers and Elsie (Phillips) Myers-Stainton; children: Ian Alister Woolford, Adam Robert Woolford, Sean Patrick Woolford. MusB, Ithaca Coll., 1967; M in Mus. Edn., Syracuse U., 1971; MA, Ohio State U., 1975; PhD, U. Edinburgh, Scotland, 1984; MPhil, Columbia U., 1993. Cert. instrumental mus. K-12, N.Y. Clarinettist Am. Wind Symphony Orch., Pitts., 1966-67; rsch. fellow Columbia U., N.Y.C., 1973-75, lectr., 1975-76; lectr. Goldsmiths' Coll. U. London, 1981-89; assoc. prof. Trinity Coll., Hartford, Conn., 1989—, St. Anthony Hall prof., 1994—. Ford Found. lectr. ethnomusicology Nat. Ctr. Performing Arts, Bombay, India, 1988; vis. assoc. prof. music Columbia U., N.Y.C., 1993; ethnomusicologist cons. Oxford U. Press, London, 1981-83, The New Grove Dictionary of Music, 7th edit., London, 1993—; resident ethnomusicologist Grove's Dictionaries of Music and Musicians, 1976-89; guest lectr. Guildhall Sch. of Music, London, 1982-89. Author: Felicity, Trinidad: Musical Portrait of a Hindu Village, 1984, (with Bruno Nettl) Folk Music in the United States: An Introduction, 1976; author introductions to facsimile reprints of Alice Cunningham Fletcher's Omaha Indian Music, 1994, Indian Games and Dances, 1994, Native Songs, 1994, others; editor, contbr.: Ethnomusicology: An Introduction, 1992, Ethnomusicology: Historical and Regional Studies, 1993; gen. editor, contbr. South Asia Vol. VI, The Garland Ency. of World Music. Grantee Am. Inst. Indian Studies, 1986-87, 88-89, Brit. Acad., 1988-89, Ford Found., 1988, Am. Philosophical Soc., 1989-90, Wenner-Gren Found. for Anthropological Rsch., 1989-90. Mem. Am. Anthropol. Assn., Am. Musciological Soc., Soc. Ethnomusicology (coun. mem. 1992—), Assn. Asian Studies, Internat. Coun. Traditional Music, Indian Musicological Soc., Sangeet Natak Akademi, Earthwatch, English Folk Dance and Song Soc. (editorial bd. Folk Music Jour.), Phi Kappa Lambda. Home: 207 Old Main St Rocky Hill CT 06067-1505 also: Grove Dictionaries Macmillan Press 4 Little Essex St London WC2R 3LF England

MYERS, JACK FREDRICK, artist, educator, author; b. Lima, Ohio, Feb. 17, 1927; s. Harold Frank and Lesta Arvilla (Ross) M.; m. Frances Dydek, Apr. 30, 1949; children: Steven Ross, David Gene, Kevin Douglas. Student, Cleve. Inst. Art, 1947-49; MFA, Kent State U., 1980. Staff artist Bill Ripley & Assocs., Cleve., 1951-57; art dir. Premier Indsl. Corp., Cleve., 1957-70; instr. Cooper Sch. Art, Cleve., 1970-80; assoc. prof. art U. Dayton, Ohio, 1982-87; ret., 1992. Author: The Language of Visual Art, 1989, Windy Side of Care, 2002, The Greatest Gift, 2002. With USNR, 1945-46, PTO. Recipient First prize in art Newsweek/Paillard S.A., 1969. Home and Office: 22269 Country Meadows Ln Strongsville OH 44149-2000

MYERS, KENNETH L(EROY), secondary education educator; b. Auburn, Nebr., Oct. 5, 1954; s. Kenneth E. and Erma F. (Hardwick) M.; m. Willo Kay Dykstra, July 1, 1995; children: Kendra, Kayla. BS in Edn., Peru State Coll., 1985, mid. sch. endorsement, 1990, MS in Edn., 1992. Cert. tchr., Nebr., Mo., Iowa. Tchr. math., coach Nodaway-Holt High Sch., Graham, Mo., 1985-87, Nebraska City (Nebr.) Lourdes High Sch., 1987-89; tchr. math., social studies, coach Newcastle (Nebr.) High Sch., 1989-97; tchr. math., coach Schaller/Crestland H.S., Early, Iowa, 1997—. Chair Newcastle Math. Curriculum Team, 1991-97; master tchr. N.E. Nebr. Masters Tchrs. Project, 1991-97; past mem. N.E. Nebr. Math. Cadre; mem. Nebr. State Coll. Evaluation Visitation Team, 1984; 1st cohort Iowa Prins. Leadership Acad.; adj. faculty math. Iowa Ctrl. C.C., 2002—. Mem. Early Iowa City Coun., 2001—. Mem. Iowa Coaches Assn., Newcastle Faculty Orgn. (pres. 1992-95), 1st Cohort Iowa Prin. Leadership Acad. Achievements include development of reverse FOIL method of factoring using grid structure. Office: Schaller Crestland HS Early IA 50535 E-mail: kenwillo@frontiernet.net.

MYERS, LEE EDWARD, elementary education educator; b. Wabash, Ind., Jan. 1, 1948; s. Herman Francis and Joanna Emmaline (Flant) M.; m. Sandra Kay Brown, June 26, 1976; children: Robin Michael, Mandy Mae. BS, Taylor U., 1970; MS, Ind. U., 1972; student, W.Va. U., 1981-82; PhD, Somerset U., 1991. Cert. tchr., Ohio. Teaching asst. Ind. U., Bloomington, 1971-72; tchr. elem. phys. edn. Marion City Schs., 1972—, coach, 1973-90; coaching asst. W.Va. U., Morgantown, 1981-82; coach Ohio State U., Marion, 1983-88. Contbr. articles to profl. jours. Pres. Keith Davis Meml. Fund, Marion, 1978—; rep. Ohio State Track and Cross Country Coaches, Ohio, 1980-86. Recipient Marion Civitan award, 1981; track scholar Taylor U., 1967. Mem. AAHPERD, Ohio Assn. Health, Phys. Edn., Recreation and Dance, Nat. Assn. Sport and Phys. Edn., Nat. Track and Field Assn., Nat. Assn. for Women in Sports, Marion Run for Fun Club (coach 1972—, pres. 1972—). Avocations: running, race walking, motorcycling, reading, traveling.

MYERS, LINDA SHAFER, secondary educator; b. Lebanon, Tenn., Apr. 12, 1943; d. Odie and Nellie Irene Shafer; m. C. Bruce Myers (div.); children: James B., Joseph C. BA, Berea Coll., 1965; MA, Austin Peay State U., 1972, postgrad., 1993. Cert. tchr., Tenn. English tchr. Montgomery County Schs., Clarksville, Tenn., 1985—; chair dept. English Clarksville H.S., 2001—. Mem. Nat. Tenn. Edn. Assn., Nat. Tenn. Coun. of Tchrs. of English, Delta Kappa Gamma Soc. Internat. Avocation: genealogy. Office: Clarksville H S 151 Richview Rd Clarksville TN 37043-4723

MYERS, MARILYN CONN, elementary education educator; b. Hannibal, Mo., Apr. 6, 1936; d. Terrell Aleshire and Catherine Marie (White) Conn; m. Earl D. Myers, Sept. 1, 1956 (wid.); children: Teresa, Toni, Traci. AA, Hannibal LaGrange Coll., 1956; BS, Quincy Coll., 1971; MA, N.E. Mo. State U., 1978. Classroom tchr. Quincy (Ill.) Dist. 172, 1971-90, Reading Recovery tchr. leader, 1990—. Adv. bd. Weekly Reader, 1989—91; adj. prof. U. Ill., 1991—96, Nat. Louis U., 1997—98, Ill. State U., 1998—. Mem. exec. bd. United Way. Recipient Literacy award Quincy Svc. League, 1992; recognized for svc. Quincy Found. for Quality Edn. Mem. N.Am. Coun. Reading Recovery, Miss. Valley Reading Coun. (pres. 1974-75 Literacy award 1989), ASCD, Nat. Assn. Edn. Young Children, Assn. Childhood Edn. Internat., Internat. Reading Assn., Phi Delta Kappa, Delta Gamma (pres. 1990-92, Beta chpt. pres. 2002—, state com. chair 1996-98). Avocations: walking, reading, travel. Home: 11 Spruce Ct Bloomington IL 61704-2782 Office: Ill State U DeGarmo Hall Normal IL 61761 E-mail: mcmyers1@aol.com.

MYERS, MARJORIE LORA, elementary school principal; b. Waco, Tex., Jan. 12, 1950; d. Duncan Clark and Dorothy (Love) M.; m. Larry Lee Brannon, Dec. 19, 1975 (div. 1979). BA in Edn. and Spanish, U. Fla., 1972; MA in Bilingual and Multicultural Edn., George Mason U., 1985; postgrad., Georgetown U., 1986-88, George Washington U., 1999—. Cert. bilingual tchr., pub. sch. adminstrn., D.C., Va. Lead ESL tchr. Rock Springs Multicultural Adult Edn. Ctr., Atlanta, 1977-81; composite K-12 tchr., adminstr. Bechtel Corp., Andes Mountains, Uribante-Caparo, Venezuela, 1981-83; rsch. asst. NSF, Washington, 1983-84; bilingual and ESL tchr. Lincoln Jr. H.S., Washington, 1984-88; bilingual counselor Deal Jr. H.S., Washington, 1988-89; Leadership in Ednl. Adminstrn. Devel. participant Francis Jr. H.S., Washington, 1989-90; coord. programs and instrn. lang. minority affairs D.C. Pub. Schs., Washington, 1990-93; asst. prin. Cardozo Sr. H.S., Washington, 1993-94; prin. H.D. Cooke Elem. Sch., Washington, 1994-95; prin. Escuela Key a Two-Way Spanish Immersion Sch. Arlington (Va.) Pub. Schs., 1995—. Mem. adv. bd. Ctr. for Immigration Policy & Refugee Assistance, Georgetown U., Washington, 1986-88; adj. prof. George Washington U., 1991, George Mason U., 1992-94, Marymount U., summer 1995. Mem. ASCD, TESOL, NABE. Independent. Episcopalian. Avocations: tennis, hunting, biking, horseback riding, skiing, racketball, swimming. Home: 1840 California St NW Apt 13A Washington DC 20009-1873 Office: Francis Scott Key Two-Way Spanish Immersion Elem Sch 2300 Key Blvd Arlington VA 22201-3415 E-mail: mlmyers@arlington.k12.va.us.

MYERS, MICHELE TOLELA, academic administrator; b. Rabat, Morocco, Sept. 25, 1941; arrived in U.S., 1964; d. Albert and Lillie (Abecassis) Tolela; m. Pierre Vajda, Sept. 12, 1962 (div. Jan. 1965); m. Gail E. Myers, Dec. 20, 1968 (div. Oct. 2003); children: Erika, David. Diploma, Inst. Polit. Studies, U. Paris, 1962; MA, U. Denver, 1966, PhD, 1967; MA, Trinity U., 1977; LHD, Wittenberg U., 1994, Denison U., 1998, U. Denver, 1999. Asst. prof. speech Manchester Coll., North Manchester, Ind., 1967—68; asst. prof. speech and sociology Monticello Coll., Godfrey, Ill., 1968—71; asst. prof. communication Trinity U., San Antonio, 1975—80, assoc. prof., 1980—86, asst. v.p. for acad. affairs, 1982—85, assoc. v.p., 1985—86; assoc. prof. sociology, dean Undergrad. Coll. Bryn Mawr Coll., Pa., 1986—89; pres. Denison U., Granville, Ohio, 1989—98, Sarah Lawrence Coll., Bronxville, NY, 1998—. Comm. analyst Psychology and Commn., San Antonio, 1974—83; bd. dirs. Sherman Fairchild Found., 1992—; mem. Fed. Res. Bank Cleve., 1995—98; pres.'s commn. Nat. Collegiate Athletic Assn., 1993—97, JSTOR, 1999—. Co-author (with Gail Myers): The Dynamics of Human Communication, 1973, The Dynamics of Human Communication, 6th and internat. edits., 1992, The Dynamics of Human Communication, French transl., 1984, Communicating When We Speak, 1975, Communicating When We Speak, 2d edit., 1978, Communication for the Urban Professional, 1977, Managing by Communicaton: An Organizational Approach, 1982, Managing by Communicaton: An Organizational Approach, Spanish transl., 1983, Managing by Communicaton: An Organizational Approach, internat. edit., 1982. Trustee Phila. Child Guidance Clinic, 1988—89; trustee assoc. The Bryn Mawr Sch., Balt., 1987—89;

v.p., bd. dirs. San Antonio Cmty. Guidance Ctr., 1979—83. Fellow in acad. adminstrn., Am. Coun. Edn., 1981—82, Columbus fellow, Bank One, 1990—94. Mem.: Am. Coun. Edn. (commn. on women in higher edn. 1990—92, bd. dirs. 1993—99, chmn. 1997—98). Home: 935 Kimball Ave Bronxville NY 10708-5507 Office: Sarah Lawrence Coll One Mead Way Bronxville NY 10708 E-mail: mmyers@sarahlawrence.edu.

MYERS, MILES ALVIN, educator, educational association administrator; b. Newton, Kans., Feb. 4, 1931; s. Alvin F. and Katheryn P. (Miles) M.; m. Celeste Myers; children: Royce, Brant, Roslyn. BA in Rhetoric, U. Calif., Berkeley, 1953, MAT in English, 1979, MA in English, PhD in Lang. and Literacy, U. Calif., Berkeley, 1982. Cert. secondary tchr. English. Tchr. English Washington Union High Sch., Fremont, Calif., 1957-59, Oakland (Calif.) High Sch., 1959-67, 69-74, Concord High Sch., Mt. Diablo, Calif., 1967-69; chmn. bd. dirs. Alpha Plus Corp. Preschs., Piedmont, Calif., 1968—; dir. All City High, 1973-74; tchr. English Castlemont High Sch., Oakland, 1974-75; mem. faculty U. Calif., Berkeley, 1975-85; adminstrv. dir. Bay Area writing project Sch. Edn. U. Calif., Berkeley, 1976-85; adminstrv. dir. nat. writing project Sch. Edn. U. Calif., Berkeley, 1979-85; pres., CEO Calif. Fedn. Tchrs., 1985-90; exec. dir. Nat. Coun. Tchrs. of English, Urbana, Ill., 1990-97, Edschool.com of Edvantage/Riverdeep, 1999—2001, Calif. Subject Matter Projects, U. Calif., 1997—98; dir. Inst. Rsch. on Learning and Tchg., Berkeley, Calif., 2001—; bd. dirs. Bay Area Sch. Reform Collabortive, 2000—. Co-dir. Nat. Standards Project for English Language Arts, 1992-96; adj. prof. English U. Ill., Champaign-Urbana, 1991-94; vis. lectr. at numerous colleges and Univs.; rschr. in field. Author: The Meaning of Literature, 1973; co-author: Writing: Unit Lessons in Composition, Book III, 1965, The English Book-Composition Skills, 1980; author: A Procedure for Holistic Scoring, 1980, Changing our Minds, 1996; co-author: Exemplars of Standards for English Language Arts, 3 vols., 1997, Asilomar Testing Report, 2001; editor Calif. Tchr., 1966-81; contbr. articles to profl. jours.; pub. monographs. Sgt. U.S. Army, 1953—55. Recipient cert. of Merit, Ctrl. Calif. Coun. Tchrs. of English, 1969, Commendation award Oakland Fedn. Tchrs., 1970, First Place award Internat. Labor Assn., 1971, Disting. Svc. award Calif. Coun. Classified Employees, 1991, Svc. award Nat. Writing Project, 1996. Fellow Nat. Conf. Rsch. in English; mem. Nat. Coun. Tchrs. of English, Nat. Conf. on Rsch. in English, Am. Fedn. of Tchrs. (legis. dir. Calif. Fedn. of Tchrs. 1971-72, Union Tchr. Press awards 1969-75, 86-89, 91, Ben Rust award Calif. Fedn. of Tchrs. 1994), Am. Edn. Rsch. Assn., Calif. Assn. Tchrs. of English (Disting. Svc. award 86), U. Calif./Berkeley Alumni Assn. Home: 5823 Scarborough Dr Oakland CA 94611-2721 Office: Dir Inst Rsch on Learning & Tchg Berkeley CA 94704 Fax: 510-531-1734. E-mail: milesmye@pacbell.net.

MYERS, RAYMOND A. government education administrator; EdD, George Washington U., 1975; M, Rowan U., 1971; BA, Rockhurst Coll. Tchr. Hyogo U. of Tchr. Edn., Yashiro, Japan, 1997; liaison, off. edn. tech. US Dept. Edn. Internat. Edn. Cmty., Wash., DC, 2002—. Contbr. articles various profl. jours. Vol. Peace Corp., Men's Tchr. Tng. Inst., Karnataka State, Dharwar, India, 1966—68. Office: US Dept Edn Internat Edn Cmty 400 Maryland Ave SW Rm FB6-7E220 Washington DC 20202 Office Fax: 202-401-3941.*

MYERS, RICHARD LEE, microbiology and immunology educator; b. Crystal Springs, Miss., July 18, 1939; s. Charles Raymond and Billie Myers; m. Mary Kathleen Feagan, Jan. 3, 1980; children: Barbra Leigh, Ashley Nichole. BS, Delta State U., 1961; MS, Memphis State U., 1965; PhD, Okla. U., 1972. Home: 4406 Congressional Cir Nixa MO 65714-8726 Office: Southwest Mo State U 901 S National Ave Springfield MO 65804-0088

MYERS, ROBERT EUGENE, writer, educator; b. L.A., Jan. 15, 1924; s. Harold Eugene and Margaret (Anawalt) M.; m. Joyce E. Daily, 1946 (div. 1949); 1 child, Kathleen; m. Patricia A. Tazer, Aug. 17, 1956; children: Edward E., Margaret A., Hal R., Karen I. AB, U. Calif., Berkeley, 1955; MA (Crown-Zellerbach fellow), Reed Coll., 1960; EdD, U. Ga., 1968. Employed in phonograph record bus., 1946-54; tchr. elem. sch., 1954-61; rsch. asst. U. Minn., 1961-62; asst. prof. Augsburg Coll., 1962-63, U. Oreg., 1963-66; elem. tchr. Eugene, Oreg., 1966-67; assoc. prof. U. Victoria, 1968-70; assoc. rsch. prof. Oreg. System of Higher Edn., 1970-73; film maker, producer ednl. filmstrips, books, recs., 1973-77; learning resources specialist Oreg. Dept. Edn., Salem, 1977-81; with Linn-Benton Edn. Svc. Dist., Albany, Oreg., 1982-87; ret., 1987. Author: (with E. Paul Torrance) Creative Learning and Teaching (Pi Lambda Theta award 1971), 1970, La Ensenanza Creativa, 1970, Can You Imagine?, 1965, Invitations to Thinking and Doing, 1964, Invitations to Speaking and Writing Creatively, 1965, Plots, Puzzles, and Ploys, 1966, For Those Who Wonder, 1966, Timberwood Tales, Vol. II, 1977, Wondering, 1984, Imagining, 1985, What Next?, 1994, Facing the Issues, 1995, Cognitive Connections, 1996, Mind Sparklers, 1997, Multiple Ways of Thinking with Social Studies, 1997, Character Matters, 1999, A Matter of Respect, 2000, It's Your Attitude That Counts, 2000, Mind Stretchers, 2001, Stories That Build Character, 2001, Think and Write, 2002, Now What, 2002, Spurs to Creative Thinking, 2002, Word Play, 2002, Developing Creative Thinking Skills, 2003; films: Feather (CINE Golden Eagle award), 1972, The Magic Net, 1972, Elephants, 1973. Mem. exec. bd. Nat. Assn. Gifted Children, 1974-77. With U.S. Mcht. Marine, 1944-45. Recipient CINE Golden Eagle award Coun. Internat. Non-theatrical Events, 1973. Mem. Internat. Reading Assn. Democrat. Home: 1357 Meadow Ct Healdsburg CA 95448-3347

MYERS, ROBERT TRUE, educational administrator; b. Wilmington, Del., Nov. 24, 1948; s. Robert True and Harriet Louisa (Beaman) M.; m. Dixie Darlene Honodel, May 22, 1949; 1 child, Bree Heather. BA, Shepherd Coll., 1971; MA in Edn., Pepperdine U., L.A., 1974; MS in Sports Medicine, U.S. Sports Acad., Mobile, Ala., 1986, MS in Sports Mgmt., 1987. Tchr., coach Washington County Bd. Edn., Hagerstown, Md., 1974-79, Martinsburg (W.Va.) H.S., 1979; div. chair health and phys. edn. Hagerstown Jr. coll., 1979-88; sales mgr. Hamilton Nissan, Hagerstown, 1988-90; tchr., coach Frederick County Bd. Edn., Frederick, Md., 1993-94, Washington County Bd. Edn., Hagerstown, 1990-93, asst. prin., 1994-98, prin., 1998—. Cons. TSS, Inc., Hagerstown, 1980—. Mem. exec. com. ARC, Hagerstown, 1983-90; bd. dirs. Hawk Triathlon for Charity, Hagerstown, 1984-91. Capt. USMC, 1971-74. Mem. AAHPERD, Md. Assn. Health, Phys. Edn., Recreation and Dance, (pres., Merit award 1992), Nat. Assn. Secondary Sch. Prins. Avocations: running, cycling, rock climbing, kayaking. Home: 12657 Old Germantown Rd Waynesboro PA 17268-9463 Office: Washington County Bd Edn PO Box 730 Hagerstown MD 21741-0730

MYERS, ROBERTA FRANCES, retired elementary school educator; b. Miller, Mo., May 30, 1945; d. Robert Clayton and Virginia Frances (Kabell) Duvall; BS in Vocat. Home Econs., Southwest Mo. State U., 1967. Cert. tchr., Mo. Tchr. home econs. Hartville (Mo.) Sch., 1967-68; tchr. kindergarten Burnett Elem., Houston, 1968-69, tchr. 2d grade, 1969-71; tchr. 1st grade Fairview Elem., Carthage, Mo., 1972—96, ret., 1996. Mem. Fairview Elem. PTA, 1972—, Fall Festival Assn., Miller Youth Baseball Assn.; sec., treas. Miller Athletic Booster Club, 1985-88; tchr. sunday sch. Gray's Point Christian Ch., Miller, Mo., 1977-83; mem. Round Grove Bap. Ch., 1990—. Mem. Mo. State Tchrs. Assn., Carthage Community Tchrs. Assn. (sec. 1980-83, 88-89). Democrat. Avocations: crocheting, crafts, quilting, mule wagon rides, country living. Home: 415 Tartar Miller MO 65707-9627

MYERS, RUSSELL DAVIS, retired technical school educator; b. Dighton, Mass., Mar. 22, 1938; s. Russell Bruce and Gwendolyn (Davis) M.; m. Anne Weld Lincoln, Jan. 28, 1961; children: Scott, Kimberly, Todd. B. Marine Sci., Maine Maritime Acad., 1958; MEd, Fitchburg Coll., 1993. Registered engr. Draftsman Nactor, Taunton, Mass., 1954-55; plumber Russell B. Myers & Sons and Churchfuel, Taunton, Mass., 1961-78; tech. instr. Bristol Plymouth, Taunton, Mass., 1978-96, ret., 1996. Mem. Raynham (Mass.) Fin. Com., 1978; cooperator Bristol County Savings Bank, Taunton. Lt. USN, 1958-61. Republican. Avocations: boating, fishing, sailing. Home: 106 Leonard St Raynham MA 02767-1127

MYERS, SHELLEY LYNN, elementary education educator; b. Williamsport, Pa., May 11, 1967; d. John Franklin and Sandra Mae (Johnson) M. BS, Shippensburg U., 1989; MEd summa cum laude, Bloomsburg (Pa.) U., 1992; postgrad., Indiana U. Pa., 1993—. Cert. elem. edn. and reading specialist. Tchr. 5th grade Williamsport Sch. Dist., 1990-91, tchr. 1st grade, 1991-93, tchr. kindergarten, 1993—. Instr. reading Pa. Coll. Tech., Williamsport, 1992-93; mem. adv. com. Lang. Arts Com., Williamsport, 1993-94; mem. various sch. coms.; presenter in field. Summer day camp dir. YMCA, Williamsport, 1989. Mem. Internat. Reading Assn., North Ctrl. Reading Coun. (v.p. 1993-94, pres. 1994-95), Keystone State Reading Assn., Delta Kappa Gamma. Methodist. Avocations: reading, travel.

MYERS, VIRGINIA LOU, education educator; b. Indpls., July 18, 1940; d. John Rentschler and Bonnie Mae (Powell) Jones; m. James W. Rose Jr., Aug. 2, 1966 (div. Nov. 1986); m. Byron P. Myers, Sept. 11, 1987. BS in Edn., U. Indpls., 1966; MS in Edn., Butler U., 1971; PhD in Edn. Psychology, U. South Fla., 1991. Cert. elem. tchr., reading specialist and prin., Ind. Tchr. Indpls. Pub. Schs., 1966-72; pvt. tutor Self, Indpls., 1972-74; tchr.'s tchr. Urban/Rural Sch. Devel. Project, Indpls, 1974-77; reading techr. Met. sch. dist. Pike Twp., Indpls., 1977-80; curriculum specialist Met. sch. dist. Washington Twp., Indpls., 1980-82; tchr. chpt. I Noblesville (Ind.) Pub. Schs., 1982-83; instr. social scis. Manatee C.C., Venice, Fla., 1983-87; asst. prof. edn. Mo. So. State Coll., Joplin, 1990-91, East Carolina U., Greenville, N.C., 1992-96; ednl. cons. Cath. Diocese of Venice, Fla., 1996-99; program mgr. child devel. and edn. Manatee Cmty. Coll., 1999—2001; sr. rsch. assoc. Fla. Inst. Edn., 2001—02; indep. early childhood cons., 2002—. Cons. Bertie County Schs., Windsor, NC, 1994—96; program mgr. early childhood and edn. Manatee C.C., 1999—2001, mem. early childhood adv. bd., 1996—2001; lead coach early literacy and learning model project Fla. Inst. Edn., 1990—2001; cons. Early Learning Accelerates Total Edn. Treas. Smart Start Initiative, Greenville, 1993—96; chair Birth Through Kindergarten Higher Edn. Consortium, 1994—96; mem. Fla. C.C. Early Childhood Network, 1999—, Manatee County Early Childhood Trainers Adv. Coun., 2000—, Lakewood Ranch H.S. Child Devel. Lab. Sch. Adv. Bd., 2000—, Sch. Readiness Coalition of Sarasota County, Inc., 2001—, exec. dir., 2002. Mem. ASCD, Nat. Assn. for Edn. Young Children, Orton Dyslexia Soc., Assn. Childhood Edn., Internat., Venice Area C. of C. (edn. com. 2001-02), Phi Theta Kappa (advisor 2000-01). Presbyterian. Avocations: needle work, reading. Home: 334 Woodvale Dr Venice FL 34293-4161 E-mail: drvmyers@comcast.net.

MYERSON, ROBERT J. radiation oncologist, educator; b. Boston, May 12, 1947; s. Richard Louis and Rosemarie M.; m. Carla Wheatley, Aug. 8, 1970; 1 child, Jacob Wheatley. BA, Princeton U., 1969; PhD, U. Calif., Berkeley, 1974; MD, U. Miami, 1980. Diplomate Am. Bd. Radiology. Asst. prof. dept. physics Pa. State U., State Coll., 1974-76; fellow Inst. Advanced Studies, Princeton, N.J., 1976-78; resident U. Pa. Hosp., Phila., 1981-84; assoc. prof. radiology Washington U. Sch. Medicine, St. Louis, 1984-97, prof. radiology, 1997—. Contbr. articles to profl. jours. Recipient Career Devel. award Am. Cancer Soc., 1985. Fellow Am. Coll. Radiology; mem. Am. Coll. Radiation, Am. Soc. Therapeutic Radiologists, Am. Phys. Soc. Democrat. Jewish. Avocation: bicycling. Office: Washington U Radiation Oncology Ctr Box 8224 4921 Parkview Pl Saint Louis MO 63110-1001 E-mail: myerson@radonc.wustl.edu.

MYERSON, ROGER BRUCE, economist, game theorist, educator; b. Boston, Mar. 29, 1951; s. Richard L. and Rosemarie (Farkas) M.; m. Regina M. Weber, Aug. 29, 1982; children: Daniel, Rebecca. AB summa cum laude, SM, Harvard U., 1973, PhD, 1976. Asst. prof. decision scis. Northwestern U., Evanston, Ill., 1976-78, assoc. prof., 1979-82, prof., 1982-2001, Harold Stuart prof. decision scis., 1986-2001, prof. econs., 1987-2001; W.C. Norby prof. econs. U. Chgo., 2001—. Guest researcher U. Bielefeld, Federal Republic of Germany, 1978-79; vis. prof. econs. U. Chgo., 1985-86, 2000-01. Author: Game Theory: Analysis of Conflict, 1991; mem. editorial bd. Internat. Jour. Game Theory, 1982-92, Games and Econ. Behavior, 1988-97; assoc. editor Jour. Econ. Theory, 1983-93; also articles. Guggenheim fellow, 1983-84; Sloan rsch. fellow, 1984-86. Fellow Econometric Soc., Am. Acad. Arts and Scis. (Midwest v.p. 1999-2002). Office: U Chgo Dept Econs 1126 E 59th St Chicago IL 60637

MYNATT, MARVIN DENNIS, utilities company training executive; b. Knoxville, Tenn., Jan. 13, 1951; s. Alvelder (Green) M.; m. Irma Littlejohn, Mar. 5, 1977; children: Stephen Christopher, Jonathan Dennis. AA, U. Tenn., Knoxville, 1970, BA, 1974, MA, 1975, PhD, 1992. Co-op. intern human resource devel. staff TVA, Knoxville, 1972-75, edn. resource planner human resource devel. staff, 1975-76, employment tng. officer div. pers., 1976-77, edn. planner div. edn. and manpower devel., 1977-79, head dept. edn. and skills devel., 1979-89, supr. skills devel. sect., 1988—, mgr. environ. tng., 1993—. Deacon New Mt. Calvary Missionary Bapt. Ch., Knoxville, 1979—, chmn. bd. trustees, 1991—; pres. Chilhowee Elem. Sch. PTA, Knoxville, 1990; adult leader, den leader, cubmaster Knoxville area Boy Scouts Am., 1990—. Mem. ASTD, Am. Vocat. Assn., Nat. Alliance Bus., Nat. Environ. Tng. Assn., Phi Lambda Theta, Kappa Delta Pi, Phi Kappa Phi, Iota Lambda Sigma. Avocations: bible study, civil war books, louis l'amour westerns. Office: TVA Environ Tng 400 E Summit Hill Dr Knoxville TN 37915-1027

MYOUPO, JEAN FRÉDÉRIC, computer science educator, researcher; b. Batoufam, Cameroon, Apr. 22, 1953; arrived in France, 1980; s. Moise Kaptchouang and Pauline Tchomikouang; m. Marie Christine Rauzy, Dec. 8, 1984; children: Debora, Magalie, Benjamin. BSc in Math., U. Yaounde, Cameroun, 1979, MSc in Math., 1980; PhD, U. Toulouse III, France, 1983; Habil, U. Paris XI, 1994. Lectr. U. Sheerbrooke, Que., 1983-85; asst. prof. U. Yaounde, 1985-90; assoc. prof. U. Paris XI, 1990-93, U. Rouen, France, 1993-94; prof. U. Amiens, France, 1994—, dir. grad. studies, 1996—, dean of faculty, 1999—2002. Mem. program com. ISCA, Eng., 1993-94. Contbr. articles to profl. jours. Mem. Human Rights Orgn., Les Ulis, France, 1992—. CNRS rsch. grantee, 1994, 96—. Mem. IEEE Computer Soc., Soc. Indsl. and Applied Math., Assn. for Computing Machinery. Christian. Avocations: jogging, tennis, fishing, reading. Office: U Picardie-Jules Verne Faculty Math-Info 33 Rue St Leu 80039 Amiens France

MYSLINSKI, NORBERT RAYMOND, medical educator; b. Buffalo, Apr. 14, 1947; s. Bernard and Amelia Joan (Lesniak) M.; m. Patricia Ann Byrne, June 19, 1970 (dec. 1980); m. René Carter, Nov. 21, 1993; children: Matthew Ryan, Kelly Lynn. BS in Biology, Canisius Coll., Buffalo, 1965-69; PhD in Pharmacology, U. Ill., Chgo., 1973. Rsch. assoc. Tufts U., Boston, 1973-75; asst. prof. U. Md., Balt., 1975-80, assoc. prof. physiology, 1980—, co-dir. Facial Pain Clinic, 1980-84, instr. nursing, 1982-84; rsch. fellow U. Bristol, Eng., 1984-85; adj. assoc. prof. U. Md. Sch. Nursing, 1997—. Instr. C.C. Balt., 1980—82; dir. grad. program dept. physiology U. Md., 1981—97, dir. h.s. biomed. rsch. program, 2000—, mem. faculty Marine-Estuarine Environ. Scis. grad. program, 1988—97; founder, dir. Patricia Byrne Nursing Scholarship Fund Trocaire Coll., Buffalo, 1985; dir. NIH Minority Rsch. Apprentice Program Balt. Coll. Dental Surgery, 1988—99; mem. grant rev. com. Nat. Inst. Nursing Rsch., 1993—94; grant reviewer Dept. Health and Human Svcs., 1993—94; cons. in field; appeared on more than 20 live TV and radio programs; founder, dir. Internat. Brain Bee, 1999—; chmn. Neuroscience Edn. Workship, Prague, Czech Republic, 2003—; mem. com. Md. Higher Edn. Commn., 2003—. Editor newsletters Med. Soc. Md. Rsch., 1977-82, Brain Storm, 1999—; author book chpts., revs. and numerous abstracts on pharmacology and neurosci.; inventor in field; reviewer 7 jours. Rep. task force on aging U. Md., 1979—84; instr. Am. Heart Assn., Balt., 1978, ARC, Balt., 1977—83; com. mem. Md. Higher Edn. Edn. Commn., 2003—; eucharistic min., pastoral visitor Cath. Ch., 1983—93; bd. dirs. Md. Brain Awareness Week, Md., 1996—, Balt. Brains Rule!, 2002—, Md. Brain Lit. Competition, 2000—, Md. Brain Art Competition, 2000—. Capt. U.S. Army, 1969—77. Grantee NIH, various drug cos. and founds.; USPHS fellow, 1969-73; recipient Alumni of Yr. award St. Mary's H.S., Lancaster, N.Y., 1996, Disting. Alumni award for outstanding career Canisius Coll., Buffalo, 1997, Time to Care Cmty. Svc. award U. Md., 1998, Founders Day Pub. Svc. award U. Md., 2000. Mem.: High Schs. Neurosci. (founder 2003), Am. Soc. Pharmacology and Exptl. Therapeutics, Soc. for Neurosci. (pres. Balt. chpt. 1990—92, editor newsletter 1990—97, neurosci. literacy com. 1997—2001), Am. Physiol. Soc., Internat. Assn. Dental Rsch. (adv. 1980—81), Md. Soc. Med. Rsch. (exec. com. 1978—86, bd. dir. 1978—86), Internat. Brain Rsch. Orgn., European Brain and Behavior Soc. (hon.). Republican. Home: 9395 Carrie Way Ellicott City MD 21042-1701 Office: U Md OCBS Dept 666 W Baltimore St Baltimore MD 21201-1510 Fax: (410) 706-0193. E-mail: nrm001@dental.umaryland.edu.

NA, TSUNG SHUN (TERRY NA), Chinese studies educator, writer; b. Beijing, Nov. 3, 1932; came to U.S., 1964; s. Chi-L and Hui (Hu) N.; m. Yen Yen Chao, 1964. BA, Taiwan Normal U., 1956; MA, U. B.C., 1970; PhD, U. Minn., 1978. Assoc. prof. Taipei Normal Coll., Taiwan, Republic of China, 1956-64; vis. lectr. Ind. U., Bloomington, 1964-66; asst. prof. U. Minn., Mpls., 1970-80; vis. prof. Sun Yat-sen U., Taiwan, 1981-84; prof., dir. Am. Inst. Chinese Studies, Charles Town, W.Va., 1985—. Author: (English books) A Linguistic Study of P'i-pa Chi, 1969, Studies on Dream of the Red Chamber: A Selected and Classified Bibliography, 1979, Supplement, 1981, Taiwan Studies on Dream of the Red Chamber: A Selected and Classified Bibliography, 1983, Chinese Studies in English: A Selected Bibliography, 1991, (Chinese) Mandarin Pronunciation, 1966, Teaching Chinese in the U.S.A., 1983, Studies on Chinese Classical Novels, 1985, A Collection of Short Stories, 1987; contbr. numerous articles, short stories, and research essays to jours. and newspapers in U.S., Taiwan, ROC, and China. Mem. MLA, Assn. Asian Studies. Office: Am Inst Chinese Studies PO Box 453 Charles Town WV 25414-0453

NACHTERGAELE, BRUNO LEO ZULMA, mathematical physics educator, researcher; b. Oudenaarde, Belgium, June 24, 1962; came to U.S., 1991; s. Arthur and Claire (VandenBorre) N.; m. Marijke L. Devos, Oct. 11, 1986; children: Sigrid, Shanti. Lic. in physics, Cath. U. Louvain, Belgium, 1984, PhD in Physics, 1987. Rschr. Cath. U. Louvain, 1984-88, rsch. assoc., 1991, U. Chile, Santiago, 1989-90; instr. physics Princeton (N.J.) U., 1991-93, asst. prof., 1993-96; assoc. prof. math. U. Calif., Davis, 1996-2000, prof. math., 2000—. Contbr. articles to sci. jours. Mem. Am. Phys. Soc., Am. Math. Soc., European Phys. Soc., Internat. Assn. Math. Physicists. Office: U Calif Davis Dept Math 1 Shields Ave Davis CA 95616-5270 E-mail: bxn@math.ucdavis.edu.

NADAS, JULIUS ZOLTAN, data processing educator; b. Ried, Austria, Oct. 1, 1945; came to U.S., 1951; s. Julius Zoltan and Ibolya (Szollosy) N.; m. Erika Marta Vietorisz, Sept. 25, 1971; children: Krisztina, Gyula, Zsolt, Tas. BS, Case Inst. Tech., Cleve., 1966; MA, U. Wis., 1968. Staff cons. Sperry Univac, Chgo., 1968-74; prof. data processing and dept. chair Wilbur Wright Coll., Chgo., 1974—. Grievance chair Cook County Coll. Tchrs. Union, Chgo., 1990; chair Dist.-Wide Faculty Coun. Com. for Distance Learning, 1993-94. Scoutmaster Hungarian Scout Assn. Troop 19, Chgo., 1981-89. Recipient Disting. Svc. Prof. award Bd. Trustees of Chgo. City Colls., 1994. Mem. Math. Assn. Am. Office: Wilbur Wright College 4300 N Narragansett Ave Chicago IL 60634-1591

NADER, SUZANNE NORA BEURER, elementary education educator; b. Detroit, July 6, 1947; d. Victor James and Patricia Kathleen (Perry) Beurer; m. Joseph Samuel Nader, Sept. 12, 1969; 1 child, Joseph Samuel Jr. BA, Eastern Mich. U., 1982, MA, 1990. Cert. elem. tchr., prin., Mich. English tchr. jr. high alternative program Wayne-Westland (Mich.) Sch. Dist., adult basic edn. tchr.; tchr. 5th grade Our Lady of Grace Sch., Dearborn Heights, Mich.; tchr. adult basic edn. Willow Run (Mich.) Sch. Dist., 1986-87; substitute tchr. Plymouth-Canton (Mich.) Sch. Dist., 1983; tchr. grades 2-3 Wayne-Westland (Mich.) Schs., 1993-94, tchr. grade 5, 1994-98, tchr. grade 3, 1998-2000, tchr. grades 2-3, 2000-01, tchr. grade 3, 2001—. Instr. Sch. Craft Coll.; English tutor for Japanese engrs.; tutor Best of Friends Learning Inst., Plymouth. Grant AAUW. Mem. ASCD, Women in Leadership Network. E-mail: JoeSueNader1@prodigy.net.

NADLER, GERALD, management consultant, educator; b. Cin., Mar. 12, 1924; s. Samuel and Minnie (Krumbein) N.; m. Elaine Muriel Dubin, June 22, 1947; children: Burton Alan, Janice Susan, Robert Daniel. Student, U. Cin., 1942-43; BSME, Purdue U., 1945, MS in Indsl. Engring, 1946, PhD, 1949. Instr. Purdue U., 1948-49; asst. prof. indsl. engring. Washington U., St. Louis, 1949-52, assoc. prof., 1952-55, prof., head dept. indsl. engring., 1955-64; prof. U. Wis., Madison, 1964-83, chmn. dept. indsl. engring., 1964-67, 71-75; prof., chmn. dept. indsl. and sys. engring. U. So. Calif., L.A., 1983-93, IBM chair engring. mgmt., 1986-93, IBM chair emeritus, prof. emeritus, 1993—; v.p. Artcraft Mfg. Co., St. Louis, 1956-57; dir. Intertherm Inc., St. Louis, 1969-85. Pres. Ctr. for Breakthrough Thinking Inc., L.A., 1989—; vis. prof. U. Birmingham, Eng., 1959, Waseda U., Tokyo, 1963, Ind. U., 1964, U. Louvain, Belgium, 1975, Technion-Israel Inst. Tech., Haifa, 1976; speaker in field. Author: The Planning and Design Approach, 1981; (with S. Hibino) Breakthrough Thinking, 1990, 2d edit., 1994, Creative Solution Finding, 1995; (with G. Hoffherr, J. Moran) Breakthrough Thinking in Total Quality Management, 1994, (with W. Chandon) Ask the Right Questions, 2003; contbr. articles to profl. jours.; reviewer books, papers, proposals. Mem. Ladue Bd. Edn., St. Louis County, 1960-63, L.A. County Quality and Productivity Commn., 1997—; chmn. planning com. Wis. Regional Med. Program, 1966-69; bd. dirs. USC Credit Union, 1994—. Served with USN, 1943-45. Gilbreth medal Soc. Advancement Mgmt., 1961, Editl. award Hosp. Mgmt. Mag., 1966, Disting. Engring. Alumnus award Purdue U., 1975, Outstanding Indsl. Engr. award, 1997; Book of Yr. award Inst. Indsl. Engrs., 1983, Frank and Lillian Gilbreth award, 1992; Phi Kappa Phi Faculty Recognition award U. So. Calif., 1990, Engring. Disting. Svc. award U. Wis. Madison, 2000. Fellow AAAS, Inst. Indsl. Engrs. (pres. 1989-90), Inst. Operations Rsch. and Mgmt. Scis., Inst. for Advancement Engrs., Am. Soc. Engring. Edn.; mem. NAE, Japan Work Design Soc. (hon. adv. 1968—), World Future Soc., Acad. Mgmt., Engring. Mgmt. Soc., Sigma Xi, Alpha Pi Mu (nat. officer), Pi Tau Sigma, Omega Rho, Tau Beta Pi. Office: Univ Park GER 240 Dept Of I&se Los Angeles CA 90089-0193 E-mail: nadler@usc.edu.

NADROTOSKA, BARBARA ANNA, art educator; b. Stamford, Conn., Aug. 25, 1938; d. Michael and Gladys Nadrotoski. BFA, Pratt Inst., 1960; M in Liberal Arts, U. South Fla., 1989. Art dir. Heim Advt., Sarasota, Fla., 1979—83, Hunt-Wilde, Tampa, Fla., 1983—84; freelance designer Tampa, 1984—85; graphic designer Hillsboro Printing, Tampa, 1985—88; art dir. AAA Auto Clubs, Tampa, 1988—91; instr. art Remington Coll., Tampa, 1991—2003. Adj. prof. humanities U. South Fla., Tampa, 1995—2003. Exhibitions include Warde-Nasse Gallery, N.Y.C., 1975—76, Lever House Gallery, 1976, Woman's Art Ctr. Gallery, Sarasota, 1979—82, Fla. Ctr. for Contemporary Art, Tampa, 1987, 1991, Lee Scarfone Gallery, 1989—99, Art Ctr. Sarasota, 1990, St. Petersburg (Fla.) Art Ctr., 1998—2001, J.J. Watts Studio Gallery, Tampa, 1999—2000, Gold Dragon Gallery, 2001—02. Scholar Pratt Inst., Scholastic Mag., N.Y.C., 1956, U. South Fla.,

Tampa, 1988. Mem.: Friday Morning Musicale, Women Artists Rising, Nat. Mus. Women in the Arts, St. Petersburg Arts Ctr., Tampa Mus. Art. Home: 8730 N Himes Ave #1010 Tampa FL 33614

NAEVE, CATHERINE ANN, secondary education educator; b. Long Beach, Calif., Aug. 20, 1946; d. Harry Naeve, Jr. and Rae Catherine (Sieler) Coyle. AA, Long Beach City Coll., 1966; BA, Calif. State U., Long Beach, 1969, Tchg. Credential, 1970, MA, 1972; Spl. Edn. Credential, Calif. State U., Turlock, 1981. Lectr. Calif. State U., Long Beach, 1972-75; tchr. Locke H.S., L.A., 1975-78, Mark Twain Jr. H.S., Modesto, Calif., 1980-84, Beyer H.S., Modesto, Calif., 1984-93, Johansen H.S., Modesto, Calif., 1993—. Chair student sect. Calif. Assn. for Health, Physical Edn., Recreation & Dance, Long Beach, 1968-70, publ. chair, 1978-82; chair women's coaches L.A. City Schs., 1978-80; chairperson spl. edn. curriculum Modesto City Sch., 1987—, chair elem. spl. edn. curriculum, 1997—. Trustee First Bapt. Ch., Linden, Calif., 1989-97, sound technician, 1983—; mentor tchr. Modesto City Sch., 1986-88; sound technician No. Calif. Youth Choir (So. Bapt. Chs.). Recipient Hall of Fame award Coaches L.A. Women's Coaches, 1989, Disting. Svc. award Calif. Girls and Women in Sports, 1989, Cert. of Appreciation and Recognition Modesto City Schs.-Project Workability, 1990, 91, CIF Pioneer award. Mem. Computer Using Educators, Coun. for Exceptional Children. Home: PO Box 22 21596 E Acampo Rd Clements CA 95227 Office: Johansen HS 641 Norseman Dr Modesto CA 95357-0405

NAFTALIS, GARY PHILIP, lawyer, educator; b. Newark, Nov. 23, 1941; s. Gilbert and Bertha Beatrice Naftalis; m. Donna Arditi, June 30, 1974; children: Benjamin, Joshua, Daniel, Sarah. AB, Rutgers U., 1963; AM, Brown U., 1965; LLB, Columbia U., 1967. Bar: N.Y. 1967, U.S. Dist. Ct. (so. dist.) N.Y. 1969, U.S. Ct. Appeals (2d cir.) 1968, U.S. Ct. Appeals (3d cir.) 1973, U.S. Ct. Appeals (D.C. cir.) 1993, U.S. Supreme Ct. 1974. Law clk. to judge U.S. Dist. Ct. So. Dist. N.Y., 1967-68; asst. U.S. atty. So. Dist. N.Y., 1968-74, asst. chief criminal divsn., 1972-74; spl. asst. U.S. atty. for V.I., 1972-73; spl. counsel U.S. Senate Subcom. on Long Term Care, 1975, N.Y. State Temp. Commn. on Living Costs and the Economy, 1975; ptnr. Orans, Elsen, Polstein & Naftalis, N.Y.C., 1974-81, Kramer, Levin, Naftalis & Frankel, N.Y.C., 1981—. Lectr. Law Sch. Columbia U., 1976-88; vis. lectr. Law Sch. Harvard U., 1979; mem. deptl. disciplinary com. Appellate div. 1st Dept., 1980-86. Author: (with Marvin E. Frankel) The Grand Jury: An Institution on Trial, 1977, Considerations in Representing Attorneys in Civil and Criminal Enforcement Proceedings, 1981, Sentencing: Helping Judges Do Their Jobs, 1986, SEC Actions Seeking to Bar Securities Professionals, 1995, SEC Cease and Desist Powers Limited, 1997, The Foreign Corrupt Practices Act, 1997, Prosecuting Lawyers Who Defend Clients in SEC Actions, 1998, Obtaining Reports from a Credit Bureau for Litigation May be a Crime, 1999, Encouraging Cooperation by Individual Respondents in SEC Enforcement Investigations, 2002, Navigating the Foreign Corrupt Practices Act, 2002, Fugitive Disentitlement in Civil Forfeiture Proceedings, 2002; editor: White Collar Crimes, 1980. Trustee Boys Brotherhood Rep., 1978—, Blueberry Treatment Ctr., 1981-91, Joseph Haggerty Children's Fund, 1991—; bd. dirs. The Legal Aid Soc., 2000—. Fellow: Am. Coll. Trial Lawyers; mem.: ABA (white collar crime com. criminal justice sect. 1985—, coun. criminal justice sect. 2002—), N.Y. Coun. Def. Lawyers (bd. dirs. 2000—01), Internat. Bar Assn. (bus. crimes com. 1988—), N.Y. Bar Assn. (com. state legis. 1974—76, exec. com. comml. and fed. litigation sect.), Fed. Bar. Coun. (com. cts. 2d cir. 1974—77), Assn. of Bar of City of N.Y. (com. criminal cts. 1980—83, com. judiciary 1984—87, coun. criminal justice 1985—88, com. on criminal law 1987—90, 1997—2001). Home: 1125 Park Ave Apt 7B New York NY 10128-1243 Office: Kramer Levin Naftalis & Frankel 919 3rd Ave New York NY 10022-3902

NAFZIGER, JAMES ALBERT RICHMOND, lawyer, educator; b. Mpls., Sept. 24, 1940; s. Ralph Otto and Charlotte Monona (Hamilton) N. BA, U. Wis., 1962, MA, 1969; JD, Harvard U., 1967. Bar: Wis. 1967. Law clk. to chief judge U.S. Dist. Ct. (ea. dist.) Wis., 1967-69; fellow Am. Soc. Internat. Law, Washington, 1969-70, adminstrv. dir., 1970-74; exec. sec. Assn. Student Internat. Law Socs., 1969-70; lectr. Sch. Law Cath. U. Am., Washington, 1970-74; assoc. prof. law Coll. Law Willamette U., Salem, Oreg., 1977-80, prof., 1980-95, Thomas B. Stoel prof., 1995—, assoc. dean, 1985-86, dir. internat. programs, 1984—. Scholar-in-residence Rockefeller Found. Ctr., Bellagio, Italy, 1985; vis. assoc. prof. Sch. Law, U. Oreg. 1974-77; vis. prof. Nat. Autonomous U. Mex., 1978; hon. prof. East China U. of Politics and Law, 1999—; lectr. tutor Inst. Pub. Internat. Law and Internat. Rels., Thessaloniki, Greece, 1982; cons. Adminstrv. Conf. U.S., 1988-90, Internat. Com. Migration, 1997—; mem. bd. advisors Denver Jour. Internat. Law and Policy, Am. Jour. Comparative Law (bd. dirs. 1985—). Editor Procs. of Am. Soc. Internat. Law 1977; Am. author: Conflict of Laws: A Northwest Perspective, 1985, International Sports Law, 1988; co-editor: Law and Justice in a Multistate World, 2002; contbr. articles to profl. jours. Bd. dirs. N.W. Regional China Coun., 1987—89. 1st lt. U.S. Army, 1962—64. Recipient Burlington No. Faculty Achievement award, 1988, Willamette U. Pres.'s award for excellence in scholarship, 2000. Mem.: ACLU (pres. chpt. 1980—81, mem. state bd. 1982—88, sec. 1983—87), ABA (legal special ctrl. and east European law initiative 1992—), Nat. Sports Law Inst. (bd. advisors 2002—), Internat. Sports Law Assn. (v.p. 1992—), Oreg. Internat. Coun. (pres. 1990—92), Am. Law Inst., Assn. Am. Law Schs. (chmn. law and arts sect. 1981—83, chmn. internat. law sect. 1984—85, chmn. law and arts sect. 1989—91, chmn. immigration law sect. 1990—91, chmn. internat. law workshop 1995, com. on sects. and ann. meeting 1995—98, chmn. law and arts sect. 1981—83), Am. Coun. Learned Socs. (conf. adminstrv. officers, exec. com. 2002—), Internat. Studies Assn. (exec. bd. 1974—77), Washington Fgn. Law Soc. (v.p. 1973—74), UNA-USA (pres. Oreg. divsn. 1987—90, bd. dirs. 1990—, exec. com. coun. chpt. and divsn. prof., v,o, 1990—94), Internat. Law Assn. (chmn. human rights com. 1983—88, Am. br. exec. com. 1986—, rapporteur cultural heritage law com. 1990—, co-dir. studies 1991—95, v.p. 1994—2000, pres. 2000—), Internat. Acad. Comparative Law (internat. law sect.), Am. Soc. Comparative Law (bd. dirs. 1985—, treas. 1997—), Am. Soc. Internat. Law (exec. coun. 1983—86, chmn. ann. meeting 1988, chmn. nominating com. 1989, exec. coun. 1992—95, exec. com. 1994—95), Phi Kappa Phi, Phi Beta Kappa. Home: 3775 Saxon Dr S Salem OR 97302-6041 Office: Willamette U Coll Law Salem OR 97301

NAGI, CATHERINE RASEH, retired educational administrator, financial planner; b. Bklyn., Oct. 13, 1940; d. Massed and Catherine (Irato) N. BS, Bklyn. Coll., 1962, MS, 1964, postgrad., 1965-67, 76, Hofstra U., 1967-76, St. Johns U., Queens, N.Y., 1976-78. Cert. dist. sch. adminstr., supr., prin., asst. prin., tchr. health/phys. edn., N.Y.; CFP. Tchr. health/phys. edn. Jr. High Sch. 211-Dist. 18, Bklyn., 1962, Bay Ridge High Sch., Bklyn., 1962-63; tchr., acting chair Jr. High Sch. 78-Dist. 22, Bklyn., 1963-70; acting asst. prin. Intermediate Sch. 302-Dist. 19, Bklyn., 1970-71; narcotics edn. tchr. trainer Dist. 19 Bd. of Edn., Bklyn., 1971-73, supr. health/drug edn./svcs., 1973-75; supr. reimbursable programs Dist. 22 Bd. of Edn., Bklyn., 1975-79, supr. comprehensive planning, 1979-84, dep. supt., 1984-90; acting prin. Pub. Sch. 217-Dist. 22, Bklyn., 1980; sch. supt. Dist. 28 Bd. of Edn., Queens, N.Y., 1990-97; ret., 1997. Tchr. Adult Edn./Community Ctrs., N.Y.C., 1959-65; presenter N.Y.C. and N.Y. State Ednl. Confs., Univs.; grant writer N.Y.C. Bd. Edn., 1973—. Co-author, cons. (math. workbook) Get Ahead in Math, 1985; creator, editor (ednl. mag.) Gateways to Learning, 1977-90; creator, developer ednl. data system, 1976; developer first N.Y.C./N.Y. State early identification learning disabilities program, 1975. Named Educator of Yr. Assn. Tchrs. N.Y., 1980; recipient City Coun. Proclamation N.Y.C. Coun., 1991, 97, Legis. resolution N.Y. State Assembly/Senate, 1991, 97, Congl. Record recognition U.S. Congress, 1991, 97, Recognition award Forestdale Foster and Adoptive Parents Assn., Queens, 1992, Queensboro Pres. Proclamation, Supts.' Network Recognition, Fordham U., N.Y.C., Recognition, 112 Pct. Cmty. Coun. Mem. ASCD, Am. Assn. Sch. Adminstrs., N.Y.C. Assn. Supts., N.Y.C. Adminstrv. Women in Edn., Bklyn./N.Y. State Reading Coun./Assn., Thomas Jefferson Dem. Club, Kings County Dem. Com. Avocations: travel, languages, sports, singing, gourmet cooking, collecting stamps, coins and pens. Office: 122 Crispell Rd Krumville NY 12461-5408

NAGLE, DONNA PAAR, middle school art educator; b. Bethlehem, Pa., Feb. 10, 1967; d. James Frank and Martha Rae (Lockey) Paar; m. Paul George Nagle, Mar. 14, 1992; children: Milo Paul, Thea Paar. BS, Pa. State U., 1988; MEd, Kutztown U., 1991. Cert. tchr., Pa. Art tchr. Pa. State U., University Park, 1987, mus. docent trainer, 1987; art tchr. Lower Dauphin Sch. Dist., Hummelstown, Pa., 1988—; jewelry tchr. Harrisburg (Pa.) Art Assn., 1991-94; jewelry designer Knogist Designs, Mechanicsburg, Pa., 1992—2002; owner Eye Biz Design Group, 2002—. Mem. arts adv. colloquium Pa. Dept. Edn., Harrisburg, 1989; appt. to Nat. Assessment Gov. Bd. Exercise Devel. Project, 1993; elected to Univ. Scholars Mortar Bd. Program, 1987-88. Vis. artist grantee Pa. Coun. for the Arts, 1989. Mem. NEA, Nat. Art Edn. Assn., Pa. Art Edn. Assn. (regional dir. 1989-93, elem. divsn. dir. 1993-94, conf. co-chairperson 1993, outstanding regional rep. award 1992), Harrisburg Art Assn, Alpha Omicron Pi (social dir. 1986-87, edn. chair 1987-88). Home: 28 Dewalt Dr Mechanicsburg PA 17050-1723 Office: Lower Dauphin Mid Sch 251 Quarry Rd Hummelstown PA 17036-2433

NAGLER, MICHAEL NICHOLAS, peace and conflict studies educator; b. N.Y.C., Jan. 20, 1937; s. Harold and Dorothy Judith (Nocks) N.; m. Roberta Ann Robbins (div. May 1983); children: Jessica, Joshua. BA, NYU, 1960; MA, U. Calif., Berkeley, 1962, PhD, 1966. Instr. San Francisco State U., 1963-65; prof. classics, peace studies and comparative lit. U. Calif., Berkeley, 1966-91, prof. emeritus, 1991—. Author: Spontaneity and Tradition, 1974, America Without Violence, 1982, Is There No Other Way: The Search for a Nonviolent Future, 2001, Am. Book award, 2002; co-author: The Upanishads, 1987; contbr. articles to profl. publs. Pres. bd. dirs. METTA Ctrs. for Nonviolence Edn. Fellow Am. Coun. Learned Socs., NIH; MacArthur Found. grantee, 1988. Mem. Am. Philolog. Soc. Office: U Calif Peace and Conflict Studies Berkeley CA 94720-0001 E-mail: mnagler@igc.org.

NAGLIERI, EILEEN SHERIDAN, special education educator; b. Queens, N.Y., Oct. 3, 1962; d. Raymond J. and Julia C. (Giusani) Sheridan; m. Raymond M. Naglieri, May 2, 1987. BA, St. Joseph's Coll., 1984; MS in Edn., St. John's U., 1987; postgrad., U. Ctrl. Fla., 1988—; EdS, Nova Southeastern U., 2003. Cert. elem. tchr., reading, mentally handicapped. Tchr. 1st grade Incarnation Sch., Queens Village, N.Y., 1984-87; tchr. exceptional students Denn John Mid. Sch., Kissimmee, Fla., 1987-91; resource compliance specialist Denn John Mid. Sch. and Ventura Elem. Sch., Kissimmee, 1991-93; resource compliance specialist, program specialist emotionally handicapped Lakeview Elem. Sch., Kissimmee, 1993—2001; program specialist for mentally handicapped and autistic Sch. Dist. Osceola County, Fla., 2001—. Instr. adult basic edn. Vocat., Adult and Community Edn. Osceola County, Kissimmee, 1988-91. Vol. spl. religious edn. program Our Lady Lourdes, Queens, 1976-85, Queens Children's Psychiat. Ctr., 1979-80; vol. counselor autism and devel. delays, Queens, 1984-86. Blanche A. Knauth scholar, 1980. Mem. NEA, Coun. Exceptional Children, Delta Epsilon Sigma. Roman Catholic. Avocations: sailing, reading, music.

NAGRIN, DANIEL, dancer, educator, choreographer, lecturer, writer; b. N.Y.C., May 22, 1917; s. Harry Samuel and Clara (Wexler) N.; m. Helen Tamiris, 1946 (dec. 1966); m. Phyllis A. Steele, Jan. 24, 1992. BS in Edn., CCNY, 1940; DFA, SUNY, Brockport, 1991; DHL, Ariz. State U., 1992; studied dance with Martha Graham, Anna Sokolow, Helen Tamiris, Mme. Anderson-Ivantzova, Nenette Charisse and Edward Caton, studied acting with Miriam Goldina, Sanford Meisner and Stella Adler,, 1936-56. Tchr. Silvermine Guild Art, New Canaan, Conn., 1957-66, SUNY, Brockport, 1967-71, U. Md., College Park, 1970, Davis Ctr. Performing Arts, CCNY, 1973-75, Nat. Theatre Inst., Eugene O'Neill Found., Waterford, Conn., 1974, Hartmann Theatre Conservatory, Stamford, Conn., 1975-77; long-term resident tchr., Nat. Endowment for Arts sponsorship U. Hawaii, 1978-80, tchr., 1981, Bill Evans Dance Workshop, Seattle, 1981; prof. dance dept. Ariz. State U., Tempe, 1982-92; tchr. grad. liberal studies program Wesleyan U., Middletown, Conn., 1984, Dance Workshop for Movement Rsch., N.Y.C., 1984, Improvisation Workshop, Seattle, 1985, Improvisation, Choreography and Acting Technique for Dancers, Seattle, 1985, Dance Workshop, Glenwood Springs, Colo., 1990; prof. emeritus dance Ariz. State U., 1992. Tchr. summer sessions Conn. Coll., New London, 1959, 74; Am. Dance Festival at Conn. Coll., 1960, 77, Duke U., Durham, N.C., 1978, 80, 82, 87, 88, 92, Balasaraswati/Joy Ann Dewey Beinecke Chair Disting. Tchg., 1992; summer dance program Conn. Coll., 1979, E. La Tour Dance Workshop, Sedgewick, 1982, 83; dance workshop U. Minn. at Mpls., 1984, Stanford U., 1990; co-dir. Tamiris-Nagrin Summer Dance Workshop, Sedgewick, 1960-61, (with Tamiris) summer dance session C. W. Post Coll., Greenville, N.Y., 1962-63; dir. summer dance workshop Johnson (Vt.) State Coll., 1972, 73, 75, 76. Dancer (featured dance soloist on Broadway) Annie Get Your Gun, Lend an Ear, Touch and Go, Plain and Fancy (Billboard Donaldson award, 1954), (appearance in film) Just for You, (adapted and performed one-man theater piece) The Fall, from novel by Albert Camus, 1977—79, choreographer (solo works) Spanish Dance, 1948, Man of Action, 1948, Strange Hero, 1948, Indeterminate Figure, 1957, With My Eye and With My Hand, 1968, Jazz: Three Ways, 1958, 1966, Path-Silence, 1965, Not Me, But Him, 1965, The Peloponesian War, 1967—68, Untitled, 1974, Ruminations, 1976, Getting Well, 1978, Poems Off the Wall, 1981, Apartment 18C, 1993, Crosscurrents, 1997, Lost and Never Found, 1998, Someone for Theater X, Tokyo, Japan, What Did You Say?, 2001, others, (for groups) Faces from Walt Whitman, 1950, An American Journey, 1962, asst. choreographer (original Broadway prodns.) Up in Central Park, Stovepipe Hat, Show Boat, Annie Get Your Gun, By the Beautiful Sea, others; dir.: (off-Broadway) Volpone, 1957, The Firebugs, 1960, The Umbrella, 1961, Emperor Jones (Boston, 1963, others; (film choreography) His Majesty O'Keefe; actor: (video) The Art of Memory, 1985; (plays) Three Stories High, others; extensive touring U.S., Europe, The Pacific and Japan, 1957—84, conceived and directed (videos) Steps, 1972, The Edge is Also a Circle, 1973, Nagrin Videotape Library of Dances, 1985; author: How to Dance Forever: Surviving Against the Odds, 1988, Dance and the Specific Image: Improvisation, 1993, The Six Questions: Acting Technique for Dance Performance, 1997, Choreography and the Specific Image: Nineteen Essays and a Workbook, 2001. With spl. svcs. Army Airforce, 1942-43. Grantee Rebekah Harkness Found., 1962, Logan Found., 1965, N.Y. State Coun. on Arts and Nat. Found. for Arts and Humanities, 1967-68, N.Y. State Coun. on Arts, 1971-72, 73-74, 75-76, 76-77, 78-79, 80-81, Anne S. Richardson Fund, 1971, 73, 74, 75, 76, 78, Nat. Endowment for Arts, 1975, 79, 81, 83, Ariz. State U., 1983, 84, 85, 86, 88; CAPS fellow N.Y. State Coun. on Arts, 1977-78; fellow NEA, 1977-78, 80, 82, 83, 90, 91, Minn. McKnight Nat. fellow, 1996-97; commd. ballet Rebekah Harkness Ballet Found., 1986. Mem. Actors' Equity, Phi Kappa Phi (hon.). Avocation: reading. Home and Office: 208 E 14th St Tempe AZ 85281-6707 Fax: (480) 829-3933. E-mail: nagrin@imap2.asu.edu.

NAGTALON-MILLER, HELEN ROSETE, humanities educator; b. Honolulu, June 27, 1928; d. Dionicio Reyes and Fausta Dumrigue (Rosete) Nagtalon-Miller; m. Robert Lee Ruley Miller, June 15, 1952. BEd, U. Hawaii, 1951; Diplôme, The Sorbonne, Paris, 1962; MA, U. Hawaii, 1967; PhD, Ohio State U., 1972. Cert. secondary education educator. Tchr. humanities Hawaii State Dept. Edn., Honolulu, 1951-63; supr. student tchrs. French lab. sch. Coll. of Edn. U. Hawaii, Honolulu, 1963-66, instr. French, coord. French courses Coll. Arts and Scis., 1966-69; teaching asst. Coll. Edn. Ohio State U., Columbus, 1970-72; instr. French lab. sch. Coll. Edn. U. Hawaii, Honolulu, 1974-76; adminstr. bilingual-bicultural edn. project Hawaii State Dept. Edn., Honolulu, 1975—76; coord. disadvantaged minority recruitment program Sch. Social Work, U. Hawaii, Honolulu, 1976—83; coord. tutor tng. program U. Hawaii, Honolulu, 1983—85; program dir. Multicultural Multifunctional Resource Ctr., Honolulu, 1985—86; vis. prof. Sch. Pub. Health, ret. U. Hawaii, Honolulu, 1986—91. Bd. dirs. Hawaii Assn. Lang. Tchrs., Honolulu, 1963-66, Hawaii Com. for the Humanities, 1977-83; mem. statewide adv. coun. State Mental Health Adv. Com., Honolulu, 1977-82; task force mem. Underrepresentation of Filipinos in Higher Edn., Honolulu, 1984-86. Author: (with others) Notable Women in Hawaii, 1984; contbr. articles to profl. jours. Chairperson edn. and counseling subcom. First Gov.'s Commn. on Status of Women, Honolulu, 1964; vice chairperson Honolulu County Com. on the Status of Women, 1975—76, Hawaii State Dr. Martin Luther King Jr. Commn., Honolulu, 1982—85; pres. Filipino-Am. Hist. Soc. of Hawaii, 1980—2000; mem. Hawaii State Adv. Com. to U.S. Commn. on Civil Rights, 1981—, chairperson, 1982—85; bd. dirs. Japanese Am. Citizens League Honolulu chpt., 1990—2001, mem. Hawaiian Sovereignty com., 1994—98, Protect Our Constitution; mem. Pro-Choice Polit. Action Com., 1989—92. Women of Distinction, Honolulu County Com. on Status of Women, 1982; recipient Nat. Edn. Assn. award for Leadership in Asian and Pacific Island Affairs, NEA, 1985, Alan F. Saunders award ACLU in Hawaii, 1986, Disting. Alumni award U. Hawaii Alumni Affairs Office, 1994. Mem. Filipino Am. Nat. Hist. Soc., Filipino Coalition for Solidarity, Gabriela Network (Hawaii chpt.), Filipino Cmty. Ctr., Philippine Centennial Coordinating Com./Hawaii, NOW, Alliance Française of Hawaii, Rainbow Peace Fund. Democrat. Avocations: social-political advocacy, reading, classical music, theater, literary presentations. Home and Office: 47-543 Halemanu St Kaneohe HI 96744-4604 E-mail: rlrmiller@earthlink.net.

NAGYS, ELIZABETH ANN, environmental issues educator; b. St. Louis; d. Dallas and Miriam (Miller) Nichols; m. Sigi Nagys, Feb. 7, 1970; children: Eric M., Jennifer R., Alex E. BS., So. Ill. U. Extenstion, Edwardsville, 1970. Cert. tchr., Mo., Ill. Announcer Sta. KMTY, Clovis, N.Mex., 1970-71; substitue tchr. Ritneour Sch. Dist., Overland, Mo., 1977-78; instr. biology, environ. issues Southwestern Mich. Coll., Dowagiac, Mich., 1988-92; exec. v.p. Profl. Sound Designers, Goshen, Ind., 1994-96; customer svc. coord. Meijer, Inc., 1995-96; constrn. adminstr. Trans Eastern Homes, Weston, Fla., 1997—98, Trafalger Assocs., 1998—99. Reviewer textbooks Harcourt, Brace & Co., 1993; notary pub. State of Fla., 1999—. Active Nat. Arbor Day Found.; hazardous waste com. Elkhart County, Ind., 1991—94; asst. dir. South Fla. Folk Festival, 1998—2003, dir., 2003—; bd. dirs. United Meth. Ch., Marvin Park, 1979—84; coord. United Meth. Women, 1980—87; bd. dirs., corr. sec. Broward Folk Club, 1998—2003; charter mem. Holocaust Meml. Mus.; assoc. mem. Art Inst. Chgo. Mem. AAUW (v.p. Goshen 1994-96), Nat. Audubon Soc., Nat. Women's History Mus. (charter mem.), Sierra Club, Welcome Wagon Club. Avocations: reading, gardening.

NAHARY, LEVIA L. campus programming director; b. Scranton, Pa., Apr. 21, 1965; d. Haim and Bracha (Seri) N. BA in Liberal Arts, U. Scranton, 1986; MS in Higher Edn. Counseling, West Chester U., 1995. Admissions counselor Widener U., Chester, Pa., 1987-89; admissions rep. Thomas Jefferson U., Phila., 1989-92; dir. on campus programming U. Pa., Phila., 1992—. Advisor, interviewer health professions adv. bd. U. Pa., 1994—, mem. new student orientation com., 1992—; presenter in field. Mem. ACA, Pa. Assn. Secondary Sch. and Coll. Admissions Counselors (mem. conf. planning com. 1992-93, 94-95, profl. devel. com. 1992-93), Nat. Assn. Coll. Admissions Counselors, Nat. Collegiate Vis. Svcs. Assn. Office: U Pa 1 College Hall Philadelphia PA 19104

NAHRWOLD, SUSAN NORMA, physical education educator; b. Ossian, Ind., May 23, 1963; d. fred C. and Norma P. (Werling) N. BA, Concordia U., River Forest, Ill., 1985; MS, Ind. State U., 1990. Cert. tchr., athletic trainer, Ind. Tchr. Immanuel Luth. Sch., Danbury, Conn., 1985-86, North Adams Community Schs., Decatur, Ind., 1986-87, substitute tchr., coach high sch. track team, 1987-89; intern Bluffton (Ind.) Sports Therapy, 1988-89; asst. athletic trainer Bellmont High Sch., Decatur, 1990-91; tchr. phys. edn. Univ. Sch., Terre Haute, Ind., 1989-90; asst. athletic trainer, instr. phys. edn. U. Evansville, Ind., 1991—. Instr. CPR, first aid, ARC, Evansville, 1992—. Treas. Aid Assn. Luths., 1987-88. Mem. AAHPERD, Nat. Athletic Trainers' Assn. (cert.). Lutheran. Avocations: volleyball, tennis, golf, travel. Office: Univ Evansville 1800 Lincoln Ave Evansville IN 47714-1586 Home: 3032 Brewaster Dr Indianapolis IN 46214-1747

NAHUMCK, NADIA CHILKOVSKY, performer, dance educator, choreographer, author; b. Kiev, Ukraine, Jan. 8, 1908; came to U.S., 1914; d. Moiseiy Nicholas and Bela (Segalova) Chilkovsky; m. Nicholas Nahumck, Mar. 1940 (dec. Nov. 1994). BS in Edn., Temple U., 1928; MusD, Combs Coll. Music, 1971; postgrad., U. Pa., 1973-74; D Dance (hon.), Phila. Coll. Performing Arts, 1979. Founder, dir. Phila. Dance Acad., 1946-77; dean sch. dance Phila. Coll. Performing Arts (now Univ. Arts), 1977-79, dean emeritus, 1979—. Instr. Curtis Inst. Music, Phila., 1946-68, Acad. Vocal Arts, Phila., 1958-78; vis. lectr. Temple U., Phila., 1944-45, 67, 69, Swarthmore (Pa.) Coll., 1958-60, Thomas Jefferson U., 1976; lectr. in dance ethnology U. Pa. Mus., 1973-76; vis. rsch. scholar Rhodes U., 1977; founder Performing Arts Sch. for combined arts and acad. edn., 1962. Author: Three R's for Dancing, book I, 1953, book II, 1956, book III, 1960, My First Dance Book, 1954, Isadora Duncan: The Dances, 1994, Ten Dances in Labanotation, 1955, Three R's for Dancing, 1955, 3d edit., 1960, Short Modern Dances in Labanotation, 1957, American Bandstand Dances, 1959, Introduction to Dance Literacy, 1978, Dance Curriculum Resource Guide, 1980, Interpretation of the Labanotated Duncan Dance Scores, 2000; contbr. articles to profl. jours.; choreographer 75 works including 5 with Phila. Orch., 1947-50; prodr. 17 dance films for classroom use. Mary Wigman Profl. Dance Sch./Steinway Hall scholar, 1931-32; grantee U.S. Office of Edn., 1965-67, Wenner-Gren Found., 1965, 73. Fellow Internat. Coun. Kinetography Laban; mem. Internat. Isadora Duncan Inst. Coun., Soc. Ethnomusicology (coun. 1958-63, Svc. award 1976, master notator 1965—), Nat. Mus. Women in the Arts (charter mem.). Avocations: language studies, music, gardening, mentoring young students, reading.

NAIDICH, THOMAS PAUL, neuroradiologist, educator; b. Bklyn., Apr. 8, 1944; s. James and Rose (Bitko) N.; m. Rochele Miriam Pudlowksi, Feb. 2, 1975 (div. Nov. 1981); children: 1 child, Sandra Rebecca; m. Michele W. Levin, Dec. 29, 1990. BA, Cornell U., 1965; MD, NYU, NY, 1969. Diplomate Am. Bd. Radiology; cert. Added Qualification Neuroradiology. Intern Bronx Mcpl. Hosp. Ctr., NY, 1969-70; resident in radiology Montefiore Hosp., Bronx, NY, 1970-73; fellow in neuroradiology NYU Sch. Medicine, NY, 1973-75; prof. radiology, neurosurgery and anatomy and functional morphology . Mt. Sinai Med. Ctr. NYU, NY, 1998—, dir. neuroradiology, 1998—, vice chmn. radiology for acad. affairs, 2001—, Irving and Dorothy Regenstreif Rsch. prof. of neurosci., 2002—; asst. prof. Albert Einstein Coll. Medicine, Bronx, NY, 1975-77; from asst. prof. to assoc. prof. Mallinckrodt Inst. Radiology, St. Louis, 1978-80; from assoc. prof. to prof. Northwestern U. Sch. Medicine, Chgo., 1980-88; clin. prof. neuroradiology U. Miami Sch. Med., Fla., 1988-98; dir. neuroradiology Bapt. Hosp. Miami, Fla., 1988-98; dir Clin. Imaging Rsch. Core, Mt. Sinai Med. Ctr., Mt. Sinai, NY, 2001—. Author: (with R. M. Quencer) Clinical Neurosonography, 1987; (with Valavanis, Schubiger) Clinical Imaging of the Cerebello-Pontine Angle, 1987; (with Daniels, Haughton) Cranial and Spinal Magnetic Ressonance Imaging, 1987; editor-in-chief Neuroradiology, 1980-91, chmn. editl. bd., 1991-93; assoc. editor Surg. and Radiol. Anatomy, 1991-97; founding editor Internat. Jour. Neuroradiology, 1994-00; contbr. articles to profl. jour. Recipient John Caffey award Soc. Pediatric Radiology, 1983. Mem. Am. Soc. Neuroradiology (treas. 1991-93, Cornelius Dyke award 1975), Am. Soc. Pediatric Neuroradiology (pres. 1994-95), European Soc. Neuroradiology (hon.) Avocation: antique furniture. Office: Mt Sinai Med Ctr Dept Radiology Box 1234 1 Gustave Levy Pl New York NY 10029 E-mail: thomas.naidich@mountsinai.org.

NAIK, PRASAD ANAND, marketing educator; b. Bombay, July 15, 1962; arrived in U.S., 1991; BSChemE, U. Bombay, 1984; MBA, Indian Inst. Mgmt., 1987; PhD, U. Fla., 1996. Sales exec. Dorr Oliver, Bombay, 1984-85; brand exec. Glaxo SmithKline, Delhi, India, 1987—91; asst. prof. mktg. U. Calif., Davis, 1996—2002, assoc. prof. mktg., 2002—. Contbr. articles to profl. jours. Recipient Frank Bass award Inst. Ops. Rsch., 1999; named Mktg. Sci. Inst. Young scholar, 2003. Mem. Am. Mktg. Assn., Assn. Consumer Rsch., Inst. for Ops. Rsch. and Mgmt. Scis. Office: U Calif One Shields Ave Davis CA 95616

NAIR, VELAYUDHAN, pharmacologist, medical educator; arrived in U.S., 1956, naturalized, 1963; m. Jo Ann Burke, Nov. 30, 1957; children: David, Larry, Sharon. PhD in Medicine, U. London, 1956, DSc, 1976, LHD n.c., 2003. Research assoc. U. Ill. Coll. Medicine, 1956-58; asst. prof. U. Chgo. Sch. Medicine, 1958-63; dir. lab. neuropharmacology and biochemistry Michael Reese Hosp. and Med. Center, Chgo., 1963-68, dir. therapeutic research, 1968-71. Vis. assoc. prof. pharmacology FUHS/Chgo. Med. Sch., 1963—68, vis. prof., 1968—71, prof. pharmacology, 1971—, vice chmn. dept. pharmacology and therapeutics, 1971—76, dean Sch. Grad. and Postdoctoral Studies, 1976—2003; vis. prof. Harvard U., 1994, Johns Hopkins Sch. Medicine, 1995; v.p. for rsch. FUHS/Chgo. Med. Sch., 1999—2003, disting. prof., 2001, v.p., dean emeritus, 2003—. Contbr. articles to profl. jours. Recipient Morris Parker award, U. Health Scis./Chgo. Med. Sch., 1972. Fellow: AAAS, Am. Coll. Clin. Pharmacology, N.Y. Acad. Scis.; mem.: AAUP, Internat. Soc. Devel. Neurosci., Am. Coll. Toxicology, Internat. Soc. Chronobiology, Soc. Neurosci., Soc. Exptl. Biology & Medicine, Pan Am. Med. Assn. (coun. on toxicology), Royal Inst. Chemistry (London), Brit. Chem. Soc., Am. Chem. Soc., Soc. Toxicology, Radiation Rsch. Soc., Am. Soc. Clin. Pharmacology & Therapeutics, Am. Soc. Pharmacology & Exptl. Therapeutics, Internat. Soc. Biochem. Pharmacology, Internat. Brain Rsch. Orgn., Cosmos Club (Washington), Alpha Omega Alpha, Sigma Xi. Office: FUHS Chgo Med Sch 3333 Green Bay Rd North Chicago IL 60064-3037

NAJARIAN, BETTY JO, music educator; b. Samson, Ala., Nov. 6, 1929; d. Edward Bryan and Ida (Cox) Murdock; m. Zovak Najarian, July 25, 1953; children: Pamela Najarian Whitehead, Brian Keith Najarian. BA in Music Edn., Troy (Ala.) State U., 1951; student, Fla. State U., Tallahassee, 1952, Auburn U., 1956. Ind. music tchr., ch. musician, Destin, Fla., 1955-99; pres. Okaloosa County Music. Tchrs., Ft. Walton Beach, Fla., 1987-89, Fla. State Music Tchrs. Assn. Dist. I, Ft. Walton Beach, Fla., 1993-95, Choctaw Bay Music Club, Ft. Walton Beach, 1983-85, Niceville, 1993-95, Fla. Fedn. Music Capital Dist., Destin, 1985-87, 95-97, Fla. Fedn. Music Clubs, Destin, 1997-99. Composer: The Auxiliary Song, 1987. Pres. Am. Legion Aux #296, Destin, Fla., 1958-2002; mem. Sarasota Music Archives, 1997-2002; mem. Fla. League of the Arts, Inc. Named Tchr. of Yr., Destin Elem. Sch., Okaloosa County Sch. Bd., Destin. Fla., 1956-57. Mem. Am. Coll. Musicians, Music Tchrs. Nat. Assn., Nat. Fedn. Music Clubs (chmn. 1999—), Am. Folk Music (chmn. 1999—2002), Fla. State Music. Tchrs. Assn., Okaloosa County Music Tchrs. Assn., Choctaw Bay Music Club (chaplain 2002-), Fla. League Arts, Fla. Fedn. of Music Clubs. (state pres., 1997-99, chmn. coun. dist. and club presidents 1999—). Democrat. Presbyterian. Avocations: collecting old music and hymn books, collecting music boxes, collecting glass bluebirds, collecting baskets, word games, crossword puzzles. Home: 130 Calhoun Ave Destin FL 32541-1504

NAKAMURA, KIMIKO, language educator; b. Fukui-Ken, Japan, Feb. 11, 1945; arrived in USA, 1966; d. Toshiji and Emiko Matsumura; m. Takamitsu Nakamura, Jan. 22, 1966; children: Takashi, Yoko. BM, Osaka Coll. Music, Japan, 1966; MusB, DePaul U., 1993; MusM, Valparaiso U., 1996. Japanese tchr. Inland/EastPack Co., Ea. Chgo., 1987—. Piano instr. O'Day Music Sch., Highland, Ind., 1999—. Mem.: Nat. Guild Piano Tchrs., Japan-Am. Soc. (Japanese lang. tchr. 1996—). Office: Japan America Soc Chgo 20 N Clark St Ste 750 Chicago IL 60602

NAKANISHI, DON TOSHIAKI, Asian American studies educator, writer; b. L.A., Aug. 14, 1949; m. Marsha Hirano; 1 child, Thomas. BA in Polit Sci. cum laude, Yale U., 1971; PhD in Polit. Sci., Harvard U., 1978. Instr. dept. urban studies Yale U., 1971; lectr. Coun. on Ednl. Devel. UCLA, 1973, instr. Asian Am. Studies Ctr., 1974, acting asst. prof. dept. polit. sci., 1975-78; vis. scholar Sophia U., Inst. Internat. Relations, Tokyo, 1978-89; adj. asst. prof. dept. polit. sci. UCLA, 1979-82, asst. rschr. Asian Am. Studies Ctr., 1979-82, from asst. prof. to full prof. Grad. Sch. Edn., 1982—, assoc. dir. Asian Am. Studies Ctr., 1985-87, chair interdepartmental program Asian Am. studies, 1989-90, dir. Asian Am. Studies Ctr., 1990—. Co-founder and publr. Amerasia Jour., 1970-75, edtl. bd., 1975—; researcher Social Sci. Rsch. Coun. of N.Y. and the Japan Soc. for the Promotion of Sci. of Tokyo Joint-Project on Am.-Japanese Mut. Images, 1971-73; mem. Asian Am. task force for social studies guideline evaluation, Calif. State Dept. Edn., 1973; guest spkr. Ctr. for the Study of Ednl. Policy, Grad. Sch. Edn., Harvard U., 1974, Metropathways, Ethni-City Sch. Desegregation Program, Boston, 1974; researcher, co-project chair Hispanic Urban Ctr., Project Sch. Desegregation, L.A., 1974; numerous coms. UCLA; numerous conf. chmns.; cons., rschr., speaker, presenter in field. Co-editor: (with Marsha J. Hirano-Nakanishi) The Education of Asian and Pacific Americans: Historical Perspectives and Prescriptions for the Future, 1983, (with Halford H. Fairchild, Luis Ortiz-Franco, Lenore A. Stiffarm) Discrimination and Prejudice: An Annotated Bibliography, 1991, (with Tina Yamano Nishida) The Asian Pacific American Educational Experience: A Sourcebook for Teachers and Students, 1995, (with James Lai) National Asian Pacific American Political Almanac, 1996, 98, 2000; contbr. numerous articles to profl. jours., monographs, book reviews and reports. Chair Yale U. Alumni Schs. Com. of So. Calif., 1978—; bd. dirs. Altamed and La Clinica Familiar Del Barrio of East L.A., 1982—; commr. Bd. Transp. Commrs., City of L.A., 1984-90; v.p. Friends of the Little Tokyo Pub. Libr., 1986-88; co-chair nat. scholars adv. com. Japanese Am. Nat. Mus., 1987—; mem., bd. govs. Assn. of Yale Alumni, 1988-91; mem. exec. coun. Mayor's LA's Best Aftersch. Program, City of Los Angeles, 1988-90. Rsch. fellow Japan Soc. for the Promotion of Sci., 1978; recipient Nat. Scholars awrd for Outstanding Rsch. Article on Asian Pacific Am. Edn., Nat. Assn. for Asian and Pacific Am. Edn., 1985, Civil Rights Impace award Asian Am. Legal Ctr. of So. Calif., 1989; grantee Chancellors' Challenge in the Arts and Humanities, 1991, Calif. Policy Seminar, 1992, U. Calif. Pacific Rim Studies, 1992; recepient numerous other research and conference grants. Mem. Nat. Assn. for Interdisciplinary Ethnic Studies (bd. dirs. 1976-79), Assn. Asian Am. Studies (nat. pres. 1983-85), Nat. Assn. for Asian and Pacific Am. Edn. (exec. bd. dirs., v.p. 1983—). Home: 4501 N Berkshire Ave Los Angeles CA 90032 Office: UCLA Asian Am Studies Ctr 3230 Campbell Ave Los Angeles CA 90024-1546 E-mail: dtn@ucla.edu.

NAKANISHI, KOJI, chemistry educator, research institute administrator; b. Hong Kong, May 11, 1925; came to U.S., 1969; s. Yuzo and Yoshiko (Sakata) N.; m. Yasuko Abe, Oct. 25, 1947; children: Keiko, Jun. BSc, Nagoya U., Japan, 1947; PhD, Nagoya U., 1954; DSc (hon.), Williams Coll., 1987, Georgetown U., 1992. Asst. prof. Nagoya U., 1955-58; prof. Tokyo Kyoiku U., 1958-63, Tohoku U., Sendai, Japan, 1963-69; prof. chemistry Columbia U., N.Y.C., 1969-80, Centennial prof. chemistry, 1980—; dir. research Internat. Ctr. Insect Physiology and Ecology, Nairobi, Kenya, 1969-77; dir. Suntory Inst. for Bioorganic Research, Osaka, Japan, 1979-91. Hon. prof. Shanghai Inst. Materia Medica, 1995. Author: Infrared Spectroscopy-Practical, 1962, rev. edit., 1977, Circular Dichroic Spectroscopy-Exciton Coupling in Organic Stereochemistry, 1983, A Wandering Natural Products Chemist, 1991; co-editor, contbr. chpt. Comprehensive Natural Products Chemistry, vol. 1-9, 1999; contbr. chpts. to books. Recipient Asahi cultural prize, 1968, Sci. Workers Union medal, Bulgaria, 1978, E.E. Smissman medal U. Kan., 1979, H.C. Urey award Columbia U., 1980, Alcon ophthalmology award, 1986, Paul Karrer gold medal U. Zurich, 1986, E. Havinga medal Havinga Found., Leiden, 1989, Imperial prize Japan Acad., 1990, Japan Acad. prize, 1990, R.T. Major medal U. Conn., 1991, L.E. Harris award U. Nebr., 1991, award in chem. scis. NAS, 1994, J. Heyrovsky hon. gold medal Czech Acad. Scis., 1995, Robert A. Welch award in chemistry, 1996, Person of Cultural Merit award Japanese Govt., 1999, T. Wang Bioorganic lectureship award, 2001, King Faisal Internat. prize for sci. King Faisal Found., Riyadh, 2003. Fellow N.Y. Acad. Scis., Nat. Acad. Sci. Italy (fgn.); mem. Chem. Soc. Japan (hon., award in pure chemistry 1954, award 1979, Nakanishi prize established 1996), Am. Chem. Soc. (E. Guenther award 1978, Remsen award Md. sect. 1981, A.C. Cope award 1990, Nichols medal N.Y. sect. 1992, Mosher award Santa Clara Valley sect. 1995, internat. award in agrochems. 1995), Biochem. Soc. Japan, Chem. Soc. Japan, Brit. Chem. Soc. (Centenary medal 1979), Swedish Acad. Pharm. Scis. (Scheele award 1992), Am. Acad. Arts and Scis., Am. Soc. Pharmacognosy (rsch. achievement award 1985), Internat. Chirality Symposium (Chirality gold medal 1995), Pharm. Sc. Japan (hon.), Am. Mus. Soc. Natural History (1st environ. award 2000, King Faisal Internat. prize in sci. 2003). Home: 560 Riverside Dr New York NY 10027-3202 Office: Columbia U Dept Chemistry Mail Code 3114 3000 Broadway New York NY 10027-6941

NAKAYAMA, MINEHARU, Japanese language professional, educator; b. Nagano, Japan, Dec. 11, 1958; s. Minematsu and Hiroko (Kuribayashi) N.; m. Jennifer E. Workman. BA in English Lang. & Lit., Waseda U., Tokyo, 1983; MA in Linguistics, U. Conn., 1986, PhD in Linguistics, 1988. Japanese Oral Proficiency Interview Tester, 1991-94. Lectr. U. Conn., Storrs, 1984-86; vis. instr. Conn. Coll., New London, 1985-88; asst. prof. Ohio State U., Columbus, 1988-94, assoc. prof., 1994—, dir. Inst. for Japanese Studies, 2002—, assoc. dir. East Asian Studies Ctr., 2002—03, acting dir. East Asian Studies Ctr., 2003—. Cultural advisor WBNS-TV Nagano Winter Olympics coverage team, 1998. Author: Acquisition of Japanese Empty Categories, 1996; co-author: Let's Play Games in Japanese, 1991; editor: Issues in East Asian Language Acquisition, 2001, Sentence Processing in East Asian Languages, 2002; co-editor: Proceedings of the Japanese Syntax Workshop, 1988, Japanese/Korean Linguistics, vol. 9, 2001. Recipient Awards for Study Papers of the Waseda Centennial Celebration, Waseda U., 1982, award for internat. understanding Rotary Found., 1983, Outstanding Internat. Faculty award Office Internat. Edn., 1998; conf. grantee N.E. Asia Coun., 1989, rsch. assistance grantee N.E. Asia Coun., 1990, Study-in-Japan grantee Japan Found., 1994, workshop and conf. grantee Japan Found. Lang. Ctr., Tchg. Material grantee Gogaku Kyoiku Shinko Zaidan, 1995, conf. grantee Japan Found., Korea Rsch. Found., 1999. Mem. Assn. for Asian Studies, Assn. Tchrs. of Japanese, Linguistic Soc. Am., Ctrl. Assn. Tchrs. of Japanese, Assn. of Lang. Sci., Ohio Assn. Tchrs. of Japanese, Japan Second Lang. Assn. Office: Dept East Asian Langs & Lits Ohio State U 1841 Millikin Rd Columbus OH 43210-1229 E-mail: nakayama.1@osu.edu.

NALE, JULIA ANN, nursing educator; b. Chgo., Oct. 27, 1948; d. Anthony John and Mary Elizabeth (Magrady) Doheny; m. Robert Douglas Nale, Feb. 27, 1971; children: Daniel, Kerry. Diploma, St. Francis Sch. Nursing, Evanston, Ill., 1969; BS, U. S.C. Coastal Carolina Coll., Conway, 1989. Staff nurse St. Francis Hosp., 1969-71; charge nurse McDonough Dist. Hosp., Macomb, ill., 1971-72; supr. surg. ICU Victory Meml. Hosp., Waukegan, ill., 1973-78; charge nurse St. Mary's Hosp., Galesburg, ill., 1978-79; assoc. dir. nursing Community Meml. Hosp., Monmouth, Ill., 1979-85; staff nurse Loris (S.C.) Community Hosp., 1987-91; instr. health occupations Horry County Sch. Dist., Conway, SC, 1985-89, 2002instr. LPNs, 1989; staff nurse Conway Hosp., 1992—, patient edn. coord., 2002—. Mem. S.C. Textbook Selection Com., 1988-90. Lectr., tchr. Tommy Trauma Program for Pub. Sch. Children, Monmouth, 1982-84; charter mem. Com. to Combat Alcohol/Drug Abuse, Monmouth, 1985. Named Tchr. of the Yr. Finklea (S.C.) Career Ctr., 1989, Aynor-Conway Career Ctr., 1991, other awards. Mem. AACN, NEA, S.C. Ednl. Assn., Horry County Vocat. Assn., S.C. Vocat. Assn. (pres. health occupations div. 1990-91), Am. Vocat. Assn. Roman Catholic. Avocations: swimming, cross-stitch, reading. Office: Conway Hosp 300 Singleton Ridge Rd Conway SC 29528

NAMBOODIRI, KRISHNAN, sociology educator; b. Valavoor, Ind., Nov. 13, 1929; s. Narayanan and Parvathy (Kutty) N.; m. Kadambari Kumari, Sept. 7, 1954; children: Unni (dec.), Sally. B.Sc., U. Kerala, 1950, M.Sc., 1953, MA, U. Mich., 1962, PhD, 1963. Lectr. U. Kerala, India, 1953-55, 58-59; tech. asst. Indian Statis. Inst., Calcutta, 1955-58; reader demography U. Kerala, 1963-66; asst. prof. sociology U. N.C., Chapel Hill, 1966-67, asso. prof., 1967-73, prof., 1973-84, chmn. dept., 1975-80; Robert Lazarus prof. population studies Ohio State U., Columbus, 1984—2000, chmn. dept. sociology, 1989-93, prof. emeritus, 2000—. Author: (with L.F. Carter and H.M. Blalock) Applied Multivariate Analysis and Experimental Designs, 1975; editor: Demography, 1975-78, Survey Sampling and Measurement, 1978, Auth. Matrix Algebra: An Introduction, 1984, (with C.M. Suchindran) Life Table Techniques and Their Applications, 1987, (with R.G. Corwin) Research in Sociology of Education and Socialization: Selected Methodological Issues, 1989, Demographic Analysis: A Stochastic Approach, 1991, (with R.G. Corwin) The Logic and Method of Macrosociology, 1993, Methods for Macrosociological Research, 1994, A Primer of Population Dynamics, 1996; contbr. articles to profl. jours. Fellow Am. Statis. Assn.; mem. Population Assn. Am. (dir. 1975-76), Internat. Union Sci. Study Population, Am. Sociol. Assn., Indian Sociol. Assn., Am. Statis. Assn., Sociol. Research Assn. Home: 3107 N Star Rd Columbus OH 43221-2366 E-mail: namboodiri.2@osu.edu.

NAMIAS, JUNE, historian, educator, writer; b. Boston, May 17, 1941; d. Foster and Helen (Needle) N.; m. Peter Edmund Slavin, June 1965 (div. Oct. 1970); 1 child, Robert Victor Slavin. BA with honors, U. Mich., 1962; MA in Tchg., Harvard U., 1963; PhD in History, Brandeis U., 1989. H.s. tchr. history Newton (Mass.) Pub. Schs., 1965-87; vis. asst prof. history MIT, Cambridge, Mass., 1988-91, Wheaton Coll., Norton, Mass., 1991-92; assoc. prof. history U. Alaska, 1992—. Author: First Generation: In the Words of Twentieth-Century American Immigrants, 1978, rev. edit., 92, White Captives: Gender and Ethnicity on the American Frontier, 1607-1862, 1993; editor: A Narrative of the Life of Mrs. Mary Jemison (by James E. Seaver), 1992, Six Weeks in the Sioux Tepees (by Sarah F. Wakefield), 1997; contbr. poetry to various jours. and encys. Mem. Orgn. Am. Historians, Am. Hist. Assn., Soc. Ethnohistory. Jewish. Office: U Alaska Anchorage Dept History 3211 Providence Dr Anchorage AK 99508-4614

NAMJOSHI, MADHAV, economist, educator; b. Bombay, Maharashtra, India, Aug. 24, 1970; arrived in U.S., 1992, permanent resident; s. Arvind and Sheela Namjoshi. BS, U. Bombay, India, 1992; MS, U. Toledo, Ohio, 1994; PhD, U. Iowa, Iowa City, 1998. Registered Pharmacist Bombay, 1992. Rsch. asst. U. Iowa, Iowa City, 1995—98; intern Hoechst-Marion-Roussel, Kansas City, Mo., 1996; sr. health economist Eli Lilly and Co., Indianapolis, Ind., 1998—2001, mgr., health outcomes rsch., 2001—. Adj. asst. prof. Butler U., Indianapolis, Ind., 2000. Contbr. articles to profl. jours., chpt. to book, 2000. Pub. policy com. mem. Nat. Alliance for the Mentally Ill (NAMI), Indpls., 2002—. Recipient Career Devel. Award, U. Toledo, 1994, Outsdanding Grad. Student, U. Iowa, 1998; grantee Grad. Tchg. Assistantship, U. Toledo, 1992-1994, U. Iowa, 1995, Grad. Rsch. Assistantship, 1996-1998. Mem.: Am. Coll. Study Methods for Clin. Trials, EuroQol Group. Avocations: photography, travel. Office: Eli Lilly and Company McCarty St 75/05 DC 1758 Indianapolis IN 46204 Office Fax: 317-433-0448. E-mail: namjoshi_madhav@lilly.com.

NANASI, MADONNA, reading educator; b. Bogalusa, La., Dec. 26, 1936; d. Maxwell Redus and Elizabeth Ann (Harkins) Pollard; m. Laszlo Nanasi; 1 child, Michael Andras. BA, U. Detroit, 1971; MAT in reading, Oakland U., 1978. Cert. elem. and secondary tchr. Past dist. dir. of compensatory edn./reading specialist Anchor Bay Sch. Dist., New Baltimore, Mich., reading cons., chpt. I instr. tchr. assistance team bldg. coord. Pres. Macomb Reading Coun. 1993-94; adj. prof. U. Detroit; invited U.S./China Joint Conf. Edn., Reading, Beijing, 1992, Oakland U., 1999—; guest presenter Oakland U., 1992; mem. state and local com. for early literacy, participant writing of Mich. Litercy Progress Profile, 1996-2001, trainer, 1998—; trainer tchrs. for Playful Literacy Program for Presch. Educators, 2001—; adj. prof. Oakland U., 1998—. Author: (handbook) Whole Language, Whole Books, Whole Child, 1991; co-author: (curriculum guide) Integrating Language Arts in Science and Math Using Children's Literature, 1994. Mem. Macomb Reading Specialist Com. Mem. Mich. Reading Assn., Internat. Reading Assn., Alpha Delta Kappa (past pres.). Home: 37017 Tamarack Dr Sterling Heights MI 48310-4159

NANCE, BETTY LOVE, librarian; b. Nashville, Oct. 29, 1923; d. Granville Scott and Clara (Mills) N. BA in English magna cum laude, Trinity U., 1957; MA in LS, U. Mich., 1958. Head dept. acquisitions Stephen F. Austin U. Libr., Nacogdoches, Tex., 1958-59; libr. 1st Nat. Bank, Ft. Worth, 1959-61; head catalog dept. Trinity U., San Antonio, 1961-63; head tech. processes U. Tex. Law Libr., Austin, 1963-66; head catalog dept. Tex. A&M U. Libr., College Station, 1966-69; chief bibliographic svcs. Washington U. Libr., St. Louis, 1970; head dept. acquisitions Va. Commonwealth U. Libr., Richmond, 1971-73; head tech. processes Howard Payne U. Libr., Brownwood, Tex., 1974-79; libr. dir. Edinburg (Tex.) Pub. Libr., 1980-91. Pres. Edinburg Com. for Salvation Army. Mem. ALA, Pub. Libr. Assn., Tex. Libr. Assn., Hidalgo County Libr. Assn. (v.p. 1989-81, pres. 1981-82), Pan Am. Round Table Edinburg (corr. sec. 1986-88, assoc. dir. 1989-90), Edinburg Bus. and Profl. Womens Club (founding bd. dirs., pres. 1986-87, bd. dirs. 1987-88), Zonta (bd. dirs. West Hidalgo Club, 1986-88, San Antonio 1996-97), Alpha Lambda Delta, Alpha Chi. Methodist. Home: 5359 Fredericksburg Rd # 806 San Antonio TX 78229-3549 E-mail: bettynance@webtv.net.

NANCE, KATHERINE ROARK, principal; b. Halifax County, Va., Mar. 14, 1950; d. Randolph Riley and Helen (Hall) Roark; m. Julian Thomas Nance Jr., Apr. 9, 1977. BA in English, Mary Washington Coll., Fredericksburg, Va., 1972; MEd in Sch. Adminstrn., Lynchburg (Va.) Coll., 1988. Tchr. Lynchburg City Pub. Schs., 1972-86, tchr., staff devel. specialist, 1986-91, asst. prin., 1991-92; acting prin. Dearington Elem., 1992-93; prin. Elon Elem. Amherst County Pub. Schs., Madison Heights, Va., 1993—. Adj. prof. Lynchburg Coll., summer 1989. Mem. ASCD, Nat. Assn. Elem. Sch. Prins., Va. Assn. Elem. Sch. Prins., Phi Delta Kappa, Kappa Delta Pi. Mem. Christian Ch. (Disciples Of Christ). Avocations: reading, piano.

NANCE, MARY JOE, retired secondary school educator; b. Carthage, Tex., Aug. 7, 1921; d. F.F. and Mary Elizabeth (Knight) Born; m. Earl C. Nance, July 12, 1946; 1 child, David Earl. BBA, North Tex. State U., 1953; postgrad., Northwestern State U. La., 1974; ME, Antioch U., 1978. Cert. bus. educator. Tchr. Port Isabel (Tex.) Ind. Sch. Dist., 1953-79; tchr. English Tex., 1965, Splendora (Tex.) H.S., 1979-80, McLeod, Tex., 1980-81, Bremond, Tex., 1981-84; ret., 1985. Vol. tchr. for Indian students, 1964—65; vol. tutor, tchr. ESL; active WAAC, 1942—43, WAC, 1945. Recipient Image Maker award Carthage C. of C., 1984; named on Meml. for Women, Washington. Mem. NEA, Tex. Tchrs. Assn., Tex. Bus. Tchrs. Assn. (Cert. of Appreciation 1978), Nat. Women's Army Corps Vets. Assn., Air Force Assn. (life), Gwinnett Hist. Soc., Hist. Soc. Panola County, Panola County Hist. & Geneal. Assn., Nat. Hist. Soc. Baptist.

NANCE, RAYMOND G. science educator; b. Hobbs, N.Mex., Aug. 13, 1960; s. Raymond Thomas and Linda Ann (Brazel) N.; m. Teresa Marie Melvin, Sept. 19, 1981. BS, Wayland Bapt. U., 1982; MS, U. No. Colo., 1993. Cert. secondary sci. tchr., N.Mex. Geologist Morco Geol. Svcs., Carlsbad, N.Mex., 1982-84; geotech. specialist Westinghouse Electric Corp., Carlsbad, 1984-85, assoc. engr., 1985-87, planning/control analyst, 1987-88; prodn. tech. Benson Mineral Group, Inc., Denver, 1988-90; grad. teaching asst. U. No. Colo., Greeley, 1990-93; sci. tchr. Hagerman (N.Mex.) Mcpl. Schs., 1993-95, Carlsbad (N.Mex.) Mcpl. Schs., 1995—. Mem. adv. bd. Realistic Applied Technology Symposiums, Carlsbad, 1993-97. Sr. ptnr. Ptnrs., Greeley, 1988-93; scoutmaster, advisor Boy ScoutsAm., Carlsbad, 1985-88, 99-2003. Named one of Outstanding Young Men Am., 1985. Mem. NEA, Nat. Speleological Soc., Nat. Sci. Tchrs. Assn., Nat. Earth Sci. Tchrs. Assn., Environ. Edn. Assn. N.Mex. Avocations: cave exploration, fly fishing, climbing, backpacking, bicycling. Home: 7112 Norris Rd Carlsbad NM 88220-8757

NANNA, ELIZABETH ANN WILL, librarian, educator; b. Rahway, N.J., Nov. 21, 1932; d. Rudolph Julius and Dorothy Ada (Haulenbeck) Will; m. Antonio Carmine Nanna, June 15, 1963. Cert. in bus. with honors, Stuart Sch. Bus. Adminstrn., 1963; AA, Ocean County Coll., 1980; BA with honors, MA, Georgian Ct. Coll., 1984, postgrad., 1984-85, Jersey City State Coll., 1988, Montclair State Coll., 1988-89. Cert. art, early childhood and spl. edn., media specialist, supr., N.J. Entrepreneur Ye Olde Cedar Inn, Toms River, N.J., 1963-78; tchr. art and history Monsignor Donovan High Sch., Toms River, 1980-82; tchr. art Whiting (N.J.) Elem. Sch./Manchester Twp. Sch. Dist., 1983-84, Ridgeway Elem. Sch./Manchester Twp. Sch. Dist., Manchester, 1985-87; gifted and talented program tchr., coord., 1984-86; tchr. spl. edn. New Egypt (N.J.) Elem. Sch./Plumsted Twp. Sch. Dist., 1988, libr. media specialist, 1988—. Author: Fostering Cognitive Growth Through Creativity, 1984; contbr. articles to profl. jours. Mem. Mounmouth Park Ball Com., Monmouth County, N.J., 1974—; dir. teen charm sch. Rutgers U. Extension Svc., Ocean County, N.J., 1965; chmn. Ocean County Fair Queen, 1967-84, Ocean County Heart of Hearts Charity Ball, 1976. Recipient Leadership and Svcs. award Ocean County Fair, Ocean County Heart Fund Assn., 1977. Mem. N.J. Reading Assn. (state coun.), N.J. Libr. Assn., N.J. Edn. Assn., Ednl. Media Assn. N.J., Ocean County Artists Guild, Edn. Media Assn. N.J., Georgian Ct. Coll. Alumni Assn. Republican. Roman Catholic. Avocations: international travel, studying arts, cultures, skiing. Home: 7211 Mystic Way Port Saint Lucie FL 34986-3259 Office: Plumsted Twp Sch Dist 44 N Main St New Egypt NJ 08533-1316

NANNA, MICHELE, cardiologist, educator; b. Mola di Bari, Puglia, Italy, Mar. 21, 1953; came to U.S., 1981; naturalized, 1985; s. Giovanni and Maria (Francese) N.; m. Barbara Luise McKnight, Aug. 5, 1981 (div. Feb. 1991); children: Michael Giovanni Jr., Anna Maria; m. Nancy J. Konovalov, Nov. 14, 1991; 1 child Giovanni Jacob Michele. MD summa cum laude, U. Bari, Italy, 1978. Diplomate in internal medicine, cardiovasc. disease, adult echocardiography Am. Bd. Internal Medicine; lic. physician, Italy, Calif., N.Y. Intern Ospedale Conzorziale, Bari, 1978-81; clin. clerkship U. Soc. Calif. Med. Ctr., L.A., 1982-83; instr. medicine, fellow in cardiovascular disease U. So. Calif., 1983-86; asst. prof. medicine U. Rochester, N.Y., 1986-88, Albert Einstein Coll. Medicine, Bronx, N.Y., 1988-94; assoc. prof. of med., 1994—; dir. care unit Bronx Mcpl. Hosp. Ctr., 1988-92; dir. lab. Montefiore Med. Ctr., Bronx, N.Y., 1988—. Cardiology cons. Monroe Community Hosp., Rochester, 1987-88; mem. coms. Bronx Mcpl. Hosp. Ctr., 1988—, chmn. com., 1990-92. Editor jour. Ultrasound in Medicine and Biology, 1986—; editor-in-chief Jour. Cardiovascular Diagnosis and Procedures, 1993-2000; contbr. chpts. to books and articles to profl. jours. Grantee NIH, 1987, Whitaker Found., Genetech Inc., Bristol-Myers Squibb, Inc. Mem. AMA, Am. Heart Assn., Am. Coll. Cardiology, N.Y. Athletic Club. Republican. Roman Catholic. Avocations: boating, swimming, jogging. Office: Albert Einstein Coll Med Montefiore Med Ctr 111 E 210th St Bronx NY 10467-2401

NANTO, ROXANNA LYNN, marketing professional, management consultant; b. Hanford, Calif., Dec. 17, 1952; d. Lawson Gene Brooks and Bernice (Page) Jackson; m. Harvey Ken Nanto, Mar. 23, 1970; 1 child, Shea Kiyoshi. AA, Chemeketa Community Coll., 1976; BSBA, Idaho State U., 1978. PBX operator Telephone Answer Bus. Svc., Moses Lake, Wash., 1965-75; edn. coord. MimiCassia Community Edn., Rupert, Idaho, 1976-77; office mgr. Lockwood Corp., Rupert, Idaho, 1977-78; cost acct. Keyes Fibre Co., Wenatchee, Wash., 1978-80; acctg. office mgr. Armstrong & Armstrong, Wenatchee, Wash., 1980-81; office mgr. Cascade Cable Constrn. Inc., East Wenatchee, Wash., 1981-83; interviewer, counselor Wash. Employment Security, Wenatchee, 1983-84; pres. chief exec. officer Regional Health Care Plus, East Wenatchee, 1986-88; dist. career coord. Eastmont Sch. Dist., East Wenatchee, 1984-90; prin. Career Cons., 1988-90; exec. dir. Wenatchee Valley Coll. Found., 1990-91; ednl. cons. Sunbelt Consortium, East Wenatchee, 1991-93; cons. CC Cons. Assocs., 1993—; ptnr. Cmty. Devel. Mktg. and Mgmt. Resource Group, Wenatchee, Wash., 1994—, also bd. dirs.; ptnr. Bus. Consulting and Rsch., Malaga, Wash., 1997-99. Speaker North Cen. Washington Profl. Women, Wenatche, 1987, Wen Career Women's Network, Wenatchee, 1990, Wenatchee Valley Rotary, 1990, Meeting the Challenge of Workforce 2000, Seattle, 1993; cons., speaker Wash. State Sch. Dirs., Seattle, 1987; speaker Wenatchee C. of C., 1989; sec. Constrn. Coun. of North Cen. Washington, Wenatchee, 1981-83; bd. dirs. Gen. Vocat. Adv. Bd., Wenatchee, 1986-88, Washington Family Ind. Program, Olympia, 1989-91; mem. econ. devel. coun. Grant County, 1992—; ptnr. low income housing devel. Bus. Cons. & Rsch., Wenatchee, 1996-99. Mem. at large career Women's Network, 1984—, mem. Econ. Devel. Coun. of No. Cen. Washington; mem. Steering Com. to Retain Judge Small. Recipient Nat. Paragon award, 1991, Wash. State Gov.'s award for achievement in farmworker housing, 2001; grantee Nat. Career Devel. Guidelines Wash. State, 1989; named Wenatchee Valley Coll. Vocat. Contbr. of Yr., 1991. Fellow Dem. Women's Club; mem. Nat. Assn. Career Counselors, Nat. Assn. Pvt. Career Counselors, Nat. Coun. Resource Devel., NCW Estate Planning Coun. Avocations: self improvement books, staff and organizational development, cmty. improvements advocate, housing development for elderly and special needs individuals. Home and Office: 2961 Riviera Blvd Malaga WA 98828-9733

NAPIER, BETH, secondary education educator; b. San Diego, July 16, 1949; d. Samuel and Vivian (Shederick) N.; children: Caitlin, McCoy. BA in Chemistry, Mills Coll., 1982; MA in Edn., U.S. Internat. U., 1988. Cert. secondary tchr., Calif. Chair sci. dept. Oakland (Calif.) Unified Sch. Dist., 1982-92, resource tchr. phys. sci., 1992—. Head Proctor Chem. Labs., Coll. of Marin, Kentfield, Calif., 1976-78; adj. instr. Holy Names Coll., Oakland, 1988-89; tchr., rschr. in astrophysics and nuclear physics Lawrence Berkeley (Calif.) Labs., 1990, in biochem. and cystic fibrosis Children's Hosp., Oakland, 1993; co-chair curriculum com. Bay Area Sci. & Tech. Edn. Consortium, Oakland, 1992—; bd. dirs. Chabot Obs. and Sci. Ctr., Oakland; presenter in field. Conf. organizer Good Schs. for Tough Times, Oakland. Carrie Copening Meml. scholar, 1980; recipient Sec. of Energy BASTEC award Dept. Energy, U.S. Govt., 1992. Mem. Oakland Edn. Assn. Avocations: planetarium operation, brazilian dance. Office: Chabot Sci Ctr 4917 Mountain Blvd Oakland CA 94619-3014

NAPLES, CAESAR JOSEPH, law and public policy educator, lawyer, consultant; b. Buffalo, Sept. 4, 1938; s. Caesar M. and Fannie A. (Occhipinti) N.; children: Jennifer, Caesar; m. Sandra L. Harrison, July 16, 1983. AB, Yale U., 1960; JD, SUNY, 1963. Bar: N.Y. 1963, Fla. 1977, Calif. 1988, U.S. Supreme Ct. 1965. With Moot & Sprague, Buffalo, 1965-69; asst. dir., employee rels. N.Y. Gov. Office, Albany, 1969-71; asst. v. chancellor SUNY, Albany, 1971-75; vice chancellor and gen. counsel Fla. State U. System, 1975-82; vice chancellor Calif. State U. System, 1983-92, vice chancellor emeritus, 1992—, prof. law and fin. emeritus, 1983—; bd. dirs., gen. counsel, corp. sec. Open U., Denver and Wilmington, Del., 1999—2003; gen. counsel Walden U., 1989—2003. Cons. Govt. of Australia, U. Nev. Sys., Assn. Can. Colls. and Univs., Que., also other univs. and colls. Contbr. articles to profl. jours.; co-author: Romanov Succession, 1989 with J. Victor Baldridge. Mem. Metlife Resources Adv. Bd., 1986-2002, chmn., 1992-2002; mem. Meml. Heart Inst. Long Beach Meml. Hosp., 1993—, bd. dirs., chmn. 1998—, found. bd., 1996—; bd. dirs. Calif. Acad. Math. and Scis., 1995—. Capt. U.S. Army, 1963-65. Mem. Acad Pers. Adminstrn. (founder), Nat. Ctr. for Study Collective Bargaining Higher Edn. (bd. dirs.). Avocations: opera, tennis. Office: 816 N Juanita Ave Ste B Redondo Beach CA 90277-2200 Fax: 310-798-0065. E-mail: cjnaples@csulb.edu.

NAPODANO, RUDOLPH JOSEPH, internist, medical educator; b. Rochester, N.Y., Oct. 16, 1933; BA, U. Buffalo, 1955; MD, SUNY-HSC, Syracuse, 1959. Diplomate Am. Bd. Internal Medicine, Am. Bd. Cardiovascular Diseases. Intern, asst. resident Highland Hosp., Rochester, 1959-61; fellow in cardiology SUNY-Upstate, Syracuse, 1961-62; chief resident in medicine Highland Hosp., 1962-63; spl. trainee in cardiology U. Rochester, 1968, clin. asst. prof. medicine, 1969-70, asst. prof. medicine, 1970-72, assoc. prof., 1972-79, prof., 1979-93, prof. emeritus, 1993—, with Sch. Medicine and Dentistry, 1970-93; ret.; prof. medicine SUNY, Syracuse, 1994-98. Fellow ACP, Am. Coll. Cardiology; mem. AAAS, Soc. Gen. Internal Medicine, Rochester Acad. Medicine (trustee 1976—, pres. 1980-81), Alpha Omega Alpha.

NAPPI, MARIE TERESA, secondary school mathematics educator; b. Bklyn., July 29, 1952; d. Gasper Raymond and Ida Beatrice (Chanice) Valenti; m. John Gondolfo Nappi, July 15, 1972; children: John, Joseph. BA in Math. and Edn. cum laude, Hunter Coll., 1974; MA in Elem. Edn., Adelphi U., 1992. Cert. tchr. math. 7-12, edn. N-6, N.Y. 5th grade tchr. St. Anthony's Elem. Sch., South Ozone Park, N.Y., 1974-80; comm.-technician tchr. AT&T, N.Y.C., 1980-82; jr. h.s. math. tchr. St. Raphael Sch., East Meadow, N.Y., 1985-92, St. Elizabeth Ann Seton, East Meadow, 1992-95, Marie Curie Mid. Sch., Bayside, NY, 1995—2002; asst. prin. Mid. Sch. 74, Bayside, 2002—. Adj. prof. math. Nassau C.C., Garden City, N.Y., 1992—; advisor student coun., nat. jr. honor soc., East Meadow, N.Y., 1992-94; math. coord., mathlete advisor Nat. Math. League, 1992—. Mem. PTA, Merrick, N.Y., 1982—. Recipient Commendation award N.Y. State Senate, 1993. Mem. Nat. Cath. Edn. Assn., Nat. Coun. of Math. Tchrs., Nassau County Math. Tchrs. Assn. (Math. Tchr. of Yr. 1992), Nat. Assn. Student Activity Advisers. Avocations: step aerobics, bowling, piano, reading, collecting autographs.

NARAGON, STEVEN SCOTT, philosophy educator; b. South Bend, Ind., May 7, 1959; s. Ralph Raymond and Ramona (Houser) N.; m. Pamela Higgins, Jan. 4, 1983; children: Natasha, Emma, Adelyn, Thomas. Student, Philipps U., Marburg, Germany, 1980-82; BA, Manchester Coll., 1982; PhD, U. Notre Dame, 1987. Instr. Ind. U.-Purdue U., Indpls., 1987, U. Indpls., 1987; asst. prof. Manchester Coll., North Manchester, 1991—, chmn. dept. philosophy, 2001—. Vis. asst. prof. U. Ark., Fayetteville, 1987-88; vis. scholar U. Notre Dame, 1989-91; book reviewer Tchg. Philosophy, 1988, Internat. Studies in Philosophy, 1991. Co-editor Bull. Peace Studies Inst., 1993-94; contbr. articles to profl. jours. Grantee NEH, 1988, 94. Mem. N.Am. Kant Soc., Am. Philos. Assn. Office: Manchester Coll 604 E College Ave North Manchester IN 46962-1225 E-mail: ssnaragon@manchester.edu.

NARASIMHULU, SHAKUNTHALA, biochemist, educator; b. Mysore, India; came to U.S., 1954; d. Ramaiya and Seethamma Madgiri. BSc, Mysore U., 1951; MS, Drexel U., 1955; PhD, Thomas Jefferson U., 1960; MS, U. Pa. Rsch. assoc. U. Pa., Phila., 1960-67, instr. biochemistry, 1966-69, asst. prof., 1967—. Comm. com. U. Pa.; lectr. and speaker in field. Contbr. articles to profl. jours.; invited reviewer. Vis. Dozent grantee Alexander Humboldt Found., Germany, 1969-71; Rsch. grantee NIH, 1975-80, Office of Naval Rsch., 1974-82. Mem. Am. Soc. Biochemistry and Molecular Biology, Endocrine Soc., N.Y. Acad. Sci., Assn. Women in Sci., Phila. Biochemists Club, John Morgan Soc. U. Pa., Sigma Xi. Achievements include first to cytochrome P450. Office: Univ Pa 36th and Hamilton Walk Philadelphia PA 19104

NARAYAN, RAMESH, astronomy educator; b. Bombay, Sept. 25, 1950; came to U.S., 1983; s. G.N. and Rajalakshmi (Sankaran) Ramachandran; m. G.V. Vani, June 6, 1977. BS in Physics, Madras U., 1971; MS in Physics, Bangalore U., 1973, PhD in Physics, 1979. Rsch. scientist Raman Rsch. Inst., Bangalore, India, 1978-83; postdoctoral fellow Calif. Inst. Tech., 1983-84, sr. rsch. fellow, 1984-85; assoc. prof. astronomy U. Ariz., Tucson, 1985-90, prof., 1990-91; prof. astronomy Harvard U., Cambridge, Mass., 1991—, chmn. dept., 1997-2001. Sr. astronomer Harvard-Smithsonian Ctr. for Astrophysics, 1991—, assoc. dir., 1996-97; adv. bd. Inst. Theoretical Physics U. Calif., Santa Barbara, 1994-98, chmn., 1996-97; com. gravitational physics NRC, 1997-99; chmn. adv. bd. Ctr. for Gravitational Wave Physics, Pa. State U., 2001—; mem. adv. bd. Max Planck Inst. for Astrophysics, 2002—, chmn., 2003—. Contbr. articles to profl. jours. Named NSF Presdl. Young Investigator, 1989. Mem. AAAS, Am. Astron. Soc., Internat. Astron. Union. Achievements include research in the general area of theoretical astrophysics, specializing in accretion disks, black holes, gravitational lenses, gamma-ray bursts, radio pulsars, image processing and scintillation. Office: Harvard-Smithsonian Ctr Astrophysics 60 Garden St # 51 Cambridge MA 02138-1516

NARDACCI, MARTHA JOYCE, elementary education educator; b. Providence, Oct. 6, 1951; d. Joseph and Martha (Bellotti) Procaccini; m. Nicholas L. Nardacci, Apr. 14, 1978; children: Nicholas, Loriann. BS cum laude, R.I. Coll., Providence, 1973, MEd in Instrnl. Tech., 1976; diploma, U. Cracow, Poland, 1974. Cert. elem. tchr., R.I. Tchr. 3d grade Brown Ave. Sch., Johnston, R.I., 1973-75, tchr. 5th grade, 1975-78, tchr. kindergarten, 1982; tchr. 6th grade Thornton Sch., Johnston, 1979; math. specialist Johnston Schs., 1980; tchr. 2d grade Sarah Dyer Barnes Sch., Johnston, 1982; tchr. 1st grade G.C. Calef Sch., Johnston, 1978-79, tchr. kindergarten, 1984-2000, Early Childhood Ctr., Johnston, 2000—. Mem. kindergarten curriculum revision com. Johnston Sch. Dept., 1990-91; adminstr. Early Prevention of Sch. Failure Test, 1988; mem. report card revision com., tchr. support team Early Childhood Ctr., 2000-01, mem. School Improvement Team, 2000-03. Active Big Sisters of R.I., Providence, 1970-72. Recipient Project Power award R.I. Found., 1986, Class award Earth Artists Program, EPA, 1994, 2003. Mem. Assn. Childhood Edn. Internat., Learning Ctrs. Club. Home: 152 Gentry Way North Scituate RI 02857-1545 E-mail: mjmnstar@home.com.

NARDOZZI, PETER MICHAEL, pharmacist, clinical educator, lecturer, entrepreneur; b. Brockton, Mass., Nov. 6, 1937; s. Michael John Nardozzi and Doris M. (MacLea) Worthington; m. Sandra Scott Boyatsis (div. 1975); 1 child, Mark; m. Sandra Scafani, Dec. 31, 1984; 1 child, Cody Abernathy. BS in Pharmacy, Northeastern U., 1960; MS in Nutrition, Hawaii Inst. for Health, Diet and Nutrition, 1982; PharmD, Southeastern Coll. Pharm. Scis., Miami, Fla., 1992. Registered pharmacist, Fla., Maine, Mass.; lic. cons. pharmacist, Fla. Exec. v.p. Nardozzi Rexall Drug and other firms, Fla. and Mass., 1960-77; propr. Bonnie & Cycles, Boston, 1974-76; treas. Columbian Enterprises Importing/Emeralds, Caribbean Salvage Diving Co., Boston, 1975-77; ptnr., v.p., pharmacist Oceanside Drug, Pompano Beach, Fla., 1965-87; pharmacist mgr. Grand Union Pharmacy Dept., Hialeah, Fla., 1977-78; chief pharmacist Shoppers Drug Mart, Ft. Lauderdale, Fla., 1978-80; pres. Carribean Salvage, Inc., Pompano Beach; dir. pharm. services Bodee Med. Facilities, Pompano Beach, 1981; founder, exec. v.p. Hawaii Diet Plan, Honolulu, 1982-84; founder, pres. Innovative Bus. Devel. Group, Albuquerque, 1984-85; pharmacist, mgr. Cunningham Drug, Singer Island, Fla., 1986-87, Popular Pharmacy, Miami, 1987—89, Pharmor Drug, Miami, 1989—93; pharmacist, clin. educator Rite Aid Corp., Bath, Maine, 1994—. Assoc. Achievement Research & Verification Systems, Albuquerque, 1984-85; bd. dirs. Alliance Enterprises, Albuquerque, Zyne Design, Taos, N.Mex.; founder, pres. ITOCAM-Alternative Medicine Cons. Co.; mem. Pharmacy in the Amazon Rainforest, Pharmacy on the Belize Reef, Internat. Expdns.; lectr. continuing ednl. alternative complementary therapies. Author weight loss booklet, 1985; editor Nat. Nutrition Newsletter, 1982-84; health columnist; co-patentee nutritional diet supplement. Youth counselor Hawaii Supreme Ct., Honolulu, 1982; lectr. drug abuse Nat. Assn. Retail Druggists. Fellow Am. Soc. Cons. Pharmacists; mem. Am. Pharm. Assn., Am. Mktg. Assn., Nat. Small Bus. Assoc., Maine Pharmacy Assn., Fla. Pharm. Assn., Hawaii Soc. Corp. Planners, Ctr. for Entrpreneurial Mgmt., Soc. Integrative Medicine, Soc. Natural Pharmacy, Venture Founders, Mortar and Pestle Soc. E-mail: docn@gwi.net.

NARDUZZI, JAMES LOUIS, college dean, consultant; b. Cleve., July 20, 1953; s. Louis James and Norma (Minor) Narduzzi; m. Bonnie Ann Sinko, Aug. 7, 1982; children: Elizabeth, Emily. BA, Miami U., Oxford, Ohio, 1975; MA, Am. U., 1977, PhD, 1985. Acad. dir. London Semester Program Am. U., Washington, 1984; asst. dir. Washington Semester Programs Washington, 1979-82; dir. Washington Semester Programs, 1982-88; dir. Summer and Spl. Programs U. Hartford (Conn.), 1988-91, asst. acad. dean, asst. v.p., 1991-94; dean Univ. Coll. Sch. Continuing Studies U. Richmond (Va.), 1994—. Cons. EPA, Chgo., 1994, Butler U., Indpls., 1993. Author: Mental Health Among Elderly Native Americans, 1994; contbr. articles to profl. jours. Participant Leadership Greater Hartford, 1989; bd. dirs. Arts Coun. Richmond; chair Greater Richmond Heart Walk. Mem. Nat. Univ. Continuing Edn. Assn. (Cmty. Involvement award 1991). Avocations: golf, swimming.

NARSAVAGE, GEORGIA ROBERTS, nursing educator, researcher, dean, associate dean; b. Pittston, Pa., Jan. 1, 1948; d. George H. Roberts and Betty (Smith) Brown; m. Peter P. Narsavage, Oct. 26, 1968; children: Peter A., Paul J., Marea L. BSN, U. Md., Washington DC, 1969; MSN, Coll. Misericordia, 1984; PhD in Nursing, U. Pa., Phila., 1990. RN, Ohio.; cert. adult nurse practitioner, Ohio, 2002. Staff nurse Mercy Hosp., Scranton, Pa., 1970-72; pvt. duty nursing Pa., 1972-79; pvt. duty nurse Community Med. Ctr., Scranton, Pa., 1979; clinical instr. Lackawanna County Vo-Tech Practical Nursing Program, Dunmore, Pa., 1979-82; clinical and theoretical instr. Mercy Hosp. Sch. of Nursing, Scranton, Pa., 1982-84; asst. prof. nursing dept. nursing U. Scranton, Pa., 1984-93, assoc. prof., 1993—99, chmn. dept., 1991-94, dir. RN program dept. nursing, 1990-92, assoc. dean Panuska Coll. Profl. Studies, 1998—99; dir. MSN program Sch. Nursing Case Western Res. U., Cleve., 1999—, assoc. prof., 1999—, assoc. dean Academic Programs, 2003—. Postdoctoral fellow U. Pa., Phila., 1995-97; cons. in field. Contbr. articles to profl. jours. Gifted program mentor Scranton Sch. Dist.; active in ch. and civic choirs. Grantee U. Scranton, 1989, 91, 94-98, grantee NIH NRSA, 1995-97; recipient Rsch. award European Respiratory Soc., 2002. Mem. ANA, APHA, Am. Thoracic Soc./Am. Lung Assn. (Abstract award 2002), Pa. Nurses Assn. (bd. dirs., chmn. com., conv. del., Excellence award 1996, Mentor award 2002), Lackawanna Nurses Assn. (bd. dirs., com. chmn., dist. pres.), Nat. League for Nursing, Coun. Nursing Informatics (chair nominating com. 1993-95), Pa. League for Nursing (chair nominating com.), Ohio Nurses Assn. (chmn. practice com.), Midwest Nursing Rsch. Soc. (chmn. membership com.), U. Md. Nurses Alumnae Assn., Ea. Nursing Rsch. Soc. (mem.-at-large bd. dirs., interim treas., rsch. grantee 1994), Theta Phi Sigma (Excellence award 1994). Lutheran. Office: FPB SON CWRU 10900 Euclid Ave Cleveland OH 44106-4904 E-mail: gln2@po.cwru.edu.

NARVER, JOHN COLIN, business administration educator emeritus; b. Portland, Oreg., Aug. 5, 1935; s. Ursel Colin and Merle (Wells) N.; children: Gregory, Allison Ann, Colin. BS, Oreg. State U., 1957; MBA, U. Calif.-Berkeley, 1960; PhD, 1965. With Boise Cascade Corp., Portland, 1960-61; asst. prof. U. B.C., Can., 1964-66; asst. prof. dept. mktg. and internat. bus. U. Wash., Seattle, 1966-68, assoc. prof., 1968-71, prof., 1971-99, chmn. dept., 1974-78. Vis. prof. Norwegian Sch. Econs., 1973, Bogazici U., Istanbul, Turkey, 1974, U. Helsinki, 1995; cons. in field. Author: Conglomerate Mergers and Market Competition, 1967, (with R. Savitt) The Marketing Economy: An Analytical Approach, 1971, (with S. Slater) The Effect of a Market Orientation on Business Profitability, 1990. Served to lt. U.S. Army, 1957-59. Mem. Phi Delta Theta. Democrat. Episcopalian. Home: 2015 Federal Ave E Seattle WA 98102-4141

NASH, ANNAMARIE, secondary education educator; b. Paterson, N.J., Dec. 26, 1937; d. Karl and Anneliese (Schmidt) Gimmel; m. James John Nash, Aug. 16, 1959; children: James, Brian, Thomas. BA, Montclair State Coll., 1959; MA, William Paterson State Coll., 1980. Cert. tchr., elem. adminstr., secondary adminstr., supr., N.J. Social studies tchr. West New York (N.J.) Bd. Edn., 1959-60, Cedar Grove (N.J.) Bd. Edn., 1968—. Active Nat. Assn. Atomic Vets., Salem, Mass., 1982, Disabled Am. Vets. Aux., Cinn., 1988, Little Falls (N.J.) Athletic Club Aux., 1972, Little Falls Jr. Women's Club, 1964-73. Recipient Project Business Program award Jr. Achievement, Inc., 1986; named to Governor's Teacher Recognition Program, 1988. Mem. NEA, N.J. Edn. Assn., Essex County Edn. Assn., Cedar Grove Edn. Assn. (treas., sec. 1968—). Avocations: reading, walking, volleyball, travel. Office: Cedar Grove Bd Edn Cedar Grove High Sch Rugby Rd Cedar Grove NJ 07009

NASH, HENRY WARREN, marketing educator; b. Tampa, Fla., Sept. 19, 1927; s. Leslie Dikeman and Mildred (Johnson) N.; m. Frances Lora Venters, Aug. 20, 1950; children: Warren Leslie, Richard Dale. BS in Bus. Adminstrn, U. Fla., 1950, MBA, 1951; postgrad., Ind. U., 1951-53; PhD, U. Ala., 1965. Student asst. U. Fla., 1948-50, grad. asst., 1950-51, Ind. U., 1951-53; salesman Field Enterprises, Inc., Chgo., 1953; assoc. prof. bus. and econs. Miss. Coll., 1953-57; assoc. prof. marketing Miss. State U., 1957-66, prof., head dept., 1966-96; emeritus prof. mktg.; emeritus head dept. mktg., quantitative analysis, bus. law; dir. Coll. Bus. and Industry Acad. Advising Ctr., 1995-2000; ptnr. Southland Cons. Assos., 1968-84; bd. dirs. Govt. Employees Credit Union, 1969-92, v.p., 1969-73, pres., 1973-78. Author: (with others) Principles of Marketing, 1961. Served with USNR, 1945-46. Loveman's Merchandising fellow U. Ala., 1961-62 Mem. Am. Mktg. Assn., Am. Acad. Advt., Acad. Internat. Bus., So. Econ. Assn., So. Mktg. Assn. (sec. 1974-75, pres. 1976-77), Sales and Mktg. Execs. (internat. chmn. educators com. 1967-70), Miss. Retail Mchts. Assn. (bd. dirs.), Pi Sigma Epsilon (Nat. educator, v.p. 1967-69, nat. pres. 1967-71), Kiwanis (treas. Starkville club 1969-70, v.p. 1973-74, pres. 1974-75, lt. gov. 1977-78, gov. 1982-83), Blue Key, Beta Gamma Sigma, Omicron Delta Kappa, Mu Kappa Tau (nat. v.p. 1977-79, 86-88, pres. 1979-81, 88-90), Alpha Kappa Psi, Phi Kappa Phi (v.p. Miss. State U. 1990-91, pres. 1991-92). Baptist (tchr., deacon). Home: 2800 W Main St Cottage 302B Tupelo MS 38801-3027

NASH, JAMES JOHN, superintendent; b. N.Y.C., Nov. 12, 1933; s. James B. and Margaret (Curnyn) N.; m. Annamarie Gimmel, Aug. 16, 1959; children: James, Brian, Thomas. BA, Montclair State U., 1956, MA, 1962. Cert. elem. tchr., adminstr., prin., supr. N.J. Tchr. Little Falls (N.J.) Bd. Edn., 1958-73, prin., 1973-85, supt., 1985—. Pres. Little Falls Recreation Commn., 1975-76. Mem. Am. Assn. Sch. Adminstrs., Nat. Assn. Atomic Vets. (life), Nat. Assn. Radiation Survivors (life), Disabled Am. Vets. (life), N.J. Coun. Edn., N.J. Assn. Sch. Adminstrs. (exec. com. 1989—), N.J. Schoolmaster's Club, Passaic County Assn. Sch. Adminstrs. (pres. 1990-91), Passaic County Assn. Prins. (pres. 1980-81). Avocations: reading, walking, travel, pub. speaking on vets affairs. Office: Little Falls Bd Edn Stevens Ave # 1 Little Falls NJ 07424-2245

NASH, JUDITH KLUCK, mathematics educator; b. Manchester, Conn., Dec. 26, 1946; d. Erwin John and Eleanor May (Starke) Kluck; m. Stephen T. Nash, Apr. 7, 1990. BS, So. Conn. State U., 1969; MS, 1976. Math. tchr. Cheshire (Conn.) Pub. Schs., 1969-93, Tunxis C.C., Farmington, Conn., 1994—. Home: 72 Tunxis Path Plantsville CT 06479-1348 Office: Tunxis CC 271 Scott Swamp Rd Farmington CT 06032-3324

NASSAR-MCMILLAN, SYLVIA C. adult education educator; b. Detroit, Aug. 29, 1963; d. Albert S. Nassar and Erika L. Strunk; m. Ian Johnson McMillan, July 17, 1994. BA, Oakland U., 1984; MA, Ea. Mich. U., 1986; PhD, U. N.C., Greensboro, 1994. Grad. asst. Ea. Mich. U., Ypsilanti, 1985-86; bi-lingual officer mgr. Motion Mfg., Detroit, 1986-87; counselor UAW/GM Human Resource Ctr., Pontiac, Mich., 1987-88; program coord. women's ctr. We. Mich. U., Kalamazoo, 1988-89, coord. career planning, 1989-90; career counselor, intern Loyola U., Chgo., 1990; counselor, site supr. Charlevoix Publ Schs., Beaver Island, Mich., 1991; asst. prof., counseling coord. Austin Peay State U., Clarksville, Tenn., 1994-96; asst. prof. counselor edn. U. N.C., Charlotte, 1996—. Mem. sexism com. Austin Peay State U., 1995-96, mem. critical incident stress mgmt., 1994-96, mem. univ. hearing bd., 1994-96. Workcamp leader Vols. for Peace, Baxter State Park, Mich., 1990, Girl Scouts Am., Kalamazoo, 1990; group counselor/cmty. edn./vol. tng. HAVEN-Domestic Violence Shelter, Oakland County Mich., 1986-88. Doctoral fellow Residence Life U. N.C., Greensboro, 1991-94; recipient Profl. Devel. award Mich. Coll. Personnel Assn., 1989-90. Mem. APA, ACA (editl. bd. Jour. of Counseling and Devel. 1996—, professionalism com. 1995-98), So. Assn. Counselor Edn. and Supervision, Assn. Counselor Edn. and Supervision, Chi Sigma Iota. Office: Dept Counselor Edn Spl Edn & Child Devel U NC Charlotte NC 28223

NASSAU, CAROL DEAN, educator; b. Omaha, Jan. 16, 1953; 1 child, William Dean Nassau. BA in Translation, U. Nebr., 1976; MA in Comparative Lit., Binghamton (N.Y.) U., 1983, MAT in Fgn. Lgn., 1987; EdD in Ednl. Theory and Practice, SUNY, Binghamton, 2003. Cert. tchr., N.Y. Translator Mutual of Omaha Ins. Co., Omaha, 1976-78; tchr. Unatego Ctrl. Schs., Wells Bridge, N.Y., 1987-88, Oneonta (N.Y.) City Schs., 1988—2000; coord. data analysis svcs. Broome-Tioga BOCES, Binghamton, NY, 2000—. Nat. trainer Generating Expectations Student Achievment. Contbr. articles to profl. jours.; actress (TV series) Susquehanna Stories, 1990. Couper fellowship Binghamton U., 1994; recipient essay contest award N.Y. State Founds. in Edn. Assn., 1998. Mem. NEA, AAUW, ASCD, Am. Ednl. Rsch. Assn., N.Y. Schs. Data Analysis Tech. Assistance Group (founding mem.). Democrat. Avocations: acting, skiing, travel. Home: 16 Hazel St Oneonta NY 13820-1307

NASSOURA, NANCY KATHRYN, special education educator; b. N.Y.C., Oct. 16, 1968; d. Robert Emmett and Winifred Kathryn (Flynn) Bozzomo; m. Khaled Nassoura, July 8, 1995. BA, Coll. St. Elizabeth, 1991; MA in Spl. Edn., Kean Coll. N.J., 1994. Tchr. handicapped, elem. edn., secondary English. Permanent substitute Clifton (N.J.) Pub. Schs., 1992; resource ctr. tchr. Bedwell Elem. Sch., Bernardsville, N.J., 1992-94, Hilltop Elem. Sch., Mendham, N.J., 1994—. Head tchr. summer program, YMCA, Livingston, N.J., 1991—, morning program, Basking Ridge, N.J., 1992-94. Mem. Coun. Exceptional Children, Coun. for Children with Behavorial Disorders, Coun. for Children with Learning Disabilities, Orton Dyslexia Soc., N.J. Edn. Assn., N.J. Coun. for Social Studies, Kappa Delta Pi. Avocations: writing, reading, rollerblading, mountain biking, music. Office: Hilltop Elem Sch 12 Hilltop Rd Mendham NJ 07945-1215

NASSTROM, ROY RICHARD, retired education educator, consultant; b. Oakland, Calif., Oct. 28, 1930; s. Roy Richard and Edith Dolores (Spilman) N.; m. Sally Louise Shaw, Aug. 29, 1964; children: Karen, Eric. AA, U. Calif., Berkeley, 1955, BA, 1956, MA, 1964, PhD, 1971. Asst. to supt. Ravenswood Sch. Dist., East Palo Alto, Calif., 1964-65; acting instr. edn. U. Calif., Berkeley, 1965-68; asst. prof. ednl. adminstrn. U. Ky., Lexington,

1969-70; asst. prof. edn. Purdue U., West Lafayette, Ind., 1971-76; mediator, fact finder Ind. Edn. Employment Rels. Bd., 1974-76; asst. grad. dean Winona (Minn.) State U., 1976-77, chmn. ednl. adminstrn. dept., 1976-88, prof., 1976-01, prof. emeritus, 2001—, chmn. ednl. leadership dept., 1998-01. Cons., spkr. various orgns. and schs., 1969—; mem. bd. abstractors Ednl. Adminstrn. Abstracts, 1976-83; dir. post-masters studies, Winona State U., 1992-99. Editor Ravenswood Report, 1964-65, U. Calif.-Berkeley Sch. Edn. Newsletter, 1965-68; editors AASA Prof., 1979-82; manuscript reviewer various jours. and pubs, 1983-87; contbr. articles and revs. to profl. jours., chpts. to books. Mem. steering com. Winona On-line Dems., 2003—. With U.S. Army, 1952—54. Recipient numerous grants, 1969-98. Mem.Am. Ednl. Rsch. Assn. (paper reviewer 1983-2000), Am. Assn. Sch. Adminstrs., Am. Assn. Colls. for Tchr. Edn. (instnl. rep., paper reviewer), Nat. Assn. Scholars, Minn. Hist. Soc., Phi Delta Kappa, Pi Sigma Alpha . Avocation: photography. Home: 1702 Edgewood Rd Winona MN 55987-2149 E-mail: nasstrom@cal.berkeley.edu., rrn@hbci.com.

NASWORTHY, CAROL CANTWELL, education and public policy researcher; b. Sapulpa, Okla., Aug. 6, 1939; d. Harlin Forrest and Margaret (Martin) Cantwell; m. Jack Edward Nasworthy. BA in English, Okla. State U., 1962; MA in English, U. Ark.; MEd in Ednl. Adminstrn., Lamar U., 1979; PhD in Ednl. Adminstrn., U. Tex., Austin, 1989. Cert. tchr., Tex. Tchr., dept. chair Tulsa Pub. Schs., 1962-74, Nederland (Tex.) Pub. Schs., 1974-84; legis. aide Tex. Ho. of Reps., Beaumont and Austin, 1982-84; adminstr. Tex. Edn. Agy., Austin, 1985; dir. programs Tex. Gov.'s Office, 1985-87; dir. programs Office Pub./Pvt. Sector Initiatives Tex. Employment Commn., Austin, 1987-93; asst. to commr. Tex. R.R. Commn., Austin, 1993-95; rsch. assoc. S.W. Edn. Devel. Lab., Austin, 1995—. Curriculum cons. Okla. State U., Stillwater and Tulsa, 1967; chair Tex. Com. Practitioners Vocat. Edn., 1990—. Contbr. to profl. publs. Trustee, vice-chair Austin C.C., 1990—. Grantee U.S. Dept. Labor, 1990—, Tex. Dept. Human Svcs., 1990—. Mem. Tex. Coun. Women Sch. Execs. (bd. dirs. 1986-90), Phi Delta Kappa. Democrat. Office: SW Edn Devel Lab 2100 E 7th St Austin TX 78702-3424

NATALE, MARLENE ELVIRA, secondary school educator; b. Jamaica, N.Y., Nov. 20, 1947; d. Enrico and Cecelia Madeline (Nardi) Cadolino; m. Michael C. Natale, Nov. 10, 1973; 1 child, Michael Enrico. BA in Math. Edn., SUNY, New Paltz, 1969; MA in Guidance and Counseling, L.I. U., 1973. Cert. math. tchr. Tchr. math. Sewanhaka Cen. High Sch. Dist., Elmont, N.Y., 1969—. Republican. Roman Catholic. Avocations: landscaping, golf, crosswords. Home: 39 Marlborough Rd West Hempstead NY 11552-1711

NATALICIO, DIANA SIEDHOFF, academic administrator; b. St. Louis, Aug. 25, 1939; d. William and Eleanor J. (Biermann) Siedhoff. BS in Spanish summa cum laude, St. Louis U., 1961; MA in Portuguese lang., U. Tex., 1964, PhD in Linguistics, 1969. Chmn. dept. modern langs. U. Tex., El Paso, 1973-77, assoc. dean liberal arts, 1977-79; acting dean liberal arts, 1979-80; dean Coll. Liberal Arts U. Tex., El Paso, 1980-84, v.p. acad. affairs, 1984-88, pres., 1988—. Bd. dirs. El Paso br. Fed. Res. Bd. Dallas, chmn., 1989; mem. Presdl. Adv. Commn. on Ednl. Excellence for Hispanic Ams., 1991; bd. dirs. Sandia Corp., Trinity Industries; bd. dirs. Nat. Action Coun. for Minorities in Engring., 1993—; mem. Nat. Sci. Bd. 1994-2000; mem. NASA Adv. Coun., 1994-96; bd. mem. Fund for Improvement of Post-Secondary Edn., 1993-97; bd. dirs. Fogarty Internat. Ctr. of NIH, 1993-96; bd. chair Am. Assn. Higher Edn., 1995-96; bd. dirs. U.S.-Mexico Commn. for Ednl. and Cultural Exch., 1994—. Co-author: Sounds of Children, 1977; contbr. articles to profl. jours. Bd. dirs. United Way El Paso, 1990-93, chmn. needs survey com., 1990-91, chmn. edn. divsn., 1989; chmn. Quality Edn. for Minorities Network in Math. Sci. and Engring., 1991-92; chairperson Leadership El Paso, Class 12, 1989-90, mem. adv. coun., 1987-90, participant, 1980-81; mem. Historically Black Colls. and Univs./Minority Instns. Consortium on Environ. Tech. chairperson, 1991-93. Recipient Harold W. McGraw. Jr. prize in edn., 1997, Torch of Liberty award Anti-Defamation League B'nai B'rith, 1991, Conquistador award City of El Paso, 1990, Humanitarian award El Paso chpt. NCCJ, 1990; mem. El Paso Women's Hall of Fame, 1990. Mem. Philos. Soc. Tex. Avocations: hiking, bicycling, skiing, skating. Home: 711 Cincinnati Ave El Paso TX 79902-2616 Office: U Tex at El Paso Office Of President El Paso TX 79968-0001*

NATHAN, LAURA E. sociology educator; b. L.A., Oct. 28, 1951; d. Monroe and Sheila (Solomon) Engelberg; m. Mark D. Nathan, April 9, 1978; children: Justin, Michael. BA in Sociology, U. Calif., Santa Barbara, 1973; MA in Sociology, U. Calif., L.A., 1975, PhD in Sociology, 1981. Teaching assoc. in sociology Univ. Calif., L.A., 1975-76; acting asst. prof. sociology Calif. State Univ., Fullerton, Calif., 1977-81; coord., instr. Univ. Calif., L.A., 1979-80; assoc. prof. sociology and psychology Antelope Valley Coll., Lancaster, Calif., 1981-82; asst. prof. sociology Mills Coll., Oakland, Calif., 1982-87, assoc. prof. sociology, 1987-93, prof. of sociology, 1993—, Robert J. and Ann B. Wert prof. of sociology, 1993-96, head dept. sociology and anthropology, 2000—01, dean social sci., 2001—02. Lectr. in sociology and womens studies Calif. State Univ., Long Beach, 1978; program evaluator U.S. Dept. Health, Edn. and Welfare, L.A., 1974-75, program dir. 1975-76; mem. conf. planning com. Womens Leadership Conf., Mills Coll., also com. chair, 1992-93; bd. dirs. Am. Cancer Soc., East Bay Region, Calif., 1985-96, Calif. divsn., 2001-; bd. dirs. Am. Cancer Soc. East Bay Metro Unit, 1996—, pres., 1999-2001, bd. dirs. Am. Cancer Soc. Calif. Div. Author: (with others) Secondary Analysis of Survey Data, 1985; contbr. chpts. to books. Regents Rsch. grantee, 1979, Mellon Found. grantee, 1983, Faculty Devel. Rsch. grantee Mills. Coll., 1985, 86, 87, 90, 91, 94, 95, 99, 2002, Barratt Found. grantee, 2002, W.K. Kellogg Nat. fellow, 1988, Thornton Bradshaw Humanities fellow Claremont Grad. Sch., 1990, Graduate Leadership Am., 1997; recipient Disting. Leadership award Am. Cancer Soc., 1995, Unit and Region Lifetime Achievement award, 2000, ten Broek Soc. award for Excellence in Teaching, 1996. Mem. Pacific Sociol. Assn. (mem. nominating com. 1985-88, mem. program com. 1995-96, exec. coun., 1997-99), Am. Sociol. Assn. (membership com. 1988-92, com. soc. and persons with disabilities 1997-2000, chair), Soc. for the Study of Social Problems (chmn. poverty, class inequality div. 1987-88). Jewish. Avocations: traveling, mysteries, vol. work, beading, pilates. Office: Mills Coll 5000 Macarthur Blvd Oakland CA 94613-1301 E-mail: laura@mills.edu.

NATHAN, LEONARD EDWARD, writer; b. Los Angeles, Nov. 8, 1924; s. Israel and Florence (Rosenberg) N.; m. Carol Gretchen Nash, June 27, 1949; children: Andrew Peter, Julia Irene, Miriam Abigail. Student, Ga. Tech., 1943-44, UCLA, 1946-47; BA summa cum laude, U. Calif.-Berkeley, 1950, MA, 1952, PhD, 1961. Instr. Modesto (Calif.) Jr. Coll., 1954-60; prof. dept. rhetoric U. Calif., Berkeley, 1960-91, ret., 1992, chmn. dept., 1968-72. Author: Western Reaches, 1958, The Glad and Sorry Seasons, 1963, The Matchmaker's Lament, 1967, The Day The Perfect Speakers Left, 1969, The Tragic Drama of William Butler Yeats, 1963, Flight Plan, 1971, Without Wishing, 1973, The Likeness, 1975, Coup, 1975, Returning Your Call, 1975, The Transport of Love: The Meghaduta by Kalidasa, 1976, Teachings of Grandfather Fox, 1977, Lost Distance, 1978, Dear Blood, 1980, Holding Patterns, 1982, Carrying On: New and Selected Poems, 1985, Diary of a Left-Handed Bird Watcher, 1996, The Potato Eaters, 1999, Tears of the Old Magician, 2003; also record: Confessions of a Matchmaker, 1973, De Meester van Het WinterLandschap, Selected Poems in Dutch transl. by Cees Nooteboom, Uitgeverij de Arbiedspers, Amsterdam, 1990, Diary of a Left-Handed Birdwatcher in Swedish Translation by Lennart Nilsson, 2002; translator: (with James Larson) Songs of Something Else, 1982, (with Clinton Seely) Grace and Mercy in Her Wild Hair, 1982; (with Czeslaw Milosz) Happy As a Dog's Tail: Poems by Anna Swir, 1985, With the Skin: Poems of Aleksander Wat, 1989, Talking to My Body, Poems of Anna Swir, 1996; (with Arthur Quinn) The Poet's Work: Study of Czeslaw Milosz, 1991. With U.S. Army, 1943-45, ETO. Recipient Phelan award, 1955; Longview prize, 1961; award in lit. Nat. Inst. Arts and Letters, 1971; Poetry medal Commonwealth Club, 1976, 80, 99; U. Calif. Creative Arts fellow, 1961-62, 73-74; U. Calif. Humanities research fellow, 1983-84; Am. Inst. Indian Studies fellow, 1966-67; Guggenheim fellow, 1976-77 Mem. Assn. of Lit. Scholars and Critics. Avocation: birdwatching. Home: 40 Beverly Rd Kensington CA 94707-1304

NATHAN, RICHARD P(ERLE), political scientist, educator; b. Schenectady, N.Y., Nov. 24, 1935; s. Sidney Robert and Betty (Green) N.; m. Mary McNamara, June 5, 1957; children: Robert Joseph, Carol Hewit. AB, Brown U., 1957; M in Pub. Adminstrn., Harvard U., 1959, PhD, 1966. Legis. asst. U.S. Senator Kenneth B. Keating, Washington, 1959-62; dir. domestic policy rsch. Nelson A. Rockefeller, 1963-64; rsch. assoc. The Brookings Instn., Washington, 1966-69, sr. fellow, project dir. monitoring studies gen. revenue sharing, community devel. block grant and pub. svc. employment programs, 1972-79; associated staff The Brookings Inst., Washington, 1980-85; asst. dir. U.S. Office of Mgmt. and Budget, Washington, 1969-71; dep. undersec. U.S Dept. Health, Edn. and Welfare, Washington, 1971-72; prof. pub. and internat. affairs Woodrow Wilson Sch. Pub. and Internat. Affairs Princeton (N.J.) U., 1979-89, also dir. Princeton Urban and Regional Rsch. Ctr., 1979-89; Disting. prof. polit. sci. and pub. policy SUNY, Albany, 1989-97; provost Rockefeller Coll. Pub. Affairs and Policy, Albany, 1989-98. Bd. dirs. Rockefeller Inst. Govt., Fleet Nat. Bank; assoc. dir. Nat. Adv. Commn. on Civil Disorders, 1967-68; vis. prof. govt. and fgn. affairs U. Va., 1972-77; chmn. Nixon Adminstrn. Transition Task Forces on Poverty and Intergovtl. Fiscal Rels., 1968, Domestic Coun. Com. on Welfare Reform Planning, 1969-70; mem. Commn. on Orgn. Govt. of D.C., 1970-72; bd. overseers New Sch. for Social Rsch., 1982-88; mem. working seminar on family and welfare Marquette U., 1986-87; selection com. Rockefeller Pub. Svc. Awards Program, 1976-78; income maintenance task force Nat. Urban Coalition, 1975-78; treas. Manpower Demonstration Rsch. Corp., 1974-81, chmn., 1981-98; mem. coun. scholars U.S. Libr. of Congress, 1989—; mem. N.Y. State Temp. Commn. Constl. Revision, 1993-94; mem. U.S. Adv. Commn. on Intergovtl. Rels., 1998-2000; vis. fellow GAO, 1998-2000; cons. U.S. Gen. Acctg. Office, 1998-2000. Author: Jobs and Civil Rights, The Role of the Federal Government in Promoting Equal Opportunity in Employment and Training, 1969, The Plot That Failed: Nixon and the Administrative Presidency, 1975, Monitoring Revenue Sharing, 1975, Revenue Sharing, The Second Round., 1977, Monitoring the Public Service Employment Program, 1978, America's Government: A Fact Book of Census Data on the Organization, Finances, and Employment of Federal, State, and Local Governments, 1979, Public Service Employment: A Field Evaluation, 1981, The Administrative Presidency, 1983, Reagan and the States, 1987, Social Science in Government Uses and Abuses, 1988, A New Agenda for Cities, 1992, Turning Promises into Performance: The Management Challenge of Implementing Workfare, 1993; co-author: (with Thomas L. Gais) Implementing the Personal Responsibility Act: A First Look, 1999, Social Science in Government, 2000; (with Gerald Benjamin) Regionalism and Realism, A Study of Governments in the New york Metropolitan Area, 2001; contbr. chpts. to books; editor: (with Harvey S. Perloff) Revenue Sharing and the City, 1968; (with John D. DiJulio, Jr.) The View From the States, Making Health Reform Work, Brookings Instn., 1994; mem. editl. bd. Urban Affairs Quar., 1978-85. Eisenhower fellow European Econ. Commn., 1977. Mem. ASPA (Intergovtl. Mgmt. award 1985), Nat. Acad. Social Inst., Nat. Acad. Pub. Adminstrn. (James E. Webb award 1986), Am. Pub. Human Svcs. Assn. (bd. dirs. 2000-02), Am. Polit. Sci. Assn. (Charles E. Merriam award 1987), Assn. for Pub. Policy Analysis and Mgmt., Assn for Pub. Policy Analysis and Mgmt. (pres.-elect 2000—), Ft. Orange Club, Phi Beta Kappa, Theta Delta Chi. Republican. Jewish. Avocations: reading, travel, movies. Home: 9 Ridgefield Dr Voorheesville NY 12186-9798 Office: SUNY Rockefeller Inst Dir Office 411 State St Albany NY 12203-1003 E-mail: nathanr@rockinst.org.

NATIVIDAD, EVANGELIA DE HITTA, Spanish educator, court interpreter, translator; b. Tigaon, The Philippines, July 9, 1936; came to U.S., 1969; d. Gregorio F. and Asuncion (de Hitta) N. BA in Spanish, LeTran Coll., Manila, 1964; MA in Spanish, Cultura Hispanica, Madrid, 1969. Elem. tchr. pub. schs., Tigaon, 1954-59; clk. and liaison officer cash div. Philippine Bur. Treasury, Manila, 1960-63; prof. Spanish, U. Santo Tomas, Manila, 1964-68; tchr. amb. Expt. Internat. Living, Balt. Pub. Schs., 1969-70; prof. Spanish, Morgan State U., Balt., 1970—. Adviser Spanish Club Foreign Language Dept.; translator, interpreter Tagalog and Spanish various cts. and schs. Vice pres. Katipunan-Filipino Assn., Balt., 1980-83, Bicol Assn., Washington, 1985-91; resource person Internat. Visitors Ctr., Balt., 1970. Govt. of Spain scholar, 1968. Mem. MLA, AAUP, Spanish Nat. Honor Soc. (founder), Bus. and Profl. Women (chmn. legis. com., corr. sec.), Xi Xi (founder, adviser). Roman Catholic. Avocations: singing, playing piano, painting, dancing, tutoring. Home: 1816 E Belvedere Ave Baltimore MD 21239 Office: Morgan State U Fgn Lang Dept Baltimore MD 21239

NAUDZIUS, ALDONA KANAUKA, pianist, music educator; b. Kaunas, Lithuania, Sept. 18, 1933; came to U.S., 1949; d. Vincas and Ona (Razmaite) Kanauka; m. Victor K. Naudzius, Dec. 1961; children: Ingrid Aldona, Renata Victoria. BA, Bennington Coll., 1955; MA, Columbia U., 1957; EdD, U. Ill., 1983; studied piano with, C. Friedberg, J. DeGray, C. Frank, V. Bacevicius, T. Richner, A. Forte, R. McDowell, S. Dorfman, S. Stravinsky, V. Leyetchkiss. Cert. music tchr. Ill., Ind., N.Y., M ass., social studies tchg. cert. Ill., N.Y. Tchr. music Pub. Schs., N.Y., 1958-59, 1959-62, East Chicago, Ind., 1963-67; tchr. piano Morton East H.S., Cicero, Ill., 1985-86; tchr. music De Lourdes Coll., Des Plaines, Ill., 1986, Chgo. Pub. Elem. Schs., 1989-94, Near North Metro H.S., Chgo., 1994-96, William Taft H.S., Chgo., 1996-98; pvt. piano tchr., 1998—. Participant internat. piano seminars, Graz, Austria, 1992, Lyon, France. Musician: Nelita True's Master Class, Dmitry Paperno's Master Class, 2000, C. Kiraly's Master Class, 2003, piano master class, 2003. Mem. Am.-Lithuanian Cmty., Lithuanian Scouts Assn. (collegiate divsn.), Am.-Lithuanian Music Soc., Wagner Music Soc. Roman Catholic. Home: 5733 N Sheridan Rd Chicago IL 60660-8767 E-mail: aldona_n@yahoo.com.

NAUGHTON, JOHN PATRICK, cardiologist, educator; b. West Nanticoke, Pa., May 20, 1933; s. John Patrick and Anne Frances (McCormick) N.; children: Bruce, Marcia, Lisa, George, Michael, Thomas. AA, Cameron State U., Lawton, Okla., 1952; BS, St. Louis U., 1954; MD, Okla. U., 1958; MD (hon.), Kosin U., 1995. Intern George Washington U. Hosp., Washington, 1958-59; resident U. Okla. Med. Center, 1959-64; asst. prof. medicine U. Okla., 1966-68; assoc. prof. medicine U. Ill., 1968-70; prof. medicine George Washington U., 1970-75, dean acad. affairs, 1973-75, dir. div. rehab. medicine and Regional Rehab. Research and Tng. Center, 1970-75; dean Sch. Medicine, SUNY, Buffalo, 1975-96, prof. medicine, physiology, social, preventive and rehab. medicine, 1975—; acting v.p. for health scis. SUNY, 1983-84, v.p. clin. affairs, 1984-96. Dir. Nat. Exercise and Heart Disease Project, 1972-83; chmn. policy adv. bd. Beta-blocker Heart Attack Trial Nat. Heart, Lung and Blood Inst., 1977-82; pres. Western N.Y. chpt. Am. Heart Assn., 1983-85, v.p. N.Y. State affiliate, 1985, pres. N.Y. State affiliate, 1988-90; chmn. clin. applications and preventions adv. com. Nat. Heart, Lung and Blood Inst., 1984; mem. Fed. COGME working group on consortia, 1996-97, N.Y. Gov.'s Commn. on Grad. Med. Edn., 1985, N.Y. State Coun. on Grad. Med. Edn., 1988-90, chmn. 1996—; pres. Assoc. Med. Schs. N.Y., 1982-84, mem. adminstrv. com. Coun. of Deans, 1983-89; mem. N.Y. State Dept. of Health Adv. Com. on Physician Recredentialing; mem. exec. coun. Nat. Inst. on Disability and Rehab. Rsch. 1991-92; v.p. James H. Cummings Found. Author: Exercise Testing and Exercise Training in Coronary Heart Disease, 1973, Exercise Testing: Physiological, Biomechanical, and Clinical Principles, 1988 Career devel. awardee Nat. Heart Inst., 1966-71; recipient Brotherhood-Sisterhood award in medicine NCCJ, N.E. Minority Educators award, 1990, Acad. Alumnus of Yr. award Okla. U., 1990, award for svc. to minorities in med. edn., 1991, Frank Sindelar award N.Y. State Am. Heart Assn., 1995, James Platt White Soc. award, 1995, Outstanding Contbns. in the field of Health Care award Sheehan Meml. Hosp., 1995, Chancellor Charles P. Norton medal, SUNY, Buffalo, 1997, AMS Disting. Svc. award, 2001. Fellow ACP, Am. Coll. Cardiology, Am. Coll. Sports Medicine (pres. 1970-71, Citation award 2000), Am. Coll. Chest Physicians; Am. Coll. Preventive Medicine, Am. Heart Assn. (epidemiology coun. 2000—, coun. on nutrition, phys. activity and metabolism), Acad. Health Profls. Ins. Assn. (hon.). Office: SUNY Buffalo 128 Farber Hall 3435 Main St Buffalo NY 14214-3099 E-mail: jpn@buffalo.edu.

NAULT, LOWELL RAYMOND, entomology educator; b. San Francisco, Apr. 4, 1940; s. Gerard H. and Helen (Lee) N.; m. Loretta Anne Kushall, July 12, 1963; children: Brian Andrew, Julie Anne. BS, U. Calif., Davis, 1962; MS, Cornell U., 1964, PhD, 1966. Prof. emeritus entomology Ohio Agr. Rsch. Devel. Ctr., Ohio State U., Wooster, 1966—, assoc. chmn. entomology, 1991-92, assoc. dir., 1995—2002, interim assoc. v.p. agrl. adminstr., dir., 1998—99. Program mgr. USDA Competitive Rsch. Grants Office, Washington, 1982. 85. Editor: The leafhoppers and planthoppers, 1985; contbr. more than 150 articles and book chpt. to profl. publ. Recipient Disting. Rsch. award, Sr. Scientist Ohio State U., 1989; Distinguished Scholar Award, Ohio State Univ., 1999. Fellow AAAS, Royal Entomol. Soc. London, Am. Phytopath. Soc., Entomol. Soc. Am. (pres. 1990-91, C.V. Riley award 2000, hon. 2002). Achievements include rsch. in characterizing transmission of plant viruses and bacteria by insects, evolutionary biology and behavior of the Homoptera. Home: 2722 Taylor Dr Wooster OH 44691-1637 Office: Dept of Entomology Ohio State U Ohio Agr Rsch Devel Ctr Dept Entomology 1680 Madison Ave Wooster OH 44691

NAUMAN, ANN KEITH, education educator, department chairman; b. Greensboro, N.C., Aug. 2, 1931; d. Erle Almon and Santa Maria Keith; m. William Logan Nauman, Sept. 15, 1951; children: Richard Logan, Gerald Keith. BA, La. State U., 1961, MA, 1965, BS, 1966, MS, 1969, PhD, 1974; postgrad., Southeastern La. U., 1976-78, Cath. U., Santiago, Chile. Sch. libr. Parish Sch. Sys., Baton Rouge, 1966-76; asst. prof. ednl. founds. Southeastern La. U., Hammond, 1976-80, assoc. prof., 1986-89, prof., 1989—; prof., head dept. St. Joseph Sem. Coll., St. Benedict, La., 1980—. Author: Biographic Handbook of Educators, 1981, Guide to Latin American Archives, 1982, Time Management for Librarians, 1991, Inés de Suarez, Conquistadora, 2000. Fellow La. State U., 1972, OAS, Santiago de Chile, 1973; Mellon grantee Tulane U. Office: Southeastern La U PO Box 659 Hammond LA 70402-0001

NAVARRO, RICHARD, educational association administrator; Masters Degree, Harvard U.; D in Internat. Devel. Edn. and Anthropology, Stanford U. Assoc. prof. dept. tchr. edn. Mich. State U., founding dir., sr. faculty assoc. Julian Samora Rsch. Inst.; dean Sch. Edn. and Integrative Studies Calif. Poly., Pomona, 1997—2003; leader UNICEF Project to Rebuild Iraq Edn. Sys., Kabul, Afghanistan, 2003—. Rsch. assoc. Nat. Ctr. for Rsch. on Tchr. Edn., Mich. State U., 1986—91; chairperson, exec. dir. Midwest Consoritum for Latino Rsch., 1990—93; co-dir. Mexico-U.S. Consortium for Acad. Cooperation, 1992—95; spl. asst. to provost Stanford U., 1993—94; mem. higher edn. adv. bd. Interstate New Tchr. Assessment and Support Consortium; chair Calif. Commn. on Tech. in Learning; mem. exec. com. Calif. State U. Deans of Edn.; vice chair Pomona Valley Ednl. Found.; co-chair East San Gabriel Valley Edn. Consortium; mem. L.A. Annenberg Met. PRoject, DELTA Governing Bd.; founding mem., sec.-treas. Inst. at Indian Hill for Edn. Reform; mem. exec. com. Ace Coun. Fellows. Mem.: Nat. Bd. for Profl. Tchg. Stds. (bd. m em., mem. exec. com.).*

NAVRATIL, GERALD ANTON, physicist, educator; b. Troy, N.Y., Sept. 5, 1951; s. Lloyd George and Frances Mary (Scalise) N.; m. Joan Frances Etzweiler, Sept. 4, 1976; children: Frances, Alexis, Paula. BS, Calif. Inst. Tech., 1973; MS, U. Wis., 1974, PhD, 1976. Project assoc. dept. physics U. Wis.-Madison, 1976-77; asst. prof. enging. sci. Columbia U., N.Y.C., 1977-78, asst. prof. applied physics, 1978-83, assoc. prof., 1983-88, prof., 1988—, chmn. 1988-94, chmn. of applied physics dept, 1997-2000, vice dean Sch. Engring. and Applied Sci., 1994-95; vis. fellow Princeton U., 1985-86, UCSD, 1995-96; cons. MIT, 1984-86, Fusion Systems, Inc., 1988, Inst. Def. Analysis, 1992—; chmn. program adv. com. TFTR, 1994-97, NSTX, 1996—, chmn. Snowmass Fusion summer study, 2002, mem. US Dept. of Energy (fusion energy adv. com. 1998-), Assoc. editor Physics of Plasmas, 1994—. Patentee in field. Cottrell Rsch. grantee, 1978; U.S. Dept. Energy High Beta Tokomak Research contract, 1982—; NSF grantee, 1978-88; Alfred P. Sloan rsch. fellow, 1984. Fellow Am. Phys. Soc., Univ. Fusion Assn. (sec./treas. 1988-89, v.p. 1990, 2003-, pres. 1991), Fusion Power Assoc. (mem. bd. dirs, 2000-), The Chubb Found. (mem. bd. trustees 1995-), Sigma Xi. Office: Columbia U Dept Applied Physics 500 W 120th St Rm 200 Mudd New York NY 10027-6623

NAYAR, BALDEV RAJ, political science educator; b. Gujrat Dist., India, Oct. 26, 1931; emigrated to Can., 1964; s. Jamna Das and Durga Devi (Marwah) N.; m. Nancy Ann Skinner, Aug. 27, 1961; children— Sheila Jane, Kamala Elizabeth, Sunita Maria. BA, Punjab U., 1953; MA, 1956, U. Chgo., 1959, PhD, 1963. Asst. prof. Calif. State Coll., Hayward, 1963-64; mem. faculty dept. polit. sci. McGill U., 1964-94, assoc. prof., 1966-71, prof., 1971-94, prof. emeritus, 1996—, assoc. chmn., 1990-93. Rsch. assoc. Internat. Devel. Rsch. Centre, 1978 Author: Minority Politics in the Punjab, 1966, National Communication and Language Policy, 1969, The Modernization Imperative and Indian Planning, 1972, American Geopolitics and India, 1976, India's Quest for Technological Independence, 1983, India's Mixed Economy, 1989, The Political Economy of India's Public Sector, 1990, Superpower Dominance and Military Aid, 1991, The State and International Aviation in India, 1994, The State and Market in India's Shipping, 1996, Globalization and Nationalism, 2001, India and the Major Powers After Pokhran II, 2001; co-author: India in the World Order, 2003. Bd. dirs. Shastri Indo-Canadian Inst., 1970-72, sr. fellow, 1978, 86. Recipient Watumull prize Am. Hist. Assn., 1966; Charles E. Merriam fellow, 1957; Carnegie Study New Nations fellow, 1962; Can. Council sr. fellow, 1967, 74; SSHRC leave fellow, 1982 Mem. Can. Asian Studies Assn. Office: McGill Univ Dept Polit Sci Montreal QC Canada H3A 2T7 E-mail: bnayar@po-box.mcgill.ca.

NAYLOR, SUSAN EMBRY, music educator; b. Huntington Park, California, Feb. 21, 1951; d. Hollie J. and Sara Mozelle (Maddox) E. MusB in piano performance, Converse Coll., 1973; MusM, Ga. State U., 1975. Cert. music tchr. Ga. Prof. piano and music theory Reinhardt Coll., Waleska, Ga., 1975—, music program coord., 1995-2000. Pvt. piano tchr. Waleska, Marietta, and Kennesaw, Ga., 1973—. Performer solo piano and ensemble recitals colls., chs. and profl. orgns., 1973—; pianist Spartanburg (S.C.) Symphony Orch., 1970-73, featured soloist, 1972; guest pianist Nat. Pub. Radio, 1988. Ch. pianist Bapt., Meth. Churches in Marietta, Dallas, and Kennesaw, 1973—. Recipient Cobb County Young Artist Award; Cobb County Arts Coun. Parks and Recreation and Jr. League, 1983, 86. Mem. Ga. Music Tchr. Assn., adjudicator 1976—, coll. faculty chair 1996-98, cert. credentials chair 1997-99, pres. elect 1998-2000, pres. 2000-2002, Finance/Advisory Comm., 2000-, Ga. Fedn. Music Clubs adjudicator 1976—, Cherokee Music Tchr. Assn. pres. 1988-91, 1st v.p. program 1997-99, Cherokee County Arts Coun. exec. bd., v.p. 1993-95, Music Tchr. Nat. Assn., Nat. coll. faculty cert., nat. cert. evaluation team 1993-96, ho. dels. 2000-2002. Baptist. Avocations: antiques, reading. Home: 109 Myrtle Ct Waleska GA 30183-4202 Office: Reinhardt Coll 7300 Reinhardt Coll Cir Waleska GA 30183-2981 E-mail: sen@reinhardt.edu.

NDIMBA, CORNELIUS GHANE, language educator; b. Ngeptang-din, Cameroon, Sept. 5, 1953; came to the U.S., 1981; s. Dominic Kimah and Sabina (Meilo) N.; 1 child, Melvynne Meilo. BS in Econs. and Mgmt., S.E. Okla. State U., 1984, M in Adminstrv. Studies, 1989; postgrad., Tex. Woman's U. Cert. tchr. bus. adminstrn. and mgmt., Tex. Customer svc. rep. Internat. Bank of West Africa, Cameroon, 1979-81; storeroom clk. S.E. Okla. State U., Durant, 1981-84, student counselor, 1989-90; purchasing asst. Las Colinas Sports Club, Irving, Tex., 1985-88; assembler GM Corp., Arlington, Tex., 1988; admissions rep. ATI Career Tng., Dallas, 1991-92; ESL tchr. Dallas Ind. Sch. Dist., 1992—. Sales cons. Am. Foods, Irving, 1989-94. Mem. com. Boy Scouts Am., Dallas, 1992, Cmty. Adv. Com., East Dallas, 1994. Mem. Internat. Reading Assn., Parent-Tchr. Assn., Sasse Old Boys Assn. (pres. 1989—). Republican. Roman Catholic. Avocations: tennis, outdoor soccer, travel, manufacturing. Office: 4800 Ross Ave Dallas TX 75204-4807

NEAL, DENNIS MELTON, middle school administrator; b. Lakeland, Fla., Feb. 7, 1966; s. M. H. and Alice Marie (Twiddy) N.; m. Christine Anne Rufo, Oct. 21, 1989; children: Lauren Elizabeth, Waverly Rose, Emma Katherine. AA, Polk C.C., Winter Haven, Fla., 1987; BS, Fla. So. Coll., 1991; MEd, Stetson U., 1995. Cert. elem. tchr., ednl. leader, prin., Fla. Guest svcs. Cypress gardens, Winter Haven, 1985-86; entertainer Boardwalk and Baseball, Baseball City, Fla., 1986-88; guest svcs. Hilton Walt Disney World, Orlando, Fla., 1988-91; tchr. Deltona (Fla.) Middle Sch., 1991-95, asst. prin., 1995-99, Heritage Middle Sch., Deltona, Fla., 1999-2000; prin. intern Pine Ridge H.S., 2000—. Chair correlate com., team leader Deltona Middle Sch., sch. adv. coun. Tchr. Lith. Ch. of Providence, Orange City, Fla., 1992-93; active Parent, Tchr., Student Assn. Named One of Top 100 Beginning Tchrs. in Nation, Sallie Mae Student Loan Assn., 1992. Avocations: soccer, racquetball, drawing, painting. Home: 2939 Owen Ct Deltona FL 32738-1846

NEAL, HOMER ALFRED, physics educator, researcher, university administrator; b. Franklin, Ky., June 13, 1942; s. Homer and Margaret Elizabeth (Holland) Neal; m. Donna Jean Daniels, June 16, 1962; children: Sharon Denise, Homer Alfred. BS in Physics with honors, Ind. U., 1961; MS in Physics (John Hay Whitney fellow), U. Mich., 1963, PhD in Physics, 1966. Asst. prof. physics Ind. U., 1967—70, assoc. prof., 1970—72, prof., 1972—81, dean research and grad. devel., 1976—81; prof. physics SUNY, Stony Brook, 1981—87, provost, 1981—86; prof. physics, chmn. U. Mich., Ann Arbor, 1987—93, v.p. rsch., 1993—97, interim pres., 1996—97, prof. of physics, 1987—2000, Samuel A. Goudsmit disting. prof. physics, 2000—, dir. of atlas project, 1997—. Bd. dirs. Ford Motor Co., Covanta Corp.; mem. Nat. Sci. Bd., 1980—86; mem. adv. coun. Oak Ridge Nat. Lab., 1993—99; mem. external adv. coun. Nat. Computational Sci. Alliance, 1997—; mem. applications strategy coun. Univ. Corp. for Advanced Internet Devel., 2000—; chmn. Argonne Zero Gradient Synchrotron Users Group, 1970—72; trustee Argonne Univs. Assn., 1971—74, 1977—80; physics adv. panel NSF, 1976—79, chmn. physics adv. panel, 1987—89; high energy physics adv. panel U.S. Dept. Energy, 1977—81. Contbr. articles to profl. jours. Mem. bd. regents Smithsonian Instn., 1989—2001; trustee Ctr. for Strategic and Internat. Studies, 1990—2000; Oak Ridge (Tenn.) Nat. Lab., 1993—; mem. bd. overseers Superconducting Super Collider, 1989—93; trustee Environ. Rsch. Inst. of Mich., 1994—96; N.Y. Sea Grant Inst., 1982—86. Recipient Stony Brook medal, 1986, Ind. U. Disting. Alumni award, 1994; fellow NSF, 1966—67, Sloan, 1968, Guggenheim, 1980—81. Fellow: AAAS, Am. Acad. Arts and Scis., Am. Phys. Soc.; mem.: Univs. Rsch. Assn. (trustee), Sigma Xi. Office: Dept of Physics Rm 2477 Randall Lab 500 East University Ann Arbor MI 48109-1120

NEAL, JOSEPH LEE, vocational school educator; b. Memphis, Feb. 17, 1948; s. James Henry and Minnie Rue (Waldrop) N.; children: Janice Celeste Neal, Mary Joanne; m. Lou Alice Smith, Apr. 10, 1999. AAS, N.W. C.C., Senatobia, Miss., 1979, AS in Bus., 1980; BS, U. S. Miss., 1984, MS, 1986. Cert. tchr. Miss. Police officer City of W. Memphis, Ark., 1970-72; customer svc. rep. Biomed. Labs., Little Rock, Ark., 1972-75; sales, svc. rep Moore Ford Co., N. Little Rock, 1975-77; electronics technician N.W. Miss. C.C., Senatobia, 1979-82, electronics inst., 1982-83; electronics engr. U. So. Miss., Hattiesburg, 1983-85; electronics instr. Tex. State Tech. Inst., Sweetwater, 1985-87, De Soto County Vo-Tech. Ctr., Southaven, Miss., 1988-97, South Panola H.S., Batesville, Miss., 1997—. Cons. engr. various radio ops., Hattiesburg, 1982-85; mem. curriculum com. De Soto County Schs., 1990-95; steering com. N.W. Miss. Tech. Prep., Senatobia, 1992-95, participant in Learn to Work Workshop Miss. St. U. and Pealey Electronics, 1997, tchr. trainer for Tech. Discovery, 1998, 99. Bd. dirs. Optimist Club, Sweetwater, Tex., 1987. Named Outstanding Tchr., Horn Lake So. C. of C., 1992. Mem. Am. Vocat. Assn., Miss. Trade and Tech. Assn. (v.p. 1994-95, pres. 1995-96), Miss. Assn. Vocat. Educators (pres. dist. 1 1991-92, 95-96, bd. dirs. 1991-92, 95-96, sec. dist. 1 1993-94, v.p. 1994-95), Vocat.-Indsl. Clubs of Am. (100% Advisor 1990, 91, 92, VICA state advisor of yr. 1993), N.Am. Hunting Club (life). Baptist. Avocations: hunting, fishing, pub. speaking. Home: PO Box 172 1578 Freeman Rd Como MS 38619 Office: South Panola HS Batesville MS 38606

NEAL, MARCUS PINSON, JR., radiologist, medical educator; b. Columbia, Mo., Apr. 22, 1927; s. M. Pinson and Mathilda (Evers) N.; m. Gail S. Fallon, May 27, 1961; children: Sandra G. Neal Dawson, M. Pinson III, Ruth-Catherine Neal Perkins. AB, U. Mo., 1949, BS, 1951; MD, U. Tenn., 1953. Intern Med. Coll. Va., Richmond, 1953-54; resident U. Wis. Hosp., Madison, 1954-57; instr. dept. radiology Sch. Medicine U. Wis., Madison, 1957-59; mem. staff U. Wis. Hosps., Madison, 1957-63; asst. prof. radiology, dir. dept. radiology Cen. Wis. Colony, Madison, 1959-63; radiologist Wis. Diagnostic Ctr., Madison, 1962-63; mem. staff Med. Coll. Va. Hosps., Va. Commonwealth U., 1963-99; assoc. prof. radiology Med. Coll. Va., Va. Commonwealth U., 1963-66, prof. radiology, 1966-97, prof. emeritus, 1997—, dir. postgrad. edn. dept. radiology, 1964-73, chmn. divsn. diagnostic radiology, 1965-68, asst. dean Sch. Medicine, dir. grad. med. edn., dir. regional med. program, 1968-71, dir. continuing edn. Sch. Medicine, 1969-72, interim dean Sch. Medicine, 1971, asst. v.p. for health scis., 1971-73, provost Health Scis. campus, 1973-78, assoc. dean for continuing med. edn. and quality assurance Sch. Medicine, 1978-79, dir. housestaff edn., dept. radiology, 1979-93, dir. section genitourinary radiology, dept. radiology, 1981-92. Bd. dirs. Common Wealth Bank, Richmond; cons., radiologist Va. Hosp., Madison, 1962-63, USAF Hosp., Truax Field, Madison, 1962-63, McGuire VA Hosp., Richmond, 1963-99; bd. forestry Commonwealth of Va., 1990-94, chmn. bd. forestry, 1993-94. Editor: Emergency Interventional Radiology: Practical Aspects, 1988; contbr. articles to profl. jours. Pres. Oxford Civic Assn., Richmond, 1965-67, Three Ridges Condominium Assn., Wintergreen, Va., 1979-84. Served as pharmacist mate USNR, 1945-47. Fellow Oak Ridge Inst. Nuc. Studies, Am. Coll. Radiology (fellow emeritus, councilor Va. chpt. 1977-83, 85-91, 93-97); mem. AMA, Radiol. Soc. N.Am., Am. Roentgen Ray Soc., Med. Soc. Va., So. Med. Assn. (pres. 1982-83, Disting. Svc. award 1994), Richmond Acad. Medicine, Capital Club (bd. dirs.), Commonwealth Club, Bull and Bear Club, Willow Oaks Country Club, Sigma Xi. Avocations: hunting, fishing, gardening. Home: 7301 Riverside Dr Richmond VA 23225-1242 Office: Med Coll Va PO Box 980615 Richmond VA 23298-0615

NEAL, RICHARD GLENN, educational management company executive; b. Washington, June 13, 1928; s. Everette Earl and Estelle Pearl (Liming) N.; m. Frances Irene Felts, Dec. 27, 1949; children: Michael, Linda, Susanna, Melanie. BA, U. Md., 1952; MA, George Washington U., 1957; advanced cert., Ohio State U., 1964; PhD, Columbia Pacific U., 1984; postgrad., U. Va., George Mason U., Am. U., Cath. U. Cert. tchr., Va. Tchr. social studies Fairfax County Pub. Schs., 1952-53; dir. spl. programs, prin., guidance, counselor, tchr. Arlington County Pub. Schs., 1953-68; dir. spl. programs, assoc. supt instrn., supr. edn./pers. Prince William County Sch. Bd., Manassas, Va., 1972-87, dir. sch.-based mgmt., 1987-90; owner, operator Neal Assocs., 1988—, Pub. Employee Rels. Svc., Falls Church, Va., 1980-87; pres. Ednl. Satellite Tng. (EDSATRA) Inc., Manassas, 1992—. Exec. dir. Arlington Edn. Assn., 1957-63; assoc. dir. Ednl. Svc. Bur., 1968-72; sr. cons. EFR Corp., 1972-88; cons. to over 300 ednl. orgns. including Va. Poly. Inst., George Mason U., Nat. Sch. Bds. Assn., Nat. Acad. Sch. Execs., So. Assn. Schs. and Colls., Sage Corp., Ky., Iowa and Va. Sch. Bds. Assn., North Ctrl. Regional Edn. Svcs. Agy., Del. Assn. Sch. Adminstrs., New Hanover County Schs., Reading (Pa.) Pub. Schs.; presenter over 300 seminars. Author 25 books including: Managing Educational Negotiations, 1968, Laws Affecting Public School Negotiations, 1970, Grievance Procedures and Grievance Arbitration, 1971, Avoiding and Controlling Teacher Strikes, 1972, Retrieval Bargaining, 1981, Negotiations Strategies, A Reference Manual, 1981, School and Government Labor Relations, 1982, Winning Grievances, 1983, Managing Time, 1983, School Based Management: A Detailed Guide for Successful Implementation, 1990, School Based Management Vol. II, 1993; editor, contbr. over 100 articles to profl. jours. Active Heritage Found., Cato Inst., Nat. Right to Work Com. With USN, 1945-47; 1st. lt. USAF, 1950-58. Recipient Medal of Merit in Edn., Order of St. John of Jerusalem, 1989. Mem. NEA, Am. Assn. Sch. Adminstrs., Assn. Sch. Pers. Adminstrs., Nat. Assn. Negotiators and Contract Adminstrs., Am. Enterprise Inst., Found. for Econ. Edn., Nat. Orgn. for Legal Problems in Edn., Internat. Pers. Mgmt. Assn., Phi Delta Kappa. Avocation: spending time with family. Home: RR 1 Box 186-f Union Hall VA 24176-9778 Office: EDSATRA Inc 8667 Sudley Rd # 303 Manassas VA 20110-4588

NEAL, TERESA SCHREIBEIS, secondary education educator; b. Wheatland, Wyo., Mar. 19, 1956; d. Gene L. and Bonnie Marie (Reed) Schreibeis; m. Michael R. Neal, Apr. 7, 1990; 1 child, Rianna Michele. BA in Am. Studies and English Edn., U. Wyo., 1978; MA in History, U. So. Calif., 1989, PhD, 1994, Cert. Studies of Women/Men in Soc., 1995. Cert. secondary edn. tchr., Wyo., Colo. Tchr. lang. arts and social studies, asst. coach Carbon County Sch. Dist. 1, Rawlins, Wyo., 1978-86; asst. lectr. freshmen writing program U. So. Calif., L.A., 1986-90; adj. prof. history Palomar (Calif.) C.C., San Diego, 1991; software support specialist Dynamic Data Systems, Westminster, Colo., 1992-93; tchr. humanities gifted and talented classes Arvada (Colo.) West H.S., 1993-98; tchr., program developer New Montessori Mid. Sch., 1998-00, Mountain Shadows Mid. Sch., Boulder, Colo., 1998-2000; adj. prof. history, humanities and English composition Red Rocks C.C., Lakewood and Arvada, Calif., 2002—. Participant critical thinking and humanities secondary edn. project NEH, Wyo., 1985-86; adj. prof. English Composition, Front Range C.C., Westminster, Colo., 2000-. Mem., chmn. Reading Is Fundamental Program, Rawlins, 1983-85, Women of the West Mus., 2001—; tchr., sponsor Denver-Metro YMCA Youth and Govt., 1994-97, Close Up, Washington, 1984-86, 97; tchr., advisor Nat. History Day Contest, 1995—; tchr., sponsor World Affairs Challenge, Denver U., 1998; vol. math. tutor Foothills Acad., Wheat Ridge, Colo., 2001-02. Mem. AAUW (Project Renew fellow 1987-88), Western Assn. Women Historians, G. Autrey Mus. Western Art, Phi Beta Kappa. Avocations: travel, fine arts, baseball, reading. E-mail: tneal@javakats.com.

NEAL-BARNETT, ANGELA MARIE, psychology educator; b. Youngstown, Ohio, Feb. 13, 1960; d. Andrew Lee and Doris Lucille Neal; m. Edgar J. Barnett Jr., July 17, 1995; 1 child, Reece. BA, Mt. Union Coll., 1982; MA, DePaul U., 1985, PhD, 1988. Lic. psychologist, Ohio. Clin. therapist ECHO Community Health Orgn., Chgo., 1985-87; post-doctoral fellow U. Pitts. (Pa.), Western Psychiat. Inst., 1988-89; asst. prof. Kent (Ohio) State U., 1989—, 1989-95, assoc. prof., 1995—. Pres., founder Rise Sally Rise Prodn.; founder, CEO Rise, Sally, Rise, Inc.; bd. dirs. King-Kennedy Ctr., Ravenna, Ohio, 1989—95; rsch. fellow Inst. African Am. Affairs, Kent, 1991—; co-chair Allied Health Edn. Com., 1994—; mem. NIMH Child Psychopathology and Treatment Rev. Panel, 1996—99; spkr. in field. Author: Forging Limits: African American Children Clinical Developmental Perspectives; contbr. articles to profl. jours.; author: Soothe Your Nerves: The Black Women's Guide to Understanding and Overcoming Anxiety, Panic and Fear; author, prodr.: CD Believe and Succeed. Mem. alumni coun. Mt. Union Coll.; mem. governing bd. Ida B. Wells Cmty. Acad., 1998-2000. Urban Rsch. grantee Ohio Bd. Regents, 1990, biomed. support grantee NIH, 1991, small grantee NIMH, 1994-96; recipient Minority Career Advancement award NSF. Mem. APA (, mem. adv. com. minority fellowship program, Kenneth & Marie Clark award), Ohio Pscyhol. Assn., Assn. Advancement Behavior Therapy, Assn. Black Psychologists, African Am. Lit. Guild Kent. Methodist. Avocations: tennis, reading. Office: Kent State U Dept Psychology 118 Kent Hl Kent OH 44242-0001 also: Rise Sally Rise Inc 361 Starr Line Dr Tallmadge OH 44278 E-mail: aneal@kent.edu.

NEALIS, JAMES GARRY THOMAS, III, pediatric neurologist, educator, author; b. N.Y.C., Mar. 7, 1945; s. James and Catherine N.; m. Arlene Dee Kramer, Feb. 6, 1981; children— Peyton Colleen, Douglas Andrew, Gregory Haynes, James Garry Thomas IV, Patrick Ryan. B.A., Fordham U., 1966; M.D., U. Miami, 1971. Diplomate Am. Bd. Psychiatry and Neurology, Am. Bd. Electroencephalography. Intern in pediatrics Babies Hosp., Columbia Presbyn. Med. Ctr., Columbia U. Sch. Medicine, N.Y.C., 1971-72, resident, 1972-73; resident in neurology Boston U. Sch. Medicine, 1973-74, 75-76, resident in neurology Harvard U. Sch. Medicine, Boston, 1975-76, instr. pediatric neurology, 1976-78; chief resident Boston City Hosp., 1975-76; asst. in neurophysiology Boston Children's Hosp., 1976-78; founder Neuro-Ednl. Evaluation Clinic, 1977-78; asst. prof. clin. neurology U. Fla., Jacksonville; chief pediatric neurology Jacksonville Children's Hosp., 1979— ; lctr. U. N. Fla.; clin. instr. neurology cons. Naval Regional Med. Ctr., Jacksonville, 1979— ; adviser Pres.'s Com. Med. Ethics, Washington, 1980; sec. Fla. Neurol. Inst., 1985; lectr. in field. Contbg. author: Physical Disabilities and Health Impairments. Contbr. chpts. to med. books, articles to med. jours. Trustee Epilepsy Found.; bd. dirs. Speech and Hearing Clinic; founder, bd. dirs. Northeast Fla. League Against Reye's Syndrome; founder, bd. dirs. Jacksonville Parents Assn. Against Gilles de la Tourette Syndrome; mem. Jacksonville Police Council, 1981— ; founder Jacksonville Alzheimer's Ctr.; profl. adviser Parents in Action Against Drugs and Substance Abuse, 1983— ; multiple TV appearances including (host) To Your Health, WJXT, 1983, The Brain, WJXT, 1985, Drugs and Your Brain, 1986; (guest) Alzheimers Disease, 1984, The 700 Club, CBN, 1985. Named Outstanding Young Man of Yr., Bold City Jr. C. of C., 1980. Mem. Am. Acad. Neurology, Eastern Assn. EEG, Am. Med. Electroencephalographic Assn. (pres. 1984), Jacksonville Assn. Children with Learning Disabilities (bd. advisers), Am. Epilepsy Soc., Duval County Med. Soc., (trustee) Child Neurology Soc. (mem. nat. com. med. ethics 1984-85, adv. 1985-86, nat. adv. pediatric brain death 1985, practice com.), Fla. Soc. Neurology (sec. 1980, v.p. 1981, pres. 1983), Fla. Med. Assn. (del. 1983-84), Council Exceptional Children, Jacksonville C. of C.

NEBERGALL, ROBERT WILLIAM, orthopedic surgeon, educator; b. Des Moines, Dec. 31, 1954; s. Donald Charles and Shirley (Williams) N.; m. Lisa Lynn; children: Nathaniel Robert Baird, Bartholomew William Campbell, Lily Kathryn Audrey. BS in Biology, Luther Coll., 1977; DO, U. Osteo. Health Scis., 1981. Intern Des Moines Gen. Hosp., 1981-82; resident orthop. surgery Tulsa Regional Med. Ctr., 1982-86; trauma fellow Assn. Osteosynthesis /Assn. Study of Internal Fixation Fellowship Program, Stuttgart and Mainz, 1986; sports medicine fellow U. Oreg. Orthop. and Fracture Clinic, Eugene, 1986; orthop. surgeon Tulsa Orthop. Surgeons, 1987—. Team physician Tulsa Ballet Theatre, 1987—, Internat. Pro Rodeo Assn., Oklahona City, 1987—96, Oklahona City, 2003—; dir. sports medicine program Tulsa Regional Med Ctr., 1990—; team physician Longhorn World Championship Rodeo, 1992—, Nathan Hale H.S. Football, 1992—, Ctrl. H.S., 1993—, Tulsa Roughnecks Soccer, 1993—96; chmn. dept. orthop. surgery Tulsa Regional Med. Ctr., 1994—2003; team physician Okla. All State Games, 1994—2001, Jim Thorpe All Star Games, 2002—; clin. asst. prof. surgery Okla. State U. Coll. Osteo. Medicine; exec. med. com. Surg. Care Tulsa, 1996—2000; clin. asst. prof. surgery Kirksville Coll. Osteo. Medicine; mem. pro tempore Okla. Bd. Osteo. Examiners; mem. governing bd. South Crest Hosp., 1999—2002; bd. mgrs. TOPS, LLC, 1999—; exec. mgmt. com. Tulsa Outpatient Surgery Ctr., 1999—, pres., 2002—. Contbr. chpt. to Epidemiology of Sports Injuries. Mem. Okla. Found. for Med. Quality Inc., Oklahoma City, 1988—; past pres. Culver (Ind.) Summer Sch. Alumni Assn., 1991; bd. trustee Culver Ednl. Found. of Culver Mil. Acad., 1991—93. Recipient Vol. award Tulsa Ballet Theatre, 1990, Physicians Recognition award AMA, 1990; named Outstanding Young Man in Am., U.S. Jaycees, 1983. Fellow Am. Osteo. Acad. Orthopedics; mem. Am. Coll. Sports Medicine, Am. Osteo. Orthopedic Soc. Sports Medicine (past pres.), N.Y. Acad. Scis., Assn. Osteosynthesis Fellowship Alumni Orgn., Green Country Ind. Practice Assn. (pres. 1994-98), Tulsa Orthop. Soc., Sigma Sigma Phi., pres. Beta Chapter, 1981. Methodist. Avocations: strength training, bicycling, hunting. Office: Tulsa Orthopedic Surgeons 802 S Jackson Ave Ste 130 Tulsa OK 74127-9010

NEBORSKY, STEPHANIE JOY, reading and language arts consultant, educator; b. Putnam, Conn., June 14, 1950; d. Stephen Frank and Dorathy Elizabeth (Angelott) Neborsky; m. John W. Thrower, Jr., Aug. 14, 2000. AS, Manchester (Conn.) C.C., 1968-70; BS in Intermediate Edn., Eastern Conn. State U., 1972, MS in Lang. Arts, 1978; cert. supervision and adminstrn., Sacred Heart U., 1991. Cert. reading and lang. arts cons., supervision and adminstrn., Conn. Tchr. English and reading Dr. Helen Baldwin Sch., Canterbury, Conn., 1972-86, 94-95, tchr. 6th-8th grade lang. arts, 1986-89, 95-97, 5th grade tchr., writing coach, 1989-90, lang. arts coord., 1990-94; adult edn. instr. Putnam (Conn.)-Thompson Cmty. Coun., 1975-76; tchr. 4th grade Cantebury Elem. Sch., Conn., 1997—. Tchr. Summer Youth Employment Tng. Program East Conn./Brandeis U., Hampton, 1993; adj. instr. Sacred Heart U., Lisbon, Conn., 1993—; presenter numerous edn. confs.; scorer and resolution reader Conn. State Dept. Edn., 1980-90. Contbr. articles to profl. jours. Named Dist. Tchr. of Yr., Canterbury Pub. Schs., 1989, Finalist Conn. Tchr. of Yr., 1989. Mem. ASCD, Ea. Conn. Reading Assn. (pres. 1995-96), Canterbury Edn. Assn. (governing bd. sec. 1995-97), Internat. Reading Assn., New Eng. Reading Assn., Nat. Coun. Tchrs. English, Whole Lang. Umbrella, Conn. TAWL, Delta Kappa Gamma (rec. sec. 1994-96). Avocations: collecting children's books, travel, tunis sheep, judging and promoting youth sheep shows, gardening. Home: 314 Main St Hampton CT 06247-1416 Office: Canterbury Elem Sch 67 Kitt Rd Canterbury CT 06331-1122

NECCO, ALEXANDER DAVID, lawyer, educator; b. Gary, Ind., Jan. 31, 1936; s. Alesandro Necco and Mary Millonovich; m. Caroline Chappel, Apr. 20, 1958 (dec. Mar. 1978); 1 child, Laurie Ann Necco Stansbury; m. Edna Joanne Painter, July 1, 1989. BA in Philosophy, U. Nev., 1958; JD, Oklahoma City U., 1965. Bar: Okla. 1965, U.S. Dist. Ct. (we. dist.) Okla. 1965, U.S. Ct. Appeals (10th cir.) 1987), U.S. Ct. Claims 1989, U.S. Ct. Vets. Appeals 1994. Assoc. Robert Jordan, Oklahoma City, 1965-66, Stuckey & Witcher, Oklahoma City, 1968-69; atty. Okla. Hwy. Dept., Oklahoma City, 1966, Oklahoma City Urban Renewal, 1966-67; ptnr. Stuckey & Necco, Oklahoma City, 1969-71, Necco & Dyer, Oklahoma City, 1978-82, Dyer, Necco & Byrd, Oklahoma City, 1982-88; pvt. practice Oklahoma City, 1965—; ptnr. Necco & Byrd, Oklahoma City, 1988—. Adj. prof. Oklahoma City U. Sch. Bus., 1965—, Webster U., 1995—. Cubmaster Boy Scouts Am., Oklahoma City. With USMC, 1953-82, lt. col. Res. ret. Named Pro-bono Atty. of Month Okla. County. Mem.: ABA, Okla. Trial Lawyers Assn., Marine Corps Res. Officers Assn. (pres. Oklahoma City chpt. 1984—85), Sigma Nu, Phi Delta Phi. Republican. Roman Catholic. Avocations: golf, swimming, tennis. Office: Necco & Byrd PC Landmark Towers W 3555 NW 58th St Ste 130 Oklahoma City OK 73112-1662 E-mail: dnecco@neccoandbyrd.com.

NEEDHAM, CHARLES WILLIAM, neurosurgeon, educator; b. Bklyn., Oct. 14, 1936; s. William and Jeanne (Studioso) N.; m. Constance Taft, June 15, 1958; children: Susan, Andrew, Jennifer, Sarah, Benjamin. BS cum laude, Wagner Coll., 1957; MD, Albany Med. Coll., 1961; MSc, McGill U., 1969. Diplomate Am. Bd. Neurol. Surgery; lic. physician, Conn. Asst. prof. neurol. surgery UCLA Sch. Medicine, 1969—71; clin. assoc. prof. neurol. surgery U. Ariz., Tucson, 1971—84; staff neurosurgeon Norwalk (Conn.) Hosp., 1996—, Bridgeport (Conn.) Hosp., 1996—; asst. prof. neurosurgery Yale U. Sch. Medicine, New Haven, 1989—. Postdoctoral fellow Nat. Inst. Neurol. Diseases & Blindness, 1967-69. Author: Neurosurgical Syndromes of the Brain, 1973, Cerebral Logic, 1978, Principles of Cerebral Dominance, 1982, Neurosurgical Signs, 1986; contbr. articles to profl. jours. Served to capt. M.C. USAF, 1963—65. Recipient numerous awards for excellence in medicine including AMA Continuing Edn. awards, 1978—, Yale U. Sch. Medicine award, 1986, Scallon Surg. award, 1999. Fellow ACS; mem. AAAS, Am. Assn. Neurol. Surgeons, Congress Neurol. Surgeons, Brain and Behavioral Scis. Assn., N.Y. Acad. Scis., New Eng. Neurosurg. Soc., Conn. State Neurosurg. Soc. (pres. 1992—), Fairfield County Med. Soc. Avocations: philosophy, physics, anthropology, writing. Office: 10 Mott Ave Norwalk CT 06850 Home: 61 E 77th St 6C New York NY 10021

NEEDHAM, JUDY LEN, artist, art educator; b. Big Spring, Tex., Dec. 1, 1941; d. Carl Granvil and Mary Louise (Grilliette) Hill; m. Andrew James Needham III, Jan. 1, 1960; children: Andy, Jack, Johnny, Joshua. Grad. high sch., Tuscola, Tex., 1960. Workshop dir., coord. Fine Arts League Coleman (Tex.) County, 1990-96, art exhbn. dir. 1992-96, pres., 1992, 93. Exhibited in group shows Citizens Nat. Bank, Brownwood, Tex., 1992, 1st Coleman (Tex.) Nat. Bank, 1992-95, Coleman County State Bank, 1992-96, Security State Bank, Abilene, Tex., 1995, John Selmon Gallery, Stamford, Tex., 1995, Gage Hotel Emporium, Marathon, Tex., 1994-95, West Tex. Art Gallery, San Angelo, 1994-95, Kendall Art Gallery, San Angelo, 1995, Breckenridge (Tex.) Fine Arts Gallery, 199.4. Troop leader Heart of Tex. coun. Girl Scouts Am., Brownwood, 1965-70; den mother, asst. camp dir. Chisholm Tr. coun. Boy Scouts Am., Abilene, 1972-79; pres. Band Boosters Coleman H.S., 1990, 91, 92. Recipient Dist. Award of Merit Boy Scouts Am. Chisholm Trail Coun., 1979, Best of Show Cross Plains (Tex.) Paint and Palett, 1993, Best of Show Coleman County Fine Arts League, 1994, Best of Show Comanche County Art Assn., 1995. Avocations: crochet, photography, reading. Home: 427 Sunrise Dr Coleman TX 76834-2107

NEEDHAM, LILLIE DULCENIA, secondary education educator, business educator; b. Chgo., June 12, 1949; d. Clarence R. Sr. and Deborah Lee (Morris) Needham; 1 child, Aston R. Needham-Watkins. BS in Edn., Chgo. State Coll., 1970, MS in Edn., 1974. Tchr. Chgo. Pub. Schs., 1970—, office occupations coord., 1976-77, 78-90, 91—, S.W.A.T. shop founder, coord. info. processing, 1992—, bus./computer dept. chair. Mem. NAFE, ASCD, Chgo. Bus. Edn. Assn. (sec. 1994-95, v.p. 1995—), Nat. Bus. Edn. Assn. Internat. Soc. Bus. Educators, Chgo. Computer Soc., Bus. Profls. Am., Am. Entrepreneur Assn.

NEEDLES, BELVERD EARL, JR., accountant, educator; b. Lubbock, Tex., Sept. 16, 1942; s. Belverd Earl and Billie (Anderson) N.; m. Marian Powers, May 23, 1976; children: Jennifer Helen, Jeffrey Scott, Annabelle Marian, Abigail Marian. BBA, Tex. Tech. U., 1964, MBA, 1965; PhD, U. Ill., 1969. CPA, Ill.; cert mgmt. acct. Asst. prof., assoc. prof. acctg. Tex. Tech. U., Lubbock, 1968-72; dean Coll. Bua. and Adminstrn., Chgo. State U., 1972-76; prof. acctg. U. Ill., Urbana, 1976-78; dir. Sch. Accountancy DePaul U., Chgo., 1978-86, prof. acctg., 1976-88, Arthur Andersen & Co. alumni disting. prof. acctg., 1988—2002, Ernst & Young dist. prof. acctg.,

2003—. Author: Accounting and Organizational Control, 1973, Modern Business, 2d edit., 1977, Principles of Accounting, 1980, 8th edit., 2002, Financial Accounting, 1982, 7th edit., 2001, The CPA Examination: A Complete Review, 7th edit., 1986, Comparative International Auditing Standards, 1985, Financial and Managerial Accounting, 5th edit., 2002; editor Accounting Instructor's Report, 1981—, The Accounting Profession and the Middle Market, 1986, Creating and Enhancing The Value of Post-Baccalareate Accounting Education, 1988, A Profession in Transition: The Ethical and Responsibilities of Accountants, 1989, Comparative International Accounting Educational Standards, 1990, Accounting Education for the 21st Century: The Global Challenges, 1994, Financial Acctg.: A Global Approach, 1999. Treas., bd. dirs. CPAs for Pub. Interest, 1978-86. Gen. Electric fellow, 1965-66, Deloitte Haskins and Sells fellow, 1966-68; named Disting. Alumnus Tex. Tech. U., 1986; recipient Award of Merit DePaul U., 1986, Faculty Award of Merit Fedn. of Schs. of Accountancy, 1990, Excellence in Tchg. Award DePaul U., 1998; named among 100 most influential accts. Acctg. Today, 2001. Fellow Am. Acctg. Assn. (sec. internat. sect. 1984-86, vice chmn. 1986-87, chmn. 1987-88, named outstanding internat. acctg. educator 1996); mem. AICPA (named Outstanding Educator 1992), Fedn. Schs. Accountancy (bd. dirs. 1980-87, pres. 1986), Acad. Internat. Bus., Ill. CPA Soc. (bd. dirs. 1994-96, vice chair 2001-02, sr. vice chair 2002-2003, chmn., 2003—, Outstanding Acctg. Educator 1990), European Acctg. Assn. (exec. com. 1986-89), Intenrat. Assn. for Edn. & Rsch. in Acctg. (v.p. 1989-92, sec.-treas. 1992-97, pres. 1997-2002), Phi Delta Kappa, Phi Kappa Phi, Beta Alpha Psi (named Acct. of Yr. for Edn. 1992), Beta Gamma Sigma.

NEEL, BARBARA ANNE SPIESS, elementary school educator, artist; b. Alexandria, Va., Feb. 19, 1945; d. Philip Daniel and Dorothy Elaine (Goepp) Spiess; m. William Barton Neel, June 6, 1966; children: Jennifer Lloyd, Elizabeth Barton. BFA, BS in Edn., U. Cin., 1967. Cert. tchr., N.J., Va. Elem. art tchr. Hamilton Twp. (N.J.) Schs., 1967-68; vol. to art tchr. Arlington (Va.) County Pub. Schs., 1977-81, elem. art tchr., 1983—2003, drawing and painting fine arts tchr., 1986-90, summer laureate art tchr., 1991. Tapestry weaver; water color and acrylic painter. One-woman art show Ellipse Gallery, Arlington, Va., 2001. Mem. NEA, Nat. Art Edn. Assn., No. Va. Art Edn. Assn., Va. Art Edn. Assn., Arlington Edn. Assn., Va. Edn. Assn., Arlington Visual Artists Coalition, Springwater Fibers Workshop (Tapestry 1st prize 1992). Presbyterian. Avocations: knitting, folk music, piano, singing. Home: 2308 N Upton St Arlington VA 22207-4045 Office: Key Elem Sch 2300 Key Blvd Arlington VA 22201-3415 E-mail: bsneel@tmail.arlington.k12.va.us.

NEEL, SPURGEON HART, JR., physician, retired army officer; b. Memphis, Sept. 24, 1919; s. Spurgeon Hart and Pyrle (Womble) N.; m. Alice Glidewell Torti, Nov. 18, 1939; children: Spurgeon Hart III, Alice Leah Neel Zartarian. Student pre-med., Memphis State U., 1939; MD, U. Tenn., 1942; MPH, Harvard U., 1958; MSBA, George Washington U., 1965. Diplomate: Am. Bd. Preventive Medicine. Intern Meth. Hosp., Memphis, 1943; resident x-ray Santa Ana (Calif.) AFB, 1944; resident aviation medicine USAF Sch. Aerospace Medicine, 1960; commd. 2d lt. U.S. Army, 1942, advanced through grades to maj. gen., 1970; various assignments U.S., 1943-44, 47-48, WWII European Theater, ETO, 1944-47; chief surgeon service Ft. McPherson, Ga., 1949; med. service Ft. McPherson Army Hosp., Ft. McPherson, Ga., 1949; div. surgeon (82d Airborne Div.), Ft. Bragg, NC, 1949-51; comdr. (30th Med. Group), Korea, 1953-54; dep. dir. div. physiology and pharmacology (WRAIR, WRAMC), 1956; chief aviation br. (OTSG), 1957; chief aviation medicine Ft. Rucker, Ala., 1960; comdg. officer U.S. Army Hosp., post surgeon, 1961-64; stationed in Vietnam, 1965-66, 68-69; dep. surgeon gen. U.S. Army, Washington, 1969-73; comdr. (U.S. Army Health Services Command), 1973-77. Clin. assoc. prof. family practice U. Tex. Health Sci. Ctr., San Antonio, now prof. emeritus occupl. and aerospace medicine U. Tex. Sch. Pub. Health; med. cons. U.S. Automobile Assn., other industries, San Antonio. Contbr. articles med. jours. Decorated D.S.M. with oak leaf cluster, Legion of Merit with 4 clusters, Bronze Star with oak leaf cluster, Air medal with 3 oak leaf clusters, Joint Service Commendation medal, USAF Commendation medal, Purple Heart, others.; recipient Seaman award Assn. Mil. Surgeons U.S., 1950, Gary Wratten award, 1967; McClelland award Army Aviation Assn. Am., 1962; named to U.S. Army Aviation Hall Fame, 1976; recipient Lyster award Aerospace Med. Assn., 1977, Nat. Soc. DAR medal of honor, 1999. Fellow ACP, Am. Coll. Preventive Medicine (past v.p.), Royal Soc. Health, Aerospace Med. Assn. (past pres., Louis H. Bauer Founders award 2003), Internat. Acad. Aviation and Space Medicine, Am. Acad. Med. Adminstrs., Am. Coll. Health Care Execs.; mem. AMA (past-sec. sect. mil. medicine), Assn. Mil. Surgeons U.S., Assn. U.S. Army, Army Aviation Assn. Am., Dustoff (Hall of Fame 2001), Phi Chi (assoc.). Home: 4106 Tarlac Dr San Antonio TX 78239-3072

NEELANKAVIL, JAMES PAUL, marketing educator, consultant, researcher; b. Anjoor, India, May 29, 1940; came to U.S., 1973, naturalized, 1985; s. Paul V. and Mary (Velara) N.; m. Salvacion Querol Pena, July 15, 1973; children: Mary Angel, Jacques Prince. BS, St. Thomas Coll., India, 1961; MBA, Asian Inst. Mgmt., Philippines, 1972; PhD, NYU, 1976. Asst. prof. N.Y. Inst., 1976-78; assoc. prof. Montclair State Coll., N.J., 1978-80; asst. prof. NYU, 1980-84; chmn. mktg. and internat. bus. dept. Hofstra U., Hempstead, N.Y., 1984-86, assoc. dean sch. bus., 1986-89, acting dean, 1989-91, prof. mktg. and internat. bus., 1991—; supr. Firestone, Bombay, India, 1961-70; cons. Internat. Advt. Assn., N.Y.C., 1979-88, GTE Inc., Stamford, Conn., 1980-85, Healthchem Inc., N.Y.C., 1980-83. Author: Global Business: Contemporary Issues, Problems and Challenges, Self-Regulation, 1980, Agency Compensation, 1982, Advertising Regulation, 1985, Advertising Regulations in Selected Countries, 1987; co-author Advertising Self-Regulation: A Global Perspective, 1980, Global Business: Contemporary Issues, Problems and Challenges; also articles. Min. Resurrection Ascension Ch., N.Y.C., 1990-98. Mem. Internat. Advt. Assn., Am. Mktg. Assn., Acad. Internat. Bus. Avocations: reading, tennis, travel.

NEELD, ELIZABETH HARPER, author, retreat and workshop leader, consultant; b. Brooks, Ga., Dec. 25, 1940; d. Tommie Frank and Rachel (Leach) Harper; m. Gregory Cowan, Feb. 24, 1975 (dec. 1979); m. Jerele Don Neeld, 1983. BS, U. Chattanooga, 1962, MEd, 1966; PhD, U. Tenn., Knoxville, 1973. Dir. English programs MLA, N.Y.C., 1973-76; prof. English Tex. A&M U., College Station, 1976-83; exec. prof. U. Houston Sch. Bus., 1992—98; internat. cons. on change, 1990—. Author: Sister Bernadette: Cowboy Nun From Texas, 1991, A Sacred Primer: The Essential Guide to Quiet Time and Prayer, 1999, Seven Choices: Finding Daylight After Loss Shatters Your World, 2003; author, editor 15 additional books; author: (audiocassette series) Yes! You Can Write; anchor and subject of PBS documentary The Challenge of Grief, 1991. Democrat. Episcopalian. Avocations: cooking, opera, art collaging. Home: 6706 Beauford Dr Austin TX 78750-8124

NEER, CHARLES SUMNER, II, orthopedic surgeon, educator; b. Vinita, Okla., Nov. 10, 1917; s. Charles Sumner and Pearl Victoria (Brooke) N.; m. Eileen Meyer, June 12, 1990; children: Charlotte Marguerite, Sydney Victoria, Charles Henry. BA, Dartmouth Coll., 1939; MD, U. Pa., 1942. Diplomate Am. Bd. Orthopaedic Surgery (bd. dirs. 1970-75). Intern U. Pa. Hosp., Phila., 1942-43; asso. in surgery N.Y. Orthopedic-Columbia-Presbyn. Med. Center, N.Y.C., 1943-44; instr. in surgery Coll. Physicians and Surgeons, Columbia U., N.Y.C., 1946-47, instr. orthopaedic surgery, 1947-57, asst. prof. clin. orthopaedic surgery, 1957-64, asso. prof., 1964-68, prof. clin. orthopaedic surgery, 1968-90, prof. clin. orthopaedic surgery emeritus, spl. lectr. orthopaedic surgery, 1990—. Attending orthopaedic surgeon Columbia-Presbyn. Med. Ctr., N.Y.C.; chief adult reconstructive svc. N.Y. Orthopaedic Hosp.; chief shoulder and elbow clinic Presbyn. Hosp.; cons. orthopaedic surgeon emeritus N.Y. Orthopaedic-Columbia-Presbyn. Med. Ctr., 1991—; chmn. 4th Internat. Congress Shoulder Surgeons; chmn. Internat. Bd. Shoulder Surgery, 1992—. Founder, chmn. bd. trustees Jour. Shoulder and Elbow Surgery, 1990—; contbr. articles to books, tech. films, sound slides. Served with U.S. Army, 1944-46. Recipient Disting. Svc. award Am. Bd. Orthopaedic Surgeons 1975. Fellow ACS (sr. mem. nat. com. on trauma), Am. Acad. Orthop. Surgeons (com. on upper extremity, shoulder com.); mem. AMA, ACS (mem. com. trauma), Am. Bd. Orthop. Surgeons (bd. dirs. 1970-75, Disting. Svc. award 1975), Am. Shoulder and Elbow Surgeons (inaugural pres.), Am. Assn. Surgery Trauma, Am. Orthop. Assn., Mid-Am. Orthop. Assn. (hon.), N.Y. Acad. Medicine, Allen O. Whipple Surg. Soc., N.Y. State Med. Soc., N.Y. County Med. Soc., Pan Am. Med. Assn., Am. Trauma Soc., Soc. Latino Am. Orthop. y Traumatology, Internat. Soc. Orthop. Surgery and Traumatology, Va. Orthop. Soc. (hon.), Carolina Orthop. Alumni Assn. (hon.), Conn. Orthop. Club (hon.), Houston Orthop. Assn. (hon.), Soc. Française de Chirurgie Orthop. et Traumatology (hon.), Soc. Italiana Orthop. Etravmatologia e Traumatologia; patron, Shoulder and Elbow Soc. Australia, South African Shoulder Soc., Giraffe Club, Internat. Bd. Shoulder Surgery (chmn. 1992—), Alpha Omega Alpha, Phi Chi. Home and Office: 231 S Miller St Vinita OK 74301-3625 E-mail: elmcreekacres@junction.com., elmcreekacres@junction.com

NEET, KENNETH EDWARD, biochemist, educator; b. St. Petersburg, Fla., Sept. 24, 1936; s. Claude Parks and Edna Francis (Keefe) N.; m. Jane Carol Bamford, June 11, 1960; children: Kerrie Elise, Kellie Estelle, Kirk Ernest, Kyle Eric. BS, U. Fla., 1958, MS, 1960, PhD, 1965. Postdoctoral fellow U. Calif., Berkeley, 1965-67; from asst. prof. to prof. Case Western Res. U., Cleve., 1967-90; prof., chair biol. chemistry Finch. U. Health Sci./Chgo. Med. Sch., North Chicago, Ill., 1990—. Vis. scientist Nat. Inst. Med. Rsch., Mill Hill, Eng., 1973-74, Stanford (Calif.) U., 1980-81; cons. Cephalon, Inc., Phila., 1990-93; mem. study sect. NIH, Bethesda, Md., 1982-86, NSF, Washington, 1976, 90. Assoc. editor Jour. Biol. Chemistry, 1996—; contbr. articles to profl. jours. Lt. (j.g.) Med. Svc. Corps, USN, 1960-63. Recipient Those Who Excel award Ill. State Bd. Edn., 1995, Morris L. Parker award FUHS/CMS, 1995; grantee NIH, 1968—, Am. Cancer Soc., 1968-73, Josiah Macy Found., 1980-81. Mem. Am. Soc. Biochemistry and Molecular Biology (treas. 2000-), Protein Soc., Soc. for Neurosci. Office: Finch U Health Sci/ Chgo Med Sch 3333 Green Bay Rd North Chicago IL 60064-3037

NEFF, DIANE IRENE, university administrator; b. Cedar Rapids, Iowa, Apr. 26, 1954; d. Robert Mariner and Adeline Emma (Zach) N. BA in Psychology and Home Econs., U. Iowa, 1976; MA in Sociology, U. Mo., 1978; MEd in Ednl. Leadership, U. West Fla., 1990; EdD in Ednl. Leadership, U. Ctrl. Fla., 2003. Contract compliance officer, dir. EEO, City of Cedar Rapids, 1979-81; commd. ensign USN, 1981, advanced through grades to lt. comdr.; asst. legal officer Naval Comm. Area Master Sta., Guam, 1982-83; comm. security plans and requirements officer Comdr.-in-Chief US Naval Forces in Europe, London, 1983-85; dir. standards and evaluation dept. Recruit Tng. Command, Orlando, Fla., 1985-89; rsch. and analysis officer Naval Res. Officers Tng. Corps Office Chief Naval Edn. and Tng., Pensacola, Fla., 1989-91; tech. tng. officer Recruit Tng. Command, Great Lakes, Ill., 1991-92, mil. tng. officer, 1992-93, dir. apprentice tng., 1993-95; coord. ednl. and tng. programs U. Ctrl. Fla., Orlando, 1995—. Founding mem. Unity of Gulf Breeze, Fla., 1990; performer various benefits for chs., mus., others, Orlando, 1988, 91, 95, 96, 97. Fellow Adminstrn. on Aging, 1977. Mem. ASTD. Unitarian Universalist. Avocation: piano. E-mail: dneff@mail.ucf.edu.

NEFF, GARY VERYL, mathematics educator, consultant; b. Altoona, Pa., Sept. 2, 1943; s. Donald Eugene and Florence Ione (Ross) N.; m. Mary Ellen Andre, Oct. 1964; children: Gary Jr., Traci. BS, Ind. U., 1964; MEd, U. Pitts., 1969; M in Math. Edn., Ind. U., 1970; MS in Math., Ohio U., 1971. Cert. tchr. math., driver's edn., prin., Pa.; tchr. math., Ohio. Tchr. West Allegheny Schs., Imperial, Pa., 1964-65; tchr., coach Greater LSD, Latrobe, Pa., 1965-87; asst. prof. Salem (W.Va.) Coll., 1987-88, Bethany Coll., W.Va., 1988-90, Ohio U. Eastern, Athens, 1990—. Mem. steering com., interim dir. S.E. region Project Discovery, Columbus, Ohio, 1992—; cons. Zanesville (Ohio) City Schs., 1992—, Cambridge (Ohio) City Schs., 1992—, Hamilton (Ohio) City Schs., 1994—, K-6 Math. Tchr. Tng., Athens, 1991-94, S.E. Region Ohio, St. Clairesville, 1991—; mem. textbook selection com. St. Clairsville Schs., 1994, curriculum writer, 1993. Councilman Latrobe Boro, 1975-80; committeeman 2d ward Latrobe Boro, 1976-82. Prison Edn. grantee Ohio State Correctional Facility, 1994. Mem. Nat. Coun. Tchrs. Math., Ohio Coun. Tchrs. Math., Pa. Coun. Tchrs. Math. (chmn. state conf. software sales 1995), Ohio Math. Educators Leadership Coun., Rural Systemic Initiative, Elks. Avocation: antiques. Home: PO Box 71 Belmont OH 43718-0071 Office: Ohio U Eastern 45425 National Rd W Saint Clairsville OH 43950-9764

NEFF, GREGORY PALL, mechanical engineer, educator; b. Detroit, Nov. 23, 1942; s. Jacob John and Bonnie Alice (Pall) Neff; m. Bonita Jean Dostal, Apr. 27, 1974; 1 child, Kristiana Dostal. BS in Physics, U. Mich., 1964, MA in Math., 1966, MS in Physics, 1967; MSME, Mich. State U., 1982. Registered profl. engr., Ind., cert. mfg. engr., mfg. technologist, sr. indsl. technologist. Rsch. asst. cyclotron lab U. Mich., Ann Arbor, 1968-72, tchg. fellow physics dept., 1973; instr. sci. dept. Lansing (Mich.) CC, 1976-82; guest lectr. Purdue U. Calumet, Hammond, Ind., 1982-83, from asst. prof. to assoc. prof., 1984—2003, prof., 2003—. Cons. Inland Steel Co., East Chicago, Ind., 1984—86, Polyurethane divsn. Pinder Industries, East Chicago, 1990—92, Elevated divsn. Pitts. Tank & Tower, Henderson, Ky., 1990—91; program evaluator tech. accreditation commn. Accreditation Bd. Engring. and Tech., 1996—2003; mem., team chair Tech. Accreditation Commn., 2003—. Contbr. chapters to books, articles to profl. jours. Mem. Tri-County Regional Planning Commn., Lansing, 1978—80; chair non-motorized adv. coun. Mich. Dept. Transp., Lansing, 1982—83; commr. Ingham County Bd. Commrs., Mason, Mich., 1977—80. Mem.: ASME (sec. MET dept. heads com. 1999, vice chair 2000, chair 2001, webmaster 1999—, bd. engring. edn. 2001—03, mem. com. tech. accreditation 2002—), ASHRAE, Order Engrs., Nat. Assn. Indsl. Tech., Am. Soc. Engring. Edn. (Merl K. Miller award 1994), Soc. Mfg. Engrs. (chpt. 112 bd. dirs. 1986—, webmaster 1999—, Appreciation award 1990, 1992, Outstanding Faculty Advisor award 1991), Tau Alpha Pi, Sigma Alpha Epsilon. Democrat. Roman Catholic. Office: Purdue U Calumet 2200 169th St Hammond IN 46323-2068 E-mail: gneff@purdue.edu.

NEFF, JOHN MICHAEL, health facility administrator, educator, dean; b. Gudalajara, Mex., Dec. 26, 1932; s. Clarence Alvin Neff and Priscilla (Holton) Fenn; m. Lee Cuninggim, Aug. 20, 1961; children: Michael Merriman, Heidi Holton, Joseph Daniel. BA, Pomona Coll., 1955; post-grad., UCLA, 1955-57; MD, Harvard U., 1960. Intern, then resident in pediatrics Sch. Medicine Johns Hopkins U., Balt., 1960-63; epidemic intelligence svc. officer Ctr. for Disease Control USPHS, Atlanta, 1963-65; chief resident in pediatrics Sch. Medicine Johns Hopkins U., Balt., 1965-66, from asst. to assoc. prof. dept. pediatrics, 1968-81, from asst. dean to assoc. dean, 1968-75; fellow in infectious diseases Med. Sch. Harvard U. Children's Hosp., Boston, 1966-68; chief pediatrics Balt. City Hosp., 1975-81; v.p., med. dir. Children's Hosp. Med. Ctr., Seattle, 1981—98; prof. pediats. U. Wash., Seattle, 1981—, assoc. dean Sch. Medicine, 1981—98; dir. Ctr. for Children with Spl. Needs Children's Hosp. and Regional Med. Ctr., Seattle, 1998—. Founding mem., bd. trustees Broadmead Life Time Care Ctr., Balt., 1975-81. Editor: Jour. Infectious Diseases-Evaluation of Smallpox Vaccine, 1977; contbr. articles to profl. jours. Lt. comdr. USPHS, 1963-65. Fellow Infectious Disease Soc. Am.; mem. Soc. Pediatric Rsch., Am. Acad. Pediatrics. Office: Childrens Hosp and Regional Med Ctr 6901 Sandpoint Way NE PO Box 50020 MS: S-219 Seattle WA 98145-5020

NEFF, KATHY S. swimming and water safety educator; b. Rochester, Ind., Apr. 24, 1959; Cert. pool operator. Head coach girls swimming, diving Rochester Cmty. Sch. Corp., 1988-97, aquatic dir., swimming and water safety instr. grades K-12, 1991—, asst. men's swim coach, 1994-97, dir. substitute svcs., 1998—; farmer Neff Farms, 1998—; coach Swim Analysis Camp Ind. U., summers 93-97; v.p. Ptnrs. in Edn., 1996-98, pres., 1998-2000. Bd. dirs. Rochester Royals Swim Team, 1992-94; asst. men's swim coach Culver Mil. Acad., 1993-94; aquatic supr. Culver (Ind.) Mil. Summer Camps, 1992, 93, 98, waterfront dir., 1999-2000; swimming and diving ofcl. Ind. H.S. Athletic Assn., 1991—. Mem. Nat. Fedn. Interscholastic Ofcls. Assn., North Ctrl. Ind. Athletic Ofcls. Assn. Avocations: sailing, horseback riding, reading. Office: Rochester Comty Schs Po Box 108 Rochester IN 46975

NEFF, MARY ELLEN ANDRE, retired elementary school educator; b. Indiana, Pa., July 6, 1943; d. Frank Vincent and Marie Isabel (Elrick) Andre; children: Gary V. Jr., Traci Dawn. BS, Indiana U. Pa., 1965, MEd, 1971. Elem. sch. tchr. Blairsville (Pa.)-Saltsburg Sch. Dist., Derry (Pa.) Area Sch. Dist.; ret., 2002. Mem. NEA, PTA, Pa. State Edn. Assn., Blairsville-Saltsburg Edn. Assn. (past sec.), Nat. Soc. DAR (vice regent), Latrobe Lions Club (pres.), Saltsburg Hist. Soc. (pres.), Westmoreland County Hist. Soc. (bd. dirs., sec.), Delta Kappa Gamma (pres. 1986-90, treas. 1992-2000); sec. to Laurel Area Partnership on Aging. Home: 17 Carriage Rd Greensburg PA 15601-9014

NEFF, RAY QUINN, electric power educator, consultant; b. Houston, Apr. 29, 1928; s. Noah Grant and Alma Ray (Smith) N.; m. Elizabeth McDougald, Sept. 4, 1982. Degree in Steam Engring., Houston Vocat. Tech., 1957; BSME, Kennedy Western U., 1986. Various positions Houston Lighting & Power Co., 1945-60, plant supr., 1960-70, plant supt. asst., 1970-80, tech. supr., 1980-85, tng. supr., 1985-87; owner, operator Neff Enterprises, Bedias, Tex., 1987—; tng. supr. Tex. A&M U., 1991—. Cons. Houston Industries, 1987-89. Author: Power Plant Operation, 1975, Power Operator Training, 1985, Power Foreman Training, 1986. Judge Internat. Sci. and Engring. Fair, Houston, 1982, Sci. Engring. Fair Houston, 1987. Mem. ASME, Assn. Chief Operating Engrs., Masons. Republican. Methodist. Avocations: farming, ranching, classic cars. Home: Hwy 90 Rte 2t PO Box 193A Bedias TX 77831-0193 Office: Tex A&M U Power Plant College Station TX 77843-0001

NEFF, ROBERT WILBUR, academic administrator, educator, minister; b. Lancaster, Pa., June 16, 1936; s. Wilbur Hildebr and Hazel Margaret (Martin) N.; m. Dorothy Rosewarne, Aug. 16, 1959; children: Charles Scott, Heather Lynn. BS, Pa. State U., 1958; BD, Yale Div. Sch., 1961, MA, 1963, PhD, 1969; DD, Juniata Coll., 1978, Manchester Coll., 1979; DHL, Bridgewater Coll., 1979. Asst. prof. Bridgewater Coll., 1964-65; mem. faculty dept. Bibl. studies Bethany Theol. Sem., 1965-77, prof., 1973-77; gen. sec. Ch. of the Brethren, Elgin, Ill., 1978-86; pres. Juniata Coll., 1986-98, pres. emeritus, 1998—2003. Vis. prof. Pa. State U., 1998—2003; assoc. for resource devel. The Village at Morrison's Cove, 1999—; mem. faculty North Park Sem., No. Bapt. Sem., Theol. Coll. No. Nigeria; bd. dirs. Mellon Bank (Ctrl.) Nat. Assn., exec. com., 1989, chair exec. com., 1993, chair CRA com., 1994-2001; mem. pres.'s com. NCAA, 1996-99; bd. dirs. Susquehanna Valley Satellite, 2002--; adj. faculty Bethany Theol. Sem., 1999—; lectr. Young Ctr. at Elizabethtown Coll., 2002; mem. USDA Del. to Baltic States, 2000. Mem. governing bd. Nat. Coun. Chs. of Christ, 1976-86, mem. exec. com., 1979-86; mem. Mid-East panel, 1980, 2d v.p., 1985-86; mem. ctrl. com. World Coun. Chs., 1983-92; rep. Assembly of World Coun. Chs., 1983, mem. exec. com. on interch. rels., 1980-84, mem. del. to China, 1981, chmn. presdl. panel, 1982-84; bd. dirs. Bethany Theol. Sem., 1978-86; campaign chmn. United Way, Huntington County, 1989; chair higher edn. com. Ch. of Brethren, 1993-98. Danforth fellow, 1958-69 Mem. Soc. Bibl. Lit., Soc. Old Testament Study, Chgo. Soc. Bibl. Rsch., Soc. Values in Higher Edn., Coun. Ind. Colls. (nat. bd. dirs. 1991-94, treas. 1995-98), Pa. Coun. Ind. Colls. and Univs. (exec. com. 1988-90, 92-96, chair ann. conf. nominating com. 1993-94), Mid Atlantic Athletic Conf. (sec., mem. exec. com. 1994-97). Democrat. Home: RR 1 Box 437 Alexandria PA 16611-9652 Office: Village at Morrisons Cove 429 Market St Martinsburg PA 16866

NEFF-ENCINAS, JULIE GAY, bilingual education specialist, consultant; b. Chgo., June 21, 1957; d. Wesley Miles and Betty Ann (Pitts) Neff; m. Ernesto Valenzuela Encinas, July 5, 1980; children: Ariella, Gerard, Martin. BA, Hanover Coll., 1978; MEd, U. Ariz., 1979. Cert. secondary tchr. with bilingual edn. endorsement. Mid. sch. tchr. Cath. Diocese of Tucson, 1979-80; tchr. bilingual edn. Tucson Unified Sch. Dist., 1980-89, bilingual edn. curriculum specialist, 1989-96, compliance project specialist, 1996—2000; mem. adj. faculty No. Ariz. U., Flagstaff, 1993-96; improvement facilitator Tucson Unified Sch. Dist.; bilingual edn. tchr. U.S. Dept. Edn., 1999—2003. Cons. S.W. Regional Lab., Los Alamitos, Calif., 1993-96. Co-author Tucson Unified Sch. Dist. Compliance Procedures Manual for Bilingual Edn., 1993, Tucson Unified Sch. Dist. Comprehensive Plan for Bilingual Edn., 1993. Title VII Short Term Tng. grantee U.S. Dept. Edn., 1991-94, Title VII Systemwide Improvement grantee U.S. Dept. Edn., 1995-00. Avocation: birdwatching. Home: 4040 S Silver Bridle Ln Tucson AZ 85735-8625 Office: Tucson Unified Sch Dist Pistor Middle Sch 1010 E 10th St Tucson AZ 85719-5813

NEGA, NANCY KAWECKI, middle school science educator; b. Chgo., Mar. 16, 1946; d. John Sebastian and Irene M. (Wantuch) Kawecki; m. Lance J. Nega, Feb. 24, 1968 (div. 1997); children: Sandi Kawecka Nenga, Todd J. BA in Biology, Ill. Coll., 1968; MS Tchg. in Elem. Math., U. Ill., Chgo., 1991. Cert. EA sci. tchr. Rschr. Morton-Norwich, Inc., Woodstock, Ill., 1968-72; tchr. Elmhurst (Ill.) Unit Dist. 205, 1986—; master tchr. DEd pre-service tchr. program Argonne Nat. Lab., Ill., 2001—. Trainer Globe Program, Washington, 1995-99; Internet trainer Argonne (Ill.) Nat. Lab., 1996-2000. Recipient Presdl. award of excellence in sci. and math. tchg. NSF, 1995, Paul DeHart Hurd award, NMLSTA, 1999 Mem. Nat. Sci. Tchrs. Assn., Ill. Sci. Tchrs. Assn. (award of excellence 1994), Nat. Mid Level Sci. Tchrs. Assn., Mid Level Sci. Tchrs. Network. Office: Churchville Mid Sch 155 Victory Pkwy Elmhurst IL 60126-1215

NEGELE, JOHN WILLIAM, physics educator, consultant; b. Cleve., Apr. 18, 1944; s. Charles Frederick and Virgil Lea (Wettich) N.; m. Rose Anne Meeks, June 18, 1967; Janette Andrea, Julia Elizabeth. BS, Purdue U., 1965; PhD, Cornell U., 1969. Research fellow Niels Bohr Inst., Copenhagen, 1969-70; vis. asst. prof. MIT, Cambridge, 1970-71, faculty mem., 1971—, prof. physics, 1979—, William A. Coolidge prof., 1991—, head nuclear and particle theory divsn., 1988-89, dir. Ctr. for Theoretical Physics, 1989-98. Cons. Los Alamos Sci. Lab., Brookhaven Nat. Lab., Lawrence Livermore Nat. Lab., Oak Ridge Nat. Lab.; mem. physics div. rev. com. Argonne Nat. Lab., (Ill.), 1977-83; mem. nuclear sci. div. rev. com. Lawrence Berkeley Lab., (Calif.), 1982—; mem. adv. bd., steering com. Inst. for Theoretical Physics, U. Calif.-Santa Barbara, 1982-86; mem. adv. bd. inst. for Nuclear Theory U. Washington, 1990—, chair 1992-94; program adv. com. Tandem Van de Graaff Accelerator, Brookhaven Nat. Lab., 1977-78, Bates Linear Accelerator, 1977-80, Los Alamos Meson Prodn. Facility, 1986-89, Brookhaven Alternating Gradient Synchraton, 1987-90. Author: Quantum Many Particle Systems, 1987; contbr. articles to profl. jours.; editor: Advances in Nuclear Physics, 1977—. Grantee NSF, 1965-69; grantee Danforth Found., 1965-69, Woodrow Wilson Found., 1965, Alfred P. Sloan Found., 1979, Japan Soc. for Promotion Sci., 1981, John Simon Guggenheim Found., 1982; Alexander von Humboldt Found. fellow, 1998. Fellow Am. Phys. Soc. (exec. com. 1982-84, program com. 1980-82, editorial bd. Phys. Rev. 1980-82, exec. com. topical group on computational physics 1992-93, chair divsn. of computational physics 1992-93, exec. com. 1992-94, Bonner prize com. 1984-85), AAAS (nominating com. 1987-91, mem. physics sect. com. 1991—), Fedn. Am. Scientists. Home: 70 Buckman Dr Lexington MA 02421-6000 Office: MIT Dept Physics 6-315 77 Massachusetts Ave Dept 6-308 Cambridge MA 02139-4307

NEGRON, JAIME, performing arts center administrator, real estate agent; b. San Juan, P.R., Dec. 23, 1939; came to U.S., 1952; s. Rito and Tomasa (Otero) N.; m. Barbara Charlotte Stovall, Nov. 5, 1959; children: Jeannette Michelle, Victoria Frances. BA in Econs., Howard U., 1987. Lic. realtor. Chief receiving and shipping Am. U., Washington, 1960-62, book dept. mgr., 1968-71; bookstore mgr. Follett Corp., Chgo., 1962-68, Cath. U., Washington, 1971-74; dir. Howard U. stores Howard U., Washington, 1974-87, dir. aux. enterprises, 1987-91; real estate agt. Long & Foster Realtors, Fairfax, Va., 1993—; asst. dir. aux. enterprises Perimeter Coll., Atlanta, 1992-96; dir. retail ops. J.F. Kennedy Ctr. for Performing Arts, Washington, 1996—2002. Cons. U. Del., Newark, 1988, Wesley Sem., Washington, 1984, R.R. Moton Meml. Inst., N.Y.C., 1974-79. Active Vienna Jaycees, 1970-80. With USN, 1958-60. Mem. Middle Atlantic Coll. Stores (pres. 1984), Nat. Assn. Coll. Stores, Nat. Bd. Realtors, Va. Bd. Realtors. Episcopalian. Avocation: dancing. Office: Long and Foster Realtors 3918 Prosperity Ave Fairfax VA 22031

NEHER, ROBERT TROSTLE, biology educator; b. Mt. Morris, Ill., Nov. 1, 1930; s. Oscar Warner and Etha Mae (Trostle) N.; m. Mary Rebecca Timmons, June 12, 1954; children: Kenneth, Jon, Daniel. BA in Sci., Manchester Coll., Ind., 1953; MAT in Biology, Ind. U., 1955, PhD in Botany, 1963; MRE in Counseling, Bethany Sem., Chgo., 1957. Assoc. Christian edn. Ch. of Brethren, Elgin, Ill., 1956; asst. prof., then assoc. prof. biology U. LaVerne, Calif., 1958-62, prof. biology, 1966—, chmn. nat. sci. divsn., 1978—, provost, v.p. acad. affairs, 2000-01; dir. U. LaVerne Field Sta. Magpie Ranch, Drummond, Mont., 1994—. Dep. dir. Nat. Energy Rsch. and Info. Inst., 1982-88, chair pre-health sci. com., program dir., academic coun., 1985—; aquaculture cons. Bolsa Aquaculture Consortium, 1973-76, AM China Corp., 1981; cons. devel. of in-svc. tchg. tng. in environ. edn. L.A. Pub. Schs.; dir. coll. level curriculum program Montclair High Sch., Van Nuys, Calif. Co-editor: Energy from Biomass, 1979; contbr. articles to profl. jours. City councilman LaVerne City Coun., 1976-84, mayor pro tem, 1980-84; commr. L.A. County Watershed Commn., 1976-91; bd. dirs. Pomona Valley Youth Svcs.; juvenile divsn. chmn. 1978-79; chmn. San Gabriel Valley Get-About Transp. Bd., 1980-84; mem. L.A. County Solid Waste Curbside Recycling Task Force, 1980-82; chmn. La Verne City Commn. on Environ. Quality, 1972-75; mem. La Verne City Planning Commn., 1966-72; moderator La Verne Ch. of Brethren, 1966-75, chmn. bd. 1977-80, mem. ch. bd. dirs., 1966-84; trustee, officer San Gabriel Valley Mosquito and Vector Control Dist., 1991—. Named Outstanding Tchr. of Yr., La Verne Coll., 1969—70; recipient Els Johnson Cmty. Svc. award, U. La Verne, 2003; grantee, NSF, 1960—61; NSF faculty fellow, Ind. U., Bloomington, 1961—62. Mem. AAAS (life mem), Am. Soc. Plant Taxonomists, Calif. Bot. Soc., San Bernardino County Mus. Assn., Audubon Soc., Sierra Club, Nat. Geog. Soc., Sigma Xi. Office: U La Verne Natural Science Divsn 1950 3rd St La Verne CA 91750-4401 E-mail: neherr@ulv.edu.

NEHLS, ROBERT LOUIS, JR., school system financial consultant; b. Berkeley, Calif., Dec. 27, 1944; s. Robert Louis and Inda May (Kean) N.; m. Diana Jean Smith, June 17, 1967; 1 child, Patrick Robert. AA, Coll. Marin, 1965; BS, San Jose State U., 1967, MA, 1976; EdD, U. San Francisco, 1991. Cert. tchr., sch. adminstr., Calif. Tchr. Diablo Valley Coll., Pleasant Hill, Calif., 1979-86; acct. Kelly and Tama, CPAs, Walnut Creek, Calif., 1978-79; tchr. Pleasanton (Calif.) Unified Sch. Dist., 1970-78, 79-81, dir. fiscal svcs., 1981-83; dep. supt. San Leandro (Calif.) Unified Sch. Dist., 1983-87, 90-2001; asst. supt. Acalanes Union H.S. Dist., Lafayette, Calif., 1987-89; supt. Orinda (Calif.) Union Sch. Dist., 1989-90; tchr. St. Marys Coll. Sch. Edn., Moraga, Calif., 1997; chief bus. official Tahoe Truckee Sch. Dist., 2001—02; interim supt. Truckee Sch. Dist., 2003. Exec. adv. com. Calif. Found. Improvement of Employee/Employer Relationships, Sacramento, 1992-97. Mem. Blarney's Irish Band, Truckee, Calif., 2001—; contbr. articles to profl. jours. Mem. Blarney's Irish Band, 2001—. Mem. Assn. Calif. Sch. Adminstrs. (comptroller 1992-95, pres. 1996-97), Calif. Assn. Sch. Bus. Ofcls. (bd. dirs. no. sect. 1984-89), No. Calif. Sch. Bus. Ofcls. (past pres.), Acad. of Sci., Phi Kappa Phi. Avocations: fishing, skiing, performing irish and scottish music. Home and Office: 19895 Wildwood West Dr Penn Valley CA 95946 Fax: 530-432-9886. E-mail: bobhehls@earthlink.net.

NEHRING, LISA MARIE, secondary school educator; b. Charleston, S.C., June 30, 1966; d. Roy Andrew and Lilian (Nunnen) Olson; m. C. Mark Nehring, June 15, 1991. BA in Math., Lake Forest Coll., 1988; MEd in Adminstrn. summa cum laude, Nat.-Louis U., 1994. Cert. tchr., Ill.; cert. supr. adminstrn., Ill. H.S. math. tchr. Wykeham Rise, Washington, Conn., 1988-89, Wamogo Regional H.S., Litchfield, Conn., 1989-90; math. tchr. Waukegan (Ill.) H.S., 1990-94, Adlai E. Stevenson H.S., Lincolnshire, Ill., 1994—. Mem. Nat. Coun. Tchrs. Math., Ill. Coun. Tchrs. Math. Avocations: skiing, tennis, travel, dance. Office: Adlai E Stevenson HS Two Stevenson Dr Lincolnshire IL 60069 E-mail: lnehring@district125.k12.il.us.

NEIBERGER, RICHARD EUGENE, pediatrician, nephrologist, educator; b. Onaga, Kans., Nov. 16, 1947; s. Earl Edward and Margaret Bell (Grim) N.; m. Mary June Chamberlin, Oct. 31, 1971; children: Ami, Eric, Chris, Robert. BS in Physics, U. Ctrl. Fla., 1971; PhD, U. Louisville, 1979, MD, 1982. Diplomate Am. Bd. Pediat., Nat. Bd. Med. Examiners. Intern, then resident in pediat. Albert Einstein Coll. Med., Bronx, N.Y., 1982-85, fellow in pediat. nephrology, 1985-88; asst. prof. U. Fla. Coll. Med., Gainesville, 1988-93, assoc. prof., 1993—; med. dir. pediatrics Renal Stone Disease Clinic, 1996—. Assoc. med. dir. Children's Kidney Ctr., Gainesville, 1989—; co-investigator on 6 rsch. studies, dir. Pediatric Rsch. Stone Disease Clin. U. Fla., rsch. peer rev. com. Am. Heart Assn., 1997-99; physician advisor Fla. Med. Quality Assurance, Tampa, 1994-2002. Contbr. articles to profl. jours. Active Children's Home Soc., Gainesville, 1994—2002, Ronald McDonald House, 1996—. Named one of Best Drs. in Am., Best Drs. in Fla., Best Pediatricians in Am.; grantee, CoInvest, Bethesda, Md., 1995—. Mem. AMA, Fla. Med. Assn., So. Med. Assn., Am. Soc. Nephrology, Internat. Pediat. Nephrology Assn., Am. Soc. Pediat. Nephrology, Fla. Soc. Pediat. Nephrology (pres. 1998). Republican. Methodist. Avocations: camping, skiing, travel. E-mail: neibere@peds.ufl.edu.

NEIDERT, KALO EDWARD, accountant, educator; b. Safe, Mo., Sept. 1, 1918; s. Edward Robert and Margaret Emma (Kinsey) N.; m. Stella Mae Vest, June 22, 1952; children— Edward, Karl, David, Wayne, Margaret. BS in Bus. Adminstrn. with honors, Washington U., St. Louis, 1949, MS in Bus. Adminstrn, 1950; postgrad., U. Minn., 1950-54. CPA, Nev. Mem. faculty U. Minn., 1950-54; mem. faculty U. Miss., 1954-57, U. Tex., Austin, 1957-61, Gustavus Adolphus Coll., St. Peter, Minn., 1961-62; prof. acctg. and info. systems U. Nev., 1962-90, prof. emeritus, 1990—; auditor Washoe County Employee Fed. Credit Union, 1969-82, dir., treas., 1982-86. Author: Statement on Auditing Procedure in Decision Tree Form, 1974. Asst. scoutmaster local Boy Scouts Am., asst. dist. commr. New Area coun.; bd. dirs. Tahoe Timber Trails, 1980-82, treas., 1981-82, v.p. fin., 1982-84; Bd. dirs. St. Johns Child Care Center, 1982-84; cen. com. mem. Washoe County Rep. Party, Reno, 1986-88, 90—. Mem. AICPA, Assn. System Mgmt. (treas. Reno chpt. 1984—), Am. Acctg. Assn., Am. Econ. Assn., Am. Fin. Assn., Fin. Mgmt. Assn., Nev. Soc. CPAs, Western Fin. Assn., Oddfellows, Beta Alpha Psi, Beta Gamma Sigma. Presbyterian. Office: U Nev Coll Bus Adminstrn Reno NV 89557-0001 E-mail: kneidert@osardtcak.net.

NEIGHBORS, PATSY JEAN, school counselor; b. Overton, Tex., May 22, 1936; d. Jackson A. and Alta Lois McQuaid; m. Richard Lon Neighbors, May 31, 1957; children: Sharon Elaine, Richard Lon Jr., Kelly Dianne. BS, East Tex. State U., 1957, MS, 1965. Lic. counselor, Tex.; cert. libr., Tex. Tchr., coach Hawkins (Tex.) Ind. Sch. Dist., 1958-60, Quitman (Tex.) Ind. Sch. Dist., 1962-91, counselor, 1991—99; ret., 1999; elem. counselor Rains Ind. Sch. Dist., Emory, Tex., 2002—. Mem. Tex. Profl. Counselors Assn., Tex. High Sch. Counselors Assn., Tex. Classroom Tchrs. Assn., Piney Woods Counselors Assn. (membership chair 1989—), Delta Kappa Gamma (chair project com. 1988—). Avocations: watching sports, classic cars, sewing, fishing.

NEIHARDT, HILDA, foundation administrator, writer, educator; b. Bancroft, Nebr., Dec. 6, 1916; d. John Gneisenau and Mona (Martinsen) N.; m. Albert Joseph Petri, Apr. 18, 1942 (div. Oct. 1963); children; Gail Petri Toedebusch, Robin, Coralie Joyce Hughes. AB, U. Nebr., 1937; postgrad., Letitia Barnum Sch. Theatre, Chgo., 1943-44; JD, U. Mo., 1963. Bar: Mo. 1963. Adminstrv. asst. Consulate of Switzerland, St. Louis, 1937-42; pvt. practice Columbia, Mo., 1963-85, Lake Ozark, Mo., 1985-88; pres. John G. Neihardt Found., Bancroft, 1987—2000. Lectr. in field. Author: Black Elk and Flaming Rainbow, 1995, Black Elk Lives, 2000; editor: The Giving Earth, 1991, The End of The Dream, 1991, The Ancient Memory, 1991. Trustee John G. Neihardt Trust, Columbia and Tekamah, Nebr., 1973-99; chmn. bd. dirs. John G. Neihardt Found., 2000-02; with USN, 1944-45. Mem. AAUW, Westerners, Internat. P.E.O. Avocations: boating, camping, horses. Home: PO Box 358 504 Pennsylvania Ave Bancroft NE 68004 also: 4235 E McDowell #88 Phoenix AZ 85008 Office: John G Neihardt Found PO Box 344 Bancroft NE 68004-0344

NEILFOROSHAN, MOHAMAD R. computer science and information systems educator; b. Isfahan, Iran, Sept. 22, 1954; s. Bagher and Khanom; m. Monireh; children: Vahideh, Hadi, Maryam, Hamed. BS in Computer Sci., Sch. of Planning Computer, Applications, Tehran, Iran, 1978; MS in Computer Sci., U. So. Miss., 1980; PhD in Computer Sci., U. Conn., 1993. Faculty U. N.C., Charlotte, 1983-85, Cen. Conn. State U., New Britain, 1985-92; dept. head Wentworth Inst. Technology, Boston, 1992—2000; prof. computer sci. and info. sys. Stockton Coll., 2000—. Manuscript editor Info. Technology, N.Y.C., 1993—; presenter in field. Contbr. articles to profl. jours. Recipient fellowship awards U. Conn., 1992. Mem.: ABET (computer sci. accreditation bd. evaluator), IEEE, Assn. for Computing Machinery, Am. Soc. Engring. Edn. (mem. exec. bd. info. sys. 1998—). Home: PO Box 200893 Mission Hill Sta Boston MA 02120

NEILL, RITA JARRETT, elementary school educator; b. Lincolnton, N.C., Oct. 20, 1950; d. George William and Mozelle (Boyles) Jarrett; m. Randy William Neill, Nov. 27, 1970; children: Jennifer Neill Huffman, Julie Neill Foster. AB, Lenoir Rhyne Coll., 1972; MA, Gardner Webb, 1987; degree in birth to kindergarten edn., U. N.C., Charlotte, 1998. Kindergarten tchr. Troutman Elem., (N.C.), 1977-96; presch. tchr. for developmentally delayed 3-4 yr. olds Wayside Elem., Statesville (N.C.)/Iredell County Schs., 1996—. Mem. ASCD, Assn. Edn. Young Children (treas. Iredell County 1994-96, membership chmn. 1996-98), N.C. Assn. Edn. (sec. 1986-88), Iredell County Assn. Edn. Young Children (chmn. 1996-98). Home: 308 Wiggins Rd Mooresville NC 28115-9393

NEILSON, JANE SCOTT, mathematics educator; b. Oakland, Calif., July 29, 1919; d. George Robert and Ethel Genevive (Smith) Scott; m. James Drake Neilson II, Sept. 24, 1955 (dec.). Student in engring., U. Mich., 1937, student in lit. and art, 1938-40; BA in Elem Edn., Calif. State U., Northridge, 1960; postgrad. in secondary edn., UCLA, 1966-67. Process engr. Brigs Mfg. Co., Detroit, 1941-43; mathematician dept. purchasing Detroit GM, 1943-44; mathematician Chrysler Corp., Highland Pk., Mich., 1944-45; dir. recreation ARC, Europe and Korea, 1945-54; assoc. engr. Dr. Betando, Santa Monica, Calif., 1954-56; tchr. math. Las Virgines Unified Sch. Dist., Calabasas, Calif., 1961-79, subs. tchr., 1984-93. Docent Getty Mus., Malibu, Calif., 1982-94. Avocations: sno-skiing, biking, painting, piano, photography. Home: 4624 Eastbourne Bay Oxnard CA 93035-3703

NEIMS, ALLEN HOWARD, university dean, medical scientist; b. Chgo., Oct. 24, 1938; s. Irving Morris and Ruth (Geller) N.; m. Myrna Gay Robins, June 18, 1961; children: Daniel Mark, Susan Roberta, Nancy Elizabeth. BA, BS, U. Chgo., 1957; MD, Johns Hopkins U., 1961, PhD, 1966. Intern, resident in pediatrics Johns Hopkins Hosp., 1961-62, 66-68; research asso. Lab. Neurochemistry, NIH, 1968-70; asst. prof. physiol. chemistry and pediatrics Johns Hopkins Med. Sch., 70-72; assoc. prof. McGill U., 1972-77, prof. pharmacology and pediatrics, 1977-78; dir. Roche developmental pharmacology unit, 1972-78; prof., chmn. dept. pharmacology and therapeutics, prof. pediatrics U. Fla., Gainesville, 1978-89, dean Coll. Medicine, 1989-96, prof. pharmcology, pediat., 1996—; dir. Ctr. for Spirituality and Health, 2002—. Dir. Ctr. Spirituality and Health; Fulton Bequest prof. U. Melbourne, Australia, 1974; mem. human embryology and devel. study sect. NIH, 1979-83; sci. cons. Can. Found. for Study of Sudden Infant Death, 1974-77, Nat. Soft Drink Assn., 1976-78, Internat. Life Scis. Inst., 1978-89; bd. sci. counsellors Nat. Inst. Child Health and Human Devel., 1984-89. Contbr. chpts. to books, articles to med. jours. Served to comdr. USPHS, 1968-70. NIH, Can. Med. Research Council grantee. Mem. Can. Assn. Research in Toxicology (pres. 1976-78), Am. Soc. Pharmacology and Exptl. Therapeutics (past mem. exec. coms. clin. pharmacology and drug metabolism), Am. Pediatric Soc., Am. Acad. Pediatrs. Office: U Fla Coll Medicine PO Box 100267 Gainesville FL 32610-0267 E-mail: ahneims@ufl.edu.

NEISWINGER, RHONDA JEAN, elementary school educator; b. Brazil, Ind., Sept. 14, 1966; d. Ronald Lee and M. Jeanne (Dalton) Travis; m. Dean Rex Neiswinger, June 7, 1986; 1 child, Grace Lanae. BS cum laude, Ind. State U., 1988. Tchr., volleyball coach Clay City (Ind.) High Sch., 1988—93; exec. dir. Ind. Land Improvement Contractors Assn., 1999—. Mem. Kappa Delta Pi. Avocations: painting, craftwork, reading. Home and Office: 248 W County Rd 650S Clay City IN 47841-9731

NELL, EDWARD JOHN, economist, educator; b. Chgo., July 16, 1935; s. Edward John and Marcella (Roach) N.; m. Onora O'Neill, Jan. 19, 1963 (div. 1975); children: Adam, Jacob; married, 1977 (div. 1986); children: Miranda, Guinevere; m. Marsha Karen Lasker, Nov. 25, 1989. BA, Princeton U., 1957; BA, MA, BLitt, Oxford (England) U., 1957-62. Tutor Nuffield Coll., Oxford, 1959-62; asst. prof. Wesleyan U., Middletown, Conn., 1962-67; lectr., sr. lectr. U. East Anglia, Norwich, United Kingdom, 1967-69; prof. econs. New Sch. for Social Rsch., N.Y.C., 1969—, dept. chair grad. faculty, 1974-75, 84-90, Malcolm B. Smith Prof., 1993—. Prof. Bennington (Vt.) Coll., 1978-79; vis. prof. U. Rome, McGill U., Montreal, U. Nice, France, U. Orleans, France, U. Bremen, Germany. Author: Historia y Economia Politica, 1980, Demanda Efectiva Precios y Salarios, 1982, Prosperity and Public Spending, 1988, Transformational Growth and Effective Demand, 1992, Making Sense of a Changing, Economy, 1995, Keynes After Sraffa; editor, author: Free Market Conservatism, 1984, Beyond the Steady State, 1992, Nicholas Kaldor and Mainstream Economics, 1991, Money in Motion, 1995, Growth Profits and Property, 1980, Economics As Worldly Philosophy, 1992; author: (with M. Hollis) Rational Economic Man, 1975; contbr. articles to profl. jours. Vice chmn. Ams. for Dem. Action, Conn., 1965-68; dir. Class Struggle, Inc., N.Y.C., 1980-85; active dir. various peace, civil rights and environ. groups, N.Y.C., 1970—. Rhodes scholar, 1957-60; Bard Ctr. fellow, 1984; Jerome Levy grantee, 1988, 90. Fellow Centro di Studi Economici Avanzati (bd. dirs. 1986-88); mem. Am. Econ. Assn., Assn. Post-Keynesian Econs. (bd. editors 1980—), Ea. Econ. Assn., U.S. Rhodes Scholar Assn., Princeton Club, Phi Beta Kappa. Avocations: writing short stories, drawing, painting. Home: PO Box 1058 Woodstock NY 12498-8058 Office: PO Box 491 Bearsville NY 12409-0491

NELLETT, GAILE H. university level educator; b. Ottawa, Ill., Nov. 5, 1941; d. Edwin Edward and Mabel Delia (Higgins) Hausaman; children: Anne Marie, James, Sarah, Susan, Julie; m. Henry H. Nellett. BSN, Governors State U., University Park, Ill., 1993; MS in Nursing Adminstrn., Loyola U., Chgo., 1995, PhD, 1998. RN, Ill. ENEC (End of Life Nursing Edn. Consortium) certified, 2001. Staff nurse med.-surg. and psychiat. units Cmty. Hosp. Ottawa, 1974-75, asst. head nurse, 1975-77, head nurse psychiat. unit, 1977-79, head nurse psychiat. and chem. dependency units, 1979-84, nursing mgr. psychiat. and chem. dependency units, 1984-92, program mgr. psychiat. and chem. dependency units, 1987-92, part-time home health nurse, 1992-94; rsch. asst. Loyola U., 1993-96; asst. prof. U. St. Francis, 1997—, sr. chmn., 2000—. Bd. dirs. Ottawa area United Way, 1976-92, v.p., 1985, sec., 1984, 86. Nursing Adminstrn. fellow Edward Hines Jr. VA, Hines, Ill., 1994, tuition fellow Loyola U., 1993-96. Mem. ANA, Nat. Nurses Soc. on Addictions, Ill. Nurses Assn. (bd. dirs. dist. 4 1974-80), Peer Assistance Network for Nurses (regional support person dist. 2 1988-), Am. Psychiat. Nurses Assn., Midwest Nursing Rsch. Soc., Sigma Theta Tau. Soc., Rogerian Scholars Roman Catholic. Avocations: archery, hunting, handcrafts, reading. Home: 2768 E 2551st Rd Marseilles IL 61341 E-mail: gnellett@stfrancis.edu.

NELSEN, EVELYN RIGSBEE SEATON, retired educator; b. Jonesboro, Ark., Nov. 9, 1930; d. Glen Brown and Ruby Beatrice (Minton) Rigsbee; m. Frank W. Seaton, Apr. 19, 1952 (div. Aug. 1980); children: Susanna, Frank, Caroline, Rebecca, Elizabeth; m. David Allen Nelsen, July 25, 1981. BS in Edn., Ark. State U., 1968, MS in Edn., 1976; postgrad., U. Miss., 1968, U. Ark., Little Rock, 1989-90, U. Ctrl. Ark., 1990-92. Cert. English, French and gifted edn. tchr., adminstrn., secondary prin., Ark. Saleswoman Fan-Craft, Inc., Plainville, Conn., 1955-61; pers. dir. St. Bernard's Hosp., Jonesboro, 1961-68; tchr. Jonesboro Pub. Schs., 1968-81, Hazen (Ark.) Schs., 1985-92; remodeler, Little Rock, 1981-85, Hazen and Jonesboro, 1992—. Tchr. Gov.'s Sch. for Gifted, summer 1983; former mem. English Planning Commn., State of Ark, former mem. Gifted Edn. Commn. Author: (novel) Tori; contbr. numerous articles to trade jours., essays to newspaper. Vol. various Dem. polit. campaigns, Ark., 1968—, Clinton Presdl. Campaign, Little Rock, 1992, Dem. Nat. Com. Grantee U. Miss., summer 1968. Mem. Am. Assn. Ret. Persons, Ark. Assn. Ret. Tchrs., Royal Trust, Nat. Trust, Phi Delta Kappa, Delta Kappa Gamma, Lambda Iota Tau. Avocations: reading, gardening, wallpapering, writing, house painting. Home: 1007 W Washington Ave Jonesboro AR 72401-2676

NELSON, ANITA JOSETTE, educator; b. San Francisco, June 10, 1938; d. George Emanuel and Yvonne Louise (Borel) N. BA, San Francisco State Coll., 1960; MA, U. Denver, 1969. Dir. Community Ctr., Nurenberg, W.Ger., 1961-63; dir. program spl. services Cmty. Ctr., Tokyo, 1964-66; resident counselor U. Denver, 1967-69; dir. student activities Maricopa (Ariz.) Tech. Coll., 1969-72, coach women's varsity tennis, coordinator campus activities, 1972-75; counselor, prof., fgn. student advisor Scottsdale (Ariz.) C.C., 1975-94, divsn. chair counseling, 1989-91, emeritus faculty, 1994. Named Phoenix Mgmt. Council Rehabilitator of Year, 1977. Republican. Home: 351 Molino Ave Mill Valley CA 94941-2767

NELSON, BARBARA ANN, elementary education educator; b. Bklyn., May 3, 1954; d. Lauritz T. and Virginia U. (Graham) N. BA, U. N.C., Greensboro, 1976; MS, Adelphi U., 1978. Lic. N.Y. State; cert. tchr. N.Y. Speech-language pathologist Charleston (S.C.) County Schs., 1978-79, United Cerebral Palsy, S.I., N.Y., 1979-82, clin. liaison, 1982-84; speech-language pathologist Levittown (N.Y.) Pub. Schs., 1984—. Instr. Coll. New Rochelle. Tchr. liaison, v.p. PTA. Dist. grantee. Mem. N.Y. State Speech-Lang.-Hearing Assn., L.I. Speech-Hearing Assn., Spl. Edn. Cadre, Staff Devel. for Tchr. Evaluations, Excellence and Accountability Initiative (chairperson Pre-sch. com. of spl. edn.). Home: 35 Jerome Dr Farmingdale NY 11735-1812

NELSON, BARBARA LOUISE, secondary education educator; b. Indpls., Apr. 18, 1935; d. Dennis Arthur Chandler and Bertha Louise (Drane) Hill; children: Edwin Robert Swanson, III, Patricia Marie Swanson, Barbara Michelle Swanson Clure. BA, Ind. U., 1956; tchrs. cert., Millikin U., 1964; MA, U. Denver, 1969. Cert. English tchr. Tchr. AL Jr. High Sch., Jefferson Co.; tchr., dept. chair O'Connell Jr. High, Jefferson Co.; tchr. Alameda High Sch., Jefferson County R-1, Lakewood, Colo. Exch. tchr. ITF, Melbourne, Australia, 1976, Lakewood-Sutherlandshire Sister City Tchr. Visitation Exch., 1989; mem. writing com. Jefferson County Commn. Chalice, min., lector, Stephen min., prayer min., mem. stewardship commn., evangelism commn. Christ Episc. Ch. Mem. NEA, Colo. Internat. Tchr. Exch. League, Colo. Edn. Assn., Jefferson County Edn. Assn., Delta Kappa Gamma (advisor, past pres., v.p., rec. sec. and treas., corr. sec. Pi chpt.), Phi Delta Kappa (scholarship chmn., svc. key 1998, Sanders scholarship com.), Delta Delta Delta. Home: 3100 S Race St Englewood CO 80113-3032 E-mail: blnelson@jeffco.k12.co.us.

NELSON, BARBARA SECREST, educational developer; b. Reidsville, N.C., Jan. 7, 1949; d. Edgar B. and Mary Elizabeth (Slate) Trent; m. Michael William Nelson, Dec. 31, 1985. BA in Edn., U. N.C., 1971, MA in Curriculum and Instrn., 1975. Cert. K-3 tchr., N.C. Kindergarten and primary tchr. Wake County Schs., Raleigh, N.C., 1971-74; rsch. and evaluation cons. N.C. Dept. Pub. Instrn., Raleigh, 1974-84; mktg. and sales mgr. edn. div. Computer South, Charlotte, N.C., 1984-85; mktg. support rep. Apple Computer, Inc., Charlotte, 1985-87, K-8 solutions mgr. Cupertino, Calif., 1987-89, account exec. Culver City, Calif., 1989-92, ednl. devel., 1990—, S.E. mktg./solutions mgr. Charlotte, N.C., 1994—. Com. mem. N.C. Effective Teaching Com., Raleigh, 1984; program chmn. N.C. Instrnl. Microcomputing Conf., Greensboro, 1985. Co-author Apple Learning Series for K-2, 1986. Mem. ASCD. Home and Office: 4908 Carmel Club Dr Charlotte NC 28226-8020

NELSON, CARL ALFRED, international business educator; b. Pitts., Oct. 11, 1930; s. Alfred Helge Nelson and Isabel Alice (Younger) Newbauer; m. Barbara Long, June 2, 1956; children: Jennifer, Allison, Monica. BS, U.S. Naval Acad., 1956; MS, U.S. Naval Post Grad., 1967; student, US Naval War Coll., 1970; D of Bus. Adminstrn., U.S. Internat. U., 1984. Enlisted USN, 1949, advanced through grades to capt., 1956-82; comdr. USS Worden CG-18, 4 others; v.p., dir. AMMEX Cons., Chula Vista, Calif., 1985-86; pres. Global Bus. & Trade, San Diego, 1982—. Prof. Calif. Sch. Internat. Mgmt.; lectr. in field. Author: Your Own Import-Export Business: Winning the Trade Game, 1988, Import-Export: How to Get Started in International Trade, 1989, 3d edit., 2000, Global Success, 1990, Managing Globally; A Complete Guide to Competing Worldwide, 1993, Protocol for Profit, 1998, International Business, 1998, Exporting, 1999, The Advisor, 1999, Secret Players, 2003; contbr. articles to profl. jours.; contbr. short stories to popular mags. Pres. Chula Vista Boys Club, 1988; exec. bd. dirs. Calif. Dem. Party, 1992-97, pres. S.D. Writers/Editors Guild, 1998, 2002; dir. Vietnam Vets.; active Econ. Devel. Commr., Chula Vista. Decorated Legion of Merit, Bronze Star, Air medals; named Alumni of Yr., U.S. Internat. U., 1989; recipient Disting. Global Educator award Calif. Sch. Internat. Mgmt., 2003. Mem. Assn. Global Bus., Acad. Internat. Bus., San Diego World Trade Assn., Authors's Guild of Am., Chula Vista C. of C. (dir. 1984-90, Internat. Focus award 1988), Optimist Club, Masons (32 deg.). Home: 1385 Don Carlos Ct Chula Vista CA 91910-7130

NELSON, CHARLES A. physicist, educator; b. Chadron, Nebr., Oct. 11, 1943; s. Arnold W. and Martha J. (Brackman) Nelson; m. Nancy Kneller, May 21, 1988; 4 children. BS in Engring. Physics, U. Colo., 1965; PhD in Theoretical Physics, U. Md., 1969. Rsch. assoc. City Coll. CUNY, N.Y.C., 1968-70; cons. Ctr. Particle Theory, U. Tex., Austin, 1970-72; rsch. assoc. La. State U., Baton Rouge, 1970-72, Nat. Bur. Stds., Gaithersburg, Md., 1972-73; prof. physics SUNY, Binghamton, 1973—. Vis. scientist Fermilab, Batavia, Ill., 1980—81, Kyoto (Japan) U., 1981. Contbr. scientific papers to confs. and jours. Grantee, NSF, 1978—81, U.S. Dept. Energy, 1982—. Mem.: Am. Phys. Soc. Office: SUNY Dept Physics Binghamton NY 13902 E-mail: cnelson@binghamton.edu.

NELSON, CHARLOTTE COLEEN, special education educator; b. Belleville, Kans., Nov. 21, 1942; d. Clarence George and Sybil Evelyn (Davidson) Rahe; m. Phillip Allen Truby, May 30, 1965 (div. 1976); children; Gregory Brent, Michelle Diane Truby; m. Maynard Eugene Nelson, Oct. 7, 1978. BS, Kans. State U., 1964; MA, U. Mo., Kansas City, 1970; MS, Kans. State U., 1981, EdD, 1994. Elem. tchr. Republic (Kans.) Elem. Sch., 1964-65, Unified Sch. Dist. # 110, Overland Park, Kans., 1966-67; chpt. 1 reading tchr. CSD # 1, Hickman Mills, Mo., 1970-73; elem. tchr. Unified Sch. Dist. # 271, Beloit, Kans., 1973-79; gifted edn. cons. Unified Sch. Dist. # 305, Salina, Kans., 1979-91, coord. for assistive tech. and gifted edn., 1991—. Mem. Nat. Assn. for Gifted Children, Delta Kappa Gamma (pres. chpt. 1988-90). Avocations: music, golf, tennis, reading. Home: 160 S Estates Dr Salina KS 67401-3562 Office: 715 N 9th St Salina KS 67401-1822 E-mail: charlotte.nelson@usd305.com.

NELSON, DAWN MARIE, middle school language arts educator; b. Norristown, Pa., Mar. 29, 1960; m. Peirce Nelson; children: Adam, Joshua. Student, Montgomery County C.C., Blubell, Pa., 1977-78, Temple U., 1979-80, Ursinus Coll.; BS in Edn. summa cum laude, Cabrini Coll., Radnor, Pa., 1992, postgrad., 1996—, St. Joseph's U., 1995. Cert. elem. tchr., Pa.; cert. ACSI. Lead tchr. lang arts, head upper sch. dept. Penn Christian Acad., Norristown, 1992-2000. Asst. curriculum and program developer; accreditation steering com.; supr. Math. Olympics, co-chmn.; mentor, student tchr. supr., mid. sch. tchr., speech meet coord. Vol. pub. and pvt. schs., ch. orgns. Mem. ASCD, ACSI, Alpha Sigma Lambda. Avocations: reading, travel, quilting, writing. Office: Penn Christian Acad 50 W Germantown Pike Norristown PA 19401-1565

NELSON, DENNIS LEE, finance educator; b. Randall, Minn., Nov. 4, 1929; s. George Otto and Emma Ida (Schwanke) N.; m. Joyce Marie Prozinski, Aug. 25, 1956; children: Constance, Kristin, Norma Joan. BS, St. Cloud State U., 1954; MA, U. Minn., 1964, PhD in Econs., 1970. Prof. econs. U. Minn., Duluth, 1964—, dir. ctr. for econ. edn., 1967-71, grad. faculty, 1970—, head dept. econs., 1971-77, assoc. chancellor, 1977-88, vice chancellor fin. ops., 1987-88. Mem. faculty Westhill Coll., U. Birmingham, Eng., 1996-97; instnl. rep. for adminstrs. on Nat. Collegiate Athletic Assn., 1978-87; adminstr., vis. faculty Oxford U., Eng., 1997, Yonsei U., Seoul, 1988, Moscow U., 1978, 84. Author econ. textbooks. Recipient Disting. Alumnus award U. Minn. Mem. Duluth Blueline Club, Duluth Quarterback Club, UMD Rasmussen Fund, UMD Hoop Club, Pres. Club U. Minn. Lutheran. Avocations: gardening, writing, reading, woodworking, bridge. Home: On the Lake 21190 Forest Rd Little Falls MN 56345-4065 Office: U Minn 10 University Dr Duluth MN 55812-2403

NELSON, DONNA JEAN, chemistry educator, researcher; b. Eufaula, Okla., Aug. 29, 1952; d. John Howard Jr. and Dorotha (Eckelkamp) Baker; 1 child, Christopher Brammer. BS in Chemistry, U. Okla., 1974; postgrad., Auburn (Ala.) U., 1974-76; PhD, U. Tex., 1979; postgrad., Purdue U., 1980-83. Robert A. Welch pre-doctoral fellow, 1977, 78, 79; Robert A. Welch postdoctoral fellow, 1980; asst. prof. U. Okla., Norman, 1983-89, assoc. prof., faculty adminstrv. fellow Provost's Office, 1989—. Jr. faculty rsch. fellow Okla. U., 1984, assocs. disting. lectr., 1985-86. Robert A. Welch grantee, 1979. Mem. Am. Chem. Soc. (women chemists com. 1988—, James Flack award com. 1987-90), Phi Lambda Upsilon, Alpha Chi Sigma, Iota Sigma Pi, Sigma Xi. Home: 1700 Winding Ridge Rd Norman OK 73072-3149 Office: U Okla Dept of Chemistry Norman OK 73072

NELSON, DORENE, secondary education educator; b. Aberdeen, SD, Jan. 29, 1945; d. Joe W. and Hazel M. (Dunker) Sager; m. Gordon C. Nelson, June 29, 1963; children; Carmel, Corey. BS, No. State Coll., 1967, MS, 1970. Cert. secondary english and social studies. English tchr. Northwestern Pub. Schs., Mellette, S.D., Groton (S.D.) Pub. Schs. Asst. debate coach. Mem. S.D. Edn. Assn. (pres., v.p., sec.), Nat. Coun. Tchrs. English, Nat. Forensic League (double diamond degree) SCASD, SDFCA (sec.). Home: PO Box 675 Groton SD 57445-0675

NELSON, DOUGLAS MICHAEL, school system administrator, educator; b. Seattle, Wash., Feb. 20, 1948; s. Donald Edgar and Helen Thomasina (Manarino) N.; m. Virginia Jude Smith, Aug. 4, 1973; children: Kourtney, Karly, Jenna. BA, Whitman Coll., 1970; MEd, U. Puget Sound, 1974; EdD, Seattle U., 1986. Tchr. history Auburn (Wash.) Sr. H.S., 1970-75; asst. prin. Pioneer Jr. H.S., Walla Walla, Wash., 1975-78; prin. Highland Middle Sch., Kennewick, Wash., 1978-80, Meridian Jr. H.S., Kent, Wash., 1980-85; asst. supt. Franklin Pierce Sch. Dist., Tacoma, Wash., 1985-89; supt. Pullman (Wash.) Sch. Dist., 1989-2000, mem. livability task force, 1998-2000. Adj. prof. Wash. State U., Pullman, 1990-2000. Pres. Wash. Sch. Admin. Polit. Action Com., State of Wash., 1996; cmty. svc. mem., bd. dirs. Pullman Cmty. Found., 1989-2000; bd. dirs. Pullman Edn. Found., 1995-2000; supt. Bend-La Pub. Schs., 2000—. Recipient Excellence in Edn. award State of Wash., 1994, Outstanding Adminstr. award Wash. State PTA Region 9, Kent, Wash., 1985, Excellence in Edn. Leadership award Univ. Coun. for Ednl. Adminstrn., 1997. Mem. Pullman (Wash.) C. of C. (pres. 1994; Mem. of Yr. 1999), Parkland-Spanaway (Wash.) C. of C. (exec. bd., pres. elect 1986-89, community growth award 1988), Northeast Washington Assn. Sch. Adminstrs. (pres. 1999), Wash. Assn. Sch. Adminstrs. (regional officer 1988-89), Future of Wash. Schs. (exec. comm. 1995-97), Wash. ASCD (outstanding educator award 1984), Rotary Club, Phi Delta Kappa (scholarship award 1985). Roman Catholic. Avocations: golf, snow skiing, reading, travel. Home: 20328 Donkey Sled Rd Bend OR 97702-2644 Office: Bend-La Pine Pub Schs 520 NW Wall St Bend OR 97701-2608 E-mail: dvnelson@bendnet.com., dnelson@bend.k12.or.us.

NELSON, HERBERT JAMES, philosophy educator; b. Grand Forks, N.D., Aug. 26, 1938; s. Herbert Cecil and Beryl (Carroll) N.; m. Nancy May Lauzau, Nov. 26, 1964; children: Catherine, Susan. PhB, Pontifical Gregorian U., Rome, 1960, PhL, 1961; PhD, SUNY, Buffalo, 1969. Instr. in philosophy Niagara U., Niagara Falls, N.Y., 1963-66; from asst. prof. to assoc. prof. philosophy Canisius Coll., Buffalo, 1968-82; prof. Canisius U., Buffalo, 1982—, chair philosophy dept., 1976-90, v.p. for acad. affairs, 1996—. Contbr. articles to profl. jours. NEH grantee, 1982. Mem. Am. Philos. Assn., Am. Cath. Philos. Assn., Philosophers in Jesuit Edn. (founding mem., pres. 1994-95). Roman Catholic. Home: 495 81st St Niagara Falls NY 14304-3305 Office: Canisius Coll 2001 Main St Buffalo NY 14208-1035 E-mail: nelson@canisius.edu.

NELSON, IVORY VANCE, academic administrator; b. Curtis, La., June 11, 1934; s. Elijah H. and Mattie (White) N.; m. Patricia Robbins, Dec. 27, 1985; children: Cherlyn, Karyn, Eric Beatty, Kim Beatty. BS with distinction, Grambling (La.) State U., 1959; PhD with distinction, U. Kans., 1963. Assoc. prof. chemistry So. U., Baton Rouge, 1963-67, head div. sci., 1966-68; prof. chemistry Prairie View (Tex.) A&M U., 1968-83, asst. acad. dean, 1968-72, v.p. rsch., 1972-82, acting pres., 1982-83; exec. asst. Tex. A&M U. System, College Station, 1983-86; chancellor Alamo C.C. Dist., San Antonio, 1986-92; pres. Cen. Wash. U., Ellensburg, 1992-99, Lincoln U., Pa., 1999—. DuPont teaching fellow U. Kans., 1959; rsch. chemist Am. Oil Co., 1962; sr. rsch. chemist Union Carbide Co., 1969; vis. prof. U. Autonomous Guadalajara, Mex., 1966, Loyola U., 1967; Fulbright lectr., 1966; cons. evaluation coms. Oak Ridge (Tenn.) Assoc. Univs., NSF, Nat. Coun. for Accreditation Tchr. Edn., So. Assn. Colls. and Schs.; mem. regional policy coms. on minorities Western Interstate Com. on Higher Edn., 1986-88; mem. exec. com. Nat. Assn. State Univs. and Land Grant Colls., 1980-82. Contbr. articles to profl. jours. Bd. dirs. Target 90, Goals San Antonio, 1987-89, coun. of pres.NAIDA,(1993-96) Commn. on Student Learning, Wash., 1992—, United Way San Antonio, 1987-89, Alamo Area coun. Boy Scouts Am., 1987-89, San Antonio Symphony Soc., 1987-91, Key Bank of Wash.; mem. bd. dirs. assn. Western U., (1995—) mem. com. for jud. reform State of Tex., 1991; mem. edn. adv. bd. Tex. Rsch. Park, 1987-89; bd. givs. Am. Inst. for character Edn., Inc., 1988-91; mem. adv. com. Tex. Ho. of Reps., 1978; chmn. United Way Campaign Tex. A&M U. System, 1984, others. Staff sgt. USAF, 1951-55, Korea. T.H. Harris scholar Grambling State U., 1959; fellow Nat. Urban League, 1969. Mem. AAAS, Am. Chem. Soc., Tex. Acad. Sci., NAACP, Phi Beta Kappa, Sigma Xi, Phi Lambda Upsilon, Beta Kappa Chi, Alpha Mu Gamma, Kappa Delta Pi, Sigma Pi Sigma, Omega Psi Phi, Sigma Pi Phi, Phi Kappa Phi. Avocations: fishing, photography, sports. Office: Lincoln U Office of Pres PO Box 179 Lincoln University PA 19352-0999 E-mail: inelson@lu.lincoln.edu.

NELSON, JILL ELAINE, nurse attorney, health care consultant, health facility administrator, instructor, researcher; b. Ashland, Ohio, Jan. 1, 1952; d. John Robert and Phyllis Rae (Williams Hardesty) N. Assoc. summa cum laude, Cuyahoga C.C., 1975; BA cum laude, Baldwin-Wallace Coll., MBA, 1993; JD, Case Western Res. U., 1999. Bar: Ohio 2000; RN, Ohio; cert. healthcare mediator, compliance profl., profl. coder. RN Emergency/Trauma rm. St. Luke's Hosp., Cleve., 1982-87; rsch. asst. div. of neurosci. Case Western Reserve U., Cleve.; RN, rsch. asst. dept. Artificial Organ Rsch. Cleve. Clinic, 1975-82; coord., adminstr. rsch. Met. Health Med. Ctr. Case Western Res. U., Cleve., 1983-93, consulting asst. dir. Office of Rsch. Adminstrn., 1993-94, project dir. dept. family medicine, 1994-95, adminstrv. dir. cancer ctr. clin. trials unit, 1994-97; cons. West Hudson, Inc., Dallas, 1997; patent coord. affiliates at STERIS Corp., 1997-98; paralegal specialist Ctr. Devices Radiol. Health, FDA, 1998; intern Food & Drug Law Inst., Washington, 1998; nurse legal cons./paralegal Krembs & Alkire LLP, 1998-99; legal intern Supreme Ct. Ohio, 1998-99; dir. corp. compliance and privacy, chmn. mgmt. engring. Comprehensive Health Care of Ohio, Inc. (EMH) Regional Healthcare Sys., 2001—. Instr. legal nurse cons. program, divsn. bus. and tech. Cuyahoga C.C. legal nurse cons. program, 2000—; instr. Baldwin-Wallace Coll., 2002-. Assoc. editor Health-Matrix: Jour. Law Medicine. Mem. ABA, AAAS, NAFE, Am. Health Lawyers Assn., Am. Coll. Healthcare Execs., Assocs. Clin. Pharmacology, Am. Trial Lawyers Assn., Am. Assn. Profl. Coders, Am. Health Info. Mgmt. Assn., Nat. Coun. Univ. Rsch. Adminstrs., Mental Health Assn., ENA (cert. clin. rsch. coord., past pres.-elect), Inst. for Personal Health Skills, Soc. of Ohio Healthcare (atty.), Ohio State Bar Assn., Cuyahoa County Bar Assn., Lorain County Bar Assn., Healthcare Compliance Assn., Internat. Assn. Privacy Profls., Alpha Sigma Lambda. Home: 19291 Trillium Trl Strongsville OH 44149-3146 E-mail: jillenelso@aol.com.

NELSON, JIMMIE DIRK, kinesiology administrator, educator, researcher; b. Wichita, Kans., July 23, 1962; s. Ronald Paul and Bonnie Lou (Horton) N.; m. Renda Joy Colglazier, May 27, 1989; children: Philip Alexander, Emalee Joy. BS, Mont. State U., 1984; MS in Edn., U. Kans., 1986, PhD, 1990. Tchg. asst. U. Kans., 1987-89; asst. prof. Mo. So. State Coll., Joplin, 1989-94, assoc. prof., 1994-99, head dept. kinesiology, 1992-99; chair divsn. kinesiology, assoc. prof. LeTourneau U., Longview, Tex., 1999—2001, asst. v.p. acad. affairs, prof., 2000—03; chair, dept. Health and Human Performance Ctrl. Mo. State U., 2003—. Dietary and fitness and health cons. Mo. Day Care Workers, 1989—99; textbook reviewer Brown & Benchmark Pubs., Allyn & Bacon Pub., Prentice Hall Pub., Brooks/Cole Pub. Co., Benjamin/Cummings Pub. Co., McGraw-Hill Cos.; acad. editor Coursewise Pub., 1997—; reviewer minority health rsch. and edn. grant program Tex. Higher Edn. Coord. Bd., 2001. Tchr. jr. and sr. high edn. coord. 4th and Forrest Ch. of Christ, Joplin, 1989-99; tchr. Pine Tree Ch. of Christ, Longview, 1999—; vol. Spl. Olympics, 1989-2000, youth sports coach, 1998-2000. Named to, Wendy's of Mont./Mont. State U. Athletic Hall of Fame, 1994, All 20th Century Football Team, Mont. State U., 2001. Mem. Nat. Acad. Advising Assn., Nat. Collegiate Honors Coun., Soc. of Centennial Alumni Mont. State U. Mem. Ch. of Christ. Avocations: aviation, zoology, military history, jazz music, old house renovation. Home: 905 Sunshine Sq Longview TX 75601-3237 Office: Ctrl Mo State U Po Box 800 Warrensburg MO 64093

NELSON, KATHERINE MACTAGGART, secondary school educator; b. Mattoon, Ill., Aug. 27, 1953; d. Leonard John and Wandalee Mae (Clodfelder) Stabler; m. John Robert Nelson; children: Scott MacTaggart, Robert John, Matthew David. BS in Edn., Eastern Ill. U., 1973; MS in Edn., Carroll Coll., 1998. Tchr. Owen Valley Schs., Spencer, Ind., 1974-76; acad. support coordinator Whitefish Bay Schs., Milw., 1976-80; dir. research Sullivan, Murphy Assoc., Milw., 1980-81; tng. specialist Northwestern Ins., Milw., 1981-84; tng. coordinator Cath. Knights Ins. Soc., Milw., 1984-87; tchr. Pewaukee (Wis.) High Sch., 1988-95, Arrowhead H.S., Hartland, Wis., 1995—; adj. prof. Cardinal Smith U. Pres., mem. bd. Cushing Elem. Sch. PTO, 1994-96; mem. Milw. Zool. Soc., Women's Fellowship Bd.; founder Mgmt. Resources Exec. Sec. Roundtable, Milw., 1986; vol. com. mem. Wis. Make-A-Wish Found.; mem. Christian edn. com. Congl. Ch., 1990-93, chair women's fellowship com., 1993-96, Bible sch. dir., 1990, 91, nomination com., 1998; vol. Cross for State Supt. campaign. Recipient Leadership award YMCA, 1986. Mem. NEA, ASTD (bd. dirs., chmn. pub. rels. 1984, vol. trainer 1982-89), Internat. Assn. Pers. Women (chmn. pub. rels. 1984-85, chmn. membership and registrar, nominating com., by-laws com., vol. trainer 1981-89), Arrowhead Union Edn. Assn. (exec. com. 1990-93), Law Wives Assn. (v.p. membership and soc. coms., PYC sidestays fin. com.), Pewaukee Yacht Club Sidestays, Wis. Club, P.E.O. Sisterhood (guard, chaplain). Republican. Home: N61W29911 Rybeck Rd Hartland WI 53029-9213 Office: Arrowhead Union High School 700 North Ave Hartland WI 53029-1143

NELSON, LINDA SHEARER, child development and family relations educator; b. New Kensington, Pa., Dec. 8, 1944; d. Walter M. and Jean M. Shearer; m. Alan Edward Nelson, Dec. 29, 1973; children: Amelia (Amy), Emily. BS in Home Econs. Edn., Pa. State U., 1966; MS in Child Devel. and Family Rels., Cornell U., 1968; PhD in Higher Edn. and Child Devel., U. Pitts., 1982. Head tchr.-lab. nursery sch. Dept. of Psychology, Vassar Coll., Poughkeepsie, N.Y., 1968-69; instr. child devel. dept. home econs. edn. Indiana (Pa.) U., 1969-72, asst. prof., 1972-77, assoc. prof., 1977-84, prof. child devel. and family rels., 1984-93, prof. child devel. and family rels., human devel. and family environ. studies dept., 1993—, chmn. dept., 1991—93, 1998—. Ind. cons., trainer Head Start Programs, Pa., 1970—, Child Care Programs and Agys., Pa., 1970—; child devel. assoc. rep. Coun. for Early Childhood Profl. Recognition, Washington, 1989—91; field rep. Keyston U. Rsch. Corp., Erie, 1990—91; spkr. in field. Co-author (with A. Nelson): Child Care Administration and Instructor's Manual, 2000; mem. adv. bd.: Early Childhood Education Annual Editions, 1985—, mem. adv. bd. interface: Home Economics and Technology Newsletter, 1993—96; contbr. articles to profl. jours. Bd. dirs. Indiana County Child Care Program, 1970-92; guest spkr. Delta Kappa Gamma, Indiana, 1990, Bus. and Profl. Women, Indiana, 1991, IUP's The Marriage Project, 1996, AAUW, Ind., 1996. Grantee in field, 1985—. Mem. Nat. Assn. for Edn. Young Children, Pitts. Assn. for Edn. Young Children (conf. co-chair 1983-85, in-svc. tng. spkr. 1995), Assn. Pa. State Coll. and Univ. Faculties, Kappa Omicron Nu, Phi Upsilon Omicron. Democrat. Presbyterian. Avocations: photography, reading, Chautauqua Instn. programs. Office: Indiana U of Pa Human Devel and Environ Studies Dept 207 Ackerman Hl Indiana PA 15705-0001 E-mail: lnelson@iup.edu.

NELSON, LYNDA P. elementary education educator; b. Brockton, Mass., Oct. 3, 1941; d. Sol and Beatrice (Baron) Zuckerman; m. Charles T. Nelson, Aug. 27, 1961; children: David, Glenn, Sarah. BA, U. Mass., 1963; MEd, Fitchburg State U., 1976. Cert. elem. edn./moderate spl. needs tchr., Mass.; lic. real estate salesperson. Libr. Berlin (Mass.) Pub. Libr., 1965-94; tutor Berlin Meml. Sch., 1976—, chpt. I dir., 1985—. Realtor, Mass., 1985—. Vol. case reviewer Div. Social Svcs., Mass., 1991—; sec. bd. dirs. Berlin Retirement Homes, 1980—; mem. Ednl. Futures Com., Berlin, 1992—; sec. Housing Partnership, Berlin, 1990—; past leader Girl Scouts U.S., Berlin. Recipient Tchg. award Clinton Area Ednl. Forum, Atlantic Union Coll., 1992. Mem. Berlin Art and Hist. Soc. Congregation B'nai Shalom. Avocations: braiding rugs, basketry. Home: 20 Linden St Berlin MA 01503-1663

NELSON, MARGUERITE HANSEN, special education educator; b. S.I., N.Y., June 23, 1947; d. Arthur Clayton and Marguerite Mary (Hansen) Nelson. AB magna cum laude, Boston Coll., 1969; MS in Edn., SUNY, Plattsburgh, 1973; cert. in gerontology, Yeshiva U., 1982; PhD, Fordham U., N.Y.C., 1995. Cert. elem. and spl. edn. tchr. N.Y. Pre-primary tchr. Pub. Sch. 22R S.I., N.Y.C. Bd. Edn., 1969—70; primary tchr. Oak Street Sch., Plattsburgh, NY, 1971—73, Laurel Plains Sch., Clarkstown Ctrl. Schs., New City, NY, 1973—78, Resource Rm. Lakewood Sch., Congers, NY, 1978—2002; assoc. prof. St. Thomas Aquinas Coll., Sparkill, NY, 2002—. Adj. faculty St. Thomas Aquinas Coll., Sparkill, 1985—89, 1995—2002, Fordham U., N.Y.C., 1990; presenter in field. Author: (book) Teacher Stories, 1993, Research on Teacher Thinking, 1993, Metaphor as a Mode of Instruction, 1995; contbr. articles to profl. jours. Recipient Impact II Tchr. Recognition award, 1984; grantee, Chpt. II, 1983—84, Clarkstown Ctrl. Schs., 1986—91, Office Spl. Edn., 1992, 1995, N.Y. Assn. Comprehensive Edn., 1997. Mem.: APA, AAUW, Coun. for Exceptional Children, Assn. Retarded Citizens, Assn. Children with Learning Disabilities, Am. Ednl. Rsch. Assn., N.Y. State Congress Parents and Tchrs. (hon.). Avocations: reading, poetry, ballet, gardening, flower arranging. Home: PO Box 395 Valley Cottage NY 10989-0395 Office: Saint Thomas Aquinas Coll Rt 340 Sparkill NY 10976 E-mail: mnelson@stac.edu.

NELSON, MARIAN EMMA, education educator; b. Brockton, Mass., Apr. 4, 1932; d. Carl V. and Lillian M. (Smith) N. AS, Boston U., 1952; BS in Edn., Bridgewater State Coll., 1956, MS in Edn., 1962. Cert. gen. tchr., elem., elem. libr. Tchr. 1st grade Brockton Pub. Schs., 1956-62; assoc. prof. edn. Bridgewater (Mass.) State Coll., 1962-96, ret., 1996. Founder, bd. dirs., pres. of bd. Children's Art Presch., Brockton. Author Primary Pod Phonics program; contbr. articles to profl. jours. Tchr. ch. sch. 1st Evang. Luth. Ch.; mem. Coun. on Aging, Town of Bridgewater, 1998—. Luth. Brotherhood grantee. Mem. NEA, Mass. Tchrs. Assn., Nat. Assn. Lab. Schs., Delta Kappa Gamma (past pres. chpt.), Phi Delta Kappa. Home: 60 Trailwood Dr Bridgewater MA 02324-2079

NELSON, MARLOW GENE, agricultural studies educator; b. Powers Lake, N.D., Aug. 16, 1946; s. Elmer Richard and Beulah Joanne (Johnson) N.; m. Joyce Marlys Dilland, June 14, 1970; children: Paul Richard, Mark Jerrod, Aaron Brent. BS in Agrl. Edn., N.D. State U., 1968. Cert. tchr., N.D. Tchr. Tioga (N.D.) High Sch., 1968-72, 1990—, Carrington (N.D) High Sch., 1972-74; owner farm Battleview, N.D., 1974—; tchr. Stanley (N.D.) High Sch., 1974-87. Pres. Burke County Weed Control, Bowbells, N.D., 1988-90. Leader 4-H Burke County, N.D., 1986-90; deacon Bethel Baptist Ch., Powers Lake, N.D., tchr. Sunday sch. Mem. N.D. Vocat. Agrl. Tchrs. Assn. (dist. v.p. 1971-72), N.D. Stockmen's Assn., N.D. Charolais Assn., N.D. Farmers Union (bd. dirs. 1989—), Burke County Farmers Union (pres. 1992—), Burke County Agrl. Improvement Assn. (bd. dirs. 1985-89, Outstanding Agriculturist award 1990, Burke County Soil Conservationist of Yr. 1993). Democrat. Avocation: hunting. Home: HC 1 Box 122 Powers Lake ND 58773-9439 Office: Tioga High Sch 303 N Linda St Tioga ND 58852

NELSON, MARY ELLEN GENEVIEVE, adult education educator; b. Milw., Sept. 13, 1948; d. William Paul and Evelyn Marie (Saduske) Naber; m. Kenneth Arthur Nelson, July 22, 1972; children: William Norris, Victoria Marie. BS in Edn., Mt. Mary Coll., 1970; MEd, Carroll Coll., 1994. Cert. tchr., Wis.; cert. in math., computers, careers Wis. Tech. Coll. Sys. Clk. Oldline Life Ins., Milw., 1967-70; math. tchr. Menomonee Falls (Wis.) East H.S., 1970-76; math. and adult basic edn. tchr. Waukesha County Tech. Coll., Pewaukee, Wis., 1978-82, math. tchr., goal instr., 1982-88, lead adult basic edn. tchr. and goal instr., 1988—. Dir. presch. program St. Agnes Cath. Ch., Butler, Wis., 1979-82, presch. tchr., 1977-79; den mother cub scout Pack 72, Boy Scouts Am., Butler, 1983-84, candy fundraiser chmn., 1985, 86; mem. Menomonee Falls Edn. Com., 1987-97; mem. Leadership Menomonee Falls, 1995-96, mem. bd. govs., 1997-2000. Recipient award, Wis. Math. Coun., 1995, YWCA, 1996. Mem. Wis. Math. Coun., Wis. Adult and Continuing Edn. Assn., Menomonee Falls C. of C. (Waukesha County Tech. Coll. rep. 1993—, edn. com. 1986—), Rotary (partnership). Roman Catholic. Avocations: crafts, golf, traveling. Home: N54W15485 Northway Dr Menomonee Falls WI 53051-6716 Office: Menomonee Falls Campus Cmty Ctr W152N8645 Margaret Rd Menomonee Falls WI 53051-3185 E-mail: mnelson@wctc.edu.

NELSON, MURRY ROBERT, education educator; b. Chgo., May 12, 1947; s. H. Cyril and Beatrice (Lissner) N.; m. Elizabeth Jane Rose, June 15, 1973; children: Rebecca Meredith, Daniel Zachary. AB in Sociology, Grinnell (Iowa) Coll., 1969; MA in Teaching, Northwestern U., 1972; MA in Anthropology, PhD in Edn., Stanford U., 1975. Tchr. Chgo. Pub. Schs., 1970-72; supr. tchr. interns Stanford (Calif.) U., 1972-75; asst. prof. edn. The Penn State U., University Park, 1975-82, assoc. prof. edn., 1982-87, coord. elem. program, 1984-90, prof. edn., 1987—, coord. grad. edn. curriculum and instrn., 1992-98, head dept. curriculum and instrn., 2000—; Fulbright lectr. in edn. U. Iceland, 1983. Disting. vis. prof. U. Wyo., 1989; Fulbright Sr. Lectureship in Am. Studies, Ministry of Edn., Norway, 1990-91; workshop presenter in field; cons. in field. Author: Law in the Curriculum, 1978, Children and Social Studies, 1992, 98, The Originals - The New York Celtics Invent Modern Basketball, 1999; editor: Critical Issues in Curriculum, 1988, Curriculum History, 1989, The Future of the Social Studies, 1994, The 1916 Report of the Committee on Social Studies of the Commission on the Reorganization of Secondary Education of the National Education Association, 1994; contbr. numerous articles to profl. jours.; mem. editorial bd. Theory and Rsch. in Social Edn., 1978-84, 87-90, Social Studies Jour., 1980-83, Social Edn., Internat. Social Studies Forum, 2000—. Named Outstanding Young Man of Am., 1975, 79; named Vis. Phi Delta Kappa scholar, 1979; recipient Harry J. Carmen Gold medal for Outstanding Achievement in Social Studies, 1985, Outstanding Rsch. award Rural Edn. Assn., 1982, Fulbright Sr. Lectureship, U. Iceland, 1983, Norwegian Ministry of Edn., 1990-91. Mem. Am. Edn. Rsch. Assn. (program chair Rsch. in Social Studies Edn. 1988, com. on spl. interest groups 1992-94, chair 1993-94), Coun. for Anthropology and Edn., Nat. Coun. for Social Studies (chmn. rural social studies com. 1979-80, bd. dirs. 1997-2000. chair acad. freedom com. 1981-82, coll. and univ. faculty assembly bd. dirs. 1981-83, chairperson 1983), Pa. Coun. for Social Studies (pres. 1987-88, bd. dirs. 1983-89), Social Sci. Edn. Consortium, Phi Delta Kappa. Avocations: basketball, skiing, baseball cards, travel. E-mail: mrn2@psu.edu.

NELSON, PATRICIA LYNN, early childhood educator; b. Burbank, Calif., Dec. 20, 1963; d. Leon Numa Bordelon and Barbara Jean Madden;

m. Brian Henry Nelson, Aug. 11, 1990. AA, AS, Mt. San Antonio Coll., Walnut, Calif., 1986; BA, Calif. State U., L.A., 1991. Interpreter for deaf East San Gabriel Valley Regional Occupation Program, West Covina, Calif., 1986; tchr. aide Covina Valley Sch. Dist., Covina, Calif., 1986-90; dir./tchr. Valley Trails Camp/Woodcrest, Tarzana, Calif., 1990-91; tchr. presch. Town and Country Sch., Westminster, Calif., 1991, Somerset Sch., Westminster, 1992—. Counselor Tom Sawyer Camp, Altadena, Calif., summer 1989; nursery aide Christ Luth. Ch., West Covina, 1989-90; camp counselor Sierra Madre coun. Girl Scouts U.S., Arcadia, Calif., 1982-88, troop leader, 1982—. Recipient Gold award Sierra Madre coun. Girl Scouts U.S., 1982, Green Angel award, 1988. Democrat. Roman Catholic. Avocations: camping, volleyball, softball, painting t-shirts, activities with children.

NELSON, PAULA MORRISON BRONSON, educator; b. Memphis, Mar. 26, 1944; d. Fred Ford and Julia (Morrison) Bronson: m. Jack Marvin Nelson, July 13, 1968; children: Eric Allen, Kelly Susan. BS, U. N.Mex., 1967; MA, U. Colo., Denver, 1985. Physical edn. tchr. Grant Union Sch. Dist., Sacramento, 1967-68, Denver Pub. Schs., 1968-74, with program for pupil assistance, 1974-80; tchr. ESL Douglas County Pub. Schs., Parker, Colo., 1982-83; chpt. 1 reading specialist Denver Pub. Schs., 1983-96, computer/reading specialist, 1996-98, reading specialist, gifted and talented tchr., 1998-99, lead tchr. in charge instrn., 1999-2001, edn. cons., 2001—02. Demonstration tchr. Colo. Edn. Assn., 1970-72; mem. curriculum com. Denver Pub. Schs., 1970-72; mem. Douglas County Accountability Com., Castle Rock, Colo., 1986-92; mem. educators rev. panel Edn. for Freedom; computer trainer Denver Pub. Schs. Tech. Team, 1992-02. Co-author: Gymnastics Teacher's Guide Elementary Physical Education, 1973, Applauding Our Constitution, 1989; editorial reviewer G is for Geography, Children's Literature and the Five Themes. 1993; producer slide shows Brotherhood, 1986, We the People...Our Dream Lives On, 1987, Celebration of Cultures, 1988. Named Pub. Edn. Coalition grantee, Denver, 1987, 88, 89, 90, grantee Rocky Mountain Global Edn. Project, 1987, Wake Forest Law Sch., Winston-Salem, N.C., 1988, 89, 90, 92, Read to Achieve grantee Colo. State Dept. Edn., 2000; recipient chpt. II grant, 1991, Tech. grant, 1993, Title VI Reading grant, 1999, 2000, Three R's of Freedom award State Dept. Edn., 1987, Nat. Recognition award Commn. on Bicentennial of Constitution., 1987, Distinguished Tchr. award City of Denver, 1994. Mem.: Denver Fedn. Tchrs., Am. Fedn. Tchrs., Tech. in Edn. Republican. Methodist. Avocations: snow and water skiing, tennis. Home: 18 Covewood Dr Norwalk CT 06853

NELSON, PHILIP EDWIN, food scientist, educator; b. Shelbyville, Ind., Nov. 12, 1934; s. Brainard R. and Alta E. (Pitts) N.; m. Sue Bayless, Dec. 27, 1955; children: Jennifer, Andrew, Bradley. BS, Purdue U., 1956, PhD, 1976. Plant mgr. Blue River Packing Co., Morristown, Ind., 1956-60; instr. Purdue U., West Lafayette, Ind., 1961-76, head dept. food sci., 1983—2003. Cons. PEN Cons., West Lafayette, 1974; chair Food Processors Inst., Washington, 1990-93; mem. adv. bd. USDA, 2002—. Editor: Fruit Vegetable Juice Technology, 1980, Principles of Aseptic Processing and Packaging, 1992. Recipient Pers. Achievement award USDA, 1997. Fellow Inst. Food Techs. (pres. 2001-02, Indsl. Achievement award 1976, Nicholas Appert award 1995, 49'er Svc. award 1995, Tanner Lectr. 1999); mem. AAAS, Sigma Xi, Phi Tau Sigma (pres. 1976-77). Achievements include 11 U.S. and foreign patents. Office: Purdue U Dept Food Sci 745 Ag Mall Drive West Lafayette IN 47907-2009 E-mail: pen@purdue.edu.

NELSON, ROBERT LOUIS, special education educator, consultant; b. Manitowoc, Wis., Sept. 14, 1927; s. Louis Robert and Germaine Emily (Moser) N.; m. Catherine Mary Wojtanowska, Oct. 2, 1948; children: Karen Marie, Christine Mary, Robert Stephen. B of Edn., U. Wis., Whitewater, 1959; MS, U. Wis., Madison, 1968; MA, Ohio State U., 1969; PhD, Mich. State U., 1974. Tchr., prin., adminstr. Bark River Elem. Sch., Nashotah, Wis., 1952-68; tchr. Ctrl. High Sch., West Allis, Wis., 1969-71, Hale High Sch., West Allis, Wis., 1972-77; lectr. Cardinal Stritch Coll., Milw., 1975-77, Milw. Area Tech. Coll., 1972-74; lectr., counselor U. Wis., LaCrosse, 1977-89; freelance speaker, cons. Manitowoc, Wis., 1990—. Cons., lectr. Luth. Hosp., LaCrosse, 1987-89. Author: Downhill to Uphill, 1980, Teaching Vocabulary in Sensible Ways, 1984; contbr. articles to profl. jours. Vol. guide Pinecrest Hist. Village, Manitowoc, 1990—; libr. asst. Manitowoc Pub. Libr., 1990—. With U.S. Army, 1945-46. Mich. State U. scholar, 1966, Calif. State U. scholar, 1967; Ohio State U. fellow, 1968-69. Mem. Internat. Reading Assn., Nat. Coun. Tchrs. English, Wis. Hist. Soc., Manitowoc County Hist. Soc., Retired Tchrs. Assn., Phi Delta Kappa. Avocations: travel, photography, model trains, walking, biking. Home: 1129 S 12th St Manitowoc WI 54220-5221

NELSON, RONALD JOHN, retired cardiothoracic surgeon, educator; b. Nov. 20, 1934; s. Clarence Oscar and Magnhild Marie (Anderson) N.; m. L. Ruth Needels, June 10, 1961; children: Daniel G., Peter J., Kristen A. BA magna cum laude, U. Minn., 1956, BS, 1957, MD, 1959. Diplomate Am. Bd. Surgery, Am. Bd. Thoracic Surgery. Intern King County Hosp., Seattle, 1959-60; resident in surgery U. Wash., Seattle, 1961-68, instr. dept. surgery, 1967-68; asst. chief cardiovasc. surgery Harbor/UCLA Med. Ctr., Torrance, 1968-73, chief cardiovasc. surgery, 1973-76, chief divsn. thoracic and cardiovasc. surgery, 1976-89; chief cardiac surgery St. John's Heart Inst., 1989-93, cardiac surgeon, 1989-98; ret., 1998. Dir. Research and Edn. Inst., 1981-82; asst. prof., assoc. prof. surgery UCLA Sch. Medicine, 1970-80, prof. surgery, 1981-89, clin. prof. surgery, 1989-98; hon. mem. staff St. John's Hosp., Santa Monica, ret., 1998. Contbr. chpts. to books, articles to sci. jours. Chmn. Rolling Hills Covenant Ch., Rolling Hills Estates, Calif., 1975-77; mem. bd. reference Fuller Theol. Sem. Ext., Pasadena, Calif., 1978-83. Postdoctoral fellow NIH, 1964-65, rsch. grantee, 1978—. Fellow ACS, Coun. of Cardiovasc. Surgery of Am. Heart Assn.; mem. Pacific Coast Surg. Assn., Am. Assn. Thoracic Surgery, Soc. Thoracic Surgeons, other profl. orgns., Phi Beta Kappa, Alpha Omega Alpha. Home: 2104 Via Rivera Palos Verdes Estates CA 90274 E-mail: ronruth@flash.net.

NELSON, ROY JAY, retired French educator; b. Pitts., July 27, 1929; s. Roy J. and Ruth Brown (Bainbridge) N.; m. Anita Lee Chandler, Aug. 16, 1954; children: Wendy Nelson Wilson, Barbara Nelson Videira. BA, U. Pitts., 1951; MA, Middlebury Coll., 1952; PhD, U. Ill., 1958. Instr. French, U. Mich., Ann Arbor, 1957-60, asst. prof., 1960-65, assoc. prof., 1965-72, prof., 1972-94, prof. emeritus, 1994—. Author: Péguy poète du sacré, 1960, Causality and Narrative in French Fiction from Zola to Robbe-Grillet, 1989; editor: 20e siècle: La Problèmatique de discours, 1986; contbr. articles to French Rev. Recipient Ruth Sinclair counseling award U. Mich., 1982, cert. for outstanding tchg., 1986; faculty tchg. award Amoco Found., 1992. Mem. MLA, Am. Assn. Tchrs. French, U. Mich. Rsch. Club. Avocation: writing fiction. Office: U Mich Dept Romance Langs and Lits Ann Arbor MI 48109-1275 E-mail: rnelson01@comcast.net.

NELSON, RUSSELL MARION, surgeon, educator; b. Salt Lake City, Sept. 9, 1924; s. Marion C. and Edna (Anderson) N.; m. Dantzel White, Aug. 31, 1945; children: Marsha Nelson McKellar, Wendy Nelson Maxfield, Gloria Nelson Irion, Brenda Nelson Miles, Sylvia Nelson Webster, Emily Nelson Wittwer (dec.), Laurie Nelson Marsh, Rosalie Nelson Ringwood, Marjorie Nelson Helsten, Russell Marion Jr. BA, U. Utah, 1945, MD, 1947; PhD in Surgery, U. Minn., 1954; ScD (hon.), Brigham Young U., 1970; DMS (hon.), Utah State U., 1989; LHD (hon.), Snow Coll., 1994. Diplomate: Am. Bd. Surgery, Am. Bd. Thoracic Surgery (dir. 1972-78). Intern U. Minn. Hosps., Mpls., 1947, asst. resident surgery, 1948-51; first asst. resident surgery Mass. Gen. Hosp., Boston, 1953-54; sr. resident surgery U. Minn. Hosps., Mpls., 1954-55; practice medicine (specializing in cardiovascular and thoracic surgery), Salt Lake City, 1959-84; staff surgeon LDS Hosp., Salt Lake City, 1959-84, dir. surg. research lab., 1959-72, chief cardiovascular-thoracic surg. div., 1967-72, also bd. govs., 1970-90, vice chmn., 1979-89; staff surgeon Primary Children's Hosp., Salt Lake City, 1960; attending in surgery VA Hosp., Salt Lake City, 1955-84, Univ. Hosp., Salt Lake City, 1955-84; asst. prof. surgery Med. Sch. U. Utah, Salt Lake City, 1955-59, asst. clin. prof. surgery, 1959-66, asso. clin. prof. surgery, clin. prof., 1966-69, research prof. surgery, 1970-84, clin. prof. emeritus, 1984—; staff services Utah Biomed. Test Lab., 1970-84. Dir. tng. program cardiovascular and thoracic surgery at Univ. Utah affiliated hosps., 1967-84; mem. policyholders adv. com. New Eng. Mut. Life Ins. Co., Boston, 1976-80 Contbr. articles to profl. jours. Mem. White House Conf. on Youth and Children, 1960; bd. dirs. Internat. Cardiol. Found.; bd. govs. LDS Hosp., 1970-90, Deseret Gymnasium, 1971-75, Promised Valley Playhouse, 1970-79; mem. adv. com. U.S. Sec. of State on Religious Freedom Abroad, 1996-99. lst lt. to capt. M.C., AUS, 1951-53. Markle scholar in med. scis., 1957-59; Fellowship of Medici Publici U. Utah Coll., 1967; Gold Medal of Merit, Argentina, 1974; named Hon. Prof. Shandong Med. U., Jinan, People's Republic of China, 1985; Old People's U., Jinan, 1986; Xi-an (People's Republic of China) Med. Coll., 1986, Legacy of Life award, 1993. Fellow A.C.S. (chmn. adv. council on thoracic surgery 1973-75), Am. Coll. Cardiology, Am. Coll. Chest Physicians; mem. Am. Assn. Thoracic Surgery, Am. Soc. Artificial Internal Organs, AMA, Dirs. Thoracic Residencies (pres. 1971-72), Utah Med. Assn. (pres. 1970-71), Salt Lake County Med. Soc., Am. Heart Assn. (exec. com. cardiovascular surgery 1972, dir. 1976-78, chmn. council cardiovascular surgery 1976-78), Utah Heart Assn. (pres. 1964-65), Soc. Thoracic Surgeons, Soc. Vascular Surgery (sec. 1968-72, pres. 1974), Utah Thoracic Soc., Salt Lake Surg. Soc., Samson Thoracic Surg. Soc., Western Soc. for Clin. Research, Soc. U. Surgeons, Am., Western, Pan-Pacific surg. assns., Inter. Am. Soc. Cardiology (bd. mgrs.), Phi Beta Kappa, Sigma Xi, Alpha Omega Alpha, Phi Kappa Phi, Sigma Chi. Mem. Ch. of Jesus Christ of Latter-day Saints (pres. Bonneville Stake 1964-71, gen. pres. Sunday sch. 1971-79, regional rep. 1979-84, Quorum of the Twelve Apostles 1984—). Office: 47 E South Temple Salt Lake City UT 84150-1200

NELSON, SARAH ELLEN, elementary music educator; b. St. Paul, Feb. 13, 1957; d. Walter Eugene and Virginia Beth (Huddleston) Nelson; children: Lucas, Kassandra. BS in Elem. Edn., S.W. State U., 1981. Cert. elem. and music edn. Rural elem. tchr. Harding County Schs., Buffalo, S.D., 1981-83, Meade Sch. Dist., Sturgis, S.D., 1983-86; tchr. 2d grade Aztec (N.Mex.) Mcpl. Schs., 1986-90; rural elem. tchr. Newell (S.D.) Schs., 1990-92; tchr. elem. band and vocal music Todd County Schs., Mission, S.D., 1992—. Ch. organist, choir dir. various locations, Minn., S.D. and N.Mex., 1978—; dep. voter registrar San Juan County, Aztec, 1988-90. Mem. NEA, Girl Scouts of Am., Aztec Edn. Assn. (bldg. rep., v.p., pres. 1987-90), Todd County Edn. Assn. Lutheran. Avocations: reading, canoeing, cooking, computers, walking. Home: Wagon Wheel Park Winner SD 57580 Office: Todd County Schs PO Box 87 Mission SD 57555-0087 E-mail: snelson@tcsdk12.org.

NELSON, SCOTT LEE, physical education educator; b. St. Louis, July 3, 1964; s. Charles Lenorad and Ola Fay (Sherrod) N.; m. Gina Brewer, June 11, 1988; 1 child, Natalie. BE, Freed-Hardeman U., Henderson, Tenn., 1986; MEd, U. Memphis, 1994. Social studies, phys. edn. specialist Mt. Dora (Fla.) Sch., 1987-88; phys. edn. specialist Nova Elem. Sch., Jackson, Tenn., 1990—. Recipient part-time Masters fellowship U. Memphis, 1994, project mentor grant U. Tenn., 1993. Mem. AAHPERD, NEA, Tenn. Assn. Health, Phys. Edn., Recreation and Dance, Tenn. Edn. Assn., Jackson-Madison County Edn. Assn. Home: 52 Driftwood Dr Jackson TN 38305-7700 Office: Nova Elem Sch 248 Bedford White Rd Jackson TN 38305-5931

NELSON, SUSANNAH MARIE, secondary school educator, literature educator; b. Ft. Worth, Dec. 29, 1953; d. Frank William and Mary Naomi (Limbaugh) Fucich; married; 1 child, Daniel Allen Green. BA in Liberal Studies, Calif. State U., Sacramento, 1975, MA in Elem. Edn., 1983. Tchr. St. Ignatius Sch., Sacramento, 1975-89, vice prin., 1986-89, prin., 1989-91, tchr., 1991—96, Loretto H.S., 1996—2000; tchr., campus min. Christian Bros. H.S., 2000—; prof. literature, writing, humanities Nat. U., 1997—. Mem. Nat. Cath. Edn. Assn., Phi Kappa Phi. Democrat. Roman Catholic. Avocations: boating, stitchery, piano, reading. Office: Christian Bros HS 4315 Martin Luther King Jr Blvd Sacramento CA 95820

NELSON, TOZA, retired elementary school educator, church administrator; b. Beaumont, Tex., Feb. 25, 1948; d. Silas Bailey and Mary Eula (Prudhomme) Estes; m. Don W. Nelson, Oct. 26, 1974; 1 child, Bryan Alan Jones. BS, West Tex. State U., 1972; MEd, Tex. Tech U., 1975. Cert. elem. tchr., reading specialist, supr., Tex. Elem. tchr. Lubbock (Tex.) Ind. Sch. Dist., 1972-78, elem. demonstration tchr., 1978-83, coord. elem. reading and lang. arts., 1983-93, elem. prin., 1993—2002; adminstr. Raintree Christian Ch., Lubbock, 2002—. Office: Raintree Christian Ch 3601 82d Lubbock TX 79423-

NELSON, WILLIAM RANKIN, surgeon, educator; b. Charlottesville, Va., Dec. 12, 1921; s. Hugh Thomas and Edith (Rankin) N.; m. Nancy Laidley, Mar. 17, 1956 (div. 1979); children: Robin Page Nelson Russel, Susan Kimberly Nelson Wright, Anne Rankin Nelson Cron; m. Pamela Morgan Phelps, July 5, 1984. BA, U. Va., 1943, MD, 1945. Diplomate Am. Bd. Surgery. Intern Vanderbilt U. Hosp., Nashille, 1945-46; resident in surgery U. Va. Hosp., Charlottesville, 1949-51; fellow surg. oncology Meml. Sloan Kettering Cancer Ctr., N.Y.C., 1951-55; instr. U. Colo. Sch. Medicine, Denver, 1955-57, asst. clin. prof., 1962-87, clin. prof. surgery, 1987—. Asst. prof. Med. Coll. Va., Richmond, 1957-62; mem. exec. com. U. Colo. Cancer Ctr.; mem. nat. bd., nat. exec. com. Am. Cancer Soc. Contbr. articles to profl. jours. and chpts. to textbooks. Capt. USAAF, 1946-48. Recipient Nat. Div. award Am. Cancer Soc., 1979. Fellow Am. Coll. Surgeons (bd. govs. 1984-89); mem. AMA, Internat. Soc. Surgery, Brit. Assn. Surg. Oncology, Royal Soc. Medicine (U.K.), Soc. Surg. Oncology (pres. 1975-76), Soc. Head and Neck Surgeons (pres. 1986-87), Am. Cancer Soc. (pres. Colo. div. 1975-77, exec. com., nat. bd. dirs., del. dir. from Colo. div. 1985-94), Am. Soc. Clin. Oncology, Western Surg. Assn. Colo. Med. Soc., Denver Med. Soc., Denver Acad. Surgery, Rocky Mt. Oncology Soc., Univ. Club, Rotary. Republican. Episcopalian. Avocations: skiing, backpacking, travel, bicycling, fly fishing. E-mail: wrn3@msn.com .

NELSON SARGEANT, SUSAN MARIE, speech pathology/audiology services professional; b. Washington, Oct. 21, 1953; d. Boyce Gerald and Mary (Murphy) Nelson; m. Robert Nolan Sargeant; children: Rachel-Marie, Rebekah-Ann. BS, James Madison U., 1976; MS, Vanderbilt U., 1979. Speech-lang. pathologist Danville (Va.) Pub. Schs., 1976-78; tchr. early childhood/spl. edn. Rockingham County Pub. Schs., Harrisonburg, Va., 1979-80; program coord. parent edn.-infant devel. Rappahannock Area Community Svcs. Bd., Fredericksburg, Va., 1980-86; pvt. practice infant and family cons. Fredericksburg, 1987—96; speech-lang. pathologist Spotsylvania Pub. Schs., 1996—. Cons. Parent Ednl. Advocacy Tng. Ctr., Alexandria, Va., 1982, 90; presenter, session leader at profl. workshops and confs. Bd.irs. Spl. Olympics, Stage Door Prodns. Recipient Outstanding Child Advocate award Va. Div. Children, 1982; named one of Ten Outstanding Young Women of Am., 1986. Mem. Coun. for Exceptional Children (local arrangements chair internat. conv. 1988, Va. pres. 1997), Va. Div. Mental Retardation of Coun. Exceptional Children (pres. 1990-93, Va. divsn. early Childhood (pres. 1980-82), Speech and Hearing Assn. Va., Assn. Retarded Citizens, Assn. for Persons with Significant Handicaps (bd. dirs.), Internat. Assn. Infant Massage Instrs. (cert.). Roman Catholic. Home and Office: 458 Laurel Ave Fredericksburg VA 22408-1519

NEMAN, BETH S. English educator; b. Detroit, Dec. 2, 1931; d. Louis I. Smilansky and Harriet (Feldman) Smilansky Plaut; m. Albert H. Neman, July 12, 1953 (dec. Feb. 2003); children: David G., Daniel L. AB, U. Mich., 1953; MA, U. Cin., 1963; PhD, Miami U., 1976. Cert. elem. and secondary tchr., Ohio, Mich. Tchr. Cleve. Pub. Schs., 1953-55, Princeton Pub. Schs., Sharonville, Ohio, 1955-57; co-head, tchr. English dept. Madeira (Ohio) High Sch., 1963-70; teaching assoc. Miami U., Oxford, Ohio, 1971-76, asst. prof., 1976-80; asst. prof. English Wilmington (Ohio) Coll., 1980-86, assoc. prof., 1986-93, prof. English, 1993—2003, head dept. English, 1996-99, prof. emerita, 2003—. Cons. in field. Author: Teaching Students to Write, 1980, 96, Writing Effectively, 1983, 90, Writing Effectively in Business, 1992; contbr. articles to encys., scholarly jours. Rsch. fellow Miami U., 1974-75; Ohio Bd. Regents grantee, 1990-91, 92-93. Mem. Nat. Coun. Tchrs. English, Coll. Composition and Communication Conf., Am. Soc. Eighteenth Century Studies, Phi Beta Kappa. Jewish. Avocations: exploring foreign lands, theatre, books, art. Home: 1101 Lois Dr Cincinnati OH 45237-5121 E-mail: beth_neman@wilmington.edu.

NEMETH, ROBERT FRED, elementary school educator; b. Ind., 1950; s. Fred Frank and Betty Jo Nemeth; m. Teresa Marie, 1973; children: James R., William J. BS, No. Ill. U., 1974, MEd, 1981, EdD, 1994. Cert. tchr., adminstr., Ill. Tchr. grades 5 and 6, intramural sports coord. Sch. Dist. # 95, Lake Zurich, Ill., 1974—. Rep., UNICEF, Lake Zurich, 1975—; coach Palatine (Ill.) Baseball, 1985—95. Mem. NEA, Ill. Edn. Assn., Lake Zurich Edn. Assn. Avocations: woodworking, painting, sports, outdoors. Office: Sarah Adams Elementary Sch 555 Old Mill Grove Rd Lake Zurich IL 60047-2819

NEMICKAS, RIMGAUDAS, cardiologist, educator; b. Kaunas, Lithuania, Mar. 10, 1938; came to U.S., 1949; s. Romualdas and Elena (Saulyte) N.; m. Joan A. McLee, Feb. 16, 1965; children: Rimas Jonas, Kristina Nemickas Tomlinson, Tomas Edward, Nikolas. Student, Ind. U., 1954-57; MD magna cum laude, Loyola U., 1961; MD (hon.), Kaunas Med. Acad., 1993. Diplomate in internal medicine and cardiovascular diseases Am. Bd. Internal Medicine; lic. physician, Ill., Ind. Intern U. Chgo. Clinics, 1961-62; med. resident U. Ill. Rsch. and Edn. Hosps., 1966—67; fellow in cardiology Cook County Hosp., Chgo., 1962-63, U. Chgo. Hosp., 1967-69; assoc. chief cardiology Loyola U., Maywood, Ill., 1972-77, clin. prof. medicine, 1979—. Dir. cardiology Ill. Masonic Med. Ctr., Chgo., 1980—2001, emeritus, 2001—. Mem. Task Force for Health Care Reform, Ministry of Health, Vilnius, Lithuania, 1994-97. Capt. USAF, 1963-66. Fellow ACP, Am. Coll. Cardiology, Am. Coll. Chest Physicians; mem. Am. Heart Assn., Chgo. Soc. Internal Medicine, Chgo. Cardiology Group. Republican. Roman Catholic. Avocations: walking, travel, fishing, collecting art. Office: Ill Masonic Med Ctr 836 W Wellington Chicago IL 60657-5188 E-mail: rnemickas@msn.com., rimgaudas.nemickas-md@advocatehealth.com.

NEMIRO, BEVERLY MIRIUM ANDERSON, author, educator; b. St. Paul, May 29, 1925; d. Martin and Anna Mae Anderson; m. Jerome Morton Nemiro, Feb. 10, 1951-75; children: Guy Samuel, Lee Anna, Dee Martin. Student, Reed Coll., 1943-44; BA, U. Colo., 1947; postgrad., U. Denver. Tchr. Seattle Pub. Sch., 1945-46; fashion coord., dir. Denver Dry Goods Co., 1948-51; fashion dir. Denver Market Week Assn., 1952-53; free-lance writer Denver, 1958—. Moderator TV program Your Presch. Child, Denver, 1955-56; instr. writing and comm. U. Colo. Denver Ctr., 1970—, U. Calif., San Diego, 1976-78, Met. State Coll., 1985; dir. pub. rels. Fairmont Hotel, Denver, 1979-80; freelance fashion and TV model. Author, co-author: The Complete Book of High Altitude Baking, 1961, Colorado a la Carte, 1963, Colorado a la Carte, Series II, 1966, (with Donna Hamilton) The High Altitude Cookbook, 1969, The Busy People's Cookbook, 1971 (Better Homes and Gardens Book Club selection 1971), Where to Eat in Colorado, 1967, Lunch Box Cookbook, 1965, Complete Book of High Altitude Baking, 1961, (under name Beverly Anderson) Single After 50, 1978, The New High Altitude Cookbook, 1980. Co-founder, pres. Jr. Symphony Guild, Denver, 1959-60; active Friends of Denver Libr., Opera Colo.; mem. Friends of Painting and Sculpture, Denver Art Mus. Recipient Top Hand award Colo. Authors' League, 1969, 72, 79-82, 100 Best Books of Yr. award NY Times, 1969, 71; named one of Colo. Women of Yr., Denver Post, 1964. Mem. Am. Soc. Journalists and Authors, Colo. Authors League (dir. 1969-79), Authors Guild, Authors League Am., Friends Denver Libr., Opera Colo. Guild, Denver Women's Press Club, Rotary, Kappa Alpha Theta. Address: Park Towers 1299 Gilpin St Apt 15W Denver CO 80218-2556

NEMIROFF, MAXINE CELIA, art educator, gallery owner, consultant; b. Chgo., Feb. 11, 1935; d. Oscar Bernard and Martha (Mann) Kessler; m. Paul Rubenstein, June 26, 1955 (div. 1974); children: Daniel, Peter, Anthony; m. Allan Nemiroff, Dec. 24, 1979. BA, U. So. Calif., 1955; MA, UCLA, 1974. Sr. instr. UCLA, 1974-92; dir., curator art gallery Doolittle Theater, Los Angeles, 1985-86; owner Nemiroff Deutsch Fine Art, Santa Monica, Calif. Leader of worldwide art tours; cons. L'Ermitage Hotel Group, Beverly Hills, Calif., 1982—, Broadway Dept. Stores, So. Calif., 1979—, Security Pacific Bank, Calif., 1978—, Am. Airlines, Calif. Pizza Kitchen Restaurants; art chmn. UCLA Thieves Market, Century City, 1960—, L.A. Music Ctr. Mercado, 1982—; lectr. in field. Apptd. bd. dirs. Dublin (Calif.) Fine Arts Found., 1989; mem. Calif. Govs. Adv. Coun. for Women, 1992; mem. art selection com. Calif. State Office Bldgs., 1997—. Named Woman of Yr. UCLA Panhellenic Council, 1982, Instr. of Yr. UCLA Dept. Arts, 1984; recipient Woman of Achievement award Friends of Sheba Med. Ctr., 2003; elected to Fashion Circle of the Costume Coun., L.A. County Mus. Art, 1997—; honoree L.A. Art Core 15th Ann. Awards Benefit, 2003. Mem. L.A. County Mus. Art Coun., UCLA Art Coun., UCLA Art Coun. Docents, Alpha Epsilon Phi (alumnus of yr. 1983). Avocations: tennis, horseback riding, skiing, piano and guitar. E-mail: mumseyart@aol.com.

NERO, ELLIE THERESA, elementary education educator; b. Buena Vista, Miss., Feb. 18, 1931; d. Bud and Levell (Baskin) Cunningham; m. Alonza James Nero, Nov. 24, 1955; children: Lolita Kay, Renata Lynette, Katherine Levell. BS, Rust Coll., 1954; MEd, Northeastern U., 1974; MA, Gov.'s State U., 1975. Cert. primary and elem. educator, Ill.; type A cert., Miss. Tchr. Chickasaw County Schs., Buena Vista, 1954-55; prin. Macedonia Sch., Buena Vista, 1955-56; tchr. Chgo. Bd. Edn., 1957-68; tchr. reading resources Grant Sch., Chgo., 1968—. Head tchr. Head Start summer program, Grant Sch., Chgo., 1965-72; dir. summer youth program Dist. 9, Chgo., 1972-89; adj. liaison U. Ill., Chgo., 1987-92; tchr. rep. local sch. coun., Chgo., 1990—; chmn. adv. com. Profl. Personnel, Chgo., 1990—. Mem. Inter-Religious Concerns Com., 1990—; Chgo. Tchrs. Union, 1993—. Grantee Joyce Found., Chgo., 1988, U. Ill., Chgo., 1990. Mem. Assn. Supervision and Curriculum Devel., Chgo. Area Reading Assn., Parents Helping Their Children (coord. program, Outstanding Svc. award 1991), Phi Delta Kappa. Avocations: reading, theatre, concerts, sightseeing. Home: 9205 S Cregier Ave Chicago IL 60617-3602

NERODE, ANIL, mathematician, educator; b. L.A., June 4, 1932; s. Nirad Ranjan and Agnes (Spencer) N.; m. Sondra Raines, Feb. 12, 1955 (div. 1968); children: Christopher Curtis, Gregory Daniel; m. Sally Riedel Sievers, May 16, 1970; 1 child, Nathanael Caldwell. BA, U. Chgo., 1949, BS, 1952, MS, 1953, PhD, 1956. Group leader automata and weapons systems Lab. Applied Sci., U. Chgo., 1954-57; mem. Inst. for Advanced Study, Princeton, 1957-58, 62-63; vis. asst. prof. math. U. Calif. at Berkeley, 1958-59; mem. faculty Cornell U., 1959—, prof. math., 1965—, Goldwin Smith prof. math., 1990—, chmn. dept. math., 1982-87, dir. Math. Sci. Inst., 1986-97; acting dir. Center for Applied Math., 1965-66; vis. prof. Monash U., Melbourne, Australia, 1970, 74, 78, 79, U. Chgo., 1976, M.I.T., 1980, U. Calif., San Diego, 1981; disting. vis. scientist EPA, 1985-87; dir. Ctr. for Found. of Intelligent Sys. Cornell U., 1997—2001. Prin. investigator numerous grants; mem. sci. adv. bd. EPA, 1988-93, chair tech. adv. panel Global Change, 1990-92; mem. sci. adv. bd. Ctr. for Intelligent Control, Harvard-MIT-Brown U., 1988-94; cons. to govt. and industry;

co-founder Hynomics Corp., 1995. Author: (with John Crossley) Combinatorial Functors, 1974, (with Richard Shore) Logic for Applications, 2d edit., 1996, (with G.A. Metakides) Principles of Logic and Logic Programming, 1996, (with B. Khoussainov) Automata Theory and its Applications, 2001; editor Advances in Mathematics, 1967-70, Jour. Symbolic Logic, 1967-82, Annals of Pure and Applied Logic, 1983-96, Future Generation Computing Systems, 1983-97, Jour. Pure & Applied Algebra, 1988—, Annals of Math. and Artificial Intelligence, 1989—, Logical Methods in Computer Sci., 1991-94, Computer Modelling and Simulation, 1991—, Constraints, 1995-2001, Grammers, 1997-2001, (with J. Remmel, S. Goncharov, Y. Ershov) Handbook of Recursive Algebra, 1998. Mem. AIII, IEEE, Assn. Computing Machinery, Am. Math. Soc. (assoc. editor procs. 1962-65, v.p. 1992-95), Soc. Indsl. and Applied Math., Math. Assn. Am., Assn. Symbolic Logic, European Assn. for Theoretical Computer Sci. Home: 406 Cayuga Heights Rd Ithaca NY 14850-1402 Office: Cornell U 545 Mallott Hall Dept Math Ithaca NY 14853-4201 E-mail: anil@math.cornell.edu.

NES, SANDRA LEE, learning disabilities educator; b. Bellefonte, Pa., Mar. 11, 1953; d. William Robert and Valerie Jean (Brown) Chubb; m. William David Nes, June 26, 1976; children: William Bradley, Michael David, Craigen Robert. BS, Pa. State U., 1976; MEd, U. Ga., 1992; Postgrad., Tex. Tech. U., 1994—. Cert. tchr. learning disabilities and mental retardation, Ga. Tchr. learning disabilities Madison County Mid. Sch., Danielsville, Ga., 1992-93; tchr. spl. edn. Bean Elem. Sch., Lubbock, Tex., 1993-94. Mem. Coun. for Exceptional Children, S.W. Ednl. Rsch. Assn., Profl. Assn. Ga. Educators, Kappa Delta Pi. Avocations: gardening, hiking, swimming, arts and crafts. Home: 5818 76th St Lubbock TX 79424-1717 Office: #170 Edn/Adminstrn Bldg Tex Tech Univ Lubbock TX 79409

NESBIT, WILLIAM TERRY, small business owner, consultant; b. Pitts., Jan. 30, 1945; s. William Frank and Glenna (Cleeton) N.; divorced. Owner, CEO Narrow Gauge Car Shop, Evergreen Outdoor Ctr., Shiremanstown, Pa., 1972—; mem. faculty Millersville (Pa.) U., 1976-81, Temple U., Phila., 1979, Nat. Aquatic and Small Craft Sch., Bemis Point, N.Y., 1980, Harrisburg (Pa.) Area C. C., 1981-82, 91, Dickinson Coll., Carlisle, Pa., 1982-83. Judge 32d Capital Area Sci., Engring. Fair, Dickinson Coll., Carlisle, Pa., 1989; mem. tech. briefs reader adv. panel NASA, 2000—. Co-developer ARC basic and whitewater canoeing programs for instrn., 1977-79; inventor, developer The Z Drag for Boat Rescues, 1980; developer, mfr. first HOn3 ready-to-run plastic rolling stock having NMRA warrant; contbg. author: The Brown Book, 2d edit., 1982. Vol. ARC, 1961—; contbr. A.C. Kalmbach Meml. Libr., Chattanooga; benefactor Carlyton Sch. Dist. Libr., Carnegie, Pa. Recipient award for Humanity ARC, 1967, award for 30 Yrs. Vol. Svc., 1991; named Class I Radiol. Protection Officer, U.S. Dept. Def. and NRC, 1993. Mem. Math. Assn. Am., Nat. Assn. Canoe Liveries and Outfitters (founding), Nat. Model Railroad Assn. (life, mid-eastern region bd. dirs. 1997-2001, supt. Susquehanna divsn. 1996-2000, edn. chair 2002-), Conewago Canoe Club (canoe tng. officer 1999—). Episcopalian. Avocation: ferroequinology. Office: Evergreen Outdoor Ctr PO Box 3081 Shiremanstown PA 17011-3081 E-mail: william.nesbit@dla.mil.

NESBITT, ROBERT EDWARD LEE, JR., physician, educator, scientific researcher, writer, poet; b. Albany, Ga., Aug. 21, 1924; s. Robert E.L. and Anne Louise (Hill) N.; m. Ellen Therese Morrissey. BA, Vanderbilt U., 1944, MD, 1947. Diplomate: Am. Bd. Ob-Gyn (asso. examiner). Asst. prof. Johns Hopkins U., 1954-56, chief obstetric pathology lab., acting chief obstetrics, 1955-56; prof., chmn. dept. ob-gyn Albany (N.Y.) Med. Coll., Union U., 1956-61, SUNY Health Sci. Ctr., Syracuse, 1961-81, dir. gen. gynecology service, 1982-84, prof. and chmn. emeritus dept. ob-gyn; obstetrician-gynecologist-in-chief Albany Hosp., 1956-61; obstetrician, gynecologist-in-chief Syracuse Meml. Hosp., 1961-65; obstetrician-gynecologist-in-chief Crouse-Irving Hosp., 1963-70, attending staff, 1970-84; prof. surgery U. South Fla., Tampa, 1988-92, prof. ob.-gyn., 1988-92. Chief ob-gyn State U. Hosp., 1964-81, chmn. med. staff and med. bd., 1964-66; attending staff St. Joseph's Hosp.; cons., chief gynecology sect. surg. service Syracuse VA Hosp., 1984-88; chief gynecology sect., asst. chief surgery, dir. uro-gynecology VA Med. Ctr., Bay Pines, Fla., 1988-92, acting chief of staff, 1990, interim chief surgery, 1991-92, chmn. O.R. com. surg. svc., 1988-92, chmn. patient care evaluation com., 1989-90, chmn. clin. exec. bd., 1990, chmn. drug usage evaluation com., 1990-91, chmn. profl. standards bd., 1990; cons. Syracuse Psychiat. Inst.; mem. cancer tng. grants and edn. com. Nat. Cancer Insts.; mem. adv. com. Bur. Maternal and Child Health, N.Y. State Dept. Health, 1957-61; nat. adviser to Children, publ. of Children's Bur., HEW, 1959-63; cons. Children's Bur., 1959-62; mem. prenatal care guide subcom. Am. Pub. Health Assn., 1962-64; cons. to regional adviser in maternal and child health Pan Am. San. Bur., WHO, 1963-65; numerous guest professorships including univs. in Mex., Chile, Uruguay, Colombia, St. Vincent (W.I.), Venezuela, People's Republic of China, Western Europe, Panama, Australia, Canada. Author: Perinatal Loss in Modern Obstetrics, 1957, Last Twig on the Bush?, 1999, In the Fullness of Time, 1999, Hearts of Flesh, 2001, (poetry collections) Chorales for Arid Souls, 1999, The Fullness Search, 2000, Visions Shared, 2000, Daily Relevance, 2000, Glimpses, 2002, Marked Off from Pagans, 2000, Puppet or Saint, 2001, Latent Harvest, 2002, Dry River Beds, 2003, over 300 published poems, also poems in numerous anthologies (15 Editor's Choice awards), sect. on ob-gyn in Rypin's Med. Licensure Exams; co-author: Infant, Perinatal, Maternal and Childhood Mortality in U.S, 1968; editor: sect. on obstetrics and gynecology Stedman's Medical Dictionary, 1958—64, sect. on fetus Funk and Wagnalls Universal Std. Ency., 1959; 1st guest editor: sect. on fetus Clinics in Perinatology, 1974; 1st editor sect. on fetus Clinical Diagnosis Quiz for Obstetrics and Gynecology, 1976, Clini-Pearls in Obstetrics and Gynecology, 1977; contbr.: sect. on fetus Attorneys' Textbook of Medicine. Capt. M.C., U.S. Army, 1952-54. Named One of Ten Outstanding Young Men in Am., U.S. Jr. C. of C., 1957; Robert E.L. Nesbitt Jr. scholarship, Sr. Resident in Ob-Gyn, and Robert E.L. Nesbitt Jr. student scholarship established in his honor, SUNY Health Sci. Ctr. at Syracuse, 1987; recipient Wisdom award, 2001, named to Hall of Fame, Wisdom Soc., 2001, Winston Churchill medal of wisdom, 2002. Fellow: A.C.S. (com. forum fundamental surg. problems 1962—67), N.Y. Acad. Scis., Am. Coll. Obstetricians and Gynecologists (chmn. com. mental retardation and perinatal health 1966), Am. Assn. Maternal and Child Health, Venezuelan Obstetrics-Gynecol. Soc. (hon.); mem.: AMA (mem. residency accreditation com., site visit team mem.), Internat. Soc. Poets (disting.), Pub. Health Council N.Y. State, Am. Soc. Cytology, Onondaga County Med. Soc., Med. Soc. N.Y. State (regional obstetrics chmn., subcom. Maternal and Child Welfare), Pan Am. Med. Assn. (med. ambassador goodwill, life mem. sect. on cancer), Soc. for Gynecol. Investigation (coun.), Alpha Omega Alpha, Southwest, Fla. obstet. and gynecol. socs. (hon.). Achievements include research and 230 publications on cytologic, cytochemical and histochemical study of early cervical cancer, perinatal and placental pathology, cytologic and hormonal studies in normal and high-risk obstetrics patients, experimental production of abruptio placentae, reproductive endocrinology, animal experimentation, induced endocrine insults upon pregnant and nonpregnant ewes and hormonal influence on placentation, invitro placenta perfusion, fetal growth and development, female urology, surgical techniques for restoration of female pelvic floor integrity; human spirituality; inspirational poetry. Home: 3743 Roscommon North Martinez GA 30907

NESHEIM, DENNIS WARREN, art educator, artist, writer, instructional materials producer, special education educator; b. Decorah, Iowa, Nov. 24, 1948; s. Kenneth H. and Adelle N.; m. Lavonne Selene Jones, Mar. 29, 1968. AA, Rochester State Jr. Coll., Minn., 1970; BS in Art/Art Edn., Winona (Minn.) State U., 1972; MA in Spl. Edn., U. Colo., Denver, 2000. cert. art tchr. K-12, Minn., Wis., Ark., Colo. Dept. Def. Dependent Schs. Tchr. art Cassville (Wis.) Pub. Schs., 1972-74, Franklin Mid. Sch., Shawano, Wis., 1974-76; substitute tchr., tchr. 4th grade Dept. Def. Dependent Schs., Neu Ulm, Germany, 1977-78, tchr. art Ulm. Am. Sch., 1978-80, tchr. art and video arts, 1980-87; tchr., artist art ctrs., Fla., 1987-89; owner, producer Nesheim Arts & Video, Lakeland Fla., Lakewood, Colo., 1989—2001; tchr. art, tchr. aide Synergy Sch., Denver; tchr. spl. edn. Euclid Mid. Sch., Littleton, Colo., 2000—. Presenter workshops and seminars, 1980-86; video tng., cons., Lakeland, 1988-93. Author, illustrator: (workbook) Making Waves, An Imagination Starter, 1994; creator, producer: (instrnl. video/handbook kits) Look and Draw series, 1990—; editor lit. quar. Onionhead, 1989-93, others; cons. writer, editor Frugal Times, 1992; writer, editor Free Shopping News, 1985-87, S&N Advertising, 1985-87; prodr. (videos) Fantastic Realism, The Video, 1989, Epic Silence, 1989, Verbal Science, 1989, October 26, 1970, 1990, See in the Dark, 1990, Look and Draw, 1990, Head in the Clouds, 1990, Look and Draw Faces and Figures, 1991, Look and Draw Space In Perspective, 1992; prodr. (with David Lee Jr.) Produce Better Video, 1989; one-man shows include Donau Casino, Neu Ulm, Germany, 1977, Maas Brothers Gallery, Lakeland, 1990; exhibited in group shows at Wurzburg (Germany) Milcom, 1979, Oberstube Gallery, Ulm, Germany, 1985-86, Ridge Art, Winter Haven, Fla. (Merit award), 1988, Arts on the Park, Lakeland, 1988-91, Arts Ctr., St. Petersburg, Fla. 1989, Art League Manatee, Bradenton, Fla., 1989, Ridge Art Assn., Winter Haven, Fla., 1990, Mt. Dora (Fla.) Ctr. for the Arts, 1990, Imperial Artists Gallery, Lakeland, 1990-91; contbr. articles to profl. jours. Mem. Arts on Park, Lakeland Ctr. for Creative Arts, 1987-95, bd. dirs., 1991-93; mem. Green Mountain Park Vols. Recipient various commendations and appreciation awards from schs. and cmty. orgns. Mem.: Fine Art Forum, Coun. Exceptional Children, Compuserve. Avocations: hiking, reading, creative cooking. Office: Euclid Mid Sch 777 W Euclid Ave Littleton CO 80120

NESHEIM, MALDEN C. academic administrator, nutrition educator; Provost emeritus Cornell U., Ithaca, N.Y., prof. emeritus nutrition, 1997—. Office: Cornell U 311 Savage Hall Ithaca NY 14853-7601 E-mail: mcn2@cornell.edu.

NESIN, JEFFREY DAVID, academic administrator; b. N.Y.C. m. Diane Garvey, 1968; children: Kate Dillon, Sarah Grace. BA in Eng. Lit., Hobart Coll., 1966; MA in Eng. Lit, SUNY, Buffalo, 1971, MA in Am. Studies, 1973. Faculty dept. humanities & scis. Sch. Visual Arts, N.Y.C., 1974-91; pres. Memphis Coll. Art, 1991—. Asst. to pres. Sch. Visual Arts, 1982-91; cons. Smithsonian Instn., IBM, 1st Tenn. Bank; panelist, speaker in field. Contbg. editor: High Fidelity, Creem; contbr. reviews, interviews, essays to mags.; adv. editor Jour. Popular Music and Society. Recipient Thomas W. Briggs Found. Cmty. Svc. award, 1998. Mem. Am. Studies Assn., Met. Am. Studies Assn. (past pres.), Assn. Ind. Colls. Art & Design (bd. dirs. 1991—), Nat. Assn. Schs. Art & Design (chair commn. on accreditation, exec. com. and bd. 1999—), Ctr. for So. Folklore (bd. and exec. com. 2000—), Memphis Rotary. Avocations: mystery novels, barbecue, baseball, american music. Office: Memphis Coll Art Office of President 1930 Poplar Ave Memphis TN 38104-2756 Home: 1545 Vinton Ave Memphis TN 38104-4923*

NESMITH, SARA, secondary education educator and counselor; b. Hondo, Tex., July 22, 1947; d. C. D. and Wilma L. (Spratt) Sadler; m. Gary J. Nesmith, July 19, 1969; 1 child: Andrea Nicole. BS in Home Econs. Edn., S.W. Tex. State U., 1968; MEd, Colo. State U., 1975. Cert. home economist, Colo. Math. tchr. Lockhart (Tex.) Sch. Dist., 1968-69; home econs. and math. tchr., FHA advisor San Marcos (Tex.) Schs., 1969-71; tchr., dept. chair, FHA advisor Jefferson County Schs., Lakewood, 1972—96; dean of students Green Mountain H.S., Jefferson County Schs., 1996—97, counselor, 1997—2003, chair counselor dept., 1998—2003. Mem. Consumer and Family Studies Task Force, Colo., 1987-2003. Mem. Littleton United Meth. Ch., 1978—. Recipient Outstanding Svc. to Home Econs., C.C. and Occupl. Edn. Sys., Colo., 1985, Colo. Vocat. Home Econs. Tchr. Yr. award, 1992 Execellence in Edn. award Green Mtn. H.S., 2001; named Outstanding Vocat. Home Econs. Tchr., Colo. Vocat. Home Econs. Tchrs., 1992. Mem. NEA, Am. Sch. Counselor Assn., Colo. Sch. Counselor Assn., Jefferson County Sch. Counselor Assn., Colo. Edn. Assn. (Colo. Outstanding Secondary Sch. Counselor 2002), Jefferson County Edn. Assn. Avocations: golf, snow skiing, scrapbooking, travel, reading. Office: Green Mountain High Sch 13175 W Green Mountain Dr Lakewood CO 80228-3512

NESMITH, SUSANNA KATHLEEN, secondary educator; b. Billings, Mont., Aug. 8, 1959; d. James Wilburn and Susanna Kay (Bach) D.; m. Jeffrey Thomas Nesmith, June 29, 1980 (div. Aug. 1984); children: James D., Christopher R. AA, Olympic Coll., 1986; BS, Ctrl. Wash. U., 1987, MEd, 1991. Bus. tchr. Eton Tech. Inst., Port Orchard, Wash., 1987-89; substitute tchr. various schs., Wash., 1990-91; bus. tchr., advisor North Beach High Sch., Ocean Shores, Wash., 1991—99; tchr., advisor Washougal (Wash.) H.S., 1999—. Adj. computer instr. Olympic Coll., Bremerton, Wash., 1988-89; adj. bus. tchr. Grays Harbor Coll., Aberdeen, Wash., 1992-99. Advisor North Beach Future Bus. Leaders chpt., Ocean Shores, 1991-99; regional advisor Capitol Region Future Bus. Leaders of Am., Olympia, 1991-93; den leader, com. mem., merit badge counselor Boy Scouts Am., Ellensburg, Port Orchard, Ocean Shores, 1989—; treas. North Beach Youth Soccer Assn. With U.S. Army, 1979-82. Mem. Future Bus. Leaders of Am. (advisor, regional advisor capitol region), Bus. Edn. Assn. Avocations: reading, crafts, children. Home: 4707 SE 314th Pl Washougal WA 98671-9231 Office: Washougal HS 1201 39th St Washougal WA 98671

NESTER, WILLIAM RAYMOND, JR., retired academic administrator and educator; b. Cin., Feb. 19, 1928; s. William Raymond and Evelyn (Blettner) N.; m. Mary Jane Grossman; children: William Raymond, Mark Patrick, Brian Philip, Stephen Christopher. BS, U. Cin., 1950, EdM, 1953, EdD, 1965; DHL (hon.), No. Ky. U., 2001, U. Nebr., 2002. Dir. student union U. Cin., 1952-53, asst. dean of men, 1953-60, dean of men, 1960-67, assoc. prof. edn., 1965-70, dean of students, 1967-69, vice provost student and univ. affairs, 1969-76, prof. edn., 1970-78, assoc. sr. v.p., assoc. provost, 1976-78; v.p. student svcs. Ohio State U., Columbus, 1978-83, prof. edn., 1978-83; pres. Kearney State Coll., Nebr., 1983-91, prof. edn., 1983-93; chancellor U. Nebr., Kearney, 1991-93, prof. emeritus, chancellor emeritus, 1993—; v.p. univ. rels. devel. No. Ky. U., 1996-99. Pres. emeritus Mus. Nebr. Art, 1991—; cons. on higher edn., 1993—. Pres. Metro-Six Athletic Conf., 1975-76. Mem. Am. Assn. State Colls. and Univs. (bd. dirs.), Ctrl. States Intercollegiate Conf. (pres. 1986-89), Nat. Assn. Student Pers. Adminstrs. (past regional v.p., mem. exec. com.), Am. Assn. Higher Edn., Ohio Assn. Student Pers. Adminstrs. (past pres.), Nat. Intrafrat. Conf. (pres. 1991-92), Frat. Scholarship Officers Assn. (past pres.), Mortar Bd., Pi Kappa Alpha (nat. pres. 1978-80, past pres. Pi Kappa Alpha Ednl. Found.), Omicron Delta Kappa, Phi Delta Kappa, Phi Alpha Theta, Phi Eta Sigma, Sigma Sigma. Episcopalian. Home: 7674 Coldstream Dr Cincinnati OH 45255-3932 E-mail: wrnchanem@cs.com.

NETER, JOHN, statistician, educator; b. Germany, Feb. 8, 1923; m. Dorothy Rachman, June 24, 1951; children: Ronald J., David L. BS, U. Buffalo, 1943; MBA, U. Pa., 1947; PhD, Columbia U., 1952. Asst. prof. Syracuse (N.Y.) U., 1949-55, chmn. dept. bus. stats., 1952-55; prof. U. Minn., Mpls., 1955-75, chmn. dept. quantitative analysis, 1961-65; C. Herman and Mary Virginia Terry prof. mgmt. sci., stats. U. Ga., Athens, 1975-89, prof. emeritus, 1990—. Supervisory math. statistician U.S. Bur. Census, 1959-60; chmn. panel on quality control of fed. assistance programs Nat. Acad. Scis., 1986-87; cons. in field. Co-author: Statistical Sampling for Auditors and Accountants, 1956, Fundamental Statistics for Business and Economics, 1956, 4th edit., 1973, Applied Linear Statistical Models, 1974, 4th edit., 1996, Applied Statistics, 1978, 4th edit., 1993, Applied Linear Regression Models, 1983, 3d edit., 1996; editor: Am. Statistician, 1976-80; assoc. editor: Decision Scis., 1973-74; contbr. articles to profl. jours. Chmn. citizens adv. com., City of St. Louis Park, Minn., 1972, mem. planning commn., 1974-75. Served with AUS, 1943-45. Ford Found. faculty research fellow, 1957-58 Fellow Am. Statis. Assn. (council 1963-64, 67-70, dir. 1975-80, pres. 1985), AAAS (chmn., sec. on statistics 1991), Decision Scis. Inst. (pres. 1978-79). Home: 310 St George Dr Athens GA 30606-3910 Office: Terry Coll Bus Univ Ga Athens GA 30602-6255

NETI, SUDHAKAR, mechanical engineering educator; b. Bapatla, India, Sept. 27, 1947; came to U.S., 1968; naturalized, 1977. s. Chiranjeeva Rao and Meenakshi Neti; m. Kathy Gibson, Jan. 11, 1974. BME, Osmania U., 1968; MS, U. Ky., 1970, PhD, 1977. Research asst. U. Ky., 1968-77; asst. prof. mech. engring. Lehigh U., Bethlehem, Pa., 1978-83, assoc. prof., 1983-92, prof., 1992—. Vis. fellow Wolfson Coll., Oxford U., Eng.; vis. rsch. assoc. U.K. Atomic Energy Rsch. Establishment, Harwell, Eng.; fallout shelter analyst Fed. Emergency Mgmt. Adminstrn.; chair Mech. Engring. Thermal-Fluids Divsn., 1996—, dir. Lehigh U. Indsl. Assessment Ctr., 2000—, mem. Lehigh Valley Planning Commn., 1996, 97, bd. dirs. ANS, PANE; cons. to industry. Contbr. articles to profl. jours. Summer faculty fellow NASA-Am. Soc. Engring. Edn., 1978; grantee electric Power Research Inst., Dept. Energy, NSF, NRC. Mem. ASME, AAAS, Sigma Xi (chpt. treas. 1997-2002), Phi Beta Delta. Office: Lehigh U Mech Engring Dept 19 Memorial Dr W Bethlehem PA 18015-3085 E-mail: sn01@lehigh.edu.

NETT, LOUISE MARY, nursing educator, consultant; b. Sept. 25, 1938; Diploma, St. Cloud Sch. Nursing, 1959; cert. in therapy program, Gen. Rose Hosp., Denver, 1967. Staff nurse med. unit Mt. Sinai Hosp., Mpls., 1959-60; staff nurse nursing registry San Francisco, 1960-61; emergency rm. staff nurse Colo. Gen. Hosp., Denver, 1961-62; head nurse Outpatient Clinic Charity Hosp., New Orleans, 1962-64; dir. respiratory care U. Colo. Health Scis. Ctr., Denver, 1965-85, pulmonary program specialist Webb-Waring Lung Inst., 1985-89; rsch. assoc. Presbyn./St. Luke's Ctr. for Health Scis. Edn., Denver, 1989—. Clins. assoc. prof. nursing U. Colo. Sch. Nursing, Denver; adj. asst. prof. U. Kans. Sch. Allied Health; instr. medicine pulmonary divsn. U. Colo. Sch. Medicine, Denver, 1980-89; mem. Nat. Heart, Lung, and Blood Inst. adv. coun., NIH, 1979-82, mem. safety and data monitoring bd. for early intervention for chronic obstructive pulmonary disease, lung divsn., 1985-91; mem. clin. practice guidelines for smoking cessation and presentation panel Agy. for Health Care Policy and Rsch., 1994; dir. numerous courses, confs. in field; worldwide lectr. assns., symposia, confs., TV, convs., meetings, workshops; internat. cons. hosps., health depts., 1975—; local, regional lectr. through med. programs Am. Lung Assn., Am. Cancer Soc. Colo., cmty. hosps., businesses. Author: (with T.L. Petty) For Those Who Live and Breathe with Emphysema and Chronic Bronchitis, 1967, 2d edit., 1971, Enjoying Life with Emphysema, 1984, 2d edit., 1987 (Am. Jour. Nursing Book of Yr. award 1987), Rational Respiratory Therapy, 1988; mem. editl. bd. Heart and Lung Jour., 1972-87, Respiratory Times Newsletter, 1986-88, Jour. Home Health Care Practice, 1988; contbr. articles to profl. jours., chpts. to books. Mem. subcom. on nursing Am. Lung Assn., 1975-76; mem. exec. bd. dirs. Colo. divsn. Am. Cancer Soc., 1984—, chairperson pub. edn. com., 1985-86; mem. exec. com. Am. Stop Smoking Intervention Study, 1991-94, mem. alliance bd. Recipient Rocky Mountain Tobacco Free Challenge Regional award for treatment of nicotine addiction program, 1989, award for ednl. seminars, 1989, award in profl. end., 1992, award for outstanding work in developing and promoting smoking cessation, 1992, profl. educator award, 1993, award for nicotine treatment network, 1993. Mem. ANA, Am. Assn. for Respiratory Care (health promotion com. 1987—, internat. liaison com. 1987-90, Charles H. Hudson Pub. Respiratory Health award 1991), Am. Assn. of Cardio Vascular and Pulmonary Rehab., Am. Thoracic Soc. (ad hoc com. role of non-physician in respiratory care 1972, respiratory therapy com. 1972-74, program planning com. 1989), Behavioral Medicine Soc., Colo. Trudeau Soc. (v.p. 1981, pres.-elect 1982, pres. 1983), Colo. Pub. Health Assn., Internat. Oxygen Club, Internat. Soc. for Humor Studies, Soc. of European Pnemonology. Office: 1850 High St Denver CO 80218-1308

NETTELS, ELSA, English language educator; b. Madison, Wis., May 25, 1931; d. Curtis Putnam and Elsie (Patterson) N. BA, Cornell U., 1953; MA, U. Wis., 1955, PhD, 1960. From instr. to asst. prof. English Mt. Holyoke Coll., South Hadley, Mass., 1959-67; from asst. prof. to prof. English Coll. William and Mary, Williamsburg, Va., 1967-97, prof. emeritus, 1997—. Author: James and Conrad, 1977 (South Atlantic Modern Lang. Assn. award 1975), Language, Race and Social Class in Howells' America, 1988, Language and Gender in American Fiction: Howells, James, Wharton, and Cather, 1997; contbr. articles to profl. jours. NEH fellow, 1984-85. Mem. MLA, South Atlantic MLA (edit. bd. 1977-83), Henry James Soc. (editl. bd. 1983—). Office: Coll William and Mary Dept English Williamsburg VA 23187 E-mail: exnett@wm.edu.

NETTLES, JOHN BARNWELL, obstetrics and gynecology educator; b. Dover, N.C., May 19, 1922; s. Stephen A. and Estelle (Hendrix) N.; m. Eunice Anita Saugstad, Apr. 28, 1956; children: Eric, Robert, John Barnwell; m. 2d, Sandra Williams, Sept. 14, 1991; stepchildren: Steven Williams, Clayton Williams. BS, U. S.C., 1941; MD, Med. Coll. S.C., 1944. Diplomate: Am. Bd. Obstetrics and Gynecology. Intern Garfield Meml. Hosp., Washington, 1944-45; research fellow in pathology Med. Coll. Ga., Augusta, 1946-47; resident in ob-gyn. U. Ill. Rsch. and Ednl. Hosps., Chgo., 1947-51; instr. to asst. prof. ob-gyn. U. Ill. Coll. Medicine, Chgo., 1951-57; asst. prof., assoc. prof., prof. ob-gyn. U. Ark. Med. Ctr., Little Rock, 1957-69; dir. grad. edn. Hillcrest Med. Ctr., Tulsa, 1969-73; prof. ob-gyn Coll. Medicine, U. Okla., Oklahoma City, 1969-78; chmn. dept. ob-gyn. U. Okla.-Tulsa Med. Coll., 1975-80, prof., 1980—, mem. coun. on residency edn. in ob-gyn., 1974-79. Dir. Tulsa Obstet. and Gynecol. Edn. Found., 1969-80; Coordinator med. edn. Nat. Def., Ark., 1961-69; mem. S.W. regional med. adv. com. Planned Parenthood Fedn. Am., 1974-78; mem. adv. com. Health Policy Agenda Am. People, 1982-85, rev. com. Accreditation Coun. for Continuing Med. Edn., 1987-92. Contbr. articles on uterine malignancy, kidney biopsy in pregnancy, perinatal morbidity and mortality, human sexuality sch. age pregnancy to profl. jours. Served as lt. (j.g.) M.C. USNR, 1945-46; as lt. 1953-54. Fellow Am. Coll. Obstetricians and Gynecologists (dist. sec.-treas. 1964-70, dist. chmn. exec. bd. 1970-73, v.p. 1977-78, Disting. Svc. award 1998), ACS (bd. govs. 1969-71, program com. 1970-71, Surg. forum 1977-84, adv. com. gyn/ob 1985-92), Royal Soc. Health, Royal Soc. Medicine; mem. Ark. Obstet. and Gynecol. Soc. (exec. sec. 1959-69), Ctrl. Assn. Obstetrics and Gynecology (exec. com. 1966-69, pres. 1978-79), Internat. Soc. Advancement Humanistic Studies in Gynecology, Assn. Mil. Surgeons U.S., AMA (sect. coun. on obstetrics and gynecology 1975-96, chmn. 1982-96, del. from Am. Coll. Obstetricians and Gynecologists 1987-96, governing coun. sr. physicians group 2003—, Young at Heart award Young Physicians sect. 1994), Nurses Assn. Am. Coll. Obstetricians and Gynecologists (exec. bd. 1970-73, assoc. 1980-95), So. Med. Assn. (chmn. obstetrics 1973-74), Okla. Med. Soc., Tulsa County Med. Soc., Chgo. Med. Soc., Am. Assn. for Maternal and Infant Health, Assn. Am. Med. Colls., Am. Public Health Assn., Am. Assn. Sex Edn. Counselors and Therapists (S.W. regional bd. 1976-79), Soc. for Gynecol. Investigation, AAAS, Am. Soc. for Study Fertility and Sterility, Internat. Soc. Gen. Semantics, So. Gynecol. and Obstet. Soc. (pres. 1981-82), Am. Cancer Soc. (pres. Okla. div. 1979-83, St. George's medal 1991), Com. on In-Tng. Exam. in Obstetrics and Gynecology, Am. Coll. Nurse Midwives (governing bd. examiners 1979-83), Sigma Xi (pres. Tulsa chpt. 1992-93), Phi Rho Sigma. Lutheran. Office: U Okla Health Sci Ctr 1145 S Utica Ave Ste 600 Tulsa OK 74104-4070

NETTROUR, LILA GROFF, biology educator; b. San Francisco; d. Arthur and Mary Ellen (Anderson) Groff; m. Lewis F. Nettrour, Oct. 22, 1966; children: John, Barbara. BA, St. Olaf Coll., 1964; MEd, U. Pitts.,

1966. Microbiologist Mayo Clinic, Rochester, Minn., 1964-65; sci. tchr. Dover Eyota (Minn.) High Sch., 1966-67; part-time instr. Community Coll. Allegheny County, Pitts., 1980-90, assoc. prof. biol. scis., 1991—. Dir. YMCA North Hills, Pitts., 1974-80, chmn. 1980; bd. dirs. St. John's Luth. Ch. Living Gifts and Meml. Fund, Pitts. Mem. AAUW, North Hills Environ. Coun. Office: Community Coll Allegheny Co 8701 Perry Hwy Pittsburgh PA 15237-5353

NEU, CHARLES ERIC, historian, educator; b. Carroll, Iowa, Apr. 10, 1936; s. Arthur Nicholas and Martha Margaret (Frandsen) N.; m. Deborah Dunning, Sept. 2, 1961 (div. 1978); children: Hilary Adams, Douglas Bancroft.; m. Sabina deWerth Tuck, Mar. 27, 1999. BA, Northwestern U., 1958; PhD, Harvard U., 1964. Instr. history Rice U., 1963-64, asst. prof., 1964-67, asso. prof., 1968-70; asso. prof. history Brown U., Providence, 1970-76, prof., 1976—2003, prof. emeritus, 2003—, chmn. dept. history, 1995—98, 1999—2002. Dir. summer seminar NEH, 1979, 1986—87, 1989, 92. Author: An Uncertain Friendship: Theodore Roosevelt and Japan, 1906-1909, 1967, The Troubled Encounter: The United States and Japan, 1975; co-editor: The Wilson Era: Essays in Honor of Arthur S. Link, 1991; editor: After Vietnam: Legacies of a Lost War, 2000. Recipient, Woodrow Wilson Found. fellowship, 1958—59, Am. Coun. Learned Socs. fellowship, 1975—76, Charles Warren Ctr. fellowship, 1971—72, Howard Found. fellowship, 1976—77, Guggenheim fellowship, 1981—82, NEH scholarship, 1968—69, guest scholarship, Woodrow Wilson Ctr., 1988, Barrett Hazeltine citation for disting. undergrad. tchg., 1998. Mem. Am. Hist. Assn., Orgn. Am. Historians, Soc. Historians of Am. Fgn. Policy, Phi Beta Kappa. Democrat. Home: 4929 SW 71st Place Miami FL 33155 E-mail: cneu@bellsouth.net.

NEU, IRENE DOROTHY, historian, educator; b. Cin. d. Frederick Francis and Mary Clara (Holterman) Neu; m. Robert Leslie Jones, Nov. 25, 1976. BA, Marietta Coll., 1944; MA, Cornell U., 1945, PhD, 1950. Fellow, Rsch. Ctr. Entrepreneurial History Harvard U., Cambridge, Mass., 1950—51; instr. Rockford (Ill.) Coll., 1951—52, Conn. Coll., New London, 1953—54; assoc. prof. history S.E. Mo. State Coll., Cape Girardeau, 1956—62, prof. history, 1962—64; assoc. prof. history Ind. U., Bloomington, 1964—70, prof. history, 1970—86, prof. emeritus history, 1986—. Author: Erastus Corning, Merchant and Financier, 1794-1872, 1960; co-author: The American Railroad Network, 1861-1890, 1956; contbr. articles to profl. jours. Fulbright fellow, Italy, 1954—55, Social Sci. Rsch. Coun. faculty fellow, 1960—61, Eleutherian Mills Hist. Libr. sr. fellow, 1970. Mem.: Ind. Hist. Soc., Bus. History Conf., Orgn. Am. Historians, Phi Beta Kappa. Home: 206 Brentwood St Marietta OH 45750-1509

NEUBERG, JOEL GARY, librarian; b. Chgo., June 11, 1945; s. LeRoy and Sari (Platt) N.; m. Pamela Susan Haas, June 12, 1970; 1 child, Jacob Michael. BA in English, U. Calif., Berkeley, 1967; MA in English and Creative Writing, San Francisco State U., 1972; AA in Forest Tech., Santa Rosa (Calif.) Jr. Coll., 1979; MLS, San Jose State U., 1997. Corres. Press Dem., Santa Rosa, 1972-74; park ranger Sonomoa County and Calif. State Parks, Bodega Bay, 1977-81; exec. dir. Holocaust Libr. & Rsch. Ctr., San Francisco, 1983-91; libr. El Molino High Sch., Forestville, Calif., 1991—2002, Sonoma Acad., Santa Rosa, Calif., 2002—. Instr. Santa Rosa Jr. Coll., 1973—, lectr. Sonoma State U., 2002—. Author: Out of the Promised Land Into the Wilderness, 1972; (with Jacob Boas) Kristallnacht: The Night of Broken Glass, 1988; editor: Kobrin Memorial Book, 1992. Vol. U.S. Peace Corps., Niger, West Africa, 1967-69; field supr., asst. dir. Student Conservation Assn., Charlestown, N.H., 1972-88; bd. dirs. Gold Ridge Resource Conservation Dist., Sebastopol, Calif., 1978-81; bd. dirs. Holocaust Ctr. No. Calif., San Francisco, 1991—, treas. 1994. Recipient Beyond War award, 1987, Cert. of Appreciation, ALA, 1991; Weyerhaeuser Lumber Co. Merit scholar, 1963-67; Calif. Coun. Humanities grantee, 1986; Mandel fellow U.S. Holocaust Meml. Mus., 1998. Mem. Alliance For Study of Holocaust (bd. dirs. 1983—, treas. 1984, pres. 1999-), Assn. of Holocaust Orgns. (bd. dirs. 1988-94). Republican. Jewish. Avocations: back-packing, cross-country skiing, swimming, photography, foreign languages. Office: Sonoma Acad 50 Mark West Springs Rd Santa Rosa CA 95403 E-mail: jneuberg@santarosa.edu.

NEUDECK, GEROLD WALTER, electrical engineering educator; b. Beach, N.D., Sept. 25, 1936; s. Adolph John and Helen Annette (Kramer) N.; m. Mariellen Kristine MacDonald, Sept. 1, 1962; children: Philip Gerold, Alexander John. BSEE, U. N.D., 1959, MSEE, 1960; PhD in Elec. Engring., Purdue U., 1969. Asst. prof. U. N.D., Grand Forks, 1960-64; grad. instr. Purdue U., West Lafayette, Ind., 1964-68, asst. prof., 1968-71, assoc. prof., 1971-77, prof. elec. engring., 1977—, asst. dean engring., 1988-90, assoc. dir. NSF/ERC Engring., 1988-94, dir. Optoelectronics Rsch. Ctr., 1993-96. Cons. in field. Author: Electric Circuit Analysis and Design, 1976, 2d edit., 1987, Junction Diode/Bipolar Transisters, 1983, 2d edit., 1989; author, editor: Modular Series on Solid State Devices, 1983; contbr. over 250 articles to profl. jours.; inventor/14 U.S. patents in field. Bd. dirs. W. Lafayette Devel. Commn., 1990—, Greater Lafayette Pub. Transp., 1975-80; pres. Lafayette Tennis, 1976-78. Recipient Dow Outstanding Faculty award Am. Soc. Engring. Edn., 1972, Western Elec. Fund award, 1974-75, D.D. Ewing award Purdue U., 1973, A.A. Potter award, 1973, Honeywell Teaching award, 1995, Aristotle award Semicondr. Rsch., 2001. Fellow IEEE (Harry S. Nyquist award 1992, editor Transactions on Electron Devices 1994-97); mem. Am. Vacuum Soc., Sigma Xi, Eta Kappa Nu, Sigma Tau, Sigma Pi Sigma. Avocations: tennis, backpacking, fishing, woodworking, bread baking. Office: Purdue U 1285 Elec Engring Bldg West Lafayette IN 47907-1285

NEUGER, SANFORD, orthodontics educator; b. Cleve., Aug. 17, 1925; s. Samuel and Ethel (Manheim) N.; m. Marjorie Odess, Sept. 8, 1963; 1 child, Howard Michael. BS, Western Res. U., 1947, DDS, 1953; MS in Orthodontics, Ind. U., 1957. Diplomate Am. Bd. Orthodontics. Orthodontics demonstrator Western Res. U., Cleve., 1957-58; asst. prof., assoc. prof. orthodontics Western Res. U./Case Western Res. U., Cleve., 1958-75; clin. prof. orthodontics Case Western Res. U., Cleve., 1975—, acting chmn. Orthodontics Dept., 1969-71. Asst. dental surgeon U. Hosp., Cleve., 1967—. Author: (syllabus) Contemporary Edgewise Mechanics-Sliding Mechanics, 1973, Limited Tooth Movement, 1970; author-presenter: (videotape) Orthodontics Soldering, 1970. Vol. United Way, 1988, Case Western Res. U. Alumni Assn., Jewish Nat. Fund. Comdr. USNR (ret. 1972). Named Man of Yr. Case Western Res. U. Orthodontics alumni, 1982. Fellow Am. Coll. Dentists; mem. Am. Dental Soc., Cleve. Dental Soc. (bd. dirs. 11965-90), Cleve. Soc. Orthodontists (pres. 1969)., Great Lakes Assn. Orthodontists Assn., Am. Assn. Orthodontists, Pierre Fauchard Soc., Alpha Omega (pres. Cleve. chpt. 1984-85), Omicron Kappa Upsilon. Jewish. Avocation: replicar building. Home: 24850 Hilltop Dr Cleveland OH 44122-1350 Office: 1500 S Green Rd Cleveland OH 44121-4080

NEULS-BATES, CAROL, business executive, musicologist; b. Bklyn., Dec. 1, 1939; d. Frederick Carl and Edith (Tindall) Neuls; m. William Boulton Jr. Bates, Sept. 1, 1962; 1 child, Julia Barstow Bates. BA cum laude, Wellesley Coll., 1961; PhD, Yale U., 1970; postgrad., NYU Sch. Bus. Adminstrn., 1979. Mng. editor RILM: Abstracts of Music Lit., Grad Ctr. CUNY, 1972—75; project dir., co-prin. investigator Women in Am. Music, 1976—79; adj. asst. prof. music Hunter Coll., CUNY, 1973—75; asst. to curator Lincoln Ctr. Libr. Performing Arts, 1975—76; asst. editor Coll. Music Symposium, 1975—78; asst. prof. music Bklyn. Coll., CUNY, 1978—82; account supr. John O'Donnell Co., N.Y.C., 1982—85, v.p., 1986—. Author: (books) Women in Music: An Anthology of Source Readings from the Middle Ages to the Present, 1982, 1995, Women in American Music: A Bibliography of Music and Literature, 1979; contbr. articles to music and women's studies jours., to New Grove's Dictionary of Music and Musicians series. Fellow, Yale U., 1962—67; grantee, Radcliffe Inst., 1968—70, Nat. Endowment for the Humanities, 1976—79, Ford Found., 1977—79, Nat. Fedn. Music Clubs, 1978. Mem.: NOW, Women in Devel., Nat. Soc. Fund Raising Execs., Nat. Women's Studies Assn., Inst. Rsch. in History, Sonneck Soc., Am. Musicol. Soc., Coll. Music Soc. (coun. 1975—78).

NEUMAN, ROBERT STERLING, art educator, artist; b. Kellogg, Idaho, Sept. 9, 1926; s. Oscar C. and Katherine (Samuelson) N.; m. Helen Patricia Feddersen, Apr. 6, 1947 (div. 1971); children— Ingrid Alexandra, Elizabeth Catherine; m. Sunne Savage, June 3, 1979; 1 dau., Christina Mary. Student, U. Idaho, 1944-46; BAA., M.F.A., Calif. Coll. Arts and Crafts, 1947-51; student, San Francisco Sch. Fine Arts, 1950-51, Mills Coll., 1951. Assoc. prof. art Brown U., 1962-63; lectr. drawing Carpenter Center for Visual Arts, Harvard, 1963-72; prof. art, chmn. dept. Keene (N.H.) State Coll., 1972-90. Exhbns. include, Mus. Modern Art, Whitney Mus. Am. Art, Carnegie Internat., San Francisco Mus. Art, Boston Mus. Fine Arts, Worcester (Mass.) Art Mus., also, Japan and Europe. Served with AUS and USAAF, 1945-46. Recipient Howard Found. award for painting, 1967; Fulbright grantee, 1953-54; Guggenheim fellow, 1956-57; Bender grantee San Francisco Art Assn., 1952. Home: 135 Cambridge St Winchester MA 01890-2411

NEUMAN, TOM S. emergency medical physician, educator; b. N.Y.C., July 23, 1946; s. Otto and Susan Ann (Baltaxe) N.; m. Doris Rubin, Aug. 24, 1969; children: Allison Rachel, Russell Solomon. AB, Cornell U., 1967; MD, NYU, 1971. Diplomate Nat. Bd. Med. Examiners, Am. Bd. Internal Medicine, Am. Bd. Pulmonary Diseases, Am. Bd. Preventive Medicine in Occupl. Medicine and Underseas and Hyperbaric Medicine), Am. Bd. Emergency Medicine. Intern Bellevue Hosp., N.Y.C., 1971-72, resident, 1972-73; commd. med. officer USN, 1973; advanced through grades to capt. USNR, 1990; instr. Naval Undersea Med. Inst., New London, Conn., 1973-74; staff med. officer Submarine Devel. Group One, San Diego, 1974-76, 78-80; emergency room physician Chula Vista (Calif.) Community Hosp., 1975-80; attending physician VA Med. Ctr., La Jolla, Calif., 1976-78; fellow in pulmonary medicine and physiology U. Calif. Sch. Medicine at San Diego, 1976-78, clin. instr., 1978-80, asst. clin. prof., 1980-84, flight physician Life Flight Aeromed. Program, 1980-86, asst. dir. dept. emergency medicine, 1980-94, assoc. dir. dept. emergency medicine, 1994—, attending physician pulmonary divsn., 1980-99, assoc. clin. prof. medicine and surgery, 1984-87, base hosp. physician, 1984—, dir. Hyperbaric Med. Ctr., 1984—; med. officer UDT/SEAL Res. Unit 119, San Diego, 1980-84, Mobile Diving and Salvage Unit One, USNR, San Diego, 1984-86, PRIMUS Unit 1942-A, U. Calif. at San Diego, 1988-90; sr. med. officer Seal Teams 1/3/5, USNR, Coronado, Calif., 1986-87; asst. officer in charge Med. Unit 1942-A U. Calif. Sch. Medicine, San Diego, 1990-95, prof. clin. medicine, 1996—. Mem. med. adv. bd. western regional underwater lab. program U. So. Calif. Marine Sci. Ctr., Catalina, 1982—85; assoc. adj. prof. medicine and surgery U. Calif. Sch. Medicine at San Diego, 1987—90, adj. prof. medicine and surgery, 1990—96, prof. clin. medicine and adj. prof. surgery, 1996—; mem. San Diego Coroner's com. for investigation of diving fatalities, 1974—; mem. diving cons. Vocat. Diver Tng. Facility, Calif. Inst. Med., Chino, 1967; mem. task force City Mgr. on Carbon Monoxide Poisoning, San Diego, 1991; mem. com. for minimal course content for recreational scuba instr. cert. Am. Nat. Stds. Inst., 1992—94, chmn. emergency med. physician quality improvement com., 1992—94; mem. undersea and hyperbaric medicine exam subcom. Am. Bd. Preventative Medicine, 1999—; mem. com. on creating vision for space medicine beyond earth orbit, mem. com. on extreme environments NAS; mem. com. longitudinal study of astronaut health NAS-IOM; cons. NASA. Author: book chpts.; contbr. articles to profl. jours.; editor: textbooks. Fellow ACP, Am. Coll. Preventive Medicine; mem. Am. Thoracic Soc., Am. Lung Assn., Undersea and Hyperbaric Med. Soc. (program com. 1981-82, nominations com. 1982-83, chmn. 1988-89, mem. edn. com. 1982-87, chmn. awards com. 1983-84, v.p. exec. com. 1983-84, co-chmn. credentials com. 1984-85, editor-in-chief Undersea and Hyperbaric Medicine 1995—2002), Profl. Assn. Diving Instrs. (emeritus), NAS-IOM (com. on extreme environment, com. on longitudinal study of astronaut health). Avocations: scuba diving, fishing, photography. Office: U Calif Med Ctr Dept Emergency Medicine 200 W Arbor Dr Dept 8676 San Diego CA 92103-8676 E-mail: tneuman@ucsd.edu.

NEUMANN, CHARLES HENRY, mathematician, educator; b. Washington, Jan. 30, 1943; s. Bernhardt Walter and Emma (Habitz) Neumann; m. Cheryl Elaine Girard, June 18, 1965; children: Matthew Roy, Kristen Elizabeth. AS, Alpena (Mich.) CC, 1962; BS in Math., Mich. State U., 1964, MAT. in Math., 1965. Sci. tchr. Alpena (Mich.) Pub. Schs., 1965-66; instr. math. Alpena CC, 1966-84, math. sci. dept. chair, 1969-84; prof. Oakland CC, Bloomfield Hills, Mich., 1984—. Scoutmaster troop 92 Boy Scouts Am., Alpena, 1981—84; bd. dirs. Luth. Social Svcs. Mich., 1996—, v.p., 1999—; trustee Mich. Edn. Spl. Svcs., 1975—93, 2002—, pres., 1976—93; mem. exec. com. Oakland County Dem. Com., Mich., 1995—96; bd. dirs. Mich. Vision Svc. Assn., Columbus, 1985—89, Ohio Vision Svc. Assn., 1988—89, Blue Cross Blue Shield Mich., 1986—94. Mem.: NEA (del. 1974—80, mem. adv. com. membership 1993—96), Oakland CC Faculty Assn. (v.p. 1994—95, 1998—2001, pres. 1995—98), Mich. Assn. Higher Edn. (v.p. two-yr. colls. 1970—96, 2002—), Mich. Math. Assn. Two-Yr. Colls., Mich. Edn. Assn. (bd. dirs. 1974—80), Am. Math. Assn. Two-Yr. Colls., Math. Assn. Am., Phi Kappa Phi. Lutheran. Avocations: collecting antique books, racquetball, cross country skiing. Home: 5871 Warbler Clarkston MI 48346-2973 Office: Oakland CC 2900 Featherstone Rd Auburn Hills MI 48326-2817

NEUMEIER, MATTHEW MICHAEL, lawyer, educator; b. Racine, Wis., Sept. 13, 1954; s. Frank Edward and Ruth Irene (Effenberger) N.; m. Annmarie Prine, Jan. 31, 1987; children: Ruthann Marie, Emilie Irene, Matthew Charles. B in Gen. Studies with distinction, U. Mich., 1981; JD magna cum laude, Harvard U., 1984. Bar: NY 1987, Mich. 1988, Ill. 1991, US Dist. Ct. (ea. dist.) Mich. 1988, US Dist. Ct. (ea., no. dists. and trial bar) Ill. 1991, US Ct. Appeals (7th cir.) 1992, US Ct. Appeals (fed. cir.) 1998, US Supreme Ct. 1991. Sec.-treas. Ind. Roofing & Siding Co., Escanaba, Mich., 1973-78; mng. ptnr. Ind. Roofing Co., Menominee, Mich., 1977-78; law clk. to presiding justice US Ct. Appeals (9th cir.), San Diego, 1984-85; law clk. to chief justice Warren E. Burger US Supreme Ct., Washington, 1985-86; spl. asst. to chmn. US Constn. Bicentennial Commn., Washington, 1986; assoc. Cravath, Swaine & Moore, NYC, 1986-88; spl. counsel Burnham & Ritchie, Ann Arbor, Mich., 1988; assoc. Schlussel, Lifton, Simon, Rands, Galvin & Jackier, P.C., Ann Arbor, Mich., 1988-90, Skadden, Arps, Slate, Meagher & Flom, Chgo., 1990-96; ptnr. Jenner & Block, Chgo., 1996—. Adj. prof. computer law and high tech. litig. John Marshall Law Sch., Chgo., 1999—. Editor Harvard Law Rev., 1982-84. Pres., bd. dir. Univ. Cellar Inc., Ann Arbor, 1979-81; bd. dir. Econ. Devel. Corp., Menominee, 1978-79, Midwestern divsn. Am. Suicide Found., sec., 1992-97, Commonwealth Plaza Condominium Assn., dir., 1999—, pres., 2000—, Harvard Law Soc. Ill., 2003-; mem. vestry Ch. Our Savior, 1997-2000; bd. dir. Chgo. Children's Mus., 1999—, sec., 2003-; chmn. Harvard Law Sch. 15 Yr. Reunion Gift Fund, 1999. Mem. ABA, State Bar Mich., Assn. of Bar of City of NY, Chgo. Bar Assn., Def. Rsch. Inst., The 410 Club, Econ. Club Chgo, City Club of Chgo. Republican. Avocations: classic automobiles, piano, choir. Office: Jenner & Block Ste 4200 One IBM Plz Chicago IL 60611 E-mail: mneumeier@jenner.com.

NEUNZIG, CAROLYN MILLER, elementary, middle and high school educator; b. L.I., May 5, 1930; kd. Stanley and Grace (Walsh) Miller; m. Herbert Neunzig, May 28, 1955; children: Kurt Miller, Keith Weidler. BA, Beaver Coll., Glen Side, Pa., 1953; MSSc, Syracuse U., 1989; postgrad., Adelphi U.; Cert., N.C. State U., Raleigh. Cert. in elem. edn., reading, history and English, N.C., permanent cert. in secondary English, N.Y. Reading tchr. grades K-6 St. Timothy's Sch., Raleigh, N.C., 1971-83, 5th grade tchr., 1983-88, 5th grade lead tchr., 1986-88; tchr. English and geography 7th grade St. Timothy's Mid. Sch., Raleigh, 1991—; tchr Am. govt. 12th grade St. Timothy's Mid. Sch./Hale H.S., Raleigh, 1991-93. Instr. continuing edn. program history Meredith Coll., Raleigh, 1990-91, spl. high sch. registration commr., 1991-93, instr. presdl. classroom, 1998, 99; mem. Ctr. for Study of Presidency, 1998-2003. Asst. election ofcl. Wake County, N.C., 2003. Mem. AAUW, Am. Acad. Polit. and Social Sci., Acad. Polit. Sci., Ctr. for Study of the Presidency, Churchill Ctr. E-mail: c.neunzig@gte.net.

NEUSCHEL, ROBERT PERCY, management consultant, educator; b. Hamburg, N.Y., Mar. 13, 1919; s. Percy J. and Anna (Becker) N.; m. Dorothy Virginia Maxwell, Oct. 20, 1944; children: Kerr Anne Ziprick, Carla Becker Neuschel Wyckoff, Robert Friedrich (Fritz). BA, Denison U., 1941; MBA, Harvard U., 1947. Indsl. engr. Sylvania Elec. Products Co., Inc., 1947-49; with McKinsey & Co., Inc., 1950-79, sr. partner, dir., 1967-79; prof. corp. governance, assoc. dean J. L. Kellogg Grad. Sch. Mgmt.; former dir. Northwestern U., assoc. dean J.L. Kellogg Sch. Mgmt. Mem. exec. bd. Internat. Air Cargo Forum, 1988—; mem. com. study air passenger svc. and safety NRC, 1989—; bd. dirs. Butler Mfg. Co., Combined Ins. Co. Am., Templeton, Kenley & Co., U.S. Freightways Co.; lectr. in field; mem. McKinsey Found. Mgmt. Rsch., Inc.; transp. task force Reagan transition team; chmn. bd. dirs. Internat. Intermodal Expn. Atlanta. Author: The Servant Leader: Unleashing the Power of Your People, 1998; co-author: Emerging Issues in Corporate Governance, 1983; contbr. over 125 articles to profl. jours. Pres. Bd. Edn., Lake Forest, Ill., 1965-70; rep. Nat. council Boy Scouts Am., 1970—, mem. N.E. exec. coun., 1969—; chmn. bd. Lake Forest Symphony, 1973; bd. dirs. Loyola U., Chgo., Chgo. Boys' Club, Nat. Ctr. Voluntary Action, Inst. Mgmt. Consultants; trustee N. Suburban Mass Transit, 1972-73, Loyola Med. Ctr.; mem. adv. coun. Kellogg Grad. Sch. Mgmt., Northwestern U., White House conferee Drug Free Am.; mem. Nat. Petroleum Coun. Transp. and Supply Com. Served to capt. USAAF, World War II. Named Transporation Man of Yr. Chitransp. Assoc., 1994; recipient Salzberg medallion Syracuse U., 1999. Fellow Acad. Advancement Corp. Governance; mem. Transp. Assn. Am., Nat. Def. Transp. Assn. (subcom. transp. tech. agenda 1990—), Intermodal Assn. N.Am. (chmn. bd. dirs.), Harvard Bus. Sch. Club (pres. 1964-65), Economic Club (named Internat. Educator of Yr., 2000), Exec. Club, Chgo. (Ill.) Club, Mid-Am. Club, Mid-Day Club. Presbyn. Home: 101 Sunset Pl Lake Forest IL 60045-1834 Office: 2001 Sheridan Rd Evanston IL 60208-0849 E-mail: cs-neuschel@nwu.edu.

NEVANS, LAUREL S. rehabilitation counselor; b. N.Y.C., Aug. 1, 1964; d. Roy N. and Virginia (Place) Nevans; m. Russell Baird Palmer III, Oct. 12, 1991 (div. Jan. 2001). BA in English, Secondary Edn. cum laude, U. Richmond, 1986, postgrad., 1989-92; MA in Edn. and Human Devel., George Washington U., 1991, cert. in job devel. and placement, 1992. Group leader S.E. Consortium for Spl. Svcs., Larchmont, NY, 1980—85; vocat. instr. Assn. for Retarded Citizens Montgomery County, Rockville, Md., 1986—89; edn. specialist George Washington U. Out of Sch. Work Experience Program, Washington, 1989—90; rsch. asst. George Washington U. Dept. Tchr. Prep. & Spl. Edn., Washington, 1989—91; employability skills tchr., rsch. intern Nat. Rehab. Hosp. Rehab. Engring. Dept., Washington, 1991; vocat./ind. living skills specialist The Independence Ctr., Rockville, Md., 1991—93; leadership team mgr. Career Choice project The Endependence Ctr. of No. Va., Arlington, 1993—94; program dir. United Cerebral Palsy of D.C. and No. Va., Washington, 1994—97; sr. assistive tech. specialist Tech., Automation & Mgmt., Inc., Greenbelt, Md., 1997—98; owner WebLaurels Designs, Silver Spring, Md., 1998—, Artist-Crafts, 2001—, Clayers with Disabilities Listserv (electronic discussion list), 2002—, Artist Crafts, Silver Spring, 2001—. Teaching asst. Rehab. Counseling Program, George Washington U., 1991; moderator FPList Electronic Discussion List, 2000—; owner Clayers with Disabilities Electronic Discussion List, 2002- . Bd. mem., newsletter editor Cameron Hill Owners Assn., 2002—. Recipient traineeship GWU Counseling Dept., 1990, 91. Mem. Nat. Rehab. Assn., Nat. Rehab. Counselors Assn., D.C. Met. Area Assn. Person's in Supported Employment (editor newsletter 1995-97), Nat. Career Devel. Assn., Nat. Employment Counseling Assn., Nat. Assn. Ind. Living, Am. Assn. Counseling and Devel., Am. Rehab. Counseling Assn., Nat. Polymer Clay Guild. Democrat. Avocations: writing, photography, music, travel, jewelry making. Home: 8501 Cameron St Silver Spring MD 20910-3466 E-mail: laurel@artistcrafts.com.

NEVILL, WILLIAM ALBERT, chemistry educator; b. Indpls., Jan. 1, 1929; s. Irwin Lowell and Mary Marie (Barker) N.; m. Nancy Neiman (Roll), May 19, 1979; children: Paul David, John Michael, Steven Joseph, Anne Marie, Deborah Ruth. BS, Butler U., 1951; PhD, Calif. Inst. of Tech., 1954. Rsch. chemist Procter and Gamble, Cin., 1954; chemistry prof., chmn. dept. Grinnell Coll., 1956-67; prof. chemistry Ind. U., Purdue, Indpls., 1967-83, chmn. dept., 1967-72, dean sch. sci., 1972-79, dir. grad. studies, 1979-83; pres. B and N Cons. Co., 1972-93; vice chancellor acad. affairs La. State U., Shreveport, La., 1983-85, prof., 1983-94; pres. Catoctin Assoc., 1993—. Arbitrator, mediator, Ind. Employment Rels. Bd., 1975-83. Author: Gen. Chemistry, 1967, Expt. in Gen. Chemistry, 1968. Bd. dir. Indpls. Sci. and Engring. Found., 1972-75, 79-82, Westminster Found., Lafayette, Ind., 1972-74, Am. Chem. Soc., 1986-92. With U.S. Army, 1954-56; col., USAR, 1956-84. Grantee NSF, 1959-74; Grantee NIH, 1963-70; Grantee Office Naval Rsch., 1953 Mem. Ind. Acad. Sci., Am. Chem. Soc., chmn. sect. 1972, counselor 1973-92. Presbyterian.

NEVINS, LYN (CAROLYN A. NEVINS), educational supervisor, trainer, consultant; b. Chelsea, Mass., June 9, 1948; d. Samuel Joseph and Stella Theresa (Maronski) N.; m. John Edward Herbert, Jr., May 1, 1979; children: Chrissy, Johnny. BA in Sociology, Edn., U. Mass., 1970; MA in Women's Studies, George Washington U., 1975. Cert. tchr., trainer. Tchr. social studies Greenwich (Conn.) Pub. Schs., 1970-74; rschr. career/vocat. edn. Conn. State Dept. Edn., Hartford, 1975-76; rschr., career/vocat. edn. Area Coop. Edn. Svcs., Hamden, Conn., 1976-77; program mgr., trainer career edn. and gender equity Coop. Ednl. Svcs., Norwalk, Conn., 1977-83, trainer, mgr., devel., Beginning Educator Support and Tng. program Fairfield, Conn., 1987—; state coord. career edn. Conn. State Dept. Edn., Hartford, 1982-83; supr. Sacred Heart U., Fairfield, 1992—. Bias com. Conn. State Dept. Edn., Hartford, 1981—; vision com. Middlesex Mid. Sch., Darien, Conn., 1993-95; mem. ednl. quality and diversity com. Town of Darien, 1993-95; cons., trainer career devel./pre-retirement planning Cohen and Assocs., Fairfield, 1981—, Farren Assocs., Annandale, Va., 1992—, Tracey Robert Assocs., Fairfield, 1994—; freelance cons., trainer, Darien, 1983-87; presenter Nat. Conf. GE, 1980, Career Edn., 1983, Am. Edn. Rsch. Assn., 1991; lectr. in field. Tennis coach Spl. Olympics, 1993—, Darien (Conn.) Girls' Softball League, 1992-96, tennis coord. Spl. Olympics Summer Games, 1997—; mem. bldg. com. Darien (Conn.) High Sch., 1999—. Mem. NOW (founder, state coord. edn. 1972-74), ASCD. Avocations: tennis, running, walking, golf, travel. Home: 4 Hollister Ln Darien CT 06820-5404 Office: Coop Ednl Svcs 40 Lindeman Drive Trumbull CT 06611-4723

NEVSIMAL, ERVIN L. elementary education educator; Phys. sci. tchr. Adams Jr. High Sch., Tampa, Fla., 1995, Gaither H.S., Tampa, 1995—. Recipient Exemplary Middle Level Sci. Teaching award, CIBA-Geigy, 1992. Office: Gaither High Sch 16200 N Dale Mabry Hwy Tampa FL 33618-1300

NEW, ELOISE OPHELIA, special education educator; b. Jeffersonville, Ind., Jan. 14, 1942; d. Ivan Foster and Nellie Katherine (Harman) Baugh; m. Paul Eugene New, Nov. 23, 1961; children: Paula, Paul Jr. BS in Elem. Edn., Eastern Ky. U., 1963; MA in Edn., Coll. Mt. St. Joseph, 1987. Cert.

elem. K-8, and developmentally handicapped tchr. K-12, Ohio. Tchr. Newport (Ky.) City Schs., 1963-69, Ross County and Chillicothe (Ohio) City Schs., 1977-78; developmentally handicapped tchr. Mt. Logan Middle Sch., Chillicothe, 1979—. Tchr. Sunday sch. Tabernacle Bapt. Ch., Chillicothe, 1987-93, chmn. elem. edn. com., 1988-93, Sunday sch. supt., 1994-2002, mem. christian Bd. Edn., 1988-2002; spokesperson for edn. selectin Chillicothe Edn. Found., 1989. Recipient Excellence in Edn. award Pllasco-Ross Adminstrn. Conf. for Spl. Educators, 1984, Ohio Jennings Scholar award, 1991-93. Mem. NEA, Ohio Edn. Assn., Chillicothe Edn. Assn. (rep. 1986-88). Baptist. Home: 614 Fawndale Pl Gahanna OH 43230 Office: Mt Logan Mid Sch 841 E Main St Chillicothe OH 45601-3509

NEW, JOHN GERARD, neuroscientist, educator; b. Detroit, Mar. 25, 1956; s. John McCaffery and Veronica Catherine (Maguire) N.; m. Katherine Anne Saxe, Apr. 18, 1981; children: Phillip Devlin, Evan Murdoch. BS in Marine Biology, U. Mass., 1978; MS in Neurobiology, U. Mich., 1981; PhD in Neurobiology, Wesleyan U., 1987. Asst. scientist Warner-Lambert/Parke-Davis, Ann Arbor, Mich., 1978-81; tchr., rsch. asst. Wesleyan U., Middletown, Conn., 1981-86; postdoctoral fellow Ctr. Nat. Rsch. Sci., Gif-sur-Yvette, France, 1987, Scripps Instn. Oceanography, La Jolla, Calif., 1987-89; asst. prof. dept. biology Loyola U., Chgo., 1989-95, assoc. prof. dept. biology, 1995—2001, prof. dept. biology, 2001—. Grass fellow Marine Biology Lab., Woods Hole, Mass., 1989; adj. assoc. prof. Parmly Hearing Inst., 1995—2001, adj. prof., 2001—; vis. scholar Scripps Instn. Oceanography, 1996, Hawaii Inst. Marine Biology, U. Hawaii, 2002. Contbr. articles to profl. jours. Recipient Fgn. Exch. fellow Found. Simone et Cino del Duca, Paris, 1987, award Capranica Found., 1991, Rsch. grant NIH, 1987—. Mem. Soc. Neurosci., Am. Elasmobranch Soc., Internat. Soc. Neuroethology, JB Johnston Club. Avocations: sailing, scuba diving, historical studies, iaido. Office: Loyola U Dept Biology 6525 N Sheridan Rd Chicago IL 60626-5344 E-mail: jnew@luc.edu.

NEW, ROSETTA HOLBROCK, home economics educator, nutrition consultant; b. Hamilton, Ohio, Aug. 26, 1921; d. Edward F. and Mabel (Kohler) Holbrock; m. John Lorton New, Sept. 3, 1943; 1 child, John Lorton Jr. BS, Miami U., Oxford, Ohio, 1943; MA, U. No. Colo., 1971; PhD, The Ohio State U., 1974; student Kantcentrum, Brugge, Belgium, 1992, Lesage Sch. Embroidery, Paris, 1995, Kent State U., 1998. Cert. tchr., Colo. Tchr. English and sci. Monahans (Tex.) H.S., 1943-45; emergency war food asst. U.S. Dept. Agr., College Station, Tex., 1945-46; dept. chmn. home econs., adult edn. Hamilton (Ohio) Pub. Schs., 1946-47; tchr., dept. chmn. home econs. East H.S., Denver, 1948-59, Thomas Jefferson H.S., Denver, 1959-83; mem. exec. bd. Denver Pub. Schs.; also lectr.; exec. dir. Ctr. Nutrition Info. U.S. Office of Edn. grantee Ohio State U., 1971-73. Mem. Cin. Art Mus., Nat. Trust for Historic Preservation. Mem. Am. Home Econs. Assn., Am. Vocat. Assn., Embroiders Guild Am., Hamilton Hist. Soc., Internat. Old Lacers, Ohio State U. Assn., Ohio State Home Econs. Alumni Assn., Fairfield (Ohio) Hist. Soc., Republican Club of Denver, Internat. Platform Assn., Phi Upsilon Omicron. Presbyterian. Lodges: Masons, Daughters of the Nile, Order of Eastern Star, Order White Shrine of Jerusalem. Home and Office: 615 Crescent Rd Hamilton OH 45013-3432

NEWBERRY, CONRAD FLOYDE, aerospace engineering educator; b. Neodesha, Kans., Nov. 10, 1931; s. Ragan McGregor and Audra Anitia (Newmaster) N.; m. Sarah Louise Thonn, Jan. 26, 1958; children: Conrad Floyde Jr., Thomas Edwin, Susan Louise. AA, Independence Jr. Coll., 1951; BEME with aero. sequence, U. So. Calif., 1957; MSME, Calif. State U., Los Angeles, 1971, MA in Edn., 1974; D.Environ. Sci. and Engring., UCLA, 1985. Registered profl. engr., Calif., Kans., N.C., Tex.; chartered engr., U.K. Mathematician L.A. divsn. N.Am. Aviation Inc., 1951-53, jr. engr., 1953-54, engr., 1954-57, sr. engr., 1957-64; asst. prof. aerospace engring. Calif. State Poly. U., Pomona, 1964-70, assoc. prof. aerospace engring., 1970-75, prof. aerospace engring., 1975-90, prof. emeritus, 1990—; staff engr. EPA, 1980-82; engring. specialist space transp. systems div. Rockwell Internat. Corp., 1984-90; prof. aeronautics and astronautics Naval Postgrad. Sch., Monterey, Calif., 1990—2002, prof. emeritus, 2002—, acad. assoc. space systems engring., 1992-94. Recipient John Leland Atwood award as outstanding aerospace engring. educator AIAA/Am. Soc. Engring. Edn., 1986, Fred Merryfield Design award ASEE, 1997. Fellow: AIAA (dep. dir. edn. region VI 1976—79, dep. dir. career enhancement 1982—91, chmn. L.A. sect. 1989—90, chmn. acad. affairs com. 1990—93, dir.tech. aircraft sys. 1990—93, chmn. Point Lobos sect. 1990—91, 1999—2001); mem.: IEEE, ASME, AAAS, NSPE, Am. Soc. Naval Engrs., Nat. Assn. Environ. Profls., Calif. Water Pollution Control Assn., Assn. Unmanned Vehicle Sys. Internat., Soc. Allied Weight Engrs., Soc. Automotive Engr., Water Environ. Fedn., Exptl. Aircraft Assn., Inst. Environ. Scis., Air and Waste Mgmt. Assn., Soc. Naval Architects and Marine Engrs., Am. Helicopter Soc., U.S. Naval Inst., Am. Meteorol. Soc., Am. Soc. Pub. Adminstrn., Am. Soc. Engring. Edn. (divsn. exec. com. 1976—80, chmn. aerospace divsn. 1979—80, exec. com. ocean, marine engring. divsn. 1982—85, newsletter editor 1982—87, divsn. exec. com. 1989—94, exec. com. ocean, marine engring. divsn. 1990—97, program chmn. 1991—93, chmn. 1993—95, chmn. Profl Interest Coun. 1995—97, bd. dirs. 1995—97, trustee 1999—2002), Am. Acad. Environ. Engrs. (cert. air pollution control engr.), Calif. Soc. Profl. Engrs., Royal Aero. Soc., Inst. Advancement Engring., Brit. Interplanetary Soc., Planetary Soc., SAFE, SID, Kappa Delta Pi, Sigma Gamma Tau, Tau Beta Pi. Democrat. Achievements include research on aircraft, spacecraft, missiles, and engine design, waveriders, aircrew centered system design and related impacts on exergy, quality, concurrent engineering, cost and environmental controls. Home: 9463 Willow Oak Rd Salinas CA 93907-1037 Office: Naval Postgrad Sch Dept Aeronautics Astronautics AA/Ne 699 Dyer Rd Monterey CA 93943-5106

NEWBERY, ILSE SOFIE MAGDALENE, German language educator; b. Darmstadt, Germany, Nov. 15, 1928; came to U.S., 1965; d. Otto and Charlotte (Brill) Brusius; m. A.C.R. Newbery, Dec. 28, 1954; children: Martin Roger, Frances Janet. Diplom akad. gepr. Übersetzer, U. Mainz, Germany, 1949; Staatsexamen Höh. Lehrfach, U. Frankfurt, Germany, 1954; PhD, U. B.C., Vancouver, Can., 1964. Part-time lectr. Queen's U., Belfast, Ireland, 1955-56; grad. asst. U. B.C., 1958-62; lectr. U. Calgary, Can., 1964-65; asst. prof. Georgetown (Ky.) Coll., 1965-67, assoc. prof., 1968-83, prof. German, 1983-94, chair langs. dept., 1989-94, prof. emeritus, 1994—. Examiner Goethe Inst., 1983-87; oral proficiency tester ACTFL, 1985-87; rsch. in German exile lit. Author software in field, 1989—. Founding mem. internat. folk ensemble Singing Hons, Lexington, 1977—. Recipient KCTFL Project award, Ky. Coun., 1994, Rollie Graves Tech. Excellence award, 1993. Mem. Am. Assn. Tchrs. German (v.p. Ky. chpt. 1979-81, pres. 1981-83), Am. Coun. Tchrs. Fgn. Langs., Ky. Coun. Tchrs. Fgn. Langs. (bd. dirs. 1979-83). Avocations: music, tennis, squash, skiing, climbing.

NEWBILL, KAREN MARGARET, elementary school educator, education educator; b. East Orange, N.J., Oct. 6, 1945; d. Richard Oliver and Edna Mae (Crook) Jacobson; m. Gary C. Newbill, Aug. 18, 1965; children: Kari L., Erick D. BA, Seattle Pacific U., 1968; MEd, City U., Bellevue, Wash., 1993. Cert. tchr., Wash. Tchr. Shoreline Pub. Schs., Seattle, 1969-71, Northshore Sch. Dist., Bothell, Wash., 1971-74; tutor, substitute tchr. Issaquah (Wash.) Sch. Dist., 1980-89, tchr., 1989—, tech. and curriculum integration cons., 1991—. Adj. prof. N.W. Coll., Kirkland, Wash., 1994—, mem. prof. edn. adv. bd., 1994—; adj. prof. Seattle Pacific U., 1994—; student tchr. supr. U. Wash., Seattle, 1991—, guest lectr., 1996—98, City U., 1998—; presenter Nat. Brain Expo, 2000—03. Mem. ASCD, NEA, Wash. Edn. Assn., Internat. Reading Assn. Avocations: decorative painting, reading, traveling, music. Home: 420 Kalmia Pl NW Issaquah WA 98027-2619 Office: Issaquah Sch Dist 565 NW Holly St Issaquah WA 98027-2899 E-mail: newbillk@aol.com.

NEWBORG, BARBARA CAROL, retired medical educator; b. N.Y.C., Apr. 14, 1921; d. Sidney and Agnes (Morgenthau) N. AB, Swarthmore Coll., 1941; MD, Johns Hopkins U., 1949. Intern Duke U. Med. Ctr., Durham, N.C., 1949-50, asst. resident, 1950-52, instr., 1952-55, assoc., 1955-71, asst. prof. of medicine, 1971-80, assoc. prof. of medicine, 1980-92, assoc. prof. medicine emeritus, 1992—; ret., 1992. Contbr. articles profl. jours. Trustee Walter Kempner Found. Mem. AMA, Durham-Orange County Med. Assn., Am. Soc. Internal Medicine. Home: 1500 Alabama Ave Durham NC 27705-3118

NEWCOMB, CAROLYN JEANNE, special education educator; b. St. Louis, June 12, 1936; d. John Mason and Dorothy Marie (Bayley) Seamans; m. Harris Denman Newcomb, Nov. 30, 1957 (dec.); children: Pamela Jeanne, Kristina Lynne, Keith Daniel. BS in Elem. Edn., Cen. Mo. State Coll., 1958; MA in Edn., Lindenwood Coll., 1978. Cert. elem. tchr., emotionally disturbed, learning disability, mentally retarded edn., Mo. Tchr. 1st grade Ferguson/Florissant (Mo.) Sch. Dist., 1959-61, Riverview Gardens Sch. Dist., St. Louis County, Mo., 1961-62; tchr. 1st, 2d and 3d grades St. Charles (Mo.) Sch. Dist., 1963-75, tchr. emotionally disturbed, 1975-85, tchr. mentally retarded and autistic, 1985-93; homebound tchr., 1993-99. Supervising tchr. Lindenwood Coll., St. Charles, 1965-93, U. Mo., St. Louis, 1965-93; spkr. on ind. behavior mgmt. St. Charles Sch. Dist., 1967-74, head coach Spl. Olympics, 1989-96. Treas. PTA, 1964; tchr. adult class St. Charles Presbyn. Ch., 1986-92, Stephen min., 1993—, 2001-, congregational care, 1997—; asst. minister, 2002-. Named Tchr. of Yr. Monroe Sch., 1974, Benton Sch., 1984; recipient awards St. Charles Sch. Dist., 1985, 86, 91, 92. Mem. Coun. for Exceptional Children (sec. 1985, v.p. 1986, pres. 1987, Chpt. 212 Tchr. of Yr. award 1987), St. Charles Edn. Assn. (v.p. 1974, pres. 1975). Avocations: piano, gardening, travel, needlework. Home: 13 Ashland Pl Saint Charles MO 63301-4605 Office: St Charles Presbyn Ch 131 Gamble St Saint Charles MO 63301-1601

NEWCOMB, JOAN LESLIE, elementary education educator; b. Castro Valley, Calif., Jan. 6, 1960; d. Blanchard Dean and Frances Jeanette (Carpenter) N.; m. James Brian Cameron, July 2, 1983 (div. Apr. 21, 1995). BA in History, Calif. State U., Hayward, 1982. Cert. K-12 tchr., Calif. Tchr. John Reed Sch., Rohnert Park, Calif., 1987-90, Monte Vista Sch., Rohnert Park, Calif., 1990—; integrated tchr./project based coach Cotati-Rohnert Park Unified Sch. Dist., 1997—. Pres. Sch. Site Coun., Rohnert Park, 1990-92, 95-97; leadership team Monte Vista Sch., Rohnert Park, 1990-96; lead tchr. North Coast Beginning Tchr. Project, Santa Rosa, Calif., 1995-96; coord. 4/5 lang. arts task force Cotati-Rohnert Park Unified Sch. Dist., 1996-97; spkr. in field. Soprano United Ch. of Christ, Petaluma, Calif., 1995—, mem. bd. Christian edn., 1996—. Recipient Fulbright award, Japan, 1997, Edn. Found. grant Rohnert Park Edn. Found., 1989, 90, 97. Mem. NEA, NSF, Internat. Tech. Educator's Assn., New Eng. Hist. Geneal. Soc. Democrat. Avocations: travel, writing, reading, needlework, history. Office: Monte Vista Elem Sch 1400 Magnolia Ave Rohnert Park CA 94928-8129

NEWCOMB, KATHY RAE, elementary education educator; b. Warren, Ohio, Nov. 4, 1952; d. Richard Franklin and Thelma Pearl (Dawson) Palmer; m. Thomas Lee Newcomb, July 28, 1984; 1 child, Matthew Ray. BS, Kent State U., 1975; MEd, Westminster Coll., 1982. Cert. elem. educator, Ohio. Tchr. 1st grade Bloomfield-Mesopotamia Local Schs., Mesopotamia, Ohio, 1975-79, tchr. 3rd grade, 1979-82, tchr. 1st grade, 1982—. Active Parkman (Ohio) Congl. Ch., 1984—; mem. James A. Garfield Scholarship Fund, Garrettsville, Ohio, 1990—. Recipient Class Act Tchr. award, 1994; grantee several tchr. grants Bloomfield-Mesopotamia Schs., 1978—. Mem. Ohio Edn. Assn., Parkman (Ohio) C. of C., N. Am. Wildlife Park Found. Avocations: reading, church work, history, execise, gardening. Office: Bloomfield-Mespo Local Schs 4466 Kinsman Rd Mesopotamia OH 44439

NEWCOMB, ROBERT WAYNE, electrical engineer educator; b. Glendale, Calif., June 27, 1933; s. Robert Dobson and Dorothy Opal (Bissinger) N.; m. Sarah Eleanor Fritz, May 22, 1954; children: Gail E., Robert. W. BSEE, Purdue U., 1955; MS, Stanford U., 1957; PhD, U. Calif., Berkeley, 1960. Registered profl. engr., Calif. Rsch. intern Stanford Rsch. Inst., Menlo Park, Calif., 1957-60; tchg. assoc. U. Calif., Berkeley, 1957-60; asst. and tenured assoc. prof. Stanford U., 1960—70; prof. elec. engring. U. Md., College Park, 1970—. Bd. dirs. PARCOR Rsch. program, Universidad Politecnica de Madrid, Spain. Author: Linear Multisport Synthesis, 1966, Active Integrated Circuit Synthesis, 1968, Concepts of Linear Systems and Control, 1968, Network Theory, 1967; editor: Neurocomputing Letters, 2002—. Recipient IEEE CAS Edn. awrd, 2001; Fulbright fellow, 1963; Fulbright-Hays fellow, 1976; Robert Wayne Newcomb Lab. opened at U. Politecnica Madrid, 1995. Fellow IEEE (life, golden jubilee medal 1999); mem. Soc. Indsl. and Applied Math., Math. Assn. Am., Acad. Am. Poets. Avocations: film, literature, poetry, guitar. Home: 13120 Two Farm Dr Silver Spring MD 20904-3418 Office: U Md Microsystems Lab Elec/Computer Engring College Park MD 20742-0001 E-mail: newcomb@eng.umd.edu.

NEWCOMB, THOMAS LEE, elementary school educator; b. Ravenna, Ohio, Dec. 7, 1954; s. Rolland Eugene and Vera May (Bell) N.; m. Kathy Rae Palmer, July 28, 1984; 1 child, Matthew Ray. BA, Hiram Coll., 1977; MEd, Lesley Coll. Grad. Sch., 1983; DLitt, Nova Coll., Calgary, Alberta, Can., 1988, PhD, 1991. Cert. elem. tchr., reading specialist, bilingual specialist, Ohio (life). Chpt. I reading tchr. Bloomfield-Mespo Local Schs., Mesopotamia, Ohio, 1977-80, 3rd grade tchr., 1980-82, spl. tutor k-5, 1982-83, 2nd grade tchr., 1983-85, learning disability tchr., 1985-86, 3rd grade tchr., 1986—. Grantsman Bloomfield-Mespo Local Schs., Mesopotamia, 1978—, coord. arts in sch., 1991—, coord. partnerships, R.I.F.; cons., researcher, pvt. practice, 1983—; adj. faculty, Nova Coll., Calgary, 1991—. Author: numerous books, poems, 1978—; contbr. articles to profl. jours. Mem. James A. Garfield Scholarship Fund, Garretsville, Ohio, 1990—. Recipient Tchr. of the Yr. award, 1992, 93, Class Act Tchr. award, 1994; grantee from numerous govt. and philanthropic foundations. Mem. Ohio Edn. Assn., World Wildlife Fund, Defenders of Wildlife. Congregationalist. Avocations: electronics, chuchwork, literature, music, historic preservation. Office: Bloomfield Mespo Local Schs PO Box 229 Mesopotamia OH 44439-0229

NEWELL, WILLIAM JAMES, sign language educator; b. Port Jefferson, N.Y., Sept. 13, 1947; s. William James and Mary Louise (Pinder) N.; m. Beverly Jo Beller, June 18, 1971; children: Eric James, Christopher Ian. BA, St. Edwards U., Austin, Tex., 1970; MS, St. Cloud State U., 1977; PhD, Greenwich U., 1994. Cert. tchr. Am. Sign Lang.; cert. Coun. on Edn. of the Deaf. Houseparent, tchr. aide Tex. Sch. for the Deaf, Austin, 1969-70; tchr. of the deaf Harris County Pub. Schs., Houston, 1970-72, Dade County Pub. Schs., Miami, Fla., 1972-74; supervising tchr. of the deaf Hennepin Tech. Ctrs., Mpls., 1974-78; instr. Am. Sign Lang. Rochester (N.Y.) Inst. Tech., 1978-81; chairperson sign communication dept. Nat. Tech. Inst. for the Deaf, Rochester, 1981-91, rsch. assoc., 1991-96, prof. Am. sign lang. and deaf studies, 1996—. Proprietor Sign Lang. Consulting Svcs., Ednl. Cons., Adult Edn. Resource. Co-developer: Sign Communication Proficiency Interview, 1981—; author: Basic Sign Communication, 1983. Recipient Outstanding Svc. award Sign Instrs. Guidance Network, Silver Spring, Md. Mem. Am. Sign Lang. Tchrs. Assn. (pres. 1986-90, chairperson evaluation and cert. com. 1990—, Veditz award 1996, 2000), Conv. of Am. Instrs. for the Deaf. Avocations: home brewing, walking for fitness, backyard birdfeeding. Home: 1103 Coralhurst Ct Webster NY 14580 Office: Nat Tech Inst for the Deaf 52 Lomb Memorial Dr Rochester NY 14623-5604 E-mail: accessld@usa.net.

NEWHALL, DAVID SOWLE, history educator; b. Burlington, Vt., July 26, 1929; s. Chester Albert and Nella Perry (Tillotson) N.; m. Edna Irene Newton, Mar. 25, 1952; children: Rebecca, John Newton, Jesslyn, Melissa, David Chester. BA, U. Vt., 1951; postgrad., Boston U., 1953—55; AM, Harvard U., 1956, PhD, 1963. Instr., asst. prof. U. Vt., Burlington, 1959-66; asst. prof., assoc. prof. history Centre Coll., Danville, Ky., 1966, prof., 1970, chmn. divsn. social studies, 1968—74, 1981—85, disting. prof. humanities, 1987, Pottinger disting. prof. history, 1994-95; Pottinger disting. prof. history emeritus, 1995—. Mem. adv. com. Danville High Sch., 1980-81; cons. dept. history Berea (Ky.) Coll., 1983, 2001; rep. Ky. Coun. on Internat. Edn., Lexington, 1984-85. Author: Clemenceau: A Life at War, 1991; contbr. to Historical Dictionary of the Third French Republic, 1988, Kentucky Ency., 1992, Historic World Leaders, 1994, Women in World History: A Biographical Encyclopedia, 1999-2002, Ency. of Appalachia, 2003-. Elder Presbyn. Ch., U.S.A., Danville, 1969—; officer Danville H.S. Band Parents Assn., 1968-82; bd. dirs. Project Opportunity, Lee and Breathitt Counties, Ky., 1968-74; mem. Citizens Com. on Coal-Hauling Traffic, Boyle County, Ky., 1982—; mem. adv. bd. Ky. Elderhostel, 1996—. With U.S. Army, 1951-53, Korea. Recipient Acorn award Ky. Advocates for Higher Edn., 1994; Nat. Meth. scholar Boston U., 1953-55. Mem. Soc. for French Hist. Studies, Nat. Coun. for History Edn., Phi Beta Kappa (officer Centre Coll. 1971-95), Omicron Delta Kappa, Phi Alpha Theta. Avocations: church choir, railroading. Home: 634 N 3rd St Danville KY 40422-1125 Office: Dept of History Centre Coll Danville KY 40422

NEWHOUSE, JOSEPH PAUL, economist, educator; b. Waterloo, Iowa, Feb. 24, 1942; s. Joseph Alexander and Ruth Linnea (Johnson) Newhouse; m. Margaret Louise Locke, June 22, 1968; children: Eric Joseph, David Locke. BA, Harvard U., 1963, PhD, 1969; postgrad (Fulbright scholar), Goethe U., Frankfort, Germany, 1963—64. Staff economist Rand Corp., Santa Monica, Calif., 1968—72, dep. program mgr., health and biosci. rsch., 1971—88, sr. staff economist, 1972—81, head econs. dept., 1981—85, sr. corp. fellow, 1985—2001; John D. MacArthur prof. health policy and mgmt., dir. div. Health Policy Rsch. and Edn., Harvard U., 1988—. Lectr. UCLA, 1970—83, adj. prof., 1983—88; mem. faculty Rand Grad. Sch., 1972—88; dir. Rand-UCLA Ctr. for Study Health Care Fin. Policy, 1984—88, co-dir., 1988—92; prin. investigator health ins. study grant HHS, 1971—86; chmn. health svcs. rsch. study sect. HHS-Agy. for Health Care Policy and Rsch., 1989—93; mem. Nat. Commn. Cost Med. Care, 1976—77; mem. health svcs. devel. grants study sect. HEW, 1978—82, Inst. Medicine of NAS, 1978—, mem. coun., 1991—97; mem. Physician Payment Rev. Commn., 1993—96; chmn. Prospective Payment Assessment Com., 1996—97; vice chair Medicare Payment Assessment Commn., 1997—2001, mem., 2001—; bd. regents Nat. Libr. Medicine, 1999—; bd. dirs. Aetna, ABT Assocs. Author: The Economics of Medical Care, 1978, The Cost of Poor Health Habits, 1991, A Measure of Malpractice, 1993, Free for All?, 1993, Pricing the Priceless, 2002; editor: Jour. Health Econs., 1981—; assoc. editor: Jour. Econ. Perspectives, 1992—98, mem. editl. bd.: New Eng. Jour. Medicine, 2003—; contbr. articles to profl. jours. Recipient David Kershaw award and prize, Assn. Pub. Policy and Mgmt., 1983, Baxter Am. Found. prize, 1988, Adminstr.'s citation, Health Care Fin. Adminstrn., 1988, Hans Sigrist Found. prize, 1995, Elizur Wright award, 1995, Zvi Griliches award, 2000, Kenneth Arrow award, 2001. Fellow: AAAS, Am. Acad. Arts and Scis.; mem.: Internat. Health Econs. Assn. (bd. dirs. 1996—, pres. 1996—98), Econometric Soc., Royal Econ. Soc., Am. Econ. Assn., Assn. for Health Svcs. Rsch. (bd. dirs. 1991—, pres. 1993—94, Article of Yr. award 1989). Office: Harvard U Health Policy Rsch and Edn 180 Longwood Ave Boston MA 02115-5821

NEWITT, JAY, construction management educator; PhD, Colo. State U., 1981. Tchr. Brigham Young U., Provo, Utah. Recipient John Trimmer Merit Shop Tchg. award Excellence Edn. Construction Found., 1992. Office: Brigham Young U PO Box 24206 Provo UT 84602*

NEWLAND, CHESTER ALBERT, public administration educator; b. Kansas City, Kans., June 18, 1930; s. Guy Wesley and Mary Virginia (Yoakum) N. BA, U. N. Tex., Denton, 1954; MA, U. Kans., 1955, PhD, 1958. Social Sci. Rsch. Coun. fellow U. Wis. and U.S. Supreme Ct., 1958-59; instr. polit. sci. Idaho State U., Pocatello, 1959-60; mem. faculty U. North Tex., Denton, 1960-66, prof. govt., 1963-66, dir. dept. govt., 1963-66; prof. polit. sci. U. Houston, 1967-68; dir. Lyndon Baines Johnson Libr., Austin, Tex., 1968-70; prof. pub. adminstrn. U. So. Calif., 1966-67, 68-71, 76-82, 84-92, Duggan disting. prof. pub. adminstrn., 1992—; prof. George Mason U., Fairfax, Va., 1982-84. Mem. faculty Fed. Exec. Inst., 1971-76, dir. 1973-76, 80-81; mgr. task force on fed. labor-mgmt. rels. U.S. Pers. Mgmt. Project, Pres.'s Reorgn., Washington, 1977-78. Editor in chief Pub. Adminstrn. Rev., 1984-90; contbr. articles to profl. jours. Chmn. Mcpl. Rsch. Coun., Denton, 1963-64; city councilman, Denton, 1964-66; mem. Pub. Sector Commn. on Productivity and Work Quality, 1974-78; trustee Sacramento (Calif.) Mus. History, Sci. and Tech., 1993-95; mem. UN Devel. Program Kazakhstan, 1997-2000, strategy review program, 2002, Moldova, 1994, Kuwait, 1991, 95-96; cons. Poland, 1990-91, Hungary, 1991, Czech and Slovak Republics, 1992, Bank of Greece, 1999-2002, Taiwan, 2001. Mem. Nat. Acad. Pub. Adminstrn., Southwestern Social Sci. Assn. (chmn. govt. sect. 1964-65), Am. Soc. Pub. Adminstrn. (pres. Dallas-Ft. Worth chpt. 1964-65, nat. coun. 1976, 78-81, editorial bd. jour. 1972-76, chmn. publ. com. 1975-79, program chmn. 1977, nat. pres. 1981-82, Dimock award 1984, Van Riper award 2002), Am. Polit. Sci. Assn., Internat. Pers. Mgmt. Assn. (program chmn. 1978, Stockberger award 1979), Am. Acad. Polit. and Social Sci., Internat. City Mgmt. Assn. (hon.), Nat. Assn. Schs Pub. Affairs and Adminstrn. (Staats Pub. Svc. award 1989). Office: Univ Southern California 1800 I St Sacramento CA 95814-3004

NEWMAN, AMY SUZANNE, psychologist, educator; b. Pitts., Oct. 10, 1954; d. William Reece Elton and Margie Ruth (Pollard) N.; m. Eric James Van Denburg, Oct. 11, 1986; children: Alyssa Newman, Miles Hall. BA in Psychology with honors, U. Utah, 1977; MA in Psychology, Washington U., St. Louis, 1980, PhD in Psychology, 1984. Intern U. Tex. Health Sci. Ctr., Dallas, 1979-80; research asst. Washington U., St. Louis, 1981-82; staff psychologist Cardinal Glennon Meml. Hosp. for Children, St. Louis, 1982-84; postdoctoral fellow Orange (Calif.) County Juvenile Ct. Evaluation and Guidance Unit, 1984-85; clin. psychologist Clin. Psychology Assocs., Bloomingdale, Ill., 1985-86; sr. psychologist, head, tm. mental health svcs. Michael Reese Hosp. and Med. Ctr., Chgo., 1986-91; clin. psychologist dept. psychiatry Katharine Wright Ctr., Ill. Masonic Med. Ctr., Chgo., 1991-97; pvt. practice Chgo., 1987—. Instr. George Warren Brown Sch. Social Work, Washington U., St. Louis, 1982-83; assoc. faculty Ill. Sch. Profl. Psychology, Chgo., 1986-91; instr. dept. psychology Loyola U., Chgo., 1994-95, 97-98, 2003; adj.faculty Roosevelt U. Sch. Psychology, Chgo., 1999—; peer reviewer Jour. Behavioral Medicine, Lynchburg, Va., 1987—. Co-author: (with others) Adherence, Generalization, and Maintenance in Behavioral Medicine, 1982; contbr. articles to profl. jours. Mem. APA, Phi Beta Kappa, Mortar Bd., Phi Kappa Phi, Phi Eta Sigma. Democrat. Mem. United Church of Christ. Avocations: running, cooking, sewing, traveling. Office: 55 E Washington St Ste 2801 Chicago IL 60602-2205

NEWMAN, ANDREA HAAS, school counselor, educator; b. N.Y.C., Nov. 17, 1947; d. Charles and Miriam (Kasdan) Haas; m. Arthur Robert Newman, July 5, 1970 (div. Apr., 1997); children: Aaron Charles, Andrew Benjamin, Alan Jacob. BS, Ohio State U., 1970; MEd, Cleve. State U., 1985. Cert. sch. counselor. English spl. edn. tchr. Roosevelt H.S., Dayton, Ohio, 1970-71; counselor Parma (Ohio) H.S., 1985-86, occupational work adjustment, sch. counselor, 1986-88; sch. counselor Hillside Jr. H.S., Seven Hills, Ohio, 1988-95, Parma Sr. H.S., 1995—. Mem. strategic planning team Parma City Schs., 1992-93, tchr. svc. planning com., 1993-94; personality fitness trainer Personality Fitness for Youth, L.A., 1987-88; advisor S.A.D.D. (Students Against Drunk Driving), Seven Hills, 1992—. Instr., group leader Systematic Tng. for Effective Parenting, Hillside Jr. High Sch., 1992-93. Mem. Ohio Sch. Counselors Assn. Jewish. Avocations: hiking, golf, fitness walking, cycling. Office: Parma Sr HS 6285 W 54th St Parma OH 44129-5259

NEWMAN, BARBARA MAE, retired special education educator; b. Rockford, Ill., July 16, 1932; d. Greene Adam and Emma Lorene (Fields) N. BS Edn., No. Ill. U., 1973. Cert. elem. edn. K-8 tchr., spl. edn. (blind and p.s.) K-12 tchr. Exec. sec. Rockford Art Assn., 1961-70; tchr. Title 1 Rockford Pub. Sch. Dist. #205, 1975-76, tchr. vision impaired, 1977-91. Feature editor (Rock Valley Coll. newpaper) The Valley Forge, 1970; contbg. writer (Rockford Coll. history) A Retrospective Look, 1980. St. Bernadette adult choir, 1958-95, Cathedral Chorale, 1995—; holder 5 offices Am. Bus. Women's Assn., Forest City chpt., 1963-70; vol. Winnebago Ctr. for the Blind, Rockford, 1965-70; mem. Rockford Diocesan Chorale, 1969—. Named Woman of Yr., Am. Bus. Women's Assn., Forest City chpt., Rockford, 1966; scholar Ill. State Scholarship Commn., No. Ill. U., 1970-73. Mem. Ill. Ret. Tchrs. Assn., Cath. Woman's League. Roman Catholic. Avocations: writing, swimming.

NEWMAN, BARBARA MILLER, psychologist, educator; b. Chgo., Sept. 6, 1944; d. Irving George and Florence (Levy) Miller; m. Philip r. Newman, June 12, 1966; children: Samuel Asher, Abraham Levy, Rachel Florence. Student, Bryn Mawr Coll.; AB with honors in Psychology, U. Mich., 1966, PhD in Devel. Psychology, 1971. Undergrad. research asst. in psychology U. Mich., 1963-64, research asst. in psychology, 1964-69, teaching fellow, 1965-71, asst. project dir. Inst. for Social Research, 1971-72, univ. lectr. in psychology and research assoc., 1971-72; asst. prof. psychology Russell Sage Coll., 1972-76, assoc. prof., 1977-78; assoc. prof. and chair dept. family rels. and human devel. Ohio State U., 1978-83, prof. and chair, 1983-86, assoc. provost for faculty recruitment and devel., 1987-92, prof., 1992-2000; prof. and chair dept. human devel. and family studies U. R.I., 2000—. Author: Development Through Life, 1975, 8th edit., 2003; author: (with P. Newman) Living: The Process of Adjustment, 1981, Understanding Adulthood, 1983; author: Adolescent Development, 1986, When Kids Go to College, 1992, Childhood and Adolescence, 1997; author: (with P. Newman, L. Landry-Meyer and B. Lohman) Life Span Development: A Case Book, 2003; contbr. articles to profl. jours. Mem. AAAS, APA, Soc. Rsch. in Child Devel., Am. Psychol. Soc., Nat. Coun. Family Rels., Groves Conf. on Marriage and Family, Soc. for Rsch. on Adolescence, Am. Assn. Family and Consumer Scis. Office: U RI Human Devel and Family Studies 112 Transition Ctr Kingston RI 02881 E-mail: bnewman@uri.edu.

NEWMAN, BRUCE ALLAN, political science educator; b. Wilmington, Del., Aug. 30, 1960; s. Thomas Allan and Ethel Mae (Stayton) N.; m. Alice BA, U. Del., 1986; MA, U. Dallas, 1990, PhD in Politics, 2000. Instr. in polit. sci. Western Okla. State Coll., Altus, 1991—. With U.S. Army, 1980-83. Earhart Found. fellow, 1987-88, 88-89. Mem. Am. Polit. Sci. Assn., Okla. Polit. Sci. Assn. (adj. scholar), Okla. Coun. Pub. Affairs. Republican. Avocations: reading, hiking, travel, movies. Home: 1812 Hollywood Dr Altus OK 73521-5410 Office: Western Okla State Coll 2801 N Main St Altus OK 73521-1310 E-mail: newmanbruce@hotmail.com.

NEWMAN, ELSIE LOUISE, mathematics educator; b. Bowling Green, Ohio, Mar. 25, 1943; d. Carroll E. and Grace G. (Underwood) Frank; m. Lawrence J. Newman, Sept. 15, 1962; children: Timothy, Jennifer. BS cum laude, Bowling Green (Ohio) State U., 1968; MEd, U. Toledo, 1992. Study supr. After Sch. Study Tutorial Program, Bowling Green, 1983-85; prof. Owens C.C., Toledo, 1987—. Office mgr. K.C. Ins. Co., Bowling Green, 1984; tutor in maths. Bowling Green City Schs., 1984-88, Bur. of Vocat. Rehab., Oregon, Ohio, 1988-91. Co-editor Jour. Tchg. and Learning, 1998—; contbr. articles to profl. jours. Advisor 4H Club, Bowling Green, 1985-98; asst. Christmas Clearing bur. Voluntary Action Ctr., United Way, Bowling Green, 1982-86, residential crusade chmn. Am. Cancer Soc., Bowling Green, 1981-82. Bowling Green U. scholar, 1966-68. Mem. Nat. Coun. Tchrs. of Math., Am. Math. Assn. Two Yr. Colls., Ohio Assn. Devel. Edn., Owens Faculty Assn. (treas. 1998-2000), Phi Kappa Phi, Kappa Delta Pi, Pi Lambda Theta. Home: 328 S Summit St Bowling Green OH 43402-3017

NEWMAN, FREDRIC ALAN, plastic surgeon, educator; b. Bklyn., Aug. 16, 1948; s. Harold Louis and Isabel (Seltzer) Newman; m. Stacey Hope Clarfield, Nov. 27, 1983; children: Benjamin, Marissa, Alexandra. BA, Yale Coll., 1970; MD summa cum laude, SUNY Downstate, Bklyn., 1974. Diplomate Am Bd Plastic Surgery, Am Bd Surgery. Resident gen. surgery Beth Israel Hosp., Boston, 1974-77; resident and chief gen. surgery SUNY Downstate, Bklyn., 1977-79; fellow plastic surgery NYU/Inst. Reconstrv. Plastic Surgery, N.Y.C., 1979-81; fellow facial reconstruction Jackson Meml. Hosp., Miami, Fla., 1981-82; asst. clin. prof. dept. plastic surgery N.Y. Med. Coll., West, 1984-95, Columbia Coll. Physicians and Surgeons, N.Y.C., 1995—. Chmn bd dirs, CEO, pres Edno Surg Devices, Inc, Del., 1998—. Author: (book) Aesthetic Plastic Surgery, 1984, Plastic Surgery, 1985; contbr. articles to profl. jours. Fellow: ACS, Int Col Surgeons; mem.: NY State Med Soc, Am Cleft Palate Asn, Am Soc Aesthetic Plastic Surg, Am Soc Plastic and Reconstructive Surgeons. Avocations: sailing, skiing, reading, computers. Office: 722 Post Rd Darien CT 06820 E-mail: drnewman@snet.net.

NEWMAN, JANET ELAINE, elementary education educator; b. Savannah, Ga., Dec. 4, 1947; d. Oral Kenneth and Mary Gertrude (Flynn) N. AA, R.I. Jr. Coll., Providence, 1967; A in B., R.I. Jr. Coll., 1976; BA, Mt. St. Joseph Coll., 1969. Elem. tchr. Coventry (R.I.) Sch. Dept., 1970-73; supr. elec. soldering Harwood Mfg., Providence, 1973-80; elem. tchr. Providence Sch. Dept., 1980—. Mem. Legal/Edn. Partnership, 1990—, Classroom Alternate Programs/Classroom Alternate Strategies of Teaching Team, 1993—; mem. adv. bd. West Broadway Schoolwide Project, 1994—, Sch. Improvement Project, 1994—; Times 2 tchr., 1997. Bd. dirs. Woodland Estates Condominium Assn., 1988—; tchr. CCD, St. Martha's Ch., 1985-87; mem. tech. com. Carl G. Lauro Elem. Sch., 1996—. Fellow R.I. Writing Consortium, 1990, Taft Inst. at R.I. Coll., 1991. Roman Catholic. Home: 1145 Hartford Ave Johnston RI 02919-7128 Office: Providence Sch Dept 797 Westminster St Providence RI 02903-4045

NEWMAN, JEANNE JOHNSON, sociolinguistic educator, researcher; b. Twin Falls, Idaho, Dec. 8, 1939; d. Glen Everett Johnson and Alta Ruth (Egbert) Kizer; children: Ronald, Javier. BA, Calif. State U., 1986, MA, 1988; PhD, U. Pa., 1993. ESL tchr., coord. edn. dept. Tulare County Community Action Agy., Visalia, Calif., 1967-69; dir. community devel., dir. planning and evaluation Kings County Community Action Orgn., Hanford, Calif., 1970-75; program planner Community Action Program Tulare County, Visalia, Calif., 1975-79; edn. rev. instr., program specialist, tchr. PROTEUS Adult Tng., Inc., Visalia, Calif., 1979-84; student asst., tutor Calif. State U., Fresno, 1985-86, rsch. asst., 1986-87, U. Pa., Phila., 1988-89; tchr., workshop facilitator Svc., Commitment, Success Bus. and Tech. Sch., Phila., 1990-93; rsch. assoc. Vocational Rsch. Inst., divsn. Jewish Employment & Vocational Svcs., Phila., 1993-95; acad. dir. Stage Lang. Acad., Seoul, Korea, 1995—. Presenter rsch. papers Second Lang. Rsch. Forum, Eugene, Oreg., L.A., 1989, 90, Boston U. Lang. Devel., 1989, 90, TESOL Internat., N.Y.C., 1991, Balt., 1994, Long Beach, Calif., 1995, Pa. chpt. PENN-TESOL East, 1994; cons. SCS Bus. and Tech. Sch., Phila., 1990-93; mem. staff Literacy Rsch. Ctr., newsletter editor, 1990; contbg. mem. Working Papers in Ednl. Linguistics, editor, 1989-91. Author rsch. papers. Visitor Presbyn. Home Elderly, Phila., 1988-91; mem., organizer Tri-County Sr. Citizens, Commn. on Aging, Fresno, Kings and Tulare County, 1980-85. Calif. State U. Alumni Assn. scholar, 1987-88, U. Pa. Grad. Sch. Edn. scholar, 1988-93. Mem. TESOL Internat. (vol. Pa. chpt. 1989-94), Am. Assn. Ret. Educators, Am. Assn. Applied Linguistics, AAUW, NAFE, Internat. Platform Assn., Modern Lang. Assn. Avocations: swimming, skiing, pottery making, camping, dressmaking. Home and Office: 831-3 Yeoksam-Dong Gangnam-Ku Seoul Republic of Korea 135-080

NEWMAN, JOHN NICHOLAS, naval architect educator; b. New Haven, Mar. 10, 1935; s. Richard and Daisy (Neumann) N.; m. Kathleen Smedley Kirk, June 16, 1956; children— James Bartram, Nancy Kirk, Carol Ann. BS Mass. Inst. Tech, 1956, MS, 1957, Sc.D., 1960; postgrad., Cambridge (Eng.) U., 1958-59; D Technicae honoris causa, U. Trondheim, Norway, 1992. Research naval architect David Taylor Model Basin, Navy Dept., Washington, 1959-67; assoc. prof. naval architecture MIT, Cambridge, 1967-70, prof., 1970—, prof. emeritus. Vis. prof. U. New South Wales, Australia, 1973, U. Adelaide, Australia, 1974, Tech. U. Norway, 1981-82; cons. Navy Dept., Dept. Justice, pvt. firms. Author: Marine Hydrodynamics, 1977; Contbr.: articles to profl. jours., including Sci. Am. Recipient prize Am. Bur. Shipping, 1956; Walter Atkinson prize Royal Instn. Naval Architects, 1973, also Bronze medal, 1976; Guggenheim fellow, 1973-74; research grantee Office Naval Research; NSF. Mem. AAAS, NAE, Soc. Naval Architects and Marine Engrs. (Davidson medal 1988), Norwegian Acad. Sci. Home: 1 Bowditch Rd Woods Hole MA 02543-1201 E-mail: jnn@mit.edu.

NEWMAN, JUSTINA ANNE, nursery school administrator, consultant; b. New Brunswick, N.J., Dec. 21, 1943; d. John S. and Louise B. (Marcks) Hilman; m. Raymond William Newman, Sept. 15, 1962; children: Raymond, Steven, Michelle. BA in Elem. Edn., nursery sch. endorse., Georgian Ct. Coll., 1982, cert. spl. edn., 1986. Dir., owner, child devel. cons. Beachwood (N.J.) Nursery Sch. Inc., 1986—. Exec. bd. Pine Beach Sch. PTA, Little League, Pine Beach/Beachwood, Cub Scouts; co-leader Brownies, Toms River (N.J.) High Sch. band Wagon. Recipient Accredation award Nat. Acad. Early Childhood Programs, 1992—. Mem. Nat. Assn. for the Edn. of Young Children (Ocean chpt., editor, founder N.J. chpt. newsletter 1988—, N.J. Assn. for the Edn. of Young Children (pres. Ocean chpt. 1984-88, corr. sec. 1990-92, fin. com. 1990—, grant program com.), Assn. for Childhood Edn. Internat. (early childhood divsn. 1990—). Roman Catholic. Avocations: music, writing, traveling. Home: 525 Admirals Cir Pine Beach NJ 08741-1413 Office: Beachwood Nursery Sch 1014 Pinewood Rd Beachwood NJ 08722

NEWMAN, LYNDA NITTSKOFF, medical/surgical nurse, nurse educator; b. Cleve., Aug. 4, 1956; d. Leo and Eileen Ruth (Glick) Nittskoff; m. Nelson S. Newman, Nov. 21, 1979; children: Ari, Daniel, Michelle. BSN, Kent State U., 1978; MSN, Case Western Res. U., 1983. Cert. specialist med.-surg. nursing, ANA. Staff nurse surg. ICU Mt. Sinai Hosp., Cleve., 1978-80; clin. nurse II med. ICU U. Hosps. Cleve., Ohio, 1980-82; clin. nurse specialist Highland View Hosp. and Metro Health Rehab., Cleve., 1983-87; clin. coord. home dialysis U. Hosps. Cleve., Ohio, 1987—. Asst. clin. instr. Frances Payne Bolton Sch. Nursing, Case Western Res. U., Cleve., 1984—; adj. clin. instr. Kent State U. Sch. Nursing, 2001--; presenter in field. Contbr. articles to profl. jours. Recipient Outstanding Profl. Achievement award Frances Payne Bolton Sch. Nursing, Alumni Assn., Case Western Res. U., Cleve., 1994, Cleve. Plain Dealer's Nurse of Yr. award, 2000, Best Abstract award 20th Ann. Conf. on Periotoneal Dialysis U. Mo., Columbia, 2000. Mem. Am. Nephrology Nurses Assn. (cert. nephrology nurse, pres.-elect North Coast chpt.), Sigma Theta Tau (Excellence in Nursing Practice award 2003). Democrat. Jewish. Avocations: reading, theatre, computers. Home: 3525 Kerndale Rd Cleveland OH 44124-5608 Office: Univ Hosps Cleve 11100 Euclid Ave Cleveland OH 44106-1736

NEWMAN, MARIE STEFANINI, law librarian, educator; b. Boston, Aug. 30, 1951; d. Mario and Elizabeth (Just) S.; m. Gary Nathaniel Newman, Sept. 30, 1978; children: Alexander, Elizabeth. AB, Smith Coll., 1973; MS, Columbia U., 1974; JD, Rutgers U., 1983. Bar: N.Y. 1984. Jr. librarian Bayonne (N.J.) Pub. Library, 1974-75; editor Microfilming Corp. Am., Glen Rock, N.J., 1975-78; circulation librarian SUNY Downstate Med. Ctr, Bklyn., 1979-80; head reference svcs. N.Y. Law Sch., N.Y.C., 1984-90, adj. assoc. prof. law, 1985-90; assoc. dir. Pub. Svcs., lectr. U. Pa. Law Sch., 1991-93; dep. libr. dir. and adj. prof. law Pace U. Sch. Law, White Plains, N.Y., 1993-99, libr. dir., assoc. prof. law, 1999—. Database mgr. Inst. Internat. Comml. Law, 1994—. Mem. Am. Assn. Law Libraries. Office: Pace Law Libr 78 N Broadway White Plains NY 10603-3710 E-mail: mnewman@law.pace.edu.

NEWMAN, MARY THOMAS, communications educator, management consultant; b. Howell, Mo., Oct. 15, 1933; d. Austin Hill and Doris (McQueen) Thomas; m. Grover Travis Newman, Aug. 22, 1952 (div. 1967); 1 child, Leah Newman Lane; m. Rodney Charles Westlund, July 18, 1981. BS, S.F. Austin State U., 1956; MA, U. Houston, 1965; PhD, Pa. State U., 1980. Cert. permanent tchr., Tex. Instr. comms. South Tex. Coll., Houston, 1965-70; assoc. prof. comms. Burlington County Coll., Pemberton, N.J., 1970-72; tchg. asst. in comms. Pa. State U., University Park, 1972-73, asst. prof. Ogontz Campus Abington, 1973-80; lectr. mgmt. and comms. U. Md., Europe and Asia, 1980-83; mem. vis. faculty dept. comms. U. Tenn., Knoxville, 1984-85; asst. prof. human factors U. So. Calif., L.A., 1985-88; assoc. prof. human factors, dir. profl. devel. U. Denver Coll. Systems Sci., 1988-92; assoc. prof. USC, Berlin, Germany, 1992-93; assoc. prof., assoc. dir. Whitworth Coll., Spokane, Wash., 1993-95; prof. comms. Houston Bapt. U., 1995—; level III assoc. Booze-Allen & Hamilton Mgt. Cons., Mc Lean, Va., 2000—. Vis. prof. speech comm. Okla. State U., 1999-2000; pres. Human Resource Comms. Group, Easton, Md., 1984—; lectr. Bus. Rsch. Inst., Toyo U., Tokyo, 1983, Saitama Med. U., Japan, 1983; scholar in residence U.S. Marine Corps., Quantico, Va., 1990-92; mem. final phase faculty USC MSSM Troop Draw Down, Berlin, Germany, 1992-93; team mem. Spokane Inter-Collegiate Rsch. & Tech. Inst., 1993-95; dir. Women's Leadership Conf., Moses Lake, Wash., 1993; mem. world svcs. com. YWCA, Spokane; Lilly fellow 1996; mgmt. trainer joint-ventures Phillips China Inc., Sealand Transp., others, China, 1997; established Mgmt. Devel. Ctr., Guanjou, PRC, 1998; vis. prof. Speech Comm., Okla. State U. Author: Introduction to Basic Speech Communication, 1969; contbr. articles to profl. jours. Program developer U.S. Army Hdqrs. Sch. Age Latch Key Program, Alexandria, Va., 1987; mem. Govt. of Guam Women's Issues Task Force, 1985; vis. prof. Jinan U., China, 1999—. Lilly fellow in humanities and arts, summer 1996. Mem. AAUW (program chair Houston chpt. 1997-98), Human Factors Soc., Speech Communication Assn. (legis. coun. 1970-73, editl. bd. jour. 1970-76), Ea. Communication Assn. (editl. bd. jours. 1975-80), Univ. Film Assn. (publicity dir. 1978-80), Indsl. Comm. Coun., Chesapeake Women's Network, Easton Bus. and Profl. Women, Asia Soc., Alpha Chi, Alpha Psi Omega, Pi Kappa Delta, Delta Kappa Gamma. Avocations: military history and women's issues research. Address: 8283 Greensboro Dr Mc Lean VA 22102-3802 E-mail: maryat@okstate.edu.

NEWMAN, PATRICIA ANNE, nurse anesthesia educator; b. New Orleans, Aug. 25, 1941; d. Merwyn James and Yvonne Louise (Cannon) Woodson; m. Robert Charles Newman Sr., Dec. 9, 1967 (div. Dec. 1975); 1 child, Robert Charles Jr. Diploma in nursing, Mercy Hosp., New Orleans, 1961; cert. in nurse anesthesia, Charity Hosp., New Orleans, 1963; BA in Health Care, Edn., Ottawa U., 1978; MS in Nurse Anesthesiology, Xavier U., 1992. Cert. RN anesthetist. Staff nurse anesthetist Hotel Dieu Hosp., New Orleans, 1963-70, Oschsner Found. Hosp., New Orleans, 1970-71, Houston Anesthesia Assocs., 1976-81, East Jefferson Hosp., Metairie, La., 1971-76; staff nurse anesthetist, chief nurse anesthetist Stamford (Conn.) Anesthesia Assocs., 1981-91; instr. clin. anesthesia Charity Hosp./Xavier U. Sch. Nurse Anesthesiology, New Orleans, 1991—. Adj. instr. in grad. sch. Xavier U., New Orleans, 1992—. Mem. Coun. for Pub. Interest in Anesthesia (chair 1991-92), Am. Assn. Nurse Anesthetists (mgmt. com. 1991-92, nominating com. 1988-89, minutes com. 1985-86, 92-93, pub. rels. com. 1995-96), La. Assn. Nurse Anesthetists (pub. rels. com. 1992, bd. dirs. 1994-95, chmn. govt. rels. com. 1994-95, 95-96, v.p. 1995-96, acting pres. 1995-96, editor LANASCOPE 1995-96), Conn. Assn. Nurse Anesthetists (pres., v.p., various chairs coms.). Roman Catholic. Avocations: tennis, bridge, aerobic exercise, walking, collecting clocks. Office: Xavier U Charity Hosp Sch Nurse Anesthesiology 1532 Tulane Ave New Orleans LA 70112-2802

NEWMAN, PHYLLIS, adult education educator, psychologist; b. N.Y.C., June 23, 1931; d. Arthur and Augusta (Cohen) Deutsch; m. Stan Newman, Dec. 10, 1967; 1 child, Allen. BS in Indsl. Labor Rels., Cornell U., 1952; MS in Edn.-Psychology, profl. diploma, St. John's U., Jamaica, N.Y., 1976. Tchr. N.Y.C. Bd. Edn., 1963-83, psychologist, 1983-86; instr. adult edn. Pima C.C., Green Valley, Ariz., 1988—92, Pima County Adult Edn., Tucson, 1989—95. Psychologist, counselor, N.Y.C., 1978-86; owner, mgr. Transitions Assocs., seminar condrs., N.Y.C.. Tucson and Green Valley, 1991-99. Author: Transitions: A Woman's Guide to Successful Retirement, 1991. Home and Office: 420 E 55th St Apt 4D New York NY 10022-5140

NEWMAN, RAYMOND MELVIN, biologist, educator; b. New Castle, Pa., June 10, 1956; s. Raymond Melvin and Sarah L. (Lawton) N.; m. Patricia Ann Scott, Nov. 22, 1989. BS in Biology, Slippery Rock (Pa.) U., 1978; MS, U. Minn., 1982, PhD in Fisheries, 1985. Grad. asst. U. Minn., St. Paul, 1979-84, rsch. specialist forest resources, 1985-86, asst. prof. fisheries, 1988-94, assoc. prof. fisheries, 1995—2002, prof. fisheries, 2002—; fellow natural resources U. Conn., Storrs, 1986-88; investigator U. Mich. Biol. Sta., Pellston, 1987-88. Exotics task force Nat. Sea Grant, Silver Spring, Md., 1991; mem. interagy. exotic species com. Minn. Dept. Natural Resources, St. Paul, 1992—; vis. scientist Inst. for Freshwater Ecology, River Lab., Dorset, U.K.; guest scientist Max Planck Inst. Chem. Ecology, Jena, Germany, 2002. Assoc. editor Jour. N.Am. Biol. Soc., 1994-98; mem. editl. bd. Ecology Freshwater Fish, 1992—; contbr. articles to profl. jours., chpts. to books. Bd. dirs. Twin Cities Trout Unltd., Mpls., 1982-87. Fellow Am. Inst. Fishery Rsch. Biologists; mem. Am. Fisheries Soc. (exec. com. Minn. chpt. 1992, 96), Ecol. Soc. Am., N.Am. Benthological Soc. Achievements include rsch. in chemical defense from herbivory by aquatic plants, control of exotic weed by native insects. Office: U Minn Fisheries Wildlife 1980 Folwell Ave Saint Paul MN 55108-1037 E-mail: rmn@fw.umn.edu.

NEWMAN, REBECCA K. principal; BA, Mich. State U., 1968; MEd, U. Kans., 1975, EdD, 1978. Cert. spl. edn. grades K-12 Md., secondary prin. and supr. Md., supt. Md., elem. edn. K-8 Mich., spl. edn. K-12 Mich., English 9-12 Mich., social studies 7-9 Mich. Head tchr. adolescent unit Lafayette Clinic, Detroit, 1968—70; asst. prin., tchr. Island View Adolescent Ctr., Detroit, 1970—71; head tchr. children's unit Lafayette Clinic, Detroit, 1971—73; ednl. dir. Mid-Continent Psychiat. Hosp., Olathe, Kans., 1973—75; program mgr. Severe Personal Adjustment Program, Kansas City, Kans., 1975—78; asst. prin. Rock Terrace H.S. Montgomery County Pub. Schs., 1978—80, prin. Regional Inst. for Children and Adolescents, 1980—86, prin. Mark Twain Mid.-Sr. H.S., 1986—90, supr. secondary instrn. Area 3, 1990—91, acting asst. prin. Wootton H.S., 1991—92, prin. Paint Branch H.S., 1992—95, prin. Wootton H.S., 1995—. Mem. Corp. Partnerships Task Force, Montgomery County, 1996; participant prin.'s view Montgomery County Pub. Schs. Pub. TV, 1989; mem. adv. bd. multidisciplinary master's degree tng. program for tchrs. of the behaviorally disordered/emotionally disturbed U. Md., College Park, 1985—86. Mem. editl. bd.: Focus on Autistic Behavior, 1990—91. Mem.: Montgomery County Assn. Adminstrv. and Supr. Pers. (mem. negotiations team 1993—96).*

NEWMAN, RITA GRAY, retired education specialist; b. Cleveland, Ohio, Aug. 27, 1929; d. Morris Howard and Fannie Schock Gray; m. Robert Joel Newman, Mar. 20, 1949 (dec. Dec. 1975); children: Jeffrey Keith, Joel David, Morris Lee. BA in Elem. Edn., So. Meth. U., 1967, MA in Edn., 1970; PhD in Edn., North Tex. State U., 1979. Tchr. 1st grade, kindergarten Dallas Ind. Sch. Dist., Tex., 1968—71, supr., curriculum writer, 1971—77, prin. McMillan Prim. Sch., 1977—86, prin. Amelia Earhart Learning Ctr., 1986—95; field asst. Tex. Edn. Agy., Richardson, Tex., 1996—98; ednl. cons. Dallas, 1998—. Adj. prof. North Tex. State U., Denton, Tex., 1995—98. Mem.: Assn. Supervision and Curriculum Devel., Nat. Assn. for Edn. of Young Children, Assn. for Childhood Edn. Internat., Rotary, Phi Delta Kappa (internat.). Home: 6349 A Bandera Ave Dallas TX 75225

NEWMAN, ROCHELLE BEVERLY, middle school educator; b. Trenton, N.J. m. Michael A. Newman; children: Daniel, Seth. Student, Mt. Holyoke Coll., 1962-64; BA magna cum laude, U. Mass., 1966. Cert. tchr. math. k-12, N.J. Tchr. N. Las Vegas Jr. H.S., 1967-68, Lawrence H.S., Lawrenceville, NJ, 1977, Ewing H.S., Trenton, N.J., 1977-87, West Windsor, Plainsboro (N.J.) Middle Sch., 1987—. Coach Odyssey of the Mind (won state and nat. competitions); item writer, com. mem. Nat. Assessment of Ednl. Progress, 1989—; item writer, reviewer VNT, coll. bd. com. on quantitative literacy; reviewer AIR PAEETM participant. Vol. religious and comty. activities. Named Outstanding Tchr. Ewing H.S., Gov.'s Program, N.J., 1986; recipient Presdl. award Excellence in Math. Tchg., 2001. Mem. Nat. Coun. Tchrs. of Math., Assn. Math. Tchrs. of N.J. Avocation: travel. Office: Grover Mid Sch 10 Southfield Rd Box 506 West Windsor NJ 08550

NEWMAN, SHARON ANN, principal; b. Denver, Sept. 25, 1946; m. John G. Newman, June 30, 1973; children: Michael, Lisa. BA in Speech, Coll. Mt. St. Joseph, Cin., 1969; MAT in Liberal Studies, Lewis and Clark Coll., Portland, Oreg., 1992. Textbook editor Nat. Textbook Co., Chgo., 1972; tchr. speech and drama Seton High Sch., Cin., 1968-69; tchr. 6th grade St. Therese Sch., Aurora, Colo., 1979-70; tchr. speech and English Seton High Sch., Pueblo, Colo., 1970-71; tchr., head speech dept. Jefferson County Pub. High Schs., Denver, 1971-74; tchr. grades 7 and 8 Shakopee (Minn.) Cath. Middle Sch., 1983-84; tchr., team leader Regis High Sch., Denver, 1985-87; dir. admissions Jesuit High Sch., Portland, 1988-90; prin. St. Thomas More Sch., Portland, 1992-98, Cedaroak Pk. Primary Sch., West Linn, Oreg., 1998—. Speaker, cons. in field. Author newspaper columns, booklets, books for local use. Mem. Cin. Human Rels. Commn., 1967. Recipient Oreg. Disting. Pvt. Sch. Prin. award Oreg. Elem. & Secondary Prins. Assn., 1995. Mem. ASCD, Nat. Assn. Elem. and Secondary Prins., N.W. Women in Ednl. Adminstrn., Confedn. Oreg. Sch. Adminstrs. Avocations: family activities, singing, reading, writing, entertaining. Office: Cedaroak Pk Primary Sch 4515 S Cedaroak Dr West Linn OR 97068

NEWMAN, SHARON LYNN, elementary education educator; b. Lewisburg, Tenn., Jan. 9, 1946; d. Hermit Taft and Martha Elizabeth (Pardue) Simmons; m. George Wynne Newman Sr., June 11, 1967; 1 child, George Wynne Jr. BS in Edn., Athens State Coll., 1979; MEd, Cumberland U., 2001. From substitute tchr. to chpt. 1 reading tchr. Giles County Bd. Edn., Pulaski, Tenn., 1979—89; title I math tchr. Elkton Elem. Sch, 1989—2000, title I reading tchr., 2000. Chpt. 1 coord. Elkton (Tenn.) Elem. Sch., 1989—, mem. steering com., 1989—, chair math. dept., 1993-95, chpt. title I com., 1995—, site dir. title I, 1996—, mem. disaster preparedness team, student learning com., 2002-,PE Curriculum comm., 2002-. Ch. libr. Elkton (Tenn.) Bapt. Ch., 1992—; vol. Giles County Hist. Soc. Libr. and Mus., 1995-,mem. Tenn. Trail of Tears Assoc., 2002-, Mem. NEA, Nat. Coun. Tchrs. Math., Giles County Edn. Assn. (rsch. chairperson 1993-95, IPD com. 1999—, sch. membership rep. 2002-),mem. Giles Coun. Hist. Soc., 1996-, mem. Elkton Hist. Soc. 2000-. Home: 1758 Old Stage Rd Ardmore TN 38449-5308 Office: Elkton Elem Sch Elkton TN 38455

NEWNAM, PHYLLIS SUE See SAND, PHYLLIS SUE NEWNAM

NEWSOM, DAVID DUNLOP, foreign service officer, educator; b. Richmond, Calif., Jan. 6, 1918; s. Fred Stoddard and Ivy Elizabeth (Dunlop) N.; m. Jean Frances Craig, Nov. 17, 1942; children: John, Daniel, Nancy, David, Catherine. AB, U. Calif., 1938; MS, Columbia U., 1940; LLD, U. Pacific, 1979. Pulitzer traveling scholar, 1940-41; pub. Walnut Creek (Calif.) Courier-Jour., 1946-47; 3d sec., info. officer Am. embassy, Karachi, Pakistan, 1948-50; 2d sec., vice consul Oslo, 1950-51; pub. affairs officer Baghdad, Iraq, 1952-55; officer-in-charge Arabian peninsula affairs Dept. State, Washington, 1955-59; with Nat. War Coll., 1959-60; 1st sec. Am. embassy, London, 1960-62; dep. dir. Office No. African Affairs, Dept. State, Washington, 1962-63, dir., 1963-65; U.S. ambassador Libya, 1965-69; asst. sec. state for African affairs, 1969-74; U.S. ambassador, 1974-77, 1977-78; undersec. state of polit. affairs, 1978-81; dir. Inst. Study of Diplomacy, Sch. Fgn. Svc., Georgetown U., 1981-90, Marshall Coyne rsch. prof. diplomacy, 1989-91; interim dean Sch. Fgn. Svc. Georgetown U., 1995-96; Cumming Meml. prof. internat. rels. U. Va., 1991-98; spl. adviser U.S. del. UN Gen. Assembly, 1972, 78, 79, 80. Sr. fellow The Miller Ctr., U. Va., 1999-2003; mem. com. on sci., tech. and health aspects of fgn. policy Nat. Rsch. Coun., 1999. Author: (book) Soviet Brigade in Cuba, Diplomacy and The American Democracy, The Public Dimension of Foreign Policy, The Imperial Mantle. Served to lt. USNR, 1942-46. Recipient Commendable Service award USIS, 1955; Dept. State Meritorious Service award, 1958; Nat. Civil Service League award, 1972; Rockefeller Pub. Service award, 1973; Lifetime award Am. Fgn. Svc. Assn., 2000. Mem. U.S. Fgn. Svc. Assn., Coun. Fgn. Rels., Cosmos Club. Presbyterian. Home: 2409 Angus Rd Charlottesville VA 22901-2631

NEWSOM, GERALD HIGLEY, astronomy educator; b. Albuquerque, Feb. 11, 1939; s. Carroll Vincent and Frances Jeanne (Higley) N.; m. Ann Catherine Bricker, June 17, 1972; children: Christine Ann, Elizabeth Ann. BA, U. Mich., 1961; MA, Harvard U., 1963, PhD, 1968. Research asst. McMath-Hulbert Obs., Pontiac, Mich., summers 1959, 61; research asst. astronomy dept. U. Mich., Ann Arbor, 1959-61; research asst. Shock Tube Lab. Harvard U., Cambridge, Mass., 1962, 64-68; research asst. dept. physics Imperial Coll., London, 1968-69; asst. prof. astronomy Ohio State U., Columbus, 1969-73, assoc. prof., 1973-82, prof., 1982—, acting chmn. dept. astronomy, 1991-93, vice chmn. dept. astronomy, 1993—, acting asst. dean, 1985-86; sr. post-doctoral research asst. Physikalisches Institut, Bonn, Fed. Republic of Germany, 1978. Author: Astronomy, 1976, Exploring the Universe, 1979; contbr. articles to profl. and scholarly jours. Fellow Woodrow Wilson Found., 1961-62, NSF, 1961-63; grantee Noble Found., 1961-64. Mem. Internat. Astron. Union, Am. Astron. Soc. Home: 46 W Weisheimer Rd Columbus OH 43214-2545 Office: Ohio State U Dept Astronomy 140 W 18th Ave Columbus OH 43210-1173 Business E-Mail: gnewsom@astronomy.ohio-state.edu.

NEWSOME, PATRICIA H. retired elementary school educator; b. Athens, Ga., July 12, 1939; d. Charles N. and Frances (Cummings) Harris; m. Paul W. Newsome; four children. BS in Edn., Auburn U., 1961; MEd, Ga. State U., 1974. Tchr. 6th grade Muscogee County Sch. Dist., Columbus, Ga., 1968—99; ret., 1999. Bd. dirs. Second Harvest Food Bank; tutor Our House; alt. South Ga. United Meth. Conf.; bd. dirs. older adult coun. St. Luke Meth. Ch. Named Reading Tchr. of Yr., Muscogee County, 1987-88. Mem. Muscogee County Coun. IRA (membership chair), Ga. Coun. IRA, IRA, Ga. Sci. Tchrs. Assn., Dist. VI Sci. Tchrs. Assn., Muscogee Ret. Educators Assn. (co-chmn.), Ga. Ret. Educators Assn., United Meth. Women (cir. III), Exec. Club, Mr. & Mrs. Club. Home: 2944 Roswell Ln Columbus GA 31906-1341

NEWSOME, SANDRA SINGLETON, elementary education educator, assistant principal; b. Bayboro, N.C., Apr. 4, 1948; d. John Wilson Singleton and Cora Lee (Beasley) Hatchel; m. Edward Newsome Jr., Feb. 14, 1971. BS, Elizabeth City State U., 1970; MS, Bowie State U., 1979; EdD, Pensacola Christian Coll., 1992. Cert. tchr., Washington. Tchr. D.C. Pub. Schs., Washington, 1970-80, reading tchr., 1980-82, reading specialist, 1982-99; asst. prin. Calvary Temple Christian Sch., Sterling, Va., 1985-86; prof. Bowie State U., Washington, 1994—; prin. Roper Middle Sch. of Math, Sci. and Tech., Washington, 1996-97; reading thcr. James Madison Middle Sch. Prince George's County Pub. Schs., 1999, sch. improvement resource tchr. Beacon Hts. Elem. Sch., 1999, asst. prin. Melwood Elem. Sch., 1999—. Adminstrv. intern Roper Mid. Sch. of Math. Sci. and Tech., Washington, 1993-95; cons. Bowie State Spl. Interest Coun., 1991-92, D.C.-Dakar Friendship Coun., 1991-92; adv. bd. Walk In Faith mag., Washington, 1991-92; dir. Acad. Tutorial Program, Temple Hills, Md., 1990-91; coord. Best Friends Nat. Orgn. Francis Jr. High, Washington. Contbr. articles to profl. jours. Mentor Teen Parenting, Inc., Hyattville, Md., 1989, Valuettes, Washington, 1990-92; dir. Adult Literacy Coun., Temple Hills, 1990; asst. dir. Jr. Toastmasters, Brightwood, 1993; program developer, dir. Visions: A Tour into Values, Washington, 1993; pres. Hellen Lee Dr. Civic Assn., Clinton, 1994-95; dir. Christian Edn., Alexandria (Va.) Christian Ctr., 1994—. Recipient Save Our Youth Am. award Soya, Inc., Washington, 1989, Literacy award Bowie State U., 1991; Teacher-to-Teacher grantee, 1990-92; fellow Cafritz Found., 1991. Mem. ASCD, AFT, AAUW, LEAD Program, Nat. Black Child Devel. Inst., Bowie State Spl. Interest Orgn., Alexandria Christian Ctr., Hellen Lee Dr. Civic Assn. (pres. 1994-95). Avocations: interpretative poetry reading, travel, african studies, photography. Home: 2319 Parkside Dr Mitchellville MD 20721-4229 Office: Melwood Elem Sch 7100 Woodyard Rd Upper Marlboro MD 20772-4316

NEWSON, ADELE SHERON, English educator; b. Inkster, Mich., Oct. 16, 1957; d. Bud and Addie Lee (Gordon) Newson; divorced; children: Alexander Sean, Anne Simone Gordon-Newson. BA, Spelman Coll., 1980; MA, Ea. Mich. U., 1981; PhD, Mich. State U., 1986. Instr. Mich. State U., East Lansing, 1968-87; adj. prof. English U. Md. Eastern Shore, Princess Anne, 1987-89; asst. prof. English Albright Coll., Reading, Pa., 1989-92; assoc. prof. English Fla. Internat. U., Miami, 1992—. Author: Zora Neale Hurston: A Reference Guide, 1987; contbr. articles to profl. jours. and encys. Juror Md. State Arts Coun., Balt., 1991. Fulbright exch. scholar Potchefstroom U., South Africa, 1992—. Mem. MLA, Nat. Coun. Tchrs. of English, Mid.-Atlantic Writers Assn., Zora Neale Hurston Soc. (sec. 1989—). Office: Fla Internat U North Campus Dept English Miami FL 33181 Home: 1022 Merritt Ave Oshkosh WI 54901-5344

NEWTON, CHARLES KENNEDY, special education educator, educator; s. Charles Newton and Nancy (Kennedy) N.; m. Vicki Ann Newton, Apr. 18, 1981; 1 child, Charles Clifford Newton. BA, Goddard Coll., 1967; MA, U.S. Internat. U., 1972; teaching credential, Calif. State U., L.A. Tchr. other health impaired Multnomah County Edn. Svc. Dist. Mem. Coun. for Exceptional Children; big brother YMCA Big Brother Program. Recipient Excellence in Spl. Edn. award, Coun. for Exceptional Children. Avocations: sailing, canoeing.

NEWTON, ELIZABETH PURCELL, counselor, consultant, author; b. Madison, N.C., June 3, 1925; d. Charles Augustus and Anna Meta (Buchanan) P.; m. William Edward Newton, June 11, 1949; children—James Purcell, Betsy Newton Hein, Christina Newton Harwood. A.A., Peace Coll., 1944; B.A., U. N.C., 1946; M.Ed., Ga. State U., 1969; Ed.S., West Ga. Coll., 1981. Tchr., counselor S. Cobb High Sch., Austell, Ga., 1965-69; counselor, dept. head Wheeler High Sch., Marietta, Ga., 1969-76; counselor, div. head guidance services Walton High Sch., Marietta, Ga., 1976—90; ret., 1990; sch. rep. Coll. Bd., Princeton, N.J., 1981—90, panelist, presenter S.E. region, Atlanta, 1983-85; presenter Ga. Sch. Counselors Assn., Atlanta, 1980—90; cons. Panhandle Area Edn. Coop., Chipley, Fla., 1985. Author: Steps to College Admissions, 1978; Student's Guide to College Admissions, 1981; Student's Guide to Career Preparation, 1982. Sch. rep. Citizens Adv. Council, Marietta, 1981, 82, 85. Ga. Dept. Edn. grantee, 1981; named Outstanding Woman in Edn., Atlanta Jour., 1985. Mem. Cobb Counselor Assn. (organizer, chmn. nominations com. 1985), Ga. Sch. Counselors Assn. (Secondary Counselor of Yr. 1983), Am. Sch. Counselors Assn. (Nat. Secondary Counselor of Yr. 1984), Phi Delta Kappa. Presbyterian.

NEWTON, JANNA SUE, elementary education educator; b. Fort Smith, Ark., Feb. 1, 1943; d. Ivor Eugene Hill and Anne Elise (Ross) Martin; m. Albert Lee Newton, June 21, 1968; children: Penelope S., Hunter Lee. BS, Ark. Tech. U., 1965. Educator Fort Smith Pub. Schs., 1965—. Mem. elem. coun. Ark. Dept. Edn., Little Rock, 1993—99. Mem. Assn. Childhood Edn. Internat. (bd. dirs. 1965—).

NEWTON, ROGER GERHARD, educator, physicist; b. Landsberg, Germany, Nov. 30, 1924; came to U.S., 1946, naturalized, 1949; s. Arthur and Margaret (Blume) Neuweg; m. Ruth Gordon, June 18, 1953; children: Rachel, Julie, Paul. Student, U. Berlin, Germany; AB summa cum laude, Harvard, 1949, MA, 1950, PhD, 1953. Teaching fellow Harvard, 1951-52; mem. Inst. Advanced Study, Princeton, 1953-55, 79; mem. faculty Ind. U., 1955-, prof. physics, 1960-78, disting. prof. physics, 1978—95, disting. prof. emeritus, 1995—, chmn. dept., 1973-80, chmn. math. physics program, 1965-86, dir. Inst. for Advanced Study, 1982-86. Vis. prof. U. Rome, Italy, 1962-63, U. Montpellier, France, 1971-72 Author: Scattering Theory of Waves and Particles, 1966, 2d edit., 1982, The Complex j-Plane, 1964, Inverse Schrödinger Scattering in Three Dimension, 1989, What Makes Nature Tick?, 1993, The Truth of Science, 1997, Thinking About Physics, 2000, Quantum Physics, 2002; assoc. editor: Jour. Math. Physics, 1967-70, 73-76, 83-86, editor 1992—; assoc. editor Am. Jour. Physics, 1986-88; assoc. editor Inverse Problems, 1985-90, internat. adv. panel 1991—; contbr. articles to profl. jours. Pres. Bloomington Civil Liberties Union, 1968. Served with AUS, 1946-47. Recipient Bowdoin prize Harvard, 1948; Jewett fellow, 1953-55; NSF sr. postdoctoral fellow, 1962-63; C.N.R.S. fellow U. Montpellier, France, 1971-72 Fellow AAAS (coun. 1987-89), Am. Phys. Soc. (chmn. Heinemann prize com. 1991-92); mem. AAUP, N.Y. Acad. Scis., Fedn. Am. Scientists, Phi Beta Kappa (pres. Gamma chpt. 1991-92), Sigma Xi.

NEZIRI, MARIA G. DE LUCIA, elementary school educator; b. Mineola, N.Y., Dec. 27, 1967; d. Salvatore and Alfonsina DeL.; m. Lulzim Neziri, Aug. 20, 1995; 1 child, Noah. BS Edn., Adelphi U., 1990; MS in Edn., Queens U., 1994; MS in Reading and Spl. Edn., Hofstra U., 1999. Cert. tchr. reading, spl. edn. K-12. Elem. tchr. Westbury (N.Y.) Pub. Schs., 1990—. Creator, coord The Write View, The Writing Club after school club; creator, instr. inservice courses Reading and Writing Workshop; mentor for new tchrs. Mem. Nat. Coun. Tchrs. Maths., Nat. Coun. Tchrs. English, Internat. Reading Assn. Avocations: gardening, cooking, reading. Home: 37 S Fulton St Westbury NY 11590-5205

NG, KWOK-WAI, physics educator; b. Hong Kong, Aug. 15, 1958; came to U.S., 1981; s. Wan-Fu and Kam-Har (Sin) N.; m. Grace Mun Yan, Dec. 28, 1987; 1 child, Nelson Eukai. BSc, U. Hong Kong, 1981; PhD, Iowa State U., 1986. Postdoctoral fellow U. Tex., Austin, 1986-88; asst. prof. physics U. Ky., Lexington, 1988-94, assoc. prof., 1994-2000, prof., 2000—. Contbr. articles to Phys. Rev. Letter, Phys. Rev. B, Japanese Jour. Applied Physics. Mem. IEEE, Am. Phys. Soc., Phi Kappa Phi. Achievements include gap anisotropy of high Tc superconductors; superconducting tunneling spectroscopy. Office: Univ Ky Dept Physics Astronomy Lexington KY 40506-0001 E-mail: kwng@uky.edu.

NG, PETER ANN-BENG, computer science educator, researcher; b. Yong-Peng, Johore, Malaysia, Dec. 31, 1941; came to U.S., 1966; s. Kim-Chong and Hwee-Kuan (Chua) Ng; m. Ida Ah-Siew-Lim, May 24, 1969; children: Eric Huai-Tsaw, Evan Hean-Tsaw. BS in Math., St. Edward's U., 1969; PhD in Computer Sci., U. Tex., 1974. Asst. prof. CUNY, N.Y.C., 1974-76, U. Mo., Columbia, 1976-81, assoc. prof., 1981-84, prof., chmn., 1984-86, U. North Tex., Denton, 1986-87, N.J. Inst. Tech., Newark, 1987-97; prof. U. Nebr., Omaha, 1998—, chair dept. computer sci., 1998-2000, dir. Inst. for Integrated Systems Rsch., 1986-97, exec. dir. Global e-Learning Project, Intl. Progs./Studies, 2000—. Founder Internat. Conf. Systems Integration; mem. acad. affairs bd. HIST, Shanghai, China, 1999—. Editor: Modern Software Engineering, 1990; mem. editorial bd. IEEE Transactions on Software Engring. 1983-90; advisory editor Data & Knowledge Engring. Jour., 1984—; editor-in-chief Jour. on Systems Integration, 1991—. Fellow Soc. for Design and Process Sci.; mem. IEEE Computer Soc., ACM. Roman Catholic. Avocations: basketball, soccer. Office: U Nebraska Omaha Coll Info Sci & Tech Dept Of Computer Science Omaha NE 68182-0001

NG, WING CHIU, accountant, educator, application developer, lawyer, educator, advocate; b. Hong Kong, Oct. 14, 1947; came to U.S., 1966; s. Bing Nuen and Oi Ying (Lee) Ng. BS, MS, Yale U., 1969; PhD, NYU, 1972; JD, U. Hawaii, 2000. Bar: Hawaii 2001; CPA, Hawaii. Rsch. assoc. SUNY, Stony Brook, 1972-74; asst. prof. U. Md., College Park, 1974-76; rsch. physicist U. Bonn, Fed. Republic of Germany, 1976-78; chartered acct. Richter, Usher & Vineberg, Montreal, Can., 1978-80; pvt. practice Honolulu, Hawaii, 1980—; pres. Bowen, Ng & Co., Honolulu, 1983-84, Asia-Am. Investment, Inc., Honolulu, 1983—, Mathematica Pacific, Inc., Honolulu, 1984—. Part-time prof. U. Hawaii, Honolulu, 1982—; ptnr. Advance Realty Investment, Honolulu, 1980—; dir. S & L Internat., Inc., Honolulu, 1987—. Creator: (computer software) Time Billing, 1984, Dbase General Ledger, 1987, Dbase Payroll, 1987, Dbase Accounts Receivable, 1989; co-author: Draft Constitution of the Federal Republic of China, 1994. Dir. Orgn. of Chinese Ams., Honolulu, 1984-86, Fedn. for a Dem. China, Honolulu, 1990—, Hong Kong, 1991—; dir. Alliance Hong Kong Chinese in U.S., 1995—. Included in Prominent People of Hawaii, Delta Pub. Co., 1988. Mem. AICPA, Hong Kong Soc. Accts., Hawaiian Trail & Mountain Club (auditor 1987—). Democrat. Buddhist. Avocations: hiking, the internet. Office: 1149 Bethel St Ste 306 Honolulu HI 96813-2210

NGUYEN, CHARLES CUONG, engineering educator, researcher, dean; b. Danang, Vietnam, Jan. 1, 1956; arrived in U.S., 1978, naturalized, 1978; s. Buoi and Tinh Thi Nguyen; m. Kim-Bang Pham, Aug. 5, 1989; children: Carissa Kim Thuy Duong, Olivia Quynh Duong, Dylan Nhat Khang, Parker Duy Khang. Diploma, Konstanz U., Fed. Rep. Germany, 1978; MS with distinction, George Washington U., 1980, DSc with superiour performance, 1982. Engr. Siemens Corp., Erlangen, Germany, 1977-78; lectr. George Washington U., Washington, 1978-82; asst. prof. engring. Cath. U. Am., Washington, 1982-85, assoc. prof. elec. engring., 1985-92, prof., 1992—, chmn. dept. elec. engring. and computer sci., 1997-2001, dean Sch. Engring., 2001—. Cons. Mitre Corp., Meridian Corp., Jet Propulsion Lab., others; dir. Ctr. Artificial Intelligence and Robotics, 1985—; mem. organizing coms. various robotics confs.; sr. rsch. assoc. NAS, 1990—; program vice chair IEE-Internat. Conf. Robotics 2d Automation, 1997, Internat. Symposium and Robotic Automation, 1997; chmn. organizing com. Robotics Internat., Internat. Symposium Robotics and Mfg. Founding editor, editor-in-chief: Jour. Intelligent Automation and Soft Computing; editor: (book) Robotics and Manufacturing, Vol. 5, 1994, Intelligent Automation and Soft Computing, Vol. 1, 1994, Intelligent Automation and Soft Computing, Vol. 2, 1994; mem. editl. bd.: Jour. Intelligent and Fuzzy Sys., Engring. Design and Automation, assoc. editor: Computers and Elec. Engring.: An Internat. Jour., 1992—, guest editor: Jour. Robotic Sys., —; contbr. scientific papers to profl. jours. Recipient Rsch. Initiation award, Engring. Found., 1985; fellow, NASA-Am. Soc. Elec. Engring., 1985, 1986, NASA-Am. Soc. Elec. Engring. Summer, Goddard Space Flight Ctr., 1994; scholar Disting. Alumni, George Washington U., 2001—02. Mem.: IEEE (sr.; program v.p. Washington chpt.), Soc. Mfg. Engrs. (sr. Robotics Internat.), Internat. Soc. Mini-and Microcomputers, Tau Beta Pi (faculty advisor), Sigma Xi. Roman Catholic. Avocations: guitar, singing, tennis, skiing, ping pong. E-mail: nguyen@cua.edu.

NGUYEN, HUONG TRAN, English language professional, federal agency official; b. Haiphong, Vietnam, Nov. 16, 1953; came to the U.S., 1971; d. Joe (Quang) Trong Tran and Therese (Nguyet-Anh) (Do) Dotran; m. Tony (Phu) The Nguyen; children: Long Tran Nguyen, Ty Tran Nguyen. B in Liberal Studies, San Diego State U., 1976, tchg. credential grades K-12, 1977; M in Curriculum Devel., Point Loma Coll., 1984; lang. devel. specialist cert., Calif. Commn. Credentialing, 1991. ESL tchr. San Diego (Calif.) Job Corps, 1978-80; resource tchr. grades K-12 San Diego (Calif.) Unified Sch. Dist., 1980-82; resource tchr. SEAL project grades K-12 Long Beach (Calif.) Unified Sch. Dist., 1982-83, ESL specialist, 1983-85, 85-92, English lang. devel. tchr., chair, 1992-95; adminstr., 1996-98; sr. fellow officer U.S. Dept. Edn., Office Bilingual & Minority Lang. Affairs, Washington, 1995-96; disting. tchr.-in-residence Calif. State U., Long Beach, 1998—. Named Outstanding Tchr. of 1994, Disney Co. Am. Tchr. Awards, Washington, 1994, Outstanding Tchr. in Fgn. Lang./ESL, Disney Co. Am. Tchr. Awards, Washington, 1994. Mem. NEA, TESOL, Calif. Lang. Tchrs. Assn., Calif. Tchr. Assn., Calif. Assn. for Bilingual Edn., Tchr. Assn. Long Beach, Assn. Curriculum and Supervision. Avocations: reading, traveling, gardening, visiting museums. Home: 6262 Cherokee Dr Westminster CA 92683-2004 Office: Calif State U Coll Edn Dept Tchr Edn 1250 N Bellflower Blvd Long Beach CA 90840-0001

NGUYEN, KING XUAN, language educator; b. Hue, Vietnam, Dec. 20, 1930; came to U.S., 1975; s. Duong Xuan Nguyen and Thi Thi Ton-Nu. BA, U. Saigon, 1960, LLB, 1963; MEd, Boise State U., 1980. Tchr. Boise Sch. Dist., 1975-95; lectr. S.E. Asian Studies Summer Inst./U. Wash., 1992, 93, U. Wis., 1994, Ariz. State U., 1996, 97. Spl. lectr. Boise State U., 1975-77. Col. Vietnamese Air Force to 1975. Recipient Red Apple Award for Outstanding Svc. to Edn., Boise, 1990. Mem. NEA, Idaho Edn. Assn., Boise Edn. Assn., Consortium Tchrs. Southeast Asian Langs., Assn. of TESOL. Home: 9674 W Pattie Ct Boise ID 83704-2824

NGUYEN, LAN THI HOANG, physician, educator; b. Hai-Duong, Vietnam, July 18, 1950; came to U.S., 1975; d. Thua Nang and Niem Thi (Do) N.; m. Khanh Vinh Quoc, Oct. 15, 1981. MD, U. Kans., 1983. Intern St. Mary Med. Ctr./UCLA, Long Beach, Calif., 1983-84; resident City of Faith Med. Rsch. Ctr.-Oral Roberts Sch. Medicine, Tulsa, 1986-88; fellow VA Med. Ctr.-Wadsworth-UCLA, 1988-90; physician Santa Ana (Calif.) Med. Ctr., Doctors Hosp. Santa Ana, Fountain Valley (Calif.) Regional Med. Ctr. Clin. assoc. prof. family medicine Keck Sch. Medicine U. So. Calif., L.A., 2002—. Contbr. articles to profl. jours. V.p. Vietnamese Am. Med. Rsch. Found. Kans. Med. scholar, 1979-81. Fellow: ACP, Am. Coll. Endocrinology, Am. Coll. Nutrition; mem.: Am. Assn. Clin. Endocrinologists (charter). Office: 14971 Brookhurst St Westminster CA 92683-5556

NGUYEN, VUNG DUY, radiologist, educator; b. Nhatrang, Vietnam, Dec. 25, 1938; came to U.S., 1975; s. Con Duy and Duc Thi Nguyen; m. Quy Tran, Nov. 10, 1963; children: Khanh Duy, Phong Duy, Lam Duy, Linhda. MD with honors, Saigon (Vietnam) U., 1964; cert., U. Tex. Health Sci. Ctr., San Antonio, 1979. Lic. radiologist, Tex. Radiologist chief Draftee Ctr., Gia Dinh, Vietnam, 1967-69; staff radiologist Cong Hoa Hosp., Saigon, 1969-74; asst. chief radiology dept. Saigon Med. Sch., Saigon, 1974-75; instr. radiology U. Tex. Health Sci. Ctr., San Antonio, 1977-79, asst. prof. radiology, 1980-84, assoc. prof. radiology, 1985—. Cons. skeletal radiology Med. Hosp. Ctr., San Antonio, 1979—; cons., chief of svc. Audie Murphy VA Hosp., San Antonio, 1979—. Contbr. chpts. to books, 30 articles to profl. jours. Advisor Vietnamese med. students, San Antonio, 1980—. maj. South Vietnamese Army Med. Corps, 1958-74. Recipient Am. Physician Recognition award AMA, 1983. Mem. AAAS, U. Radiologists Assn., Radiol. Soc. N.Am., Internat. Skeletal Soc., N.Y. Acad. Scis. Avocations: soccer, swimming, fishing, gardening, traveling. Home: 3511 Hunters Sound St San Antonio TX 78230-2838 also: Woodward/White Inc 129 1st Ave Aiken SC 29801-4862

NICELY, DENISE ELLEN, elementary education educator; b. Fort Carson, Colo., Apr. 28, 1966; d. Dallas Lorenzo and Elizabeth Mae (Thurston) Nicely. BS, Radford U. Cert. elem./mid. sch. tchr., Va. Tchr. kindergarten Basics Primary Sch., Chesapeake, Va., 1989-90; tchr. third grade B.M. Williams Elem., Chesapeake, 1990-91, tchr. second grade, 1991—. Math. curriculum devel., Chesapeake Pub. Schs., 1992—; sci. lead tchr. B.M. Williams Primary, 1992—, math. lead tchr., 1992—. Spl. Olympics Vol., Chesapeake Spl. Olympics, 1990—; supporter Va. Paralyzed Vets. Assn., 1992—. Mem. Chesapeake Edn. Assn., Nat. Coun. Tchrs. Math., PTA. Presbyterian. Avocations: volleyball, softball. Office: BM Williams Primary 1100 Battlefield Blvd N Chesapeake VA 23320-4736

NICELY, ROBERT FRANCIS, JR., education educator, administrator; b. Greensburg, Pa., Jan. 10, 1940; s. Robert Francis and Jean Isabelle (Baird) N.; m. Donna Comnale, Dec. 29, 1962; children: Lisa Ann, Scott Alan. BS, Pa. State U., 1961; MEd, Indiana U. Pa., 1965; PhD, U. Pitts., 1970. Cert. tchr. math and sci., Pa. Tchr. math. and chemistry Norwin and Gateway Schs., 1961-67; instrnl. cons. Pitts. Sch. Dist., 1967-68; lectr., asst. prof., rsch. assoc. U. Pitts., 1968-72; from asst. prof. edn. to prof. emeritus, assoc. dean and acting dean to assoc. dean emeritus Pa. State U., 1972—2002, prof. emeritus, assoc. dean emeritus, 2002—. Contbr. articles to profl. jours.; spkr. in field. Mem. ASCD (bd. dirs. 1981-85, 95-99, chair nominating com. 1986-87, chair conf. com. 1990, exec. coun. 2001-03, assoc. editor, co-editor, mem. editl. bd. Jour. Curriculum and Supervision 1985-92, Outstanding Affiliate Newsletter and Jour. awards 1993, 94, 96, 98, 2000, 02), Pa. ASCD (pres. 1982-84, exec. bd. 1978-, editor PASCD Update and Pa. Ednl. Leadership, Outstanding Rsch. and Pub. award 1985, 99, Disting. Svc. award 1986, Spl. Leadership award 1990, 97, Pres. award 2002), Cen. Pa. ASCD, Coun. Profs. Instrnl. Supervision, Nat. Coun. Tchrs. Math. (chair instrnl. issues adv. com. 1992-94), Pa. Coun. Tchrs. Math. (pres. 1988-90, Outstanding Leadership and Svc. award 1983, Outstanding Contbns. to Math. Edn. award, 1991, co-editor 4 PCTM Yearbooks), Pa. Edn. Rsch. Assn. (pres. 1987-88, 94-95, editor Pera-Scope 1985-95), Phi Delta Kappa (pres. Pa. state chpt. 1984-85). Avocations: aerobic conditioning, golf, landscape design and construction, genealogy. Home: 2266 Sagamore Dr State College PA 16803-2420 Office: Pa State U 314 Rackley University Park PA 16802-7023 E-mail: bobnicely@psu.edu.

NICHOLAS, DAVID, history educator; AB, U. N.C., Chapel Hill, 1961; AM, U. Calif., Berkeley, 1963; PhD, Brown U., 1967. Asst. prof. history U. Nebr., Lincoln, 1967—71, assoc. prof. history, 1971—76, prof. history, 1976—89, Clemson (S.C.) U., 1989—2001, Kathryn Calhoun Lemon prof. of history, 2001—, head dept. history, 1985—95. Mem. editl. bd. The Oxford Dictonary of the Middle Ages. Fellowship for younger scholars, NEH, 1969—70, fellow, Am. Coun. Learned Socs., 1978, John Simon Guggenheim Meml. Found., 2003, Grant-in-aid, Am. Coun. Learned Socs., 1969. Office: Clemson U Kathryn and Clahoun Lemon Prof History Clemson SC 29634-0527

NICHOLAS, RALPH WALLACE W. anthropologist, educator; b. Dallas, Nov. 28, 1934; s. Ralph Wendell and Ruth Elizabeth (Oury) N.; m. Marta Ruth Weinstock, June 13, 1963. BA, Wayne U., 1957; MA, U. Chgo., 1958, PhD, 1962. From asst. prof. to prof. Mich. State U., East Lansing, 1964-71; prof. anthropology U. Chgo., 1971—, chmn. dept., 1981-82, dep. provost, 1982-87, dean of coll., 1987-92, dir. Ctr. Internat. Studies, 1984-95, William Rainey Harper prof. anthropology and social scis., 1992-2000, William Rainey Harper prof. emeritus, 2000—; pres. Internat. House of Chgo.,

1993-2000. Cons. Ford Found., Dhaka, Bangladesh, 1973 Author: (with others) Kinship Bengali Culture, 1977, The Fruits of Worship, 2003; editor: Jour. Asian Studies, 1975-78. V.p. Am. Inst. Indian Studies, 1974-76, treas., 1993-2001, pres.-elect 2001-02, pres. 2002—; trustee Bangladesh Found.; dir. Indo-Am. Ctr., Chgo. Ford Found. fgn. area tng. fellow, India, 1960-61; Sch. Oriental and African Studies research fellow, London, 1962-63; sr. Fulbright fellow, West Bengal, India, 1968-69 Fellow AAAS, Am. Anthrop. Assn., Royal Anthrop. Inst. (Eng.); mem. Assn. Asian Studies, India League of Am. Found. (trustee). Office: U Chgo Dept Anthropology 1126 E 59th St Chicago IL 60637-1580 also: Am Inst Indian Studies 1130 E 59th St Chicago IL 60637

NICHOLERIS, CAROL ANGELA, music educator, composer, conductor; b. Cambridge, Mass., Oct. 15, 1955; d. Menelaus and Sophia (Flecca) N. BMusic, Boston U., 1977, D in Mus. Arts, 1997; MAT, Bridgewater State Coll., 1983, CAGS Edn. Adminstrn., 1991. Cert. music specialist, supr./dir. music edn. Dir. music Hingham Congl. Ch., 1976-95; tchr. music Silver Lake Regional H.S., Kingston, Mass., 1977-79, Hingham (Mass.) Pub. Schs., 1982, Whitman (Mass.) Pub. Schs., 1982-88; asst. prof. elem. music edn. Bridgewater (Mass.) State Coll. Lab. Sch., 1988-98, asst. prof. music composition and gen. studies, 1998-2000, assoc. prof. music composition & gen. studies, 2000—. Asst. condr. Harbour Chora Arts Soc., Hanover, Mass., 1988—93; music dir. Braintree Choral Soc., 1998—2001, Bridgewater State Coll. Alumni Chamber Choir, 2000—. Pub. composer of choral music. Mem. NEA, Am. Choral Dirs. Assn. (life), Music Educators Nat. Conf., Pi Kappa Lambda (life). Avocations: winter mountaineering, hiking, fishing, skiing. Office: Bridgewater State Coll Music Dept Maxwell Libr Bridgewater MA 02325-0001 E-mail: cnicholeris@bridgew.edu.

NICHOLLS, RICHARD ALLEN, middle school social studies educator; b. Chgo., Sept. 1, 1944; s. Harry Allen and Rita Mae (O'Connell) N.; m. Linda Lee Soderberg, Mar. 27, 1969 (div. 1979). AA, Lincoln Coll., 1964; BA, MacMurray Coll., 1966; postgrad., Loyola U., 1967; MA, Nat. Lewis U., 1991. Cert. volleyball coach. 6th grade tchr. Chgo. Pub. Schs., 1966-67; 7th & 8th grades tchr. Palos Sch. Dist. 118, Palos Park, Ill., 1967—. Sponsor student govt. Palos Sch. Dist. 118, 1971-73, sponsor pompon squad, 1971-73, mem. curriculum devel. com., 1970-72; writer (with others) curriculum for devel. of thematic units for transition of Palos South Jr. H.S. to Palos Mid. Sch., summer 1995; volleyball coach Palos South Jr. H.S. (now Palos South Mid. Sch.), 1977-90, Victor J. Andrew H.S., 1981-84, Carl Sandburg H.S., 1985-91; mem. Ill. Goals Assessment Program com. for sch. stds., 1992-93. Mem. NEA, Ill. Edn. Assn., U.S. Volleyball Assn., Palos Edn. Assn., Am. Athletic Union (volleyball coach, nat. champions 1981, 82, 95, finalists 1984, 85, 87 jr. Olympics Nat. Tournament, 5th pl. jr. Nats., 1994) Am. Legion (Citizenship award 1964), Phi Theta Kappa. Avocations: coaching volleyball, sponsoring school trips, personal training for physical fitness. Office: Palos Sch Dist 118 8800 W 119th St Ste 1 Palos Park IL 60464-1099

NICHOLLS, STEPHEN CHARLES, surgeon, educator; b. New Zealand, Oct. 8, 1950; came to U.S., 1976; BS, U. Auckland, New Zealand, MD, 1975. Diplomate Am. Bd. Surgery, Am. Bd. Vascular Surgery. Intern Auckland Pub. Hosp., 1975; resident in surgery Albert Einstein Med. Ctr., N.Y.C., 1976-77, Mt. Sinai Hosp., N.Y.C., 1979-83, fellow vascular surgery, 1985-86; fellow clin. rsch. U. Wash., Seattle, 1983-85, surgeon, 1986—; chief vascular surgery, dir. vascular lab. Harborview Med. Ctr., Seattle; assoc. prof. U. Wash., Seattle, 1986—. Fellow AHA Stroke Coun., Wellcare Networks; mem. Internat. Soc. Cardiovascular Surgery, Soc. Vascular Surgery. Home: 726 12th Ave E Seattle WA 98102-4622 Office: U Wash Dept Surgery 359796 325 9th Ave Seattle WA 98104-2499 Business E-Mail: stevenic@u.washington.edu.

NICHOLS, CALEB LEROY, lawyer, educator, employment consultant; b. Sedley, Va., Oct. 19, 1947; s. Alfred Manry and Sylvia Lee (Young) N. BA, Norfolk State U., 1970; JD, U. Conn., West Hartford, 1973; LLM, Georgetown U., 1977; grad. Exec. Mgmt. Program, Yale Sch. Mgmt., 1988. Bar: Pa. 1974, U.S. Ct. Customs and Patent Appeals 1974, U.S. Ct. Mil. Appeals 1974, U.S. Ct. Claims 1974, U.S. Customs Ct. 1974, U.S. Tax Ct. 1974, U.S. Dist. Ct. (ea. dist.) Pa. 1977, U.S. Ct. Appeals (9th cir.) 1977, U.S. Supreme Ct. 1977, U.S. Ct. Appeals (4th cir.) 1978, U.S. Ct. Internat. Trade 1981. Legal asst. First Nat. Bank, Portland, Oreg., 1977-78; securities examiner Corp. Commn., Salem, Oreg., 1978-79; examiner atty. Nat. Assn. Securities Dealers, Chgo., 1979-80; legal asst. Legal Svc. Corp. Iowa, DesMoines, 1980; asst. counsel Pa. Dept. Revenue, Harrisburg, 1981-83; dir. Conn. Dept. Banking, Hartford, 1983-87; prof. Western Conn. State Coll., Danbury, 1987-93, Ancell Sch. Bus. Western Conn. State U., 1987-93; dir. affirmative action Western Conn. State U., 1993-95; pres. Nichols Consulting Svcs., 1994—. Atty. Office of James W. Harris, York, Pa., 1992-2002; adj. prof. Pace U. Law Sch., 1989; mem. task force Bd. Accountancy Conn. Sec. of State; mem. World Affairs Ctr., Hartford, 1987. Mem. bd. adv. inst. fin. planning Quinnipiac Coll., 1987. Lt. USCG, 1973-77. Mem. FBA, N.Am. Securities Adminstrs. Assn. (chmn. disclosure com. 1983-85), Nat. Assn. Securities Dealers, Inc. (arbitrator 1982—), Westchester-Fairfield Corp. Counsel Assn., Practising Law Inst., Inst. Fin. Planning (bd. advisers). Home and Office: PO Box 1585 Erie PA 16507

NICHOLS, CAROL JEAN, nurse educator; Diploma in nursing, Greenville (S.C.) Gen. Hosp., 1963; BS in Vocat. Edn. cum laude, Ga. State U., 1978, MEd, 1980, EdS, 1987. Staff nurse psychiat. unit Greenville Gen. Hosp., 1963-68; nurse educator/instr. Shands Teaching Hosp., Gainesville, Fla., 1968-69, asst. head nurse radiation therapy dept., nurse educator, 1969-71; from staff nurse to head nurse Drs. Meml. Hosp., Atlanta, 1971-73; supr. psychiat. area, responsible for staff/patient edn. Touro Infirmary, New Orleans, 1973; staff nurse operating rm. N.E. Ga. Med. Ctr., Gainesville, Ga., 1974; asst. supr. operating rm. Joan Glancy Hosp., Duluth, Ga., 1974; instr. pediatrics Atlanta Tech. Inst., 1974—2001, also coord. infection control, 1993—2000; ret., 2000. Mem. Ga. Nurses Assn. (treas. 4th dist.), Am. Heart Assn., Ga. Vocat. Assn. (past v.p. and 1st v.p. region I), Am. Vocat. Assn., Mortar Bd., Golden Key, Blue Key, Kappa Delta Pi.

NICHOLS, CHARLES EDWARD, secondary education administrator; b. Charleston, W. Va., Feb. 1, 1947; s. Clarence H. and Sybil A. (Carpenter) N.; m. Pamela K. Lytle, June 10, 1967; children: Charles E. II, Christopher F. AB in Edn., Music and Math., Glenville State Coll., 1970; MA in Edn. Adminstrn., W. Va. Grad. Coll., 1978. Cert. tchr. secondary level, music, math., adminstrn. County music coord., band dir. Clay (W. Va.) County Schs., 1970-76; adminstr. Elk Valley Christian Sch., Elkview, W. Va., 1976-77; choral dir., music tchr. Clay County High Sch., 1977-82, dean of students, 1982-85; dir., transp. and student svcs. Clay County Schs., 1985-89, dir. fed. and spl. projects, 1989-94; staff devel. dir. Regional Edn. Svc. Agy., Dunbar, W.Va., 1994-98, exec. dir., 1998—. Adult base edn. instr. Clay County Schs., 1980-85; extension instr. Glenville (W. Va.) State Coll., 1982, 85; adj. instr. W. Va. Grad. Coll., Institute, W. Va., 1991—; presenter IBM Schs. Exec. Conf., Atlanta, 1993, Nat. Ednl. Computer Conf., Balt., 1994. Author: Elk Valley Student/Parent Handbook, 1977. Sec. Reamer Hill Cemetery Assn., Inc.; elder King's Way Christian Ch., Nitro, W.Va. Mem. W.Va. Assn. Sch. Adminstrs., Am. Assn. Edn. Svc. Agys., W.Va. Regional Edn. Svc. Agys. (mem. exec. com., chmn., legis. liaison). Home: 204 Ehman Dr Charleston WV 25302-4213 Office: Regional Edn Svc Agy III 501 22nd St Dunbar WV 25064-1711

NICHOLS, DIANE LINDA CLARK, French language educator; b. Barre, Vt., Dec. 29, 1947; d. Harold Orlando and Bertha Marie (Bjorn) Clark; m. Ernest F. Nichols, July 10, 1971; children: Heather, Lisa, Erica. BS in Secondary Edn., U. Vt., 1969; MA in Liberal Studies, Keene State Coll., 1992. French tchr. Champlain Valley Union H.S., Hinesburg, Vt., 1969-70; tchr. English and reading Hartford (Vt.) H.S., 1970-73; tchr. French Monadnock Regional H.S., East Swanzey, N.H., 1988—. Past advisor Key Club, Monadnock Regional H.S., East Swanzey, 1993-94, advisor French Club, 1993—. Mem. Am. Assn. Tchrs. French (sec. 1992-94), N.H. Assn. Tchrs. Fgn. Langs. (N.E. Conf. on Tchg. Fgn. Langs. fellow 1991). Unitarian Universalist. Avocations: yoga, walking, reading, sewing, travel. Home: 61 Adams St Keene NH 03431-4107 Office: Monadnock Regional H S 580 Old Homestead Hwy Swanzey NH 03446-2308

NICHOLS, EUGENE DOUGLAS, mathematics educator; b. Rovno, Poland, Feb. 6, 1923; came to U.S., 1946, naturalized, 1951; s. Alex and Anna (Radchuk) Nichiporuk; m. Alice Bissell, Mar. 31, 1951. BS, U. Chgo., 1949, postgrad., 1949-51; MEd, U. Ill., 1953, MA, 1954, PhD, 1956. Instr. math. Roberts Wesleyan Coll., North Chili, N.Y., 1950-51, U. Ill., 1951-56; assoc. prof. math. edn. Fla. State U., 1956-61, prof., head dept., 1961-73; dir. Project for Mathematical Devel. of Children, 1973-77; dir. math program NSF, 1958-61; dir. Math. Inst. Elem. Tchrs., 1961-70; pres. Nichols Schwartz Pub., 1992—; prof. math. edn. Fla. State U., 1974-90. Chmn. U. Ill. Com. on Sch. Math., 1954-55; cons. editor math McGraw-Hill Book Co., summer 1956 Co-author: Modern Elementary Algebra, 1961, Introduction to Sets, 1962, Arithmetic of Directed Numbers, 1962, Introduction to Equations and Inequalities, 1963, Introduction to Coordinate Geometry, 1963, Introduction to Exponents, 1964, Understanding Arithmetic, 1965, Elementary Mathematics Patterns and Structure, 1966, Algebra, 1966, Modern Geometry, 1968, Modern Trigonometry, 1968, Modern Intermediate Algebra, 1969, Analytic Geometry, 1973, Holt Algebra 1, 1974, 78, 82, 86, 92, Holt Algebra 2, 1974, 78, 82, 86, 92, Holt Geometry, 1974, 78, 82, 86, Holt School Mathematics, 1974, 78, 81, Holt Pre-Algebra Mathematics, 1980, 86, Holt Mathematics, 1981, 85, Elementary School Mathematics and How to Teach It, 1982, Geometry, 1991, Holt Pre-Algebra, 1992, Mathematics Dictionary and Handbook, 1993, 95, 98, 99; author: Pre-Algebra Mathematics, 1970, Introductory Algebra for College Students, 1971, Mathematics for the Elementary School Teacher, 1971, College Mathematics, 1975, College Mathematics for General Education, rev. edit., 1975. Named Fla. State U. Disting. Prof., 1968-69; recipient Disting. Alumni award U. Ill. Coll. Edn., 1970. Mem. Am. Math. Soc., Math. Assn. Am., Sch. Sci. and Math. Assn., Nat. Coun. Tchrs. Math., Coun. Basic Edn., Text and Acad. Authors Assn., Pi Mu Epsilon, Phi Delta Kappa. Home: 3386 W Lakeshore Dr Tallahassee FL 32312-1305 E-mail: eunichols@aol.com.

NICHOLS, LEE ANN, library media specialist; b. Denver, Apr. 27, 1946; d. Bernard Anthony and Margaret Mary (Pughes) Wilhelm; m. Robert Joseph Nichols, July 12, 1975; children: Rachel, Steven, Sarah. BS in Edn., St. Mary of the Plains, Dodge City, Kans., 1968; MA in Edn., Colo. U., 1978. Cert. type B profl. tchr., Colo. Tchr. So. Tama Sch. Dist. Montour, Iowa, Iowa, 1968-70, Strasburg (Colo.) Sch. Dist., 1970-73; svc. rep. Montain Bell, Denver, 1973-75; libr., tchr. Simla (Colo). Sch. Dist., 1976-78; dir. Simla Br. Libr., 1978-81; dir. Christian edn. St. Anthony's Ch/, Sterling, Colo., 1983-84; libr. cons. Rel Valley Sch., Iliff, Colo., 1984-98, Plateau Sch. Dist., Peetz, Colo., 1986-99; dir. Fleming Cmty. Libr., Colo., 1997—. Mem. Colo. Coun. for Libr. Devel., Denver, 1986-92, chmn. 1991; instr. Northeastern Jr. Coll., Sterling; del. Gov.'s Conf. on Libr. and Info. Scis., 1990. Author: Computers 101. . .in a Nutshell, 2002; contbr. articles to profl. jours. Active Sterling Arts Coun., sec., 1982-85, v.p., 1985, pres., 1986-87; chair Northeastern Jr. Coll. Found., Sterling, 1983-87, mem. 1981-91; mem. community adv. coun. Northeastern Jr. Coll., 1991-93, chair, 1993; bd. dirs. Wagon Wheel chpt. Girl Scouts Am., 1975-78. Mem. ALA, Am. Assn. Sch. Librs., Assn. Libr. Svcs. to Children, Colo. Ednl. Media Assn., Colo. Libr. Coun., Internat. Reading Assn. (Colo. Coun.). Avocations: reading, sewing. Home: 12288 County Road 370 Sterling CO 80751-8494 Office: Fleming Cmty Libr 506 N Fremont Ave Fleming CO 80728-9520

NICHOLS, MARCI LYNNE, gifted education coordinator, educator, consultant; b. Cin., July 7, 1948; m. James G. Nichols, June 19, 1970; children: Lisa, Jeannette. B in Arts and Sci., Miami U., Oxford, Ohio, 1970, MEd, 1990, PhD, 1997. Cert. Secondary English, elem. gifted edn., computer edn., Ohio. Secondary English tchr. West Clermont Local Schs., Cin., 1970-71; coord. gifted edn. and tchr. Batavia (Ohio) Local Schs., 1981—. Spkr., cons. Local Gifted Orgns., Cin., 1988—; vis. instr. dept. ednl. psychology Miami U., Oxford, Ohio, 1991-98, assoc./adj. prof. 1998—; presenter Nat. Rsch. Symposium on Talent Devel., 1991. Author, presenter: (videotape series) Parenting the Gifted Parts I and II, 1992; columnist, contbr. Resources for Everyday Living; contbr. articles to profl. jours; creator attitude assessment instrument. Speaker Christian Women's Club, Ohio, Ind., Ky., W.Va., 1981—; deacon First Presbyn. Ch. of Batavia, Ohio, 1986-88; bd. trustee Super Saturday program gifted edn. com. Miami U., 1995—. Recipient Douglas Miller Rsch. award Miami U., 1991. Mem. ASCD, Am. Ednl. Rsch. Assn. (presenter 1997, 98), Nat. Assn. for Gifted Children, Consortium Ohio Coords. of Gifted, Parents Assn. for Gifted Edn. (trustee 1997), Midwest Ednl. Rsch. Assn. (presenter), Internat. Platform Assn., Mensa (ann. gathering presenter 1998), Phi Kappa Phi. Home: 110 Wood St Batavia OH 45103-2923 Office: Batavia Local Schs 800 Bauer Ave Batavia OH 45103-2837

NICHOLS, ROGER SABIN, genealogist, retired school counselor; b. Ames, Iowa, Oct. 21, 1938; s. Sabin Alfred and Margaret Pauline (Andrew) N.; m. Glendene Donna Greta, June 12, 1960; children: Margaret Emily, Charles Sabin II. BS, Iowa State U., 1960; MA in Edn., U. No. Iowa, 1965, EdS, 1976. Cert. tchr. sci., social studies, lang. arts, counselor K-12, dir. pupil svcs., Iowa. Tchr., counselor Bridgewater-Fontanelle (Iowa) Cmty. Sch. Dist., 1960-66; counselor, guidance dir. Sioux City (Iowa) Cmty. Sch. Dist., 1966-98. Human rels. cons. Western Hills Area Edn. Agy., Sioux City, 1979-82, spl. edn. transition adv. com., 1987-97, chmn. career devel. unit writing com., 1989-90; mem., chmn. spl. needs adv. com. Western Iowa Tech. Cmty. Coll., Sioux City, 1982-87, area planning coun. for vocat. edn., 1986-90; com. mem. Sioux City Cmty. Sch. Dist., 1967-89; evaluation team N. Ctrl. Assn. Colls. and Schs., 1983; brief counseling rsch. project Iowa State U., 1989-90; counselor's adv. com. office of admissions U. S.D., 1990-92; state conf. presenter Iowa Assn. Counseling and Devel., 1990, 94; local coord. Counseling for Higher Skills Rsch. Project, Kans. State U., 1994-96; primary rschr. Berning Family book project, 1999—. Contbg. author: Critical Incidents in School Counseling, 1973, Simmerman Family Record, 1995; author: William Fawcett Thompson as William Fawcett, Actor, 1999; contbr. poetry to Lyrical Iowa, 1965, 67; contbr. articles to profl. jours. On-air friendraiser host Friends of FM-90, Sioux City, 1982-2000; mem. 4-H subcom. Woodbury County Extension Svc., Sioux City, 1984-96; 4-H departmental fair departmental supt. Woodbury County Fair Assn., Moville, Iowa, 1984-89, mem. Scholarship Com. Waitt Family Found., 1999—; voting mem. Iowa Ann. Conf., United Meth. Ch., 1999—. Named Iowa Counselor of Yr., Iowa Assn. Coll. Admissions Counselors, 1995; recipient Nat. Def. Edn. Act Stipend, U. S.D., 1968. Mem. ACA, NEA (life), Nat. Geneal. Soc., Internat. Suzuki Assn., Iowa State Edn. Assn. (del. assembly 1965), Sioux City Edn. Assn. (chmn. profl. rights and responsibilities com. 1967-68, rep. assembly 1968-69), Iowa Counseling Assn., Am. Sch. Counselors Assn., Iowa Sch. Counselors Assn. (chair ethics com. 1997-98), Nat. Career Devel. Assn. (career info. rev. svc. 1970-73), Iowa Career Devel. Assn. (state membership chmn. 1975-76), Iowa Specialists in Group Work, Am. Vocat. Assn., Iowa State Hist. Soc., Iowa State Geneal. Soc., Conn. Soc. Genealogists, Czechoslovak Geneol. Soc. Internat., N.E. Historic Geneal. Soc., Nat. Geneal. Soc. (contbg. author NGS Newsmag.), Derbyshire Family History Soc. (contbg. author Branch News 1993), Siouxland Master Chorale (pres. 1968-71, v.p. 1977-80, 88-90, treas. 1982-83), Sioux City Chamber Music Assn. (pres. 1980-81), Phi Delta Kappa (pres. Siouxland chpt. 1996-97). Republican. Methodist. Avocation: church musician. Home: 3819 Peters Ave Sioux City IA 51106-1813 E-mail: rngnichols@aol.com.

NICHOLS, RONALD LEE, surgeon, educator; b. Chgo., June 25, 1941; s. Peter Raymond and Jane Eleanor (Johnson) N.; m. Elsa Elaine Johnson, Dec. 4, 1964; children: Kimberly Jane, Matthew Bennett. MD, U. Ill., 1966, MS, 1970. Diplomate Am. Bd. Surgery (assoc. cert. examiner, New Orleans, 1991), Nat. Bd. Med. Examiners. Intern U. Ill. Hosp., Chgo., 1966-67, resident in surgery, 1967-72, instr. surgery, 1970-72, asst. prof. surgery, 1972-74; assoc. prof. surgery U. Health Scis. Chgo. Med. Sch., 1975-77, dir. surg. edn., 1975-77; William Henderson prof. surgery Tulane U. Sch. Medicine, New Orleans, 1977—2002, vice chmn. dept. surgery, 1982-91, staff surgeon, 1977—2002, prof. microbiology, immunology and surgery, 1979—, William Henderson prof. surgery emeritus, 2003—. Cons. surgeon VA Hosp., Alexandria, La., 1978-93, Huey P. Long Hosp., Pineville, La., 1978-2002, Lallie Kemp Charity Hosp., Independence, La., 1977-85, Touro Infirmary, New Orleans, Monmouth Med. Ctr., Long Branch, N.J., 1979-88; mem. VA Coop. Study Rev. Bd., 1978-81, VA Merit Rev. Bd. in Surgery, 1979-82; sci. program com. 3d Internat. Conf. Nosocomial Infections, Ctr. Disease Control, sci. program and fundraising com. 4th Internat. Conf.; bd. dirs. Nat. Found. Infectious Diseases, 1989-2003, v.p., 1994-97, pres.-elect., 1997-99, pres., 1999-2001, trustee, 2003—; hon. fellow faculty Kasr El Aini Cairo U. Sch. Medicine, 1989; adv. com. on infection control Ctrs. for Disease Control, 1991-97; disting. guest, vis. prof. Royal Coll. Surgeons Thailand, 1989, 1992; infectious diseases adv. bd. Roche Labs., 1988-95, Abbott Labs., 1990-92, Kimberly Clark Corp., 1990-99, SmithKline Beecham Labs., 1990-95, Fujisawa Pharm., chmn., 1990-99, Bayer Pharm., 1994-2001, Merck Sharpe Dohme, 1996, Depotech, 1996, Zeneca Pharm., 1997—, Rhone-Poulenc Rorer, 1997-99, Wyeth-Ayrest Labs., 1998—, Pfizer Pharm., 1999, Searle Pharm., 1999-2001, GlaxoWellcome, 1999, Aventis, 1999-2000, Cubist Pharm., 2000—, others; study group Prophylaxis Antibiotic Project La. Health Care Rev., Inc., 1995-2000, Nat. Com. Study Blood Borne Disease Transmission make Nat. Policy, Rockefeller Brothers Fund, 2001-03; lectr. Royal Coll. Physicians and Surgeons Can., 1998, Internat. Infectious Disease Soc. Ob-gyn., 1998, 20th N.Y. State Surg. Symposium, 1998, dept. surgery Dept. U. Ark., 1998; apptd. by gov. La. commn. HIV and AIDS, 1999—2003; nat. policy com. study innovative surgery reg. Greenwall Found., 2003—. Author: (with Gorbach, Bartlett and Nichols) Manual of Surgical Infection, 1984; author, guest editor: (with Nichols, Hyslop Jr. and Bartlett) Decision Mking in Surgical Sepsis, 1991; guest editor, author: Surgical Sepsis and Beyond, 1993; mem. editl. bd. Current Surgery, 1977—, Hosp. Physician, 1980—, Infection Control, 1980-86, Guidelines to Antibiotic Therapy, 1976-81, Am. Jour. Infection Control, 1981-99, Internat. Medicine, 1983—, Confronting Infection, 1983-86, Current Concepts in Clin. Surgery, 1984—, Fact Line, 1984-91, Host/Pathogen News, 1984—, Infectious Diseases in Clin. Practice, 1991—, surg. sect. editor, 1992—, Surg. Infections: Index and Revs., 1991—, So. Med. Jour., 1992-97, ANAEROBE, 1994—, Surg. Infections, 1998—, Clin. Infectious Diseases, 1999—; editl. adv. bd. MD Consult Infectious Diseases, 2002—; mem. adv. bd. Physician News Network, 1991-95; patentee (with S.G. schoenberger and W.R. Rank) Helical-Tipped Lesion Localization Needle Device; patentee in field. Elected faculty sponsor graduating class Tulane Med. Sch., 1979-80, 83, 85, 87, 88, 91-92. Maj. USAR, 1972-75. Recipient House Staff tchg. award U. Ill. Coll. Medicine, 1973, Rsch. award Bd. Trustees U. Health Scis.-Chgo. Med. Sch., 1977, Owl Club Tchg. award, 1980-86, 90; named Clin. Prof. of Yr. U. Health Scis., Chgo. Med. Sch., 1977, Clin. Prof. of Yr., Tulane U. Sch. Medicine, 1979; Douglas Stubbs Lectr. award Surg. Sect. Nat. Med. Assn., 1987, Prix d'Elegance award Men of Fashion, New Orleans, 1993, Annual La. Laureate Emeritus lectureship, 2002; named Brit. Jour. of Surgery Lectr., 1997, 1st Annual Warren Cole lectr., 2001, 2d Annual La. Laureate Emeritus lectr., 2002. Fellow Infectious Disease Soc. Am. (mem. FDA subcom. to develop guidelines in surg. prophylaxis 1989-93, co-recipient Joseph Susman Meml. award 1990), Am. Acad. Microbiology, Internat. Soc. Univ. Colon and Rectal Surgeons, ACS (mem. operating rm. environ. com. 1978-80, vice chair operating rm. environ. com. 1980-81, chmn. operating rm. environ. com. 1981-83, sr. mem. operating rm. environ. com. 1983-87, mem. internat. rels. com. 1987-93, sr. mem. internat. rels. com. 1993-97); mem. AMA, Nat. Found. for Infectious Diseases (bd. dirs.), Joint Commn. on Accreditation of Health Care Orgn. (Infection Control adv. group, 1988-98, sci. program com. 3d internat. conf. nosocomial infections CDC/Nat. Found. Infectious Diseases 1990, FDA Subcom. to Develop Guidelines in Surg. Prophylaxis, 1989-93; prophylactic antibiotic study group La. Health Care Rev. Inc. 1996-2000, clin. advisor, mem., 2001—, AIDS commr. State of La. 1992-94, mem., La. Commn. HIV and AIDS, 1999—), 5th Nat. Forum on AIDS (sci. program com.), U.S. Pharmacopeial Convention Inc. (adv. panel surg. drugs and devices 1995-2000, nominating com. The Heinz Awards 1995-96), Assn. Practitioners in Infection Control (physician adv. coun. 1991-98), Internat. Soc. Anaerobic Bacteria, So. Med. Assn. (vice chmn. sect. surgery 1980-81, chmn. 1982-83), Assn. Acad. Surgery, N.Y. Acad. Sci., Warren H. Cole Soc. (pres.-elect 1988, pres. 1989-90), Assn. VA Surgeons, Soc. Surgery Alimentary Tract, Inst. Medicine Chgo., Midwest Surg. Assn., Cen. Surg. Assn., Ill. Surg. Soc., European Soc. Surg. Rsch., Collegium Internationale Chirugiae Digestivae, Chgo. Surg. Soc. (hon.), New Orleans Surg. Soc. (bd. dirs. 1983-87), Soc. Univ. Surgeons, Surg. Soc. La., Southeastern Surg. Soc., Phoenix Surg. Soc. (hon.), Hellenic Surg. Soc. (hon.), Cen. N.Y. Surg. Soc. (hon.), Tulane Surg. Soc., Alton Ochsner Surg. Soc., Am. Soc. Microbiology, Soc. Internat. de Chirugie, Surg. Infection Soc. (sci. study com. 1982-83, fellowship com. 1985-87, ad hoc sci. liaison com. 1986-89, program com. 1986-87, chmn. ad hoc com. rels. with industry 1990-93, mem. sci. liaison com. 1995-96), Soc. for Intestinal Microbial Ecology and Disease, Soc. Critical Care Medicine, Am. Surg. Assn., Kansas City Surg. Soc., Bay Surg. Soc. (hon.), Cuban Surg. Soc. (hon.), Panhellenic Surg. Soc. (hon.), Tacoma Surg. Club (hon.), Sigma Xi, Alpha Omega Alpha. Episcopalian. Home: 1521 7th St New Orleans LA 70115-3322 Office: 1430 Tulane Ave New Orleans LA 70112-2699 E-mail: RLNMD@yahoo.com.

NICHOLS, SANDRA JEAN, reading specialist; b. Dallas, Oct. 25, 1940; d. Cecil Vernon and Hazel Virginia (House) Crumrine; m. Jess Willard Nichols, Nov. 15, 1957; children: D. Annette, Paul E. (dec.). AA, Eastfield Coll., Mesquite, Tex., 1972; BA magna cum laude, North Tex. State U., 1974, MEd, 1977; MS, East Tex. State U., 1986. Cert. profl. tchr., earl childhood tchr., reading specialist and supervision, Tex. Kindergarten and elem. tchr. Lawrence Elem. Sch., Mesquite, Tex., 1974-77; tchr. reading Wilkinson Mid. Sch., Mesquite, 1977-86; reading specialist West Mesquite H.S., 1986—2001; ret., 2001; v.p. Conditioned Air Svcs., 1977—. Instr. Eastfield Coll., Dallas County C.C. Dist., 1980-85; mem. curriculum coun. Mesquite Ind. Sch. Dist., 1986-2001; presenter numerous staff devel. programs, 1983-2001. Photographer, author audio-visuals Volcanic Geology of the Northwest, 1980, Off the Beaten Trail in Big Bend, 1989, Signs, 1991. Instr. swimming ARC, Mesquite, 1964-68; vol. counselor Cystic Fibrosis Summer Camps, Dallas Children's Med. Ctr., 1983-85; vol. Polit. Action Com., Mesquite, 1990-92. Grantee NSF, Tex. A&M U., 1986. Mem. Assn. Profl. Tex. Educators (pres. Mesquite chpt. 1990-91), Mesquite Edn. Assn. (pres. 1990-91), Tex. Archaeol. Soc., Dallas Archaeol. Soc., Dallas Paleontol. Soc., Alpha Delta Kappa (sec. chpt. 1992-94, v.p. 1996-1998, chpt. pres. 1998-2000). Mem. Ch. Of Christ. Avocations: reading, camping, backpacking, travel.

NICHOLS, STEPHEN GEORGE, Romance languages educator; b. Cambridge, Mass., Oct. 24, 1936; s. Stephen George and Marjorie (Whitney) N.; m. Mary Winn Jordan, June 22, 1957 (div. 1972); children: Stephen Frost (dec.), Sarah Winn; m. Edith Karetzky, 1972; stepchildren: Laura Natalie Karetzky, Sarah Karetzky Rothman. AB cum laude, Dartmouth

Coll., 1958; PhD, Yale U., 1963; LittD (hon.), U. Genève, 1992. Asst. prof. French UCLA, 1963-65; assoc. prof. comparative lit. U. Wis.-Madison, 1965-68, chmn. dept., 1967-68; prof. Romance langs. and comparative lit. Dartmouth Coll., 1968-84, chmn. dept. comparative lit., 1969-72, 74, 79-82, chmn. dept. romance langs., 1974-77, Edward Tuck prof. French, 1984-85, chmn. dept. French and Italian, 1982-85, liaison officer Sch. Criticism and Theory, 1983-85; faculty Dartmouth Inst., 1980-85, faculty dir., 1984-85; prof. romance langs. U. Pa., 1985-86, Edmund J. Kahn Disting. prof. humanities, 1986-92; James M. Beall prof. French and humanities Johns Hopkins U., Balt., 1992—; grad. group chmn. French and Italian U. Pa., 1986-88, chmn. dept. romance langs., 1987-88, assoc. dean for humanities, 1988-91; acting chair French, 1993-94; dir. grad. studies dept. French The Johns Hopkins U., Balt., 1992-94; R. Champlin and Debbie Sheridan interim dir. Eisenhower Libr., Johns Hopkins U., 1994-95, chmn. dept. French, 1995—. Dir. sch. Criticism and Theory, 1995-2000; vis. prof. U. Tel Aviv, 1977, NYU, 1979-81, Exeter (Eng.) U., 1980, Ariz. State U., 1982, U. Calif., Irvine, 1985, Sch. Criticism and Theory, 1989, 95, Humanities Rsch. Inst. U. Calif., 1990, Ecole Pratique des Hautes Etudes, Paris, 1995, U. Pa., 1995, Dartmouth Coll., 1995-96, Cornell U., 1996—, Ecole Normale Superieure, Paris, 1996, 98, 2000, 02, U. Paris, 1997; rev. panelist NEH, 1979-81, 84, 91, Guggenheim fellow, 1987-88; ACLS sr. fellow, 2001-02; Phi Beta Kappa vis. scholar, 1983-84; Lauder fellow Aspen Inst. for Humanistic Study, 1988; adv. bd. Inst. d'Etudes Francaises d'Avignon, Bryn Mawr Coll., 1965—; dir. seminar NEH, 1975-79, Mellon summer seminar in humanities Johns Hopkins U., 1993, 94; exec. com. Ea. Comparative Lit. Conf.; mem. adv. coun. dept. comparative lit. Princeton U., 1982-88, chmn., 1984-88; co-dir. Ctr. Cultural Study, U. Pa., 1986-92; co-dir. Louis Marin Ctr. for French Studies, 1992—; advisor Waverly Consort, 1987-95; adv. bd. Soc. Humanities Cornell U., 1993—; reviewer Guggenheim Fellowship applications, medieval sect., 1995—, French, 1996—; chair task force on artifact in libr. collections Coun. on Libr. Info. Resources, 1999-2001. Author: Formulaic Diction and Thematic Composition in the Chanson de Roland, 1961, The Songs of Bernard de Ventadorn, 1962, 2d edit., 1968, Le Roman de la Rose, 1967, 72, Comparists at Work, 1968, The Meaning of Mannerism, 1972, Mimesis: From Mirror to Method, Augustine to Descartes, 1982, Medieval and Renaissance Theories of Representation, 1984, Romanesque Signs: Early Medieval Narrative and Iconography, 1983, 85, Images of Power: History/Text/Discourse, 1986, The Legitimacy of the Middle Ages, 1988, The New Philology, 1990, Boundaries and Transgressions, 1991, The New Medievalism, 1991, Commentary as Cultural Artifact, 1992, Medievalism and the Modernist Temper: On the Discipline of Medieval, 1996, The Whole Book: Miscellany and Order in the Medieval Manuscript, 1996, The Evidence in Hand: The Artifact in Library Collections, 2001, L'Altérité du Moyen Age, 2003; editor: (book series) Parallax: Revisions of Culture and Society, 1987—; asst. editor French Rev., 1968-88; mem. editl. bd. Olifant, 1974-94, Medievalia et Humanistica, 1974-95, Medievalia, 1975—, Comparative Lit. Studies, 1986, Publ. of the MLA, 1988-89, Recentiores, 1991—, Modern Lang. Notes, 1992; adv. bd. Colleagues Press, 1986-96, Exemplaria: A Jour. Medieval Theory, 1987—; adv. com. PMLA, 1980-84; adv. editor Romanic Rev., 1986—, Storia della Storiographia, 1992—. Rotary Found. fellow U. d'Aix Marseilles, France, 1958-59; fellow Inst. Rsch. in Humanities, 1966-67, NEH fellow, 1978-79, sr. fellow Sch. of Criticism and Theory, 1988—. Fellow Medieval Acad. Am.; mem. Acad. Lit. Studies (nominating com. 1974-78, sec.-treas. 1978-87), Dante Soc., Internat. Comparative Lit. Assn., New Eng. Medieval Assn. (adv. com. 1981-85), MLA (chmn. com. on careers 1985-86, James Russell Lowell prize com. 1986-88, com. on profl. ethics 1987-88, del. assembly 1994-97), Medieval Acad. Am., Soc. Rencesvals (sec.-treas. Am. sect. 1964-69). Home: 5 Saint Martins Rd Baltimore MD 21218-1815

NICHOLS, STEVEN PARKS, mechanical engineer, lawyer, educator; b. Cody, Wyo., July 1, 1950; s. Rufus Parks Nichols and Gwen Sena (Frank) Keyes; m. Mary Ruth Barrow, Aug. 5, 1990; 1 child, Nicholas Barrow Nichols. PhD, U. Tex., Austin, 1975, JD, 1983. Assoc. dir. Tex. Space Grant Consortium, Austin, 1989-91, dir. Design Projects Program, 1989—2002; dep. dir. Ctr. for Energy Studies, U. Tex., Austin, 1988-91, dir. of Ctr., 1991-99, acting dir. Ctr. for Electromechanics, 1994-99, assoc. prof. mech. engring., 1996—, assoc. chair dept. mech. engring., 1999—2001, dir. Ctr. for Energy and Environ. Resources, 1998—99, dir. Chair of Free Enterprise, 2001—, fellow, 2001—, assoc. v.p. rsch., 2002—. Bd. dirs. Assn. Mfg. Excellence; chmn. Nat. Coun. Space Grant Dirs., NASA, 1989-92; bd. dirs. So. Coalition for Advanced Transp., 1994-99, chair elect 1998-99, chair 1998-2000; bd. dirs. Nat. Inst. for Engring. Ethics, 1996-2001; chmn. mgmt. divsn. ASME Internat., 1999-2001, exec. com. engring. and tech. mgmt., 1999-. Patentee (with others) pulsed welding techniques, railgun igniter, inert burner, rail thruster, other patents pending. Fellow ASME; mem. NSPE, ABA, Am. Soc. Engring. Edn. (Fred Merryfield Design award 2001), Nat. Inst. Engring. Ethics (bd. govs. 1987-93, 96-2001), N.Y. Acad. Scis. Home: 1400 Lorrain St Austin TX 78703-4023 Office: U Tex Dept Mech Engring Austin TX 78712

NICHOLS, VIRGIL, special education educator; b. Memphis, Tenn., Apr. 1, 1946; s. John Adam and Vera Elizabeth (Betts) Goempler; m. Susan Carol Underhill (div.); children: William Joss, Travis John. BA, U. West Fla., 1975; MS, Iowa State U., 1982; PhD, U. So. Miss., 1992. Cert. tchr., Iowa, Fla. Acad. tchr. Beggs Vocat. Sch., Pensacola, Fla., 1976-77; tchr. second grade Escambia County Schs., Pensacola, 1977-78; learning disabilities tchr. Ogden (Iowa) Community Schs., 1978-82; behavior disability thcr. Maquoketa (Iowa) Community Schs., 1982-84, South Tama County Schs., Tama, Iowa, 1984-89; instr. U. So. Miss., Hattiesburg, 1991-92; asst. prof. Peru (Nebr.) State Coll., 1992—. Adj. prof. U. So. Miss., 1992. With USN, 1965-69. Mem. Coun. Exceptional Children (tchr. edn. div.), Coun. Children with Behavior Disorders. Avocations: swimming, soccer, tennis, running. Office: Peru State Coll Peru NE 68421

NICHOLSON, JUNE C. DANIELS, retired speech pathologist; b. Augusta, Maine, Dec. 28, 1938; d. Sumner T. and Bernadette (Dulac) Daniels; m. Kenneth E. Nicholson, June 27, 1964; children: Jeffrey Scott, Daren Patrick. BS, Abilene Christian U., 1963; MS, U. Vt., 1980. Cert. ASHA CCC, Vt. Dept. Edn.; cert. tchr., Vt. Speech pathologist grades K-12 Arlington (Vt.) Pub. Sch., ret., 1996. Vol. Peace Corp., Shumen, Bulgaria, 2001—03, St. Lucia, West Indies, 1971—73. Mem. NEA, Ret. Tchrs. Assn. of NEA, Am. Speech/Hearing Assn., Vt. Speech/Hearing Assn., Vt. Edn. Assn., Vt. Ret. Tchrs. Assn., Delta Kappa Gamma.

NICHOLSON, THEODORE H. educational administrator; b. Chgo., July 27, 1929; B.S., Loyola U., Chgo., 1951; M.S. (State of Ill. Vets scholar), No. Ill. U., 1955; postgrad., Rockford Coll., 1955; Ph.D. (NDEA fellow, 1966-67), U. Wis.-Madison, 1967; children— Craig, Kimberlee, Christine, Rhonda, Katrina, Alexandra. Tchr., Morris Kennedy Sch., Winnebago County, Ill., 1951-53, Rockford (Ill.) Public Schs., 1953-55, evening sch., 1955-59; prin. Marsh Schs., Dist. 58, Winnebago County, 1959-65, supt., 1959-66; supt. Dearborn Twp. Sch. Dist. 8, Dearborn Heights, Mich., 1967-68, Wilmington (Ohio) City Sch., 1968-72; supr. schs., Wausau, Wis., 1972-90; assoc. prof. edn. leadership U. No. Colo., 1990-93; vis. prof. Central State U., Wilberforce, Ohio, 1969-70; assoc. Univ. of Wis.-Madison, 1993-94; teaching asst., rsch. asst., lectr. U. Wis., summer 1976; assoc. prof. to assocs. U. Wis., Madison, 1993-94; lectr., cons. Univ. Council Ednl. Adminstrn.; mem. coordinating com. Partnership Schs.; v.p. N.C. Data Processing Ctr., 1974-81. Active Cen. Wausau Progress, 1973-82; mem. Pvt. Industry Coun.; bd. dirs. Wausau Performing Art Found., 1986-91, Wausau Area Community Found., 1988-91. Served with USN, 1943-46. Recipient Citizenship award City of Rockford, 1960, 64, Recognition award State Wis. Dept. Pub. Instr., 1989, Wausau Bd. Edn., 1989; Community Leader award Sta. WXCO, Wausau, 1974. Mem. Am. Assn. Sch. Adminstrs., Wis. Assn. Sch. Dist. Adminstrs. (state bd. dirs., Adminstr. of Yr. award spl. edn. dept., 1986, Recognition award 1989), Am. Assn. Supervision and Curriculum Devel., C. of C. (bd. dirs., edn com., Businessman's Roundtable), Phi Delta Kappa. Contbr. articles in field to profl. publs.

NICKA, BETTY LOU, secondary education educator; b. Madison, Wis., June 2, 1937; d. Marvin J. and Tilla S. (Haakinson) Lindberg; m. John George Nicka, June 27, 1970; 1 child, Karyn Theresa. BS, U. Wis., LaCrosse, 1959. Tchr. Mitchell Jr. High Sch., Racine, Wis., 1959-63, Cherokee Jr. High Sch., Madison, Wis., 1963-65, East High Sch., Madison, Wis., 1965-92. Coach tennis, volleyball, basketball & track Madison East High Sch., 1965-73, dir. dance, performing arts, 1965-92, choreographer theatre plays and musicals, 1970-73. Coord. com. performing arts in dance Tower Twirler Dancers, Wis., 1978-92. Mem. NEA, Am. Assn. Health, Phys. Edn., Recreation and Dance, Wis. Edn. Assn. (coun. 1959—), Wis. Assn. Health, Phys. Edn., Recreation and Dance, So. Wis. Edn. Insvc. Orgn. (chair phys. sec. 1966-67), Madison Area Retired Educators Assn. Democrat. Lutheran. Home: 2105 Sheridan Dr Madison WI 53704-3844

NICKEL, ROSALIE JEAN, reading specialist; b. Hooker, Okla., Oct. 10, 1939; d. Edwin Charles and Esther Elizabeth (Wiens) Ollenburger; m. Ted W. Nickel, June 3, 1960; 1 child, Sandra Jean. BA, Tabor Coll., 1961; MA, Calif. State U., Fresno, 1970. Cert. tchr., Calif. Elem. tchr. Visalia (Calif.) Pub. Schs., 1961-62; overseas tchr. Kodaikanal Internat. Sch., Madras State, India, 1963-65; tchr. Mendota (Calif.) Jr. H.S., 1966; elem. tchr. Fresno Pub. Schs., 1966-68, Inglewood (Calif.) Pub. Schs., 1968-73; spl. reading tchr. Tulsa Pub. Schs., 1974-81; salesperson, mgr. Compag, Marion, Kans., 1981-85; gifted student tchr. Wichita (Kans.) Pub. Schs., 1986; reading specialist, resource tchr. Fresno (Calif.) Unified Schs., 1987—, coord. sch. tech., 1989-95, mem. dist. K-3 literacy task force, 1995-97. Mem. quality rev. team Birney Elem. Sch., Fresno. Newsletter editor Marion County Arts Council, 1981-82. Co-dir. Am. Field Svc., Tulsa, 1980-81; v.p. Women's Federated Clubs Am., Marion, 1985-86; pres. Butler Mennonite Brethern Women's Fellowship, 1989-91. Mem. Internat. Reading Assn., Fresno Area Reading Council. Avocations: travel, sewing, baking, computers, piano. Home: 2821 W Compton Ct Fresno CA 93711-1181 Office: Fresno Unified Schs Tulare and M Sts Fresno CA 93721-2287

NICKELS, RUTH ELIZABETH, band director; b. Warsaw, Ind., Nov. 21, 1955; d. Marjorie Jane Shipley; m. David Brent Nickels, July 7, 2001. MusB in Performance, DePauw U., 1978; MusM in Performance, Ithaca Coll., 1980; cert. in edn., Grace Coll., 1986; post-master credits, Ind. U., 1986. Profl. tchg. lic. music edn. Dir. bands Fairfield Jr.-Sr. H.S., Goshen, Ind., 1986—92; H.S. band dir. Yorktown (Ind.) H.S., 1992—93; dir. bands Orleans (Ind.) Jr.-Sr. H.S., 1993—97, Southwestern Jr.-Sr. H.S., Hanover, Ind., 1997—. Music judge Ind. State Music Assn., Indpls. Mem.: NEA, Ind. State Tchrs. Assn., Ind. Bandmasters Assn., Music Educator's Nat. Conf., Women Band Dirs. Assn., Nat. Band Assn. Avocations: reading, travel, cooking, walking. Home: PO Box 337 Hanover IN 47243 Office: Southwestern Jr-Sr HS 167 S Main Cross St Hanover IN 47243 Home Fax: 812-866-6233; Office Fax: 812-866-6233. Personal E-mail: renickels@msn.com. Business E-Mail: rnickels@swjcs.k12.in.us.

NICKENS, HARRY CARL, medical association administrator; b. Monterey, Tenn., June 25, 1944; s. Van B. and Martha (Winningham) N.; m. Alicia Beck, Aug. 26, 1967; children: Kimberly, Cassidee, Brad. BS, Tenn. Tech. U., 1966, MS, 1968; EdD, U. Tenn., 1972. Counselor Va. Western Community Coll., Roanoke, 1972-76, dir. student devel., 1977-78, dean students, 1979-84, exec. dir. community devel. and tng., 1985-89; pres. Coll. Health Scis., Roanoke, 1989—2001; v.p. cmty. rels. and devel. Ephraim McDowell Health, Danville, Ky., 2003—. Chair Roanoke Valley Chamber's Sch., originator Grad, Ctr.; pres. Ephraim McDowell Health Care Found., 2003—. Pres. Roanoke Valley Career Edn.; bd. dirs. Va. Cares, Adult Care Ctr., Am. Heart Assn., Va. Amateur Sports.; active mem. First Bapt. Ch.; sr. mem. Roanoke County Bd. Suprs. Mem. Kiwanis (pres. Roanoke chpt. 1990—2002). Avocation: gardening. Home: 4179 Toddsbury Dr Vinton VA 24179-1113 Office: Ephraim McDowell Health 217 South 3rd St Danville KY 40422*

NICKERSON, GARY LEE, secondary school educator; b. Cleve., Nov. 7, 1942; s. Alto Lee and Louise Evelyn (Watson) N.; m. Barbara Marie Butler, Aug. 17, 1968; 1 child, L'Oreal. BS, Ohio U., 1966; MA, Atlanta U., 1971. Cert. secondary tchr., Ohio. With Cleve. Pub. Schs., 1966-98; sci. dept. chmn. John F. Kennedy High Sch., Cleve., 1985-98; youth edn. coord. Cleve. Bot. Garden, 1999—2002; sci. mgr. Cleve. Mcpl. Schs., 2002—. Physics instr. Case Western Res. U., Cleve., summer 1988; sci. instr. Std. Oil Elem. Teaching Retraining Program summer 1986; mem. adv. panel Ednl. Devel. Ctr., Inc., Newton, Mass., 1989-98; sci. instr. Cleve. Ednl. Found. Elem. Teaching Retraining Program, 1990—, Baldwin Wallace U. Upward Bound Program, 1992; engring. project instr. MEIOP Summer Program Case Western Res. U., 1991; tchr. trainer Kent State U. Trivet program, 1991-98; sci. tchr. Gov.'s Inst. for Gifted and Talented, Cleve. State U., 1992-98. Co-author curriculum guides. Trustee N.E. Ohio Sci. and Engring. Fair, 2001—. Recipient Cert. of Excellence in Teaching Rotary, 1990. Mem. NAACP, Urban League, Cleve. Regional Coun. Sci. Tchrs. (bd. dirs. 1986-87, pres. 2002--), Metrocabse Assn., Nat. Sci. Tcrhrs. Assn., Sci. Edn. Coun. Ohio, Kappa Alpha Psi. Democrat. Baptist. Avocations: ice skating, tennis, swimming, singing, weight lifting. Home: 5871 White Pine Dr Cleveland OH 44146-3075 Office: Cleve Bot Garden 11030 East Blvd Cleveland OH 44106-1706

NICKLIN, GEORGE LESLIE, JR., psychoanalyst, educator, physician, author; b. Franklin, Pa., July 25, 1925; s. George Leslie and Emma (Reed) N.; m. Katherine Mildred Aronson, Sept. 30, 1950 BA, Haverford Coll., 1949; MD, Columbia U., 1951; cert. in psychoanalysis, William A. White Inst., N.Y.C., 1962. Diplomate Am. Bd. Psychiatry and Neurology. Resident, then chief resident Bellevue Psychiat. Hosp., N.Y.C., 1953-56; pvt. practice specializing in psychoanalytic psychiatry, 1956—; staff Bellevue Hosp., 1956—; assoc. clin. prof. psychiatry NYU Med. Sch., 1970—; dir. L.I. Inst. Psychoanalysis, 1978-88, dir. emeritus, 1988—, dir. emeritus. Mem. Com. to Award Martin Luther King Peace Prize. Author: Doctors In Peril, 2000. Mem. Corp. Haverford Coll., 1957-2003; trustee Westbury Friends Sch., 1957-2000; founder Friends World Coll., 1958. With AUS, 1943-46, ETO. Decorated Purple Heart with oak leaf cluster, Bronze Star with oak leaf cluster and three battle stars. Fellow Am. Acad. Psychoanalysis, Am. Psychiat. Assn. (disting. life fellow, 2003); mem. AAAS, NAACP, Soc. Med. Psychoanalysts (pres. 1986-87), White Psychoanalytic Soc., Assn. for World Edn. (charter trustee, treas. 1970-78), 9th Inf. Divsn. Assn., Vets. of the Bulge, Mil. Order of the Purple Heart. Clubs: Gardiner's Bay Country (Shelter Island, N.Y.); Penn (London). Mem. Soc. Of Friends. Home and Office: 6 Butler Pl Garden City NY 11530-4603

NICOL, MALCOLM F. physical chemistry educator; b. N.Y.C., Sept. 13, 1939; s. John and Hilda E. (Foertner) N.; m. Ann Carolyn Tryon, Aug. 25, 1963 (div. May 1990); children: Barbara, Katherine, Virginia; m. Julia Thacher, Aug. 14, 2002. BA, Amherst Coll., 1960; PhD, U. Calif., Berkeley, 1963. Postdoctoral chemist UCLA, 1963-64, asst. prof. phys. chemistry, 1965-70, assoc. prof., 1970-75, prof., 1975-99; vis. prof. chemistry and physics U. Nev., Las Vegas, 1998—, exec. dir. High Pressure Sci. and Engring. Ctr., 1998—. Cons. Lawrence Livermore (Calif.) Nat. Lab., 1985—, Los Alamos Nat. Lab., 1990—. Assoc. editor Jour. Phys. Chemistry, 1981-90, sr. editor, 1991-98; contbr. over 100 articles on chemistry, physics and geophysics to sci. jours. Fellow Alfred P. Sloan Found., 1973-77. Fellow AAAS, Am. Phys. Soc.; mem. Am. Chem. Soc. (councilor 1986-88, 91-95), Internat. Assn. for the Advancement of High Pressure Rsch. and Tech. (treas. 1999—), Am. Geophys. Union. Home: 1663 E Gabriel Dr Las Vegas NV 89119 Office: U Nev Las Vegas Dept Physics Box 454002 Las Vegas NV 89154-4002

NIDER, MICHAEL EDWARD, elementary school educator; b. Montevideo, Minn., Mar. 26, 1954; s. Edward John and Phyllis Mae (Schiltz) N.; m. Lou Ann Pfleger Nider, July 21, 1979; children: Alexis Marie, Anthony Edward. BS, Moorhead State U., 1978; Elem. Endorsement, U. Mary, Bismarck, N.D., 1982. 7th-8th grade tchr. Leahy Elem. Sch., Raleigh, N.D., 1978-79, St. Vincent Sch., Mott, N.D., 1979-81; 5th-6th grade tchr. St. Joseph Sch., Mandan, N.D., 1981-91; 8th grade health tchr. Mandan Pub. Schs., 1991—. Office: Mandan Jr HS 406 4th St NW Mandan ND 58554-2912

NIECE, RICHARD DEAN, academic administrator; b. Oberlin, Ohio, Nov. 1, 1946; s. Lewis H. and Dortha (Geyer) N. BS in Edn., Ohio State U., 1968; MEd, Kent State U., 1976, PhD, 1988. Cert. supt., prin., tchr. Curriculum dir. Brunswick (Ohio) City Schs., 1982-85; asst. prof. Kent (Ohio) State U., 1985-87; sr. v.p. and provost Walsh U., North Canton, Ohio, 1987—, assoc. prof. Contbr. articles to profl. jours. Mem. ASCD, Phi Delta Kappa. Home: 3311-E Mariners Island DrNW Canton OH 44708-3091 Office: Walsh U 2020 Easton St NW Canton OH 44720-3336

NIELSEN, BARBARA STOCK, state educational administrator; State supt. S.C. Dept. Edn., Columbia, 1991—99; vis. prof. sch. edn. Coll. at Charleston; sr. fellow Strom Thurmond Inst. Clemson U., 2000—; dir. Schs. Around the World. Office: Strom Thurmond Inst Govt and Pub Affairs Clemson U Perimeter Rd Clemson SC 29634-0125*

NIELSEN, CHERIE SUE, elementary educator; b. Bingham Canyon, Utah, Nov. 9, 1947; d. Merrill Abindadi and Eva Elizabeth (Christensen) Nelson; m. Mark Andrew Nielsen, June 27, 1969; children: Travis, Jennifer, Trent, Denise, Marlene. AS, Snow Coll., 1968; BS, Brigham Young U., 1988. Cert. elem. tchr., gifted and talented endorsement, Utah. 4th grade tchr. Granite Sch. Dist., Salt Lake City, 1988-92, 5th grade tchr., 1992—. Tchr. asst. Pioneer Elem. Sch., West Valley, Utah, 1992-94, art tchr., 1990—. V.p. coun. level PTA, Salt Lake City, 1993-94. Named Disting. Tchr. Utah State Senate, 1994. Republican. Mem. Lds Ch. Avocations: reading, quilting, watercolor, art, crafts. Office: Pioneer Elem Sch 3860 S 3380 W Salt Lake City UT 84119-4442

NIELSEN, ELOISE WILMA SOULE, elementary education educator; b. Sanilac County, Mich., Apr. 24, 1923; d. Stanley and Jessie Christina (Hacker) Soule; m. Harald Christian Nielsen, Dec. 19, 1953; children: Brenda Mae Nielsen Stone, Judy Ann (dec.), Paul Eric, Gloria Lynn Nielsen Iannucci. Student, Cen. Mich. U., Mt. Pleasant, 1942, BS, 1946; MA, Mich. State, 1953; postgrad., Bradley U I.S.U., U. Ill. Cert. Mich. perman, Ill. all grades, Jr. Coll. Ill. spl. edn., learning disabilities, behavior disorder. Tchr. Appin Rural Sch., Ubly, Mich., 1942-44, Mt. Pleasant (Mich.) Pub. Schs., 1944-46, Mt. Clemens Pub. Schs., Dickinson and Grant, 1946-52; social worker, psychologist, remedial reading Lansing (Mich.) Pub. Schs., 1953-57; spl. edn. programmer Dist. 150, Peoria, Ill., 1967-87; pioneered learning disability and behavior disorder Peoria, 1988—. Organizer: (booklet for tchrs.) Day Brighteners, 1989; editor ann. Soule-Nielsen Notebook, 1984-99. Vol. Friendship Ho. Computer Lab. Mem. NEA, Coun. for Exceptional Children, Alpha Delta Kappa (pres.). Democrat. Lutheran. Avocations: music, crafts, genealogy, square dance, camping, touring. Home: 2318 N Gale Ave Peoria IL 61604-3229

NIELSEN, LYNN CAROL, educational consultant; b. Perth Amboy, N.J., Jan. 11, 1950; d. Hans and Esther (Pucker) N.; m. Russell F. Baldwin, Nov. 22, 1980; 1 child, Blake Nielsen Baldwin. BS, Millersville U., 1972; MA, NYU, 1979; JD, Rutgers U., 1984. Bar: N.J. 1984; cert. tchr. handicapped, reading specialist, learning disability tchr. cons., elem. edn. supr. Instr. Woodbridge (N.J.) Twp. Bd. Edn., 1972-83; legal intern appellate sect. divsn. criminal justice Atty. Gen. State N.J., Trenton, 1983, dep. atty. gen. divsn. civil law, 1985; assoc. Kantor & Kusic, Keyport, N.J., 1984-86, Kantor & Linderoth, Keyport, N.J., 1986-92. Officer Fords (N.J.) Sch. # 14 PTO, 1974-75; elder First Presbyn. Ch. Avenel, N.J., 1985-88, Flemington (N.J.) Presbyn. Ch., 1997-99; bd. dirs. New Beginnings Nursery Sch., Woodbridge, 1989-90, Flemington Presbyn. Nursery Sch., 1991-93; elder Flemington Presbyn. Ch., 1997-99; bd. mem. Woodside Farms Homeowners Assn., 1996-99. Mem. ABA, N.J. Bar Assn., Monmouth County Bar Assn., Hunterdon County Bar Assn. Avocations: reading, skiing, sailing. Home and Office: 3 Buchannan Way Flemington NJ 08822-3205

NIELSON, BARBARA BROADHEAD, special education administrator; b. Nephi, Utah, Apr. 9, 1931; d. Elmer Robert and Anna Else (Rassmussen) Broadhead; m. Gordon Leon Nielson, Jan. 5, 1953; children: Victoria, Ellen, Margo, Peggy, Thomas, Lyle, Clark. BS cum laude, Brigham Young U., 1965-67, MS, 1972-74, DEd, 1988-92. Cert. prof. elem., early childhood and spl. edn. tchr., adminstr. Elem. and kindergarten tchr. Tintic Sch. Dist., Eureka, Utah, 1966-68; spl. edn. tchr. Millard Sch. Dist., Delta, Utah, 1968-77, elem. prin., 1977-91, chpt. I dir., 1991-92, spl. edn. dir., coord. at-risk programs, 1992—. Co-owner Booster Edn. Svc., Delta, 1973-75; mem. Utah Sch. Accreditation Com., Salt Lake City, 1980-85, Career Ladder Coun., Delta, 1984-92; dir. Millard Sch. Dist. Edn. Found., Delta, 1991-92. Author: A Systematic Instructional Reading Approach for Parent of School Age Children, 1973, (games) Tic-Tac-Toe Phonics, 1973; co-author: Booster Math Materials, 1973; contbr. articles to profl. jours. Active Sierra club, Utah, 1990-94, Ashgrove Cement County Community Coun., Nephi-Delta, 1990-94, West Millard Recreation Coun., Delta, 1980-90; lobbyist, co-writer hazardous waste siting criteria Millard County Concerned Citizens for State of Utah, 1988-94. Named Outstanding Spl. Edn. Tchr., Utah State Office Edn., Salt Lake City, 1973, 74-75; recipient Disting. Svc. in Edn. award Utah State Legis., Salt Lake City, 1991. Mem. Utah Edn. Assn. (profl. rights and responsibility com. 1977-79), So. Utah Educators Assn. (coun. mem. 1974-78), U. Adminstrv. Womens Assn., Delta Rotary, Prins. Acad. of Utah, Delta Kappa Gamma (regional dir. 1973-74). Republican. Mem. Latter Day Saints. Avocations: environmentalist, reading, gardening, travel, history/genealogy. Office: Millard Sch Dist PO Box 666 Delta UT 84624-0666 Home: Apt 308 2244 N Canyon Rd Provo UT 84604-5868

NIEMANN, BIRGIE ANN, university fundraiser; b. Ainsworth, Nebr., Aug. 28, 1951; d. Ralph Sidney and Norma June (Smith) Collins; m. Michael Victory Houston, Aug. 20, 1971 (div. Dec. 1992); children: John, Mark; m. Scott Thomas Niemann, Dec. 11, 1993. AA in Speech, York Coll., 1971; BA in Communication, Pepperdine U., 1975; MS in Counseling, Calif. State U., 1982; postgrad., U. Nebr., 1996-97. Sec., adminstrv. asst. Pepperdine U., Malibu, Calif., 1971-75, asst. dean of students, 1976; bus. mgr. Wayne-Ferrell, Inc., Iowa City, 1980-82; parent counselor Systems Unlimited Inc., Iowa City, 1982-84; adminstrv. asst. U. Iowa Found., Iowa City, 1984-87; assoc. dean of students Mich. Christian Coll., Rochester Hills, Mich., 1987-89, dean of students, 1989-91; asst. to pres., 21st century advance campaign dir. York (Nebr.) Coll., 1991-94, dir. devel. and pub. rels., 1995-96; remedial advisor Structure of Intellect, Glenwood Springs, Colo., 1998—2000; assoc. v.p. corp. and found. rels. Rochester Coll., Rochester Hills, 2000—. Contbr. articles to religious publs. Vol. Drug Free Cmty. Task Force, Oakland County, 1989; v.p. External Relations Rochester Coll., Rochester Hills, 2003—; lectr., guest spkr. Ch. of Christ, Calif., 1976—; bd. dirs. Assocs. of Rochester Coll. Mem. Ch. of Christ. Avocations: hiking, cross-stitch, writing. Office: 800 W Avon Rd Rochester Hills MI 48307

NIEMCZYK, KAREN SUE, special education educator; b. Beloit, Kans., May 26, 1964; d. Kenneth Duane and Mary Ellen (Vaughn) Bader; m. Andrew Francis Niemczyk, July 20, 1991; children: Alex John, Tanner Andrew. BS in Edn., Ft. Hays State U., 1986. Cert. tchr., Kans. Paraprofl. Early Childhood Devel. Ctr., Hays, Kans., 1983-85; instr. aerobics Cloud County C.C., Concordia, Kans., 1988—; tchr. self-contained interrelated classrooms Beloit Spl. Edn. Coop., Unified Sch. Dist. 273, 1986—. Coord., Beloit, 1986—; mem. tchr. awards com. Beloit Schs. Unified Sch. Dist. 273, 1991—, sch. site coun., 1992—, mem. spl. edn. and adv. coun. Coach, bd. dirs. Beloit Area Spl. Olympics, 1986—. Mem. ASCD, Coun. Exceptional Children, Phi Eta Sigma. Republican. Roman Catholic. Avocations: aerobics, swimming, camping, sports. Home: 411 E 3rd St Beloit KS 67420-2407 Office: Beloit Elem Sch 12th And Bell St Beloit KS 67420

NIERATH, DEBRA ANN, elementary education educator; b. Detroit, Oct. 25, 1954; d. Ernest Arthur and Joan Mary (Torchia) N. BS, Wayne State U., Detroit, 1976, postgrad. Cert. elem. tchr. Tchr. 4th grade Assumption Grotto Sch., Detroit; tchr. 2d and 3d grade St. John Berchman Sch., Detroit, St. Joan of Arc Sch., St. Clair Shores, Mich. Recipient C.C. Barnes Meml. award; recipient scholarships. Mem. Nat. Coun. Social Studies, Coun. Exceptional Children. Avocations: arts, crafts, swimming, boating. Home: 11823 Brougham Dr Sterling Heights MI 48312-3977

NIES, KATHERINE ANN, English teacher; b. Ridgeway, Pa., Jan. 28, 1958; d. Charles John and Marjorie Ann (Allen) Dangelo; m. Joseph Anthony Nies II, July 17, 1982; children: Alexander Joseph, Elizabeth Grace. BS, Indiana U. Pa., 1989. Cert. tchr. secondary English. English tchr. Middletown (Mo.) H.S., 1979-82; English tchr., dept. chair Mercyhurst Preparatory Sch., Erie, Pa., 1982-92; English tchr. North East (Pa.) H.S., 1992—. Fin. com. Mercyhurst Preparatory Sch., 1988-92. Mem. N.W. Coun. Tchrs. of English. Home: 649 W Arlington Rd Erie PA 16509-2268

NIES, KEVIN ALLISON, physics educator; b. N.Y.C., Apr. 23, 1949; d. Russell Albert and Signe Marie (Rasmussen) N. BS in Physics, U. Calif., Santa Barbara, 1972; postgrad., UCLA, 1979, Pasadena City Coll., 1980-81, Calif. State U., Northridge, 1985-90. Tchg. credential, Calif.; lic. FCC radio telephone 2d class. Rsch. assoc. level 2 UCLA Brain Inst., L.A., summer 1973; TV technician, engr. NBC, N.Y.C., 1978; founder, dir. Calif. Video Inst., L.A., 1980—; tchr. secondary edn. L.A. Unified Sch. Dist., 1985—. Judge sci. fair San Fernando H.S., Slymar, Calif., 1994; instr. video prodn. Calif. Video Inst., L.A., 1982-85; mem. Assn. Women in Sci., L.A., 1978-83, 94, NSTA, 1985-88, Nat. Orgn. Broadcasting Engrs. and Technicians, 1978-80. Author: From Priestess to Physician, 1996; author, dir.: (video series) Women Physicists and Their Research, 1981, (video programs) Voyager: The Inside Story, 1982, Scientists in Space, 1983, Working Under Volcanos, 1984, Rendezvous with a Comet, 1985; author, illustrator: (book) From Sorceress to Scientist, 1990; webmaster The Hypatia Inst. Mem. Mus. of Tolerance, L.A., 1995-96. Mem. NOW, United Tchrs. L.A., Nat. Alliance of Breast Cancer Orgns., UCLA Alumni Assn. Democrat. Office: The Calif Video Inst PO Box 572019 Tarzana CA 91357-2019

NIESWIADOMY, ROSE MARIE, nursing educator, researcher; b. Ft. Worth, July 7, 1935; d. Hugo Charley and Marie Elizabeth (Franklin) Mieth; m. Benedict Louis Nieswiadomy, June 5, 1955; children: Michael, Anne, Patricia, Andrew. BS, MS, Tex. Woman's U., 1974; PhD, U. North Tex., 1980. Coord. grad. nursing Tex. Woman's U., Dallas, 1986—93, prof. emerita, 2003—. Author: Foundations of Nursing Research, 4th edit., 2002. Mem. ANA (coun. nurse rschrs.), Tex. Nurse's Assn. (dist. 4 v.p. 1993-94, bd, dirs. 1989-94), Nat. League for Nursing, So. Nursing Rsch. Soc., Sigma Theta Tau (Beta Beta chpt., v.p. 1994—). Roman Catholic. Avocations: sewing, bridge. Home: 11350 Drummond Dr Dallas TX 75228-1947

NIETO, BEATRIZ CHAVEZ, nursing educator; b. Edinburg, Tex., Apr. 14, 1958; d. Ruben and Amelia (Guerra) Chavez; m. Roy Munoz Nieto, June 17, 1983; 1 child, Vincent Michael. BSN, Incarnate Word Coll., 1981; MSN, U. Tex. Health Sci. Ctr., 1993. Cert. clin. nurse specialist in med.-surg. nursing. Charge nurse Santa Rosa Children's Hosp., San Antonio, 1981-82; asst. DON Beverly Enterprises Home Health, McAllen, Tex., 1982-83; staff nurse St. David's Comty. Hosp., Austin, Tex., 1983-84; instr. for nurse asst. program Tex. State Tech. Inst., Harlingen, 1984-87; insvc./infection control dir. Mission (Tex.) Hosp., Inc., 1987-90; specialist nursing dept. U. Tex. Pan Am., Edinburg, 1990-93, asst. prof. nursing, 1993—. Adv. bd. nurse asst. program Tex. State Tech. Inst., Harlingen, 1987-88; mem. Am. Heart Assn./CPR Valley task Force, Rio Grande Valley, Tex., 1992-94; peer advisor U. Tex. Health Sci. Ctr., San Antonio, 1992-93; planning com. workshop in field, 1993. Co-author: Healing and the Grief Process, 1996. Instr., instr. trainer Am. Heart Assn., 1992-93. Mem. ANA, Assn. Practitioners in Infection Control (pres. 1987-90), Tex. Nurses Assn., 1984—, Sigma Theta Tau (Delta Alpha chpt. 1993—). Democrat. Avocations: reading, writing, needlepoint, spending time with family. Home: 423 W Samano St Edinburg TX 78539-4448 Office: U Tex Pan Am 1201 W University Dr Edinburg TX 78539-2909

NIEUWENDORP, JUDY LYNELL, special education educator; b. Sioux Center, Iowa, Jan. 3, 1955; d. Leonard Henry and Jenelda Faith (Van't Hul) N. BA in Religious Edn., Reformed Bible Coll., 1977; BA in Secondary Edn. and Social Scis., Northwestern Coll., 1980; degree edn. of emotional disabilities, Mankato State U., 1984; MEd, Marian Coll., 1989. Tutor, counselor The Other Way, Grand Rapids, Mich., 1976-77; sr. counselor Handicap Village, Sheldon, Iowa, 1978-79; florist Sheldon Greenhouse, 1979-80; K-6 summer sch. tchr. Worthington (Minn.) Sch. Dist., 1982-83; tchr. of emotional/behavioral disabilities class Worthington Sr. H.S., 1981-85, White Bear Lake (Minn.), 1985-89, Northland Pines H.S., Eagle River, Wis., 1989—. Negotiator Coop. Edn. Svcs. Agy., Tomahawk, Wis., 1994—; instr. workshop Advanced Learning, Cedar Falls, Iowa, 1991-92; regional rep. for coun. of spl. program devel. Den. Coop. Svc. Unit, 1983-85; basketball/volleyball coach Worthington, White Bear Lake and Three Lakes, Wis., 1981-89; founder, pres. Angel Whispers jewelry collection, 1997—. Mem. scholarship com. Profl. Bus. Women Am., Worthington, 1984-85; asst. devel. mem.Hosp. Mental Health Unit, Worthington, 1983-84; founder parent support group for parents of spl. edn. students Worthington Sch. Dist., 1983-84. Mem. Nat. Edn. Coun., Wis. Edn. Assn., Coun. for Exceptional Children, Minn. Educators for Emotionally Disabled, AKF Martial Arts. Avocations: kuy-ky-do, golf, gardening, reading, angel jewelry. Home: 5148 Hwy G Eagle River WI 54521

NIEWIAROSKI, TRUDI OSMERS (GERTRUDE NIEWIAROSKI), social studies educator; b. Jersey City, Apr. 30, 1935; d. Albert John and Margaret (Niemeyer) Osmers; m. Donald H. Niewiaroski, June 8, 1957; children: Donald H., Donna, Margaret Anne, Nancy Noel. AB in History and German, Upsala Coll., East Orange, N.J., 1957; MEd, Montgomery County Pub. Schs., Rockville, Md., 1992. Cert. tchr., Md. Tchr. geography Colego Americano, Quito, Ecuador, 1964-66; bd. dirs. Cotopaxi Acad., Quito, 1964-65; tchr. speed reading Escuela Lincoln, Buenos Aires, Argentina, 1966-67; substitute thcr. Montgomery County Pub. Schs., Rockville, 1978-83, tchr. social studies, 1984—. Del. Eisenhower People to People Educators' Del. Vietnam, 1993; pres. Fulbright Meml. Fund Program, 1997; resident tchg. fellow Russia-Ukraine Excellence in Tchg. Program, 1997; resident scholar in Korea, The Korea Soc., 1999. Author curricula; contbr. chpts. to books, articles to profl. jours.; lectr. at workshops. Bd. dirs. Cotopaxi Acad., Quito, 1964-65; pres. Citizens Assn., Potomac, Md., 1977-81; leader Girl Scouts U.S., 1975-76; adv. coun. Milken Found; pres. Fulbright Meml. Fund Program Japan Alumni, 1999—. Recipient Md. Tchr. of Yr. award State of Md. Edn. Dept., 1993, finalist nat. Tchr. of Yr., 1993, Disting. Alumni award Upsala Coll., 1993, Nat. Educator award Milken Found., 1994, Summer Fellowship Korean Studies Program, 1999, Joseph Malone fellowship Sultanate of Oman, 2003, Goethe Inst. fellowship, Germany, 2003; Fulbright fellow, India, 1985, China, 1990, Japan Keizai Koho Ctr. fellow, 1992, Fulbright Meml. Fund Tchr. Program fellow, Japan, 1997, Fulbright fellow, South Africa, 2001, Malone fellow, Oman, 2003; UMBC-U. Mex. Art and Culture scholar, 1995; Goethe Inst. fellow, Germany, 2003. Mem. AAUW, ASCD, Nat. Coun. Social Studies, Md. Coun. for Social Studies, Asia Soc., Smithsonian Instn., Montgomery County Hist. Soc., Spl. Interest Groups-China, Japan and Korea, Md. Bus. Roundtable for Edn., Nat. Social Studies Suprs. Assn., Kappa Delta Pi. Avocations: cake and cookie decorating, travel. Office: R Montgomery High Sch Rockville MD 20852 E-mail: trudi_niewiaroski@fc.meps.kil.md.us.

NIGHTINGALE, EDMUND JOSEPH, clinical psychologist, educator; b. St. Paul, Jan. 10, 1941; s. Edmund Anthony and Lauretta Alexandria (Horejs) N.; m. Marie Arcara, Apr. 9, 1978 (dec. April 1992); one child: Edmund Bernard. Student, Nazareth Hall Prep. Sem., 1959-61; AB, St. Paul Sem., 1963; AB magna cum laude, Catholic U. of Louvain, Belgium, 1965; MA, S.T.B. cum laude,, 1967; postgrad., U. Minn., 1971; MA, Loyola U., Chgo., 1973; PhD in Clin. Psych., 1975. Lic. clin. psychologist, Ill., Minn., cert. Nat. Registry of Health Svc. Providers in Psychology; diplomate clin. psychology Am. Bd. Profl. Psychology. With Cath. Archdiocese of St. Paul and Mpls., 1967-73; int. in clin. psychology Michael Reese Hosp. and Med. Ctr., Chgo., 1973-74; with W. Side VA Hosp., Chgo., 1974-75; staff psychologist Student Counseling Ctr., Loyola Univ., Chgo., 1975; staff psychologist, clin. coord. inpatient unit Drug Dependency Treatment Ctr., 1975—80; chief psychology VA Med. Ctr., Danville, IL, 1980-86, VA Med. Ctr. Mpls., 1986—. Mem. personnel bd. Archdiocese of St. Paul and Mpls., 1968-70; lectr. psychology, Loyola U., Chgo., 1975; asst. professorial lectr. psychology, St. Paul Xavier Coll., Chgo., 1975-78; adj. asst. prof. psychology in psych., Abraham Lincoln Sch. Med., Med. Ctr. U. Ill., Chgo., 1977-82; adj. prof. psychology, Purdue Univ., 1981-87; asst. prof. psych. Med. Sch., U. Minn., 1987—, clin. assoc. prof. psychology Coll. Liberal Arts, 1986-90; adj. asst. prof., 1990—; clin. asst. prof. U. Ill. Sch. Med., Urbana/Champaign, 1982-87; mem. grad. fac. in counseling psychology Ind. State U., Terre Haute, 1983-86. Founding editor: Louvain Studies, 1966; editor: VA Dir. of Psychology Staffing and Svcs., 1982, 83, 84, 85, 87. Bd. dirs. Inst. Postgrad. Studies, Ill. Psychol. Assn. Recipient Outstanding Leadership awd., Assn. VA Chief Psychologists, 1992. Fellow APA (clin. psychology, pub. svc., psychol. hypnosis, sec. treas. pub. svc. 1990-91, coun. reps. 1999—); mem. AAAS, Am. Psychol. Soc., Assn. for Advancement of Psychology, Ill. Psychol. Assn. (clin. psychology and acad. sects., sec. 1982-83, pres.-elect 1983-84, pres. 1984-85), Am. Group Psychotherapy Assn., Am. Soc. Clin. Hypnosis, Minn. Psychol. Assn. (pub. svc.-pres. 1997-99), Eagle Scout, Assn. VA Chief Psychologists (sec., treas. 1987-90, pres.-elect 1990-91, pres. 1991-92, past pres. 1992-93), Minn. Soc. of Clin. Hypnosis (bd. dirs. 1999-2001). Home: 2281 Ocala Ct Mendota Heights MN 55120-1646 Office: VA Med Ctr Minneapolis MN 55417

NIJMAN, JAN, geographer, educator; b. Heemskerk, The Netherlands, Oct. 15, 1957; arrived in U.S., 1987; BA in Human Geography, U. Amsterdam, 1980, MA in Human Geography, 1985; PhD in Geography, U. Colo., 1990. Freelance journalist, Netherlands, 1981—87; cons., rschr. Regioplan, Amsterdam, 1985, U. Amsterdam Sch. Environ. Scis., 1986; tchg. asst. dept. geography U. Ill., Champaign-Urbana, 1987—88; instr. dept. geography U. Colo., Boulder, 1988—90; asst. prof. geography U. Miami, Fla., 1990—94, assoc. prof. geography, 1994—98, prof. dept. geography and regional studies, 1998—, dir. internat. studies program Coll. Arts and Scis., 1993—98. Cons. internat. dvisn. Moran, Stahl & Boyer, Boulder, 1989—90; disting. vis. rsch. prof. Amsterdam Study for the Met. Environment U. Amsterdam, 1996; mem. sr. panel geography and regional sci. program NSF, Washington, 1998—2000; mem. com. for rsch. and exploration Nat. Geog. Soc., Washington, 2001—; presenter in field. Author: The Geopolitics of Power and Conflict: Superpowers in the International System, 1993, The Global Moment in Urban Evolution, 1996; editor (with R. Grant): The Global Crisis in Foreign Aid, 1998, 2000. Grantee, U. Miami, 1990—92, 1993, 1996, 1997, 2000, 2002, 2002, Assn. Am. Geographers, 1997, Nat. Geog. Soc., 1998—2000, NSF, 1998—2001, 1999, 2002—, 2003—; Knight Jr. fellow, U. Miami, 1990—92, John Simon Guggenheim Meml. Found., 2003. Mem.: Koninklijk Nederlands Aardrijkskundig Genootschap, Internat. Studies Assn., Assn. Am. Geographers (Warren Nystrom award 1991). Office: Univ Miami Dept Geography and Regional Studies PO Box 8067 Coral Gables FL 33124-2221

NIKOLAI, LOREN ALFRED, accounting educator, writer; b. Northfield, Minn., Dec. 14, 1943; s. Roman Peter and Loyola (Gertrude) N.; m. Anita Carol Baker, Jan. 15, 1966; children: Trishia, Jay. BA, St. Cloud State U., 1966, MBA, 1967; PhD, U. Minn., 1973. CPA, Mo. Asst. prof. U. N.C., Chapel Hill, 1973-76; assoc. prof. U. Mo., Columbia, 1976-80, prof., 1980-82, Ernst & Young Disting. prof. Sch. Accountancy, 1982—, dir. masters programs, 2002—. Author: Financial Accounting: Concepts and Uses, 1988, 3d edit., 1995, Intermediate Accounting, 1980, 9th edit., 2003, Accounting Information for Business Decisions Recipient Faculty award of merit Fedn. Schs. of Accountancy, 1989, Disting. Alumni award St. Cloud U., 1990, Coll. of Bus. Faculty Mem. of Yr. award, 1991, Mo. Outstanding Acctg. Educators award, 1993; Kemper fellow U. Mo., 1992, Alumni award MU Faculty, 1996, UM Presdl. awd. for Outstanding Teaching, 1999; Coll. of Bus. Teacher of the Yr., 1999. Mem. AICPA, Am. Acctg. Assn., Mo. Soc. CPAs, Fedn. Schs. of Acctg. (pres. 1994). Office: U Mo Sch Accountancy 303 Cornell Hall Columbia MO 65211-0001

NIKOLICH-ZUGICH, JANKO, biomedical scientist, educator; b. Belgrade, Serbia, Serbia-Monteneg (Yugoslavia), Nov. 25, 1960; MD, U. Belgrade, 1984, MS, 1987, PhD, 1993. Cert. gen. practice Yugoslavia, 1985. Rsch. assoc. Scripps Clinic and Rsch. Found., La Jolla, Calif., 1987—90; asst. mem., asst. prof. Meml. Sloan-Kettering Cancer Ctr. and Cornell U. Grad. Sch. Med. Scis., N.Y.C., 1990—96, assoc. mem., assoc. prof., 1996—2000; prof., sr. scientist dept. molecular microbiology and immunology Vaccine and Gene Therapy Inst., Oreg. Primate Rsch. Ctr., Oreg. Health & Sci. U., Portland, 2000—. Dir. flow cytometry core faculty MSKCC, N.Y.C., 1990—2000. Editor: Intrathymic T-cell Development, 1994; mem. editl. bd.: Cellular Immunology, 1996—, Jour. Immunology, 1996—; contbr. articles to profl. jours. Recipient Preclincal Prostate Cancer award, Cancer Rsch. Inst., 1999—2002; scholar, PEW Charitable Trust, 1991—95. Mem.: Am. Assn. Immunologists. Office: Vaccine and Gene Therapy Inst OHSU 505 NW 185th Ave Beaverton OR 97229 Business E-Mail: nikolich@ohsu.edu.

NILSSON, MARY ANN, music educator; b. N.Y.C., Jan. 5, 1944; d. Gerhard Eugene and Selma Christine (Landy) N.; m. June 19, 1988. BS with honors, New Paltz State U., 1965; MA, NYU, 1983; MM, Meredith Coll., 2000; student, The Christian U., 2003. LPN, N.Y. Piano tchr. New Paltz (N.Y.) State U. Coll., 1983-85, Ulster County C.C., Stone Ridge, N.Y., 1983-85; music instr. Piedmont C.C., Roxboro, N.C., 1999, Durham Tech. Coll., 1999, Durham (N.C.) C.C., 2000—02; coll. instr. Vance-Granville C.C., Henderson, NC, 2002, Mt. Olive Coll., Research Triangle Park, NC, 2002—. Music history tchr. Family of Ellenville, N.Y., 1990-91; tchr. music appreciation Long Meml. Music Acad., Roxboro, N.C., 2001, tchr. music course continuing edn., 2001; music instr. Mt. Olive Coll., Research Triangle Park, N.C., 2002. Musician (Performances): New Paltz State U., 1992, Town of Lumberland, N.Y., 1993, Lunch & Listen series, 1994, Hudson Valley Sr. Residence, 1995, South Winds Sr. Residence, 1995, Forest at Duke, 1997, Long Meml. Ch., 1997; musician: (pianist competition) Meredith Coll., 1999; musician: (master class) Walter Hautzig Meredith Coll., 1999; musician: (recital) Meredith Coll., Durham Regents, 2001, Forest at Duke, Carolina House, 2001, Carol Woods, Croasdale, Chapel Heill Sr. Ctr., 2003; contbr. articles to profl. jours. Choir dir., organist First Presbyn. Ch., Monticello, N.Y., 1985-86; vol. Durham (N.C.) Hosp., 1996—. Named one of 12 winners, Van Cliburn Tchrs. program, Ft. Worth Tex., 2003; grantee, Ulster County Office of Aging, 1983, Sullivan County Office of Aging, Nat. Music Tchrs. Assn., 2001, Music Tchrs. Nat. Assn., 2001. Mem. Nat. Guild Piano Tchrs. (adjudicator 1983—, chmn. piano audition ctr. 1988-95), Durham Music Tchrs. Assn., Pi Kappa Lambda. Avocations: reading german, walking, fitness. Home and Office: 214 Equestrian Chase Rougemont NC 27572-9351

NIMEROFF, PHYLLIS RUTH, electronic engineer, visual artist; b. Washington, Apr. 22, 1951; d. Isadore and Anne (Schultz) N. BFA, Md. Inst. Coll. Art, 1973; BS in Electronic Engring. Tech., Capitol Coll., 1988. Exhibiting vis. artist East Coast, 1968—; art tchr. D.C. Schs., Washington, 1974-75; ops. tech. TV Stas., Mont., Nebr., Md., Washington, 1978-85; engr. PRC, Inc., Suitland, Md., 1988-1997; multimedia communicator Lockheed Martin, Washington, 1998—. Mem. Alpha Chi, Tau Alpha Pi. Avocation: gardening. Home: 6505 Greentree Rd Bethesda MD 20817-3325 E-mail: primeroff@zdnetonebox.com.

NIPPER, HENRY CARMACK, toxicologist, educator; b. Mar. 31, 1940; s. Henry Lee and Zackie Irene (Carmack) N.; m. Margaret Anne Gilbreth, June 10, 1966; children: Zachary Gilbreth, Gregory Lee Gilbreth. AB, Emory U., 1960; MS, Purdue U., 1966; PhD, U. Md., 1971. Diplomate Am. Bd. Clin. Chemistry. Analytical chemist E.I. DuPont de Nemours Co., Wilmington, Del., 1960-63; instr. pathology U. Md. Sch. Medicine, Balt., 1973-74, asst. prof., 1974-83; dir. chemistry VA Med. Ctr., Balt., 1973-83; instr. pathology Harvard Med. Sch., Boston, 1983-86; sci. dir. clin. chemistry Beth Israel Hosp., Boston, 1983—; assoc. prof. Creighton U., Omaha, 1986—, asst. dean med. admissions, 1996—. Dir. Creighton Univ. Med. Ctr., Clin. Chemistry and Forensic Toxicology Labs., 1986-96, 99—, dir. Creighton Forensic Lab., 1989-96; mem. clin. adv. bd. Beckman Inst., Brea, Calif., 1982-83; mem. panel on clinchem. and toxicology FDA Ctr. for Devices and Radiologic Health, 1989-92, cons., 1992-96, 2000—, chair, 1996-2000. Editor: Clinician and Chemist, 1979, Selected Papers on Clinical Chemistry Instrumentation, 1985; chair editl. bd. Forensic Urine Drug Testing, 1993-96; contbr. articles to profl. jours. Soccer coach Wellesley Soccer, Mass., 1984; scout leader Boy Scouts Am., Cub Scouts, Omaha, Wellesley, and Balt., 1982-93; bd. dirs. Ruxton-Riderwood Cmty. Assn., Balt., 1983, Omaha Morning Rotary, 1987—; pres. Nat. Registry Clin. Chemistry, 1992-93. VA rsch. grantee, 1979; Gillette-Harris rsch. fellow U. Md., 1968-69. Fellow Nat. Acad. Clin. Biochemistry; mem. Am. Assn. for Clin. Chemistry (Roe award 1978), Am. Acad. Forensic Scis., Assn. Clin. Biochemists (U.K.), Alpha Tau Omega. Democrat. Avocations: railroad photography, collecting old trains. Office: Creighton U Dept Pathology 2500 California Plz Omaha NE 68178-0001 E-mail: nipper@creighton.edu.

NISBETT, WILMA CONSTANCE, elementary education educator; b. Basseterre, St. Kitts, West Indies, Nov. 22, 1950; Came to U.S., 1968. d. Carlyle Winston Stephenson and Henrietta L. Ham; m. Calvin Terrence Nisbett, July 12, 1980. BA, Coll. V.I., 1975; MA, U. V.I., 1992. Cert. tchr., V.I. Tchr. St. Croix (V.I.) Bd. Edn., 1975—. Mem. adv. bd. St. Croix Moravian Sch., 1990-92, sec., 1992—. Recipient Achievement cert. U. Hartford, 1978, Appreciation cert. Ednl. Support Systems, Inc., 1982, St. Croix Parent-Tchr. Student Coun., 1988, Recognition cert. Bay Area Summer Writing Inst., 1988, Academic Achievement cert. U.S. Virgin Islands, 1990-93. Mem. ASCD (John Amos Comenius award 1993).

NIXON, RALPH ANGUS, psychiatrist, educator, research neuroscientist; b. Somerville, Mass., Jan. 29, 1947; s. Ralph Angus and Eleanor Nixon; m. Katharine Sangree Faulkner, Aug. 20, 1974; children: Abigail, Rebecca. AB, Brandeis U., 1968; PhD in Cell and Devel. Biology, Harvard U., 1974; MD, U. Vt., 1976. Intern Mass. Gen. Hosp., 1976, Salem Hosp., 1977; resident in psychiatry Mass. Gen. Hosp., 1977-79, McLean Hosp., 1979-80; clin. assoc. in psychiatry Mass. Gen. Hosp., Boston, 1980-97; assoc. in neurosci. Children's Hosp Med. Ctr., Boston, 1982-88; staff physician Rehab. Ctr. for Aged, Boston, 1984-90; asst. prof. psychiatry Harvard Med. Sch., Boston, 1982-86, assoc. prof., 1986-96; assoc. neuropathologist McLean Hosp., Belmont, Mass., 1982-90, assoc. psychiatrist, 1988-93, neuropathologist, 1991; psychiatrist, 1993-97; prof. psychiatry and cell biology NYU Med. Sch., N.Y.C., 1997—, vice chmn. dept. psychiatry, 2001—; dir. dept. neurosci., dir. dementia rsch. program Nathan Kline Inst.-NYU Med. Ctr., Orangeburg, 1997—. Mem. sci. rev. com. Am. Fedn. for Aging Rsch., 1990-92; mem. neurosci., behavior and sociology of aging rev. com., subcom. A, Nat. Inst. on Aging, NIH, 1991-95, chmn., 1994-95; dir. labs. for molecular neurosci. McLean Hosp., 1992; mem. adv. bd. Internat. Congress Alzheimer's Disease, 1993—. Mem. editl. bd. Jour. Neurochemistry, 1986-96, Neurochem. Rsch., 1988—, Harvard Rev. Psychiatry, 1992—, Neurobiology of Aging, 1994—, Alzheimer's Disease Rev., 1997—; contbr. over 200 biol. articles to Sci. Jour. Cell Biology, Jour. Biol. Chem., Annals N.Y. Acad. Sci., Proc. NAS, chpts. to books; Proteases and Protease Inhibitors Banner C Nixon R.A. eds. Annals Acad. Sci. vol. 67, 1992. Hon. bd. dirs. Ch. League for Civic Concerns, Boston, 1987-89. Recipient Merit award NIH, 1990, Leadership and Excellence in Alzheimer Disease award, Nat. Inst. Aging, 1992, Temple Discovery award Alzheimers ASsn., 1999, N.Y. State OMH Rsch. award, 1999, others; Ethel DuPont Warren fellow, 1979-80, rsch. felolw Med. Found., 1980-82, Alfred P. Sloan Found., 1981-83, Scottish Rite Schizophrenia Rsch. Program, 1983-85. Mem. AAAS, Soc. for Neurosci., Fedn. Am. Scientists, Am. Soc. for Neurochemistry, Internat. Soc. for Neurochemistry, Am. Psychiat. Assn., Am. Soc. for Cell Biology, Am. Assn. for Geriatric Psychiatry, Gerontol. Soc. Am., Am. Assn. Neuropathologists, N.Y. Acad. Sci. Achievements include 5 patents (with others) on diagnosis and treatment of Alzheimer's disease. Office: Nathan Kline Inst NYU Med Ctr 140 Old Orangeburg Rd Orangeburg NY 10962-1157

NIXON, ROBERT OBEY, SR., business educator; b. Pitts., Feb. 14, 1922; s. Frank Obey and Margurite (Van Buren) N.; m. Marilyn Cavanagh, Oct. 25, 1944 (dec. 1990); children: Nan Nixon Friend, Robert Obey, Jr., Dwight Cavanagh. BS in bus. adminstrn., U. Pitts., 1948; MS, Ohio State U., 1964; MBA, U. Phoenix, 1984. Commd. 2d lt. USAF, 1943, advanced through grades to col., 1970, master navigator WWII, Korea, Vietnam; sales, adminstrn. U.S. Rubber Corp., Pitts., 1940-41; asst. engr. Am. Bridge Corp., Pitts., 1941-42; underwriter, sales Penn Mutual Life Ins. Corp., Pitts., 1945-50; capt., nav. instr. USAF Reserves, 1945-50; ret. USAF Col., divsn. chief Joint Chiefs of Staff, 1973; educator, cons. U. Ariz., 1973-79; bus. dept. chmn., coord., founder weekend coll. Pima C.C., Tucson, 1979-90, prof. mgmt., 1991-98, coord. weekend coll. program, 1991—. Adj. faculty Pima C.C., 1998—; founder, pres. Multiple Adv. Group ednl. cons., Tucson, 1978—. Author: Source Document: On Accelerated Courses and Programs at Accredited Two- and Four-Year Colleges and Universities, 1996; contbr. articles to profl. jours. Mem. Soc. Logistics Engrs. (sr., charter mem.), Phi Delta Theta. Presbyterian. Avocations: tennis, hiking, swimming. Home: 1824 S Regina Cleri Dr Tucson AZ 85710-8664 Fax: 520-885-2378. E-mail: eb58271@goodnet.com., bnixon@pimacc.pima.edu.

NIZNIK, CAROL ANN, electrical engineer, educator, consultant; b. Saratoga Springs, N.Y., Nov. 10, 1942; d. John Arthur Niznik and Rosalia Sopko; m. Donald H. Walter, Jan. 11, 1964. AAS in Engring. Sci., Alfred (N.Y.) State Coll., 1962; BSEE, U. Rochester, N.Y., 1969, MSEE, 1972; PhD in Elec. Engring., SUNY, Buffalo, 1978. Technician Taylor Instrument Corp., Rochester, 1962-64; sr. technician IBM Corp., Poughkeepsie, N.Y., 1964-68; rsch. scientist Eastman Kodak Corp., Rochester, 1969-70; sr. engr. Xerox Corp., Webster, N.Y., 1971-74; rsch. asst. prof. SUNY, buffalo, 1979-80; assoc. prof. elec. engring. U. Pitts., 1980-83; pres., cons. NW Systems, Rochester, 1975—. Adj. prof. math. Rochester Inst. Tech., 1993-94; vis. assoc. prof. Ctr. for Brain Rsch., Sch. Medicine, U. Rochester,

1983-84. Author tech. monograph on cerebellum prosthesis component; contbr. some 70 articles to profl. jours.; patentee in field. Recipient fellowships, grants and U.S. govt. contracts. Mem. IEEE (sr.), Sigma Xi, Eta Kappa Nu, Tau Beta Pi. Roman Catholic. Avocations: doll collecting, care of pets, gardening. Office: NW Sys PO Box 18133 Rochester NY 14618-0133

NJIE, VERONICA P.S. nurse educator, clinical nurse; d. Edward G. Njie and Grace B.S. Daniels-Njie. BSN, Howard U., Washington, 1992; MSN, The Cath. U. Am., Washington, 1996. RN Washington, clin. specialist in med.-surg. nursing. Tchr. Dept. Edn., Banjul, The Gambia, 1980—82; state registered nurse (SRN) Royal Victoria Hosp., Banjul, 1985—86; rsch./field asst. Med. Rsch. Coun., Fajara, 1986—87; nurse technician Howard U. Hosp., Washington, 1988—90, clin. nurse II, 1990—96; clin. nurse N.W. Health Care Ctr. Beverly Enterprise, 1990—98; clin. instr. Montgomery Coll., Tacoma Park, Md., 1996; asst. prof. nursing Balt. City C. C., Balt., 1997. Contbr. articles to profl. jours. Recipient Intramural Rsch. Tng. award, NIH, 2000. Mem.: Md. Assn. Higher Edn., ANA, Nat. League Nursing, Sigma Theta Tau. Democrat. Roman Catholic. Avocations: reading, travel, theater, dancing, movies. Office: Cath U Am Michigan Ave NE Washington DC 20064 Office Fax: 202-319-6485. E-mail: vpnjie@aol.com.

NNAEMEKA, OBIOMA GRACE, French language and women's studies educator, consultant, researcher; b. Agulu, Anambra, Nigeria; came to U.S., 1974; d. Christopher Egbunike and Jessie Ifemelue (Ogbuefi) Obidiegwu; children: Ike, Uchenna. BA with honors, U. Nigeria, Nsukka, 1972; MA, U. Minn., 1977, PhD with distinction, 1989. Rsch. fellow U. Nigeria, 1972-74, lectr., 1982-87; asst. prof. Concordia Coll., Minn., 1988-89, Coll. Wooster, Ohio, 1989-91; assoc. prof. Ind. U., Indpls., 1991—. Cons. Govt. Senegal, Dakar, 1990-92; commentator Internat. Svc. Radio Netherlands, Hilversum, 1990—; Edith Kreeger Wolf Disting. prof. Northwestern U., 1992. Author: Agrippa d'Aubigné: The Poetics of Power and Change, 1998; editor: The Politics of Mothering, 1996, Sisterhood, Feminisms, & Power, 1997; contbr. articles to profl. jours. Founder, pres. Assn. African Women's Scholars, 1995; convener, organizer First Internat. Conf. Women in Africa & African Diaspora, 1992. Named Achiever of Yr. Leadership Nigeria Network, 1994; grantee from McArthur Found., Rockefeller Found., Swedish Internat. Devel. Agy., Swedish Agy. for Rsch. Cooperation with Developing Countries, 1991-92. Mem. Am. Assn. Tchrs. French, Ind. Fgn. Lang. Tchrs. Assn., Modern Langs. Assn., African Studies Assn., African Lit. Assn. Avocations: reading, travel. Office: Ind U Dept Fgn Langs Cultrs 425 University Blvd Indianapolis IN 46202-5148 E-mail: waad@iupui.edu.

NOAKES, BETTY LAVONNE, retired elementary school educator; b. Oklahoma City, Okla., Aug. 28, 1938; d. Webster L. and Willie Ruth (Johnson) Hawkins; m. Richard E. Noakes, Apr. 22, 1962 (dec.); 1 child, Michele Monique. Student, Oklahoma City U., MEd, 1971; BS, Cen. State U., 1962; postgrad., Cen. State U., Okla. State U. Elem. tchr. Merced (Calif.) Pub. Schs., 1966-67, Oklahoma City Schs., 1971-73, Mid-Del Schs., Midwest City, Okla., 1973-95; founder, owner Noakes-I Care Day Care, 1995—2002. 2d v.p. PTA, Pleasant Hill, 1991, cert. recognition, 1992-93; active Nat. PTA, 1991-92; charter mem. Nat. Mus. of Am. Indian-Smithsonian Instn.; chmn. stewardship com. Quayle U. Meth. Ch., 1997—; mem. Wesley Found. bd. Langston U.; mem. Urban League, Urban League Guild, YWCA. Recipient Cert. Appreciation YMCA, 1992-92, Disting. Svc. award Mid-Del PTA, 1992. Mem. NEA, AAUW, NAACP, NAFE, LWV, Okla. Edn. Assn., Nat. Ret. Tchrs. Assn., Okla. Ret. Tchrs. Assn., Smithsonian Instn., Oklahoma City U. Alumni Assn., Nat. Trust for Hist. Preservation, United Meth. Women Assn., Ctrl. State U. Alumni Assn., Okla. Order Ea. Star, Order of the Golden Cir. (aux. of Great We. Consistory # 34 Dorcas-LL Golden Ci. assembly # 41), Daus. of Isis, Phi Delta Kappa (sgt.-at-arms), Zeta Phi Beta (1st v.p.). Avocations: aerobics, singing, piano, clarinet, folk dancing. Home: 5956 N Coltrane Rd Oklahoma City OK 73121-3409 E-mail: nblnzeta@aol.com.

NOBACK, CHARLES ROBERT, anatomist, educator; b. N.Y.C., Feb. 15, 1916; s. Charles Victor and Beatrice (Cerny) N.; m. Eleanor Louise Loomis, Nov. 23, 1938 (dec. Mar. 24, 1981); children: Charles Victor, Margaret Beatrice, Ralph Theodore, Elizabeth Louise. BS, Cornell U., 1936; MS, NYU, 1938; postgrad., Columbia U., 1936-38; PhD, U. Minn., 1942. Asst. prof. anatomy U. Ga., 1941-44; faculty L.I. Coll. Medicine, 1944-49, asso. prof., 1948-49; mem. faculty Columbia Coll. Phys. and Surg., 1949—, assoc. prof. anatomy, 1953-68, prof., 1968-86, prof. emeritus, 1986—, spl. lectr., 1986-92, acting chmn. dept., 1974-75, lectr., 1996—. Author: The Human Nervous System, 1967, 75, 81, Spinal Cord, 1971, The Nervous System Introduction and Review, 1982, 77, 86, 91, (with R. Demarest) Human Anatomy and Physiology, 1990, 2d edit., 1992, 3d edit., 1995, (with D. Van Wyseberghe and R. Carola) Human Anatomy, 1992, (with N. Strominger and R. Demarest) The Human Nervous System, Structure and Function, 5th edit., 1996; editor: with R. Carola and H. Harley) The Primate Brain, 1970, Sensory Systems of Primates, 1978; sr. editor: Advances in Primatology: series editor: Contbns. to Primatology; contbr. articles to profl. jours., sects. to Ency. Britannica, McGraw Hill Ency. Sci. and Tech., Collier's Ency. Recipient Physicians and Surgeons Disting. Svc. award, 1999. Fellow N.Y. Acad. Scis. (past rec. sec.), AAAS; mem. Am. Assn. Anatomists, Histochem. Soc., Internat. Primatological Soc., Am. Soc. Naturalists, Cajal Club Am. (past pres.), Assn. Phys. Anthropologists, Harvey Soc., Am. Acad. Neurology, Soc. Neurosci., Sigma Xi. Home: 116 7th St Cresskill NJ 07626-2005 Office: Columbia U Anatomy And Cell Dept New York NY 10032

NOBLE, DIANE KAY, education specialist; b. Kansas City, May 24, 1950; d. William Gene and Lora Kathleen (Norris) DePugh; m. David Craig, Apr. 2, 1988; children: Jeffrey William, Matthew Ryan. BA in Elem. Edn., William Jewell Coll., 1972; MEd, N.E. Mo. State U., 1986. Cert. elem. tchr., Mo., Tex.; cert. elem. adminstr., Tex. Tchr. Carrollton (Mo.) R-VII Sch. Dist., 1972-78; libr., instr. gifted and talented Bucklin (Mo.) R-II Sch. Dist., 1982-83; tchr. grades 6 and 7 Kirkwood (Mo.) R-VII Sch. Dist., 1983-84, instr. gifted, 1984-89, Denton (Tex.) Ind. Sch. Dist., 1989-91, curriculum specialist, 1991—. Mem. ASCD, Nat. Mid. Sch. Assn., Nat. Coun. Tchrs. Maths., Nat. Coun. Tchrs. English, Nat. Sci. Tchrs. Assn., Phi Delta Kappa (local v.p. 1988-89), Delta Kappa Gamma. Office: Denton Ind Sch Dist 1307 N Locust St Denton TX 76201-3037

NOBLE, ERNEST PASCAL, pharmacologist, biochemist, educator; b. Baghdad, Iraq, Apr. 2, 1929; came to U.S., 1946; s. Noble Babik and Barkev Grace (Kasparian) Babikian; m. Inga Birgitta Kilstromer, May 19, 1956; children— Lorna, Katharine, Erik BS in Chemistry, U. Calif.-Berkeley, 1951; PhD in Biochemistry, Oreg. State U., 1955; MD, Case Western Res. U., 1962. Diplomate Nat. Bd. Med. Examiners. Sr. instr. biochemistry Western Res. U., Cleve., 1957-62; intern Stanford Med. Ctr., Calif., 1962-63, resident in psychiatry, 1963-66, research assoc., asst. prof., 1965-69; assoc. prof. psychiatry, psychobiology and pharmacology U. Calif.-Irvine, 1969-71, prof., chief neurochemistry, 1971-76, 79-81; dir. Nat. Inst. Alcohol Abuse and Alcoholism HEW, 1976-78, assoc. adminstr. sci., alcohol, drug abuse and mental health, 1978-79; Pike prof. alcohol studies, dir. Alcohol Research Ctr. UCLA Sch. of Medicine, 1981—. Mem. various med./sci. jour. editorial bds.; contbr. numerous articles to profl. jours., chpts. to books V.p. Nat. Coun. on Alcoholism 1981-84; pres. Internat. Commn. for the Prevention of Alcoholism and Drug Dependency, 1988. Fulbright scholar, 1955-56; Guggenheim fellow, 1974-75; Sr. Fulbright scholar, 1984-85; recipient Career Devel. award NIMH, HEW, 1966-69 Fellow Am. Coll. Neuropsychopharmacology; mem. Internat. Soc. Neurochemistry, Am. Soc. Pharmacology and Exptl. Therapeutics, Research Soc. on Alcoholism. Office: UCLA 760 Westwood Plz Los Angeles CA 90095-8353

NOBLE, NELDA KAYE, elementary education educator; b. Lumberton, N.C., Jan. 4, 1952; d. Albert T. and Nelle T. (Kizer) N. BS in Christian Edn., Atlanta Christian Coll., 1974; BA in Elem. Edn., Fla. Atlantic U., 1980, M in Counselor Edn., 1988. Cert. elem. tchr., early childhood tchr., guidance counseling, ESOL. Kindergarten tchr., asst. dir. Circle D Day Care and Kindergarten, College Park, Ga., 1974-76; tchr. Putnam County Schs., Palatka, Fla., 1980-84, Coral Springs Christian Sch., Coral Springs, Fla., 1984-85, Palm Beach County Schs., Boca Raton, Fla., 1985-95, Gwinnett County Pub Schs., Tucker, Ga., 1995—. Chairperson Instructional Innovation Team-J.C. Mitchell Elem., Boca Raton, 1992-95, mem. sch. adv. coun., 1992-95. Bd. dirs. 1st Christian Pre-Sch., Boca Raton, 1985-88, 94. Mem. Palm Beach County Reading Coun. Avocations: reading, crafts. Home: 515 Crane Dr Lawrenceville GA 30045-6122 Office: Nesbit Elem Sch 6575 Cherokee Dr Tucker GA 30084-1618

NOBLE, RONALD MARK, sports medicine facility administrator; b. Atlanta, Dec. 28, 1950; s. Dexter Ron and Judy (Puckett) N.; m. Teresa Lowder, Sept. 20, 1975; children: Kimberly, Heather, James, Ashlee. AS, Ricks Coll., 1974; BS cum laude, Troy State U., 1976; MS, U. Tenn., 1977. Grad. asst. U. Tenn., Knoxville, 1976-77; lectr. Tex. A&M U., College Station, 1977-79; asst. prof. U.S. Mil. Acad., West Point, N.Y., 1979-80; dir. clin. phys. NASA Med. Ctr., MSFC, 1980-85; exec. dir. Total Wellness Ctr., Huntsville, Ala., 1986-90, Preventive and Rehab. Sports Medicine Assocs., Huntsville, 1990—; clin. advisor Huntsville Med. Sch., U. Ala., 1990—, exec. dir. preventive and clin. advisor, preceptor, 1992—. Adj. prof. U. Ala., Huntsville, 1982-85, 2000—; sports medicine cons. Mex. Olympic Com., San Luis Potosi, 1980, Duke U. Basketball, Durham, N.C., 1987—, U.S. Olympic Team, 1994-96; coord. U.S. Olympic Com. Nat. Rehab. Network, 1992—; cons. USAF Dept. Manned Space Flight Ops., L.A., 1983-84, USFSA, 1996—; cons. sports sci. and tech. athletic dept. Ala. A&M U., 1994-97; asst. coach U.S. Olympic Com., Colorado Springs, 1979-83; spl. advisor Pres. Coun. on Phys. Fitness and Sports, Huntsville, 1991-94; clin. advisor, preceptor U. Ala. Huntsville Med. Sch., 1991—; cons., Sport Sci. & Tech. Divsn., U.S. Figure Skating Assn., 1998-2000. Developer computer software in field; contbr. articles to profl. jours., also to USAF manual. Campaign mgr. Brooks for State Legislature, Huntsville, 1992; bd. dirs. Huntsville Boys Club, 1988-89, Big Bros./Sisters of No. Ala., Huntsville, 1988-89, Ala. affiliate Am. Heart Assn., Huntsville, 1980-88; commr. Ala. Gov.'s Com. on Phys. Fitness, 1991-94; mem. U.S. Olympic Com. Spkrs. Bur., 1978-80; U.S. Olympic Com., Nat. Rehab. Network for Elite Athletes. With U.S. Army, 1970-73, Vietnam. Named Outstanding Leader Jaycees of Ala., 1983; Paul Harris fellow Huntsville Rotary Club, 1987—. Mem. Huntsville Rotary (Paul Harris fellow), Kappa Delta Pi. Mem. Lds Ch. Avocations: family activities, sports, woodworking, gardening, service to others. Office: PRSM Sports Therapy 4715 Whitesburg Dr S Ste 200 Huntsville AL 35802-1632

NOBLES, DARLENE ADELE, elementary education educator; b. Chgo., Dec. 12, 1949; d. Mae Schaller; m. Joseph T. Nobles, Jan. 29, 1972; 2 children. AA, Fla. Jr. Coll., Jacksonville, 1974; BA, U. South Fla., Tampa, 1979; MA, U. South Fla., 1982; postgrad., U. Md., 1990—. Cert. early childhood, elem. tchr., supervision, adminstrn., Fla., Ga., Md. Tchr., kindergarten, 2d grade Hillsborough Pub. Sch., Dover, Fla., 1979-82; tchr., grades 1 & 2 Cobb County Pub. Sch., Marietta, Ga., 1982-87; magnet tchr. Wicomico County Pub. Schs., Salisbury, Md., 1987-88, tchr., 2d grade, 1988—. Cooperating tchr. for student tchrs. Salisbury State U. Dept. Edn., 1989—, first program facilitator. Mem. Mothers and Others for a Safe Planet, 1989, Jr. Woman's Club of Wicomico (edn. com. 1988-92). Named Suncoast Area Tchr. Training clin. tchr. for excellence in teaching U. South Fla., 1982. del. to Russia as part of U. Nebr. Tchrs. Coll. People to People Ednl. Orgn., 1995. Mem. AAUW, Nat. Assn. for Edn. of Young Children, Assn. for Childhood Edn. Internat. (pres. Betty Brantly br. 1980-82). Methodist. Avocations: oil painting, gardening.

NODDINGS, NEL, education educator, writer; b. Irvington, N.J., Jan. 19, 1929; d. Edward A. Rieth and Nellie A. (Connors) Walter; m. James A. Noddings, Aug. 20, 1949; children: Chris, Howard, Laurie, James, Nancy, William, Sharon, Edward, Vicky, Timothy. BA in Math., Montclair State Coll., 1949; MA in Math., Rutgers U., 1964; PhD in Edn., Stanford U., 1973; PhD (hon.), Columbia Coll., S.C., 1995. Cert. tchr., Calif., N.J. Tchr. Woodbury (N.J.) Publ Schs., 1949-52; tchr. math. dept. Matawan (N.J.) High Sch., 1958-62, chair, asst. prin., 1964-69; curriculum supr. Montgomery Twp. Pub. Schs., Skillman, N.J., 1970-72; dir. precollegiate edn. U. Chgo., 1975-76; asst. prof. Pa. State U., State College, 1973; from asst. prof. to assoc. prof. Stanford (Calif.) U., 1977-86, prof., 1986—, assoc. dean, 1990-92, acting dean, 1992-94, Lee L. Jacks prof. child edn., 1992-98, prof. emeritus, 1998—; prof. philosophy and edn. Columbia U., N.Y.C., 1998—. Bd. dirs. Ctr. for Human Caring Sch. Nursing, Denver, 1986-92; cons. NIE, NSF and various other sch. dists. Author: Caring: A Feminine Approach to Ethics and Moral Education, 1984, Women and Evil, 1989; author: (with W. Paul Shore) Awakening the Inner Eye: Intuition in Education, 1984; author: (with Carol Witherell) Stories Lives Tell, 1991; author: The Challenge to Care in Schools, 1992, Educating for Intelligent Belief or Unbelief, 1993, Philosophy of Education, 1995; author: (with Suzanne Gordon and Patricia Benner) Caregiving, 1996; author: (with Michael Katz and Kenneth Strike) Justice and Caring, 1999; author: Starting at Home: Caring and Social Policy, 2002, Educating Moral People, 2002, Happiness and Education, 2003. Mem. disting. women's adv. bd. Coll. St. Catherine. Recipient Anne Roe award for Contbns. to Profl. devel. of Women, Harvard Grad. Sch. Edn., 1993, medal for disting. svc. Tchrs. Coll. Columbia, 1994, Willystine Goodsell award, 1997, Laureate chpt. Kappa Delta Pi, Pi Lambda Theta award, 1999; Spencer Mentor grantee, Spencer Found., 1995-97. Fellow Philosophy of Edn. Soc. (pres. 1991-92); mem. Am. Ednl. Rsch. Assn. (Div B, 2000, Lifetime achievment award), Am. Philos. Assn., Nat. Acad. Edn. (pres. 2001—), John Dewey Soc. (pres. 1994-96), Phi Beta Kappa (vis. scholar). Avocation: gardening. E-mail: noddings@stanford.edu.

NODORFT, REBECCA ANN, school administrator; b. Lancaster, Wis., Sept. 18, 1950; d. Chester Merle and Pearl Elizabeth (Frankland) Boardman; m. Rexford Wayne Nodorft, July 15, 1972; children: Randy, Renee, Ryan. BS, U. Wis., Platteville, 1986; MEd, U. Wis., Whitewater, 1990; cert. in ednl. adminstrn., U. Wis., Madison, 1991. Cert. tchr., sch. adminstr., Wis. Tchr. Beloit (Wis.) Sch. Dist., 1987-90, program coord., 1990-92; mid. sch. prin. Clinton (Wis.) Middle Sch., 1992—. Mem., pres. Beloit Jr. Woman's Club, 1976-87. Mem. ASCD, Asns. Wis. Sch. Adminstrs., Rock Valley Prins.' Assn., Wis. Math. Coun. (presenter), Delta Kappa Gamma. Home: RR 1 Box 335 1920 Town Hall Rd Beloit WI 53511-9770 Office: Clinton Community Sch Dist 313 Mill St Clinton WI 53525-9480

NOETZEL, ARTHUR JEROME, business administration educator, management consultant; b. East Cleveland, Ohio, July 2, 1916; s. Arthur John and Margaret (Weinfurtner) N.; m. Dorothy Elizabeth McKeon, Oct. 23, 1945 (dec. March 1988); children: Catherine Ellen Noetzel Levitt, Gretchen Marie Noetzel Walsh. BSBA, John Carroll U., 1938; MBA, Northwestern U., 1940; PhD, U. Mich., 1955; LittD (hon.), John Carroll U., 1985. Instr. John Carroll U., Cleve., 1941-42, asst. prof., 1942-46, prof. bus. adminstrn., 1955—; asst. dean Sch. Bus. John Carroll U., Cleve., 1945-56, dean, 1956-70, academic v.p., 1970-84. Bd. dirs. Ctr. for Family Bus., Cleve., Ohio Coll. Podiatric Medicine, Cleve. Contbr. articles and book reviews to profl. jours. Bd. dirs. St. Vincent Charity Hosp., Cleve., 1970-82, Borromeo Coll., Wickliffe, 1978-84; chmn. Communication and Devel. Commn., Univ. Heights, Ohio, 1980—. Named Citizen of Yr., City of Univ. Heights, Ohio, 1983; recipient Alumni award John Carroll U., 1984, Cert. of Merit, Minority Developers Council, Cleve., 1985, You're The Top award, Golden Age Ctrs. of Cleve., 1997; Danforth Found. fellow, 1956. Roman Catholic. Avocation: reading. Office: John Carroll U University Hts Cleveland OH 44111 Home: 111 Hamlet Hills Dr Apt 24 Chagrin Falls OH 44022

NOFFSINGER, WILLIAM BLAKE, computer science educator, academic administrator; b. Atlanta, July 5, 1950; s. M.F. and Winifred (Blake) N.; m. Kathy A. Golden, Apr. 27, 1985; children: Margeaux Jones-Golden, William Blake Jr. BS in Exptl. Psychology, U. Fla., 1974, MS in Exptl. Psychology, 1984; postgrad. in Computer Sci., Fla. State U., 1993—. Sys. mgr. Santa Fe C.C., Gainesville, Fla., 1974-77, instnl. rschr., instr., 1977-79; sys. analyst U. Fla., Gainesville, Fla., 1979-82, sys. coord., 1982-88, sr. computer coord., 1988—, computer sci. instr., 1985—, asst. dir. info. tech. bus. svcs. divsn., 1999—. Computing and rsch. cons. Ctr. for Climacteric Studies, Gainesville, 1986, VA Hosp., Gainesville, 1986-87, U. Fla. Pediat. Neurology, Gainesville, 1991—. Contbr. articles to profl. jours. Judge computer sci. entries Alachua county Sci. Fair, Gainesville, 1981. Recipient Davis Productivity award State of Fla., 1992, 93, 96, 97; grantee Santa Fe C.C., 1978, U. Fla., 1989, 90. Mem. IEEE, Data Processing Mgmt. Assn. (chpt. v.p. 1982), Assn. for Computing Machinery, Phi Delta Kappa (chpt. treas. 1981). Episcopalian. Avocations: running, audio, electronics, equestrian. Office: U Fla 33 Tigert Hall Gainesville FL 32611-2073 Home: 13271 NW 93rd Ln Alachua FL 32615-6757

NOFSINGER, JOHN, finance educator, consultant; b. Hampton, Va., Nov. 25, 1965; m. Suzzanna Frenier. BSEE, Wash. State U., 1988, PhD in Fin., 1996; MBA, Chapman U., 1991. Engr. Pacific Gas, San Francisco, 1988—89; fin. prof. Marquette U., Milw., Wash. State U., Pullman. Cons. N.Y. Stock Exch., Assn. for Investment Mgmt. Rsch. Author: Investment Madness, 2001, Investment Blunders, 2002, Infectious Greed, 2003; contbr. articles to profl. jours. Capt. USAF, 1989—92. Named winner acad. paper competition, Chgo. Quantitative Alliance, 1997. Mem.: Fin. Mgmt. Assn. (Best of the Best Paper award 1997, Best Paper in Investments award 1997), Am. Fin. Assn. Office: Wash State Univ Dept Fin/Coll Bus Pullman WA 99164-4746 Business E-Mail: john_nofsinger@wsu.edu.

NOGA, EDWARD JOSEPH, aquatic animal veterinary medicine educator; b. Chgo., Sept. 14, 1953; s. Edward Francis and Gwendolyn Honore (Boucher) N. BS, Fla. Atlantic U., 1974, MS, 1977; DVM, U. Fla., 1982. Asst. prof. aquatic medicine N.C. State U., Raleigh, 1982-88, assoc. prof., 1988-94, prof., 1994—. Cons. Profl. Testing Svc., N.Y.C., 1984, 88, Fla. Dept. Environ. Regulation, Tallahassee, 1987-88, WHO, Barbados, Dominican Republic, 1987, EPA, Sandy Hook, N.J., 1988-89, Coun. on Agriculture, Taipei, China, 1989, Environ. Protection Agy., 1989, 90, 91, 94, 96, Hebrew U., Israel, 1992, Nat. U. Singapore, 1999; adj. prof. marine sci. U. N.C., Wilmington. Contbr. articles to profl. jours. Faculty scholar Fla. Atlantic U., 1971-74, Howell Lancaster (Fla.) scholar Farm Bur., 1978; Sea grantee, 1997. Mem. AVMA, Tissue Culture Assn. (Wilton Earle award 1977), Fla. Atlantic U. Alumni Hall of Fame, Internat. Assn. Aquatic medicine, World Mariculture Soc., Phi Zeta, Sigma Xi, Phi Kappa Phi. Achievements include development of invitro culture systems for ectoparasites; discovery of new toxic alga; discovery of novel antibiotics; patents in vaccine for channel catfish disease and administration; method for inhibiting growth of melanin pigmented cells. Office: NC State U Coll Vet Med 4700 Hillsborough St Raleigh NC 27606-1428

NOHRNBERG, JAMES CARSON, English language educator; b. Berkeley, Calif., Mar. 19, 1941; s. Carson and Geneva Gertrude (Gibbs) N.; m. Stephanie Payson Lamport, June 14, 1964; children: Gabrielle L., Peter Carson L. Student, Kenyon Coll., 1958-60; BA, Harvard Coll., 1962, postgrad., 1965-68; PhD, U. Toronto, 1970. Tchg. fellow dept. English U. Coll., U. Toronto, 1963-64; jr. fellow Soc. of Fellows Harvard U., 1965-68; acting instr. dept. English Yale U., New Haven, 1968-69, lectr., 1969-70, asst. prof., 1970-75, assoc. prof., 1975; prof. English U. Va., Charlottesville, 1975—. Adj. instr. English Harvard U., Cambridge, 1967; Gauss Seminars in Criticism lectr. Princeton U., 1987; lectr. various univs., 1974—2002. Author: The Analogy of The Faerie Queene, 1976, 80, Like Unto Moses: The Constituting of an Interruption, 1995; mem. editl. bd. Spenser Ency., 1977-90, Spenser Studies, 1977—; contbr. articles to profl. jours. and poems to mags.; editor vols. on allegory, Bible, Homer, Dante, Boiardo, Spenser, Milton, Thomas Pynchon, Northrop Frye, among others. Recipient Am. Acad. Poets prize Harvard U., 1962; Woodrow Wilson fellow, 1962, jr. fellow Harvard U., 1965-68, Morse fellow Yale U., 1974-75, U. Va. Ctr. for Advanced Studies fellow, 1975-78, Guggenheim fellow, 1981-82, Ind. U. Inst. for Advanced Studies fellow, 1991, U. Va. Sesquicentennial Fellow, 2003—. Mem.: MLA, Milton Soc., Spenser Soc., Phi Beta Kappa. Presbyterian. Avocations: writing poetry, collecting books and records. Home: 1874 Wayside Pl Charlottesville VA 22903-1631 Office: U Va Dept English Bryan Hall Charlottesville VA 22903 E-mail: jcn@virginia.edu.

NOLAN, DONALD JAMES, retired state educational commisioner; b. Cohoes, N.Y., May 14, 1934; s. John T. and Henrietta M. (Courteau) N.; m. Marguerite Ellen Hastings, June 20, 1959; children: Mark Andrew, David Matthew, Laura Ellen, Barbara Anne, Gwyn Margaret, Stephen James, Jay Robert, Kelly Elizabeth, Donald Joseph. AB, SUNY, Albany, 1960, MA, 1961; PhD, U. Ill., 1967. Instr. French U. Ill., 1965-67; asst. prof. romance langs. SUNY, Albany, 1968-69; dir. Coll. Proficiency Examinations N.Y. State Edn. Dept., 1969-71; dir. regents external degree program U. State of N.Y., 1971-78; asst. commr. higher edn. N.Y. State Edn. Dept., 1978-82, dep. commr. higher, profl. edn., 1982—96, ret., 1996. Mem. Pres.'s Adv. Panel Accreditation, 1977-79, Commn. Higher Edn. and the Adult Learner, 1986-89, steering com. Outcomes Analysis in Accreditation, 1990-92; chair task force expectation external publs., 1990-92; cons., lectr. in field. Author: The History of Regents College: The Early Years, 1998. 1st Lt. U.S. Army, 1954-57. Mem. State Higher Edn. Exec. Officers (pres. 1992-93). Home: 10 Belmonte Ln Clifton Park NY 12065-5723*

NOLAN, JAMES FRANCIS, JR., education educator; b. Scranton, Pa., July 3, 1950; s. James Francis and Mary Kathryn (Fitzpatrick) N.; m. Ellen M. Landers, Apr. 22, 1977; children: Geoffrey, Daniel. BS, U. Scranton, 1972; MS, Marywood Coll., 1978; PhD, Pa. State U., 1983. Cert. secondary sch. German tchr., guidance counselor. Elem. tchr., Dunmore, Pa., 1972-74; German tchr. Wyoming Valley West Schs., Kingston, Pa., 1974-78; guidance counselor W. Branch Sch. Dist., Morrisdale, Pa., 1978-80; asst. prof. Lafayette Coll., Easton, Pa., 1983-86, U. Scranton, Pa., 1986-87; grad. asst. Pa. State U., University Park, 1980-83, asst. prof., 1987-92, dir. student teaching, 1992—95, assoc. prof., 1992—2000, prof., 2000—. Co-dir. Elem. Profl. Devel. Sch. Collaborative, 1999—. Author (with James Levin): Classroom Management: A Professional Decision Making Model, 4th edit., 1999; author: (with Denise Meister) Teachers and Educational Change: The Lived Experience of Secondary School Restructuring, 2000; assoc. editor Jour. Curriculum and Supervision, 1987—93; contbr. articles; editor: Pennsylvania Educational Leadership, 2002. Mem. ASCD, Pa. ASCD (pres. 1991-92), Am. Edn. Rsch. Assn., Coun. Profs. Instrnl. Supervision, Assn. Tchr. Educators, Phi Delta Kappa. Home: 502 Orlando Ave State College PA 16803-3478 Office: Pa State Univ 148 Chambers Bldg University Park PA 16802-3205 E-mail: jimnolan@psu.edu.

NOLAN, JOHN PATRICK, mathematician, educator; b. Patterson, N.J., Mar. 22, 1954; s. William James and Anne (Zemitus) N.; m. Martha Roberts, Mar. 6, 1993; children: Julia Martha, Erin Laura. BS in Math., U. Md., 1975; PhD in Math., U. Va., 1982. Lectr. U. Zambia, Lusaka, Zambia, 1982-84; asst. prof. Kenyon Coll., Gambier, Ohio, 1984-86, U. N. Fla., Jacksonville, 1986-87; software cons. Quantitative Medicine Inc., Annapolis, Md., 1987-89; asst. prof. Am. U., Washington, 1989-92, assoc. prof., 1992-98, prof., 1998—, dept. chair, 1999—2001; founder, pres. Robust Analysis, Inc., 2002—. Contbr. articles to profl. jours. Mem. AAAS, Am. Math. Soc., Math. Assn. Am., Inst. Math. Stats. Avocations: traditional music and dance, outdoor activities. Office: Am U Dept Math 4400 Massachusetts Ave NW Washington DC 20016-8050 E-mail: jpnolan@american.edu.

NOLAN, PATRICK JOSEPH, screenwriter, playwright, educator; b. Jan. 2, 1933; children: Patrick, Christian, Mark. BA, Villanova U., 1955; MA, U. Detroit, 1961; PhD, Bryn Mawr Coll., 1973. Teaching fellow and mem. faculty dept. English U. Detroit, 1959-62; instr. English Villanova (Pa.) U., 1962-80, prof., 1980—. Playwright: Chameleons, 1980, Midnight Rainbows, 1991; TV screenwriter: The Jericho Mile, 1979 (Emmy award). Vol. dir. devel. Daemion House Cmty. Counseling Ctr. Served to lt. (j.g.) USNR, 1955-59, PTO. Recipient teaching excellence award Philadelphia mag., 1980, Alumni Medallion award Villanova U., 1986. Mem. Writers Guild Am. (West chpt.), Dramatists Guild. Roman Catholic. Avocations: swimming, biking.*

NOLAN, PETER JOHN, physics educator; b. N.Y.C., Mar. 25, 1934; s. Peter John and Nora (Gleeson) Nolan; m. Barbara Nolan, 2000; children from previous marriage: Thomas, James, John, Kevin. BS in Physics, Manhattan Coll., 1956; cert. in meteorology, UCLA, 1958; MS in Physics, Adelphi U., 1966, PhD in Physics, 1974. Engr. various corps., N.J., N.Y., 1956-63; systems analysis engr. on lunar module Gruman Aircraft Engring. Corp., Bethpage, N.Y., 1963-66; asst. prof. Physics SUNY, Farmingdale, 1966-68, assoc. prof. Physics, 1968-71, prof. Physics, 1971—. Chmn physics dept SUNY, Farmingdale, 1970—77. Author: Experiments in Physics, 1982, 2d edit., 1995, Electromagnetic Theory for Electrical Technology Students, 1995, Fundamentals of College Physics, 1993, Italian Version, Fundementi Di Fisica, 1996. Mem.: Am Asn Physics Teachers. Home: 59 Parnell Dr Smithtown NY 11787-2428 Office: SUNY Dept Physics Farmingdale NY 11735 E-mail: nolanpj@farmingdale.edu., pjnolan@optonline.net.

NOLAN, RICHARD THOMAS, clergyman, educator; b. Waltham, Mass., May 30, 1937; s. Thomas Michael and Elizabeth Louise (Leishman) N.; life ptnr. Robert C. Pingpank, Sept. 14, 1955. BA, Trinity Coll., 1960; cert. in clin. pastoral edn., Conn. Valley Hosp., 1962; diploma, Berkeley Divinity Sch., 1962; MDiv., Hartford Sem. Found., 1963; postgrad., Union Theol. Sem., N.Y.C., 1963; MA in Religion, Yale U., 1967; PhD, NYU, 1973; postgrad., Ctr. Career Devel. and Ministry, Newton Center, Mass., 1987, Harvard U., 1991. Ordained deacon Episcopal Ch., 1963, priest, 1965; cert. in death, dying and bereavement Waterbury Hosp. Health Ctr., Conn., 1977. Instr. Latin and English Watkinson (Conn.) Sch., 1961-62; instr. math. Choir Sch. of Cathedral of St. John the Divine, N.Y.C., 1962-64; instr. math. and religion, assoc. chaplain Cheshire (Conn.) Acad., 1965-67; instr. Hartford (Conn.) Sem. Found., 1967-68, asst. acad. dean, lectr. philosophy and edn., 1968-70; instr. Mattatuck C.C., Waterbury, Conn., 1969-70, asst. prof. philosophy and history, 1970-74, assoc. prof., 1974-78, prof. philosophy and social sci., 1978-92, prof. emeritus, 1992—; vicar St. Paul's Parish, Bantam, Conn., 1974-88, pastor emeritus, 1988—; pres. Litchfield Inst., Conn. and Fla., 1984-96; adj. lectr. in philosophy Palm Beach C. C., Fla., 2000—02. Ethics com. Waterbury Hosp. Health Ctr., 1984—88; vis. and adj. prof. philosophy, theology and religious studies Trinity Coll., Conn., L.I. U., U. Miami, St, Joseph Coll., Conn., Pace U., Teikyo Post U., U. Conn., Hartford Grad. Ctr., Ctrl. Conn. State U., 1964—95, Broward C.C., Fla.; lectr. philosophy and theology Barry U., Fla., 1973, 1989—92, 1997—98; adj. assoc. in continuing edn. Berkeley Div. Sch. Yale U., 1987—89; Rabbi Harry Halpern Meml. lectr., Southbury, Conn., 1987; adj. prof. philosophy Fla. Atlantic U., 1999; adj. prof. The Union Inst., Fla., 1999; faculty of cons. examiners Charter Oak State Coll., Conn., 1990—93; assoc. for edn. Christ Ch. Cathedral, Hartford, Conn., 1988—94, hon. canon, 1991—; cons. Dept. Def. Activity Non-Traditional Ednl. Support, Ednl. Testing Svc., Princeton, NJ, 1990; vis. scholar Coll. Preachers, Washington Nat. Cathedral, 1994; supply priest Episcopal Diocese of S.E. Fla., 1994—2002; ret. priest-in-residence St. Andrew's Ch., Lake Worth, Fla., 2002—; bd. regents Cathedral Church of St. John the Divine, 2002—. Author: (with H. Titus and M. Smith) Living Issues in Philosophy, 7th edit., 1979, Indonesian edit., 1984, 9th edit., 1995, (with F. Kirkpatrick) Living Issues in Ethics, 1982, 2d edit., 2000, Chinese edit., 1988 (Honored Author for Books Exceeding 100,000 Copies award 1986); editor, contbr. Diaconate Now, 1968; host Conversations with ..., 1987-89. Notary pub., Fla. Rsch. fellow Yale U., 1978, 87; recipient Founder's Day award NYU, 1973. Mem. Am. Acad. Religion, Am. Philos. Assn., Authors Guild, Hemlock Soc. Fla. (adv. bd. 1998—), Interfaith Alliance, Integrity, Boston Latin Sch. Alumni Assn., Tabor Acad. Alumni Assn., McCook Fellows Soc. Trinity Coll., Cavalier King Charles Spaniel Club, Am. Friends of Anglican Centre in Rome, Anglican Assn. Bibl. Scholars, Phi Delta Kappa. Avocation: Cavalier King Charles spaniels. Home: 2527 Egret Lake Dr West Palm Beach FL 33413-2161 E-mail: canon@rtnolan.com.

NOLAND, CHARLES DONALD, lawyer, educator; b. Tulsa, July 31, 1946; s. Clyde Earl and Birdeen Elizabeth (White) N.; m. Elisabeth Hooper Reynolds, June 27, 1987; 1 stepchild, Richard G. Reynolds. BA in Journalism, U. N.Mex., 1972, JD, 1978. Bar: N.Mex. 1978, U.S. Dist. Ct. N.Mex. 1979, U.S. Ct. Appeals (10th cir.) 1991, U.S. Supreme Ct. 1991. Reporter, copy editor New Mexican, Santa Fe, 1968, 69; newsman AP, Des Moines, 1969-71, Albuquerque, 1968-69, 73-74; editor programmed instrn. materials Systema Corp., Albuquerque, 1974-75; pvt. practice Albuquerque, 1978-79; from asst. gen. counsel to gen. counsel N.Mex. Dept. Edn., Santa Fe, 1979-83; asst. atty. gen. State of N.Mex., Santa Fe, 1984-85; pvt. practice Santa Fe, 1985-95; dep. gen. counsel N.Mex. Dept. Corrections, Santa Fe, 1995-97; legal counsel Spl. Edn. Office N.Mex. Dept. Edn., Santa Fe, 1997—2003, asst. gen. counsel, 2003—. Adj. prof. U. N.Mex. Grad. Sch. Edn., 1981, 92, 98, N.Mex. Highlands U. Grad. Sch. Edn., 1985, Coll. Santa Fe, 1984-89; pvt. practice, of counsel Simons, Cuddy & Friedman, Santa Fe, 1985-95; hearing officer tchr. termination appeals N.Mex. Bd. Edn., 1980, 81; presenter N.Mex. Sch. Bds., Assn. Law Conf., 1980-95, 98, 2002; panelist pub. sch. reduction in force Nat. Sch. Bds. Assn. Conv., Dallas, 1981; participant Lawyers Adv. Opinion Project, N.Mex. Ct. Appeals, 1986-87. Contbr. articles to profl. jours. Founding bd. dirs. Santa Fe Symphony Orch., 1984-85, corp. sec., 1985-88; community musician Santa Fe Concert Band, Santa Fe Brass Ensemble, 1983-89; mem. audit com. Christ the King Episc. Mission, 1996, chair 1997, treas., 1998; mem. Holy Faith Episc. Ch., 1998—, mem. choir, 1999— Mem. State Bar N.Mex. (pub. advocacy sect., alt. dispute resolution), N.Mex. Assn. Sch. Bd. Attys. (treas. 1980-83, pres. 1987-88, 90-93). Avocation: trombone. Home: 2 Pino Pl Santa Fe NM 87508-8750 Office: NMex Dept Edn Office Gen Counsel 300 Don Gaspar Ave Santa Fe NM 87501-2786 E-mail: cnoland@sde.state.nm.us.

NOLAND, GARY LLOYD, vocational school educator, administrator; b. Lindsborg, Kans., July 29, 1942; s. Willard L. and Florence L. (Waggoner) N.; m. Deborah L. Homan, Mar. 20, 1981; children: Krista L., Timothy L. BSBA, Cen. Mo. State U., 1971, MEd, 1974. Cert. vocat. dir., Mo. V.p. sales First Nat. Land Co., Scottsdale, Ariz., 1961-66; student grad. asst. Cen. Mo. State U., Warrensburg, 1968-72; instr. State Fair CC., Sedalia, Mo., 1972-74, dir. job placement, 1974-79; dir. Statewide Job Placement Svc., Sedalia, 1979-84, State Fair Area Vocat. Sch., Sedalia, 1984—. Dir. State Fair C.C. Found., Sedalia, 1986—; mgr. State Fair Coll. Farm, Sedalia, 1987-92. Author: Help Yourself to Successful Employment, 1980; author instructional modules. Mem., chmn. ctrl. Mo. chpt. March of Dimes, Sedalia, 1979; v.p. Pettis County Farm Bur., Sedalia, 1987-91, pres., 1991-95; bd. dirs. Mo. Farm Bur., 1995—, Am. Cancer Soc., Sedalia, 1989-92. Named Outstanding Young Man Am., 1979, Outstanding Placement Specialist, Mo. Guidance and Placement, 1980, Outstanding Vocat. Program Area VII, U.S. Dept. Edn., 1982. Mem. VFW (life), Am. Simmental Assn., Am. Legion, Mo. Coun. Local Adminstrs., Mo. Assn. Secondary Prins., Mo. Cattleman's Assn., Pettis County Cattleman's Assn., Lions (pres. Sedalia 1979-80), Masons, Sedalia Area C. of C. (amb. 1975-92). Baptist. Avocations: farming, golfing, fishing. Home: 1985 W Timber Ridge Dr Sedalia MO 65301-8917 Office: State Fair Area Vocat Sch 3201 W 16th St Sedalia MO 65301-2188

NOLAND, MONICA GAIL, elementary school educator; b. Macon, Ga., Oct. 14, 1950; d. Millard Joseph and Josephine Francis (Gawrysiak) Parrish; m. Wayne Douglas Noland, Aug. 16, 1973; children: Bryce Douglas, Karyn Marie. BA in Edn. with honors, Ariz. State U., 1972; postgrad., U. Nev., Las Vegas, 1973-80, U. Nev., Reno, 1985; MA in Elem. Edn., Adams State Coll., 1989; student U.S. Space Acad., Kennedy Space Ctr. Cert. tchr., Nev., Colo. Tchr. elem. sch. Clark County Sch. Dist., Las Vegas, 1972-75, 86-87, Nye County Sch. Dist., Tonopah, Nev., 1985, Mancos (Colo.) Sch. Dist., 1987-92, Montezuma-Cortez (Colo.) Sch. Dist., 1992—. Vice-chair Mancos Curriculum Coordinating Coun., 1989-92; bd. dirs. Noland Electric, Inc. Dist. rep. REACH Com. (educating gifted & talented). Climax fellow Amoco Melibdenum Edn. Found., 1988. Mem. ASCD, Nat. Coun. Tchrs. Math., Nat. Assn. Edn. of Young Child, VFW Aux. Avocations: oil painting, gardening, fitness, travel. Office: Montezuma-Cortez Sch Dist RE 1 Cortez CO 81321

NOLD, AURORA RAMIREZ, business and economics educator; b. Honolulu, Apr. 21, 1958; m. Allan Jeffrey Nold, Aug. 1, 1995. BSBA cum laude, St. Louis U., 1969, MS in Bus. Adminstrn. magna cum laude, 1975, PhD summa cum laude, 1986. Exch. prof., dept. chairperson mgmt. St. Louis U., Baguio City, Philippines, 1980-86, dean Coll. Bus., 1980—86; rsch. asst. East/West Ctr. for Am. Studies, Honolulu, 1986-87; dir. Am. studies USIS, Washington, 1987-89; fin. cons. Shadow Hill Samaritan, Long Beach, Calif., 1989-93; dir. A&A Edu Care Consultancy Programs, Inc., Las Vegas, Nev., 1993—. Bd. advisors Am. Biog. Inst., Raleigh, N.C., 1995—, Internat. Biog. Ctr., Cambridge, Eng., 1995—; rschr. S.H.S. Inc., Las Vegas, 1995—; prof. econs., bus and mgmt. C.C. So. Nev.; prof. stats. U. Nev., Las Vegas; tutor C.C. So. Nev. Author: Business Education in the Philippines, 1986; contbr. articles to profl. jours. Pres. Rep. Presdl. Task Force, Las Vegas, 1995—. Cultural Exch. grant Fulbright Am. Studies, 1987, scholarship grant St. Louis U., 1979-86; recipient Appreciation award Nat. Humane Edn. Soc., 1996, Nat. Park Trust, 1996, Nat. Law Enforcement Officers Meml. Fund, 1997, Oustanding Cmty. and Profl. Achievement Commemorative medal Am. Biog. Inst., 1997, internat. cultural diploma of honor, 2000. Mem. AAUW, NAFE, Asian Am. Studies Assn., U.S. Profl. Bookkeepers Assn., Nev. Faculty Alliance. Republican. Mem. Lds Ch. Avocations: collecting rare coins, writing, reading, music and coin collecting. Office: A&A Edu Care Consultancy Programs Unit 657-10 7812 Clarkdale Dr Las Vegas NV 89128-3866 E-mail: auroranold@cs.com.

NOLL, JEANNE C. retired music educator; b. Reading, Pa., Aug. 12, 1935; d. Carl Foreman and Barbara Rebecca (Mengel) Winter; m. Clair W. Noll; children: Eric W., Douglas C. BS in Music Edn., Lebanon Valley Coll., Annville, Pa., 1957; music student, West Chester U., Milligan U., Lehigh U., MIT. Cert. tchr Pa., 1961. Elem. music Tchr. N. Coventry Elem. Sch., Chester County, Pa., Yokohama (Japan) Army Sch., 1957—58; jr. HS vocal tchr. Reading (Pa.) Sch. Dist., 1959—61; organist, choir dir. St. Paul's United Ch. of Christ, Fleetwood, Pa., 1967—2001, organist/choir dir. emerita, 2002—; vocal music tchr., elem., jr. and sr. HS Kutztown (Pa.) Area Sch. Dist., Kutztown, 1981—94. Accompanist Kutztown Cmty. Choir, 1999—2001; dir. award-winning show choir Kutztown Area Sch. Dist., 1981—94. Del. Rep. Nat. Conv. Pa. 6th Congl. Dist., Phila., 2000—00; committeewoman Berk County Rep. Party, Fleetwood, 1982—; state Rep. committeewoman Pa. Rep. state com., Harrisburg, 1998—; mem. Berks Area Muhlenberg Coun. of Rep. Women, 1996, 2d v.p., 2003—. Mem.: East Penn Valley Kiwanis Club (Director, Key Club Advisor 1994—. Kiwanian of the Year 2000). United Ch. Of Christ. Avocations: travel, singing, reading, politics.

NOLL, LAURIE JANE, secondary school educator; b. Alton, Ill., Aug. 27, 1961; d. David Richard and Shirley Ann Bliven; m. Tim Joseph Noll, Mar. 22, 1982; children: Emily, Ian, Eileen. BA, MacMurry Coll., Jacksonville, Ill., 1982; MA, Western Ill. U., 1994. Cert. elem. tchr. Tchr. Davenport Schs., Iowa, 1982—85, AEA, Bettendorf, Iowa, 1985—92; spl. svc. tchr., dept. chmn. Burlington Cmty. Schs., Iowa, 1992—, dept. chmn., 1997—, interpreter, 1984—92. Bd. dirs. Players Workshop, 2000—, interpreter, 1999—, City of Burlington, 1998—. Named Local Tchr. of Yr., Wal-Mart, 2002. Mem.: PEO, Pi Lambda Theta. Home: 1639 Madison Ave Burlington IA 52601 Office: Burlington Community Schs 421 Terrace Dr Burlington IA 52601

NOLL, ROGER GORDON, economist, educator; b. Monterey Park, Calif., Mar. 13, 1940; s. Cecil Ray and Hjordis Alberta (Westover) Noll; m. Robyn Schreiber, Aug. 25, 1962 (dec. Jan. 2000); 1 child, Kimberlee Elizabeth; m. Ann Seminara, Dec. 2, 2001. BS, Calif. Inst. Tech., 1962; AM, Harvard U., 1965, PhD in Econs, 1967. Mem. social sci. faculty Calif. Inst. Tech., 1965-84, prof., 1973-82, inst. prof., 1982-84, chmn. div. humanities and social scis., 1978-82; prof. econs. Stanford U., 1984—, Morris M. Doyle centennial prof. of pub. policy, 1990—2002, dir. pub. policy program, 1986—2002, dir. Am. Studies Program, 2001—02, dir. Stanford Ctr. for Internat. Devel., 2002—; Jean Monnet prof. European U. Inst., 1991; vis. fellow Brookings Instn., 1995-96, non-resident sr. fellow, 1996—2000. Sr. staff economist Coun. Econ. Advisors, Washington, 1967—69; sr. fellow Brookings Instn., Washington, 1970—73; mem. tech. adv. bd. Com. Econ. Devel., 1978—82; mem. adv. coun. NSF, 1978—89, NASA, 1978—81, SERI, 1982—90; mem. Pres.'s Commn. Nat. Agenda for Eighties, 1980; chmn. L.A. Sch. Monitoring Com., 1978—79; mem. Commn. Behavioral Social Scis. and Edn. NAS, 1984—90, mem. bd. sci., tech. and econ. policy, 2000—; mem. energy rsch. adv. bd. Dept. Energy, 1986—89; mem. Sec. Energy Adv. Bd., 1990—94, Calif. Coun. Sci. and Tech., 1995—2000. Author: (book) Reforming Regulation, 1971, The Economics and Politics of Deregulation, 1991, The Economics and Politics of the Slowdown in Regulatory Reform, 1999; co-author: Economic Aspects of Television Regulation, 1973, The Political Economy of Deregulation, 1983, The Technology Pork Barrel, 1991; editor: Government and the Sports Business, 1974, Regulatory Policy and the Social Sciences, 1985, Challenges to Research Universities, 1998; co-editor: Constitutional Reform in California, 1995, Sports, Jobs and Taxes, 1997, A Communications Cornucopia, 1998; supervisory editor: Info. Econs. and Policy Jour., 1984—92. Recipient 1st ann. book award, Nat. Assn. Ednl. Broadcasters, 1974; fellow Guggenheim, 1983—84; grantee NSF, 1973—82. Mem.: Am. Econ. Assn. Democrat. Home: 4153 Hubbartt Dr Palo Alto CA 94306-3834 Office: Stanford U Dept Econs Stanford CA 94305

NOLLER, HARRY FRANCIS, JR., biochemist, educator; b. Oakland, Calif., June 10, 1939; s. Harry Francis and Charlotte Frances (Silva) N.; m. Betty Lucille Parnow, Nov. 25, 1964 (div. 1969); 1 child, Maria Irene; m. Sharon Ann Sussman; 1 child, Eric Francis; stepchildren: Django Sussman, Seb Sussman. AB, U. Calif., Berkeley, 1960; PhD, U. Oreg., 1965. Postdoctoral fellow MRC Lab. of Molecular Biology, Geneva, Switzerland, 1966-68; asst. prof. biology U. Calif., Santa Cruz, 1968-73, assoc. prof., 1973-79, prof. biology, 1979—, Robert Louis Sinsheimer prof. molecular biology, 1987—. Dir. Ctr. Molecular Biology of RNA, 1992—; lectr. in field. Named Spkr. of Yr., Dutch Biochemical Soc., 2002; recipient Newcomb-Cleve. Prize, 2001, Rosensteil award in Basic Biomed. Sci., 2002, Judd award, Sloan Kettering, 2003; Sherman Fairchild Disting. scholar Calif. Inst. Tech., 1990. Fellow Am. Acad. Arts and Scis.; mem. NAS, The RNA Soc. (pres.-elect 1997, pres. 1998, Lifetime Achievement award 2003), Russian Acad. Scis. Office: Sinsheimer Labs U Calif Santa Cruz High St Santa Cruz CA 95064-1099

NORA, JAMES JACKSON, physician, writer, educator; b. Chgo., June 26, 1928; s. Joseph James and Mae Henrietta (Jackson) N.; m. Barbara June Fluhrer, Sept. 7, 1949 (div. 1963); children: Wendy Alison, Penelope Welbon, Marianne Leslie; m. Audrey Faye Hart, Apr. 9, 1966; children: James Jackson Jr., Elizabeth Hart Nora. AB, Harvard U., 1950; MD, Yale U., 1954; MPH, U. Calif., Berkeley, 1978. Diplomate Am. Bd. Pediatrics, Am. Bd. Cardiology, Am. Bd. Med. Genetics. Intern Detroit Receiving Hosp., 1954-55; resident in pediatrics U. Wis. Hosps., Madison, 1959-61, fellow in cardiology, 1962-64; fellow in genetics McGill U. Children's Hosp., Montreal, Can., 1964-65; assoc. prof. pediatrics Baylor Coll. Medicine, Houston, 1965-71; prof. genetics, preventive medicine and pediatrics U. Colo. Med. Sch., Denver, 1971—, prof. emeritus, 1986. Dir. genetics Rose Med. Ctr., Denver, 1980—; dir. pediatric cardiology and cardiovascular tng. U. Colo. Sch. Medicine, 1971-78; mem. task force Nat. Heart and Lung Program, Bethesda, Md., 1973; cons. WHO, Geneva, 1983—; mem. U.S.-U.S.S.R. Exchange Program on Heart Disease, Moscow and Leningrad, 1975. Author: The Whole Heart Book, 1980, 2d rev. edit., 1989; author: (with F.C. Fraser) Medical Genetics, 4th Rev. edit., 1994; author: Genetics of Man, 2d rev. edit., 1986, Cardiovascular Diseases: Genetics, Epidemiology and Prevention, 1991; author: (novels) The Upstart Spring, 1989; author: The Psi Delegation, 1989, The Hemingway Sabbatical, 1996, Panacea, 2002; author: (poetry) Songs from a Brazen Bull, 2001. Mem. com. March of Dimes, Am. Heart Assn., Boy Scouts Am. 2nd lt. USAAC, 1945—47. Grantee Nat. Heart, Lung and Blood Inst., Nat. Inst. Child Health and Human Devel., Am. Heart Assn., NIH; recipient Virginia Apgar Meml. award. Democrat. Presbyterian. Avocations: writing fiction, poetry.

NORBERG-CALIENDO, LYNDA JOY, school system administrator; b. Bklyn., Oct. 16, 1941; d. Harold I. and Shirley Claire (Karp) Levy; m. Jon Norberg (div. 1988); children: Paige, Toby, Hilary; m. Richard Caliendo, July 28, 1990. BFA, Ohio U.; MS in Reading, postgrad., Hofstra U. Cert. supt., Conn.; cert. adminstr., N.Y.; cert. tchr., Mass., Ohio. Reading cons., asst. prin. Stagecoach Elem. Sch., Centereach, N.Y., 1972-83; dir. curriculum and instruction Elmont (N.Y.) Union Free Sch. Dist., 1983-86; edn. cons. Scott, Foresman & Co., Oakland, N.J., 1986-87; asst. supt. instruction Valley Stream (N.Y.) Union Free Sch. Dist. 30, 1987-90; dep. supt. Hamden (Conn.) Pub. Schs., 1990—. Mem. adv. bd. Global Edn., Early Childhood Edn., N.Y. State Coun. Social Studies; ednl. coord. Internat. Games for the Disabled; commr. World Games of Spl. Olympics-Spkrs. Bur.; mem. adv. and steering coms. Habitat for Humanity. Mem. ASCD, AASA, Anti Defamation League-A World of Difference, Phi Delta Kappa. Home: 631 Whitney Ave New Haven CT 06511-2218 Office: Womens Bldg Spring Glen Sch 1908 Whitney Ave Hamden CT 06517-1206

NORCEL, JACQUELINE JOYCE CASALE, educational administrator; b. Nov. 19, 1940; d. Frederick and Josephine Jeanette (Bestafka) Casale; m. Edward John Norcel, Feb. 24, 1962. BS, Fordham U., 1961; MS, Bklyn. Coll., 1966; 6th yr. cert., So. Conn. State U., 1980; postgrad., Bridgeport U. Elem. tchr. pub. schs., N.Y.C., 1961-80; prin. Coventry (Conn.) Schs., 1980-84, Trumbull (Conn.) Schs., 1984—2003, Frenchtown Elem. Sch., 2003—. Guest lectr. So. Conn. State U., 1980; cons. Monson (Mass.) Schs., 1984; mem. Conn. State Prin. Acad. Adv. Bd., 1986-88; mem. adj. faculty Sacred Heart U., Fairfield, Conn., 1985—, So. Conn. State U., summer 1991; fed. rels. coord. Nat. Assn. Elem. Sch. Prins., Conn., 1999-2002. Editor: Best of the Decade, 1980; mem. editl. adv. bd. Principal Matters; contbr. articles to profl. jours. Chmn. bldg. com. Trumbull Bd. Edn., 1978-80; chmn. Sch. Benefit Com., Trumbull, 1985-86; catechist Bridgeport Diocese, Roman Cath. Ch., Conn., 1975-85, youth min., 1979-84, coord., evaluator leadership tng. workshops for teens and adults, 1979-84; mem. St. Stephen's Parish Coun., 1993-97, trustee, 1997—, Eucharist minister, 1999—, lector, 1990—; com. mem. New Sch. Bldg. Town of Trumbull, 2001—. Recipient Town of Trumbull Svc. award, 1982, Nat. Disting. Prin. award, 1988, Joseph Formica Disting. Svc. award EMSPAC, 1994. Mem.: ASCD, Assoc. Tchrs. Math. in Conn., New Eng. Coalition Ednl. Leaders, Ea. Conn. Coun. Internat. Reading Assn., Conn. Assn. Elem. Sch. Prins., Trumbull Adminstrs. Assn. (pres.-elect 1989—91, pres. 1991—93, 2002—), Conn. Assn. Supervision and Curriculum Devel., Nat. Assn. Elem. Sch. Prins. (del. to gen. assemblies 1984—90, zone I dir. 1987—90, del. to gen. assemblies 1999—), Hartford Area Prins. and Suprs. Assn. (local pres. 1981—82), Conn. Assn. Schs. (bd. mem. 2000—), Adminstrn. and Supervision Assn. (sec. 1980—81, pres. 1981—82, exec. bd. 1982—93), Elem. Mid. Sch. Prins. Assn. (pres. 1985—86, state elected rep. 1989—90, fed. rels. coord. 1990—94, dists. 1, 2 and 3 dir. 1995—98, commr. 1997—2000, fed. rels. coord. 1999—2002, Citizen of Yr. award 1991, Pres.'s award 1981—85), N.E. Regional Elem. Prins. Assn. (rep. 1984—86, sec. 1986—87), Delta Kappa Gamma (v.p. 1996—2000), Pi Lambda Theta, Phi Delta Kappa (v.p. rsch. and projects 1993—95, Disting. Fellow award 1992). Home: 5240 Madison Ave Trumbull CT 06611-1016 Office: Tashua Sch 401 Stonehouse Rd Trumbull CT 06611-1651 E-mail: norcelJ98@Yahoo.com.

NORCROSS, BARBARA BREEDEN, retired educator; b. Stanardsville, Va., Mar. 11, 1934; d. John Ray and Orphia Virginia (Caldwell) Breeden; m. George M. Norcross, Jr., Dec. 18, 1954; children: Teresa Rae Norcross Bibb, Angelea Caldwell Norcross Foster. BS, U. Va., 1955. Cert. tchr., Va. Sec. to asst. dir. U. Va. Hosp., Charlottesville, 1955-56; tchr. Greene County Schs., Stanardsville, 1956-61, Charlottesville Pub. Schs., 1962-91; retired, 1991. Writer, organizer, tchr. self-paced instr. for at-risk students Charlottesville High Sch., 1989. Author: (with others) Individualized Progress in Driver Education, 1966. Exec. mgr. Joe Wright for State Senate, Va., 1984; dir., chmn. Va. Student Aid Found., 1987-88. Mem. Va. Assn. Driver Edn. and Traffic Safety, Assn. Driver Tng. and Safety Educators Am. (exec. bd.), Va. Basketball Club (sec. 1980-85), U. Va. Women's Basketball Club (pres. 1987-88). Avocations: gardening, sports, music, sewing. Home: 2608 Northfield Rd Charlottesville VA 22901-1233

NORD, BERYL ANNETTE, judge, educator; b. Frederic, Wis., Oct. 12, 1948; d. Francis Gustaf and Irene Marian N.; 2 children. BA cum laude, U. Minn., 1970, JD cum laude, 1973. Bar: Minn. 1973, U.S. Dist. Ct. Minn. 1973, U.S. Ct. Appeals (8th cir.) 1977. Law clk. to assoc. justice Minn. Supreme Ct., St. Paul, 1973-74; asst. city atty. City of St. Paul, 1974-83; mcpl. judge County of Hennepin, Mpls., 1983-86, dist. ct. judge, 1986—. Adj. prof. U. Minn. Law Sch., Mpls., 1983—87. Big sister St. Paul YWCA Big Sister Program, 1973-76; bd. dirs. 58th Dist. DFL, 1976-80, chairperson, 1980-82; mem. DFL Feminist Caucus, 1974-83, bd. dirs., 1976-78, Criminal Justice Coordinating Coun., 1978-80; mem. DFL Cen. Com., 1980-83; past mem. Minn. Women's Polit. Caucus. Mem. Minn. Judges Assn. (bd. dirs. 1989-96), Nat. Assn. Women Judges (nat. bd. dirs. 10th dist. 1984-87), Hennepin County Bar Assn. (del. state bar convs., governing coun. 1989-91), Minn. Bar Assn. (criminal law sect. 1978-80, 83-88, civil litigation sect. 1982-83, bd. govs. 1989-91), Pi Kappa Delta. Office: 4th Jud Dist Ct 300 S 6th St Minneapolis MN 55487-0001

NORD, G. DARYL, computer science educator; BS, Mayville State Coll., 1969; PhD, U. N.D., 1976. Grad. tchg. asst. U. N.D.; asst. prof. info. sys. U. N.Mex., 1976—77; vis. prof. mgmt. info. sys. Coll. Bus. San Diego State (Calif.) U., 1984—85; computer tchr. Okla. State Univ. Mem. nat. pubs. com. Decision Scis. Inst., 1990—92, mem. nat. membership rels. com., 1992—94. Editor: The Jour. Computer Info. Sys., 1982—86, Jour. Computing and Info., 1995. Recipient Computer Educator of the Yr. award Internat. Assn. for Computer Info. Systems, 1992; scholar Fulbright Found. Mem.: Internat. Bus. Schs. Computer Assn., Inst. Mgmt. Sci. and Ops. Rsch. Soc. Am., Info. Resource Mgmt. Assn., ACM. Office: Okla State U Mgmt Info Sy 220 Business Bldg Stillwater OK 74078-0555*

NORDENBERG, MARK ALAN, law educator, academic administrator; b. Duluth, Minn., July 12, 1948; s. John Clemens and Shirley Mae (Tappen) N.; m. Nikki Patricia Pirillo, Dec. 26, 1970; children: Erin, Carl, Michael. BA, Thiel Coll., 1970; JD, U. Wis., 1973. Bar: Wis. 1973, Minn. 1974, U.S. Supreme Ct. 1976, Pa. 1985. Atty. Gray, Plant, Mooty & Anderson, Mpls., 1973-75; prof. law Capital U. Law Ctr., Columbus, Ohio, 1975-77, U. Pitts., 1977—, acting dean Sch. Law, 1985-87, dean Sch. Law, 1987-93, interim univ. sr. vice chancellor and provost, 1993-94, Univ. Disting. Svc. prof., 1994—, interim univ. chancellor, 1995-96, univ. chancellor, 1996—. Mem. U.S. Supreme Ct. Adv. Com. on Civil Rules, Washington, 1988-93, Pa. Supreme Ct. Civil Procedure Rules Com., Phila., 1986-92; reporter civil justice adv. group U.S. Dist. Ct., Pitts., 1991-96; bd. dirs. Mellon Fin. Corp. Author: Modern Pennsylvania Civil Practice, 1985, 2d edit., 1995. Bd. dirs. Urban League of Pitts., Allegheny Conf. on Cmty. Devel., Pitts., Pitts. Coun. on Higher Edn., Pa. Assn. Colls. and Univs., Assn. of Am. Univs., Nat. Collegiate Athletic Assn.; trustee Thiel Coll., Greenville, Pa., 1987—97; bd. dirs. Inst. for Shipboard Edn. Found., Pitts. Digital Greenhouse, Pitts. Life Scis. Greenhouse, Pitts. Robotics Foundry, Coun. on Competitiveness. Named Vectors Pitts. Person of Yr. in Edn., 1996, Person of Yr., 1997, Pitts. Mag. Person of Yr., 2001. Fellow Am. Bar Found.; mem. ABA, Pa. Bar Assn., Allegheny County Bar Assn., Pitts. Athletic Assn., Assn. Am. Univs., Nat. Collegiate Athletic Assn., Law Club Pitts., Univ. Club, Duquesne Club, Wildwood Golf Club, Pitts. Golf Club. Office: U Pitts Cathedral of Learning Pittsburgh PA 15260

NORDGREN, LYNN LIZBETH, elementary education educator, educational administrator; b. Mankato, Minn., Jan. 29, 1951; d. Lee Adolph and Donna Lou (Charles) N.; 1 foster child, Nathan. BS in Tchg., Mankato State U., 1975, M in Experiential Edn., 1996. Cert. tchr. 1-6, spl. edn. k-12, experiential edn., k-12, Minn. Tchr. EMH/TMH (intermediate) Spl. Edn. Lincoln Sch., Mpls, 1975-77, 4th grade Lincoln Sch., Mpls, 1977-79, EMH (primary) Spl. Edn. Standish Sch, Mpls, 1979-80, Omega Math. Lab. Holland Sch., Mpls, 1983-84, gifted and talented Olson Elem. Sch., Mpls, 1983-88, 3d and 4th grades Pub. Sch. Acad., Mpls, 1988-91; profl. devel. facilitator Mpls. Pub. Schs., Mpls, 1991—. Mem., tchr. rep. dist. leadership team Mpls. Schs., 1990—; creator, producer, owner The Learning Bridge (ednl. products), 1992-96; field test coord. Nat. Bd. Profl. Tchg. Stds.; state and nat. profl. trainer. Author: Assuring Professional Excellence, 1998; prodr.: (films) Inside Out: The Professional Development Process, 2002. Pres. People Acting for Indigenous Rights, Mpls., 1990-96; network leader Am. Fedn. Tchrs., 1991-93; sec. Hawthorne Area Cmty. Coun., 1995-97; leader Cmty. Block Club, 1995-2001. Recipient Tchr. Venture Fund awards Econ. Project, 1985-86, World Hunger Project, 1986-87, cert. of commendation in edn. State of Minn. Gov.'s Office, 1990; grantee Minn. Environ. Svcs. Found., 1991-96, Nat. Bd. for Profl. Tchg. Standards, 1992-94, 94, Saturn Partnership award, Best Block Club award, 2000, Citizenship award City Mpls., 2000; grantee for tchg. quality and improving student achievement. Mem. Am. Fedn. Tchrs., Mpls. Fedn. Tchrs. (steward 1991-97, exec. bd. 1996—, dist. adv. bd. 2001—), Edn. Minn. Democrat. Avocations: gardening, travel, reading, movies. Home: 2810 N 4th St Minneapolis MN 55411-1512 Office: 2225 E Lake St Minneapolis MN 55407

NORDGREN, MARY KATHLEEN, secondary school educator; b. Minn. d. Robert J. and Ihla L. Ellingson; m. Richard B. Nordgren; children: Stephanie, Erik. BS in Home Econ., U. Minn., Mpls., 1973, MEd, 1987. Home econ. educator Lake Superior Sch. Dist., Silver Bay, Minn., 1973—82; banker Union State Bank, Hazen, ND, 1982—92; family & consumer sci. educator Golden Valley (N.D.) H.S., 1992—. Del. leader People to People Student Ambassadors, 2001. Advisor Kids on the Block; bd. dirs. English Luth., fin. sec. Recipient Prevention Through Edn. award, Mental Health Assn., 2001. Mem.: Jaycees, Lions (charter pres.), Phi Upsilon Omicron, Alpha Delta Kappa. Office: Golden Valley High Sch 10 3rd St NW Golden Valley ND 58541

NORDLOH, DAVID JOSEPH, English language educator; b. Cin., May 3, 1942; s. Joseph Westerman and Josephine (Fusz) N.; m. Barbara Jane Beddow, June 29, 1968; children: Geoffrey David, Jennifer Ellen Blum. AB in English, Coll. of Holy Cross, 1964; PhD in English, Ind. U., 1969. Asst. prof. English Ind. U., Bloomington, 1969—75, assoc. prof. English, 1975—81, prof. English, 1981—, assoc. dean faculties, 2003—. Vis. assoc. prof. U. Va., Charlottesville, 1978; dir. Am. Studies Program, Ind. U., 1987-94. Gen. editor: A Selected Edition of W.D. Howells, 1974—; editor: Twayne's United States Author's Series, 1978-90; co-editor: American Literary Scholarship, 1986—; mem. editl. bd. Walter Scott Edition, 1984—; adv. bd. The Writings of James Fenimore Cooper, 1995—. Pres. Bloomington Symphony Orch., 1986-88, 93-94. Fulbright scholar, 1982-83. Mem. Am. Lit. Assn. Home: 3123 E Diana Ct Bloomington IN 47401-4407 Office: Ind U English Dept 442 Ballantine Hall Bloomington IN 47401-5048

NORDYKE, ROBYN LEE, primary school educator; b. Dodge City, Kans., Aug. 20, 1948; d. Donald L. and Lois O. (Blattner) Dansel; m. Rod E. Nordyke, July 11, 1970; children: Alisha, Kelsey, Gina. AA, Dodge City Cmty.Coll., 1968; BS in Edn., Fort Hays State U., 1970. First grade tchr. Unified Sch. Dist. #214, Ulysses, Kans., 1970-76, kindergarten tchr., 1976-79, 92—; dir., owner Robyn's Nest Pre-Sch., Ulysses, 1980-92; sch. improvement reading chmn. North Ctrl. Accreditation, 2001—03. Cons. Discovery Toys, Livermore, Calif., 1984-90. 4-H project leader, 1988—, cmty. leader, 1999—; bd. mem. Unified Sch. Dist. #214 Bd. Edn., Ulysses, 1981-85; bd. mem., treas. and chmn., sec. libr. bd. Grant County, Ulysses, 1986-95, mem. extension exec. bd., 1997-98; mem. Grant County 4-H Program Devel. Com., 1997-98; mem. adv. bd. Parents as Tchrs., 1998—; mem. steering team NCA, 2001—. Avocations: skiing, walking, reading. E-mail: rnordyke@pld.com.

NORGAARD, RICHARD BRUCE, economist, educator, consultant; b. Washington, Aug. 18, 1943; s. John Trout and Marva Dawn (Andersen) N.; m. Marida Jane Fowle, June 19, 1965 (div.); children: Kari Marie, Marc Anders; m. Nancy A. Rader, June 5, 1993; children: Addie Nelle, Mathiesen Rader. BA in Econs., U. Calif., Berkeley, 1965; MS in Agrl. Econs., Oreg. State U., 1967; PhD in Econs., U. Chgo., 1971. Instr. Oreg. Coll. Edn., 1967-68; asst. prof. agrl. and resource econs. U. Calif., Berkeley, 1970-76, assoc. prof., 1976-77, 80-87, assoc. prof. energy and resources, 1987-92, prof. energy and resources, 1992—. Project specialist Ford Found., Brazil, 1978-79; environ. cons. to internat. devel. agencies; mem. sci. com. on problems of the environment U.S. Nat. Rsch. Coun.; chmn. bd. Redefining Progress, 1993-97; mem. sci. adv. com. U.S. EPA, 2000-. Author: Development Betrayed: The End of Progress and a Coevolutionary Revisioning of the Future, 1994; contbr. articles to profl. jours. Active civil rights, environ., and peace orgns. Mem. AAAS, Am. Econs. Assn., Internat. Soc. Ecol. Econs. (pres. 1998-2001, past pres. 2002-), Fedn. Am. Scientists, Assn. Environ. and Resource Econs., Am. Inst. Biol. Scis. (bd. dirs. 2000-). Home: 1198 Keith Ave Berkeley CA 94708-1607 Office: U Calif Energy & Resources Program 310 Barrows Hall Berkeley CA 94720-3050

NORGARD, MICHAEL VINCENT, microbiology educator, researcher; b. Glenridge, N.J., Oct. 5, 1951; s. Bernard Raymond and Marion C. (Testa) N.; m. Gabriella Rosella Lombardo, July 18, 1976; 1 child, Gina Gabriella. AB, Rutgers U., 1973; PhD, U. Medicine and Dentistry, N.J., 1977. Postdoctoral fellow Roche Inst. Molecular Biology, Nutley, N.J., 1977-79; asst. prof. U. Tex. Southwestern Med. Sch., Dallas, 1979-86, assoc. prof., 1986-91, prof., 1991—, vice chmn. microbiology, 1994-98, chmn. microbiology, 1998—. Cons. U.S. Dept. Justice, Washington, 1986-92; mem. study sect. on bacteriology and mycology NIH, Bethesda, Md., 1990-94, chmn., 1994, panelist Internat. Sexually Transmitted Diseases Diagnostics Network, 1990—; panelist Congenital Syphillis Policies Ctrs. for Disease Control, Atlanta, 1987, Trepenol Vaccines, WHO, Birmingham, Eng., 1989. Mem. editl. bd. Jour. Sexually Transmitted Diseases, 1988-98, Jour. Infection and Immunity, 1993-96; contbr. articles to profl. publs., including Infection and Immunity, Jour. Infectious Diseases, Current Opinion Infectious Diseases, 1989—. Grantee NIH, 1980—, Robert A. Welch Found., 1982—, Austin, Tex., 1982—, Serex Internat., Van Nuys, Calif., 1983, 86, 89, Dallas Biomed. Corp., 1988-89, Tex. Higher Edn. Coordinating Bd., Austin, 1990. Fellow Infectious Diseases Soc. Am., Am. Acad. Microbiology; mem. AAAS, Am. Venereal Disease Assn., Am. Soc. Microbiology, Tex. Infectious Diseases Soc. Roman Catholic. Achievements include U.S. patents for monoclonal antibodies against Treponema, methods for Diagnosing Syphilis, cloning of the 47-KDa antigen of Treponema pallidum; first to develop monoclonal antibodies against the syphilis bacterium; discoverer of membrane lipoproteins in T pallidum. Office: U Tex Southwestern Med Ctr Dept Microbiology 5323 Harry Hines Blvd Dallas TX 75390-7208

NORMAN, ARLENE PHYLLIS, principal; b. Seattle; d. Samuel Edward and Connie Solveig (Jorgensen) Hendricksen; m. Charles Edward Norman; children: Tamara, Mark, Todd, Lisa. BA, Wash. State U.; MAT, Lewis and Clark Coll., 1980; postgrad., Portland State U. Tchr. Salem (Oreg.) Sch. Dist., 1956, Beaverton (Oreg.) Sch. Dist., 1973-83, prin. Terra Linda Sch., 1984-94; prin. Aloha Park Sch., 1994. Prof. Portland State U.; presenter children's seminar Nat. Coun. Tchrs. Eng. Confs. Contbr. articles to mags. Mem. selection com. Associated Oreg. Industries, 1994, 95. Named Prin. of Excellence, Assoc. Oreg. Industries, 1991, sch. named Sch. of Excellence, 1991. Mem. NASEP, N.W. Women in Ednl. Adminstrn., Profl. Assistance Com. for State of Oreg., Toastmasters (pres.), Phi Delta Kappa, Pi Lambda Theta (pres.).

NORMAN, CHARLENE WILSON, secondary school educator; b. Ft. Campbell, Ky., Apr. 19, 1949; d. Charles B. and Mary (Powe) Wilson; m. John D. Norman, Mar. 21, 1971; children: David, Mary Katharine. AS, Mid. Ga. Coll., 1969; BS in Edn., Ga. So. U., 1971; MEd in Math., Ga. Coll., 1979. Cert. tchr., Ky., Ga. Tchr. Tabor Jr. H.S., Warner Robbins, Ga., 1971-72, Windsor Acad., Macon, Ga., 1972-78, North Cobb H.S., Acworth, Ga., 1978-79, Campbell H.S., Smyrna, Ga., 1979-81, U. Ky., Lexington, 1981—, Bryan Sta. H.S., Lexington, 1982—. Insvcs. presenter Fayette County Bd. Edn., Lexington, 1988—; presider Nat. Coun. Tchrs. Math., Paducah, Ky., 1993; state conf. presider Ky. Coun. Tchrs. Math., Lexington. Asst. Sunday sch. tchr. First United Meth. Ch., Paris, Ky., 1989—. Named outstanding tchr., Tandy Corp., 1991-92, FAME outstanding tchr., Nat. City Bank and Fayette County Schs., 1994, 96, Star Tchr., 1978. Mem. Nat. Coun. Tchrs. Math., Ky. Coun. Tchrs. Math., Lexington Coun. Tchrs. Math. (pres. 1990). Avocations: reading, crafts. Home: 173 Northland Dr Paris KY 40361-9133 Office: Bryan Sta HS 1866 Edgeworth Dr Lexington KY 40505-2010 E-mail: cnorman@fayette.k12.ky.us.

NORMAN, CHRISTINA REIMARSDOTTER, secondary education language educator; b. Stockholm, Jan. 7, 1947; came to U.S., 1968; d. Leif Reimar and Hilma Birgitta (Berg) Norman; m. Geoffrey Robert Norman, May 27, 1968; children: Catarina, Camilla. Fil. Mag., Stockholm U., 1968; MA, SUNY, Albany, 1973. Cert. tchr., N.Y., Conn. Tchr. French Our Lady of Grace Sch., Stratford, Conn., 1970-71; tchr. French, German Burnt Hills (N.Y.)-Ballston Lake Jr. High Sch., 1971-74; tchr. English Colegio Ayalde, Lujua, Vizcaya, Spain, 1975-78; tchr. French, English, Spanish Hillcrest Jr. High Sch., Trumbull, Conn., 1979-83; tchr. Spanish and French Saxe Mid. Sch., New Canaan, Conn., 1983-94; tchr. Spanish and German New Canaan H.S., 1994—. Mem. Conn. Orgn. Lang. Tchrs. Avocations: travel, skiing, reading. Office: New Canaan High Sch Farm Rd New Canaan CT 06840

NORMAN, DONALD ARTHUR, cognitive scientist; b. N.Y.C., Dec. 25, 1935; s. Noah N. and Miriam F. N.; m. Martha Karpati (dec.); children—Cynthia, Michael; m. Julie Jacobsen; 1 child, Eric BSEE, MIT, 1957; MSEE, U. Pa., 1959, PhD in Psychology, 1962; degree in psychology (hon.), U. Padua, Italy, 1995. Lectr. Harvard U., 1962-66; prof. dept. psychology U. Calif.-San Diego, La Jolla, 1966-92, prof. emeritus, 1992—, prof., chair dept. cognitive sci., 1988-92, chair dept. psychology, 1974-78; Apple fellow Apple Computer Inc., Cupertino, Calif., 1993-97, v.p. advanced tech., 1995-97; exec. info. appliances Hewlett Packard, Palo Alto, Calif., 1997-98; co-founder, prin. Nielsen Norman Group, Mountain View, Calif., 1998—; pres. learning sys. UNext, 1999—2001; prof. dept. computer sci. Northwestern U., 2001—. Cons. to industry on human computer interaction and user-centered design. Author: Human Information Processing, 2d edit., 1977, Learning and Memory, 1982, User Centered System Design, 1986, The Psychology of Everyday Things, 1988, The Design of Everyday Things, 1989, 2002, Turn Signals Are the Facial Expressions of Automobiles, 1992, Things That Make Us Smart, 1993, The Invisible Computer, 1998. Recipient Excellence in Rsch. award, U. Calif., 1983, Lifetime Achievement award, Computer Human Interaction. Fellow: Assn. Computing Machines, Cognitive Sci. Soc. (chmn., founding mem.), Human Factors & Ergonomics Soc., Am. Psychol. Soc., Am. Acad. Arts and Scis.; mem.: Inst. Design, IIT Chicago (trustee). E-mail: norman@nngroup.com.

NORMAN, MARY MARSHALL, educator, counselor, therapist; b. Auburn, N.Y., Jan. 10, 1937; d. Anthony John and Zita Norman. BS cum laude, LeMoyne Coll., 1958; MA, Marquette U., 1960; EdD, Pa. State U., 1971. Cert. alcoholism counselor. Tchr. St. Cecilia's Elem. Sch., Theinsville, Wis., 1959-60; vocat. counselor Marquette U., Milw., 1959-60; dir. testing and counseling U. Rochester (N.Y.), N.Y., 1960-62; dir. testing and counseling, dean women, assoc. dean coll. Corning (N.Y.) C.C., Corning (N.Y.) C.C., 1962-68, asst. dean students, dir. student activities, asst. prof. ps University Park, 1962-68; rsch. asst. Ctr. for Study Higher Edn. Pa. State U., University Park, Pa., 1969-71; dean faculty South Campus C.C. Allegheny County, West Mifflin, Pa., 1971-72, campus pres., coll. v.p., 1972-82; pres. Orange County C.C., 1982-86; alcohol counselor Sullivan County Alcohol Drug Abuse Svc., 1985-90; sr. counselor Horton Family Program, 1990-96, ednl. cons., writer, 1996—. Cons. Boricua Coll., N.Y.C., 1976-77; reader NSF, 1977-78; mem. govtl. commn. com. Am. Assn. Cmty. and Jr. Colls., 1976-79, bd. dirs., 1982—; mem. and chmn. various middle state accreditation teams. Contbr. articles to profl. jours. Mem. Econ. Devel. Seneca County, Seneca County Tourism Bd.; active St. Patrick's Ch.; bd. dirs. Orange County United Way; bd. dirs. Orange County Alcoholism and Drug Abuse Coun., 1993—96; bd. dirs. Seneca County Hist. Soc., 1997—, Guild and Altar Soc., 1999. Mem. Nat. Women's Hall of Fame. Mem.: Pa. Coun. on Higher Edn., Nat. Am. Coun. on Edn. (Pa. rep. identification women for adminstrn. 1978—82, bd. dirs., pres. 1980—96), Pitts. Coun. Women Execs. (charter), Pa. Assn. Acad. Deans, Pa. Assn. Two-Yr. Colls., Am. Assn. Women in Cmty. and Jr. Colls. (charter, Woman of the Yr. 1981), Nat. Assn. Women Deans and Counselors, Am. Assn. Higher Edn., Seneca County C. of C. (bd. dirs., mem. tourism com.), Orange County C. of C. (bd. dirs.), Amnesty Internat. (charter mem. women's coun. 2000—), Concerned Citizens for Good Govt. (charter), Kiwanis (bd. dirs. Seneca Falls), Gamma Pi Epsilon. Home: 9 S Park St Seneca Falls NY 13148-1423

NORMAN, PEGGY ROCKER, retired secondary school educator; b. Richland, Ga., Aug. 14, 1938; d. Evelyn (Rigdon) Bland Womack; m. L. Roy Norman; children: Cecilia McAllister, Rodney. BSE, Ga. So. U., 1959; MEd, U. Ga., 1976, EdS, 1985. Tchr., dept. head Dekalb County Schs., Decatur, Ga., 1962-65; tchr. Marietta (Ga.) City Schs., 1966; tchr., dept. head Cobb County Schs., Marietta, 1966-80; tchr. Lafayette (La.) Parish Schs., 1980-84; tchr., dept. head Cobb County Schs., Marietta, 1984-94; ret., 1994. Supervising student tchrs. U. Ga., Marietta, 1985—. Outreach leader Holt Rd. Bapt. Ch., Marietta, 1990-92; active textbook adoption com., 1989, curriculum revision com. Parenting grantee Fed., 1987-90; named Tchr. of Yr., 1993. Mem. Am. Vocat. Assn., Ga. Vocat. Assn., Ga. Home Econs. Assn., Parent-Tchr.-Student Assn., 4-H Club (life), Phi Delta Kappa (treas. 1987, 88, 89), Alpha Delta Kappa. Republican. Avocations: sewing, gourmet cooking, spectator sports, shopping, playing cards. Home: 517 Chapman Ln Marietta GA 30066-3670

NORMAN, SHERI HANNA, artist, educator, cartographer; b. Chgo., Dec. 15, 1940; d. L. J. and Margaret Maxine (Kuyper Fleischer) Hanna; m. Donald Lloyd Norman, Feb. 28, 1963 (div. 1996); 1 child, Ronald Wayne. BA, U. Wyo., Laramie, 1963; postgrad., Dayton Art Inst., 1975; MFA, San Francisco Art Inst., 1993. Substitute tchr. Arlington, Va. and Yellow Springs, Ohio Pub. Sch. Dists., 1965-71; tech. illustrator, draftsperson U. Tex. Austin, Geotek, Inc., Denver, 1976-85; cartographer British Petroleum, San Francisco, 1985-87; draftsperson Earth Scis. Assocs., Palo Alto, Calif., 1988-92; intern, printmaking asst. Crown Point Press, San Francisco, 1991-92; freelance cartographer San Francisco and Napa, 1993—; educator pub. printmaking and papermaking workshops, San Francisco, 1995-96, Napa, Calif., 1997—; pub. printmaking demonstrations San Francisco Women Artists Gallery, 1995—96; book-arts workshops Calistoga, Calif., San Francisco, 1999; tchr. Napa Valley Adult Sch., Napa, Calif., 1999-2001; staff artist Bergin Glass Impressions, Napa, Calif., 2002—. Leader pub. nature/women's ceremony-ritual, San Francisco, 1991—93; artist in residence Villa Montalvo Ctr. Arts, Saratoga, Calif., 1996, Dorland Mountain Arts Colony, Temecula, Calif., 1996; vis. faculty Art Inst. Boston, 2002. Author, illustrator: Envisioning An Unbroken Arc, vol. I, vol. II, 1992; book, Garden Haven Reminiscences, a Collection, 2002, San Francisco Bay Area Presses, Visual Arts Ctr., Bluffton (Ohio) Coll., 1996, Bay Area Art II, Created Spaces, Nature as a Point of Departure, 1999, Napa Valley Coll. Art Gallery, 2002, Florence Crittenton Svcs., San Francisco, 1995, San Francisco Women Artists Gallery, 1995—97, Visual Aid's BIG DEAL, San Francisco, 1996—98, Napa Artists for People with AIDS, The Art of Giving, The Giving Art, Calistoga, 1999, 2000, St. Helena, Calif., 2001; curator, participating book artist A Display of Contemporary Book Arts Main Libr., Napa, 2000. Mem. Arts Coun. Napa Valley, Land Trust Napa County. Mem.: Calif. Coun. Adult Edn. (grantee North Coast chpt. 2000), Calif. Soc. Printmakers (exhbn. com. 1995). Avocations: ongoing nature studies and nature advocacy, early mythologies and meditative practice. Home: 423 Cross St Napa CA 94559-3335 E-mail: inklings@napanet.net.

NORMANN, MARGARET ELLA, deacon, educator; b. Providence, Jan. 13, 1931; d. Parker Edward and Margaret Millard (McDowell) Monroe; m. Conrad Neil Normann, July 17, 1953; children: Andrea Kristin Mudge, Margaret Ingrid Wierdsma, Conrad Neil, Parker Monroe. BA in Drama, Vassar Coll., 1952; MA in English, NYU, 1966; MS in Recreation and Leisure, So. Conn. State U., 1978. Ordained deacon Protestant Episcopal Ch., 1993. Human svc. officer, dir. recreation programs Town of Bedford, NY, 1975—83; cmty. edn. coord., writer, cons. Cmty. Residences Info. Svc. Program, White Plains, NY, 1983—91; initiator, exec. dir. Apropes Housing Opportunities and Mgmt. Enterprises, Inc., Bedford/Mount Kisco, NY, 1985—93; deacon Ch. of the Holy Communion, Mahopac, NY, 1993—; chaplain Four Winds Hosp., Cross River, NY, 1993—. Writing instr., tutor, evaluator SUNY Empire State Coll., Hartsdale, NY, 1984—. Mem. comprehensive planning com., Bridgton, Maine; v.p. Heritage Village Condo. Assn., Southbury, Conn. Recipient Disting. Svc. Alumnae award, Lincoln Sch., Providence, 1988, Cert. of Merit, State of N.Y., Albany, 1991, Mickey Leland Home for the Homless award, 1991. Republican. Home (Winter): 888 B Heritage Village Southbury CT 06488 Home (Summer): Margaret House Box 591 Route 107 Bridgton ME 04009

NORRIS, CAROL BROOKS, librarian, educator; b. Porterdale, Ga., Dec. 22, 1943; d. James P. and Georgia E. (Queen) Brooks; m. Frederick W. Norris, Aug. 30, 1963; children: Lisa C., Mark F. Student, Milligan Coll., Tenn., 1961—63; BA, Phillips U., Enid, Okla., 1965; MLS, U. Md., 1982; postgrad., East Tenn. State U., 1978—80, postgrad., 1991, U. Tenn., 1988, postgrad., 1990. Caseworker Dept. Child Welfare, Enid, 1966-67; homebound tchr. New Haven (Conn.) Pub. Schs., 1967-70; English tchr. Putnam (Okla.) High Sch., 1965-66, U.S. Army, Boeblingen, Germany, 1975-77, Cen. Tex. State Coll., 1977; tchr. adult basic edn. Johnson City (Tenn.) Schs., 1977-79; systems analyst East Tenn. State U., Johnson City, 1980-82, libr., assoc. prof., 1982—, mem. univ. coun., 1989-91, mem. tchr. edn. adv. coun., 1989-92, mem. faculty senate, 1985-88, sec. senate, 1986-87, mem. women's studies steering com., 1993—2001, writing com., rsch. devel. com., 1993-96, mem. commn. women, 2001—. Author: (with others) Library Hi Tech Bibliography, 1987, 90, Read More About It, 1989, Notable Women in the Life Sciences, 1996, Tennessee Landscape, People and Places, 1996, Notable Women in the Physical Sciences, 1997; editorial advisor Nat. Forum jour., 1981-86; contbr. articles to profl. jours. Mem. ALA, Tenn. Libr. Assn., East Tenn. Online Users Group (pres. 1984-85, v.p. 1983-84, sec. 1982-83), Boone Tree Libr. Assn. (v.p. 1986-88), Delta Kappa Gamma, Phi Kappa Phi, Kappa Delta Pi. Democrat. Mem. Christian Ch. Avocations: reading, writing, travel, photography. Office: East Tenn State Univ 70665 Johnson City TN 37614

NORRIS, CHARLEY WILLIAM, retired otolaryngologist, educator; b. Morganville, Kans., Jan. 3, 1933; s. George P. and Mary (Kaiser) N.; m. Linda Larson, Nov. 30, 1963; children: Andrew William, Erik Christopher. BA, U. Kans., 1960, MD, 1964. Intern Latter Day Saints Hosp., Salt Lake City, 1964-65, resident gen. surgery, 1965-66; ear, nose and throat resident Tufts Univ., Boston, 1966-69; jr. mem. staff Tufts U. Med. Sch., Boston, 1968-69; attending staff physician Boston City Hosp., 1969-71; asst. prof. U. Kans., Kans. City, 1971-75, assoc. prof., 1975-81, prof., chmn., 1981-90; chief of staff U. Kans. Hosp., 1989-92; prof. otolaryngology U. Kans., 1992-99, prof. emeritus, 1995—. Instr. Tufts U., Boston, 1969-71; cons. Vets. Hosp., Kans. City, Mo., 1971—. Contbr. chpt. to book and articles to profl. jours. With USN, 1951-56. Fellow ACS, Am. Soc. for Head and Neck Surgery, Am. Laryngol., Rhinological and Otological Soc., Am. Acad. Otolaryngic Allergy, Am. Soc. Head and Neck Surgery, Am. Acad. Otolaryngology, N.Y. Acad. Sics.

NORRIS, DOLORES JUNE, elementary school educator; b. Belmore, N.Y., Feb. 10, 1938; d. Abe and Doris Cyril (Stahl) Wanser; m. William Dean Norris, June 11, 1960; children: William Dean II, Ronald Wayne, Darla Cyrille. BS in Elem. Edn., So. Nazarene U., 1959; MS in Computer Edn., Nova U., 1988, EdS in Computer Applications, 1990. Cert. elem. edn. and computer sci. tchr., Fla. Tchr. 4th and 5th grades Ruskin (Fla.) Elem. Sch., 1959-61; tchr. 5th grade Emerson Elem. Sch., Kansas City, Kans., 1961-63; tchr. 1st grade Hickman Mills, Mo., 1964-65; tchr. 3d and 4th grades Lake Mary Elem. Sch., Sanford, Fla., 1968-72; tchr. 1st grade St. Charles Cath. Sch., Port Charlotte, Fla., 1976-77; primary tchr. Meadow Park Elem. Sch., Port Charlotte, 1977-89; computer specialist Vineland Elem. Sch., Rotanda West, Fla., 1989-90, Myakka River Elem. Sch., Port Charlotte, 1990—, tech. trainer, 1995—. Reading coun. Charlotte County Schs., Port Charlotte, 1987—, rep., 1989-90, in-svc. com. 1990-93, 98; program planner Meadow Park Elem. Sch., 1988-89; program planner Myakka River Elem. Sch. 1991-93. Mem. Rotary, Punta Gorda, Fla., 1982-86; co-dir. teens Touring Puppet Group, Punta Gorda, 1982-86; puppet co-dir. NOW Teens, Punta Gorda, 1976-80. Mem. Fla. Assn. Computers in Edn, pres. Southwest Florida Assn. Computers in Edn. Avocations: piano, swimming, travel. Home: 1171 Richter St Port Charlotte FL 33952-2870

NORRIS, GERALD LEE, dean; b. Effingham, Ill., Feb. 2, 1940; s. Howard C. and Phyllis C. (Koester) N.; m. Ruth E. Norris, Aug. 13, 1961 (div. 1980); 1 child, Heather Raye; m. Joye Kaye Hall, Jan. 1, 1981; 1 child, Jackson Clay. BS in Edn., Ea. Ill. U., 1962, MS in Edn., 1967; EdD, Ill. State U., 1976. Art tchr. Robinson (Ill.) Cmty. Schs., 1962-67; art tchr. univ. high sch. Ill. State U., Normal, 1967-73, prin., asst. prin., 1973-79; dean coll. edn., prof. Western N.Mex. U., Silver City, 1979-86; prof. sch. adminstrn. U. Ctrl. Ark., Conway, 1986-87; dean coll. profl. studies Bemidji

(Minn.) State U., 1987—. CEO Norris Enterprises, Bemidji, 1980—. Mem. cabinet United Way, Bemidji, 1993—. Grantee U.S. Office Edn., 1988-91. Mem. Bemidji Cmty. Arts Coun. (bd. dirs. 1988—), Rotary (pres. Sunrise of Bemidji chpt. 1994—). Avocation: antique automobiles. Office: Bemidji State U Dean Coll Profl Studies 1500 Birchmont Dr NE Bemidji MN 56601-2699

NORRIS, JOAN CLAFETTE HAGOOD, retired assistant principal; b. Pelzer, SC, June 26, 1951; d. William Emerson and Sarah (Thompson) Hagood; divorced; 1 child, Javiere Sajorah. BA in History and Secondary Edn., Spelman Coll., 1973; MA in Teaching in Edn., Northwestern U., 1974; MA in Adminstrn. and Supervision, Furman U., 1984. Cert. elem. edn. tchr., elem. prin., social studies tchr., elem. supr., S.C.; notary pub., S.C. Clk. typist Fiber Industry, Greenville, SC, 1970, Spelman Coll. Alumni Office, Atlanta, 1970-73; tchr. Chgo. Bd. Edn., 1973-74, Greenville County Pub. Schs., Greenville, S.C., 1974-97, Hollis Acad., Greenville, S.C., 1996-97; asst. prin. Nevitt Forest Elem. Sch., Anderson, SC, 1997—2002; ret., 2002. Dir. elem. summer sch. Anderson Sch. Dist. 5, 1998, asst. prin. acad., 2001—02; mem. steering com. N.W. area Greenville County Sch. Dist., 1994—95, chmn. elem. steering com., 1996, participant Curriculum Leadership I, 96, participant potential adminstrs. internship program, 1997—; participant Asst. Prins. Inst. Furman U., summer, 1999; flagship status application reader S.C. Sch., 2000. Contbr. articles to profl. jours. Staff devel. com. summer sch. program Anderson County Elem. Sch. Dist. 5, 2000—02; bd. dirs. Girl Scouts of Old 96 Coun. Inc., 2001—; sec. Webette's Temple 1312, Greenville, 1985, parliamentarian, 1986; bus. ptnr. contact person Nevitt Forest Elem. Sch., 1997—2000, comm. contact person, 1997—2000. Selected to Potential Adminstrs. Acad., Furman U., 1991; named Tchr. of Yr., Armstrong Elem. Sch., 1982, 91; grantee Alliance of Quality Edn., 1989-90, 97-98, Chick-A-Fil-A extended day program in math and reading, 1998; grantee Publix Charities Media Ctr. Books, 2000. Mem. NEA, AAUW (exec. bd. cmty. rep. Greenville br. 1993-94, v.p. programs 1994-96, pres.-elect. 1996-97, pres. 1997-98, nominating com., gift honoree, 5 Star Recognition award 1998), S.C. Assn. Sch. Adminstrs. (nom. Disting. Asst. Prin. 2000, Sch. of Promise application reader 2000), S.C. Coun. Sci., S.C. Assn. Curriculum Devel. (nat. mem.), Spelman Alumni Assn., Northwestern Alumni Assn., S.C. Coun. Sci., Phi Delta Kappa (chpt. alt. del. 1992-93, sec. chpt. 1993-94, v.p. membership 1996-97). Democrat. Baptist. Avocations: reading, talking to older people, listening to blues music, travel, playing basketball. Home: 219 Barrett Dr Mauldin SC 29662-2030 E-mail: jhagoodnorris@hotmail.com.

NORRIS, JOHN ANTHONY, health products executive, lawyer, educator; b. Buffalo, Dec. 27, 1946; s. Joseph D. and Maria L. (Suite) Norris; m. Kathleen E. Mullen, July 13, 1969; children: Patricia Marie, John Anthony II, Joseph Mullen, Mary Kathleen, Elizabeth Mary. BA, U. Rochester, 1968; JD, MBA with honors, Cornell U., 1973; cert., Harvard U., 1986. Bar: Mass. 1973. Assoc. Peabody, Brown, Boston, 1973-75; from assoc. to ptnr., exec. com., v.p., dir. Powers Hall, Boston, 1975-80; chmn. bd., pres., CEO, founder Norris & Norris, Boston, 1980-85; dep. commr., COO FDA, Washington, 1985-88, chmn. action planning and cap coms., 1985-88, chmn. reye syndrome com., 1985-87, chmn. trade legis. com., 1987-88; corp. officer, exec. v.p. Hill & Knowlton, Inc., N.Y.C., 1988-93; worldwide dir. Health Scis. Cons. Group., 1988-93; chmn. health scis. policy coun. Health Scis. Cons. Group, 1989-93; chmn. bd., pres., CEO, founder John A. Norris, Esq., PC, Boston, 1993—; pres., CEO Nat. Pharm. Coun., Reston, Va., 1995-96. Instr. Tufts Dental Sch., 1974—79, Boston Coll. Law Sch., 1976—80, Boston U. Law Sch., 1979—83, Harvard U. Pub. Health Sch., 1988—; mem. bd. editors FDA Drug Bull., FDA Consumer Report, 1985—88; bd. dirs. Summit Tech., Inc., Cytologics, Inc., Horus Therapeutics, Inc., Nat. Applied Scis., Med. Knowledge Processing, Inc.; trustee Caritas Christi Healthcare Sys. Editor-in-chief: Cornell Internat. Law Jour., 1971—73, founder, faculty editor-in-chief: Am. Jour. Law and Medicine, 1973—81, assoc. editor: Medicolegal News, 1973—75, reviewer: New Eng. Jour. Medicine Law-Medicine Notes, 1980—81. Mem. U.S. Pres. Chernobyl Task Force, 1986, vice-chmn. health affects sub-com.; mem. Fed. Pain Commn.; chmn. Mass. Stuatory Adv. Com. Regulation Clin. Labs., 1977—83; mem. Mass. Gov.'s blue ribbon task force hosp. determination of need DON, 1979—80; chmn. Mass. Clin. Lab. Regulatory Commn.; mem. U.S. Intra-Govtl. AIDS Task Force, 1987; chmn. bd. dirs. Boston Holiday Project, 1981—83; bd. dirs. Mass. 4-H Found., 1982—2002, vice-chmn. bd. dirs., 1996—2002; chmn. U.S. del. Japan, Austria, Saudi Arabia, 1987, Finland, Denmark, Italy, 1986; chmn. Boston alumni and scholarship com. U. Rochester, 1979—85, mem. trustees coun., 1979—85, chmn. reunions; mem. exec. com. Cornell Law Sch. Assn., 1982—85, class pres., chmn. reunions; trustee Jordan Hosp., 1978—80, mem. exec. com., 1979—80, chmn. CEO search com., 1980; chmn. Joseph D. Norris, Esq. Health Law and Pub. Policy Fund, 1979—; mem. IOM Drug Devel. Forum, 1986—88, co-chmn. end points sub-com., 1987—88. With U.S. Army, 1972—73. Named one of Ten Outstanding Young Leaders award, Jaycees, 1982; recipient Kansas City Hon. Key award, 1988, award Merit, FDA, 1987—88, PHS award, 1987, HHS Sec. award, 1988; Comprehensive Health Planning fellow, 1970—73. Mem.: ABA (vice-chmn. medicine and law com. 1977—80), Internat. Coun. Global Health Progress (bd. dirs. 1989—95), Soc. Computer Applications Med. Care Informatics (bd. dirs. 1984—85), Am. Soc. Law and Medicine (1st v.p. 1975—80, chmn. bd. dirs. 1981—84, life mem. award 1981), Nat. Health Lawyers, Am. Soc. Hosp. Attys., Mass. Bar Assn., Phi Kappa Phi. Home: 531 W Washington St Hanson MA 02341-1067

NORRIS, KAREN W. grants specialist; b. Washington, Mar. 5, 1950; d. Jerome J. and Lillian (Pittle) N.; children: Elysa, Mindy. BA, George Washington U., 1972; MBA, Hood Coll., 1994. Tchr. journalism, TV and English Montgomery County Pub. Schs., Rockville, Md., 1972-80; broadcast engr. CBS TV-WDVM-TV, Washington, 1980-83; pvt. practice comm. cons. Washington, 1983-88; grants specialist Prince George's County Pub. Schs., Upper Marlboro, Md., 1988—. Mem. cultural arts adv. com. Montgomery County Govt., Rockville, 1975; mem. performing arts adv. com. Prince George's County Pub. Schs., Upper Marlboro, 1994-98; panel chair U.S. Dept. Edn. 21st Century Sch., 2001 Bd. dirs. Journalism Edn. Assn., Balt., 1972-75. Recipient Excellence in H.S. Journalism award Montgomery County C. of C., Rockville, 1978; named Md. Journalism Tchr. of Yr., Md. Journalism Edn. Assn., Rockville, 1972. Mem. AAUW (mem. pub. policy com. 1998). Office: Baltimore City Pub Sch Grants Adminstrn 200 E North Ave Baltimore MD 21202

NORRIS, KATHY HORAN, school counselor; b. Perryton, Tex., Jan. 31, 1944; d. Shirley Coppoc and Margaret Z. (George) Horan; m. Kenneth L. Haralson, July 3, 1965 (dec. May 1983); children: Dale Kirk, Dana; m. Vernon Lee Norris, Apr. 5, 1984. BS in Elem. Edn., Hardin-Simmons U., 1966; MEd, Wayland Bapt. U., 1986. Cert. sch. counselor, Tex.; lic. profl. counselor, Tex. Elem. tchr. Lubbock (Tex.) Ind. Sch. Dist., 1966-69, Colorado Springs County Sch. Dist., 1969-73, Plainview (Tex.) Ind. Sch. Dist., 1974-85, 87-89, counselor, 1989-92; grad. asst. Wayland Bapt. U., Plainview, 1985-86; owner, operator The Tchr. Store, Plainview, 1986-87; sch. counselor College Hill Elem. Sch., Plainview, 1992—. Asst. prof. Wayland Bapt. U., 1989-94; mem. adv. coun. College Hill Sch., Plainview, 1993—; ind. cons. on tchr. expectations and student achievement, Plainview, 1989—; mkem. sch. collaboration initiative Region 17 Sci. Ctr., Lubbock, 1994—; presenter in field. Contbr. 1st grade math. textbook Riverside Pub. Co., 1985; author curriculum materials in field. Mem. choir First Bapt. Ch., Plainview, 1994—. Mem. Tex. Counseling Assn., Assn. Tex. Profl. Educators (bldg. rep. 1975-85), Plainview Counseling Assn. (pres. 1990-91, 94-95). Republican. Avocations: sewing, gardening, yard work, reading. Office: College Hill Elem Sch 707 Canyon St Plainview TX 79072-6756

NORRIS, LOIS ANN, elementary school educator; b. Detroit, May 13, 1937; d. Joseph Peter and Marguerite Iola (Gourley) Giroux; m. Max Norris, Feb. 9, 1962 (div. 1981); children: John Henry, Jeanne Marie, Joseph Peter. BS in Social Sci., MA, Ea. Mich. U., 1960; cert. adminstr., Calif. State U., Bakersfield, 1983. Kindergarten tchr. Norwalk-LaMirada Unified Sch. Dist., 1960-62; tchr. various grades Rialto Unified Sch. Dist., 1962-66; kindergarten tchr. Inyokern (Calif.) Sch., 1969-82; 1st grade tchr. Vieweg Basic Sch, 1982-92, kindergarten tchr., 1992-96; retired, 1996. Head tchr. Sierra Sands Elem. Summer Sch.; adminstrv. intern Sierra Sands Adult Sch., master tchr., head tchr., counselor. Ofcl. scorekeeper, team mother, snack bar coord. China Lake Little League; team mother, statistician Indian Wells Valley Youth Football; bd. mem. PTA; pres. Sch. Site Coun.; treas. Inyokern Parents Club; run coord. City of Hope; timekeeper, coord. Jr. Olympics; mem. planning com. Sunshine Festival; active Burros Booster Club; docent Maturango Mus.; mem. Pink Lady orgn., mem. hosp. corp. bd. Ridgecrest Regional Hosp.; mem. Women's Aux. for Commd. Officers Mess. Recipient Hon. Svc. award PTA, 1994. Mem. NEA, AAUW, Calif. Tchr. Assn., Desert Area Tchr. Assn., Assn. Calif. Sch. Adminstr., Inyokern C. of C. (sec.), Am. Motorcycle Assn., NRA, AOPA, Bakersfield Coll. Diamond Club, Inyokern Rotary, Beta Sigma Phi. Republican. Mem. Lds Ch. Avocations: swimming, physical fitness, music, American history, gardening. Home: PO Box 163 201 N Brown Rd Inyokern CA 93527 E-mail: anorris@iwvisp.com.

NORSKOG, EUGENIA FOLK, elementary education educator; b. Staunton, Va., Mar. 23, 1937; d. Ernest and Edna Virginia (Jordan) Folk; m. Russell Carl Norskog, Nov. 25, 1967; children: Cynthia, Carl, Roberta, Eric. BA, King Coll., 1958; MEd, George Mason U., 1977. Cert. tchr., Va. Tchr. elem. Bristol (Va.) Pub. Schs., 1958-61, 62-65, Staunton (Va.) Pub. Schs., 1961-62, Fairfax (Va.) County Pub. Schs., 1965-68; with Project 100,000, USAFI, Fort Ord, Calif., 1969; tchr. elem. Monterey (Calif.) Peninsula Sch. Div., 1970-71, Prince William County Schs., Manassas, Va., 1972-2001, ret., 2001; Va. rehab. sch. Prince William County, Richmond, Va., 1979-82. V.p. Fauquier Gymnastics, Warrenton, Va., 1982-83, pres., 1983-85; coach, bd. dirs., referee Warrenton Soccer Assn., 1980-88; soccer referee Piedmont Referee Assn., Manassas, 1990-95. Mem. NEA, Va. Edn. Assn. Prince William Edn. Assn. (bd. dirs. 1974-77). Home: 7160 Airlie Rd RR 8 Box 398 Warrenton VA 20187-9448

NORSTRAND, IRIS FLETCHER, psychiatrist, neurologist, educator; b. Bklyn., Nov. 21, 1915; d. Matthew Emerson and Violet Marie (Anderson) Fletcher; m. Severin Anton Norstrand, May 20, 1941; children: Virginia Helene Norstrand Villano, Thomas Fletcher, Lucille Joyce. BA, Bklyn. Coll., 1937, MA in Biochemistry, 1965, PhD in Biochemistry, 1972; MD, L.I. Coll. Medicine, 1941. Diplomate Am. Bd. Psychiatry and Neurology, cert. geriat. psychiatry. Intern Montefiore Hosp., Bronx, N.Y., 1941-42; asst. resident in neurology N.Y. Neurol. Inst.-Columbia-Presbyn. Med. Ctr., N.Y.C., 1944-45; pvt. practice Bklyn., 1947-52; resident in psychiatry Bklyn. VA Med. Ctr., 1952-54, resident in neurology, 1954-55, staff neurologist, 1955-81, asst. chief neurol. svc., 1981-91, staff psychiatrist, 1991-95. Neurol. cons. Indsl. Home for Blind, Bklyn., 1948-51; clin. prof. neurology SUNY Health Sci. Ctr., Bklyn., 1981—; attending neurologist Kings County Hosp., Bklyn., State U. Hosp., Bklyn.; cons. in field. Contbr. articles to profl. jours. Mem. Nat. Rep. Congl. Com., Rep. Senatorial Inner Circle. Recipient Spl. plaque Mil. Order Purple Heart, 1986, Spl. Achievement award PhD Alumni Assn. of CUNY, 1993, Lifetime Achievement award Bklyn. Coll., 1995, others. Fellow Am. Psychiat. Assn., Am. Acad. Neurology, Internat. Soc. Neurochemistry, Am. Assn. U. Profs. Neurology, Am. Med. EEG Soc. (pres. 1987-88), Nat. Assn. VA Physicians (pres. 1989-91, James O'Connor award 1987), N.Y. Acad. Scis., Sigma Xi. Republican. Presbyterian. Avocations: writing, piano, travel, reading. Home: 7624 10th Ave Brooklyn NY 11228-2309

NORTH, ANITA, secondary education educator; b. Chgo., Apr. 21, 1963; d. William Denson and Carol (Linden) N. BA, Ind. U., 1985; MS in Edn., Northwestern U., 1987. Cert. tchr., Ill. High sch. social studies and English tchr. Lake Park High Sch., Roselle, Ill., 1987-89; high sch. social studies tchr. West Leyden High Sch., Northlake, Ill., 1989—. Exch. program coord. West Leyden High Sch., 1989-98, head coach boys' tennis team, 1989-97, asst. coach girls' tennis team, 1994-2000, asst. speech coach, 1992-93; adj. prof. Orgnl. Mgmt. program Concordia U., River Forest, Ill., 2000—. Docent, Chgo. Architecture Found., 2000—. Humanities fellow Nat. Coun. Humanities, 1995; recipient Fern Fine Tchg. award West Leyden H.S., 1992. Mem. Nat. Coun. for Social Studies, Ill. Coun. for Social Studies, Orgn. Am. Historians, Ill. Tennis Coaches Assn., Phi Delta Kappa. Christian. Avocations: wilderness backpacking, tennis, orienteering, gardening, antique books and maps.

NORTH, CAROL SUE, psychiatrist, educator; b. Keokuk, Iowa, May 6, 1954; d. Ray Stemen and Doris Ethelyn (Wood) N. BS in Gen. Sci., U. Iowa, 1976; MD, Washington U., St. Louis, 1983, M in Psychiat. Epidemiology, 1993. Resident in psychiatry Barnes Hosp., Washington U. Med. Sch., St. Louis, 1983—87; rsch. fellow dept psychiatry Washington U., St. Louis, 1987-90, instr. dept. psychiatry, 1987-89, asst. prof. dept. psychiatry, 1989-97, assoc. prof. psychiatry, 1997-2001, prof., 2001—; staff psychiatrist Grace Hill Neighborhood Health Ctr., St. Louis, 1987-96, Midwest Psychiatry, 1993-95, Adapt of Am., 1995—. Author: Welcome, Silence, 1987, Multiple Personalities, Multiple Disorders: Psychiatric Classification and Media Influence, 1993; contbr. articles to profl. jours. Bd. Dirs. St. Louis Met. Alliance for the Mentally Ill, 1992-2000; trustee Rosati Stblzn. Ctr. for Homeless and Mentally Ill, 1992-94; bd. med. advisors Grace Hill Neighborhood Health Ctr., 1997—. Nat. Inst. Alcoholism and Alcohol Abuse grantee, 1988-93, Nat. Hazards Rsch. Applications Info. Ctr. grantee, 1987-88, NIMH grantee, 1991-95, 97-99, 2002-03, Ctr. Substance Abuse Treatment grantee, 1997-2002, Nat. Inst. on Drug Abuse grantee, 1998-2003. Fellow Am. Psychiat. Assn., Am. Psychopathol. Assn.; mem. AMA, Life History Rsch. Soc., Ea. Mo. Psychiat. Soc. (exec. coun. and pres. 1996-98), Internat. Soc. Traumatic Stress Studies, Am. Acad. Clin. Psychiatrists (bd. dirs. 1999-2003), Nat. Alliance for Mentally Ill, Am. Assn. Cmty. Psychiatrists, St. Louis Track Club. Presbyterian. Avocations: distance running, oil painting, historic home rehabilitation. Office: Washington U Sch Medicine Dept Psychiatry Campus Box 8134 660 S Euclid Saint Louis MO 63110-1002

NORTH, KATHRYN E. KEESEY (MRS. EUGENE C. NORTH), retired educator; b. Columbia, Pa., Jan. 25, 1916; d. Isaac and Elizabeth (French) Keesey; B.S., Ithaca Coll., 1938; M.A., N.Y. U., 1950; m. Eugene C. North, Aug. 18, 1938. Dir. music Cairo (N.Y.) Central Sch. Dist., 1938; music edn. cons. Argyle (N.Y.) Central Sch. Dist., 1939; dir. gen. music curriculum Hartford (N.Y.) Central Sch. Dist., 1939; mem. staff Del. Dept. Pub. Instrn., Dover, 1943; dir. music edn. Herricks (N.Y.) Pub. Schs., 1944-71; ret., 1971. Vis. lectr. Ithaca Coll., summers 1959, 60, 62-65, Fairleigh-Dickinson U., Rutherford, N.J., summer 1966, Albertus Magnus Coll., New Haven, summer 1968; instr. Adelphi Coll., 1954-55, Sch.. Edn., N.Y.U., 1964-65. Mem. Music Educators Nat. Conf., N.E.A., N.Y. State Sch. Music Assn., N.Y. State Tchrs. Assn., Nassau Music Educators Assn. (exec. bd. 1947-58), N.Y. State Council Adminstrs. Music Edn. (chpt. v.p. 1967-68), Herricks Tchrs. Assn. (pres. 1948), Sigma Alpha Iota. Mem. Order Eastern Star. Home: 1645 Calle Camille La Jolla CA 92037-7107

NORTHCRAFT, SHIRLEY LOUISE, elementary school educator; b. Eugene, Oreg., June 8, 1950; d. Robert Eugene and Aline Mae (Jennings) Kischel; m. Ronald Owen Northcraft, June 12, 1976; children: Lori Diane, Daniel Adam. BS in Elem. Edn., Western Oreg. U., 1973; MS in Curriculum, Instrn., U. Oreg., 1975. Cert. tchr., Oreg. Tchr. Hucrest Elem. Sch., Roseburg, Oreg., 1972—. Cons., participant revisions in curriculum materials, evaluation materials; mem. Wellness Cadre. Judge, cons., com. chmn. Jr. Miss Scholarship Program, Roseburg, 1974—, judge Miss Douglas County Scholarship Pagent; bd. dirs. Doug County Schs. Fed. Credit Union, Roseburg, 1980-82, Roseburg Boys Lacross Team, 2002—; bd. dirs., chmn. publicity com. Celebration of Literacy, 2001—; leader, judge 4-H Club; elder, meml. com. sec., handbell choir mem. Presbyn. Ch. Fellow Oreg. State Schs. Standardization Cadre; mem. Altrusa Internat. (chpt. pres. elect), Friends of Crater Lake Nat. Pk. (life), Alpha Delta Kappa (past chpt. pres.). Republican. Home: 1685 NW Hopper St Roseburg OR 97470-1837 Office: Hucrest Elem Sch 1810 NW Kline St Roseburg OR 97470-6043

NORTHCUTT, KATHRYN ANN, elementary school and gifted-talented educator, reading recovery educator; b. Ft. Worth, Nov. 11, 1953; d. Lawrence William and Eva Jo (McCormick) Lloyd; m. Frank E. Northcutt, Aug. 28, 1980; 1 child, Matthew Adam. Student, North Tex. State U., 1972-75; BS in Edn., U. Tex., Tyler, 1980, MEd, 1986. Cert. elem. educator, music educator, supr. K-8; cert. curriculum and instrn. supr. Tchr. grade 1 Longview (Tex.) Ind. Sch. Dist., Longview, 1980-87, tchr. gifted and talented reading, 1990-92, tchr. 3d grade, 1992-93, tchr. 4th grade, 1993-95, reading recovery tchr., 1995—; tchr. 1st grade Pine Tree Ind. Sch. Dist., 1987-90. Mem. Gregg County Hist. Soc., Longview Opera Guild (pres.). Mem. ASCD, Nat. Coun. Tchrs. Math., Assn. Tex. Profl. Educators, Reading Recovery Coun. N.Am., Jr. League of Longview (sustaining), Phi Beta Kappa, Sigma Alpha Iota. Home: 1206 Rosewood Ct Longview TX 75604-2872 Office: Longview Ind Sch Dist PO Box 3268 Longview TX 75606-3268

NORTHCUTT, MARIE ROSE, elementary, secondary, & special education educator; b. White Plains, N.Y., Feb. 2, 1950; d. Carlo and Marcelline Marie Rose (Benoit) DeMarco; m. Kenneth Walter Northcutt, Mar. 17, 1984; children: James Lee, Thomas Joseph. BA, Lynchburg Coll., 1972; MA, Columbia U., 1977. Cert. elem. and secondary tchr., N.Y. Tchr. Petersburg (Va.) Pub. Schs., 1972-74; asst. relocation mgr. Ticor Co., White Plains, 1974-75; 3rd grade tchr. Resurrection Sch., Rye, 1975-76; 6th grade tchr. Harrison (N.Y.) Cen. Sch. Dist., 1976-78, learning disabilities specialist, 1981—; tchr. of emotionally handicapped N.Y.C. Schs., 1978-80; learning evaluator Empire State Coll., White Plains, 1981-82. Ind. evaluation cons., White Plains, 1981—; chair Mid. States Sub-com. Active Harrison H.S. PTA. Mem. Assn. for Children with Learning Disabilities, Westchester County Assn. for Children with Learning Disabilities, Spl. Edn. Parents Tchrs. Assn., Orton Soc., Phi Delta Kappa. Roman Catholic. Avocations: reading, cooking. Home: 81 Griffin Pl White Plains NY 10603-3609 Office: Harrison Cen Sch Dist Union Ave Harrison NY 10528-2108

NORTON, BRYAN G. environmental scientist, educator, philosopher; b. Marshall, Mich., July 19, 1944; s. Kenneth Lucien and Lida M. (Miller) N. BA in Polit. Sci., U. Mich., 1966, PhD in Philosophy, 1970. Tchg. fellow, lectr. U. (Ann Arbor) Mich., 1967-70; from asst. to assoc. to prof. New Coll. of U. South Fla., Sarasota, 1970-88; rsch. assoc. U. (Coll. Pk.) Md. Inst. for Philosophy and Pub. Policy, 1981-83; prof. pub. policy Ga. Inst. Tech., Atlanta, 1988—, coord. philosophy of sci. and tech. program, 1997—99, 2000—02; assoc. scientist Zoo Atlanta, 1989—. Cons. Ea. Rsch. Group, 1992-94, Rsch. Triangle Inst., Rsch. Triangle Pk., N.C., 1996—; mem. environ. econs. adv. com., sci. adv. bd. U.S. EPA, 1994-97; bd. dirs. Defenders of Wildlife, Washington, 1996—. Author: Why Preserve Natural Variety?, 1987, Toward Unity Among Environmentalists, 1991, Searching for Sustainability, 2003; contbr. articles to Philosophy of Sci., Environ. Ethics, Land Econs., Biosci., Ecol. Econs., Duke Environ. Law and Policy Jour., Conservation Biology, Monist. Active in numerous species protection efforts. Recipient Nat. Winner award (essay contest) Environ. Affairs, 1978; Gilbert White fellow Resources for the Future, Washington, 1985, 86. Fellow Hastings Ctr.; mem. Internat. Soc. Environ. Ethics, Soc. for Conservation Biology (bd. govs. 1989-94, 2002—), Internat. Soc. Ecol. Econs., Pi Sigma Alpha. (Nat. Polit. Sci. Hon. award 1966). Achievements include devel. of environ. ethics position "weak anthropocentrism"; of "risk decision squares" for environ. policy analysis; first to show influences of am. pragmatists on Aldo Leopold and environmentalism. Office: Ga Inst Tech Sch Pub Policy Atlanta GA 30332-0001

NORTON, GLYN PETER, French literature educator; b. Exeter, Deaconshire, England, May 22, 1941; s. Trevor Thomas and Betty (Marshall) N.; m. Victoria Josefina Perez, Oct. 28, 1966; children: Alexandra, Leslie. AB, U. Mich., 1963, AM, 1965, PhD, 1968. Asst. prof. Dartmouth Coll., Hanover, N.H., 1968-71; prof. French lit. Pa. State U., University Park, 1971-88; prof. French lit., chmn. dept. romance langs., dir. Ctr. Fgn. Langs., Lits. and Cultures, Williams Coll., Williamstown, Mass., 1988-93, Willcox B. and Harriet M. Adsit prof. internat. studies, 1993—. Author: Montaigne and the Introspective Mind, 1975, The Ideology and Language of Translation in Renaissance France, 1984; editor: The Cambridge History of Literary Criticism, vol III, 1999; contbr. articles to ednl. jours. Recipient medal City of Melun, France, 1985; NEH fellow, 1973-74, Guggenheim fellow, 1986-87; Am. Coun. Learned Socs. grantee, 1980-81, 85. Fellow Camargo Found.; mem. MLA, Renaissance Soc. Am., Soc. Francaise des Seiziemistes. Avocations: music, gardening, travel. Office: Williams Coll Dept Romance Langs Weston Hall Williamstown MA 01267

NORTON, MARY BETH, history educator, writer; b. Ann Arbor, Mich., Mar. 25, 1943; d. Clark Frederic and Mary Elizabeth (Lunny) N. BA, U. Mich., 1964; MA, Harvard U., 1965, PhD, 1969; DHL (hon.), Siena Coll., 1983, Marymount Manhattan Coll., 1984, De Pauw U., 1989; DLitt (hon.), Ill. Wesleyan U., 1992. Asst. prof. history U. Conn., Storrs, 1969-71; from asst. prof. to prof. Cornell U., Ithaca, NY, 1971-87, Mary Donlon Alger prof. Am. history, 1987—. Author: The British-Americans: The Loyalist Exiles in England, 1774-1789, 1972, Liberty's Daughters: The Revolutionary Experience of American Women, 1750-1800, 1980 (Berkshire prize for Best Book Woman Historian 1980), Founding Mothers and Fathers: Gendered Power and the Forming of American Society, 1996 (finalist Pulitzer prize in history 1997), In the Devil's Snare: The Salem Witchcraft Crisis of 1692, 2002 (Amb. Book award of English-Speaking Union 2002); co-author: A People and A Nation, 1982, 6th rev. edit., 2001; editor: AHA Guide to Hist. Literature, 3d rev. edit., 1995; co-editor: Women of America: A History, 1979, To Toil the Livelong Day: America's Women at Work, 1790-1980, 1987, Major Problems in American Women's History, 1989, 3d rev. edit., 2003; contbr. articles to profl. jours. Trustee Cornell U., 1973-75, 83-88; mem. Nat. Coun. Humanities, Washington, 1979-84. Woodrow Wilson Found. fellow, 1964-65, NEH fellow, 1974-75, Shelby Cullom Davis Ctr. fellow Princeton U., 1977-78, Rockefeller Found. fellow, 1986-87, Soc. for Humanities fellow Cornell U., 1989-90, John Simon Guggenheim Meml. Found. fellow, 1993-94, Starr Found. fellow Lady Margaret Hall, Oxford U., 2000, Mellon postdoctoral fellow Huntington Libr., 2001. Fellow Soc. Am. Hist. (exec. bd. 1974-87, 2003—, Allan Nevins prize 1970); mem. Am. Hist. Assn. (v.p. for rsch. 1985-87), Am. Acad. Arts and Sci., Orgn. Am. Hist. (exec. bd. 1983-86), Berkshire Conf. Women Hist. (pres. 1983-85) Democrat. Methodist. Office: Cornell U Dept History 325 Mcgraw Hall Ithaca NY 14853-4601 E-mail: mbn1@cornell.edu.

NORTON, ROBERT LEO, SR., mechanical engineer, educator, researcher; b. Boston, May 5, 1939; s. Harry Joseph and Kathryn (Warren) Norton; m. Nancy Auclair, Feb. 27, 1960; children: Robert L. Jr., MaryKay, Thomas J. AS in Mechanical Engring. cum laude, Northeastern U., 1962, BS in Indsl. Tech. summa cum laude, 1967; MS in Engring. Design, Tufts U., 1970. Registered profl. engr., Mass. Engr. Polaroid Corp., Cambridge, Mass., 1959-66, sr. engr. Waltham, Mass., 1979-81; project engr. Jet Spray Cooler, Inc., Waltham, 1966-69; bio-med. engr. Tufts surg. rsch. dept. N.E. Med. Ctr. Hosps., Boston, 1969-71; rsch. assoc. Tufts surg. svc. Boston City

Hosp., 1971-74; lectr. bio-med. engring. Franklin Inst., Boston, 1973-76; instr. dept. surgery Tufts U., Boston, 1970-82, asst. prof. engring. design Medford, 1974-79; prof. mech. engring. Worcester Poly. Inst., Mass., 1981—; pres. Norton Assocs. Engring., Norfolk, Worcester, 1970—. Presenter in field. Author: (textbook) Design of Machinery: An Introduction to the Synthesis and Analysis of Mechanisms and Machines, 2d edit., 1999, Design of Machinery: An Introduction to the Synthesis and Analysis of Mechanisms and Machines, Korean transl., 1995, Design of Machinery: An Introduction to the Synthesis and Analysis of Mechanisms and Machines, Spanish transl., 1996, Design of Machinery: An Introduction to the Synthesis and Analysis of Mechanisms and Machines, Chinese transl., 1997, Machine Design: An Integrated Approach, 1996—98, Machine Design: An Integrated Approach, internat. edit., 1996, Cam Design and Manufacturing Handbook, 2001, others; contbr. articles to profl. jours.; reviewer: IFTOMM Mechanism and Machine Theory. Fellow: ASME (reviewer Jour. Mech. Design, reviewer Jour. Applied Mechanics, Machine Design award 2002); mem.: Am. Soc. Engring. Edn. (program chmn. computers in edn. divsn. 1985—86, sec. computers edn. divsn. 1986—87, pres. computers edn. divsn. 1988—90, reviewer Jour. Prism, J. F. Curtis award 1984, Merle Miller award 1987, 1992), Soc. Automotive Engrs., Sigma Xi, Pi Tau Sigma. Achievements include patents in field. Avocations: sailing, computers, motorcycling. Office: Worcester Poly Inst Dept Mechanical Engring 100 Institute Rd Worcester MA 01609-2247 E-mail: norton@wpi.edu., norton@designofmachinery.com.

NORTON, RUTH ANN, education educator; b. Sioux City, Iowa, Mar. 7, 1947; d. Burton Ellwood and Mildred Ruth (Schneider) Norton; m. Jack William Moskal, May 30, 1985. BA, U. No. Iowa, 1969; MS, Syracuse U., 1984, EdD, 1985. Cert. tchr. Iowa, Vt. Tchr. Cedar Falls (Iowa) Unified Sch. Dist., 1969-79; asst. didr. Area 7 Tchr. Ctr., Waterloo, Iowa, 1979-80; tchr. Moretown (Vt.) Elem. Sch., 1980-81; prof. Calif. State U., San Bernardino, 1985—, dir. student tchg., 1989-95, coord. elem. intern program, 1996-99, dir. elem. edn. program, 1999—. Cons. Tech. Tng. Inst. Calif. State U., San Bernardino, trainer supervision workshops; cons. Constl. Heritage Inst., Lime St. Elem. Sch., Hesperia, Calif. Contbr. articles to profl. jours. Bd. dirs. Redlands Ednl. Partnership Found.; chairperson reflections com. Redlands PTA Coun. Recipient Outstanding Prof. in Svc. award, Coll. Edn., 2003. Mem.: ASCD, So. Calif. Assn. Tchr. Educators, Nat. Coun. Social Studies, Calif. Coun. Social Studies, Calif. Assn. Supervision and Curriculum Devel., Assn. Tchr. Educators, Am. Ednl. Rsch. Assn., Phi Kappa Phi, Phi Delta Kappa. Avocations: gardening, swimming, needlepoint, reading. Office: Calif State U 5500 University Pkwy San Bernardino CA 92407-2318 E-mail: rnorton@csusb.edu.

NORTWEN, PATRICIA HARMAN, music educator; b. New Ulm, Minn., Mar. 6, 1930; d. Joseph Absolom and Viola Maureen (Stroud) Harman; m. Dallas Ernest Andrew Nortwen, Dec. 22, 1956; children: Laura Lee, Daniel Harman. BA magna cum laude, U. Minn., 1952, BS in Edn., MA, U. Minn., 1956. Tchr. music N.W. Sch., U. Minn., Crookston, 1952-54; instr. music S.D. State U., Brookings, 1954-56; tchr. music Robbinsdale (Minn.) Jr. H.S., 1956-57; music dir. Bethlehem Luth. Ch., Mpls., 1957-67; instr. music Golden Valley Luth. Coll., Mpls., 1967-85; ind. music tchr., Mpls., 1957—. Performer Early Music Consort, also others; prodr. (cable TV series) Women/Music, 1984-85; author, mng. editor: Music Theory Workbook, Vols. 1-6, 1993-96. Bd. dirs., sec., pres. Civic Orch. Mpls., 1989-94; cmty. adv. bd. U. Minn. Sch. Music, 1998—. Mem.: Thursday Mus. (pres. 1988—92, various offices 1992—97, devel. chair 1997—), Young Peoples Symphony Concert Assn. (v.p. 1992—2000), U. Minn. Sch. Music Alumni Coun. (chair 1997—99), Minn. Music Tchrs. Assn. (chair edn. found. 1995—97, pres.-elect 1997—99, pres. 1999—2001, found. bd. dirs. 2000—02, found. treas. 2002), Frederic Chopin Soc. (sec. 1992—96, bd. dirs. 1992—), Music Tchrs. Nat. Assn., Phi Beta Kappa, Sigma Alpha Iota (province officer 1975—85, nat. dir. 1975—89, 1998—, Nat. Leadership award 1952, Ring of Excellence award 1990). Avocations: reading, singing, hiking, fishing, knitting. Home: 210 W Grant St Apt 313 Minneapolis MN 55403-2244 E-mail: pdnortwen@juno.com.

NORWOOD, CAROLE GENE, retired middle school educator; b. Odessa, Tex., Feb. 27, 1943; d. Perry Eugene and Jeffie Lynn (Stephens) Knowles; m. James Randall Norwood, Aug. 4, 1973. BA, U. Tex., 1966; MA, U. North Tex., 1975; cert. ESL, Our Lady of the Lake U., San Antonio, 1988. Cert. Sec. Edn. English, Spanish, ESL. Student intern Dept. of the Interior, Washington, 1962; receptionist Senate Chambers, Austin, Tex., 1965; English instr. Universidade Mackenzie, Sao Paulo, Brazil, 1966-67, Uniao Cultural Brasil-Estados Unidos, Sao Paulo, 1966-67; tchr. Terrell (Tex.) Jr. Sr. High Sch., 1967-68, Agnew Jr. High Sch., Mesquite, Tex., 1968-70; teaching asst. U. North Tex. Denton, Tex., 1970-71; sec. to pres. The Village Bank, Dallas, 1971-72; tchr. Plano (Tex.) High Sch., 1972-74; ESL adult edn. tchr. Dallas, 1972-73; tchr., yearbook sponsor Brentwood Middle Sch., San Antonio, 1975-90; instructional specialist Gus Garcia Jr. High Sch., San Antonio, 1990-98, interdisciplinary team leader, 1992-93, 96-97, instrnl. facilitator, 1998-2000. Yearbook and newspaper sponsor, Agnew Jr. High Sch., 1969-70. Contbr. articles to profl. jours. Mem. World Wildlife Fund, Audubon Soc., Nat. Wildlife Fedn., Nature Conservancy, San Antonio Museum Assn., San Antonio Zoological Soc., Los Padrinos (Mission Rd. Devel. Ctr.); U.I.L. coach 1976-87, 92-93. Named Outstanding Young Woman of Am., 1972. Mem. AAUW, NEA, ASCD, Nat. Coun. Tchrs. English, San Antonio Area Coun. Tchrs. English, Tex. State Tchrs. Assn., Edgewood Classroom Tchrs. Assn. (faculty rep. 1991-94), Longhorn Singers Alumni Assn., Delta Kappa Gamma (chpt. pres. 1990-92, San Antonio coord. coun. chair 1995-96, state program com. mem. 1995-97), Lions. Presbyterian. Office: Edgewood Ind Sch Dist Gus Garcia Jr School 3306 Ruiz St San Antonio TX 78228-6226

NORWOOD, CAROLYN VIRGINIA, business educator; b. Florence, S.C., Dec. 11; d. James Henry and Mildred (Jones) N. BS, N.C. A&T State U., 1956; MA, Columbia U., 1959; postgrad., Seton Hall U., Temple U.; cert. scholarly distinction, Nat. Acad. Paralegal Studies, 1991. Instr. Gibbs. Jr. Coll., St. Petersburg, Fla., Fayetteville State U., N.C.; asst. prof. C.C. Phila.; prof. Essex County Coll., Newark, 1968—. Cons. Mercer County Coll., Trenton, N.J.; mem. assessment team Lehman Coll., Bronx, N.Y., Mid.-States Commn., Phila., 1980—; vol. tutor Newark Literacy Campaign, 1998—. Co-author: Alphabetic Indexing, 6th edit., 1999. Mem. Nat. Coun. on Black Am. Affairs, AACC; vol. tutor Newark Literacy Campaign. Recipient EDDY award Gregg/McGraw-Hill Co., N.Y.C., 1986, cert. of recognition of outstanding and dedicated svc. Mid. States Assn. Colls. and Schs., Commn. on Higher Edn., 1994; profiled in NBEA Yearbook chpt. on Leadership in Bus. Edn., 1993; postdoctoral fellow Temple U., 1977-78. Mem. AAUW, NAACP, Nat. Coun. Black Am. Affairs, Nat. Bus. Edn. Assn. (bd. dirs. 1982-85), Ea. Bus. Edn. Assn. (pres. 1986-87, membership dir. 1976-85, Educator of the Yr. 1994), Nat. Coun. Negro Women, N.J. Bus. Edn. Assn., Alpha Kappa Alpha, Phi Delta Kappa, Delta Pi Epsilon. Avocations: bowling, photography. Office: Essex County Coll 303 University Ave Newark NJ 07102-1719

NOSKO, MICHAEL GERRIK, neurosurgeon, educator; b. Montreal, Feb. 24, 1957; came to U.S., 1991; s. Joseph John and June Elizabeth (Salter) N.; m. Deborah Anne Branciere, May 23, 1981; children: Douglas Joseph, Denise Elizabeth, Keith Michael. BS, McMaster U., 1978; MD, U. Toronto, 1982; PhD, U. Alberta, 1986. Intern U. Toronto (Ont., Can.) Gen. Hosp., 1982-83; resident U. Alberta Hosps., Edmonton, Can., 1986-91; assoc. prof. neurosurgery Robert Wood Johnson Med. Sch., New Brunswick, N.J., 1991—, chief, divsn. neurosurgery, 1991—. Cons. and presenter in field. Contbr. articles to profl. jours., chpts. to books. Rsch. fellow Alberta Heritage Found., 1983-86; Chancellor' scholar McMaster U., 1975, Univ. scholar, 1976, Edwin Marwin Dalley Meml. scholar, 1977; recipient Acad. award Am. Acad. Neurol. Surgery, 1986. Fellow Am. Coll. Surgeons (Resident Rsch. award 1986), Royal Coll. Surgeons Can., Acad. Medicine N.J.; mem. AMA, Am. Assn. Neurol. Surgeons, Can. Neurosurg. Soc., N.J. Neurosurg. Soc., N.Y. Acad. Scis., Middlesex County Med. Soc., Soc. Critical Care Medicine, Congress Neurol. Surgeons, Alpha Omega Alpha. Anglican. Avocations: aircraft/helicopter pilot/instructor, fishing. Office: Divsn Neurosurgery 125 Paterson St Ste 2100 New Brunswick NJ 08901-1962 E-mail: nosko@umdnj.edu.

NOVAK, JAUNITA KATHYL, retired music educator; b. Iberia, Mo., May 3, 1928; d. Arthur Hobert and Clarice (Gardner) Perkins; m. Joseph Thomas Novak, Aug. 7, 1965. BS in Edn., Central Mo State U., 1954, BS in Music, 1960, postgrad., 1966. Tchr. Iberia (Mo.) Pub. Sch., 1948-55, elem., h.s. music tchr., 1955-59; tchr. Cons Sch. Dist. #2, Raytown, Mo., 1959-80; sec. Farm Bureau & Midwest Mgmt., Liberty, Mo., 1980-82; bank teller Centerre Bank, Liberty, Mo., 1982-83; office mgr. Bedingers Ethan Allen Gallery, Liberty, Mo., 1983-84; Fashion Coordinator Donly & Co., Liberty, Mo., 1984-92; substitute tchr. Iberia R.V. Schs., 1992-96. Dir. Girls Scouts, Iberia, 1948-49; PTA pres. Iberia H.S., 1956; bd. dirs., sec. Iberia City Cemetery, 1990-96. Valedictorian scholarship Drury Coll., 1946. Mem. AAUW (life), Am. Bus. Women's Assn. Liberty Belles (life), Mo. State Tchrs. Assn. (life), Raytown Ret. Tchrs. (life), Music Edn. Assn. (life), Iberia Garden Club (pres. 1994-95), Iberia Cmty. Betterment Assn. (bd. dirs. 1995—), Iberia Acad.-Jr. Coll. Alumni Assn. (pres. 1994-96), Kappa Kappa Iota. Republican. Baptist. Avocations: playing piano & organ, singing, sewing, knitting, tennis. Home: PO Box 201 Iberia MO 65486-0201

NOVAK, MARLENA, artist, educator, writer, curator; b. Brownsville, Pa., Mar. 6, 1957; d. Anthony Edward and Mary Margaret (Shader) N.; m. Jay Alan Yim, June 28, 1990. BFA in Painting, Carnegie-Mellon U., 1982; MFA in Art Theory and Practice (Painting), Northwestern U., 1986. Tchr. art, Northwestern U., Evanston, Ill., 1985, 89, 96-00, De Paul U., Chgo., 1986-92, 94, 96-99, Amsterdams Inst. voor Schilderkunst, The Netherlands, 1996; asst. prof. U.N.Mex., Albuquerque, 1992-93. One person shows include Handled With Care Gallery, Provincetown, Mass., 1983, Dittmar Gallery, Evanston, 1986, Carson Street Gallery, Pitts., 1989, C.G. Jung Inst. Chgo., Evanston, 1990, Wabash Coll., Crawfordsville, Ind., 1990, Esther Saks Gallery, Chgo., 1991, MC Gallery, Mpls., 1992, Ruschman Gallery, Indpls., 1993, Kay Garvey Gallery, Chgo., 1994, 95, Three Ill. Ctr., Chgo., 1994, Galerie Vromans, Amsterdam, 1995, Galerie Waszkowiak, Berlin, 1997; Galerie Ucher, Cologne, 1998, Roy Boyd Gallery, Chgo., 1999; exhibited in group shows at Harrisburg (Pa.) Mus., 1984, Govt. Ctr., Boston, 1984, Univ. Kobe (Japan), 1985, Union Art Gallery, Milw., 1986, Rockford (Ill.) Mus., 1986, Gracie Mansion Gallery Mus. Store, N.Y.C., 1987, George Walter Vincent Smith Art Mus., Springfield, Mass., 1988, East West Contemporary Art Gallery, Chgo., 1989, Provincetown Art Assn. and Mus., 1989, 94, Eve Mannes Gallery, Atlanta, 1990, Mary and Leigh Block Gallery, Northwestern U., Ill., 1990, Deson-Saunders Gallery, Chgo., 1990, Chgo. Cultural Ctr., 1990, Art Inst. Chgo., 1990, Esther Saks Fine Art, Chgo., 1991, 92, DePaul U. Art Gallery, Chgo., 1992, Ruschman Gallery, 1992, 94, MC Gallery, 1992, Lowe Gallery, Atlanta, 1992, Kay Garvey Gallery, 1992, 93, 95, Charlotte Jackson Fine Art, Santa Fe, 1993, John Sommers Gallery, 1993, CWCA, Chgo., 1993, Klein Art Works, 1993, Greenpeace Fund Benefit, Chgo., 1994, Bethany Coll. Fine Art Ctr., Mankato, Minn., 1994, Galerie Vromans, 1994, 95, Wabash Coll., 1994, Global Focus, Beijing, 1995, Stichting Amazone, Amsterdam, 1995, Galerie Beeld & Ambeeld, Enschede, The Netherlands, 1996, Galerie Waszkowiak, Berlin, 1996, Mindy Oh Gallery, N.Y., 1997, Barnes Inst., Stuttgart, 1997; Roy Boyd Gallery, Chicago, 1998, Mary and Leigh Block Mus., Evenston, Ill., 1998; Gallery 312, 'Chicago Artists,' Chicago, 1998, Klein Art Works, Abstract, Chgo., 1998, Roy Boyd Gallerym 1999, UNESCO-ICSU Conf. on Sci. Exhbn., 1999, Galerie Beeld and Aabeold, Enschede, Netherlands, 1999, Margin Gallery, Chgo., 1999, N.Y. Polish Consulate, 1999, Galerie Ucher, Köln, Germany, 1999; contbr. articles to various publs. Avocations: travelling, sailing, contemporary music festivals and concerts. Home: 835 N Wood St Apt 102 Chicago IL 60622-5044

NOVAK, MARTHA LOIS, elementary education educator; b. Cape Girardeau, Mo., Sept. 14, 1938; d. Roy Edward and Mable Mae (Clinton) Partain; m. Raymond Victor Novak, Nov. 29, 1968; children: Carolyn, Edward. BA, U. Calif., Fresno, 1964. Cert. tchr., Calif. Tchr. kindergarten Clovis (Calif.) Unified Sch. Dist., 1964; tchr. Magnolia Sch. Dist., Anaheim, Calif., 1964-69, Burr Oak Sch. Dist., Chgo., 1969-70, Buttonwillow (Calif.) Sch. Dist., 1970-72, Richland Sch. Dist., Shafter, Calif., 1972-80, St. Francis Sch., Bakersfield, Calif., 1980-84, Standard Sch. Dist., Bakersfield, 1984-93, St Joseph Sch., Pekin, Ill., 1994—. Chmn. honor chorus Kern County Schs., Bakersfield, 1974-75; 2d v.p. cen. sect. Calif. Music Educators Assn., 1976-78; pres. Standard Sch. Dist. Tchrs. Assn., Bakersfield, 1988-92; mentor tchr. Standard Sch. Dist., 1990-93; presenter Kern County Music Educators, 1986, Kern County Reading Assn., 1986-90, Calif. State Reading Assn., 1988; presenter music workshops Kern County Spl. Edn. Tchrs., 1989-93. Author manuals. Female lead in musical prodns. Shafter (Calif.) High Patrons Orgn., 1978-83; grand marshall Potato Festival parade City of Shafter, 1979; commr. of heritage Kern County Govt., Bakersfield, 1990-93. Recipient Tchr. of Yr. award Tchrs. Assn. Standard Sch. Dist., 1992; named Citizen of Yr. City of Shafter, 1979. Fellow ASCD, PTA (past officer), Nat. Tchrs. Assn., Calif. Tchrs. Assn. (local pres. 1988-92), Delta Kappa Gamma (local music chmn. 1988-92). Avocations: singing, golf, camping, reading. Home: Apt 13 507 Mccord Ave Bakersfield CA 93308-8030

NOVAKOV, GEORGE JOHN, JR., gifted and talented educator, consultant, administrative assistant; b. New Orleans, Apr. 1, 1945; s. George John Novakov Sr. and Gloria (Edwards) Frost; m. Ann Marie Mariano, Dec. 27, 1969; children: Jay, Jaime. BA, U. New Orleans, 1967, MEd, 1970, postgrad., 1985, Tulane U., Loyola U., 1985. Tchr. New Orleans Pub. Schs., 1967—, adminstrv. asst., dir. admission Edna Karr Secondary Sch., 1994—, student data mgr. Edna Karr Secondary Sch., 1994—. Grant writer asst. Edna Karr Secondary Sch., New Orleans Pub. Libr., 1987-99. Author: (play) The Christmas Caper, 1980. Ind. Study Humanities fellow, 1991. Mem. La. Assn. of Computer Using Educators (assoc. editor newsletter, 1992), Greater New Orleans Coun. of Tchrs. of English, Presenter at Nat. Edn. Computer Conf., 1998, 2002. Democrat. Roman Catholic. Avocations: opera, science fiction, computers. Home: 7340 Edward St New Orleans LA 70126-2012 Office: Edna Karr Secondary Sch 3332 Huntlee Dr New Orleans LA 70131-7046 E-mail: george_novakov@nops.k12.la.us.

NOVARA MURPHY, AMY, court reporter; b. Murphysboro, Ill., Jan. 24, 1962; d. Andrew C. and Alice Jane (Arbeiter) Novara; m. James R. Murphy, Dec. 31, 1993. AA, So. Ill. U., 1983, BS, 1985. Cert. shorthand reporter, Ill. Ct. reporter Amy A. Novara Reporting Svc., Murphysboro, 1991—. Interviewer: When the Whole World Changed, 1993. Sec. BPW, Murphysboro, 1991-93; vol. So. Ill. Hosp. Assn., Murphysboro, 1995-97; mem. Murphysboro H.S. Booster Club, 1995—; sec. Murphysboro Pride Group, 1991-96. Mem. Nat. Ct. Reporters Assn., Ill. Shorthand Reporters Assn., Ill. Ofcl. Ct. Reporters Assn., So. Ill. U. Alumni Club, Alpha Gamma Delta (pres. BH Alumnae chpt. 1995-97, adviser undergrad. chpt. 1990—, province dir. alumnae 1997, bd. dirs. house assn. 1992—, sec. house assn. 2000-03, pres. house assn. 2003—). Roman Catholic. Avocations: antique collecting, travel, baseball, hockey. Home and Office: Amy A Novara Reporting Svc 32 Herring Dr Murphysboro IL 62966-1530

NOVINSKA, DEIRDRE ANN, special education educator; b. West Plains, Mo., Nov. 24, 1960; d. Delbert Bruce and Genevieve Mae (Diels) Wells; m. James Joseph Novinska, Aug. 20, 1983; children: Megan Ann, Justin James. BS, U. Wis., Eau Claire, 1982, MS, 1983; MS in Edn. Adminstrn., U. Wis., Superior, 1996. Lic. speech-lang. pathologist, Wis. Speech/lang. therapist Wauzeka (Wis.) Pub. Sch., 1983-84, Iowa-Grant Pub. Schs., Livingston, Wis., 1984-85, Medford Area (Wis.) Pub. Schs., 1985-92, speech/lang. therapist, early edn. coord., 1992-94, spl. edn. coord., early edn. coord., 1994—. Speech/lang. pathologist Taylor County (Wis.) Birth-3 Program, 1992-93. Bd. dirs. Parent Resource Ctr., Medford, 1994—, Black River Industries, Medford, 1994—; co-chair Early Childhood Coun., Medford, 1992—. Mem. Am. Speech/Lang. Assn., Coun. for Exceptional Children, Wis. Speech Hearing Assn., Jaycettes, Optimists. Avocations: skiing, reading, collecting, walking. Office: Medford Pub Schs 1015 W Broadway Ave Medford WI 54451-1311

NOVITSKI, CHARLES EDWARD, biology educator; b. Rochester, N.Y., Oct. 3, 1946; s. Edward and Esther Ellen (Rudkin) N.; m. Margaret Thornton Sime, June 15, 1968; children: Nancy Ellen, Linda Nicole, Elise Michelle. BA in Biology, Columbia Coll., 1969; PhD in Biophysics, Calif. Inst. Tech., 1979. Rsch. fellow and assoc. City of Hope Nat. Med. Ctr., Duarte, Calif., 1977-80; sr. tutor in biochemistry Monash U., Victoria, Australia, 1980-82, lectr. in biochemistry, 1982-84; program leader and rsch. scientist in nematode control Agrigenetics Advanced Sci. Co., Madison, Wis., 1985-88; assoc. prof. molecular biology Cen. Mich. U., Mt. Pleasant, 1989—. Assoc. editor Jour. Nematology, 1994-97; contbr. articles to various profl. jours. Mem. Soc. of Nematologists, Internat. Soc. of Plant Molecular Biology. Achievements include patent for Nematode Control; research in the molecular genetics of mitochondria and of nematodes. Home: 1208 E Preston Rd Mount Pleasant MI 48858-3927 Office: Cen Mich U Dept Biology Mount Pleasant MI 48859-0001

NOWAK, FELICIA VERONIKA, endocrinologist, molecular biologist, educator; b. Camden, N.J. d. Walter Ignatius and Felicia Valeria (Krukowska) N. AB cum laude, Trinity Coll., Washington, D.C., 1970; PhD, U. Wis., 1975; MD, Washington U., 1978. Resident in internal medicine Washington U. Med. Ctr., St. Louis, 1978-80; fellow in endocrinology Harbor/UCLA Med. Ctr., L.A., 1980-83; asst. prof. medicine Columbia U., N.Y.C., 1985-87; asst. prof. molecular cell biology U. Conn., Storrs, 1988-92; asst. prof. medicine div. endocrinology St. Louis U., 1992—99; assoc. prof. molecular neuroendocrinology Ohio U., 1999—. Contbr. articles to profl. jours. Tutor Ctr. for Acad. Programs U. Conn., 1991-92. Recipient grants March of Dimes Rsch. Found., NIH, Pharm. Rsch., Mfrs. Am. Found. Mem. Endocrine Soc., Soc. for Neurosci., Sigma Xi. Achievements include discovery of the porf-1 and porf-2 genes and elucidation of their roles in mammalian brain development and hormonally determined function in extraneural organs including testes.

NOWAK, MARY LEONARDA, school administrator, principal; b. Springfield, Ill., Apr. 25, 1942; d. Leonard Louis and Agnes Bridget (Kowalski) N. BS in Edn., U. Akron, 1971; MS in Edn., Boston Coll., 1987; postgrad., Marquette U., 1990-91, postgrad., 1992-93. Cert. adminstr., Wis. Religious edn. tchr. Mary Queen of Heaven Sch., Greensburg, Ohio, 1976-78; tchr. Christ the King Sch., Akron, Ohio, 1976-78; dir. religious edn., tutor, organist Visitation of BVM, Pitts., 1978-79; 1st and 2d grade tchr. St. Anthony Sch., Sharon, Pa., 1979-85, Sacred Heart Sch., Milw., 1985-87; 5th and 6th grade tchr. St. Augustine Sch., West Allis, Wis., 1987-89, adminstr., prin., 1989-93, St. Mary of Good Counsel Sch., Mayville, Wis., 1993-97; prin. St. Paul Cath. Sch., Milw., 2000—02; dir. assocs. for Daughters of Divine Charity St. Mary Province, 2002—. Ch. musician, organist St. Adalbert Ch., Milw., 1987-2000; ch. musician Holy Cross Ch., 1997—, St. Emeric's Ch., 1997—; sec. Sch. Task Force East West Allis, 1990-93; chair Polit. Action Task Force of Region VI Prins., Milw., 1991-92; regional rep. Nat. Regional Congress of Cath. Schs., Mpls., 1991. Chair Seneca Grant Com., 1993-97. Grantee, Youth Gardens for All, 1984, Milw. Found., 1986, Marquette U., 1991-92, 93-94, CESA #1 Youth Svcs. Learning Tng., 2000-01, Youth Svc. Learning Curriculum Rev., 2000-01; Reading Disability scholar Marquette U., 1987; recipient Exemplary award Cath. Mission Archdiocese Milw., 1990. Mem. ASCD, Nat. Cath. Edn. Assn., Assn. Liturgical Musicians of Archdiocese of Milw., Milw. Archdiocesan Elem. Prin.'s Assn. (dist. chair 1990-91), Milw. Art Mus., Diabetes Assn., Nat. Jr. Hon. Soc., Nat. Mid. Sch. Assn. Roman Catholic. Avocations: piano, organ, needlecraft, gardening, tennis. Home: 6763 W Rogers St West Allis WI 53219-1345 Office: St Augustine Sch 6763 W Rogers St West Allis WI 53219-1397 E-mail: leonardas@archmil.org.

NOWELL, LINDA GAIL, organization executive; b. Ft. Worth, Apr. 24, 1949; d. Jesse Wayne and Bennie Dale (Flint) Stallings. BA in English, North Tex. State U., 1970. Cert. secondary edn. tchr., Tex. Ind. sales rep. Jostens Printing & Pub. Div., Owatona, Minn., 1980-84; v.p. Nowell Equipment Co., Cranfils Gap, Tex., 1984-89; edn. coord. Tex. Farm Bur., Waco, Tex., 1987-90; account exec. MAC Printing, Las Vegas, 1991-94; mgr. frontier health outreach program Nev. Rural Health Ctrs., Inc., 1994-97; state coord. Nev. 5-A-Day Coalition, 1995-96; exec. dir. No To Abuse, Pahrump, Nev., 1999—. Grant manager, writer, newsletter editor Participant Landmark Edn., Inc. Mem. NAFE, United Way Pioneer Territory (bd. dirs.), Fam/Fam Connection (adv. bd.). Home: PO Box 790 Pahrump NV 89041-0790

NOWOCIN, DEBRA TERESE, gifted and talented secondary education educator; b. Chicago Heights, Ill., Aug. 4, 1951; d. Anthony F. and Anita G. (Cioe) N. BS in Edn., Ea. Ill. U., 1973; gifted cert., Nat. Coll. Edn., 1978; MS in Edn., No. Ill. U., 1981. Cert. tchr., gifted tchr., gen. administrv. Tchr., grades 4-6 Sch. Dist. 170, Chicago Heights, 1973-76, tchr. title I summer sch., 1974-76, tchr. summer enrichment program, various yrs., sci. and gifted enrichment tchr., grade 7, 1976—. Tchr. Worlds of Wisdom and Wonder program for gifted and talented children Ctr. for Gifted, Nat.-Louis U., Evanston, Ill., 1990-93; coord. sci. fair Washington Jr. High Sch. (team sponsor); co-sponsor Spartan Explorers Social Studies Club. Appeared in video Team Up With TV: Using Video in the Classroom, 1991. Active various dist. curriculum coms. Recipient Presdl. award for excellence in sci. teaching nominee, 1984. Mem. NSTA, Ill. Coun. for Gifted,, Ill. Sci. Tchrs. Assn., Ill. Jr. Acad. Sci. (sec., treas. region 9, asst. to state safety chmn.), South Suburban Sci. Coun., Kappa Delta Pi. Home: 121 E 24th St Chicago Heights IL 60411-4248 Office: Washington Jr High Sch 25 W 16th Pl Chicago Heights IL 60411-3475

NOYES, DEBRA ROSE, dance educator; b. Elyria, Ohio, Sept. 4, 1955; d. James M. and Jenetta M. (White) Cahl; m. John R. Noyes, Sept. 9, 1989. AA, Peninsula Coll., 1987; BA, U. Wash., 1989; MEd, Seattle Pacific U., 1992. Cert. in elem. lab. notation; cert. aerobics instr. Peninsula Coll., Port Angeles, Wash., 1984-86; teaching asst. U. Wash., Seattle, 1988-89; instr., choreographer Seattle Pacific U., 1990-92, adminstrv. asst., 1990-92; exec. asst., tng. and project coord. Bell Atlantic Pub. Sector Systems, Clearwater, Fla., 1992-93; ballroom dance instr., choreographer Tampa, 1994—. Contbr. articles to profl. jours. Dir. Arts Edn. Advocacy Coalition, Seattle, 1992-93. Recipient Associated Student Coun. scholarship Peninsula Coll., 1986-87, Wash. Alliance for Health, Physical Edn., Recreation and Dance award Peninsula Coll., 1986-87, U. Wash. U.G. Merit scholarship, 1988-89, U. Wash. Devries Dance scholarship U. Wash., 1988-89, Outstanding Dance award (First Places) Calif. Star Ball, 1988, Supreme Dance award (First Places) Oreg. Star Ball, 1988; named to Nat. Dean's list, 1988-89. Mem. AAHPERD, Dance Educators Assn. of Wash. (pres. 1992-93, pres.-elect 1990-92, conf. chair 1990-92), Nat. Dance Assn. (mem. higher edn. com. 1991-93), Congress on Rsch. in Dance, Dance Notation Bur., Wash. Alliance for Health, Physical Edn., Recreation and Dance. Avocations: dancing, outdoor activities, reading, writing, sewing. Home: 11732 Branch Mooring Dr Tampa FL 33635-6278 Address: 11732 Branch Mooring Dr Tampa FL 33635-6278

NOYES, DIRK ARNOLD, special education educator, education educator; b. Coral Gables, Fla., July 13, 1961; s. Donald Arthur and Wilma (Royce) N. BS in Elem. Edn., Nova U., 1986, MS in Specific Learning Disabilities, 1990. Cert. tchr., Fla. Drop-out prevention tchr. jr. high sch. Dade County Pub. Schs., Miami, Fla., 1986-87, jr. high sch. spl. edn. tchr., 1987-88, elem. sch. spl. edn. tchr., 1988-91; chair exceptional edn. dept. Kendale Lakes Elem. Sch., Miami, 1990-91; placement specialist Region 6 Ops., Miami, 1991—. Adj. prof. Nova U., 1992—; regional and state judge Odyssey of the Mind, 1991—; presenter at profl. confs. Contbr. articles to profl. publs. Mem. Coun. Exceptional Children (chpt. treas. 1986-87), Dade County Nova Alumni (chair membership 1990-92, parlimentarian 1992—). Avocations: photography, skiing.

NUESSE, CELESTINE JOSEPH, retired university official; b. Sevastopol, Wis., Nov. 25, 1913; s. George and Salome Helen (Martens) N.; m. Margaret O'Donoghue, 1969. B.E., Central State Tchrs. Coll., Stevens Point, Wis., 1934; MA, Northwestern U., 1937; PhD, Cath. U. Am., 1944, L.H.D., 1982; LL.D., Merrimack Coll., 1960. Tchr. social studies Pub. High Sch., Antigo, Wis., 1934-40; instr. sociology Coll. St. Catherine, St. Paul, 1943, Marquette U., Milw., 1943-45; instr. Cath. U. Am., Washington, 1945-48, asst. prof., 1948-52, assoc. prof., 1952-64, prof., 1964-81, prof. emeritus, 1981—, dean Sch. Social Sci., 1952-61, exec. v.p., 1967-81, provost, 1968-79, provost emeritus, 1981—. Spl. rep. in Germany, Nat. Cath. Welfare Conf., 1950-51; mem. U.S. Nat. Commn. for UNESCO, 1950-56, 63-69, exec. com., 1954-56; mem. gov. bd. UNESCO Youth Inst., Munich, Germany, 1955-59; mem. U.S. Bd. Fgn. Scholarships, 1954-58, chmn., 1956-58; mem. D.C. Commr.'s Coun. on Human Relations, 1958-64, D.C. Commn. on Postsecondary Edn., 1975-80 Author: The Social Thought of American Catholics, 1634-1829, 1945, The Catholic University of America: A Centennial History, 1990; co-author, co-editor: The Sociology of the Parish, 1951; staff editor New Cath. Ency., 1963-66, chmn. editl. bd. supplements, 1973-79; contbr. articles to profl. jours. Mem. Am. Cath. Hist. Assn., Am. Cath. Sociol. Soc. (pres. 1954), Am. Sociol. Assn., Cath. Assn. Internat. Peace (pres. 1954-56), Cath. Commn. Intellectual and Cultural Affairs, Inst. Internat. Sociologie, Internat. Conf. on Sociology of Religion (past v.p.), Nat. Cath. Ednl. Assn., Cath. Interracial Council Washington (pres. 1962-66), Cosmos Club (Washington), KC, Phi Beta Kappa (hon.), Alpha Kappa Delta, Pi Gamma Mu, Sigma Tau Delta, Phi Sigma Epsilon. Home: 8108 River Crescent Dr Annapolis MD 21401

NUESSEL, FRANK HENRY, linguistics educator; b. Evergreen Park, Ill., Jan. 22, 1943; s. Frank Henry and Rita Elizabeth (Aspell) N. AB, Ind. U., 1965; MA, Mich. State U., 1967; PhD, Ill. U., 1973. Instr. No. Ill. U., Dekalb, 1967-70; asst. prof. Ind. State U., Terre Haute, 1973-75; prof. linguistics U. Louisville, 1975—, dir. program linguistics, 1980-86; assoc. dean Coll. Arts and Scis., 1986-88. Mem. editorial bd. Hispanic Linguistics U. Pitts., 1983— ; assoc. editor Lang. Problems and Lang. Planning, U. Tex., 1983—. Author: Theoretical Studies in Hispanic Linguistics, 1988, The Study of Names, 1992, The Image of Older Adults in the Media, 1992, The Semiotics of Ageism, 1992, The Esperanto Language, 2000, Linguistic Approaches to Hispanic Literature; editor: Linguistic Approaches to the Romance Lexicon, 1978, Contemporary Studies in Romance Languages, 1980, Current Issues in Hispanic Phonology and Morphology, 1985, (with Marcel Danesi) The Imaginative Basis of Thought and Culture, 1994; mem. editl. bd. Diálogos Hispánicos de Amsterdam, 1987—; contb. articles to profl. jours. Mem. exec. bd. Understanding Aging Inc., Acton, Mass., 1984-87. Julius J. Oppenheimer fellow, 1985-86; Pres. award Dist. Rsch., 1997, Metroversity Instrnl. Devel. award, 2002. Fellow Gerontol. Soc. Am. (Disting. Educator Achievement award); mem. MLA, Linguistic Soc. Am., Am. Assn. Tchrs. Spanish and Portuguese (exec. coun. 2003-), Am. Assn. of Tchrs. of Esperanto (pres. 1996-2000), Nat. Coun. on Aging, Ky. Assn. Gerontology (exec. bd. 1987—), Am. Name Soc. Home: 912 Pennwood Dr New Albany IN 47150-2132 Office: U Louisville Dept Modern Languages Louisville KY 40292-0001 E-mail: fhnues01@athena.louisville.edu.

NUGENT, MARY KATHERINE, elementary education educator; b. Terre Haute, Ind., Aug. 15, 1953; d. Thomas Patrick and Jeanne (Butts) N. BS, Ind. State U., Terre Haute, 1975, MS, 1978. Cert. in elem. edn., spl. edn., Ind. Tchr. 6th grade Cloverdale (Ind.) Sch. Corp., 1976-79; tchr. 4th-6th grades Glenwood Sch., Richardson, Tex., 1986-88; tchr. intermediate mentally handicapped class Meadows Elem. Sch., Terre Haute, 1988-89, tchr. 5th grade, 1989-90, tchr. 4th grade, 1990-93; tchr. 6th grade lang. arts and reading Woodrow Wilson Mid. Sch., Terre Haute, 1993—. Mem. steering com. Tchr. Applying Whole Lang., Terre Haute, 1989-91. Avocations: reading, gardening, computers. Office: Vigo County Sch Corp 961 Lafayette Ave Terre Haute IN 47804-2929

NUGENT, S. GEORGIA, academic administrator; m. Thomas J Scherer. B cum laude, Princeton U., 1973; PhD in classics, Cornell U. Instr. Swarthmore Coll.; assoc. prof. Brown U., 1985; asst. prof. Princeton U., 1979, dean, Harold McGraw Jr. Ctr. for tchg. and learning, asst. to pres., 1992—95; assoc. provost, 1995; pres. Kenyon Coll., 2003—. Author books. Recipient Wriston award for excellence in tchg. Office: President Ransom Hall Kenyon Coll Gambier OH 43022

NUGENT, WALTER TERRY KING, historian; b. Watertown, N.Y., Jan. 11, 1935; s. Clarence A. and Florence (King) Nugent; m. Suellen Hoy, 1986; children from previous marriage: Katherine, Rachel, David, Douglas, Terry, Mary. AB, St. Benedict's Coll., 1954, DLitt, 1968; MA, Georgetown U., 1956; PhD, U. Chgo., 1961. Instr. history Washburn U., 1957-58; asst. prof. Kans. State U., 1961-63, Ind. U., 1963-64, assoc. prof., 1964-68, prof., 1968-84, assoc. dean Coll. Arts and Scis., 1967-71, dir. overseas study, 1967-76, chmn. history dept., 1974-77; Andrew V. Tackes prof. history U. Notre Dame, 1984-00, Andrew V. Tackes prof. emeritus, 2000—. Paley lectr., Fulbright vis. prof. Hebrew U., Jerusalem, 1978—79; summer seminar dir. NEH, 1979; vis. prof. U. Hamburg, U. Warsaw, 1982; Mary Bell Washington Fulbright prof. U. Coll., Dublin, 1991—92. Author: (book) The Tolerant Populists, 1963, Creative History, 1967, The Money Question During Reconstruction, 1967, Money and American Society 1865-1880, 1968, Modern America, 1973, From Centennial to World War: American Society 1876-1917, 1977, Structures of American Social History, 1981, Crossings: The Great Transactlantic Migrations 1870-1914, 1992; author: (with Martin Ridge) The American West: The Reader, 1999, Into the West: The Story of Its People, 1999 (Caughey award, 2000); author: Making Our Way: A Family History, 2003. Bd. dirs. U.S.-Israel Ednl. Found., 1985—89. Recipient medal of Merit, Warsaw U., 1992; Newberry Libr. fellow, 1962, Guggenheim fellow, 1964—65, Huntington Libr. fellow, 1979, 1985, Beinecke fellow, Yale U., 1990. Mem.: Soc. Historians the Gilded Age and Progressive Era (pres. 2000—02), Soc. Am. Historians, Western Hist. Assn. Democrat. Catholic. E-mail: wnugent@nd.edu.

NUMBERE, DAOPU THOMPSON, petroleum engineer, educator; b. Buguma, Nigeria, Mar. 30, 1951; came to the U.S., 1975; s. Thompson and Norah (West) N.; m. Tonye Eugenia Higgwe, Dec. 29, 1987. BS in Mech. Engring., U. Coll. Swansea, 1975; MS in Petroleum Engring., Stanford U., 1977; PhD, U. Okla., 1982. Asst. prof. U. Mo., Rolla, 1982-88, assoc. prof., 1988-96, prof., 1996—, head dept. petroleum engring., 1996-2000. Cons. Sigma Cons., Mattoon, Ill., 1987-93, Marathon Oil Co., 1998; chmn. Mo. Oil and Gas Coun., 1996-2000. Author: Petroleum Reservoir Class Manual, 1991, Principles of Waterflooding, 1998. Recipient Shell-BP award, 1971-75, Selwyn Caswell prize U. Coll. Seansea, 1975, Okla. Rsch. award Okla Rsch. Coun., 1981. Mem. ASME, Internat. Soc. for Computer Methods and Adv. in Geomechanics, Soc. Petroleum Engrs., Sigma Xi. Achievements include development of an innovative method for streamline generation for oil recovery prediction, simultaneous prediction of oil recovery and water influx for oil and gas reservoirs. Office: U Mo Rolla 119 Mcnutt Hall Rolla MO 65401

NUNES, PRICILLA O. special education educator, artist; b. Acushnet, Mass., Aug. 6, 1928; d. George Mendall and Rose Blanche (Pepin) Nunes; m. Joseph Nunes, Apr. 19, 1949; children: Jay Joseph, Tod Albert, Marc Truman. BA, U. Mass., Dartmouth, 1977; MEd, Worcester State Coll., 1981. Advisor spl. edn. New Bedford, Mass., 1993—. Exhibited works with Bierstadt Art Soc., 1993; exhibited at Davoll Country Store, 1997-98. Active in various charity events. Mem. AAUW, Mass. Ret. Tchrs. Assn., Ret. State, County and Mcpl. Employees Assn., Internat. Porcelain Artists and Tchrs. Inc., New Bedford Art Mus., Friends of Free Pub. Libr., Friends of Zeitarian Theater, Coll. Club of New Bedford. Avocation: china and porcelain painting. Home: 37 Lawrence St New Bedford MA 02745-5521

NUNLEY, MALINDA VAUGHN, retired elementary school educator; b. Tenn. d. William D. and Callie (Ross) Vaughn; m. Harry H. Nunley, Dec. 24, 1940 (dec.); chidlren: Jerry Michael, Sally Coleen. BS in Edn., Mid. Tenn. State U., 1961; MEd in Psychology, Middle Tenn. State U., 1972; postgrad., U. Tenn., Chattanooga, 1974-80, Mid. Tenn. State U. Cert. art tchr., spl. edn. tchr., guidance counselor and cons., individual testing and diagnostics in spl. edn. Tenn. Tchr. Panama Canal Co, Balboa, Panama Canal Zone, 1954-56; adult tchr. U.S. Army, Ft. Davis, Panama Canal Zone, 1956-60; elem. tchr. Ancon Elem. Panama Canal Zone Sch., Tenn., 1961-64; tchr. South Pitts. High Sch., 1964-66, Normal Park Elem. Sch., Chattanooga, Tenn., 1966-71; spl. edn. tchr. Griffith Creek Elem. Sch., Tenn., 1971-83; ret. Tenn. Tutor, substitute tchr., speaker to groups, Tenn., 1994—; homebound tchr. for alcohol and drug abuse adolescents, 1989-90; spl. speaker to class groups 4th-7th, 1993-94. Mem. NEA, Tenn. Edn. Assn., Marion County Tchrs. Assn., Tenn. Ret. Tchrs. Assn., Chattanooga Edn. Assn. (past faculty rep.). Home: 6555 Highway 27 Chattanooga TN 37405-7288

NUNNALLY, DOLORES BURNS, retired physical education educator; b. Strong, Ark., Jan. 2, 1932; d. Marion Saunders Burns and Emma Jo (Burns) Baca; m. Curtis Jerome Nunnally, Apr. 16, 1954; 1 child, Jo Lynn Nunnally Blair. BSE, Ark. State Tchrs. Coll., 1953; MSE, State Coll. Ark., 1964; EdD, U. Sarasota, 1981. Phys. edn. tchr. El Dorado (Ark.) Pub. Schs., 1953-72; real estate salesman Continental Real Estate, Downers Grove, Ill., 1972-74; phys. edn. instr. Triton Coll., River Grove, Ill., 1973-74; substitute tchr. DuPage and Kane County Schs., Ill., 1972-74; phys. edn. tchr. Wheeling (Ill.) Sch. Dist. 21, 1974-91. Tennis coach El Dorado Pub. Schs., 1953-73; tennis pro El Dorado Racquet Club, City of El Dorado, summers 1965-72. Contbr. articles to profl. jours. Pres. Ark. Sq. Dance Fedn., Little Rock, 1971-72, Progressive Sunday Sch., El Dorado, 1994—. Recipient All Star Coaches Clinic award Ark. H.S. Coaches Assn., 1971. Mem. NEA, AAHPERD (pres. 1969-70, State Honor award 1972), Ark. Assn. Health, Phys. Edn., Recreation and Dance (life), Ill. Assn. Health, Phys. Edn., Recreation and Dance (Quarter Century award 1981, Svc. award 1991), U.S. Tennis Assn., Order Eastern Star, Delta Phi Kappa. Methodist. Avocations: league tennis, swimming. Home: PO Box 641 1415 Huttig Hwy Strong AR 71765-9783

NUNZ, GREGORY JOSEPH, aerospace engineer, program manager, educator, entrepreneur; b. Batavia, N.Y., May 28, 1934; s. Sylvester Joseph and Elizabeth Marie (Loesell) N.; m. Georgia Monyea Costas, Mar. 30, 1958; children: Karen, John, Rebecca, Deirdre, Jaimie, Marta. BSChemE, Cooper Union, 1955; postgrad., U. So. Calif., Calif. State U.; MS in Applied Math., Columbia Pacific U., 1991, PhD in Mgmt. Sci., 1993. Adv. design staff, propulsion mgr. U.K. project Rocketdyne div. Rockwell, Canoga Park, Calif., 1955-65; mem. tech. staff Aerospace Corp., El Segundo, Calif., 1965-70; mem. tech. staff propulsion div. Jet Propulsion Lab., Pasadena, Calif., 1970-72; chief. monoprop. engring. Bell Aerospace Corp., Buffalo, N.Y., 1972-74; group supr. comb. devices Jet Propulsion Lab., Pasadena, 1974-76; dep. group leader, asst. div. leader, program mgr. internat. HDR geothermal energy program, program mgr. space-related projects Los Alamos (N.Mex.) Nat. Lab., 1977—. Assoc. prof. electronics L.A. Pierce Coll., Woodland Hills, Calif., 1961-72; instr. No. N.Mex. C. C., Los Alamos, 1978-80, div. head scis., 1980-92; adj. prof. math. U. N.Mex., Los Alamos, 1980—; sr. mgmt. rep. Excel Telecom., Inc., 1995-98; ptnr. JRB Rsch., 2000—. Author: Electronics Lab Manual I, 1964, Electronics in Our World, 1972; co-author: Electronics Mathematics, vol. I, II, 1967, Imotep to Khufu: How It Can Be Done, 2001; contbg. author Prentice-Hall Textbook of Cosmetology, 1975, Alternative Energy Sources VII, 1987; contbr. articles to profl. jours.; inventor smallest catalytic liquid N2H4 rocket thrustor, co-inventor first monoprop/biprop bimodal rocket engine, tech. advisor internat. multi-prize winning documentary film One With the Earth. Mem. Aerial Phenomena Research Orgn., L.A., 1975. Fellow AIAA (assoc., liquid propellants com. on stds.); mem. Arista, Math. Assn. Am. Avocations: travel, archaeology, foreign languages, golf. Office: Los Alamos Nat Lab PO Box 1663 Los Alamos NM 87545-0001 also: U NMex Los Alamos Br 4000 University Dr Los Alamos NM 87544-2233 E-mail: gnunz@lanl.gov.

NUSS, SHIRLEY ANN, computer coordinator, educator; b. Madison, Minn., Oct. 22, 1946; d. Woodland Henry and Aileen Thelma (Mattox) Cover; divorced; 1 child, Melissa Ann. BEd, Trinity U., Washburn U., 1969; MA, Mich. State U., 1982, PhD, 1990. 3d grade tchr. Topeka Pub. Schs. System, 1969-70; 6th grade tchr. McCune (Kans.) Middle Sch., 1970-72; 7th grade English tchr. Muskego (Wis.) Norway Sch. Dist., 1972-78; intermediate level. tchr. Gibson Sch. for Gifted Children, Redford, Mich., 1979-82; 3d grade tchr. Cranbrook Edn. Community, Bloomfield Hills, Mich., 1982-89, multi media/computer coord., instr., 1989—. Adj. prof. ednl. tech. cert. program and master's degree in tech. edn. Mich. State U., 2000-01. tchr. Space Pioneer Learning Adventure design camp, 2003; ednl. adv. bd. Henry Ford Mus. and Greenfield Village, Dearborn, 1988-91; Renaissance Outreach for Detroit Area Schs; task force Mich. Coun. for the Humanities, Lansing, 1991-92; speaker, presenter on tech. Mich. Sci. Tchr. Assn., Lansing, 1992-96, Mich. Assn. Computer Users in Learning, Ind. Sch. Assn. Ctrl. States; tchr. adv. bd. Teaching and Computer Magazine, 1988-90; developer grades 1-5 multimedia/computer curriculum Brookside Sch., Cranbrook, 1995-96. Author: (museum activities) Henry Ford Museum, Greenfield Village, 1991. Space camp fellowship Mary Bramson award Huntsville, Ala., 1992; Detroit Edison Conservation grantee Detroit Edison, 1992, ROADS Mimi grant Mich. Coun. for Humanities, Lansing, 1993. Mem. Cranbrook Schs. Faculty Coun. (pres., v.p. 1993-95). Republican. Presbyterian. Avocations: antique collecting, reading, gardening, computers and technology. Home: 1715 Shankin Dr Walled Lake MI 48390-2446 Office: Cranbrook Schs Brookside 550 Cranbrook Rd # 801 Bloomfield Hills MI 48301 E-mail: snuss@cranbrook.edu., drnuss@aol.com.

NUSSBAUM, LEO LESTER, retired college president, consultant; b. Berne, Ind., June 27, 1918; s. Samuel D. and Margaret (Mazelin) N.; m. Janet Nell Gladfelter, Nov. 25, 1942; children: Felicity Ann, Luther James, Margaret Sue. BS, Ball State U., 1942, MA, 1949; PhD, Northwestern U., 1952; postgrad., U. Mich., 1963. Tchr. Monmouth H.S., Decatur, Ind., 1946-48; dean men, asst. prof. bus. Huntington (Ind.) Coll., (Ind.), 1948-51; dean coll. liberal arts, assoc. prof. edn. and psychology U. Dubuque, Iowa, 1952-60; dean coll., prof. edn. and psychology Austin Coll., 1960-67; dean coll., prof. psychology Coe Coll., 1967-82, pres., 1970-82, pres. emeritus, 1982—; dir. Acad. Sr. Profls. Eckerd Coll., 1983-87; dir. PEL-ASPEC Project, 1988-95; coord. faculty ASPEC Colleagues, St. Petersburg, 1992-97. Cons. pvt. practice St. Petersburg, Fla., 1982—; Fulbright lectr. U. Mysore, India, 1958-59; cons., evaluator So. Assn. Colls. and Schs., Atlanta, 1963-67, North Cen. Assn. Colls. and Schs., 1959-60, 67-82, dir. I.E. Industries and Iowa Electric Light and Power Co., Cedar Rapids, 1982-91, dir. emeritus, 1991-92. Contbr. articles to profl. jours. Bd. dirs. Cedar Rapids Symphony, 1968-70; mem. cabinet Cedar Rapids United Way, 1980-82; elder Presbyn. Ch., moderator Presbytery of S.W. Fla., 1989. Sgt. U.S. Army, 1942-46. Recipient Disting. Alumnus award Ball State U., 1976, Alumni Merit award Northwestern U., 1977. Mem. Assn. Colls. Midwest (chmn. 1975-77), Iowa Assn. Ind. Colls. and Univs. (chmn. 1976-77), Danforth Assocs., Rotary (Cedar Rapids pres. 1975-76), Phi Delta Kappa, Blue Key, Pi Gamma Mu Home: 6909 9th St S Apt 336 Saint Petersburg FL 33705-6207 E-mail: cnussbau@tampabay.ar.com.

NUSSENBAUM, SIEGFRIED FRED, chemistry educator; b. Vienna, Nov. 21, 1919; came to U.S., 1939; s. Marcus and Susan Sara (Rothenberg) N.; m. Celia Womark, Feb. 20, 1951; children; Deborah M., Evelyn R. BS in Chemistry, U. Calif., Berkeley, 1941, MS in Food Tech., 1948, PhD in Comparative Biochemistry, 1951. Analytical chemist Panam. Engring. Co., Berkeley, 1942-43; asst. chief chemist Manganese Ore Co., Las Vegas, 1943-45; rsch. assoc. U. Calif., Berkeley, 1951-52, dir. master clin. lab. sci. program San Francisco, 1969-87; from instr. to prof. Calif. State U., Sacramento, 1952-90, chair dept. chemistry, 1958-65. Cons. biochemist Sacramento County Hosp., 1958-70; lectr. U. Calif. Davis Med. Ctr., 1970-93, guest lectr., 1993-95. Author: Organic Chem-Principles and Applications, 1963; contbr. articles to profl. jours. Sgt. U.S. Army, 1945-47. Fellow AAAS; mem. Am. Chem. Soc., Am. Assn. Clin. Chemistry (Outstanding Contbn. in Edn. award no. sect. 1991), Nat. Acad. Clin. Biochemistry. Achievements include research in pectic enzymes, mechanism of amylopectin formation and differentiation from amylose, phenotyping of lipemias. Home: 2900 Latham Dr Sacramento CA 95864-5644

NUSZ, PHYLLIS JANE, not-for-profit fundraiser, consultant, educational consultant; b. Lodi, Calif., Dec. 16, 1941; d. Fred Henry and Esther Emma (Enzminger) Nusz. BA, U. Pacific, 1963, MA, 1965; EdD, Nova Southeastern U., 1987. Cert. fund raising exec. Prof. speech comm. Bakersfield (Calif.) Coll., 1965-86; from asst. dir. student activites to found. exec. dir. Bakersfield (Calif) Coll., 1965-86; mgmt. seminar dir. Delta Kappa Gamma Soc. Internat., Austin, 1983-86; loaned exec. United Way San Joaquin County, Stockton, Calif., 1990; fundraising and edn. cons. PJ Enterprises, Lodi, 1987—. Bd. dirs. U. Calif. Sch. Medicine Surg. Found., San Francisco, 1989—92; mem. Heritage Cir. and Chancellor's Assn. U. Calif., San Francisco, 1987—. Recipient Archives award of merit, Evang. Luth Ch. Am., 1988; fellow, Calif. Luth. U., 1985—. Mem.: NEA, Nat. Assn. Parliamentarians, Nat. Soc. Fund Raising Execs. (bd. dir. 1988—91, chmn. mentor program Calif. Capital chpt. 1991, chmn. acad. fund raising 1991, chmn. mentor program Golden Gate chpt. 1991, founding pres. San Joaquin chpt. 1992—93, Pres.'s award for Meritorious Svc., Golden Gate chpt. 1991), Rotary Internat. (North Stockton bd. dir. 1993—99, treas. 1994—96, pres.-elect 1996—97, pres. 1997—98, dist. 5220 membership devel. com. 1997—98, immediate past pres. 1998—99, membership task force 1998—99, dist. membership chmn. 1999—2000, dist. gov. elect 2000—01, dist. gov. 2001—02, mem. Internat. Afghan refugee relief com. 2001—02, Zone 24 avoidable blindness task force 2002—03, Zone 24 RI Convention Promotion Coun. 2002—03, Zone 23 & 24 leadership devel. task force 2002—04, chair Zone Inst. Prog. 2003, nat. adv. TRF Permanent Fund 2003—, internat. coord. 2003, Internat. Poverty Task Force 2003—04, chmn. Far West PETS 2004, coord. zone 24, multiple Paul Harris fellow, RI Found. Bequest Soc., RI Found. major donor benefactor), U. Pacific Alumni Assn. (bd. dir. 1974—82), Delta Kappa Gamma (chpt. pres. 1976—78, Chi State parliamentarian 1979—81, chair Internat. Golden Gift Fund 1982—86, sec. 1985—87). Republican. Lutheran. Avocations: photography, travel, swimming, walking, fishing. Office: PJ Enterprises 1300 W Lodi Ave Ste A11 Lodi CA 95242-3000 E-mail: pjnursz@aol.com.

NUTTER, JAMES RANDALL, management educator; b. Stephenville, Tex., Nov. 11, 1945; s. Coleman Evan and Mary Frances (Jay) N.; m. Marilyn Grace Marotta, Aug. 23, 1969; children: Heather Elizabeth, Susan Mary, Katherine Grace. BS, No. Ill. U., 1968, MEd, 1969; DSc, Nova U., 1991; DBA, Nova S.E. U., 1995. Tchr. social studies Hinsdale (Ill.) South H.S., 1968-69, Govt. U.S. V.I., St. Thomas, 1969-71; dir. employee rels. Shuron divsn. Textron Corp., Rochester, N.Y., 1971-73; dir. corp. tng. Sybron Corp., Rochester, 1973-75; dir. human resources Red Wing Co., Fredonia, N.Y., 1975-82; assoc. prof., dept. chair Liberty U., Lynchburg, Va., 1982-92; prof., chair bus. dept., dir. grad. bus. studies Geneva Coll., Beaver Falls, Pa., 1992—. Pres. Nutter/Forbus Group, Inc., Lynchburg, 1982-92; bd. dirs. Lynchburg Preheater Inc.; commr. Assn. Collegiate Bus. Schs. and Programs, 1998—; mem. acad. adv. coun. Pacific Inst. for Bus. Mgmt.; vis. prof. Peoples Republic of China Fgn. Experts Bur., N.W. Nazarene U. MBA Mex. Program. Mem. Am. Mgmt. Assn., Soc. Strategic Mgmt., Acad. Mgmt., Soc. Human Resource Mgmt. (faculty advisor 1972—), Christian Bus. Faculty Assn., Assn. Collegiate Bus. Schs. and Programs (nat. chair 2002-03, bd. dirs. 2002—). Republican. Avocations: fishing, travel, reading. Home: 108 Dana Dr Monaca PA 15061-2871 E-mail: jrn@geneva.edu.

NUTTER, JUNE ANN KNIGHT, exercise physiologist, educator; b. Des Moines, Iowa, Jan. 22, 1947; d. Joseph Willard and Jean Roena (Eyestone) Knight; m. Lester Albert Nutter, Aug. 25, 1968; children: Melissa Ann, Jacqueline Christine. BS in Phys. Edn. with distinction, U. Okla., 1969; MA in Exercise Sci., U. Nebr., 1982, PhD in Exercise Physiology, 1987. Exercise test technologist. Tchr. phys. edn. Douglas Sch. Sys., Ellsworth AFB, SD, 1979-80; grad. tchg. asst. U. Nebr., Omaha and Lincoln, 1980-82, 83-85; intern St. Joseph's Hosp., Omaha, 1985; instr. Denver Tech. Coll., Colo. Springs, Colo., 1988, Chapman Coll., Colo. Springs, 1987-88; asst. prof. Wake Forest U., Winston-Salem, NC, 1988-89; asst. prof., coord. exercise sci. program R.I. Coll., Providence, 1989—. Cons. R.I. Dept. Edn., Providence, 1990, Measurement, Inc., Durham, N.C., 1990, Warwick (R.I.) Pub. Schs., 1996-97; book reviewer Simon & Schuster, 1991, WCB/McGraw-Hill, 1997; mem. R.I. Govs. Coun. on Health and Phys. Fitness, 1992-95. Contbr. articles to profl. jours. Com. chmn. Family Svcs., Ellsworth AFB, 1978-79. Recipient Inspiration award Nat. Assn. for Sport and Phys. Edn.; grantee U. Nebr., 1982, 86, NIH, 1986, RI Coll., 1990. Mem. AAHPERD, Am. Coll. Sports Medicine, R.I. Assn. for Health, Phys. Edn., Recreation and Dance (Presdl. citation award), Nat. Strenght & Conditioning Assn.

NUTTING, KATHLEEN S. elementary education educator; b. Enid, Okla., May 18, 1948; d. Johnie and Esther L. (Schweer) Mittelstet; m. Francis L. Nutting, Mar. 7, 1981; children: Sara Kathleen, Gina Lynn, Lisa Kristine. BS, Okla. State U., 1970; MA, Phillips U., 1980, Colo. U., 1985; postgrad., U. Denver, 1986. Cert. elem. tchr., elem. adminstr. From elem. tchr. to prin. Jefferson County Schs., Golden, Colo., 1972—95, prin., 1995—98; program dir. Regis U., Denver, 1998—. Mem. Nat. Staff Devel. Coun. Mem. ASCD, Internat. Reading Assn., Phi Delta Kappa. Home: 13888 W 59th Pl Arvada CO 80004-3748

NUWER, HENRY JOSEPH (HANK NUWER), journalist, educator; b. Buffalo, Aug. 19, 1946; s. Henry Robert and Teresa (Lysiak) N.; m. Alice May (Cerniglia), Dec. 28, 1968 (div. Mar. 1980); 1 child, Henry Christian; m. Jenine (Howard), Apr. 9, 1982 (sep. 2003); 1 child, Adam. BS English, State Univ. Coll. of N.Y., Buffalo, 1968; MA English, Highlands U., N. Mex., 1971; PhD equivalency, Ball State U., Muncie, Ind., 2002—. Freelance author; journalist, 1969—; asst. prof. Clemson Univ., SC, 1982-83; assoc. prof. Ball State Univ., Muncie, Ind., 1985-89; sr. editor Rodale Press, Emmaus, Pa., 1990-91; editor in chief Arts Ind. Mag., Indpls., 1993-95; assoc. prof. journalism U. Richmond, Va., 1995-97. Hazing (expert lectr.), 1990—; hazing cons. NBC Movie-of-the-Week, Moment of Truth: Broken Pledges, Indpls., 1994; adj. prof. journalism Ind. U. Sch. Journalism, Indpls., 1995—; Anderson U., 1998-2002; asst. prof. journalism, Franklin Ind. Coll., 2002--; nat. advisor NCAA study and survey on hazing in coll. athletic groups Alfred U., 1999; hazing cons. U.S. Dept. Edn., 2002--. Author: Steroids, 1990; Broken Pledges: The Deadly Rite of Hazing, 1990; How to Write Like an Expert, 1995; The Legend of Jesse Owens, 1998; Wrongs of Passage, 1999, revised edit., 2002; High School

Hazing, 2000; To the Young Writer, 2002; The Hazing Reader, 2003; mem. editl. staff Chic Mag., 1976-77; contbg. articles to profl. jour. Grantee: Nat. Endowment for the Arts, 1976; Idaho Humanities Coun., 1985; Gannett Found., 1988; named New Mag. Adviser of Yr., Coll. Media Advisers, 1988; Disting. Alumnus, Buffalo State Coll., 1999. Mem. Soc. Profl. Journalists;(3d. pl.) Best Bus. Article, Ind. competion 2002; Investigative Reporters and Editors; Soc. Profl. Journalism. Democrat. Roman Catholic. Office: Franklin Coll Journalism Dept 501 E Monroe St Franklin IN 46131-2598 also: Ind Univ Sch Journalism 902 W New York St ES 4104 Indianapolis IN 46202 E-mail: hnuwer@hanknuwer.com.

NWAGBARA, CHIBU ISAAC, industrial designer, consultant; b. Umuahia, Abia, Nigeria, Apr. 24, 1957; s. Marcus and Catherine (Onyemairo) N.; m. Chioma Adamma Ariwodo, Apr. 26, 1997; children: Obinna Alex, Amara Joy. BS, No. Ill. U., 1984, MS, 1986, Purdue U., 1990, PhD, 1993. Cert. indsl. technologist. Tech. mgr. 3M Internat., Lagos, Nigeria, 1977-80; founder, pres. ChiMarc Assocs., DeKalb, Ill., 1981-84; rsch. asst. No. Ill. U., DeKalb, Ill., 1985-86; assoc. editor Purdue U., West Lafayette, Ind., 1987-89, rsch. assoc., 1990-91, grad. lectr., 1990-93; cons. Arthur Andersen & Co., St. Charles, Ill., 1993-95; program mgr. Allen-Bradley Co., Milw., 1995-96; project mgr. BellSouth Telecom. Inc., Atlanta, 1997—. Cons. Arnett Clinic, Lafayette, 1992-93, Chimarc Assocs., DeKalb, 1986—, GoldMark Ltd., Lagos, 1985-90. Coord. community outreach program Purdue U. Afro-Am. Studies and Rsch. Ctr., West Lafayette, 1990-91; coach Am. Youth Soccer Orgn., West Lafayette, 1987-90. Named one of Outstanding Young Men of Am., 1989, Men of Achievement, 1995. Mem. Inst. Indsl. Engrs., Am. Soc. for Quality Control, Am. Edn. Rsch. Assn., Nat. Assn. Indsl. Tech., Internat. Soc. for Performance and Instrn., World Future Soc. Methodist. Avocations: enjoys travel, reading, meeting people, music, sports. Office: BellSouth Telecom Inc 675 W Peachtree St NW Atlanta GA 30375-0001 Home: Apt 1008 1435 Boggs Rd Duluth GA 30096-9002

NWAGBARAOCHA, JOEL ONUKWUGHA, academic administrator, educator; b. Victoria, Cameroons, Nov. 21, 1942; came to U.S., 1964; naturalized, 1974; s. John O. and Christiana (Ihejeihu) N.; m. Patsy Coleman, Aug. 27, 1977; children: Jason, Jonathan, John, Eric. BS in Math., cert. in physics, Norfolk State U., 1969; EdM, Harvard U., 1970, EdD (Univ. fellow), 1972. Tchr. math. and physics Emmanuel Coll., Owerri, Nigeria, 1960-64; asst. dir. Manpower Rsch. Inst./Norfolk (Va.) State Coll., 1969-70; rsch. assoc. Harvard U. Grad. Sch. Edn., 1969-72; assoc. dir. co-op acad. planning program Inst. for Svcs. to Edn., Washington, 1972-74, dir. instnl. planning and mgmt. program, 1974-76, dir. divsn. acad. planning and faculty devel., 1976-78; assoc. prof. edn., v.p. planning and ops. analysis Morgan State U., Balt., 1978-87; v.p. acad. affairs Voorhees Coll., Denmark, S.C., 1987-80; pres. Barber-Scotia Coll., Concord, N.C., 1990-94; prof. edn., bus. adminstrn. Strayer U., Washingtn, 1994—, dir. grad. studies, 2000—. Dean Tacoma Park Campus, Strayer Coll., Washington; cons. in higher edn. planning and evaluation system devel., 1972—. Co-author: Operational Manual for ollege Planning Development, 1977, Planning Management and Evaluation System, 1979; mem. editl. bd. Spartan Echo, 1967-69; contbr. articles to profl. jours. Mem. AAAS, Am. Coun. on Edn., Nat. Coun. on Social Studies, Am. Assn. for Higher Edn., Am. Humanist Assn., Soc. for Coll. and Univ. Planning, Am. Assn. Univ. Adminstrs., Am. Mgmt. Assn., Higher Edn. Group of Washington, Smithsonian Nat. Assoc., Alpha Kappa Mu, Phi Beta Sigma, Beta Kappa Chi, Phi Delta Kappa. Home: 10928 Battersea Ln Columbia MD 21044-2701 Office: Strayer Univ Washington DC Campus 1025 15th St NW Washington DC 20005-2601

NWANGWU, JOHN TOCHUKWU, epidemiologist, public health educator; b. Ogidi, Anambra, Nigeria, Apr. 16, 1952; came to U.S., 1973; s. Sidney N. and Phoebe Nwangwu; m. Chioma Ugonwa Nwokolo, Sept. 3, 1988; children: Nmadinobi, Tobenna, Kamsiyo. MB, U. Nebr., Omaha, 1979; MPH, Loma Linda U., 1981; PhD, Columbia U., 1988; postgrad., Erasmus U., Rotterdam, The Netherlands, 1991. Cons. WHO, 1982-87; instr. Columbia U., N.Y.C., 1983-85, St. Joseph's Coll. Hosp., Bklyn., 1986-88; asst. prof. SUNY, 1988-89; chief epidemiologist Kern County Health Dept., Bakersfield, Calif., 1989-90, dir. epidemiology and data mgmt., 1990; assoc. prof. pub. health Conn. State U., New Haven, 1991-95, prof. pub. health, 1995—. Vis. prof. Calif. State U., Bakersfield, 1990, Yale U., New Haven, 1992, adj. prof. epidemiology Sch. Medicine, 1995—; epidemiologist/rsch. affiliate faculty Yale U. Sch. Medicine, 1993—; cons. Hosp. of St. Raphael, New Haven, 1995—; cons. to fgn. countries, 1982—; presenter in field; adj. prof. cmty. medicine Sch. Medicine U. Conn., 1995—; vis. prof. Harvard Sch. Pub. Health, 1998; vis. scholar Dana-Farber Cancer Inst., Harvard U., Boston; cons. in infectious disease VA Hosp., Rocky Hill, Conn., 1998. Contbr. articles to profl. publs. Erasmus U. fellow, 1991. Fellow Royal Soc. Medicine, Am. Coll. Epidemiology; mem. APHA, Internat. Epidemiol. Assn., N.Y. Acad. Scis., Assn. Tchrs. Preventive Medicine. Avocations: badminton, squash, reading. Home: 898 Greenway Rd Woodbridge CT 06525-2413 Office: Conn State U Dept Pub Health 144 Farnham Ave Dept Pub New Haven CT 06515-1202 also: Yale U Sch Medicine Dept Epidemiology and Pub Health 60 College St New Haven CT 06510-3210 E-mail: Nwangwu@scsu.ctstateu.edu.

NWEKE, WINIFRED CHINWENDU, education educator; b. Ogbunike, Anambra, Nigeria, Dec. 8, 1947; came to U.S., 1980; d. Gabriel Abanobi and Grace Nonyem (Ezeani) Ejeckam; m. Ernest Ekeneme Nweke, Oct. 25, 1980; children: Jennifer, Jeffrey, Nkiruka, Chukwuma. BSc in Edn., U. Nigeria, 1974; MA, U. Ottawa, Ont., Can., 1977; PhD, U. Ottawa, 1980; MBA, Ea. Mich. U., 1984. Tchr. high sch. Govt. Coll., Ikorodu, Lagos, Nigeria, 1974-75; fed. edn. officer Women Tchrs' Coll., Aba, Nigeria, 1975-76; lectr. II U. Benin, Benin City, Nigeria, 1980; postdoctoral fellow U. Mich., Ann Arbor, 1984-85; asst. prof. Tuskegee (Ala.) U., 1987-89, assoc. prof., 1989-97; coord. for rsch. Ga. Profl. Standards Commn., Atlanta, 1997—. Author book and chpts. in books; contbr. articles to profl. jours. Mem. tech. adv. bd. State of Ala. Dept. Edn., Montgomery, 1991-97; measurement and evaluation specialist Al Consortium for Minority Tchr. Edn., Tuskegee, Ala., 1989-94; fund raiser Girl Scouts Am., Auburn, 1992-93. Faculty fellow U. Ottawa, 1978-79; Dept. Def. Dep. Schs. grantee, 1990-92. Mem. Am. Ednl. Rsch. Assn., Nat. Coun. Measurement in Edn., Midsouth Edn. Rsch. Assn. (membership com. 1990, program com. 1995), Phi Delta Kappa. Episcopalian. Avocations: photography, reading. Office: Ga Profl Standards Commn Two Peachtree St Ste 6000 Atlanta GA 30303 E-mail: winifred.nweke@gapsc.com.

NWOFOR, AMBROSE ONYEGBULE, vocational assessment evaluator; b. Amandugba, Nigeria, Dec. 7, 1947; came to the U.S., 1975; s. Wewe Ogbuihe and Nwanyi-Ihuoma (Olujie) N.; m. Clara Chinyere, June 14, 1975; children: Chiugo, Chiedoziem, Uzonna, Nnanaka, Ozioma. Diploma in elec. engring., Inst. Mgmt. & Tech. Engring., Enugu, Nigeria, 1973; BS in Electronics, Norfolk State U., 1977; MS in Ind. Tech., Ea. Mich. U., 1978; MEd in Ednl. Adminstrn., Ariz. State U., 1980. Electronic engr. Geoservices (Nigeria) Ltd., Nigeria, 1973-74, Taylor Electronics, Ariz., 1979-80; internat. svcs. engr. Dowell Schlumberger Overseas, Brazil, 1981-82; engring. lab. dir. U. Port Harcourt, Nigeria, 1982-83; sr. rsch. fellow, computer cons. Fed. U. Tech., Nigeria, 1983-89; pvt. specialist N.Y., 1989-91; elec. vocat. tchr. N.Y. Bd. Edn., 1991-93, vocat. assessment evaluator, 1993—. H.S. bd. mem. Amandugba Tech. Sch., Nigeria, 1984-88; pvt. vocat. assessment cons., 1989—. Inventor in field. Active Amandugba (Nigeria) Alms, 1973—, Amandugba (Nigeria) Dynamic Front, 1987—; chmn. Amandugba (Nigeria) Water Project, 1982-89; pres. Amandugba Fed. Union, Inc., 1992—. Mem. IEEE, Am. Vocat. Assn., Soc. Mfg. Engrs., Nat. Tech. Assn., Sci. Assn. Nigeria, N.Y. State Occupl. Assn. Roman Catholic. Avocation: video recording. Home: 702 Sturgis Pl Baltimore MD 21208-5840

NYE, DANIEL WILLIAM, retired elementary school educator; b. Harrisburg, Pa., Apr. 14, 1942; s. Daniel J. and Clarice L. (Stonesifer) N.; m. Carol A. Stewart, Aug. 10, 1968; 1 child, Michael S. BS in Health Edn., West Chester (Pa.) U., 1964; MEd in Elem. Edn., Towson (Md.) U., 1970. Cert. tchr., Md. Tchr. phys. edn. elem. sch. Harford County Pub. Schs., Bel Air, Md., 1964-72, tchr. phys. edn. mid. sch., 1972-73, tchr. phys. edn. elem. sch., 1974-2000, ret., 2000. Rep. United Rep. Life Ins. Co., Harrisburg, Pa., 1981-85. Mem. AAHPERD, NEA, Md. State Tchrs. Assn., Harford County Edn. Assn., Md. AAHPERD, Harford County Ret. Sch. Personnel Assn. Republican. Avocations: avid golfer, antique car collector and restorer, stamp collector. Home: 1119 Carrs Mill Rd Bel Air MD 21014-2414 Office: Harford County Pub Schs 45 E Gordon St Bel Air MD 21014-2915

NYE, ERIC WILLIAM, English language and literature educator; b. Omaha, July 31, 1952; s. William Frank and Mary Roberta (Lueder) N.; m. Carol Denison Frost, Dec. 21, 1980; children: Charles William, Ellen Mary. BA, St. Olaf Coll., 1974; MA, U. Chgo., 1976, PhD, 1983; postgrad., Queens' Coll., Cambridge, England, 1979-82. Tutor in coll. writing com. U. Chgo., 1976-79, tchg. intern, 1978; tutor Am. lit. Cambridge (Eng.) U., 1979-82; asst. prof. English and religious studies U. Wyo., Laramie, 1983-89, assoc. prof., 1989—, dir. English honors program, 1985—89, 1992—93, 2002—. V.p., bd. dirs. Plainview Tel. Co., Nebr.; hon. vis. fellow U. Edinburgh (Scotland) Inst. for Advanced Studies in the Humanities, 1987; guest lectr. NEH summer Inst., Laramie, Wyo., 1985, Carlyle Soc. of Edinburgh, 1987, Wordsworth summer Conf., Grasmere, Eng., 1988, cons. NEH. Contbr. articles and reviews to profl. jours. Mem. Am. Friends of Cambridge U., Friends of Cambridge U. Libr. (life), Gen. Soc. Mayflower Descendants; elected mem. Wyo. Coun. for Humanities, 1992-96, mem. exec. com., 1993-94; mem. adv. bd. Wyo. Ctr. for the Book, 1995—; mem. Peripatetics, 1989-, leader Boy Scouts Am. Named Nat. Merit Scholar St. Olaf Coll., 1970-74; recipient Amb. Fellowship, Rotary Found., 1979-80, grant Am. Coun. of Learned Socs., 1988, Disting. Alumnus award, Lincoln (Neb.) E. High Sch., 1986. Mem.: MLA (del. assembly 1991—93), Bibliog. Soc. London (hon. sec.-treas. for N.Am. 2002—), Soc. History of Authorship, Reading, and Pub., Assn. Lit. and Linguistic Computing, Assn. Computers and the Humanities, Assn. Literary Scholars and Critics (life), Queens' Coll. Club (Cambridge), Wyo. State Hist. Soc. (life), Jane Austen Soc. N.Am. (life), Coleridge Soc. (life), Friends of Dove Cottage (life), Carlyle Soc. (life), Tennyson Soc. (life), Penn Club (London), Royal Oak Found., Charles Lamb Soc., The Victorian Inst., Phi Beta Kappa (pres., v.p., sec. Wyo. chpt. 1988—). Home: 1495 Apache Dr Laramie WY 82072-6966 Office: U Wyo Dept English PO Box 3353 Laramie WY 82071-3353

NYE, REBA RHODES, science and home economics educator; b. Orange, Va., Jan. 16, 1921; d. Roscoe Edward and mattie Gertrude (Ruckman) Rhodes; m. William Lyman Nye, June 2, 1946; children: Thomas Lyman, Gertrude Ellen. BS in Home Econs., W.Va. U., 1943; postgrad., Temple U., 1948-49. Cert. secondary tchr., W.Va., Calif. Tchr. Greenbrier County Ssch., Williamsburg, W.Va., 1943-45; farm home supr. U.S. Govt., Princeton, W.Va., 1945-46; home economist Pierce Phelps Co., Phila., 1947-50; tchr. Mountain View (Calif.) Sch. Dist., 1963-81. Moderator and other offices Presbyn. Women, Los Altos, Calif., 1983-95; pres., bd. dirs. Sr. Coordinating Coun., Los Altos, 1990-97. Recipient Vol. award Mayor of Los Altos, 1994. Mem. AAUW (bd. dirs. 1978-85), Calif. Ret. Tchrs. Assn. (pres. and other offices 1981—, Area IV chmn. resources, Pres.'s award 1990-92), Fedn. Women (bd. dirs., v.p., 1993-96), Phi Upsilon Omicron (pres. 1942-43). Democrat. Avocations: quilting, gardening, volunteer work, skiing, fishing. Home: 364 Alicia Way Los Altos CA 94022-2348

NYENHUIS, JACOB EUGENE, college official; b. Mille Lacs County, Minn., Mar. 25, 1935; s. Egbert Peter and Rosa (Walburg) N.; m. Leona Mae Van Duyn, June 6, 1956; children: Karen Joy, Kathy Jean, Lorna Jane, Sarah Van Duyn. AB in Greek, Calvin Coll., 1956; AM in Classics, Stanford U., 1961, PhD in Classics, 1963; LittD (hon.), Hope Coll., 2001. Asst. in classical langs. Calvin Coll., Grand Rapids, Mich., 1957-59; acting instr. Stanford (Calif.) U., 1962; from asst. prof. to prof. Wayne State U., Detroit, 1962-75, dir. honors program, 1964-75, chmn. Greek and Latin dept., 1965-75; prof. classics, dean for humanities Hope Coll., Holland, Mich., 1975-78, dean for arts and humanities, 1978-84, provost, 1984—2001, prof. and provost emeritus, 2001—; sr. rsch. fellow A.C. Van Raalte Inst., 2001—02, dir., 2002—. Cons. Mich. Dept. Edn., Lansing, 1971-72, Gustavus Adolphus Coll., St. Peter, Minn., 1974, Northwestern Coll., Orange City, Iowa, 1983, Whitworth Coll., Spokane, Wash., 1987, The Daedalus Project, 1988, Albion Coll., 2002-03, Kalamazoo Coll., 2003-4; reviewer NEH, Washington, 1986-87, panelist, 1991; reviewer Lilly Endowment, Indpls., 1987-89, U.S. Dept. Edn., 1993, Mich. Humanities Coun., 1999-2001; vis. assoc. prof. U. Calif., Santa Barbara, 1967-68, Ohio State U., Columbus, 1972; vis. rsch. prof. Am. Sch. Classical Studies, Athens, Greece, 1973-74, mng. com.; vis. scholar Green Coll. Oxford U., 1989; mem. edit. adv. bd. Christianity and The Arts, 1998, chmn., 1999-2001. Co-author: Latin Via Ovid, 1977, rev. edit., 1982, A Dream Fulfilled: The Van Raalte Sculpture in Centennial Park, 1997; editor: Petronius: Cena Trimalchionis, 1970, Plautus: Amphitruo, 1970; author: Centennial History of 14th Street Christian Reformed Church, Holland, Michigan, 2002, Myth and the Creative Process: Michael Ayrton and the Myth of Daedalus, the Maze Maker, 2003; contbr. articles to profl. jours. Elder Christian Ref. Ch., Palo Alto, Calif., 1960—62, elder, clk. Grosse Pointe, Mich., 1964—67, Holland, Mich., 1976—85, v.p., 1988—91, exec. com., 1994—95; trustee Calvin Theol. Sem., 2001—, mem. exec. com., 2002—, v.p., 2003; chmn. human rels. coun. Open Housing Com., Grosse Pointe, 1971—73. Mem. Am. Philol. Assn., Danforth Assocs. (chmn. regional com. 1975-77), Mich. Coun. for Humanities (bd. dirs., 1976-84, 88-92, 96-99, chmn. 1980-82, Disting. Svc. award 1984), Nat. Fedn. State Humanities Couns. (bd. dirs. 1979-84, pres. 1981-83), Gt. Lakes Colls. Assn. (bd. dirs. 1991-93), Coun. on Undergrad. Rsch. (councilor-at-large 1993-99), Green Coll. Soc., Mortar Board, Phi Beta Kappa, Eta Sigma Phi. Democrat. Avocations: photography, carpentry. Office: Hope Coll Van Raalte Inst PO Box 9000 Holland MI 49422-9000 E-mail: nyenhuis@hope.edu.

NYHUS, LLOYD MILTON, surgeon, educator; b. Mt. Vernon, Wash., June 24, 1923; s. Lewis Guttorm and Mary (Shervem) N.; m. Margaret Goldie Sheldon, Nov. 25, 1949; children: Sheila Margaret, Leif Torger. BS, Pacific Luth. Coll., 1945; MD, Med. Coll. Ala., 1947; Doctor honoris causa, Aristotelian U., Thessalonika, Greece, 1968, Uppsala U., Sweden, 1974, U. Chihuahua, Mex., 1975, Jagallonian U., Cracow, Poland, 1980, U. Gama Filho, Rio de Janeiro, 1983, U. Louis Pasteur, Strasbourg, France, 1984, U. Athens, 1989. Diplomate Am. Bd. Surgery (chmn. 1974-76). Intern King County Hosp., Seattle, 1947-48, resident in surgery, 1948-55; practice medicine specializing in surgery Seattle, 1956-67, Chgo., 1967—; instr. surgery U. Wash., Seattle, 1954-56, asst. prof., 1956-59, assoc. prof., 1959-64, prof., 1964-67; Warren H. Cole prof., head dept. surgery U. Ill. Coll. Medicine, 1967-89, emeritus head, 1989—, prof. emeritus, 1993. Emeritus surgeon-in-chief U. Ill. Hosp.; sr. cons. surgeon Cook County, West Side VA, Hines (Ill.) VA hosps.; cons. to Surgeon Gen. NIH, 1965-69. Author: Surgery of the Stomach and Duodenum, 1962, 4th edit., 1986, named changed to Surgery of the Esophagus, Stomach and Small Intestine, 5th edit., 1995, Hernia, 1964, (book name change) Nyhus and Condon's Hernia, 5th edit., 2002, Abdominal Pain: A Guide to Rapid Diagnosis, 1969, 95, Spanish edit., 1996, Russian edit., 2001, Manual of Surgical Therapeutics, 1969, latest rev. edit., 1996, Mastery of Surgery, 1984, 3d edit., 1997, Spanish edit., 1999, Surgery Ann., 1970-95, Treatment of Shock, 1970, 2d rev. edit., 1986, Surgery of the Small Intestine, 1987; editor-in-chief Rev. of Surgery, 1967-77, Current Surgery, 1978-90, emeritus editor, 1991—; assoc. editor Quar. Rev. Surgery, 1958-61; editl. bd. Am. Jour. Digestive Diseases, 1961-67, Scandinavian Jour. Gastroenterology, 1966-97, Am. Surgeon, 1967-89, Jour. Surg. Oncology, 1969-99, Archives of Surgery, 1977-86, World Jour. Surgery, 1977-95; contbr. articles to profl. jours. Served to lt. M.C. USNR, 1943-46, 50-52. Decorated Order of Merit (Poland); postdoctoral fellow USPHS, 1952-53; recipient M. Shipley award So. Surg. Assn., 1967, Rovsing medal Danish Surg. Soc., 1973; Disting. Faculty award U. Ill Coll. Medicine, 1983, Disting. Alumnus award Med. Coll. Ala., 1984, Disting. Alumnus award U. Wash., 1993, 99; Guggenheim fellow, 1955-56. Fellow ACS (1st v.p. 1987-88), Assn. Surgeons Gt. Brit. and Ireland (hon.), Royal Coll. Surgeons Eng. (hon.), Royal Coll. Surgeons Ireland (hon.), Royal Coll. Surgeons Edinburgh (hon.), Royal Coll. Physicians and Surgeons Glasgow (hon.), Internat. Soc. Surgery Found. (hon., sec.-treas. 1992-2001); mem . Am. Gastroent. Assn., Am. Physiol. Soc., Pacific Coast Surg. Assn., Am. Surg. Assn. (recorder 1976-81, 1st v.p. 1989-90), Western Surg. Assn., Ctrl. Soc. Clin. Rsch., Chgo. Surg. Soc. (pres. 1974), Ctrl. Surg. Assn. (pres. 1984), Seattle Surg. Soc., St. Paul Surg. Soc. (hon.), Kansas City Surg. Soc. (hon.), Inst. Medicine Chgo., Internat. Soc. Surgery (hon. fellow 2001, pres. U.S. sect. 1986-88, pres. 34th World Congress 1991, internat. pres. 1991-93), Internat. Soc. for Digestive Surgery (pres. III world congress Chgo. 1974, internat. pres. 1978-84), Soc. for Surgery Alimentary Tract (sec. 1969-73, pres. 1974), Soc. Clin. Surgery, Soc. Surg. Chmn., Soc. U. Surgeons (pres. 1967), Duetschen Gesellschaft für Chirurgie (hon.), Polish Assn. Surgeons (hon.), L'Academie de Chirurgie (France) (corr.), Nat. Acad. of Medicine (France, Argentina and Brazil, hon.), Swiss Surg. Soc. (hon.), Brazilian Coll. Surgeons (hon.), Surg. Biology Club, Warren H. Cole Soc. (pres. 1981), Japan Surg. Soc. (hon.), Assn. Gen. Surgeons of Mex. (hon.), Columbian Surg. Soc. (hon.), Costa Rican Coll. Medicine & Surgery (hon.), Assn. Surgeons Costa Rica (hon.), Internat. Fedn. Surg. Colls. (hon. treas. 1992-99), Sigma Xi, Alpha Omega Alpha, Phi Beta Pi. Home: 310 Maple Row Winnetka IL 60093-1036 Office: U Ill Coll Medicine Dept Surgery MC 958 840 S Wood St Chicago IL 60612-7322 E-mail: lmn_23@msn.com.

NYIEN, PATRICIA, music educator; b. Kenosha, Wis., May 16, 1953; d. David Arne and Sarah Viola (Molgaard) Dissmore; m. Phillip Dwayne Nelson, Aug. 16, 1973 (div. Oct. 1995); children: Phillip Kirk Nelson, Kindra Lynn Nelson; m. Harvey David Nyien, Apr. 20, 1996; 1 child, Kevin Patrick Nelson. Student, LaSalle Extension U., 1971; B Music Edn., Belmont U., 1977. Pvt. piano tchr., Avilla, Mo., 1973—75, Hendersonville, Tenn., 1975—77, Clarksville, Tenn., 1977—79, Hinsdale, Ill., 1979—86, Westmont, Ill., 1986—; choral dir. Greenwood Annex/Jr. H.S., Clarksville, 1977—79; presch. music/jr. choir dir. Oak Brook (Ill.) Christian Sch., 1981—95. Mem.: The Internat. Cat Assn., Am. Choral Dirs. Assn., Music Tchrs. Nat. Assn. (theory chmn. 2001—03, cert.), Salt Creek Music Tchrs. Assn. (publicity com. 1990—94, membership com. 1994—98, treas. 1998—2000, theory chmn. 2001—, pres. 2003—), Internat. Bengal Cat Assn., Ill. state music tchr. assoc. (treas. 1998—2000). Republican. Mem. Assemblies Of God. Avocations: needlepoint, skiing, singing, knitting, breeding Bengal cats. Home: 830 Franklin St Westmont IL 60559

NYIRI, JOSEPH ANTON, sculptor, art educator; b. Racine, Wis., May 24, 1937; s. Joseph Anton Nyiri and Dorothy Marion (Larson) Zink; m. Laura Lee Primeau, Aug. 29, 1959 (dec. Mar. 1982); children: Krista, Nicole, Page; m. Melissa Trent, July 28, 1985. BA, U. Wis., 1959, MS, 1961. Tchr. art Madison (Wis.) Sch. Dist., 1959-62; art cons. San Diego Unified Schs., 1962-65, dist. resource tchr., 1965-73, regional tchr. occupational art, 1973-76, mentor tchr., 1985-95; sculptor San Diego, 1962—; fine arts cons., 1966—; head dept. art edn. Serra H.S., San Diego, 1976—; tchr. art Zool. Soc. San Diego, 1991—. Cons. gifted and talented edn. program San Diego City Schs., 1995—, gifted programs Escondido, Calif. and Poway, Calif. Schs., 1995—, Boston Schs., 1996-98, Romona, Calif. Pub. Schs., 1996—; instr. art U. Calif. at San Diego, La Jolla, 1967-80, San Diego State U. Extension, 1969—; fine art restorer, 1963—, lectr. art and art edn., 1963—; pvt. art tchr. San Diego City Zoo. Exhibited sculpture in numerous one-man, two-person, juried and invitational shows, 1960—, U. Mex.-Baja Calif., 1983; rev. Calif. Art Rev., 1989. Active Art Guild San Diego Mus. Art; bd. dirs. San Diego Art Inst. Sgt. Wis. N.G., 1955-61. Named One of 3 Tchrs. of Yr., San Diego County, 1983, One of Outstanding Art Tchrs. in U.S., RISD, 1984, Secondary Tchr. of Yr., San Diego City Schs., 1982; recipient creativity award Pacific Inst., 1969; named to Horlick H.S. Grads. of Distinction, Racine, Wis. Mem. Arts/Worth: Nat. Coun. Art (charter), Allied Craftsmen San Diego, Internat. Platform Assn., San Diego Art Inst. (bd. dirs.), San Diego Mus. Art (mem. Art Guild), Zool. Soc. San Diego. Democrat. Mem. Christian Ch. Avocations: running, hiking, travel, reading, writing poetry. Office: 3525 Albatross St San Diego CA 92103-4807 also: Zool Soc San Diego Edn Dept PO Box 551 San Diego CA 92112-0551

NYKIEL, KAREN ANN, development administrator; b. Chgo., July 27, 1945; d. John Marion and Dorothy Ann (Lasko) N. BA, Coll. St. Benedict, St. Joseph, Minn., 1969; MSNS, Seattle U., 1975; MA, Mundelein Coll., Chgo., 1989. Tchr. science Benet Acad., Lisle, Ill., 1969-73; adult edn. coord. St. Joan of Arc Ch., Lisle, 1973-77; adj. faculty chemistry Coll. DuPage, Glen Ellyn, Ill., 1975—; campus min. Diocese of Joliet, Ill., 1982-92; adminstr. Queen of Peace Ctr., Lisle, 1992-97; devel. dir. St. Mary of Providence, Chgo., 1998—. Cons. Nat. Fusion Co., Plainfield, Ill., 1980-82; mem. Benedictine Sisters Sacred Heart, Lisle, 1965—, bd. dirs., 1980-92; state coord. Pax Christi Ill., 1994—; pres. Queen of Peace Ctr., Inc., Lisle, 1992-97; adj. faculty religious studies Coll. DuPage, Benedictine U., Coll. St. Francis; mem. med. team Republic of the Congo, 1996. Mem. C. of C., Lisle, 1992—. Grantee NSF, 1971, 72, 73, 74. Mem. Am. Chemical Soc., Assn. Sr. Svc. Providers, Rotary Internat. (Lisle chpt. chair internat. com., pres. 1997-98). Democrat. Roman Catholic. Avocations: playing guitar, reading, lecturing. Home and Office: Sacred Heart Monastery 1910 Maple Ave Lisle IL 60532-2164

NYLANDER, DONNA MARIE, educational administrator; b. Chicago Heights, Ill., July 23, 1950; d. Ralph and Josephine (Portelli) Talamonti; m. Rick Nylander, Sept. 4, 1971; children: Ricky, Joey, Steve. BS in Edn., Western Ill. U., 1972; MA in Edn., Govs. State U., University Park, Ill., 1985, postgrad., 1992. Tchr. Sch. Dist. 151, South Holland, Ill., 1973-88; instr. Prairie State Coll., Chicago Heights, 1986-88; grant coord. Ill. Bd. Edn., Flossmoor, Ill., 1988—. Cons. midwest ter. Discover Intensive Phonics, 1986-88; facilitator Region 6 Adv. Coun., Joliet, Ill., 1988—. Editor newsletter The Bear Facts, 1988-90. Pres. St. Kieran's Sch. Bd., Chicago Heights, 1986—; mem. Glenwood (Ill.) Human Rels. Commn., 1988; v.p. Glenwood Jr. Women's Club, 1977-80. Mem. South Suburban Assn. for Edn. Young Children (bd. dirs. 1980-86). Roman Catholic. Home: 3080 Serenity Ln Naperville IL 60564-4669 Address: Starnet Region VI 6020 151st St Oak Forest IL 60452-1841

NYQUIST, WYMAN ELLSWORTH, biometry educator; b. Scobey, Mont., June 13, 1928; s. Rudolph Ephraim and Alyce Maria (Nordberg) N.; m. Ruth Malene Suneson, June 15, 1952; 1 child: Craig Evan. BS, Mont. State U., 1950; PhD, U Calif., Davis, 1953. Instr. U. Calif., Davis, 1953-57, asst. prof., 1957-63; assoc. prof. Purdue U., West Lafayette, Ind., 1963-68, prof. dept. agronomy, 1968—. Spl. rsch. fellow NIH, Raleigh, N.C., 1969-70. 1st lt. USAF, 1954-56. Fellow Am. Soc. Agronomy, Crop Sci. Soc. Am.; mem. Internat. Biometric Soc., Coun. Agr., Sci. and Tech., Genetics Soc. Am., Sigma Xi. Avocations include research on methods in biometry, experimental design, statistical genetics and quantitative genetics. Home: 1600 Ravinia Rd West Lafayette IN 47906-2362 Office: Purdue U Dept Agronomy 915 W State St West Lafayette IN 47907-2054 E-mail: wnyquist@purdue.edu.

OAKES, ANITA GWYNNE, physical therapist, educator; b. Glen Cove, N.Y., Aug. 1, 1952; d. Gardner and Maud (Shaddock) O. BA, SUNY, Potsdam, 1974; MS in Physical Therapy, Beaver Coll., Glenside, Pa., 1985. Reg. physical therapist, N.Y., Pa. Phys. therapist Nittany Valley Rehab. Hosp., Pleasant Gap, Pa., 1985-86, Northstar, Malone, N.Y., 1986-87, Alice

Hyde Hosp., Malone, 1986-92, chief phys. therapist, 1992-97; home health phys. therapist Clinton County Health Dept./Franklin County Health Dept. Instr. Malone Exercise Racquette Club, 1990-92; clin. instr. Dyouville (N.Y.) Coll., 1995, Herkimer (N.Y.) C.C., 1996—, Canton (N.Y.) Coll. Tech., 1997. Mem. Am. Phys. Therapy Assn., N.Y. Phys. Therapy Assn., Veterinary Phys. Therapy Spl. Interest Group (orthop. sect.). Avocations: aerobics instruction, gardening. Office: Franklin County Health Dept Court Malone NY 12953-

OAKES, ROBERT JAMES, physics educator; b. Mpls., Jan. 21, 1936; s. Sherman E. and Josephine J. (Olson) O.; children: Cindy L., Lisa A. BS, U. Minn., 1957, MS, 1959, PhD, 1962. NSF fellow Stanford U., 1962-64; asst. prof. physics, 1964-68; assoc. prof. physics Northwestern U., 1968-70, prof. physics, 1970-76, prof. physics and astronomy, 1976—. Vis. staff mem. Los Alamos Sci. Lab., 1971-92; vis. scientist Fermi Nat. Accelerator Lab., 1975—, CERN, 1966-67; mem. Inst. for Advanced Study, Princeton, 1967-68; vis. scientist DESY, 1971-72; faculty assoc. Argonne Nab. Lab., 1982— ; U.S. scientist NSF-Yugoslav joint program, 1982-92; panelist Nat. Rsch. Coun., 1990-98. A.P. Sloan fellow 1965-68; Air Force Office Sci. Rsch. grantee, 1969-71, NSF grantee 1971-87, Dept. Energy grantee, 1987—; named Fulbright-Hays Disting. prof. U. Sarajevo, Yugoslavia, 1979-80; recipient Natural Sci. prize China, 1993. Fellow Am. Phys. Soc., AAAS; mem. N.Y. Acad. Sci., Ill. Acad. Sci., Physics Club (Chgo.), Sigma Xi, Tau Beta Pi. Clubs: Physics (Chgo.). Office: Northwestern U Dept Physics 2145 Sheridan Rd Evanston IL 60208-0834

OAKES, WALTER JERRY, pediatric neurosurgeon; b. De Soto, Mo., July 10, 1946; s. Marvin Melton and Mildred Florene (Link) O.; m. Linda Helen Maas (div. Jan. 1985); 1 child, Kathleen Suzanne; m. Jean Evans, Dec. 1988; children: Matthew Marvin, Peter Clifford. BA in Chemistry, U. Mo., 1968; MD, Duke U., 1972. Diplomate Am. Bd. Neurol. Surgeons. Neurosurgery resident Duke U., Durham, N.C., 1972-78, asst. prof. neurosurgery, 1979-90, assoc. prof. neurosurgery, 1991—, asst. prof. pediatrics, 1981-92, assoc. prof. pediatrics, 1992; pediatric neurosurgery resident U. Toronto Hosp. for Sick Children, Ont., Can., July-Dec., 1975; registrar pediatric neurosurgery U. London Hosp. for Sick Children, Eng., Sept., 1978-Feb., 1979; prof. neurosurgery and pediat. U. Ala., Birmingham, 1992—, Dan Hendley chair pediatric neurosurgery, 2002—. Fellow: ACS. Office: Children's Hosp of Ala 1600 7th Ave S Ste 400 Birmingham AL 35233-1785 Business E-Mail: wjomd@uab.edu.

OAKLAND, VELMA LEANE, elementary school educator; b. Moorhead, Minn., Dec. 29, 1939; d. Alfred J. and Annie (Klusman) Kuvaas; m. Aug. 17, 1959; 1 child, Terry Lee. BS in Edn., Mayville State U., 1966; MS in Edn., N.D. State U., 1969. Cert. elem. tchr., Minn. Tchr. Granville (N.D.) Pub. Schs., 1960-62, Tappen (N.D.) Pub. Schs., 1962-64, Hughes Elem. Sch., Red Lake Falls, Minn., 1964—; commr. Red Lake County, Minn. Heat Start dir. Inter County Community Coun., Red Lake Falls, Minn., 1970-73; commr. HUD, 1988; mem. Red Lake County Fair Bd., 1988—; mem. exec. com. 7th Congl. Dist., 1988; mem. N.W. Regional Devel. Commn., 1990—; mem. adv. com. N.W. Minn. Global Studies Inst., 1990-91; pres. Red Lake County Eocn. Devel. Corp., 1991-92; sec.-treas. N.W. Regional Devel. Commn. Enterprise Loan Fund. Named Tchr. of Yr., Red Lake Falls Civic and Commerce Assn., 1985; named Outstanding D.F.L.er Red Lake County, 1994. Mem. Minn. Edn. Assn. (sec. 1979—, treas. 1983—, exec. com. 1983—, Impace bd. dirs. 1994, Creative Leadership award 1993), Red Lake Falls Edn. Assn. (Tchr. of Yr. 1985, pres. 1994-95), Delta Kappa Gamma. Avocations: reading, fishing, softball, basketball. Home: 502 Chicago Ave SW Red Lake Falls MN 56750-4008

OAKLEY, DAVID STERLING, physics educator, consultant; b. Denver, Apr. 2, 1958; s. Gary Addison and JoAnn (Winans) O.; m. Barbara JoAnn Quinn, Apr. 5, 1986; children: David Addison, Andrew Timothy, Madeleine. BA, Colo. U., 1981; MA, Tex. U., 1985, PhD, 1987. Rsch. assoc. Colo. U., Boulder, 1987-89; asst. prof. Lewis and Clark Coll., Portland, Oreg., 1989-93; assoc. prof. Colo. Christian U., Lakewood, 1993—. Dir. rsch. Safe Air Monitoring Systems, Inc., Denver, 1989—. Contbr. articles to profl. jours. Youth counselor Young Life, Austin, Tex., 1981-87; mem. So. Utah Wilderness Alliance, Salt Lake City, 1986—, Oreg. Rivers Coun., Portland, 1992—. Mem. Am. Phys. Soc. Presbyterian. Achievements include patent in method for detecting hydrogen containing compounds, detection of natural gas and household radon; research in correlation between solar neutrino flux and solar magnetic fields, in nuclear structure, role of space-time in Christian theology. Office: Colo Christian Univ 180 S Garrison St Lakewood CO 80226-1053

OAKLEY, FRANCIS CHRISTOPHER, history educator, former college president; b. Liverpool, Eng., Oct. 6, 1931; came to U.S., 1957, naturalized, 1968; s. Joseph Vincent and Siobean (NiCurean) O.; m. Claire-Ann Lamenzo, Aug. 9, 1958; children: Deirdre, Christopher, Timothy, Brian. BA, Corpus Christi Coll., Oxford U., 1953, MA, 1957; postgrad., Pontifical Inst. Medieval Studies, Toronto, 1953-55; MA, Yale U., 1958, PhD, 1960; LLD, Amherst Coll., 1986, Wesleyan U., 1989; LHD, Northwestern U., 1990, North Adams State Coll., 1993, Bowdoin Coll., 1993; LittD, Williams Coll., 1994. Mem. faculty Yale U., 1959-61, Williams Coll., Williamstown, Mass., 1961—, prof. history, 1970—2002, dean faculty, 1977-84, Edward Dorr Griffin prof. history of ideas, 1984—85, pres., 1985-94, pres. emeritus, 1994—, Edward Dorr Griffin prof. history of ideas, 1994—2002, prof. emeritus, 2002—; interim pres. Am. Coun. Learned Socs., 2002—03; hon. fellow Corpus Christi Coll., Univ. Oxford, 1991—; pres. emeritus Am. Coun. Learned Socs., 2003—; sr. fellow Oakley Ctr. Humanities, Williams Coll., 2002. Vis. lectr. Bennington (Vt.) Coll., 1967, Sir Isaiah Berlin vis. prof. Oxford U., 1999-2000; Merle Curti lectr. U. Wis., Madison, 2001; Étienne Gilson lectr Pontifical Inst. Medieval Studies, Toronto, 2002; mem. Inst. Advanced Study Princeton, 1981-82; assoc. Nat. Humanities Ctr., 1991; guest scholar Woodrow Wilson Internat. Ctr. for Scholars, 1994; chair bd. dirs. Am. Coun. Learned Socs., 1993-97; trustee Sterling and Francine Clark Art Inst., 1985—, pres. 1998—; trustee MassMoCA Found., 1995—, Willamstown Art Conservation Ctr., 1995-98, Williamstown Theatre Festival, 1985-93, Nat. Humanities Ctr., 1996-02, 2003—, Lake Forest Coll., 1997-2001; trustee Inst. Advanced Cath. Studies, 1998—, vice chair, 2002—; mem. MassMoCA Cultural Devel. Commn., 1988—; mem. adv. coun. Ctr. for Study of Religion, Princeton U., 1999—. Author: The Political Thought of Pierre d'Ailly: The Voluntarist Tradition, 1964, Kingship and the Gods: The Western Apostasy, 1968, Council over Pope?, Towards a Provisional Ecclesiology, 1969, Medieval Experience: Foundations of Western Cultural Singularity, 1974, rev. England edit., The Crucial Centuries, 1979, Spanish edit., 1980, 95, Medieval Acad. edit., 1988, 93, The Western Church in the Later Middle Ages, 1979, rev. edit., 1985, 88, 91, Natural Law, Conciliarism and Consent in the Late Middle Ages, 1984, Omnipotence, Covenant and Order: An Excursion in the History of Ideas, 1984, Community of Learning: The American College and the Liberal Arts Tradition, 1992, Scholarship and Teaching: A Matter of Mutual Support, 1996, Politics and Eternity: Studies in the History of Medieval and Early Modern Political Thoughts, 1999, The Leadership Challenges of a College Presidency, 2002, The Conciliarist Tradition, 2003; editor: (with Daniel O'Connor) Creation: The Impact of an Idea, 1969, (with Bruce Russett Governance, Accountability and the Future of the Catholic Church, 2003; contbr. articles to profl. jours; co-editor: Governance Accountability and the Future of the Catholic Church, 2003. Lt. Brit. Army, 1955-57. Goldsmith's Co. London fellow, 1953-55, Social Sci. Rsch. Coun. fellow, 1963, Am. Coun. Learned Socs. fellow, 1965, 69-70, Weil Inst. fellow, 1965, Folger Shakespeare Libr. fellow, 1974, NEH fellow, 1976, 81-82; recipient Wilbur Lucius Cross medal Yale Grad. Sch., 1997. Fellow Medieval Acad. Am. (pres. fellows 1999-2002), Am. Acad. Arts and Scis.; mem. Am. Hist. Assn., Am. Cath. Hist. Assn., Am. Ch. History Soc., New Eng. Medieval Conf. (pres. 1983-84), The Century Assn., Am. Cusanus Soc. (adv. bd. 1997—). Democrat. Roman Catholic. Office: Williams Coll Oakley Ctr Humanities & Soc Sci Williamstown MA 01267 E-mail: francis.c.oakley@williams.edu.

OAKLEY, WANDA FAYE, management consultant, educator; d. Joe and Doris Oakley. BSBA, U. N.C., 1971, postgrad., 1972-73. CPA, N.C.; cert. fraud examiner, cert. govt. fin. mgr. Acct. Oakley Motors, Durham, 1965-73; controller Airheart Ins. Agy., Inc., Durham, 1973-75; controller, owner Quality Car Wash, Durham, 1974-83; acct. computer svcs. dept. William H. Mitchell, P.A. and CPAs, Durham, 1983-84; mgr. John Anderson & Assocs., Inc., Durham, 1984-85; v.p. CMS Svcs., Inc., York, S.C., 1985-86; adminstr. N.C. State U., Raleigh, 1986-89; pvt. practice bus. cons. Raleigh, 1989—. Instr. Wake Tech. Community Coll., Raleigh, 1985—, Small Bus. Ctr., Johnston Community Coll, Smithfield, N.C., 1990—; proctor N.C. State Bd. CPA Examiners, Raleigh, 1986—; bus. cons. in field. Fellow N.C. Assn. CPAs, AICPA; mem. NAFE, Assn. Cert. Fraud Examiners, Exersafety Internat. (master's cert. 1984), Assn. Govt. Accts., U. N.C. Alumni Assn. (life). Home: PO Box 3257 Durham NC 27715-3257 Office: 4404 Ryan St Durham NC 27704-1808

OATES, EDITH LUNSFORD, secondary education mathematics educator; b. Pine Bluff, Ark., Mar. 3, 1948; d. Woodrow W. and Alta L. (Worthen) Lunsford; m. Jerry L. Oates, Jule 12, 1987; children: Carolyn, Dana, Cary, Keith. BS in Math., U. Ark. Cert. elem. tchr., secondary math., Ark. Tchr. Sheridan (Ark.) Jr. High Sch., 1980—. Chmn. bldg. planning coun. Sheridan (Ark.) Jr. High Sch., 1991-92. Mem. Nat. Coun. Tchrs. Math., Ark. Coun. Tchrs. Math., Delta Kappa Gamma, Beta Sigma Phi. Home: PO Box 366 Sheridan AR 72150-0366 Office: 400 N Rock St Sheridan AR 72150-2228

OATES, MAUREEN KATHERINE, environmental educator; b. San Diego, Dec. 11, 1923; d. Daniel Louis and Mary Lynch; m. James Martin Oates Jr., May 12, 1946; children: James Martin III, Daniel L., Kathleen M., Laurence E., Kevin J., Patrick W. BA in Biology, San Diego State U., 1944; MEd in Sci. Edn., Northeastern U., Boston, 1964; Cert. of Advanced Study, Harvard U., 1969. Lic. sci. tchr., supr., Mass. Sci. tchr. Concord (Mass.)-Carlisle High Sch., 1964-66; dir. Project Lighthouse 9 Sch. Dist. Consortium, Marshfield, Mass., 1966-67; dir. environ. edn. The Edn. Collaborative, Wellesley, Mass., 1967-68; rsch. assoc. Edn. Devel. Ctr., Newton, Mass., 1969-71, cons. to Teen Age Health Project, 1982-84; evaluation cons., 1972-73; dir., developer Charles River Project, Newton, 1974-76; dir. environ. edn. EdCo, Brookline, Mass., 1976-81; dir. mus. consortium Boston Mus. Sci., 1986-88; dir. edn. Maine Audubon Soc., Falmouth, Maine, 1988—. Evaluation cons. Mass. Dept. Edn., Boston, 1971-74; mem. adv. bd. Maine Energy Edn. Project, Gorham, 1988-90, Maine Environ. Edn. Assn., Lewiston, 1990—, Sch. Systemic Initiative, Augusta, Maine, 1992—. Author: (tchr. guides) Project WALSE, 1978-80 (Mass. Dept. Edn. award 1980), Water Watchers, 1987; co-author ednl. unit Acting to Create a Healthy Environment, 1983. Cub Scout den mother Boy Scouts Am., Watertown, Mass., 1955-65; mem., chair Watertown Conservation Commn., 1969-83; chair Watertown Arsenal Alternative Use Com., 1971-74; mem. Watertown Town Meeting, 1973-78; bd. mem. Charles River Watershed Assn., Newton, 1974-76. With USN, WAVES, 1944-46. Grantee Mass. Dept. Edn., Marshfield, 1967, Newton, 1973, Boston, 1976, Brookline, 1978, NSF, Falmouth, Maine, 1988, 90. Mem. ASCD, N.Am. Alliance Environ. Edn., Nat. Sci. Tchrs. Assn., Nat. Wildlife Fedn., New Eng. Environ. Edn. Assn., Maine Environ. Assn. (bd. mem. 1990—). Avocations: gardening, piano, writing for children, beach. Office: Maine Audubon Soc PO Box 6009 118 Us Route 1 Falmouth ME 04105-2140

O'BAIRE, MARIKA, community health nurse, writer; b. Manila, Oct. 3, 1947; d. Gerald John and Giovanna (BelForti) Barry; children: Matthew, Alexei, Rita, D. Patrick. Student, U. Conn., 1964-65; diploma, Ellis Hosp. Sch. Nursing, 1977; BSN, Russell Sage Coll., 1980, postgrad., 1983, 94; grad. ontological design, Logonet Inc. ODC-J, 1993; postgrad. in humanities, Calif. State U., Dominguez Hills, 1995—; postgrad., Univ. Dundee, 2000—. RN N.Y.; lic. avatar master/wizard Star's Edge Internat., 1999. English tchr. Lang. Inst., Taipei, Taiwan, 1971-73; team leader, staff nurse in acute psychiatry Samaritan Hosp., Troy, N.Y., 1978-80; staff nurse, pediatric ICU Albany (N.Y.) Med. Ctr., 1980-84, 97—; rsch. nurse Commn. on Quality Care for Mentally Disabled, Albany, 1984; staff nurse Columbia-Greene Med. Ctr., Catskill, N.Y., 1984-89; night charge nurse Conifer Park, Scotia, N.Y., 1991-92; nursing educator St. Clare's Hosp., Schenectady, N.Y., 1992-96; adjunct clin. educator Albany Med. Ctr. So. Vt. Coll., Bennington, 1997—2001. Philosophy coaching Cmty. Hospice Saratoga, N.Y., 1998—; founder Future Design: Create What You Prefer, Avatar Tech. & Skills, 2000; Favorite Nurses, Colonie, N.Y., 2002—. Contbr. Echo Mag.; author: (screenplays) Dragon, 2002, About Love, (novels) Future Joyous, 2002, (screenplays) Syin. Vol. curriculum designer in gifted and talented programs; mem. Red Cross Disaster Team. Mem. Amnesty Internat. Childreach Plan Internat., Upstate Independent Filmakers/Screenwriters, Thorobred Toastmasters. Home and Office: 214 Liberty St Apt 563 Schenectady NY 12305 E-mail: mobaire@earthlink.net.

OBEAR, FREDERICK WOODS, academic administrator; b. Malden, Mass., June 9, 1935; s. William Fred and Dorothea Louise (Woods) O.; m. Patricia A. Draper, Aug. 30, 1959 (dec. Dec. 1993); children: Jeffrey Allan, Deborah Anne, James Frederick; m. Ruth Crowley Sundell, Feb. 21, 1998. BS with high honors, U. Mass., Lowell, 1956, LHD, 1985; PhD, U. N.H., 1961. Mem. faculty dept. chemistry Oakland U., Rochester, Mich., 1960-81, prof., 1979-81, v.p. for acad. affairs, provost, 1970-81; chancellor U. Tenn., Chattanooga, 1981-97, univ. prof., chancellor emeritus, 1997—. Mem. nat. adv. panel Nat. Commn. on Higher Edn. Issues, 1981; mem. pres. commn. NCAA, 1991-94. Trustee Marygrove Coll., 1973-79. Am. Council Edn. fellow, 1967-68 Mem. AAAS, Am. Assn. State Colls. and Univs. (bd. dirs. 1992-96, chair 1995), Am. Chem. Soc., Am. Assn. Higher Edn., Sigma Xi. Roman Catholic. Office: 417H Fletcher Hall 615 McCallie Ave Chattanooga TN 37403-2504 E-mail: frederick-obear@utc.edu.

OBENHAUS, KATHY ANN, special education educator; b. Columbus, Ind., Dec. 1, 1954; d. Ivan Dale and Marcella Ruth (Krienke) Van Reenan; m. Fredericus Theodorus Hagenbeek, 1975; children: Matthew Van Hagenbeek, Cristian Van Hagenbeek; m. Ernest Derrell Obenhaus, Mar. 5, 1988; 1 child, Rachel M. BA summa cum laude, U. Guam, 1976; MS in Edn. Deaf, Idaho State U., 1993. Cert. elem. edn. tchr. K-12 aurally handicapped. Tchr. of deaf Guam Dept. Edn., 1976-78, Clark County Sch. Dist., Las Vegas, Nev., 1979—. Chmn. Task Force on Deaf Edn., Las Vegas, 1990-92. Editor: Intermountain Deaf Education Advocates of Learning. Mem. sch. bd. First Good Shepherd Luth. Sch., 1992-95, ch. coun., 1993-95. Named Outstanding Spl. Educator Clark County Sch. Dist., 1991. Mem. Am. Soc. Deaf Children, Calif. Educators of Deaf, Independently Merging Parent Assns. Calif.-Together. Lutheran. Avocations: child rearing, reading, needlework, writing. Office: Clark County Sch Dist 1560 Cherokee Ln Las Vegas NV 89109-3106

OBER, JOSIAH, history educator; b. Brunswick, Maine, Feb. 27, 1953; s. Nathanial and Patricia Wilder (Stride) Ober. BA, U. Minn., 1975, MA, 1977; PhD, U. Mich., 1980. Asst. prof. history Mont. State U., Bozeman, 1980—84, assoc. prof., 1984—88, prof., 1988—90; prof. classics Princeton (NJ) U., 1990—, chmn. dept. classics, 1994—2001. Vis. prof. U. Mich., Ann Arbor, 1986—87; sr. rsch. assoc. Am. Sch. Classical Studies, Athens, Greece, 1981, Athens, 83, Athens, 85, Athens, 88; vis. lectr. Archeol. Inst. Am., 1985—87; Martin Classical lectr. Oberlin Coll., 1994; Magie chair in classics, 1994—; bd. dirs. Princeton U. Press., 1995—2000. Author: Fortress Attica, 1985, Mass and Elite in Democratic Athens, 1989, The Athenian Revolution, 1996, Political Dissent in Democratic Athens, 1998; contbr. articles to profl. jours. Grantee, Am. Coun. Learned Socs., 1981, 1989, NEH, 1981, 1989, 1996, Nat. Humanities Ctr. NC, 1983—84, Ctr. Hellenic Studies, 1989—90, Guggenheim Found., 1996. Mem.: Am. Sch. Classical Studies, Am. Philol. Assn. (bd. dirs.), Archaeol. Inst. Am. Home: 55 Aiken Ave Princeton NJ 08540-5257 Office: Princeton U Dept Classics Princeton NJ 08544-0001 E-mail: jober@princeton.edu.

OBERG, LYLE, physician, academic administrator; b. Forestburg, Alberta, Can. m. Evelyn Oberg; children: Jillian, Scott. Pre-med studies, Red Deer Coll.; MD, U. Alberta, Can. Physician Gen. Practice; elected to legis. assembly Alberta Parliament, Edmonton, 1993—, appointed minister of learning, 1999—. Chmn. standing policy com. on health restructuring Alberta Legis. Assembly, Edmonton, Canada, 1995—97, minister of family and social svcs., 1997—99; Alberta rep. Ministerial Coun. on Social Policy Renewal; mem. treasury bd, and standing com. on learning and employment Alberta Legislative Assembly, 1999—. Bd sch, trustees. Avocations: golf, hunting, sailing. Office: Legislative Bldg 10800 97 Ave Edmonton AB T5K 1E4 Canada

OBERMEYER, THERESA NANGLE, sociology educator; b. St. Louis, July 25, 1945; d. James Francis and Harriet Clare (Shafer) Nangle; m. Thomas S. Obermeyer, Dec. 23, 1977; children: Thomas Jr., James, Margaret, Matthew. BA, Maryville U., St. Louis, 1967; MEd, St. Louis U., 1970, PhD, 1975. Lic. real estate broker Alaska, 1979, cert. Type A teacher Alaska, 1979. Dir. student activities Lindenwood Univ., St. Charles, Mo., 1969-70; asst. dean of students Loyola Coll., Balt., 1972-73; asst. dir. student activities St. Louis C.C., 1973-78; dir. student activities U. Alaska, Anchorage, 1978-79; instr. sociology Chapman U., Anchorage, 1981-93; secondary tchr. McLaughlin Youth Ctr. for Juvenile Delinquents, 1984-90. Mem Anchorage Munic Health Commn., 1980—81; elected alt. coun. urban bd edn. Nat Sch. Bds. Assn., 1994; maj. party nominee US Senate Gen. Election, 1996; founder, mem. Alaska Women's Polit. Caucus, 1979—; elected Anchorage Sch. Bd., 1990—94, treas., 1993. Recipient Fed Women's Equity Act, US Dept Educ Univ Alaska, 1978—79; fellow Fulbright, Project India, 1974, Project Jordan, 1977; grantee Title I, Univ Md and Loyola Col, 1972—73; scholar NDEA, 1968—70. Mem.: AAUW (bd. dirs. Anchorage br. 1980—81), DAR (regent Coll. John Mitchell chpt. 1992—94), Am. Soc. Pub. Adminstrn. (pres., bd. dirs. south ctrl. chpt. 1981). Avocations: athletics, swimming, horseback riding, skiing, running. Home: 3000 Dartmouth Dr Anchorage AK 99508-4413 Fax: 907-278-9455. E-mail: tobermeyer@gci.net.

OBERNE, SHARON BROWN, elementary education educator; b. Lakeland, Fla., Sept. 2, 1955; d. Morris C. and Amy (Beecroft) Brown; m. Ronald Allan Oberne, Mar. 29, 1980; children: Laura, Aaron, Kelley. AA in Pre-tchg., Hillsborough C.C., Tampa, Fla., 1975; BA in Elem. Edn., U. South Fla., 1976, cert., AA in Acctg., U. South Fla., 1980. Cert. tchr. K-8. 3rd grade tchr. Zolfo Springs Elem., Wauchula, Fla., 1976-77, 2nd grade tchr., 1977-79; 1st grade tchr. Westgate Christian Sch., Tampa, Fla., 1979-80; 5th grade tchr. Pasoc Elem., Dade City, Fla., 1980-81; 3rd grade tchr. San Antonio Elem., Dade City, 1981-86; temporary reading tchr. Chesterfield Heights Elem., Norfolk, Va., 1986-87; 2nd grade tchr. Ocean View Elem., Norfolk, 1987—. Dir. Ocean View Writing Club, Norfolk, 1992—. Author: Pink Monkey, 1994, Space Traveler, 1995, Daisy Dolphin (Spelling in Context). Pres. USS Guam's Wife's Club, Norfolk Naval Base, 1990-91; amb. of goodwill USS Guam, 1990-91; founder AmeriKids of Ocean View, Norfolk, 1991-93; liaison Adopt-A-Sch. Program, Norfolk, 1991—. Recipient Good Neighbor award NEA, 1994, Second Place award Cox Cable, 1996, First Place award, 1997, Inspiration award, 1998. Mem. CHADD, Internat. Platform Assn., Norfolk Reading Coun., Nat. Autism Soc. Avocations: writing, reading, swimming, walking. Home: 8243 Briarwood Cir Norfolk VA 23518-2862

O'BRIANT, MARGARET DENNY, retired elementary school educator; b. Durham, NC, Aug. 23, 1948; d. John Howard and Myrtle Ruth (Lunsford) Denny; divorced; children: Guenevere Anjanette, Chadwick Sean; m. Wallace W. O'Brient. BS in Spanish, Appalachian State U., 1970; BS in Early Childhood Edn., Brenau Coll., 1976; postgrad., N.C. Cen. U., 1981-83. Cert. tchr. Spanish, 7-12, early childhood edn., K-4, N.C. Tchr. Spanish/English North Wilkes High Sch., Hays, N.C., 1970-71; tchr. coll.-level basic English Army Edn. Ctr. Lang. Sch., Fort Bragg, N.C., 1972; tchr. Spanish/English North Hall High Sch., Gainesville, Ga., 1976-77; Title 1 1st-grade tchr. Hall County Schs., Gainesville, 1978-79; tchr. asst. Durham (N.C.) County Schs., 1979-86, tchr. third grade, 1986—2000, team leader 3d grade, 1991-93, sch. sci. liaison, 1995-98. Sch. rep. N.C. Sci. Tchr. Assn. Conf., 1996; tchr. Computertots, 2000—. Active PTA, Durham, 1979—2000; pianist, Sunday Sch. tchr., adminstrv. bd. Rougemont (NC) United Meth. Ch., 1979—2001, bd. dirs., 1979—; v.p. Rougemont United Meth. Women, 1994—96, pres., 1997—; den leader Boy Scouts Am., Durham, 1984—85, 1987—94, Ruritan, 2002—. Named Sch. Recycling Educator of Yr., 1996. Mem. NEA, NC Assn. Educators, Durham Assn. Educators, Rougemont Ruritan Nat. (song leader 2003—). Democrat. Avocations: quilting, knitting, sewing, piano, reading. Home: 12507 Roxboro Rd Rougemont NC 27572-7817 Office: Computertots Ambassador Dr Durham NC 27703 E-mail: craftymaggie@msn.com.

O'BRIEN, ANNMARIE, education educator; b. N.Y.C., Nov. 10, 1949; d. Hugh and Margaret (Doherty) O'B.; m. William James McGinty, Dec. 30, 1976; children: Michael Hugh, Liam Patrick. BS in Elem. Edn., Boston U., 1971; MS in Early Childhood Edn., Queens Coll., 1976; EdD in Ednl. Leadership, Portland State U., 1994. Tchr. St. Gerard Majella Elem. Sch., Hollis, N.Y., 1972-76, Lower Kuskokwim Sch. Dist., Bethel, Alaska, 1977-85; child sexual abuse prevention coord. Resource Ctr. for Parents and Children, Fairbanks, Alaska, 1986; grad. asst., project evaluator Portland (Oreg.) State U., 1989-92, student tchr. supr., 1992; prof. edn., rsch. assoc. Inst. Social and Econ. Rsch. U. Alaska, Anchorage, 1993-96; prin. Old Harbor Sch., Kodiak Island Borough Sch. Dist., Kodiak, Alaska, 1996-99; dir. curriculum and instr. Northwest Arctic Borough, Kotzebue, Alaska, 1999—. Author: A Child Abuse Prevention Training Manual for Educators, 1976; co-author: The Academy for Future Educators Guidebook, 1992. Recipient scholarship Portland State U., 1991. Mem. ASCD, Kappa Delta Pi. Office: NWA BSD PO Box 51 Kotzebue AK 99752-0051 E-mail: aobrien@nwarctic.org.

OBRIEN, BARBARA ANN, speech and language pathologist; b. Albany, N.Y., Nov. 13, 1946; d. William Henry and Katherine (Garrow) O. BA, SUNY, Albany, 1969; MEd, U. Va., 1971. Lic. speech pathologist; cert. tchr., Va. Speech pathologist Fairfax County Pub. Schs., Falls Church and McLean, Va., 1971—, autism resource tchr., 1994—, merit tchr., peer observer, 1989—, colleague lead clinician, 1990—. Writer, presenter Future Directions, Arlington, Va., 1984; pvt. practice, Falls Church, 1987-89; assoc. Nelson Ctr., Annandale, Va., 1990—; mem. speech and lang. adv. coun. Fairfax County Pub. Schs., 1993. Mem. NEA, Am. Speech Hearing Lang. Assn., Va. Speech Hearing Assn. Home: 8360 Greensboro Dr Mc Lean VA 22102-3511 Office: Cooper Intermediate Sch 977 Balls Hill Rd Mc Lean VA 22101-2020

O'BRIEN, DAVID MICHAEL, law educator; b. Rock Springs, Wyo., Aug. 30, 1951; s. Ralph Rockwell and Lucile O'Brien; m. Claudine M. Mendelovitz, Dec. 17, 1982; children: Benjamin, Sara, Talia. BA, U. Calif., Santa Barbara, 1973, MA, 1974, PhD, 1977. Fulbright lectr. Oxford (Eng.) U., 1987-88; lectr. U. Calif., Santa Barbara, 1976-77; asst. prof. U. Puget Sound, Tacoma, Wash., 1977-79; Spicer prof. U. Va., Charlottesville, 1979—. Fulbright rschr., Tokyo, Kyoto, Japan, 1993-94, Fulbright chair, Bologna, Italy, 1999; jud. fellow U.S. Supreme Ct., Washington, 1982-83; vis. postdoctoral fellow Russell Sage Found., N.Y.C., 1981-82; lectr. USIA, Burma, Japan, France, 1994-95. Author: Supreme Court Watch, 1991—,

Constitutional Law and Politics, 2 vols., 5th edit., 2003, Storm Center: The Supreme Court in American Politics, 6th edit., 2003, To Dream of Dreams: Constitutional Politics in Postwar Japan, 1996, To Dream of Dreams: Religious Freedom in Postwar Japan, 1996; editor: Views from the Bench, 1985, Judges on Judging, 1997, Government by the People, 19th edit., 2002. Rappatour, jud. selection 20th Century Fund Task Force, N.Y., 1986-87. Tom C. Clark Jud. Fellow, Jud. Fellows Commn., Washington, 1983. Mem. ABA (Silver Gavel award 1987), Am. Judicature Soc., Am. Polit. Sci. Assn., Supreme Ct. Hist. Soc. (editl. bd. 1982—), Internat. Polit. Sci. Assn. Democrat. Avocations: painting, travel. Home: 916 Tilman Rd Charlottesville VA 22901-6338 Office: U Va 232 Cabell Hall Charlottesville VA 22901

O'BRIEN, ELMER JOHN, librarian, educator; b. Kemmerer, Wyo., Apr. 8, 1932; s. Ernest and Emily Catherine (Reinhart) O'B.; m. Betty Alice Peterson, July 2, 1966. AB, Birmingham So. Coll., 1954; Th.M., Iliff Sch. Theology, 1957; MA, U. Denver, 1961. Ordained to ministry Methodist Ch., 1957; pastor Meth. Ch., Pagosa Springs, Colo., 1957—60; circulation-reference librarian Boston U. Sch. Theology, 1961—65; asst. librarian Garrett-Evang. Theol. Sem., Evanston, Ill., 1965—69; librarian, prof. United Theol. Sem., Dayton, Ohio, 1969—96, prof. emeritus, 1996—; abstractor Am. Bibliog. Center, 1969—73; dir. Ctr. for Evang. United Brethren Heritage, 1979—96; acting libr. Iliff Sch. Theology, 2000—01. Chmn. div. exec. com. Dayton-Miami Valley Libr. Consortium, 1983-84; rsch. assoc. Am. Antiquarian Soc., 1990. Author: Bibliography of Festschriften in Religion Published Since 1960, 1972, Religion Index Two: Festschriften, 1960-69; contbg. author: Communication and Change in American Religious History, 1993, Essays in Celebration of the First Fifty Years, 1996; pub. Meth. Revs. Index, 1818-1985, 1989-91; contbr. essay to profl. jour. Recipient theol. and scholarship award Assn. Theol. Schs. in U.S. and Can., 1990-91; Assn. Theol. Schs. in U.S. and Can. library staff devel. grantee, 1976-77, United Meth. Ch. Bd. Higher Edn. and Ministry research grantee, 1984-85 Mem. ALA, Acad. Libr. Assn. Ohio, Am. Theol. Libr. Assn. (head bur. personnel and placement 1969-73, dir. 1973-76, v.p. 1977-78, pres. 1978-79), Am. Antiquarian Soc. (rsch. assoc. 1990), Delta Sigma Phi, Omicron Delta Kappa, Eta Sigma Phi, Kappa Phi Kappa. Clubs: Torch Internat. (v.p. Dayton club 1981-82, pres. 1982-83). Home: 4840 Thunderbird Dr Apt 281 Boulder CO 80303-3829 E-mail: Ejobr@aol.com.

O'BRIEN, JAMES ALOYSIUS, foreign language educator; b. Cin., Apr. 7, 1936; s. James Aloysius and Frieda (Schirmer) O'B.; m. Rumi Matsumoto, Aug. 26,1961. BA, St. Joseph's Coll., 1958; MA, U. Cin., 1960; PhD, Ind. U., 1969. Instr. English, St. Joseph's Coll., Rensselaer, Ind., 1960-62; asst. prof. Japanese, U. Wis., Madison, 1968-74, assoc. prof., 1974-81, prof., 1981—2003, prof. emeritus, 2003—, chmn. East Asian langs and lit., 1979-80, 82-85, 1996—2000. Author: Dazai Osamu, 1975, Akutagawa and Dazai: Instances of Literary Adaptation, 1988; translator: Selected Stories and Sketches (Dazai Osamu), 1983, Three Works (Muro Saisei), 1985, Crackling Mountain and Other Stories (Dazal Osamu), 1989. Mem. MIddleton City Common Coun., 1996—. Ford Found fellow, 1965-66; Fulbright-Hays and NDEA fellow, 1966-68; Social Sci. Research Council fellow, 1973-74; Japan Found. fellow, 1977-78 Mem. Assn. Asian Studies, Assn. Tchrs. of Japanese (exec. com. 1981-84, dir. devel. 1981-83, pres. 1984-90) Home: 2533 Branch St Middleton WI 53562-2812 Office: U Wis Dept East Asian Langs-Lit 1220 Linden Dr Madison WI 53706-1525

O'BRIEN, JAMES FRANCIS, chemistry educator; b. Phila., July 4, 1941; s. Francis J. and Marie D. (Smith) O'B.; m. Barbara L. Wiley, June 6, 1970; children: Ted, Michael. BS, Villanova U., 1964; PhD, U. Minn., 1968. Postdoctoral fellow Los Alamos (N.Me.) Sci. Lab., 1968-69; disting. prof. of chemistry S.W. Mo. State U., Springfield, 1969—.

O'BRIEN, JOHN CONWAY, economist, educator, writer; b. Hamilton, Lanarkshire, Scotland; s. Patrick and Mary (Hunt) O'B.; m. Jane Estelle Judd, Sept. 16, 1966; children: Kellie Marie, Kerry Patrick, Tracy Anne, Kristen Noël. B.Com., U. London, 1952, cert. in German lang., 1954; tchr.'s cert., Scottish Edn. Dept., 1954; AM, U. Notre Dame, 1959, PhD, 1961. Tchr. Scottish High Schs., Lanarkshire, 1952-56; instr. U. B.C., Can., 1961-62; asst. prof. U. Sask., Can., 1962-63, U. Dayton, Ohio, 1963-64; assoc. prof. Wilfrid Laurier U., Ont., Can., 1964-65; from asst. to full prof. Econs. and Ethics Calif. State U., Fresno, 1965—. Vis. prof. U. Pitts., 1969-70, U. Hawaii, Manoa, 1984, U. Queensland, Brisbane, Australia, 1994; keynote speaker Wageningen Agrl. U., The Netherlands, 1987; presenter papers 5th, 6th, 10th World Congress of Economists, Tokyo, 1977, Mexico City, 1980, Moscow, 1992; presenter Schmoller Symposium, Heilbronn am Neckar, Fed. Republic Germany, 1988, paper The China Confucius Found. and "2540" Conf., Beijing, 1989, 6th Internat. Conf. on Cultural Econs., Univ. Umeå, Sweden, 1990, Internat. Soc. Intercommunication New Ideas, Sorbonne, Paris, 1990, European Assn. for Evolutionary Polit. Economy, Vienna, Austria, 1991; active rsch. U. Göttingen, Fed. Republic Germany, 1987; acad. cons. Cath. Inst. Social Ethics, Oxford; presenter in field. Author: Karl Marx: The Social Theorist, 1981, The Economist in Search of Values, 1982, Beyond Marxism, 1985, The Social Economist Hankers After Values, 1992; editor: Internat. Rev. Econs. and Ethics, Internat. Jour. Social Econs., Ethical Values and Social Econs., 1981, Selected Topics in Social Econs., 1982, Festschrift in honor of George Rohrlich, 3 vols., 1984, Social Economics: A Pot=Pourri, 1985, The Social Economist on Nuclear Arms: Crime and Prisons, Health Care, 1986, Festschrift in honor of Anghel N. Rugina, Parts I and II, 1987, Gustav von Schmoller: Social Economist, 1989, The Eternal Path to Communism, 1990, (with Z. Wenxian) Essays from the People's Republic of China, 1991, Festschrift in Honor of John E. Elliott, Parts I and II, 1992, Communism Now and Then, 1993, The Evils of Soviet Communism, 1994, Ruminations on the USSR, 1994, The Future Without Marx, 1995, Essays in Honour of Clement Allan Tisdell, 1996, Essays in Honor of Clement Allan Tisdell, Part I, 1996, Part II and III, 1997, Part IV and V, 1998, Part VI, 1999, Part VII and VIII, 2000, Social Economists at Work, 1999, Our Fragile Civilization, 2001; translator econ. articles from French and German into English; contbr. numerous articles to profl. jours. With British Royal Army Service Corps, 1939-46, ETO, NATOUSA, prisoner of war, Germany. Recipient GE Corp. award Stanford U., 1966, Ludwig Mai Svc. award Assn. for Social Econs., Washington, 1994; named Disting. Fellow of Internat. Soc. for Intercomm. of New Ideas, Paris, 1990. Fellow Internat. Inst. Social Econs. (mem. coun., program dir. 3d World Cong. Social Econs. Fresno Calif. 1983, keynote spkr. 4th conf. Toronto 1986), Internat. Soc. for Intercomm. New Ideas (disting.); mem. Assn. Social Econs. (dir. west region 1977—, pres.-elect 1988-89, program dir. conf. 1989, pres. 1990, presdl. address Washington 1990, Thomas Divine award 1997), Western Econ. Assn. (organizer, presenter 1977-95), History Econs. Soc., Soc. Reduction Human Labor (exec. com.), European Assn. Evolutionary Polit. Econs., Ga. Acad. Econ. Scis. (Republic of Ga. fgn. mem.). Roman Catholic. Avocations: jogging, collecting miniature paintings, soccer, tennis, photography. Home: 9000 E San Victor Rd 112 Scottsdale AZ 85258 Office: Calif State U Econs And Ethics Dept Fresno CA 93740-0001 E-mail: john_obrien@csufresno.edu.

O'BRIEN, JOHN WILLIAM, JR., investment management company executive, finance educator; b. Bronx, N.Y., Jan. 1, 1937; BS, MIT, 1958; MS, UCLA, 1964. Sr. assoc. Planning Rsch. Corp., L.A., 1962—67; dir. fin. systems group Synergetic Scis., Inc., Tarzana, Calif., 1967—70; dir. analytical svcs. divsn. James H. Oliphant & Co., L.A., 1970—72; chmn. bd., chief exec. officer, pres. Wilshire Assocs. (formerly O'Brien Assocs. Inc.), Santa Monica, Calif., 1972—75; v.p. A.G. Becker Inc., 1975—81; chmn., chief exec. officer Leland O'Brien Rubinstein Assocs., 1981—97; mng. dir. Credit Suisse Asset Mgmt., N.Y.C., 1997—2000; adj. prof. finance U.C. Berkeley Haas Sch. Bus., 2000—. Recipient Graham and Dodd award Fin. Analysts Fedn., 1970; named Businessman of Yr. Fortune Mag., 1987. Mem.: Delta Upsilon. Home: 119 Jasmine Creek Dr Corona Del Mar CA 92625-1418 E-mail: obrien@jwobrien.com.

O'BRIEN, KATHY MOSDAL, educator; b. Billings, Mont., Nov. 10, 1951; d. Thelmer and Grace Ruth (McCaskie) Mosdal; m. Wayne Robert Moist, June 16, 1979 (div. May 1981); m. Curtis Charles O'Brien, Oct. 19, 1985. BA, Wartburg Coll., 1974; MA, Western Wash. U., 1992. Tchr. Dawson County Sch. Dist., Glendive, Mont., 1974—75, Crook County Sch. Dist., Sundance, Wyo., 1975—87, Albany County Sch. Dist., Laramie, Wyo., 1987—90; tchg. asst. Western Wash. U., Bellingham, 1990—92; English instr. Bellingham Tech. Coll., Whatcom C.C., Bellingham, Wash., 1992—94, Skagit Valley Coll., Mt. Vernon, Wash., 1992—94, Miles C.C., Miles City, Mont., 1994—99; curator of edn. Western Heritage Ctr., Billings, Mont., 2000—01; asst. dir. Acad. Support Ctr. Mont. State U., Billings, 2001—. Mem. State Hist. Records Adv. Bd., Helena, Mont., 2000—02, Mont. Com. for the Humanities, Missoula, 2001—. Contbr. articles to profl. jours. Recipient Celebrate Literacy award, Internat. Reading Assn., Laramie, 1989. Democrat. Avocations: quilting, reading.

O'BRIEN, MARYANN ANTOINETTE, retired nursing educator; b. Keiser, Pa., Jan. 30, 1938; d. John James and Antoinette Phyllis (St. Mary) Rugalla; m. Vincent Dennis O'Brien, Nov. 15, 1958; children: Vincent, John, Therese, Joseph. Diploma, Temple U. Hosp., 1958; BA in Profl. Arts., St. Joseph's Coll., 1988; postgrad., Nova U., 1990—. Cert. emergency nurse; cert. BCLS; cert. ACLS. Vis. nurse Vis. Nurse Assn. of Jersey City, 1958-59; staff nurse Bayonne (N.J.) Hosp., 1961-66, Alexian Bros. Hosp., Elizabeth, N.J., 1966-76, Clearbrook Adult Community, Cranbury, N.J., 1976-78; asst. dir. nursing Cen. Jersey Jewish Home for the Aged, Somerville, N.J., 1978-79; surg. nurse S.W. Regional Med. Ctr., Fort Myers, Fla., 1980; staff, asst dir. nursing Cape Coral (Fla.) Hosp., 1980-89; assoc. exec. dir. nursing Humana McFarland Hosp., Lebanon, Tenn., 1989-90; nurse educator James Lorenzo Walker Inst. Tech., Naples, Fla., 1990—2002, mem. CISD team; ret., 2002. Mem. sch. adv. com., 1994—98; chair, 1996—97, 1997—98; sec., 1998—99. Reviewer, author: (with others) Practical Nurse Textbook, 1994, ECG Workbook, 1995; item writer NCLEX-PN, 1994, 96; author: (videos) Enteral Nutrition, 1999, Infection Control, 2000, Prevention and Medical Errors, 2001. Recipient Tchr. of Distinction Collier County Edn. Found., 1999, 2000, 01, Golden Apple Tchr. award, 2001. Mem. NEA, Fla. Nurses Assn., Fla. Vocat. Assn., Fla. Tchg. Profl. Assn., Collier County Vocat. Adult Assn., Assn. Practical Nurse Educators of Fla., Temple U. Alumni Assn., Acad. of Tchrs. E-mail: vinman@swfla.rr.com.

O'BRIEN, NANCY A. youth counselor; b. Watertown, Minn., July 4, 1945; d. Julius Vitus and Viola Frances (Rieland) Hardt; m. Robert S. O'Brien, June 8, 1968; children: Sean, Scott. BS, Coll. St. Teresa, Winona, Minn., 1967; MS, Iowa State U., 1978. Lic. tchr., counselor, Iowa. Tchr. Colorado Springs (Colo.) Community Schs., 1967-68; counselor Title 1 Des Moines Pub. Schs., 1978-79, Waukee (Iowa) Community Schs., 1980-85; guidance cons. Heartland Area Edn. Agy., Johnston, Iowa, 1985-88; counselor Des Moines (Iowa) Pub. Schs., 1988—. Conf. coord., trainer, cons. Children's Health Market. Active Honolulu Symphony, Hawaii Assistance League. Mem. Iowa Assn. For Counseling and Devel. (editor newsletter 1981-83, editorial bd. jour. 1983-85, pres. local chpt. 1985, pub. relations com. 1986, sec. 1987-95), Iowa Sch. Counselors Assn. (sen. 1985, del. to nat. conv. 1987), Am. Assn. for Counseling and Devel., Am. Sch. Counselors Assn. Roman Catholic. Avocation: reading. Home: 94-511 Lumiauau St Waipahu HI 96797-5055

O'BRIEN, TIMOTHY ANDREW, writer, journalist, lawyer, educator; b. N.Y.C., July 11, 1943; s. Timothy Andrew and Hildegarde J. (Schenkel) O'B.; m. Maria de Guadalupe Margarita Moreno, Jan. 15, 1971; children: Theresa Marie, Tim A. BA in Comm., Mich. State U., 1967; MA in Polit. Sci., U. Md., 1972; postgrad., Tulane U., 1974-75; JD, Loyola U., New Orleans, 1976. Bar: La. 1976, D.C. 1977, U.S. Supreme Ct 1981. News writer, reporter, anchor WKBD-TV, Detroit, 1968-69, WTOP-TV, Washington, 1969-72, WDSU-TV, New Orleans, 1972-74, WVUE-TV, New Orleans, 1974-77; law corr. ABC News, 1977-99; corr. Cable News Network (CNN), 2001—. Leo Goodwin Prof. Law Southeastern U., 1997; disting. prof. law Hofstra U., Sch. Law, 2000, St. Thomas Sch. Law, Miami, 2001, Nova U., 2002; disting. vis. prof. law, Nova Southeastern U., 1999, 2001, Loyola Sch. of Law, 2003. Contbr. articles to profl. jours. Bd. govs. Woodward Acad., College Park, Ga.; bd. visitors Loyola U. Sch. Law., 1997—. Recipient AP award for outstanding reporting of extraordinary event, 1976, New Orleans Press Club award for non-spot news reporting, 1976, Emmy award for documentary on D.C., 1969, ABA awards of merit, 1979 (2), 80, 85, Gavel award for documentary, 1980, Nat. award for human rights reporting Women in Comm., 1981, Disting. Alumnus award Mich. State U., 1996. Mem. Am. Law Inst., Radio-TV Corrs. Assn. Washington, Am. Judicature Soc. (bd. dirs. 1991-97). Office: CNN 820 First St NE Washington DC 20002

O'BRIEN, WALTER FENTON, mechanical engineering educator; b. Roanoke, Va., Feb. 4, 1937; s. Walter Fenton and Lorraine Estelle (Doolin) O'B.; m. Nancy Brooks, Mar. 20, 1959; children: Julia, Kelly. BSME, Va. Poly. Inst. & State U., 1960; MSME, Purdue U., 1961; PhD in Mech. Engring., Va. Poly. Inst. & State U., 1968. Registered profl. engr., Va. Engring. specialist Aerospace Rsch. Corp., Roanoke, 1961-64; instr. in mech. engring. Va. Poly. Inst. & State U., Blacksburg, 1964-67; mgr. new products Litton Industries, Blacksburg, 1967-70; asst. prof. mech. engring. Va. Poly. Inst. & State U., Blacksburg, 1970-72, assoc. prof. mech. engring., 1972-78, prof. mech. engring., 1978-85, J. Bernard Jones prof. mech. engring., 1985—, assoc. dean rsch. and grad studies coll. engring., 1990-93, head dept. mech. engring., 1993—. Cons. to various cos. and govt., 1970—; vis. scientist aeropropulsion lab. USAF, Wright AFB, Ohio, 1987-88; lectr. NATO, Boston, Munich, Paris, 1992, mem. propulsion and energetics panel, 1993—. Contbr. over 80 articles to profl. jours. Bd. dirs. Va. Mus. Transp., Roanoke, 1985-92. Fellow ASME (chmn. internat. gas turbine inst. 1983-89, v.p. 1994-97); assoc. fellow AIAA. Achievements include work in propulsion engineering and turbine compressors. Home: 1602 Carlson Dr Blacksburg VA 24060-5553 Office: Mech Engring Dept 100 S Randolph Hall Va Tech Blacksburg VA 24061

O'BRIEN, WILLIAM JOSEPH, materials engineer, educator, consultant; b. N.Y.C., July 25, 1940; s. William P. O'Brien; divorced; children: Anne Marie, Matthew. BS, CCNY, 1960; MS, NYU, 1962; PhD, U. Mich., 1967. Assoc. dir. rsch. J.F. Jelenko Inc., N.Y.C., 1956-61; from asst. to assoc. prof. Marquette U., Milw., 1961-67; mech. engr., dir. Biomaterials Rsch. Ctr., Milw., 1967-70; prof. biologic and materials scis. U. Mich., Ann Arbor, 1970—, dir. Biomaterials Rsch. Ctr., 1994—. Cons. WHO, N.Y.C., 1967-70, Johnson & Johnson, Inc., New Brunswick, N.J., 1970-83; chmn. rsch. com. Sch. Dentistry U. Mich., 1987-91. Editor: (book) Dental Materials, 1989; inventor Magnesia Ceramic, 1985. Recipient UN Cert., 1967, Disting. Contbn. award Mexican Prosthodontics Soc., 1991. Mem. Materials Rsch. Soc., Acad. Dental Materials, Adhesion Soc., Dental Materials Group (pres. 1985). Office: U Mich Biomaterials Rsch Ctr 1011 N University Ave Ann Arbor MI 48109-1078

O'BRIEN-CROTHERS, JANICE LOUISE, elementary education educator; b. La Grange, Ill., Feb. 2, 1957; d. Robert Allen and Carolyn Louise (Wittmann) Jones; children: David, Aaron, Carly; m. James Crothers; 1 stepchild, Calvin. BA in Early Childhood Edn. with honors, Elmhurst Coll., 1989; MEd in Ednl. Leadership, Concordia U., 1999. Cert. tchr., Ill. Tchr. La Grange Day Care Ctr., 1975-77; sales rep. Carson Pirie Scott, Hillside, Ill., 1977-78; printer Papermate, La Grange Park, Ill., 1978-79; self-employed home day care provider La Grange, 1979-84; elem. tchr. Brook Park Sch., La Grange Park, 1989—2000; tchr. 3rd grade Komensky Sch., 2000—01; tchr. K/EC Central Rd. Sch., 2001—. Adv. panel for spl. edn. and early childhood edn. Elmhurst (Ill.) Coll., 1990—, mentor tchr. 1992—; adj. prof. Elmhurst Coll., 1999-. Pianist Elmhurst Christian Reformed Ch., Elmhurst, Ill., 2001—. Recipient Ill. Pride of Headstart award, State Capitol, 1990. Mem. NEA, Ill. Edn. Assn., ASCD. Avocations: wedding coord., musician, vocalist, writing children's books, drawing.

O'BRYANT, CECYLE ARNOLD, secondary English language educator; b. Middlesex, N.C. d. Hubert Leon and Oma Cecyle (Sugg) Arnold; children: Charles III, Hubert A., Patrick C. BA in English and Polit. Sch., Wake Forest U.; MEd in English Edn., U. N.C., Greensboro; postgrad., various schs. and subjects.; degree in academically gifted students, U. N. Carolina. English tchr. Broadway High Sch., N.C., Hepzibah High Sch., Ga., High Point Cen. High Sch, N.C.; 10th grade advanced placement English tchr. Atkins High Sch., N.C.; tchr. academically gifted students Atkins Mid. Sch. Sponsor Nat. Honor Soc., Hepzibah High Sch., High Point Cen., Great Books Club High Point Cen.; adv. coun. sch. improvement team, Atkins Sch. Mem. Winston-Salem, Forsyth Tchrs. Adv. Coun. on Exceptional Children; tchr. Sunday Sch.; pres. Bapt. Women; ind. vol. work for charitable and civic causes; chmn. So. Assn. of Credentials Comml. Dept. Grantee PTA Coun.; recipient N.C. Sch. of Arts Drama scholarship two consevutive summers; tchr. winner N.C. Ctr. for Advancement of Teachers, 1989, 93; named Atkins Tchr. of Yr.; semifinalist W.S. Forsyth County Schs. Tchr. of Yr. Mem. ASCD, Forsyth Assn. Classroom Tchrs., World Coun. of Exceptional Children, N.C. Assn. Educators, N.C. Tchrs. of English, Arts Coun. (sch. rep), Internat. Honorary Ednl. Orgn., Delta Kappa Gamma. Office: Atkins Middle School N Cameron Ave Winston Salem NC 27107

OBST, NORMAN PHILIP, economist, educator; b. Bklyn., May 25, 1944; s. Joseph J. and Pearl L. (Newmark) O.; m. Barbara E. Brudevold, Dec. 23, 1970; children: Lindora, Jannise, Laara, Benjamin. BA, SUNY, Binghamton, 1965; MS in Econs., Purdue U., 1967, PhD in Econs., 1970. Asst. prof. U. Wash., 1970-73, Mich. State U., East Lansing, 1973-77, assoc. prof., 1977-92, prof. econs., 1992—, dir. undergraduate programs, 2000—. Cons. in field. Referee Am. Econ. Rev., Internat. Econ. Rev., Jour. of Money, Credit and Banking, Eastern Econ. Jour., Jour. of Econ. Issues, Jour. of Macroeconomics, Jour. of Econs. and Bus., Zentralblatt fur Mathematik; contbr. articles to profl. jours. Supr., assessor Williamstown Twp., 1988—2000, sec. bd. appeals, 1988—2000, planning commn. mem. 1974-88, vice chmn. 1985-88; chief adminstrv. officer, Williamstown Twp. Budget, 1989—2000; cen. adminstr. Williamstown Twp. Sewer System, 1988—2000; bd. determination Ingham County Drain Commn., 1989; co-chair govt. com. I-96 strategic econ. plan with Lansing area bus. leaders, 1990. Mem. Am. Econ. Assn., Am. Fin. Assn., Midwest Econ. Assn., Mich. Assessors Assn. Avocations: chess, table tennis, financial markets. Office: Mich State Univ Marshall Hall Dept Econs East Lansing MI 48824-1038

OCHSENWALD, WILLIAM LEO, history educator, consultant; b. Columbus, Ohio, June 18, 1943; s. William Theodore and Corinne (Herderick) O. BA in History, Ohio State U., 1964, MA, 1966; PhD, U. Chgo., 1971. Asst. prof. history Va. Poly. Inst. and State U., Blacksburg, 1971-77, assoc. prof., 1977-86, prof., 1986—. Assoc. fellow Middle East Centre, Cambridge (Eng.) U., 1979-80. Author: The Hijaz Railroad, 1980, Religion, Society and State in Arabia, 1984; reviewer for jours. Grantee Am. Rsch. Inst. in Turkey, 1973, 75, Social Sci. Rsch. Coun., 1975, 79; Fulbright-Hays fellow, 1969-70. Mem. Middle East Studies Assn., Middle East Inst., Turkish Studies Assn., Soc. for Gulf Studies. Office: Va Poly and State U Dept History Blacksburg VA 24061-0117

OCKERMAN, HERBERT W. agricultural studies educator; b. Chaplin, Ky., Jan. 16, 1932; m. Frances Ockerman (dec.). BS with Distinction, U. Ky., 1954, MS, 1958; PhD, N.C. State U., 1962; postgrad., Air U., 1964-70, Ohio State U., 1974, postgrad., 1983, postgrad., 1987, postgrad., 2001, postgrad., 2003. Asst. prof. Ohio State U., Columbus, 1961-66, assoc. prof., 1966-71, prof., 1971—. Former mem. Inst. Nutrition and Food Tech.; judge regional and state h.s. sci. fairs, 1965—, Ham Contest, Ky. State Fair, Sausage and Ham Contest, Ohio Meat Processing Groups; cons. Am. Meat Inst., 1977-88, USDA, 1977-2003, CRC Press., Inc., 1988—; bd. examiners U. Calcutta, 1987-88; examiner U. Mysore, India, 1990-97; expert witness, various firms, 1992—, UN expert 95; mem. expert com. FAO/WHO; presenter, cons. in field. Contbr. more than 196 articles to profl. jours., 76 chpts. to books. Comdr. USAF, 1955-58. Fisher Packing scholar; named Highest Individual in Beef Grading, Kansas City Meat Judging Contest, 1952; recipient Cert. of Appreciation, Ohio Assn. Meat Processors, 1987-2003, Profl. Devel. award Cahill faculty, commendation for internat. work in agr. Ohio Ho. of Reps., badge of merit for svc. to agr. Polish Govt., plaque Argentina Nat. Meat Bd., animal sci. award Roussel UCALF, France, U. Assiuit, Egypt, silver platter Nat. Meat Bd., Sec. Agr., Livestock and Fishery, Argentina, Svc. award Coun. Grad. Students, Pomerance Tchg. award, Outstanding Alumni award U. Ky., also named to Hall of Disting. Alumni, 1995, award for outstanding ednl. achievements Argentine Soc. Agr., Coop. award vet. faculty U. Cordoba, Svc. award Panoma Legis. Br., Brazil; veterinary faculty U. Cordoba, Spain, 1982, 94, Nat. Chung-Hsing U., 1982, 95, Vet. Mus. Ciechanowcu, Poland, Internat. award Assn. Nat. Tech. en Alimentos de Mexico, Can. Indst. Food Sci. and Tech., 1998, Appreciation plaque Republic of Argentina, 1999, Candle Stick of Knowledge, Ludhiana U., Punjab, India, 1999, Internat. award Am. Meat Sci. Assn., 1999, 2000, Appreciation Plaque Am. Coll. Commerce, 1999, Appreciation Plaque, Taiwan, 1999, Plaque, Selcuk U., Turkey, 1999, Folklore and Cultural memento Sudanese Socs., Sudan U., 1999, Homage and Acknowledgment, Argentine Sec. Agr., 2000, Most Honored Guest, Weifang, China, 2001, World History award Jhadong U. Taiwan, China, 2001, plaque Congress of Hon., Cordoba, Spain, 2001, Michal Oczapowski award Polish Acad. Sci., 2002, Sausage Maker award, Poland, 2001, Great Educator award, China, 2001, Silver Medallion award INTA Argentina, 2001, Pub. award Taiwan, 2002, Animal Sci. Plaque, China, 2002, Food award, China, 2002, Michal Oczapowski medal 2002. Mem. NAS, NCR, ASTM, Am. Meat Sci. Assn., Am. Soc. Animal Sci. (Rsch. award 1987), Reciprocal Meat Conf., European Meeting of Meat Rsch. Workers, Polish Vet. Soc. (hon.), Inst. Food Technologists (nat. and OVS chpts.), Inst. Food Tech. (Internat. award 1998, 2000), Can. Meat Sci. Assn., Internat. Congress Meat Sci. and Tech., Rsch. in Basic Sci., Phi Beta Delta (treas. 1987, pres. 1991, Internat. scholar award 1991, Internat. Faculty award 1991, Presdl. medallion award), Gamma Sigma Delta (Rsch. award 1977, Internat. award of merit 1988), Sigma Xi (outstanding advisor in coll. award 1995), Phi Beta Kappa (Outstanding Tchg. award 1997, Extension Diversity award 1997, Pomerene Tchg. Enhancement award 1997, Outstanding Internat. Faculty award 1997), Internat. Gamma Sigma Delta (Disting. Achievement Nat. award 1998), Phi Kappa Phi. Office: Ohio State U Meat Lab Animal Sci 2029 Fyffe Rd Columbus OH 43210-1007 E-mail: ockerman.2@osu.edu.

O'CONNELL, DANIEL CRAIG, psychology educator; b. Sand Springs, Okla., May 20, 1928; s. John Albert and Letitia Rutherford (McGinnis) O'C. BA, St. Louis U., 1951, Ph.L., 1952, MA, 1953, S.T.L., 1960; PhD, U. Ill., 1963. Joined Soc. of Jesus, 1945; asst. prof. psychology St. Louis U., 1964-66, asso. prof., 1966-72, prof., 1972-80, trustee, 1973-78, pres., 1974-78; prof. psychology Loyola U., Chgo., 1980-89, Georgetown U., Washington, 1990-98, emeritus, 1998—, chmn., 1991-96. Vis. prof. U. Melbourne, Australia, 1972, U. Kans., 1978-79, Georgetown U., 1986, Loyola U., Chgo., 1998-2003; Humboldt fellow Psychol. Inst. Free U. Berlin, 1968; sr. Fulbright lectr. Kassel U., W. Ger., 1979-80. Author: Critical Essays on Language Use and Psychology, 1988; contbr. articles to profl. jours. Recipient Nancy McNeir Ring award for outstanding teaching St. Louis U., 1969; NSF fellow, 1961, 63, 65, 68; Humboldt Found. grantee,

1973; Humboldt fellow Tech. U. of Berlin, 1987. Fellow Am., Mo. psychol. assns., Am. Psychol. Soc.; mem. Midwestern, Southwestern, Eastern psychol. assns., Psychologists Interested in Religious Issues, Psychonomic Soc., Soc. for Scientific Study of Religion, N.Y., Mo. acads. sci., AAUP, AAAS, Phi Beta Kappa. Home and Office: Hallahan House 4511 W Pine Blvd Saint Louis MO 63108-2191 E-mail: doconnell1@jesuits-mis.org.

O'CONNELL, JACK, school system administrator; b. Glen Cove, N.Y., Oct. 8, 1951; m. Doree O'Connell; 1 child, Jennifer Lynn. Student, Ventura Coll.; BA, Calif. State U., Fullerton; cert. secondary tchr., Calif. State U., Long Beach, 1975. Tchr. various high schs.; mem. Calif. State Assembly, 1982—94, Calif. State Senate, 1994—2002, chair budget sucbom. on edn., chair majority caucus and coastal caucus, mem. bus. and professions com., constnl. amendments com., mem. edn. com., environ. quality com., others; Calif. State supt. of pub. instrn., 2003. Recipient awards Small Bus. Assn., Calif. State U. Alumni Coun., Faculty Assn. Calif. C.C., Hispanic C. of C., Internat. Sr. Citizens Assn., Planning and Conservation League, Calif. Sch. Bds. Assn., Calif. Bldg. Industry Assn., Doris Day Animal League, Calif. assn. for the Physically Handicapped, Bus. and Profl. Women, MADD, Calif. Healthcare Inst. Democrat. also: 228 W Carrillo St Ste F Santa Barbara CA 93101-6162 also: 1260 Chorro St Ste A San Luis Obispo CA 93401-3669 also: 89 S California St Ste E Ventura CA 93001-2897 Office: Calif Dept Edn 1430 N St Sacramento CA 95814

O'CONNELL, JOHN F. lawyer, retired law educator; b. Mahanoy City, Pa., Jan. 4, 1919; s. Thomas Vincent O'Connell and Mary Elizabeth Cunningham; m. Rosemary Teresa O'Connell, Jan. 9, 1943 (dec. June 1990); children: Paul, Rosemarie, Dennis, Michael, Patricia, Kevin; m. Yvonne Louise O'Connell, Dec. 2, 1993. BA, La Salle Coll., 1940; JD, Western Reserve U., 1950; MA, U. Md., 1960; PhD, So. Calif. U., 1995. Commd. 2d lt. USAF, 1943, advanced through grades to col., ret., 1968; dean, law prof. Western State U. Coll. Law, Fullerton, Calif., 1975-87; law prof. Am. Coll. Law, Brea, Calif., 1987-89; dean So. Calif. Coll. Law, Brea, 1989-91, ret., 1991. Author: Remedies in a Nutshell, 1985. Decorated Legion of Merit, Bronze Star, Army Commendation medal, Air Force Commendation medal. Mem. Air Force Office Spl. Agts., Delta Theta Phi. Republican. Roman Catholic. Home: 8764 Captains Pl Las Vegas NV 89117-3516

O'CONNELL, WILLIAM RAYMOND, JR., educational consultant, retired academic administrator; b. Richmond, Va., Jan. 4, 1933; s. William Raymond and Mary Helen (Wenenger) O'C.; m. Peggy Annette Tucker, June 29, 1957; 1 child, William Raymond III. BMusEd, Richmond Profl. Inst., 1955; MA, Columbia U., 1962, EdD, 1969; HLD (hon.), New Eng. Coll., 1995. Asst. to provost Richmond (Va.) Profl. Inst., 1955-57, dean of men, 1957-59, dean of students, dean of men, 1959-61; asst. to provost, dir. student info. ctr. Tchrs. Coll. Columbia U., N.Y.C., 1962-65, rsch. asst. inst. of higher edn. Tchrs. Coll., 1965-66; rsch. assoc. So. Regional Edn. Bd., Atlanta, 1966-69, dir. spl. programs, 1969-73, project dir., undergrad. edn. reform, 1973-79; dir. curriculum and faculty devel. Assn. Am. Colls., Washington, 1979-80, v.p. for programs, 1980-82, v.p., 1982-85; pres. New Eng. Coll., Henniker, NH, 1985-95, pres. emeritus, 1995—; vis. sr. fellow Assn. Am. Colls. and Univs., 1995—97; dir. health edn. and leadership program Nat. Assn. Student Pers. Adminstrs., 1996—2002. Cons. Coun. for Advancement Small Colls., 1975; mem. adv. com. project on instnl. renewal through improvement of tchg. Soc. for Values in Higher Edn., 1975-78; mem., evaluator N.H. Postsecondary Edn. Commn., 1987-95, vice chmn., 1990-92, chmn., 1992-94; evaluator Nat. Ctr. for Rsch. to Improve Postsecondary Tchg. and Learning, 1987-90, New Eng. Assn. Schs. and Colls., 1988, 91; mem. higher edn. rev. panel awards for pioneering achievements in higher edn. Charles A Dana Found., 1988, 89. Author, editor: articles to profl. publs. Pres. Richmond Cmty. Amb. Project, 1958-60, bd. dirs., 1960-61; bd. dirs. Alumni Assn. Acad. divsn. Va. Commonwealth U., 1970-73; trustee Atlanta Boys Choir, Inc., 1978-79, chmn. fundraising com., 1976-77; trustee Atlanta Coun. for Internat. Visitors, 1973-76, 78-79; pres. UN Assn., Atlanta, 1976, 77; mem. steering com. Nat. Coun. chpt. and divsn. pres. UN Assn. U.S., 1977-79, nat. coun., 1980-90; mem. steering com. Leadership Concord, 1992-95, chmn., 1994-95. Named Cmty. Amb. to Sweden Cmty. Amb. Project of the Experiment in Internat. Living, 1956. Fellow Royal Soc. of the Arts (U.K.); mem. N.H. Coun. on World Affairs (bd. dirs. 1993-95), Greater Concord C. of C. (bd. dirs. 1989-93), Coordinating Coun. for Internat. Univs. (bd. dirs. 2001—), Phi Delta Kappa. Methodist. Avocations: antiques, travel.

O'CONNELL-POPE, MARY ANNE PRUDENCE, diagnostic special educator; b. Danbury, Conn., Aug. 7, 1958; d. Eugene William and Georgiana (Conklin) O'Connell; m. Frank V. Pope, May 23, 1987; children: Spencer, Siobhanne, Madelinne. BS in Edn., Westfield (Mass.) State Coll., 1979, MEd, 1981, cert. advanced gen. studies, 1988. Tchr. mentally retarded Stearn Elem. Sch., Pittsfield, Mass., 1979-80, Hibbard Elem. Sch., Pittsfield, 1980-81, Westside Community Sch., Pittsfield, 1981-82, William Elem. Sch., Pittsfield, 1982-85; work-study tchr. Pittsfield High Sch., 1985-87, unit leader, 1987-89; resource room tchr. Reid Mid. Sch., Pittsfield, 1987-89, Camel's Hump Mid. Sch., Richmond, Vt., 1989—2000; diagnostic special educator Chittenden East Supervisory Union, 2000—. Mem. Coun. for Exceptional Children. Home: 31 Aspen Dr Essex Junction VT 05452-4375 Office: Camel's Hump Mid Sch Jericho Rd Richmond VT 05477

O'CONNOR, FRANK M. business educator, sales professional; b. N.Y.C., Oct. 11, 1938; s. Patrick Joseph and Margaret M. (Tully) O'C.; m. Veronica Jane Marie, Oct. 10, 1987. BS, Fordham U., 1969, MBA, 1973. Mktg. adminstr. Am. Can Co., N.Y.C., 1961-71; sales rep. Pfizer Pharms., N.Y.C., 1971-75; mgr. mktg. UN Postal Adminstrn., N.Y.C., 1975-77; regional dir. Roxane Labs., N.Y.C., 1977-87; account mgr. Quad Pharms., N.Y.C., 1987-92; regional mgr. Vangard Labs., Inc., 1992—. Adj. faculty Coll. Bus. Adminstrn., Fordham U., N.Y.C. With USAF, 1957-61. Mem. AAUP, Friendly Sons St. Patrick, Met. Mus. Art. Roman Catholic. Avocations: golf, tennis. Home: 81-12 Courtland Ave Apt 99 Stamford CT 06902

O'CONNOR, KAREN, political science educator, researcher, writer; b. Buffalo, Feb. 15, 1952; s. Robert J. and Norma (Wilton) O'C.; m. F. Allen McDonogh, June 7, 1974 (div. 1986). 1 child, Meghan; m. Richard Cupitt, July 31, 1992. B.A., SUNY-Buffalo, 1973, J.D., 1977, Ph.D., 1979. Bar: Ga. 1978. Instr. polit. sci. Emory U., 1977-78, asst. prof., 1978-83, assoc. prof., 1983-88; prof., 1988-95; prof. Am. Univ., 1995—, dir. Women & Politics Inst., 1999—. Author: Women's Organization's Use of the Courts, 1980; (with N.E. McGlen) Women's Rights, 1983, (with La Sabato) American Government, 8th edit., 2004; Mem. editorial bd. Women & Politics, 1980—, editor, 1999-2003, Law & Policy, 1982—. Jour. of Politics, 1984-87, Am. Politics Quarterly, 1987-90. Contbr. articles to profl. jours. Mem. Am. Polit. Sci. Assn. (exec. council 1985-87), So. Polit. Sci. Assn. (pres. 2000-01), Nat. Capitol Area Pol. Sci. Assn. (pres. 2001-02), Cosmos Club. Home: 4383 Westover Pl NW Washington DC 20016-5555

O'CONNOR, KATHRYN MACVEAN, elementary educator; b. Middletown, NY, Aug. 9, 1960; d. Kenneth Alpin and Anna Margaret (Daley) MacVean; m. Shawn Richard O'Connor, Oct. 15, 1988; children: Andrew Kenneth, Matthew John, Emily Ann. BS, Syracuse U., 1982; MA, SUNY, New Paltz, 1984. Educator Mt. Carmel Sch., Middletown, 1982-85; asst. prof. SUNY, New Paltz, 1985-90; tchr. Minisink Valley Ctrl. Sch., Slate Hill, N.Y., 1987—. Active Jr. League of Orange County, Middletown, 1985—2003, Leadership Orange Class of 2003; bd. dirs. People for People, 1989—98, Sarah Wells Girl Scout Coun., Middletown, 1999—. Named Vol. of Yr., Jr. League of Orange County, 2003. Mem.: Phi Delta Kappa. Avocations: walking, sewing, crafts. Home: PO Box 249 Slate Hill NY 10973-0249 Office: Minisink Valley Elem Sch PO Box 217 Slate Hill NY 10973-0217

O'CONNOR, PATRICIA RANVILLE, secondary and special education educator; b. Flint, Mich., Feb. 24, 1951; d. Marcel L. and Ruth Ellen (Smith) Ranville. BS, Ea. Mich. U., 1973, MA, 1978; MS in Adminstrn., Pepperdine U., 1995. Cert. tchr. (life) Calif., severely handicapped and learning handicapped, multiple subject, resource specialist. Spl. edn. tchr. Genessee Intermediate Sch. Dist., Flint, 1974-78, Barstow (Calif.) Unified Sch. Dist., 1978-81, Westport Sch., L.A., 1981-83; resource specialist Culver City (Calif.) Unified Sch. Dist., 1983-96, mentor tchr., chair dept. spl. edn., coord. sch. improvement program; asst. prin. mid. sch. El Segundo (Calif.) Unified Sch. Dist., 1996-97; prin. El Segundo Mid. Sch., 1997—. Chair sch. site coun., self review com. Coordinated Compliance Review; chair lang. arts curriculum com. dist. El Segundo; team leader dept. edn. program quality rev. State of Calif.; mem. C.A.R.E. Team; reader, scorer Calif. Assessment Program; coord. sch. wide goal setting esteem program Striving for My Personal Best. Recipient Hon. Svc. award PTA. Mem. NEA, Calif. Tchrs. Assn. Home: 5460 White Oak Ave Unit C210 Encino CA 91316-4554

O'CONNOR, PATRICK JOSEPH, writer, musician, university educator; b. Wichita, Kans., Dec. 27, 1948; s. Rubie Nell Bishop; m. Carolyn Sue Drummond-Hay (div. Apr. 1, 1979); 1 child, Dalton. MA in Comm., Wichita State U., 1989. Lectr. Wichita State U., 1994—; instr. Embry-Riddle U., Wichita, 1996—98, Friends U., Wichita, 1997—98; artist in residence Wichita Pub. Schs., 1998—99; music reviewer for popular music and soc. Bowling Green (Ohio) State U., 1996—98. Dir. mus. exhibit Traditions of the Blues in Wichita First Nat. Black Hist. Soc. Kans. and Kans. Interpretive Traveling Exhibit, Kans. State Hist. Society/Kansas Humanities Council/National Endowment for the Humanities, Wichita, Kansas City, 1996—; dir. prodn. for panel and happening Wichita Art Mus., 1999—99; interviewer/writer Documentary: The Wichita Blues History Project, 1999—; panelist Friends U., Wichita, 2002—. Author: Tales From A Blackout, 1997, Wichita Blues: Discovery, 1998, Moody's Skidrow Beanery, 1999, Delano/ Stories From The Neighborhood, 2001, short stories; musician: (cassette tape) Upscale Blues, 1994, (compact disc) Blue Heaven: Bill Garrison with Jimmy D. Lane, 2000; actor: (musical revue) Pump Boys and Dinettes, 1998, Twin Lakes Playhouse; contbr. articles to profl. jours. Grantee Delano Maggard Scholarship grant, Wichita State U., 1989, Profl. Devel. grant, Kans. Arts Commn., 1994, Heritage Program grant, Kans. Humanities Coun.l/NEH, 1996, Rsch. grant, Wichita Cmty. Found., 1996, Multicultural Activity grant, Kans. Arts Commn./Nat. Endowment for the Arts, 1997, Folk Arts Apprenticeship grant, Kans. State Hist. Soc./Nat. Endowment for the Arts, 1997. Mem.: Wichita Blues Soc. (archivist 2003), Kans. Folklore Soc., Am. Fedn. Musicians Local #297 (bd. dirs. 2003). Personal E-mail: Rowfant@hotmail.com.

ODDEN, ALLAN ROBERT, education educator; b. Duluth, Minn., Sept. 16, 1943; s. Robert Norman and Mabel Eleanor (Bjornnes) Odden; m. Eleanor Ann Rubottom, May 28, 1966; children: Sarina, Robert. BS, Brown U., 1965; MDiv, Union Theol. Sem., 1969; MA, Columbia U., 1971, PhD, 1975. Tchr. N.Y.C. Pub. Schs., 1967-72; rsch. assoc. Teachers' Coll. Columbia U., N.Y.C., 1972-75; dir. policy Edn. Commn. of the States, Denver, 1975-84; prof. U. So. Calif., L.A., 1984-93, U. Wis., Madison, 1993—. Rsch. dir. Sch. Fin. Commns., Conn., 1974—75, SD, 1975—76, Mo., 1975—76, Mo., 1993, Mo., 94, NY, 1978—81, NJ, 1991—92, Ark., 2003; co-dir. Consortium Policy Rsch. Edn.; cons. Nat. Govs. Assn., Nat. Conf. State Legislatures, U.S. Sec. Edn., U.S. Senate, U.S. Dept. Edn., many state legislatures and govs.; nat. rsch. coun. task force sch. fin. equity adequacy and productivity, 1996—99; ct. master Superior Ct. N.J. in Abbott V. Burke Sch. Fin. Case, 1997—98. Author: (book) Education Leadership for America's Schools, 1995; co-author: Financing Schools for High Performance, 1998, Paying Teachers for What They Know and Do, 1997, Paying Teachers for What They Know and Do, 2d edit., 2002, School Finance: A Policy Perspective, 1992, School Finance: A Policy Perspective, 2d edit., 2000, Reallocating Resources: How to Boost Student Achievement Without Spending More, 2001; editor: Education Policy Implementation, 1991, Rethinking School Finance, 1992, School-Based Financing, 1999; contbr. articles to profl. jours., chapters to books. Mem. L.A. Chamber Edn. and Human Resources Commn., 1986, Gov.'s Sch. Fin. Commn., Calif., 1987, Calif. Assessment Policy Com., Gov.'s Edn. Task Force, Wis., 1996, Carnegie Corp. Task Force Edn. in the Early Yrs., 1994—96; mem. nat. rsch. coun. com. sch. fin. equity, adequcy and productivity, 1996—99; mem. Gov.'s Blue Ribbon Commn. State and Local Partnerships 21st Century, Wis., 2000. Grantee, Dept. Edn., Carnegie Corp., Spencer Found., Ford Found., Atlantic Philanthropic Svcs., Mellon Found., Carnegie Corp., Pew Charitable Trusts. Mem.: Nat. Soc. Study Edn., Politics Edn. Assn., Am. Ednl. Fin. Assn. (pres. 1979—80), Am. Ednl. Rsch. Assn. Avocations: Lionel training collecting, youth soccer, baseball coach. Home: 3128 Oxford Rd Madison WI 53705-2224 Office: U Wis Sch Edn Wis Ctr Edn Rsch 1025 W Johnson St # 653E Madison WI 53706-1706 E-mail: arodden@facstaff.wisc.edu.

ODEGAARD, DANIEL OWEN, dentist, educator; b. Jan. 22, 1949; s. Carroll O. and Gladys R. (Ihnot) O.; m. Mary Jo Zelenovich, June 3, 1978; children: Andrew, Paul, Kristin. BS, U. Minn., 1970, DDS, 1972. Pvt. practice, Mpls., 1974—. Clin. prof. U. Minn. Sch. Dentistry, Mpls., 1974—. Capt. USAF, 1972—74. Mem.: ADA, Mpls. Dist. Dental Soc., Minn. Dental Assn., Minn. Acad. Restorative Dentistry, Am. Acad. Fixed Prosthodontics, Campus Club (Mpls.). Lutheran. Avocation: musician. Office: 1001 Med Arts Bldg 825 Nicollet Ave Minneapolis MN 55402

O'DELL, BERNICE VINSON (KATHY O'DELL), elementary school educator; b. Ware Shoals, S.C., Dec. 3, 1954; d. William Bryant and Rubye (Medlin) Vinson; m. Robert Keith O'Dell, Feb. 14, 1983; children: Tonya (dec.), Kim. BS, Erskine Coll., Due West, S.C., 1977; MA, Furman U., 1986, 90. Cert. biology and sci. tchr., early childhood edn., educable and trainable mentally handicapped, emotionally handicapped edn., learning disabilities, S.C.; nat. bd. cert. tchr. Speech and hearing asst. Whitten Ctr., Clinton, S.C., 1978-83, tchr. spl. edn., 1983—84, Anderson County Sch. Dist. 2, Honea Path, 1984—. Mem. English Lang. Arts Leadership Team, 2002. Sunday sch. tchr. Mt. Gallagher Bapt. Ch., Ware Shoals, 1989-99. Recipient tchr. incentive award Anderson County Sch. Dist. 2, 1990. Mem.: Internat. Reading Assn. Avocation: handicrafts. Home: PO Box 548 Ware Shoals SC 29692-0548 Office: Marshall Primary Sch 218 Bannister St Belton SC 29627-1831 E-mail: katbug@earthlink.net.

ODELL, DANIEL H. science educator, scuba instructor; b. Chgo., Ill., Feb. 20, 1940; s. Harold Gilliam and Agnes (Rholes) O.; m. Janice Thompson Odell, Jan. 9, 1971 (div. Sept. 1, 1978); 1 child, Jesse Daniel Odell; m. Kathleen Garcia Husted Odell, Jan. 9, 1982; 1 child, David Husted Odell. AA, N. Mex. Mil. Inst., 1960; BS, U. N. Mex., 1964; MEd, Oreg. State U., 1968. Tchr. gen. sci.grade 8 Lincoln Sr. Elem., Stockton, Calif., 1965-67, Sunset Jr. H.S., Coos Bay, Oreg., 1968-79; tchr. advanced biology Robinson Sch., San Juan, P.R., 1979-82; marine environ. tchr. Ctrl. H.S., St. Croix, U.S. Virgin Is., 1982—. Dive instr. NAUI, St. Croix, U.S. Virgin Is., 1984—; water safety instr. Red Cross, St. Croix, U.S. Virgin Is., 1992—; Woodrow Wilson Nat. Fellowship Found. environ. tchr. workshop leader Princeton, 1998; presenter workshops in field; recon instr. trainer coral reef surveys Ctr. for Marine Conservation, 2000. Mem. nat. spiritual assembly Bahai, Virgin Is., 1995—. Recipient: Presdl. award Excellence in Sci. Tchg. Nat. Sci. Tchr. Assn. 1994. Mem. St. Croix Dive Assn. (pres.), St. Croix Power Squadron (exec. officer), St. Croix Environ. Assn. (Environ. Tchr. of the Year 1993), Nat. Sci. Educator Assn., St. Croix Yacht Club. Avocations: diving, sailing, traveling, reading. Home: PO Box 3613 Christiansted VI 00822-3613

O'DELL, JOAN ELIZABETH, lawyer, mediator, business executive, educator; b. East Dubuque, Ill., May 3, 1932; d. Peter Emerson and Olive (Bonnet) O'D.; children: Dominique R., Nicole L. BA cum laude, U. Miami, 1956, JD, 1958. Bar: Fla. 1958, DC 1974, Ill. 1978, Va. 1987, U.S. Supreme Ct. 1972; lic. real estate broker Ill., Va., W.Va. Trial atty. SEC, Washington, 1959-60; asst. state atty. Office State Atty., Miami, Fla., 1960-64; asst. county atty. Dade County Atty.'s Office, Miami, 1964-70; county atty. Palm Beach County Atty.'s Office, West Palm Beach, Fla., 1970-71; regional gen. counsel Region IV EPA, Atlanta, 1971-73, assoc. gen. counsel Washington, 1973-77; sr. counsel Nalco Chem. Co., Oakbrook, Ill., 1977-78; v.p., gen. counsel Angel Mining, Washington and Tenn., 1979-96; pres. S.W. Land Investments, Miami, 1979-88; v.p. Events U.S.A., Washington, 1990—. Mem. Exec. Women's Coun., Tucson, 1982—85; co-chmn. sch. improvement coun. Harpers Ferry Jr. H.S., 2000—; bd. dirs. Tucson Women's Found., 1982—84, U. Ariz. Bus. and Profl. Women's Club, Tucson, 1981—85, LWV, Tucson, 1981—85, pres., 1984—85; bd. dirs. LWV Ariz., 1984—85, chmn. nat. security study; bd. dirs. LWV, Palm Beach County, Fla., 1990—92, Jefferson County Visitors and Conv. Bur., Harpers Ferry, W.Va., 2001—. Mem. Fla. Bar Assn., D.C. Bar Assn., Va. State Bar Assn., Ill. Bar Assn. Avocations: camping, hiking, skiing. E-mail: treetopsjodell@yahoo.com.

ODELL, WILLIAM DOUGLAS, endocrinologist, educator; b. Oakland, Calif., June 11, 1929; s. Ernest A. and Emma L. (Mayer) O.; m. Margaret F. Reilly, Aug. 19, 1950; children: Michael, Timothy, John D., Debbie, Charles. AB, U. Calif., Berkeley, 1952; MD, MS in Physiology, U. Chgo., 1956; PhD in Biochemistry and Physiology, George Washington U., 1965. Intern, resident, chief resident in medicine U. Wash., 1956-60, postdoctoral fellow in endocrinology and metabolism, 1957-58; sr. investigator Nat. Cancer Inst., Bethesda, Md., 1960-65; chief endocrine service NICHD, 1965-66; chief endocrinology Harbor-UCLA Med. Center, Torrance, Calif., 1966-72, chmn. dept. medicine, 1972-79; vis. prof. medicine Auckland Sch. Medicine, New Zealand, 1979-80; prof. medicine and physiology U. Utah Sch. Medicine, Salt Lake City, 1980-99, chmn. dept. internal medicine, 1980-96, prof. medicine and physiology, 1996-99, emeritus prof. medicine and physiology, 1999—. Pres. med. staff U. Utah Sch. Medicine, 1995-96. Mem. editorial bds. med. jours.; author, editor 8 books in field; contbr. over 330 articles to med. jour. With USPHS, 1960-66. Recipient Disting. Svc. award U. Chgo., 1973, Pharmacia award for outstanding contbn. to clin. chemistry, 1977, Gov. award State of Utah Sci. and Tech., 1988, also rsch. awards, Mastership award ACP, 1987. Mem.: Soc. Exptl. Biol. Medicine (councillor), Western Soc. Clin. Rsch. (Mayo Soley award), Western Assn. Physicians (pres.), Pacific Coast Fertility Soc. (pres.), Soc. Study of Reprodn. (bd. dirs.), Endocrine Soc. (v.p., Robert Williams award 1991), Am. Soc. Andrology (pres.), Assn. Am. Physicians, Am. Physiol. Soc., Am. Soc. Clin. Investigation, Alpha Omega Alpha. E-mail: owodell@aol.com.

ODEN, ROBERT A., JR., academic administrator; m. Teresa Oden; children: Robert, Katherine. BA in History and Lit., Harvard Coll.; MA in Religious Studies/Oriental Langs., Cambridge U.; MA in Theology, Harvard Divinity, 1972; D in Near Eastern Langs. and Lit., Harvard U., 1975; MA (hon.), Dartmouth Coll., 1987. Faculty Dartmouth Coll., 1975—89, prof., 1985—89, chair dept. of religion, 1983—89; dir., founder Dartmouth's Humanities Inst.; headmaster Hotchkiss Sch., Lakeville, Conn., 1989—95; pres. Kenyon Coll., Gambier, Ohio, 1995—2002, Carleton Coll., Northfield, Minn., 2002—. Chmn. com. on orgn. and policy Dartmouth Coll., com. on admissions and fin. aid; lectr. in field. Author: The Bible Without Theology, 1987. Mem.: Conn. Assn. Ind. Schs. (bd. dors.). Avocations: fishing, running, religious studies, archaeology. Office: Carleton Coll 1 North College St Northfield MN 55057

ODER, BROECK NEWTON, school emergency management consultant; b. Ill. s. Bruce Newton and Mary Louise Oder; m. Jolene Marie Peragine, 1975 (dec. June 1979). BA in History, U. San Diego, 1974, MA in History, 1975; postgrad., U. N.Mex., 1976-79. Life C.C. tchg. credential, Calif. Rsch. asst. to pres. U. San Diego, 1975; grad. asst. U. N.Mex., Albuquerque, 1976-79; tchr. history, chmn. dept. Santa Catalina Sch., Monterey, Calif., 1979—, asst. dean students, 1981-83, dir. ind. study, 1981-95, dean students, 1983-91, dir. emergency planning, 1986—, dean campus affairs, 1991-94, dir. security, 1994—. Disaster preparedness coun. Monterey County Office Edn., 1988-99; chair Diocesan Sch. Emergency Preparedness Coun, 1991-98. Mem. bd. of tchrs. The Concord Rev.; contbr. articles to profl. publs. including American National Biography. Participant Jail and Bail, Am. Cancer Soc., Monterey, 1988, 89; reviewer sch. emergency plans, Monterey, 1989—. Recipient award of merit San Diego Hist. Soc., 1975, Outstanding Tchr. award U. Chgo., 1985, Outstanding Young Educator award Monterey Peninsula Jaycees, 1988, resolution of commendation Calif. Senate Rules Com., 1988, cert. of commendation Calif. Gov.'s Office Emergency Svcs., 1991, nat. cert. of achievement Fed. Emergency Mgmt. Agy., 1991, Outstanding High Sch. Tchr. award Tufts U., 1998, High Sch. Tchr. of Excellence, U. Calif. at San Diego, 1998, Outstanding Tchr. of Am. History award Calif. DAR, 2001-02; nominee Disney Tchr. award, 2002. Mem. ACLU, NAACP, NRA (life), Am. Hist. Assn., Orgn. Am. Historians, Nat. Coun. on History Edn., Soc. for History Edn., Second Amendment Found., Law Enforcement Alliance Am., Calif. State Sheriffs Assn., Phi Alpha Theta. Avocations: reading, sports, target shooting. Office: Santa Catalina Sch 1500 Mark Thomas Dr Monterey CA 93940-5291

ODISHOO, SARAH A. English language educator; b. Chgo., July 12, 1939; d. Saul Eshoo and Nanajan Odishoo; divorced; children: Elizabeth, Leslie. BA in English Lit., Ill. Wesleyan U., 1961; MA in Poetry and English Lit., N.E. Ill. U., 1980. Instr. English composition No. Ill. U., 1982-85; prof. English, world lit., mythology and writing Columbia Coll., Chgo., 1985—, prof. lit., 1992—. Co-dir. freshman writing program, dir. profl. writing program and seminars Columbia Coll., 1985-89, pres. faculty orgn., 1990-92, dir. myth. workshops, 1998, guest poet/collaborator CD/sound collaboration, dept. sound, 1999, liaison to bd. trustees, CCFO rep., 1999-2000; faculty adv. coun. Ill. Bd. Higher Edn., 1985-89; coord. PEN Midwest Reading Series, 1988-89; archeol. dig for study of mythology of early Jewish and Christian nomadic cultures, Nitzana, 1992; artist in-residence Nitzana (Israel) Ednl. Project, dept. history Ben Gurion U. Negev, 1993, U. Wyo., 1999, Byrdcliffe Colony, Woodstock (NY) Guild, 2000; lectr. River Oaks Art Coun., Oak Pk., Ill., 2000, Chgo. Cultural Ctr., 2003; guest lectr. Hyde Sch., Bath, Maine, 2003; Mythic Path Instr., Hyde Sch., Bath, Maine, 2003. Office: Columbia Coll Chgo 600 S Michigan Ave Chicago IL 60605 E-mail: sodishoo@colum.edu.

ODOM, PATRICIA ANN (PATT ODOM), artist, educator; b. Hattiesburg, Miss., Nov. 21, 1942; d. Charles Casey and Katie Clara (Stringer) O.; m. Robert Frank Drake, Aug. 25, 1964 (div. Jan. 1970); children: Robert Charles, Thomas Casey. BS in Drawing and Painting, U. So. Miss., 1964, M in Art Edn., 1975; studied with Hon Chee Hee, U. Hawaii, 1968; studied with Douglas Walton, La. Tech. U., 1982; student, Ringling Sch. Art & Design, 1994; postgrad., U. Tenn., Arrowmont, 1994-96; numerous art workshops, 1987-98; studied with, Wolf Khan, Barbara Brainard, 2002, Hugh Williams, Santa Fe, Ron Pokrasso, Cynthia Knapp, 2003. Tchr. art E. Elem. Sch., Ocean Springs, Miss., 1966-67, Pecan Park, Ocean Springs, Miss., 1971-75, Ocean Springs H.S., 1975-79; art instr., gallery dir. Gulf Coast C.C., Gautier, Miss., 1980-99. Guest lectr. Hinds C.C., 1997, George Ohr Mus., 2002, Walter Anderson Mus., 2003; guest spkr. Miss. Art Mus., Pascagoula Garden Club; panelist spkr. Miss. Assn. Colls. Conf., 1997; moderator Cmty. Bridges Project, Biloxi, Miss., 1997; tchr. workshops John

Campbell Folk Sch., NC, 2002—03, Pensacola (Fla.) Art Club, 2002—03, Isle of Pines (SC) Sch. Figure and Design, 2003—. Designed logo for Gulf Coast YMCA, Hattiesburg Racquetball and Fitness Ctr.; executed mural at Keesler Air Force Base, 1992; one-woman shows include: William Carey Coll., Gulfport, Miss., 2003, Wolf Face Gallery, Ocean Springs, 2003; exhibited in group shows Meridian Mus., Walter Anderson Mus., Miss. Mus. Art, Shane Sekul Gallery, Attic Gallery, Vicksburg, Miss., 2003; represented in permanent collections 1st Magnolia Bank, Biloxi, Miss., Mobile Mus. Art, Lamar Bank, U. So. Miss., William Carey Coll., Cottonlaudia Mus. Art; prin. works include sculpture Sen. John Stennis, Seabees Base, Gulfport, Miss., 1988; works appear in numerous calendars, (book) In Harmony with Nature, 1989 (Pen and Ink book), Art in Mississippi, 1720-1980; group exhbn: Walter Anderson Mus., Miss. Mus. of Art, Meridian Mus. Art, Mobile, Ala. So. Drawing Exhbn. Recipient Nat. Tchrs. Award of Excellence, 1989, Purchase award, Cottonlandia Mus. Art, 1996, 1st place, Miss. Art Colony Traveling Show, 1997, Honored artist and educator of Miss., Nat. Mus. of Women in the Arts, 2001, Merit award, Cottonlandia Mus. Art, 2002, 3d pl. in exhbn., Art Wave, 2002, 3d pl. Geo Ohr Mus. Nat. Show, Pen and Quill, 2001, 2d pl. award, Cottonlandia Mus. Art, 2002, Grand prize, George Ohr Nat. Challenge, 2002, 2d pl. award, Miss. Art Colony Show, 2002, Best of Show 2-D award, George Ohr Nat. Challenge, 2003, Exceptional Color award, OSAA Exhibit, 2003, Best Acrylic award, Singing River Art Show, 2003. Mem.: Miss. C.C. Art Instrs., Nat. Art Edn. Assn., Gulf Coast Art Assn., Biloxi Art Assn., Ocean Springs Art Assn. (bd. dirs. 1986—87, 1995—96, 1999, pres. 1994, 2002, receiving chair 1988, receiving chair for ann. show 1984—86, past v.p. 1980—81, Exceptional Merit award for color), Singing River Art Assn. (show chair 1988), Jackson County Arts Coun., Miss. Women in Arts, Art Wave (show chair 1980—99), South Miss. Art Assn. (1st pl. printmaking, 1st pl. mixed media, 2d pl. oil, 3d pl. mixed media), Delta Psi Omega, Kappa Kappa Iota. Avocations: painting, gardening, commercial art. Home: 306 Porter St Ocean Springs MS 39564-3714 E-mail: patto@ametro.net.

ODOM, WILLIAM ELDRIDGE, army officer, educator; b. Cookeville, Tenn., June 23, 1932; s. John Albert and Callie Frances (Everhart) O.; m. Anne Weld Curtis, June 9, 1962; 1 child, Mark Weld. BS, U.S. Mil. Acad., 1954; MA, Columbia U., 1962, PhD, 1970; DSc (hon.), Middlebury Coll., 1987. Commd. 2nd lt. U.S. Army, 1954, advanced through grades to lt. gen., 1984; mem. U.S. Mil. Liaison Mission to Soviet Forces, Germany, 1964-66; from asst. prof. to assoc. prof. govt. U.S. Mil. Acad., West Point, 1966-69, 74-76; asst. Army attache U.S. embassy, Moscow, 1972-74; nat. security staff mem. White House, 1977-81; asst. chief of staff for intelligence Dept. Army, Washington, 1981-85; dir. Nat. Security Agy., Fort Meade, Md., 1985-88; dir. nat. security studies Hudson Inst., 1988—. Adj. prof. pol. sci. Yale U., 1989—; chmn. bd. dirs. Am. Sci. and Engring., V-ONE (Virtual Open Network Environment). Author: The Soviet Volunteers, 1973, On Internal War, 1992, Trial After Triumph, 1992, America's Military Revolution, 1993, (with Robert Dujarric) Commonwealth or Empire? Russia, Central Asia and The Transcaucasus, 1995, The Collapse of the Soviet Military, 1998, Fixing Intelligence, 2003. contbr. articles to profl. jours. Trustee Middlebury Coll. Bd. 1987-97. Decorated Def. D.S.M. with oak leaf cluster, D.S.M. with oak leaf cluster, Legion of Merit, Nat. Security medal, Nat. Intelligence D.S.M.; grand cross Order of Merit with Star (Fed. Republic Germany); Order Nat. Security Merit (Republic of Korea), officer Nat. Order of Merit (France). Mem. Coun. on Fgn. Rels., Am. Assn. for Advancement of Slavic Studies, Internat. Inst. for Strategic Studies, Am. Polit. Sci. Assn., Acad. Polit. Sci. Congregationalist. Office: Hudson Inst 1015 18th St NW Ste 300 Washington DC 20036-5200

O'DONNELL, EDITH J. educational and information technology consultant, writer, musician; b. Proctorville, Ohio, Mar. 26, 1929; d. John Jordan and Florence Amber (Banks) Black; m. Edward Kennedy O'Donnell, Dec. 8, 1950; children: Kathleen Marie, Michael Edward. AA, Cerritos Coll., 1963; BA, Calif. State U., Long Beach, 1965, MA, 1973; MLS, U. So. Calif., 1977, EdD, 1991. Libr., tchr. St. Joseph's H.S., Lakewood, Calif., 1968-72; libr., media dir. Los Altos H.S., Hacienda Heights, Calif., 1972-93; faculty libr. info. sci. San Jose State U., Fullerton, Calif., 1991-94; ednl. tech. cons., spkr., 1994—. Condr. workshops and cons. in field; instr. North Orange County C.C. Dist., 1988-90; cons., writer Consolidated Program divsn. State of Calif. Dept. Edn., 1981. Author: Integrating Computers Into the Classroom: The Missing Key, Integrating Internet Into the Classroom: The Missing Icon; contbr. articles to profl. publs.; prod. TV ednl. programs. Del. Gov.'s Coun. on Librs. and Info. Sci., White House Conf., 1980; active La Mirada Symphony Orch., La Mirada Pops Orch. City of Buena Park grantee. Mem. DAR, Computer Using Educators, Calif. Tchrs. Assn., Calif. Sch. Assn. (sect. exec. bd. 1980-86), Sons and Daus. Pioneer River Men, Kappa Delta Pi. Methodist. Address: PO Box 2062 Fullerton CA 92833-0062

O'DONNELL, BROTHER FRANK JOSEPH, principal; b. Phila., Aug. 6, 1942; s. Francis J. and Eleanor E. (Doney) O'D. BA, U. Dayton, 1963; MLS, Cath. U. Am., 1964; MEd, Loyola Coll., 1971; JD, U. Md., 1991. Faculty mem. Cardinal Gibbons High Sch., Balt., ednl. media coord., libr., 1964—, prin., 1969—. Legis. aide, Md. Gen. Assembly, 2000-; dep. dir. Commn. Law Ctr., Balt., 1998; prov. dir. of edn., 1993; spl. asst. to sec. Dept. Juvenile Justice, Md., 2003—. Mem. ABA, Nat. Assn. Secondary Sch. Prins., Nat. Cath. Edn. Assn., Nat. Lawyers Guild, Nat. Ctr. for Non-Profit Bds.

O'DONNELL, MARK PATRICK, writer, drama educator; b. Cleve., July 19, 1954; s. Hubert John and Frances (Novak) O'D. BA magna cum laude, Harvard U., 1976. Faculty dept. drama NYU, N.Y.C., 1984—; faculty New Sch., N.Y.C., 1984—, Yale U., 1998—2003. Author: Elementary Education, 1985, Vertigo Park, 1992, Getting Over Homer, 1996; playwright: Fables for Friends, 1980, That's It, Folks!, 1983, The Nice and the Nasty, 1986, Strangers on Earth, 1988, Vertigo Park, 1990, Scapin, 1996, Let Nothing You Dismay, 1998, Hairspray, 2002; contbg. editor Esquire mag., 1977-78, Spy mag., 1987—, Seven Days mag., 1988-90. Cons. Nat. Gay Task Force, Washington, 1987. Recipient Le Comte Du Nuoy prize, 1980; Guggenheim fellow, 1986. Mem. Dramatists Guild, Writers Guild Am. Home and Office: 202 Riverside Dr Apt 8E New York NY 10025-7280

O'DONNELL, VICTORIA, communication educator; b. Greensburg, Pa., Feb. 12, 1938; d. Victor C. and Helen A. (Detar) O'D.; children from previous marriage: Christopher O'Donnell Stupp, Browning William Stupp; m. Paul M. Monaco, Apr. 9, 1993. BA, Pa. State U., 1959, MA, 1961, PhD, 1968. Asst. prof. comm. Midwestern State U., Wichita Falls, Tex., 1965-67; prof. dept. chair comm. U. No. Tex., Denton, 1967-89; prof., dept. chair comm. Oreg. State U., Corvallis, 1989-91; prof. comm., basic course dir. Mont. State U., Bozeman, 1991-93, prof. comm., dir. honors program, 1993—. Prof. Am. Inst. Fgn. Studies, London, 1988; cons. Arco Oil & Gas, Dallas, 1983-86, Federal Emergency Mgrs. Agy., Salt Lake City, 1986; speechwriter Sen. Mae Yih, Salem, Ore., 1989-91; steering com. Ore. Alliance Film & TV Educators, 1990-91; expert witness tobacco litig., Tex., 1997; participant Western Regional Honors Conf.; panelist Nat. Rsch. Coun. for Ford Found. Author: Introduction to Public Communication, 1992, 2d edit., 1993; co-author: Persuasion, 1982, Propaganda and Persuasion, 1986, 3d edit., 1999; rschr., writer, prodr.: (video) Women, War and Work, 1994; scriptwriter: The Howl of the Wolf, 1997; narrator (PBS TV) Gary Strobel, Bison in the Killing Field. Bd. dirs. Friends of the Family, Denton, 1987-89; bd. dirs. Bozeman Film Festival, 1991-2000, v.p., 1997-98, pres., 1998-00; del. Tex. Dem. Conv., Denton, 1976. Grantee Mont. Com. for the Humanities, 1993, Oreg. Coun. for the Humanities, 1991, NEH, 1977. Mem. Nat. Collegiate Honors Coun. (co-chair Portz Fund com.), Nat. Comm. Assn., Internat. Comm. Assn., Western States Comm. Assn. Home: 290 Low Bench Rd Gallatin Gateway MT 59730-9741 Office: Mont State U U Honors Program Bozeman MT 59717-0001 E-mail: vodonnel@montana.edu.

O'DONOVAN, LEO JEREMIAH, former academic administrator, priest, theologian; b. N.Y.C., Apr. 24, 1934; s. Leo J. O'Donovan Jr.. AB, Georgetown U., 1956; Licentiate in Philosophy, Fordham U., 1961; STB, Woodstock Coll., 1966, Licentiate in Sacred Theology, 1967; ThD, U. Münster, Fed. Republic Germany, 1971; LittD (hon.), Sogang U., Seoul, 1993; DHL, Loyola Coll., 1991, Coll. St. Rose, 2000; MD (hon.), Georgetown U., 2001. Ordained to ministry Cath. Ch., 1966. Instr. philosophy Loyola Coll., Balt., 1961—63; asst. prof. Woodstock Coll., Woodstock, 1971—74; assoc. prof. Weston Sch. Theology, Cambridge, Mass., 1974—81, prof., 1981—89; pres. Georgetown U., Washington, 1989—2001, prof., 2001—. Provincial asst. formation Md. Province S.J., Balt., 1985—88; cons. Nat. Conf. Cath. Bishops, Washington, 1986—89; bd. dirs. The Riggs Nat. Bank, Walt Disney Co., 2001—, MedStar Health, Inc. Bd.. dirs. U. Detroit Mercy, 1986—95; mem. Consortium of Univs. Washington Met. Area, 1989—2001, chair, 1994—96; mem. Fed. Cuty Coun., 1993—2001, Bus.-Higher Edn. Forum, 1989—2001, Nat. Coun. Arts, 1994—98, Consortium Fin. Higher Edn., 1990—98, chmn., 1995—97; mem. Am. Reads Stery Com., 1997—. Recipient Knight Comdr.'s Crodd, Germany; fellow, Danforth Found., 1956—71, vis. fellow, Woodstock Theol. Ctr.; grantee teaching grantee, Assn. Theol. Schs., 1978—79; scholar, Fulbright Found., U. Lyon, France, 1956—57. Fellow: Soc. Values in Higher Edn. (bd. dirs. 1989—); mem.: Boston Theol. Soc., Assn. Cath. Colls. and Univs. (bd. dirs. 1994—2000), Assn. Jesuit Colls. and Univs., Univ. Club. Office: Georgetown U 37th and O St NW Washington DC 20057-1789

O'DRISCOLL, MARILYN LUTZ, elementary school educator; b. L.A. d. Robert Thomas and Helen Mary (Cardamone) Lutz; m. John P. O'Driscoll Jr., Jan. 15, 1966 (dec. 1978); children: Kelley, John, Patrick. BS in Edn., U. So. Calif., 1961, cert. lang. devel. specialist, 1990. Cert. tchr., Calif. Tchr. kindergarten Montebello (Calif.) Sch. Dist., 1961-64, Garvey Sch. Dist., Rosemead, Calif., 1964—2003. Program quality reviewer San Gabriel Consortium, 1988-94; mem. parent bd. Incarnation Sch., Glendale, Calif., 1990-92, chmn. sch. site coun., 1990-93; participant ednl. TV program, 1989; dist. cons., 1995-04, Emerson leadership team, 1990-03, master tchr., 1995-2003; consulting tchr., 2003-. Pres. Incarnation Parish Coun., 1993-95. Mem. ASCD, NEA, Garvey Edn. Assn., Calif. Tchrs. Assn., Women of Troy (life), Spirit of Troy (life), Trojan Guild, Kappa Delta.

OE, EMILY NORENE, counselor, play therapist; b. Dickinson, N.D., Nov. 12, 1942; d. Nicholas George and Eunice Norene (Wilson) O. BEd, U. Alaska, Fairbanks, 1977; MA, Gonzaga U., 1978; PhD, U. North Tex., 1989. Lic. profl. clin. counselor, N.D.; registered play therapist and play therapy supr.; nat. cert. counselor. Child care worker Home of Good Shepherd, St. Paul, 1972-73; counselor Emmaus Sch. for Girls, King George, Va., 1973-74; guidance counselor Immaculate Conception Sch., Fairbanks, 1974-76, 78-80; child counselor Fairbanks Counseling and Adoption Agy., 1978-80; elem. counselor Fairbanks North Star Borough Sch. Dist., 1980-86; assoc. prof., counselor edn. Sam Houston State U., Huntsville, 1989-96; pvt. practice Huntsville, 1991-96; pvt. practice, play therapist, cons. Houston, 1995—. Co-author: Counseling Program Handbook, 1993; co-editor: Kaleidoscope of Play Therapy Stories, 1996; guest editor Internat. Newsletter, 1991; contbr. articles to profl. jours. Named Counselor Educator of Yr., Tex., 1995. Mem. N.D. Counseling Assn., N.D. Mental Health Counseling Assn., Assn. for Play Therapy (bd. dirs. 1989-99, sec. 1989-96, 97-99), Tex. Assn. Play Therapy (Nancy Guillory award 1997), Sam Houston Assn. Play Therapy. Roman Catholic. Office: 12890 49th St SW Belfield ND 58622-9216

OELBERG, DAVID GEORGE, neonatologist, educator, researcher; b. Waukon, Iowa, May 26, 1952; s. George Robert and Elizabeth Abigail (Kepler) O.; m. Debra Penuel, Aug. 4, 1979; children: Anna Elizabeth, Benjamin George. BS with highest honors, Coll. William and Mary, 1974; MD, U. Md., 1978. Diplomate in pediatrics and in neonatal-perinatal medicine Am. Bd. Pediatrics. Intern U. Tex. Med. Br., Galveston, 1978-79, resident, 1979-81, house pediat. staff, 1978-81; postdoctoral fellow in neonatal Medicine U. Tex. Med. Sch., Houston, 1981-84, asst. prof. dept. pediat., 1984-90, assoc. prof., 1990-93; assoc. prof. pediat., head perinatal rsch. Ctr. Pediat. Rsch., Ea. Va. Med. Sch., 1993-2001, prof., interim chmn. dept. pediats., 2001—; dir. divsn. neonatal-perinatal medicine Ea. Va. Med. Sch. Mem. hosp. staff Hermann Hosp., Houston, 1983-93; physician Crippled Children's Svcs. Program, Houston, 1985-93; mem. hosp. staff Lyndon B. Johnson County Hosp., 1990-93; vis. prof. Wyeth-Ayerst Labs., 1992; med. dir. Office Rsch., Children's Hosp. of King's Daus., 1993—, v.p. for acad. devel., 2001—; med. dirs. Office of Rsch., Sentara-Norfolk Gen. Hos., 1993—. Mem. editl. adv. bd. jour. Neonatal Intensive Care; contbr. articles to profl. jours.; ad hoc reviewer profl. jours.; patentee in field. Physician cons. Parents of Victims of Sudden Infant Death Syndrome, Houston, 1984; chmn. Instl. Animal Care and Use Com. Recipient award in analytica chemistry Am. Chem. Soc., 1974, NIH Clin. Investigator award NHLBI, 1989-94; rsch. grantee Am. Lung Assn., 1989-90, NIH, 1989-94. Fellow Am. Acad. Pediat. N.Y. Acad. Scis.; mem. AMA, NAS, Soc. Exptl. Biology and Medicine, So. Soc. Pediat. Rsch. (councilor, pres.), Soc. Pediat. Rsch. Achievements include a method for optical measurement of bilirubin in tissue. Home: 1624 W Little Neck Rd Virginia Beach VA 23452-4720 Office: Ea Va Med Sch Ctr Pediatric Rsch 855 W Brambleton Ave Norfolk VA 23510-1005

OERDING, JAMES BRYAN, military educator; b. Roseburg, Oreg., June 21, 1935; s. William Arthur and Naomi Eileen Oerding. BS, U.S. Mil. Acad., 1960; MA, U. Fla., 1975-77; candidate in philosophy, U. Calif., Davis, 1978-80. Cert. community coll. tchr., Calif. Commd. 2nd lt. U.S. Army, 1960, advanced through grades to maj., various assignments, officer 7th Spl. Forces Group, 1973-74, research specialist 1st Psychol. Ops. Bn., 1975-78; internat. plans & tng. specialist U.S. Army Western Command Hdqrs., Ft. Shafter, 1980-85; internat. security assistance analyst U.S. Army, Washington, 1985-86, dir. Army sr. fellowship program, 1986-89; comdt. U.S. Army Mgmt. Engring. Coll., Rock Island, Ill., 1989-91, dep. for strategic plans, 1991-92, regional rep. East Coast D.M.E.C., 1992-94; ret., 1994. Cons. on travel and mgmt. Escapes Unltd., Greencastle, Pa., 1988—; cruise lectr., 1994-2001. Regents' fellow U. Calif. at Davis, 1978, Chancellor's fellow, 1980. Mem. Spl. Forces Assn. (life), Am. Indochina Vets. Legion (N.C. state chmn. 1975-76), VFW, Disabled Am. Vets. Republican. Avocations: stamp collecting, writing. E-mail: escapesunlimited@hotmail.com.

OERTEL, GOETZ KUNO HEINRICH, physicist, professional science administrator; b. Stuhm, Germany, Aug. 24, 1934; came to U.S., 1957; s. Egon F.K. and Margarete W. (Wittek) O.; m. Brigitte Beckmann, June 17, 1960; children: Ines M.H. Oertel Downing, Carsten K.R. Abitur, Robert Mayer, Heilbronn, Fed. Republic Germany, 1953; vordiplom, U. Kiel, Fed. Republic Germany, 1956; PhD, U. Md., 1963. Aerospace engr. Langley Ctr. NASA, Hampton, Va., 1963-68, chief solar physics Washington, 1968-75; policy analyst for sci. advisor to Pres. Office of Mgmt. and Budget, Washington, 1974-75; head astronomy divsn. NSF, Washington, 1975; dir. def. and civilian nuc. waste programs U.S. Dept. Energy, Washington, 1975-83; acting mgr. sav. river ops. office Aiken, S.C., 1983-84; dep. mgr. ops. office Albuquerque, 1984-85; dep. asst. sec. of energy for EH, Washington, 1985-86; pres., CEO Assn. Univs. for Rsch. in Astronomy, Inc., Washington, 1986-99; also bd. dirs. Assn. Univs. for Rsch. in Astronomy, Inc. (AURA, Inc.), Washington, disting. advisor, 2000—. Cons. Los Alamos Lab., N.Mex., 1987-92, Westinghouse Electric, 1988—, Lampadia Found., Fundacion Andes of Santiago de Chile, Vitae Found. Sao Paulo, Brazil; bd. dirs. Inst. for Sci. and Soc., Ellensburg, Wash., IUE Corp.; mem. bd. internat. sci. orgns. NRC; chmn. bd. Sch. of Computational Sci., George Mason U., 2000-03; mem. U.S. Com. for CODATA, 1993-2003, chmn. 1997-2000; U.S. nat. del. CODATA ICSU, 1999-2003; mem. peer rev. com. ASME, 1996—; cons. conicyt, Govt. of Chile, 2000—, VIFAE Found., Brazil, 2001—, Fundacion Andes, Chile, 2000—; interim bd. dirs. Ctr. of Excellence for Hazardous Materials Mgmt., Carlsbad, N.Mex., 2003—. Fulbright grantee, 1957. Fellow AAAS; mem. Am. Phys. Soc., Am. Astron. Soc., Internat. Astron. Union, N.Y. Acad. Scis., Internat. U. Exch., Inc. (bd. dirs.), Cosmos Club, Sigma Xi. Lutheran. Achievements include patents in field. Avocations: fitness, chess, computing, genealogy. Home: 8833 Watts Mine Ter Potomac MD 20854-5439 Office: PO Box 388 Cabin John MD 20818-0388 E-mail: goetz@oertel.org.

OETINGER, DAVID FREDERICK, biology educator; b. Buffalo, Apr. 25, 1945; s. Clayton Henry and June Marguerite Oetinger; m. Madeline Anne Ivosevic; children: Wayne David, Mark David. BA, Houghton Coll., 1967; MS, U. Nebr., 1969, PhD, 1977. Asst. prof., then assoc. prof. biology Houghton (N.Y.) Coll., 1977-84; assoc. prof., now prof. biology Ky. Wesleyan Coll., Owensboro, 1984—. Contbr. articles prof. jours. Comdr. USNR, ret. Mem. Am. Soc. Parasitologists, Helminthological Soc. Washington, Ky. Acad. Sci., Southeastern Soc. Parasitologists. Office: Ky Wesleyan Coll 3000 Frederica St Owensboro KY 42302-1039 E-mail: acantho@kwc.edu.

OETTINGER, ANTHONY GERVIN, mathematician, educator; b. Nuremberg, Germany, Mar. 29, 1929; came to U.S., 1941, naturalized, 1947; s. Albert and Marguerite (Bing) O.; m. Marilyn Tanner, June 20, 1954; children: Douglas, Marjorie. AB, Harvard U., 1951, PhD, 1954; Henry fellow, U. Cambridge, Eng., 1951-52; Litt.D. (hon.), U. Pitts., 1984. Mem. faculty Harvard, 1955—, asso. prof. applied math., 1960-63, prof. linguistics, 1963-75, Gordon McKay prof. applied math., 1963—, chmn. program on info. resources policy, 1972—, mem. faculty of govt., 1973—, prof. info. resources policy, 1975—. Mem. command control comm. and intelligence bd. Dept. Navy, 1978-83; mem. sci. adv. group Def. Comm. Agy., 1979-90; chmn. bd. visitors Joint Mil. Intelligence Coll., 1986—; chmn., dir. Ctrl. Intelligence Advanced Tech. Panel, 2002—; cons. Arthur D. Little, Inc., 1956-80, Office Sci. and Tech., Exec. Office of Pres., 1960-73, Bellcomm, Inc., 1963-68, Sys. Devel. Corp., 1965-68, Nat. Security Coun., Exec. Office of Pres., 1975-81, Pres.'s Fgn. Intelligence Adv. Bd., 1981-90; chmn. Computer Sci. and Engring. Bd., Nat. Acad. Scis., 1968-73; mem. Mass. Cmty. Antenna TV Commn., 1972-79, chmn., 1975-79; mem. rsch. adv. bd. Com. for Econ. Devel., 1975-79; trustee Babbage Inst., 1991—; panel mem. Naval Studies Bd. NAS/NRC, 1993-95; mem. banking and fin. team Pres.' Commn. on Critical Infrastructure Protection, 1998; mem. Def. Sci. Bd., 2003—. Author: A Study for the Design of an Automatic Dictionary, 1954, Automatic Language Translation: Lexical and Technical Aspects, 1960, Run Computer Run: The Mythology of Educational Innovation, 1969, High and Low Politics: Information Resources for the 80s, 1977, Behind the Telephone Debates, 1988, Mastering the Changing Information World, 1993; editor: Proc. of a Symposium on Digital Computers and Their Applications, 1962; contbr. chpts. to The Information Resources Policy Handbook: Research for the Information Age, 1999. Fellow Am. Acad. Arts and Scis., AAAS, IEEE, Assn. Computing Machinery (mem. coun. 1961-68, chmn. com. U.S. Govt. Rels. 1964-66, editor computational linguistics sect. Commn. 1964-66, pres. 1966-68); mem. Soc. Indsl. and Applied Math. (mem. coun. 1963-67), Coun. on Fgn. Rels., Phi Beta Kappa, Sigma Xi. Clubs: Cosmos (Washington); Harvard (N.Y.C.). Home: 65 Elizabeth Rd Belmont MA 02478-3819 Office: Harvard U Maxwell Dworkin 125 33 Oxford St Cambridge MA 02138-2901 E-mail: anthony@deas.harvard.edu.

O'FARRELL, TIMOTHY JAMES, psychologist, educator; b. Lancaster, Ohio, Apr. 22, 1946; s. Robert James and Helen Loretta (Tooill) O'F.; m. Jayne Sara Talmage, May 19, 1973; 1 child, Colin. BA, U. Notre Dame, 1968; PhD in Psychology, Boston U., 1975. Instr. Harvard U. Med. Sch., Boston, 1977-82, asst. prof., 1982-86, assoc. prof., 1986-2000, prof., 2000—. Chief Harvard Families and Addiction Program, 1991—; staff psychologist VA Med. Ctr., Brockton, Mass., 1975-78, dir. Alcoholism Clinic, 1978-83, dir. Counseling for Alcoholics' Marriages Project, 1978—, chief Alcohol and Family Studies Lab., 1981-91; chief, Harvard Families and Addiction Program, 1991—; assoc. chief psychology svc., 1988—; VA predoctoral grantee, 1969-72; rsch. grantee VA, 1978—, Nat. Inst. on Alcohol Abuse and Alcoholism, 1991—, Smithers Found., 1991—, Guggenheim Found., 1993-94. Author: Alcohol and Sexuality, 1983, Treating Alcohol Problems: Marital and Family Interventions, 1993, Accreditation Guide for Substance Abuse Treatment Programs, 1997; editl. bd. numerous scientific jours.; contbr. articles to profl. jours. Fellow APA, Behavior Therapy and Rsch. Soc.; mem. NIAAA (psychosocial rsch. rev. group 1989-93), Assn. Advancement Behavior Therapy, Eastern Psychol. Assn. Home: 14 Wadsworth Ln Duxbury MA 02332-5116 Office: VA Med Ctr 116B1 Brockton MA 02301 E-mail: timothy_ofarrell@hms.harvard.edu.

O'FARRILL, FRANCISCA JOSEFINA, early childhood educator; b. Havana, Cuba, Oct. 4, 1931; d. Eusebio and Rosalinda Lidia (Leon) Sosa; m. Mateo Ernesto O'Farrill, Oct. 4, 1951; children: Marta O'Farrill-Iribar, Sonia O'Farrill-Barranco. BA, Escuela Normal de Kindergarten, Havana, Cuba, 1952; PhD in Edn., U. Havana, 1956; MS in Psychology, Caribbean Ctr. Advance Studies, 1987. Tchr. Head Start Program, Miami, Fla., 1972-83, lead tchr., 1983-87; adminstr. St. Luke's Day Care Ctr., Miami, Fla., 1987-89; ctr. dir. Head Start Program, Miami, Fla., 1989—. Recipient Most Prestigious award Head Start, 1987, Outstanding Svc. award Metro-Dad C.A.A., 1988, Merit award Profs. and Students of Havana Schs. Assn., 1980, Proclamtion City of Miami, 1993, Cert. Appreciation City of West Miami, 1993. Mem. ASCD, Am. Assn. for Counseling, Nat. Head Start Assn., Fla. Assn. for Community Action, Fla.'s Concern for Children, ZONTA Club of Miami, Nat. Guild of Piano Tchrs. Roman Catholic. Avocations: singing, playing piano, reading, listening to classical music. Home: 6227 SW 10th St Miami FL 33144-4901

OFFEN, KAREN MARIE, historian, educator; b. Pocatello, Idaho, Oct. 10, 1939; d. Norman V. and Ella Mae (McAlister) Stedtfeld; m. George R. Offen, Dec. 30, 1965; children: Catherine, Stephanie. BA, U. Idaho, 1961; AM, Stanford U., 1963, PhD, 1971. Lectr. History U. Santa Clara, Calif., 1973, U. San Francisco, 1975-76, Stanford (Calif.) U., 1978, 1982, 1984, 1986, 1989, 1992, 2002, Ctrl. European U., Budapest, 1999, U. of Konstanz, 2000. Ind. scholar affiliated with Inst. Rsch. Women & Gender, Stanford U., 1978—; dir. summer seminar NEH, 1984, 86, 89, 92, 2002; founding mem., sec. treas. Internat. Fedn. Rsch. Women's History, 1987-95; pres. Western Assn. Women Historians, 1991-93. Mem. editl. adv. bd. French Hist. Studies, Arenal, L'Homme, Jour. Women's History, European Legacy, Hist. Reflections; contbr. articles to profl. jours. Bd. dirs. Internat. Mus. Women, San Francisco, 1999—. Recipient Disting. Alumni Achievement award U. Idaho, 1994, Sr. Scholar award, 1995, Internat. Mus. of Women (bd. dirs., 1999—); NEH Ind. Study & Rsch. fellow, 1980-81, Rockefeller Found. Humanities fellow, 1985-86, J.S. Guggenheim fellow, 1995-96. Mem. AAUW, Am. Hist. Assn. (com. women historians 1983-86, chair com. internat. hist. activities 1986-90), Soc. French Hist. Studies (exec. com. 1983-86), P.E.O., Kappa Kappa Gamma. Democrat. Avocations: skiing, travel, hiking. Office: Stanford U Inst Rsch Women & Gender Stanford CA 94305-8640

OFFENBERG, ROBERT M. educational psychologist; b. Bklyn., Mar. 27, 1942; s. Irving S. O. and Gertrude Thelma (Gershman) Babitz; m. Susan M. Shapiro, July 11, 1965; children: Joel David, Diane Beth Offenberg-

Rose. BA, NYU, 1964; MA, The New Sch. Social Rsch., 1967; EdD, Temple U., 1973. Lic. psychologist Pa. Caseworker N.Y. Bur. Child Welfare, N.Y.C., 1965-67; statistician Phila. State Hosp., 1967-69; rsch. assoc. Sch. Dist. Phila., 1969-93, sr. rsch. assoc., 1993-2000, sr. policy rschr., 2000—. Adj. faculty Antioch U., Phila., 1987-89, Trenton (N.J.) State Coll., 1986; rsch. auditor New Orleans Pub. Schs., 1970-73; cons. in field. Contbr. chpts. to books and articles to profl. jours. Mem., bd. dirs., v.p. Phila. chpt. Epilepsy Found. Am., 1982-87. NDEA fellow Temple U., 1968-71. Mem. Am. Psychol. Assn., Am. Edn. Rsch. Soc. Avocations: classical music, photography, stero equipment. Home: 137-B N 22nd St Philadelphia PA 19103-1046 Office: Sch Dist Phila Office of Accountability and Assessment Office of Assessment Franklin Pky and 21st Philadelphia PA 19103 Business E-Mail: roffenbe@phila.k12.pa.us.

OFFUTT, DREW GRIFFITH, physicial education educator; b. Bethesda, Md., May 9, 1969; s. Ralph Worthington Jr. and Suzanne Clements (Griffith) O. AA in Phys. Edn., Montgomery Jr. Coll., Rockville, Md., 1992; BS in Kinesiology, Phys. Edn., U. Md., 1996. Supr. dept. intramurals Montgomery Coll., Rockville, 1992; head coach boys basketball St. Johns H.S., Washington, 1992—; head coach, dir. Camp Laurel, Laurel, Maine, 1993—; personal trainer Sport & Health Assocs., Rockville, 1993—. Tutor U. Md., College Park, 1992—, tchr. fitness/wellness dept., 1994—; head coach freshman baseball, asst. varsity coach baseball Potomac Sch., McLean, Va., 1995. Mem. AAPERD, Md. Alliance Phys. Edn., Recreation and Dance, World Wildlife. Roman Catholic. Avocations: baseball, camping, weight training, writing, reading biographies. Home: Apt M 144 Pasture Side Way Rockville MD 20850-5968

O'FLAHERTY, LUCY LOUISE, secondary education educator; b. Bklyn., Dec. 13, 1941; d. Louis Charles and Carmela (De Luca) Aufiero; m. James Jerome O'Flaherty, May 26, 1973; children: Michael Sean, Alison Marie. BA in Edn., Social Studies, Fordham U., 1970; MS in Edn., Hofstra U., 1984; M in Social Work, Adelphi U., 1992. Cert. tchr., N.Y. Pers. recruiter Merrill, Lynch, Pierce, Fenner & Smith, Inc., N.Y.C., 1967-71, program adminstr., 1971-72; coord. and tchr. social studies St. Agnes Sch., Rockville Centre, N.Y., 1982-88; tchr. social studies Holy Trinity High Sch., Hicksville, N.Y., 1988—; psychiatric social worker Sunrise Psychiatric Clinic, 1990-91, 93—. Med. social work intern Ctrl. Gen. Hosp., Plainview, 1990-91; pvt. practice counseling and psychotherapy. Bereavement counselor and group facilitator YWCA-YMCA, Plainview, N.Y., 1990-91, 92-94. Mem. NASW, Nat. Assn. Cath. Educators, N.Y. State Social Studies Assn., Kappa Delta Pi. Home: PO Box 113 Malverne NY 11565-0113 Office: 98 Cherry Ln Hicksville NY 11801-6232

OFSTAD, EVELYN LARSEN BOYL, retired primary school educator, radio announcer, video producer; b. Laurel, Oreg., Sept. 11, 1918; d. Walter Winfred and Nellie Lyle (Gellatly) Larsen; m. Robert Morris Boyl (dec.); children: Kathleen Roberta, Robert Morris Jr., Shannon Gae, Brian Larsen; m. Olaf Ofstad, Nov. 15, 1988. BS, Oreg. State U., 1940; MS in Tchg., Portland State U., 1968. Cert. learning specialist. Radio announcer Sta. KOAC, Corvallis, Oreg., 1939-40; announcer, script writer Sta. KWIL, Albany, Oreg., 1940-42, operator, announcer, 1941-42; sec. Higgins Ship Bldg., New Orleans, 1943-44; elem. tchr. Portland Pub. Schs., 1968-71; learning specialist North Clackamas Schs., Milw., Ore., 1972-85, home instr. Milwaukie, Oreg., 1985-86. Prodr., actor video travelogues on Portland Cable Access, 1987—; mem. Oreg. Sr. Theater, 1987-95; actor plays and mus. prodns. Plaza Players, 1999—. Co-leader Girl Scouts Am., Oak Grove, Oreg., 1954-55, Webelos Boy Scouts Am., 1956-57, 70-71; videographer Ptnrs. of Ams., Oreg. and Costa Rica, 1990-91; head video prodn. Channel 29 In-House TV of Retirement, Holladay Park Plz.; prodr. biweekly travel show, weekly activities show. Mem. AAUW (pres. Albany chpt.). Avocations: painting, video production, bell playing, travel, synchronated swimming.

OGAWA, DENNIS MASAAKI, American studies educator; b. Manzanar, Calif., Sept. 7, 1943; s. Frank M. and Alice T. (Tanaka) O.; m. Amy Ranko, Jan. 1, 1973; children: Quin, Owen, Autumn. BA, UCLA, 1966, MA, 1967, PhD, 1969. Prof. Am. studies U. Hawaii at Manoa, Honolulu, 1969—. Dir. Nippon Golden Network, Honolulu, 1982—; chmn. Dept. Am. Studies, U. Hawaii, Honolulu, 2003—. Author: Jan Ken Po, 1973, Kodomo No Tame Ni, 1978; co-author: Ellison Onizuka: Remembrance, 1986. Dir. Japanese Cultural Ctr., Hawaii, 1992-98, Olelo: Corp. Cmty. Television, 1994-98, Hawaii Internat. Film Festival, 1994-97. Danforth Found. assoc., 1975; named Disting. Historian Hawaiian Hist. Soc., 1992; sr. fellow Japan Soc. Promotion of Sci., 1978, East West Ctr., Honolulu, 1979. Democrat. Office: Univ Hawaii Am Studies Dept 1890 E West Rd Honolulu HI 96822-2318

OGBONNAYA, CHUKS ALFRED, entomologist, agronomist, environmentalist; b. Akoli-Imenyi, Abia, Nigeria, June 30, 1953; came to U.S., 1975; s. Alfred Agbaeze and Christy (Agubuche) Ogbonnaya; m. Joyce Elizabeth Belgrave, Mar. 30, 1985; children: Latoya, Oluchi, Kelechi, Chioma. BS, U. Nebr., 1979, PhD, 1985; MS, N.W. Mo. State U., 1981. Cert. profl. crop scientist, profl. agronomist. Lab. asst. U. Nebr., Lincoln, 1976-78, rsch. asst., 1978-80, 82-85, postdoctoral fellow, 1985; asst. prof., postdoctoral fellow Mountain Empire Coll., Big Stone Gap, Va., 1985-90, prof., 1990—, coord., prof. environ. sci. dept., 1986—; prof., 1990. Disting. scholar-in-residence Pa. State U., summer 1990, vis. prof., 1990. Soccer coach Parks and Recreation, Big Stone Gap, 1989; mem. Va. Water Resources Statewide Adv. Bd., govt.-mined land reclamation adv. bd. Recipient Times Teaching award, 1990, Chancellor's Profs. award Va., 1990; Fulbright sr. scholar, 1993-94. Mem. Am. Soc. Agronomy, Crop Sci. Soc. Am., Entomol. Soc., Va. Acad. Sci., Va. Mining Assn. (Outstanding Contbn. to Comty. award 1993), Internat. Platform Assn., Phi Beta Kappa. Methodist. Avocations: tennis, soccer. Home: 520 Bays View Rd Kingsport TN 37660-3202 Office: Mountain Empire Coll PO Box 700 Big Stone Gap VA 24219-0700

OGDEN, HUGH, English literature educator, poet; b. Erie, Pa., Mar. 11, 1937; s. Harold S. and Ethel (Yokes) O.; m. Ruth Simpson, Mar. 19, 1960 (div. 1975); children: Cynthia, David, Katherine. BA, Haverford Coll., 1959; MA, NYU, 1961; PhD, U. Mich., 1967. Asst. prof. Trinity Coll., Hartford, Conn., 1967-76, assoc. prof., 1976-92, prof. English, 1992—. Author: Two Roads and This Spring, 1991, Looking for History, 1993, Windfalls, 1996, Natural Things, 1998, Gift, 1998. Sec. Glastonbury (Conn.) Land Heritage Coalition, 1990-94. NEA Poetry fellow 1993, Residency fellow UCross Found., 1994, MacDowell Colony, 1995, 2003; poetry grant Conn. Commn. on Arts, 1990, 2003. Home: 331 Chestnut Hill Rd Glastonbury CT 06033-4103 Office: Trinity Coll Hartford CT 06106

OGDEN, JAMES RUSSELL, marketing educator, consultant, lecturer, writer; b. Paris, Ill., Nov. 4, 1954; s. Russell Lee and Marianne (Johnson) O.; children: David James, Anne Marie, Kari Kristine; m. Denise T. Alarid, 1989. B of Bus. Edn., Ea. Mich. U., 1978; MS, Colo. State U., 1981; PhD, U. No. Colo., 1986. With acctg. and fin. dept. Hydra-Matic Divsn. GM Motors, 1978; dir. mktg. Mich. Tech. Inst., 1979; grad. fellow Colo. State U., Ft. Collins, 1979-81, asst. mgr. family housing, 1979-81; placement counselor U. No. Colo., Greeley, 1981-83, mktg. instr., 1982-83; CEO, pres. Ogden, Ogden Latshaw & Assocs., Coopersburg, Pa., 1982—; chair advt. and mktg. dept., assoc. prof. Adams State Coll., Alamosa, Colo., 1983-89; dept. chair, prof. mktg. Coll. Bus., Kutztown (Pa.) U., 1989—, bd. bus. advisors Students in Free Enterprise, 1996—. Interim dir. Small Bus. Devel. Ctr., Adams State Coll., 1988-89; adj. prof. Ctrl. Mich. U., Mt. Pleasant, 1987—, Cedar Crest Coll., Allentown, 1989—, Pa. State U., 1994-95, Nova Southeastern U., doctoral com. chair, Ft. Lauderdale, Fla., 1995—; spkr. in field; mktg. and advt. cons.; corp. trainer; textbook reviewer, editl. cons. Merrill Pub. Co., Allyn & Bacon, Inc., Richard Irwin, Inc., Macmillan Pub., John Wiley & Sons, Inc., Prentice-Hall, Houghton & Mifflin Co., Austen Press, Simon & Schuster; textbook reviewer Fairchild Books and Visuals, Inc.; tech. editor Rsch. and Edn. Assn.; doctoral com. mem. Nova Southeastern U., Drexel U., Phila., Pace U., N.Y.C., Temple U., Phila.; bd. dirs. Z-Coil, Inc., Albuquerque Author: Developing a Creative and Innovative Integrated Marketing Communication Plan, 1998; co-author: The Best Test Preparation for the CLEP College-Level Examination Program Principles of Marketing, 1996; contbg. author, editor: Principles of Business, 1991, Essentials of Advertising, 1992, rev. edit., 1994, Marketing's Powerful Weapon: Point-of-Purchase Advertising, 2001; editor: Essentials of Marketing, 1994; contbr. over 40 articles to profl. jours. Treas. Com. to Elect Jorge Amaya County Commr., Colo., 1985, Bob Pastore for Senate Com.; senator Assoc. Student and Faculty Senate, Adams State Coll., 1984-85; bd. dirs. Am. Advt. Fedn. Acad. Com., 1991-97, Alamosa Personnel Bd., 1986-88, Alamosa County Devel. Corp., 1987-89, Alamosa Tourism Com., 1988-89, trustee bd. dirs. Creede Repertory Theatre, 1987-89; expert witness in tourism and mktg. State of Colo.; advisor team entries into Nat. Student Advt. Competition, Coll. World Series of Advt., 1989-90, 93—; trustee Dr. R.L. Ogden Meml. Scholarship, Colo. State U. Found., 1992—; faculty advisor Students in Free Enterprise Nat. Competition, 1997—, faculty advisor, bus. adv. bd. Kutztown U. chpt. Recipient award for Excellence in Econ. Edn., Freedoms Found. Valley Forge, 1986, Capital award for contbn. to edn., Nat. Leadership Coun., 1991-92; named Outstanding Educator of Sch. Bus., Adams State Coll., 1987-88; Sam Walton fellow Students in Free Enterprise, 1997, 98, Outstanding Educator award, 1998. Fellow Direct Mktg. Assn.; mem. Am. Advt. Fedn. (faculty advisor 1987—, bd. dirs. acad. com. 1991-97), Western Mktg. Educators Assn. (paper reviewer), Nat. Guild Hypnotists (cert.), Acad. Mktg. Sci., Advt. Club N.Y., Point of Purchase Advt. Inst., Am. Collegiate Retailing Assn., Assn. Nat. Advertisers, Nat. Assn. Hispanic Profs. of Bus. Adminstrn. and Econs., New Eng. Bus. Adminstrn. Assn., Ctrl. Pa. Advt. Club, Phi Kappa Phi, Alpha Sigma Alpha (fin. advisor 1992—), Alpha Kappa Psi (dist. dir.). Democrat. Avocations: scuba, music, traveling. Office: Kutztown U Coll Bus Dept Mktg Kutztown PA 19530 E-mail: ogden@kutztown.edu.

OGDEN, WILLIAM MICHAEL, school system administrator; b. Wooster, Ohio, Oct. 29, 1944; s. Raymond Job and Vinnie Lena (Ensminger) O.; m. Norena Faith Parker, June 4, 1966 (div. 1978); children: Michele Rae, John Michael; m. Mary Ann Pusey, Oct. 6, 1978; 1 stepchild, Jeffrey Clare Applegate. BA, Coll. Wooster, 1968; MEd, LaVerne (Calif.) Coll., 1975; postgrad., Akron U., Ashland (Ohio) Coll. Cert. elem. tchr., prin., spl. edn. tchr. Tchr. Mansfield (Ohio) City Schs., 1968-77, adminstr., 1977—, dist. energy officer, 1980-83, dir. elem. summer reinforcement program, 1986-88. Martha Holden Jennings Found. scholar, 1977. Mem. ASCD, Ohio Assn. Elem. Sch. Prins., Mansfield Adminstrs. Assn., Ashland-Richland-Morrow County Assn. Elem. Sch. Prins. (pres. 1990-91), Mohican Assn. Edn. of Young Children, Mansfield Univ. Club, Jaycees, Elks, Phi Delta Kappa (Mohican Area Ohio chpt., area chpt. 1231, divsn. V). Republican. Presbyterian. Avocations: reading, travel, snow skiing, tennis, camping. Home: 4575 E Fontenoy Rd Boyne City MI 49712-9385 Office: Mansfield City Schs 53 W 4th St Mansfield OH 44902-1205

OGILVIE, KELVIN KENNETH, university president, chemistry educator; m. Emma Roleen; children: Kristine, Kevin. BS with honors, Acadia U., 1964, DSc (hon.), 1983; PhD, Northwestern U., 1968; DSc (hon.), U. N.B., Can., 1991, McGill U., 1998. Assoc. prof. U. Man., Winnipeg, 1968-74; prof. chemistry McGill U., Montreal, 1974-88, Can. Pacific prof. biotech., 1984-87; bd. dirs. Sci. Adv. Bd., Biologicals, Toronto, Ont., 1979-84; dir. Office of Biotech. McGill U., 1984-87; prof. chemistry Acadia U., Wolfville, 1987—, v.p. acad. affairs, 1987—93, pres., vice-chancellor, 1993—2003. Invited lectr. on biotech. Tianjin, People's Republic of China, 1985; Snider lectr. U. Toronto, 1991; Gwen Leslie Meml. lectr., 1991; Centennial Mossman lectr. McGill U., 1998; mem. Nat. Adv. Bd. Sci. and Tech., 1994-95; chair selection com. Indsl. Postgrad. Scholarship program NSERCC, 1994; mem. Coun. N.S. Univ. Pres. 1993-2003; mem. Coun. of Applied Sci. and Tech. for N.S., 1988-93; mem. Nat. Biotech. Adv. Com., 1988-99; mem. Fisher (Can.) Biotech. Adv. Ctr., 1989-92; mem. sci. adv. bd. Allelix Biopharms., 1991-93; chair adv. bd. NRC Inst. for Marine Bioscis., 1990-93; mem. steering com. on biotech. labor Can., 1990-92; mem. Atlantic regional com. Prime Min.'s Awards for Tchg. Excellence in Sci., Tech. and Math., 1993—; chair regional planning forum for a pharm. industry, Atlantic, Can., 1993; mem. Atomic Energy Control Bd., Can., 1997-99; chair sci. adv. bd. Quanta Nova Can., 1998-2001; mem. Can. Electronic Bus. Roundtable, 1999-2002, Can. Global Bus. Dialogue on Electronic Commerce, 1999, Coun. of Ministers Com. on Online Learning, 2000-01; mem. IBM Global Edn. Policy Coun., 2000--, The Can. e-Bus. Initiative, 2002—. Mem. editl. bd. Nucleosides and Nucleotides, 1981-92; contbr. over 150 articles to profl. jours.; holder 14 patents. Bd. dirs. Plant Biotech. Inst., 1987-90. Decorated Order of Can., Knight of Malta; named Hon. Col. 14th Air Maintenance Squadron, RCAF, 1995-2000; recipient Commemorative medal for 125th Anniversary of Confedn. Can., 1992, Buck-Whitney medal, 1983, Manning Prin. award, 1992, Queen Elizabeth Golden Jubilee medal, 2002; named to McLean's Honor Roll of Canadians Who Made a Difference, 1988; E.W.R. Steacie Meml. fellow, 1982-84; inducted into Discovery Ctr. Sci. and Tech. Hall of Fame, 2002. Fellow Chem. Inst. Can.; mem. Am. Chem. Soc., Ordre des Chemists of Que., Assn. Univs. and Colls. Can. (standing com. on rsch. 1993-2000), Atlantic Univ. Athletic Assn. (pres. 1995-97). Achievements include inventing of BIOLF-62 (ganciclovir), antiviral drug used worldwide; developed general synthesis of RNA; developed original 'gene machine'; developer complete chemical synthesis of large RNA molecules. Home: PO Box 307 Canning NS Canada B0P 1HO Office: Acadia U Dept Chemistry Wolfville NS Canada B4P 2R6 E-mail: kelvin.ogilvie@acadiau.ca.

OGILVIE, T(HOMAS) FRANCIS, engineer, educator; b. Atlantic City, Sept. 26, 1929; s. Thomas Fleisher and Frances Augusta (Wilson) O.; m. Joan Husselton, Sept. 11, 1950; children: Nancy Louise, Mary Beth, Kenneth Stuart. BA in Physics, Cornell U., 1950; M.Sc. in Aero. Engring., U. Md., 1957; PhD in Engring. Sci., U. Calif., Berkeley, 1960; D in Naval Arch./Marine Engring. (hon.), Nat. Tech. U. Athens, 1996. Physicist, David Taylor Model Basin, Dept. Navy, Bethesda, Md., 1951-62, 64-67; liaison scientist Office of Naval Research, London, 1962-63; asso. prof. naval architecture and marine engring. U. Mich., Ann Arbor, 1967-70, prof. fluid mechanics, 1970-81, chmn. dept. naval architecture and marine engring., 1973-81; prof. ocean engring. MIT, Cambridge, 1982-96, prof. emeritus, 1996—, head dept., 1982-94. Vis. prof. naval architecture Osaka (Japan) U., 1976; vis. prof. math. U. Manchester, Eng., 1976; founding mem. Ariz. Sr. Acad., Tucson, 1997. Contbr. articles to profl. jours. Recipient Meritorious Pub. Svc. award U.S. Dept. of Transp., 1982. Fellow Soc. of Naval Architects and Marine Engrs. (coun. 1977-82, exec. com. 1978-80, 83-84, William H. Webb medal 1989); mem. Sigma Xi, Phi Beta Kappa. Home: 7559 S Eliot Ln Tucson AZ 85747-9627

OGLE, ROBBIN SUE, criminal justice educator; b. North Kansas City, Mo., Aug. 28, 1960; d. Robert Lee and Carol Sue (Gray) O. BS, Ctrl. Mo. State U., 1982; MS, U. Mo., 1990; PhD, Pa. State U., 1995. State probation and parole officer Mo. Dept. Corrections, Kansas City, 1982-92; collector J.C. Penney Co., Mission, Kans., 1990-92; instr. U. Mo., Kansas City, 1990-92; grad. lectr. Pa. State U., University Park, 1992-95; prof. criminal justice dept. U. Nebr., Omaha, 1995—. Author: Battered Women Who Kill: A New Framework, 2002; contbr. articles to profl. jours. Athletic scholar Ctrl. Mo. State U., Warrensburg, 1978-82. Mem. AAUW, ACLU, NOW, Am. Soc. Criminology, Acad. Criminal Justice Scis., Am. Correctional Assn., Phi Kappa Phi. Avocations: reading, watching basketball, walking dog. Office: U Nebr Dept Criminal Justice 1100 Neihardt Lincoln NE 68588-0630 Home: 2410 N 99th St Omaha NE 68134-5642 E-mail: RSOgle@webtv.net.

OGLE, TERRI J. BRYANT, elementary education educator; b. St. Louis, Sept. 17, 1961; d. Robert Eugene and Elsie Marie (Wilson) Bryant; m. James Alan Ogle, June 12, 1982; children: Alexandra Brooke, Jamieson Spencer. BA, Columbia Coll., 1982; MA, Maryville Coll., 1989. 1st grade tchr. New Haven (Mo.) Sch. Dist.; 4th grade tchr. Washington (Mo.) Sch. Dist. Mem. Delta Kappa Gamma. Home: 233 Timber Ridge Ln Marthasville MO 63357-1584

OGLESBY, BEVERLY CLAYTON, kindergarten educator; b. Jacksonville, Fla., Mar. 11, 1950; d. Willie Edward Clayton and Venetta (Preston) Singleton; m. Eugene Oglesby, June 23, 1974; children: Venetta, Erin. BS, Fla. Meml. Coll., 1971; MEd, U. North Fla., 1982. Cert. tchr., Fla. 3d grade tchr. S. Bryan Jennings Elem. Sch., Orange Park, Fla., 1971-75, kindergarten tchr., 1975-77, 83-90, 1993-94, 2d grade tchr., 1977-82, 1st grade tchr., 1982-83, devel. 1st grade tchr., 1990-92, devel. 2d grade tchr., 1992-93, devel. kindergarten tchr., 1994—. Kindergarten team leader S. Bryan Jennings Elem. Sch. 1975-90; mem. instrnl. material coun. Clay County Schs., Green Cove Springs, Fla., 1989, devel. dist. com. 1990-92; presenter Clay County Whole Lang. Clay County Reading Coun., Orange Park, 1988-89, So. Early Childhood Assn. and Early Childhood Assn. of Fla. Confs. SACS com. mem. Forest Hill Elem. Sch., Jacksonville, 1973; SECA rep. State of Fla.; mem. PTA bd. Oceanway Jr. High Sch., Jacksonville, 1980. Named S. Bryan Jenning Elem. Sch. Tchr. of Yr., 1989-90. Mem. Early Childhood Assn. Fla. (pres. 1992-93, SECA rep. 1995—), So. Early Childhood Assn. (chair membership com. 1993-95, rep. to Early Childhood Assn. Fla., 1995—, pres.-elect 2003-04, pres. 2004-06), Nat. Assn. for Edn. Young Children, Assn. Childhood Edn. Internat., North Fla. Assn. Young Children (pres. 1986-87), Early Childhood Assn. Fla. (pres. 1993-94), Phi Delta Kappa. Avocations: reading and collecting children's books, walking. Home: 215 Corona Dr Orange Park FL 32073-3219

OGLESBY, JERRI BURDETTE, elementary education educator; b. Olney, Md., Oct. 13, 1953; d. Herbert M. and Ellen (Miller) Burdette; m. Albert C. Oglesby Jr., Nov. 18, 1978; children: Matthew Jacob, Nathan Bryan. BA in Elem. Edn., Shepherd Coll., 1975; MEd, Johns Hopkins U., 1995, cert. adminstrn., 1999. Cert. elem. tchr., Md.; cert. adminstrn. and supervision, Md. Tchr. elem. Montgomery County Pub. Schs., Rockville, Md., 1976-97, asst. prin., 1997-99, prin., 1999—; assoc. faculty mem. Johns Hopkins U., 1995—. Deacon Boyds (Md.) Presbyn. Ch., 1980—. Mem. NEA, ASCD, Nat. Coun. Tchrs. Math., Montgomery County Edn. Assn., Elem. Prins. Assn., Nat. Reading Assn., Tchrs. of English, Montgomery County Admintrs. Assn.

O'GORMAN, TARA ANN, elementary education educator; b. Yonkers, N.Y., July 22, 1965; d. John T. O'Gorman and Josephine M. (Corneila) O'G. BA in Communication Arts, Iona Coll., 1987, MS in Multicultural Edn., 1994. Cert. tchr., N.Y. Presch. asst. head tchr. Bright Horizons, Yonkers, N.Y., 1991-93, summer reading program specialist, 1992-93; 2nd grade tchr. St. Ann Sch., Bronx, N.Y., 1993—. Acad. cons., Yonkers, 1990—. Recipient Partial Tuition scholarship N.Y. State Archdiocese, 1993-94. Mem. Phi Delta Kappa. Roman Catholic. Avocations: reading, acting, music, crafting, tennis. Office: Saint Ann Sch 3511 Bainbridge Ave Bronx NY 10467-1497

OH, KEYTACK HENRY, industrial engineering educator; b. Hamduk, Korea, Mar. 16, 1938; s. DalPyong and Kee-Sook (Yang) O.; m. Youngsim Lee, Sept. 15, 1967; children: Jeanne, Susan. BS, Hanyang U., Seoul, Korea, 1962; MS, Okla. State U., 1966; PhD, The Ohio State U., 1974. Supr. East Gate Telephone Exch., Seoul, Korea, 1958-61; ops. rschr. Western Elec. Co., Oklahoma City, 1966-68, MIS staff mem. Columbus, Ohio, 1968-72; logistics engr. Ross Labs., Columbus, Ohio, 1972-75; asst. prof. U. Mo./St. Louis Grad. Engring. Ctr., Rolla, 1975-82; assoc. prof. U. Toledo, 1982-98, prof. emeritus, 1999—. Pres. Oh Enterprises Corp., Toledo, 1995—. Author: The Perfect Wedding—Starting with Proper Invitations and Announcements, 1980, Computers and Industrial Engineering, 1994, Productivity and Quality Research Frontiers, 1995. Chmn. bd. trustees Korean Acad., Toledo, 1995-98. Recipient presdl. fellowship Okla. State U., 1965. Mem. Inst. Indsl. Engrs. (pres. Toledo chpt. 1984), Am. Soc. for Engring. Edn., Anthony Wayne Toastmasters (pres. 1994), Toastmasters Internat. (area gov. 1995, divsn. gov. 1996), Korean Assn. of Greater Toledo (pres. 1996-98), Fedn. Korean Assns. U.S.A. (bd. dirs. 1997-99). Republican. Presbyterian. Avocations: tennis, golf. Home: 2817 Westchester Rd Toledo OH 43615-2245 Office: U Toledo Dept Mech/Indsl & Mfg Engrg Toledo OH 43606

OHANIAN, HANS CHRISTOPH, physicist, author, educator; b. Leipzig, Germany, Apr. 29, 1941; s. Helmut and Emilie Ohanian; m. Susan Farnsworth, June 28, 1966. BA, U. Calif., Berkeley, 1963; PhD, Princeton U., 1968. Asst. prof. Rensselaer Poly. Inst., Troy, N.Y., 1968-76, adj. prof., 1979—; sr. scientist Dudley Observator, Schenectady, N.Y., 1990—. Vis. fellow Princeton (N.J.) U., 1976-77; assoc. prof. Union Coll., Schenectady, N.Y., 1977-83; vis. prof. U. Rome, 1985-86; vis. rsch. prof. Rensselaer Poly. Inst., Troy, 1998—. Author: Gravitation and Spacetime, 1976, Physics, 1985, Modern Physics, 1987, Classical Electrodynamics, 1988, Principles of Quantum Mechanics, 1990, Principles of Physics, 1993, Relativity: A Modern Introduction, 2001; assoc. editor Am. Jour. Physics, 1993-97; contbr. articles on gravitation to profl. publs. Mem. Am. Phys. Soc., Text and Acad. Authors Assn., Phi Beta Kappa, Sigma Xi. Home: PO Box 370 Charlotte VT 05445-0370 Office: Rensselaer Poly Inst Dept Physics Troy NY 12180

OHANIAN, SUSAN, freelance education writer; b. Sacramento, Feb. 19, 1941; d. Will Franklin and Martha (Jones) Farnsworth; m. Hans Christoph Ohanian, June 28, 1966. BA, San Francisco State U., 1962; MA, U. Calif., 1964. Cert. reading and English tchr. N.Y. Instr. Mercer County Community Coll., Trenton, N.J., 1967-69, Rensselaer Polytech Inst., Troy, N.Y., 1968-69; tchr. Troy Pub. Schs., 1969-83; staff writer Learning Mag., Belmont, Calif., 1983-88; freelance writer Schenectady, N.Y., 1988-94, Charlotte, Vt., 1994—. Author: Garbage Pizza Patchwork Quilts and Math Magic, Within the Forest, Dates with the Greats, Who's in Charge?, 1994, Math at a Glance, 1995, Math Cross-Sections, 1995, One Size Fits Few, 1999, Caught in the Middle, 2001, What Happened to Recess and Why Are Our children Struggling in Kindergarten?, 2002, The Great Word Catalogue, 2002; contbr. articles to profl. jours. Home and Office: PO Box 370 Charlotte VT 05445-0370 E-mail: susano@gmatv.net.

O'HARE, JOSEPH ALOYSIUS, academic administrator, priest; b. N.Y.C., Feb. 12, 1931; s. Joseph Aloysius and Marie Angela (Enright) O'H. AB, Berchmans Coll, Cebu City, Philippines, 1954, MA, 1955; STL, Woodstock Coll., Md., 1962; PhD, Fordham U., 1968; DHL (hon.), Fairfield U., 1980, Rockhurst Coll., Kansas City, Mo., 1984, Ateneo de Manila U., 1990, CUNY, 1991, Coll. of St. Rose, Albany, N.Y., 1995, St. Francis Coll., Bklyn., 1996, St. Peter's Coll., 1997; DLitt (hon.), Coll. of New Rochelle, 1984; D.D. (hon.), Muhlenberg Coll., 1998; DLitt (hon.), Fordham U., 2003. Joined S.J., 1948, ordained priest Roman Cath. Ch., 1961. Instr. Ateneo de Manila U., 1955-58, prof. philosophy, 1968-72; assoc. editor Am. Mag., N.Y.C., 1972-75, editor-in-chief, 1975-84; pres. Fordham U., Bronx, NY, 1984—2003. Author weekly column Of Many Things (Best Original Column award Cath. Press Assn. 1976, 78, 81, 84) E-mail: johare@fordham.edu.

O'HARE, SANDRA FERNANDEZ, education educator; b. N.Y.C., Mar. 19, 1941; d. Ricardo Enrique and Rosario de Los Angeles (Arenas) Fernandez; m. S. James O'Hare, Oct. 12, 1963; children: James, Richard, Michael, Christopher. BA, Marymount Coll., 1962; MA, U. San Francisco, 1980. Cert. elem. and coll. tchr.; bilingual and lang. devel. specialist. Instr.

adult edn., Guam, 1964-66, Spanish Speaking Ctr., Harrisburg, Pa., 1977-79; tchr. Colegio Salesiano, Rota, Spain, 1973-74, 84, Alisal Sch. Dist., Salinas, Calif., 1977-79, Liberty Sch., Petaluma, Calif., 1981-85, Cinnabar Sch., Petaluma, 1985—; instr. Chapman U., 1994-98; also summer migrant edn. programs, 1990-91. Instr. Santa Rosa (Calif.) Jr. Coll., 1982-83; mem. math. curriculum com. Sonoma County Office Edn., Santa Rosa, 1988; mem. Summer Sci. Connections Inst., Sonoma State U., 1994, Redwood Empire Math. Acad., summer 1995; mem. Sonoma County Math Project, 1995-96; summer '96 NEH stipend to Harvard U. Translator: Isabel la Catolica, 1962. Mem. Asian relief com. ARC, Harrisburg, 1975, Boy Scouts Am., Petaluma, 1983, Mechanicsburg, Pa., 1974, Monterey, Calif., 1971, Sonoma County Adult Literacy League, 1996—. Sarah D. Barder fellow Johns Hopkins U., 1990. Mem. NEA, AAUW (chair edn. founds. com. 1985-86), Calif. Assn. Bilingual Educators, Club Hispano-Americano Petaluma (pres. 1987-89), M3 Investment Club. Roman Catholic. Avocation: travel. Home: 1289 Glenwood Dr Petaluma CA 94954-4326

O'HERN, JANE SUSAN, psychologist, educator; b. Winthrop, Mass., Mar. 21, 1933; d. Joseph Francis and Mona (Garvey) O'H. BS, Boston U., 1954, EdD, 1962; MA, Mich. State U., 1956. Instr. Mercyhurst Coll., 1954-55, Hofstra Coll., 1956-57, State Coll., Salem and Boston, 1957-60; asst. prof. Boston U., 1962-67, assoc. prof., 1967-75, prof. edn. and psychiat. (psychology), 1975-95, prof. emeritus, 1995—, chmn. dept. counseling psychology, 1972-75, 88-89, dir. mental health edn. program, 1975-81, dir. internat. edn., 1978-81, asst. v.p. internat. edn., 1981; prof. emeritus mental health and behavioral medicine program Boston U. Sch. Medicine, 2001—. Pres. ASSIST Internat., Inc., 1989—98; adv. bd, Internat. Study Cons., 1994—98; founder BettyBoston LLC, 2002—. Contbr. articles to profl. jours. Trustee Boston Ctr. Modern Psychoanalytic Studies, 1980-92. Recipient grants U.S. Office Edn., NIMH, Dept. of Def. Mem. Assn. Counselor Edn. and Suprs., Am. Counseling Assn., North Atlantic Assn. Counselor Edn. and Supervision (past pres.), Mass. Psychol. Assn., Am. Psychol. Assn., Mortar Bd., Pi Lamda Theta, Sigma Kappa, Phi Delta Kappa, Phi Beta Delta. Home: 111 Perkins St Apt 287 Boston MA 02130-4324

OHL, RONALD EDWARD, academic administrator; b. Warren, Ohio, May 30, 1936; s. Howard Edward and Ella May (Van Auker) O.; m. Joan Ann Elizabeth Eschenbach, June 29, 1974. BA, Amherst Coll., 1958; MA, Columbia U., 1961; M in Divinity, Union Theol. Sem., N.Y.C., 1964; PhD, U. Pa., 1980. Ordained minister Congregationalist Ch., 1964. Counselor to grad. students Columbia U., N.Y.C., 1960-62; asst. dean students, asst. prof. history Elmhurst (Ill.) Coll., 1964-67; spl. asst. to dean of men Temple U., Phila., 1967-68; assoc. dean coll., dean student affairs, instr. in edn. Colo. Coll., Colorado Springs, 1968-74; with Fairleigh Dickinson U., Rutherford, N.J., 1975-83, successively acting v.p. for external relations, asst. to pres., acting chmn. and cons. relations div. univ. resources and pub. affairs; pres. Salem (W.Va.)-Teikyo U., 1983—, trustee, 1989—, also bd. dirs. Bd. dirs. One Valley Bank. Contbr. articles to profl. jours. Bd. dirs. Sta. WNPB-TV, 1992-98. Recipient Edward Poole Lay Traveling fellowship award Amherst Coll., 1958-59, Young Am. Artists' Dirs. award U.S. Embassy, Rome, 1959-60; Rockefeller Bros. Fund fellow, 1961-62; named Research Asst., U. Pa., 1967-68. Mem. W.Va. Assn. Ind. Colls. (pres. 1985-89), North Ctrl. Assn. Colls. and Schs. (cons.-evaluator 1987—), W.Va. Found. for Ind. Colls. (acad. vice chmn. 1992-94, sec., treas. 1999-00), Clarksburg C. of C. (bd. dirs. 1985-91, 93-96, 97—), Univ. Club (N.Y.C.), W.Va. Christopher Quincentenary Commn., Martin Luther King Centenary, Rotary. Avocations: reading, writing, aviation, skiing, backpacking. Home: 603 Horizon Way Martinsburg WV 25401-1032

OHL, THOMAS ANTHONY, school counselor; b. N.Y.C., Mar. 22, 1956; s. Daniel John and Theresa (Prusko) O. AAS in Bus. Adminstrn., Broome C.C., Binghamton, N.Y., 1976; BA in Sociology, SUNY Binghamton, 1979; MS in Counselor Edn., SUNY Oneonta, 1992; CAS in Counseling Svcs., Suny Oswego, 1999. Cert. sch. counselor. Tchr. aide, child care worker Children's Home Wyoming Conf., Binghamton, 1987-93; sch. counselor Hillside Children's Ctr., Auburn, N.Y., 1993—. Substitute sch. counselor Del.-Chenango-Madison-Otsego BOCES, Norwich, N.Y., 1992-93. Mem. com. Boy Scouts Am., Auburn, 1996—. Mem. Cayuga Area Counselors Assn. Democrat. Roman Catholic. Avocations: camping, fishing, woodcarving, hiking. Office: Hillside Children's Ctr 7432 County House Rd Auburn NY 13021-8299 Business E-Mail: tohl@hillside.com.

OHMART, SALLY JO, elementary education educator; b. Wheeling, W.Va., Dec. 19, 1938; d. M. James and Ruth I. (Gary) Welton; m. Paul E. Ohmart, June 6, 1960; children: Kim Ohmart Laurin, Karen Ohmart McAvoy. BS in Edn., Miami U., Oxford, Ohio, 1960; MS in Edn., Ind. U., 1975. Cert. tchr., Ohio, Ind. Tchr. Crooked Creek Elem. Sch., Met. Dist. of Washington Twp. Schs., Indpls., 1960-61; tchr. Ctrl. Sch., Lebanon (Ind.) Cmty. Sch. Dist., 1970-92; state cadre Connected Learning Assures Successful Students, 1992-94, regional historian, 1994-96, regional edn. chmn., 1997—. Past pres. Smile Awhile Home Econs., Lebanon, 1983; mem. Indpls. Symphony, 1991; chair edn. com. Centenary United Meth. Ch., 1967-68. Mem. AAUW, Order Eastern Star (past worthy matron), Alpha Delta Kappa (pres. Lebanon chpt. 1984-86, state rec. sec. 1988-90, state corr. sec. 1990-92, state pres. 1994-96), Tri Kappa, Delta Kappa Gamma (chpt. pres. 1998—). Republican. Avocations: reading, ceramics, cross-stitch, boating. Home: 12561 Medalist Pkwy Carmel IN 46033-8934 Office: Ctrl Elem Sch 515 E Williams St Lebanon IN 46052-2259

OHN, JONATHAN K. business educator; b. Jeonju, Republic of Korea, Apr. 15, 1961; s. Hyung S. and Sun J. Ohn; m. Grace K. Kim, Mar. 31, 1964; children: Stephanie, Jennifer. BS, Seoul Nat. U., 1984, MBA, 1987, Lehigh U., 1993, PhD, 1998. Tchg. asst. Lehigh U., Bethlehem, Pa., 1994—96; instr. Muhlenberg, Allentown, Cedar Crest Coll., Allentown, Pa., 1996—98; investment cons. Allexander Wescott, Allentown, Pa., 1998; asst. prof. Va. State U., Petersburg; assoc. prof. Wagner Coll., Staten Island, NY, 2002—. Adviser econs. and fin. student club Va. State U., Petersburg, 2000—01, mem. info. resources and tech. com., 2001—02, mem. fin. curriculum devel. com., mem. Phillip Morris scholarship com.; vis. prof. Lehigh U., Bethlehem, 2000—02. Contbr. articles and papers to profl. jours. (1998's Highly Commented award, 1998). 1st lt. Korean Air Force, 1988—91. Grantee Competiitve Rsch. grantee, Va. State U., 1999, Competitive Rsch. grantee, 2000, 2001. Mem.: Fin. Mgmt. Assn., Am. Econ. Assn., Am. Fin. Assn. Avocations: tennis, golf, basketball, music. Home: 38 Park St 26 A Florham Park NJ 07932 Personal E-mail: jo02@lehigh.edu. Business E-Mail: john@vsu.edu.

OIKAWA, HIROSHI, college president, materials science educator; b. Sakhalin, Japan, Oct. 15, 1933; s. Torao and Tomi (Kumagai) O.; m. Ayako Otomo, May 4, 1963; children: Makoto, Junko. BE, Tohoku U., Sendai, Japan, 1956, ME, 1958, D in Engring., 1961. Instr. Tohoku U., 1961-63, lectr., 1963-64, assoc. prof., 1964-82; rsch. fellow U. Fla., Gainesville, 1966-68; prof. Tohoku U., 1982-97, councilor, 1993-97, dean faculty engring., 1995-97; prof. emeritus Tohuku U., 1997—; prof. Nat. Instn. Acad. Degrees, Yokohama, Japan, 1997-98; pres. Coll. Indsl. Tech., Amagasaki, Japan, 1998—. Co-editor: Metals Handbooks, 1990, Metals Databook, 1993. Mem. Engring. Acad. Japan (bd. dirs. 2000—), Japan Inst. Metals (bd. dirs. 1992-94, 96-97, chief dir. Tohoku chpt. 1991-93, pres. 1996-97), Iron and Steel Inst. Japan (bd. dirs. 1990-92), Japan Inst. Light Metals (bd. dirs. 1989-95), Minerals, Metals and Materials Soc., ASM Internat., Inst. Materials. Office: Coll Indsl Tech Nishikoya 1 Amagasaki 661-0047 Japan E-mail: oikawa@cit.sangitan.ac.jp.

OJINNAKA, CHUKWUNONYE MOSES, chemistry educator; b. Akpulu, Imo, Nigeria, June 6, 1948; s. Samuel Ezelefeanya and Janet Abiazuba (Ejiofor) O.; 1 child, Chukwudi Aham Samuel Jr. BSc in Chemistry, U. Ibadan, Nigeria, 1973, PhD in Chemistry, 1978; Cert. in NMR Instrumentation, Varian AG Switzerland, Ibadan, 1975. Chartered chemist. Rsch. officer Fed. Inst. Indsl. Rsch., Oshodi, Lagos, Nigeria, 1974; grad. asst. in chemistry U. Ibadan, 1975, demonstrator in chemistry, 1976-77; head rsch. divsn. Leather Rsch. Inst. Nigeria, Zaria, Kaduna, 1978-79; rsch. assoc. U. Ill. Med. Ctr., Chgo., 1981; lectr. chemistry U. Port Harcourt, Rivers State, Nigeria, 1979-85, sr. lectr., 1985-94, head dept. pure and indsl. chemistry, 1988-90, prof. chemistry, 1995—. Chief cons. Kemispect Assocs., 1994—. Author: Introduction to Principles of Organic Chemistry, 1994, Infrared Spectroscopy: Technique and Applications, 1996, Tanners' Guide to Nigerian Plants, 1987, African Herbal Medicine, 1985; contbr. articles to profl. jours.; asst. editor Acad. Scis. Jour. Scientia Africana, 1994—. Capt. Biafran Army, 1967-70. Fed. Govt. Nigeria Univ. scholar, 1970-73, U. Ibadan Grad. scholar, 1975-77; Swedish Govt. fellow, U. Stockholm, 1984-85. Fellow Chem. Soc. Nigeria, 1997; mem. Inst. Chartered Chemists of Nigeria (vice chmn. 1990-91), Soc. for Medicinal Plants Rsch. (Europe), Nigerian Soc. Pharmacognosy. Roman Catholic. Achievements include research in molluscicidal activity of napoleonaside from Napoleonaea Imperialis. Office: U Port Harcourt Dept Chemistry Box 149 Port Harcourt, Post Office Choba Rivers Nigeria E-mail: cmojinnaka@yahoo.co.uk.

O'KEEFE, RAYMOND PETER, lawyer, educator; b. N.Y.C., Jan. 16, 1928; s. William Bernard and Catherine Irene (Smith) O'Keefe; m. Stephanie Ann Fitzpatrick, June 19, 1954; children: Raymond, William, Ann, Kevin, Mary, James, John. AB cum laude, St. Michael's Coll., 1950; JD, Fordham U., 1953. Bar: N.Y. 1954, Fla. 1976, U.S. Dist. Ct. (so. dist.) : N.Y. 1955, U.S. Ct. Claims : 1960, U.S. Ct. Appeals (2d cir.) : 1963, U.S. Supreme Ct. : 1971. Assoc. Thayer & Gilbert, N.Y.C., 1953—55; prof. law Fordham U. Sch. Law, N.Y.C., 1955—63; sr. assoc. Carter, Ledyard & Milburn, N.Y.C., 1963—68; ptnr. Ide & Haigney, N.Y.C., 1968—74; sr. ptnr. McCarthy, Fingar, Donovan, Drazen & Smith, White Plains, NY, 1974—. Adj. prof. Pace U. Sch. Law, White Plains, 1979—, Fordham U. Sch. Law, 1983—; lectr. N.Y. Med. Coll., Valhalla, NY, 1979—; prof. St. Thomas of Villanova Miami Sch. Law, 1984—; vis. prof. Thomas M. Cooley Sch. Law, Lansing, 1991, Fordham U. Sch. Law, 1992; justice State of N.Y. Justice Ct., 1978—81. Trustee Am. Irish Hist. Soc.; chmn. bd. Westchester Halfway House, 1974—78; bd. dirs. Westchester Youth Shelter, 1980. With USN, 1945—48. Recipient Alumni award, St. Michael's Coll., 1961, Humanitarian award, Fordham Law Sch., 1999. Mem.: ABA (commn. on youth, drugs and alcoholism 1984), Assn. of Bar of City of N.Y., N.Y. State Trial Lawyers Assn., Assn. Trial Lawyers Am., Fla. Bar Assn., N.Y. State Bar Assn. (chmn. spl. com. on lawyer alcoholism and drug abuse 1979—), Surf Club, Harbor View Club, Larchmont Shore Club. Home: 802 Kure Village Way Kure Beach NC 28449-4900

OKESON, DOROTHY JEANNE, educational association administrator; b. Garden City, Kans., Aug. 31, 1931; d. Arthur E. and Thelma Lucille (McGraw) Clements-Newman; m. Arnold Leroy Okeson, Dec. 20, 1953; 1 child, Michael Leroy. BA, U. No. Colo., 1961. Cert. jr. high and secondary tchr. Tchr. Weskan (Kans.) Consolidated Sch., 1952-54, Weskan Unified Sch. Dist., 1962-70; corr. sec. Sherman-Wallace Assn. Retarded Children, Goodland, Kans., 1968-95. Mem. Gov.'s Adv. Planning Council, Topeka, 1976-80, Kans. Planning Council Devel. Disabilities, Topeka, 1980-87, chmn., 1985-87. Contbr. articles to Western Times newspaper. Bd. dirs. Assn. Retarded Citizens, Merriam, Kans., 1969-79; asst. campaign mgr. county gubernatorial candidates, Sharon Springs, Kans., 1986; vol. Kans. Spl. Olympics. Mem. NEA (ret. life), AAUW (legis. chmn. 1980-89, pres. 1989-91), Nat. Assn. Devel. Disabilities (chmn. subcom. child devel. 1976-87, mem. coun., by-laws and pub. policy com. 1987), Cheyenne/Rawlins County Assn. for Retarded Citizens. Republican. Lutheran. Avocations: reading, antiques, bird watching. Home: 906 Logan St Apt 106 Atwood KS 67730-1645

OKHAMAFE, IMAFEDIA, English literature and philosophy educator; b. Otuo, Nigeria; s. Obokhe and Olayemi Okhamafe. Double PhD, Purdue U., 1984. Prof. philosophy and English U. Nebr., Omaha, 1993—. Office: U Nebr Annex 26 Omaha NE 68182-0001 also: U Nebr Philosophy Dept Omaha NE 68182-0001 E-mail: imafedia@unomaha.edu.

OKINO, WENDY JEAN, special education educator; b. Montebello, Calif., Nov. 1, 1957; d. Douglas Harold and Betty Maria (Segerra) Holmes; m. Philip Betram Okino, Sept. 15, 1979 (div. June 1990); 1 child, Laina Kikumi. BA in Phys. Edn., Calif. State U., L.A., 1980, MA in Ednl. Adminstrn., 1993. Cert. multiple subject teaching, specialist severely handicapped, Calif., preliminary administrv. svcs. credential, Calif. Mgr. food svc. Szabo Food Svc. Co., Anaheim, Calif., 1981-83; tchr. ESL Montebello (Calif.) Sch. Dist., 1980-82, Chaffey Adult Sch., Ont., Calif., 1984-86; tchr. personal hygiene Baldwin Park (Calif.) Adult Sch., 1984-86; substitute tchr. handicapped toddlers, children with hearing impairments, autistic children San CLASS Regional Sch. Dist., San Bernadino, Calif., 1985-87, tchr. high sch. multi-handicapped, 1987=88, tchr. pre-school multi-handicapped, 1988-91, tchr. multi-handicapped Dominga High Sch., 1991—. Mem. Calif. Tchrs. Assn. (treas. 1989-91, sec. 1991-93, area rep. 1993—). Democrat. Roman Catholic. Avocations: outdoor exercise, cooking, crafts, reading, aerobics. Home: 15941 Winbrook Dr Chino Hills CA 91709-3860 Office: San CLASS Regional Sch Dist 601 N E St San Bernardino CA 92410-3012

OKPEWHO, ISIDORE O, education educator; BA with honors, London U., 1964; PhD in english, U. of Denver, 1976; DLitt, U. of London, 2000. Asst. prof. SUNY Buffalo, 1974—76; lectr. to full, English Ibadan U., Nigeria, 1976—90; vis. prof. Harvard U., 1990—91; prof., Africana studies, English and comparative lit. Binghamton U., 1991—. Assoc. dean, faculty of arts Ibadan U., 1979—81, chmn., dept. of English, Nigeria, 1987—90; hmn., dept. of Africana studies SUNY Binghamton, 1991—97; sr. vis. St. Anthony's Coll., Oxford U., 1993; fellow Nat. Humanities Ctr., Rsch. Triangle Pk, 1997—98; Ford found. vis. scholar WEB DuBois Inst. for Afro-American Rsch., Harvard U., 1990—91; fellow of the ctr. for advanced study in the behavioral sci., 1988; fellow of the Woodrow Wilson Internat. Ctr. for Scholars, Washington, 1982—83; dir. for Africa Internat. Assn. for Oral Lit. in Africa Budapest, 1984; mem., adv. com. Internat. Comparative Lit., 1982—83; v.p. Nigerian Assn for African and Comparative Lit., 1981—90; mem. Presdl. Planning Com. for Open U. of Nigeria, 1980. Author: (novels) Tides, 1993 (Brit. Commonwealth Writers prize for Africa, 1993), (book) The African Diaspora: African Originas and New World Identities, 1999, Once Upon a Kingdom: Myth, Hegemony and Identity, 1998, African Oral Literature: Backgrounds, Character and Continuity, 1992, The Oral Performance in Africa, 1990, A Portrait of the Artist as a Scholar, 1990, The Heritage of African Poetry: An Anthology of Oral and Written Poetry, 1985, Myth in Africa: A Study of its Aesthetic and Cultural Relevance, 1983, The Epic in Africa: Toward a Poetics of the Oral Performance, 1979, The Last Duty, 1976, The Victims, 1970; contbr. articles to profl. jours.; mem. editl. bd. Rsch. in African Literatures, Oral Tradition; editor: Journal of African and Comparative Literature. Mem., bd. dirs. African Studies Assn., 1994—97; mem., bd. cons. Guthrie Theater, Mpls., 1992—94; mem., rsch. adv. coun. Ctr. for the Study of World Religions, 1992—96; chmn. Task Force for the 40th Anniversary of Ibadan U., Nigeria, 1986—88. Grant, Rockefeller Found., 1999, Ford Found. grant. Mem.: George Moses Horton Soc. for the Study of African Poetry, Coun. of Black Studies, Am. Folklore Soc., African Lit. Assn., African Studies Assn., Internat. Soc. for Folk Narrative Rsch., Folklore Fellows Internat. Office: PO Box 6000 Binghamton NY 13902

OKULSKI, JOHN ALLEN, principal; b. Mineola, N.Y., July 28, 1944; s. John Joseph and Rose (Zebrowski) O.; m. Martina Carol Schoneboom, July 16, 1966; children: Richard, Peter, John. BS, Rutgers U., 1966; MS, C.W. Post Coll., 1972; postgrad., Hofstra U., 1975-76, Queens Coll., 1973. Social studies tchr. Long Beach (N.Y.) Jr. H.S., 1966-67, Lynbrook (N.Y.) H.S., 1967-69, Herricks H.S., New Hyde Park, N.Y., 1969-72; guidance counselor Herricks Jr. H.S., 1972-75; dept. chmn. sec. sch. guidance Herricks pub. schs., 1975-78; asst. prin. Herricks H.S., 1978-87; prin. Bay Shore (N.Y.) H.S., 1987-92, Garden City (N.Y.) H.S., 1992—. Cubmaster Boy Scouts Am., New Hyde Park, 1975-83; v.p. New Hyde Park Little League, 1978-83. Recipient Outstanding Achievement award Garden City C. of C., 1995. Mem. L.I. Pers. and Guidance Assn. (officer), Mid. States Accreditation Assn. (adv. com. N.Y. chpt.), Garden City C. of C. (Outstanding Achievement award 1995). Presbyterian. Home: 8528 264th St Floral Park NY 11001-1132 Office: Garden City High Sch 170 Rockaway Ave Garden City NY 11530-1499

OLAGUNJU, AMOS OMOTAYO, computer science educator, consultant; b. Igosun, Kwara, Nigeria, Nov. 27, 1954; came to U.S., 1980; s. Solomon Atoyebi and Ruth Ebun (Adegoke) O.; m. Janet; 1 child, Amanda. EdD, U. N.C., Greensboro, 1987; PhD, Kensington U., 1990; cert. in cryptography and info. systems, MIT, 1996, cert. in design and analysis experiments, cert. in digital comm. networks, MIT, 1999, cert. in bioinformatic principles, 2001. Cert. bioinformatic prins. MIT, 2001. Mgmt. info. system dir. Barber-Scotia Coll., Concord, NC, 1981-82; lectr. NC A&T State U., Greensboro, NC, 1982-87, asst. prof., 1987-90; mem. tech. staff Bell Communications Rsch., Piscataway, NJ, 1986-90; vis. prof. Mich. State U., East Lansing, Mich., 1990-91; coord. acad. computing, assoc. prof. Del. State U., 1991-92, prof., chair dept. math. and computer sci., 1992—2001; collegiate prof. UMUC-Asia, 2001—02; prof. computer networking and applications St. Cloud State U., 2002—. Cons. NSF, Washington, 1991-93, Edn. Testing Agy., Princeton, NJ, 1995—. Author: Lecture Notes Series in Language C, Systems Programming, Database Systems, Theoretical Aspects of Computing, File Structures, Introduction to Computer Science and Scientific and Engineering Applications of Fortran, 1991-96; mem. editl. bd. Sci. World Jour., 2003—; contbr. articles to Software Metrics, Automatic Indexing, Perfect Hashing, Number Theory, Efficient Statis. Algorithms, Del. State News. Pres. Ahmadu Bello Assn. Computer Univ. Students, Zaria, Nigeria, 1976, Orgn. United Africans, Concord, NC, 1982. Recipient Queen's Grad. award Queen's U., Kingston, Ont., 1979; Navy-Am. Soc. for Engring. Edn. fellow, 1997, sr. fellow 1998, 2000. Mem. Internat. Assn. Sci. Tech. Devel. (reviewer 2001—), Assn. for Modelling and Simulation in Enterprises (program chair 1989-90, editor), Assn. for Computing Machinery (reviewer), NC Acad. Sci. (program chair 1991—, mem. editl. bd. 1999—), NY Acad. Sci. Achievements include invention of the Bell Communication Rsch. Software Daily Software Report and Analysis Measurement System and Generic Administrative Quantitative Decision Support System. Home: 1617 Highland Trail Saint Cloud MN 56301

OLAH, GEORGE ANDREW, chemist; b. Budapest, Hungary, May 22, 1927; arrived in U.S., 1964, naturalized, 1970; s. Julius and Magda (Krasznai) Olah; m. Judith Agnes Lengyel, July 9, 1949; children: George John, Ronald Peter. PhD, Tech. U. Budapest, 1949, D (hon.), 1989; DSc (hon.), U. Durham, 1988, U. Munich, 1990, U. Crete, Greece, 1994, U. Szeged, Hungary, 1995, U. Veszprem, 1995, Case Western Res. U., 1995, U. So. Calif., 1995, U. Montpellier, 1996, SUNY, 1998, U. Pecs, Hungary, 2001, U. Debrecen, 2003. Mem. faculty Tech. U. Budapest, 1949—54; assoc. dir. Ctrl. Chem. Rsch. Inst., Hungarian Acad. Scis., 1954—56; rsch. scientist Dow Chem. Can. Ltd., 1957—64, Dow Chem. Co., Framingham, Mass., 1964—65; prof. chemistry Case Western Res. U., Cleve., 1965—69, C.F. Mabery prof. rsch., 1969—77; Donald P. and Katherine B. Loker disting. prof. chemistry, dir. Hydrocarbon Rsch. Inst., U. So. Calif., LA, 1977—. Vis. prof. chemistry Ohio State U., 1963, U. Heidelberg, Germany, U. Colo., 1969, Swiss Fed. Inst. Tech., 1972, U. Munich, 1973, U. London, 1973—79, Louis Pasteur U., Strasbourg, 1974, U. Paris, 1981; hon. vis. lectr. U. London, 1981—95; cons. to industry. Author: Friedel-Crafts Reactions, Vols. I-IV, 1963—64; author: (with P. Schleyer) Carbonium Ions, Vols. I-V, 1969—76; author: Friedel-Crafts Chemistry, 1973, Carbocations and Electrophilic Reactions, 1973, Halonium Ions, 1975; author: (with G.K.S. Prakash and J. Somer) Superacids, 1984; author: (with Prakash, R.E. Williams, L.D. Field and K. Wade) Hypercarbon Chemistry, 1987; author: (with R. Malthotra and S.C. Narang) Nitration, 1989; author: Cage Hydrocarbons, 1990; author: (with Wade and Williams) Electron Deficient Boron and Carbon Clusters, 1991; author: (with Chambers and Prakash) Synthetic Fluorine Chemistry, 1992; author: (with Molnar) Hydrocarbon Chemistry, 1995; author: (with Laali, Wang, Prakash) Onium Ions, 1998; author: A Life of Magic Chemistry, 2001; chpts. to books, numerous papers to profls. jours., patentee in field; author (with Pranash): Across Conventional Lines, 2003. Recipient Alexander von Humboldt Sr. U.S. Scientist award, 1979, Calif. Scientist of Yr. award, 1989, Pioneer of Chemistry award, Am. Inst. Chemists, 1993, Mendeleev medal, Russian Acad. Scis., 1992, Kapitsa medal, Russian Acad. Natural Scis., 1995, Order of the Hungarian Corvin-Chain, 2001, Albert Einstein medal, Russian Acad. Natural Scis., 2002, Bolyai prize, Hungarian Acad. Sci., 2002; Guggenheim fellow, 1972, 1988. Fellow: AAAS, Chem. Inst. Can., Brit. Chem. Soc. (hon.; hon./centenary lectr. 1978, Centenary lectr. 1978); mem.: NAS, Can. Royal Soc., Royal Soc. Sci. Arts Barcelona, Royal Acad. Sci. and Arts, Am. Acad. Arts and Sci., Am. Philos. Soc., Hungarian Acad. Sci. (hon.), Royal Chem. Soc. (hon.), Italy Chem. Soc. (hon.), Chem. Soc. Japan (hon.), Am. Chem. Soc. (award petroleum chemistry 1964, Leo Hendrik Baekeland award N.J. sect. 1966, Morley medal Cleve. sect. 1970, award Synthetic Organic Chemistry 1979, Roger Adams award in organic chemistry 1989, Arthur C. Cope award 2001), European Acad. Arts, Sci. and Humanities, Royal Soc. London (fgn. mem.), Italian Nat. Acad. Sci. Lincei. Home: 2252 Gloaming Way Beverly Hills CA 90210-1717 Office: U So Calif Labor Hydrocarbon Rsch Inst Los Angeles CA 90007 E-mail: olah@usc.edu.

OLBIS, KAREN, elementary education educator, musician, vocalist; b. Freehold, N.J., Oct. 18, 1964; d. John Anthony and Caroline Dorothy (Faber) O. BA, Rutgers U., 1987, M of Ednl. Adminstrn., 1991; postgrad., Juilliard Sch. Music, N.Y.C., 1987-88. Cert. tchr. of nursery sch., elem. sch., English and music, N.J.; cert. paralegal. Pub. sch. tchr., Freehold, n.J., 1984—. Cantor, soloist St. Robert Bellarmine Ch., Freehold, 1982—; voice tchr. in pvt. studio, Freehold, 1990—; free-lance soloist, 1984—. Soloist Orch. St. Peter-by-the-Sea, others. Singer, actress in community theater, 1983—; singer in community and profl. choral orgns., 1983—. Roman Catholic. Avocations: reading, antiques, theater, golf, piano. Home: 113 Monmouth Rd Freehold NJ 07728-7926

OLCZAK, PAUL VINCENT, psychology educator; b. Buffalo, N.Y., May 25, 1943; s. Vincent Henry and Helen (Babula) O.; m. Marie Rose Oliveri, Oct. 20, 1973; children: Paul V. II, Patrick J., Drew M. MA, No. Ill. U., 1969, PhD, 1972. Clin. psychologist Family Ct. Psychiat. Clinic, Buffalo, 1975-77, cons. supervisory psychologist, 1977—; supr. psychol. svcs. Hopevale, Inc., Hamburg, N.Y., 1977-89; clin. psychologist Amherst (N.Y.) Police Dept., 1989—; asst. prof. psychology SUNY, Geneseo, 1977-83, assoc. prof. psychology, 1983-90, prof. psychology, 1990—, chairperson, 1999—; clin. psychologist child and adolescent psychiatry Niagara Falls Meml. Hosp., 1996—. Co-editor: Community Mediation, 1991; contbg. author: The POI in Clinical Situations: A Review, 1991, Self-actualization-Polemics Surrounding Its Use, 1991; contbr. articles to profl. jours./publs. Mem. APA, Ea. Psychol. Assn., Midwestern Psychol. Assn., Psychonomic Soc., Soc. Exptl. Social Psychology, Internat. Assn. for Conflict Mgmt., Psi Chi, Sigma Xi. Home: 150 Briarhill Rd Buffalo NY 14221-1811 Office: SUNY Dept Psychology Geneseo NY 14454 E-mail: olczak@geneseo.edu.

OLDANI, NORBERT LOUIS, mathematician, educator, composer; b. Detroit, Nov. 16, 1936; s. Louis and Lillian Oldani. BA, U. Detroit, 1958, MA, 1960. Teaching fellow U. Detroit, 1958-59; analyst AC Spark Plug, Milw., 1961-62; tchr. St. John's U., N.Y.C., 1962-66, Mohawk Valley

Community Coll., Utica, NY, 1967—99. Contbr. several articles to profl. jours. Regional music composer Ctrl. N.Y. area. NSf grantee, 1968, 70. Mem. Am. Math. Soc., Math. Assn. Am., N.Y. State Math. Assn. Two-Yr. Colls. (chair curriculum com. 1977-79). Roman Catholic. Achievements include composition of several electronic musical pieces.

OLDENHAGE, IRENE DOROTHY, retired elementary school educator; b. Jersey City, May 9, 1941; d. Herman Albert and Emma Rose (Scozzafava) Hespos; divorced; 1 child, David George. BA in Elem. Edn., Paterson State Coll., 1962; postgrad., Seton Hall U., 1986; Master's Equivalency, St. Peter's U., Jersey City, 1996; postgrad., U. San Fancisco, 1976, St. Peter's U., 1990-91. Elem. tchr. Fairview Bd. Edn., NJ, 1962-67, Bogota Bd. Edn., NJ, 1969—2002; ret., 2002. Rep. Bogota Libr. Bd., 1984-85; vol. Hands Across Am., Bogota, 1986, Ithaca Coll., 1982. Recipient Gov.'s Tchr. Recognition award, State of NJ, 1989. Mem. NEA, NJ Edn. Assn., Bergen County Edn. Assn., Bogota Edn. Assn. (bldg. rep. 1982—, Svc. to Youth award 1996). Lutheran. Avocations: crafts, reading. Home: 98 Palisade Ave Bogota NJ 07603-1724

OLDER, RICHARD SAMUEL, elementary school music educator; b. Cuba, N.Y., Aug. 10, 1947; s. Laurence Charles and Ann Nell (Reese) O.; m. Helen Mary DiOrio, Nov. 8, 1986; 1 child, Michelle Ann. B in Music Edn., Westminster Choir Coll., 1971. Cert. tchr. of music, N.J. Tchr. 8th grade vocal and gen. music Columbia Jr. H.S., Berkeley Heights, N.J., 1971-81; tchr. vocal and gen. music Woodruff and Mountain Park elem. schs., Berkeley Heights, 1981-88, Woodruff and T.P. Hughes schs., Berkeley Heights, 1988—. Recipient 20 Yrs. of Svc. award PTA Woodruff Sch., 1990. Mem. N.J. Edn. Assn. (local rep. 1986-87), Foxhollow Golf Club. Republican. Presbyterian. Avocations: golf, bowling, swimming, piano, guitar. Home: 43 River Bend Rd Berkeley Heights NJ 07922-1812 Office: TP Hughes Elem Sch Snyder Ave Berkeley Heights NJ 07922 E-mail: oldernj@comcast.net.

OLDHAM, ELAINE DOROTHEA, retired elementary and middle school educator; b. Coalinga, Calif., June 29, 1931; d. Claude Smith Oldham and Dorothy Elaine (Hill) Wilkins AB in History, U. Calif., Berkeley, 1953; MS in Sch. Adminstrn., Calif. State U., Hayward, 1976; postgrad., U. Calif., Berkeley, Harvard U., Mills Coll. Tchr. Piedmont Unified Sch. Dist., Calif., 1956-94, ret., 1994. Pres., bd. dirs. Camron-Stanford House Preservation Assn., 1979-86; adminstrv. v.p., bd. dirs. Achievement Rewards for Coll. Scientists Found., Inc., San Francisco; active various civic and cmty. support groups; bd. dirs. Anne Martin Children's Ctr., Lincoln Child Ctr.; pres. Acacia br. Children's Hosp., Oakland, 1996-2001, No. Light Sch. Aux., East Bay League II of San Francisco Symphony. Mem. Am. Assn. Mus. (bd. dirs.), Am. Assn. Mus. Trustees, Internat. Coun. Mus., Inst. Internat. Edn., Am. Assn. State and Local History, Am. Decorative Arts Forum San Francisco, Oakland Mus. Assn. (women's bd.), DAR (Piedmont chpt., regent 1997-2000, Outstanding Tchr. Am. History award), Nat. Soc. Colonial Dames Am. (pres., 2003—, 1st Pres. Gens. award), Magna Charta Dames, Daus. of Confederacy (v.p., scholarship chair), Calif. Hist. Soc., Hugeunot Soc. (v.p., scholarship chair), Plantagenent Soc., Order of Washington, Colonial Order of Crown, Ams. of Royal Descent, Order St. George and Descs. of Knights of Garter, San Francisco Garden Club, San Francisco Antiques Show (com. mem.), U. Calif. Alumni Assn. (co-chmn. and chmn. 10th, 25th and 50th yr. class reunion coms., com. 45th and 50th reunions), Piedmont Hist. Soc. (sec., v.p.), Internat. Diplomacy Coun. (San Francisco chpt.), Internat. Churchill Soc., English Spkg. Union, Pacific Mus. Soc., Am. Women for Internat. Understanding (No. Calif. chpt.), Prytanean Alumnae Assn. (bd. dirs.), Harvard Club (San Francisco), Bellevue Club (Oakland), San Francisco Garden Club, San Francisco Breakfast Club, Phi Delta Kappa, Delta Kappa Gamma. Republican. Episcopalian. E-mail: ElaineO972@aol.com.

OLDHAM, JOHN MICHAEL, physician, psychiatrist, educator; b. Muskogee, Okla., Sept. 6, 1940; s. Henry Newland and Alice Gray (Ewton) O.; m. Karen Joan Pacella, Apr. 24, 1971; children: Madeleine Marie, Michael Clark. BS in Engring., Duke U., 1962; MS in Neuroendocrinology, Baylor U., 1966, MD, 1967. Licensed physician N.Y., N.J., S.C., Tex.; diplomate in psychiat. and forensic psychiatry Am. Bd. Psychiatry and Neurology. Intern pediatrics St. Luke's Hosp., N.Y.C., 1967-68; resident psychiat. Columbia U. Dept. Psychiat., N.Y.S. Psychiatric Inst., N.Y.C., 1968-70, chief resident in psychiat., 1970-71; candidate Columbia Psychoanalytic Ctr., N.Y.C., 1969-77; dir. psychiatric emergency svcs. Roosevelt Hosp., N.Y.C., 1973-74, dir. residency tng. dept. psychiat., 1974-77; dir. short term diagnostic and treatment unit N.Y. Hosp. Westchester Divsn., White Plains, N.Y., 1977-80, dir. divsn. acute treatment svcs., 1980-84; deputy dir. N.Y. State Psychiatric Inst., N.Y.C., 1984-89, acting dir., 1989-90, dir., 1990—2002; assoc. chmn. dept. psychiatry Columbia U. Coll. Physicians & Surgeons, N.Y.C., 1986-96, vice chmn., 1996-2000, acting chmn., 2000—02; chief med. officer N.Y. State Office Mental Health, Albany, 1989—2002; chmn. dept. psychiatry and behavioral sci. Inst. Psychiatry, Med. U. SC, 2002—, exec. dir., 2002—. Chmn. dept. psychiatry and behavioral scis., exec. dir. Med. U. S.C. Inst. Psychiatry, 2002-; instr. clin. psychiat. Columbia U. Coll. Physicians & Surgeons, 1974-76, assoc. clin. psychiat., 1976-77, lectr. psychiat., 1977-84, assoc. prof. clin. psychiat., 1984-88, prof. clin. psychiat., 1988-96, Elizabeth K. Dollard prof. clin. psychiatry medicine & law, 1996-2002, prof. psychiatry Med. U. S.C., 2002-; asst. prof. psychiat. Cornell U. Med. Coll., N.Y.C., 1977-83, assoc. prof. clin. psychiat., 1983-84; attending staff dept. psychiat. Roosevelt Hosp., N.Y.C., 1973-77; assoc. attending psychiat., N.Y. Hosp., 1977-84, Presbyn Hosp., N.Y.C., 1984-88, attending psychiat., 1988-2002; tng., supervising psychoanalyst Columbia Psychoanalytic Ctr., N.Y.C., 1983-2002; coord. med. student edn., Cornell U. Med. Coll. Dept. Psychiat., Westchester Divsn., White Plains, N.Y., 1977-84; coord. clin. clerkships in psychiat. Roosevelt Hosp., Columbia U. Coll. Physicians & Surgeons, N.Y.C., 1974-77; spl. adv. bd. Freedom From Fear, Inc.; examiner Am. Bd. Psychiatry and Neurology; chmn. acute divisin rsch. group, Westchester Divsn., N.Y. Hosp., 1981-84, co-project dir. borderline rsch. group, 1982-84, co-prin. investigator familial transmission DSM III personality disorders, 1982-84; prin. investigator personality disorders in bulimia, N.Y.S. Psychiatric Inst., 1985-90, structured DSM III assessment psychoanalytic patients, Columbia Psychoanalytic Ctr., 1986-91; co-prin. investigator validity DSM III R personality disorders, N.Y. State Psychiatric Inst., 1987-94; co=investigator NIMH, 1996—. Author: (with L.B. Morris) The Personality Self-Portrait, 1990; editor Jour. Psychia. Practice; contbg. editor Jour. Personality Disorders; sect. editor Psychiatry; dep. editor Am. Psychiat. Pub., Inc.; mem. exec. editl. bd. Psychiat. Quar.; reviewer Psychiat. Svcs., Jour. of Neuropsychiatry; contbr. numerous articles to profl. jours.; more than 100 presentations in field. Recipient John J. Weber prize Excellence in Psychoanalytic Rsch. Columbia Psychoanalytic Ctr., 1990. Fellow Am. Coll. Psychiatrists (disting.), Am. Psychiat. Assn. (chmn. com. psychoanalytic liaison N.Y. County dist. br. 1986-87, pres. 1989-90, com. rsch. psychiat. treatment 1987-93, coun. rsch., steering com. practice guidelines, chmn. sci. program com. 1992-95, cons. 1991-92, 95-96, chmn. com. quality indicators 1999-2003, chmn. coun. quality care 2003—), Am. Psychopath. Assn., N.Y. Acad. Medicine;mem. Am. Psychoanalytic Assn. (cert.), Assn. Psychoanalytic Medicine (pres. 1989-91), Internat. Psychoanalytical Assn., N.Y. Acad. Sci., N.Y. State Med. Soc., Assn. Rsch. Personality Disorders (bd. dirs.), Internat. Soc. for Study of Personality Disorders (pres. 2000—). Office: Med Univ SC Dept Psychiatry and Behavioral Sci PO Box 250861 67 President St Charleston SC 29425 Office Fax: 843-792-3187. Business E-Mail: oldhamj@musc.edu.

OLEARCHYK, ANDREW, cardiothoracic surgeon, educator; b. Peremyshl, Ukraine, Dec. 3, 1935; s. Symon and Anna (Kravéts) O.; m. Renata M. Sharan, June 26, 1971; children: Christina N., Roman A., Adrian S. Grad., Med. Acad., Warsaw, Poland, 1961; grad., U. Pa., 1970. Diplomate Am. Bd. Surgery, Am. Bd. Thoracic Surgery. Chief divsn. anesthesiology, asst. dept. surgery Provincial Hosp., Kielce, Poland, 1963-66; resident in gen. surgery Geisinger Med. Ctr., Danville, Pa., 1968-73; resident in thoracic, cardiac surgery Allegheny Gen. Hosp., Pitts., 1980-82; pvt. practice medicine specializing in cardiac, thoracic and vascular surgery Phila. and Camden, N.J., 1982—. Contbr. articles to profl. jours., book A Surgeons Universe, 2003. Achievements include recognition of a triad of the absence of rheumatic fever, severea therosclerosis of the aortic valve and a low incidence of coronary artery disease in patients with a congenital bicuspid aortic valve (2002); modification of a vertical reduction aortoplasty by a distal external synthetic grafting for surgical treatment of aneurysms of the ascending aorta (2002); treatment of a bullous emphysema of the lung by a conservative resection of bullae and a local application of a biological glue (2001); applied a staged treatment of the left subclavian steal syndrome and coronary artery disease by the left carotid-subclavian and coronary artery bypasses (1999); establishing that in patients with coronary artery disease, the causes of congestive heart failure in those with a mild to moderate reduction of the left ventricular ejection fraction were hypertension, myocardial infarction or ishemic insufficiency of the mitral valve, and in those with severe reduction of the left ventricular ejection fraction were left ventricular dysfunction alone, or in combination with ischemic mitral regurgitation (1999); repair of a pseudoaneurysm of the ascending aorta on a beating heart (1997); ligation of bilateral coronary-pulmonary artery fistulas on a beating heart (1996); internal repair of the coronary sinus (Valsalva) aneurysm (1996); grafting of the internal thoracic to coronary arteries without touching the atherosclerotic ascending aorta, on cardiopulmonary bypass with a beating, warm and vented heart and bradycardia induced by beta-blockers (1994); design of Olearchyk R Triple Ringed Cannula Spring Clip to secure vein grafts over blunted cannulas in coronary artery bypass surgery (1989); combined right femoral and iliac retroperitoneal surgical approach to remove retained intraaortic balloon device (1989); technique for early antegrade flow from an axillary to main graft during replacement of the ascending aorta in proximal aortic dissection (1989); intro. of endarterectomy and external prostetic grafting of ascending and transverse aorta under hypothermic circulatory arrest (1987); first to combine insertion of the inferior vena cava filter with a protected iliofemoral venous thrombectomy (Olearchyk's operation. 1986); pioneering promotion of grafting of diffusely diseased coronary arteries with the internal thoracic artery (1980-82) and of the left anterior descending coronary artery sys. during resection of cardiac aneurysms (1979-80); recognized that alcoholism and smoking were common habits of patients with stomach cancer (1975); description of a combined treatment of advanced gastic carcinoma by resection and chemotherapy (1975); demonstration of safety of simultaneous use of fluothane and curare as gen. anesthesia (1966); description of combined treatment of advanced testicular seminoma with chemotherapy, resection and radiotherapy (1961). Address: 129 Walt Whitman Blvd Cherry Hill NJ 08003-3746

O'LEARY, DAVID MICHAEL, priest, educator; b. Lynn, Mass., Mar. 11, 1958; BA, St. John's Sem., Boston, 1981, MDiv, 1985; MEd, Boston Coll., 1986; STL, Weston Jesuit Sch. Theology, 1990; DPhil, Oxford U., Eng., 1999; Cert. in Alcohol Counseling/Substance Abuse, Boston Coll Sch. Social Work, 1982; Cert. in Spiritual Direction, St. Mary's Sem. and U., Balt., 1995; Cert. in Human Sexuality, Christian Inst. for Study of Human Sexuality, Bosotn, 1995. Ordained priest Boston Archdiocese, 1985. From spl. edn. tchr. to dir. spl. edn. program St. John's Sem., Boston, 1977—81; rschr., film editor, and writer Office Religious Edn. Arcdiocese Boston, 1981—82; co-leader group therapy, case worker Brigham & Women's Hosp., Kenmore Sq. De-Tox, Boston, 1982—83; substance abuse counselor St. John/St. Hugh, Roxbury, Mass., 1983—84; deacon intern Immaculate Conception Ch., Malden, Mass., 1984—85; parochial vicar Immaculate Conception Parish, Everett, Mass., 1986-91; parochial vicar, dir. religious edn. St. Augustine's Parish, South Boston, 1991-93, St. Theresa's Ch., North Reading, Mass., 1993-95; asst. prof. moral theology, spirituality-,sexual ethics St. Mary's Sem. and U., Balt., 1995—; assoc. U. chaplain, dir. Cath. Ctr. Tufts U., Medford, Mass., 1998—2002, U. chaplain, 2002—, 2nd prof. Adj. faculty lectr. in moral theology and social ethics St. John's Sem. Pastoral Inst., 1991; vis. lectr. in social ethics USAF Acad., Denver, 1992, USAF Chaplain Sch., Squadron Oficer Sch.,Air Command and Staff Coll., Air War Coll., Maxwell AFB, Ala., summer, 1992; adj. faculty Christian Inst. for Study of Human Sexuality and St. Luke's Inst., Silver Springs, Md., 1995—98; theol. cons. Md. Cath. Conf. of Bishops and St. Luke's Inst., Silver Springs, Md., 1995—98; mem. Human Investigation Rev. Com. New Eng. Med. Ctr. and Tufts U., 1998; chmn. instn. rev. bd. Tufts U., Medford, Mass., 2001; elected to bd. ministry Harvard U., Cambridge, Mass., 2002. Author: (Book) A Vision of Catechesis for Today and Pointers on Catechetical Instruction, 1996, Roman Catholic Beliefs and Prayers: A Handbook for Those on a Spiritual Journey, 1999, The Roman Catholic Perspective on the Morality of Withdrawing or Witholding Food and Fluid Administered Artificially to an Individual in the Persistent Vegitative State, 2001, Seeking the Path of God's Justice: an Analysis of the U.S. Bishop's Letter on Economic Justice, 2001; contbr. articles to profl. jours. Resident dir. Exceptional Citizens Week for disadvantaged, Gilmanton, N.H., 1990-94; bd. dirs. Camp Giving summer camp for physically and mentally challenged, 2001. Chaplain, major USAF, 1982—94. Mem.: Nat. Assn. of Coll. and Univ. Chaplains, Cath. Theol. Soc. Am., Am. Acad. Religion, USAF Assn., Soc. Biblical Lit. Republican. Avocation: long distance running. Office: Office of Univ Chaplain Tufts U Goddard Chapel 3 The Green Medford MA 02155

O'LEARY, ROSEMARY, law educator; b. Kansas City, Mo., Jan. 26, 1955; d. Franklin Hayes and Mary Jane (Kelly) O'L; m. Larry Dale Schroeder; 1 child, Meghan Schroeder O'Leary. BA, U. Kans., 1978, JD, 1981, MPA, 1982; PhD, Syracuse U., 1988. Bar: Kans. 1981. Gov.'s fellow Office of Gov., Topeka, 1981-82; asst. gen. counsel kans. Corp. Com., Topeka, 1982-83; dir. policy, lawyer Kans. Dept. Health and Environment, Topeka, 1983-85; asst. prof. Ind. u., Bloomington, 1988-90; assoc. prof. Ind. U., Bloomington, 1994—; asst. prof. Syracuse (N.Y.) U., 1990-94. Author: Environmental Change: Federal Courts and the EPA, 1993, Public Administration and the Law, 2d edit., 1996; contbr. more than 50 articles to profl. jours. Bd. govs. U. Kans. Sch. Law, Lawrence, 1980-82, devel. bd., 1981-85; bd. dirs. League Women Voters Syracuse, 1986-88; vol. Habitat for Humanity, Mex., 1990; cons. NSF, 1990; panel mem. Nat. Acad. Scis., Washington, 1990-96. Recipient Outstanding Rsch. award Lily Found., 1992, Best Article award PAR, 1993, 94, Prof. of Yr. award NASPAA, 1996. Mem. ABA (editorial bd. Natural Resources and Environment jour. 1989-95, Award for Excellence 1981), ASPA (exec. com. law and environ. sects., chair environment sect., Rsch. award 1991, Best Conf. Paper award 1991), Am. Polit. Sci. Assn. (nat. chair pub. adminstrn. sect., exec. com. sect. publ.), Acad. Mgmt., Law and Soc. Assn., Assn. Pub. Policy Analysis and Mgmt. Avocations: kayaking, hiking, swimming, canoeing. Office: Ind U SPEA 410J Bloomington IN 47405

OLEJARZ, HAROLD, art educator; b. Bklyn., Oct. 23, 1952; s. Leijb and Sigrid (Hoffman) O.; m. Susan Joan Rosen, Nov. 22, 1980. BA, Bklyn. Coll., 1975; MFA, Pratt Inst., 1977. Pres. 14 Sculptors Gallery, N.Y.C., 1977-84; writer, critic Arts Mag., N.Y.C., 1978-83; art tchr. Ben Franklin Middle Sch., Ridgewood, NJ, 1991—2001, Eisenhower Mid. Sch., Wyckoff, NJ, 2001—. Dodge Found. fellow, 1993, N.J. State Arts Coun. fellow, 1992, 87; performance grantee Franklin Furnace, 1990, artist grantee Wis. Arts Bd., 1990. Mem. Ridgewood Edn. Assn. (chief negotiator 1995). Home: 13 Esmond Pl Tenafly NJ 07670-1608 Office: Eisenhower Mid Sch 334 Calvin Ct Wyckoff NJ 07481 E-mail: harold@olejarz.com.

OLEJNICZAK, JULIAN MICHAEL, lawyer, publications executive; b. Chgo., Oct. 27, 1939; s. Edward Francis and Clara Evelyn (Zatarga) O.; m. Sylvia Ann Graham, June 11, 1971; children: Julian Michael Jr. (dec.), Julie Ann, Edward Francis II. BS, U.S. Mil. Acad., 1961; MA, U. Wis., 1969; MBA, JD, U. N.C., 1988. Bar: Tenn. 1988, U.S. Dist. Ct. (mid. dist.) Tenn. 1988, U.S. Dist. Ct. (we. dist.) Tenn. 1990. Commd. officer U.S. Army, 1961, advanced through grades to lt. col., 1977, retired, 1984; assoc. Baker, Worthington, Crossley, Stansberry & Woolf, Nashville, 1988-91; v.p. publs. Assn. Grads. U.S. Mil. Acad., West Point, N.Y., 1991—. Mem. Beta Gamma Sigma. Republican. Roman Catholic. Avocations: writing, art collector. Office: Assn of Grads US Mil Acad 698 Mills Rd West Point NY 10996-1611

OLENICK, SANDRA LEIGH, elementary education educator; b. Pitts., Sept. 4, 1950; d. Christopher Richard and Theresa Mary Kosor; m. Gerald James Olenick, Apr. 26, 1975; children: Terrilyn, Lindsay. BS in Elem. Edn., Calif. State U. Pa., 1971; MA in Elem. Edn., W.Va. U., 1973; postgrad., U. Pitts., 1977-80. Tchr. elem. grades 5 and 6 Greater Latrobe (Pa.) Sch. Dist., 1971-74, tchr. elem. and mid. sch., 1974-81, tchr. elem. grade 6, 1981—. Mem. St. Mary Ch. Coun., Forbes Road, Pa.; tchr. rep. Mt. View PTO. Mem. NEA, TIMMS Collaboration for S.N. Pa., Nat. Coun. Tchrs. Math., Math. Coun. Western Pa., Pa. State Edn. Assn., Pa. Coun. Tchrs. Math., Smithsonian Assocs., W.Va. U. Alumni Assn., Nat. Coun. Tchrs. English. Democrat. Roman Catholic. Avocations: reading, swimming, coaching novice basketball for girls, walking. Office: Mt View Elem Sch 3110 Mountain View Dr Greensburg PA 15601-3740

OLESEN, CAROLYN MCDONALD, dance educator, choreographer; b. Blytheville, Ark., Aug. 27, 1963; d. Travis Eugene and Barbara Jean (Myers) McDonald; m. Donald John Olesen Jr., Nov. 3, 2001. BA in Dance, U. Calif., Irvine, 1987; MA in Edn., U. Iowa, 1998; choreographer, Coe Coll., 1998. Instr. dance Kirkwood C.C., Cedar Rapids, Iowa, 1987-90, choreographer, 1987—2001, artistic dir., 1990—2001; owner, pres. McDonald Arts Ctr., Marion, Iowa, 1988—2001; instr. dance Coe Coll., Cedar Rapids, 1989—2001; choreographer show choir All Saints Mid. Sch., Marion, Iowa, 1998-2000; choreographer color guard dance ensemble Washington H.S., Cedar Rapids, 1996-97; instr. fitness, gourmet cooking S.E. C.C., Lincoln, Nebr., 2002—, instr., 2002—; choreographer The Lofte Theatre, Manley, Nebr., 2002. Cons. Jane Boyd Cmty. House, Cedar Rapids, 1993—94; dir. Auburn Dance Team, 2003—. Singer/songwriter Rockit Science, 2000-01, Split Decision, 2001, Dark Horse, 2001--. Avocations: wine tasting, gourmet cooking, gardening, song writing.

OLEXY, JEAN SHOFRANKO, English language educator; b. Plymouth, Pa., Oct. 23, 1938; d. John Andrew and Elizabeth (Lawrence) Shofranko; m. Joseph P. Olexy Jr., Oct. 29, 1960; children: Lysbeth Olexy Kilcullen, Joseph P. Olexy III, Douglas L. Olexy. BA in English, Wilkes U., Wilkes-Barre, Pa., 1960; MEd in Teaching and Curriculum, Pa. State U., Harrisburg, 1992. Secondary English tchr. Wilkes-Barre (Pa.) City Schs., 1960-61, Brick Township Sch. Dist., Brick Town, N.J., 1964-66, Upper Merion Area Sch. Dist., King of Prussia, Pa., 1968—99; ret. Lectr., cons. dept. fgn. langs. Safarik U., Slovak Republic, 1992; mem. strategic plan steering com. Ctrl. Montgomery County Area Vocat. Tech. Ctr., Norristown, Pa., 1995-96, bd. dirs., 1996—; curriculum cons. Evang. Lyceum, Bratislava, Slovakia, 1992; vol. reading specialist, mem. Norristown Literacy Coun.; mem. Middle States Evaluation team and com. secondary schs. accreditation Parkland Sch. Dist., Pa., 1996. Co-author: (multi media presetation) Slovak Story telling and Folktales; translator: Slovak Folktales; contbr. articles to profl. jour. Mem. Balch Inst. for Ethnic Studies, Phila., 1982-93; mem. N.E. Pa. Slovak Heritage Soc., Wilkes-Barre, Pa., 1982—; sec. Valley Forge-Exch. Club, King of Prussia, Pa., 1985-89; bd. dirs. Francisvale Home for Smaller Animals, Wayne, Pa., 1987-88; mem. bd. strategic planning Montgomery County Area Vocat.-Tech. Ctr., Norristown, Pa., 1996—. Named Outstanding Educator of Yr. Beta Pi Chpt. Delta Kappa Gamma, King of Prussia, Pa., 1988; Nat. Faculty Acad. fellow Pa. State U., 1993. Mem. NEA, ASCD, Nat. Coun. Tchrs. English, Pa. Edn. Assn., N.E. Pa. Slovak Heritage Soc., Czech and Solvak Soc. (Balt./Phila.), Czech and Slovak Geneal. Soc. Internat., Ratain Valley Slavic Cultural Soc., Nat. Storytelling, Readin gPub. Mus., Penn State Almuni Assn. (life), Upper Merion Edn. Assn., Delta Kappa Gamma (pres. Beta Pi chpt. 1994-96). Lutheran. Avocations: music, reading, genealogy research, handcrafts. Home: 382 Maiden Ln King Of Prussia PA 19406-1803 E-mail: jsolexy@aol.com.

OLHEISER, MARY DAVID, lawyer, educator; b. Dickinson, N.D., Jan. 13, 1918; d. Rudolph and Magdalen (Goetz) O. BA, Holy Names Coll., Spokane, Wash., 1942; MA, St. Louis U., 1952; PhD, Boston Coll., 1962; M in Ch. Adminstrn., Cath. U., 1976, Licentiate in Canon Law, 1977. Joined Sisters of the Order of St. Benedict, 1932. Elem. sch. tchr. Holy Rosary Sch., Tacoma, 1936-50; instr. edn. Coll. of St. Benedict, St. Joseph, Minn., 1952-62, prof. edn., 1962-77, v.p. for acad. affairs, 1972-74; defender of the bond St. Cloud (Minn.) Diocesan Tribunal, 1974-83, judge, 1983-97. Jud. cons. St. Benedicts Monastery, St. Joseph Carmelite Hermits, Alexandria, 1974—, Fedn. St. Benedict, St. Joseph, 1976—; lectr. on rights of women and code of canon law. Author: From Autonomy to Federations: An Historical Survey of Constitutional Development in Benedictine Monasteries, 1977. Trustee Coll. St. Benedict, St. Joseph, 1980-93; bd. dirs. Cath. Charities of the Diocese of St. Cloud, 1992-94; bd. dirs. Carmelite Hermits of Adoration, Inc., 1998—; dir. Eremitic Life Diocese of St. Cloud, 2001—. Mem. Canon Law Soc. Am. Home: 104 Chapel Ln Saint Joseph MN 56374-2020 Office: St Benedicts Monastery Saint Joseph MN 56374 E-mail: molheiser@csbsju.edu.

OLIM, AUGUST SOUZA, counselor; b. Honolulu, Aug. 11, 1940; s. Frank Souza and Hilda Lucy (Leong) O; m. Sharon Jean Warren, Dec. 28, 1963; children: Warren Kalani Olim, Tamera Meilani Olim. BA, U. N. Colo., 1958-63; MS, Pepperdine U., 1973-75. Cert. Exceptional Children (Life), Educable Mentally Retarded Gen. Elem. (Life), Pupil Pers. Ryan Adminstrn. Clear, Learning Handicapped. Tchr. Educable Mentally Retarded Centennial Intermediate, Norwalk-LaMirada, Calif., 1963-65, Walton Intermediate, Garden Grove, Calif., 1965-67; tchr. Learning Handicapped Ralston Intermediate, Garden Grove, Calif., 1967-70; tchr. Learning Disability Group Chapman Jr. High Sch., Garden Grove, Calif., 1970-74, 9th grade English tchr., 1974-76, 7th, 8th, 9th grade counselor, 1976-81; project facilitator Clinton Elem. Sch., Garden Grove, Calif., 1981-84; counselor, co-adminstr. Lake Continuation High Sch., Garden Grove, Calif., 1984-95; prin. Cook Elem., Jordan Spl. Edn., Garden Grove, Calif., 1988, Lincoln Adult Edn. Ctr., Garden Grove, Calif., 1992, Chapman Adult Edn., 1995—2000. Pres. Coun. for Exceptional Children, Orange County, Calif., 1976-80; regional dir. Pacific Am. Concerns HEW, Wash., 1977-81; treas. Asian/Pac/Islander Nat. Edn. Assn., Wash., 1977-81; v.p. Very Spl. Arts, So. Calif., 1989-90. Dir. Jr. Miss Pageant Fountain Valley (Calif.) Jaycees, 1970—72; treas., v.p. Fountain Valley Jaycees, 1972—74; state dir. Calif. Jaycees, 1975; dir. Jr. Miss Inc. Dist. Eight Jaycees Orange County, Calif., 1976; sch. bd. Speech Lang. Ctr., Buena Park, 1994—99; bd. Crippled Children Soc. Orange County, 1995—; bd. dirs. Ainahau o Kaleponi Hawaiian Civic Club, 1997—; co-founder Asian Pacific Islander Cultural Heritage Coun., 1999—. Recipient Life Hon. PTA Lampson, Garden Grove, Calif., 1967, Spoke award Fountain Valley (Calif.) Jaycees, 1972; named Outstanding State Dir. Calif. Jaycees, 1976, Outstanding Bd. Mem. Asian Pacific Islander Tchrs., HI, 1979. Mem. Calif. State Fedn. Coun. for Exceptional Children (mem. ethnic and multicultural concerns com.), Garden Grove Pupil Pers. Assn., Very Spl. Arts Calif., Spl. Olympics Beauty Pageant, Minority Affairs Commn. Nat. Edn. Assn., Interagy. for Legis. of Spl. Edn., Phi Delta Kappa. Roman Catholic. Avocations: music, tennis, cooking, gardening. Home: 25535 Sun City Blvd Sun City CA 92586-3846

OLIN, MARILYN, secondary school educator; b. Rochester, N.Y. BA in English, Nazareth Coll. Rochester, 1965; MS in English Edn., SUNY, Brockport, 1971. Nat. bd. cert. tchr. 1999. Tchr. Paxon Sch. for Advanced Studies, Jacksonville, Fla., 1996—. Mem.: Nat. Forensic League, Nat. Bd. for Profl. Tchg. Stds. (bd. mem.). Office: Paxon Sch for Advanced Studies 3239 Norman E Thagard Blvd Jacksonville FL 32254

OLIPHANT, JODIE JENKINS, secondary school consultant; b. Huntsville, Tex., May 1, 1945; d. Lewis George and Mydusta (McGuire) Jenkins; m. Lou Cal Oliphant, Nov. 8, 1963; children: Rosalind, Patrick, Liranda, Ashley. BS, Tex. So. U., 1970; MEd, Prairie View A&M U., 1972. Cert. sch. adminstr. Tchr. bus. Houston Ind. Sch. Dist., 1970-79, sch. counselor, 1979-85, sch. cons., 1985—. Chmn., bd. dirs. Oliphant Found., Houston; co-owner FOLKTALES African Am. Bookstore, Austin. Co-author 7th grade typewriting curriculum, 1979. Vol. Voter Registration Campaign, Houston, 1979, 80, 83, United Negro Coll. Fund, 1983, Girl Scouts U.S., Houston, 1986-94, Jesse Jackson for Pres. Campaign, Houston, 1988, Ann Richards for Gov. Campaign, Houston, 1990; del. State Dem. Conv., Houston, 1988; mem. Brentwood Bapt. Ch., Houston, Dowling Mid. Sch. PTA Bd., 1990-91. Recipient Cert. of Appreciation Mayor of Houston, 1979. Mem. Nat. Coun. Negro Women (exec. bd. Dorothy I. Heights sect. 1979-80, Svc. award 1977, Human Rels. award 1979, Community Svc. award 1991), Nat. Women of Achievement (v.p. Galena Pk. Metroplex chpt. 1991, pres. 1995, Golden Apple Ednl. Svc. award 1993), Eta Phi Beta (past. pres. and cons. Xi chpt., exec. bd. 1973—, nat. fin. sec. 1986-90), Alpha Kappa Alpha (exec. bd. Alpha Kappa Omega chpt. 1979-82, 87), Phi Delta Kappa, Top Ladies of Distinction, Inc. Avocations: travel, reading, modeling. Office: Houston Ind Sch Dist 3830 Richmond Ave Houston TX 77027-5802

OLIVA, LAWRENCE JAY, former academic administrator, history educator; b. Walden, N.Y., Sept. 23, 1933; s. Lawrence Joseph and Catherine (Mooney) Oliva; m. Mary Ellen Nolan, June 3, 1961; children: Lawrence Jay, Edward Nolan. BA, Manhattan Coll., 1955; MA, Syracuse U., 1957, PhD, 1960; postgrad., U. Paris, 1959; DHL (hon.), Manhattan Coll., 1987; LLD (hon.), St. Thomas Aquinas Coll., 1988; DHL (hon.), Hebrew Union Coll., 1992; DLitt, Univ. Coll., Dublin, 1993; PhD, Tel Aviv U., 1994. Prof. history NYU, 1969—, assoc. dean, 1969—70, vice dean, 1970—71, dean faculty, 1971—72, dep. vice chancellor, 1970—75, v.p. acad. planning and services, 1975—77, v.p. acad. affairs, 1977—80, provost, exec. v.p. acad. affairs, 1980—83, chancellor, exec. v.p., 1983—91, pres., 1991—2002, pres. emeritus, 2002—. Author: Misalliance: A Study of French Policy in Russia during the Seven Years' War, 1964, Russia in the Era of Peter the Great, 1969; editor: Russia and the West from Peter to Kruschev, 1965, Peter the Great, 1970, Catherine the Great, 1971; contbr. articles to profl. jours. Trustee Inst. Internat. Edn.; active Onassis Found., UN Assn. of N.Y. Adv. Coun., N.Y.C. Partnership, Assn. for Better N.Y., Am. Mus. Immigration; adv. bd. U. Athletic Assn.; bd. dirs. Chatham House, Royal Inst. Internat. Affairs, Am. Bd. Dirs. Coun. for U.S. and Italy Nat. Collegiate Athletic Assn., Pres.'s Commn.; adv. bd. Pres.'s Coun.; bd. dirs. N.Y. State Commn. on Nat. and Cmty. Svc. Recipient Medal of Sorbonne, U. Paris, 1992, Man. in Edn. award, Italian Welfare League, medal of honor, Ellis Island; fellow Fribourg fellow, 1959. Mem.: Irish-Am. Cultural Inst., Assn. Colls. and Univs. of State of N.Y, Am. Coun. Edn., Soc. Fellows NYU, Phi Gamma Delta, Phi Beta Kappa. Home: 33 Washington Sq W New York NY 10011-9154 Office: 60 Wash Square S 503 New York NY 10012*

OLIVA, TERENCE ANTHONY, marketing educator; b. Rochester, N.Y., Feb. 21, 1943; s. Anthony J. and Teresa (Savasta) O.; children: Mark, Andrea. BA in Math. and Art, St. Mary's Coll., Calif., 1964; MBA with distinction, Fresno State U., 1971; PhD, U. Ala., 1974. Assoc. prof. mgmt. La. State U., Baton Rouge, 1974-82; vis. assoc. mktg. Columbia U., N.Y.C., 1982-83; assoc. prof., mktg. Rutgers U., Newark, 1983-88; vis. assoc. prof. Wharton Sch., U. Pa., Phila., 1985-87, assoc. prof., 1989-90; prof., dep. dir. Ctr. for Electronic Mktg. Temple U., 1990—. Mem. editl. bd. Org. Sci., 1993—. Author, editor: Production Mgmt., 1981; assoc. editor Mgmt. Sci. Dept. Tech., 1989-91; editl. bd. mem. Org. Sci.; contbr. 32 articles to profl. jours. Capt. USAF, 1965-69, Vietnam. Decorated Bronze Star; recipient Andrisani/Frank Undergrad Tchg. award, Leadership in Rsch. award SBM, 1998, Lindback Found. Tchg. award, 2001. Mem. Am. Mktg. Assn., INFORMS, Sigma Kappa Phi (Prof. of Yr. award), Phi Delta Kappa, Omicron Delta Epsilon, Mu Kappa Tau. Home: 605 S 48th St Philadelphia PA 19143-2010

OLIVAREZ, CELINDA, elementary education educator; b. Rio Grande City, Tex., Sept. 8, 1964; d. Rogerio and Benilde (Garcia) O. BS, Pan Am. U., 1987. Cert. tchr., Tex. Tchr. San Benito (Tex.) Ind. Sch. Dist., 1988-89; bilingual tchr. Los Fresnos (Tex.) Ind. Sch. Dist., 1989—. Instr. English as 2d lang. adult edn. programs, Brownsville, Tex., 1989—; poetry instr. Universal Interscholastic League, Los Fresnos, 1989—; mem. Dist. Bilingual Edn. Com., Los Fresnos, 1990—. Recipient Region I Educator of Yr. award, 1992. Mem. Assn. Tex. Profl. Educators (Tchr. of Yr. award Region I 1992, state finalist Tchr. of Yr. award 1992), Hispanic Cultural Orgn. Avocations: writing poetry, reading, crochet, baking. Home: 317 Carter Ct Brownsville TX 78526-9488 Office: Los Fresnos Ind Sch Dist PO Box 309 Los Fresnos TX 78566-0309

OLIVE, ALICIA NORMA JOHNSON, retired elementary school educator; b. Phila., Mar. 25, 1922; d. Emmett McCoy and Anna Johnson; m. John Mancheon Olive, Dec. 14, 1942; children: Alicia Carlma and Edna Clarisse. BA, Howard U., 1942; MA, George Washington U., 1977. English and reading tchr. Miller Jr. H.S., Washington, 1961-62, Evans Jr. H.S., Washington, 1962-64, MacFarland Jr. H.S., Washington, 1964-66; English, reading and spl. edn. tchr. Rabaut Jr. H.S., Washington, 1966-76, English tchr., 1981-84, chmn. English dept., 1970-76; curriculum writer Langdon Elem. Sch., Washington, 1976-81; reading tchr. Episcopal Ctr. for Children, Washington, 1987-93; ret., 1993. Cons., demonstrator D.C. Pub. Schs. Sys., 1976-84, evaluator of tchr.'s programs, 1976-81. Author handbooks: Meeting Ind. Needs Daily, 1970, Rabaut Reading Bulletins 1-12, 1975; editor curriculum materials; contbr. articles to profl. publs. Vestry mem. St. George's Ch., Washington, 1992—, pres. Parish Guild, 1975, pres. Sunday Sch. Tchrs., 1973, sec./pres. Women of Ch., 1976. Grantee D.C. Pub. Schs. Sys., 1984. Mem. D.C. Tchrs. Retiree Orgn., Internat. Reading Assn., Nat. Coun. English Tchrs., D.C. Coun. English Tchrs. Democrat. Episcopalian. Avocation: writing fiction and educational articles.

OLIVE, KARL WILLIAM, elementary education educator, secondary educator; b. Colorado Springs, Colo., Feb. 18, 1969; s. Kermit Floyd and Betty Jean (Anderson) O. BA in Studio Art, Centre Coll., Danville, Ky., 1991; MA in Art Edn., Western Ky. U., 1993; MA in Ceramics, U. Louisville, 2001. Studio glassblowing asst to Stephen Powell Centre Coll., 1990-91; art tchr., track coach Ft. Knox (Ky.) Cmty. Schs., 1991—. Elem. art edn. instr. Western Ky. U., 1995-99. Recipient Class A Coach of the Yr. in Track and Field, 2003. Mem. Nat. Art Edn. Assn., Ky. Art Edn. Assn., Coll. Art Assn., Louisville Visual Art Assn., Am. Craft Coun. Republican. Methodist. Avocations: sports, stock market, ceramics. Office: Fort Knox H S Bldg 7501 Fort Knox KY 40121

OLIVEIRA, MARY JOYCE, university official; b. Oakland, Calif., Feb. 16, 1954; d. Joseph and Vivian (Perry) O. BA, U. Calif., Berkeley, 1978; student, Holy Names Coll., Oakland, 1992; grad. in math., Calif. State U., Hayward, 1994-96. Cert. tchr., Calif.; cert. single subject math. credential, Hawaii; notary public, Calif.; notary pub. Recreation specialist Oakland Parks and Recreation, 1977-89; substitute tchr. Diocese of Oakland, 1989-90; tutor Oakland Pub. Schs., 1991; substitute tchr. Alameda (Calif.) Unified Sch. Dist., 1991-97, Piedmont (Calif.) Unified Sch. Dist., 1993-96; tchr. math. summer program Lincoln Mid. Sch., Alameda, 1997; tchr. math. and sci. Wood Mid. Sch., Alameda, 1997-98; adminstrv. asst. II, U. Calif., Berkeley, from 2000. Tchr. summer program Wood Mid. Sch., Alameda, 1993, 96, Chipman Mid. Sch., Alameda, 1994, Encinal H.S., Alameda, 1995; math. tutor Calif. State U., Hayward, 1996, Intersession, Bay Farm Sch., Alameda, 1996; math tutor, 1996-99. Creator children's sock toys Oliveira Originals, 1985; author numerous poems. Vol. in art therapy oncology ward Children's Hosp., Oakland, 1985; vol. Berkeley Unified Sch. Dist., 1990-91. Mem. Nat. Coun. Tchrs. Math., Calif. Math. Coun., Math. Assn. Am., Nat. Notary Assn., Avocations: swimming, weight lifting, reading, arts and crafts. Home: Alameda, Calif. Died Jan. 6, 2002.

OLIVER, ANN BREEDING, secondary education educator; b. Hollywood, Fla., Sept. 21, 1945; d. Harvey James and Ruth (Lige) Breeding; m. John Russell Kelso, July 22, 1972 (div. Feb. 1984); 1 child, Anna Liege; m. Ted J. Oliver, June 29, 1996. BA in Fgn. Lang., U. Ky., 1967; MA in History of Art, Ohio State U., 1971. Curatorial intern Lowe Art Mus., Coral Gables, Fla., 1972; adj. faculty Fla. Atlantic U., Boca Raton, Fla., 1972-73, 78; lectr. Miami (Fla.) Dade C.C., 1974, with art-music workshop, 1980-81, lectr.-cons., 1972—, adj. faculty music dept., 1991; curator of edn. Ctr. for the Fine Arts, Miami, 1987-92, High Mus. of Art, Atlanta, Ga., 1992-96; Spanish tchr. Sprayberry H.S., Cobb County Bd. Edn., Marietta, Ga., 1997—. Mem. Artists in Edn. Panel, Ga. Coun. for Arts, 1994; field reviewer Inst. Mus. Svcs., 1994; adj. faculty in art history Kennesaw State U., Marietta, Ga., 1996—; Spanish tchr. Cobb County Bd. Edn., Atlanta, Spray H.S., Marietta, Ga. Contbg. editor African Art: An Essay for Teachers, 1993; project mgr. and contbg. author: Rings: Five Passions in World Art: Multicultural Curriculum Handbook, 1996. Mem. Cobb County Com. for Fgn. Lang. Curriculum Alignment. Recipient Nat. award for graphics Mead Paper Co., 1989, Gold Medal of Honor publication design S.E. Mus. Educators Publ. Design, 1994. Mem. Am. Assn. of Mus., Inst. Mus. Svcs., Nat. Art Edn. Assn., Am. Mus. Tchrs. Fgn. Langs., Fla. Art Edn. Assn. (dir. mus. divsn.), Ga. Art Edn. Assn. (dir. mus. divsn., Mus. Educator of Yr. 1993), Fgn. Lang. Assn. of Ga. Home: 2420 Mitchell Rd NE Marietta GA 30062-5321

OLIVER, BERNARD, academic dean; b. Berkeley, Calif., Mar. 28, 1949; s. Joseph M. and Emma Mae (Ashby) O.; married; children: Kenneth G., Joseph J., Rachel A., Deborah S. BS, Calif. State U., Hayward, 1971; MA, Stanford U., 1972, EdD, 1978. Tchr. Jefferson Union High Sch. Dist., Daly City, Calif., 1972-75; asst. prof. U. Tex., Austin, 1978-82; cons. rsch. Commn. on Tchr. Credentialing, Sacramento, 1982-85; chairperson, assoc. prof. Syracuse (N.Y.) U., 1985-88; dean St. Cloud (Minn.) State U., 1988-91; dean, prof. Wash. State Univ., 1991—97; prof. Ctr. Ednl. Partnerships U. Mo., Kans. City, 1997—. Cons. pub. schs., Tex. N.Y., Calif., 1978—; presenter in field. Author: (with others) Education 1978-89; contbr. articles and revs. to profl. jours. Mem. coms. United Way, St. Cloud, 1988-91, com. ARC, Syracuse, 1985-88; vol. NAACP, St. Cloud, 1988-90. Fellow Coun. So. Univs., 1982, Ford Found., 1976-78, Stanford U., 1975-76. Mem. Am. Ednl. Rsch. Assn., Nat. Assn. Black Sch. Educators, Assn. Tchr. Educators, Assn. for The Study Higher Edn., Am. Assn. Colls. of Tchr. Edn. (exec. bd. mem. 1992-95, Future Tchr. Recruitment 1992—). Avocations: racquetball, basketball, cycling. Office: Ctr Ednl Partnerhsips Sch Edn Univ Mo 5100 Rockhill Rd Kansas City MO 64110-2499 Office Fax: 816-235-5270. E-mail: oliverb@umkc.edu.*

OLIVER, BEVERLY GAIL, special education educator; b. Anderson, Ind., Sept. 9, 1953; d. Lloyd John and Elizabeth Maxine (Vance) Cain; m. Larry Dale Oliver, Jan. 31, 1974; 1 child, Jeremy. BA, Calif. State U., Bakersfield, 1987, MA in Spl. Edn. Learning, 1994. Tchr.'s aide Bakersfiled City Sch. Dist., 1983-84; spl. edn. tchr. Greenfield Union Sch. Dist., Bakersfield, 1988—, technology specialist, 1995—. Ind. cons. on tech. in edn., 1990-94; math. cons. San Joaquin Math. Project, Fresno-Bakersfield, 1991-94. Recipient Presdl. award for Elem. Math., 1995. Mem. Nat. Coun. Tchrs. of Math., Cen. Math. Coun., Calif. Tchrs. Assn., Computer Using Educators. Avocations: reading, roller blading, cross-country skiing, personal computing. Office: Greenfield Union Sch Dist 425 E Fairview Rd Bakersfield CA 93307-5322 E-mail: oliverb@gfusd.k12.ca.us., boliver@ncinternet.net.

OLIVER, BRUCE LAWRENCE, information systems specialist, educator; b. Westfield, Mass., Nov. 20, 1951; s. Ernest Lawrence and Elizabeth (Welchek) O. AS, Greater Hartford C.C., 1972; BS, U. Mass., 1974; MBA, U. Hartford, 1989. Cert. tchr. sec. and vocat. edn., Mass., Conn.; cert. asset protection and fin. privacy cons. Comml. sales Gordon Realty, Enfield, Conn., 1972-75; forestry tech. rsch. Dept. Environ. Protection, State of Conn., Hartford, 1973-1974; res. sales Forsman Realty, Enfield, 1975-77; substitute sec. tchr. Enfield Sch. Systems, 1975-78; collections mgr. New Eng. Bank & Trust, Enfield, 1978-79; ops. CCEC/McCullahg Leasing, Inc., S. Windsor, Conn., 1979-81; pres. Ollie & Ike's, Inc., Enfield, 1985-86; MBA Adj. U. Hartford, West Hartford, Conn., 1988-89; workstation engr. Travelers, Hartford, 1982-89. V.p. 1st Class Expert Sys., Inc., Wayland, Mass., 1989-90, Microsoft Corp., Boston, 1991-94; cons., pres. Profl. Office Solutions, Enfield, 1981—; pres. New Venture Inc., Enfield, 1994—; owner, nvi: Ednl. Multimedia Group, nvi: Webmaster Internet Devel.; del. leader Comparative Studies Assn.; Internat. Cultural Exch. with China, Washington; pub. spkr. Spkrs. Bur., U. Hartford; vis. mem. faculty mgmt. info. sci. U. Hartford, 1989-91. Author: A Novice's Guide to Personal Computer Buying, New Ventures to Egypt, New Ventures to China, Faith, Hope and Love: Coping With Life and Death. Gubernatorial appointee Conn. bd. trustees Reg. C.C.s, 1985-89; vice chmn. Student Affairs and Acad. Policies Com. Hartford, 1987; chmn., trustee Conn. Data Processing Curriculum Com., Hartford, 1989; elected com. mem. Enfield Dem. Com., 1975; chmn. regional adv. coun. Asnuntuck C.C.; notary pub. Conn., 1972—; gubernatorial appointee Conn. bd. trustees Community Tech. Colls., 1990-93. Recipient CTM degree Toastmaster Internat., Hartford, 1987, State Farmer degree Conn. Future Farmers Am., DeKalb Agrl. Accomplishment award, cert. of recognition Bicentennial (USA) Commn., Enfield, 1976, Vigil Hon. BSA Order of the Arrow, Hartford, 1972, Merit award State of Conn. Community-Tech. Colls. Bd. of Trustees, 1994. Mem. World Affairs Coun. of Hartford, Computer Soc. of IEEE, Am. Assn. for Artificial Intelligence, Assn. C.C. Trustees, Am. Assn. Cmty. and Tech. Colls., Microsoft AlumNet Assn., Internat. Platform Assn., Oldefield Farms Homeowners' Assn. (residence com. sec. 1990-91), Hartford County Soil and Water Conservation Dist., Nat. Press Club Found., Robert Schueller's Eagles Club, Masons. Democrat. Roman Catholic. Avocations: travel, refinishing antiques, tennis, hiking, real estate investment, photography. Home: 71 Oldefield Farms Enfield CT 06082-4565 E-mail: Bruce@Oliver.ws.

OLIVER, DAVID FRANCIS, music educator, director; b. Chattanooga, June 21, 1959; s. David F. and Christine (Jones) O. MusB, Wheaton Coll., 1982; MusM in Organ Performance, New Eng. Conservatory of Music, 1984; postgrad., Eastman Sch. Progress, 1984—. Asst. prof. music, dir. music Barber-Scotia Coll., Concord, N.C., 1986-89; assoc. prof. music, dir. music Voorhees Coll., Denmark, S.C., 1990—. Sophomore class advisor, 1987-88; organist Men's Glee Club, Wheaton (Ill.) Coll., Glen Ellyn (Ill.) Covenant Ch., Coll. Ch., Wheaton, St. Andrews Episcopal Ch., Downers Grove, Ill., Lookout Mountain (Tenn.) Presbyn. Ch., Browncroft Community Ch., Rochester, N.Y., Friendship Bapt. Ch., Charlotte, N.C., Trinity Episcopal Ch., Rochester, Emmanuel Luth. Ch., Columbia. Performer in numerous recitals including Wheaton Coll., 1980, 81, 82, 83, Trinity Episcopal Ch., Boston, 1983, New Eng. Conservatory of Music, Boston, 1984, Johnson C. Smith U., Charlotte, 1987, 90, Seacrest Presbyn. Ch., Delray Beach, Fla., 1989, Paine Coll., Augusta, Ga., 1992, St. Thomas Ch., N.Y.C., 1993; solo performances include Lincoln Ctr., N.Y.C., Kennedy Ctr., Washington, Notre Dame, Paris, Grossmunster, Zurich, Switzerland. Bd. dirs., sec. Cabarrus Arts Coun., Concord, 1987-89. Recipient Sears-Roebuck Teaching Excellence award, 1990-81; grantee Mclelland Found., 1989; Eastman Sch. Music fellow, 1984-86. Mem. Am. Guild Organists, Alpha Phi Alpha, Phi Mu Alpha. Office: Voorhees Coll Voorhees Rd Denmark SC 29042

OLIVER, DEBBIE EDGE, elementary education educator; b. Houston, Jan. 8, 1953; d. John Orval and Charlotte (Laird) Edge; m. Lawrence Allen Oliver, July 21, 1973; 1 child, Kelly Dawn. BA in Teaching, kindergarten cert., Sam Houston State U., 1975. Cert. elem. tchr., Tex. Tchr. 3rd grade Big Sandy Ind. Sch. Dist., Livingston, Tex., 1975—. Mem. site-based decision group, mem. textbook com., tech. com., gifted and talented com., U.I.L. sponsor Big Sandy Ind. Sch. Dist., 1989—; H.E.B. Edn. 2000 rep., 1993—; mem. grant writing com. Telecomms. Infrastructure Fund, 1997. Hon. mem. Future Farmers Am., Livingston, 1987; rodeo sec. Polk County Youth Rodeo Assn., Livingston, 1984—; adult leader 4-H, Livingston, 1984—; rodeo sec. Coldspring Lions Rodeo, 1997, 98. Recipient Disting. Svc. award Future Farmers Am., 1989; Title II math./sci. mini-grantee Edn. Svc. Ctr., Huntsville, Tex., 1992. Mem. Ch. of Christ. Home: RR 3 Box 60 Livingston TX 77351-9501 Office: Big Sandy Ind Sch Dist RR 3 Box 422 Livingston TX 77351-9507

OLIVER, DOMINICK MICHAEL, business educator; b. Niagara Falls, N.Y., Apr. 12, 1962; s. Dominick Jr. and Priscilla (Prenatt) O.; m. Vicki Anne Sellig, May 18, 1991. AAS, Niagara County C.C., Sanborn, N.Y., 1982; BS in Bus., Niagara U., N.Y., 1984, MS in Edn., 1986. Lic. tchr. bus. and distributive edn., N.Y.; bus. sch. lic. bus., mgmt., acctg., gen. academics, N.Y. Temporary instr. Niagara County C.C., Sanborn, 1986-87; tchr. on spl. assignment LaSalle Sr. H.S., Niagara Falls, N.Y., 1986-87; instr. St. Joseph Parochial Elem. Sch., Niagara Falls, 1987-88; instr., acad. dean Kelley Bus. Inst., Niagara Falls, 1988-91; instr. Cheryl Fell's Sch. Bus., Niagara Falls, 1991-92; instr., advisor Bryant and Stratton Bus. Inst., Buffalo, 1992—99, sr. mentor, portfolio textbook curriculum com., 1996—99; sr. instr., math coordinator The Huntington Learning Ctr., 1999—2000; adj. instr. comp. sci. SUNY Buffalo, 2000—, Niagara County Cmty. Coll., 2001—; asst. prof. office mgmt. and admin. Erie Cmty. Coll., 2002—. Bus. mgr. Dove Artworks, Buffalo, 1996—; instr. Adopt-A-H.S., Seneca Vocat. H.S., Kensington H.S., Lafayette H.S., Riverside H.S., Buffalo, 1996-1999; evaluator Empire State Coll., 2003—. Life mem. Buffalo and Erie County Naval and Servicemen's Park, Buffalo, 1991—. Republican. Roman Catholic. Avocations: sports (baseball, football, hockey), political history of united states, reading classical literature. Home: 119 Wendover Ave Buffalo NY 14223-2731 Office: Erie CC 4041 Southwestern Blvd Orchard Park NY 14127-2199

OLIVER, DONNA H. secondary education educator; AB, Elon Coll.; MEd, U. N.C.; MS, N.C. State U.; PhD, U. N.C. Tchr. biology Hugh M. Cummings High Sch., Burlington, NC; v.p. academic affairs Bennett Coll., Greensboro, NC, 1989—. Recipient Nat. Biology Tchr. of Yr. award, 1986, Nat. Teacher of the Yr. awd., Coun. of Chief State School Offices, 1987. Office: Bennett College 900 E Washington St Greensboro NC 27401*

OLIVER-WARREN, MARY ELIZABETH, retired library science educator; b. Hamlet, N.C., Feb. 23, 1924; d. Washington and Carolyn Belle (Middlebrooks) Terry; m. David Oliver, 1947 (div. 1971); children: Donald D., Carolyn L.; m. Arthur Warren, Sept. 14, 1990 (dec. Feb. 1995). BS, Bluefield State U., 1948; MS, South Conn. State U., 1958; student, U. Conn., 1977. Cert. tchr., adminstr. and supr., Conn.; cert. pub. sch. substitute tchr., K-12, N.J. Media specialist Hartford (Conn.) Pub. Schs., 1952-86; with So. Conn. State U., New Haven, 1972—, asst. prof. Sch. Libr. Sci. and Instructional Tech., 1987-95, ret., 1995; substitute tchr. K-12 Windsor, Conn., 1999—. Mem. dept. curriculum com. So. Conn. State U., 1987-95, adj. prof., 1995—; cert. substitute tchr. Somerset County Pub. Schs., 1997—; cert. substitute tchr. Windsor, Conn. Sch. Sys., 1999-. Author: My Golden Moments, 1988, The Elementary School Media Center, 1990, Text Book Elementary School Media Center, 1991, I Must Fight Alone, 1991, (textbook) I Must Fight Alone, 1994. Mem. ALA, Conn. Ednl. Media Assn., Black Librs. Network N.J. Inc., Assn. Ret. Tchrs. Conn., Black and Hispanic Consortium, So. Conn. State U. Women's Assn., Cicuso Club (v.p.), Friends Club (v.p.), Delta Kappa Gamma, Alpha Kappa Alpha. Avocations: reading, music, piano, walking. Home: 224 High Path Rd Windsor CT 06095-4103 Office: So Conn State U 501 Crescent St New Haven CT 06515-1330

OLKERIIL, LORENZA, English language educator; b. Koror, Palau, Oct. 10, 1948; d. Ngiratewid and Modekngei Olkeriil; children: Kevin O. Chin, Renee Chin. BA in Elem. Edn., U. Guam, 1982; MA in Instnl. Tech. in Edn., San Jose State U., 1989. Classroom tchr. Ministry of Edn., Koror, 1972-76, 78—, curriculum specialist, 1976-78, edn. trainer, 1988—, coord. bilingual program, 1988—; chair English dept. Palau High Sch.; elem. sch. prin., 1999—. Tng. dir. Peace Corp, Palau, summer 1987; GED instr., Palauan lang. instr. Micronesian Coll., Koror; cons. to pvt. sch., Koror. Speaker Ngiwal State Legis., Koror, 1992, 98; mem. Ngiwal State Constitution, 1983. San Jose State U. fellow, 1987. Mem. Didil Belau (pres. 1992-93), Ngaraboes (treas.-sec. 1980—). Avocations: farming, fishing, softball, weaving, dancing. Home: PO Box 966 Palau PW 96940-0843 Office: PO Box 159 Palau PW 96940-0159

OLMAN, GLORIA, secondary education educator; Tchr. Utica High Sch., Mich. Named Nat. H.S. Journalism Tchr. of Yr., 1992, Spl. Recognition advisor, 1981, Disting. Advisor Dow Jones Newspaper Fund Inc., 1987; named to Mich. Journalism Hall of Fame, 1997. Office: Utica High Sch 47255 Shelby Rd Utica MI 48317-3156

OLMSTED, AUDREY JUNE, communications educator, department chairman; b. Sioux Falls, S.D., June 5, 1940; d. Leslie Thomas and Dorothy Lucille (Else) Perryman; m. Richard Raymond Olmsted; 1 child, Quenby Anne. BA, U. No. Iowa, 1961, MA, 1963; PhD, Ind. U., 1971. Comm. instr. Boston U., 1964-71, acting chair comm., 1972-73, asst. prof. comm., 1971-74; debate coach R.I. Coll., Providence, 1978-92, asst. prof. comm., 1987—, chmn. dept. of comm., 1999—, internat. student advisor, 1980—. Text editor Prentice-Hall Pub., 1986-88. Recipient Faculty award R.I. Coll. Alumni Assn., 1987. Mem. Nat. Assn. Fgn. Student Advisors, Eastern Comm. Assn., Nat. Comm. Assn. Democrat. Office: RI Coll Dept Comm 600 Mount Pleasant Ave Providence RI 02908-1924

OLMSTED, PATRICIA PALMER, educational researcher; b. Chgo., Sept. 19, 1940; d. Richard O. and Marion E. (Huffman) Palmer. BA in Psychology, Mich. State U., 1962; postgrad. Stanford U., 1962-63; MA, Columbia U., 1965; PhD, U. Fla., 1977. Grad. research asst. Columbia U., N.Y.C., 1964, pub. health trainee psychopathology, 1964-65; assoc. rsch. scientist dept. med. genetics Psychiat. Inst., N.Y.C., 1965-66; asst. rsch. coord. Merrill-Palmer Inst., Detroit, 1966-68, instr., 1966-69, rsch.coord., 1966-69; instr. Coll. Edn. U. Fla., Gainesville, 1969-71, asst. in edn., 1971-73, assoc. in edn., 1973-77; clin. asst. prof. Sch. Edn., U. N.C., Chapel Hill, 1977-82, clin. assoc. prof., 1982-86, dir. parent edn. follow-through program, 1977-86; rsch. assoc. High/Scope Ednl. Rsch. Found., 1986-91, sr. rsch. assoc., 1991—, dep. coord. internat. child care study, 1986—; grantee, 1977-86, cons. various pub. schs., 1969—. Contbr. articles on rsch. in edn. to profl. jours., chpts. to books. Dept. Edn. grantee, 1977-84. Mem. APA, Soc. Rsch. Child Devel., Am. Ednl. Rsch. Assn., Nat. Assn. Edn. Young Children, Phi Delta Kappa. Office: High/Scope Ednl Rsch Found 600 N River St Ypsilanti MI 48198-2898

OLNEY, JAMES, English language educator; b. Marathon, Iowa, July 12, 1933; s. Norris G. and Doris B. (Hawk) L.; children: Nathan, Marina Gobnait. BA, U. Iowa, 1955; MA, Columbia U., 1958, PhD, 1963. Asst. prof. Drake U., Des Moines, 1963-67; Fulbright lectr. Cuttington Coll.,

Liberia, 1967-69; prof. English N.C. Central U., Durham, 1970-83; Voorhies prof. English La. State U., Baton Rouge, 1983—. Vis. prof. Northwestern U., 1974, Amherst Coll., 1978—79. Author: Metaphors of Self, 1972, Tell Me Africa, 1973, the Rhizome & the Flower, 1980, The Language(s) of Poetry, 1993, Memory and Narrative, 1998 (Christian Gauss award 1999); editor: Autobiography, 1988; editor So. Rev., 1983—. Fellow NEH, 1975-76, Guggenheim Found., 1980-81, Nat. Humanities Ctr., Research Triangle Park, N.C., 1980-81 Mem. MLA (exec. coun. 1983-87), Am. Acad. Arts & Scis. Office: La State U Southern Review 43 Allen Hall Baton Rouge LA 70803-0001 Home: 8 Whistler Ct Irvine CA 92612

O'LOUGHLIN, JUDITH BERYL, elementary and special education educator; b. N.Y.C., July 4, 1944; d. Sol and Mary (Testa) Bernstein; m. Joseph John O'Loughlin; children: Jennifer, Amy. BA, Montclair State U., 1966; MEd, William Paterson U., 1990; post-masters certs., Montclair State U., 1995, 97. Cert. tchr., N.J., English 7-12, 1966, ESL K-12, 1990, elem. edn. K-8, 1990, handicapped K-12, 1995, learning disabilities tchr. cons., 1997. English tchr. grades 9-12 Kearny (N.J.) H.S., 1966-67; English tchr. grade 9 West Brook Jr. H.S., Paramus, N.J., 1967-73; ESL adult educator Evening Sch. for the Fgn. Born, Hackensack, N.J., 1977-95; ESL tchr. Spl. Svcs. Sch. Dist., Ridgewood, N.J., 1986-88; ESL and spl. edn. tchr. Ho-Ho-Kus (N.J.) Pub. Sch., 1988—. Workshop coord. Fall ESL/Bilingual Ann. Conf., William Paterson U., Wayne, N.J., 1990—. Cons. writing process books for ESL students; presenter workshops and demonstrations in field, various regional and nat. confs. ESL trainer Lit. Vols. of Am., Englewood, N.J., 1990. Title VII Bilingual-ESL Tchr. Tng. grantee Fed. Govt., Washington, 1986-90. Mem. NEA, N.J. Edn. Assn., TESOL (awards com. coord. 1995-97, chair 1999—, bd. dirs. 2003), N.J. Tchrs. English to Spkrs. Other Langs.-N.J. Bilingual Educators (sec. exec. bd. 1992-96, v.p. 1997-99, pres. 1999-2001, past pres. 2001-03, sec. Perth Amboy chpt. 1992-96, co-founder, past chair North Region Paramus 1989—), Internat. Reading Assn., Coun. for Exceptional Children, Kappa Delta Pi, Pi Lambda Theta (Excellence in Tchg. Multicultural Edn. award 2003). Home: 104 Kaufman Dr Westwood NJ 07675-2715 Office: Ho-Ho-Kus Pub Sch 70 Lloyd Rd Ho Ho Kus NJ 07423-1550

OLSEN, CARL FRANKLIN, school superintendent; b. Conway, Ark., Dec. 5, 1950; s. Leo William and Norma G. (Patton) O.; m. Carol Jean Panter, Apr. 13, 1974; children: Amanda, Daniel. Student, Biola U., La Mirada, Calif., 1969-72; BA, Calif. State U., Fullerton, 1973; MA, Calif. State U., Bakersfield, 1979; EdD, U. So. Calif., 1984. Cert. in adminstrv. svcs., Calif. Tchr. jr. high sch. Wasco (Calif.) Union Sch. Dist., 1975-77, elem. tchr., 1977-79, spl. projects coord., 1979-81; prin. Fairfax Sch. Dist., Bakersfield, Calif., 1981-85; supr./prin. Maple Sch. Dist., Shaffer, Calif., 1985-87; supt. Fruitvale Sch. Dist., Bakersfield, 1987—. Adj. prof. Calif. State U., Bakersfield, 1991-2000, Point Loma Nazarene U., 2000—; exec. dir. Fruitvale Ednl. Found., Bakersfield, 1990—; bd. dirs. Kern County Spl. Edn. Consortium, Bakersfield, 1987—, Schs. Legal Svc., 1998—. Byram Meml. scholar, U. So. Calif., 1982. Mem. Assn. Calif. Sch. Adminstrs., Phi Delta Kappa, Kappa Delta Pi. Avocations: basketball, films, reading, tennis. Office: Fruitvale Sch Dist 7311 Rosedale Hwy Bakersfield CA 93308-5738

OLSEN, DAVID MAGNOR, chemistry and astronomy educator; b. Deadwood, S.D., July 23, 1941; s. Russell Alvin and Dorothy M. Olsen; m. Muriel Jean Bigler, Aug. 24, 1963; children: Merritt, Chad. BS, Luther Coll., 1963; MS in Nat. Sci., U. S.D., 1967. Instr. sci., math. Augustana Acad., Canton, S.D., 1963-66; instr. chemistry Iowa Lakes Community Coll., Estherville, Iowa, 1967-69, Merced (Calif.) Coll., 1969—2003, instr. astronomy, 1975—2003, div. chmn., 1978-88, coord. environ. hazardous materials tech., 1989—2003; ret., 2003. Trustee Merced Union High Sch. Dist., 1983—, pres., 1986-87, 97, 2002. Mem. NEA, Am. Chem. Soc., Astron. Soc. of the Pacific, Calif. Tchrs. Assn., Planetary Soc., Calif. State Mining and Mineral Mus. Assn. (bd. dirs., sec. 1990-93), Nat. Space Soc., Merced Coll. Faculty Assn. (pres. 1975, 93, 94, treas. 1980-90, 96, 97, bd. dirs., sec. 1990-91), Castle Challenger Learning Ctr. Found. (bd. dirs., pres. 2003-), Merced Track Club (exec. bd. 1981), M Star Lodge, Sons of Norway (v.p. 1983), Rotary Internat. (pres. Merced Sunrise 2000-01). Democrat. Lutheran. Home: 973 Idaho Dr Merced CA 95340-2513 E-mail: dmolsen@elite.net.

OLSEN, GLENN WARREN, historian, educator; b. Mpls., Nov. 27, 1938; s. Warren Spandet and Alice Elvira (Lionstone) O.; m. Suzanne Miltner, Aug. 27, 1966; children: Teresa, Catherine, Gregory, John. BA, North Park Coll., Chgo., 1960; MA, U. Wis., 1962, PhD, 1965. Asst. prof. Seattle U., 1965-66, assoc. prof., 1969-72; asst. prof. Fordham U., Bronx, N.Y., 1966-69; prof. U. Utah, Salt Lake City, 1972—. Vis. prof. U. Notre Dame, Ind., 1990; v.p. Kairos Found., Erie, Pa., 1970—. Adv. editor: Cath. Hist. Rev., 1971—; cons. editor: Communio: Internat. Cath. Rev., 1988—; contbr. articles to profl. jours. Lectr. internat. sci. bd., confs. on European culture, U. Navarre, Pamplona, 1992—; regent St. Mary's Coll., Notre Dame, 1973-79. Fulbright grantee, 1963-65, travel grantee Am. Coun. Learned Socs., 1979, NEH grantee, 1990; David Piermont Gardner fellow U. Utah, 1977, fellow Inst. for Ecumenical and Cultural Rsch., 1978-79. Mem. Medieval Acad. Am., Am. Hist. Assn., Am. Cath. Hist. Assn., Soc. for Italian Hist. Studies, Medieval Assn. Pacific (pres., councillor 1976-79, 92-95, pres. 1996-98), Rocky Mountain Medieval and Renaissance Assn. (pres., councillor 1984-85), Am. Soc. Ch. History (councillor 1981-84). Roman Catholic. Avocations: travel, music, reading. Home: 2233 Bryan Cir Salt Lake City UT 84108-0311 Office: U Utah Dept History 208 Carlson Hall Salt Lake City UT 84112-1127

OLSEN, INGER ANNA, psychologist, educator; b. Copper Mountain, B.C., Can., Dec. 25, 1926; BS, Wash. State U., 1954, MS, 1956, PhD, 1962. Psychiat. nurse Provincial Mental Health Svcs. B.C., 1947-51, psychologist, 1956-58, Vancouver (B.C.) City Met. Health Svcs., 1958-60; psychologist Student Counseling Ctr., Wash. State U., Pullman, 1960-62; sr. psychologist Met. Health Svcs., Vancouver, 1962-66; instr. psychology Langara Coll., Vancouver, 1966—87. Contbr. articles to profl. jours. Docent Vancouver Aquarium Assn.; bd. dirs. Second Mile Soc., 1975—89. Mem. APA, Gerontol. Soc. Am., Can. Assn. Gerontology, Phi Beta Kappa, Sigma Xi, Alpha Kappa Delta. Home: 1255 Bidwell St Apt 1910 Vancouver BC Canada V6G 2K8

OLSEN, M. KENT, lawyer, educator; b. Denver, Mar. 10, 1948; s. Marvin and F. Winona (Wilker) O.; m. Shauna L. Casement; children: Kristofor Anders, Alexander Lee, Nikolaus Alrik, Amanda Elizabeth. BS, Colo. State U., 1970; JD, U. Denver, 1975. Bar: Colo., U.S. Dist. Ct. Colo. 1982, U.S. Tax Ct. Law clk. Denver Probate Ct., 1973-75; assoc. ptnr. Johnson & McLachlan, Lamar, Colo., 1975-80; assoc. Buchanan, Thomas and Johnson, Lakewood, Colo., 1981-82, William E. Myrick, P.C., Denver, 1982-83; referee Denver Probate Ct., Denver, 1983-89; ptnr. Haines & Olsen, P.C., Denver, 1989-95; pvt. practice Denver, 1995—2001; ptnr. Olsen & Traeger, LLP, 2001—. Adv. bd. Denver Paralegal Inst., 1993—, Elder Law Inst., 1994—. Mem. Gov.'s Commn. on Life and the Law, Denver, 1991-2000; bd. dirs. Adult Care Mgmt., Inc., Denver, 1985-95; bd. dirs. Arc of Denver, Inc., 1990—, pres., 1995-97; bd. dirs. Colo. Guardianship Alliance, Denver, 1990-91; bd. dirs. Colo. Fund for People with Disabilities, 1994—, pres., 1994-2000. Recipient Outstanding Vol. Svc. award Adult Care Mgmt., 1990, Outstanding Svc. award The Arc of Denver, 1991, Vol. Svc. award Colo. Gerontol. Soc., 1997, Pres.'s award Arc of Denver, 1998. Mem. ABA, Colo. Bar Assn. (past chair probate sect.), Acad. Elder Law Attys., Colo. Assn. Homes and Svcs. to the Aging, Denver Bar Assn., Denver Estate Planning Coun. Avocations: running, skiing, racquetball, art, hiking. Home: 3030 S Roslyn St Denver CO 80231-4153 Office: 650 S Cherry St Ste 850 Denver CO 80246-1805 E-mail: mkolsen@olsentraeger.com.

OLSHEN, RICHARD A. statistician, educator; b. Portland, Oreg., May 17, 1942; s. A.C. and Dorothy (Olds) O.; m. Susan Abroff, 1979. AB, U. Calif., Berkeley, 1963; PhD, Yale U., 1966. Rsch. staff statistician, lectr. Yale U., New Haven, 1966-67; asst. prof. stats. Stanford (Calif.) U., 1967-72; assoc. prof. stats. and math. U. Mich., Ann Arbor, 1972-75; assoc. prof. math. U. Calif., San Diego, 1975-77, prof. math., 1977-89, dir. lab. for math. and stats., 1982-89; prof. biostats. Sch. Medicine Stanford U., 1989—, prof. by courtesy dept. stats., 1990—, prof. by courtesy dept. elec. engring., 1995—, chief divsn. biostats., 1998—, assoc. chair dept. health rsch. and policy, 1999-2001.

OLSON, ANN MARTIN, language education specialist; b. N.Y.C., Apr. 3, 1933; d. Arthur Francis and Jane Frances (Ryan) Martin; m. Peter Byrne Olson, Feb. 11, 1967; children: Sven Martin, Katrin Ann, Gunnar Byrne. Superior degree, Sorbonne, Paris, 1954; BA, Coll. New Rochelle, 1955; MS in Edn., SUNY, Oswego, 1993. Cert. tchr. French, N.Y.; cert. ESOL tchr., N.Y. Tchr. French Scarsdale (N.Y.) Pub. Schs., 1959-67; instrnl. specialist Bilingual/ESL Assistance Ctr., Syracuse, N.Y., 1987—. Coord. multicultural assessment conf., Binghamton, 1994; coord., presenter Colloquium on Bilingual Exceptional Students, 1993, 94. Editor (student anthology) Visions and Voices, 1988-95. Mem. Concord Coalition, Washington, 1994, Social Justice Com., Fayetteville, N.Y., 1994; active area French club. Recipient Cert. of Recognition divsn. bilingual edn. N.Y. State Dept. Edn., Albany, 1992, Cert. of Appreciation, Hispanic Task Force N.Y. State Assembly, Albany, 1993. Mem. Tchrs. of English to Speakers of Other Langs. (workshop presenter 1994), N.Y. State Tchrs. of English to Speakers of Other Langs. (workshop presenter 1994). Avocations: bridge, reading, bicycling, swimming, cooking. Home: 309 Elm St Fayetteville NY 13066-1413

OLSON, BETTYE JOHNSON, artist, retired educator; b. Mpls., Jan. 16, 1923; d. Emil Antonious and Irene Irina (Wandtke) J.; m. Howard Einar Olson, July 16, 1949; children: Martha, Jeffrey, Barbara, Virginia. BS in Art Edn., U. Minn., 1945, MEd in Art Edn., 1949; student, U. N.Mex., Taos, 1947; student summer sch., Cranbrook Summer Art, Mich., 1948. Tchr. art grades 3-12 Summit Sch. for Girls, St. Paul, 1945-47; instr. art U. Minn., Mpls., 1947-49; instr. painting and design Concordia Coll., St. Paul, 1975-78, 83-84; instr. summer sch. Art Inst., 1983—89; instr. painting summer sch. Augsburg Coll., Mpls., 1988—89, instr. painting prints, 1988—89; lectr. art Augsburg Coll. of 3rd Age, Mpls., 1984—2003, dir., 1993-98; ret.; instr. painting elder learning inst. U. Minn., 2000—03. Mem. staff Walker Art Ctr., summer 1947; instr. Grunewald Guild, Wash., summer 1990; lectr. women in liturgical arts Luther Northwestern Sem., 1985, lectr. theology and the arts, 1987, 89; lectr. art and lit. series AAUW, 1986-89; artist-in-residence Holden Village Luth. Retreat Ctr., Chelan, Wash., summers 1967-68, 70-71, 73, 78-79, 86-90, 94-97. One-woman shows include Met. Med. Ctr., Mpls., 1974, Concordia Coll., St. Paul, 1975, St. Olaf Coll., Northfield, Minn., 1977, West Lake Gallery, 1964, 67, 71, 75, 78, 82, Inver Hills Coll., Inver Grove Heights, Minn., 1978-, House of Hope Ch., St. Paul, 1978, 1998, Plymouth Congl. Ch., Mpls., 1978-97, Jerome Gallery, Aspen, Colo., 1978, Osborn Gallery, St. Paul, 1979, Augsburg Coll., 1979, 96, Luther Coll., Decorah, Iowa, 1980, Wilson Libr., U. Minn., 1981, St. Paul Campus Gallery, U. Minn., 1981, Am. Swedish Inst., 1978, 1982, Smaland Mus., Vaxjo, Sweden, 1982, Luth. Brotherhood Co., 1983, Phipps Gallery, Hudson, Wis., 1985, Luther Sem., St. Paul, 1998, Berge Gallery, Stillwater, Minn., 1995, 2000, Augsburg Coll., 1978, 1996, Luther Sem., St. Paul, 1998, Johnson Heritage Gallery, Grand Marias, Minn., 2002, Heritage; participant juried exhbns., including Walker Art Ctr., 1947, Mpls. Art Inst., 1947, St. Paul Gallery, 1961, Sky Gallery, 1975, Minn. Arts Assn., 1975 (Merit award 1975, 76), 76, Minn. Mus. Art, 1976, Watercolor U.S.A., Springfield, Mo., 1977, Minn. State Fair, 1947, 64, 66-68, 74-79, 90, 93 (Merit award 1976, 3rd prize 1977, 93), Lakewood Coll., White Bear Lake, Minn., 1974-79, 81 (Grand prize 1977, Purchase prize 1977), Butler Inst. Am. Art, Youngstown, Ohio, 1977, W.A.R.M. Gallery, Mpls., 1977, Calif. Women's Conf., Pasadena, Calif., 1978, AAUW, 1981; exhibited in group shows at Friends of Art Inst., 1979, West Lake Gallery, 1964-83, Kuopio Art Mus., Finland, 1982, St. Paul Co., 1983, Augsburg Coll., 1988, 89, Minn. Mus. Art, 1988, Nash Gallery, U. Minn., 1994, Hill Mansion-History Soc., 1995, 96, Sosin and Sosin Gallery, Mpls., 2002, Stillwater Print Show, 2002; others; represented in permanent collections: 3M Co., Minn. History Soc., Minn. Mus. Am. Art, Employers Ins. Co. of Wausau, Concordia Coll., Nothern States Power Co., Cray Rsch., Pillsbury World Headquaters, Luther Coll., Kuopio Art Mus. Finland, Am. Swedish Inst., Smaland Mus. Sweden, Augsburg Coll., Luther Sem., St. Paul, and many others. Mem. bd. congl. life Evang. Luth. Ch. Am., St. Paul, 1989-91; coop. mem. West Lake Gallery, Mpls., 1963-83; mem. Mpls. Art Inst., 1945—, Minn. Mus. Am. Art, Walker Art Ctr.; juror, Minn. State Fair, 2001. Mentor tchg. scholar Met. Arts Coun. to Woman's Art Registry Minn., St. Paul, 1990-94; grantee liberal arts programs Minn. Humanities Commn., St. Paul, 1995-96, 97-98. Mem. AAUW (bd. dirs. 1992-94), Woman's Art Registry Minn. (bd. dirs. 1992-95). Avocations: attending concerts, theater, skiing, hiking, reading. Home: 1721 Fulham St Apt H Saint Paul MN 55113-5251

OLSON, BETTY-JEAN, retired elementary education educator; b. Camas, Wash., Apr. 26, 1934; d. Earl Raymond and Mabel Anna (Burden) Clemons; m. Arthur H. Geda, Dec. 31, 1957; children: Ann C. Geda, Scott A. Geda; m. Conrad A. Olson, June 14, 1980. AA, Clark Coll., 1954; BA in Edn., Cen. Wash. Coll. Edn., 1956; MEd, No. Monn. Coll., 1975. Cert. elem. tchr. class I, Mont., supr. K-9 class III. Supervising tchr., demo. teaching No. Mont. Coll.; kindergarten, 1st grade instr. Glasgow, Mont.; supervisor, head tchr. Reading Lab, Glasgow AFB, Mont.; 1st grade instr., kindergarten tchr., elem. adminstr. K-7 Medicine Lake (Mont.) Dist. 7; mem. ret. Certification stds. and practices Adv. Coun. to the State Bd. Pub. Edn.; mem. bd. examiners Nat. Coun. for Accred. of Tchr. Edn., adv. com. Western Mont. Coll., U. Mont.; grad. spkr. Medicine Lake, 1998; v.i.p. Day Spkr., Plentywood; workshop leader and presenter in field. Mem. Sheridan County Cmty. Protective Svcs. Com., Med-Lake Scholarship Com.; mem. Treasure State coun. Girl Scouts U.S.A., 1998, Mo. River Tourism bd.; trustee Sheridan County Meml. Scholarship Com.; bd. dirs. Glenwood Inc. Vol. Mus. Recipient Golden Key Profl. award Glasgow Edn. Assn., Outstanding Svc. award NE Mont. Reading Coun., State Merit Award Tchr. Nat. Coun. of Geographic Tchrs., Outstanding Svc. award Fort Peck Fine Arts Coun.; named Tchr. of Mo. KUMV-TV Channel 8, 1998. Mem. NEA, ASCD, Internat. Reading Assn., Nat. Coun. Social Studies, Nat. Elem. Prin. Assn., Medicine Lake Edn. Assn. (past pres.), Mont. Edn. Assn. (rev. bd., officerships), Mont. Elem. Prin., N.E. Mont. Reading Coun. (v.p.), Delta Kappa Gamma (state pres., chpt. pres., exec. bd., committeeships, mem. internat. exec. bd., inspirational spkr.). Home: 108 E Antelope Antelope MT 59211-9607

OLSON, CAROL LEA, lithographer, educator, photographer; b. Anderson, Ind., June 10, 1929; d. Daniel Ackerman and Marguerite Louise Olson. AB, Anderson Coll., 1952; MA, Ball State U., 1976. Pasteup artist Warner Press, Inc., Anderson, 1952-53, apprentice lithographer stripper, 1953-57, journeyman, 1957-63, lithographic dot etcher, color corrector, 1959-73, prepres coord. art dept., 1973-81, prepres tech. specialist, 1981-83, color film assembler, 1983-96. Part-time photography instr. Anderson Univ.; tchr. photography Anderson Fine Arts Ctr., 1976-79; instr. photography, photographics Anderson U., 1979-2003; mag. photographer Bd. Christian Edn. of Ch. of God, Anderson, 1973-86; freelance photographer. One person show Anderson U., 1979; exhibited in group shows Anderson U., 1980—, Purdue U., 1982. Instr. 1st aide ARC, Anderson, 1969-79; sec. volleyball Anderson Sunday Sch. Athletic Assn., 1973-2000. Recipient Hon. mention, Ann Arbor, Mich., 1977, Anderson Fine Arts Ctr., 1977, 78, 83, 1st Pl., 1983, Hon. Mention, 1983, 2d Pl., 1988, Hon. Mention, 1988, 93, Best of Show, 1983, 91, 92, Best Nature Catagory Anderson Fine Arts Ctr., 1994. Mem. AAUW, Associated Photographer Internat., Nat. Inst. Exploration, Profl. Photographers Am. Mem. Ch. of God. Avocations: camping, travel, canoeing. Home: 2604 E 6th St Anderson IN 46012-3725

OLSON, CHERYL ANN, reading educator; b. Oslo, Nov. 26, 1957; d. Charles C. and Sally Ann (Bowen) Olson; divorced; children: Alexis Lima, Anastasia Lima. BS, U. Maine, 1979; MA, U. R.I., 1988. Cert. mid. sch. tchr., 1-12 reading cons., Mass. Cons., tutor Gloucester (Mass.) Pub. Schs., 1984-88; gen. tchr. St. Ann's Sch., Gloucester, 1988-89; reading tchr. O'Maley Mid. Sch., Gloucester, 1989-92, reading cons., 1992-94, chpt. 1 reading tchr., 1994—98, social studies tchr., 1998—2001, math. tchr., 2001—. Advisor youth group West Gloucester Congl. Ch., 1993-97, deacon, 1990; encampment chair Girl Scouts U.S., 1990-95. Mem. Internat. Reading Assn., Order Ea. Star. Avocations: camping, skiing, reading.

OLSON, DIANE LOUISE, secondary education educator; b. Ft. Dodge, Iowa, Dec. 15, 1951; d. Ralph Leroy and Donna Marie (Solbeck) O.; m. Michael John Schroeder, June 1, 1991. BA in English Edn., U. No. Iowa, 1974; MA in English Edn., N.E. Mo. State U. (now Truman, State U.), 1986. Cert. tchr., Iowa, Nat. Bd. Tchrs., 2000. Tchr. English, drama, composition and speech, journalism Lamoni (Iowa) Community Schs., 1974-76; tchr. English Rockwell (Iowa)-Swaledale Community Schs., 1977-80; tchr. various subjects Wayne Cmty. Schs., Corydon, Iowa, 1980—. Evaluator Dept. Edn., 2002—; mentor for tchrs. Iowa Office for Staff Devel., 2001—02; adj. instr. Graceland U., Lamoni, Iowa, 2001—, Indian Hills C.C., Centerville, Iowa, 2001—, Morningside Coll., Sioux City, Iowa, 2003—. Author pamphlets for workshops; editor, writer: The Story of Cambria, 1990; columnist, editor, photographer Humeston New Era, 1995—99; contbr. articles to profl. jours. Mem. adminstrv. bd. Christian-United Meth. Ch., Humeston, 1982—, lay leader, 1994, 95, youth group leader, 1996—, chmn., 2001—, PEO 96—, guard 1998-99, chaplain, 2002—; actress, reader Wayne County Arts Coun., Corydon, 1987-93; actress, dir. Humeston Theater Group, 1992, 96, 98; writer, actress Wayne County Sesquicentennial Pageant, 1994-96. Recipient Ednl. Achievement award Corydon Optimist Club, 1996; named Outstanding Young Woman of Am., 1986, Outstanding Writing Tchr., Writing Conf., 1991; State of Iowa grantee, 1980. Mem. NEA, AAUW (pres. 1993-95), Nat. Coun. Tchrs. English, Iowa Edn. Assn., Iowa Coun. Tchrs. English, Wayne Cmty. Edn. Assn. (sec. 2002-03), Mormon Trail Chamber and Devel. Corp., Beta Sigma Phi (treas., v.p.). Democrat. Avocations: reading, writing, hiking, biking, travel. Home: 511 Guy Porter St Humeston IA 50123-1004 Office: Wayne Community Schs 102 N Dekalb St Corydon IA 50060-0308

OLSON, DOROTHY BERNICE, retired elementary and secondary school educator; b. Lakeville, Minn., Oct. 9, 1925; d. Albert Olaus and Ann (Bergstrom) Ellingboe; m. Herman Clarence Olson, Dec. 26, 1960 (dec. May 1974). BS, Mankato State U., 1951; MA, St. Cloud State U., 1980. Cert. elem. tchr., secondary tchr. Elem. tchr. Dist. 65, Lakeville, 1943-44, Ledger (Mont.) Sch., 1945, Helena (Mont.) Sch., 1945—46; sec. Comml. Nat. Bank & Trust Co., N.Y.C., 1946-48; English tchr. Lakeville High Sch., 1948; tchr. Lakeville Pub. Sch., 1948-50; English and vocal music tchr. Comfrey (Minn.) Pub. Sch., 1951—60; English tchr. Tech. High Sch., St. Cloud, Minn., 1966-85. Mem. League Women Voters, St. Cloud, 1989—; active Bethlehem Luth. Ch., St. Cloud, 1961—. Recipient 1st place Spelling Bee award Cen. Minn. Coun. Aging, 1991. Mem. NEA (life), AAUW, Minn. Edn. Assn., Retired Educators Assn., Sons of Norway (pres., v.p., social dir., trustee publicity), Trollhim Lodge (Outstanding Lodge Mem. 1977), Delta Kappa Gamma (1st v.p., musician 1971—), PEO (chmn. yearbook com. 1981—, pres. 2001-03). Avocations: painting, languages, singing, writing, reading. Home: 18940 Fall Ridge Rd Richmond MN 56368-8145

OLSON, FERRON ALLRED, metallurgist, educator; b. Tooele, Utah, July 2, 1921; s. John Ernest and Harriet Cynthia (Allred) O.; m. Donna Lee Jefferies, Feb. 1, 1944; children: Kandace, Randall, Paul, Jeffery, Richard. BS, U. Utah, 1953, PhD, 1956. Ordained bishop LDS Ch., 1962. Research chemist Shell Devel. Co., Emeryville, Calif., 1956-61; assoc. research prof. U. Utah, Salt Lake City, 1961-63, assoc. prof., 1963-68, chmn. dept mining, metall. and fuels engring., 1966-74, prof. dept. metallurgy and metall. engring., 1968-96, prof. emeritus, 1996—. Cons. U.S. Bur. Mines, Salt Lake City, 1973-77, Ctr. for Investigation Mining and Metallurgy, Santiago, Chile, 1978; dir. U. Utah Minerals Inst., 1980-91. Author: Collection of Short Stories, 1985, (hist. book) Seymour Brunson: Defender of the Faith, 1998, (novel) Harriet Cynthia Allred Olson, 1995; contbr. articles to profl. jours. Del. State Rep. Conv., Salt Lake City, 1964; bishop, 1962-68, 76-82, missionary, 1988. With U.S. Army, 1943-46, PTO. Named Fulbright-Hayes lectr., Yugoslavia, 1974-75, Disting. prof. Fulbright-Hayes, Yugoslavia, 1980, Outstanding Metallurgy Instr., U. Utah, 1979-80, 88-89, Disting. Speaker U. Belgrade-Bor, Yugoslavia, 1974. Mem. Am. Inst. Mining, Metall. and Petroleum Engrs. (chmn. Utah chpt. 1978-79), Am. Soc. Engring. Edn. (chmn. Minerals div. 1972-73), Fulbright Alumni Assn., Am. Bd. Engring. and Tech. (bd. dirs. 1975-82). Republican. Achievements include research on explosives ignition and decomposition; surface properties of thoria, silica gels, silicon monoxide in ultra high vacuum; kinetics of leaching of Chrysocolla, Malachite and Bornite; electrowinning of gold; nodulation of copper during electrodeposition. Home: 1862 Herbert Ave Salt Lake City UT 84108-1832 E-mail: donnaolson1@mailstation.com.

OLSON, GARY DUANE, history educator; b. Spring Grove, Minn., July 30, 1939; s. Raymond G. and Ethel N. (Storlie) O.; m. Rosaaen Marie Skifton, Sept. 4, 1960; children: Erik Lee, Timothy Karl, Lars Christian. BA, Luther Coll., 1961; MA, U. Nebr., 1965, PhD, 1968. Tchr. social studies Kerkhoven Pub. Schs., Minn., 1961-63; asst. prof. history Augustana Coll., Sioux Falls, S.D., 1968-73, assoc. prof., 1973-79, prof., 1979—, dean acad. svcs., 1981-87, v.p. acad. affairs, dean, 1987-95. Cons.-evaluator North Ctrl Assn., 1992—. Author: (with H. Krause) Prelude to Glory, 1974, (with E.L. Olson) Sioux Falls, South Dakota: A Pictorial History, 1985; contbr. articles to profl. jours. Mem. Orgn. Am. Historians, S.D. Hist. Soc., Vesterheim Mus. Assn., Norwegian-Am. Hist. Assn. Home: 2505 S Main Ave Sioux Falls SD 57105-4820 Office: Augustana Coll Sioux Falls SD 57197-0001 E-mail: gary_olson@augie.edu.

OLSON, GREGORY BRUCE, materials science and engineering educator, academic director; b. Bklyn., Apr. 10, 1947; s. Oscar Gustav Fritz and Elizabeth Rose (Dorner) Olson; m. Jane Ellen Black, May 10, 1980; 1 child, Elise Marie. BS, MS in Materials Sci. and Engring., MIT, 1970, ScD in Materials Sci. and Engring., 1974. Rsch. assoc. dept. materials sci. and engring. MIT, Cambridge, 1974-79, prin. rsch. assoc., 1979-85, sr. rsch. assoc., 1985-88; prof. materials sci. and engring. Northwestern U., Evanston, Ill., 1988—, Wilson-Cook prof. engring. design, 1999—. Cons. Army Materials Tech. Lab., Watertown, Mass., 1975-88, Lawrence Livermore (Calif.) Nat. Lab., 1983-89; Jacob Kurtz Exchange Scientist Technion-Israel Inst. Tech., 1979; SERC vis. prof. U. Cambridge, 1992; assoc. chmn. dept. materials sci. and engring. Northwestern U., 1992-98, dir. materials tech. lab.-steel rsch.group, 1985—; founding mem. Questek Innovations LLC, 1997—. Editor: Innovative UHS Steel Technology, 1990, Martensite, 1992; contbr. numerous papers and articles to jours., encys., and symposia; inventor hydrogen-res. UHS steels, stainless bearing steel, ultrahard carburizing steels. Fellow AMAX Found., 1972-74; named N.Mex. Disting. lectr. in Materials, 1983; recipient Creativity Extension award NSF, 1983-85; Wallenberg grantee Jacob Wallenberg Found., Sweden, 1993; recipient Tech. Recognition award NASA, 1994, Tech. of Yr. award Industry Week mag. 1998, Pollution Prevention Project of Yr. award SERDP, 2003, Innovation of Yr. award Sun-Times Chgo., 2003. Fellow ASM (chmn. phase transformation com. 1987-90, Boston chpt. Saveur Meml. lectr. 1986, Phila. chpt. 1998, Alpha Sigma Mu lectr. 1996), AIME (student affairs com., M.R. Tenebaum award 1993); mem. AAAS, Materials Rsch. Soc., Internat. Soc. Martensitic Transformation, Assn. Univ. Related Rsch. Parks (Tech. Transfer award 1998). Lutheran. Avocations: sports cars, jazz trumpet. Office: Northwestern U Dept Materials Sci and Engring 2225 N Campus Dr Evanston IL 60208-3108

OLSON, JOANNE J. artist, art educator; b. Morristown, N.J., July 11, 1942; d. Eads Johnson Jr. and Jane Cook Johnson; m. Robert F. Rogel, Apr. 30, 1966 (div.); children: Tyler, Tori, Dan, Mac; m. Eric A. Olson, Oct. 18, 1996. AA, Colby Sawyer Coll., 1962. Part-time art dir. The Whitney Shop, New Canaan, Conn., 1960—64; asst. mgr. Johnny Seesaws, Peru, Utah, 1963—64; ski instr. Star Skiers, Crystal Mountain, Wash., 1978—84; clk., creative dir. Lindon Bookstore, Enumclaw, Wash., 1984—94; owner, dir. Apple Hill Art Sch., Enumclaw, 1992—96, itinerant art tchr., 1996—2003. Sec., v.p. Maple Valley (Wash.) Co-op Presch., 1973—75. Sec. Maple Valley Arts Commn., 1975—77; arts coord. Westwood PTSA, Enumclaw, 1979—83. Recipient Golden Acorn award, Nat. PTSA, 1986, Excellence in Cmty. Svc. award, Enumclaw Arts Commn., 1993. Episcopalian. Avocations: skiing, hiking, reading, creative activities.

OLSON, JULIE ANN, systems consultant, educator; b. Oklahoma City, May 14, 1957; d. Willard Alton and Ruth Harriet (Ehlers) O.; m. Kevin Peter McAuliffe, Oct. 12, 1985; children: Scott Andrew, Shannon Elizabeth, Kathryn Victoria, Ryan Douglas. BA in History, Augustana Coll., 1979; MBA, Keller Grad. Sch. Mgmt., Chgo., 1989. Sys. analyst Continental Bank, Chgo., 1979-82; prin., staff mgr. west regional tng. mgr., profl. devel. mgr Computer Scis. Corp. (formerly Computer Ptnrs.), San Bruno, Calif., 1982—, chmn. nat. orgn. change mgmt. SIG, 1982—. Instr. data processing Oakton C.C., Des Plaines, 1982-96, faculty coord. accelerated data processing cert. program, 1983-92. Exec. dir., chmn. scholarship Miss N.W. Cmtys. Inc., Des Plaines, 1984-88; bd. dirs. Mt. Prospect Hist. Soc., 1994-96, Mt. Prospect chpt. Am. Cancer Soc., Peninsula Quilt Guild; pres. women's group Hope Luth. Ch., 1999; bd. dirs., registrar Am. Youth Soccer Orgn. Recipient Grand prize for quilt, San Mateo County Fir, 2002. Mem. ASTD, NAFE, IAF, Data Processing Mgmt. Assn. (asst. faculty coord. Student chpt. 1985-87). Lutheran. Avocations: classical pianist, reading, flamenco dancing, scrapbooking, quilting. Home: 409 Castilian Way San Mateo CA 94402-2327 Office: Computer Sci Corp 1111 Bayhill Dr Ste 250 San Bruno CA 94066-3041 E-mail: mcaulke_409@yahoo.com.

OLSON, KEITH WALDEMAR, history educator; b. Poughkeepsie, N.Y., Aug. 4, 1931; s. Ernest Waldemar and Elin Ingeborg (Rehnstrom) O.; m. Marilyn Joyce Wittschen, Sept. 10, 1955; children— Paula, Judy. BA, SUNY, Albany, 1957, MA, 1959; PhD, U. Wis., 1964; PhD (hon.), U. Tampere, Finland, 2000. Mem. history faculty Syracuse U., N.Y., 1963-66; mem. history faculty U. Md., College Park, 1966—, prof. history. Fulbright prof. U. Tampere, Finland, 1986-87, U. Oulu, Finland, 1993, U. Jyväskylä, Finland, 1994. Author: The G.I. Bill, the Veterans and the Colleges, 1974; Biography of a Progressive: Franklin K. Lane, 1979, Watergate: The Presidential Scandal That Shook America, 2003. Pres. Am. Scandinavian Found., Washington, 1977-79. Served with U.S. Army, 1952-54. U.S. Office Edn. grantee, 1965-66; U. Md. grantee, 1971, 76, 78. Mem. Am. Hist. Assn., Orgn. Am. Historians, Wis. Hist. Soc., Swedish Am. Hist. Soc., Finnish Hist. Soc. (hon.), Soc. Historians of Am. Fgn. Rels., Cen. Study of Presidency, Am. Scandinavian Assn. (pres. 1998-99). Unitarian Universalist. Home: 10746 Kinloch Rd Silver Spring MD 20903-1226 Office: U Md Dept History College Park MD 20742-0001 E-mail: KO6@umail.umd.edu.

OLSON, LYNN, editor; m. Steve Olson; 2 children. Grad., Yale U. Sr. editor Edn. Week, 1990—. Author: The School to Work Revolution: How Employers and Educators Are Joining Forces to Prepare Tomorrow's Skilled Workforce, 1997. Recipient award, Edn. Writers Assn., Nat. Assn. Secondary Sch. Prins., Internat. Reading Assn.; grantee, Alfred P. Sloan Found., N.Y., 1995. Mem.: Carnegie Found. for Advancement Tchg. (bd. mem.). Office: Editl Projects in Edn Inc Ste 100 6935 Arlington Rd Bethesda MD 20814-5233*

OLSON, MAXINE LOUISE, artist, lecturer; b. Kingsburg, Calif., June 29, 1931; d. Alfred and Lena A. Marshall; divorced; children: Todd Olson, Terry Olson. BA, Calif. State U., Fresno, 1973, MA, 1975. Asst. prof. U. Ga., Athens, 1986-89; lectr. Coll. of Sequoias, Visalia, Calif., 1973-96. Lectr. Fresno City Coll., 1990, Calif. State U., Fresno, intermittently 1973-96; tchr. U. Ga., Contona, Italy, 1987, 93; 6th Annual MicroPubl. Graphics, San Francisco, 1998, The World's Women On-Line United Nations Conf., Beijing, China, 1995. Exhibited works at Oakland Mus., Palazzo Casali, Venice, Italy, Forum Gallery, N.Y.C., Soho 20, N.Y., The World's Women on-line/UN 4th World Conf. on Women, Beijing, China, William Sawyer Gallery, Palm Springs Mus., Calif., Silicon Gallery, Pa., Calif. Dept. Fish and Game, Fresno, 2001. Recipient Gold award Art of Calif. Mag., 1992, IDN Design award, 1997-98. Mem. Coll. Art Assn. Roman Catholic. Avocations: painting, drawing, digital art. Home: 1555 Lincoln St Kingsburg CA 93631-1804 E-mail: molson@mobynet.com.

OLSON, MYRNA RAYE, education educator; b. Lakota, North Dakota, Mar. 11, 1947; d. Merlin W. and Ruby A. (Tufte) Munson; children: Nathan, Austin. BS in edn., No. Mont. Coll., 1969; MEd, Mont. State U., 1971; EdD, U. N.D., 1975. Prof. of higher edn., dir. of teaching and learning doctoral program, U. N.D.; tchr. Mont. Sch. for the Deaf and Blind, Gt. Falls, Mont., N.D. Sch. for the Blind, Grand Forks, ND. Speaker in field of higher edn. Author: Collaboration Handbook for Educators, 1995, Women's Journeys Through Crisis, 1988, others. Mem. Assn. for the Study of Higher Edn. Home: 3602 Chestnut St Grand Forks ND 58201-7654

OLSON, NORMAN FREDRICK, food science educator; b. Edmund, Wis., Feb. 8, 1931; s. Irving M. and Elva B. (Rhinerson) O.; m. Darlene Mary Thorson, Dec. 28, 1957; children: Kristin A., Eric R. BS, U. Wis., 1953, MS, 1957, PhD, 1959. Asst. prof. U. Wis.-Madison, 1959-63, assoc. prof., 1963-69, prof., 1969-93, dir. Walter V. Price Cheese Research Inst., 1976-93; dir. Ctr. Dairy Research, 1986-93; disting. prof. U. Wis.-Madison, 1993-97, prof. emeritus, 1997—. Cons. to cheese industry, 1997—. Author: Semi-soft Cheeses; inventor enzyme microencapsulation; sr. editor Jour. Dairy Sci., 1996-2000. Lt. U.S. Army, 1953-55. Recipient Laureate award Nat. Cheese Inst., 1998, Disting. Svc. award Coll. Agrl. Life. Sci., U. Wis., 2002; named Highly Cited Rschr. ISI, 2002. Fellow Inst. Food Technologists (Macy award 1986), Am. Dairy Sci. Assn. (v.p. 1984-85, pres. 1985-86, Pfizer award 1971, Dairy Rsch. Inc. award 1978, Borden Found. award 1988, Hon. award 1997); mem. Inst. Food Technologists. Democrat. Lutheran. Avocation: cross country skiing. Home: 114 Green Lake Pass Madison WI 53705-4755 Office: U Wis Dept Food Sci Babcock Hall Madison WI 53706

OLSON, PETER WESLEY, international business educator; b. Amityville, N.Y., June 13, 1950; s. Wesley Harry and Mildred Constance (Petersen) O.; m. Donna Marie Marmorale, July 13, 1974; children: Jessica Marie, Jacqueline Nicole, Stephanie Anne. BA, L.I. Univ., 1972, MBA, 1977; PhD, Columbia U., 2002. Svc/sales rep. Otis Elevator Co., L.I. City, N.Y., 1973-75, internat. sales rep. N.Y.C., 1975-79; exec. asst. to v.p. NAO United Techs., Inc., Farmington, Conn., 1979-81; internat. sales mgr. Allied Bronze Corp., L.I. City, 1981-83; pres. Internat. Techs., Inc., Windsor, Conn., 1983-88; prof., curriculum chair, internat. mgmt. Hartford Grad. Ctr., Hartford, Conn., 1988—92; exec. dir. internat. devel. Conn. World Trade Inst. (subs. Conn. World Trade Assn., Hartford, 1989—95; prof. internat. mgmt. Rensselaer Poly. Inst. Lally Sch. Mgmt. and Tech., Hartford. Bd.dirs. China Investment Group, N.Y.C.; mem. adv. bd. dirs. Conn. World Trade Assn., Hartford, 1988-95, mem. edn. com., 1988-95; chief fin. officer Women's Health Internat., New Haven, 1995--. Bd. dirs. Antiquarian Landmark Soc., Hartford, mem. exec. fin. com., pub. rels. com.; chmn. Spl. Olympics, Windsor, 1983-84; bd. dirs. Earthside Found., Ocala, Fla., 1984-86; elder, mem. edn. com. Trinity Luth. Ch.; capt. Engine # 1 Locust Valley Vol. Fire Dept., 1987—. Mem. Am. Mgmt. Assn., Entrepreneurs Assn., Fireman's Exempt Assn., Masons, Master of Roome Lodge #742, Kiwanis (v.p. Windsor club 1984), Delta Mu Delta (Nu chpt. pres. 1977-78). Republican. Lutheran. Avocations: skiing, golf, tennis, flying. Home: 6 Cedar Ave Locust Valley NY 11560-2341 Office: Rensselaer Poly Inst 275 Windsor St Hartford CT 06120-2910 Office Fax: 860-547-0866.

OLSON, PRISCILLA ANN, elementary education; b. Pittsfield, Mass., Oct. 4, 1934; d. Arthur L. and Gladys Elizabeth (Hayn) Walters; m. Paul A. Olson, Aug. 8, 1959; children: David, Cheryl, Eric. Student, Emmanual Coll.; BS in Edn., Bridgewater Tchrs. Coll., 1956. Cert. elem. tchr., reading tchr., supr. reading. Permanent substitute tchr., remedial reading tchr. Town of Easton, Mass.; 1st grade tchr. Town of West Bridgewater, Mass., 1956-60; reading specialist Town of Easton, Mass., 1981—99. Recipient Horace Mann grant. Mem. Internat. Reading Assn., Mass. Reading Assn., Local Reading Assn., Kappa Delta Pi. Home: 325 Purchase St South Easton MA 02375-1674 Office: Town of Easton Lincoln St North Easton MA 02356

OLSON, ROBERTA JEANNE MARIE, art historian, author, educator, curator; b. Shawano, Wis., June 1, 1947; d. Robert Bernard Olson and Emma Pauline (Dallmann) Hoops; m. Alexander Buchanan Vance Johnson, June 15, 1980; 1 child, Allegra Alexandra Olson Johnson. BA, St. Olaf Coll., 1969; MA, U. Iowa, 1971; MFA, Princeton U., 1973, PhD, 1976. Preceptor Princeton U., 1972-74; contbg. editor Arts Mag., N.Y.C., 1973-75; art news editor The Soho Weekly News, N.Y.C., 1976-78; from asst. prof. to assoc. prof. Wheaton Coll., Norton, Mass., 1975-88, prof., 1988-2000, chmn. art dept., 1987-89, 92-93, 97-98, A. Howard Meneely chair, 1990-92. Mary L. Heuser faculty chair in the arts Wheaton Coll., 1997—2000; assoc. curator of drawings The N.Y. Hist. Soc., N.Y.C., 1999—; cons. Smithsonian Instn., Washington, 1984—86; bd. dirs. The Drawing Soc., N.Y.C., 1989—94, The Friends of Art; bd. advisers Halley's Comet Soc., 1986—; mem. collections com. drawing and print dept. Met. Mus. Art, 1993—; coll. com. drawing dept. Fogg Art Mus., Harvard U., 1997—; presenter in field. Author: Italian Nineteenth Century Drawings and Watercolors: An Album, 1976, Italian Drawings 1780-1890, 1980 (N.Y. Times Best Art Book award, 1981, Whole Earth Book award), Fire and Ice: A History of Comets in Art, 1985, Italian Renaissance Sculpture, 1992, French edit., 1993, Ottocento: Romanticism and Revolution in 19th Century Italian Painting, 1993; editor: The Art of Drawing: Selections from the Wheaton College Collection, 1997, Fire in the Sky: Comets and Meteors, the Decisive Centuries, in British Art and Science, 1998, The Florentine Tondo, 2000, Seat of Empire, 2002; guest curator Art Mus. Princeton U., 1974, Nat. Gallery of Art, 1980, N.-Y. Hist. Soc., 1990; author: (art exhbn. catalogs) Six Centuries Sculptor's Drawings, 1981, Disegni di Tommaso Minardi, 2 vols., 1982, Galleria Nazionale d'Arte Moderna, (songs) Old Master Drawings from the Mus. Art RISD, 1983; contbr. articles various prof. publications. Fellow Samuel H. Kress Found., 1973—74, Whiting Found. for Humanities, 1974—75; grantee, NEH, 1982—83, 1987—88, Am. Philos. Soc., 1989, Am. Coun. Learned Socs., 1990—91, Getty sr. rsch. grantee, 1994—95, Samuel H. Kress Found., 1996, 1999—2000, Getty sr. rsch. grantee, 2003—05. Fellow: The Morgan Libr.; mem.: Art Table, Coll. Art Assn., Italian Art Soc., Drawing Soc., Assn. Univ. Profs. Italian, Phi Beta Kappa (pres. Kappa chpt. 1980—82). Avocations: running, yoga, collecting, horseback riding. Home: 1220 Park Ave Apt 3-c New York NY 10128-1733 Office: N-Y Hist Soc Two West 77th St New York NY 10024 E-mail: rolson@nyhistory.org.

OLSON-HELLERUD, LINDA KATHRYN, elementary school educator; b. Wisconsin Rapids, Wis., Aug. 26, 1947; d. Samuel Ellsworth and Lillian (Dvorak) Olson; m. H. A. Hellerud, 1979; 1 child, Sarah Kathryn Hellerud. BS, U. Wis., Stevens Point, 1969, tchg. cert., 1970, MST, 1972; MS, U. Wis., Whitewater, 1975; EdS, U. Wis., Stout, 1978. Cert. K-12 reading tchr. and specialist. Clk. U. Counseling Ctr. U Wis., Stevens Point, 1965—69; elem. sch. tchr. Wisconsin Rapids, Wis., 1970-76; sch. counselor, 1976-79; dist. elem. guidance dir., 1979-82; elem. and reading tchr., K-2 early intervention team, reading assessment team, 1982—; instr. summer remedial reading program. Cons. in field; instr. Summer Literacy Program. Advocate Literacy Tutoring Program; adv. Moravian Ch. Sunday Sch. Mem.: NEA, Internat. Reading Assn., Wood County Lit. Coun. (cons.), Wood County Hist. Soc., Wis. State Hist. Soc., Wis. Reading Assn. (early intervention com.). United Ch. Christ. Avocations: literacy activities, piano, foreign languages, technology, tennis. Home: 1011 16th St S Wisconsin Rapids WI 54494-5371 Office: Howe Elem Sch Wisconsin Rapids WI 54494

OLSZEWSKI, SHARON ANN, adult education educator; b. Wausau, Wis., Nov. 20, 1956; d. Florian Edward and Elizabeth (Grochmal) O.; Romatowski; m. Robert Adam Olszewski, Aug. 12, 1978; children: Elissa Beth, Andrew Robert, Adam Michael. BS, U. Wis., La Crosse, 1978; MA, Marian Coll., 1993. Cert. tchr., sch. adminstr., Wis. Elem. sch. instr. pvt. sch., Mosinee, Wis., 1979-81, 86-93; comty. edn. coord., adult comty. edn. instr. North Cen. Tech. Coll., Wausau, 1993—, ESL adult edn. instr., 1994—. Asian-Am. tutor The Neighbor's Pl., Wausau, 1993—; mem. strategic planning com. Mosinee Sch. Dist., 1994, Alcohol and Other Drugs com., 1992; organizer, supr. Coll. Camp '94, Mosinee, 1994-95; chief instr. Shorei Kempo Larate, Yin Yang Do Assn., 1985—. Leader Am. Spirit Wis. 4-H, Wausau, 1994-95, mem. cultural arts com., 1994—. Mem. AAUW, ASCD, Am. Assn. Cmty. Coll. Women, Assn. Wis. Sch. Adminstrs., Delta Epsilon Sigma, Kappa Delta Pi. Democrat. Avocations: bicycling, youth and adult karate, softball, baseball. Home: 3403 Swan Ave Wausau WI 54401-0417

OLUBADEWO, JOSEPH OLANREWAJU, pharmacologist, educator; b. Oroago, Kwara, Nigeria, Apr. 16, 1945; came to U.S., 1980; s. Solomon Akanbi and Leah Ifanike (Omodara) O.; m. Victoria Ibidunni Balogun, Aug. 20, 1972; children: Oludele, Oluseyi, Olubunmi, Oluwole. BSc with honors, Ahmadu Bello U., Zaria, Nigeria, 1970; PhD, Vanderbilt U., 1976. Asst. lectr. Ahmadu Bello U., 1970-75, lectr. II to lectr. I, 1975-80, sr. lectr., 1980; rsch. scientist U. Tenn. Ctr. Health Scis., Memphis, 1980-84, asst. prof., 1984-85; assoc. prof. Xavier U., New Orleans, 1985-91, prof., 1991—; adj. rsch. prof. physiol. dept. Higher Sch. Cert. La. State U., New Orleans, 1999—. Spl. reviewer NIH, 1989-92. Mem. editorial bd. Jour. Nat. Pharm. Assn., 1989; reviewer Annals of Pharmacotherapy, Cellular and Molecular Biology; contbr. articles to profl. jours. Fellow African-American Inst. Grad. Program, 1971-75, Am. Heart Assn., 1983, 84, NIH, 1987, 88. Mem. AAUP, Am. Soc. for Pharmacology and Exptl. Therapeutics, Southeastern Pharmacology Soc. (life), Am. Assn. Colls. Pharmacy, N.Y. Acad. Scis., West African Soc. Pharmacology (life). Baptist. Avocations: basketball, volleyball, aerobics, chess, writing poetry. Home: 13510 Dwyer Blvd New Orleans LA 70129-1530 Office: Xavier U La 7325 Palmetto St New Orleans LA 70125-1056

OLUYITAN, EMMANUEL FUNSO, communications educator; b. Efon-Alaye, Nigeria, July 25, 1940; BA cum laude in Polit. Sci., Bowie (Md.) State U., 1972; MPA in Policy Analysis and Journalism, Ind. U., 1975, EdD in Instructional Tech., 1980. News reporter Nigerian Nat. Press, Lagos, 1964-65; music libr., news translator, news reporter Nigerian Broadcasting Corp., 1965-69; pub. info. coord. Aerospace Rsch. Ctr., Sch. Pub./Environ. Affairs, Ind. U., Bloomington, 1973-75; victim assistance officer Indpls. Police Dept., 1975-76; prin. lectr. Nigerian TV Authority, Lagos, 1978-81; assoc. prof. dept. edn. Ahmadu Bello U., Zaria, Nigeria, 1981-88, asst. dean postgrad. studies, 1985-88, head instructional tech. divsn., 1983-88; program officer Nat. Assn. for Equal Opportunity in Higher Edn., Washington, 1988-93; dir. Office of Pub. Rels. and Pubs. Lincoln University, Pa., 1993-96; dir. integrated info. tech. Bennett Coll., Greensboro, N.C., 1996-97; asst. prof. of comm. Wilberforce (Ohio) U., 1997—. Staff writer Office of Pub. Info., Bowie State U., 1973; vice chmn. bd. Adventures in Health, Edn. and Agrl. Devel., Inc., Rockville, Md., 1993—; bd. dirs. Anthony J. Cebrun Journalism Ctr., Nashville; CEO, ASE African Ctr., Dayton, Ohio. Photographer, fgn. news editor Ebony Tree, 1970-72; editor: African Insight, 1973, Nigeria Audio-Visual Newsletter, 1982-86, Nigeria Audio-Visual Jour., 1982-86, Global Vision, 1988-93, Update, 1988-93; assoc. editor Black Excellence, 1988-93; editor-in-chief Weekly Calendar, 1993-96, LU Newsletter, 1993-96, The Lincoln Lion, 1993-96, The Lincoln-Jour., 1993-96; contbr. articles to profl. jours., newspapers; contbr. photographs to books, jours.; prodr. numerous ednl. materials (videos, slides, pictures) Recipient Dir. Gen.'s Commendation, Nigerian TV Authority, 1987, Fed. Govt. of Nigeria's Postgrad. award, 1977-80, Award of Accomplishment and Worthiness, Indpls. Police Dept., 1976, Contr.'s Citation, Nigerian Broadcasting Corp., 1967. Mem. Assn. of Nigerians Against Corruption (founder), Nigerian Assn. for Ednl. Media and Tech., Internat. Assn. Black Profls. in Internat. Affairs, Assn. of Ednl. Comm. and Tech., Oxford Rotary Club (v.p. 1995-96). Avocations: tennis, ping-pong, photography, travel. Office: Wilberforce U LRC 115 Comm Divsn Wilberforce OH 45384 E-mail: eoluyita@wilberforce.edu.

O'MALLEY, JOHN PATRICK, retired dean; b. Hoosick Falls, N.Y., Nov. 27, 1928; s. Thomas Joseph and Mary Alice (Mulvihill) O.'M.; m. Margaret Parlin, June 24, 1989. BA, Villanova U., 1950; MA, PhD, Cath. U., 1969. Tchr. Archbishop Carroll High Sch., Washington, 1954-68, prin., 1987-89; asst. prof. Cath. U., Washington, 1968-69, Merrimack Coll., North Andover, Mass., 1969-74, dean humanities, 1976-78; chair edn. dept. Emmanuel Coll., Boston, 1974-76; dean coll. arts and scis. Villanova (Pa.) U., 1978-84; provost St. Thomas U., Miami, Fla., 1985-86; assoc. prof. Widener U., Chester, Pa., 1990-99, ret., 1999. Editor: Non-Fiction, Books I and II, 1968. Home: PO Box 586 Norfolk CT 06058-0586 E-mail: momalley@snet.net.

O'MALLEY, MARY KAY, elementary education educator; b. East Cleveland, Ohio, Feb. 12, 1959; d. Patrick Joseph and Ruth Mary (Friedmann) O'M. BA, Notre Dame Coll., 1980; MEd, John Carroll U., 1988. Cert. elem. tchr., Ohio. Asst. prin., tchr. 4th grade St. Francis of Assisi Sch., Gates Mills, Ohio, 1980—. Instr. dept. edn. John Carroll U., University Heights, Ohio, 1990—; adj. instr. dept. edn. Notre Dame Coll., South Euclid, Ohio, 1990—; presenter in field. Recipient Cleve. Diocese award, 1992, Ea. Region Diocese award, 1988, Diocese Excellence in Edn. award, 2000. Mem. ASCD, Internat. Reading Assn., Nat. Cath. Edn. Assn. Avocations: gardening, photography, bicycling, walking. Office: St Francis of Assisi Sch 6850 Mayfield Rd Gates Mills OH 44040-9635

O'MALLEY, THOMAS PATRICK, academic administrator; b. Milton, Mass., Mar. 1, 1930; s. Austin and Ann Marie (Feeney) O'M. BA, Boston Coll., 1951; MA, Fordham U., 1953; STL, Coll. St.-Albert de Louvain, 1962; LittD, U. Nijmegen, 1967; LLD (hon.), John Carroll U., 1988, Sogang U., Seoul, Rep. of Korea, 1996. Entered Soc. of Jesus, 1952. Instr. classics Coll. of Holy Cross, Worcester, Mass., 1956-58; asst. prof., chmn. dept. classics Boston Coll., 1967-69, assoc. prof., chmn. dept. theology, 1969-73; dean Boston Coll. (Coll. Arts and Scis.), 1973-80; pres. John Carroll U., Cleve., 1980-88; vis. prof. Cath. Inst. W. Africa, 1988-89; assoc. editor AMERICA, N.Y.C., 1989-90; rector Jesuit Com. Fairfield U., 1990-91; pres. Loyola Marymount U., L.A., 1991-99. Author: Tertullian and the Bible, 1967. Trustee Boston Theol. Inst., 1969-73, Fairfield U., 1971-82, 89-91, John Carroll U., 1976-88, Xavier U., 1980-86, U. Detroit, 1982-88, Boston Coll. H.S., 1986-88, Boys Hope, 1986-88, Loyola Marymount U., 1991—, St. Joseph's U., 1996—, Loyola U., Chgo., 1998—. Mem. AAUP, Soc. Bibl. Lit., N.Am. Patristic Soc.

O'MARA, KEVIN JOSEPH, principal; b. Chgo., Nov. 28, 1958; s. Patrick J. and Joan K. (Kramer) O'M.; m. Sharon A. Lindberg, Sept. 3, 1988; 1 child, Amanda. BA in Math., Rosary Coll., River Forest, Ill., 1991. Cert. secondary math. tchr. Mgr. Lettuce Entertain You Restaurant Group, 1985-91; tchr. Oak Park-River Forest High Sch., Ill., 1991-94; dean of students West Leyden High Sch., North Lake, Ill., 1994—2001; asst. prin. Ridgewood H.S., Norridge, Ill., 2001—03, prin., 2003—. Recipient Sallie Mae award Student Loan Mktg. Assn., 1993. Mem. Nat. Coun. Tchrs. Math., Kappa Mu Epsilon. Democrat. Roman Catholic. Avocation: soccer. Home: 827 S Lombard Ave Oak Park IL 60304-1609 Office: Ridgewood HS 7500 W Montrose Ave Harwood Heights IL 60706*

O'MEARA, ONORATO TIMOTHY, academic administrator, mathematician; b. Cape Town, Republic of South Africa, Jan. 29, 1928; arrived in U.S., 1957; s. Daniel and Fiorina (Allorto) O'M.; m. Jean T. Fadden, Sept. 12, 1953; children: Maria, Timothy, Jean, Kathleen, Eileen. B.Sc., U. Cape Town, 1947, M.Sc., 1948; PhD, Princeton U., 1953; LLD (hon.), U. Notre Dame, 1987. Asst. lectr. U. Natal, Republic South Africa, 1949; lectr. U. Otago, New Zealand, 1954-56; mem. Inst. for Advanced Study, Princeton, N.J., 1957-58, 62; asst. prof. Princeton U., 1958-62; prof. math. U. Notre Dame, Ind., 1962-76, chmn. dept., 1965-66, 68-72, Kenna prof. math., 1976-98, provost, 1978-96, provost emeritus, 1996—, Kenna prof. emeritus, 1998—. Vis. prof. Calif. Inst. Tech., 1968; Gauss prof. Göttingen Acad. Sci., 1978; mem. adv. panel math. scis. NSF, 1974-77, cons., 1960—. Author: Introduction to Quadratic Forms, 1963, 71, 73, 2000, Lectures on Linear Groups, 1974, 2d edit., 1977, 3d edit., 1988, Russian translation, 1976, Symplectic Groups, 1978, 82, Russian translation, 1979, The Classical Groups and K-Theory (with A.J. Hahn), 1989; contbr. articles on arithmetic theory of quadratic forms and isomorphism theory of linear groups to Am. and European profl. jours. Mem. Cath. Commn. Intellectual and Cultural Affairs, 1962—, Commn. on Cath. Scholarship, 1997-99; life trustee U. of Notre Dame, 1996—. Recipient Marianist award U. Dayton, 1988; Alfred P. Sloan fellow, 1960-63. Mem. Am. Math. Soc., Am. Acad. Arts and Sci., Collegium (bd. dirs. 1992-96). Roman Catholic. Home: 1227 E Irvington Ave South Bend IN 46614-1417 Office: U Notre Dame Office of Provost Emeritus Notre Dame IN 46556

O'MEARA, PATRICK O. political science educator; b. Cape Town, South Africa, Jan. 7, 1938; came to U.S., 1964. s. Daniel and Fiorina (Allorto) O'M. BA, U. Capetown, 1960; MA, Ind. U., 1966, PhD, 1970. Dep. dir. African studies program, asst. prof. polit. sci. Ind. U., Bloomington, 1970-72, dir. African studies program, 1972—, assoc. prof. polit. sci. and pub. and environ. affairs, 1972-81, prof. polit. sci. and pub. and environ. affairs, 1981—, dean office of internat. programs, 1993—. Cons. in field Author: Rhodesia: Racial Conflict or Coexistence?, 1975; editor (with Gwendolen M. Carter): Southern Africa in Crisis, 1977; editor: African Independence: The First Twenty-Five Years, 1985, Southern Africa: The Continuing Crisis, 1979, International Politics in Southern Africa, 1982; editor: (with Phyllis M. Martin) Africa, 1977, 3d edit., 1995; editor: (with C.R. Halisi and Brian Winchester) Revolutions of the Late Twentieth Century, 1991; editor: (with Howard D. Mehlinger and Matthew Krain) Globalization and the Challenges of a New Century, 2000; editor: (with Howard D. Mehlinger and Roxanna Ma Newman) Changing Perspectives on International Education, 2001; contbr. articles to profl. jours., chapters to books. Recipient Cross of St. George, Govt. of Catalonia, Spain, 1997, Amicus Poloniae, Embassy of Poland, 2003. Mem. African Studies Assn., Pi Alpha Alpha. Roman Catholic. Office: Ind U Bryan Hall 205 Bloomington IN 47405

O'MEARA, THOMAS FRANKLIN, priest, educator; b. Des Moines, May 15, 1935; s. Joseph Matthew and Frances Claire (Rock) O'M. MA, Aquinas Inst, Dubuque, Iowa, 1963; PhD, U. Munich, Germany, 1967. Ordained priest Roman Cath. Ch., 1962. Assoc. prof. Aquinas Inst. of

Theology, Dubuque, Iowa, 1967-79; prof. U. Notre Dame, South Bend, Ind., 1981-84, William K. Warren prof. of theology, 1985—. Author 14 books, including: Romantic Idealism and Roman Catholicism, 1983, Theology of Ministry, 1985, revised edit., 1999, Church and Culture, 1991, Thomas Aquinas: Theologian, 1997, Erich Przywara, S.J., His Theology and His World, 2002, A Theologian's Journey, 2002. Mem. Catholic Theol. Soc. Am. (pres. 1980). Roman Catholic. Office: St Thomas Aquinas Priory 7200 Division St River Forest IL 60305 E-mail: tomeara@nd.edu.

OMER, GEORGE ELBERT, JR., orthopaedic surgeon, educator; b. Kansas City, Kans., Dec. 23, 1922; s. George Elbert and Edith May (Hines) O.; m. Wendie Vilven, Nov. 6, 1949; children: George Eric, Michael Lee. BA, Ft. Hays Kans. State U., 1944; MD, Kans. U., 1950; MSc in Orthopaedic Surgery, Baylor U., 1955. Diplomate Am. Bd. Orthopaedic Surgery, 1959, (bd. dirs. 1983-92, pres. 1987-88), re-cert. orthopaedics and hand surgery, 1983, cert. surgery of the hand, 1989. 2nd lt. U.S. Army, 1945; advanced through grades to col., 1967; ret. U.S. Army, 1970; rotating intern Bethany Hosp., Kansas City, 1950-51; resident in orthopaedic surgery Brooke Gen. Hosp., San Antonio, 1952-55, William Beaumont Gen. Hosp., El Paso, Tex., 1955-56; chief surgery Irwin Army Hosp., Ft. Riley, Kans., 1957-59; cons. in orthopaedic surgery 8th Army, chief orthop. surgery 121st Evacuation Hosp. Republic of Korea, 1959-60; asst. chief orthopaedic surgery, chief hand surgeon Fitzsimons Army Med. Center, Denver, 1960-63; dir. orthopaedic residency tng. Armed Forces Inst. Pathology and Walter Reed Army Med. Ctr., Washington, 1963-65; chief orthopaedic surgery and chief Army Hand Surg. Center, Brooke Army Med. Center, 1965-70; cons. in orthopaedic and hand surgery Surgeon Gen. Army, 1967-70; prof. orthopaedics, surgery, and anatomy, chmn. dept. orthopaedic surgery, chief div. hand surgery U. N.Mex., 1970-90, med. dir. phys. therapy, 1972-90, acting asst. dean grad. edn. Sch. Medicine, 1980-81. Mem. active staff U. N.Mex. Hosp., Albuquerque, 1970—, chief of med. staff, 1984-86; cons. staff other Albuquerque hosps.; cons. orthopedic surgery USPHS, 1966-85, U.S. Army, 1970-92, USAF, 1970-78, VA, 1970-2000; cons. Carrie Tingley Hosp. for Crippled Children, 1970-99, interim med. dir., 1970-72, 86-87, mem. bd. advisor 1972-76, chair, 1994-96. Mem. bd. editors Clin. Orthopaedics, 1973-90, Jour. AMA, 1973-74, Jour. Hand Surgery, 1976-81; trustee Jour. Bone and Joint Surgery, 1993-99, sec., 1993-96, chmn., 1997-99; contbr. more than 300 articles to profl. jours., numerous chpts. to books. Decorated Legion of Merit, Army Commendation medal with 2 oak leaf clusters; recipient Alumni Achievement award Ft. Hays State U., 1973, Recognition plaque Am. Soc. Surgery Hand, 1989, Recognition plaque N.Mex. Orthopaedic Assn., 1991, Recognition award for hand surgery Am. Osteo. Acad. Orthopaedics, 1982, Pioneer award Internat. Socs. for Surgery Hand, 1995, Rodey award U. N.Mex. Alumni Assn., 1997, Cornerstone award U. N.Mex. Health Scis. Ctr., 1997; recognized with Endowed Professorship U. N.Mex. Sch. Medicine, 1995; recognized with named Annual Orthop. Seminar and Alumni Day Brooke Army Med. Ctr., 1999. Fellow ACS, Am. Orthopaedic Assn. (pres. 1988-89, exec. dir. 1989-93), Am. Acad. Orthopaedic Surgeons, Assn. Orthopaedic Chmn., N.Mex. Orthopaedic Assn. (pres. 1979-81, 1999-2000), La. Orthopaedic Assn. (hon.), Korean Orthopaedic Assn. (hon.), Peru Orthopaedic Soc. (hon.), Caribbean Hand Soc., Am. Soc. Surgery Hand (pres. 1978-79), Am. Assn. Surgery of Trauma, Assn. Bone and Joint Surgeons, Assn. Mil. Surgeons U.S., Riordan Hand Soc. (pres. 1967-68), Sunderland Soc. (pres. 1981-83), Soc. Mil. Orthopaedic Surgeons, Brazilian Hand Soc. (hon.), S.Am. Hand Soc. (hon.), Groupe D'Etude de la Main, Brit. Hand Soc. (hon.), Venezuela Hand Soc. (hon.), South African Hand Soc. (hon.), Western Orthopaedic Assn. (pres. 1981-82), AAAS, Russell A. Hibbs Soc. (pres. 1977-78), 38th Parallel Med. Soc. (Korea) (sec. 1959-60); mem. AMA, Phi Kappa Phi, Phi Sigma, Alpha Omega Alpha, Phi Beta Pi. Achievements include pioneer work in hand surgery. Home: 316 Big Horn Ridge Rd NE Sandia Heights Albuquerque NM 87122 Office: U N Mex Dept Orthopaedic Surgery 2211 Lomas Blvd NE Albuquerque NM 87106-2745

OMMAYA, AYUB KHAN, neurosurgeon, educator; b. Pakistan, Apr. 14, 1930; came to U.S., 1961, naturalized, 1968; s. Sultan Nadir and Ida (Counil) Khan; m. Ghalazala Nangiana, 1984; children: David, Alexander, Shana, Aisha, Iman, Sinan. MD, U. Punjab, Pakistan, 1953; MA, Oxford U., Eng., 1956; DSc (hon.), Tulane U. Diplomate Am. Bd. Neurological Surgery. Intern Mayo Hosp., Lahore, Pakistan, 1953-54; resident in neurosurgery Radcliffe Infirmary, Oxford, Eng., 1954-61; vis. scientist NIH, Bethesda, Md., 1961-63, assoc. neurosurgeon, 1963-68, head sect. applied rsch., 1968-74, chief neurosurgery, 1974-79; clin. prof. George Washington U. Med. Sch., 1970—. Cons. VA, Armed Forces Radiobiology Rsch. Inst.; chmn. Inter-Agy. Com. for Protection Human Rsch. Subjects of Fed. Coordinating Coun. for Sci., Engring. and Tech., NAS; chmn. biomechanics adv. com. com. Nat. Hwy. Traffic Safety Adminstrn.; mem. adv. com. Nat. Ctr. Injury Control & Prevention, Atlanta; inaugural Lewin Meml. lectr. U. Cambridge, Eng., 1983; mem. adv. coun. CDC; Snively lectr. Am. Assn. Auto. Medicine, 1988; Ibn-Sina lectr. Islamic Med. Assn. N.Am.; clin. prof. Georgetown U. Med. Ctr. Contbr. articles to profl. jours.; inventor, patentee spinal fluid flow driven artificial organs for diabetes and degenerative diseases of the nervous system. Pres. Ctr. Integrative Neurosci., Bethesda; v.p., dir. rsch. Cyborgan, Inc., Bethesda. Recipient J. W. Kirkdaldy prize Oxford U., 1956, Lifetime Achievement award Internat. Coll. Surgeons, 1996; recipient Sitara-i-Imtiaz for Achievements in Neurosurgery Govt. Pakistan, 1981; Hunterian prof. Royal Coll. Surgeons, 1968; Rhodes scholar, 1954-60 Fellow ACS, Third World Acad. Scis. (assoc., med. scis. com.), Royal Coll. Surgeons Eng.; mem. ASME (exec. affiliate), Soc. for Neurosci., Am. Assn. Neurol. Surgeons, Rsch. Soc. Neurosurgeons, Brit. Soc. Neurol. Surgeons, Am. Assn. Pakistani Physicians (pres.), Internat. Brain Rsch. Orgn. (life), Pan-Am. Med. Assn. Home: 8901 Burning Tree Rd Bethesda MD 20817-3007 Office: 8006 Glenbrook Rd Bethesda MD 20814-2608

OMTVEDT, IRVIN THOMAS, academic administrator, educator; b. Rice Lake, Wis., June 12, 1935; s. Thomas and Irene M. (Nelson) O.; m. Wanda Ruth Rank, Aug. 15, 1959; children: Mark, Penny. BS in Agr., U. Wis., Madison, 1957; MS in Animal Science, Okla. State U., Stillwater, 1959, PhD in Genetics and Animal Breeding, 1961. Fieldman livestock program, Meat and Animal Science Dept. U. Wis., 1956-57; grad. rsch. asst., Animal Science Dept. Okla. State U., 1958-61; extension livestock specialist U. Minn., 1962-64; assoc. prof. animal science Okla. State U., 1964-70, prof. animal science, 1970-73; asst. dean agr., assoc. dir. Ala. Agrl. Experiment Sta. Auburn U., 1973-75; grad. faculty fellow U. Nebr., Lincoln, 1975-2000, prof. animal science, 1975-2000, head animal science dept., 1975-82, dean agrl. rsch., dir. Nebr. Agrl. Experiment Sta., 1982-88, interim vice chancellor for agr. and natural resources, 1987-88, vice chancellor Inst. Agr. and Natural Resources, 1988-2000, v.p. agr. and natural resources, 1992-2000, interim sr. vice chancellor for acad. affairs, 1996-97, vice chancellor for extended edn., 1997-99; prof. emeritus animal sci., 2000—. Commr. Nebr. Rural Devel. Commn., 2000—03; sec. Agr. Builders of Nebr., 2000—; mem. task force NASULGC Food & Soc. Project, 2000—. Author: 1 textbook; contbr. numerous articles to profl. jours. Bd. dirs. Kiwanis Club of Lincoln, Capital City, 1980-83, 2002—, pres. 1982; mem. Lincoln Agribusiness Club, 1982—; bd. dirs. St. Mark's United Meth. Ch. Found., 1989-95, adminstrv. bd., 2000—; bd. dirs. Nebr. Human Resources Found., 1990-91, ADEC Distance Ed Consortium, 1989-95, Nebr. Cmty. Founds., 2002—; mem. staff parish com. St. Mark's Ch., 2000—. Named to NE Hall Agr. Achievement, 1997; recipient Appreciation award, Nebr. SPF, 1981, Booster award, Nebr. Pork Producers, 1983, Agrl. Achievement award, Ak-Sar-ben, 1989, ADEC Leadership award, 1995, NE Rural Radio Assn. Svc. to Agr. award, 1999, Pound-Howard Disting. Career award, 2000, NE Agribus. Club Svc. to Agr. award, 2001, NE Farm Bur. Silver Eagle award, 2001. Fellow AAAS, Am. Soc. Animal Sci. (editl. bd. Jour. Animal Sci. 1970-73, intersociety coun. rep. 1984-86, mem. bd. dirs. 1980-86, sec.-treas. 1980-83, pres. 1984-85, 88); mem. Nat. Assn. State Univ. and Land Grant Colls. (bd. dirs. bd. on agr. 1992-97), Am. Registry of Profl. Animal Scientists (gov. bd. 1985-88, pres. 1986-87), Coun. for Agrl. Sci. and Tech. (bd. dirs. 1986-89, chair nat. concerns com. 1986-89), Innocents Soc. U. Nebr.-Lincoln (hon.), Sigma Xi, Alpha Zeta, Gamma Sigma Delta (Merit award 1993), Phi Beta Delta. Avocations: travel, gardening. Office: U Nebr Inst Agr & Natural Resources 202 Agrl Hall Lincoln NE 68583 E-mail: iomtvedt1@unl.edu.

OMURA, GEORGE ADOLF, medical oncologist; b. N.Y.C., Apr. 30, 1938; s. Bunji K. and Martha (Pilger) O.; m. Emily Fowler, Dec. 27, 1962; children: June Ellen, Susan, Ann, George Fowler. BA magna cum laude, Columbia U., 1958; MD, Cornell U., 1962. Intern Bellevue Hosp., N.Y.C., resident, 1965-67; fellow Meml. Sloan Kettering Cancer Ctr., N.Y.C., 1967-70; asst. prof. medicine U. Ala., Birmingham, 1970-73, assoc. prof. medicine, 1973-78, prof. medicine, 1978-95, prof. emeritus, medicine, 1995—, prof. ob-gyn., 1991-95; v.p. clin. devel. BioCryst Pharms., Inc., Birmingham, 1995-99, med. dir., 1996-99; prof. emeritus, ob-gyn U. Ala., Birmingham, 1996—. Cons. Nat. Cancer Inst., 1975-97; chmn. Southeastern Cancer Study Group, 1983-87; cons. to FDA, 1994-95; cons. to pharm. industry, 2000—; prin. investigator cancer and leukemia Group B for Ala., 1986-95. Contbr. articles to profl. jours. Served with USNR, 1963-65. Am. Cancer Soc. jr. faculty clin. fellow, 1971-74. Fellow: ACP; mem.: Am. Assn. Cancer Rsch., Am. Soc. Hematology, Am. Soc. Clin. Oncology, Gynecol. Oncology Group (co-prin. investigator Ala. 1988—2003, bd. dirs. 2003—), Alpha Omega Alpha, Phi Beta Kappa. Home: 3621 Crestside Rd Birmingham AL 35223-1514 Office: University Sta Birmingham AL 35294-0001 E-mail: geoaomura@aol.com.

OMURA, YOSHIAKI, physician, educator; b. Tomari, Toyama-ken, Japan, Mar. 28, 1934; arrived in U.S., 1959, naturalized, 1979; s. Tsunejiro and Minako (Uozu) Omura; m. Rose Ninon Alexander, Sept. 8, 1962; children: Alexander Kenji, Vivienne Midori, Richard Itsuma. Assoc. degree, Nihon U., 1952—54; BSc in Applied Physics, Waseda U., 1957; MD, Yokohama City U., 1958; postgrad. exptl. physics, Columbia U., 1960—63; ScD (Med.), Coll. Physicians and Surgeons, Columbia U., 1965. Diplomate Internat. Coll. Acupuncture and Electro-Therapeutics, Am. Acad. Pain Mgmt., Am. Bd. Forensic Medicine, Am. Acad. Experts in Traumatic Stress. Rotating intern Tokyo U. Hosp., 1958, Norwalk (Conn.) Hosp., 1959; rsch. fellow cardiovasc. surgery Columbia U., N.Y.C., 1960; resident physician in surgery Francis Delafield Hosp., Cancer Inst., Columbia U., 1961—65; asst. prof. pharmacology and instr. surgery N.Y. Med. Coll., 1966—72; vis. prof. (summers) U. Paris, 1973—77; Maitre de recherche, Disting. Fgn. Scientist program of INSERM Govt. of France, 1977. Rsch. cons. orthop. surgery Columbia U., 1965—66; part-time emergency rm. physician Englewood Hosp., 1965—66; rsch. cons. pharmacology dept. N.Y. Downstate Med. Ctr., SUNY, 1966; co-founder, cons. Lincoln Hosp. Acupuncture Drug Detoxification Program, 1974—75; chmn. Columbia U. Affiliation and Cmty. Medicine com., Cmty. Bd. Francis Delafield Hosp., 1974—75; vis. rsch. prof. dept. elec. engring. Manhattan Coll., 1960—99; chmn. Sci. Divsn. Children's Art & Sci. Workshops, N.Y.C., 1971—92; dir. med. rsch. Heart Disease Rsch. Found., Bklyn., 1972—; adj. prof. dept. pharmacology Chgo. Med. Sch., 1982—93; adj. prof. physiology Sch. Med. Showa U., Tokyo, 1988—96; adj. prof. preventive medicine N.Y. Med. Coll., 1997—; vis. prof. Inst. Anesthesiology and Reanimation (summer) U. Padua, Italy, 1999; prof. dept. non-orthodox medicine Ukrainian Nat. Med. U., Kiev, 1993—; attending physician dept. neurosci. L.I. Coll. Hosp., 1980—88; cons. NY Pain Ctr., 1988—92, NIH Rsch. Grant Evaluation, 1994—96; v.p. Internat. Kirlian Rsch. Assn., 1981—; mem. N.Y. State Bd. Medicine, 1984—94; mem. alumni coun. Coll. Phys. and Surg. Columbia U., 1986—. Author: 6 books; contbr. chpts. to books, over 190 articles to profl. jours.; mem. editl. bd. Alternative Medicine, 1985—93, Scandinavian Jour. Acupuncture and Electrotherapy, 1987—, Functional Neurology, 1988—2002, editl. cons. Jour. Electrocardiology, 1980—86; founder, editor-in-chief: Acupuncture & Electro-Therapeutics Rsch. Internat. Jour., 1974—. Recipient Acupuncture Scientist of Yr. award, Internat. Congress of Chinese Medicine, 1989, World 1st Qi Gong Scientist of Yr. award, Internat. Congress of Chinese Medicine & Qi Gong, 1990; fellow, Columbia U., 1960; grantee, Am. Cancer Soc. Inst., 1961—63, John Polacek Found., 1966—72, NIH, 1967—72, Heart Disease Rsch. Found., 1972—. Fellow: Internat. Coll. Angiology, N.Y. Cardiol. Soc., Am. Coll. Angiology, Am. Assn. Integrative Medicine (life), Am. Coll. Forensic Examiners (life), Royal Soc. Medicine (life), Internat. Coll. Acupuncture and Electro-Therapeutics (pres. 1980—), Am. Coll. Acupunture (life); mem.: N.Y. Japanese Med. Soc. (pres. 1963—73), Am. Soc. Artificial Internal Organs, Japan Bi-Digital O-Ring Test Med. Soc. (pres. 1990—), Japan Bi-Digital O-Ring Test Assn. (pres. 1986—), N.Y. Acad. Sci., Internat. Assn. for Study of Pain (founding mem. 1975—). Achievements include 5 U.S. patents and 5 Japanese patents. Home and Office: 800 Riverside Dr Ste 8I New York NY 10032-7400 Fax: 212-923-2279. Personal E-mail: dromura@aol.com. Business E-Mail: icaet@yahoo.com.

ONAK, THOMAS PHILIP, chemistry educator; b. Omaha, July 30, 1932; s. Louis Albert and Louise Marie (Penner) O.; m. Sharon Colleen Neal, June 18, 1954. BA, Calif. State U., San Diego, 1954; PhD, U. Calif., Berkeley, 1957. Research chemist Olin Mathieson Chem. Corp., Pasadena, Calif., 1957-59; asst. prof. Calif. State U., Los Angeles, 1959-63, assoc. prof., 1963-66, prof. chemistry, 1966-99, prof. emeritus, 1999. Author: Organoborane Chemistry, 1975; Contbr. articles to profl. jours., chpts. to books. Recipient Rsch. Career award NIH, 1973-78, Nat. award Am. Chem. Soc., 1990, Outstanding Prof. award Calif. State U., System, 1993-94; named Calif. Prof. of Yr. Carnegie Found. and Coun. for the Advancement and Support of Edn., 1995; Fulbright Rsch. fellow U. Cambridge, Eng., 1965-66. Home: 230 E Highcourte Ln Tucson AZ 85737-6859 Office: Calif State U Dept Chemistry 5151 State U Dr Los Angeles CA 90032

O'NEAL, LYMAN HENRY, biology educator; b. Princeton, Ind., Jan. 18, 1942; s. Henry and Eleanor Anne (Reibold) O'N.; m. Cynthia Sue Woods, June 13, 1964; children: Michael Lyman, Cheri Sue. BA, Oakland City Coll., 1963; MS, U. Minn., 1970, PhD, 1973. Secondary sch. tchr. Francisco (Ind.) High Sch., 1963-66; prof. biology Oakland City (Ind.) Coll., 1973-89, Edison C.C., Punta Gorda, Fla., 1989—. Rsch. asst. U. Minn., St. Paul, 1967-73; adj. prof. Henderson (Ky.) C.C., 1982, Fla. So. Coll., Port Charlotte, 1989, Fla. Gulf Coast U., 1998—; bd. dirs. Ecol. Consortium Mid Am. Hancock Biol. Sta. Murray State U., 1982-89; mem. validation study panel Ind. State Dept. Edn., 1986; mem. Mote Marine Lab. Charlotte Harbor Adv. Coun., 1994—; mem. curriculum task force Fla. Gulf Coast U., 1994—. Contbr. articles to profl. jours. Mem. cmty. adv. bd. Fawcett Meml. Hosp. Mem. Am. Inst. Biol. Sci., Fla. Acad. Scis., Nat. Sci. Tchrs. Assn., Nat. Assn. Biology Tchrs. Avocations: hiking, camping, painting, multimedia, cartooning. Home: 23 Amazon Dr Punta Gorda FL 33983-5208 Office: Edison CC 26300 Airport Rd Punta Gorda FL 33950 E-mail: loneal@edison.edu., Lyoneal@cs.com.

O'NEAL, NELL SELF, retired principal; b. Glenwood, Ark., Feb. 19, 1925; d. Jewell Calvin and Nannie May (Bankston) Self; m. Billie Kenneth O'Neal, Apr. 1, 1943 (div. Jan. 1976); children: Kenneth Dan O'Neal, Rikki Devin O'Neal, Teresa Lynn Severson Gordon. BA, Little Rock U., 1964; MS in Edn., Ark. State Tchrs. Coll., 1965. Cert. tchr. mentally retarded, blind; cert. elem. sch. prin. Spl. edn. tchr. Little Rock Pub. Schs., 1961-65; prin. exceptional unit Ark. Sch. for the Blind, Little Rock, 1965-95; retired, 1995. Mem. LWV, AARP, NOW, NEA, AAUW, Assn. for the Edn., and Rehab. of Blind and Visually Impaired (J. Max Woolly Superior Svc. award 1990), Ark. Edn. Assn., Ark. Retired Tchrs. Assn., Sierra Club, Alpha Delta Kappa. Democrat. Methodist. Avocations: dancing, swimming, gardening, reading, writing. Home: 6513 Cantrell Rd Little Rock AR 72207-4218

O'NEAL, VICKI LYNN, elementary education educator; b. Joplin, Mo., Feb. 20, 1950; d. Alven Rush Hall and Betty June (Cochran) Berry; m. Larry Dean O'Neal, June 17, 1977; children: Valerie Renee, Natalie Michelle. BS in Elem. Edn., Mo. So. Coll., 1972; MS in Edn., Pittsburg State U., 1979. Tchr. elem. Lincoln Elem. Sch., Baxter Springs, Kans., 1972—. Elder First Presbyn. Ch., Baxter Springs, 1989-91, 92-94, 2002—. Grantee Southeast Kans. Ednl. Found., 1993-94, 94-95, 98-99, 2001—; named Educator of Yr. Baxter Springs C. of C., 1994; Peruvian Rainforest scholar, 1996, Fulbright Meml. Fund. Tchr. Japanese scholar, 1998, NASA Edn. Workshop scholar, 2000, Kans. Geography summer scholar, 2001, Internat. Space Sta. Conf. scholar, 2002; named Walmart Tchr. of Yr., 2001; nominee Kans. Tchr. of Yr., 2003. Mem. BT-PEO (corr. sec. 1994-96), Girl Scouts U.S.A. (leader/co-leader 1986-94, Green Angel 1992), Kans. Chpt. PEO Sisterhood, Beta Sigma Phi (scholarship co-chair 1993-95), Delta Kappa Gamma (pres. 2002—). Avocations: travel, walking, reading. Home: 3032 Edgewood Ave Baxter Springs KS 66713-2281 Office: Lincoln Elem Sch 801 Lincoln Ave Baxter Springs KS 66713-2429 E-mail: onealv1@usd508.org.

O'NEIL, CHARLOTTE COOPER, environmental education administrator; b. Chgo., Sept. 21, 1949; d. Adolph H. and Charlotte Waters (Edman) Cooper; m. William Randolph O'Neil, Nov. 18, 1972; children; Sean, Megan. BA in Polit. Sci., Okla. State U., 1969; BS in Edn., U. Tenn., 1988. Cert. tchr., Tenn. Intern Senator Charles H. Percy, Washington, 1969; state treas., state hdqrs. office mgr. Jed Johnson for U.S. Senate, Okla., 1972; mem. acct. staff Pacific Architects & Engrs., Barrow, Alaska, 1973; tchr. social studies Jefferson Jr. High Sch., Oak Ridge, Tenn., 1988; edn. specialist Sci. Applications Internat. Corp., Oak Ridge, Tenn., 1988-94, mgr. environ. edn. and info. tech. sect., 1994-95, mgr. comm. edn. and pub. info. sect., 1995-96, mgr. pub. rels., edn. and multimedia/engring. design, 1996-99, comms. and tech. support svcs. divsn. mgr., 1999—. EEMG spl. responsibility com. chmn., publicity chmn., mem. steering com. 1st ann. ASME tribute to tech. competition Am. Mus. Sci.and Energy, 1996-97. Author: Science, Society and America's Nuclear Waste, 1992, 2d edit., 1995, Technical Career Opportunities in High-Level Waste Management, 1993, The Environmental History of the Tonawanda Site, 1994, FAA Community Involvement Training: Better Decisions through Consensus, 1996, Public Involvement in the Lake Cumberland Debris Management Project, 1997, Rock Island Arsenal Community Relations Plan, 1997, St. Louis FUSRAP Site Fact Sheet Series and Community Relations Plan, 1998, rev., 2000, IT Solutions Fact Sheet series, 1999, Water Resource Management Fact Sheet, 1999, Winds of Change Promotional Brochure, 1999; contbr. articles to profl. jours. Mem. Tenn. Geography Alliance, Nat. Coun. for Social Studies (culture, sci. and tech. com., sci. and society com., sec.-treas. 1991-94), Golden Key, Atomic City Aquatic Club (chair constl. rev. com. 1991-93). Office: Sci Applications Internat PO Box 2502 Oak Ridge TN 37831-2502

O'NEIL, DANIEL JOSEPH, scientist/engineer, research executive, educator; b. Boston, June 5, 1942; s. Daniel Joseph and Grace Veronica (Francis) O'N.; m. Elizabeth Noone, Nov. 14, 1964; children: Elizabeth Grace, Daniel Joseph, Dara Veronica. BA, Northeastern U., 1964; MS, So. Conn. State U., 1967; PhD, U. Dublin, 1972. Sr. rsch. chemist Raybestos-Manhattan Advanced Rsch. Lab., Stratford, Conn., 1964-67; unit leader Hitco Materials Sci. Ctr., Gardena, Calif., 1967-68; tech. dir. Euroglas Ltd., Middlesex, Eng., 1970-72, Kildare, Ireland, 1970-72; founding faculty mem., dir. external liaison and coop. edn., lectr. polymer sci. U. Limerick, Ireland, 1972-75; chief exec. European Rsch. Inst. Ireland, Limerick, 1981-83; sr. rsch. scientist Ga. Tech. Rsch. Inst., Atlanta, 1975-78, prin. rsch. scientist, 1978-91, dir. energy and materials sci. lab., 1988-90, group dir. office of dir., 1990-91; v.p. and dean grad. coll. U. Okla., Norman, 1991-93, prof. chemistry, 1991-93; pres., dir. Sarkeys Energy Ctr. Univ. Okla. Rsch. Corp., Norman, 1992-93; founder, mng. dir. Okla. Energy Rsch. Ctr., Atlanta, 1992-93; chmn., pres. CRADA Corp., Atlanta, 1993-98, chmn., 1998—; dir. N.Mex. Engring. Rsch. Inst., 1998—; rsch. prof. Sch. Engring., U. N.Mex., 1998—. Bd. dirs. U. Okla. Rsch. Corp., Okla. Ctr. for Advancement of Sci. and Tech., Okla. Exptl. Program Stim. Comp. Res.; mem. adv. bd. Gov.'s Energy Coun.; mem. Okla. Higher Edn. State Regents Coun. on Rsch. and Grad. Edn., 1991-93; mem. exec. coun., treas./contr. com. N.Mex. Critical Infrastructure Assurance Coun., 1998—; mem. adv. bd. Lovelace Respiratory Rsch. Inst., 1998-2000, N.Mex. Biotch and Biomed. Assn., 1999—; edn. chair Profl. Aerospace Contractors Assn., 1998—. Author, co-author of 100 reports and publs. including Research Innovation and the University, 1992, University Research and Economic Development, 1992, University Strategic Planning, 1993, Institutional Strategy for Increasing Sponsored Research, 1996, Accessing Technology, 1998, Critical Infrastructure Protection for States, 1998, Development and Acquisition of Industry-Sponsored Research at U.S. Universities, 1999, Industry-University Collaboration in the U.S.A., 1999, Transportation Critical Infrastructure Protection, 2000, Chemical Biological Sensors, 2000, NMCIAC-State Model for CIP, 2000, CIP Threats—Hype or Fact, 2001. Pres. U. Okla. Res. Corp, 1992-93, bd. dirs., 1992-93; mng. dir. Okla. Energy Res. Ctr., 1992-93; mem. Okla. Ctr. Advancement of Sci. and Tech., 1991-94; mem. Team Ireland com. Atlanta Olympics, 1995-96; mem. White House Conf. Trade and Investment, Ireland, 1995—; mem. No. Ireland and Border Countries Trade and Investment Coun., Inc. Fellow Soc. Rsch. Adminstrs., Profl. Aerospace Contractors Assn. (exec. com. 1998—); mem. AAAS, Am. Chem. Soc., Biomass Energy Rsch. Assn. (bd. dirs. 1990-2000, v.p. 1998-2000), Trinity Coll. Dublin Alumni Assn., Internat. Club of Atlanta (founder), Husky Club Northeastern U., So. Conn. State U. Alumni Assn., Sigma Xi. Address: 6200 Eubanu Blvd SE No 1228 Albuquerque NM 87111 Office: U NMex NMex Engring Rsch Inst 901 University Blvd SE Albuquerque NM 87106-4339

O'NEIL, HAROLD FRANCIS, psychologist, educator; b. Columbia, SC, Jan. 26, 1943; s. Harold Francis Sr. and Margaret Mary (Ryan) O'Neil; m. Eva L. Baker, Sept. 15, 1984; children: Tristan, Christopher. PhD, Fla. State U., 1969; MS, Hollins Coll., 1970. Asst., assoc. prof. U. Tex., Austin, 1971-75; program mgr. Def. Advanced Rsch. Projects Agy., Arlington, Va., 1975-78; from team chief to dir. Tng. Rsch. Lab. Army Rsch. Inst., Alexandria, Va., 1978-85; prof. U. So. Calif., L.A., 1985—. Cons. Army Rsch. Inst., Alexandria, 1985—, Inst. Def. Analyses, Alexandria, 1985—, Amry Sci. Bd., Washington, 1994—2001, Def. Sci. Bd. Task Force on Tng., Washington, 1999—2002. Editor: (book) Academic Press Education and Technology Series, 1977—92; editl. adviser Lawrence Erlbaum Assocs., Inc., Pubs., 1992—; contbr. chapters to books, articles to profl. jours.; founding editor Japanese Jour. Edn. Fellow: APA, Am. Psychol. Soc. Achievements include research in role of cognition and affect in computer-based instruction, role of motivation in testing, cross-cultural rsch. in Japan on the role of test anxiety and performance; Taiwan and Korea on the role of self-regulation anc achievement, games for tng; development of measures for metacognition, effort, and anxiety. Office: Univ So Calif 600 Wph University Park Los Angeles CA 90089-0001

O'NEIL, J(AMES) PETER, computer software designer, educator; b. Rockville Center, N.Y., Apr. 2, 1946; s. Clement Lee and Frances Rita (Theis) O'N.; m. Carol Ann Sypniewski, June 8, 1968; children: Kelly Ann, Thomas Joseph. BA in Psychology, Loyola U., Chgo., 1968; MA in Sci. Edn., Webster Coll., St. Louis, 1972. Cert. elem. tchr. K-8, Mo., elem. tchr. K-8, Wis., dir. instruction, Wis. Tchr., student tchr. Sacred Heart Sch., Florissant, Mo., 1968-73; tchr. sci. Waunakee (Wis.) Mid. Sch., 1973-96, chmn. K-8 sci. dept., chmn. K-12 dept., 1984-92; learning coord. Deforest (Wis.) Area Sch. Dist., 1992—. Dir. Waunakee Summer Sci. Program, 1975-91; dir. instrn./tech. Brodhead Wis., 1996-99; designer sci. curriculum computer CD-ROM programs Sci. Curriculum Assistance Program and Elem. Sci. Curriculum Assistance Program, 1990—; dir. instrn. DeForest (Wis.) Area Sch. Dist., 2000--. Feature editor: Science Scope, 1989-96;

contbr. over 30 activities and articles to profl. jours. Group worker settlement houses Chgo., St. Louis; mem. Parish Coun.; dir. Waunakee Area Edn. Found. Named Master Tchr. NSF, Waunakee, 1986-96; recipient Tchr. of Yr. award Waunakee, 1984, 90, 92, Kohl Found. award, 1992, Mid. Sch. Tchr. of Yr. award Wis., 1992-93. Mem. Nat. Sci. Tchrs. Assn., Wis. Soc. Sci. Tchrs., Wis. Elementary Sci. Tchrs., NEA, Wis. Ednl. Assn. Roman Catholic. Avocations: computers, sports, writing, jogging. Home: 119 Simon Crestway Waunakee WI 53597-1721 Office: Deforest Area Sch Dist 520 E Holum St De Forest WI 53532-1316 E-mail: jponeil@deforest.k12.wi.us.

O'NEIL, ROBERT MARCHANT, university administrator, law educator; b. Boston, Oct. 16, 1934; s. Walter George and Isabel Sophia (Marchant) O'N.; m. Karen Elizabeth Elson, June 18, 1967; children— Elizabeth, Peter, David, Benjamin AB, Harvard U., 1956, AM, 1957, LLB, 1961; LLD, Beloit Coll., 1985, Ind. U., 1987. Bar: Mass. 1962. Law clk. to Justice William J. Brennan Jr. U.S. Supreme Ct., 1962-63; acting assoc. prof. law U. Calif.-Berkeley, 1963-66, prof., 1966-67, 69-72; exec. asst. to pres., prof. law SUNY-Buffalo, 1967-69; provost, prof. law U. Cin., 1972-73, exec. v.p., prof. law, 1973-75; v.p., prof. law Ind. U., Bloomington, 1975-80; pres. U. Wis. System, 1980-85; prof. law U. Wis.-Madison, 1980-85, U. Va., Charlottesville, 1985—, pres., 1985-90; gen. counsel AAUP, 1970-72, 91-92. Author: Civil Liberties: Case Studies and the Law, 1965, Free Speech: Responsible Communication Under Law, 2d edit., 1972, The Price of Dependency: Civil Liberties in the Welfare State, 1970, No Heroes, No Villians, 1972, The Courts, Government and Higher Education, 1972, Discriminating Against Discrimination, 1976, Handbook of the Law of Public Employment, 1978, 2d rev. edit., 1993, Classrooms in the Crossfire, 1981, Free Speech in the College Community, 1997, The First Amendment and Civil Liability, 2001; co-author: A Guide to Debate, 1964, The Judiciary and Vietnam, 1972, Civil Liberties Today, 1974. Trustee Tchrs. Ins. and Annuity Assn.; bd. dirs. Commonwealth Fund, Nat. Coalition Against Censorship, Am. Law Inst. Home: 1839 Westview Rd Charlottesville VA 22903-1632 Office: Thomas Jefferson Ctr Protection Free Expression 400 Peter Jefferson Pl Charlottesville VA 22911-8691

O'NEIL, WAYNE, linguist, educator; b. Kenosha, Wis., Dec. 22, 1931; s. L.J. and Kathryn (Obermeyer) O'N.; married; children: Scott Leslie, Patrick Sean, Elizabeth Erla. AB, U. Wis., 1955, AM, 1956, PhD, 1960; AM (hon.), Harvard U., 1965. Asst. prof. linguistics and lit. U. Oreg., 1961-65; prof. linguistics and edn. Harvard U., 1965-68, lectr. edn., 1968-72, vis. prof. edn., 1978-86; prof. linguistics MIT, 1968—, chmn. lit. faculty, 1969-75, chmn. linguistics program, 1986-97, head dept. linguistics and philosophy, 1989-97. Lectr. human devel. Wheelock Coll., Boston, 1991—; lectr. Beijing Normal U., 1980, Beijing and Shanghai Fgn. Lang. Insts., 1981; lectr. linguistics Shandong (China) U., 1982-83, prof., 1984—; prof. Summer Inst. on Lang. Change, NEH, 1978; vis. prof. Tsuda Coll., Tokyo, 1983, Kanda U. Internat. Studies, Makuhari, Japan, 1997, Am. Indian Lang. Devel. Inst., 2000—, Kanazawa Inst. of Tech., Japan, 2001—; co-dir. MIT-Japan Sci. and Tech. mind articulation project, 1996—. Mem. editorial group Radical Teacher, 1975— ; author: (in Chinese) English Transformational Grammar, 1981, Linguistics and Applied Linguistics, 1983, (with S.J. Keyser) Rule Generalization and Optionality in Language Change, 1985, (with S. Flynn) Linguistic Theory in Second Language Acquisition, 1988, (with S. Flynn and G. Martohardjono) The Generative Study of Second Language Acquisition, 1998, (with A. Marantz and Y. Miyashita) Image, Language, Brain, 2000. Mem. steering com. Resist, 1967—, Peoples Coalition for Peace and Justice, 1970-72; co-founder, mem. Linguistics for Nicaragua, 1985—. With U.S. Army, 1952-54. Fulbright fellow in Iceland, 1961; Am. Council Learned Socs. study fellow M.I.T., 1964-65; George Watson fellow U. Queensland, Brisbana, Australia, 1998. Mem. AAAS, Linguistic Soc. Am., Nat. Coun. Tchrs. English, Am. Assn. Applied Linguistics. Office: MIT Dept Linguistics and Philosophy Cambridge MA 02139-4307 E-mail: waoneil@mit.edu.

O'NEIL, WILLIAM FRANCIS, academic administrator; b. Worcester, Mass., Mar. 26, 1936; s. John J. and Mary A. (Trahant) O'N.; m. Mary Elizabeth Dillon, Aug. 22, 1959; children: Kathleen, Mary Elizabeth. BS, Boston U., 1960; MEd, Worcester State Coll., 1963; diploma, U. Conn., 1970; EdD, Wayne State U., 1972; PhD in Pub. Edn. (hon.), Bridgewater State Coll., 2002; BFA (hon.), Montserrat Coll. Art, 1994. Tchr. Worcester Pub. Schs., 1960—68, cmty. sch. dir., 1968—73; assoc. prof., dir. community edn. devel. ctr. Worcester State Coll., 1973-75, dir. community svc., 1975—77, dean grad. and continuing edn., 1977—83, exec. v.p., 1983—85, Mass. Coll. Art, Boston, 1985—86, acting pres., 1986—87, pres., 1987—96; exec. officer Mass. State Coll. Coun. Pres., 1996—2002. Contbr. articles to profl. jours. Mem. Worcester Dem. City Com., Ward I Dem. Com., 1980—; pres., trustee Worcester Pub. Libr., 1977-82; mem. Mass. Bd. Libr. Commrs., 1984-89; bd. dirs. Worcester State Coll. Found., 2001—. Recipient Outstanding Alumni award field of edn. Worcester State Coll., 1996, citation Mass. Ho. of Reps., 1977, key City of Worcester, 1982; Mott fellow Charles Stewart Mott Found., 1971; Godine Cmty. Svc. medal, Mass. Coll. Art, 2002. Mem. Mass. Pub. Colls. and Univs. Pres. and Chancellors Assn. (chair 1991-92), Assn. Ind. Colls. Art and Design (bd. dirs. 1988-96), Mass. Cmty. Edn. Assn. (life; bd. dirs. 1972-77), Mass. State Colls. Pres. Assn. (chair 1992-93), Profl. Arts Consortium (v.p. Boston 1986-96, pres. 1993-94). Roman Catholic. E-mail: woneil@worcester.edu.

O'NEILL, KATHRYN J. librarian, educator; b. Flint, Mich., Oct. 28, 1942; d. Edward Robert and Mary Elizabeth (Day) Zahn; m. A. Michael O'Neill, June 1964 (div. 1984); children: Daniel Sean, Margaret Anne, Matthew M. (dec.). Student, Ctrl. Mich. U., 1960-62; BA in Edn., U. Mich., 1964, MLS, 1969. Tchr. English Ann Arbor (Mich.) Pub. Schs., 1964-69, libr., media specialist, 1970-71, Ladue Sch. Dist., St. Louis, 1977—. Cons. in field. Contbg. editor: Down-to-Earth Publs. Mem. Brentwood (Mo.) Planning and Zoning Commn., 1987-93; alt. mem. Brentwood Bd. Adjustment, 1990-95; bd. dirs. Brentwood Libr., 1995-2000, v.p., 1997-1998, pres., 1999-2000; elder Richmond Heights Presbyn. Ch.; mem. supervisory com., Vantage Credit Union, 2000—; participant FOCUS St. Louis Cmty. Leadership for Tchrs., 1997—. Recipient Tchr.-Libr. Collaboration award Mo. Assn. Sch. Librs., 1995, Bright Idea award, 2001. Mem. AAUW (bd. dirs. Ann Arbor and Kirkwood-Webster Groves chpts.), U.S. Orienteering Fedn. (level I coach U.S. Olympic Com. 1989—, 4th ranked U.S. woman in master's category U.S. championship 1991, 96, Mo. state orienteering champion 1986, 91, 95, 97), St. Louis Orienteering Club (v.p. 1985-87, editor 1990-92), Hosteling Internat.-Am. Youth Hostel (trip leader), Phi Kappa Phi, Beta Phi Mu, Alpha Chi Omega. Avocations: music, theater, hiking, travel, canoeing. Home: 1716 Blue Jay Cv Brentwood MO 63144-1604

O'NEILL, MARY BONIFACE, alternative education administrator; b. Limerick, Ireland, Jan. 16, 1916; came to U.S., 1935; d. Daniel J. and Ellen (O'Connor) O'N. BA, Incarnate Word Coll., 1942; MA, U. Tex., 1943, Our Lady of Lake U., 1956, 58. Joined Holy Spirit Sisters, Roman Cath. Ch., 1934. Tchr. St. Peter Claver Acad., San Antonio, 1950-63, prin., 1964-70; exec. dir. Healy Murphy Ctr., San Antonio, 1970—. Recipient Recognition award Nat. Coun. Jewish Women, 1984, Martin Luther King award, Humanitarian award Women in Communications, 1988, Spl. Community Svc. award NAACP, 1988, Pro Ecclesia et Pontiface award Pope John Paul II, 1989, Citation of Excellence cert. Tex. Ho. of Reps., San Antonio Light Woman of Yr. award, Irishman of Yr. Cuchulainn award, 1987, others. Democrat. Office: 618 Live Oak San Antonio TX 78202-1932

O'NEILL, MICHAEL, management educator; b. Washington, Sept. 2, 1938; s. John Patrick and Mary Lou (Maginnis) O'N.; m. Elfrieda Langemann, Apr. 10, 1993; 1 child, Susan Ewens. BA, St. Thomas Coll., 1960; MA, Cath. U., 1964; EdD, Harvard U., 1967. Supt. Cath. Diocese of Spokane (Wash.), 1967-76; assoc. prof., dir. pvt. sch. adminstrn. U. San Francisco, Sch. Edn., 1976-78, dean, prof., 1978-81, prof., 1981-82; dir. fundraising No. Calif. Nuclear Weapons Freeze, 1982; prof., dir. inst. non-profit orgn. mgmt. U. San Francisco, Coll. Profl. Studies, 1983—2000; prof. U. San Francisco, 2000—. Tchr. Boston Coll., 1984, Ft. Wright Coll., 1970, 75, U. Notre Dame, 1968, 69. Author: How Good are Catholic Schools?, 1967, New Schools in a New Church, 1971, The Third America: Emergence of the Nonprofit Sector in the United States, 1989, Ethics in Nonprofit Management: A Collection of Cases, 1990, Nonprofit Nation: A New Look at the Third America, 2002; co-author: (with Dennis R. Young) Educating Managers of Nonprofit Organizations, 1988, (with Herman Gallegos) Hispanics and the Nonprofit Sector, 1991, (with Teresa Odendahl) Women and Power in the Nonprofit Sector, 1994, (with Kathleen Fletcher) Nonprofit Management Education: U.S. and World Perspectives, 1998, (with William L. Roberts) Giving and Volunteering in California, 2000; assoc. editor Nonprofit Mgmt. and Leadership, 1989-2000; mem. editl. bd. Harvard Ednl. Review, 1965-67; contbr. articles to profl. jours. Mem. membership com. Ind. Sector, 1993-98, rsch.com., 1989-92; bd. dirs. Nat. Acad. Ctrs. Coun., 1989-2000. Teaching fellow Harvard U., 1965-67. Mem. Assn. for Rsch. Non-profit Orgns. and Vol: Action (bd. dirs. 1993-99, pres. 1996-98). Roman Catholic. Office: U San Francisco Coll Profl Studies 2130 Fulton St San Francisco CA 94117-1047

O'NEILL, SHEILA, principal; Prin. Cor Jesu Acad., St. Louis. Recipient Blue Ribbon award U.S. Dept. Edn., 1990-91. Office: Cor Jesu Acad 10230 Gravois Rd Saint Louis MO 63123-4099

O'NEILL, WALTER JOHN HUGH, university director, consultant; b. Freeport, N.Y., May 31, 1962; s. John Hugh and Mary Adele (Crawford) O'N. BS, SUNY, Binghamton, 1986. Counselor aid fin. aid SUNY, Binghampton, 1983-86, dir. fin. aid Old Westbury, 1987-91; adminstr. fin. aid Columbia U., N.Y., 1986-87; dir. fin. aid Chgo. State U., 1991-92, Ill. Inst. Tech., Chgo., 1992—. Enrollment, aid cons. O'Neill Cons., Freeport, N.Y., 1987-89, Chgo., 1993—. Active Chgo. Alternative Policing Strategy, 1994—. Named one of Outstanding Young Men of Am., 1986-87. Mem. Nat. Assn. Student Fin. Aid Adminstrs., Ill. Assn. Student Fin. Aid Adminstrs. Roman Catholic. Home: 7711 S Sawyer Ave Chicago IL 60652-1918 Office: Ill Inst Tech 3300 S Federal St Rm 212 Chicago IL 60616-3793

ONET, VIRGINIA C(ONSTANTINESCU), research scientist, educator, writer; b. Sarmasag, Salaj, Romania, Mar. 17, 1939; came to U.S., 1986; naturalized, 1991. d. Virgil and Eugenia (Marinescu) Constantinescu; m. Gheorghe Emil Onet, Sept. 3, 1981. DVM, U. Agriculture Scis., Cluj-Napoca, Romania, 1966; PhD, Coll. Vet. Med., Bucharest, Romania, 1974. Asst. prof., then assoc. prof. Coll. Vet. Medicine, Cluj-Napoca, 1966-81, lectr., 1981-85; pvt. rschr. Germany, 1985-86; ind. cons., 1986-88; rsch. group leader Grand Labs., Inc., Larchwood, Iowa, 1988-92, mgr. R&D dept. parasitology, 1992-95, mgr. R & D dept. spl. rsch. projects, 1995—. Mem. profl. bd. Coll. Vet. Medicine, Cluj-Napoca, 1970-72, mem. faculty com., 1980-81; mem. Exam. Bd. for Screening Vet. Medicine Candidates, Cluj-Napoca, 1974-85. Author: Diagnosis Guide for Parasitic Disease, 1983; co-author: Laboratory Diagnosis in Veterinary Medicine, 1978; author 7 textbooks; contbr. over 45 articles to profl. jours. Merit scholar Coll. Vet. Medicine, Bucharest, 1964. Mem. AAAS, Am. Soc. Parasitologists, Am. Vet. Med. Assn., Am. Assn. Vet. Parasitologists, World Vet. Poultry Assn., World Assn. for Advancement Vet. Parasitology, Romanian Vet. Medicine Soc., Romanian Soc. Biologists, World Assn. Buiatrics, N.Y. Acad. Scis. Avocations: music, poetry, travel, crocheting, reading. Home: 4509 Mountain Ash Dr Sioux Falls SD 57103-4959 Office: Grand Labs Inc PO Box 193 Larchwood IA 51241-0193

ONG, MICHAEL KING, mathematician, educator, banker; b. Manila, Philippines, Dec. 16, 1955; s. Sanchez and Remedios (King) O. BS in Physics cum laude, U. Philippines, 1978; MA in Physics, SUNY, Stony Brook, 1979, MS in Applied Math., 1981, PhD in Applied Math., 1984. Asst. prof. Bowdoin Coll., Brunswick, Maine, 1984-91; sr. mathematician, fin. analyst Chgo. Rsch. & Trading Group Ltd., 1990-92; v.p., sr. rsch. analyst First Chgo. NBD, 1993-94; head market risk analysis unit First Chgo. Corp., 1994—, 1st v.p., head corp. rsch. unit, 1996-97; sr. v.p., head treasury bus. rsch. ABN-AMRO Bank, Chgo., 1997—, head of enterprise risk mgmt., 1999-2000; exec. v.p., chief risk officer Credit Agricole Indosuez, 2000—03; prof. fin. Stuart Grad.Sch. Bus. Ill. Inst. Tech., 2003—, dir. fin. program, exec. dir. Ctr. Law and Fin. Markets, Stuart Grad. Sch. Bus., 2003—. Adj. prof. fin. markets and trading program Stuart Sch. Bus. Ill. Inst. Tech., 1990—, bd. dirs. Carr Global Advs., 2000—. Author: Internal Credit Risk Models--Performance Measurement and Capital Allocation, 1999, Credit Ratings - Methodologies, Rationale and Default Risk, 2002; mem. editl. bd. Jour. Fin. Regulation & Compliance, Jour. of RISK; contbr. articles to profl. jours. Mem. Am. Fin. Assn., Am. Math. Soc., Math. Assn. Am., Soc. Indsl. and Applied Math., Consortium for Math. and Its Applications, Am. Phys. Soc., Phi Kappa Phi. Avocations: writing, singing, traveling, painting. Home: 2650 N Lakeview Ave Apt 4106 Chicago IL 60614-1833 Office: Ill Inst Tech Stuart Grad Sch Bus 565 W Adams St Chicago IL 60661-3691 Office Fax: 312-906-9649. Business E-Mail: ong@stuart.iit.edu. E-mail: michaelong123@aol.com.

ONG, TONG-MAN, microbiologist, educator; b. Tainan, Taiwan, June 9, 1935; came to U.S., 1965; s. Kar and Tsai (Tsai) Ong.; m. Shu-hui Huang, Jan. 14, 1967; children: Fiona, Kara. BS, Taiwan Normal U., Taipei, 1960; MS, Ill. State U., 1967, PhD, 1970. Faculty asst. Taiwan Normal U., Taipei, Taiwan, 1961-64; rsch. asst. Ill. State U., Normal, Ill., 1965-70; postdoctoral fellow Oak Ridge (Tenn) Nat. Lab., 1970-72; fellow Nat. Inst. Environ. Health, Rsch. Triangle Pk., N.C., 1972-77, geneticist, 1977-78; vis. prof. Shanghai Med. U., China, 1986-92; adj. prof. West Va. U., Morgantown, 1985—; disting. vis. prof. Guanzhou Med. Coll., China, 1988-97; microbiology sect. chief Nat. Inst. Occup. Safety & Health, Morgantown, W. Va., 1979-97, molecular epidemiology team leader, 1997—. Contbr. over 250 articles to profl. jours. Recipient Rsch. Fellowship Damon Runyon Rsch. Inc., 1971, '72, Achievment award Ill. State U. Alumni Assn., Normal, Ill., 1988. Mem. AAAS, Environ. Mutagen Soc., Environ. Health Inst., Sigma Xi, Phi Sigma Soc. (outstanding grad. student Ill. State U. 1968). Home: 149 Lamplighter Dr Morgantown WV 26508-8649 Office: Nat Inst Occupational Safety Health 1095 Willowdale Rd Morgantown WV 26505-2845

ONGKINGCO, FLORENCE KAGAHASTIAN, health facility educator; b. Laguna, The Philippines, July 29, 1945; d. Leopoldo Kagahastian and Cresenciana Quesada; m. Prospero Ongkingeo, July 10, 1976; 1 child Michelle Ann. Diploma in nursing with honors, Philippine Gen. Hosp. Sch. Nursing, 1966; BSN, U. Philippines, 1967; MA in Nursing, NYU, 1975; cert. in computer programming, Queens Computer Coll., 1986. RN, N.Y.; cert. profl. in healthcare quality. Supr., clin. instr. Operations Brotherhood, Vientiane, Laos; team leader NYU Med. Ctr., N.Y.C.; coord. nursing care Luth. Med. Ctr.; clin. instr. Queens Hosp. Ctr., Jamaica, N.Y.; dir. staff devel. St. John's Queen's Hosp., Elmhurst, N.Y.; dir. quality assurance and staff devel. Westchester Sq. Med. Ctr., Bronx, N.Y.; dir. nursing edn., staff devel. Booth Meml. Med. Ctr., Flushing, NY; dir. Edn. Cabrini Ctr. for Nursing and Rehab., N.Y.C. Mgmt. devel., workshop leader nursing process and nursing standards; amb. to Nursing Spectrum; presenter in field. Producer, dir. slide-tape program, video program in field. Mem. Ednl. Assn. Hartford Inst. for Geriatric Nursing, Internat. Honor Soc. of Nursing, Sigma Theta Tau.

ONOKPISE, OGHENEKOME UKRAKPO, agronomist, educator, forest geneticist, agroforester; b. Lagos, Nigeria, May 10, 1951; came to U.S., 1981; s. Jerome Esagwu and Margaret E. (Agbanobi) O.; m. Lucy Omotaka Edemo, Jan. 31, 1977; children: Oghenemaro, Omurhu, Oghogho, Onori-ode. BS, U. Ife, Ile-Ife, Nigeria, 1974; MS, U. Guelph, Ont., Can., 1980; PhD, Iowa State U., 1984. Tutor Sch. Agrl., Yandev, Nigeria, 1974-75; rsch. officer Rubber Rsch. Inst. Nigeria, Benin City, 1975-81; rsch. asst. Iowa State U., Ames, 1981-85; rschr. Ohio State U., Wooster, 1985-86; asst. prof. Fla. A&M U., Tallahassee, 1986-91, assoc. prof., 1991-94, prof., 1994—. Mem. Germplasm Collection Team Internat. Rubber R&D Bd. London, Eng. in Brazil, 1981; team leader Cocoyam Breeding Team USAID, Cameroon, Republic of West Africa, 1988-90, coord. weed control project, Ghana, 1996—; sabbatical leave Inst. Forest Genetics and Tree Breeding U. Gottingen, Germany, 2002. Contbr. articles to Commonwealth Forestry Rev. Jour., Annals Applied Biology, Plant Breeding, Acta Agronomca, Seed Sci. and Tech., African Jour. Genetics, Am. Jour. Enology and Viticulture, Indian Jour. Plant Breeding and Genetics, Silvae Genetica, Agronomie, Jour. Plantation Crops, African Tech. Forum, Women in Natural Resources Jour., Natural Resources, Salem Press, Restoration Ecology, Internat. Jour. Tropical Agr. Editor Pack 104 Club Scouts Newsletter, Boy Scouts Am., Tallahassee, 1986-88; mem. Parish Coun. St. Louis Parish, Tallahassee, 1987-88; tutor Bapt. H.S., Buea, Cameroon, 1988-89; mem. choir St. Louis Cath. Ch., 1991—. Recipient Sci. Paper award Assn. Rsch. Dirs., Washington, 1987; named Best Agrl. Instr., Agrl. Sci. Club FAMU Students, Tallahassee, 1988, 93; grantee USAID-FAMU, Cameroon, 1988-90, NASA-Fla. A&M U., 1988-91, Internat. Paper Co., 1994, USAID-Fla. A&M U.-U. Fla., Ghana, 1996-98, USDA-Fgn. Agrl. Svcs.-Fla. A&M U., Ghana, 1998—, USDA-Rsch. and Sci. Exch. Divsn.-Fla. A&M U., Ghana, 1999—; German Acad. Faculty Exch. fellow, 2002. Fellow Indian Soc. Genetics and Plant Breeding; mem. Am. Soc. Agronomy, Commonwealth Forestry Assn., Soc. of Am. Foresters (campus faculty rep., diversity com.). Achievements include development of concepts of moving forest for the tropical rain forest; growth of carrots in hydroponic system within growth chambers, inbreeding depression in polyploids with emphasis on forages. Home: 2810 Kennesaw Pl Tallahassee FL 32303-1202 Office: Fla A&M U Martin Luther King Blvd Tallahassee FL 32307 E-mail: o.onokpise@worldnet.att.net.

ONORATO, NICHOLAS LOUIS, retired program director, economist; b. South Barre, Mass., Feb. 24, 1925; s. Charles and Amalia (Tartaglia) O.; m. Elizabeth Louise Settergren, July 19, 1947; children: Gary, Deborah, Nicholas, Jeffrey, Glenn, Charles (dec.), Lisa. BS in Pub. Relations, Boston U., 1951; MA in Econs, Clark U., 1952, PhD, 1959. Mem. faculty Becker Jr. Coll., Worcester, Mass., 1952-54; prof. econs. Worcester Poly. Inst., 1955-68, chmn. dept. econs., govt., bus., 1968-74, dir. Sch. Indsl. Mgmt., 1972-99; prof. emeritus Worcester (Mass.) Poly Inst., 1994. Vis. prof. Clark U., Worcester, 1964-66; fin. cons. Coz Chem. Co., Northbridge, Mass., 1959-95. Contbr. to newspapers and mags. Trustee Bay State Savs. Bank, Worcester. Served with USNR, 1943-46. Mem. Am. Finance Assn., Am. Econ. Assn., Am. Accounting Assn., Phi Kappa Theta. Clubs: Torch (pres. Worcester 1967, 87, 95). Home: 39 Knollwood Dr Shrewsbury MA 01545-3329

OORT, ABRAHAM HANS, meteorologist, researcher, educator; b. Leiden, The Netherlands, Sept. 2, 1934; came to U.S., 1961; s. Jan Hendrik and Johanna Maria (Graadt Van Roggen) O.; m. Bineke Pel, May 20, 1961; children: Pieter Jan, Michiel, Sonya. MS, MIT, 1963; PhD in Meteorology, U. Utrecht, The Netherlands, 1964. Rsch. meteorologist Koninklyk Nederlands Meteorologisch Instituut, De Bilt, The Netherlands, 1964-66, Geophys. Fluid Dynamics Lab/NOAA, Washington, 1966-68, Princeton, N.J., 1968-77, sr. rsch. meteorologist, 1977-96, ret., 1996. Prof. dept. geol. and geophys. scis. Princeton U., 1971-96; Shiatsu tchr. Kushi Inst. for Macrobiotic Studies, Becket, Mass., 1999--. Author: Physics of Climate, 1992; contbr. monographs in field. 2nd lt. Netherlands Air Force, 1959-61. NATO sci. fellow MIT, Cambridge, 1961-63; 10th Victor P. Starr Meml. lectr. MIT, 1988; recipient Gold medal U.S. Dept. Commerce, Washington, 1979. Fellow N.Y. Acad. Scis., Am. Meteorol. Soc. (Jule G. Charney award 1993), Royal Meteorol. Soc.; mem. Am. Geophys. Union. Democrat. Avocations: sculpture, shiatsu, meditation, Cranio-Sacral Therapy.

OOTES, JAKE, minister education, culture and employment; b. Renfrew, Ontario, Can. 1 child, Luke. Grad. H.S., Renfrew, Ont., Can.; comm. studies, St. Paul and Carleton Univs., Ottawa, Can. Reporter Comty. newspapers in Ont.; pub, info. officer Fed. Dept. Indian and Northern Affairs, Ottawa, 1962—67; exec. asst. to commr. Northwest Territories, 1967—70, dir. territorial dept. info., 1970—75; owner, publisher Fort Saskatchewan Record and two other newspapers, 1975—82; publisher, editor Northwest Explorer, 1983—88, Above and Beyond, 1988—; elected min. Legis. Assembly of Northwest Territories, 1995—; min. of education, culture and employment Northwest Territories, 2000—. Founding sec. St. Johns Ambulance Svc. in Northwest Territories; Wade Hamer Found. Yellowknife; bd. dirs. Northwest Territories Tourism Industry Assn. Named (His Saskatchewan Record) Best Comty. Paper in Canada.; recipient Medal of Merit and Bar, Northwest Territories and Alberta Scouts. Office: Northwest Territories Dept Edn PO Box 1320 Yellowknife NT X1A 2L9 Canada

OPELA, MARIAN MEADE, principal, consultant; b. Sharon, Conn., July 5, 1941; d. Jerry Roselle and Ruth Bean (Wills) Meade; m. H. Terry Opela, July 1, 1967; children: Stephen, Glenn, H. Kevin. BA, Middlebury Coll., 1962; MEd, SUNY, Buffalo, 1968; postgrad., Coll. of St. Rose, 1993—. Cert. tchr. social studies, N.Y.; cert. SAS. Tchr. Cheektowaga (N.Y.) Ctrl. High Sch., 1963-67; nursery sch. dir. Magic Dragon Pre-Sch., Stockport, N.Y., 1979-81; tchr. Acad. of the Holy Names, Albany, N.Y., 1981-84, Ichabod Crane Ctrl. Sch., Valatie, 1984-94, strategic planning coord., 1991-94; asst. prin. Ravena (N.Y.)-Coeymans-Selkirk Mid. Sch., 1994—, summer sch. prin., 1996. Cons. N.Y. State Edn. Dept., Albany, 1990, 92, 94. Lay leader, speaker North Chatham (N.Y.) Meth. Ch., 1990—; del. Columbia County Environ. Mgmt. Coun., Hudson, N.Y., 1984-92; candidate for Kinderhook Town Bd., 1991. Mem. N.Y. State Coun. for Social Studies, Kinderhook Rep. Club, Nat. Campers and Hikers Assn. (exec. bd. 1968-93, Nat. plaque 1980), Delta Kappa Gamma, Phi Delta Kappa. Avocations: camping, hiking, reading, mentoring. Home: 309 Rt 28 B Valatie NY 12184-9782

OPFER, NEIL DAVID, construction educator, consultant; b. Spokane, Wash., June 1, 1954; s. Gus Chris and Alice Anna (Nibbe) Opfer. BS in Bldg. Theory cum laude, Wash. State U., 1976, BA in Econs. cum laude, BA in Bus. cum laude, Wash. State U., 1977; MS in Mgmt., Purdue U., 1982; PD in Engring., U. Wis., 2003. Cert. cost engr., project mgr., profl. constructor; lic. gen. contractor. Estimator Standard Oil (Chevron), Richmond, Calif., 1975; gen. carpenter forman Opfer Constrn. Corp., Spokane, 1976; assoc. engr. Inland Steel Corp., East Chgo., Ind., 1977-78, millwright supr., 1978-79, field engr., 1979-82, project engr., 1982-84, sr. engr., 1984-87; asst. prof. construction and construction mgmt. Western Mich. U., Kalamazoo, 1987-89, U. Nev., Las Vegas, 1989-95, assoc. prof. construction and construction mgmt., 1995—. Contbr. articles to profl. jours. Bd. dirs. Christmas in April, 1993—98, Habitat for Humanity, 1991—. Mem. Am. Welding Soc. (bd. dirs. 1982-87), Am. Inst. Constructors, Am. Assn. Cost Engrs. (nat. bd. dirs. 1995-97, Order of Engr. award 1989), Project Mgmt. Inst., Constrn. Mgmt. Assn., Tau Beta Pi (life), Phi Kappa Phi (life). Methodist. Avocations: biking, running, marathons, triathlons. Home: 1920 Placid Ravine St Las Vegas NV 89117-5961 Office: Univ Nev Civil Engring 4505 S Maryland Pkwy Las Vegas NV 89154-4015 E-mail: opfern@ce.unlv.edu.

OPLER, LEWIS ALAN, psychiatrist, educator, researcher; b. LA, Apr. 16, 1948; s. Marvin Kaufmann and Charlotte (Fox) D.; m. Annette Arcario; children: Mark, Daniel, Michelle, Douglas. BA magna cum laude, Harvard U., 1969; PhD in Pharmacology, Albert Einstein Coll. Medicine, 1975, MD, 1976. Diplomate Am. Bd. Psychiatry and Neurology. Asst. prof. dept.

psychiatry Albert Einstein Coll. of Medicine, Bronx, 1979-85, assoc. clin. prof., 1985-87; clin. dir. Bronx Psychiat. Ctr., Bronx, 1985-87; assoc. clin. prof. dept. psychiatry Coll. Physicians Columbia U., N.Y.C., 1987-91, clin. prof. Coll. Physicians, 1991-99; unit chief Presbyn. Hosp., N.Y.C., 1987-90, dir. psychiat. rsch., 1987-94; med. dir. N.Y.C. regional office N.Y. State Office Mental Health, 1994-95, med. dir. N.Y.C. region, 1995-99, dir. rsch. divsn., 1999—. Psychopharmacology cons. Columbia U., 1987—; adj. prof. Coll. Physicians, 1999—; clinical prof. psychiatry NYU Sch. Medicine, 2001—. Contbr. articles to profl. jours. Nat. Merit scholar, 1965; recipient Spl. Achievement award N.Y. State Office Mental Health, 1987, Exemplary Psychiatrist award Nat. Alliance for Mentally Ill, 1992, 93. Mem. Nat. Alliance for the Mentally Ill of N.Y. State (hon.), Am. Pychiat. Assn., N.Y. Acad. Scis. Avocation: musician. Office: Bronx Psychiatric Ctr 1500 Waters Pl Bronx NY 10461-2723

OPPENHEIM, IRWIN, chemical physicist, educator; b. Boston, June 30, 1929; s. James L. and Rose (Rosenberg) O.; m. Bernice Buresh, May 18, 1974; 1 child, Joshua Buresh. AB summa cum laude, Harvard U., 1949; postgrad., Calif. Inst. Tech., 1949-51; PhD, Yale, 1956. Physicist Nat. Bur. Standards, Washington, 1953-60; chief theoretical physics Gen. Dynamics/Convair, San Diego, 1960-61; assoc. prof. chemistry MIT, Cambridge, 1961-65, prof., 1965—. Lectr. physics U. Md., 1953-60; vis. assoc. prof. physics U. Leiden, 1955-56, Lorentz prof., 1983; vis. prof. Weizmann Inst. Sci., 1958-59, U. Calif., San Diego, 1966-67; Van der Waals prof. U. Amsterdam, 1966-67. Author: (with J.G. Kirkwood) Chemical Thermodynamics, 1961; editor: Phys. Rev. E, 1992-2001. Recipient Hildebrand award, 1998. Fellow Am. Phys. Soc., Am. Acad. Arts and Scis., Washington Acad. Sci.; mem. Phi Beta Kappa, Sigma Xi. Achievements include research in quantum statis. mechanics, statis. mechanics of transport processes, thermodynamics. Home: 140 Upland Rd Cambridge MA 02140-3623 Office: MIT 77 Massachusetts Ave #6-223 Cambridge MA 02139-4307 E-mail: irwin@mit.edu.

OPPENHEIM, PAUL, vocational educator; Tchr. Sch. Bldg. Construction U. Fla., now asst. prof. Rinker Sch. Bldg. Constrn. Recipient John Trimmer Merit Shop Tchg. award Excellence Edn. Construction Found., 1993. Office: U Fla Sch Bldg Constrn PO Box 115703 Gainesville FL 32611-5703

ORAN, GERALDINE ANN, assistant principal; b. Burleson, Tex., June 27, 1938; d. Clyde Lloyd and Ruth (Baxley) Renfro; m. Francis Larry Oran, Dec. 18, 1960; children: Angelique Michelle, Jeremy Lloyd. AS summa cum laude, Roane State Community Coll., Harriman, Tenn., 1976; BS summa cum laude, U. Tenn., 1978, MS summa cum laude, 1990. IBM instr., office mgr. Kelsey-Jenney Bus. Coll., San Diego, 1958-61; exec. sec. Bendix Corp., San Diego, 1961-62; ednl. adminstr. South Harriman Bapt. Ch., 1964-74; sec. West Hills Presbyn. Ch., 1974-78; tchr. Midtown Elem., Harriman, 1979-89; adminstrv. intern, prin. preparation program Danforth Found. Leadership 21, 1989; asst. prin. Cherokee Mid. Sch., Kingston, Tenn., 1990—. Mem., sec., treas., pres. PTA and PTO, Harriman, 1967-81; active Cancer, Heart Fund and March of Dimes, Harriman, 1979—; dir. vacation Bible sch. South Harriman Bapt. Ch., 1983-86, tchr. women's Bible sch., 1965—; club sponsor Tenn. Just Say No to Drugs Team, Roane County, 1985-87; mem. Task Force on Mid. Schs., Tenn. Dept. Edn., 1990; selection com. Tenn. Mid. Sch. Tchr. of Yr., 1992. Named Tchr. of Yr., Roane County, 1987. Mem. ASCD, NEA (del. rep. 1985-86), Tenn. Assn. Supervision and Curriculum Devel., Tenn. Assn. Middle Schs., Nat. Assn. of Secondary Sch. Prins., Tenn Edn. Assn. (del. rep. 1984-86, Outstanding Svc. award 1985-86), Roane County Edn. Assn. (membership chair 1984-85, pres. 1985-86), Roane County Adminstrs. Assn. (pres. 1993), Gamma Phi Beta, Kappa Delta Pi, Phi Kappa Phi, Delta Kappa Gamma. Baptist. Avocations: reading, painting, crafts, sculpting, walking. Home: PO Box 917 Harriman TN 37748-0917 Office: Cherokee Mid Sch Paint Rock Ferry Rd Kingston TN 37763-2914

ORAVEC, EDWARD PAUL, secondary school educator; b. Elmira, N.Y., June 2, 1958; s. Andrew and Margaret (Andrasko) O. BA in History, SUNY, Buffalo, 1980; MEd in Social Studies, SUNY, 1988. Cert. social studies tchr. grades 7-12. Tchr. North Sargent Sch., Gwinner, N.D., 1980-83, Cairo-Durham (N.Y.) H.S., 1983-85; grad. asst. SUNY, Buffalo, 1985-86; tchr. Chelsea (Vt.) Sch., 1986-88; middle sch. tchr., social studies dept. chair Harwood Union H.S., Moretown, Vt., 1988-2001; dir. Twinfield Learning Ctr., Plainfield, Vt., 2001; tchr. grades 7-8 Twinfield Union Sch., Plainfield, 2001—. Author: Elder Friends, 1998, Making Prejudice Visible, 1999. Named Tchr. of the Yr., Washington West Supervisory Union, Moretown, 1988. Fellow Power of the Pen; mem. NEA, Nat. Coun. for the Social Studies, Vt. Assn. of Middle Level Educators. Avocations: hiking, walking, reading. Office: Twinfield Union Sch Dept Social Studies Plainfield VT 05667 E-mail: Ed.Oravec@twinfield.net.

ORAZEM, MARK EDWARD, chemical engineering educator; b. Ames, Iowa, June 7, 1954; s. Frank and Slava (Furlan) O. BSChemE, Kans. State U., 1976, MSChemE, 1978; PhD in Chem. Engring., U. Calif., Berkeley, 1983. Asst. prof. dept. chem. engring. U. Va., Charlottesville, 1983-88; assoc. prof. dept. chem. engring. U. Fla., Gainesville, 1988-92, prof. dept. chem. engring., 1992—. Contbr. articles to profl. jours. Mem. AIChE (area chmn. 1990-92), Nat. Assn. Corrosion Engrs. (rsch. com. 1992—), Electrochem. Soc. (assoc. editor, Electrochem. and Solid State Letters). Achievements include development of measurement model techniques for electrochemical impedance spectroscopy and optically stimulated deep-level impedance spectroscopy for characterization of semiconductors. Office: Univ Fla Dept Chem Engring Gainesville FL 32611

ORAZI, ATTILIO, anatomic pathologist, researcher, educator; b. Milan, Aug. 2, 1954; came to U.S., 1992; naturalized, 2001; s. Luigi Mario and Giulia (Formiga) O.; m. Maria Lupieri; children: Giulia, Rita. MD cum laude, U. Milan, 1979; specialist in anatomic pathology, U. Pavia, Italy, 1987; specialist in hematology, U. Milan, 1991. Diplomate Am. Bd. Pathology. Intern U. Milan, 1979-80; resident physician Ballochmyle Hosp., Mauchline, Scotland, 1980-81; sr. house officer Leicester (Eng.) Royal Inf., 1981-82; registrar in pathology Northampton (Eng.) Gen. Hosp., 1982-83; postdoctoral fellow Nat. Cancer Inst., Milan, 1983-85, staff pathologist, 1985-92; assoc. prof. pathology, dir. immunohistochemistry Ind. U. Sch. Medicine, Indpls., 1992-97, prof. pathology, 1997-98, Coll. Physicians and Surgeons, Columbia U., 1998—2001; dir. divsn. hematopathology Columbia U., The Presbyn. Hosp., N.Y.C., 1998—2001; dir. divsn. hematopathology Sch. of Medicine Ind. U., Indpls., 2001—. Contbr. numerous sci. reports, book chpts., editls. to profl. jours. including Nature Genetics, Lab. Invest., Procs. NAS USA, Am. Jour. Physiology, Blood, Am. Jour. Surg. Pathology, Am. Jour. Clin. Pathology, Cancer Rsch., Jour. Clin. Oncology, Exptl. Hematology, Brit. Jour. Haematology. Fellow, Royal Coll. Pathology, 1995. Fellow Royal Coll. Pathology; mem. Internat. Acad. Pathology, Royal Coll. Pathology, European Assn. for Haematopathology, Am. Soc. Hematopathology. Republican. Roman Catholic. Achievements include research on clinical and experimental hematology; on diagnostic hematopathology; spleen and bone marrow pathology. Office: Ind U Sch Medicine Riley Hosp Ind U Med Ctr 702 Barnhill Dr Rm 0969 Indianapolis IN 46202 E-mail: aorazi@iupui.edu.

ORBACH, RAYMOND LEE, physicist, educator; b. Los Angeles, July 12, 1934; s. Morris Albert and Mary Ruth (Miller) O.; m. Eva Hannah Spiegler, Aug. 26, 1956; children: David Miller, Deborah Hedwig, Thomas Randolph. BS, Calif. Inst. Tech., 1956; PhD, U. Calif., Berkeley, 1960; PhD in Policy Analysis (hon.), The Rand Grad. Sch., Santa Monica, Calif., 2002. NSF postdoctoral fellow Oxford U., 1960-61; asst. prof. applied physics Harvard U., 1961-63; prof. physics UCLA, 1963-92, asst. vice chancellor acad. change and curriculum devel., 1970-72, chmn. acad. senate L.A. divsn., 1976-77, provost Coll. Letters and Sci., 1982-92; chancellor U. Calif., Riverside, 1992—2002, chancellor emeritus, Disting. Prof. Physics emeritus, 2002—; dir. office sci. U.S. Dept. Energy, Washington, 2002—. Mem. physics adv. panel NSF, 1970-73; mem. vis. com. Brookhaven Nat. Lab., 1970-74; mem. materials rsch. lab. adv. panel NSF, 1974-77; mem. Nat. Commn. on Rsch., 1978-80; chmn. 16th Internat. Conf. on Low Temperature Physics, 1981; Joliot Curie prof. Ecole Superieure de la Physique et Chimie Industrielle de la Ville de Paris, 1982, chmn. Gordon Rsch. Conf. on Fractals, 1986; Lorentz prof. U. Leiden, Netherlands, 1987; Raymond and Beverly Sackler lectr. Tel Aviv U., 1989; faculty rsch. lectr. UCLA, 1990; Andrew Lawson lectr. U. Calif., Riverside, 1992; mem. external rev. com. Nat. High Magnetic Fields Lab., 1994—. Author: (with A.A. Manenkov) SpinLattice Relaxation in Ionic Solids, 1966; divsn. assoc. editor Phys. Rev. Letters, 1980-83, Jour. Low Temperature Physics, 1980-90, Phys. Rev., 1983—; contbr. articles to profl. jours. Recipient Whitney M. Young Humanitarian award Urban League of Riverside and San Bernardino, 1998, El Sol Azteca award La Prensa Hispana, 2000; Alfred P. Sloan Found. fellow, 1963-67; NSF sr. postdoctoral fellow Imperial Coll., 1967-68; Guggenheim fellow Tel Aviv U., 1973-74. Fellow Am. Phys. Soc. (chmn. nominations com. 1981-82, counselor-at-large 1987-91, chmn. divsn. condensed matter 1990-91); mem. AAAS (chairperson steering group physics sect.), NSF (mem. rsch. adv. com. divsn. materials 1992-93), Phys. Soc. (London), Univ. Rsch. Assn. (chair coun. pres. 1993), Sigma Xi, Phi Beta Kappa, Tau Beta Pi. Home: 2950 Van Ness St NW Apt 212 Washington DC 20008 Office: Office of Sci Dept Energy 1000 Independence Ave SW Washington DC 20585

ORBACZ, LINDA ANN, physical education educator; b. Schenectady, N.Y., June 29, 1948; d. Victor and Genevieve (Stempkowski) O. AAS, Ulster C.C., Stone Ridge, N.Y., 1969; BS, So. Ill. U., 1972; MA, George Washington U., 1982. Cert. permanent tchr., N.Y. Tchr., coach Ellenville (N.Y.) Ctrl. Sch., 1972-73, New Fairfield (Conn.) Sch., 1973-75, Middletown (N.Y.) City Sch., 1975-84, Liberty (N.Y.) Ctrl. Sch., 1984-86; dir. athletics, phys. edn. tchr., coach Newburgh (N.Y.) Enlarged City Sch., 1986—. Alumni adv. Ulster County C.C., Stone Ridge, 1981—. Softball, soccer and basketball coach, Newburgh, 1987-92, softball, field hockey, basketball and cheerleading coach Ellenville, Middletown, New Fairfield, Liberty, 1972-86. Recipient Presdl. Sports award Sports Fitness, Washington, 1988, 94. Mem. Am. Alliance Health, Phys. Edn., Recreation and Dance, N.Y. State Alliance Health, Phys. Edn., Recreation and Dance. Avocations: nautilus weight tng., phys. conditioning, in-line skating, skiing, aerobic exercise. Office: Gardnertown Fundamental Magnet Sch 6 Plattekill Tpke Newburgh NY 12550-1708

ORCUTT, BEN AVIS, retired social work educator; b. Falco, Ala., Oct. 17, 1914; d. Benjamin A. and Emily Olive Adams; m. Harry P. Orcutt, 1946 (dec.). AB, U. Ala., 1936; MA, Tulane U., 1939, MSW, 1942; DSW, Columbia U., 1962. Social worker ARC, Lagarde Gen. Hosp., New Orleans; social worker, acting field dir. Fort Benning (Ga.) Regional Hosp., 1942-46; chief social work svc. VA Regional Office, Phoenix, 1946—51; chief social work svc. unit outpatient office VA, Birmingham, Ala., 1954-57, 58; rsch. asst. Rsch. Ctr. Sch. Social Work, Columbia U., N.Y.C., 1960-62, field advisor social work, 1962, assoc. prof. social work, 1965-76, La. State U., Baton Rouge, 1962-65; prof. social work, dir. doctoral program U. Ala., University, 1976-84; ret. Rsch. cons. Tavistock Centre, London, 1972; cons. sch. social work U. Houston, 1990, Troy State System, 1992. Author: Science and Inquiry in Social Work Practice, 1990, (with Harry P. Orcutt) America's Riding Horses, 1958, (with Elizabeth R. Prichard, Jean Collard, Austin H. Kutscher, Irene Seeland, Nathan Lefkowitz) Social Work with the Dying Patient and the Family, 1977, (with others) Social Work and Thanatology, 1980; editor: Poverty and Social Casework Services, 1974; mem. editl. bd. Jour. Social Work, 1982-84; contbr. articles to profl. books and jours. Mem. alumni bd. Sch. Social Work Columbia U., 1985—88, 1991—94. Recipient Centennial award for edn. Columbia U. Sch. Social Work, 1998; named to Ala. Social Work Hall of Fame, 1999; NIMH fellow, 1957-60. Mem. NASW, Ala. Conf. Social Welfare, Group for Advancement Doctoral Edn. (steering com., editor newsletter 1980-83), Zonta, others. Episcopalian. Home: 222 Fox Run Tuscaloosa AL 35406 Office: PO Box 870314 Tuscaloosa AL 35487-0314

ORDINACHEV, JOANN LEE, educator; b. Rogers, Ark., Mar. 17, 1936; d. Floyd Andrew and Irene Elnora Elizabeth (Slinkard) Walkenbach; m. J. Dean Harter, Dec. 24, 1953 (div. 1977); m. Miles Donald Ordinachev, Mar. 11, 1978. B.S. cum laude, U. Mo., 1971; M.A.T., Webster U., 1974; PhD, St. Louis U., 1989. Cert. spl. ed. adminstr., dir., counselor. Office mgr. Edwards Constrn. Co., Joplin, Mo., 1954-58; with Jasper Welfare Office, Joplin, 1958-61; tchr. St. Louis Archdiocean, 1963-68, 70-71; TV personality, tchr. Sta. KDMO Cablevision, Carthage, Mo., 1968-69; tech. reading and remedial math. specialist applied tech. divsn. Spl. Sch. Dist., St. Louis, 1974-89, crisis counselor and co-chair guidance office, 1989-90, chair guidance office, 1990—; owner Jody's Dyslexia Lab., Concord Village, Mo., 1982—. Bd. dirs. Heritage House Apts., Heritage Housing Found., Inc., Metro St. Louis Tchrs. Housing Corp., 1989-92; bd. trustees St. Louis C.C., 1995; active League of Women Voters. Mem. NEA, Am. Vocat. Assn., Mo. Vocat. Assn., Spl. Dist. Tchrs. Assn. (pres. 1980-81), Orton Dyslexia Soc., Sch. Psychologists Assn., Council Exceptional Children, Network for Women Psychologist. Democrat. Eastern Orthodox. Office: Spl Sch Dist 1700 Derhake Rd Florissant MO 63033-6419

ORDORICA, STEVEN ANTHONY, obstetrician, gynecologist, educator; b. N.Y.C., Jan. 4, 1957; s. Vincent and Rose (Goiricelaya) O. BA magna cum laude, NYU, 1979; MD, Stony Brook U., 1983. Diplomate Am. Coll. Obstetrics and Gynecology, speciality cert. maternal-fetal medicine; lic. Nat. Bd. Med. Examiners. Resident obstetrics and gynecology NYU-Bellevue Hosp. Ctr., 1983-87, fellow maternal-fetal medicine, 1987-89, instr. obstetrics-gynecology, 1989-91; clin. instr. obstetrics-gynecology NYU, 1986-89, asst. prof. ob/gyn., 1989—2001, clin. assoc. prof. ob/gyn., 2001—; dir. perinatal clinics and prenatal diagnostic unit Gouverneur Hosp., N.Y.C., 1989-94. Perinatal cons. Bellevue Hosp. Ctr., N.Y.C., 1989—; faculty mem. perinatal div. NYU Med. Ctr., 1989—; presenter in field. Contbr. articles to Surgery, Am. Jour. Obstetrics and Gynecology, Am. Jour. Perinatal, Surgery, Obstetrics and Gynecology, Jour. Reproductive Medicine, Acta Geneticae Medicae et Gemellologiae, Jour. Rheumatology. Named NYU scholar; recipient Founder's Day award, NYU, Wash. Sq. Alumni award. Mem. Am. Coll. Obstetrics and Gynecology, Soc. Perinatal Obstetricians, N.Y. Acad. Scis., N.Y. State Perinatal Soc., AMA, Phi Beta Kappa, Beta Lambda Sigma. Achievements include research in investigating aspects of maternal-fetal physiology. Office: NYU Med Ctr 530 1st Ave Ste 10Q New York NY 10016-6402

O'REAR, EDGAR ALLEN, III, chemical engineering educator; b. Jasper, Ala., Feb. 24, 1953; s. Edgar Allen O'Rear Jr. and Edith Idzorek. BSChemE, Rice U., 1975; SM in Organic Chemistry, MIT, 1977; PhD, Rice U., 1981. Rsch. engr. Exxon Rsch. and Engring., Baytown, Tex., summer 1975; asst. prof. to assoc. prof. U. Okla., Norman, 1981-91, Conoco disting. lectr., 1987-92, prof., 1991—, dir. Bioengring. Ctr., 1999—, assoc. dean rsch. Coll. Engring., 1995-99. Vis. sr. rschr. Hitachi Cen. Rsch. Lab., Kokubunji, Japan, summer 1988; vis. scientist RIKEN-Inst. for Phys. and Chem. Rsch., Wako-Shi, Japan, summer 1992; vis. prof. Chulalongkorn U., Bangkok, Thailand; cons. Boehringer-Mannheim, Indpls., Baxter-Travenol, Deerfield, Ill., Associated Metallurgists, Norman; co-founder Inst. for Applied Surfactant Rsch.; organizer symposia; reviewer for funding agys. and profl. jours. Co-author: Fluid Mechanics Exam File, 1985; contbr. tech. articles to profl. jours. Usher, mem. parish coun. St. Thomas More U. Parish, Norman, GlenMary Home Missioners; People to People Phys. Scientist Del. to China; mentor Big Bros.,Big Sisters, Norman, 1984-86. Recipient Faculty Rsch. award Sigma Xi, 1986, 2003; rsch. grantee NSF, NIH, Whitaker Found., NASA, AHA, OCAST, Dept. of Def. Fellow Am. Inst. for Med. and Biol. Engring.; mem. AIChE, AAAS, Internat. Soc. Biorheology (sec. gen. 1992-99, v.p. 1999-2002, pres. 2002—), Am. Chem. Soc., Tau Beta Pi. Roman Catholic. Achievements include patent for production of polymeric films from a surfactant template; method and composition for treatment of thrombosis in a mammal. Office: U Okla Dept Chem Engring SEC T335 100 E Boyd St Norman OK 73019-1000

O'REILLY, FRANCES LOUISE, academic administrator; b. Great Falls, Mont., Feb. 20, 1947; d. Francis Joseph and Bernadine Madeline (DeRose) O'R. BA in Sociology and English, Carroll Coll., 1969; MBA, U. Mont., 1977. Head Start tchr. Rocky Mountain Devel. Coun., Helena, Mont., 1969, social svc. dir. Head Start, 1970-76; rsch. asst. U. Mont., Missoula, 1976, teaching asst., 1976-77; broker, owner Manning & O'Reilly Realty Inc., Great Falls, 1977-81; dir. residence hall Carroll Coll., Helena, 1981—. Dir. residential life Carroll Coll., 1992—, coord. residential life, 1991-92, adj. faculty mem. dept. bus. acctg. & econs., 1982-86, dept. communications, 1991—, dir. summer programs, 1983—, mem. adv. bd. student affairs com., 1983—; social work cons. Office Children Devel. Region #8, Denver, 1970-76; supr. social work practicums Head Start Rocky Mountain Devel. Coun., 1970-76. Vol. Diabetes Found., Helena, 1993-94, various polit. campaigns, Helena, 1993-94. Mem. Mont. Assn. Student Affairs, Beta Gamma Sigma. Avocations: reading, symphony, yoga, aerobics, theater. Office: Carroll Coll PO Box 64 Helena MT 59624-0064

O'REILLY, PATTY MOLLETT, psychometrist, consultant; BA in Psychology, U. Ala., 1978, MA in Devel. Learning and Psychometrics, 1979. Resource tchr. pub. schs., Madison, Ala., 1979-86, Huntsville, Ala., 1986-90; owner, mgr. Huntsville Ednl. Svc., cons., diagnostics, tutoring, 1988—. Supr. grad. teaching students U. Ala., summers 1985-87, lectr. psychology, summer 1993. Mem. Coun. for Exceptional Children. Office: Huntsville Ednl Svc PO Box 1131 Huntsville AL 35807-0131

OREM, CASSANDRA ELIZABETH (SANDRA OREM), small business owner, educator, holistic health consultant and practitioner; b. Balt., Sept. 26, 1940; d. Ira Julius and Mabel Ruth (Peeples) O. Diploma, Ch. Home and Hosp. Sch. Nursing, 1962; BSN with honors, Johns Hopkins U., 1968; MSN, U. Md., 1972; cert., Balt. Sch. Massage, 1988; MA in Applied Psychology, U. Santa Monica, 1991, cert. in advanced applied psychology, 1992; cert., Waitley Masters Coaching Prog., 1996; postgrad., U. of the South, 2000—. Staff, charge nurse Ch. Home and Hosp., Balt., 1962-63; asst. instr. Ch. Home and Hosp. Sch. Nursing, Balt., 1963-64, instr., 1964-70; student rschr., clin.-primary investigator U. Md. Sch. Nursing, Balt., 1971-72; clin. nurse specialist Johns Hopkins Hosp., Balt., 1972-77, rsch., clin. co-investigator, 1975, asst. dir. nursing, 1977-79, asst. adminstr., DON, 1979-87; clin. assoc. faculty Johns Hopkins U. Sch. Nursing, 1984-87; program dir., instr. intermediate massage course Balt. Sch. Massage, 1988-98, instr., 1988—2001, instr. advanced massage course, 1991-98, program dir. advanced massage course, 1995-98, curriculum devel. coord., 1996-98, network mktg. cons., 1991—; ptnr., educator UBP Assocs., 1990-91. Pres. Nursing Edn. and Cons. Svc., Inc., Balt., 1976-78, Oasis Health Systems, Inc., Balt., 1987—; spkr. workshop facilitator, cons. profl. topics, Health and Wellness, Personal Growth, Time Mgmt., 1973—; mem. adv. bd. Integrative Medicine Nursing Consult Integrative Medicine Comm., 1999-2000. Author: (profl. booklet, audio publs.) Patient Education Book and Related Materials, 1977, Time Management/Organizing Sys., 1995; contbr. chpts. and articles to profl. jours. Vol. Office on Aging, Balt., 1982-83, Boy Scouts Am., Balt., 1984-85, Cathedral of the Incarnation, Children's Peace Ctr., Balt., 2000-01, Help Increase the Peace Program for/with Children, 2000—. Mem. Am. Holistic Nurses' Assn., Ch. Home and Hosp. Sch. Nursing Alumni Assn. (treas. 1970-72, pres.-elect 1975-76), Am. Massage Therapy Assn., Md. Massage Therapy Assn., U. Md. Alumnae Assn., Sigma Theta Tau (Pi chpt.). Democrat. Episcopalian. Avocations: camping, photography, pets, birding, music.

ORENSTEIN, JANIE ELIZABETH, educational association administrator, educator; b. Winston-Salem, N.C., Mar. 3, 1961; d. William Ralph and Mary Elizabeth (Brantley) Mauney; m. Gary Stephen Catarina, Sept. 10, 1983 (div. Oct. 1991); m. Alan Jay Orenstein, Feb. 13, 1993; children: Sara, Becky. Student, Westchester (N.Y.) C.C., 1985-87. Cert. YMCA sch. age child care dir., Child Devel. Assn. Tchg. asst. The Cottage Sch., Pleasantville, N.Y., 1984-87; program dir. Broward YMCA, Ft. Lauderdale, Fla., 1989—; south teen cluster co. dir. YMCA of USA, Ft. Lauderdale, 1994—. Advisor, coach Spl. Olympics, Ft. Lauderdale, 1992—; presenter Fla. Sch. Age Childcare Coalition, Orlando, Fla., 1992; assessing schoolage quality advisor Wellsley (Mass.) Coll., 1993—, Childcare Connection, North Lauderdale, 1994—; com. mem. Broward County Schs., Ft. Lauderdale, 1993—. Co-mem. United Way, 1989; vol. Safe Place, 1994. Recipient Good Samaritan award Coral Springs Handicapped Com., Coral Springs, Fla., 1990. Mem. Coun. for Exceptional Children. Democrat. Episcopalian. Avocations: youth coaching, soccer, dance, theater. Home: 9815 NW 48th Dr Coral Springs FL 33076-2617 Office: YMCA 7718 Wiles Rd Coral Springs FL 33067-2075

ORENSTEIN, MICHAEL (IAN ORENSTEIN), philatelic dealer, columnist; b. Bklyn., Jan. 6, 1939; s. Harry and Myra (Klein) O.; m. Linda Turer, June 28, 1964; 1 child, Paul David. BS, Clemson U., 1960; postgrad., U. Calif., Berkeley, 1960-61. Career regional mgr. Minkus Stamp & Pub. Co., Calif., 1964-70; mgr. stamp div. Superior Stamp & Coin Co., Inc., Beverly Hills, Calif., 1970-90; dir. stamp divsn. Superior Galleries, Beverly Hills, Calif., 1991-94; dir. space memorabelia Superior Stamp and Coin. Co., Inc., Beverly Hills, Calif., 1992-94; dir. stamp and space divsn. Superior Stamp & Coin an A-Mark Co., Beverly Hills, Calif., 1994-97; sr. buyer, appraiser Superior Stamp & Coin, Beverly Hills, Calif., 1997-2000; v.p., COO Superior Galleries, 2001; co-founder, ptnr., prin., pres. AuroraGalleries Internat., 2002—; pres. Aurora Galleries, 2002—. Cons. Office of Insp. Gen. NASA; cons., expert witness Nassay County Dist. Atty. Author: Stamp Collecting Is Fun, 1990; philatelic advisor/creator The Video Guide To Stamp Collecting, 1988; columnist LA Times, 1965-93; contbr. Brookman Times, Scott Stamp Monthly. With AUS, 1962-64. Recipient Medal of Yuri Gagarin, Fedn. Supporting Russian Cosmonauts, 2002. Mem. AAIA, Am. Stamp Dealers Assn., C.Z. Study Group, German Philatelic Soc., Confederate Stamp Alliance, Am. Philatelic Soc. (writers unit 1975-80, 89-93), Internat. Fedn. Stamp Dealers, Internat. Soc. Appraisers: Stamps, Space Memorabilia. Republican. Avocation: fishing. Address: 19546 Minnehaha Northridge CA 91326

ORESKES, SUSAN, private school educator; b. N.Y.C., May 24, 1930; d. Morris and Sarah (Rudner) Nagin; m. Irwin Oreskes, June 19, 1949; children: Michael, Daniel, Naomi, Rebecca. BA, Queens Coll., 1952; dance student, Eddie Torres Sch., Manhattan, N.Y., 1984-90. Organizer Strycker's Bay Neighborhood Coun., N.Y.C., 1961-75; dir. weekly column cmty. newspaper Enlightenment Press, N.Y.C., 1975-85; assoc. tchr. Riverside Ch. Weekday Sch., N.Y.C., 1985-95. Organizer, v.p. F.D.R.-Woodrow Wilson Polit. Club, Manhattan, 1961-71; organizer Hey Brother Coffee House, 1968; tchg. vol. Am. Mus. Natural History, N.Y.C., 1999—. Democrat. Jewish. Avocations: music, dance, travel. Home: 670 W End Ave New York NY 10025-7313

ORGANEK, NANCY STRICKLAND, nursing educator; b. Middletown, Conn., June 19, 1937; d. Warren Luther and Anna Augusta (Nordquist) Strickland; m. Joseph Richard Organek, May 27, 1961; children: Melissa Lynne, Kelly Anne. BS with honors, U. Conn., 1959, MS, 1979, PhD, 1985; MEd, U. Buffalo, 1967. RN, Conn. Staff nurse, asst. head nurse VA Hosp., West Haven, Conn., 1959-60, Portland (Conn.) Convalescant Ctr., 1976-78; staff nurse VA Hosp., Newington, Conn., 1961; elem. tchr. Balt. Bd. Edn., 1961-62, Buffalo Bd. Edn., 1962-65, Burlington (Mass.) Bd. Edn., 1965-66, Middletown Bd. Edn., 1966-68; asst. prof. nursing U. Conn., Storrs,

1979—. Cons. Mt. Sinai, Hartford, Conn., 1981-90; researcher on adolescent pregnancy; presenter at internat., nat. and local meetings. Contbr. articles to profl. publs. Advisor Portland Bd. Edn./Health Coun., 1980-84; rep. Task Force on Domestic Violence, Hartford, 1979-80; speaker Portland High Sch., 1981. Mem. ANA, NAACOG, Nat. Assn. Neonatal Nurses, N.Am. Nursing Diagnosis Assn., Ea. Nursing Rsch. Soc., Conn. Perinatal Assn., Conn. Nurses Assn. (Svc. award 1984), Conn. Assn. Neonatal Nurses, Sigma Theta Tau (officer 1985-87), Pi Lambda Theta (honors 1981). Avocations: skiing, ceramics. Home: 179 E Cotton Hill Rd Portland CT 06480-1036 Office: U Conn 26u231 Glenbrook Rd Storrs Mansfield CT 06268

ORIANS, GORDON HOWELL, biology educator; b. Eau Claire, Wis., July 10, 1932; s. Howard Lester and Marion Meta (Senty) O.; m. Elizabeth Ann Newton, June 25, 1955; children: Carlyn Elizabeth, Kristin Jean, Colin Mark. BS, U. Wis., 1954; PhD, U. Calif., Berkeley, 1960. Asst. prof. zoology U. Wash., Seattle, 1960-64, assoc. prof., 1964-68, prof., 1968-95, prof. emeritus, 1995—. Active Wash. State Ecol. Commn., Olympia, 1970-75, ecology adv. com. EPA, Washington, 1974-79; assembly life scis. NAS/NRC, Washington, 1977-83, environ. studies and toxicology bd., 1991—. Author: Some Adaptations of Marsh Nesting Blackbirds, 1980, Blackbirds of the Americas, 1985, Life: The Science of Biology, 2000; editor: Biodiversity and Ecosystem Processes in Tropical Forests, 1996. 1st lt. U.S. Army, 1955-56. Mem. AAAS, NAS, Am. Inst. Biol. Scis. (Disting. Svc. award 1994), Am. Ornithologists Union (Brewster award 1976), Am. Soc. Naturalists, Animal Behavior Soc., Royal Netherlands Acad. Arts and Scis., Orgn. for Tropical Studies (pres. 1988-94), Ecol. Soc. Am. (v.p. 1975-76, pres. 1995-96, Eminent Ecologist award 1998). Avocations: hiking, opera. Office: U Wash Dept Zoology PO Box 351800 Seattle WA 98195-1800 E-mail: blackbrd@serv.net.

ORIJI, GIBSON K. medical educator, medical researcher; b. Port Harcourt, Rivers, Nigeria, Dec. 13, 1960; arrived in U.S., 1981; s. Frank M. and Cecilia N. Oriji; m. Mary A. Bates, May 13, 1985; children: Gordon, Guyton, Gilbert. BSce/trf in Med. Tech., Rivers State U. Sci. and Tech., Port Harcourt, Nigeria, 1980; BS in Biology, Tex. So. U., 1983; PhD in Physiology, Howard U., 1992. Med. tech. bd. cert. Instr. dept. biology Tex. So. U., Houston, 1983—85; instr., grad. tchg. asst. dept. physiology and biophysics Howard U. Coll. Medicine, Washington, 1987—92; postdoctoral fellow Health Sci. Ctr., Coll. Medicine U. Tenn., Memphis, 1992—94; intramural rsch. fellow NIH, Bethesda, Md., 1994—98; asst. prof. biology William Paterson U., Wayne, NJ, 1998—. Sci. dir. Pre-Colege Acad. Program, Wayne, 1998—; adj. prof. biology Prince George's CC, Largo, Md., 1997—98, Largo, 2002. Sci. rsch. faculty liaison Pathways to Acad. Success, Wayne, 1998—2002. Biochemist Army Med. Svc. Commn. Corps. Res., 1997—. Walter Reed Army Med. Ctr., Washington. Grantee Rsch., Ctr. Rsch., 2002. Mem.: Am. Physiol. Soc. (sci. rsch. faculty liaison 1998—2002, Undergraduate Summer Rsch. 2001-2002). Office: William Paterson U 300 Pompton Rd Wayne NJ 07470 Office Fax: 973-720-2338. Business E-Mail: Orijig@wpunj.edu.

O'RILEY, KAREN E. principal; b. L.A. BA, Loyola Marymount U., L.A., 1981; MPA, Calif. State U., 1983. Home: PO Box 261005 Encino CA 91426-1005

ORITSKY, MIMI, artist, educator; b. Reading, Pa., Aug. 14, 1950; d. Herbert and Marcia (Sarna) O. Student, Phila. Coll. Art, 1968-70; BFA, Md. Inst. Coll. Art, 1975; MFA, U. Pa., 1979. Artist, supr. subway mural projects Crisis Intervention Network, Phila., 1978-83; instr. painting U. Arts, Phila., 1984, 89-93, Abington Art Ctr., Jenkintown, Pa., 1989—, Main Line Art Ctr., Haverford, Pa., 1993—. One-woman shows include Gross McCleaf Gallery, 1980-82, Callowhill Art Gallery, Reading, Pa., Amos Eno Gallery, N.Y.C., 1986, 89, 91, 94, 96, 98, 2001, 03, Hahnemann U. Gallery, Phila., 1988, Kauffman Gallery, Shippensburg, Pa., 1989, 97, Kimberton (Pa.) Gallery, 1990, Rittenhouse Galleries, Phila., 1992-94, A.I.R. Gallery, N.Y.C., 2003; exhibited in group shows at Current Representational Painting in Phila., 1980, Gross McCleaf Gallery, 1980-82, Yearsley Spring Gallery, Phila., 1998, Phila. Art Alliance, 1998, Coll. Art Gallery, Trenton, NJ, 1996, 98, 2000, Abington Art Ctr., 1999, Brattleboro Mus., TW Wood Mus., Montshire Mus., Phila. Art Alliance, Florence Griswold Mus., 2002-03; pub. in NewAmerican Paintings, 2000. Recipient Purchase award Pa. Coun. Arts and Arcadia Coll., 1983, Reading Pub. Mus., 1984, Best of Show award Abington Art Ctr. Juried Annual, 1998; fellow Environment Found., 1980, Millay Colony for Arts, 1983. Mem. Coll. Art Assn. E-mail: gill1313@aol.com.

ORKAND, RICHARD KENNETH, neurobiologist, researcher, educator; b. N.Y.C., Apr. 23, 1936; BS, Columbia U., 1956; PhD, U. Utah, 1961; MA, U. Pa., 1974. Fellow U. Coll. London, 1961-64, Harvard U., Boston, 1964-66; asst. prof. U. Utah, Salt Lake City, 1966-68; prof. UCLA, 1968-74; prof., chmn. U. Pa., Phila., 1974-86; prof. U. P.R., San Juan, from 1986, dir. Inst. Neurobiology, 1986-96; Benjamin Meaker prof. U. Bristol, 1993; adj. prof. biology Calif. Poly. U., San Luis Obispo, from 1993. Exec. dir. Caribbean Neurosci. Found., 1987-97; mem. adv. coun. Conservation Trust of P.R., 1990-94; councilor AAAS, Caribbean, 1990-95. Co-author: Introduction to Nervous Systems, 1977; contbr. over 80 articles to profl. jours. Mem. com. Dem. Party, Phila., 1981. Recipient Laufberger medal Czech Physiology Soc., 1997; Fulbright grantee, 1999. Fellow AAAS. Achievements include research in studies of physiology of neuroglia and neuron-glia interaction. Home: San Juan, PR. Died Jan. 13, 2002.

ORLANDO, KATHERINE KAY, elementary education educator; b. Washington, Sept. 24, 1963; d. Samuel Paul and Mary Jean (Ruby) O. BS in Elem. Edn., U. Md., 1985, MEd in Curriculum and Instrn., 1990; postgrad., Johns Hopkins U. Cert. tchr., adminstr., supr., Md. Tchr., team leader Howard County Pub. Schs., Ellicott City, Md., 1986—. Adj. prof. early childhood edn. Frederick (Md.) C.C., 1992—. Author sci. curriculum materials. Leader Youth Cath. Edn., 1988-90; tchr. Sunday sch. Black Student Achievement Program, Ellicott City, 1991. Mem. ASCD, Tchrs. Applying Whole Lang. (bd. dirs. 1992—), Pi Lambda Theta. Roman Catholic. Avocations: crafts, tennis, dancing. Home: 1607 Fallston Rd Fallston MD 21047-1625

ORLIK, CHRISTINA BEAR, music educator; b. Detroit, Nov. 10, 1945; d. Robert William and Olive Marie (Evans) Bear; m. Peter Blythe Orlik, Aug. 18, 1967; children: Darcy Anne, Blaine Truen. BS in Edn., Wayne State U., 1967, MS in Edn., 1969. Tchr. clarinet pvt. practice, Detroit, 1961-69; elem. band dir. City Recreation Dept., Troy, Mich, 1964-67; dir. bands Crary Jr. High Sch., Waterford, Mich, 1967-69; instr. woodwind pvt. practice, Mt. Pleasant, Mich, 1970-84; dir. bands Montabella Jr. High Sch., Blanchard, Mich, 1974-76; substitute tchr. Mt. Pleasant Schs., 1976-84, libr. media profl., 1984-85, tchr. gen. music, 1985—, orch. dir., 1987—. Part-time instr. Ctrl. Mich. U. Tchr. Edn., 1989—91; organizing mem., mgr. Ctrl. Mich. Cmty. Band, Mt. Pleasant, 1973—75; clarinetist, bassoonist Alma (Mich.) Symphony Orch., 1973—86, Eddy Concert Band, Saginaw, Mich., 1973—2000; founder, mgr. Four for Strings orch. festival, 1991—. Tchr. Sunday sch. St. Andrew's Episcopal Ch., Clawson, Mich., 1966-67; treas., mem. chair LWV, Mt. Pleasant, 1972-73; chair Child Care Adv. Com., Mt. Pleasant, 1973-74. Mem. Am. String Tchrs. Assn. (program review grantee 1990), Mich. Edn. Assn., ch. Sch. Band and Orch. Assn. (Dist. 5 Orch. Tchr. of Yr. 2000), Music Educators Nat. Conf. Avocation: dancing. Home: 613 Kane St Mount Pleasant MI 48858-1949 Office: West Intermediate Sch 440 S Bradley St Mount Pleasant MI 48858-3052

ORLOWSKA-WARREN, LENORE ALEXANDRIA, art educator, fiber artist; b. Detroit, May 22, 1951; d. William Leonard and Aloisa Clara (Hrapkiewicz) Orlowski; m. Donald Edward Warren, May 11, 1990. AA, Henry Ford C.C., 1972; BS in Art Edn., Wayne State U., 1974, M in Spl. Edn., 1978; BFA, Ctr. for Creative Studies, 2000. Tchr. arts and crafts Detroit Pub. Schs., 1974—2002; fiber artist Detroit Inst. Arts. Cons. Arts Detroit Cmty. Plan, TRIACO Arts & Crafts, 1996—; instr., demonstrator weaving Detroit Inst. Arts; represented by Gallery Five, Tequesta, Fla., Ann Arbor Art Ctr. One-woman show at Dearborn C. of C., Ctr. for Creative Studies, 2000; exhibited in group shows, including alumni exhibit Henry Ford C.C., 1989, Detroit Artist Market, 1995-2000, Scarab Club, 1996, Lansing Art Gallery, 1997, Ctr. for Creative Studies, 1997, Yr. of the Woman Exhibit, 1998, Tom Thompson Meml. Art Gallery Juried Ontario Artists Exhibit, 1998, 2001, One Focus, Two Worlds Exhibit, 1999, Fashion Exhibit and Felt the Feeling of Fiber, U.245 Gallery, 1999, Ctr. Creative Studies, 2000, Ann Arbor Art Ctr., 2001, Downriver Coun. for the Arts, 2001, Alumni Fiber Artist exhibit Coll. Creative Studies, 2002, Ann Arbor Art Ctr. All Media Exhbn., 2002 (Barbara Dorr Meml. award), Outside The Lines Gallery, 2001, 02, Padziewski Gallery, 2003, Scarab Club, 2003; contbr. to Sch. Arts Mag.; represented in permanent collections Gallery Five, Tequesta, Fla., Ann Arbor Art Ctr. Mem. exec. bd. Springwells Pk. Assn., 1989-99, pres., 1994-96, chairperson youth act workshops; com. mem. Dearborn cmty. art coun. Art on the Ave., 1993-99, Gallery Crawl chairperson, 1998; chair Nat. Woman's History Month workshop, 1995. Mem.: Cranbrook Acad. Art, Am. Tapestry Alliance, Art Inst. of Chgo., Downriver Coun. for Arts, Surface Design Assn., The Textile Mus., The Nat. Mus. Women in Art Williamsburg Burgesses, Met. Mus. Art, Norton Mus. Art (Williamsburg assoc.), Mich. Surface Design, Friends of Fiber Art Internat. Assn., Coll. Art Assn., Birmingham Bloomfield Art Assn., Detroit Inst. Arts-Founders Soc., Am. Craft Coun., Mich. Art Edn. Assn. (presenter art advocacy workshop), Nat. Art Edn. Assn. (electronic gallery coord. 1992—99). Avocations: fiber art, travel, colonial gardening, reading colonial history and biographies. Home: 10 Berwick Ln Dearborn MI 48120-1102

ORLOWSKI, KAREL ANN, elementary school educator; b. Fremont, Ohio, Dec. 22, 1949; d. Karl and Angeline Marie (Oudersluys) Kooistra; m. Paul Joseph Orlowski, Apr. 28, 1973; 1 child, Jennifer Frann. BA in Music Edn., U. Mich., 1971; MS in Elem. Edn., Dowling Coll., Oakdale, N.Y., 1978. Cert. tchr., N.Y. Tchr. vocal music Patchogue (N.Y.)-Medford Schs., 1971—, lead tchr. music dept., 1986-88, 91-94; dir. of musicals Eagle Elem. Sch., 1990-94. Dir. drama dept. River Elem. Sch., Patchogue, 1974-90, Chosen Few show choir South Ocean Mid. Sch., Patchogue, 1984-90, Notation! show choir Eagle Elem. Sch., 1990-94, 95—, A Chords show choir Barton Elem. Sch., 1994-95. Mem. N.Y. State Sch. Music Assn., Suffolk County Music Educators Assn. (co-chmn. so. divsn. I chorus 1993-95, divsn. II S.W. chorus 1996-97; asst. v.p. divsn. I festivals 1997-98, exec. v.p. for festivals 1998-2000, mem. standing coms. 1999-2000, co-chmn. membership 2003—). Republican. Episcopalian. Avocations: reading, renaissance music, vocal jazz, nascar sk class and figure-eight racing. Home: 37 Detmer Rd East Setauket NY 11733-1912 Office: Patchogue-Medford Schs 241 S Ocean Ave Patchogue NY 11772-3787

ORME, MELISSA EMILY, mechanical engineering educator; b. Glendale, Calif, Mar. 12, 1961; d. Myrl Eugene and Geraldine Irene (Schmuck) O.; m. Vasilis Zissis Marmarelis, Mar. 12, 1989; children: Zissis Eugene and Myrl Galinos (twins). BS, U. So. Calif., L.A., 1984, MS, 1985, PhD, 1989. Rsch. asst. prof. U. So. Calif., 1990-93; asst. prof. U. Calif., Irvine, 1993-96, assoc. prof., 1996—2002, prof. engring., 2002—. Panel reviewer NSF, Arlington, Va., 1993—; cons. MPM Corp., Boston, 1993-97. Contbr. articles to profl. jour. Recipient Young Investigator award NSF, 1994, Arch T. Colwell Merit award SAE, 1994. Mem. AAUW, AIAA, ASME, Am. Phys. Soc., Minerals, Metals and Materials Soc. Achievements include 14 US patents. Office: U Calif Dept Mech Engring Irvine CA 92697-0001

ORMISTON, PATRICIA JANE, elementary education educator; b. Flint, Mich., Aug. 22, 1938; d. Elmer A. and Katheryn Lucille (Day) Knudson; m. Lester Murray Ormiston, June 13, 1964; 1 child, Brian Todd. BS, Minot State U., 1962; postgrad., U. Mont., 1963—, Mont. State U., 1963—, Western Mont. Coll., 1987. Elem. tchr. Lowell Sch., Gt. Falls, Mont., 1958, Webster Sch., Williston, N.D., 1958-59, Plaza (N.D.) Pub. Sch., 1959-61, Cen. Sch., Helena, Mont., 1962-63, Elrod Sch., Sch. Dist. 5, Kalispell, Mont., 1963—. Core team Onward to Excellence, Sch. Dist. 5, Kalispell, 1989-92; participant Rocky Mountain Nat. Outcome-Based Edn. Conf., Greeley, Colo., 1990; presenter Kendall Hunt Lit. Reading Unit, Phi Delta Kappa, Kalispell, 1991, Mont. Assn. Gifted Talented Edn., 1991, Word Conf., Seattle, 1993; inst. presenter, symposium spkr. Utah Coun. Internat. Reading Assn. 28th Ann. State Reading Conf., Salt Lake City, 1994; univ. supr. student tchrs. Mont. State U., Bozeman, 1994—; mem. adv. bd. Kendall Hunt Pub. Co., Dubuque, Iowa, 1991—; symposium spkr., mem. reading coun., coun. tchrs. English S.D. State Conf., Mitchell, 1994; symposium spkr. Five Valleys Reading Conf. U. Mont., Missoula, 1994; insvc. presenter South Whidbey Intermediate Sch., Langley, Wash., 1994. Contbr. author lit. based reading units 2d grade level Kentall Hunt Pub. Co., Dubuque, Iowa, 1989—; author: PEGASUS Integrating Themes in Literature and Language Correlated to Gages Lake, Illinois State Goals for Learning Language Arts, Grades K-6, 1993, PEGASUS Integrating Themes in Literature and Language Correlated to State of Georgia Quality Core Curriculum for English and Language Arts, Grades K-6, 1994, PEGASUS Integrating Themes in Literature and Language Correlated to State of Indiana Essential Skills English/Language Arts, Grades K-6, 1994, PEGASUS Integrating Themes in Literature and Language Correlated to Dade County Public Schools Competency-Based Curriculum for Language Arts, Grades K-5, 1994. Vol. Conrad Mansion Restoration, Kalispell, 1976—; presenter 34th ann. conv. Lit. Base Reading Internat. Reading Assn., New Orleans, 1989. Named Tchr. of Yr., Kalispell Sch. Dist. 5, 1986; Chpt. 2 grantee, 1987-88; Gertrude Whipple Profl. Devel. grantee IRA, 1988. Mem. NEA, Internat. Reading Assn. (symposium speaker 38th ann. conv. San Antonio 1993), Nat. Coun. Tchrs. English, Kalispell Edn. Assn. (bldg. rep. 1987-88, chmn. profl. acknowledgement com. 1988-93), Nat. Hist. Preservation, Phi Delta Kappa, Delta Kappa Gamma. Avocations: reading, writing, hiking, skiing, golf. Home: PO Box 64 Kalispell MT 59903-0064 Office: Elrod Sch 3rd Ave W Kalispell MT 59901-4426

ORNSTEIN, DONALD SAMUEL, mathematician, educator; b. N.Y.C., July 30, 1934; s. Harry and Rose (Wisner) O.; m. Shari Richman, Dec. 20, 1964; children— David, Kara, Ethan. Student, Swarthmore Coll., 1950-52; PhD, U. Chgo., 1957. Fellow Inst. for Advanced Study, Princeton, N.J., 1955-57; faculty U. Wis., Madison, 1958-60, Stanford (Calif.) U., 1959—, prof. math., 1966—. Faculty Hebrew U., Jerusalem, 1975-76 Author: Ergodic Theory Randomness and Dynamical Systems, 1974. Recipient Bocher prize Am. Math. Soc., 1974 Mem. NAS, Am. Acad. Arts and Sci. Jewish. Office: Stanford U Dept Math Stanford CA 94305

ORNSTEIN, LIBBIE ALLENE, primary school educator; b. Miami, Fla., Mar. 3, 1949; d. Raymond Gerald and Rose Elaine (Feinberg) Blasberg; m. Morton Jay Ornstein, June 16, 1978; children: Randy Brian, Mark Justin. BEd, U. Miami, Coral Gables, Fla., 1971; MS in Early Childhood Edn., Fla. Internat. U., 1980. Cert. elem., early childhood and spl. edn. tchr., Fla. Spl. edn. tchr. F. Douglas Elem. Sch., Phila., 1973-75; 4th grade tchr. Lorah Park Elem. Sch., Miami, Fla., 1975-76; kindergarten tchr. Charles Drew Elem. Sch., Miami, 1976-79; nursery sch. tchr. Temple Beth Ahm, Cooper City, Fla., 1982-83; 2d grade tchr. Myrtle Grove Elem. Sch., Miami, 1983-86; pk 4 tchr. Univ. Sch., Nova U., Davie, Fla., 1986-88; kindergarten tchr. Pines Lakes Elem. Sch., Pembroke Pines, Fla., 1988—. Cub scout den mother Boy Scouts Am., Plantation, Fla., 1987; mem. ORT, Plantation, 1990. Democrat. Jewish. Avocations: reading, needlework, crafts, sewing. Home: 145 NW 98th Ter Plantation FL 33324-7215 E-mail: kindercop7@aol.com.

OROSZ, PATRICIA ANN, elementary education educator; b. Plainfield, N.J., Mar. 2, 1954; d. Russell and Angelina (Tagliferro) Pagano; m. Ronald Stephen Orosz, Aug. 22, 1980; children: Kevin, Danielle, Marc. Student, Marietta Coll., 1973; BA, BS, Rider Coll., 1976; postgrad., William Paterson Coll., 1977. Cert. K-8 tchr., N.J. Elem. tchr. A.a. Anastasia sch., Long Branch, N.J., 1976-77; tchr. math. and reading Mt. Hebron Sch., Montclair, N.J., 1978-79; tchr. math. and drama Glenfield Sch., Montclair, 1979-80; tchr. gifted and talented Belleville (N.J.) Bd. Edn., 1979-82; elem. tchr., chmn. adv. bd. Pemberton (N.J.) Twp. Bd. Edn., 1986—. Advisor PTA, Marlton and Pemberton, 1990—, Big Sister Program, Marlton, 1992—. Recipient award Gov. of N.J., 1992. Mem. ASCD, N.J. Edn. Assn., N.J. Tchrs. Math. Assn. Home: 29 Buckley Ln Marlton NJ 08053-4925 Office: Emmons Sch Scrapetown Rd Pemberton NJ 08000

O'ROURKE, JAMES, ophthalmologist, pathologist, educator; b. Trenton, N.J., Mar. 2, 1925; s. James Joseph and Mary Francis (Fitzgerald) O'R.; m. Marita Florence Howard, June 12, 1954; children: James, Mary Carol, Elizabeth, Margaret. MD, Georgetown U., 1949; MS, U. Pa., 1954. Diplomate Am. Bd. Ophthalmology. Intern St. Francis Hosp., Trenton, 1949-50; postdoctoral fellow U. Pa., Phila., 1950-52; resident in surgery Wills Eye Hosp., Phila., 1952-54; clin. assoc. NIH, Bethesda, Md., 1954-57; asst. prof. surgery Georgetown U., Washington, 1957-60, assoc. prof., 1960-65, prof. surgery, 1965-69, U. Conn. Health Ctr., Farmington, 1969-83, prof. pathology, 1984—; dir. U. Conn. Vision Ctr., Farmington, 1985—. Adj. prof. engring. Trinity Coll., Hartford, Conn., 1978—; bd. dirs. Fidelco Found., Bloomfield, Conn., Conn. Eye Bank, New Britain. Author: Nuclear Ophthalmology, 1976; contbr. articles to profl. jours. With USNR, 1943-46. NIH grantee, 1957-69, 69-90, 87-92. Mem. Am. Ophthalmology Soc., Am. Soc. for Exptl. Pathology, Soc. Vascular Medicine and Biology, Cosmos Club, Rotary (Paul Harris fellow 1990). Episcopalian. Avocations: american jazz, history, hiking. Home: 113 Main St Farmington CT 06032-2237 Office: U Conn Health Ctr 263 Farmington Ave Farmington CT 06030-0002

O'ROURKE, JOAN B. DOTY WERTHMAN, retired school system administrator; b. N.Y.C., June 7, 1933; d. George E. Doty and Lillian G. Bergen; 10 children. BA summa cum laude, Marymount Manhattan Coll., 1953; MA, Columbia U., 1958; PhD, St. John's U., 1971. Tchr. history Marymount HS, N.Y.C., 1953-55; instr. history Marymount Manhattan Coll., 1957-59; acting chmn. history dept. Nassau C.C., Mineola, NY, 1959-60; prof. history Westchester CC, Valhalla, NY, 1963-74; prin. Pius X Sch., Scarsdale, NY, 1974-77; assoc. dir. alumni rels. Fordham U., N.Y.C., 1980-84; co-founder, dir. Assn. for Profl. Psychol. and Ednl. Counseling, Wilmette, Ill., 1987-91; ptnr., pres. O'Rourke and Assocs., 1993-97; ret., 1997. Dir., writer Sta. WFAS, White Plains, 1963—64; adj. prof. social sci. Fordham U., N.Y.C., 1974—76. Mem. resident bd. Del Webb, Sun City, Calif., 2001—03; mem. fin. com. St. Francis of Assisi Ch., LaQuinta, Calif., 2001—; bd. dirs. Cath. Charities Diocese of San Bernardino, 2001—, Sun City, Palm Desert, 2001—03, Cath. Charities of San Bernardino, Calif., 1999—. Recipient Alumni award, Marymount Coll., 1988, Mother Raymunde McKay Cmty. Svc. award, Marymount Manhattan Coll., 1993; Tchg. fellow, St. John's U., Jamaica, N.Y., 1968. Mem.: Mich. Shores Club, Order of Holy Sepulchre (lady), Soc. Mayflowers Descs. Ill. Democrat. Roman Catholic. E-mail: doctorjoan@web.tv.net.

O'ROURKE, ROBERT A. cardiologist, educator; b. San Francisco, Calif., June 12, 1936; m. Suzann Reiter, June 8, 1963; children: Michael, Kevin, Sean, Kathleen, Ryan. Student, Santa Clara U., 1954-55; BS, Creighton U., 1957, MD, 1961. Diplomate Am. Bd. Internal Medicine, Am. Bd. Cardiology. Straight med. internship Georgetown U. Hosp., Washington, 1961-62, jr. asst. resident internal medicine, 1962-63, sr. asst. resident internal medicine, 1963-64, med. houseofficer internal medicine, 1961-65, fellow cardiology dept., 1964-65, instr. in medicine cardiology, 1968-69; fellow U. Calif Cardiovasc. Rsch. Inst., Washington, 1965-66; staff cardiologist Madagan Army Hosp., Washington, 1966-68; asst. prof. medicine cardiology coll. medicine U. Ariz., Tucson, 1969-70; asst. prof. medicine cardiology, dir. clin. cardiology section, dir. heart station U. Calif., San Diego, 1970-73, assoc. prof. medicine cardiology, dir. clin. cardiology section, dir. coronary care unit, assoc. dir. myocardial infarction rsch. unit, 1973-76; acting chief medicine Audie L. Murphy Vets. Adminstrn. Hosp., 1977-78; Charles Conrad Brown disting. prof. cardiovasc. disease, dir. cardiovasc. divsn. U. Tex. Health Sci. Ctr., San Antonio, 1976—. Cons. in field for various hosps.; vis. professorships to various med. ctrs./univs. Mem. editl. bd.: Jour. Am. Coll. Cardiology, 1983-87, Am. Jour. Cardiology, 1976-81, 83—, Am. Heart Jour., 1980—, Clin. Cardiology, 1985—, Jour. Intensive Care Medicine, 1985—, Internat. Jour. Cardiology, 1981—, Annals of Internal Medicine, 1979-82, Med. Month, 1983—, Weekly Update: Cardiology, 1978-80, Cardiovasc. Medicine, 1976-80, Cardiologic Consultation, 1980—, Cardiovasc. Drugs and Therapy, 1989-90, Coronary Artery Disease, 1990—, Cardiology, 1990—, Jour. Heart Valve Disease, 1992, Current Problems in Cardiology, 1975—, assoc. editor, 1980-83, editor-in-chief, 1984—, Circulation, 1977-80, 81-83, 83-86, 86—, consulting editor, 1993, Yr. Book Cardiology, 1986-92, assoc. editor, 1986-92; assoc. editor: Jour. Applied Cardiology, 1985-90, Am. Jour. Cardiovasc. Pathology, 1985—. Recipient Sinsheimer award for Cardiovasc. Rsch., 1969-70; grantee from various sponsors. Fellow Am. Coll. Physicians, Am. Coll. Cardiology; mem. Am. Soc. Clin. Investigation, Am. Fedn. Clin. Rsch., Am. Heart Assn., Am. Physiological Soc., Assn. Army Cardiologists, Southern Soc. Clin. Rsch., Am. Soc. Echocardiography, Assn. U. Cardiologists, Alpha Omega Alpha, others. Office: The Univ Tex Health Sci Ctr VAH Rm C644 7703 Floyd Curl Drive San Antonio TX 78229-3900*

O'ROURKE, SUZAN MARIE, secondary education educator; b. Evergreen Park, Ill., Sept. 19, 1951; BA in English, St. Joseph's Coll., Rensselaer, Ind., 1972. Cert. 6-12 lang. arts tchr., Ill. Substitute tchr. Mother McAuley H.S., Chgo., 1972; tchr. St. Margaret of Scotland Sch., Chgo., 1973-75; tchr. lang. arts Park Jr. H.S., La Grange, Ill., 1975-77, St. Barnabas Grammar Sch., Chgo., 1977-80, St. Thomas More Grammar Sch., Chgo., 1980—. Recipient Heart of Sch. award St. Thomas More Grammar Sch.-Archdiocese of Chgo., 1993. Mem. ASCD, Nat. Coun. Tchrs. English, Nat. Cath. Edn. Assn. (tchr. assoc.). Roman Catholic. Avocations: sewing, art, indian artifact research, horse shows, creative writing. Office: St Thomas More Grammar Sch 8130 S California Ave Chicago IL 60652-2716

OROZCO, LUZMARIA, language educator, educator; b. Mexico City, Nov. 3, 1933; came to U.S., 1953; BA in French and English, Marycrest Coll., Davenport, Iowa, 1956; MA in English, Marquette U., 1958; PhD in Comparative Lit., U. Minn., 1973. Chair humanities divsn. Marycrest Internat. U., Davenport, Iowa, 1975-78, prof. English and Spanish. Humanities rep. human rights commn. Palmer Sch. Chiropracters, 1979—; official translator Latin Am. affairs Diocese of Davenport, 1978; vis. prof. St. Agnes Coll., Md., 1978, St. Jerome Coll., Waterloo, Ontario, Canada, 1976, Yale U., New Haven, Conn., 1986-87; cons., participant Iowa Program in Humanities, 1975-79; translator, cons. testing program on bilingual edn. U. Iowa, 1978. Editor of publs. Sister of Humility of Mary, 1960-85; contbr. numerous poems to competitions. Danforth Instn. grantee, 1967-69, Fulbright grantee, 1970-72; recipient award for teaching excellence and campus leadership Sears-Roebuck and Found. for Ind. Higher Edn., 1990. Mem. MLA, Popular Culture Assn., Spanish-Speaking Commn., Chaparral Poetry Assn. Roman Catholic. Avocations: tennis, swimming, fighting illiteracy. Office: Marycrest Internat U Dept English Davenport IA 52804

ORPHANIDES, NORA CHARLOTTE, ballet educator; b. N.Y.C., June 4, 1951; d. M.T. and Mary Elsie (Tilly) Feffer; m. James Mark Orphanides, July 1, 1972; children: Mark, Elaine Orphanides Mastrosimone, Jennine. BA, CUNY, 1973; student, Joffrey Ballet Sch., N.Y.C., 1970-75; postgrad., Princeton Ballet Sch., 1976-86. Cert. speech and hearing handicapped tchr. With membership dept. M.M.A., N.Y.C., 1987—2002; mem. faculty Princeton (N.J.) Ballet Sch., 1983—, trustee emeritus, 1992—. Mem. cast Princeton Ballet ann. Nutcracker, 1985-90, now Am. Repertory Ballet Co., 1993—; appeared in Romeo & Juliet, 1995-96, 2000. Fundraising gala chmn. Princeton Ballet, 1985, 86, 91-92, chmn. spl. events, 1987—, trustee, 1986—, chmn. Nutcracker benefit, 1990—, Dracula benefit, 1991, honoree, 1999; dept. chmn. June Fete to benefit Princeton Hosp., 1988, 90-91, 92, 96, 2000, trustee, 1995-99; vol. Nat. Hdqrs. Recording for the Blind, 1991-93; dinner chmn. Nassau Ch. Music Festival, 1992, Handel Festival, Nassau Ch., 1993, Princeton Chamber Symphony, 1993; hon. chmn. Princeton Ballet Gala, 1993; chmn. Christmas Boutique, Princeton Med. Ctr., 1993; trustee, Princeton Med. Ctr. Aux. Bd., 1992—, trustee 1995—, pres., 1997-99, past pres., 2000—; choreographer Stuart Country Day Sch., Princeton, 1996-99, 2001; chmn. benefit dinner Eden Inst., 2000. Named honoree Princeton Ballet, 1999, recipient Edward R. and Irene D. Farley Cmty. Stewardship award, Eden Inst. Found., 2003. Democrat. Avocations: piano, skiing, tennis. Office: 301 N Harrison St Princeton NJ 08540-3512

ORR, BETSY, business education educator; b. Dermott, Ark., Nov. 24, 1954; d. Doy and Peggy (Johnson) Ogles; m. Gary Orr, July 10, 1976; children: Brent, Shane. BA, U. Ark., 1975, bus. edn. cert., 1978, MEd, 1987, EdD, 1994. Cert. tchr., Ark. Tchr. Springdale (Ark.) High Sch., 1978-89; instr. bus. edn. U. Ark., Fayetteville, 1989-94, asst. prof., 1994-2000, assoc. prof., 2000, assoc. dean, 2000—. Mem. Nat. Bus. Edn. Assn., Assn. Tchr. Educators, Ark. Bus. Edn. Assn. (editor 1989-92), Delta Pi Epsilon (pres. 1992—), Phi Delta Kappa, Delta Kappa Gamma. Avocations: walking, reading. Home: 1006 NW N St Bentonville AR 72712-4526 Office: U Ark Peabody II Fayetteville AR 72701 E-mail: borr@uark.edu.

ORR, JOSEPH ALEXANDER, educational administrator; b. West Palm Beach, Fla., Nov. 20, 1929; s. Joseph Alexander and Eula (Terry) O.; m. Ardis W. Orr (div.); children: Eric, Pamela, Tracey; m. Linda F. Orr. BS, Fla. A&M U., 1951; MS, Mich. State U., 1953; MEd, Fla. Atlantic U., 1965; PhD, Fla. State U., 1972. Sci. tchr. Roosevelt Sr. H.S., West Palm Beach, Fla., 1953-68; counselor, coord. Adult Edn. Dept. Sch. Sys., Palm Beach County, Fla., 1960-72; dean of students Palm Beach H.S., West Palm Beach, 1968-70; asst. dean Fla. A&M U., Tallahassee, 1970-72; adj. prof. Ind. U., Bloomington, 1972-73; prin. Ctrl. Sr. H.S., Louisville, 1972-74, Jupiter (Fla.) H.S., 1974-78; adj. prof. Fla. Atlantic U., Boca Raton, 1978—; asst. supt. Palm Beach County (Fla.) Sch. Bd., 1978-84, assoc. supt., 1984-92, dep. supt., chief acad. officer, 2001—; exec. dir. Palm Beach County Sch. Adminstrs. Assn., 1992-2001. Chair State Adv. Bd. for Severely Emotionally Disturbed. Contbr. articles to profl. jours. Bd. dirs. Children's Home Soc. Fla., Palm Beach County Coun. Arts; past chair Health and Human Svcs. Bd., Palm Beach County, Inst. New Dimensions, Palm Beach C.C., Assn. Retarded Citizens, Inc., West Palm Beach; past pres. Scholastic Achievement Found. Palm Beach County, Edn. Found. Palm Beach County. Recipient Disting. Svc. award NEA, Pioneer award for excellence in pub. svc. Nat. Forum of Pub. Adminstrn., Outstanding Achievement award Fla. Assn. Cmty. Educators, Four Seasons award Nat. Assn. for Year Round Edn. Mem. ASCD, Fla. Assn. Sch. Adminstrs., Am. Assn. Sch. Adminstrs., Nat. Assn. Secondary Sch. Prins., Nat. Cmty. Edn. Assn. (Sch. Leadership award), Kiwanis Internat. Democrat. Episcopalian. Avocation: boating. Office: Palm Beach County Sch Adminstrs Assn PO Box 31511 Palm Beach Gardens FL 33420

ORR, KENNETH BRADLEY, academic administrator; b. Charlotte, N.C., Mar. 15, 1933; s. Frank Wylie and Kate Harriett O.; m. Ruth Douglas Currie; children: Kevin, Jeffrey, Jonathan. BA, Duke U., 1954; MDiv, Union Theol. Sem., 1960, ThM, 1961; PhD, U. Mich., 1978; LittD, Carroll Coll., 1990; DD, Presbyn. Coll., 1997. Ordained to ministry, Presbyn. Ch., 1961. Minister West End Presbyn. Ch., Roanoke, Va., 1961-64; asst. to pres. Union Theol. Sem., Richmond, Va., 1964-68, v.p., 1968-74; pres. Presbyn. Sch. Christian Edn., Richmond, 1974-79, Presbyn. Coll., Clinton, S.C., 1979-97, pres. emeritus, 1997—; sr. v.p. John McRae & Assocs., Atlanta, 1997—. Past mem. coun. presidents Nat. Assn. Intercollegiate Athletics, Kansas City, Mo., chmn. S. Atlantic Conf., 1989—91; mem. nat. adv. com. on instnl. quality and integrity U.S. Dept. Edn., 1995—2001. Contbr. to religious and ednl. publs. Mem. Assn. Presbyn. Colls. and Univs. (pres. 1994, exec. com.), Coun. Ind. Colls. (bd. dirs. 1993-96), Laurens County C. of C. (past pres.), Kiwanis. Democrat. Avocations: reading, travel, tennis, classical music.

ORSCHELN, SHERYL JANE, art educator; b. Moberly, Mo., Nov. 21, 1948; m. Edward Gary Orscheln, Sept. 6, 1969; children: Eric, Karl, Emily. BAE, U. Kans., Lawrence, 1970; MEd in Curriculum and Instrn., U. Mo., 1997. Art tchr. No. Callaway C1 Sch. Dist., 1997—. Avocations: painting, reading, travel, bridge.

ORSI, MARTHA D. literature educator, language educator; b. Newark, Apr. 15, 1941; d. Paul D'Alessandro and Viola Ciufi; children: James P., Michael D., David G. BS in Secondary Edn., Bucknell U., 1963; MA equivalent, Rutgers U., 1965. Cert. English tchr. grades 9-12 N.J., 1965, Pa., 1991. English tchr. Edison Jr. H.S., NJ, 1965—69, Valley Stream North H.S., Franklin Square, NY, 1969—70; long-term substitute French tchr. Moravian Acad. Upper Sch., Bethlehem, Pa., 1989—90; adj. prof. English Northampton C.C., Bethlehem, 1989—. Adj. prof. English Moravian Coll., Bethlehem, 1994, Cedar Crest Coll., 2002. Mem.: AAUW (legis. chair 1976—78, ednl. founds. chair 1975—77, lit. study group leader 1978—80), Phi Beta Kappa. Home: 2019 Hilltop Rd Bethlehem PA 18015-5122 Office: Northampton CC 3835 Green Pond Rd Bethlehem PA 18020 Personal E-mail: morsi@fast.net. Business E-Mail: morsi@northampton.edu.

ORSINI, MYRNA J. sculptor, educator; b. Spokane, Wash., Apr. 19, 1943; d. William Joseph Finch and Barbara Jean (Hilby) Hickenbottom; m. Donald Wayne Lundquist, Mar. 31, 1962 (div. Mar. 1987); children: Laurie Jeanine Winter, Stephanie Lynne Lundquist. BA, U. Puget Sound, 1969, MA, 1974; postgrad., U. Ga., 1987. Tchr. Tacoma (Wash.) Pub. Schs., 1969-78; owner, pres. Contemporary Print Collectors, Lakewood, Wash., 1978-81, Orsini Studio, Tacoma, 1985—. Sculptor: works include Vartai symbolic gate for Ctrl. Europas Park, Vilnius, Lithuania, 1994; Menat steel and neon corp. commn. completed in Tacoma, Wash. 1995. Chair Supt.'s Supervisory Com., Tacoma, 1978-79; lobbyist Citizens for Fair Sch. Funding, Seattle, 1979; art chair Women's Pres. Coun., Tacoma, 1987-88; founder, bd. dirs. Monarch Contemporary Art Ctr., Wash.; bd. mem. Nisqually Regional Arts Coun., 1997—. Recipient 1st pl. sculpture award Pleinair Symposium Com., Ukraine, 1992, Peron Symposium Com., Kiev, Ukraine, 1993; recognized 1st Am. sculptor to exhibit work in Ukraine, 1993; prin. works include ten monumental sculptures worldwide. Mem. N.W. Stone Sculptors Assn. (coun. leader 1989—), Nat. Assn. Women Artists, Pacific Gallery Artists, Internat. Sculpture Ctr., Tacoma City Club, Nat. Assn. Pen Women, Womens Caucus for the Arts, Olympia Arts Assn. Avocations: reading, sailing, biking. Office: Orsini Studio PO Box 1125 Tenino WA 98589-1125

ORSINI, PAUL VINCENT, music educator; b. Albany, N.Y., Oct. 4, 1955; s. Paul Vincent and Lucia (Rutolo) O. MusB in Music Edn., SUNY, Potsdam, 1977; MusM in Performance, Syracuse U., 1979. Cert. K-12 music tchr., N.Y. Musician Mirage, 1978-79; entertainer The Carmen Canavo Show, Tampa, Fla., 1979-83; freelance entertainer Albany, 1983-86; substitute tchr. Suburban Coun. Schs., Albany, 1983-86; tchr. Corinth (N.Y.) Sch. Dist., 1986-87, Shenendehowa Sch. Dist., Clifton Park, N.Y., 1987—. Owner, leader High Society Big Band, Clifton Park, 1988-91. Premiered trumpet compositions of Dr. Brian Israel Syracuse Univ., 1977-79. Advisor Shenendehowa Crisis Intervention Team, Clifton Park, 1988-93; faculty rep., exec. bd. Friends of Music of Shenendehowa, Clifton Park, 1993; active Shenendehowa Partnership Team, 1995-97; lead trumpet Greg Nazarian Big Band, 1998-2002, The Starliters Big Band, 2002--; rep. Unified Arts, Shenendehowa, 1999; prin. trumpet South Colonie Meml. Wind Ensemble, 2000—. Mem. Albany Musicians Assn., Internat. Trumpet Guild, N.Y. State Congress of Parents and Tchrs. (hon. life mem.). Avocations: fishing, sports, travel, reading, jazz. Home: 54 Via Da Vinci Clifton Park NY 12065-2906

ORTEGA, GINKA GEROVA, concert flutist; b. Preslav, Bulgaria; came to U.S., 1962; d. George and Lucy Gerov; m. Jesus Ortega, 1969; children: Irena, Julian. Student, Varna State Sch. Music, 1962; BA, Oberlin Conservatory of Music, 1967; MA, U. Mich., Detroit, 1970. Mem. faculty Cranbrook Schs., Bloomfield Hills, Mich., 1971, Wayne State U. Sch. Fine and Performing Arts, Detroit; soloist Mich. Touring Arts and Arts Midwest, 1987—; founder, artistic dir. Musica Viva Internat. Concerts. Faculty Sch. Fine and Performing Arts, Wayne State U., 1980—. Carnegie Hall debut, 1983; guest artist, performer internat. festivals incl. Juventudes Musicales, Spain, Musica da Camera, Mex., 1986—; concert tours to Europe, 1988-90, Far East and Japan, 1988, Middle East, 1988-89, Cayman Island, Brit. W.I., 1990-97, C.Am., S.Am., Carribean Island, Hong Kong, Brazil, China, Finland, France, Japan, Spain, Italy, Can., Argentina; solo recitalist incl. Carnegie Hall, N.Y. Orch. Hall, St. Lawrence Ctr., Internat. Concerts, Mallorca Amb., Toronto, Bellas Artes, Mex., Compidoglio, Rome, Palacio Benacazon, Spain, Meiji Geikwin, Japan, 1996; founder, artistic dir. Musica Viva; Internat. Concerts. Named Mich. Musical Amb. and Arts award, State of Mich.; named one of Michigan's Most Influencial Women, Corp Mag., 2003; recipient Mich. Mus. Amb. and Arts award, Gov. of State of Mich., The Arts award, State of Mich. Avocations: art, literature, flamenco, travel, film. E-mail: ginkaflutist@cs.com.

ORTEL, THOMAS LEE, oncologist, hematologist, educator; b. Greenfield, Ind., Aug. 27, 1957; s. Donald William and Shirley Radine (Abbott) O. BS with high distinction, Ind. U., 1979, PhD in Chemistry, 1983, MD, 1985. Diplomate Am. Bd. Internal Medicine, Hematology Subspeciality. Intern Duke U. Med. Ctr., Durham, N.C., 1985-86, resident, 1986-88, fellow in hematology and oncology, 1988-91, assoc. in medicine, 1991-93, asst. prof. medicine, 1993-98, med. dir. Clin. Coagulation Lab., 1994—, assoc. prof. medicine, 1999—, asst. prof. pathology, 1994—. Med. dir. Platelet Antibody Lab., 1999—. Recipient Am. Heart Assn. Clinician Scientist award, 1991-96, Pew Scholar award, 1995-2000, Medforte Innovation award Am. Soc. of Artificail Internal Organs, 2000. E-mail: ortel001@mc.duke.edu.

ORTINAU, DAVID JOSEPH, marketing specialist, educator; b. Harvey, Ill., Dec. 14, 1948; s. Harold Raymond and Lois Agnice (Reich) O.; m. Shirley Keating, Aug. 15, 1975 (div. Nov. 1979); m. Renee Susan Hess, Apr. 30, 1983 (div. Aug. 1993). BS in Mgmt., So. Ill. U., 1970; MS in Bus. Adminstrn., Ill. State U., 1971; PhD in Mktg., La. State U., 1979. Sr. rsch. analyst, dir. projects Rabin Rsch. Co., Chgo., 1971-73; adminstrv. asst., instr. mktg. Coll. Bus., Ill. State U., Normal, Ill., 1973-76; grad. teaching assoc., instr. mktg. Coll. Bus., La. State U., Baton Rouge, Fla., 1976-79; from asst. prof. mktg. to assoc. prof. Coll. Bus., U. South Fla., Tampa, Fla., 1979-84; dir. mktg. and rsch. Market Rsch. Group, Tampa, Fla., 1980-83; assoc. prof. U. South Fla., Tampa, Fla., 1984-95, coord. PhD program dept. mktg., 1989-91, prof., 1995—. V.p. mktg. Neaves, Neaves and Ortinau, Normal, 1974-77. Co-author: Marketing Research: A Practical Approach in the New Millennium, 2000, Marketing Research: Within a Changing Information Environment, 2003; mem. editl. rev. bd. Jour. Acad. Mktg. Sci., 1989— (Disting. Merit award for Outstanding Reviewer 1992-93, Outstanding JAMS Rev. 1997-2000), Jour. Bus. Rsch., 2000— (Outstanding Editl. Rev. 2002); contbr. articles to Jour. Health Care Mktg., Jour. Mktg. Edn., Jour. Bus. Rsch., Jour. Svcs. Mktg., Jour. Acctg. Horizons, Jour. Retailing, others. Recipient Disting. Merit award Advt. Fedn. SW Fla., 1983, Coba Outstanding Rsch. award U. South Fla., 1987, Outstanding Tchg. award, 1980, 81, 82, 86, 90, 95, 2001. Fellow Soc. for Mktg. Advances, 2001, (bd. dirs. 1998—, co-chair doctoral consortium 1998-99); mem. Am. Mktg. Assn. (doctoral consortium fellow 1978, reviewer 1982—), Assn. Consumer Rsch., So. Mktg. Assn. (reviewer 1975—, chmn. 1976—, sec. 1990-91, treas. 1992-95, pres. elect 1995-96, pres. 1996-97, chmn. Svcs. Mktg. Customer Satisfaction Track Program 1990-92, co-chair doctoral consortium 1998, 99, Outstanding Articles award 1981, 86, 87, 90, 92), Acad. Mktg. Sci. (reviewer 1988—, chmn. 1989, 92, Reviewer of Yr. 1992, session chair new tech. and retail store images at 1999, 2003 confs.), retailing svcs. mktg. track program chair, 2003), Acad. Bus. Adminstrn. (track program chmn. 1993), Beta Gamma Sigma (pres. Fla. chpt. 1990-91). Avocations: all sports, reading, gardening, the arts. Research and consulting specializations focus on attitudinal, motivational, multivariate measurement and data analysis methods in areas of services marketing and quality, customer satisfaction and evaluation models, advertising, marketing education topics/issues, diffusion and diagnostic performance processes of product innovations, consumer services and interactive marketing technologies. Home: 2305 Windsor Oaks Ave Lutz FL 33549-5880 Office: U South Fla Mktg Dept Tampa FL 33620 E-mail: dortinau@coba.usf.edu.

ORTIZ, GERMAINE LAURA DE FEO, secondary education educator, counselor; b. Astoria, N.Y., Aug. 6, 1947; d. Andrew and Germaine Laura (Fournier) De Feo; m. Dennis Manfredo, June 6, 1970 (annulled July 1975); m. Angel Manuel Ortiz, July 11, 1975; 1 child, Germaine Angela. AA, Suffolk County C.C., Selden, N.Y., 1969; BA magma cum laude, SUNY, Stony Brook, 1971, MALS, 1974; MS in Edn. with distinction, Hofstra U., 1989. Cert. N-6, 7-12 social studies tchr., sch. counselor, N.Y.; cert. rank II social studies, jr. coll. tchr., sch. counselor, Fla. Tchr. social studies, guidance counselor Connetquot Cen. Sch. Dist. Islip, Bohemia, N.Y., 1971—. Guidance counselor Connetquot Ctrl. Sch.; adj. prof. psychology Nassau C.C., Garden City, NY. Mem. ASCD, NEA, N.Y. State Unified Tchrs., Connetquot Tchrs. Assn., Nat. Coun. for Social Studies, N.Y. Coun. for Social Studies, L.I. Coun. for Social Studies, Hofstra U. Alumni Assn., Suffolk County C.C. Alumni Assn., DAV Aux., Vietnam Vets. Am. Aux. Roman Catholic. Avocations: swimming, exercise, meteorology. Home: 5 Honey Ln W Miller Place NY 11764-1719 Office: Connetquot Cen Sch Dist Islip 780 Ocean Ave Bohemia NY 11716-3631

ORTIZ, MARY THERESA, biomedical engineer, educator; b. N.Y.C., Mar. 25, 1957; d. Henry and Viola (Rega) O. BS, Wagner Coll., 1979; MS, Rutgers U., 1981, PhD, 1987. Emergency med. technician, N.Y. Adj. lectr. N.Y.C. Tech. Coll., Bklyn., 1981-89; teaching/rsch. asst. Rutgers U., New Brunswick, N.J., 1982-86; rsch. scientist N.Y. State Inst. for Basic Rsch., S.I., 1988-93; assoc. prof. Kingsborough C. C., Bklyn., 1993—. Adj. asst. prof. Coll. S.I., 1989-94, NASA SLSTP faculty counselor, 1994, NASA/ASEE summer faculty fellow, 1995. Contbr. articles to sci. jours. Mem. youth adv. coun. N.Y.C. Youth Bd. Beame Adminstrn., 1970's; participant N.Y.C. Tech. Coll. Access for Women, Bklyn., 1980's, Rutgers U. Coll. Engrs. Open House, Piscataway, 1985-86. Grad. Prof. Opportunities Program fellow Rutgers U., 1979-82, Grad. Student Dissertation and Research Support grantee, 1986; Women's Rsch. and Devel. Fund grantee CUNY, 1988. Mem. IEEE, N.Y. Acad. Scis. (judge city and boro sci. fairs), Nat. Engrs. Honor Soc., IEEE, ASEE, NSPE, Kappa Mu Epsilon, Beta Beta Beta. Democrat. Roman Catholic. Home: 31 Ruth Pl Staten Island NY 10305-2430 Office: Kingsborough C C 2001 Oriental Blvd Brooklyn NY 11235-2333 E-mail: MOrtiz@kbcc.cuny.edu.

ORTIZ, VICTOR RAÚL, parochial school educator; b. Barranquitas, P.R., Feb. 25, 1959; s. Wilfredo and Gladys (Ortiz) O. ThM summa cum laude, MDiv summa cum laude, St. Vicente de Paul Seminary, Fla.; MEd summa cum laude, U. Pheonix, Ariz, P.R.; Lic. Fil., U. Católica Madre y Maestra, Santo Domingo, Dominican Republic. Tchr. theology, history Colegio Valvanera, Coamo, P.R., 1980-83, asst. prin., 1981-83, tchr. Spanish, 1982-83; supt. catholic schs. Diócesis de Caguas, 1986-89; vicario cooperador-párroco San Andrēs Apóstol, Barranquitas, 1986-89; vicario episcopal de educaciOn Diócesis de Caguas, 1989—. Author (with P. Victor) Concepto del Pecado, 1987, Desarrollo de la Conciencia Moral, 1992. Mem. Alianza Pro-Ley de Cierre, San Juan, P.R., 1991; v.p. Grupo Cívico Contra El Crimen Naranjito, P.R., 1992. Recipient Primer Alto Honor Escuela Superior Dr. Jose N Gandara, 1977, Cuadro Alto Honor del Decano Univ. Pontificia Catholica, 1982. Mem. Assn. Tchrs. of P.R. Office: Superintendencia de Escuelas Catolicas PO Box 8699 Caguas PR 00726-8699

ORTIZIO, DEBRA LOUISE, elementary education educator; b. Hoboken, N.J., Mar. 2, 1955; d. Louis Mario and Mary Evelyn (Borra) O. BA in Elem. Edn., Jersey City State Coll., 1977, MA in Reading, Reading Specialist, Jersey City State Coll., 1985, postgrad., 1986. Lic. elem. edn. tchr., reading specialist, N.J. Remedial reading tchr. St. Joseph Man Power Program, Union City, N.J., 1977-78; basic skills tchr. Gilmore Sch.-Union City (N.J.) Bd. Edn., 1978-86, 4th grade tchr., 1997—2002, 5th grade tchr., 2002—03, 6th grade tchr., 1986-97, 2003—. Coach advisor rifles and flag twirlers Emerson H.S., Union City, 1981-83; Students Awareness of Substance Abuse advisor Gilmore Sch., Union City, 1991-92, 93-98, Earth Day coord., 1990, 91; fund raiser advisor Christmas Gifts for Christ Hosps., Gilmore Sch., Union City, 1989-98, student coun. advisor, 1993-94. Ednl. task force Sch. Mgmt. Team, 1999—. Recipient Tchr. Recognition award Hudson County, 1993, Tchr. Recognition award State of N.J., 1993. Roman Catholic. Home: 308 Passaic Ave Hasbrouck Heights NJ 07604-1704 Office: Gilmore Sch Union City NJ 07087

ORTMANN, DAVID C. secondary school educator; b. Kittanning, Pa., Apr. 11, 1951; s. Jacob J. and Mary (Czjnar); m. Brandi McNease, June 7, 1997; children: Avery, Jacob. BS in Edn., Slippery Rock U., 1973. Tchr. Ford City (Pa.) Cath. Sch., 1973-77, Armstrong Ind. Sch. Dist., Ford City, 1977-79, Houston Ind. Sch. Dist., 1979-88, Klein Ind. Sch. Dist., Spring, Tex., 1988—, head varsity coach girls basketball, jr. varsity girls track, 1994-95, coach 9th grade basketball, coach girls varsity softball, coach boys jr. varsity soccer, 1998—2001. Avocations: coaching, officiating, running road races. Office: Klein Oak HS 22603 Northcrest Dr Spring TX 77389-4451

ORUMA, FRANCIS OBATARE, mechanical engineering educator, consultant; b. Jimeta-Yola, Nigeria, Nov. 28, 1948; s. Chief W.O. Oruma and Margaret A. Abramita; m. roseline Taino Cookey, Aug. 5, 1978; children: Frenka, Essee, Alima, Erthel. BSME, Ind. Tech., Ft. Wayne, 1977; PhD in Mech. Engring., N.C. State U., Raleigh, 1984; MBA, Ashland (Ohio) U., 1990. Mech. engr. ITT, Raleigh, 1978-80; cons. Raleigh, 1984-86; assoc. prof. mech. engring., dir. PC-CAD Ohio No. U., Ada, 1988—, Leroy H. Lylte Disting. chair in mech. engring., 1990-91, 93—. Vis. prof. U. Okla., Norman, 1987. Trustee Food Bank/Artspace, Lima, Ohio, 1993—, Allen-Lima Econ. Devel. Consortium, Vet.'s Meml. Conv. and Civic Ctr. of Lima/Allen County. Mem. ASME (faculty advisor 1992—), Bradfield Lions, Masons, Rotary Club (trustee 1993-95, v.p. 1994-95), Cavalier Club of Lima (pres. 1994-95). Home: 3307 Roundtree St Lima OH 45805-4021

ORWIG, TIMOTHY THOMAS, academic administrator, writer; b. Ft. Dodge, Iowa, Mar. 11, 1959; s. Clarence Francis and Mary Isabell (Van Alstine) O. BA, Morningside Coll., 1980; MA, U. Ark., 1982, Boston U., 2001. Instr. Augustana Coll., Rock Island, Ill., 1983-85; dir. learning ctr. Morningside Coll., Sioux City, Iowa, 1986-97, asst. dean, 1997-99, dir. found. rels., 1999. Cons. US Fish and Wildlife Svc., Cayuga, ND, 1995—97; lectr. Simmons Coll., 2002. Author: Morningside College: A Centennial History, 1994; co-editor: The Augustana Reader, 1985; columnist 4th St. Revue, 1996-99; contbr. articles to profl. jours. Bd. dirs. Iowa Hist. Preservation Alliance, Des Moines, 1996-99; pres. Woodbury County Conservation Found., Sioux City, 1997-99. Rsch. fellow Soc. for the Preservation New Eng. Antiquities, 2001, 03; recipient Outstanding Vol. of Yr. award Iowa chpt. Nature Conservancy, 1995, Disting. Alumni award Morningside Coll., 1995, Dir.'s award Sioux City Pub. Mus., 1994. Fellow: New Eng. Soc. Arch. Historians (bd. dirs. 2003—04); mem.: SiouxLandmark (founder, vice-chair 1994—99). Democrat. Episcopalian. Avocation: hiking. Home: 421A Grafton St Worcester MA 01604-3801 E-mail: ttorwig@aol.com.

ORY, STEVEN JAY, physician, educator; b. Houston, Aug. 4, 1950; s. Edwin Marvin and Norma Gertrude O.; m. Kathleen Higgins, Jan. 10, 1981; children: Eleanor Claire, Edward Michael. BA, Washington and Lee U., 1972; MD, Baylor Coll., 1976. Diplomate Am. Bd. Obstetrics and Gynecology, subsplty. cert. in Reproductive Endocrinology and Infertility. Asst. prof. Duke U., Durham, N.C., 1981-82, Northwestern U., Chgo., 1982-85; assoc. prof., cons. Mayo Clinic, Rochester, Minn., 1985-95, chmn. sect. reproductive endocrinology and infertility, 1985-95; pvt. practice reproductive endocrinology and infertility; mem. ob-gyn. staff N.W. Ctr. for Infertility and Reproductive Endocrinology, Margate, Fla., 1995—; assoc. clin. prof. obstets. and gyn. U. Miami, Fla., 1999—. Assoc. dir. Am. Fertility Soc., Birmingham, Ala., 1986-87; bd. trustees Northwest Med. Ctr., Margate, Fla., 2003—. Asst. editor: Fertility and Sterility, 1988-96; contbr. articles to profl. jours. Mem. Internat. Soc. for Advancement of Humanistic Studies in Medicine (bd. dirs. 1999-2002), Am. Soc. Reproductive Medicine (chmn. practice com. 1998-2000, bd. dirs., 1999-2002), Soc. Reproductive Endocrinologists (sec.-treas., pres. 2001-2002), Ft. Lauderdale Ob-Gyn. Soc. (pres. 1998-2000). Address: 2825 N State Road 7 Ste 302 Margate FL 33063-5737

ORYSHKEVICH, ROMAN SVIATOSLAV, retired physician, physiatrist, dentist, educator; b. Olesko, Ukraine, Aug. 5, 1928; came to U.S., 1955, naturalized, 1960; s. Simeon and Caroline (Deneszczuk) O.; m. Oksana Lishchynsky, June 16, 1962; children: Marta, Mark, Alexandra. DDS, Ruperto-Carola U., Heidelberg, Ger., 1952, MD, 1953, PhD cum laude, 1955. Cert. Am. Assn. Electromyography and Electrodiagnosis, 1964; diplomate Am. Bd. Phys. Medicine and Rehab., 1966, Am. Bd. Electrodiagnostic Medicine, 1989. Research fellow in cancer Exptl. Cancer Inst., Rupert-Charles U., 1953-55; rotating intern Coney Island Hosp., Bklyn., 1955-56; resident in diagnostic radiology NYU Bellevue Med. Ctr.-Univ. Hosp., 1956-57; resident, fellow in phys. medicine and rehab. Western Res. U. Highland View Hosp., Cleve., 1958-60; orthopedic surgery Met. Gen. Hosp., Cleve., 1959; asst. chief rehab. medicine service VA West Side Med. Ctr., Chgo., 1961-74, acting chief, 1974-75, chief, 1975-99; dir., coord. edn. U. Ill. Integrated Residency Program, Phys. Medicine & Rehab, 1974-89; clin. instr. U. Ill., 1962-65, asst. clin. prof., 1965-70, asst. prof., 1970-75, assoc. clin. prof., 1975-94, clin. prof., 1994-99; ret., 1999. Author, editor: Who and What in U.W.M.M., 1978; contbr. articles to profl. jours; splty. cons. in phys. medicine and rehab. to editl. bd. Chgo. Med. Jours., 1978-89. Founder, pres. Ukrainian World Med. Mus., Chgo., 1977; founder, 1st pres. Am. Mus. Phys. Medicine and Rehab., 1980-91. Fellow AAUP, Am. Acad. Phys. Medicine and Rehab.; mem. AAAS, Assn. Acad. Physiatrists, Am. Assn. Electromyography and Electrodiagnosis, Ill. Soc. Phys. Medicine and Rehab. (pres., dir. 1979-80), Ukrainian Med. Assn. N.Am. (dir., pres. chpt. 1977-79, fin. mgr. 17th med. conv. and congress Chgo. 1977, adminstr. and conv. chmn. 1979), World Fedn. Ukrainian Med. Assns. (co-founder and 1st exec. sec. research and sci. 1977-79), Internat. Rehab. Medicine Assn., Rehab. Internat. U.S.A., Nat. Assn. VA Physicians, Assn. Med. Rehab. Dirs. and Coordinators, Nat. Rehab. Assn., Nat. Assn. Disability Examiners, Am.

Med. Writers Assn., Biofeedback Rsch. Soc. Am., Chgo. Soc. Phys. Medicine and Rehab. (pres., founder 1978-79), Ill. Rehab. Assn., Ukrainian Acad. Med. Scis. (founder, pres. 1979-80), Gerontol. Soc., Internat. Soc. Electrophysiol. Kinesiology, Internat. Soc. Prosthetics and Orthotics, Fedn. Am. Scientists. Ukrainian Catholic. Avocations: research in prosthetics, amputations, normal and pathological gaits, bracing orthotics. Home: 1819 N 78th Ct Elmwood Park IL 60707-3502

OSAITILE, ANDY ELDO, English language and literature educator; b. Benin City, Bendel, Nigeria, Apr. 24, 1956; came to U.S., 1981; s. Igiebor and Alice (Idubor) O.; m. Mabel Efe Atekha, Nov. 3, 1990. BS, Mid. Tenn. State U., 1985; MA, Tenn. State U., 1989; MSSW, U. Louisville, 1993. Asst. prof. Vol. State C.C., Gallatin, Tenn., 1990—. Rschr. Kent Sch. of Social Work, U. Louisville, 1993; presenter in field. Contbr. articles to newspapers. Vol. Nashville Cares, 1990—, ARC, 1991—. Mem. AAUP (sec. Vol. State C.C. chpt. 1994), NASW, Nat. Coun. Tchrs. English, Conf. on Coll. Composition and Comm., Alpha Phi Omega (pres. 1985). Baptist. Avocations: Karate, writing stories, reading. Home: 1931 Pinehurst Dr Nashville TN 37216-4107 Office: Vol State C C 1360 Nashville Pike Gallatin TN 37066-3146

OSAKWE, CHRISTOPHER, lawyer, educator; b. Lagos, Nigeria, May 8, 1942; came to U.S. 1970, naturalized 1979; s. Simon and Hannah (Morgan) O.; m. Maria Elena Amador, Aug. 19, 1982; 1 child, Rebecca E. LLB, Moscow State U., 1967, PhD, 1970; JSD, U. Ill., 1974. Bar: Moscow, 1967, Kazakhstan, 1997. Prof. sch. law Tulane U., New Orleans, 1972-81, 86-88; ptnr. firm Riddle and Brown, New Orleans, 1989—; Eason-Weinmann prof. comparative law, dir. Eason-Weinmann Ctr. for Comparative Law Tulane U., New Orleans, 1981-86. Vis. prof. U. Pa., 1978, U. Mich., 1981, Washington and Lee U., 1986; vis. fellow St. Anthony's Coll., Oxford U., Eng., 1980, Christ Ch. Coll., Oxford U., 1988-89, Lomonosov Moscow State U., 1999-2003; cons. U.S. Dept. Commerce, 1980-85. Author: The Participation of the Soviet Union in Universal International Organizations, 1972, The Foundations of Soviet Law, 1981, Joint Ventures with the Soviet Union: Law and Practice, 1990, Soviet Business Law, 2 vols., 1991, (with others) Comparative Legal Traditions in a Nutshell, 1982, Comparative Legal Traditions--Text, Materials and Cases, 1985, 2d edit., 1994, The Russian Civil Code Annotated: Translation and Commentary, 2000, Comparative Law in Diagrams: General and Special Parts, 2000, 2d edit., 2002; editor Am. Jour. Comparative Law, 1978-85. Carnegie fellow Hague Acad. Internat. Law, 1969; Russian Rsch. fellow Harvard U., 1972; USSR Sr. Rsch. Exch. fellow, 1982, Rsch. fellow Kennan Inst. for Advanced Russian Studies, 1988. Mem. ABA, Am. Law Inst., Am. Soc. Internat. Law, Supreme Ct. Hist. Soc., Soc. de Legislation Comparée, Order of Coif. Republican. Roman Catholic. Home: 339 Audubon Blvd New Orleans LA 70125-4124 Office: 201 S Charles Ave Ste 3100 New Orleans LA 70170 E-mail: osakwec@aol.com.

OSBORN, SUSAN CHANEY, educator, writer; b. Ft. Campbell, Ky., Jan. 7, 1953; d. Lawrence Elvie and Wilma Barbara (Powell) Howard; m. Nicholas Lourick, Aug. 1, 1976 (div. Oct. 1981); m. Steve Osborn, Mar. 20, 1993; 1 child. BS, Ga. State U., 1989; MS, U. Colo., 1997. Lic. tchr., Colo, pvt. occupational tchr., Colo. Owner, photographer Creative Assistance, Atlanta, 1979-89; educator St. Mary's Acad., Cherry Hills Village, Colo., 1989-90, Denver Pub. Schs., 1990-92; internet resource coord. Nat. Renewable Energy Lab., Golden, Colo., 1993-95; writer Diners Club Internat., Englewood, Colo., 1995-96; owner, writer, coord. Publs. Resolution, Denver, 1996—. Website advisor Colo. Dept. Pub. Health and Environment, Denver, 1998-99; advisor Houghton-Mifflin Co., Boston, 1992; mem. math. text seclection com. Denver Pub. Schs., 1991; cons. Hauser Chem. Co., Boulder, Colo., 1994. Author: Public Service Company Classroom Connection, 1992, photography manual. Art/photography dir. Boy's Club, Marietta, GA., 1987; art show sect. organizer Girl's Club, Atlanta, 1988; implementor Bear Creek Blvd. Civic Assn., Lakewood, Colo., 1995; pub. rels. coord. Resolve Rocky Mountain Assn., Denver, 1996. Fellow Colo. Writing Project; mem. NEA, Golden Key. Avocations: creative writing, creative photography, theatre, hiking, mountain biking. Office: Publs Resolution PO Box 37263 Denver CO 80237

OSBORNE, GLENNA JEAN, social and health services administrator; b. East Rainelle, W.Va., Jan. 5, 1945; d. B.J. and Jean Ann (Haranac) Osborne; m. Thomas Joseph Ferrante Jr., June 11, 1966 (div. Nov. 1987); 1 child, Thomas Joseph Osborne; m. Brian Mark Popp, Aug. 13, 1988 (div. Oct. 1999). BA cum laude, U. Tampa, 1966; MA, Fairleigh Dickinson U., 1982; cert., Kean Coll., 1983. Cert. English, speech, dramatic arts tchr., prin./supr.; cert. nursing child assessment feeding scale and nursing child assessment tchg. scale, DENVER II cert., HOME cert. Tchr. Raritan H.S., Hazlet, N.J., 1966, Keyport (N.J.) Pub. Schs., 1968-86, coord. elem. reading and lang. arts, 1980-84, supr. curriculum and instrn., 1984-86; prin. Weston Sch., Manville, N.J., 1986-88, The Bartle Sch., Highland Park, N.J., 1988-91, Orange Ave. Sch., Cranford, N.J., 1991-92; dir. The Open Door Youth Shelter, Binghamton, N.Y., 1992-94; child protective investigator supr. Dept. Health and Rehab. Svcs., Orlando, Fla., 1994-95; program supr. Children's Home Soc., Sanford, Fla., 1995; clin. supr. Healthy Families-Orange, Orlando, Fla., 1995-98; dir. program ops. Children's Home Soc., Tavares, Fla., 1998—. Regional trainer Individualized Lang. Arts, Weehawken, N.J., 1976-86; cons. McDougal/Littel Pubs., Evanston, Ill., 1982-83; chair adv. bd. women's residential program Ctr. for Drug Free Living, Orlando, 1996. Contbr. chpt.: A Resource Guide of Differentiated Learning Experiences for Gifted Elementary Students, 1981. V.p. Sch. Readiness Coalition for Lake County, 1999; mem. adv. coun. Lake Cmty. Action Agy., Head Start, 1999; bd. mem. Mount Dora Cmty. Trust, 2002—; bd. dirs., sec. Ctrl. Healthy Start Coalition, 1999—2003; Sunday sch. tchr. Reformed Ch., Keyport, 1975—80, supt. Sunday sch., 1982—84. Mem.: Elks, Order Ea. Star, Kiwanis (Mt. Dora bd. dirs. 2000, pres. 2002—), Phi Delta Kappa. Republican. Methodist. Avocation: writing. Office: Children's Home Soc 1300 S Duncan Dr Bldg D Tavares FL 32778-4223

OSBORNE, MARTHA P. secondary school educator; b. Bellaire, Ohio, Nov. 19, 1937; d. H.S. and Velma L. (Archer) Colvin; m. Roscoe B. Osborne, June 17, 1981; children: Ward L. Petrey, Brian A. Petrey. BA, Asbury Coll., Wilmore, Ky., 1961; MA, Union Coll., Barbourville, Ky., 1984. Cert. life tchr., Ky.; cert. tchr., Fla. Tchr. social studies Anderson County Bd. Edn., Lawrenceburg, Ky.; elem. tchr. Grant County Bd. Edn., Dry Ridge, Ky., Kenton County Bd. Edn., Independence, Ky., secondary tchr. English; tchr. Sch. Bd. Nassau County, Fernadina Beach, Fla. Home: Whitley Co Mid Sch Whitley Co Bd Edn 6101 Cumberland Falls Hwy Corbin KY 40701-8636

OSBURN, ELLA KATHERINE, elementary education educator; b. Waycross, Ga., Nov. 25, 1961; d. William Daniel and Mabelle Irene (Tatum) O. BS in Home and Consumer Econs., Freed-Hardeman Coll., Henderson, Tenn., 1984, MEd in Curriculum and Instrn., 1992. Cert. in elem. edn. K-8, Ga. Tchr. 1st grade South Ga. Christian Acad., Albany, 1986-88; substitute tchr. Gwinnett County Schs., Lawrenceville, Ga., 1988-89; childcare worker The Children's Home, Valdosta, Ga., 1989-90; sec. Ga. Christian, Valdosta, 1990-91; tchr. 1st grade S.W. Elem.-Hancock County Schs., 1994-96. Author: (curriculum guide) Log of Intervention and Curriculum Guides for Reading Difficulties, 1991-92. Mem. NEA, ASCD, Ga. Assn. Educators, Smithsonian Inst. Mem. Ch. of Christ. Avocations: collecting and saving pennies, travel, collecting antiques, playing putt-putt golf. Home: PO Box 575 Hoschton GA 30548-0575

OSCHMANN, JOAN EDYTHE, gifted and elementary education educator; b. N.Y.C., July 27, 1936; d. Jesse Melchior and Edythe Martha (Fritsche) Budacz; m. Herbert V. Oschmann, Dec. 14, 1957 (div. Dec. 1971); children: Penney Joan Werner, John Peter. BA in Early Childhood Edn., Queens Coll., 1957; MS in Edn., Hofstra U., 1975, CAS, 1980, postgrad. Cert. tchr., adminstr., N.Y. Tchr. kindergarten East Meadow (N.Y.) Schs., 1957-59; tchr., dir. nursery sch. Wesleyan Sch., Smithtown, N.Y., 1962-67; tchr. gifted, elem. edn., home-based enrichment program Three Village Schs., Setauket, N.Y., 1967-95, 4th grade gifted tchr., 1995—. Mem. writing inst. Three Village Schs., 1976—, kindergarten com., 1984, gifted adv. com., 1986. Mem. Ea. Star, Amaranth Orgn. Triangles (jr. dep. 1974-80). Avocations: ceramics, crewel stitchery, writing. Home: 6 Clifford Blvd Hauppauge NY 11788-2506

OSGOOD, RUSSELL KING, academic administrator; b. Fairborn, Ohio, Oct. 25, 1947; s. Richard M. and Mary Russell Osgood; m. Paula Haley, June 6, 1970; children: Mary, Josiah, Micah, Iain. BA, Yale U., 1969, JD, 1974. Bar: Mass. 1974, U.S. Dist. Ct. Mass. (admitted to) 1976. Assoc. Hill & Barlow, Boston, 1974—78; assoc. prof. Boston U., 1978—80; prof. Cornell U., Ithaca, NY, 1980—88, dean law sch., 1988—98; pres. Grinnell (Iowa) Coll., 1998—. Lt. USNR, 1969—71. Mem.: Selden Soc., Stair Soc., Mass. Hist. Soc. Office: Grinnell Coll 1121 Park St Grinnell IA 50112-1640 E-mail: osgood@grinnell.edu.

OSGUTHORPE, JOHN DAVID, otolaryngologist, educator; b. Fairbanks, Alaska, 1948; MD, U. Utah, 1973; grad., Med. Ed. in Otolaryngology. Intern UCLA, 1973-74, resident surgery, 1974-75, resident otolaryngology, 1975-78; prof. Med. U. SC, Charleston, SC, 1979—; otolaryngologist Med. U. Hosp., Charleston, SC. Accreditation coun. Skull Base fellowship U. Zurich. Mem.: HNS, AMA (del. 1998—), Residence Rev. Comm., Sinus Allergy Health Partnership (bd. dir. 1998—), Am. Rhinologic Soc. (bd. dir. 1998—2001, editor 1998—2001), Am. Laryngological Assn., Am. Acad. Otolarynologic Allergy (pres. 1995), Am. Acad. Otolaryngology, Head and Neck Surgery (bd. dirs. 1997—, coord. continuing edn. 2000—, Disting. Svc. award 1995). Office: Med Univ SC Dept Otolaryngology 150 Ashley Ave Charleston SC 29401-5803 E-mail: osguthjd@att.net.

O'SHEA, DONALD C. physicist, educator, optical engineer; b. Akron, Ohio, Nov. 14, 1938; s. Donald Joseph and Sarah O'S.; m. Helen Rose Spustek, Oct. 20, 1962; children: Sean Stanley, Kathleen Susan, Sheila Sarah, Patrick Donald. BS, U. Akron, 1960; MS, Ohio State U., 1963; PhD in Physics, Johns Hopkins U., 1968. Rsch. fellow McKay Lab., Harvard U., Cambridge, Mass., 1968-70; asst. prof. Ga. Inst. Tech., Atlanta, 1970-75, assoc. prof., 1975-87, prof. physics, 1987—. Author: Elements of Modern Optical Design, 1978; co-author: Introduction to Lasers and Their Applications, 1978; editor Optical Engring., 1998-99, 2001—; contbr. some 40 articles to profl. jours. Fellow Internat. Soc. Optical Engring. (sec. 1997, v.p. 1999, pres. 2000), Optical Soc. Am. (Esther Hoffman Beller award 1996). Democrat. Roman Catholic. Achievements include creation of the optics discovery kit for children; 3 patents in optical design. Office: Ga Inst Tech Sch Physics Atlanta GA 30332-0430 E-mail: doshea@prism.gatech.edu.

OSHEROFF, DOUGLAS DEAN, educator, physicist, researcher; b. Aberdeen, Wash., Aug. 1, 1945; s. William and Bessie Anne (Ondov) Osheroff; m. Phyllis S.K. Liu, Aug. 14, 1970. BS in Physics, Calif. Inst. Tech., 1967; MS, Cornell U., 1969, PhD in Physics, 1973. Mem. tech. staff Bell Labs., Murray Hill, NJ, 1972—82, head solid state and low temperature physics research dept., 1982—87; prof. Stanford (Calif.) U., 1987—, J.G. Jackson and C.J. Wood prof. physics, 1992—, chair physics, 1993—96, 2001—. Mem. Columbia Accident Investigation Bd., 2003. Rschr. on properties of matter near absolute zero of temperature, co-discoverer of superfluidity in liquid 3He, 1971, nuclear antiferromagnetic resonance in solid 3He, 1980. Co-recipient Simon Meml. prize, Brit. Inst. Physics, 1976; recipient Oliver E. Buckley Solid State Physics prize, 1981, Nobel prize in Physics, 1996; fellow John D. and Catherine T. MacArthur prize, 1981. Fellow: Am. Acad. Arts and Scis., Am. Phys. Soc.; mem.: NAS. Office: Stanford U Rm 150 Varian Physics Bldg 382 Via Pueblo Mall Stanford CA 94305-4060

OSIYOYE, ADEKUNLE, obstetrician, attorney medical and legal consultant, gynecologist, educator; b. Lagos, Nigeria, Jan. 5, 1951; came to U.S., 1972; s. Alfred and Grace (Apena) Oshiyoye; m. Toyin Osinowo Oshiyoye, Dec. 28, 1991; children: Adekunle Jr., Adedayo Justice. Student, Howard U., 1972-73; BS, U. State of N.Y., 1974; postgrad., Columbia U., 1974-78; MD, Am. U., Montserrat, West Indies, 1979; JD, Thomas Cooley Law Sch., Lansing, Mich., 1997. Bar: Mich. 1998. Intern South Chgo. Community Hosp., 1980-81; intern dept. obstetrics-gynecology Cook County Hosp., Chgo., 1981-82, resident physician, 1982-84, chief resident physician dept. obstetrics-gynecology, 1984-85; assoc. prof. dept. obstetrics-gynecology Chgo. Osteo. Coll. Medicine, 1986—; health physician, cons. physician City of Chgo. Dept. Health, 1989—. Attending physician St. Bernard Hosp., Chgo., 1985—, Hyde Park Hosp., Chgo., 1986—, Mercy Hosp., Chgo., 1987—, Roseland Hosp., Chgo., 1985—, Columbus Hosp., Chgo., 1985—, Jackson Park Hosp., Chgo., 1985—; coord. emergency rm. Cook County Hosp., 1983-85, cons. medical, legal residential care, CEO, pres., atty. Law Offices Dr. Emmanuel Oshiyo M.D., J.D., P.C., 1998—. Med. editor African Connections, 1990—; med. columnist Newsbreed Mag., 1990—; founding mem. Ob-Gyn Video Jour. Am. Organizer Harold Washington Coalition, Chgo., 1983-87; operation mem. Operation P.U.S.H., Chgo., 1987—; active Chgo. Urban League, 1989—, Cook County Dem. Party, 1988—; mem. Mayor's Commn. on Human Rels., Chgo., 1990—, State of Ill. Inaugural Com., 1991. Shell scholar, 1965-69; recipient Fed. Govt. scholarship award, 1972, Howard Univ. scholarship award, 1973, Fed. Govt. Nigeria grad. med. scholarship award, 1975-79, Cerebral Palsy rsch. award, 1977, Ob-gyn. Video Jour. award, 1989, Role Model award Chgo. Police Dept., 1991, 92, Chgo. Bd. Edn., 1991, Chgo. 100 Black Men, 1991, Gov.'s Recognition award, 1992; named one of Best Dressed Men in Chgo., Chgo. Defender, 1990, 91. Fellow Am. Coll. Internat. Physicians, Am. Coll. Obstetricians & Gynecologists; mem. AMA (physician recognition award 1986), Am. Coll. Glegal Medicine (edn. com.), Am. Soc. Law Medicine, Am. Pub. Heart Assn., Nat. Med. Assn., Ill. Med. Soc., Chgo. Med. Assn., Chgo. Gynecol. Soc., Cook County Physician Assn., Nigerian Am. Forum (chmn. health com., chmn. election com.), Cook County Hosp. Surg. Alumni Assn., Howard U. Alumni Assn. (regent, chmn. scholarship com. Chgo. chpt.), Eureka Lodge (investigating com.), Masons, Shriners, Order of Eastern Star, Alpha Phi Alpha (life mem., mem. Labor Day com., dir. ednl. programs Xi Lambda chpt. 1990—, co-chmn. courtesy Black & Gold com. 1989, 90, Recognition award 1991), Pan Hellenic Action Coun. (chmn. pub. rels. com.), Ill. Maternal and Child Health Coalition, Beta Kappa Chi, ABA, State Bar Mich., Oakland County Bar, Mich. Trial Lawyers Assn., Am. Immigration Lawyers Assn., Wayne County Med. Soc. (Legislative Com.), Mich. State Med. Soc. Apostolic. Avocations: ping pong, fishing, golf, basketball, swimming. Home: PO Box 2940 Southfield MI 48037-2940 Office: Dept Health 37 W 47th St Chicago IL 60609-4657

OSKIN, JOELLEN ROSS, special education educator, school librarian; b. McKeesport, Pa., Apr. 26, 1943; d. Clarence Melvin Ross and Ada Mae Oliver; m. David William Oskin, Sept. 5, 1964; children: David William, Steven Ross. BS in Spl. Edn. magna cum laude, 1980, MLS So. Conn. U., 1987. Spl. edn. tchr. Greenwich (Conn.) Bd. Edn., 1980—89, Darien (Conn.) Bd. Edn., 1989—91; libr. Automated Kings Coll. Libr., Kings Coll., Auckland, New Zealand, 1992—94. Bd. dirs. Vis. Nurse/VNC Network, Wilton, Conn.; mem. adv. bd. Kids In Crisis, Greenwich, 2001—02. Mem.: AAUW. Avocations: golf, reading, travel.

OSKOUI, R. cardiologist, educator; b. Washington; BS summa cum laude, Georgetown U., 1985; MD, Columbia U., 1989. Diplomate Am. Bd. Internal Medicine, Nat. Bd. Med. Examiners, Am. Bd. Cardiovascular Disease; cert. instr. ACLS. Resident in internal medicine Georgetown U. Med. Ctr., 1989-92, clin. instr. divsn. cardiology, 1995—; fellow in cardiovascular disease Washington Hosp. Ctr., 1992-95; cardiologist Capital Heart Assocs., P.C., Washington, 1995—; asst. clin. prof. medicine George Washington U. Med. Ctr., 1996—; dir. non-invasive cardiology Sibley Meml. Hosp., 1997—. Mem. pharmacy and therapeutics com. Sibley Meml. Hosp., 1996-97, med. edn. com. Washington Hosp. Ctr., 1997—; interviewer admissions com. Georgetown U. Sch. Medicine, 1996-99. Contbr. articles to profl. jours. Fellow Am. Coll. Cardiology, Am. Soc. Echocardiography, Internat. Soc. Adult Congenital Cardiac Disease, Phi Beta Kappa. Avocations: horseback riding, scuba diving. Office: Capital Heart Assocs PC 3301 New Mexico Ave NW Ste 202 Washington DC 20016-3622

OSNES, PAMELA GRACE, behavior analyst; b. Burke, S.D., Sept. 10, 1955; d. John Ruben and Dortha Grace (Wilson) O.; children: Jocelyn Fern, Logan John. BS in Spl. Edn., BS in Elem. Edn., U. S.D., 1977; MA in Clin. Psychology, W.Va. U., 1981; PhD in Spl. Edn., 1998. Spl. edn. tchr. Sioux Falls (S.D.) Sch. Dist., 1977-79; instr. psychology dept. W.Va. U., Morgantown, 1982-85; dir. Carousel Preschool Program, Morgantown, 1982-85; assoc. prof. U. South Fla., Tampa, 1986-93, adminstrv. coord. advanced grad. programs dept. spl. edn., 1994-97, instr. dept. spl. edn., 1997-98, assoc. prof., 1999—, coord. Master's Program in Applied Behavior Analysis, 2000—03; asst. prof. spl. edn. Ohio State U., 2003—. Mem. Assn. for Behavior Analysis, Coun. for Exceptional Children (div. early childhood, div. rsch., tchr. edn. div.), Coun. Adminstrs. Spl. Edn., Coun. for Children with Behavior Disorders.

OSOWIEC, DARLENE ANN, clinical psychologist, educator, consultant; b. Chgo., Feb. 16, 1951; d. Stephen Raymond and Estelle Marie Osowiec; m. Barry A. Leska. BS, Loyola U., Chgo., 1973; MA with honors, Roosevelt U., 1980; postgrad. in psychology, Saybrook Inst., San Francisco, 1985-88; PhD in Clin. Psychology, Calif. Inst. Integral Studies, 1992. Lic. clin. psychologist, Mo., Ill., Calif. Mental health therapist Ridgeway Hosp., Chgo., 1978; mem. faculty psychology dept. Coll. Lake County, Grayslake, Ill., 1981; counselor, supr. MA-level interns, chmn. pub. rels. com. Integral Counseling Ctr., San Francisco, 1983-84; clin. psychology intern Chgo.-Read Mental Health Ctr. Ill. Dept. Mental Health, 1985-86; mem. faculty dept. psychology Moraine Valley C.C., Palos Hills, Ill., 1988-89; lectr. psychology Daley Coll., Chgo., 1988-90; cons. Gordon & Assocs., Oak Lawn, Ill., 1989; adolescent, child and family therapist Orland Twp. Youth Svcs., Orland Park, Ill., 1993; psychology fellow Sch. Medicine, St. Louis U., 1994-95; pvt. practice Geneva and St. Charles, Ill., 1996—; founder Maximum Potential, Chgo., 1996—. Contbr., author: Transpersonal Hypnosis, 1999. Chair program com. Lincoln Park Bus. Devel. Inst., 2003—. Ill. State scholar, 1969-73; Calif. Inst. Integral Studies scholar, 1983. Mem. APA (chair edn. and tng. com. divsn. 30 1998-2000, chair mem. svcs. 2001—), Am. Psychol. Soc., Am. Women in Psychology, Ill. Psychol. Assn., Calif. Psychol. Assn., Mo. Psychol. Assn., Fla. Psychol. Assn., Am. Soc. Clin. Hypnosis, Chgo. Soc. Clin. Hypnosis, NOW (chair legal adv. corps, Chgo. 1974-76), Lincoln Park C. of C. (chair program com. 2003—). Avocations: playing piano, gardening, reading, backpacking, writing. Office: 2210 Dean St Ste E-1 Saint Charles IL 60175 E-mail: d.osowiec@att.net.

OSSENBERG, HELLA SVETLANA, psychoanalyst; b. June 10, 1930; came to U.S., 1957, naturalized, 1964; d. Anatole E. and Tatiana N. (Dombrovski) Donath; m. Carl H. Ossenberg, June 7, 1958. Diploma langs. and psychology, U. Heidelberg, Germany, 1953; MS, Columbia U., 1968. cert. Nat. Psychol. Assn. Psychoanalysis, 1977; diplomate Am. Bd. Examiners. Sr. psychiat.. social worker VA Mental Hygiene Clinic, N.Y.C., 1975-88. Mem. Theodor Reik Cons. Center 1978—; field instr. Columbia U., Fordham U. schs. social work. Mem. NASW, Acad. Cert. Social Workers, Nat. Psychol. Assn. Psychoanalysis, Nat. Assn. Advancement Psychoanalysis (Am. Bds. Accreditation and Certification), Coun. Psychoanalytic Psychotherapists. Office: 345 W 58th St New York NY 10019

OSSERMAN, ROBERT, mathematician, educator, writer; b. N.Y.C., Dec. 19, 1926; s. Herman Aaron and Charlotte (Adler) O.; m. Maria Anderson, June 15, 1952; 1 son, Paul; m. Janet Adelman, July 21, 1976; children—Brian, Stephen. BA, NYU, 1946; postgrad., U. Zurich, U. Paris; MA, Harvard U., 1948, PhD, 1955. Tchg. fellow Harvard U., 1949-52, vis. lectr., rsch. assoc., 1961-62; instr. U. Colo., 1952-53; mem. faculty Stanford U., 1955-94, prof. emeritus, 1994—, prof. math., 1966—, chmn. dept. math., 1973-79, Mellon Prof. Interdisciplinary Studies, 1987-90; dep. dir. Math. Scis. Rsch. Inst., Berkeley, Calif., 1990-95, dir. spl. projects, 1995—. Mem. NYU Inst. Math. Scis., 1957-58, Math. Scis. Rsch. Inst., Berkeley,., 1983-84, head math. br. Office Naval Rsch., 1960-61; researcher and author publs. on differential geometry, complex variables, differential equations, astronomy, cosmology, especially minimal surfaces, isoperimetric inequalities. Author: Two-Dimensional Calculus, 1968, A Survey of Minimal Surfaces, 1969, 1986, Poetry of the Universe, 1995; author: (videos) Fermat's Last Theorem, 1994, Mathematics in Arcadia, 1999, Galileo: A Dialog, 2000; co-author (with Steve Martin): Funny Numbers, 2003. Fulbright lectr. U. Paris, 1965-66; Guggenheim fellow, 1976-77; vis. fellow U. Warwick, Imperial Coll., U. London. Fellow AAAS; mem. Am. Math. Soc., Math. Assn. Am., Astrom. Soc. Pacific. Office: Math Sci Rsch Inst 17 Gauss Way Berkeley CA 94720

OSSIP-KLEIN, DEBORAH JANN, psychologist, educator; b. Miami Beach, Fla., June 2, 1955; d. Albert Edward and Kathrine (Freidkin) Ossip; m. Andrew Mark Ossip-Klein, Aug. 22, 1982; children: Jenna Eve, Alison Gwen. BA in Psychology and Sociology, U. Miami, Fla., 1975; MS in Clin. Psychology, U. Pitts., 1978, PhD in Clin. Psychology, 1981. Intern U. Miss. and Jackson VA Med. Ctr., 1980-81; asst. prof. psychology U. Rochester, N.Y., 1981-88, assoc. prof. psychology, 1988—; sr. scientist comty. and preventive medicine, 1994—. Dir. smoking rsch. program U. Rochester, 1984—. Contbr. 25 articles to profl. jours., 5 chpts. to books. Research dir., co-founder Smoking Relapse-Prevention Hotline, 1981—; mem. smoking or health com. Am. Lung Assn., Rochester and Albany, N.Y., 1983-85; chmn. strategic planning com., Albany, 1984-85. Recipient Outstanding Performance award Dept. VA Med. Ctr., Canandaigua, N.Y., 1993; grantee Nat. Cancer Inst., 1984-91, Am. Cancer Soc., 1989-91, Nat. Inst. Aging, 1992-93, Dept. VA, 1993—. Mem. AAUP, APA, Soc. Behavioral Medicine. Jewish. Home: 12 San Rafael Dr Rochester NY 14618-3702

OSTAR, ALLAN WILLIAM, academic administrator, higher education consultant; b. East Orange, N.J., Sept. 4, 1924; s. William and Rose O.; m. Roberta Hutchison, Sept. 10, 1949; children. Cert. engring., U. Denver, 1943; BA, Pa. State U., 1948; postgrad., U. Wis., 1949-55; LL.D., U. No. Colo., 1968, Eastern Ky. U., 1972, Whittier Coll., 1973; L.H.D., U. Maine, 1975; D.Letters, Central Mich. U., 1975; D.P.S., Bowling Green State U., 1975, R.I. Coll., 1983; D.Higher Edn., Morehead State U., 1977; L.H.D., Appalachian State U., 1977, No. Mich. U., 1978, Dickinson State Coll., N.D., 1979, Towson State U., 1980, Salem State Coll., 1980, Mont. Coll. Mineral Sci. and Tech., 1983, Ball State U., 1984; LL.D., U. Alaska, 1978, Ill. State U., 1983, Western Mich. U., 1984; D. Polit. Sci., Kyung Hee U., Korea, 1984; L.H.D., Fitchburg State Coll., 1986, Bridgwater State Coll., 1988, No. State Coll., 1988, Harris-Stowe State Coll., 1986; LLD, Edinboro U. Pa., 1987, Loch Haven U., Pa., 1989; LHD, No. Ariz. U., 1990, Shepherd (W.Va.) Coll., 1992, SUNY, 1993, Lincoln U., Mo., 1995. Dir. nat. pub. relations U.S. Nat. Student Assn., 1948-49; exec. asst. Commonwealth Fund, N.Y.C., 1952-53; asst. to dean extension div. U. Wis., 1949-52, dir. office communications services, 1954-58; dir. Joint Office Instnl. Research, Nat. Assn. State Univs. and Land Grant Colls., Washington, 1958-65; pres. Am. Assn. State Colls. and Univs., Washington, 1965-91, pres. emeritus, 1991—; sr. cons. Acad. Search Consultation Svc., 1991—. Adj. prof. edn.

Pa. State U., 1990—. Co-author: Colleges and Universities for Change, 1987; contbr. chpts. in books. Mem. 42d (Rainbow) div. U.S. Army, 1943-46. Decorated 2 Bronze Stars; recipient Centennial award for disting. svcs. to edn. U. Akron, 1970, Fogelsanger award Shippensburg (Pa.) State Coll., 1974, World Peace Through Edn. medal Internat. Assn. U. Pres., 1975, Disting. Achievement award, U. So. Colo., 1979, Chancellor's award U. Wis., 1985, Chancellor's medal CUNY, 1986, Disting. Alumnus award Pa. State U., 1989, svc. award Coun. on Internat. Ednl. Exch., 1990, Chancellor's medal Internat. Svc. U. Ark., Little Rock, 1990, Disting. Pub. Svc. medal Dept. of Def., 1991; Alumni fellow Pa. State U., 1975. Unitarian-Universalist. Home: 5500 Friendship Blvd Chevy Chase MD 20815-7219

OSTEN, MARGARET ESTHER, librarian; b. Mukacevo, Czechoslovakia; came to U.S., 1949; Profl. Diploma, Prague and Budapest, 1944, PhD, 1946; Indsl. Engr. Diploma, Vysoka Skola Obchodni, Prague, 1948; MS in Libr. Sci., Columbia U., 1952. Cert. pub. libr., N.Y. Prof. Prague Coll., Czechoslovakia, 1945-48; various to sr. cataloguer, libr. Columbia U., N.Y.C., 1952-59; sr. libr. Bklyn. Pub. Libr., 1959-62; libr., asst. prof. Manhattanville Coll., Purchase, N.Y., 1962-65; supr. libr., asst. sect. head; acting head of post 51 Nat. Union Catalog, 1965-69; head, cataloguing dept. CUNY Grad. Ctr., 1969-71; chief libr. Leo Baeck Inst., N.Y.C., 1971-72; libr.-in-charge, Engring. Libr. CUNY, 1972-75. Tchr. St. John's Univ. Grad. Sch. Libr. Sci., 1972; lectr. 3rd World Congress of Czechoslovak Soc. Arts, Sci., Columbia U., 1966; curator of an exhibit, 50th anniversary of Czechoslovak Republic, 1968; Czechoslovakian del. to Coun. of European Women in Exile, pres., 1959; others. Contbr. articles to newspapers. Served on elections com. Morningside Heights Consumers Co-operative Columbia U. area, Manhattan, N.Y. Mem. ALA, SLA, N.Y. Libr. Club, AAUP, Nat. Coun. Women of Free Czechoslovakia (bd. dirs.), Nat. Coun. Women of U.S. Avocations: libr. sci., polit. econs., langs., skiing, tennis. Home: 80 La Salle St New York NY 10027-4711

OSTERHOLM, J(OHN) ROGER, humanities educator; b. Worcester, Mass., Nov. 24, 1936; s. Walfred Anders and Ellen Olivia (Hendrickson) O.; m. Jo-Ann M. Doiron, Dec. 22, 1962 (div. 1981); children: Doreen, Jon R., Don J.; m. Diane Jane Ungerer, May 1, 1982 (div. 2002). BA, Upsala Coll., 1959; MA, CCNY, 1966; PhD, U. Mass., 1978; postgrad., Tex. Tech U., 1961-62, Worcester (Mass.) State Coll., 1965-66, Clark U., 1972. Announcer, disk jockey Sta. WFMU, East Orange, N.J., 1957-59; instr. Worcester Jr. Coll., 1962; supr. Aetna Life Ins. Co., N.Y.C., 1963-65; tchr. Wachusett Regional H.S., Holden, Mass., 1965-66; assoc. prof. Ctrl. N.E. Coll., Worcester, 1966-79, chmn. humanities, 1977-79; prof. Embry-Riddle Aero. U., Daytona Beach, Fla., 1979—2002, prof. emeritus, 2002—. Cons. Am. Pub. U., 1998—; spkr. on journalism, aviation films and Bing Crosby; advisor to coll. student publs., 1969-94, 1997-2002; designer on-line comm. and humanities courses Integrated Curriculum in Engring, Embry-Riddle Aero. U., 1998-2002. Author: Literary Career of Isaiah Thomas, 1978, Bing Crosby: A Bio-bibliography, 1994; editor: The Riddle Reader, 1988; co-author: MiG-15 to Freedom, 1996; contbr. articles to profl. jours. and Guide to U.S. Popular Culture (Encyclopedia); performer, actor Daytona Beach Playhouse, 1980-83, Embry-Riddle Aero. U., 1985-89, Ormond Beach Performing Arts Ctr., 2002. Dirs. Daytona Playhouse, Daytona Beach, 1980-83; lector Grace Luth. Ch., Ormond Beach, Fla., 1989—; pres. Civility at Large, 1998—. With USAF, 1960-62. Recipient Best Supporting Actor award Daytona Playhouse, 1981. Mem.: Ormond Beach Theatre Workshop, Internat. Crosby Cir., Air Force Assn., Popular Culture Assn., Rho Tau Sigma, Alpha Phi Omega. Republican. Avocations: acting, airplane models, computer simulations. E-mail: DocJollyR@aol.com.

OSTERKAMP, DALENE MAY, psychology educator, artist; b. Davenport, Iowa, Dec. 1, 1932; d. James Hiram and Bernice Grace Simmons; m. Donald Edwin Osterkamp, Feb. 11, 1951 (dec. Sept. 1951). BA, San Jose State U., 1959, MA, 1962; PhD, Saybrook Inst., 1989. Lectr. U. Santa Barbara (Calif.) Ext., 1970-76, San Jose (Calif.) State U., 1976—82; prof. Bakersfield (Calif.) Coll., 1961-87, prof. emerita, 1987—; adj. faculty, counselor Calif. State U., Bakersfield, 1990—95. Gallery dir. Bakersfield Coll., 1964-72. Juried group shows include Berkeley (Calif.) Art, Ctr., 1975, Libr. of Congress, 1961, Seattle Art Mus., 1962. Founder Kern Art Edn. Assn., Bakersfield, 1962, Bakersfield Printmakers, 1976. Staff sgt. USAF, 1952-55. Recipient 1st Ann. Svc. to Women award Am. Assn. Women in C.C., 1989. Mem. APA, Assn. for Women in Psychology, Assn. for Humanistic Psychology, Calif. Soc. Printmakers. Home: PO Box 387 Glennville CA 93226-0387 Office: Calif State Univ Stockdale Ave Bakersfield CA 93309

OSTHOFF, PAMELA BEMKO, secondary education educator; b. Orange, N.J., Nov. 6, 1953; d. Julian Boris and Olga Donelik Bemko; children: Joseph, Kathryn. BA in Spanish and Secondary Edn., Fla. So. Coll., 1975. Sci. tchr. Kathleen Jr. H.S., Lakeland, Fla., 1975-76; Spanish and English tchr. Lake Gibson Jr. H.S., Lakeland, 1976-83; Spanish tchr. Lakeland Sr. H.S., 1983—. Recipient 1st Pl. Nat. award for econ. edn. Nat. Coun. Econ. Edn., 1995, 97, Govs. award for excellence in econ. edn. State Econ. Coun., Tampa, Fla., 1995, 96, 97, 99, 2000, 01, 03, Leavey award for econ. edn. Freedoms Found., Valley Forge, Pa., 1997, Lakeland High Tchr. of the Yr, 1998, Walmart Tchr. of the Yr., 2000, World Lang. Tchr. of Yr., 2002; semi-finalist NASDAQ Edn. Found. and NCEE regional, 1999, 2000, 01. Mem. Am. Assn. Tchrs. Spanish and Portuguese, Fla. Fgn. Lang. Assn., Polk County Fgn. Lang. Coun. (past pres.), Kappa Delta Pi. Republican. Presbyterian. Avocations: traveling, reading, gourmet cooking. Home: 5327 Lisa Ave Lakeland FL 33813-3038 Office: Lakeland Sr HS 726 Hollingsworth Rd Lakeland FL 33801-5818

OSTRIKER, JEREMIAH PAUL, astrophysicist; b. N.Y.C., Apr. 13, 1937; s. Martin and Jeanne (Sumpf) Ostriker; m. Alicia Suskin, Dec. 1, 1958; children: Rebecca, Eve;1 child, Gabriel. AB, Harvard, 1959; PhD (NSF fellow), U. Chgo., 1964; postgrad., U. Cambridge, Eng., 1964—65; degree (hon.), U. Chgo., 1992. Rsch. assoc., lectr. astrophysics Princeton (N.J.) U., 1965—66, asst. prof., 1966—68, assoc. prof., 1968—71, prof., 1971—, chmn. dept. astronomy, dir. obs., 1979—95, Charles A. Young prof. astronomy, 1982—2002, provost, 1995—2001; Plumian prof. astronomy and exptl. philosophy U. Cambridge, England, 2001—. Author: Development of Large-Scale Structure in the Universe, 1991; editl.bd., trustee Princeton U. Press; contbr. articles to profl. jours. Recipient Vainu Bappu Meml. award, Indian Nat. Sci. Acad., 1993, Karl Schwarzschild medal, Astronomische Gesellschaft, 1999, U.S. Nat. medal of Sci., 2000; fellow Alfred P. Sloan, 1970—72. Fellow: AAAS; mem.: NAS (counselor 1992—95, bd. govs. 1993—95), Royal Netherlands Acad. Arts and Scis. (fgn.), Am. Acad. Arts and Scis., Am. Philos. Soc., Internat. Astron. Union, Am. Astron. Soc. (councilor 1978—80, Warner prize 1972, Russel prize 1980), Royal Astron. Soc. (assoc.), Am. Mus. Natural History (trustee 1997—). Home: 33 Philip Dr Princeton NJ 08540-5409 E-mail: jpo@astro.princeton.edu.

OSTROFSKY, ANNA, music educator, violinist; b. NYC, June 27, 1953; d. Joseph and Lena (Cipollone) Simeone; m. Frederick Ostrofsky, May 26, 1975; 1 child, Jacqueline. MusB, Manhattan Sch. Music, 1974, MusM, 1975; profl. diploma, Fordham U., 1990. Orch. dir., tchr. Harlem Sch. Arts, NYC, 1975-76; first violinist NJ Symphony Orch., Newark, 1975-76; string instr. Hoff-Barthelson Sch. Music, Scarsdale, NY, 1976-79; concertmaster Chappaqua Chamber Orch., NY, 1976-89; orch. dir./string instr. City Sch. Dist. New Rochelle, NY, 1978-83; first violinist Hudson Valley Philharm. Orch., Poughkeepsie, NY, 1981-89; 1st violinist Ea. Philharm. Orch., Greensboro, NC, 1982-83; orch. dir. Briarcliff Union Free Sch. Dist., Briarcliff Manor, NY, 1983—; 1st violinist Concert Soc. Putnam and No. Westchester, 1982—; first violinist New Rochelle Opera, NY, 1997, 98; adj. prof. violin/viola King's Coll., Briarcliff Manor, 1989-94. Coord. employment opportunities Westchester County (NY) Sch. Music Assn., Dist. coord. for Performing Arts, 2002-. Debut Carnegie Recital Hall, 1976; conductor Westchester Elem. All-County Orch., 1997. Recipient First prize Artists' Internat. Mgmt., 1975, Excellence in Chamber Music Teaching award Chamber Music Am., 1991. Mem. NY State Acad. Teaching and Learning. Democrat. Roman Catholic. Avocations: writing music composition and orchestration, reading, swimming, walking, cooking. Home: PO Box 396 Somers NY 10589-0396 Office: 444 Pleasantville Rd Briarcliff Manor NY 10510-1922 Fax: 914-769-2509.

OSTROFSKY, BENJAMIN, business and engineering management educator, industrial engineer; b. Phila., July 26, 1925; s. Eli and Edith (Segal) O.; m. Shirley Marcia Welcher, June 2, 1956; children: Keri Ellen Pearlson, Marc Howard. BSME, Drexel U., 1947; M in Engring., UCLA, 1962, PhD in Engring., 1968. Registered profl. engr., Tex., Calif. Lectr. Engring. Systems Design, UCLA, L.A., 1962-68; dir. ctr. mgmt. studies and analyses Coll. Bus. Adminstrn., Houston, 1970-72, prof. prodn. and logistics mgmt., 1969-73, chmn. dept., 1972-74; prof. indsl. engring. Cullen Coll. Engring., Houston, 1970—2003; prof. ops. mgmt. Coll. of Bus. Adminstrn., Houston, 1973-98, prof. emeritus, 2003—. Lectr. Army Rsch. Inst., others; v.p. Tech. Soc. Logistics Engrs., 1974-76; nat. dir. Logistics Edn. Found., 1980-98, acad. advisor, 1990—. Author: Design, Planning and Development Methodology, 1977; co-author: Manned Systems Design: Methods, Equipment and Applications, 1981. Program mgr. USAF Office of Sci. Rsch. project, 1977-86. Lt. U.S. Army, 1943-45, USAF, 1950-53. Fellow AAAS, Soc. Logistics Engrs. (cert. profl. logistician, chmn. nat. edn. com. 1972-74, sr. editor Annals 1986-98, mng. editor 1986-98, Armitage medal 1978, Eccles medal 1988, Founders medal 1993); mem. NSPE, Inst. Indsl. Engrs., Ops. Rsch. Soc. Am., Decision Scis. Inst., Am. Soc. for Engring. Edn., IEEE Engring. Mgmt. Soc., Blue Key, Sigma Xi, Tau Beta Pi, Phi Kappa Phi, Alpha Iota Delta, Alpha Pi Mu. Home: 14611 Carolcrest Dr Houston TX 77079-6405

OSTROM, KATHERINE ELMA, retired educator; b. LA, Dec. 30, 1928; d. Charles W. and Mabel M. (Christensen) Shults; m. Carl R. Ostrom, Jan. 29, 1949 (dec.); children: Margaret K. Larson, Carl R. Jr. BA cum laude, U. Wash., 1966, MA in Tchg. English, 1973, EdD, 1994. Std. tchg. cert. grades K-12, Wash.; continuing prin. cert.-secondary, Wash. Substitute tchr. Renton, Kent & South Ctrl. Sch. Dist., 1966; tchr. Foster HS, Tukwila, Wash., 1966-67, 75-76, Showalter Mid.Sch., Tukwila, 1967-79; dept. chair Showalter Mid. Sch., Tukwila, 1968-87, vice prin., 1979-87; tchr., supr. student tchr. U. Wash., Seattle, 1989-91; subs. tchr. Tukwila Sch. Dist., 1999—. Tchr. Western Wash. State Coll., Bellingham, 1967-68; liaison, supr. Jr. Achievement, Seattle, 1988-89; cons., trainer Nat. Assn. Elem. Sch. Prins., 1992-98; vol. tchr. Immigrant & Refugee Resources Ctr., Seattle, 1996-2003; dir. Forum on Edn., PDK, Seattle, 1997; mem. Citizen Adv. Com. in Curriculum, Renton, S.D., 2001-2003, chair, 2002-03. Host del. Tukwila-Ikawa (Japan) Sister Cities, Seattle, 1980; chair Tukwila-Ikawa (Japan) Sister City, Seattle, 1999—2002; block-watch organizer King County, Wash., 1994—2001; key communicator Renton (Wash.) Sch. Dist., 1996—2003; tutor Skyway Meth. Ch., Seattle, 1997—2000, staff parish com., 1996—. Named Vol. of Yr., BPW, Tukwila, Wash., 1990; Coll. scholar U. Puget Sound, Tacoma, Wash., 1946; Pathfinder award, 1997. Mem. Assn. Wash. Sch. Prin. (chair state vice prin. conf. 1986, regional dir. 1986-88), Wash. Physicians for Social Responsibility (del. to Mid. East 1994), Key Players, Prosser Piano and Organ, Phi Delta Kappa (pres. chpt. 1991-95, newsletter editor 1988-90, 1995-2003, area coord. 1995-2001), Phi Beta Kappa (bd. dirs., trustee Puget Sound Assn., 2000—, pres. Puget Sound Assn., 2003—). Democrat. Home: 12817 80th Ave S Seattle WA 98178-4911 E-mail: kateostrom@aol.com.

OSTROVSKY, LEV ARONOVICH, physicist, oceanographer, educator; b. Vologda, USSR, Dec. 10, 1934; s. Aaron L. Ostrovsky and Lidiya A. (Warshawskaya) Khvilivitskaya; children: Svetlana, Alexander. Cert. rsch. physicist in radiophysics, U. Gorky, USSR, 1957; PhD, U. Gorky, 1964; Dr Sci, Acoust. Inst., Moscow, 1973. Lead engr. Design Bureau, Gorky, 1957-59; asst. prof., then assoc. prof. physics Poly. Inst., Gorky, 1962-65; sr. researcher Radiophys. Rsch. Inst., Gorky, 1965-77; chief scientist and head lab. Inst. Applied Physics Russian Acad. Sci., Nizhni Novgorod (formerly Gorky), 1977—; assoc. prof to prof. U. Nizhni Novgorod, 1966-94; prof. sr. rsch. scientist U. Colo./NOAA Environ. Tech. Lab., Boulder, 1994-2001; Orson Andersen fellow Inst. Geophys. and Planet. Physics Los Alamos Nat. Lab., 1998-99; sr. scientist Zel Tech./NOAA Environ. Tech. Lab., 2001—. Co-author: Nonlinear Wave Processes in Acoustics, 1990, English edit., 1998, Modulated Waves, 1999; author or co-author 3 lectr. notes; editor 4 book translations from English to Russian, 3 paper collection books, a topical dictionary; mem. editl. and adv. bds. including Chaos; contbr. articles to various Russian sci. jours.; patentee in field. Recipient State Prize of USSR, 1985, USSR State Discovery Cert., 1982. Fellow Acoustical Soc. Am.; mem. Acoustical Soc. Russia, European Geophys. Soc., Am. Geophys. Union. Office: Zel Tech/NDAA ETL R/ETL-O Boulder CO 80305 E-mail: lev.a.ostrovsky@noaa.gov.

OSTROW, RONA LYNN, librarian, educator; b. N.Y.C., Oct. 21, 1948; d. Morty and Jeane Goldberg; m. Steven A. Ostrow, June 25, 1972; 1 child, Ciné Justine. BA, CCNY, 1969; MS in LS, Columbia U., 1970; MA, Hunter Coll., 1975; PhD., Rutgers U., 1998. Cert. libr., N.Y. Br. adult and reference libr. N.Y. Pub. Libr., N.Y.C., 1970-73, rsch. libr., 1973-78; asst. libr. Fashion Inst. Tech., N.Y.C., 1978-80; assoc. dir. Grad. Bus. Resource Ctr., Baruch Coll., CUNY, 1980-90, assoc. prof., 1980-90; assoc. dean of librs. for pub. svcs. Adelphi U., Garden City, N.Y., 1990-94; chief libr. Marymount Manhattan Coll., N.Y.C., 1994-98; asst. provost Fairleigh Dickinson U., Teaneck, N.J., 1998-2000; chief libr. Lehman Coll. CUNY, Bronx, 2000—. Author: Dictionary of Retailing, 1984, Dictionary of Marketing, 1987; co-author: Cross Reference Index, 1989. Mem.: ALA, Assn. Coll. and Rsch. Librs. Office: CUNY Lehman Coll Libr 250 Bedford Park Blvd W Bronx NY 10468-1589 E-mail: rostrow@lehman.cuny.edu.

O'SULLIVAN, GERALD JOSEPH, association executive; b. Chgo., Dec. 9, 1941; s. Gerald Thomas and Norine Rita (Herbert) O'S.; m. Joan Griffin, June 14, 1992; children from previous marriage: Stacey Marie, Lauren Ann; 1 stepchild, Kelly. Student, Chgo. Tchrs. Coll., Roosevelt U., MPA, 1974. Cert. tchr., Ill.; cert. law enforcement officer, Ill. Pub. health adminstr. Chgo. Dept. Health, 1968-76, dir. fiscal svcs., 1976-78, dir. mgmt. and ops., 1978-81, adminstrv. dir., 1981-83; dir. personnel Ill. Atty. Gen. Office, Chgo., 1983-86, dir. ops., 1986-91; dir. program devel. Genesis Schs., Inc., Chgo., 1991-93; sr. v.p. ops. World Trade Ctr. Chgo. Assn., 1993-94; sr. ops. mgr. Chgo. Mfg. Tech. Ctr., 1994-95; supt. Impact Incarceration Cook County Sheriff's Office, 1995-96; exec. dir. Cook County Sherrif's Tng. Acads., 1997—. Community prof. Gov. State U., Chgo., 1986-88; prof. grad. program Roosevelt U., Chgo., 1974-81; cons E.W. Lynch Vocat. Sch., Chgo. Mem. steering com. Ill. Juvenile Justice Inst., 1992-93; bd. dirs. Apple Canyon Lake Property Owners' Assn., Apple River, Ill., 1988-90; mem. City of Chgo. Task Force Brownnfields Land Redevel., 1995. Staff sgt. U.S. Army, 1964-66. Mem. Soc. Human Resource Mgmt., Nat. Sheriff's Assn., Law Enforment Tng. Mgrs. Assn., Ill. Chiefs Police Assn., Ill. Juvenile Justice Inst. (steering com. 1992-93), Chgo. Bar Assn. (justice for youth com. 1992-93), Ill. C. of C., Sierra Club, City of Chgo. Exec. Alumni (past v.p.), Thunderbird Internat. Sch. Mgmt. Alumni. Roman Catholic. Office: Cook County Sheriffs Tng Inst 2000 N 5th Ave River Grove IL 60171-1907

OSUNDE, EGERTON OYENMWENSE, social studies and social sciences educator, curriculum studies educator; b. Kano City, Kano, Nigeria, July 6, 1950; s. Gabriel Osagbovo and Beatrice Ayi (Eke) O.; m. Awawu Kuru Yesufu, July 8, 1980; children: Ifueko, Isoken, Enoghama, Osagie, Osayimwense. BSc with honors, Ahmadu Bello U. Zaria, Nigeria, 1975; MA, MSc LS, Case Western Reserve U., 1979; MA, PhD, Ohio State U., 1984. Tchr. Oguola Elem. Pub. Sch., Benin City, Nigeria, 1967-68, asst. prin., 1969; tchr. Edaiken Grammer Sch., Benin City, Okhuaihe, Nigeria, 1970-72; lecturer II U. Benin, Benin City, Nigeria, 1980-81; grad. teaching assoc. Ohio State U., Columbus, Ohio, 1982-84; lecturer I faculty of edn. U. Benin, 1988-86, sr. lectr., 1988-91; post-doctoral teaching assoc. Ohio State U., Columbus, 1990-91; asst. prof. U. Bloomsburg, Bloomsburg, Pa., 1991—. Manuscript reviewer Journal Higher Edn., Ohio State U., Columbus, 1987, Social Edn. Nat. Coun. Social Studies, Wash., 1992; mem internat. edn. advisory bd. Bloomsburg U., Pa., 1991— Author: High School Social Studies, 1992; contbr. (chapt. in book) Education and Development, 1987; founding editor: Nigeria Journal of Social Studies, 1987-90; contbr. to profl. jours. Recipient Imokhumw's prize Holy Trinity Grammer Sch., Nigeria, 1965, AAHE prize Am. Assn. Higher Edn., 1984, Pa. SSHE award Pa. Office Social Equity, 1993; Fulbright Hays scholar U.S. Dept. Edn., 1993. Mem. Assn. Supervision and Curriculum Studies, Comparative and Internat. Edn. Soc., Nat. Coun. Social Studies, Ind. Coun. Social Studies, Nat. Soc. for Study of Edn., Phi Delta Kappa, Social Studies Assn. Nigeria, Avocations: table tennis, photography, listening to music, reading. Office: Bloomsburg U Dept Curr & Found 3103 McCormick Hall Bloomsburg PA 17815

OSWALD, JAMES MARLIN, education educator; b. Plainview, Tex., Aug. 17, 1935; s. James Buchanan and Eula Bea (Marlin) O.; m. Dorothy Anne Veigel, Dec. 27, 1956; children: Richard, Ramona, Roberta. BS, West Tex. State Coll., 1957, MA, 1958; EdD, Stanford U., 1970. Tchr., supr. Salt Lake City Pub. Schs., 1958-66; curriculum specialist Am. Insts. Rsch., 1966-68; staff assoc. Nat. Coun. Social Studies, 1968-69; asst. prof. social studies and social sci. edn. Syracuse (N.Y.) U., 1969-72; rschr.-writer, dir. global cultural studies edn. projects Am. Univs. Field Staff, 1972-75; asst. supt. instrn. East Penn Sch. Dist., Emmaus, Pa., 1975-78; field coord. Pa., Del. and N.J. citizen edn. Rsch. for Better Schs., Phila., 1978-80; instrnl. devel. specialist C.C. Phila., 1980-96; energy conservation cons., 1959—; edn. cons., 1963—. Propr. Energy Cons. and Main Line Stoves, 1972—; pres. N.Y. State Coun. Social Studies, 1971-72; co-founder, pres. Inst. Plant Based Nutrition, 1996—; pres. PlantKingdomGourmet.com, VeganFund-.com, VeganQuality.com, 2000—. Author: The Monroe Doctrine: Does It Survive?, 1969; Research in Social Studies and Social Science Education, 1972; co-author: Earthship, 1974, Planet Earth, 1976, Our Home, the Earth, 1980, Marco Polo Vegan Cuisine, 1998, Christopher Columbus Vegan Cuisine, 1999, Criteria for Nutritional Guidelines for Century 21, 1999, Ferdinand Magellan Vegan Cuisine, 2000, Commemoration of Heroic Produce Grower Sacrifices, Death and Survival on September 11, 2001, 2001, Garden of Eden Vegan Cuisine, 2003, Astronaut Vegan Cuisine, 2003, New York City Vegan Cuisine, 2003, Philadelphia Vegan Cuisine, 2003; introduced concepts of global cultural studies, 1972, humanself, 1972, zero runoff landscaping, 1979, veganomics, 1998, veganocracy, 1998, veganagro, 1998, microagro, 2003; editor quar. newsletter Plant Based Nutrition, website www.plantbased.org; contbr. articles to profl. jours.; cons. on energy efficiency, ecol. conservation, plant based econ. devel., zero runoff landscaping, solar energy utilization, solid-fuel heating, natural air conditioning, human phys. devel., weight and energy mgmt., life coaching, vegan nutrition, veganic-organic gardening, home farming, kitchen and comml. seed sprouting, welfare to work food prodn., fin., life, career and retirement planning. With U.S. Army, 1957-58, USAR, 1958-68. Recipient Sertoma Svc. to Mankind award, Salt Lake City, 1966; grantee Stanford U., NSF, U.S. Office Edn., Inst. Internat. Studies; Henry Newell fellow Stanford U., 1966-68; Fulbright-Hays SEAsia U. Singapore Study Program fellow, 1967. Mem. Am. Vegan Soc. (life), Vegan Soc. (U.K.), Vegan Organic Network Horticulture-Agr. (U.K.), Hastings-Halliburton Vegetarian Assn. (Can.), Inst. Nutrition Edn. and Rsch. (bd. advisor), Inst. Plant Based Nutrition, N.Am. Vegetarian Soc. (life), Physicians Com. for Responsible Medicine, Vegetarians of Phila., Vegetarian Resource Group, Toronto Vegetarian Assn., Main Line Vegetarian Soc. (founding pres.), Ctr. for Cancer Edn., Hindu Temple Soc. Am., Internat. Soc. Kirsna Consciousness, Food for Life Internat., Internat. Oak Soc., Social Sci. Edn. Consortium (life), Tex. Panhandle-Plains Hist. Soc., Utah Hist. Soc. (life), Desc. Founders of Ancient Windsor, Windsor Hist. Soc., Pa. Assn. for Sustainable Agr., Farm Animal Reform Mvmt., Pa. Hort. Soc., Pa. Forestry Assn., Pa. State Hort. Assn., Pa. Fruit Grower Assn., Pa. Vegetable Growers Assn., Pa. Nut Growers Assn., Vegetable Growers Assn. N.J., Lower Merion Hist. Soc., Va. Nut Growers Assn., Stanford Club Phila., Keystone Trails Assn., Phi Delta Kappa (emeritus). Home and Office: 333 Bryn Mawr Ave Bala Cynwyd PA 19004-2606 E-mail: jmoswald@bellatlantic.net.

OSWALT, (EUGENE) TALMADGE, educational administrator; b. Tuscaloosa, Ala., Sept. 3, 1935; s. James Carl and Ethel (Kemp) O.; m. Katherine Johnson, Apr. 2, 1954; 1 child, Eugene T. Jr. BS, U. Ala., 1958; MAT, U. Montevallo, 1963; EdD, Auburn U., 1975. Cert. tchr., supr., adminstr., Ala. Tchr., adminstr. Montgomery (Ala.) Pub. Schs., 1958-63, supr. instrn., 1963-74, asst. supt., 1974-91; tchr. St. John Resurrection Cath. Sch., Montgomery, 1991-92; acads. dir. Ala. Ind. Schs. Assn., Montgomery, 1992—. Adj. assoc. prof. Auburn U. at Montgomery, 1974—; adj. asst. prof. Troy State U., Montgomery, 1981-91. Mem. ASCD, NEA. Democrat. Baptist. Home: 6021 Meridian Ln Montgomery AL 36117-2759 Office: Ala Ind Schs Assn Huntingdon College Montgomery AL 36106

OSZAJCA, SHARON-ANN ELIZABETH, elementary education educator; b. Providence, Oct. 5, 1946; d. Matthew Joseph and Genevieve (Zommer) O. BS, R.I. Coll., 1968, MEd, 1971. Cert. tchr., Spl. edn. tchr., N.H.; cert. tchr., R.I. Tchr. Stone Hill Elem. Sch., Cranston, R.I., 1968-71, Edgewood Highlands, Cranston, 1971-75, Beulah Elem. Sch., Richmond, Va., 1975-79, Tunbridge (Vt.) Cen. Sch., 1980-86; tchr. resource rm. Stevens High Sch., Claremont, N.H., 1986-88; coord. secondary spl. edn. Claremont Sch. Dist., 1988-89; tchr. resource rm. Claremont Jr. High Sch., 1989-90; learning specialist Cornish (N.H.) Elem. Sch., 1990—. Mem. aux. Tunbridge Fire Dept., 1982-84. Mem. NEA, Coun. Exceptional Children (divsn. learning disabilities, divsn. early childhood, divsn. children with communication disorders, coun. children with behavioral disorders), Cornish Edn. Assn., N.H. Edn. Assn. Avocations: reading, creative writing, needlework. Home: PO Box 108 Cornish Flat NH 03746-0108 Office: Cornish Sch Dist RR 2 Box 400 Cornish NH 03745-9801

OTHERSEN, HENRY BIEMANN, JR., pediatric surgeon, physician, educator; b. Charleston, S.C., Aug. 26, 1930; s. Henry and Lydia Albertine (Smith) O.; m. Janelle Lester, Apr. 4, 1959; children: Megan, Mandy, Margaret, Henry Biemann III. BS, Coll. Charleston, 1950; MD, Med. Coll. S.C., 1953. Diplomate: Am. Bd. Surgery, Am. Bd. Thoracic Surgery, Am. Bd. Pediatric Surgery. Intern Phila. Gen. Hosp., 1953-54; postgrad. U. Pa., 1956-57; resident in gen. surgery Med. Coll. S.C., Charleston, 1957-62; resident in pediatric surgery Ohio State U. and Columbus Children's Hosp., 1962-64; research fellow Harvard U., Mass. Gen. Hosp., Boston, 1964-65; asst. prof. pediatric surgery Med. U. S.C., Charleston, 1965-68, assoc. prof., 1968-72, prof., 1972—, chief pediatric surgery, 1972-98; med. dir. Med. U. S.C. Hosp., 1981-85, Children's Hosp., 1985—2001, med. dir. profl. staff, 1996—2001, physician liaison for documentation, 2002—; acting chief surgery VA Hosp., 2002—. Editor The Pediatric Airway; mem. editorial bd. Jour. Pediatric Surgery, Jour. Parenteral and Enteral Nutrition; contbr. articles on pediatric oncology, esophageal, tracheal strictures to profl. jours. Bd. dirs., pres. S.C. divsn. Am. Cancer Soc., 1977-79. Served with USN, 1954-56, Korea. Fellow ACS, Am. Acad. Pediatrics; mem. Am. Pediatric Surg. Assn. (bd. govs. 1986-89, pres.-elect 1996, pres. 1997), Brit. Assn. Pediatric Surgeons (overseas coun.), Am. Surg. Assn., So. Surg. Assn., Am. Trauma Soc., Charleston County Med. Soc. (pres. 1980), Alpha Omega Alpha (councilor 1978-94). Office: Pediatric Surgery PO Box 250613 96 Jonathan Lucas St Ste 418 CSB Charleston SC 29425 Fax: 843-792-3858. E-mail: othershb@musc.edu.

OTT, C(LARENCE) H(ENRY), citizen ambassador, accounting educator; b. Richmond, Mich., Jan. 20, 1918; s. Ferdinand and Wilhelmina (Radkte) O.; m. Helen Louise McKay, Oct. 29, 1942 (dec. Apr. 1994); children: James Richard, Dennis McKay, Richard Darrel, Delene Michelle. BA, Valparaiso U., 1940; MBA, Northwestern U., 1970; PhD, Southeastern U., 1980. CPA, N.Y.; cert. mgmt. acct., N.Y. Chief acct. G.E. X-Ray Corp., Chgo., 1940-41; pub. auditor Arthur Andersen & Co., Chgo., 1941-43; renegotiator contracts U.S. Army Air Corps, Chgo., 1943-45; internal auditor David Bradley Mfg. (Sears), Bradley, Ill., 1945-48; contr., treas. Manco Mfg. Co., Bradley, 1948-59; owner, operator Yellow-Checker Cab Co., Kankakee, Ill., 1959-70; chmn. acctg., prof. Rochester (N.Y.) Inst. Tech., 1970-73, Southwestern Mich. Coll., Dowagiac, Mich., 1973—; citizen amb. People to People Internat., Kansas City, Mo., 1992—. Curriculum advisor Southwestern Mich. Coll., Dowagiac, 1992—. Del. to Russia to faciliate their transition to Dem. form of govt.; del. leader Wharton Sch. Fin., U. Pa., Phila., 1992, Citizen Ambassador to many countries including Tahita, Bora Bora, Moorea, Cuba, Quebec, Can., Ecuador, Galapagos Islands, Israel, Egypt, Hong Kong, Mainland China, Greece, Greek Islands, Turkey, Singapore, India, Japan, France, Morocco, Portugal, Spain, Russia, British Isles, Italy, Iceland, Greenland. Mem. Nat. Assn. Accts., Inst. Cert. Mgmt. Accts., Planning Execs. Inst. (spkr., chmn.), Alpha Kappa Psi, Pi Kappa Alpha, Pi Gamma Mu. Republican. Avocations: travel, golf, bowling, reading, exercise. Home: 30992 Middle Crossing Rd Dowagiac MI 49047-9268

OTT, PAULA NISBET, nursing and emergency medical technician educator; b. Peoria, Ill., Nov. 21, 1944; d. Paul McCracken and Melcena Ellen (Arvin) Nisbet; m. Franklin Leo Ott, Nov. 8, 1966; children: Penelope, Jason, Cynthia. BSN, Ill. Wesleyan Coll., 1966; MEd, Northeast La. U., 1977. Cert. Indsl. Audiometric Tech., ARC Instr. First Aid and CPR, Basic and Advanced EMT Instr. Operating room supr. Glenwood Regional Med. Ctr., West Monroe, La., 1966; staff RN Rockford (Ill.) Meml. Hosp., 1966; mental health community nurse H. Douglas Singer Zone Ctr., Rockford, 1966-69; instr. Delta Ouachita Regional Tech. Inst., West Monroe, 1969-88, dept. head health occupations, 1988—2003. Nursing cons. GM Fisher Guide, Monroe, 1989—; regional faculty Am. Heart Assn. Author: (with others) Cole's Basic Nursing Skills, 1991, Instructor's Guide and Concepts, 1991. La. Lung Assn. scholar, New Orleans, 1980; named Educator of Yr., La. Votech. Tchr. of Yr. State Dept. Edn., Baton Rouge, 1986. Mem. Am. Vocat. Assn. (policy com., region IV educator of yr., 1982), Nat. Assn. Health Occupation Tchrs. (treas., 1980-82, outstanding svc. award, 1983), La. Vocat. Assn. (parlimentary historian exec. coun., outstanding svc. award, 1982), La. Assn. Health Occupations Edn. (pres., past pres., exec. coun., tchr. of year, 1982), La. Soc. EMT Instr. Coords. (edn. com. chair, 1986—), Sigma Theta Tau Internat. Republican. Mem. Assembly of God Ch. Avocations: swimming, crafts, cooking, travel, drawing. Home: 462 Bailey Rd Farmerville LA 71241-5544 Office: La Tech Coll Delta Ouachita Campus 609 Vocational Pky West Monroe LA 71292-0127

OTT, SABINA, art educator; b. N.Y.C., Oct. 8, 1955; d. Aaron and Rita (Schwartz) O.; m. Bruce Robert Gluck, Dec. 16, 1978 (div. Apr. 1982). BFA, San Francisco Art Inst., 1979, MFA, 1981. Assoc. prof. Calif. State U., L.A., 1990-94; mem. grad. faculty Art Ctr. Coll. of Design, Pasadena, Calif., 1985-95; assoc. prof., dir. grad. program Washington U., St. Louis, 1996—. Bd.. dirs. L.A. Contemporary Exhbns.; mem. bd. advisors Found. for Art Resources, L.A., 1991—. Solo exhbns. include San Francisco Mus. Art, 1988, The Corcoran Gallery of ARt, 1990, L.A. County Museum of Art, 1992, 200 Gertrude St., Melbourne, Australia, 1996, Forum for Contemporary Art, 1997. Mem. fundraisng com. Coalition for Freedom of Expression, 1989-90; activist WAC, L.A., 1989-91. Grantee NEA, 1990; recipient New Talent award L.A. County Museum of ARt, 1986. Mem. Coll. Art Assn., Forum for Contemporary Art, Critical Mass (bd. dirs. 1997—, St. Louis). Office: Washington U Sch Art Room 100 CB1031 One Brookings Dr Saint Louis MO 63130

OTT, WALTER RICHARD, academic administrator; b. Bklyn., Jan. 20, 1943; s. Harold Vincent and Mary Elizabeth (Butler) Ott; m. Carla M. Narrett, May 27, 2002; children: Regina Winter Burrell, Christina W. Chiappetta, Walter R. Jr. BS in Ceramic Engring., Va. Poly. Inst. and State U., 1965; MS in Ceramic Engring., U. Ill., 1967; PhD in Ceramic Engring., Rutgers U., 1969; DSc (hon.), Alfred U., 2001. Registered profl. engr., Pa. Process engr. Corning Inc., Buckhannon, W.Va., 1965-66; staff research engr. Champion Spark Plug Co., Detroit, 1969-70; prof. engring. Rutgers U., New Brunswick, N.J., 1970-80; dean, assoc. provost N.Y. State Coll. Ceramics, Alfred, 1980-88; provost, chief acad. officer Alfred U., Alfred, 1988-2000; pres. Predictive Edge, Inc., West Orange, NJ, 2000—; v.p. enrollment mgmt. Caldwell (N.J.) Coll., 2002—. Rsch. assoc. Atomic Energy Commn.-E.I. duPont de Nemours, Aiken, S.C., 1971; cons. Haight & Hofeldt Inc., Chgo., 1984-88, Pillsbury, Mpls., 1977-79, Ctr. for Profl. Advancement, New Brunswick, 1971-79, Hammond (Ind.) Lead Products, 1970-80; bd. dirs. Victor (N.Y.) Insulator Inc., UNIPEG, 1987-88; treas.. Alfred Tech. Resources N.Y.; bd. dirs. Grads Found., N.Y.C. Contbr. articles to profl. jours.; patentee in field. Recipient Ralph Teetor award Soc. Automotive Engrs., 1973, PACE award Nat. Inst. Ceramic Engrs., 1975, Ann. award Ceramic Assn. N.J., 1980; named to Greaves Walker Roll, Keramos, 1991. Fellow Am. Ceramic Soc. (trustee 1980-83, v.p. 1988-89); mem. Ceramic Ednl. Coun. (pres. 1976-77), Ceramic Assn. N.Y. (treas. 1980-88, bd. dirs.), Ceramic Assn. N.J. (bd. dirs. 1974-80), Keramos (pres. 1982-84, Greaves-Walker Roll of Honor 1991), Tau Beta Pi. Avocations: tennis, reading. Home: 165 Clarken Dr West Orange NJ 07052-3429 Office: Caldwell College Caldwell NJ 07006

OTTE, PAUL JOHN, academic administrator, consultant, trainer; b. Detroit, July 10, 1943; s. Melvin John Otte and Anne Marie (Meyers) Hirsch; children: Deanna Kropf, John. BS, Wayne State U., 1968, MBA, 1969; EdD, Western Mich. U., 1983. With Detroit Bank and Trust Co., 1965-68; teaching fellow Wayne State U., Detroit, 1968-69; auditor, mgr. Arthur Young & Co., Detroit, 1969-75; contr., dir. Macomb Community Coll., Warren, Mich., 1975-79, v.p. bus., 1979-86; pres. Franklin U., Columbus, Ohio, 1986—, prof. undergrad. and grad. programs, 1986—. Author various tng. manuals, 1982. Cpl. USMC, 1961-65. Teaching fellow Wayne State U., 1968-69. Mem. AICPA, Mich. Assn. CPAs (chmn. continuing profl. edn. com. 1980-82, leadership com. 1981-83), Nat. Assn. Coll. and Univ. Bus. Officers (acctg. prins. com. 1986), Assn. Ind. Colls. and Univs. Ohio (bd. dirs.), Greater Detroit C. of C. (leadership award 1983), Columbus C. of C. (info. svc. com.). Roman Catholic. Avocations: travel, speaking engagements. Office: Franklin U 201 S Grant Ave Columbus OH 43215-5399

OTTINO, JULIO MARIO, chemical engineering educator, scientist; b. La Plata, Buenos Aires, Argentina, May 22, 1951; came to U.S., 1976; naturalized, 1990; s. Julio Francisco and Nydia Judit (Zufriategui) O.; m. Alicia I. Löffler, Aug. 20, 1976; children: Jules Alessandro, Bertrand Julien. Diploma in Chem. Engring., U. La Plata, 1974; PhD in Chem. Engring., U. Minn., 1979; exec. program Kellogg Sch. Mgmt., Northwestern U., 1995. Instr. in chem. engring. U. Minn., Mpls., 1978-79; asst. prof. U. Mass., Amherst, 1979-83, adj. prof. polymer sci., 1979-91, assoc. prof. chem. engring., 1983-86, prof., 1986-91; Chevron vis. prof. chem. engring. Calif. Inst. Tech., Pasadena, 1985-86; sr. rsch. fellow Ctr. for Turbulence Rsch. Stanford (Calif.) U., 1989-90; Walter P. Murphy prof. chem. engring. Northwestern U., Evanston, Ill., 1991-2000, chmn. dept. chem. engring., 1992-2000; McCormick Inst. prof., 2000—; George T. Piercy Disting. prof. U. Minn., 1998, prof. mech. engring., 2001—. Cons. to U.S. and European corps.; Allan P. Colburn Meml. lectr. U. Del., 1987; Merck Sharp & Dohme lectr. U. P.R., 1989, Stanley Corrsin lectr. Johns Hopkins U., 1991; Centennial lectr. U. Md., 1994, William N. Lacey lectr. Calif. Inst. Tech., 1994, P. V. Danckwerts Meml. lectr. Inst. Chem. Engring., Eng., 1999; Robb lectr. Pa. State U., 2002; mem. tech. adv. bd. Dow Chem.; mem. bd. dirs. Coun. Chem. Rsch. Author: The Kinematics of Mixing: Stretching, Chaos and Transport, 1989; contbr. articles to profl. jours.; assoc. editor Physics Fluids A, 1991—; mem. editl. bd. Internat. Jour. Bifurc. Chaos, 1991—; assoc. editor Am. Inst. Chem. Engring. Jour., 1991-95, assoc. editor., 1995—; one man art exhibit, La Plata, 1974. Recipient Presdl. Young Investigator award NSF, 1984, Alpha Chi Sigma award AIChE, 1994, W.H. Walker award AIChE, 2001, E.W. Thiele award AIChE, Chgo., 2002; Univ. fellow U. Mass., 1988, J.S. Guggenheim fellow, 2001; Lacey lectureship, Calif. Inst. Tech., 1994, Danckwerts lectureship Royal Instn., 1999, Robb lectr. Pa. State U. Fellow Am. Phys. Soc.; mem. AAAS, NAE, Am. Acad. Arts and Scis., Am. Chem. Soc., Am. Phys. Soc., Soc. Rheology, Am. Soc. Engring. Edn., Sigma Xi (disting. lectr. 1997-99), Coun. for Chem. Rsch.(gov. bd. coun. 1999-2001). Achievements include research in granular dynamics, chaos, complex systems and mixing. Avocations: visual arts, painting. Home: 1092 Crescent Ln Winnetka IL 60093-1501 Office: Northwestern U Dept Chem Engring 2145 Sheridan Rd Evanston IL 60208-0834 E-mail: jm_ottino@northwestern.edu.

OTTO, FRED BISHOP, retired physics educator; b. Bangor, Maine, Aug. 17, 1934; s. Carl Everett and Edna Rosena (Bishop) O.; m. Alma Merrill, June 23, 1957; children: Janet, Nancy, Robert, Kathryn. BS, U. Maine, 1956; MA, U. Conn., 1960, PhD, 1965. Asst. prof. physics Colby Coll., Waterville, Maine, 1964-68; asst. prof. elec. engirng. U. Maine, Orono, 1968-74; design engr. Eaton W. Tarbell & Assocs., Bangor, Maine, 1974-79; quality control engr. Pyr-A-Lavm, Brewer, Maine, 1979-80; cons. engr., Orono, 1980-84; instr. physics Maine Maritime Acad., Castine, 1982-89, 1989-93, assoc. prof., 1993-96, prof., 1996-98; asst. prof. Husson Coll., Bangor, 1998—2000; ret., 2000. Editor: Instructor's Resource Manual to Accompany Wilson's Physics, 1992, (contbg. editor) The Castle Electrical Curriculum, 1992; contbr. articles to profl. jours. Mem. Am. Phys. Soc., Am. Assn. Physics. Tchrs., Illuminating Engring. Soc. Methodist. Home: 430 College Ave Orono ME 04473-4230

OTWELL, DONNA SHARON, history educator; b. Hot Springs, Ark., June 3, 1951; d. Woodrow James and Elsie (Randolph) O. BSE, Ouachita Bapt. U., Arkadelphia, Ark., 1973, MSE, 1977; EdD, U. Memphis, 1994. Tchr. devel. reading, geography, Am. history and psychology North Little Rock (Ark.) Sch. Dist., 1979—. Recipient Educator of the Yr. award, 1987, PTA Lifetime award 1988; named All-Am. scholar Nat. Coll. award U.S. Achievement Acad., 1995. Mem. Phi Delta Kappa (past pres.), Alpha Delta Kappa, Delta Kappa Gamma, Alpha Delta Kappa (v.p.).

OU, LO-CHANG, physiology educator; b. Shanghai, Oct. 16, 1930; came to U.S., 1964; m. Cynthia Chin Ou, June 10, 1960; children; Winnie, Edward, Emily, Joseph. BS, Peking U., Beijing, 1954; PhD, Dartmouth Coll., 1971. Tchg. asst., dept. biochemistry Peking U., Beijing, 1954-60, lectr., dept. biochemistry, 1960-62; demonstrator, dept. physiology Hong Kong U., 1962-64; asst. prof. dept. physiology Dartmouth Med. Sch., Hanover, N.H., 1977-80, assoc. prof., 1980-85, rsch. prof., 1985—, prof. emeritus (active), 1998—. NIH rsch. grantee, 1977-94. Mem. Am. Physiol. Soc. Achievements include research on pathophysiology of high altitude. Office: Dartmouth Med Sch Dept Physiology Lebanon NH 03756 E-mail: Lo.Chang.Ou@Dartmouth.edu.

OURS, MARIAN LEAH, elementary education educator; b. Tallmansville, W.Va., Apr. 6, 1937; d. Mayford Thaddeus and Leila Joy (Tenney) O. BS, W.Va. U., 1960, MA, 1965. Tchr., libr. Monongalia County Schs., Morgantown, W.Va., 1960-68; tchr., dept. head Fremont (Calif.) Unified Sch. Dist., 1968—. Mem. libr. task force Fremont Unified Sch. Dist., 1989-90, dist. and secondary math. com., 1980—, tech. task force, 1992, 93. Mem. Santa Clara County Libr. Commn., San Jose, Calif., 1991—, chair, 1989-90; mem. Milpitas (Calif.) Libr. Commn.; treas. Friends of Milpitas Libr., 1990, 92,93, pres., 1987-89. Recipient Ednl. Leadership award Fremont Sch. Adminstrs. Assn., 1985, Cert. of Appreciation PTA, 1984, Tchr. of Month Fremont Bd. Edn., 1988. Mem. Nat. Coun. Tchrs. Math., Calif. Math. Coun., Computer Using Educators, Fremont Unified Dist. Tchrs. Assn., Calif. Tchrs. Assn. Methodist. Office: Walters Jr High 39600 Logan Dr Fremont CA 94538-1990

OUSLEY, LAURIE M. English educator; b. Providence, Sept. 21, 1969; d. Clifford Roger and Mildred Louise (Hemberger) O. BA in English, R.I. Coll., 1993; MA in English, Clark U., 1997; PhD, SUNY, Buffalo, 2003. Tchg. asst. Clark U., Worcester, Mass., 1994-96; instr. composition Becker Coll., 1996; writing tutor Anna Maria Coll., 1996-97; instr. lit. Becker Coll., 1997; tchg. asst. SUNY, Buffalo, 1997—2003; mem. faculty dept. English and philosophy Monroe C.C., Rochester, NY, 2003—. Asst. Huxley Libr., 1994-95; mem. editl. staff Worcester Hist. Mus., 1995; conf. presenter in field. Contbr. to Dictionary of Literary Biography, 1997. Reading and writing tutor Literacy Vols. Am., 1990-92. Presdl. fellow SUNY, 1997-01. Mem. MLA, N.E. MLA, Children's Lit. Assn., Constitution Island Assn. Office: Monroe CC Dept English and Philosophy 1000 E Henrietta Rd Rochester NY 14623

OUTEN, DAWN, secondary education educator; b. L.A., Mar. 4, 1942; d. Jesse Lee and Joe Anna (Joshua) Williams; m. Wilbert Outen Jr., Sept. 1, 1964; children: JohAnna, Clarence, Christy. B of Human Studies, Dominguez Hills U., Carson, Calif., 1976; MEd, U. LaVerne, Calif., 1986; postgrad., Nova U., Ft. Lauderdale, Fla., 1992—. Tchr. L.A. Unified Sch. Dist., 1977-81, Compton (Calif.) Unified Sch. Dist., 1981-86; multi-cultural coord. Chino (Calif.) Unified Sch. Dist., 1986—. Part-time faculty Calif. Poly. State U., Pomona, 1990-92; mem. steering com. Los Angeles County Bd. Edn., L.A., 1984—; lectr. multi cultural, child and youth studies and tech. in edn. Contbr. articles to profl. jours. Mem. steering com. on interracial unity YWCA, Pomona, 1992—; v.p. Parents Against Violence in Edn., Chino, 1992. Recipient Outstanding Contbns. award Constl. Rights Found., L.A., 1987, Recognition of Svc. award County of Los Angeles, 1992. Mem. ASCD, Calif. Tchrs. Assn., Chino Valley C. of C., Notary Assn., Coun. of Negro Women, Univ. Women, Phi Delta Kappa. Republican. Christian. Avocations: music, theater, reading, computer. Office: Chino Unified Sch Dist 5130 Riverside Dr Chino CA 91710-4130

OUZTS, EUGENE THOMAS, minister, secondary education educator; b. Thomasville, Ga., June 7, 1930; s. John Travis and Livie Mae (Strickland) O.; m. Mary Olive Vineyard, May 31, 1956. BA, Harding U., Searcy, AR, 1956, MA, 1957; postgrad., Murray State U., KY, U. Ark., U. Ariz., Ariz. State U., No. Ariz. U. Cert. secondary tchr., Ark., Mo., Ariz.; cert. c.c. tchr., Ariz.; ordained minister Church of Christ, 1956. Min. various chs., 1957—65; tchr. various pub. schs., 1959—92; min. Ch. of Christ, Ariz., 1965—; 1st lt. CAP/USAF, 1980, advanced through grades to lt. col., 1989, chaplain, 1982—, asst. wing chaplain, 1985—. Adviser student activities Clifton (Ariz.) Pub. Schs., 1965-92; bd. dirs. Ariz. Ch. of Christ Bible Camp, Tucson, 1966—. Mem. airport adv. bd. Greenlee County, Clifton, Ariz., 1992—. Recipient Meritorious Svc. award, 1994, Exceptional Svc. award, 1997, Civil Air Patrol; named Ariz. Wing Chaplain of Yr, 1984, Thomas C. Casaday Unit Chaplain of Yr., 1985, Ariz. Wing Safety Officer of Yr., 1989, Ariz. Wing Sr. Mem. of Yr., 1994, Southwest Region Sr. Mem. of Yr., 1995, Civil Air Patrol. Mem. Mil. Chaplains Assn., Air Force Assn., Disabled Am. Vets., Am. Legion, Elks. Democrat. Avocations: flying, building and flying model aircraft, reading. Home and Office: HC 1 Box 557 Duncan AZ 85534-9720

OVEDOVITZ, ALBERT CHESTER, economist, educator; b. Bklyn., Jan. 23, 1944; s. Louis Charles Ovedovitz and Bella (Greenberg) Shamaskin; m. Rita Lee Forman, May 27, 1967; children: Lon Alan, Eric Neal. BA in Econs., Stats., CUNY Queens Coll., 1964, MA in Econs., 1966; PhD of Econs., CUNY, 1974. Asst. prof. econs. SUNY, Fredonia, 1967-68, Elmira (N.Y.) Coll., 1968-70; statistician Statis. Office UN, N.Y.C., 1970-74; prin. rsch. analyst County of Suffolk, N.Y., 1975-82; prin. rsch. officer Ctr. for Labor and Urban Programs CUNY Queens Coll., Flushing, 1982-83; assoc. prof. computer info. sys./decision scis. St. John's U., Jamaica, N.Y., 1984—. Cons. statis., forensic econ., 1970—; cons. World Trade Ctr. Victims Compensation Fund. Author: Business Statistics in Brief, 2001; editor: Crisis in Population, 1969; contbr. articles to profl. jours. Fellow Nat. Def. Edn. Act, 1964. Mem. AAUP, Am. Statis. Assn. (Meritorious Achievement award 1987), Nat. Assn. Forensic Econs. Office: Saint John's Univ Grand Central And Utopia Pkwy Jamaica NY 11439-0001 E-mail: rial527@optonline.net.

OVERTON, EDWIN DEAN, campus minister, educator; b. Dec. 2, 1939; s. William Edward and Georgia Beryl (Fronk) O. BTh, Midwest Christian Coll., 1963; MA in Religion, Ea. N.Mex. U., 1969, EdS, 1978; postgrad., Fuller Theol. Sem., 1980. Ordained to ministry Christian Ch., 1978. Min. Christian Ch., Englewood, Kans., 1962-63; youth min. 1st Christian Ch., Beaver, Okla., 1963-67; campus min. Cen. Christian Ch., Portales, N.Mex., 1967-68, Christian Campus House, Portales, 1968—; tchr. religion, philosophy, counseling Ea. N.Mex. U., Portales, 1970—, acting chmn. religion dept., 2000. Dir. Campus Christian House, 1980—; farm and ranch partner, Beaver, Okla., 1963—. State dir. Beaver Jr. C. of C., 1964-65; pres. Beaver H.S. Alumni Assn., 1964-65; elder Cen. Christian Ch., Portales, 1985-88, 90-93; chmn. Beaver County March of Dimes, 1966; neighborhood chmn. Portales March of Dimes, 1997; pres. Portales Tennis Assn., 1977-78. Mem. U.S. Tennis Assn., Am. Assn. Christian Counselors, Ea. N.Mex. U. Faith in Life Com., Lions Club. Republican. Home: 1129 Libra Dr Portales NM 88130-6123 Office: Christian Campus House 223 S Avenue K Portales NM 88130-6643 E-mail: campusmin@juno.com.

OVERTON, ELIZABETH NICOLE, elementary school educator, aerobics instructor; b. Fayetteville, NC, Dec. 22, 1966; d. Hilton Rudolph and Pearl Elizabeth (Jackson) Barefoot; m. Stephen Mark Overton, Mar. 29, 1997; children: Jessup Colton, Caden Jackson. BA in English, Campbell U., 1989, MEd in English Edn., 1996, MEd in Elem. Edn., 1999. Lic. tchr., N.C.; cert. fitness instructor, Nat. Dance Exercis Instr.'s Tng. Assn. Tutor gifted students Campbell U., Buies Creek, N.C., 1987-88; tchr. secondary English and journalism Sampson County Schs., Clinton, N.C., 1989-97; tchr. 2d grade reading Harnett County Schs., Lillington, N.C., 1997-2000; instr. aerobics Hardbodies, Erwin, N.C., 1997—; tchr. 3d grade Harnett County Schs., Dunn, NC, 2000—03, tchr. 2d grade, 2003—. Advisor yearbook Raider, Sampson County Schs., 1990-97, asst. editor lit. mag. Lyricist, 1987-88; editor, pub. newsletter Tiger Times, 1997—; entertainer as Belkie Bear, Easter Bunny, Chelsie the Clown, Dunn, N.C., 1983-89. Judge Miss Erwin Denim (Little Miss), 1996; mem., soloist adult choir Stoney Run Ch., Dunn, 1981—, tchr. vacation Bible sch., 1988—, tchr. Sunday sch., 1990-91, 1999-2001. Mem. Nat. Coun. Tchrs. of English, N.C. Assn. Educators (bldg. rep. 1991-92), Woodmen of the World, Omicron Delta Kappa, Kappa Delta Pi, Phi Kappa Phi, Delta Kappa Gamma. Republican. Baptist. Avocations: fitness training, hiking, reading, travel. Home: 13339 Harnett-Dunn Hwy Dunn NC 28334 Office: Harnett Primary Sch 800 W Harnett St Dunn NC 28334

OVREBO, JUDITH, retired physical education educator; b. Wausau, Wis., Mar. 28, 1950; d. Donald Irving and Rozella Eileen (Boggs) O.; m. Harold Marvin Oberg, July 5, 1975 (div.); children: Jessica Kristine, Deborah Elisabeth. BS, U. Conn., 1972; MS in Phys. Edn., U. R.I., 1978; grad., So. Conn. State U., 1986, postgrad., 1992. Tchr. phys. edn. Fitch Jr. High Sch., Groton, Conn., 1972-79, Fitch Sr. High Sch., Groton, Conn., 1979-97. Mentor co-op. tchr. State of Conn., Groton, 1988—; evaluator New Eng. Assn. Schs. and Colls., 1993. Chairperson phys. edn. sub-com. New Eng. Assn. of Schs. and Colls., Groton, Conn., 1988-90; bd. dirs. Ledyard (Conn.) Girls Softball League, 1989—, mgr., coach, 1989—; coach Ledyard Youth Basketball League, 1991—; mentor Take Stock in Children, Ocala, Fla.; organizer Connections, 2000—; vol. Hospice Marion County, Gerla, Fla., 2002-. Mem. AAHPERD, NEA, Am. Softball Assn., Conn. Assn. Health, Phys. Edn., Recreation and Dance, Conn. Edn. Assn., Groton Edn. Assn., Nat. Assn. Sports and Phys. Edn., Nat. Assn. Girls and Women Sports, Phi Kappa Phi. Avocations: swimming, organ. church involvement, reading. Home: 7598 SW 81st Pl Ocala FL 34476-6924 E-mail: jovrebo@cs.com.

OWEN, BERNICE DOYLE, nursing educator; BS, U. Iowa, 1963; MS in Pub. Health Nursing, U. Minn., 1964; PhD, U. Wis., 1982. Staff nurse VA Hosp., Madison, Wis., 1964-65; pub. health nurse Dane County Health Dept., Madison, 1965-66; instr. pub. health nursing U. Wis. Madison Sch. Nursing, 1966-69, asst. prof., head pub. health nursing, 1969-72, assoc. clin. prof. pub. health nursing, 1972-77, chairperson primary health care div., 1975-77, lectr., 1977-82, asst. prof., 1982-88, assoc. prof., 1988-91, prof., 1991—. Part time asst. prof. U. Wis.-Milw., Sch. Nursing, 1984; mem. expert panel to develop clin. guidelines for low back disorders Agy. for Health Care Policy and Rsch., U.S. Dept. Health and Human Svcs., 1991-92; cons. and presenter in field. Ad hoc reviewer: Rsch. in Nursing and Health, 1987-88, 92; reviewer for manuscripts: Nat. Inst. for Occupational Safety and Health, 1985-91, Lippincott, Inc.; contbr. articles to profl. jours. Recipient scholarship Fireman's Fund Ins. Co., 1980-81, 1981-82, Schering award for occupational health nursing for WIs., 1990, Pres. Vol. Action award Point of Light Found., 1993; numerous rsch. and ednl. grants. Mem. ANA, APHA, Wis. Nurses' Assn., Madison Dist. Nurses Assn., Am. Assn. Occupational Health Nurses, Am. Assn. Occupational Health Nurses of South Cen. Wis. (treas. 1984-88, sec. 1994-96), Wis. State Assn. Occupational Health Nurses (bd. dirs. 1988-90), Wis. Pub. Health Assn. (legis. com. 1968-69, bd. dirs. 1973-75, aging com. 1974-75, injury prevention com. 1984—, co-chair membership com. 1991-93, v.p. 1994-96). Assn. Comty. Health Nursing Educators, Sigma Theta Tau (Beta Eta chpt. chair eligibility com. 190-92, others). Avocations: photography, swimming, reading, fishing, gardening. Home: 1001 Pflaum Rd Madison WI 53716-2827 Office: U Wis Sch Nursing 600 Highland Ave # H6242 Madison WI 53792-3284

OWEN, CAROL THOMPSON, artist, educator, writer; b. Pasadena, Calif., May 10, 1944; d. Sumner Comer and Cordelia (Whittemore) Thompson; m. James Eugene Owen, July 19, 1975; children: Kevin Christopher, Christine Celese. Student, Pasadena City Coll., 1963; BA with distinction, U. Redlands, 1966; MA, Calif. State U., L.A., 1967; MFA, Claremont Grad. Sch., 1969. Cert. cmty. coll. instr., Calif. Head resident Pitzer Coll., Claremont, Calif., 1967-70; instr. art Mt. San Antonio Coll., Walnut, Calif., 1968-96, prof. art, 1996—, 1996-97, prof. emeritus, 1997, dir. coll. art gallery, 1972-73. Group shows include Covina Pub. Libr., 1971, U. Redlands, 1964, 65, 66, 70, 78, 88, 92, Am. Ceramic Soc., 1969, 97, 99, 2000, Mt. San Antonio Coll., 1991, The Aesthetic Process, 1993, Separate Realities, 1995, Sequence 1, 2001, San Bernardino County Mus., 1996, 97, 98, 99, Tampa Fla. Black, White & Gray, Artists Unltd., 1998, Current Clay VII, La Jolla, Calif., 1998, Westmoreland Art Nat., 1998, 99, Riverside Art Mus., 1998, Fine Art Inst. Juried Show, San Bernardino, 1998, 99, 2000, Parham Gallery, L.A., 1998, 99, Angels Gate Cultural Ctr., San Pedro, Calif., 1998, Los Angeles County Fair, Pomona, Calif., 1998, Monrovia, Arts Festival, 1998, Art for Heavens Sake Festival, 1998, 99, Riverside Art Mus., 1998, 99, 2000, Birger Sandzen Meml.Gallery McPherson, Kans., 1998, 2000, Earthen Art Works Gallery, LA, 1999, State Polytechnic U., Pomona, 1999, 2001, Mo. State U., Warrensburg, 1999, City, of Brea Gallery, 1999, 2000, All Media Exhibit, Chico, Calif.. 1999, Period Gallery, Omaha, 1999, 2000, 01, 02, Mixed Media, Period Gallery, 2002, Franklin Square Gallery, Southpoet, NC, 1999, 2000, Judson Gallery, LA, 1999, San Angelo (Tex.) Mus. Fine Arts, 2000, So. Calif. Juried Art Exhbn., San

Bernardino, Calif., 2000, Gallery 212, Ann Arbor, Mich., 2000, Judson Gallery, LA, 2000, Artists Unltd., Inc., Tampa, Fla., 2000, Urban Inst. Contemporary Arts, Grand Rapids, Mich., 2000, Tri-Lakes Ctr. for Arts, Palmer Lake, Colo., 2000, Santa Cruz Art League, Calif., 2000. Fine Arts Inst., San Bernardino County Mus., Redlands Calif. 2000, Vermont Artisan Designs, Brattleboro, 2000, USA Craft '99, New Caanan, Cons., 1999, Keith Gallery, Dexter, Mich., 1999, Claremont Forum Gallery, 1999, Parham Gallery, Santa Monica, Calif., 1999 (Grand prize 1999), City of Brea Galleries, Calif., 2000, 01, Chiarosouro Galleries, Chgo., 2000, TLD Design Ctr. and Gallery, Westmont, Ill., 2000, 2001, North Tahoe Art Ctr., Calif., 2000, Palos Verdes Art Ctr., Rancho Palos Verdes, Calif., 2000, Peck Gallery, Providence, 2000, Alder Gallery, Oreg., 2001, Rocky Mt. Arts Ctr., NC, 2001, Esmay Fine Art Gallery, Rochester NY, 2001, Hillcrest Festival, 2001, Dysfunctional, Business of Art Ctr., Manitou Springs, Colo., 2001, Nat. Juried Exhbn., Gallery 214, Montclair, NJ, 2002, Mt. San Antonio Coll., Walnut, Calif., 2001, Gallery Mia Tyson, Wilmington, NC, 2002, Millard Sheets Gallery, Pomona, Calif., 2002 (Honorable mention), Period Gallery, "Abstraction", Omaha, 2002, "Cup: The Intimate Object", Rocky Mount Art Ctrs., Rocky Mount, NC, 2003, Ink & Clay 29 Exhbn., Kellogg U. Art Gallery, Calif. State Poly. U., Pomona, 2003, Period Gallery, Omaha, 2003, Feats of Clay XVI Lincoln (Calif.) Arts, 2003, Sanchez Art Ctr., Pacifica, Calif., 2003, "Containment", SKH, Great Barrington, Mass., 2003, Charlie Cummings Clay Studio, Ft. Wayne, Ind., 2002, numerous others; ceramic mural commd. U. Redlands, 1991; represented in permanent collections Redlands Art Assn Gallery, Redlands; artwork in (book) Collectible Teapots, 2000; Group Internat. Exhbn. Internationale Wertbewerb Salzbrand Keramic, 2002, der Handwerks Kammer Koblenz, Galerie Handwerk, Germany, 2002. Recipient San Bernardino County Mus., 1996, Hon. Mention, 1998, 1999,; Past Pres. Monetary award, 1997, Jack L. Conte Design Cons. Purchase award Westmoreland Art Nat., 1998, 3rd Pl. Monetary award All Calif. City of Brea Galleries, 2000, Honorarium for teapots Urban Inst. Contemporary Arts, Grand Rapids, Mich., 2000. Mem. Am. Ceramic Soc. (design divsn., Design chpt. monetary award 1999), Calif. Scholarship Fedn., Coll. Art Assn. Am., Friends of Huntington Library, L.A. County Mus. Art, Redlands Art Assn., Heard Mus. Assn., Riverside Art Mus., Fine Arts Inst., Sigma Tau Delta. Republican. Presbyterian.

OWEN, CAROLYN SUTTON, educator; b. Shreveport, La., Jan. 7, 1932; d. S.T. and Kathleen Willard (Judkins) Sutton; m. Donald Curtiss Owen, Aug. 6, 1955 (dec. May 2003); children: Judith Kathleen Owen Moen, Kyle Curtiss. BA, La. Tech., 1953; MA, Tex. Woman's U., 1988. Cert. Tchr., Tex. Tchr. Calcasieu Parish, Lake Charles, La., 1953-54, Calcasien Parish, Westlake, La., 1955-56, San Antonio Independent Sch. Dist., 1954-55, Dallas Independent Sch. Dist., 1968-94; ret. Recipient Carolyn Owen Patio dedication J.L. Long Middle Sch. Faculty, 1980. Mem.: AAUW, NEA (life). Republican. Episcopalian. Avocations: horticulture, reading, travel. Home: 7737 El Santo Ln Dallas TX 75248-4316

OWEN, LARRY GENE, academic administrator, educator, electronic and computer integrated manufacturing consultant; b. Pine Bluff, Ark., Oct. 2, 1932; s. Cecil Earl and Helen Marie (Jacks) O.; m. Ruth MyrNewton, Sept. 3, 1953; children: Deborah, Patricia, Larry Gene, Shea. BS in Physics and Math., U. So. Miss., 1967; postgrad., Inst. Tech., 1974-75; MS n Ops. Mgmt., U. Ark., 1987. Enlisted USAF, 1951, advanced through ranks to master sgt., 1968, electronic technician, 1951-61, comms. supt., 1961-71, ret., 1971; tchr. math. and Physics Southwestern Tech. Inst., Camden, Ark., 1971-72, tchr. electronics, 1972-75; dean tech. engring.omputer Integrated Mfg. Ctr. So. Ark. U. Tech., Camden, 1988-89, dean, dir. divsn. Computer Integrated Mfg. Ctr., 1989-91, dean, prof., 1991-97, assoc. vice chancellor, 1996-98, dean emeritus, 1996—. Adj. asst. prof. So. Ark. U.; project dir. Ark. Consortium for Mfg. Competitiveness So. Growth Policies Bd., 1988-98; vice chair South Ark. Fiber Optics Coun., 1997. Contbr. articles to profl. jours. Mem. Rep. Task Force; chair Atea Coll. Cons., 1991—. Mem. Instrumentation Soc. Am. (sr.), Am. Assn. Physics Tchrs. Am. Tech. Edn. Assn. (rep. Ark. 1989-91, 95-96, pres. so. region 1992-93, chair Coll. of Cons.), Soc. Mfg. Engrs. (sr., chmn. South Ark. chpt. 1991-92, mem. govs. mfg. network adv. com.), Am. Legion (fin. dir. post 45). Baptist. Home: 306 Lakeside Ave Camden AR 71701-3237

OWEN, LARRY LESLI, management educator, retired military officer, small business owner; b. Dothan, Ala., Sept. 21, 1945; s. Lesley Homer and Doris (Teuten) O.; m. Betty Aldredge, Aug. 4, 1966; children: Kimberley, Larry Allen, Jonathan. BA in Human Resources, Pepperdine U., 1979; MS in Personnel Mgmt., Troy State U., Ala., 1986. Enlisted U.S. Army, 1963, advanced through grades to maj., battlefield commn., commd. 2d lt., 1970, inf. officer, 1970-85, ret., 1985. Instr. mgmt. Chattahoochee Valley State Coll., Phenix City, Ala., 1987-90, Patrick Henry Jr. Coll., 1990-94; instr. tng. for bus. and industry program Ala. So. Coll. Sys., 1992-94, Wallace C.C.-Selma, 1994—; tng. mgr., Riverdale Mill, 1994—; cons. Mil. Profl. Resources, Inc.; mem. Boise Cascade Tng. Task Force, 1992, chmn. Mgr.'s Roundtable, 1992; mem. Wallace C.C. Selma Tech. Prep Consortium. Designer, developer interactive video disc Combat Decision-Making, 1986 (Designer of Yr. award 1986), Mortar Tactical Tng., 1987. Chmn. Ft. Mitchell Nat. Cemetery, Phenix City, 1986-87, trustee, 1988-90; chmn. Vietnam Wall Com., Columbus, Ga., 1986-87; trainer Econ. Improvement Project, Phenix City, 1987-90; chmn. Nat. Am. Flag Run Com., 1989; chmn. tourism com. Phenix City C. of C., 1989; mem. scholarship and recruitment com. Auburn U. Paper/Pulp Found.; tech. adv. com. State of Ala., Dept. Edn. Named Instr. of Yr. U.S. Army, 1982. Mem. TAPPI (career devel. com. 1991—), ASTD, Soc. Human Resource Mgrs., Soc. Applied Learning Tech., Internat. Paper Maintenance Selection/Testing Com., Ala. State Dept. of Edn. Technology/Tech. Adv. com., Ala. State Workforce Devel Com., Jackson C. of C (pride com.), Phenix City/Russell County C. of C. (chmn. tourism com., bd. dirs.), 1st Cav. Assn. (Follow Me chpt., pres. 1985-87, 88-90), Chattahoochee Valley Vets. Coun. (co-chmn. 1986-90). Baptist. Avocations: fishing, hunting. Home: 1634 Northpointe Dr Deatsville AL 36022-2557

OWEN, SALLY ANN, gifted and talented education educator; b. Columbus, Wis., Aug. 14, 1932; d. Willard Ervin and Marian (Thomas) O.; m. Thomas. BS, U. Wis., 1955; MA, Pepperdine U., L.A., 1978; postgrad., U. Calif., La Jolla, San Diego State U. Cert. gifted edn. tchr., Calif. Tchr. humanities Am. Community Schs., Athens, Greece; tchr. English, counselor Dept. Def., Tokyo; secondary tchr. English history and phys. edn., counselor San Diego Unified Sch. Dist.; tchr. gifted and talented edn. ind. study seminar Point Loma High Sch., San Diego; tchr. interdisciplinary team, tchr. gifted and talented edn. ind. study seminar Standley Jr. High Sch. Mentor tchr., 1983—; presenter in lang. arts field. Recipient svc. award PTA, Latin Am. studies award. Mem. Assn. San Diego Educators for the Gifted (Tchr. of Yr. award 1991, Excellence in Gate Edn. award 1993, Gate New Voices in the Humanities award 1994-95), Calif. Assn. Tchrs. English, Nat. Coun. Tchrs. English (Lit. Mags. Excellence award). Home: 7295 Charmant Dr San Diego CA 92122-4384

OWEN, VIRGINIA BONNIE, secondary school educator; b. Madison, Wis., Dec. 17, 1945; d. Duane T. and HAzel (Eastman) Bonnie; m. John T. Owen, June 3, 1967; children: Jennifer, Shelly, David. B of Edn., U. Hawaii, 1969; postgrad., Colo. State U. Cert. tchr. Colo. Tchr. Poudre R-1, Ft. Collins, Colo., 1986—, dept. chmn. social studies, 1991—. Tchr. spl. administrv. assignment, 1993—. Leadership Ft. Collins C. of C., 1986—.

OWEN-RIESCH, ANNA LOU, economics and history educator; b. West Bend, Wis., Apr. 16, 1919; d. Louis J. and Emily (Dexheimer) Riesch; children: Deann, Todd, John. BE, U. Wis., Whitewater, 1940; PhM, U. Wis., 1942, PhD, 1952. Mem. faculty U. Wis., Milw., 1948-52, asst. dean L. and S. Madison, 1954-57, mem. faculty, 1954-56; vis. lectr. U. Colo., Boulder, 1958-69, asst. prof., 1969-83, assoc. prof., 1983-89, prof., 1989—. Social dir. Meml. Union, U. Wis., Madison, 1948-49; faculty advisor to student groups, U. Colo., Boulder, 1965-81; chmn. social studies Intedisciplinary Studies U. Colo., Boulder, 1983-85, honors dir., 1984-85. Author: Perlman's Lectures on Capitalism and Socialism, 1970, Conservation Under F.D. Roosevelt, 1983; contbr. articles to profl. jours. Lectr., workshop leader Benevolent Corps., West Bend, Wis., 1976-81; lectr. Intensive English Ctr., Boulder, 1978-82; vol. YMCA, Heart Assn., Cancer Found., Boulder, 1982-89. Named Hyde Park scholar, 1950; recipient Disting. Alumni Svc. award, U. Wis., Whitewater, 1983. Mem. AAUP, Miss. Valley Hist. Assn., Orgn. Am. Historians, Am. Hist. Assn., Am. Econ. Assn., Acad. Ind. Scholars, Delta Kappa Pi. Avocations: swimming, canoeing, hiking, boating, gardening, travel. Home: 200 Devon Pl Boulder CO 80302-8033 also: U Colo Honors-Norlin Libr University Of Colorado CO 80309

OWENS, CHERYL MICHELLE, behavior specialist; b. Fairbanks, Alaska, June 19, 1959; d. Billy J. and Reba J. (Cox) O. BS, Wright State U., 1981; MEd, Xavier U., 1985. Cert. learning disabled tchr., elem. edn. tchr., sch. counselor Ohio. Tchr. Ohio Vets. Children's Home, Xenia, 1981-86, Marburn Acad., Columbus, Ohio, 1986-88; ednl. specialist Ohio State U. Hosp.'s, Columbus, 1988-89; behavior specialist Columbus Pub. Schs., 1989—. Martha Holden Jennings Found. scholar, 1992-93. Mem. Coun. for Exceptional Children, Coun. for Children with Behavior Disorders, Coun. Adminstrs. Spl. Edn.

OWENS, GARLAND CHESTER, accounting educator; b. Wilson, N.C., Dec. 12, 1922; s. James F. and Leona (Owens) O.; m. Mary Elizabeth Wade, June 19, 1948; 1 dau., Lynn Carol. BS, U. Richmond, 1947; MS, Columbia U., 1948, PhD, 1956. C.P.A., N.Y. State. Acct. Arthur Young & Co. (C.P.A.s), N.Y.C., 1950-53; mem. faculty Columbia Grad. Sch. Bus., N.Y.C., 1956-86, prof., 1964-86; prof. emeritus Columbia U., 1986; assoc. dean Columbia Grad. Sch. Bus., 1962-70; prof. Mercer U. Sch. Bus., 1986-93; prof. emeritus Mercer U., 1993; program dir. Mgmt. Devel. Center, Belo Horizonte Minas Gerais, Brazil, 1973-75. Controller Arctic Inst. N.Am., 1957-77 Author: Cost Basis in Business Combinations, 1956, (with James A. Cashin) Auditing, 1963; former reading editor: Jour. Accountancy. Mem. bd. edn. Union Free Sch. Dist. 5, Greenburgh, N.Y., 1964-69, v.p., 1965-68, pres., 1968-69; mem. N.E. Regional Postmaster Selection Bd., U.S. Postal Service, 1969-75. Served to capt. USAAF, 1942-45. Decorated D.F.C., Air medal Mem. Am. Inst. C.P.A.s, N.Y. State Soc. C.P.A.s, Ga. State Soc. C.P.A.'s, Am. Acctg. Assn., Beta Gamma Sigma. Methodist. Home: 12 Cole Pl Palm Coast FL 32137

OWENS, HELEN DAWN, elementary school educator, reading consultant; b. Eastman, Ga., Oct. 9, 1949; d. Eli B. and Irene (Harrell) Branch; m. Bobby Lee Owens, Dec. 9, 1967; children: Leslie Owens-Blankenship, Monica Dawn. AA, Miami (Fla.) Dade Jr. Coll., 1969; BS, Fla. Internat. U., 1978; MEd, Mercer U., 1986, EdS, 1991. Cert. presch.-12th grade, reading specialist, early childhood edn. specialist, Ga. Youth ctr. dir. Dept. Def., Clark AFB, Philippines, 1969-70; English lang. instr. Chinese Mil. Acad., Feng Shan, Taiwan, 1973-75; tchr., music instr. ABC Presch., Miami, 1976-78; kindergarten and music tchr. Berkshire Sch., Homestead, Fla., 1978-79; tchr., reading specialist Perdue Elem. Sch. Houston County Bd. Edn., Warner Robins, Ga., 1979—. Mem. nominating com. mem. Ga. picture book of yr. U. Ga., Athens, 1990-91; reading cons. for schs., county edn. bds., regional reading ctrs., Ctrl. Ga., 1990—. Author: With Loving Hands and Tender Hearts, 1975. Exec. bd. dirs. Ladies Ministries, Ch. of God., Warner Robins, 1990-94; dir. Internat. City Girls' Club, Warner Robins, 1990-96. Recipient 25-Yr. Bible Tchr. Svc. award Internat. City Ch. of God., 1991; named Fla. State Family Tng. Dir. of Yr., Fla. Ch. of God, 1979, Ga. Girls' Club Coord. of the Year, 1995. Mem. Internat. Reading Assn. (Ga. coun. 1979-96, dir. mem. devel. 1993-96, v.p. 1996-97, pres. elect 1997-98, pres. 1998-99, past pres. HOPE coun. 1990-92, Annette Hopson Svc. award 1998), Profl. Assn. Ga. Edn., Internat. Platform Assn. Republican. Avocations: reading, sewing, touring foreign countries, swimming, storytelling. Home: 111 Crestwood Rd Warner Robins GA 31093-6803 Office: Perdue Elem Sch 856 Highway 96 Warner Robins GA 31088-2222

OWENS, HILDA FAYE, management and leadership development consultant, human resource trainer; b. Fountain, N.C., Mar. 23, 1939; d. Floyd Curtis and Essie Lee (Gay) O. BS in Edn. and Psychology, East Carolina U., 1961, MA in Edn., 1965; PhD in Higher Edn., Fla. State U., 1973; postgrad., Western Carolina U., 1962, U. Louisville, 1967, U. N.C., 1968. Tchr. New Bern (N.C.) City Schs., 1961-65; dir. counseling svcs., prof. Mt. Olive (N.C.) Coll., 1965-71, dean students, prof., 1973-77; coord. student affairs, rsch. assoc. bd. regents State Univ. System Fla., Tallahassee, 1971-73; assoc. prof. higher edn. U. S.C., Columbia, 1977-83; v.p. acad. affairs, prof. Spartanburg (S.C.) Meth. Coll., 1985-90; exec. asst. to pres. for planning and rsch., cons. Spartanburg (S.C.) Meth. Coll., 1990-91; pres., sr. cons. Excel Resource Assocs., Spartanburg, 1991—. Mem. bd. dirs. The Haven; numerous presentations in field; speaker bus., ednl., civic and ch. meetings, confs. and workshops; prof. psychology Spartanburg Meth. Coll., S.C., 1990-91. Editor: Risk Management and the Student Affairs Professional, 1984, (with Witten and Bailey) College Student Personnel Administration: An Anthology, 1982; mem. editl. bd. Jour. Staff, Orgn. and Program Devel., Assn. Student Pers. Adminstrs. Jour., Nat. Assn. Student Pers. Adminstrs. Monograph Bd., Coll. Student Affairs Jour.; contbr. articles to profl. jours., over 40 chpts. to books. Grad. Leadership Spartanburg, 1987; adminstrv. bd. Bethel United Meth. Ch.; mem. exec. bd. Tuscarora coun. Boy Scouts Am. S.C. Coll. Pers. Assn. named Rsch. and Writing award in her honor, 1995; named One of 45 Outstanding S.C. Women, 1980, Disting. Grad. award Fla. State U., 1981, Outstanding Bus. and Profl. Woman of Yr. Spartanburg Bus. and Profl. Women, 1986, Capital Bus. and Profl. Women, 1992, Mt. Olive Bus. and Profl. Women, 1977; recipient Meritorious Svc. award S.C. Coll. Pers. Assn., 1990; Rotary Paul Harris fellow, 1998. Mem. NAFE, ASTD, Am. Mgmt. Assn., Nat. Assn. Student Pers. Adminstrs. (adv. bd. region III, Disting. Svc. award), Am. Assn. Higher Edn., Carolinas Soc. Tng. and Devel., Nat. Orgn. on Legal Problems in Edn., S.C. Pers. Assn. (pres., award named in honor 1994), Bus. and Profl. Women S.C. (pres., bd. dirs. Ednl. Found.), Internat. Platform Assn., Spartan West Rotary Club (officer, bd. dirs.), Pi Delta Kappa (pres. U. S.C. chpt.). Democrat. Avocations: coin collecting, golf, movies, basketball, reading. Office: Excel Resource Assocs PO Box 1087 Spartanburg SC 29304-1087

OWENS, JULIA MARIE, mathematics educator; b. Chgo., Sept. 18, 1959; d. Stanley and Frankie (Quarterman) Obuchowski; m. Christopher Glenn Owens, Aug. 5, 1989. B, Nat. Coll. Edn., Evanston, Ill., 1981; M, U. Cen. Fla., Orlando, 1989. Spl. edn. tchr. Hampshire (Ill.) Mid. Sch., 1981-82, St. Cloud (Fla.) Mid. Sch., 1983-85, math. tchr., 1985—. Peer tchr. Profl. Orientation Program of Fla., St. Cloud, 1986—. Named Tchr. of Yr. St. Cloud Middle Sch., 1991, Most Popular Educator, 1991; recipient Tchr. Merit award Walt Disney World Co., 1990. Mem. Nat. Coun. Tchrs. Math.

OWENS, MARILYN MAE, elementary school educator, secondary school educator; b. Poland, Ohio, Nov. 17, 1932; d. S. Reed and Vernice Mae (Flickinger) Johnson; m. J. Edward Owens, July 23, 1953; children: Charlene, Preston, Lorraine. BS in Art Edn., Millersville State U., 1970, elem. cert., 1983; MEd in Art, Towson U., 1975; elem. prin. cert., Western Md. U., 1984. Cert. elem. and secondary tchr. art, elem. tchr., Pa.: art supr. elem. and secondry, prin. elem., Md. Tchr art. k-12 Northeastern Sch. Dist., Manchester, Pa., 1970-99; ret., 1999. Adj. instr. humanities, art appreciation York Coll. of Pa., 1977-81; mem. long range planning com., Northeastern Sch. Dist., Manchester, 1988-90, supt.'s adv. bd., 1990-91, elem. adv. bd. Orendorf Sch., 1990-92, 97-98, dist. budget com., 1991-92, elem. budget com. Conewago Elem. Sch., 1993-98, computer tech. elem. com., 1993-95, instrnl. and profl. devel. com., 1994-98, calligraphy tchr. Northeastern Adult Cmty. Edn., 1988-90. Leader Girl Scouts of U.S., Penn Laurel, York, Pa., 1963-67; mem. Northeastern Art Out-Reach program, Northeastern Edn. Assn. Comty. Rels. Com., Northeastern Sch. Dist.'s Portfolio Com.; vol. Susan B. Byrnes Health Ctr., Conewago Elem. Sch., Northeastern Sch. Dist., Spl. Olympics, York, York Co. Heritage Trust (life mem., bd. dirs. 2003—). Recipient scholarship Ind. (Pa.) State Coll., 1950; grantee Northeastern Sch. Dist., Manchester, 1989-90. Mem. AAUW, Nat. Art Edn. Assn., Northeastern Edn. Assn. (v.p. 1987-88, pres. 1988-89, cmty. rels. program 1998-99), Pa. Art Edn. Assn. (ret., Ret. Art Educator of Yr. 1999), Pa. Guild of Craftsmen (Yorktowne chpt., mailing com. 2001—), Pa. Inst. CPA (Women's Aux. S. Ctrl. chpt.), York Quilters Guild, Clearfield Hist. Soc. (life), York Art Assn., Kiwanis Club York, Phi Delta Kappa (scholarship com. 1990-94, scholarship chair 1998-99, 2000-02, Disting. Svc. award 1999). Avocations: painting, crafts, hiking, camping, sewing. Home: 2505 Schoolhouse Ln York PA 17402-3918

OWENS, PATRICIA ANN, history educator; d. James William and Loretta (Fuller) O. BA, Ill. State U., 1972; MS, MA, So. Ill. U., 1975, PhD, 1986; MA, U. Wyo., 1991. Cert. tchr., Ill. Park interpreter Nat. Park Svc., various locations, 1974-76, 77-78; program dir. U.S. Forest Svc., Huron, Mich., 1977; acad. counselor Wabash Valley Coll., Mt. Carmel, Ill., 1978-84, div. chair, 1987-88, instr., 1984—. Summer instr. Yellowstone Nat. Pk., 1995—99. Avocation: photography. Office: Wabash Valley Coll 2200 College Dr Mount Carmel IL 62863-2657

OWENS, SUE GASTON, middle school educator; b. Greenville, S.C., Nov. 6, 1955; d. Dearman Samuel and Harriet (Gaston) O. BS, Winthrop U., 1976; MEd, Converse Coll., 1981. Tchr. Whitlock Jr. H.S., Spartanburg, S.C., 1977—. Bd. dirs. Bethlehem Cmty. Ctr., Spartanburg, 1991-96; dist. rep. Wallace (S.C.) Family Life Ctr., 1992-97; cert. lay spkr. S.C. conf. United Meth. Ch., 1991—; pres. Spartanburg dist. United Meth. Women, 1993-96, coord. membership, nurture and outreach of S.C. conf., 1996-2000; mem. South Atlantic Regional Sch. of Christian Mission Planning Team, 1997-2000; dir. women's divsn. Gen. Bd. of Global Ministries, United Meth. Ch., 2000—. Mem. AAHPERD, NEA, S.C. Alliance for Health, Phys. Edn., Recreation and Dance, S.C. Edn. Assn.

OWENS, WALLACE, JR., art educator; b. Muskogee, Okla., Dec. 28, 1932; s. Wallace Arthur and Sarah (Evans) O. BA in Art Edn., Langston U., 1959; M. in Teaching Art, Cen. State U., Edmond, Okla., 1965; MFA, Instituto Allende, San Miguel de Allende, Mex., 1966; postgrad., North Tex. STate U., 1970-71. Chmn. art dept. Langston U., Okla., 1966-80; asst. prof. art Cen. State U., Edmond, 1980—. One-man shows include: Langston U., 1980, Okla. Territorial Mus., 1983, Art Assn., Oklahoma City, 1985; exhibited paintings and sclupture in group shows throughout Midwest; represented in State of Okla. Collection. Served with U.S. Army, 1953-55, Fed. Republic Germany. Fulbright scholar U. Rome, summer 1970; study tour grantee African Am. Inst., 1973. Mem. Higher Edn. Alumni Coun., Okla. Edn. Assn., Lions. Democrat. Baptist. Home: 3374 Sunny Acres Ln Guthrie OK 73044

OWINGS, SUZANN M. school system administrator, educator; b. L.A., Jan. 26, 1947; d. Theodore Raymond and Elizabeth Marie O'Malley. BA, Calif. State Coll., L.A., 1969; MAT, Ind. U., 1971; PhD, U. N.Mex., 1978. Adminstr. Ind. U., Bloomington, 1970-71; tchr. Compton (Calif.) Sr. High Sch., 1971-75; cons. Owings, Albuquerque, 1975-78; assoc. dir. Energy Consumers of N.Mex., Albuquerque, 1978-79; statewide comprehensive planner CES, N.Mex. State U., Albuquerque, 1979; strategic planner Bechtel Inc., San Francisco, 1979-83; dean Golden Gate U., San Francisco, 1983-84; cons. Bitn Assocs., Corrales, N.Mex. and L.A., 1984—; coord. Albuquerque Pub. Schs., 1992—. Instr. mgmt. Troy State U., U. Phoenix, Chapman U.. Co-author, co-editor: Southwest Images and Trends: Factors in Community Development, 1979, numerous others. Co-organizer Rio Rancho 2000, 1992-93; mem., chmn. Sandoval County Intergovtl./Bus. Adv. Coun., Bernalillo, N.Mex., 1993—; mem. Sandoval County Econ. Devel. Com., 1991—. Mem. ASTD (pres.- elect, v.p., bd. dirs.), Am. Soc. for Pub. Adminstrn. (pres.-elect, chairperson Pub. Policy Inst.), Optimist (bd. dirs., pres. N.W. Albuquerque club). Avocations: walking, cycling, gardening. Home: PO Box 872 Placitas NM 87043-0872

OWINGS, THALIA KELLEY, elementary school educator; b. Franklin, N.H., Apr. 11, 1948; d. James Warren and Elizabeth Louise (Chadwick) Kelley; m. Alan Morritt, June 25, 1966 (div. June 25, 1990); children: Manderlee, Tiffany, Brooke; m. Frederick Richard Owings, Dec. 31, 1994; children: Jennifer, Lisa. AA, Harvard U. Ext., 1982, BA, 1989; postgrad., Calif. State U., San Bernardino, 1996—. Cert. tchr., Calif., emergency tchr. Instr. CEA Internat., Providence, 1971-77; adminstrv. asst. Gulf Oil/Cumberland Farms, Norwood, Mass., 1989-91, So. Calif. Edison Co., Rosemead, Calif., 1991-96; substitute tchr. Palm Springs (Calif.) Unified Sch. Dist., 1996—2000. Tutor Calif. for Literacy!, Pasadena, Chino, and Palm Springs, Calif., 1991—; applicant interviewer Harvard U.; mem. edn. com. Shelter From the Storm, 2000-03, tutor com. chair, 2000—, vol. coord., 2002-03. Mem. So. Calif. Harvard/Radcliff Club, Toastmasters Internat. (v.p. pub. rels. 1995-96), Edison's Roundtable. Avocations: screenplay writing, photography, bicycling, dancing, golfing. Home: 407 E Laurel Cir Palm Springs CA 92262-2236

OWSLEY, TINA KATHLEEN, special education educator; b. Ponca City, Okla., Apr. 3, 1953; d. Lindsey C. Jr. and Nina Jane (Lotts) O. BA in Edn., Northeastern Okla. State U., 1975, MS in Edn., 1978; cert. in deaf edn., Tex. Woman's U., 1981; cert. in spl. edn. adminstrn., Gallaudet U., Washington, 1984. Cert. speech correction, learning disabilities, Mo., speech therapy, learning disabilites, deaf edn., Okla., speech pathology, learning disabilities, deaf edn., educable mentally handicapped, physically impaired, Kans. Tchr. learning disabilities, speech pathologist Perry County Schs., Perryville, Mo., 1975-77; tchr. learning disabilities Vinita (Okla.) Pub. Schs., 1977-78; cons. hearing impaired Sequoyah County Spl. Edn. Coop., Sallisaw, Okla., 1978-80; tchr. hearing impaired Ft. Gibson (Okla.) Pub. Schs., 1980-83; asst. to the v.p. Gallaudet U., 1983-84; coord., tchr. hearing impaired Shawnee County Spl. Edn. Coop., Topeka, 1984—. Parent advisor Project ECHO, Okla. Dept. Edn., Oklahoma City, 1978-83; early interventionist Hearing Cons., Topeka, 1989—. Co-author: Curriculum Guide - Presch. Hearing Impaired Children, 1991. Bd. dirs. Florence Crittendon, 1995—2000. Mem. AAUW (corr. sec. 1998—2002, vice pres. membership 2003-05), Nat. Assn. for Edn. of Young Children (Kans. chpt., pres. Topeka Assn. 1988-89), NEA (Kans. chpt., mem. Topeka spl. edn. com. 1991—, polit. action com. 1991—2001, bldg. rep. 1993-95), Coun. for Exceptional Children (pres. Chpt. 204 1989—2000, v.p. Kans. Fedn. 1991-92, pres.-elect Kans. Fedn. 1992-93, pres. 1993-94, immediate past pres. 1994-95, chmn. Spl. Edn. Day at the Legis. Kans. Coun. 1991, 95), Kans. Divsn. Early Childhood (pres. 1989-90, mem. chair 1993—2000), Kans. Educators of Hearing Impaired (pres. 1989-90, Kans. Educator of the Yr.-Deaf/Hard of Hearing 1996), Kans. Commn. for Deaf and Hearing Impaired (chair Early Identification and Intervention Coun. 1990-95), Soroptimist Internat. Am. (corr. sec. local chpt. 1991-92, cmty. svc. chair 1991-95, del. 1992-94, bd. dirs. 1992-93, 95-97, rec. sec. 1993-94, chair Youth Citizenship Award/Tng. Award Program 1995—99, growth and devel. co-chair 1996—2000, v.p. 1998—2000, Soroptimist of the Yr. 1993, 97, Soroptimist Woman of Distinction, 2000), Sertoma Internat. (publicity chair 1992-94), Topeka Tots Team (sec. 1991-97), Jr. Deaf Club (sponsor 1992-96), Camp Fire Coun. (bd. dirs. 1993-96, chair program/membership 1993-96). Republican. Mem. Christian Ch. (Disciples Of Christ). Avocations: counted cross-stitch, reading, gardening. Home: 2806 SW Engler Ct Topeka KS 66614-4317 Office: Shawnee County Spl Edn Coop 1725 SW Arnold Ave Topeka KS 66604-3306

OXELL, LOIE GWENDOLYN, fashion and beauty educator, consultant, columnist; b. Sioux City, Iowa, Nov. 17, 1917; d. Lyman Stanley and Loie Erma (Crill) Barton; m. Eugene Edwin Eschenbrenner, Aug. 8, 1936 (dec. 1954); children: Patricia Gene, Eugene Edward (dec. Feb. 1994); m. Henry J. Oxell, Nov. 3, 1956 (dec. July 1994). AS in Fashion Merchandising, Broward C.C., Davie, Fla., 1978. Fashion rep. Crestmoor Suit & Coat Co., St. Louis, 1951-56; appeared on "To the Ladies" weekly TV show KSD-TV, St. Louis, 1950s; cons./instr. Miami-Herald Newspaper Glamor Clinic, Miami, Fla., 1957-71; pres./owner Loie's (Loy's) Inc., Miami, Fla., 1958-71; pres., owner West Coast East Talent Agy.; instr./lectr. Charron-Williams Coll., Miami, 1973-77; instr. Fashion Inst. Ft. Lauderdale, Fla., 1977-86; pres./owner Image Power Unltd., Plantation, Fla., 1992—. Lectr. in field; columnist Sr. Life and Boomer Times, Fla., 1993-97, Sr. Life, 1997-98, The Entertainer, 1997-98 Author: I'd Like You to Meet My Wife, 1964, Executive Wives, A.C. Sparkplug Co., So! We're in Our 60's, 70's, 80's Plus; regularly appeared in comedy skits, fashion segments, commentary, and TV comms. Del Russo Beauty Show, 1960s; actress Red Skelton TV show, Miami, Fla., also fashion show prodns., TV comms. Lectr., instr. Work Force, AARP Sr. Cmty. Svc. Employment Program, Ft. Lauderdale and Hollywood, Fla., 1987—, keynote spkr. nat. conv., Charlestown, S.C., 1986; life mem. women's com. Miami Children's Hosp. Aux.; faculty adv. Nu Tau Sigma Charron Williams Coll., 1973-77; pres. Venice of Am. chpt. Am. Bus. Women's Assn., 1975-76. Recipient Cert. of Appreciation Dade County Welfare Dept. Youth Hall, Miami, 1966, Community TV Found., Miami, 1966, 71, Woman of the Yr. award Am. Bus. Women's Assn. (Venice of Am. chpt.), 1976-77, Award for Svc. AARP Sr. Community Svc. Program, 1993. Mem. The Fashion Group Internat. Avocations: bridge, golf.

OXLEY, MARGARET CAROLYN STEWART, elementary education educator; b. Petaluma, Calif., Apr. 1, 1930; d. James Calhoun Stewart and Clara Thornton (Whiting) Bomboy; m. Joseph Hubbard Oxley, Aug. 25, 1951; children: Linda Margaret, Carolyn Blair Oxley Greiner, Joan Claire Oxley Willis, Joseph Stewart, James Harmon, Laura Marie Oxley Brechbill. Student, U. Calif., Berkeley, 1949—51; BS summa cum laude, Ohio State U., 1973, MA, 1984, postgrad., 1985, postgrad., 1988, postgrad., 1992, Ohio State U, 2003. Cert. tchr., Ohio. 2d grade tchr. St. Paul Sch., Westerville, Ohio, 1973—. Presenter in field. Mem. editl. bd. Reading Tchr., vol. 47-48, 1993-94, Jour. Children's Lit., 1996—; co-author: Reading and Writing, Where it All Begins, 1991, Teaching with Children's Books: Path to Literature-Based Instruction, 1995, Adventuring With Books, vol. 12, 2000, vol. 13, 2002. Active Akita Child Conservation League, Columbus, Ohio, 1968-70. Named Columbus Diocesan Tchr. of Yr., 1988; Phoebe A. Hearst scholar, 1951, Rose Sterheim Meml. scholar, 1951; recipient Mary Karrer award Ohio State U., 1994. Mem. Nat. Coun. Tchrs. English (Notable Children's Books in the Lang. Arts com. 1993-94, chair 1995-96, treas. Children's Literature Assembly bd. dirs. 1996-99, co-chair fall breakfast children's lit. assembly, 2000-03, co-chair excellence in poetry for children com. 2003--), Internat. Reading Ass (Exemplary Svc. in Promotion of Literacy award 1991), Literacy Connection (pres.), Children's Lit. Assembly, Ohio Coun. Tchrs. English Lang. Arts (Outstanding Educator 1990), Phi Kappa Phi, Pi Lambda Theta (hon.). Democrat. Roman Catholic. Avocations: reading, writing, travel, gardening, working with children. Home: 298 Brevoort Rd Columbus OH 43214-3826

OXLEY, MARY BOONE, early childhood education educator; b. Brownwood, Tex., June 18, 1928; d. Virgil Earl and Olive (Boone) Wheeler; m. William R. Oxley, June 8, 1950 (dec. Sept. 1987); children: Paul, Claire. BS, Tex. Women's U., 1949; MS, Tex. A&M U., 1967. Cert. tchr., Tex. Tchr. grade 2 El Paso (Tex.) Ind. Sch. Dist., 1949-50, Antioch (Calif.) Ind. Sch. Dist., 1950-52; tchr. grades 1-3 Richmond (Calif.) Ind. Sch. Dist., 1952-54; tchr. kindergarten St. Thomas Early Learning Ctr., College Station, Tex., 1967-85; lectr. early childhood edn. Tex. A&M U., College Station, 1985—. Presenter workshops in field. Author: Illustrated Guide to Kindergarten Instruction, 1976; contbr. articles to profl. jours. Bd. dirs. Magination Station (children's theater), Bryan, Tex., 1990-94; cons. St. Thomas Early Learning Ctr., College Station, 1985-94. Mem. Nat. Assn. for Edn. Young Children (chmn. program 1976), Tex. Assn. for Edn. Young Children, Assn. Childhood Edn. Internat. (advisor 1990-94), Nat. Coun. Social Studies, Phi Delta Kappa. Democrat. Episcopalian. Avocations: bird watching, travel, youth camps. Home: 1005 Arboles Cir College Station TX 77840-4817 Office: Tex A&M Univ Edn Curriculum Instrn College Station TX 77843-0001

OXTOBY, DAVID WILLIAM, college president, chemistry educator; b. Bryn Mawr, Pa., Oct. 17, 1951; s. John Corning and Jean (Shaffer) O., m. Claire Bennett, Dec. 17, 1977; children: Mary-Christina, John, Laura. BA, Harvard, 1972; PhD, U. Calif., Berkeley, 1975. Asst. prof. U. Chgo., 1977-82, assoc. prof., 1982-86, prof., 1986—2003, Mellon prof., 1987-92, dir. James Franck Inst., 1992-95, dean phys. scis. divsn., 1995—2003, William Rainey Harper prof., 1996—2003; pres., prof. chemistry Pomona Coll., Claremont, Calif., 2003—. Co-author: Principles of Modern Chemistry, 1986, Chemistry: Science of Change, 1990. Trustee Bryn Mawr Coll., 1989—, Tchrs. Acad. Math. and Sci., 1999-2003, Toyota Technol. Inst., Chgo., 2002—; mem. bd. govs. Argonne Nat. Lab., 1996-2002, Astrophys. Rsch. Consortium, 1998-2003. Recipient Quantrell award U. Chgo., 1986, Alumni award of merit William Penn Charter Sch., 2003; Alfred P. Sloan Found. fellow, 1979, John Simon Guggenheim Found. fellow, 1987; Camille and Henry Dreyfus Found. tchr.-scholar, 1980. Fellow Am. Phys. Soc.; mem. Am. Chem. Soc., Royal Soc. Chemistry (Marlow medal 1983), Phi Beta Kappa. Office: Office of the Pres Pomona Coll 550 N College Ave Claremont CA 91711

OYLER, BERTHA JEANNE, elementary school educator; b. Columbus, Ind., Feb. 3, 1943; d. Jean Hamilton and Julia Louise (Koch) LaSell; m. Michael Paul Oyler, Aug. 8, 1965 (dec. Mar. 1984); children: David, Joanthon, Sarah, Samantha. BS in Edn., Concordia Tchrs. Coll., 1965, MEd, 1988. Tchr. St. Peter's Luth. Sch., Hampton, Nebr., 1965-66, Mt. Calvary Luth. Sch., Milw., 1966-68, Nazareth Luth Sch., Milw., 1969-70, Luth. Children's Friend Soc., Wauwatosa, Wis., 1971, Trinity Luth. Sch., Sheboygan, Wis., 1985—. Advisor Student Coun. Trinity, Sheboygan, 1991-92, Trinity Scholastic Olympics, Sheboygan, 1986-2002. Advisor Sheboygan Area Luth Singles, 1986, Widow's Brunch, Sheboygan, 1987—; resource adminstr. Internat. Luth Singles, 1989—. Mem. Wis. Assn. Student Coun. (advisor), Luth. Edn. Assn. Avocations: home remodeling, travel, singles ministry, church choir. Office: Trinity Luth Sch 824 Wisconsin Ave Sheboygan WI 53081-4030

OZAKI, NANCY JUNKO, performance artist, performing arts educator; b. Denver, Feb. 14, 1951; d. Joe Motoichi and Tamiye (Saki) O.; m. Gary Steven Tsujimoto, Nov. 12, 1989. BS in Edn., U. Colo., 1973; postgrad., U. Colo., Denver, 1977, Metro State Coll., 1982, Red Rocks C.C., 1982-83, U. No. Colo., 1982, U. N.Mex., 1985, U. No. Colo., 1988. Elem. tchr. Bur. Indian Affairs, Bloomfield, N.Mex., 1973—75, Aurora Pub. Schs., Colo., 1977—83, Albuquerque Pub. Schs., 1983—84, Denver Pub. Schs., 1984—87, Oak Grove Sch. Dist., San Jose, Calif., 1988—89, San Mateo City Elem. Dist., Calif., 1990—92; performing artist Japanese drums Young Audiences, San Francisco, 1992—93, Denver, 1994—97; performing artist Japanese drums Epcot Ctr. Walt Disney World, Orlando, Fla., 1993—97; co-dir., mgr., performer One World Taiko Japanese Drum Troupe, Denver, 1997—2001, Seattle, 2001—; artist-in-residence Washington States Arts Commn., 2003—. Artist-in-residence Wash. State Arts Commn., 2003—; mem. Touring Arts Roster, King County. Vol. worker with young Navajo children; co-sponsor girl's sewing and camping groups. Mem. Kappa Delta Pi (Theta chpt.). Avocations: reading, sewing, skiing, hiking, snorkeling. Office: PO Box 80158 Seattle WA 98108 E-mail: oneworldtaiko@earthlink.net.

OZELLI, TUNCH, economics educator, consultant; b. Ankara, Turkey, May 18, 1938; came to U.S., 1962; s. Sufyan and Saziye (Ozmorali) O.; m. Lale A. Baymur, Dec. 30, 1960 (div. Mar. 1972); children: Selva, Kerem; m. Nancy Ann Goldschlager, Feb. 3, 1974 (div. Dec. 1984); m. Meral Ozdemir, May 9, 1992. MBA, Fla. State U., 1963; PhD, Columbia U., 1968. Rsch. fellow Harvard U., Cambridge, Mass., 1969-70; econ. advisor Office Prime Minister, Ankara, 1970-72; prof. mgmt. N.Y. Inst. Tech., N.Y.C., 1972—. Spl. advisor State Planning Orgn., Ankara, 1989-92. Contbr. articles to profl. jour. Ford Found. scholar, 1963-64, Found. for Econ. Edn. fellow, 1968. Mem. Am. Econ. Assn., Middle East Studies Assn., Turkish Mgmt. Assn., Delta Mu Delta. Avocation: equestrian activities. Office: Dept of Economics NY Inst Tech Old Westbury NY 11568

OZI, ELIZABETH, private school administrator; b. Sáo Paulo, Brazil, Aug. 5, 1959; d. Heni and Firmina O. BA in Psychology, U. Las Vegas, 1987; postgrad., NOVA U., Fla., 1989—; cert. of continuing profl. edn., U. Nev., 1988. Cert. tchr. Tchr. Clark County Sch. Dist., Las Vegas, Nev., 1990-94; owner, sch. dir. Parent's Choice, Las Vegas, Nev., 1993—. Dir. Home Base Bus., Las Vegas, Nev., 1993—. Interviewer (Radio Show Series) Recognizing Signs to Prevent Suicide, 1990. Counselor Suicide Prevention, Nev., 1988-90. Recipient Cert. of Leadership award Nat. U., Las Vegas, 1990. Mem. Psi Chi. Avocation: writing. Home: 4646 Grasshopper Dr Las Vegas NV 89122-6123

OZKAN, UMIT SIVRIOGLU, chemical engineering educator; b. Manisa, Turkey, Apr. 11, 1954; came to U.S., 1980; d. Alim and Emine (Ilgaz) Sivrioglu; m. H. Erdal Ozkan, Aug. 13, 1983. BS, Mid. East Tech. U., Ankara, Turkey, 1978, MS, 1980; PhD, Iowa State U., 1984. Registered profl. engr., Ohio. Grad. rsch. assoc. Ames Lab. U.S. Dept. Energy, 1980-84; asst. prof. Ohio State U., Columbus, 1985-90, assoc. prof. chem. engring., 1990-94, prof., 1994—, assoc. dean for rsch. Coll. Engring., 2000—. Contbr. articles to profl. jours. French Ctr. NAt. Rsch. Sci. fellow, 1994-95; recipient Women of Achievement award YWCA, Columbus, 1991, Outstanding Engring. Educator Ohio award Soc. Profl. Engrs., 1991, Union Carbide Innovation Recognition award, 1991-92, NSF Woman Faculty award in sci. and engring., 1991, Engring. Tchg. Excellence award Keck Found., 1994, Ctrl. Ohio Outstanding Woman in Sci. & Tech., 1996, Pitts.-Cleve. Catalysis Soc. Outstanding Rsch. award, 1998, Achievement award SWE, 2002, Columbus Outstanding Rsch. award ACS, 2002. Fellow Am. Inst. Chemists; mem. NSPE, N.Am. Catalysis Soc., Am. Inst. Chem. Engring., Am. Soc. Engring. Edn., Am. Chem. Soc., Combustion Inst., Sigma Xi. Achievements include research in selective oxidation, hydrogenation, NO reduction, hydrodesulfurization, hydrodeoxygenation, hydrodenitrogenation, fuel reformulation, in-situ spectroscopy. Office: Ohio State U Chem Engring 140 W 19th Ave Columbus OH 43210-1110

OZMENT, STEVEN, historian, educator; b. McComb, Miss., Feb. 21, 1939; s. Lowell V. and Shirley M. (Edgar) O.; children by previous marriage: Joel, Matthew, Katherine, Amanda, Emma. BA, Hendrix Coll., 1960; BD, Drew Theol. Sch., 1964; PhD, Harvard U., 1967; MA (hon.), Yale U., 1975. Asst. prof. Inst. Late Medieval and Reformation Studies, U. Tübingen, Fed. Republic Germany, 1966-68; asst. prof. history and religious studies Yale U., New Haven, 1968-72, assoc. prof., 1972-75, prof., 1975-79; prof. history Harvard U., 1979—, McLean prof. ancient and modern history, 1991—, assoc. dean undergrad. edn., 1984-87. Bonsall vis. prof. Stanford U., 1991. Author: Homo Spiritualis, 1969, The Reformation in Medieval Perspective, 1971, Mysticism and Dissent, 1973, The Reformation in the Cities, 1975; author: (with others) The Western Heritage, 1979, The Western Heritage, 7th edit., 2000, The Age of Reform, 1980, Reformation Europe: A Guide to Research, 1982, When Fathers Ruled: Family Life in Reformation Europe, 1983, The Heritage of World Civilizations, 1985, The Heritage of World Civilizations, 6th edit., 2002; author: Magdalena and Balthasar: An Intimate Portrait of Life in 16th Century Europe, 1986, Three Behaim Boys: Growing Up in Early Modern Germany, 1990, Protestants: The Birth of a Revolution, 1992, The Burgermeister's Daughter: Scandal in a 16th Century German Town, 1996, Flesh and Spirit: Private Life in Early Modern Germany, 1999, Ancestors: The Loving Family in Old Europe, 2001; mem. editl. bd.: Archive for Reformation History, 1976—93, Sixteenth Century Jour., 1976—, Jour. Am. Acad. Religion, 1972—77, Jour. Hist. Ideas, 1986—, Netherlands Archive for Ch. History, 1987—. Recipient Disting. Alumnus award Hendrix Coll., 1997; Morse fellow, 1970-71, Guggenheim fellow, 1978, Cabot fellow, 1992. Mem. Am. Soc. Reformation Rsch. (dir. 1979-83). Home: 69 High Rd Newbury MA 01951-1725 Office: Harvard Univ Robinson Hall Cambridge MA 02138 E-mail: steven0z@juno.com.

OZUMBA, BENJAMIN CHUKWUMA, obstetrician, gynecologist; b. Onitsha, Anambra, Nigeria, Mar. 21, 1954; s. Arthur Nwabunwanne and Alice chiebonam (Igebuike) O.; m. Chinelo Obianuju Udokwu, Jan. 29, 1994; children: Benjamin Chukwumdindu, Sarah Onyinyechukwu, Elizabeth Chimfumnanya, Rached Chidinma. MB, BChir, U. Lagos, Nigeria, 1979; FMCOG, Post Grad. Med. Coll., Nigeria, 1987; MRCOG, Royal Coll. Ob.-Gyn., London, 1993; FICS, Internat. Coll. Surgeons, U.S., 1991; FWACS, W. African Coll. Surgeons, Lagos, Nigeria, 1993. Intern Lagos U. Tchg. Hosp., 1979—80; med. officer Coll. of Edn., Minna, Nigeria, 1980—81; sr. house officer Univ. Nigeria Tchg. Hosp., Enusu, 1981—82, registrar, 1982—83, sr. registrar, 1983—88, sr. lectr./ cons., 1988—93; prof. ob./gyn. U. Nigeria, Nsukka, 1993—. Chmn. Enugu Med. Soc., 1993-95; coord. Tutorial System Internat., Nigeria, 1993-95. Editor: Tropical Pediatrics and Child Health, 1999; assoc. editor Orient Jour. Medicine, 1988—, Nigerian Jour. Surgical Scis., 1991—; contbr. articles to profl. jours. V.p. Enugu chpt. Full Gospel Businessmen's Fellowship Internat., 1994-95, chpt. pres., 1997—; chmn. Harvest and Love Feast Com., Chapel of Redemption, Enugu, Nigeria, 1994-95. Takemi fellow Internat. Health Harvard U., 1995-96. Fellow Internat. Coll. Surgeons, W. African Coll. of Surgeons, Nigerian Postgrad. Med. Coll.; mem. AAAS (internat. mem.), Royal Coll. Obstetricians and Gynecologists. Born Again Christian. Achievements include measuring: serum concentrations of alphafetoprotein in mormal pregnancy and in pregnancy induced hypertensions; ivermectin levels in human breast milk. Home: 115 Agbani Rd Enugu 400001 Nigeria Office: Univ Nigeria Teaching Hosp Dept Ob-gyn Enugu Anambra Nigeria E-mail: BenOzumba@hotmail.com.

PAARMANN, LARRY DEAN, electrical engineering educator; b. Maquoketa, Iowa, Feb. 3, 1941; s. Arthur Herman Paarmann and Blanche Caroline (Lozenzen) Earles. BS, No. Ill. U., 1970; MS, U. Ill., 1977; PhD, Ill. Inst. Technology, 1983. Instr. Kishwaukee Coll., Malta, Ill., 1970-75; rsch. asst. U. Ill., Urbana, 1975-76; engr. IIT Rsch. Inst., Chgo., 1977-78; instr. IIT, Chgo., 1978-83; asst. prof. Drexel U., Phila., 1983-90; assoc. prof. Wichita (Kans.) State U., 1990—. Reviewer IEEE Transactions on Signal Processing. Author Design and Analysis of Analog Filters: A Signal Processing Perspective, 2001; contbg. author: Wiley Encyclopedia of Biomedical Enginerring, 2003; assoc. editor IEEE Signal Processing Mag.; contbr. articles to profl. jours. IEEE (sr., chpt. chmn. 1989-90, tech. program chmn. 1994 Wichita conf. on comm., networking and signal processing), European Assn. for Signal Processing. Achievements include contbns. to modeling and signal processing techniques. Home: 2615 N Parkwood Ln Wichita KS 67220-2625 Office: Wichita State U Dept Elec Engring Wichita KS 67260-0044

PAAS, JOHN ROGER, language educator; b. Chgo., Mar. 14, 1945; s. Walter V. and Doris (Marinoff) P.; m. Martha Clem White, Aug. 24, 1968; children: Emily, Anne. BA summa cum laude, Hamilton Coll., Clinton, N.Y., 1967; PhD, Bryn Mawr Coll., 1973. Part-time asst. prof. Bryn Mawr (Pa.) Coll., 1973-74; prof. German Carleton Coll., Northfield, Minn., 1974—, dept chair, 1985-88. Author: The German Political Broadsheet 1600-1700, 7 vols., 1985—, Effigies et Poesis: An Illustrated Catalogue of Printed Portaits with Laudatory Verses by German Baroque Poets, 2 vols., 1988; editor: Unbekannte Gedichte und Lieder des Sigmund von Birken, 1990, Hollstein's German Engravings, Etchings and Woodcuts, 1400-1700, vols. 38-41, 1994-95, Der Franken Rom: Nürnburgs Blütezeit in der zweiten Hälfte des 17 Jhts., 1995, Augsburg, die Bilderfabrik Europas, 2001, (with Wolfgang Harms, Michael Schilling and Andreas Wang) Illustrierte Flugblätter des Barock: Eine Auswahl, 1983; contbr. articles to profl. jours. Sgt. U.S. Army, 1969—71. Summer grantee German Acad. Exch. Svc., 1975, 78, 83, Andrew W. Mellon Found., 1976, Faculty Devel. grantee Bush Found., 1978, Carleton Coll., 1985, NEH grantee, 1990, 92-93; vis. fellow Beinecke Libr., Yale U., 1991, IREX fellow, 1978, Fulbright sr. rsch. fellow, 1988-89, Humboldt Rsch. fellow, 2000-01. Mem. MLA, Am. Assn. Tchrs. German, Soc. German Renaissance and Baroque Lit., Internationaler Arbeitskreis für Barockliteratur, Frühe Neuzeit Interdisziplinär. Home: 107 College St Northfield MN 55057-2222 Office: Carleton College 1 N College St Northfield MN 55057-4044

PAASWELL, ROBERT EMIL, civil engineer, educator; b. Red Wing, Minn., Jan. 15, 1937; s. George and Evelyn (Cohen) P.; m. Rosalind Snyder, May 31, 1958; children: Judith Marjorie, George Harold. BA (Ford Found. fellow), Columbia U., 1956, BS, 1957, MS, 1961; PhD, Rutgers U., 1965. Field engring. asst. Spencer White & Prentis, Washington, 1954-56, engr. N.Y.C., 1957-59; rsch. scientist Davidson Lab., N.J., 1964; rsch. fellow Greater London Council, 1971-72; rsch. and teaching asst. Columbia U., 1959-62; asst. prof. civil engring. SUNY, Buffalo, 1964-68; chmn. bd. govs. Urban Studies Coll., 1973-76, assoc. prof., 1968-76, prof. civil engring., 1976-82; dir. Center for Transp. Studies and Research, 1979-82, chmn. dept. environ. design and planning, 1980-82; prof. transp. engring. U. Ill., Chgo., 1982-86, 89-90, dir. Urban Transp. Ctr., 1982-86; exec. dir. Chgo. Transit Authority, 1986-89; dir. transp. rsch. consortium, prof. civil engring. CCNY, 1990—, disting. prof., 1991—; dir. CUNY Inst. Urban Systems, 2000—. Faculty-on-leave Dept. Transp., 1976-77, cons., 1981—; v.p. Faculty Tech. Cons., Inc., Midwest Sys. Scis., Inc., 1982-86; dir. Urban Mass Transp. Adminstrn. Summer Faculty Workshop, 1980, 81; cons. transp. planning, energy and soil mechanics; spl. cons. to Congressman T. Dulski, 1973; vis. expert lectr. Jilin U. Tech., Changchun, Peoples Republic of China, 1985, hon. prof. transp., 1986—; bd. dirs. E'Escuto Archs. and Engrs., Chig, Hickling Co., Ottawa, Can., Transic Devel. Corp.; chmn. transp. steering adv. bd. Office of Tech. Assessment for Infrastructure and the Urban Core Project, 1994—; faculty Lincoln Inst. of Land Policy, 1994-95; vis. scholar Tel Aviv U., Israel, 1995—; arbitrator in productivity Met. Transp. Authority, N.Y.C., 1996—; mem. exec. com. Coun. on Transp., 1996—, NSF Ctr. for Infrastructure Sys.; cons. Coun. of North East Govs., 1997—; faculty "Conflict Resolution," NYU, 1998—; mem. exec. com. Inst. for Civil Infrastructure Sys. (NSF), 1998—; chair panel new paradigms in transit Transp. Rsch. Bd.; bd. dirs. Transit Stds. Consortium, chmn., 2000—. Author: Problems of the Carless, 1977; contbg. author: Transport and Urban Development, 1995, Panels for Transportation Planning, 1997, Studies in Israel Planning, 1996, Dynamic Networks and Spatial Change, 1999, After the World Trade Center, 2002; editor: Site Traffic Impact Assessment, 1992; contbg. author: Decisions for the Great Lakes, 1982, World Book Encyclopedia, 1992, 93, 94, Transport and Urban Development, 1995, Israel Planning Studies, 1996, 97, Panels for Transportation Planning, 1997, New Contributions to Transportation Analysis in Europe, 1999; mem. bd. editors Jour. Environ. Systems, 1974—, Transp., 1978—, Jour. Urban Tech., 1992—; contbr. articles to profl. jours. Mem. Buffalo Environ. Mgmt. Commn., 1972-74; mem. Area Com. for Transit, Mayor's Energy Adv. Bd., 1974, Block Grant Rev. Com., City of Buffalo; chmn. com. on transp., mem. rev. adv. bd. Rsch. and Planning Coun. Western N.Y.; mem. transp. com. Chgo. 1992 Worlds Fair; mem. citizens' adv. bd. Chgo. Transit Authority, 1985—; mem. strategic planning com. Regional Transp. Authority, 1985; mem. steering com. Nat. Transit Coop. Rsch. Program, 1991—, Borough pres. (Manhattan) Trans. Adv. Bd., Bronx Ctr. Devel. Project; bd. dirs. Transit Devel. Corp., 1992—; exec. bd. Transp. Coun., 1996—; mem. exec. com. Colin Powell Ctr.; bd. dirs. York Aviation Inst., 2003—; chmn. adv. bd. Cmty. Transp. Devel. Ctr., 2003—. Recipient Dept. Transp. award, 1977; SUNY faculty fellow, 1965-66 Fellow ASCE (past pres. Buffalo sect., chmn. steering com. 1992 splty. conf. traffic impact analysis); mem. AAAS, Transp. Rsch. Bd. (chmn. com. on transp. disadvantaged, mem. exec. com., peer rev. com. nat. transp. ctrs. 1988—), Inst. Transp. Engrs. (transit coun., exec. com., chmn. legis. policy com., rsch. com. surface transp. policy project 1995—), Coun. on Transp. (bd. dirs. 1996—), N.Y. Acad. Scis., Sigma Xi. Office: CCNY Inst Transp Systems Rm 220-Y 135th St and Convent Ave New York NY 10031

PACE, KAREN YVONNE, mathematics and computer science educator; b. Jefferson City, Mo., Dec. 29, 1957; d. William John and Georgia (Loesch) Sippel; m. Charles Edward Pace, Dec. 27, 1982. EdB, Mo. State U., 1980; EdM, Drury U., 1985. Cert. secondary tchr. Tchr. Salem (Mo.) Sch. Dist., 1980—, Southwest Bapt. U., Boliver, Mo., 1985—. Dist. chair Career Ladder Com., Salem, 1991-92; treas. Cmty. Tchrs. Orgn., Salem, 1992-93; assessment expert Salem Sch. Dist., 1993-94; sr. leader Mo. Assessment Project 2000, 1994. Pres. Community Cause Club, Salem, 1994. Mem. Salem Tchrs. Assn. (budget com. chair 1992-94). Democrat. Avocation: music. Home: PO Box 795 Salem MO 65560-0795 Office: Salem Sch Dist 1400 W 3rd St Salem MO 65560-1769

PACHAN, MARY JUDE KATHRYN DOROTHY, guidance counselor; b. East Otto, N.Y., Jan. 29, 1933; d. Nicholas and Mary (Podolinsky) P. BS in Edn., Medaille Coll., 1964; MS in Edn., St. Bonaventure U., 1972. Cert. guidance counseling, N.Y., elem. edn. tchr., N.Y. 3d grade tchr. Holy Cross Sch., Buffalo, 1955-56; 3d and 4th grade tchr. Immaculata Heart of Mary Sch., Buffalo, 1956-60; 8th grade tchr. Our Lady of Loretta Sch., Buffalo, 1960-64; tchr. English DeSales High Sch., Lockport, N.Y., 1964-68; counselor campus ministry SUNY, Buffalo, 1968-72; counselor St. Joseph's Collegiate Inst., Buffalo, 1973—99; ret., 1999. Dir. guidance svcs. St. Joseph's Collegiate Inst., Buffalo, 1989-96. Grantee in English, Nazareth Coll., Rochester, N.Y., 1965, journalism grantee Wall St., Boston U., 1966. Mem. N.Y. State Pers. and Guidance Assn., Counseling and Devel. Hospice Tng., AACD. Avocations: cross country skiing, horseback riding, concerts. Home: 557 Burroughs Dr Amherst NY 14226-3900

PACHECO, MANUEL TRINIDAD, retired academic administrator; b. Rocky Ford, Colo., May 30, 1941; s. Manuel J. and Elizabeth (Lopez) Pacheco; m. Karen M. King, Aug. 27, 1966; children: Daniel Mark, Andrew Charles, Sylvia Lois Elizabeth. BA, N.Mex. Highlands U., 1962; MA, Ohio State U., 1966, PhD, 1969. Mem. faculty Fla. State U., 1968—71, U. Colo., 1971; prof. edn., univ. dean Tex. A&I U., Laredo, 1972—77; prof. multicultural edn., chmn. dept. San Diego State U., 1977—78; prof. Spanish and edn. Laredo State U., 1978—80; exec. dir. Bilingual Edn. Ctr., Kingsville Tex. A&I U., 1980—82; assoc. dean Coll. Edn. U. Tex., El Paso, 1982—86, exec. dir. for planning, 1984; pres. Laredo State U., 1984—88, U. Houston-Downtown, 1986—97, U. Ariz., Tucson, 1991—97, U. Mo. Sys., Columbia, 1997—2002; ret., 2002. Cons. lang. divsn. Ency. Britannica, 1965—72; bd. dirs. Valley Nat. Bank Corp., Nat. Security Edn. Program, ASARCO; mem. exec. com. Bus.-Higher Edn. Forum. Co-editor: Handbook for Planning and Managing Instruction in Basic Skills for Limited English Proficient Students, 1983; prodr.: (videotapes) Teacher Training, 1976. Named, Most Prominent Am.-Hispanics Spanish Tchr. Mag., 1984, one of 100 Outstanding Hispanics Hispanis Bus., 1988, Man of Yr., Hispanic Profl. Action Com., 1991; recipient Disting. Alumnus award, Ohio State U., Columbus, 1984, Disting. Leadership in Higher Edn. award, Sec. of Edn. Richard Riley, 1997; Fulbright fellow, U. de Montepellier, France, 1962. Mem.: Tex. Assn. Chicanos in Higher Edn., Hispanic Assn. Colls. and Univs., Nat. Acad. Pub. Adminstrn., Am. Assn. State Colls. and Univs., Rotary, Phi Delta Kappa.*

PACHER, PAL, pharmacologist, educator, researcher; b. Budapest, Hungary, Aug. 7, 1969; s. Pál and Irén (Bolfert) P. Med. Diplomate, Semmelweis U. Medicine, Budapest, 1994; diploma holistic medicine, U.K., 2000; PhD, Hungarian Acad. of Sci., 2001. Diplomate. Lectr. asst. dept. pharmacology Semmelweis U. Medicine, 1994—; postdoctoral rsch. fellow Thomas Jefferson U., Phila., 1999-2001; pharmacologist Inotek Corp., Beverly, Mass., 2001—, dir. cardiovasc. pharmacology, 2002—; sr. rsch. scientist NIAAA, NIH, Bethesda, 2002—. Mem.: Inst. of Holistic Medicine (U.K.), Am. Heart Assn., Am. Diabetes Assn., Juvenile Diabetes Assn., Biophys. Soc., NY Acad. Scis., Internat. Soc. for Heart Rsch., Worldwide Hungarian Med. Acad., Hungarian Cardiol. Soc., Hungarian Chamber Physicians, Hungarian Pharmacol. Soc. Achievements include research in cardiovascular pharmacology and physiology. Avocations: computers, chess, excursions, swimming. Home: 5578 Burnside Dr #5 Rockville MD 20853 Office: NIAAA Park Bldg Rm 445 12420 Parklawn Dr MSC 8115 Bethesda MD 20815

PACIENCIA, DAVID A. school superintendent; b. Baldwinsville, N.Y., June 16, 1950; s. Jose and Stella M. Paciencia; m. Nancy D. Lutze, Aug. 26, 1972; children: Susan, Keri, Todd. BA, Potsdam (N.Y.) Coll., 1972; MEd, Syracuse U., 1975. Tchr. Rome (N.Y.) City Schs., 1972-76, adminstrv. intern, 1976-77; mid. sch. prin. Cassadaga Valley Consol. Sch. Dist., Sinclairville, NY, 1977; h.s. sch. prin. Oneida (N.Y.) City Schs., 1979-86; supt. Mt. Morris (N.Y.) Consol. Sch. Dist., 1986-90, South Jefferson Ctrl. Sch. Dist., Adams, N.Y., 1990-98, Kenmore-Town of Tonawanda U.F.S.D., 1998—2001; supt. schs. Taconic Hills Ctrl. Sch. Dist., Craryville, NY, 2001—. Contbr. articles to profl. jours. Eucharistic min., lector, 1976—. Recipient Disting. Svc. award SUNY Potsdam, 1996, hon. degree South Jefferson Future Farmers Assn., 1992; Outstanding Sch. Adminstr. award Jefferson-Lewis County Music Tchrs. Assn., 1994, Buffalo Pathfinder 2000 award, St. Lawrence Acad. medal, 2003. Mem. N.Y. State Coun. Supts. (v.p., treas. commr.'s adv. bd. 1992—, pres. 2002-03,), Mid. States Assn. (chmn. 1982—), No. Bus. Coun., Ducks Unltd. (charter, treas. 1993-94), Rotary (past pres.), KC, Phi Delta Kappa. Avocations: boating, fishing, photography. Office: Taconic Hills Ctrl Sch Dist PO Box 482 Craryville NY 12521

PACINO, FRANK GEORGE, physician, educator; MD, U. Calif, Irvine, Coll. of Medicine, 1962; M.P.H., Loma Linda U., 1970. Intern Glendale Community Hosp., Calif., 1961-62; control physician, STD div. Los Angeles County Dept. Health, 1963-64, asst. chief, STD div., 1964-66; dist. health officer San Antonio Health District, 1966—92, Harbor Health Dist., 1972—92; practice medicine specializing in public health San Pedro, Calif., 1972—; med. dir. South Coast Alcohol Program, 1972—. Served with AUS, 1954-56. Recipient cert. of appreciation Los Angeles County Health Dept., 1966; commendation Los Angeles County Bd. Suprs., 1975, Patient Svcs. Improvement award Dept. Health Svcs. Los Angeles County, 1987, 88, 89. Mem. Physicians Assn. Los Angeles County (pres. 1972-73, 81-82, Physician Recognition award 1972), Am. Assn. Public Health Physicians (pres. 1975-76, pres. Calif. chpt. 1977-78, 81-82), So. Calif. Public Health Assn. (chmn. fins.), Public Health Physicians Assn. (pres. 1970-71), Am. Med. Assn. Office: 16662 Intrepid Ln Huntington Beach CA 92649-2826

PACK, NANCY J. special education educator, speech therapist; b. Santa Monica, Calif., May 28, 1952; d. James Neil and Muriel Elaine (Stone) Hess; m. Albert Richard Pack, Mar. 22, 1986; children: Ember, Andrea, Galen. BA in Speech/Drama, Chico State U., 1975, MA in Speech Pathology, 1977. Cert. in early childhood spl. edn., Wash. Lang. disorders specialist Shasta County Office of Edn., Redding, Calif., 1977-80; tchr. hearing impaired Tehama County Dept. Edn., Red Bluff, Calif., 1983-89, speech and lang. pathologist, 1983-89, spl. edn. tchr., 1989-94, North Kitsap Sch. Dist., Poulsbo, Wash., 1994—. Mem. adv. bd. Spl. Edn. Steering Com., Poulsbo, 1996-97, Spl. Edn. Tech. Com., Poulsbo, 1997-98; presenter in field. Tchr. adult edn. Tehama County Dept. Edn., Red Bluff, 1980-82. Recipient Tchr. of Yr. award Tehama County Edn. Found., 1992-93, Exemplary Educator award Calif. Coun. for Edn. Exceptional Children, 1993-94."Who" award Redd ing Svc. Ctr. Coun. of Calif. Tchrs. Assn., 1993. Mem. Am. Speech and Lang. Assn. (cert. clin. competence), Tehama County Cert. Employees Assn. (pres. 1988-94), Coun. for Exceptional Children, Nat. Assn. Edn. of Young Children, Wash. Educators Assn. Avocations: backpacking, mountain climbing, cross country skiing, windsurfing, camping. Home: 2255 Dalarna Ct NE Poulsbo WA 98370-7590

PACKARD, LINDA LEE, elementary education educator; b. Columbus, Ohio, July 28, 1955; d. Paul Richard and Wilma Laverta P.; children: Michael Keller, Amanda Keller. BS summa cum laude, Ohio State U., 1992; MEd, Ashland U., 2002. Tchr. Hilliard (Ohio) City Schs., 1992—. Rep. Math and Sci. Leadership Acad.; mid. sch. Math tchr. leader. Recipient Meritorious Svc. award Columbus State C.C., 1983; named Woman of Woodcraft, Woodmen of the World, Columbus, 1983. Mem.: NEA, Central Ohio Coun. Tchrs. Math., Ohio Coun. Tchrs. Math., Nat. Coun. Tchrs. of Math., Golden Key, Pi Lambda Theta, Phi Kappa Phi. Republican. Methodist. Avocations: softball, volleyball, computers, reading, horseback riding. Home: 1568 Buck Trail Ln Worthington OH 43085-4761 Office: Weaver Mid Sch 4600 Avery Rd Hilliard OH 43026-8287

PACKARD, MILDRED RUTH, middle school educator; b. Boulder, Colo., Sept. 8, 1947; d. Peter L.M. and Jane G. Packard. BA, Lynchburg Coll., 1969; MS, Va. Poly. Inst. and State U., 1973. Cert. phys. edn. tchr., Va. Tchr., basketball, gymnastics and track coach Osbourn High Sch., Manassas, Va., 1969-73; tchr., coach girls softball, basketball and volleyball Rippon Mid. Sch., Woodbridge, Va., 1973-89, athletic dir., 1982-89; tchr., athletic dir., volleyball coach Lake Ridge Mid. Sch., Woodbridge, 1989—2003; ret. Mem. NEA, AAHPERD, Va. Edn. Assn., Prince William Edn. Assn., Va. Assn. Health, Phys. Edn., and Recreation. Avocations: volleyball, golf, reading. Office: Lake Ridge Mid Sch 12350 Mohican Rd Woodbridge VA 22192-1757

PACKARD, ROCHELLE SYBIL, elementary school educator; b. June 25, 1951; d. Dave Wallace and Jeanette (Goddy) P. BA in Early Childhood Edn., Point Park Coll., 1973; MEd in Elem. Edn., U. Pitts., 1975. Instrnl. II permanent tchg. cert., Pa. Substitute tchr. Pitts. Pub. Bd. Edn., 1973-77, tchr. kindergarted, 1st grade, 2d grade, 1977—92, tchr. kingergarten, 1992—. Chair Israel Day Parade, Pitts., 1981; mem. Hadassah, Pitts., 1983—, Pioneer Women, Pitts., 1982—, ORT, Pitts., 1975—. Mem. Pitts. Fedn. Tchrs., Pitts. State Edn. Agy. Democrat. Jewish. Home: 4100 Lydia St Pittsburgh PA 15207-1135

PACKARD, SANDRA PODOLIN, education educator, consultant; b. Buffalo, Sept. 13, 1942; d. Mathew and Ethel (Zolte) P.; m. Martin Packard, Aug. 2, 1964; children: Dawn Esther, Shana Fanny BFA, Syracuse U., 1964; MSEd, Ind. U., 1966, EdD, 1973. Cert. tchr. art K-12, N.Y. Asst. prof. art SUNY-Buffalo, 1972-74; assoc. prof. art Miami U., Oxford, Ohio, 1974-81, spl. asst. to provost, 1979-80, assoc. provost, spl. programs, 1980-81; dean Coll. Edn. Bowling Green State U., Ohio, 1981-85; provost and vice chancellor for acad. affairs U. Tenn., Chattanooga, 1985-92; pres. Oakland U., Rochester, Mich., 1992-95, prof. edn., 1995—, dir. higher edn. doc. cognate; sr. fellow, dir. tech. in edn. Am. Assn. State Colls. and Univs., 1995; coord. Nat. Coun. for Accreditation of Tchr. Edn., Washington, 1995—2001. Cons. Butler County Health Ctr., Hamilton, Ohio, 1976-78; vis. prof. art therapy Simmons Coll., 1979, Mary Mount Coll., Milw., 1981; bd. dirs. SE Ctr. for Arts in Edn., 1994-96; mem. corp. adv. com. Corp. Detroit Mag., 1994-95; cons. Univ. of the North, South Africa Project of the Am. Coun. on Edn., 1995; bd. mem. Fellows Coun. Am. Coun. on Edn., 1994-96. Sr. editor Studies in Art Edn. jour., 1979-81; mem. editl. adv. bd. Jour. Aesthetic Edn., 1984-90; editor: The Leading Edge, 1986; contbr. articles to profl. jours., chpts. to conf. papers Chmn. com. Commn. on Edn. Excellence, Ohio, 1982-83, Tenn. State Peformance Funding Task Force, 1988, Tenn. State Task Force on Minority Tchrs., 1988; reviewer art curriculum N.Y. Bd. Edn., 1985; mem. supt. search com. Chattanooga Pub. Schs., 1987-88; mem. Chattanooga Met. Coun., 1987-88, Chattanooga Ballet Bd., 1986-88, Fund for Excellence in Pub. Edn., 1986-90, Tenn. Aquarium Bd. Advisors, 1989-92, Team Evaluation Ctr. Bd., 1988-90; mem. Strategic Planning Action Team, Chattanooga City Schs., 1987-88, Siskin Hosp. Bd., 1989-92, Blue Ribbon Task Force Pontiac 2010: A New Reality, City of Pontiac Planning Divsn., 1992—; steering com., cultural action bd. Chattanooga, planning com United Way, 1987; Jewish Fedn. Bd., 1986-91; mem. coun. for policy studies Art Edn. Adv. Bd., 1982-91; ex-officio mem. Meadow Brook Theatre Guild, 1992-95; bd. chair Meadow Brook Performing Arts Co., 1992-95; chair World Cup Soccer Edn. Com./Mich. Host Com. 1993-95; bd. dirs. Ptnrs. for Preferred Future, Rochester Cmty. Schs., 1992-95, Traffic Improvement Assn. Oakland County, 1992-95, Oakland County Bus. Roundtable, 1993-95; Rochester C. of C. host com. chair on edn. World Cup, 1992-95; mem. fin. adv. com. Jewish Fedn. Detroit, 1995-97; bd. dirs. United Way Southeastern Mich., 1992-95: bd. dirs. United Way Oakland County, 1992-95, Pontiac 2010: A New Reality, mayor's transition team city/sch. rels. task force: team evaluation leader Dept. of State Am. Univ. Bulgaria, 1995; bd. trustees Cohn's & Colitis Found., 1996-97. Am. Coun. on Edn. and Mellon fellow Miami U., 1978-79; recipient Cracking the Glass Ceiling award Pontiac Area Urban League, 1992. Fellow Nat. Art Edn. Assn. (disting.); mem. Nat. Coun. Profs. of Ednl. Adminstrn. (technology com., 2000-03), Am. Assn. Colls. for Tchr. Edn. (com. chair 1982-85), Am. Art Therapy Assn. (registered), Nat. Art Edn. Assn. Women's Caucus (founder, pres. 1976-78, McFee award 1986), Am. Assn. State Colls. and Univs. (com. profl. devel. 1993-95, state rep. 1994-95), Econ. Club Detroit (bd. dirs. 1992-95), Rotary Club, Great Lakes Yacht Club (social chmn. 1996-97, ground chmn., bd. dirs. 1997-98), Phi Delta Kappa (Leadership award 1985), Nat. Assn. Profs. of Edn. Adminstrn. (com. chair 1998-), Great Lakes Yacht Club, 1995 (bd. dir. 1996-1998). Avocation: sailing. Home: 10471 Scout Trail White Lake MI 48386 Office: Oakland U 475 Education Bldg Rochester MI 48309-4423 E-mail: packard@oakland.edu.

PACKARD, SHEILA ANNE, nursing educator, researcher; b. Hartford, Conn., July 15, 1949; d. Charles David and Anne Irene (Moriarity) P. BS in Nursing, Boston Coll., 1971, PhD in Sociology, 1986; MSN, Yale U., 1974. RN, Mass. Staff nurse Boston VNA, 1971-72, dir. edn., 1978-79; instr. Westchester (Pa.) State Coll. dept. nursing; clinician Wilmington (Del.) Med. Ctr., 1975-76; instr. Boston U. Sch. of Nursing, 1976-78, Boston Coll. Sch. of Nursing, Chestnut Hill, Mass., 1979-81; assoc. prof. U. Conn. Sch. of Nursing, Storrs, 1983—. Active in many rsch. projects in field of nursing. Contbr. articles to profl. jours. Recipeint Manchester Meml. Hosp. scholarship, 1967, Boston Coll. scholarship, 1967-70, 1980-82, Mary Lawrence Rsch. award, U. Conn. Sch. of Nursing, 1986, 87. Mem. Am. Nurses Assn., Am. Sociological Assn., Phi Kappa Phi, Sigma Theta Tau. Democrat. Roman Catholic. Home: 28 Cold Spring Dr Vernon Rockville CT 06066-5005 Office: Univ Conn U 59 175 Auditorium Rd Storrs Mansfield CT 06269-0001

PACKER, LEE ANN, special education educator; b. Keene, N.H., Dec. 31, 1948; d. Lee Dascombe and Frances Hazel (Edwards) Bowman; m. Robert Michael Packer, Nov. 27, 1982; children: Meredith Ryan, Michael Bowman. AA, Green Mountain Coll., 1968; BA, Boston U., 1970, postgrad., 1978-83, Rivier Coll., 1984-85. Cert. tchr., N.H. Resource rm. tchr. Fall Mountain Regional Sch. System, Walpole, N.H., 1972-74; learning disabled program specialist Nashua (N.H.) Sch. Dist., 1974-81, Oyster River Sch. Dist., Durham, N.H., 1981-82; ednl. evaluator Sch. Adminstrv. Unit # 63, Wilton, N.H., 1983-88, dir. spl. edn., 1988—. Instr. Keene (N.H.) State Coll., summer 1973; mem. state evaluation team N.H. State Dept. Edn., 1986—, state alternative cert. team, 1986—; coord. Ams. Disabilities Act sect. 504, 1991—, Sch. Adminstrv. Unit # 63. Bd. dirs. YWCA Nashua, 1978-80. Mem. N.H. Spl. Edn. Dirs. Assn. (affiliate). Mem. Lds Ch. Avocations: arts and crafts, cooking, gardening. Office: Sch Adminstrn Univ # 63 Livermore St Wilton NH 03086

PACKHAM, MARIAN AITCHISON, biochemistry educator; b. Toronto, Ont., Can., Dec. 13, 1927; d. James and Clara Louise (Campbell) A.; m. James Lennox Packham, June 25, 1949; children: Neil Lennox, Janet Melissa. BA, U. Toronto, 1949, PhD, 1954; DSc honoris causa, Ryerson Poly. U., 1997. Sr. fellow dept. biochemistry U. Toronto, 1954-58, lectr. dept. biochemistry, 1958-63, 66-67; rsch. assoc. dept. physiol. scis. Ont. Vet. Coll., U. Guelph, 1963-65; rsch. assoc. blood and cardiovascular disease rsch. unit U. Toronto, 1965-66, asst. prof. dept. biochemistry, 1967-72, assoc. prof., 1972-75, prof., 1975—, acting chmn. dept. biochemistry, 1983. Contbr. articles to profl. jours. Royal Soc. Can. fellow, 1991; recipient Lt. Govs. Silver medal Victoria Coll., 1949; co-recipient J. Allyn Taylor Internat. prize in Medicine, 1988. Mem.: Can. Soc. Biochemistry and Molecular and Cellular Biology, Can. Atherosclerosis Soc., Internat. Soc. Thrombosis and Haemostasis, Can. Soc. Clin. Investigation, Can. Soc. Hematology, Am. Soc. Hematology. Office: U Toronto Dept Biochemistry Toronto ON Canada M5S 1A8

PADDOCK, SANDRA CONSTANCE, music educator; b. Buffalo, Sept. 20, 1972; d. Walter Robert and Susan Elizabeth Wloch; m. Darren Ennis Paddock, July 20, 1996; children: Leanne Kristine, Robert Duane. B in Music Edn. cum laude, SUNY, Buffalo, 1994, M in Arts and Humanities, 1997. Cert. tchr. N.Y. Music tchr. Niagara Wheatfield (N.Y.) Schs., 1995—96; orchestra dir. Kenmore-Tonawanda Schs., 1996—2000; orch. dir., string tchr. Orchard Park (N.Y.) Mid. Sch., 2000—. String adjudicator Erie County Elem. and Jr. High Festivals, 1998, 2002; co-chairperson Erie County (N.Y.) Jr. High Music Festivals, 2001, 02. Musician (solo violinist): faculty recital, 2001. 1st violin Amherst Symphony Orch., 1997—. Mem.: Erie County Music Educator's Assn., Music Educator's Nat. Conf. Avocations: reading, attending concerts.

PADILLA, ELSA NORMA, retired school system administrator; b. Guines, Havana, Cuba, Feb. 25, 1947; came to U.S., 1962; d. Regulo and Esther (Beato) Cuesta; m. Pedro Manuel Padilla, June 10, 1967; children: Jorge Alberto, Alejandro Manuel. BA, U. Ariz., 1970, MEd, 1972, cert. administration, 1982. Cert. elem. tchr. bilingual endorsement, spl. edn., adminstrn., Ariz. Spl. edn. tchr. Tucson Unified Sch. Dist., 1970, 1972-76, spl. edn. program specialist, 1976-78, spl. edn. tchr., 1978-81, bilingual diagnostician, 1981-84, asst dir. spl. edn., 1984-89; principal Ochoa Elem. Sch. Tucson Unified Sch. Dist., 1989-96, compliance coord., 1996-99; ednl. cons. Tucson Unified Sch. Dist., 1999—. Part time instr. Ariz. Dept. Edn., 1980-87, No. Ariz. U., 1983-89, U. Ariz., Tucson, 1983-88; mem. bilingual diagnostic team Tucson Sch. Dist., 1978, author Bilingual Spl. Edn. Program, 1980; prin. in restructuring of sch. project funded by Charles Stewart Mott Found.; grant reader Office Bilingual Edn. and Minority Lang. Affairs, U.S. Dept. Edn., 1995—; cons. in field. Co-author: Courage to Change. Bd. dirs. TETRA Corp., Tucson, 1988-94, Vista Adv. Coun., Tucson, 1990-93; mem. City of South Tucson Econ. Devel. Adv. Bd., 1993-96. Grantee: U.S. Dept. Edn., Tucson, 1984; recipient NEA Excellence award, 1994. Democrat. Avocations: cooking, swimming. E-mail: enpadilla@aol.com.

PADOVANO, ANTHONY THOMAS, theologian, educator; b. Harrison, N.J., Sept. 18, 1934; s. Thomas Henry and Mary Rose (Cierzo) P.; m. Theresa Lackamp, 1974; children— Mark, Andrew, Paul, Rosemarie BA magna cum laude, Seton Hall U., 1956; S.T.B. magna cum laude, Pontifical Gregorian U., Rome, Italy, 1958, S.T.L. magna cum laude, 1960, S.T.D. magna cum laude, 1962; Ph.L. magna cum laude, St. Thomas Pontifical Internat. U., Rome, 1962; MA, NYU, 1971; PhD, Fordham U., 1980. Ordained priest Roman Cath. Ch., 1959. Asst. chaplain Med. Center, Jersey City, 1960; asst. St. Paul of the Cross Ch., Jersey City, 1962, St. Catharine Ch., Glen Rock, N.J., 1963; prof. systematic theology Darlington Sem., Mahwah, N.J., 1962-74; disting. prof. Am. lit. Ramapo Coll., NJ, 1971—; founding faculty mem., disting. prof. theology/religious studies Fordham U., 1973-93. Mem. Archdiocesan Commn. Ecumenical and Interreligious Affairs, 1965, Commn. Instrn. Clergy in Documents Vatican II, 1966; del. dialogue group Luth.-Roman Cath. Theol. Conversations, 1969; del.-at-large senate of priests Archdiocese of Newark; Danforth assoc., 1975—; Cath. pastor Inclusive Cmty. World Coun. Chs., 1986—; lectr. in field, also appearances on radio and TV; parish min. St. Margaret of Scotland, Morristown, N.J. Author: The Cross of Christ, the Measure of the World, 1962, The Estranged God, 1966, Who is Christ, 1967, Belief in Human Life, 1969, American Culture and the Quest for Christ, 1970, Dawn Without Darkness, 1971, Free to be Faithful, 1972, Eden and Easter, 1974, A Case for Worship, 1975, America: Its People, Its Promise, 1975, Presence and Structure, 1975, The Human Journey, 1982, Trilogy, 1982, Contemplation and Compassion, 1984, Winter Rain: A Play, 1985, His Name is John: A Play, 1986, Christmas to Calvary, 1987, Love and Destiny, 1987, Summer Lightening: A Play, 1988, Conscience and Conflict, 1989, Reform and Renewal, 1990, A Celebration of Life, 1990, The Church Today: Belonging and Believing, 1990, Scripture in the Streets, 1992, A Retreat with Thomas Merton, 1996, Hope is a Dialogue, 1998, Resistance and Renewal, 2002; editor: Centenary Issue Roman Echoes, 1959; editl. bd. The Advocate, 1966-73; contbr. articles to mags., Padovano Papers, personal and profl. papers, Archives, U. Notre Dame. With Diocese Paterson Ecumenical Commn.; founding pres. Justice and Peace Commn., Diocese of Paterson, active Resigned Priests Com. Mem. Cath. Theol. Soc. Am., Mariological Soc. Am., Nat. Fedn. Priests Councils (ofcl. rep. to Constl. Conv., Chgo. 1968), Corpus (pres.), Fedn. Christian Ministries, Internat. Fedn. of Married Cath. Priests (v.p. for N.Am.). Home: 9 Millstone Dr Morris Plains NJ 07950-1536 Office: Sch of Am Internat Studies Ramapo Coll NJ Mahwah NJ 07430 E-mail: tpadovan@optonlime.net.

PAFF, JOHN WILLIAM, public relations executive; b. Columbus, Ohio, Nov. 14, 1962; s. John Dale and Sarah Jeanette (Newton) P.; m. Jeanne Carolyn Schramm Paff, June 6, 1987; children: John David, Mark Cannon, Joshua Mitchell, Michael Caleb. BA, Oral Roberts U., Tulsa, 1985; MA, Regent U., Virginia Beach, Va., 1987. Pub. liaison Nat. Legal Found., Chesapeake, Va., 1987-89, pub. affairs dir., 1989-91, adminstr., 1991-93; dir. pub. rels. Huntington (Ind.) Coll., 1993—2002, exec. dir. comm., exec. asst. to pres., 2003—. Freelance web developer, comms., cons., 1996—. Editor: National Legal Found. Minuteman, 1989-93, HC Alumni Newsletter, 1993-97, Huntington College Parent, 1994-97, Huntington College News and Views, 1993-97, Huntington College Magazine, 1997—. Participant Huntington (Ind.) County Leadership, 1995. Republican. Methodist. Office: Huntington College 2303 College Ave Huntington IN 46750-1299 E-mail: jpaff@johnpuff.com., jpaff@huntington.edu.

PAFFENBARGER, RALPH SEAL, JR., epidemiologist, educator; b. Columbus, Ohio, Oct. 21, 1922; s. Ralph Seal and Viola Elizabeth (Link) P.; m. Mary Dale Higdon, Sept. 19, 1943 (dec.); children: Ralph, James (dec.), Ann, Charles, John (dec.), Timothy; m. Jo Ann Schroeder, July 20, 1991. AB, Ohio State U., 1944; MB, Northwestern U., 1946, MD, 1947; MPH, Johns Hopkins U., 1952, DrPH, 1954; ScD honoris causa, U. Laval, 1998. Intern Evanston (Ill.) Hosp., 1946-47; research asst. pediatrics La. State U. and Charity Hosp., New Orleans, 1949-50; practice medicine, specializing in geriatrics Framingham, Mass., 1960-68; clin. asst. prof. preventive medicine U. Cin., 1955-60; lectr. biostatistics Sch. Pub. Health, Harvard U., 1961-62, clin. assoc. preventive medicine Med. Sch., 1963-65, lectr. epidemiology Sch. Pub. Health, 1965-68, vis. lectr., 1968-83, vis. prof. epidemiology, 1983-85, vis. lectr., 1986-88, adj. prof. epidemiology, 1988—; prof. epidemiology in-residence U. Calif. Sch. Pub. Health, Berkeley, 1968-69, adj. prof., 1969-80; prof. epidemiology Stanford U., 1977-93, prof. emeritus, 1993—; rsch. epidemiologist U. Calif., Berkeley, 1993—. Commd. officer USPHS, 1947, med. dir., Atlanta, Ga., 1947-53, Bethesda, Md., 1953-55, Cin., 1955-60, Framingham, 1960-68, ret., 1968; mem. epidemiology and disease control study sect. NIH, 1972-76 Assoc. editor: Am. Jour. Epidemiology, 1972-75, 80-98, editor, 1975-79; contbr. articles to profl. publs. Founding mem. Internat. Olympic Com. Olympic Acad. Sport Scis., 1999. Recipient prize for Sports Scis. Internat. Olympic Com., 1996. Fellow Royal Soc. Physicians (hon.); mem. AAAS, AMA, APHA, Am. Epidemiol. Soc., Am. Heart Assn., Internat. Epidemiol. Assn., Soc. Epidemiol. Rsch., Rsch. Soc. Am., Internat. Soc. Cardiology, Am. Assn. Suicidology, Marcé Soc., Am. Coll. Sports Medicine, Am. Acad. Sports Physicians, Nat. Fitness Leaders Assn., Royal Soc. Medicine (hon.), Phi Eta Sigma, Pi Kappa Epsilon, Delta Omega. Home: 892 Arlington Ave Berkeley CA 94707-1938 Office: Stanford U Sch Medicine Stanford CA 94305

PAGAN, KEITH AREATUS, music educator, academic administrator; b. Beggs, Okla., June 7, 1931; s. Areatus and Opal Gail (Facker) P.; m. Betty Lois Wallace; children: Melva Joy, Lisa Lynne, Beryl Kay. B in Music Edn., Bethany Nazarene Coll., 1952; M in Music Edn., Okla. U., 1953; D in Music Edn. with honors, Ind. U., 1970. Asst. prof. music Bethany (Okla.) Nazarene Coll., 1952-53, 55-58; prof. music Pasadena (Calif.) Coll., 1961-76; acad. dean, v.p. acad. affairs Point Loma Nazarene Coll., San Diego, 1976-88, prof. music, chair dept. music., 1989—98. Dir. S.W. Music Symposium, San Diego, 1991—; cons. Sch. for Creative and Performing Arts, San Diego, 1990—, Chula Vista, Calif., 1992—; mem. vis. team Western Coll. Assn., Calif., 1977-82. Arranger (choral) To God be the Glory, (brass) Keith A. Pagan Brass Quintet Series, The King Shall Come; mem. editorial bd. Christian Scholars Rev., 1986—, EverGreen Morning Music Press. Trustee Christian Scholars Rev., 1994—; dir. music Village Ch., Rancho Santa Fe, Calif. With U.S. Army, 1953-55. Recipient WHO award Calif. Higher Edn. Assn., 1971, Lawrence Vredevoe Disting. Leadership award 1986, Spl. Svc. to Music award Calif. Music Educators Assn., 1991; winner 4th ann. anthem contest Choral Condrs. Guild; grantee Danforth Found., 1960. Mem. Calif. Coll. and Univ. Faculty Assn. (pres. 1969-70), Music Tchrs. Assn. Calif. (parliamentarian 1971-73), Western Assn. Schs. and Coll. (accreditation liaison 1976-88). Avocations: travel, photography. Home: 7450 Margerum Ave San Diego CA 92120-2025

PAGANO, ALICIA I. education educator; b. Sidney, N.Y., June 29, 1929; d. Neil Gadsby Leonard and Norma (Carr) Collins; m. Thomas McNutt, Feb. 20, 1954 (div. Nov. 1962); m. LeRoy Pagano, Feb. 26, 1963 (div. Oct. 1985); children: Janice, Daniel, Jack, Pier. BA in Music, Barrington Coll., 1952; MAT in Music, Rollins Coll., 1964; EdD in Edn. Adminstrn., Am. U., 1972. Tchr. music Prince Georges County Pub. Schs., Beltsville, Md., 1966-69; asst. prof. Medgar Evers Coll., Bklyn., 1973-78; nat. program dir. Girl Scouts USA, N.Y.C., 1978-83; nat. dir. vol. development U.S. Com. UNICEF, N.Y.C., 1983-84; pres. Pagano Consulting Internat., Jersey City, 1984—; asst. prof. mgmt. Coll. Staten Island, CUNY, 1985-89; adj. prof. museum studies NYU, N.Y.C., 1986-91; assoc. exec. dir. Louis August Jonas Found., Red Hook, N.Y., 1988-89; assoc. prof. edn. N.J. City U., 1990—. Chair Wingspread Nat. Conf./Nat. Collaboration for Youth, Washington, 1982; adv. bd. dirs. Early Childhood Ctr.; rschr., cons. in early childhood edn. in West Africa, 1988—. Author, editor: Social Studies in Early Childhood, 1979; author: The Future of American Business, 1985, (with others) Learning Opportunities Beyond School, 1987; co-editor: International Early Childhood Teacher Education, 1999; contbr. articles to profl. jours. Judge annual awards Girls, Inc., N.Y.C., 1985-90; reader Jersey City Spelling Bee, 1991; vol. Girl Scouts USA, Essex/Hudson Counties, N.J., 1995—, Boys & Girls Clubs, Hudson County, N.J., 1995—. Mem. ASCD, AAUW, Am. Ednl. Rsch. Assn., Nat. Assn. Early Childhood Tchr. Edn. (bd. dirs. 1995—), N.J. Assn. Early Childhood Tchr. Educators (v.p.

1994-97, pres. 1997-99), Orgn. Mondiale pour l'Edn. Prescolaire (N.J. regional dir. 1996-98). Avocations: hiking, swimming, international travel. Home: PO Box 413 Mastic Beach NY 11951-0413 E-mail: apagano@njcu.edu.

PAGANO, JOSEPH STEPHEN, physician, researcher, educator; b. Rochester, N.Y., Dec. 29, 1931; s. Angelo Pagano and Marian (Vinci) Signorino; m. Anna Louise Reynolds, June 8, 1957; children: Stephen Reynolds, Christopher Joseph. AB with honors, U. Rochester, 1953; MD, Yale U., 1957. Resident Peter Bent Brigham Hosp. Harvard U., Boston, 1960-61; fellow Karolinska Inst., Stockholm, 1961-62; mem. Wistar Inst., Phila., 1962-65; from asst. to assoc. prof. medicine & microbiology U. N.C., Chapel Hill, 1965-73, prof., 1974—, dir. divsn. infectious diseases, 1972-75; founder, dir. U. N.C. Lineberger Comprehensive Cancer Ctr., Chapel Hill, 1974-97, dir. emeritus, 1997—. Attending physician U. Hosps., Chapel Hill; vis. prof. Swiss Inst. Cancer Rsch., Lausanne, 1970-71, Lineberger prof. cancer rsch., 1986—; mem. virology study sect. NIH, Bethesda, Md., 1973-79; recombinant DNA adv. com. USPHS, 1986-90; bd. dirs. Burroughs Wellcome Fund, 1993-2001; chmn., adv. com. N.C. Cancer Coord. and Control, 1993—; Mclaughlin vis. prof. U. Tex. Med. Br., 1996; Norma Berryhill Disting. lectr. U. N.C., 1997; Harry Eagle lectr. Albert Einstein Coll. Medicine, 1997; Harry F. Dowling lectr. U. Ill. Sch. Med., 1991; Gertrude & Werner Henle lectr. in viral oncology, 1990, Joseph and Ruth McCartney Hauck lectr. Mayo Clinic, 2002. Mem. editorial bd. Jour. Virology, Jour. Immunology, Cancer Rsch., Jour. Gen. Virology, Antimicrobial Agts. and Chemotherapy, 1974-93; contbr. articles to profl. jours., chpts. to books. Mem. awards assembly GM Cancer Rsch. Found., 1997-2001; chair sci. adv. bd. Trimeris; mem. sci. adv. bd. AlphaVax. Recipient USPHS Rsch. Career award NIH, 1968-73, N.C. award in sci., 1996. Mem. Inst. Med., Am. Assn. Cancer Rsch., Am. Assn. Cancer Insts. (bd. dirs. 1992-99, pres., chmn.), Internat. Assn. for Rsch. in Epstein-Barr Virus (pres. 1990-94), Sci. Adv. Bd. Alphavax; chair Sci. Adv. Bd. Trimeris, Chapel Hill Tennis Club (pres. 1980-82), Carolina Club, Baldhead Island Club. Episcopalian. Avocations: tennis, squash. Home: 114 Laurel Hill Rd Chapel Hill NC 27514-4323 Office: U NC CB7295 Lineberger Comp Cancer Ctr Chapel Hill NC 27599-0001

PAGE, ANNE RUTH, gifted education educator, education specialist; b. Norfolk, Va., Apr. 13, 1949; d. Amos Purnell and Ruth Martin (Hill) Bailey; m. Peter Smith Page, Apr. 24, 1971; children: Edgar Bailey, Emmett McBrannon. BA, N.C. Wesleyan Coll.; student, Fgn. Lang. League; postgrad., N.C. State U.; student, Overseas Linguistic Studies, France, Spain, Eng., 1978, 85, 86. Cert. tchr., N.C. Tchr. Cary (N.C.) Sr. High Sch., 1971-72; tchr., head dept. Daniels Mid. Sch., Raleigh, N.C., 1978-83; chmn. fgn. lang. dept. Martin Mid. Gifted and Talented, Raleigh, N.C., 1983—. Leadership team Senate Bill 2 Core co-chair; dir. student group Overseas Studies, Am. Coun. for Internat. Studies, France, Spain, Eng., 1982, 84, 86, 88; bd. dirs. N.T.H., Inc., Washington; cert. mentor tchr. Wake County Pub. Schs., 1989; dir. student exchs. between Martin Mid. Sch. and Sevigné Inst. of Compiegne, France. Sunday sch. tchr. Fairmont United Meth. Ch., Raleigh, 1983-85. Mem. Alpha Delta Kappa. Democrat. Home: 349 Wilmot Dr Raleigh NC 27606-1232 Office: Martin Mid Sch GT 1701 Ridge Rd Raleigh NC 27607-6737

PAGE, CHERYL MILLER, elementary school educator; Cert. health edn. specialist. Health educator Salem (Oreg.)-Keizer Sch. Dist. Named Nat. Health Edn. Profl. Yr., Oreg. Outstanding Secondary Health Educator of Yr., Vol. of Yr., Am. Cancer Soc.; recipient Tambrands award, Am. Assn. Health Edn., 1996. Mem.: Oreg. Alliance Health, Phys. Edn., Recreation and Dance (treas. 1992—96), Oreg. Assn. for the Advancement of Health Edn. (sec./treas. 1990—92), Nat. Bd. for Profl. Tchg. Stds. (bd. mem.). Avocations: running, reading. Office: Salem-Keizer Sch Dist PO Box 12024 Salem OR 97309*

PAGE, ELLIS BATTEN, psychologist, educator; b. San Diego; s. Frank Homer and Dorothy (Batten) P.; m. Elizabeth Latimer Thaxton, June 21, 1952 (dec. 2000); children: Ellis Batten (Tim), Elizabeth Page Sigman, Richard Leighton. AB, Pomona Coll.; MA, San Diego State U.; EdD, UCLA, 1958. Tchr. secondary schs., Calif.; dean Coll. Edn., prof. edn. and psychology Tex. Woman's U., 1960-62; prof. ednl. psychology U. Conn., 1962-79; prof. ednl. psychology and research Duke U., 1979—. Vis. prof. U. Wis., 1960, 62, Stanford U., 1965, Harvard U., 1968-69, U. Javeriana, Bogotá, 1975; leader Ford Found. rsch. adv. team Venezuelan Ministry Edn., Caracas, 1969-70; vis. prof. Spanish Ministry Edn., 1972, 80, 82-85; rsch. cons. U.S. Office Edn., USN, Nat. Inst. Edn., Bur. Edn. Handicapped; chmn. nat. planning com. Nat. Ctr. Edn. Stats.; adviser Brazilian Ministry Edn., 1973, 80; chief Ministerial Commn. Edn., Bermuda, 1983-85; mem. Adv. Coun. for Edn. Stats., U.S. Dept. Edn., 1987-90; pres. TruJudge, Inc., 1993—. Author, editor in field. Capt. USMCR. Recipient Disting. Alumnus award San Diego State U., 1980; NSF fellow, 1959, IBM fellow, 1966-67. Fellow AAAS (life), APA (pres. ednl. psychology 1976-77), Am. Psychol. Soc., John Dewey Soc., Am. Assn. Applied and Preventive Psychology, Nat. Conf. Rsch. English, Philosophy Edn. Soc.; mem. Am. Coun. Assn., Am. Ednl. Rsch. Assn. (pres. 1979-80), Am. Statis. Assn. (officer N.C. chpt.), Assn. Computational Linguistics, Nat. Assn. Scholars, N.C. Assn. Rsch. Edn. (Disting. Rsch. award 1981, 91, pres. 1984-85), Rhetoric Soc. Am. (dir.), Psychometric Soc., Sociedad Española de Pedagogia (hon.), Sigma Xi, Phi Kappa Phi, Phi Gamma Delta, Psi Chi, Kappa Delta Pi, Phi Delta Kappa (life, svc. key). Episcopalian. Home: 110 Oakstone Dr Chapel Hill NC 27514-9585 E-mail: EBPage@Duke.edu.

PAGE, JOSEPH ANTHONY, law educator; b. Boston, Apr. 13, 1934; s. Joseph E. and Eleanor M. (Santosuosso) P.; m. Martha Gil-Montero, May 18, 1984. AB, Harvard U., 1955, LLB, 1958, LLM, 1964. Asst. prof. coll. law U. Denver, 1964-67, assoc. prof., 1967-68; assoc. prof. law ctr. Georgetown U., 1968-73, prof., 1973—, dir. Ctr. for the Advancement of the Rule of Law n the Ams., 2003—. Bd. dirs. Pub. Citizen, Inc., Washington. Author: The Revolution That Never Was, 1972, The Law of Premises Liability, 1976, Peron: A Biography, 1984, The Brazilians, 1995, Torts: Proximate Cause, 2003; co-author: Bitter Wages, 1973. Lt. USCGR, 1959-67. Office: Georgetown U Law Ctr 600 New Jersey Ave NW Washington DC 20001-2075 E-mail: page@law.georgetown.edu.

PAGE, LINDA JEWEL, professional coaching and mental health care educator; b. Quanah, Tex., Mar. 18, 1941; d. Wesley Lee and Eddie Lea (Fiero) P.; m. Roger Hollander, June 10, 1963 (div. Sept. 1973); children: Malika Jewel, Chantal Louise. BA, Mills Coll., 1963; MA, Princeton U., 1967, PhD in Sociology, 1973; MA in Counseling Psychology, Alfred Adler Inst. (now Adler Sch. Profl. Psychology), 1989. Lic. clin. profl. counselor, Ill. Assoc. prof. Northridge (Calif.) State U. (formerly San Fernando Valley State Coll.), 1964-68; lectr., assoc. prof. Concordia U. (formerly Sir George Williams), Montreal, Quebec, Can., 1970-73; teaching master Sir Sandford Fleming Coll., Lindsay, Ont., 1977-79; intern Rudolf Dreikurs Centre, Toronto, Ont., 1979-81; pvt. practice Toronto, 1981-87; dir., founder Psychotherapy Inst. Toronto, 1987-92. Dean faculty counselling and psychotherapy Alfred Adler Inst. Ont., 1990-92, pres. Adler Profl. Schs., 1992, core faculty, Adler Sch. Profl. Psychology, 1992-97; pres. Adler Sch. Profl. Coaching, 1998. Co-editor: For What Time I Am In This World, 1978; writer poems: (children's album) Musical Chairs, 1980; scriptwriter (children's albums) Big Bird and Oscar Go Camping in Canada, 1979, Kids on the Block, C'mon Along, We All Belong, 1986; editor, writer, broadcaster Can. Broadcasting Corp., Kids Records, 1974-77; columnist G.P. Psychotherapist Newsletter, 1989-93. Woodrow Wilson Found. fellow, 1963, NSF fellow, 1963-66. Mem. N.Am. Soc. Adlerian Psychology (rsch. com. 1989-93, del. assembly 1991), Soc. for Exploration of Psychotherapy Integration, Soc. for Psychotherapy Rsch., Ont. Assn. Cons., Counselors, Psychotherapists and Psychometrists (cert.), Internat. Coach Fedn., Phi Beta Kappa. Buddhist. Avocations: canoeing, music. Home: 134 Dovercliffe Rd Guelph ON Canada N1G 3A6 Office: Adler Sch Profl Coaching 180 Bloor St W Ste 502 Toronto ON Canada M5S 2V6 E-mail: ljpage@adler.ca.

PAGE, MAX, education educator; BA magna cum laude, Yale U., 1988; PhD in history, U. Penn., 1995. Lectr., dept. history U. Penn., 1995—96; asst. prof. of history and dir., heritage preservation program Ga. State U., 1996—99; leverhulme vis. rsch. prof. U. Nottingham, Sch. of Am. and Canadian Studies, 1998—99; vis. prof., dept. history Yale U., 1999—2001; asst. prof. architecture and history U. of Mass., 2001—. Bd. dirs. Urban History Assn., 2003—; program com. mem. Soc. of Am. City and Regional Planning Historian, 2002—03; bd. adv. Gotham Ctr., N.Y.C., 2000—; trustee Atlanta Preservation Ctr., 1998—2000; lectr. U. Penn., 1994, tchg. asst., 1990—93, instr., tchg. asst. program, 1993. Editl. collective mem. Radical History Review, 2001—, referee Am. Studies, The Pub. Historian, Jour. of Am. History, U. of Chgo. Press, U. Penn. Press, MIT Press, 1999—, cons. editor Atlanta Mag., 1997—99. Curator N.Y. Hist. Soc., 2003—; mem. town commn. Amherst Hist. Commn., 2001—; hist. cons. People's Light and Theater Co., Malvern, Pa., 2002—03; hist. rsch. and cons. Am. History Workship, Bklyn., 1993—; leader Big Onion Walking Tours, N.Y.C., 1994—2000. Recipient Healey Faculty Rsch. award, U. Mass, 2003—03; fellowship, John Simon Guggenheim Meml. Found., 2003, Graham Found. Pub. grant, 2002, Gilder Lehrman Inst. of Am. History fellowship, 2002, Spiro Kostof award, Soc. of Arch. Historians, 2001. Office: Dept of Art U Mass 151 Presidents Dr, Office I Amherst MA 01003

PAGE, SALLY JACQUELYN, university official; b. Saginaw, Mich., 1943; d. William Henry and Doris Effie (Knippel) P. BA, U. Iowa, 1965; MBA, So. Ill. U., 1973. Copy editor C.V. Mosby Co., St. Louis, 1965-69; editl. cons. Editl. Assocs., Edwardsville, Ill., 1969-70; rsch. adminstr. So. Ill. U., 1970-74, asst. to pres., affirmative action officer, 1974-77; officer of instn. U. N.D., Grand Forks, 1977—, lectr. mgmt., 1978—. Polit. comentator Sta. KFJM, Nat. Public Radio affiliate, 1981-90; mem. mayor's com. Employment of People With Disabilities, 1980-97. Contbr. articles to profl. jours. Chmn. N.D. Equal Opportunity Affirmative Action Officers, 1987-2003; chmn. N.D. U.S. Diversity Coun.; pres. Pine to Prairie coun. Girl Scouts U.S., 1980-85; mem. employment com. Ill. Commn. on Status of Women, 1976-77; mem. Bicentennial Com., Edwardsville, 1976, Bikeway Task Force, Edwardsville, 1975-77, Bus. Leadership Network, ARC Upper Valley; bd. dirs. Grand Forks Homes, 1985—, pres., 1996-2001; mem. Civil Svc. Rev. Task Force, Grand Forks, 1982, civil svc. commr., 1983-98, chmn., 1984, 86, 88, 92, 96; ruling elder 1st Presbyn.; mem. Grand Forks Mayor's Adv. Cabinet, 1998-2000. Mem. AAUW (dir. Ill. 1975-77), PEO, Coll. and Univ. Pers. Assn. (rsch. and publs. bd. 1982-84), Soc. Human Resource Mgmt., Am. Assn. Affirmative Action. Democrat. Presbyterian. Home: 3121 Cherry St Grand Forks ND 58201-7461 Office: U ND Grand Forks ND 58202 E-mail: Sally-Page@mail.und.nodak.edu.

PAGE, TAMMY, assistant principal; b. Bklyn., May 26, 1960; d. Jesse and Carolyn Page. BA, Hunter Coll., 1987; MA, Adelphi U., 1988. Cert. adminstr./supr. Adminstr. CUNY, N.Y.C., 1979-83; tchr. multi-cultural sch. N.Y.C. Bd. Edn., Bklyn., 1987-90, tchr. sch. for gifted, 1990-93, staff developer for curriculum and instrn., cons. N.Y.C., 1993—. Tchr. liaison with parents, N.Y. Bd. Edn., 1989-91, workshop coord., N.Y.C., 1990-91, 91-93; presenter in field. Recipient Pres.'s Excellence in Teaching award City U. Avocations: reading, poetry writing, chess. Office: Spl Educator Support Progrm United Fedn of Tchrs 260 Park Ave S New York NY 10010-7214

PAGILLO, CARL ROBERT, elementary school educator; b. Bklyn., Apr. 11, 1950; s. Nicholas and Rachel (Rhyne) P.; m. Joanne Ferro, Aug. 1, 1992. BA, Queens Coll., 1973, MS in Elem. Edn., 1975; advanced in edn. adminstrn., Bklyn. Coll., 1993. Tchr. grade 3, 5, and 6 Pub. Sch. 207 Queens, Howard Beach, N.Y., 1983-93; tchr. multimedia PS 20 YQ, Howard Beach, N.Y., 1983-93; tchr. lang. arts PS 56 Q, Richmond Hill, N.Y., 1993—. Pres., founder Catherine St. Block Assn., Lynbrook, 1987-91; baseball coach, mgr. Little League, Pony League and Baby Ruth League, Nassau County, 1974-92; capt. Lynbrook 4.0. tennis team, 1984-93. Recipient Ely Trachtenberg award United Fedn. of Tchrs., 1986. Mem. Phi Delta Kappa. Avocation: tennis. Home: 17 Catherine St Lynbrook NY 11563-1207

PAGLIA, CAMILLE, writer, humanities educator; b. Endicott, N.Y., 1947; d. Pasquale John and Lydia (Colapietro) P. BA in English summa cum laude with highest honors, SUNY, Binghamton, 1968; MPhil, Yale U., 1971, PhD in English, 1974. Mem. faculty Bennington (Vt.) Coll., 1972-80; vis. lectr. Wesleyan U., 1980, Yale U., New Haven, 1980-84; prof. humanities U. Arts, Phila., 1984-2000, univ. prof. and prof. humanities and media studies, 2000—. Author: Sexual Personae: Art and Decadence from Nefertiti to Emily Dickinson, 1990, Sex, Art, and American Culture, 1992, Vamps and Tramps: New Essays, 1994, Alfred Hitchcock's "The Birds", 1998; columnist: Salon.com, 1995—2001; contbg. editor: Interview Magazine, 2001—. Office: Univ Arts 320 S Broad St Philadelphia PA 19102-4994

PAGLIARULO, MICHAEL ANTHONY, physical therapy educator; b. Amityville, N.Y., May 15, 1947; s. Anthony and Louise (Cipriani) P.; m. Patricia Marilyn Salm, Mar. 22, 1975; children: Michael, David, Elisa. BA in Biology, SUNY, Buffalo, 1969, BS in Phys. Therapy, 1970; MA in Phys. Therapy, U. So. Calif., 1974; EdD in Postsecondary Edn. Adminstrn., Syracuse U., 1988. Lic. phys. therapist, N.Y., Calif. Staff phys. therapist Brunswick Hosp. Ctr., Amityville, 1970; lectr. U. So. Calif., L.A., 1974-75, U. Calif., San Francisco, 1975-80; curriculum coord. Ithaca (N.Y.) Coll., 1980-82, asst. prof., 1982-89, acting dir., 1986-89, assoc. prof., dir., 1989-94, assoc. prof. phys. therapy, 1994—, chair, 1989-94, 97-98. Author: Introduction to Physical Therapy, 1996, 2d edit., 2001. Bd. dirs. Marin/Roundtree Homeowners Assn., San Rafael, Calif., 1978-80; cubmaster Boy Scouts Am., Ithaca, 1989-91. Capt. U.S. Army, 1970-72. Named to Copiague H.S. Hall of Achievement, 1998. Mem.: Am. Phys. Therapy Assn. (bd. dirs. Calif. chpt. 1979—80, treas. N.Y. chpt. 1989—91, speaker del. assembly 2001—03, Merit award 1988, Norma Chadwick award 1993, Merit award 1995, 1997, Outstanding Svc. award 1997, Dr. Marilyn Moffat Disting. Svc. award 1998, Baethe-Carlin award for acad. tchg. excellence 2002), Phi Kappa Phi. Congregationalist. Avocations: scuba diving, water and snow skiing, model trains. Office: Ithaca Coll Dept Phys Therapy Danby Rd Ithaca NY 14850

PAGON, ROBERTA ANDERSON, pediatrics educator; b. Boston, Oct. 4, 1945; d. Donald Grigg and Erna Louise (Goettsch) Anderson; m. Garrett Dunn Pagon Jr., July 1, 1967; children: Katharine Blye, Garrett Dunn III, Alyssa Grigg, Alexander Goettsch. BA, Stanford U., 1967; MD, Harvard U., 1972. Diplomate Am. Bd. Pediatrics, Am. Bd. Med. Genetics. Pediatric intern U. Wash. Affiliated Hosp., Seattle, 1972-73, resident in pediatrics, 1973-75; fellow in med. genetics U. Wash. Sch. Medicine, Seattle, 1976-79, asst. prof. pediatrics, 1979-84, assoc. prof., 1984-92, prof., 1992—. Prin. investigator, editor in chief GeneTests (www.genetests.org), Seattle, 1992—; bd. dirs. Am. Bd. Med. Genetics, 1998—2003, pres., 2002—03; bd. sci. counselors Nat. Human Genome Rsch. Inst., NIH, 2000—. Sponsor N.W. region U.S. Pony Club, 1985-94. Mem. Am. Soc. Human Genetics, Am. Coll. Med. Genetics, Western Soc. Pedat. Rsch., Phi Beta Kappa. Avocations: hiking, backpacking, horseback riding. Office: Children's Hosp & Reg Med Ctr Divsn Genetics & Devel 4H-4 4800 Sand Point Way NE Seattle WA 98105-0371

PAGOTTO, LOUISE, English language educator; b. Montreal, June 22, 1950; came to U.S., 1980; d. Albert and Elena (Tibi) P. BA, Marianopolis Coll., Montreal, 1971; TESL Diploma, U. Papua New Guinea, 1975; MA, McGill U., 1980; PhD, U. Hawaii at Manoa, Honolulu, 1987. Tchr. Yarapos H.S., Wewak, Papua New Guinea, 1971-73, Electricity Commn. Tng. Coll., Port Moresby, Papua New Guinea, 1975-76, Coll. of Marshall Islands, Majuro, summers 1983-91, Leeward C.C., Pearl City, Hawaii, 1988-89, Kapiolani C.C., Honolulu, 1989—, interim asst. dean instrn., 1996-98, chair dept. lang. arts, 1998—2000, interim asst. dean of arts and scis., 2000—02, acting dean arts and scis., 2002—. Presenter in field. Contbr. articles to profl. jours. McConnell fellow McGill U., 1979, Can. Coun. fellow, 1980-83; recipient Excellence in Teaching award Bd. of Regents, 1993. Mem. AAUW, Linguistic Soc. Am., Nat. Coun. Tchrs. English, Hawaii Coun. Tchrs. English. Avocations: water sports (swimming, bodyboarding), walking. Office: Kapiolani CC 4303 Diamond Head Rd Honolulu HI 96816-4421

PAIGE, RODERICK R. secretary of education; b. Monticello, Miss., June 17, 1933; BS, Jackson State U., 1955; MS, Ind. U., 1964, Ph.D, 1969. Head football coach Jackson St. Univ., 1962—69; dean Coll. Edn. Tex. So. U., developer Ctr. Excellence in Urban Edn.; supt. Houston Ind. Sch. Dist., 1994—2000; sec. U.S. Dept. Edn., Washington, 2001—. Est. Ctr. for Excellence in Urban Edn., Tex. Southern U.; created Peer Exam., Evaluation, Redesign (PEER) program. Co-author: A Declaration of Beliefs and Visions. Mem. NAACP; mem. adv. bd. Tex. Commerce Bank, Am. Leadership Forum. Recipient Harold W. McGraw, Jr. Prize in Edn., 2000; named Supt. Yr. award, Nat. Assn. Black Sch. Educators', 2000, Nat. Supt. Yr., Am. Assn. Sch. Adminstr., 2001. Mem. review coms. Tex. Edn. Agy., State Bd. Edn. Task Force H.S. Edn.; chair, Youth Employment Issues Nat. Com. Employment Policy U.S. Dept. Labor subcom.; mem. Nat. Assn. Advancement Colored People, Edn. Com. States, Coun. Great City Schs.(recipient Richard R. Green award for Outstanding Urban Educator, 1999). Office: Dept Edn Office of Sec 400 Maryland Ave SW Washington DC 20202-0100

PAIKOWSKY, SAMUEL G. civil engineering educator; b. Petah Tikva, Israel, Sept. 17, 1954; came to U.S., 1982; s. Rubin and Zehava (Garber) P.; m. Lynn Gariepy, July 15, 1988; children: Oren, Guy, Dan, Tamar. BSc, Technion, Haifa, Israel, 1979, MSc, 1982; ScD, MIT, 1989. Prof. civil/environ. engrng. geotech. engrng. rsch. lab. U. Mass., Lowell, 1979—. Registered profl. engr., Israel. Recipient NSF Young Investigator award, 1993—, Hogentogler award ASTM, 1996. Achievements include research relevant to granular material behavior; research related to pile foundation design and construction. Office: U Mass at Lowell Dept Civil and Environ Engring Lowell MA 01854

PAINO, RONALD THOMAS, education consultant; b. Passaic, N.J., July 10, 1945; s. Eugene Joseph and Josephine Ann (Cellini) P. BS, Monmouth Coll., 1969; cert., Newark State Coll., 1974, Georgian Ct. Coll., 1982, 85, Princeton U., 1993. Cert. tchr., N.J. Tchr. math. and sci. Freehold Twp. (N.J.) Bd. Edn., 1969-80; math. content specialist East Windsor Bd. Edn., Hightstown, N.J., 1982-88; edn. cons. Control Data Corp., Mpls., 1988-89; edn. specialist Roach Orgn., Inc., Atlanta, 1989-93; tchr., dir. Coop. Math. Lab. East Windsor Bd. Edn., Hightstown, N.J., 1993—. Edn. cons. in devel. studies Richmond Community Coll., Hamlet, N.C., 1990-91, Morris Brown Coll., Atlanta, 1990-92, Sampson C.C., Clinton, N.C., 1990-91; sch.-based cons. N.J. Dept. Edn., Trenton, 1986; edn. specialist TVA, 1992. Mem. ASCD. Avocations: sailing, gardening, swimming.

PAINTER, LORENE HUFFMAN, retired education educator, psychologist; b. Hickory, NC, Aug. 16, 1932; d. Horace Clifton and Jennie Ozelle (Lineberger) Huffman; m. Hanley Hayes Painter, June 11, 1950; children: Charles Nathan, Janet Fern. AB, Lenoir-Rhyne Coll., Hickory, 1953; MA, Appalachian State U., Boone, N.C., 1959; EdD, U. N.C., Greensboro, 1980. Tchr. English and French, Taylorsville (N.C.) High Sch., 1953-54; tchr. English and social studies College Park Jr. High Sch., Hickory, 1954-59; instr. edn. Lenoir-Rhyne Coll., 1959-62, asst. prof., 1962-69, assoc. prof., 1969-80, prof., 1980—2000, chmn. dept., 1989-94, dir. Curriculum Lab., 1960—2000; ret., 2003. Evaluator sch. programs So. Assn., Piedmont, N.C., 1970—; edn. cons. Catawaba,Burke, Caldwell, Alexander and Iredell counties, N.C., 1970—; mem. career devel. team Catawba County Schs., 1986—. Author: Student Teaching Guidebook, 1968—, Elective English in Secondary Schools, 1980. Scholar Luth. Ch. in Am., 1976, 78. Mem. AAUP, Nat. Coun. for Accrediation Tchr. Edn., N.C. Assn. Tchr. Educators, Delta Kappa Gamma (officer 1963—, state scholar 1977-78), Mu Sigma Epsilon. Advent Christian. Avocations: reading, travel, needlework, gardening, family recreation. Home: 1137 11th Street Cir NW Hickory NC 28601-2254

PAINTER, NELL IRVIN, historian, author; b. Houston, Aug. 2, 1942; BA, U. Calif., Berkeley, 1964; student, U. Bordeaux, France, 1962-63, U. Ghana, 1965-66; MA, UCLA, 1967; PhD, Harvard U., 1974. Teaching fellow Harvard U., Cambridge, Mass., 1969-70, 72-74; asst. prof. history U. Pa., Phila., 1974-77, assoc. prof., 1977-80; prof. history U. N.C., Chapel Hill, 1980-88, Princeton (N.J.) U., 1988-91, acting dir. Afro-Am. Studies Program, 1990-91, Edwards Prof. Am. History, 1991—. Russell Sage vis. prof. history Hunter Coll., CUNY, N.Y.C., 1985-86. Author: Exodusters: Black Migration to Kansas After Reconstruction, 1976, The Narrative of Hosea Hudson: His Life as a Negro Communist in the South, 1979, Standing at Armageddon: The United States 1877-1919, 1987, Sojourner Truth: A Life, A Symbol, 1996, Southern History Across the Color Line, 2002; editor: Gender and Am. Culture Series; mem. editl. bd. Jour. Women's History, Ency. Americana; contbr. articles to profl. jours. Ford Found. fellow, 1971-72, Am. Coun. Learned Soc. fellow, 1976-77, Charles Warren Ctr. Studies in Am. History fellow, 1976-77, Radcliffe/Bunting Inst. fellow, 1976-77, Nat. Humanities Ctr. fellow, 1978-79, Guggenheim fellow, 1982-83, Ctr. Advanced Study in Behavioral Scis. fellow, 1988-89, Kate B. and Hall J. Peterson fellow Am. Antiquarian Soc., 1991, NEH fellow, 1992-93; recipient Ccoretta Scott King award AAUW, 1969-70, Grad. Soc. medal Radcliffe Coll. Alumnae, 1984, Candace award Nat. Coalition One Hundred Black Women, 1986; named U. Calif. at Berkeley Alumnae of Yr., 1989. Mem. Am. Coun. Learned Soc., Am. Antiquarian Soc., Am. Hist. Assn. (mem. program com. 1976-78, J. Franklin Jameson fellowship com. 1978-79, Beveridge and Dunning prizes com. 1985-87, mem. coun. 1991-93), Am. Studies Assn. (mem. internat. com. 1983-88, mem. nat. coun. 1989-92, mem. adv. coun. 1991-92), Assn. Study Afro-Am. Life and History (mem. program com. 1976), Assn. Black Women Historians (mem. rsch. com. 1980—, nat. dir. 1982-84, chair Brown pub. prize com. 1983-86, 88-91), Berkshire Conf. Women Historians (mem. program com. 1976), Inst. So. Studies (mem. exec. com. 1987-88), Orgn. Am. Historians (mem. com. status women 1975-77, mem. program com. 1977-79, 83-85, Frederick Jackson Turner award com. 1983, mem. exec. bd. 1984-87, chair ad hoc com. on minority historians 1985-87, chair Avery O. Craven award 1994-95), Nat. Book Found. (chair non-fiction jury, Nat. Book awards 1994), Social Sci. Rsch. Coun. (mem. com. social sci. pers. 1977-78), So. Hist. Assn. (chair Syndor prize com. 1991-92), So. Regional Coun. (mem. Lillian Smith Book prize com. 1986, mem. exec. com. 1987), Soc. Am. Historians (chair Parkman prize com. 1993—). Office: Princeton U History Dept Princeton NJ 08544-0001

PAJUNEN, GRAZYNA ANNA, electrical engineer, educator; b. Warsaw, Dec. 15, 1951; d. Romuald and Danuta (Trzaskowska) Pyffel; m. Veikko J. Pajunen (div. 1990); children: Tony, Thomas, Sebastian. MSc, Warsaw Tech. U., 1975; PhD in Elec. Engring., Helsinki (Finland) U., 1984. Grad. engr. Oy Stromberg Ab, Helsinki, 1974, design engr., 1975-79; teaching/rsch. asst. Helsinki U. Tech., 1979-85; vis. asst. prof. dept. elec. and computer engring. Fla. Atlantic U., 1985-86, asst. prof. elec. and computer engring., 1986-90, assoc. prof. elec. engring., 1990—; vis. asst. prof. dept elec. engring. UCLA, 1988-89. Cons. Motorola; lectr. in field. Author: Adaptive Systems - Identification and Control, 1986; contbr.

articles to profl. jours.; holder 14 patents in field. Grantee Found. Tech. in Finland, Ahlstrom Found., 1982, Wihuri Found., 1982, Foun.d Tech. in Finland, 1983, Acad. Finland, 1984, EIES Seed grantee, 1986, Finnish Ministry Edn., 1985, NSF, 1988-89, 93-94, State of Fla. High Tech. and Industry Coun., 1989. Mem. IEEE, Control Sys. Soci., N.Y. Acad. Sci., AAUW, SIAM, Control and Sys. Theory Group. Roman Catholic. Avocations: jazz, ballet, piano, jogging, skiing. Office: Fla Atlantic U Dept Elec Engring Boca Raton FL 33431

PAK, NOMYON, biologist, educator; b. Chungju, Korea, Aug. 5, 1931; came to U.S., 1973; s. Bong Hwa and Taek Soon (Seo) P.; m. Jungill Seo; children: Wonkyu, Christie Kyonghae. BS math., Kongju U., 1950; BS in Biology, Seoul Nat. U., 1954; MS in Biology, Yonsei U., 1958; AA Liberal Art, DeAnza Coll., 1978; EdD, U. San Francisco, 1984. Lic. ESL tchr. Calif., life agent Korean Interpreter. Math. tchr. Chungju Tchrs. H.S., Korea, 1950, Busan YMCA Sch., Korea, 1952, Haesung Inst., Seoul, Korea, 1953-54; dir. Somun Inst., Seoul, 1955-56; tchg. asst. biology Dongguk U., Seoul, Korea, 1954-57; tchr. biology Sangmyung Girl's High, Seoul, 1960-67; asst. prof. biology Inchon (Korea) Tchrs. Coll., 1966-72; instr. ESL Belmont Adult Sch., L.A., 1989-93; instr. sci. Chinese Med. Coll., Oakland, Calif., 1996; prin. Contra Costa Korean Sch., 1993—; dir. Nomyon Inst., Commn. Agy. and Ins. Agy., Campbell, Calif., 1981—. Interpreter, Campbell, Calif.; translator Dept. of Army, Silver Spring, Md., 1987; life agt. Blue Cross, Jackson Nat. Life, 1973—; instr. Japanese, West Valley Coll., Saratoga, Calif., 1992. Asia Found. fellow, 1962. Mem. AAAS, AIBS, Am. Sociol. Assn., Am. Polit. Assn., Am. Assn. Ednl. Rsch., Comparative and Internat. Edn. Soc., Biophys. Soc. Japan, Japanese Minyo Club, Japanese Poetry Club. Home: 1270 Nadine Dr Campbell CA 95008-1725 Office: Nomyon Inst 1270 Nadine Dr Campbell CA 95008-1725

PALAFOX, MARI LEE, private school educator; b. Des Moines, Sept. 22, 1952; d. Ronald Lester and Maxine Lucille (Miller) Watts; m. René Jose Palafox, July 13, 1974; 1 child, Rebecca Leigh. BA, U. Calif.-San Diego, La Jolla, 1975. Multiple subjects credential, Calif., Assn. Christian Schs. Internat. Teaching credential, 1990. Mid. sch. tchr. Santee (Calif.) Sch. Dist., 1975-80; tchr. math., softball coach Christian Jr. High Sch., El Cajon, Calif., 1980-89, Christian High Sch., El Cajon, 1989-95, Linfield Christian Sch., Temecula, Calif., 2000—. Math. specialist Christian Unified Schs. San Diego. Recipient Cert. of Recognition, Ednl. Testing Svc., 1991; named Disting. Tchr., U. Calif., San Diego, 1996, Tandy Tech. Outstanding Tchr., 1996-97. Mem. Calif. Tchrs. Math., Greater San Diego Math. Coun. (pvt. sch. rep. 1982-83), Nat. Coun. Tchrs. Math. Avocations: softball, volleyball, basketball, cross-stitch. Office: Linfield Christian Sch 31950 Pauba Rd Temecula CA 92592 Home: 42477 Swoboda Ct Temecula CA 92591

PALAGI, ROBERT GENE, college administrator; b. Chgo., Aug. 20, 1948; s. Gene and Stella (Vasick) P.; m. Diane Joyce Sanderson, July 31, 1971; children: Melissa, Jason. AS, So. Ill. U., 1969, BS, 1972; MEd, DePaul U., 1975; MS, No. Ill. U., 1994. Cert. secondary tchr., cert. counselor. Educator Dept. Mental Health, Tinley Park, Ill., 1972-75, mental health specialist, 1975-77, grant coord., 1977-80; vocat. therapist Our Lady of Mercy Hosp., Dyer, Ind., 1980-81, mgr. edn. and tng., 1981-84; edn. cons. devel. St. Mary of Nazareth Hosp.; instr., counselor Chgo. City Colls., 1986-89, assoc. dir., 1989-90, coord. career devel., 1990-91, dir. acad. support, 1991-94; indsl. arts. specialist Ingalls Hosp., 1994-99; dir. funded ednl. programs Moraine Valley C.C., Palos Hills, Ill., 1999—. Cons. Chgo. Merc. Exch., Chgo., 1985-86; faculty Ind. U. N.W., Gary, Ind., 1981-82; mgr. evening svcs. Ind. Vocat. Tech. Coll., Hammond, Ind., 1990—. Chairperson pub. rels. Pullman Civic Orgn., Chgo., 1983, bd. dirs., 1993; bd. dirs. Pullman Historic Found., 1991-94. Mem. Am. Vocat. Assn., Coop. Edn. Assn., Midwest Coop. Edn. Assn., Ill. Vocat. Assn., Ill. Coop. Edn. Assn. Home: 11316 S Langley Ave Chicago IL 60628-5126 Office: Ingalls Ctr for Otpt Rehab Dawson Tech Inst 1551 Huntington Dr Calumet City IL 60409-5440

PALEOLOGOS, EVANGELOS, hydrologist, educator; b. Athens, Greece, June 26, 1958; came to U.S., 1983; s. Constantine E. and Kathy A. (Michos) P.; m. Cleo L. Kalemkeris, Apr. 30, 1989; children: Katrina, Demi. BSCE, MSCE, Poly. U., 1986; PhD in Hydrology, U. Ariz., 1994. Sr. staff cons. Intera Inc., Las Vegas, Nev., 1992-95; asst. prof. U. S.C., Columbia, 1995-2001, assoc. prof., 2001—. Organizer internat. confs. Author: Environmental Risk Analysis, Environmental Risk and Liability Management; contbr. articles to profl. jours.; mem. editl. bd. Jour. Stochastic Hydrology and Hydraulics, Stochastic Environ. Rsch. and Risk Assessment, 1998—. Mem. adv. bd. Global Alliance for Disaster Reduction. Dept. Energy Nat. Water Rsch. Ctr. and Environ. Mgmt. grantee, 1997; recipient Initializers award S.C. Rsch. Inst., 1998. Mem. Am. Geophys. Union, European Geophys. Soc. Greek Orthodox. Avocations: art collecting, gardening. Office: Dept Geol Scis U Sc Columbia SC 29208-0001 E-mail: epal@geol.sc.edu.

PALER, PEGGY LOUISE D'ARCY, elementary education educator, education educator; b. Wink, Tex., Nov. 23, 1936; d. T. Earl and Mable Louise (Blair) D'Arcy; m. Abraham D. Paler, May 27, 1955 (dec. Jan. 1990). BS, Howard Payne U., Brownwood, Tex., 1958; MA, U. Guam, 1975; EdD, U. So. Calif., 1982. Cert. tchr., Guam, Tex., N.Mex. Tchr. 1st grade Jayton (Tex.) Sch. Dist., 1958-59, Albuquerque Pub. Schs., 1959-65; tchr. kindergarten-2d grade Guam Pub. Schs., Agana, 1966-87; assoc. prof. edn. U. Guam, Mangilao, 1983-88, Coll. St. Joseph, Maasin, Philippines, 1988-89; asst. prof. edn. Sul Ross State U., Alpine, Tex., 1989-91; assoc. prof. edn. Howard Payne U., 1991-92; presch. tchr. Del Norte Bapt. Weekday Sch., 1997-98. Edn. cons. World Vision Internat., Maasin, 1986, Gen. Bapt. Kindergarten, Maasin, 1987-90; com. mem. Guam Dept. Edn., 1984-87; presenter Internat. Reading Assn., 1970-86. Chmn. bd. Calvary Bapt. Ch. Day Care, Guam, 1975-80; conf. leader Gen. Bapt. Ch., Maasin, 1988-89. Recipient numerous awards. Mem. ASCD, Assn. Childhood Edn., Tex. Soc. Coll. Tchrs. of Edn., Internat. Reading Assn., Ind. Order of Odd Fellows and Rebekahs, Phi Delta Kappa. Avocations: international travel, reading, arts and crafts, sewing. Home and Office: PO Box 9662 Albuquerque NM 87119-9662

PALERMO, JUDY HANCOCK, elementary school educator; b. Longview, Tex., Sept. 7, 1938; d. Joseph Curtis and Bennie Lee (Deason) Hancock; m. Donald Charles Palermo, Apr. 1, 1961; 1 child, Donald Charles Jr. (dec.). BS in Secondary Edn., 1960. Cert. secondary and elem. edn. tchr., Tex. Art tchr. Dallas Ind. Sch. Dist., 1960-62, 65-67; asst. dir. freshmen orientation program North Tex. State U., Denton, summer 1969, dormitory dir. Oak St. Hall, 1968-71, tchr. part-time, 1970-77; substitute tchr. Denton Ind. Sch. Dist., 1975-78, tchr. 5th grade, 1979-87, art tchr., 1987—; tchr. kindergarten Kiddie Korral Pre-Sch., Denton, 1978-79; ret., 1999. Trained gifted tchr. Woodrow Wilson Elem. Sch., Denton, 1980, grade level chmn., 1980; grade level chmn. Eva S. Hodge Elem. Sch., Denton, 1988-89, 92-93; mem. rsch. bd. advisors Am. Biog. Inst., 1991—. Active Denton Humane Soc., 1982—, Denton Educators Polit. Action Com., 1984—85; Eva S. Hodge historian PTA, 1992—99. Mem. NEA, NAFE, Tex. State Tchrs. Assn., Denton Classroom Tchrs. Assn. (faculty rep. 1984-85), Denton Edn. Assn., Denton Area Art Edn. Assn. (program chmn. 1990-91), Greater Denton Arts Coun., Numismatic Assn. (sec. Greater Denton chpt.), Denton Sq. Athletic Club, Denton Greater Univ. Dames Club (treas. 1970), Bus. and Profl. Women's Assn. (treas. 1990-91, chair audit com. 1992-93, chmn. 1993—), Delta Kappa Gamma (treas. 1986-88, comms. com. 1994—). Democrat. Avocations: painting, ceramics, drawing, calligraphy, photography. Home: 3405 Nottingham Dr Denton TX 76209-1281

PALISCA, CLAUDE VICTOR, musicologist, educator; b. Rijeka, Croatia, Nov. 24, 1921; came to U.S., 1930; s. Matthew and Gisella (Fleischhacker) P.; m. Jane Agnes Pyne, June 12, 1960 (div. Feb. 1987); children: Carl Pyne, Madeline Grace; m. Elizabeth Ann Keitel, Apr. 4, 1987. BA, Queens Coll., 1943; MA, Harvard U., 1948, PhD, 1954; MA (hon.), Yale U., 1964. Instr., then asst. prof. music U. Ill. at Urbana, 1953-59; asso. prof. history music Yale U., New Haven, 1959—, prof., 1964-80, Henry L. and Lucy G. Moses prof. music, 1980-92, emeritus, from 1992, dir. grad. studies music, 1967-69, 87-92, chmn. music dept., 1969-75, chmn., dir. grad. studies in Renaissance studies, 1977-80. Chmn. council on humanities Yale U., 1977-79, fellow Silliman Coll., 1963— ; sr. fellow council humanities Princeton U., 1961; cons. U.S. Office Edn., 1963—, NEH, 1967— ; dir. Nat. Seminar Music Edn., 1963 Author: Girolamo Mei: Letters on Ancient and Modern Music, 1960, 2d edit., 1977, (with others) Musicology, 1963, Baroque Music, 1968, 3d edit., 1991, (with Donald Grout) History of Western Music, 5th edit., 1996, Humanism in Italian Renaissance Musical Thought, 1985 (Internat. Musicol. Soc. award 1987), The Florentine Camerata, 1989, Studies in the History of Italian Music and Music Theory, 1994; translator: (with Guy Marco) Zarlino, The Art of Counterpoint, 1968; editor: Hucbald, Guido and John on Music: Three Medieval Treatises, 1978, Norton Anthology of Western Music, 1980, 3rd edit., 1996, (with D. Kern Holloman) Musicology in the 1980's, 1982, Zarlino, On the Modes, 1983, Yale Music Theory Translation Series, Boethius, Fundamentals of Music, 1989, The Theory of Music, Franchino Gaffurio, 1993, Nicola Vicentino, Ancient Music Adapted to Modern Practice, 1996; mem. editl. and adv. bds. Studies in Music (Western Australia), Jour. Mus. Theory, Musical Quar.; mem. exec. com.: New Grove Dictionary, Jour. History of Ideas; contbr. articles to publs. Bd. dirs., exec. com. Arts Council Greater New Haven, 1964-77, Neighborhood Music Sch., 1966-69; mem. exec. com. Ednl. Center for Arts, New Haven, 1973-83, chmn., 1979-80; bd. dirs., chmn. edn. com. New Haven Symphony Soc., 1966-72, v.p., 1968-72; mem. edit. adv. bd. J.S. Guggenheim Meml. Found., 1983-92. Served with AUS, 1943-46. John Knowles Paine traveling fellow, 1949-50; Fulbright fellow, 1950-52; Guggenheim fellow, 1959-60, 81-82; Nat. Endowment for the Humanities sr. fellow, 1972-73; Misha Strassberg sr. fellow in creative arts U. Western Australia, summer, 1984. Fellow AAAS, Am. Coun. Arts in Edn. (pres. 1967-69); mem. Internat. Musicol. Soc. (dir., v.p. 1977-82), Am. Musicol. Soc. (hon., pres. 1970-72), Coll. Music Soc. (coun.), Renaissance Soc. (coun. 1973-74, exec. com. 1978-87), ACLS-Soviet Union of Composers Commn. on Music Composition and Musicology (co-chmn. 1986-90). Home: Hamden, Conn. Died Jan. 11, 2001.

PALLADINO-CRAIG, ALLYS, museum director; b. Pontiac, Mich., Mar. 23, 1947; d. Stephan Vincent and Mary (Anderson) Palladino; m. Malcolm Arnold Craig, Aug. 20, 1967; children— Ansel, Reed, Nicholas. BA in English, Fla. State U., 1967; grad., U. Toronto, Ont., Can., 1969; MFA, Fla. State U., 1978, PhD in Humanities, 1996. Editorial asst. project U. Va. Press, Charlottesville, 1970-76; instr. English Inst. Franco Americain, Rennes, France, 1974; adj. instr. Fla. State U., Tallahassee, 1978-79, dir. Four Arts Ctr., 1979-82, dir. U. Mus. of Fine Arts, 1982—, prof. mus. studies. Mem. grad faculty Mus. Studies Cert. Program Fla. State U. Curator, contbg. editor: articles and exhbn. catalogues Nocturnes and Nightmares, Monochrome/Polychrome, Chroma; contbg. editor (articles and exhbn. catalogues) Body Language; guest curator, author: Mark Messersmith: New Mythologies; curator, editor Albert Paley--Sculpture, Drawings, Graphics and Decorative Arts, Trevor Bell: A British Painter in America, and Trial by Fire: Contemporary Glass; curator, author: The Abridged Walmsley--Selections from the Career of William Aubrey Walmsley; author: Jack Nicholson: Micro-Theatres, Alexa Kleinbard: Talking Leaves, Jake Fernandez--Ethereal Journeyman, Jim Roche-Sense of Place; gen. editor: Athanor I-XXII, 1980—; Represented in permanent collections Fla. Ho. of Reps., Barnett Bank, IBM. Individual artist fellow Fla. Arts Coun., 1979 Mem. Am. Assn. Mus., Fla. Art Mus. Dirs. Assn. (sec. 1989-91), Phi Beta Kappa. Democrat. Avocation: antique american fountain pen collecting. Home: 1410 Grape St Tallahassee FL 32303-5636 Office: Fla State U Mus of Fine Arts 250 Fine Arts Bldg Tallahassee FL 32306-1140 E-mail: apcraig@mailer.fsu.edu.

PALLOTTA, JOHANNA ANTONIA (JOHANNA STEPHEN), physician, educator, researcher; b. Boston, May 7, 1937; d. John and Antonia (Lanni) P.; m. Michael John Stephen, Aug. 13, 1966; children: Jacqueline, Antonia, Michael, Andrew. BS in Chemistry magna cum laude, Boston Coll., 1958; MD, N.Y. Med. Coll., 1962. Diplomate Am. Bds. Internal Medicine, Endocrinolgoy and Metabolism; lic. N.Y., Mass., Calif. Intern St. Elizabeth's Hosp., Boston, 1962-63; resident in medicine N.Y. Med. Coll. Metro. Hosp., N.Y.C., 1963-64; resident in medicine, fellow radioisotope svc. VA Hosp., Bronx, 1964—66; fellow metabolism and endocrinology Yale U. Sch. Medicine, 1966-67; instr. medicine Harvard Med. Sch., 1967-69, Beth Israel Deaconess Hosp. Harvard Med. Sch., Boston, 1969-70; asst. prof. medicine Harvard Med. Sch., Boston, 1970—. Tutor med. scis. Harvard Med. Sch., 1972-73; dir. endocrinology clinic Beth Israel Deaconess Hosp., Boston, 1967—, dir. radioimmunoassay lab., 1972-83, clin. cons., 1984—, asst. in medicine, 1967-69, assoc. in medicine, 1969-70, asst. physician, 1970-79, assoc. physician, 1979-87, sr. physician, 1987—, dir. clin. rsch. ctr. core radioimmunoassay lab., 1984-93; cons. staff Mount Auburn Hosp., Cambridge, 1974-90; mem. numerous other coms., 1969—. Researcher in field; contbr. articles to profl. jours. Named Carl Shapiro scholar, BIDMC-Harvard Med. Sch., 2000—; recipient S. Robert Stone Harvard Med. Sch.-BIDMC tchg. award, 1998. Fellow: ACP; mem.: Am. Fedn. Clin. Rsch., Am. Thyroid Assn., Am. Assn. Clin. Endocrinology, Endocrine Soc., Harvard Aesculapian Club, Alpha Omega Alpha. Roman Catholic. Home: 16 Fresh Pond Ln Cambridge MA 02138-4616 Office: Beth Israel Hosp Harvard Med Sch 330 Brookline Ave Boston MA 02215-5491 E-mail: jpallott@BIDMC.harvard.edu.

PALLOWICK, NANCY ANN, special education educator; b. Milw., May 27, 1953; d. William Bower and Harriette Ann (Lozar) P.; m. Douglas Richard Pugh, Aug. 11, 1990; children: Mikhail Richard, Senia Bower. B of Edn., U. South Fla., 1978; postgrad., Fla. Atlantic U., 1981-89; MS in Human Resource Devel., Fla. Internat. U., 1999. Tchr. emotionally handicapped Ramblewood Mid. Sch., Coral Springs, Fla., 1978-83; freelance artist Ft. Lauderdale, Fla., 1983-85; tchr. emotionally handicapped Hunt Elem. Sch., Coral Springs, 1985-86; tchr. learning disabled Rock Island Elem. Sch., Ft. Lauderdale, 1986-92; tchr. emotionally handicapped Margate (Fla.) Mid. Sch., 1992-94, behavior specialist, 1994-95, North Area Exceptional Student Edn., 1995-97; master trainer Profl. Crisis Mgmt., 1996—; exceptional student edn. specialist Hollywood Hills H.S., 1997-98; behavior specialist Ft. Lauderdale High Zone, 1998—2001; behavior resource tchr. area 2 Palm Beach County Sch. Dist., 2001—. Dept. head Margate Mid. Sch., 1992—95, peer tchr., 1988—95, insvc. facilitator, 1993—95; dist. trainer Broward County Sch. Bd., 1994—2001. Steward Broward Tchrs. Union, 1994-95. Broward County Sch. Bd. grantee, 1989-90, 91-92, 93-94. Mem. ASCD, Am. Fedn. Tchrs., Am. Craft Coun., Mich. Artists Guild, Tchr. Edn. Alliance, Teams Project, Fla. Craftsment, S. Fla. Fiber Artists, Assn. Behavior Analyst, Coun. for Exceptional Children. Democrat. Roman Catholic. Avocations: art, weaving, handmade paper, silk screen, batik. Home: 1110 SW 15th St Boca Raton FL 33486-6704 Office: Area 2 Exceptional Student Edn 505 S Congress Ave Boynton Beach FL 33426 E-mail: npallowick@aol.com.

PALM, CHARLES GILMAN, university official; b. Havre, Mont., Apr. 25, 1944; s. Victor F. and Laura (McKinnie) P.; m. Miriam Willits, Sept. 15, 1968. AB, Stanford U., 1966; MA, U. Wyo., 1967; MLS, U. Oreg., 1970. Asst. archivist Stanford (Calif.) U., 1971—74, dep. archivist, 1974-84, archivist, 1984-87, head libr., 1986-87, assoc. dir., 1987-90; dep. dir. Stanford U., Palo Alto, Calif., 1990—2001, dep. dir. emeritus, 2002—. Co-author: Guide to Hoover Institution Archives, 1980, Herbert Hoover, Register of His Papers in the Hoover Institution Archives, 1983. Mem. Calif. Heritage Preservation Commn., Sacramento, 1988—, vice chmn., 1993-97, chmn., 1997-2003; mem. Nat. Hist. Records and Publs. Commn., Washington, 1990-96; mem. history & edn. ctr. adv. bd. ARC, 1994—; trustee Golden State Mus. Corp., 1997-2003. Fellow Soc. Am. Archivists; mem. Soc. Calif. Archivists (pres. 1983-84), Bohemian Club. Republican. Office: Hoover Instn Stanford CA 94305

PALM, MARION, educator; b. Aug. 6, 1940; children: Peter, Mari, Noah. BA, U. Minn., 1978; MS, Bank Street, 1995. Founder, dir. Poets Under Glass, Bklyn., 1987—. Dir. Proclamation for literacy programs, Borough Pres. Bklyn., N.Y.C., 1998; featured reader, various instns. and orgns., N.Y.C.; adj. prof. Bklyn. Coll. Author books of poetry. Recipient Cornell U., N.Y.C.; liasion dir. Cmty. Coun. Police Precinct #72, Bklyn. Recipient Cmty. Svc. awards Chase Bank, N.Y.C., 1991-93; Bklyn. Arts Coun. grantee, 1986, 88, 90. Mem. Poetry Soc. Am., Acad. Am. Poets, U.Minn. Alumni Assn. Home: 705-41 St Brooklyn NY 11232 E-mail: marionpalm@aol.com.

PALMER, BARBARA JEAN, special education administrator; b. Louisiana, Mo., Dec. 14, 1939; d. Charles Mountjoy and Mary Margaret (Barnett) Crank; m. Lewis William Palmer, Nov. 23, 1961; children: Sidney Justin, Nathan Randolph. BA, Phillips U., 1961; MS, Ft. Hays State U., 1987, EdS, 1989; EdD, Kans. State U., 1992. Cert. tchr. secondary sci., tchr. spl. edn., adminstr., Kans. Tchr. sci. North Kansas City (Mo.) Pub. Schs., 1961-63, Independence (Mo.) Pub. Schs., 1963-64, Ottowa (Kans.) Pub. Schs., 1966-67, Hugoton (Kans.) Unified Sch. Dist., 1968-69; dir. Grant County Day Care Ctr., Ulysses, Kans., 1969-74; tchr. behavior disorders High Plains Ednl. Coop., Ulysses, 1985-88, asst. dir., 1988—. Mem., past pres. Unified Sch. Dist. 214 Bd. Edn., Ulysses, 1979-87; mem., past pres. bd. dirs. High Plains Ednl. Coop., 1980-86. Mem. ASCD, Coun. for Exceptional Children, Kans. Assn. for Spl. Edn. Adminstrs., Kans. Coun. for Children with Behavior Disorders (state sec. 1988-90), Phi Kappa Phi. Democrat. Methodist. Avocations: candle making, travel, hiking, reading, church activities. Office: High Plains Ednl Coop 621 E Oklahoma Ave Ulysses KS 67880-2819

PALMER, BARBARA LOUISE MOULDEN, elementary education educator; b. Winchester, Va., Nov. 20, 1941; d. Howard Kemper and Mary Elethia (Jones) Moulden; m. Staymon Eli Palmer, Aug. 9, 1958; children: Mark Eli, Nancy Louise. AB in Elem. Edn., Shepherd Coll., 1972; MA in Edn. Adminstrn., W.Va. U., 1992. Cert. tchr., W.Va. Tchr. Gerrardstown (W.Va.) Elem. Sch., 1972-90; tchr. lang. arts, computer edn. Pikeside Learning Ctr., Martinsburg, W.Va., 1991-94; computer skills tchr. Musselman Middle Sch., Bunker Hill, W.Va., 1995—2003; technology resource tchr. substitute Frederick County Pub. Schs., Winchester, Va., 2003—. Demonstrator use of computers in edn. Gerrardstown Homemakers' Club; tchr. computer skills to youth orgns.; designer computer programs Gerrardstown Men's Club, presenter computer learning experience sessions. Past adult leader 4-H Club; past sec., past pres. Gerrardstown PTA; past mem. Musselman High Sch. Band Boosters Assn., Musselman High Sch. Athletic Booster Club; parent mem. Sch. Improvement Coun. Musselman Middle Sch., 1993, 94. Named lifetime mem. Gerradstown PTA, 1990. Mem. NEA, ASCD, W.Va. Edn. Assn., Berkeley County Edn. Assn., Gerrardstown Elem. Faculty Senate (chair 1990-91), Pikeside Learning Ctr. Faculty Senate (vice-chair 1992-93, chair 1993-94, 94-95), Phi Delta Kappa. Avocations: reading, computer technology, travel. Home: 736 Loop Rd Gerrardstown WV 25420 Office: Musselman Middle Sch 8784 Winchester Ave Bunker Hill WV 25413-9601

PALMER, BRENT DAVID, environmental physiology educator, biologist; b. Burbank, Calif., May 13, 1959; s. Warren Thayer and Yvonne Lita (McKelvey) P.; m. Sylvia Irena Karalius, June 26, 1982. BA, Calif. State U., Northridge, 1985; MS, U. Fla., 1987, PhD, 1990. Grad. asst. U. Fla., Gainesville, 1985-90; asst. prof. Wichita (Kans.) State U., 1990-91, Ohio U., Athens, 1991-97; asst. prof. environ. physiology U. Ky., Lexington, 1997-98, assoc. prof. environ. physiology, 1998—. Cons. U.S. EPA, 1992—, Environment Can., 1995-96; vice chmn. Gordon Rsch Conf. Environ. Endocrine Disruptors, 1998, chmn., 2000. Contbr. chpts. to books, articles on vertebrate reproductive biology and toxicology to profl. jours.; reviewer U.S. EPA, Nat. Sci. Found., Biology of Reproduction, Champaign, Ill., Harper Collins pubs., N.Y.C., Reproduction, Fertility and Devel., Australia, Comments on Toxicology, Ind. Press, Jour. Morphology, N.Y.C., Environ. Health Perspectives, Biology of Reproduction, Gen. and Comparative Endocrinology, Am. Jour. Anatomy, Environ. Toxicology. Coord. Sci. Olympiad, Wichita, 1991, So. Ohio Dist. Sci. Day, 1992-94, Sci. and Engring. Fair, 1992-94. Recipient Best Student Paper award, Herpetologists League, 1988, Stoye award, Am. Soc. of Ichthyologists and Herpetologists, 1988, Student Rsch. award, Soc. Study of Amphibian and Reptiles, 1989, Grants-in-aid of Rsch., Sigma Xi, 1989; grantee rsch., NIH, 1995—, NSF, 1998—, EPA, 2001—. Mem. AAAS, Am. Soc. Zoologists (organizer symposia on environ. endocrine disruptors 1995), Soc. Study Reproduction, Phi Beta Kappa. Achievements include description of functional morphology, physiology, and biochemistry of reptilian and amphibian oviducts; establishment of the evolution of an archosaurian reproductive system that may have implications for dinosaur reproduction; description of the effects of environmental endocrine disrupters on wildlife and humans. Office: U Ky TH Morgan Sch Biol Scis 101 Morgan Bldg Lexington KY 40506-0001

PALMER, BRUCE HARRISON, academic administrator; b. Hartford, Conn., Apr. 13, 1955; s. David Alan and Marilyn Elaine (Shelburne) P. BA, Gordon Coll., 1977; MA, Gordon-Conwell Sem., 1979; MEd, Harvard U., 1982. Mng. publs. editor, asst. to fin. aid dir. Gordon-Conwell Sem., South Hamilton, Mass., 1979-81; dir. student fin. aid Roberts Wesleyan Coll., Rochester, N.Y., 1982-86, v.p. staff, 1983-84; assoc. dir. student fin. aid, coord. Info. and Data Svcs., lectr., gen. faculty U. Va., Charlottesville, 1986-94; dir. fin. aid Ea. Coll., St. Davids, Pa., 1994-95, Franklin Pierce Coll., Rindge, N.H., 1995—. Deacon Congl. Ch. Temple, N.H., 1997—. Contbr. articles to newspapers. Program devel. Cmty. Outreach Park Street Ch., Boston, 1981; student pastor Park Street Bapt. Ch., Framingham, Mass., 1982; mem. Ivy Creek Found., Charlottesville, 1988—; vol. John Heinz Nat. Wildlife Refuge, Phila., 1994. Mem. Nat. Assn. Student Pers. Adminstrs., Nat. Assn. Student Fin. Aid Adminstrs. (editor jour.), Va. Assn. Student Fin. Aid Adminstrs. (tng. com., instr., automated svcs.), N.H. Assn. Student Fin. Aid Adminstrs., Phi Delta Kappa. Democrat. Office: Franklin Pierce Coll College Rd Rindge NH 03461 Home: 6 Sleepy Hollow Rd North Dartmouth MA 02747-1330

PALMER, C(HARLES) HARVEY, physicist, educator; b. Milw., Dec. 8, 1919; s. Charles Harvey and Grace Hambleton (Ober) P.; m. Elizabeth Hall Machen, Sept. 11, 1948; children: Charles Harvey III, Helen Palmer Stevens. SB in Physics magna cum laude, Harvard U., 1941, MA in Physics, 1946; PhD in Physics, Johns Hopkins U., 1951. Staff mem. MIT Radiation Lab., Cambridge, 1942-45; asst. prof., then assoc. prof. physics Bucknell U., Lewisburg, Pa., 1950-54; rsch. assoc. Lab. Astrophysics and Phys. Meteorology, Balt., 1954-60; asst. prof. elec. engring. Johns Hopkins U., Balt., 1960-64, assoc. prof., 1964-79, prof. elec. engring., 1979-92, prof. emeritus, 1992—. Cons. Caterpillar Tractor Co., Aberdeen Proving Ground, Bendix Radio. Author: Optics: Experiments and Demonstrations, 1962; contbr. papers on ultrasonics, anomalous behavior of diffraction gratings, infrared spectrum of water vapor and measurement of ultrasmall angles to profl. publs. Fellow Optical Soc. Am.; mem. Am. Phys. Soc., N.Y. Acad. Scis., Sigma Xi. Democrat. Mailing: c/o Johns Hopkins U Dept Elec and Computer Engr 3400 N Charles St Baltimore MD 21218-2680

PALMER, CHRISTINE (CLELIA ROSE VENDITTI), operatic singer, pianist, vocal educator; b. Hartford, Conn., Apr. 02; d. John Marion and Immacolata (Morcaldo) Venditti; m. Raymond Smith, Oct. 5, 1949 (div. June 1950); m. Arthur James Whitlock, Feb. 25, 1953. Student, Mt. Holyoke Coll., 1937-38, New Eng. Conservatory of Music, 1941-42; pvt. studies, Boston, Hartford, N.Y.C., Florence and Naples, Italy; RN with honors, Hartford Hosp. Sch. Nursing, 1941. Artist-in-residence El Centro Coll., Dallas, 1966-71. Pvt. vocal instr.-coach, specializing in vocal technique for opera, mus. comedy, supper club acts, auditions, Dallas, 1962-94; voice adjudicator San Francisco Opera Co., 1969-72, Tex. Music Tchrs. Assn., 1964-75, others; lectr. in field; appearances with S.M. Chartocks' Gilbert and Sullivan Co.; now performing lecture/entertainment circuit. Leading operatic soprano N.Y.C. Opera, Chgo., San Francisco, San Carlo, other cities, 1944-62; presented concert N.Y. Town Hall, 1951; soloist with symphony orchs. maj. U.S. Cities, 1948-62; soloist Marble Collegiate Ch., Holy Trinity Ch.; coast-to-coast concert tour, 1948; numerous appearances including St. Louis MUNY Opera, Indpls. Starlight Theatre, Lambertville Music Circus; soloist Holiday on Ice, 1949-50; TV performer, including Home Show on NBC, Telephone Hour on NBC, Holiday Hotel; performer various supper clubs, N.Y.C., Atlanta, Bermuda, Catskills, others, including Number One Fifth Avenue, The Embers, The Carriage Club, Viennese Lantern. Hon. mem. women's bd. Dallas Opera Assn.; mem. adv. bd. Tex. Opera News; mem. Tex. Music Tchrs. Cert. Bd., Collegiate Chorale, Don Craig Singers, The Vikings; mem. women's bd., Dallas Bapt. Univ. Oliver Ditson scholar, 1942; recipient Phi Xi Delta prize in Italian, 1937; named Victor Herbert Girl, ASCAP; Spl. Recognition Gold book of Dallas Soc. Mem. Nat. Assn. Tchrs. of Singing (pres. Dallas chpt. 1972-74), Nat. Fedn. Music Clubs, Tex. Fedn. Music Clubs, Dallas Fedn. Music Clubs (pres. 1972-74), Dallas Symphony League, Dallas Music Tchrs. Assn. (pres. 1971-72, Tchr. of Yr. 1974), Thesaurus Book Club (pres. 1990-91, 97-98), Friday Forum (Dallas, bd. dirs.), Dallas Women's C. of C., Eagle Forum, Pub. Affairs Luncheon Club, Dallas Fedn. Music Club, Pro Am., Wednesday Morning Choral Club, Dallas Knife and Fork Club, Prestoncrest Rep. Club. Presbyterian. Home: 6232 Pemberton Dr Dallas TX 75230-4036

PALMER, DANNA SWAIN, special education educator; b. Greenville, N.C., Nov. 16, 1955; d. Thomas Ryan and Kristina (Massie) Swain; m. Charles Edward Palmer, July 26, 1980; children: Thad Edward, Kyle Thomas, Cory Leonard. BS in Music Edn., East Carolina U., 1978; M in Elem. Edn. with high honors, Wilmington Coll., 1993; spl. edn. cert., U. Del., 1994, Del. State U., 1994. Typing, swimming and music tchr. Norfolk (Va.) Acad., 1979-80; pvt. piano tchr. Seaford, Del., 1981-88; choral music tchr. Crusader Christian Acad., Salisbury, Md., 1989; 3d grade tchr., French tchr. Epworth Christian Sch., Laurel, Del., 1990-91; elem. tchr., asst. Woodbridge Schs., Greenwood, Del., 1992-93; spl. edn. tchr. Seaford (Del.) Sch. Dist., 1993—. Mem., parent rep. Prin.'s Adv. Coun., Seaford, 1991-92, Supt.'s Adv. Coun., Seaford, 1993-94; mem., profl. rep. Supt.'s Profl. Adv. Coun., Seaford, 1994; del., spl. edn. rep. Project 21 Team Rsch., Dover, Del., 1994; swimming instr. ARC, Georgetown, Del., 1973-80, Seaford Jaycee Pool, 1974-94. Song leader, co-chair Pioneer Clubs, Seaford, 1986-91; choir dir. children's ministries St. John's United Meth. Ch., Seaford, 1980-85; V.p., sec. PTA of Seaford Mid. Sch., 1992-94, sec. 1992—; legislative liaison Seaford Mid. Sch., 1994—. Mem. Music Educator's Nat. Conf., Del. Music Educator's Assn., Music Tchr.'s Nat. Assn., Nat. Coun. for Tchrs. of Lang. Arts, Coun. for Exceptional Children, TESOL, Del. Limited English Proficiency Speakers. Republican. Avocations: music, biking, swimming, writing, sewing. Home: 531 N Phillips St Seaford DE 19973-2307 Office: Seaford Sch Dist 500 E Stein Hwy Seaford DE 19973-1528

PALMER, DORA DEEN POPE, English and French language educator; b. Jackson, Miss., June 26, 1946; d. Melvin Sr. and Gladys (Wolfe) Pope; m. Carey Palmer Jr.; 1 child, Cawandra V. AA, Utica Jr. Coll., 1966; BS in Edn., Jackson State U., 1968, MA in Edn., 1976. Cert. English and French tchr. Tchr. English and French McCullough H. S., Monticello, Miss., 1968-69, Topeka-Tilton H.S., Monticello, 1969-70, Crystal Springs (Miss.) H.S., 1971-93; tchr. French Jackson (Miss.) Pub. Sch. Dist., 1993—. Chair English Dept., Crystal Springs, 1983-93; lectr. Jackson State Upward Bound, Jackson, 1984—; chair Crystal Springs H.S. steering and editing com. So. Assn. Colls. and Schs.; prodr., sponsor black history projects. Drama coach N.W. Mid. Sch., Jackson, 1993—; sponsor Beta Club, Crystal Springs, 1979; sec. Expo-Social & Civic Club, Jackson, 1988—; pianist Mount Wade Missionary Bapt. Ch., 1965-80, Terry Mission Missionary Bapt. Ch., 1979-87. Named Tchr. of Month, Tiger Pause newspaper, 1989, Star Tchr. Jackson State Upward Bound, 1992, Tchr. of Yr. Crystal Springs H.S., 1993; recipient Tchr. Appreciation award The Tiger ann., 1987, Outstanding Svc. award Terry Mission Bapt. Ch., 1983. Mem. ASCD, Nat. Assn. Edn., Miss. Assn. Edn. Democrat. Avocations: playing piano, reading, cooking southern dishes, sewing. Home: 316 S Denver St Jackson MS 39209-6303 Office: Provine HS N W Jackson 2400 Robinson St Jackson MS 39209-7019

PALMER, DOW EDWARD, JR., secondary educator; b. Del Rio, Tex., Jan. 26, 1951; s. Dow E. and Mary G. P.; m. Debra Kay Hall, Aug. 24, 1971; children: Angela Jean, Lysbeth Anne. BS in Edn., U. Tex., 1972. Cert. tchr., Tex. Tchr. Johnston High Sch., Austin, Tex., 1973-85, tchr., dept. chair, 1978-85; tchr. Dripping Springs (Tex.) High Sch., 1985—, tchr., dept. chair, 1987-93, campus tech. coord., 1989-98, dist. tech. dir., 1998—. Mem. AFT, Tex. Computer Edn. Assn. Avocations: home construction, music. Home: 4210 Mcgregor Ln Dripping Springs TX 78620-3350 Office: Dripping Springs Ind Sch Dist 111 Tiger Ln Dripping Springs TX 78620-3451

PALMER, EDWARD L. social psychology educator, television researcher, writer; b. Hagerstown, Md., Aug. 11, 1938; s. Ralph Leon and Eva Irene (Brandenburg) P.; children: Edward Lee, Jennifer Lynn. BA, Gettysburg Coll., 1960; BD, Luth. Theol. Sem., Gettysburg, 1964; MS, Ohio U., 1967, PhD, 1970. Asst. prof. Wetern Md. Coll., Westminster, 1968-70, Davidson Coll., N.C., 1970-77, assoc. prof., 1977-86, chair, 1985—99, prof., 1986—, Watson prof., 1991—. Guest rschr. Harvard U., Cambridge, Mass., 1977; vis. scholar UCLA, 1984, UNC Chapel Hill, 1991, Univ. Exeter, UK, 2000; cons. Council on Children, Media, Merchandising, 1978-79, 1st Union Bank Corp., Charlotte, N.C., 1975-79; NSF proposal reviewer, 1978—. Editl. reviewer Jour. Broadcasting and Electronic Media, 1978—; editor: Children and the Faces of TV, 1980, Faces of Televisual Media, 2003; author: Children in the Cradle of TV, 1987; contb. to Wiley Ency. of Psychology, 1984, 2002, Lawrence Erlbaum Assocs., 1991, Sage Pub., 1993-96; author jour. articles and book chpts. Sec. A. Mecklenburg Child Devel. Assn., Davidson and Cornelius, N.C., 1974-78; bd. mem. pub. radio Sta. WDAV, 1970-90, Telecomms. task force Rutgers U., 1981. Recipient Thomas Jefferson Tchg. award Robert Earl McConnell Found., 1993. Mem. APA, Am. Psychol. Soc., Assn. Heads Depts. Psychology (chair 1994-96), Am. Psychol. Assn. (task force on advt. and children 2001-03), Southeastern Psychol. Assn., Southeastern Soc. Social Psychologists, Phi Beta Kappa (pres. Davidson chpt. 1985-86). Avocations: sunrise and sunset walks, writing poetry, bird watching, music composition and performance. Office: Davidson Coll PO Box 7007 Davidson NC 28035-7007 E-mail: edpalmer@davidson.edu.

PALMER, JAMES DANIEL, information technology educator; b. Washington, Mar. 8, 1930; s. Martin Lyle and Sarah Elizabeth (Hall) P.; m. Margret Kupka, June 21, 1952; children: Stephen Robert, Daniel Lee, John Keith. AA, Fullerton Jr. Coll., 1953; BS (Alumni scholar), U. Calif., Berkeley, 1955, MS, 1957; PhD, U. Okla., 1963; DPS (hon.), Regis Coll., Denver, 1977. Chief engr. Motor vehicle and Illumination Lab. U. Calif., Berkeley, 1955-57; assoc. prof. U. Okla., Norman, 1957-63, prof., 1963-66, asst. to dir. Rsch. Inst., 1960-63, cons. Rsch. Inst., 1966-69, dir. Sch. Elec. Engring., 1963-66, dir. Systems Rsch. Center, 1964-66; dean sci. and engring., prof. elec. engring. Union Coll., Schenectady, 1966-71; pres. Met. State Coll., Denver, 1971-78; rsch. and spl. programs adminstr. Dept. Transp., Washington, 1978-79; v.p., gen. mgr. rsch. and devel. div. Mech. Tech., Inc., Latham, N.Y., 1979-82; exec. v.p. J.J. Henry Co., Inc., Moorestown, N.J., 1982-85; BDM internat. prof. info. tech. George Mason U., Fairfax, Va., 1985-95, prof. emeritus, 1995—; software cons., 1995—. Bd. dirs. J.J. Henry Co., Inc.; cons. Sym Mgmt. Co., Boston, Higher Edn. Exec. Assocs., Denver, PERI, Princeton; adj. prof. U. Colo. Co-author: (with A.P. Sage) Software Systems Engineering, (with Aseltine, Beam and Sage) Introduction to Computer Systems, Analysis, Design and Application. Bd. dirs., exec. v.p. adv. com. U.S.A. Vols. for Internat. Tech. Assistance, 1967-83, exec. v.p., 1970-71, chmn. exec. com.; trustee, vice chmn. Nat. Commn. on Coop. Edn.; mem. exec. policy bd. Alaska Natural Gas Pipeline, 1978-79; trustee Auraria Higher Edn. Program, Denver; mem. Fulbright fellow Selection Com., Colo.; bd. mgrs., mem. exec. com. Hudson-Mohawk Assn. Colls. and Univs., trustee, chmn. bd., 1970-71; adv. com. USCG Acad., 1972-82, chmn. adv. com., 1979-82; mem. Colo. Gov.'s Sci. and Tech. Adv. Council; pres. Denver Cath. Community Services Bd.; mem. Archdiocesan Catholic Charities and Community Services; mem. bd. U. Okla. Rsch. Inst.; mem. adv. com. Mile-Hi Red Cross. With USMC, 1950-51. Named James D. Palmer scholarship in his honor, George Mason U., 2002; recipient U.S. Coast Guard medal, 1983; Centennial scholar, Case-Western Res., 1981. Fellow IEEE (exec. and adminstrv. coms., v.p. long-range planning and finance, chmn. com. on large scale systems, Joseph E. Wahl Outstanding Career Achievement award 1993, Millennium medal 2000); mem. Systems, Man and Cybernetics Soc. (pres., Outstanding Contbns. award 1981), alumni assns. U. Calif. and U. Okla., Inst. Internat. Edn. (bd. dir. Rocky Mt. sect.), Soc. Naval Architects and Marine Engrs., Am. Soc. Engring. Edn., Am. Mil. Engrs., N.Y. Acad. Sci., Navy League, Sigma Xi, Eta Kappa Nu, Pi Mu Epsilon, Alpha Gamma Sigma. Home: 860 Cashew Way Fremont CA 94536-2646 Office: George Mason U Sch of Info Tech & Engring Fairfax VA 22030 E-mail: jdpalmer@ix.netcom.com.

PALMER, JEANNETTE URSULA, counselor, educator; b. Mare Island, Calif., June 21, 1941; d. Edward and Jeannette (Wilkon) Jaurszewski; div.; 1 child, Michelle. BA in History and Edn., Salve Regina Coll., 1963; postgrad., Colo. State Coll., 1968; MS in Rehab. Counseling, U. Ariz., 1971; postgrad., U. Tex. Health Sci. Ctr., 1979, North Tex. State U., 1980; EdD in Spl. Edn. and Counseling, East Tex. State U., 1989. Lic. profl. counselor, rehab. counselor, marriage and family counselor; nat. cert. counselor. Tchr. pub. sch. system, New Eng., Colo., 1963-69; substitute tchr. Amphitheatre Dists., Tanque Verde Dists., Tucson, 1969-70; counselor, coordinator intern Rehab. Dept. U. Ariz., 1971; asst. dir., counselor Goodwill Rehab. Ctr., Winston-Salem, N.C., 1972-73; prof. deafness and psychology, svc. learning coord. Eastfield Coll., Mesquite, Tex., 1973—; pvt. practice counseling Dallas, 1977—; clin. dir. The Listening Ctr., 1992. Cons. to def. attys., 1971-72, Tex. Commn. for the Deaf, Tex. Edn. Agy., Guatemala Dept. Edn., Parent Edn. Groups; adj. prof. Sch. Allied Health of Southwestern Med. Sch. U. Tex., 1975-76; pres. Tex. Cultural Alliance, 1987, 88. Mem. Nat. Rehab. Assn. Am. Counseling Assn. Avocations: travel, music, arts. Home: 1242 N Selva Dr Dallas TX 75218-3261 Office: Eastfield Coll 3737 Motley Dr Mesquite TX 75150-2033

PALMER, JUDITH GRACE, university administrator; b. Washington, Ind., Apr. 2, 1948; d. William Thomas and Laura Margaret (Routt) P. BA, Ind. U., 1970; JD cum laude, Ind. U., Indpls., 1973. Bar: Ind. 1974, U.S. Dist. Ct. (so. dist.) Ind. 1974. State budget analyst State of Ind., Indpls., 1969-76, exec. asst. to gov., 1976-81, state budget dir., 1981-85; spl. asst. to pres. Ind. U., 1985-86, v.p. for planning, 1986-91, v.p. for planning and fin. mgmt., 1991-94, v.p., CFO, 1994—. Bd. dirs. Ind. Fiscal Policy Inst., Kelley Exec. Ptnrs.; bd. dirs., treas. Advanced Rsch. and Tech. Inst. Bd. dirs., sec.-treas. Columbian Found., 1990-94, 2000—; bd. dirs. Columbia Club, 1989-98, pres. 1995; bd. dirs. Commn. for Downtown, 1984, mem. exec. bd., 1989-92, chmn. cmty. rels. com., 1989-93; mem. State Budget Commn., 1981-85. Named one of Outstanding Young Women in Am., 1978; recipient Sagamore of the Wabash award, 1977, 85, Citation of Merit, Ind. Bar Assn. of Young Lawyers, 1978, Appreciation award, 1980. Mem. ABA, Ind. Bar Assn., Indpls. Bar Assn. Roman Catholic. Office: Ind Univ Bryan Hall Rm 204 Bloomington IN 47405 E-mail: jgpalmer@indiana.edu.

PALMER, LARRY ISAAC, lawyer, educator; b. 1944; AB, Harvard U., 1966; LLB, Yale U., 1969. Bar: Calif. 1970. Asst. prof. Rutgers U., Camden, N.J., 1970-73, assoc. prof., 1973-75, Cornell U., Ithaca, N.Y., 1975-79, prof. law, 1979—2002, vice provost, 1979-84, v.p. acad. programs, 1987-91, v.p. acad. program and campus affairs, 1991-94; endowed chair Dept. Urban Health Policy U. Louisville, 2003—. Vis. fellow Cambridge U., 1984-85. Author: Law, Medicine, and Social Justice, 1989, Endings and Beginnings: Law, Medicine and Society in Assisted Life and Death, 2000. Mem. Am. Law Inst. Office: Inst Bioethics Health Law and Policy Sch Medicine 501 E Broadway Ste 310 Univ Louisville Louisville KY 40292 E-mail: lip1@cornell.edu.

PALMER, MARILYN JOAN, English composition educator; b. Mahoning County, Ohio, Mar. 3, 1933; d. Rudolph George and Marian Eleanor Wynn; m. Richard Palmer, Nov. 10, 1956 (dec. 1987); children: Ricky, Larry, Kevin. Phys. therapy cert., UCLA, 1954, BS, 1955; MA in Philosophy, Ohio State U., 1969; PhD, U. Okla., 1996. Phys. therapist Neil Ave. Sch. for Handicapped, Columbus, Ohio, 1968-69; instr. philosophy Ohio State U., Columbus, 1969; instr. English Youngstown (Ohio) State U., 1970-71; writer, editor The Economy Co., ednl. publs., Oklahoma City, 1977-81; grad. asst. in English U. Okla., Norman, 1981-87, lectr. in English, 1988-90, tech. writing instr. ind. studies, 1988-97. Free-lance editing and cons.; cons. for on-line CD-ROM to accompany a textbook, 2002. Author: Technical Writing for Science, Business and Industry, 1988, An Enthymeme as a Platform for Understanding Audience Values, 1997; editor: Kindergarten Keys Teacher's Guidebook, 1982, author parochial supplement, 1982. Fund-raiser Easter Seal Soc., 1965-68; den mother coord. Boy Scouts Am., 1966, 67. Dept. Energy grantee, 1976. Mem. AAUP, Am. Phys. Therapy Assn., Soc. for Women in Philosophy, Alpha Xi Delta (nat. editor Quill 1984-86). E-mail: doclynn@cox.net.

PALMER, MARTHA H. counseling educator, executive; b. Chgo., Jan. 10, 1954; d. Thomas Manuel Palmer Sr. and Marie Louise (Cranford-Crawford) Palmer; stepchildren: Kwasi Asimeng-Boahene, Betty Boahene, Shirley Boahene. BA in Psychology, Ea. Ill. U., 1976, MS, 1977; cert. in cmty. law, John Marshall Law Sch., Chgo., 1981; student, U. Ill., Chgo., 1992; postgrad., No. Ill. U., 1995—. Med. asst. health svcs. Ea. Ill. U., Charleston, 1976-77; dir. sch. age and sr. citizen programs YMCA, Chgo., 1978-80; site dir., facilities mgr. Ctr. for New Horizons, Chgo., 1980-85; counselor No. Ill. U., DeKalb, 1985-89; lectr. Malcolm X Coll., Chgo., 1989, recruitment coord., 1989-90; dir. Bethel Self Sufficiency Program, Chgo., 1989-90; asst. prof. counseling Harold Washington Coll. City Coll. Chgo., 1990—, acting chair, chmn. dept. counseling, 1999—. Developer Harold Washington Coll. Sisters Academic Scholarship Program, 1997. Creator of character Marty The Clown (U.S. patent, trademark 1998); author poems; contbr. articles to profl. jours. Coord. Afrikan Cultural Pageant, Ea. Ill. U., Charleston and No. Ill. U., DeKalb, 1972-86; mem. Sojourners United Political Action Com.; immediate past pres., pres., mem. Sojourners United Polit. Action Commn., Chgo., 1993-99; founder Harold Washington Coll., Black Women's Caucus, Chgo., 1991—; edn. rep. Task Force for Black Polit. Empowerment, Chgo., 1994—; coord. Coll. Support Groups for Self Help, 1991; co-founder Black Maleness Program, 1991; vol. La Rida Hosp., Chgo.; co-convenor Rainbow PUSH Coalition City Coll. Chgo. divsn.; co-founder Sisters in Scholarship Program, Harold Washington Coll., 1997; co-chair 150th Commemoration Women's Rights Nat. Womens Polit. Caucus Greater Chgo. Recipient Sharps and Flats Music Club Adv. award, 1994, BSU award, 1996, Hospitality Adv. Bd. Acknowledgement, Roman Cath. Ch. Mem. NOW, Nat. Assn. Black Psychologists, Ill. Assn. Black Psychologists, Ladies of Peter Claver (Court 129), Delta Sigma Theta. Democrat. New Thought Christian. Avocations: singing, dancing, designing, drawing. Office: Jordan Evans Inst Inc PO Box 21177 Chicago IL 60621-0177

PALMER, PATRICIA ANN TEXTER, English language educator; b. Detroit, June 10, 1932; d. Elmer Clinton and Helen (Rotchford) Texter; m. David Jean Palmer, June 4, 1955. BA, U. Mich., 1953; MEd, Nat.-Louis U., 1958; MA, Calif. State U., San Francisco, 1966; postgrad., Stanford U., 1968, Calif. State U., Hayward, 1968-69. Chmn. speech dept. Grosse Pointe (Mich.) Univ. Sch., 1953-55; tchr. South Margerita Sch., Panama, 1955-56, Kipling Sch., Deerfield, Ill., 1955-56; grad. level chmn. Rio San Gabriel Sch., downey, Calif., 1957-59; tchr. newswriting and devel. reading Roosevelt H.S., Honolulu, 1959-62; tchr. English, speech and newswirint El Camino H.S., South San Francisco, Calif., 1963-68; chmn. ESL dept. South San Francisco Unified Sch. Dist., 1968-81; dir. ESL Inst., Millbrae, Calif., 1978—. Adj. faculty New Coll. Calif., 1981—, Skyline Coll., 1990—; Calif. master tchr. ESL Calif. Coun. Adult Edn., 1979-82; cons. in field. Past chair Sister City Com., Millbrae. Recipient Concours de Francias prix, 1947; Jeanette M. Liggett Meml. award for excellence in history, 1949. Mem. AAUW, NAFE, TESOL, ASCD, Am. Assn. Intensive English Programs, Internat. Platform Assn., Calif. Assn. TESOL, Nat. Assn. for Fgn. Student Affairs, Computer Using Educators, Speech Comm. Assn., Faculty Assn. of Calif. C.C., U. Mich. Alumnae Assn., Nat.-Louis U. Alumnae Assn., Ninety Nines (Golden West chpt.), Cum Laude Soc., Soroptimist Internat. (dir., Millbrae-San Bruno Women Helping Women award 1993), Rotary Club, Chi Omega, Zeta Phi Eta. Home: 2917 Franciscan Ct San Carlos CA 94070-4304

PALMER, RAYETTA J. technology coordinator, educator; b. Tribune, Kans., Dec. 9, 1949; d. Raymond H. and Helen Jean (Whittle) Helm; children: Carol Lynn, Eric Lee. BA in Bus. Edn., U. No. Colo., 1970; MA in Computer Edn., Lesley Coll., 1990. Cert. vocat. educator, Colo. Bus./computer tchr. Dept. Def. Schs., Mannheim, Germany, 1983-87; vocat.-tech. tchr. and coord. Cheyenne County Sch. Dist., Cheyenne Wells, Colo., 1987—. Instr. Lamar C.C., 1987—; instr. Colo. Online Learning, 1999—; bookkeeper Scherler Sales, Inc., 2000—. Treas. Cheyenne County Rep. Ctrl. Com., Colo., 1989—; elected mem. Cheyenne Wells City Coun., 2000. Mem. Internat. Soc. for Tech. in Edn., Pi Omega Pi. Republican. Avocations: reading, bridge, travel, church organist. Home: PO Box 771 Cheyenne Wells CO 80810-0771 Office: Cheyenne County Sch Dist PO Box 577 Cheyenne Wells CO 80810-0577

PALMER, ROBERT ALAN, lawyer, educator; b. Somerville, N.J., June 29, 1948; BA, U. Pitts., 1970; JD, George Washington U., 1976. Bar: Va. 1977. Dir. labor relations Nat. Assn. Mfrs., Washington, 1976-79; assoc. gen. counsel Nat. Restaurant Assn., Washington, 1979-85, gen. counsel, 1985-87; assoc. prof. Pa. State U., State College, 1987-88, Calif. State Poly. U., 1988-92, prof., 1992—. Mem. ABA, Va. State Bar Assn. Home: 557 Fairview Ave Arcadia CA 91007-6736 Office: 3801 W Temple Ave Pomona CA 91768-2557

PALMER, ROBERT JEFFREY, special education educator; b. Clarksburg, W.Va., June 25, 1961; s. Robert Edward and Katherine Elizabeth (Snopps) P. BS in Phys. Edn., W.Va. U., 1984, MA in Spl. Edn., 1994. Cert. tchr. phys. edn. 7-12, safety edn. 7-12, spl. edn. K-12. Tchr. Berkeley County Schs., Martinsburg, W.Va., 1988-89; tchr. spl. edn. Morgan County Schs., Berkeley Springs, W.Va., 1989—. Athletic dir. Paw Paw Schs., 1994—, head baseball coach, 1996—. Mem. Coun. for Exceptional Children, Moos, Lions. Democrat. Mem. Christian Ch. (Disciples Of Christ). Avocations: motorcycles, music, reading, golf, baseball. Home: PO Box 455 435 Moser Ave Paw Paw WV 25434-0455 Office: Paw Paw High Sch 422 Moser Ave Paw Paw WV 25434-9501 E-mail: wvu1994@aol.com.

PALMER, ROSEMARY GUDMUNDSON, education educator; b. Logan, Utah, July 19, 1946; d. Melvin P. and Mary Mae Gudmundson; m. Frederick W. Palmer, July 15, 1971; children: Christopher W., Melanie. BS, Utah State U., 1968, MEd, 1973; PhD, U. Wyo., 1997. Cert. elem. tchr. grades K-8, reading tchr. grades K-12, English tchr. grades K-12, remedial reading tchr. grades K-12, audio visual tchr. grades K-12. 5th grade tchr. Granite Sch. Dist., Granger, Utah, 1968-69; 6th grade tchr. Mesa (Ariz.) Pub. Schs., 1969-70, Davis Sch. Dist., Bountiful, Utah, 1970-71; supr. corrective reading grades 1-5 Spencer (Iowa) Cmty. Schs., 1973-74; jr. high reading, lang. arts tchr., study skills developer Sweetwater Sch. Dist. #1, Rock Springs, Wyo., 1981-96. Instr. reading in content area U. Wyo. Ext., Rock Springs, 1984-91; instr. children's lit. Western Wyo. C.C., Rock Springs, 1992, 94, 96; asst. prof. Boise State U., 1998—; liaison to elem. sch., 1998—; mem. Idaho State Literacy Assessment Com., 2001—, Idaho Curriculum Selection Com., 2002. Author: Children's Voices from the Trail: Narratives from the Platte River Road, 2002; author column Sweetwater County Guide, 1987-91; contbr. articles to profl. jours. Story reader Nat. Libr. Week, Rock Springs (Wyo.) Pub. Libr., 1990-97; bd. dirs. Love Reading Com., Rock Springs, 1993-97. Mem. Internat. Reading Assn. (presenter confs., mem. content literacy subcom., del. People to People program to Russia and Ukraine 1992), Soc. Children's Book Writers and Illustrators (area coord. 2002—), Nat. Coun. Tchrs. English (presenter confs.), Phi Delta Kappa, Phi Kappa Phi. Avocations: reading, writing, singing, sewing, doing historical research. Office: EESS Boise State U 1910 University Dr Boise ID 83725 E-mail: rpalmer@boisestate.edu.

PALMER, VERNON VALENTINE, law educator; b. New Orleans, Sept. 9, 1940; s. George Joseph and Juliette Marie (Wehrmann) P. BA, Tulane U., 1962, LL.B., 1965; LL.M., Yale U., 1966; PhD, Pembroke Coll., Oxford U., 1985. Bar: La. 1965, U.S. Supreme Ct. 1981. Asst. prof. law Ind. Sch. Law, Indpls., 1966-70; lectr. law U. Botswana, Lesotho & Swaziland, Roma, Lesotho, 1967-69; prof. Tulane Law Sch., New Orleans, 1970—, Clarence Morrow research prof. law, 1980—, Thomas Pickles prof. law, 1989—; external examiner Nat. U. Lesotho, Roma, 1978-81. Dir. Tulane Paris Inst. European Legal Studies, European Legal Studies; reporter for revision of civil code La. Law Inst. 1979; vis. prof. Faculty Law, U. Strasbourg, 1988, The Sorbonne, U. Paris, 1986, 92, Universite des Antilles, Martinique, 1998, Universidad Ramon Llull, Barcelona, 1998, U. Trento, 1999—, U. Laussanne, 2000, U. Geneva, 2000. Author: The Roman-Dutch and Lesotho Law of Delict, 1970, The Legal System of Lesotho, 1971, The Paths to Privity, 1992, The Civil Law of Lease in Louisiana, 1997, Louisiana: Microcosm of a Mixed Jurisdiction, 1999, Mixed Jurisdictions Worldwide: The Third Legal Family, 2001; (with Bussani) Pure Economic Loss Europe, 2003; contbr. numerous articles to profl. jours. Pres. French Quarter Residents Assn., 1973-75, Alliance for Good Govt., 1974-75; del. Nat. Democratic Conv., N.Y.C., 1976; chmn. World Congress on Mixed Jurisdictions, 2002, pres., pres. WOrld Soc. of Mixed Jursdiction Jurists, Titulary Mem. Internat. Acad. of Compatative Law, 2003. Decorated chevalier L'ordre des Palmes Académiques. Mem. La. Law Inst., World Soc. Mixed Jurisdiction Jurists (pres.), Titulaire Internat. Acad. Comparative Law The Hague. Democrat. Roman Catholic. Home: 3311 Coliseum St New Orleans LA 70115-2401 Office: 6329 Freret St New Orleans LA 70118-6231 E-mail: vpalmer@law.tulane.edu .

PALMER-CALLICOTT, DEBORAH DAWN, educational examiner; b. Searcy, Ark., Jan. 3, 1958; d. Derrel M. and Julia (Owen) Palmer; m. Richard D. Callicott, June 9, 1990. BS in Spl. Edn., East Tex. State U., 1981, MS in Lang., Learning Disabilities and Diagnostic, 1983. Cert. spl. edn. supr., Ark. Tchr. spl. edn. Ark. Sch. Dist. 7, Texarkana, 1981-89, ednl. examiner, 1989—. Sponsor y-Teens, Texarkana, Tex., 1985—. Mem. Coun. for Exceptional Children (pres. Texarkana chpt. 1984-87), AAUW (treas. Texarkana 1987), Texarkana (Tex.) Jaycees, Texarkana (Tex.) C. of C., Optimists, Phi Delta Kappa (sec. Texarkana 1987-89). Home: 2206 College Dr Texarkana TX 75503-3806

PALMERI, MARLAINA, school executive; b. Rochester, N.Y., Feb. 20, 1950; d. Joseph Michael and Eleanor Louise (Polisseni) P. BA, SUNY, Plattsburgh, 1971; MA, SUNY, Brockport, 1984; EdD, U. Rochester, 1998; student, U. Matlock, England, U. Copenhagen, Denmark, U. Moscow, Russia. Cert. Sch. Dist. Adminstr., Sch. Adminstr. Supr., N-6, N.Y. Tchr. Rochester (N.Y.) City Schs., 1972-86, supr. elem. magnet schs., 1986-88, vice prin., 1988-92, prin., 1992-99; sr. v.p. Edison Schs. Inc., N.Y.C., 1999—. Named Disting. Educator, N.Y. State, 1996. Mem. ASCD, Nat. Assn. Elem. Sch. Prins., Phi Delta Kappa. Avocations: tennis, golf. Home: 147 Pond Rd Honeoye Falls NY 14472-9352 Office: Edison Schs Inc 521 5th Ave New York NY 10175-1600

PALMER-SACCHITELLA, KELLEY ANNE, special education educator; b. Rochester, N.Y., Aug. 24, 1967; d. James Arthur Palmer and Shirley Anne (Owens) Broderick; m. Nicholas Sacchitella, Sept. 4, 1992. BS, St. Bonaventure, 1989; MEd, Nazareth Coll., 1994. Child habilitation specialist Mary Cariola Child Ctr., Rochester, 1989-90, sr. mgr., 1990-93; grad. asst. Nazareth Coll., Rochester, 1993-94; teaching asst. Mary Cariola Pre-sch., Rochester, 1993-94; tchr. spl. edn. Letchworth Cen. Sch., Gainesville, N.Y., 1994-98, Honeoye (N.Y.) Ctrl. Sch., 1998—. Coach Odyssey of the Mind, 1998—. Recipient N.Y. State Family Svc. award, 1991, Rochester Guild for Children scholarship, 1994. Mem. Coun. for Exceptional Children, Phi Delta Kappa, Kappa Delta Pi (sec. 1994—). Avocations: hiking, camping, skiing, reading. Home: 9631 Lawrence Hill Rd W Springwater NY 14560-9611 E-mail: kelley@honeoye.org.

PALMISANO, SISTER MARIA GORETTI, principal; b. Balt., Nov. 6, 1929; d. Theodore Michael and Agnes Marie (Wheeler) P. BS in Edn., Duquesne U., 1966; MEd in Adminstrn. and Supervision, Towson State U., 1974; postgrad., Loyola Coll., 1976-83. Cert. advanced profl., Md. Tchr. St. Michael Sch., Forstburg, Md., 1952-59; music tchr. Holy Name Sch., Pitts., 1959-64; music tchr., tchr. jr. high St. Margaret Mary Sch., Harrisburg, Pa., 1964-69; prin. St. Brigid Sch., Balt., 1969-73, Bishop John Neumann Sch., Balt., 1973-83; adminstr. SSND Motherhouse, Balt., 1983-91; prin. St. Mary Sch., Hagerstown, Md., 1991—. Mem. St. Maria Goretti Recruitment, Hagerstown, 1992-93. Named Woman of Yr., Highlandtown Exch. Club, 1983. Mem. ASCD, Nat. Cath. Prins. Assn., Elem. Sch. Prins. Assn.-Archdiocese of Balt. (v.p. 1979-83, chairperson Mid. States Accreditation Elem. Sch. 1996). Avocations: reading, playing piano/organ, walking, crossword puzzles. Home and Office: 218 W Washington St Hagerstown MD 21740-4712

PALMREUTER, KENNETH RICHARD LOUIS, principal; b. Vassar, Mich., Feb. 8, 1939; s. Clarence L. and Louise M. (Koch) P.; m. Martha Marie Zoellick, June 16, 1962; children: Pauline, Karen, Joel. BS in Edn., Concordia Tchrs. Coll., 1962; MA in Elem. Sch. Adminstrn., U. Mich., 1967; postgrad., Wayne State U., 1976-78, U. Colo., 1988-89; LLD, Concordia Tchrs. Coll., Seward, Nebr., 1993. Tchr. Grace Luth. Sch., River Forest, Ill., 1960-61, Calvary Luth. Sch., Lincoln Park, Mich., 1962-63, prin., tchr. jr. high, 1963-76; asst. prin. Luth. High Sch. West, Detroit, 1976-78, prin., 1978-87; exec. dir. Luth. High Sch., Denver, 1987—. Mem. Commn. on Theology and Ch. Rels., Luth. Ch.-Mo. Synod, 1995—, mem. planning coun. for mission and ministry, 1988-90; adv. team Luth. High Schs., 1984-88, 94—, Concordia Centennial adv. com., 1992; day sch. com. Rocky Mountain Dist., 1990-94, tchrs. conf. chmn., 1990-94, dist. conv. com., 1988, 91; nominations com. Mich. Dist., 1987, bd. social ministry, 1980-84, dist. conv. com., 1972, student aid com., 1974-78; conf. program com. Mich. Assn. Non-Pub. Schs., 1984-85; adv. coun. Wayne County Cmty. Coll., 1986-87. Named Outstanding Young Educator, Lincoln Park Jaycees, 1973; nominated Nat. Disting. Luth. Prin., 1992. Mem. NASSP, ASCD, Assn. Luth. Secondary Schs., Luth. Edn. Assn. Home: 2783 S Depew St Denver CO 80227-4106 Office: N Lutheran High Sch 3031 W 144th Ave Broomfield CO 80020*

PALMS, JOHN MICHAEL, academic administrator, physicist; b. Rijswijk, The Netherlands, June 6, 1935; naturalized, 1956; s. Peter Joannes and Mimi Adele (DeYong) P.; m. Norma Lee Cannon, June 2, 1958; children: John Michael, Danielle Maria, Lee Cannon. BS in Physics, The Citadel, 1958, DSc (hon.), 1980; MS in Physics, Emory U., 1959; PhD, U. N.Mex., 1966. Commd. 2d lt. USAF, 1958, retired capt. Res., 1970; lectr. physics dept. U. N.Mex., 1959-60; instr. physics dept. USAF Acad., 1961-62; staff mem. Western Electric Sandia Lab., 1961-62, U. Calif. Los Alamos Sci. Lab., 1962-66, Oak Ridge Nat. Lab., 1966; asst. prof. Emory U., Atlanta, 1966-69, assoc. prof., 1969-73, chmn., assoc. prof. dept. physics, asso. prof. radiology dept. Med. Sch., 1973-74, prof., chmn. dept. physics, 1969-74, dean Coll. Arts. and Scis., 1974-80, acting chmn. dept. math. and computer sci., 1976-77, v.p. arts and scis., acting chmn. dept. anthropology, 1979-80, acting dean Emory Coll., 1979-80, acting dir. Emory U. Computing Ctr., 1980-82, v.p. acad. affairs, 1982-88, interim dean Grad. Sch., 1985-86, Charles Howard Candler prof. nuclear, radiation and environ. physics, 1988-90; pres., prof. physics Ga. State U., Atlanta, 1989-91, U. S.C., Columbia, 1991—. Bd. dirs. Fortis, Inc., N.Y.C., Exelon Corp., Chgo., NCAA, Simcom Internat. Holdings, Inc., Atlanta; adv. com. Oak Ridge Nat. Lab., 1985-89; mem. nat. nuclear accredititng bd. Inst. Nuclear Power Ops., 1985-91, mem. nat. adv. coun., 1997-2001; mem. panel for semicondr. detectors NAS/NRC, 1963-74; cons. Acad. Natural Scis., Phila., Hughes, Inc., Santa Barbara, Calif., Tennelec, Inc., Three Mile Island Environ. Study, TRW Space Sys. Divsn., L.A., Ga. Dept. Human Resources, Nat. Cancer Inst.; mem. high tech. task force Atlanta C. of C. Contbr. articles on nuclear, atomic, med. and environ. physics to profl. jours. Mem. adv. bd. The Citadel, Oak Ridge Nat. Lab.; mem. exec. bd. Atlanta Area Coun. Boy Scouts of Am., 1989-90; mem. cmty. rels. bd. U.S. Penitentiary, Atlanta; trustee, chmn. Inst. Def. Analyses, Wesleyan Coll., 1984-89, Pace Acad., 1984-89, St. Joseph's Hosp., Atlanta, 1987-89, Ga. Rsch. Alliance, 1988-89; mem. S.C. Univs. Edn. Found., Devel. Found. and Rsch. Found., S.C. Rsch. Inst. Bds.; bd. dirs. Civic-Atlanta Partnership Bus. and Edn., Inc., 1988-90, United Way; chair Rhodes scholar selection com., 1987, S.C., 1995-99; bd. dirs. Nat. Merit Scholarship Corp. Mem. AAAS, Am. Phys. Soc., Am. Assn. Physics Tchrs., IEEE (Nuclear Sci. Group), Am. Nuclear Soc., Am. Coun. Edn., Coun. Provosts and Acad. V.P.s, Am. Conf. Acad. Deans, Soc. Nuclear Medicine, Health Physics Soc., Greater Columbia C. of C. (bd. dirs.), Rotary, Columbia C. of C., Phi Beta Kappa, Sigma Xi, Phi Kappa Phi, Omicron Delta Kappa, Sigma Pi Sigma. Home and Office: Pres U SCO Osborne Bldg Columbia SC 29208-0001

PALOCHKO, ELEANOR LARIVERE, retired secondary education educator; b. Woonsocket, R.I., May 8, 1924; d. Albert E. and Rosella (Hernan) LaRivere; m. Raymond Francis Palochko, June 26, 1948; children: Ellen, David, Gary, Peggy. BS, U. Conn., 1945; postgrad., Columbia U., 1946, U. Conn., 1982, Cen. Conn. State U. Tchr. bus. Morgan High Sch., Clinton, Conn., 1945-46, Bassick High Sch., Bridgeport, Conn., 1947-49, Jonathan Law High Sch., Milford, Conn., 1961-92; ret., 1992. Former leader Girl Scouts U.S.A., Brownie Scouts; former treas., sec., v.p., pres. PTA, Milford; advisor Keyettes; vol. Milford Hosp. Aux., Bloodmobile drives ARC; sec. Friends of Counted Embroidery, Milford Sr. Ctr.; treas. Milford Hosp. Aux. Mem. NEA, AAUW (exec. bd., past v.p., sec., treas., Ednl. Found. gift in her name 1984-85), Conn. Edn. Assn., Milford Edn. Assn. (bldg rep.), New Eng. Bus. Educators Assn. (rep. profl. devel. com.), Conn. Bus. Educators Assn., Ret. Tchrs. of Bridgeport and New Haven, U. Conn. Alumni Assn., Ret. Profl. Women's Club (sec.), Conn. State Ret. Tchrs. Roman Catholic. Avocations: counted cross-stitch, reading, golf, elderhostels travel. Home: 134 Corona Dr Milford CT 06460-3514

PALOCZY, SUSAN THERESE, elementary school principal; b. Dayton, Ohio, Nov. 17, 1953; d. William Michael and Elfriede Meckel (Adkisson) P. BA, Our Lady of the Lake U., San Antonio, 1975, MA in Edn., 1978, cert. in mid-mgmt., 1979; EdD, Tex. A&M U., 1997. Cert. mid-mgmt. adminstr., supr., elem. and secondary tchr., Tex. Elem. acad. coord., tchr., summer sch. prin. Harlandale Ind. Sch. Dist., San Antonio, elem. prin. Mem. ASCD, Tex. Coun. Women Sch. Execs., Tex. Elem. Prins. and Suprs. Assn., Tex. Congress Parents and Tchrs., Kappa Delta Pi. Address: 321 Tuttle Rd San Antonio TX 78209-6146 Office: Wright Elem 115 E Huff Ave San Antonio TX 78214-2230

PALOMINO, KRISTI SUZANN, elementary school educator; b. Garden Grove, Calif., Mar. 19, 1970; d. Stephen James and Jeanne Frances (Prelesnik) T.; m. Jessie Palomino Jr.; children: Sophia, Sebastian. BA in Liberal Studies, San Francisco State U., 1992, credentials in multiple subject edn., 1993. Cert. elem. tchr., Calif., crosscultural lang. acquisition devel. Tchg. asst. San Francisco State U., 1988-92; substitute tchr. Newark (Calif.) Unified Sch. Dist., 1992-93, New Haven Unified Sch. Dist., Union City, Calif., 1992-93; tchr. after-sch. program Milpitas (Calif.) Unified Sch. Dist., 1993, elem. substitute tchr., elem. tchr., 1994, elem. tchr., 1994-95, Newark (Calif.) Unified Sch. Dist., 1995-99, literacy coord., 1998-99, prin., 2001, kindergarten tchr., 2001—. After-sch. tutor Chpt. 1 program Milpitas Unified Sch. Dist., 1994-95. Mem. Calif. Tchrs. Assn. Democrat. Avocations: exercise, reading, gardening, theatre, scrapbooking. Home: 6324 Lafayette Ave Newark CA 94560-2435 E-mail: kpalomino@nusd.k12.ca.us.

PALOVICH, MARILYN LEE, elementary education educator; b. Trinidad, Colo., Apr. 24, 1943; d. Raymond Leon and Mary (Swigle) Swift; m. Joseph Lawrence Palovich, June 6, 1964; children: Milena Jo, Chad Michael. AA, Trinidad State Jr. Coll., 1963; BA, Adams State Coll., Alamosa, Colo., 1966. Cert. elem. edn. Tchr. grades 1-2-3-4 North Garcia Sch. Dist. No. 5, Trinidad, 1963-65; tchr. kindergarten Trinidad Sch. Dist. No. 1, 1965-68, tchrs. grades 3 and 5, 1970—. Mem. adv. bd. Louden/Henritze Archaeology Mus., Trinidad, 1993—. Author: (poetry) Treasured Poems of America, 1994. Pres. Assn. Retarded Citizens, Trinidad, 1987-89; pres., v.p. So. Colo. Assn. to Aid the Handicapped, Trinidad, 1989—; mem. adv. bd., treas. So. Colo. Devel. Disability Svcs., Trinidad, 1987-89. Recipient Outstanding Elem. Tchr. award, 1974, 1st Pl. Nat. 5th Grade award Weekly Reader Editors, Middletown, 1994, Grand Prize Nat. 5th Grade award, 1995. Mem. NRA, Western Slavonic Assn., Colo. Fedn. Tchrs., Trinidad Fedn. Tchrs. Avocations: leather sewing and tooling, gun engraving, reading, writing poetry, handcrafts. Home: 733 Pine St Trinidad CO 81082-2314

PALTER, ROBERT MONROE, humanities educator; b. N.Y.C., June 19, 1924; s. Meyer and Mildred (Gilder) Palter; m. Ruth Rappeport, July 15, 1945 (div. 1953); 1 child, Alixe Daphne Cielo; m. Toni Ann Inman, Apr. 5, 1955 (div. 1977); children: Geoffrey Meyer, Jennifer Thorn Allan, Nicholas Trask, Adam Finch; m. Annette B. Weiner, May 21, 1979 (dv. 1982). AB, Columbia U., 1943; PhD, U. Chgo., 1952. From instr. to assoc. prof. phys. scis. and philosophy U. Chgo., 1949-64; prof. philosophy and history U. Tex., Austin, 1964-82; Dana prof. history of sci. Trinity Coll., Hartford, Conn., 1983-91, prof. emeritus, 1991—. Author: (book) Whitehead's Philosophy of Science, 1960; editor: Toward Modern Science, 1961, The Annus Mirabilis of Sir Isaac Newton, 1971, The Duchess of Malfi's Apricots and Other Literary Fruits, 2002. With U.S. Army, 1944—46. Mem.: Phi Beta Kappa.

PALVINO, NANCY MANGIN, retired librarian; b. Rochester, N.Y., Nov. 22, 1937; d. John Bernard and Miriam Lucille (Fox) Mangin; m. Lawrence Robert Palvino, July 2, 1960; children: Mark, Laurie, Lisa, Katharine, Thomas. BS, SUNY, Geneseo, 1959; MLS, U. Buffalo, 1993. Cert. libr., N.Y. Libr. Spencerport (N.Y.) Elem. Sch., 1959-60; tchr. East Greenbush (N.Y.) Elem. Sch., 1960-63; libr. # 41 Sch., Rochester, 1993—2001; ret., 2001. Author: (bibliography) Autism, 1991. Fundraiser Rochester Philharm. Orgn., 1970; mem. women's bd. dirs. St. Mary's Hosp., Rochester, 1980—, giftshop chairperson, 1989-92, exec. coun., 1989-92, chmn. of ball, 1985, Imperial Ball Meml. Art Gallery, 1987, Holiday Open House, 1988; v.p. women's coun. Meml. Art Gallery, Rochester, 1989-91. Grantee DeWitt Wallace Reader's Digest Fund, 1994. Mem. ALA, N.Y. Libr. Assn. (scholarship 1992), Greater Rochester Areas Media Specialists (chmn. scholarship com. 1994-95, scholarship 1992), Phi Delta Kappa. Avocations: golf, reading, walking, knitting. Home: 345 Kilbourn Rd Rochester NY 14618-3632

PAM, ELEANOR, behavorial sciences educator; b. Bklyn., June 24, 1936; d. Simon and Berta (Field) Pam; m. Robert Emanuel Juceam, May 24, 1970; children: Daniel James, Jacquelyn Brooke, Gregory Andrew. BA, Brandeis U., 1958; MA, NYU, 1960, MA, 1963, PhD, 1969. Exec. asst. to pres. Queensboro C.C., CUNY, 1969-72, assoc. dean coll., 1969-72, univ. dir. spl. programs, 1972-73, 1978-79; dept. chair, prof. behavioral scis. Hostos C.C., CUNY, 1981-96; prof. John Jay Coll. Criminal Justice, CUNY, 1996-2000, dir. Domestic Violence Rsch. and Resource Ctr. Inmate Edn., 1997—2000. Pres. coun. Brandeis U., Waltham, Mass., 1972—. Active Mayor's Commn. Combat Domestic Violence. Recipient Founders Day award, NYU, 1969, Appreciation award, CUNY, 2000. Mem.: NOW (founding), Vet. Feminists of Am. (hon. bd. mem., medal of honor 2001, 2002), City U. Women's Coalition, Women and Soc. Jewish. Home: 106 Hemlock Rd Manhasset NY 11030-1214 E-mail: EleanorPam@aol.com.

PAN, ROSALIE JIA-LING, English educator; b. Shanghai, Aug. 16; came to U.S., 1979; d. You-Yuan Pan and Ruth Li. BA in English Lang. and Lit., Shanghai Fgn. Langs. U., 1967; MA in Linguistics, SUNY, Stony Brook, 1981, D of Arts in Linguistics, 1989. Lectr. English, Beijing No. 2 Fgn. Langs. U., 1968-79; tchr. asst. SUNY, 1980-85, 88-89, grad. asst., 1981-85, 88-89; lang. specialist High Tech. Solutions, Inc., Poughkeepsie, N.Y., 1985-88; instr. ESL and linguistics Pierce Coll., Lakewood, 1989—. U. Pitts. scholar, 1979-80. Mem. TESOL, MLA,, Am. Assn. Applied Linguistics, Internat. Assn. World English, Linguistics Soc. Am. Avocations: swimming, traveling, playing piano, dancing, reading. Office: Pierce Coll 9401 Farwest Dr SW Tacoma WA 98498-1919 E-mail: 1-pan@pierce.ctc.edu.

PAN, YI, computer science educator; b. Wujiang, Jiangsu, China, May 12, 1960; came to U.S., 1987; s. Jun and Xiuzhen (Fei) P.; m. Hong Miao, Aug. 4, 1986; children: Marissa, Anna. BEng, Tsinghua U., Beijing, 1982, MEng, 1984; MSc, U. Pitts., 1988, PhD, 1991. Rsch. asst. Tsinghua U., 1982-86; tchg. asst. U. Pitts., 1987-89, tchg. fellow, 1989-91; asst. prof. computer sci. U. Dayton, Ohio, 1991-96, assoc. prof., 1996-2000; assoc. prof. computer sci. Ga. State U., Atlanta, 2000—. Director of Graduate Studies in Computer Science University of Dayton, Dayton, 1998—2000. Contbr. articles to profl. jours. Recipient Rsch. Opportunity award NSF, 1995, Investment Competition Fund award Ohio Bd. Regents, 1996, World Acad. Scis. Achievement award, 2002; Mellon Found. fellow 1990, Summer Rsch. fellow U. Dayton Rsch. Coun., 2000, Air Force Office for Sci. Rsch., JSPS fellow, 1998. Mem.: IEEE (sr.; Secretary of the IEEE Computer Society Dayton Chapter 1996—97, IEEE Computer Society Distinguished Visitor Program Speaker 2000). Home: 615 Summer Breeze Ter Alpharetta GA 30005-6431 Office: Ga State U Computer Sci Dept Atlanta GA 30303 E-mail: pan@cs.gsu.edu.

PANAGOS, REBECCA JEAN HUFFMAN, university educator, researcher, consultant; b. Shreveport, La., Aug. 19, 1952; d. Richard Herbert and Betty Jean (Lilly) Huffman; m. Dennis Lee Panagos, Dec. 12, 1976; children: Ryan Edward, Anne Rebecca, Alexander. BA, La. Tech. U., 1973, MA in Edn., 1974; PhD, U. Mo., 1996. Cert. vocat. evaluator, tchr., Mo. Tchr. civics, English, journalism Bethel Christian Sch., Ruston, La., 1973-74; counselor Goodwill Industries Denver, 1975-76; guidance counselor Spl. Sch. Dist. St. Louis County, Mo., 1976-95; assoc. prof. tchr. preparation Lindenwood U., St. Charles, Mo., 1995—. Ednl. cons., 1993—. Author: Career Self-Efficacy for Adolescents with Learning Disabilities, 1996; editor Nat. Vocal. Assessment in Edn. Profile, 1993-96; contbr. articles to profl. jours. in spl. edn. Mem. Order of Ea. Star, 1970—, Order of Rainbow for Girls, 1970—, Internat. Families, 1984—. Recipient Outstanding Tchr. of Yr. award Nat. Assn. Vocat. Spl. Needs Edn., 1995, Outstanding Rsch. of Yr. award Am. Vocat. Assn., 1996. Mem. Coun. for Exceptional Children (interdisciplinary com. for vocat. assessment and evaluation 1993-97, faculty advisor student chpt. 1996—, pres. chpt. 212). Democrat. Methodist. Avocations: promoting international adoptions, research, publishing, jogging. Office: Lindenwood Univ 209 S Kingshighway St Saint Charles MO 63301-1693

PANARETOS, JOHN, mathematics and statistics educator; b. Kythera, Lianianika, Greece, Feb. 23, 1948; s. Victor and Fotini (Kominu) P.; m. Evdokia Xekalaki; 1 child, Victor. First degree, U. Athens, 1972; MSc, U. Sheffield, Eng., 1974; PhD, U. Bradford, Eng., 1977. Lectr. U. Dublin, Ireland, 1979-80; asst. prof. U. Mo., Columbia, U.S, 1980-82; assoc. prof. U. Iowa, Iowa City, U.S., 1982-83, U. Crete, Iraklio, Greece, 1983-84; assoc. prof. div. applied math., Sch. Engring. U. Patras, Greece, 1984-87, prof., 1987-91, assoc. dean sch. engring., chmn. div. applied math., 1986-87, vice-rector, 1988-91; prof. Athens U. Econs., 1991—, dir. grad. program, chair dept. stats., 1993-96, 2000—02; pres. Nat. Coun. Edn. of Greece, 1996—2000. Sec.-gen. Ministry Edn. and Religious Affairs, Greece, 1988-89, 95-96. Contbr. articles to profl. jours. Mem. Sci. Coun. of Greek Parliament, 1987—; mem. ednl. com. OECD, 1994-97; mem. governing bd. CERI of OECD, 1994-97; chmn. rsch. com., pers. com. U. Patras, 1988-91. Mem. N.Y. Acad. Sci., Am. Statis. Assn., Inst. Math. Stats., Bernoulli Soc. for Probability and Math. Stats., Greek Math. Soc., Greek Statis. Inst., Internat. Statis. Inst. Office: Athens U Econs 76 Patision St 10034 Athens Greece E-mail: jpan@aueb.gr.

PANCELLA, PAUL VINCENT, physics educator; b. St. Louis, Oct. 10, 1959; s. Frank Victor and Lorraine Dorothy (Pelletier) P. BA with honors, St. Louis U., 1981; MA, Rice U., 1984, PhD, 1987. Rsch. assoc. Bonner Lab.-Rice U., Houston, 1986-87, Cyclotron Facility Ind. U., Bloomington, 1987-90; asst. prof. Western Mich. U., Kalamazoo, 1990—, prof., chair dept. physics, 2002. Contbr. articles to Phys. Rev. Letters and Phys. Rev. C. Fellowship Rice U., 1981. Mem. Am. Phys. Soc., Phi Beta Kappa. Roman Catholic. Office: Physics Dept Western Mich U Kalamazoo MI 49008-5252

PANDIT, SUDHAKAR MADHAVRAO, engineering educator; b. Gherdi, India, Dec. 3, 1939; came to U.S., 1968; s. Madhavrao Dhondopant and Ramabai P.; m. Maneesha Sudhakar Mangala Nulkar, May 12, 1966; children: Milind, Devavrat. MS in Indsl. Engring., Pa. State U., 1970; MS in Statistics, U. Wis., 1972, PhD in Mech. Engring., 1973. Trainee engr. Kirloskar Oil Engines Ltd., Pune, India, 1961-62; engr. East Asiatic Co., Bombay, India, 1962; asst. engr. Heavy Engring. Corp., Ranchi, India, 1962-68; teaching asst. Pa. State U., State College, 1968-70; rsch. asst. U. Wis., Madison, 1970-73, lectr., 1973-76; prof. Mich. Technol. U., Houghton, 1976—. Faculty rep. Nat. Tech. U., Mpls., 1991—; ASA/NSF/NIST sr. rsch. fellow, 1993-94. Author: Time Series and System Analysis with Applications, 1983, Modal and Spectrum Analysis: Data Dependent Systems in State Space, 1991; contbr. articles to profl. jours. Recipient faculty rsch. award Mich. Technol. U., 1994; honored by Mich. Assn. Governing Bds. State Univs., 1995. Mem. ASME, Soc. Mfg. Engrs., Sigma Xi. Achievements include developed a new philosophy and methodology of system analysis, prediction and control called data dependent systems. Home: 22218 Ridge Rd Houghton MI 49931-9801 Office: Mich Technol U ME-EM Dept 1400 Townsend Dr Houghton MI 49931-1200

PANDIT, VINAY YESHWANT, business educator; b. Bombay, Dec. 28, 1943; came to U.S., 1969; s. Yeshwant Sakharam and Kusum (Barave) P.; m. Rajashree A. Agharkar, Aug. 16, 1980; children: Ungira, Meghana. BTech, Indian Inst. Technology, Bombay, 1967; MSc, King's Coll., London, 1969; MBA, Columbia U., 1971, M in Philosophy, 1975, PhD, 1978. Cert. Mgmt. Acct. Reader Columbia U., N.Y.C., 1975; asst. prof. SUNY, Fredonia, 1976-77, assoc. prof., 1981-83, asst. prof. Buffalo, 1977-81; assoc. prof. St. Bonaventure (N.Y.) U., 1983-89, chmn. faculty senate, 1988-91, prof., chmn. of mktg. and mgmt. sci., 1989-92. Cons. in field. Contbr. articles to profl. jours. Recipient Merck Sharp and Dome award, 1968, 69, Dorab Tata Travel Grant, 1967, British Ministry Technology Fellow, 1969, Columbia U. doctoral scholar, 1971-75, Kennecott Copper Fellow, 1970-71. Fellow Acad. Mktg. Sci. (award for paper 1984); mem. Decision Scis. Inst., Inst. Mgmt. Acctg., Inst. Mgmt. Sci. Office: St Bonaventure U Sch Bus Saint Bonaventure NY 14778

PANIAN, BARBARA ANNE MARIE, special education educator; b. Verona, N.J., June 12, 1951; d. Francis X.J. and Mary Catherine (Dwyer) Coughlin; m. Frank A. Panian, Aug. 17, 1974; children: Francis Xavier, George Christopher. BA in Edn., Marywood Coll., Scranton, Pa., 1973. Cert. tchr. of handicapped, N.J. Dir., counselor Camp Hope, Essex County Assn. for Retarded Citizens, East Hanover, N.J., 1963-90; tchr. spl. edn. Parsippany (N.J.)-Troy Hills Bd. Edn., 1973—. Rec. sec., life mem. Lake Parsippany Sch. PTA, 1985-89; chmn. tuition com. King of Kings Presch., Mountain Lakes, N.J., 1991-93. Named Outstanding Tchr., Parsippany-Troy Hills Bd. Edn., 1989. Mem. N.J. Edn. Assn., Essex County Assn. for Retarded Citizens (life). Avocations: sewing, embroidery, crocheting. Office: Knollwood Sch Vail Rd Parsippany NJ 07054

PANKEY, GEORGE ATKINSON, internist, educator, researcher; b. Shreveport, La., Aug. 11, 1933; s. George Edward and Annabel (Atkinson) P.; m. Patricia Ann Carreras, Sept. 22, 1972; children: Susan Margaret, Stephen Charles, Laura Atkinson, Edward Atkinson. Student, La. Poly. Inst., 1950-51; BS, Tulane U., 1954, MD, 1957; MS, U. Minn., 1961. Diplomate Am. Bd. Internal Medicine, Am. Bd. Infectious Disease. Intern U. Minn. Hosps., 1957-58, resident in internal medicine, 1958-60, Mpls. VA Hosp., Mpls. Gen. Hosp., 1960-61; practice medicine New Orleans, 1961—; partner Ochsner Clinic, New Orleans, 1968-99; asst. vis. physician Charity Hosp. La., New Orleans, 1961-62, vis. physician, 1962-75, sr. vis. physician, 1975-95; cons. infectious diseases Ochsner Clinic Found., 1963—, head sect. infectious diseases, 1972-94, dir. infectious disease training program, 1972—94, dir. infectious disease rsch., 1999—; instr. dept. medicine, div. infectious diseases Tulane U. Sch. Medicine, New Orleans, 1961-63, clin. instr., 1963-65, clin. asst. prof. medicine, 1965-68, clin. assoc. prof., 1968-73, clin. prof., 1973—; clin. prof. dept. medicine La. State U. Sch. Medicine, 1979—; clin. prof. oral diagnosis, medicine and radiology La. State U. Sch. Dentistry, 1983—. Cons. World Health Info. Services Inc., 1974; dir., founder Century Nat. Bank, New Orleans; mem. medicine test com. Nat. Bd. Med. Examiners, 1979-83; mem. infectious diseases adv. bd. Hoffman-LaRoche, 1982—; cons. Federal Air Surgeon, 1997—. Author: A Manual of Antimicrobial Therapy, 1969, (with Charles W. Gross and Michael G. Mendelsohn) Contemporary Diagnosis and Management of Sinusitis, 1997, 2d edit., 1998, 3d edit., 2000; editor: (with Geoffrey A. Kalish) Outpatient Antimicrobial Therapy - Recent Advances, 1989, Infectious Diseases Digest, 1983-95, So. Med. Assn. Program for Infectious Diseases Dial-Access, 1983-92, Ochsner Clinic Reports on Serious Hosp. Infections, 1985—, Ochsner Clinic Reports on Geriatric Infectious Diseases, 1990-93, Ochsner Clinic Reports on the Management of Sepsis, 1991-93, Infectious Disease Clinics of North America, 1994; bd. editors: Patient Care, 1969-75, Today in Medicine, 1990; mem. editl. bd. Nat. Infectious Disease Info. Network, 1983; mem. editl. adv. bd. Compendium Continuing Edn. in Dentistry, 1984—, Quinolones Bull., 1985-93,

Ochsner Jour., 1999—, Infectious Disease News, 2001—; contbr. numerous articles to profl. jours. Dir. Camp Fire Inc.; Pres. New Orleans Young Republican Club, 1969-71; adv. bd. Angie Nall Sch. Hosp., Beaumont, Tex.; trustee Nall Found. for Children, Beaumont. Recipient cert. merit Am. Acad. Gen. Practice, 1969, 70 Master ACP-ASIM (laureate award La. chpt. 1997); fellow Am. Coll. Preventive Medicine, Infectious Disease Soc. Am. (Clinician award 1996), Am. Coll. Chest Physicians, Royal Soc. Medicine; mem. Am. Soc. of Transplantation, Assn. Contamination Control (chpt. pres. 1968-70), Am. Fedn. Med. Rsch., So. Med. Assn. (certificate of award 1970), Am. Soc. Internal Medicine (del. ann. meeting 1971-72), Am. Soc. Microbiology, Am. Thoracic Soc., New Orleans Acad. Internal Medicine (pres. 1977-78, 96-97), AMA, Aerospace Med. Assn., Am. Soc. Tropical Medicine and Hygiene, Am. Venereal Disease Assn., Am. Soc. Parasitologists, Internat. Travel Medicine Soc., La. Soc. Internal Medicine (pres. 1972-73), La. Med. Soc., La. Thoracic Soc. (chmn. program com. 1968, governing council 1976-80), Surg. Infection Soc., Immunocompromised Host Soc., Musser Burch Soc., Orleans Parish Med. Soc., N.Y. Acad. Scis., Pan Am. Med. Assn. (diplomate mem. sect. internal medicine 1971, sect. pres. infectious diseases and virology 1978-85), SAR, Huguenot Soc. Founders Manakin in Colony of Va., Aviation Med. Examiner, Masons (32 deg), Shriners. Home: 5910 Prytania St New Orleans LA 70115-4348 Office: Ochsner Clinic Found 1514 Jefferson Hwy New Orleans LA 70121-2483 E-mail: gpankey@ochsner.org.

PANKO, JESSIE SYMINGTON, education educator; b. Jan. 19, 1935; Student, Hunter Coll., N.Y., 1959-62; BA, MS, SUNY, 1969; PhD, Syracuse U., 1974. Tchr. Anderson Elem. Sch., Mariana Islands, Guam, 1964-65; tchr. Herman Ave. Elem. Sch., Auburn, N.Y., 1969-71; asst. prof. edn. dept. SUNY, Cortland, N.Y., 1971-76, Utica, Rome, N.Y., 1974-76; asst. prof. applied scis. dept. Loop Coll., Chgo., 1976-77; assoc. prof. social scis. dept. Truman Coll., Chgo., 1977-81; dir. student teaching St. Xavier Coll., Chgo., 1976—, dir. undergrad. edn., 1977-79, dir. grad. edn., 1979-81, prof. edn. ctr., 1981-83, dir. grad. prog. in edn., 1983-86, dir. edn. ctr., 1986-89, dean sch. edn., 1989-92. Bd. dirs. Queen of Peace, Acad. of Our Lady; mem. com. grad. programs St. Xavier Coll., 1986-89, tchr. edn. coun., 1976—, early childhood adv. bd., 1976-92. Moffett SUNY scholar, 1969. Mem. AAUP, ASCD, Am. Assn. Colls. of Tchr. Edn. (instnl. rep. 1987-92), Assn. Ind. Liberal Arts Colls. of Tchr. Edn. (instl. rep. 1986-92), Ill. Assn. of Tchr. Edn. in Pvt. Colls. (instnl. rep. 1985-98), Ill. Assn. Colls. Tchr. Edn. (coll. rep. 1981-98, sec. 1990-92), Assn. Tchr. Educators, Nat. Assn. Educatos Young Children, Ill. Dirs. Student Tchg., Chgo. Consortium Dirs. Student Tchg. (chairperson 1976-79), Ill. Assn. Tchr. Educators, Chgo. Area Dir. Student Tchg. (chmn. 2002—), Pi Lambda Theta, Kappa Delta Pi. Office: St Xavier U 3700 W 103rd St Chicago IL 60655-3105

PANNAPACKER, WILLIAM ALBERT, III, humanities educator; b. Camden, N.J., Apr. 25, 1968; s. William Albert Jr. and Gertrude Cecelia (Rieck) P.; m. Teresa Jenkins, May 30, 1992; children: Rebecca, Jessica. BA in English, St. Joseph's U., Phila., 1990; MA in English, U. Miami, Coral Gables, Fla., 1993; AM in English and Am. lit., Harvard U., 1997, PhD History Am. Civilization, 1999. Lectr. English U. Miami, 1992-93, Miami-Dade C.C., 1993; lectr. Am. Studies Brandeis U., Waltham, Mass., 1996; project supr. W.E.B. DuBois Inst., Cambridge, Mass., 1995-97; tchg. fellow history and lit., English, fine arts, comparative literature Harvard U., Cambridge, 1995-98, lectr., 1999-2000; asst. prof. English, Towsley rsch. scholar Hope Coll., Holland, Mich., 2000—. Sr. cons. History Assocs., Inc., Washington, Rockville, Md., 2000. Author: Revised Lives: Whitman, Religion, and Constructions of Identity in Nineteenth-Century Anglo-American Culture, 2003; contbr. articles to lit., hist., polit. ednl. (pedagogy) and reference publs.; columnist Chronicle of Higher Edn., 1998—; mem. editl. bd. Mickle St. Rev. Recipient Bowdoin prize, 1994, 99, Bell prize, 1995, 98, Hofer prize, 1996, Arnold prize, 1998; Whiting fellow, 1998-99; Mellon Faculty Devel. grantee, 2001-2002, 2002—; Mellon Found. Curriculum Devel. grantee, 2002—; Towsley Rsch. scholar, Hope Coll., 2003—. Mem. AAUP, MLA (mem. del. assembly 2000-2003), Am. Studies Assn. (task force on employment in higher edn. 1999-2003), Am. Lit. Assn. Avocations: book collecting, gardening, art. Office: Hope Coll Dept English 321 Lubbers Hall Holland MI 49422-9000

PANNELL, SYLVIA JO HILLYARD, drama/theatrical designer, educator; b. Phillipi, W.Va., Jan. 12, 1945; d. William David and Forest (Stewart) H.; m. Clifton Wyndham Pannell, Dec. 9, 1994; stepchildren: Alexander, Richard, Charles, Thomas. AA, Central Fla. Jr. Coll., 1965; BS, Fla. State U., 1967, MFA, 1970. Instr. drama S.W. Mo. State U., Springfield, 1970-74; asst. prof. U. New Orleans, 1974-77; drama prof., costume designer, head design program U. Ga., Athens, 1977—, assoc. dept. head, 1979-95. Costume designer Asolo State Theater, Sarasota, Fla., 1968, Coll. Light Opera Co., Falmouth, Mass., 1970, ABC-TV Breaking Away, Athens, 1979, Highlands (N.C.) Playhouse, 1989-95; costume designer, theater mgr. Jekyll Island (Ga.) Musical Comedy Fest, 1984-88, Highlands Playhouse, 1989-94 Co-author: Varieties of Theatrical Art, 1985; contbr. articles to profl. jours.; book review editor Theater Design & Tech., 1991—. Bd. mem. Helios Arts Found., 1993-95, Torch Club Internat., 1992—. Recipient Creative Rsch. award, U. Ga. Rsch. Found., 1985, Sandy Beaver Teaching award Franklin Coll. Arts and Sci., 1982, purchase prize, prague quadrinnele recognition for costume designs for HMS Pinafore, 1986. Fellow U.S. Inst. for Theatre Tech. (bd. dirs. 1979-85, 90—); mem. Costume Soc. Am., U.S. Inst. for Theater Tech., U. & Coll. Theater Assn. (v.p. design & tech. 1982-84), Southeastern Theater Conf., U. Ga. Tchg. Acad., Phi Kappa Phi, Phi Beta Delta. Avocations: jogging, hiking, yoga. Home: 520 W Cloverhurst Ave Athens GA 30606-4216 Office: U Ga Dept Drama Baldwin St Athens GA 30602 E-mail: hillyard@arches.uga.edu.

PANUSKA, JOSEPH ALLAN, academic administrator; b. Balt., Md., July 3, 1927; s. Joseph William and Barbara Agnes (Preller) P. BS, Loyola Coll., Balt., 1948; PhD, St. Louis U., 1958; STL, Woodstock Coll., 1961; LLD (hon.), U. Scranton, 1974; LHD (hon.), Marywood Coll., 1992; degree (hon.), Trnava (Slovakia) U., 1997. Joined S.J., 1948; ordained priest Roman Cath. Ch., 1960. Instr. dept. physiology Emory U. Sch. Medicine, 1962-63; asst. prof. biology Georgetown U., 1963-66, assoc. prof., 1966-72, prof., 1973; provincial, bd. dir. Jesuit Conf. Md. Province (S.J.), 1973-79; acad. v.p., dean faculties, prof. biology Boston Coll., 1979-82; pres. U. Scranton, Pa., 1982-98, pres. emeritus, 1998—; rector Jesuit Ctr., 1998—. Mem. Pa. Commn. Ind. Colls. and Univs., 1982-98, mem. exec. com., treas., 1987-91, vice chmn., 1988-89, chmn., 1990-91; mem. President's Commn., NCAA, 1989-90. Mem. editl. bd. Crybiology, 1968-88, editor-in-chief, 1971-74; contbr. chpts. to books, articles to sci. rsch. jours. Mem. corp. Am. Found. Biol. Rsch., 1967-85, pres. bd. dirs., 1974-79, v.p., 1979-83; trustee Loyola Coll., 1979-85, St. Joseph's U., 1979-84, U. Scranton, 1970-73, 1982-98, St. Peter's Coll., 1971-72, Woodstock Coll., 1973-76, Fordham U., 1982-88, Cambridge Ctr. for Social Studies, 1973-79 (pres. 1973-79), Corp. Roman Cath. Clergymen, 1973-79 (pres. 1973-79); rector Jesuit Community at Georgetown U., 1970-73; bd. dirs. United Way Pa., 1985-87, Scranton Preparatory Sch., 1984-90, Scranton Area Found., 1997-98; chmn. Pa. Commn. for Ind. Colls. and Univs., 1990-91; bd. dirs. John Carroll U., 1992-98, Nat. Inst. Environ. Renewal, 1992-98, Woodstock Theol. Ctr., Washington, 1998-2001, St. Joseph's Prep. Sch., Phila., 1998-2001, Alvernia Coll., 2001—; bd. visitors Panuska Coll. Profl. Studies, U. Scranton, 1998--. NIH postdoctoral fellow, 1962-63; recipient Danforth Found. Harbison prize for disting. teaching, 1969, B'nai B'rith Americanism award, 1997, recipient from 2001, Michelini award Outstanding Svc. to Higher Edn. AICUP (Assoc. Indep. C and U. Pa.), 2001; vis. fellow St. Edmunds Coll., Cambridge U., 1969; college named J.A. Panuska College of Professional Studies, Univ. at Scranton. Mem. Am. Physiol. Soc., Soc. for Cryobiology, Soc. Exptl. Biology and Medicine, Assn. Jesuit Colls. and Univs. (bd. dirs. 1982-98, treas. 1993-96), Pa. Assn. Colls. and Univs. (exec. com., adv. com. to State Bd. Edn. 1990-91), Scranton C. of C. Home and Office: Jesuit Ctr PO Box 223 Wernersville PA 19565-0223 E-mail: jescntsec@talon.net.

PAOLINI, GILBERTO, literature and science educator; b. L'Aquila, Italy; naturalized citizen, 1954; s. John and Assunta Angela (Turavani) P.; m. Claire Jacqueline Landro; children: Angela Janet, John Frank. BA, U. Buffalo, 1957, MA, 1959; postgrad., Middlebury Coll., summer 1960, 61; PhD, U. Minn., 1965. Lectr. Spanish Rosary Hill Coll., Buffalo, 1957-58; instr. Italian and Latin lit. U. Mass., Amherst, 1958-60; instr. Spanish and Italian Syracuse U., 1962-65, asst. prof., 1965-67; assoc. prof. Spanish lit. Tulane U., New Orleans, 1967-76, prof., 1976—, dir. Tulane scholars and honors program, 1981-83, chmn. colloquia dept., 1981-83. Originator Spanish Culture Week, New Orleans, 1977, 79; chmn. adv. com. Jambalaya program Nat. Endowment Humanities, New Orleans, 1975-80; Spanish essay reader Ednl. Testing Svc., Princeton, 1979-85; founder, gen. chmn. La. Conf. on Hispanic Langs. and Lits., 1981, 83, 85, 87, 89, 93, 95, 97, 99. Author: Bartolome Soler: novelista: Procedimientos estilísticos, 1963; An Aspect of Spiritualistic Naturalism in the Novel of B.P. Galdos: Charity, 1969, La Vita Transecolare nel Contado Aquilano, 2003; mem. editl. bd.: Forum Italicum, 1967-71, Critica Hispanica, 1979—, Discurso Literario, 1985—, Letras Peninsulares, 1987—, Ojáncano, 1994—; assoc. editor: South Central MLA Bull, 1978-80; editor: La Chispa: Selected Procs., 1981-99, Papers on Romance Literary Relations, 1983; cons. editor South Central Rec., 1988-99; contbr. articles to profl. jours. With AUS, 1952-54, USAFRES, 1954-57. Recipient Disting. Service award Sociedad Espanola, 1979, Knight Cross of Order of Isabel the Catholic, 1984; subject of Festscrift Studies, Honor of Gilberto Paolini, 1996. Mem. MLA, AAUP, Am. Assn. Tchrs. Spanish and Portuguese (chmn. pub. rels. com. 1981-86, pres. La. chpt. 1979-81, 88-89), Am. Assn. Tchrs. Italian, Am. Assn. Advancement Humanities, Soc. for Lit. and Sci., Asociacion Internacional de Hispanistas, Southeastern Am. Soc. 18th Century Studies (exec. v.p.), Assn. Internat. Galdosistas, Soc. Literatura Española del Siglo XIX, Phi Sigma Iota, Sigma Delta Pi (v.p. for S.W. 1989-92). Office: Tulane Univ 304 Newcomb Hall New Orleans LA 70118 E-mail: gpaolini@tulane.edu.

PAOLUCCI, ANNE ATTURA, playwright, poet, English and comparative literature educator, educational consultant; b. Rome; d. Joseph and Lucy (Guidoni) Attura; m. Henry Paolucci(dec.). BA, Barnard Coll; MA, Columbia U., PhD, 1963; hon. degree, Lehman Coll., CUNY, 1995. Mem. faculty English dept. Brearley Sch., NYC, 1957-59; asst. prof. English and comparative lit. CCNY, 1959-69; univ. rsch. prof. St. John's U., Jamaica, NY, 1969-75, prof. English, 1975-77, acting head dept. English, 1973-74, chmn. dept. English, 1982-91, dir. doctor of arts degree program in English, 1982-97; ednl. cons.; editl. cons. Bagehot Coun. Fulbright lectr. in Am. drama U. Naples, Italy, 1965-67; spl. lectr. U. Urbino, summers 1966-67, U. Bari, 1967, univs. Bologna, Catania, Messina, Palermo, Milan, Pisa, 1965-67; disting. adj. vis. prof. Queens Coll., CUNY; bd. dir. World Centre for Shakespeare Studies, 1972— ; spl. guest Yugoslavia Ministry of Culture, 1972; rep. US at Internat. Poetry Festival, Yugoslavia, 1981; founder, exec. dir. Council on Nat. Lits., 1974— ; mem. exec. com. Conf. Editors Learned Jour.-MLA, 1975—85; del. to Fgn. Lang. Jours., 1977—85; mem. adv. bd. Commn. on Tech. and Cultural Transformation, UNESCO, 1978—80; vis. fellow Humanities Rsch. Centre, Australian Nat. U., 1979; rep. US woman playwright Inter-Am. Women Writers Congress, Ottawa, Ont., Can., 1978; organizer, chmn. profl. symposia, meetings; TV appearances; hostess Mag. in Focus, Channel 31, NYC, 1971-72; mem. N.Am. Adv. Council Shakespeare Globe Theatre Ctr., 1981— ; mem. Nat. Grad. Fellows Program Fellowship Bd., 1985—87; mem. Nat. Garibaldi Centennial Com., 1981; trustee Edn. Scholarship, Grants Com. of NIAF, 1990-94; guest speaker with E. Albee Ohio No. State U., 1990; Appointed by Pres. Reagan to Nat. Council on the Humanities, 1986-1993; One of the 10 top Women in Bus. in Queens, 2003. Author (with H. Paolucci) books, including: Hegel On Tragedy, 1962, new edition, 2001, From Tension to Tonic: The Plays of Edward Albee, 1972, new edit., 2000, Pirandello's Theater: The Recovery of the Modern Stage for Dramatic Art, 1974, 2d edit. 2002, Henry Paolucci: Selected Writings on Literature and the Arts; Sci. and Astronomy; Law, Govt., and Pol. Sci., 1999, Dante's Gallery of Rogues, 2001, Do Me a Favor (and other short stories), 2001 (nominated for the Pulitzer Prize), Poems Written for Sbek's Mummies, Marie Menken, and Other Important Persons, Places, and Things, 1977, Eight Short Stories, 1977, Sepia Tones, 1985, 2nd edit., 1986; plays include: Minions of the Race (Medieval and Renaissance Conf. of Western Mich. U. Drama award 1972), video version, 2002, Cipango!, 1985, pub. as book, 1985, 86, videotape excerpts, 1986, revision, 1990; performed NYC and Washington, 1987-88, Winterthur Mus., U. Del., 1990; The Actor in Search of His Mask, 1987, Italian translation and prodn., Genoa, 1987, The Short Season, Naples, 1967, Cubiculo, NY, 1973, German translation, Vienna, 1996, mini-prodn. of Minions of the Race, The Players, 1999, video prodn. 2002, In the Green Room (play), 1999, Three Short Plays, 1995; poems Riding the Mast Where It Swings, 1980, In the Green Room (orig. play), 1999; Gorbachev in Concert, 1991, Queensboro Bridge (and other Poems), 1995 (Pulitzer prize nominee 1995-96), Terminal Degrees, 1997; contbr. numerous articles, rev. to profl. jour.; editor, author intro. to: Dante's Influence on Am. Writers, 1977; gen. editor tape-cassette series China, 1977, 78; founder Coun. on Nat. Lit.; gen. editor series Rev. Nat. Lit., 1970-2000, CNL/Quar. World Report, 1974-76, semi-ann., 1977-84, ann., 1985-2000; full-length TV tape of play Cipango! for pub. TV and ednl. TV with original music by Henry Paolucci, 1990; featured in PBS psl. Italian-Americans II: A Beautiful Song, 1998; translations of Poems by Leopardi (with Thomas Bergin), 2003; In Wolf's Clothing, (mystery), 2003. Pres. Reagan appointee Nat. Grad. Fellows Program Fellowship Bd., 1985—86, Nat. Coun. Humanities, 1986—, Ann. award FIERI, 1990; bd. dirs. Am. Soc. Italian Legions of Merit, chmn. cultural com., 1990—; bd. dirs. Italian Heritage and Culture City-wide com., 1986—; pres. Columbus: Countdown 1992 Fedn.; mem. Gov. Cuomo's Heritage Legacy Project for Schs., 1989—; trustee CUNY, 1996—, chairwoman bd. trustees, 1997—99; mem. adv. com. on edn. N.Y. State Senate, 1996—. Decorated cavaliere Italian Republic, commendatore Order of Merit (Italy); named one of 10 Outstanding Italian Ams. in Washington, awarded medal by Amb. Rinaldo Petrignani, 1986; recipient Notable Rating for Mags. in Focus series N.Y. Times, 1972, Woman of Yr. award Dr. Herman Henry Scholarship Found., 1973, Amita award, 1970, award Women's Press Club N.Y., 1974, Gold medal for Quincentenary Can. trustee NIAF, 1990, ann. awards Consortium of Italian-Am. Assns., 1991, Am.-Italian Hist. Assn., 1991, 1st Columbus award Cath. Charities, 1991, Leone di San Marco award Italian Heritage Coun. of Bronx and Westchester Counties, 1992, Children of Columbus award Order of Sons of Italy in Am., 1993, 1st Nat. Elena Cornaro award Order of Sons of Italy, 1993, Golden Lion award, 1997, Ann. award Am. Italian Cultural Roundtable, 1997, Am. Italian Tchrs. Lifetime Achievement award, 1997, Italian-Am. Legislator's award, Albany, 1997, N.Y. State Italian-Am. Legis. Lifetime Achievement award, 1997, Columbus Citizens Fedn. Ann. award, 1997, Italian Welfare League award, 1998, Queens Coun. on Arts award, 1998, N.Y. State Conservative Party Bronx com. award, 1998, Woman of Distinction award Kingsborough C.C./CUNY, 1999; named one of "Ten Top Queens Women in Bus., 2003; Columbia U. Woodbridge hon. fellow, 1961-62; Am. Coun. Learned Socs. grantee Internat. Pirandello Congress, Agrigento, Italy, 1978; recipient Woman of Distinction award N.Y. State Senate, 2000. Mem. Internat. Shakespeare Assn., Shakespeare Assn. Am., Renaissance Soc. Am., Internat. Comparative Lit. Assn., Am. Comparative Lit. Assn., MLA, Am. PEN, Hegel Soc. Am., Dante Soc. Am. (v.p. 1976-77), Am. Found. Italian Arts and Letters (founder, pres.), Pirandello Soc. (pres. 1978-85), Am. Soc. Italian Legions of Merit (bd. dir. 1990-93). Achievements include pioneering work in multi-comparative literary studies.

PAONESSA, M. SUZANNE, budget analyst; b. Albany, N.Y., May 1, 1974; d. Thomas and Mary Laura (Maresca) Paonessa. BS in Fin., Siena Coll., 1996. Fin. mgmt. specialist U.S. Dept. Energy, Schenectady (N.Y.) Naval Reactors Office, 1996-99; assoc. dir. fin. aid Siena Coll., 1999-2001; assoc. dir. budget and bus. svcs. U. Maine, Orono, 2001—, instr., Profl. Employees Adv. Coun. (PEAC). Treas. Schenectady Naval Reactors Office Employee Assn., 1997—98. Vol. YMCA; ch. lector, greeter; co-dir. Siena Coll. Friendly's Fanfest, 1997—98; mem. Siena Coll. Career Adv. Network. Mem.: Nat. Youth Sports Coaches Assn., DOE Women's Golf League (treas. 1998—, named Most Improved Player 1998), Fin. Mgmt. Assn., 21st Century Leaders Soc., Kensho-Do Karate Club (asst. instr. 1998—2000, brown belt), Sigma Beta Delta, Delta Epsilon Sigma, Alpha Kappa Alpha. Roman Catholic. Avocations: Karate, golf, softball, soccer, volleyball. E-mail: sqboo@yahoo.com.

PAPACHRISTOU, PATRICIA TOWNE, economics educator; b. Hartford, Conn., Oct. 16, 1946; d. George Robert and Lois Katherine (Stretch) Towne; m. Gerald Christopher Papachristou, Aug. 23, 1969; children—Mark Andrew, Angela Marie. BA in Polit. Sci. cum laude, Trinity Coll., Washington, 1968; MA in Polit. Sci., Duke U., 1970; MA in Econs., Memphis State U., 1975, MBA, 1979; postgrad. U. Miss., 1979— . Tchr., chair social studies dept. Immaculate Conception HS, Memphis, 1971-78; instr. Christian Bros. Coll., Memphis, 1980-84, asst. prof. economics, 1984-87, assoc. prof. econ., 1988-95, prof. econs., 1995—; intern Kaiser-Permanente Health Services Research Ctr., Portland, Oreg., 1984. Contbr. articles to profl. jours. Non-service fellow U. Miss., 1979-80; Jane Cassels Record scholar Kaiser Health Rsch. Ctr., 1983. Mem. Am. Econ. Assn., Atlantic Econ. Soc., MidSouth Economists, Missouri Valley Econ. Assn. (v.p. 2003—), Omicron Delta Epsilon, Pi Gamma Mu, Delta Sigma Pi. Roman Catholic. Avocations: bridge, camping. Home: 2858 Shelley Cv Memphis TN 38115-1814 E-mail: ppapachr@cbu.edu.

PAPADAKOS, PETER JOHN, critical care physician, educator; b. Bklyn., Feb. 4, 1957; s. John and Irene (Vahaviolos) P.; m. Susan E. Dantoni; 1 child, Yanni. BA, NYU, 1979; MD, CUNY, 1983. Intern, then resident in surgery Roosevelt Hosp., N.Y.C., 1983-85; resident in anesthesiology Mt. Sinai Hosp., N.Y.C., 1985-87, fellow in critical care medicine, 1987-88; prof. anesthesiology and surgery U. Rochester (N.Y.) Sch. Medicine, 1988—2003, also dir. divsn. critical care medicine, 2000—, prof. anesthesiology and surgery, 2003—. Prof. respiratory care SUNY. Editor: (textbook) The Intensive Care Manual, 2001; editor-in-chief Controversies in Critical Care; sect. editor Intensive Care Medicine Jour. Applied Cardiopulmonary Pathophysiology, Internet Jour. Emergency and Intensive Care Medicine, Intensive Care & Shock; contbr. articles to profl. jours., numerous chpts. to books. Trustee Incurable Illness Found., N.Y.C., 1986-88. Recipient rsch. award USN, 1975, Pres.'s citation Soc. Critical Care Medicine, 1996. Fellow Coll. Critical Care Medicine, Am. Coll. Chest Physicians; mem. Shock Soc., Soc. Critical Care, Thoracic Soc. Achievements include research on effect of inverse ratio ventilation and pressure regulated volume control on acute respiratory distress syndrome, research on septic shock and oxygen delivery, basic science work on pulmonary pathophysiology of acute lung failure; research on nitric oxide in treatment of lung failure and acute respiratory distress syndrome; research on open lung concept. Office: U Rochester 601 Elmwood Ave Rochester NY 14642-0001 E-mail: peter_papadakos@urmc.rochester.edu.

PAPADIMITRIOU, DIMITRI BASIL, economist, college administrator; b. Salonica, Greece, June 9, 1946; came to U.S., 1965, naturalized, 1974; s. Basil John and Ellen (Takas) P.; m. Rania Antonopoulos. BA, Columbia U., 1970; PhD, New Sch. U., 1986. V.p., asst. sec. ITT Life Ins. Co. N.Y., N.Y.C., 1970-73; exec. v.p., sec., treas. William Penn Life Ins. Co. N.Y., N.Y.C., 1973-78, also dir.; exec. v.p., provost Bard Coll., 1978—, Jerome Levy prof. econs., 1978—; exec. dir. Bard Ctr., 1980—; pres. Levy Econs. Inst., 1988—; disting. scholar Shanghai Acad. Social Scis., 2002. Adj. lectr. econs. New Sch. U., 1975-76; fellow Ctr. for Advanced Econ. Studies, 1983; Wye fellow Aspen Inst.; bd. dirs. William Penn Life Ins. Co. N.Y.; bd. govs. Levy Econs. Inst., 1986—; mem. subcoun. capital allocation Competitiveness Policy Coun.; mem., vice-chmn. Congrl. Commn. to Rev. the Trade Deficit, 2000-2002; mem. adv. com. Women's World Banking; radio econs. commentator Sta. WAMC, NPR, PRI, Money Radio, Marketplace. Author: Employment Policy Community Development and the Underclass, 1997, Employment Policy: Theory and Practice, 1998; co-author: Community Development Banking, 1993, A Path to Community Development, 1993, An Alternative in Small Business Finance, 1994, Monetary Policy Uncovered: The Federal Reserve's Experiment with Unobservables, 1994, Targeting Inflation: The Effects of Monetary Policy on the CPI and Its Housing Component, 1996, The Fed Should Lower Interest Rates More, 1998, What to Do With the Surplus, 1998, How Can We Provide for the Baby Boomers in their Old Age?, 1999, Can Social Security Be Saved, 1999, Fiscal Policy for the Coming Recession, 2001, Is Personal Debt Sustainable?, 2002, Deflation: Treating the Disease not the Symptom, 2003; editor, contbr. Profits, Deficits and Instability, 1992, Aspects of Distribution of Wealth and Income, 1994, Stability in the Financial System, 1996, Modernizing Financial Systems, 1998, Employment Policies: Theories and Evidence, 1999; co-editor, contbr.: Poverty and Prosperity in the USA in the Late Twentieth Century, 1993, Financial Conditions and Macroeconomic Performance, 1992; bd. editors Ea. Econ.Jour., Rev. of Income and Wealth; book reviewer Econ. Jour., Ea. Econ. Jour. Trustee, treas. Am. Symphony Orch. Mem. Am. Econ. Assn., Am.-Hellenic Banker Assn., Royal Econ. Soc., Am. Fin. Assn., Econ. Club N.Y. (The Bretton Woods com.), European Econ. Assn., Eastern Econ. Assn., Econ. Sci. Chamber of Greece, Assn. for Evolutionary Econs. Home and Office: Bard Coll Annandale On Hudson NY 12504

PAPAGEORGE, TOD, photographer, educator; b. Portsmouth, N.H., Aug. 1, 1940; s. Theodore and Eileen Elizabeth (Flanigan) P.; m. Pauline Whitcomb, Feb. 3, 1962 (div. 1970); m. Deborah Flomenhaft, June 21, 1987; 1 child, Theo. BA in English Lit., U. N.H., 1962; MA, Yale U., 1979. Lectr. in photography MIT, Cambridge, Mass., 1974-75; lectr. in visual studies Harvard U., Cambridge, 1975-76; Walker Evans prof. of photography Yale U., New Haven, 1978—. Vis. instr. in photography The Parsons Sch. Design, N.Y.C., 1969-72, The Pratt Inst. of Art, N.Y.C., 1971-74, The Cooper Union Sch. Art, N.Y.C., 1971-74; adj. lectr. in photography Queens Coll., N.Y.C., 1972-74. Guest dir. exhbn., Mus. Modern Art, N.Y.C., 1977, Yale Art Gallery, 1981; one-man shows include Light Gallery, N.Y.C., 1973, 79, Cronin Gallery, Houston, 1977, Art Inst. Chgo., 1978, Galerie Zabriskie, Paris, 1979, Stills Photography Group, Edinburgh, Scotland, 1980, Daniel Wolf Gallery, N.Y.C., 1981, 85, Akron (Ohio) Art Mus., 1981, Sheldon Meml. Art Gallery, Lincoln, Nebr., 1981, Franklin Parrasch Gallery, N.Y.C., 1991; group shows include Mus. Modern Art, N.Y.C., 1971, 73, 74, 76, 77, 78, 79, 91, 97, 99, 2002, Lowe Art Mus., Coral Gables, Fla., 1974, Balt. Mus. Art, 1975, Mus. Fine Arts, Boston, 1976, 91, Thomas Gibson Gallery, London, 1976, Galerie Zabriskie, Paris, 1977, 87, U. Colo., 1977, Houston Mus. Fine Arts, 1977, Art Inst. Chgo., 1979, Corcoran Gallery Art, Washington, 1980, Fraenkel Gallery, San Francisco, 1981, Daniel Wolf Gallery, N.Y.C., 1982, 83, 86, Albright-Knox Mus., Buffalo, 1983, The Whitney Mus. Art, N.Y.C., 1983, The Photographer's Gallery, London, 1983, Nat. Mus. Am. Art, Washington, 1984, The Dog Mus., N.Y.C., 1984, The Barbican Nat. Gallery, London, 1985, Light Gallery, N.Y.C., 1985, Centro Reina Sophia, Madrid, Spain, 1987, N.Y. State Mus., Albany, 1987, Worcester (Mass.) Art Mus., 1990, 94, Jewish Mus. Art, Wellesley, Mass., 1990, Musee De La Photographie, Mont-Sur-Marchienne, Belgium, 1991, Franklin Parrasch Gallery, N.Y.C., 1992, Yale Art Gallery, New Haven, 1999, Greenberg Van Doren Gallery, N.Y.C., 1999, others; represented in permanent collections Mus. Modern Art, Art Inst. Chgo., Boston Mus. Fine Arts, Yale U. Art Gallery, Bibliothéque Nationale, Paris, Mus. Fine Arts, Houston, Dallas Mus. Fine Arts, Nat. Mus. Am. Art, Washington, J.B. Speed

Mus., Louisville, Seattle Art Mus., Kunsthaus, Zurich, Switzerland, others; commd. by Seagrams Corp., 1975, Mus. Modern Art, N.Y., 1977, AT&T, 1978, Yale U. Art Gallery, 1981, Warner Comm., 1983; author: Walker Evans and Robert Frank: An Essay on Influence, 1981, What We Bought: The Photographs of Robert Adams, 2002; editor: Public Relations: The Photographs of Garry Winogrand, 1977. Guggenheim fellow, 1970, 77; Nat. Endowment Arts fellow, 1973, 76 Achievements include being subject of numerous articles and publs. Home: 122 Cottage St New Haven CT 06511-2406 Office: Yale U Sch Art PO Box 208339 New Haven CT 06520-8339 E-mail: tod.papageorge@yale.edu.

PAPANEK, GUSTAV FRITZ, economist, educator; b. Vienna, July 12, 1926; s. Ernst and Helen Papanek; m. Hanna Kaiser, June 13, 1947; children: Thomas H., Joanne R. Papanek Orlando. BA in Agrl. Econs, Cornell U., 1947; MA in Econs, Harvard U., 1949, PhD, 1951. Economist, dep. dir. program planning for Asia, tech. coop. adminstrn. Dept. State, 1951-53; from econ. adv. to dir. adv. group to planning commn. Harvard U., Pakistan, 1954-58, from dep. dir. to dir. devel. adv. svc., 1958—70, dir. adv. group to planning commn., 1971—73; prof. econs. Boston U., 1974-92, prof. emeritus, 1992—, chmn. dept., 1974-83, interim dir., 1977-80, dir. Ctr. Asian Devel. Studies, 1983-90, dir. Asian program, 1991-92; dir., cons. team devel. studies to planning commn. Govt. of Indonesia, 1987-89; pres. Boston Inst. Developing Econs., Ltd. (BIDE), 1987—; dir. policy adv. team to Federated States of Micronesia, 1995—2002. Cons. econ. crisis Govt. of Indonesia, 1998—2002; co-dir. pro-poor growth study U.S. AID, 2002—; cons. in field. Author: (book) Pakistan's Development: Social Goals and Private Incentives, 1967, The Indonesian Economy, 1980, Development Strategy, Growth Equity and the Political Process in Southern Asia, 1986; co-author: Decision Making for Economic Development, 1971, The Indian Economy, 1988, others; contbr. articles to profl. jours. With U.S. Army, 1944—46. Grantee, Ford Found., AID, World Bank, UN Devel. Program, UN Univ., HEW, Asian Devel. Bank. Mem.: Pakistan Econ. Assn., Assn. Asian Studies (pres. New Eng. conf. 1975—77), Assn. Comparative Econ. Studies (pres. 1982), Soc. Internat. Devel. (past mem. exec. com.), Am. Agrl. Econs. Assn., Am. Econs. Assn. Home and Office: 2 Mason St Lexington MA 02421-6315 E-mail: papanek@bide.com.

PAPAS, IRENE KALANDROS, English language educator, poet, writer; b. Balt., Mar. 16, 1931; d. Louis and Kounia (Stamatakis) Kalandros; m. Steve S. Papas, Sept. 10, 1952; children: Fotene Stephenie Tina, Barbara Counia. AA with highest honors, Balt. C.C.; BA magna cum laude, Goucher Coll., 1968; MA in English Lang. and Lit., U. Md., 1974, postgrad., 1980—. Lic. theology profl. Tchr./tutor various schs., Balt., 1965—; tchr. theology U. Md. Free Univ., College Park, 1979—; author/pub. Ledger Publs., Silver Spring, Md., 1982—; TV producer Arts and Humanities Prodns., Silver Spring, 1991—. Lectr. in English, philosophy, Montgomery Coll., Goucher Coll.; instr. English Composition, World Literature, U. Md., College Park, 1968—; adj. faculty various colls.; White House duty, 1997—. Author: Irene's Ledger Songs of Deliverance, 1982, Irene's Ledger Song at Sabbatyon, 1986, Small Meditations, Leaves for Healing, 1996; prodr./dir. tv. progs. Election judge, Montgomery County (Md.) Suprs. Bd. of Elections, 1980's, 90's; tutor in literacy, 1989. Recipient First Prize Arts and Culture Category Smithsonian Inst., 1991; honored 6th Annual Awards Ceremony Montgomery Community, 1991. Mem. AAUP, Internat. Platform Assn., Nat. Poetry Assn., Phi Beta Kappa. Democrat. Greek Orthodox. Avocations: art/iconography, calligraphy, music, needlepoint. Office: PO Box 10303 Silver Spring MD 20914-0303

PAPENTHIEN, RUTH MARY, fiber artist, retired educator; b. Milw., Aug. 30, 1924; d. Roy Oliver and Hazel Mary (Heyer) P. BA, U. Wis., 1946; student, The Konstfackskolan, Stockholm, 1959-60; MFA, Cranbrook Acad. Art, Bloomfield Hills, Mich., 1965. Elem. sch. tchr. Milw. Pub. Schs., 1948-63; instr. fiber art Alverno Coll., Milw., 1966-67; vis. instr. fiber art Sch. Fine Arts Ohio State U., Columbus, 1967-72; fiber art instr. Arrowmont Sch. Arts and Crafts, Gatlinburg, Tenn., summer 1970; vis. artist fiber art Ball State U., Muncie, Ind., 1972; asst. prof. fiber art Tyler Sch. Art Temple U., Phila., summer 1973. Tchr. Cheley Colo. Camps, Estes Park, 1956-59, 64, 65. One-woman shows include Alverno Coll., Milw., 1967, Ohio State U. Union, Columbus, 1968, The Liturgical Arts, St. Luke's Meth. Ch., Oklahoma City, 1974; exhibited in group shows in Wis. Designer Craftsmen exhbns. at Milw. Arts Ctr. (Anonymous Donor award 1963, 64, Court of Honor 1965, 66, 70, 71), Miss. River Craft Exhbn., Brooks Meml. Art Gallery, Memphis, 1963, Detroit Art Inst., 1964, Rockford (Ill.) Art Assn. Burpee Gallery of Art, 1964, 65 (1st pl. and hon. mention 1966), Rochester (Minn.) Art Ctr., 1967, Capital U., Columbus, Ohio (Liturgical Art award 1967, 71, 73), Coll. of Wooster, Ohio, 1970, Midland (Mich.) Art Ctr., 1972, Ball State U., Muncie, Ind., 1972, S.C. Johnson Collection Contemporary Crafts, 1970-72, Ohio State U., 1972, Huntington Nat. Bank and Trust Co., Columbus, 1972, Ozaukee Art Ctr., Cedarburg, Wis., 1976, West Bend (Wis.) Gallery Fine Arts, 1978, Peninsula Mus. Art, Newport News, Va., 1995, Blue Skies Gallery, Hampton, Va., 1997, 98; represented in permanent collections Alverno Coll., Milw., Ohio Hist. Ctr., Columbus, Ohio Med. Indemnity Inc., Columbus, Karlsberger and Assoc. AIA, Columbus, U. Rochester (N.Y.) Meml. Gallery, IBM Bldg., Columbus, The Prairie Archives, Milw. Art Ctr.; represented in pvt. collections in Ohio, Wis., Fla., La., Calif., Va.; contbr. artwork to jours. Home: 208 Woodmere Dr Williamsburg VA 23185-3935

PAPI, LIZA RENIA, artist, writer, educator; b. Malacacheta, Minas Gerais, Brazil, Jan. 19, 1949; came to U.S., 1978; d. Rivadavia and Lair Bronzon P.; 1 child, Mourrice O. BA, Inst. Fine Arts Rio de Janeiro, 1974; MFA, CUNY, 1992. Art instr. CUNY, Henry St. Settlement, N.Y.C., Third St. Music; illustrator Studio T. Graphics. Artist in residence Mus. del Barrio, N.Y.C.; dir. publicity Art Sphere Cultural Ctr., N.Y.C., 1990-91; coord. Americanos, N.Y.C., 1990-94. Author: The Vanishing Beetles, 1991, Carnavalia, African Brazilian Folklore and Crafts, 1994. Residency planning grantee N.Y. Found. Arts, 1994, Anneberg Art-in-Edn. grantee, 1998—. Mem. Soka Gakkai Internat., Coll. Art Assn., The Fgn. Press. Buddhist. Avocations: contemprary dance, biking. Office: Apt 6P 400 Chambers St New York NY 10282-1006

PAPIN, NANCY SUE, educational computer coordinator; b. Long Beach, Calif., Apr. 5, 1951; d. Emil Richard and Marjorie (Wright) DeSmet; m. Robert N. Papin, Oct. 5, 1971; children: Karina L., Brianne M. Student, Apple Computer Co., 1987-91, Cypress Coll., 1997—; BA in History, postgrad., U. Nev., Las Vegas, 2003—. Sec. Sebring Products, Inc., L.A., 1970—74, bus. owner, 1970—, Sebring Internat. of Hollywood, Calif., 1971-74; computer coord. Centralia Sch. Dist., Buena Park, Calif., 1986-95; Apple edn. advisor Apple Computer Co., 1993-95. Mem. edn. tech. com. Centralia Sch. Dist., Buena Park, 1991-95; mem. sch. site coun. Los Coyotes Sch., La Palma, Calif., 1986-92, San Marino Sch., Buena Park, 1991-94; mem. grant writing com. Kennedy H.S., La Palma, 1991-99; mem. Vision 21 coordinating counsel Centralia Sch. Dist.; mem. sch. site coun. Walker Jr. H.S., 1994-95; mem. tech. com. J.F. Kennedy H.S., 1996-2000. Author: History/Social Science Frameworks Correlation, 1991. Republican. Roman Catholic. Avocations: computers, sewing, needlepoint, reading.

PAPINEAU, PATRICIA AGNES, special education educator; b. Balt., Feb. 14, 1951; d. Patrick Joseph and Catherine (Herb) McHugh; m. Ronald George Papineau, Nov. 25, 1971; children: Scott, Patrick. BS in Spl. Edn. and Early Childhood, Bowie (Md.) U., 1988; MEd in Elem. Math., Salisbury U., 1992; EdD, Wilmington Coll., 1999. Tchr. days Caroline County Schs., Denton, Md., 1988—; adj. prof. Chesapeake Community Coll., Wye Mills, Md., 1988—97. Co-author: Number Curiosity. Coach, mem. com. Spl. Olympics, Denton, 1990—; leader Girl Scouts for Spl. Students, Denton, 1990-95; sec. VFW Aux., Greensboro, Md., 1989—; b. dirs. Caroline Adult Med. Day Care; mem. Friends of Caroline Libr. Named Nat. Vol. of Yr., Am. Legion, 2002; recipient Nat. Outstanding Cmty. Svc. Vol. of Yr. award, VFW Aux., 2003. Mem. NEA, Kappa Delta Pi. Roman Catholic. Avocations: reading, cross stitch, travel.

PAPLAUSKAS, LEONARD PAUL, academic administrator, health science educator; b. Wiesbaden, Germany, June 22, 1949; came to U.S., 1950; s. Leonardas and Emilija (Sadauskas) P.; m. Lynn Ellen Verhoeven, Nov. 24, 1972 (div. Jan. 1988); 1 child, Grant Peter; m. Judith Ann Jones, June 30, 1990. BS, Loyola U., 1970; masters equivalent, So. Ill. U., 1972, postgrad. Asst. sec. U.S. adopted names coun. AMA, Chgo., 1974-75; rsch. adminstr. Health & Hosp. Governing Commn., Chgo., 1975-76; asst. dir. Office Rsch. & Sponsored Programs Northwestern U., Evanston, Ill., 1976-84, dir. Office Rsch. & Sponsored Programs, Med. Sch. Chgo., 1977-84, instr. div. biol. sci. Evanston, 1983-84; instr. dept. natural sci. Loyola U., Chgo., 1982-84; asst. v.p. rsch. U. Conn. Health Ctr., Farmington, 1984-2000, assoc. v.p. rsch. adminstrn., 2000—. Cons. NIH, Bethesda, Md., 1977—, Am. Assn. for Accreditation of Human Rsch. Programs, 2002—, assn. for the Accreditation of Human Rsch. Programs, 2002-; leader 5 piece jazz combo Siezure, 2002. Contbr. articles to profl. jours. Bd. dirs.,pres. Currier Woods Assoc./Currier Woods Tax Dist., Cheshire, Conn., 1991—; bd. dirs., exec. com., v.p., corp. sec. Conn. United for Rsch. Excellence, 2002—, founder, leader Seizure Jazz Quintet, 1990-99. NIH grantee, 1987—. Mem. AAAS, Nat. Coun. Univ. Rsch. Adminstrs., Soc. Rsch. Adminstrs., Mus. of Natural History, Smithsonian Instn. Avocations: skiing, fishing, mountain biking, music. Office: U Conn Health Ctr 263 Farmington Ave Farmington CT 06030-0002 E-mail: paplauskas@adp.uchc.edu.

PAPP, LEANN ILSE KLINE, respiratory therapy educator; b. Niles, Ohio, June 18, 1944; d. Lee Andrew and Mildred Alice (Vaughan) Kline; m. Roger John Papp, July 11, 1964; 1 child, Lisa Marie. AAS in Respiratory Therapy, Sinclair C.C., Dayton, Ohio, 1975; ASN, Manatee Jr. Coll., Bradenton, Fla., 1983; B in Allied Health Edn., Ottawa U. of Kansas City, Overland Park, Kans., 1988; MS in Health and Wellness, Calif. Coll. Health Scis., 1995. RN, Fla., Ark.; cert. respiratory therapy technologist, registered respiratory therapist, BCLS instr., Am. Heart Assn., cert. hypnotherapist. Staff therapist Childrens' Med. Ctr., Dayton, 1975-79; staff therapist L.W. Blake Hosp., Bradenton, Fla., 1979; chief therapist The Breath Ctr., Sarasota, Fla., 1979-83; mem. clin. faculty Sarasota Meml. Hosp., 1983-84; spl. procedures therapist, mem. clin. faculty North Little Rock (Ark.) Meml. Hosp., 1984-85; clin. edn. coord. St. Vincent Infirmary, Little Rock, 1985-86; dir. clin. edn. for respiratory therapy tech. Pulaski Vo-Tech, North Little Rock, 1986-88; staff therapist Cobb Gen. Hosp., Austell, Ga., 1988-89; program dir. respiratory therapy tech. Coosa Valley Tech. Inst., Rome, Ga., 1989—. Cons. Applied Measurement Profls., Lenexa, Kans, 1991-92, 93-94; faculty Am. Heart Assn., Marietta, Ga., 1989-96, Am. Heart Assn., Floyd County, Ga., 1997—; advisor Ga. Coun. on Vocat. Edn., Atlanta, 1991-94; mem. ednl. commn. Author: Nosocomial Infection and Control, 1993; co-author: Georgia State Standards-Respiratory Therapy Technology, 1989-90, 93-94, 97-98. Co-chairperson Cystic Fibrosis Found., Atlanta, 1990; mem. Am. Lung Assn. (Ga. chpt.), 1995, bd. dirs., 1995. Recipient Commr.'s award of Excellence Ga. Dept. Tech. and Adult Edn., 1994. Mem. Am. Assn. Respiratory Care (sec. 2001—), Ga. Soc. Respiratory Care (mem. edn. com. 1993—, mem. health care reform com. 1995, chair election com. 1996—), Ga. Vocat. Assn., Health Occupations Educators (Outstanding New Tchr. award 1992), Lambda Beta Soc. Office: Coosa Valley Tech Coll 1 Maurice Culberson Dr SW Rome GA 30161-7603

PAPPAS, CHARLES NICHOLAS, III, dentist, educator; b. Phila., Jan. 14, 1936; s. Charles Nicholas, Jr. and Marie (Pero) Pappas; m. Edith Basedow, Aug. 24, 1974. Student, U. Colo., 1953—55; DDS, Northwestern U., 1959. Assoc. practice dentistry, South Weymouth, Mass., 1962; pvt. practice dentistry Weymouth Heights, Mass., 1962—65; public health dentist Dept. Health and Hosps., Boston, 1965—70; assoc. practice Weymouth, 1965—68, Brookline, Mass., 1969; practicing clin. dentist Harvard U., 1970—71, clin. instr. operative dentistry, 1967—71; clin. rsch. asst. Forsyth Dental Ctr., 1972; asst. prof. restorative dentistry U. Pa., 1972—83; dentist Dept. Pub. Health, City of Phila., 1984—. Clin. instr. Tufts U., 1965. Author: The Life and Times of G.V. Black, 1983, (pamphlet) Self-Control of Tooth Decay, 1967; contbr. articles to profl. publs. Program, fund-raising chmn. Phillips Brooks Club Boston Trinity Ch., 1965—66. Capt. AUS, 1960—62. Recipient Earle Banks Hoyt award for excellence in tchg., 1980. Mem.: AAAS, ADA, Christian Dental Soc., NY Acad. Scis., Pa. Assn. Dental Surgeons, Mass. Dental Soc., Philadelphia County Dental Soc., Harvard Odontological Soc., Yale Libr. Assocs., U.S. Submarine Vets WWII (assoc. Cert. of Appreciation 1982), Goethe Soc. New Eng., English-Speaking Union, 4001 Lit. Union (founder, faculty advisor), New Haven Colony Hist. Soc., Hist. Soc. Pa., Ill. State Hist. Soc., G.V. Black Soc., Northwestern U. of Delaware Valley Club (pres. 1978), Xi Psi Phi, Lambda Chi Alpha. Home: 5723 Charles St Philadelphia PA 19135-3806 Office: City of Phila Dist Health Ctr # 10 Dental Clinic 2230 Cottman Ave Philadelphia PA 19149

PAPPAS, EFFIE VAMIS, English and business educator, writer, poet, artist; b. Cleve., Dec. 26, 1924; d. James Jacob and Helen Joy (Nicholson) Vamis; m. Leonard G. Pappas, Nov. 3, 1945; children: Karen Pappas Morabito, Leonard J., Ellen Pappas Daniels, David James. BBA, Western Res. U., 1948; MA in Edn., Case Western Res. U., 1964, postgrad., 1964-68; MA in English Lit., Cleve. State U., 1986; postgrad., Indiana U. Pa., 1979-86. Cert. elem. and secondary tchr., Ohio. Tchr. elem. schs., Ohio, 1963-70; office mgr. Cleve. State U., 1970-72, adminstr. pub. relations, 1972-73; med. adminstr. Brecksville (Ohio) VA Hosp., 1974-78; lectr. English, econs./bus. mgmt., math., comm., composition Cuyahoga C.C., Cleve., 1978-92. Tchg. asst. Case Western Reserve U., 1979-80; lectr. bus. comms. Cleve. State U., 1980; participant in Sci. and Cultural Exch. dels. Am. Inst. Chemists, to Peoples Republic of China, 1984 and to Soviet Union, 1989. Feature writer The Voice, 1970-78; editor, writer Cleve. State U. newsletter and mag., 1970-73. Cub scout leader Boy Scouts Am., Brecksville, 1960; mem. local coun. PTA, 1965-70; sec. St. Paul's Coun., 1990-91; Sunday Sch. tchr., mem. choir Brecksville United Ch. of Christ, 1975-76, mem. bd. missions, 1966-67, membership com. 1993, St. Paul Ladies Philoptohos, 1990-2003; active Women's Equity Action League, 1995-2003; mem. planning com. for edn. Case Western Res. U., Cleve. Coll. 75th Anniversary steering com.; mem. Greater Cleve. Learning Project. Recipient Editor's Choice award for outstanding achievement in poetry Nat. Libr. of Poetry, 1995, 2000; grantee Cuyahoga C.C., 1982. Mem. NEA, NAFE, AAUW (legis. chair, del. Ohio meetings 1993-94, del. Ohio Coalition for Change, 1993-94, mem. Ohio and Cleve. br. del. Gt. Lakes regional meeting 1994, co-chair Cleve. br. 1994, 96-97, legis. chair 1997-98, del. to S.W. regional meeting 1995, del. to Internat. Fedn. Univ. Women triennial meeting Stanford U. 1992), AARP, Ohio Edn. Assn. (rep. assembly Columbus 1994, 99-2001, 2002-03), Nat. Mus. Women in Arts (hon. roll mem.). Avocations: travel, art, legal studies, theater, correspondence with national and international friends. Home: 8681 Brecksville Rd Brecksville OH 44141-1912

PAPPAS, JOHN GEORGE, secondary school educator; b. Munich, May 8, 1962; parents U.S. citizens; s. Michael Thomas and Sophie Athens (Stambolis) P. BS in Bus. Adminstrn. and Mgmt., La Roche Coll., 1985; math./secondary education cert., California U. Pa., 1993. Acct., bookkeeper South Hills Anesthesia Assocs., Pitts., 1986-87; personal fitness instr. and sales profl. Prince's Gym, Canonsburg, Pa., 1988-92; math. tchr. Baldwin-Whitehall Sch. Dist., Pitts., 1993—. Sponsor Freshmen Class, Pitts., 1993—. Asst. coord. Spl. Olympics, Baldwin H.S., 1994. Mem. Nat. Coun. Tchrs. Math., Baldwin Transition Team.

PAPPAS-SPEAIRS, NINA, financial planner, educator; d. Steve E. and Martha (Hicks) Kalfas; m. Harry J. Pappas, 1951 (div.); children: John J., Nicholas S., Vivian E. Pappas Unger, Mark A., Carol A. Pappas Siegel; m. Mitchell F. Speairs, 1992 (dec. 2001). BS, U. Cin., 1950; MA, Northwestern U., 1957; PhD, U. Ill., 1978. Faculty St. Mary's H.S., Chgo., Sch. Dist. 102, LaGrange, Ill., U. Ill., Chgo., 1969-79, U. Tex., Arlington, 1979-82, Tex. Wesleyan Coll., Ft. Worth, 1982-83; realtor Merrill Lynch Realty, Ft. Worth, 1983-84; fin. planner Cigna Corp., Irving, Tex., 1984-90; pvt. practice fin. planning and investments, Ft. Worth, 1990—. Organizer, condr. 1st U.S. Olympic Acad., Chgo., 1977; collaborator Internat. Olympic Acad., Olympia, Greece, 1977, guest lectr., 77, 78; chief of mission to Greece U.S. Olympic Com., 1977; guest lectr. Nat. Olympic Acad. Republic of China, 1982. Author: History and Development of the International Olympic Academy: 1927-1977, 1978; editor: Perspectives of the Olympic Games, 1979; also articles. Vice chair Edn. Coun. U.S. Olympic Com., 1977—85; mem. sch. bd. Dist. 107, LaGrange, Ill., 1971—74; pres. Opera Guild Ft. Worth, 1982. Recipient Silver Medal Internat. Olympic Acad., Olympia, Greece, 1981. Mem. Lecture Found. Ft. Worth, Ft. Worth Sister Cities Internat., Symphony League, Opera Guild, RoundTable Women's Wednesday Club (pres. 2003—), Woman's Club, River Crest Country Club, Ft. Worth Boat Club, Ridglea Rejebian Club, Carousel, Woman's Wednesday Club (pres. 2003-04). Republican. Greek Orthodox. Avocations: golf, reading, sailing, dancing. Home: 7705 Lake Highlands Dr Fort Worth TX 76179-2809 E-mail: nspeairs@earthlink.net.

PARADYSZ, MARSHA L. academic administrator; b. Clinton, Ind., May 1, 1957; d. Claude Derrill and Bessie Faye (Brown) Wilson; children: Matthew Dustin Hickman, Jessica Faye Hickman; m. William David Paradysz; 1 child, Tara Star. BS in Mgmt. of Human Resources, Oakland City (Ind.) Coll., 1991; postgrad., Ind. U. S.E., New Albany. Asst. dist. mgr. Avon Products, Cin., 1978-87; asst. to English and math. profs. Oakland City U., Bedford, 1987-89; admissions counselor Bedford (Ind.) Coll. Ctr., 1994-96; adminstrv. asst. Orange County Child Care Cooperative, Paoli, Ind., 1988-90, dir. youth svcs., 1990-93; dir. Lawrence County First Steps and Step Ahead, 1996; exec. dir. Orange County Child Care Coop., Paoli, 1997-98; asst. dir. devel. Sarasota Ballet of Fla., 1998-99; instr. Ind. Bus. Coll., 1999—2002, dir. continuing edn., 2002—. Mem. svc.-learning adv. com. Middle Grades Improvement, Paoli, 1992-93; mem. gifted and talented adv. com. Paoli Schs., 1990-98; asst. property mgr. Meridian Mgmt., 1999—. Actor, singer, dancer Orange County Players, Paoli, 1985-98; bd. dirs. Internat. Network for Children and Families, 1998-99; elder Presbyn. Ch., 1998—. Named one of Outstanding Young Women Am., 1986; Youth as Resources grantee Nat. Crime Prevention Coun., 1992, 91, Cmty. Guidance for Youth grantee Lilly Endowment, 1993; recipient Gov.'s Voluntary Action award State of Ind., 1992, 93. Presbyterian. Avocations: music, canoeing, writing, reading, theater. Home: 5508 E Rawles Ter Indianapolis IN 46219-7121

PARAISO, JOHNNA KAYE, elementary education educator; b. Wyandotte, Mich., Nov. 17, 1961; d. John Calvin and Ruth (Hughes) Underwood; m. Normandy Paraiso, Oct. 6, 1984; children: Sophia Elisabeth, Abigail Mahalia, Genevieve Christine. BS, Bob Jones U., 1983. Cert. ACSI, educator K-8 (all subjects). Tchr. fifth grade Temple Christian Sch., Redford, Mich., 1983-86; music tchr. Fairlane Christian Sch., Dearborn Heights, Mich., 1986-90; tchr. 2d grade Internat. Christian Sch., San Francisco, 1992-93, dept. head primary childhood edn., 1992-93. Freelance musician children's concerts; leader Curriculum Selection Com.; initiator Elem. Music Program; dir. several dramatic prodns.; tchr. piano, guitar. Children's minister 1st Bapt. Ch., San Francisco, 1991-94. Mem. Pi Lambda Theta. Home: 2024 Stonebrook Dr Murfreesboro TN 37128-5334

PARCHMENT, YVONNE, nursing educator; b. Kingston, Jamaica, July 2, 1943; came to U.S., 1979; d. George Augustus Leslie and Evelyn Maude (Brown) Mitchell; m. Neville McDonald Parchment, Feb. 2, 1963; children: Suzanne Marie, April A. Parchment-Knight, Neville Wade, Everton Jerome. AA, AS, Miami (Fla.) Dade Cmty. Coll., 1982; BSN, U. Miami, 1984, MS in Nursing, 1989; postgrad., Fla. Internat. U., 1996—. RN, Fla. Tchr. elem. sch. Alpha Infant Sch., Kingston, 1974-79; nurse South Miami Hosp., 1979-95; clin. nurse specialist Mt. Sinai Med. Ctr., Miami, 1989-95; clin. asst. prof. Fla. Internat. U., Miami, 1995—. Contbr. articles to profl. jours. Bd. dirs. mental health com. Cmty. Health Ctr., Miami, 1996—. Capt. Army Nurse Corps., USAR, 1989—. Rsch. grantee Fla. League Nursing, 1996. Mem. AACN, Fla. Nurses Assn. (bd. dirs. dist. 5), Jamaica Nurses Assn. of Fla. (past v.p., v.p. 1997—, mem. edn. com., cultural diversity com.), Sigma Theta Tau (mem. by-laws com.). Episcopalian. Avocations: dancing, reading, sewing. Office: Fla Internat U North Campus Miami FL 33181

PARDAVI-HORVATH, MARTHA MARIA, physicist, educator; b. Budapest, Hungary, Feb. 3, 1940; came to U.S., 1985; d. Elek and Katalin (Sattelberger) H.; m. Ferenc Pardavi, July 7, 1967; 1 child, Martha. PhD in Physics, Hungarian Acad. Sci., Budapest, 1985, R. Eotvos U., 1988. Rsch. assoc. Hungarian Acad. Sci., Budapest, 1967-75, head lab., 1975-85; rsch. assoc. Ohio State U., Columbus, 1988; vis. prof. NRC, Rome, 1989; prof. George Washington U., Washington, 1989—. Author: Microelectronic Technology, Magnetic Multilayers, Nonlinear Microwave Signal Processing, Magnetic Systems; contbr. more than 150 articles to profl. jours. Mem. IEEE (chpt. chair 1989, editor Newsletter), AAAS, N.Y. Acad. Scis., Am. Phys. Soc., Internat. Soc. Interdisciplinary Study of Symmetry (sec.), Sigma Xi. Office: George Washington U Dept ECE 801 22nd St NW Washington DC 20052

PARDEE, MARGARET ROSS, violinist, violist, educator; b. Valdosta, Ga., May 10, 1920; d. William Augustus and Frances Ross (Burton) P.; m. Daniel Rogers Butterly, July 4, 1944. Diploma, Juilliard Sch. Music, 1940, grad. diploma, 1942; diploma, Juilliard Grad. Sch., 1945. Instr. violin and viola Manhattanville Coll. Sacred Heart, N.Y.C., 1942-54, Juilliard Sch., N.Y.C., 1942, Meadowmount Sch. Music, Westport, N.Y., 1956-84, 88-92, Bowdoin Coll. Music Festival and Sch., Maine, summer 1987. Mem. faculty Estherwood Sch. and Summr Festival, 1984-86, Killington (Vt.) Music Festival, 1993—, Mannes Sch. Music, 1996—; concert master Gt. Neck (L.I., N.Y.) Symphony, 1954-85; adj. assoc. prof. Aaron Copeland Sch. Music, Queens Coll., CUNY, Flushing, 1978—, Adelphi U., Garden City, N.Y., 1979-83; adj. prof. SUNY, Purchase, 1980-93; vis. prof. Simon Bolivar Youth Orch. and Conservatory, Caracas and Barquisimeto, Venezuela, 1988, 89, Conservatorio Orch. Nat. Juvenil, Caracas, 1988, 89; mem. jury for internat. competitions; guest artist prof. 1st Internat. Festival for Young Violinists, Caracas, 1988; guest vis. prof. Orch. Filarmonica Nat. y Mcpl. Sinfonica Caracas, 1992, 97. Debut N.Y. Town Hall, 1952; toured U.S. as soloist and in chamber music groups; soloed with symphony orchs., Miss., N.J., D.C., N.Y. Bd. dirs. Meadowmount Sch. Music. Recipient Andres Bello award Venezuela Min. Edn., 1993. Mem. Soc. for Strings (dir. 1965-92), Assoc. Music Tchrs. League N.Y. (cert.), N.Y. State Music Tchrs. Assn. (cert., citation 1989), Music Tchrs. Nat. Assn., Am. String Tchrs. Assn. (citation for exceptional leadership 1990), Am. Fedn. Musicians, Viola Rsch. Soc. Office: care Juilliard Sch Lincoln Ctr Plz New York NY 10023

PARDEN, CINDY MARIA, elementary school educator; b. Pensacola, Fla., Aug. 6, 1957; d. Leroy and Helen Lorene (Earnest) Rigby; m. Stephen Anthony Parden, July 11, 1998. AA, Pensacola Jr. Coll., 1977; BS, U. West Fla., 1979; MEd, U. South Ala., 1987. Cert. elem. tchr., Ala. Tchr. 4th-5th grades Escambia Cty Sch. Bd., Pensacola, Mobile (Ala.) City Schs., tchr. 4th grade, tchr. 1st grade and basic skills. Named one of 2,000 Notable Am. Women, 1994, 1996, 2000, 2002, 2,000 Outstanding People of 20th Century, 1995, 1996; named to Dictionary of Internat. Biography, 1994,

1995, 1996, 1998, Internat. Directory of Disting. Leadership, 1994, 1996, 2001, 2002. Mem. NEA (del. 1992-95), Assn. Classroom Tchrs., Ala. Edn. Assn. (state del. 1988-95), Mobile Edn. Assn. Home: 250 Border Dr E Mobile AL 36608-2752

PARDES, HERBERT, psychiatrist, educator; b. Bronx, N.Y., July 7, 1934; s. Louis and Frances (Bergman) P.; m. Judidth Ellen Silber, June 9, 1957; children: Stephen, Lawrence, James. BS, Rutgers U., 1956; MD, SUNY, Bklyn., 1960; DSc (hon.), SUNY, 1990. Straight med. intern Kings County Hosp., 1960-61, resident in psychiatry, 1961-62, 64-66; asst. prof. psychiatry Downstate Med. Ctr., Bklyn., 1968-72, prof., chmn. dept., 1972-75; dir. psychiat. svcs. Kings County Hosp., Bklyn., 1972-75; prof., chmn. dept. psychiatry U. Colo. Med. Sch., 1975-78; dir. psychiat. svcs. Colo. Psychiat. Hosp., Denver, 1975-78; dir. NIMH, Rockville, Md., 1978-84; asst. surgeon gen. USPHS, 1978-84; prof. psychiatry Columbia U., N.Y.C., 1984—, chmn. dept., 1984—, dir. Psychiat. Inst., 1984-89, v.p. for health scis., dean faculty medicine, 1989—99; pres., CEO N.Y.-Presbyn. Hosp., N.Y.C., 2000—. Contbr. articles to med. jours. Pres. sci. bd. Alliance for Rsch. on Schizophrenia and Depression. Capt. M.C., AUS, 1972-74. Named Ann. Hon. Lectr. Downstate Med. Ctr. Alumni Assn., 1972; recipient Alumni Achievement medal, 1980, William Menninger award ACP, 1992, Dorothy Dix award Mental Illness Fedn., 1992, Vester Mark award, 1994, Salmon award, 1996. Mem. Assn. Am. Med. Colls. (chair 1995-96), Am. Psychiat. Assn. (v.p. 1986-88, pres. 1989-90, Disting. Svc. award 1993), Inst. Medicine, Am. Psychoanalytic Assn., Coun. of Deans (adminstrv. bd., chair-elect 1993-94, chair 1994-95), Assoc. Med. Schs. N.Y. (pres. 1995-2000), Phi Beta Kappa, Alpha Omega Alpha. Office: NY Presbyn Hosp Pres and CEOs Office 161 Ft Washington Ave New York NY 10032 also: 525 E 68th St New York NY 10021

PARDUE, KAREN REIKO, elementary education educator; b. Honolulu, June 13, 1947; d. Rex Shinzen and Ruth Fujiko (Arakawa) Ishiara; m. Jerry Thomas Pardue, Oct. 21, 1978 (dec. Sept. 1994); 1 child, Holly; m. Nicholas Lambiase, Mar. 17, 1998 (div. July 1999). BS, Western Ill. U., 1969; MA, U. No. Colo., 1971, 72. Tchr. home econs. Galesburg (Ill.) H.S., 1969-70; tchr. spl. edn. Jefferson County Pub. Schs., Golden, Colo., 1973-85, 87-94; tchr. 2d and 3d grade Englewood (Colo.) Christian Sch., 1985-86; tchr. 2d grade Jefferson County Pub. Schs., 1994—. Adj. instr. Colo. Christian U., Lakewood, 1989—; mem. recommended basic list com. Jefferson County Pub. Schs., 1993-95. Grantee Colo. Dept. Edn., 1976, Jefferson Found. Venture, 1988. Mem. ASCD, Colo. Coun. Learning Disabilities, Jefferson County Ednl. Assn., Jefferson County Internat. Reading Assn., Delta Kappa Gamma (rec. sec. 1988-89, pres. 1990-92, treas. 1994-96, Values award for exemplary performance 2001-2002). Avocations: reading, sewing. Home: 6827 S Webster St Unit D Littleton CO 80128-4469

PARDUE, MARY-LOU, biology educator; b. Lexington, Ky., Sept. 15, 1933; d. Louis Arthur and Mary Allie (Marshall) P. BS, William and Mary Coll., 1955; MS, U. Tenn., 1959; PhD, Yale U., 1970; D.Sc. (hon.), Bard Coll., 1985. Postdoctoral fellow Inst. Animal Genetics, Edinburgh, Scotland, 1970-72; assoc. prof. biology MIT, Cambridge, 1972-80, prof., 1980—, Boris Magasanik prof. biology, 1995—. Summer course organizer Cold Spring Harbor Lab., NY, 1971—80; mem. rev. com. NIH, 1974—78, 1980—84, nat. adv. gen. med. scis. coun., 1984—86; sci. adv. com. Wistar Inst., Phila., 1976—; mem. health and environ. rsch. adv. com. U.S. Dept. Energy, 1987—94; bd. trustees Associated Univs., Inc., 1995—97; mem. Burroughs Wellcome Adv. Com. on Career Awards in Biomed. Scis., 1996—2000, now bd. dirs.; chair Inst. of Medicine Com. on Biol. Basis of Sex and Gender Differences, 1999—2001. Mem. editorial bd. Chromsoma; contbr. articles to profl. jours. Mem. rev. com. Am. Cancer Soc., 1990-93, Howard Hughes Med. Inst. Adv. Bd., 1993-2000. Recipient Esther Langer award Langer Cancer Rsch. Found., 1977, Lucius Wilbur Cross medal Yale Grad. Sch., 1989; grantee NIH, NSF, Am. Cancer Soc. Fellow AAAS, NAS (chmn. genetics sect. 1991-94, coun. 1995-98), Am. Acad. Arts and Sci. (coun. mem. 1992-96); mem. NRC (bd. on biology 1989-95), Genetics Soc. Am. (pres. 1982-83), Am. Soc. Cell Biology (coun. 1977-80, pres. 1985-86), Phi Beta Kappa, Phi Kappa Phi, Sigma Xi. Office: MIT Dept Biology 68-670 77 Massachusetts Ave Dept 68-670 Cambridge MA 02139-4307

PARHAM, LINDA DIANE, occupational therapist, researcher, educator; b. Guantanamo, Cuba, Aug. 28, 1952; d. Gerald Dathel and Shirley (Melzer) Parham; m. Harry Edward Trigg III, June 1, 1985; 1 child, Dorothy Helen Trigg. BS, U. Fla., 1974; MA, U. So. Calif., L.A., 1980; PhD, U. Calif., L.A., 1989. Asst. dir. occupl. therapy Bayberry Psychiat. Hosp., Hampton, Va., 1974-75; sr. occupl. therapist Maryview Cmty. Mental Health Ctr., Portsmouth, Va., 1975-78; pvt. practice L.A., 1980-84; asst. prof. U. So. Calif., L.A., 1986-92, assoc. prof., 1992—. Adj. instr. Univ. So. Calif., 1979—80, 1985—86; dir. edn. Ayres Clinic, Torrance, Calif., 1985—96; dir. edn. and rsch. Pediatric Therapy Network, Torrance, Calif., 1996—. Editor: (book) Play in Occupl. Therapy for Children; mem. editl. rev. bd.: Occupl. Therapy Jour. Rsch., 1988—90; contbr. articles to profl. jours. and textbooks. Recipient Jean Ayres Award, Am Occupl. Therapy Found, 1998, Leadership Commendation, 1999; fellow Am. Occupl. Therapy Found, 1988; scholar Ctr. Study Sensory Integrative Dysfunction, 1980. Fellow: Am. Occupl. Therapy Assn.; mem.: Assn. Study of Play (v.p. 2000—01, pres. 2001—02), Soc. Rsch. Child Devel., Sensory Integration Internat. (faculty emeritus, sec. 1986—87), World Fedn. Occupl. Therapists, Occupl. Therapy Assn. Calif. Office: U So Calif 1540 Alcazar St # 133 Los Angeles CA 90089 Personal E-mail: ldiane@pacificnet.net. Business E-Mail: lparham@hsc.usc.edu.

PARHI, KESHAB KUMAR, electrical and computer engineering educator; b. Balasore, Orissa, India, June 15, 1959; came to U.S., 1983; s. Budhiram and Kamalini Parhi; m. Jagruti Mahapatra, Dec. 11, 1988; children: Megha, Rahul. B of Tech., Indian Inst. Tech., Kharagpur, 1982; MSEE, U. Pa., 1984; PhD, U. Calif., Berkeley, 1988. Teaching and rsch. asst. U. Pa., Phila., 1983-84; postgrad. researcher U. Calif., Berkeley, 1984-88; mem. tech. staff T.J. Watson Rsch. Ctrs. IBM, Yorktown Heights, N.Y., 1986, AT&T Bell Labs., Holmdel, N.J., 1987; asst. prof. U. Minn., Mpls., 1988-92, assoc. prof., 1992-95, prof., 1995—, Edgar F. Johnson prof., 1997—, Disting. McKnight U. prof., 2000—. Tech. dir. DSP Sys., Broadcom Corp., Irvine, Calif., 2000-02; vis. rschr. NEC Computer Comm. Lab., Kawasaki, Japan, 1992, 96-97; cons. AT&T Bell Labs., 1987, U.S. West Sci. and Techs., Boulder, Colo., 1989. Editor Jour. VLSI Signal Processing, 1993—; contbr. articles to profl. jours. Recipient NSF Young Investigator award, 1992, Eliahu Jury award U. Calif., Berkeley, 1987, Demetri Angelakos award U. Calif., Berkeley, 1987; IBM grad. fellow, 1987-88, Regents fellow U. Calif., 1986-87. Fellow IEEE (assoc. editor transactions on cirs. and sys. 1990-91, assoc. editor transactions on signal processing 1993-95, assoc. editor transactions on cirs. and sys. part II 1995-97, 2002—, transactions on VLSI syss. 1997-98, signal processing letters 1997—, signal processing mag 2003—, signal processing soc. paper award 1991, Browder J. Thompson Meml. Prize Paper award 1991, W.R.G. Baker prize 2001, Kiyo Tomiyasu Tech. Field award 2003), Cirs. and Sys. Soc. (Guillemin-Cauer award 1993, Darlington award 1994, Golden Jubilee medal 1999, Disting. lectr. 1994-99, Design Automation Conf. Best Paper award 1996). Avocations: swimming, gardening, hiking, traveling. Office: U Minn Dept Elec/Computer Engring 200 Union St SE Minneapolis MN 55455-0154

PARIS, KATHLEEN, secondary school educator; Biology tchr. Bethel High Sch., Spanaway, Wash. Named Wash. State Biology Tchr. of Yr., 1993; recipient Presdl. award in secondary sci., 1997. Office: Bethel High Sch 22215 38th Ave E Spanaway WA 98387-6824

PARIS, KEVIN, English educator; b. N.Y.C., Oct. 14, 1953; s. Ferdinand and Minerva (Alicea) P.; m. Miriam Celeste Pérez, Dec. 20, 1975; children: Kevin, Miriam. BA in English and Secondary Edn., U. P.R., 1977, MEd in English and Secondary Edn., 1979. Cert. tchr., P.R., Tex. Instr., tchr. trainer Cath. U. P.R., Ponce, 1980-82, asst. prof., tchr. trainer, 1983-85; tchg. asst. East Tex. State U., Commerce, 1982-83; secondary tchr., tchr. trainer Dallas Ind. Sch. Dist., 1985—98; prof. ESL and English Brookhaven Coll., Farmers Branch, Tex., 1998—, dir. intensive English program, 2002—03. Writing cons. region 10 Edn. Svc. Ctr., Richardson, Tex., 1986; mem. adv. bd. Tex. Higher Edn. Coordinating Bd., Austin, 1994—; writer curricula in field. Founding pres. Mesquite (Tex.) H.S. Band Parent Orgn., 1993-94. Mem. Tex. TESOL, TESOL, Nat. Inst. for Staff and Orgnl. Devel. Office: Brookhaven Coll 3939 Valley View Ln Dallas TX 75244-4906

PARIS, VIRGINIA HALL (GINGER PARIS), principal; b. Talladega, Ala., Sept. 25, 1962; d. Robert Dorch and Bonnie (Green) Hall; m. Walter Kevin Paris, June 8, 1985; children: Taylor Ray, Tyger Jean. AS, Jefferson State Jr. Coll., 1982; BS, Auburn U., 1984; MS, Jacksonville State U., 1991, U. Ala., Birmingham, 1994, EdS in Ednl. Leadership/Adminstrn., 1997. Cert. ednl. leadership. Tchr. gifted program Talladega County Schs., 1984-85, tchr. learning disabled program, 1988-89; tchr. Big Bend C.C., Vicenza, Italy, 1986-87; tchr., dir. Villagio Child Devel. Ctr., Vicenza, 1987-88; tchr. social studies Dixon Mid. Sch., Talladega, 1989-91, tchr. sci., 1991-99, prin., 1999—; insvc. edn. cons. U. Montevallo, 1994-96; self-employed insv. cons., 1996—. Self employed insvc. edn. cons., 1996—; tchr. rep. spl. edn. screening com. Talladega City Schs., 1989-93; vis. com. So. Assn. Colls. and Schs., Montgomery, Ala., 1992; dir. Thundering Speed, Inc. Vol. instr. ARC, Vicenza, 1986, Talladega, 1988; coord. Adopt-a-Grandparent program Talladega Health Care, 1991-96; media chmn. Talladega Pilgrimage; mem. Friends of Libr., Talladega, 1992; coord., sponsor March for Parks, Talladega, 1994, 95, 96, 97; bd. dirs. Talladega Parks and Recreation, chair, 1994-98; mem. planning com. Talladega 2000 Edn. Task Force, 1998-99, mem. steering com., 1996, 97; ofcl. host Internat. Motorsports Hall of Fame; chairperson and ednl. supv., Talladega/Texaco Walk of Fame, 2000—. Recipient Tchr. of Yr. award Dixon Rep. Ala., 1991-92, Pilot Club Tchr. of Yr 1995, Tchr. of Yr. award Dixon Rep. Jacksonville State U., 1992-93; Tchr. of the Yr. Jaycees 1994-95; Talladega Jaycees Outstanding Talladegan, 1999, Ala. Jr. C. of C. Outstanding Alabamian, 1999. Mem. NEA, Ala. Edn. Assn., Nat. Sci. Tchrs. Assn., Talladega City Edn. Assn., Anniston Mus. Natural History, Ala. Cattlewomen's Assn., Environ. Edn. Assn., Nat. Pks. and Conservation Assn., Nat. Audubon Soc., Nat. Arbor Day Found., Nat. Wildlife Assn., Auburn U. Alumni Assn., Ala. Middle Sch. Assn. (program dir. region VI 1995-96), Pilot Club, Kappa Delta Pi, Delta Zeta Alumni. Republican. Baptist. Avocations: softball, volleyball, swimming, aerobics, animals. Office: Dixon Mid Sch 415 Elm St Talladega AL 35160-2704 Home: 620 Cherry St Talladega AL 35160-2716

PARISH, SYNTHIA LEE, special education educator; b. Pullman, Wash., Aug. 27, 1958; d. Curtis Lee and Maureen (Bonham) P.; m. Max W. Williams, Sept. 9, 1978 (div. June 1986); children: Jeremiah James, Sarah Rose. AA, Wenatchee (Wash.) Valley Coll., 1978; BA in Edn., Cen. Wash. U., 1981; postgrad., various colls., Wash., 1981—. Tchr. art and spl. edn., dir. spl. edn. Creston (Wash.) Sch. Dist., 1981-84; tchr. spl. edn. and music, dir. spl. edn., track coach Bickleton (Wash.) Sch. Dist., 1984-85; tchr. spl. edn. Wapato (Wash.) Sch. Dist., 1985—, social skills program instr., dir., 1992—. Instr. Upward Bound., Yakima, Wash., 1990. Tutor Equal Opportunities Program, Ellensburg, Wash., 1980-81; actress, singer Creston Community Players, 1981-84; dir. Miss Creston Pageant, 1983-84; coach Spl. Olympics, Wapato, 1989—; cheerleading coach, pep club advisor Creston Sch. Dist., 1981-84; cheerleading coach, jr. class advisor Bickleton Sch. Dist., 1984-85; counselor AIDS Coalition, Yakima, 1988-90; bd. dirs. March of Dimes, Yakima, 1989—, sec., 1991—; bd. dirs. Health Profls. Adv. Coun., Yakima, 1990, co-chmn., 1991—. Mem. NEA, Wash. Educators Assn., Eagles. Avocations: music, painting, writing poetry. Office: Wapato Sch Dist PO Box 33 Wapato WA 98951-0033 Home: 502 Concord Ave Grandview WA 98930-1502

PARISH, THOMAS SCANLAN, human development educator; b. Oak Park, Ill., Jan. 24, 1944; s. Robert S. and Florence Catherine (Fleming) P.; children: Robert V., Kimberly E., David G., Thomas P., Kathryn E., Lydia E.; m. Jocelyn G. Parish, Dec. 29, 2000. BA, No. Ill. U., 1968; MA, Ill. State U., 1969; PhD, U. Ill., 1972. Instr. psychology Parkland Coll., Champaign, Ill., 1971-72; asst. prof. Okla. State U., Stillwater, 1972-76; assoc. prof. Kans. State U., Manhattan, 1976-80, prof., 1980—, asst. to dean of edn., 1992-97; assoc. dir. ARIOS-Kan., 1994-96. Rsch. coord. for Midwest Desegration Asst. Ct., 1994-96; regional dir. Excel Comm., 1997—. Assoc. editor Jour. of Social Studies Rsch., 1994-98; cons. editor Jour. Genetic Psychology, 1984—, Internat. Jour. Reality Therapy, 1992—, The Genetic, Social and General Psychology Monographs, 1984—; contbr. articles to profl. jours. Bd. dirs. Friendship Tutoring Program, Manhattan, 1982-91, Stillwater Awareness Coun., 1973-74; co-founder, bd. dirs. Youth Alternatives, Inc., Champaign, 1971-72; pres. Mid-Western Edn. Rsch. Assn., 1998-99. Fellow Am. Psychol. Soc.; mem. Am. Ednl. Rsch. Assn., APA, Assn. Reality Therapists, Soc. for Rsch. in Child Devel., Phi Delta Kappa, Phi Kappa Phi. Office: Kans State U Coll of Edn Bluemont Hall Manhattan KS 66506 Home: PO Box 516 Fayette IA 52142-0516 E-mail: thomas_s_parish@hotmail.com., tparish@ksu.edu.

PARISI, CHERYL LYNN, elementary school educator; b. Hackensack, N.J., Aug. 26, 1955; d. Elza A. and Constance Leah (Sculley) Sockey; m. Albert J. Parisi, Apr. 18, 1981; 1 child, Christopher Thomas. BA, Fairleigh Dickinson U., 1977; postgrad., Columbia U., N.Y.C., 2002—. Cert. tchr., N.J. Piano instr., Bergen County, N.J., 1972-79; art tchr. Meml. Sch., South Hackensack, N.J., 1979-80, Hackensack Mid. Sch., 1980-84, Nellie K. Parker Sch., Hackensack, 1984—. Exhibited in group shows at The Jacob Javits Conv. Ctr., N.Y.C., 1990, The Designer Craftsmen's Gallery, New Brunswick, N.J., 1993, Gloucester County Coll., Sewell, N.J., 1993, Johnson and Johnson Corp., Titusville, N.J., 1993, Arts Coun. Princeton, N.J., 1993, Montclair State U., Upper Montclair, N.J., 1992, 94, named to panel for selection of educators for the NEH seminar Amer. and Brit. Chldrns. Lit., Princeton, 1999. Author and co-dir. of chldrns. musical: Claude Monet: A Bridge to the Past, 1999. Recipient Art Educator Achievement award Fantasy Fund Inc. at the Cathedral of St. John the Divine, N.Y.C., 1992; grantee Hackensack Edn. Found., 1991; grantee Hackensack Small Grants Program, 2003; NEH fellow Princeton U., 1991. Mem. Art Educators N.J. (chairperson 1993 Yr. of the Am. Craft 1991-93, publicity 50th anniversary conf. 1990; pres. Bergen County chpt. 1984-86, Achievement award 1989), Nat. Art Edn. Assn. Avocations: playing the piano, reading. Home: 167 Godwin Ave Wyckoff NJ 07481-2004 Office: Nellie K Parker Sch 261 Maple Hill Dr Hackensack NJ 07601-1497

PARK, CHAN HYUNG, cell biologist, physician; b. Seoul, Korea, Aug. 16, 1936; s. Chung Suh and Yoon Sook Yuh; m. Mary Hyungrok Kim, Apr. 16, 1966; 1 child, Christopher Myungwoo. MD, Seoul Nat. U., 1962, MS, 1964; PhD, U. Toronto, 1972. Diplomate in internal medicine and med. oncology Am. Bd. Internal Medicine. Asst. prof. U. Kans. Med. Ctr., 1974-80, assoc. prof., 1980-86, prof., 1986-89; prof., chief divsn. oncology/hematology, dept. internal med. Tex. Tech U. Health Scis. Ctr., 1989—94; dir. Cancer Ctr., Samsung Med. Ctr., Seoul, 1994—2001, cons. physician, 2001—, head divsn. hematology/oncology dept. medicine, 1994-99, cons. physician, 2001—; sr. rsch. scientist The Ctr. for the Improvement of Human Functioning Internat., Inc., Wichita, Kans., 2001—; cons. physician Aidan, Inc., Tempe, Ariz., 2001—. Transl. novel from German to Korean; mem. editl. bd. Jour. Nutrition, Growth and Cancer, 1986-87; mem. editl. bd. Internat. Jour. Hematology, 1999—; contbr. articles to biomed and sci. jours. Recipient Rsch. Career Devel. award USPHS, NIH, 1979-84. Fellow: ACP; mem.: Am. Soc. Hematology, Internat. Soc. Exptl. Hematology, Am. Soc. Clin. Oncology, Am. Assn. Cancer Rsch. Home: 8814 E Churchill Cir Wichita KS 67206 Office: The Ctr for the Improvement Human Functioning Internat Inc 3100 N Hillside Wichita KS 67219

PARK, DUK-WON, mining/civil engineer, educator; b. Ki-San, Kyong-Book, Korea, Mar. 8, 1945; came to U.S., 1969; s. Sung-Ui and Sang-Soon Park; m. Sun-Ja Kim, Dec. 6, 1974; children: Jeanie, Jason, Eunice. BS in Mining Engring., Inha U., Inchon, Korea, 1967; MS in Geol. Engring., U. Mo., Rolla, 1971, PhD in Geol. Engring., 1975. Asst. project engr. D'Appolonia Cons. Engrs., Pitts., 1975-76; asst. prof., assoc. prof. W.Va. U., Morgantown, 1976-81; prof. dept. mineral engring. U. Ala., Tuscaloosa, 1981—96, prof. dept. civil engring., 1996—. Short course instr. W.Va. U., Morgantown, 1977-79; cons. Continental Conveyor Equipment Co., Winfield, Ala., 1982-84, Law Engring. Co., Birmingham, Ala., 1988-89, Gallet and Assocs., Birmingham, 1996, Starnes and Atchison, 2002, P.E. LaMoreaux Assocs., 2001, Maynard, Cooper and Gale, 2002. Contbr. over 120 articles to profl. jours. and conf. procs. Achievements include patents on borehole strss meter and apparatus and roof bolt hole groover. Office: U Ala Box 870205 Tuscaloosa AL 35487-0154

PARK, JOHN THORNTON, academic administrator; b. Phillipsburg, N.J., Jan. 3, 1935; s. Dawson J. and Margaret M. (Thornton) P.; m. Dorcas M Marshall; June 1, 1956; children: Janet Ernst, Karen Daily. BA in Physics with distinction, Nebr. Wesleyan U., 1956; PhD, U. Nebr., 1963. NSF postdoctoral fellow Univ. Coll., London, 1963-64; asst. prof. physics U. Mo., Rolla, 1964-68, assoc. prof. physics, 1968-71, prof., 1971-2000, prof. emeritus, 2000—, chmn. dept. physics, 1977-83, vice chancellor acad. affairs, 1983-85, 86-91, interim chancellor, 1985-86, 91-92, chancellor, 1992-2000, chancellor emeritus, 2000—. Vis. assoc. prof. NYU, 1970-71; pres. Talema Electronics, Inc., St. James, Mo., 1983-99, Tortran Corp., 1990—; prin. investigator NSF Rsch. Grants, 1966-92; bd. dirs. Mo. Tech. Corp., Jefferson City, Mo., 1994—, Mo. Enterprise, 1990—. Phelps County Bank, 1997—. Contbr. articles to profl. jours. Recipient Most Disting. Scientist award Mo. Acad. Sci., 1994. Fellow Am. Phys. Soc. (mem. divsn. elec. and atomic physics); mem. Am. Assn. Physics Tchrs., Rotary. Methodist.

PARK, JON KEITH, dentist, educator; b. Wichita, Kans., May 26, 1938; DDS, U. Mo., 1964; BA, Wichita State U., 1969; MS in Dental Hygiene Edn., U. Mo., 1971; MS in Oral Pathology, U. Md., 1982; cert. in dental radiology, U. Pa. Sch. Dental Medicine, 1982. Diplomate Am. Bd. Oral and Mixillo-facial Radiology. Pvt. practice dentistry, Wichita, 1964-67; chmn. dept. dental hygiene Wichita State U., 1967-72; assoc. prof. oral diagnosis, dir. oral radiology Balt. Coll. Dental Surgery, U. Md., 1972—. Program dir. U. Md. dental externship, 1974-77; lectr. Essex C.C., Harford County C.C.; cons. in radiology VA Hosp., Medix Sch. Dental Assisting; mem. Md. StateRadiation Control Adv. Bd., 1981—; chmn. devel. com. Introduction to Basic Concepts in Dental Radiography, Dental Assisting Nat. Bd., Inc., Am. Dental Assts. Assn., 1991 Editor Am. Acad. Oral and Maxillofacial Radiology Newsletter; patentee pivotal design dental chair. Mem. Ute Pass Hist. Soc. Recipient U. Md. Media Achievement award, 1977, 78. Fellow Am. Coll. Dentists, Am. Acad. Dental Radiology; mem. ADA, Md. State Dental Assn., Balt. City Dental Soc. (ad hoc com. radiation safety, exec. coun.), Am. Acad. Oral Pathology, Am. Acad. Oral and Maxillofacial Radiology (ednl. standards com., editor newsletter), Orgn. Tchrs. oral Diagnosis, Am. Theater Organ Soc., Kans. Dental Hygienists Assn. (hon.), Balt. Music Club, Am. Assn. Dental Schs., Internat. Assn. Dental and Maxillofacial Radiology, Balt. Opera Guild, Engring. Soc. Balt., Met. Opera Guild, Balt. Symphony Orch. Assn., Ute Pass Cmty. Assn., Univ. Club, Omicron Kappa Upsilon, Psi Omega. Episcopalian. E-mail: jpark@umaryland.edu.

PARK, ROGER COOK, law educator; b. Atlanta, Jan. 4, 1942; s. Hugh and Alice (Cook) P.; m. Rosemarie J. Lilliker, June 14, 1967 (div. 1979); 1 child, Matthew; m. Suzanne Nicole Howard, Feb. 18, 1984; stepchildren: Sophie Currier, Nicolas Currier. BA cum laude, Harvard U., 1964, JD magna cum laude, 1969. Bar: Mass. 1969, Minn. 1973. Law clk. to Hon. Bailey Aldrich U.S. Ct. Appeals (1st Cir.), Boston, 1969-70; with Zalkind & Silverglate, Boston, 1970-73; prof. Law Sch. U. Minn., Mpls., 1973-95, Fredrikson and Byron prof. law, 1990-95; Disting. James Edgar Hervey prof. law U. Calif./Hastings Coll. Law, San Francisco, 1995—. Vis. prof. Law Sch. Stanford U., Palo Alto, Calif., summer 1977, Sch. Law Boston U., 1981-82, Law Sch. U. Mich., Ann Arbor, fall 1984; bd. dirs. Ctr. for Computer-Aided Legal Instrn., 1982-96; reporter adv. group Civil Justice Reform Act, Dist. of Minn.; mem. evidence adv. com. Minn. Supreme Ct., 1988-95. Author: Computer Aided Exercises in Civil Procedure, 1979, 4th edit., 1995, (with McFarland) Trial Objections Handbook, 1991, Waltz and Park Casebook on Evidence, 8th edit., 1994, (with Leonard and Goldberg) Evidence Law, 1998; contbr. articles to profl. jours. Lt. U.S. Army, 1964-66, Vietnam. Mem. ABA (mem. subcom. on fed. rules of evidence, mem. rules of criminal procedure adn evidence com. criminal justice sect. 1988—), Am. Law Inst., Am. Assn. Law Schs. (chairperson evidence sect. 1994). Office: Hastings Coll of Law 200 Mcallister St San Francisco CA 94102-4707

PARK, WILLIAM LAIRD, agricultural economics educator, consultant, college associate dean; b. Mar. 29, 1931; s. William D. and Ardella (Laird) Park; m. Ann Payne, Aug. 7, 1953; children: Leslie, David W., Wayne I., Andrea, John L. BS, Utah State U., 1957, MS, 1958; PhD, Cornell U., 1963. Dep. chief coop. rels. NY/NJ Milk Mktg. Adminstrn., N.Y.C., 1958—65; assoc. prof. agrl. econs. Rutgers U., New Brunswick, NJ, 1965—68, chmn. dept. agrl. econs. and mktg., 1970—75; sr. agrl. economist Devel. and Resources Corp., Sacramento, 1969—70; chmn. dept. agrl. econs. Brigham Young U., Provo, Utah, 1977—83, prof., 1983—, assoc. dean agr., 1988—98, dir. Agrl. Sta., 1995—98, ret., 1998. Pres. Ag-Econ Rsch. Assocs., Orem, Utah, 1978—; bd. dirs. N.E. Agrl. Econs. Coun., 1972—77; cons. agr., agribus. Author: Estimating Demand and Price Structures by Residual Analysis, 1970; author: numerous bulls., reports on dairy econs., feasibility analysis, internat. econ. devel.; contbr. articles to profl. jours. Cpl. U.S. Army, 1953—55. Mem.: Am. Agrl. Econs. Assn., Western Agrl. Econs. Assn., Phi Kappa Phi, Sigma Xi. Republican. Mem. Lds Ch. Home: 7807 White Pine Way Sandy UT 84094-0256

PARK, WILLIAM WYNNEWOOD, law educator; b. Phila., July 2, 1947; s. Oliver William and Christine (Lindes) Park. BA, Yale U., 1969; JD, Columbia U., 1972; MA, Cambridge U., 1975. Bar: Mass. 1972, DC 1980. Law practice, Paris, 1972-79; prof. law Boston U., 1979—. V.p. London Ct. Internat. Arbitration; dir. Boston U. Ctr. Banking Law Studies, 1990-93; vis. prof. U. Dijon, France, 1983-84, Inst. U. Hautes Etudes Internat., Geneva, 1983, U. Hong Kong, 1990; fellow Selwyn Coll., Cambridge, Eng., 1975-77; arbitrator Claims Resolution Tribunal for Dormant Accts., Switzerland. 1998-2002. Author: International Chamber of Commerce Arbitration, 3d edit., 2000, International Forum Selection, 1995, International Commercial Arbitration, 1997, Annotated Guide to the 1998 ICC Arbitration Rules, 1998, Arbitration in Banking and Finance, 1998; contbr. articles to profl. jours. Trustee Mass. Bible Soc.; sr. warden King's Chapel, Boston. Fellow Chartered Inst. Arbitrators (U.K.), Coll. Comml. Arbitrators; mem. ABA (chmn. internat. dispute resolution com.). Home: 36 King St Cohasset MA 02025-1304 Office: Boston U Law Sch 765 Commonwealth Ave Boston MA 02215-1401

PARKER, ADRIENNE NATALIE, art educator, art historian; b. NY, May 23, 1925; d. Benjamin and Bertha (Levine) Lefkowitz; m. Norman Richard Parker, July 22, 1945; children: Dennis, Jonathan W., Steven L. BA cum laude, Hunter Coll., 1945; MFA, Montclair Coll., 1975; postgrad., Instituto Des Artes, San Miguel, Mex., 1987. Instr. art, English Granby High Sch., Norfolk, Va., 1945-46; instr. art Mahwah (N.J.) Bd. Edn., 1970-75, Daus. of

Miriam Home for the Aged, Clifton, N.J., Fedn. Home, Paterson, N.J.; instr. art, history Bergen C.C., Paramus, N.J., 1980—. One-woman show Bergen C.C., Woodstock Artists Assn.; exhibited in group shows at N.J. Art Educators, Bergen County Art Educators, N.J. Tercentenary (1st place), Pine Libr., Sara Delano Roosevelt House, Hunter Coll., Woodstock Art Assn., 1990-95, 99-2003, Fair Lawn Art Assn., 1991 (award), Palisade Guild Spinners and Weavers, 1994, Bergen C.C., 1994-95, 1999-2001. Editor Fairlawn H.S. PTA, Thomas Jefferson Jr. H.S.; pres., bd. dirs. The Cmty. Sch., Fairlawn, 1983—86; mem. art adv. exhbn. com. Pine Libr., 1992, 1993, 1994, 1995, 1996, 1997, 1998, 1999, 2000, 2001, 2002, 2003. Mem. N.J. Art Educators, Bergen County Art Educators, Wood Stock Art Assn., Fairlaw Art Assn., Hunter Coll. Alumni Assn. (bd. dirs. no. N.J. chpt. 1970—, pres. 1977-79, program chmn./v.p. 1993-94), Palisade Guild Spinners and Weavers (founder, editor, charter) Phi Beta Kappa. Avocations: hiking, cross country skiing, travel, archeology, study of primitive cultures. Home: 3827 Fair Lawn Ave Fair Lawn NJ 07410-4325 E-mail: aishelet@aol.com.

PARKER, BONNIE GAE, social science educator; b. El Paso, Tex., Oct. 12, 1958; d. Joel Tracy and Clara Sadie (Martin) Williamson; m. William Dorsey Parker III, May 16, 1981; children: Gisela Clare, William Dorsey IV. BA in History, U. Houston, 1980. Cert. secondary sch. tchr., Tex. Tchr. history and govt. Jesse H. Jones H.S., Houston, 1981-83; tchr. history Willowridge H.S., Missouri City, Tex., 1983-86; substitute tchr. Ft. Bend Ind. Sch. Dist., Sugarland, Tex., 1986-89; tchr. social sci. St. Mark's Episcopal Sch., Houston, 1989—. Dir. religious edn. St. Stephen's Episcopal Ch., 1988-90. Pres. St. Mark's Daus. of the King, Houston, 1992-94; mem. sch. bd. St. Mark's Episcopal Sch., 1985-87; mem. vestry St. Mark's Episcopal Ch., 1987-90; del. local Rep. 25th dist., Harris County, Tex., 1984, 86, 88, 92, 94, 96, 98, 2000, 2002; alt. del. Tex. state Rep. convention, 1996; del., 1998, 2000, 2002. Avocations: Karate, golf. Home and Office: 6501 Kenyon Ln Bellaire TX 77401-3701

PARKER, BRENDA JEAN, secondary education educator; b. Red Oak, Iowa, Apr. 26, 1967; d. James Edward and Sandra Selene (Ferguson) Bates; m. John Eli Parker. BS in Edn., N.W. Mo. State U., 1989; MS in Tchg., Webster U., 1997. Tchr. English and French Leavenworth (Kans.) H.S. Mem. NEA. Home: 119 S Prairie Rose St Smithville MO 64089-8345

PARKER, CAROL TOMMIE, psychotherapist, educator; b. Birmingham, Ala. d. Estes Carter and Anny May (Skinner) Thompson; m. John W. Hill; children: Patrick, Laurie, Annette (dec.), Timothy, Gail, Daniel. BSW, U. Nebr., Omaha, 1977; MSW, U. Nebr., Lincoln, 1978. Diplomate Am. Bd. Med. Psychotherapists; cert. master social worker. Practice psychotherapy specializing in individual and family therapy, Omaha, 1980—. Family therapist Med. Coll. U. Nebr., Omaha, 1978-94; asst prof., adj. faculty sch. social work U. Nebr., Omaha, 1987-94, asst. prof. courtesy faculty Coll. Medicine Dept. Psychiatry, Dept. Family Practice U. Nebr. Med. Ctr., 1988—; practicum instr. sch. social work U. Nebr., Omaha, 1980-94. Bd. dirs. Advocacy Office Children and Youth, Omaha, 1984-85. Fellow Nat. Assn. Social Workers; mem. Acad. Cert. Social Workers, Internat. Acad. Behavioral Medicine, Counseling and Psychotherapy, Inc. (diplomate), Am. Assn. Marriage and Family Therapy (clin., approved supr.), Omaha Club., Omaha Press Club. Democrat.

PARKER, CHARLES BRAND, JR., training company executive; b. Washington, Sept. 15, 1936; s. Charles Brand and Annie Laura (Chambers) P.; m. Grace Carolyn McGunigal, Sept. 8, 1959; children: Christopher Arlen, Shannon James. AB, George Washington U., 1960; BD, Southeastern Sem., Wake Forest, N.C., 1963, ThM, 1969; EdD, N.C. State U., 1978. Coll. minister Meredith Coll., Raleigh, 1967-71; exec. dir. Triangle Complex, Inc., Raleigh, 1971-72; project dir. N.C. Manpower Coun., Raleigh, 1972-74; dir. Office Employment & Tng., Raleigh, 1974-80; rsch. dir. Thad Green Enterprises, Inc., Raleigh, 1980-83; pres. Tng. Resources, Inc., Raleigh, 1983—. Cons. N.C. Adv. Coun. on Vocat. Edn., Raleigh, 1984-91; initiator Fed. Job Corps Ctr., Kittrell, N.C.; dir. N.C. Employment & Tng. Coun., Raleigh, 1978-80. Author: Youth Labor Market Prospects for the 1980x, 1982, Establishing Employment and Training Performance Criteria for Youth: Trends and Techniques, 1982, Entrepreneurship: Implications for Training Economically Disadvantaged Youth, 1982; editor: An Analysis of the Major Elements of Transition of Youth From School to Work, 1982, Employment and Training of Minority Youth in the 1980s, 1982, Public Funding for Education in North Carolina, 1984, Biennial Rev. North Carolina's Achievement in Accomplishing the Purposes of the Vocational Education Act and the Job Training Partnership Act 1986-88, 1989, companion vol. 1988-90, 1991. With USNR, 1954-62. Southeastern Sem. fellow, Wake Forest, N.C., 1965; recipient Outstanding Adminstrn. award U.S. Dept. Labor, Raleigh, 1975, Boss of Yr. award Am. Bus. Woman's Assn., Raleigh, 1979. Mem. Raleigh C. of C., Raleigh Civitan Club. Democrat. Baptist. Avocations: gardening, entrepreneurship, historic preservation, phys. fitness, writing. Home: 4717 Stanford St Raleigh NC 27609-5333 Office: Tng Resources Inc 214 New Bern Pl Raleigh NC 27601-1416

PARKER, CHERI ANN, elementary education educator; b. Mpls., Sept. 14, 1964; d. John Richard and Corinne Elizabeth (Vasseur) Steinbauer; m. Michael Jamison Parker, Mar. 12, 1988; 1 child, Nicholas Richard. BS, Jacksonvile U., 1986; MS in Elem. Edn., Fla. Internat. U., 1994. Elem. tchr. Kenwood Elem. Sch., Miami, Fla., 1986-99, tchr. hearing impaired, 1989-90, tchr. edn. rep., 1987-99, Fairforest Elem. Sch., Spartanburg, SC, 1999—. Kindergarten tchr. Air Base Elem. Sch., Homestead, Fla., 1987. Named Outstanding Young Educator, Fla. Jaycees, 1988, Tchr. of Yr., Kenwood Elem. Sch., 1989. Mem. Coral Gables Jaycees (membership v.p. 1987-88, sec. 1988-89), Alpha Delta Kappa (Gamma Theta chpt. v.p. 1994-96, pres. 1996-98, chaplain 1998-99). Republican. Roman Catholic. Avocations: cross-stitch, running, swimming. Home: 992 Shoresbrook Rd Spartanburg SC 29301-6500 Office: Fairforest Elem Sch PO Box 1001 Fairforest SC 29336-1001

PARKER, CHERYL JEAN, small business owner; b. Kansas City, Kans., Feb. 3, 1948; d. Mildred Eileen (Mayer) Ross; m. Jack W. Parker, June 25, 1977; children: Brian Scott, Kimberly Michelle. BS, Kans. State U., 1970; MA, U. Mo., Kansas City, 1975; postgrad., Dept. Def. Info. Sch., 1984. Cert. tchr. Mo., Kans. Migrant tchr. Piper Unified Schs. 203, Kansas City, Kans., 1970-72; tchr. North Kansas City Pub. Schs., Kansas City, 1970-75; elem. guidance counselor Excelsior (Mo.) Springs Pub. Schs., 1975-77; rsch. asst. foster parent rsch. project Coll. Human Ecology, Manhattan, Kans., 1977-78; test examiner 1st Inf. Div., Fort Riley, Kans., 1980-82, pub. affairs specialist, 1983-85; pers. clerk 3rd ROTC Div. Hdqrs., Fort Riley, 1982-83; tchr. Living Word Christian Sch., Manhattan, 1985-86; program mgr., career counselor Army Community Svcs., Army War Coll., Carlisle, Pa., 1987-90; elem. guidance counselor Shawnee Mission (Kans.) Pub. Schs., 1990-96; small bus. owner, 1996—. Recording sec. Career Edn. Com., Excelsior Springs, 1975-77; career counselor personal contacts and referrals, Carlisle, 1986-90; career counselor relocation/outplacement, U.S. Army, Carlisle, 1987-90; job fair coord. Army Community Svcs., Carlisle, 1989-90; guest speaker various clubs, confs., Carlisle, Excelsior Springs. Author: (with others, catalog) Foster Parent Resources, 1977-78; contbr. articles to profl. jours. Violinist Christ Community Ch. Orch., Camp Hill, Pa., 1986-89, Full Faith Ch. Psalm 150 Orch., 1993; mem. hospitality com. PTA, Carlisle, 1987-88; mem. Suggestion Awards Rev. Com., Fort Riley, 1983-85. Hollis Award scholar Kans. State U., 1968, Kansas City Star scholar Kansas City Star Newspaper, 1966-70. Mem. Kans. NEA, Kans. Assn. Counseling and Devel. (Spurs Acad. hon. mem.), Carlisle Area Pers. Assn., Federally Employed Women (nomination chmn. 1989—), Federal Women's Program (program mgr. 1988-89, certificate 1989), Alpha Lambda Delta. Mem. Christian Ch. Avocations: christian and classical music, reading, needlework, travel, swimming. Home: 9824 W 132nd Ter Overland Park KS 66213-3319

PARKER, CYNTHIA MARY, economist, educator; d. Gene Albert and Minna Edna Fabbri; m. Jeffrey Alan Parker, Apr. 15, 1982; 1 child, Lisa Marie. BA in Econ., Calif. State U., Fullerton, 1980, MBA in Econ., 1989. Estimator Gen. Dynamics Corp., Pomona, Calif., 1980-81; administrv. asst. Jeffrey A. Parker, Montclair, Calif., 1982—; instr. skating Skate Junction, West Covina, Calif., 1986-94; rsch. economist, cons. Formuzis & Pickersgill, Inc., Santa Ana, Calif., 1987-90; instr. econ. Sunny Hills H.S., Fullerton, Calif., 1991-93, Calif. State U., Fullerton, 1991-93; forensic economist QED Rsch., Inc., Palo Alto, Calif., 1992—; instr. econ. and fin. Nat. U., Riverside, Calif., 1993—. Assoc. prof. Chaffey Coll., Rancho Cucamonga, Calif., 1993—, Mt. San Antonio Coll., Walnut, Calif., 1994—, mem. paralegal adv. com., 1994—. Mem. Nat. Assn. Bus. Economists, Nat. Assn. Forensic Economists, Omicron Delta Epsilon, Zeta Tau Alpha Alumni.

PARKER, DIANA MARIE, parochial school educator, administrator; b. Mpls., Feb. 7, 1946; d. John Paul and Dorothy Marie (Dawson) Smith; m. Dennis Edward Parker, Aug. 12, 1967; children: Katherine, Rebecca. Student, No. Ill. U., 1968-72; BS in Journalism, U. V.I., 1991. Cert. tchr., Ill. Tchr., dept. chair C. F. Simmons Jr. High Sch., Aurora, Ill., 1968-73; substitute tchr. Ill. Sch. Dist. 131, Aurora, Ill., 1974-76; tchr. Antilles Sch., St. Thomas, V.I., 1977-78, adminstr., 1978-87; prin. Sts. Peter and Paul High Sch., St. Thomas, V.I., 1987-90; dir. catholic sch. Diocese St. Thomas, V.I., 1990—. Bd. dirs. Antilles Sch. St. Thomas, 1990—; dir. Sts. Peter & Paul Cathedral Religious Edn. Program, St. Thomas, 1981—. Contbr. articles to profl. jours. . Mem. consumers coop of V.I., St. Thomas, 1976—, pres. 1982-89. Recipient Outstanding Virgin Islander award 17th Legislture for V.I., 1988. Mem. Nat. Catholic Ednl. Assn., Nat. Assn. Secondary Sch. Prin., St. Thomas-St. John Interscholastic Atletic Assn. (sec. 1985—). Roman Catholic. Avocations: reading, swimming, cooking, sewing. Home: 7775 Upper Lerkenlund Charlotte Amalie VI 00802-3606

PARKER, DONALD FRED, college dean, human resources management educator; b. Oilton, Okla., Nov. 7, 1934; s. Robert Fred Parker and Georgia Marie (Culley) Meek; m. Jo Ellen Dunfee, Apr. 6, 1963; children: Margaret Elizabeth, Emily Lyle. BA in Sociology, U. Okla., 1957; MS in Personnel Adminstrn., George Washington U., 1966; PhD in Human Resource Mgmt., Cornell U., 1974. Commd. ensign USN, 1957, advanced through grades to capt., 1977, staff officer with chief naval ops., 1969-71, comdg. officer, exec. officer, Patrol Squadron Ten Brunswick, Maine, 1974-76, prof. Naval War Coll. Newport, R.I., 1976-78, comdg. officer Navy Personnel Research & Devel. Ctr. San Diego, 1978-80, ret., 1980; asst. prof. Grad. Sch. Bus., U. Mich., Ann Arbor, 1980-84; prof., dean Coll. Commerce and Industry U. Wyo., Laramie, 1984-91; Sara Hart Kimball dean bus., prof. human resources mgmt. Oreg. State U., Corvallis, 1991—2001. Advisor U.S. West Wyo. State Bd. Advisors, Cheyenne, 1986-91; ex-officio dir. Wyo. Indsl. Devel. Corp., Casper, 1987; vis. prof. Acad. Internat. Econ. Affairs, Hsinchu, Taiwan, 1986-91. Author numerous articles, book chpts., case studies. Mem. Acad. of Mgmt. (human resource mgmt. divsn. dir. 1983-85), Midwest Assn. Deans and Dept. Chairs in Bus. (pres.), Western Assn. Collegiate Schs. Bus. (bd. dirs., pres. 1999), Phi Kappa Phi, Beta Gamma Sigma (pres. 1998-2000, past pres. 2000—02). Avocations: jogging, hiking. Home: 4400 NW Honeysuckle Dr Corvallis OR 97330-3355 Office: Oreg State U Coll Bus 200 Bexell Hall Corvallis OR 97331-8527 E-mail: parker@bus.orst.edu.

PARKER, EUGENE NEWMAN, retired physicist, educator; b. Houghton, Mich., June 10, 1927; s. Glenn H. and Helen (MacNair) Parker; m. Niesje Meuter, 1954; children: Joyce, Eric. BS, Mich. State U., 1948, DSc (hon.), 1975; PhD, Calif. Inst. Tech., 1951; DHC in Physics and Math. (hon.), U. Utrecht, The Netherlands, 1986; DHC in Theoretical Physics (hon.), U. Oslo, 1991. Instr. math. and astronomy U. Utah, 1951—53, asst. prof. physics, 1953—55; mem. faculty physics U. Chgo., 1955—95, prof. dept. physics, 1962—95, prof. dept. astronomy and astrophysics, 1967—95, prof. emeritus, 1995—. Author: Interplanetary Dynamical Processes, 1963, Cosmical Magnetic Fields, 1979, Spontaneous Current Sheets in Magnetic Fields, 1994. Recipient Space Sci. award, AIAA, 1964, Chapman medal, Royal Astron. Soc., 1979, Gold medal, 1992, Disting. Alumni award, Calif. Inst. Tech., 1980, Karl Schwarzschild award, Astronomische Gesselschaft, 1990, Bruce medal, Astron. Soc. Pacific, 1997, medal, Assn. Internat. Devel. Nice (France) Obs., 1997, Kyoto prize, Inamori Found., 2003, Maxwell prize, plasma physics divsn., Am. Phys. Soc., 2003. Mem.: NAS (H. K. Arctowski award 1969, U.S. Nat. medal of Sci. 1989), Norwegian Acad. Sci. and Letters, Am. Geophys. Union (John Adam Fleming award 1968, William Bowie medal 1990), Am. Astron. Soc. (Henry Norris Russell lectr. 1969, George Ellery Hale award 1978). Achievements include development of theory of the origin of the dipole magnetic field of Earth; prediction and theory of the solar wind and heliosphere; theoretical basis for the X-ray emission from the Sun and stars. Home: 1323 Evergreen Rd Homewood IL 60430-3410 E-mail: parker@odysseus.uchicago.edu.

PARKER, GEORGE ERNEST, secondary mathematics educator; b. Willimantic, Conn., Nov. 4, 1940; s. J. Ernest and Alice C. (Costello) P.; m. Cynthia Ann Nucci Parker, Oct. 16, 1965; children: Kimberly, Geoffrey, Christopher. BS, Ea. Conn. State U., 1964; MA, Wesleyan U., 1971, student, 1973, 81, 84, 85, 86, U. Conn., 1982, 83, 89. Cert. secondary sch. tchr. math, sci., Conn. Math. tchr. Valley Regional H.S., Deep River, Conn., 1964-65, Sweeney Sch., Willimantic, Conn., 1965-66, Coventry (Conn.) H.S., 1966-76; math dept. head Edwin O. Smith Sch., Storrs, Conn., 1976—2002. Lectr. secondary math. edn. U. Conn., Storrs, 1976—87; adj. prof. Ea. Conn. State U., Willimantic, 1982—90, 2002—; cons. curriculum Project to Increase Mastery Math. & Sci., Middletown, Conn., 1984—; pres. Foxbrush Consultants. Author: (with others) Computer Integrated Lessons for the Math Classroom, 1989, Math Connections Book III, 1995. V.p. Conn. Jr. Soccer Assn., 1970-75; pres. Mansfield (Conn.) PTA, 1984-86. G.E. Vanguard Fellow, 1984; recipient Outstanding Tchr. award MIT, 1992, Presidential award Nat. Found. Sci., 1994. Mem.: Nat. Coun. Tchrs. Math. (state rep. 1968—), Assn. Tchrs. Math. in Conn., Assn. Tchrs. Math. in New Eng., Conn. Coun. Suprs. Math. (pres. 1995—2001, exec. bd. 1990—), Math. Assn. Am., Conn. Soccer Coaches Assn. (pres., founder 1973—77). Roman Catholic. Avocations: running, reading, hiking, boating, soccer referee.

PARKER, JAMES FLETCHER, middle school educator; b. Washington, Aug. 13, 1951; s. Clifford Marion and Martha Lois (McPhail) P. Student, Shenandoah Coll., 1969-71; BS, Old Dominion U., 1973. Cert. tech. edn., Va. Tchr. Spratley Jr. High Sch., Hampton, Va., 1974, Lindsey Jr. High Sch., Hampton, 1974, East Suffolk (Va.) Mid. Sch., 1974-79, Driver Intermediate Sch., Suffolk, 1979-90, John Yeates Mid. Sch., Suffolk, 1990—. Contbr.: (state curriculum guide) Introduction to Technology, 1988. Vol. Suffolk Young Dems., 1976-78; mem. Driver Intermediate Sch. PTA, 1979-90, John Yeates Mid. Sch. PTA, Suffolk, 1990—. Mem. ASCD, NEA, Va. Edn. Assn., Edn. Assn. of Suffolk (v.p. 1997—), Am. Vocat. Assn., Va. Vocat. Assn., Internat. Tech. Edn., Assn., Va. Tech. Edn. Assn., Suffolk Tech. Edn. Assn., Edn. Assn. Suffolk (exec. bd. 1996-97), Tech. Student Assn. (chpt. adv. 1979—), Tidewater Tech. Tchrs., Va. Mid. Sch. Assn., Coun. Tech. Tchr. Edn. Avocations: golf, reading, computers. Home: 95 Bolling Rd Portsmouth VA 23701-2061 Office: John Yeates Mid Sch 4901 Bennetts Pasture Rd Suffolk VA 23435-1405

PARKER, JOHN RANDOLPH, pathologist, educator; b. Rochester, Minn., Apr. 29, 1967; s. Joseph Corbin and Patricia (Singleton) P. BA, U. Mo., Kansas City, MD, 1993. Diplomate in anatomic pathology, forensic pathology and neuropathology Am. Bd. Pathology; diplomate Am. Coll. Forensic Medicine. Rsch. asst. U. Tenn. Meml. Hosp., Knoxville, 1985; pathology student fellow U. Mo. Sch. Medicine, 1989-90; intern in diagnostic radiology U. Okla. Health Scis. Ctr., Oklahoma City, 1993-94, resident in anatomic pathology, 1994-96; fellow in forensic pathology office of chief med. examiner State of Okla., Oklahoma City, 1996-97; chief fellow in surg. pathology U. Tex.-M.D. Anderson Cancer Ctr., Houston, 1997-98, mem. faculty dept. pathology, 1998-99; neuropathology fellow dept. pathology Baylor Coll. Medicine, Houston, 1999-2000, Vanderbilt U. Med. Ctr., Nashville, 2000-01, mem. faculty dept. pathology, 2001—. Contbr. articles to Annals of Clin. and Lab. Sci., Archives of Pathology, Jour. Okla. State Med. Assn., Gynecologic Oncology, others. Organizer 4-H Summer Scholars Med. Terminology, Lakewood Hosp., 1989-91; co-chmn. Impaired Med. Student Coun., 1990-91. Recipient Richardson K. Noback Clin. Excellence award, 1993, Gov.'s commendation State of Okla., 1995, cert. of appreciation Office of Chief Med. Examiner, State of Okla., 1995, U. Okla. Lloyd and Ruth Rader Trust Scholarship award, 1996, AMA/Glaxo Wellcome Leadership award, 1997. Mem. AMA, Am. Coll. Forensic Examiners, Coll. Am. Pathologists, Am. Soc. Clin. Pathologists, Nat. Assn. Med. Examiners, U.S. and Can. Acad. Pathology, Mortar Board, Golden Key, Alpha Omega Alpha, Omicron Delta Kappa. Office: Vanderbilt U Med Ctr Dept Pathology C-3321 Medical Center North Nashville TN 37232-2562 E-mail: winoglue@aol.com.

PARKER, JUDITH ANN KELLEY, secondary school educator; b. Honolulu, Jan. 11, 1942; d. Charles Robert and Gladys Marion (Bartlett) Kelley; m. Kenneth Alfred Parker, June 24, 1963; children: Cheryl, Christopher. BS in Home Econs., U. Mass., 1963, MS in Home Econs., 1983. Vocat. tchr. Spl. Needs Smith Vocat., Northampton, Mass., 1982-85; tchr. Peck Middle Sch., Holyoke, Mass., 1985-91, Agawam (Mass.) H.S., 1991-92, Holyoke (Mass.) H.S., 1992—2001. Clk., supper, deacon 1st Congrl. Ch., 1979—. Mem. Western Mass. Home Econs. (v.p. 1987-89), Mass. Home Econs. Assn. (fin. chmn. 1993-94), Assn. Family and Consumer Scis. Avocations: needlework, stained glass, swimming, camping, rafting. Office: Holyoke HS 500 Beech St Holyoke MA 01040-2202

PARKER, KEITH DWIGHT, sociology educator; b. Phila., Oct. 15, 1954; s. Emery Woodruff, June 20, 1981; children: Narroyl, Malcolm. BA, Delta State U., Cleveland, Miss., 1978; MA, Miss. State U., 1982, PhD, 1986. Asst. dean students Delta State U., 1979-82; asst. prof. sociology Auburn (Ala.) U., 1986-89, U. Nebr., Lincoln, 1989-94, assoc. prof., 1994—2003, dir. African Am. studies, 1993—98; prof. sociology U. Ga., 2003—, assoc. provost Instl. Diversity, 2003—. Mem. editl. adv. bd. Jour. Social and Behavioral Scis., 1990-91; cons. editor Internat. Jour. Contemporary Sociology, 1991-95; contbr. articles to profl. jours. Bd. dirs. Lincoln-Lancaster Drug Project, 1992-96, Salvation Army, Lincoln, 1993-2003. Recipient Barbara Jordan award Big 8 Conf. on Student Govt., 1991. Mem. Midwest Sociol. Soc., Am. Soc. Criminology. Office: U Ga 119 Holmes Hunter Bldg Athens GA 30602

PARKER, LISA E. developmental studies educator; b. Decatur, Ga., May 28, 1963; d. Estil Wayne Evans and Ethelene 9Beasley) Allen; m. Donald Wayne Parker, Sept. 29, 1983; childern: Donald Wesley, Matthew Carrson. BS in Edn. cum laude, Tift Coll., 1984; BS in Edn., Ga. So. U., 1984, MEd, 1987, EDS, 1989. Cert. gifted educator; cert. learning disabilities. Tchr. Vidalia (Ga.) City Schs., 1984-86, 1986-88, Treutlen County Bd. Edn., Soperton, Ga., 1988-91, Southeastern Tech. Inst., Vidalia, 1991, instr. devel. studies, 1991—. Instr. devel. studies, 1991—; mem. Devel. Studies Adv. Com. Vidalia, Ga., 1991—; chair S.E. Consortia Devel. Educators, Vidalia, 1993—, vice chair state level; mem. Sex Equity Com., Vidalia, 1991—, Dress Com., Vidalia, 1992, Workroom Orgn., Vidalia, 1992, chairperson state level, 1994-96; commr. faculty forum, 1994-96. V.p. PTO, Vidalia, 1991-93; leader Boy Scouts Am., Vidalia, 1992—; mem. MADD, Vidalia, 1992—; vol. Spl. Olympics, Vidalia, 1984—. Mem. ASCD, Am. Vocat. Assn., Ga. Vocat. Assn., Nat. Assn. Devel. Educators. Republican. Baptist. Avocations: bible study, cross stitch, interior decorating, softball, camping. Office: Southeastern Tech Inst 3001 E 1st St Vidalia GA 30474-8817 Home: 1245 Salem Rd Mount Vernon GA 30445-2407

PARKER, LYNDA CHRISTINE RYLANDER, secondary education educator; b. Bremerton, Wash., Apr. 21, 1949; d. Richard Algot and Marian Ethelyn (Peterson) Rylander; m. Joseph Hiram Parker, Feb. 7, 1981; 1 child, Joseph Hiram IV. BA in English, Sociology, Pacific Luth. U., 1971, MA in Ednl. Administrn., 1981, prin.'s credential, 1982, postgrad. Tchr. lang. arts Cen. Kitsap Schs., Silverdale, Wash., 1971-74; tchr. English gifted Okanagan Schs., Kelowna, B.C., Can., 1974-78; tchr. lang. arts gifted Federal Way (Wash.) Schs., 1978-86; tchr. lang. arts, remedial reading, humanities gifted Bethel Sch. Dist., Spanaway, Wash., 1986—. Counselor Okanagan Sch. Dist., Kelowna, 1974-78; advisor Ski Club, Cheerleaders, Svc. Club, Pep Club, Kitsap Schs., Silverdale, 1971-74, Cheerleaders, Pep Club, Svc. Club, Ski Club, annual, newspaper, class advisor, Okanagan Sch. Dist., Kelowna, 1974-78, newspaper, Cheerleaders, Bethel Schs., Spanaway, 1986—; multimedia, at-risk program, gifted program, 1996-; presenter of workshops for parents, tchrs., adminstrs., 1988—. Named Christa McAuliffe Outstanding Tchr. of Yr. State of Wash., 1988. Mem. NEA, ASCD, NAFE, Nat. Assn. Secondary Sch. Prins., Wash. Edn. Assn., Wash. Assn. Secondary Sch. Prins., Bethel Educators Assn. Republican. Lutheran. Avocations: piano, snow skiing, body building. Home: 1721 169th Street Ct S Spanaway WA 98387-9141

PARKER, MARILYN, elementary school and education educator, assistant principal, school/special education counselor, entrepreneur; b. Port Arthur, Tex., June 4, 1969; d. Joseph and Mildred (Detiege) P. BBA in Fin., Prairie View A&M U., 1994, MEd in Curriculum and Instrn., 1997, MA in Counseling, 1998, MEd in Ednl. Adminstrn., 2002. Lic. profl. counselor. Customer svc. tng. asst. MCI Telecom., Sugarland, Tex., 1992-94; 5th grade tchr. Isaacs Elem., Houston, 1994—, 5th grade chair, 1997—98; co-tchr., resource tchr. Cypress-Fairbanks Ind. Sch. Dist., 1998—; asst. prin. Houston Ind. Sch. Dist., 2002—; prof. LeTourneau U. Owner The Scribe Co., Sch. Related Svcs. Houston, Inc.; prof. edn. Le Tourneau Christian U.; after-sch. study hall supr., detention hall supr. Cypress Fairbanks Ind. Sch. Dist.; webmaster, coun. mem. Houston Ind. Sch. Dist. Tech. Coun., 1997-98, spelling textbook adoption agent; spelling bee coord. Houston Chronicle Newspaper, 1997-98. Food drive recruiter Isaacs Elem. Houston Ind. Sch. Dist., 1996—97; cmty. police activity league liaison Houston Police Dept., 1997—98; leader Girl Scouts San Jacinto, Houston, 1997; editl. list and exec. asst. Higher Dimension Ch., 2001—; min. The Fountain of Praise Ch. Mem. CEC, NAFE, Assn. Notaires, Tex. Counseling Assn., Chi Sigma Iota, Phi Delta Kappa. Avocations: dance, aerobics, reading, community involvement, mentoring. E-mail: mparker31@yahoo.com.

PARKER, MARION HAWKINS, retired librarian; b. Lawrenceville, Va., June 6, 1942; d. John Lee and Alice Louise (Pearson) Hawkins; m. Ammie Parker Jr., Dec. 6, 1959; children: Anthony, Johnnye, Kenneth. Student, Hampton Inst., 1958-59; AA cum laude, Orange County C.C., 1971; BS in Elem. Edn., SUNY, New Paltz, 1974; MLS, L.I. U., 1976. Cert. elem. tchr., pub. libr., sch. libr. media specialist, N.Y. From clk. to head children's dept. libr. Newburgh (N.Y.) Free Libr., 1964-86; libr. media specialist West St. Sch., Primary Sch., Newburgh, 1986-87, Vails Gate High Tech Magnet Sch., Newburgh, 1987—2000; ret., 2000. Co-author: (with Stella Denton) 1776; A Bicentennial Bibliography, 1976. Bd. dirs. United Fund, Meals on Wheels, fundraising chmn.; acting chmn. bd. dirs. Head Start of Ea. Orange County; past chmn. Bd. Christian Edn., Ebenezer Bapt. Ch. Mem. N.Y. Libr. Assn., Order Ea. Star (past grand matron, Star of Hope, past 1st v.p. supreme coun. grand chpt.), Royal and Exalted Order Amaranth (past supreme grand assoc. matron, past state dep.), Newburgh Area Zonta Club (past pres.), Rose of Seven Seals (past state dep.). Democrat. Home: 414 Bingham Rd Marlboro NY 12542-5921 E-mail: mottl@juno.com.

PARKER, NORMAN NEIL, JR., software systems analyst, mathematics educator; b. Chgo., June 23, 1949; s. Norman Neil and Sarah Anne Parker; m. Rowena Robles, June 27, 1987. BS with honors, Iowa State U., 1971, MS with honors, 1974. Cert. secondary math. tchr., Ill. Grad. teaching asst. math. dept. Iowa State U., Ames, 1971-72; tchr. math. dept. Thornwood High Sch., South Holland, Ill., 1972-81; software system analyst, space shuttle software IBM, Houston, 1981-94; software system analyst Loral Space Info. Systems, Houston, 1994-96; sr. software sys. analyst Lockheed Martin Space Mission Systems & Svcs., Houston, 1996-98, chmn. software architecture rev. bd. for onboard shuttle, 1994—; computer scientist staff IV United Space Alliance, Houston, 1998—. Cons. Atomic Energy Commn., Iowa State U., Ames, 1970-72; Iowa State U. rep. NSF Regional Conf., Northfield, Minn., 1972. Contbr. articles to profl. jours. Life mem. Order of Demolay, 1963—; gymnastic judge Ill. High Sch. Assn., Nat. Gymnastics Judges Assn., Internat. Gymnastics Fedn., 1971-81; gymnastics coach Thornwood High Sch., South Holland, Ill., 1972-80; gymnastics program dir. South Holland Park Dist., 1976-80; devel. coord Spaceweek Corp., Houston, 1983-87; officer Filipino-Internat. Families Tex., Houston, 1989-93; mem. retreat team Christ Renews His Parish, 1994-2000, eucharistic min., 2001—, min. to the sick, 2001—; active Christian Action program, 1998-2001; active foster-adoption program Assoc. Cath. Charities, 2000—. Recipient Achievement award, NASA, 1994. Mem. AIAA (sr.), Clear Lake Area Spl. Interest Group Ada, Space Ctr. Object-oriented Projects and Engring. (charter), Johnson Space Ctr. Employees Activities Assn. (assoc.), Gong Yuen Chuan Fa Fedn. (sr.), Seiei Kan Shaolin Kung Fu (sr.). Republican. Roman Catholic. Home: 4307 Alysheba Ln Friendswood TX 77546-2464 Office: United Space Alliance 1st Fl-1H3 600 Gemini St Houston TX 77058-2783 E-mail: norman.n.parker@usa.space-ops.com.

PARKER, PAULETTE ANN, academic administrator; b. Detroit, Sept. 17, 1951; d. Charles Louis and Vera Ernestine (Dobiyash) Payor; m. James Hodges Parker Jr.; children: J. Daniel, Rebekah, Joshua. Student, U. Mich., 1969-71; BA in Govt. cum laude, Coll. William and Mary, 1992, MA in Govt., 1995. Intern U.S. Congress Ho. of Reps., Washington, summer 1971; adminstr. fgn. lang. houses Coll. of William and Mary, Williamsburg, Va., 1988-90, sec. dept. econs., 1990-93. Vol. Am. Cancer Soc., Am. Lung Assn., Am. Heart Assn., Va. Arthritis Found.; tchr. Williamsburg Comty. Ctr. Sunday Sch., 1988-91; vol. Am. Cancer Soc., Newport News chpt., 1990-91, PTA Breton H.S., 1990-91; active Union of Couns. for Soviet Jews, Washington, 1983-91. Mem. AAUW, Internat. Studies Assn. (presenter papers), So. Polit. Sci. Assn. (presenter papers), Women in Internat. Security (presenter papers), Women's Caucus for Polit. Sci., Am. Polit. Sci. Assn., Pi Sigma Alpha. Avocations: reading, tennis, water sports, gardening, traveling.

PARKER, PETER D.M. physicist, educator, researcher; b. N.Y.C., Dec. 14, 1936; s. Allan Ellwood and Alice Francis (Heywood) P.; m. Judith Maxfield Curren, Dec. 27, 1958; children: Stephanie, Gregory, Gretchen. BA, Amherst Coll., 1958; PhD, Calif. Tech., 1963. Physicist Brookhaven Nat. Labs., Upton, N.Y., 1963-66; prof. Yale U., New Haven, Conn., 1966—. Office: Yale U Physics Dept Wright Nuclear Structure 272 Whitney Ave New Haven CT 06520-8124 E-mail: peter.parker@yale.edu.

PARKER, REBECCA MARY, special education facility administrator, educator; b. Biloxi, Miss., Sept. 1, 1961; d. Peter John and Mary Laura (Whittington) Pitalo; m. David Alan McKee, Oct. 5, 1985 (div. Mar. 1992); 1 child, Daniel Owen McKee; m. Charles L. Parker, Feb. 3, 1994; 1 child, Mary Caroline, 1 child, Jessica Hart. BS in Spl. Edn., U. So. Miss., 1985, M of Behavioral Disorders, 1992; postgrad., Boston U., Berlin. Double A cert. Miss. State Dept. Edn. Tchr. learning disabilities Jackson County Schs., Biloxi, 1985-86; learning impaired specialist Dept. of Def. Dependent Schs., Berlin, 1986-89; tchr. day treatment program Gulf Oaks Psychiat. Facility, Biloxi, 1989-95; behavioral interventionist Jackson County Schs., Vancleave, Miss., 1986-89; exec. dir. recreation integration program O'Keefe Found., New Hope Ctr., Ocean Springs, Miss., 1997—. Adj. faculty U. So. Miss., Gautier, 1993—; spkr. on attention deficit Ctr. for Child Abuse, Gulfport, Miss., 1997; spkr. on applied behavioral analysis Juvenile Shelter Staff, Pascagoula, Miss., 1997; spkr. on recreational integration Gulfport Exch. Club, 1997; cons. on behavior issues Ocean Springs Schs., 1997-98; condr. parenting classes New Hope Ctr., Ocean Springs, 1997; mem. tng. staff on inclusion YMCA, Jackson, and Gulf Coast region, 1997-99; presenter in field. Conductor tng. sems. YMCA's, Jackson and Gulf Coast. Acad. scholar Miss. Gulf Coast Jr. Coll., 1981. Mem. CEC, Assn. for Retarded Citizens (audit bd. 1997—), Assn. for Severe Handicap, Ocean Springs C. of C. Methodist. Avocation: raising three children. Home: 4701 Gibson Rd Ocean Springs MS 39564-6009 Office: New Hope Ctr 1904 Government St Ocean Springs MS 39564-3933

PARKER, ROBERT GEORGE, radiation oncology educator, academic administrator; b. Detroit, Mich., Jan. 29, 1925; s. Clifford Robert and Velma (Ashman) P.; m. Diana Davis, June 30, 1977; children by previous marriage: Thomas Clifford, James Richardson. BS, U. Wis., 1946, MD., 1948. Diplomate Am. Bd. Radiology (trustee 1978-90, pres. 1988-90). Intern U. Nebr. Hosp., Omaha, 1948-49; resident in pathology Western Res. U., Cleve., 1949-50; resident in radiology U. Mich., Ann Arbor, 1950, 52-54, instr. in radiology, 1954-55; staff radiotherapist Swedish Hosp. Tumor Inst., Seattle, 1955-58; prof. radiology U. Wash., Seattle, 1958-77; prof. radiation oncology UCLA, 1977—. Lt. USNR, 1950-52. Fellow Am. Coll. Radiology (gold medalist 2001); mem. AMA (radiology residence rev. com.), Am. Soc. Therapeutic Radiologists (pres. 1975-76, gold medalist 1989), Radiol. Soc. N.Am. (bd. dirs. 1984-90, pres. 1991-92, gold medalist 1996), Am. Radium Soc. (bd. dirs. 1988-92, pres. 1992, Janeway medalist 1997). Office: UCLA 200 Ucla Medical Plz Ste B265 Los Angeles CA 90095-8344

PARKER, SCOTT JACKSON, theatre manager; b. Ft. Bragg, N.C., July 28, 1945; s. John William and Darice Lee (Jackson) P. MA, U. N.C., 1971; MFA, U. Va., 1978. Mng. dir. Duke U. Theatre, Durham, N.C., 1970-76; gen. mgr. East Carolina U. Theatre, Greenville, 1980-85; producer The Lost Colony Outdoor Drama, Manteo, N.C., 1986-89; dir. Inst. of Outdoor Drama U. N.C., Chapel Hill, N.C., 1990—. V.p. Paul Green Found., nationwide, 1989—. Producer, mgr., dir., scene designer. With U.S. Army, 1969-70. Mem. Nat. Theatre Conf. (pres. 1999-2000), Assn. for Theatre in Higher Edn. (founding mem. 1987), Coll. of Fellows of the Am. Theatre (bd. dirs.), Southeastern Theatre Conf. (pres. 1982), Arts Advs. of N.C. (pres. 1993-94), The Players Club N.Y.C. Democrat. Baptist. Avocations: white water kayaking, camping, hiking. Office: U NC Inst Outdoor Drama Cb # 3240 Chapel Hill NC 27599-0001

PARKER, SKEETER, secondary school educator; b. Hahira, Ga., Jan. 15, 1967; s. Arlie Jr. and Norma Jean (Rich) P. BBA, Valdosta (Ga.) State Coll., 1989, MEd in Secondary Math., 1993. Cert. secondary mid. grades math. tchr., Ga. Sportswriter The Berrien Press, Nashville, Ga., 1987—; tchr. high sch. math., dir. sports info. Tiftarea Acad., Chula, Ga., 1990-92; tchr. math., Mathcounts and Math. Olympics coach Berrien Mid. Sch., Nashville, 1993—2002; tchr. math. Berrien H.S., Nashville, Ga., 2002—, head math. dept., 2003—. Asst. baseball coach Berrien Mid. Sch., Nashville, 1997-2002; cross country coach Berrien H.S., 2001—. Author, editor: Rebel Football History, 1985, Rebel Baseball Record Book, 1987, Tiftarea Academy Football History, 1990, The Ancestry and Descendants of Charles Walter Nash and Martha Ann Harper, 1994. Baseball umpire Ga. High Sch. Assn., 1990-95; mem. instrumental ensemble 1st Bapt. Ch., Nashville, 1990—; operator electric clock for football Valdosta State U., 1990-99. Named Tchr. of Month, Tiftarea Acad., 1991, STAR Tchr. for Berrien County, 2001, Region @-AA Coach of Yr. for cross country, 2001, 02. Mem. Nat. Coun. Tchrs. Math., Profl. Assn. Ga. Educators. Office: Berrien High Sch 500 E Smith Ave Nashville GA 31639-0008

PARKER, STEPHEN JAN, Slavic language and literature educator; b. N.Y.C., Aug. 5, 1939; s. Irving and Fan (Magarik) P.; m. Marie-Luce Monferran, June 15, 1965; children: Sandra, Richard. BA, Cornell U., 1960, MA, 1962, PhD, 1969. Asst. prof. U. Okla., Norman, 1966-67, U. Kans., Lawrence, 1967-73, assoc. prof., 1973-86, prof. Slavic langs. and lits., 1986—, chmn. dept. Slavic langs. and lits., 1987—2000. Co-author: Russia on Canvas, 1981; author: Understanding Vladimir Nabokov, 1987; coeditor The Achievements of Vladimir Nabokov, 1984; editor, publisher: The Nabokovian, 1978—. Chmn. bd. dirs. Lawrence Preservation Fund, 1979-82. NEH fellow, 1970-71. Mem. Am. Assn. for the Advancement of Slavic Studies, Am. Assn. Tchrs. of Slavic and East European Langs., MLA, Vladimir Nabokov Soc. (founder, sec., treas. 1978—), Am. Coun. of Slavists, Am. Dept. of Fgn. Langs. Office: U Kans Dept Slavic Languages Lawrence KS 66045-0001

PARKER-BROILES, DIANA MARIE, school counselor; b. Kansas City, Mo., May 17, 1947; d. Darmon Donnie and Wilma Fern (Ross) Parker; m. James Lafayette Broiles, Jr., June 16, 1973; 1 child, James Damon. BA, Baker U., 1969; MA, U. Mo., Kansas City, 1973. Cert. tchr., counselor, Mo., Okla. Tchr. English, Unified Sch. Dist. 259, Wichita, Kans., 1973-76, counselor, 1976-86; tchr. English, Kansas City Pub. Schs., 1969-73, 89-90, counselor, 1990-91, Oklahoma City Pub. Schs., 1992—. Mem. adv. bd., cons. Student Adv. Coun., Wichita, 1975-80. Active local polit. campaigns, Wichita, 1978-86, vol. voter registration; bd. dirs. Hope Inc. Recipient excellence award Wichita Pub. Sch., Outstanding Sponsor and Work award Student Adv. Coun., 1976-80. Mem. NAFE, ACA, Am. Vocat. Assn., Okla. Counseling Assn., Jack and Jill, Oklahoma City Met. Alliance Black Sch. Educators, Phi Delta Kappa, Alpha Kappa Alpha (former pres. local chpt.). Avocations: reading, traveling, crafts, gardening. Home and Office: PO Box 50271 Oklahoma City OK 73140-5271

PARKEY, ROBERT WAYNE, radiology and nuclear medicine educator, research radiologist; b. Dallas, July 17, 1938; s. Jack and Gloria Alfreda (Perry) P.; m. Nancy June Knox, Aug. 9, 1958; children: Wendell Wade, Robert Todd, Amy Elizabeth. BS in Physics, U. Tex., 1960; MD, S.W. Med. Sch., U. Tex., Dallas, 1965. Diplomate Am. Bd. Radiology, Am. Bd. Nuclear Medicine. Intern St. Paul Hosp., Dallas, 1965-66; resident in radiology U. Tex. Health Sci. Ctr., Dallas, 1966-69, asst. prof. radiology, 1970-74, assoc. prof., 1974-77, prof., chmn. dept. radiology, 1977—, Effie and Wofford Cain Disting. chair in diagnostic imaging, 1994—. Chief nuc. medicine Parkland Meml. Hosp., Dallas, 1974-79, chief dept. radiology, 1977—. Contbr. numerous chpts., articles and abstracts to profl. pubs. Served as catp. M.C., Army N.G., 1965-72. NIH fellow Nat. Inst. Gen. Med. Sci., U. Mo., Columbia, 1969-70; Nat. Acad. Scis.-NRC scholar in radiol. rsch. James Picker Found., 1971-74. Fellow Am. Coll. Cardiology, Am. Coll. Radiology; mem. Am. Coll. Nuclear Physicians (charter, ho. of dels. 1974—), Coun. on Cardiovascular Radiology of Am. Heart Assn., AMA, Assn. Univ. Radiologists, Dallas County Med. Assn., Dallas Ft. Worth Radiol. Soc., Radiol. Soc. N.Am., Soc. Chmn. of Acad. Radiology Depts., Soc. Nuclear Medicine (acad. coun.), Tex. Med. Assn., Tex. Radiol. Soc., Sigma Xi, Alpha Omega Alpha. Achievements include Achievements include academic research on nuclear cardiology, development of new imaging technologies, medical education. Avocations: gardening, golf, tennis. Office: U Tex Southwestern Med Ctr Dept Radiology 5323 Harry Hines Blvd Dallas TX 75390-8896

PARKHURST, CONNIE LOU, audiologist; b. Bay City, Mich., Mar. 15, 1953; d. John Anthony and Betty Lou (VanPopplen) Horner; m. Steven Michael Parkhurst, Dec. 21, 1974; children: Sean, David, James. Assoc., Delta C.C., University Center, Mich., 1973; BS summa cum laude, Western Mich. U., Kalamazoo, 1975; MA in Audiology, La. State U., 1982. Clin. cert. competence Am. Speech & Hearing Assn. Speech therapist Carrollton (Mich.) Pub. Schs., 1975-78, East Baton Rouge Parish Schs., Baton Rouge, La., 1978-81; audiologist, deaf educator State of La. and East Baton Rouge Schs., 1981-84; clin. supr. grad. students Ctrl. Mich. U., Mt. Pleasant, 1984-89; clin. audiologist/hearing aid dealer Mich. Ear Clinic, Saginaw, 1989-92; cons. audiology Midland (Mich.) Intermediate Sch. Dist., 1992—; clin. audiologist Narendra Kumar, M.D., Saginaw, Mich., 1992-95; clin. supr. in audiology Cen. Mich. U., Mt. Pleasant, 1995—. Com. mem. Head Start Mid Mich., Mt. Pleasant, 1985-88; presenter state conv., 1983, state and nat. convs., 1987-89, 90, 99. Leader Campfire Assn., Midland, 1986-88; com. mem. Homer Twp. Govt. Wage Com., Midland, 1989-94; pres. Chippewassee Parent-Tchr. Group, Midland, 1993-95; baseball coach Westown League, Midland, 1992; trustee Midland County Edn. Svc. Agy. Sch. Bd., 2001—. Dept. Edn. grantee Cen. Mich. U., 1988. Mem. Am. Speech and Hearing Assn. (award for continuing edn. 1989-92, 96-99), Am. Acad. Audiology, Mich. Speech and Hearing Assn., La. Speech and Hearing Assn., Phi Delta Kappa. Avocations: reading, sewing, sailing, participating in son's sports. Home: 4304 Oakridge Dr Midland MI 48640-2164 Office: Cen Mich U 425 Moore Hl Mount Pleasant MI 48859-0001 E-mail: connie.l.parkhurst@cmich.edu.

PARKIN, JAMES LAMAR, otolaryngologist, educator; b. Salt Lake City, June 2, 1939; s. Elmer Lamar and Mary Ilene (Soffe) Parkin; m. Bonnie Dansie, July 1, 1963; children: Jeffrey, Brett, Matthew, David. BS, U. Utah, 1963, MD, 1966; MS, U. Wash., 1970. Diplomate Am. Bd. Otolaryngology. Resident in otolaryngology U. Wash., Seattle, 1968—72; practice medicine specializing in otolaryngology Salt Lake City, 1972—; chmn. divsn. otolaryngology U. Utah Sch. Medicine, Salt Lake City, 1974—93, prof. surgery, 1981—, acting chmn. dept. surgery, 1984—84, 1993—94, chmn., 1994—96. Pres. med. bd. Univ. Med. Ctr., Salt Lake City, 1983—85, chmn. exec. com. faculty practice orgn., 1994—96, assoc. v.p. health scis., 1996—97; bd. govs. Utah Med. Ins. Assn., Salt Lake City, 1979—81. Guest editor Ear, Nose and Throat Jour., 1982, assoc. editor Archives of Otolaryngology. Leader Boy Scouts Am.; bishop Ch. of Jesus Christ of Latter-Day Saints, Salt Lake City, 1983—86, stake pres., 1986—96, pres. Eng. London South Mission, 1996—2000. Recipient Honor award, Am. Acad. Otolaryngology, 1980. Fellow: ACS, Am. Neurotology Soc., Am. Soc. Laser Medicine and Surgery, Am. Laryngol, Rhinol. and Otol. Soc., Am. Plastic and Reconstructive Surgery, Am. Otol. Soc.; mem.: Soc. Otolaryngology-Maxillofacial Surgery (pres. Utah chpt. 1979), Am. Cancer Soc. (pres. Utah chpt. 1984—86), Soc. Univ. Otolaryngologists (pres. 1984—85), Assn. Acad. Depts. Otolaryngology (chmn. nat. faculty survey com. 1980—90, sec.-treas. 1982—84, pres. 1986—88). Home: 2390 Bernadine Dr Salt Lake City UT 84109-1206 Office: U Utah Health Scis Ctr 50 N Medical Dr Salt Lake City UT 84132-0001

PARKINSON, WILLIAM HAMBLETON, physics, educator; b. Trenton, N.J., June 26, 1932; s. William and Norma Elizabeth (Thompson) P.; m. Phyllis Thurlow Smith, Sept. 2, 1954; children: William Richard Cameron, Daniel Dougald Lee. BSc in Physics, U. Western Ontario, London, Can., 1956, MSc in Physics, 1957, PhD in Physics, 1959. Lectr. in astronomy Harvard Coll. Observatory, Cambridge, Mass., 1961—2001, sr. rsch. assoc., 1969—2001; assoc. dir. atomic and molecular physics divsn. Harvard-Smithsonian Ctr. Astrophysics, Cambridge, 1973-87; physicist Smithsonian Inst., Cambridge, 1973-87, supervisory physicist, 1987-91, sr. physicist, 1991—. Recipient scholarship Ont. Rsch. Found., 1956-59; post-doctoral overseas fellow Nat. Rsch. Coun. Can., 1959-61. Fellow Am. Phys. Soc.; mem. Internat Soc. Optical Engring., Internat. Astron. Union (commn. 14 v.p. 1991-94, pres. 1994—), Am. Astron. Soc. Anglican. Avocations: aviculture, gardening. Office: Harvard Coll Observatory 60 Garden St # 50 Cambridge MA 02138-1516

PARKO, EDITH MARGARET, special education educator; b. Sanford, Fla., Sept. 1, 1943; d. Clarence Robert Jones and Domarious (LeCroy) Varn; m. Joseph Edward Parko Jr., Apr. 16, 1966; 1 child, Kimberly Graham. AA, U. Fla., 1963; BA, Stetson U., 1965; MA, Atlanta U., 1970; PhD, Ga. State U., 1984. Lic. tchr., sch. counselor, instrnl. leadership, dir. spl. edn. Ga. Tchr. sci. Seminole County Bd. Edn., Sanford, Fla., 1965-66; tchr. sci./math. Atlanta City Schs., 1966-68; tchr. emotionally disturbed Ga. Mental Health Inst., Atlanta, 1972-79; tchr. learning disabilities The Howard Sch., Atlanta, 1983-87; cons. Ga. Dept. Edn., Atlanta, 1987-88; tchr. emotionally disturbed Atlanta City Schs., 1988-90, rschr., 1990-91, coord. learning disabilities, 1991-94, coord. youth svcs., 1994—2001; program mgr. for rsch., evaluation, and testing Ga. Dept. of Edn., 2001—03; cons. edn. rsch. and evaluation Mgmt. of Am., 2003—. Author children's lit. Named Outstanding Adminstr., Met. Atlanta CEC, 1995, Ga. Fedn. CEC, 1995. Mem. AEA, CEC (pres. 1998-2000), Learning Disabilitis Assn., Profl. Assn. Ga. Educators. Avocations: golf, writing, reading, trout fishing, travel. Home: 325 Elmira Pl NE Atlanta GA 30307-2039

PARKO, JOSEPH EDWARD, JR., emeritus educator; b. St. Louis, May 15, 1938; s. Joseph Edward Sr. and Florence Evelin (Graham) P.; m. Edith Margaret Jones, Apr. 16, 1966; 1 child, Kimberly Graham. BA, Stetson U., 1966; MBA, Ga. State U., 1972. Asst. to dean (Sch. Urban Life) Ga. State U., 1972-73, dir. (Urban Community Svc.), 1974-86, dir. (non-profit studies program), 1987-97. Cons. United Way, Atlanta, 1985-89, Met. Atlanta Rapid Transit Authority, 1986; trainer workshops non-profit and govt. orgns., 1974—; bd. dirs. Progressive Healthcare Providers, Inc., pres. Progressive Healthcare Providers Charities, Atlanta rep. Friends com. on nat. legislation, 2002—. Editor: Organizing for Action, 1976; editor Community Info. Clearinghouse newsletter, 1972-82; contbr. articles to profl. jours., mags. and newspapers. Mem. housing task force Atlanta Regional Commn., 1975, Human Svcs. Adv. Coun., Atlanta, 1976, Planning Zoning Commn., Avondale, Ga., 1984, Leadership Atlanta, 1980, Non-profit Mgmt. Assn.; bd. dirs. Nat. Assn. of Neighborhoods, D.C., 1977-80, Urban Life Assn., Atlanta, 1972-80; chmn. United Way Strategic Planning subcom., 1989. With USAF, 1957-61. Woodrow Wilson fellow, 1966; Higher Edn. Act grantee, 1973, 76; recipient Outstanding Atlantan award, 1975, Merit award Ga. Adult Edn. Assn., 1982. Mem. Amnesty Internat., ACLU, Greenpeace, Leadership Atlanta Alumni Assn., Am. Friends Svc. Com. Democrat. Mem. Soc. Of Friends. Avocations: golf, fly fishing, travel, photography, working for peace.

PARKS, BEATRICE GRIFFIN, elementary school educator; b. Columbus, Miss., Jan. 03; d. James D. and Jimmie (McCottrell) Griffin; m. Orbia Ray Parks, Aug. 12, 1956 (div. May 1987); children: Donna Raye, Monica Lynn, David Griffin. BS in Edn., Lincoln U., Jefferson City, Mo., 1954. Elem. tchr. Cape Girardeau (Mo.) Pub. Schs., 1954-55, East St. Louis (Ill.) Bd. Edn., 1955-56; tchr. U.S. Army, Germany, 1956-57; elem. tchr. St. Louis Bd. Edn., 1960—, art specialist, 1980-94; floral designer Silk Expressions by Bea, St. Louis, 1991—; interior decorator Trans Designs, St. Louis, 1987-89. Arts chairperson Visual/Performing Arts Ctr., St. Louis, 1985-90; mem. Phyllis Wheatley YWCA. Recipient Svc. award Visual and Performing Arts Ctr., St. Louis, 1983-84, Art Excellence award, 1985-86. Mem. Nat. Art Edn. Assn., Mo. Art Edn. Assn., St. Louis Tchrs. Assn., Nat. Lincoln U. Alumni Assn., Greater St. Louis Lincoln U. Alumni Assn., Alpha Kappa Alpha (Founders award 1985, Arts and Heritage award 1988-89, Soror of Yr. 1992). United Ch. of Christ. Avocations: music, theater, writing. Home: 7192 White Oak Ln Saint Louis MO 63130-1816 Office: Silk Expressions by Bea PO Box 3087 Saint Louis MO 63130-0487

PARKS, DARRELL LEE, vocational education contultant, administrator; b. Richmond, Ind., Apr. 16, 1937; s. Garland H. and Goldie J. (Kimmel) P.; m. Naomi Joan Rust, Aug. 16, 1958; children: Pamela Sue, Patricia Jo, Rebecca Ann, Brian Lee. BS in Agr., Ohio State U., 1959, MS in Agrl. Edn., 1965, PhD in Agrl. Edn., 1968; postdoctoral student, Miami U., Oxford, Ohio, 1974-75. Tchr. agr. Parkway Local Schs., Mercer County, Ohio, 1959-62, Canal Winchester Local Schs., Franklin County, Ohio, 1963-65; supr. itinerant tchrs. Ohio State U., Columbus, 1965-66; supr. agrl. edn. Ohio State Dept. Edn., Columbus, 1966-70, asst. dir. vocat. edn., profl. staff and curriculum devel., 1970-71, 75-78, asst. dir. vocat. edn., dir. div. planning and evaluation, 1971-72, dir. vocat. and career edn., 1982-95, ret., 1995; adminstrv. specialist instrnl. program mgmt. Gt. Oaks Joint Vocat. Sch. Dist., Cin., 1972-75; dir. Nat. Acad. Vocat. Edn. Nat. Ctr. Rsch. in Vocat. Edn., Columbus, 1978-79. Adj. prof., lectr. Grad. Sch. Ohio State U., 1979-95; cons. in field; presenter at profl. confs. Contbr. articles to nat. jours. and mags. Trustee Northwest Civic Assn., Columbus, 1978-79; trustee, Little League baseball coach North Columbus Sports Assn., 1990. Recipient Disting. Alumni award Ohio State U. Coll. Agr., 1991. Mem. Am. Vocat. Assn. (life), Nat. Assn. Surps. Agrl. Edn., Nat. Vocat. Agr. Tchrs. Assn., Ohio Vocat. Agr. Tchrs. Assn., Ohio Vocat. Assn. (life), Ohio Vocat. Dirs. Assn., Am. Vocat. Edn. Pers. Devel. Assn. (pres. 1976-77), Nat. Assn. State Dirs. Vocat. Edn. (pres. 1990), Nat. Future Farmers Am. Alumni Assn. (life, hon. Am. Farmer degree 1984), Mason (Ohio) Lions (charter), Phi Delta Kappa, Gamma Sigma Delta. Republican. Methodist. Avocations: nature study, woodworking. Home: 1355 Slade Ave Columbus OH 43235-4058

PARKS, GEORGE BROOKS, land development consultant, university dean; b. Lebanon, Ky., Feb. 18, 1925; s. George W. and Eleanor B. (Brooks) P.; children— Paula, William. Student N.C. Central Coll., 1942-44; LL.B., Howard U., 1948; LL.M., George Washington U., 1949. Bar: U.S. Dist. Ct. D.C. 1948, U.S. Ct. Appeals 1949, Ky. 1951, U.S. Supreme Ct. 1952. Assoc. Coleman, Parks & Washington, Washington, 1948-60; sr. title officer Security Title Ins. Co., 1960-63; founder, pres. Mchts. Title Co., Los Angeles, 1963-69; dir. urban affairs Title Ins. & Trust Co., Los Angeles, 1969-70; exec. dir. Housing Opportunity Ctr., Los Angeles, 1970-73; asst. to councilman David Cunningham, Los Angeles, 1973-74; dep. county supr. Los Angeles County, 1974-76; asst. dean South Bay U. Sch., Carson, Calif., 1976-78, Glendale U. Sch. Law, Los Angeles, 1978— ; cons. Summa Corp., Los Angeles, 1978-84; pvt. practice cons., Los Angeles, 1978— . Appointed to Productivity Adv. com. City of Los Angeles by Mayor Tom Bradley, 1986. Recipient Cert. of Appreciation, City of Los Angeles, 1979, Outstanding Leadership award Lutheran Housing Corp., 1980; named Disting. Lectr., Nat. Soc. Real Estate Appraisers, 1981, Disting. Alumni, Howard U. Alumni Assn., 1982. Mem. ABA. Democrat. Lutheran. Home: 1149 S Alfred St Los Angeles CA 90035-2503 Office: George B Parks & Assocs 1122 S La Cienega Blvd Ste 104 Los Angeles CA 90035-2500

PARKS, HAROLD RAYMOND, mathematician, educator; b. Wilmington, Del., May 22, 1949; s. Lytle Raymond Jr. and Marjorie Ruth (Chambers) P.; m. Paula Sue Beaulieu, Aug. 21, 1971 (div. 1984); children: Paul Raymond, David Austin; m. Susan Irene Taylor, June 6, 1985; 1 stepchild, Kathryn McLaughlin. AB, Dartmouth Coll., 1971; PhD, Princeton U., 1974. Tamarkin instr. Brown U., Providence, 1974-77; asst. prof. Oreg. State U., Corvallis, 1977-82, assoc. prof., 1982-89, prof. math., 1989—, chmn. dept. math., 2001—. Vis. assoc. prof. Ind. U., Bloomington, 1982-83. Author: Explicit Determination of Area Minimizing Hypersurfaces, vol. II, 1986, (with Steven G. Krantz) A Primer of Real Analytic Functions, 1992, 2d edit., 2002, (with G. Musser, R. Burton, W. Siebler) Mathematics in Life, Society and the World, 1997, 2d edit., 2000, (with Steven G. Krantz) The Geometry of Domains in Space, 1999, (with Krantz) The Implicit Function Theorem: History, Theory, and Applications, 2002; contbr. articles to profl. publs. Cubmaster Oregon Trail Coun. Boy Scouts Am., 1990-92. NSF fellow, 1971-74. Mem. Am. Math. Soc., Math. Assn. Am., Soc. Indsl. and Applied Math., Phi Beta Kappa. Republican. Mem. Soc. Of Friends. Home: 33194 Dorset Ln Philomath OR 97370-9555 Office: Oreg State U Dept Math Corvallis OR 97331-4605 E-mail: parks@math.orst.edu.

PARKS, JULIA ETTA, retired education educator; b. Kansas City, Kans., Apr. 5, 1923; d. Hays and Idella Long; m. James A. Parks, Aug. 10, 1941; 1 child, James Hays. BEd, Washburn U., 1959, MEd, 1965; EdD, U. Kans., 1980. Tchr., concert vocalist Lowman Hill Elem. Sch., 1959-64; faculty Washburn U., Topeka, Kans., 1964-93, prof. edn., 1981-92, mem. pres.'s adv. coun., 1981-84, chair edn., phys. edn., health and recreation divsn., multicultural com., dept. edn., 1986-92. Insvc. lectr. reading instrns. Kans. Pub. Schs., 1960-93; lectr. Topeka Pub. Schs.; mem. acad. sabbatical com. Washburn U., 1987-90, vis. teams Nat. Coun. for Acreditation of Tchr. Edn., 1974-86, prof. emeritus, 1993. Bd. dirs. Children's Hour, 1981-84, Mulvane Art Ctr., 1974-78; judge All Kans. Spelling Bees, 1982-86; sec. Brown Decision Sculpture Com., 1974-85; oral record account of experiences as a minority student in integrated Topeka H.S., 1984; mem. multicultural non-sexist com. Topeka Pub. Sch., 1967—; apptd. to Kans. Equal Edn. Opportunities Adv. Com., 1988; marshall Washburn U. Commencements, 1980-92; mem. State of Kans. Task Force in Edn., 1991-92; presenter in field. Recipient Educator's award Living the Dream Com., Local award for Excellence in Equity in Edn., The Brown Found.; named to Topeka H.S. Hall of Fame, 1991; The Julia Etta Parks Honor Award created in her honor, Edn. Dept. Washburn U. Mem. Kans. Intergenerational Network, Washburn U. Alumni Assn. (contbr. alumni mag. 1989, recipient Tchg. Excellence award 1983), Internat. Reading Assn., Kans. Inst. Higher Edn. (mem. pres. adv. coun. 1981-83), Kans. Reading Assn., Kans. Reading Profls. Higher Edn., Topeka H.S. Hist. Soc., Links Club (pres. 1982-84, chairperson scholarship com. 1984-93), Topeka Back Home Reunion Club (historian, v.p. 1991—), Delta Kappa Gamma, Phi Delta Kappa, NONOSO Women's Hon. Sorority.

PARKS, PATRICK, English language educator, humanities educator; BA in Lit. and Mass Comms., Southwest State U., 1975; BS in English Edn. and Journalism, Bemidji State U., 1977; MFA in English, U. Iowa, 1982. Instr. English and journalism, newspaper advisor Harris-Lake Park H.S., Lake Park, Iowa, 1977-78, Ely (Minn.) H.S., 1978-79; tchg. asst. in rhetoric and lit. U. Iowa, Iowa City, 1981-82; instr. English and Journalism, pubs. advisor Muscatine (Ill.) C. C., 1982-86; prof. English and Humanities, dir. writers ctr. Elgin (Ill.) C. C., 1986-98, disting. prof. English and Humanities, 1998—. Instr. creative writing and composition evening program Southeastern C. C., Burlington, Iowa, 1979-80, creative writing Arts Outreach program U. Iowa, Iowa City, 1981, fiction writing The Writer's Workshop weekend program, 1982; facilitator No. Ill. Network Stff Devel., Lake Geneva, Wis., 1992, 1994; co-coord. ALA and Lila Wallace/Reader's Digest pilot program, Elgin, Ill., 1993; faculty adv. The Sarajevo Project, Elgin C. C., 1992—; presenter, lectr. in field. Editor, adv. (literary jour.) Farmer's Market; contbr. numerous stories, poems to literary jours., articles to profl. jours. Artist fellow Ill. Arts Coun. 1988; recipient Outstanding C. C. Professor of the Year award Carnegie Foun. Advancement of Tchg. and Coun. Advancement an Support of Edn. 1994, Outstanding Faculty award Ill. Cmty. Coll. Trustees Assn. 1994, Honorable Mention Fla. State U. World's Best Short Story Contest 1992, writing contest Rambunctious Review 1991, Excellence in Tchg. award Nat. Inst. Staf and Orgnl. Devel. 1991, First Place fiction writing contest Roselle Pub. Lib. 1988. Mem. Ill. Writers, Inc. (chair, bd. dirs.), Assoc. Writing Programs, C. C. Humanities Assn., Nat. Coun. Tchrs. English, Campus Compact Ctr. Cmty. Coll., Tchrs. and Writers Collaborative. Office: Elgin Comm Coll English Dept 1700 Spartan Dr Elgin IL 60123-7189

PARKS, SUZANNE LOWRY, psychiatric nurse, educator; b. Columbus, Ohio, Feb. 29, 1936; d. Frank Carson and Mabel (Brown) Lowry Morris; children: Jennifer, Kristin, Greg. BS, Emory U., 1958; MS, U. Md., 1959; postgrad., U. Hawaii, 1983-85, Columbia Pacific U., 1981-83, 86—. Asst. prof. psychiat. nursing U. Va., 1959-61, U. N.C., Chapel Hill, 1961-63, grad. faculty, 1975-81; asst. prof., dir. div. psychiat. nursing edn. sch. nursing Duke U., 1964-66; clin. nurse specialist Duke U. Hosp., 1966-68; clin. instr. psychiatry Sch. Medicine Emory U., Atlanta, 1968-71; asst. prof., nursing coord. Appalachian Area Nursing Insvc. project Clemson (S.C.) U., 1973-75; clin. staff Northside Mental Health Ctr., Chapel Hill, 1975-81; dir. staff devel. Hawaii State Hosp., Kaneohe, 1981-83; nurse Lainolu Retirement Ctr., Wakakii, 1983-85; asst. prof. Hawaii Loa Coll., Kaneohe, 1985-88; nurse chem. dependancy sect. Charter Winds Hosp., Athens, Ga., 1988-89; clin. specialist psychiat. inpatient svc. VA Med. Ctr., Atlanta, 1990-93; asst. clin. prof. psychiat. nursing East Carolina U., Greenville, N.C., 1993-97. Owner Suzanne's Selections 1988-89; travel nurse Flying nurses Med. Express Calif. and Alaska, 1989-90. Mem. ANA, NAFE, Am. Assn. Marriage and Family Counselors, Friends and Families of Schizophrenics, Mental Health Assn., Nurses Naturally Inc. (pres.). Home: 509 Glenwood Ave #627 Raleigh NC 27603

PARKS, WILLIAM RAYMOND, II, criminal justice educator; b. Fayetteville, N.C., May 28, 1948; s. William R. Parks and Darlene (Jamanis) Naylor; m. Sybil Richardson; 1 child, Stacy. BS in Criminal Justice, Valdosta State U., 1974, MS, 1975; JD, U. S.C., Columbia, 1987. Bar: S.C. 1994. Shift supr. Ga. Dept. Corrections, Valdosta, 1972-73; patrolman Lowndes County, Valdosta, 1973-74; capt. Cumberland County, Fayetteville, 1975-77; dir. Criminal Justice Dept., Fayetteville, 1975-78; asst. prof. Shaw U., Fayetteville, 1978-80; postal inspector U.S. Postal Svc., Washington, 1979-85; atty. State of S.C., Columbia, 1988-90; asst. prof. J.C. Smith U., Charlotte, N.C., 1991-94; pvt. practice Atlanta, 1994—. Sgt. U.S. Army, 1967-70, Vietnam. Recipient Am. Jurisprudence award Lawyers Coop. and U. S.C. Sch. Law, 1986; fellow U.S. Dept. Justice, 1974-75. Mem. Nat. Social Sci. Honor Soc. (dir. 1976-78), S.C. Bar (ethics com. 1989-91). Office: 14 Ocean Blvd PO Box 14923 Surfside Beach SC 29587-4923

PARLER, ANNE HEMENWAY, elementary education educator, horse trainer; b. Rochelle, Ill., July 15, 1931; d. William Merwin and Edith Florence (Ranger) Hemenway; m. William Carlos Parler, Aug. 13, 1955; children: William Jr., Blair Hemenway, Bethanie Parler Detar, B. Carolyn. BS in Edn., No. Ill. U., 1953; postgrad., Long Beach State U., 1953-54, U. S.C., 1956-58, U. Md., 1969-71. Cert. tchr. Music (K-12), Md. Tchr. Long Beach (Calif.) Sch. Dist., 1953-54, West Covina (Calif.) Sch. Dist., 1954-55, Columbia (S.C.) Sch. Sys., 1955-58, U. Md., College Park, 1970-71, St. Patrick's Episcopal Sch., Washington, 1971-73, Montgomery County Pub. Schs., Rockville, Md., 1973-95; ret., 1995; owner Sunny Meadows Horse Farm, Ocean View, Del., 1994—. Pvt. voice and piano tchr., Rockville, 1960-90. Contralto soloist Faith Meth. Ch., Rockville, 1968-90, dir. handbell choirs, 1985—; Dem. election judge, Rockville. Mem. NEA, MCEA (union rep.), Music Educators Nat. Conf., Met. Opera Guild, Nat. Women in the Arts Mus., Am. Guild English Handbell Ringers, Malice Domestic Mystery Writers Conv., Am. Quarter Horse Assn., Ill. State Soc., Harvard Law Wives, Navy Wives Club, Sigma Sigma Sigma, Sigma Alpha Iota. Democrat. Methodist. Home: PO Box 204 Ocean View DE 19970-0204 Office: Sunny Meadows Horse Farm PO Box 204 Ocean View DE 19970-0204

PARLOS, ALEXANDER GEORGE, systems and control engineering educator; b. Istanbul, Turkey, July 12, 1961; came to U.S., 1980; s. George Alexander and Helen (Stavridis) P.; m. Dalila Marcia Vieira, Aug. 25, 1985. BS, Tex. A&M U., 1983; MS, MIT, 1985, DSc, 1986. Rsch. asst. MIT, Cambridge, Mass., 1984-86; sr. rsch. assoc. U. N.Mex., Albuquerque, 1986-87; rsch. asst. Tex. A&M U., College Station, 1982-83, asst. prof., 1987-92, assoc. prof., 1993—2002, prof., 2003—. Co-founder, pres. ANN Engring., Inc., 1992-96; co-founder, chmn. Orasis Software, Inc., 1997-99; co-founder Veros Systems, Inc., 2001—; cons. engr. BDM Internat., Inc., McLean, Va., 1988—; sr. engring. assoc. API, Albuquerque, 1990—; cons. engr. Northrop-Grumman Corp., Bethpage, N.Y., 1994—; cons. engr. Kevin Kennedy & Assoc., Inc., Indpls., 1995—. Contbr. articles to Internat. Jour. Control, IEEE Trans. on Nuc. Sci., AIAA Jour. Guidance, Control and Dyamics, AIAA Jour. Propulsion and Power, Space Nuc. Power Sys., Nuc. Tech., Nuc. Sci. Engring., IEEE Trans. on Neural Networks, IEEE Trans. Automatic Control, IEEE Trans. on Industry Applications, also others. Treas. S.W. Crossing Assn., College Sta., 1990-91; advisor Hellenic Student Assn., College Station, 1988-91. Grantee NASA, 1988—, Dept. Energy, 1989—, Lockheed Missile Co., 1989, Electric Power Rsch. Inst., 1988, Am. Pub. Power Assn., 1993—, Advanced Rsch. Projects Agy., 1993—, Tex. Advanced Tech. Program, 1995—, NSF, 2000—; recipient Tech Brief Invention awards (3), NASA, 1999, Best Paper award Internat. Joint Conf. on Neural Networks, 1999. Mem. IEEE (sr., assoc. editor Trans. on Neural Networks 1994—), AIAA (sr.), ASME, Am. Nuc. Soc. (exec. com. human factors divsn. 1993—, chair tech. program com. human factors divsn. 1993—, chair program planning remote sys. divsn. 1989-90), Internat. Neural Networks Soc. (mem. conf. tech. program com. 1995—, mem. editl. bd. trans. on ctrl. automation and sys. 2000—). Achievements include 2 patents in field; 8 patents pending; research in neural information processing. Office: Tex A&M U 116 Engring Phys College Station TX 77843-0001

PARRINO, ROBERT, finance educator; b. N.Y.C., Sept. 4, 1957; s. Dominick Paul Parrino and Gertrude (Rainer) Wieczorek; m. Emily Allen Parrino, July 12, 1980. BSChemE, Lehigh U., Bethlehem, Pa., 1979; MBA, Coll. William and Mary, 1980; MS, U. Rochester, 1991, PhD in Fin., 1992. CFA. Sr. analyst Marriott Corp., Bethesda, Md., 1984-85; pres. Sprigg Lane Fin. Corp., Charlottesville, Va., 1985-88; faculty dept. fin. U. Tex., Austin, 1992-96, 97—; faculty U. Chgo., 1996-97. Dir. The Bentley Group, Charlottesville, 1987-88, Hicks, Muse, Tate & Furst Ctr. for Pvt. Equity Fin., Austin, 2000—. Contbr. articles to profl. jours. Capt. U.S. Army, 1981-84, lt. col. USAR. ret. Mem. Assn. for Investment Mgmt. and Rsch. (cand. curriculum com. 1994-99), Am. Econ. Assn., Fin. Mgmt. Assn., Am. Soc. Appraisers 1988-96 (Richmond chpt. treas. 1987-88), Beta Gamma Sigma. Office: U Texas Dept Fin 21st and Speedway Austin TX 78712 E-mail: parrino@mail.utexas.edu.

PARRIS, DONNA SANDS, secondary school educator; b. Winter Haven, Fla., July 30, 1951; d. Maxwell Lloyd and Thelma Desmond (Darby) Sands; 1 child, Brad; m. Jack Andy Parris, June 5, 1992; 1 stepchild, Andy. BS in Edn., Western Carolina U., 1973. Cert. tchr., N.C. Mgr. Alfredo's Restaurant, Maggie, N.C., 1981-85; tchr. health, phys. edn. Haywood County Schs., Waynesville, N.C., 1973-81, 89—, tchr. dropout prevention, 1985-88, mentor, trainer, 1989—, mem. staff devel. cadre, 1991—; health, phys. edn. and 7-8 lang. arts tchr. Ctrl. Haywood H.S., 1994—. Co-author: (textbook) Making Life Choices; editor ednl. handbooks and teaching resources. Named N.C. Health Tchr. Yr., N.C. Assn. Health Edn., 1992. Mem. AAHPERD, ASCD, N.C. Assn. Educators (officer various coms. including polit. action com. for edn. 1974-81), Waynesville Bus. and Profl. Women. Democrat. Methodist. Avocations: camping, water sports, reading, textile painting, horseback riding. Office: Haywood Ctrl HS PO Box 249 Clyde NC 28721-0249

PARRIS, FLORENCE MAE, elementary education educator; b. Waynesboro, Ga., Dec. 7, 1959; d. John Sr. and Ina Mae (Bowles) Rogers; m. David Anderson Parris, May 12, 1984; children: David II, India. BS in Early Childhood Edn., Paine Coll., 1983; MEd in Adminstrn. and Supervision, Trevecca Nazarene Coll., 1992. Film processor Colorcraft-Augusta (Ga.) Divsn.; switchboard operator Meharry-Hubbard Hosp., Nashville; vol. tchr. Meharry Day Care, Nashville; kindergarten tchr. Cousins Elem., Sardis, Ga.; first grade tchr. Mary Ann Garber Elem., Chattanooga; office mgr. Your Family Dentist, Chattanooga; kindergarten tchr. Lakeside Elem., Chattanooga; non-graded sch. tchr. Piney Woods Elem., Chattanooga. Elem. tchr. Waynesboro (Ga.) Elem.; vol. tchr. Reading Summer Program, Nevis, West Indies, 1994. Named Educator of Month, Tchr. Retirement Assn., Waynesboro, 1990, Tchr. of Yr. Cousins Elem. Sch., 1989-90, 90-91. Mem. Tenn. Assn. Educators, Chattanooga Edn. Assn., Zeta Phi Beta Sorority Inc., Ea. Stars. Avocations: drawing, reading, aerobics. Home: 234 Anderson Rd Waynesboro GA 30830-7414

PARRISH, ALMA ELLIS, elementary school educator; b. Peoria, Ill., Mar. 28, 1929; d. William Edward and Marie (Allton) Ellis; m. Clyde R. Parrish, Jr., Nov. 20, 1949; children: Clyde R. III, Charles, Donald, Royce, Christopher. BS, Bradley U., Peoria. Cert. elem. tchr., S.C., Ill. Tchr. Community Consol. Sch. Dist. 59, Elk Grove Village, Ill., Sipp Sch. Dist., Peoria, Kershaw County Sch. Dist., Camden, S.C. Vol. Guardian ad Litum of S.C. Mem. DAR, ACLU, Unitarian Universalist Assn., S.C. Ret. Edn. Assn., Tchrs. Coun. Dist. 59 (pres., com.), Ill. Ret. Tchrs. Assn., Kershaw County Ret. Edn. Assn., S.I. Coun., S.C. Master Gardeners Assn.

PARRISH, CARMELITA B. retired secondary school educator; b. Varina, N.C., Mar. 19, 1934; d. James Robert and Nita Mae (Webb) Beal; m. John J. Parrish, July 24, 1953 (dec.); children: Deborah Joy Parrish White, Toni Lynne Parrish Altenburg. AA, Mid. Ga. Coll., 1979; BS in Edn., Ga. So. U., 1981; MEd, Valdosta State U., 1988, U. Ga., 1993. Secondary tchr. English, graphic arts, Spanish Ware County Bd. Edn., Waycross, Ga., 1981-91; tchr. Spanish, English Telfair County Bd. Edn., McRae, Ga., 1991-92, Pickens County H.S., Jasper, Ga., 1992-98. Co-advisor Spanish Club; advisor yearbook; tchr. Spanish, journalism; adj. instr. Spanish, Macon (Ga.) State Coll., 1999—. Former leader Girl Scouts U.S., Spain; tchr. area Sunday sch.; band chaperone; tour leader student travel in Europe, 1985—. Recipient Star Tchr. award, Waycross-Ware County C. of C., 1987. Mem. NEA, Nat. Coun. Tchrs. of English, Ga. Assn. Educators (local assoc. pres., legislator contact team, Ga. Assn. Educators-Polit. Action Com.), So. Assn. Colls. and Schs. (mem. evaluation com.), Phi Kappa Phi. Home: 6229 Thomaston Rd #103 Macon GA 31220-7715 Office: 100 College Station Dr Macon GA 31206-5100

PARRISH, EDWARD ALTON, JR., electrical and computer engineering educator, academic administrator; b. Newport News, Va., Jan. 7, 1937; s. Edward Alton and Molly Wren (Vaughn) Parrish; m. Shirley Maxine Johnson, Oct. 26, 1963; children: Troy Alton, Gregory Sinton. BEE, U. Va., 1964, MEE, 1966, DScEE, 1968. Registered Tenn., Va. Group leader Amerad Corp., Charlottesville, Va., 1961—64; asst. prof. elec. engring. U. Va., Charlottesville, 1968—71, assoc. prof. elec. engring., 1971—77, prof. elec. engring., 1977—86, chmn. dept. elec. engring., 1978—86; dean, centennial prof. electrical engring. Vanderbilt U., Nashville, 1987—95; pres., prof. elec. and computer engring. Worcester Poly. U., 1995—. Cons. U.S. Army, Charlottesville, Va., 1971—77, ORS, Inc., Princeton, NJ, 1973—74, Sperry Marine Systems, Charlottesville, 1975—76, Hajime Industries Ltd., Tokyo, 1978—84. Contbr. articles to profl. jours. With USAF, 1954—58. Grantee numerous rsch. grants. Fellow: IEEE (bd. dirs. 1990—91, v.p. ednl. activities 1992—93, engring. accreditation commn. 1989—96, exec. com. 1991—96, officer 1993—96, chmn. elect 1994—95, chmn. 1995—96, past chmn. 1996—97, editor-in-chief IEEE Computer 1995—98), ABET (bd. dirs. 2000—); mem.: IEEE Computer Soc. (sec. 1997, v.p. 1978—81, pres. 1988), Tau Beta Pi, Eta Kappa Nu, Sigma Xi. Baptist. Avocations: music, woodworking. Office: Office of Pres Worcester Polytechnic Institue 100 Institute Rd Worcester MA 01609-2247 E-mail: eap@wpi.edu.

PARRISH, SHERRY DYE, elementary school educator; b. Birmingham, Ala., Oct. 18, 1957; d. Charles Max and Peggy Gail (Doss) Dye; m. James Wiley Parrish, June 13, 1987; 1 child, Taylor Austin Shaw. BS in Elem. Edn., Samford U., 1979; MS in Elem. Edn., U. Ala., 1995. Cert. tchr. Rank I, Class A., Ala. Tchr. Franklin Acad., Birmingham, Ala., 1979-83, Shades Cahaba Elem. Sch., Homewood, Ala., 1986-94, Trace Crossings Sch., Hoover, Ala., 1994-95, South Shades Crest Sch., Hoover, Ala., 1995—. Chairperson sci. fair Shades Cahaba Elem. Sch., Homewood, 1990-94; mem. accreditation team, Warrior (Ala.) Sch., 1990; presenter Homewood City Schs., 1988, Constructivist Conf., Birmingham, 1994, 95, co-presenter NCTM regional conf., 1995, presenter Mid-South Whole Lang. Conf., Birmingham, 1995. Rsch. participant (book) Theme Immersion: Inquiry Based Curriculum in Elementary and Middle Schools, 1994. Founder, tchr. Women in Transition, Shades Mt. Baptist Ch., Birmingham, 1993—; presenter Festival of Marriage, Ridgecrest N.C, 1994, Dayspring Women's Conf., Birmingham, 1994. Mem. Nat. Coun. Teachers of Math., Am. Edn. Rsch. Assn., Educator's Forum. Avocations: reading, tennis, travel. Office: South Shades Crest Elem 3770 S Shades Crest Rd Hoover AL 35244-4123

PARROTT, SHARON LEE, retired elementary educator; b. Ostrander, Ohio, Oct. 15, 1949; d. Fay Llewellyn and Thelma Irene (Reed) P. BS in Elem. Edn., Ind. Wesleyan U., 1975. From kindergarten assoc. tchr. to asst. tchr. Columbus (Ohio) Children's Coll., 1975; 1st grade tchr. Kayenta (Ariz.) Unified Sch. Dist. 27, 1975-84, presch. tchr., 1986-95, 1st grade tchr., 1995-97; substitute tchr. Delaware and Union County Schs., Ohio, 1984-86. Tchr. Kayenta Bible Ch., 1981-92, recorder, 1991-93. Avocations: cooking, reading, outdoor activities. Home: 4375 Canyon Trail #2 Cottonwood AZ 86326-5900

PARRY, ROBERT WALTER, chemistry educator; b. Ogden, Utah, Oct. 1, 1917; s. Walter and Jeanette (Petterson) P.; m. Marjorie J. Nelson, July 6, 1945; children: Robert Bryce, Mark Nelson. BS, Utah State Agr. Coll., 1940; MS, Cornell U., 1942; PhD, U. Ill., 1946; DSc (hon.), Utah State U., 1985, U. Utah, 1997. Rsch. asst. NDRC Munitions Devel. Lab. U. Ill., Urbana, 1943-45, tchg. fellow, 1945-46; mem. faculty U. Mich., Ann Arbor, 1946-69, prof. chemistry, 1958-69; Disting. prof. chemistry U. Utah, Salt Lake City, 1969-97, prof. emeritus, 1997—. Chmn. bd. trustees Gordon Rsch. Conf., 1967-68; cons. in field. Founding editor Inorganic Chemistry, 1960-63. Recipient Mfg. Chemists award for coll. tchg., 1972, Sr. U.S. Scientist award Alexander Von Humboldt-Stiftung, West Germany, 1980, First Govs. medal of Sci., State Utah, 1987. Mem. AAAS (chmn. chemistry sect. 1983), Internat. Union Pure and Applied Chemistry (chmn. U.S. nat. com., chmn. com. tchg. chemistry 1968-74), Am. Chem. Soc. (bd. editors jour. 1969-80, dir. 1973-83, pres.-elect 1981, pres. 1982, Disting. Svc. to Inorganic Chemistry award 1965, Disting. Svc. to Chem. Edn. award 1977, Utah award Utah sect. 1978, Priestly medal 1993), Sigma Xi. Achievements include research in structural problems of inorganic chemistry and incorporation results into theoretical models, chemistry of phosphorus, boron and fluorine. Home: 5002 Fairbrook Ln Salt Lake City UT 84117-6205 Office: U Utah Dept Chemistry 315 South 1400 East Salt Lake City UT 84112-0850 Fax: 801-581-8433. Business E-Mail: parry@chemistry.chem.utah.edu.

PARRY-GILL, BARBARA DREPPERD, retired educational administrator; b. Coral Gables, Fla., Sept. 6, 1935; d. Clarence Hartsel and Mildred (Orme) Drepperd; children: William H. Glassford Jr., Robert K. Glassford. BEd, U. Miami, 1957; MS in Ednl. Leadership, Nova U., 1993. Tchr. Dade County Pub. Schs., Miami, Fla., Montpelier (Vt.) Pub. Schs., Longmeadow (Mass.) Pub. Schs.; prin. Lower Sch. Gulliver Acad., Coral Gables; ret. Mem.: AAUW, Delta Kappa Gamma. E-mail: bdparry@aol.com.

PARSONS, CHARLES DACRE, philosophy educator; b. Cambridge, Mass., Apr. 13, 1933; s. Talcott and Helen B. (Walker) P.; m. Marjorie Louise Wood, Sept. 6, 1968; children: Jotham Wood, Sylvia Anne. AB, Harvard U., 1954, A.M., 1956, PhD, 1961; postgrad., U. Cambridge, Eng., 1954-55. Jr. fellow Soc. Fellows, Harvard U., 1958-61, asst. prof. philosophy, 1962-65, Cornell U., 1961-62; assoc. prof. philosophy Columbia U., N.Y.C., 1965-69, prof., 1969-89, chmn. dept., 1976-79, 85-89; prof. Harvard U., Cambridge, Mass., 1989—, Edgar Pierce prof. philosophy, 1991—. George Santayana fellow in philosophy Harvard U., 1964-65; vis. fellow All Souls Coll., Oxford, Eng., 1979-80 Author: Mathematics in Philosophy, 1983; editor: (with S. Feferman et al) Kurt Goedel, Collected Works, vol. III, 1995, vols. IV-V, 2003; editor Jour. Philosophy, 1966-90, cons. editor, 1990—; contbr. articles to profl. jours. NEH fellow, 1979-80, Guggenheim fellow, 1986-87, Netherlands Inst. Advanced Study fellow, 1987, Ctr. for Advanced Study in the Behavioral Scis. fellow, 1994-95. Fellow Am. Acad. Arts and Scis.; mem. Norwegian Acad. Sci. and Letters (fgn.), Assn. for Symbolic Logic (sec. 1971-76, v.p. 1986-89, pres. 1989-92), Am. Philos. Assn. Home: 16 Ellery Sq Cambridge MA 02138-4229 Office: Harvard U Emerson Hall Cambridge MA 02138

PARSONS, DANIEL LANKESTER, pharmaceutics educator; b. Biscoe, N.C., Sept. 10, 1953; s. Solomon Lankester and Doris Eva (Bost) P. BS in Pharmacy, U. Ga., 1975, PhD, 1979. Asst. prof. pharmaceutics U. Ariz., Tucson, 1979-82; asst. prof. Auburn (Ala.) U., 1982-86, assoc. prof., 1986-91, prof., 1991—, chmn. divsn., 1990—. Cons. Wyeth-Ayerst, Phila., 1989—93, Technomics, Ardsley, NY, 1990—93, Murty Pharm., Lexington, Ky., 1996—99; presenter in field. Author: (with G.V. Betageri and S.A. Jenkins) Liposome Drug Delivery Systems, 1993. Named Disting. Alumni Sandhills Coll., 1990, Tchr. of Yr., Pharmacy Student Coun., 1987, Grad. Faculty Mem. of Yr., Grad. Student Orgn., 1994, Prof. of Yr., Kappa Psi Fraternity, 2000. Mem. Am. Pharm. Assn., Am. Assn. Pharm. Scientists, Phi Kappa Phi, Kappa Psi (advisor 1990-95, nat. grad. devel. com. 1993-95, nat. scholarship com. 1995-99, nat. grand coun. dep. com. 1997—, Svc. award 1990, 95, Advisor award 1992). Achievements include research on plasma protein binding of drugs and effects of perfluorochemical blood substitutes on such binding. Office: Auburn U Sch Pharmacy Auburn AL 36849 E-mail: parsodl@auburn.edu.

PARSONS, HARRIET JEAN, mathematics educator; b. Moorhead, Minn., May 21, 1940; d. Karl Alfred and Eleanor (Nesheim) P.; m. John Robert Brundage, June 25, 1977. BA in Math., U. Mich., 1963, MA in Math., 1965. Cert. secondary tchr., Mich. Math. tchr. Crestwood H.S., Dearborn Heights, Mich., 1966-67; secondary math. tchr. Ann Arbor (Mich.) Pioneer H.S., 1967—2001. Cooperating tchr. U. Mich., Ann Arbor, Ea. Mich. U., Ypsilanti. Mem. ACLU, The Drug Policy Alliance, Planned Parenthood Fedn. of Am., Nat. Resources Def. Coun., Sierra Club. Avocations: bicycling, hiking, playing piano, astronomy.

PARSONS, JEFFREY ROBINSON, anthropologist, educator; b. Washington, Oct. 9, 1939; s. Merton Stanley and Elisabeth (Oldenburg) P.; m. Mary Thomson Hrones, Apr. 27, 1968; 1 child, Apphia Hrones. BS, Pa. State U., 1961; PhD, U. Mich., 1966. Asst. prof. anthropology U. Mich., Ann Arbor, 1966-71, assoc. prof., 1971-76, prof., 1976—, dir. mus. anthropology, 1983-86. Vis. prof. Universidad Nacional Autonoma de Mexico, 1987; vis. prof. Universidad Buenos Aires, 1994, Univ. Nac de Catamarca, Argentina, 1996, Univ. Nac de Tucuman, Argentina, 1996, Univ. Mayor de San Andres, Bolivia, 1999. Author: Prehistoric Settlement Patterns in the Texcoco Region, Mexico, 1971; (with William T. Sanders and Robert Stanley) The Basin of Mexico: The Cultural Ecology of a Civilization, 1979; (with E. Brumfiel) Prehispanic Settlement Patterns in the Southern Valley of Mexico, 1982; (with M. Parsons) Chinampa Agriculture and Aztec Urbanization in the Valley of Mexico, 1985; (with Mary H. Parsons) Maguey Utilization in Highland Central Mexico, 1990; The Production of Consumption of Salt During Postclassic Times in the Valley of Mexico, 1994; (with E. Brumfiel and M. Hodge) The Developmental Implications of Earlier Dates for Early Aztec in the Basin of Mexico, 1996; (with C. Hastings and R. Matos) Rebuilding the State in Highland Peru, 1997; A Regional Perspective on Inca Impact in the Sierra Central, Peru, 1998; (with C. Hastings and R. Matos) Prehispanic Settlement Patterns in the Upper Mantaro-Tarma Drainage, Peru, 2000; The Last Saltmakers of Nexquipayac, Mexico, 2001. Rsch. grantee NSF, 1967, 70, 72-73, 75-76, 81, Nat. Geog. Soc., 1984, 86, 88, 2003. Mem. Am. Anthrop. Assn. (Alfred V. Kidder award 1998), Soc. Am. Archaeology, AAAS, Inst. Andean Rsch., Inst. Andean Studies, Sociedad Mexicana de Antropologia, Sociedad Argentina de Antropologia. Office: Museum of Anthropology U Mich Ann Arbor MI 48109

PARSONS, JOHN GORDON, dairy chemistry educator; b. Manitoba, Can., Dec. 3, 1939; s. Gordon P. and Thelma (Smith) P., m. Penelope Rae Dugdale, Aug. 8, 1963; children: Kevin, Nancy. BS, U. Manitoba, 1961, MS, 1963; PhD, Pa. State U., 1968. Grad. asst. U. Man., Winnipeg, 1961-63; rsch. asst. Pa. State U., University Park, 1963-68; asst. prof. S.D. State U., Brookings, 1968-73, assoc. prof., 1973-78, assoc. prof., head dept. dairy sci., 1978-79, prof., 1979—2001, prof. and head emeritus, 2001—. Contbr. articles to profl. jours. and popular mags. Lectr. nat. meetings. Mem. Am. Dairy Sci. Assn. (1994 Milk Industry Foundn. award), Inst. Food Tech., Am. Cultured Dairy Products Inst., Coun. Agrl. Sci. and Tech., Sigma Xi (Brookings chpt. pres. 1978-79). Republican. Presbyterian. Lodge: Rotary. Home: 790 Main Ave Brookings SD 57006-1425 Office: Dairy Sci Dept Sd State Univ Brookings SD 57007-0001*

PARSONS, LORRAINE LEIGHTON, nurse, child care professional; b. Albany, Maine, Feb. 7, 1939; d. Alfred Elmer Leighton and Arlene Rachael Winslow; m. Jack Arnol Greig (div. July 1982); children: Scotty, Kim; m. Robert Davis Parsons, Dec. 20, 1991. Student, U. Maine. RN, Maine. Office nurse Charles Hannigan, MD, Auburn, Maine, 1961-64; with Stephens Meml. Hosp., Norway, Maine, 1964-69; tchr. spl. edn. W. Paris (Maine) Sch., 1969-73; tchr. reading and math. Buckfield (Maine) Sch., 1974-78; nurse Ledgeview Nursing Home, W. Paris, 1979-80, Central Maine Med. Ctr., Lewiston, 1980-96; child care profl. Marwin Cons. Co., Raymond, Maine, 1996—. Author: Families of the Fox and Geese Quilt, 1997, Homesteads of Hartford, 1997, Quilting is Qumforting, 1999, Town of Hartford, 2000, Military Service, 2000, Marston Homestead, 2000, Crazy Quilt, 2000, Winslow Home, 2001, The Alfred E. Leighton Family, 2001, Rokomeko - Native Americans, 2002, Life - 1870, 1879 & 1881, 2003; co-author: Hartford in Pictures, 1984; author: Rokomeko Indians Native Americans, 2002. Pres., founder Hartford (Maine) Heritage Soc., 1976; program chairwoman Hartford Bicentennial, 1997-98. Recipient Cert. of Honor Bicentennial, State of Maine, 1998, Double-Trouble Nature category Internat. Libr. Photography, 2000; grantee Maine Arts, 1998. Avocations: dolls, stamps, town histories. Home: RR 1 Box 207 Canton ME 04221-9714

PARSONS, MARY LOUISE BRITTON, elementary educator; b. Hamilton, Ohio, July 6, 1937; d. Harvey Oscar and Christina M. (Benge) Britton; m. Bill R. Parsons, Apr. 11, 1957; children: Harold David, Richard Cameron, Cynthia Jean, Christina Lou. Assoc. in Bus. Adminstrn., Ashland (Ky.) Jr. Coll.; BS in Edn., Miami U., Oxford, Ohio; MA in Edn., Mount St. Joseph, Cin. Cert. elem. tchr. Acctg. stenographer Proctor & Gamble, Cin., 1958-59; substitute tchr. Fairfield (Ohio), Ross, Butler Co., 1968-70; kindergarten tchr. First Bapt. Ch., Fairfield, 1971-72, day care dir., 1972-73; substitute tchr. Fairfield City Schs., 1973-74, elem. tchr., 1974—99; reading tutor Fairfield Ctrl. Sch., 1974; pvt. tutor Fairfield, 1972-76; sci. curriculum coord. Fairfield West, 1980-82, drug free schs. coord., 1988-90; ret., 1999. Mem. adv. com. First Baptist Daycare, 1979-80; bond issue/levy coms. Fairfield City Schs. Vol. Am. Cancer Soc.; tchr. vacation bible sch., Sunday sch. First Bapt. Ch., Hamilton, 1962-70; tchr. infant-adult edn. First Bapt. Ch., Fairfield, 1970-92, choir mem., 1970—. Mem. Internat. Reading Assn., Retired Tchrs. Am. (life), Tchrs. Applying Whole Lang., Fairfield Classroom Tchrs. (recording sec., bd. dirs. 1980, extracurricular contract com. 1982—). Republican. Avocations: poetry, needlework & crafts, walking, swimming, reading. Home: 827 Vinnedge Ave Fairfield OH 45014-1751

PARSONSON, PETER STERLING, civil engineer, educator, consultant; b. Reading, Mass., Oct. 18, 1934; s. Alfred Horace and Elvera (Moran) P.; m. Marilyn Shepherd, July 6, 1962 (div. Mar. 1984); children: Sheryl Elaine Parsonson Peeples, Ellen Marie Parsonson Milberger, Peter Shepherd; m. Sarah Irby, Oct. 6, 1990. BS, MIT, 1956, MS, 1959; PhD, N.C. State U., 1966. Registered profl. engr., Ga., Fla., Calif. Civil engr. Fay, Spofford and Thorndike, Boston, 1956-57, Ingenieria de Suelos, S.A., Caracas, Venezuela, 1959-61, Tippetts-Abbett-McCarthy-Stratton, N.Y.C., 1961-64; asst. prof. Coll. Engrng. U. S.C., Columbia, 1966-69; assoc. prof. dept. civil engrng. Ga. Inst. Tech., Atlanta, 1970-82, prof. dept. civil and environ. engrng., 1982-2000, prof. emeritus dept. civil and environ. engrng., 2000—, group leader Transp. Engrng. faculty, 1995-99. Pres. Parsonson and Assocs., Inc., Atlanta, 1976—; cons. hwy. engrng. litigation; instr., rschr. hwy. design, constrn., operation and maintenance; vis. prof. Simón Bolívar U., Caracas, 1994, Nat. U. Colombia, Medellín, 1996; prof. ad honorem U. P.R., Mayagüez, 1995, 96; vis. lectr. on intelligent transp. systems Jiangsu and Hebei Provinces China, 1999; presenter in field. Author: Management of Traffic-Signal Maintenance, 1984, Signal Timing Improvement Practices, 1992; co-author: Traffic Detector Handbook, 1985; contbr. chpts. to books and articles to profl. jours. Fellow Inst. Transp. Engrs. (life; Marble J. Hensley Outstanding Individual Activity award 1974, Herman J. Hoose Disting. Svc. award, 1984, Karl A. Bevins Traffic Ops. award, 1992); mem. NSPE, Transp. Rsch. Bd., Nat. Acad. Forensic Engrs. Episcopalian. Home: 105 Mark Trl NW Atlanta GA 30328-2102 Office: Ga Inst Tech Civil And Environ Engring Atlanta GA 30332-0355 E-mail: peter.parsonson@ce.gatech.edu.

PARSONT, MINA RAINÈS-LAMBÉ, retired language educator; b. Paris, Apr. 11, 1935; came to U.S., Jan. 1950; d. Léon and Anna (Lentzner) Rainès-Lambé; m. Michael Allen Parsont, July 4, 1959; children: Marc Sheldon, Todd Jamie. AA, Sacramento City Coll., 1954; BA with honors, U. Calif., Berkeley, 1956; postgrad., La Sorbonne, Paris, 1958; MAT in French, Colo. State U., 1966; postgrad., U. Md., 1975. Cert. secondary tchr., Md., Calif. Tchr. Spanish Sacramento Sr. High Sch., 1956-57; asst. English Ecole de Jeunes Filles, Suresnes, France, 1958; tchr. French Beverly Hills (Calif.) Elem. Sch., 1962-63; teaching asst., instr. Colo. State U., 1963-66; tchr. French, Spanish Montgomery County (Md.) Pub. Schs., 1971-95; ret., 1995. Tchr. adult edn., Albany, Calif. and L.A., 1960-61, Montgomery County, 1972—; tutor French, 1955—. Creator (with others) Let's Talk Cards for fgn. lang. students. French Govt. scholar, 1987—; recipient Thanks to Tchrs. award Sta. WJLA-TV, Washington, 1991; named Chevalier, Ordre des Palmes Académiques, 1997. Mem. AAUW, Am. Assn. French tchrs., Md. Fgn. Lang. Assn. (past bd. dirs.), Greater Washington Assn. Fgn. Lang. Tchrs. (Disting. Fgn. Lang. Educator award 1989), Na'amat. Avocations: travel, family activities, reading, theater, singing.

PARTHEMORE, JACQUELINE GAIL, internist, educator, hospital administrator; b. Harrisburg, Pa., Dec. 21, 1940; d. Philip Mark and Emily (Buvit) Parthemore; m. Alan Morton Blank, Jan. 7, 1967; children: Stephen Eliot, Laura Elise. BA, Wellesley Coll., 1962; MD, Cornell U., 1966. Diplomate Am. Bd. Internal Medicine. Resident in internal medicine N.Y. Hosp./Cornell U., 1966-69; fellow in endocrinology Scripps Clinic and Rsch. Found., La Jolla, Calif., 1969-72; rsch. ednl. assoc. VA Hosp., San Diego, 1974-78; staff physician VA San Diego Health Care Sys., 1978-79, asst. chief, med. svc., 1979-83, acting chief, med. svc., 1980-81, chief of staff, 1984—; asst. prof. medicine U. Calif. Sch. Medicine, San Diego, 1974-80, assoc. prof. medicine, 1980-85, prof. medicine, assoc. dean, 1985—. Mem. nat. rsch. resources coun. NIH, Bethesda, Md., 1990-94. Contbr. chapters to books, articles to profl. jours. Mem. adv. bd. San Diego Opera; mem. Roundtable and Channel 10 Focus Group, San Diego Millennium Project, 1999; bd. dirs. San Diego Vets. Med. Rsch. Found., Nat. VA Rsch. and Edn. Found. Recipient Bullock's 1st Annual Portfolio award, 1985, San Diego Pres.'s Coun. Woman of Yr. award, 1985, YWCA Tribute to Women in Industry award, 1987, San Diego Women Who Mean Bus. award, 1999, Excellence in Leadership award Am. Hosp. Assn., 2002. Fellow ACP, Am. Assn. Clin. Endocrinologists; mem. Endocrine Soc., Nat. Assn. VA Chiefs Staff (pres. 1989-91), Wellesley Coll. Alumnae Assn. (1st v.p. 1992-95), San Diego Wellesley Club (pres. 1997-99). Avocations: gardening, reading, sailing, cooking, travel. Office: VA San Diego Healthcare Sys 3350 La Jolla Village Dr San Diego CA 92161-0002 E-mail: jparthemore@ucsd.edu.

PARTLOW, MADELINE, principal; Degree in early and mid. childhood edn., Ohio State U.; M in Early and Mid. Childhood, 1995, M in Ednl. Adminstrn., 1997. Prin. Blacklick Elem., Gahanna, New Albany (Ohio) Mid. Sch., 2001—. Office: New Albany Mid Sch 6600 E Dublin-Granville Rd New Albany OH 43054-8740*

PARTLOW, SHARA SUE, nursing educator; b. Amarillo, Tex., Apr. 24, 1951; d. William Frank and Lillie Ruth (Chambers) Partlow; divorced; children: David Ray, Daniel Mathis. Diploma of Nursing, N.W. Tex. Hosp., Amarillo, 1972; AAS, Amarillo Jr. Coll., 1978; BSN, W. Tex. State U., 1979, MSN, 1980. RN, Tex. Operating room supr. S.W. Osteopathic Hosp., Amarillo, Tex., 1973-75; team leader High Plains Bapt. Hosp., Amarillo, 1976-79; chmn. nursing leadership dept. N.W. Tex. Hosp., Amarillo, 1979-81; part-time staff nurse Okla. Teaching Hosp., Oklahoma City, 1986-87; instr. Southwestern Okla. State U., Weatherford, 1986-87; instr. sch. nursing Meth. Hosp., Lubbock, Tex., 1987—. Instr./trainer Am. Heart Assn., Amarillo, 1980-83. Recipient N.W. Tex. Hosp. Community Svc. award, 1982, Estelle Munn award Toastmistress, 1982, 83; named Outstanding Young Woman of Am., 1982; winner regional contest Toastmistress, 1982. Mem. ANA, ARC, Nursing Oncology Edn. Programs. Roman Catholic. Office: Meth Hosp Sch Nursing 2002 Miami Ave Lubbock TX 79410-1010

PASACHOFF, JAY MYRON, astronomer, educator; b. NYC, July 1, 1943; s. Samuel S. and Anne (Traub) P.; m. Naomi Schwartz, Mar. 31, 1974; children: Eloise Hilary, Deborah Donna. AB, Harvard U., 1963, AM (NSF fellow), 1965, PhD (NSF fellow, N.Y. State Regents fellow for advanced grad. study), 1969. Rsch. physicist Air Force Cambridge Rsch. Labs., Bedford, Mass., 1968-69; Menzel rsch. fellow Harvard Coll. Obs., Cambridge, Mass., 1969-70; rsch. fellow Hale Obs., Carnegie Instn., Washington, and Calif. Inst. Tech., Pasadena, 1970-72; from asst. prof., dir. Hopkins Obs. to prof. Williams Coll., Williamstown, Mass., 1972—84, Field Meml. prof. of astronomy, 1984—, chmn. astronomy dept., 1972—77, 1991—92, 1997—2001. Adj. asst. prof. astronomy U. Mass., Amherst, 1975-77, adj. assoc. prof., 1977-83, adj. prof., 1986-90; vis. colleague and vis. assoc. prof. astronomy Inst. for Astronomy, U. Hawaii, 1980-81; vis. scientist Inst. d'Astrophysique, Paris, 1988; mem. Inst. Advanced Study, Princeton, 1989-90, Harvard-Smithsonian Ctr. for Astrophysics, 1993-94, 2001-02; total and other solar eclipse expdns., Mass., 1959, Que., Can., 1963, Mex., 1970, asst. dir. Harvard-Smithsonian-Nat. Geog. Expdn., P.E.I., Can., 1972, NSF expdn., Harvard-Smithsonian-Williams Expdn., Kenya, 1973; NSF expdn., Colombia, 1973 (annular eclipse), Australia, 1974, Pacific Ocean, 1977, Man., Can., 1979, NSF expdn., India, 1980, Pacific Ocean, 1981, Java, Indonesia, 1983, Miss., 1984 (annular eclipse), Papua New Guinea, 1984, Sumatra, Indonesia, 1988, Hawaii 1989 (partial eclipse), Finland, 1990, Hawaii, 1991, Calif., 1992 (annular eclipse), Pacific near Africa, 1992, N.H., 1994 (annular eclipse), Chile, 1994, India, 1995, Israel, 1996 (partial eclipse), Mongolia, 1997, Aruba, 1998, Malaysia, 1998 (annular eclipse), Australia, 1999, Romania, 1999, Seattle, 2000, Calif., 2000, Zambia, 2001, Costa Rica, 2001, Mex., 2002, Australia, 2002, Iceland, 2003; guest investigator NASA Orbiting Solar Obs.-8, 1975-79, NASA Solar and Heliospheric Obs., 1999-2000; Carter lectr., New Zealand, 1998. Author: Contemporary Astronomy, 1977, 4th edit., 1989, Astronomy Now, 1978, Astronomy: From Earth to the Universe, 1979, 6th edit., 2002, A Brief View of Astronomy, 1986, First Guide to Astronomy, 1988, First Guide to the Solar System, 1990, Journey Through the Universe, 1992; co-author: (with Marc L. Kutner, Naomi Pasachoff) Student Study Guide to Contemporary Astronomy, 1977, (with Kutner, Pasachoff and N.P. Kutner) Student Study Guide to Astronomy Now, 1978; (with M.L. Kutner) University Astronomy, 1978, Invitation to Physics, 1981; (with N. Pasachoff, T. Cooney) Physical Science, 1983, 2d edit., 1990, Earth Science, 1983, 2d edit., 1990; (with D.H. Menzel) A Field Guide to the Stars and Planets, 4th edit., 2000; (with R. Wolfson) Physics, 1987, 3rd edit., 1999 (Extended with Modern Physics, 1989, 3rd edit. 1999), (with N. Pasachoff, R.W. Clark, M.H. Westermann) Physical Science Today, 1987; (with N. Pasachoff and others) Discover Science, 7 vols., 1989; (with Michael Covington) Cambridge Eclipse Photography Guide, 1993; (with Len Holder and James DeFranza) Calculus, 1994, Single Variable Calculus, 1994, Multivariable Calculus, 1995; (with Edward Cheng, Patrick Osmer and Hyron Spinrad) The Farthest Things in the Universe, 1994; editor (with J. Percy) The Teaching of Astronomy, 1990, (with Leon Golub) The Solar Corona, 1997, 2d edit., 1998, (with Roberta J. M. Olson) Fire in the Sky: Comets and Meteors, the Decisive Centuries, 1998, 2d edit., 1999, Astronomy, 1998, Sound and Light, 1999; (with Alex Filippenko) The Cosmos: Astronomy at the New Millennium, 2000, 2d edit., 2003, The Complete Idiot's Guide to the Sun, 2003; assoc. editor: Jour. Irreproducible Results, 1972-94, Annals of Improbable Rsch., 1994—; abstractor from Am. jours. for Solar Physics, 1968-78; cons. editor McGraw-Hill Ency. Sci. and Tech., 1983—; co-editor-in-chief (with S.P. Parker), McGraw-Hill Ency. of Astronomy, 1993; cons. Random House Dictionary, 1983-86, Nat. Geographic Atlas, 5th edit., 1981, 6th edit., 1990; phys. sci. com. World Book Ency., 1989-95, cons., 1996—; contbr. articles to profl. jours. Recipient bronze medal Nikon Photo Contest Internat., 1971, photograph aboard NASA Voyagers, 1977, Dudley award Dudley Obs., 1985; grantee NSF, 1973-75, 79-83, 88—2002, Nat. Geog. Soc., 1973-86, 91—2001, Rsch. Corp., 1973-78, 82-88, 2001, Getty Found., 1994-95, NASA, 1999-2000. Fellow AAAS (chair sect. D 1987-88, 97-98), Royal Astron. Soc., Am. Phys. Soc. (mem.-at-large Am. Phys. Soc./Am. Assn. Physics Tchrs. Forum on Edn. 1995-98), NY Acad. Sci., Internat. Planetarium Soc.; mem. AAUP (chpt. pres. 1977-80), Internat. Astron. Union (U.S. nat. rep. Commn. on Tchg. Astronomy 1976-2000, chair eclipse working group 1991—, rep. to Com. on Tchg. Sci. of Internat. Coun. Sci. Unions 1991-93, v.p. com. on edn. and devel. 2000-2003, pres. 2003—, US nat. liaison commn. on edn. and devel., 2000—, pres. com. on edn. and devel., 2003—), Am. Astron. Soc. (astronomy edn. adv. bd. 1990-97, astronomy news com. 1991-96, Edn. prize 2003), Astron. Soc. Pacific, Union Radio Sci., Am. Assn. Physics Tchrs. (astronomy com. 1983-87), Sigma Xi (chpt. pres. 1973-74, 95—, nat. lectr. 1993-97), Phi Beta Kappa. Home: 111 Park Street Williamstown MA 01267-2116 Office: Williams Coll Hopkins Obs 33 Lab Campus Dr Williamstown MA 01267-2565 E-mail: jay.m.pasachoff@williams.edu.

PASCH, ALAN, philosopher, educator; b. Cleve., Dec. 1, 1925; s. P. Jerome and Esther (Broverman) P.; m. Eleanor Kudlich Berna, Dec. 27, 1950; 1 child, Rachel. BA, U. Mich., 1949; MA, New Sch. Social Research, 1952; PhD, Princeton U., 1955; Bamford fellow, 1955-56. Instr. philosophy Ohio State U., 1956-59, asst. prof., 1959-60; assoc. prof. philosophy U. Md., College Park, 1960-67, prof., 1967-97, prof. emeritus, 1997—. Author: Experience and the Analytic, 1958; also articles, revs. Served with AUS, 1944-46, PTO. Mem. Am. Philos. Assn. (exec. dir. 1969-72, sec.-treas. Eastern div. 1965-68), Metaphys. Soc. Am., Washington Philosophy Club (pres. 1978-79), Washington Rare Book Group. Office: 6910 Wake Forest Dr College Park MD 20740-7615 E-mail: ap3@umail.umd.edu.

PASCHAL, JAMES ALPHONSO, counselor, educator secondary school; b. Americus, Ga., Aug. 11, 1931; s. Bouie L. and Mary L. (Jackson) P.; widower Mar. 24, 1988; 1 child, Maret E. BA, Xavier U., New Orleans, 1957; MS, Ft. Valley State Coll., 1963; EdD, U. S.C., 1977. Cert. adminstr., tchr. counselor, social worker, S.C. Tchr. grade 5 East View Elem. Sch., Americus, Ga., 1957-59; libr., counselor Staley Jr. H.S., Americus, 1959-65; sch. social worker Americus City System, 1965-67; coord. student svcs. Augusta (Ga.) Tech., 1967-78; dir. student affairs Benedict Coll., Columbia, S.C., 1978-82; coord. facilities S.C. Commn. on Higher Edn., Columbia, 1982-89; counselor Swainsboro (Ga.) H.S., 1990-91, Monroe H.S., Albany, Ga., 1991—. Vol. Caritas, New Orleans, 1953-57, Friendship House, New Orleans, 1955-56. With U.S. Army, 1951-53, Korea. Recipient scholarship Ft. Valley (Ga.) State Coll., 1948, grad. assistantship, Ft. Valley State Coll., 1962-63. Mem. NEA, ACA. Ga. Counseling Assn., Alpha Phi Alpha (v.p. 1972-74). Republican. Roman Catholic. Avocations: reading, walking, helping others. Home: PO Box 5523 Albany GA 31706-5523

PASCHKE, TERESA ANN, artist, educator; b. Mpls., Dec. 1, 1962; d. Kenneth George and Joan Marie (Schreader) P. BFA, Mpls. Coll. Art and Design, 1985; MFA, U. Kans., 1998. Instr. art and design U. Kans., Lawrence, 1995-97, asst. to grad. dir., 1995-98; asst. prof. Iowa State U., Ames, 2000—, Miller faculty fellow, 2001, Wakonse fellow ctr. tchg. excellence, 2003. Homebound vol. Mpls. Pub. Libr., 1992, Homeward vol., 2002; bd. dirs. Textile Ctr. of Minn. Dendel scholar Handweavers Guild Am., 1996, Nolte scholar U. Minn., 1991, Allis scholar North Hennepin C.C., 1982; grad. honors fellow U. Kans., 1996. Mem. Foundns. in Art: Theory and Edn., Nat. Honor Soc., Surface Design Assn., Am. Craft Coun., Textile Ctr. Minn. (bd. dirs.). Democrat. Avocations: camping, bicycling. Address: 225 S Hazel Ames IA 50010 E-mail: tpaschke@iastate.edu.

PASCUAL, MATILDA PEREDA, vocational program coordinator; b. Tamuning, Guam, Jan. 15, 1957; d. Matias Ortez and Josefa Cruz (Pereda) Pascual; m. William Howard Brooks, Feb. 2, 1982 (div. Feb. 1994); 1 child, Toni Marie Brooks. AS in Hotel/Airline Mgmt., Internat. Bus. Coll. Guam, 1979; BA in Edn., U. Guam, 1990. Cert. tchr., Guam. Waitress Old Rip & Bottle, Maite, Guam, 1976-77; clk. trainee Gross Receipt Tax Dept. Dept. Revenue and Tax, Govt. Guam, Agana, 1976-79; front desk clk. Guam Horizon Hotel, Tumon, 1983—89; phys. edn. tchr. Dept. Edn., Govt. Guam, Piti, 1989—90; adminstrv. asst. Pacific Star Hotel, Tumon, 1990—99; instr. hotel/motel operation and food and beverage Guam C.C., Mangilao, 1990—. Advisor Tourism/Distributive Edn. Club Am. Orgn. Simon Sanchez H.S., Yigo, Guam, 1990—93; prof. tourism tng., cons. secondary/post-secondary hotel ops. John F. Kennedy H.S./Guam C.C., 1999—; program coord. IV vocat. edn., PVEIP project dir., state dir. skills USA-VICA Guam Dept. Edn., Divsn. Curriculum and Instrn., 1998—; advisor tourism and distributive edn. club Guam C.C./George Washington H.S. Pres. Vicente Borja Cruz Clan Orgn. Recipient Disting. Svc. award Nat. Jr. Honors Soc., 1986-88. Mem. Am. Vocat. Assn., Am. Fedn. Tchrs., Distributive Edn. Club Am. (bd. advisor 1991—). Roman Catholic. Avocations: travel, meeting new friends, socializing, golf. Home: Sunset Apt #107 Barrigada GU 96913-5752 E-mail: mattiepascual@yahoo.com.

PASELK, RICHARD ALAN, chemist, educator; b. Inglewood, Calif., July 20, 1945; s. Robert Arthur and Doris Mae (Miller) P.; m. Gail Annette Gulliver, Mar. 18, 1967; children: Laura Ann, Deborah Ailene. BS in Biophysics, Calif. State U., Los Angeles, 1968; PhD in Biochemistry, U. So. Calif., 1975. Research tech. U. So. Calif. Sch. Medicine, Los Angeles, 1968-69; lectr. Calif. State U., Long Beach, 1974-76; asst. prof. Humboldt State U., Arcata, Calif., 1976-81, assoc. prof., 1981-86, prof., 1986—, chmn. dept. chemistry, 1986-89, 95—, cur., Webmaster Robert A. Paselk Sci. Instrument Mus., 1998—. Bd. dirs., Webmaster Humboldt State U. Natural History Mus., 1998—. Tech. editor Zymed Corp., S. San Francisco, 1984-85; developer, publisher multimedia ednl. chemistry software; contbr. articles to profl. jours. Bd. dirs. Sierra-Cascade Girl Scouts U.S., Eureka, Calif., 1977-80; docent Clark Meml. Mus., Eureka, 1980-86; panelist NSF, 1994, 96, 97. Avocations: wood and metal working, history, reproducing ancient sci. instruments. Home: 1624 Hyland St Bayside CA 95524-9302 Office: Humboldt State U Chemistry Dept Arcata CA 95521 E-mail: rapl@humboldt.edu.

PASIC, MARY ROSE, principal; b. Crested Butte, Colo., Oct. 19, 1937; d. John Louis and Rose Mary (Kuretich) P. BA, Mt. St. Mary's Coll., 1959, MS in Edn., 1966. Cert. tchr., Calif. Tchr. Los Angeles Unified Sch. Dist., 1959-73, asst. prin., tchr. tng. and demonstration, 1973-78, prin., 1978—. Holder numerous offices Jrs. League Crippled Children, Los Angeles, 1961-72. Mem. Mt. St. Mary's Coll. Alumnae Assn., Euclan, Phi Delta Kappa (v.p., chmn. membership UCLA chpt. 1983-84), Delta Kappa Gamma (pres. 1975-76, scholar 1975), Kappa Delta Pi (sec. So. Calif. Alumni chpt. 1984-85). Avocations: painting, tennis, dressmaking, travel.

PASSAGLIA, CANDACE V. special education educator; b. Woodstock, Ill., Nov. 17, 1951; d. Vaughn D. and Phyllis (Higgins) Heidenreich; m. Roger Michael Passaglia, Dec. 29, 1973; children: Ryan James, Shannon Marie. BS in Edn./Spl. Edn., No. Ill. U., 1973, MS in Spl. Edn. Adminstrn., 1995; learning disabilities/physically handicapped cert., U. Calif., Irvine, 1986. Cert. elem. edn., Ill., Calif.; cert. spl. edn. K-12. Tchr. grade 4 Woodstock (Ill.) Cmty. Sch. Dist. 200, 1973; exec. sec. various cos., 1974-83; instrnl. aide, substitute tchr. various sch. dists., Calif., 1984-87; resource specialist Irvine Unified Sch. Dist., 1987-89; learning disabilities tchr. Cary (Ill.) Elem. Sch. Dist. # 26, 1989-95; learning disabilities specialist Wilmette (Ill.) Sch. Dist. 39, 1995-96; tchr. grade 5 Cary Elem. Sch. Dist. 26, 1996—; instr. No. Ill. U. Grad. Sch., 1996—. Tech. com., sys. operator computer network, mem. sch. improvement com. Cary (Ill.) Sch. Dist. # 26, 1990—; lectr. No. Ill. U., DeKalb, 1993, 94; keynote spkr. Kans. State U., Manhattan, 1994, 95. Author, editor: (nat. newsletter) Co-Teaching Network News, 1992—. Bd. dirs. Mission Viejo (Calif.) Little League Assn., 1985-87; mem. Cary (Ill.)-Grove H.S. Baseball Parent's Assn., 1990-94; oboist Crystal Lake Cmty. Band, 1989-91; 1st soprano The New Oratorio Singers, 1991-92; mem. Cary Cmty. Theatre, 1995—. Mem. ASCD, United Learning Disabilities Assn. Avocations: computers, writing, gardening, family time, reading. Office: Three Oaks Sch Cary Elem Sch Dist 26 15 S 2nd St Cary IL 60013-2872

PASSANANTE, PATRICIA MARIE, middle school educator; b. Bklyn., Apr. 27, 1948; d. Charles and Auriela (Mauro) Casoria; m. Joseph John Passanante, Aug. 8, 1970; children: Laurie Adriana, Kristen Elizabeth. BA, CUNY, 1969; MA in Liberal Studies, SUNY, Stony Brook, 1989. Cert. tchr. Latin 7-12, math. 7-12, N.Y., sch. adminstr., supr. Latin/math. instr. 7-12 Franklin Sch., N.Y.C., 1969-72; Latin/math. instr. 6-8 Harbor Country Day Sch., St. James, N.Y., 1972-76; Latin instr. grades 9-12 Acad. St. Joseph's, Brentwood, N.Y., 1986-89; Latin instr. grades 7-8 Riverhead (N.Y.) Ctrl. Sch., 1989-94, instr. math. grade 8, 1994—, asst. chmn. math., 2003—. 8th grade advisor Riverhead Mid. Sch., 1994-2002, facilitator site-based mgmt. team, 1994-98, conflict mediator, 1993-96. Item writer Latin Proficiency Exam, 1990-95, Tests for Latin Conv., 1989-96. Catechist, Infant Jesus Parish, Port Jefferson, N.Y., 1982-93; jr. leader cons. Girl Scouts U.S., Coram, N.Y., 1983-86, leader, 1982-86. Named to Pres.'s Cir., Girl Scouts U.S., 1986; recipient St. Pius X award Diocese of Rockville Ctr., 1992. Mem. Classical Assn. of Empire State (scholar award 1989), N.Y. State Classical League (Co-chair's award 1993), Am. Classical League, Nat. Coun. Math. Tchrs., Suffolk County Classical Soc., Suffolk County Math. Tchrs. Roman Catholic. Office: Riverhead Middle School 600 Harrison Ave Riverhead NY 11901-2786

PASSEY, GEORGE EDWARD, psychology educator; b. Stratford, Conn., Sept. 28, 1920; s. Henry Richard and Elizabeth (Angus) P.; m. Algie Aldridge Ashe, Nov. 18, 1950; children— Richard Ashe, Elizabeth Aldridge, Mary Louise. BS, Springfield Coll., 1942; MA, Clark U., 1947; PhD, Tulane U., 1950. Asst. prof. U. Ala., Tuscaloosa, 1952-55, assoc. prof., 1955-56, 57-59, prof., 1959-63, prof. psychology, chmn. div. social and behavioral scis., 1967-73, prof. engring., 1969-84, Disting. Service prof. psychology, 1984-85, Disting Service prof. emeritus, 1985—; dean U. Ala. (Sch. Social and Behavioral Scis.), 1973-84. Research scientist Lockheed Ga. Co., Marietta, Ga., 1956-57, 63-65, cons., 1965-67; prof. Ga. Inst. Tech., 1965-67 Served with USNR, 1942-46, PTO; with USAF, 1951-52. Fellow Am. Psychol. Assn.; mem. So. Soc. for Philosophy and Psychology, Southeastern Psychol. Assn., Ala. Psychol. Assn., Pine Harbor Golf and Racquet Club, Sigma Xi. Home: 7141 Skyline Dr Pell City AL 35128-6936

PASSON, RICHARD HENRY, English language educator, former administrator; b. Hazleton, Pa., Aug. 18, 1939; s. Henry Richard and Grace Miriam (Bernstein) P.; m. Margaret Rose Ferdinand, Aug. 14, 1965; children— Michael, Rebecca, Christopher. BA (Bishop Hafey scholar), King's Coll., Pa., 1961; MA, U. Notre Dame, 1963, PhD (NDEA fellow), 1965. From instr. to prof. English U. Scranton, 1964-73, chmn. English dept., 1970-73, fgn. student adviser, 1965-67; dean Coll. Arts and Scis., Creighton U., Omaha, 1973-77; acad. v.p. St. Joseph's U., Phila., 1977-84; provost U. Scranton, Pa., 1984-2000, prof. English, 2000—02; interim acad. v.p. St. Joseph's U., Phila., 2002—. Contbr. articles profl. jours. Recipient grant Nat. Assn. Fgn. Students, 1966 Mem. Modern Lang. Assn., Am. Assn. Higher Edn., Am. Assn. Acad. Deans, Nat. Coun. Tchrs. English. Democrat. Roman Catholic. Office: U Scranton 402 Brennan Hall Scranton PA 18510 E-mail: passonr1@scranton.edu.

PASSTY, JEANETTE NYDA, English language educator, writer; b. LA, Calif., Jan. 19, 1947; d. Walter Isaac and Mollie Sarah Nyda; m. Gregory Bohdan Passty, June 18, 1976; 1 child, Benjamin. AA, L.A. Valley Coll., 1966; BA, UCLA, 1968; MA, U. So. Calif., 1974, PhD, 1982. Cert. c.c. instr., Calif. Tchg. asst., lectr., assoc. dir. freshman English program U. So. Calif., 1971-78; lectr. English dept. U. Tex., Austin, 1983-85; vis. asst. prof., adj. assoc. prof. Tex. Luth. U., Seguin, 1983, 85-87; from instr. to asst. prof. St. Philip's Coll., San Antonio, Calif., 1988-92, assoc. prof., 1992—. Lectr. UCLA, U. Tex., Austin, Western Mich. U., U. Louisville, Salisbury State U., Morehead State U., Tex. Tech. U., U. Wales, Bangor; humanities book reviewer CHOICE (ALA Jour.), 1985—86; manuscript reviewer Fairleight Dickinson U. Press, 1991—; editl. cons. CONNECTIONS: Online Distance Learning Faculty Forum, 2002—. Author: Eros and Androgyny: The Legacy of Rose Macaulay, 1988, The Lion Tells Her Story: A Biography of the Honorable N.P. Brooks Hinton, 1998, Bringing Denis Home: The Hero from Hope, Kansas, 2001; annotator: Alice Crawford's Paradise Pursued, 1995; contbr. articles to encyclopedia and profl. jours.; guest Sta. KSPL Radio In Touch With, 1989; appearance Sta. KENS-TV, 1992, Channel 12 Morehead, KY, 1998, CNN, 1995, Roadside (entr'acte with G.S. Bailey), 2000. Mem. Nat. Abortion Rights Action League, Tex. Abortion Rights Action League, Greenpeace, Environ. Def. Fund, The Nature Conservancy, Sierra Club, Handgun Control Inc., Orgn. Internat. Conf. on the Holocaust, San Antonio, 2000. Nominee excellence award, Nat. Inst. Staff and Orgnl. Devel., 2003; recipient Elizabeth K. Pleasants Tchg. award, U. So. Calif., 1974, letters of appreciation, Lord Bonham-Carter, 1987, HRH Princess Margaret, 1989—90, Oustanding Acad. Book award, ALA, 1989, Women Honoring Women award, Am. Assn. Women in C.C.s, 1997, Katherine Anne Porter Lit. prize, 1999, NISOD Internat. Conf. on Tchg. and Leadership Excellence Award, 2003; Viering Kersey scholar, L.A. Valley Coll., 1964—66, NEH grantee, Tex. Luth. U., 1986. Mem. AAUW, NOW, MLA, Nat. Coun. Tchrs. of English, South Ctrl. Soc. 18th Century Studies, Virginia Woolf Soc. Avocations: academic decathlon, taekwondo, arctic travel. Office: St Philip's Coll English Dept 1801 Martin Luther King Dr San Antonio TX 78203-2098

PASTERNACK, ROBERT HARRY, school psychologist; b. Bklyn., Nov. 30, 1949; s. William and Lillian Ruth (Levine) P.; m. Jeanelle Livingston, Apr. 10, 1980; children: Shayla, Rachel. BA, U. South Fla., 1970; MA, N.Mex. Highlands U., 1972; PhD, U. N.Mex., 1980. Dir. Eddy County Drug Abuse Program, Carlsbad, N.Mex., 1972-73; adminstrv. intern U.S. Office Edn., Washington, 1975-76; exec. dir. Villa Santa maria, Cedar Crest, N.Mex., 1976-78; clin. dir. Ranchos Treatment Ctr., Taos, N.Mex., 1978-79; sch. psychologist N.Mex. Boys Sch., Springer, 1980—, supt., 1991; pres. Ensenar Health svcs., Inc., Taos, 1980—; CEO Casa de Corazon, Taos, N.Mex., 1994-98; state dir. spl. edn. N.Mex. State Dept. Edn., Santa Fe, 1998—. Instr. N.Mex. Highlands U., Las Vegas, 1980—, U. N.Mex., Albuquerque, 1980—; cons. N.Mex. Youth Authority, Santa Fe, 1988—, N.Mex. Devel. Disabilities Bur., Santa Fe, 1986—, various sch. dists.; state dir. spl. edn., N.Mex., 1998—; asst. sec. spl. edn. and rehab. svcs. U.S. Dept. Edn., 2001—. Author: Growing Up: The First Five Years, 1986; contbr. articles to profl. publs. Pres., bd. dirs. Children's Lobby, N.Mex., 1978, N.Mex. Spl. Olympics, 1986-88, Child-Rite, Inc., Taos, 1990; mem. Gov.'s Mental Health Task Force, Albuquerque, 1988—. Mem.: N.Mex. Coun. on Crime and Delinquency, Nat. Alliance Mentally Ill, Correctional Edn. Assn., Nat. Assn. Sch. Psychologists. Avocations: tennis, racquetball, skiing, cooking. Home and Office: 6235 5th St NE Apt 14 Washington DC 20002*

PASTERNAK, JOANNA MURRAY, humanities educator; b. Houston, Feb. 9, 1953; d. Lee Roy and Evelyn Mary (Kirmss) Murray; children: Sheila Ann Tanner, Lawrence Ross Tanner IV; m. Allen Pasternak, Jan. 9, 1993. BA in Liberal Arts with honors, Our Lady of the Lake, San Antonio, 1990; MA in Liberal Arts, U. St. Thomas, Houston, 1998. Acctg. clk. Houston Post, 1981-85; owner, art cons. Tanner Fine Art, Houston, 1985-92; spl. edn. tchr. Houston Ind. Sch. Dist., 1991-94, dept. chmn., 1994—, secondary social studies tchr., 2000—02; prof. and dept. chair humanities U. Phoenix, Houston, 2001—. Art cons. Plz. Gallery, Houston, 1985; mem. benefits com. Houston Ind. Sch. Dist., 1992-2001; presenter Am. Fedn. Tchrs. Nat. Edn. Conf., 1994. Contrb. articles to profl. jours. Vol. legis com. nat. health care campaign AFL-CIO; bd. dirs. PTA, SDMC; Dem. campaign worker, 1993—; precinct and state del. Dem. Senate, 1994-96, 98; sec. Dist. 13 Dem. Com., 1998; v.p. Houston Ind. Sch. Dist. Elem. Chess League, 1996-99; mem. edn. com. Harris County Dem. Com., mem. exec. com.; sec.-treas. Coalition of Cmty. and Commerce, 1997-2000; commr. Houston Bldg. and Stds. Commn., 1999-2002; precinct judge, chmn. precinct 139, Houston. Recipient Vick Driscoll award Tex. Commerce Bank, 1996. Mem. Am. Assn. Children with Learning Disabilities, Tex. Fedn. Tchrs. (bd. dirs. quality ednl. stds. in tchg. 1993, legis. com., chmn. 1993-99), Houston Fedn. Tchrs. (chmn. legis. liaison com. 1993-99, v.p. 1992-99), River Oaks Roadwomen, Delta Mu Delta. Democrat. Avocation: civic and political activities. Home: 2141 Colquitt St Houston TX 77098-3310

PASTIN, MARK JOSEPH, association executive; b. Ellwood City, Pa., July 6, 1949; s. Joseph and Patricia Jean (Camenite) Pastin; m. Joanne Marie Reagle, May 30, 1970 (div. Mar. 1982); m. Carrie Patricia Class, Dec. 22, 1984 (div. June 1990); m. Christina M. Brecto, June 15, 1991. BA summa cum laude, U. Pitts., 1970; MA, Harvard U., 1972, PhD, 1973. Asst. prof. Ind. U., Bloomington, 1973-78, assoc. prof., 1978-80; founder, bd. Compliance Resource Group, Inc., 1983—; chmn., CEO, pres. Coun. Ethical Orgns., Alexandria, Va., 1986—; prof. mgmt., dir. Ariz. State U., Tempe, 1988-92, prof. emeritus, 1996—; chair Health Ethics Trust, 1995—. Mem. adv. bd. Aberdeen Holdings, San Diego, 1988-90; dir. Learned Nicholson, Ltd., 1990-91; bd. Japan Am. Soc. Phoenix, Found. for Ethical Orgns.; cons. GTE, Interim Healthcare, 1997-2000, U.S. Dept. Edn., 2002, Tex. Instruments, MicroAge Computers, Med-Tronic, Blood Sys., Inc., Opus Corp., GTE, NyNex, Am. Express Bank, Kaiko Bussan Co., Japan, Arex Co., Japan, Century Audit Co., U.S. Dept. Edn., Japan, Scottsdale Meml. Hosp., Consanti Found., Lincoln Electric Co., Tenet Healthcare, The Williams Co.; vis. faculty Harvard U., 1980; invited presenter Australian Inst. Mgmt., Nippon Tel. & Tel., Hong Kong Commn. Against Corruption, 1984, Young Pres.'s Orgn. Internat. U., 1990, Nat. Assn. Indsl. & Office Parks, 1990, ABA, 1991, Govt. of Brazil, 1991. Author: Hard Problems of Management, 1986 (Book of Yr. Armed Forces Mil. Comtrs. 1986, Japanese edit. 1994), Power by Association, 1991, The Hotline Handbook, 1996, Planning Forum, 1992; editor: Public-Private Sector Ethics, 1979; mem. editl. bd. Report on Medicare Compliance; pub. Pastin Report on Best Compliance Practices, 1998—, Guerin Lect. on Philanthropy, 1996. Founding bd. mem. Tempe Leadership, 1985-89; bd. mem. Ctr. for Behavioral Health, Phoenix, 1986-89, Tempe YMCA, 1986—, Valley Leadership Alumni Assn., 1989-92; mem. Clean Air Com., Phoenix, 1987-90. Nat. Sci. Found. fellow, Cambridge, Mass., 1971-73; Nat. Endowment for the Humanities fellow, 1975; Exxon Edn. Found. grant, 1982-83. Mem.: Found. Ethical Orgns. (chmn. 1988, pres.), Am. Soc. Assn. Execs. (invited presenter 1987—97), Mt. Vernon Country Club, Harvard Club D.C., Phi Beta Kappa, Golden Key. Avocations: golf, running. Office: 214 S Payne St Alexandria VA 22314-3530 Home: 7205 Regent Dr Alexandria VA 22307-2044 E-mail: councile@aol.com.

PASTOR, STEPHEN DANIEL, chemistry educator, researcher; b. New Brunswick, N.J., Feb. 15, 1947; s. Stephen and Irene (Bors) P.; m. Joan Ordemann, Apr. 3, 1971 (div. 1979); 1 child, Melanie; m. Joanne Behrens, July 13, 1985 (div. 1990). BA in Chemistry, Rutgers U., 1969, MS in Chemistry, 1978, PhD in Chemistry, 1983. Chemist Nat. Starch and Chem. Corp., Bridgewater, N.J., 1972-79; rsch. group leader CIBA-Geigy Corp., Ardsley, N.Y., 1979-84, rsch. mgr., 1985-87; group leader Cen. Rsch. Labs. CIBA-Geigy Ag, Basel, Switzerland, 1987-89, rsch. fellow Ardsley, 1989-90, rsch. mgr., 1990-97, sr. rsch. fellow, 1998—. Asst. adj. prof. PACE U., Pleasantville, N.Y., 1984—, assoc. adj. prof., 1989-93, adj. prof., 1994—. Contbr. articles to profl. jours.; 100 patents in field. 1st lt. U.S. Army, 1969-71. Mem. Am. Chem. Soc. (Westchester sect. Disting. Scientist award 1997). Achievements include research on organophosphorous and organosulfur chemistry, conformational analysis, germanium chemistry, organometallic chemistry, asymmetric synthesis, homogeneous catalysis. Home: 27 Crows Nest Ln Unit 4F Danbury CT 06810-2005

PASTORE, DONNA LEE, physical education educator; BA in Phys. Edn., U. Fla., 1981, MA in Phys. Edn., 1983; PhD, U. So. Calif., 1988. Instr. Pa. State U., Beaver, Pa.; asst. prof. Sch. Health Ohio State U., assoc. prof. Advisor Sports Mgmt. Club. Editl. bd. Jour. Sport Mgmt.; rev. Strategies. State coord. Nat. Girls and Women in Sport Day, 1992. Recipient NAGWS Linds to to Leadership award, 1982, NAGWS Rsch. award, 1983, Mabel Lee award, 1995. Mem. Ohio AHPERD (chair rsch. sect. higher edn., v.p.-elect sports sci. divsn., eastern dist. bylaws & oper. code com.), N. Am. Soc. Sports Mgmt. Office: Ohio State U Sch Phys Activity and Ednl Svcs 455 Larkins Hall 337 W 17th Ave Columbus OH 43210 E-mail: pastore.3@osu.edu.*

PASTOREK, PAUL G. federal agency administrator; Undergrad., Loyola U., 1976, JD, 1979. Former ptnr. Adams and Reese, New Orleans; gen. counsel NASA, Washington, 2002—. Pres. La. State Bd. Elem. and Secondary Edn., 2000—; mem. various state bds. and commns. Office: NASA Hdqrs Mail Code A 300 E St SW Washington DC 20546

PASTRANA, RONALD RAY, Christian ministry counselor, Biblical theology educator, former school system administrator; b. N.Y.C., Sept. 5, 1939; s. Anthony and Mildred Pastrana; m. Josephine Pastrana; children: Christine, Therese. BA in History/Sci. Edn., Queens Coll., 1963; advanced sci. cert., Pace U., 1964-68; MS in Counseling Edn., St. John's U., 1967; diploma, U.S. Acad. of Health Sci., 1975, U.S. Army Command and Gen. Staff Coll., 1979; D Ministry, Sch. Bible Theology Sem., 1996, ThD, 2000. Lic. min. Pentecostal Assemblies of God of Am.; cert. life support sys. in internat. space NOAA, NASA. Tchr. sci. Marie Curie Jr. High Sch., Bayside, N.Y., 1963-68; guidance counselor Half Hollow Hills High Sch., Dix Hills, N.Y., 1969-71, Walt Whitman High Sch., Huntington Station, N.Y., 1968-69, coord. occupational svcs., 1971-74; guidance coord. Dutchess County Bd. Coop. Ednl. Svcs. Tech. Edn. Ctr., Poughkeepsie, N.Y., 1974-86; coord. guidance and related acads. Dutchess County BOCES Tech. Edn. Ctr., Poughkeepsie, N.Y., 1986-96; asst. dir. Reach Out Sch. of Ministry, Hyde Park, N.Y., 1996—; prof. Biblical theology Sch. Bible Theology Sem., San Jacinto, Calif., 1999—. Ednl. cons. N.Y. State Edn. Dept., Albany, 1975-83, Armed Forces Vocat. Testing Group, Dept. of Def., Washington, 1975-77; cert. educator Lunar Edn. Project, NASA, 1986-87, Asteroids, Lunar Rocks, Meteorites Edn. Projects, 1999—; sci., math. and tech. cons., 1998; pub. Reach Out Ministries. Author: Career Guidance in the Classroom, 1974, A Curriculum Guide to the Study of the Seven Dispensations and Eight Covenants, 1996, Dispensational Theology, 1997, Pentecostal Doctrine and Theology, 1998, Student Guide to the Seven Dispensations and Eignt Covenants, 1999, The Greek Fathers of the Early Christian Church, 2000, The Latin Fathers of the Early Christian Church, 2000, The Reformers of the Christian Church, 2001, Reach Out Ministries. Lt. col. USAR, ret. 1992. NSF sci. study grantee, 1964-68, grantee NASA and Nat. Ocean. and Atmos. Adminstrn., 1999; recipient: Dutchess County Counselor of the Year award, 1995; decorated Joint Svc. Commendation medal, Army achievement medal, Selective Svc. Meritorious medal, Army Res. Components Achievement medal, Nat. Def. Svc. medal, N.Y.S. medal for Meritorious Svc., Meritorious Svc. award for civilian svc. USN, 2000. Mem. Am. Counselors Assn., Am. Mental Health Counselors Assn., Nat. Career Devel. Assn., Am. Assn. Christian Counselors, N.Y. Acad. Scis., N.Y. State Assn. for Counseling and Devel., Sch. Adminstrs. Assn. N.Y. State, Dutchess County Counseling Assn. (exec. bd. 1989-96), Phi Delta Kappa. Avocations: rock and mineral collecting, fitness activities, canoeing, hiking. Office: Wappingers Ctrl Sch Dist Office of Sci & Tech 6 Hillside Lake Rd Wappingers Falls NY 12590 Home: 23 North Loop Rhinebeck NY 12572-1920

PASVOLSKY, RICHARD LLOYD, parks, recreation, and environment educator; b. Englewood, NJ, Feb. 16, 1924; s. Valentine and Ellen Isabel (Stoughton) P.; m. Jo Anne Evans, June 16, 1968. BEd, Panzer Coll., 1950; MA in Edn., NYU, 1955; D in Recreation, Ind. U., 1973. Asst. supt. recreation City of Rutland, Vt., 1951-53; supt. recreation City of Montpelier, Vt., 1953-55; dir. parks and recreation Twp. of Parsippany-Troy Hills, NJ, 1955-62; asst. prof. outdoor and environ. edn. NJ State Sch. Conservation, Branchville, NJ, 1962-71; assoc. prof. edn. Ramapo Coll. NJ, Mahwah, NJ, 1972-84, coach archery, 1973-84; adj. prof. Kean Univ., Union, NJ, 1985—. Instr. archery, dir. dance and recreation World Archery Ctr., Pomfret, Conn., 1964-92; dir. NJ State Coll. divsn. Nat. Archery Assn., 1978-84. Advisor to choreographer, cons. prodn. office closing ceremonies Statue of Liberty Centennial Celebration, 1986; rec. artist: Square Dances, 1961, 91, mag. articles, 1954-66; columnist Lines About Squares, 1983—. Instr. dance camp staff Lloyd Shaw Found., 1981—, bd. dirs., 1982-88; bd. trustees Sussex County Sr. Legal Resources Ctr., 1992-94. With U.S. Army, 1943-46, ETO. Recipient Alumni award Panzer Coll. NJ, 1979, Spl. Alumni award, 1987; named to Ramapo Coll. Athletic Hall of Fame, 1993, Lakewood (NJ) HS Hall of Fame, 1998. Mem. AAHPERD (Recreator of Yr. Ea. Dist. 1977), NJ Alliance Health, Phys. Edn., Recreation and Dance, Callers Coun. NJ, Callerlab, Phi Delta Kappa. Avocations: calling square dances, ballroom dancing, skiing, golf, tennis. Home: 31 Newton Ave Branchville NJ 07826-4203 Office: Kean U NJ Phys Edn Dept Union NJ 07083

PATE, JOHN GILLIS, JR., financial consultant, accounting educator; b. Chattanooga, Jan. 27, 1928; s. John Gillis Pate and Iona Estelle (Bowman) Pate Ketchman; m. Daphne Mae Davis, Feb. 8, 1946; children: John Gillis III, Daphne Iona, Donna Gay. Student, U. Tampa, 1947-48; AA with highest honors, U. Fla., 1950; BS cum laude, Fla. State U., 1953, MS, 1958; PhD, Columbia U., 1968. CPA, S.C. Mgr. Grocery Concession, Albany, Ga., 1944-45, Variety Store, Panama City, Fla., 1946-47; asst. to CPA Standard Brands, Inc., Birmingham, Ala., 1951-53; acctg. supervisory trainee Birmingham, Ala., 1953-54; grad. asst. Fla. State U., Tallahassee, 1957-58; asst. to CPA Pensacola, Fla., 1956-58; CPA, 1958; asst. prof. U. Ga., Athens, 1958-60; lectr. Columbia U., N.Y.C., 1961-64; asst. prof. Bernard M. Baruch Coll. of CUNY, 1963-69; prof. acctg. U. Tex.-El Paso, 1969-85, U. S.C., Spartanburg, 1988-93. Cons. resource person fin. and human resources Charles Lea Ctr., Spartanburg, 1988—, dir. Internal Audit and Spl. Projects, 1994-2002. Author: Index C.P.A. Exams and Unofficial Answers, 1974-81; co-author: Accounting Trends and Techniques, 1967-88, Index to Accounting and Auditing Services, 1971; contbr. articles to ann. profl. publs. Tither, Coronado Bapt. Ch., El Paso, 1969-86, Buck Creek Bapt. Ch., Spartanburg, 1987—; cons. Alderman of El Paso, 1982, County Councilman of Spartanburg, 1991-98. With lt. j.g. USN, 1955-56. Columbia U. fellow, 1960; Earhart Found. fellow, 1960, Am. Acctg. Assn. fellow, 1960, Found fellow, 1961-62; recipient Haskins and Sells award, 1960. Mem. AICPA (cons. 1961-88), Am. Acctg. Assn., Moose, Masons, Shriners, Beta Alpha Psi, Beta Alpha Chi. Republican. Home and Office: 106 Lori Cir Spartanburg SC 29303-5527

PATE, ROBERT HEWITT, JR., counselor educator; b. Abingdon, Va., Apr. 5, 1938; s. Robert Hewitt and Esther Frances (Kirk) P.; m. Ellen O'Neal Pope, Dec. 11, 1960; children: Robert Hewitt III, Mary Ellen Pate Barton. AB, Davidson Coll., 1960; MEd, U. Va., 1965; PhD, U. N.C., 1968. Lic. prof. counselor, Va. Marketer Sinclair Refining Co., Abingdon, Va., 1960-61, 63-64; counselor St. Andrews Presbyn. Coll., Laurinburg, N.C., 1965-66; prof. counselor edn. U. Va., Charlottesville, 1968—, interim dean, 1994-95, assoc. dean, 1995—. Mem. adj. faculty Fed. Exec. Inst., Charlottesville, 1978—. Author: Being A Counselor, 1983. Elder local Presbyn. ch. 1st lt. U.S. Army 1961-63. Mem. Am. Counseling Assn., Va. Counselors Assn. (pres. 1983-84), Nat. Bd. Cert. Counselors (chair 1996-97). Avocation: reading. Home: 552 Dryden Pl Charlottesville VA 22903-4666 Office: Curry Sch Dean's Office 405 Emmet St S PO Box 400260 Charlottesville VA 22904-4260

PATERIK, FRANCES SUE, secondary school educator, actress; b. Bloomington, Ill., Feb. 10, 1953; d. Francis LaVerne and Magaline Wilken. Student, Am. Cons. Music, Chgo., 1976—78, N.W. Ind. Opera Co., 1980, Hinsdale Opera Co., Ill., 1981; BA, MA, Western Ill. U., 1984. Tchg. asst. Western Ill. U., Macomb, 1982—84; music tchr. Cardinal Cmty. Schs., Eldon, Iowa, 1985—89, Johnston (Iowa) Cmty. Schs., 1990—94; music/performing arts tchr. Colfax (Iowa)-Mingo Cmty. Sch., 1995—2002, Merrill Middle Sch., Des Moines, 2002—. Dir. handbell choir First Christian Ch., Des Moines, 1996—2000; soprano soloist Des Moines Concert Singers, 1989—, Des Moines Choral Soc., 2002—. Actress : (various comedic roles) Ingersoll Dinner Theatre; Playhouse; Drama Workshop; Stage West. Mem.: Iowa Choral Dirs. Assn., Am. Choral Dirs. Assn., Music Educators Nat. Conf., Nat. Wildlife Fedn., Sierra Club. Democrat. Avocations: gardening, animal welfare, dancing. Office: Des Moines Pub Schs Des Moines IA 50312

PATERSON, PATRICIA MCDONNOUGH, secondary school educator, sports official; b. Chgo., July 25, 1918; d. James Martin and Minnie (Gronseth) McDonnough; m. Andrew Allan Paterson, Apr. 26, 1941 (dec.); children: Andrew Jr., John James, Margaret Murray. BA, Mundelein Coll., 1939; MEd, Concordia, 1976. Cert. primary physically handicapped tchr. Tchr. Chgo. Pub. Schs., 1950-83; coach women's swimming DePaul U., Chgo., 1956-59; coach synchronized swim team Oak Park, Ill., 1964-72; adminstrv. chmn. Ill. Synchronized Swim Assn., 1960—. Chmn. awards & opening & closing ceremonies Pan Am Games, 1959, U.S. Olympic Com., Portage Park, Chgo., U.S. Swim Trials, Chgo., 1972; history chmn. U.S. Synchronized Swimming, Indpls., 1978-94. Contbr. articles to profl. jours. Judge Official Level 4 Synchronized Swim, 1988—. Recipient Asua Pan Am medal, 1959; Found. Rsch. grantee, 1985—. E-mail: patersonsynswim@aol.com.

PATILLO, SYLVIA JANE, human resources executive, educator; b. Kansas City, Mo., Nov. 15, 1946; d. John W. and Lola Mae (Williams) Jamierson; divorced; children: Rochelle D. Brown, Jason L. Patillo. AA, Penn. Valley C.C., Kansas City, 1981; BS, Park Coll., 1988; MA, Ottawa U., 1992, cert. sr. profl. in human resources, 1994. Computer operator Interstate Brands Corp., Kansas City, 1976-85, sec., 1986-88, personnel asst., 1988-89; employment specialist Gov. Employees Hosp. Assn., Independence, Mo., 1989-95; human resources mgr. Torotel Products, Inc., 1998—. Adj. prof. Baker U., 1993-96, Park Coll., 1996—. Recording sec. Nat. Black MBA Assn., Kansas City, 1993—; vol. Urban League of Kansas City, 1986—; bd. dirs. Rose Brooks Ctr. Shelter for Women, Kansas City, 1987-90. Recipient scholarship Am. Bus. Womens Assn., 1987, 88. Mem. Soc. Human Resource Mgrs.

PATNODE, LYNNE MARIE, childcare center owner; b. Milw., May 31, 1955; d. Richard and Eloise (Jessup) Farmer; m. John Gerald Patnode, Apr. 2, 1982; children: Krista, Gerainne, Cynthia, Angela. BS, Montclair State U., 1978; MS, Nova U., 1992. Tchr. Oak Hill Sch. for Blind, Hartford, Conn., 1978-80; customer svc. rep. Amica Ins., Wethersfield, Conn., 1980-82; ins. rep. Kenny Webber & Lowell, Inc., Canton, Conn., 1982-83; owner, dir. Gymtots Child Care Ctr., Inc., Torrington, Conn., 1985—. Owner BP Assocs., Torrington, 1991—; cons. Sunny Days Child Care, Inc., Canton, 1991—, Dona-Rache Child Care Ctr., Harwinton, Conn., 1990—, Early Learning, Inc., Torrington, 1992—; speaker, workshop trainer in field. Leader Girl Scouts U.S.A., Torrington, 1983-89. Mem. Nat. Assn. for Self Employed (award 1992), Nat. Assn. Edn. of Young Children, N.W. Conn. Assn. for Edn. of Young Children (v.p. 1987—), Nat. Found. Ind. Bus., U.S. C. of C. Democrat. Roman Catholic. Avocations: stained glass windows, music, soccer. Office: 10 North Rd Harwinton CT 06791-1901

PATON, DAVID, ophthalmologist, educator; b. Balt., Aug. 16, 1930; s. Richard Townley and Helen (Meserve) P.; m. Diane Johnston Brokaw, Mar. 9, 1985; 1 child from previous marriage, D. Townley. BA, Princeton U., 1952; MD, Johns Hopkins U., 1956; DSc (hon.), Bridgeport U., 1984, Princeton U., 1985. Diplomate Am. Bd. Ophthalmology. Intern Cornell Med. Sch.-N.Y. Hosp., 1956-57; rsch. fellow in ophthalmology NIH, Bethesda, Md., 1957-59; resident Wilmer Inst., Johns Hopkins Sch. Medicine, Balt., 1959-64; assoc. prof. Wilmer Inst., 1964-71; asst. prof. Johns Hopkins Sch. Medicine, 1964-71; prof., chmn. dept. ophthalmology Baylor Coll. Medicine, Houston, 1971-82, prof. emeritus ophthalmology, 1998—; med. dir. King Khaled Eye Specialist Hosp., Riyadh, Saudi Arabia, 1982-84; chmn., chief med. officer OcuSystems, Inc., Greenwich, Conn., 1985-87; prof. Cornell U. Coll. Medicine, 1986-92; chmn., program dir. dept. ophthalmology Cath. Med. Ctr. of Bklyn. and Queens, 1986-92. Founder Project ORBIS, Inc., N.Y.C., 1971, med. dir., 1971-87; founder, bd. pres. The EXCEL Found., 1989-99; mem. com. med. sci. USIA, 1991-94; bd. dirs. Eye Bank for Sight Restoration, N.Y.C., One World Sight Project, Southhampton Hosp., 1998—, East Hampton Healthcare Found., 1998—; bd. pres. World Eye Orgn., Hong Kong, 1999—; mem. med. adv. bd. Johns Hopkins Sch. Pub. Health, 1988-2003. Author of several books; contbr. articles to profl. jours. Recipient Royal Decoration 3d Order, Royal Decoration 2d Order (Jordan), Pres.'s Citizen medal, 1987, Legion of Honor (France); Markle scholar in acad. medicine, 1967-72; named honoree Manhattan League Helen Keller Svcs. for the Blind, 2002. Fellow Am. Acad. Ophthalmology (sec. continuing edn. 1977-82, 1st v.p. 1982, Honor award 1975, Sr. Honor award 1992), ACS (bd. govs. substitute 1972-73); mem. Am. Bd. Ophthalmology (chmn. 1982), Assn. Univ. Profs. Ophthamology (trustee 1978-81), Md. Ophthalmol. Soc. (pres. 1969-70), Pan Am. Assn. Ophthalmology (coun. 1973-75). Home: PO Box 5015 East Hampton NY 11937-6096 E-mail: dpaton1@aol.com.

PATRICK, BRENDA JEAN, educational consultant; b. Dallas, Aug. 24, 1955; d. Gene Everett and Peggy Rose (Tanzy) Patrick; children: Michael Everett, Tray Riley. BS in Elem. Edn., Tex. A&M U., Commerce, 1981, MS, 1984, postgrad., 1989—. Cert. profl. supr., mid-mgmt. adminstr. Tchr. Garland Ind. Sch. Dist., 1982-87, acad. coach, 1983-86; with Austin Acad. for Excellence, 1987-88; program coord., master cons. Region 10 Edn. Svc. Ctr., 1988—. Coord. Tchr. Expectation Student Achievement; trainer Devel. Capable People; trainer of trainers Profl. Devel. and Appraisal Sys.; developer, presenter workshops and seminars in field. Author: Better Teaching, Texas Secretary. Past bd. dirs. Dallas Arboretum's Fan Club.

Recipient Tex. History Tchr. award Daus. of Republic of Tex., Am. History Tchr. award DAR; named Vol. with a Heart, YWCA. Mem. Tex. PTA (hon. life), Tex. Staff Devel. Coun., Phi Delta Kappa.

PATRICK, HUGH TALBOT, economist, educator; b. Goldsboro, N.C., Feb. 22, 1930; s. Talbot and Paula (Miller) P.; children: Stephen, Matthew, Catherine. BA, Yale U., 1951; MA in Far Eastern Studies, U. Mich., 1955, MA in Econs., 1957, PhD in Econs., 1960; MA (hon.), Yale U., 1968; PhD (hon.), Lingnan U., 2000. Econ. analyst U. S. Govt., 1951-52; lectr. econs. U. Mich., 1958-60; asst. prof. econs. Yale U., New Haven, 1960-64, assoc. prof., 1964-68, prof. Far Eastern econs., 1968-84; dir. Yale U. Econ. Growth Ctr., 1976-79, 80-83; R.D. Calkins prof. internat. bus. Columbia U., N.Y.C., 1984—2001, prof. emeritus, 2001—. Vis. prof. U. Bombay, 1961-62; mem. Japan-U.S. Econ. Rels. Group, 1978-81, U.S. Com. for Pacific Econ. Coop.; dir. Ctr. on Japanese Econ. and Bus., Columbia U., 1986—. Editor: Japanese Industrialization and Its Social Consequences, 1976, Japanese High Technology Industries-Lessons and Limitations of Industrial Policy, 1986; contbr. chpt. and co-editor (with Henry Rosovsky): Asia's New Giant-How the Japanese Economy Works, 1976; contbr. chpt., co-editor (with Masahiko Aoki): The Japanese Main Bank System: Its Relevance for Developing and Transforming Economies, 1994, co-editor (with Larry Meissner): Pacific Basin Industries in Distress: Structural Adjustment and Trade Policy in Nine Industrialized Economies, 1991 (Masayoshi Ohira Meml. prize 1992), (with Yung Chul Park) The Financial Development of Japan, Korea nad Taiwan: Growth, Repression and Liberalization, 1994, (with Takeo Hoshi) Crisis and Change in the Japanese Financial System, 2000. Ford Found. fellow 1957-58; grantee Am. Coun. Learned Socs., 1962; Guggenheim fellow, 1964-65; Fulbright rsch. prof., 1964-65; Fulbright-Hays NDEA fellow, 1968-69; Assn. Asian Studies Disting. lectr., 1977. Mem. Japan Soc. (dir. 1973-79, 81-2000), Social Sci. Rsch. Coun. (dir., chmn. 1985-88), Pacific Trade and Devel. Confs. (chmn.). Democrat. Office: Columbia U 320 Uris Hall 3022 Broadway New York NY 10027-6945

PATRICK, JOHN JOSEPH, social sciences educator; b. East Chicago, Ind., Apr. 14, 1935; s. John W. and Elizabeth (Lazar) P.; m. Patricia Grant, Aug. 17, 1963; children— Rebecca, Barbara AB, Dartmouth Coll., 1957; Ed.D., Ind. U., 1969. Social studies tchr. Roosevelt High Sch., East Chicago, 1957-62; social studies tchr. Lab. High Sch., U. Chgo., 1962-65; research assoc. Sch. Edn., Ind. U., Bloomington, 1965-69, asst. prof., 1969-74, assoc. prof., 1974-77, prof. edn., 1977—, dir. social studies devel. ctr., 1986—, dir. ERIC clearinghouse for social studies, social sci. edn., 1986—2003. Bd. dirs. Biol. Scis. Curriculum Study, 1980-83; ednl. cons. Author: Progress of the Afro-American, 1968, The Young Voter, 1974; (with L. Ehman, Howard Mehlinger) Toward Effective Instruction in Secondary Social Studies, 1974, Lessons on the Northwest Ordinance, 1987; (with R. Remy) Civics for Americans, 1980, rev. edit. 1986; (with Mehlinger) American Political Behavior, 1972, rev. edit. 1980, (with C. Keller) Lessons on the Federalist Papers, 1987; America Past and Present, 1983; (with Carol Berkin) History of the American Nation, 1984, rev. edit., 1987; Lessons on the Constitution, 1985, James Madison and the Federalist Papers, 1990, How to Teach the Bill of Rights, 1991, Ideas of the Founders on Constitutional Government: Resources for Teachers of History and Government, 1991, Young Oxford Companion to the Supreme Court of the United States, 1994, Founding the Republic: A Documentary History, 1995, (with Gerald Long) Constitutional Debates on Freedom of Religion: A Documentary History, 1999, (with Richard M. Pious and Donald A. Ritchie) The Oxford Essential Guide to the U.S. Government, 2000, The Bill of Rights: A History in Documents, 2002. Bd. dirs. Law in Am. Soc. Found., 1984-88, Social Sci. Edn. consortium, 1984—; mem. Gov.'s Task Force on Citizenship Edn., Ind., 1982-87; active Ind. Commn. on Bicentennial of U.S. Constn., 1986-92; bd. dirs. Coun. for the Advancement of Citizenship, Nat. History Edn. Network, 1994-96; mem. Natr. Coun. for History Standards, 1991-94. Recipient John W. Ryan award for disting. svc. in internat. programs and studies, Ind. U., 2002. Mem. ASCD, Nat. Coun. Social Studies, Social Sci. Edn. Consortium (v.p. 1985-87), Coun. for Basic Edn., Am. Polit. Sci. Assn., Am. Hist. Assn., Orgn. Am. Historians, Phi Delta Kappa. Home: 1209 E University St Bloomington IN 47401-5045 Office: Ind U 2805 E 10th St Bloomington IN 47408-2601

PATRICK, PAMELA ANN, research consultant; b. Dallas, June 10, 1963; d. Gene Everett and Peggy Rose (Tanzy) P. AAS, Eastfield Coll., 1982; BA in English, Tex. A&M U.-Commerce, 1987, MS in Edn., English, 1988. Tex. provisional cert. 1990. Sales clk. Sears, Mesquite, 1982-84; substitute tchr. various Ind. Sch. Dists., Tex., 1988—. Contbr. articles to profl. jours. Mem. UDC, DAR, Daus. Republic Tex., Daus. Union Vets. Civil War, Dallas County Heritage Soc., Dallas Geneal. Soc., Nat. Trust for Historic Preservation, Dallas Hist. Soc., Green County Hist. Geneal. Soc., Snyder Kennedy Cemetery Preservation Soc. (pres.), Robert Morris Hist. Soc. (pres.), Humane Soc. U.S., DAV Aux., Phi Delta Kappa, Sigma Tau Delta. Republican. Methodist. Avocations: photographer, gardener, genealogist, corvette enthusiast. Home: PO Box 870668 Mesquite TX 75187-0668

PATRICK, SUSAN D. government agency administrator; B in English, Colo. Coll.; M in Comm. Mgmt., U. So. Calif. Dir. distance learning campus Old Dominion U.; coord. Digital State Survey 2002 State of Ariz.; dep. dir. Office Edn. Tech. U.S. Dept. Edn., Washington. Office: US Dept Edn Rm FB6-7E208 400 Maryland Ave SW Washington DC 20202*

PATRICKS, EDWARD JOHN, elementary education educator; b. Chgo., Jan. 19, 1958; s. John Anthony and Marion Nora (Kinnavy) P. Ed, Ill. Benedictine, Lisle, Ill., 1981. Cert. tchr., Ill. Sci. tchr. St. Pius X, Stickney, Ill., 1981-84; dept. chair, sci. tchr. St. Giles Junior High, Oak Park, Ill., 1984-98; sci. tchr. Hyde Park Mid. Sch., Las Vegas, 1998—, coach boys' basketball. Commr. City of Berwyn, 1991—, North Berwyn Pk. Dist., 1995—; past commr. St. Mary of Celle Little League; sponsor Berwyn Playground and Recreation Commn., Berwyn Blazers Taveling Soccer; coach Redrock Little League, Las Vegas; bd. dirs. Dem. Orgn. Berwyn, St. Mary of Celle, St. Vincent De Paul Conf. Mem. ASCD, NSTA, Nat. Cath. Educators Assn., Ill. Assn. Pk. Dists., Ill. Sheriffs Assn., Suburban Pks. and Recreation Divsn., Nat. Recreation and Pk. Assn., Berwyn Devel. Corp., KC (4 degree). Home: 1344 Angel Falls St Las Vegas NV 89142-1323 Office: Hyde Park Mid Sch 900 Hinson St Las Vegas NV 89107-4452 E-mail: ejpcommish@msn.com.

PATRIE, CHERYL CHRISTINE, elementary education educator; b. Dobbs Ferry, N.Y., June 8, 1947; d. Edward F. and Antoinette C. (Patrie) P. BA in Edn., U. Fla., 1969; MS in Edn., U. Miami, 1979. Cert. assoc. master tchr., Fla. Tchr. Marion County Sch. Bd., Ocala, Fla., 1970, Dade County Sch. Bd., Miami, 1973—. Mem. faculty coun. Lorah Park lem. Sch., Miami, 1979-89, 1991—, career lab. cons., 1983-85, human growth and devel. cons., 1983—, phys. fitness co-chmn., 1984-90, chair dept., 1993—; coord. quality instrn. incentives program, 1984-89; mem. Dade County Elem. Sch. Day Task Force, 1987-88. Mem. United Tchrs. Dade (bldg. union steward 1979-89, mem. crisis in inner city task force 1984-85, Disting. Svc. award 1984). Home: 1127 Robin Ave Miami FL 33166-3129 Office: Lorah Park Elem 5160 NW 31st Ave Miami FL 33142-3439

PATRIZIO, LILIANA, educator; b. Woburn, Mass., Oct. 7, 1964; d. Nicodemo and Angela Patrizio. BS in Edn., Lesley Coll., 1986. Cert. middle sch. and moderate spl. needs tchr., Mass. Spl. edn. instr. Marshall Middle Sch., Billerica, Mass., 1986-87, English High Sch., Lynn, Mass., 1987-88; learning specialist Shawsheen Tech. Sch., Billerica, 1988-91; head tchr. Dearborn Acad., Arlington, Mass., 1991—. Brownie patrol leader Girl Scouts U.S.A., Burlington, 1990-91; CCD tchr. St. Charles Ch., Woburn, 1990-91; support vol. Students Against Drunk Driving, Billerica, 1990-91. Mem. Mass. Tchrs. Assn. Avocations: travel, writing, family.

PATRON, NICHOLAS VICTOR, special education educator; b. Canton, Ohio, Mar. 26, 1951; s. Nicholas Victor and Mary Josephine (Ottavio) P. BA, Walsh U., Canton, Ohio, 1973. Elem. tchr. Diocese of Youngstown Schs., Canton, 1973-87; spl. edn. tchr. Plain Local Schs., Canton, 1987—. Bus. dir. Head of the Class, Canton, 1992—. Libr. substitute Stark County Libr., Canton, 1990—. Named Canton's Best Tchr., City of Canton, 1983; recipient Nat. Honor Soc. award Glen Oak H.S., 1994. Fellow NEA, Ohio Tchr.'s Retirement Assn. Avocations: art, reading, crafts, gardening, walking.

PATTAK, KATHY KRAMER, elementary physical education educator; b. Pitts., Nov. 9, 1951; d. Elliott Burton and Marilyn Lucille (Mendoza) Kramer; m. Alan Jay Pattak, July 13, 1975; 1 child, Cory. BS, Ind. U., 1973; MS in Counseling, Duquesne U., 1975. Cert. tchr., Pa. Elem. health and phys. edn. tchr. Stephen Foster Sch., Mt. Lebanon, Pa., 1973—, Lincoln Sch., 1999—. Adv. bd. Power in Edn., Castle Shannon, Pa., 1991-93, strategic planning com. Mt. Lebanon Sch. Dist., 1990-93. Pres. Pitts. region women's Am. Ort, 1989-91; pres. Keystone Oaks Steel Band Parent Assn., 1997-2000. Mem. NEA, AAHPERD, Pa. Assn. Health, Phys. Edn., Recreation and Dance, Bower Hill Civic League and Swim Club (v.p. 1991-93, bd. dirs 1987—), Delta Psi Kappa. Avocations: sewing, needlepoint, golf, musicals. Office: 700 Vermont Ave Pittsburgh PA 15234-1220

PATTEN, BEBE HARRISON, minister, chancellor; b. Waverly, Tenn., Sept. 3, 1913; d. Newton Felix and Mattie Priscilla (Whitson) Harrison; m. Carl Thomas Patten, Oct. 23, 1935; children: Priscilla Carla and Bebe Rebecca (twins), Carl Thomas. D.D., McKinley-Roosevelt Coll., 1941; D.Litt., Temple Hall Coll. and Sem., 1943. Ordained to ministry Ministerial Assn. of Evangelism, 1935; evangelist in various cities of U.S., 1933-50; founder, pres. Christian Evang. Chs. Am., Inc., Oakland, Calif., 1944—, Patten Acad. Christian Edn., Oakland, 1944—, Patten Bible Coll., Oakland, 1944-83; chancellor Patten Coll., Oakland, 1983—; founder, pastor Christian Cathedral of Oakland, 1950—. Held pvt. interviews with David Ben-Gurion, 1972, Menachim Begin, 1977, Yitzhak Shamir, 1991; condr. Sta. KUSW world-wide radio ministry, 70 countries around the world, 1989-90, Stas. WHRI and WWCR world coverage short wave, 1990— Founder, condr.: radio program The Shepherd Hour, 1934— ; daily TV, 1976—, nationwide telecast, 1979— ; Author: Give Me Back My Soul, 1973; Editor: Trumpet Call, 1953— ; composer 20 gospel and religious songs, 1945— . Mem. exec. bd. Bar-Ilan U. Assn., Israel, 1983; mem. global bd. trustees Bar-Ilan U., 1991. Recipient numerous awards including medallion Ministry of Religious Affairs, Israel, 1969; medal Govt. Press Office, Jerusalem, 1971; Christian honoree of yr. Jewish Nat. Fund of No. Calif., 1975; Hidden Heroine award San Francisco Bay coun. Girl Scouts U.S.A., 1976, Golden State award Who's Who Hist. Soc., 1988; Ben-Gurion medallion Ben-Gurion Rsch. Inst., 1977; Resolutions of Commendation, Calif. Senate Rules Com., 1978, 94, Disting. Leadership award Ch. of God Sch. of Theology, 1996; hon. fellow Bar-Ilan U., Israel, 1981; Dr. Bebe Patten Social Action chair established Bar-Ilan U., 1982. Mem. Am. Assn. for Higher Edn., Religious Edn. Assn., Am. Acad. Religion and Soc. Bibl. Lit., Zionist Orgn. Am., Am. Assn. Pres. of Ind. Colls. and Univs., Am. Jewish Hist. Soc., Am.-Isreal Pub. Affairs Com. Address: 2433 Coolidge Ave Oakland CA 94601-2630

PATTEN, BERNARD MICHAEL, neurologist, writer, educator; b. N.Y.C., Mar. 23, 1941; s. Bernard M. and Olga (Vaccaro) P.; m. Ethel Doudine, June 18, 1964; children: Allegra, Craig. AB summa cum laude, Columbia Coll., 1962; MD, Columbia U., 1966. Med. intern N.Y. Hosp. Cornell Med. Ctr., N.Y.C., 1966-67; resident neurologist Columbia Presbyn. Med. Ctr., N.Y.C., 1967-69, chief resident neurologist, 1969-70; assoc. prof. neurology Baylor Coll. Medicine, Houston, 1973-95; ret., 1995. Asst. chief med. neurology NIH, Bethesda, Md., 1970-73; mem. med. bd. Nat. Myasthenia Gravis Found., 1973—, Nat. AmyoTrophic Lateral Sclerosis Found., 1982—, Nat. Myositis Assn., 1995—; invited faculty Rice U., 1999—; faculty Women's INst. Houston. Author: One or Two Things I Remember About Her, 1999, Tristan and Iseult: Modern Version, 2000, Investment Pearls for Modern Times Expressed in Meter and in Rhymes, 2000, The Great Cotzias, 2001, Ascent to Heaven, 2001, Quia Imperfectum, 2001; contbr. more than 200 articles to profl. jours. With USPHS, 1970-73. Rsch. grantee NIH, pvt. founds., nat. health orgns. Fellow ACP, Royal Coll. Physicians, Tex. Neurol. Soc. Achievements include discoverer (with others) L-Dopa for Parkinson's disease; pioneered use of immune suppression for myasthenia gravis, diagnosis and treatment of medical and neurologcal complications of breast implants. Home: 1019 Baronridge Dr Seabrook TX 77586-4001 E-mail: DADPATTEN@aol.com.

PATTENAUDE, RICHARD LOUIS, university administrator; b. Seattle, Feb. 22, 1946; s. Joseph Arthur and Alice June (Vrooman) P.; m. Michele Arlen Stevenson, May 31, 1975; children: Lauren, Lisa, Dylan, Joshua. BA with honors in Econs., Calif. State U., San Jose, 1968; PhD in Polit. Sci., U. Colo., 1974. Asst./assoc. prof. Drake U., Des Moines, 1974-80, assoc. dean liberal arts, 1976-80; asst. v.p. acad. affairs SUNY-Binghamton, 1980-82, assoc. v.p., 1982-86; v.p. acad. affairs; prof. polit. sci. Ctrl. Conn. State U., New Britain, 1986-91; pres., prof. polit. sci. U. So. Maine, Portland, 1991—. Cons. in field; panelist, presenter various nat. higher edn. meetings. Contbr. numerous articles to profl. jours., chpts. to books in field. Commr. Occupational and Licensing Commn., Iowa, 1978-80; mem. Gov.'s Com. Efficiency, 1979; mem. adv. coun. planning dept. City of Binghamton, 1984-1986; bd. dirs. Broome County United Way, 1985, Greater Hartford Red Cross, 1991-93, Mercy Hosp., Portland, 1992-94, Portland Symphony Orch., Maine Devel. Found., 1991-97, Maine Sci. & Tech. Found., 1992-98, Portland Mus. Art, 1993-99, Pmt. Symphony 1998-, Maine Med. Ctr., 2002-, Inst. Civic Leadership, 1992-94, Greater Portland United Way, Maine Med. Ctr., 2002—. With U.S. Army, 1969-71, Vietnam. Fanny W. Ames scholar, 1965; Title II fellow, 1970. Mem. Assn. Instl. Rsch. and Planning Officers (v.p. 1983-84, pres. 1984-85), Am. Assn. State Colls. and Univs. (state rep. 1995—, bd. dirs. 1999—), Greater Portland C. of C. Office: U So Maine Office of Pres 707 Law Building 96 Falmouth St Portland ME 04103-9300 Address: U So Maine PO Box 9300 Portland ME 04104-9300

PATTERSON, CAROLYN F. retired English educator; b. Winnsboro, S.C., Nov. 7, 1935; d. William Lyle and Alma (Wilson) Ferguson; m. Marion Symmes Patterson, Dec. 16, 1956; 1 child, Marion. AB, Lander U., 1957; MEd, Clemson U., 1973. English tchr. Greenwood (S.C.) Sch. Dist. #50, 1958-89; asst. prin. Greenwood H.S., 1989-94, Emerald H.S., 1994-97. Mem. Ch. of Jesus Christ of Latter-Day Saints. Home: 2350 W Shaw Ave Ste 123 Fresno CA 93711-3412

PATTERSON, CLAIRE ANN, career techincal educator; b. Cin., Dec. 28, 1950; d. Lloyd E. and Ruth T. (Flaherty) Lachtrupp; m. Calvin Stanley Patterson, Jr., July 14, 1973; children: Christopher, Alicia. BS, U. Cin., 1973, MEd, 1980. Cert. elem. tchr., elem. supr., secondary math, secondary prin., asst. supt., Ohio., Va., P.R. Third grade tchr. Acadamia de Aguidilla, P.R., 1973-74; fifth grade tchr. Our Lady of the Rosary, Norfolk, Va., 1974-76; jr. high math and sci. tchr. Yavneh Hebrew Day Sch., Cin., 1976-79; math tchr. Winton Woods City Schs., Cin., 1979-80; math. coord. Great Oaks Inst. of Tech. and Career Devel., Cin., 1980-86, benefits coord./personnel profl., 1986-88, career devel. mgr., 1987-93, asst. dir., 1993-97, dean of instrn., 1998-99, mgr. testing and assessment, 1999—2001, mgr. profl. devel., 2001—03, dir. human resources, 2003—. Ednl. cons. schs. in Ohio, 1988—. Author: Let's Celebrate Math, 1991; contbr. articles to profl. jours. Mem. Ohio Career Devel. Task Frce, 1991-93. Recipient Career Coord. award State of Ohio, 1993. Mem. Ohio Vocat. Assn. (com. chmn. 1990-93, pres. 1997-2000, Pacesetter award 1991, 92, 93, Trendsetter award 1998, 99), Career Edn. Assn. (pres. 1992-93), Nat. Coun. Local Adminstrs., S.W. Career Coun. (pres. 1991-92), Ohio Vocat. Edn. Leadership Inst. (grad. 1993). Republican. Roman Catholic. Avocations: writing murder-mystery plays, travel, reading. Office: Great Oaks Inst Tech and Career Devel 3254 E Kemper Rd Ste 3 Cincinnati OH 45241-1581 Home: 279 Beechridge Dr Cincinnati OH 45216

PATTERSON, DONALD FLOYD, human, medical and veterinary genetics educator; b. Maracaibo, Venezuela, Feb. 2, 1931; came to U.S., 1932; s. Carl Earl and Dayne (Murphy) P.; children: Russell H., Wade D. DVM, Okla. State U., 1954; DSc, U. Pa., 1967. Diplomate Am. Coll. Vet. Internal Medicine, Am. Bd. Vet. Internal Medicine, Am. Bd. Vet. Cardiology. Intern Angell Meml. Hosp., Boston, 1954-56; instr. Okla. State U., Stillwater, 1956; instr., asst. prof. Vet. Sch. U. Pa., Phila., 1958-64, from assoc. prof. to prof. Vet. Sch., 1966-73, chief sect. med. genetics, 1966-95, Sheppard prof. med. genetics Vet. Sch., 1973-97, prof. human genetics Med. Sch., 1974—; NIH spl. fellow divsn. med. genetics Johns Hopkins U., Balt., 1964-66; founder Ctr. for Comparative Med. Genetics U. Pa., Phila., 1995—98, prof. med. genetics. Established 1st formal course med. genetics Sch. Vet. Medicine, 1968. Contbr. over 600 papers to sci. and med. jours. Capt. USAF, 1956-58. Recipient Merit award Am. Animal Hosp. Assn., 1982, NIH Merit award, 1989, 91, Med. Rsch. award World Congress Vet. Medicine, 1992. Fellow Am. Coll. Cardiology, Phila. Coll. Physicians; mem. AVMA (Gaines Rsch. award 1972, Career Rsch. Achievement award 1995), Am. Soc. Human Genetics. Democrat. Avocations: canoeing, poetry, literature. Office: U Pa Sch Vet Medicine 3900 Delancey St Philadelphia PA 19104-4107

PATTERSON, DONALD ROSS, lawyer, educator; b. Sept. 9, 1939; s. Sam Ashley and Marguerite (Robinson) P.; m. Peggy Ann Schulte, May 1, 1965; children: D. Ross, Jerome Ashley, Gretchen Anne. BS, Tex. Tech U., 1961; JD, U. Tex., 1964; LLM, So. Meth. U., 1972. Bar: Tex. 1964, U.S. Ct. Claims 1970, U.S. Ct. Customs and Patent Appeals 1970, U.S. Ct. Mil. Appeals 1970, U.S. Supreme Ct. 1970, U.S. Dist. Ct. (ea. dist.) Tex. 1982, U.S. Ct. Appeals (5th cir.) 1991, U.S. Ct. Appeals (D.C. cir.) 1994; bd. cert. in immigration and naturalization law, Tex. Commd. lt. (j.g.) USN, 1964, advanced through grades to lt. comdr., 1969; asst. officer in charge Naval Petroleum Res., Bakersfield, Calif., 1970-72; staff judge adv. Kenitra, Morocco, 1972-76; officer in charge Naval Legal Svcs. Office, Whidbey Island, Wash., 1976-79; head mil. Justice divsn., Subic Bay, The Philippines, 1979-81; ret. USN, 1982; pvt. practice Tyler, Tex., 1982—. Former instr. U. Md., Chapman Coll., U. LaVerne, Tyler Jr. Coll., Jarvis Christian Coll., U. Tex., Tyler. Mem. East Tex. Estate Planning Coun. Mem. Coll. of State Bar of Tex., Tex. Bar Assn., Smith County Bar Assn., Am. Immigration Lawyers Assn., Masons, Rotary (past pres.), Shriners, Toastmasters (past pres.), Phi Delta Phi. Republican. Baptist. Home: 703 Wellington St Tyler TX 75703-4666 Office: 777 S Broadway Ave Ste 106 Tyler TX 75701-1648 E-mail: oneworld2gether@cs.com.

PATTERSON, DOUGLAS MACLENNAN, finance educator; b. Jan. 16, 1945; s. Thomas and Ruth (MacLennan) P.; m. Sara Louise Lucas; children: Cara Beth, John Douglas. BSEE, U. Wis., 1968, MBA, 1972, PhD, 1978. Elec. engr. Westinghouse Electric, Balt., 1968-71; asst. prof. U. Mich., Ann Arbor, 1976-80, Va. Tech., Blacksburg, 1980—, dir. PhD program in fin., 1991-95, assoc. prof., 1986-98, prof., 1998—. Vis. prof. U. Calif., Santa Barbara, 1989; vis. scholar U. Tex., Austin, 1994; presenter numerous seminars; participant Fin. Time Series Conf., Isaac Newton Inst. for Math. Scis., Cambridge, Eng., 1998. Co-author: A Nonlinear Times Series Workshop: A Tool Kit for Detecting and Identifying Nonlinear Serial Dependence; contbr. articles to profl. jours. Mem. ad hoc com. Detroit Area Hosp. Assn., 1978-79. Recipient Tchg. Excellence award Va. Tech., 1983; U. Mich. fellow, 1979; USN grantee, 1984, 85, 90. Mem. Am. Fin. Assn., Am. Econ. Assn., Fin. Mgmt. Assn., Beta Gamma Sigma. Methodist. Home: 702 Crestwood Dr Blacksburg VA 24060-6006 Office: Va Poly Inst Dept Finance 0221 Blacksburg VA 24061 E-mail: amex@vt.edu.

PATTERSON, HAROLD DEAN, retired superintendent of schools; b. Alexander City, Ala., May 29, 1932; s. Obed Howard and Sara Bell (Joiner) P.; m. Shirley Bryant, May 31, 1958; children: Lisa Jane, Anne Leslie, Harold Dean Jr. BS, Auburn U., 1954; MA, Vanderbilt U., 1957, EdD, 1964. Cert. sch. adminstr., Ala., S.C., Ill. Tchr. Bessemer (Ala.) H.S., 1957-63, asst. prin., 1959-62; prin. North Hall, Evanston (Ill.) Twp. H.S., 1964-66; prin. Mountain Brook (Ala.) H.S., 1966-71; assoc. supt. Greenville County Schs., Greenville, S.C., 1971-74; supt. schs. Sumter County Sch. Dist. 17, Sumter, S.C., 1974-82, Spartanburg County Sch. Dist. 7, Spartanburg, S.C., 1982-88, Guntersville (Ala.) City Schs., 1988-95, legis. liaison, 1995-98; ret., 1998. Mem. S.C. Gov.'s Com. on Financing Edn., Columbia, 1983, S.C. Pvt. Industry Coun., Columbia, 1984-88, S.C. Legis. Oversight Com., Columbia, 1984; pres. Peabody alumni bd. Vanderbilt U., Nashville, 1989-90. 2d lt. U.S. Army, 1954-56. Recipient Outstanding Educator award Florence chpt. Phi Delta Kappa, 1981, The Exec. Educator 100 award The Exec. Educator mag., 1987. Mem. Am. Assn. Sch. Adminstrs. (chmn. legis. corp. 1985-95, mem. exec. com. 1988-91, James R. Kirkpatrick award 1987, Disting. Svc. award 2000), Ala. Assn. Sch. Adminstrs., Nat. Assn. Secondary Sch. Prins., Rotary (dist. 6860 gov. 1995-96). Methodist. Avocation: golf. Home: 5020 Neely Ave Guntersville AL 35976-8102 E-mail: hdpat54@aol.com.

PATTERSON, HOWARD YATES, academic athletics administrator; b. Boston, Aug. 22, 1950; s. Charles F. and Dorothy M. (Smith) P.; m. Cathi Dawn Cuba, Dec. 27, 1987; children: Jori, MacKenzie, Coleman. BS, Springfield (Mass.) Coll., 1973; MS, Midwestern State U., 1975; PhD, U. North Tex., 1995. Instr., coach soccer Midwestern State U., Wichita Falls, Tex., 1973-89; dir. athletics U. Incarnate Word, San Antonio, 1990—2001; dir. athletics, interim dean student affairs U. Tex., Tyler, 2001—. Business E-Mail: hpatterson@uttyler.edu.

PATTERSON, JAMES WILLIS, pathology and dermatology educator; b. Takoma Park, Md., Dec. 29, 1946; s. James Clark and Helen (Hendricks) P.; m. Julie Wyatt, Dec. 30, 1989; 1 child, James Wyatt. BA, Johns Hopkins U., 1968; MD, Med. Coll. Va., 1972. Diplomate Am. Bd. Dermatology, Am. Bd. Dermatopathology, Nat. Bd. Med. Examiners; recert. in dermatology. Fellow dermatopathology Armed Forces Inst. Pathology, Washington, 1979—80; clin. instr. dermatology U. Colo. Med. Ctr., Denver, 1980—82; rotating intern in medicine Med. Coll. Va., Richmond, 1972-73, resident in dermatology, 1973-76, assoc. prof. pathology and dermatology, 1982-89, prof., 1989-92, dir. dermatopathology, 1982-92; with Dermatology Assocs. of Va., 1992-96, Va. Dermatopathology Svcs., Richmond, 1992-96; clin. prof. pathology Med. Coll. of Va., 1992—; prof. pathology and dermatology U. Va., 1996—. Cons. in pathology McGuire VA Hosp., Richmond, 1982-92; cons. in pathology and dermatology Kenner Army Hosp., Ft. Lee, Va., 1982-95. Author: Dermatology: A Concise Textbook, 1987; contbr. over 100 articles on dermatology and pathology to med. jours.; asst. editor Jour. Cutaneous Pathology, 1989-94. Mem. nat. alumni schs. com. Johns Hopkins U., 1986—. With M.C., U.S. Army, 1976-82, col. Res. (ret.). Recipient Stuart McEwen award Assn. Mil. Dermatologists, 1980, 82. Fellow: ACP, Am. Soc. Dermatopathology (sec.-treas. 2001—), Am. Acad. Dermatology; mem.: Va. Dermatol. Soc. (sec.-treas. 1984—88, v.p. 1988—89, pres. 1989—90), Johns Hopkins U. Alumni Assn. (pres. ctrl. Va. chpt. 1989), Res. Officers' Assn. (life), Tau Epsilon Phi (life). Republican. Presbyterian. Avocations: american history, baseball, golf.

PATTERSON, KELLEY RENÉ, special education educator; b. Herrin, Ill., Mar. 9, 1961; d. William Ray and Glenda Sue (Spiller) Colp; m. William Mark Patterson, Sept. 8, 1979; children: Kara Nicole, Jessica Marie, Markella Ann. BA in Spl. Edn. and Elem. Edn., So. Ill. U., 1994. Cert. spl. edn. tchr., elem. tchr., Ill. K-2nd grade tchr. Buncombe (Ill.) Sch., 1994-97, spl. edn. tchr., 1997-2000; cons. tchr. JAMP Spl. Edn. Svcs., Olmsted, Ill., 2000—03; spl. edn. tchr. Williamson Co. Spl Educ. Co-op.,

2003—. Cheerleading sponsor Buncombe Sch., 1994-95. Sunday sch. tchr. First Apostolic Ch., Marion, Ill., 1981—. George B. and Edith Wham scholar So. Ill. U., 1993, Madelyne Treece Elem. Edn. scholar, 1993; recipient Mil. Order of Purple Hearts award, 1989, 93. Mem. Coun. for Exceptional Children, Kappa Delta Pi, Golden Key Nat. Honor Soc. Apostolic. Home: 1635 Eagle Point Bay Rd Goreville IL 62939-2268 Office: Williamson Co Spl Educ Co-op 411 S Court Marion IL 62959

PATTERSON, MADGE LENORE, elementary education educator; b. Vandergrift, Pa., Nov. 9, 1925; d. Paul Warren and Lucy Mae (Lemmon) Schaeffer; m. Stanley Clair Patterson, June 19, 1948 (dec.); 1 child, Stanley Kent. BS in Edn., Indiana State Tchrs. Coll., Pa., 1946, MEd, 1971. Elem. tchr. New Kensington (Pa.) Pub. Schs., 1946-49, Armstrong Sch. Dist. Schs., Ford City, Pa., 1951-52, kindergarten tchr., 1967-93, Rural Valley (Pa.) Presbyn. Ch., 1957-67; vol. tutor Adult Lit., Kittanning, Pa., 1993—; co-owner dairy farm. Sunday sch. tchr., choir mem., 1949—; sec. Rural Valley Presbyn. Ch. Women's Assn., 1988-92; vol. tutor Big Bros. and Sisters of Armstrong County, ARIN GED students. Mem. NEA, Pa. Assn. Sch. Retirees, Clara Cockerille Reading Coun. (treas. 1994-98), Pa. State Edn. Assn., Internat. Reading Assn. (Literacy award 2000), Keystone Reading Assn., Assn. Early Childhood Edn., Rural Valley Bus. and Profl. Club, Women's Civic Club (Woman of Yr. 1994), Am. Assn. Ret. Persons, Rural Valley Grange (lectr.). Democrat. Avocations: dancing (line, square, ballroom), reading, camping, music, travel. Home: RR 2 Box 182 Dayton PA 16222-8813

PATTERSON, MARIA JEVITZ, microbiology-pediatric infectious disease educator; b. Berwyn, Ill., Oct. 23, 1944; d. Frank Jacob and Edna Frances (Costabile) Jevitz; m. Ronald James Patterson, Aug. 22, 1970; children: Kristin Lara, Kier Nicole. BS in Med. Tech. summa cum laude, Coll. St. Francis, Joliet, Ill., 1966; PhD in Microbiology, Northwestern U., Chgo., 1970; MD, Mich. State U., 1984. Diplomate Am. Bd. Med. Examiners, Am. Bd. Pediatrics Gen. Pediatrics, Am. Bd. Pediatrics Infectious Diseases. Lab. asst., instr. med. microbiology for student nurses Med. Sch. Northwestern U., Chgo., 1966-70; postdoctoral fellow in clin. microbiology affiliated hosps. U. Wash., Seattle, 1971-72; asst. prof. microbiology and pub. health Mich. State U., East Lansing, 1972-77, assoc. prof., 1977-82, assoc. prof. pathology, 1979-82, lectr. dept. microbiology and pub. health, 1982-87, resident in pediatrics affiliated hosps., 1984-85, 86-87, clin. instr. dept. pediatrics and human devel., 1984-87, assoc. prof. microbiology-pub. health-pediatrics-human devel., 1987-90, prof., 1990—. Staff microbiologist dept. pathology Lansing Gen. Hosp., 1972-75; dir. clin. microbiology grad. program. Mich. State U., 1974-81, staff microbiologist, 1978-81; postdoctoral fellow in infectious diseases U. Mass. Med. Ctr., Worcester, 1985-86; asst. dir. pediatrics residency Grad. Med. Edn. Inc., Lansing, 1987-90; med. dir. Pediatrics Health Ctr. St. Lawrence Hosp., Lansing, Mich., 1987-90, Ingham Med. Ctr., 1990-94; cons. clin. microbiology Lansing Gen. Hosp., 1972-75, Mich. State U., 1976-82, Mich. Dept. Pub. Health, 1976—, Ingham County Health Dept., 1988—, Am. Health Cons., 1993, State of Mich. Atty. Gen. Office, 1994-98, Lansing Sch. Dist., 1998—, Mich. Antibiotic Residence Reduction, 1998—; cons. to editl. bd. Infection and Immunity, 1977; cons. Mich. State U. AIDS Edn. Tng. Ctr, 2001—; presenter seminars. Contbg. author: Microbiology: Principles and Concepts, 1982, 4th edit., 1995, Pediatric Emergency Medicine, 1992, Principles and Practice of Emergency Medicine, 1997, Rudolph's Pediatrics, 2002; item writer certifying bd. examination Bd. Am. Acad. Pediats., 1990—, Am. Bd. Osteopathy, 1997—; contbr. articles to profl. jours. and publs. Mem. hon. com. Lansing AIDS Meml. Quilt, 1993. Recipient award for tchg. excellence Mich. State U. Coll. Osteo. Medicine, 1977, 78, 79, 80, 83, Disting. Faculty award Mich. State U., 1980, Woman Achiever award, 1985, excellence in pediatric residency tchg. award, 1988, 2001, Alumni Profl. Achievement award Coll. of St. Francis, 1991, excellence in diversity award Mich. State U., 2000, Weil Endowed Disting. Pediat. Faculty award, 2001; grantee renal disease divsn. Mich. Dept. Pub. Health 1976-82. Fellow Pediatric Infectious Diseases Soc., Infectious Diseases Soc. Am., Am. Acad. Pediatrics; mem. Am. Coll. Physician Execs., Am. Soc. Microbiology, Am. Soc. Clin. Pathologists (affiliate, bd. registrant), South Ctrl. Assn. Clin. Microbiology, Mich. Infectious Diseases Soc., N.Y. Acad. Scis., Kappa Gamma Pi, Lambda Iota Tau. Roman Catholic. Home: 1520 River Ter East Lansing MI 48823-5314 Office: Mich State Univ Microbiology/Molecular Genetics/Pediat East Lansing MI 48824-4320

PATTERSON, MARTHA ELLEN, artist, art educator; b. Anderson, Ind., Mar. 12, 1914; d. Clarence and Corrine Ringwald; m. John Downey, Nov. 27, 1935 (div. 1946); 1 child, Linda Carol; m. Raymond George Patterson, May 6, 1947. Student, Dayton Art Inst., Bendell Art Sch., Bradenton, Fla. Beauty operator WRENS, Springfield, Ohio, 1932-40; co-owner Park Ave. Gallery, Dayton; window decorator, art tchr. Tchr. art; judge art shows. One-woman shows Springfield (Ohio) Mus. Art, 1998, as well as N.C.R. Country Club, Bill Turner Interiors, U. Dayton, High Street Gallery, Trails End Club, The Designerie, Riverbend Park, Statesman Club, State Fidelity Bank, Wegerzyn Hort. Ctr., Pebble Springs, Backstreet, First City Fed. Bank, Bradenton, Fla., Alley Gallery, Merrill Lynch, Miami U., Gem. City Bank, Dayton, Ohio, Winters Bank, Dayton, Sherwin Williams, Howard Johnsons, Dayton Woman's Club, Bergamo, Dayton Meml. Hall, Bob and Arts, Del Park Med. Soc., The Dayton Country Club, Christ Methodist Ch., Unitarian Ch., The Metropolitan, Rikes, Dr. Pavey's, Dr. Chaney's, Dayton Convention Ctr., The Yum Yum, Jan Strunk Interiors, Park Avenue Gallery, Ohio Mus. of Art, Springfield, 1997, New Carlisle Chiropractic Ctr., 2003, Springfield Art Mus. Yearly Show, 2003; artist: (water colors, oils, acylics, inks and pastels); group exhbns. include: Dayton Art Inst., Meml. Hall of Dayton, Dayton Country Club, Bergamo, Women's Club of Dayton, Am. Watercolor Soc., Sarasota Art Ctr., Art League of Manatee County, Butler Inst., Riverbend Park, First City Fed., NCR Country Club, Springfield (Ohio) Mus., Longboat Key Art Ctr., others; represented in permanent collections of Mr. and Mrs. Richard Nixon, Virginia Graham, Les Brown, Paul Lynde, Air Force Mus. at Wright Patterson, U. Dayton-Ohio, Dr. Stephen House, Doug Yeager and others. Vol. Christian Woman's Soc. of Am., Twig Children's Hosp., Dayton, The Utopians; mem. Tri Art Dayton, Long Boat Key Art Ctr., Fla. Recipient first prize Dayton Soc. Painters and Sculptors Show Rikes, First Prize, 1976, 77, First Prize, Best in Show, 1978, Beavercreek Art Assn. First Place, Best in Show, Artist and Sculpture Yearly Show, 1966, 68 2d place, Dayton Art Inst. 2d prize, Tri County Hon. Mention, Walker Motor Sales 2d place, Bendell Art Gallery 2d and 3d, Montgomery County Fair Best in Show, Springfield Art Mus. Big Show, 2003. Mem. Art League of Manatee County (Fla.), Nat. Mus. Women in Art, Nat. Soc. Altrusa, Am. Watercolor Soc., Springfield Mus. Art, Dayton Soc. Painters, Long Boat Key Art League, Tri Art. Republican. Methodist. Avocations: art mus., books, music, travel, gourmet cooking. Home: 3853 Lawrenceville Dr Springfield OH 45504-4459

PATTERSON, MELISSA, elementary education educator; b. Grand Island, Nebr., Nov. 24, 1956; d. John Abbott and Mabel Edith (Schimmer) P. BA, So. Calif. Coll., Costa Mesa, 1979; postgrad., San Diego State U., Imperial (Calif.) Valley Coll. Cert. multiple subject tchr., learning handicapped specialist, Calif., life sci. tchr., resource specialist. Dir., tchr. It's a Small World Presch., Imperial, Calif., 1980-82; prin., tchr. Faith Acad. Christian Sch., Imperial, 1982-87; tchr. 2d grade Imperial Unified Sch. Dist., 1988-90, secondary tchr. biology and chemistry, elem. reading specialist, 1990-91, reading, resource specialist, 1991-96; resource specialist, spl. edn. tchr. Calexico (Calif.) Unified Sch. Dist., 1996-98; program devel. specialist edn./disabilities Migrant Head Start, El Centro, Calif., 1998—2000; resource specialist Brawley (Calif.) Elem. Sch. Dist., 2000—. Mem. NEA, Coun. for Exceptional Children, Calif. Edn. Assn., Nat. Assn. Edn. Young Children, Calif. Assn. Edn. Young Children, Calif. Assn. Resource Specialists. Office: Miguel Hidalgo Elementary School Brawley CA 92227 Home: 1930 Woodside Dr El Centro CA 92243

PATTERSON, MILDRED LUCAS, retired teaching specialist; b. Winston-Salem, N.C., Jan. 24, 1937; d. James Arthur and Lula Mae (Smith) Lucas; m. James Harrison Patterson Jr., Mar. 31, 1961; children: James Harrison III, Roger Lindsay. BA, Talladega Coll., 1958; MEd, St. Louis U., 1969; postgrad., Webster U., 1970. Classroom tchr. Winston-Salem (N.C.) Pub. Schs., 1959-61, St. Louis Bd. Edn., 1961-72, reading specialist, 1972-88, co-host radio reading show, 1988-91; tchr. specialist Reading to Achieve Motivational Program, St. Louis, 1991-99; ret., 1999—. Bd. dirs. Supt.'s Adv. Com., University City, Mo., 1994—; presenter Chpt. I Regional Conf. Co-author: Wearing Purple, 1996. Bd. dirs. Gateway Homes, St. Louis, 1989-93; mem. com. University City Sch. Bond Issue, 1994; mem. Univ. City Arts and Letters Commn., 1998-99. Recipient Letter of Commendation, Chpt. I. Regional Conf., 1991, Founders' award Gamma Omega chpt. Alpha Kappa Alpha, 1985. Mem. Internat. Reading Assn. (Broadcast Media award for radio 1990, Bldg. Rep. award St. Louis chpt. 1990). Avocations: reading, arts and crafts, storytelling, motivational speaking. E-mail: mildred9@bellsouth.net.

PATTERSON, MYRNA NANCY, secondary education educator; b. Cambridge, Mass., July 20, 1942; d. Samuel Daniel and Ann Freda (Katz) Hark; children: Daniel Charles, Sara Rachel. BA cum laude, Syracuse U., 1964; MA, Harvard U., 1966; postgrad. clin. tng. Zinburg Ctr., Harvard Med. Sch., 1992. Cert. tchr. French and English, Mass., N.Y. French and drama tchr., grade 6 Buckingham, Browne and Nichols Schs., Cambridge, 1978-86; tchr. Belmont (Mass.) Day Sch., 1987; dir., tchr. acad. talented program Lynnfield (Mass.) Pub. Schs., 1988-90; enrichment coord. K-8 Edgartown and Tisbury Schs., Martha's Vineyard, 1992-93; dir. Martha's Vineyard Hebrew Ctr. Religious Sch., 1996-97; tchr. English and French New Jewish H.S., Waltham, Mass., 1997-98. Writer-in-residence Wellesley Chelmsford Edgartown Schs., Mass. Cultural Coun., 1995-98; intern Radcliffe Career Svcs., Cambridge, 1987-88; studied with poets at Vt. Studio Ctr., 1995, Fine Arts Work Ctr., 1996, 98, Squaw Valley Cmty. of Writers, summers 1994, 97, writing workshops. Author (poetry) Family Reunion, 2003; contbr. articles, poetry to lit. mags., curriculum guides including The Secret Garden, 1991, Sing Down the Moon, 1995, Taking Sides, 1996, photography to Pariswalks, 1999. Vol. Peace Corps, Tchad, Africa, 1966-67. Grantee Buckingham, Browne & Nichols Sch., Cambridge. Mem. Phi Sigma Iota, Phi Kappa Phi. Avocations: gardening, birding, bicycling, photography.

PATTERSON, OSCAR, III, university program administrator; b. July 25, 1945; s. Oscar Jr. and Frances (Killian) P.; m. Kathy E. Gibson, June 6, 1966 (div. Apr. 1979); 1 child, Elizabeth Anne Patterson Cassel; m. Julie Ann Holmes, Dec. 28, 1990. BA, Pfeiffer U., 1967; MFA, U. Ga., 1973; PhD, U. Tenn., 1982. Asst. prof. architecture and fine arts Auburn (Ala.) U., 1972-75; chairperson BFA in Theatre program Western Carolina U., Cullowhee, N.C., 1975-79; dir. telecom. U. N.C., Pembroke, 1984-88; chair comm. and visual arts U. North Fla., Jacksonville, 1998—. Juvenile probation officer Cleveland Ct. Sys., Shelby, N.C., 1967-68; gen. mgr., news dir. WNCP-TV, N.C., 1984-98. Contbr. articles to profl. jours.; host pub. tv program, 1989-98. U.S. Army, 1968-75, Vietnam. Mem. AEJMC, Soc. Profl. Journalists, Phi Kappa Phi. Republican. Avocations: historical reenactment, beach exploration. Home: 248 Patrick Mill Cir Ponte Vedra Beach FL 32082-4013 E-mail: opatters@unf.edu.

PATTERSON, PAUL M. school administrator; b. Aberdeen, S.D., Sept. 29, 1946; s. Robert M. and Esther M. (Wellman) P.; 1 child, Jennifer K. BS, No. State U., 1964; MS, U. Ill., 1976, EdD, 1994. Tchr. Rapid City (S.D.) Pub. Schs., 1968-75, Rock Island (Ill.) Pub. Schs., 1975-76, Sch. Dist. U-46, Elgin, Ill., 1976-85, coord. fine arts, 1985-92, dir. instructional programs, 1992—. Cons. Chgo. Pub. Schs., 1990, North Palos Dist. 117, North Palos Hills, Ill., 1993. Contbr. articles to profl. jours. Adv. bd. Ill. Arts Coun., Chgo., 1994—, Ill. Alliance for Arts Edn., Chgo., 1987—, Ill. State Bd. Edn. Fine Arts Com., Springfield, 1986-94; mem. Heritage Commn., Elgin, 1985-88. Ill. Adminstr. scholar Ill. Bd. Edn. and Nat. Gallery of Art, Washington, 1991. Mem. ASCD, Ill. ASCD, Am. Assn. Sch. Adminstr., Phi Delta Kappa, Kappa Delta Pi. Office: School District 46 355 E Chicago St Elgin IL 60120-6500

PATTERSON, POLLY JONES, academic director, marriage and family therapist; b. Kinston, Ala., Aug. 25, 1944; d. Horace Woodrow and Dora Lee (Kendrick) Jones; m. Max Rhodes Patterson, May 5, 1963; 1 child, Lee Patterson Martin. BS in Edn., Troy State U., 1991, MS in Edn., 1992, M in Psychology, 1993. Cert. tchr., Ala. Dir., counselor workplace literacy MacArthur State Tech. Coll., Opp, Ala., 1991—2003, dir. student support svcs., 1994—; dir. student svcs., counselor, dir., student support svcs. Lurleen B. Wallace Cmty. Coll., MacArthur campus, 2003—. Adj. psychology instr. MacArthur State Tech., Troy State U., Dothan. Mem. NEA, Ala. Edn. Assn., Ala. Assn. for Instnl. Rsch., Ala. Assn. for Devel. Edn., Bus. and Profl. Women, Ala. Assn. Ednl. Opportunity Programs, Coun. for Opportunity in Edn., S.E. Assn. Edn. Opportunity Programs, Alpha Delta Kappa, Phi Kappa Phi. Baptist. Avocations: spending time with grandson, reading, crochet, collecting and refinishing antiques. Office: Lurleen B Wallace MacArthur Campus N Main St Opp AL 36467 E-mail: 2grans@alaweb.com.

PATTERSON, WILLIAM BROWN, dean, history educator; b. Charlotte, N.C., Apr. 8, 1930; s. William Brown and Eleanor Selden (Miller) P.; m. Evelyn Byrd Hawkins, Nov. 27, 1959; children: William Brown Patterson, Evelyn Byrd Donatelli, Lucy Patterson Murray, Emily Patterson Higgs. BA, U. South, 1952; MA, Harvard U., 1954, PhD, 1966, cert. ednl. mgmt., 1982; BA, Oxford (Eng.) U., 1955, MA, 1959; MDiv, Episc. Div. Sch., Cambridge, Mass., 1958. Ordained to ministry Episcopal Ch. as deacon, 1958, as priest, 1959. Asst. prof. history Davidson (N.C.) Coll., 1963-66, assoc. prof., 1966-76, prof. history, 1976-80, U. of South, Sewanee, Tenn., 1980—, dean Coll. Arts and Scis., 1980-91. Author: (with others) Discord, Dialogue, and Concord, 1977, This Sacred History: Anglican Reflections for John Booty, 1990, King James VI and I and the Reunion of Christendom, 1997; mem. bd. editors St. Luke's Jour. Theology, Sewanee, 1982-90; contbr. numerous articles to profl. jours. Trustee U. South, 1968-71; mem. internat. adv. com. U. Buckingham, Eng., 1977-93; pres. So. Coll. and Univ. Union; organizer Associated Colls. of South, 1988-89. Danforth Found. grad. fellow, 1952, Mellon Appalachian fellow U. Va., 1992-93, rsch. fellow NEH, 1967, Folger Shakespeare Libr., Washington, 1975, Inst. for Rsch. in Humanities, U. Wis., Madison, 1976, Newberry Libr., Chgo., 1979; Rhodes scholar, 1953. Mem. Am. Hist. Assn., Am. Soc. Ch. History (Albert C. Outler prize for best book in ecumenical ch. history 1999), N.Am. Conf. on Brit. Studies, Eccles. History Soc. Eng., Royal Hist. Soc. Eng., Renaissance Soc. Am., So. Hist. Assn., Soc. for Values in Higher Edn., Episcopal Div. Sch. Alumni/ae Assn. (mem. exec. com. 1984-87), Phi Beta Kappa, Beta Theta Pi. Avocations: gardening, tennis. Home: 195 N Carolina Ave Sewanee TN 37375-2040 Office: U of South Dept History 735 University Ave Sewanee TN 37383-0001 E-mail: bpatters@sewanee.edu.

PATTI, MARCO GIUSEPPE, surgeon, educator; b. Catania, Italy, Apr. 15, 1956; came to U.S., 1983; s. Francesco P. and Ada (Travali) P.; m. Verna C. Gibbs, Nov. 30, 1985; 1 child, Verna Ada. MD, U. Catania, 1981. Resident in gen. surgery U. Calif., San Francisco, 1986—93, dir. swallowing ctr., assoc. prof. surgery, 1994—. Fellow ACS, Assn. Acad. Surgery, Internat. Soc. Diseases of Esophagus, San Francisco Surg. Soc., Italian Surg. Assn., Esophageal Club. Avocations: classical music, swimming, languages, travel. Office: Univ Calif San Francisco 533 Parnassus Ave Rm U-122 San Francisco CA 94122-2722

PATTISON, DELORIS JEAN, retired counselor, university official; b. Logansport, Ind., Oct. 3, 1931; d. John R. and Grace I. Gallagher (Yocum) Taylor; m. John A. Pattison, July 3, 1952; children: Traci (dec.), John A. II, Scott, Becky. BS in Secondary Edn., Goshen Coll., 1973; MA in Edn., Ball State U., 1977. Life cert. vocat. edn. tchr., Ind. Tchr. home econs. Marion (Ind.) H.S., 1973-78; dir. youth employment Logansport Cmty. Schs., 1979-83; substitute tchr. Ft. Wayne (Ind.) Cmty. Schs., 1983-87; employment counselor Ind. Dept. Employment, Marion, 1987-90; counselor, coord. adminstrv. career svcs. Ind. Wesleyan U., Marion, 1990-95; ret., 1995. News reporter Woodridge News, United Meth. Meml. Home Newsletter. Editor: A Teen Trace, 1971; also articles. Bd. dirs. Ind. Christian Coll. Consortium, 1990-1995. Named Outstanding Employee, Ind. Dept. Employment and Tng., 1989. Mem. Nat. Assn. Colls., Midwest Coll. Placement Assn., Coll. and Univ. Staffing, Dist. Min. Spouse Assn. (sec. 1987-89), Am. Legion Aux., Elegant Dames (charter), Red Hatters Assn. Methodist. Avocations: reading, walking, writing, travel. Home: 801 N Huntington #47 Hippensteel Dr Warren IN 46792

PATTON, ALTON DEWITT, electrical engineering consultant; b. Corpus Christi, Tex., Feb. 1, 1935; s. Alton G. and Civilia Louise (Taylor) P.; m. Nancy Jo Elder, Mar. 1, 1959; children: Elizabeth, Carolyn. BEE, U. Tex., Austin, 1957; MEE, U. Pitts., 1961; PhD in Elec. Engring., Tex. A&M U., 1972. Registered profl. engr., Tex.; diplomate Am. Bd. of Forensic Engring. and Tech. Engr. Westinghouse Electric Corp., Pitts., 1957-65; prof. elec. engring. dept. Tex. A&M U., College Station, 1965-79, 82-2000, head elec. engring. dept., 1992-96, Brockett prof., 1986, Dresser prof., 1987, dir. Electric Power Inst., 1976-79, 85-92; rsch. fellow Tex. Engring. Expt. Sta., College Station, 1985, dir. Ctr. for Space Power, 1987-92; pres. Associated Power Analysts Inc., College Station, Tex., 1973—. Mem. panel for assessment of NIST Elec. and Electronics Engring. Lab., 1995-2000, NRS. Contbr. articles to elec. engring. jours., 1960—. V.p. Emerald Forest Home Owners Assn. Fellow IEEE (life, tech. com., aerospace policy com., prize paper award 1975, 94, Richard Harold Kaufmann award 2000); mem. NSPE. Republican. Presbyterian. Avocations: fishing, hunting, photography, stamp and coin collecting. Home: 8411 Spring Crk College Station TX 77845-4608 Office: Associated Power Analysts Inc 303 Anderson St College Station TX 77840-3114 E-mail: adpatton@myriad.net.

PATTON, CARL ELLIOTT, physics educator; b. San Antonio, Sept. 14, 1941; s. Carl Elliott and Geraldine Barnett (Perry) Patton. BS, MIT, 1963; MS, Calif. Inst. Tech., 1964, PhD, 1967. Sr. scientist Raytheon Co., Waltham, Mass., 1967-71; assoc. prof. physics Colo. State U., Ft. Collins, 1971-75, prof., 1975—. IEEE Magnetics Soc. Disting. lectr., 1993, sec. treas. 2003-2004; chair Am. Phys. Soc. Topical Group on Magnetism and its Applications, 1998-99. Editor-in-chief IEEE Transactions on Magnetics, 1987-91. Fellow IEEE (sec./treas., 2003—, Third Millenium medal 2000, Magnetics Soc. Lifetime Achievement Award 2003), Am. Phys. Soc. Office: Colo State Univ Dept Physics Fort Collins CO 80523-0001

PATTON, CARL VERNON, academic administrator, educator; b. Coral Gables, Fla., Oct. 22, 1944; s. Carl V. and Helen Eleanor (Benkert) Patton; m. Gretchen West, July 29, 1967. BS in Community Planning, U. Cin., 1967; MS in Urban Planning, U. Ill.-Urbana, 1969, MS in Pub. Adminstrn., 1970; MS in Pub. Policy, U. Calif.-Berkeley, 1975, PhD in Pub. Policy, 1976. Instr. to prof. U. Ill., 1968—83, dir. Bureau of Urban and Regional Planning Rsch., 1977—79, prof., chmn. dept., 1979—83; prof., dean Sch. Architecture and Urban Planning U. Wis., Milw., 1983—89; v.p. acad. affairs, prof. polit. sci., geography and urban planning U. Toledo, 1989—92; pres. Ga. State U., Atlanta, 1992—. Author: Academia in Transition, 1979; co-author: The Metropolitan Midwest, 1985; co-author: (with David Sawicki) Basic Methods of Policy Analysis and Planning, 1986, rev. 2d edit., 1993 Chinese translations, 2001, 2002; co-author: (with Kathleen Reed) Guide to Graduate Education in Urban and Regional Planning, 1986, 1988; editor: Spontaneous Shelter: International Perspectives and Prospects, 1988; co-editor (with G. William Page): Quick Answers to Quantitative Problems: A Pocket Primer, 1991; assoc. editor: Jour. of Planning Edn. and Rsch., 1983—87, editl. bd.: Habitat International, 1993—99, Intertrade and Investment (formerly Atlanta Internat. Mag.), 1993—2000; contbr. articles to profl. jours. Fellow NIMH, 1973—75; Chmn. Community Devel. Commn., Urbana, 1978—82; mem. Civic Design Ctr., Milw., 1983—87, City of Milw. Art Commn., 1988—89, Toledo Vision, 1989—92, City of Toledo Bd. Cmty. Rels., 1990—92; chair Centennial Olympic Park Area Inc., 1998—2000, Ctrl. Atlanta Progress, 2000—03; mem. Ga. Rsch. Alliance, Atlanta Convention and Vis. Bur., Woodruff Art Ctr., Fox Theatre; chair Grady (Hosp.) Healthcare, Inc., 1998—2000, Atlanta Reg. Consortium for Higher Edn., 1998—; mem. Ga. Coun. on Econ. Edn., Atlanta Neighborhood Devel. Ptnrship., U.S. Disabled Athletes Fund Bd.; fellow U. Ill. Ctr. for Advanced Studies, 1973—74; bd. dirs., chair The Atlanta Downtown Partnership, 1997—2000. Fellow: Am. Inst. Cert. Planners; mem.: Met. Atlanta C. of C., Assn. Collegiate Schs. of Planning (v.p. 1985—87, pres. 1989—91), Am. Planning Assn. Avocation: racquetball, photography, travel.. Home: 250 Park Ave West NW # 908 Atlanta GA 30313- Office: Ga State U Office of Pres University Plz Atlanta GA 30303-3083

PATTON, CHARLES HENRY, lawyer, educator; b. Asheville, N.C., Jan. 13, 1953; s. Charles Robert and Sarah (Gulledge) P. BA, Memphis State U., 1975, JD, 1979. Bar: Tenn. Assoc. Holt, Bachelor, Spicer & Ryan, Memphis, 1979-80; fin. exec. Felsenthal Planning Service Co., Memphis, 1980-81; sole practice Memphis, 1981—; prof. Memphis State U., 1982—. Planned giving dir. Christ United Meth. Ch., Memphis, 1986; mem. Planned Giving Coun. Memphis. Mem. S.E. Regional Bus. Law Professors Assn., Memphis Bar Assn., Estate Planning Coun. Memphis. Republican. Avocations: classic automobile restoration, model trains. Office: 5100 Poplar Ave Ste 2701 Memphis TN 38137-4000

PATTON, CINDY ANNE, biology educator; b. Portsmouth, Va., Aug. 31, 1956; d. James Clark and Nancy Elizabeth (Bell) P. BS in Biology, Fitchburg (Mass.) State Coll., 1986; M in Health Edn., Worcester (Mass.) State Coll., 1993. Cert. sci., biology, gen. sci. and health tchr., Mass. Tchr. earth sci. Leominster (Mass.) High Sch., 1987-88; tchr. sci. Grey Jr. High Sch., Acton, Mass., 1989-93, cheerleading coach, 1989-93; tchr. South Mid. Sch., Braintree, Mass., 1993-94, student coun. advisor, 1993-94; biology prof. Middlesex C.C., Bedford, Mass., 1994—. Advisor tennis intramurals, Acton, 1990-93. Bd. dirs. Minutemen Assn. Retarded Citizens, Concord, Mass., 1989; coach Acton Cmty. Basketball, 1990-93; EMT, 1991—; CPR instr. Am. Heart Assn., 1993—; mem. Acton (Mass.) Bd. Health, 1994—. Recipient resolution Mass. Ho. of Reps., 1991, Portrait of Tchr. award Campbell Soup Co., 1991, Am. Hero in Edn. award Reader's Digest, 1991. Mem. NAST. Avocations: tennis, basketball. Office: Middlesex CC Springs Rd Bedford MA 01730

PATTON, DIANA LEE WILKOC, artist, educator; b. New Rochelle, N.Y., June 28, 1940; d. August E. and Meta Diane (Neuburg) Wilkoc; m. Gardner C. Patton, Aug. 10, 1963; children: Michael, Talryn, Shawn. AB cum laude, Brown U., 1962; postgrad., Pan-Am. Art Inst., 1962-63. Svc. mgr. Lord and Taylor, N.Y.C., 1962-63; tchr. adult edn., Mountain Lakes, N.J., 1972-74, Somerville, N.J., 1978-82, Jointure for Cmty. Adult Edn., 1982—. Artist in watercolors, pen and ink and acrylics; creator jewelry. One-woman and group shows N.E. U.S., Perth, Australia, 1977, spl. bicentennial exhibit, Trenton, N.J., 1976, Rutgers U., 1980, Brookdale Coll., 1982, Camden County Coll., 9186, Moris County Coll., 1988, Bergen Mus. Arts and Scis., 1987, 88, 90, 91, Princeton Med. Ctr., 1993, 94, 96, Madison Gallery--Morristown Hosp., 2001, 03, Salmagundi Club, N.Y.C., 2002; one-woman show SAA Pluckemin Galleries, 1998; represented in pvt. and pub. collections in U.S., Australia, N.Z., Germany, Luxembourg, Japan, Eng.; designer ofcl. poster N.J. Festival Ballooning, 1990, Arc Challenge Races, 1993, 94; instr. in field; developer art appreciation courses for children and adults; toymaker, 1973-76. Winner bronz medal in watercolor Nat. Mystic (Conn.) Outdoor Art Festival, 1977, mayor's purchase prize Franklin Twp., 1976, Tri-State Watercolor award Somerset

County Coll., 1978, Best in Show award Raritan Valley Art Assn., 1978, 94, award Garden State Watercolor Soc., 1979, 84, 85, 1st, 2d and Best in Show award Somerset and Westfield Art Assns. shows, 1st place for profl. watercolor Plainfield Tri-State Arts Festival, 1983, 85, 87, 96, N.E. Art Festival, Caldwell Coll., 1990, 95, Tewksbury award, 1990, 2d place in watercolor Internat. Miniature Art Show, Washington, 1983, Best in Show and Grumbacher award Caldwell State show, 1984, 1st place Carrier Clinic Tri-State, 1984, Grumbacher bronze award, 1984, Grumbacher silver award, 1985, 88, 94, watercolor award Artists League Ctrl. N.J. Show, Cornelious Lowe Mus., 1986, Winsor-Newton award Am. Artists Pro-league, 1987, Robert Simmons award, 1989, Basking Ridge Environ. Ctr. award, 1994, Best in Show award N.J. State Juried, Piscataway, 1988, 2d place N.J. Miniature Art Soc., 1989, 1st pro award Raritan Valley, 1992, 93, 1st mixed media award Basking Ridge Environ. Ctr., 1994, award Essex Watercolor Club, 1999, Grumbacher Gold award Essex Watercolor Club, 2000; artist-in-residence grantee Middlesex Librs., 1983-92, watercolor demonstrator, 1983—; TV appearances State of Arts-N.J., 1986, Midday (spl. art shows), 1986, TKR, 1995; Elisha Benjamin scholar Brown U., 1960. Mem. Garden State Watercolor Soc. (writer, editor 1994—), Miniature Art Soc. Fla., Miniature Art Soc., Washington, N.J. Watercolor Soc., AAUW (life, various offices 1963-73), Art Assn. Raritan Valley (pres. 1980-82, writer, editor newsletter 1993—), Art Assn. Somerset, Art Assn. Westfield, Art Assn. North Haven (Maine), Essex Watercolor Club, Am. Artists Profl. League, Hanover Squares Club (co-pres. 1972-73), Creative Artist's Guild. Presbyterian. Home: 497 Stony Brook Dr Bridgewater NJ 08807-1945

PATTON, NANCY MATTHEWS, elementary education educator; b. Pitts., Apr. 7, 1942; d. Thomas Joseph and Sara Theresa (Jocunskas) Matthews; m. Jack E. Patton, July 20, 1974; children: Susan, Steven. BS in Edn., Ind. U. of Pa., 1963; postgrad., U. Pitts., 1986. 4th grade tchr. Elroy Sch., Pitts., 1980-91; 6th grade tchr. Brentwood Mid. Sch., Pitts., 1991—2003. Sponsor Brentwood Mid. Sch. newspaper; coach Brentwood varsity cheerleaders, 1981-93, mid. sch. cheerleaders, 2000—. Mem. Brentwood Borough Coun., 1988—99, v.p., 1994—97, pres., 1998—99; trustee Brentwood Libr., 1988—, pres. bd. trustees, 2002—; mem. Brentwood Econ. Devel. Corp., 1995—99; sec. Brentwood Dem. Com., 1989—95. Mem.: NEA, Pa. State Edn. Assn., Lithuanian Citizens' Soc. (bd. dirs.), Brentwood Century Club. Democrat. Roman Catholic. Avocations: reading, community service. Home: 105 Hillson Ave Pittsburgh PA 15227-2941

PATTON, THOMAS EDWARD, artist, educator; b. Sacramento, Calif., May 17, 1954; s. Edward Clyde and Joan (Dall) P. BFA, San Francisco Art Inst., 1976; MA, U. New Mex., 1977, MFA, 1982. Instr. Millersville (Pa.) State Coll., 1979, New Mex. Inst. Mining & Tech., Socorro, 1981-82, Skidmore Coll., Saratoga Springs, N.Y., 1982-83; prof. U. Mo., St. Louis, 1983—. Author: (monograph) The Isolation and Intrusion Series, 1979, (catalogue) New Views: Photgaphs from Two Continents, 1985; one-man shows include Blue Sky Gallery, Portland, Oreg., 1982, U. N.Mex. Art Mus, 1982, Brockton (Mass.) Art Mus., 1984, UCLA, 1987, Mitchell Mus., Mt. Vernon, Ill., 1991, Kansas City Art Inst., 1994; exhibited in group shows at San Francisco Mus. Modern Art, 1985, St. Louis Art Mus., 1989, Mus. Photographic Art, San Diego, 1991, Downey Mus. Art, 1992, Wright State U., 1994; represented in public collections at Australia Nat. Gallery, Milw. Art Mus., Okland Mus., Portland Art Mus., Seattle Art Mus., St. Louis Art Mus., San Francisco Mus. Modern Art, U. N.Mex. Recipient Visual Artists fellowship NEA, Washington, 1990-91, James D. Phelan award, 2001-02. Mem. Soc. for Photographic Edn. Office: Calif State U Chico CA 95929

PATTY, ANNA CHRISTINE, tax specialist; b. Atlanta, Aug. 25, 1937; d. Henry Richard and Gertrude Johnson; children: Robert E., C. Wayne Jr., Christine E. BS in Math., U. Ga., 1959; MA in Curriculum and Instrn., Va. Poly. Inst. and State U., 1991. Cert. tchr., Va. Mgr. Steak and Ale Restaurants, Inc., Dallas, 1982-84; bus. mgr. Nova Plaza Corp., Charlotte, N.C., 1984-86; asst. mgr. WoodLo, Inc., Charlotte, 1986-87; food activity mgr. Army and Air Force Exch. Svc., Schweinfurt, Germany, 1987-89; substitute tchr. Montgomery County Schs., Christiansburg, Va., 1989-91; rsch. asst. Va. Poly. Inst. and State U., Blacksburg, 1990-91; mid. sch. tchr. math. and sci. Hampton (Va.) City Schs., 1991-93, mid. sch. tchr. sci., 1993-97, mid. sch. tchr. Advancement Via Individual Determination, 1997-98; tax preparer Jackson-Hewitt, Christiansburg, Va., 2001—. Mem. NSTA/APST Summer Inst., U.Md., 1992, NSTA Summer Inst., Sci. and Tech., SUNY, Stoney Brook, N.Y., 1995; EXCEL coach Christopher Newport U., 1993-95. With Operation Path Finders, Sandy Hook, N.J., 1994. Mem. NEA, Va. Educators Assn., Nat. Sci. Tchrs. Assn. (summer inst. participant 1992), Va. Middle Sch. Assn., Va. Sci. Tchrs., Nat. Coun. Tchrs. Math. Democrat. Unitarian Universalist. Avocations: hiking, camping, herbs, wine tasting, cooking. Home: 3327 Springview Dr Christiansburg VA 24073-6867 E-mail: annajpatty@hotmail.com.

PATWA, HUNED S. neurology educator; b. Godhra, India, July 26, 1966; s. Saifuddin and Mehfuza Patwa; m. Zehra Patwa, July 1995. BS in Biology, Carnegie Mellon U., 1988; MD, NYU, 1992. Intern Beth Israel Hosp., NYC, 1992-93; resident in neurology Sch. Medicine Yale U., New Haven, 1993-96, clin. instr., 1996-97, asst. prof. dept. neurology, 1997—. Dir. neurology clerkship Yale U., dir. clin. neurosci. physician assoc. program. Mem. AMA, Am. Acad. Neurology, Am. Assn. Electrodiagnostic Medicine. Office: Yale U Sch Medicine Dept Neurology PO Box 208018 New Haven CT 06520-8018

PAUL, ALIDA RUTH, arts and crafts educator; b. San Antonio, May 30, 1953; d. Richard Irving and Anne Louise (Holman) Paul. B.S. in Edn., Southwest Tex. State U., 1975; M.Ed., U. Houston, 1984. Cert. tchr., Tex. Tchr. art and crafts Houston Ind. Sch. Dist., 1975—. Republican. Episcopalian. Home: 16830 Grampin Dr Houston TX 77084-1945

PAUL, ARA GARO, university dean; b. New Castle, Pa., Mar. 1, 1929; s. John Hagop and Mary (Injejikian) P.; m. Shirley Elaine Waterman, Dec. 21, 1962; children: John Bartlett, Richard Goyan. BS in Pharmacy, Idaho State U., 1950; MS, U. Conn., 1953, PhD in Pharmacognosy, 1956. Cons. plant physiology Argonne (Ill.) Nat. Lab., 1955; asst. prof. pharmacognosy Butler U., Indpls., 1956-57; faculty U. Mich., Ann Arbor, 1957—, prof. pharmacognosy, 1969—; dean U. Mich. Coll. Pharmacy, 1975-96; dean emeritus, Hans W. Vahlteich prof. pharmacognosy, 2001—. Vis. prof. microbiology Tokyo U., 1965-66; mem. vis. chemistry faculty U. Calif., Berkeley, 1972-73; del. U.S. Pharmacopeial Conv., 1980, 90; scholar-in-residence Am. Assn. Colls. Pharmacy, 1996; bd. grants Am. Found. Pharm. Edn., 1997—, chmn., 1999, co-chmn. endowment com., 2002—, bd. dirs., 2003—; mem. organizing com. Millennial World Congress Pharm. Scis., 1996-2000; mem. FIP Found., 2000—, chmn. bd. trustees, 2001—. Contbr. articles to profl. jours. Recipient Outstanding Tchr. award Coll. Pharmacy, U. Mich., 1969, Outstanding Alumnus award Idaho State U., 1976, Profl. Achievement award Coll. Pharmacy, Idaho State U., 1990; G. Pfeiffer Meml. fellow Am. Found. Pharm. Edn., 1965-66, Disting. Svc. Profile award Am. Found Pharm. Edn., 1992; fellow Eli Lily Found., 1951-53, Am. Found. Pharm. Edn., 1954-56, NIH, 1972-73. Fellow AAAS; mem. Am. Pharm. Assn., Am. Soc. Pharmacognosy, Acad. Pharm. Scis., Am. Assn. Colls. Pharmacy, Am. Assn. Pharm. Scientists, Phi Lambda Upsilon, Sigma Xi, Phi Delta Chi, Phi Sigma Kappa, Rho Chi. Home: 1415 Brooklyn Ave Ann Arbor MI 48104-4496 Office: U Mich Coll Pharmacy Ann Arbor MI 48109-1065 E-mail: arapaul@umich.edu.

PAUL, CAROL ANN, retired academic administrator, biology educator; b. Brockton, Mass., Dec. 17, 1936; d. Joseph W. and Mary M. (DeMeulenaer) Bjork; m. Robert D. Paul, Dec. 21, 1957; children: Christine, Dana, Stephanie, Robert. BS, U. Mass., 1958; MAT, R.I. Coll., 1968, Brown U., 1970; EdD, Boston U., 1978. Tchr. biology Attleboro (Mass.) High Sch., 1965-68; asst. dean., mem. faculty biology North Shore Community Coll., Beverly, Mass., 1969-78; master planner N.J. Dept. for Higher Edn., Trenton, 1978-80; assoc. v.p. Fairleigh Dickinson U., Rutherford, N.J., 1980-86; v.p. acad. affairs Suffolk Community Coll., Selden, N.Y., 1986-94, prof. biology, 1994-98; ret. Faculty devel. cons. various colls., 1979-98, title III evaluator, 1985-98. Author: (lab. manual and workbook) Minicourses and Labs for Biological Science, 1972 (rev. edit., 1975); (with others) Strategies and Attitudes, 1986; book reviewer, 1973-77, 94-98. V.p. LWV, Beverly, 1970—74, Cranford, NJ, 1982—83; alumni rep. Brown U., 1972—92; mem. Cape Cod Area LWV, 2001—; bd. dirs. YMCA of Cape Cod, clk. of bd., 1998—. Commonwealth Mass. scholar, 1954-58; recipient Acad. Yr. award NSF, 1968-69, Proclamation for Leadership award Suffolk County Exec., 1989. Mem.: AAUW, AAWCC, AAHE, Nat. Coun. for Staff (nat. exec. bd. 1979—80), Profls. and Orgn. Developers (planning com. 1977—79), Brown Alumni Club of Cape Cod (bd. dirs. 2001—, sec. 2001—), Pi Lambda Theta, Phi Theta Kappa. Roman Catholic. Avocation: swimming. Address: 26 Martin Circle Winslowe's View at Pine Hills Plymouth MA 02360

PAUL, DONALD ROSS, chemical engineer, educator; b. Yeatesville, N.C., Mar. 20, 1939; s. Edgar R. and Mary E. (Cox) P.; m. Sally Annette Cochran, Mar. 28, 1964 (dec. Jan. 1995); children: Mark Allen, Ann Elizabeth; m. Barbara Louise Wilson, Apr. 20, 2002. BS, N.C. State Coll., 1961; MS, U. Wis., 1963, PhD, 1965. Rsch. chem. engr. E.I. DuPont de Nemours & Co., Richmond, Va., 1960-61; instr. chem. engring. dept. U. Wis., Madison, 1963-65; rsch. chem. engr. Chemstrand Rsch. Ctr., Durham, N.C., 1965-67; asst. prof. chem. engring. U. Tex., Austin, 1967-70, assoc. prof., 1970-73, prof., 1973—, T. Brockett Hudson prof., 1978-85, Melvin H. Gertz Regents chmn. chem. engring., 1985—, chmn. dept. chem. engring., 1977-85, dir. Ctr.'for Polymer Rsch., 1981—, dir. Tex. Materials Inst., 1998—. Turner Alfrey vis. prof. Mich. Molecular Inst., 1990-91; cons. in field. Author: (with F.W. Harris) Controlled Release Polymeric Formulations, 1976, (with S. Newman) Polymer Blends, 2 vols., 1978, (with Y.P. Yampolskii) Polymeric Gas Separation Membranes, 1994, (with C.B. Bucknall) Polymer Blends: Formulation and Performance, 2 vols., 2000. Recipient award Engring. News Record, 1975, Ednl. Svc. award Plastics Inst. Am., 1975, awards U. Tex. Student Engring. Coun., 1972, 75, 76, award for engring. tchg. Gen. Dynamics Corp., 1977, Joe J. King Profl. Engring. Achievement award, 1981, Holcott Engring. Rsch. award, 1994, Disting. Engring. Alumnus award N.C. State U., 1994, Outstanding Grad. Tchg. award U. Tex., 1994, Malcolm E. Pruitt award Coun. Chem. Rsch., 1998, Disting. Svc. citation U. Wis., 2000; named Donald L. Katz lectr. U. Mich., 2000. Fellow AIChE (South Tex. best fundamental paper award 1984, Materials Engring. and Scis. Divsn. award 1985, William H. Walker award 1998); mem. NAE, Mex. Acad. Scis. (corr. mem.), Am. Chem. Soc. (Doolittle award 1973, Phillips award in applied polymer sci. 1984, E.V. Murphree award in indsl. and engring. chemistry 1999), Soc. Plastics Engrs. (Outstanding Achievement in Rsch. award 1982, Internat. Edn. award 1989, Internat. award 1993), Fiber Soc., Nat. Materials Adv. Bd., Phi Eta Sigma, Tau Beta Pi, Phi Kappa Phi, Sigma Xi. Home: 7001 Valburn Dr Austin TX 78731-1818 Office: U Tex Ctr Polymer Rsch Dept Chem Engring Austin TX 78712

PAUL, NORMAN LEO, psychiatrist, educator; b. Buffalo, N.Y., July 5, 1926; s. Samuel Joseph and Tannie (Goncharsky) P.; m. Betty Ann Byfield, June 6, 1951 (dec. May 1994); children: Marilyn, David Alexander; m. Janet Athos, Aug. 16, 2002. MD, U. Buffalo, 1948. Fellow pharmacology U. Cin. Coll. Medicine, Ohio, 1949-50; resident psychiatry Mass. Mental Health Ctr., Boston, 1952-55; fellow child psychiatry James Jackson Putnam Children's Ctr., Boston, 1957-59, Mass. Gen. Hosp., Boston, 1958-59; chief psychiatrist Day Hosp. Mass. Mental Health Ctr., Boston, 1960-64; dir. conjoint family therapy Boston State Hosp., 1964-65, cons. in family psychiatry, 1965-70; assoc. clin. prof. dept. neurology Boston U. Sch. Medicine, 1977—. Cons. Mental Health Ctr., Alaska Native Hosp., Anchorage, 1967-68; cons. in family psychiatry Boston VA Hosp., 1967-71, Mass. Soc. for the Prevention of Cruelty to Children, Boston, 1993—; vis. family therapist St. George's Med. Sch., London, 1996-97; lectr. in psychiatry Harvard Med. Sch., Boston, 1976-2003; faculty assoc. Mgmt. Analysis Corp., Cambridge, Mass., 1979-82; presenter paper Internat. Conf. on Telemedicine and Telecare, London, 1996. Family therapist: (tv documentary) PBS-Trouble in the Family, 1965 (George Foster Peabody award 1965); co-author A Marital Puzzle, 1977, 86, German edit., 1987, French edit., 1995, Chinese edit., 1997. Sponsor Mass. Orgn. to Repeal Abortion Laws, Boston, 1965-70; chair Audio Unit of Child Devel. and Mass Media, White House Conf. on Children and Youth, Washington, 1970; bd. trustees Cambridge (Mass.) Coll., 1977-89; bd. dirs. Let's Face It, 1990—, Ctr. for Family Connections, 1998—. Capt. USAF, 1950-52. Recipient Edward A. Strecker, M.D. award for young psychiatrist of yr., 1966, Cert. of Merit, Mass. Coun. on Family Life, Boston, 1967, Cert. of Commendation, Mass. Assn. for Mental Health, Boston, 1967, Disting. Achievement award Soc. for Family Therapy and Rsch., Boston, 1973, Lifetime Achievement award Mass. Assn. for Marriage and Family Therapy, 1998, Disting. Svc. award Physician Health Svcs., 1998. Fellow Royal Soc. Medicine, Am. Psychiat. Assn. (life); mem. Am. Assn. Marriage and Family Therapy (bd. dirs. 1983-86), Am. Family Therapy Assn. (v.p. 1982-83, Disting. Contbn. award 1984), Assn. for Rsch. in Nervous and Mental Disorders, Group for the Advancement Psychiatry (chair com. on the family 1982-84). Avocations: study of codes, travel. Office: 394 Lowell St Ste 6 Lexington MA 02420-2549 E-mail: NPAUL@SAN.RR.COM.

PAUL, OUIDA FAY, music educator; b. Deatsville, Ala., Jan. 18, 1911; d. Elza Bland and Martha Eleanor (Hinton) P. AB in Math. and English, Huntingdon Coll., 1930, BS in Music Edn., 1933; MA in Music and Music Edn., Columbia U., 1943, EdD in Music and Music Edn., 1957; postgrad., U. Ill., 1968; studied oil painting, Gloria Foss Sch. of Art, 1978—83. Tchr. math., English and music pub. schs., Ala., 1930—42; tchr. math. Sacred Heart Convent Sch., N.Y.C., 1942-43; tchr. h.s. choral music Kingsport, Tenn., 1943-45; instr., asst. prof. music edn. Greensboro (N.C.) Coll., 1945-49; asst. prof. U. Fla., Gainesville, 1949-61, U. Hawaii, Honolulu, 1961-68; tchr. musicology and voice Leeward C.C., Pearl City, Hawaii, 1968-77; pvt. tchr. voice, Honolulu, 1977-95, Gainesville, 1996—. Choir dir. 1st Presbyn. Ch., Gainesville, 1950-61, Protestant Chapel, USN, Honolulu, 1962-68, Cmty. Ch., Honolulu, 1969-78, Wesley United Meth. Ch., Honolulu, 1978-94; contralto soloist various chs., 1950-94; adjudicator solo and choral auditions and festivals, 1945-94. One-woman shows include Honolulu Cmty. Theatre, 1980, 84, First United Meth. Ch., 1980; group shows with Honolulu Artists, others; permanent collections René Malmezac, Tahiti; contbr. articles to profl. jours. Cons. to com. on edn. Hawaii Gov.'s Commn. on Status of Women, 1965; English lang. tutor Hawaii Literacy, Inc., Honolulu, 1978-95. Recipient Alumni Achievement award, Huntingdon Coll. Alumnae Assn., 1998. Mem. Music Educators Nat. Conf. (1st v.p. Hawaii 1969-70), Am. Choral Dirs. Assn. (Hawaii chmn. 1963-66), Nat. Assn. Tchrs. Singing, Altrusa (pres. Gainesville 1960-61, past pres. Honolulu), Delta Kappa Gamma (pres. Hawaii Theta chpt. 1963-64, past state music chmn., named one of Makers of Destiny Hawaiian Style 2002.). Methodist. Avocation: oil painting. Home: 8015 NW 28th Pl Apt B210 Gainesville FL 32606-8607 E-mail: weefae@webtv.net.

PAUL, ROCHELLE CAROLE, special education educator; b. East Liverpool, Ohio, July 8, 1951; d. Homer Neil and Dolores Elizabeth (Seiler) P. BS, Clarion State Coll., 1973; MS, Clarion U., 1987; MDiv, Trinity Luth. Sem., Columbus, Ohio, 1992. Cert. tchr., Pa., Ohio. Spl. edn. tchr. Dorchester County Bd. Edn., Cambridge, Md., 1973-78, Forest Area Sch. Dist., Tionesta, Pa., 1979-88; edn. coord. juvenile-probate divsn. Common Pleas Ct. of Licking County, Newark, Ohio, 1993-95; instr. Ctrl. Ohio Tech. Coll., Newark, 1994—, program dir. for early childhood assoc. degree, 1999-2000; prevention specialist Ctr. Alternative Resources, Newark, 1996-98; program dir. early childhood devel. Ctrl. Ohio Tech. Coll., Newark, 1999-2000; exec. dir. Literacy Network Ctrl. Ohio, 2000—; intervention specialist Treca Digital Acad., 2002—. Rep. Pres.'s adv. bd. Trinity Luth. Sem., 1991-92; active St. Paul's Evang. Luth. Ch., Newark, Ohio; mem. head start cmty. assessment com., LEADS, 1999—, trustee, 2000—, policy coun. chair head start, 2000—. Mem. ASCD, AAUW, Coun. Exceptional Children (chpt. pres. 1972-73, 98—), Nat. Assn. Edn. of Young Children, Alcohol and Drug Abuse Prevention Assn. Ohio, Ohio Coalition of Assoc. Degree Early Childhood Programs. Avocations: tai chi, reading, writing, vocal and instrumental music, travel. Home: 164 Newton Ave Newark OH 43055-4758 Office: Literacy Network Ctrl Ohio COTC Baker House 1179 University Dr Newark OH 43055-1707 E-mail: rcpaulteacher@netscape.net.

PAUL, VERA MAXINE, mathematics educator; b. Mansfield, La., Dec. 14, 1940; d. Clifton and Virginia (Smith) Hall; m. Alvin James Paul III, June 14, 1964; children: Alvin J., Calvin J., Douglas F. BS, So. U., 1962; MS, Roosevelt U., 1975. Tchr. Shreveport (La.) Bd. Edn., 1962-64, Chgo. Bd. Edn., 1964-81, asst. prin., 1981—; tchr. South Bend (Ind.) Cmty. Sch., 1967-68. Mem. Chgo. Bd. Edn., 1964-92. Recipient Disting. Vol. Leadership award March of Dimes, Chgo., 1982, Mayoral Tribute award City of Pontiac (Mich.), 1987, Disting. Svc. award City Coun. Detroit, 1988, Svc. award City Coun. Cleve., 1990, State of Mich. Cert. of Merit Sen. Jackie Vaughn III, Great Lakes Svc. award, 1992, Svc. award Mich. Senate, 1992, Outstanding Svc. award U. Ill., Chgo., Women Connecting Project, 1997, Outstanding Leadership and Dir. award Chgo. Women Connecting-U. Ill. Chgo. Ctr. for Rsch. on Women and Gender, 1997. Mem. NAACP, Am. Fedn. Tchrs., Chgo. Tchr. Union, Ill. Coun. Affective Reading Edn., Ill. Coun. Tchrs. Math., Nat. Coun. Tchrs. Math., Nat. Alliance Black Sch. Educators, Zeta Phi Beta (regional dir. 1986-90, Zeta of Yr. 1988, Disting. Svc. award 1992, 95, Outstanding Svc. award 1996), Ret. Tchrs. Assn. Chgo. (bd. dirs. 2002). Lutheran. Avocations: reading, computer games, walking, piano.

PAUL, WILLIAM, physicist, educator; b. Deskford, Scotland, Mar. 31, 1926; came to U.S., 1952; s. William and Jean (Watson) P.; m. Barbara Anderson Forbes, Mar. 28, 1952; children: David, Fiona. MA, Aberdeen U., Scotland, 1946; PhD, Aberdeen U., 1951; A.M. (hon.), Harvard U., 1960; D Honoris Causa, Paris, 1994. Asst. lectr., then lectr. Aberdeen U., 1946-52; mem. faculty Harvard U., 1953—, Gordon McKay prof. applied physics, 1963-91, Mallinckrodt prof. applied physics, 1991-2000, prof. physics, 1980-2000, Mallinckrodt rsch. prof. applied physics, 2000—, rsch. prof. physics, 2000—. Professeur associé U. Paris, 1966-67; cons. solid state physics, 1954—; Ripon prof., Calcutta, 1984 Author: Handbook on Semiconductors: Band Theory and Transport Properties, 1982; co-editor: Solids Under Pressure, 1963, Amorphous and Liquid Semiconductors, 1980, Physics of Semiconductor Materials and Applications, 1986, High Pressure in Semiconductor Physics, Vols. 1 and 2, 1998. Carnegie fellow, 1952-53; Guggenheim fellow, 1959-60; Humboldt awardee, 1990; fellow Clare Hall Cambridge U., 1974-75. Fellow Am. Phys. Soc., Brit. Inst. Physics, N.Y. Acad. Scis., Royal Soc. Edinburgh; mem. AAUP, Sigma Xi. Home: 2 Eustis St Lexington MA 02421-5612 Office: Harvard U Pierce Hall Cambridge MA 02138 E-mail: paul@deas.harvard.edu.

PAULINA, DIANA, alternative school educator; b. Detroit; d. Walter and Marie (Hrit) P.; m. Kevin Crawley, Aug. 23, 1981. BA in German and English Edn., U. Mich., 1969; MA in Edn. Alternative Sch., Ind. U., 1979. Cert. tchr., German, English and reading. Various tchg. positions USAF/Lang. Inst., Germany, 1970-74; instr. Marshalltown (Iowa) C.C., 1974-79; dir., counselor Unbound, Inc., Iowa City, Iowa, 1980-90; instr. Cmty. Edn. Ctr. Alternative Schs., Iowa City, 1984—; sponsor Iowa City (Iowa) Student Computer Club, 1993—. Internet cons. Iowa City Cmty. schs., 1991—; v.p., bd. dirs. Response TV, Inc., Iowa City, 1992—; policy bd. chair Iowa Student Computer Assn. bull. Bd. Svc., 1992—. Mem. ASCD, ALA, AAUW, NEA, Iowa State Edn. Assn. (internet cons. 1992—, Mem. of Yr. East Ctrl. Uniserve unit 1996), Iowa City Edn. Assn. (pres., v.p., tech. chair, Mem. of Yr. 1996), Internat. Reading Assn., Nat. Coun. Tchrs. English, Iowa Coun. Tchrs. Lang. Arts, Iowa Assn. Alternative Educators (Educator of Yr. award 1996), Iowa City Ednl. Cable Consortium, Iowa City Pub. Access (cmty. cable prodr. 1983—), Iowa Student Computer Assn., Assn. Computing Machinery, U. Mich. Alumni Assn., Ind. U. Alumni Assn. Avocations: reading, bowling, internet exploration, handcrafts, wallyball. Home: PO Box 1963 Iowa City IA 52244-1963 Office: CEC Alternative Schs 509 S Dubuque St Iowa City IA 52240-4228

PAULINO, SISTER MARY MCAULEY, principal; b. Inarajan, Guam, Aug. 24, 1934; d. Mariano Torres Paulino. BA in Edn., U. Guam, 1974; M in Pvt. Sch. Adminstrn., U. S.F., 1992; postgrad., U. Guam. tchr. religious edn., Guam. V.p. Archdiocese of Agana, Guam; prin. Santa Barbara Sch., Dededo, Guam, 1978-81, Cathedral Grade Sch., 1986-90, 92-95, Baumgartner Meml. Sch., 1995—. Coach math Olympiad and spelling bee; mem. peace and justice com. Agana Cathedral Parish Coun. Recipient Appreciation award for support of Guam historic preservation, faithful and valuable svc. to edn., commendation and congratulatory resolution 20th Guam Legis., Gov.'s Art award 1989. Mem. Nat. Cath. Educators Assn., ASCD, Internat. Reading Assn., Civic Ctr. Guam Found., Phi Delta Kappa.

PAULOVKIN, JOSEPH MATTHEW, middle school educator; b. Pitts., Feb. 26, 1954; s. Joseph and Olga Helen (Blistan) P.; m. Elvira Maria Barriga, Oct. 13, 1984; children: Jason, Jeremy, Jonathan. Student, Bucknell U., 1972-74; MusB magna cum laude, Duquesne U., 1977; MusM, U. Miami, 1979. Tchr. music North Miami (Fla.) Beach Sr. Sch., 1987-90, Ruben Dario Mid. Sch., Miami, 1990—. Adj. faculty Fla. Internat. U., Miami, 1986-87. Performed guitar in concert with Engelbert Humperdinck, Liza Minelli, Vicki Carr, Bill Cosby, Carol Lawrence, Milton Berle, Bernadette peters, Maureen McGovern, Howie Mandel, Bob Hope, Bill Conti, 1979-94; performed at Superbowl 23/NBC TV. Tchr. Sunday sch. Jesus Fellowship Ch., Miami, 1992-98, praise band musician, 1978—. Avocations: computers, music, camping, hiking. Home: 7509 SW 141st Ave Miami FL 33183-3056 E-mail: playloud@earthlink.net.

PAULSEN, LINDA GRAYSON, contract consultant, artist, poet; b. Salt Lake City, July 31, 1951; d. George Albert and Phillis Lucille (Samuelson) Grayson; m. Steven Earl Paulsen, July 25, 1972; children: Shannon Lee, Jeffrey David, Eric Steven, Timothy George, Jacob Scott. Student, Brigham Young U., 1969-72, Western Wyo. C.C., 1985—86, student, 1997, student, 2000. Substitute tchr., contract cons. Sweetwater County Sch. Dist. No. 1, Rock Springs, Wyo., 1989—; co-pub. The Friend mag., Fla., Jack and Jill mag., Fla. Tchr. creative writing workshops, Rock Springs, Wyo., 1980—; pvt. tchr. piano, Rock Springs, Wyo., 1974—; tutor lang. arts and music, Rock Springs, Wyo., 1974-91; writer-composer dramatic/musical prodns. LDS Ch., Provo, Utah, Rock Springs, Wyo., 1970—. Composer humorous musical plays, road shows; exhbns. include Sweetwater County Libr. Sys., Rock Springs, Wyo., Cmty. Fine Arts Ctr., Out West Gallery, Rock Springs, Wyo., Kimball Art Ctr., Park City, Utah. Mem.: Sweetwater Artists Assn. Avocations: literature, drama, dance, music, art. Home and Office: 281 E Winchester Springville UT 84663

PAULSON, RONALD HOWARD, English and humanities educator; b. Bottineau, N.D., May 27, 1930; s. Howard Clarence and Ethel (Tvete) P.; m. Barbara Lee Appleton, May 25, 1957 (div. 1982); children: Andrew Meredith, Melissa Katherine. BA, Yale U., 1952, PhD, 1958. Instr. U. Ill., 1958-59, from asst. to assoc. prof., 1959-63; prof. English Rice U., Houston, 1963-67, Johns Hopkins U., Balt., 1967-75, chmn. dept., 1968-75, Andrew W. Mellon prof. humanities, 1973-75, Mayer prof. humanities,

1984—, chmn. dept., 1985-91; prof. English Yale U., New Haven, Conn., 1975-84, Thomas E. Donnelly prof., 1980-84, Ward Phillips lectr., 1978, Alexander lectr., 1979, Brown and Haley lectr., 1979, Hodges lectr., 1980. Author: Theme and Structure in Swift's Tale of a Tub, 1960, Fielding, 1962, Hogarth's Graphic Works, 1965, rev. edits., 1970, 89, Fictions of Satire, 1967, Satire and the Novel, 1967, (with Thomas F. Lockwood) Fielding: The Critical Heritage, 1969, Satire: Modern Essays in Criticism, 1971, Hogarth: His Life, Art and Times, 1971, Rowlandson: A New Interpretation, 1972, Emblem and Expression: Meaning in Eighteenth Century English Art, 1975, The Art of Hogarth, 1975, Popular and Polite Art in the Age of Hogarth and Fielding, 1979, Literary Landscape: Turner and Constable, 1982, Book and Painting: Shakespeare, Milton and the Bible, 1983, Representations of Revolution, 1983, Breaking and Remaking, 1989, Figure and Abstraction in Contemporary Painting, 1990, Hogarth Vol. 1: The Making of the Modern Moral Subject, 1991, Hogarth Vol. 2: High Art and Low, 1991, Hogarth Vol. 3: Art and Politics, 1993, The Beautiful, Novel, and Strange: Aesthetics and Heterodoxy, 1996, Don Quixote in England: The Aesthetics of Laughter, 1998; editor: The Analysis of Beauty, 1997, The Life of Henry Fielding: A Critical Biography, 2000, Hogarth's Harlot: Sacred Parody in Enlightenment England, 2003; mem. editl. bd. ELH, 1967—, sr. editor, 1985-2002. 1st lt. AUS, 1952-54. Sterling fellow 1957-85, Guggenheim fellow 1965-66, 1986-87, NEH fellow 1977-78. Fellow Am. Acad. Arts and Scis.; mem. Am. Soc. for 18th Century Studies (pres. 1986-87). Home: 2722 Saint Paul St Baltimore MD 21218-4332 Office: Johns Hopkins U Dept English Baltimore MD 21218

PAULSTON, CHRISTINA BRATT, linguistics educator; b. Stockholm, Dec. 30, 1932; arrived in US, 1951; d. Lennart and Elsa Bratt; m. Rolland G. Paulston, July 26, 1963; children: Christopher-Rolland, Ian Rollandsson. BA, Carleton Coll., 1953; MA in English and Comparative Lit., U. Minn., 1955; Ed.D., Columbia U., 1966. Cert. tchr., Minn. Tchr. Clara City and Pine Island High Schs., Minn., 1955-60, Am. Sch. of Tangier, Morocco, 1960-62, Katrineholm Allmanna Laroverk, Katrineholm, Sweden, 1962-63, East Asian Library, Columbia U., N.Y.C., 1963-64; asst. instr. Tchrs. Coll., Columbia U., 1964-66; instr. U. Punjab, Chandigarh, India, summer 1966, Pontificia Universidad Catolica Del Peru, Lima, 1966-67; cons. Instituto Linguistico de Verano, Lima, 1967-68; asst. prof. linguistics U. Pitts., 1969-75, prof., 1975-99, prof. emerita, tchg. pro bono, 1999—, asst. dir. English Lang. Inst., 1969-70, dir. English Lang. Inst., 1970-97, acting dir. Lang. Acquistion Inst., fall 1971, acting chmn. dept. gen. linguistics, 1974-75, chmn., 1975-89. Apptd. internat. advisor in sociolinguistics to Summer Inst. of Linguistics, 1997. Author numerous books and articles on linguistics. Recipient research award Am. Ednl. Research Assn., 1980; Fulbright-Hays grantee, Uruguay, 1985. Mem. Assn. Tchrs. English to Speakers of Other Langs. (2d v.p., conv., chmn. 1972, exec. com. 1972-75, rsch. com. 1973-75, 78-80, chmn. 1973-75, 1st v.p. 1975, pres. 1976), Linguistics Soc. Am. (com. linguistics and pub. interest 1973-77), Internat. Assn. Tchrs. of English as a Fgn. Lang., Am. Coun. on Tchg. of Fgn. Langs., MLA (exec. com. lang. and soc. 1975-76), Ctr. Applied Linguistics (trustee 1976-81, exec. com. 1980, publs. com. 1981, rsch. com. 1981). Democrat. Episcopalian. Office: U Pitts Linguistics Pittsburgh PA 15260

PAULUS, NORMA JEAN PETERSEN, lawyer; b. Belgrade, Nebr., Mar. 13, 1933; d. Paul Emil and Ella Marie (Hellbusch) Petersen; m. William G. Paulus, Aug. 16, 1958; children: Elizabeth, William Frederick. LL.B., Willamette Law Sch., 1962; LL.D. (hon.), Linfield Coll., 1985; LittD (hon.), Whitman Coll., 1990; LHD (hon.), Lewis & Clark Coll., 1996. Bar: Oreg. 1962. Sec. to Harney County Dist. Atty., 1950-53; legal sec., 1953-55; sec. to chief justice Oreg. Supreme Ct., 1955-61; of counsel Paulus and Callaghan, Salem; mem. Oreg. Ho. of Reps., 1971-77; sec. of state State of Oreg., Salem, 1977-85; supt. pub. instrn., 1990-99; of counsel Paulus, Rhoten & Lien, 1985-86. Mem. Oreg. exec. bd. U.S. West, 1985-97; adj. prof. Willamette U. Grad. Sch., 1985; mem. N.W. Power Planning Com., 1986-89. Mem. adv. com. Def. Adv. Com. for Women in the Svc., 1986, Nat. Trust for Hist. Preservation, 1988-90; trustee Willamette U., 1978—; bd. dirs. Oreg. Grade Instn. Sci. and Tech., 1985-2001, Edn. Commn. States, 1991-99, Coun. Chief State Sch. Officers, 1995-98, Nat. Assessment Governing Bd., 1996-99, Oreg. Garden Found., 1997—, Oreg. Coast Aquarium, 1999—; bd. dirs., adv. bd. World Affairs Coun. Oreg., 1997—; overseer Whitman Coll., 1985—; bd. cons. Marion-Polk Boundary Commn., 1970-71; mem. Presdl. Commn. to Monitor Philippines Election, 1986; dir. Oreg. Hist. Soc., 2001—. Recipient Disting. Svc. award City of Salem, 1971, LWV, 1995, Path Breaker award Oreg. Women's Polit. Caucus, 1976; named One of 10 Women of Future, Ladies Home Jour., 1979, Woman of Yr. Oreg. Inst. Managerial and Profl. Women, 1982, Oreg. Women Lawyers, 1982, Woman Who Made a Difference award Nat. Women's Forum, 1985; Eagleton Inst. Politics fellow Rutgers U. Mem. Oreg. State Bar, Nat. Order Women Legislators, Women Execs. in State Govt., Women's Polit. Caucus Bus. and Profl. Women's Club (Golden Torch award 1971), Delta Kappa Gamma.

PAUP, DONALD C. psychology educator; b. L.A., Apr. 2, 1939; s. Marvin K. and Corinne (Vincent) P.; m. Helen Jon Sands, Aug. 10, 1963; children: Elizabeth, Jennifer. BA, Occidental Coll., 1961; MA, Tulane U., 1969, PhD, 1970. Postdoctoral fellow Mich. State U., East Lansing, 1971-72, UCLA, 1972-73; from faculty to prof. George Washington U., Washington, 1973—. Program dir. exercise science Am. Coun. on Internat. Sports, Washington, 1978-84; pres. Employee Fitness Assocs., Washington, 1979-90; clinician Pres.'s Coun. Phys. Fitness & Sports, Washington, 1976—. Dir. cardiovascular com. Nat. Capital YMCA, Washington, 1986-88; dir. Cardinal Hill Swim & Racquet Club, Vienna, Va., 1981-86. Mem. AAHPERD, Am. Coll. Sports Medicine, U.S. Badminton Assn. (dir. 1980-86, Ken Davidson sportsmanship award 1974, coach internat. teams 1971-75). Office: Exercise Sci George Washington U 817 23rd St NW Washington DC 20037-2517 E-mail: dpoup@gwu.edu., dcpaup@aol.com.

PAUPP, TERRENCE EDWARD, research associate, educator; b. Joliet, Ill., Aug. 10, 1952; s. Edward Theodore and Mary Alice (Combs) P. BA in Social Scis., San Diego State U., 1974; ThM, Luth. Sch. Theology, 1978; JD, U. San Diego, 1990. Instr. philosophy San Diego City Coll., 1983-86, Southwestern Coll., Chula Vista, Calif., 1980-83; law clerk Sch. Law U. San Diego, 1987-88; law clerk Office of Atty. Gen., San Diego, 1988-89; rsch. assoc. Frank & Milchen, San Diego, 1989, Dougherty & Hildre, San Diego, 1990-95; sr. rsch.-assoc. Inst. for Ctrl. and Ea. European Studies, San Diego State U., 1996-98; sr. policy analyst Nuc. Age Peace Found., Santa Barbara, Calif., 2001—. Cons. Cmty. Reinvestment Act, San Diego, 1993-95; sr. rsch. assoc. Inst. Ctrl. and Ea. European Studies San Diego State U., 1994-95; adj. faculty in criminal justice and polit. sci. Nat. U.; cons., contbr. Inst. for Policy Studies, Washington, Interhemispheric Resource Ctr., N.Mex., The Ctr. of Concer, Washington, Global Exch., San Francisco. Author: Achieveing Inclusionary Governance: Advancing Peace and Development in First and Third World Nations, 2000; contbr. articles to law jours. Appointed National Chancellor of the USA Internat. Assn. of Educators for World Peace, 2001; cons. Neighborhood House 5th Ave., 1994—95, PBS Frontline documentary The Nicotine Wars, 1994, Bethel Baptist Ch., 1994—95. Mem. ATLA, N.Y. Acad. Scis. Democrat. Lutheran. Avocation: tennis. E-mail: tpaupp@aol.com.

PAVALON, DONNA MAE, librarian; b. Hutchinson, Minn., May 11, 1948; d. Loraine Frances and Lucy Gertrude (Woller) Schandel; m. Norman B. Pavalon, Aug. 27, 1977; children: Kerri A., Kelli L. BS, U. Wis., Milw., 1973; MS, libr. cert., U. Nev., Las Vegas, 1988. Cert. reading specialist, libr. specialist. Tchr. Milw. Pub. Schs., 1974-78; tchr., libr. Clark County Sch. Dist., Las Vegas, Nev., 1978-86, libr., 1987—. Mem. ALA, Nev. Libr. Assn., Clark County Sch. Librs. Assn. (pres. elect 1990-91, pres. 1991-92). Home: 2357 Viewcrest Rd Henderson NV 89014-3628

PAVELKA, ELAINE BLANCHE, mathematics educator; b. Chgo. d. Frank Joseph and Mildred Bohumila (Seidl) P. BA, MS, Northwestern U.; PhD, U. Ill. With Northwestern U. Aerial Measurements lab., Evanston, Ill.; tchr. Leyden Cmty. H.S., Franklin Park, Ill.; prof. math. Morton Coll., Cicero, Ill. Invited prof. Internat. Congress on Math. Edn., Karlsruhe, Germany, 1976. RecipientSci. Talent award Westinghouse Electric Co. Mem. Am. Edn. Rsch. Assn., Am. Math. Assn. 2-Yr. Colls., Am. Math. Soc., Assn. Women in Math., Can. Soc. History and Philosophy of Math., Ill. Coun. Tchrs. Math., Ill. Math. Assn. C.C., Math. Assn. Am. Math. Action Group, Ga. Ctr. Study and Tchg. and Learning Math., Nat. Coun. Tchrs. Math., Sch. Sci. and Math. Assn., Northwestern U. Alumni Assn., U. Ill. Alumni Assn., Am. Mensa Ltd., Intertel, Sigma Delta Epsilon, Pi Mu Epsilon. Home: PO Box 7312 Westchester IL 60154-7312

PAWL, RONALD PHILLIP, neurosurgery educator; b. Chgo., July 26, 1935; s. Phillip Joseph and Ruby Helen (Graham) P.; m. Mary M. Rohner, July 11, 1959; children: Mary, Linda, Diane, Julie, Matthew, Michael. BS in Neurosurgery, Loyola U., Chgo., 1957, MD, 1961. Diplomate Am. Bd. Neurol. Surgery. Intern Resurrection Hosp., 1961-62; resident in gen. surgery and orthopedics Hines VA Hosp., 1962-63; resident in neurology and neurosurgery U. Ill., Chgo., 1963-66, asst. prof. neurosurgery, 1968-73; asst. chief neurosurgery Tripler Army Med. Ctr., Honolulu, 1966-68; assoc. prof. neurosurgery U. Ill., Chgo., 1973—; dir. pain treatment ctr. Lake Forest (Ill.) Hosp., 1978—. Pres. Am. Bd. Pain Medicine, 1995, residency rev. com. chmn., 1997—. Author: Chronic Pain Primer, 1979; editor Seminars in Neurology, 1989; editor Clin. Jour. Pain, 1988—, Surg. Neurology, 1994—, Clin. Rev. of Pain, 1997—, Currant Rev. of Pain, 1995—; contbr. articles to profl. jours. Capt. U.S. Army, 1966-68. Named Physician of Yr., Ill. Masonic Med. Ctr., Chgo., 1973. Mem. Ctrl. Neurosurg. Soc. (pres. 1979), Midwest Pain Soc. (pres. 1986), Am. Acad. Pain Medicine (treas. 1990), Ill. Neurosurg. Soc. (pres. 1982). Roman Catholic. Office: 900 N Westmoreland Rd Lake Forest IL 60045-1674 E-mail: ron@pawl.com.

PAWLICZKO, GEORGE IHOR, academic administrator; b. Rochester, N.Y., Oct. 26, 1950; s. Roman and Irene Olha (Zubryckyj) P.; m. Ann Maria Lencyk, June 10, 1978. BA, St. John Fisher Coll., 1972; MA, Fordham U., 1974, MBA, 1986, PhD, 1989. Admissions counselor Fordham U., Bronx, N.Y., 1977-78, asst. dean Grad. Sch. of Bus. N.Y.C., 1978-81; asst. to pres., dir. mgmt. info. systems Marymount Coll., Tarrytown, N.Y., 1981-82; exec. dir. N.Y. Inst. Credit, N.Y.C., 1982-94, The Global Inst. Fin. and Banking (formerly Am. Inst. Banking Greater N.Y.), N.Y.C., 1994—. Trustee St. Andrew's Ch., Hamptonburgh, N.Y., 1986-2002. Mem. Shevchenko Scientific Soc., Beta Gamma Sigma, Phi Alpha Theta. Office: The Global Inst Fin and Banking 80 Maiden Ln New York NY 10038-4811

PAXTON, JUANITA WILLENE, retired university official; b. Birmingham, Ala. d. Will and Elizabeth (Davis) P. AB, Birmingham So. Coll., 1950; MA, Mich. State U., 1951; EdD, Ind. U., 1971; postgrad., U. Tex., summer 1965. Dormitory dir. Tex. Tech U., Lubbock, 1951-53; dir. univ. ctr. and housing SUNY, Fredonia, 1953-56, assoc. dean of students, 1956-57; asst. dean of women U. N.Mex., Albuquerque, 1957-63; dean of women East Tenn. State U., Johnson City, 1963-68, 70-78, dir. Counseling Ctr., 1978-93. Tng. dir. CONTACT Teleministries, Tenn., 1984-92, chmn. bd. dirs., 1986, 95. Chmn. social concerns Munsey United Meth. Ch., 1989-92, sec. adminstrv. bd., 1980-84, vice chairperson, 1993, chair, 1994, mem. coun. on ministries, 1980-94, chair stewardship campaign, 1995, chair promotion and publicity subcom. building campaign, 1996-2001, chair scholarship com., 1997—, lay leader, 2001—, sec. staff parish rels. com., 2001—, sec. ch. coun., 2003—, mem. nominations com., 2001—, mem. SEND team, Circle tchr., 2000—. U.S. Ednl. Profl. Devel. Act grantee, 1968-69. Mem.: Watauga Pers. and Guild Assn. (pres.-elect 1967—68, chair ETEA guidance divsn. 1968), Tenn. Assn. Women Deans Counselors (pres. 1966—68), Tenn. Coll. Pers. Assn. (legis. chair 1974), Am. Coll. Pers. Assn. (media com. 1977—79, newsletter editor com. XVI 1977—79), East Tenn. State U. Retirees Assn. (bd. dirs. 1993—2000, program com. 1994, 1995, pres.-elect 1995, pres. 1996, chair com. to compile Tales of the Univ. 1999—, sec. 2000, chair Tales of U. com. 2000—, bd. dirs. 2003—), Asbury Retirement Ctrs. Tenn. and Va. (bd. dirs. 1991—96, policy com. 1991—96, nomination com. 1994—96, chair 1995—96, fin. com. 1996), Monday Club Aux. (corr. sec. 1979—80, pres. 1980—81, 1988—89, v.p. 1993—95, pres. 1995—96, v.p. 1996—99, pres. 1999—2000), Gen Federated Woman's Club, Univ. Women's Club (pres. 1994—96), Delta Kappa Gamma Soc. Internat. (chpt. pres. 1972—74, state rec. sec. 1975—77, state v.p. 1977—79, chair state nominating com. 1979—81, internat. rsch. com. 1982—84, chair state ad hoc com. to study feasibility exec. sec. 1987—89, exec. bd. 1989—91, state pres. 1989—91, internat. chair rules com. 1992, constn. com. 1992—94, pers. com. 1995—97, chair 1997—99, archives com. 1999—2001, pers. com. 2001—03, State Achievement award 1987). Avocations: reading, bridge, travel, needlework. E-mail: willenepj@charter.net.

PAXTON, LAURA BELLE-KENT, English language educator, management professional; b. Lake Charles, La., Feb. 8, 1942; d. George Ira and Gladys Lillian (Barrett) Kent.; m. Kenneth Robert Paxton Jr., Jan. 2, 1962. BA, McNeese U., Lake Charles, 1963, MA in English, 1972; EdD, East Tex. U., 1983. cert. English, social studies instr., prin., supt., ednl. adminstr., Ariz. Tchr. Darrington (Wash.) High Sch., 1966-70; English instr. Maricopa C.C., Phoenix, 1974-92; migrant program instr. Phoenix Union High Sch., 1984-88; English instr. Embry-Riddle Aeronautical U., Luke AFB, Ariz., 1985-87; sales rep. Merrill Lynch Realty, Phoenix, 1985-88; co-owner Paxton Mgmt. Co., Phoenix, 1985-92; prof., program chair gen. edn. Western Internat. U., Phoenix, 1992—; instr. U. Phoenix, 1999—. Author Ariz. corr. courses, 1987-88; presenter migrant worker program confs., 1987—; reviewer Prentice-Hall, 1985. Author: Handbook for Middle Eastern Dancers, 1978, The Kent Family History From 1787-1981, 1981, A Handbook of Home Remedies, 1981, Elements of Effective Writing: A Composition Guidesheet, 1994, Documentation for Business Papers: A Guidesheet, 1995, (textbook) Writing Power, 1998. Mem. Everett, Wash. Opera Guild, 1966-70, Ariz. State U. Opera Guild, Tempe, 1978-80; mem. City of Darrington Council, 1969-70; ESL instr. Friendly House, Phoenix, 1978-79. Mem. Ariz. English Assn., Phi Delta Kappa.

PAXTON, LISA ANN, speech language pathologist; b. Laramie, Wyo., Feb. 29, 1968; d. LeRoy Dean and La Donna Mae (Roblyer) Smith; m. Camron Lee Paxton, Aug. 12, 1989; 1 child, Cy Hunter. BGS, Fort Hays State U., 1991, MS, 1992. Lic. speech lang. pathologist, Kans. Speech lang. pathologist N.W. Kans. Ednl. Svc. Ctr., Oakley, 1991-92, Unified Sch. Dist. # 352, Goodland, Kans., 1992—. Mem. Am. Speech Lang. Hearing Assn., Kans. Speech Lang. Hearing Assn. Home: 107 Harrison St Goodland KS 67735-2149

PAXTON, MARY JEAN WALLACE, science educator; b. Gary, Ind., Nov. 10, 1930; d. John James Wallace and Ruth Isobel Johnson; m. Robert Gerard Haagens, Dec. 27, 1971 (dec. Feb. 14, 1976); 1 child, Jan Gerard Haagens; m. David Grant Paxton, Dec. 27, 1978. BS, St. Mary's Coll., 1957; PhD, U. Notre Dame, 1964. Asst. then assoc. prof. St. Mary's Coll., Notre Dame, Ind., 1964—69; rsch. fellow Harvard Sch. Pub. Health, Boston, 1969—71, Mass. Gen. Hosp., Boston, 1971—73; asst. prof. biology R.I. Coll., Providence, 1973—78; asst. to full prof. biology Jacksonville (Ala.) State U., 1978—93, dir., in service edn., 1990—93, acting dir. continuing edn., 1990—93; adj. instr. life scis. Palomar Coll., San Marcos, Calif., 1994—. Co-author: Biological and Medical Aspects of Contraception, 1965; author: The Female Body in Control, 1981, Endocrinology: Biological and Medical Perspective, 1986. Fellow coop. grad. fellow, NSF, 1962. Mem.: AAUW. Avocations: gardening, reading, crossword puzzles, fitness. Home: 3050 Skyline Dr Oceanside CA 92056 E-mail: mjw-paxton@cox.net.

PAXTON, ROBERT OWEN, historian, educator; b. Lexington, Va., June 15, 1932; s. Matthew W. and Nell B. (Owen) P.; m. Sarah Plimpton, Dec. 9, 1983 BA, Washington and Lee U., 1954, LittD (hon.), 1974; BA, Oxford (Eng.) U., 1956, MA, 1961; PhD, Harvard U., 1963; DHL (hon.), SUNY, Stony Brook, 1994; DL (hon.), U. Caen, France, 1994; DL, U. Lyon, France, 2003. Instr. history U. Calif., Berkeley, 1961-63, asst. prof., 1963-67; asso. prof. SUNY, Stony Brook, 1967-69; prof. history Columbia U., 1969—, chmn. dept., 1980-82, dir. Inst. on West Europe, 1991-95. Author: Parades and Politics at Vichy, 1966, Vichy France: Old Guard and New Order, 1940-44, 1972, 2d edit., 2001, Europe in the Twentieth Century, 1975, 4th edit., 2001, French Peasant Fascism, 1997; co-author: Vichy France and the Jews, 1981, 2d edit., 1995; co-editor: De Gaulle and the U.S., 1995. Served with USNR, 1956-58. Decorated comdr. Ordre National des Arts et des Lettres (France), officer Ordre Nat. du Mérite (France); recipient Scholarly Distinction award Am. Hist. Soc., 1998; Rhodes scholar, 1954-56; Am. Coun. Learned Socs. fellow, 1974-75; Rockefeller Found. fellow, 1978-79; German Marshall Fund fellow, 1986. Fellow Am. Acad. Arts and Letters; mem. Am. Philos. Soc., Linnaean Soc. N.Y. (pres. 1978-80). Home: 460 Riverside Dr Apt 72 New York NY 10027-6801 Office: Columbia U Dept History New York NY 10027 E-mail: rop1@columbia.edu.

PAYNE, ALMA JEANETTE, English language educator, author; b. Highland Park, Ill., Oct. 28, 1918; d. Frederick Hutton and Ruth Ann (Colle) P. BA, Wooster (Ohio) Coll., 1940; MA, Case Western Res. U., 1941, PhD, 1956. Tchr. English, history, Latin Ohio Pub. Schs., Bucyrus and Canton, 1941-46; from instr. to prof. English and Am. studies Bowling Green (Ohio) State U., 1946-79, dir. Am. studies program, 1957-79, chair Am. culture PhD program, 1978-79, prof. emerita English, Am. studies, 1979—; adj. prof. Am. studies U. South Fla., 1982—. Author: Critical Bibliography of Louisa May Alcott, 1980, Discovering the American Nations, 1981; contbr. articles to profl. jours.; editor Nat. Am. Studies Assn. Newsletter; contbr. articles to profl. jours. Nat. Coun. for Innovation in Edn. grantee, Norway, U.S. Embassy and Norwegian Dept. Ch. and State, 1978-79; recipient MAry Turpie award in Am. studies, 1996. Mem. AAUW (pres. 1982-84), Soc. Mayflower Descs in Fla. (state treas. 1985), Nat. Am. Studies Assn. (v.p. 1977-79), Zonta, Phi Beta Kappa, Phi Kappa Phi, Kappa Delta Pi, Alpha Lambda Delta. Republican. Presbyterian. Avocations: travel, gardening, baseball, photography, reading. Home and Office: 2164 Cj Ln Labelle FL 33935-6632

PAYNE, ANITA HART, reproductive endocrinologist, researcher; b. Karlsruhe, Baden, Germany, Nov. 24, 1926; came to U.S., 1938; d. Frederick Michael and Erna Rose (Hirsch) Hart; widowed; children: Gregory Steven, Teresa Payne-Lyons. BA, U. Calif., Berkeley, 1949, PhD, 1952. From rsch. assoc. to prof. U. Mich., Ann Arbor, 1961-96, prof. emeritus, 1996—; assoc. dir. U. Mich. Ctr. for Study Reprodn., Ann Arbor, 1989-94; sr. rsch. scientist Stanford (Calif.) U. Med. Ctr., 1995—. Vis. scholar Stanford U., 1987-88; mem. reproductive biology study sect. NIH, Bethesda, Md., 1978-79, biochem. endocrinology study sect., 1979-83, population rsch. com. Nat. Inst. Child Health and Human Devel., 1989-93. Assoc. editor Steroids, 1987-93; contbr. book chpts., articles to profl. jours. Recipient award for cancer rsch. Calif. Inst. for Cancer Rsch., 1953, Acad. Women's Caucus award U. Mich., 1986, Mentor award Women in Endocrinology, 1999. Mem. Endocrine Soc. (chmn. awards com. 1983-84, mem. nominating com. 1985-87, coun. 1988-91), Am. Soc. Andrology (exec. coun. 1980-83), Soc. for Study of Reprodn. (bd. dirs. 1982-85, sec. 1986-89, pres. 1990-91, Carl G. Hartman award 1998). Office: Stanford U Med Ctr Dept OB GYN Divsn Reproductive Biology Stanford CA 94305-5317

PAYNE, ARLIE JEAN, parent education administrator; b. Priest River, Idaho, Oct. 9, 1920; d. Charles Ross and Novella (Person) Randall; m. Edgar E. Payne, July 18, 1942; children: Randy, Nancy, Kathleen, Charles, Stacy. BA, East Washington U., 1942, MEd, 1968. Tchr. Rainier (Wash.) Pub. Schs., 1941-42; tchr. phys. edn. George Dewey Jr. High Sch., Bremerton, Wash., 1946; coll. dir. nursery sch. Farragut, Idaho, 1946-47; tchr. kindergarten West Valley Pub. Schs., Dishman, Washington, 1951-52, Mercer Island, Washington, 1952-53; active devel. and op. pvt. child care ctr., 1957-63; tchr. pvt. nursery sch. Community Colls. of Spokane, Mercer Island, Washington, 1964-65; developer 1st program for presch. age handicapped children Lake Washington Spl. Edn. Ctr., Kirkland, Washington, 1965-67; cons. parent edn. Lake Wash. Sch. Dist., Kirkland, Washington, 1967-68; legis. chairperson A.H.E., 1970-72; coord. family life Shoreline Community Coll., Seattle, 1968-72; dir. parent cooperative program Community Colls. of Spokane, 1973-85; mem. Gov.'s Commn. for Child Care, 1985; owner Whimsical Jean's Books. Author: We're Driving Our Kids Crazy, 1993; editor, publisher Lake Spokane News Forum. Recipient Crystal Apple award for Support for Edn. Wash. State Pub. Rels. Assn., 1995. Home: 16094 N Saddlebrook Rd Nine Mile Falls WA 99026-9352 Office: Lake Spokane News Forum/ Whimsical Jean's Books 5978 Hwy 291 # 3 Nine Mile Falls WA 99026

PAYNE, FRANCES ANNE, literature educator, researcher; b. Harrisonburg, Va., Aug. 28, 1932; d. Charles Franklin and Willie (Tarvin) P. BA, B.Mus., Shorter Coll, 1953; MA, Yale U., 1954, PhD, 1960. adj. fellow St. Anne's Coll., Oxford Eng. Instr. Conn. Coll., New London, 1955-56, U. Buffalo, 1958-60, lectr., 1960, asst. prof., 1960-67; assoc. prof. SUNY, Buffalo, 1967-75, prof. English and medieval lit., 1975—. Adj. fellow St. Anne's Coll., Oxford, Eng., 1966—. Author: King Alfred and Boethius, 1968; Chaucer and Menippean Satire, 1981. Contbr. articles to scholarly publs. AAUW fellow, Oxford, 1966-67; Research Found. grantee SUNY Central, Oxford, 1967, 68, 71, 72; recipient Julian Park award SUNY-Buffalo, 1979. Mem. Medieval Acad. Am., New Chaucer Soc., Internat. Soc. Anglo-Saxonists, Pi Kappa Lambda Office: SUNY-Buffalo 306 Clemens Hall Buffalo NY 14260-4600 E-mail: fapayne@buffalo.edu.

PAYNE, GARELD GENE, vocal music educator, medical transcriptionist; b. Colony, Okla., Aug. 27, 1931; s. Eugene A. and Agnes D. (Chastain) P.; children: Gareld, S. Raymond, Lynn Dita, Jana Lee. MusB, Oklahoma City U., 1965; MusM in Edn., North Tex. State U. (name change to U. North Tex.), 1969; ednl. specialist, Pitts. State U., 1989; EdD, Okla. State U., 2003. Ind. organist, pianist numerous nightclubs, nationwide, 1956-64; instr. vocal, instrumental music Muenster (Tex.) Ind. Sch. Dist., 1965-69; tchr. vocal music Dallas Ind. Sch. Dist., 1966-74, Carrizo Springs (Tex.) Ind. Sch. Dist., 1976-79, Coffeyville (Kans.) Unified Sch. Dist., 1979-91; tchr. elem. vocal music Oklahoma City Pub. Schs., 1996—. Rec. artist (album) Evening With Gareld, 1984; composer publ. anthems. With USAF, 1950—53. Scholar Oklahoma City U., 1949. Mem. Am. Fedn. Musicians, NEA, Am. Orff-Schulwerk Assn., Am. Recorder Soc., Am. Theater Organ Soc., Am. Guild Organist Orgns. of Am. Kodaly Educators, Phi Mu Alpha Sinfonia Frat., Phi Delta Kappa. Republican. Methodist. Avocations: astrology, oil and water color painting, cooking, reading, computers. Home: 3643 NW 15th St Oklahoma City OK 73107-4423 E-mail: pgareld_osu@brightok.net.

PAYNE, GEORGE FREDERICK, academic administrator; b. Summerville, S.C., Jan. 29, 1941; s. Fred N. and Lota (Griffith) Payne; m. Kay Martin, June 23, 1963; children: John F., Mark C., Janet E. Student, Ga. Inst. Tech., 1959-60, U.S. Naval Acad., 1960-62; BS, U. S.C., 1963, MA, 1966; MRE, Luth. Theol. Sem., 1968; postgrad., U. Ga., 1969-71; LLD (hon.), Lincoln Meml. U., 1988. Cert. fund raising exec. 2000. From instr. to asst. prof. Ga. So. Coll., Statesboro, 1966-78; dir. admission Brewton-Parker Coll., Mt. Vernon, Ga., 1978-80; v.p. devel. North Greenville Coll., Tigerville, SC, 1980-86; pres. Limestone Coll., Gaffney, SC, 1986-91, dir. various grants, 1976-91; spl. agt., registered rep. Prudential Fin. Svcs., 1991-92; dir. ITT Tech. Inst., Greenville, SC, 1992-95; exec. dir. Inst. Adv.

Greenville Tech. Coll./ Greenville Tech. Found., 1996—, GTF McAlister LLC, 2003—. Author: (book) An Introduction to the Principles of Geography: Facts, Skills, Concepts, and Models, 1973; contbr. articles to profl. jours. Active Leadership Greer, SC, 1980—81, regent, 1982—84; active AACTion Consortium, 1980—82, Leadership Greenville, 1982—83; bd. dirs. Greenville County unit Am. Cancer Soc., 1985—86; advisor Cherokee County Arts Coun., 1986—91; trustee Rolling Green Village Continuing Care Ret. Cmty., 1996—, sec., 1998, 2003; trustee Baptist Found. S.C., 2001—. With USN, 1960—62. Recipient Disting. Svc. award, Brewton-Parker Coll., 1980, North Greenville Coll., 1986. Mem.: Nat. Soc. Fund Raising Execs., Greater Greer C. of C. (bd. dirs. 1981—84), Roatry. Baptist. Avocation: reading. Office: Greenville Tech Coll PO Box 5616 Greenville SC 29606-5616 E-mail: paynegfp@GulTec.edu.

PAYNE, GLORIA MARQUETTE, business educator; b. Elkins, W.Va., Dec. 21, 1923; d. Anthony and Roselyn Marquette; m. Carl Wesley Payne, Mar. 6, 1950; 1 child, Mary Debra Payne Moore. BA, MHL (hon.), Davis and Elkins Coll.; MA, W.Va. U.; PhD, U. Pitts., 1975; postgrad., NYU Fashion Inst. Tech. Cert. designed appearance cons. Sec. Equitable Ins. Co., Elkins, 1943-44; tchr., dept. head Spencer (W.Va.) H.S., 1944-45; prof. bus. Davis & Elkins Coll., Elkins, 1945-93; image cons. Elkins, 1988-93; bus. cons., 1970-93; mgr. Elkins Wallpaper Shop, 1945-65; owner Merle Norman Cosmetic Studio, Elkins, 1950-56. Dir. tchr. workshops W.Va. U., Marshall U., State Dept. Edn., Charleston, W.Va., summers; dir. machine shorthand workshops for tchrs. throughout the U.S.; dir. designer appearance World Modeling Assn., N.Y.C., 1989—; instr. modeling Davis & Elkins Coll., 1980-93. Author: A Methods Class is Interesting and Challenging, 1970, The Oak or the Pumpkin; mem. editl. bd. Nat. Assn. of Business Teachers Edn. Pub., 1993, 94; contbr. articles to profl. jours. Chair Bi-Centennial, City of Elkins; dir. Elkins Fair, City of Elkins; pres. St. Brendans Parish; judge Mountain State Forest Festival Parades, 1988-94; rep. Region I at Dallas Nat. Conv., 1994 (one of five nat. finalists); div. chair bus., econs., and tourism. Recipient Outstanding Prof. award Sears-Roebuck Co., Lois Latham award for Excelence in Tchg., Cmty. Svc. award Elkins C. of C., 1992, Outstanding Educator award BPW, 1997, WVBEA, W.Va. Vocat. Assn., 1994, 97, Region I award for Outstanding Vocational Educator, Outstanding Collegiate Tchr. Bus. award, 1997, 1st recipient James S. McDonnell Found. Fully Endowed Acad. Chair in Bus. and Econs.; named Educator of Yr., W.Va. Women's Club, Outstanding Educator AAUW, Randolph County C. of C. Citizen of Yr., 1998. Mem. Am. Bus. Writers Assn., W.Va. Edn. Assn. (past pres., Outstanding Prof., Outstanding Svc. award, Outstanding Bus. Educator award), Tri-State Bus. Edn. Assn. (historian, outstanding svc. award, Tchr.-Educator of the South award 1991), World Modeling Assn. (v.p. 1988-95, modeling award 1989), Designed Appearance U.S. (dir. 1990-98), W.Va. Bus. Edn. Assn. (award 1977, 85, 94, 97), Bus. & Profl. Women's Orgn., W.Va. C. of C., The Fashion Club (advisor), Beta Sigma Phi (advisor), Beta Alpha Beta (advisor), Pi Beta Phi, Phi Beta Lambda (advisor). Democrat. Roman Catholic. Avocations: flower arranging, modeling. Home: 301 Davis St Elkins WV 26241-4030 Office: Davis & Elkins Coll 100 Sycamore St Elkins WV 26241-3996

PAYNE, HARRY CHARLES, historian, educator; b. Worcester, Mass., Mar. 25, 1947; BA, MA, Yale U., 1969, PhD, 1973, MPhil, 1970; degree (hon.), Hamilton Coll., 1988, Colgate U., 1989, Williams Coll., 1993, Amherst Coll., 1994, U. of the South, 1997. Mem. faculty Colgate U., Hamilton, NY, 1973—82, prof. history, 1982—85; provost, acting pres. Haverford Coll., Pa., 1985—88; pres. Hamilton Coll., Clinton, NY, 1988—93, Williams Coll., Williamstown, Mass., 1994—99, Woodward Acad., College Park, Ga., 2000—. Contbr. scientific papers. Bd. dirs. Barnard Coll. Fellow Overseas fellow, Churchill Coll., Cambridge U., Eng., 1977. Mem.: Am. Coun. Edn., Am. Soc. 18th-Century Studies (pres. 1984—85, Article prize 1977). Office: Woodward Acad 1662 Rugby Ave College Park GA 30337-2199

PAYNE, JOYCE TAYLOR GILLENWATER, art specialist, art museum consultant, educator; b. Charleston, W.Va., Oct. 4, 1932; d. Clyde Matthew and Bessie Francis (Summers) Taylor; m. Jack W. Gillenwater, Aug. 26, 1950 (div. Mar. 1980); children: Jack William Gillenwater Jr., Brenda Joyce Gillenwater, Kevin David Gillenwater, Todd Gregory Gillenwater; m. Roy B. Payne Jr., Mar. 19, 1982. BS cum laude, W.Va. State Coll., Institute, 1969; MA in Art Supervision, W.Va. U., 1976, postgrad., 1976-89. Tchr. art Herbert Hoover H.S., Elkview, W.Va., 1970-71, Andrew Jackson Jr. H.S., Cross Lanes, W.Va., 1971-90; art specialist Cabell County Bd. Edn., Huntington, W.Va., 1990-94; instr. art edn. Shawnee State U., Portsmouth, Ohio, 1994—2003. Mem. adv. bd. W.V.a Bd. Edn., Charleston, 1986-87, Kanawha County Bd. Edn., Charleston, 1986. Artist, working in painting, sculpture, pottery, fiber works. Mem. NEA (rep.), W.Va. Edn. Assn., W.Va. Art Edn. Assn., Kanawha County Tchrs. Assn., Kanawha County Art Edn. Assn., Cabell County Tchrs. Assn., Nat. Art Edn. Assn. Avocations: scuba diving, art works, reading, travel. Home: 283 Oakwood Ave Portsmouth OH 45663-8908 E-mail: royb@zoomnet.net.

PAYNE, LISA MOSSMAN, middle school educator; b. Chula Vista, Calif., May 9, 1966; d. William George Jr. and Lynne (Burke) Mossman; m. Charles Alan Payne, June 2, 1990; children: Molly Alexandra, Max Emerson. BA in English, U. Calif., Irvine, 1988; MA in English, Chapman U., 1990. Cert. jr. coll. tchr., Calif. Tchr. Chapman U., Orange, Calif., 1989-90, Orange Coast Coll., Costa Mesa, Calif., 1990, Riverside (Calif.) C.C., 1990; tchr. English, head dept. St. John's Sch., Rancho Santa Margarita, Calif., 1990-94, dir. middle sch. summer program, 1993. Leader Jr. Great Books Found., Chgo., 1992—; mem. Middle Sch. Restructuring Team, 1993; Library Accreditation Team, 1993-94. Author curriculua in field; writer children's books. Mem. Soc. Children's Bookwriters and Illustrators. Avocations: star trekking, coffee, world mythology, middle ages, drama. Home: 17632 Jordan Ave Apt 37B Irvine CA 92612-2933

PAYNE, LUCY ANN SALSBURY, law librarian, educator, lawyer; b. Utica, N.Y., July 5, 1952; d. James Henry and Dorothy Eileen (Seavy) Salsbury; m. Albert E. Payne, June 2, 1973 (div. 1983); 1 child, Joni Eileen. MusB, Andrews U., 1974; MA, Loma Linda (Calif.) U., 1979; JD, U. Notre Dame, Ind., 1988; MLS, U. Mich., 1990. Bar: Ind. 1988, Mich. 1988, U.S. Dist. Ct. (no. and so. dists.) Ind. 1988, U.S. Ct. Appeals (7th cir.) 1992. Rsch. specialist Kresge Libr. Law Sch. U. Notre Dame, 1988—90, asst. libr., 1990—91, assoc. libr., 1991—96, libr., 1996—2002. Vis. prof. Notre Dame London Law Programme, 2001. Contbr. articles to profl. jours. Recipient Rev. Paul J. Foik award, 2001, Commitment award Notre Dame Black Student Law Assn., 2002. Adventist. Home and Office: 4420 Barrett NW Albuquerque NM 87114

PAYNE, MICHAEL DAVID, English language educator; b. Dallas, Jan. 17, 1941; s. Fred G. Payne and Jocie Marie (Kirkham) Lundberg; children: Jeffrey, Jennifer, Albert, Edward. Student, U. Calif.-Berkeley, 1958-59, 61; BA, So. Oreg. Coll., 1962; PhD, U. Oreg., 1969. Tchr. English, Medford (Oreg.) Sr. High Sch., 1962-63; instr. English, U. Oreg., Eugene, 1963-69; asst. prof. to prof. English, Bucknell U., Lewisburg, Pa., 1969—, chmn. dept. history, 1980-82, chmn. dept. English, 1982-88, 92-94, chair faculty, 2000—, Presdl. prof., 1982-86, John P. Crozer prof. English lit., 1986—, chmn. faculty, 1999—; dir. Bucknell Univ. Press, 1972-76; assoc. editor Bucknell Rev., 1970-85, editor, 1985-88. Author: Irony in Shakespeare's Roman Plays, 1974, Reading Theory, 1993, Reading Knowledge, 1997; editor: Contemporary Essays on Style, 1969, Shakespeare: Contemporary Critical Approaches, 1979, Text, Interpretation, Theory, 1985, Self, Sign and Symbol, 1986, Perspective, 1986, Criticism, History and Intertextuality, 1987, New Interpretations of American Literature, 1987, The Senses of Stanley Cavell, 1988, Blackwell Dictionary of Cultural and Critical Theory, 1996, Renaissance Literature: An Anthology, 2003, Life.after.theory, 2003; gen. editor Bucknell Lectures in Lit. Theory, 1990-95. Recipient Lindback award for disting. teaching, 1976, Disting. Svc. award CEA, 1988, Profl. Achievement award, 1993; Folger Shakespeare Libr. fellow, 1973, NEH fellow, 1974, Bucknell Alumni fellow, 1978-79. Mem.: MLA, Children's Lit. Assn., Coll. English Assn., Inst. Romance Studies (U. London), Johnson Soc. London, Phi Beta Kappa (hon.). Home: 9 Market St Apt A Lewisburg PA 17837-1562 E-mail: payne@bucknell.edu.

PAYNE, NANCY SLOAN, retired visual arts educator; b. Johnstown, Pa., Aug. 5, 1937; d. Arthur J. and Esther Jenkins (Ashcom) Sloan; m. Randolph Allen Payne, Nov. 19, 1970; 1 child, Anna Sloan. BS in Art Edn., Pa. State U., 1959; MFA in Sculpture, George Washington U., 1981. Visual arts tchr. Alexandria (Va.) Schs., 1960-61; art tchr. sch. program Corcoran Gallery of Art, Washington, 1962; visual arts tchr. Montgomery County Schs., Rockville, Md., 1965-67; instr. No. Va. C.C., Alexandria, 1971-73, Mt. Vernon Coll., Washington, 1971-73; visual arts tchr. Arlington (Va.) County Schs., 1967-79; edn. coord. The Textile Mus., Washington, 1982-87; mid. sch. visual arts tchr., K-12 dept. chair St. Stephen's and St. Agnes Sch., Alexandria, 1988-97; ret. Co-founder Fiber Art Study Group, Washington, 1988—; co-owner Art Gallery, Chincoteague Island, Va., 1989—. Exhibited in group shows at Craftsmen's Biennial Va. Commonwealth U. (Excellence in Textiles award), 1973, Va. Craftsmen Biennial The Va. Mus., 1980, Creative Crafts Coun. 15th Biennial, 1982, Alexandria's Sculpture Festival, 1983, 84, 13 Fiber Artists Exhbn. Foundry Gallery, Washington, 1985. Founding mem. Alexandria Soc. for Preservation Black Heritage, Alexandria, 1982—. Mem. Nat. Art Edn. Assn. Democrat. Avocations: growing flowers, collecting hub caps, McDonald toys, and polit./campaign items. Home: 6258 Circle Dr Chincoteague Island VA 23336-2222 Office: Clouds/Folly Gallery Chincoteague Island VA 23336

PAYSON, MARTIN SAUL, secondary school educator, mathematician; b. N.Y.C., May 18, 1945; s. Harry and Beatrice Clare (Garber) P.; m. Joan Patricia Thompson, Sept. 11, 1969 (div. 1983); 1 child, Susan Elizabeth; m. Ilene Debbie Gellman, Apr. 10, 1983; 1 child, Howard Jeffrey. BA in Philosophy, Monmouth Coll., 1969; MS in Elem. Edn., CUNY, 1975. Tchr. math. Frederick Douglass Intermediate Sch., N.Y.C., 1970-84, John Philip Sousa Jr. H.S., Bronx, N.Y., 1984-91; leader math. team John Philip Souxa Jr. H.S., Bronx, N.Y., 1990-91; tchr. math. Michael Angelo Mid. Sch., Bronx, 1991—, Pub. Sch. #89, Bronx, 1998—2002; ret., 2002. Asst. head philosophy dept. Monmouth (Ill.) Coll., 1968-69. N.Y. State Edn. Dept. Regents scholar, 1963. Mem. Assn. Math. Tchrds. N.Y. State, Nat. Coun. Tchrs. Math., United Fedn. Tchrs. N.Y.C. Avocations: sports, camping, fishing, gardening, duplicate bridge. Home: 42 Chief Ninham Dr Carmel NY 10512-3624 Office: Michael Angelo Mid Sch 2545 Gunther Ave Bronx NY 10469-6105

PAYUK, EDWARD WILLIAM, elementary education educator; b. St. Louis, July 19, 1948; s. Stanley Eli and Lillian (Bluestein) P.; m. Pamela Karen Miller, Sept. 5, 1970 (div. Oct. 1986); children: Stacy Lynne, Lori Michelle; m. Judith Ann Cohen, Dec. 4, 1986; stepchildren: Jeffrey Alan Kieffer, Kimberly Beth Kieffer. AA, Meramec C.C., St. Louis, 1969; BS, U. Mo., St. Louis, 1971; MA, Webster U., 1973, postgrad., 1976. Tchr. Ferguson-Florissant Sch. Dist., St. Louis, 1971-2001, lang. arts com. dist. level, 1997—2001; prof. geology St. Charles CC, St. Peters, Md., 2001—03, prof. coll. enhancement, 2003—; Purina Product cons., educator Nestle-Purina Quality Mktg., Fresno, Calif., 2002—. Tutor, St. Louis, 1984-91. Contbr. articles to profl. jours. Sci. literacy com. St. Louis Sci. Acad., 1991—; rep. Tchrs., Industry & Environment Conf., Jefferson City, Mo., 1995; mem. Little Creek Nature Study Adv. Com., 1997. With U.S. Army, 1969-70. Mem. NEA, Mo. Edn. Assn., Ferguson-Florissant Edn. Assn. Jewish. Avocation: collector of einsteinia. Home: 13660 Amiot Dr Saint Louis MO 63146-3608 E-mail: epayuk@yahoo.com., epayuk@swbell.net.

PAZ, HAROLD LOUIS, dean, medical educator, internist; b. N.Y.C., Jan. 3, 1955; BA in Biology and Psychology, U. Rochester, 1977, MD, 1982; MS in Life Sci. Engring., Tufts U., 1979. Diplomate subspecialty in pulmonary medicine Am. Bd. Internal Medicine. Intern in internal medicine Northwestern U. Med. Ctr., Chgo., 1982—83, resident in internal medicine, 1983—85, chief med. resident, 1985—86; instr. clin. medicine Northwestern U., Chgo., 1985—86; fellow in pulmonary and critical care Johns Hopkins U., Balt., 1986—88, fellow in environ. health scis., 1986—88; asst. prof. medicine Hahnemann U., Phila., 1988—92, asst. prof. anesthesia, 1989—92, assoc. dean grad. med. edn., 1992—94, assoc. prof. medicine, 1992—94, dir. med. ICU, 1988—94, assoc. hosp. med. dir., 1992—94, dir. Ctr. for Clin. Outcomes, 1992—94; med. dir., assoc. dean for clin. affairs, assoc. prof. U. Medicine and Dentistry N.J. Robert Wood Johnson Med. Sch., New Brunswick, 1994—95, dean, CEO, assoc. prof. medicine, 1995—. Editor: Jour. Undergrad. Rsch., 1976, Med. Staff News newsletter, 1992—94; cons.: Annals Internal Medicine, Clin. Immunology and Immunopathology, Chest, Intensive Care Medicine, Physician Execs., N.Y. State Med. Jour., mem. editl. bd.: Jour. Disease Mgmt. and Clin. Outcomes, 1996—, Chest, 1998—. Recipient Disting. Svc. award, Motolinsky Rsch. Found., 1998, Cmty. Leaders of Distinction award, County C. of C., 1999; Eudowood fellow, Johns Hopkins U., 1987—88, U. Rochester scholar, 1979. Fellow: ACP, Am. Coll. Chest Physicians; mem.: AMA, Laennec Soc. (pres. 1994—95), Philip Drinker Soc. for Critical Care (pres. 1992—94), Am. Thoracic Soc. Office: UMDNJ Robert Wood Johnson Med Sch 125 Paterson St New Brunswick NJ 08901-1962

PAZNOKAS, LYNDA SYLVIA, elementary and middle school education educator; b. Portland, Oreg., Feb. 19, 1950; d. Marley Elmo and Undine Sylvia (Crockard) Sims. BA, Wash. State U., 1972; MS, Portland State U., 1975; EdD, Oreg. State U., 1984. Cert. tchr., Oreg. Tchr. 5th grade, outdoor sch. specialist Clover Park Sch. Dist. 400, Tacoma, 1971-72; tchr. 6th grade, outdoor sch. specialist Hillsboro (Oreg.) elem. Dist. 7, 1972-78, Bend (Oreg.)-La Pine Sch. Dist., 1978-82, elem. curriculum specialist, 1983-85, tchr. 4th grade gifted and talented, 1985-90; grad. teaching asst. Oreg. State U., Corvallis, 1982-84; asst. prof., assoc. prof. No. Ariz. U., 1990-99, chair instnl. leadership, 1997-98; Boeing disting. prof. sci. edn. Wash. State U., Pullman, 1999—. Ednl. cons., tchr. workshops, 1973—; presenter workshop Soviet-Am. Joint Conf., Moscow State U., 1991, Meeting of Children's Culture Promoters, Guadalajara, Mex., 1994, Internat. Conf. Sci., Tech. and Math. Edn. for Human Devel., UNESCO, Panaji, India, 2001, Nishinomiya Joint Rsch. Conf., Japan, 2001, and others; faculty Ariz. Journey Schs. for Math. and Sci. Tchg. Improvement; coord. Odyssey of the Mind, Bend, 1985-89, tchr.-mentor program for 1st-yr. tchrs., Beaverton, Oreg., 1982-83; presenter Social Edn. Assn. of Australia, 1997. Author: Pathways of America: Lewis and Clark, 1993, Pathways of America: The Oregon Trail, 1993, Pathways of America: The California Gold Rush Trail, 1994, Pathways of America: The Santa Fe Trail, 1995, Fifty States, 1997, U.S. Presidents, 1997, U.S. Map Skills, 1997, Human body, 1998, National Parks and Other Park Service Sites, 1999, Our National Parks, 1999, Pathways of America: The California Mission Trail, 2000, Circling the World: Festivals and Celebrations, 2000, Endangered Species, 2001; contbr. articles to profl. jours. Vol., leader, bd. dirs. Girl Scouts U.S., 1957—; elder First Presbyn. Ch., Bend, 1980—; vol. hist. interpretation High Desert Mus., Bend, 1987-91; docent Mus. No. Ariz.; pres. bd. dirs. The Arboretum at Flagstaff; sec. bd. dirs., pres. bd. dirs. Palouse Discovery Sci. Ctr., 2000—, past pres. Arboretum bd.; mem. Ptnrs. Achieving Leadership in Sci., Wash., D.C., Leadership and Assistance for Sci. Edn. Reform, Wash., D.C. Recipient Excellence in Teaching award Bend Found., 1985-86, 86-87; named Tchr. Yr. Oreg. Dept. Edn., 1982, Higher Edn. Tchr. Yr., Wash. Sci. Tchrs. Assn. (WSTA), 2003; Celebration Teaching grantee Geraldine Rockefeller Dodge Found., 1989, 90, 91, 92, 93, 94, 95, EPA grantee, 1997-99, Eisenhower Math and Sci. Edn. Act grantee, 1997, 99, Grand Canyon Assn. grantee, 1996, 97, 98; commd. Ky. Col., 1993. Mem. NEA, Internat. Coun. Assns. Sci. Edn. (newsletter advisor), Nat. Coun. Tchrs. Math., NSTA (past mem. nat. supervision com., internat. com.), Nat. State Tchrs. of Yr. (nat. pres. 1988-90), Nat. Assn. Rsch. in Sci. Tchg., Oreg. Coun. Tchrs. Math. (bd. dirs. 1981-82), Oreg. Coun. Tchrs. English (bd. dirs. 1981-82), Ariz. Reading Assn. (bd. dirs.), Nat. Coun. for Social Studies, Coun. for Elem. Sci. Internat. (bd. dirs. 1995-98, 99—, chair informal edn. com.), Internat. Reading Assn., Oreg.-Calif. Trails Assn., Nat. Sci. Edn. Leadership Assn., Assn. for Edn. of Tchrs. in Sci., Nat. Assn. for Rsch. in Sci. Tchg., Assn. for Sci. Edn., N.W. Oreg.-Calif. Trails Assn., Lewis and Clark Trail Heritage Found., Delta Kappa Gamma (1st v.p.), Phi Delta Kappa (found. rep. 1991-92, v.p. programs 1992-93, historian 1993-94, v.p. membership 1994-95), Golden Key Hon., Pi Lambda Theta, Phi Kappa Phi, Phi Epsilon Omicron (corr. sec.), Kappa Delta Pi (chpt. counselor, mem. spkrs. bur., nat. Web com., sci. specialist), others. Avocations: cross-country skiing, photography, hiking, researching immigrant trails, gardening. Home: 101 Enman-Kincaid Rd Pullman WA 99163 E-mail: lpaznokas@wsu.edu.

PEA, ROY, education educator; BA in Philosophy and Psychology, Mich. State U., 1974; DPhil Oxon. in Developmental Psychology, Oxford (Eng.) U., 1978. NIMH postdoctoral fellow psycholinguistics Rockefeller U., 1978—79; asst. prof. psychology Clark U., 1979—81; assoc. dir. Ctr. for Children and Tech., Bank St. Coll. Edn., 1984—86, sr. rsch. scientist, 1981—86, Inst. for Rsch. on Learning, 1988—91; John Evans prof. edn. an dlearning scis. Northwestern U., 1991—96, dean Sch. Edn. and Social Policy, 1992—96; dir. Ctr. for Tech. in Learning SRI Internat., 1996—2001; prof. edn. and learning scis. Stanford (Calif.) U., 2001—. Co-founder Teachscape, 1999, bd. dirs.; established, dir. Stanford Ctr. for Innovations in Learning. Office: Stanford U Sch Edn 485 Lasuen Mall Stanford CA 94305-3096*

PEABODY, DEBBIE KAY, elementary school educator; b. Wooster, Ohio, Apr. 9, 1954; d. Walter L. and Carolyn E. (Lee) Mussatto; m. David Leslie Peabody, Jan. 6, 1973; children: Dawn Kathleen, Lesli Kay. BS in Elem. Edn., Southwestern Adventist Coll., Keene, Tex., 1986. Cert. tchr. K-8, Ariz. Head tchr. SDA Elem. Sch., Camp Verde, Ariz., 1986-89; tchr. 6th grade Roosevelt Sch. Dist., Phoenix, 1989-93, jr. high reading tchr., 1993-94, collaborative peer tchr., 1994-96, 2d grade tchr., 1996-97, 3d grade tchr. Cologne model, 1997—. Dist. assessment plan co-chair Roosevelt Sch. Dist., 1993—; mem. Greater Phoenix Curriculum Coun. Dist. Assessment Plan Writing Team, 1994—; CHAMPS coord. Sunland Elem. Sch., Phoenix, 1991-94. Co-author: (activity book) Explosion of ASAP Activities, 1994. Recipient Edn. of Merit award Southwestern Union Coll., 1985, 86. Mem. ASCD, NEA, Ariz. Edn. Assn., Roosevelt Edn. Assn., Nat. Coun. Tchrs. Math. Avocations: quilting, embroidery, biking, hiking, canoeing. Office: Southwest School 1111 W Dobson Phoenix AZ 85041

PEABODY, MERLE ANDREW, education educator; b. Stoneham, Mass., May 21, 1944; s. Warren Marcus and Dorothy Isabella (Oliver) P.; m. Alice Antoinette Sardegna, Sept. 29, 1979; 1 child, Amy Star. BS in Edn., Northeastern U., Boston, 1972; MA in Teaching History, Bridgewater (Mass.) State Coll, 1989. Permanent substitute Melrose (Mass.) Pub. Schs., 1971-81, Stoneham (Mass.) Pub. Schs., 1973-76, 79-81; social studies and English tchr. Bethel Christian Acad., Rockland, Mass., 1981-94, asst. prin., 1992-94, mem. governance mgmt. team, 1993-94. Adj. prof. history, philosophy and polit. sci. Quincy (Mass.) Coll., 2000—; substitute tchr. Middleboro Pub. Schs., Freetown-Lakeville Regional Sch. Sys., Bristol County Agrl. Sch., 1994—. Mem. Middleboro (Mass.) Hist. Commn., 1988-99—. Sgt. Mass. N.G., 1962-68. Mem. Orgn. Am. Historians, New Eng. History Tchrs. Assn., Mass. Coun. for the Social Studies, Old Colony Hist. Soc., Middleboro Hist. Assn., Phi Alpha Theta. Republican. Baptist. Avocation: reading.

PEACE, BARBARA LOU JEAN, education educator; b. Valdosta, Ga., Jan. 11, 1939; d. Billington Philip and Hattie Lougene (Dollar) Peace. Student, Valdosta State Coll., 1956-58; BA in English, Tenn. Temple U., 1961; postgrad., Fla. State U., 1962-63; MS in Indsl. and Orgnl. Psychology, Valdosta State U., 1994. Receptionist ITT, Thompson Industries, Valdosta, Ga., 1961; child welfare worker Lowndes County Welfare Dept., Valdosta, 1961-62; supr. child welfare divsn. Muscogee County Dept. Family & Children Services, Columbus, Ga., 1963-66; dir. social work Valdosta-Lowndes County Headstart Program, 1966-67; tchr. English & Remedial Reading Valdosta City Sch. System, 1966-73; tchr. advisor English & Psychology Valdosta Technical Inst., 1973—; chmn. dept. psychology Valdosta Tech. Inst., 1994—. Chair South Ga. Consortium Psychology Tchrs., 1994-95; advisor Vocat. Indsl. Clubs Am., 1981-88, 90—, adv. coun., 1982-86, planning com. regional leadership conf., 1984, coord. state leadership contests, state advisor officer tng., presenter leadership confs., 1986; advisor Valdosta Tech. Inst. 1981-88, 90—, quality coun. mem. 1994, quality coun. team leader 1995-96, chair blood drive, 1994-95; past vica craft adv. bd. Valdosta H.S., Lowndes H.S. Sponsor ARC Blood Drive, Valdosta, 1984-88, Ga. Sheriffs' Boys' Ranch, Arts, Inc.; vol. Am. Heart Assn., Am. Lung Assn., 1994—; contbr. Am. Cancer Soc., United Way; active personnel, finance, nominating and kindergarten and kitchen coms. Azalea City Bapt. Ch., adult choir, dir. children's choir, tchr. Sunday Sch., nursery worker; bd. dirs., pianist, advisor/counsellor, tutor Valdosta Korean Bapt. Ch., 1985-92. Mem. Am. Vocational Assn., Ga. Vocational Assn., Vocat. Ga. Assn., Vocational Edn. Spl. Needs Personnel, Action Travelers (bd. dirs. 1970—), Adventuretour Exchange Club (sponsor 1981-85). Republican. Baptist. Avocations: traveling, music, stamp collecting, gourmet cooking. Office: Valdosta Tech Inst 4089 Val Tech Rd Valdosta GA 31602-0929

PEACOCK, CHARLES H. agricultural studies educator; From asst. to assoc. prof. turfgrass sci. U. Fla., extension turfgrass specialist; sr. agronomist Anheuser-Busch Co.; prof. Agriculture N.C. State U., Raleigh. Fellow Nat. Assn. Colls. Tchrs. Agriculture 1992. Office: N C State U Dept Crop Sci Williams Hall 1215 PO Box 7620 Raleigh NC 27695-7620*

PEACOCK, JANIE JOAN, retired elementary school educator; b. Saltillo, Miss., Apr. 28, 1932; d. Henry Oliver and Lillie Belle (Moffitt) Branyan; m. Hugh Clarence Peacock Jr., Aug. 26, 1956; children: Hugh Christopher, Alan Branyan. BA in History, Miss. Coll., 1954; MRE, So. Bapt. Sem., 1956; MEd, U. Ga., 1973; EdS, Ga. State U., 1987. Tchr. 1st grade Jefferson County Schs., Louisville, 1956-59; tchr. English and social studies Bremen (Ga.) City Schs., 1959-60; tchr. 5th grade Rome (Ga.) City Schs., 1971-72; tchr. lang. arts Darlington Sch., Rome, 1973-74, West Point (Ga.) City Schs., 1974-75, LaGrange (Ga.) Acad., 1975-86; mid. sch. tchr. LaGrange City Schs., 1987-94, Troup County Schs., 1994-98, ret., 1998. Treas. Kaluska Garden Club, West Point, 1974-87; pres. Ga. Bapt. Min.'s Wives; moderator-elect Ga. Coop. Bapt. Fellowship, 1995-96, moderator, 1996-97. Mem. NEA, AAUW, Nat. Coun. Tchrs. of English, Ga. Assn. Educators, Assembly on Adolescent Lit., Delta Kappa Gamma Soc. (pres. Beta Mu chpt. 1992). Democrat. Avocations: music, sewing, needlework, reading.

PEACOCK, MARILYN CLAIRE, primary education educator; b. Harvey, Ill., Aug. 2, 1952; d. Carmen Anthony and Helen Elaine (Welch) R. AA with high honors, Thornton C.C., 1972; BS in Edn. with high honors, Ill. State U., 1974; MEd, Nat.-Louis U., 1990. Cert. K-9, Ill. Tchr. kindergarten Primary Acad. Ctr., Markham, Ill., 1976-91, tchr. K-3, 1991—. Ill. State scholar, 1969. Mem. Ill. Edn. Assn. (assn. rep. 1976-88), Kappa Delta Pi, Phi Theta Kappa. Republican. Avocations: music, travel. Home: 2447 Clyde St Homewood IL 60430-3103 Office: Acad Ctr 3055 W 163rd St Markham IL 60426-5626 E-mail: mcrpeacock@hotmail.com.

PEAKE, FRANK, middle school educator; b. Elgin, S.C., Oct. 25, 1939; s. Barney and Elrie (Branham) P. AA, Anderson Coll., 1966; BS, U. S.C., 1968; MA in Teaching, The Citadel, 1976. Cert. tchr., S.C. Classroom tchr. Berkeley Jr. High, Moncks Corner, S.C., 1968-70, Berkeley Middle Sch., Moncks Corner, 1970-85, 90-95, ret., 1995; classroom tchr. Macedonia Middle Sch., Moncks Corner, 1986-88, North Ctrl. High, Kershaw, S.C., 1988-89. With S.C. Air Nat. Guard, 1959-65. Mem. Nat. Coun. Tchrs. Math., Mensa. Republican. Baptist. Avocations: reading, gardening. Home: 1201 Peake Rd Elgin SC 29045

PEAL, CHRISTOPHER JOHN, educational administrator; b. Moline, Ill., Dec. 17, 1963; s. Gerald J. and Annette M. Peal. BA, Olivet Nazarene U., 1986; MA, U. Mich., 1989; PhD, Loyola U., 1996. Cert. supt., adminstr., tchr., Ill., Mich. English, lang. arts, speech, journalism tchr., newspaper advisor Plymouth-Canton High Sch., Mich., 1986-90; asst. prin. Muskegon Catholic Ctrl. Jr./High Sch., Mich., 1990-91; dean students Canton Mid. Sch., Streamwood, Ill., 1991-94; prin. North Elem. Sch., Watervliet, Mich., 1994-97, Mary Helen Guest Elem. Sch., Walled Lake, Mich., 1998—. Mem. Watervliet Sch. Improvement Team, 1994-97; mem. Elgin (Ill.) Sch. Dist. U-46 Mid. Sch. Task Force, 1991-94; advisor to student newspaper, adj. instr. Lake Mich. Coll., 1997; mem. Mary Helen Guest Elem. Sch. PTA, 1998—; mem. Walled Lake Consolidated Schs. Adminstrs. Assn., 1998—, mem. exec. bd., 2000—; mem. Mary Helen Guest Elem. Sch. North Ctrl. Accreditation Team, 1998—; chair Walled Lake Schs. Strategic Safety Plan, 2003-. Mem. Watervliet PTO, 1994-97; short-term missionary work, Turkey, 2000, China, 2001. Recipient Spl. Tribute award State of Mich., 1987, Gold Apple Teaching Excellence award Wayne County (Mich.) Intermediate Sch. Dist., 1987, 88, 89, Dist. Svc. award Walled Lake PTA, 2003; dean's merit fellow U. Mich., 1987, 88, Dow Jones Newspaper Fund fellow, 1988. Mem. ASCD, Mich. Elem. and Mid. Sch. Prins. Assn., Nat. Assn. Elem. Sch. Prins., Mich. Interscholastic Press Assn. (judge 1988-90), Columbia Scholastic Press Assn. (bd. judges 1987-90, conv. speaker), Gt. Lakes Interscholastic Press Assn. (judge 1988-90), Journalism Edn. Assn., U. Mich. Alumni Assn. (life), Walled Lake Colson. Schs. Adminstrs. Assn. (exec. bd. 2000—), Gallileo Leadership Consortium. Avocations: antiquing, computers, golf. Office: Mary Helen Guest Elem Sch 1655 Decker Rd Walled Lake MI 48390-2627

PEARCE, BELINDA ALLEN, elementary reading recovery educator; b. Clinton, Ky., May 16, 1951; d. Billie Todd and Ramona (Boswell) Allen; m. Woody D. Pearce, Aug. 23, 1970; children: Kristie Michaela, Jessica Lynne. BS in Elem. Edn., Blue Mountain Bapt. Coll. Women, 1972; MEd in Elem. Edn., U. So. Miss., 1976; postgrad., Jackson State U., 1995. 3d grade tchr. Rienzi (Miss.) Sch., 1972-73; 5th and 6th grade reading tchr. Hancock North Ctrl. Elem. Sch., Pass Christian, Miss., 1973-74, 3d and 4th grade reading tchr., 1974-75, 3d grade tchr., 1975-79, North Bay Elem. Sch., Bay St. Louis, Miss., 1979-86; 2d grade tchr. Waveland Elem. Sch., Bay St. Louis, Miss., 1986-94; Chpt. I reading recovery tchr. North Bay Elem. Sch., 1994-99; tchr. 3d grade Charles B. Murphy Elem. Sch., Pearlington, Miss., 1999—2001; spl. populations coord. Hancock County Vocat. Sch., Kiln, Miss., 2001—. Dept. chmn. Hancock North Ctrl. Elem. Sch., Waveland Elem. Sch. Vol. Bible sch. tchr. First Bapt. Ch., Brazil, summer 1989. Mem. Miss. Profl. Educators, Miss. Edn. Assn. (numerous offices), Reading Recovery Coun. N.Am. Avocations: swimming (tchr. Red Cross lessons), walking, reading. Home: 916 Victoria St Waveland MS 39576-2635

PEARCE, ROBERT BRENT, agricultural studies educator; BS, U. Calif., 1963; MS, Va. Polytechnic Inst., 1965, PhD, 1967. Prof. agr. Iowa State U., Ames, prof. agr. emeritus, 1999—. Fellow Nat. Assn. Colls. Tchrs. Agriculture, 1992. Office: Iowa State U Dept Agronomy 120 Agronomy Ames IA 50011-0001*

PEARCY, LEE THERON, secondary education educator, writer; b. Little Rock, Aug. 20, 1947; s. Lee Theron and Janet Gillum (Jackson) P.; m. Kathryn Ellen Eyre, Aug. 15, 1970; children: Benjamin Theron, Sarah Gillum. BA, Columbia U., 1969, MA, 1971; PhD, Bryn Mawr Coll., 1974. Tchr. Englewood (N.J.) Sch. for Boys, 1969-71; asst. prof. St. Olaf Coll., Northfield, Minn., 1973-77, U. Tex., Austin, 1977-85; tchr., chmn. dept. classics Episcopal Acad., Merion, Pa., 1985-2001, dir. curriculum, 2001—. Author: Mediated Muse, 1984, Shorter Homeric Hymns, 1989, New First Steps in Latin, 2000; asst. editor Classical World, 1993-2000, assoc. editor, 2000-; founding editor Ancient Medicine/Medicina Antiqua, 1996—; contbr. articles, revs. and poetry to scholarly jours. Fellow Am. Coun. Learned Socs., 1979; tchr.-scholar NEH, 1990-91. Mem. Am. Philol. Assn., Soc. for Promotion Roman Studies, Classical Assn. Atlantic States (pres. 1996-97), Soc. for Ancient Medicine. Methodist. Avocations: tennis, squash, fishing, cycling, walking. Home: 223 Upland Rd Merion Station PA 19066-1821 Office: Episcopal Acad 376 N Latches Ln Merion Station PA 19066-1797 E-mail: lpearcy@ea1785.org.

PEARLMAN, ALISON, art educator; b. W. Long Br., N.J., Oct. 7, 1968; d. Daniel David Pearlman and Paula Itaya. AB, U. Calif., Berkeley, 1990; MA, U. Chgo., 1991, PhD with departmental honors, 1997. Asst. curator Mus. Contemporary Art, Chgo., 1998—2001; mem. faculty Art Ctr. Coll. Design, Pasadena, Calif., 2001—. Freelance editor, 2001—. Fellow Am. Art, Henry Luce Found./Am. Coun. Learned Socs., 1994, Chgo. Humanities Inst. Dissertation fellow, U. Chgo., 1995. Mem.: Assn. Art Editors, Coll. Art Assn. Home: 1750 N Harvard Blvd Hollywood CA 90027

PEARLMAN, BARBARA, artist, educator; b. N.Y.C., Apr. 25, 1938; d. Henry and Edith (Stein) P.; 1 child, Alexandre Yulish. BA, Parsons Sch. Design, 1960. Illustrator Neiman Marcus, Dallas, 1960-61, Vogue, Marie Claire, France, Eng., Germany, 1961-65, Galey & Lord, N.Y.C., 1965-78, Vogue, Harpers, N.Y. Mag., Glamour, N.Y. Art, N.Y.C., 1965-78; tchr. Parsons Sch. Design, N.Y.C., 1975-79, Fashion Inst. Tech., N.Y.C., 1979-95, Nassau Fine Arts Mus., 1980-81. Spkr. NYU Phenomenology in the Arts. Exhbns. N.Y.C., Germany, 1978-95; featured in Russian and Polish mags.; works featured in History of Fashion (Eunic Sloane), numerous others; contbr. articles to Gebracht Graphic mag. Recipient award Soc. Illustrators, 1976, 69, 70. Mem. Nat. Orgn. Women Artists. Home: 2259 Edsall Ave Bronx NY 10463-6202

PEARLMAN, MITZI ANN, elementary education educator; b. Houston, July 21, 1951; d. Bernard Joseph and Annie Mae (Gollob) P. BA in Sociology, U. Colo., Boulder, 1975; MA in Elem. Edn., U. Colo., Denver, 1988. Cert. elem. tchr., Colo. Tchr. 2d grade Cherry Creek Schs., Englewood, Colo., 1987-88; tchr. 2d and 3d grades Douglas County Schs., Castle Rock, Colo., 1988-2000. Vol. Denver Zoo. Recipient Douglas County NOVA awards for Creative Excellence in Teaching, 1988, 89, 90, 91, 92, Innovative Instrn. award Bus. Week mag., 1990, Douglas County Edn. Found. grants, 1993, 97, 98, Pub. Svc. Intergenerational grant, 1993, Classroom Connection Disseminator grants, 1992, 93, 2000Classroom Connection Adaptor grants, 1992, 93, 94, 95, 96, 97, 98, Douglas County mini grant, 1989; named Channel 7 Tchr. of the Week, 1993. Mem. Internat. Reading Assn., Douglas County Reading Assn. (treas. 1992-94), Colo. Assn. Sci. Tchrs., Phi Delta Kappa. Avocations: reading, pets, relaxing, travel. Office: Wheeling Elem Sch 472 S Wheeling Dr Aurora CO 80012

PEARMAN, REGINALD JAMES, educational administrator; b. N.Y.C., May 23, 1923; s. William H. Astoria Arabell (Webb) P.; children: Jeanita, Lydia, Reginald. B.S., NYU, 1950; Ed.D., U. Mass., 1974. Cert. tchr., N.Y. Tchr., N.Y.C. Pub. Schs., 1951-55, supr., 1955-62; with Fgn. Service, State Dept., Caracas, Venezuela, 1962-65, Peace Corps, Washington, 1965-67, AID, Washington, 1967-69; dir. job devel. N.Y.C. Human Resources Adminstrn., 1969-71; ednl. program specialist U.S. Dept. Edn., Washington, 1971-74; mem. adv. com. women's equity U.S. Office of Edn., 1974, task force arts and humanities, 1975-76, task force edn. of gifted, 1976-77, basic edn., 1977, urban edn., 1978, pub. sch. adminstrn., 1979; mem. adv. bd. internship program Am. Pub. Transit Assn., 1977-79; mem. White House Initiative for Historically Black Colls. and Univs., 1982-83; tchr. Calif. State Coll.-Los Angeles, 1966, Cornell U./N.Y. State Sch. Labor and Indsl. Relations, 1968, 70, U. Md., College Park, 1974-76; with Md. Dept. Employment and Tng., Wheaton, 1985-86; counseling coord. Montgomery Coll., 1987—; mem. scholarship selection com. Creative Edn. Found., 1991-92; discussion leader Creative Problem Solving Inst., SUNY, Buffalo, 1991-92; grad. adviser U. Mass./D.C. Publ. Sch. project; also cons. Served with U.S. Army, 1944-47; PTO. Bd. dirs. D.C. Striders youth sports club, Inst. Scholar Athletes, 1992; mem. Pres.'s Coun. Youth Opportunity, 1968; mem. D.C. ofcls. com. Nat. Youth Games, 1983; ofcl. Potomac Valey Track and Field Assn.; mem. platform com. N.Y. State Liberal Ind. party, 1968. Mem. NCAA All Am. Track Team, 1949, U.S. Olympic Team, Helsinki, 1952. NCCJ fellow, 1953; U. Havana scholar, 1955; U. Pitts. fellow, 1967; named to NYU Hall of Fame, 1974, Pa. Relay Carnival Hall of Fame, 1994, N.Y. Pioneer Club Hall of Fame, 1996; recipient Disting. Alumni award, 1977, Brotherhood in Sports award B'nai B'rith, 1954. Mem. Nat. Alliance Black Sch. Educators (higher edn. commn.), Inst. Scholar Athletes (bd. dirs.), Phi Delta Kappa. Lutheran. Established 4 Am. records and 3 world records in running events in middle distances. Home: 9118 September Ln Silver Spring MD 20901-3705

PEARSE, GEORGE ANCELL, JR., chemistry educator, researcher; b. Stoneham, Mass., May 18, 1930; s. George Ancell and Marguerite Mae (Velmure) P.; m. Janet Rose Chaves, June 13, 1953; children: William, Kathleen, Nancy, Susan, James. BS, U. Mass., 1952; MS, Purdue U., 1956; PhD, U. Iowa, 1959. Rsch. chemist E.I. DuPont, Seaford, Del., 1959-60; asst. prof. chemistry Le Moyne Coll., Syracuse, N.Y., 1960-64, assoc. prof. chemistry, 1964-70, chmn. dept. chemistry, 1965-72, prof. chemistry, 1970-96, prof. emeritus, 1996—; part-time prof. Syracuse U., 1989—. Vis. rsch. prof. U. Stockholm, Sweden, 1978-79, Cambridge (Eng.) U., 1985-86, James Cook U., Townsville, Australia, 1993. Mem. editorial bd. Microchemical Jour., 1984—. Mem. Am. Chem. Soc., Sigma Xi, Phi Lambda Upsilon, Alpha Chi Sigma. Republican. Roman Catholic. Office: Le Moyne Coll Dept Chemistry Syracuse NY 13214

PEARSON, KAREN LEITER, speech and language pathologist; b. Syracuse, N.Y., Sept. 1, 1947; d. Leo A. and Gladys Leiter; m. Jeffrey S. Pearson, Aug. 16, 1970; 1 child, Wendy Elizabeth. BS, Syracuse U., 1969; MA, U. Conn., 1971. Cert. speech and lang. pathologist. Speech and lang. pathologist New Britain (Conn.) Meml. Hosp., 1971-72, Gaylord Hosp., Wallingford, Conn., 1972-76, Wethersfield (Conn.) Bd. Edn., 1976-78, St. Francis Hosp. and Med. Ctr., Hartford, Conn., 1975-80, Marlborough (Conn.) Elem. Sch., 1980-94, Rham High Sch., Hebron, Conn., 1985-86, Rham High Sch. and Mid. Sch., Hebron, 1994—2002, Wethersfield Sch. Sys., 2002—03. Contbr. articles to profl. jours. Bd. dirs. Glastonbury (Conn.) Recreational Swimming, 1985; ofcl. U.S. Swimming Assn., 1986-88. Mem. NEA, Am. Speech and Hearing Assn. (Ace award 1994, 95, 97), Conn. Speech and Hearing Assn., Conn. Edn. Assn. Avocations: travel, walking, photography. Home: 180 Shoddy Mill Rd Glastonbury CT 06033-3519 E-mail: karenp901@cs.com.

PEARSON, ROY LAING, business administration educator; b. Victoria, Hong Kong, Oct. 18, 1939; s. Roy Ross and Martha Ann L.; m. Louise Elliott Johns, June 11, 1960; 1 child, Cynthia Laing. BS in Commerce, U. Va., 1961, PhD in Econs., 1968. Asst. prof. U. Ark. Sch. Bus. Adminstrn., Fayetteville, 1964-68; assoc. prof. Centenary Coll. La., Shreveport, 1968-71; assoc. prof. bus. adminstrn. Coll. William and Mary, Williamsburg, Va., 1971-76, prof. bus. adminstrn., 1976-87, dir. Bur. Bus. Rsch., 1985-98, Chancellor prof. bus. adminstrn., 1987—. V.p. Wessex Group, Inc., Williamsburg, Va., 1979—; sec.-treas. McKinley land Co., Inc., Williamsburg, 1969-2001. Editor, author: (newsletter) Virginia Business Report, Virginia Outlook, 1984-99. Bd. dirs. Williamsburg Community Hosp., 1985-90; gov.'s adv. bd. economists Commonwealth of Va., Richmond, 1984-98, 2002-; mem. trust fund adv. com. Va. Employment Comm., 1984—. NSF fellow, 1963. Mem. Va. Assn. Economists (pres. 1990-91, bd. dirs. 1985-91, disting. fellow 1998), Assn. for Univ. Bus. and Econ. Rsch. (bd. dirs. 1991-92, v.p. 1992-94, pres. 1994-95, hon. mem. 1999—), Nat. Assn. Bus. Economists, Internat. Inst. Forecasters (bd. dirs. 2001-), Richmond Assn. Bus. Economists, Nat. Economists Club. Avocations: scuba diving, underwater photography, science fiction. Office: Coll William & Mary Sch Bus Adminstrn Williamsburg VA 23185 Home: 4400 Chickasaw Ct Williamsburg VA 23188-8020

PEARSON, SCOTT ROBERTS, economics educator; b. Madison, Wis., Mar. 13, 1938; s. Carlyle Roberts and Edith Hope (Smith) P.; m. Sandra Carol Anderson, Sept. 12, 1962; children: Sarah Roberts, Elizabeth Hovden. BS, U. Wis., Madison, 1961; MA, Johns Hopkins U., 1965; PhD, Harvard U., 1969. Asst. prof. Stanford U., Calif., 1968-74, assoc. prof., 1974-80; assoc. dir. Food Rsch. Inst., 1977-84, dir., 1992-96, prof. food econs., 1980—. Cons. AID, World Bank, Washington, 1965—; staff economist Commn. Internat. Trade, Washington, 1970-71. Author: Petroleum and the Nigerian Economy, 1970; (with others) Commodity Exports and African Economic Development, 1974, (with others) Rice in West Africa, Policy and Economics, 1981, (with others) Food Policy Analysis, 1983, (with othersO The Cassava Economy of Java, 1984, (with others) Portuguese Agriculture in Transition, 1987, (with Eric Monke) The Policy Analysis Matrix, 1989, (with others) Rice Policy in Indonesia, 1991, (with others) Structural Change and Small-Farm Agriculture in Northwest Portugal, 1993, (with others) Agricultural Policy in Kenya, 1995, (with others) Small Farm Agriculture in Southern Europe, 1998. Mem. Am. Agrl. Econs. Assn., Am. Econ. Asn. Home: 691 Mirada Ave Stanford CA 94305-8477

PEARSON, SUSAN WINIFRED, dean, consultant; b. Wasco, Calif., Oct. 8, 1941; d. Gerald Thomas and Maxine (Jensen) P. BS, Tex. Christian U., 1963, MEd, 1971; EdD, U. Houston, 1982. Tchr. history, chmn. dept. Spring Br. Ind. Sch. Dist., Houston, 1963-68; personnel asst. Tenneco, Inc., Houston, 1969-70; grad. asst. Tex. Christian U., 1970-71; dir. student activities Navarro Jr. Coll., Corsicana, Tex., 1972-73; dir. counseling svcs. Horth Harris County Coll., Houston, 1973-84, divsn. head bus., comm. & fine arts, devel. studies, 1984-86, dean instrn./student svcs., 1986—. Ednl. cons., 1994—. Contbr. articles to profl. jours. Mem. Am. Pers. & Guidance Assn., Am. Coll. Pers. Assn., Nat. Assn. Women Deans, Adminstrs. and Counselors, So. Coll. Pers. Assn., Tex. Assn. Women Deans, Adminstrs. and Counselors, Tex. Assn. Coll. and Univ. Student Pers. Adminstrs., Tex. Assn. Jr. Coll. Instructional Adminstrs., Tex. Assn. C.C. Chief Students Pers. Adminstrs., Phi Kappa Phi, Delta Gamma. Presbyterian. E-mail: spea445025@aol.com.

PEASE, ELLA LOUISE, elementary education educator; b. Kokomo, Ind., May 31, 1928; d. James E. and Carrie Alice (Ringer) Earnest; m. Harold Edwin Pease, Aug. 10, 1985; children: Charles Miller, James Miller, Ricky Ensley, Wanda Cisna. BS, Ball State U., 1956, MA, 1959; postgrad., Ind. U., Ft. Wayne. Tchr. 1st grade Union Twp. (Ind.) Pub. Schs., 1953-56, Wells City (Ind.) Pub. Schs., Forest Park Sch., Ft. Wayne, Ind., 1956-93. Docent Ft. Wayne Art Mus. Mem. NEA-Ret., Ret. Ind. Tchrs. Assn., Ft. Wayne Ret. Tchrs. Assn. Methodist. Home: 5108 E State Blvd Fort Wayne IN 46815-7467

PEASE, ROGER FABIAN WEDGWOOD, electrical engineering educator; b. Cambridge, Eng., Oct. 24, 1936; came to U.S., 1964; s. Michael Stewart and Helen Bowen (Wedgwood) P.; m. Caroline Ann Bowring, Sept. 17, 1960; children: Emma Ruth, Joseph Henry Bowring, James Edward. BA, Cambridge U., Eng., 1960, MA, PhD, Cambridge U., Eng., 1964. Rsch. fellow Trinity Coll., Cambridge, 1963-64; asst. prof. U. Calif., Berkeley, 1964-67; mem. tech. staff AT&T Bell Labs., Murray Hill, N.J., 1967-78; prof. elec. engring. Stanford (Calif.) U., 1978—. Cons. IBM, San Jose, Calif., 1964-67, Xerox Corp., Palo Alto, Calif., 1978-84, Perkin Elmer Co., Hayward, Calif., 1979-90, Lawrence Livermore (Calif.) Labs., 1984-92, Affymax Rsch. Inst., 1989-93, Affymetrix, 1993—; mem. tech. adv. bd. Ultratech. Stepper, 1993—; with Dept. of Def. Advanced Rsch. Project Agy., 1996-98. Contbr. more than 200 articles to profl. jours. Patentee (8) in field. Scoutmaster Boy Scouts Am., Holmdel, N.J., 1977-78. Pilot officer RAF, 1955-57. Fellow IEEE (Rappaport award 1982); mem. Nat. Acad. Engring., San Jose Sailing Club. Avocations: sailboat racing, windsurfing. Office: Stanford U Dept Elec Engring Stanford CA 94305

PEASLEE, JAYNE MARIE, computer scientist, educator; b. Corning, N.Y., Mar. 1, 1958; d. Frank and Alice Joyce (Thresher) Walters; m. Kenneth Stewart Peaslee, June 28, 1980; children: Mary Alice, Brent Kenneth. BA, SUNY, Geneseo, 1980; postgrad., SUNY Binghamton, 1984-86; MS, Elmira Coll., 1987. Tchg. asst. Corning-Painted Post (N.Y.) Sch. Dist., 1980-81; instr. computer sci. Corning C.C., 1981—, mid. states chmn. Profl. cert. nat. chair Acad. Leadership Tng., 1996. Leader Seven Lakes Girl Scouts U.S. Council, Corning, 1994-2000. Recipient Honor plaque Data Processing Mgmt. Assn., 1985. Mem. AAUW, Assn. Computer Machinery, Nat. Mus. Women in Arts, Math. Assn., Corning Quilters Guild. Methodist. Avocations: sewing, ice skating, swimming, drawing, painting. Office: Corning CC 1 Academic Dr Corning NY 14830-3297

PEASLEE, MARGARET MAE HERMANEK, zoology educator; b. Chgo., June 15, 1935; d. Emil Frank and Magdalena Bessie (Cechota) Hermanek; m. David Raymond Peaslee, Dec. 6, 1957; 1 dau., Martha Magdelena Peaslee-Levine. AA, Palm Beach Jr. Coll., 1956; BS, Fla. So. Coll., 1959; med. technologist, Northwestern U., 1958, MS, 1964, PhD, 1966. Med. technologist Passavant Hosp., Chgo., 1958-59; med. technologist St. James Hosp., Chicago Heights, Ill., 1960-63; asst. prof. biology Fla. So. Coll., Lakeland, Fla., 1966-68; asst. prof. of biology U. S.D., Vermillion, SD, 1968-71, assoc. prof., 1971-76, prof., 1976, acad. opportunity liaison, 1974-76; prof., head dept. zoology La. Tech. U., Ruston, La., 1976-90, assoc. dean, dir. grad. studies and rsch., prof. biol. scis. Coll. Life Scis., 1990-93; v.p. for acad. affairs U. Pitts. at Titusville, Titusville, Pa., 1993—. Contbr. articles to profl. jours. Fellow AAAS; mem. AAUP, Am. Inst. Biol. Scis., Am. Soc. Zoologists, S.D. Acad. Sci. (sec.-treas. 1972-76), N.Y. Acad. Scis., Pa. Acad. Sci., La. Acad. Sci. (sec. 1979-81, pres. 1983), Sigma Xi, Phi Theta Kappa, Phi Rho Pi, Phi Sigma, Alpha Epsilon Delta. E-mail: peaslee@pitt.edu.

PEAVY, JOHN WESLEY, III, investment advisor, educator, investment advisor, educator, consultant, financial consultant; b. Dallas, July 3, 1944; s. John Wesley Jr. and Ermine Palmer (Arnold) P.; m. Linda Ann Ruesewald, Nov. 15, 1997. BBA, So. Methodist U., 1966; MBA, U. Pa., 1968; PhD, U. Tex., Arlington, 1978. CLU, chartered fin. analyst, chartered fin. cons. Securities salesman Goldman, Sachs & Co., N.Y.C. and Dallas, 1970—75; instr. fin. U. Tex., Arlington, 1976—77; instr. Tex. Christian U., Ft. Worth, 1977—78; asst. prof. Ariz. State U., Tempe, 1978—79; prof. So. Meth. U., Dallas, 1979—94, Vaughan-Rauscher prof. fin. investments, 1991—94, chmn. fin. dept., 1986—88. Pres. Peavy Fin. Svcs., Inc., Dallas, 1983—; chmn. Founders Trust Co., Dallas, 1993-98; adj. prof. Am. Grad. Sch. Internat. Mgmt., Glendale, Ariz.; mem. investment adv. com. Tchrs. Retirement System Tex., 1992-99, chief investment officer, 1999-2002; prof. Tex. Christian U., 2002—; mng. dir., Dana Investment Advisors, Inc., Brookfield, Wis., 2002—; trustee Rsch. Fund CFAs, 1990—94, rsch. dir., 1992-94. Author: Hyperprofits, 1985, Case Studies in Portfolio Management, 1990; editor: Takeovers and Shareholders: The Mounting Controversy, 1985; exec. editor CFA Digest; cons. editor Fin. Analysts Jour., Rev. Fin. Econs., Jour. Investing; contbr. articles on fin. to profl. jours. Recipient Disting. Prof. award So. Meth. U.; Columbia U. fellow, 1983, 85, So. Meth. U. fellow, 1981-90. Mem. Fin. Mgmt. Assn. (honor soc. pres. 1985, 88), Inst. CFAs (bd. examiners 1984-88, curriculum com. 1988-94, chmn. curriculum com. 1992-94, coun. on edn. and rsch. 1991—94), Southwestern Fin. Assn. (bd. dirs. 1985-86, v.p. 1987-88, pres. 1988-89). Home: 7512 Glenshannon Cir Dallas TX 75225-2052

PEAVY, SALLY HUDGINS, special education educator, diagnostician, school psychologist; b. Macon, Ga., Nov. 30, 1948; d. Jack W. and Lillian T. (Bloodworth) Jenkins; m. Luke L. Hudgins, Sept. 5, 1970 (dec. Apr. 13, 1978); 1 child, Emily W.; m. Donald P. Peavy, Nov. 18, 1970; 1 child, Dallas L. BS in Elem. Edn. and Mental Retardation, Auburn U., 1970; MEd in Learning Disabilities and Behaviour Disorders, Ga. State U., 1972, postgrad., 1990—. Cert. tchr. T-5 in spl. edn., T-4 in mental retardation, T-6 in sch. psychology, Ga. Spl. edn. instr. Smith Station (Ala.) Elem. Sch., 1970-71; spl. edn. instr., resource tchr. Sagamore Hills and Montclair Elem. Schs. De Kalb County Schs, Atlanta, 1972-75; spl. edn. instr. Panola Way Elem. Sch., Atlanta, 1987-90, Gwinnet County Summerour Middle Sch., Lawrenceville, Ga., 1990-92, sch. psychologist, 1994—. Leader Girl Scouts Am., Dekalb County, Ga., 1983-88; guide Mus. of Art, Atlanta, 1983; bd. dirs. PTA, Dekalb County, 1984; chmn. tutorial reading program, Jr. League of Dekalb County, 1986-87; team parent Tucker Baseball Assn.; nursery tchr. Mt. Carmel Christian Ch.; Specific Learning Disabilities vol. DeKalb County, Jolly Elem. Recipient Bob Clarke Meml. scholarship Gwinnet County Sch. System, 1992; grantee U.S. Govt., Auburn U., 1969-70, Ga. State U., 1971-72. Mem. Nat. Assn. Sch. Psychologists, Ga. Assn. Sch. Psychologists, Coun. Exceptional Children (diagnostic div.), Kappa Delta Pi.

PECH, ROSE ANN, special education educator; b. Edwardsville, Ill., Oct. 16, 1942; d. Battista and Helen Justine (Menoni) Boccaleoni; m. James O. Pech, Oct. 23, 1965 (dec. Jan. 1974; 1 chid, Timothy James; m. Nelson K. Reese, May 15, 1976 (div. Apr. 1984). Student, So. Ill. U., Alton, 1960-62; BS with high honors, Ill. State U., Normal, 1964; postgrad., Northwestern U., Evanston, Ill., 1966; MS in Edn., No. Ill. U., DeKalb, 1968-72. Tchr. educable mentally handicapped Spl. Edn. Dist. Lake County, Gurnee, Ill., 1964-66, tchr. learning disabled, 1966-67; tchr. cons. Maine Twp. High Sch. Dist. 207, Des Plaines, Ill., 1967-69; itinerant tchr. learning disabled Spl. Edn. Dist. Lake County, Gurnee, 1969-70; substitute tchr. Glenbrook High Sch., Wheeling, Ill., 1971-73; instr. gen. ednl. devel. Coll. Lake County, Grayslake, Ill., 1973-76; tchr. learning disabled Lake Villa (Ill.) Sch. Dist. 41, 1976—94; ret., 1994; part-time tchr. lng. disabled Spring Grove (Ill.) Sch., 1997—. Cons. Maine Twp. Diagnostic and Remedial Learning Ctr., Park Ridge, Ill., 1967-69; IFT rep. Lake County Inst. Adv. Com., Waukegan, Ill., 1988—94; tchr. rsch. linker Am. Fedn. Tchrs.-Ill. Fedn. Tchrs. Local 504, Waukegan, 1988—; mem. Dist. 41 Curriculum Coun., Lake Villa, 1978-82, chmn., 1979-81. Chmn. youth ministry team United Protestant Ch., Grayslake, Ill., 1983-89, 92-94, mem. Christian edn. commn., 1991-94, chair cradle roll com., 1994-2000, adminstrv. coun., 2000—; vol. Am. Cancer Soc., Am. Legion, Chgo.-Lake Bluff Children's Home, Heart Fund, Salvation Army, Pub. Assistance to Deliver Shelter to Homeless, Lake County, Ill., 1988—; site mgr. Pub. Action Deliver Shelter, 1994—. Spl. edn. fellow State Ill., 1966. Mem. ASCD, Am. Fedn. Tchrs., Ill. Fedn. Tchrs., NEA, Ill. Edn. Assn., Lake Villa Fedn. Tchrs. (corr. sec. 1978-80, 92—94, bldg. pres. 1983-84), Orton Dyslexia Soc., Lake County Fedn. Tchrs., Kappa Delta Epsilon, Kappa Delta Pi, Women of Moose. Avocations: travel, photography, geneology, reading, cross-country skiing. Home: 68 Wesley Ave Lake Villa IL 60046-9056 Office: Nippersink School Dist 2 10006 N Main St Richmond IL 60071

PECHUKAS, DIANA GISOLFI See GISOLFI, DIANA

PECK, ALEXANDER NORMAN, elementary education educator; b. Akron, Ohio, Sept. 6, 1934; s. Kenneth Owen and Elizabeth (Leckie) P.; m. Joan katherine Lombardi, Oct. 19, 1958; children: Alexander Norman II,

Gregory C., Glenn P., Douglas A. BS, SUNY, Cortland, 1957; MA, NYU, 1988. Tchr. phys. edn. Hewlet-Woodmere (N.Y.) Schs., 1959-60, Syosset (N.Y.) Pub. Schs., 1960-62, North Street Elem. Sch., White Plains, N.Y., 1962-68; tchr., chair dept., coord. athletics, coach football and wrestling Highlands Jr. H.S., White Plains, 1968-79; tchr. phys. edn., team leader White Plains Mid. Sch., 1979—, mem. sch. based coun., 1995-98. Group leader Mohawk Day Camps, White Plains, 1960-69, dir. boys program, 1970-87, asst. dir. camp., 1988-94, head counselor MVP Baskeball Camp, 1995-96; pres. Gray Fox Cons., 1996—; sports dir., cons. 1st Ch. Day Camp, Old Greenwich, Conn., 1996—. Cubmaster Boy Scouts Am., Mamaroneck, N.Y., asst. dist. commr., White Plains; chair site utilization com. Rye Neck Schs., Mamaroneck; active White Plains PTA; chmn. ch. coun. Mamaroneck United Meth. Ch., 1996-98, trustee, 1999—. Recipient svc. award White Plains PTA, 1963. Mem. Am. Assn. Health, Phys. Edn., Recreation and Dance, N.Y. State Assn. Health, Phys. Edn., Recreation and Dance (zone pres., chair state legislature), N.Y. State Tchrs. Assn. (zone v.p.), N.Y. State United Tchrs., N.Y. State High Sch. Athletic Assn. (zone chair modified sports, svc. award), White Plains Tchrs. Assn. (treas. 1966-68), Am. Camping Assn. (presenter tri state camping conv. 1986, 89, 93, 94). Avocations: antiques, photography, military history. Home: 1 Overdale Rd Rye NY 10580-1022 Office: White Plains Middle Sch 128 Grandview Ave White Plains NY 10605-3225

PECK, CLAUDIA JONES, associate dean; b. Ponca City, Okla., Feb. 1, 1943; d. Claude W. and Josephine Jones; children: Jody Athene, Cameron Guthrie. BS, U. Okla., 1972; MS, U. Mo., 1976; PhD, Iowa State U., 1981. Instr. econs. Iowa State U., Ames, 1980-81; asst. prof. consumer studies Okla. State U., Stillwater, 1981-85, assoc. prof., 1985-88, prof., 1988-89; assoc. dean for rsch. and grad. studies U. Ky., Lexington, 1989—, faculty assoc. Sanders-Brown Ctr. on Aging, 1991. Contbr. articles to profl. jours. Recipient Lela O'Toole Rsch. award Okla. Home Econs. Assn., 1988, Merrick Found. Teaching. award Okla. State U., 1987. Mem. Am. Assn. Family and Consumer Scientists (v.p. 1990-92), Am. Coun. on Consumer Interests (pres. 1994-95, Applied Rsch. award 1985), Missouri Valley Econ. Assn. (v.p. 1994-96), Sigma Xi (pres. 1993-94). Office: U Ky 102 Erikson Hall 0050 Lexington KY 40506-0001

PECK, ERNEST JAMES, JR., academic administrator; b. Port Arthur, Tex., July 26, 1941; s. Ernest James and Karlton Maudean (Luttrell) P.; children from previous marriage: David Karl, John Walter; m. Frances R. Taylor; 1 stepchild, Michael R. Peck. BA in Biology with honors, Rice U., 1963, PhD in Biochemistry, 1966. Rsch. assoc. Purdue U., West Lafayette, Ind., 1966-68, asst. prof., 1968-73, Baylor Coll. Medicine, Houston, 1973-74, assoc. prof., 1974-80, prof., 1980-82; prof., chmn. biochemistry Sch. Med. Sci., U. Ark., Little Rock, 1982-89; dean sci. and math. U. Nev., Las Vegas, 1989-95; vice chancellor acad. affairs U. Nebr., Omaha, 1995-98; exec. dir. Coun. Colls. of Arts and Scis., rsch. prof. Ariz. State U., Tempe, 1998—. Adj. prof. U. Ark., Pine Bluff, 1986-88; program dir. NSF, Washington, 1988-89; mem. editl. bd. Jour. Neurosci. Rsch., N.Y.C., 1982-92. Co-author: Female Sex Steroids, 1979, Brain Peptides, 1979. Recipient Rsch. Career award NIH, Nat. Inst. of Child Health and Human Devel., 1975-80; NIH fellow, 1964-66. Fellow AAAS; mem. Am. Chem. Soc., Am. Soc. Biochemistry and Molecular Biology, Sigma Xi. Avocations: fishing, hunting. Office: Ariz State U Coun Coll Arts Scis PO Box 873108 Tempe AZ 85287-3108

PECK, FRED NEIL, economist, educator; b. Bklyn., Oct. 17, 1945; s. Abraham Lincoln and Beatrice (Pikholtz) P.; m. Jean Claire Ginsberg, Aug. 14, 1971; children: Ron Evan, Jordan Shefer, Ethan David. BA, Binghamton (NY) U., 1966; MA, SUNY, Albany, 1969; PhM, NYU, 1984; PhD, Pacific Western U., 1984; MS in Edn., Coll. New Rochelle, 1993. Lectr. SUNY, Albany, 1969-70; research asst. N.Y. State Legislature, Albany, 1970; sales and research staff Pan Am. Trade Devel. Corp., N.Y.C., 1971; v.p., economist The First Boston Corp., N.Y.C., 1971-88; mng. dir. Sharpe's Capital Mkt. Assocs. Inc., N.Y.C., 1988-89; pres., chief economist Hillcrest Econs. Group, N.Y.C., 1989-93; dir. edn. The Ednl. Advantage, Inc., New City, N.Y., 1990-95; dir. Robert F. Kennedy Acad., N.Y.C. Dept. Edn., 1998—. Adj. prof. Hofstra U., Hempstead, N.Y., 1975; lectr. NYU, 1982; mem. faculty New Sch. for Social Rsch., N.Y.C., 1974-94; coord. ednl. tech. N.Y.C. Bd. of Edn., 1990-98. Author, editor: (biennial publ.) Handbook of Securities of U.S. Government, 1972-86. Mem. ASCD, Am. Econ. Assn., Ea. Econ. Assn., Econometric Soc., Nat. Assn. Bus. Economists, Am. Statis. Assn., Coun. Exceptional Children, Doctorate Assn. of N.Y. Educators, Beta Gamma Sigma (hon. soc.), Phi Delta Kappa. Lodges: Knights Pythias, Knights Khorassan. Democrat. Jewish. Office: Robert F Kennedy Acad 420 E 12th St New York NY 10009-4019 E-mail: docfnp@bigfoot.com.

PECK, ROBERT DAVID, educational foundation administrator; b. Devil's Lake, N.D., June 1, 1929; s. Lester David and Bernice Marie (Peterson) P.; m. Lylia June Smith, Sept. 6, 1953; children: David Allan, Kathleen Marie. BA, Whitworth Coll., 1951; MDiv, Berkeley (Calif.) Bapt. Div. Sch., 1958; ThD, Pacific Sch. Religion, 1964; postgrad., U. Calif., Berkeley, 1959-60, 62-63, Wadham Coll., Oxford U., Eng., 1963. Music tchr. pub. schs., Bridgeport, Wash., 1954-55; prof., registrar Linfield Coll., McMinnville, Oreg., 1963-69; asst. dir. Ednl. Coordinating Coun., Salem, Oreg., 1969-75; assoc. prof. Pacific Luth. U., Tacoma, 1976-79, U. Puget Sound, Tacoma, 1977; v.p. John Minter Assocs., Boulder, Colo., 1979-81, Coun. Ind. Colls., Washington, 1981-84; adminstrv. v.p. Alaska Pacific U., Anchorage, 1984-88; pres. Phillips U., Enid, Okla., 1988-94, chancellor, 1994-95; chmn. The Pres. Found. for Support of Higher Edn., Washington, 1995—; sr. assoc. InterEd, Phoenix, 1998—. Pres. Phillips U. Ednl. Enterprises Inc., 1994-95; cons. Higher Edn. Exec. Assocs., Denver, 1984—; owner Tyee Marina, Tacoma, 1975-77; yacht broker Seattle, 1977-79. Author: Future Focusing: An Alternative to Strategic Planning, 1983, also articles. Dem. county chmn., McMinnville, 1968, Dem. candidate for state Ho. of Reps., McMinnville, 1969; pres. McMinnville Kiwanis, 1965-69. Cpl. Signal Corps, U.S. Army, 1952-54. Carnegie Corp. grantee, 1982, 84. Mem. Okla. Ind. Coll. Assn. (sec. 1989—). Mem. Christian Ch. Avocations: sailing, sculpting. E-mail: robertpeckb@cs.com.

PECK, WILLIAM ARNO, physician, educator, university official and dean; b. New Britain, Conn., Sept. 28, 1933; s. Bernard Carl and Molla (Nair) P.; m. Patricia Hearn, July 10, 1982; children by previous marriage: Catherine, Edward Pershall, David Nathaniel; stepchildren: Andrea, Elizabeth, Katherine. AB, Harvard U., 1955; MD, U. Rochester, N.Y., 1960; DSc (hon.), U. Rochester, 2000. Intern, then resident in internal medicine Barnes Hosp., St. Louis, 1960-62; fellow in metabolism Washington U. Sch. Medicine, St. Louis, 1963; mem. faculty U. Rochester Med. Sch., 1965-76, prof. medicine and biochemistry, 1973-76, head divsn. endocrinology and metabolism, 1969-76; John E. and Adaline Simon prof. medicine, co-chmn. dept. medicine Washington U. Sch. Medicine, St. Louis, 1976-89; physician in chief Jewish Hosp., St. Louis, 1976-89; prof. medicine and exec. vice chancellor med. affairs, dean sch. medicine, pres. univ. med. ctr. Washington U., St. Louis, 1989—2003, Wolff disting. prof., dean emeritus and dir. ctr. for health policy, 2003—. Chmn. endocrinology and metabolism adv. com. FDA, 1976-78; chmn. gen. medicine study sect. NIH, 1979-81; chmn. Gordon Conf. Chemistry, Physiology and Structure of Bones and Teeth, 1977, Consensus Devel. Conf. on Osteoporosis, NIH, 1984; co-chmn. Workshop on Future Directions in Osteoporosis, 1987; chmn. Spl. Topic Conf. on Osteoporosis, U.S. FDA, 1987; bd. dirs. Angelica Corp., Allied Healthcare Products, Hologic, Reinsurance Group of Am., TIAA-CREF Trust Co. Editor Bone and Mineral Rsch. Anns., 1982-88. Pres. Nat. Osteoporosis Found., 1985-90. Served as med. officer USPHS, 1963-65. Paul Harris fellow Rotary Found., 2001; recipient Lederle Med. Faculty award, 1967, Career Program award NIH, 1970-75, Commr.'s Spl. citation FDA, 1988, Humanitarian award Arthritis Found. Ea. Mo., 1995, Crohn's and Colitis Fedn. Am., 1999, Founders award Nat. Osteoporosis Found., 1996, Huntington Disease Soc. Am. award, 2002, Juvenile Diabetes Rsch. Found. Lifetime Achievement award, 2003, Internat. Brotherhood award Bikur Cholim Hosp., Jerusalem, 2003. Fellow AAAS, ACP; mem. Internat. Bone & Mineral Soc., Royal Soc. Medicine, Am. Assn. Clin. Endocrinologists, Am. Geriatrics Soc., Am. Soc. Biochemistry & Molecular Biophysics, Am. Soc. Bone and Mineral Rsch. (councilor 1978-81, pres.-elect 1982-83, pres. 1983-84), Am. Soc. Clin. Investigation, Am. Soc. Internal Medicine, Assn. Am. Med. Colls. (coun. deans adminstrv. bd. 1992—, chmn. 1996-97, chair elect 1997-98, chair 1998—, immediate past chair 1999), Assn. Am. Physicians, Endocrine Soc., Orthopaedic Rsch. Soc., Soc. Med. Adminstrs., St. Louis Metro. Med. Soc., St. Louis Soc. Internal Medicine (pres. 1986), Inst. Medicine Nat. Acad. Sci., Washington U. Health Adminstrn. Program Alumni Assn. (hon.), Research! Am. (vice chair 1999—), Pi Theta Epsilon (hon.), Sigma Xi, Alpha Omega Alpha (bd. dirs 1992-95). Home: 32 Huntleigh Downs Saint Louis MO 63131 Office: Washington U Sch Medicine #1 Brookings Dr Box 1133 Saint Louis MO 63130

PECKENPAUGH, DONALD HUGH, psychologist, consultant, writer; b. East Chicago, Ind., Aug. 11, 1928; s. George Martin and Thelma Mentia P.; m. Mary Frances Dreesen, Sept. 2, 1950; children: Ann Dreesen, Eve Louise. PhB, U. Chgo., 1948, AM, 1954, PhD, 1968. Lic. psychologist, Ill., Ind., Minn. Author: A School System's Role in Social Renewal, 1966, A Comprehensive Concept for Vocational Educational Facilities, 1967, Partners in Education, 1967, Exemplary Programs in Multi-Cultural Education, 1974, Population and You, 1975, Moral Education, 1976, The Public School as Moral Authority, 1977, Psychoeducational Evaluation, 1984. Nat. Inst. Mental Health fellow, 1965-67. Mem. Am. Psychol. Assn., Am. Assn. Sch. Adminstrs. (life), Phi Delta Kappa. Office: 3 Brook Ln Palos Park IL 60464-1289

PECKHAM, JOYCE WEITZ, foundation administrator, former secondary education educator; b. Rochester, N.Y., Oct. 11, 1937; d. Clarence Christian and Mildred Emma (Knapp) Weitz; m. Lauren Augustus Peckham, Dec. 20, 1958; children: David, Kent. BS, Elmira Coll., 1959, MS, 1967. Tchr. science Horseheads (N.Y.) Cen. Sch., 1959-71; sec.-treas. Peckham Pipe Organs, Breesport, N.Y., 1971—. Trustee and sec. electronic coms. Antique Wireless Assn., Bloomfield, N.Y., 1986—, sec. and mem. sec. 1986—, mem. bd. dirs. 1981—. Mem. Horseheads Hist. Soc., Internat. Majolica Soc., First United Methodist Ch. (trustee, choir mem.). Avocations: collecting antiques, reading, travel. Home: 194 Ormiston Rd Breesport NY 14816-9702

PEDERSEN, KNUD GEORGE, economics educator, academic administrator; b. Three Creeks, Alta., Can., June 13, 1931; s. Hjalmar Neilsen and Anna (Jensen) P.; m. Joan Elaine Vanderwarker, Aug. 15, 1953 (dec. 1988); children: Greg, Lisa; m. Penny Ann Jones, Dec. 31, 1988. Diploma in Edn., Provincial Normal U., 1952; BA, U. B.C., 1959; MA, U. Wash., 1964; PhD, U. Chgo., 1969; LLD (hon.), McMaster U., 1996; DLitt (hon.), Emily Carr Inst. of Art and Design, 2003; LLD (hon.), Simon Fraser U., 2003. Asst. prof. econs. of edn. U. Toronto; asst. prof. econs. of edn., assoc. dir. U. Chgo., 1970-72; dean, assoc. prof., then prof. U. Victoria, B.C., 1972-75, acad. v.p., prof., 1975-79; pres., vice-chancellor, prof. Simon Fraser U., Vancouver, B.C., 1979-83; pres., prof. U. B.C., Vancouver, 1983-85; pres., vice-chancellor U. Western Ont., London, Can., 1985-94, prof. econs. of edn., 1985-96; interim pres. U. No. B.C., 1995; founding pres., vice-chancellor Royal Roads U., 1995-96; chancellor U. No. B.C., 1998—. Bd. dirs. Assn. Univs. and Colls., Canada, 1979—84, chmn., Canada, 1989—91; bd. dirs. Vancouver Bd. Trade, 1983—85; pres. Can. Club Vancouver, 1983—84; mem. coun. trustees Inst. for Rsch. on Pub. Policy, Ottawa, Ont., Canada, 1983—89; chmn. Coun. Ont. Univs., 1989—91. Author: The Itinerant Schoolmaster, 1972; contbr. chpts. to books, numerous articles to profl. jours. Decorated officer Order of Can., Order of Ont., Order of B.C.; recipient 125th Anniversary of Confedn. of Can. medal, Queen's Jubilee medal; fellow Ford Found., 1965-68, Can. Coll. Tchrs., 1977, Royal Soc. for Encouragement of Arts, 1984; also 11 major scholarships. Mem. Semiahmoo Golf and Country Club. Avocations: golf, fishing, gardening, cooking, carving. E-mail: pedersen@sfu.ca.

PEDERSEN, RICHARD FOOTE, diplomat and academic administrator; b. Miami, Ariz., Feb. 21, 1925; s. Ralph Martin and Gertrude May (Foote) P.; m. Nelda Newell Napier, May 9, 1953; children: Paige Elizabeth, Jonathan Foote, Kendra Gayle. BA summa cum laude, Coll. of Pacific, 1946; MA, Stanford U., 1947; PhD, Harvard U., 1950; LLD (hon.), George Williams Coll., 1964, U. of Pacific, 1966; DHL (hon.), Am. U., Cairo, 1997. Teaching fellow, tutor Harvard U., Cambridge, Mass., 1949-50; with UN econ. and social affairs Dept. State, Washington, 1950-53; adviser econ. and social affairs U.S. Mission to UN, N.Y.C., 1953—55, adviser polit. and security affairs, 1956-59, sr. advisor polit. and security affairs, 1959-64, minister, counselor, 1964-66, ambassador, sr. adviser to U.S. rep., 1966-67; ambassador, dep. U.S. rep. UN Security Coun., N.Y.C., 1967—69; counselor Dept. State, 1969-73; ambassador to Hungary, 1973-75; sr. v.p. internat. U.S. Trust Co., 1975-78; pres. Am. U., Cairo, 1978-90; dir. internat. programs Calif. Poly Pomona U., 1990-95. Mem. adv. bd. Nat. Coun. U.S.-Arab Rels., 1985—; trustee Consortium for Internat. Devel., 1990—95; mem. adv. bd. Ctr. Near Eastern Studies UCLA, 1996—99; adv. bd. Sch. Internat. Studies, U. Pacific, 1997—. Mem. Nat. Coun. YMCAs, 1961-73; bd. dirs. Ctr. for Civic Edn., 1995—, Physicians for Peace, 1988-90; mem. Fulbright bd., Egypt, 1980-82, adv. bd. Fulbright Cultural Enrichment Program, So. Calif., 1991—. With AUS, 1943-45 ETO. Recipient Sumner Peace prize Harvard U., 1950, Outstanding Alumnus award U. Pacific, 1962, Order of Sacred Treasure, Gold and Silver Star, Govt. of Japan, 1987; named One of 10 Outstanding Young Men, U.S. Jr. C. of C., 1956; awarded Order of Scis. and Arts, first class Govt. of Egypt, 1990. Mem. Coun. Fgn. Rels., Am. Soc. Internat. Law, L.A. World Affairs Coun., Am. Fgn. Svc. Assn., Mid. East Inst., Oriental Inst., UN Assn. Am., Internat. Assn. Univ. Pres., Pacific Coun. Internat. Policy, Asia Soc. Clubs: Harvard (N.Y.); Cosmos (Washington). Democrat. Congregationalist. Avocations: swimming, tennis, egyptology, local history. Home: 2503 N Mountain Ave Claremont CA 91711-1545 E-mail: rfpdrsn@earthlink.net.

PEDERSON, WILLIAM DAVID, political scientist, educator; b. Eugene, Oreg., Mar. 17, 1946; s. Jon Moritz and Rose Marie (Ryan) P. BS in Polit. Sci., U. Oreg., 1967, MA in Polit. Sci., 1972, PhD in Polit. Sci., 1979. Tchg. asst. polit. sci. dept. U. Oreg., Eugene, 1975-77; instr. govt. dept. Lamar U., Beaumont, Tex., 1977-79; asst. prof. polit. sci. dept. Westminster Coll., Fulton, Mo., 1979-80; asst. prof., head polit. sci. and pre-law Yankton Coll. U. S.D., 1980-81; prof., Am. Studies Chair, dir. Internat. Lincoln Ctr. La. State U., Shreveport, 1981—; program analyst NIH, Bethesda, Md., summer 1973; assoc. prof. jr. state program Am. U., Washington, summer 1984; prof. jr. state program Georgetown U., 1997—2002; rsch. assoc. Russian and East European Ctr./U. Ill., Urbana, summers 1982—; founding dir. Washington semester La. State U., Shreveport, 1982-91, 96—, with Presdl. Conf. Series, 1992—, with ann. Abraham Lincoln lecture series/Am. Studies program, 1982—. Mem. nat. adv. com. Presdl. commn. on the Bicentennial of Abraham Lincoln, 2002—. Editl. staff writer: The Times, Shreveport, 1990; columnist: Red Rooster, 2002; author: The Rating Game in American Politics, 1987; editor: The Barberian Presidency, 1989, Morality and Conviction in American Politics, 1990, Congressional-Presidential Relations: Governmental Gridlock, 1991, Great Justices of the U.S. Supreme Court: Ratings and Case Studies, 1993, 2d edit., 1994, Lincoln and Leadership: A Model for a Summer Teachers Inst., 1993, Abraham Lincoln: Sources and Style of Leadership, 1994, Abraham Lincoln: Contemporary, 1995, 2d edit., 1996, FDR and the Modern Presidency: Leadership and Legacy, 1997, Lincoln Forum: Abraham Lincoln, Gettysburg and the Civil War, 1999, George Washington's Image in American Culture, 2001, George Washington and the Origins of the American Presidency, 2000, George Washington: Foundations of Leadership and Character, 2001, Franklin D. Roosevelt and the Shaping of American Culture, 2001, Franklin D. Roosevelt and Congress, 2001; The New Deal and Public Policy, 1998; co-editor: Grassroots Constitutionalism, 1988; editor The Polit. Sci. Educator, 1996-98, Abraham Lincoln Abroad, 1998—; co-editor Jour. Contemporary Thought, 1997—; guest editor: Quarterly Jour. Ideology, 1994; founding editor Washington Semesters and Internships, 1998—, Internat. Abraham Lincoln Jour., 2000—, Classic Cases in American Constitutional Law, 2001, Franklin D. Roosevelt and the Transformation of the Supreme Court, 2003, Franklin D. Roosevelt and Abraham Lincoln, 2003, Franklin D. Roosevelt and the Shaping of the Modern World, 2003, Leaders of the Pack: Polls and Case Studies of Great Supreme Justices, 2003; contbr. articles to profl. jours.; founder La. Lincolnator, 1994. Mem. Mayor's Comm. on the Bicentennial U.S. Constn., 1987; active Barnwell Ctr., Shreveport, 1984, Am. Rose Soc., Shreveport, 1982. With U.S. Army, 1968-70. Recipient Tng. award NIH, 1973, Outstanding Prof. award Westminster Coll. 1980, La. State U., 1984, 2001-02, Cultural Olympiad award, 1995, Page Shreveport Rose Shreveport Times Jour., 1995; grantee La. State U., 1982, La. Endowment for Humanities, 1987, 93, 95-97; NEH fellow, 1981-85. Fellow Am. Polit. Sci. Assn., Am. Judicature Soc.; mem. Abraham Lincoln Assn. (mem. bd. dirs. 1994, Achievement award 1994, dir. conf. in the south, 1992, dir. 1st summer Inst. on Abraham Lincoln, 1993, grantee 1992, 93), Ctr. Study Presidency, Internat. Soc. Polit. Psychology, Washington Semesters and Internship Assn., Internat. Lincoln Assn. (bd. dirs. 1994-95, pres. 1990-93, chair bd. dirs. 1998—), La. Hist. Assn. (bd. dirs. 2001—). Office: La State U Internat Lincoln Ctr One University Pl BH Shreveport LA 71115-2301 E-mail: wpederso@pilot.lsus.edu.

PEDRAM, MARILYN BETH, reference librarian; b. Brewster, Kans., Apr. 3, 1937; d. Edgar Roy and Elizabeth Catherine (Doubt) Crist; m. Manouchehr Pedram, Jan. 27, 1962 (Oct. 28, 1984); children: Jaleh Denise, Cyrus Andre. BS in Edn., Kans. State U., 1958; MLS, U. Denver, 1961. Cert secondary educator, Mo. 7th grade tchr. Clay Ctr. (Kans.) Pub. Schs., 1958-59, Colby (Kans.) Pub. Sch. System, 1959-60; reference libr. Topeka (Kans.) Pub. Libr., 1961-62, extension dept. head, 1963-64, reference libr., 1964-65; br. libr. asst. Denver Pub. Libr., 1965-67; reference libr. Kansas City (Mo.) Pub. Libr., Plaza Br., 1974-79, Kansas City (Mo.) Main Libr., 1979—. Mem. AARP, ALA, Mo. Libr. Assn., Pub. Libr. Assn., Celiac Sprue Assn., Kans. State U. Alumni Assn., Nat. Parks and Conservation Assn. Avocations: flower gardening, gourmet cooking, travel, reading, walking. Office: Kansas City Pub Libr 311 E 12th St Kansas City MO 64106-2412

PEEBLES, LUCRETIA NEAL DRANE, policy and administration educator; b. Atlanta, Mar. 16, 1950; d. Dudley Drane and Annie Pearl (Neal) Lewis; divorced; 1 child, Julian Timothy. BA, Pitzer Coll., 1971; MA, Claremont Grad. Sch., 1973, PhD, 1985. Special edn. tchr. Marshall Jr. High Sch., Pomona, Calif., 1971-74; high sch. tchr. Pomona High Sch., 1974-84; adminstr. Lorbeer Jr. High Sch., Diamond Bar, Calif., 1984-91; prin. Chapparal Mid. Sch., Moorpark, Calif., 1991-92, South Valley Jr. High Sch., Gilroy, Calif., 1992—95; asst. prof. dept. edn. Spelman Coll., Atlanta, 1995—97; asst. prof. Coll. Edn. U. Denver, 1997—. Co-dir. pre-freshman program, Claremont (Calif.) Coll., 1974; dir. pre-freshman program, Claremont Coll., 1975; cons., Claremont, 1983—. Author: Negative Attendance Behavior: The Role of the School, 1985, Teaching Children Proactive Responses to Media Violence, 1996, Validating Children: A Collaborative Model, 1996, The Challenge of Leadership in Charter Schools, 2000, Charter School Equity Issues: Focus on Minority and At-Risk Students, 2000, Millennial Challenges for Educational Leadership: Revisiting Issues of Diversity, 2000. Active Funds Distbn. Bd.-Food for All, 1987—, Funds Distbn. Task Force-Food for All, 1986; mem. Adolescent Pregnancy Childwatch Task Force. Named Outstanding Young Career Woman Upland Bus. and Profl. Women's Club, 1978-79; Stanford U. Sch. Edn. MESA fellow, 1983, NSF fellow Stanford U., 1981, Calif. Tchrs. Assn. fellow, 1979, Claremont Grad. Sch. fellow, 1977-79, fellow Calif. Edn. Policy Fellowship Program, 1989-90; recipient Woman of Achievement award YWCA of West Edn., 1991. Mem. Assn. Calif. Sch. Adminstrs. (Minigrant award 1988), Assn. for Supervision and Curriculum Devel., Nat. Assn. Secondary Sch. Principals, Pi Lambda Theta. Democrat. Am. Baptist. Home: 1470 S Quebec Way # 166 Denver CO 80231-2660

PEEBLES, RUTH ADDELLE, secondary education educator; b. Livingston, Tex., Dec. 9, 1929; d. Andrew Wiley and Addelle (Green) P. BA, East. Tex. Baptist Coll., 1951; M of Religious Edn., Southwestern Baptist Seminary, Ft. Worth, 1955; MA, Sam Houston State U., 1968. Instr. of religion and Baptist student dir. Ea. N.Mex. U., Portales, 1955-58; Baptist student dir. Madison Coll., Harrisonburg, Va., 1958-60; youth dir. Garden Oaks Baptist Ch., Houston, 1960-62; history tchr. Livingston Ind. Sch. Dist., 1962-84. Editor: Pictorial History of Polk County, Texas, 1976; author: There Never Were Such Men Before, 1987. Bd. dirs. Polk County Libr. and Mus., Livingston, 1980-83, Polk County Heritage Soc., 1987-89, Polk County Hist. Found., 1997—. Recipient Cmty. Svc. award Polk County C. of C., 1980, Hist. Preservation awards Polk County Heritage Soc., 1987, Tex. State Hist. Commn., 1989, SCV Cert. of Appreciation, 1993, Ladies Appreciation medal SCV, 1994; named Outstanding Grad. Livingston H.S., 1999. Mem. Daughters of the Republic of Tex., Tex. State Hist. Assn., Tex. State Hist. Found., Hood's Tex. Brigade Assn., Polk County Heritage Soc., Atascosito Hist. Assn. Baptist. Avocations: hist. rsch., wood carving.

PEEKEL, ARTHUR K. secondary school educator; Tchr. social scis. Rolling Meadows (Ill.) High Sch. Recipient State Tchr. of Yr. Social Scis. award Ill., 1992. Office: Rolling Meadows High Sch 2901 W Central Rd Rolling Meadows IL 60008-2536

PEELER, RICHARD NEVIN, internist, educator; b. Salisbury, N.C., Sept. 9, 1926; s. Banks Joseph and Agnes Goldie (Andrew) P.; m. Frances Anne Signorelli, Dec. 27, 1951; children: Lauren Marie, Anne Sullivan, Karen Andrew, Matthew George, Mark O'Brien. AB, Catawba Coll., 1947; MD, Johns Hopkins U., 1951. Intern Johns Hopkins Hosp., Balt., 1951-52, resident, 1952-53, 55-56, fellow in medicine, 1956-57, instr. medicine, 1952-57, asst. prof., 1977—; pvt. practice in internal medicine and infectious disease Annapolis, Md., 1957-96; mem. staff Anne Arundel Med. Ctr., 1957-99, emeritus staff, 1999—. Pres. med. staff, 1969-71, dir. outpatient intravenous svcs., 1988-99, sr. epidemiologist, 1993-99; instr. physicians asst. course Anne Arundel C.C.; sr. ptnr. Annapolis (Md.) Med. Specialists, LLP, ret. 1996. Contbr. articles to med. jours. Bd. dirs. Annapolis Life Care Ctr., 1981-84. With U.S. Army, 1954-56. Fellow ACP, Am. Soc. for Microbiology, So. Med. Assn., Md. Med. and Chirurgical Faculty, Johns Hopkins Med.-Surg. Soc., Anne Arundel County Med. Soc., Annapolis Yacht Club, Johns Hopkins Club, Officers and Faculty Club.

PEELER, SCOTT LOOMIS, JR., foreign language educator; b. Rome, Ga., Aug. 25, 1947; s. Scott Loomis Sr. and Emily Willis P. BA in Spanish and French, U. South Fla., 1969, MA in Spanish and Edn., 1974; EdD candidate, Ariz. State U., 1982-91. Cert. tchr., Fla. Tchr. Spanish Polk County Sch., Lakeland, Fla., 1969—2000, Bloomingdale HS, Valrico, Fla., 2002. Tchr. Brandon (Fla.) Adult and Cmty. Sch., 1978-79, Hillborough C.C., Fla., 1986; grad. rsch. asst. Ctr. Indian Edn., Ariz. State U., Tempe, 1983-84; bi-lingual census worker U.S. Dept. Census, Tampa, 1980; tchr. tribal mgmt. program Scottsdale (Ariz.) C.C., 1988; asst. dir. Portuguese Lang. Study Inst. in Brazil, U. South Fla., Curitiba, Paraná, Brazil, 1998, 2000, conversational English tchr., 1999; tour guide Customized Historic Tours of Ybor City, Tampa Bay Destinations, Destination Tampa Bay; lectr. in field. Author: Historical Markers and Monuments in Tampa and Hillsborough County, Florida, 1994; contbr. articles to profl. jours. Donor Peeler Am. Indian Scholarship U. South Fla., 1986; active Ptnrs. of Ams., Sister Cities Internat., Tampa, 1972—, chair edn. com., bd. dirs., 1990-98; mem.

Tampa Hist. Soc., 1972—; bd. dirs. Tampa Bay History Ctr., 1994-99, Mus. Cherokee Indian, Ybor City Mus.; started ptnr. city relationship between Lakeland, Fla. and Valledupar, Cesar, Colombia, 1977; co-chair Ariz. Indian Edn./Native Am. Lang. Issues Conf., 1984; mem. pres.'s coun. U. South Fla.; mem. Sister Cities Com., Lakeland, Fla., del. on ofcl. visit to Japan, 1993; mem. minority task force Tampa Bay Area Blood Marrow Donor Program; vol. Tampa/Hillsborough County Conv. and Visitors Ctr; chair Granada, Nicaragua Com., 1996-98. Recipient Teaching Incentive award Carnation Milk Corp., Phoenix, 1984, named one of Outstanding Young Men of Am., Montgomery, Ala., 1984; Am. Indian Leadership prog. grantee Ariz. State U., 1982-84; Newberry Library fellow Am. Indian Ctr. History, Chgo., 1981. Mem. SCV, Nat. Indian Edn. Assn. (Ariz. steering com. 1984), Huguenot Soc. SC (life), Fla. Geneal. Soc. (pres. 2002-03, U. South Fla. Alumni Assn., Christian Hope Indian Eskimo Fellowship, Cajun Connection, Alliance Francaise, L'Unione Italiana, Tampa Bay History Ctr. (charter), Ybor City Mus. (charter), Nat. Congress Am. Indians, Tampa Trolley Soc., Krewe of the Knights of Sant 'Yago, (knighted in 2003), Tampa Bay Area Camellia Soc., Nat. Mus. Am. Indians (charter), Nat. Indian Adult Edn. Assn., Brandon Area Geneal. and Hist. Soc. (2003). Home: 433 Summit Chase Dr Valrico FL 33594-3841 Office: Bloomingdale HS 1700 E Bloomingdale Ave Valrico FL 33594 E-mail: slpeelerjr@yahoo.com.

PEENO, LARRY NOYLE, state agency administrator, consultant; b. Evansville, Ind., Dec. 24, 1941; s. Paul Albert and Marcella (Imogene) Franz; m. Margaret Marie Graf, June 8, 1973. AB, Western Ky. U., 1968, MA, 1969; EdD, U. Mo., 1977. Cert. tchr. Mo. Art tchr. Normandy Sr. High Sch., St. Louis, 1974-90, chmn. art dept., 1976-89; dist. art coord. Normandy Sch. Dist., St. Louis, 1988-92; fine arts cons. Dept. Elem. and Secondary Edn., Jefferson City, Mo., 1990—. Mem. adv. bd. St. Louis Art Mus., 1988—. Contbg. author: Supervision and Administration: Programs, Positions, Perspectives, 1991, Nat. Standards For Arts Edn.: What Every Young American SHould Know and Be Able To Do in The Arts, 1994, Nat. Visual Arts Standards, 1994; editor Show-Me-Art newsletter, 1983-84. With USAF, 1959-62. Fellow Nat. Art Edn. Assn. (disting., nat. program coord. 1993, bd. dirs. 1995-97, trustee found. 1998—, Nat. Newsletter award 1983-84, Award of Excellence 1983-84, Educator of Yr. for supervision and adminstrn. 1998); mem. ASCD, Nat. Assn. State Dirs. Art Edn., Mo. Art Edn. Assn. (Secondary Art Tchr. of Yr. 1987-88, Outstanding Art Educator award 1983-84), Music Educators Nat. Conf., Mo. Music Educators Assn. Office: Dept Elem and Secondary Edn 205 Jefferson State Ofc Jefferson City MO 65102

PEEPLES, MARK EDWARD, virology researcher, educator; b. Lancaster, Pa., Sept. 26, 1952; s. Robert Fred and Ruth Jane (Walters) P.; m. Rebecca Ann Brumberg, Nov. 5, 1977. BS, Heidelberg Coll., 1974; PhD, Wayne State U., 1978. Postdoctoral fellow Univ. Mass. Med. Sch., Worcester, 1978-80, instr., 1980-83; asst. prof. Rush Med. Coll., Chgo., 1983-88, assoc. prof., 1988-92, prof., 1992—, assoc. chmn., 1990-99, head, sect. of virology, dept. immunology/microbiology, 1989—. Cons. Wellstat, Inc., Rockville, Md., 1995—, Apath LLC, St. Louis, 1999—, Trimeris, Inc., Durham, N.C., 2000—; ad hoc mem. Exptl. Viology Study Sect. and Virology Study Sect., NIH, 1991—; mem. Step 1 microbiology test com. Nat. Bd. Med. Examiners, 1995-97; sabbatical at NIH, 1995-96. Assoc. editor Virology, 1987-99; contbr. chpt. to The Paramyxoviruses; contbr. articles to Virology, Jour. Virology, Jour. Exptl. Medicine, Cancer Rsch., Jour. Nat. Cancer Inst., Jour. Gen. Physiology, Gene, Neurology, Jour. Infectious Diseases, Jour. Clin. Microbiology, Proc. NAS. NIH Postdoctoral fellow, 1978-81, NIH Rsch. Career Devel. awardee, 1988-93, grantee NIH, 1985-93, 90-98, 2001-06, 2002-07; NSF U.S.-Australia Coop. Rsch. grantee, 1993-95. Mem. AAAS, Am. Soc. Virology, Am. Soc. for Microbiology, Sigma Xi (pres. Rush U. chpt. 1988-90, 2001-03). Achievements include identification and localization of the proteins in viral particles from respiratory syncytial virus proteins; devised a system to limit respiratory syncytial virus minigenome replication to a single cycle; identified iduronic acid and N-sulfation as critical components of respiratory syncytial virus attachment to target cell surface heparan sulfate; determined that the respiratory syncytial virus fusion protein functions efficiently independent of the viral attachment protein; demonstrated specific targeting of respiratory syncytial virus to the ciliated cells lining the human respiratory tract; demonstrated hepatitis B virus receptor sites on human liver plasma membranes; identified apolipoprotein H as a protein that binds Hepatitis B virus; cloned the apolipoprotein H gene; demonstrated lipid binding activity and nuclear localization of the Newcastle disease virus matrix protein and its nuclear localization signal; identified of the importance of an amphipathic alpha helix in the Newcastle disease virus fusion protein. Office: Rush-Pres-St Luke Med Ctr Dept Immunology/Microbiol 1653 W Congress Pkwy Chicago IL 60612-3833 Business E-Mail: mpeeples@rush.edu.

PEEPLES, WILLIAM DEWEY, JR., mathematics educator; b. Bessemer, Ala., Apr. 19, 1928; s. William Dewey and Thelma Jeannette (Chastain) P.; m. Katie Ray Blackerby, Aug. 30, 1956; children: Mary Jeannette, William Dewey III, Gerald Lewis, Stephen Ray. BS, Samford U., 1948; MS, U. Wis., 1949; PhD, U. Ga., 1951. Rsch. mathematician Ballistics Rsch. Lab., Aberdeen, Md., summer 1951; mem. faculty Samford U., Birmingham, Ala., 1951-56, prof. math., 1959-95, head dept., 1967-95; prof. emeritus, 1995; mem. faculty Auburn U., 1956-59. Cons. Hayes Internat. Corp. Co-author: Modern Mathematics for Business Students, 1969, Finite Mathematics, 1974, Modern Mathematics with Applications to Business and the Social Sciences, 4th edit, 1986, Finite Mathematics with Applications to Business and the Social Sciences, 1981, 2d edit., 1987; Contbr. articles to profl. publs. Served to 1st lt. AUS, 1954-56. Mem. Am. Math. Soc., Math. Assn. Am., Nat. Council Tchrs. Math., Ala. Coll. Tchrs. Math. (pres. 1969), Sigma Xi, Pi Mu Epsilon, Phi Kappa Phi (pres. 1977), Lambda Chi Alpha. Baptist (deacon, chmn. 1986). Club: Mason (Shriner). Home: 419 Poinciana Dr Birmingham AL 35209-4129 E-mail: wdpeeples@peoplepc.com.

PEERADINA, SALEEM, English educator, poet; b. Bombay, Oct. 5, 1944; came to U.S., 1988; s. Habib and Noorunnisa Peeradina; m. Mumtaz Peeradina, May 11, 1978; children: Shoneizi, Lail. MA, Bombay (India) U., 1969, Wake Forest U., 1973. Lectr. in English St. Xavier Coll., Bombay, India, 1976-77, Sophia Coll., Bombay, 1977-80, dir. open classroom, 1978-84; copywriter Hindustan Thompson, Bombay, 1984-87; vis. prof. Adrian/Alma (Mich.) Colls., 1988-89; assoc. prof. Siena Heights U., Adrian, Mich. Revs. editor Express Mag., Bombay, 1982-88; poetry readings East West Ctr., Univ. Hawaii, Third World Arts Festival, London, The Commonwealth Inst., London, U. Sussex and Milan, as well as numerous readings at instns. in continental U.S. author: (poetry) First Offence, 1980, Group Portrait, 1992, Meditations on Desire, 2003; editor: (poetry anthology) Contemporary Indian Poetry in English: An Assessment and Selection, 1972; contbr. poetry to many anthologies. Mem. MLA. Avocations: cooking, photography, travel, walking. Home: 1110 Bent Oak Ave Adrian MI 49221-1509 Office: Siena Heights U 1247 E Siena Heights Dr Adrian MI 49221-1755 E-mail: speerad2@sienahts.edu.

PEET, PHYLLIS IRENE, women's studies educator; b. Winnipeg, Man., Can., Mar. 3, 1943; came to the U.S., 1948; d. Harold Parsons and Gladys Mae (Riley) Harrison; m. Thomas Peter Richman, June 14, 1963 (div. 1969); m. Charles Francis Peet, Sept. 9, 1972. BA in Art, Calif. State U., Northridge, 1972; MA in Art History, U. Calif., L.A., 1976, PhD in Art History, 1987. Sec. L.A. County Supr. Kenneth Hahn, 1960-68; assoc. in art history L.A. County Mus. Art, 1974-75; asst. dir., curator Grunwald Ctr. for the Graphic Arts, U. Calif., L.A., 1975-78; Am. art scholar High Mus. Art, Atlanta, 1984-90; instr. women's studies Monterey (Calif.) Peninsula Coll., 1986—, dir., instr. women's programs/women's studies, 1989—. Dirs.' adv. com. The Art Mus. of Santa Cruz County, 1981-84, 89-94; vis. lectr. Calif. State U., Fresno, fall 1984; program coord. conf. Inst. for Hist. Study, San Francisco, 1987; lectr. bd. studies in art U. Calif. Santa Cruz, 1991-95. Author, co-curator, editor, compiler: (book and exhbn.) The American Personality: The Artist Illustrator of Life in the United States, 1860-1930, 1976; author, curator: (book and exhbn.) American Women of the Etching Revival, 1988; co-author: American Paintings in the High Museum of Art, 1994; contbr. articles to profl. publs. including Am. Nat. Biography, Fitzroy Dict. of Women Artists, 1997, Dict. of Literary Biography, 1998. Vol., activist Dem. Party, L.A., 1960-66, Peace and Freedom Party, L.A., 1967-71; vol. Dem. Party Candidates, Santa Cruz, Calif., 1979-96, Santa Cruz Action Network, 1980-85; mem. nominating com. Girl Scouts of Am., Monterey Bay, 1991-93. Rockefeller Found. fellow U. Calif. L.A., 1978-79, 79-80, Dickson grantee U. Calif. L.A., 1981-82; recipient Women Helping Women award Soroptimists, Monterey and Carmel, Calif., 1991, 95, Allen Griffin for Excellence in Edn. award Cmty. Found. of Monterey County, 1993, Quality of Life award Econ. Devel. Corp., Monterey, 1994. Mem.: NAACP, ACLU, NOW, AAUW, Coll. Art Assn., Western Assn. Women Historians, Inst. for Hist. Study, Nat. Women's Studies Assn., Planned Parenthood, Monterey Bay Women's Caucus for Art (founder, bd. dirs. 1988—93), Women's Internat. League for Peace and Freedom. Avocations: print collecting, photography. Office: Womens Programs Monterey Peninsula Coll 980 Fremont St Monterey CA 93940-4704

PEET, ROBERT KRUG, ecology educator; b. Beloit, Wis., Feb. 14, 1947; s. Joseph Lockwood and Severa (Krug) P.; m. Mary Monnig, Apr. 8, 1971; children: Matthew, Jeffrey. BA, U. Wis., 1970, MS, 1971; PhD, Cornell U. 1975. Asst. prof. U. N.C., Chapel Hill, 1975-80, assoc. prof., 1980-88, prof., 1988—. Editor Jour. Vegetation Sci., 1990-95; editor-in-chief Ecology and Ecol. Monographs, 1996-2001. Fellow AAAS; mem. Ecol. Soc. Am. (sec. 1992-95, Disting. Svc. award 1995), Internat. Assn. Vegetation Sci. (governing bd. 1990—). Office: U NC Dept Biology CB #3280 Chapel Hill NC 27599-3280

PEGUES, KATHLEEN GARCIA, gifted and talented educator; b. Gainesville, Fla., Apr. 4, 1949; d. Robert C. Garcia and Joy (Stevens) Garcia Wood; m. John K. Pegues IV, Aug. 13, 1977; children: Emily, Adam. BA, Sweet Briar Coll., Va., 1971; MEd, U. Va., 1974. Cert. devel. teaching specialist Devel. Skills Inst., 1987. Lang. arts tchr. for gifted/talented Fauquier County Pub. Schs., Warrenton, Va., 1974—2000; tchr. gifted and talented Loudoun County Pub. Schs., Hamilton, Va., 2000—. Bd. dirs. Fauquier Soc. Prevention Cruelty to Animals, 1976-82; deacon Warrenton Presbyn. Ch., Va., 1980-83; coord. Ch. World Svc. Crop Hunger Walk, Warrenton, 1983-88; rep. alumnae admissions Sweet Briar Coll. Recipient Fauquier County Excellence in Edn. fellowship, 1984, 96. Mem. Sweet Briar Coll. Alumnae Assn. (pres. 1998-2001). Home: PO Box 3006 Warrenton VA 20188-1706 Office: Harmony Intermediate Sch 38174 W Colonial Hwy Hamilton VA 20158 E-mail: kgpegues@msn.com.

PEIFFER, RANDEL AARON, agricultural sciences educator, researcher; b. Ligonier, Pa., Aug. 4, 1944; s. Tony and Emma E. (Leighty) P. BS, Delaware Valley Coll., 1968; MS, Pa. State U., 1970, PhD, 1976. Rsch. asst. prof. Del. State U., Dover, 1986; asst. prof. Del. State Coll., Dover, 1986-93, assoc. prof., 1993—. Vis. prof. Farmers Home Adminstrn. Advisor carpentry adv. com. Vocat. Tech. Sch., Kent County, Del., 1987—; mem. Del. Agr. Mus., Dover, 1986—; mem. tech. com. NE-SARE, 1994—. Recipient First Pl. Sci. Poster in Plant and Soil Sci., 9th Biennial Rsch. Symposium, Assn. Rsch. Dirs. 1890 Land-Grant Colls. and Univs., Atlanta, 1992—. Mem. Am. Soc. Agronomy, Crop Sci. Soc. Am., Fraternal Order Police, Silver Lake Fishing Club (editor newsletter Dover chpt. 1984—). Achievements include research inforage management and utilization, biological control of gypsy moth in urban forest and crop ecology. Office: Del State U Dept Agr Natural Resources Dover DE 19901

PEIRCE, CAROLE, elementary school educator; b. Oshkosh, Wis., June 11, 1943; d. Charles J. and Bernadette (Graf) P.; m. Jack McDowell, Nov. 18, 1982. BS, U. Wis., Oshkosh, 1965; MA, U. Wis., Madison, 1966. Instr. U. Wis. Ctr. System, Marinette & Fond Du Lac, 1966-70, Concordia Coll., Milw., 1970-71; tchr. of French Behavioral Rsch. Labs., Palo Alto, Calif., 1971-73; elem. tchr. Nido De Aguilas Internat. Sch., Santiago, Chile; elem. bilingual tchr. Alum Rock Sch. Dist., San Jose, Calif., 1978-87; elem. tchr. Huntsville (Ark.) Sch. Dist., 1987-95; French, Spanish, and ESL tchr. Huntsville (Ark.) H.S., 1995-2000. Presenter Bay Area Sch. Dists. Calif. 1984-87, Springdale Tchrs. Co-op, Little Rock, Arkadelphia, Ark., Dallas, Albuquerque, St. Paul, Dominican Republic; tchr., cons. Nat. Geog. Soc., 1990-96. Author Social Studies Review Article 1985. Grantee Environ. Edn. State of Calif., 1986, NSTA to Internat. Geographical Congress, Washington, 1992, NASA Ednl. Workshop for Elem. Sci. Tchrs., 1993; Christa McAuliffe fellow, 1993-94; recipient Nat. Disting. Teaching award Nat. Achievement Coun. Geographic Edn., 1993. Mem. NEA, Nat. Coun. for Social Studies, Nat. Coun. for Geog. Edn., Ark. Geog. Alliance (newsletter editor, Geography Tchr. of Yr., 1993-94), Ozark Soc. Avocations: global studies, geography, outdooring, travel. Home: 2046 Madison 8325 Hindsville AR 72738-9727

PEIRCE, DONALD OLUF, retired elementary education educator; b. Boulder, Colo., Mar. 5, 1939; s. James Girdwood and Ruth Julia (Wagner) P.; m. Joyce Arleen Kovatch. BS, Temple U., 1971, MEd, 1978. Cert. elem. tchr., reading specialist, Pa. Remedial reading tchr. Bartram High Sch., Phila., 1975-80; piano, reading, lang. arts tchr. Locke Elem. Sch., Phila., 1981—. Tutoring project coord. With USMCR, 1963-68. Mem.: Internat. Dyslexia Assn. (bd. dirs.), Internat. Reading Assn. (Phila. chpt.), Del. Valley Reading Assn. Republican. Episcopalian. Avocations: music composition, piano, swimming, cinema, travel. Office: Locke Elementary School 46th & Haverford Ave Philadelphia PA 19139

PEIRCE, JAMES WALTER, secondary school educator, historian, educator; b. Aug. 8, 1933; s. Kenneth Adelbert and Helen Virginia Peirce; m. Nancy Anne Kratovil, Apr. 14, 1962; 1 child, Mark Andrew. Cert. social studies tchr., secondary prin. Md. History tchr., adminstr. Prince George's County Bd. Edn., Upper Marlboro, Md., 1967—. Vol. fireman Chillum-Adelphi (Md.) Fire Dept., 1960—65; vol. ranger Pasapsco River Valley State Pk., Ellicott City, Md., 1991—99. Author: Pasapsco Valley Mill Sites, 1995, Four Hundred Years of Dicken, 2001, (poems) History of Post #28, 1997, The People Call it Chesapeake, 1999, History of the Prince George's Council of the American Legion, 2003. Life mem. Md. Congress of Parents and Tchrs., 1976—. With USN, 1951—56. Named Outstanding Educator of Am., Acad. Am. Edn., 1974; recipient Outstanding Svc. award, Prince George County. Mem.: U. Md. Alumni Assn., Am. Legion (life; historian 1995—). Republican. Avocations: history, genealogy, research, poetry, writing. Home: 5900 Whaleboat Dr Clarksville MD 21029

PELAVIN, SOL HERBERT, research company executive; b. Detroit, Dec. 16, 1941; s. Norman J. and Alice A. Pelavin; m. Diane Christine Blakemore, Aug. 14, 1966; 2 children. BA in Math., U. Chgo., 1965, MAT in Math., 1969; MS in Stats., Stanford U., 1974, PhD candidate in mathematical models of edn. research, 1975. Tchr. pub. schs., 1965-70. teaching rsch. asst. Stanford (Calif.) U., 1972-74; cons. Rand Corp., Santa Monica, Calif., 1975; policy analyst SRI Internat., Menlo Park, Calif., 1975-78; exec. officer NTS Research Corp., Durham, N.C., 1978-82; pres. Pelavin Assocs., Inc., Washington, 1982-94; exec. v.p., COO Am. Inst. Rsch., 1994-2001, pres., CEO, 2001-; dir. Data Analysis and Tech. Support Ctr., Washington, 1989-93, Policy Analysis Support Ctr., Washington, 1993—; expert witness to U.S. Congress, 1977, 79, Cabinet briefing, 1983; cons. Frank, Bernstein, Conway and Goldman, Balt., 1980-81; dir. Ednl. Analysis Ctr., Washington, 1982-85. Author: (with P. Barker) A Study of the Generalizability of the Results of Standardized Achievement Tests, 1976, (with J.L. David) Research on the Effectiveness of Compensatory Education Programs: A Reanalysis of Data, 1977, (with others) Federal Expenditures for the Education of Children and Youth With Special Needs, 1981, (with D.C. Pelavin) An Evaluation of the Fund for the Improvement of Postsecondary Education, 1981, 83, (with others) Evaluation of the Commodity Supplemental Food Program, 1982, An Evaluation of the Bilingual Education Evaluation, Dissemination and Assessment Centers, 1984, A Study of a Year-Round School Program, 1978, Teacher Preparation: A Review of State Certification Requirements, 1984, Analysis of the National Availability of Mathematics and Science Teachers, 1983, Minority Participation in Higher Education, 1988, Changing the Odds, 1990, others; contbr. articles to profl. jours. NSF fellow U. Chgo., 1968-69; Cuneo fellow Stanford U., 1973. Mem. Am. Ednl. Research Assn., Am. Psychol. Assn. Democrat. Jewish. Office: American Inst Rsch 1000 Thomas Jefferson Washington DC 20007-3500 E-mail: spelavin@air.org.

PELC, KAROL IGNACY, engineering and technology management educator, researcher; b. Czestochowa, Poland, July 29, 1935; came to U.S., 1985; s. Stanislaw Pelc and Kamilla (Hecko) Pelc-Kosna; m. Ryszarda Lidia Ryglewicz, Sept. 24, 1959; 1 child, Dariusz. MScEE, Tech. U. Wroclaw, Poland, 1958, PhD in Econs., 1976; PhD in Electronics, U. Uppsala, Sweden, 1968. Prodn. & engring. mgr. Energopomiar Co., Wroclaw, 1960-65; rsch. asst. dept. electronics U. Uppsala, 1961-62; assoc. dir. divsn. Inst. Electric Power Industry, Wroclaw, 1966-68; founder, dir. Forecasting Rsch. Ctr., Wroclaw, 1971-81; electronic design engr. Rsch. Inst. Tech. U. Wroclaw, 1957-60, rsch. dir., 1968-77, lectr., dir. Jelenia Gora Coll. br., 1982-85; prof. Mich. Technol. U., Houghton, 1985—; dir. Ctr. for Technol. Innovation, Leadership & Entrepreneurship, 2001—02. Vis. prof. Indian Inst. Tech., Bombay, 1981, Stevens Inst. Tech., Hoboken, N.J., 1993, U. Sci. and Tech., Beijing, 2002; vis. scholar Japan Ctr. for Mich. Univs., Hikone, 1992; mem. innovation task force Internat. Inst. for Applied Sys. Analysis, Laxenburg, Austria, 1983-84; chmn. forecasting seminar Polish Acad. Scis., Warsaw, 1974-81; v.p. divsn. Soc. Mgmt. and Orgn., Wroclaw, 1979-80. Author: Planning of Research and Development, 1981; co-author: Technological Challenges, 1999, Technology Strategies and Forecasts, 2003; mem. editl. bd. U.S. R&D Mgmt., Eng., Transformations, Poland; contbr. over 100 articles to scholarly jours.; patentee in field. Mem. Internat. Assn. Mgmt. Tech., Internat. Assn. for Rsch. and Devel. Mgmt., Engring. Mgmt. Soc. of IEEE. Roman Catholic. Avocations: classical music, tourism, cross-country skiing, bicycling, swimming. Office: Mich Technol Univ Sch Bus & Econ Houghton MI 49931

PELCYGER, IRAN, retired principal; b. Bklyn., Feb. 26, 1937; s. Jacob and Yetta (Nabridge) P.; m. Elaine Morley, June 4, 1956; children: Stuart Lawrence, Gwynne Ellice, Wayne Farrol. BS, CCNY, 1959, MA in Sci. and Edn., 1962; postgrad., Yeshiva U., 1963, Adelphi U. and NYU, 1964-67, 68-74. Cert. tchr., ednl. adminstr., N.Y. Tchr., adminstr. various pub. schs., Bklyn., 1959—; tchr., acting chmn. sci. dept., chmn. program dept. Jr. High Sch. 265, Bklyn., 1959-66; tchr. aerospace and gen. sci., chmn. sci. dept. Jr. High Sch. 111, Bklyn., 1966-71, asst. prin., 1971-74; prin. Frances E. Carter Sch., Bklyn., 1974-98; ret. 1998. Adj. instr. Sch. Edn., CCNY, 1988—; mem. ad-hoc com. elem. edn., N.Y. Dept. Edn., 1987, mem. organizing com., moderator edn. conf., 1986—; adj. prof. York Coll., 1998, Bronx C.C., 1998—, Iona Coll., New Rochelle, N.Y., 2000—; site mgr. Tech. Prep. Program Bronx C.C., 2002—. Contbg. editor: A Guide for Elementary Sch. Prins., 1985, Proceedings of the Mainstream Conf.: Opening Doors to a Brighter Future, 1988; co-writer: Mainstreaming Handbook: A Guide to Implementing. Mem. N.Y.C. Elem. Sch. Prins. Assn. (past pres.), Coun. Suprs. and Adminstrs. (past v.p., exec. bd. 1983—, trustee Welfare Fudn 1986-90), N.Y. Acad. Pub. Edn., Nat. Assn. Elem. Sch. Prins., Network for Effective Schs., ASCD, Phi Delta Kappa. Home: 79 Sheryl Cres Smithtown NY 11787-1321 E-mail: iran.pelcyger@bcc.cuny.edu

PELCZYNSKI, SUZETTE ELIZABETH, elementary school educator; b. Milw., Nov. 1, 1950; d. Chester Roman and Florence E. (Sanasac) P. BA, CArdinal Stritch Coll., 1972. 3d grade tchr. Port Washington (Wis.)-Saukville Pub. Schs., 1972—, insvc. instr., 1989-91, spl. events chair, 1984-92. Insvc. instr. Comprehensive Ednl. Svcs. Agy., Mils., 1990-91 Mem. Nat. Coun. Tchrs. Math., Wis. Math. Coun. (named to Top 50 Math. Educators 1987), Wis. Edn. Assn., Port Washington-Saukville Edn. Assn. (chief negotiator 1976-77). Home: 423 S Spring St Port Washington WI 53074-2329

PELHAM, FRAN O'BYRNE, writer, teacher; b. Phila., Oct. 16, 1939; d. Frederick Thomas and Frances Rebecca (Johns) O'Byrne; m. Donald Lacey Pelham, June 15, 1968; children: Mary Frances, Michael. BA, Holy Family Coll., 1967; M in English Edn., Trenton Coll., 1974; EdD, U. Pa., 1993. Cert. secondary tchr. Tchr. Sch. Dist. Bristol (Pa.) Twp., 1967-70; feature writer various publs., Phila. and others, 1980—; prof., dir. Writing Ctr. Holy Family Coll., Phila., 1982-89; asst. prof. lit. and writing LaSalle U., Phila., 1989-93, Beaver Coll., Glenside, Pa., 1994—; dir. tech. communications Internat. Chem. Co., Phila. 1985-90. Speaker, workshop leader various orgns. Author: Search for Atocha Treasure, 1989, Downtown America: Philadelphia, 1989, Moon Journal: Prayer Poems, 1998; contbr. articles to mags. Participant Jenkintown Arts Festival, 1984; Campus Ministry Team Holy Family Coll., Phila., 1986-89, Alliance for a Living Ocean, 1991—, Phila. Children's Reading Roundtable, Authors Guild, Franciscan Adult Sch. Bd., 1995, A Non-denominational Cmty. Harvesting Our Resources, Support Police Immediate Response Intervention Team; bd. dirs. U. Pa. Edn. Alumni Assn. Recipient Citation Mayor's Commn., 1988. Mem. AAUW, Nat. Coun. Tchrs. Eng., Am. Conf. Irish Studies, Nat. League Am. Pen Women (br. pres. 1982-84), Phila. Writers' Conf. (bd. dirs. 1982-86), Pi Lambda Theta, Lambda Iota Tau, Phi Delta Kappa. Democrat. Roman Catholic. Avocations: scuba diving, tennis, boating, travel. Office: Dept of Lit Beaver College Glenside PA 19120

PELIKAN, JAROSLAV JAN, history educator; b. Akron, Ohio, Dec. 17, 1923; s. Jaroslav Jan and Anna (Buzek) P.; m. Sylvia Burica, June 9, 1946; children: Martin, Michael, Miriam. Grad. summa cum laude, Concordia Jr. Coll., Ft. Wayne, Ind., 1942; BD, Concordia Theol. Sem., St. Louis, 1946; PhD, U. Chgo., 1946; MA (hon.), Yale U., 1961; DD (hon.), Concordia Coll., Moorehead, Minn., 1960, Concordia Sem., 1967, Trinity Coll. Hartford, Conn., 1987, St. Vladimir's Orthodox Theol. Sem., 1988, Victoria U., Toronto, 1989, U. Aberdeen, Scotland, 1995; LittD (hon.), Wittenberg U., 1960, Wheeling Coll., 1966, Gettysburg Coll., 1967, Pacific Luth. U., 1967, Wabash Coll., 1988, Jewish Theol. Sem., 1991; HHD (hon.) Providence Coll., 1966, Moravian Coll., 1986, Jewish Theol. Sem., 1991; LLD (hon.), Keuka Coll., 1996, Notre Dame, 1979, Harvard U., 1998, U. Regina, 1998; LHD (hon.), Valparaiso U., 1966, Rockhurst Coll., 1967, Albertus Magnus Coll., 1973, Coe Coll., 1976, Cath. U. Am., 1977, St. Mary's Coll., 1978, St. Anselm Coll., 1983, U. Nebr.-Omaha, 1984, Tulane U., 1986, Assumption Coll., 1986, LaSalle U., 1987, Carthage Coll., 1991, U. Chgo., 1991, So. Meth. U., 1992, SUNY, Albany, 1993, Fla. Internat. U., 1997; ThD (hon.), U. Hamburg, 1971, St. Olaf Coll., 1972, Charles U., Prague, 1999, STD, Dickinson Coll., 1986; DSc in Hist., Comenius U., Bratislava, 1992; ScD (hon.), Loyola U., Chgo., 1995. Faculty Valparaiso (Ind.) U., 1946-49, Concordia Sem., St. Louis, 1949-53, U. Chgo., 1953-62; Titus Street prof. eccles. history Yale U., 1962-72, Sterling prof. history, 1972-96, William Clyde DeVane lectr., 1984-86, dir. humanities, 1974-75, chmn. Medieval studies, 1974-75, 78-80, dean Grad. Sch., 1973-78; Joseph chair Boston Coll., 1996-97, Annenberg Sch. Comm., U. Pa., 1998-2001; Disting. Vis. Scholar Libr. Congress, Washington, 2001—02. Vis. prof. Boston Coll., 1996-97, Annenberg Sch. Comm., U. Pa., 1998; Gray lectr. Duke U., 1960, Ingersoll lectr. Harvard U., 1963, Gauss lectr. Princeton U., 1980, Jefferson lectr. NEH, 1983, Richard lectr. U. Va., 1983, Rauschenbusch lectre. Colgate-Rochester Divinity Sch., 1984, Gilson lectr. U. Toronto, 1985, 98, Hale lectr. Seabury-Western Sem., 1986, Mead-Swing lectr. Oberlin Coll., 1986, Gross lectr. Rutgers U., 1989; adv. bd. Ctr. Theol.

Inquiry, 1984-90; mem. coun. The Smithsonian Instn., 1984-90; US chmn. US Czechoslovak Commn. on Humanities and Social Scis., 1987-92; scholarly dir. instns. of democracy project Annenberg Found Trust, Sunnylands, 2002—. Author: From Luther to Kierkegaard, 1950, Fools for Christ, 1955, The Riddle of Roman Catholicism, 1959 (Abingdon award 1959), Luther the Expositor, 1959, The Shape of Death, 1961, The Light of the World, 1962, Obedient Rebels, 1964, The Finality of Jesus Christ in an Age of Universal History, 1965, The Christian Intellectual, 1966, Spirit Versus Structure, 1968, Development of Doctrine, 1969, Historical Theology, 1971, The Christian Tradition, 5 vols., 1971-89, Scholarship and Its Survival, 1983, The Vindication of Tradition, 1984, Jesus through the Centuries, 1985, The Mystery of Continuity, 1986, Bach Among the Theologians, 1986, The Excellent Empire, 1987, The Melody of Theology, 1988, Confessor Between East and West, 1990, Imago Dei, 1990, Eternal Feminines, 1990, The Idea of the University: A Reexamination, 1992, Christianity and Classical Culture, 1993, Faust the Theologian, 1995, The Reformation of the Bible/ The Bible of the Reformation, 1996, Mary through the Centuries, 1996, The Illustrated Jesus Through the Centuries, 1997, What Has Athens to do with Jerusalem?, 1997, Divine Rhetoric, 2001, Credo, 2003; editor, translator: Luther's Works, 22 vols., 1955-71, The Book of Concord, 1959; editor: Makers of Modern Theology, 5 vols., 1966-68, The Preaching of Chrysostom, 1967, Interpreters of Luther, 1968, Twentieth-Century Theology in the Making, 3 vols., 1969-70, The Preaching of Augustine, 1973, The World Treasury of Modern Religious Thought, 1991, Sacred Writings, 7 vols., 1992; (with Valerie Hotchkiss) Creeds and Confessions of Faith in the Christian Tradition, 3 vols., 2003; mem. editl. bd. Collected Works of Erasmus, Classics of Western Spirituality, Evangelisches Kirchenlexikon, Emerson's Nature, 1986, The World Treasury of Modern Religious Thought, 1990; departmental editor Ency. Britannica, 1958-69; adminstrv. bd. Papers of Benjamin Franklin; chmn. publs. com. Yale U. Press, 1979-90, 92—, v.p. bd. govs., 1988—; contbr. articles to profl. jours. Pres. 4th Internat. Congress for Luther Research, 1971, New Eng. Congress on Grad. Edn., 1976-77. Recipient Abingdon award, 1959; Pax Christi award St. John's U., Collegeville, Minn., 1966, Colman J. Barry award, 1995; John Gilmary Shea prize Am. Cath. Hist. Assn., 1971, nat. award Slovak World Congress, 1973, religious book award Cath. Press Assn., 1974, Christian Unity award Atonement Friars, 1975, Bicentennial award Czechoslovak Soc. Arts and Scis., 1976, Wilbur Cross medal Yale U. Grad. Sch. Assn., 1979, Profl. Achievement award U. Chgo. Alumni Assn., 1980, Shaw medal Boston Coll., 1984, Comenius medal Moravian Coll., 1986, Alumnus of Yr. award U. Chgo. Div. Sch., 1986, Bicentennial medal Georgetown U., 1989, award for excellence Am. Acad. Religion 1989, Umanità award Newberry Libr., 1990, Jacques Barzun award Am. Acad. for Liberal Edn., 1997, Festschriften: Schools of Thought in the Christian Tradition, 1984, The Unbounded Community, 1996; sr. fellow Carnegie Found. for Advancement Tchg., 1982-83. Fellow Medieval Acad. Am. (councillor, Haskins medal 1985); mem. Am. Hist. Assn., Am. Soc. Ch. History (pres. 1965, Achievement award 1998), Internat. Congress Luther Rsch. (pres. 1971), Am. Acad. Arts and Scis. (v.p. 1976-94, pres. 1994-97), Am. Philos. Soc. (councillor 1984-87, Moe prize 1997), Am. Acad. Polit. and Social Sci. (pres. 2000—), Coun. Scholars of Libr. of Congress (founding chmn. 1980-83), Elizabethan Club, Mory's, Phi Beta Kappa (senator United chpts. 1985-90). Home: 156 Chestnut Ln Hamden CT 06518-1604

PELKEY, TEENA FERRIS, elementary education educator, consultant; b. San Rafael, Calif., Dec. 3, 1949; d. Ernest Herbert and Fern Cleone Simmons; children: April F., Allison M. AA, Solano Coll., 1970; BA, Calif. State U., 1987. Credential multiple subject profl. clear, Calif. Lectr. to high sch. civics classes, Vallejo, Calif., 1986; substitute tchr. Vallejo Unified Sch. Dist., 1987, instr. jr. high level, 1988, substitute tchr., 1992—; 1st grade instr. St. Apollinaris Sch., Napa, Calif., 1988-90; substitute Del Norte Unified Sch. Dist., Crescent City, Calif., 1991-92; substitute tchr. Vallejo Unified Sch. Dist., 1992—; 1st and 2nd grade instr. Cooper Sch., Vacaville Unified Sch. Dist., 1996-97, 1st grade tchr., 1997—. Del. to Napa/Solano PTA Coun., Vallejo, 1986-87; bd. dirs. Interagy. Commn., Vallejo, 1987-90; gen. mgr. Teena Ferris Pelkey Prodns., TFP Enterprises-Polit. Coords.; long-term substitute tchr. 3rd grade Notre Dame Sch., Vacaville, Calif., Highland Elem. Sch., Vallejo; 2nd grade instr., lang. arts instr. Al-Noor Elem. Sch., Vallejo. Author: Policy Manual Affirmative Action, 1989, 90. Bd. dirs. Greater Vallejo Recreation Dist., 1987-90, vice chair, 1990; bd. dirs. North Bay Opera Assn., Sister City Assn. of Vallejo, 1989-90, 92, v.p. fund raising, 1993; coord. United Dem. Campaign, Lower Solano County, Calif., 1992; Solano County coord. spl. election campaign for Senator Mike Thompson, Solano County, 1993; Dem. del. 7th Assembly Caucus; pres. Vallejo Sister City Assn., 1995—; apptd. bd. dirs. Vallejo Alcohol Policy Coalition; assembly dit. del. Calif. State Party Conv. Recipient award for svc., 1990, Challenge the Future award, 1989, Dare 2 B Different award, Cert. of Appreciation, Assembly Dems. of Calif., 1992, Cert. of Gratitude Akashi, Japan (sister city to Vallejo), Plaque of Gratitude Greater Vallejo Recreation Dist. Mem. Internat. Reading Assn., Solano County League of Women Voters, Vallejo Sister City Assn., United Dems. of Vallejo, Women In the Arts. Democrat. Roman Catholic. Avocations: 1st edit. books, art, sister city activities, reading, walking, collecting art glass. Home: 216 Sandy Neck Way Vallejo CA 94591-7850

PELLEGRINO, JAMES WILLIAM, college dean, psychology educator; b. N.Y.C., Dec. 20, 1947; s. Vincent and Emily (Nicosia) P.; m. Barbara Jo Sposato, June 6, 1970 (div. 1975); 1 child, Christopher Michael; m. Susan Rosen Goldman, Dec. 23, 1978; children: Joshua Goldman, Seth Goldman. BS in Psychology, Colgate U., 1969; MS in Experimental, Quantitative Psychology, U. Colo., 1970, PhD in Experimental, Quantitative Psychology, 1973. Asst. prof. U. Pitts., 1973-78, assoc. prof., 1978-79, U. Calif., Santa Barbara, 1979-83, prof., 1983-89; Frank Mayborn prof. Vanderbilt U., Nashville, 1989—2001, dean Peabody Coll. Edn. and Human Devel., 1991-98; disting. prof. cognitive psychology and edn. U. Ill., Chgo., 2001—, co-dir. Ctr. for Study of Learning, Instrn. and Tchr. Devel., 2001—. Co-dir. Learning Tech. Ctr. Vanderbilt U., 1989-91; proposal reviewer NSF, Can. Rsch. Coun., Australian Rsch. Coun.; chmn. com. on evaluation of nat. assessment of ednl. programs, Nat. Acad. Scis., com. on found. of assesment, com. on learning rsch. and ednl. practice; presenter in field. Author: (with others) Cognitive Psychology and Instruction, 1978, Handbook of Semantic Word Norms, 1978, Memory Organization and Structure, 1979, Aptitude, Learning and Instruction: Cognitive Process Anayses, How Much and How Can Intelligence Be Increased, 1982, Advances in Instructional Psychology, vol. II, 1982, Handbook of Research Methods in Human Memory and Cognition, 1982, Advances in the Psychology of Human Intelligence, 1982, Individual Differences in Cognition, 1983, Human Abilities: An Information Processing Approach, 1984, Test Design: Developments in Psychology and Psychometrics, 1985, International Encyclopedia of Education, 1985, What is Intelligence?, 1986, Arthur Jensen: Consensus and Controversy, 1987, Intelligence and Cognition: Contemporary Frames of Reference, 1987, Metacognition, Motivation and Understanding, 1987, Test Validity, 1988, Learning and Individual Differences: Abilities, Motivation and Methodology, 1989, The Psychology of Learning and Motivation, 1989, The Proceedings of the 22nd Annual Hawaii International Conference on System Sciences, 1989, Vision and Action: The Control of Grasping, 1990, Learning Disabilities: Theoretical and Research Issues, 1990, Intelligence: Reconceptualization and Measurement, 1991, Philosophy of Science, Cognitive Psychology, and Educational Theory and Practice, 1992, New Approaches to Testing: Rethinking Aptitude, Achievement and Assessment, 1992, Cognitive Approaches to Automated Instruction, 1992; co-author: Human Intelligence: Perspectives and Prospects, 1985, Testing: Theoretical and Applied Perspectives, 1989, Instruction: Theoretical and Applied Perspectives, 1991, Jasper Project: Lessons in Curriculum, Instruction, Assessment and Professional Development, 1997, Grading the Nation's Report Card, 1999, How People Learn: Building Research and Practice, 1999; contbr. numerous articles to profl. jours. Named Lifetime Nat. Assoc., NAS; recipient Austen Colgate award, Phil R. Miller award, Outstanding Young Men in Am. award. Mem. AAAS, NRC, Am. Ednl. Rsch. Assn. (various coms.), Midwestern Psychol. Assn., Rocky Mountain Psychol. Assn., N.Y. Acad. Sci., European Assn. Rsch. on Learning and Instrn., Cognitive Sci. Soc., Soc. Multivariate Experimental Psychology, Computers in Psychology, Soc. Mathematical Psychology, Soc. Rsch. and Child Devel., Psychonomic Soc., Sigma Xi, Phi Beta Kappa, Psi Chi. Avocations: sports, gardening, music. Home: 175 N Harbor Dr # 4703 Chicago IL 60601 Office: U Ill at Chgo Dept Psychology (MC285) 1007 W Harrison St Chicago IL 60607 E-mail: pellegjw@uic.edu.

PELLEGRINO, NANCY DAVIS, middle school educator; b. Newark, Feb. 10, 1944; d. William Francis and Doris (Williams) Davis; m. Donald Nicholas Spano (dec. May 1980); children: Donna, Donald; m. Anthony Joseph Pellegrino Jr., Mar. 17, 1984. BA in Sci., Rutgers U., 1965; MEd, Nat.-Louis U., 1994. Cert. tchr. biology, gen. sci. Biology tchr. Our Lady of Good Coun., Newark, N.J., 1964-67; 4th grade tchr. Most Holy Name of Jesus, Gulfport, Fla., 1974-80; tchr. dropout prevention Pinellas Park (Fla.) Mid. Sch., 1988-93, tchr. sci.-tech. edn. lab., 1993—. Chmn. Sch. Adv. Coun., Pinellas Park, 1992-95, pro edn. facilitator, 1993—; presenter Sci.-Tech. Conf., St. Petersburg, Fla., 1993, Edn. at Tech. Conv., Innisbrook, Fla., 1994; curriculum writer Fla. Dept. Edn., Tallahassee, 1994, Improving Edn. in Orlando, 1995; mem. Sch. Adv. Coun.; presenter Quality Expo. Sapp Bookfair scholar Bookfair Assn., 1992; finalist Cigna Tchr. of Yr., 1996. Mem. ASCD, Fla. Assn. Sch. Tchrs., Pinellas Assn. Sci. Tchrs. (Outstanding Sci. Tchrs. Assn. 1997). Avocations: model airplane building, computers. Office: Pinellas Park Mid Sch 6940 70th Ave Pinellas Park FL 33781-3999

PELLEY, SHIRLEY NORENE, library director; b. Raymondville, Tex., Oct. 9, 1931; d. Llloyd Marshall and Lillian Norene (Southall) Ayres; m. May 14, 1954 (div.); children: Michael, Cynthia, Katheryne. BA in Music Edn., Bethany Nazarene Coll., 1954; MLS, U. Okla., 1966. Tchr. Hilldale Elem. Sch., Oklahoma City, 1954-56; music tchr. self-employed, Okla., Mo., 1956-64; circulation clk. Bethany (Okla.) Pub. Libr., 1964-65; libr. reference U. Okla. Libraries, Norman, 1966-83; dir. learning resource ctr. So. Nazarene U., Bethany, 1983—. Mem. ALA, Okla. Libr. Assn., Assn. Coll. and Rsch. Librs., Met. Librs. Network of Ctrl. Okla., Assn. Christian Librs. Republican. Nazarene. Avocations: reading, walking, travel. Office: So Nazarene U Learning Resource Ctr 4115 N College Ave Bethany OK 73008-2671

PELTASON, JACK WALTER, foundation executive, educator; b. St. Louis, Aug. 29, 1923; s. Walter B. and Emma (Hartman) P.; m. Suzanne Toll, Dec. 21,1946; children: Nancy Hartman, Timothy Walter H., Jill K. BA, U. Mo., 1943, MA, 1944, LLD (hon.), 1978; AM, Princeton U., 1946, PhD, 1947; LLD (hon.), U. Md., 1979, Ill. Coll., 1979, Gannon U., 1980, U. Maine, 1980, Union Coll., 1981, Moorehead (N.D.) State U., 1980; LHD (hon.), 1980, Ohio State U., 1980, Mont. Coll. Mineral Scis. and Tech., 1982, Buena Vista Coll., 1982, Assumption Coll., 1983, Chapman Coll., 1986, U. Ill., 1989. Asst. prof. Smith Coll., Mass., 1947-51; asst. prof. polit. sci. U. Ill., Urbana, 1951-52, assoc. prof., 1953-59, dean Coll. Liberal Arts and Scis., 1960-64, chancellor, 1967-77; vice chancellor acad. affairs U. Calif., Irvine, 1964-67, chancellor, 1984-92; pres. U. Calif. System, Oakland, 1992-95, Am. Coun. Edn., Washington, 1977-84; prof. emeritus dept. politics and soc. U. Calif., Irvine, 1995—2003; pres. Bren Found., 1997—2003; ret., 2003. Cons. Mass. Little Hoover Commn., 1950 Author: The Missouri Plan for the Selection of Judges, 1947, Federal Courts and the Political Process, 1957, Fifty-eight Lonely Men, 1961, Understanding the Constitution, 15th edit., 2000, orig. edition, 1949, (with James M. Burns) Government By the People, 1952, 20th edit., 2003; contbr. articles and revs. to profl. jours. Recipient James Madison medal Princeton U., 1982 Fellow Am. Acad. Arts and Scis.; mem. Am. Polit. Sci. Assn. (coun. 1952-54), Phi Beta Kappa, Phi Kappa Phi, Omicron Delta Kappa, Alpha Phi Omega, Beta Gamma Sigma. Home: 18 Whistler Ct Irvine CA 92612-4069 Office: U Calif Dept Politics & Society Social Sci Plz Irvine CA 92697-0001 E-mail: jwpeltas@uci.edu.

PELTON, M LEE, academic administrator; B magna cum laude, Wichita U., 1974; D, Harvard U., 1984. Tchg. fellow, English instr. Harvard U., 1980—86; sr. tutor Winthrop Ho., 1986; dean of student to dean of coll. Colgate U., 1986—91; dean of coll., adj. prof. Dartmouth Coll., 1991—98; pres. Williamette U., 1998—. Mem. bd. Oregon Ind. Coll. Fund, 1998—, Oregon Ind. Coll. Assn., 1998—; bd. overseers Harvard U., 2000; mem. Commn. on Minorities in Higher Edn., 2000—02. Mem.: Governor's Commn. on Financing Higher Edn. (Ore.), President's Coun. of Nat. Collegiate Athletic Assn. (Div. III), Nat. Assn. of Ind. Colleges and Universities (com. on policy analysis and pub. rels. 2000—03), Am. Coun. on Edn., Am. Assn. of Higher Edn. Office: Williamette U 900 State St Salem OR 97301

PEMBERTON, CYNTHIA LEE A. educational leadership educator; b. Portland, Oreg., Oct. 2, 1958; d. Ronald E. and Patricia E. (Schars) Pemberton. BS in Biology and Psychology, Willamette U., 1980; MS in Interdisciplinary Studies, So. Oreg. State U., 1983; EdD in Ednl. Leadership-Higher Edn. Adm., Portland State U., 1996. Instr. Trucker Meadows C.C., Nev., 1985-87; instr., swimming coach U. Nev., Reno, 1984-89; asst. athletic dir. women's sports Linfield Coll., McMinnville, Oreg., 1989-95, assoc. prof., aquatics dir., sr. women adminstr., 1989-98; asst. prof. grad. faculty dept. sport sci., phys. edn. and dance Idaho State U., 1998—2001, assoc. prof. grad. faculty, dept. chmn. edn. leadership, 2001—. Hannah Kennan scholar, Peck scholar. Mem. AAUW, NOW, AAHPERD, NAGWS, NASPE, AERA, Women's Sports Found., Alpha Chi Omega, Omicron Delta Kappa, Psi Chi, Kappa Delta Pi, Pi Kappa Phi. Avocations: exercise, reading. Office: Idaho State U Dept Ednl Leadership PO Box 8059 Pocatello ID 83209-8059 Fax: 208-282-5324. E-mail: pembcynt@isu.edu.

PEMBERTON, JANETT E. MATTHEW, language educator; b. Trinidad, W.I.; came to U.S., 1961, naturalized, 1974; d. Cecil E. and A. Elaine Matthew; m. Sandi Macpherson Pemberton. BA, Howard U., 1965, MA, 1967; D of Arts, Cath. U. Am., 1978. Asst. instr. Howard U., Washington, 1967; instr. Bowie State Coll., 1968; asst. prof. Prince George's Community Coll., 1968-71, assoc. prof. dept. English, 1971-82, prof., 1982-89, mem. acad. standards and regulations com., 1979, chmn. Afro-Am. studies com., 1976-78, mem. affirmative action com., 1973-74; dir. SP JP Consulting Svcs., Inc.; guest instr. Cath. U. Am., Washington, 1975-78. Author: Transcendatalism and the Promise of Educational Reform, 1980, The Teaching of Afro-American Poetry: An Aesthetic Approach, 1978, Discussions on Aristotle's Ethics: Implications for Teachers and Administrators, 1980. Nat. Teaching fellow, 1968; recipient Teaching award Cath. U. Am., 1975, Community Leadership award, 1976, Disting. Women's award, 1980, Outstanding Service and Achievement award, 1981, medal of honor, 1985; named to Hall of Fame for contbns. to edn., 1985, Bd. Govs., ABI, 1986. Mem. Washington Soc. Performing Arts, Nat. Symphony Orch., Internat. Platform Assn., Nat. Council Tchrs. English, Edn. Writers Assn., MLA, Am. Assn. Advancement of Humanities, AAUP, Nat. Soc. Lit. and Arts, Presdl. Roundtable, Senatorial Inner Circle. Seventh-day Adventist. E-mail: JEMPemberton@aol.com.

PEMBERTON, MELISSIE COLLINS, retired elementary education educator; b. Pembroke, Va., Dec. 25, 1907; d. Walter Wingo and Grace Moore (Musselman) Collins; m. Oakland Herbert Pemberton, May 17, 1930; children: Oakland Herbert Jr., Walter Scott, William Durwood. BA in Edn., George Washington U., 1962; MA equivalency, Md. Bd. Edn., 1968. Tchr. Giles County Bd. Edn., Newport, Va., 1925-30, D.C. Pub. Schs., Washington, 1945-47, Montgomery County Pub. Schs., Rockville, MD, 1955-59, 63-75. Tchr. rep. Curriculum Materials Rev., Rockville, Md., 1967-68, Elem. Spl. Edn. Rev. and Evaluation Com. for Textbooks, Rockville, 1970; del. Montgomery Edn. Assn., Rockville, 1967. Leader Montgomery County Govt., Rockville, 1988, advisor, 1994-95; sponsor Rep. Nat. Com., Washington, 1988; radio operator U.S.A. FCC, Washington, 1942, mem. Vol. Svc. Motor Corps, Richmond, Va., 1942; sec. Bon Air Heights Civic Assn., 1994-95; sec. Ben Aid Heights Civic Assn., 1994—; adv. Montgomery County Govt., Rockville, Md., 1994—, Md. State Hwy. Adminstrn. Dept. Transp., 1994—. Named Civitan Internat. scholar, 1964. Mem. Bon Air Heights Civic Assn., Montgomery County Edn. Assn. (emeritus life mem. 1975), NEA, Md. State Tchrs. Assn., Pi Lamba Theta. Republican. Methodist. Avocations: stamp, coin and plate collecting, gardening, painting. Home: PO Box 741 Gainesville VA 20156-0741

PEMBERTON, MERRI BETH MORRIS, special education educator; b. Tahlequah, Okla., July 26, 1959; d. Roger C. and Evelyn A. (Mercer) Morris; m. Larry Jay Pemberton, Nov. 22, 1986; children: Eric Michael, Ciara Elise, Andrew Levi. BS, Midwestern State U., 1986, MEd, 1989. Receptionist YMCA, Wichita Falls, Tex., 1984-91; tchr. resource spl. edn. Petrolia (Tex.) Ind. Sch. Dist., 1986-89; tchr. spl. edn. emotionally disturbed Wichita Falls Ind. Sch. Dist., 1989-91; diagnostician Cookson Hills Christian Schs., Kansas, Okla., 1991-92, spl. edn. cons., 1992—. Contbr. article to profl. jour. Named to Outstanding Young Women of Am., 1991. Mem. Coun. for Exceptional Children (pres. 1989-90), Tex. Coun. for Exceptional Children (sec. 1990-91), Kappa Delta Pi. Home: RR 3 Box 200 Kansas OK 74347-9533

PENA, DIANA C. mathematics educator; b. El Paso, Oct. 8, 1960; d. Rodolfo D. and Rosalie Pena. BSME, U. Tex., El Paso, 1986, MS in Mfg. Engring., 1994, MEd in Adminstrn., 1995. Cert. secondary math. tchr. Rschr. Honeywell Optoelectronics, Dallas, 1990-92; math. tchr. Ysleta Ind. Sch. Dist., El Paso, 1991-92, El Paso Ind. Sch. Dist., 1992—. Supr. SEE Inst., El Paso, 1990-91; subsitute tchr. El Paso Ins. Sch. Dist., 1989-90; math. and computer sci. tchr. Crestline Sch., El Paso, 1989-91. Mem. St. Patrick's Ladies Altar Soc., El Paso, 1988—; funds solicitor Operation Noel, El Paso, 1991—. Mem. Kappa Delta Pi. Avocations: reading, tennis, badmitton, computers, jogging. Home: 1608 Winslow Rd El Paso TX 79915-1430

PENA, MARIA GEGES, academic services administrator; b. Torrance, Calif., Nov. 27, 1964; d. Nicholas John and Dina Connie (Vengel) Geges; m. Vicente Gregorio Pena, June 22, 1991. AA, El Camino Coll., 1985; BA, U. Calif., San Diego, 1987; MS, San Diego State U., 1989, postgrad., Claremont Grad. Sch., 1990—, Western State U., 1995—. Peer counselor El Camino Coll., Torrance, Calif., 1982-85; peer advisor U. Calif., San Diego, 1985-87, vice chancellor student affirmative action rsch. intern, 1986-87, outreach asst. disabled student svcs., 1986-89; coord. student svcs. Mira Costa Coll., Oceanside, Calif., 1989—. Contbr. articles to profl. jours. Mem. Calif. Assn. Postsecondary Educators of Disabled. Democrat. Greek Orthodox. Avocations: law, education, cd collecting, collecting beatles memorabilia. Office: Mira Costa Coll 1 Barnard Dr Oceanside CA 92056-3820

PEÑA, MARIA TERESA, surgeon, educator, otolaryngologist; b. Chgo., Dec. 20, 1962; d. Gilbert and Maria Teresa Peña. BA, U. Fla., 1985; MD, Wayne State Med. Sch., 1991. Diplomate Am. Bd. Otolaryngology. Attending surgeon dept. otolaryngology Children's Nat. Med. Ctr., Washington, 1998—, dir. Oromotor Dysfunction Clinic, 1999—, asst. prof., 2000—. Contbr. articles to profl. jours. Spkr. Nat. Youth Leadership Forum, Washington, 2000, 2001. Recipient Discovery Fund award, Children's Nat. Med. Ctr., 1997, Minority Supplement award, ROL NIH, 2000, award, Am. Soc. Pediat. Otolaryngology, 2000, Bd. of Lady Visitors award, 2002; fellow Rsch. fellow, Wayne State U., 1990. Mem.: ACS, Am. Acad. Otolaryngology, Am. Coll. Women Surgeons. Avocations: travel, sports, theatre. Office: Childrens Nat Med Ctr 111 Michigan Ave NW Washington DC 20010 Business E-Mail: mpena@cninc.org.

PENA, MODESTA CELEDONIA, retired principal; b. San Diego, Tex., Mar. 3, 1929; d. Encarnacion E. and Teofila (Garcia) P. BA, Tex. State Coll. for Women, 1950, MA, 1953. Cert. sch. supr., prin., supt., Tex. Tchr. English San Diego H.S., 1950-76; asst. supt. curriculum and instrn. San Diego Ind. Sch. Dist., 1976-80; gifted edn. resource tchr. William Adams Jr. H.S., Alice, Tex., 1980-83, asst. prin. for instrn., 1983-88; ret., 1988. Faculty Bee County Coll., 1975-76. V.p. San Diego PTA, 1963; charter mem. Duval County Hist. Commn., 1975—; reporter Duval Co. Hist. Com., 1988—; chmn. Com. to Establish Local Pub. Libr., 1993; trustee Duval County-San Diego Pub. Libr., pres., 1993-98, mem., 1999—, dir. Duval County literacy program, 1994—; cmty. rep. site-based dist. mgmt. com. San Diego Ind. Sch. Dist., 1995-97. Newspaper Fund Inc. fellow, 1964; recipient Adolfo Arguijo Day award, 1990; named Outstanding Sr. of Duval County, Grayfest, 1992; named to San Diego Hall of Honor, 1995. Mem. Tex. State Tchrs. Assn. (local unit rec. sec. 1952-53, 63-64, 1st v.p. 1957-58, 66-67, pres. 1961), Delta Kappa Gamma (rec. sec. chpt. 1972-74, 1st v.p. 1974-76, pres. 1976-78, chpt. parliamentarian 1984-88, 2003-2004, state com. constn./bylaws 1979-81, state com. Eula Lee Carter Meml. Fund, 1987-89, area coord., 1989-1991, state com. pers. 1991-93, state rec. sec. 1993-95, state com. nominations 1995-97, chmn. 1997-99, state conv. chair 1999-2000, state com. necrology 2001-03, state com. ceremonials 2003-05, Chpt. Achievement award 1985, Internat. Golden Gift award 1994, State Achievement award 1996, Internat. Mem. in Print award 2002), Phi Delta Kappa (treas. chpt. 1978-79, rec. sec. chpt. 1983-84). Home: PO Box 353 306 W Gravis Ave San Diego TX 78384-2604

PENCE, HARRY EDMOND, chemistry educator; b. Martins Ferry, Ohio, Feb. 4, 1937; s. Harry and Mary (Bell) P.; m. Virginia Walliser, Sept. 5, 1959; children: Lynn, Laura, Heather. BS, Bethany (W.Va.) Coll., 1958; MS, W.Va. U., 1962; PhD, La. State U., 1968. Instr. Washington & Jefferson Coll., Washington, Pa., 1961-65, asst. prof., 1965-66; assoc. prof. SUNY, Oneonta, 1967-69, prof., 1969—97, dist. tchg. prof., 1997—. Pres. faculty senate SUNY, 1975-77. Author: Study Guide to Accompany Kotz and Purcell's General Chemistry, 2d edit., 1991, (with John Kotz and William Vining) Test Bank to Accompany Kotz and Purcell's General Chemistry, 1991. Mem. AAAS, Am. Chem. Soc., History Sci. Soc., Soc. for Lit. and Sci. Office: SUNY Oneonta Dept Chemistry Oneonta NY 13820

PENCE, IRA WILSON, JR., material handling research executive, engineer; b. Pontiac, Mich., June 18, 1939; s. Ira Wilson and Fern Elizabeth (Fraser) P.; m. JoAnna Springer, Sept. 5, 1959; children: Ira W. III, Teresa Ann, Deidre Lynn. BS, U. Mich., 1962, MSEE, 1964, PhD, 1970. Rsch. engr. Willow Run Labs., Ypsilanti, Mich., 1960-67, Dow Lab., Ann Arbor, Mich., 1967-70, GE, Schenectady, N.Y., 1970-80, engring. mgr. Charlottesville, Va., 1980-83; v.p. engring. Unimation, Inc., Danbury, Conn., 1983-87; dir. MHRC Ga. Inst. Tech., Atlanta, 1987-97, dir., pres. Intelligent Integrated Info. Sys., 1999—. Cons. Superior Motor, Hartford, 1987-89; bd. dirs. Wesley Found.; mem. adv. coun. Westinghouse, Pitts., 1983-87, treas. Wesley Comm. Ctrs., Inc., 1999-2003; dir. 21iii.com, 2000—; exec. pres. Intelligent Integrated Info. Sys., 1999—. Editor: Progress in Material Handling and Logistics, 1988; Material Handling for 90's, 1990. Trustee United Meth. Ch., 1988—, Camp Wesley, 1998—. Recipient New Product of Yr. award Innovation Today, 1985. Mem. IEEE (sr., sect. chmn. 1978), ASME (Materials Handling Engring. divsn. chair 1994). Republican. Methodist. Avocations: cabinet making, golf. Office: Ga Inst Tech 765 Ferst Dr Atlanta GA 30332-0001 Fax: (770) 435-0493. E-mail: ipence@isye.gatech.edu.

PENCEK, CAROLYN CARLSON, treasurer, educator; b. Appleton, Wis., June 13, 1946; d. Arthur Edward and Mary George (Notaras) Carlson; m. Richard David Pencek, July 10, 1971; children: Richard Carlson, Mallory Barbara Rowlinds. BA in Polit. Sci., Western Coll., 1968; Ma in Polit. Sci., Syracuse U., 1975; EdD, Temple U., 1999. Investment analysts asst. Bankers Trust Co., N.Y.C., 1969-71; substitute tchr. Lackawanna Trail Sch. Dist., Factoryville, Pa., 1971-81; instr. polit. sci. Keystone Coll., La Plume, Pa., 1972-73; USGS coding supr. Richard Walsh Assocs., Scranton, Pa., 1975-76; instr. polit. sci. Pa. State U., Dunmore, 1976-77; treas. Creative Planning Ltd., Dunmore, 1988—. Bd. trustees Lourdesmont Sch., Clarks Summit, Pa., 1989—, v.p., 2000—. Bd. dirs. Lackawanna County Child and Youth Svcs., Scranton, 1981—, pres., 1988-90; founding mem., sec. Leadership Lackawanna, 1982-84; bd. dirs. N.E. Pa. Regional Tissue and Transplant Bank, Scranton, 1984-88, Vol. Action Ctr., Scranton, 1986-91; founding mem. Women's Resource Ctr. Assn., Scranton, 1986—, pres., 1986-87; v.p. sch. improvement coun. Lackawanna Trail Sch. Dist., 1995-96, sec., 1996-97; mem. adv. bd. Pa. State U., Worthington Scranton, 1998—. Named Vol. of Yr. nominee, Vol. Action Ctr., 1985; Temple U. fellow, Phila., 1991-92. Mem. AAUW (sec. 1973-75, state sel. com. 1979-81), Assn. Jr. Leagues Internat. (area II coun. mem. 1978-79), Jr. League Scranton (v.p. 1980, pres. 1981-83, Margaret L. Richards award 1984), Philharmonic League (v.p. 1976, pres. 1977). Episcopalian. Home: RR 2 Box 2489 Factoryville PA 18419-9649 Office: Creative Planning Ltd 1100 Dunham Dr Dunmore PA 18512-2653 E-mail: spot717@aol.com.

PENDLETON, GAIL RUTH, newspaper editor, writer, educator; b. Franklin, N.J., May 8, 1937; d. Waldo A. and Ruby (Bonnett) Rousset; m. John E. Tyler, Mar. 10, 1956 (div. 1978); children: Gwenneth, Victoria, Christine; m. Jeffrey P. Pendleton, Oct. 1, 1978 (dec. 1992). BA, Montclair (N.J.) State Coll., 1959; M in Div., Princeton (N.J.) Theol. Sem., 1973; MA in English, William Paterson Coll., 1998. Ordained minister Presbyn. Ch., 1974. Tchr. Epiphany Day Sch., Kaimuki, Oahu, Hawaii, 1956-58; editor Women's Sect. Daily Record, Morristown, N.J., 1959-62, reporter, 1963-65; tchr. Hardystown Twp. Sch., Franklin, 1968-69; asst. pastor 1st Presbyn. Ch., Sparta, N.J., 1973-74; reporter N.J. Herald, Newton, 1976-78, editor lifestyle sect., 1978-93, editor Friday entertainment sect., 1993-95, editor spl. sect., 1995-97; pres. Crystal Palace Networking Inc., Newton, 1995—. Adj. prof. Ramapo Coll. of N.J., Mahwah, 1998, County Coll. of Morris, Randolph, N.J., 1998, Sussex County C.C., Newton, N.J., 1998—, Centenary Coll., Hackettstown, N.J., 1999—; tchr. Univ. H.S., Newark, 1999-2000. Recipient Ruth Cheney Streeter award Planned Parenthood N.W. N.J., 1985. Mem. N.J. Press Assn. (family sect. layout award 1985, 87, 88, 89, 91, 2nd feature columns award 1986).

PENDLETON, MARIE PEARSON, school administrator, educator; b. Urbana, Ill., Oct. 11, 1953; d. John E. and Maxine L. (Harrell) Pearson; m. Mark E. Pendleton, Jan. 12, 1974; children: Emily, Anna. BS, U. Ill., 1976; MEd, Xavier U., Cin., 1977. Cert. elem. tchr. grades pre-K to 3, Ohio, Am. Montessori Soc., 3-6, 6-12. Tchr. Barrie Day Sch., Silver Spring, Md., 1977-78; tchr. kindergarten North Baltimore (Ohio) Pub. Schs., 1978-79; founder, tchr., dir. The Montessori Sch. of Bowling Green, Ohio, 1980—. Instr. Bowling Green State U., 1986, 99, spl. spkr., 1982—. Trustee Bowling Green Pregnancy Ctr., 1986-91; trustee Bowling Green Ch. of the Nazarene, 1980-2003, mem. children's ministries bd. 1986—; leader Girl Scouts U.S., 1990-97. Named to Outstanding Young Women of Am., 1988. Mem. Am. Montessori Soc. (trustee, nat. bd. dirs. 1999-2003), Nat. Coun. Tchrs. Math., Nat. Soc. Daus. of Am. Revolution. Avocations: reading, swimming, drama, home decorating. Home: 707 Mckinley Dr Bowling Green OH 43402-1538 Office: The Montessori Sch of BG 515 Sand Ridge Rd Bowling Green OH 43402-3700 E-mail: mpendle@wcnet.org.

PENDRAK, ROBERT FRANCIS, internist, insurance company executive; b. Phila., June 26, 1946; s. Frank Joseph and Julia Ann (Kozlecki) P.; m. Jacqueline Celeste Kulpinski, June 15, 1968; children: Brian Todd, Erica Lynn. BS in Biology, St. Joseph U., Phila., 1968; MD, Hahnemann U., 1972; Assoc. in Risk Mgmt., Ins. Inst. Am., Malvern, Pa., 1995; MS in Healthcare Mgmt., Finch U., 2000. Diplomate Am. Bd. Quality Assurance and Utilization Review Physicians; lic. physician. Pa. Intern in internal medicine Hahnemann Med. Coll. and Hosp., Phila., 1972-73, resident in internal medicine, 1973-74, Polyclinic Med. Ctr., Harrisburg, Pa., 1974-75; pvt. practice in internal medicine Pendrak, Kandra, Fierer, Kuskin Assocs., Ltd., Harrisburg, 1975-87; acting med. dir. Silver Spring health plan Phico Ins. Co., Mechanicsburg, Pa., 1987, assoc. med. dir., 1987-88, med. advisor risk mgmt., 1988-94, med. dir. risk mgmt., 1994-95; v.p., med. dir., employee health physician Phico Group, Inc., Mechanicsburg, 1996—2001; med. dir. Pa. Blue Shield, Camphill, 2001—. Med. dir. Commonwealth Pa. Bur. Vocat. Rehab. (Visual), Harrisburg, 1974-87; clin. asst. prof. medicine, Pa. State Coll. Medicine Med. Ctr., Hershey, Pa., 1978-89, clin. assoc. prof., 1989—; plant physician Harrisburg Steel Corp., divsn. of Harsco, 1982-86; vice chmn. Polyclinic Med. Ctr. Quality Assurance Utilization Rev. Com., 1978, 79, chmn., 1980-97; cons. to Dept. Defense, Armed Forces Medical-Legal Chest Pain Spcl. Rsch. Project. Contbr. articles to ins. and med. jours.; made presentations to over 500 groups including CEOs, Bds. of Trustees, med. staff, residents, nurses. Mem. five yr. planning com. Ctrl. Dauphin Sch. Dist., Pa., 1983-84; bd. dirs. Assn. for Retarded Citizens of Dauphin County (Pa.), 1993—, Lakevue Athletic Assn., 1987-95. Fellow Am. Soc. Healthcare Risk Mgmt., Am. Coll. Med. Quality; mem. Soc. Ins. Trainers and Educators, Am. Coll. Physician Execs. Avocations: train collecting, snow skiing, walking, coaching softball. Home: 4787 Sweetbrier Ter Harrisburg PA 17111-3616 Office: Pa Blue Shield 1800 Center St PO Box 890089 Camp Hill PA 17089-0089 E-mail: robert.pendrak@highmark.com.

PENICK, GEORGE DIAL, pathologist; b. Columbia, SC, Sept. 4, 1922; s. Edwin Anderson and Caroline Inglesby (Dial) P.; m. Marguerite Murchison Worth, Feb. 7, 1947; children: George Dial, Hal Worth, David Williams, Anderson Holladay, Marguerite Worth. Student, U. N.C, 1939-42, BS, 1944; MD, Harvard U., 1946. Intern in pathology Presbyn. Hosp. City Chgo., 1946-47; instr. pathology U. N.C., Chapel Hill, 1949-53, asst prof. pathology, 1953-56, assoc. prof. pathology, 1956-63, prof. pathology, 1963-70; prof., head dept. pathology U. Iowa, Iowa City, 1970-81, prof. pathology and dermatology, 1981-93. Cons. Watts Hosp., Durham, N.C., 1949-70; attending pathologist N.C. Meml. Hosp., Chapel Hill, 1953-70; dir. Nat. Heart Inst. Program, Project U. N.C.,1962-70; cons. lab. svc. VA Med. Ctr., Iowa City, 1970-93. Contbr. articles to profl. jours. Capt. U.S. Army, 1947—49. Med. Sci. scholar John and Mary Markle Found., N.Y.C., 1953-58; recipient Disting. Svc. award Sch. of Med. U. N.C., 1979. Fellow Coll. Am Pathologists; mem. AMA, Am. Soc. Clin. Pathologists, Am. Assoc. Pathologists, Internat. Acad. Pathology, Phi Beta Kappa. Democrat. Episcopolian. Avocations: bicycling, tennis, computing, christian education. Home: The Penick Village Unit 270 PO Box 2001 Southern Pines NC 02388 E-mail: gpenick2@earthlink.net.

PENICK, JOHN E. education educator; b. Langley, Va., Jan. 2, 1944; s. Edgar Cohen and Bessie (Beene) P.; m. Nell Inman, July 23, 1966; children: Lucas T., Megan J. Penick. BS, U. Miami, 1966, MA, 1969; PhD, Fla. State U., 1973. Sci. dept. head Miami (Fla.) Jackson High Sch., 1967-70; instr. Miami-Dade Community Coll., 1968, Fla. State U., Tallahassee, Fla., 1970-73; dir. tchr. edn. Loyola U., Chgo., 1973-75; prof. U. Iowa, Iowa City, 1975-97, head Sci. Edn. Ctr., 1982, 89-93; prof., head dept. math., sci. and tech. edn. N.C. State U., Raleigh, 1998—. Editor monograph series Focus on Excellence, 1983-89; author: Biology: A Community Context, 2003; contbr. numerous articles to profl. jours. Named Disting. Alumnus Fla. State U., 1987; recipient Burlington No. award for outstanding career achievement U. Iowa, 1992; Fulbright fellow USIA, Portugal, 1985. Fellow Iowa Acad. Sci.; mem. ASCD, NSTA (bd. dirs. 1986-88, pres. 2003, Ohaus awards), Nat. Assn. for Rsch. in Sci. Tchg. (assoc. editor 1979-84), Coun. Sci. Soc. Prs. (sec. 1991-92, treas. 2003—), Nat. Assn. Biology Tchrs. (pres. 1989), Assn. for Edn. of Tchrs. in Sci. (Outstanding Sci. Educator 1987, Outstanding Mentor 1997, pres. 2002), Sigma Xi. Office: NC State U 326 Poe Hl Raleigh NC 27695-0001

PENIN, LINDA MARGARET, elementary education educator; b. N.Y.C., May 18, 1946; d. Santos Rodriquez and Dorothea May (Fink) P. BA, Jersey City State Coll., 1969, MA, 1973. Cert. elem. tchr., reading tchr., reading specialist. Tchr. elem. Leonia (N.J.) Bd. Edn., 1969—2003, ret., 2003. Recipient Gov.'s Tchr. Recognition award State of N.J., 1989. Mem. NEA, N.J. Edn. Assn., Bergen County Edn. Assn., Leonia Edn. Assn., Order Ea. Star N.J. (officer, sec. local chpt.). Republican. Methodist. Avocations: reading, bike riding, relaxing at beach. Home: 24 Kimble Ct Pompton Plains NJ 07444-1656 Office: Leonia Bd Edn 500 Broad Ave Leonia NJ 07605-1598

PENKALA, ANTOINETTE MARIE, mortgage company executive; b. N.Y.C., July 12, 1952; d. Peter Paul Michael and Mary Ann (Popu) P.; m. Richard Williams, May 27, 1978 (div. Sept. 1981). BA in Econs., Albertus Magnus Coll., 1974. Credit and collections clk. State Nat. Bank, Bridgeport, Conn., 1976-77; supr. accounts payable, accounts receivable Sanitas Svc. Corp., Bethany, Conn., 1977-78; supr. work order control Textron Lycoming, Stratford, Conn., 1978-93; asst. to accessory merchandise mgr. Wayside of Milford, Conn., 1993-94; asst. to dir. facilities U. New Haven, 1994—2003; broker coord. Am. Mortgage Network, 2003—. Democrat. Roman Catholic. Avocations: gardening, reading, classical plays, classical music, amateur car racing. Home: 118 Bertrose Ave Milford CT 06460-5907

PENN, HUGH FRANKLIN, JR., psychology educator; b. Hartselle, Ala., Jan. 28, 1941; s. Hugh Franklin and Marynelle (Walter) P.; m. Susan Irwin Adams, June 5, 1976; children: Charles Bracken, Caryn Elizabeth. BS, Florence State Coll., 1964; MA, Florence State Univ., 1967; grad. ednl. specialist, U. Ala., 1972, PhD, 1982. Psychology tchr. Hartselle (Ala.) H.S., 1964-89, sch. counselor, 1989-91, spl. svcs. counselor, 1991—; psychology instr. Calhoun C.C., Decatur, Ala., 1970—; counseling psychologist/disabilities coord. Hartselle City Schs., 1996—. Chmn. bd. North Ctrl. Ala. Mental Health Bd., 1984-87, v.p. bd. dirs., 1998—, pres., 2001—; pres. of advisors Ala. Assn. Student Couns., 1970; ea. states head advisor So. Assn. Student Couns., 1973-74; mem. adv. bd. Mental Health Assn. Morgan County, 1996—; sec. mem. adv. bd. Juvenile Cts. of Morgan County, 2002--; mem. quality assurance com. Morgan County Dept. Human Resources, 2001--. Named Outstanding Young Educator of Ala., Ala. Jaycees, 1973; recipient Georgia Vallery award for outstanding svc. in cmty. mental health State of Ala., 2000. Mem. APA, ACA, Coun. for Exceptional Children, Learning Disabilities Assn., Am. Sch. Counselor Assn., Autism Soc. Am., Internat. Dyslexia Assn., Hartselle C. of C. (Thomas Guyton Humanitarian award 1994). Methodist. Home: 412 Aquarius Dr SW Hartselle AL 35640-4000 Office: Hartselle City Schs 305 College St NE Hartselle AL 35640-2357

PENN, PATRICIA WHITLEY, education educator; b. Richmond, Va., Aug. 4, 1953; d. Hugh G. and Peggy D. (Dymacek) Whitley; m. Robert Alan Penn, Aug. 16, 1975; children: Ginny, Lindsay. BS in English Edn., David Lipscomb U., Nashville, 1975; MEd in Reading, Va. Commonwealth U., Richmond, 1978; PhD in Curriculum and Instrn., Kans. State U., 2000. Cert. English edn. tchr. grades 5-12, reading specialist K-Adult, Kans., Va. Instr. lang. arts Hanover County Pub. Schs., Ashland, Va., 1975—80; reading specialist, spl. needs coord. Sherman Mid. Sch., Hutchinson, Kans., 1980—89, Liberty Mid. Sch., Hutchinson, 1990—92; grad. tchg. asst. Kans. State U., Manhattan, 1992—94; assoc. prof. edn., chair divsn. edn. Friends U., Wichita, Kans., 1994—. Named Davis Found. Educator of Yr. Mem. Internat. Reading Assn., Ark Valley Reading Assn., Kans. Reading Assn., Kans. Assn. Middle Level Edn., North Ctrl. Kans. Reading Assn., Phi Kappa Phi, Phi Delta Kappa. Mem. Ch. of Christ. Avocations: reading, sewing, gardening, cooking. Home: 407 N Valley Stream Dr Derby KS 67037-8728 Office: Friends University 2100 W University St Wichita KS 67213-3397 E-mail: ppenn@friends.edu.

PENN, SHERRY EVE, communication psychologist, educator; b. Jersey City, Nov. 25, 1941; d. Herman Joseph and Ida (Eventoff) P.; m. Donald Eugene Crawford, Aug. 15, 1987; stepchildren: Dan, Helen, David. BA in Psychology and Theatre, U. Louisville, 1963; MA in Theatre and Music History, U. Fla., 1967; PhD in Communication Psychology, Performing Arts, Union Inst., 1975. Dir. dance, assoc. prof. Miami (Fla.)-Dade Community Coll., 1967-78; assoc. dean baccalaureate program World U., Miami, 1978; press sec., dir. comm. Jefferson County (Ky.) Judge Exec. A. Mitch McConnell, 1979-81; assoc. dean, asst. v.p. Union Inst. Grad. Sch., 1984-87, core faculty prof., 1984—; v.p. communication Penn-Crawford Assocs., 1987—. Chair program policy bd., external masters degree program in psychology Lone Mountain Coll., Miami, 1975-76; cons. in pub. rels., comm., 1970—; vis. prof. U. Fla., 1969, Calif. State U., San Francisco, 1973, 74, Fla. Internat. U., 1975-76, U. Louisville, 1982-84, Webster U., 1983-84; presenter, speaker in field. Artistic dir., producer Miami Jazz Dance Ensemble, Miami Mime Artists, 1967-79; writer, producer pub. TV programs, 1980; exec. producer weekly pub. affairs series Consumer Corner, 1980-81; choreographer for various dance, mime and operatic prodns. Fellow Ford Found., 1961. Mem. ASTD, Pub. Rels. Soc. Am., Am. Women in Radio and TV, Women in Communication. Home: 100 Uno Lago Dr Apt 405 Juno Beach FL 33408-2699

PENNACCHIO, LINDA MARIE, secondary school educator; b. Boston, Oct. 8, 1947; d. Antonio and Florence (Delano) P. BA in Math., U. Mass., 1969; MEd in Guidance, Boston State Coll., 1974, cert. advanced study in adminstrn., 1976. Cert. math., guidance counselor, prin. Math. tchr. Abraham Lincoln Sch., Revere, Mass., 1969-91; office asst. Mass. Gen. Hosp., Bunker Hill Health Ctr., Charlestown, Mass., 1982-96; computer tchr. grades K-8 Abraham Lincoln Sch., Revere, 1985-91; math. tchr. Beachmont Middle Sch., Revere, 1991-97, guidance counselor, equity coord., mentor tchr., 1995-98; dean of students Revere H.S., 1998—. Adviser Nat. Jr. Honor Soc., Revere, 1985-94; mem. math. Curriculum Revision Com., Revere, 1985-86, 94-95, Com. to Establish Gifted and Talented Program, Revere, 1988; participant U.S. Dept. Edn. Tech. Grant, Revere, 1989-92; mem. math. portfolio pilot study Commonwealth of Mass. Dept. Edn., 1992-98, mem. palms leadership team, chair textbook selection com. for elem. sch. math., coach advisor-advisee program; co-adviser Beachmont Sch. Aspirers Club. Mem. ASCD, Nat. Coun. Tchrs. Math., Mass. Tchrs. Assn., Assn. Tchrs. Math. in Mass., Nat. Assn. Student Activity Advisers. Democrat. Roman Catholic.

PENNEL, MARIE LUCILLE HUNZIGER, retired elementary education educator; b. Oregon, Mo., Jan. 16, 1934; d. William Henry and Milree (Huff) Hunziger; m. Berres H. Pennel, Mar. 6, 1955; children: Patricia Lu Pennel Wolfe, Pamela Cille Pennel Ginther. BS, Northwest Mo. State U., 1954; MS, Kans. U., 1959; postgrad., Kans. State U. Cert. elem. tchr., Kans. 1st grade tchr., Lawrence, Kans.; kindergarten tchr. Atchison, Kans., Unified Sch. Dist. 415, Hiawatha, Kans., 1972-94. Recipient Outstanding Svc. award, Lawrence Jaycees, 1958, 59. Mem. ASCD, NEA, Kans. Edn. Assn., Assn. for Childhood Edn. Internat., PEO, Kappa Delta Pi, Delta Kappa Gamma. Home: 403 Woodbury Ln Hiawatha KS 66434-1525

PENNELL, LINDA BENNETT, secondary school educator; b. Macon, Ga., Nov. 30, 1947; d. Frank Autrelle and Blance (Fraser) Bennett; m. John Clarence Pennell, Dec. 28, 1969; children: John Jacob, Frank McClinton. BA, Valdosta State Coll., 1969; MEd, Ga. State U., 1974. Cert. reading specialist, Tex.; mid-mgmt. cert. Tchr. Freehome Elem. Sch., Canton, Ga., 1973-74, Cypress-Fairbanks Ind. Sch. Dist., Houston, 1975—; team leader Cook Jr. High, Houston, 1988-91, dept. chair, 1991-95; asst. prin. Truitt Jr. High, Houston, 1995—. Presenter in field. Ruling elder Windwood Presbyn. Ch., Cypress, Tex., 1986-89, 90-91. Recipient Guiding Star award Star Furniture and Houston Chronicle, 1993, Middle Sch. Start Educator Achievement award Jr. Achievement, 1993. Mem. ASCD, Nat. Assn. Secondary Sch. Prins., Assn. Tex. Profl. Educators (membership chair 1985, treas. 1988-89, pres. 1991), Tex. Reading Assn., Internat. Reading Assn. Presbyterian. Avocations: riding horses, reading, traveling, singing, theater. Home: PO Box 610 Cypress TX 77410-0610 Office: Truitt Jr High 6600 Addicks Satsuma Rd Houston TX 77084-1520

PENNEY, JACQUELINE, artist, educator; b. Roslyn, N.Y., Mar. 26, 1930; d. Laurent Lariviere and Francoise (DeLisle) Gaultney; m. William A. Penney, Mar. 14, 1953 (div. Apr. 1981); children: Deborah Lynne, William Arthur III; m. Kenneth Gerald Moore, Sept. 7, 1985 (div. June 1998). Student, Phoenix Sch. Design, 1948-49, Black Mountain Coll., 1949, Inst. Design, Chgo., 1949-50; student of Charles Reid, Robert E. Wood, Daniel Green, Mario Cooper, Barbara Nechis. Tchr. studio workshops, Venice, Fla., 1983-85, Vero Beach, Fla., 1985, Huntington Art League. Author: Painting Greeting Cards in Watercolor, 1997, Discover the Joy of Acrylic Painting, 2001; co-author: The Artful Journal: A Spiritual Quest, 2002; one-woman shows at Plandome Gallery, N.Y., 1982, Gallery East, East Hampton, N.Y., 1980-81, 83-84, 88, East End Arts Coun., Riverhead, N.Y., 1980-81, 84; exhibited in group shows at Audubon Artists, 1975-76, 82, Guild Hall, East Hampton, 1979-82, 84, East End Arts Coun., 1980-83, 88, Nat. League Am. Pen Women, 1981, Nat. Soc. Painters in Casein and Acrylic, N.Y.C., 1981, Heckscher Mus., Huntington, N.Y., 1981, 83-84, 87-88, others; represented in permanent collections Stony Brook Sch., N.Y., Eastern L.I. Hosp., Greenport, Unitarian/Universalist Ch., Oak Park, Ill., Banka Commerciale Italiana, Milan, Cutchogue (N.Y.) Free Libr., Suffolk County Nat. Bank, Cutchogue, Rutger State U. Zimmerly Art Mus. Mem. Nat. Assn. Women Artists. Home and Office: Jacqueline Penney Art Gallery and Studio 270 North St PO Box 959 Cutchogue NY 11935

PENNEY, LINDA HELEN, music educator; b. Poquonnock, N.J., Mar. 22, 1958; d. John J. and Edith (Cook) P. B in Music cum laude, U. Hartford, 1979; MS in Edn., Fordham U., 1986; MMusic, U Conn., 1996. Cert. tchr., N.Y., Conn.; cert. adminstr., N.Y. Choral dir. Middletown (Conn.) High Sch., 1979-82, Bronxville (N.Y.) Mid. Sch.-High Sch., 1983-87; dir. music Canaan (Vt.) Pub. Sch., 1987-88; dir. chorus, drama Ardsley (N.Y.) Mid. Sch.-High Sch., 1988-92; vocal and choral dir., instr. music theory, theater Port Chester (N.Y.) High Sch., 1992—. Dir. performing arts Woodside on the Move-N.Y.C. Cultural Youth Bd., 1983-85; mem. faculty Ossining (N.Y.) Studio Music, 1989-91. Mem. Am. Choral Dirs. Assn., Music Educators Nat. Conf. (nat. registry), Internat. Assn. Jazz Edn., Westchester Coun. for Arts, N.Y. State Schs. Music Assn., Westchester County Schs. Music Assn. (chair area all-state music festival 1985-87). Avocations: concerts, reading, hiking. Home: 37 Willow Lake Dr Holmes NY 12531-5443 Office: Port Chester High Sch Tamarack Rd Port Chester NY 10573

PENNEY, SHERRY HOOD, university president, educator; b. Marlette, Mich., Sept. 4, 1937; d. Terrance and B. Jean (Stoutenburg) Hood; m. Carl Murray Penney, July 8, 1961 (div. 1978); children: Michael Murray, Jeffrey Hood; m. James Duane Livingston, Mar. 30, 1985. BA, Albion Coll., 1959, LLD (hon.), 1989; MA, U. Mich., 1961; PhD, SUNY, Albany, 1972; hon. degree, Quincy Coll., 1999. Vis. asst. prof. Union Coll., Schenectady, N.Y., 1972-73; assoc. higher edn. N.Y. State Edn. Dept., Albany, 1973-76; assoc. provost Yale U., New Haven, 1976-82; vice chancellor acad. programs, policy and planning SUNY System, Albany, 1982-88; acting pres. SUNY, Plattsburgh, 1986-87; chancellor U. Mass., Boston, 1988-95; pres. U. Mass. Sys., Boston, 1995; chancellor U. Mass. Boston, 1996-2000, endowed prof., 2001—. Chmn., bd. dirs. Nat. Higher Edn. Mgmt. Sys., Boulder, Colo., 1985-87; mem. commn. on higher edn. New Eng. Assn. Schs. and Colls., Boston, 1979-82, Mid. States Assn. Schs. and Colls., Phila., 1986-88; mem. commn. on women Am. Coun. Edn., Washington, 1979-81, commn. on govt. rels., 1990-94; bd. dirs. NSTAR, Boston Edison Co., 1990—, Carnegie Found. for Advancement of Teaching, 1994-2002. Author: Patrician in Politics, 1974; editor: Women and Management in Higher Education, 1975; contbr. articles to profl. jours. Nat. adv. com. Nat. Initiative for Women in Higher Edn., 2001—; mem. Internat. Trade Task Force, 1994—96; mem. exec. com. Challenge to Leadership, 1988, chair, 1995—98; mem. Mid-Am. adv. bd. HERS, 1992—, Mary Baker Eddy Libr., Boston, 2001—; trustee Berkeley Div. Sch., Yale U., 1978—82, John F. Kennedy Libr. Found., 1988—2001; bd. dirs. Albany Symphony Orch., 1982—88, U. Mass. Found., 1988—2000, Mcpl. Rsch. Bur., Boston, 1990—2001, New Eng. Coun., 1990—2000, Greater Boston C. of C., 1989—2002, Met. Affairs Coalition, chair, 1999—2001; bd. dirs. New Eng. Aquarium, 1990—, Greater Boston One to One Leadership Coun., 1990—2000, NASULGC Commn. Urban Affairs, 1990—2000, The Ednl. Resource Inst., chair, 1996—; bd. dirs. The Environ. Bus. Coun., 1991—97. Recipient Disting. Alumna award Albion Coll., 1978, Disting. Citizen award for racial harmony Black/White Boston, 1994, Am. Coun. on Edn./Nat. Identification Program Mass. Leadership award, 1995, New Eng. Women's Leadership award, 1996, Pinnacle award for Lifetime Achievement Greater Boston C. of C., 1998, Abigail Adams award, Mass. Women's Polit. Caucus, 2003. Mem. Am. Assn. Higher Edn., Orgn. Am. Historians, St. Botolph Club, Comml. Club (Boston). Unitarian Universalist. Office: U Mass Boston 100 Morrissey Blvd Boston MA 02125-3300 E-mail: sherry.penney@umb.edu.

PENNING, PATRICIA JEAN, elementary education educator; b. Springfield, Ill., Sept. 3, 1952; d. Howard Louis and Jean Lenore (Hartley) P. AA, Lincoln Land C.C., Springfield, 1972; BA, Millikin U., 1975. Cert. tchr. grades K-9. Receptionist Drs. Penning, Marty & Teich, Springfield, 1968-72; child care asst. La Petite Acad., Springfield, 1970-72; tchr. St. Agnes Sch., Springfield, 1975—. Mail clk. St. John's Hosp., Springfield, 1977-88; mem. dir. instrnl. tv St. Agnes Sch., Springfield, 1981—, sec. primary level, 1993—, mem. reading com., 1994—, mem. social com., 1994—. Mem. St. Agnes Folk Choir, Springfield, 1976—; cantor, St. Agnes Ch., Springfield, 1976—, creator butterfly garden. Recipient Outstanding Tchr. award Office Cath. Edn., Springfield, 1988, Golden Apple award Ch. 20 and Town and Country Bank, Springfield, 1993; named Apprentice Cathechist, Diocese of Springfield, Ill., 1992. Mem. Internat. Reading Assn., Nat. Coun. Math., Nat. Cath. Edn. Assn. (Grad. award 1991), Ill. State Assn. Curriculum and Devel. Roman Catholic. Avocations: reading, crafts, gardening, classical music. Home: 22 Westminster Rd Chatham IL 62629-1254 Office: St Agnes Sch 251 N Amos Ave Springfield IL 62702-4792

PENNINGER, FRIEDA ELAINE, retired English language educator; b. Marion, N.C., Apr. 11, 1927; d. Fred Hoyle and Lena Frances (Young) P. AB, U. N.C., Greensboro, 1948; MA, Duke U., 1950, PhD, 1961. Copywriter Sta. WSJS, Winston-Salem, N.C., 1948-49; asst. prof. English Flora Macdonald Coll., Red Springs, N.C., 1950-51; tchr. English Barnwell, S.C., 1951-52, Brunswick, Ga., 1952-53; instr. English U. Tenn., Knoxville, 1953-56; instr., asst. prof. Woman's Coll., U. N.C., Greensboro, 1956-58, 60-63; asst. prof., assoc. prof. U. Richmond (Va.), 1963-71; chair., dept. English Westhampton Coll., Richmond, 1971-78; prof. English U. Richmond, 1971-91, Bostwick prof. English, 1987-91; ret., 1991. Author: William Caxton, 1979, Chaucer's "Troilus and Criseyde" and "The Knight's Tale": Fictions Used, 1993, (novel) Look at Them, 1990; compiler, editor: English Drama to 1660, 1976; editor: Festschrift for Prof. Marguerite Roberts, 1976. Fellow Southeastern Inst. of Mediaeval and Renaissance Studies, 1965, 67, 69. Democrat. Presbyterian. Home: 2701 Camden Rd Greensboro NC 27403-1438

PENTKOWSKI, RAYMOND J. principal; Former supt. Battenkill (Vt.) Valley Supervisory Union, Addison-Rutland (Vt.) Supervisory Union; formerly prin. Ludlow (Vt.) Elem. Sch.; prin. Poultney (Vt.) Elem. Sch. Named state finalist Nat. Supt. of Yr. award, 1989. Office: PoultneyElem Sch Poultney VT 05764 E-mail: Ray.Pentkowski@rswsu.org.

PENWELL, PATRICIA LEE, special education educator; b. Oregon, Mo., Nov. 22, 1935; d. Paul Olen and Dorothea Ruth (Bigley) Crouse; m. David Wayne Penwell, Aug. 28, 1955 (div. Feb. 1989); children: Todd Randall, David Wayne, Cynthia Suzanne. BSEd, Miami U., Oxford, Ohio, 1973; MA in Edn., U. No. Iowa, Cedar Falls, 1983. Cert. tchr. in elem. edn., learning disabilities, mental disabilities, emotional handicaps, Iowa. Tchr. 3d grade Piti (Guam) Elem. Sch., 1957-58, Villisca (Iowa) Elem. Sch., 1973-75, multi-category resource tchr., 1975-77; substitute tchr. K-6 Pinellas County (Fla.) Schs., 1981-82, 83-84; multi-category resource tchr. Cedar Falls Schs., 1985-87; tchr. emotionally handicapped Waterloo (Iowa) Elem. Schs., 1987-88; emotionally handicapped rsch. tchr. Washington Sch. Dist., Phoenix, 1988-95, 4th grade tchr., 1995-99, ret., 1999. Grad. asst. U. No. Iowa, 1982-83, student tchr. supr., 1986-87. Elder Covenant Presbyn. Ch., Phoenix, 1991-2000. Recipient Lamp of Learning award Washington Sch. Dist., 1994. Mem. Coun. for Exceptional Children (pres., Tchr. of Yr. 1993). Avocations: hiking, reading, travel. Home: 2631 N 26th St Phoenix AZ 85008-1908 Office: Desert View Sch 8621 N 3rd St Phoenix AZ 85020-3185

PEOPLES, ESTHER LORRAINE, elementary education educator, writer, publisher; b. Ames, Iowa, Sept. 18, 1933; d. Henry Francis and Hildred Cecile (Jacques) Gulliver; m. Ralph William Hill, Dec. 1951; m. Graydon Peoples, Dec. 11, 1970; children: Cathryn Louise Hill, Charles Henry Hill, Stephen Edward Hill; 6 stepchildren. BS in Elem. Edn., Drake U., 1962, MS in Edn., Curriculum and Instruction, 1967, postgrad., 1978. Cert. elem. tchr., Iowa; cert. elem. tchr., elem. prin., Ariz. Primary tchr. Glick Elem., Marshalltown, 1962-63, Grant Elem., Des Moines, 1963-65, Fisher Elem. Sch., Marshalltown, 1965-78, student tchr., coop. tchr., 1966-77, 90, intern prin., 1978; elem. tchr. Phoenix Country Day Sch., Paradise Valley, 1978-88, acting head lower sch. K-5, 1985; elem. program dir. Tesseract, Paradise Valley, 1988-91, tchr. grade 2, 1988-96; ret., 1996. Spkr. in field. Author: You Can Teach Someone to Read, A How-To Book for Friends, Parents and Teachers, 2000; contbr. articles to profl. jours. Honored by Paradise Valley Tesseract named sci. bldg. The Lorraine Peoples Sci. Ctr. Mem. NEA, Ariz. Edn. Assn., Iowa State Edn. Assn., Assn. Childhood Edn., Ariz. Pub. Assn., Small Pubs. Assn. N.Am., Ariz. Book Pubs. Assn., Mobile In Svc. Tng. Lab., Mortar Bd. Home: PMB 185 2487 S Gilbert Rd 106 Gilbert AZ 85296 E-mail: gelpeoples@aol.com., globkspub@aol.com.

PEPE, LOUIS ROBERT, lawyer, educator; b. Derby, Conn., Mar. 7, 1943; s. Louis F. and Mildred R. (Vollaro) P.; m. Carole Anita Roman, June 8, 1969; children: Marissa Lee, Christopher Justin, Alexander Drew. B in Mgmt. Engring., Rensselaer Poly. Inst., 1964, MS, 1967; JD with distinction, Cornell U., 1970. Bar: Conn. 1970, U.S. Dist. Ct. Conn. 1970, U.S. Ct. Appeals (2d cir.) 1971, U.S. Supreme Ct. 1975, U.S. Ct. Claims 1978. Assoc. Alcorn, Bakewell & Smith, Hartford, Conn., 1970-75, ptnr., 1975-82; sr. ptnr. Pepe & Hazard, Hartford, 1983—. Adj. assoc. prof. Hartford Grad. Ctr., 1972-87; adj. prof. U. Conn. Law Sch., 2000—. Mem. New Hartford Housing Authority, 1971-72, New Hartford Planning Zoning Commn., 1973-84, chmn., 1980-84, New Hartford Inland Wetlands Commn., 1975-78; mem. dean's adv. coun. Cornell Law Sch., 1990—; dir. Capitol Area Found. Equal Justice, 1993—, pres., 1999-2001. 1st lt. U.S. Army, 1964-66. Decorated Army Commendation medal. Fellow Am. Bar Found., Conn. Bar Found., Am. Coll. Constl. Lawyers, Am. Coll. Trial Lawyers; mem. ABA, Am. Bd. Trial Advocates, Conn. Bar Assn. (chmn. constrn. law sect. 1989-92, chmn. standing com. on professionalism 2000-2003, v.p. 2003—, chmn. probono com. 2003-), Conn. Trial Lawyers Assn., Hartford County Bar Assn., Phi Kappa Phi. Home: 3 Metacom Dr Simsbury CT 06070-1851 Office: Pepe & Hazard Goodwin Sq Hartford CT 06103-4300 E-mail: lpepe@pepehazard.com.

PEPPAS, NIKOLAOS ATHANASSIOU, chemical and biomedical engineering educator, consultant; b. Athens, Greece, Aug. 25, 1948; s. Athanassios Nikolaou Peppas and Alice Petrou Rousopoulou; m. Lisa Brannon, Aug. 10, 1988; 1 dau., Katherine. Diploma in Engring., Nat. Tech. U., Athens, 1971; ScD, MIT, 1973; D hon. causa, U. Parma, Italy, 1999, U. Ghent, Belgium, 1999, U. Ghent, U. Athens, 2000. Asst. prof. chem. engring. Purdue U., West Lafayette, Ind., 1976-78, assoc. prof., 1978-81, prof., 1981—2002, Showalter Disting. prof. of chem. and biomed. engring., 1993—2002; prof. chem. engring. U. Tex., Austin, 2003—, prof. biomed. engring., 2003, prof. pharmaceutics, 2003—, Robertson Meek disting. prof., 2003—, chair biomed. engring., 2003. Vis. prof. U. Geneva, 1982-83, Calif. Inst. Tech., Pasadena, 1983, U. Paris, 1986, Hoshi U., Japan, 1994, Hebrew U., Jerusalem, 1994, U. Naples, 1995, Free U. Berlin, 2001, Complutense U. Madrid, 2001; adj. prof. U. Parma, Italy, 1987; cons. in field; mem. adv. bd. several cos. Author: Biomaterials, 1982, Hydrogels in Medicine and Pharmacy, 1987, One Hundred Years of Chemical Engineering, 1989, Pulsatile Drug Delivery, 1993, Biopolymers, 1993, Superabsorbent Polymers, 1994, Polymer/Inorganic Interfaces, 1995, Biomaterials for Drug and Cell Delivery, 1994; contbr. over 845 articles and over 300 abstracts to jours. Active Austin Symphony Orch., Transfiguration Orthodox Ch. Austin. Recipient APV medal, Herbert McCoy award Purdue U., 2000. Fellow: AIChE (chmn. materials divsn. 1988—90, dir. bioengring. divsn. 1994—97, bd. dirs. 1999—2002, Materials Engring. Sci. award 1984, Bioengring. award 1994, Best Paper award 1994), Am. Phys. Soc., Italian Soc. Medicine and Scis., Am. Phys. Soc., Am. Assn. Pharm. Scientists (Rsch. Achievements Pharm. Tech. award 1999, Dale Wurster award 2002), Am. Inst. Med. Biol. Engrs., Soc. Biomaterials (pres.-elect 2002, pres. 2003—); mem.: Biomed. Engring. Soc. (Best Rsch. award 2002), Polymer Pioneer, Am. Soc. Engring. Edn. (AT&T award 1982, Curtis McGraw award 1988, G. Westinghouse award 1992), Soc. Biomaterials (Clemson award 1992), Controlled Release Soc. (pres. 1987—88, Founders award 1991, Eurand award 2002), N.Y. Acad. Scis., Am. Chem. Soc. (Newsmaker of Yr. award 2002), Sigma Xi. Avocations: linguistics, opera, rare maps, classical record collecting, wine collecting. Office: U Tex Dept Chem Engring Austin TX 78712

PEPPER, FLOY CHILDERS, educational consultant; b. Broken Arrow, Okla., Mar. 14, 1917; d. James Alexander and Louise Lena (Barber) Childers; m. James Gilbert Pepper, Mar. 23, 1940; children: James G., Suzanne Pepper Henry. BS, Okla. State U., Stillwater, 1938; MS, Okla. State U., 1939; postgrad., Oreg. U. Home econs. tchr. Bur. Indian Affairs, Ft. Sill, Okla., 1939-40, Chemawa, Oreg., 1940-42, Portland (Oreg.) Pub. Schs., 1945-65; instr. Portland State U., 1967-85; supr. spl. edn. Multnomah Ednl. Svc. Dist., Portland, 1965-83; orientation specialist N.W. Regional Ednl. Lab., Portland, 1983-85; curriculum writer Oreg. State Bd. Edn., Salem, 1987-90; evaluator Native Indian Tchr. Edn. Program U. B.C., Vancouver, 1987-89; cons. Indian edn. Portland Pub. Sch., 1989—. Coauthor: Maintaining Sanity in the Classroom, 1971, revised edit., 1982; contbr. articles to profl. jours. Recipient Ed Elliot Human Rights award Oreg. Edn. Assn., 1996 Mem. Indian Curriculum Com. (alternative chmn. 1990-99), Oreg. Soc. of Individual Psychology, Multicultural Task Force (co-chmn. 1990-99, Dist. Svc. award 1990-91). Republican. Avocations: writing, reading, dancing, presenting workshops. Home and Office: Remembrance LLC 2200 SW Scenic Dr Portland OR 97225-4015

PEPPER, ROLLIN ELMER, microbiology educator, consultant; b. Glens Falls, N.Y., June 8, 1924; s. Henry Orville and Ruby Mae (Tucker) P.; m. Lucille Blackman, May 30, 1953 (dec.); children: Roger R., Barbara Pepper Moquin, Susan Pepper Aisenberg; m. Martha Charles, Mar. 3, 1990. BA, Earlham Coll., 1950; MS, Syracuse U., 1953; PhD, Mich. State U., 1963. Assoc. scientist Ethicon, Inc., Somerville, N.J., 1951-60; rsch. assoc. Mich. State U., East Lansing, 1963-64; prof. biology Elizabethtown Coll., Pa., 1964-90, chmn. dept., 1967-77, prof. emeritus, 1990—. Vis. prof. biology U. Zambia, Lusaka, 1972-73; microbiology cons. Sporicidin Co., Rockville, Md., 1971-94, Baums Bologna, Elizabethtown, 1976-83; health officer Borough of Elizabethtown, 1981-97. Contbr. chpt. to book, articles to profl. jours.; patentee in field. Pres. Elizabethtown Bd. Health, 1976-77. Mem. Elizabethtown Club, Rotary (pres. 1983-84, dist. youth exch. chmn. 1978-81, Presdl. citation 1984, pres. chpt. Friendship Force 1991-92, Vincent W. O'Connor Cmty. Svc. award 1997), Sigma Xi. Mem. Brethren in Christ Ch. Avocations: travel, camping, photography. Home: 420 N Mount Joy St Elizabethtown PA 17022-1634 Office: Elizabethtown Coll Dept Biology Elizabethtown PA 17022

PEPPERDENE, MARGARET WILLIAMS, English educator; b. Vicksburg, Miss., Dec. 25, 1919; d. O.L. and Jane (Stocks) Williams. BS, La. State U., 1941; MA, Vanderbilt U., 1948, PhD, 1953. Div. Instr. English U. Oreg., 1946-47; teaching fellow Vanderbilt U., 1948-50; instr., then asst. prof. Miami U., Oxford, Ohio, 1952-56; mem. faculty Agnes Scott Coll., 1956—, prof. English, chmn. dept., 1967—. Author articles.; Editor: That Subtile Wreath: Lectures Presented at the Quartercentenary Celebration of the Birth of John Donne, 1973. Served to lt. USNR, 1943-46. Fulbright fellow, 1950-51; Ford Found. grad. fellow, 1951-52; AAUW fellow, 1954-55; research fellow Dublin Inst. Advanced Studies, 1954-55; Guggenheim fellow, 1956-57; recipient Gov.'s Award in Humanities, Ga., 1987. Home: 418 Glendale Ave Decatur GA 30030-1922

PERADOTTO, JOHN JOSEPH, classics educator, editor; b. Ottawa, Ill., May 11, 1933; s. John Joseph and Mary Louise (Giacometti) P.; m. Noreen Doran, Aug. 29, 1959 (div. 1982); m. Marlene Rosen, Aug. 29, 1992; children: Erin, Monica, Noreen, Nicole. BA, St. Louis U., 1957, MA, 1958; PhD, Northwestern U., 1963. Instr. classics and English Western Wash. U., Bellingham, 1960-61; instr. Georgetown U., 1961-63, asst. prof. classics, 1963-66, SUNY, Buffalo, 1966-69, asso. prof., 1969-73; prof., chmn. classics U. Tex., Austin, 1973-74; prof. classics SUNY-Buffalo, 1974-2000, Andrew V.V. Raymond prof. classics, 1984-99, Disting. tchg. prof., 1990-2000, Disting. tchg. prof. emeritus, 2000—, chmn. dept., 1974-77, dean div. undergrad. edn., 1978-82. Benedict Disting. vis. prof. Carleton Coll., 2003; Martin lectr. Oberlin Coll., 1987; dir. summer seminar for coll. tchrs. NEH, 1976, for secondary sch. tchrs., 1984; vis. scholar winter quarters UCSD, 2000—; Benedict disting. vis. prof. Carleton Coll., 2003. Author: Classical Mythology: An Annotated Bibliographical Survey, 1973, Man in the Middle Voice: Name and Narration in the Odyssey, 1990, also articles and revs.; founding assoc. editor: Arethusa, editor-in-chief:, 1974—95, mem. bd. editors: SUNY Press, 1978—81; editor: SUNY Press Classical Series, 1981—2000, Classical Literature and Contemporary Literary Analysis, 1977, Women in the Ancient World, 1978, 1983, Studies in Latin Literature, 1984, Under the Text; co-editor: Population Policy in Plato and Aristotle, 1975, The New Archilochus, 1976, Augustan Poetry Books, 1980, Indo-European Roots of Classical Culture, 1980, Vergil: 2000 Years, 1981, Texts and Contexts: American Classical Studies in Honor of J.P. Vernant, 1982, Semiotics and Classical Studies, 1983, Audience-oriented Criticism and the Classics, 1986, Herodotus and the Invention of History, 1987, Gonimos: Neoplatonic and Byzantine Studies Presented to L.G. Westerlink at 75, 1988, The Challenge of Black Athena, 1989, Pastoral Revisions, 1990, Reconsidering Ovid's Fasti, 1992, Bakhtin and Classical Studies, 1993, Rethinking the Classical Canon, 1994, Horace: 2000 Years, 1995, The New Simonides, 1996, The Iliad and its Contexts, 1997. Fellow Center for Hellenic Studies, 1972-73; recipient Chancellor's award for teaching excellence State U. N.Y., 1975, Disting. Retiring Editor award Coun. of Editors of Learned Jours., 1995. Mem. Am. Philol. Assn. (dir. 1974-77, pres. 1990), Classical Assn. Atlantic States (exec. com. 1976-78). Office: Dept Classics State U Ny Buffalo NY 14261-0011 E-mail: peradott@buffalo.edu.

PERCAS DE PONSETI, HELENA, foreign language and literature educator; b. Valencia, Spain, Jan. 17, 1921; came to U.S., 1940, naturalized, 1950; m. Ignacio V. Ponseti, 1961. Baccalaureat, Paris, France, 1939; BA, Barnard Coll., 1942; MA, Columbia, 1943, PhD, 1951. Tchr. lang. and lit. Barnard Coll., 1942-43, Russell Sage Coll., 1943-45, Columbia U., 1945-47, Queens Coll., 1946-48; mem. faculty Grinnell Coll., 1948—, prof. lang. and lit., 1957—, Roberts Honor prof. modern fgn. langs., 1961-62, Richards prof. modern fgn. langs., 1963-82, prof. emerita, 1982—. Author: La Poesia Femenina Argentina, 1810-1950, 1958, Cervantes y su concepto del arte, 1975, Cervantes the Writer and Painter of Don Quijote, 1988; contbr. articles to profl. jours. Mem.: Asociacion de Cervantistas Alcala de Henares Spain (charter 1987), Cervantes Soc. Am. (founding mem.), Hispanic Soc. Am. (hon.; hon. assoc. 2001). Home: 110 Oakridge Ave Iowa City IA 52246-2935

PERCY, JOHN REES, astronomer, educator; b. Windsor, Berkshire, Eng., July 10, 1941; arrived in Can., 1946; s. George Francis and Christine (Holland) P.; m. Maire Ede Robertson, June 16, 1962; 1 child, Carol Elaine. BSc, U. Toronto, Ont., Can., 1962, MA, 1963, PhD, 1968. Asst. prof. U. Toronto, 1968-72, assoc. prof., 1973-78, prof., 1978—; assoc. dean., vice prin. Erindale Coll., U. Toronto, Mississauga, Canada, 1989-94; cross apptd. to Ont. Inst. Studies in Edn., 2000—. Co-author: Science 10: An Introductory Study, 1988; editor: The Study of Variable Stars Using Small Telescopes, 1986; co-editor: The Teaching of Astronomy, 1990, Variable Star Research: An International Perspective, 1991, Astronomy Education, 1996, New Trends in Astronomy Teaching, 1998, Amateur-Professional Partnerships in Astronomy, 2000. Vice-chair, bd. trustees Ontario Sci. Ctr., 1992-98. Recipient Royal Jubilee medal Govt. of Can., 1977, Disting. Educator award Ont. Inst. Studies in Edn., 1998, Jack Bell award, 1999, Northrop Frye award U. Toronto, 2003; named hon. pres. Sci. Tchrs. Assn. of Ont., 1988-91. Fellow AAAS; mem. Astronomy Soc. Pacific (pres. 1997-99), Am. Assn. Variable Star Observers (pres. 1989-91), Royal Can. Inst. (pres. 1985-86, Sandford Fleming medal 1997), Royal Astron. Soc. Can. (pres. 1978-80, Svc. award 1977), Internat. Astron. Union (pres. commn. 27-variable stars 1991-94, pres. commn. 46 teaching of astronomy 1994-97, coord. travelling telescope project, editor newsletter on teaching astronomy), Am. Astron. Soc. (edn. bd. 1999-2002), Can. Astron. Soc. (chair edn. com. 2000—). Achievements include research on variable stars, stellar evolution, and science education. Office: U Toronto Erindale Campus Mississauga ON Canada L5L 1C6

PERDEW, JOHN PAUL, physics educator, condensed matter and density functional theorist; b. Cumberland, Md., Aug. 30, 1943; BS, Gettysburg Coll., 1965; PhD, Cornell U., 1971. Postdoctoral fellow U. Toronto, 1971-74, Rutgers U., New Brunswick, N.J., 1974-77; prof. physics Tulane U., New Orleans, 1977—, chair physics dept., 1991—94, 2001—03. Vis. scientist Nordita, Copenhagen, Argonne Nat. Lab., ETH Zurich, ITP Santa Barbara, Naval Rsch. Lab., Washington; invited lectr. more than 65 internat. confs. Contbr. more than 185 sci. articles to profl. jours. NSF Rsch. grantee, 1978—, Petroleum Rsch. Fund grantee 1998-2000; recipient Tulane LAS award for excellence in rsch., 1990. Fellow Am. Phys. Soc.; mem. Am. Chem. Soc., Am. Assn. Physics Tchrs., Internat. Acad. Quantum Molecular Sci., Phi Beta Kappa. Office: Tulane U Dept Physics New Orleans LA 70118 E-mail: perdew@tulane.edu.

PERDIGO, LUISA MARINA, foreign language and literature educator; b. Havana, Cuba, Dec. 25, 1947; came to U.S. 1962; d. Mario and Hortensia Dolores (Alvarez) P. AB, CUNY, 1971, MA, 1974, PhD, 1981; MA, Columbia U., 1987. Cert. translator English/Spanish, Am. Translators Assn. Asst. prof. Spanish, asst. dean St. Thomas Aquinas Coll., Sparkill, N.Y., 1982-87; asst. prof. Spanish and French CUNY, La Guardia, 1987-88, asst. prof. Spanish, City Coll., 1988-89; asst. prof. Spanish St. Peter's Coll., Jersey City, N.J., 1989-91; asst. prof. Spanish and French Clarion U., Pa., 1992-94, Rockland Coll. SUNY, 1995-96, Mercy Coll., 1998—. Author: La Estética de Octavio Paz, 1975, The Origins of Vicente Huidobro's Creacionismo (1911-1916) and its Evolution (1917-47), 1994, The Lyrics of the Troubadour Perdigon, 2002, (poetry) Desde el Hudson/From the Hudson, 1993, Huellas/Footprints, 1997, America at the Millenium, 2000, The Best Poems and Poets of 2002, Theatre of the Mind, 2003; author numerous poems; contbr. articles to profl. jours. Participant seminar in poetry, NEH, U. Kans., 1991; Rsch. fellow Orgn. Am. States, Chile, 1981; grantee CUNY, 1975; scholar Columbia U., 1982-84. Mem. MLA, Clarion Hist. Soc., Circulo de Cultura Panamericano, Sigma Delta Pi, Pi Delta Phi.

PERDREAU, CORNELIA RUTH WHITENER (CONNIE PERDREAU), English as a second language educator, international exchange specialist; b. Beacon, N.Y. d. Henry Kato Whitener and Mazie Althea (Martin) Whitener-Johnson; 1 child, Maurice Laurence Henri. BA, SUNY, Potsdam, 1969; MA, Ohio U., 1971, 72. French/Latin tchr. Walt Whitman Jr. High Sch., Yonkers, N.Y., 1969-70; French teaching asst. Ohio U., Athens, 1970-71, ESL tchr., 1976—; English/French tchr. Lycee de Chambery, France, 1972. English tchr. Acad. de Paris, France, 1984; study abroad coord. Ohio U., Athens, 1988-98, dir. edn. abroad office U. Athens, 1998—. Contbr. articles to profl. jours. Chair Tri-County Community Action Agy., Sugarcreek, Ohio, 1982; mem. bd. Dairy Barn Arts Ctr., Athens, 1985-91; trustee Ohioana Bd. Trustees, Columbus, 1987-96; mem. TOEFL Policy Coun., 1998—. Mem. NAFSA Assn. Internat. Educators (pres. 1996-97), TESOL (chair rules and resolutions com. 1993-95), Internat. Assn. Black Profls. in Internat. Affairs (founder), Adminstrs. and Tchrs. in ESL (chair 1992-93), Internat. Black Profls. in TESOL (founder, chair 1992-95), Ohio TESOL (pres. 1986-87), Assn. Internat. Educators (pres.-elect 1995). Office: Ohio U Study Abroad Office 107 Gordy Hall Athens OH 45701

PERDUE, CHARLES L., JR., social sciences educator, language educator; b. Panthersville, Ga., Dec. 1, 1930; s. Charles L. Sr. and Eva Mae (Samples) Perdue; m. Nancy J. Martin; children: Martin Clay, Marc Charles, Kelly Scott, Kevin Barry(dec.). Student, North Ga. Coll., 1948-49, Santa Rosa (Calif.) Jr. Coll., 1953; AB in Geology, U. Calif., Berkeley, 1958, postgrad., 1958-59; MA in Folklore, U. Pa., 1968, PhD in Folklore, 1971. Engring. writer Convair Astronautics, Vandenberg AFB, Calif., 1959-60; geologist, mineral classification br. U.S. Geol. Survey, Washington, 1960-67; asst. prof. English dept. U. Va., Charlottesville, 1971-72, asst. prof. English, sociology and anthropology depts., 1972-73, from asst. prof. to assoc. prof. English and anthropology depts., 1973—92, prof., 1992—. Cons. in field. Author (with others): (book) Weevils in the Wheat: Interviews with Virginia Ex-Slaves, 1976; author: Outwitting the Devil: Jack Tales from Wise country, Virginia, 1987, Pig's Foot Jelly and Persimmon Beer: Foodways from the Virginia Writers' Project, 1992; author: (with Nancy J. Martin-Perdue) Talk About Trouble: A New Deal Portrait of Virginians in the Great Depression, 1996; contbr. articles to profl. jours. With U.S. Army, 1951—54. Recipient award for Outstanding Book Using Oral History, Nat. Oral History Assn., 1997; Univ. Predoctoral fellow, U. Pa., 1967—71, Wilson Gee Inst. Rsch. grantee, U. Va., 1974, 1975, Rsch. grantee, NEH, 1980—81, 1984. Mem.: Va. Folklore Soc. (archivist, editor 1974—89, archivist 1990—94, archivist, pres. 1995—96, archivist 1997—), Nat. Coun. Traditional Arts (bd. dirs. 1971—87, pres. 1973—79), Mid. Atlantic Folklore Assn. (founding mem., bd. dirs.), Am. Folklore Soc. (exec. bd. 1980—83, book rev. editor jour. 1986—87). Office: U Va Dept Anthropology PO Box 400120 Charlottesville VA 22904-4120 E-mail: clp5a@virginia.edu.

PERDUE, JULIE DIANE, special education educator; b. Kalamazoo, Mich., Aug. 22, 1965; d. Eugene R. and Delores J. (Nifong) Cheh; m. Joe William Perdue, Aug. 10, 1991. BS, Ball State U., 1987; MEd, Memphis State U., 1990. Cert. tchr., Tenn. Tchr. West Tenn. Sch. for Deaf, Jackson, 1987-91, Union U., Jackson, 1990-91, Ringgold (Ga.) Elem. Sch., 1991-92, Red Bank Mid. Sch., Chattanooga, 1992—, Chattanooga State Coll., 1991—. Parent advisor Tenn. Infant Parent Svcs., Chattanooga, 1991—. Mem. NEA, Tenn. Edn. Assn, Tenn. Regis. Interpreters for the Deaf. Republican. Methodist. Avocations: cross-stitch, reading, walking, cooking. Home: 13200 Carters Way Rd Chesterfield VA 23838-3000

PEREIRA, JULIO CESAR, middle school educator; b. Vila Nova Sintra, Cape Verde, Cape Verde, Oct. 12, 1937; came to U.S., 1983; s. Julio Feijoo Pereira and Beatriz Feijoo Pereira. Student, Mil. Sch., Coimbra, Portugal, 1958-61; MAEE, U. Lisbon, Portugal, 1976; cert. in teaching, Afonso Domingues, Lisbon, 1979, Ea. Nazarene Coll., Quincy, Mass., 1988. Registered profl. engr., Portugal. Vocat. sch. tchr. Portuguese Sch., Lisbon, 1969-83, dir. instrn., 1980-81; social studies tchr. Madison Park H.S., Boston, 1984-85; math. tchr. Dearborn Mid. Sch., Boston, 1985—. Inventor slide model for algebraic addition. Lt. Portuguese Army, 1961-65. Recipient Tchr. Appreciation award Algebra Project Boston, 1992, Multicultural Recognition award Mass. Dept. Edn., 1992, Ofcl. citation Mass. Senate, 1993, Presdl. award for Excellence in Math. Teaching, Pres. of U.S., 1994. Mem. Coun. Presdl. Awardees in Math. Avocations: reading, research, computer programming, gardening, travel. Office: Dearborn Mid Sch 35 Greenville St Boston MA 02119-2315 Mailing: PO Box 2450 Mashpee MA 02649-8450

PEREL, JAMES MAURICE, pharmacology and psychiatry educator, researcher; b. Buenos Aires, Mar. 30, 1933; came to U.S., 1947, naturalized, 1954; s. Aria and Bella (Silverberg) P.; m. July 18, 1959 (div. 1971); 1 child, Allan B.; m. Audrey Feldman, Apr. 9, 1972; children: Alissa A., Stephen M. BS, CUNY, 1956; MS, NYU, 1961, PhD, 1964. Nuclear chemist N.Y. Naval Shipyard Lab., Bklyn., 1956-58; assoc. rsch. scientist NYU, Goldwater Meml. Hosp., N.Y.C., 1964-67; asst. prof. medicine and chemistry Emory U., Atlanta, 1967-70; asst. prof. psychiatry, pharmacology Columbia U. Coll. Physicians and Surgeons, N.Y.C., 1970-76; assoc. prof. clin. pharmacology, chief psychiat. rsch. N.Y. State Psychiat. Inst., N.Y.C., 1976-80; chief clin. pharmacology VA Med. Ctr. Highland Drive, Pitts., 1979-83; prof. psychiatry and pharmacology U. Pitts. Sch. Medicine, 1980—, acting chmn. dept. pharmacology, 1985-88; dir. clin. pharmacology Western Psychiat. Inst. and Clinic, Pitts., 1980—; prof. grad. neurosci., 1988—; postdoctoral fellow in clin. pharmacology NIH and NYU, 1964-67. Lectr. chemistry CUNY, 1963-67; assoc. rsch. scientist N.Y. State Psychiat. Inst., 1970-76; cons., mem. grant-awarding study sects. NIH, NIMH. Mem. editorial bd. Psychopharmacology, Neuropsychobiology, Therapeutic Drug Monitoring; contbr. over 400 articles to sci. jours., chpts. to books. Recipient Founders Day award NYU, 1974, Julius Koch Meml. award Rho Chi, 1983; named Psychopharmacologist of Yr., U. Toronto, 1993; predoctoral fellow NSF, 1958-60; numerous rsch. grants, including NIH, NIMH, Founds. Fund for Rsch. in Psychiatry, pharm. cos., pvt. founds. Fellow Am. Inst. Chemists; mem. Am. Soc. Clin. Pharmacology and Therapeutics, Am. Soc. Pharmacology and Exptl. Therapeutics, Am. Chem. Soc., Internat. Assn. Therapeutic Drug Monitoring and Clin. Toxicology, Soc. for Biol. Psychiatry, Sigma Xi. Jewish. Achievements include discovery of several widely-used pharmacotherapeutic agents. Office: U Pitts Sch Medicine 3811 Ohara St Pittsburgh PA 15213-2593 E-mail: pereljm@upmc.edu., pereljm@pitt.edu.

PERELLE, IRA B. psychologist, educator; b. Mt. Vernon, NY, Sept. 16, 1925; s. Joseph Yale and Lillian (Schaffer) P.; m. Diane A. Granville, 1982; 1 child, Jessica Eve. Student, U. Tex., 1943; grad. in elec. engring, R.C.A. Inst., 1951; student, Iona Coll.; BS, Fordham U., 1969, MS, 1970, PhD, 1972. Prodn. mgr. Arden Jewelry Case Co., 1946-49; became chief engr. Westlab Electronic Service Engrs., 1949; ptnr. Westlab, 1954; pres. Westlab, Inc., 1955-64, chmn. bd., 1956; pres. Westchester Research and Devel. Labs., 1953-65; exec. dir. Interlink, Ltd., 1966—; dir. Atlantic Research

Inst., 1975—. Cons. higher edn. divsn. U.S. Dept. of Edn., 1994—; cons. ednl. research Fordham U., Catholic U. of P.R., Bayamon (P.R.) Central U., World U., San Juan, P.R., John Jay Coll., N.Y.C., Rockland C.C., N.Y.; rsch. cons. So. Westchester County Bd. Coop. Ednl. Services; stats. cons. City of Mt. Vernon (N.Y.), Reader's Digest, Pleasantville, N.Y., GT&E Inc., CUNY; devel. dir. Animal Behavior Soc.; served as expert witness for N.Y. State Tax Ct.; assoc. Columbia U. Seminars; prof. dept. psychology NYU; prof. dept. bus. and econs., dept. psychology Mercy Coll., Dobbs Ferry, N.Y.; prof. Grad. Sch. Bus., L.I. U.; adj. prof. SUNY-Purchase, Fordham U., N.Y.C.; vis. prof. Fairleigh Dickenson U.; faculty adv. com. Mercer County Coll., 1969-73; conf. leader Nat. Conf. Ednl. Tech., 1971-73. Author: A Practical Guide to Educational Media for the Classroom Teacher, 1974; also articles; research on laterality for evolutionary biology. Discoverer Perelle Phenomenon, psychology-attention. Mem. staff Civil Def., 1954-74; bd. dirs. Mid-Hudson Inst., Dobbs Ferry, N.Y. Served as radio instr. USAAF, 1943-46. With USN, 1943—45. Mem. IEEE, AAAS, N.Y. Zool. Soc., Assn. Ednl. Communication and Tech., N.Y. State Ednl. Communication Assn., Audio Engring. Soc., Acoustical Soc. Am., Am. Inst. Physics, Am. Psychol. Assn., Am. Ednl. Rsch. Assn., Am. Statis. Assn., Animal Behavior Soc., Am. Genetic Soc., N.Y. Acad. Scis. Office: Mercy Coll Dept of Psychology & Bus Econ Dobbs Ferry NY 10522 Business E-Mail: iperelle@mercy.edu.

PEREZ, FRANCISCO IGNACIO, clinical psychologist, educator; b. Havana, Cuba, May 21, 1947; came to U.S., 1960; s. Francisco J. and Maria F. (Villa) P.; m. Georgina Montero, Aug. 27, 1971; children: Francisco A., Teresa M. BA, U. Fla., 1969, MA, 1971, PhD, 1972. Lic. psychologist, Tex. Asst. prof. edn. U. Houston, 1972-74; asst. prof. neurology & psychiatry Baylor U. Coll. Medicine, Dallas, 1974-80; pvt. practice clin. psychology, Houston, 1980—; clin. asst. prof. neurology and phys. medicine Baylor Coll. Medicine, Houston, 1980—; asst. prof. occupational psychology Health Sci. Ctr. Sch. Pub. Health U. Tex., 1993— Bd. dirs. Houston Community Youth Ctr., Stroke Club, Houston. NIMH research grantee, 1976-77; mem. med. adv. bd. Multiple Sclerosis Soc., Crons & Ilietis Found. Mem. Am. Psychol. Assn., Internat. Neuropsychology Soc., Assn. Advancement Behavior Analysis, Biofeedback Soc. Am. Roman Catholic. Contbr. articles to profl. jours. Home: 2315 Golden Pond Dr Kingwood TX 77345-1602 Office: 6560 Fannin Suite 1224 Houston TX 77030

PEREZ, MARY ANGELICA, bilingual specialist, educational administrator; b. San Benito, Tex., Sept. 03; d. Refugio P. and Maria G. (Guerra) P. AA, Tex. Southmonost Coll., Brownsville, Tex., 1955; BS in Elem. Edn., Tex. A&I U. (now Tex. A&M U.), 1959. Cert. elem. tchr., Tex., Calif. Substitute tchr. Bassett Unified Sch. Dist., La Puente, Calif.; tchr. kindergarten West Covina (Calif.) Unified Sch. Dist., ret.; tchr. ESL Tulane U., New Orleans; tchr. bilingual kindergarten San Benito (Tex.) Consolidated Sch. Dist.; tchr. bilingual 4th grade Brownsville (Tex.) Consolidated Sch. Dist.; tchr., head coord. Headstart St. Benedict Ch., San Benito, Tex. SCORE cons. to local sch. dist. Mem. L.A. World Affairs Coun., Nat. Dem. Club. Delta Kappa Gamma scholar, 1953; grantee NDEA, 1963, EEOC, 1969, U. Madrid, 1991; Congl. Recognition for 27 Yrs. of Tchrs. Calif. Mem. NEA, Nat. Assn. Bilingual Edn., Calif. Tchrs. Assn., Calif. Assn. Bilingual Educators, Tex. Tchrs. Assn. (pres. 1966), Calif. State Sheriff's Assn., Catholic Tchrs. Guild (pres. Brownsville Diocese 1965), Hispanic Women's Coun., L.A. World Affairs Coun. Democrat. Roman Catholic. Avocation: making and selling crafts. Home: 1900 S 77 Sunshine Strip Harlingen TX 78550-8273

PEREZ, MARY CHRISTINE, guidance counselor, small business owner; b. Miami, Fla., Dec. 5, 1967; d. Marta Miranda Perez. BA, Fla. Internat. U., 1989, MS, 1995. Cert. K-12 tchr., sch. guidance counselor, Fla. Tchr.'s aide Dade County Pub. Schs., Miami, 1986-87, tchr.'s asst., 1987-89, elem. tchr., 1989-95, guidance counselor, 1995—, chmn. student svcs. dept. Ruben Dario Mid. Sch., 1996—, mem. curriculum coun., 1996—. Sec.-treas., part owner K Lucky Transp. Svc., Miami, 1997—. Active Young Rep. Club, Miami, 1997. Named Role Model, 1st Union Nat. Bank and Hot Wheels Skating Ctr., 1997. Mem. Fla. Counseling Assn., Dade County Counseling Assn. Roman Catholic. Avocations: animals, music, sports, creative writing. Home: 14855 SW 39th Ct Miramar FL 33027-3324 Office: Ruben Dario Mid Sch 350 NW 97th Ave Miami FL 33172-4107

PEREZ, RENAE LEWIS, elementary education educator; b. Tyler, Tex., July 19, 1959; d. Paul Lawrence Lewis and Johnnie (Jackson) Harris; m. Philip Perez, Aug. 4, 1990. BS, U. North Tex., 1981; MEd, East Tex. State U., 1985. Cert. tchr. ESL, early childhood edn., Tex. Tchr. kindergarten B.F. Darrell, Dallas, 1981-82, C.F. Carr, Dallas, 1982-85; tchr. 1st grade R.L. Thornton, Dallas, 1985-92, A. Kramer, Dallas, 1992—. Mem. Phi Delta Kappa, Alpha Kappa Alpha. Avocations: world travel, arts and crafts painting, interior decorating. Office: 732 Pulitzer Ln Allen TX 75002-5239

PEREZ-CRUET, JORGE, physician, psychopharmacologist, psychophysiologist, psychiatrist, educator, addictionologist, geropsychiatrist; b. Santurce, P.R., Oct. 15, 1931; s. Jose Maria Perez-Vicente and Emilia Cruet-Burgos; m. Anyes Heimendinger, Oct. 4, 1958; children: Antonio, Mick, Graciela, Isabelle. BS magna cum laude, U. P.R., 1953, MD, 1957; diploma in psychiatry, McGill U., Montreal, Que., Can., 1976. Diplomate Am. Bd. Psychiatry and Neurology, Nat. Bd. Med. Examiners, Am. Bd. Geriat. Psychiatry; lic. Can. Coun. Med. Examiners, Med. Coun. Canada; cert. in quality assurance; cert. CHPQ by HQCB; cert. specialist in psychiatry RCPC, 1976. Rotating intern Michael Reese Hosp., Chgo., 1957-58; fellow in psychiatry Johns Hopkins U. Med. Sch., 1958-60, instr., then asst. prof. psychiatry, 1962-73; lab. neurophysiology and psychomatic lab. Walter Reed Army Inst. Rsch., Washington, 1960-62, cons., 1963-65; rsch. assoc. lab. chem. pharmacology NHI, NIH, Bethesda, Md., 1969-71; adult psychiatry sect. lab. clin. sci. NIMH, Bethesda, Md., 1971-73; psychiatry resident diploma course in psychiatry McGill U. Sch. Medicine, Montreal Gen. Hosp., 1973-76, Montreal Children's Hosp., 1975; prof. psychiatry, cief psychopharmacology lab. U. Mo.-Mo. Inst. Psychiatry, St. Louis, 1976-78; chief psychiatry svc. San Juan (P.R.) VA Hosp., pharmacy and therapeutic com., 1978-92; also prof. psychiatry U. P.R. Med. Sch., 1978-92; prof. psychiatry U. Okla. Health Sci. Ctr., Oklahoma City VA Med. Ctr., 1992—. Spl. cons. NASA, Moffettfield, Calif., 1965-69; cons. divsn. narcotic addition and drug abuse NIDA, 1972-73; mem. drug adv. com. FDA/NIDA, 1976-80, mem. pharmacy and therapeutic com., 1992—; local organizer Internat. Coll. Neuropsychiatry, San Juan, P.R., 1986; spl. advisor mental health P.R. Senate, P.R. sec. health, 1989; prin. investigator NASA biosatellite project JH Sch. Med., 1963-65.; staff psychiatrist mental health svcs., VAMC, Oklahoma City, 1992—, med. dir. opivid treatment program, 2001--. Editor: Catholic Physicians Guild Archiocese of Okla., 1997-98. Mem. Rep. Nat. Com., 1995; mem. Eisenhower Commn., 2001. Capt. M.C. USAR, 1960-62; sr. surgeon USPHS, 1969-71, med. dir., 1971-73. Recipient Coronas award, 1957, Ruiz-Arnau award, 1957, Diaz-Garcia award 1957, Geigy award, 1975, 76, AMA Recognition award 1971, 76, 81, Horner's award 1975, 76, Pavlovian award, 1978, Recognition cert. VA Svc. awards and commendations, 1980-98, Senate of P.R., 1986, Cert. of Merit Gov. of P.R., 1986, Cert. Recognition, Sec. Health, San Juan, Puerto Rico, Appreciation plaque Fifth World Congress or Irma, Manila, Philippines, Eisenhower Commn., 1995. Disting. fellow APA (life); fellow Interam. Coll. Physicians and Surgeons, Royal Coll. Physicians and Surgeons Can. (sr., cert.), Am. Psychiat Assn. (life, disting. life fellow, 2003); mem. Am. Coll. Med. Quality, Am. Physiol. Soc., Am. Coll. Psychiatrists, Pavlovian Soc., Am. Fedn. Clin. Rsch., Am. Fedn. Med. Rsch., Am. Assn. Geriat. Psychiatry, Am. Soc. Clin. Pharmacology and Therapeutics, Am. Soc. Pharmacology and Exptl. Therapeutics, Am. Soc. Addiction Medicine (cert. 1998), Am. Acad. Addiction Psychiatry (dir. Area VIII, 2002), Soc. Neurosci., Am. Coll. Med. Quality, Nat. Assn. Healthcare Quality, Internat. Soc. Rsch. Aggression, Okla. Psychiat. Assn., Am. Soc. Clin. Psychopharmacology, Menninger Found., Charles F. Menninger Soc., Okla. Assn. Health Care Quality, Alumni, UPR Sch. Med., Johns Hopkins Med. Surg. Inst., NIH Alumni (life), McGill, Okla. Hist. Soc. Republican. Roman Catholic. Home: 3304 Rosewood Ln Oklahoma City OK 73120-5604 Office: Oklahoma City VA Med Ctr 921 NE 13th St Oklahoma City OK 73104-5007 Fax: 405-270-1566. E-mail: jperezcrue@aol.com.

PEREZ-CRUET, MICK JORGE, neurological surgeon, educator; b. Washington, May 3, 1961; s. Jorge Fortunato and Anyes Lilly (Heimendinger) Perez-Cruet; m. Donna Jeanne Roggenbuck, July 9, 1994; children: Kristin Magdalene, Joshua Michael, Rachel Elizabeth, David Gabriel. BA, Grinell Coll., 1983; MSc in Chemistry, U. South Fla., 1986; MD, Tufts U., 1991. Intern surg. svc. Baylor Coll. Medicine, Houston, 1991-92, resident in neurosurgery, 1992-97; attending neurosurgery, v. chmn. Wilford Hall Med. Ctr., San Antonio, 1997—2001; spinal fellow Rush U./CINN, Chgo., 2001—02; asst. prof., dir. minimally invasive spine surgery Rush U., Chgo., 2002—03; assoc. dir. Inst. Spine Care/CINN; dir., spinal surgery Mich. Head and Spine Inst., 2003—. Prin. investigator clin. trials; presenter in field; appointee Coun. State Neurosurg. Socs., 1997, chmn. young physicians com., chmn. workforce com.; chmn. workforce com., scientific adv. bd. Neospine; chmn. workforce com., scientific adv. bd., cons. CBYON. Editor: (textbook) Outpatient Spinal Surgery; author: An Anatomical Approach to Minimally Invasive Spine Surgery; asst. editor: Neurosurgery News; contbr. chapters to books, articles to profl. jours. Chmn. class reunion Tufts Sch. Medicine, 1995-96; dir. class fund Grinnell Coll., 1999—. Air Force Health Professions scholar, 1987-91. Mem. AMA, ACS, AAAS, Congress Neurol. Surgeons, Am. Assn. Neurol. Surgeons, Mass. Med. Soc., Tex. Med. Assn., Maj. USAF Med. Corp, Fla. Acad. Sci., Am. Fedn. Clin. Rsch., Sigma Xi (grantee 1985). Avocations: hunting, fishing, scuba diving, underwater photography, biking. Home: 1070 Timberlake Dr Bloomfield Hills MI 48302 Office: Mich Head and Spine Inst 22250 Providence Dr Ste 300 Southfield MI 48075 Office Fax: 248-440-2201. E-mail: perezcruet@yahoo.com.

PÉREZ-GONZALEZ, ESMERALDA, principal, educator; b. Alice, Tex., Sept. 7, 1963; d. Felipe Perez and Cora Cantu Perez Carrillo. BS, Corpus Christi State U., 1987, MS, 1993; AA, Del Mar Coll., 1987. Tchr. Holy Family Sch., Corpus Christi, Tex.; prin. Archbishop Oscar Romero Middle Sch., Corpus Christi, Tex. Title VII Bilingual Edn. Fellowship grantee, Gov. Fellowship award, 1994, Tchr. of Yr. nominee, 1998, First runner-up Hispanic Educator of Yr., 1998. Mem. Tex. Assn. Bilingual Edn., PTA, Nat. Cath. Edn. Assoc., Assoc. Supervision, Curriculum Devel., Nat. Assoc. Secondary Sch. Prin., Year Round Edn., Tex. Middle Sch. Assoc., Nat. Middle Sch. Assoc., Nat. Coun. of tchrs. of Math., tex. Coun. of Tchrs. of Math. Avocations: continuing education, walks on the beach, collecting sanddollars, family. Home: 7130 Everhart Rd Apt 23 Corpus Christi TX 78413-2470

PEREZ-SILVA, GLAISMA, special education teacher; b. Mayagüez, P.R., Oct. 19, 1957; d. Ismael Pérez and Gladys (Silva) Valentin; 1 child, Andrés Guillermo Figueroa. BA in Spl. Edn., Catholic U., Ponce, P.R., 1980; MS in Spl. Edn. summa cum laude, Interam. U., Rio Piedras, P.R., 1987. Spl. edn. tchr. Manuel G. Tavarez Sch., Ponce, P.R., 1980-81, Amalia Marin Sch., Rio Piedras, P.R., 1981-82, 83-87, Carmen Gomez Tejera Sch., Rio Piedras, 1982-83, Victor Pares Sch., Rio Piedras, 1987-88; bilingual spl. edn. tchr. R. J. Kinsella Cmty. Sch., Hartford, Conn., 1988-96, spl. edn. monitor, 1993-95, program coord. enrichment program, 1994-95, coord. cultural and artistic program, 1991-96, governance team, 1994-96; bilingual spl. edn. tchr. T.J. Quirk Middle Sch., 1996—, Hartford Public High Sch., 1998—. Spl. edn. tchr. Hartford Bd. Edn. Summer Camp, 1989; site supr. Ctr. City Chs. Summer Camp, Hartford, 1992, 94; tchr. coord. The Village for Families and Children Summer Program, 1995, Charter Oak Cultural Ctr. Arts Enrichment Camp, 1996— (founder, dir.); staff writer El Extra News, Hartford, 1992-95, adv. bd., 1997—; Spanish music dir. WFCS-FM, New Britain, Conn., 1993-97; spl. reporter WFCR-Tertulia, Amherst, Mass., 1994—; lectr. in field. Tchr. Spanish Noah Webster Enrichment Program, Hartford, 1991, bd. dirs. PTA, 1991-92; collaborator D.J. WRTC, Hartford, 1991-93, Guakia, Inc., Hartford, 1991-96, vis. artist, 1996-97, ARTS program cons., 1997-98; bd. dirs. Kinsella's Union Sch. Com., Hartford, 1991-93, Padres Abriendo Puertas, 1994-97; adv. bd. The Writers Voice, Fairfield, Conn., 1995-96, El Extra News, 1997—; advisor Kinsella Sch. and Cmty. Partnership, 1992-96; ednl. advisor cultural and cmty. issues Charter Oak Cultural Ctr., Hartford, 1993, bd. dirs., 1995; mem. steering com. P.R. Cultural Day Wadsworth Atheneum, Hartford, 1993-96, co-chair, 1994-95, bd. electors, 1995; bd. dirs. Cimarrona: Centro de la Mujer Puertorriquena (Puerto Rican Woman Center), Hartford, 1995, pres., 1996-97; cons. creative writing Spanish Am. Union, Mass., 1996. Mem. Hartford Fedn. Tchrs. Avocations: reading, drawing, crafts, music, poetry. Office: Hartford Pub High Sch 55 Forest St Hartford CT 06105-3243

PEREZ-VALDES, YVONNE ANN, nurse, educator; b. Tampa, Fla., May 18, 1946; d. Raimundo Abal and Encarnita (Perez) P. ASN, St. Petersburg Jr. Coll., 1978. Cert. ob-gyn., pediatric ICU nurse, RN, Fla. Nurse St. Joseph Hosp., Tampa, Fla., 1966-71, cardiologist office nurse mgr., 1976-78; ICCU nurse U. Community Hosp., Tampa, Fla., 1979-80; emergency rm. charge nurse, Intensive Coronary Care Unit asst. head nurse Centro Asturiano Hosp., Tampa, Fla., 1980-85; mem. faculty, head dept. nursing Tampa Coll., 1985-88; supr., dir. edn. Oakwood Nursing Home, Tampa, 1988-89; instr. health Hillsborough County Schs., Tampa, 1989-95; developer staff, mgr. risk, dir. edn. safety and pers. Meadowbrook Manor Tampa, 1994-95. Faculty mem. Health Industry & Adv. Bd., Tampa, 1992-95; bilingual instr. for refugee asst. program Ideal Sch., Miami, Fla., 1980—; pvt. duty home health nurse, 1972-75; office nurse mgr. for cardiologist/internist, 1975-76. Author: Cry Out, I'm Listening. Mem.-at-large Nat. Rep. Com., Washington, 1991-92; mem. Presdl. Com., Washington, 1991-95, Senatorial Com., Washington, 1991-95. Name included Benefactor's Wall Am. Nursing Found. Bldg., Washington. Mem. ANA, ARC, Am. Cancer Assn., Am. Hispanic Nurses (chmn. 1992), Fla. Nurses Assn., Tampa Nurses Assn., St. Joseph's Hosp. Devel. Coun., Nat. Audubon Soc., Am. Diabetes Assn. Democrat. Roman Catholic. Avocations: photography, reading, boating, travel, writing. Office: Hillsborough County Schs Ctr for Tng 5410 N 20th St Tampa FL 33610-8213 also: Meadowbrook Manor Tampa 8720 Jackson Springs Rd Tampa FL 33615-3210

PERFETTI, ROBERT NICKOLAS, educational consultant; b. Staples, Minn., Jan. 8, 1937; s. Nickolas Albert and Lila Bertha (Beurge) P. BS, St. Cloud State U., 1960; postgrad., Bemidji State U., 1961-62, Calif. State U., L.A., 1964-68, Pepperdine U., 1967-68; MA, La Verne U., 1970; postgrad., U. So. Calif., 1972-73, Point Loma U., Pasadena, Calif., 1974-75; EdD, Pacific States U., 1975. Cert. admistr., counselor, secondary, community coll., jr. high sch., adult, and elem. edn. Calif. Prin. Richmond (Minn.) Pub. Schs., 1960-62; elem. tchr. Sebeka (Minn.) Sch. Dist., 1962-63; team leader lang. arts, social sci. and summer sch. Rowland Unified Sch. Dist., Rowland Heights, Calif., 1965-76, coord. math. lab., 1976-79, secondary counselor, 1979-81, coord. work experience edn., career edn. and career ctr., 1981-95, home ind. study coord., ednl. cons., 1992-95; mental health counselor St. Gabriel's Hosp., Little Falls, Minn., 1999. Coord. Gender Equity, 1980-95, Job Tng. Partnership Act, 1980-95; advisor Nat. Vocat. Tech. Honor Soc., 1991-95; alumni dir. Sacred Heart Sch., Staples. Editor: (profl. newspaper) Reaction. Officer parish coun. Our Lady of the Assumption Ch., Claremont, Calif., chmn. edn. com.; chmn. PTA, Rowland Heights; rep. fed. project, Rowland Heights; scoutmaster, chmn. troop com. Boy Scouts Am. Recipient Svc. Commendation Rowland Unified Sch. Dist., 1978; named. L.A. County Tchr. of Yr. Calif. State Dept. Edn., 1975, Outstanding Secondary Educator of Am., 1974, Giano Tchr. of Yr. Giano Intermediate Sch., 1973, Tchr. of Yr. Rowland Unified Sch. Dist., 1974. Mem. NEA (life), Calif. Tchrs. Assn., Assn. Rowland Educators (v.p.), Calif. Assn. Work Experience Educators (Alpha chpt. v.p.), Alpha Phi Omega (pres.), Pi Delta Epsilon (pres.), KC (3d degree). Roman Catholic. Avocations: water sports, traveling, research, writing. Home: 4318 320th St Cushing MN 56443-2115 E-mail: perfetti@brainerd.net., drnickolas@yahoo.com.

PERGER, DONNA SPAGNOLI, retired secondary school mathematics educator; b. Portsmouth, Va., Apr. 24, 1951; d. Delmo John and Lurline M. (Smith) Spagnoli; m. Steve John Perger Jr., June 9, 1980; 1 stepchild, Stephanie Lee. BS in Secondary Edn., Old Dominion U., 1973. Tchr. math. Manor H.S., Portsmouth, Va., 1973-74, Bettie Williams Sch., Virginia Beach, Va., 1974-78, Virginia Beach Jr. H.S., 1978-80, Queens Lake Sch., York County, Va., 1980—2003, chair dept. math. Lead tchr. VQUEST. Art work published in Stampers Sampler, Somerset Studio and Gallery mags. Elder Olive Br. Christian Ch. Named Mid. Sch. Tchr. of Yr. Daily Press Newspaper, Newport News, 1993. Avocations: paper embossing (repousse), needlework, sewing, gardening. E-mail: dperger@ycsd.york.va.us.

PERHACS, MARYLOUISE HELEN, musician, educator; b. Teaneck, N.J., June 15, 1944; d. John Andrew and Helen Audrey (Hosage) P.; m. Robert Theodore Sirinek, Jan. 27, 1968 (div. Jan. 1975). Student, Ithaca (N.Y.) Coll., 1962-64; BS, Juilliard Sch., 1967, MS, 1968; postgrad., Hunter Coll., 1976, St. Peter's Coll., Jersey City, N.J., 1977. Cert. music tchr., N.Y., N.J. Instr. Carnegie Hall, N.Y.C., 1966-69; program developer, coord., instr. urban edn. program Newburgh (N.Y.) Pub. Sch. System, 1968-69; adj. prof. dept. edn. St. Peter's Coll., Jersey City, 1976-92; tchr. brass instruments Indian Hills High Sch., Oakland, N.J., 1976; tchr. Jersey City Pub. Schs., 1976-77, N.Y.C. Pub. Sch., Bronx, 1980-84; pvt. tchr. Cliffside Park, N.J., 1976—; vocal music tchr. East Rutherford, N.J., 1990; tchr. music Bergen County Spl. Svcs. Sch. Dist., 1990-91; tchr. gen. music Little Ferry (N.J.) Pub. Schs., 1991-92; tchr. mid. sch. instrumental Paramus (N.J.) Pub. Schs., 1993-94; tchr. vocal music West New York (N.J.) Pub Schs., 1995—. Tchr. music summer enrichment program, West New York, NJ, 1999, 2000, summer instrumental music program Park Ridge (N.J.) H.S., 1995, 96, Waldwick Concert Band, 2003; tchr., singer, trumpeter Norwegian Caribbean Lines, 1981-82, Jimmy Dorsey Band, Paris and London, 1974; music and edn. lecture cir., 1992—. Singer with Original PDQ Bach Okay Chorale, 1966, Live from Carnegie Hall Recordings, 1970, St. Louis Mcpl. Opera, 1970, Ed Sullivan Show, 1970; singer, dancer, actress (Broadway shows) Promises, Promises, 1969-71, Sugar, 1971-72, Lysistrata, 1972; trumpeter (Broadway shows) Jesus Christ Superstar, 1973, Debbie!, 1976, Sarava!, 1979, Fiddler on the Roof, Lincoln Ctr., 1981, Sophisticated Ladies, 1982; writer, host series on women in music Columbia Cable/United Artists, 1984; recordings: Carnegie Hall Live, Avery Fisher Hall, Lincoln Ctr. Cons. to cadette troop Girl Scouts U.S., Jersey City, 1967-68, Bergen County N.J. Coun., 1995—. Mem. NEA, AFTRA, Actors Equity Assn., Am. Fedn. Musicians (mem. theatre com. local 802 N.Y.C. 1972—, chmn. 1973), Music Educators Nat. Conf., N.J. Music Educators Assn., N.J. Sch. Music Assn., N.J. Edn. Assn., Internat. Women's Brass Conf. (charter mem.), Internat. Trumpet Guild, Mu Phi Epsilon. Democrat. Episcopalian. Avocations: cats, cake decorating, food sculpting, horticulture, sewing. Home and Office: 23 Crescent Ave Cliffside Park NJ 07010-3003

PERI, WINNIE LEE BRANCH, educational director; b. Dallas; d. Floyd Hamilton and Eula Dee (Richardson) Branch; m. Fred Ronald Peri; children: Kenneth Michael, Michael Anthony, Desiree Denise. BA in Psychology, Calif. State U., Long Beach, 1978, English teaching credential, 1988; social sci. teaching credential, Calif. State U., Northridge, 1979. Republic of South Africa tchr. Internat. Sch. Svcs., Princeton, N.J., 1980-82; tchr. English, St. Jeanne de Lestonnac Sch., Tustin, Calif., 1988-91; dir. edn. Sylvan Learning Ctr., Mission Viejo, Calif., 1993-94; ESL tchr. Capistrano Unified Sch. Dist., San Juan Capistrano, Calif., 1998-2000; self-employed tutor, 1995—97, 2001—03. Facilitator Rainbows for All God's Children, 1989; mem. team experience sch. evaluation com. WASC/WCEA. Mem. adv. bd. Thomas Paine Sch. PTA; dep. sheriff Los Angeles County. Mem. Psi Chi.

PERICH, TERRY MILLER, secondary school educator; b. Greensburg, Pa., Sept. 22, 1948; s. Miller and Eleanor Ann (Schmuck) P.; m. Kathleen Ann Ferrari, July 26, 1975. BA in Elem. Edn., Edinboro U., 1970; elem. cert., Pa. State U., 1973; Masters equivalency degree, U. Pitts., 1994; postgrad., Carlow Coll., 1994. Trained student assistance prof., Pa.; cert. tchr. elem. edn. Tchr. sci. and math. Penn Trafford Schs., Harrison City, Pa., 1970—. Mentor, tchr. Tchr. Enhancement Inst. St. Vincent Coll., Latrobe, Pa.; selected tchr. Watershed Restoration St. Vincent Coll., Latrobe. County committeeman Dem. Party, Penn Twp., Pa., 1994—; lion tamer Bushy Run Lions Club, Claridge, Pa., 1993—, 3rd v.p., 1995, 2d v.p., 1996, 1st v.p., 1997—. Recipient Commendation, Pres.-elect Clinton, Student Assistance Program award for working with students at risk St. Vincent Coll. Prevention Projects, 1991. Mem. NEA, ASCD, PACE, Nat. Sci. Tchrs. Assn., Pa. Tchrs. Edn. Assn., Pa. Sci. Tchrs. Assn., Westmoreland County Assn. Student Assistance Profls. (bd. dirs. 1992-94, mem. Westmoreland county student assistance team 1995-96, 96-97), Penn Trafford Edn. Assn. (exec. bd. dirs. 1990-91). Roman Catholic. Avocations: travel, education. Home: 13 Rizzi Dr Irwin PA 15642-8902 Office: Penn Mid Sch PO Box 368 Watt Rd Claridge PA 15623

PERINELLI, MARGUERITE ROSE, women's health nurse, educator; b. Bklyn., Dec. 20, 1947; d. Joseph and Carmela (Conti) Perinelli; children: Joseph, Philip, Kathryn, Thomas, Mary Sarah, Rosemarie. Diploma, St. Vincent Med. Ctr. Richmond, S.I., N.Y., 1968; student, Coll. S.I., 1969-74; BSN, Wagner Coll., 1991. Lamaze certified childbirth educator. Nursery staff nurse St. Vincent's Med. Ctr. Richmond, 1968-72; obstetrics staff nurse S.I. Univ. Hosp., 1973—, maternal child nurse labor and delivery, 1993—; staff nurse Carmel Richmond Nursing Home, 1992-93; per diem nurse U. Hospice, 1995—. Vol. Pax Christi Hospice, 1992—96; sec. CNP SIUH North, 1994—, S.I. chpt. NYCRNA, 1997—99, 2002—. Recipient Distinguished Leadership award, Nightingale Soc., Nat. Collegiate Nursing award. Mem.: ANA, Internat. Childbirth Edn. Assn., NY State Nurses Assn., Lamaze Internat.

PERKES, VICTOR ASTON, science education educator; b. Oakland, Calif., July 17; s. Charles and Helen Carroll (Marshall) P.; m. Barbara Jackson, Dec. 27, 1953; children: Mark, Kent, Allison, Emily. BA, Calif. State U., San Jose, 1956, MA, 1960; PhD, Stanford U., 1967. Elem., secondary tchr., adminstrn. credentials, Calif. Tchr. Ravenswood Sch. Dist., East Palo Alto, Calif., 1954-56, San Mateo (Calif.) Union High Sch. Dist., 1956-58; tchr., sci. coord. Hillsborough (Calif.) Schs., 1958-63; research asst. Stanford (Calif.) U., 1963-66; prof. sci. edn. U. Oreg., Eugene, 1965-67, U. Calif., Davis, 1967—. Mem. numerous coll. and dist. accreditation coms. Contbr. numerous articles to profl. jours. Scholar ASCD, 1963; fellow Stanford U., 1964; over 30 state and fed. grants. Mem. NSTA (various offices), Nat. Assn. for Sci. Supervision (coms.), Nat. Assn. Biology Tchrs. (coms.), Nat. Geog. Soc. (coms.), Nature Conservancy, Save Redwoods League, Commonwealth Club Calif. Avocations: camping, travel, gardening, politics.

PERKINS, ARTHUR LEE, SR., retired principal, real estate broker, insurance agent; b. Denham Springs, La., Feb. 24, 1935; s. Joe I. and Elma (Jackson) P.; m. Nora L. Johnson, Dec. 20, 1958; children: Arthur Jr., Michael, Jeffrey, Tonya. BS, So. U., Baton Rouge, 1957, MEd, 1965, postgrad., 1972. Cert. secondary edn. tchr., La.; lic. ins. agt., real estate broker, La. Prin. West Livingston H.S., Denham Springs, La., 1957-70; tchr., prin. Albany (La.) H.S., 1970-98; ret., 1998; real estate broker State of La., 1972—; ins. agt. Profl. Inc., Baton Rouge, 1997—. Treas. local chpt. NAACP, Denham Springs, 1993—; mem. Livingston Parish Voters League, Denham Springs, 1954—, treas.; commr. Recreation and Parks, Denham Springs, 1980-96, La. H.S. Athletic Assn., Baton Rouge, 1995-97; councilman City of Denham Springs, 1975-91, 95—. 2nd lt. U.S. Army, 1957-58, capt. 951st Ref. Co., 1957-72, ret. lt. col. USNG, 1988. Mem. Capital City Lodge (3d D. award 1968), Kappa Alpha Psi (lt. stratugus 1984—). Democrat. Protestant. Avocation: hunting. Home: 906 Hatchell Ln Denham Springs LA 70726-2621

PERKINS, BRADFORD, history educator; b. Rochester, NY, Mar. 6, 1925; s. Dexter and Wilma (Lord) P.; m. Nancy Nash Tucker, June 18, 1949 (dec.); children: Dexter III, Matthew Edward, Martha Nash. James Bradford (dec.). AB, Harvard U., 1946, PhD, 1952. From instr. to asso. prof. history U. Calif. at, Los Angeles, 1952-62; prof. history U. Mich., 1962-97, chmn. dept., 1971-72, 80-81, prof. emeritus, 1997—. Commonwealth Fund lectr. Univ. Coll., London, Eng., 1964; vis. prof. history Brandeis U., 1970, Ecole des Hautes Etudes en Sciences Sociales, Paris, 1983; Albert Shaw lectr. Johns Hopkins U., 1979; mem. council Inst. Early Am. History and Culture, 1968-71; program dir. Nat. Endowment for Humanities Fellowships in Residence for Coll. Tchrs., 1974-75 Author: The First Rapprochement: England and the United States, 1795-1805, 1955, Youthful America, 1960, Prologue to War: England and the United States, 1805-1812, 1961, Causes of the War of 1812, 1962, Castlereagh and Adams: England and the United States, 1812-1823, 1964, The Great Rapprochement: England and the United States, 1895-1914, 1968, The Creation of a Republican Empire, 1993. Served with AUS, 1943-45, ETO. Decorated Bronze Star.; Recipient Bancroft prize, 1965, Disting. Faculty award U. Mich., 1986; Warren fellow, 1969-70; Faculty Rsch. fellow Social Sci. Rsch. Council, 1957-60; Guggenheim fellow, 1962-63 Mem. Am. Hist. Assn., Soc. Am. Historians, Orgn. Am. Historians (coun. 1969-72), Soc. Historians Am. Fgn. Rels. (coun. 1967-72, pres. 1974, Graebner award 1992), Mass. Hist. Soc., Am. Antiquarian Soc. Home: 827 Asa Gray Dr # 458 Ann Arbor MI 48105 E-mail: bperkins@umich.edu

PERKINS, DWIGHT HEALD, economics educator; b. Chgo., Oct. 20, 1934; s. Lawrence Bradford and Margery (Blair) P.; m. Julie Rate, June 15, 1957; children: Lucy Fitch, Dwight Edward, Caleb Blair. BA, Cornell U., 1956; AM, Harvard U., 1961, PhD, 1964. From instr. to assoc. prof. Harvard U., Cambridge, Mass., 1963-69, prof. econs., 1969-81, assoc. dir. East Asian Rsch. Ctr., 1973-77, chmn. dept. econs., 1977-80, H.H. Burbank prof. polit. economy, 1981—, dir. Asia Ctr., 2002—; dir. Harvard Inst. Internat. Devel., Cambridge, 1980-95. Trustee China Med. Bd., 1995—, chair, 2000—; cons. permanent subcom. on investigations US Senate, 1974-80; H.M. Jackson vis. prof. Chinese studies U. Wash., 1985, Phi Beta Kappa lectr., 1992-93, Faculty Salzburg seminar, 1996; lectr. Fulbright tchg. policy program, Vietnam, 1997-2003; mem. Internat. Adv. Group to Prime Min. of Papua, New Guinea, 1991-92, 2000-02; cons. Korea Devel. Inst., 1972-80, Govt. Malaysia, 1968-69. Author: (with M. Halperin) Communist China and Arms Control, 1965, Agricultural Development in China, 1368-1968, 1969, Market Control and Planning in Communist China, 1966, China: Asia's Next Economic Giant?, 1986, (with E.S. Mason and others) The Economic Modernization of Korea, 1980, (with S. Yusuf) Rural Development in China, 1984, (with M. Gillis and others) Economics of Development, 1983, 5th edit., 2001; editor: China's Modern Economy in Historical Perspective, 1975, (with M. Roemer) Reforming Economic Systems in Developing Countries, 1991, (with J. Stern and others) Industrialization and the State: The Korean Heavy and Chemical Industry Drive, 1995; (with others) Assisting Development in a Changing World, 1997, Industrialization and the State: The Changing Role of the Taiwan Government in the Economy, 1945-1998, 2001, Innovative East Asia: The Future of Growth, 2003. Mem. Vis. Com. Far Ea. Studies, U. Chgo., 1973-77; mem. bd. govs. East-West Ctr., Honolulu, 1979-82; co-moderator Aspen Inst. Seminar on Korea, Colo., 1980-83. Lt. (j.g.) USNR, 1956-58. Fgn. Area Tng. fellow Ford Found., N.Y., 1958-62; NSF Sci. Faculty fellow Tokyo, 1968-69 Mem. Am. Philos. Soc., Assn. Asian Studies, Assn. Comparative Econ. Systems (pres. 1999-2000), Am. Econ. Assn., Phi Beta Kappa. Home: 64 Pinehurst Rd Belmont MA 02478-1504 Office: Harvard Univ Dept Econs Cambridge MA 02138-5781 E-mail: dwight_perkins@harvard.edu.

PERKINS, FLOYD JERRY, retired theology educator; b. Bertha, Minn., May 9, 1924; s. Ray Lester and Nancy Emily (Kelley) P.; m. Mary Elizabeth Owen, Sept. 21, 1947 (dec. June 1982); children: Douglas Jerry, David Floyd, Sheryl Pauline; m. Phyllis Genevra Hartley, July 14, 1984. AB, BTh, N.W. Nazarene Coll., 1949; MA, U. Mo., 1952; MDiv, Nazarene Theol. Sem., 1952; ThM, Burton Sem., 1964; PhD, U. Witwatersrand, Johannesburg, South Africa, 1974; ThD, Internat. Sem., 1994. Ordained to Christian ministry, 1951. Pres. South African Nazarene Theol. Sem., Florida Transvaal, Africa, 1955-67, Nazarene Bible Sem., Lourenco Marques, Mozambique, 1967-73, Campinas, Brazil, 1974-76; prof. missions N.W. Nazarene Coll., Nampa, Idaho, 1976; prof. theology Nazarene Bible Coll., Colorado Springs, Colo., 1976-97. Chmn., founder com. higher theol. edn. Ch. of Nazarene in Africa, 1967-74; sec. All African Nazarene Mission Exec., 1967-74; ofcl. Christian Council Mozambique, 1952-74. Author: A History of the Christian Church in Swaziland, 1974. Served with USN, 1944-46. Mem. Soc. Christian Philosophers, Evang. Theol. Soc., Am. Schs. Orientan Rsch., Am. Soc. Missiology, Assn. Evang. Missions Profs. Republican. Avocation: golf. Home: 6355 Oak Ave Apt 21 Temple City CA 91780-1300

PERKINS, JAMES ASHBROOK, English language educator; b. Covington, Ky., Feb. 7, 1941; s. Harry Dimmit and Juanita (Ashbrook) P.; m. Jane Crabtree Allen, Aug. 17, 1963; children: James Allen, Jeffrey Ashbrook. BA, Centre Coll., 1963; MA, Miami U., Oxford, Ohio, 1965; PhD, U. Tenn., 1972. Tchg. asst. in English Miami U., 1964-65; instr. Memphis State U., 1965-67; tchg. asst. U. Tenn., Knoxville, 1967-69, asst. prof., 1971-73; instr., chair All Sts. Episcopal Sch., Vicksburg, Miss., 1969-71; prof. English Westminster Coll., New Wilmington, Pa., 1973—, chmn. dept. English and pub. rels., 2000—. Vis. Fulbright prof., Korea, 1998; co-founder Westminster PR Group, 2000. Author: (poetry) The Woodcarver, 1978, The Amish 2, Perceptions 2, 1981; (short stories) Snakes, Butterbeans and the Discovery of Electricity, 1990, 2003; author, co-editor: (essays) Southern Writer's at Century's End, 1997; co-editor: All the King's Men: Three Stage Versions, 2000, For the Record: A Robert Drake Reader, 2001; collaborator: Brother Enemy: Poems of the Korean War, 2002; author numerous poems. NEH fellow, 1978, 81, 87, 89. Mem. MLA, Am. Lit. Assn., South Atlantic MLA, Robert Penn Warren Cir. (pres. 2002-03). Democrat. Avocations: racquetball, writing. Office: Westminster Coll Dept English and Pub Rels New Wilmington PA 16172-0001 E-mail: jperkins@westminster.edu.

PERKINS, LEEMAN LLOYD, music educator, musicologist; b. Salina, Utah, Mar. 27, 1932; s. Milton Lloyd and Ida Margaret (Johnson) P.; m. Marianne Suzanne Contesse, Nov. 14, 1956; children: Eric Raymond, Bruce Philippe, Marc Christian (dec.), Patrick Thierry. BFA, U. Utah, 1954; PhD, Yale U., 1965. Instr. Boston U., 1964, Yale U., 1964-67, asst. prof., 1967-71, dir. undergraduate studies in music history, 1969-70; assoc. prof. music history, coord. for musicology U. Tex., Austin, 1971-75, grad. adv. for musicology, 1976; prof. music Columbia U., N.Y.C., 1976—2003, prof. emeritus, 2003—, chmn. dept music, 1985-90. Instr. advanced seminar in Medieval History, Smith Coll., 1968; vis. assoc. prof. music Columbia U., 1975; vis. prof. Boston U., 1978; dir. NEH Summer Seminar, 1977. Editor: Johannes Lheritier Opera Omnia, 1969, (with Howard Garey) The Mellon Chansonnier, 1979, Music in the Age of the Renaissance, 1999; gen. editor: Masters and Monuments of Renaissance Music, 1978—. Chmn. grad. musicology com., Columbia U., 1980-84, 1993-96, 97-2001. Sgt., 7th Army Symphony, U.S. Army, 1957-59. Recipient James Morris Whiton Fund award Yale U., 1965, The Otto Kinkeldey award Am. Musicological Soc., 1980, la Médaille de la Ville de Tours, 1997; Trumbull Coll. fellow Yale U., 1966-71, Lewis-Farmington fellow Yale U., 1962-63, Morse fellow Yale U., 1967-68, Am. Coun. Learned Soc. fellow, 1973-74, NEH fellow, 1979, 1984-85, French Archival Scis. fellow Newberry Libr. Center for Renaissance Studies, 1991; Martha Baird Rockefeller grantee, 1963-64, Paul Mellon Found. grantee, 1972, Am. Coun. Learned Soc., 1972, 82, U. Tex. grantee, 1975, Mem. Am. Musicological Soc. (chmn. program com. 1979, bd. dirs. 1980-81, adv. bd., 1985-86, chmn. ad hoc sub com., 1985-86, exec. com. delegate, 1989-92, mem. fellowship com. 1995-98), Internat. Musicological Soc., The Renaissance Soc. of Am., Phi Beta Kappa, Phi Kappa Phi. Mem. Lds Ch. E-mail: LLP1@columbia.edu.

PERKINS, LILY LEIALOHA, humanities educator, writer; b. Lahaina Maui, Hawaii, Mar. 5, 1930; d. Samuel Umi and Margaret Malia (Kaa'a) Apo; m. Stephen G. Mark, 1954 (1966); m. Roland Francis Perkins, 1971; children: Mark 'Umi, Kele Douglas. AB in English Lit. cum laude, Boston U., 1957; MS in Libr. Sci., Simmons Coll., 1959; MA in English Lit., Mt. Holyoke Coll., 1966; PhD in Folklore and Folklife, U. Pa., 1978. Catalogue libr. Mus. Fine Arts, Boston, 1959-61, Smith Coll., Northampton, Mass., 1965-66; instr. English Northeastern U., Boston, 1966-68; libr. Boston Psychoanalytic Inst., 1973-74; assoc. prof. English and Anthropology Atenisi U., Nuku'alofa, Tonga, 1980-86; instr. Hawaiian studies U. Hawaii-Leeward, Pearl City, 1989-94; asst. prof. Hawaiian studies U. Hawaii-West Oahu, Pearl City, 1994—99; ret. Coord. Internat. Oral Traditions Program, Honolulu, 1994; exec. bd. mem. Hawaii Literary Arts Coun., Honolulu, 1995X. Author: Natural, 1979, Kingdoms of the Heart, 1980, Cyclone Country, 1987, Other Places, 1987, The Firemakers, 1987, The Oxridge Woman, 1998, Histories in Stone, Wood & Bone, 1999, How the Iwa Flies, 2003; founder, editor Jour. Hawaiian and Pacific Folklore and Folklife Studies, 1990X, Kamalu'uluolele Pubs., 1979X. Recipient Funding award for initiating Jour. HawnPac Folklore Folklife Studies, Hawai'i State Legis., 1984-86; named First Joint Doctoral Interne in Culture Learning Inst., U. Pa. to East-West Ctr., 1974-76, Hawaii award for Lit., Hawaii State Found. Culture and Arts, 1998; grantee for oral tradition studies Nat. Endowment for the Humanities, 1994. Mem. Assn. Social Anthropology Oceania, Assn. Literary Scholars and Critics, Soc. for Hawaiian Archaeology, Assn. Asian Am. Studies, Pacific Arts Assn., U. Pa. Alumni Assn. (Hawaii chpt.), Mt. Holyoke Alumni Assn. (Hawaii chpt.). Democrat. Avocations: music playing violin, swimming, walking, traveling, meeting people. Home: 85-175 Farrington Hwy Apt A334 Waianae HI 96792-2169

PERKINS, WILLIAM CLYDE, business educator; b. Lebanon, Ind., Aug. 2, 1938; s. Clyde Philip and Dorothy May (Finch) P.; m. Phyllis Louise Swinford, June 18, 1960; children: Bonnie Michele, Betsy Anne Hawkins, Jeffrey William. BS in Civil Engring., Rose Polytech. Inst., 1960; MBA, Ind. U., 1962, D of Bus. Adminstrn., 1966. Instr. U.S. Mil. Acad., West Point, N.Y., 1964-65, asst. prof., 1965-66, Ind. U., Bloomington, 1966-69, assoc. prof., 1969-74, prof., 1974—. Author: Managing Information Technology, 1991, 94, 99, 2002, FORTRAN for Business Students, 1981, Computers and Information Systems, 1973. Capt. U.S. Army, 1964-66. Fellow Decision Scis. Inst. (treas. 1984-86, v.p. 1982-84, pres. 1992-93, disting. svc. award 1988); mem. Midwest Decision Scis. Inst. (pres. 1984-85, 25 yr. disting. svc. award 1994), Assn. for Info. Sys. Mem. United Ch. of Christ. Avocations: hiking, traveling, reading. Home: 4308 E Cambridge Dr Bloomington IN 47408-3109 Office: Ind U Kelley Sch Bus Bloomington IN 47405

PERKOWSKI, JAN LOUIS, language and literature educator; b. Perth Amboy, N.J., Dec. 29, 1936; m. Liliana Asenova Daskalova, May 24, 1989. AB magna cum laude, Harvard U., 1959, AM, 1960, PhD, 1965. Asst. prof. U. Calif., Santa Barbara, 1964-65; assoc. prof. U. Tex., Austin, 1965-74; prof. U. Va., Charlottesville, 1974—. Author: A Kashubian Idiolect in U.S., 1969, Vampires, Dwarves & Witches Among the Ontario Kashubs, 1972, Vampires of the Slavs, 1976, Gusle & Ganga Among the Hercegovinians of Toronto, 1978, The Darkling-A Treatise on Slavic Vampirism, 1989; contbr. over 65 articles to profl. jours. Grantee, fellow Ford Found., Harvard U., Kościuszko Found., U. Tex., Am. Philos. Soc., Nat. Mus. Man, U. Va., NEH, Kennan Inst., I.R.E.X., Fulbright, others. Mem. Am. Assn. for the Advancement of Slavic Studies, Am. Assn. Tchrs. of Slavic and East European Langs., Am. Assn. S.E. European Studies. Office: U Va Dept Slavic Langs & Lits 109 Cabell Hall Charlottesville VA 22903

PERKOWSKI, MAREK ANDRZEJ, electrical engineering educator; b. Warsaw, Oct. 6, 1946; came to U.S., 1981; s. Adam Perkowski and Hanna (Zielinska) Mystkowska; m. Ewa Kaja Wilkowska, Oct. 26, 1974; 1 child, Mateusz Jan. MS in Electronics with distinction, Tech. U. Warsaw, 1970, PhD in Automatics with distinction, 1980. Sr. asst. Inst. Automatics, Tech. U. Warsaw, 1973-80, asst. prof., 1980-81; vis. asst. prof. dept. elec. engring. U. Minn., Mpls., 1981-83; assoc. prof. elec. engring. Portland (Oreg.) State U., 1983-94, prof., 1994—. Co-author: Theory of Automata, 3d edit., 1976, Problems in Theory of Logic Circuits, 4th edit., 1986, Theory of Logic Circuits-Selected Problems, 3d edit., 1984; contbr. 134 articles to profl. jours., 11 chpts. to books. Mem. Solidarity, Warsaw, 1980-81. Recipient Design Automation award SIGDA/ACM/DATC IEEE, 1986-91; Rsch. grantee NSF, 1991, 94, Commn. for Familites Roman Cath. Ch., Vatican, 1981, Air Force Ofice Sci. Rsch., 1995. Mem. IEEE (Computer Soc.), Polish Nat. Alliance, Assn. for Computing Machinery, Am. Soc. for Engring. Edn. Roman Catholic. Avocations: tourism, philosophy, woodcarving. Home: 15720 NW Perimeter Dr Beaverton OR 97006-5391 Office: Portland State U Dept Elec & Comp Engring PO Box 751 Portland OR 97207-0751 E-mail: mperkows@ece.pdx.edu.

PERKYNS, JANE ELIZABETH, music educator, composer, actress; b. St. John, New Brunswick, Can., Jan. 17, 1960; arrived in U.S., 1990, naturalized, 2000; d. Joseph Archibald Gormley, Carmelita Anne Gormley; m. John Stephen Perkyns, Aug. 20, 1983; children: Stephen, Nicholas. MusB, Dalhousie U., Halifax, N.S., Can., 1982; MusM, Juilliard Sch., 1983; D in Musical Arts, U. B.C., Vancouver, B.C., Can., 1990. Music adminstr., tchr. Jewish Cmty. Ctr., Houston, 1990—94; adj. music faculty Tex. So. U., Houston, 1990—96, asst. prof. music, 1996—2001, assoc. prof. music, 2001—. Founder, dir. Curtyn Calls Theatre and Pub. Co., Houston, 1995—; co-dir. spl. edn. programs Theatre Under the Stars, Houston, 2000—; dir. Charles P. Rhinehart Piano Festival, 2001—03. Composer: (Musical) The Gift, 1994, Pinnojokio, 1996, Love is a Disability, 1998, Medea's Children, 1999, musician Solo/collaborative recitals. Panelist Cultural Arts Coun. Houston/Harris County, 2000—02. Grantee Mayor's Initiative Grant, Cultural Arts Coun. Houston/Harris County, 2001, Gen. Assistance Grant, Cultural Arts Coun., 2003, Office Civil Rights, 2003. Mem.: Am. Musicological Soc., Royal Conservatory Music (coord. of exams Houston area 1994—2003), Houston Music Tchrs. Assn. (bd. mem., chair scholarship event 1995—2002), Tex. Music Tchrs. Assn., Music Tchrs. Nat. Assn. (cert.), Coll. Music Soc., Houston Tuesday Musical Club. Avocations: children's arts and crafts, cooking, yoga. Home: 5634 Benning Dr Houston TX 77096 Office: Tex So Univ 3100 Cleburne Houston TX 77004 Office Fax: 713-313-1869. Personal E-mail: perkyns_je@tsu.edu. Business E-Mail: perkyns-je@tsu.edu.

PERLINGIERI, ILYA SANDRA, art history scholar, writer; b. N.Y.C. d. Nathaniel Gordon and Dr. Naomi Miller Coval-Apel; children: Blake Andrew, Chemynne Alida. BA, U. Mo., 1966; MA, San Diego State U., 1984; PhD, Columbia Pacific U., 1999. Cert. life C.C. credential, Calif. Dir. Ilya Sandra Perlingieri Sewing and Design Sch., San Diego and Miami, Fla., 1973-92; asst. prof., chmn. dept. fashion design Marist Coll., Poughkeepsie, N.Y., 1984-85; mem. faculty Fashion Inst. Design, San Diego, 1986-87, L.A., 1999—2000. Adj. prof. San Diego State U., 1989-92; dir. Textile Arts and Conservation Ctr., San Diego, 1979-83; guest lectr. Met. Mus. Art, N.Y.C., Nat. Gallery, London, Art Inst. Chgo., Los Angeles County Mus. Art, Nat. Gallery, Washington, NYU, Yale U., others; guest PBS-TV, Sta. NPR, NBC-TV, BBC, London. Author: Sofonisba Anguissola: The First Great Woman Artist of the Renaissance, 1992 (transl. into French 1992), The Uterine Crisis, 2003; contbg. editor Threads mag.; contbr. numerous articles on costume and art history to profl. jours. and mags. Dir. edn. Nomad Mus. Tribal Art, Portland, 1999-2001. Recipient award Prague Quadriennale, 1979, Gildred Found., 1980, Samuel H. Kress Found., 1989, 99; French Fgn. Ministry Lecture grantee, 1995, grantee The Thanks be to Grandmother Winifred Found., 2001. Mem. Renaissance Soc. Am., Costume Soc. Am. (charter), Royal Horticultural Soc., Victoria and Albert Mus., Royal Bot. Gardens, Met. Mus. Art, Huntington Libr. and Art Collections, Early Modern Women (charter). Avocations: playing classical piano, lyric soprano, organic gardening, needlework, gourmet cooking.

PERLMAN, BARRY ARNOLD, astronomy educator; b. New Bedford, Mass., July 21, 1947; s. Louis and Lorainne Rhoda (Bendit) P. BS, Boston U., 1970; MS, Nova U., 1989. Cert. tchr. Fla. Adminstrv. law judge Fla. Dept. Labor, Miami, 1972-82; planetarium specialist, adj. prof. Broward County C.C., Ft. Lauderdale, Fla., 1982-87; planetarium dir. Mus. Sci. & History, Jacksonville, Fla., 1987-88, Dade Pub. Schs., Miami, 1989-94; asst. prof. Broward County C.C., 1994—; dir. edn. South Fla. Sci. Mus., West Palm Beach, 1996-98; dir. Sci. Explorium, Boca Raton, Fla., 1998—2000. Ptnr. Rocket Tech. Fla., Ft. Lauderdale, 1982-87; pres. Ft. Lauderdale Acad. Sci., 1979; dir. Fox Observatory, Ft. Lauderdale, 1977-78; bd. of directors, Graves Museum of Natural History, 1995. Author: Applied Physical Science, 1989. Mem. Fla. Planetarium Assn., Fla. Rocket Soc. (pres. 1989-90). Avocation: collecting ancient art. Home: Apt 107 3950 N 56th Ave Hollywood FL 33021-1680

PERLMAN, BELLA BEACH, retired elementary school educator; b. Chgo., Mar. 12, 1931; d. Samuel and Eula Pearl (Hicks) Beach; m. Noel B. Perlman, June 29, 1963; 1 child, Samuel B. BA, Ky. State Coll., 1954; MEd, Nat. Coll. Edn., 1982. Cert. tchr., Ill. Tchr. Posen-Robbins (Ill.) Pub. Schs., 1957-67; substitute tchr. Chgo. Pub. Schs., 1973-75, Faulkner Pvt. Sch., Chgo., 1973-76, tchr., 1976-97, Chgo. Pub. Schs., 1997—, ret., 2003. Mem. Phillips 49 (sec. reunion com. 1989-98). Democrat. Baptist. Avocation: travel. Home: 400 E 33rd St Apt 514 Chicago IL 60616-4219 Office: Dela Cruz 2317 W 23rd Pl Chicago IL 60608-3805

PERLMAN, JOHN NIELS, retired elementary school educator, poet; b. Alexandria, Va., May 13, 1946; s. Ellis Sherman and Birthe Elaine P.; m. Janis Lynn, May 26, 1967; 1 child, Nicole Jeanne Kachina. BA, Ohio State U., 1969; MS in Edn., Iona Coll., 1981. Cons. NEA, Washington, 1971-72; tchr. Mamaroneck (N.Y.) Pub. Schs., 1973—2002; ret., 2002—. Author: (poetry books) Kachina, 1971, Homing, 1981, The Natural History of Trees, 1995, 2003, Edward-John, 1998, Legion Their Numbers, 2003. Recipient Acad. Am. Poets prize, 1969; N.Y. Found. Arts fellow, 1991. Buddhist. Avocations: hiking, canoeing, gardening. Home: 38 Ferris Pl Ossining NY 10562-3510 E-mail: johnperl@aol.com.

PERLMAN, MARK, economist, educator; b. Madison, Wis., Dec. 23, 1923; s. Selig and Eva (Shaber) P.; m. Naomi Gertrude Waxman, June 7, 1953; 1 child, Abigail Ruth Williams. BA, MA, U. Wis., 1947; PhD, Columbia, 1950. Asst. prof. U. Hawaii, 1951-52, Cornell U., 1952-55; asst. prof., then assoc. prof. Johns Hopkins U., 1955-63; prof. econs., history and pub. health U. Pitts., 1963-94, chmn. dept., 1965-70, univ. prof., 1969-94, univ. prof. emeritus, 1994—. Co-chmn. Internat. Econ. Assn. Conf. on Econs. of Health in Industrialized Nations, Tokyo, Japan, 1973, Conf. on Orgn. and Retrieval Econs. Data, Kiel, West Germany, 1975; vis. fellow Clare Hall U. Cambridge, 1977; ofcl. visitor faculty econs. and politics, U. Cambridge, 1976-77; co-chmn., co-editor Internat. Congress on Health Econs., Leyden, The Netherlands, 1980; mem. Princeton Inst. Adv. Study, 1981-82; adj. scholar Am. Enterprise Inst., 1981—; Österreichischer Länderbank Joseph Schumpeter prof. Technische Universität, Vienna, 1982; disting. vis. scholar Beijing Chinese Nat. Acad. Social Scis., 1983; Rockefeller Found. resident scholar Villa Serbelloni, Bellagio, Como, Italy, 1983; vis. prof. Inst. für Weltwirtschaft U. Kiel, 1987, U. Augsburg, 1992, U. Chemnitz, 1996; mem. Internat. Com. for Documentation in the Social Scis., UNESCO, 1988-94, exec. com. 1993-94. Author: Judges in Industry: A Study of Labor Arbitration in Australia, 1954; editor (with C.E. Barfield): Capital Markets and Trade: The United Statres Faces a United Europe, 1991; author: Labor Union Theories in America, 1958, 2nd edit., 1978, The Machinists: A New Study in American Trade Unionism, 1961, Democracy in the I.A.M., 1962; author: (with T.D. Baker) Health Manpower in a Developing Economy, 1967; author: The Character of Economic Thought, Economic Characters, & Economic Institution, 1996, Festschrift: Editing Economics: Essays in Honour of Mark Perlman, 2001; author: (with Bela Gold, et al) Techonological Progress and Insutraial Leadership: The Growth of the U.S. Steel Industry, 1900-1970, 1984; author: (with Charles R. McCAnn, Jr.) Pillars of Economic Understanding: Ideas & Traditions, 1998; author: (with Charles R. McCann, Jr.) Pillars of Economic Understanding: Factors and Markets, 2000; editor: Human Resources in the Economy, 1963; editor: (with Reuben E. Slesinger and Asher Isaacs) Contemporary Economics and Selected Readings, 1967; author (with Benjamin Chinitz and Charles Levin): Spatial, Regional, and Population Economics: Essays in Honor of Egar M. Hoover, 1972; editor (with Norval Morris): Law and Crime: Essays in Honor of Sir John Barry, 1972; editor: Economics of Health and Medical Care, 1974, The Organization and Retrieval of Economic Knowledge, 1977; editor: (with G.K. MacLeod) Health Care Capital: Competition and Control, 1978; editor: (with Arnold Heertje) Evolving Technology and Market Structure: Studies in Schumpeterian Economics, 1990; editor: (with Klaus Welermair) Studies in Economic Rationality: X-Efficency Examined and Extolled. Essays Written in the Tradition of and to Honor Harvey Lelbenstein, 1990; editor: (with C.E. Barfield) Capital Markets and Trade: The United States Faces a United Europe, 1991; editor: (with N.H. Ornstein) Political Power and Social Change: The United States Faces a United Europe, 1991; editor: (with C.E. Barfield) Industry, Services, and Agriculture: The U.S. Faces a United Europe, 1991; editor: (with F.M. Scherer) Entrepreneurship, Technological Innovation, and Economic Growth: Studies in the Schumpeterian Tradition, 1992; editor: (with Yuichi Shionoya) Innovations in Technology, Industries, and Institutions, 1994, Schumpeter in the History of Ideas, 1994; editor: (with Ernst Helstadter) Behavioral Norms, Technological Progress, and Economic Dynamics: Studies in Schumpeterian Economics, 1996; editor: (with Kenneth Arrow, Enrico Colombatto, and Christian Schmidt) The Rational Foundations of Economic Behaviour, 1996; editor: (with Francisco Louca) Is Economics an Evolutionary Science?, 2000; editor: Cambridge Surveys of Economic Institutions and Policies, 1991—96, articles, essays on health, population change, econ. devel., orgn. econ. knowledge and methodology, econ. productivity, history of econ. discipline; cons. editor, later editl. cons. (USIA publ.) Portfolio on Internat. Econ. Perspectives, 1972—83, mng. co-editor Jour. Evolutionary Econs., 1989—96, corr. Am. editor Revue d'Economie Politique, 1990—, series editor Great Economists of the World, 1990—96. With U.S. Army, 1943—46. Social Sci. Rsch. Coun. fellow, 1949-50; Ford Found. fellow, 1962-63; Fulbright lectr. Melbourne U., 1968 Fellow: History Econs. Soc. (hon.; v.p. 1979—80, pres. elect 1983—84, pres. 1984—85); mem.: J.A. Schumpeter Gesellschaft (editor 1986—96), Verein fuer Sozial-Politik, Ausschuss fuer Dogmengeschichte, Royal Econ. Soc., Am. Econ. Assn. (founding and mng. editor Jour. Econ. Lit. 1968—81), European Assn. History Econ. Thought Soc. (hon.), Athenaeum (London), Phi Beta Kappa. Jewish. Home: 302 Fox Chapel Rd Apt 414 Pittsburgh PA 15238-2337

PERLMUTTER, DAWN, art and philosophy educator, aesthetics researcher; b. Phila., Oct. 10, 1959; d. Abraham Perlmutter and Joan Rocco Sutton. BFA in Interior Archtl. Design, Moore Coll. Art, 1980; MFA in Painting, Am. U., Washington, 1988; PhD in Arts & Humanities, N.Y. U., 1993. Docent edn. dept. gen. and specialized collection tours Hirshhorn Mus. & Sculpture Garden, Washington, 1985-88; instr. dept. fine arts The Art League Sch., Alexandria, Va., 1988-89; adj. asst. prof. dept. art & art history Mercer County C.C., Trenton, N.J., 1993; adj. lectr. dept. arts & humanities Richard Stockton Coll. N.J., Pomona, 1994; instr. dept. graphic design Del. County C.C., Media, Pa., 1994-95; adj. asst. prof. dept. philosophy U. Del., Newark, 1994—; asst. prof. art and philosophy dept. fine arts Cheyney U. Pa., 1995—. Mem. exec. bd. Assn. Pa. State Coll. & U. Facilities, Harrisburg, 1995—. One-woman shows include Embassy of Sweden, Washington, 1983, Galerie Triangle, Washington, 1984 (best painting for the theme of children cash award 1983), Lansburghs Cultural Ctr., Washington, 1984, Washington Project for the Arts, 1985, 86, 87, Newmans Gallery, Washington, 1986, 90, 92, 94; exhibited in group shows at Please Touch Children's Mus., Phila., 1977, Gallery West, Alexandria, Va., 1984, Long Beach Mus. Art, L.A., 1984, Circle Theatre Gallery, Washington, 1986, Washington Consulting Group Art Gallery, 1988, Watkins Gallery Am. U., 1986, 87, 88, Studio Gallery, Washington, 1988, The Art League Gallery, Alexandria, Va., 1983, 87, 88, 89 (equal award of excellence 1983), The Capitol Hill Art League Gallery, Washington, 1988, 89 (cash award fall arts festival 1988, 3rd place 1989), Art East Gallery N.Y. U., 1991, Del. County C.C. Art Gallery, Media, Pa., 1994, Richard Hall Art Gallery Dixon U. Ctr., Harrisburg, Pa., 1995; exhibited in permanent collections at Please Touch Children's Mus., Phila., Hope Village, Inc., Washington, also in pvt. collections. Recipient Smithsonian Resident Assoc. scholarship, 1986, Grad. fellowship Am. U., 1987-88, Campus Faculty Profl. Devel. grant, Cheyney U. Pa., 1995. Mem. Am. Soc. for Aesthetics, Coll. Art Assn., Am. Acad. Religion, Internat. Soc. for the Advancement of Living Traditions in Art, The Greater Phila. Philosophy Consortium. Avocations: archery, fencing. Office: Cheyney U Pa Dept Fine Arts Box 526 Cheyney PA 19319

PERLOFF, JEFFREY MARK, agricultural and resource economics educator; b. Chgo., Jan. 28, 1950; s. Harvey S. and Miriam (Seligman) P.; m. Jaqueline B. Persons, Aug. 15, 1976; 1 child, Lisa. BA, U. Chgo., 1972; PhD, MIT, 1976. Asst. prof. U. Pa., Phila., 1976-80, U. Calif., Berkeley, 1980-82, assoc. prof., 1982-89, prof., 1989—. Author: (with Dennis Carlton) Modern Industrial Organization, 1990, 3d edit., 2000, Microeconomics, 1999, 2d edit., 2001; contbr. numerous articles to profl. jours. Fellow: Am. Agrl. Econs. Assn. Office: U Calif Dept Agrl Econs 207 Giannini Hall Berkeley CA 94720-3310 E-mail: perloff@are.berkeley.edu.

PERLOFF, MARJORIE GABRIELLE, English and comparative literature educator; b. Vienna, Sept. 28, 1931; d. Maximilian and Ilse (Schueller) Mintz; m. Joseph K. Perloff, July 31, 1953; children— Nancy Lynn, Carey Elizabeth. AB, Barnard Coll., 1953; MA, Cath. U., 1956, PhD, 1965. Asst. prof. English and comparative lit. Cath. U., Washington, 1966-68, asso. prof., 1969-71, U. Md., 1971-73, prof., 1973-76; Florence R. Scott prof. English U. So. Calif., Los Angeles, 1976—; prof. English and comparative lit. Stanford U., Calif., 1986—, Sadie Dernham prof. humanities, 1990—, prof. emerita, 2000. Vis. prof. U. Utah, 2002. Author: Rhyme and Meaning in the Poetry of Yeats, 1970, The Poetic Art of Robert Lowell, 1973, Frank O'Hara, Poet Among Painters, 1977, 2nd edit., 1998, The Poetics of Indeterminacy: Rimbaud to Cage, 1981, 2d edit., 1999, The Dance of the Intellect: Studies in the Poetry of the Pound Tradition, 1985, 2d edit., 1996, The Futurist Moment: Avant-Garde, Avant-Guerre and the Language of Rupture, 1986, 2d edit., 2003, Poetic License: Essays in Modern and Postmodern Lyric, 1990, Radical Artifice: Writing Poetry in the Age of Media, 1991, Wittgenstein's Ladder: Poetic Language and the Strangeness of the Ordinary, 1996, Frank O'Hara, 2d edit., 1998, Poetry On and Off the Page: Essays for Emergent Occasions, 1998, Twenty-first Century Modernism, 2001; editor: Postmodern Genres, 1990; co-editor: John Cage: Composed in America, 1994; contbg. editor: Columbia Literary History of the U.S., 1987; contbr. preface to Contemporary Poets, 1980, A John Cage Reader, 1983. Guggenheim fellow, 1981-82, NEA fellow, 1985; Phi Beta Kappa scholar, 1994-95. Fellow Am. Acad. Arts and Scis.; mem. MLA (exec. coun. 1977-81, Am. lit. sect. 1993—), Comparative Lit. Assn. (pres. 1993-94, mem. adv. bd. Libr. of Am.), Lit. Studies Acad. Home: 1467 Amalfi Dr Pacific Palisades CA 90272-2752 Office: Stanford U Dept English Stanford CA 94305 E-mail: mperloff@earthlink.net.

PERLOFF, ROBERT, psychologist, educator; b. Phila., Feb. 3, 1921; s. Myer and Elizabeth (Sherman) P.; m. Evelyn Potechin, Sept. 22, 1946; children: Richard Mark, Linda Sue, Judith Kay. AB, Temple U., 1949; MA, Ohio State U., 1949, PhD, 1951; DSc (hon.), Oreg. Grad. Sch. Profl. Psychology, 1984; DLitt (hon.), Calif. Sch. Profl. Psychology, 1985. Diplomate Am. Bd. Profl. Psychology. Instr. edn. Antioch Coll., 1950-51; with pers. rsch. br. Dept. Army, 1951-55, chief statis. rsch. and cons. unit., 1953-55; dir. R & D Sci. Rsch. Assos., Inc., Chgo., 1955-59; vis. lectr. Chgo. Tchrs. Coll., 1955-56; mem. faculty Purdue U., 1959-69, prof. psychology, 1964-69; field assessment officer univ. Peace Corps Chile III project, 1962; Disting. Svc. prof. bus. adminstrn. and psychology U. Pitts. Joseph M. Katz Grad. Sch. Bus., 1969-90, Disting. Svc. prof. emeritus, 1991—; dir. rsch. programs U. Pitts. Grad. Sch. Bus., 1969-77; dir. Consumer Panel, 1980-83. Bd. dirs. Book Ctr.; cons. in field, 1959—; adv. com. assessment exptl. manpower R & D labs. Nat. Acad. Scis., 1972-74; mem. rsch. rev. com. NIMH, 1976-80, Stress and Families rsch. project, 1976-79; mem. adv. bd. Cornell Inst. for Rsch. on Children, 2002—. Contbr. articles to profl. jours.; editor Indsl. Psychologist, 1963-65, Evaluator Intervention: Pros and Cons; book rev. editor Personnel Psychology, 1952-55; co-editor: Values, Ethics and Standards Sourcebook, 1979, Improving Evaluations; bd. cons. editors Jour. Applied Psychology; bd. advs. Archives History Am. Psychology, Psychol. Svc. Pitts., Recorded Psychol. Jours.; guest editor Am. Psychologist, 1972, Edn. and Urban Soc., 1977, Profl. Psychology, 1977; adv. editor Contemporary Psychology, 1994—. Bd. dirs., v.p. Sr. Citizens Svc. Corp., Calif. Sch. Profl. Psychology; bd. dirs. Greater Pitts. chpt. ACLU, sec., 1997-98; chmn. nat. adv. com. Inst. Govt. and Pub. Affairs, U. Ill., 1986-89, sec. nat. adv. com., 1997—; mem. adv. com. Cornell Inst. for Rsch. on Children, 2002—. Decorated Bronze Star; named in his honor, Robert Perloff Grad. Rsch. Assistantship in Inst. Govt. and Pub. Affairs, U. Ill., 1990, in his honor, Robert Perloff Career Achievement award, Knowledge Utilization Soc., 1991; recipient Legacy award, Greater Pitts. Psychol. Assn., 2001, Hist. Preservation award, City of Pitts., 2002. Fellow: APA (mem.-at-large exec. com. divsn. consumer psychology 1964—67, coun. reps. 1965—68, pres. divsn. 1967—68, chmn. sci. affairs com., divsn. consumer psychology 1968—69, edn. and tng. bd. 1969—72, mem.-at-large exec. com. divsn. consumer psychology 1970—71, coun. reps. 1972—74, dir. 1974—82, chmn. fin. com., treas. 1975—84, chmn. investment com. 1977—82, pres. 1985, adv. bd., bd. sci. affairs 1994—96, task force intelligence and Intelligence Tests, author column Std. Deviations in jour., pres. address selected as one of 50 over 50 yrs.), AAAS, Ea. Psychol. Assn. (dir. 1977—80, pres. 1980—81); mem.: Coun. of Sci. Soc. (found. alumnus, pres. 1998—), Knowledge Utilization Soc. (pres. 1993—95), Soc. Psychologists in Mgmt. (pres. 1993—94, Disting. Contbn. to Psychology Mgmt. award 1989), Am. Evaluation Assn. (pres. 1977—78), Am. Psychol. Found. (v.p. 1988—89, pres. 1990—92, trustee 1995—98, Lifetime Achievement in Psychology Gold Medal award 2000), Assn. for Consumer Rsch. (chmn. 1970—71), Pa. Psychol. Assn. (Disting. Svc. award 1985), Internat. Assn. Applied Psychology, Am. Psychol. Soc., Phi Beta Kappa, Psi Chi, Beta Gamma Sigma, Sigma Xi (pres. U. Pitts. chpt. 1989—91). Home: 815 Saint James St Pittsburgh PA 15232-2112 E-mail: rperloff@katz.pitt.edu.

PERNICIARO, CHARLES VINCENT, dermatologist, educator, entrepreneur; b. New Orleans, June 15, 1957; s. Ernest Gabriel and Phereby Sheppard Perniciaro; children: Jamie Lynn, Kelly Gabrielle. BS, U. La., Lafayette, 1979; MD, La. State U., New Orleans, 1983. Diplomate Am. Bd. Dermatology, Am. Bd. Dermatology and Pathology. Staff physician Ochsner Clin. of Baton Rouge, La., 1987-90; sr. assoc. cons. and staff dermatologist Mayo Clinic, Jacksonville, Fla., 1990-93, cons., staff dermatologist and dermatopathologist, 1993-99; pvt. practice dermatology Brunswick, Ga., 1999—, Neptune Beach, Fla., 1999—. Pres., CEO Holiday Lighting Concepts, Inc., 1996-2000; lectr., presenter in field; adj. clin. assoc. prof. pathology U. Fla. Shands Jacksonville Med. Ctr., 1999-2001. Contbr. articles to profl. jours. Founder, bd. dirs. S.W. La. Skin Cancer Found., 1987. Recipient Resident-in-Tng. award So. Med. Assn., 1994, Outstanding Paper award Noah Worcester Dermatol. Soc., 1993, First Place Poster award 17th Internat. Colloquium Dermatopathology, 1996. Fellow: Am. Soc. Dermatopathology (chmn. membership com., bd. dirs. 2000—01), Am. Acad. Dermatology (com. on preventive dermatology 1988—90, task force on dermatologic oncology 1990—93, environ. coun. 1994—96, adv. coun. 1995—2001); mem.: So. Med. Assn. (vice chair sect. dermatology 1995—96, chair-elect 2001—03), Fla. Soc. Dermatology (bd. dirs. 1998—, chmn. membership com. 1999—2002, v.p. 2002—03, pres. 2003—), Jacksonville Dermatology Soc. (sec.-treas. 1995, pres. 1996), Lions (charter, bd. dirs. Ponte Vedra Beach 1997—98). Avocations: tennis, computers. Home: 514 Midway St Neptune Beach FL 32266 Office: Brunswick Dermatology Clinic 3008 E Park Ave Brunswick GA 31520-4241

PERNICK, MARTIN STEVEN, history educator; b. N.Y.C., June 2, 1948; s. Louis W. and Florence P. (Goldberg) P. m. Marie R. Deveney, July 8, 1983; 1 child, Benjamin William. BA, Brandeis U., 1968; MA, Columbia U., 1969, PhD, 1979. Lectr. Coll. Medicine Pa. State U., Hershey, 1972-79; from asst. prof. to prof. U. Mich., Ann Arbor, 1979—. Vis. lectr. Harvard U., Cambridge, Mass., 1975-76; creator, dir. Hist. Health Film Collection, Ann Arbor, 1986—. Author: A Calculus of Suffering, 1985, The Black Stork, 1996; contbr. chpt. to Death: Beyond Whole-Brain Criteria, 1988. Nat. Libr. Medicine fellow, 1984-85, NEH fellow, 1985-88. Mem. Am. Assn. History Medicine (exec. coun. 1992-95). Office: U Mich Dept History Ann Arbor MI 48109-1003

PERONI, PETER A., II, psychologist, educator; b. Trenton, N.J., Nov. 14, 1942; s. Peter A. and Mary D. (DiLeo) P. BA, LaSalle U., 1964; MA, Trenton State Coll., 1967, MAT, 1969; EdD, Rutgers U., 1977. Cert. secondary sch. social studies, student pers. svcs.; lic. psychologist, Pa. Tchr. St. Anthony High Sch., Trenton, 1964-67, Lawrence Twp. (N.J.) Pub. Schs., 1967-68; counselor Bucks County C.C., Newtown, Pa., 1968-72, prof., 1972-95; cons. psychologist, 1995—. Consulting psychologist N.J. Dept. Health, Trenton, 1977-84; dir. clin. svcs. New Horizon Treatment Svcs., Trenton, 1984-88. Author: The Burg: An Italian-American Community at Bay in Trenton, 1979; writer, co-producer (TV): The Burg: A State of Mind, 1980; author: Academic Success Through Self-Conditioning, 1982. N.J. Commn. for Humanities grantee, 1980. Avocation: motorcycle touring. Home: 52 Hollynoll Dr Trenton NJ 08619-2208

PERREGO, VIRGINIA, mathematics educator; b. Wilkes-Barre, Pa., May 19, 1945; d. Harold Paul adn Frances (Austin) Trethaway; m. William Charles Perrego, Aug. 3, 1968; children: David, Melissa, Mark. BS, Marywood Coll., 1967, MLS, 1968. Cert. tchr., N.Y.. Tchr., sch. libr. Taft Elem. Sch., Washingtonville, N.Y., 1968-73; tchr., math. I instr. Round Hill Elem. Sch., Washingtonville, 1983—; math instr. Washingtonville Middle Sch., 1992-93; fam. math. trainer 4th grade Round Hill, 1993-94. Mem. Philosophy Com., Washingtonville, 1989-91; math. tchr. rep. Congruency Com.-Dist., Washingtonville, 1989—. Tchr. bd. rep. PTA, Washingtonville; bldg. camp group leader St. Mary's Ch., Washingtonville, 1990—. Grantee for grad. study Nat. Dept. Def. Mem. Assn. Math. Tchrs. of N.Y., Nat. Coun. Tchrs. of Math. Republican. Roman Catholic. Office: Round Hill Elem Sch Rt 208 S Washingtonville NY 10992

PERRILL, REBECCA LAURAN, elementary school educator; b. Columbus, Ohio, Mar. 20, 1954; d. Charles Howard and Helen Marie (Simons) P. BA in Elem. Edn., Ohio Wesleyan U., 1976; postgrad., Ohio State U., 1977-78, U. Dayton, Wright State U., Ashland U., Portland State U. Cert. elem. edn. tchr., Ohio. Tchr. 2nd and 4th grades Washington Court House (Ohio) City Schs., elem. tchr., grade 5. Mem. Kappa Delta Pi, Delta Kappa Gamma, Phi Delta Kappa. Home: 329 Gregg St Washington Court House OH 43160-1449

PERRIMAN, WENDY KAREN, poet, educator; b. Stamford, England, July 9, 1958; d. David Wathen Blower and Heather Boulton Unwin; m. Steven Ralph Perriman, Aug. 8, 1981; 1 child. BA, U. Lancaster, Eng., 1979; postgrad. Cert. Edn., U. Bristol, Eng., 1980; MA, Drew U., 2000, MPhil, 2001, PhD, 2003. Probationary tchr. Eastbrook Comprehensive Sch., London, 1980-81; English and drama tchr. Cornwall Sch., Dortmund, West Germany, 1981-83, King's Sch., Gutersloh, West Germany, 1983-85; acting head English and drama Weston Park Girls' Sch., Southampton, England, 1989-92; head drama, asst. head English Bitterne Park Sch., Southampton, 1992-94; freelance poet Madison, NJ, 1994—; adj. asst. prof. English Drew U., Madison, NJ, 2002—. Pub., editor Inka Publs., N.J., 1996—; adj. asst. prof. English Drew U., Madison, NJ, 2002--. Author: Collected Experience, 1996, Show and Tell, 1997, Free Fall, 1998. Mem. MLA, Poetry Soc. Am., Acad. Am. Poets, Modern Poetry Assn. Office: Inka Publs PO Box 53 Madison NJ 07940-0053

PERRIN, JANICE HELEN DAVIS, special education educator; b. Port Arthur, Tex. d. Albert Otho and Helen (Anderson) Davis. BS in Early Childhood Edn./Reading, U. So. Miss., 1978; M. Elem. Edn., spl. edn. K-12 cert., reading specialist cert., Mansfield U., 1987. Cert. reading elem., early childhood and spl. edn., Pa., N.Y., early childhood edn., MS, W.Va., Mo, reading, elem. edn., Mo. Adult basic edn./GED tchr. JTPA, Mansfield (Pa.) U.; remedial reading and math. tchr. Columbia (Miss.) Pub. Schs., 1979-81; remedial reading tchr. Sikeston R-6 Sch., Morehouse, Mo., 1978-79; optional I spl. edn. tchr. Corning Painted Post Sch. Dist., Painted Post, N.Y., 1985-86, 88-89; optional IV spl. edn. tchr. Bur. of Coop. Ednl. Svcs., Williamsport, Pa., 1989-90; tchr. Apalachin (N.Y.) Alternative Learning Program Broome-Deware-Tioga Bur. Coop. Ednl. Svcs., 1991, 92-93; opt. II tchr. Bur. Coop. Ednl. Svcs.-Broome-Tioga Chenago Forks Sch. Dist., Binghamton, N.Y., 1992—. Presenter on children's safety issues. Mem. N.Y. State U. Tchrs., Am. Fedn. Tchrs., Internat. Student Affairs (past pres., v.p.), Order of Rainbow for Girls (past worth advisor). Home: 26 Addison Ave Buffalo NY 14226-2323

PERRIN, NANCY ANN, elementary music educator; b. Dayton, Ohio, June 13, 1948; d. Eugene Clark and Geneva Louise (Sease) Maupin; 1 child, Mike J. Brown; m. Keith A. Perrin, Dec. 5, 1987. MusB, Ohio State U., 1970; MusM in Edn., Wright State U., 1984, MEd, 1991. Cert. tchr., supr., elem. prin., h.s. prin., staff pers. adminstr., asst. supt., supr. instrnl. svcs., Ohio. Tchr. Tecumseh Local Schs., New Carlisle, Ohio, 1976—, head dept. music, 1989—; instr. Sinclair C.C., Dayton, 1980—. Mem. ASCD, Am. Mathay Assn. (archivist 1986-91), Music Educators Nat. Conf., Ohio Assn. Elem. Sch. Adminstrs., Dayton Music Club. Avocations: playing keyboard and guitar, bicycling, ballroom dancing. Home: 270 Banbury Rd Centerville OH 45459-1706 Office: Tecumseh Local Bd Edn Park Layne Sch 9760 W National Rd New Carlisle OH 45344-9290 E-mail: nancyp@woh.rr.com.

PERRON, ANNE MICHELLE, physical education educator; b. Mamou, La., Mar. 28, 1959; d. Buford Joseph and Madge Marie (Soileau) P. BS, U. Southwestern La., 1982, MEd, 1984. Cert. tchr., La. Tchr. Plantation Elem. Sch., Lafayette, La., 1982—. Bd. dirs. The Extra Mile, Lafayette, 1992; youth team capt. March of Dimes Walk Am., Lafayette, 1990—; coord. Am. Heart Assn. Jump Rope for Heart, Lafayette, 1989—. Mem. La. Assn. Educators (rep. 1982), La. Assn. Health, Phys. Edn., Recreation and Dance, Phi Delta Kappa, Alpha Delta Kappa, Delta Psi Kappa. Home: 132 N Meyers Dr Lafayette LA 70508-7342 Office: Plantation Elementary Sch 1801 Kaliste Saloom Rd Lafayette LA 70508-6113

PERRONE, RUTH ELLYN, university administrator; b. Hearne, Tex., July 2, 1951; d. John Paul Perrone and Ellen Gayle (Sullivan) Perrone-Robertson. BS, Stephen F. Austin State U., 1973; MPA, Tex. A&M U., 1986. Social worker Tex. Dept. Pub. Welfare, Nacogdoches, Tex., 1974-76; licensing rep. Tex. Dept. Human Resources, Bryan, 1976-85; spl. asst. to vice chancellor for state affairs Tex. A&M Univ. System, Austin, 1987-90; asst. to pres. Tex. A&M U., College Station, 1990-92. dir. external rels., 1992-99, v.p. govt. affairs, 1999—2002; v.p. govt. rels. Ohio State U., 2003—. Advisor legis. study group Tex. A&M U., 1992-2002; bd. dirs. Scott & White Hosp. Health Plan, 1995-2000. Chair governing bd. John Ben Shepperd Pub. Leadership Found., Odessa, Tex., 1993-94; bd. dirs. Tex. Lyceum, Austin, 1992-97; assoc. mem. St. Joseph Hosp. Aux., Bryan, 1993—. Named Best of Show, Greater Omaha Am. Mktg. Assn., 2002. Mem.: Assn. Am. Univs., Council of Fed. Relations, Bryan/College Station C. of C. (coun. on govtl. affairs), Assn. Am. Univs. (coun. fed. rels. 2001—), Coun. ADvancement and Support Edn., Nat. Assn. State Univ. and Land Grant Coll. (exec. com. mem., coun. on govtl. affairs). Avocations: ballet, theatre, reading, dinner parties. Office: Ohio State U 205 Bricker Hall 190 N Oval Mall Columbus OH 43210-1394 E-mail: perrone.4@osu.edu.

PERROS, THEODORE PETER, chemist, educator; b. Cumberland, Md., Aug. 16, 1921; s. Peter G. and Christina (Sioris) P.; m. Electra Paula Zolotas, July 21, 1973 (div.). BS, George Washington U., 1946, MS, 1947, PhD, 1952; postgrad., Technische Hochschule, Munich, Germany. Analyst research div. U.S. Naval Ordnance Lab., 1943-46; mem. faculty George Washington U., Washington, 1946—, prof. chemistry and forensic scis., 1960-91, prof. emeritus in residence, 1991—, chmn. dept. forensic sci., 1971-73, chmn. dept. chemistry, 1980-88; v.p. Meridian-West Assos., 1978—. Rsch. chemist Bur. Ordnance, 1949; rsch. dir. Air Force Office Sci. R&D, 1958-59; cons. U.S. Naval Ordnance Lab., 1953-56; fed. commr., chmn. bd. dirs. Interstate Commn. Potomac River Basin, 1980; sec. Ahepa Ednl. Found., 1969-78; mem. Chesapeake Bay Sci. and Tech. Adv. Com., 1993; Washington rep. tax advocacy panel Dept. Treas., 2002. Author: (with William F. Sager) Chemical Principles, 1961, (with C.R. Naeser, W. Harkness) Experiments in General Chemistry, 1961, College Chemistry, 1966; Contbr. (with C.R. Naeser, W. Harkness) articles to profl. jours. Pres. So. Intercollegiate Athletic Conf., 1968, Hellenic Rep. Club of Washington, 1968-70, D.C. Heritage Groups Coun., 1980; campaign chmn. Nat. Rep. Heritage Groups Coun., 1977-78, recipient Kurt Voldemars Meml. award for disting. svc., 1985; mem. D.C. Rep. State Com., 1980—; exec. com. Rep. Nat. Com., 1994-95; chmn. Nat. Rep. Heritage Groups Coun., 1994-95; elected Bob Dole del. San Diego Rep. Conv., 1996, Gov. Bush del. Phila. Rep. Conv., 2000; apptd. to taxpayer adv. panel as Washington rep. to IRS, 2002. Named Disting. Prof. in Edn. George Washington U., 1990, Award of Distinction, CHS Alumni Assn., 1992; NSF fellow, 1959; AEC grantee, 1951-53, Rsch. Corp. grantee, 1953-54. Fellow Am. Inst. Chemists (Honor Scroll award 1997), Am. Acad. Forensic Scis., Washington Acad. Scis.; mem. Am. Chem. Soc., Soc. Applied Spectroscopy, German Lang. Soc., Chem. Soc. London, Gesellschaft Deutscher Chemiker, Philos. Soc. Washington, Am. Hellenic Ednl. Progressive Assn. (pres. Inst. Arts and Scis., pres. Washington chpt. 1976-78, dist. gov. 1982-83, supreme gov. 1985-86, Am. Hellenic Ednl. Progressive Assn. (AHEPAN) Acad. Achievement award 1984, editor AHEPAN mag. 1997—), Sigma Xi, Omicron Delta Kappa, Alpha Chi Sigma (pres. 1964, bd. gov.'s 1986-88, Profl. Merit award 1985, Profl. Chemistry award 1985). Achievements include research on stabilities of inorganic coordination polymers, preparation and characterization fluorine containing compounds transition metals. E-mail: (home) (office). Home: 500 23d St NW B-606 Washington DC 20037 E-mail: tperros@att.net., tpp@gwu.edu.

PERRY, ARTHUR WILLIAM, plastic surgeon, educator; b. Cornwall, NY, Jan. 2, 1957; s. Michael Martin and Harriet (Estrin) P. AB magna cum laude, Rutgers U., 1977; MD with distinction, Albany Med. Coll., 1981. Diplomate Am. Bd. Plastic Surgery. Clin. fellow in surgery Harvard Med. Sch., Boston, 1981-84; fellow in burn surgery Cornell U. Med. Coll., N.Y.c., 1984-85; resident in plastic surgery U. Chgo., 1985-87; clin. asst. prof. surgery U. Medicine and Surgery N.J.-Robert Wood Johnson Med. Sch., New Brunswick, 1987-97, clin. assoc. prof. plastic surgery, 1997—; clin. assoc. in surgery U. Pa., Phila., 1993—2003; chief plastic surgery Somerset Med. Ctr., Somerville, Pa., 2003—, chief of plastic surgery, 2003. Mem. N.J. Bd. Med. Examiners, Trenton, 1995—, treas., 2002—, mem. exec. com., 2002, chmn. advt. com., 1997—; chmn. preliminary evaluation com., 1997—2001; vice chmn., mem. devel. com. Carnegie Bank, Princeton, NJ, 1990—98; mem. body art steering com. N.J. Dept. health and Sr. Svcs., 1999—2001; designee State Bioterrorism Task Force, 2001; mem. N.J. Hosp. Assn. Bioterrorism Task Force, 2001—. Co-author: Cosmetic Surgery, 1997; contbr. chpt. to books, articles to profl. jours. Mem. health adv. bd. to Congressman Mike Ferguson, 2001. Recipient Gingrass award Plastic Surgery Rsch. Coun., 1981, best paper award Midwestern Assn. Plastic Surgeons, 1987. Fellow ACS; mem. Am. Soc. Plastic Surgeons, Am. Soc. Aesthetic Plastic Surgery (award for vol. svc.), Alpha Omega Alpha. Office: 3055 State Route 27 Franklin Park NJ 08823-1315 E-mail: dr.perry@perryplasticsurgery.com.

PERRY, DONALD E. principal; Student, Lewis U., Ill. State U.; BS in Elem. Edn., Olivet Nazarene U., 1976; MS in Edn. Adminstrn., Ill. State U., 1988. Tchr. Alan Shephard Sch. and Shabbona Elem. Sch., Bourbonnais, Ill., 1977—80, Crete (Ill.) Elem. Sch., 1980—85; asst. prin., asst. to bus. mgr. Dist. 118 Palos West Elem. Sch., Palos Park, Ill., 1985—98; prin. Dist. 203 Schs. Beebe Elem. Sch., Naperville, Ill., 1988—98, Kennedy Jr. H.S., Naperville, 1998—. Police and fire commr. City of Napervillle; mem. coll. edn. adv. bd. Benedictine U.; mem. adv. bd. Edwards Hosp.; village clk. Bourbonnais; village trustee.*

PERRY, EDNA BURRELL, retired elementary school principal; b. Washington, July 30, 1934; d. Harold Flowers and Annie Mae (Harrison) Burrell; m. Sidney Lee Perry, Jr., June 5, 1954; children: Angela, Andrea R. BME magna cum laude, Howard U., Washington, 1956; MA in Adminstrn./Supervision, Roosevelt U., Chgo., 1972. Cert. prin., nat. cert. counselor. Tchr. Healy Sch., Chgo., 1959-62; from asst. prin. to prin., counselor C.H. Wacker Sch., Chgo., 1962-94; ret.; team dir. Golden NeoLife Diamite Internat., Milpitas, Calif., 1986—. Vol. Am. Cancer Soc., Chgo., 1960-80; minister of music Ch. of the Good Shepherd, Chgo., 1959—, condr. choir, 1959—. Named Lay Person of the Yr., Ch. of Good Shepherd, 1980, Woman of the Yr., 1992, Music award, 1994. Mem. Nat. Assn. Negro Musicians, Nat. Pharm. Assn. Aux. (nat. pres. 1977-79, 90-93), Delta Sigma Theta. United Ch. of Christ. Avocation: nutritional counseling. Home: 9201 S Cregier Ave Chicago IL 60617-3602

PERRY, ELISABETH ISRAELS, historian, educator, administrator; b. N.Y.C., Mar. 29, 1939; d. Carlos Lindner Israels and Irma (Commanday) Bauman; m. Lewis Curtis Perry, Nov. 26, 1970; children: Susanna, David. BA in History, UCLA, 1960, PhD in History, 1967. Lectr. history Calif. State Coll., Long Beach, 1966-67; asst. prof. history U. Colo., Boulder, 1967-69; asst. prof., part-time adminstr. SUNY, Buffalo, 1970-78; vis. asst. prof. history Univs. Iowa, Ind., Cin., 1981-84; vis. prof. history Vanderbilt U., Nashville, 1984-85, assoc. prof. history, 1985-93; vis. prof. Am. history Bklyn. Coll., CUNY, 1991-92; dir. grad. program in women's history Sarah Lawrence Coll., Bronxville, N.Y., 1993-97; John Francis Bannon prof. history St. Louis U., 1999—. Dir. seminars NEH, Washington, 1987, 90, 91, 95, 2000. Author: From Theology to History, 1973, Belle Moskowitz, 1987; co-author: The Challenge of Feminist Biography, 1992, America: Pathways to Present, 1994, 5th edit., 2002, Women in American Party Politics, 1999. Humanities scholar Cumberland Valley Girl Scouts, Nashville, 1991. Fulbright scholar U. Paris, 1964; NEH sr. fellow, 1980-81; recipient

Grant-in-Aid award Am. Coun. Learned Socs., 1991. Mem. Soc. for Historians of the Gilded Age and Progressive Era (pres. 1998-2000). Office: St Louis U Dept History Saint Louis MO 63108 E-mail: perrye@slu.edu.

PERRY, GLEN JOSEPH, school system administrator, educator; b. Oakland, Calif., May 3, 1953; s. Joseph and Lucille (Piccarelli) P.; children: Glen Jr., Nicholas. AA, Chabot Coll., 1973; BS, Calif. State Univ., 1975. Police officer, detective City of San Leandro, San Leandro, Calif., 1975-81, City of Woodland, Woodland, Calif., 1981-85; tchr. Woodland Unified Sch. Dist., Woodland, Calif., 1988-92, discipline coord., 1992—2002; ret., 2002. Chair dept. math. Woodland Unified Sch. Dist., 1990-92, discipline behavior assigns, 1988-2002; discipline seminars, 1997-98. Author: Contractual Accountability System, 1996. Elder Victory Family Fellowship, Woodland, Calif., 1997; Bible tchr., Sacramento, Woodland, Calif., 1987-99. Named Outstanding Law Enforcement Officer of Yr. Woodland C. of C., 1981, Resolution of Appreciation award Woodland City Coun., 1981, Tchr. of Yr. award Douglass Jr. H.S., 1989.

PERRY, HELEN, medical/surgical nurse, secondary school educator; b. Birmingham, Ala., Mar. 4, 1927; d. Van Mary Ellenol (Thornton) Curry; m. Charlie Pitts, May 1960 (div.); 1 child, Charlenia Pitts; m. George Perry (dec. 1989); children: Hattie Mae(dec.), George Jr., Bishop, Jose Sr. Student, LaSalle Extension U., Chgo., 1968, Georgetown U., 1979; Doctorate/Mayanuis Mosaic Soc., Duke Univ., San Antonio, 1979. Cert. paramedic; LPN. Tchr. Wenona HS City Bd. Edn., Birmingham, 1977—. Notary pub., Ala., 1975—; home health nurse U. Ala. Birmingham Hosp., 1988—. Trustee Nat. Crime Watch, 1989; mem. adv. bd. Am. Security Coun., Va., 1969—91; mem. Coalition for Desert Storm; others; vol. ARC, Birmingham, 1970—; mem. crime watch Am. Police, Washington, 1989; mem. Hall of Fame Pres. Task Force, Washington, 1983—91, Image Devel. Adv. Bd.; nominee Nat. Rep. Com., Washington, 1991, 1992; selected VIP guest del. Rep. Nat. Conv., Houston, 1992; life mem. Rep. Presdl. Task Force, Washington, 1992; mem. Jefferson Com., 2001; mem. adv. bd. Nat. Congl. Com., Washington; mem. fin. com. fundraiser Middleton for Congress Campaign, 1994, Dist. # 59 Bd. Reps.; mem. exec. com. Jefferson County Rep., chairperson legis. dist. 52; chair Harriet Tubman Rep. Com.; del. Commonwealth of Ky. So. Rep. Leadership Conf., 2000; min. Greater Emmanuel Temple Holiness Ch., Birmingham, 1957—, ordained elder, vice champion mother bd.; mem. Nat. Law Enforcement Assn., 1989. Nominee Presdl. Election Registry, Rep. Presdl. Task Force, 1992; named Good Samaritan, Law Envforcement Officers; recipient award, Ala. Sheriff Assn., 1989, Navy League, 1989—91, cert. of appreciation, Pres. Congl. Task Force, 1990, Rep. Nat. Com., 1994, Diamond award, U.S.A. Serve Am., 1992, Rep. Presdl. award, Legion of Merit, 1994, Royal Proclamation, Royal Highness Kevin, Prince Regent of Hutt River Province, 1994, Royal Ceremonial jewel, Svc. award, Ala. Bd. Nursing, Outstanding Sr. Citizen's cert. of recognition. Mem.: Ala. Nurses Assn., Nat. Assn. Unknown Players, Nat. Rep. Women Assn., LaSalle Ext. U. Alumni (life). Avocations: singing, writing, speaking, reading, planting flowers. Home: 201 W Ann Dr SW Birmingham AL 35211-4935

PERRY, JAMES ALFRED, environmental scientist, consultant, science educator, director; b. Dallas, Sept. 27, 1945; BA in Fisheries, Colo. State U., 1968; MA, Western State Coll., 1973; PhD, Idaho State U., 1981. Sr. water quality specialist Idaho Div. Environ., Pocatello, 1974-82; area mgr. Centrac Assocs., Salt Lake City, 1982; H.T. Morse disting. prof. water quality U. Minn., St. Paul, 1982—, head dept. fisheries, wildlife, conservation biol., 2000—, dir. natural resources policy and mgmt., 1985—2002, dir. grad. studies in water resources, 1988—92, 1999—2001; dep. dir. AID-funded Environ. Tng. Project for Ctrl. and Ea. Europe, 1992-96; spl. asst. to dean grad. sch. U. Minn., St. Paul, 1996-2000. Vis. scholar Oxford U., Green Coll., England, 1990—91; cons. in field. Author: Water Quality Management of a Natural Resource, 1996, Ecosystem Management for Central and Eastern Europe, 2001; editor: Jour. Natural Resources and Life Scis. Edn.; mem. editl. bd. Mitigation and Adaptation Strategies for Global Change. Charter mem. Leadership Devel. Acad., Lakewood, Minn., 1988; bd. dirs. Minn. Ctr. for Environ. Advocacy, 1995–. Recipient Richard C. Newman Art of Tchg. award, 1998, Morse-Alumni award, 1999, Outstanding Svc. award U. Minn., 2001, CISW award, 2003; ACOP/ESCOP nat. leadership fellow, 1995-96, CIC acad. leadership fellow, 2000-01; PALI fellow, 2003—. Fellow: Am. Inst. Fish Resource Biology; mem.: The Soc. for Conservation Biology, The Wildlife Soc., Am. Fisheries Soc., N.Am. Benthol. Soc. (exec. bd. Albuquerque 1990—91), Internat. Soc. Theoretical and Applied Limnology, Internat. Water Resources Assn., Am. Water Resources Assn., Minn. Acad. Scis. (bd. dirs. 1987—90), Gamma Sigma Delta (merit award 2001), Xi Sigma Pi, Sigma Xi. Office: U Minn Dept Fisheries Wildlife and Conservation Biology 204 Hodson Hall 1980 Folwell Ave Saint Paul MN 55108-1037 E-mail: jperry@umn.edu.

PERRY, JAMES FREDERIC, philosophy educator, writer; b. Washington, Jan. 21, 1936; s. Albert Walter and Helene Anna Maria (Neumeyer) P.; m. Sandra Jean Huizing, Feb. 18, 1957 (div. May 1972); children: Sandra Elaine, James Frederic Jr., Bartholomew; m. Roberta Schofield, June 6, 1984. Student, Princeton U., 1953-56, Marietta (Ohio) Coll., 1958-60; BA with honors in Philosophy, Ind. U., 1962, PhD in Philosophy of Edn., 1972. NDEA fellow in philosophy U. N.C., 1962—65; instr. N.C. State U., Raleigh, 1965-66; Univ. fellow Ind. U., 1971, adj. lectr., 1972-75; prof. philosophy Hillsborough Community Coll., Tampa, Fla., 1975-97, hons. prof. philosophy, 1997—. Adj. prof. philosophy U. South Fla., 2000—. Author: Random, Routine, Reflective, 1989; contbr. articles to profl. jours. Precinct committeeman Dem. Party, Tampa, 1988—. Mem. AAUP (pres. Fla. conf. 1986-89, chair com. "A" on acad. freedom 1989-2002), C.C. Humanities Assn. (so. divsn. exec. bd. 1981-89), Am. Philos. Assn., Fla. Philos. Assn., Internat. Soc. Philos. Enquiry, Internat. Congress for Critical Thinking and Moral Critiques (founding mem. S.E. coun. 1991), World Congress Philosophy (Boston 1998, Istanbul 2003), Princeton Alumni Assn. of Fla. Suncoast (sec. 1983-86, pres. 1986-95), Mensa, Authors Guild, Textbook and Acad. Authors Assn., Nat. Collegiate Honors Coun. Avocations: travel, foreign travel, genealogy. Office: Hillsborough C C PO Box 10561 Tampa FL 33679-0561 E-mail: philart@gte.net.

PERRY, JEANNE ELYCE, principal; b. Ft. Collins, Colo., Jan. 23, 1953; d. Franklin Clyde and Ruth Caroline (Skoglund) Stewart; m. William Kay Perry, Dec. 28, 1974; children: Belinda Eve, Angela Marie. BA in Elem. Edn., Western State Coll., 1975; MA in Ednl. Leadership, U. No. Colo., 1992. Tchr. elem. sch. Soroco Sch. Dist., Oak Creek, Colo., 1977-86, L.A. Unified Sch. Dist., 1986-88; coord. elem. computer Weld RE-1 Sch. Dist., Gilcrest, Colo., 1988-93; prin. Delta (Colo.) Coun. Sch. Dist., 1993—. Leader Girl Scouts Am., Yampa, Colo., 1984-86, Platteville, Colo., 1988-89; precinct committeewoman Rep. Party, Platteville, 1991-93. Colo. Gov.'s grantee, 1990, 91. Mem. ASCD, NAESP. Baptist. Avocations: hiking, skiing, gardening, crafts. Office: Hotchkiss Elem Sch PO Box 309 Hotchkiss CO 81419-0309

PERRY, JOHN WESLEY, SR., psychotherapist; b. Elleville, Ga., Mar. 30, 1934; s. West Charles and Mary (Willie) P.; m. Alma Perry, Dec 25, 1956; children: Sheranda Pearl, John Wesley Jr., Sheree Denise. AA, Edward Waters Coll., 1955; BS, Paul Quinn Coll., 1962; MEd, Prairie View U., 1967, 74; EdD, Calif. Coast U., 1989. Cert. clinical therapist, Tex., counselors tng., U. Ark., U.S. Dept. Labor; lic. profl. counselor Tex. State Bd. Profl. Counselors. Tchr. phys. edn., coach Bremond (Tex.) High Sch., 1962-65; counselor coord. Dept. of Labor, San Marcos, Tex., 1965-70; tchr. hist. Austin (Tex.) I.S.D., 1970-71, 71-72; sch. administr. Pearce Jr. High Sch., Austin, 1971-87; state parole officer Tex. State Parole Bd., Austin, 1987-88; psychotherapist child behavior Killeen, Tex., 1988—. Trustee bd. pro tempo A.M.E. Ch., Austin; active Boy Scouts, Austin. With U.S. Army, 1955-57. Recipient Stewart certificate Grant Chapel A.M.E. Ch., Austin, 1965, Bus. Mgr. award Nat. Alumni Paul Quinn Coll. Alumni, Waco, Tex., 1978, 79, v.p. award, 1980, Outstanding Civic award United Negro Coll. Fund, 1984; grantee Chapel A. M. E. Ch. Office: Dr J Wesley Perry Therapy Clinic 600 S Gray St Killeen TX 76541-7140

PERRY, JOYCE FITZWILLIAM, secondary school educator; b. San Francisco, Aug. 12, 1946; d. Leo Matthew and Mildred E. (McBain) Fitzwilliam; m. Robert James Perry, June 21, 1969 (div. Apr. 1980); children: Dominic Matthew, Alex Michael. BA, Gonzaga U., 1968; M in Counseling, U. Phoenix, 1995. Cert. tchr., nat. cert. counselor, Ariz. Middle sch. lang. arts and social studies tchr. Frank Odle Jr. High, Bellevue, Wash., 1969-72, Greenway Middle Sch., Phoenix, 1979-82, Sunrise Middle Sch., Scottsdale, Ariz., 1982—2002, Mountain Trail Middle Sch., Phoenix, 2002—. Mem. evaluation team North Ctrl. Schs. Accreditation, Ariz., 1988-90. Author: Seasons of the Heart, 1982. Named Middle Level Educator of Yr., Ctrl. Ariz. Middle Level Assn., 1994. Mem. ACA, Phi Delta Kappa.

PERRY, MARION J.H. English educator; b. Takoma Park, Md., June 2, 1943; d. Armin Werner and Adah Hubbard (Porter) Helz; m. Franklyn Alfred Perry, Jr., July 17, 1971; children: Aurelia, Scott. BA, Ripon (Wis.) Coll., 1964; MA, U. Iowa, 1966; MFA, 1969; MA, U. Buffalo, 1979, PhD, 1986. Instr. West Liberty (W.Va.) State Coll., 1966-68, Albright Coll., Reading, Pa., 1968-70; lectr. SUNY-EOC, Buffalo, N.Y., 1970-74; mentor Empire State Coll., Buffalo, N.Y., 1978-81; prof. English Lit. Erie C.C., Orchard Park, N.Y., 1980—. Dir. Women's Ctr. Erie C.C., Orchard Park, N.Y., 1989-95. Author: (poetry) Establishing Intimacy, 1982, Dishes, 1989, The Mirror's Image, 1981, Icarus, 1980; pub., founder (on-line mag) Word Worth. Mem., v.p. League of Women Voters, E. Aurora, N.Y., 1987-92; sec. bd. dirs. ECC Found., Buffalo, N.Y., 1989-99. Recipient Woman of Yr. award Bus. and Profl. Women, Orchard Park, N.Y., 1994, All Nations Poetry Contest Triton Coll., River Grove, Ill., 1980-81. Mem. Nat. Coun. Tchrs. English, Poetry Soc. Am., Phi Delta Kappa. Office: Erie Community College S 4041 SW Blvd Orchard Park NY 14127-2199 E-mail: mhperry@www.word-worth.com.

PERRY, PAMELA JO, mathematician, educator; b. Little Rock, May 10, 1962; d. C.B. and Patricia Jo (Swindle) White; m. Nathan Lee Perry, Oct. 24, 1981; children: Cortney Lynn, Jesse Lee, Jared Lane. BS in Edn., U. Ctrl. Ark., 1985. Cert. tchr. math. and sci. Tchr. migrant Pangburn (Ark.) Sch., 1985-86; tchr. math./sci. Midland H.S., Pleasant Plains, Ark., 1987-90, Pangburn H.S., 1990—. Mem. Nat. Coun. Tchrs. Math. Republican. Baptist. Avocations: swimming, basketball, reading, horseback riding, teaching sunday school. Office: Pangburn HS 1100 Short St Pangburn AR 72121-8836

PERRY, RAYMOND CARVER, education educator; b. Anaheim, Calif., July 6, 1906; s. Arthur Raymond and Helen (Carver) P.; m. Evelyn Lucile Wright, July 7, 1940; children: Douglas Wright, David Wright. AB, Stanford U., 1926; MA, U. So. Calif., L.A., 1928, EdD, 1933. Cert. psychologist, Calif. Secondary tchr. Mexia (Tex.) Sch. Dist., 1926-27; elem. tchr. Artesia (Calif.) Sch. Dist., 1927-28; tchr. jr. high L.A. Sch. Dist., 1928-30, tchr. jr. coll., 1930-35; prof. and dean San Diego State Coll., 1935-40; divsn. chief Calif. Dept. Edn., Sacramento, 1940-45; prof. edn. U. So. Calif., L.A., 1945-72, prof. edn. emeritus, 1972—. Curriculum cons., psychologist Fontana (Calif.) Sch. Dist., 1947-51; curriculum survey staff Melbo Assocs., L.A., 1948-71; curriculum cons. Sulphur Springs Sch. Dist., L.A. County, 1965-69. Author: Basic Mathematics for College Students, 1957, Group Factor Analysis of Adjustment Questionnaire, 1934, Cross My Heart, 1990; co-author: Review of Educational Research, 1965. Svc. group rep. City Coordination Coun., Long Beach, Calif., 1933-35. Lt. comdr. USNR, 1942-45. Mem. Nat. Coun. Tchrs. Math., Andrus Ctr. Assocs., U. So. Calif. Ret. Faculty, Phi Delta Kappa (San Diego chpt. pres. 1935-40). Republican. Presbyterian. Avocations: photography, travel.

PERRY, RICHARD LEE, retired academic administrator, physics educator; b. Portland, Oreg., Jan. 22, 1930; s. William McGuire and Emily Ruth Perry; m. Ruth Corrine Ferrell, June 13, 1952; children: Dawn, Glenn, Craig, Stella. BA, Linfield Coll., 1952; MS, Oreg. State Coll., 1955; PhD, Oreg. State U., 1961. Assoc. physicist Linfield Rsch. Inst., McMinnville, Oreg., 1956-61; asst. prof. U. of the Pacific, Stockton, Calif., 1961-65, assoc. prof., 1965-71, prof., 1971-97, prof. emeritus, 1997—, chair physics dept., 1987-96. Cons. Thompson Ramo-Wooldridge, Inc., Canoga Park, Calif., 1962-63; cons. physicist Tektronix, Inc., Beaverton, Oreg., summers 1963, 64, U.S. Army Nuclear Def. Lab., Edgewood Arsenal, Md., 1968-69; rsch. scientist, cons. NASA/Ames Rsch. Ctr., Moffett Field, Calif., summers 1978, 79, 80, 81, 83, 84. Contbr. articles to profl. jours. AEC fellow, 1967, NASA/ASEE fellow, 1975, 76. Republican. Avocations: church, travel. Home: PO Box 48 Valley Springs CA 95252-0048

PERRY, ROBERT, fine arts and performing arts educator; b. New Bedford, Mass., July 13, 1938; s. Antone and Mary (Sousa) P.; m. Elaine Delores Amaral, Sept. 5, 1959; children: LeslieAnn, Robert Jr., John Robert. B Music Edn. magna cum laude, U. Mass., Lowell, 1965; MusM, Boston U., 1972; EdD, U. Mass., Amherst, 1993. Cert. music tchr., supr., Mass. Jr. H.S. music tchr. Somerset (Mass.) Pub. Schs., 1965-66, supr. music grades K-8, 1966-69, supr. music grades K-12, 1969-94, coord. find and performing arts, 1994—2001; coord. music edn. U. Mass., Lowell, 1992-93. Asst. student tchrs. Barrington (R.I.) Coll., 1973-77, Westfield (Mass.) State Coll., 1978-83; condr. marching band workshops Boston Conservatory, 1977-78; mem. focus com. Edn. Reform, Mass., 1993—; adj. faculty R.I. Coll., 2000—; cons. in field, 1993—. Contbr. articles to profl. publs. Bd. dirs. Somerset Friends of Music, 1972—; pres. Somerset Arts Coun., 1980-82; founder Carl McDermott Scholarship, Somerset, 1987—; condr. R.I. All State Jr. H.S. Band, 1987, All Star Brasses, Zeiterion Theatre, New Bedford, Mass., 1994-95; organizer Somerset Friends of Music, Musictown Festivals, 1972; asst. mgr. Mass. All State Band, 1981, mgr., 1982; chair Mass. All State Concert, 1992; mem. Touch of Brass Quintet, 1980—. Mem. Mass. Music Educators Assn. (pres. elect 1993-95, pres. 1995—, Lowell Mason award 1992, Disting. Svc. award 1998), Internat. Trumpet Guild, Somerset Adminstrs. Assn. (treas. 1982—2000), Educators Nat. Conf. Avocations: running, painting, Aikido, reading, camping. Home: 51 Robin Ln Somerset MA 02726-3540 Office: Somerset Pub Schs 580 Whetstone Hill Rd Somerset MA 02726-3702

PERRY, RUTH ANNA, English language educator; b. Edenton, N.C., Nov. 22, 1937; d. Walter H. and Agnes E. (Bond) Perry. BS, Hampton (Va.) Inst., 1959, MA, 1967; PhD, Auburn (Ala.) U., 1980. Tchr. English Nash County (N.C.) Pub. Schs., 1959-64, Virginia Beach (Va.) Pub. Schs., 1964-68; coord. English Norfolk (Va.) State U., 1968—. Author: Materials for English 207, 1992; co-author, editor: Variations on Humankind: An Introduction to World Literature, 1992. Judge for pub. speaking 4-H Clubs Ann. Contest, Suffolk, Va., 1986—; organist Mineral Spring Bapt. Ch., Suffolk, 1968—; vol. SHARE, Norfolk, Va., 1990. Recipient Cert. of Recognition, Edn. Achievement Award, Service award, Norfolk State U.; named Outstanding Auburn Woman Graduate, 1992. Mem. MLA, South Atlantic MLA, Coll. Lang. Assn., Va. Assn. Tchrs. English, Mid Atlantic Writers Assn., Nat. Coun. Tchrs. English, Order Eastern Star (star point 1989—), Zeta Phi Beta (local pres. 1984-88, Achievement award 1980, Appreciation Svc. award 1979, 89). Avocations: reading, playing the piano, attending sports events and musical concerts. Home: 2610 Beachmont Ave Norfolk VA 23504-3704

PERRY, WILLIAM JAMES, education educator, former federal official; b. Vandergrift, Pa., Oct. 11, 1927; s. Edward Martin and Mabelle Estelle (Dunlap) Perry; m. Leonilla Green, Dec. 29, 1947; children: David, William, Rebecca, Robin, Mark. BS in Math., Stanford U., 1949, MS, 1950; PhD, Pa. State U., 1957. Instr. math. Pa. State U., 1951—54; sr. mathematician HRB-Singer Co., State College, Pa., 1952—54; dir. electronic def. labs. GTE Sylvania Co., Mountain View, Calif., 1954—64; founder & pres. ESL, Inc., Sunnyvale, Calif., 1964—77; tech. cons. Dept. Def., Washington, 1967—77, under sec. def. for research and engring., 1977—81; mng. dir. Hambrecht & Quist (investment bankers), San Francisco, 1981—85; chmn. Tech. Strategies & Alliances, Menlo Park, Calif., 1985—93; prof., co-dir. Ctr. for Internat. Security and Arms Control Stanford U., 1989—93; appt. Dep. Sec. Def. Pentagon, Washington, 1993—94, appt. Sec. Def., 1994—97; prof. engring.-econ. sys. and ops. rsch. Stanford (Calif.) U., 1997—, sr. fellow, Hoover Inst., 1997—, co-dir., Preventive Defense Project, 1997—; chmn. Global Tech. Ptnrs. With U.S. Army, 1946—47. Recipient Def. Disting. Svc. medal, U.S. Govt., 1980, 1981, Achievement medal, Am. Electronics Assn., 1980, Forrestal medal, 1994, Henry Stimson medal, 1994, Arthur Bueche medal, NAE, 1996, Eisenhower award, 1996, Presdl. Medal Freedom, 1997, Outstanding Civilian Svc. medals, U.S. Army, 1997, USN, 1997, USAF, 1997, USCG, 1997, NASA, 1981, Def. Intelligence Agy., 1997; fellow sr. fellow, Inst. Internat. Studies, Stanford U., 1997—. Mem.: bd. dirs., Anteon Internat. Corp. Office: Stanford University CISAC Encina Hall Stanford CA 94305 Fax: 650-725-0920. E-mail: wjperry@stanford.edu.*

PERRYMAN, BILLY PAT, elementary educator; b. San Antonio, July 17, 1959; s. Billy J. and Patricia (Baker) P. BS, S.W. Tex. State U., 1982, MEd, 1983. Cert. elem. tchr., Tex. Tchr. reading Bulverde Mid. Sch. Comal Ind. Sch. Dist., New Braunfels, Tex., 1983-84, tchr. Frazier Elem. Sch., 1984-88; tchr. Stahl Elem. Sch., N.E. Ind. Sch. Dist., San Antonio, 1988-91, tchr. Oak Meadow Elem. Sch., 1991—, mem. dist. ednl. improvement coun., 1991-93. Recipient Ray Berdelen award for excellence in teaching Stahl Elem. Sch., 1990, Elem. Tchr. of Yr. award N.E. Ind. Sch. Dist., 1990, Disting. Educator of Bexar County award N.E. Ind. Sch. Dist. and Trinity U., Supt.'s award, 1992-93. Mem. N.E. Alamo Area Coun. Social Studies (pres. 1992-93), San Antonio Conservation Soc. (assoc.), Oil City A's Antique Car Club (sec. 1989—). Avocations: travel, antique cars, trains, history. Office: BJP Inc RR 2 Box 194 Luling TX 78648-9506

PERRYMAN-JOINES, KEITH (KEITH P. JOINES), school counselor; b. N.Y.C., Sept. 15, 1948; s. James Leslie Perryman Sr. and Alydia Louisa (Frank) Joines; m. Agnes Louise Cruse, July 7, 1977; 1 child, Keith Perryman-Joines II. BA, U. Bridgeport, 1970, MS, 1972, CAS, 1983. Group dynamics coord. Upward Bound, Bridgeport, Conn., 1971-75; head tchr., project dir. Spred Learning Ctr., Wilton, Conn., 1972-73; job developer, counselor Harding Prep. Program, Bridgeport, 1973-75; deputy dir. G.W. Carver Found., Norwalk, Conn., 1975-76; program dir. Hall Neighborhood House, Bridgeport, Conn., 1976-77; ops. coord. CETA-ETA Summer Youth Program, Bridgeport, 1977-79, dir., 1979-81; guidance counselor East Side Mid. Sch., Bridgeport, 1976-81; sch. counselor Bassick High Sch., Bridgeport, 1981—; coll. counselor Housatonic Community Tech. Coll., Bridgeport, 1983-94. Summer N.Y.C. supr. Hall Neighborhood House, Bridgeport, 1975-77; cons. Kolbe Alt. Sch., Bridgeport, 1976-77, Effectiveness Tng. Assocs., Trumbull, Conn., 1976-81; recreation leader Parks and Recreation Dept., Bridgeport, 1977-79; tutor Orcutt Boys Club, Bridgeport, 1976-77; presenter in field. Bd. dirs. Youth Outreach & Prevention Ctrs., Bridgeport, 1975, Planned Parenthood, Bridgeport, 1973-77, New Haven, Conn., 1974; mem. com. to elect Mullane, Bridgeport, 1976; presenter N.E. Regional Coll. Bd., 1989, 95. Recipient Cmty. Svc. Plaque Big Bros./Big Sisters, 1995. Mem. New England Assn. Coll. Admission Counselors (scholar 1989), Conn. Coun. Personel Assocs., Conn. Assn. Latin Ams. Higher Edn. (Community Svc. plaque 1988), Conn. Sch. Counselor Assn., Bridgeport Edn. Assn. (v.p. 1984-86, Save Our Babies award, Community Svc. plaque 1990). Republican. Roman Catholic. Avocations: bicycling, travel. Home: 100 Weaver St Torrington CT 06790-5721 Office: Bassick High Sch 1181 Fairfield Ave Bridgeport CT 06605-1100

PERSAUD, TRIVEDI VIDHYA NANDAN, anatomy educator, researcher, consultant; b. Port Mourant, Berbice, Guyana, Feb. 19, 1940; arrived in Canada, 1972; s. Ram Nandan and Deen (Raggy) P.; m. Gisela Gerda Zehden, Jan. 29, 1966; children: Indrani Uta and Sunita Heidi (twins), Rainer Narendra. MD, Rostock U., Germany, 1965, DSc, 1974; PhD in Anatomy, U. West Indies, Kingston, Jamaica, 1970. Intern, Berlin, Germany, 1965-66; govtl. med. officer, 1966-67; lectr., sr. lectr. anatomy dept. U. West Indies, 1967-72; assoc. prof. anatomy dept. U. Man., Winnipeg, 1972-75, prof., 1975—, prof. ob-gyn., reproductive scis., 1979-99, prof. emeritus, 1999—, prof. pediatrics and child health, 1989—, prof., chmn./head dept. human anatomy & cell sci., 1977-93, dir. Teratology Rsch. Lab., 1972-97. Cons. in teratology, Children's Centre, Winnipeg, 1973—; mem. sci. staff Health Scis. Centre, Winnipeg, 1973—. Author, editor 22 med. textbooks, including: Early History of Human Anatomy: From Antiquity to the Beginning of the Modern Era, 1984, (with others) Basic Concepts in Teratology, 1985, Environmental Causes of Human Birth Defects, 1991, History of Human Anatomy: The Post-Vesalian Era, 1997, (with K.L. Moore) The Developing Human, 7th edit., 2003, Before We Are Born, 6th edit., 2003; rev. Medical Embryology, 6th edit., 2003; contbr. numerous chpts. to books, over 200 articles to profl. jours. Recipient Carveth Jr. Scientist award Can. Assn. Pathologists, 1974, Albert Einstein Centennial medal German Acad. Scis., 1975, Dr. & Mrs. H.H. Saunderson award U. Manitoba, 1985, 12th Raymond Truex Disting. Lectureship award Hahnemann U., 1990, Queen Elizabeth II Golden Jubilee medal Govt. Can., 2003. Fellow Royal Coll. Pathologists of London; mem. Can. Assn. Anatomists (pres. 1981-83, J.C.B. Grant award 1991), Am. Assn. Anatomists, Teratology Soc., European Teratology Soc. Office: U Man Dept Anatomy & Cell Sci 730 William Ave Winnipeg MB Canada R3E OW3 E-mail: persaud@ms.umanitoba.ca.

PERSINGER, HOWARD MOSES, JR., educational association administrator; b. Williamson, W.Va., Apr. 18, 1937; m. Jeanne Chafin; children: Howard III, Holly, Courtney. B in English, Davidson Coll., 1959; JD, U. Va., 1964. Mem. W.Va. State Bd. Edn., Charleston, 2000—, pres., 2002—; lawyer Williamson, 1964—. Mem. Mingo County Bd. Edn., 1977—82, 1998—2002, pres., 1998—2000; mem. County Redevelopment Authority; mem., trustee First Presbyn. Ch., Williamson; bd. dirs. Fellowship Christian Athletes. With U.S. Army, 1959—61, capt. USAR. Mem.: W.Va. Bar Assn. (pres. 2000—01, mem. ethics com. 1986—87, bd. govs. 1987—90, mem. character com. 1995—2000), Va. Bar Assn., Pa. Bar Assn., Ky. Bar Assn., Kiwanis Club Williamson (bd. dirs., Kiwanian of the Yr. 1992). Office: State Bd Edn Bldg 6 Rm 351 1900 Kanawha Blvd Charleston WV 25305-0330*

PERSON, RUTH JANSSEN, academic administrator; b. Washington, Aug. 27, 1945; d. Theodore Armin and Ruth Katherine (Mahoney) Janssen. BA, Gettysburg (Pa.) Coll., 1967; AMLS, U. Mich., 1969, PhD, 1980; MS in Adminstrn., George Washington U., 1974. Head of reference/asst. prof. Thomas Nelson C.C., Hampton, Va., 1971-74; lectr. U. Mich., Ann Arbor, 1975-79, coord. of continuing edn., 1977-79; asst. prof. Cath. U., Washington, 1979-85, assoc. prof., 1985-86, assoc. dean Sch. of Libr. and Info. Sci., 1983-86; dean Coll. Libr. Sci. Clarion (Pa.) U., 1986-88; assoc. vice chancellor U. Mo., St. Louis, 1988-93; v.p. for acad. affairs Ashland (Ohio) U., 1993-95; v.p. acad. affairs, prof. bus. adminstrn. Angelo State U., San Angelo, Tex., 1995-99; chancellor, prof. bus. Ind. U., Kokomo, Ind., 1999—. Reviewer U.S. Dept. Edn., Washington, 1987-89, 92; trustee Pitts. Regional Libr. Ctr., 1986-88; chair publs. com. Assn. of Coll. and Rsch. Librs., Chgo., 1986-90; cons. United Way, Alexandria, Va., 1985; cons.-evaluator North Ctrl. Assn., 1993-95, 2000—; nat. vis. com. Southwest Ctr. Advanced Tech. Edn., 1996-98; Health Profs. Edn. Adv. Com.; faculty workload com. Tex. Higher Edn. Coord. Bd., 1998-99; Higher Edn. Info. Sys. Com.; mem. adv. bd. KeyBank, 1999-2001; bd. dirs. Steak n Shake Co.

Co-editor: (book) Academic Libraries: Their Role and Rationale in Higher Education, 1995; editor: (book) The Management Process, 1983; editl. bd. Coll. & Rsch. Librs., 1990-96; contr. articles to profl. jours. Mem. Strategic Planning Task Force, Ashland C. of C., 1994; bd. dirs. Alternatives for Living in Violent Environs., Inc., St. Louis, 1992-94, San Angelo Cultural Affairs Coun., 1998-99; commr. Commn. for Women, Anne Arundel County, Md., 1984-86; mem. Citizens Adv. Bd., Clarion, Pa., 1986-88; mem. Olivette, Mo. Human Rels. Commn., 1992-94, San Angelo Bus. and Profl. Women's Club, 1995-99, pres.-elect, 1996-97, pres., 1997—; mem. bldg. design oversight com. San Angelo Mus. Fine Arts, 1995-99; mem. com. Cactus Jazz Festival, 1995-99; bd. dirs. San Angelo Bus. and Edn. Coalition, 1997-99, San Angelo Cultural Affairs Coun., 1998-99; bd. dirs. Ind. Tech. Partnership, 2001-03, YWCA, Kokomo, 2000-02, Workforce Investment Bd., 2002—; mem. adv. bd. St. Joseph's Hosp., 2000, Ind. SDBC, 2002—; trustee Howard County Pub. Libr., 2002—. Fellow Am. Coun. Edn., 1990, Harvard Inst. Ednl. Mgmt., 1989, Rackham fellow U. Mich., 1976; ACE fellow Ariz. Bd. Regents, 1990-91; recipient Washington Woman award Washington Woman mag., 1986. Mem.: ALA (com. on accreditation 1993—97), Am. Assn. State Colls. and Univs. (mem. profl. devel. com. 2001), Howard County C. of C. (women's bus. coun. 2000—), Coun. for the Preservation of Anthropol. Records (bd. dirs.), Am. Assn. Univ. Adminstrs. (bd. dirs. 1993—95, v.p. elect 2001—), Beta Gamma Sigma, Phi Alpha Theta, Kappa Delta Pi, Pi Lambda Theta, Beta Phi Mu, Psi Chi. Lutheran. Avocations: piano, herb gardening, antiques, cooking, sailing. Office: Ind U Kokomo PO Box 9003 2300 S Washington St Kokomo IN 46904

PERSONETTE, LOUISE METZGER (SISTER MARY ROGER METZGER), mathematics educator; b. Indpls., Dec. 21, 1925; d. Frank Alexander and Frances Lee Ann (Durham) Metzger; m. Marlen William Personette, Dec. 9, 1967 (div. Dec. 1985); 1 stepson: Lyle Scott. BS in Elem. Edn., Athenaeum of Ohio, 1952; MEd, Xavier U., 1964. Nun St. Francis Convent, Oldenburg, Ind., 1942—67; elem. tchr. Cath. Schs., Cin., 1945-56, secondary math tchr. Middletown, Ohio, 1957-63, Evansville, Ind., 1964-65, Hamilton, Ohio, 1966-67; elem. tchr. Kent (Wash.) Schs., 1968-72, math specialist, 1973-82;. math cons. greater Seattle Schs., 1983—; GED instr. Muckleshoot Indian Tribe, Auburn, Wash., 1998—2000. Dir. Heatherhill Edn. Ctr., Kent, 1982—, Homework House, Kent, 1987—90; adj. instr. Seattle Pacific U., 1975—95, City U., Seattle, 1975—95; SAT prep. math tutor, 2002—. Co-author: S.O.S. Story Problems, 1980. Mem. Nat. Coun. Tchrs. Math., Math. Assn. Am., Washington State Math Coun., Puget Sound Coun. Tchrs. Math., New Horizons. Home and Office: Heatherhill Education Ctr 11830 SE 263rd Ct Kent WA 98031-8407 E-mail: louisamath@msn.com.

PERTEET, ICY D. secondary education educator; b. Kosciusko, Miss., Nov. 28, 1952; d. Claude Sr. and Katie Joiner; m. Ray Kenny Perteet, Sept. 17, 1971; children: Kenny De Von, Iginar De Mentria. AA, Holmes C.C., Goodman, Miss., 1973; BS, Miss. U. for Women, 1976. Vocat. preperation tchr. Choctaw County Sch., Ackerman, Miss., 1976-83, family and consumer sci. instr. Weir, Miss., 1983-97; family and consumer sci./career discovery instr. Attala County Sch. and Ethel H.S., McAdams, Miss., 1997—. Advisor Family career, Cmty. Leader of Am., McAdams, Miss., 1997—; pres. Tech. Prep. Adv. Bd., McAdams, 1999—. Book reviewer: Family Today, 1999. Life Attala County Youth Choir, Kosciusko, 1990-91; life mem., troop leader Girl Scouts, Kosciusko, 1991-2000; mem. adv. bd. Partnership for a Health Attala County, Kosciusko, 1997-2000. Mem.: NEA, Miss. Assn. Educators, Attala County Assn. Educators (bldg. contact person 1998—2003, sec.), Miss. Assn. Family and Consumer Sci. Educators (pres. 1996—97), Toastmasters Internat., Coun. Christian Women (pres. 1987—), Gamma Beta Phi, Phi Upsilon Omicron (sec. 1975—2003). Baptist. Avocations: reading, collecting angels, gardening, traveling. Home: RR 1 Box 232C Sallis MS 39160-9753 Office: Attala County Sch Dist RR 1 Box 2320 Sallis MS 39160-9801

PERTUZ, MARCIA JANE, primary school educator; b. Buffalo, Nov. 18, 1945; d. Richard Lee and Betty Jeanne (Gazdick) Fleming; m. Alvaro E. Pertuz, Aug. 19, 1967; children: Juliana Lee Abbott, Brett Alan. B of Edn., SUNY, 1967; MEd, U. Minn., 1993, Harvard U., 2000. Cert. elem. tchr., Mass.; nat. bd. cert. early childhood generalist. Tchr. Coconut Grove Elem. Sch., Miami, Fla., 1967-68, Cedar Lake Elem. Sch., Oscoda, Mich., 1968-69, St. Francis Sch., Rochester, Minn., 1980-82; dir. Hugs and Hearts Day Care Ctr., Edina, Minn., 1983-87; tchr. Woods Acad., Maple Plain, Minn., 1987-88, Longfellow Internat. Fine Arts Magnet Sch., Mpls., 1988-89, Ramsey Internat. Fine Arts Sch., Mpls., 1989-91, Downtown Open Sch., Mpls., 1991-93, La Escuela Fratney, Milw., 1993-95, Amigos Sch., Cambridge, Mass., 1995—. Vol. proof reader Rethinking Schs., Milw., 1993-95; mem. Jr. League, Mpls., Milw. and Mass., 1993-2002; sec. bd. dirs. Olmstead County Coun. Coordinated Child Care, Rochester, 1976-78; mem. adv. bd. Parents Anonymous, Mpls., 1978-79. Named Wis. Tchr. World Wis. Dept. Edn., LaCrosse, 1994. Home: 46 Concord Sq # 3 Boston MA 02118-3102 E-mail: marcia_pertuz@post.harvard.edu.

PERUMPRAL, JOHN VERGHESE, agricultural engineer, administrator, educator; b. Trivandrum, Kerala, India, Jan. 14, 1939; came to U.S., 1963; s. Verghese John and Sarah (Geverghese) P.; m. Shalini Elizabeth Alexander, Dec. 27, 1965; children: Anita Sarah, Sunita Anna. BS in Agrl. Engring., Allahabad (UP India) U., 1962; MS in Agrl. Engring., Purdue U., 1965, PhD, 1969. Postdoctoral rsch. assoc. agrl. engring. dept. Purdue U., West Lafayette, Ind., 1969-70; asst. prof. agrl. engring. dept. Va. Poly. Inst. and State U., Blacksburg, 1970-78, assoc. prof., 1978-83, prof., 1983-86, Wm. S. Cross Jr. prof., head dept. biol. systems engring., 1986—. Author more than 100 tech. publis. including articles in scholarly and profl. jours. Mem. Am. Soc. Agrl. Engring. (outstanding faculty award student br. 1976, 81, cert. teaching excellence 1979, assoc. editor, transaction of ASAE 1985-86), Fluid Power Soc., Sigma Xi, Alpha Epsilon. Presbyterian. Office: Va Poly Inst and State U Biol Sys Engring Dept Blacksburg VA 24061

PERUZZI, WILLIAM THEODORE, anesthesiologist, intensivist, educator; b. Sharon, Pa., Aug. 31, 1956; MD, Ohio State U., 1984. Diplomate Am. Bd. Anesthesiology. Rotating intern Ohio State U., Columbus, 1984-85, resident in anesthesiology, 1985-87; fellow in critical care medicine Northwestern Meml. Hosp., Chgo., 1987-88, chief sect. critical care medicine, 1991—; assoc. prof. anesthesiology Northwestern U. Sch. Medicine, Chgo., 1991—. Fellow Am. Coll. Critical Care Medicine, Am. Coll. Chest Physicians; mem. AMA, Am. Soc. Anesthesiologists, Am. Soc. Critial Care Anesthesiologists, Am. Assn. Respiratory Care, Soc. Critical Care Medicine, Chgo. Med. Soc., Ill. Med. Soc., Ill. Soc. Anesthesiologists. Office: Northwestern Meml Hosp Feinberg Pavilion 251 E Huron St Ste 8-336 Chicago IL 60611-2908

PERYON, CHARLEEN D. education educator, consultant; b. Milw., Apr. 29, 1931; d. Raymond James Dolphin and Violet Selma Solheim Dolphin Berendes; m. Robert Edward Peryon, Nov. 21, 1953; children: Anne Marie Peryon Noonan, Robert Louis, Lynne Marie Peryon Lang. BA in Biology, Clarke Coll., Dubuque, Iowa, 1953; cert. med. tech., St. Anthony Hosp. Sch. Med. Technology, Rockford, Ill., 1954; MEd in Clin. Reading, U. Guam, 1972; PhD in Spl. Edn., Utah State U., 1979. Cert. tchr. Ill., Iowa; cert. cons. Iowa; cert. sch. adminstr. Utah. Tchr. sci. LaGrange (Ill.) Schs., 1966-68, Washington Sr. High Sch., Mangiloa, Guam, 1968-70; asst. prof. edn. U. Guam, Mangiloa, 1970-71; reading specialist Dept. Edn. Territory of Guam, Agana, 1971-73, state curriculum cons., 1973-75; assoc. prof. reading and spl. edn. U. Guam, Mangiloa, 1975-85; assoc. prof. reading and learning disabilities Clarke Coll., Dubuque, 1985-86; spl. edn. cons. Keystone Area Edn. Agy., Dubuque, 1986-89; prof. spl. edn. U. Dubuque, 1989—. Cons. in field. Author: Distar Teacher Aide's Handbook, 1974; co-auuthor: Reading Specialist's Handbook, 1973; mem. editorial bd. U. Guam Press, Manigloa, 1983-85; contbr. numerous articles to profl. jours. Trustee Cascade Libr. Bd. Recipient spl. award U.S. Dept. Def. Sch. Dist., Manila, 1976, Internat. Reading Assn. of Newark, 1975. Mem. Internat. Reading Assn. (pres. Guam chpt. 1973-74, chmn. Pacific area 1973-75), Coun. for Exceptional Children (pres. 1992-93), Am. Soc. Clin. Pathologists, Phi Delta Kappa (historian 1977-78, 83-84), Chi Omicron Gamma (pres. 1982-84), Kappa Delta Pi (counselor 1993) Roman Catholic. Avocations: reading, music, cooking, camping, tennis, riding. Home: PO Box 127 Cascade IA 52033-0127

PESCE, PHYLLIS ANNE, elementary education educator; b. N.Y.C., Apr. 14, 1956; d. Paul and Anna F. Pesce. BS in Edn., Slippery Rock (Pa.) State U., 1979; student, Kutztown (Pa.) State U.; postgrad., Kean Coll., Union, N.J., William Paterson Coll., Wayne, N.J., Pace U. Cert. elem and art tchr., N.Y., N.J., Pa. Tchr. family living and sex edn. N.Y.C. Bd. Edn., Bronx, 1985-93; tchr. art edn., art specialist K-8 Jersey City Bd. Edn., 1993—. Workshop leader; presenter for N.E. Regional Ctr. to Phila. and Syracuse (N.Y.) Sch. Dists., Nat. Art Edn. Assn. conv., San Francisco, 1996, Chgo., 1998, Art Educators N.J., 1993—. Mem. adv. com. dist. 12BX AIDS, Substance, Child, and Sexual Abuse Prevention; presenter, mem. AIDS Outreach Project Bronx Teams. Arts for Every Kid grantee, 1995; Tchr. as Artist Participant grantee, 1993-97. Mem. ASCD, SABE, PSA, AAHPERD and SAFE Inst., Nat. Art. Edn. Assn., Art Educators N.J. (curriculum com. 1998), N.J. Edn. Assn., League of Schs. (presenter), Responsive Edn. Inst. (liaison, accelerated schs. tnr., NE Regional Ctr. presenter), Delta Zeta. Avocations: pottery, painting. Office: Pub Sch 39 Plainfield Ave Jersey City NJ 07306

PESCH, LEROY ALLEN, physician, educator, health and hospital consultant, business executive; b. Mt. Pleasant, Iowa, June 22, 1931; s. Herbert Lindsey and Mary Clarissa (Tyner) P.; children from previous marriage: Christopher Allen, Brian Lindsey, Daniel Ethan; m. Donna J. Stone, Dec. 28, 1975 (dec. Feb. 1985); stepchildren: Christopher Scott Kneifel, Linda Suzanne Kneifel; m. Gerri Ann Cotton, Sept. 27, 1986; 1 child, Tyner Ford. Student, State U. Iowa, 1948-49, Iowa State U., 1950-52; MD cum laude, Washington U., St. Louis, 1956. Intern Barnes Hosp., St. Louis, 1956-57; rsch. assoc. NIH, Bethesda, Md., 1957-59; asst. resident medicine Grace-New Haven Hosp., New Haven, 1959-60; clin. fellow Yale Med. Sch., New Haven, 1960-61, instr. medicine, 1961-62, asst. prof. medicine, 1962-63, asst. dir. liver study unit, 1961-63; assoc. physician Grace-New Haven Hosp., 1961-63; assoc. prof. medicine Rutgers U., New Brunswick, N.J., 1963-64, prof., 1964-66, chmn. dept. medicine, 1965-66; assoc. dean, prof. medicine Stanford Sch. Medicine, 1966-68; mem. gen. medicine study sect. NIH, 1965-70, chmn., 1969-70; dean, dir. univ. hosps. SUNY, Buffalo, 1968-71; dep. asst. sec. manpower HEW, 1970-72, spl. cons. to sec. for health, 1970-75; prof. div. biol. scis. and medicine U. Chgo., 1972-77; prof. pathology Northwestern U., 1977-79; health and hosp. cons.; chmn., chief exec. officer Health Resources Corp. Am., 1981-84; chmn. bd. dirs. Republic Health Corp., 1985-88; chmn., chief exec. officer The Bora Health Group, Seattle, 1987-92; pres. Genus Tech. Corp., 1987—; chmn., chief exec. officer The Pesch Group Cos., Sun Valley, Idaho, 1989—. Contbr. articles on internal medicine to profl. jours. Bd. dirs. Buffalo Med. Found., 1969-72, Health Orgn., Western N.Y., 1968-71, Joffrey Ballet, N.Y.C., 1980—; trustee Michael Reese Hosp. and Med. Ctr., Chgo., 1971-76, pres., CEO, 1971-77; mem. exec. bd. Auditorium Theatre Coun., Chgo.; trustee W. Clement and Jessie V. Stone Found.; mem. adv. com. Congl. Awards; pres. Pesch Found. Sr. asst. surgeon USPHS, 1957-59. Mem. AAAS, Am. Assn. Study of Liver Diseases, Am. Fedn. Clin. Rsch., Am. Soc. Biol. Chemists, Quadrangle Club, Acapulco Yacht Club, Sigma Xi, Alpha Omega Alpha. E-mail: allenp@cox-internet.com.

PESCHEL, JO ANN, secondary school educator; b. New Ulm, Tex., July 24, 1939; d. Lloyd Otto and Hertha (Blezinger) P. BS, U. Houston, 1962, MEd, 1972. Cert. tchr. health and phys. edn., Tex. Tchr., coach Hungerford (Tex.) Ind. Sch. Dist., 1962-64, Klein (Tex.) Ind. Sch. Dist., 1964-72, tchr., 1972—. Mem. NEA, Tex. State Tchrs. Assn., Iota Epsilon (Delta Kappa Gamma legis. chmn.). Mem. Dr. Evangelical Lutheran Ch. E-mail: joannp1038@aol.com.

PESTERFIELD, LINDA CAROL, retired school administrator, educator; b. Pauls Valley, Okla., May 3, 1939; d. D.J. and Geneva Lewis (Sheegog) Butler; m. W.C. Peterfield, Aug. 30, 1958; children: Ginger Carol, Walt James, Jason Kent. Student. E. Cen. State U., Ada, Okla., 1957, 76, 79; BS, Okla. State U., 1961; postgrad., Ottawa U., Ottawa, Kans., 1970, Okla. U., 1979. Tchr. Sumner Elem. Sch., Perry, Okla., 1961-62; tchr. Whitebead D-16, Pauls Valley, Okla., 1964-65, Cen. Heights Unified, Ottawa, Kans., 1969-71; prin., tchr. Whitebead D-16, Pauls Valley, 1975-91; adminstrv. asst., curriculum dir. Pauls Valley Sch., P.V., 1991—2003; ret., 2003. Mem. profl. standard bd. State Dept. Edn., Okla., 1988—; presenter in field. Bd. dirs. Positively Pauls Valley, 1987-97; county chmn. Nat. and Okla. 4-H Fund Drive, Garvin County, Okla., 1987-88; mem. organizational com. C-CAP-Child Abuse Prevention Orgn., Pauls Valley, 1987—; mem. vision 2000 com. Garvin County Assn. Svcs. Named to Gov.'s Honor Roll Recognition and Appreciation for Community Activities, Pauls Valley, Okla., 1985-86; named Pauls Valley Citizen of Yr., 1996. Mem. Cooperative Coun. Okla. Sch. Adminstrn., Whitebead Ednl. Assn., Okla. Orgn. Dependent Sch., Okla. Assn. Elem. Sch. Prins., AAUW, All Sports Club (v.p. 1984-89, pres. 1985, 90), Okla. Heritage Assn., Pauls Valley Hist. Soc., Rotary (bd. dirs. 1993-96, Paul Harris fellow 1997), Pauls Valley C. of C. (pres. 1997, pres. exec. bd. dirs. 1998—), State Found. for Acad. Excellence Forum Com., Rotary (bd. dirs. 1993-96, 1999-2001, 2003—), Delta Kappa Gamma (past local auditor, parliamentarian, v.p., pres. 1979-96), Phi Delta Kappa. Democrat. Mem. Ch. of Christ. Home: RR 3 Box 306 Pauls Valley OK 73075-9232 E-mail: wlpest@itlnet-net.

PETER, KENNETH SHANNON, elementary school educator; b. Chgo., Apr. 2, 1945; s. Joseph Francis and Kathleen Daley (Shannon) P.; m. Susan Ann Richardson, Aug. 27, 1977; children: Megan Elyse, Evan Michael. BA in Elem. Edn., Occidental Coll., L.A., 1967; MA in Phys. Edn., U. Laverne, Calif., 1978; MA in Ednl. Adminstrn., Calif. State U., L.A., 1988. Cert. in elem. edn., gifted and talented, ednl. adminstrn., Calif. Elem. tchr. L.A. Unified Sch. Dist., 1968, Pasadena (Calif.) Unified Sch. Dist., 1969-77, phys. edn. specialist, 1978-90, project tchr., 1990—. Cons. in phys. edn.; mem. program quality rev. Pasadena Unified Sch. Dist., 1990—; bd. dirs., presenter Calif. Poly Elem. Workshop Com., 1981-89. Author monographs: Characteristics of Elementary Physical Education Specialists, 1978, Comparison of Specialist and Non-Specialist Taught Studies, 1988. Mem. nat. sch. site com. Am. Heart Assn., Dallas, 1994-97, mem. Jump for Heart task force, So. Calif., 1978-89; area dir. Dem. Party, Calif., 1963-74; mem. sch. site coun. Washington Sch., Glendora, Calif., 1993-95. Named Outstanding Vol., Am. Heart Assn., 1994, Tchr. of the Yr., Pasadena Unified Schs., 1985; recipient Award of Distinction, Calif. Dept. Health Svcs., 1992. Mem. Calif. Acad. Phys. Edn. (sr. assoc.), Calif. Assn. Health, Phys. Edn., Recreation and Dance (elem. phys. edn. chair 1978—), Phi Kappa Phi, Phi Alpha Theta, Delta Phi Epsilon. Democrat. Roman Catholic. Avocations: tennis, fitness. Home: 1665 S Calmgrove Ave Glendora CA 91740-5907 Office: Pasadena Unified Sch Dist 351 S Hudson Ave Pasadena CA 91101-3599

PETERS, BARBARA AGNES, principal; b. Lockport, N.Y., Aug. 11, 1952; d. Raymond Charles Betsch and Evelyn Mae (Ehmke) Soulvie; m. Victor Waldorf Baker, June 17, 1978 (div.); children: Alexander, Erik; m. Robert Emerson Peters, Nov. 3, 1990; children: Brian, Jennifer. BS in Edn., SUNY, Fredonia, 1974; MEd, U. Wales, Cardiff, 1979; EdD, SUNY, Buffalo, 2002. Cert. tchr. N, K-6, secondary English, reading, CAS-sch. dist. adminstr., N.Y. CAS Ednl. Adminstrn., SAS, SDA. Tchr. English Emmet Belknap Jr. H.S., Lockport, N.Y., 1974-76; exec. dir. Dept. of Youth and Recreation Svcs., Lockport, 1978-89; instr. Empire State Coll., Lockport, 1983—; tchr. English Akron (N.Y.) Cen. Sch. Dist., 1989-95; asst. prin. West Seneca East Middle Sch., 1995-97; prin., mem. numerous dist. coms. Winchester Elem. Sch., 1997—. Mem. dist. planning team Akron Sch., 1990-95, mem. tech. long-range planning com., 1992-94. Team owner's mgr. Buffalo Bills Football Club, Orchard Park, N.Y., 1978—; mem. Bd. Performing and Visual Arts,Tonawanda, 1992. Recipient Erie County Youth Best award, 1995; honoree Internat. Women's Decade, 1985; named to Outstanding Young Women of Am., 1986, Educator of Yr. West Seneca C. of C., 2000; Rotary grad. fellow, 1975. Mem. ASCD, N.Y. State Middle Sch. Assn., Swiftwater Power Squadron Advanced Pilot and Bridg eOfficer, LaSalle Yacht Club, Western N.Y. Women in Adminstrn. (treas. 1998, bd. dirs. 1999—, Excellence in Ednl. Leadership award 1996), Phi Delta Kappa (award innovative ednl. program 1996). Avocations: boating, golf. Office: Winchester Elem Sch 350 Harlem Rd West Seneca NY 14224 E-mail: Barbara_Peters@westseneca.wnyric.org.

PETERS, CATHY J. nurse practitioner, education consultant; b. Niagara Falls, N.Y., Dec. 9, 1951; d. Walter Anthony and Phyllis (La Barber) P. BSEd, SUNY, Cortland, 1973; AAS, SUNY, Syracuse, 1975; MS in Nursing, U. Rochester, 1981. Cert. adult nurse practitioner, N.Y. Nursing instr. SUNY, Brockport, 1981-82; dir. health edn. Group Health of Blue Cross/Blue Shield, Rochester, N.Y., 1985-88; dir. edn. Health Psychology Assocs., Rochester, 1988-91; nurse practitioner AC Rochester/GM, 1991-92. Condr. stress mgmt. workshops, Rochester; editor, grant writer, dept. women's health and ob-gyn. Rochester Gen. Hosp., 1991-93; cons. health edn. adv. bd. Monroe County Health Dept., Rochester, 1989-90; mem. med. team Inst. for Shipboard Edn., U. Pitts., 1993. Author (column in Rochester Bus. mag.) Mind/Body, 1996—. Vol. Blessed Sacrement Ch., Rochester, 1991—. Robert Wood Johnson grantee, 1979-81; Civil Svc. Employees' Assn. scholar, 1975. Mem. APHA, N.Y. State Coalition Nurse Practitioners, Internat. Patient Edn. Coun., Rochester Nurses' Registry. Avocations: painting, yoga, travel, reading. Home and Office: PO Box 18555 Rochester NY 14618-0555

PETERS, ELIZABETH ANN HAMPTON, retired nursing educator; b. Detroit, Sept. 27, 1934; d. Grinsfield Taylor and Ida Victoria (Jones) Hampton; m. James Marvin Peters, Dec. 1, 1956; children: Douglas Taylor, Sara Elizabeth. Diploma, Berea Coll. Hosp. Sch. Nursing, 1956; BSN, Wright State U., Dayton, Ohio, 1975; MSN, Ohio State U., Columbus, 1978. Therapist, nurse Eastway, Inc., Dayton, Ohio, 1979-81; therapist, family counseling svc. Good Samaritan-Cmty. Mental Health Ctr., Dayton, Ohio, 1981-83; instr. Wright State U. Sch. Nursing, Dayton, 1983-84; clin. nurse specialist, pain mgmt. program UPSA, Inc., Dayton, 1983-86; staff nurse Hospice of Dayton, Inc., 1985-86, dir. vol. svcs., 1986-89, dir. bereavement svcs., 1986-87; asst. prof. Cmty. Hosp. Sch. Nursing, Springfield, Ohio, 1990-93, prof., 1993-97; ret., 1997; parish nurse Honey Creek Presbyn. Ch., 1998—2003. Co-author (with others): Oncologic Pain, 1987. Mem. Clark County Mental Health Bd., Springfield, 1986-95; mem. New Carlisle (Ohio) Bd. Health, 1990-2003. Mem.: Sigma Theta Tau. Home: 402 Flora Ave New Carlisle OH 45344-1329

PETERS, JACQUELINE MARY, secondary education educator; b. Milw., Oct. 6, 1947; d. Arnold Martin and Rosalie Ellen (Mulherin) Fladoos; divorced; children: Casey Martin, Ann Marie. Student, Clarke Coll., Dubuque, Iowa, 1965-67; BA, Calif. State U., Long Beach, 1970; MA in History and Tchg., LaVerne (Calif.) U., 1973. Reading tchr. Chaffey H.S., Ontario, Calif., 1971-78, tchr. phys. edn., 1976-78, English tchr., 1978-90, tchr. history, 1990—. Mentor AAUW, cmty. schs., 1997-99. State rep. Trans Nat. Golf Assn., 1963-75; bd. dirs. Cmty. Challenge Grants, Ontario, 1996-00. Named to Sports Hall of Fame, Dubuque Sr. H.S., 1996; Med-Cal grantee, 1996, Project Yes grantee, 1997-99. Mem. AAUW (bd. dirs., br. pres. 1995-99, Edn. Foun. Gift Honoree 1998), Calif. Tchrs. Assn. Republican. Roman Catholic. Avocations: golf, fly fishing, pysanka, poetry, bridge. Home: 320 W 21st St Upland CA 91784-1413 Office: Chaffey HS 1245 N Euclid Ave Ontario CA 91762-1923

PETERS, JUDITH GRIESSEL, foreign language educator; b. Albany, N.Y., Sept. 30, 1939; d. Edward Ernest and Miriam Anne Griessel; m. Howard Nevin Peters, Aug. 24, 1963; children: Elisabeth Anne, Nevin Edward. BA, Valparaiso (Ind.) U., 1961; PhD, U. Colo., 1968. Internat. svc. program chair Valparaiso U., 1993—98, dept. fgn. langs. chair, 1995—98, prof. emerita fgn. langs. and lit. Faculty fellowship Lilly Endowment, 1989, NDEA Title IV fellowship U.S. Govt., 1961-64. Avocations: canoeing, gardening, travel, volunteering. Home: 860 N 500 E Valparaiso IN 46383-9743

PETERS, LEON, JR., electrical engineering educator, research administrator; b. Columbus, Ohio, May 28, 1923; s. Leon P. and Ethel (Howland) Pierce; m. Mabel Marie Johnson, June 6, 1953; children: Amy T. Peters Thomas, Melinda A. Peters Todaro, Marta C. Cohee, Patricia D., Lee A., Roberta J. Peters Cameruca, Karen E. Peters Ellingson. BSE.E., Ohio State U., 1950, MS, 1954, PhD, 1959. Asst. prof. elec. engring. Ohio State U., Columbus, 1959-63, assoc. prof., 1963-67, prof., 1967-93, prof. emeritus, 1993—, assoc. dept. chmn. for rsch., 1990-92, dir. electro sci. lab., 1983-94. Contbr. articles to profl. jours. Served to 2d lt. U.S. Army, 1942-46, ETO. Fellow IEEE Home: 2087 Ellington Rd Columbus OH 43221-4138 Office: Ohio State U Electrosci Lab 1320 Kinnear Rd Columbus OH 43321-1156

PETERS, MILTON EUGENE, educational psychologist; b. Anderson, Ind., July 22, 1938; s. Olen A. and Dorothy LaVerne (Lambert) P.; m. Carol Ann Dudycha, Aug. 27, 1960. BA, Wittenburg U., 1960; M in Div., Hamma Sch. Theology, 1963; MA, Bowling Green State U., 1965; PhD, U. Toledo, 1975. Lic. psychologist, Ohio. Pastor Luth. Ch. Am., 1966-69; instr. psychology Defiance (Ohio) Coll., 1969-70, Bluffton (Ohio) Coll., 1970-72; tchr., rsch. asst. U. Toledo, 1973-75, prof., 1975-76; dir. instl. rsch., asst. prof. psychology U. Findlay, Ohio, 1976-85, assoc. prof. psychology, 1985-89, prof., 1989—. Cons., lectr. in field; ednl. rschr. Contbr. articles to profl. and religious jours. Mem. APA, Am. Assn. Univ. Prof. (pres. U. Findlay), Midwestern Psychol. Assn., Creative Edn. Found. (colleague), Findlay Beacon Club, Fostoria Power Squadron. Home: 1130 Country Club Dr Findlay OH 45840-6342 Office: 1000 N Main St Findlay OH 45840-3653 E-mail: peters@findlay.edu.

PETERS, PATRICIA L. elementary education educator; b. Alton, Ill., Oct. 20, 1954; d. Golden D. Jr. and Patricia A. (Elmore) Zike; m. M.L. Peters, Dec. 14, 1979; 1 child, Goldie Lee. BA in Bus., William Woods Coll., Fulton, Mo., 1976; MS in Edn., So. Ill. U., 1987. Cert. elem. and early childhood tchr., Mo. Corp. officer, stockholder Am. Marine Svcs., Inc., Alton, 1980—; elem. tchr. computers, lang. arts and math. Ferguson (Mo.)-Florissant Sch. Dist. Program presenter edn. seminars. Contbr. articles to profl. publs. Lit. sets grantee, Intermediate sci. grantee; recipient William Walter Griffith award, 1991, Citicorp Ednl. award. Mem. NEA, ASCD, MSTA (pres., v.p., treas.) Nat. Assn. for Edn. Young Children, Internat. Reading Assn., Ferguson-Florissant Edn. Assn. (rep.), Kappa Delta Pi, Alpha Chi Omega.

PETERS, RALPH MARTIN, academic administrator; b. Knoxville, Tenn., May 9, 1926; s. Tim C. and Alma (Shannon) P.; m. Lorraine Daniel, 1949; children— Teresa, Marta. BS, Lincoln Meml. U., 1949; MS, U. Tenn., 1953, EdD, 1960. Tchr. pub. schs. Lincoln Meml. U., 1956-63, prof., dept. chmn., v.p., 1956-63, 92-97, interim pres., 1997-98; prof. edn., dean students, dean Grad. Sch. Tenn. Tech. U., Cookeville, 1963-89, dean emeritus, 1989. Editor publs. Served with Armed Forces, World War II. Mem. Phi Kappa Phi, Phi Delta Kappa, Omicron Delta Kappa. Clubs: Rotary. Baptist. Home: PO Box 3231 Cookeville TN 38502-3231

PETERS, SUE ELLEN, elementary school educator; b. Rock Springs, Wyo., Oct. 1, 1951; d. Vernon A. Martin and Betty E. McCloy Honadel; m. Gary M. Peters, Sept. 5, 1980; children: David Blaine, Tessa Ellen. BS in Edn., Black Hills State Coll., 1973; MS in Natural Sci., U. Wyo., 1988. Substitute tchr. K-12 Edgemont (S.D.) Ind. Sch. Dist., 1973-77, tchr., 1977-79, Campbell County Sch. Dist 1, Gillette, Wyo., 1979—. Math curriculum com. Campbell County Sch. Dist., Gillette, 1982—, math. standards team, 1989-91, family math. team, 1993—, 6 traits of reading team, 2001-02, Wyo. Edgate team, 2002-03. Recipient Vol. award St. Jude Children's Rsch. Hosp., Memphis, Tenn., 1988, '89, '90, '91. Mem. NEA, PEO (recording sec., chpt. AR, 2002—, Wyo. state del., 2002), Wyo. Edn. Assn. (human rights com. mem. 1980-82), Campbell County Edn. Assn., Nat. Coun. Tchrs. of Math., Campbell County Reading Coun., Wyo. Coun. Tchrs. of Math., Epsilon Sigma Alpha (2nd v.p. Wyo. chpt. 1991, sec. Omega Chi chpt. 1988-90). Avocations: travel, reading, vol. work. Office: Conestoga Elem Sch 4901 Sleepy Hollow Blvd Gillette WY 82718-7496

PETERS, THOMAS GUY, surgeon, educator; b. Cin., Oct. 3, 1945; s. Robert Lewis and Martha (Renter) P.; m. Dorothy Jean (Ruby) Geers; children: Elizabeth Jan, Andrew Thomas, Joseph Geers, Sarah Jane. BA, Miami U., Oxford, Ohio, 1966; MD, U. Cin., 1970. Diplomate Am. Bd. Surgery. Surg. intern Milwaukee County Gen. Hosp., 1970-71; resident in surgery Med. Coll. Wis., Milw., 1971-72, 74-77; fellow in transplantation U. Colo., Denver, 1977-78; asst. prof. surgery U. Tenn., Memphis, 1978-84, assoc. prof. surgery, 1984-87, prof. surgery, 1987-88; dir. Jacksonville Transplant Ctr., Methodist Med. Ctr., Fla., 1988—; clin. prof. surgery U. Fla., 1989—, Uniformed Svcs. U. of the Health Scis., 1995—. Clin. fellow Am. Cancer Soc., N.Y.C., 1975-76; assoc. examiner Am. Bd. Surgery, Phila., 1983, 2001, tchg. physician in residence Miami U., 1999-2000. Editor: National Transplantation Resource Directory, 1987, Organ and Tissue Donation: A Reference Guide for Clergy, 1989; contbr. articles to profl. jours., chpts. to books. Col. M.C. USAR. Recipient Resident Rsch. award Wis. Surg. Soc., 1976, 77, Outstanding Tchr. award U. Tenn. Alumni Assn., The Disting. Svc. awrad U. Tenn. Med. Ctr., 1984, The Trustees award Nat. Kidney Found., N.Y.C., 1987, Miami U. Student Found. honoree, 1990, others. Fellow AMA, ACS, Am. Soc. Nephrology; mem. Am. Soc. Transplant Surgeons, Am. Soc. Trasnplantation, Assn. Mil. Surgeons U.S., Soc. Med. Cons. to Armed Forces, Transplantation Soc., United Network for Organ Sharing. Home: 3601 River Hall Dr Jacksonville FL 32217-4277 Office: Jacksonville Transplant Ctr 580 W 8th St Ste 8000 Jacksonville FL 32209-6533

PETERSDORF, ROBERT GEORGE, physician, medical educator, academic administrator; b. Berlin, Feb. 14, 1926; s. Hans H. and Sonja P.; m. Patricia Horton Qua, June 2, 1951; children: Stephen Hans, John Eric. BA, Brown U., 1948, DMS (hon.), 1983; MD cum laude, Yale U., 1952; ScD (hon.), Albany Med. Coll., 1979; MA (hon.), Harvard U., 1980; DMS (hon.), Med. Coll. Pa., 1982, Brown U., 1983; DMS, Bowman-Gray Sch. Medicine, 1986; LHD (hon.), N.Y. Med. Coll., 1986; DSc (hon.), SUNY, Bklyn., 1987, Med. Coll. Ohio, 1987, Univ. Health Scis., The Chgo. Med. Sch., 1987; DSc (hon.), St. Louis U., 1988; LHD (hon.), Ea. Va. Med. Sch., 1988; DSc (hon.), Sch. Medicine, Georgetown U., 1991, Emory U., 1992; DSc (hon.), Tufts U., 1993; DSc (hon.), Mt. Sinai Sch. Medicine, 1993, George Washington U., 1994; other hon. degrees. Diplomate Am. Bd. Internal Medicine. Intern, asst. resident Yale U., New Haven, 1952—54; sr. asst. resident Peter Bent Brigham Hosp., Boston, 1954—55; fellow Johns Hopkins Hosp., Balt., 1955—59; chief resident, instr. medicine Yale U., 1957—58; asst. prof. medicine Johns Hopkins U., 1958—60, physician, 1958—60; assoc. prof. medicine U. Wash., Seattle, 1960—62, prof., 1962—79, chmn. dept. medicine, 1964—79; physician-in-chief U. Wash. Hosp., 1964—79; pres. Brigham and Women's Hosp., Boston, 1979—81; prof. medicine Harvard U. Med. Sch., Boston, 1979—81; dean, vice chancellor health scis. U. Calif.-San Diego Sch. Medicine, 1981—86; clin. prof. infectious diseases Sch. Medicine Georgetown U., 1986—94; pres. Assn. Am. Med. Colls., Washington, 1986—94, pres. emeritus, 1994—; prof. medicine U. Wash., 1994—, disting. prof., sr. advisor to dean, 1998—; disting. physician Vets. Health Adminstrn., Seattle, 1995—98, sr. physician, 1998—. Cons. to surgeon gen. USPHS, 1960—79; cons. USPHS Hosp., Seattle, 1962—79; mem. spl. med. adv. group VA, 1987—94. Editor: Harrison's Principles of Internal Medicine, 1968—90; contbr. numerous articles to profl. jours. With USAAF, 1944—46. Named Disting. Internist of 1987, Am. Soc. Internal Medicine; recipient Lilly medal, Royal Coll. Physicians, London, 1978, Wiggers award, Albany Med. Coll., 1979, Robert H. Williams award, Assn. Profs. Medicine, 1983, Keen award, Brown U., 1980, Disting. Svc. award, Baylor Coll. Medicine, 1989, Scroll of Merit, Nat. Med. Assn., 1990, 2d Ann. Founder's award, Assn. Program Dirs. in Internal Medicine, 1991, Flexner award, Assn. Am. Med. Coll., 1994. Master: ACP (pres. 1975—76, Stengel award 1980, Disting. Tchr. award 1993, Laureate award Wash. chpt.); fellow: AAAS, Execs. Assn. (hon.); mem.: Assn. Am. Physicians (pres. 1976—77, Kober medal 1996), Inst. Medicine of NAS (councillor 1977—80), Rainier Club, Cosmos Club. Home and Office: 8001 Sand Point Way NE C71 Seattle WA 98115

PETERSEN, EVELYN ANN, education consultant; b. Gary, Ind., July 2, 1936; d. Eric Maxwell and Julia Ann (Kustron) Ivany; m. Ozzie G. Hebert, Feb. 27, 1957 (div. July 1963); children: Heather Lynn Petersen Hewett, Eric Dean Hebert; m. Jon Edwin Petersen, June 13, 1964; children: Karin Patricia, Kristin Shawn. BS, Purdue U., 1964; MA, Cen. Mich. U., 1977. Cert. tchr. elem. edn. with early childhood and vocat. edn. endorsements, Mich. Elem. tchr. Harford Day Sch., Bel Air, Md., 1958-62, Interlochen (Mich.) Elem. Sch., 1964-67; dir., tchr. Traverse City (Mich.) Coop. Presch., 1969-77; off-campus instr. grad. level Cen. Mich. U., Mt. Pleasant, 1977-92; Child Devel. Assoc. nat. rep. Coun. for Early Childhood Profl. Recognition, Washington, 1981—. Instr. N.W. Mich. Coll., Traverse City, 1974-75, 78, U. Wis., Sheboygan, 1981-83; project dir., instr. West Shore C.C., Scotville, Mich., 1984-86, 89; edn. cons., 1980—; parenting columnist Detroit Free Press, Knight Ridder Tribune Wire, 1984—; bd. mem. Children's Trust Fund, Lansing, Mich., 1983-85; mem. ad hoc adv. com. Bd. Edn. State of Mich., Lansing, 1985-86, child care provider trainer Dept. Social Svcs., 1988; chairperson adv. bd. Traverse Bay Vocat. Edn. Child Care Program, 1976-79; panelist Nat. Parenting Ctr., L.A., 1992—. Author: A Practical Guide to Early Childhood Planning, Methods and Materials: The What, Why and How of Lesson Plans, 1996, The Seeds of Success series: Growing Happy Kids, Growing Creative Kids, Growing Thinking Kids, Growing Responsible Kids, 1997; author, co-prodr. (audio and video cassette series) Parent Talk, 1990, Effective Home Visits: Video Training, 1994. County coord. Week of the Young Child, Traverse City, 1974-78; vol. probate ct. Traverse City, 1973-83; commr. Traverse City Human Rights Commn., 1981-82. Mem. AAUW (chairperson, coord. Touch & Do Exploratorium 1974-76), Nat. Fedn. Press Women, Nat. Assn. for Edn. of Young Children, Children's Trust Fund for Abuse Prevention, Mich. Assn. for Edn. of Young Children, Mich. Mental Health Assn., Assn. for Childhood Edn. Internat., Author's Guild. Avocations: writing, reading, travel, snorkeling. Home and Office: 843 S Long Lake Rd N Traverse City MI 49684-9078

PETERS-LAMBERT, BETTY A. assistant principal; b. Clifton, Ill., Aug. 24, 1958; d. Clarence Henry and Margaret Pauline (Hebert) P. AA, Kankakee C.C., Ill., 1978; BS, Ill. State U., Normal, 1980, MS, 1990; CAS in Ednl. Adminstrn., U. Ill., Urbana-Champaign, 1998. Cert. tchr. phys. edn., K-12, Ill. Substitute tchr. various schs., Iroquois/Kankakee County, 1981-83; tchr.'s aide for gifted Alan Shepard Sch., Bourbonnais, Ill., 1983-84; phys. edn. tchr. Noel LeVasseur Elem. Sch., Bourbonnais, 1984—2002; asst. prin. John F. Kennedy Mid. Sch., Kankakee, Ill., 2002—. Bd. dirs. AHA, 1985-99, pres. 1993-98, mem. Jump Rope for Heart Task Force, AHA, Springfield, Ill., 1994-2002; mem. PTA, Bourbonnais, 1991-2002; bd. dirs. Bradley Bourbonnais Schs. Fed. Credit Union, 1993—; mem. Jr. League of Kankakee, 1993—. Mem.: Ill. Assn. for Health, Phys. Edn., Recreation and Dance (Eastern dist. pres. 2002), Kappa Delta Pi. Roman Catholic. Avocation: walking. Home: 1548 Bittersweet Dr Saint Anne IL 60964-4462 Office: John F Kennedy Mid Sch 1550 W Calista Kankakee IL 60901

PETERSON, BARBARA ANN BENNETT, history educator, television personality; b. Portland, Oreg., Sept. 6, 1942; d. George and Hope Bennett; m. Frank Lynn Peterson, July 1, 1967. BA, BS, Oreg. State U., 1964; MA, Stanford U., 1965; PhD, U. Hawaii, 1978; PhD (hon.), London Inst. Applied Rsch., 1991, Australian Inst. Coordinated R, 1995. From prof. history to prof. emeritus U. Hawaii, 1967—95, prof. emeritus, 1995—; prof. history Oreg. State U., 2000—. Prof. Asian history and European colonial history and world problems Chapman Coll. World Campus Afloat Semester At Sea, 1974, European overseas exploration, expansion and colonialism U. Colo., Boulder, 1978, Modern China, Modern East Asia, The West in the World U. Pitts., 1999; assoc. prof. U. Hawaii-Manoa Coll. Continuing Edn., 1981; Fulbright prof. history Wuhan (China) U., 1988-89; Fulbright rsch. prof. Sophia U., Japan, 1967; rsch. assoc. Bishop Mus., 1995-98; lectr. Capital Spkrs., Washington, 1987—; prof. world civilization Hawaii State Ednl. Channel, U. Hawaii Sys., 1993-97; adj. fellow East-West Ctr., Honolulu, 1998-99; prof. history U. Pitts. Semester at Sea, fall 1999; adj. prof. Hawaii Pacific U., East-West Ctr., Hawaii, 1998-99. Co-author: Women's Place is in the History Books, Her Story, 1962-1980: A Curriculum Guide for American History Teachers, 1980; author: America in British Eyes, 1988, John Bull's Eye on America, 1995, Sarah Childress Polk, First Lady of Tennessee and Washington, 2002 (nominated for Pulitzer prize 2003, Avery O. Craven award 2003, Merle Curti award 2003); editor: Notable Women of Hawaii, 1984, (with W. Solheim) The Pacific Region, 1990, 91, American History: 17th, 18th and 19th Centuries, 1993, America: 19th and 20th Centuries, 1993, Notable Women of China, 2000 (nominated for Pulitzer prize 2001), Hawaii in the World, 2000; assoc. editor Am. Nat. Biography, 1998 (Dartmouth medal); contbr. articles to profl. publs. Participant People-to-People Program, Eng., 1964, Expt. in Internat. Living Program, Nigeria, 1966; chmn. 1st Nat. Women's History Week, Hawaii, 1982; pres. Bishop Mus. Coun., 1993-94; active mem. Hawaii Commn. on Status of Women; fundraiser local mus. and children's activities. Fulbright scholar, Japan, 1967, sr. tchg. Fulbright scholar, China, 1988-89; NEH-Woodrow Wilson fellow Princeton U., 1980; recipient state proclamations Gov. of Hawaii, 1982, City of Honolulu and Hawaii State Legis., 1982, Outstanding Tchr. of Yr. award Wuhan (China), U., 1988, Woman of Yr. award, 1991; inducted into the Women's Hall of Fame, Seneca Falls, N.Y., 1991; co-champion Hawaii State Husband and Wife Mixed Doubles Tennis Championship, 1985. Fellow: World Lit. Acad. (Eng.); mem.: AAUW, Am. Studies Assn. (Hawaii chpt. pres. 1984—85), Women in Acad. Adminstrn., Hawaii Found. History and Humanities (mem. editl. bd. 1972—73), Am. Coun. on Edn., Fulbright Assn. (founding pres. Hawaii chpt. 1984—88, mem. nat. steering com. chairwomen ann. conf. 1990, pres. 1998—99), Am. Hist. Assn. (mem. numerous coms., Albert J. Beveridge award 2003), Maison Internat. des Intellectuals, Phi Kappa Phi, Pi Beta Phi. Avocations: writing, cooking, fund raising for charity and children's organizations and museums, gardening, travel. Office: East West Ctr Burns Hall 1601 East West Rd Honolulu HI 96848-1601 also: Oreg State U History Dept 306 Milam Hall Corvallis OR 97331

PETERSON, BONNIE LU, mathematics educator; b. Escanaba, Mich., Jan. 19, 1946; d. Herbert Erick and Ruth Albertha (Erickson) P. AA, Bay de Noc C.C., 1966; BS, No. Mich. U., 1968, MA in Math., 1969; EdD, Tenn. State U., 1989. Tchr. Lapeer (Mich.) High Sch., 1969-70, Nova High Sch., Ft. Lauderdale, Fla., 1970-79, Hendersonville (Tenn.) High Sch., 1979—. Adj. faculty Vol. State C.C., Gallatin, Tenn., 1989—; chair Sumner County Schs. Tchrs. Insvc., Gallatin, 1990-92; mem. math. specialist team State of Tenn., 1991-93; reader for advanced placement calculus exam. Coll. Bd., 1994, 95, 96, 97, 98, 99; chair equipment com. Tchrs. Tchg. with Tech., 1998; spkr. in field. Mem. edn. com. Vision 2000-City of Hendersonville, 1993-94. Recipient State-Level Presdl. award, 1994, 95, 96, 98, Nat. Presdl. award for Excellence in Math. and Sci. Tchg., 1998; Tenn. State Bd. grantee, 1989-92; Woodrow Wilson fellow, 1993; Tandy scholar, 1995. Mem. ASCD, Nat. Coun. Tchrs. Math. (chair workshop support com. 1990), Tenn. Math. Tchrs. Assn. (v.p. for secondary schs.), Mid. Tenn. Math. Tchrs. Assn. (past pres.), Tenn. Alliance Presdl. Awardees (treas. 2000—, Tenn. co-coord. Presdl. award in Math. 2000—), Phi Delta Kappa (past pres.). Avocations: cooking, counted cross stitch. Home: 1081 Coon Creek Rd Dickson TN 37055-4014

PETERSON, BRADLEY MICHAEL, astronomy educator; b. Mpls., Nov. 26, 1951; s. Harry C. and Dona M. (Erickson) P.; m. Janet R. Cook, Oct. 19, 1978; children: Evan, Erika, Elizabeth, Ellyn. B Physics, U. Minn., 1974; PhD in Astronomy, U. Ariz., 1978. Postdoctoral rschr. U. Minn., Mpls., 1979; postdoctoral fellow Ohio State U., Columbus, 1979-80, instr. astronomy, 1980, asst. prof., 1980-84, assoc. prof., 1984-91, prof., 1991—. Assoc. rsch. astronomer Lick Obs., U. Calif., Santa Cruz, 1989; mem. IUE users com. astrophysics div. NASA, Washington, 1992-96, mem. ultraviolet and optical mgmt. ops. working group, 1993-96, chmn. astrophysics working group, 1997-2000; mem. structure and evolution of Universe subcom. NASA, 1998-2003, mem. nat. astronomy and astrophysics adv. com., 2002—; mem. xoun. Space Telescope Inst., 2003—. Author: Introduction to Active Galactic Nuclei, 1997; contbr. over 170 articles to sci. jours. Grantee NSF, 1981—, NASA, 1986—. Mem. Am. Astron. Soc., Internat. Astron. Union, Astron. Soc. Pacific. Roman Catholic. Office: Ohio State U Dept Astronomy 140 W 18th Ave Columbus OH 43210-1106 E-mail: peterson@astronomy.ohio-state.edu.

PETERSON, DAN, secondary school educator; Grad., San Jose State U.; student, U. Hawaii. Science tchr. Henry M. Gunn High Sch., Palo Alto, Calif., 1965—. Master tchr. San Jose State Coll., Stanford U.; mentor tchr., instrnl. supr. Designed an interactive computer-laser system for classroom use. Recipient Outstanding Earth Sci. Tchr. award, 1992. Mem. BAESI (sterring com.).

PETERSON, DONALD DEAN, secondary school educator; b. Iowa Falls, Iowa, Jan. 2, 1943; s. Lawrence Bert and Martha Marie (Lawson) P.; m. Josette Dee Duprez, Feb. 1, 1963; children: Jeffrey Justin, Danielle Michelle. BA, U. No. Iowa, 1965, MA in Geography, 1975. Tchr. Allison-Bristow (Iowa) Pub. Schs., 1965-68, Marshalltown (Iowa) Schs., 1968—2000, head social studies dept., 1994—2000; adj. instr. No. Iowa Univ., 2000—. Trained as tchr. cons. Geog. Alliance of Iowa, Cedar Falls, 1991—; participant Summer Geography Inst., 1991. Named tchr. of yr. Iowa Secondary Social Studies, 1994, Nat. Coun. for Social Studies, 1995. Mem. NEA, Iowa State Edn. Assn., Iowa Coun. Social Studies (planning com. 1992—), Nat. Coun. Geog. Edn. (Cram award 1993), Geog. Alliance of Iowa, Marshalltown Edn. Assn. Republican. Lutheran. Avocations: baseball card collecting, travel, photography. Office: Marshalltown High Sch 1602 S 2nd Ave Marshalltown IA 50158-4081

PETERSON, DOROTHY HAWKINS, artist, educator; b. Albuquerque, Mar. 14, 1932; d. Ernest Lee and Ethel Dawn (Allen) Hawkins; m. John W. Peterson, July 9, 1954; children: John Richard, Dorothy Anne. BS in Edn., U. N.Mex., Albuquerque, 1953; MA, U. Tex., 1979. Freelance artist, 1960—; educator, instr. Carlsbad (N.Mex.) Ind. Elem. Sch. Dist., 1953-54; instr. Charleston (S.C.) County Schs., 1955-56; instr. in painting Midland (Tex.) Coll., 1971-76, Roswell (N.Mex.) Mus. Sch., 1981-83, 91—; instr. in art history Ea. N.Mex. U., Roswell, 1989—2000; instr. painting N.Mex. Mil. Inst., Roswell, 1992—94. Bd. dirs. N.Mex. Arts Commn., Santa Fe; cons. Casa de Amigos Craft Guild, Midland, Tex., 1971-73. One woman shows include Art Inst., Permian Basin, Odessa, Tex., 1994. Tutor Roswell Literacy Coun., 1988-89; bd. dirs. N.Mex. Arts & Crafts Fair, Albuquerque, 1983-85. Named Best of Show, Mus. of the S.W., 1967, 69; recipient Top award, 1973, 75, Juror award N.Mex. Arts & Crafts Fair, 1986, 1st pl. award Profl. Watercolor N.Mex. State Fair, 1988; Talens-d' Arches award, Tex. Watercolor Soc., 1998; Bd. Dirs. award, San Diego Watercolor Soc., 1998, N. Mex. Watercolor Soc., 1998. Mem. Nat. Watercolor Soc. (signature mem.), N.Mex. Watercolor Soc. (signature mem.; 2d pl. award 1981, San Diego Watercolor Soc. award 1988, 1st pl. award state fair 1988, Grumbacher award 1993, Wingspread award 1994, 1st pl. award 1995, 1st, 3rd and Graham award 1997, Best of Show 2001). Office: Dorothy Peterson Studio PO Box 915 Roswell NM 88202-0915

PETERSON, ELMOR LEE, mathematical scientist, educator; b. McKeesport, Pa., Dec. 6, 1938; s. William James and Emma Elizabeth (Scott) P.; m. Sharon Louise Walker, Aug., 1957 (div. Jan. 1961); 1 child, Lisa Ann Peterson Loop Baker; m. Miriam Drake Mears, Dec. 23, 1966; 1 child, David Scott. BS in Physics, Carnegie Mellon U., 1960, MS in Math., 1961, PhD in Math., 1964. Technician U.S. Steel Rsch. Ctr., Monroeville, Pa., summer 1959; engr. Westinghouse Atomic Power, Forest Hills, Pa., summer 1960; rsch. engr. Atomics Internat., Canoga Park, Calif., summer 1961; physicist Lawrence Radiation Labs., Livermore, Calif., summer 1963; sr. math. Westinghouse R & D, Churchill Boro, Pa., 1963-66; asst. prof. math. U. Mich., Ann Arbor, 1967-69; assoc. prof. math. and mgmt. sci. Northwestern U., Evanston, Ill., 1969-73, prof. math. and mgmt. sci., 1973-77, prof. applied math. and mgmt. sci., 1977-79; prof. math. and ops. rsch. N.C. State U., Raleigh, 1979—, co-dir. ops. rsch., 2000—. Vis. asst. prof. W.Va. U., dept. Math., Morgantown, 1966; vis. assoc. prof. U. Wis. Math. Rsch. Ctr., Madison, 1968-69; vis. prof. Stanford U. Ops. Rsch. Dept., 1976-77. Author: (with others) Geometric Programming, 1967, Russian trans., 1971; contbr. articles to profl. jours. Mobil Found. Rsch. grantee, 1967-69, Air Force Office Sci. Rsch. grantee, 1973-75, 76-78, NSF grantee, 1985-86. Mem. Soc. for Indsl. and Applied Math., Ops. Rsch. Soc. Am., Am. Math. Soc., Math. Assn. Am. Avocations: aerobic exercise, antique furniture. Home: 3717 Williamsborough Ct Raleigh NC 27609-6357 Office: NC State U Hillsborough St Raleigh NC 27695-0001 E-mail: elpeters@eos.ncsu.edu.

PETERSON, FRANCIS, physicist, educator; BEE, Rensselaer U., 1964; PhD, Cornell U., 1968. Prof. physics dept. Iowa State U., Ames, prof. emeritus, 2003—. Recipient Disting. Svc. Citation award, 1993. Mem. Am. Assn. of Physics Tchrs. (v.p. 2002). Office: Iowa State U A 325 Physics Dept Ames IA 50011-0001*

PETERSON, GINGER, secondary education educator; b. Patrick AFB, Fla., Apr. 18, 1951; m. George E. Peterson Jr., Aug. 12, 1972; children: Jason, Jory, Jake. BS in Math., Religion, Ea. N.Mex. U., 1973, MEd, 1991. Cert. tchr., N.Mex. Jr. high/high sch. math. tchr., dept. head math. Floyd (N.Mex.) Schs., 1991-93; math. tchr., head dept. Dora (N.Mex.), 1993—. Adv. bd. mem. Floyd High Sch., 1991-92; interview com. mem. Dora H.S., 1994-99. Mem.: Delta Kappa Gamma.

PETERSON, JILL SUSAN, elementary school educator; b. Richland, Wash, July 26, 1946; d. Clarence Edward and Doris Edeline (Ostby) Lange; m. Wallace Peterson Jr., Aug. 10, 1968 (dec. Jan. 1991); 1 child, Dawn Sa Ra. BA, Pacific Luth. U., 1968; MA, U. St. Thomas, 1984; post grad., Augsburg Coll., U. Minn., U. St. Thomas, U. Calif., Irvine. Tchr. Little Can. Elem. Sch., 1968—74; title I tutor Red Oak Elem., St. Paul, 1975—79; lead tchr. Sand Creek Elem., Mpls., 1979—88, Andover Elem., Mpls., 1988—. Adj. instr. multicultural edn. Hamline U., 1995—99; instr. Seeking Ednl. Equity and Diversity, 1995—, 2003—. Human rights commr. City Arden Hills, Minn., 1987—90; pres. Children of the World, 1995—99; vol. Ctr. for Victims of Torture, Mpls., 2000; mem. coun. Roseville Luth. Ch., Minn., 1986—88, 1994—96. Recipient Award of Excellence, Minn. Elem. Sch. Prin. Assn., 1992. Mem.: NEA, Anoka-Hennepin Edn. Minn., Edn. Minn., Alpha Delta Kappa (pres. Alpha Omicron chpt. 1993—94, Regional Scholar of Merit 1994, Tchr. Outstanding Performance 2000). Avocations: reading, swimming, travel, volunteering. Home: 3061 Highpointe Curve Roseville MN 55113 Office: Andover Elem Sch 14950 Hanson Blvd NW Andover MN 55304

PETERSON, KENNETH ALLEN, SR., superintendent, retired; b. Hammond, Ind., Jan. 20, 1939; s. Chester E. and Bertha (Hornby) P.; B.Ed. cum laude, Chgo. State U., 1963; M.S., Purdue U., 1970; NSF grantee U. Iowa, 1964-65; postgrad. U. Ill., 1977-81; Vanderbilt U.; m. Marilyn M. Musson, Jan. 3, 1961; children: Kimberly, Kari, Kenneth Allen Jr. Tchr., Markham (Ill.) Sch. Dist. 144, 1961-67; prin. Brookwood Sch., Glenwood (Ill.) Sch. Dist. 1967, 1967-77, prin. Hickory Bend Sch., 1977-78, dir. spl. edn., 1978-80, asst. supt. schs., 1981-83, ret. supt schs., 1983-94; prof. Govs. State U., 1994—, now emeritus superintendent of schools; mem. No. Ill. Planning Commn. for Gifted Edn. Chmn. Steger (Ill.) Bicentennial Commn., 1976; vice chmn. Ashkum dist. Boy Scouts Am., 1981-83, lodge advisor, sect. advisor, exec. bd., area advisor Vigil honor mem. Order of Arrow Calumet council Boy Scouts Am.; v.p. Calumet Coun. Boy Scouts of Am., 1989—; program com. South Cook County council Girl Scouts U.S.A., 1971-73, 80-81, mem. fin. com., 1981-86, also bd. dirs., nat. del.; mem. Steger Community Devel. Commn. Recipient Order of Arrow Service nat. founders award, Silver Beaver award, Dist. award of merit Boy Scouts Am., Disting. Svc. award Nat. Order of Arrow. Mem. ASCD, Coun. Exceptional Children, P.T.A. (life), Am. Assn. Sch. Adminstrs., Kappa Delta Pi. Republican. Lutheran. Home: 3208 Phillips Ave Steger IL 60475-1161 Office: Coll of Edn Governors State Univ University Park IL 60466

PETERSON, LINDA H. English language and literature educator; b. Saginaw, Mich., Oct. 11, 1948; BA in Lit. summa cum laude, Wheaton Coll., 1969; MA in English, U. R.I., 1973; PhD in English, Brown U., 1978. From lectr. to assoc. prof. Yale U., New Haven, 1977-92, prof., 1992—, dir. undergrad. studies English, 1990-94, chair, 1994-2000, acting chair, 2003, Niel Gray Jr. prof. of English, 2002—. Dir. Bass writing program Yale Coll., 1979-89, 90—; mem. various departmental and univ. coms. Yale U., 1977—; presenter in field. Author: Victorian Autobiography: The Tradition of Self-Interpretation, 1986, Traditions of Victorian Women's Autobiography: The Poetics and Politics of Life Writing, 1999; co-author: Writing Prose, 1989, A Struggle for Fame: Victorian Women Artists and Authors, 1994; co-editor: Wuthering Heights: A Case Study in Contemporary Criticism, 1992, The Norton Reader, 10th edit., 2000, Instructor's Guide to the Norton Reader, 2000; mem. editl. bd. Writing Program Adminstrn., 1983-85, Coll. Composition and Comm., 1986-88, Auto/Biography Studies, 1990—;, Victorian Poetry, 2002—; contbr. articles to profl. jours. Resident fellow Branford Coll., 1979-87, Mellon fellow Whitney Humanities Ctr., 1984-85, fellow NEH, 1989-90, fellow Harry Ransom Humanities Rsch. Ctr., U. Tex., 1997; life fellow Clare Hall, Cambridge, Eng., 1998—. Mem. MLA (del. assembly 1984-86, mem. program com. 1986-89, mem. nonfiction divsn. com. 1988-92, mem. nominating com. 1993-94, mem. teaching of writing divsn. 1993-98), Nat. Writing Program Adminstrs. (mem. cons.-evaluator program 1982-95, mem. exec. bd. 1982-84, 89-90, v.p. 1985-86, pres. 1987-88), Nat. Coun. Tchrs. English (mem. CCCC nominating com. 1985, mem. coll. sect. com. 1987-90). Home: 53 Edgehill Rd New Haven CT 06511-1343 Office: Yale U Dept English PO Box 208302 New Haven CT 06520-8302

PETERSON, LORNA INGRID, library educator; b. Buffalo, July 22, 1956; d. Raymond George and Sybil Odette (Lythcott) P. BA, Dickinson Coll., 1977; MSLS, Case Western Res. U., 1980; PhD, Iowa State U., 1992. Reference libr. Wright State U., Dayton, Ohio, 1980-81; cataloger Ohio U., Athens, 1981-82, Iowa State U., Ames, 1983-85, libr. instr., 1985-89, bibliographic instrn. libr., 1989-90; vis. asst. prof. SUNY Sch. Info. and Libr. Studies, Buffalo, 1990, assoc. prof., 1991—. Contbr. articles to profl.

jours. Bd. dirs. YWCA, Ames, 1984-86. Mem. ALA, N.Y. Libr. Assn., Assn. of Libr. and Info. Sci. Educators, African Am. Libr. Assn. of Western N.Y. Office: SUNY-Buffalo 534 Baldy Hall Buffalo NY 14260-1000

PETERSON, LORRAINE ELIZABETH, retired librarian, educator; b. Newport, R.I., July 24, 1935; d. Philip W. and Barbara Simmons Mosher; m. Francis A. Peterson, Jr. (div. Sept. 1972); children: Elizabeth Bentley, Erica, Cara Matthews. BA, U. R.I., 1957, MLS, 1972. Cert. library sci. tchr. Social dir. R.I. Hosp. Sch. Nursing, Providence, 1957-58; social case worker State of R.I. Pub. Asst., Providence, 1958-60; librarian, tchr. Rogers High Sch., Newport, 1972—2000. Newsletter editor TAN Newport, 1986-88. Mem.: Newport Retired Tchr. Assn., R.I. Libr. Assn., R.I. Ednl. Media Assn., AARP. Episcopalian. Avocations: bowling, sports. Office: George H Norman Library Rogers High Sch Wickham Rd Newport RI 02840-4233

PETERSON, MARILYN ANN WHITNEY, journalism educator; b. Holdrege, Nebr., July 22, 1933; d. Claude Francis and Esther (Soderholm) Whitney; m. Richard Fay Peterson, June 17, 1956. BA, U. Nebr., Kearney, 1955; MA, U. No. Colo., 1963; LHD (hon.), Midland Luth. Coll., 1998. Tchr. Gothenburg (Nebr.) N.H., 1955-56, Kearney Jr. H.S., 1956-57, Cozad (Nebr.) H.S., 1957-60, Wheatridge H.S., Denver, 1960-62, Eustis (Nebr.) H.S., 1962-64; prof. Journalism Midland Luth. Coll., Fremont, Nebr., 1964-94. Faculty chairperson Midland Luth. Coll., 1992-94. Author: The Mimeographed Newspaper, 1972; co-author: Transformational Grammar, 1964; contbr. articles and poetry to profl. jours., mags. and newspapers. Bd. dirs. Nebr. Humanities Coun., Cozad Comty. Hosp.; chairperson Cozad Hosp. Found. Recipient Zimmerman Disting. Professorship Midland Luth. Coll., 1993-94. Mem.: P.E.O., Soc. Collegiate Journalists (nat. 2nd v.p. 1992—94), Nat. Journalism Hall of Fame (charter coll./univ. advisers 1994), Am. Scholastic Press Assn., Am. Scholastic Press Assn., Nebr. Collegiate Media Assn. (charter), Columbia Scholastic Press Assn. (Gold Key 1993), Assoc. Collegiate Press. (Hall of Fame 1988), Coll. Media Advisers Inc. (nat. sec. 1986—92, Nat. Disting. Newspaper Adviser 1975, Nat. Disting. Yearbook Adviser 1980, Nat. Disting. Multi-Media Adviser 1991). Republican. Methodist. Avocations: writing, music, art, creating unusual celebrations. Home: 102 W 11th St Cozad NE 69130-1401

PETERSON, MARY ELIZABETH, retired elementary school educator; b. Wellsville, Ohio, Aug. 2, 1930; d. Guy Emmett and Edith Ellen (Todd) P. BS, Malone Coll., 1961; MA, Kent State U., 1968; postgrad., Akron (Ohio) U., 1970—. Cert. elem. tchr., Ohio. With C.B. Hunt Co., Salem, Ohio, 1952-55; bookkeeper Fred & Co., Cleve., 1955-57; billing clk. Comml. Motor Freight, Canton, Ohio, 1957-58; bookkeeper part-time Waltz the Camera Man, Canton, 1958-68; tchr. Canton City Schs., 1961-91, ret., 1991. Computer liaison Canton City Schs., 1983—, book adoption com., 1985-86. McGregor Sch. liaison ARC, Canton, 1970; tchr. adult Sunday Sch., First Ch. of the Nazarene. Mem. Stark County Ret. Tchrs. Assn., Ohio Ret. Tchrs. Assn., Malone's Women's Club. Republican. Avocations: music, writing poetry, painting. Home: 806 41st St NW Canton OH 44709-2539

PETERSON, MARY KAY, elementary education educator; b. Concordia, Mo., Sept. 17, 1946; d. Raymond A. and Marie Kathryn (Welch) Burrow; m. James G. Peterson, Jan. 27, 1968; 1 child, Jeffrey James. BS, Cen. Mo. State U., 1967, MS, 1975. 1st grade tchr. Raytown (Mo.) Schs., 1967-69; elem. tchr. Blue Springs (Elem.) Schs., 1969—. Mem.: Mo. State Tchrs. Assn., Cmty. Educators Assn., Internat. Reading Assn. (Mo. state coun., v.p., pres.-elect, pres.), Delta Kappa Gamma (sec., v.p., pres.). Office: Thomas Utica Sch 1813 W Main St Blue Springs MO 64015-3563 E-mail: mpeterson@bssd.net.

PETERSON, MYRA M. special education educator; b. Eagle Bend, Minn., July 1, 1937; children: Randy E., Vicky L. Rholl. Assoc. in Edn., St. Cloud State U., 1957, BS in Elem. Edn., 1963; cert. in learning disabilities, Bemidji State U., 1979. Cert. edn. Elem. instr. Wadena (Minn.) Pub. Sch., 1957-60; supplemental edn. and secondary level reading Bertha-Hewitt (Minn.) Sch., 1964-75, learning disabilities instr., 1975—. Coord. for local sch. Minn. Basic Skills Program, Bertha-Hewitt (Minn.) Sch., 1980-85; adv. bd. for spl. needs N.W. Tech. Coll., Wadena, 1992—. Mem., edn. com. United Meth. Ch., Wadena; pres. Am. Legion Aux., Wadena, 1990—. Named Tchr. of Yr., Bertha-Hewitt (Minn.) Edn. Assn., 1981. Mem. NEA, Minn. State Edn. Assn., Bertha-Hewitt Edn. Assn., N.W. Reading Coun. (pres. 1987-88), Delta Kappa Gamma Internat. (pres. Alpha Eta chpt. 1993-95, Woman of Achievement 1991). Office: Bertha-Hewitt Sch PO Box 8 Bertha MN 56437-0008

PETERSON, NANCY, special education educator; AS, Webster State Coll., 1963; BS in Elem. Edn. magna cum laude, Brigham Young U., 1964, MS in Ednl. Psychology, 1966, PhD in Ednl. Psychology, 1969. Instr. in tchr. edn. Brigham Young U., Provo, Utah, 1966-69; asst. prof. edn. dept. spl. edn. U. Kans., Lawrence, 1969-74, dir. spl. edn. classes for handicapped children Clin. Tng. Ctr., 1969-89, project dir. head start tng., 1973-74, coord. edn. univ. affiliated facility Clin. Tng. Ctr., 1969-74, coord. pers. tng. programs in mental retardation, 1973-76, assoc. prof. edn., 1974-88, project dir. pers. tng. programs, 1986-93, prof. edn. dept. spl. edn., 1988—, dept. chair, 1994—. Rsch. sci. Bur. Child Rsch., U. Kans., 1969—; prin. investigator for Kans. U. Kans. Early Childhood Rsch. Inst., 1977-82 Recipient J.E. Wallace Wallin award Internat. Coun. Exceptional Children, 1993. Office: U Kans Dept Spl Edn 3001 Dole Bldg Lawrence KS 66045-0001

PETERSON, VERONICA MARIE (RONNIE PETERSON), clinical nurse manager; b. Washington, Feb. 29, 1956; BA, U. Wis., Eau Claire, 1978; BSN, U. Wis., Madison, 1990, MS, 1993. Oncology staff nurse U. Wis. Hosp. and Clinics, Madison, 1990-93, nursing supr., 1993-97, nurse mgr., 1998—. Author: Just the Facts: A Pocket Guide to Basic Nursing, 1994, 2d edit., 1998; author: (poetry) SunFlowers, 1997, Listen, 1996, Learning to Soar, 1997, Alone, 1997, My Grandmother's Quilt, 1998, Sisters, 1998, others; author/dir. videos: Understanding Changes in Your Health After Cancer Treatment, 1993, Reflections on Nursing, 1994; contbr. articles to profl. jours.; compiled, dir., participant dinner theatre prodn.: Reflections on Nursing. Recipient Nat. Presdl. award for Lit. Excellence Iliad Press, 1997, 98. Mem. Wis. Nurses Assn. (bd. dirs. 1993-97, nurse liaison to Wis. State Med. Soc.994-97, Image of Nursing award 1993, 95), Madison Dist. Nurses Assn. (2d v.p. 19-94, pres. 1995-97), Internat. Soc. Poets, Oncology Nursing Soc., Pi Kappa Delta (nat. oratory champion 1978).

PETERSON, WILLARD JAMES, Chinese history educator; b. Oak Park, Aug. 1, 1938; s. Otto Stewart and Catherine (Esin) P.; m. Toby Black, Aug 27, 1960. BA, U. Rochester, 1960; MA, U. London, 1964; PhD, Harvard U., 1970. Asst. prof. Dartmouth Coll., Hanover, N.H., 1970-71; prof. East Asian Studies and History Princeton (N.J.) U., 1971—, Gordon Wu '58 prof. chinese studies, 2002—. Author: Bitter Gourd, 1979, Power of Culture, 1994, Ways with Words, 2000, Cambridge History of China, vol. 9, 2002. Office: Dept of East Asian Studies & Hist Princeton U Princeton NJ 08544-0001

PETESCH, NATALIE L. MAINES, English language educator, author; BS magna cum laude, Boston U., 1955; MA, Brandeis U., 1956; PhD, U. Tex., 1962. Teaching fellow U. Tex., Austin, 1956-59, spl. instr., 1959-60; asst. prof. dept. English San Francisco State U., 1961-62, Southwest Tex. State U., 1962-65; author short stories, novels. Disting. vis. prof. in creative writing, U. Idaho, 1982; presenter readings and fiction workshops nationwide. Author: After the First Death, There is No Other, 1974 (winner U. Iowa Sch. Letters award for Short Fiction, 1974), The Odyssey of Katinou Kalokovich, 1974, Two Novels: The Leprosarium and The Long Hot Summers of Yasha K., 1979 (winner New Letters Summer Prize book award, 1978), Soul Clap Its Hand and Sing, 1981 (literary fellowship Pa. Coun. on Arts, 1980), Duncan's Colony, 1982, Wild With All Regret, 1986 (winner Swallow's Tale competition, 1985), Flowering Mimosa, 1987, Justina of Andalusia and Other Stories, 1990, (autobiographical memoir) Contemporary Authors, 1990, The immigrant Train and Other Stories, 1996, biog. essay in Lessons in Persuasion, 2000; short stories included in anthologies. Recipient Pitts. Cultural Trust award for Outstanding Established Artist, 1991, Harvey Curtis Webster award for Best Story, 1989; Main Street Morning included in Best American Short Stories, 1979, other writing awards. Avocations: travel, walking, reading, music. Home: 6320 Crombie St Pittsburgh PA 15217-2511

PETIT, SUSAN YOUNT, French and English language educator; b. Fairfield, Ohio, Aug. 25, 1945; d. Howard Wesley and Elizabeth R. Yount; m. John M. Gill, June 22, 1984. BA in English, Knox Coll., 1966; MA in English, Purdue U., 1968; MA in French, Coll. of Notre Dame, Belmont, Calif., 1983. Prof. French and English Coll. of San Mateo, Calif., 1968—. Mem. exec. com. Calif. C.C. Acad. Senate, Sacramento, 1984-86; pres. acad. senate San Mateo County C.C. Dist., 1981-82, Coll. of San Mateo, 1978-79. Author: Michel Tournier's Metaphysical Fictions, 1991, Françoise Mallet-Joris, 2001; contbr. articles and revs. to profl. publs., chpts. to books. Mem. MLA, Am. Assn. Tchrs. French, Simone de Beauvoir Soc., Conseil Internat. d'Etudes Francophones, Women in French, Calif. Lang. Tchrs. Assn., F. Scott Fitzgerald Soc., Am. Name Soc., Phi Beta Kappa. Office: Coll of San Mateo 1700 W Hillsdale Blvd San Mateo CA 94402-3757 E-mail: petit@smccd.net.

PETITAN, DEBRA ANN BURKE, educator, education counselor, design engineer, writer, author; b. Chgo., Mar. 12, 1932; d. James Marcellus and Susan Florence (Hines) Burke; m. Kenneth Charles Petitan, Aug. 9, 1952; 1 child, Susan Florence. AA, Wilson Jr. Coll., Chgo., 1951, N.Y. Inst. Photography, 1952; BS in Primary Edn., Chgo. State U., 1956, MS in Indsl. Edn., 1967; DSc in Applied Sci. and Tech., London Inst. Tech., 1971; postgrad., U. Wis., Bradley U., U. Calif., U. Ill.; grad., Inst. Children's Lit., West Redding, Conn., 1991; cert. in Childrens' Portraiture, North Light Art Sch., 1997. Tchr. Chgo. Bd. Edn., 1958-71, guidance counselor, 1976-84, now tchr., cons.; nat. dir. edn. Nation of Islam, 1971-75; design engr. Fed. Sign and Signal Corp., Chgo., 1975-76; CEO, owner Petitan's Creative Projects, Inc. Nat. adv. bd. Nat. Right to Work Orgn., 1976-85; cons. ednl. devel., 1978; computer libr. cons.; owner, CEO, Fayzah's Fin. Svcs., Instrn. Svcs. in Trading and Investing, Fayzah's Creative Projects, Inc.; ednl. cons. tech. analysis and chart reading stock market; participant summer writing festival U. Iowa, 1991. Photographer VISTA News, 1969-70; writer children's lit.; author curriculum introducing computer-aided design techniques in the pub. schs., 1965. Cmty. svc. rec. sec. 9600 Block Club; navigator, pub. rels. officer IL wing Squadron 8, capt. CAP, 1953—56; chmn. Career Women for Johnson/Humphrey, Chgo., 1965; dir. Christian edn. Trinity United Ch. Christ, Chgo., 1978—81, family counselor, 1978—81; organizer, leader family counseling ministry, lic. lay Eucharistic min. Episcopal Ch. St. Edmund, Chgo. Episc. Diocese, 1989. Named Woman of Yr. Iota Phi Lambda, 1978; recipient 250 Hr. medal Ground Observer Corps, 1952, 25 Yr. Service medal Chgo. Bd. Edn., 1987. Mem. Off-Campus Writer's Workshop (editor newsletter), Soc. of Children's Book Writers, Am. Contract Bridge League, Am. Bridge Assn. (life master, rec. sec.), Children's Reading Roundtable, Green River Writers, Epsilon Pi Tau. Achievements include introduction of Computer Aided Design curriculum to field of education. Office: Fayzah's Fin Ednl Svc Chicago IL 60603 E-mail: drdap1@ameritech.net.

PETLICHKOFF, LINDA MARIE, physical education educator; b. Dearborn, Mich., Sept. 25, 1950; d. Mike and Margaret Aileen Petlichkoff. BS, Mich. State U., 1972, MA, 1982; PhD, U. Ill., 1988. Secondary math. tchr. Wayne (Mich.)-Westland Cmty. Schs., 1973-83; head volleyball coach Henry Ford C.C., Dearborn, 1980-83; asst. prof. phys. edn. Boise (Idaho) State U., 1987-92, assoc. prof. phys. edn., 1992-95, prof. phys. edn., 1995—. Mem. nat. faculty Am. Sport Edn. Program—Coaching Principles, Champaign, Ill., 1989—. Contbr. articles to profl. jours. Grantee Idaho State Bd. Edn., 1989, Coll. Edn. Infrastructure, Faculty Rsch. Funding, 1993, Boise State U. Found., 1997. Mem. AAHPERD, APA (divsn. 47), Assn. for Advancement of Applied Sport Psychology (cert. cons., publ. dir. 1993-95, pres. 2002-03). Avocations: mountain biking, golf, snow skiing. Office: Boise State U Dept Kinesiology 1910 University Dr Boise ID 83725-1710 E-mail: lpetlic@boisestate.edu.

PETOSKEY, THOMAS W. secondary school educator; b. Bay City, Mich., Feb. 17, 1955; s. Walton R. and Henrietta (Wesolowski) P. BS, U. Detroit, 1977; MS, Oklahoma City U., 1982, EdD, 1984. Cert. tchr., Okla., Mich., Calif. Tchr. sci. Oklahoma City Pub. Schs.; now tchr. sci. Archdiocese of L.A. Com. mem. Loyola Marymount U. Named Vol. of Yr., Oklahoma City Pub. Schs., 1982, 83, Tchr. of Yr., 1992. Mem. ASCD, Am. Fedn. Tchrs., Calif. Sci. Tchrs. Assn., Nat. Cath. Edn. Assn., Nat. Sci. Tchrs. Assn.

PETRAIT, BROTHER JAMES ANTHONY, secondary education educator, clergy member; b. Phila., May 4, 1937; s. John Joseph and Antonina Frances (Cizek) P. BA, U. Detroit, 1969; MEd, U. Ga., 1971; postgrad. in Scis. and Edn., 8 Univs. and Colls. in U.S., 1971—. Joined Oblates of St Francis de Sales, Roman Cath. Ch., 1957. Sci. tchr. Salesian H.S., Detroit, 1961-70, Judge Meml. H.S., Salt Lake City, 1972-76, Benedictine H.S., Detroit, 1976-82, St. Joseph H.S., Ogden, Utah, 1983-88, Fredriksted, V.I., 1988—; tchr. resource agt. Am. Astron. Soc., 1995—. Pres. Mich. Assn. of Biology Tchrs., 1978-82, Utah Biology Tchrs. Assn., 1985-88; bd. dirs. Utah Sci. Tchrs. Assn., 1985-88; presenter at workshops, speaker in Chgo., New Orleans, Las Vegas, Detroit, Phila., Salt Lake City, Layton, Orlando, Purdue U., Anaheim, Australian Nat. Univ., Canberra; participant in 8 NSF-funded programs: U. Ga., Christian Bros. Colls., Vanderbilt U., St. Lawrence U., Ball State U., W. Va. U., No. Ariz. U. Contbr. article to teacher's mags. and ednl. jours. including The Am. Biology Tchr., The Sci. Tchr., The Cath. Digest., Congrl. Record. Anti nuclear weapons activist, founder and leader Nuclear Free Utah, Ogden, 1986-88; led boycott against Morton Salt Co., maker of nuclear weapons.. Recipient Outstanding Biology Tchr. award Nat. Assn. Biology Tchrs., 1975, Nat. Finalist in Presdl. awards for excellence in sci. and math. tchg. Nat. Sci. Tchrs. Assn./NSF/The White House, 1995, finalist and alt. in the Albert Einstein fellowship for Disting. Educators, 1997; fellow Access Excellence fellow Genentech Inc. program for Outstanding Biology Tchrs., 1996, 97. Mem. AAAS, Nat. Sci. Tchrs. Assn. (cert. in biology and gen. sci., Star award 1976, Ohaus awards, 1980, 84), Am. Astron. Soc. (tchr. resource agt. 1995—, leadership inst. participant U. Tex. and McDonald Observatory 1998), Soc. of Amateur Radio Astronomers, Nat. Sci. Edn. Leadership Assn., Soc. For Sci. Exploration, Inst. of Noetic Scis., Soc. Scientific Exploration, Seti League (V.I. coord.), Nat. Assn. Biol. Tchrs., Phi Delta Kappa. Avocations: radio amateur, computers, photography, videography. Home and Office: Saint Joseph H S Plot 3 Rte 2 Frederiksted VI 00840 E-mail: jpetrait@earthling.net.

PETRAK, CLIFF MATTHEW, secondary school educator; b. Chgo., Sept. 6, 1942; s. Joseph Petrak and Josephine Marcella (Jedlinski) Petrak. BS in Math., De Paul U., Chgo., 1964; MS in Math., Chgo. State U., 1970, MS in Edn. Libr. Sci. and Comms., 1981. Mem. math. faculty Brother Rice H.S., Chgo., 1964—, head libr., 1976—89, asst. libr, 1975—76, 1990—, frosh-soph baseball coach, 1966—89, varsity baseball coach, 1990—2000, varsity and jr. varsity bowling coach, 1987—. Author: The Art and Sci. of Aggressive Base Running, 1986, The Complete Guide to Outfield Play, 1998; contbr. articles to profl. jours. Named to Coaches Hall of Fame, Chgo. Cath. League, 2002; recipient Tony Lawless award, Chgo. Cath. League (baseball), 1991, 1993, 1994, 2000, Chgo. Cath. League (bowlingl), 2003. Mem.: Nat. Coun. Tchrs. of Math. Roman Catholic. Avocations: dancing, hiking, bicycling, baseball, white-water rafting. Office: Brother Rice HS 10001 S Pulaski Rd Chicago IL 60655 E-mail: cpetrak1@hotmail.com.

PETRALIA, RONALD SEBASTIAN, entomologist, neurobiologist; b. Lawrence, Mass., Nov. 7, 1954; s. Samuel and Rosalie (Zanfagna) P. BS in Entomology summa cum laude, U. Mass., 1975; PhD in Entomology and Biology, Tex. A&M U., 1979. Rsch. asst. Tex. A&M U., College Station, 1975-79, rsch. assoc., 1979-80; asst. prof. biology St. Ambrose Coll., Davenport, Iowa, 1980-85; rsch. fellow dept. anatomy George Washington U., Washington, 1985-90; sr. staff fellow Nat. Inst. Deafness and Other Comm. Disorders, NIH, Bethesda, Md., 1991-97, staff scientist, 1997—. Presenter in field. Contbr. chpts. to books: Excitatory Amino Acids, 1992, The Mammalian Coclear Nuclei: Their Role in Neuroendocrine Function, 1996, The Ionotropic Glutamate Receptors, 1997, Ionotropic Glutamate to Receptors in the CNS, 1999, Handbook of Chemical Neuroanatomy: Glutamate, 2000; contbr. articles to profl. jours. Mem. AAAS, Chesapeake Soc. Microscopy (coun. mem., newsletter editor, past pres.), Soc. Neurosci., Entomol. Soc. Am., Microscopy Soc. Am., Assn. Rsch. Otolaryngology, Cambridge Entomol. Club, Sigma Xi. Roman Catholic. Home: 3 Pooks Hill Rd Apt 218 Bethesda MD 20814-5404 Office: NIDCD NIH Rm 50/4142 9000 Rockville Pike Bethesda MD 20892-8027 E-mail: petralia@nidcd.nih.gov.

PETREA, PATRICIA BETH, special education educator; b. Seaford, Del., Sept. 8, 1966; d. Zeb William and Joan Marie (Fluharty) P.; 1 child, Zeb Charles. BA in Social Sci., Salisbury State U., 1989; cert. in spl. edn., U. Md. Ea. Shore, 1991; M in Spl. Edn., Wilmington Coll. Cert. tchr., spl. edn. tchr., Md., social sci., spl. edn., Del. Tchr. spl. edn Laurel (Del.) Sch. Dist., 1991—. Mem. NEA. Avocations: travel, reading, cooking. Home: 105 S Dual Hwy Seaford DE 19973-1817

PETRILLI, MICHAEL J. federal agency administrator; B honors in polit. sci., U. Mich., 1995. Assoc. dep. under sec. US Dept. Edn., Innovation and Improvement, Wash., 2002—, spec. asst. to dep. sec. edn., 2001—02; dir. US Dept. Edn., Strategic Planning Process; vp Cmty. Partnerships at K12; program dir. Thomas B. Fordham Found., Dayton, Ohio; dir. student leadership programs Joy Outdoor Edn. Ctr., Clarksville, Ohio. Office: US Dept Edn Innovation and Improvement 400 Maryland Ave SW FOB-6 Rm 4W314 Brant Rock MA 02020 Office Fax: 202-401-4123. E-mail: michael.petrilli@ed.gov.*

PETRILLO, ANNA, elementary school educator; b. Roccoromana, Caserta, Italy, July 21, 1952; came to U.S., 1954; d. Carmine Antonio and Anna (Ricciardi) P. BS in Edn., Youngstown State U., 1974; MEd, U. Houston, 1982, cert. supervision and mid-mgmt., 1991, postgrad., 1986—; endorsement ESL, Tex. So. U., 1984. Cert. elem. tchr., ESL tchr., supr., midmgmt. adminstr., Tex. Tchr. ESL for adults Girard (Ohio) Pub. Schs., 1976-78; tchr. 3d and 4th grades Diocese of Youngstown, Ohio, 1975-78; tchr. 1st grade, math. specialist, reading specialist Houston Ind. Sch. Dist., 1978-86, tchr. technologist, career ladder level III, 1986—. Adj. prof. Houston C.C., 1986—; mem. career ladder com. Houston Ind. Sch. Dist., 1984-93, grant writing cons., 1991—, mem. Houston's task force for edn. excellence, 1983-84; textbook reviewer Merrill Pub. Co., 1985. Mem. Houston Proud Community Involvement, 1990—; cert. ombudsman Harris County Area Agy. on Aging, Houston, 1991-92; instr. first aid ARC, Youngstown, 1972-78. Grantee NSF, 1982, Impact II replicator 1984, 91, 94, developer 1985, 87, 89, Houston Bus. Com. for Ednl. Excellence, 1992-93, mini-grantee. Mem. ASCD, Congress of Houston Tchrs., Assn. Tex. Profl. Educators, Houston Assn. for Childhood Edn. (pres. 1992-94, v.p. for later childhood 1990-92), Houston Area Apple Users Group (edn. SIG chair 1985-91), U. Houston Alumni Orgn. (life), Phi Delta Kappa (newsletter editor 1990). Democrat. Roman Catholic. Avocations: travel, reading, community volunteer. Office: Lovett Elem Sch 8814 S Rice Ave Houston TX 77096-2622 Home: 5406 Beechnut St Houston TX 77096-1216

PETROSKY, REGINE, art educator; b. Ihlauschen, Germany, Oct. 28, 1937; came to U.S., 1951; d. Bruno Max and Hedwig Louise (Ambrosius) Mallwitz; m. Anthony William Petrosky, Feb. 2, 1957; children: Debora, Phylis (dec.). Grad., N.Y. Sch. Indsl. Art, 1956; postgrad., Queens (N.Y.) C.C., 1973, Columbia Greene C.C., Hudson, N.Y., 1989. Staff art and pattern making dept. Simplicity Patterns, N.Y.C., 1956-57; staff expediting Bucilla Co., L.I., N.Y., 1972-73; clk., dispatcher United Parcel Svc., Maspeth, N.Y., 1973-84; instr. art Columbia Greene C.C., Hudson, 1985—. Dir. activities St. Joseph's Villa, Catskill, N.Y., 1995—; freelance designer numerous mags., 1977—. Recipient award Grumbacher/Koh-I-Noor, 1993, Winsor and Newton Co., 1989, 93. Mem. Bethlehem Art Assn. (chair prize and show 1996), Kent Art Assn., Hudson River Watercolor Soc., Hudson-Athens Lighthouse Preservation Soc. (cons. interior restoration), Greene County Photography Club (trustee, bd. dirs.). Greene County Arts and Crafts Guild, Inc. (trustee, pres., Art award 1993, 94, 95). Lutheran. Avocations: gardening, trout fishing, needlework, nature crafts, tai chi. Home: 356 State Route 385 Catskill NY 12414-6019 Office: Saint Josephs Villa 38 Prospect Ave Catskill NY 12414-1599

PETROU, ANASTASIS D. consultant, adjunct faculty; b. Kato Varosi, Famagusta, Cyprus, Oct. 6, 1961; s. Androula and Demetrios Theodotou. B.S, Mankato State U., Mankato, MN, 1981—84; MBA, Mankato State U., Mankato, MN, USA, 1985—89; MA in Polit. Sci., Mankato State Univesity, Mankato, MN, USA, 1989—94; MLIS, UCLA, 1996—2000, PhD in Libr. and Info. Sci., 1996. Faculty mem. / tenured asst. prof. Mankato (Minn.) State U., 1988—94; grad. student rschr. UCLA, Los Angeles, Calif., 1996—99; adj. faculty Woodury U., Burbank, Calif., 2000—01. Author: (manual) PALS Personal Computer Disaster Prevention and Recovery Plan, 1991; contbr. articles to profl. jours. and confs.

PETROU, JUDITH ELLEN, retired secondary school educator; b. Hammond, Ind., Nov. 6, 1938; d. Gerhardt Herman and Hazel Bertha (Weseloh) Busch; m. Raymond Harry Ernest, Dec. 21, 1963 (div. Nov. 1988); children: Gregory, Patricia; m. John D. Petrou, June 23, 1990. BA, Valparaiso U., 1960; MA, Northwestern U., 1966. Cert. secondary tchr., Ind. Tchr. social studies Portage (Ind.) Schs., 1961, Hammond Schs., 1961-67; tchr. computer sci. Gary (Ind.) Schs., 1974—2001; sci. dept. chair, 1992—2001; ret., 2001. Lectr. NW Ind. Symphony. Mem. park bd. Town of Cedar Lake, Ind., 1985-88; trustee Lake County Pub. Library System, Merrillville, Ind., 1979-90, bd. pres., 1985-88, vol.; sec. Lake County Library Found., 1985, bd. dirs., 1985—; vol. Portage Libr. Friends. Mem. ALA, NEA, Am. Fedn. Tchrs., Am. Libr. Trustees Assn. (intellectual freedom com. 1979-90, chmn. 1990), Ind. Libr. Trustees Assn. (pers. com. 1982-83, membership com. task force 1987-90), No. Ind. Libr. Bds. Assn. (pres. 1981). Lutheran. Avocations: reading, baking, travel, writing.

PETROVICH, DOROTHY, elementary school educator; b. N.J., July 14, 1931; d. Nicholas and Freida (Kleva) Frantin; m. Walter Petrovich, Aug. 22, 1954; children: David, Amy. BS, Jersey City State Tchrs. Coll., 1953. Tchr. Bd. Edn., Middletown, N.J., 1953-54; substitute tchr. various schs., 1954-70; remedial math. tchr. Monmouth Beach (N.J.) Bd. Edn., 1970-72, 1st-4th grade tchr., 1972-91, ret., 1991. Editorial asst. to Socialist Republic, winner writing awards, cons. to editorial bd. internat. mag. Mem. N.J. Edn. Assn., NEA, Monmouth Beach Edn. Assn. (sec.-treas.). Home: 165 S Manor Ct Belmar NJ 07719-3658

PETROZZINO, JANE A. learning consultant; b. Newark, Oct. 5, 1947; d. Anthony Frank and Janet Louise Petrozzino. BA, William Paterson Coll., 1969, MEd, 1974; PhD, Fordham U., 1982. Elem. tchr. Wayne (N.J.) Pub. Schs., 1969-74, learning disabilities specialist, 1974-75, learning cons., 1975-84; pvt. practice as learning cons. Kinnelon and Wayne, N.J., 1981—; supr. spl. edn. Ramapo Ctrl. Sch. Dist., Hillburn, N.Y., 1984-87; prin./asst. to regional exec. dir. spl. edn. Region VII Coun. Spl. Edn., Bergen County, N.J., 1987-88; supr. instrn./asst. to supt. Moonachie Bd. Edn., Bergen County, N.J., 1987-88; supr. spl. svcs. Totowa (N.J.) Bd. Edn., 1988-89. Adj. prof. William Paterson Coll., Wayne, 1978—: panelist/cons. U.S. Dept. Edn., Washington, 1982—; lectr., in-svc. staff trainer various bds. edn., N.Y., N.J., 1982—; mem. U.S. world team in field of dyslexia Orton Dyslexia Soc./Pres.'s Com. U.S. Amb. Program, 1993. Mem. N.J. Assn. Learning Cons., N.Y. State Adminstrs. Assn., Orton-Dyslexia Soc., Assn. Children with Learning Disabilities, Fordham U. Sch. Adminstrs. Assn., Phi Delta Kappa. Roman Catholic. Avocations: piano, dance, foreign languages, skating. Home: 77 Old Cow Pasture Ln Kinnelon NJ 07405-2413

PETRUSKI, JENNIFER ANDREA, speech and language pathologist; b. Kingston, NY, Jan. 28, 1968; d. Andrew Francis and Judith (Cruger) Petruski. BS, SUNY, Buffalo, 1990, MSEd, 1992. Cert. tchr. speech-hearing handicapped N.Y., lic. speech-lang. pathology N.Y. Speech-lang. pathologist Kingston (N.Y.) City Schs., 1992—, student rev. team facilitator, 2002—; clin. practicum supr. SUNY, New Paltz, 1996—. Cooperating tchr. SUNY, New Paltz, 1995—2002; ind. contr. speech svcs. Ulster County, 1997; cooperating tchr. Coll. St. Rose, 1997; summer sch. tchr. New Paltz Sch. Dist., 2002. Mem.: Speech and Hearing Assn. Hudson Valley, Bd. Regional Assn. Pres., N.Y. State Speech-Lang. and Hearing Assn., Am. Speech and Hearing Assn., Speech and Hearing Assn. Hudson Valley (corr. sec. 1995—98, newsletter editor 1995—2002, membership com. 1995—2002, treas. 1997, pres. 1999—2000, nominating com. 1999—2000, membership chair 2000—02, legis. chair 2000—, website designer 2001—02, past. pres. 2001—, historian 2001—, continuing edn. adminstr. 2002, program com. 2003), Bd. Regional Presidents (membership chair 2000—02, public info. chair 2003). Home: PO Box 88 Hurley NY 12443 E-mail: jpetruski@aol.com.

PETRUSKI, MARY THERESA, secondary school educator; b. Balt., Mar. 21, 1951; d. Joseph Oscar and Mary Louise (James) Robison; m. Robert Michael Petruski, Dec. 21, 1974; 1 child, Michael Joseph. BA, Shepherd Coll., Shepherdstown, W.Va., 1973; MEd, Coll. of NJ, 1980. Cert. tchr., W.Va., N.J.; cert. supr., N.J. Sales assoc. WBAL-TV, Balt., 1973-74; exec. sec. N.Am. Phillips Lighting, Robbinsville, N.J., 1975-76; tchr. history Toms River (NJ) Regional Schs., 1976-87; tchr. history, supr. dept. social studies, prin. gen. studies Hillel H.S., Ocean, NJ, 1988—. Travel cons. AIFS, Greenwich, Conn., 1978-87; travel cons. ACIS, 1999—; mem. panel dept. on women's studies Rutgers U., New Brunswick, N.J., 1987; mem. women's studies program Wellesley Coll.; advisor Model UN, Yeshiva U., N.Y.C., 1992—; advisor Model Congress, 1999—. Contbr. articles to profl. jours. Mem. Interfaith Hospitality Network; participant Christmas for the Children, Ocean County Criminal Justice System, Toms River, 1992; mem. Chapel of the Four Chaplains, Valley Forge, Pa., 1991—. Mem. AAUW, NOW, Nat. Coun. for History Edn., NJ Coun. for History Edn., Nat. Coun. of the Social Studies, NJ Coun. of Social Studies, Orgn. Am. Historians, Supervision and Curriculum in Secondary Schs., Sigma Sigma Sigma. Democrat. Presbyterian. Avocations: foreign travel, playing piano, hiking, white water rafting. Home: 1188 Windham Ct Toms River NJ 08755-1373 Office: Hillel HS 1027 Deal Rd Ocean NJ 07712-2503

PETRUZZI, CHRISTOPHER ROBERT, business educator, consultant; b. Peoria, Ill., July 28, 1951; s. Benjamin Robert and Mary Katherine (Urban) P.; m. Georgina Sailer, June 20, 1992; 1 child, Lillian Caroline. BA, Wabash Coll., 1972; MBA, U. Chgo., 1974; PhD, U. So. Calif., 1983. Lectr. bus. U. Wis., Milw., 1975-77; cons. H.C. Wainwright, Boston, 1978-79; lectr. U. So. Calif., 1978-81; prof. bus. U. Pa., Phila., 1981-84; prof. acctg. NYU, 1984-89, Calif. State U., Fullerton, 1989—. Pres. ECON Investment Software, San Clemente, Calif., 1987-2000; pres. Euronet Securities Corp., N.Y.C., 2000-2001, Smart Execution LLC, 2001-02 Earhart fellow, 1972-73, U. Chgo. fellow, 1974-76. Libertarian. Christian. Office: Ste 302B 629 Caminode los Mares San Clemente CA 92673 Home: 1527 Via Tulipan San Clemente CA 92673

PETRY, BARBARA LOUISE CROSS, elementary educator; b. Canton, Ohio, Jan. 8, 1954; d. Glenn Griffin and Mary Lucille (Bamberger) Cross; m. Thomas Alan Petry Sr., July 23, 1983; 1 child, Thomas Ala Jr. BA, BS, U. Tampa, 1975; MEd, U. Akron, 1978; cert. tchr. of gifted, Ashland Univ., 1988. Lic. pvt. pilot. Tchr. Our Lady of Peace, Canton, 1975-78; prin. St. Paul Sch., Canton, 1978-82; tchr. Canton City Schs., 1984—2000; tchr. gifted students Collier County Publ. Sch., 2000—. Sec., treas. Petry and Assocs. Mem. Jr. League of Canton, Aircraft and Owners and Pilots Assn., Aviation Days, Inc., East Cen. Ohio Pilots Assn., Ninety Nines, Nat. Alumni Assn. Univ. Tampa (bd. mem.), Omicron Delta Kappa, Alpha Chi Omega, Kappa Delta Pi, Phi Delta Kappa. Republican. Roman Catholic. Home: 150 June Ct Marco Island FL 34145-3533

PETTENGILL, GORDON H(EMENWAY), physicist, educator; b. Providence, Feb. 10, 1926; s. Rodney Gordon and Frances (Hemenway) P.; m. Pamela Anne Wolfenden, Oct. 28, 1967; children: Mark Robert, Rebecca Jane. BS, MIT, 1948; PhD, U. Calif., Berkeley, 1955. Staff mem. Lincoln Lab. MIT, Lexington, 1954-63, 65-68, prof. planetary physics, dept. earth, atmospheric and planetary scis. Cambridge, 1971—2001, dir. Ctr. Space Rsch., 1984-90; assoc. dir. Arecibo (P.R.) Obs., 1963-65, dir., 1968-71. Served with inf., Signal Corps AUS, 1944-46. Decorated Combat Inf. badge; recipient Magellanic Premium, Am. Philos. Soc., 1994. Fellow Am. Geophys. Union (Whipple award 1995, Charles A. Whitten award 1997); mem. AAAS, Am. Phys. Soc., Am. Astron. Soc., Internat. Astron. Union, Internat. Radio Sci. Union, Nat. Acad. Sci., Am. Acad. Arts and Sci. Achievements include pioneering several techniques in radar astronomy for describing properties of planets and satellites; discovering 59-day rotational period of planet Mercury. Office: MIT 77 Massachusetts Ave Rm 37-582D Cambridge MA 02139-4307

PETTIEGREW, HENRY, assistant principal; b. Hollandale, Miss., Nov. 17, 1948; s. Erma Lee (Loften) P.; m. Velma Jean, Aug. 23, 1970; children: Toya Rhnay, Henry II. BS, Jakcson State U., 1972; MA, Kent State U., 1978. Tchr., dept. chair person Cleve. Pub. Schs., 1972-86, tchr. vocat. edn., 1986-87, asst. prin., 1987-90, acting prin., 1991-92, asst. prin., 1992—. Bd. dirs. Canaan Ednl. Enhancement Community Ctr., Cleve., 1988-89. Named Outstanding Young Men of Am., 1983. Mem. ASCD, Ohio Assn. Secondary Sch. Adminstr., Ohio Network and Asst. for Sch. and Community, Cleve. Indsl. Edn. Club (sec. 1981-82, treas. 1982-83, v.p. 1983-84, pres. 1984-86). Democrat. Baptist. Avocations: reading, woodcraft, music. Home: 32147 Hamilton Ct Apt 103 Cleveland OH 44139-5739

PETTIGREW, CLAIRE RUDOLPH, music educator; b. Chambersburg, Pa., Aug. 3, 1961; d. Herman Leon and Helen Frances (Tobey) Rudolph; m. Daniel Pettigrew III, Mar. 10, 1991; stepchildren: Christine, Sara. BS in Edn. in Music, West Chester U., 1983, MEd in Elem. Edn., 1991. Tchr. music West Chester (Pa.) Area Sch. Dist., 1984—. Co-dir. summer music program West Chester Cmty. Ctr., 1986. Mem. West Chester Cmty. Band, 1987—, sec., 1993-97, pres., 1997—; charter mem. Gilbert and Sullivan Soc. Chester County. Mem. NEA, Pa. Sch. Edn. Assn., Music Educator Nat. Conf., Am. ORFF-Schulwerk Assn., Phi Delta Kappa, Sigma Alpha Iota (Coll. Honor award 1983). Avocations: counted cross-stitch, playing flute and piccolo. Office: Starkweather Elem Sch 1050 Wilmington Pike West Chester PA 19382-7300

PETTIGREW, FRANK EDWIN, JR., assistant dean, physical education educator; b. Ravenna, Ohio, Mar. 6, 1950; s. Frank Edwin Sr. and Darlene Marie (Carver) P.; m. Amy Allen Atkinson, Nov. 4, 1978; children: Emily Erin, Hallie Allyn. BS in Edn., Ashland Coll., 1972; MA in Phys. Edn., Kent State U., 1977; PhD in Edn., U. Idaho, 1984. Tchr. phys. edn. Canton (Ohio) City Schs., 1972-74, Lake Placid (Fla.) Schs., 1974-76; grad. asst. Kent (Ohio) State U., 1976-77, asst. prof., 1985-90, assoc. prof., 1990—, asst. dean Sch. Phys. Edn., Recreation and Dance, 1992—, dir. Sch. Exercise, Leisure and Sport, 1995—; instr. phys. edn. Northwestern U., Evanston, Ill., 1977-81; asst. prof. U. Idaho, Moscow, 1981-85. Author: Secondary Physical Education, 1993; contbr. chpt. to: Preventing Catastrophic Injuries in Recreation, 1985; contbr. articles to profl. jours. Softball coach Lake Youth Sport Programs, Hartville, Ohio, 1992-93. Recipient Outstanding Alumni award Ashland Coll., 1987. Mem. AAHPERD (fellow Rsch. Consortium 1990), Ohio Assn. Health, Phys. Edn., Recreation and Dance (v.p. 1989-91, chairperson rsch. grants 1991—). Republican. Mem. Brethren Ch. Avocations: golf, softball. Home: 12898 Williamsburg Ave NW Uniontown OH 44685-8299

PETTIGREW, JO ARNOLD, educational association administrator; MA in Speech and Drama, North Tex. State U.; EdD in Ednl. Adminstrn., Okla. State U. Asst. exec. dir. Okla. State Sch. Bds. Assn., 1983—95; exec. dir. United Suburban Schs. Assn., 1996—. Bd. dirs. S.W. Ednl. Lab., Austin, Tex., 2002—, sec. bd. dirs., 2003—. Mem.: Okla. Edn. Coalition. Office: SEDL 211 E 7th St Austin TX 78701-3281*

PETTIGREW, JOHNNIE DELONIA, educational diagnostician; b. Electra, Tex., July 2, 1948; d. John Drew and Dolly Marie (Watkins) Chester; divorced; 1 child, Jan Elise. B Elem. Edn., U. North Tex., 1970, MEd, 1982; postgrad., Tex. Woman's U., 1993—, EdD, 1998. Cert. elem., kindergarten, learning disabilities, spl. edn. early childhood, gifted edn. tchr., ednl. diagnostician, adminstr., Tex. 2d grade tchr. Azle (Tex.) Ind. Sch. Dist., 1969-70; 3d grade tchr. Decatur (Tex.) Ind. Sch. Dist., 1970-72; kindergarten, spl. edn. tchr. Boyd (Tex.) Ind. Sch. Dist., 1972-74, kindergarten, gifted edn., spl. edn. tchr., 1981-93; spl. edn. tchr. Springtown (Tex.) Ind. Sch. Dist., 1977-81; gifted edn. tchr. Denton (Tex.) Ind. Sch. Dist., 1993-94, ednl. diagnostician, 1994—. Cons. in gifted edn., early childhood and drama to various sch. dists., Tex.; rsch. cons. various HeadStrt programs; adj. prof. U. North Tex., Denton, 1993—, Tex. Woman's U., 1997—; bd. dir. Denton (Tex.) Area Assn. Edn. Young Children. Author: (play) The Monks Tale: Romeo and Juliet, 1990, also ednl. materials. Co-founder children's story hour Decatur Pub. Libr., 1970; bd. dirs., dir. Wise County Little Theatre, Decatur, Off 380 Players, Wise County, Tex.; life mem. Boyd Ind. Sch. Dist. PTA, 1989, Tex. PTA. Mem. Am. Assn. for Tchg. and Curriculum, Assn. for Childhood Edn. Internat., Am. Edn. Rsch. Assn., Tex. Assn. for Gifted and Talented, Nat. Assn. for the Edn. of Young Children, Denton Area Assn. for Edn. of Young Children (bd. dirs.), So. Early Childhood Assn., Phi Delta Kappa, Phi Kappa Phi. Avocations: theater, needlecraft, sewing. Home: PO Box 91 Decatur TX 76234-0091 Office: 1205 W University Dr Denton TX 76201-1753 E-mail: jpettigrew@dentonisd.org., jpettigrew@twu.edu.

PETTIGREW, L. EUDORA, retired academic administrator; b. Hopkinsville, Ky., Mar. 1, 1928; d. Warren Cicero and Corrye Lee (Newell) Williams; children: Peter W. Woodard, Jonathan R. (dec.). MusB, W.Va. State Coll., 1950; MA, So. Ill. U., 1964, PhD, 1966; PhD honoris causa, U. Pretoria, South Africa, 2002, Holy Family Coll., 2002. Music/English instr. Swift Meml. Jr. Coll., Rogersville, Tenn., 1950-51; music instr., librarian Western Ky. Vocat. Sch., Paducah, 1951-52; music/English instr. Voorhees Coll., Denmark, S.C., 1954-55; dir. music and recreation therapy W.Ky. State Psychiatric Hosp., Hopkinsville, 1956-61; research fellow Rehab. Inst., So. Ill. U., Carbondale, 1961-63, instr., resident counselor, 1963-66, coordinator undergrad. ednl. psychology, 1963-66, acting chmn. ednl. psychology, tchr. corps instr., 1966; asst. prof. to assoc. prof. dept. psychology U. Bridgeport, Conn., 1966-70; prof., chmn. dept. urban and met. studies Coll. Urban Devel. Mich. State U., East Lansing, 1974-80; assoc. provost, prof. U. Del., Newark, 1981-86; pres. SUNY Coll. at Old Westbury, 1986-98. Cons. for rsch. and evaluation Hall Neighborhood House Day Care Tng. Project, Bridgeport, 1966-68, U.S. Ea. Regional Lab., Edn. Devel. Ctr., Newton, Mass., 1967-69; coordinator for edn. devel., 1968-69; cons. Bridgeport Public Schs. lang. devel. project, 1967-68, 70; Lansing Model Cities Agy., Day Care Program, 1971; U. Pitts., 1973, 74, Leadership Program, U. Mich. and Wayne State U., 1975, Wayne County Pub. Health Nurses Assn., 1976, Ill. State Bd. Edn., 1976-77; assoc. prof. U. Bridgeport, 1970, Ctr. for Urban Affairs and Coll. of Edn., Mich. State U., East Lansing, 1970-73; trustee L.I. Community Found.; program devel. specialist Lansing Public Schs. Tchr. Corps program, 1971-73; coord. workshop Conflict Resolution The Woman's Role in Our World, 4th Internat. UN Conf. on Women, Beijing, China, 1995; lectr. in field; condr. workshops in field; mem. adv. com. Economists Allied for Arms Reduction, 1996; guest spkr. Internat. Conf. on The New Role of Higher Edn. in the Context of an Ind. Palestinian State, An-Najah Nat. U., Nablus, Palestine, 1996. Tv/radio appearances on: Black Women in Edn, Channel 23, WKAR, East Lansing, 1973, Black Women and Equality, Channel 2, Detroit, 1974, Women and Careers, Channel 7, Detroit, 1974, Black Women and Work: Integration in Schools, WITL Radio, Lansing, 1974, others; editor: Universities and Their Role in World Peace, 2003; contbr. articles to profl. jours. Mem. Commn. U. Peace, Costa Rica; bd. dirs. U. Pretoria (South Africa) Found., Nat. Peace Garden Found. Recipient Diana award Lansing YWCA, 1977, Outstanding Profl. Achievement award, 1987, award L.I. Ctr. for Bus. and Profl. Women, 1988, Educator of Yr. 100 Black Men of L.I., 1988, Black Women's Agenda award, 1988, Woman of Yr. Nassau/Suffolk Coun. of Adminstrv. Women in Edn., 1989, Disting. Ednl. Leadership award L.I. Women's Coun. for Equal Edn. Tng. and Employment, 1989, L.I. Disting. Leadership award L.I. Bus. News, 1990, Disting. Black Women in Edn. award Nat. Coun. Negro Women, 1991; named Outstanding Black Educator, NAACP, 1968, Oustanding Woman Educator, Mich. Women's Lawyers Assn. and Mich. Trial Lawyers Assn., 1975, Disting. Alumna, Nat. Assn. for Equal Opportunity in Higher Edn., 1990, Woman of Yr., Nassau County League of Women Voters, 1991, Disting. Alumna So. Ill. U., 1997, N.Y. State Senate resolution of commendation, 1998; Elected to Achievers Hall of Fame: Long Island Bus. and Profl. Women's Orgn., 2001 Mem. AAAS, Nat. Assn. Acad. Affairs Adminstrs., Internat. Assn. Univ. Pres. (exec. com., v.p.), Phi Delta Kappa.

PETTIGREW, THOMAS FRASER, social psychologist, educator; b. Richmond, Va., Mar. 14, 1931; s. Joseph Crane and Janet (Gibb) Pettigrew; m. Ann Hallman, Feb. 25, 1956; 1 child, Mark Fraser. AB in Psychology, U. Va., 1952; MA in Social Psychology, Harvard U., 1955, PhD, 1956; DHL (hon.), Governor's State U., 1979. Rsch. assoc. Inst. Social Rsch., U. Natal, Republic South Africa, 1956; asst. prof. psychology U. N.C., 1956-57; asst. prof. social psychology Harvard U., Cambridge, Mass., 1957-62, lectr., 1962-64, assoc. prof., 1964-68, prof., 1968-74, prof. social psychology and sociology, 1974-80; prof. social psychology U. Calif., Santa Cruz, 1980-94, rsch. prof. social psychology, 1994—; prof. social psychology U. Amsterdam, 1986-91. Adj. fellow Joint Ctr. Polit. and Econ. Studies, Washington, 1982—; adv. bd. women's studies program Princeton (N.J.) U., 1985-2001; vis. prof. Westfaelishe Wilhelms-U., Germany, 1993, Philipps U., Germany, 2000, Schiller U., Germany, 2002; disting. vis. prof. Flinders U., Australia, 1997; sr. fellow Rsch. Inst. for the Comparative Study of Race and Ethnicity, Stanford U., 2001-02. Author: (with E.Q. Campbell) Christians in Racial Crisis: A Study of the Little Rock Ministry, 1959, A Profile of the Negro American, 1964, Racially Separate or Together?, 1971; (with Fredrickson, Knobol, Glazer and Veda) Prejudice, 1982; (with Alston) Tom Bradley's Campaigns for Governor: The Dilemma of Race and Political Strategies, 1988, How to Think Like a Social Scientist, 1996; editor: Racial Discrimination in the United States, 1975, The Sociology of Race Relations: Reflection and Reform, 1980; (with C. Stephan & W. Stephan) The Future of Social Psychology: Defining the Relationship Between Sociology and Psychology, 1991; mem. editorial bd. Jour. Social Issues, 1959-64, Social Psychology Quarterly, 1977-80; assoc. editor Am. Sociol. Rev, 1963-65; adv. bd. Integrated Edn, 1963-84, Phylon, 1965-93, Edn. and Urban Society, 1968-90, Race, 1972-74, Ethnic and Racial Studies, 1978-95, Rev. of Personality and Social Psychology, 1980-85, Cmty. and Applied Social Psychology, 1989—, Individual and Politics, 1989-93, Jour. Ethnic and Migration Studies, 1994—, 21st Century Afro Rev., 1994—; contbr. articles to profl. jours. Chmn. Episcopal presiding Bishop's Adv. Com. on Race Relations, 1961-63; v.p. Episcopal Soc. Cultural and Racial Unity, 1962-63; mem. Mass. Gov.'s Adv. Com. on Civil Rights, 1962-64; social sci. cons. U.S. Commn. Civil Rights, 1966-71; mem. White House Task Force on Edn., 1967; mem. nat. task force on desegregation policies Edn. Commn. of States, 1977-79; trustee Ella Lyman Cabot Trust, Boston, 1977-79; Emerson Book Award com. United Chpts. Phi Beta Kappa, 1971-73; com. status black Ams. NRC, 1985-88. Guggenheim fellow, 1967-68, Sr. Scientist fellow NATO, 1974, Ctr. Advanced Study in Behavioral Scis. fellow, 1975-76, Sydney Spivack fellow Am. Sociol. Assn., 1978, Netherlands Inst. Advanced Study fellow, 1984-85, Bellagio (Italy) Study Ctr. resident fellow, Rockefeller Found., 1991; Fulbright New Century scholar, 2003; recipient Kurt Lewin Meml. award Soc. for Psychol. Study Social Issues, 1987, (with Martin) Gordon Allport Intergroup Rels. Rsch. prize, 1988, Faculty Rsch. award U. Calif., Santa Cruz, 1988, (with Tropp) Gordon Allport Intergroup Rels. Rsch. prize, 2003. Fellow APA, Am. Sociol. Assn. (coun. 1979-82); mem. Soc. Psychol. Study Social Issues (coun. 1962-66, pres. 1967-68, Disting. Svc. award 1998), Soc. Exptl. Social Psychology (Disting. Scientist award 2002), European Assn. Social Psychology. Home: 524 Van Ness Ave Santa Cruz CA 95060-3556

PETTIT, JOHN DOUGLAS, JR., management educator; b. Alice, Tex, Aug. 19, 1940; s. John Douglas and Vivian Iola (Beaman) P.; m. Suzanne McLeod, Aug. 23, 1964; children: Melanie Ann Wilson, David Bryant. BBA, U. North Tex., 1962, MBA, 1964; PhD, La. State U., 1969. Instr. mgmt. Miss. State U., Starkville, Miss., 1964-65; grad. asst. La. State U., Baton Rouge, 1965-67, instr. mgmt., 1967-68; asst. prof. bus. Tex. Tech. U., Lubbock, Tex., 1968-69; assoc. prof. mgmt. U. North Tex., Denton, Tex., 1969-78, prof. mgmt., 1978-95; chair excellence in free enterprise Austin Peay State U., Clarksville, Tenn., 1995-96; interim chair and prof. dept. info. and decision scis. U. Tex., El Paso, Tex., 2000-2001. Bd. dirs. Capital Instnl. Svcs., Dallas and N.Y.C., mem. audit com., 2003—; cons. various orgns., 1969-98; mgr., co-owner Pettit's Cleaners/Hatters, Alice, 1992-96; vis. prof. mgmt. Wichita State U., Kans., 1994-95; vis. prof. Ecole Superieure de Commerce et de Management, Poitier, France, 2002-03, U. Kuopio, Finalnd, 2003. Kuopio, Finland, 2002, Co-author: Business Communication: Theory and Application, 7th edit. 1993, Report Writing for Business, 10th edit. 1998, Lesikar's Basic Business Communication, 8th edit. 1999; mem. editl. bd. Organl. Comm. Abstracts, 1980-85; mem. editl. bd. Jour. Bus. Comm., 1987-90, mng. editor, 1990-94. Mem. choir Trinity Presbyn. Ch., Denton, 1985-1996, 2002—; actor, singer Denton Cmty. Theater Summer Prodn., 1988-95. Recipient Master's Degree award Chgo. Bd. Trade, 1963. Fellow Assn. Bus. Comm. (pres., 1st v.p., exec. dir., 1990-94); mem. Southwestern Fedn. Adminstrv. Disciplines (pres., v.p.), Acad. Mgmt., Denton Country Club (bd. dirs.), Blue Key Nat. Hon. Fraternity, Beta Gamma Sigma (hon.), Phi Kappa Phi (hon.), Delta Sigma Pi. Presbyterian. Avocations: music, tennis. Home: 9122 David Fort Rd Argyle TX 76226-2953

PETTIT, LAWRENCE KAY, university president; b. Lewistown, Mont., May 2, 1937; s. George Edwin and Dorothy Bertha (Brown) P.; m. Sharon Lee Anderson, June 21, 1961 (div. Oct. 1976); children: Jennifer Anna, Matthew Anderson, Allison Carol, Edward McLean; m. Elizabeth DuBois Medley, July 11, 1980 (div. Dec. 1998). BA cum laude, U. Mont., 1959; AM, Washington U., St. Louis, 1962; PhD, U. Wis., 1965. Legis. asst. U.S. Senate, 1959-60, 62; asst. & assoc. prof. dept. polit. sci. Pa. State U., 1964-67; assoc. dir. fed. rels. Am. Council Edn., Washington, 1967-69; chmn. dept. polit. sci. Mont. State U., 1969-72; adminstrv. asst. to gov. State of Mont., 1973; chancellor Mont. Univ. System, Helena, 1973-79; pvt. practice ednl. cons. Mont., 1979-81; dep. commr. for acad. affairs Tex. Coordinating Bd. for Higher Edn., 1981-83; chancellor Univ. System of South Tex., 1983-86; chancellor (now pres.) So. Ill. U., Carbondale, Edwardsville, 1986-91, Disting. svc. prof., 1991-92; pres. Indiana U. Pa., 1992—2003, ret., 2003. Adv. bd. S & T Bancorp., 1997—; regional adv. bd. Nat. City Bank, 1997-99; bd. dirs. Ind. Healthcare Corp. Author: (with H. Albinski) European Political Processes, 2d edit., 1974, (with E. Keynes) Legislative Process in the U.S. Senate, 1969, (with S. Kirkpatrick) Social Psychology of Political Life, 1972, (with J. Goetz and S. Thomas) Legislative Process in Montana, 1975; mem. editl. bd. Ednl. Record, 1985-98. Adv. bd. Leadership Ctr. Ams., 1988-90, Ill. Coalition, 1989-92; candidate for 2d dist. U.S. Ho. of Reps., Mont., 1980; mem. Ill. Gov.'s Com. on Sci. and Tech., 1986-90; bd. dirs. Tex. Guaranteed Student Loan Corp., 1985-86, Reschini Found., 2003—; chmn. Ill.-Niigata Commn. on Edn. and Econ. Devel., 1990-92; chair bd. dirs. Nat. Environ. Edn. and Tng. Ctr., 1994—; mem. adv. bd. Princeton Review, 2003—. U. Wis. fellow 1962-63, Vilas fellow U. Wis., 1963-64. Mem. AAUP (pres. Mont. conf. 1971-72), Nat. Assn. Sys. Heads (pres. 1989), Am. Coun. on Edn. (chmn. leadership commn. 1989-90, sr. fellow 1991-92), Am. Assn. Higher Edn., Am. Assn. State Colls. and Univs. (Disting. Svc. award 1991), Newcomen Soc., Duquesne Club Pitts., Allegheny Club Pitts., World Affairs Coun. Pitts., Univ. Club Pitts., Pa. Soc. (life), Ind. Country Club, Rotary (Paul Harris fellow), Ind. C. of C. (bd. dirs. 1992—2003), Sigma Chi (Significant Sig award 1988), Phi Kappa Phi. Episcopalian. Home: 209 Saddlebrook Dr Indiana PA 15701 Office: NEETC Inc 1179 Grant St Indiana PA 15701 E-mail: lpettit@iup.edu.

PETTUS, KAREN ROSENBALM, elementary education educator; b. Ft. Oglethorpe, Ga., Aug. 3, 1954; d. William N. and Burmah Jo (Cannon) Rosenbalm; m. James Lee Pettus, Aug. 25, 1973; children: Michael, Jennifer. BS, U. Tenn., 1976; postgrad., U. Kans., Kans. State U., Cameron U., Lawton, Okla.; MEd, U. S.C., 1996, postgrad., 1996—. Cert. tchr., Tenn., Okla., Kans., S.C., Dept. Def. Dependent Schs. Tchr. hearing impaired and multiply handicapped Tenn. Sch. for Deaf, Knoxville, 1982-83; tchr. trainable mentally retarded Lawton Pub. Schs., 1983-84; tchr. multiply handicapped Unified Sch. Dist. 383, Manhattan, Kans., 1984-87; elem. tchr. Dept. Def. Dependent Sch., Augsburg, Fed. Republic Germany, 1989-91; elem. tchr. profoundly mentally handicapped Fairwold Sch., Columbia, S.C., 1991—; tchr. orthopedically handicapped Spring Valley High Sch., Columbia, S.C., 1991-94; dir. Office of Disability Svcs. U. S.C., Columbia, 1994—. Tchr. clinic for coaches, area devel. sports dir., area tng. dir. Spl. Olympics; chmn. Augsburg Elem. Sch. Improvement Coun. Mem. ASCD, AEA, Internat. Reading Assn. Office: U SC Office Disability Svcs Leconte Coll Rm 106 Columbia SC 29208-0001

PETTY, JOHN ERNEST, education specialist, consultant; b. Vernon, Tex., May 11, 1930; s. Ernest Clifton and Lou (Crow) P.; m. Nancy Jones, June 9, 1950; children: Jay, Patti, Jeff. BS, Southwestern U., 1954. Enlisted U.S. Army, 1947, advanced through grades to 1st sgt., 1970, ret., 1970; bus. mgr. High Plains Bapt. Hosp., Amarillo, Tex., 1970-72; area mgr. Sperry Hutchinson Co., Amarillo, 1972-74; gen. mgr. Lien Chem. Co., Amarillo, 1974-82; edn. specialist U.S. Govt., Amarillo, 1982—. Pres. elect Tex. Assn. Measurement and Evaluation in Counseling and Devel., Amarillo, 1989-90. Mem. Tex. Assn. for Counseling and Devel., Masons (sec.). Avocations: golfing, fishing, tennis, reading. Home: 6210 Hanson Rd Amarillo TX 79106-3412 Office: Mil Entrance/Processing Sta 1100 S Fillmore St Amarillo TX 79101-4318

PETZEL, FLORENCE ELOISE, textiles educator; b. Crosbyton, Tex., Apr. 1, 1911; d. William D. and Eloise Petzel. PhB, U. Chgo., 1931, AM, 1934; PhD, U. Minn., 1954. Instr. Judson Coll., 1936-38; asst. prof. textiles Ohio State U., 1938-48; assoc. prof. U. Ala., 1950-54; prof. Oreg. State U., Corvallis, 1954-61, 67-75, 77, 77, prof. emeritus, 1975—, dept. head, 1954-61, 67-75; prof., divsn. head U. Tex., 1961-63; prof. Tex. Tech. U., 1963-67. Vis. instr. Tex. State Coll. for Women, 1937; vis. prof. Wash. State U., 1967. Author: Textiles of Ancient Mesopotamia, Persia and Egypt, 1987; contbr. articles to profl. jours. Effie I. Raitt fellow, 1949-50. Mem. Met. Opera Guild, Sigma Xi, Phi Kappa Phi, Omicron Nu, Iota Sigma Pi, Sigma Delta Epsilon. Home: 150 Downs Blvd Apt A206 Clemson SC 29631-2043

PEYA, PRUDENCE MALAVA, retired elementary education educator; b. Rochester, Pa., July 27; d. George and Mildred (Tesla) P. BS, Duquesne U., 1965, MEd, 1967, MS, 1977. Permanent substitute tchr. Montour Area Sch. Dist., Coraopolis, Pa., 1965; tchr. elem. Ctr. Area Sch. Dist., Monaca, Pa., 1965-76, gifted support tchr., 1977-97, coord. gifted program, 1977-98, coord. spl. edn., 1995-98; ret., 1999. Local coach Odyssey of the Mind, 1985-97; sponsor Beaver County Acad. Games League, 1988—. Author: (handbook) Instructional Areas Appropriate for Gifted Students, 1987. Active Logstown Assocs. Hist. Soc., Ambridge, Pa., 1990—. Mem. AAUW, Greek Cath. Union U.S.A. (life), Pa. Assn. for Gifted Edn. (Elem. Gifted Tchr. of Yr. award 1984), 4th grade tchr., Beaver County Gifted Tchrs. (pres. 1993-94), Alpha Delta Kappa (past pres. Delta chpt.) Democrat. Byzantine Catholic. Avocations: michael ricker pewter collector, travel, calligraphy. Home: 341 Beaver Ave West Aliquippa PA 15001-2415

PEYSER, JAMES, state agency administrator; BA, Colgate U.; MA in Law and Diplomacy, Tufts U. With Teradyne, Inc., Boston; exec. dir. Pioneer Inst. for Pub. Policy Rsch., 1993—2001; Govs. sr. advisor on edn. and worker tng. State of Mass., 2001—. Chmn. Mass. State Bd. Edn., 1999—; acting chair Edn. Mgmt. Audit Coun.; mem. bd. overseers WGBH; mem. policy bd. Nat. Coun. on Tchr. Quality. Office: State House Rm 271M Boston MA 02133*

PEZACKA, EWA HANNA, biochemist, educator; b. Lodz, Poland, May 22, 1949; came to U.S., 1981; d. Wincenty and Janina (Andrzejewska) Pezacki; m. Jerzy Perkitny, Mar. 14, 1981. BA, Coll. of Helena Modrzejewska, Poznan, 1965; MS with highest honors, U. Adam Mickiewicz, Poznan, 1971; PhD with highest honors, U. Agrl., Poznan, 1976; postgrad., Case Western Res. U., 1981-85. Faculty asst. Biochemistry Inst. U. Agriculture, Poznan, 1971-74, sr. faculty asst., 1974-77, asst. prof., 1977-81; rsch. assoc. Case Western Res. U. Sch. Medicine, Cleve., 1981-85, sr. rsch. assoc., 1985-88; project staff Dept. Lab. Hematology, Cleve. Clinic Found., 1988-91, asst. staff, 1991-92, asst. staff dept. brain and vascular rsch., 1993-95, asst. staff dept. cell biology, 1993-95; assoc. rsch. scientist Allegheny-Singer Rsch. Inst., Pitts., 1995—; assoc. prof. Allegheny U. of the Med. Scis., 1995—. Vis. asst. U. Humboldt, Berlin-Buche, Germany, 1973-74; co-investigator Inst. Food Tech., Poznan, 1977-81, MacDonald Hosp. for Women, Cleve., 1985-88; presenter in field. Contbr. more than 60 articles to profl. jours. Fellow Univ. Humboldt, Berlin, 1973-74; grantee Polish Acad. Sci./Polish Soc. Biochemistry, 1976, NIH, 1991—, travel grantee Internat. Union Biochemistry, 1991; recipient Excellence in Biochemistry award Polish Acad. Sci., 1971, Norwegian Rsch. Coun. Internat. award, 1994. Mem. Am. Chem. Soc., Am. Soc. for Biochemistry and Molecular Biology, Internat. Union Biochemistry, N.Y. Acad. Sci., Polish Soc. Biochemistry. Avocations: sailing, horse-back riding, skiing, yard work and travel. Office: ASRI/Dept Human Genetics 11th Floor South Tower 320 E North Ave Pittsburgh PA 15212-4756

PEZESHKI, S. REZA, education educator; m. Fataneh Farmani. BS, U. Tehran, Iran, 1971; MS, U. Wash, 1977, PhD, 1982. Cert. profl. wetland scientist 1997. Rsch. faculty La. State U., Baton Rouge, 1983—90, assoc. prof., 1990—94, U. Memphis, 1994—98, prof. biology, 1998—. Editor-in-chief: Americas & Australia, Environmental and Experimental Botany, 1998—. Mem.: Soc. Wetland Scientists (mem. exec. bd., pres.-elect, pres. Southcentral chpt. 1995—2000), Am. Soc. Plant Biologists, Sigma Xi. Office: U Memphis Dept Biology 3706 Alumni St Memphis TN 38152

PFALMER, CHARLES ELDEN, secondary school educator; b. Trinidad, Colo., Aug. 9, 1937; s. Arthur Joseph and Nettie Mildred (Powell) P.; m. Margaret Christine La Duke, June 25, 1964; children: Betholyn Ann, Garret. AA, Trinidad State Jr. Coll., 1957; BA, Adams State Coll., 1959, MA, 1962. Cert. tchr., Colo. Tchr. Olathe (Colo.) H.S., 1959-60, Yuma (Colo.) H.S., 1960-98. Instr. Northeastern Jr. Coll., Sterling, Colo., 1990-97. Precinct chmn. Dem. Orgn., Yuma, 1992-96, del. to state conv., 1984-86, 88-90, 92-94, 96, Dem. county chair, 2001—; ch. treas. Yuma Episcopal Ch., 1985—; v.p. Citizens Action Com., Yuma, 1994. Recipient Outstanding Educator award West Yuma Sch. Dist., 1987, Colo. State Ho. of Reps., 1987, Local Disting. Svc. award Colo. H.S. Activities Assn., 1991, Outstanding Cmty. Svc. award Colo. Athletic Dirs. Assn., 1990; named Citizen of Yr., Yuma C. of C., 1999. Mem. NEA, Am. Polit. Collectors, Nat. Coun. for the Social Studies, Colo. Edn. Assn., Phi Delta Kappa. Avocations: collecting political buttons, antiques, sports. Home: 321 E 10th Ave Yuma CO 80759-3001 E-mail: cmpfalmer@plains.net.

PFEFFER, CYNTHIA ROBERTA, psychiatrist, educator; b. Newark, May 22, 1943; d. Edward I. and Ann Pfeffer. BA, Douglas Coll., 1964; MD, NYU, 1968. Assoc. dir. child psychiatry inpatient unit Albert Einstein Coll. Medicine, Bronx, N.Y., 1973-79; chief child psychiatry inpatient unit N.Y. Hosp. Cornell Med. Ctr., White Plains, N.Y., 1979-95; assoc. prof. clin. psychiatry Weill Med. Coll. Cornell U., N.Y.C., 1984—. Prof. psychiatry Cornell U. Med. Coll., 1989—; pres. N.Y. Coun. on Child and Adolescent Psychiatry, N.Y.C., 1989—; dir. childhood bereavement program Weill Med. Coll. Cornell U., 1999—. Author: The Suicidal Child, 1986, Difficult Moments in Child Psychotherapy, 1988; editor: Youth Suicide: Perspectives on Risk and Prevention, 1989, Intense Stress and Mental Disturbance in Children, 1996; co-editor: Neurologic Disorders: Developmental and Behavioral Sequelae for Child and Adolescent Psychiatric Clinics of North America, 1999. Recipient Erwin Stengel award Internat. Assn. Suicide Prevention, 1987, Wilford Hulse award N.Y. Coun. on Child & Adolescent Psychiatry, 1989, Sigmund Freud award Am. Soc. Psychoanalytic Physicians, 1994. Fellow Am. Psychiat. Assn., Am. Acad. Child and Adolescent Psychiatry (councillor-at-large 1989—, Norbert Rieger award 1988), Am. Psychopathological Assn.; mem. Am. Assn. Suicidology (pres. 1987, Young Contbrs. award 1981, 82). Office: NY Hosp Westchester Div 21 Bloomingdale Rd White Plains NY 10605-1504 also: 1100 Madison Ave New York NY 10028-0327

PFEFFER, JEFFREY, business educator; b. St. Louis, July 23, 1946; s. Newton Stuart and Shirlee (Krisman) P.; m. Kathleen Frances Fowler, July 23, 1986. BS, MS, Carnegie Mellon U., 1968; PhD, Stanford U., 1972. Tech. staff Research Analysis Corp., McLean, Va., 1968-69; asst. prof. U. Ill., Champaign, 1971-73; from asst. prof. to assoc. prof. U. Calif., Berkeley, 1973-79; prof. Grad. Sch. Bus., Stanford U., Calif., 1979—. Vis. prof. Harvard U. Sch. Bus., Boston, 1981-82; dir., mem. compensation com. Portola Packaging, Inc.; dir. SonoSite, Inc., Audible Magic, Inc., Actify, Inc., Unicru, Inc. Author: The External Control of Organizations, 1978, Organizational Design, 1978, Power in Organizations, 1981, Organizations and Organization Theory, 1982 (Terry Book award 1984), Managing with Power, 1992, Competitive Advantage Through People, 1994, New Directions for Organization Theory, 1997, The Human Equation, 1998, The Knowing-Doing Gap, 1999, Hidden Value, 2000. Fellow Acad. Mgmt. (bd. govs. 1984-86, New Concept award 1979, Richard D. Irwin award for scholarly contbns. to mgmt. 1989); mem. Indsl. Rels. Rsch. Assn. Jewish. Avocations: cooking, music. Home: 425 Moseley Rd Hillsborough CA 94010-6715 Office: Stanford U Grad Sch Bus Stanford CA 94305 E-mail: pfeffer_jeffrey@gsb.stanford.edu.

PFEFFER, RICHARD LAWRENCE, meteorology and geophysics educator; b. Bklyn., Nov. 26, 1930; s. Lester Robert and Anna (Newman) P.; m. Roslyn Ziegler, Aug. 30, 1953; children— Bruce, Lloyd, Scott, Glenn. BS cum laude, CCNY, 1952; MS, Mass. Inst. Tech., 1954, PhD, 1957. Research asst. MIT, 1952-55, guest lectr., 1956; atmospheric physicist Air Force Cambridge Research Center, Boston, 1955-59; sr. scientist Columbia U., 1959-61, lectr., 1961-62, asst. prof. geophysics, 1962-64; assoc. prof. meteorology Fla. State U., Tallahassee, 1964-67, prof. meteorology, 1967-96, disting. rsch. prof., 1997—, Carl-Gustav Rossby prof. meteorology, 1999—; dir. Geophys. Fluid Dynamics Inst., 1967-93. Cons. NASA, 1961-64, N.W. Ayer & Son, Inc., 1962, Ednl. Testing Service, Princeton, N.J., 1963, Voice of Am., 1963, Grolier, Inc., 1963, Naval Research Labs., 1971-76; Mem. Internat. Commn. for Dynamical Meteorology, 1972-76 Editor: Dynamics of Climate, 1960; Contbr. articles to profl. jours. Bd. dirs. B'nai B'rith Anti-Defamation League; chmn. religious concern and social action com. Temple Israel, Tallahassee, 1971-72. Fellow Am. Meterol. Soc. (program chmn. ann. meeting 1963); mem. Am. Geophys. Union, N.Y. Acad. Scis. (chmn. planetary scis. sect. 1961-63), Sigma Xi, Chi Epsilon Pi, Sigma Alpha. Home: 9042 Shoal Creek Dr Tallahassee FL 32312 E-mail: pfeffer@gfdi.fsu.edu.

PFEFFER, ROBERT, chemical engineer, academic administrator, educator; b. Vienna, Nov. 26, 1935; came to U.S., 1938, naturalized, 1944; s. Joseph and Gisela (Aberbach) P.; m. Marcia Borenstein, Dec. 24, 1960; children— Michael, Jacqueline. BChE, NYU, 1956, MChE, 1958, DEngSc, 1962. Mem. faculty CCNY, 1957-92, asst. prof. chem. engring., 1962-66, assoc. prof., 1966-71, prof., 1971-92, chmn. dept. chem. engring., 1973-87, Herbert Kayser prof., 1980-92, dean grad. studies and research, dep. provost, 1987-88, provost, v.p. acad. affairs, 1988-92; v.p. rsch. and grad. studies, prof. chem. engring. N.J. Inst. Tech., Newark, 1992-97, disting. prof. chem. engring., 1997—. Vis. prof. Imperial Coll., London, 1969; Fulbright scholar Technion-Israel Inst. Tech., 1976-77; cons. in field. Contbr. articles to tech. pubs. Fulbright Hays awardee, 1976-77; DuPont faculty fellow, 1962; NASA faculty fellow, 1964-65 Mem. AIChE (Particle Tech. Forum Nat. award 1995, Thomas Baron Nat. award 2000), Am. Soc. Engring. Edn., Sigma Xi, Tau Beta Pi, Phi Lambda Upsilon. Jewish. Office: PO Box 37 Teaneck NJ 07666 E-mail: pfeffer@njit.edu.

PFEFFERKORN, LAURA BIGGER, middle school educator; b. Spartanburg, S.C., May 24, 1963; d. Samuel Patrick Jr. and Laura Christine (Smith) Bigger; m. James W. Pfefferkorn, June 1, 1982. BS in Banking and Fin., U. S.C., Aiken, 1987; MAT in Health Edn., U. S.C., Columbia, 1993. Account rep. NCR Corp., Charleston, S.C., 1988; grad. asst. U. S.C. Sch. Pub. Health, Columbia, 1990-93; tchr. sci. Dent Mid. Sch., Columbia, 1993—, team leader, 1994—. Forum on quality edn. mem. Richland Dist. 2, Columbia, 1993-94; tchr. grad. courses Sch. Pub. Health/U. S.C. Contbr. chpt. to textbook. Roper Mountain Sci. Ctr. scholar, 1994. Mem. APHA, AAHPERD, S.C. Alliance for Health, Phys. Edn., Recreation and Dance, S.C. Mid. Sch. Assn., S.C. Assn. for Health Edn., Phi Delta Kappa. Avocations: mountain biking, running, weight training, reading. Home: 4117 Cassina Rd Columbia SC 29205-2021 Office: Dent Mid Sch 2719 Decker Blvd Columbia SC 29206-1704

PFEFFERKORN, MICHAEL GENE, SR., secondary school educator, writer; b. Delano, Calif., July 19, 1939; s. E. Michael and N. Ruth (Ervin) P.; m. Sandra J. Carter, June 15, 1963; children: Michael Jr., Patricia. AB, BS in Secondary Edn., S.E. Mo. State, 1961; MEd, U. Mo., 1963. Cert. Eng., life Social Studies tchr., Mo. Tchr. De Soto (Mo.) Pub. Schs., 1961-62, Cleveland H.S., St. Louis, 1963-84, S.W. H.S., St. Louis, 1984-86, tchr., history dept. head, 1987-92; tchr. Gateway Inst. of Tech. H.S., St. Louis, 1992—. Cons. Internat. Edn. Consortium, St. Louis, 1989-92. Co-author: Chits, Chiselers, and Funny Money, 1976; editor Mo. Jour. Numismatics; contbr. articles to numis. jours. Pres. Carondelet Hist. Soc., 1977-78, mem., 1970-90; mem. Landmarks and Urban Design Com., St. Louis, 1976-80. St. Louis Pub. Schs. Secondary Tchr. of Yr., 1999-2000; recipient Emerson Electric's Excellence in Tchg. award, 2000. Mem. ASCD, Am. Fedn. Tchrs., Nat. Coun. Social Studies Tchrs., State Hist. Soc. Mo., Am. Numis. Assn., Mo. Numis Soc. (bd. dirs. 1997—), Numis. Lit. Guild, World Coin Club Mo. Roman Catholic. Avocations: numismatics, writing, genealogy. Home: 6803 Leona St Saint Louis MO 63116-2833 Office: Gateway Inst of Tech 5101 McRee Ave Saint Louis MO 63110-2019

PFEFFERKORN, SANDRA JO, secondary school educator; b. St. Louis, Jan. 14, 1940; d. Albert A. and Alice C. (Lowell) Carter; m. Michael G. Pfefferkorn, June 15, 1963; children: Michael G. Jr., Patricia A. BS in Secondary Edn., S.E. Mo. State Coll., 1961; MEd, U. Mo., 1966. Cert. life English, Spanish, French, and reading tchr., Mo. Tchr. English, head English and fgn. lang. dept. St. Louis Bd. Edn./Cen. H.S., 1961-89; English tchr., head dept. Cleveland Naval Jr. Res. Officer Tng. Corps H.S., St. Louis, 1989—. Asst. editor Mo. Jour. Numismatics. Regents scholar, 1957; fellow Mo. Writing Project, 1981. Mem. AAUW, Nat. Coun. Tchrs. English, Internat. Reading Assn., Mo. Assn. Tchrs. English, Delta Kappa Gamma (pres. Beta Theta chpt.), Phi Delta Kappa. Roman Catholic. Avocations: writing, reading, ceramics. Home: 6803 Leona St Saint Louis MO 63116-2833 Office: Cleve Naval Jr ROTC 4352 Louisiana Ave Saint Louis MO 63111-1046

PFEIFER, PETER MARTIN, physics educator; b. Zurich, Switzerland, Apr. 19, 1946; came to U.S., 1986; s. Max and Eva (Korrodi) P.; m. Therese M. Abgottspon, June 13, 1980; children: Anne, Helen. MS in Chemistry, Swiss Fed. Inst. Tech., 1969, PhD in Natural Scis., 1980. Rsch. assoc., instr. Swiss Fed. Inst. Tech., Zurich, 1975-80; rsch. fellow Hebrew U. Jerusalem, 1981-82; asst. prof. chemistry U. Bielefeld, West Germany, 1982-86, habilitation, 1986; assoc. prof. physics U. Mo., Columbia, 1986-95; vis. prof. physics Swiss Fed. Inst. Tech., 1993-94; vis. scientist Ecole Poly., Palaiseau, France, 1994; prof. physics U. Mo., Columbia, 1995—; sr. assoc. Inst. Phys. Scis., Inc., Los Alamos, 1997—; vis. scientist Los Alamos Nat. Lab., 2000-01. Mem. adv. bd. Symposium on Probability Methods in Physics, Bielefeld, 1984, Symposium on Small Irregular Particles, Cuernavaca, Mex., 1988, Conf. on Fractals in Natural Scis., Budapest, Hungary, 1993, 22d Midwest Solid-State Theory Symposium, Columbia, 1994, 2d Internat. Symposium on Surface Heterogeneity, Zakopane, Poland, 1995, 3d conf. Fractals in Engring., Arcachon, France, 1997; spkr. in field. Mem. editl. bd. Internat. Jour. Fractals, 1992-97, Heterogeneous Chemistry Revs., 1992-98; contbr. over 100 articles to profl. jours. Recipient Gränacher Grad. fellowship Found. of Swiss Chem. Industry, 1970-71, fellowship for jr. scientists Swiss Nat. Sci. Found., 1981-82, Outstanding Rsch. prize U. Bielefeld, 1986; grantee Petroleum Rsch. Fund, 1987-99, Rsch. Leave award U. Mo., 1993-94, Inst. Phys. Sics., Los Alamos, 1999—. Mem. AAAS, N.Y. Acad. Scis., Am. Phys. Soc., Materials Rsch. Soc. Achievements include development of fractal analysis in surface science; discovery of first fractal materials, of numerous structure-function relationships (diffusion, scattering, wetting and transport properties), and of optimal performance of fractal lung; fundamental research in quantum theory: discovery of chiral superselection rule in molecules, unified framework for reduced quantum dynamics, generalized time-energy uncertainty relations, variational bounds for transition probabilities, quantum computing. Office: Univ Mo Dept Physics Columbia MO 65211-0001

PFEUFFER, DALE ROBERT, secondary school social studies educator; b. Pitts., May 23, 1955; s. Francis Jerome and Dorothy Jean (Hankey) P.; m. Mary Elizabeth Hunter, June 4, 1983 (div. 1992); 1 child, Elberta Hunter. AA, C.C. Allegheny County, 1976; BA, U. Pitts., 1977, MEd, 1983. Cert. tchr. secondary comprehensive social studies, Pa. Tchr. secondary social studies Sto-Rox Sch. Dist., McKees Rocks, Pa., 1980-81, Avonworth Sch. Dist., Pitts., 1983-84, Harford County Sch. Dist., Bel Air, Md., 1984-86. Tchr. of homebound Penn Hills Sch. Dist., 1979-80, Sto-Rox Sch. Dist., McKees Rocks, Pa., 1980-84, 86-87, Avonworth Sch. Dist., Pitts., 1983-84. Fund raiser Community Redevel. Fund, Ethnic Festival Sponsor, ARC, 1980-81; sponsor Speech and Debate Club, Harford County Sch. Dist., 1985-86. Mem. NEA, Nat. Coun. Social Studies, Assn. Undergrad. Edn. (subcom. student rsch. grants), Pa. State Edn. Assn., Md. State Tchrs. Assn., Coun. Grad. Students Edn., Nat. Geograph. Soc., Nat. Trust Historic Preservation, The Smithsonian Assocs. Democrat. Roman Catholic. Avocations: racquetball, golf, volleyball, softball, swimming. Home: 5703 Kingfish Dr Apt C Lutz FL 33558-5932

PFINGSTON, ROGER CARL, writer photographer, retired educator; b. Evansville, Ind., Apr. 6, 1940; s. Walter Carl and Esther Ora (Sandage) P.; m. Nancy Lee Weber, Dec. 15, 1962; children: Brett, Jenna. BA in Journalism, Ind. U., 1962, MS in Edn., 1967. English tchr. Kempsville Jr. H.S., Virginia Beach, Va., 1964-65, Univ. H.S., Bloomington, Ind., 1967-72; English, photography tchr. Bloomington H.S. North, 1972-97. Author: (books of poetry), Nesting, 1978, Hazards of Photography, 1980, The Circus of Unreasonable Acts, 1982, Something Iridescent, 1987, Grady's Lunch, 1988, Singing to the Garden, 2003, Earthbound, 2003. Bd. dirs. Friends of Art, Bloomington, 1994-97. 3d class Petty Officer USN, 1962-64. Recipient fellowship for poetry, Nat. Endowment for the Arts, 1978, Syndicated Fiction award PEN, 1983, 84, Tchr. Creativity fellowship Lilly Endowment, 1989. Mem. NEA, Ind. Retired Tchrs. Assn. Avocations: reading, travel, gardening. Home: 4020 W Stoutes Creek Rd Bloomington IN 47404-1332

PFISTER, DONALD HENRY, biology educator; b. Kenton, Ohio, Feb. 17, 1945; s. William A. and Dorothy C. (Kurtz) P.; m. Cathleen C. Kennedy, July 1, 1971; children: Meghan, Brigid, Edith. AB, Miami U., Oxford, Ohio, 1967; PhD, Cornell U., 1971; AM (hon.), Harvard U., 1980. Asst. prof. biology U. P.R., Mayaguez, 1971-74; asst. prof. biology, asst. curator Farlow Herbarium Harvard U., Cambridge, Mass., 1974-77, assoc. prof. biology, assoc. curator Farlow Herbarium, 1977-80, prof. biology, curator Farlow Herbarium, 1980—, dir. univ. herbaria, 1983-95, Asa Gray prof. botany, 1984—, dir. univ. herbaria, 1999—. Vis. mycologist U. Copenhagen, 1978; vis. prof. field station U. Minn., Itasca, 1979; master Kirkland House Harvard U., 1982-00. Contbr. over 80 articles to profl. jours. Grantee NSF, 1973-75, 81-85, 85—, Am. Philos. Soc., 1975-76, Whiting Found., 1986. Fellow AAAS, Linnean Soc. London; mem. Mycol. Soc. Am. (sec. 1988-91, v.p. 1993-94, pres.-elect 1994-95, pres. 1995-96), Am. Phytopath. Soc., Am. Microbiol. Soc., New Eng. Bot. Club, Sigma Xi. Office: Harvard U Herbarium 22 Divinity Ave Cambridge MA 02138

PFLUEGER, M(ELBA) LEE COUNTS, academic administrator; b. St. Louis, Sept. 2, 1942; d. Ross and Edna Mae (Russell) Counts; m. Raymond Allen Pflueger, Sept. 14, 1963 (div. June 1972); children: Salem Allen, Russell Counts. BS in Home Econs., Univ. Mo., 1969; MEd in Guidance and Counseling, Washington Univ., St. Louis, 1973. Ednl. psychologist Ozark Regional Mental Health Ctr., Harrison, Ark., 1974-75; from account mgr. to mgr. pers. Enterprise Leasing Co., St. Louis, 1977-79; mgr. employee rels. Eaton Corp., Houston, 1979-80; owner Nature's Nuggets Fresh Granola, St. Louis, 1980-83; dir. corp. ednl. svcs. Maryville Coll., St. Louis, 1983-84; adminstr. mgmt. skills devel. McDonnell Douglas, St. Louis, 1984-85, mgr. employee involvement, 1985-86, prin. specialist human resources mgmt., 1988-89, mgr. human resources Houston, 1986-88; dir. devel. sch. engring. U. Mo., Rolla, 1989-93, dir. devel., corp. and found. rels., 1992-93; regional dir. devel., assoc. dir. maj. gifts and capital projects Washington U., St. Louis, 1994—. Part-time leader trainer Maritz Motivation, St. Louis, 1984-89. Chair United Fund Campaign for U. Mo., Rolla, 1991. Mem. PEO. Avocations: reading, theatre, yoga, travel. Office: Washington U Office Maj Gifts and Capital Projects Campus Box 1228 One Brookings Dr Saint Louis MO 63130-4899

PFLUGHAUPT, JANE RAMSEY, secondary school educator; b. Houston, Dec. 19, 1940; Sidney Clarence and Lillian Bess (Melton) Ramsey; m. Louis Elliott Pflughaupt, Aug. 11, 1962; children: Cheryl Diane, Russell Alan. BA, U. Tex., 1962; MA, Stanford U., 1971. Cert. life secondary tchr., Calif., Tex. Tchr. math. Austin (Tex.) Ind. Sch. Dist., 1962-65, San Jose (Calif.) Unified Sch. Dist., 1967—, mentor tchr., 1985-90, dist. math task force, 1985—, prin.'s cabinet, 1997. Pioneer Bay Area Reform Sch. Coalition Leadership Team, 1997—; dist. curriculum adv. com. San Jose (Calif.) Unified Sch. Dist., 1991-93, dist. profl. devel. coach, 2000—; textbook rev. com. State of Calif., Sacramento, 1988-89; writer of textbook correlations for State of Oreg., 1995; chair math. dept. Pioneer H.S., 1990—, cons. McDougal Littel-Houghten Mifflin, 1993—, City of San Jose Math. Coalition, 2000—; profl. devel. coach 2000-02. Author: Integrated Math Teacher's editions, 1, 2, and 3, 1993-95, Algebra I, 1995, Algebra II, 1996, Geometry, 1997, Heath Algebra I, 1997, Algebra II, 1997, D.C. Heath Passport Series grades 6, 7, and 8, 1997. Vol. Indian Guides, Girl Scouts U.S.A., Lyceum, Los Madres, San Jose and Los Gatos, Calif., 1974-88; participant Coll. Bds. Project Equity 2000, 1991-96; demonstration tchr. NSF/Equity 2000, 1992; grant writer Pioneer H.S. Bay Area Reform Sch. Coalition, 1997, mem., 1997—. Named Tchr. of Yr. Pioneer H.S., 1990, 95; grantee Hewlett-Packard Co., 1989, 91, 92, Inst. Computer Aided Math., 1989, Tandy Co., 1994; fellow, grantee Semicondr. Rsch. Corp., 1990; Tandy Tech. Math. nat. scholar, 1994. Mem. NEA, Math. Assn. Am., Nat. Coun. Tchrs. Math., Calif. Math. Coun., Calif. Tchrs. Assn., Santa Clara Valley Math. Assn., San Jose Tchrs. Assn., Beginning Tchrs. Support Assn. (mentor 2001-02). Avocations: calligraphy, graphic design. Office: Pioneer High Sch 1290 Blossom Hill Rd San Jose CA 95118-3193

PHAM, KINH DINH, electrical engineer, educator, administrator; b. Saigon, Republic of Vietnam, Oct. 6, 1956; came to U.S., 1974; s. Nhuong D. (dec.) and Phuong T. (Tran) P.; m. Ngan-Lien T. Nguyen, May 27, 1985; children: Larissa, Galen. BS with honors, Portland State U., 1979; MSEE, U. Portland, 1982; postgrad., Portland State U., 1988-90. Registered profl. engr., Oreg., Calif., Ariz., Fla., Wash., Mass., Conn., R.I., Tex. Elec. engr. Irvington-Moore, Tigard, Oreg., 1979-80, Elcon Assocs., Inc., Beaverton, Oreg., 1980-87, from sr. elec. engr., assoc. ptnr., 1987-96, v.p., 1996—. Adj. prof. Portland (Oreg.) C.C., 1982—; mem. adv. bd. Mass Transit System Compatibility, 1994. Co-author: FE/EIT Exam: Electrical Engineering Review and Study Guide, 2000, Electrical Engineering Professional Engineer License Exam Review Handbook, 2001; pub.: Research and Education and Association, 2000; cons. tech. editor Rsch. and Edn. Assn., 1998—; contbr. articles to profl. jours. Recipient Cert. Appreciation Am. Pub. Transit Assn. and Transit Industry, 1987. Sr. mem. IEEE, Industry Applications, Power Engring. and Vehicular Tech. Soc.; mem N.Y. Acad. Scis., Mass Transit Sys. Compatibility Adv. Bd, Eta Kappa Nu. Buddhist. Avocation: reading. Office: Elcon Assocs Inc 12670 NW Barnes Rd Portland OR 97229-9001 E-mail: kinhlien@aol.com., kpham@elconassoc.com.

PHAN, PHILLIP HIN CHOI, business educator, consultant; b. Singapore, Feb. 23, 1963; came to U.S., 1982; s. Bryan K. and Rosaline (Teo) P.; m. Soo-Hoon Lee-Phan, Feb. 13, 1988. BBA with distinction, U. Hawaii, 1984; PhD, U. Wash., 1992. Cost contr. Westin Hotels & Resorts, Dallas and Singapore, 1984—88; assoc. prof. York U., Toronto, 1992—2000; cons. World Bank, 1998—2001, OECD, 1998—2000; Bruggeman chaired assoc. prof. Rensselaer Poly. Inst., Troy, NY, 1998—. Asst. prof. CUNY, 1997; adj. assoc. prof. Nat. U. Singapore, 1998-2003, Singapore Mgmt. U., 2003—; vis. prof. Thammasat U., Thailand, 1997; ptnr. Core Competence Cons., Inc., Toronto, 1993-98; dir. Blood Trac Sys. Internat., Edmonton, 1996-98; mem. Multi-Nat. Enterprises and Investment com. Can. Coun. Internat.

Bus., 1993-2000. Mem. editl. bd. Jour. Bus. Venturing, 1998—, Acad. Mgmt. Jour., 2002—; co-editor Asia Pacific Jour. of Mgmt., 1999-2001. Recipient Endowment for Excellence award Boeing Corp., Seattle, 1992, Schulich Sch. Faculty Rsch. award, 1996; Rsch. grantee Social Scis. and Humanities Rsch. Coun. Can., 1997, John Broadbent Rsch. Fund, 2000—, Kauffman Entrepeneur Found., 2002; Edna G. Benson fellow, Seattle, 1992, Michael G. Foster fellow, Seattle, 1992; George W. Tyler scholar, Seattle, 1992. Mem. Acad. Mgmt., Inst. Mgmt. Scis., Acad. Internat. Bus. Republican. Avocations: reading, cycling, tennis, scuba. Office: Lally Sch M&T 110 8th St Troy NY 12180-3522 Home: 220 S President St # 900 Baltimore MD 21202

PHAN, TÂM THANH, medical educator, psychotherapist, consultant, researcher; b. Hue, Vietnam, June 10, 1949; d. Quê'Dinh and Chánh Thi (Tô) P. BA, Adams State Coll., 1979; MA, Western State Coll., 1980; PhD in Nutrition, Am. Coll. Nutrition, 1983; D of Nutrimedicine, John Kennedy Nutrisci., Gary, Ind., 1986; PhD in Counseling, Columbus Pacific U., 1988; DSc, Lafayette U., 1989. Lic. profl. counselor, marriage and family therapist; cert. nutrimedicine specialist. Counselor Lamar U., Beaumont, Tex., 1980-82; cons. Vietnamese Cmty., Golden Triangle, Tex., 1980—, The Wholistic Clinic, Beaumont, 1980—. Mem. adv. bd. Internat. Homeopathic Clearance, Mo., 1993—. Author: How Western Culture..., 1988, Natural Preventive Medicine, The Wholitic Approach, 1992, How to Prevent Mental Illness, 1995, How to Prevent Diabetes, 1996. Fellow Internat. Nutrimedicine Assn., Am. Nutrimedicine Assn.; mem. Interant. Alliance of Nutrimedical Therapists, Internat. Holistic Med. Soc. (bd. dirs. 1996, Cert. of Merit 1996). Avocations: writing, reading, swimming, cooking, knitting. Office: The Wholistic Clinic 1995 Broadway St Beaumont TX 77701-1941

PHARR, DAVID MASON, horticulture educator; BS in Horticulture, U. Ark., 1964, MS in Food Sci., 1967; PhD in Horticulture, U. Ill., 1971; postdoctorate, Purdue U., 1971-72. Asst. prof. horticultural sci. N.C. State U., 1972-75, assoc. prof. horticultural sci., 1975-81, prof. horticultural sci., 1981—. Contbr. articles to profl. jours.; patents in field. Recipient L.M. Ware Rsch. award Southern Region Am. Soc. Horticultural Sci., 1986, ASHS Ornamentals Pub. award Am. Soc. Horticultural Sci., 1987, ASHS Outstanding Grad. Educator award, 1995, Disting. Grad. Prof., Alumni Assn., 1995. Office: NC State U Dept Hort Sci PO Box 7809 Raleigh NC 27695-0001

PHARR, JACQUELINE ANITA, biology educator; b. Charlotte, N.C., July 18, 1931; d. Sidney Marion and Gladys Zenobia (Graves) P. BS, Johnson C. Smith U., 1954; MEd, Columbia U., 1961. Tchr., chmn. sci. dept. Mecklenburg Coll., Charlotte, N.C., 1954-64, West Charlotte-Charlotte-Mecklenburg Schs., 1964-87, ret., 1987. Mem. Phi Delta Kappa, Alpha Kappa Alpha. Democrat. Methodist. Home: 2501 Senior Dr Charlotte NC 28216-4349

PHARR, NAOMI H. MORTON, business educator; b. Randolph, Va. d. Charles Henry and Mattie (Curiton) Morton. BS, Hampton (Va.) Inst., 1942; MA, NYU, 1948; EdD, No. Ill. U., 1977; postgrad., Harvard U., 1958, 59, 60, postgrad., 1961, 62, 84, postgrad., 1994. Bus. educator Norfolk (Va.) State U., 1942-92; grad. teaching asst. No. Ill. U., DeKalb, 1974-75. Participant U.S. confs. in comms., summer 1962, internat. confs. in comms., Honolulu, summer 1974, Vancouver, B.C., Can., summer 1979, Auckland, New Zealand, summer 1990; participant People-to-People Internat. Del. to South Africa, 1995. Contbr. chpt. to Nat. Bus. Edn. Yearbook, 1978. Workshop presenter to chs. and recreation ctrs., Norfolk, 1980-82; mem. choir Grace Episc. Ch., Norfolk, 1978-88; mem. U.S. del. to China, People-to-People Internat., 1993. Naomi Pharr Day proclaimed by Norfolk State U., May 18, 1992. Mem. ASCD, AAUP (mem. exec. bd. Va. Conf. 1992-94), Nat. Bus. Edn. Assn., So. Bus. Edn. Assn., Va. Bus. Edn. Assn., Am. Vocat. Assn., Internat. Tng. in Comm., Phi Delta Epsilon, Beta Gamma Sigma, Alpha Kappa Alpha. Democrat. Avocations: tennis, golf, bowling, badminton, dancing. Office: Norfolk State U 2401 Corprew Ave Norfolk VA 23504-3993

PHELAN, THOMAS, clergyman, academic administrator, educator; b. Albany, N.Y., Apr. 11, 1925; s. Thomas William and Helen (Rausch) P. AB (N.Y. State Regents scholar 1942, President's medal 1945), Coll. Holy Cross, Worcester, Mass., 1945; S.T.L., Catholic U. Am., 1951; postgrad., Oxford (Eng.) U., 1958-59, 69-70. Ordained priest Roman Cath. Ch., 1951; pastor, tchr., adminstr. Diocese of Albany, 1951-58; resident Cath. chaplain Rensselaer Poly. Inst., Troy, N.Y., 1959-72, prof. history, 1972—, dean Sch. Humanities and Social Scis., 1972-95, inst. historian, inst. dean, sr. adviser to pres., 1995—. Chmn. architecture and bldg. commn. Diocese Albany, 1968— ; cons. in field. Author: Hudson Mohawk Gateway, 1985, Achieving the Impossible, 1995; author monographs, articles, revs. in field. Treas. The Rensselaer Newman Found., 1962—; pres. Hudson-Mohawk Indsl. Gateway, 1971-84, bd. dirs. exec. com. 1984—; mem. WMHT Ednl. Telecomm. Bd., 1966-77, 84-90, chmn. 1973-77; chmn. Troy Hist. Dist. and Landmarks Rev. Commn., 1975-86, chmn. hist. adv. com., 1987—; v.p. Preservation League N.Y. State, 1979-82, mem. trustees coun., 1982-87, 89—, pres. 1987-89; sec. and bd. dirs. Ptnrs. for Sacred Places, 1989—; bd. dirs. Hall of History Found., 1983-87; trustee Troy Pub. Libr., 1992—. With USN, 1943-46. Recipient Paul J. Hallinan award Nat. Newman Chaplains Assn., 1967, Ann. award Albany Arts League, 1977, Disting. Cmty. Svc. award Rensselaer Poly. Inst., 1979, Edward Fox Demers medal Alumni Assn. Rensselaer Poly. Inst., 1986, Disting. Svc. award Hudson-Mohawk Consortium of Colls. and Univs., 1988; named Acad. Laureate of the SUNY Found. at Albany, 1988; Danforth Found. fellow, 1969-70; grantee Homeland Found., 1958-59, Dorothy Thomas Found., 1969-70. Fellow Soc. Arts, Religion and Contemporary Culture; mem. Ch. Soc. Coll. Work (dir., exec. com. 1970—), Am. Conf. Acad. Deans, Liturgical Conf., Soc. Indsl. Archaeology, Assn. Internat. pour l'Etudes des Religions Prehistoriques et Ethnologiques, Cath. Campus Ministry Assn., Cath. Art Assn., Assn. for Religion and the Intellectual Life (bd. dirs. 1987—), Soc. History of Tech. Clubs: Ft. Orange, Troy Country; Squadron A (N.Y.C.). Home: 5 Whitman Ct Troy NY 12180-4732 Office: Rensselaer Poly Inst Troy NY 12180 E-mail: phelan@rpl.edu.

PHELPS, CAROLYN SUE, educational consultant; b. Revelo, Ky., June 30, 1936; d. James W. and Maude E. (Roudntree) Ball; m. Arvine Phelps, June 8, 1957; children: Amy J., Jeffrey A., Karen S. AA, Cumberland U., 1954; B, U. Ky., 1957; M, Ohio State U., 1960; PhD, Ga. State U., 1975. Tchr. various schs., Ky., Ohio, 1954-61; asst. supt. R&D Whitfield County (Ga.) Schs., 1961-67, maths. coord. asst. supt. inst., prin., 1967-89; cons. Phelps & Assocs., Rocky Face, Ga., 1989—. Prof. Morehaed (Ky.) State U., 1989—. Author math. book; contbr. articles to profl. jours. Named Woman of Yr., Nat. Assn. Sch. Adminstrs., 1984, Daily Citizen News, 1994. Mem. ASCD, Dalton C. of C., Phi Delta Kappa. Avocations: reading, exercise. Office: Phelps & Assocs 2706 Clearview Dr Rocky Face GA 30740-9439

PHELPS, DEANNE ELAYNE, educational counselor, consultant; b. Cin., Sept. 4, 1949; d. Carlie Earthel and Marcella (Johnson) Smith; m. Jack L. Phelps, Aug. 9, 1969; children: Lisa Michele Phelps Turner, Amy Kristen Phelps Grantland. BA, Eastern Ky. U., 1971; MS in Counseling Edn., Jacksonville (Ala.) State U., 1990. Cert. secondary and English edn. tchr., Ala. Tchr. English Trinity Christian Acad., Oxford, Ala., 1976-79; dir., tchr. Bynum (Ala.) Bapt. Kindergarten, 1979-80; instr. in English Cen. Tex. Coll., Ft. McClellan, Ala., 1983-84, Jacksonville State U., 1985-88; tchr. English Wellborn H.S., Anniston, Ala., 1989-90; owner, cons. The Communication Factor, Anniston, 1990-93; pers. counselor Temporary Resources, Inc., Anniston, Ala., 1991-92; resource cons., career, transition counselor Orkand Corp., Ft. McClellan, 1992-93; mgr., sr. counselor Resource Cons., Inc., Ft. McClellan, 1993-99. Mem. ACA, NAFE, Ala. Counseling Assn., Nat. Employment Counselors Assn., Nat. Career Devel. Assn., Calhoun County C. of C., Leadership Calhoun County (vice-chair 1996-97, bd. dirs.), Chi Sigma Iota. Home: 7908 Dabney Ct Frisco TX 75034

PHEMISTER, ROBERT DAVID, veterinary medical educator; b. Framingham, Mass., July 15, 1936; s. Robert Irving and Georgia Nora (Savignac) P.; m. Ann Christine Lyon, June 14, 1960; children: Katherine, David, Susan. D.V.M., Cornell U., 1960; PhD, Colo. State U., Ft. Collins, 1967. Diplomate: Am. Coll. Vet. Pathologists. Research assoc. U. Calif., Davis, 1960-61, vis. rsch. pathologist, 1974-75; staff scientist Armed Forces Inst. Pathology, Washington, 1962-64; sect. leader to dir. collaborative radiol. health lab. Colo. State U., 1964-77; mem. faculty Coll. Vet. Medicine and Biomed. Scis., 1968-85, prof. vet. pathology, 1973-85, assoc. dean, 1976-77, assoc. dir. expt. sta., 1977-85, dean, 1977-85, interim acad. v.p. Univ., 1982, interim pres. Univ., 1983-84, spl. counselor to pres., 1984-85; vis. prof. Colo. State U., 1995-96; prof. vet. pathology Cornell U., 1985-99, dean and prof. emeritus, 1999—, dean Coll. Vet. Medicine, 1985-95. Cons. Miss. State U., 1977-81; commr. Colo. Advanced Tech. Inst., 1983-84; mem. governing bd. N.Y. Sea Grant Inst., 1985-95, vice chmn., 1990-92; mem. vet. medicine adv. com. FDA, 1984-88; mem. joint coun. on food and agrl. scis. USDA, 1988-92, mem. exec. com., 1989-92; chmn. Zweig Meml. Fund for Equine Rsch., 1985-95; mem. adv. panel for vet. medicine Pew Health Professions Commn., 1991-93. Author papers in field. Served to comdr. USPHS, 1960-68. Recipient Charles A. Lory award and Disting. Univ. Leadership award Colo. State U., 1984, Disting. Practitioner award Nat. Acad. Practice, 1985, Regional Health Adminstr.'s award, 1985; named Honor Alumnus, Colo. State U., 1989. Mem. AVMA (coun. on edn. 1985-91, adv. bd. vet. specialities 1985-89), Assn. Am. Vet. Med. Colls. (pres. 1982-83), Colo. Vet. Med. Assn. (Disting. Svc. award 1985), N.Y. State Vet. Med. Soc. (Centennial award 1990), Sigma Xi, Phi Zeta, Phi Kappa Phi, Gamma Sigma Delta (Merit award for Adminstrn. 1995). Home: 5110 Hogan Ct Fort Collins CO 80528-8801

PHENIS-BOURKE, NANCY SUE, educational administrator; b. Anderson, Ind., Oct. 29, 1943; d. Wilma (Anderson) Baker; m. Richard W. Phenis, June 11, 1966; 1 child, Heidi L. BA, Ind. State U., 1965; MA, Ball State U., 1974, postgrad., 1985. Elem. tchr. Highland Park (N.J.) Schs., 1966-68, Anderson City Schs., 1969-71; elem. tchr., tchr. gifted and talented South Madison Schs., Pendleton, Ind., 1974-85, elem. prin., 1985—. K-12 curriculum dir. South Madison Schs., 1984; mem. CAPE grant com. Eli Lilly Found., 2000. Bd. dirs. South Madison Community Found., Pendleton, 1991, First Am. Bank FirstGrant; devel. bd. St. John's Health Care Systems; mem. Prin.'s Leadership Summit, U.S. Dept. Edn., 2000. Recipient Outstanding Contbn. award Internat. Reading Assn., 1991; grantee Eli Lilly Found., 1993. Mem. NAESP (Ind. state rep. 1998—, membership adv. com. 1999), AAUW (pres. 1985-87), Ind. Assn. Sch. Prins. (bd. dirs. 1994—), First Am. (bd. dirs. 1992-95), Phi Delta Kappa (historian 1987, Leadership award 1994), Delta Kappa Gamma (sec. 1990-92, pres. 1992-94, Leadership/Adminstr. award 1993). Office: East Elem Sch 893 E Us Highway 36 Pendleton IN 46064-9580

PHENIX, GLORIA GAYLE, educational association administrator; b. Dallas, Mar. 4, 1956; m. Douglas William Phenix, Aug. 8, 1987; children: David William, Duncan Kenneth. BA, U. North Tex., 1979, postgrad., 1979-81; PhD, ABD, U. Minn., 1981-89. Dean Jordan Coll., Benton Harbor, Mich., 1990; pres. Phenix & Assocs. Tng. Cons., St. Joseph, Mich., 1991—, Topeka, Kans., 1993—. Bd. dirs. Cornerstone, Inc. Mem. allocation com. United Way, 1990-92, Literacy Coun., 1991-93; mem. Topeka Race Rels. Task Force, 1994; Mayor's Commn. Status Women, 1996— Fulbright-Hayes fellow Africa, 1990; Hewlett Mellon Found. grantee, 1987, Benton Found. grantee, 1988. Mem. Am. Polit. Sci. Assn., Minn. Polit. Sci. Assn. (bd. dirs. 1989-90), Midwest Polit. Sci. Assn., Am. Assn. Trainers and Developers, Am. Soc. for Quality Control. Presbyterian. Office: Phenix & Assocs 505 Pleasant St Ste 200 Saint Joseph MI 49085-1269 also: Phenix Assocs 530 S Kansas Ave Topeka KS 66603-3403

PHILBERT, ROBERT EARL, secondary school educator; b. Anderson, Ind., Nov. 17, 1946; s. James William and Lois Louise (Hartman) P.; m. Cheryl Toney, July 24, 1976. BS, Ball State U., Muncie, Ind., 1969, MA, 1974, EdD, 1987. Cert. social sci. tchr., Ind. Ret. tchr. chair dept. social sci. Marion (Ind.) Cmty. Schs., 1969—2003; instr. social sci. methods Ball State U., 1983. Cons. St. Paul-Bennett Schs., St. Paul's Sch. Bd., Marion, 1990-93, I.S.T.E.P. validation com., Indpls., 1992; mem. Ind. State Textbook Adv. Bd., Indpls., 1992; participant NASA Tchr. in Space program; Marion Police Dept. candidate interview com., 1997. Mem. Citizen's Amb. Program, Social Studies Delegation to the Republic of Vietnam. Sgt. U.S. Army, 1970-72. Named Outstanding Educator, Marion High Sch., 1977-80. Mem. NEA, VFW, Nat. Coun. Social Studies, Ind. Coun. for the Social Studies, Ind. Tchrs. Assn., Marion Tchrs. Assn. (pres., v.p., award), Vietnam Vets Am., Am. Legion, Elks, Phi Alpha Theta, Pi Gamma Mu, Kappa Delta Pi, Phi Delta Kappa, Delta Tau Delta. Democrat. Roman Catholic. Avocations: white water rafting, traveling, dog training, photography. Home: 1703 W 32nd St Marion IN 46953-3435 Office: 750 W 26th St Marion IN 46953

PHILBRICK, DOUGLAS ROBERT, principal, librarian, educator, mental health professional; b. St. Louis, Mar. 17, 1942; s. Robert Gilbert and Alice Hazel (LaRoche) P.; m. Lynda J. Harmon; children: Alma Robert, Amber, David, Mark, Holly, Amos, June. B of Pub. Address, Brigham Young U., 1969, MLS, 1972; MA in Secondary Adminstrn., No. State Coll., 1977; EdS, U. S.D., 1991. Cert. EMT, N.Mex.; cert. supt. specialty, edn. specialist U. S.D. Libr. dir. Inst. of Am. Indian Arts, Santa Fe, 1973, D.Q. Univ., Davis, Calif., 1973—74; tchr., libr. Lower Brule (S.D.) High Sch., 1974—75; prin. Crow Creek Sioux Tribe, Fort Thompson, SD, 1975, Bur. Indian Affairs, Lower Brule, 1975—76, Kinlichee, Ariz., 1977—79, edn. supt. Stewart, Nev., 1979—80, Sells, Ariz., 1980, Fort Thompson, SD, 1981—85, edn. specialist Phoenix, 1985—91, prin. Keam Canyon, Ariz., 1992—94; mental health tech/counselor, tchr. Indian Health Svc., Sacaton, Ariz., 1994—98, tchr. substance abuse and regular, 1998—2003. Farmer/rancher, Chamberlain, S.D., 1956-61; chmn. curriculum com. Inst. Am. Indian Arts, Santa Fe, 1973; fed. intern Washington, 1971. Author adapted Libr. of Congress classification system for Indians, 1973, Bibliography of Indian Newspapers and Periodicals, 1974. Leader 4-H, Crow Creek Indian Reservation, 1956-61; scout master Boy Scouts Am., Chamberlain, 1984, Mesa, 1995-98. With USAF, 1961-64. Recipient scholarship Libr. Adminstrn. Devel. Program, U. Md., 1972. Republican. Mem. Lds Ch. Home: 1014 E 8th Pl Mesa AZ 85203-5610

PHILIPP, ANITA MARIE, computer sciences educator; b. Evergreen Park, Ill., Sept. 7, 1948; d. Benedict Anthony and Anne Therese (Bolf) Butkus; m. Leslie Howard Philipp, Sept. 6, 1975; children: Leslie Aaron, Renée Marie. BA in Elem. Edn., St. Norbert Coll., 1969; MEd in Ednl. Media, U. Okla., 1978; postgrad., Okla. City C.C., 1980-93, U. Ctrl. Okla., 1994-2000. Cert. tchr., Okla., audio-visual specialist, Okla.; Microsoft cert. profl. in visual basic 6.0. Tchr. fifth grade Green Bay (Wis.) Bd. Edn., 1970; social ins. rep. Social Security Adminstrn., Chgo., 1970-73, ops. supr. Evanston, Ill., 1973, employee devel. specialist Chgo., 1973-76, claims rep. Oklahoma City, 1976-77, ops. analyst, 1977-78; adj. instr. computer sci. Okla. City C.C., 1985-96; dir. computer edn. St. James Sch., Oklahoma City, 1987-93; adj. instr. computer sci. U. Ctrl. Okla., Edmond, 1996; prof. computer sci. Okla. City C.C., 1996—, computer sci. votech liaison. Ednl. computer cons., 1989—; faculty advisor St. James Light Newspaper; mem. restaurant evaluation team Dunn-Farley Enterprises, San Marcos, Calif., 1978-85; computer sci. votech liaison Oklahoma City C.C., 1996—. EEO counselor Social Security Adminstrn., Chgo., 1972-73, coord. info. and referral svcs., 1982-83; leader Campfire Girls, Oklahoma City, 1986-89; mem. St. James Sch. Bd. Edn., Oklahoma City, 1987 (St. James sch. devel. com., 1990—, chairperson, interim devel. dir., 1994-96); eucharistic min. St. James Ch. Named among Top 25 Tchrs., Apple Computer/Homeland Stores, 1990; recipient Excellence in Tchg. award Nat. Inst. for Staff and Orgnl. Devel., 1999. Roman Catholic. Avocations: computers, crafts, sewing, shopping. Home: 2209 Laneway Cir Oklahoma City OK 73159-5827 Office: Okla City CC 7777 S May Ave Oklahoma City OK 73159-4419 E-mail: aphilipp@okccc.edu.

PHILIPP, WALTER VIKTOR, mathematician, educator; b. Vienna, Dec. 14, 1936; came to U.S., 1963, naturalized, 1974; s. Oskar and Anna Julie (Krasucky) P.; m. Ariane Randell, Dec. 10, 1984; children: Petra, Robert, Anthony, Andre. MS in Math. and Physics, PhD in Math., U. Vienna, 1960. Asst. U. Vienna, 1960-63, 65-67, dozent, 1967; asst. prof. U. Mont., 1963-64; vis. asst. prof. U. Ill., Urbana, 1964-65, mem. faculty, 1967—2002, prof. math., 1973—2002, prof. stats., 1988—2000, chmn. dept. stats., 1990-95, prf. emeritus, 2000—. Vis. prof. U. N.C., Chapel Hill, 1972, 88, MIT, 1980, Tufts U., 1981, U. Göttingen, 1982, 85, Imperial Coll., London, 1985; vis. rsch. prof. Beckman Inst., U. Ill., 2000—; mem. adv. bd. Monatshefte für Mathematik, 1994-2001. Assoc. editor Annals of Probability, 1976-81. Fellow Inst. Math. Stats.; mem. Am. Math. Soc., Austrian Math. Soc., Austrian Acad. Scis. (corr. mem.). Avocation: mountaineering. Home: 1922 Maynard Dr Champaign IL 61822-5265 Office: U Ill Dept Stats Champaign IL 61820

PHILIPPI, DIETER RUDOLPH, retired academic administrator; b. Frankfurt, Germany, July 26, 1929; arrived in U.S., 1956, naturalized, 1961; s. Alfred and Ellen Marguerite (Glatzel) Philippi; m. Helga Philippi, May 29, 1982; children: Stephan Andreas, Michael Joachim;children from previous marriage: Bianca Maria, Christopher Thomas. BBA, Johann Wolfgang Goethe U., 1952; postgrad., Sorbonne, summers, 1951—52, U. Omaha, U. Tex.; MBA, Canadian Inst. Banking, 1953—55. With Toronto-Dominion Bank, Calgary, Edmonton, Canada, 1953—56; chief acct. Baylor U. Coll. Medicine, Houston, 1956—63; contr. Wittenberg U., Springfield, Ohio, 1963—68; bus. mgr. Park Coll., Kansas City, Mo., 1968—70; bus. mgr., treas. Lone Mountain Coll., San Francisco, 1970—75; v.p. bus. affairs Findlay (Ohio) Coll., 1975—76; bus. mgr. Bologna (Italy) Ctr., The Johns Hopkins U., 1976—78; dir. bus. and fin. Mt. St. Mary's Coll., LA, 1978—81; asst. to v.p. overseas programs Boston U., Mannheim, Germany, 1981—85; dir. adminstrn. and fin. Overseas programs Boston U., Mannheim, Germany, 1985—93; bus. mgr., contr. Schiller Internat. U., Ingersheim, Germany, 1993—95. Lectr. Laurence U., Santa Barbara, Calif., 1973—75; fin. cons. various charitable orgns. Active Boy Scouts, Canada, 1952—56, 1956—86; pres. German Sch. of East Bay, 1970—75; campaign coord. United Appeals Fund, 1968; active Boy Scouts, Germany, 1948—52, exec. bd. Tecumseh coun., 1967—68; bd. dirs. Bellaire Gen. Hosp.; Greenland Hills Sch.; Chaminade Coll. Prep. Sch. Recipient Disting. Svc. award, United Appeals Fund, 1970, Silver Beaver award, Boy Scouts, Wood badge, 1968. Mem.: Coll. and Univ. Pers. Assn., Am. Assn. Higher Edn., Nat. Assn. Accts., Western Coll. and Univ. Bus. Officers Assn., Nat. Coll. and Univ. Bus. Officers Assn., Am. Assn. Univ. Adminstrs., Am. Mgmt. Assn., Eastern Fin. Assn., Am. Fin. Assn., Am. Acctg. Assn., Univ. Club (Kansas City), San Francisco Consortium, Commonwealth Club of Calif. (San Francisco), Alpha Phi Omega. Home: 124 Las Palmas Blvd North Fort Myers FL 33903

PHILLIPS, ALMARIN, economics educator, consultant; b. Port Jervis, N.Y., Mar. 13, 1925; s. Wendell Edgar and Hazel (Billett) P.; m. Dorothy Kathryn Burns, June 14, 1947 (div. 1976); children: Almarin Paul, Frederick Peter, Thomas Rock, David John, Elizabeth Linett, Charles Samuel; m. Carole Cherry Greenberg, Dec. 19, 1976. BS, U. Pa., 1948, MA, 1949; PhD, Harvard, 1953. Instr. econs. U. Pa., 1948-50, 51-53, asst. prof. econs., 1953-56, prof. econs. and law, 1963-91; Hower prof. pub. policy U. Pa, 1983-91; chmn. dept. econs. U. Pa., 1968-71, 72-73, assoc. dean Wharton Sch., 1973-74, dean Sch. Pub. and Urban Policy, 1974-77, chair faculty senate, 1990-91. Teaching fellow Harvard, 1950-51; assoc. prof. U. Va, 1956-61, prof., 1961-63; vis. prof. U. Hawaii, summer 1968, U. Warwick, London Grad. Sch. Bus. Studies, 1972, Ohio State U., McGill U., 1978, Calif. Inst. Tech, Northwestern U., 1980, Ariz. Coll. Law, 1981, Inst. Europeén d'Adminstrn. des Affairs (INSEAD), France, spring 1990; co-dir. Pres.'s Commn. Fin. Structure and Regulation, 1970-71; mem. Nat. Commn. Electronic Fund Transfers, 1976-77; chmn. bd. Econsult Corp., 1990-96. Author: (with R.W. Cabell) Problems in Basic Operations Research Methods for Management, 1961, Market Structure, Organization and Performance, 1962, Technology and Market Structure: A Study of the Aircraft Industry, 1971, (with P. Phillips and T.R. Phillips) Biz Jets: Technology and Market Structure in the Corporate Jet Aircraft Industry, 1994; Editor: Perspectives on Antitrust Policy, 1965, (with O.E. Williamson) Prices: Issues in Theory, Practice and Policy, 1968, Promoting Competition in Regulated Markets, 1975 ; editor Jour. Indsl. Econs., 1974-90; Contbr. articles to tech. lit. Served with AUS, 1943-45. Decorated Purple Heart, Bronze Star. Fellow: AAAS, Am. Statis. Assn.; mem.: Internat. Telecomms. Soc. (bd. dirs. 1990—2002), European Econ. Assn., Econometric Soc., Am. Econ. Assn. Home: 1115 Remington Rd Wynnewood PA 19096-4021

PHILLIPS, BERNICE CECILE GOLDEN, retired vocational education educator; b. Galveston, Tex., June 30, 1920; d. Walter Lee and Minnie (Rothsprack) Golden; m. O. Phillips, Mar. 1950 (dec.); children: Dorian Lee, Loren Francis. BBA cum laude, U. Tex., 1945; MEd, U. Houston, 1968. cert. tchr., tchr. coord., vocat. tchr., Tex. Dir. Delphian Soc., Houston, 1955-60; bus. tchr. various private schs., Houston area, 1960-65; vocat. tchr. coord. office edn. program Pasadena (Tex.) Ind. Sch. Dist., 1965-68, Houston Ind. Sch. Dist., John H. Reagan High Sch., 1968-85, ret., 1985. Bd. dirs. Regency House Condominium Assn., 1991-93. Recipient numerous awards and recognitions for vocat. bus. work at local and state levels. Mem. AAUW (life, 50 yr. mem., Houston Br. v.p. edl. found. 1987-90, pres. 1992-94, bd. dirs. 1987-96, 50-Yr. mem. cert.), NEA, Nat. Bus. Edn. Assn., Am. Vocat. Assn. (life), Tex. State Tchrs. Assn. (life), Tex. Classroom Tchrs. Assn. (life), Tex. Bus. Edn. Assn. (emeritus, Life Mem. award, numerous other awards), Vocat. Office Edn. Tchrs. Assn. Tex. (past bd. dirs.), Greater Houston Bus. Edn. Assn. (reporter), Houston Assn. Ret. Tchrs., Tex. Assn. Ret. Tchrs., Delta Pi Epsilon (emeritus), Beta Gamma Sigma. Avocations: bridge, reading, arts, crafts, travel. Home: 1123 Royston Pl Apt D Bel Air MD 21015-4614

PHILLIPS, DOROTHY LOWE, nursing educator; b. Jacksonville, Fla., June 3, 1939; d. Clifford E. and Dorothy (MacFeeley) Lowe; m. Dale Bernard Phillips, Feb. 14, 1973; children: Francis D., Sean E., Dorothy F. AA in Nursing, Ventura Coll., 1969; BSN, Calif. State U. Consortium, San Diego, 1984; M. Nursing, UCLA, 1987; EdD, Nova Southeastern U., 1995. Cert. community colls. tchr., Calif.; RN, Calif., pub. health nurse, Calif., clin. nurse specialist maternal/child. Staff nurse Cmty. Meml. Hosp., Ventura, Calif., 1969-70; charge nurse women and children's clinic Ventura County Regional Med. Ctr., Ventura, 1974-76; staff nurse, RN II Pleasant Valley Hosp., Camarillo, Calif., 1978-85; lead instr. cert. nursing asst. program div. adult edn. Oxnard (Calif.) Union H.S. Dist., 1984-89; staff rsch. assoc. UCLA, 1988; clin. instr. Ventura C.C. Sch. Nursing, 1988; college nurse Ventura Community Coll., 1989; lectr. Sch. of Nursing UCLA, 1989, lectr., coord. maternity nursing Sch. of Nursing, 1989-90, 90-91; vocat. nursing dir., health scis. coord. Oxnard Union H.S. Dist., 1990-99; assoc. dean health occupations Allan Hancock Coll., 1999—. Vis. educator health careers unit Calif. Dept. Edn., 1992-94; cons. Oxnard Adult Sch.; mem. adv. com. nursing asst./home health aide program Ventura County Regional Occupational Program; presenter in field. Competitive events judge !st Annual Leadership Conf., Health Occupations Students of Am., Anaheim, Calif.; active St. John's Regional Med. Ctr. Health Fair, 1991, Pleasant Valley Hosp. Health Fair, 1991; seminar leader "Babies and You", March of Dimes, 1988. Grad. Div. Rsch. grantee UCLA, 1986; Calif.

State PTA scholar UCLA, 1986, Ventura County Med. Secs. scholar, 1967, Audrienne H. Mosley Grad. scholar, 1987. Mem. Nat. League for Nursing, Calif. Assn. Health Career Educators (pres. 1994), So. Calif. Dirs. Vocat. Nursing Programs (rec. sec. 1996—), So. Calif. Vocat. Nurse Educators (exec. bd.), Assn. Calif. C.C. Adminstrs., Nat. Coun. Instrnl. Adminstrs., Calif. C.C. Assn. Occupl. Edn., No. Calif. ADN Dirs., Santa Maria Valley Leadership Class, Sigma Theta Tau. Republican. Lutheran. Avocations: skiing, reading, exercise, travel, backpacking. Home: 1448 Oakridge Park Rd Santa Maria CA 93455-4560 Office: Allan Hancock Coll 800 S College Dr Santa Maria CA 93454-6399

PHILLIPS, DOROTHY ORMES, elementary education educator; b. Denver, July 26, 1922; d. Jesse Edward and Belle (Noisette) Ormes; m. James Kermit Phillips, Apr. 28, 1945; children: William K., Dorothy E., Valerie A. BBA, Case Western Res. U., 1946, MA, 1959; PhD, U. Akron, 1989. Cert. tchr., adminstr., Ohio. Tchr. Cleve. Pub. Schs., 1955-68, math. cons., 1968-83, adminstrv. intern, 1970-73; grad. asst. U. Akron, Ohio, 1983-85, lectr. elem. edn., supr. student tchrs., 1985—. Math. workshop presenter Norton (Ohio) Pub. Schs., 1986, presenter career day, 1997. Bd. dirs. Centerville Mills YMCA Camp, Chagrin Falls, Ohio, chmn., 1996-99. Grantee NDEA, 1960, NSF, 1966. Mem. ASCD, Nat. Coun. Tchrs. Math., Ednl. Computer Consortium Ohio, Cleve. Pub. Schs. Math. Cons. (assoc.), Alpha Kappa Alpha, Pi Lambda Theta. Avocations: swimming, camping, reading. Home: 8746 Crackel Rd Chagrin Falls OH 44023-1807 Office: U Akron Ednl Field Experiences Zook Hl # 228 Akron OH 44325-0001

PHILLIPS, EDUARDO, surgeon, educator; b. Guadalajara, Mex., Oct. 25, 1943; m. Marion Paulette Khan; children: Mark, Anthony, Cynthia. MD with honors, Nat. U. Mexico City, 1967. Diplomate Am. Bd. Surgery. Rotating intern Hosp. Frances, Mexico City, 1966, resident in gen. surgery, 1967-69; rotating intern Sinai Hosp., Detroit, 1969, resident in gen. surgery, 1970-73, coord. surg. edn., 1974-76, chief surg. endoscopy, 1984-99, acting chmn. dept. surgery, 1991, chmn. dept. surgery, 1992-98; clin. asst. prof. surgery Wayne State U., Detroit, 1992-97, clin. assoc. prof., 1997—; chief dept. surgery N.W. region Detroit Med. Ctr./Sinai-Grace Hosp., 1998—, dir. med. affairs Northwest Region, 1998-99. Contbr. articles to profl. jours. Fellow Internat. Coll. Surgeons (pres. Mich. divsn. 1995-99, vice regent Mich 1993-95, regent Mich. 1995—, Vice Regent of Yr. 1993), Am. Coll. Surgeons; mem. AMA, Am. Soc. Abdominal Surgeons, Am. Soc. Gastrointestinal Endoscopy, Am. Soc. Bariatric Surgery, Acad. Surgery Detroit (coun mem., chmn. membership com. 1995-97, pres.-elect 1997, pres. 1998-99), Detroit Gastroent. Soc. (pres. 1985-86), Detroit Surg. Assn., Mich. State Med. Soc., Soc. Laparoendoscopic Surgeons, Mich. Soc. Gen. Surgeons, Wayne County Med. Soc., Mich. Soc. Gastrointestinal Endoscopy, Frederick A. Coller Surg. Soc., Southeastern Mich. Surg. Soc. Jewish. Avocations: outdoor activities, classical music, reading classics. Office: Sinai-Grace Hosp 6071 W Outer Dr Detroit MI 48235-2624

PHILLIPS, ELIZABETH VELLOM, social worker, educator; b. Visalia, Calif., Nov. 7, 1922; d. Ralph Cauble and Mary Amelia (Cole) Vellom; m. William Clayton Phillips, Sept. 10, 1950 (div. 1976); children: Peter Clayton, David Cole, Ann Harper. BA, UCLA, 1943; MSW, Columbia U., 1950; MPH, Yale U., 1970; PhD, Union Grad. Sch., 1980. Lic. clin. social worker; diplomate Am. Bd. Examiners Clin. Social Work. Psychiat. social worker Jewish Bd. Guardians, N.Y.C., 1950-51, Cmty. Svc. Soc. Family Camp, N.Y.C., 1955-57, Jewish Family Svc., New Haven, 1962-64, New Haven Family Counseling, 1964-68; ass. clin. prof. psychiatry Sch. Medicine Yale U., New Haven, 1973—; pvt. practice New Haven, 1981—. Sr. social work supr. mental health dept. Hill Health Ctr., New Haven, 1973-81; prof. Sch. Social Work Smith Coll., Northampton, 1981-84; initiator teen pregnancy program Hill Health Ctr., 1977-81, cons., 1975-79. Found. Women's Health Svcs., New Haven, 1985, Inner City Co-op Farm, New Haven, 1978; organizer Big Brother/Big Sister program Yale U., 1976. Named Disting. Practitioner Nat. Acads. Practice, 1996. Mem. NASW, Am. Group Psychotherapy Assn., Nat. Fedn. Socs. Clin. Social Work (sec. 1988, v.p. 1993, pres.-elect 1994-96, pres. 1996-98), Conn. Soc. Clin. Social Work (pres. 1987-88). Democrat. Jewish. Avocations: playing musical instruments, writing poetry, hiking, bridge, travel. Home: 13 Cooper Rd North Haven CT 06473-3001

PHILLIPS, FLORENCE TSU, lawyer, choreographer, dance educator; b. Taipei, Republic of China, May 2, 1949; came to U.S., 1957; d. Victor Z.M. and Dulcie (Ling) Tsu; m. Patrick J. Phillips; 1 child, Roderick James. Student, NYU, 1967-69; BA summa cum laude, UCLA, 1971, JD, 1974. Bar: Calif. 1974. Dancer Imperial Japanese Dancers, N.Y.C., 1965-70, Ballet de Paris, Paris and Montreal, Que., Can., 1967-68, Grands Ballets Canadiens, Montreal, 1968-69; atty. HUD, Washington, 1974, L.A. Pub. Defender's Office, 1975-77, Minami, Lew & Tamaki, LLP, San Francisco, 1997—. Choreographer, dir. Sinay Ballet, L.A., 1979—; owner, dir. Danceworks Studio, L.A., 1978-99. Choreographer over 30 ballets, 1979—. Trustee Westminster Prebyn. Ch., 2003—; bd. dir. West Hollywood Fine Arts Adv. Bd., 1995—97. Mem. Bar Assn. San Francisco, Phi Beta Kappa, Pi Gamma Mu. Avocations: reading, needle crafts.

PHILLIPS, JEFFREY TAYLOR, secondary school music educator; b. Florence, S.C. s. Clifford Taylor and Dottie Jean (Berry) P. B of Music Edn., Mid. Tenn. State U., 1984; MA in Edn., Western Ky. U., 1986; EdS, Austin Peay State U., 1999. Asst. dir. bands Western Ky. U., Bowling Green, 1984-86, instr. low brass, 2001—; dir. bands and orch. Hendersonville (Tenn.) H.S., 1986—2002; dir. instrumental music Pope John Paul II H.S., Hendersonville, 2002—. Mem. ACLU, 1986—, Dem. Nat. Com., 1994—. Named Young Band Dir. of Yr. Am. Sch. Band Dirs. Assn., 1992. Mem. Internat. Assn. of Jazz Educators (v.p. 1992-93, pres. 1993-96), Am. Sch. Bd. Dirs. Assn., Am. String Tchrs. Assn., Mid. Tenn. Sch. Band and Orch. Assn. (exec. bd. dirs. 1988-90, pres. 1998-2001), Am. Fedn. Musicians, Nat. Band Assn., Music Educators Nat. Conf., Phi Beta Mu. Democrat. United Methodist. Avocations: music, biking, reading, caring for dogs. Office: Pope John Paul II HS 117 Caldwell Dr Hendersonville TN 37075 Home: 128 Allen Dr Hendersonville TN 37075-3804 E-mail: jpband@bellsouth.net.

PHILLIPS, JERRY JUAN, law educator; b. Charlotte, N.C., June 16, 1935; s. Vergil Ernest and Mary Blanche (Wade) P.; m. Anne Butler Colville, June 6, 1959; children: Sherman Wade, Dorothy Colville. BA, Yale U., 1956, JD, 1961; BA, Cambridge (Eng.) U., 1958, MA (hon.), 1964. Bar: Tenn. bar 1961. Assoc. firm Miller & Martin, Chattanooga, 1961-67; asst. prof. law U. Tenn., 1967-72, assoc. prof., 1972-73, prof., 1973—, W.P. Toms prof., 1980—. Advisor Tenn. Law Revision Commn., 1968-70; mem. Tenn. Jud. Council, 1970-74; adv. Fed. Interagy. Task Force on Products Liability, 1976-77; lectr. in field. Author: Products Liability in a Nutshell, 5th edit., 1998, Products Liability Cases and Materials on Torts and Related Law, 1980, Products Liability Treatise, 3 vols., 1986, Cases and Materials on Tort Law, 1992, 2d edit., 1997, Products Liability-Cases, Materials, Problems, 1994; advisor Tenn. U. Law Rev., 1977—. U. Tenn. grantee, 1978 Mem. ABA, Am. Law Inst., Knoxville Bar Assn., Am. Assn. Law Schs., Order of Coif, Phi Beta Kappa. Clubs: Knoxville Racquet. Democrat. Episcopalian. Office: 1505 Cumberland Ave Knoxville TN 37996-0001 E-mail: jphilli2@utr.edu.

PHILLIPS, JOHN ROBERT, political scientist, educator; b. Henderson, Ky., Dec. 16, 1942; s. Leander Armstead and Ann Reid (Brown) P. Diploma, Lang. Inst., Chateauroux, France, 1966; BA, Centre Coll., Danville, Ky., 1969; MA, Western Ky. U., Bowling Green, 1973. Instr. Drury Coll., Springfield, Mo., 1971-73, Western Ky. U., Bowling Green, 1975-79; asst. prof. Thiel Coll., Greenville, Pa., 1979-83, scholar-in-residence, 1983-85; pvt. cons., 1985—; adj. prof. Lockyear Coll., Evansville, Ind., 1987-88, prof. adminstrv. and social scis., 1988-91, acad. dean, 1988-90, v.p. acad. affairs, dean coll., 1990-91, Helen Hoffman disting. svc. prof., 1990-91; exec. dir. Henderson County Human Rels. Commn., 1991-93; dean acad. affairs, prof. political studies/govt. Springfield (Ill.) Coll., 1993-97, acting pres., 1996-97, provost, dean coll., 1997-98, prof. polit. and social scis., 1998—, Rose and H. Paul LaFata Endowed Chair for Disting. Tchg., 2003. Adj. prof. pub. adminstrn. Ind. State U., Terre Haute, 1991-92; field investigator on religion and culture in ancient city of Taxila, Pakistan, 1968, on indsl. pollution of hist. bldgs. and monuments, France, Italy, Austria, 1969; rschr. on nationalism, Scotland, 1972, 2002, on local Scottish govt. and urban deves., 1993; participant in internat. confs. on The Future of a United Germany, 1991; mem. adv. coun. St. John's Hosp. Sch. Respiratory Therapy, 1993-97, Ursuline Acad Sch. Bd., v.p., 1995-97, pres., 1997-99, Cen. Ill. Fgn. Lang. and Internat. Studies Consortium, 1993—, chmn., 1994-96; cons.-evaluator Higher Learning Commn., North Ctrl. Assn. Colls. and Schs., 1999—. Mem. editl. bd. Jour. Urban Affairs, 1985-89, Pub. Voices, 2003—; manuscript referee Pub. Adminstrn. Rev., 1985-87; contbr. chpts. to mult-vol. reference series The Small City and Regional Cmty. 1981, 85, 87, 95, 99; asst. editor Pub. Voices, 2001-2003; contbr. articles on urban affairs, ednl. policy and practice, the Am. Presidency, policy planning, and federalism/intergovtl. rels. to profl. jours. Policy advisor Lt. Gov.'s Office, Frankfort, Ky., 1985-86; cons. Commn. on Ky.'s Future, Frankfort, 1985-87; mem. Bd. Cath. Edn., Diocese of Springfield, 1994-97; trustee Springfield Coll., 1996-97, commn. on human sexuality Episcopal Diocese of Springfield, 1997-98; bd. dirs. Liturgical Arts Festival of Springfield, 1998-2001. With USAF, 1963-68. Mem. Am. Polit. Sci. Assn. (Leon Weaver Award com. 1990-93), Am. Soc. Pub. Adminstrn. (publs. com. 1984-88, 92-95), Urban Affairs Assn. (publs. com. 1985-89, nominating com. 1984-85, 88-89), Pi Sigma Alpha, Alpha Sigma Lambda. Democrat. Episcopalian. Home: 2605 Delaware Dr Springfield IL 62702-1213 Office: Springfield College L-106 Becker Libr 1500 N 5th St Springfield IL 62702-2643 E-mail: phillips@sci.edu.

PHILLIPS, KAREN, secondary education educator; Physical edn. tchr., adminstr. Walter D. Johnson Jr. H.S., Las Vegas, 1993-97; asst. prin. Lied Mid. Sch., Las Vegas, 1997-99; prin. Clifford J. Lawrence Jr. High Sch., 1999—. Recipient Middle Sch. Physical Edn. Tchr. of the Yr. Nat. Assn. for Sport and Physical Edn., 1993. Office: Clifford J Lawrence Jr High Sch 4410 S Juliano Rd Las Vegas NV 89147-8691

PHILLIPS, KEITH, Spanish language educator; b. Sept. 21, 1971; BA, Ball State U., 1994; MA, Mich. State U., 1998. Multilingual claims rep. Social Security Adminstrn., Anderson, Ind., 1995-96; instr. Spanish, Mich. State U., East Lansing, 1996-98, Trinity Christian Coll., Palos Heights, Ill., 1998-99, internat. dir. semester in Spain, 1998-99; instr. Spanish Moraine Valley C.C., Palos Hills, Ill., 1999—. Office: 10900 S 88th Ave Palos Hills IL 60465 E-mail: keith.phillips@trnty.edu.

PHILLIPS, KEVIN G. education educator; b. Middletown, N.Y., Apr. 22, 1960; s. Myron Arthur and Esther May (Whorrall) P.; m. Sarah Prescott, May 28, 1983. BA, Wheaton Coll., 1982, MA, 1983; EdD, Columbia U., 2003. Dir. Christian edn. 1st United Meth. Ch., Bradenton, Fla., 1983-84; youth dir. Lakewood United Meth. Ch., North Little Rock, Ark., 1985-86; student govt. coord. Tchrs. Coll., Columbia U., N.Y.C., 1987-89; adj. prof. Nyack (N.Y.) Coll., 1988, asst. prof., 1988—93, dept. chmn., 1989—93. Lectr. King's Coll., Briarcliffe Manor, N.Y., 1987; cons. Met. Missions, Andhra Pradesh, India, 1988—; presenter seminars; treas. Leadership Devel. Cons., 1988-93; youth dir. Hopewell Reformed Ch., 1992-2001, mission coord., 2001—; instr. NY Sch. of Bible, 1999—; internat. trainer Reign Ministries of Minn., 2001—; pres. Restoring Rockland, Inc., 1993—; bd. dirs. Nyack Ambulance, 1996-2003. Contbr. articles, book revs. to profl. publs. Tng. chmn. N.Y.C. area Boy Scouts Am., 1987-2002, scoutmaster, 1988-2002. Recipient Good Shepherd award Boy Scouts Am., 1982, Silver Beaver award, 1990. Mem. Nat. Assn. Profs. Christian Edn., Kappa Delta Pi. Republican. Avocations: stamp collecting, coin collecting, hiking, backpacking, reading. Office: PO Box 959 Nyack NY 10960-0959

PHILLIPS, KIMBERLY KAY, elementary school educator; b. Atlanta, Jan. 27, 1966; d. James H. and Brenda K. (White) Reynolds; m. Roy A. Phillips Jr. BS in Middle Grades Edn., Mercer U., 1988; MEd in Middle Grades Edn., West Ga. Coll., 1994. Tchr. mid. grade math. and reading Haralson County Sch. Sys., Buchanan, Ga., 1988-94; head tchr. before and after program Loveland Sch., Omaha, 1994-95, staff mem., 1996—; instr. study skills and test taking skills course Offutt AFB, 1996—. Adult basic edn./gen. edn. diploma program instr. Met. C.C., Omaha, 1995, part-time faculty mem., 1995—. Mem. Kappa Delta Epsilon. Address: 9205 Park View Blvd La Vista NE 68128-2318

PHILLIPS, MARGARET, retired school system administrator; b. Sandusky, Ohio, Mar. 19, 1943; d. Armenio and Lidia Phillips. BS, Bowling Green State U., 1965; MA, George Washington U., 1969; postgrad., Firelands Coll., 1973-78, Kent State U., 1981-86, U. Toronto, 1987, Cambridge (Eng.) U., 1988. Cert. English, elem. tchr., Ohio. Instr. Landover (Md.) Pub. Schs., 1965—69, Bataan Elem. Sch., Port Clinton, Ohio, 1969—70, Portage Elem. Sch., Gypsum, Ohio, 1970—77, Port Clinton High Sch., 1977—2000, chair dept. English/lang. arts/reading, 1994—2000; ret., 2000. Cons. positive control communications system Intern Program, Port Clinton, 1987-2000; talk show host; juvenile ct. mediator. Mem. crisis intervention team; sec. Port Clinton (Ohio) City Tree Commn., 2000—; tchr. 7th grade confirmation classes. Named Tchr. of Yr. Key Club-Kiwanis, 1986. Mem. Stratford Festival Assn., Port Clinton C. of C. Avocation: photography. Home: 11th St Port Clinton OH 43452

PHILLIPS, MARGARET CROUSE, gifted and talented educator; b. Denton, Md., Oct. 19, 1937; d. Earl Monroe and Ida Ruth (Jones) Crouse; m. Bobby Jack Phillips, July 5, 1960. BS, Towson State U., 1959; postgrad., U. Md., 1961-65; cert. gifted edn., U. Fla., 1968. Lic. tchr., Fla. Tchr. 5th grade Caroline County Bd. Edn., Denton, Md., 1959-60; tchr. 1st grade Talbot County Bd. Edn., Easton, Md., 1960-64; tchr. 4th grade Caroline County Bd. Edn., Denton, 1964-65, tchr. 5th grade, 1965-69, Marion County Bd. Edn., Ocala, Fla., 1969-77, tchr. 1st grade, 1977-80, tchr. gifted, 1980—. Lead tchr. Peer Tchr. Program, Marion County, 1985-89; elem. rep. Comprehensive Health Coun. State Fla., 1976; tchr., coord. Parents Aid Sch. Success, Ocala, 1978-79; del. to Russia for gifted edn. People to People Internat., 1991. Bd. dirs. Ocala Community Concerts, 1982-83; choir mem. Ctrl. Bapt. Ch., Ocala, 1969-92, Sunday Sch. decoration com.; dir. Community Concert Assn., 1992-93. Named Tchr. of Yr. Marion County Coun. Exceptional Edn., Ocala, 1983, Tchr. of Yr. Gifted Marion County Exeptional Student Edn., Ocala, 1991, Woman of Yr. Marion County Woman's Club, Ocala, 1990. Mem. Exceptional Student Edn., Fla. Talented and Gifted (Tchr. of Yr. Marion County 1992), Greater Ocala Woman's Club (bd. dirs. 1989-92), Ocala Woman's Club (evening div. pres. 1979-89), Gifted Orgn. Moscow, Alpha Delta Kappa. Democrat. Avocations: music, art, travel, reading. Home: 1851 NE 40th Cir Ocala FL 34470-5039

PHILLIPS, OWEN MARTIN, oceanographer, geophysicist, educator; b. Parramatta, Australia, Dec. 30, 1930; s. Richard Keith and Madeline (Lofts) P.; m. Merle Winifred Simons, Aug. 8, 1953; children: Lynette Michelle, Christopher Ian, Bronwyn Ann, Michael Stuart. B.Sc., Sydney (Australia) U., 1952; PhD, U. Cambridge (Eng.), 1955. Rsch. fellow Imperial Chem. Industries, U. Cambridge, 1955-57; prize fellow St. John's Coll., Cambridge; asst. prof., then assoc. prof. Johns Hopkins, 1957-61; asst. dir. rsch. U. Cambridge, 1961-64; prof. geophys. mechanics Johns Hopkins, 1964—, chmn. dept. earth and planetary scis., 1971-77, 88-89, Decker prof. sci. and engring., 1975—98, Decker prof. emeritus, 1998—. Cons. to industry, 1960— ; Mem. council mems. Nat. Center Atmospheric Research, 1964-67, chmn. rev. and goals, 1965-67; mem. com. global atmospheric research project Nat. Acad. Sci., 1967-69; mem. Waterman award com. NSF, 1975-77 Author: The Dynamics of the Upper Ocean, 1966, 2d edit., 1968, 3d edit., 1977, Russian edit., 1969, 2d Russian edit., 1980, Chinese edit., 1986, The Heart of the Earth, 1968, Italian edit., 1970, 74, 77, The Last Chance Energy Book, 1979, 2d edit., 1980, Japanese edit., 1986; editor: Wave Dynamics and Radio Probing of the Ocean Surface, 1986, Flow and Reactions in Permeable Rocks, 1991; assoc. editor Jour. Fluid Mechanics, 1964-95; regional editor Proc. Royal Soc., 1990-96; mem. editl. bd. Ann. Rev. Fluid Mechanics, 1994-97; contbr. articles to profl. jours. Trustee Roland Park Country Sch., 1974-81; trustee Chesapeake Research Consortium, 1972-76, sec., 1972. Recipient Adams prize U. Cambridge, 1965, Sverdrup Gold medal Am. Meteorol. Soc., 1974; hon. fellow Trinity Coll., Cambridge, Eng., 1997. Fellow Royal Soc. (London), Am. Meteorol. Soc. (publs. commn. 1971-77, planning com. 1983-84), Am. Geophys. Union; mem. Nat. Acad. Engring. (audit com. 2000-02, Gibbs Bros. medal com. 2002), Md. Acad. Sci. (sci. coun. 1974-85, pres. 1979-85, trustee 1985-87), Phi Beta Kappa, Sigma Xi, Pi Tau Sigma. Home: 23 Merrymount Rd Baltimore MD 21210-1908

PHILLIPS, PATRICIA ANNA, principal, educator; b. Hutchinson, Kans., Mar. 19, 1962; d. Hugh William and Mary Pauline (Smith) P. AA, Hutchinson C.C., 1982; BA, Sch. of the Ozarks, 1985; MEd, Drury Coll., 1994. Cert. prin., 1999. Tchr. high sch. sci. Pierce City (Mo.) R-6 Sch. Dist., 1985-94, 95-98, Purdy (Mo.) R-2 Sch. Dist., 1994-95; adminstr. Pierce City (Mo.) R-6 Sch. Dist., 1998-2000; prin. Bronaugh R-VII Sch. Dist., 2000—. Mem. adv. bd. Regional Profl. Devel. Com., Springfield, Mo., 1996-2000; chair Profl. Devel. Com., Pierce City, 1994-99. Mem. AAUW, ASCD, NEA (local pres., dist. chair, state women's issues com., state by-laws com.), Nat. Sci. Tchrs. Assn., Mo. NEA (govt. rels. team 1996—), Nat. Assn. Secondary Sch. Prins. Democrat. Avocations: arts & crafts, travel, reading, sports, music. Office: Bronaugh R-7 Sch Dist PO Box 8 Bronaugh MO 64728-0008 Home: PO Box 5 Bronaugh MO 64728-0005

PHILLIPS, PATRICIA JEANNE, retired school system administrator; b. Amarillo, Miss., Jan. 13, 1935; d. William Macon and Mary Ann (Cawthon) Patrick; m. William Henry Phillips, June 22, 1962; 1 child, Mary Jeanne. BA, Millsaps Coll., 1954; MA, Vanderbilt/Peabody U., 1957; EdD, U. So. Miss., 1978. Tchr. Jackson (Miss.) Pub. Schs., 1954-73, prin., 1973-75, asst. prin., 1975-77; dir. ednl. program Eden Prairie (Minn.) # 272, 1977-80; dir. elem. edn. Meridian (Miss.) Pub. Schs., 1980-91, asst. supt. curriculum, 1991; ret., 1991. Prof. Miss. Coll., Clinton, 1977, Miss. State U., Meridian, 1981-2000; cons. in field. Co-author: (testing practice) Test Taking Tactics, 1987; developer tng. materials Best Practices, Brain Growth: Applications for the Classroom; contbr. articles to profl. jours. Pres. Meridian Symphony Orch., 1987, 2000—; v.p. Meridian Coun. Arts, 1986; bd. dirs. Meridian Art Mus. Named Boss of Yr., Meridian Secretarial Assn., 1985, Arts Educator of Yr., Meridian Coun. Arts, 1991; recipient Excellence award Pub. Edn. Form, 1993. Mem. ASCD, Miss. ASCD, Miss. Assn. Women (pres.), Rotary, Phi Kappa Alpha, Phi Delta Kappa (pres. 1986-87), Alpha Delta Kappa Gamma (pres. 1962), Kappa Delta Phi. Republican. Methodist. Avocations: grant writing, computers, golf. Home: 322 51st St Meridian MS 39305-2013 E-mail: bjphill@mississippi.net.

PHILLIPS, PETER CHARLES BONEST, economist, educator, researcher; b. Weymouth, Dorset, Eng., Mar. 23, 1948; came to U.S., 1980; s. Charles Bonest and Gladys Eileen (Lade) P.; m. Emily Dowdell Birdling, Feb. 10, 1971 (div. 1980); 1 child, Daniel Lade; m. Deborah Jane Blood, June 13, 1981; children: Justin Bonest, Lara Kimberley. BA, Auckland (New Zealand) U., 1969, MA, 1971; PhD, London U., 1974; MA (hon.), Yale U., 1979. Teaching fellow U. Auckland, 1969-70, jr. lectr., 1970-71; lectr. in econs. U. Essex, Colchester, Eng., 1972-76; prof. econs. U. Birmingham, Eng., 1976-79, Yale U., New Haven, Conn., 1979-85, Stanley Resor prof. econs., 1985-89, Sterling prof. econs., 1989—; Alumni disting. prof. econs. U. Auckland, 1991—; pres. Predicta Software Inc., Madison, Conn., 1994—. Vis. scholar Ecole Polytechnique, Paris, 1977; univ. vis. prof. Monash U., Melbourne, Australia, 1986; vis. prof. Inst. Advanced Studes, Vienna, Austria, 1989; disting. visitor London Sch. Econs., 1989. Editor Econometric Theory jour., 1985; joint editor Asia Pacific Economic Review, 1995—; contbr. over 180 articles, book revs., notes to profl. jours. Recipient award for promotion of sci. Japan Soc., 1983, New Zealand medal Sci. and Tech., 1998, Plura Scripsit, 1997, Plurima Scripsit Econometric Theory award, 2000, Nzier Qantas Economist of Yr., 2000; Commonwealth Grants Com. scholar, Eng., 1971, Guggenheim fellow, N.Y., 1984-85. Fellow Am. Acad. Arts & Scis., Royal Soc. New Zealand (hon.), Econometric Soc., Jour. Econometrics, Am. Statis. Soc.; mem. Inst. Math. Stats., Modsim Soc. (Biennial Medal, 2003). Avocations: running, building, poetry, reading. Home: 133 Concord Dr Madison CT 06443-1814 Office: Cowles Found PO Box 208281 New Haven CT 06520-8281 E-mail: peter.phillips@yale.edu.

PHILLIPS, RICHARD A. English educator; b. Chester, Pa., June 6, 1949; s. Albert Phillips and Florence (Dunn) P. BS, Cheyney (Pa.) U., 1971. Cert. tchr., Del. Tchr. Colonial Sch. Dist., New Castle, Del., 1971-87, 1991—, HighCroft Sch., Williamstown, Mass., 1986; exec. dir. Sylvan Learning Ctrs., Wilmington, Del., 1987-90. Mem. NEA, ASCD, Nat. Coun. Tchrs. English, Internat. Reading Assn., Del. Assn. for Curriculum Devel., Colonial Edn. Assn., Del. Assn. for Tchrs. of English, New Castle County Edn. Assn., Del. State Edn. Assn. Home: 202 Red Fox Ln Newark DE 19711-5905

PHILLIPS, RONALD LEWIS, plant geneticist, educator; b. Huntington County, Ind., Jan. 1, 1940; s. Philemon Lewis and Louise Alpha (Walker) P.; m. Judith Lee Lind, Aug. 19, 1962; children: Brett, Angela. BS in Crop Sci., Purdue U., 1961, MS in Plant Breeding and Genetics, 1963, Doctorate (hon.), 2000; PhD in Genetics, U. Minn., 1966; postgrad., Cornell U., 1966-67. Rsch. and tchg. asst. Purdue U., 1961—62, U. Minn., St. Paul, 1962—66, rsch. assoc., 1967—68, asst. prof., 1968—72, assoc. prof., 1972—76, prof. genetics and plant breeding, 1976—93, Regents prof., 1993—, McKnight presdl. chair in genomics, 2000—. Program dir. Competetive Rsch. Grants Office USDA, Washington, 1979; mem. adv. grant panels NSF, USDA, DOE, AID; chmn. Gordon Conf. on Plant Cell and Tissue Culture, 1985; mem. sci. adv. coun. U. Calif. Plant Gene Expression Ctr., Berkeley, 1986—93, chair, 1992—93; program adv. com. Palm Oil Rsch. Inst. Malaysia, 1992—2001; sci. adv. bd. Donald Danforth Plant Sci. Ctr., St. Louis, 2000—; sci. liaison officer Internat. Rice Rsch. Inst. USAID; vis. prof., Italy, 1981, Canada, 83, China, 86, Japan, 90, Morocco, 96; dir. Plant Molecular Genetics Inst., 1991—94; chief scientist USDA, 1996—98; trustee Biol. Stain Commn.; mem. Nat. Plant Genetic Resources Bd.; dir. Ctr. Microbial and Plant Genomics, 2000—. Co-editor: Cytogenetics, 1977, Molecular Genetic Modification of Eucaryotes, 1977, Molecular Biology of Plants, 1979, The Plant Seed: Development, Preservation and Germination, 1979, Genetic Improvement of Crops: Emergent Techniques, 1980, DNA-Based Markers in Plants, 1994, 2d edit., 2001; assoc. editor Genetics, 1978—81, Can. Jour. Genetics and Cytology and Genome, 1985—90, mem. editl. bd. Maydica, 1978—, In Vitro Cellular and Devel. Biology, 1988—92, Cell Culture and Somatic Cell Genetics of Plants, 1983—91, Jour. of the Oil Palm, 1994—, Proc. NAS, 1996—98; contbr. chpts. to Maize Beeding and Genetics, 1978, Staining Procedures, 1981, Chromosome Structure and Function, 1987, Corn and Corn Improvement, 1988, Plant Transposable Elements, 1988, Chromosome Engring. in Plants, 1991, Maize Handbook, 1994, sci. articles to profl. jours. Mem. chmn. coun. on ministries, lay leader United Meth. Ch., 1968, dir. Project AgGrad, 1983—; Cub Scout Pack co-chmn. Boy Scouts Am., 1976-77; judge Minn. Regional and State Sci. Fair, 1970-80. Recipient Purdue Agrl. Alumni Achievement award, 1961, Purdue Disting. Agrl. Alumni award, 1993; NSF fellow, 1961; NIH fellow, 1966-67; recipient Northrup King Oustanding Faculty Performance award, 1985, Crop Sci. Rsch. award, 1988, DeKalb Genetics Crop

Sci. Disting. Career award, 1997. Fellow: AAAS (chair sect. O), Crop Sci. Soc. Am. (awards com., divsn. chmn., bd. rep. 1988—91, pres.-elect 1998—99, pres. 1999—2000, past pres. 2000—01), Am. Soc. Agronomy (Caleb-Dorr award); mem.: NAS (chair sect. 62 1999—2002, nominating com. 2002), Am. Soc. Agronomy (award student sect.), Genetics Soc. Am., Sigma Xi, Alpha Zeta, Gamma Sigma Delta (award of merit 1994), Gamma Alpha (nat. treas.). Office: U Minn Dpt Agronomy-Plant Genetics Saint Paul MN 55108 E-mail: phill005@umn.edu.

PHILLIPS, SANDRA ALLEN, retired primary school educator; b. Newport News, Va., Mar. 10, 1943; d. Cecil Lamar and Mary (Schenk) Allen. BS, Appalachian State U., Boone, N.C., 1965; MEd, U. N.C., Charlotte, 1990. Tchr. Rockwell (N.C.) Elem. Sch., 1964-65, Granite Quarry (N.C.) Elem. Sch., 1965-68, Lillian Black Elem. Sch., Spring Lake, N.C., 1970, Berryhill Elem. Sch., Charlotte, N.C., 1970-71, 77-99, ret., 1999; tchr. J.C. Roe Sch., Wilmington, N.C., 1974-76. Elected to tchr.'s adv. coun. Charlotte-Mecklenburg Schs., 1995-96, 96-97, 97-98, 98-99; title I tchr., 1999. Named Tchr. of Yr., Berryhill Elem. Sch., 1989. Mem. Profl. Educators N.C., Classroom Tchrs. Assn. Office: Berryhill Elem Sch 10501 Walkers Ferry Rd Charlotte NC 28278-9721

PHILLIPS, SUSAN DIANE, secondary school educator; b. Shelbyville, Ky., Aug. 28, 1955; d. James William and Catherine Elizabeth (Jones) P. B of Music Edn., Eastern Ky. U., 1977; postgrad., U. Ky., 1987. Tchr. music Breckinridge County Schs., Hardinsburg, Ky., 1978, Perry County Schs., Hazard, Ky., 1980-83, Music on the Move, Louisville, 1985-86, Cooter (Mo.) R-4 Sch., 1987-90, Lewis County Schs., Vanceburg, Ky., 1990—. Staff-cavalcade of bands Ky. Derby Festival, Louisville, 1984-86; christian min. Dir. Simpsonville (Ky.) United Meth. Ch. Handbell Choirs, 1985-86; mem. grand coun. Order of St. Isidore of Seville. Named Ky. Colonel Gov. Commonwealth of Ky., 1979. Mem. NEA, Ky. Educators Assn., Ky. Music Educators Assn., Music Educators Nat. Conf., Internat. Soc. Tech. in Edn., Order of St. Isadore of Seville (grand coun.). Office: Lewis County Mid Sch Lions Ln Vanceburg KY 41179 E-mail: sphillips@lewis.k12.ky.us.

PHILLIPS, THEODORE LOCKE, radiation oncologist, educator; b. Phila., June 4, 1933; s. Harry Webster and Margaret Amy (Locke) Phillips; m. Joan Cappello, June 23, 1956; children: Margaret, John, Sally. BSc, Dickinson Coll., 1955; MD, U. Pa., 1959. Intern Western Res. U., Cleve., 1960; resident in therapeutic radiology U. Calif., San Francisco, 1963, clin. instr., 1963—65, asst. prof. radiation oncology, 1965—68, assoc. prof., 1968—70, prof., 1970—, chmn. dept. radiation oncology, 1973—98. Rsch. radiobiologist U.S. Naval Radiologic Def. Lab., San Francisco, 1963—65; rsch. physician Lawrence Berkeley Lab. Contbr. numerous articles to profl. publs. With USNR, 1963—65. Grantee, Nat. Cancer Inst., 1970—99. Mem.: Inst. Medicine, No. Calif. Radiation Oncology Assn., Radium Soc., Radiation Rsch. Soc. (pres. 1977), Am. Coll. Radiology, Calif. Med. Assn., Am. Assn. Cancer Rsch., N.Am. Hyperthermia Soc. (pres. 1994), Radiol. Soc. N.Am., Am. Soc. Clin. Oncology, Am. Soc. Therapeutic Radiology and Oncology (pres. 1984), Alpha Omega Alpha, Phi Beta Kappa. Republican. Office: U Calif San Francisco Dept Radiation Oncology 1600 Divisidero St ste H1031 San Francisco CA 94143-1708

PHILLIPS, VICKI L. school system administrator; b. Marion, Ind., Jan. 15, 1958; d. Denver Phillips and Vivian (Burnette) Fuqua. BS in Edn., Western Ky. U., 1980, MA in Psychology, 1987; doctoral student, U. Ky., 1988—; EdD in instrnl. leadership, U. of Lincoln, Eng., 2002. Dir. devel. tng. dept. Panorama, Bowling Green, Ky., 1978—80; tchr. learning and behavior disorders Simpson County Bd. Edn., 1981—85; exceptional child cons. Ky. Dept. Edn. Office Edn. for Exceptional Children, 1986—90; chief exec. asst. to edn. commr. Ky. Dept. of Edn., 1986—93; dep. dir./chief of staff Nat. Alliance for Restructuring Edn., Wash., DC, 1993—95; dir. Greater Phila. First Partnership for Reform; exec. dir. Children Achieving Challenge; supt. Sch. Dist. of Lancaster, 1998—2003; sec. of edn. Pa. Dept. Edn., Harrisburg, 2003—. Mem. ASCD, Nat. Coun. for Exceptional Children, Coun. for Behavior Disorders, Nat. Assn. for Sch. Psychologists, Ky. Assn. Sch. Adminstrs., Ky. Assn. for Psychology in the Schs., Ky. Assn. for Family-Based Svcs., Ky. Families for Family-Based Svcs., Ky. Families as Allies. Office: 333 Market St Harristown 2 Harrisburg PA 17126-0333

PHILLIPS, WANDA CHARITY, secondary education educator, writer; b. Gettysburg, Pennsylvania, Apr. 1, 1947; d. Roy Homer and Frances Marie (White) Kuykendall; m. James E. Phillips; children: Jenny, Peter, Micah. BS in secondary edn., Shippensburg U., 1968; cert. elem. edn., Grand Canyon Coll., 1973; MA in Adminstrn., No. Ariz. U., 1993. Tchr. Littlestown H.S., Pa., 1969, Phoenix, Ariz. Indian Sch., 1971-72, Peoria Sch. Dist., Ariz., 1973—; author ISHA Enterprises, Inc., Scottsdale, Ariz., 1985—. Ednl. seminar presenter ISHA Enterprises, Scottsdale, Ariz., 1986—, Assn. Christian Sch. Internat., Calif., 1988—. Author: Easy Grammar, 1986, Daily Grams: Guided Review Aiding Mastery Skills, 1986, Daily Grams: Guided Review Aiding Mastery Skills for Grades 4-5, 1987, Grades 3-4, 1988, Grades 5-6, 1993, Easy Writing, 1991, Daily Grams: Guided Teaching and Review for Grades 2 and 3, 1992, Easy Grammar, Grades 5 and 6, 1994 (children's book) My Mother Doesn't Like to Cook, 1993, Easy Grammar Plus, 1995, Easy Grammar: Grades 4 and 5, 1996, Easy Grammar: Grades 3 and 4, 1998. Daily Grams: Grades 3, 4, 5, 6, and 7, 2002. Hopes and Dreams Charity, Phoenix Found. for the Homeless Children. Mem.: Nat. Trust for Hist. Preservation, Paradise Valley Women's Club. Office: ISHA Enterprises Inc PO Box 12520 Scottsdale AZ 85267-2520

PHILLIPS, WINFRED MARSHALL, dean, biomedical research executive, mechanical engineer, educator; b. Richmond, Va., Oct. 7, 1940; s. Claude Marshall and Gladys Marian (Barden) P.; children: Stephen, Sean. BSME, Va. Poly. Inst., 1963; MA in Engring., U. Va., 1966, DSc, 1968. Mech. engr. U.S. Naval Weapons Lab., Dahlgren, Va., 1963; NSF trainee, tchg., rsch. asst. dept. aerospace engring. U. Va., Charlottesville, 1963-67, rsch. scientist, 1966-67; asst. prof. dept. aerospace engring. Pa. State U., University Park, 1968-74, from assoc. prof. to prof., 1974-80, assoc. dean rsch. Coll. Engring., 1979-80; head Sch. Mech. Engring., Purdue U., West Lafayette, Ind., 1980-88; dean Coll. Engring., U. Fla., Gainesville, 1988-99, assoc. v.p. engring., 1989-99, v.p. rsch., dean Grad. Sch., Don & Ruth Eckis prof., 1999—2002. Bd. dirs. 1st Union Bank, Gainesville, Enterprise North Fla. Corp., Gainesville, Wachovia; vis. prof. U. Paris, 1976—77; chmn. Fla. Tech. Devel. Bd., Southeastern Coalition for Minorities in Engring., vice-chmn., 1995—2000, chmn., 2001—; adv. com. Nimbus Corp., 1985—90, Hong Kong U. Sci. and Tech., 1990—93; co-founder, v.p. CEO Inc., 1990—; acad. adv. coun. Indsl. Rsch. Inst., 1990—93; sci. adv. com. Electric Power Rsch. Inst., 1994—99; adv. com. AvMed Inc.; exec. com. Accreditation Bd. on Engring. and Tech., 1991—96, internat. revs. for univs. in Saudi Arabia, USSR, The Netherlands, Kuwait, pres., 1995—96; mem. U.S. Pres.'s Commn. on Nat. Media of Sci., 2003—. Sect. editor Am. Soc. Artificial Internal Organs Jour., 1985-99; contbr. over 175 articles to profl. jours., chpts. to books. Mem. Ind. Boiler and Pressure Vessel Code Bd., 1981—88; bd. dirs. Ctrl. Pa. Heart Assn., 1974—80, U. Fla. Found., 1989—91, 1995—2001. Named Disting. Hoosier Ind., 1987, Sagamore of the Wabash, 1988; recipient Career Rsch. award, NIH, 1974—78, NIH Surgery and Bioengring. Study sect., 1988—91, Fla. High Tech. and Industry Coun., 1990—94, Nat. Engring. award, Am. Assn. Engr. Socs., 2000, Linton Grinter award, 2000, Global Messenger award, SECME, 2003. Fellow AAAS, AIAA, ASEE (chair-elect 2000—, vice chair 2001-2002, chmn. bd. 2002—, Lamme award 2003), ASME (sr. v.p. edn. 1986-88, bd. dirs. 1995-2000, pres. 1998-99, Dedicated Svc. award 2001), ORAU (chair coun., bd. and exec. com. 2002—), N.Y. Acad. Scis., Am. Astron. Soc., Am. Inst. Med. and Biol. Engring. (founding fellow, chair coll. fellows 1994-95, pres. 1996-97), Am. Soc. Engring. Edn. (past chmn. long range planning soc. awards 1990-92, vice chmn. engring. deans coun. 1991-93, chair 1993—, bd. dirs. 1994-98, 1st v.p. 1994-95, pres. 1996-97), Royal Soc. Arts; mem. Am. Soc. Artificial Internal Organs (trustee 1982-90, sec.-treas. 1986-87, pres. 1988-89, adv. bd. 1998—), Nat. Assn. State Univs. and Land-Grant Colls. (com. quality of engring. edn.), Univ. Programs in Computer-Aided Engring., Design and Mfg. (bd. dirs. 1985-91), Am. Phys. Soc., Biomed. Engring. Soc., Internat. Soc. Biotheology, Fla. Engring. Soc., Cosmos Club, Fla. Blue Key, Rotary (pres. Lafayette 1987-88), Sigma Xi, Phi Kappa Phi, Phi Tau Sigma, Sigma Gamma Tau, Tau Beta Pi (eminent engr.). Achievements include research and development of artificial heart pumps; research in reentry aerodynamics, on blood rheology, on modelling blood flow, on fluid dynamics of artificial hearts, on the use of smooth blood contacting surfaces, on prosthetic valve fluid dynamics and on laser Doppler studies of unsteady biofluid dynamics. Home: 4140 NW 44th Ave Gainesville FL 32606-4518 Office: U Fla Rsch and Grad Programs 223 Grinter Hall Gainesville FL 32611 E-mail: wphil@ufl.edu.

PHILLIPS-SCHEUERMAN, ELIZABETH SNEDEKER, educator; b. New Castle, Del., Apr. 27, 1911; d. George and Eleanor Elizabeth (McCoy) Snedeker; m. Robert W. W. Phillips, Apr. 22, 1975; m. John P. Scheuerman III, Apr. 26, 1991. BS, U. Del., 1933, postgrad., 1989. Tchr. Del. Bd. of Edn., Wilmington, 1933-48, Fla. Bd. of Edn., Ft. Lauderdale, 1948-60, ret. Vice pres. awards, publicity and membership coms. Broward County (Fla.) chpt. Freedom Found. of Valley Forge, Ft. Lauderdale, 1982-89; treas. Coral Ridge Home Owners Assn., 1975-90. Named Outstanding Alumnus U. Del., 1983; recipient Medal of Merit U. Del., 1989, Dr. Nan S. Hutichison Sr. Hall of Fame, Broward County, Fla., 2001. Mem. AAUW (Fla. state pres. 1971-73, pres. Ft. Lauderdale br. 1964-67, 81-83), Broward County Ret. Tchrs., Sea Ranch Club (bd. dirs. 1989-91). Avocations: bridge, travel, reading. Home: 631 SW 6th St # LS1004 Pompano Beach FL 33060-7744

PHILLIS, JOHN WHITFIELD, physiologist, educator; b. Port of Spain, Trinidad, Apr. 1, 1936; came to U.S., 1981; s. Ernest and Sarah Anne (Glover) P.; m. Pamela Julie Popple, 1958 (div. 1968); children: David, Simon, Susan; m. Shane Beverly Wright, Jan. 24, 1969. B in Vet. Sci., Sydney (Australia) U., 1958, D in Vet. Sci., 1976; PhD, Australian Nat. U., Canberra, 1961; DSc, Monash U., Melbourne, Australia, 1970. Lectr./sr. Monash U., 1963-69; vis. prof. Ind. U., Indpls., 1969; prof. physiology, assoc. dean rsch. U. Man., Winnipeg, Can., 1970-73; prof., chmn. dept. physiology U. Sask., Saskatoon, Can., 1973-81, asst. dean rsch., 1973-75; prof. physiology Wayne State U., Detroit, 1981—, chmn. dept. physiology, 1981-97. Mem. scholarship and grants com. Can. Med. Rsch. Coun., Ottawa, Ont., 1973-79; mem. sci. adv. bd. Dystonia Med. Rsch. Found., Beverly Hills, Calif., 1980-85, Curtis Rsch. Inst., Risingsun, Ohio, 1998-2000; mem. sci. adv. panel World Soc. for Protection of Animals, 1982-98; Wellcome vis. prof. Tulane U., 1986; mem. acad. scholars Wayne State U., 1995. Author: Pharmacology of Synapses, 1970; editor: Veterinary Physiology, 1976, Physiology and Pharmacology of Adenosine Derivatives, 1983, Adenosine and Adenine Nucleotides as Regulators of Cellular Function, 1991, The Regulation of Cerebral Blood Flow, 1993, Novel Therapies for CNS Injuries: Rationales and Results, 1996; editor Can. Jour. Physiology and Pharmacology, 1978-81, Progress in Neurobiology, 1973-97. Mem. grants com. Am. Heart Assn. of Mich., 1985-90, mem. rsch. coun., 1991-92, mem. rsch. forum com., 1991-96, chair, 1992-93; mem. Brain/Stroke Consortium Study Group, Am. Heart Assn., 1998. Wellcome fellow London, 1961-62; Can. Med. Rsch. Coun. grantee, 1970-81, rsch. prof., 1980; NIH grantee, 1983-2000. Mem. Brit. Pharmacol. Soc., Physiol. Soc., Am. Physiol. Soc., Soc. Neurosci., Internat. Brain Rsch. Orgn. Office: Wayne State U Dept Physiology 540 E Canfield St Detroit MI 48201-1928 E-mail: jphillis@med.wayne.edu.

PHILOGENE, BERNARD J. R. academic administrator, science educator; b. Beau-Bassin, Mauritius, May 4, 1940; came to Can., 1961; s. Raymond Pierre and Simone Marie (Ruffier) P.; m. Hélène Marie Lebreux, July 7, 1964; children: Simone, Catherine. BS, U. Montreal, 1964; MS, McGill U., 1966; PhD, U. Wis., 1970; DSc (hon.), Compiègne, 1995. Research officer Can. Forestry Service, Que., 1966-70, research scientist, 1970-71; asst. prof. U. B.C., Vancouver, 1971-74; asst. prof., assoc. prof., then prof. entomology U. Ottawa, Can., 1974—, vice dean sci. and engring., 1982-85, acting dean, 1985-86, dean faculty of sci., 1986-90, acad. vice rector, 1990-97; pres. Can. Consortium of Sci. Socs., 1992-94. Cons. OAS, Washington, 1979-80, Agence de Coop. Culture & Tech., Paris, 1982-83, Can. Internat. Devel. Agy., Ottawa, 1983-85, UN Environ. Program, Geneva, Switzerland, 1985-86, Internat. Devel. Research Ctr., Ottawa, 1985—. Mem. Ont. Pesticide Adv. Com., 1987-91. Decorated commandeur de l'Ordre des Palmes Académiques (France); knight of merit Order of St. John of Jerusalem. Fellow Entomol. Soc. Can. (bd. dirs. 1977-80); mem. Am. Inst. Biol. Scis., Entomol. Soc. Am., Can. Pest Mgmt. Soc., Assn. Can.-Française Advancement Sci. (bd. dirs. 1984-86), Internat. Soc. Chem. Ecology, Entomol. Soc. of Can. (Gold Medal 2000). Office: U Ottawa PO Box 450 30 Marie Curie St Ottawa ON Canada K1N 6N5 E-mail: bphilog@science.uottawa.ca.

PHILPOTT, LINDSEY, civil engineer, researcher, educator; b. Bridestowe, Devonshire, Eng., Aug. 2, 1948; came to U.S., 1983; s. George Anthony and Joyce Thirza (Teeling) P.; m. Christine May Pembury, Aug. 20, 1974 (div.); children: David, Elizabeth; m. Kathleen Linda Matson, Feb. 17, 1982 (div.); children: Nicholas, Benjamin; m. Kim Elaine Moore, Nov. 24, 1991. Higher Nat. Cert. in Civil Engring., Bristol (Eng.) Poly., 1973; BSCE, U. Ariz., 1986, MSCE, 1987. Registered profl. engr., Calif.; lic. water treatment plant operator, Calif.; USCG lic. operator 100 ton master. Area structural engr. Dept. Environment (Property Svcs. Agy.), Bristol, 1971-73; civil engr. Webco Civil Engring., Exeter, Eng., 1973-75; tech. mgr. Devon & Cornwall Housing Assn., Plymouth, Eng., 1975-79; prin., architect S.W. Design, Plymouth, 1979-81; archtl. engr. United Bldg. Factories, Bahrain, 1981-83; jr. engr. Cheyne Owen, Tucson, 1983-87; civil engr. Engring. Sci. Inc., Pasadena, Calif., 1987-89; project engr. Black & Veatch, Santa Ana, Calif., 1989-90; sr. engr. Brown & Caldwell, Irvine, Calif., 1990-91; environ. engr. Met. Water Dist. So. Calif., L.A., 1991—2002; instr. USCG and marlinespike seamanship Orange Coast Coll. Sailing Ctr., Newport Beach, Calif., 1999—; mgr. vol. support svcs. Ocean Inst., Dana Point, Calif., 2002—03; instr. Calif. Sailing Acad., Marina del Rey, 2003—. Adj. prof. hydraulics and instrumentation, San Antonio Coll., Walnut, Calif., 1995-, USCG, BCC instr., Calif. Sailing Acad., Marina del Rey, 2002—; cons. forensic specialist, Garrett Engrs., Inc., Long Beach, Calif., 2003—. Foster parent Foster Parents Plan, Tucson, 1985-87; vol. reader tech. books Recording for the Blind, Hollywood, Calif., 1988-89, South Bay, Calif., 1990-91, Pomona, Calif., 1991—; vol. sailor/tchr. L.A. Maritime Inst. Topsail Youth Program, 1994—, Ocean Inst., 1998—; instr. Calif. Sailing Acad., Marina delRay, Calif., 2002—. Mem.: ASCE, Engrs. Soc. (pres. 1985—96), Water Environment Fedn., Am. Water Resources Assn. (water quality com. 1990—), Am. Water Works Assn., Santa Monica Bay Power Fleet (sec. Marina del Rey chpt. 2000—), Mensa, Internat. Guild of Knot Tyers (pres. Pacific Am. br. 2000), Marina Venice Yacht Club (commodore 1999), South Bay Yacht Racing Club (Marina del Rey, Calif., commodore 1996), Internat. Order of Blue Gavel (treas. dist. 11 2002). Avocations: hiking, cycling, sailing, crosswords, knot-tying. Office: Calif Sailing Acad Panay Way Marina Del Rey CA 90292

PHIPARD, NANCY MIDWOOD, retired special education educator, poet; b. Boston, Jan. 31, 1929; d. William Henry and Jean Estelle (Dubbs) McAdams; m. Kenneth E. Brown, June 17, 1949 (div.); children: Christopher M. Brown, Jennifer Progodich, Michael H. Brown, Jeffrey D. Brown; m. Arnold J. Midwood, Jr., July 2, 1980 (dec.); m. Harvey F. Phipard, Jan. 14, 1998. Student, Mt. Holyoke Coll., 1946-48; BA, Wellesley Coll., 1973; MEd, Boston Coll., 1975. Dir. confs. and insvc. tng., chmn. bd. Mass. Assn. for Children with Learning Disabilities, Waltham and Framingham, 1969-75; chmn. core edn. teams, cons. to spl. programs, grant writer Needham (Mass.) Pub. Schs., 1974-79; ret., 1979; pres., feature writer S.D. Assocs., Inc., Wellesley, Mass., 1980-81; dir. pub. rels., women's career conf. Babson Coll., Wellesley, 1982. Mem. program evaluation team Mass. Dept. Edn., Quincy, 1978. Author (as Nancy Brown, with Louis Dickstein): Psychological Reports, 1974; author: (poems) Portraits of a Life, 1996, Fields of Gold, 1996, Ever-Flowing Stream, 1997, Best Poems of 1998, 1998, Colors of the Past, 2000, Echoes of Yesteryear, 2000, America at the Millennium, The Best Poems and Poets of the 20th Century, 2000, Memories of Tomorrow, 2000, Journey to Infinity, 2000, The Best Poems of 2002. Bd. dirs., fundraiser Hospice Palm Beach (Fla.) County S., 1993—97; bd. dirs. La Coqueille Villas, Inc., Manalapan, Fla., 1994—98; bd. dirs., chair cmty. rels. Lincoln Child Ctr., Oakland, Calif., 1983—85; docent Calif. Hist. Soc., San Francisco, 1982—87. Recipient Editor's Choice award, Internat. Libr. Poetry, 1996, 1998, 2000, 2003. Mem.: Internat. Soc. Poets (disting. mem.), Phi Beta Kappa. Avocations: tennis, travel, duplicate bridge. Home: 1630 Lands End Rd Manalapan FL 33462-4762

PHIPPS, LYNNE BRYAN, interior architect, educator, minister; b. Chapel Hill, N.C., Sept. 23, 1964; d. Floyd Talmadge and Sandra Patricia (McLester) Bryan. BFA, R.I. Sch. Design, 1986, B in Interior Architecture, 1987; cert. in parent edn., Wheelock Coll., Boston, 1989; MDiv, Andover Newton Theol. Sem., 1997. Ordained to ministry UCC Ch., 1997. Apprentice Thompson Ventulett Stainback, Atlanta, 1983-85; jr. designer Flansberg & Assocs., Boston, 1985—86; sr. designer Andrew Samataro & Assocs., Boston, 1986-87; prin. Innovative Designs, Duxbury, Mass., 1987—97; prin. Design One Consortium LLC, 2001—. Parent educator Families First, Cambridge, Mass.; guest lectr., jurist Auburn (Ala.) U., 1988, R.I. Sch. Design, Providence, 1990; guest jurist U. Memphis, 1995; assoc. prof. Mass. Bay C.C., Wellesley, 1997-2000; mem. adv. bd. U. R.I. Chamberlyne Sch. Design Alumni Coun., 1996—; guest lectr. Architectural and Family Issues; mem. adv. bd. Sch. Design IDA Coll., Newton, Mass. Youth min. St. Andrew's Episcopal Ch., Hanover, Mass., 1992—95; youth and family min. St. Stephen's Episcopal Ch., Cohasset, Mass., 1993—96; pastor Kingston Congl. Ch. UCC, 1997—2001. Mem. AIA (assoc.), Internat. Interior Design Assn., Internat. Platform Assn. Avocations: sailing, tennis, antique boats. Office: Design One Consortium LLC 422D South Rd Wakefield RI 02879

PHIPPS, SUSAN, retired elementary school educator; b. Plainfield, NJ, July 11, 1947; d. Warren Odell and Lucile (James) Shepard; m. James N. Brooks, June 15, 1969 (div. Nov. 1981); m. Harold Wayne Phipps, Feb. 14, 1986. BS, U. Va., 1969; MA, Appalachian State U., 1970, Edn. Splst. 6th yr. degree, 1983. Early childhood edn. splst. Classroom tchr. Watauga County Schs., Boone, N.C., 1970-71, 84-00, Avery County Schs., Newland, N.C., 1971-84. Bd. examiners Nat. Coun. Accreditation of Tchr. Edn., Washington, 1989-92; leader summer inst. N.C. Dept. Pub. Edn., Hickory and Banner Elk, 1974-79; site mgr. NC Tchr. Acad. Appalachian State U., Boone, summer 1994, 95; profl. rev. com. NC Dept. Pub. Instrn., Raleigh, 1991-94; adj. faculty Appalachian State U., Boone, NC, 2003—; cons. Nat. Bd. Profl. Tchg. Stds. N.W. Carolina U.; presenter in field. Contbr. articles to profl. jours. Bd. trustees NC Tchr. Acad., Durham, 1995-2000; co founder, bd. dirs. Avery Arts Coun., Newland, NC, 1977-84. Named Woman of Yr., Avery County C. of C., 1984. Mem. N.C. Assn. Educators (local pres. 1975-76, 85-86, dist. officer, various coms. 1976-2000, Leader, Terry Sanford award 1990, bd dirs. 1985-88, 97-2000, Delta Kappa Gamma (sec., v.p., pres. 1996-2002, Golden Apple award 1999). Avocations: travel, hiking, reading, needlecrafts, sketching. Home: 191 Winding Way Boone NC 28607-5141 Personal E-mail: suephipps@msn.com.

PHOON, COLIN KIT-LUN, pediatric cardiologist, medical educator; b. London, Dec. 7, 1963; came to U.S., 1968; s. Wai Wor and Alice Phoon; m. Janet Rose. BA in Biophysics, Johns Hopkins U., 1985; MPhil in Pharmacology, Cambridge (Eng.) U., 1986; MD, U. Pa., 1990. Diplomate in pediatrics and pediatric cardiology Am. Bd. Pediatrics. Intern, then resident in gen. pediatrics Johns Hopkins Hosp., Balt., 1990-93; fellow in pediatric cardiology U. Calif. Med. Ctr., San Francisco, 1993-96; asst. prof. pediat./pediatric cardiology NYU Sch. Medicine, N.Y.C., 1996—2003, assoc. prof., 2003—; attending physician NYU Med. Ctr./Bellevue Hosp. Ctr., N.Y.C., 1996—, NYU Downtown Hosp., N.Y.C., 1998—2001, Hosp. for Joint Diseases, N.Y.C., 1999—; dir. pediatric echocard. lab. NYU Hosps. Ctr., 2002—. Cons. Charles B. Wang Cmty. Health Ctr., N.Y.C., 1998—. Author: Guide to Pediatric Cardiovascular Physical Examination or How to Survive an Outreach Clinic, 1998; contbr. chapters to books, articles to profl. jours. Mem. Johns Hopkins Nat. Alumni Schs. Com. Recipient Dr. A.O.J. Kelly prize U. Pa., 1990, Francis Schwentker award Johns Hopkins Hosp.,1993, Clin Sci. Devel. award NIH/NHLBI, 2001—; Winston Churchill Found. scholar, 1985-86; Am. Heart Assn. fellow, 1995-96; rsch. career grantee NIH, 2001—. Fellow: Am. Acad. Pediatrics (Hon. Mention award resident rsch. competition 1993, 2d prize Young Investigator award competition 1998, Young Investigator Basic Sci. award sect. cardiology 1999), Am. Coll. Cardiology; mem.: Soc. Pediatric Rsch., N.Y. Pediatric Echocardiography Soc. (steering com. 1997, sec. 1999—), Am. Soc. Echocardiography (mem. Echo Challenge Champion Team 2001), Am. Heart Assn. (mem. coun. basic cardiovascular scis. 1984—, mem. coun. on cardiovasc. disease in the young 1991—, program com. Coun. on Cardiovascular Disease in the Young 2002—, Scientist Devel. grantee 2000—01), Alpha Omega Alpha, Phi Beta Kappa, Churchill Scholars Soc. Avocations: reading, music, history of medicine, lacrosse, choral singing. Office: NYU Med Ctr Pediatric Echo Lab 530 First Ave FPT Ste 9U New York NY 10016-6402

PIAN, CARLSON CHAO-PING, mechanical engineering educator, researcher; b. Beijing, Dec. 31, 1945; came to U.S., 1957; s. Charles H.C. and Juliette (Fan) P.; m. Sally Tseng, Aug. 23, 1969; children: Kevin, Phillip, Timothy. BS in Aerospace Engring., U. Mich., 1968, MS in Aerospace Engring., 1969, PhD in Aerospace Engring., 1974. Instr. dept. aerospace engring. U. Mich., Ann Arbor, 1965-74; vis. scientist dept. elec. engring. Eindhoven (Netherlands) Tech. U., 1974-75; rsch. engr. Lewis Rsch. Ctr. NASA, Cleve., 1975-79; prin. rsch. engr. Avco Everett (Mass.) Rsch. Lab., Inc., 1979—94, dir. magnetohydrodynamic power generation, 1987-94; with Miss. State U., 1994-95, prof., rschr., 1997-2000; sr. scientist Molten Metal Tech., Mass., 1995-97; prof. and chair mech. engring. divsn. Alfred (N.Y.) U., 2000—. Assoc. editor, Jour. Propulsion and Power, 1993—; contbr. over 95 articles to profl. jours. Assoc. Fellow AIAA (terrestial energy systems tech. com. 1982-84, plasmadynamics and lasers tech. com. 1984-86, Space Shuttle Flag award 1984); mem. ASME, Sigma Xi. Avocations: bicycling, sailing, photography. Office: Alfred U Mech Engring Divsn Alfred NY 14802 E-mail: piancp@alfred.edu.

PIASECKI, DAVID ALAN, social studies educator; b. Marquette, Mich., Sept. 14, 1956; s. Vincent Jerome and Irene Beatrice (Tousinant) P.; m. Linda Marie Anderson Piasecki, Aug. 2, 1985; children: Andrew Jacob, Zachary David. BA, No. Mich. U., 1978, MA, 1982, MA, 1984. Cert. 7-12 Social Studies, Sch. Adminstrn. and Prin. Supt., Alaska. Social studies tchr. Galena (Alaska) City Sch., 1978-80, Tanana (Alaska) H.S., 1980-85, activities dir., 1984-85; social studies tchr. Denali Borough Sch. Dist., Healy, Alaska, 1985-99; prin. Upsala (Minn.) H.S., 1999—. Student Taft Seminar For Tchrs., U. Alaska. Named Alaska Tchr. of Yr., Dept. Edn., Juneau and Anchorage, 1992, Railbelt Sch. Dist. Tchr. of Yr., NEA, Healy, 1992; recipient Secondary Econ. award Alaska Coun. on Econ. Edn., Fairbanks, Alaska, 1988, 91-92. Mem. NEA, Holy Mary of Guadalupe Cath. Ch., Nat. Alaska Coun. on Social Studies, Alaska Geographic Alliance, Nat. Coun. for Geographic Edn. Democrat. Roman catholic. Avocations: cross county skiing, basketball, tennis, hunting, travel. Home: PO Box 11 Upsala MN 56384-0011 Office: Upsala HS 415 S Main St PO Box 190 Upsala MN 56384-0190*

PIATT, ALBERT EARL, educator, researcher, consultant; b. Bellaire, Ohio, Feb. 13, 1948; s. Albert Maxwell and Evelyn Lorena (St. John) P.; m. Linda Ruth Shirley, July 18, 1969; children: Ruth Lorraine, Bonita Nicole, Dorothy Elizabeth. BS, U. Tenn., Chattanooga, 1970; EdM, Wayne State U., 1973; MA in Edn., East Carolina U., 1976; EdD, U. Tenn., 1995. Cert. secondary tchr., Tenn. Commd. 2d lt. USAR, 1970; advanced through grades to lt. col. U.S. Army, 1987, ret., 1992; adminstrv. intern Challenger Ctr., Chattanooga, 1993-94, grad. asst., 1994-95; ednl. cons. Chattanooga; 7th grade math. tchr. Brown Mid. Sch., Harrison, Tenn., 1997-2000; math. and sci. tchr. David Brainerd Christian Sch., Chattanooga, 2000—. Deacon MacPherson Presbyn. Ch., Fayetteville, N.C., 1981-84; elder Clk. of Sessiion New Hope Presbyn. Ch., Chattanooga, 1995-98. Named Disting. grad. U.S. Army JFX Inst. for Mil. Assistance, Ft. Bragg, N.C., 1980. Mem. ASCD, Nat. Mid. Sch. Assn., Res. Officers Assn., Am. Legion, VFW, DAV, Nat. Coun. Tchrs. Math., Mil. Officers Assn., Pi Lambda Theta, Phi Kappa Phi. Avocations: photography, reading, music. Home: 1721 Julian Ridge Rd Chattanooga TN 37421-3321 Office: David Brainard Christian Sch 7553 Igou Gap Rd Chattanooga TN 37421 E-mail: apiatt@dbcs.org.

PIATT, RICHARD C., II, senior pastor, educator; b. Dayton, Ohio, Nov. 5, 1953; s. Richard C. and Mildred E. (Hahn) P.; m. Susan E. Kreitzer, July 17, 1976; children: Eileen, Emily, Rich. BS in Biology, Wright State U., Dayton, 1976; MDiv, Grace Theol. Sem., Winona Lake, Ind., 1979, ThM, 1981; student, Reformed Theol. Sem., Orlando, Fla., 1998—. Ordained to ministry Gen. Assn. Regular Bapts., 1982. Pastor Palestine (Ind.) Ch., Wildwood Chapel, Upper Sandusky, Ohio; pastor, missionary Amb. Bapt. Ch., Jacksonville, Fla., 1988-94; sr. pastor Fellowship Bapt. Ch., Lakeland, Fla., 1994—. Tchr. Univ. Christian Sch., Jacksonville, 1988-94; prof. Luther Rice Sem., Jacksonville, 1991-2002; interviewer Sta. WJFR, Jacksonville, 1990-94. Coach springboard h.s. diving, 1996—. Avocation: exotic animal breeding. Home: 1209 Valley Hill W Lakeland FL 33813-2281 Office: Fellowship Baptist Church 4625 Cleveland Heights Blvd Lakeland FL 33813-2199

PIAZZA-HARPER, ANNA FRANCES, elementary education educator; b. Bridgeport, Conn., Jan. 16, 1947; d. Joseph Blaise and Josephine Adele (Lopresti) Piazza; m. Wren Joseph Paul Harper Jr., July 9, 1978; 1 child, Jonathan Joseph. BA in English, Sacred Heart U., 1968; MA in Gen. Edn., Fairfield U., 1972; student, San Jose U., 1981. Cert. tchr., Conn., adminstrn., supervision., 1981. Tchr. Bridgeport (Conn.) Pub. Schs., 1968-74, 77-78; tchr. arts and crafts Action for Bridgeport Community Devel., 1971-72; tchr. kindergarten Dept. of Def., Goeppingen, Germany, 1974-77; tchr. Monterey (Calif.) Peninsula Unified Sch. Dist., 1978-81; tng. mgr. G. Fox, Trumbull, Conn., 1981-84; mortgage svc. counselor People's Bank, Bridgeport, Conn., 1984-88; substitute tchr. Easton-Redding, Fairfield, Shelton Sch. Dists., 1989-91; tchr. grade 1 Ezra Acad., Woodbridge, Conn., 1991-93, Bridgeport Pub. Sch. Sys., 1993—. Named Outstanding Elem. Tchr., 1973. Mem. Tchrs. Acquiring Whole Lang. Avocations: wax craft designs, jewelry craft, gourmet cooking, wood crafts. Home: 15 Stephen Dr Huntington CT 06484-1865

PICARD, CECIL, school system administrator; b. Maurice, La. m. Gaylen David; children: Tyron, Layne. BA in Upper Elem. Edn., Southwestern La. Inst.; MA in Adminstrn. and Supervision, Sam Houston Tchrs. Coll.; postgrad., La. State U.; HHD (hon.), McNeese State U., 1996. Cert. tchr. elem. edn., secondary edn., prin., city/parish supr., La. Tchr., coach Vermilion Parish Sch. System, 1959-66, h.s. prin., 1966-80; mem. La. Senate, 1979-96, chmn., mem. numerous coms.; mem. La. Ho. of Reps., 1976-79; supt. of edn. State of La., 1996—. Mem. Nat. Conf. of State Legislatures, La. Ednl. TV Authority Bd., La. Ednl. Assessment Testing Commn., So. Regional Edn. Bd., Edn. Commn. of the States, La. Commn. on the Deaf. Bd. trustees Tchrs. Retirement System of La.; bd. dirs. La. Sch. for Math, Sci. and the Arts, Acadiana United Way; mem. St. Alphonse Cath. Ch.; mem. Acadian Heritage and Culture Found., Inc., La. Teenage Pregnancy Commn. Recipient Disting. Legislator award La. Assn. of Educators, 1986, Disting. Svc. award, 1989, Senator of Yr. award La. Fedn. of Tchrs., 1988, Friend of Edn. award, 1996, Legislator of Yr. award La. Assn. of Prins., 1994-95. Mem. La. Farm Bur. and Cattleman's Assn., Vermilion Assn. for Retarded Citizens, Greater Abbeville C. of C., Jaycees, Kiwanis Club, La. H.S. Athletic Assn. (exec. com.). Office: Edn Dept PO Box 94064 Baton Rouge LA 70804-9064*

PICCIRILLO, LOU ANNE, special education educator; b. Port Jervis, N.Y., Dec. 9, 1953; d. Louis Anthony and Louise Mary Piccirillo; m. Richard Frazier Jones, Oct. 13, 1985; children: Natalie Jones, MacKenzie Jones. BA in Edn., St. Joseph U., Rutland, Vt., 1975, MA in Edn., 1981. Tchr. spl. edn. BOCES Washington Warren, Hudson Falls, NY, 1976—80; coord. N.Y. State Mental Healtn and N.Y. State Edn. Depts., Albany, 1980—81; tchr., spl. edn. BOCES, Saratoga, NY, 1981—86; tchr., chair dept. spl. edn. Saratoga Springs (N.Y.) H.S., 1986—. Mem. horse show com. St. Clcments Ch., Saratoga Springs, 1996—2001; bd. dirs. AIM Adult Facility, Saratoga, 1981—84; mem. com. spl. edn. Saratoga Springs City Sch., 1998—2001. Democrat. Roman Catholic. Avocations: golf, boating, swimming. Home: 11 Meadow Ln Saratoga Springs NY 12866 Office: Saratoga City Sch Dist 186 W Circular St Saratoga Springs NY 12866

PICCOLO, JO ANNE, elementary education educator, reading consultant; b. Denver, May 5, 1951; d. Leonard and Annette (Pavone) P. BA in Edn., Regis Coll., 1973; MA in Curriculum & Instrn./Reading, U. Colo., 1986. Cert. K-6 elem. sch. tchr., endorsement in reading K-12. Math tchr. Clayton St. Elem., Thornton, Colo., 1973-74; reading tchr. Western Hills Elem., Denver, 1974-78, Centennial Elem., Broomfield, Colo., 1978-88; tchr. Skyview Elem., Thornton, 1988-90; literacy resource tchr. Westview Elem., Thornton, 1990—. Recipient Chpt. II grant Adams Five Star Schs., 1990, Innovative grant Adams Five Star Schs., 1990. Mem. ASCD, Internat. Reading Assn., Nat. Coun. Tchrs. English, Alpha Sigma Nu. Avocations: playing piano, spectator sports, curriculum devel. Home: 8100 W 41st Ave Wheat Ridge CO 80033-4434 Office: Adams 12 Five Star Schs Dist Lit Team 1500 E 128th AVe Thornton CO 80241

PICCOLO, JOSEPH ANTHONY, hospital administrator; b. Phila., Aug. 1, 1953; s. Rudolph and Mary C. (Mellela) P.; m. Elizabeth J. Mullarkey, Mar. 24, 1984; children: Mary E., Sarah C., Theresa N. BA, U. Pa., 1975; MBA, LaSalle U., 1992. Cert. in healthcare compliance, Healthcare Compliance Bd. Mgr. health sci. store U. Pa., Phila., 1973-76; mgr. univ. store Hahnemann U., Phila., 1976-86, adminstr., clin. sr. instr. dept. pathology lab. medicine, 1986-94; assoc. adminstr., compliance officer, chief privacy officer, v.p. health svcs. Fox Chase Cancer Ctr., Phila., 1994—. V.p. Hahnemann Found. Pathology, Phila., 1986-94. Author: (with others): Health Science Store Manual, 1985; mem. editl. bd. Assn. Cancer Execs., 1999—. Mem. Med. Group Mgmt. Assn., Am. Mgmt. Assn., Healthcare Fin. Mgmt. Assn., Hahnemann Pathology Assocs., Inc. (v.p., treas. 1986-94), Big Sisters of Phila. Inc. (bd. dirs., 1996-98). Avocations: golf, music, reading. Office: Fox Chase Cancer Ctr 7701 Burholme Ave Philadelphia PA 19111-2497 E-mail: J_Piccolo@fccc.eou.

PICHA, KENNETH GEORGE, mechanical engineering educator; b. Chgo., July 24, 1925; s. George and Sylvia (Beran) P.; m. Vivien O. Crawford, May 1, 1948; children: Kenneth George, Kevin Crawford, Katrina Alison. B.Mech. Engring., Ga. Inst. Tech., 1946, MS in Mech. Engring, 1948; PhD, U. Minn., 1957. Research scientist NACA, 1948-49; instr., then asso. prof. Ga. Inst. Tech. Sch. Mech. Engring., 1949-58; dir. Ga. Inst. Tech. Sch. Mech. Engring. (Sch.), 1960-66; program dir. engring. sci. program NSF, 1958-60; dean U. Mass. Sch. Engring., Amherst, 1966-76, dir. Office to Coordinate Energy Rsch. and Edn., 1977-80, prof. mech. engring., 1980-89, prof. emeritus, 1989—, dir. Office Univ. Programs, ERDA, 1976-77. Vis. prof., cons. U Puerto Rico, Mayaguez, 1982-83; cons. in field, 1959—; cons. Govt. Singapore on U. Singapore master planning, 1970-71; mem. adv. bd. Internat. Tech. Edn. Cons., 1978; chmn. engring. edn. and accreditation com. Engrs. Council for Profl. Devel., 1973-74; chmn. commn. edn. engring. profession Nat. Assn. Land Grant Colls. and Univs.; chmn. manpower devel. com. Nat. Air Pollution Control Agy., 1970-71; vice chmn. Council for Specialized Accreditation, 1973-77; vice-chmn. mem. exec. com. Council on Post Secondary Accreditation, 1974-77; NSF adv. com. Worcester Poly. Inst., 1972-75; mem. Fulbright scholar adv. com. Univ. Coll. Galway, Ireland, 1986-87, Australia, 1995-97, New Zealand, 1995-97. Bd. govs. Mass. Sci. and Tech. Found., 1970-76; bd. visitors Sch. Engring. U. Pitts.; mem. Discipline Adv. Com. for Fulbright Scholar Awards, 1991-95. Served with USNR, 1943-46. Fulbright scholar, Australia, New Zealand, 1995-97. Fellow ASME, AAAS, Am. Soc. Engring. Edn. (dir., mem. exec. com. 1974-76); mem. Ga. Inst. Tech. Nat. Alumni Assn., Sigma Xi, Tau Beta Pi, Phi Kappa Phi, Pi Tau Sigma. Clubs: Cosmos. Home: 1256 Ingleside Dr Auburn AL 36830-6600

PICK, JAMES BLOCK, business educator, demographer; b. Chgo., July 29, 1943; s. Grant Julius and Helen (Block) Pick. BA, Northwestern U., 1966; MS in Edn., No. Ill. U., 1969; PhD, U. Calif., Irvine, 1974. Cert. computer profl. Asst. rsch. statistician, lectr. Grad. Sch. Mgmt., U. Calif., Riverside, 1975-91, dir. computing, 1984-91; co-dir. U.S.-Mex. Database Project, 1988-91; assoc. prof. mgmt. and bus., dir. info. mgmt. program U. Redlands, Calif., 1991-95, 99-01, prof. bus., 1995—, chair dept. mgmt. and bus., 1995-97, 98-99, chair faculty assembly Sch. Bus., 2001—. Vis. prof. U. Iberoam., Mexico City, 1997, Mexico City, 2001; cons. internat. divsn. U.S. Census Bur., 1978; mem. Univ. Commons. Bd., 1982—86; mem. nat. curriculum task force IS, 1997; mem. U. Commn. Future Bus. Programs, 1998—2000; pres. Orange County chpt. Assn. Sys. Mgmt., 1978—79; mem. bd. govs. PCCLAS, Assn. Borderlands Studies, 1989—92, v.p., 2000—01, pres., 2002—; bd. profls. advisors demographic analysis U. Calif, Irvine, 2002—03. Author: (book) Geothermal Energy Development, 1982, Computer Systems in Business, 1986, Atlas of Mexico, 1989, The Mexico Handbook, 1994, Mexico Megacity, 1997, Mexico and Mexico City in the World Economy, 2001; mem. editl. bd. Jour. Borderlands Studies, 1999—, Jour. Info. Tech. Cases and Applications, 2002—, condr. rsch. info. sys., population, environ. studies; contbr. articles to profl. jours. Trustee Newport Harbor Art Mus., 1981—87, 1988—96, Berkeley Art Mus. and Pacific Film Archives, 2003—; chmn. permanent collection com. Newport Harbor Art Mus., 1987—91, v.p., 1991—96; trustee, chmn. collection com. Orange County Mus. Art, 1996—; mem. com. Block Mus., 1999—2001. Recipient Thunderbird award, Bus. Assn. L.Am. Studies, 1993; Ford Found. grantee, 1998—99, Sr. Fulbright scholar, 2001. Mem.: AAAS, Am. Assn. Geographers, Sociedad de Demografia Mexicana, Internat. Union Sci. Study Population, Population Assn. Am., Am. Statis. Assn., Am. Sociol. Assn., Assn. Info. Sys., Assn. Computing Machinery, Standard Club (Chgo.). Office: U Redlands Sch Bus 1200 E Colton Ave Redlands CA 92374-3755

PICKARD, CAROLYN ROGERS, secondary school educator; b. Steubenville, Ohio, Dec. 13, 1945; d. Thomas Orlando and Alice Marie (Romick) Rogers; 1 child, Carri Alyce. BA, Fla. State U., 1967; AA, Stephens Coll., Columbia, Mo., 1965. Cert. English tchr., Fla. Tchr. English, chair dept. New World Sch. Arts, Dade County Pub. Schs., Miami, Fla., 1969—. Vol. Shores Performing Arts Theater Soc. Recipient Tchr. of Yr. award North Miami Beach High Sch., 1982, Presdl. Scholars Tchr. of Excellence award, 1984. Mem. Nat. Coun. Tchrs. English, United Tchrs. Dade County, Delta Kappa Gamma. Home: 20 S Oak Forest Dr Asheville NC 28803-3311

PICKEN, EDITH DARYL, school administrator; b. Washington, Jan. 19, 1955; d. Edward George and Edith Kellog (Jones) P. BS, Towson State U., 1978; MS, CAS, Johns Hopkins U., 1985. Cert. English tchr., guidance counselor, prin. and supervision, advanced profl. I, Md. English tchr. Balt. City Pub. Schs., 1979-83; guidance counselor Anne Arundel County Pub. Schs., Md., 1985-94, asst. prin., 1994—. Guest speaker and presenter in field. Named Md. Sch. Counselor of Yr., 1989. Mem. NEA, ASCD, ACA, AAUW, Md. ASCD, Nat. Assn. Secondary Sch. Prins., Md. Assn. Secondary Sch. Prins., Assn. Ednl. Leaders, Chi Sigma Iota, Pi Lambda Theta. Office: Severna Park HS 60 Robinson Rd Severna Park MD 21146-2899

PICKERIGN, ROGER, superintendent; b. Wisc., June 6, 1947; s. Leo and Bernice P.; m. Deyonne, June 6, 1970; children: Mikical, Milissa. BS, U. River Falls, 1969, MA, 1975; Ed, Western Colo. State U., 1977; postgrad., U. Minn., 1978. Supt. WD 452, Johnson City, Kans.

PICKERING, BECKY RUTH THOMPSON, special education educator; b. Springfield, Mo., Nov. 20, 1949; d. Ray Herman Thompson and Virginia Ruth (Baily) Peterson; m. Gary Joe Pickering, Oct. 22, 1967; children: Summer Pickering Austin, Shane Gary, Slade Thompson. BS in Edn. cum laude, S.W. Mo. State U., 1983. Cert. spl. edn. tchr., Mo. Spl. edn. tchr. Marshfield (Mo.) Schs., 1997—98, Fair Grove (Mo.) Schs. RX, 1983-97, 1998—. Mem. Profl. Devel. Com., 1989—. Mem. ASCD, Cmty. Tchrs. Orgn. (pres. local 2001-02), Mo. State Tchrs. Assn. Democrat. Avocations: reading, walking, farming, writing. Home: 9254 E Farm Road 2 Fair Grove MO 65648-8147 Office: Fair Grove Schs 310 N Main St Fair Grove MO 65648

PICKERING, JAMES HENRY, III, academic administrator, educator; b. N.Y.C., July 11, 1937; s. James H. and Anita (Felber) P.; m. Patricia Paterson, Aug. 18, 1962; children: David Scott, Susan Elizabeth. BA, Williams Coll., 1959; MA, Northwestern U., 1960, PhD, 1964. Instr. English Northwestern U., 1963-65; mem. faculty Mich. State U., East Lansing, 1965-81, prof. English, 1972-81, grad. and asso. chmn. dept., 1968-75, dir. Honors Coll., 1975-81; dean Coll. Humanities and Fine Arts U. Houston, 1981-90, sr. v.p., provost, 1990-92, pres., 1992-95. Author: Fiction 100, 1974, 78, 82, 85, 88, 92, 95, 98, 2001, 04, The World Turned Upside Down: Prose and Poetry of the American Revolution, 1975, The Spy Unmasked, 1975, The City in American Literature, 1977, Concise Companion to Literature, 1981, Literature, 1982, 86, 90, 94, 97, Mountaineering in Colorado, 1987, Wild Life on the Rockies, 1988, A Mountain Boyhood, 1988, The Spell of the Rockies, 1989, Purpose and Process, 1989, Poetry, 1990, In Beaver World, 1990, Rocky Mountain Wonderland, 1991, A Summer Vacation in the Parks and Mountains of Colorado, 1992, Fiction 50, 1993, Knocking Round the Rockies, 1994, Drama, 1994, Frederick Chapin's Colorado, 1995; This Blue Hollow: Estes Park, The Early Years, 1859-1915, 1999, Mr. Stanley of Estes Park, 2000, In the Vale of Elkanah, 2003. Mem. Coll. English Assn. (pres. 1980-81), Phi Beta Kappa, Phi Kappa Phi, Omicron Delta Kappa. Office: U Houston Dept English Houston TX 77204-0001

PICKERING, MARY BARBARA, history educator, writer; b. San Francisco, June 22, 1954; d. Robert Alexander and Helen Veronica (Blasko) P.; m. Francis Edward Lauricella, Sept. 2, 1979; children: Nicolas Pickering, Natalia Pickering, Michael Pickering. AB in History magna cum laude, Harvard U., 1975, AM in History, 1976; Diplôme d'Études Approfondies, Inst. d'Etudes Politiques, 1984; PhD in History, Harvard U., 1988. Teaching asst., teaching fellow Harvard U., Cambridge, Mass., 1977-79; adj. asst. prof. history Manhattan Coll., N.Y.C., 1988, Pace U., N.Y.C., 1988-89, lectr., 1989-90, asst. prof. history, 1990-94; asst. prof. European history San Jose (Calif.) State U., 1994—96, assoc. prof., 1996—2000, prof., 2000—. Author: Auguste Comte: An Intellectual Biography vol. 1, 1993; contbr. articles to profl. jours. Gilbert Chinard scholar Inst. Français de Washington, 1983; French Govt. fellow, 1983-84; Exch. scholar Harvard U., Inst. d'Etudes Politiques, 1983-84; NEH fellow, 1991-92. Fellow The Pierpont Morgan Libr.; mem. AAUW, Am. Hist. Assn., N.Y. State Assn. European Historians, Berkshire Conf. Women Historians, Soc. French Hist. Studies, Southeastern Nineteenth-Century Studies Assn., Coord. Com. Women in the Hist. Profession-N.Y. Met. Region (chair program com. 1991-93, pres. 1993-94), Phi Beta Kappa. Democrat. Home: 2360 Vallejo St San Francisco CA 94123-4712 Office: San Jose State U History Dept San Jose CA 95192-0117

PICKETT, PHYLLIS ASSELIN, physical education educator; b. Marshfield, Wis., Apr. 22, 1947; d. Lyle Francis and Florence Dorothy (Wiernasz) Asselin; m. James Frederick Pickett, Aug. 10, 1974; children: Christopher, Ryan, J.T. BS in Phys. Edn., U. Wis., La Crosse, 1969; MS in Edn. Adminstrn., Northern Ill. U., 1978. Tchr. Lake Park High Sch., Roselle, Ill., 1969—2002, coord. women's athletics, 1970-77, tchr., supr., 1975-89; supr. student tchrs. No. Ill. U., DeKalb, 2002—. Chmn. O'Hare Suburban Conf., 1973; speaker in field. Named Coca Cola Educator of Month, 1999. Mem. NEA, Am. Alliance Health Phys. Edn. & Dance, Ill. Edn. Assn., Ill. Assn. Health Phys. Edn. & Dance (Quarter Century award 1994, N.E. dist. Tchr. of Yr. 1999, waiver response coord. 2001-, Secondary Tchr. of Yr. 2001, ednl. cons. 2002-). Home: 1112 Aegean Dr Schaumburg IL 60193-3800 E-mail: ppickett1@yahoo.com.

PICKETT, STEPHEN WESLEY, academic administrator, consultant; b. Billings, Mont., May 27, 1956; s. Wesley William and Carol Ann (Bollum) P. BA, Houston Bapt. U., 1980; MS, U. North Tex., 1988. Cert. elem. tchr., rehab. counselor, Tex. Hosp. tchr. Houston Ind. Sch. Dist., 1981-85; asst. to assoc. dean of students U. North Tex., Denton, 1988-90, asst. coord. disabled student svcs., Office Student Devel., 1990-91, dir. Office Disability Accommodation, 1991—2001, univ. mentor/advisor, 1992—2001; dir. disability svcs. U. Oreg., Eugene, 2002—, assoc. dir. office of acad. advising, 2002—. Co-author: curriculum guide The Newspaper as a Student Communicator, 1982 (winner Exxon Found.'s Impact Two award for creative teaching). Chair Mayor's Com. on Employment of Persons with Disabilities, Denton, 1990; mem. coun.-at-large Sam Houston Area Coun. Boy Scouts Am., Houston, 1975—; grad. Denton C. of C. Leadership Program, 1992; pub. rels. chair leadership Denton Steering Com , 1993-94; mem. ad. bd. city of Denton Transit, 1990-2001; exec. bd. Svc. provision for Aging Needs, a United Way Agy., 1997-2001; mem. U. of North Tex. Adv. Bd. for ADA Access, 1992-2001, co-chair UNT ADA adv. com., 2000-01; mem. budget com. Denton County United Way, 1998-2001. Recipient Cmty. Svc. award U. North Tex., 1992, award for svcs. to persons with disabilities North Tex. Rehab. Assn., 1993, Disting. Alumnus award Houston Bapt. U., 1994, Outstanding Alumnus award Ctr. for Rehab. Studies, U. North Tex., 1995. Mem. Assn. Higher Edn. and Disability, Nat. Assn. Student Pers. Adminstrs., Tex. Assn. Coll. and Univ. Student Pers. Adminstrs. (chair multicultural com. 1994-95, v.p. 1995-96, co-chair endowment found. com. 1996-97), Tex. Assn. Higher Edn. and Disabilities (sec. 1998-99, conf. co-chair 1999). Presbyterian. Avocations: reading, travel, stamp collecting. Office: U Oreg Disability Svc 164 Oregon Hall 5278 U Oreg Eugene OR 97403-5278 Office Fax: 541-346-6013. E-mail: stevewp@att.net.

PICKETT, STEVEN HAROLD, retired elementary school educator; b. Danville, Ill., Sept. 15, 1946; s. Harold George and Mary Margaret (Watson) P.; m. Marlene Mae Brumleve, June 23, 1973; children: Vincent Steven, Ryan Stephen, Alexander Maurice (dec.). AS, Danville Jr. Coll., 1966; BS, U. Ill., 1968, MEd, 1970. Cert. secondary tchr., Ill. Self-contained 8th grade classroom tchr. Gifford (Ill.) Grade Sch., 1968-70; 8th grade tchr. lang. arts, reading Effingham (Ill.) Ctr. Sch., 1970-98, Effingham (Ill.) Jr. H.S., 1998—2003; ret., 2003; owner Trophies Unlimited, 2003—. Coach basketball and track teams Effingham Cen. Sch., 1970—83; operator Trophies Unltd., 1978—. Active Effingham Pk. Dist. Bd., 1973—, v.p., 1978-88, 91, pres., 1979-80; basketball coach Effingham County Youth Commn., 1972-73; coach Small Fry Baseball Team, 1985-89, 93-96, Effingham Pony League, 1971-73, Effingham Bambino Little League, 1990-91, 99-2000, Effingham Babe Ruth Prep League, 1992, 2001, Effingham Park Dist. Khoury League Team, 1997-98; coach track team Effingham Flyers, AAU, 1977-78; coach Effingham Jr. Babe Ruth League, 2002-03. Mem. NEA, Nat. Assn. English Tchrs. (life), Ill. Edn. Assn., Effingham Classroom Tchrs. Assn., Elks. Avocations: traveling, swimming, biking, basketball, baseball. Home: 703 N Cardinal St Effingham IL 62401-3210

PICKETT, WENDY LYNN, secondary education educator; b. Indpls., Feb. 17, 1966; d. Sandra Kay (Baldwin) Gish. Student, Bob Jones U., 1984-86; BA in English, Mars Hill Coll., 1989. Cert. secondary English educator, N.C. English instr. Mars Hill (N.C.) Upward Bound, 1989—90; English tchr. Sheridan Hills Christian Sch., Hollywood, Fla., 1989-92, Mountain View Christian Acad., 1992-93, Faith Christian Sch., Hendersonville, NC, 1993—96; English tchr., yearbook advisor Tabernacle Christian Sch., Martinsville, Ind., 1996—99, Chapel Hill Christian Sch., Indpls., 1999—. Yearbook advisor Sheridan Hills Christian Sch., Hollywood, 1989-92, trip coord., 1991; yearbook advisor Faith Christian Sch., Mountain View Christian Acad.; camp counselor Sheridan Hills Bapt. Ch., Hollywood, 1991, VBS dir., worker, 1991-92; girls' basketball coach Mountain View Christian Acad. Treas. Voice of Praise-Sheridan Hills Bapt. Ch., Hollywood, 1991, sect. leader, 1992; sec. Circle K Club, Mars Hill, 1988; GA leader Ebenezer Bapt. Ch., Hendersonville, N.C., 1986; mem. ensemble Martinsville Bapt. Tabernacle, Hope Bapt. Ch., Indpls. Baptist. Avocations: volleyball, softball, crochet, reading, choir.

PICKHOLTZ, RAYMOND LEE, electrical engineering educator, consultant; b. N.Y.C., Apr. 12, 1932; s. Isidore and Rose (Turkish) P.; m. Eda Rebecca Mittler, June 30, 1957; children: Robin, Andrew, Julie. BEE, CUNY, 1954, MEE, 1958; PhD, Poly. U. N.Y., 1966. Research engr. RCA Labs., Princeton, N.J., 1954-57, ITT Labs., Nutley, N.J., 1957-61; assoc. prof. Poly. Inst. Bklyn., 1962-71; prof. elec. engring., chmn. dept. George Washington U., Washington, 1977-80, prof., 1971—; pres. Telecommunication Assocs., Fairfax, Va., 1963—; cons. Inst. Def. Analyses, 1971-90, IBM Research, Yorktown Heights, N.Y., 1968-72; del. Union Radio Scientifique, Geneva, 1979—, vice chmn., 1987; del. NRC, Washington, 1980-83; cons. Motorola, CBC, NAB, USADR, Lucent, Verizon, 1996—. Vis. prof. U. Que., 1977; vis. scholar U. Calif., 1983; chmn. U.S. Nat. Commn. C, Union Radio Sci. Internat., 1990-92; mem. sci. and indsl. adv. bd. Telecom. Inst. Ont., Can. and Inst. Nacionale de la Recherches Scientique; vice chair, wireless panel World Tech. Evaluation Ctr. Editor: book series Computer Science Press, 1979— ; IEEE Trans., 1975-80; co-editor-in-chief Jour. of Comms. and Networks, 2003—; author: Local Area and Multiple Access Networks, 1986; contbr. articles to profl. jours.; patentee in field. Recipient rsch. award RCA Labs., 1955; rsch. grantee Office of Naval Research, Washington, 1982, E-Systems, Falls Church, Va., 1983-96, MCI, Falls Church, Va., Intelsat, Washington, Nortel Networks, 1996—, DARPA, NSF, 1999—. Fellow IEEE (bd. govs. 1979-82, digital comm. com., Centennial medal 1984), AAAS, Washington Acad. Scis.; mem. IEEE Comm. Soc. (v.p. 1986-88, pres. 1990-92, Donald W. McLellan award, 1994, Erskine fellow New Zealand 1997, Third Millennium medal 2000, ACM MSWIN prize paper award, 1999, Best paper of 1999 in Jour. of Comms. and Networks, 2000, gen. chair, Infocom, Kobe, Japan 1997, gen. chair, ACM Mobicom Y2K, Boston, 2000), Math. Assn. Am., Cosmos Club, Sigma Xi, Eta Kappa Nu. Home: 3613 Glenbrook Rd Fairfax VA 22031-3210 Office: George Washington U Dept Elec Computer Engring Washington DC 20052-0001

PIDGEON, JOHN ANDERSON, headmaster; b. Lawrence, Mass., Dec. 20, 1924; s. Alfred H. and Nora (Regan) P.; children: John Anderson, Regan S., Kelly; m. Barbara Hafer, May 1986. Grad., Phillips Acad., 1943; BA, Bowdoin Coll., 1949; Ed.D., Bethany Coll., 1973; D.Litt., Washington and Jefferson Coll., 1979. Instr. Latin, adminstrv. asst. to headmaster Deerfield Acad., 1949-57; headmaster Kiskiminetas Springs Sch., Saltsburg, Pa., 1957—. Dir. Saltburg Savs. & Trust. Trustee Winchester-Thurston Sch.

Served as ensign USNR, 1943-46. Mem. New Eng. Swimming Coaches Assn. (pres. 1956-57), Cum Laude Soc., Delta Upsilon. Home and Office: Kiski Sch 1888 Brett Ln Saltsburg PA 15681-8951

PIEPKE, SUSAN L. foreign language educator, researcher, writer; b. Kerrville, Tex., Mar. 5, 1949; d. Charles and Stella S. Leedecke; m. Walter J. Piepke, June 20, 1975. BA, SUNY, Albany, 1971; MA in Linguistics, U. Rochester, 1975; MA in Spanish, Middlebury Coll., 1984, D of Modern Langs., 1986. Cert. postgrad. profl. tchr., Va.; cert. tchr., N.Y. Tchr. Spanish and French Brockport (N.Y.) H.S., 1971-83; asst. prof. fgn. langs. Elon Coll., N.C., 1984-88; assoc. prof. Bridgewater (Va.) Coll., 1988-98, prof., 1998—, acting chair dept. fgn. langs., 1992, 99, chair dept. fgn. langs., 2002—. Mem. selection com. Gov.'s German Acad., Va., 1989, 91-97. Transl., author introduction: (book) Women and Their Vocation: A 19th-Century View by Luise Büchner, 1999; contbr. articles to profl. jours. NEH grantee, 1992; Flory Humanities grantee Bridgewater Coll., 1993; Mednick grantee Va. Found. for Ind. Colls., 1999; Faculty rsch. grantee Bridgewater Coll., 2002-03. Mem.: MLA, AAUW (edn. chair 1997—99, 2000—03), Am. Assn. Tchrs. Spanish, Fgn. Lang. Assn. Va., Am. Coun. on the Tchg. of Fgn. Langs., Am. Assn. Tchrs. German. Avocation: classical music (especially opera). Office: Bridgewater Coll E College St Bridgewater VA 22812 E-mail: spiepke@bridgewater.edu.

PIERCE, CHESTER MIDDLEBROOK, retired psychiatrist, educator; b. Glen Cove, N.Y., Mar. 4, 1927; s. Samuel Riley and Hettie Elenor (Armstrong) P.; m. Jocelyn Patricia Blanchet, June 15, 1949; children: Diane Blanchet, Deirdre Anona. AB, Harvard U., 1948, MD, 1952; ScD (hon.), Westfield Coll., 1977, Tufts U., 1984; D Engring. Tech. (hon.), Wentworth Inst. Tech., 1997. Instr. psychiatry U. Cin., 1957-60; asst. prof. psychiatry U. Okla., 1960-62, prof., 1965-69; prof. edn. and psychiatry Harvard U., 1969—; pres. Am. Bd. Psychiatry and Neurology, 1977-78; ret. Mem. Polar Research Bd.; cons. USAF. Author publs. on sleep disturbances, media, polar medicine, sports medicine, racism; mem. editorial bds. Advisor Children's TV Workshop; chmn. Child Devel. Assn. Consortium; bd. dirs. Action Children's TV. With M.C. USNR, 1953-55. Fellow: Brit. Royal Coll. Psychiatrists (hon.), Royal Australian and N.Z. Coll. Psychiatrists (hon.); mem.: Am. Orthopsychiat. Assn. (pres. 1983—84), Black Psychiatrists Am. (chmn.), Inst. Medicine at NAS, Am. Acad. Arts and Scis. Democrat. Home: 17 Prince St Jamaica Plain MA 02130-2725

PIERCE, DEBORAH MARY, educational administrator; b. Charleston, W. Va. d. Edward Ernest and Elizabeth Anne (Trent) P.; m. Henry M. Armetta, Sept. 1, 1967 (div. 1981); children: Rosse Matthew Armetta, Stacey Elizabeth Pierce. Student, U. Tenn., 1956-59, Broward Jr. Coll., 1968-69; BA, San Francisco State U., 1977. Cert. elem. tchr., Calif. Pub. relations assoc. San Francisco Internat. Film Festival, 1965-66; account exec. Stover & Assocs., San Francisco, 1966-67; tchr. San Francisco Archdiocese Office of Cath. Schs., 1980-87; part-time tchr. The Calif. Study, Inc. (formerly Tchr's. Registry), Tiburon, Calif., 1988—; pvt. practice as paralegal San Francisco, 1989—; tchr. Jefferson Sch. Dist., Daly City, Calif., 1989-91. Author: (with Frances Spatz Leighton) I Prayed Myself Slim, 1960. Pres. Mothers Alone Working, San Francisco, 1966, PTA, San Francisco, 1979, Parent Tchr. Student Assn., San Francisco, 1984; apptd. Calif. State Bd. Welfare Cmty. Rels. Com., 1964-66; block organizer SAFE, 1996; active feminist movement. Named Model of the Yr. Modeling Assn. Am., 1962. Mem. People Med. Soc., Assn. for Rsch. and Enlightenment, A Course in Miracles, Commonwealth Club Calif, Angel Club San Francisco, San Diego Chat Club, Deepak Chopra 7 Spiritual Laws Group. Mem. Unity Christ Ch. Avocation: chess. Address: 3346 Taravel St San Francisco CA 94116 E-mail: deborahmpierce@hotmail.com.

PIERCE, DONALD SHELTON, retired orthopedic surgeon, educator; b. Castine, Maine, May 21, 1930; s. Frederick Ernest and Jeannie (Emmet) P.; m. Janet Ten Broeck, Dec. 29, 1956; children: Donald Shelton, Stanton ten Broeck, Frederick Ernest, Jennifer Emmet. AB cum laude, Harvard U., 1953, MD, 1957. Diplomate Am. Bd. Spine Surgery, Am. Bd. Orthop. Surgery. Intern U. Hosp., Cleve., 1957-58, resident, 1958-62; rsch. assoc. biomechanics lab. U. Calif., San Francisco, 1962-64; practice medicine specializing in orthopedic surgery San Francisco, 1962-64; instr. orthopedic surgery U. Calif. Med. Sch., San Francisco, 1962-64, Harvard Med. Sch., 1964-66; clin. and rsch. assoc. J.P. Kennedy Jr. Meml. Hosp., Brighton, Mass., 1964-66; clin. assoc. in orthopedics Harvard Med. Sch., 1966-67, clin. asst. prof. orthopaedic surgery, 1979-87, clin. assoc. prof., 1987-2000; ret., 2000; sr. orthopedic surgeon Mass. Gen. Hosp., Boston. Chief dept. rehab. medicine Mass. Gen. Hosp., Boston, 1965-72, assoc. orthopedic surgeon, 1969—, vis. orthopedic surgeon, 1969—; lectr. dept. mech. engring. MIT, 1970-72. Co-author: Amputees and Their Porstheses, 1971; author: The Total Care of Spinal Cord Injuries, 1977; contbr. articles in field to profl. jours. Pres. Wellesley (Mass.) Friendly Aid Assn., 1965-67, dir., 1967-70; dir. Family Svc. Counseling Region West, Wellesley, 1965-67; exec. com., task force chmn., adv. bd. Mass. State Rehab. Planning Commn., 1966-68. With USAF, 1951-52. Fellow ACS, Am. Acad. Orthopedic Surgeons, Royal Soc. Health, Pan Am. Med. Assn., Soc. Internat. Chirurgerie, Ortopaedie et Traumatologie; mem. Othopedic Rsch. Soc., Am. Orthopaedic Assn., NRC (musculosbeletal com.), Cervical Spine Rsch. Soc. (pres. 1986), Fedn. Spine Assns. (pres. 1987), N.E. Med. Assn. (pres.). Home: 22 Lathrop Rd Wellesley MA 02482

PIERCE, GREGORY LEE, criminal justice educator; b. Renton, Wash., Apr. 2, 1946; s. Gene O. and Fay (Baker) P.; children: Ingri K., Mari B., Chris Edward. BS, Oreg. Coll. Edn., 1973; MA Police Sci./Adminstrn., Wash. State U., 1975; MS Correctional Adminstrn., Western Oreg. State Coll., 1987. Chmn. dept. criminal justice Bluefield (W.Va.) State Coll., 1975-76; dir. pub. svcs. Southwestern Oreg. C.C., Coos Bay, Oreg., 1976-80; chmn. dept. criminal justice Blue Mountain C.C., Pendleton, Oreg., 1980—2001; assoc. prof., dir. criminal justice Bethany Coll., Lindsborg, Kans., 2001—. Judge mcpl. ct. Stanfield, Oreg., 1993—. Chmn. Community Corrections, Pendelton, Oreg., 1984—, Juv. Svcs., Pendleton, 1980-80; mem. County Reorganization, Pendleton, Fed. Community on Jails, Portland, 1986-90. With U.S. Army, 1966-68, Vietnam. Mem. Acad. Criminal Justice Scis., Lions (pres. Pendleton club 1980—, Cap Casperson award 1980). Home: 209 N Pine Ct Lindsborg KS 67456 Office: Bethany Coll 421 N 1st St Lindsborg KS 67456 E-mail: pierceg@bethanylb.edu.

PIERCE, ILONA LAMBSON, educational administrator; b. Blackfoot, Idaho, Dec. 3, 1941; d. Merlin A. Wright and Loa (Adams) Lambson; m. Sherman D. Pierce, Mar. 19, 1960. IBM cert., LDS Bus. Coll., Salt Lake City, 1960; BS, U. Utah, 1969, MEd, 1974, EdD, 1978. Cert. elem. tchr., adminstrv. endorsement, Utah; cert. tchr. ESL, Utah; lic. real estate agt., Utah. Key punch operator Mountain Bell Telephone Co., Salt Lake City, 1960-61; key punch supr. Hercules Powder Co., Bacchus, Utah, 1961-66; tchr. Cottonwood Heights Elem. Sch., Jordan Sch. Dist., Sandy, Utah, 1969-74; tchr. Willow Canyon Elem. Sch., Jordan Sch. Dist., Sandy, Utah, 1974-76; postdoctoral fellow, grad. rsch. asst. U. Utah, Salt Lake City, 1976-78; tchr. Silver Mesa Elem. Sch. Jordan Sch. Dist., Sandy, Utah, 1978-79, tchr. specialist, 1979-80, asst. prin. Mt. Jordan Mid. Sch., 1980-84, prin. Union Mid. Sch., 1984-86, dir. instrnl. media and bilingual edn., 1986-97; retired. Mem. Utah Network Ednl. TV, 1986—; chmn. tech. adv. bd., chmn. bd. dirs. Math. Engring. Sci. Achievement, 1989, bd. dirs., 1987—; treas. State Film Depository Consortium, 1986—; mem. Utah Info. Tech. Consortium, 1987—; mem. prin. mentor program Brigham Young U., 1986. Sch. dist. co-chmn. United Way, 1986—. Recipient recognition award Math Engring. Sci. Achievement, 1991, Valuable Svc. award Emergency Preparedness Action Com., 1988, Disting. Svc. award Utah Ednl. Libr. Media Assn., 1988. Mem. ASCD, Utah ASCD (bd. dirs., editor 1986-89), NEA (life), Utah Edn. Assn., J'rdan Edn. Assn., Alpha Delta Kappa (state treas. 1980-84, state pres. 1984-86), Delta Kappa Gamma. Avocations: fossil hunting, travel, reading. Home: 8895 S 540 E Sandy UT 84070-1728

PIERCE, LISA MARGARET, telecommunications executive, product and market development manager, lecturer; b. Nyack, NY, June 2, 1957; d. William and Elizabeth Pierce. BA with honors, Gordon Coll., Wenham, Mass., 1978; MBA, Atkinson Sch., Salem, Oreg., 1982. Campaign mgr. Carter/Mondale, Manchester, Mass., 1976; investigator Dept. Social Svcs., Nyack, 1977-78; paralegal Beverly, Mass., 1978-79; campaign mgr. Reagan Presdl. Primary, Rockland County, N.Y., 1980; cons. Sidereal, Portland, Oreg., 1981-82; performance analyst Dept. Social Svcs., Pomona, N.Y., 1982; market analyst Momentum Techs., Parsippany, N.J., 1983; cons. Booz Allen & Hamilton, Florham Park, N.J., 1984, Deloitte-Touche, Morristown, N.J., 1985; market researcher, forecaster AT&T, Bedminster, N.J., 1985-87, asst. pvt. line product mgr., 1987-89, Integrated Svcs. Digital Network product mgr., 1989-93; dir. Telecom. Rsch. Assocs., St. Marys, Kans., 1994-98; v.p., rsch. fellow Giga Info. Group/Forrester Rsch., Cambridge, Mass., 1998—. Panelist, contbr. TeleComms. Assn., San Diego, Internat. Comm. Assn., Atlanta, Ea. Comm. Forum, NY, Nat. Engring. Consortium, Chgo., Super Comm., Soc. Telecom. Consultants, MPLS Forum, Mid Atlantic Venture Assn., GSA Fed. Telecom. Svc. Forums, others; contbr. NY State ISDN/Internat User's Group; feature commentator Nat. Pub. Radio (All Things Considered), Pub. Broadcasting Svc. (Nightly Bus. Report), MSNBC, CNN and CNBC, Radio Wall Street, CBS Evening News. Columnist Network World, 2001—02, Bus. Comm. Rev., 2002—. Grantee in field. Mem.: IEEE.

PIERCE, MARY E. retired educator, public relations consultant; b. Chgo. d. Henry Harris and Eva Irene (Hanes) P. BE, Chgo. Tchrs. Coll., 1944. One room sch. tchr. Will County, Monee, Ill.; tchr. 5th grade Peotone (Ill.) Sch. Dist.; tchr. elem. and jr. h.s. Steger (Ill.) Sch. Dist., chair lang. arts dept.; ret., 1979; chair sch. improvement plan; pub. rels. cons. Former pres. Steger Edn. Assn.; chmn. bd. dirs. #194 Employee Credit Union, Steger, 1972-95. Village clk. Village of Richton Park, 1992—; pres. Friends of Libr., Richton Park, 1980—, v.p.; bd. dirs. So. Suburban Cancer Soc., Tinley Pk., Ill., 1994—, S.E. Chpt. Ill. Credit Union, Calumet City, Ill., 1994-95. Recipient Cmty. Svc. award Cook County Sheriff's Office, Chgo. Mem. Delta Kappa Gamma (treas. 1979—). Avocation: golf. Home: 22147 Karlov Ave Richton Park IL 60471-1725

PIERCE, SUSAN RESNECK, academic administrator, English language educator; b. Janesville, Wis., Feb. 6, 1943; d. Elliott Jack and Dory (Block) Resneck; m. Kenneth H. Pierce; 1 child, Alexandra Siegel. AB, Wellesley Coll., 1965; MA, U. Chgo., 1966; PhD, U. Wis., 1972. Lectr. U. Wis., Rock County, 1970-71; from asst. prof. to prof. English Ithaca (N.Y.) Coll., 1973-82, chmn. dept., 1976-79; program officer Nat. Endowment for Humanities, 1982-83, asst. dir., 1983-84; dean Henry Kendall Coll. Arts and Scis. U. Tulsa, 1984-90; v.p. acad. affairs, prof. English Lewis and Clark Coll., Portland, Oreg., 1990-92; pres. U. Puget Sound, Tacoma, 1992—2003. Vis. assoc. prof. Princeton (N.J.) U., 1979; bd. dirs. Janet Elson Scholarship Fund, 1984-1990, Tulsa Edn. Fund, Phillips Petroleum Scholarship Fund, 1985-90, Okla. Math. & Sci. High Sch., 1984-90, Hillcrest Med. Ctr., 1988-90, Portland Opera, 1990-92, St. Joseph's Hosp., 1992—, Seattle Symphony, 1993—; cons. U. Oreg., 1985, Drury Coll., Springfield, Mo., 1986; mem. Middle States and N. Cen. Accreditation Bds.; mem. adv. com. Fed. Women's Program, NEH, 1982-83; participant Summit Meeting on Higher Edn., Dept. Edn., Washington, 1985; speaker, participant numerous ednl. meetings, sems., commencements; chair Frederick Ness Book Award Com. Assn. Am. Colls., 1986; mem. award selection com. Dana Found., 1986, 87; mem. Acad. Affairs Council, Univ. Senate, dir. tchr. edn., chmn. adv. group for tchr. preparation, ex-officio mem. all Coll. Arts and Scis. coms. and Faculty Council on Internat. Studies, all U. Tulsa; bd. dirs. Am. Conf. Acad. Deans; bd. trustees Hillcrest Med. Ctr.; participant Aspen Inst. Md. 1999, Annapolis Group Media Roundtable, 1996, Harvard Seminar, 1992; former bd. dirs. Assn. Am. Colls. and Univs., 1989-92, Am. Conf. of Academic Deans, 1988-91, Am. Assn. Colls., 1989-92. Author: The Moral of the Story, 1982, also numerous essays, jour. articles, book sects., book revs.; co-editor: Approaches to Teaching "Invisible Man"; reader profl. jours. Bd. dirs. Arts and Humanities Coun., Tulsa, 1984-90; trustee Hillcrest Hosp., Tulsa, 1986-90; mem. cultural series com., community rels. com. Jewish Fedn., Tulsa, 1986-90; bd. dirs. Tulsa chpt. NCCJ, 1986-90, Kemper Mus. 1996—, Seattle Symphony, 1993-96, St. Joseph Hosp., 1992-93, Portland Opera, 1990-92. Recipient Best Essay award Arix. Quar., 1979, Excellence in Teaching award N.Y. State Edn. Council, 1982, Superior Group Service award NEH, 1984, other teaching awards; Dana scholar, Ithaca Coll., 1980-81; Dana Research fellow, Ithaca Coll., 82-83; grantee Inst. for Ednl. Affairs, 1980, Ford Found., 1987, NEH, 1989. Mem. MLA (adv. com. on job market 1973-74), South Ctrl. MLA, NIH (subcom. on college drinking), Assn. Governing Bds. (coun. of pres.), Nat. Inst. on Alcohol Abuse (presl. advisory group), Soc. for Values in Higher Edn., Assn. Am. Colls. (bd. dirs.), Am. Conf. Acad. Deans (bd. dirs. 1988-91), Coun. of Presidents, Assn. Governing Bds., Phi Beta Kappa, Phi Kappa Phi, Phi Gamma Kappa.

PIERIK, MARILYN ANNE, retired librarian, piano teacher; b. Bellingham, Wash., Nov. 12, 1939; d. Estell Leslie and Anna Margarethe (Onigkeit) Bowers; m. Robert Vincent Pierik, July 25, 1964; children: David Vincent, Donald Lesley. AA, Chaffey Jr. Coll., Ontario, Calif., 1959; BA, Upland (Calif.) Coll., 1962; cert. in teaching, Claremont (Calif.) Coll., 1963; MSLS, U. So. Calif., L.A., 1973. Tchr. elem. Christ Episcopal Day Sch., Ontario, 1959-60; tchr. Bonita High Sch., La Verne, Calif., 1962-63; tchr., libr. Kettle Valley Sch. Dist. 14, Greenwood, Can., 1963-64; libr. asst. Monrovia (Calif.) Pub. Libr., 1964-67; with Mt. Hood C.C., Gresham, Oreg., 1972-98, reference libr., 1983-98, chair faculty scholarship com., 1987-98, campus archivist, 1994-98; ret., 1998; pvt. piano tchr., 1998—. Pvt. piano tchr., 1998; mem. site selection com. Multnomah County (Oreg.) Libr., New Gresham br., 1987, adv. com. Multnomah County Libr., Portland, Oreg., 1988-89; bd. dirs. Oreg. Episcopal Conf. of Deaf, 1985-92. Bd. dirs. East County Arts Alliance, Gresham, 1987-91; vestry person, jr. warden St. Luke's Episc. Ch., 1989-92; vestry person St. Aidan's Episcopal. Ch., 2000—; founding pres. Mt. Hood Pops, 1983-88, orch. mgr., 1983-91, 93—, bd. dirs., 1983-88, 91—. Recipient Jeanette Parkhill Meml. award Chaffey Jr. Coll., 1959, Svc. award St. Luke's Episcopal Ch., 1983, 87, Edn. Svc. award Soroptimists, 1989. Mem. AAUW, NEA, Oreg. Edn. Assn., Oreg. Libr. Assn., ALA, Gresham Hist. Soc. Avocations: music, reading. E-mail: pierikm@teleport.com.

PIERRE, CHARLES BERNARD, mathematician, statistician, educator; b. Houston, Dec. 2, 1946; s. Rufus and Charles (Ellis) P.; m. Patsy Randle, Aug. 28, 1970 (div. 1971); m. Cynthia Gilliam, June 28, 1980 (div. 1994); 1 child, Kimberly Keri. BS, Tex. So. U., 1970, MS in Edn., 1974; PhD in Math./Math. Edn., Am. U., 1992. Cert. tchr., Tex., D.C. Comml. photographer Photographics Labs., Houston, 1968-69; elec. engr., mathematician Sta. KPRC-TV, Houston, 1970-71; instr. math. Houston Ind. Sch. Dist., 1971-72, Meth. Secondary Sch., Kailahun, Sierra Leone, West Africa, 1972-73; math. researcher West African Regional Math Program, Freetown, Sierra Leona, West Africa, 1973-77; instr. math. Houston Ind. Sch. Dist., 1977-80, 81-87, Episcopal Acad., Lower Merion, Pa., 1980-81, D.C. Pub. Schs., Washington, 1987-91. Instr. math. Houston C.C., 1985-87; asst. prof. math. and computer sci. San Jose State U., 1992-94; assoc. prof. math. scis. Clark Atlanta U., 1994—; African cons. Peace Corps, Phila., 1977, Sierra Leone, West Africa; lectr. math. Tex. So. U., U. Sierra Leone, U. Liberia, Bunambu Tchrs. Coll., Port Loko Tchrs. Coll., Inst. Edn., West Africa; assessment coord. Calif. State U. Alliance for Minority Participation, San Jose, 1994; advisor design team SKYMATH Project, Boulder, Colo., 1994-96; assoc. dir. Park City/Inst. for Advanced Study Math. Inst. Clark Atlanta U., 1994-97; participant Inst. History Math. Am. U., 1994-96; cons. in field. Author: Introduction to Coordinate Analytic Geometry, 1974, Mathematics for Elementary School Teachers, 1976; co-author: The Modern Approach to Trigonometry, 1975, A Resource Book for Teachers, 1975, Picture Book for the West African Regional Math. Program, 1975, textbook 6th grade STEM project U. Mont., 1997. Vol. Peace Corps., Sierra Leone. NSF fellow. Mem.: Math. Assn. Am., NAM, Phi Mu Epsilon (reader Jour.). Democrat. Baptist. Avocations: writing, tennis, French horn, photography, travel. Home: 4867 Wilkins Station Dr Decatur GA 30035-4321 E-mail: cpierre@cau.edu.

PIERRET, ROBERT F. electrical engineering educator; b. E. Cleveland, Ohio, Aug. 20, 1940; s. Frank Sylvester and Elsie Ann (Svoboda) P.; m. Linda Jane Pierz, Aug. 22, 1965; children: Ross, Suzanne, John. BS, Case Inst. of Technology, 1962; MS, U. Ill., 1963, PhD, 1965. Rsch. assoc. U. Ill., Urbana, 1966-67, asst. prof., 1967-70; assoc. prof. Purdue U., West Lafayette, Ind., 1970-77, prof., 1977—, asst. head of ECE, 1996—. Cons. editor Addison-Wesley Pub. Co., Reading, Mass., 1984—; editl. adv. bd. Solid-State Electronics jour., 1985—. Author: (book) Semiconductor Device Fundamentals, 1996, (four vols.) Modular Series on Solid State Devices, 1983, 87, 91. Grad. fellow NSF, 1962-66. Mem. IEEE (sr.). Avocations: personal computer, playing accordion. Office: Purdue U/Sch ECE 465 Northwestern Ave West Lafayette IN 47907-2035

PIERSON, DOUGLAS H. special education educator; b. Newark, Jan. 24, 1951; s. John Henry and Isabella Davie (Ferguson) P. BE cum laude, Boston State Coll., 1975; MEd cum laude, Fitchburg (Mass.) State Coll., 1977, Keene (N.H.) State Coll., 1985; EdD, Clark U., 1993. Tchr. Concord State Prison, Boston, 1975-79; elem. prin. and tchr. Conval Sch. Dist., Peterborough, N.H., 1979-88; instr. spl. edn. Clark U., Worcester, Mass., 1987-89; tchr. emotionally disturbed Nazareth Home for Boys, Leicester, Mass., 1988-89; ednl. supr. Eagle Hill Sch., Hardwick, Mass., 1989-92; asst. prin. Ware (Mass.) Elem. Sch., 1992-93; prin. North Lincoln Elem. Sch. and St. James Elem. Sch., Lincoln, R.I., 1993-98, Hamilton Elem. Sch., North Kingston, RI, 1998—2003, Fishing Cove Sch., North Kingstown, RI, 2003—. With USN, 1969-71. Named R.I. Elem. Prin. of Yr., 2001; named Nat. Disting. Prin., 2001. Mem. ASCD, NAESP, Coun. Exceptional Children, Nat. Assn. Edn. Young Children, R.I. Assn. Sch. Prins., Kappa Delta Pi. Home: 19 S River Dr Narragansett RI 02882-2700 E-mail: ride2223@ride.ri.net.

PIERSON, ELLERY MERWIN, retired psychometrist; b. Eugene, Oreg., Mar. 31, 1935; s. Russell Alford and Doris Amanda P.; m. Barbara Suzannah Weber, Nov. 27, 1958; children: Suzanne Christine, Audrey Elaine. BS, Portland State Coll., 1957; MEd, Rutgers U., 1965; PhD, U. Pa., 1975. Rsch. asst. Columbia Coll. Physicians and Surgeons, N.Y.C., 1957-58; lab. asst. RCA, Somerville, N.J., 1958-60; welfare investigator Middlesex County Welfare Bd., New Brunswick, N.J., 1960-61; rsch. asst. Ednl. Testing Svc., Princeton, N.J., 1961-66; rsch. psychologist Franklin Inst. Rsch. Labs., Phila., 1966-67; rsch. assoc. Sch. Dist. Phila., 1967-75, mgr. in rsch., 1975-96, dir. assessment, 1996; ret., 1996. Cons. Livingford Assocs. Mem. Am. Ednl. Rsch. Assn., Nat. Coun. Measurement in Edn., Lions (club sec. 1984-96, 98—). Avocations: personal computers, recreational vehicle travel. Home and Office: Livingford Assocs 347 Bluestone Ct Collegeville PA 19426-3941 E-mail: bepierson@msn.com.

PIERSON, KATHLEEN MARY, child care center administrator, consultant; b. Detroit, Apr. 17, 1949; d. Peter and Elsa (Stanke) Kornberger; m. David Alan Pierson, Aug. 23, 1980 (div. Nov. 1981). AS, Macomb Coll., Mich., 1974; BS, Central U. Mich., 1976. Model, Detroit, 1970-74, also piano player, lounges; horse jockey, Detroit, 1974-78; recreation therapist Rehab. Inst., Detroit, 1978-81; exec. dir. Kreative Korners, Warren, Mich., 1981—, founder Kreative Korners Adult Day Care Ctr., 1987; cons. low income child care centers Mich., 1986—. Producer: children's ednl. video tapes Miss Kathy's Back to Basics, 1992. Bd. dirs. Macomb Coll., Warren, Mich., 1984—. Guest of Honor, Mich. Opportunity Soc., 1985, Easter Seal Soc., 1976; speaker United Found., 1987, 88. Mem. South Warren Cmty. Orgn., Nat. Exec. Female Assn., Internat. Platform Assn. (speech competition). Lutheran. Avocations: Doberman breeding; playing classical music; horseback riding. Home: 5487 Southlawn Dr Sterling Heights MI 48310-6565 Office: Kreative Korners Inc 5487 Southlawn Dr Sterling Heights MI 48310-6565 E-mail: kkorn5487@aol.com.

PIEST, KENNETH LEE, ophthalmic plastic surgeon, educator; b. 1954; BS in Biol. Scis., U. Ill., Chgo., 1978, postgrad. studies in genetics, 1978—79, MD, 1984. Diplomate Nat. Bd. Med. Examiners, Am. Bd. Ophthalmology. Intern Weiss Meml. Hosp., Chgo., 1984-85; fellow U. Utah Med. Ctr., Salt Lake City, 1985-86; resident U. Tex. Health Sci. Ctr., San Antonio, 1986-89; fellow U. Pa., Phila., 1989-91, asst. chief svc., 1991; assoc. prof. U. Tex. Health Sci. Ctr., San Antonio, 1991—. Dir. Oculoplastic Orbit and Oncology Svc., San Antonio, San Antonio Craniofacial Clinic, Neurofibromatosis Clinic, San Antonio, Retinoblastoma Clinic, San Antonio. Contbr. chpts. in books and articles to profl. jours. Fellow Am. Acad. Ophthalmology (Honor award 1996); mem. AMA (Physicians Recognition award 1987, 90), Am. Soc. Ophthalmic Plastic and Reconstructive Surgery, Am. Coll. Physician Execs., Tex. Med. Assn., Phi Kappa Phi. Office: 540 Madison Oak Dr San Antonio TX 78258-3928

PIFER, ELLEN I. literary critic, educator; b. N.Y.C., June 26, 1942; m. Drury L. Pifer, Dec. 30, 1962; 1 dau., Rebecca. Student, Mills Coll., 1960-62; BA in English with distinction, U. Calif., Berkeley, 1964; MA in Comparative Lit., U. Calif., 1969, PhD, 1976. Instr. U. Calif., Berkeley, 1974-76; asst. prof. U. Del., Newark, 1977-81, assoc. prof., 1981-89, prof., 1989—, dir. grad. studies English, 2002—. Theatre critic The Berkeley Gazette, 1975-76; columnist New West Mag., San Francisco, 1976-77; cons. various univ. presses, 1979—; disting. vis. prof. Am. Lit. U. Jean Moulin, Lyon, France, 1992; vis. prof. comparative lit. U. Calif., Berkeley, 1990; Rector's disting. lectr. Am. Lit. U. Helsinki, 1993. Author: Nabokov and the Novel, 1980, Saul Bellow Against the Grain, 1990 (Outstanding Acad. Book Choice Mag.), Demon or Doll: Images of the Child in Contemporary Writing and Culture, 2000; editor: Critical Essays on John Fowles, 1986, Vladimir Nabokov's Lolita: A Casebook, 2003; mem. internat. editl. bd. Nabokov Studies, 1993—; contbr. chpts. to books and articles and revs. to books and profl. jours. Undergrad. scholar Mills Coll., 1960-62; recipient Phi Beta Kappa award to freshman student Mills Coll., George Stewart prize Mills Coll., 1962, Nat. Def. Fgn. Lang. fellow, 1968-71; grantee, fellow U. Calif., U. Del.; grantee U. Del., 1978, 81, 86, 90, 99; Del. Humanities Forum Rsch. fellow, 1987-88, Del. Arts Coun. Individual Artists fellow, 1989-90, Ctr. Advanced Studies fellow U. Del., 1993-94, NEH summer rsch. fellow, 1991; Fulbright scholar, 1992. Mem. ALA, MLA, Vladimir Nabokov Soc. (pres. 1998-2000). Office: U Del Dept English Newark DE 19716

PIGNO, MARK ANTHONY, prosthodontist, educator, researcher; b. Lake Charles, La., May 17, 1960; s. Frank Anthony and Geraldine (Carnahan) Pigno; m. Eileen Marie Failla, May 18, 1991; children: Constance, Nathaniel Anthony, Frank Anthony. BS, McNeese State U., 1983; DDS, La. State U., 1989, cert. in prosthodontics, 1991; cert. in maxillofacial prosthetics, MD Anderson Cancer Ctr., Houston, 1992. Diplomate Am. Bd. Prosthodontics. Asst. prof. U. Mo., Kansas City, 1992-93, U. Tex. Health Sci. Ctr., San Antonio, 1993—2000; assoc. prof., 2000—; dir. maxillofacial prosthetics tertiary care ctr. U. Tex. Health Sci. Ctr., San Antonio, 1997—. Mem. Craniofacial Anomalies Bd. U. Tex. Health Sci. Ctr., San Antonio, 1995—, Head and Neck Tumor Bd., 1997—. Contbr. articles to dental jours. Grantee U. Tex. Health Sci. Ctr., 1995. Fellow Internat. Coll. Maxillofacial Prosthetics, Am. Coll. Prosthodontists (mem. com. 1991—), Am. Acad. Maxillofacial Prosthetics (Ann. Rsch. award 1992); mem. ADA, Omicron

Kappa Upsilon. Roman Catholic. Avocations: fishing, gardening. Office: U Tex Health Sci Ctr Dept Prosthodontics 7912 7703 Floyd Curl Dr San Antonio TX 78229-3900

PIGOTT, GEORGE MORRIS, food engineering educator, consulting engineer; b. Vancouver, Wash., Oct. 25, 1928; s. Alexander William and Moreita (Howard) P.; m. Joyce Burroughs (div. 1980); children: George Jr., Roy K., Randall E., Julie M., Becky L.; m. Barbee W. Tucker. BS in Chem. Engring., U. Wash., 1950, MS in Chem. Engring., 1955, PhD in Food Sci. and Chemistry, 1962. Registered profl. engr., Wash., Oreg. Field engr. Continental Can Co., Seattle, 1951-53; rsch. engr. Fish and Wildlife Svc., Seattle, 1947-51, Nat. Canners Assn., Seattle, 1953-55, Boeing Corp., Seattle, 1957-60; cons. engr., 1957—; prof. food engring. Inst. Food Sci. and Tech. U. Wash., Seattle, 1962—99, dir. Inst. Food Sci. and Tech., 1990—; pres. Sea Resources Engring. Inc., Bellevue, Wash., 1965—; prof. emeritus U. Wash, 1999—. Bd. dirs. various cos. Author: Pathway to a Healthy Heart, 1983, Fish and Shellfish in Human Nutrition, 1988, Seafood: The Effect of Technology on Nutrition, 1990; contbr. more than 200 tech. papers; patentee in field. Served to lt. U.S. Army, 1951-53. Mem. NSPE, Am. Inst. Chem. Engrs., Am. Chem. Soc., Inst. Food Technologists, Am. Inst. Chemistry, Am. Soc. Agrl. Engrs., World Aquaculture Soc. Avocations: skiing, fishing, boating, scuba diving. Address: 4525 105th Ave NE Kirkland WA 98033-7637 Office: Sea Resources Engring Inc 4525 105th NE Kirkland WA 98033

PIGOTT, IRINA VSEVOLODOVNA, educational administrator; b. Blagoveschensk, Russia, Dec. 4, 1917; came to U.S., 1939, naturalized, 1947; d. Vsevolod V. and Sophia (Reprev) Obolianinoff; m. Nicholas Prischepenko, Feb., 1945 (dec. Nov. 1964); children: George, Helen. Grad., YMCA Jr. Coll., Manchuria, 1937; BA, Mills Coll., 1942; cert. social work, U. Calif.-Berkeley, 1944; MA in Early Childhood Edn., NYU, 1951. Dir.-owner Parsons Nursery Sch., Flushing, N.Y., 1951-59; dir. Montessori Sch., N.Y.C., 1966-67; dir., tchr. Head Start Program, Harlem, 1967-68; founder, dir. East Manhattan Sch. for Bright and Gifted, N.Y.C., 1968—, The House for Bright and Gifted Children, Flushing, N.Y., 1988-93. Organizer, pres., exec. dir. Non-Profl. Children's Performing Arts Guild, Inc., N.Y.C., 1961-65, 87—. Organizer Back Yard Theatre, Bayside, N.Y., 1959-61. Democrat. Greek Orhtodox. Avocations: music, dance, theatre, art, sports. Office: East Manhattan Sch 201 E 17th St 2H New York NY 10003

PIGOTT, JOHN DOWLING, geologist, geophysicist, geochemist, educator, consultant; b. Gorman, Tex., Feb. 2, 1951; s. Edwin Albert and Emma Jane (Poe) P.; m. Kulwadee Lawwongngam, May 28, 1994. BA in Zoology, BS in Geology, U. Tex., 1974, MA in Geology, 1977; PhD in Geology, Northwestern U., 1981. Ordained deacon Roman Cath. Ch., 2002, ordained Theravada Buddhist monk 2002. Geologist Amoco Internat., Chgo., 1978-80, sr. petroleum geologist Houston, 1980-81; asst., then assoc. prof. U. Okla., Norman, 1981—. Vis. prof. Mus. Natural History, Paris, 1988, Sun Yat Sen U., Kaohsiung, Taiwan, 1991; rsch. dir. 5 nation Red Sea-Gulf of Aden seismic stratigraphy and basis analysis industry consortium, 1992—; internat. energy cons., 1981—; instr. I.H.R.D.C., Boston, 1987-91, O.G.C.I., Tulsa, 1991—; energy advisor Ministry of Oil and Mineral Resources, Republic of Yemen, 1998—; advisor Prime Min. Rep. Yemen, 1998-2000; energy advisor Empresa Colombiana de Patroleos, Colombia, 2001, Petroleos de Venezuela, 2002. Mem. editl. bd. Geotectonica et Metallogenin Jour., 1992—2000. Mem. Am. Assn. Petroleum Geologists, Soc. Exploration Geophysicists, Soc. Petroleum Engrs., Geol. Soc. Am., Indonesian Petroleum Assn., Sigma Xi. Theravada Buddhist. Achievements include discovering relationship between global CO2 and natural tectonic cycles on the scale of millions of years showing previous greenhouse times during the Phanerozoic, processing first three-dimensional amplitude variation with offset seismic survey to quantify rocks, fluids, and pressures in rocks, processing and displaying first ground penetrating radar survey as a seismic section for ultrahigh resolution sequence stratigraphy, developing tectonic subsidence analysis as a practical tool for investigating the comparative anatomy of a sedimentary basins, their tectonic history, and evolving hydrocarbon potential, and constructing first paleo-heatflow maps of the Red Sea for the past 25 ma. Office: U Okla Sch Geology & Geophysics 100 E Boyd St Norman OK 73019-1000

PIIPPO, STEVE, director; Dir. material sci. tech. program Richland (Wash.) High Sch. Creator, author Materials Sci.Tech. Recipient A+ Sites Recognition award U.S. Dept. Edn. Office: Richland High Sch Math Sci Tech Program 930 Long Ave Richland WA 99352-3399

PIKA, JOSEPH A. political scientist, educator, educational association administrator; m. Mary Pika. BA in Internat. Rels., MA in Internat. Rels., Johns Hopkins U., 1970; PhD in Polit. Sci., U. Wis., 1979. Tchr. Gilman Sch., Balt., 1970—73; instr. Western Md. Coll., 1976—77; vis. lectr. U. Wis., 1977—78; asst. prof. SUNY, Buffalo, 1978—81; asst. prof. dept. polit. sci. and internat. rels. U. Del., 1981—87, assoc. prof. dept. polit. and internat. rels., 1987—93, prof. dept. polit. sci., 1993—, assoc. chair, 1989—94, dept. chair, 1994—99, acting chair, 2000—02, faculty dir. Del. Social Studies Edn. Project, 1999—2001. Exec. dir. Govs. Commn. on Govt. Reorganization and Effectiveness, 1993; mem. State Bd. Edn., 1997—2001, pres., 2001—; presenter in field. Co-author (with N.C. Thomas and J. Maltese): The Politics of the Presidency, 2001; co-author: (with R. Watson) The Presidential Contest, 1996; contbr. chapters to books, articles to profl. jours. Trustee U. Del.; active Jobs for Del. Grads., Del. Law-Related Edn.; mem. H. Fletcher Brown scholarship com. Mem.: Omicron Delta Kappa, Phi Kappa Phi, Phi Beta Kappa, Golden Key. Address: State Bd Edn Townsend Bldg PO Box 1402 Dover DE 19901 Office: U Del Dept Polit Sci 468 Smith Hall 28 Bridle Brook Ln Newark DE 19711*

PIKE, CHARLENE HELEN, retired secondary school educator; b. Detroit, Feb. 26, 1947; d. Burt A. and Lorraine J. (Dobro) Engstrom; m. David Pierce Pike, July 5, 1969. BA in Social Sci., Mich. State U., 1969; MEd, Wayne State U., 1974. Tchr. L'Anse Creuse Pub. Schs., Mt. Clemens, Mich., 1969—99, ret., 1999. Mem. Birmingham (Mich.) Power Squadron, 1975—. Mem. NEA, Nat. Mid. Sch. Assn. (trustee 1985-92, pres.-elect 1993, pres. 1994), Mich. Assn. Mid. Sch. Educators (treas. 1995—, Outstanding Svc. award 1979), Mich. Coun. for Social Studies (Outstanding Tchr. of Yr. award 1985), Mich. Edn. Assn. (Mich. Tchr. of Yr. runner-up 1987), Mich. Assn. Learning Disabled Educators, L'Anse Creuse Edn. Assn. (local exec. bd. 1980-99). Home: 325 S Maple Ave Royal Oak MI 48067-2426

PIKE, RALPH WEBSTER, chemical engineer, educator, university administrator; b. Tampa, Fla., Nov. 10, 1935; s. Ralph Webster and Macey (Adams) P.; m. Patricia Jennings, Aug. 23, 1958. B Chem. Engring., Ga. Inst. Tech., l957, PhD, l962. Rsch. chem. engr. Exxon R & D Co., Baytown, Tex., l962-64; Paul M. Horton prof. chem. engring. and sys. sci. La. State U., Baton Rouge, 1964—, assoc. vice chancellor for rsch., 1975-96, dir. La. Mineral Inst., 1979—, dean engring., 1999-2001. Cons. to chem. and petroleum refining industry, fed. govt. and State of La., 1964—. Author: Formulation and Optimization of Mathematical Models, 1970, Optimization for Engineering Systems, 1986, Optimizacion en Ingenieria, 1989. Active various civic, ch. and community orgns., Baton Rouge, l964—. 2d lt. U.S. Army, 1958-60. Recipient over 80 rsch. grants, including NASA, NSF, Dept. Interior, EPA, NOAA, state agys. and pvt. industry, 1964—. Fellow Am. Inst. Chem. Engrs. (chmn. nat. program com. l984, local sect. l985); mem. Am. Chem. Soc. (Charles E. Coates Mem. Award, 1994, univ. and profl.), Sigma Xi. Democrat. Methodist. Avocation: skiing. Home: 6063 Hibiscus Dr Baton Rouge LA 70808-8844 Office: La State U 1139 Energy Cost and Environment Bldg Baton Rouge LA 70803-0001 E-mail: pike@lsu.edu.

PILAT, JANET LOUISE B. OBERHOLTZER, adult education educator; b. Cleve., Apr. 7, 1942; d. Merton Bradley and Shirley Adeline (Jasper) Bartter; m. John Clayton Oberholtzer, June 20, 1965 (div. 1989); children: Julie Lynne Oberholtzer Chatfield, John Jacob, Joy Ellen; m. Paul Michael Pilat, Jr., May 20, 1995. BS in Edn., Baldwin Wallace Coll., 1964, MEd, 1987. Cert. reading tchr., Ohio. Tchr. Buckeye Schs., Medina, Ohio, 1964-65, East Cleveland (Ohio) Schs., 1965-67; substitute tchr. Medina City Schs., 1983-87; adj. prof. U. Akron, Ohio, 1987-95, Lorain County C.C., 1993-98. Adj. prof. Lorain County C.C., Elyria, Ohio, 1993—, Ashland U. at Grafton (Ohio) Prison, 1994; pvt. tutor and cons., Medina, 1992—. Officer bd. dirs. Girl Scouts U.S.A., Akron, 1968-83; water safety instr. ARC, Medina, 1962-97, trainer, 1976-97, bd. dirs., 1975-83, 91-93; dep. dir. Bd. Elections, 1995—. Recipient Western Res. award Girl Scouts U.S.A., 1983, Thanks Badge, 1978, Disting. Svc. award ARC, 1989, Jaycees, 1978. Mem. Internat. Reading Assn., Nat. Assn. Devel. Edn., Delta Kappa Gamma. Democrat. Methodist. Avocations: swimming, reading, sewing, baking. Home: 875 Damon Dr Medina OH 44256-2009 Office: Box 506 Medina OH 44258 E-mail: jbp5644p@aol.com.

PILKINGTON, FRANCES JEAN, secondary school educator; b. N.Y.C., Feb. 17, 1936; d. John and Emily (Grogan) P. BA in English, Ohio Dominican Coll., 1958; MA in English, St. John's U., Jamaica, N.Y., 1964; student, Laval (Que.) U., Can., 1957. Tchr. English, St. Ann's Elem. Sch., Bronx, N.Y., Cathedral High Sch., N.Y.C., Dominican Acad., N.Y.C., N.Y.C. Bd. Edn. Mem. editorial bd. The Letter newsletter. Ohio Dominican Coll. grantee Laval U., 1957. Mem. Cath. Tchrs. Assn. (del.), Bklyn. Cath. Tchrs. Assn. (editorial bd., illustrator newspaper). Home: 351 Hill Ave Elmont NY 11003-3020

PILLARELLA, DEBORAH ANN, fitness program manager, elementary education educator, consultant; b. Chgo., Oct. 2, 1960; d. Richard J. and Josephine A. (Miceli) Ban; m. James J. Pillarella, Sept. 1, 1989; children: Joseph, Luke. BA in Edn., U. Ill., 1983, MEd in Ednl. Leadership, 1992. Tchr. elem. sch. Chgo. Bd. Edn., 1983-98; fitness program mgr., program developer Cmty. Hosp. Fitness Pointe, Munster, Ind., 2001—. Youth and adult cons. Bodyworks, Chgo., 1982-98; sec. Profl. PPAC, Chgo., 1990-94; cons. IDEA Health and Fitness Assn., San Diego, 1989-99; adv. bd. Am. Coun. on Exercise, 1995, youth fitness spokesperson, 2001—. Author: Healthy Choices for Kids, 1993, Step Fitness, 1995, Adventures in Fitness, 1995. Vol. activist City of Hope, Chgo., 1990-99; side coord. Cystic Fiborsis Found., Chgo., 1988; vol. Chgo. Heart Assn., 1989. Mem. AAHPERD, Am. Coll. Sports Medicine, Chgo. Tchrs. Union, Phi Kappa Phi. Avocations: biking, hiking, swimming, walking, reading. Home: 8409 Castle Dr Munster IN 46321-1933 Office: Cmty Hosp Fitness Pointe 9950 S Calumet Ave Munster IN 46321 E-mail: dpillarella@comhs.org.

PILLAY, PRAGASEN, engineering educator; b. Durban, South Africa, Nov. 9, 1958; came to U.S., 1984; s. Somasundarum and Savatri P.; m. Raamitha Devi Pershad; children: Kamentha, Surika. B of Engring., U. Durban, South Africa, 1981; MS in Engring., U. Natal, South Africa, 1983; PhD, Va. Polytech & State U., 1987. Chartered elec. engr. Lectr. U. Natal, Durban, South Africa, 1982-83; elec. engr. Electricity Supply Commn., Durban, South Africa, 1984; grad. rsch. teaching asst. Va. Poly. Inst. and State U., Blacksburg, 1984-87; lectr. U. Newcastle-Upon-Tyne, England, 1988-90; asst. prof. U. New Orleans, 1990-93, assoc. prof., 1993-95; Jean Newell disting. prof. engring. Clarkson U., Potsdam, N.Y., 1995—. Cons. in field. Author, editor: Performance and Design of Permanent Magnet Motor Drives, 1991; contbr. articles to profl. jours. Rsch. grantee Elec. Power Rsch. Inst., 1992, State of La., 1993. Mem. IEEE (vice chmn. indsl. drs. com. 1995-97), Inst. Elec. Engrs. Achievements include use of ABC/DQ model to calculate reclosing transients in induction machines, use of wavelets to model power system disturbances; development of a technique for improving the ride-through capability of drives; mathematical modeling of permanent magnet motor drives; modeling of slip energy recovery induction motor drives. Home: 23 Haggerty Rd Potsdam NY 13676-3204 Office: Clarkson U Box 5720 8 Clarkson Ave Potsdam NY 13676-1403

PIMLEY, KIM JENSEN, financial training consultant; b. Abington, Pa., Apr. 29, 1960; d. Alvin Christian Jensen and Helen Marie (Kairis) Meinken; m. Michael St. John Pimley, Nov. 10, 1988; 1 child, Oliver Jensen Pimley. BA, MA magna cum laude, Emory U., 1982; postgrad., U. Chgo., 1985—. Mgr. tng. ops. Continental Bank, Chgo., 1986-88, mgr. coll. rels., 1988-90; mgr. client svcs. The Globecon Group, N.Y.C., 1990-92; prin. Pimley & Pimley, Inc., Princeton, N.J., 1992-93; pres. P&P Tng. Resources, Inc., Princeton, 1993—. Owner Jr. League Designer Showhouse, 1997. Contbr. poetry to various jours. 27012079en's leadership forum Dem. Nat. Com., 1997—; chmn. silent auction Princeton Friends Sch., 1997, 99, 2000; trustee Opera Festival N.J., 2000-03; bd. dirs./v.p. fin. Jewish Ctr. of Princeton, 1999—. Scholarship U. Chgo., 1984. Mem. ACLU, Oxford and Cambridge Club, Poetry Soc. Am. Office: P&P Tng Resources Inc 117 Library Pl Princeton NJ 08540-3019

PINCHING, DEBORAH ANNE ODELL, special education educator; b. Travis AFB, California, June 28, 1954; d. John R. and Ruth A. (Patchell) Dawson; married, Jan. 6, 1996. BS in edn., N.Mex. State U., Las Cruces, N. Mex., 1976; post grad., U. N.Mex. Cert. in elem. and spl. edn. teaching, N.Mex. Tchg. asst. Las Cruces Pub. Sch., Las Cruces, N.Mex., 1976-77; tchr. spl. edn. Ft. Stanton Sch. and Hosp., N.Mex., 1977-79, Carlsbad Mcpl. Sch., N.Mex., 1979—. Ednl. assistive technologist Carlsbad Mcpl. Sch., 1991—; instr. assistive teaching courses U. N.Mex., Albuquerque, 1992; presenter at profl. conf. Foster parent trainer, N.Mex. Human Svc. Dept., Carlsbad, N Mex., 1988-91, foster parent, 1984-91. Mem.: NEA (bd. mem.), Choices (bd. mem.), Coun. Exceptional Children, Pilot Club Internat. Mem.Nazarene. Avocations: crochet, computer programming, cooking. Home: 919 Franklin St Carlsbad NM 88220-5142 Office: Carlsbad Mcpl Sch 408 N Canyon St Carlsbad NM 88220-5812 E-mail: dpinching@hotmail.com.

PINCKLEY, FRANCES ANN, middle school language arts educator; b. Lawrenceburg, Tenn., Jan. 12, 1941; d. Henry Walter and Velma Lorene (Appleton) Mitchell; m. David Allen Pinckley, June 12, 1966. Postgrad., David Lipscomb U., 1959-61; BS, Mid. Tenn. State U., 1965, MS, 1984, Tenn. State U., 1989. Cert. elem. tchr., music tchr., curriculum and instrn., Tenn. English, music tchr., band and choral dir. Summertown (Tenn.) H.S., 1965-78; 11th grade English, speech, drama tchr., band/choral dir. Lawrence County H.S., Lawrenceburg, 1978-80; history, lang. arts, choral, drama tchr. Coffman Mid. Sch., Lawrenceburg, 1980—. Career ladder II tchr. Tenn. State Bd. Edn., Nashville, 1990—; tutor. Soloist, mem. Lawrence County Oratorical Soc., Lawrenceburg, 1988—; bd. dirs. Lawrenceburg Cmty. Theatre, 1976-82; Sunday sch. tchr. Pulaski St. Ch. of Christ, Lawrenceburg, 1952—, youth sponsor, 1990—; in-svc. tng. tchr. Lawrence County Bd. Edn. Named Tchr. of Yr., Lawrence County, 1973, 93. Mem. NEA, Tenn. Edn. Assn., Lawrence County Edn. Assn., Delta Kappa Gamma (treas. Phi chpt. 1981-91, 2d v.p. 1992-94, 1st v.p. 1994-96, pres. 1996-98, State Music Dir. 1988-90, Outstanding Mem. 1991, Xi State Nom. com. chmn. 1999-2001), Delta Omicron (life), Alpha Delta Kappa (1st v.p., pres.-elect Beta Nu chpt. 1997-98, pres. 2000—). Avocations: gardening, crocheting, knitting, reading, travel, singing. Home: 405 Waldon Rd Lawrenceburg TN 38464-3075 E-mail: dpfp@charter.net.

PINEDA, ANSELMO, neurosurgery educator; b. Lima, Peru, Apr. 3, 1923; s. Anselmo Vicente and Juana (Munayco)P.; m. Monique Yvonne Martin, Mar. 15, 1955; children: Patricia M., Richard A., Gilbert V., Katherine A. MD, San Marcos U., Lima, 1951; MS, Northwestern U., 1962. Diplomate Am. Bd. Neurol. Surgery. Rotating intern Loayza Hosp., Lima, 1950-51; head histology sect. Leprosy dept. Ministry Pub. Health, Lima, 1951; asst. pathologist Nat. Inst. Neoplastic Diseases, 1952; vol. asst. lab. normal and path. histology nervous system San Marcos U. Sch. Medicine, 1953; rotating intern Augustana Hosp., Chgo., 1954, resident in gen. surgery, 1955; jr. asst. resident in neurosurgery U. Chgo., 1955-56, sr. asst. resident in neurosurgery, 1956-57, chief resident in neurosurgery, 1957-58; assoc. instr. neurosurgery U. Tex., 1958-61; assoc. neurosurgeon John Sealy Hosp., Galveston, Tex., 1960-61, attending neurosurgeon, 1961; acting chief neurosurgery VA Hosp., Long Beach, Calif., 1962-63; asst. clin. prof. dept. biology UCLA, 1963-82, assoc. clin. prof. divsn. neurobiology/neurosurgery, 1982—. Cons. VA Hosp., Long Beach, 1966-67. NIH spl. fellow in Neuroanatomy Northwestern U., 1961-62. Fellow ACS, Am. Coll. Angiology, Royal Soc. Medicine; mem. AAUP, AAAS, AMA, Congress of Neurol. Surgeons, World Med. Assn., Am. Assn. Neurol. Surgeons, Calif. Med. Assn., Orange County Med. Assn., Am. Acad. Neurology, Am. Assn. Neuropathologists, Internat. Coll. Surgeons, Am. Assn. Anatomists, Am. Assn. Trauma, Am. Soc. Stereotaxic and Functional Neurosurgery, N.Y. Acad. Scis., Internat. Assn. Study Pain, U. Chgo. Surg. Soc., L.A. Surg. Soc., Sigma Xi. Home: 16571 Carousel Ln Huntington Beach CA 92649-2115 Office: 2880 Atlantic Ave Long Beach CA 90806-1714 E-mail: mp128@aol.com.

PINEDO, MYRNA ELAINE, psychotherapist, educator; b. Riverton, Wyo., Apr. 28, 1944; d. Pedro Berumen and Ruth Jama (Kuriyama) P.; m. Alan P. Schiesel, Sept. 9, 1964 (div. July 1973); 1 child, Elaine Marie (Schiesel) Thompson; m. Wallace Vern Calkins, Aug. 31, 1990. BA in Psychology, Calif. State U., Northridge, 1980; MA in Cmty. Clin. Psychology, Calif. Sch. Profl. Psychology, 1982; PhD in Cmty. Clin. Psychology, Calif. Sch. Profl. Psychiatry, 1987. Lic. marriage, family and child counselor, Calif.; cert. mental health counselor, Wash.; cert. marriage and family therapist, Wash. Pychiat. asst. William Newton, M.D., Marine del Rey, Calif., 1983-84; psychologist forensic svcs. dept. Kern County Mental Health, Bakersfield, Calif., 1984-88; alcohol counselor Spl. Treatment Edn. Program Svcs., Bakersfield, 1985-87; marriage and family therapist Jay Fisher & Assocs., Bakersfield, 1986-87; therapist program devel. Correctional Specialties, Bellevue, Wash., 1988-90; pvt. practice HAP Counseling Svcs., Bellevue, 1990—. Adj. faculty Calif. State U., Bakersfield, 1986, Kern County Mental Health, 1987, Bellevue C.C., 1989, Antioch U., 1992, 93; instituted various treatment programs for adolescents, Spanish speaking adults and Spanish speaking sex offenders; spkr. in field; expert witness in ct. Panelist EastSide Domestic Violence Com., 1991-93; bd. dirs. Kern County Child Abuse Coun., 1986-88; mem. treatment com. Kern County Child Abuse Task Force, 1985-88; mem. Stop-Abuse by Counselors, 1993—. Mem. Am. Counseling Assn., Am. Assn. Christian Counselors, Assn. Orthopsychiatry, Wash. Assn. Mental Health Counselors, Assn. Marriage and Family Therapists. Avocations: gardening, hiking, cooking.

PINES, ALEXANDER, chemistry educator, researcher, consultant; b. Tel Aviv, June 22, 1945; came to U.S., 1968. s. Michael and Neima (Ratner) P.; m. Ayala Malach, Aug. 31, 1967 (div. 1983); children: Itai, Shani; m. Ditsa Kafry, May 5, 1983; children: Noami, Jonathan, Talia. BS, Hebrew U., Jerusalem, 1967; PhD, MIT, 1972; D (hon.), U. Paris, 1999, U. Rome "La Sapienza", 2001. Asst. prof. chemistry U. Calif., Berkeley, 1972-75, assoc. prof., 1975-80, prof., 1980—. Pres.'s chair, 1993-97, Chandellor's rsch. prof., 1997-99, Miller rsch. prof., 1998-99, Glenn T. Seaborg chair chemistry, 1999—. Faculty sr. scientist materials scis. div. Lawrence Berkeley Nat. Lab., 1975—; cons. Mobil Oil Co., Princeton, N.J., 1980-84, Shell Oil Co., Houston, 1981—; chmn. Bytel Corp., Berkeley, Calif., 1981-85; vis. prof. Weizmann Inst. Sci., 1982; adv. prof. East China Normal U., Shanghai, People's Rep. of China, 1985; sci. dir. Nalorac, Martinez, Calif., 1986-92; Joliot-Curie prof. Ecole Superieure de Physique et Chemie, Paris, 1987; Walter J. Chute Disting. lectr. Dalhousie U., 1989, Charles A. McDowell lectr. U. B.C., 1989, E. Leon Watkins lectr. Wichita State U., 1990; Hinshelwood lectr., U. Oxford, 1990, A.R. Gordon Disting. lectr. U. Toronto, 1990, Venable lectr. U. N.C., 1990, Max Born lectr. Hebrew U. of Jerusalem, 1990; William Draper Harkins lectr. U. Chgo., 1991, Kolthoff lectr. U. Minn., 1991; Md.-Grace lectr. U. Md., 1992; mem. adv bd. Nat. High Magnetic Field Lab., Inst. Theoretical Physics, U. Calif. Santa Barbara, Ctr. Pure and Applied Math. U. Calif., Berkeley; mem. adv. panel chem. Nat. Sci. Found.; Randolph T. Major Disting. Lectr. U. Conn., 1992; mem. bd. sci. govs. Weizemann Inst. Sci., 1997—; Peter Smith lectr. Duke U., 1993, Arthur William Davidson lect. U. Kansas, 1992, Arthur Birch lect. Australian Nat. U., 1993, Richard C. Lord Meml. lectr. MIT, 1993, Steacie lectr. Nat. Rsch. Coun. Can., 1993, Centenary lectr. Royal Soc. Chemistry, 1994, Morris Loeb lectr. Harvard U., 1994, Jesse Boot Found. lectr., U. Nottingham, 1994, Frontiers in Chemistry lectr. Tex. A&M U., 1995, Bergman lectr. Weizmann Inst. Sci., 1995, faculty rsch. lectr. U. Calif., Berkeley, 1996, Raymond & Beverly Sackler lectr. Tel Aviv U., 1996; Priestley lectr. Pa. State U., 1997; Amy Mellon lectr. Purdue U., 1997; Rsch. frontiers chemistry lectr. U. Iowa, 1998, Moses Gomberg lectr. U. Mich., 1998, J and N Max T. Rogers, Mich. State U., 1998, Frontiers in Chemistry lectr., Wayne State U., 1998, Abbot lectr., U. N.D., 2000, John D. Roberts lectr., Calif. Tech. U., 2000, Willard lectr., U. Wis., 2000, Cliford lectr., U. Pitts., 2000, William Lloyd Evan lectr. Ohio State U., 2000, Jacob Bigeleisen lectr. Stony Brook U., 2001, Laird lectr. U. B.C., 2001; Alan S. Tetelman fellow Yale U., 2001, Regitze Vold Meml. lectr. U. Calif., San Diego, 2001, Sammet guest prof. Goëethe U., Frankfurt, 2001. Editor Molecular Physics, 1987-91; mem. bd. editors Chem. Physics, Chem. Physics Letters, Nmr: Basic Principles and Progress, Advances in Magnetic Resonance, Accounts Chemistry Research, Concepts in Magnetic Reson; adv. editor Oxford U. Press; contbr. articles to profl. jours.; patentee in field. Recipient Strait award North Calif. Spectroscopy Soc., Outstanding Achievement award U.S. Dept. of Energy, 1983, 87, 89, 97, 98, R & D 100 awards, 1987, 89, Disting. Teaching award U. Calif., E.O. Lawrence award, 1988, Pitts. Spectroscopy award, 1989, Wolf Prize for chemistry, 1991, Donald Noyce Undergrad. Teaching award U. Calif., 1992, Robert Foster Cherry award for Great Tchrs. Baylor U., Pres.'s Chair for undergrad. edn. U. Calif., 1993-97, Dickson prize Carnegie Mellon U., 2001; Guggenheim fellow, 1988, Christensen fellow St. Catherine's Coll., Oxford, 1990. Fellow Am. Phys. Soc. (chmn. divsn. chem. physics), Inst. Physics; mem. NAS, Am. Chem. Soc. (mem. exec. com. divsn. phys. chemistry, Signature award, Baekeland medal, Harrison Howe award 1991, Irving Langmuir award 1998, ACS Remsen award 2000, Dickson prize 2001), Royal Soc. Chemistry (Bourke lectr.), Internat. Soc. Magnetic Resonance (v.p., pres. 1993-96), Lawrence Hall Sci. Outreach Com. Office: U Calif Chemistry Dept D 64 Hildebrand Hill Berkeley CA 94720-0001

PING, CHARLES JACKSON, philosophy educator, retired university president; b. Phila., June 15, 1930; s. Cloudy J. and Mary M. (Marion) P.; m. Claire Oates, June 5, 1951; children: Andrew, Ann Shelton. BA, Rhodes Coll., 1951; B.D., Louisville Presbyn. Theol. Sem., 1954; PhD, Duke, 1961. Assoc. prof. philosophy Alma Coll., 1962-66; prof. philosophy Tusculum Coll., 1966-69, v.p., dean faculty, 1967-68, acting pres., 1968-69; provost Central Mich. U., Mt. Pleasant, 1969-75; pres. Ohio U., Athens, 1975-94, pres. emeritus, Trustee prof. philosophy and edn., 1994—, co.- dir. Manasseh Cutler Scholars Program, dir. Ping Inst. for Tchg. Humanities, 1994-99, dir. emeritus, 1999—. Bd. dirs. Wing Lung Bank Internat. Inst. for Bus. Devel., Hong Kong; trustee Louisville Presbyn. Theol. Sem., Muskingum Coll., Ohio; mem. adv. bd. Inst. Ednl. Mgmt. of Harvard U.; chair Commn. Planning for Future of Higher Edn., Kingdom of Swaziland; mem. Commn. on Higher Edn. Republic of Namibia. Author: Ohio University in Perspective, 1985, Meaningful Nonsense, 1966, also articles. Fulbright Sr. Rsch. scholar for So. Africa, 1995. Mem. Coun. on Internat. Ednl. Exch. (chair bd.), David C. Lam Inst. for East-West Studies (bd. dirs.), Coun. Internat. Exch. Scholars (bd. dirs., chair Africa com.). Office: Ohio U Office of Pres Emeritus Athens OH 45701 E-mail: ping@ohio.edu.

PINGREE, DIANNE, psychotherapist; b. Dallas; BFA magna cum laude, So. Meth. U., 1976, MLA, 1989; PhD in Sociology, Tex. Woman's U., 1994. Diplomate Am. Psychotherapy Assn.; lic. marriage and family therapy assoc., cert. family life educator. Found., editor, pub. Tex. Woman Mag., 1977-80; pres. Tex. Woman Inc., 1980-85; owner, pres. Dianne Pingree & Assoc., 1985-88; pub. cons. Tex. Elite Publications, Dallas, 1988-89; mediator Ctr. for Dispute Resolution Denton County, 1991; grad. tchng. assoc. Tex. Woman's U., 1990-92; postgrad. clin. intern SW Family Inst., Dallas, 1993-94; therapist J&L Human Sys. Devel., Dallas, 1994-95; psychotherapist Child and Family Svc. Inc., Austin, 1995-96; cons. Austin, 1996-98; dir. Liaison Assocs. Profl. Devel. Consultants, 1998—2001; psychotherapist, assoc. clin. staff mem. Austin Acad. for Individual and Relationship Therapy, 2001—03; psychotherapist Capital Area Mental Health Ctr., 2003—. Spkr. in field. Vol., vice chmn. mental health com. United Way Capital Area, 1998—99; vol., legal adv. Safeplace; mem. Leadership Austin, 2000—01. Recipient Matrix award Women in Comms., Women Helping Women award, Women's Ctr. Dallas, Dallas Press Club award. Mem.: Nat. Coun. on Family Rels., Tex. Assn. for Marriage and Family Therapy, Am. Assn. for Marriage and Family Therapy, Internat. Soc., Alpha Kappa Delta (pres. TWU chpt. 1992). Office: PO Box 160277 Austin TX 78716-0277

PING-ROBBINS, NANCY REGAN, musicologist, educator; b. Nashville, Dec. 19, 1939; d. Charles Augustus and Ruby Phyllis (Perdue) Regan; m. Robert Leroy Ping, June 19, 1959 (div. 1980); children: Robert Alan, Michael Regan, Bryan Edward; m. William Edward Robbins, Jr., Mar. 14, 1981. BMusic, Ind. U., 1964; MA, U. No. Colo., 1972; PhD, U. Colo., 1979. Organist Armed Forces Chapels, Frankfurt, Kaiserslautern, Germany, 1962-66; staff pianist u.S. Armed Forces Spl. Svcs. Theater, Frankfurt, 1963-65; music tchr. Fayetteville (Ind.) Pub. Schs., 1966-67, Stratton (Colo.) Pub. Schs., 1967-70; instr. piano, staff piano accompanist U. No. Colo., Greeley, 1970-72; instr. music history U. Colo., Boulder, 1974; instr., asst. prof. music U. N.C., Wilmington, 1974-79; assoc. prof. music, coord. music Shaw U., Raleigh, N.C., 1979-87; adj. prof. Atlantic Christian Coll., 1987-88, assoc. prof. part-time, 1987-90, 95—, full-time, 1990-95; dir. Atlantic C.C. Com. Arts Sch., 1987-88; pvt. instr. piano and flute, 1960—. Profl. harpsichord accompanist Internat. Inst. in Early Music, summer 1983; mem, pianist Chekker Duo, 1996—. Recs. include Early Popular Music on Piano/Harpsichord, 1984, En Blanc et Noir, 2001; author: The Piano Trio in the Twentieth Century, 1984, Scott Joplin: A Guide to Research, 1998; editor, compiler: The Music of Gustave Blessner, 1985; music reviewer News and Observer, Raleigh, 1981—, head music critic, 1989-95; contbr. articles to profl. jours. Sec. Bach Festival Com., Raleigh, 1984. John H. Edwards fellow Ind. U., 1961; U. Colo. grad fellow, 1972-74; Mellon Found. grantee, 1982; N.C. Arts Coun. grantee, 1985; NEH summer seminar fellow, 1984. Mem. Am. Musicol. Soc. (sec.-treas. chpt. 1981-83), Soc. for Ethnomusicology (chmn. regional chpt. 1983-84), Wilson Piano Tchrs. Assn. (pres. 1988-90, 95-98), Soc. Am. Music (formerly Sonneck Soc., program com. 1999), Alpha Lambda Delta, Pi Kappa Lambda, Sigma Alpha Iota.

PINGS, CORNELIUS JOHN, educational consultant, director; b. Conrad, Mont., Mar. 15, 1929; s. Cornelius John and Marjorie (O'Loughlin) P.; m. Marjorie Anna Cheney, June 25, 1960; children: John, Anne, Mary. BS, Calif. Inst. Tech., 1951, MS, 1952, PhD, 1955. Inst. chem. engring. Stanford U., 1955-56, asst. prof., 1956-59; assoc. prof. chem. engring. Calif. Inst. Tech., 1959-64, prof., 1964-81, exec. officer chem. engring., 1969-73, vice-provost, dean grad. studies, 1970-81; provost, sr. v.p. acad. affairs U. So. Calif., 1981-93; pres. Assn. Am. Univs., Washington, 1993-98. Mem., dir. Nat. Commn. on Rsch., 1978—80; mem. bd. mgmt. Coun. on Govtl. Rels., 1980—83; bd. dirs. Nations Funds, Edelbrock, Inc., L.A.; pres. Assn. Grad. Schs., 1977—78, Western Coll. Assn., 1988—90; mem. sci. engring. and pub. policy com. NAS, 1987—92, chmn., 1988—92; bd. dirs. Amervest Inc. Contbr. articles to tech. jours. Mem., chmn. bd. trustees Mayfield Sr. Sch. Bd., 1979-85; mem. Pasadena Redevel. Agy., 1968-81, chmn., 1974-81; bd. dirs. Huntington Meml. Hosp., Pasadena, 1986-92; chmn. L.A. Ctrl. City Assn., 1992. Recipient Arthur Nobel medal, City of Pasadena, 1981, Disting. Alumni award Calif. Inst. Tech., 1989, Presdl. medallion U. So. Calif., 1993. Fellow AIChE, Am. Acad. Arts and Scis.; mem. NAE, Calif. Club, Twilight Club, Bohemian Club, Cosmos Club, Valley Hunt Club. Roman Catholic. Office: 480 S Orange Grove Blvd # 6 Pasadena CA 91105-1736 E-mail: cjpings@usc.edu.

PINHEIRO, AILEEN FOLSON, secondary education educator; b. Park River, N.D., Oct. 24, 1921; d. Morris Bernard and Clara Christine (Olson) Folson; m. Eugene Arthur Pinheiro, Sept. 9, 1948. BA, Concordia Coll., 1942; MA, Whittier (Calif.) Coll., 1963. Cert. secondary edn. tchr. Tchr. Kiester (Minn.) High Sch., 1942-44, Wasco (Calif.) Jr. High Sch., 1944-45, Taylors Falls (Minn.) High Sch., 1945-47, Baldwin Park (Calif.) Unified Sch. Dist., 1947-52, 53-73, ret., 1973. Author: (handbook) The Heritage of Baldwin Park, 1981, (pamphlets) The Heritage of Baldwin Park, 1982-88. Volunteer mus. dir. City of Baldwin Park, 1983—. Recipient Older Am. Recognition award L.A. County Bd. Suprs., 1991, Woman of Yr. award San Gabriel Valley District Women's Club, 1997. Mem. AAUW (pres. 1967-69), Baldwin Park Hist. Soc. (bd. dirs. 1981-91, Trophy 1983, chmn. 1985-94), Baldwin Park C. of C. (Golden Heritage award 1983, Citizen of Yr. award 1993), Baldwin Park Women's Club (program chmn. 1990-91, treas. 1991-92, internat. chmn. 1989-96, publicity chmn. 1992-96, Club Woman of Yr. award 1997). Presbyterian. Avocations: arts and crafts, golf, bridge, travel. Home: 13009 Amar Rd Baldwin Park CA 91706-5702 Office: Baldwin Park Mus 4061 Sterling Way Baldwin Park CA 91706-4249

PINHEY, FRANCES LOUISE, retired physical education educator; b. Canton, Ohio, Apr. 18, 1927; d. Frederick Otto and Rose June (Wolf) Sengleitner; m. Donald Charles Pinhey, June 13, 1952; children: Val Don, Shauna Rae, Kaye Dorrell, Lon Pernell. BA, Muskingum Coll., 1949; MS, U. R.I., 1977; postgrad., Ind. U., 1958. Cert. tchr., Ohio. Tchr. Canton Pub. Schs., 1949-50; instr. Muskingum Coll., New Concord, Ohio, 1950-52; tchr. New Concord Pub. Schs., 1950-52, Barberton (Ohio) High Sch., 1952-53, Ottawa (Ont., Can.) Pub. Schs., 1954-57, Ottawa YMCA, 1954-57; instr. Dakota Wesleyan U., Mitchell, S.D., 1959-63, Wilmington (Ohio) Coll., 1963-67; tchr. New London (Conn.) Pub. Schs., 1967-68; asst. prof. phys. edn., coach Mitchell Coll., New London, 1968-96; asst. instr. badminton, tennis Coast Guard Acad., 1996-99; asst. coach mens baseball USCG Acad., New London, Conn., 1999; ret., 1999. Chair, mem. Conn. Sports Officiating Rating Bd., 1968-78. Nat. ofcl. women's volleyball & basketball, 1958-80; pres. PTA, Wilmington, 1967, PTA mem., New London, Conn., 1968-77; vol. New London Recreation Dept., 1986, Little League, 1970-75; vol. condr. CBA Badminton Tournaments. Inducted into Mitchell Coll. Hall of Fame, 1993. Mem. AAHPERD, Nat. Jr. Coll. Field Hockey Coaches Assn. (pres. 1991—), Nat. Jr. Coll. Men's Tennis Assn. (pres. 1978-91), U.S. Badminton Assn., Nat. Assn. Sport and Phys. Edn., Nat. Dance Assn., Nat. Dance-Exercise Instrs. Tng. Assn., Nat. Jr. Coll. Athletic Assn. (chmn. New Eng. region XXI field hockey com. 1975-89, women's field hockey Coach of Yr. region XXI 1975, 78-84, 90, nat. championships and Nat. Coach of Yr. 1979, 81, 83, 84, 90, Men's Tennis Coach of Yr. Region XXI 1983, 87, 89, 90). Avocations: badminton (ranked player, singles and doubles Conn. Badminton Assn. Top 10, 1981, 83, 84, 85, 86 and 87), tennis, gardening, dance. Home: 43 Bellevue Pl New London CT 06320-4701

PINKAVA, DONALD JOHN, botany educator, researcher; b. Cleve., Aug. 29, 1933; s. Yaroslav Joseph and Agnes (Stovicek) P.; m. Mary Jane Klements, May 14, 1976; 1 child, Michelle Marie. BS, Ohio State U., 1955, MS, 1961, PhD, 1964. Tchr. sci. Solon (Ohio) High Sch., 1955-60; instr. Ohio State U., Lakewood, 1963; asst. to assoc. prof. plant biology Ariz. State U., Tempe, 1964—, prof., 1978—, prof. emeritus, 2000—, dir. herbarium, 1964—2000. Team leader Ariz. recovery team for endangered and threatened plants U.S. Fish and Wildlife Svc. Region II, Albuquerque, 1983-2000. Author: (with E. Lehto) A Vegetative Key to Cultivated Woody Plants of Salt River Valley, Arizona, 1970; editor (with H.S. Gentry): Symposium on Agaves, Desert Bot. Garden, Phoenix, 1985; mem. editorial bd. Vascular Plants of Ariz. Manual; contbr. articles to sci. jours. Trustee Desert Bot. Garden, 1978-85. Fellow NSF, 1961-63, DuPont fellow Ohio State U., 1957, Systematic Inst. at Smithsonian Instn., 1968. Fellow AAAS, Ariz.-Nev. Acad. Sci. (co-editor jour. 1992-2000), Cactus & Succulent Soc. Am.; mem. Sigma Xi (pres., sec. Ariz. State U. chpt. 1975-80). Achievements include research in systematics of Cactaceae and Compositae, in chromosome studies of vascular plants, in floristics of Arizona and Mexico. Home: 2704 S Estrella Cir Mesa AZ 85202-7203 Office: Ariz State U Dept Plant Biology Tempe AZ 85287-1601

PINNEY, THOMAS CLIVE, retired English language educator; b. Ottawa, Kans., Apr. 23, 1932; s. John James and Lorene Maude (Owen) P.; m. Sherrill Marie Ohman, Sept. 1, 1956; children— Anne, Jane, Sarah. BA, Beloit Coll., Wis., 1954; PhD, Yale U., New Haven, 1960. Instr. Hamilton Coll., Clinton, N.Y., 1957-61; instr. English Yale U., New Haven, 1961-62; asst. prof. to prof., chmn. dept. English Pomona Coll., Claremont, Calif., 1962-97; ret., 1997. Editor: Essays of George Eliot, 1963, Selected Writings of Thomas Babington Macaulay, 1972, Letters of Macaulay, 1974-81, Kipling's India, 1986, A History of Wine in America, 1989, Kipling's Something of Myself, 1990, Letters of Rudyard Kipling, 1990, The Vineyards and Wine Cellars of California, 1994, The Wine of Santa Cruz Island, 1994. Guggenheim fellow, 1966, 84,Recipient Disting. Svc. citation Beloit Coll., 1984; fellow NEH, 1980; grantee Am. Coun. Learned Socs., 1974, 84, Am. Philos. Soc., 1968, 82, 94. Mem. MLA, Elizabethan Club (New Haven), Zamorano Club (L.A.), Phi Beta Kappa. Home: 228 W Harrison Ave Claremont CA 91711-4323 Office: Pomona Coll Dept English Claremont CA 91711

PINSKER, TILLENE GILLER, retired special education administrator; b. Omaha, Oct. 29, 1936; d. Hyman Herman and Rebecca (Winokur) Giller; m. Walter Pinsker, June 15, 1958; children: Neil, Andrew, Susann. BA, Roosevelt U., 1958; MS, Post U., 1977, PD, 1981. Cert. tchr., adminstr., supr., spl. edn. tchr., N.Y., tchr., Calif., Ill. Tchr. Massapequa (N.Y.) Sch. Dist., 1958-60, Westminster (Calif.) Sch. Dist., 1960-62; resource tchr. West Islip (N.Y.) Sch. Dist., 1975-77; coord. infant svcs. Boces 111, Deer Park, N.Y., 1977-83; dir. direction ctr. SCDC, Smithtown, N.Y., 1983-85; dir. early intervention program Adults and Children with Learning Devel. Disabilities, Bay Shore, N.Y., 1985—; ret. Lectr. C.W. Post Coll., Westbury, N.Y., Dowling Coll., Oakdale, N.Y.; mem. various panels in field; cons. Camp NYABIC, ACLD Kramer Learning Ctr., 1999; spkr. in field. Mem. Suffolk Network of Adolescent Pregnancy; bd. dirs. Office Mental Retardation; mem. subcom. Devel. Dist.; v.p. Good Samaritan Hosp. Aux., West Islip; active polit. orgns. Named Woman of Yr., NOW, 1975-76, Co-Humanitarian of Yr., Adults and Children with Learning and Devel. Disabilities, 1994. Avocations: tennis, golf. Address: 4448 James Estate Ln Lake Worth FL 33467-8116 Office: ACLD Kramer Learning Ctr 1428 5th Ave Bay Shore NY 11706-4147

PINSON, ARTIE FRANCES, retired elementary school educator; b. Rusk, Tex., June 20, 1933; d. Tom and Minerva (McDuff) Neeley; m. Robert H. Pinson, Dec. 14, 1963 (div. Nov. 1967); 1 child, Deidre R. BA magna cum laude, Tex. Coll., 1953; postgrad., U. Tex., 1956, North Tex. U., 1958, 63, New Eng. Conservatory, 1955, 57, 59, 62, Tex. So. U., 1971-72; MEd, U. Houston, 1970. Music tchr. Bullock High Sch., LaRue, Tex., 1953-59; music tchr., 9th grade English tchr. Story High Sch., Palestine, Tex., 1959-64; 6th grade tchr. Turner Elem. Sch., Houston, 1964-66; 3d, 5th and 6th grade tchr. Kay Elem. Sch., Houston, 1966-70; 6th grade tchr. Pilgrim Elem. Sch., Houston, 1970-75; 3d to 6th grade gifted and talented math. tchr. Pleasantville Elem. Sch., Houston, 1975-79; kindergarten to 5th grade computer/math. tchr. Betsy Ross Elem. Sch., Houston, 1979—2003. Instnl. coord.; lead tchr. math./sci. program Shell/Houston Ind. Sch. Dist., 1986-87, Say "Yes" program, 1988-89; math. tchr. summer potpourri St. Francis Xavier Cath. Ch., 1991; math. tchr. sci. and engring. awareness and coll. prep. program Tex. So. U., 1993-2003; participant Project Sail math. curriculum devel., Prairie View U., 1997-98, 99; presenter confs. in field; condr. tchr. tng. workshops.= Author computer software in field; contbr. articles to mags. Musician New Hope Bapt. Ch., Houston, 1991—. Sunday sch. tchr.; pianist Buckner Bapt. Haven Nursing Home, Houston, 1990-91, inspirational spkr.; mem. N.E. Concerned Citizens Civic League. Recipient Excellence in Math. Teaching award Exxon Corp., 1990. Mem. Assn. African Am. Math. Educators (Salute to Math. Tchrs. award 1991, treas. 1991-93, sec. 1993-95), Nat. Coun. Tchrs. Math., Tex. Coun. Tchrs. Math. (Excellence in Math. Tchg. award 1988), Houston Coun. Tchrs. of Math. (Excellence in Math. Tchg. award 1993), Heoines of Jericho, Palestine Negro Bus. and Profl. Women (charter mem.). Avocations: needlework, number puzzles, piano, photography, gardening. Home: 5524 Makeig St Houston TX 77026-4021 Office: Betsy Ross Elem Sch 2819 Bay St Houston TX 77026-3203 E-mail: artpin@msn.com.

PINTO, ROSALIND, retired educator, civic volunteer; b. NYC; d. Barney and Jenny Abrams; m. Jesse E. Pinto (dec.); children: Francine, Jerry, Evelyn. BA in Polit. Sci. cum laude, Hunter Coll.; MA in Polit. Sci., History, Columbia U.; postgrad., Queens Coll., LaGuardia C.C. Lic. social studies tchr. jr. HS, NY, per diem lifetime substitute; cert. secondary sch. social studies grades 7-12, NY. Substitute tchr., 1966-69, 90, 91—; tchr. social studies I.S. 126Q, LI, NY, 1969-88, Jr. HS 217 Briarwood, NYC, 1988-89; ret., 1989; part-time cluster tchr. social studies and communication arts Pub. Sch. 140, Bronx, NY, 1990-92; substitute tchr. I.S. 227Q, 1992-93. Participant seminars and workshops. Author curriculum materials; contbr. study guide for regent's competency test, 1990; contbr. poems to anthologies, Nat. Libr. Poetry including Tears of Fire, 1994, Dance on the Horizon, 1994, Outstanding Poets of 1994, Best Poems of 1995, Seasons to Come, 1995, The Voice Within, 1996, Best Poems of 1996, Best Poems of 1997, 98; recorded poem for The Sound of Poetry, Nat. Libr. Poetry, 1992, 98 (Editor's Choice award 1993-94, 96, 2001), recorded poem for Sound of Poetry, 2001, American at the Millenium: The Best Poems and Poets of the 20th Century, Poetry Elite, 2001; contbr. poems on Internet, 2001, 02; 2 poems and articles in 112th Police Precinct Newsletter, 2001, poem and article in Newsletter, 2002, contr. poem to Noble House Poetry Divsn., London, 2003. Enrollment asst. Insight Heart Team, 1989; vol. receptionist Whitney Mus., N.Y.C.; mem. com. on pub. transp. Cmty. Bd. 6, Queens, 1990—96, mem. com. on history, 1990—, chmn. beautification com., 1992—, mem. com. on planning and zoning, 1996—, mem. com. on environ. sanitation, 1999—; mem. Forest Hills Action League, 1999; advocate Census 2000 participation; active Gt. Smokies Song Chase Warren-Wilson Coll., NC, 1992; mem. Queens Hist. Soc., Forest Hills Van Ct. Homeowners Assn.; bd. dirs. Ctrl. Queens Hist. Soc.; past mem.. Rego Park Coalition Against Crime; mem. Forest Hills Civic Assn., 1996—97; vol. local polit. campaigns. Recipient Cert. Appreciation for participation, Dept. Probate Cmty. Svc. Project, 1993, award for participation in Make a Difference Day, 1994—95, award for projects, Beautification Com., 1995, Rosemary Gunning award, Queens Borough Pres. for Women's History month, 2000, Editor's Choice award, Best Poems and Poets of 2001, 2002, Poet of Merit award, Poetry Conv., 2002, 2003, Cert. Appreciation for joining graffiti cleanup, 112th Precinct Cmty. Coun., 2002—03, Cert. of Appreciation for help in Night Out Against Crime, 2002—03, 2003. Fellow Mcpl. Art Soc. (hon. mention design 2000 award); mem. NAFE, Internat. Soc. Poets (life mem. adv. panel, Internat. Poet of Merit award 1993, 2000, Editor's Choice award 2001), NY Insight Alumni Assn., Columbia U. Grad. Sch. Arts and Scis. Alumni Assn., Hunter Coll. Alumni Assn., Robert F. Kennedy Dem. Assn. (bd. dir.), Ctr. for Sci. in the Pub. Interest. Avocations: poetry, reading, long distance walking, art shows, plays.

PIONK, RICHARD CLETUS, artist, educator; b. Minn., Apr. 26, 1936; s. Franz E. Spielmann and Esther (Dufrane) Pionk. Cert. in fine arts painting, Art Students League, 1983. Tchr. Art Students League, N.Y.C., 1991—. Mem. bd. control Art Students League, 1983-90. Exhibited in one-man shows Moran Gallery, Tulsa, 1985, Connoisseur Gallery, Rhinebeck, N.Y., 1987, 88, 89, 90, Bklyn. Pub. Libr.; exhibited in group shows Queens Mus., N.Y.C., 1982, Hermitage Found., Norfolk, Va., 1985, Monmouth Mus., Lincroft, N.J., 1985, La Societe des Pastellistes de France, Lille, 1987, Canton (Ohio) Art Inst., 1987, Friends Art Mus., Naples, Fla., 1987, Mel Vin Gallery Southern Coll., Lakeland, Fla., 1987, Wind Borne Gallery, Southport, Conn., 1987, 89, Gregory Gallery, Darien, Conn., 1990, 91, 92, 93, 94, 95, 96, Geary Gallery, Darien, 1997, 98, 99, 2000, 01, 02, The Food Show at Grand Cen. Art Gallery, N.Y.C., 1989, Quincy (Ill.) Art Club, 1989, 90, Jordane Art Gallery, Ft. Myers, Fla., 1990, Pastel Soc., N.Y.C., 1991, Allied Artists, N.Y.C., 1991, Harman-Meek Gallery, Naples, 1992, Butler Inst. Art, 2000, 2003. Recipient Salzman award, 1999, 2001, Bernhardt Gold medal for pastel, 2002, numerous awards, including medal, Artist's Fellowship, 2002, medal, The Pastel Soc., 2002, 2003. Mem. Pastel Soc. Am. (1st v.p. 1978-91, exhbn. chmn. 1978—, master pastellist, Hall of Fame 1997), Allied Artists Am. (bd. dirs. 1986-91, asst. corr. sec. 1986—), Audubon Artists (juror 1989—), Artists Fellowship Inc. (bd. dirs. 1988—), Nat. Arts Club, Salmagundi Club (mem. curators com., chmn. art com. 1981—, pres. 1994—), Dutch Treat Club. Roman Catholic. Avocations: collecting 17th, 18th, and 19th century paintings and drawings. Home: 1349 Lexington Ave Apt 8B New York NY 10128-1511 Office: Studio 611 41 Union Sq W New York NY 10003-3208

PIOTROWSKI, SANDRA A. elementary education educator; b. Buffalo, May 8, 1949; d. Edward and Loretta (Kasprzyk) Grabowski; m. Daniel J. Piotrowski, June 1, 1970; 1 child, Mark. BS, Rosary Hill Coll., Buffalo, 1971; postgrad., U. North Fla. Cert. tchr., Fla. Elem. tchr. Sacred Heart Sch., Jacksonville, Fla., Spurlin Sch., Jacksonville, St. Paul's Sch., Jacksonville. Mem. ASCD, Fla. Assn. Supervision and Curriculum Devel. Home: 4625 Herta Rd Jacksonville FL 32210-6949

PIPER, ADRIAN MARGARET SMITH, philosopher, artist, educator; b. N.Y.C., Sept. 20, 1948; d. Daniel Robert and Olive Xavier (Smith) P.; m. Jeffrey Ernest Evans, June 27, 1982 (div. 1987). AA, Sch. Visual Arts, 1969; BA in Philosophy, CCNY, 1974; MA, Harvard U., 1977, PhD, 1981; student, U. Heidelberg, Germany, 1977-78; LHD (hon.), Calif. Inst. Arts, 1992, Mass. Coll. Art, 1994. Asst. prof. U. Mich., Ann Arbor, 1979-86; Mellon rsch. fellow Stanford (Calif.) U., 1982-84; assoc. prof. Georgetown U., Washington, 1986-88, U. Calif., San Diego, 1988; prof. philosophy Wellesley (Mass.) Coll., 1990—. Disting. scholar Getty Rsch. Inst., 1998—; speaker, lectr. on both philosophy and art. Artist: one-woman exhbns. include N.Y. Cultural Ctr., N.Y.C., 1971, Montclair (N.J.) State Coll., 1976, Wadsworth Atheneum, Hartford, Conn., 1980, Nexus COntemporary Art Ctr., Atlanta, 1987, The Alternative Mus., N.Y.C., 1987, Goldie Paley Gallery, Phila., 1989, Power Plant Gallery, Toronto, 1990, Lowe Art Mus., Coral Gables, Fla., 1990-91, Santa Monica (Calif.) Mus. Contemporary Art, 1991, John Weber Gallery, N.Y.C., 1989, 90, 91, 92, Whitney Mus. Am. Art, N.Y.C., 1990, Hirschorn Mus., Washington, 1991, Ikon Gallery, Birmingham, Eng., 1991, Cornerhouse, Manchester, Eng., 1992, Cartwright Hall, Bradford, Eng., 1992, Kunstverein, Munich, Germany, 1992, Indpls. Ctr. Contemporary Art, 1992, Manasterio de Santa Clara, Moguer, Spain, 1992, Grey Art Gallery, N.Y.C., 1992, Paula Cooper Art Galler, 1992, 94; group exhbns. include Paula Cooper Gallery, 1969, Dwan Gallery, N.Y.C., 1969, 70, Seattle Art Mus., 1969, Stadtisches Mus., Leverkusen, Germany, 1969, Kunsthalle Berne, Berne, Switzerland, 1969, N.Y. Cultural Ctr., 1970, Allen Mus., Oberlin, Ohio, 1970, Mus. Modern Art, N.Y.C., 1970, 88, 91, Musee d'Art Moderne, Paris, 1971, 77, 89, Inhibodress Gallery, New South Wales, Australia, 1972, Calif. Inst. Arts, Valencia, 1973, Samuel S. Fleischer Art Meml., Phila., 1974, Mus. Contemporary Art, Chgo., 1975, Newberger Mus., Purchase, N.Y., 1978, Mass. Coll. Art, Boston, 1979, Artemesia Gallery, Chgo., 1979, A.I.R. Gallery, N.Y.C., 1980, Inst. Contemporary Arts, London, 1980, The New Mus., N.Y.C., 1981, 83, 85, Kenkeleba Gallery, N.Y.C., 1983, The Studio Mus. Harlem, N.Y.C., 1985, 89, Mus. Moderner Kunst, Vienna, Austria, 1985, Intar Gallery, N.Y.C., 1988, Whitney Mus. Downtown, N.Y.C., 1988, Art Gallery Ont., Toronto, 1988, Long Beach (Calif.) Art Mus., 1989, Simon Watson Gallery, N.Y.C., 1990, Feigen Gallery, Chgo., 1990, Barbara Krakow Gallery, Boston, 1990, Milw. Art Mus., 1990, Contemporary Arts Ctr., Houston, 1991, John Weber Gallery, 1991, Anne Plumb Gallery, N.Y.C., 1991, Hirschorn Mus., 1991, The Albuquerque Mus. Art, 1991, The Toledo Mus. Art, 1991, Denver Art Mus., Fukui Fine Arts Mus., Fukyui-ken, Japan, 1992-93, N.J. State Mus., Trenton, 1992-93, Philippe Staib Gallery, N.Y.C., 1992, New Loom House, London, 1992, Espace-Lyonnais D'Art Contemporain, Lyon, France, 1993, Am. Acad. Inst. Arts and Letters, N.Y.C., 1993; permanent collections include Met. Mus. Art, Whitney Mus., L.A. Mus. Contemporary Art, San Francisco Mus. Modern Art, The Bklyn. Mus., Denver Art Mus., Kunstmuseum Berne, Musee d'Art Moderne, The Mus. Contemporary Art, Chgo., The Wadsworth Atheneum, Met. Mus. Art; art performances include RISD, 1973, The Whitney Mus. Am. Art, 1975, Kurfurstendamm, Berlin, 1977, Hauptstrasse, Heidelberg, Germany, 1978, Allen Meml. Mus., Oberlin, Ohio, 1980, Contemporary Art Inst. Detroit, 1980, San Francisco Art Inst., 1985, Calif. Inst. Art, 1984, The Studio Mus. Harlem, 1988; performances on video, 1987—; contbr. articles to profl. jours. Recipient N.Y. State Coun. on Arts award, 1989, Visual Arts award, 1990, Skowhegan medal for sculptural installation, 1995, Dance Theatre Workshop award for New Genres, 2000; NEH Travel fellow, 1979, NEA Visual Artists' fellow, 1979, 82, Andrew Mellon Postdoctoral fellow, 1982-84, Woodrow Wilson Internat. Scholars fellow, 1988-89, Guggenheim Meml. fellow, 1989, non-resident fellow N.Y. Inst. for Humanities, NYU, 1996—; NEA Artists Forums grantee, 1987; rsch. fellowship NEH, 1998, Getty Rsch. Inst. Disting. scholarship, 1998—, Internat. Forschungszentrum Kulturwissenschaften fellow Vienna. Mem. AAUP, Am. Philos. Assn. (mem. ea. divsn.), Am. Soc. Polit. and Legal Philosophy, N.Am. Kant. Soc. Avocations: medieval and renaissance music, fiction, poetry, yoga, German. Office: Wellesley Coll 106 Central St Wellesley MA 02481-8268

PIPER, CHRISTINE MARIE, elementary education educator; b. Pitts., Nov. 11, 1953; d. Anthony and Eleanor Lilian Auretto; 1 child, Luke. BA, So. Calif. Coll., 1983; MA, Calif. State U., Long Beach, 1989. Cert. tchr., Calif., Wash. K-1st grade tchr. Marantha Acad., Costa Mesa, Calif., 1977-81, 5th grade tchr., 1984-85; tchr. gifted program Vancouver (Wash.)/Cornerstone Sch., 1985-86; 1st grade Cambodian bilingual tchr. Long Beach Unified Sch. Dist., 1986-92; 2d grade tchr. Battleground (Wash.) Sch. Dist., 1992-93; 1st grade tchr. Vancouver Sch. Dist., 1993-94, reading specialist, 1994-2000; 1st grade tchr. Hockinson Sch. Dist., 2000—. Hanake Edn. scholar, 1982. Mem. ASCD, Internat. Reading Assn., Phi Delta Kappa. Avocations: reading, writing, fine arts, camping, biking. Office: Hockinson Hts Primary Sch 2000 164th St Brush Prairie WA 98606

PIPER, CLAUDIA ROSEMARY, assistant principal; b. Washington, Nov. 17, 1958; d. Thomas Irving Sr. and Mildred (McCoy) P. BA in Spl. Edn., Math. Edn., Providence Coll., 1981; postgrad., James Madison U., 1982-83; MEd, U. New. Orleans, 1993. Tchr. spl. edn. Grafton Sch., Berryville, Va., 1981-83, PARC Spl. Sch., Kenner, La., 1983-86, Waggaman (La.) Spl. Sch., 1989-93, disciplinarian, 1989-93; dean spl. svcs. John H. Martyn H.S., Jefferson, La., 1993—. Spl. edn. chmn. Waggaman Spl. Sch., 1986—, substance abuse prevention bd. chmn., 1988—. Mem. chapel choir Mission Circle, editor monthly newsletter. Mem. Assn. Black Psychologists (historian 1991—, program dir. Teen Pregnancy Prevention Program 1991—), Assn. Supervision and Curriculum Devel. Democrat. Baptist. Home: 2840 27th St NE Washington DC 20018-2522 Office: Haynes Mid Sch 1416 Metairie Rd Metairie LA 70005-3921

PIPER, FREDESSA MARY, school system administrator; b. Monroe, La., June 19, 1945; d. Floyd Preston and Zona Mary (Jones) P.; m. Robert John Parks, Mar. 20, 1969 (div. 1980); m. Zebedee Taylor Jr., Dec. 1996. BS, Ill. State U., 1964; MEd with distinction, DePaul U., 1972; EdD, Loyola U., Chgo., 1984. Cert. tchr., gen. adminstr., sch. supt., Ill. Tchr. secondary schs. Chgo. Pub. Schs., 1964-73, staff asst., 1974-76, coord., 1977-83, tchr., coord., 1984-87; asst. supt. Ednl. Svc. Region Cook County, Chgo., 1987-95. Project coord. Malcolm X City Coll., Chgo., 1973-74; coord. Athletes for Better Edn., Chgo., 1975-77; cons. Community Reading is Rewarding Program, Chgo., 1989—; author radio scripts, speeches. Project coord. Local Ward Back to Sch. Fun-Fest, Chgo., 1983—; program coord. Pre-Thanksgiving Day Srs. Dinner, Chgo., 1983—; asst. to chmn. Re-election Campaign, Chgo., 1986, 88; promotional dir. Unity in Community Boat Cruise, Chgo., 1987—. Mem. ASCD, Nat. Alliance Black Sch. Educators, Am. Assn. Sch. Adminstrs., Phi Delta Kappa, Delta Epsilon Sigma. Democrat. Baptist. Avocations: cooking, writing, computers, public speaking.

PIPER, MARGARITA SHERERTZ, retired school administrator; b. Petersburg, Va., Dec. 20, 1926; d. Guy Lucas and Olga Doan (Akers) Sherertz; m. Glenn Clair Piper, Feb. 3, 1950; children: Mark Stephen, Susan Leslie Piper Weathersbee. BA in Edn., Mary Washington Coll U. Va., Fredericksburg, 1948; MEd, U. Va., 1973, EdS, 1976. Svc. rep. C&P Telephone, Washington, 1948-55, adminstrv. asst., 1955-56, svc. supr., 1956-62; tchr. Culpeper (Va.) County Pub. Schs., 1970-75, reading lab dir., 1975-80; asst. prin. Rappahannock (Va.) County Pub. Schs., 1980-81, prin., 1981-88, dir. pupil pers., spl. programs, 1988-95; ret., 1995. Chair PD 9 regional transition adv. bd. Culpeper, Fauquier, Madison, Orange and Rappahannock Counties, Va., 1991-94; vice chair Family Assessment and Planning Team, Washington, 1992-95. Recipient Va. Gov. Schs. Commendation cert. Commonwealth of Va., 1989-93. Mem. NEA, Va. Edn. Assn., Va. Coun. Adminstrs. Spl. Edn., Va. Assn. Edn. for Gifted, Rappahannock Edn. Assn. Democrat. Methodist. Avocations: creative writing, music, walking, crosstitch, knitting.

PIPER, SUSIE E. elementary and secondary school educator, counselor, writer; AA, St. Phillips Jr. Coll., 1942; BS, Samuel Houston, 1946; M Edn., Prairie View A&M, 1956. Tchr. Rockdale I.S.D, Tex.; tchr. middle/high sch., 1944—84. Recipient Role Model Award, 2001, Tchr. Decade, 2002. Home: 5904 Coolbrook Dr Austin TX 78724

PIPERATO, DAVID F. principal; BS in Bus. Edn., Bloomsburg U. Pa., 1984; MEd in Computers in Edn., Allentown Coll. St. Francis De Sales, 1996; prin. cert. in ednl. adminstrn., Pa. State U., 1997; postgrad., Lehigh U. Bus. tchr. Palisades Jr./Sr. H.S., Kintnersville, Pa., 1984—86, Northampton (Pa.) Area Sr. H.S., 1986—88; bus. and tech. tchr. Bethlehem Area Sch. Dist., 1990—97; bus. intern J&J Flock, Inc., Easton, Pa., 1995; bus. house coord. Liberty H.S., Bethlehem, Pa., 1995—97; asst. prin. Palisades H.S., Kintnersville, Pa., 1997—2000, prin., 2000—. Presenter in field. Contbr. articles to profl. publs. Coll. and h.s. basketball coach. Mem.: Palisades Youth Aid Panel, Palisades Youth/Adult Comty. Partnerships, Pa. Assn. Secondary Sch. Prins., Nat. Assn. Secondary Sch. Prins.*

PIPES, RICHARD, historian, educator; b. Cieszyn, Poland, July 11, 1923; came to U.S., 1940, naturalized, 1943; s. Mark and Sophia (Haskelberg) P.; m. Irene Eugenia Roth, Sept. 1, 1946; children— Daniel, Steven. Student, Muskingum (Ohio) Coll., 1940-43; AB, Cornell U., 1945; PhD, Harvard U., 1950; LLD (hon.), Muskingum Coll., 1988; LHD (hon.), Adelphi U., 1991; Doctor honoris causa, U. Silesia, Poland, 1994. Mem. faculty Harvard U., 1950—, prof. history, 1958-75, Frank B. Baird Jr. prof. history, 1975-96, Baird prof. emeritus, 1996-98, Baird Rsch. Prof., 1998-2001, Baird prof. emeritus, 2001—. Assoc. dir. Russian Rsch. Ctr., 1962-64, dir., 1968-73; sr. cons. Stanford Research Inst., 1973-78; expert Russian Constl. Ct., 1992; dir. East European and Soviet affairs NSC, 1981-82. Author: Formation of the Soviet Union, rev. edit., 1964, Karamzin's Memoir on Ancient and Modern Russia, 1959, Social Democracy and the St. Petersburg Labor Movement, 1963, Europe Since 1815, 1970, Struve: Liberal on the Left, 1870-1905, 1970, Russia Under the Old Regime, 1974, Struve: Liberal on the Right, 1905-1944, 1980, U.S.-Soviet Relations in the Era of Detente, 1981, Survival Is Not Enough, 1984, Russia Observed, 1989, The Russian Revolution, 1990, Communism: The Vanished Specter, 1993, Russia Under the Bolshevik Regime, 1994, A Concise History of the Russian Revolution, 1995, Three "Whys" of the Russian Revolution, 1996, Property and Freedom, 1999, Communism: A History, 2001, The Degaev Affair: Terror and Treason in Tsarist Russia, 2003; editor: Russian Intelligentsia, 1961; (with John Fine) Of the Russe Commonwealth (Giles Fletcher), 1966, Revolutionary Russia, 1968, Collected Works in Fifteen Volumes (P.B. Struve), 1970, Soviet Strategy in Europe, 1976, The Unknown Lenin, 1996; mem. editl. bd. Strategic Rev., Orbis, Comparative Strategy, Jour. Strategic Studies, Internat. Jour. Intelligence and Counterintelligence, Continuity, Nuova Storia Contemporanea. Mem. exec. com. Com. on Present Danger, 1977-92; chmn. Govt. Team B to Rev. Intelligence Estimates, 1976; mem. Reagan transition team Dept. State, 1980. Served with USAAF, 1943-46. Guggenheim fellow, 1956, 65, Walter Cabot Channing fellow Harvard U., 1990-91; fellow Am. Coun. Learned Socs., 1965; fellow Ctr. for Advanced Study in Behavioral Scis., Stanford, Calif., 1969-70; lectr. Spring lecture Norwegian Nobel Peace Inst., Oslo, 1993; recipient George Louis Beer prize Am. Historical Assn., 1955, Comdr.'s Cross of Merit, Republic of Poland, 1996; hon. consul Republic of Ga., 1997—, hon. citizen, 1997—. Fellow Am. Acad. Arts and Scis.; mem. Coun. Fgn. Rels., Polish Acad. (fgn. mem.). Home: 17 Berkeley St Cambridge MA 02138-3409 E-mail: rpipes23@aol.com.

PIPPENGER, WILMA JEAN, secondary school educator, principal; b. Benton, Tenn., Sept. 5, 1940; d. Albert T. Cochran and Nellie A. (Watson) Beckler; m. Johnny Hoyt Pippenger Jr., June 2, 1969; 1 child, John Hoyt III. BS, Tenn. Technol. U., 1962; MS, Tusculum Coll., 1997; ednl. specialists degree, Lincoln Meml. U., 1998. Cert. tchr. Tenn. Tchr. Polk County Bd. Edn., Benton, 1962-63, 65—, prin. Linsdale, Tenn., 1963-65. Mem. NEA, Tenn. Edn. Assn., Polk County Edn. Assn. (treas. 1967-68, exec. com. 1987-88, 91-92), East Tenn. Edn. Assn., Beta Sigma Phi, Delta Kappa Gamma (v.p.). Methodist. Avocations: photography, working with young people. Home: PO Box 307 Baker Bridge Rd Benton TN 37307 Office: Polk County High Sch PO Box 188 Benton TN 37307-0188

PIPPIN, JAMES ADRIAN, JR., middle school educator; b. Rockingham, N.C., Aug. 6, 1954; s. James A. Sr. and Essie Juanita (Rorie) P. BS, Appalachian State U., 1976; MEd, Columbus Coll., 1982. Tchr. Eddy Jr. H.S., Columbus, Ga., 1976-89; dir. N.C. Agrl. Extension Svc., Penn 4-H Ctr., Reidsville, 1980-89, Millstone 4-H Camp, Ellerbe, N.C., 1993; tchr. Arnold Mid. Sch., Columbus, Ga., 1989-99, Rockingham (N.C.) Jr. High Sch., 1999—. Mem. multicultural curriculum com., sick leave bank com., textbook adoption com. and tech. com. MCSD; tchg. program participant Found. Internat. Edn., Inverness, Scotland, 1986, Dunedin, New Zealand, 1989; curriculum devel. program participant Ga. Dept. Edn., Germany, 1989, 91; adv. com. Deutsche Welle Video, 1992, 95; internat. edn. adv. com. Ga. Dept. Edn., 1993—; tchr. cons. N.C. Geographic Alliance. Author: The Physiological and Psychological Effects of Space Flight Environments on Blood Glucose and Circadian Rhythms of the Human Body; contb. author: (curricuums) World Studies, Germany and Georgia: The Search for Unity, Education in Thailand, Germany Unity and Disunity: Ubersichten; Overview of the Federal Republic of Germany, Images of Germany: Past and Present, The Olympic Spirit; A Worldwide Connection, Vol. III. Mem. discovery gallery com. Columbus Mus. Arts & Scis., curriculum devel. com. Atlanta Com. for Olympic Games. Named Ga. State semi-finalist, NASA Tchr. Space Program, 1985, Richmond County Tchr. of Yr., 2003; named to USA Today All-U.S.A. 1st Tchr. Team, 1998; recipient Project award TV Worth Tchg., CBS, 1987; Fulbright scholar, Taiwan and Thailand, 1992. Mem. ASCD, NEA (congl. contact team), Columbus Social Sci. Alliance (bd. dirs.), Ga. Assn. Educators, Nat. Coun. Social Scis., Ga. Coun. Social Scis. (bd. dirs.), N.C. Assn. Educators, Musogee Assn. Edn. (v.p., 2d v.p., chmn. policies and grievences com., legis. com., chmn. officer nominating com.), Columbus Hist. Soc., Columbus Hist. Dist. Preservation Soc. (bd. dirs.), Chattahoochee Valley Archaeol. Soc., Phi Alpha Theta, Phi Delta Kappa.

PIRAINO, ANN MAE, seminar trainer, leader, vocational counselor; b. Vancouver, Wash. d. Elsworth Wallace Schmoeckel and Alice Marie (Blankenbickler) Avalos; m. Michael Salvatore, Nov. 19, 1983. BA in Edn., Seattle U., 1972; MA in Appl. Behavioral Sci., City U. Leadership Inst of Sea, 1987. Cert. rehab. counselor. Sec. to supt. Pasco (Wash.) Sch. Dist. No. 1, 1972-74; adminstrv. asst. Burns and Roe, Inc., Richland, Wash., 1974-81; exec. sec. UNC Nuclear Industries, Inc., Richland, Wash., 1981-83, Fairchild Semiconductor, Inc., Puyallup, Wash., 1984-87; instr. Eton Tech. Inst. (ETI), Federal Way, Wash., 1987-89; trainer, cons. Piraino Prodns., Wash., 1985—. Seminar leader and cons. Profl. Sec. Internat., Wash., Alaska and Oreg. state chpts., 1985—; cons. Fed. Way Women's Network and Career Devel. Network, Wash., 1985-88; employment coord. Bus. Computer Tng. Inst., Tacoma, 1989-90; adj. faculty Office Automation Griffin Coll., Tacoma, 1990; vocat. rehab. counselor Total Care Svcs., 1990-92, 94-95, Favorite Cons., 1990-94, Genex Svcs. Inc., 1995-97, VRC, Internat. Assn. for Machinists/Ctr. for Re-Employment Safety Tng./Boeing, 1996—. Editor: (newsletter) The Circuit Writer, 1985-87, (pub. assn. newsletters) Hear Ye, Hear Ye, 1986-88, Training Wheels, 1987-90, Speak Up!, 1991-92, Reflections, 1991-94; role expert: (competency study) ASTD Competency and Standards Project, 1988. Co. rep. United Way/Fairchild Semiconductor, Wash., 1986; team co-leader March of Dimes/Fairchild Semiconductor, Wash., 1986; team leader March of Dimes/Town Criers Toastmasters, Wash., 1989, 90. Recipient Xi Alpha Epsilon and Beta Sigma Phi Woman of Yr. award, 1979-81; named Sec. of Yr. Pas-Ric-Ken/Sea Tac Chpts., Profl. Secs. Internat., Richland/Fed. Way, Wash., 1979, 90; Sec. of Yr. Wash.-Alaska Div. Profl. Secs. Internat., Spokane, 1980. Mem. NAFE, ASTD (chpt. v.p. 1988-89, pres. 1990), Profl. Secs. Internat. (chpt. pres. 1985-86, 91-92, pres.-elect Wash./Alaska divsn. 1986-87, pres. 1987-88), Internat. Platform Soc., Toastmasters (area gov. 1991-92, dean Leadership Inst. dist. 32 1992-94), Nat. Assn. Rehab. Profls. in Pvt. Sector, Wash. Women in Worker's Compensation, Internat. Case Mgmt. Assn., NRA-Nat. Rehab. Assn. Avocations: reading, volksmarching.

PIRANI, CONRAD LEVI, pathologist, educator; b. Pisa, Italy, July 29, 1914; came to U.S., 1939, naturalized, 1945; s. Mario Giacomo Levi and Adriana P.; m. Luciana Nahmias, Mar. 12, 1955; children: Barbara, Sylvia, Robert. Diploma, Ginnasio-Liceo Beccaria, 1932; MD, U. Milano, Italy, 1938. Intern Columbus Meml. Hosp., Chgo., 1940-42; resident Michael Reese Hosp., Chgo., 1942-45; dir. exptl. pathology sect. U.S. Army Med. Nutrition Lab., Chgo., 1947—52; instr. pathology U. Ill., Chgo., 1945-48, asst. prof., 1948-52, asso. prof., 1952-55, prof., 1955-70; chmn. dept. pathology Michael Reese Hosp., Chgo., 1965-72; prof. pathology Coll. Physicians and Surgeons, Columbia U., N.Y.C., 1972-84, prof. emeritus, 1985—. Cons. Armed Forces Inst. Pathology; dir. Renal Pathology Lab., 1972-84; mem. sci. com. Kidney Found., N.Y., 1973-80; cons. and spl. lectr. Columbia U., 1985-95; mem. pathology study sect. NIH, 1973-78. Contbg. author various books.; assoc. editor Lab. Investigation, 1972-82, Nephron, 1975-92, Clin. Nephrology, 1989-92; contbr. numerous articles to profl. jours. USPHS, NIH grantee. Mem. Am. Assn. Pathologists, AAAS, Internat. Acad. Pathology (counselor 1966-69), Am. Soc. Nephrology (John P. Peters award 1987), Internat. Soc. Nephrology. Home: 235 Walker St Apt 233 Lenox MA 01240-2748 Office: 235 Walker St Apt 233 Lenox MA 01240-2748

PIRKLE, WILLIAM ARTHUR, geologist, educator; b. Atlanta, May 11, 1945; s. E.C. and Valda Nell (Armistead) P.; m. Rachel Isabel Batts, Aug. 25, 1968; children: Owen William, Elizabeth Anne. BS, Emory U., 1967; MS, U. N.C., 1970, PhD, 1972. Reg. profl. geologist, Ga., S.C. Geologist Rosario Resources, Inc., Ocala, Fla., 1969; chmn. divsn. natural scis. U. S.C., Aiken, 1984-86, dean Coll. Scis., 1986-93, dir. Office Sponsored Rsch., 1993—, from asst. prof. to prof. geology, 1972—. Project geologist S.C. Geological Survey, Columbia, 1973-84. Contbr. articles to profl. jours. NSF grantee, 1986-89, U.S. Dept. Energy grantee, 1989—. Mem. AIME, Geol. Soc. Am., S.C. Acad. Scis. (pres. 1994-95, 2002-2003), Carolina Geol. Soc., Sigma Xi. Methodist. Home: 318 Lakeside Dr Aiken SC 29803-7523 Office: U SC Aiken 471 University Pkwy Aiken SC 29801-6309

PIRO, JOSEPH MARTIN, school system administrator; b. N.Y.C., Apr. 20, 1949; s. Jerry John and Theresa Piro. BA, St. Francis Coll., N.Y.C., 1970; MS, Fordham U., 1975; MA, CUNY, 1978; MA, PhD, Columbia U., 1983, 86. Cert. tchr. and adminstr., N.Y. Tchr. Sch. Dist. 24, Queens, 1970-87, adminstr. L.I. U. Ctr. for Gifted Youth, 1987—. Instr. humanities L.I. U., Brookville, N.Y., 1982—; cons. Nat. Geog., 1983-84. Contbr. articles to profl. jours. Fellow Columbia U., 1981, Japan Found. fellow, 1989, Fulbright Hays fellow, 1990. Mem. APA, ASCD, Am. Edn. Rsch. Assn., Nat. Assn. for Gifted Children, Nat. Coun. Social Studies, Nat. Staff Devel. Coun., World Coun. Gifted and Talented. Home: 80 55 212 St Queens Village NY 11427-1014 Office: Sch Dist 24 8000 Cooper Ave Glendale NY 11385-7734

PIRODSKY, DONALD MAX, psychiatrist, educator; b. Freeport, N.Y., Feb. 2, 1945; s. Max and Doris Geilhard (Biedermann) P.; m. Gail Giufre Pallotta, Jan. 4, 1997; children: Laura Anne, Jason Donald. BA, Hofstra U., 1966; MD, SUNY, Syracuse, 1970. Diplomate Am. Bd. Psychiatry and Neurology, Nat. Bd. Med. Examiners. Intern Northwestern U. Med. Ctr., Chgo., 1970-71; resident in psychiatry Strong Meml. Hosp., Rochester, N.Y., 1973-74, U. Ariz. Med. Ctr., Tucson, 1974-76; instr. psychiatry SUNY Health Sci. Ctr., Syracuse, 1976-78, attending psychiatrist, 1976-91, asst. prof. psychiatry, 1978-85, mem. exec. com. of med. coll. assembly, 1979-82, clin. assoc. prof., 1985—, adj. attending psychiatrist, 1991—; pvt. practice Syracuse and Fayetteville, N.Y., 1976—; staff psychiatrist, dir. consultation/liaison svc. Syracuse VA Med. Ctr., 1976-87, chmn. pharmacy rev. and therapeutic agts. com., 1980-86. Psychiat. cons. Ariz. Sch. for Deaf and Blind, Tucson, 1975-76, Syracuse Devel. Ctr., 1977—, Rochester Sch. for Deaf, 1978-81; ex-officio mem. Family Counseling Agy., Tucson, 1975-76; adj. attending psychiatrist SUNY Health Sci. Ctr., Syracuse, 1991—. Author: Primer of Clinical Psychopharmacology: A Practical Guide, 1981, (with Jerry S. Cohn) Clinical Primer of Psychopharmacology: A Practical Guide, 2d edit., 1992; contbr. articles to profl. jours., chpts. to med. books. Lt. comdr. USPHS, 1971-73. Fellow Am. Psychiat. Assn. (Disting., mem. cen. N.Y. dist. br.); mem. Am. Psychosomatic Soc., Am. Assn. Mental Retardation, Med. Soc. State of N.Y., N.Y. State Psychiat. Assn., Onondaga County Med. Soc. Episcopalian. Avocations: sports, collecting baseball cards and other sports memorabilia. Office: 7000 E Genesee St Fayetteville NY 13066-1131

PISARCHICK, SALLY, special education educator; Tchr. spl. edn. Cuyahoga Spl. Edn. Svc. Ctr., Parma, Ohio, 1973-2000; dir. Ohio State Initiative Cuyahoga Spl. Edn. Regional Resource Ctr., Parma, Ohio, 2000—. Recipient Slesnick award, Coun. of Admin. of Spec. Edn., 1994. Office: Cuyahoga Special Edn Regional Resource Ctr 15983 W 54th St Parma OH 44129

PISTELLA, CHRISTINE LEY, public health educator; b. Pitts., July 11, 1949; d. David Adam and Mary Louise (Barrett) Ley; m. Frank Joseph Pistella; 1 child, Lauren Nicole. BA in Edn., U. Pitts., 1970, MSW, 1972, MPH, 1977, PhD with distinction, 1979. Lic. social worker, Pa. Program counselor/supr. Transitional Svcs., Inc., Pitts., 1972-74; mental health profl. St. Francis Med. Ctr., Pitts., 1974-75; sr. rsch. social worker Magee-Women's Hosp., Pitts., 1976-78; rsch. assoc. Sch. Pub. Health U. Pitts., 1976-80, rsch. coord. Sch. Social Wk., 1978-79; asst. prof. pub. health U. Pitts. Sch. Pub. Health, 1980—. Rsch. cons. USPHS Region V, Chgo., 1985-88, Washington-Greens Human Svcs., 1982-84, Southwestern Pa. Area on Aging, Monessen, 1980-83; rsch. dir. Family Health Coun. of Western Pa., Pitts., 1982-87. Contbr. articles to profl. jours., chpts. to books; editor/co-editor more than 10 rsch. monographs on family health, social wk. Active Mayors Commn. on Families, Pitts., 1988-94, Infant Mortality Rev. Team, Pa. Perinatal Assn., Pitts., 1990-93, Injury Prevention Adv. Bd. Allegheny County, Pitts., 1989—, Venango-Forest Cmty. Health Action Com., 1992-95; steering com. Pa. Area Health Edn. Ctr., 1994—. Mem. NASW, APHA, Nat. Rural Health Assn., Pa. Forum for Primary Health Care, Pa. Pub. Health Assn., Assn. of Tchrs. of Maternal and Child Health, Assn. Cert. Social Workers, Greater Pitts. C. of C. (alumni bd. of leadership Pitts. 1991-94), Delta Omega. Democrat. Roman Catholic. Avocations: photography, travel, art appreciation, genealogy, antiques, history of western pa. Office: U Pitts Grad Sch Pub Health 216 Parran Hl Pittsburgh PA 15261-0001

PISTER, KARL STARK, engineering educator; b. Stockton, Calif., June 27, 1925; s. Edwin LeRoy and Mary Kimball (Smith) P.; m. Rita Olsen, Nov. 18, 1950; children: Francis, Therese, Anita, Jacinta, Claire, Kristofer. BS with honors, U. Calif., Berkeley, 1945, MS, 1948; PhD, U. Ill., 1952. Instr. theoretical and applied mechanics U. Ill., 1949-52; faculty U. Calif., Berkeley, 1952-62, prof. engrng. scis., 1962-96, Roy W. Carlson prof. engrng., 1985-90, dean Coll. Engrng., 1980-90, chancellor Santa Cruz, 1991-96, pres., chancellor emeritus, Roy W. Carlson prof. emeritus Berkeley, sr. assoc. to pres. Oakland, 1996-99, v.p. ednl. outreach, 1999-2000. Richard Merton guest prof. U. Stuttgart, W. Ger., 1978; cons. to govt. and industry; bd. dirs. Monterey Bay Aquarium Rsch. Inst.; trustee Am. U. of Armenia; chmn. bd. Calif. Coun. Sci. and Tech. Contbr. articles to profl. jours.; mem. editl. bd. Jour. Optimization Theory and Applications, 1982, Encyclopedia Phys. Sci. and Tech. Regent Franciscan Sch. Theology, Grad. Theol. Union, Berkeley, Calif. With USNR, WWII. Fulbright scholar, Ireland, 1965, West Germany, 1973; recipient Wason Rsch. medal Am. Concrete Inst., 1960, Vincent Bendix Minorities in Engrng. award Am. Soc. for Engrng. Edn., 1988, Lamme medal, 1993, Alumni Honor award U. Ill. Coll. Engrng., 1982, Disting. Engrng. Alumnus award U. Calif. Berkeley Coll. Engrng., 1992, Berkeley medal, 1996, U. Calif. Presdl. medal, 2000, World Tech. Network award for policy, World Tech. Coun., London, 2002. Fellow: AAAS, ASME (Applied Mechanics award 1999, Internat. Pres.'s award 2000), Am. Acad. Arts & Sci., Am. Acad. Mechanics, Calif. Acad. Sci. (hon.); mem.: ASCE, NAE, Soc. Engrng. Sci. Office: U Calif Dept Civil & Environ Engr Berkeley CA 94720 E-mail: pister@ce.berkeley.edu.

PISTORIUS, GEORGE, language educator, educator; b. Prague, Czechoslovakia, Mar. 19, 1922; came to U.S., 1958, naturalized, 1964; s. Theodor and Blazena (Jiranek) P.; m. Marie Skokan, June 30, 1945; 1 dau., Erika. Student, Charles U., Prague, 1945-48; postgrad., Université de Paris, 1948-50; certificats d'etudes superieures, Université de Strasbourg, France, 1950, 1951; PhD, U. Pa., 1963. Asst. dept. comparative lit. Charles U., 1946-48; instr. Lafayette Coll., Easton, Pa., 1958-61, asst. prof. French, 1961-63; asso. prof. Williams Coll., 1963-68, prof. Romanic langs., 1968-92, chmn. dept., 1971-82, prof. emeritus, 1992—. Instr. French, Colby Coll. Summer Sch. Lang., 1959-65 Author: Bibliography of the works of F.X. Salda, 1948, Destin de la culture francaise dans une democratie populaire, 1957, L'Image de l'Allemagne dans le roman francais entre les deux guerres (1919-1939), 1964, Marcel Proust und Deutschland, Eine Bibliographie, 1981, 2d edit. 2002, André Gide und Deutschland: Eine internationale Bibliographie, 1990. Home: 54 Cluett Dr Williamstown MA 01267-2805

PITALE-SAMPSON, MARIA, special education educator; b. Mt. Holly, N.J., Mar. 9, 1963; d. Anthony William and Marianne Antoinette P. BS, Trenton State Coll., 1985; MA, Glassboro State Coll., 1992. Cert. devel. handicapped tchr., reading tchr., N.J., Pa., K-8 tchr., N.J., reading specialist, N.J., Pa., supr. Substitute tchr., Burlington, Florence, N.J., 1983-85; tchr. aide Burlington County Summer Migrant Program, Burlington, N.J., 1984, 1985; special edn. instr. Edgewater Park (N.J.) Bd. Edn., 1985-86, Riverside (N.J.) Bd. Edn., 1986-93; instr. spl. instr. Mt. Laurel (N.J.) Bd. Edn., 1994—. Tutor Riverside (N.J.) Bd. Edn., 1989-90; adj. prof. Burlington County Coll., Pemberton, N.J., 1993-94. Mem. Riverside Sch. and Family Assn., 1989--. Recipient N.J. State Scholarship, 1981-85. Mem. NEA, Mount Laurel Edn. Assn., N.J. Edn. Assn., West Jersey Reading Coun, Trenton State Coll. Alumni Assn. Avocations: fashion, travel, reading, exercise, music.

PITCOCK, LINDA HART, middle school educator; b. Leitchfield, Ky., Dec. 16, 1952; d. Bert Wesley Hart and Barbara Dean Fuqua Bishop; m. Philip David Pitcock, June 20, 1970; children: Bronson David, Brandon Chafin, Bridget Lynette. BS in Bus. Edn., Western Ky. U., 1975, MA in Secondary Edn., 1977. Cert. bus. edn. tchr. 7-12; rank I reading specialist 1-12; elem. endorsement of secondary cert. 1-8. Tchr. 1st grade Monroe County Bd. Edn., Tompkinsville, Ky., 1981-82, 86-89, tchr. 2d grade, 1982-83, 85-86, tchr. 3d grade, 1983-84, Chpt. I reading tchr., 1990-91, tchr. 6th grade, 1989-90, 91—, tchr. 2d and 3d grades, 1984-85; dept. head social studies Monroe County Middle Sch., 2000. Cons. Ky. Coun. of Econs., Louisville, 1987-88; sponsor/coach Acad. Team, Joe Harrison Carter Elem. Sch., 1990-91; sponsor Y-Club, Monroe County Mid. Sch., 1993—. Sec. Monroe County Rescue Squad, Tompkinsville, Monroe County H.S. Band Boosters, 1995-02, Boosters reporter, 2001-02; mem. Monroe County-Old Mulkey State Shrine C.B. Club; pres. Civitan Club, Monroe County, 1986-88 (Nat. Award Disting. Pres. 1987-88), mem., officer, reporter Gamaliel Elem. PTA, 1990-91 (PTA Mem. of Yr. 1986); sec. Monroe County H.S. Band Boosters, 1994-95; mem. Parents and Tchrs. Who Care Orgn., Monroe County Mid. Schs., 1993—. Mem. NEA, Ky. Edn. Assn., Ky. Coun. of Social Studies, Internat. Reading Assn., Nat. Mid. Sch. Assn. Republican. Ch. of Christ. Avocations: reading, travel, movies, entertaining, shopping. Home: 4982 Gamaliel Rd Tompkinsville KY 42167-6720 Office: Monroe County Middle School 759 Old Mulkey Rd Tompkinsville KY 42167-7701 E-mail: lpitcock@hotmail.com., lpitcock@monroe.k12.ky.us.

PITEO, CAROL ANN, elementary education educator; b. Northampton, Mass., June 7, 1950; d. Albert Samuel and Kathleen (Griffith) Vachula; m. Rickey Lawrence Piteo, Oct. 7, 1972; children: Dianna, Nicholas, James. BA in English, U. Mass., 1972; MSEd in Reading, L.I. U., Dobbs Ferry, 1989. Cert. reading tchr., N.Y. Substitute tchr. secondary English various high schs. in we. Mass. and Westchester County, N.Y., 1972-73; instructional asst. in sci. Mohansic Elem. Sch., Yorktown Heights, N.Y., 1988-89; remedial reading tchr. Ives Sch.-Lincoln Hall, Lincolndale, N.Y., 1989-93; chairperson English dept. Ives Sch., 1998—. Cub Scout leader Boy Scouts Am., Yorktown, N.Y., 1990-92; Sunday sch. and Bible sch. tchr. Yorktown Coop. Vacation Bible Sch. and St. Andrews Luth. Ch., Yorktown, 1983-91. Avocations: creating reading study guides, computers, walking, cross-country skiing. Home: 3074 Radcliffe Dr Yorktown Heights NY 10598-2534

PITERA, DOREEN ANN, pre-school educator; b. Morristown, N.J., Jan. 16, 1971; d. George John and Eileen Dorothy (Sexton) R. AA in Liberal Arts, group tchr. cert., County Coll. of Morris, Randolph, N.J., 1992. Pre-sch. tchr. Teddy and Me Day Care, Morristown, N.J., 1988—. Mem. Nat. Child Care Assn. (cert.) Roman Catholic.

PITOT, HENRY CLEMENT, III, pathologist, educator; b. N.Y.C., May 12, 1930; s. Henry Clement and Bertha (Lowe) Pitot; m. Julie S. Schutten,

July 29, 1954; children: Bertha, Anita, Jeanne, Catherine, Henry, Michelle, Lisa, Patrice. BS in Chemistry, Va. Mil. Inst., 1951; MD, Tulane U., 1955, PhD in Biochemistry, 1959, DSc (hon.), 1995. Instr. pathology Med. Sch. Tulane U., New Orleans, 1955-59; postdoctoral fellow McArdle Lab. U. Wis., Madison, 1959-60, mem. faculty Med. Sch., 1960—, prof. pathology and oncology, 1966-99, prof. emeritus, 1999—, chmn. dept. pathology, 1968-71, acting dean Med. Sch., 1971-73, dir. McArdle Lab., 1973-91. Recipient Borden Undergrad. Rsch. award, 1955, Leaderle Faculty award, 1962, Career Devel. award, Nat. Cancer Inst., NIH, 1965, Parke-Davis award, 1968, Noble Found. Rsch. award, 1984, Esther Langer award, U. Chgo., 1984, Hilldale award, U. Wis., 1991, Founders award, Chem. Industry Inst. Toxicology, 1993, Midwest Regional chpt. Soc. Toxicology award, 1996, Emeritus Faculty award, U. Wis. Med. Sch., 2001, Disting. Lifetime Toxicology award, Soc. Toxicology, 2003. Fellow: AAAS, N.Y. Acad. Scis.; mem.: Soc. Toxicologic Pathologists, Soc. Toxicology, Soc. Surg. Oncology (Lucy J. Wortham award 1981), Soc. Exptl. Biology and Medicine (pres. 1991—93), Am. Soc. Investigative Pathology (pres. 1976—77), Am. Cancer Soc. (life), Japanese Cancer Soc. (hon.), Am. Chem. Soc., Am. Soc. Biochemistry and Molecular Biology, Am. Assn. Cancer Rsch., Am. Soc. Cell Biology. Roman Catholic. Home: 314 Robin Pkwy Madison WI 53705-4931 Office: U Wis McArdle Lab Cancer Rsch 1400 University Ave Madison WI 53706-1599 E-mail: pitot@oncology.wise.edu.

PITRELLI, ELLEN JANE, secondary school educator; b. Bklyn., July 18, 1950; d. Robert Martin and Margaret (Carlo) Timm; m. Fred Pitrelli, Aug. 29, 1971; children: Timothy Robert, Kimberly Marie. BS, St. John's U., 1971; MA, Hofstra U., 1975. Cert. secondary tchr., N.Y., bus. and math tchr. Bus. tchr. Bellport (N.Y.) Sr. High Sch., 1971-72, Longwood Sr. High Sch., Mid. Island, N.Y., 1972—. Mem. Suffolk County Tchrs. Assn., Bus. tchrs. assn., Assn. of Supr. and Curriculm Devel., Phi Delta Kappa. Avocation: reading.

PITT, BERTRAM, cardiologist, educator, consultant; b. Kew Gardens, N.Y., Apr. 27, 1932; s. David and Shirley (Blum) P., m. Elaine Liberstein, Aug. 10, 1962; children: Geoffrey, Jessica, Jillian BA, Cornell U., 1953; MD, U. Basel, Switzerland, 1959. Diplomate Am. Bd. Internal Medicine, Am. Bd. Cardiology. Intern Beth Israel Hosp., N.Y.C., 1959-60, resident Boston, 1960-63; fellow in cardiology Johns Hopkins U., Balt., 1966-67, from instr. to assoc. prof., 1967-77; prof. medicine, dir. div. cardiology U. Mich., Ann Arbor, 1977-91, prof. medicine Sch. Medicine, 1991—. Author: Atlas of Cardiovascular Nuclear Medicine, 1977; editor: Cardiovascular Nuclear Medicine, 1974; co-editor: Clinical Trials in Cardiology, 1997, Current Controlled Trials in Cardiovascular Medicine, 1999—. Served to capt. U.S. Army, 1963-65 Mem. ACP, Am. Coll. Cardiology, Am. Soc. Clin. Investigation, Assn. Am. Physicians, Am. Physiol. Soc., Am. Heart Assn., Assn. Univ. Cardiologists, Am. Coll. Chest Physicians, Johns Hopkins U. Soc. Scholars. Home: 24 Ridgeway St Ann Arbor MI 48104-1739 Office: U Mich Divsn Cardiology 1500 E Medical Center Dr Ann Arbor MI 48109-0005 E-mail: bpitt@umich.edu.

PITT, ROBERT ERVIN, environmental engineer, educator; b. San Francisco, Apr. 25, 1948; s. Wallace and Marjorie (Peterson) P.; m. Kathryn Jay, Mar. 18, 1967; children: Gwendolyn, Brady. BS in Engring. Sci., Humboldt State U., 1970; MSCE, San Jose State U., 1971; PhD in Civil and Environ. Engring., U. Wis., 1987. Registered profl. engr., Wis.; diplomate Am. Acad. Environ. Engrs. Environ. engr. URS Rsch. Co., San Mateo, Calif., 1971-74; sr. engr. Woodward-Clyde Cons., San Francisco, 1974-79; cons. environ. engr. Blue Mounds, Wis., 1979-84; environ. engr. Wis. Dept. Natural Resources, Madison, 1984-87; prof. depts. civil and environ. engring. and environ. health scis. U. Ala., Birmingham, 1987—2002, prof., dir. environ. engring. program Tuscaloosa, 2000—. Mem. mem. com. on augmenting natural recharge of groundwater with reclaimed wastewater NRC, 1991-94; Ala. state dir. for energy and environment U.S. DOE EPSCOR, 1992-94; guest lectr. U. Gesamthochschule, Essen, Germany, 1994; mem. value engrng. com. Combined Sewer Overflow, Cleve., 1993, mem. tech. adv. com., N.Y.C., 1997—. Author: Investigation of Inappropriate Pollutant Entries into Storm Drainage Systems, 1994, Potential Groundwater Contamination from Intentional and Non-Intentional Stormwater Infiltration, 1994, Groundwater Contamination from Stormwater, 1996, Stormwater Effects Handbook, 2001; co-author: Stormwater Effects Handbook: A Tool Box for Watershed Managers, Scientists, and Engineers, 2002; author software in field; mem. editl. bd. Ctr. Watershed Protection, 1994—. Asst. scoutmaster Boy Scouts Am., Birmingham, 1988-94. Recipient Disting. Svc. citation, U. Wis., 2002, 1st Pl. Nat. award U.S. Soil Conservation Svc. Earth Team, 1989, 94, award of recognition USDA, 1990, 1st Pl. Vol. award Take Pride in Am., 1991; Fed. Water Pollution Control Adminstrn. fellow, 1970-71, GE Engring. Edn. fellow, 1984-86. Mem. ASCE, Soc. for Environ. Toxicology and Chemistry, N.Am. Lake Mgmt. Soc. (Profl. Speakers award 1992), Water Environ. Fedn. (1st Pl. Nat. award 1992), Am. Water Resources Assn., Ala. Acad. Sci., Internat. Assn. Water Quality (mem. com. on solids in sewers 1996-96), Sigma Xi. Achievements include development of small storm urban hydrology prediction methods, toxicant control devices for stormwater source flows, methods to identify and correct inappropriate. Office: U Ala Dept Civil/Environ Engring Tuscaloosa AL 35487-2684

PITTENGER, ARTHUR O., JR., mathematics educator; b. Indpls., Oct. 24, 1936; s. Arthur O. Sr. and Barbara (Sherman) P.; m. Judith MacGillivray, Apr. 24, 1965; children: Laurence, Christopher, Elise. BS, Stanford U., 1958, PhD, 1967. Vis. scholar Moscow State U., 1967-68; rsch. assoc. Rockefeller U., N.Y.C., 1968-70; asst. prof. U. Mich., Ann Arbor, 1970-72; assoc. prof., then prof. U. Md. Baltimore County, Balt., 1972—, dean Arts and Scis., 1988-93, interim provost, 1993-94. Cons. IDA, Princeton, N.J., 1973-75; vis. prof. Oxford U., Eng., 1999-2000. Contbr. articles to profl. jours. Lt. U.S. Army, 1960. Fellow Inst. Math. Stats.; mem. Am. Math. Soc., Phi Beta Kappa, Phi Kappa Phi. Office: U Md Baltimore County Dept Math Baltimore MD 21250-0001

PITTMAN, CATHERINE SYLVIA, secondary school educator; b. Brunswick, Ga., Apr. 24, 1962; m. David Pittman; children: Drew, Meghan. BS, Ga. So. Coll., 1984, MEd, 1989, EdS, 1993. Tchr. grade 7,8 Risley Middle Sch., Glynn County, 1985-89; tchr. grades 9-12 Brunswick High Sch., Glynn County, 1989—. Named Ga. Tchr. of Yr., 1995, 1996, Milken Faminly Found. Nat. Educator, 1995; recipient YMCA Tribute to Women's Leaders, 1999. Mem. Glynn County Assn. of Educators, Ga. Assn. of Educators, Nat. Edn. Assn., Ga. Council of Social Studies, So. Assn. of Student Councils, Nat. Assn. of Student Activity Advisors. Home: 103 Marsh Landing Dr Brunswick GA 31523-9387 Office: Brunswick High Sch 3920 Habersham St Brunswick GA 31520-2799

PITTMAN, CONSTANCE SHEN, physician, educator; b. Nanking, China, Jan. 2, 1929; came to U.S., 1946; d. Leo F.-Z. and Pao Kong (Yang) Shen; m. James Allen Pittman, Jr., Feb. 19, 1955; children: James Clinton, John Merrill. AB in Chemistry, Wellesley Coll., 1951; MD, Harvard U., 1955. Diplomate Am. Bd. Internal Medicine, sub-bd. Endocrinology. Intern Baltimore City Hosp., 1955-56; resident U. Ala., Birmingham, 1956-57; instr. in medicine U. Ala. Med. Ctr., Birmingham, 1957—59, fellow dept. pharmacology, 1957-59, from asst. prof. to assoc. prof., 1959-70, prof., 1970—. Prof. medicine Georgetown U., Washington, 1972-73; mem. diabetes and metabolism tng. com. NIH, Bethesda, Md., 1972-76, mem. nat. arthritis, metabolism and digestive disease coun., 1975-78, mem. gen. clin. rsch. ctrs. com., 1979-83, 87-90; dir. Internat. Coun. for the Control of Iodine Deficiency Diseases, 1994—. Master ACP; mem. Assn. Am. Physicians, Am. Soc. for Clin. Investigation, Endocrine Soc. (coun., 1978-79, pres. women's caucus 1978-79), Am. Thyroid Assn. (pres. 1990-91), Kiwanis (mem. iodine deficiency disorders steering com.). Achievements include research in activation and metabolism of thyroid hormone; kinetics of thyroxine conversion to triiodothyrine in health and disease states; control of iodine deficiency disorders. Emails. Office: U Ala Div Endocrinology/Metab Lab Med Ctr Birmingham AL 35294-0001 E-mail: cpittman@endo.dom.uab.edu.

PITTMAN, JACQUELYN, retired mental health nurse, nursing educator; b. Pensacola, Fla., Dec. 22, 1932; d. Edward Corry Sr. and Hettie Oean (Wilson) P. BS in Nursing Edn., Fla. State U., 1958; MA, Columbia U., 1959, EdD, 1974. Physician asst. Med. Ctr. Clinic, Pensacola, 1953-55; clin. instr., asst. dir. nursing svc. Sacred Heart Hosp., Pensacola, 1955-56; instr. psychiat. nurse Fla. State Hosp., Chattahoochee, 1958; instr. psychiat. nursing Pensacola Jr. Coll., 1959-60, 62-63; chmn. div. nursing Gulf Coast C.C., Panama City, Fla., 1963-66; asst. prof. U. Tex., Austin, 1970-72, assoc. prof., 1972-80; prof. nursing, coord. curriculum and tchg. grad. program La. State U. Med. Ctr., New Orleans, 1980-99, rep. faculty senate, 1997-99; pres.-elect faculty assembly Sch. Nursing La. State U. Med. Ctr. Sch. Nursing, New Orleans, 1997-98, pres., 1998-99; ret., 1999. Curriculum cons. Nicholls State U., Thibodaux, La., 1982, Our Lady of Lake Sch. Nursing, Baton Rouge, 1983; rsch. liaison So. Bapt. Hosp., New Orleans, 1987-89, Med. Ctr. La., 1992-99; mem. adv. bd. Sister Henrietta Guyot Professorship; mem. planning com. Nichols State U./La. State U. Med. Ctr. Partnership, 1996-99. Mem. ethics com., trustee Hotel Dieu Hosp., New Orleans, 1987—91; judge Internat. Sci. and Engring. Fair Assn., 1990, 1992; del. La. State Nurses' Assn. State Conv., 1992, 1994; assoc. Libr. of Congress, Smithonian Instn.; mem. Dem. Nat. Comm., Presdl. Task Force, 1992, Ctr. for Study of Presidency; tchr. Christian edn. program for mentally retarded St. Ignatius Martyr Ch., 1979—80; tchr. initiation team Rite of Christian Initiation of Adults, Our Lady of the Lake Cath. Ch., Mandeville, La., 1983—86; v.p., bd. dirs. St. Tammany Guidance Ctr., Inc., Mandeville, 1987—91; mem. parish outreach meals-on-wheels program St. Tammany, Covington, La., 2001—02. Mem. ANA, LWV, Am. Assn. Adv. Sci. Directory, N.Y. Acad. Scis., Acad. Polit. Sci., Libr. of Congress Assocs., Nat. Trust for Hist. Preservation, La. Endowment for Humanities, La. Nurses Assn. (archivist 1987-99, state task force com. to preserve hist. documents 1987-99), So. Nursing Rsch. Soc., Nat. League Nursing, Boston U. Nursing Archives, Women's Inner Cir. Achievement N.Am. Cmtys., Internat. Order of Merit, World Found. Successful Women, Wilson Ctr. Assocs., Kappa Delta Pi, Sigma Theta Tau. Democrat. Roman Catholic. Avocations: swimming, golf, travel, reading, louisiana history. Address: 204 Woodridge Blvd Mandeville LA 70471-2604

PITTMAN, JAMES ALLEN, JR., physician, educator; b. Orlando, Fla., Apr. 12, 1927; s. James Allen and Jean C. (Garretson) Pittman; m. Constance Ming-Chung Shen, Feb. 19, 1955; children: James Clinton, John Merrill. BS, Davidson Coll., 1948; MD, Harvard, 1952; DSc (hon.), Davidson Coll., 1980, U. Ala., Birmingham, 1984. Intern, asst. resident medicine Mass. Gen. Hosp., Boston, 1952—54; tchg. fellow medicine Harvard U., 1953—54; clin. assoc. NIH, Bethesda, Md., 1954—56; instr. medicine George Washington U., 1955—56; chief resident U. Ala. Med. Ctr., Birmingham, 1956—58, instr. medicine, 1956—59, asst. prof., 1959—62, assoc. prof., 1962—64, prof. medicine, 1964—92, dir. endocrinology and metabolism divsn., 1962—71, co-chmn. dept. medicine, 1969—71, also prof., physiology and biophysics, 1967—92, dean, 1973—92, U. Ala. Birmingham Disting. prof., 1992—. Mem. endocrinology study sect. NIH, 1963—67; mem. nat. adv. rsch. resources coun. NIH, 1991—95; asst. chief med. dir. rsch. and edn. in medicine U.S. VA, 1971—73; prof. medicine Georgetown U. Med. Sch., Washington, 1971—73; mem. grad. med. edn. nat. adv. com. HEW, 1976—78; mem. HHS Coun. on Grad. Med. Edn., 1986—90; hon. prof. Chung Shan Med. and Dental Coll., Taiwan, 1994; sr. advisor Internat. Coun. on Ctrl. of Iodine Deficiency Diseases, 1994—96. Author: Diagnosis and Treatment of Thyroid Diseases, 1963; contbr. articles in field to profl. jours. Master: Am. Coll. Endocrinology, ACP; fellow: AAAS; mem.: So. Soc. Clin. Investigation (Founder's medal 1993), Am. Fedn. Clin. Rsch. (pres. So. sect., nat. coun. 1962—66), Am. Chem. Soc., Am. Diabetes Assn., Soc. Nuclear Medicine, Endocrine Soc. Ecuador (hon.), N.Y. Acad. Scis. (life), Am. Ornithologists Union (life), Am. Thyroid Assn., Am. Assn. Clin. Endocrinologists, Endocrine Soc., Assn. Am. Physicians, NAS Inst. Medicine, Harvard U. Med. Alumni Assn. (pres. 1986—88), Wilson Ornithol. Club (life), Omicron Delta Kappa, Alpha Omega Alpha, Phi Beta Kappa. Office: U Ala Sch of Med Pittman CAMS 1924 7th Ave S Birmingham AL 35294-0007

PITTMAN, KATHERINE ANNE ATHERTON, elementary education educator; b. Baytown, Tex., Aug. 20, 1956; d. William Clifford Sr. and Pauline (High) Atherton; children: Richard Neil, Angela Christine, William Charles. Student, Lee Coll., 1973-75, 76, 87; BA in Liberal Arts and History, Tex. A&M U., 1977; cert. in secondary edn., Stephen F. Austin State U., 1978; cert. elem. and secondary edn., U. Houston, 1989, MS in Elem. Edn., 1991. Cert. elem. and high sch. tchr., Tex. Catalog clk. J.C. Penney Co., Baytown, Tex., 1974-75; substitute tchr. San Augustine (Tex.) Ind. Sch. Dist., 1978; math. tchr. Brookeland (Tex.) Ind. Sch. Dist., 1980-81; substitute tchr. Deer Park (Tex.) Ind. Sch. Dist., 1988-89; tchr. 6th grade Channelview (Tex.) Ind. Sch. Dist., 1989-94; tchr. 7th grade English and ESL Houston Ind. Sch. Dist., 1994-95, tchr. 8th grade English, 1996—. Substitute tchr. Goose Creek Consol. Ind. Sch. Dist., Baytown, 1987-89; tchr. ESL, Harris County Dept. of Edn./Lee Coll., Baytown, 1989-90, substitute ESL tchr., 1990-91; customer svc. assoc. Montgomery Ward Co., Baytown, 1988-89. Mem. Tex. Computer Edn. Assn., Houston Fedn. Tchrs. Avocations: knitting, crocheting, computers, guitar, reading. Office: Jackson Middle Sch 5100 Polk St Houston TX 77023-1420

PITTS, CHARLES CAREY, music educator; b. Thomaston, Ga., June 8, 1944; s. Charles Milas and Addie Louise (Hunt) P.; m. Angela Jean Wheless, Aug. 4, 1968; children: Dana Caroline, Erin Elizabeth. AB, Mercer U., 1966; M of Ch. Music, So. Bapt. Theol. Sem., Louisville, 1969. Cert. music tchr. Ga. Minister of music, youth First Bapt. Ch., Forsyth, Ga., 1970-73, Rose Hill Bapt. Ch., Columbus, Ga., 1973-77, First Bapt. Ch., Cuthbert, Ga., 1977-85; minister of music Madison (Ga.) Bapt. Ch., 1985-87; sales assoc. Daniel's Men's Shop, Thomaston, 1987-89; tchr. Westwood Acad., Thomaston, 1989-90; tchr. music Upson-Lee South Primary Sch., Thomaston, 1990—. Youth chairperson Kiwanis Club, Forsyth, 1981-82; minister of music Mt. Olive Bapt. Ch., Molena, Ga., 1988-2000. Mem. Music Ministers Ga. Bapt. Conv. (regional dir. 1979-80). Baptist. Home: 300 Upson Ave Thomaston GA 30286-4518 Office: Upson Lee South Primary Sch 172 Knight Trl Thomaston GA 30286-3929

PITZER, ELIZABETH ANN, elementary school educator; b. Union City, Ind., Mar. 18, 1963; d. Gerald Neil and Dixie Lee (Miles) Marshall; m. Frank Henry Perkins, II, July 31, 1982 (div.); children: Frank Henry III, Kyle Alexander; m. James Robert Pitzer, Aug. 5, 2000; 1 child, Chand Andrew. BS, Ball State U., 1984, MA, 1988. Substitute tchr. Mississinawa Valley Schs., Union City, Ohio, 1984-85; 2d grade tchr. Randolph Ea. Sch., Union City, 1985-87, substitute tchr., 1987-88; 5th grade tchr. Arcanum (Ohio) Butler LSD, 1988—. Asst. math. lab. Project Discovery, West Region Ohio, 1994, mem. coun., Dayton, Ohio, 1994; mem. standard setting com. State Dept Edn., 4th grade math. proficiency, Ohio, 1994; presenter tchr. workshops and meetings, 1990—. V.p. TWIG # 35 Arcanum, 1990—; treas. PTO, Arcanum, 1992—; math. coord. St. Jude's Mathathon, Arcanum, 1993—; coach Odyssey of the Mind, Arcanum, 1994—; mem. Criterion Lit. Club, 1995—. Recipient Ednl. Rsch. grant Ball State U., 1993, Resource Tchr. grant, 1995, Timewarner Cable in Classroom award, 1996, Ashland Inc. Golden Apple Achiever award, 1996, Ashland Oil Individual Tchr. Achievement award, 1994, Milken Educator, 1998. Mem. NEA, Nat. Coun. Tchrs. of Math., Ohio Coun. Tchrs. of Math., Arcanum-Butler Classroom Tchrs. Assn. (bldg. rep. 1988—), Mississinawa Alumni Assn (bd. dirs. 1991—), Phi Delta Kappa (mem. math. video project com. western Ohio chpt. 1994). Roman Catholic. Avocations: reading, playing cards, family, writing, theater. Office: Arcanum Butler LSD 310 Main St Arcanum OH 45304-9524

PITZSCHLER, KATHRYN VAN DUREN, secondary school educator; b. Buffalo, Nov. 22, 1945; d. William and Olive Rasbridge (Decker) Van Duren; m. Robert B. Pitzschler, Aug. 30, 1971; 1 child, Molly Lynn. BA, Bucknell U., 1967; MS, Fairfield (Conn.) U., 1972. Cert. secondary English tchr., Conn. Tchr. English, Trumbull (Conn.) High Sch.; tchr. lang. arts, team leader Hillcrest Mid. Sch., Trumbull. Presenter, workshop leader in interdisciplinary teaching; beginning educator support tchr.-mentor, Conn. Mem. NEA, ASCD, Nat. Assn. Secondary Sch. Principals, Nat. Coun. Tchrs. English, Conn. Edn. Assn., Conn. Assn. Curriculum Devel., Trumbull Edn. Assn., Conn. Coun. Tchrs. English, NEATE, Delta Kappa Gamma. Home: 225 Edgemoor Rd Apt B Bridgeport CT 06606-2110

PIVERONUS, PETER JOHN, JR., education educator; b. Boston, Nov. 29, 1941; s. Peter John Sr. and Rose Camella (Pasciuto) P.; m. Bonnie Jean Kennedy, June 7, 1969 (div. 1981); children: Elizabeth Schaeffler, William Schaeffler, Michelle Montesano; m. Elisabeth Doris Roth, Nov. 21, 1988; children: Shannon Roth, Sara Roth. BA, Boston U., 1964, MA, 1966; PhD, Mich. State U., 1972. Asst. prof. SUNY, Buffalo, 1967-69, Claflin Coll., Orangeburg, S.C., 1969-70; adj. prof. Lansing C.C., Lansing, Mich., 1972—, Montcalm C.C., Sidney, 1973—2000, Jackson C.C., Jackson, 1979—, Baker Coll., Owosso, Mich., 2002—. Vis. prof. Mich. State U., East Lansing, 1986, Alma (Mich.) Coll., 1987. Editor, contbr.: Conflict in Ireland, 1976; contbr. articles to profl. jours. Precinct del. Ingham County Dems., Lansing, 1980-81; trustee Southland Complex Condo Assn., Lansing, 1987-90; pres. Gaelic League of Lansing, 1981-82. HEW fellow Claflin Coll., 1969-70; postdoctoral rsch. grantee U. Mich. Ctr. for Russian and East European Studies, 1985. Mem. Am. Com. for Irish Studies, Ohio Employee Ownership Ctr., Capital Ownership Group, Nat. Ctr. for Employee Ownership, Irish-Am. Cultural Inst., Soc. for History of Discoveries, Mich. Assn. Higher Edn. (faculty senator 1978-79), Mich. Edn. Assn., Econ. and Bus. Hist. Soc. Unitarian Universalist. Avocations: reading, traveling, camping, boating. Home: 201 West Jolly Rd Lansing MI 48910 Office: Lansing Community Coll 419 N Capitol Ave Lansing MI 48933-1207

PIVINSKI, SISTER MARY LORENE, academic administrator; b. Wilkes Barre, Pa., Dec. 6, 1936; d. Stanley and Sophie (Kulikowski) P. BA in Elem. Edn., Felician Coll., 1970; MA in Reading, William Paterson U., 1977. Cert. elem. sch. tchr. Tchr. various schs., N.J., Md., 1957-63; tchr. grade 7 Immaculate Conception Sch., Spotswood, N.J., 1963-64, St. Mary Sch., Closter, N.J., 1964-66; teaching prin. grade 8 St. Joseph Sch., Demarest, N.J., 1966-72; tchr. grade 8 Claremont (Va.) Acad., 1972-73; prin. St. Paul Sch., Prospect Park, N.J., 1973-80; tchr. grade 7 St. John Kanty Sch., Clifton, N.J., 1980-81, prin., 1981-88, 1998—2001; dir. edn. Felician Sisters, Lodi, NJ, 1988—2001. Avocations: needlepoint, crewel, walking, wrestling, baseball. Office: Felician Sisters 260 S Main St Lodi NJ 07644-2117

PIZER, DONALD, author, educator; b. N.Y.C., Apr. 5, 1929; s. Morris and Helen (Rosenfeld) P.; m. Carol Hart, Apr. 7, 1966; children— Karin, Ann, Margaret. BA, UCLA, 1951, MA, 1952, PhD, 1955. Mem. faculty Tulane U., 1957—, prof. English, 1964-72, Pierce Butler prof. English, 1972—2001, Mellon prof. humanities, 1978-79. Author: Hamlin Garland's Early Work and Career, 1960, Realism and Naturalism in Nineteenth-Century American Literature, 1966, The Novels of Frank Norris, 1966, The Novels of Theodore Dreiser, 1976, Twentieth-Century American Literary Naturalism: An Interpretation, 1982, Dos Passos "USA": A Critical Study, 1988, The Theory and Practice of American Literary Naturalism, 1993, American Expatriate Writing and the Paris Moment, 1996. Served with AUS, 1955-57. Guggenheim fellow, 1962; Am. Council Learned Socs. fellow, 1971-72; Nat. Endowment Humanities fellow, 1978-79 Mem. MLA. Home: 6320 Story St New Orleans LA 70118-6340

PIZZO, PIA, artist, educator; arrived in U.S., 1982, permanent resident, 1985; d. Rosario Pizzo and Rosa Greco; m. Chin Hsiao, Apr. 28, 1962 (div. May 1979); 1 child, Samantha Hsiao (dec.); m. Delbert O. Thompson, June 18, 1985. Diploma, Coll. of Art Orsoline, Milano, Italy, 1956; student, Brera Acad. Art, Milano, Italy, 1957—60; BFA, Ministry Pub. Instrn., Roma, Italy, 1957. Founder, propr. Sama Press, Long Beach, Calif., 1995—. Instr. design and color theory Brooks Coll. Design, Long Beach, Calif., 1998—; instr. art and creativity Dept. Parks, Recreation, Marine, Long Beach, Calif., 1987—; lectr. Dept. Art and Tech. Calif. State U., Long Beach, Calif., 1995—96. Exhibitions include 32 solo exhbns., Europe and USA, 1962—2003, 83 group shows, Europe, USA, Brasil, Taiwan, 1957—2002; author: The World is Waiting for the Sunrise, 1985 (hon. mention, 1987); co-author (with blind students): 6'x 8' tactile sculptural book-perm. pub. art, 1988; contbr. articles to profl. publs.; author (designer): adult and children books, 1970, 1981. Named Artist of Yr., Disting. Visual Artist, PCA Pub. Corp. for Arts, 1989; recipient Cert. Recognition award, Accademia Tiberina, Roma, Italy, 1957, cert. of Appreciation in Recognition of Outstanding Svc., City of Long Beach, Calif., 2000, permanent pub. art sign project, City of Gardena, Calif., 2001; fellow, Pollock-Krasner Found., NYC, 1984, Calif. Arts Coun., Sacramento, 1987, Pub. Corp. for the Arts, Long Beach, Calif., 2000. Mem.: Long Beach Mus. Art Artist's Coun. (solo exhbn. 1998), The Smithsonian Inst., Internat. Campaign for Tibet, Children Internat., Amnesty Internat. Avocations: classical piano, reading, concerts, museums, languages. Home and Studio: Artist's Studio 1022 E 1st St # 7 Long Beach CA 90802

PIZZURO, SALVATORE NICHOLAS, special education educator; b. Passaic, N.J., Jan. 25, 1945; s. John G. and Mary F. (Interdonato) P. BA, Jersey City State Coll., 1970, MA, 1973; prof. diploma, Fordham U., 1980; EdD, Columbia U., 1991. Tchr. spl. edn. Garfield (N.J.) Pub. Schs., 1970-71, Lodi (N.J.) Pub. Schs., 1971-75, 76-78; learning cons. Mt. Carmel Guild, Newark, 1976-76; instr. Columbia U., N.Y.C., 1988-91; asst. prof. spl. edn. Jersey City State Coll., 1990—; learning cons. Elmwood Park (N.J.) Dept. Special Svcs., 2000—02, Passaic County Ednl. Svcs. Commn., 2002—; cons. com. on edn. and workforce U.S. House of Reps., 2003; dir. Transition Adv. Svcs., 2003—; cons. Jersey city Pub. Schs., 2003—. Rsch. chmn. Transition Coords. Network NJ; cons. Congressmen Rush Holt and Pete Stark, 2002-03; post-doctoral fellow U. Ky., 1993-94; dir. Learning Consultation Svcs., N.Y.C., 1990—; coord. pre-svcs. program in mental retardation Tchrs. Coll., Columbia U., 1990-91; rsch. assoc. U. Ill., 1991-92; chmn. Early Childhood Inclusion Conf., Phila., 1993; dir. United Learning Consultants, 1994—; chmn. conf. "Assessment: Impact on Svc. Delivery", N.J., 1995; cons. Ind. Child Study Teams, Inc., 1995—; mem. task force com. on econ. and ednl. opportunities U.S. Ho. of Reps., 1994-96, chair, cons. Com. Edn. & Workforce, 1997—; chmn. the Future of Edn. in N.J. Conf., 1996; adj. faculty mem. Kean Coll. of N.J., 1997—; cons. Ednl. Resource Ctr., N.J., 1998; learning cons. Elmwood Park Dept. Spl. Svcs., 2000-02, Rutherford Dept. Spl. Svcs., 2002—; chmn. symposium on edn. funding Eagleton Inst. Politics Rutgers U., 1997; chmn. N.J. Com. on Pers. Stds. in Edn.; cons. U.S. Ho. of Reps. com. on edn. and workforce, 2002—; learning cons. Rutherford Pub. Schs., 2002-03, Jersey City Pub. Schs., 2003; chmn. symposium on sch. constrn. Kean U., 1998, chmn. symposium on urban edn., 1998, chmn. symposium on legis. initiatives in edn., 1998; chmn. congl. symposium on disability issues Capitol Hill, 2003; founder, dir. Transition Adv. Svcs., 2003—. Author: The Individuals with Disabilities Education Act and the Nature of American Politics, 1999, (textbook) The Individuals with Disabilities Education Act and the Nature of American Politics, 2001, 2d edit., 2003; editor: Learning Consultant Journal, 1995, 96, Policy Statement on Education in New Jersey,

N.J. Coalition for the Study for School Reform, 1998; cons. editor Diagnostique, 1997—. Chmn. Walk for Hunger, 1979, NE Regional Legis. Coalition, 1984-86, Nat. AD HOC Comm. on the Reauthorization of the Individuals with Disabilities Edn. Act, chmn. Nat. Forum on Reauthorization, 1996, Conf. on Future of Edn. in N.J., 1996—, N.J. Coalition on Study of Sch. Reform, 1996—; staff mem. for U.S. Congressman Major Owens, 1997—; chmn. press conf. with U.S. Congressman Robert Menendez on sch. constrn., 1998, with U.S. Congressman Donald Payne on urban edn., 1998; polit. cons. Dem. election orgn., 1999-2000; cons. Legis. Initiatives in Edn., 2000. Recipient award for dedication to mentally retarded Mt. Carmel Guild, 1972. Mem. Coun. for Exceptional Children, N.J. Coun. for Exceptional Children (pres. 1984-85), N.J. Divsn. on Mental Retardation (pres. 1986-87), Jersey City State Coll. Alumni Assn. (pres. 1974-75), Tchrs. Coll. Christian Fellowship (pres. 1988-90), Rehab. Engring. Soc. N.Am., Correctional Edn. Assn., Internat. Ctr. for Study of Psychiatry and Psychology. Roman Catholic. Avocations: writing nonfiction, jogging.

PIZZUTO, DEBRA KAY, mathematics educator; b. Camden, N.J., Nov. 25, 1957; d. Edward John and Kathryn Mary (Kegolis) Andrews; m. Victor Bruce Pizzuto, Nov. 28, 1981. BA in Bus. Adminstrn., Rutgers U., 1980. Cert. math. tchr., N.J., N.H. Tchr. math. Parkside Jr. H.S., Manchester, N.H., 1985-87, Cumberland Regional H.S., Seabrook, N.J., 1987-88, St. James H.S., Carney's Point, N.J., 1988-92, Ocean City (N.J.) H.S., 1993-96; instr. math. Atlantic C.C., Mays Landing, N.J., 1996-98; ctr. dir. Sylvan Learning Ctr., High Point, N.C., 1999-2000. Ednl. cons. Class Ideas, Bridgeton, N.J. Author, instr. (video tapes) Algebra One in Superstar Tchr. Series; contbr. articles to profl. jours. Named Superstar Tchr. for H.S. Video Instrn., The Teaching Co. Mem. ASCD, Math. Assn. Am., Nat. Coun. Tchrs. Math. Roman Catholic. Avocations: music, physical fitness, creative writing, theater, nutrition.

PLACEK-ZIMMERMAN, ELLYN CLARE, school system administrator, educator, consultant; b. Chgo., Sept. 3, 1951; d. Clarence Joseph and Jerrine LaMarr (Ruhlow) Placek; m. Allan John Zimmerman, Aug. 10, 1974; 1 child, Alissa Jan. BS, No. Ill. U., 1973, MS, 1977, cert. in advanced study, 1978, EdD, 1982. Tchr. Arlington Heights (Ill.) Pub. Schs., 1973-75, 75-76, dir. libr. and learning ctr., 1976-81, tchr. lang. arts and reading jr. high sch., 1981-84, tchr. kindergarten, 1984-86; prin. Orchard Street Sch., Fox River Grove, Ill., 1988-89, Pritchett Sch., Buffalo Grove, Ill., 1989-90, Round Lake (Ill.) Pub. Schs., 1992-93, asst. supt. curiculum and instrn., 1993-2001; asst. to supt. curriculum and instrn. Wood Dale (Ill.) Pub. Schs., 2001—03, prin., 2003—. Dir. Ill. State grant "At Risk Program" for pre-sch. children, Cary Pub. Schs., 1986-87; mem. part-time faculty Coll. Edn., Roosevelt U., Chgo., 1983-84, 88-89; tchr. jr. high social, reading and lang. arts studies, 1988; cons. in field; mem. steering com. Curriculum 2000 Conf., De Kalb, Ill., 1985; lectr. in field; supr. student tchrs. Ill. State U., Normal, 1986, Roosevelt U., Chgo., 1988-89, Elmhurst Coll., 1992; freelance writer Daily Herald newspaper. Contbg. author: Feeling Good About Food. Sec. Scarsdale Estates Homeowners Assn., Arlington Heights, 1983; bd. dirs. ABC/25 Found., 1991-92. Mem. Ill. ASCD (registration com. for fall conf. 1987, triple I arrangements com. 1988), Ill. Assn. Tchrs. English (cons., spkr. conf. 1984), Ill. Women Adminstrs. (publicty com. conf. 1985), PTA (hon. life). Avocations: playing guitar, calligraphy. Home: 402 E Orchard St Arlington Heights IL 60005-2660

PLAGMAN, RALPH, principal; Prin. George Washington High Sch., Cedar Rapids, Iowa, 1981—. Recipient Blue Ribbon Sch. award Dept. Edn., 1983, 91, 2000. Office: George Washington High Sch 2205 Forest Dr SE Cedar Rapids IA 52403-1653

PLAISTED, CAROLE ANNE, elementary education educator; b. Meredith, N.H., Apr. 3, 1939; d. Morris Holman and Christina Martin (Dunn) Plaisted. BEd with honors, Plymouth (N.H.) Tchrs. Coll., 1960; MA, Columbia U., 1966; cert., N.Y. Inst. Photography, 1990. Cert. tchr., N.H. Tchr. Lang St. Sch., Meredith, 1960-61, Mechanic St. Sch., Laconia, N.H., 1961-62, Wheelock Lab. Sch., Keene, N.H., 1963-94; asst. prof. emeritus Keene State Coll. Summer tchr. Cheshire County Headstart, Hinsdale, N.H., 1965; tchr. children's lit. Keene State Coll., 1974, 75; classroom evaluator D.C. Heath Co., Lexington, Mass., 1985-86; dist. trainer for drug edn. supervisory unit, Keene, 1988-94. Author: The Graduates Speak, 1990; co-author curriculum materials; contbr. Kindergarten: A Sourcebook for School and Home, 1984. Trustee Reed Free Libr., Surry, N.H., 1988-2000; program chair Wheelock Sch. PTA, 1964-65. Named Outstanding Elem. Tchr. of Am., 1973. Mem. Cheshire County Ret. Tchrs. Assn., Delta Kappa Gamma (pres. Alpha chpt. 1996-98, 2000-02, corr. sec. Alpha chpt. 1972-76, state scholarship chmn. 1985—, Beta Alpha state scholarship 1989, Founders award, 2001). Avocations: reading, gardening, photography.

PLANO, SANDRA KAY, secondary school educator; b. Bucyrus, Ohio, July 30, 1949; d. Doyle Michael and Freda Marie (Niedermier) Coder; m. C. Raymond McNutt, Nov. 20, 1971 (div. Dec. 1986); m. Ronald R. Plano, May 1, 1992. BS in Secondary Edn., Kent State U., 1971; MEdn, Youngstown State U., 1981. Cert. tchr., Ohio. Tchr. English Cloverleaf High Sch., Lodi, Ohio, 1971-73, West Br. High Sch., Beloit, Ohio, 1974—. Team mem. Project Arete Youngstown State U., 1983-87; mem. composition competency testing com. Mahoning County Schs., course study com. English, 1983-84, 89. Author: (with others) Teacher to Teacher, 1985, 2d edit., 1987. Lector, eucharistic minister. Recipient Gold award Herff Jones Yearbook Co., 1987, Showcase awards (2) Herff Jones Yearbook Co., 1987, 1st Pl. award Ohio State Grow Tchr. Contest Youngstown Vindicator, 1990, Golden Apple award, 2000. Mem. NEA, Ohio Edn. Assn., Quota Club (sec. 1988, 2d v.p. 1989, 1st v.p. 1990—), Kappa Delta Pi. Roman Catholic. Avocations: antique collecting, sports, reading. Office: West Branch High Sch 14277 S Main St Beloit OH 44609-9500

PLANTE, ROBERT DONALD, management educator, university dean; b. Providence, Feb. 7, 1948; s. Robert Annaclet and Grace Joan Plante; m. Jean Karole Hostetler, May 29, 1982; children: Michael, Eric, Jason. BS in Physics, Worcester Poly. Inst., 1970; PhD in Mgmt., U. Ga., 1980. Electronic intelligence officer Army Security Agy., 1970-76; asst. prof. mgmt. Purdue U., West Lafayette, Ind., 1980-84, assoc. prof., 1985-89, prof., 1990—, assoc. dean, 1999-2000, sr. assoc. dean, 2000—. Area editor Prodn. and Ops., 1990—; mem. editl. bd. Strategic Mgmt., 1995—; contbr. over 50 articles to profl. jours. Mem. Elks. Roman Catholic. Office: Purdue U Krannert Grad Sch Mgmt 1310 Krannert Bldg West Lafayette IN 47907-1310

PLANTS, WALTER DALE, retired elementary school educator, minister; b. Middlefield, Ohio, June 8, 1942; s. William E. and Hazel A. Plants; m. Sarah A. Gaddis, July 5, 1962; children: Dale Anthony, Jeanette Marie. BD, Azusa Pacific U., 1967; MEd, U. Nev., 1970. Cert. elem. tchr., ednl. adminstr. Elem. tchr. Churchill County Sch. Dist., Fallon, Nev., 1967—69, 1970—72, elem tchr., 1988—2001; grad. asst. U. Nev., Reno, 1969-70; tchr. Kingman (Ariz.) Elem. Sch. Dist. #4, 1972-77; head sci. program E. C. Best Elem. Sch., Fallon, 1988—2001; ret., 2001. Adj. instr. Ariz. State U., Tempe, 1973-77; cons. sci. Ariz. State Dept. Edn., 1975-77. Bd. dirs. Solar Energy Commn. Mohave County, Ariz., 1974; coord. County Sci. Fair, 1988-93; active Western Regional Sci. Fair Com.; sci. fair coord. Churchill County, 1989-94; mem. com. Regional Sci. Fair, 1992-94. HEW fellow, 1969; NSF grantee, 1973; AIMS Found. scholar, 1988; recipient Ariz. State PTA award, 1977, Ruth Neldon award Ariz. State Dept., 1977, Conservation award Big Sandy Natural Resources Conservation Dist. Ariz., 1976, Community Builder Svc. award Masons, Fallon, 1991, Disting. Leadership award, 1991-93; named State Tchr. of Yr. Nev. PTA, 1991, Conservation Tchr. of Yr., 1991; named to Congl. Select Edn. panel U.S. Congress, 1993. Mem. NEA, AAAS, Nat. Sci. Tchrs. Assn., Nat. Coun. Tchrs. Math., Internat. Reading Assn., Churchill County Edn. Assn. (Tchr. of Yr. 1989), Internat. Platform Assn., Nat. Arbor Day Found., World Wildlife Fund, Nat. Parks and Conservation Assn., Nat. Audubon Soc., Nev. State Tchrs. of Yr. Assn. (pres. 1994-96, pres. 1996-97), Phi Delta Kappa.

PLATA, MIRIAM RUTH, English language and ESL educator; b. Bronx, N.Y., July 18, 1951; d. Juan (John) Eugenio and Elena (Monllor) P.; m. Jaime Luis Muñoz, Dec. 24, 1972; children: Jessica Muñoz, Eleana Muñoz. Bachelors, U. P.R., 1972, Masters, 1985. Cert. tchr., P.R. Tchr. English Pub. Dept. Edn., Carolina, P.R., 1972-86; asst. prof. English U. P.R., Rio Piedras, 1986—. Cooperating tchr. faculty of edn. U. P.R., Rio Piedras, 1976—. Recipient Author of Yr. award Am. Edn. Inst., 1993; grantee U. P.R., 1992. Mem. ASCD, NEA, Nat. Coun. Tchrs. of English, Tchrs. of English to Speakers of Other Langs. (P.R. chpt.), Speech Comm. Assn. P.R., P.R. Tchrs. Assn., P.R. Coun. Internat. Reading Assn. Roman Catholic. Avocations: reading, music, movies, spending time with family. Office: U P R Secondary Sch Box 23319 U PR Sta Rio Piedras PR 00931

PLATE, JANET MARGARET DIETERLE, immunology educator, scientist; b. Minot, N.D., Nov. 27, 1943; d. David and Bertha (Hoffer) Dieterle; m. Charles Alfred Plate, June 12, 1964; children: Jason, Stacey, Aileen, Derek. BA, Jamestown Coll., 1964; postgrad., Syracuse U., 1964—65; PhD in microbiology and immunology, Duke U., 1970. Am. Cancer Soc. postdoctoral fellow Mass. Gen. Hosp., Boston, 1970-72; assoc. in immunology Harvard U.-Mass. Gen. Hosp., Boston, 1972-77; asst. prof. Harvard U. Sch. Pub. Health, Boston, 1977-78; asst. prof. immunology dept. immunology and microbiology Rush-Presbyn.-St. Luke's Med. Ctr., Chgo., 1978-80, assoc. prof. immunology dept. immunology and microbiology, 1980-89, asst. prof. medicine dept. internal medicine, 1978-82, assoc. prof. medicine dept. internal medicine, 1982-89, prof. medicine dept. internal medicine and immunology, 1989—. Sci. reviewer immunobiology study sect. NIH, Bethesda, Md., 1979-83, mem. allergy, immunology and transp. com.; mem. rsch. rev. com. Ill. divsn. Am. Cancer Soc., Chgo., 1979-90; mem. sci. adv. bd. Nat. Cancer Cytology Ctr., N.Y., 1982—; med. adv. bd. Leukemia Rsch. Found., Inc., Chgo., 1986-88; mem. com. sr. faculty appointments and promotions Rush Med. Coll., 1987-90, 93-96, instnl. rev. bd., 1998—. Mem. editl. bd. Transplantation, 1976-79, Immunopharmacology, 1978-90, Jour. Immunology, assoc. editor, 1989-93; contbr. articles to books and jours. Mem. cancer ctrs. support revs. com. Nat. Cancer Inst. Cancer Ctrs., NIH, Bethesda, Md., 1990—; mem. ad hoc student sect. rev. com. NASA, 1994; ruling elder Cmty. Presbyn. Ch., 1980-83; sec. Hornet Swim Club, 1985-88, co-v.p., 1988-89, co-pres., 1989-90, elected bd. mem. Sch. Dist. #62, 1989-93, pres., 1993—; bd. dirs., sec. Hinsdale Twp. H.S. #86, 2001-03, pres., 2003—. Grantee Nat. Cancer Inst./NIH, 1975, 78—. Mem. Am. Assn. Immunologists, Am. Soc. Histocompatibility and Immunogenetics, Transplantation Soc., Chgo. Assn. Immunologists (chmn. 1980-82), Am. Assn. Cancer Rsch., Mid-West PCR Discussion Group (charter bd. dirs. 1992—). Office: Rush-Presbyn St Luke's Med Ctr 1753 W Congress Pky Chicago IL 60612-3809

PLATER, WILLIAM MARMADUKE, English language educator, academic administrator; b. East St. Louis, Ill., July 26, 1945; s. Everett Marmaduke and Marguerite (McBride) P.; m. Gail Maxwell, Oct. 16, 1971; children: Elizabeth Rachel, David Matthew. BA, U. Ill., 1967, MA in English, 1969, PhD in English, 1973. Asst. dir. Unit One, asst. to dean Coll. Liberal Arts and Scis. U. Ill., Urbana, 1971-72, acting dir. Unit One, 1972-73, asst. dean Coll. Arts and Scis., 1973-74, asst. dir. Sch. Humanities, 1974-77, assoc. dir., 1977-83, assoc. coordinator interdisciplinary programs, 1977-83; prof. English, dean Sch. Liberal Arts Ind. U., Indpls., 1983-87; dean of faculties Ind. U.-Purdue U., Indpls., 1987—, exec. vice chancellor, 1988—, acting chancellor, 2003. Bd. dirs. Met. Indpls. Pub. Broadcasting, Inc.; cons. in field. Author: The Grim Phoenix: Reconstructing Thomas Pynchon, 1978, also articles, revs., poetry. Trustee Coun. for Adult and Experiential Learning, 1995—; bd. dirs. Ind. Com. for Humanities, 1986—92, Ind. Repertory Theatre, 1987—93, Children's Mus., 1992—2001, U. Ill. YMCA, Urbana, 1982—83, Herron Gallery Contemporary Art, 1987—93; bd. govs. Ind. U. Ctr. on Philanthropy, 1997—; bd. dirs. Midwest Univs. Consortium for Internat. Activities, Inc., 1996—98. Recipient Program Innovation prize Am. Acad. Ednl. Devel., 1982. Home: 6477 Oxbow Way Indianapolis IN 46220- Office: IUPUI Adminstrn Bldg A0108 Indianapolis IN 46202 E-mail: wplater@iupui.edu.

PLATIS, JAMES GEORGE, secondary school educator; b. Detroit, Mar. 23, 1927; s. Sam and Myra (Theodore) P.; m. Mary Lou Campbell, Aug. 16, 1974. BS in Physical Edn., Ind. U., 1955, MS in Edn., 1965; postgrad., Ind. State U., 1967. Cert. physical edn. tchr., Ind. Foreman Cast Armor, Inc., East Chicago, Ind., 1951-53, Youngstown Sheet & Tube, East Chicago, 1953-54; dir., tchr. East Chicago Pub. Schs., 1955—. Sports editor East Chicago Globe/Calumet News, 1973-78, Herald Newspapers, Merrillville, Ind., 1973-78; asst. dir. No. Ind. State Sports Mus., 1984-99. Contbr. articles to newspapers, jours. Founder East Chicago Hall of Fame, 1975, Little Olympics, East Chicago, 1956; pres. Ind. Am. Amateur Baseball Congress, 1954-57, commr., 1984-98; dir. No. Ind. State Sports Mus., 1988-00. With AUS, 1945-47, ETO. Named to Ind. Amateur Baseball Hall of Fame, 1962, East Chicago Hall of Fame, 1976, All-Am. Amateur Baseball Congress, 1955, 56, The Athletic Congress Masters All-Am., 1986-98, 99, 2000, 2001-02; selected to 90 Yr. Greatest Athletes in East Chicago History, Nat. Athletic Congress, 1990; named Amateur Coach of Yr., U.S. Baseball Fedn. Ind., 1990, Amateur Runner-up Coach of Yr., 1988; recipient 53 World and 61 Nat. No. 1 track rankings, Athletic Congress Masters, 1989-98, 2000, 2001-02, 14 League Batting Titles, 12 MV League Players awards; Ind. Jr. Legion State Champions, All-State Batting Champions, MVP in tournament, Conf. Baseball Champions, 1943, 44, 45, All-Conf. Team, 1944-45, Conf. Batting Champion, 1944, Team Cptn., 1945, All-Midwest team, Best Outfielder, 1944; 18 times Ind. all-state team; Ind. Nat. Baseball State Champions; mem. team won 53 League Championships, 54 Playoff championships, 41 Ind. State Baseball Championships, 5 Ind. State Champions Runner Up, 7 World Regional Titles, 5 World Finalists, 2 runner-up World Champions, Big Ten baseball champions Ind. U., 1949, Best Outfielder Congress All-State team, Ill., Ind. Bi-State Champions, 1950; Nat. C.I.O. Baseball Championship, 1951, 12 Times League Mgr. Of The Year, 1982-96; Big Ten Baseball Champions, Ind. U., 1949; named Athlete of Yr. Ind. Masters Track and Field, 1992, World Sr. Olympic Masters Track & Field Champion, Spain, 6 gold medals, named Best Performer, 3 Masters Track & Field World Records, 1992, Fla. Masters Track and Field Athlete of Yr., 1994-98; recipient 74 State Ind. Track and Field Individual Gold medals, 1983-99, 2000-02, 84 Ind. state regional individual gold medals, 1983-98, 2000-02, 291 All Am. Masters Track and Field Certs., 1986-99, 2000-02, 39 Ill. Grand Prix individual titles, 1989-92, 45 Mid-West Track and Field individual titles, 1989-92, 5 gold medals, silver medal World Sr. Olympic Masters Track & Field, 1996, Ga., 5 Masters Track & Field World Records, 1997, 2 Masters Track & Field World Records, 1998, Nat. Senior Olympics Qualifer, 1991, 93, 95, 97, 99, 2001, 03, 4 Gold medals, 2 World Records Nat. Sr. Olympics, 1999-2001, 7 gold medals World Sr. Olympic Masters Track and Field, Sydney, Australia, 2000, 5 World Records, selected Best Performer; named Internat. Man of the Yr. in Edn., 1991-92, 93, Professional of the Yr. in Edn., 1991, Master Track and Field All-Am., 1986-2003, Northwest Ind. Intriguing Family of the Yr., 2002. Fellow Nat. Assn. Basketball Coaches, Am. Assn. Health, Phys. Edn. and Recreation; mem. Athletic Dirs. Assn. Sportswriters Guild, VFW, Am. Legion, WWII Meml. (82nd Airborne Divsn., 1st Inf. Divsn. 1998), Mens Club Ind. U. Republican. Avocations: reading, running, baseball, writing.

PLATT, LESLIE OLIVER, psychologist; b. Atlanta, Jan. 17, 1960; d. Andrew Gordon and Zonna Laurece (Williams) Oliver; m. James William Platt, Aug. 14, 1982. BS, Presbyn. Coll., 1982; MEd, Ga. State U., 1984; PhD, U. Ga., 1993. Cert. sch. psychology, mental retardation, S.C. Spl. edn. tchr. Fulton County Bd. Edn., Atlanta, 1982-83, Alexander City (Ala.) Bd. Edn., 1984-86, Tallassee (Ala.) City Bd. Edn., 1986-88; psychometrist Wilkes County Bd. Edn., Washington, Ga., 1988-89; grad. asst. U. Ga., Athens, 1989-92; psychology intern N.W. Ga. Regional Hosp., Rome, 1992-93; psychologist Beckman Mental Health Ctr., Greenwood, S.C., 1993-94, Whitten Ctr., Clinton, S.C., 1994—. Contbr. articles to profl. jours. Scholar Presbyn. Coll., 1982. Mem. APA, Nat. Assn. Sch. Psychologists, Assn. Mental Retardation, Coun. Exceptional Children, Assn. Retarded Citizens Ea. Elmore County (bd. dirs. 1987-88, chair membership 1987-88), Kappa Delta Pi. Presbyterian. Avocations: cross-stitch, photography, reading, nature walks, pets. Home: 135 Woodland Dr Chester SC 29706-1905

PLATTI, RITA JANE, secondary school educator, draftsman, writer, inventor; b. Stockton, Calif., Aug. 29, 1925; d. Umbert Ferdinand and Concettina Maria (Natoli) Strangio; m. Elvin Carl Platti, July 27, 1955; 1 child, Kimberley Jane. Student, Dominican Coll., 1943-45; AB in Math, U. Pacific, 1947, postgrad., 1947-52, 68. Farmer, almond grower, Escalon, Calif., 1943—; tchr. math St. Mary's High Sch., Stockton, 1947-49, 52, 54; chem. analyst Petri Winery, Escalon, 1949; draftsman Kyle Steel Co., Stockton, 1950-52; pvt. practice as draftsman Stockton, 1952-66; tchr. math Montezuma Sch., Stockton, 1956-57, Davis Elem. Sch., Stockton, 1957-58; with rental bus., 1958-81; tchr. math Amos Alonzo Stagg High Sch., 1961-80, Humphreys Coll., 1981-83, Hamilton Jr. High Sch., 1984-90. Owner, involved in prodn. and mktg. R.J. Creations, 1991—; farm realtor Century 21, Escalon, Calif., 1996-97; spkr. workshops Stanislaus State U., 1992, Calif. Math. Coun., Fresno State U., 1992, Nat. Sci. Found. Conf., 1993; spkr. math./sci. conf. Calif. State U., Bakerfield, 1994-96; evaluator Math. Framework (K-12) Calif. State Dept. Edn. Author: Math Proficiency Plateaus, 1979, Preparing Fundamentals of The Use of Sound in the Teaching of Mathematics, 1994, Book of Poems, 2002; author, pub. series, 1979-86; 3 patents in field. Mem. NEA, Calif. Tchrs. Assn. Democrat. Roman Catholic. Avocations: inventing, mathematics theoretical development, poetry, piano, environmental clean up.

PLATZER, MAX F. aeronautics and astronautics educator; b. Vienna, June 26, 1933; came to U.S., 1960; s. Josef and Stefanie (Hopfgartner) P.; m. Dorothea Helene Ortner, June 28, 1958; children: Michaela, Christopher, Susan. Diploma ing., Tech. U., Vienna, 1957, D in Tech. Sci., 1964. Asst. prof. aeronautics Tech. U., Vienna, 1957-60; aerospace engr. NASA Marshall Space Flight Ctr., Huntsville, Ala., 1960-66; rsch. scientist Lockheed-Ga. Rsch. Ctr., Marietta, 1966-70; prof. Naval Postgrad. Sch., Monterey, Calif., 1970—. Mem. editl. bd. Progress in Aerospace Scis. Co-editor 3 books on aerodynamics and aeroelasticity; contbr. articles to profl. jours. Fellow AIAA (assoc. editor 1990-93, 90—), ASME. Achievements include patents in field. Office: Naval Postgrad Sch Dept Aero Astronautics Monterey CA 93943

PLAUD, JOSEPH JULIAN, psychology educator; b. Worcester, Mass., Mar. 25, 1965; s. Henry Emile and Barbara Ann (Perry) P.; m. Christine Marie Therlault, Mar. 14, 1987 (div. Mar. 1990); 1 child, Brianna Marie; m. Deborah Muench, Jan. 30, 1999. BA summa cum laude, Clark U., 1987; PhD in Psychology, U. Maine, 1993. Lic. clin. psychologist, Mass.; bd. cert. behavior analyst Behavior Analyst Certification Bd. Psychology resident U. Miss. Med. Ctr., Jackson, 1992-93; asst. prof. psychology U. N.D., Grand Forks, 1993-97; dir. rsch., webmaster Cambridge (Mass.) Ctr. for Behavioral Studies, 1999—; exec. dir. Franklin D. Roosevelt Am. Heritage Ctr., Inc. Cons. N.D. Devel. Ctr., Grafton, 1994—, State of N.H., 1999—; forensic cons., 1993—; vis. scholar Brown U., 1998—; COO New Sch. for Learning Scis.; forensic psychology cons. Applied Behavioral Cons., Inc.; exec. dir. Franklin D. Roosevelt Am. Heritage Ctr., Inc. Author: From Behavior Theory to Behavior Therapy, 1997; editor-in-chief Jour. Behavioral Analysis and Therapy; contbr. articles to profl. jours. Exec. dir. Franklin D. Roosevelt Am. Heritage Ctr., Inc. Lt. Med. Svc. Corps, USNR, 1997. Fellow APA, Behavior Therapy and Rsch. Soc. (clin.); mem. AAAS, Assn. for Advancement of Behavior Therapy, Am. Psychol. Soc., Am. Psychol. Assn., Phi Beta Kappa, Psi Chi. Democrat. Roman Catholic. Home: 44 Hickory Ln Whitinsville MA 01588-1356

PLAUT, JANE MARGARET, art educator; b. Bklyn., Mar. 31, 1948; d. Charles and Jane Elizabeth (Moore) Rifenberg; m. Harold J. Plaut, Dec. 14, 1968 (div. 1981); 1 child, Harold Jonathan Jr. AAS, N.Y.C. C.C., Bklyn., 1968; BA, Bklyn. Coll., 1978; MA, NYU, 1986. Permanent cert. H.S. art tchg. Staff artist Pastarnack Assn., N.Y.C., 1968, 69; tchr. St. Joseph's Coll., Yokohama, Japan, 1970, St. Maur Internat. Sch., Yokohama, 1970, Good Shepherd Sch., Bklyn., 1978-82, Our Lady Help of Christians, Bklyn., 1978-82, Bishop Kearney H.S., Bklyn., 1982—. Tchr. Saturday humanities enrichment program St. John's U., 2000. One-woman shows include 80 Washington Square East, N.Y.C., 1985, 39 5th Ave., N.Y.C., 1996; works exhibited in group shows at The Paul VI Inst. for Arts, Washington, 1982, 86, Querini Stampali, Venice, Italy, 1983, 84, Bishop Kearney H.S., Bklyn., 1988, 89, Selena Gallery-L.I. U., Bklyn., 1988, St. John's U., Queens, N.Y., 1990, Cathedral Basilica St. James, Bklyn., 2000, others; author, illustrator (children's book): Pierre Le Car, 2001. Recipient commendation for outstanding contbn. to edn. St. Francis Coll., 1991, 92, 94, Gold Photo award Bay Ridge Cmty. Coun., 1999; Fashion Inst. Tech. fellow, 1997. Mem. Internat. Ctr. Photography, Nat. Art Edn. Assn., Nat. Mus. Women in the Arts (charter) Met. Mus. Art, Bklyn. Mus. Avocations: painting, photography, reading. Office: Bishop Kearney HS 2202 60th St Brooklyn NY 11204-2599

PLEACHER, DAVID HENRY, secondary school educator; b. Reading, Pa., Dec. 29, 1946; s. John K. and Isabel Kathleen (Moyer) P.; m. Carol Elizabeth Jackson, June 8, 1968; children: Amy Elizabeth, Michael David, Sarah Catherine. BA in Math., Hartwick Coll., 1968; MS in Edn., James Madison U., 1971. Cert. tchr., Va. Tchr. Arlington (Va.) County Pub. Schs., 1968, Fairfax County Pub. Schs., Herndon, Va., 1968-73; tchr., dept. chair Winchester (Va.) City Schs., 1973—. Instr. James Madison U., Harrisonburg, Va., 1982-87; lectr., instr. Lord Fairfax C.C., Middletown, Va., 1986-89; project mem. Computer Software Devel. Project, 1985-90; participant Math. Inst. Woodrow Wilson Found., Princeton, 1986. Co-editor: (computer column) Va. Math. Tchr., 1982-84; author computer programs; contbr. articles to profl. jours. Recipient Presdl. award in excellence in math and sci. teaching NSF, Washington, 1985, Homer "Pete" Ice Svc. award Handley High Athletic Dept., 1991, Tandy Tech. Scholars award Tandy Corp./T.C.U., Washington, 1992. Mem. NEA (life), Va. Edn. Assn., Winchester Edn. Assn., Nat. Coun. Tchrs. Math. (presenter at confs.), Va. Coun. Tchrs. Math. (presenter at confs., William Lowry Outstanding Math Tchr. 1987), Valley Va. Coun. Tchrs. Math., Coun. Presdl. Awardees in Math. Presbyterian. Avocations: model railroading, sports, games, computer programming. Home: 304 Caroline Ave Stephens City VA 22655-5925 Office: John Handley High Sch PO Box 910 Winchester VA 22604-0910

PLEIN, KATHRYN ANNE, retired secondary school educator; b. Ashland, Wis., Jan. 28, 1945; d. Donald and Frances (Tankersly) Smith; m. Arvid Arthur Plein, Dec. 19, 1970; children: Marty, Michelle. BS in Broadfield Sci., Northland Coll., 1967; MS in Tchg., U. Wis., Superior, 1973. Cert. secondary science tchr., Wis. 7th grade sci. tchr. Wausau (Wis.) Sch. Dist., 1967-73; tchr. John Muir Mid. Sch., Wausau, 1977; ret., 2000. Mem.: AAUW (pres.-elect 1997—2000). Roman Catholic. Home: R 8800 Hwy J Schofield WI 54476

PLINE, JAMES LEONARD, civil engineer, educator; b. Nampa, Idaho, Nov. 18, 1931; s. John Clinton and Marlys H. (Hartzell) P.; m. Beverly J. Stewart, Jan. 30, 1954; 1 son, Patrick James. BSCE, U. Idaho, 1954; cert. traffic engring., Yale U., 1959; MPA, Boise State U., 1978. Registered profl. engr., Idaho, land surveyor, Idaho; cert. profl. traffic ops. engr. Asst. traffic engr. Idaho Hwy. Dept., Boise, 1963-65, asst. dist. engr. Shoshone,

1965-69; traffic engr. Idaho Transp. Dept., Boise, 1969-79, environ. and coord. planning engr., 1979-81, concept rev. engr., 1981-83, design engr., 1983-87; pres. Pline Engring., Inc., 1987—. Affiliate prof. dept. civil engring. U. Idaho, 1982— ; mem. nat. adv. com. on uniform traffic control devices, 1971—, vice chmn., 1987-98, chmn. rsch., 1987-98. Author: ITE Traffic Engineering Handbook, Expert Witness Information Notebook, Traffic Control Devices Handbook; contbr. articles to profl. jours. Mem. Idaho Traffic Safety Commn., 1970—, City Design Rev. Com., Boise, 1977-85; scoutmaster Boy Scouts Am., Boise, 1974-76. Served to lt. col. USAF. Recipient Outstanding Engring. award Idaho, 1985, Burton Marsh award, 1993, Edward Ricker Safety award, 1997; Auto Safety Found. fellow, 1958. Mem. NSPE (nat. dir. 1982-84; Outstanding Contbn. award 1974), Inst. Transp. Engrs. (hon., internat. dir. 1976-78, chmn. tech. coun. 1984—, internat. pres., 1989, Disting. Mem. award Intermountain sect. 1984, Wayne T. Van Waggoner award, 1992, Lifetime Achievement award, 2001), Idaho Soc. Profl. Engrs. (pres. 1979), Transp. Rsch. Bd., Order of Engr. (sec. Idaho chpt. 1977—), Idaho N.G. Assn. (pres. 1972, 73). Home: 2520 Fry Cir Boise ID 83704-6179 Office: 2520 Fry Cir Boise ID 83704-6179

PLISCHKE, ELMER, political science educator; b. Milw., July 15, 1914; s. Louis and Louise (Peterleus) P.; m. Audrey Alice Siehr, May 30, 1941; children: Lowell Robert, Julianne. Ph.B. cum laude, Marquette U., 1937; MA, Am. U., 1938; certificate Carnegie summer session internat. law, U. Mich., 1938; PhD (fellow), Clark U., 1943; certificate, Naval Sch. Mil. Govt. and Civil Affairs, Columbia, 1944. Instr. Springfield Coll., 1940; dist. supr., state dir. Wis. Hist. Records Survey, 1940-42; exec. sec. War Records Commn., Wis. Council Def., 1942; asst. prof. DePauw U., 1946-48, U. Md., College Park, 1948-49, assoc. prof., 1949-52, prof., 1952-79, prof. emeritus, 1979—, head dept. govt. and politics, 1954-68; adj. prof. Gettysburg (Pa.) Coll., 1979-85. Spl. historian Office U.S. High Commr. for Germany, 1950-52; cons. Dept. State, summer 1952; adj. scholar Am. Enterprise Inst. Pub. Policy Research, 1978— ; lectr. Air War Coll., Armed Forces Staff Coll., Army War Coll., Def. Intelligence Sch., Indsl. Coll. Armed Forces, Inter-Am. Def. Coll., Nat. War Coll.; lectr. Sr. Officers Seminar Fgn. Service Inst. Dept. State; lectr. Instituto de Altos Estudios Nacionales, Quito, Ecuador.; mem. adv. com. fgn. relations of U.S. Dept. State, 1967-72, chmn., 1969-70; assoc. fellow Gettysburg Coll., 1993—. Author 30 books and monographs including: Conduct of American Diplomacy, 3d edit, 1967, reissued, 1974, (with Robert G. Dixon, Jr.) American Government: Basic Documents and Materials, 1950, reissued, 1971, Berlin: Development of Its Government and Administration, 1952, reissued, 1970, The Allied High Commission for Germany, 1953, International Relations: Basic Documents, rev, 1962, American Foreign Relations: A Bibliography of Official Sources, 1955, reissued, 1966, American Diplomacy: A Bibliography of Biographies, Autobiographies, and Commentaries, 1957, Summit Diplomacy: Personal Diplomacy of the President of the United States, 1958, reissued, 1974, Contemporary Governments of Germany, 1961, rev. edit., 1969, Government and Politics of Contemporary Berlin, 1963, Foreign Relations Decisionmaking: Options Analysis, 1973, United States Diplomats and Their Missions: A Profile of American Diplomatic Emissaries Since 1778, 1975, Microstates in World Affairs: Policy Problems and Options, 1977, Neutralization as an American Strategic Option, 1978, Modern Diplomacy: The Art and the Artisans, 1979, U.S. Foreign Relations: A Guide to Information Sources, 1980, Presidential Diplomacy: A Chronology of Summit Visits, Trips and Meetings, 1986, Diplomat in Chief: The President at the Summit, 1986, Foreign Relations: Analysis of Its Anatomy, 1988, Contemporary United States Foreign Policy: Documents and Commentary, 1991, U.S. Department of State: A Reference History, 1999, others; contbr. more than 80 articles to profl. and lit. jours., and encyclopaedias; Americana Ann., 1972-83; also editorials in newspapers; editor, contbr. Systems of Integrating the International Community, 1964; mem. bd. editors Jour. Politics, 1966-68. Served from ensign to lt. USNR, 1943-46; exec. asst., then exec. officer Civil Affairs div., comdr. U.S. Naval Forces for Europe, London, 1944-45; charge denazcification policy coordination Office Dir. Polit. Affairs, Office Mil. Govt. for Germany 1945. Recipient research awards U. Md. Gen. Research Bd., 1956, 58, 69, Eliza Dodd and Henry White Ford rsch. award Clark U., 1940; research grantee Earhart Found., 1982-83, 86-87; book Interaction: Foreign Policy and Public Policy (Piper and Terchek) dedicated in honor, 1983; elected Knight Mark Twain, Mark Twain Jour., 1970. Mem. AAUP, Am. Soc. Internat. Law, Am. Polit. Sci. Assn. (coun.), D.C. Polit. Sci. Assn. (coun. mem., pres. 1961), So. Polit. Sci. Assn. (coun.), Internat. Studies Assn., Com. Study Diplomacy, Inst. Study Diplomacy, Internat. Torch Club (sec. Gettysburg club 1985-91, archivist 1991—, bd. mem. 1995-97), Eclectic Club, Phi Beta kappa, Phi Kappa Phi, Pi Sigma Alpha, Sigma Tau Delta. Home: 227 Ewell Ave Gettysburg PA 17325-3108

PLITT, DORIS SMITH, elementary education educator; b. Clarksdale, Miss., Feb. 15, 1949; d. Eldrew Polk and Mavis Melissa (Bates) Smith; m. Milton Christian Plitt, Feb. 7, 1971; children: Matthew, Laren. BS in Elem. Edn., Delta State U., Cleveland, Miss., 1970, MEd, 1972; cert. in gifted and talented edn., U. North Tex., 1994. Cert. tchr. ESL. Tchr. Claibourne Edn. Found., Port Gibson, Miss., 1971-72, Manhattan Sch., Jackson, Miss., 1972-75, Madison (Miss.) Ridgeland Acad., 1975-77, Jackson (La.) Elem. Sch., 1977-78, Walker (La.) Elem. Sch., 1978-80, St. Thomas More Sch., Baton Rouge, 1980-88; tchr., team leader Christie Elem. Sch., Plano, Tex., 1988—99; facilitator for ESL Eastside Elem., Rogers, Ark., 2001—. Region level judge Odyssey of the Mind, 1993—99. Master Bible story teller Hunters' Glen Bapt. Ch., 1992—99, mem. evangelism explosion team. Named Tchr. of Yr., Christie Elem. Sch., 1994; recipient Excellence in Tchg. award Plano Ind. Sch. Dist., 1994. Mem. Delta Kappa Gamma (editor Mu Beta chpt. newsletter), Delta Delta Delta. Baptist. Avocations: travel, reading. Home: 15514 Putman Rd Rogers AR 72756-7873 Office: Eastside Elem 505 New Hope Rogers AR 72756

PLONUS, MARTIN ALGIRDAS, electrical engineering educator; b. Trumpininken, Lithuania, Dec. 21, 1933; came to U.S., 1949, naturalized, 1955; s. Christopher and Anna (Sliupas) P.; m. Martina Rauer, Feb. 20, 1965; children— Sabine, Jacqueline, Marcus, Michelle BS, U. Ill., 1956, MS, 1957; PhD, U. Mich., 1961. Asst. prof. elec. engring. Northwestern U., Evanston, Ill., 1961-64, assoc. prof., 1964-69, prof., 1969—, dir. grad. program, 1989—; rsch. mathematician U. Mich., summers 1964-66. Bd. dirs. Ctr. Integrated Microelectronic Systems. Author: Applied Electromagnetics, 1978; contbr. articles to profl. jours. Grantee OSRD, 1964, NSF, 1967, 75-77, 94—, U.S. Air Force, 1980-85. Fellow IEEE (chmn. group antennas and propagation Chgo. sect. 1966-67, spl. recognition award 1971); mem. Internat. Sci. Radio Union, AAUP, U. Mich. Rsch. Club,, Electromagnetics Acad., Sigma Xi, Eta Kappa Nu, Sigma Tau, Tau Beta Pi. Nat. sailing champion Shields class. Home: 2525 Orrington Ave Evanston IL 60201-2427 Office: Northwestern U Dept Elec Engring & Comp Sci Evanston IL 60201

PLORDE, JAMES JOSEPH, physician, educator; b. Brewster, Minn., Feb. 16, 1934; s. James Arthur and Mary Jeanette (Lutz) P.; m. Diane Sylvia Koenigs, Aug. 28, 1964 (div. July 1974); children: Lisa Marie, Michele Louise, James Joshua; m. Jo Ann Gates, Dec. 22, 1986. BA, U. Minn., 1956, BS, 1957, MD, 1959. Diplomate Am. Bd. Internal Medicine, Am. Bd. Pathology. Vol. leader Peace Corps, Gondar, Ethiopia, 1964-66; intern King County Hosp., Seattle, 1959-60; resident U. Wash., Seattle, 1960-62, fellow infectious diseases, 1962-64; chief med. resident King County Hosp., Seattle, 1966-67; asst. prof. medicine U. Wash., Seattle, 1967-71, assoc. prof., 1971-78; fellow clin. microbiology, 1972-73; prof. medicine, lab. medicine U. Wash. Sch. Medicine, Seattle, 1978-98 (ret.), prof. emeritus medicine, lab. medicine, 1998—; head clin. investigation U.S. Naval Med. Research, Addis Ababa, Ethiopia, 1968-71; chief infectious diseases VA Hosp., Seattle, 1973-89, chief clin. microbiology, 1973-98; ret., 1998. Instr. U. Wash., 1966-67; cons. WHO, 1975, Suez Canal U. Faculty of Medicine, Ismailia, Arab Republic of Egypt, 1981-85. Contbr. numerous articles to profl. jours., chpts. to books. Fellow Infectious Disease Soc., ACP; mem. AAAS, Am. Soc. Microbiology, Acad. Clin. Lab. Physicians and Scientists. Home: 3164 W Laurelhurst Dr NE Seattle WA 98105-5346 Fax: 206-523-3541. E-mail: jjplorde@u.washington.edu.

PLOSSER, CHARLES IRVING, economist, educator; b. Birmingham, Ala., Sept. 19, 1948; s. George Gray and Dorothy (Irving) P.; m. Janet Schwert, June 26, 1976; children: Matthew, Kevin, Allison. B.E. cum laude, Vanderbilt U., 1970; MBA, U. Chgo., 1972, PhD, 1976. Cons. Citicorp Realty Cons., N.Y.C., 1972-73; lectr. Grad. Sch. Bus., U. Chgo., 1975-76; asst. prof. Grad. Sch. Bus. Stanford (Calif.) U., 1976-78; asst. prof. econs. W.E. Simon Grad. Sch. Bus., U. Rochester (N.Y.), 1978-82, assoc. prof., 1982-86, prof., 1986-89; Fred H. Gowen prof. econs. U. Rochester, N.Y., 1989-92, John M. Olin Disting. prof. econs. and pub. policy, 1992—, acting dean W.E. Simon Grad. Sch. Bus., 1990-91, 92-93, dean, 1993—2003. Chmn. bd. Consortium for Grad. Study in Mgmt., 1995-97; bd. dirs. ViaHealth, Inc., 1995-2000, Rochester Gas & Electric Corp, RGS Energy Group, 1996-2002, dir. adv. bd., 2002-; bd. dirs. Grad. Mgmt. Admission Coun., 1997-2003, chmn. bd., 2002-03. Editor, Jour. Monetary Econs., 1983—, Carnegie-Rochester Conference Series on Public Policy, 1989—; contbr. articles to profl. jours. 1st lt., U.S. Army, 1972-73. NSF research grantee, 1982, 84. Mem. Am. Econs. Assn., Econometrics Soc., Am. Fin. Assn., Tau Beta Pi, Beta Gamma Sigma. Home: 95 Ambassador Dr Rochester NY 14610-3402 Office: U Rochester Simon Grad Sch Rochester NY 14627

PLOTKIN, ALLEN, aerospace engineer, educator; b. NYC, May 4, 1942; s. Oscar and Claire (Chasick) P.; m. Selena Berman, Dec. 18, 1966; children: Samantha Rose, Jennifer Anne. BS, Columbia U., 1963, MS, 1964; PhD, Stanford U., 1968. Asst. prof. aerospace engring. U. Md., College Park, 1968-72, assoc. prof., 1972-77, prof., 1977-85; prof. dept. aerospace engring. San Diego State U., 1985—, chmn. dept., 1985-90, 93-96. Vis. assoc. Calif. Inst. Tech., Pasadena, 1975-76; cons. Naval Surface Weapons Ctr., White Oak, Md., 1981-84. Co-author: Low-Speed Aerodynamics, 1991, 2d edit., 2001. Recipient Engring. Sci. award Washington Acad. Scis., 1981; rsch. grantee NASA, NSF; NASA-Am. Soc. Engring. Edn. summer faculty fellow, 1969, 70. Fellow AIAA (assoc., assoc. editor jour. 1986—, Young Engr.-Scientist award Nat. Capital sect. 1976, Sustained Svc. award 2003), ASME; mem. Soc. Naval Architects and Marine Engrs., Am. Soc. Engring. Edn., Aerospace Dept. Chairmen's Assn. (chmn. 1989-90), Sigma Xi, Tau Beta Pi. Democrat. Jewish. Avocations: jogging, reading, country music. Home: 17364 St Andrews Dr Poway CA 92064-1231 Office: San Diego State U Dept Aerospace Engring San Diego CA 92182

PLOTKIN, JUDY ANN, special education educator; b. L.A., Apr. 9, 1949; d. Donald Olaus and Georgia Maye (Burrus) Nelson; m. Phillip Harold Plotkin, Feb. 11, 1970; children: Amy Louise, Mark Andrew. AA in Religious Studies, Valley Coll., San Bernardino, Calif., 1979; BA in Religious Studies, U. Calif., Riverside, 1982; MEd, Calif. State U., San Bernardino, 1987; EdD, U.S. Internat. U., 1998. Cert. tchr., spl. edn. tchr., Calif. Tchr. spl. edn. Advocate Sch., San Bernardino, 1983-84, Colton (Calif.) Sch. Dist., 1984-85, Carmack Sch., San Bernardino, 1985-91, Harmon Sch., San Bernardino, 1991-92, North Verdemont Sch., San Bernardino, 1992—. Head tchr. Harmon Sch., 1991-92. Rsch. asst. Adoptees Liberty Movement Assn., Redlands-Riverside, Calif., 1982—; active Bike-A-Thon, Epilepsy Soc., San Bernardino, 1982. Mem. Coun. for Exceptional Children (sec. 1983-84), AAUW, San Bernardino Epilepsy Soc., Phi Kappa Phi. Republican. Avocations: bowling, swimming, camping, arts and crafts. Office: N VerdemontSch 3555 W Meyers Rd San Bernardino CA 92407-1911

PLOTNICK, ROBERT DAVID, educator, economic consultant; b. Washington, Aug. 3, 1949; s. Theodore and Jean (Hirshfeld) P.; m. Gay Lee Jensen, Dec. 22, 1972. BA, Princeton U., 1971; MA, U. Calif., Berkeley, 1973, PhD, 1976. Rsch. assoc. Inst. Rsch. on Poverty, Madison, Wis., 1973-75; asst. prof. Bates Coll., Lewiston, Maine, 1975-77, Dartmouth Coll., Hanover, N.H., 1977-84; assoc. prof. U. Wash., Seattle, 1984-90, prof., 1990—, assoc. dean, 1990-95; acting dean, 1994-95. Vis. scholar Russell Sage Found., 1990, U. New South Wales, 1997; rsch. affiliate Inst. for Rsch. on Poverty, 1989—; chmn. Population Leadership Program, 1999—, dir. Ctr. for Studies in Demography and Ecology, 1997-2002; adj. fellow Pub. Policy Inst. Calif., 1998-2000; cons. Wash. Dept. Social and Health Svcs., Olympia, 1984-86, 90-96, 2000; cons. in field. Author: Progress Against Poverty, 1975; contbr. articles to profl. jours. Recipient Teaching Excellence award U. Wash., 1985, 89. Mem. Am. Econ. Assn., Assn. Policy Analysis and Mgmt., Population Assn. Am. Avocations: tennis, hiking, bird watching, scuba. Office: U Wash Evans Sch Pub Affairs PO Box 353055 Seattle WA 98195-3055 E-mail: plotnick@u.washington.edu.

PLOTTEL, JEANINE PARISIER, foreign language educator; b. Paris, Sept. 21, 1934; came to U.S., 1943; m. Roland Plottel, 1956; children: Claudia S., Michael E., Philip B. Baccalauréat lettres, Lycée Français de N.Y., 1952; BA with honors, Barnard Coll., 1954; MA, Columbia U., 1955, PhD with distinction, 1959. Lectr. dept. French and Romance philology Columbia U., N.Y.C., 1955-59; rsch. assoc. fgn. lang. program MLA of Am., N.Y.C., 1959-60; lectr. dept. romance langs. CUNY, N.Y.C., 1960; asst. prof. div. humanities Julliard Sch. Music, N.Y.C., 1960-65; dir. lang. labs. Hunter Coll. CUNY, N.Y.C., 1965-69; asst. prof. dept. romance langs. Hunter Coll. CUNY, N.Y.C., 1965-69, assoc. prof. dept. romance langs., 1969-81, prof. dept. romance langs., 1981—2000, assoc. prof. French doctoral program grad. sch., univ. ctr., 1980-81, prof. French doctoral program grad. sch., univ. ctr., 1981—2000, prof. emeritus, 2000—. Extensive adminstrv. experience in CUNY including chairperson Dept. Romance Langs. Author: Les Dialogues de Paul Valéry, 1960; pub., editor N.Y. Literary Forum, 1978-88; contbr. articles to profl. jours., chpts. to books. Pres. Maurice I. Parisier Found., Inc. Named Officer des Palmes Acad., 1999; recipient NEH fellowship, 1979; grantee N.Y. Coun. for the Humanities, 1986, Helena Rubenstein Found., 1986, Florence J. Gould Found., 1986, 88, N.Y. Times Found., 1986. Mem. AAUP (exec. dir. N.Y. State Conf.2002—), Maison Française (bd. dirs. Columbia U.), Peyre Inst., CUNY, Soc. French Am. Cultural Svcs. & Ednl. Aid, Hunter Coll. Art Galleries. Home: 50 E 77th St Apt 14A New York NY 10021-1836 Office: Hunter Coll-CUNY 695 Park Ave New York NY 10021-5024 E-mail: plottel@worldnett.att.net.

PLOVNICK, MARK STEPHEN, business educator; b. N.Y.C., June 8, 1946; s. Jacob and Dorothy Edith (Berger) Plovnick; m. Daisy Shulan Chan, Mar. 13, 1982. BSME, Union Coll., 1968; BA in Econs., Union Coll., 1968; MS in Mgmt., MIT, 1970, PhD in Mgmt., 1975. Instr., rschr. MIT, Cambridge, 1970—76; asst. prof. Clark Univ., Worcester, Mass., 1976—79, assoc. prof., 1979—89, chmn. dept. mgmt., 1979—82, assoc. dean Grad. Sch. Mgmt., 1982—89; prof., dean Sch. Eberhardt Sch. Bus. U. Pacific, Stockton, Calif., 1989—. Cons. to various orgns., 1970—; dir. Devel. Rsch. Assocs., Reston, Va., 1979—82; adj. assoc. prof. U. Mass. Med. Sch., Worcester, Mass., 1982—89; adj. asst. prof. Boston Univ. Sch. Medicine, 1974—75; clin. instr. Harvard Med. Sch., Boston, 1977—78. Author: 5 books; contbr. numerous articles to profl. jours. Mem. Civil Svc. Commn., San Joaquin County, 1989—94; bd. dirs. United Way, 1991—94, Goodwill Industries, 1992—, Stockton Symphony, 1995—2001. Mem.: Greater Stockton C. of C. (bd. dirs. 1990—94). Office: U Pacific Eberhardt Sch Bus Stockton CA 95211-0001 E-mail: mplovnic@uop.edu.

PLUCINSKY, CONSTANCE MARIE, school counselor, supervisor; b. Passaic, N.J., Sept. 17, 1937; d. Stephen and Beatrice (Ruby) Goralski; m. William Plucinsky, June 29, 1957; 1 child, Carolyn. BS, Paterson State Coll., 1959; MA, Seton Hall U., 1970, postgrad., 1975, William Paterson Coll., 1989—. Tchr. Garfield (N.J.) Bd. Edn., 1959-61, Paramus (N.J.) Bd. Edn., 1961-71, Bergen Gifted Child Soc., Ridgewood, N.J., 1965-71; guidance counselor grades 9-12 Paramus Bd. Edn., 1971-89, 91—, adminstrv. asst. to supt., 1989-91, counselor, coord. sex equity grades 7-12, 1990—; S.A.T. program supr. Ednl. Testing Svc., Princeton, N.J., 1992—. Mem. adv. bd., 1990—, project dir., 1993—. Editor: (newsletter) PEN, 1989-94 (pub. rels. asst., 1991—); author: (brochure) All That You Can BEEEEEE, 1991, 92, 93; contbr. articles to profl. jours. Mem. steering com. Bergen County Intercultural Task Force, 1991—; facilitator trainer Achieving Sex Equity Through Students, 1991—. Named Guidance Counselor of Yr., Bergen County Profl. Guidance Assn., 1989, N.J. Equity Hall of Fame, 1993; recipient N.J. Dept. Edn. Best Practices award Paramus Acad. Sex Equity, 1993-94, Harassment Reduction Project, 1994-95; N.J. Exemplary Equity Program grantee divsn. vocat. edn. N.J. Dept. Edn., 1991-93. Mem. AAUW, N.J. Edn. Assn., Bergen County Profl. Guidance Assn. (exec. com. 1994, first v.p. 1996—), Edn. Assn. Paramus. Democrat. Roman Catholic. Avocations: equestrian competitive rider, instructor, horse trainer. Home: 1030 Ramapo Valley Rd Mahwah NJ 07430-2413 Office: Paramus High Sch 99 E Century Rd Paramus NJ 07652-4399

PLUMMER, ORA BEATRICE, nursing educator, trainer; b. Mexia, Tex., May 25, 1940; d. Macie Idella (Echols); childeren: Kimberly, Kevin, Cheryl. BSN, U. N.Mex., 1961; MS in Nursing Edn., UCLA, 1966. Nurse's aide Bataan Meml. Meth. Hosp., Albuquerque, 1058-60, staff nurse, 1961-62, 67-68; staff nurse, charge nurse, relief supr. Hollywood (Calif.) Cmty. Hosp., 1962-64; instr. U. N.Mex. Coll. Nursing, Albuquerque, 1968-69; sr. instr. U. Colo. Sch. Nursing, Denver, 1971-74, asst. prof., 1974-76; staff assoc. III, Western Interstate Commn. for Highr Edn., Boulder, Colo., 1976-78; DON, Garden Manor Nursing Home, Lakewood, Colo., 1978-79, nurse surveyor, cons., 1979-87; ednl. coord. Colo. Dept. Health, Denver, 1987—96. Active in faculty devel. Colo. Cluster of Schs.; bd. dir. Domestic Violence Initiative, 2000—. Contbr. articles to profl. jours. Mem. adv. bd. Affiliated Children's and Family Svcs., 1977; mem. Colo. Instnl. Child Abuse and Neglect Adv. Com., 1984-92; trustee Colo. Acad., 1990-96; mem. planning com. State Wide Conf. on Black Health Concerns, 1977; mem. staff devel. com. Western Interstate Commn. for Higher Edn., 1978, mem. minority affairs com., 1978, mem. coordinating com. for baccalaureate program, 1971-76; active in minority affairs, U. Colo. Med. Ctr., 1971-72; mem. ednl. resources com., pub. rels. com., rev. com. for reappointment, promotion and tenure U. Colo. Sch. Nursing, 1971-76, mem. regulatory tng. com., 1989-93; mem. gerontol. adv. com. Met. State Coll., 1989-94; mem. expert panel long term care tng. manual Health Care Financing Adminstrn., Balt., 1989; mem. employee diversity com. Colo. Dept. Health, 1989-96. Mem. ANA, ASTD, NAFE, Colo. Nurses Assn. (affirmative action com. 1977-79, 93—), Phi Delta Kappa. mem. Nurse Delegation to Cuba, 2000. Nightingale Nominee, Colorado, 2003. Avocations: public speaking, training. Office: 4300 Cherry Creek South Dr Denver CO 80246-1523

PLUMMER, PATRICIA LYNNE MOORE, chemistry and physics educator; b. Tyler, Tex., Feb. 26; d. Robert Lee and Jewell Ovelia (Jones) Moore; m. Otho Raymond Plummer, Apr. 10, 1965; children: Patrick William Otho, Christina Elisa Lynne. BA, Tex. Christian U., Ft. Worth, Tex., 1960; postgrad., U. N.C., 1960-61; PhD, U. Tex., Austin, 1964; grad., Bryn Mawr Summer Inst., 1992. Instr., Welch postdoctoral fellow U. Tex., Austin, 1964-66; postdoctoral fellow Dept. Chemistry, U. Ark., Fayetteville, 1966-68; rsch. assoc. Grad. Ctr., Cloud Phys. Rsch., Rolla, Mo., 1968-73; asst. prof. physics U. Mo., Rolla, 1973-77; assoc. dir. Grad. Ctr. Cloud Phys. Rsch., 1977-79, sr. investigator, 1980-85; assoc. prof. physics U. Mo., 1977-85, prof. dept. chemistry and physics, 1986—. Mem. internat. sci. com. Symposium on Chemistry and Physics of Ice, 1982—, vice chair, 1996—; nat. judge Siemens-Westinghouse Sci. Projects, 1999—. Assoc. editor Jour. of Colloid and Interface Sci., 1980-83; contbr. articles to profl. jours., chpts. to books. Rsch. grantee IBM, 1990-92, Air Force Office Rsch., 1989-91, NSF, 1976-86, NASA, 1973-78; Air Force Office Rsch. summer fellow, 1988, Bryn Mawr Summer Inst., 1992, Faculty fellow Cherry Emerson Ctr. for Sci. Computation, Emory U., 1998-99. Mem. Am. Chem. Soc., Am. Phys. Soc., Am. Geophys. Union, Sigma Xi (past pres., UM-Rolla chptr.). Democrat. Baptist. Avocations: sailing, gardening, tennis, photography. Office: U Mo 201 Physics Bldg Columbia MO 65211-0001 Fax: (573) 882-4195. E-mail: plummerp@missouri.edu.

PLYLER, CHRIS PARNELL, university administrator, dean; b. Washington, Mar. 21, 1951; s. Glenn Parnell and Doris Eleanor (Oswald) P.; m. Allison Rose Lord, Aug. 4, 1979; children: Benjamin, Patrick, Christen. BA, Clemson U., 1973; MEd, U. S.C., 1975; PhD, Fla. State U., 1978. Dir. male housing Coll. Charleston, S.C., 1975-76; asst. to pres. Fla. State U., Tallahassee, 1976-77; asst. to assoc. chancellor faculty and pers. rels. State U. System Fla., Tallahassee, 1977-78; assoc. dean acad. affairs U. S.C.-Salkehatchie, Allendale, 1978-82; dir. grad. regional studies U. S.C., Aiken, 1982-84, assoc. chancellor student svcs., 1984-90, dean Beaufort, 1990-99, vice provost, exec. dean regional campuses/continuing edn. Columbia, 1999—. Adv. bd. S.C. Nat. Bank, Aiken, 1988-90, Palmetto Fed. Savs. and Loan Assn. Treas. bd. dirs. ARC, Aiken, 1984-90; bd. dirs. Boys and Girls Club, Beaufort, 1990—, Hitchcock Rehab. Ctr., Aiken, 1988-90. Mem. Am. Assn. for Higher Edn., Nat. Assn. for Student Pers. Adminstrn., S.C. Coll. Pers. Assn., So. Assn. for Coll. Student Affairs, Nat. Inst. Conf. for Regional Campus Adminstrn., Sea Island Rotary, Aiken Sunrise Rotary (bd. dirs. 1986-90), Aiken Sertoma Club, Phi Delta Kappa, Omicron Delta Kappa. Home: 7 Davant Pl Columbia SC 29209-0842 Office: U SC Regional Campuses Cont Edn 508 Carolina Plz Columbia SC 29208

POAD, FLORA VIRGINIA, retired librarian and educator; b. Roanoke, Va., Oct. 8, 1921; d. Thomas Franklin and Ethlind (Wertz) Huff; m. Stanley Theodore Benton, Dec. 24, 1942 (div. Oct. 1983); children: Peggy, Betty, Mary Jo, Lucy; m. James Joseph Poad, June 6, 1986. Student, Radford Coll., 1939-41, Ohio U., 1956-57; BS in Edn., Ohio No. U., 1960; MA in LS, U. Toledo, 1964; postgrad., Kent State U., 1964-66, 71. Reference asst. Roanoke Pub. Libr., 1939-42; catalog asst. Univ. Libr., Emory U., Atlanta, 1942; sec. ARC, Atlanta, 1943; catalog asst. Pickerington (Ohio) Pub. Libr., 1950-51; tchr. Celina (Ohio) Pub. Schs., 1957-62; tchr., libr. Toledo Pub. Schs., 1962-64; libr. supr. Oregon (Ohio) Pub. Schs., 1964-85; instr. U. Toledo, 1970, reference libr., 1971-86; tchr. Sylvan Learning Ctr., Toledo, 1985-92; ret., 1992. Mem. evaluation team Ohio Dept. Edn., Columbus, 1973; rep. Ohio Gov.'s Conf. on Librs., Columbus, 1974; chmn., mem. adv. bd. libr. sci. dept. Cmty.-Tech. Coll., 1965-69. Editor Ohio Assn. Sch. Librs. Bull., 1968-71. Vol. Am. Cancer Soc., Toledo, 1946—48, 1986—87, Mobile Meals, Toledo, 1986—93, Helping Hands, Toledo, 1994—2001. Mem. Am. Assn. Ret. Persons, Delta Kappa Gamma, Pi Lambda Theta, Kappa Delta Pi, Phi Kappa Phi. Avocations: reading, walking, crafts.

POARCH, MARY HOPE EDMONDSON, science educator; b. Columbia, S.C., July 1, 1958; d. Homer Vincent and Janis (Bland) Edmondson; m. Robert Daniel Poarch, June 4, 1983; 1 child, Matthew Vincent. BS, Tex. A&M U., 1982; MEd, U. Tex., 1985; PhD, Our Lady of the Lake U., 2003. Sci. tchr. Evant (Tex.) Ind. Sch. Dist., 1982-83, Copperas Cove (Tex.) Ind. Sch. Dist., 1983-85, Northside Ind. Sch. Dist., San Antonio, 1985-90, Alamo Heights Ind. Sch. Dist., San Antonio, 1990—. Selected as Urban/Systemic Initative Master Mentor Tchr.; regional dir. Sci. Tchrs. Assn. Tex., 1992—; instr. Univ. of Incarnate Word, 1997—; mem. Regional Collaborative for Excellence in Sci. Tchg., 1998—; mem. adv. bd. Merrill Pub. Co., 1980-90. Vol. San Antonio Zoo, 1991—. Named Outstanding Sci. Educator, Sigma Xi, 1995; P.A.C.T. grantee Am. Chem. Soc., 1992. Mem. Sch. Sci. and Math. Assn., Nat. Sci. Tchrs. Assn. (Honors Tchr. award 1988), Coun. for Elem. Sci. Internat., Nat. Mid. Level Sci. Tchrs. Assn.,

Texas State Bd Educator Cert Standards Com. Methodist. Home: 1425 Wiltshire Ave San Antonio TX 78209-6050 Office: Alamo Heights Jr Sch 7607 N New Braunfels Ave San Antonio TX 78209-2799

POATS, LILLIAN BROWN, education educator; b. Gary, Ind., Dec. 4, 1951; d. Joe Freeman and Jimmye Marie (Jones) Brown; m. Greyling Byron Poats, June 30, 1973; 1 child, Greyling Byron II. BA, Purdue U., 1972; MEd, Tex. So. U., 1975, EdD, 1984. Tchr. Gary (Ind.) Cmty. Sch. Corp., 1972-74; univ. psychometrist Tex. So. U., Houston, 1974-77, 81-84; coord. acad. advising Purdue U., Hammond, Ind., 1977-79; educator, counselor Planned Parenthood-Northwest Ind., Merrillville, 1979-81; dir. student support U. Tex. Health Sci. Ctr., Houston, 1984-89; prof. edn. Tex. So. U., 1989—. Chair black caucus exec. bd. Am. Assn. Higher Edn., Washington, 1995-97; faculty fellow U.S. Dept. Def., Pentagon, Washington, 1993. Contbr. articles to profl. jours., chpts. to books. Mem. Ft. Bend Edn. Found., Ft. Bend County CPS Bd. Named Woman of Excellence Suburban Sugarland (Tex.) Women's Assn., 1994. Mem. Purdue U. Alumni Assn., Phi Delta Kappa, Delta Sigma Theta (pres. suburban Houston-Ft. Bond chpt. 1991-92). Avocations: reading, sewing. Home: 3702 Pin Oak Ct Missouri City TX 77459-7017 Office: Tex Southern U 3100 Cleburne St Houston TX 77004-4501 E-mail: Poats_lb@tsu.edu., Poats2@cs.com.

POBLETE, RITA MARIA BAUTISTA, physician, educator; b. Manila, May 19, 1954; came to U.S., 1980; d. Juan Gonzalez and Rizalina (Bautista) Poblete. BS, U. Philippines, 1974, MD, 1978. Diplomate Am. Bd. Internal Medicine and Infectious Disease. Intern, resident Wayne State U./Detroit Med. Ctr., 1982-85, fellow in infectious disease, 1986-87, Chgo. Med. Sch./VA Hosp., North Chicago, Ill., 1985-86; fellow in spl. immunology U. Miami (Fla.)-Jackson Meml. Hosp., 1987-89; adj. clin. instr. dept. of medicine U. Miami, 1989-90, asst. prof. medicine, 1990-94. Infectious disease cons. Cedars Med. Ctr. and Mercy Hosp., Miami, 1994—. Contbr. articles to med. jours. Mem. Am. Soc. for Microbiology, Am. Soc. Internal Medicine, World Found. Successful Women. Avocations: tennis, swimming, playing guitar. Office: Cedars Med Ctr 1295 NW 14th St Ste E Miami FL 33125-1600

POCCIA, DOMINIC LOUIS, biology educator; b. Utica, N.Y., Aug. 8, 1945; s. Louis Joseph and Frances Marie (Surace) P.; m. Alison Gordon, May 18, 1971 (div. 1979); 1 child, Joseph; m. Clara Pinto Correia, Aug. 20, 1994; children: Michael, Ricky. BS, Union Coll., 1967; AM, Harvard U., 1968, PhD, 1971; AM (hon.), Amherst Coll., 1987. Asst. prof. Wellesley (Mass.) Coll., 1971-72, SUNY, Stony Brook, 1974-78, Amherst (Mass.) Coll., 1978-82, assoc. prof., 1982-87, chair biology dept., 1983-85, prof., 1987—, chair biology dept., 1989—90. Vis. scholar U. Calif., Berkeley, 1986-87; vis. prof. Stanford U. Hopkins Marine Sta., Pacific Grove, Calif., 1988; adj. prof. U. Mass., Amherst, 1984—. Author: Molecular Aspects of Spermatogenesis, 1994; contbr. articles to profl. jours.; assoc. editor Jour. Exptl. Zool., Molecular Reprodn. Devel. Recipient grants NIH, 1975-86, 89, 91, 93-94, 96—, NSF, 1990-96. Mem. Am. Soc. Cell Biology, Phi Beta Kappa, Sigma Xi. Avocation: jazz musician.

PODGOR, ELLEN SUE, law educator; b. Bklyn., Jan. 30, 1952; d. Benjamin and Yetta (Shilensky) Podgor. BS magna cum laude, Syracuse U., 1973; JD, Ind. U., Indpls., 1976; MBA, U. Chgo., 1987; LLM, Temple U., 1989. Bar: Ind. 1976, N.Y. 1984, Pa. 1987. Dep. prosecutor Lake County Prosecutor's Office, Crown Point, Ind., 1976-78; ptnr. Nicholls & Podgor, Crown Point, 1978-87; instr. Temple U. Sch. Law, 1987-89; assoc. prof. law St. Thomas U., Miami, Fla., 1989-91, Ga. State U., Atlanta, 1991—. Vis. scholar Yale Law Sch., 1998; vis. prof. U. Ga., 2000; John S. Stone vis. endowed chair U. Ala., 2000. Author: (with Israel) White Collar Crime in a Nutshell, (with Israel, Borman, Henning) White Collar Crime: Law and Practice, (with Wise) International Criminal Law: Cases and Materials; assoc. editor Ind. Law Rev., 1975-76; contbr. articles to legal jours; mem. adv. bd. BNA Criminal Practice Manual. Del. Ind. Dem. Conv., 1982. Mem. ABA, NACDL (bd. dirs.), Am. Law Inst., Ind. Bar Assn. Democrat. Jewish. Office: Ga State U Coll Law PO Box 4037 Atlanta GA 30302-4037

PODWALL, KATHRYN STANLEY, biology educator; b. Chgo., Oct. 14; d. Frank and Marie C. Stanley. BS, U. Ill.; MA, NYU. Prof. biology Nassau C.C., Garden City, NY. Developmental reviewer West Ednl. Pub., Amesbury, Mass. and Highland Park, Ill., 1989, 91-92; reviewer AAAS, Washington, 1970—; exec. bd., advisor Women's Faculty Assn., Nassau C.C., 1990—, pres, 2000-2002; lectr. in field. Author: Tested Studies for Laboratory Teaching, vol. 5, 1993; editor: (books and cassettes) Rhyming Simon Books and Cassettes, 1990, Sight Reading Syncopation, 1998, Today's Way To Play the Standards, 2000, Today's Way To Play the Classics, 2000, (book and CD) Cartoons & Car Tunes, 2001, Cartoons & Kid Tunes, 2002, Cartoons and Christmas Tunes, 2003. Recipient L.I. Alzheimer's Found. Svc. award, 2002, Excellence award, Nat. Inst. for Staff and Orgnl. Devel., 2003. Mem. AAUW, Nat. Assn. Biology Tchrs. (life), Nat. Sci. Tchrs. Assn. (life), Soc. for Coll. Sci. Tchrs., Am. Women in Sci., Met. Assn. Coll. and Univ. Biologists, Nat. Cathedral Assn., N.Y. Acad. of Scis., Friends of Archives (charter), Xerces Soc., Southampton Colonial Soc., LaSalle County Hist. Soc. (life), Garden City Hist. Soc. (life), Soroptimists (bd. dirs. dist. 1 1994-96, club pres. 1992-94, Nassau County Pres. award 2001), U. Ill. Alumni Assn. (life). Avocations: travel, gardening, zoological pursuits. Office: Nassau Community College One Education Dr Garden City NY 11530 E-mail: podwalk@ncc.edu.

POE, (LYDIA) VIRGINIA, reading educator; b. Bklyn., Jan. 19, 1932; d. Harold Waldemar and Lydia Beatrice (Doswell) Lind; m. Harold Weller Poe, Sept. 11, 1954; children: Michael Lind, David Harold, Timothy Claude. BA, Beloit Coll., 1954; MEd, U. Southwestern La., 1961, EdS, 1972; EdD, U. So. Miss., 1983. Cert. tchr., Fla., La., Ill., Wis. Elem. tchr. Caroline Brevard Sch., Tallahassee, 1961-64; supervising tchr. Fla. State U., Tallahassee, 1962-64; elem., supervising tchr. Hamilton Lab. Sch., Lafayette, La., 1965-67; prof. reading U. Southwestern La., Lafayette, 1968—, head Dept. Curriculum and Instrn., 1986-91, assoc. dir. Hawthorne Ctr. Spl. Edn. and communicative disorders, 1988—. Co-originator field experiences U. Southwestern La., 1970—; observer in elem. sch. Ecole de Charlemagne, Nancy, France, 1967; cons. Lafayette Parish Schs., 1968—. Mem. editorial rev. panel The Ednl. Forum, 1992-94; contbg. author: Reading Research Review, 1984; contbr. articles to profl. jours.; presenter in field. Organizer Conf. on Women in Politics, Lafayette, 1976 (recipient scholarship 1974); treas. State of La. ERA United, 1977; organizer, pres. First Luth. Ch. Day Care Ctr., Lafayette, 1977-80; chair quality edn. svcs. Lafayette Parish Year Round Schs. Study Com. Recipient research grant, U. Southwestern U., 1986-87. Mem. ASCD, Internat. Reading Assn., Am. Reading Assn., Coll. Reading Assn., AAUW, (fellowship contribution 1976), United Fedn. Coll. Tchrs., Nat. Assn. Yr. Round Edn., Phi Delta Kappa, Phi Kappa Phi, Kappa Delta Pi, Beta Sigma Phi. Democrat. Lutheran. Office: U Southwestern La PO Box 42051 Lafayette LA 70504-0001

POEHLEIN, GARY WAYNE, retired chemical engineering educator; b. Tell City, Ind., Oct. 17, 1936; s. Oscar Raymond and Eva Lee (Dickman) P.; m. Sharon Eileen Wood., Jan. 1, 1958; children: Steven Ray, Timothy Wayne, Valorie Ann, Sandra Lee. BSChemE, Purdue U., 1958, MSChemE, 1961, PhD, 1966. Design engr. Proctor & Gamble, Cin., 1958-61; from asst. prof. to assoc. prof. Lehigh U., Bethlehem, Pa., 1965-75, prof. chem. engring., 1975-78, co-dir. emulsion polymers inst., 1973-78; dir. sch. chem. engring. Ga. Inst. Tech., Atlanta, 1978-86, assoc. v.p. rsch., dean grad, studies, 1986-91, v.p. interdisciplinary programs, prof. chem. engring., 1991-95; prof. chem. engring., 1978-96; dir. Chem. and Transport Systems Divsn. NSF, 1996-2000; ret., 2000. Bd. dirs. Flexible Products Co., Marietta, Ga.; interim chair chem. engring. dept., vis. prof. Lehigh U., 2001—02. Contbr. over 100 articles to tech. publs. Mem. sch. bd. Bethlehem Area Sch. Dist., 1969-75. Recipient Honor Scroll award Phila. br. Am. Inst. Chemists, 1977, Mac Pruitt award Coun. for Chem. Rsch., 1989. Fellow AIChE; mem. Am. Chem. Soc., Am. Soc. Engring. Edn., Sigma Xi. Avocations: woodworking, sailing. Home: 407 S Henry St Alexandria VA 22314-5901 E-mail: gspoehlein@aol.com.

POEHLER, THEODORE OTTO, university provost, engineer, researcher; b. Balt, Oct. 20, 1935; s. Theodore O. and Marion E. (Rohde) P.; m. Anne Otter Evans, Dec. 30, 1961; children: Theodore, Jeffrey. BS, Johns Hopkins U., 1956, DEng, 1961. Mem. sr. staff Applied Physics Lab., Laurel, Md., 1963-68, prin. staff physicist, 1969-73, supr. Quantum Electrons Group, 1974-83; dir. Eisenhower Rsch. Ctr. Johns Hopkins U., Laurel, Md., 1983-89, assoc. dean rsch. Sch. Engring. Balt., 1990-92, vice provost for rsch., 1992—. Chmn. bd. dir. Tech. Devel. Ctr., Balt., 1991—. Author: (with others) Detectors in Methods of Experimental Physics, 1990; contbr. more than 150 articles to profl. jour. including Phys. Rev., Applied Physics. Capt. US Army, 1962-63. Recipient Nat. Capital award Coun. Engring. and Archtl. Soc. Mem. AAAS, IEEE, Am. Phys. Soc., Am. Chem. Soc., Materials Rsch. Soc. Achievements include 8 patents in optical information storage field and 4 patents on all-polymer batteries. Office: Johns Hopkins U 34th and Charles St Baltimore MD 21218 E-mail: top@jhu.edu.

POEPPELMEIER, KENNETH REINHARD, chemistry educator; b. St. Louis, Mo., Oct. 6, 1949; BS in Chemistry, U. Mo., 1971; PhD in Inorganic Chemistry, Iowa State U., 1978. Rsch. chemist, corp. rsch. sci. labs. Exxon Rsch. & Engring. Co., Annandale, N.J., 1978-80, sr. chemist, corp. rsch. sci. labs., 1980-81, staff chemist, corp. rsch. sci. labs., 1981-84, sr. staff chemist, corp. rsch. sci. labs., 1984; assoc. prof. chemistry Northwestern U., Evanston, Ill., 1984-88, assoc. dir. sci. and tech. ctr. for superconductivity, 1989—2000, prof., 1988—. Contbr. articles in organic, solid-state and materials chemistry to numerous profl. publs.; patentee in field. Iowa State U. fellow, 1977-78; Iowa State scholar, 1975-76. Mem. AAAS, ACS (chmn. solid state subdivsn. of divsn. inorganic cChemistry 1988-89), Materials Rsch. Soc., Catalysis Club (Chgo.). Office: Northwestern U Dept Chemistry 2145 Sheridan Rd Evanston IL 60208-0834

POIANI, EILEEN LOUISE, mathematics educator, college administrator, higher education planner; b. Newark, Dec. 17, 1943; d. Hugo Francis and Eileen Louise (Crecca) P. BA in Math., Douglass Coll., 1965; MS in Math., Rutgers U., 1967, PhD in Math., 1971. Tchg. asst., grad. preceptor Rutgers U., New Brunswick, N.J., 1966-67; asst. counselor Douglass Coll., New Brunswick, 1967, 69-70; instr. math. St. Peter's Coll., Jersey City, 1967-70, asst. prof., 1970-74, dir. of self-study, 1974-76, assoc. prof., 1974-80, prof., 1980—, asst. to pres., 1976-80, asst. to pres. for planning, 1980-96, exec. asst. to pres., 1996-98, v.p. for student affairs, 1999—. Chair U.S. Commn. on Math. Instrn., NRC of NAS, Washington, 1983-90; founding nat. dir. Women and Math. Lectureship Program, Washington, 1975-81, adv. bd., 1981—; project dir. Consortium for Advancement of Pvt. Higher Edn., Washington, 1986-88; mem. N.J. Math. Coalition, 1991—, Nat. Seminar on Jesuit Higher Edn., 1990-94, strategic planning com. N.J. Assn. Ind. Colls. and Univs., 1990-92; charter trustee Rutgers U., 1992-2004; Nutley panelist Centennial Celebration, 2002; advisor NSF Funded Project of Bank St. Coll. and EDC/Ctr. for Children and Tech., 2003—. Author: (with others) Mathematics Tomorrow, 1981, Encyclopedia of Mathmatics Education; contbr. articles to profl. jours. Mem. Newark Mus., Nutley (N.J.) Hist. Soc., Friends of Newark Libr.; trustee Nutley Free Pub. Libr., 1974-77, St. Peter's Prep. Sch., Jersey City, 1986-92; active fee arbitration commn. N.J. Supreme Ct., 1983-86, ct. ethics com., 1986-90; U.S. nat. rep. Internat. Congress Math. Edn., Budapest, Hungary, 1988; statewide planning com. NCCJ, 1988-92, youth leadership coun., 1992—; chair evaluation teams Mid. States Assn. Coll. and Schs.; U.S. del. Internat. Congress on Math; trustee The Cath. Advocate, 1993-2003; adv. NSF Funded Project Bank St. Coll. & Ed. Ctr. for Children & Tech., 2003-. Recipient George F. Johnson, S.J. Alumni Faculty award, 1976, Douglass Soc. award Douglass Coll., 1982, Outstanding Cmty. Svc. award Christopher Columbus Found., N.J., 1994, Outstanding Svc. award Middle States Assn. Colls. and Schs., 1994, Cert. of Appreciation for outstanding contbns. as nat. dir. women and math. program, 1993, Varsity Letter plaque for leadership and svc. St. Peter's Prep, 1997; named Danforth Assoc., Danforth Found., 1972-86, SPC Legend, Students of St. Peters Coll., 2002, Humanitarian award NCCJ, 2003, N.J. Women of Achievement award N.J. State Fedn. Women's Clubs, 2003, Alumnae Recognition award Douglass Coll., 2003; named to Nutley Hall of Fame, 2003. Mem. AAUP, Math. Assn. Am. (bd. dirs. lectureship program, gov. N.J. chpt. 1972-79, chair human resources coun. 1991—96, Outstanding Coll. Tchg. award 1993), Nat. Coun. Tchrs. Math. (spkr. 1974—), Soc. Coll. and Univ. Planning (program com. 1989—, spkr. nat. conf. 1986, 88, 89, 90, judge grad. paper competition), Com. on Math. with Disabilities, Com on Devel. of Man, Pi Mu Epsilon (1st woman pres. in 75 yrs. 1987-90, C.C. MacDuffee award for disting. svc. to math. 1995), Phi Beta Kappa, Alpha Sigma Nu. Roman Catholic. Avocations: gourmet cooking, travel, golf. Office: St Peter's Coll 2641 Kennedy Blvd Jersey City NJ 07306-5997

POINDEXTER, BARBARA GLENNON, secondary school educator; b. Dallas, Oct. 19, 1937; d. Victor and Ruth (Gaskins) Ward; m. Noble Turner Poindexter, Aug. 2, 1994; 1 child, Victoria Angela Russo. BS, Tex. Woman's U., 1958; postgrad., Kans. State U., 1969-70; grad., U. Northern Iowa, 1986. Cert. tchr. S.C., Kans., N.Mex., Tex. Drama and English tchr. Linn (Kans.) H.S., 1968-69; tchr. Mosquero (N.Mex.) H.S., 1973-74, Sumter (S.C.) Sch. Dist., Maywood Sch., 1974-76, Harleyville (S.C.) H.S., 1976-78, Hampton (S.C.) H.S., 1978-79, Centerville Sch., Cottageville, S.C., 1979-80; tchr. English Scurry-Rosser Sch., Scurry, Tex., 1981-82; tchr. French and Spanish Christ the King, Dallas, 1982-83; tchr. French and English, chmn. fgn. lang. dept. Wilmer-Hutchins H.S., Dallas, 1983-94; tchr. French and English Molina H.S., Dallas, 1997—. Mem.: Theta Alpha Phi. Democrat. Methodist. Home: 5315 Maple Springs Blvd Dallas TX 75235-8326 Office: Molina HS 2355 Duncanville Rd Dallas TX 75211-6532

POINDEXTER, TONYA DAWN, special education educator; b. Stilwell, Okla., Dec. 6, 1958; d. Judson and Norma Jean (Keys) Richards; m. Ricky Darrell Poindexter, June 17, 1977. AA in Edn., Connors State Coll., 1985; BS in Edn., Northeastern State U., 1987, M Spl. Edn., 1989, M in Curriculum and Instruction, 1993. Cert. tchr., Okla., Ark. Tchr. spl. edn. Liberty Sch., Muldrow, Okla., 1988-90; resource tchr. Van Buren (Ark.) High Sch., 1990—. Scotopic sensitivity screener Irlen Inst. Perceptual and Learning Devel., Long Beach, Calif., 1990—. Mem. Coun. Exceptional Children (div. learning disabilities and mental retardation). Democrat. Pentecostal. Avocations: antique glassware, native american artifacts. Home: PO Box 6823 Siloam Springs AR 72761-6823

POINSETT-WHITE, SADIE RUTH, retired elementary education educator; b. Chgo., May 11, 1934; d. Alexander Abraham and Adele Marie (Prindle) Poinsett; m. Robert Eli White, Sept. 11, 1955; children: Susan Murray, Michael L. White. BS in elem. edn., U. Ill., 1954; MA in early childhood edn., U. Md., 1980. Cert. elem. edn. tchr., Md. Head start tchr. San Bernadino (Calif.) Pub. Sch., 1966, kindergarten tchr., 1967; day care tchr. Kensington (Md.) Day Care, 1970; head start tchr. Montgomery County Pub. Sch., Rockville, Md., 1972-84, kindergarten tchr. Silver Spring, Md., 1984-99. Mem. tchr. evaluation adv. task force Montgomery County Pub. Sch., 1996-97; mem. adv. bd. African Voices project Smithsonian Instn. Nat. Mus. Natural History, 1995—. Mem. adv. bd. Noyes Libr., Kensington, 1980-84, 90-93; mem. NAACP Nat. Black Child Devel. Inc.; mem. Vol. Ptnrship. Montgomery, Inc., United Coun. of African-Am. Orgns. Rsch. fellow U. Md., College Park, 1980. Mem. Nat. Sci. Tchrs. Assn. (conf. presenter 1991-96), Md. State Dept. Edn. (conf. presenter 1991-96), Md. Assn. Sci. Tchrs. (conf. presenter 1991-96), Montgomery County Edn. Assn. (poll vol. 1986—, precinct capt. 1994—), Nat. Coun. Negro Women, Zeta Phi Beta (Basileus 1996). Avocation: 4th degree black belt tae kwon do.

POINTON, MARY LOU, special education educator; b. Ft. Smith, Ark., Aug. 1, 1933; d. Clyde Morgan and Rilla Belle (Prater) Dollar; m. Vernie Rodney Pointon, Oct. 24, 1954; children: Pamela Kaye Pointon McDonald, Susan Gail Pointon Friberg. Assoc. BA, Ft. Smith Jr. Coll., 1953; BS Ed in Speech and English, Tex. Tech U., 1962; MEd in Spl. Edn., Tex. A&M U., 1989. Cert. real estate agt., appraiser Tex. Real Estate Commn. English and drama tchr. Wolforth (Tex.) H.S., 1962-63; drama tchr. Monterrey H.S., Lubbock, Tex., 1963-64; English and history tchr. Meml. Cath. H.S., Enid, Okla., 1964-66; reading and drama tchr., libr. Covington (Okla.) H.S., 1966-68; spl. edn. tchr. drug abuse unit Mercer Island (Wash.) H.S., 1968-69; English, bus. and drama tchr. LaConner (Wash.) H.S., 1969-72; English tchr. Tehran (Iran) Am. Sch., 1972; v.p., dir. tng. and devel. Mary Lou English Tng. Ctr., Tehran, 1972-78; spl. edn. tchr. Mills Elem. Sch., Midlothian, Tex., 1987-88; tchr. learning difference students Fairhill Sch., Dallas, 1988-93; tutor learning difference students Masterpiece Co., Plano, Tex., 1993—98. Owner, v.p. Masterpiece Real Estate Co., Duncanville, Tex., 1978-89. Author: Teacher Training Manual/Individual English Training, 1973, also lang. program, 1972-78. V.p. Duncanville C. of C., 1983-85; mem. polit. action com. Dallas Assn. Realtors, 1982-84. Named Outstanding Mem. of Yr. Duncanville C. of C., 1983. Mem. DAR (v.p., founding mem. Duncanville chpt. 1980-88), NAFE, Nat. Safety Assn. Dallas Coop. (outstanding sales team 1994), Nat. Chrysanthemum Soc., N.W. Ark. Chrysanthemum Club (v.p., founding mem. 1988—), Ft. Smith Garden Club (pres. 2001-, master gardner 1999). Avocations: plants, flowers, music, reading. Home and Office: 1400 N 52nd St Fort Smith AR 72904-7310

POIRIER, HELEN VIRGINIA LEONARD, elementary education educator; b. Worcester, Mass., Oct. 2, 1954; d. Robert O'Donnell and Rose C. (Pepper) Leonard; m. Paul Nelson Poirier, Aug. 3, 1985; 1 child, Joseph Paul Robert. BS, Worcester State Coll., 1976. Cert. tchr. K-6, reading supr. K-12, adminstrn. K-8. Tchr. grade 5-6 reading and social studies Quabbin Regional Sch. Dist., Oakham, Mass., 1980—. Sec. Local Cable Access Com., Auburn, 1985-92. NEH grantee, 1986; town history grantee Oakham Hist. Soc., 1986, Oakham Hist. Commn., 1986. Mem. Cen. Mass. Coun. Social Studies (bd. dirs., sec. 1986-90, treas. 1990—), Hodges Village Environ. Edn. Assn., Tanheath Hunt Club (pres. 1995-96, sec./newsletter editor 1988-95). Avocations: horseback riding, fox hunting. Office: Oakham Center Sch Deacon Allen Dr Oakham MA 01068

POIRIER, LOUIS JOSEPH, neurology educator; b. Montreal, Que., Can., Dec. 30, 1918; s. Gustave Joseph and Calixta (Brault) P.; m. Liliane Archambault, June 11, 1947; children: Guy, Michel, Louise, Esther. BSc, U. Montreal, 1942, MD, 1947; PhD, U. Mich., 1950; D (hon.), U. Rennes, France, 1973. Asst. prof. U. Montreal, 1950-55, assoc. prof., 1955-58, prof. faculty of medicine, 1958-65; chmn. dept. anatomy Faculty of Medicine, Laval U., Cité Universitaire, Que., 1970-78, prof. exptl. neurology, 1970-83; dir. Centre de Research in Neurobiology, Laval U. and Hosp. de l'Enfant-Jesus, 1977-85, prof. emeritus, 1985—. Contbr. articles to profl. jours.; editor the extrapyramidal system and its disorders in: Advances in Neurology, vol. 24, 1979. Pres. Que. Health Scis. Research Council, 1978-81. Decorated officer Order of Can.; recipient Que. sci. award, 1975; Killam commemorative scholar, 1977, 78 Mem. AAAS, Royal Soc. Belgium (hon.), Neurol. Soc. France (hon.), Am. Assn. Anatomists, Am. Physiol. Soc., Soc. for Neurosci., Internat. Brain Research Orgn., Can. Med. Assn. (emeritus). Address: 603 Chemin Caron Lac Simon Montpellier QC Canada J0V 1M0

POLAK, ELIJAH, engineering educator, computer scientist; b. Bialystok, Poland, Aug. 11, 1931; came to U.S., 1957, naturalized, 1977; s. Isaac and Fruma (Friedman) P.; m. Virginia Ann Gray, June 11, 1961; children: Oren, Sharon. BSE.E., U. Melbourne, Australia, 1957; MSE.E., U. Calif., Berkeley, 1959, PhD, 1961. Instrument engr. ICIANZ, Melbourne, Australia, 1956-57; summer student IBM Research Labs., San Jose, Calif., 1959-60; vis. asst. prof. M.I.T., fall 1964; asso. dept elec. engring. and computer scis. U. Calif., Berkeley, 1958-61, asst. prof. elec. engring. and computer scis., 1961-66, asso. prof., 1966-69, prof., 1969-94, prof. Grad. Sch., 1994—. Author: (with L.A. Zadeh) System Theory, 1969, (with E. Wong) Notes for a First Course on Linear Systems, 1970, (with others) Theory of Optimal Control and Mathematical Programming, 1970, Computational Methods in Optimization, 1971, Optimization: Algorithms and Consistent Approximations, 1997. Guggenheim fellow, 1968; U.K. Sci. Research Council sr. fellow, 1972, 76, 79, 82 Fellow IEEE; mem. Soc. Indsl. and Applied Math. (asso. editor Jour. Theory and Applications Optimization 1972—), Soc. Math. Programming. Home: 38 Fairlawn Dr Berkeley CA 94708-2106 Office: U Calif Dept Elec Engring Cp S Berkeley CA 94720-0001 E-mail: polak@eecs.berkeley.edu.

POLAND, DONNA LEE, elementary education educator; b. Appleton City, Mo. d. Earnest Loyd and Evon Gladys (Medearis) Reed; m. Gary Keel Poland, May 24, 1969; children: Christina Lynn Wilkerson, Matthew Keel, Gari Dawn Jackson. BA in Bus. Edn., S.W. Bapt. U., 1967; elem. cert., Ottawa (Kans.) U., 1992. Cert. secondary bus., Mo., Kans.; cert. elem., Kans. Bus. edn. tchr. Butler (Mo.) H.S., 1967-72; substitute tchr. USD 368 Schs., Lakemary Ctr. for Exceptional Students, Paola, Kans., 1974-90; part-time libr. Paola (Kans.) Free Libr., 1993-94; chpt. one math tchr. 3rd and 4th grade Osawatomie (Kans.) East Elem., 1994-95, title one math and comms. tchr. 3rd and 5th grade, 1995-96. Mem. Nat. Coun. Tchrs. Math., East Ctrl. Kans. Reading Assn. Baptist. Avocations: genealogy, reading, knitting, gardening. Home: 1009 N Pearl St Paola KS 66071-1141 Office: East Elem Sch Fifth and Pacific Osawatomie KS 66064

POLAND, PHYLLIS ELAINE, secondary school educator, consultant; b. Norwood, Mass., May 10, 1941; d. Kenneth Gould Vale and Mildred Eloise (Fisk) Arnold; m. Thomas Charles Poland, June 6, 1968 (div. Nov. 1991); 1 child, Sherilyn Ann Poland Colon. AB in Math., Ea. Nazarene Coll., 1963; MS in Math., Nova U., 1986. Cert. secondary tchr., Fla. H.S. math. tchr., Burrillville, R.I., 1963-64; jr. H.S. math. tchr. Quincy, Mass., 1964-65; math. tchr. Seekonk (Mass.) H.S., 1965-68, Howard Jr. H.S., Orlando, Fla., 1968-74, Lake Highland Prep. Sch., Orlando, Fla., 1977-81, Lake Brantley H.S., Altamonte Springs, Fla., 1981—. Mem. coun. Joy Club Ctrl. Nazarene Ch., 1988—, adult edn. sec., 1990—, mem. choir, 1986—. Grantee NSF, 1969, 70, 71, 72. Mem. NEA. Home: 401 Navarre Way Altamonte Springs FL 32714-2224

POLANIN, W. RICHARD, engineering educator; b. Chgo., Apr. 14, 1952; s. Walter R. and Marie F. (Zents) P.; m. Terryl Ann Bush, July 22, 1978; children: Joshua R., Bradley J., Krista A. BS, Ill. State U., 1974, MS, 1977; EdD, U. Ill., 1990. Cert. tchr., Ill., welding insp., mfg. engr. Classroom tchr. Ill. Valley Cen. H.S., Chillicothe, 1974-79; prof. mfg. Ill. Ctrl. Coll., East Peoria, 1979—, v.p. precision laser mfg., 1995—. Pres. WRP Assocs., Metamora, Ill., 1978—; lectr. Lakeview Mus., Peoria, Ill., 1985-88; mem. adj. faculty Bradley U.; mfg. engr. Nat. Inst. Stds. and Tech.; presenter in field. Co-author: Welding Print Reading, 2001; contbr. articles to profl. jours.; tech. reviewer. Citizens adv. bd. Germantown Hills (Ill.) Sch., 1991—; mem. indsl. adv. bd. Goodwill Industries, 1999—. Recipient Excellence award Nat. Inst. for Staff and Organizational Devel., 1998. Mem. Am. Welding Soc.-Peoria (chmn. 1987-89, D16 com. internat. robot and automated welding), Soc. Mfg. Engrs. (v.p. Peoria sect. 1994—), Am. Soc. for Metals, Ill. Indsl. Edn. Assn. Home: 702 Bayside Dr Metamora IL 61548-8998 Office: Ill Ctrl Coll 1 College Dr Peoria IL 61635-0001 E-mail: rpolanin@icc.cc.il.us.

POLANSKY, BARBARA CAROL CROSBY, physical education educator; b. Ft. Worth, Aug. 3, 1955; d. Richard Hill and Patty Gene (Hoke) Crosby; m. George Alexander Polansky Jr., July 22, 1978. BS in Phys. Edn., U. North Tex., 1977, postgrad., 1981—. Cert. tchr., Tex. Tchr., coach Westwood Jr. High, Richardson (Tex.) Ind. Sch. Dist., 1977-81, tchr., dept. chair, coach, women's athletic dir., 1981-87, tchr., dept. chair, 1981—. Adv. bd. Tex. Edn. Agy., Austin, 1991—; adv. com. Richardson Ind. Sch. Dist. Edn. Coun., 1991-93, facilitator site based mgmt., 1991—; sponsor, coach Tex. Acad. Pentathlon Teams, Richardson, 1987-91; water safety instr. ARC, Richardson, 1977—. Author curriculum guides Richardson Ind. Sch. Dist., 1986—. Mem. Tex. Gov's. Commn. for Phys. Fitness and Health, 1993—, sponsor Fellowship of Christian Athletes, 1981-90, mem. First United Meth. Ch. of Richardson, 1968—. Named Outstanding Alumni Univ. of North Tex., Kinesiology Dept., 1992. Mem. Am. Alliance for Health Phys. Edn., Recreation & Dance (com. mem. 1992—, named one of top six secondary phys. educators in nation, 1992), Tex. Assn. for Health, Phys. Edn., Recreation & Dance (sec. 1985, chair/com. mem. 1990—, named outstanding secondary phys. educator 1991-92), Assn. of Tex. Profl. Educators, Richardson Health and Phys. Edn. Assn. (rep. 1988-90, v.p. 1990-91, pres. 1991-93), Richardson Edn. Assn. Avocations: swimming, crafts. Office: Westwood Jr High 7630 Arapaho Rd Dallas TX 75248-4498

POLASKI, ANNE FAITH, elementary education educator; b. Springfield, Mass., June 9, 1948; d. Paul Louis and Chrisanthe G. (Tatamanis) Kertiles; m. Thomas Stanley Polaski, Sept. 13, 1969; children: William Thomas, Sara Elizabeth. BA in Sociology, U. Mass., 1969; MEd in Curriculum and Instrn., U. Lowell, 1989. Cert. elem. tchr., Mass. Social worker Dept. Pub. Welfare, Westfield, Mass., 1970-71; tutor title I Long Branch (N.J.) Sch. System, 1971-72; social worker Freeman Nursing Home, Pepperell, Mass., 1980-89; subs. tchr. Groton (Mass.)/Dunstable Schs., 1984-88; tchr. Swallow Union Sch., Dunstable, Mass., 1989—, also mem. planning team and coun., instr. aerobics, 1990—. Math. cons. learning disabilities unit Children's Hosp., Boston, 1992—; mem. ambs. network U. Mass., Amherst, 1993—. Scriptwriter (video) Massapoag by Canoe, 1992 (Environ. Svc. award 1992). Active World Wildlife Fund, Nat. Geographic Soc., Greenpeace, Masspirg, Friends of the Groton Tree Warden, Groton/Dunstable Booster Club. Recipient recognition for honoring Am.'s 1st woman chemist, 1992, Peter Farrelly tchr. recognition award for math. and sci. practices, 1994; Horace Mann grantee Groton-Dunstable Sch. System, 1991; Dennett scholar Garden Club Fedn. Mass., 1992. Mem. ASCD, NEA, Mass. ASCD, Mass. Tchrs. Assn., Groton-Dunstable Educators Assn. (rep., mem. assembly 1992-93), Friends of Groton Tree Warden. Greek Orthodox. Avocations: aerobics, gardening, reading, skiing. Home: PO Box 426 37 Old Orchard Rd West Groton MA 01472 Office: Swallow Union Sch Main St Dunstable MA 01827

POLESE, MARY LUCRETIA, art educator; b. Hoboken, N.J., May 7, 1949; d. Ben A. and Antoinette (Corrado) P. BA in Art, Mt. Mercy Coll., 1971; postgrad., U. Florence, Italy, 1972; M in Art Edn., Kean Coll., 1986; M in Edn. Adminstrn., Capella U., 2003. Cert. art educator Kindergarten thru grade 12, elem. educator, supr., N.J. Asst. dir. Title XX After Sch. Program, Plainfield, N.J., 1975-80; classroom tchr. St. Mary's Sch., Plainfield, N.J., 1971-79; art tchr. Plainfield Pub. Schs., 1979-86, Tinton Falls (N.J.) Schs., 1986—. Mem. Bd. Edn., Red Bank, N.J., 1985-88. Named Tchr. of the Yr., Plainfield Pub. Sch., 1985, N.J. Tchr. of Yr. Atchison Sch., Tinton Falls, 1994-95, Momouth County N.J. Tchr. of Yr., 1998-99; recipient N.J. State Hist. Soc. grant State of N.J. Dept. Edn., 1988, Teaching grant State of N.J. Dept. Edn., 1990, Nat. Tchr. Inst. grant Nat. Gallery Art, Washington, 1993, Tinton Falls Edn. Assn. award, 1999-2000. Roman Catholic. Avocations: gardening, running. Office: Mahala F Atchison Sch 961 Sycamore Ave Tinton Falls NJ 07724-3131

POLIN, COLLEEN MARIE, special education educator; b. Detroit, Feb. 3, 1954; d. Henry George and Lorraine Cynthia (Spisz) Geppert. BA in Spl. Edn., Ea. Mich. U., 1975, M.Early Childhood Edn., 1981. Tchr. austically impaired Wayne County Intermediate Schs., 1976-78, Garden City (Mich.) pub. schs., 1978—. Internat. speaker in field. Active Boy Scouts Am., Garden City, 1986-87; host children's program "Alphabet Soup", MacLean Hunter Cable TV, Garden City, 1988—; bd. dirs. Mich. Partnership for New Edn. Named Tchr. of the Yr., Wayne County Soc. Autistic Citizens, 1988, Golden Apple Teaching award, Wayne County Intermediate Sch. Dist., 1989, Disting. Alumni award, Schoolcraft Coll., Livonia, 1990, Flag of Lng. and Liberty, 1992. Mem. Autism Sch. Soc., Autism Soc. Am., Coun. for Exceptional Children. Avocations: calligraphy, antique restoration, gardening. Home: 1028 Church St Plymouth MI 48170-1149 Office: Burger School 30922 Beechwood St Garden City MI 48135-1993

POLISI, JOSEPH W(ILLIAM), academic administrator; b. N.Y.C., Dec. 30, 1947; married. BA in Polit. Sci., U. Conn., 1969; MA in Internat. Relations, Tufts U., 1970, MusM, 1973, M of Mus. Arts, 1975; DMA, Yale U., 1980; DHL (hon.), Ursinus Coll., Collegetown, Pa., 1986; MusD (hon.), Curtis Inst. Music, 1990; DMA, New England Conservatory Music, 2001. Exec. officer Yale Sch. of Music, New Haven, 1976-80; dean of faculty Manhattan Sch. of Music, N.Y.C., 1980-83; dean Coll. Conservatory of Music U. Cin., 1983-84; pres. The Juilliard Sch., N.Y.C., 1984—. Performances as bassoonist throughout the U.S.; contbr. articles to various publs. in U.S. and France. Mem.: Royal Acad. Music London (hon.). Office: Juilliard Sch Office of the Pres 60 Lincoln Center Plz New York NY 10023-6588

POLITE, EVELYN C. retired middle school educator, counselor, evangelist; b. Pineland, S.C., Dec. 25, 1937; d. Martin and Mary Brantley Coger; m. Horace Polite, Jan. 1, 1958 (dec. Jan. 1987); children: Horace Lenton, Tracy Polite Floyd. BS, Allen U., 1960; M in Elem. Edn., Armstrong-Savannah (Ga.) State U., 1976; cert. specialist of arts in theology, Zoe U., Jacksonville, Fla., 2000; PhD in Christian Counseling, Zoe U., 2001. Tchr. math. Beaufort County Bd. Edn., Bluffton, SC, 1960—61, Florence County Bd. Edn., Florence, SC, 1961—63, Jasper County Bd. Edn., Ridgeland, SC, 1963—64, 1991—92, Savannah Pub. Schs., 1964—90; math. tutor Dept. Family and Children, Savannah, 1992—94. Mem. curriculum devel. com. Savannah Pub. Schs., 1983—84, mem. staff devel. coun., 1983—84; test-item writer Ednl. Testing Svc., Princeton, NJ, 1990. Pres. 42d St Civic Club, Savannah, 2000—; exec. v.p. Cuyler-Brownsville Neighborhood Orgn., Savannah, 2001—. Recipient Outstanding Tchr. award, Math.-Sci. Roundtable, Atlanta, 1990. Mem. Ch. Of God. Avocations: world missions, travel, physical fitness, reading Christian literature. Home: 1107 W 42d St Savannah GA 31415 Office: Coastal Cathedral Ch of God 2208 E DeRenne Ave Savannah GA 31406

POLITZER, HUGH DAVID, physicist, educator; b. N.Y.C., Aug. 31, 1949; s. Alan A. and Valerie T. (Diamant) P. BS, U. Mich., 1969; PhD, Harvard U., 1974. Jr. fellow Harvard U. Soc. Fellows, 1974-77; mem. faculty Calif. Inst. Tech., 1977—, prof. theoretical physics, 1979—, exec. officer for physics, 1986-88. Recipient J.J. Sakurai prize, 1986, High Energy and Particle Physics prize European Phys. Soc., 2003; fellow NSF, 1969-74, Sloan Found., 1977-81, Woodrow Wilson grad. fellow, 1969-74, Guggenheim fellow, 1997-98. Mem. Phi Beta Kappa. Address: 452-48 Calif Inst Tech Pasadena CA 91125-0001 E-mail: politzer@theory.caltech.edu.

POLKA, WALTERS S. school superintendent; b. Niagara Falls, N.Y., Nov. 5, 1945; s. Frank W. and Josephine B. (Ziblut) P.; m. Victoria M. Homiszczak, Aug. 3, 1968; children: Jennifer Marie, Monica Jo. BA, U. Buffalo, 1968; MA, Niagara U., 1970, MS, 1971; EdD, U. Buffalo, 1977; postgrad., Harvard U., 1989-98, Fla. State U., 1993. Cert. sch. dist. adminstr., tchr. social studies, N.Y. Asst. supt. Lewiston-Porter Cen. Schs., Youngstown, N.Y., 1986-90; curriculum coord. Williamsville (N.Y.) Cen. Schs., 1973-86; tchr., high sch. Lewiston-Porter Cen. Schs., 1968-73; supt. Lewiston-Porter Sch. Dist., 1990—. Adj. prof. Niagara U., Buffalo State Coll., Medaille Coll., U. Buffalo; curriculum advisor Hudson Inst., 1981-84. Scholar Niagara U. Grad. Sch., 1968-70; Filene Found. fellow Harvard U., summer 1989. Mem. ASCD, Am. Assn. Sch. Adminstrs., Am. Mgmt. Assn., Internat. Soc. Ednl. Planning (treas., past pres.), Phi Delta Kappa, Phi Alpha Theta, Pi Lambda Theta. Office: Lewiston-Porter Cen Schs 4061 Creek Rd Youngstown NY 14174-9609

POLK-MATTHEWS, JOSEPHINE ELSEY, school psychologist; b. Roselle, N.J., Sept. 24, 1930; d. Charles Carrington and Olive Mae (Bond) Polk; m. Donald Roger Matthews, Aug. 29, 1959 (div. 1974); children: John Roger, Alison Olivia; m. William Y. Delaney, Sept. 17, 1994 (div. 1997). AB, Mt. Holyoke Coll., 1952; credential in occupational therapy, Columbia U., 1954; MA, U. So. Calif., L.A., 1957; Cert. Advanced Study, Harvard U., 1979, MS, 1980; postgrad., Coll. William & Mary, 1995—. Cert. elem. edn. life teaching credential, Calif; cert. ednl. adminstrn. life credential, Calif.; cert. pupil personnel svcs., counseling life credential, sch. psychology credential, Calif.; sch. psychology credential, Nev. Occupational therapist VA Hosp., Northport, N.Y., 1953-55, L.A., 1955-57; health svcs. adminstr. John Wesley County Hosp., L.A., 1957-59; elem. tchr. L.A. (Calif.) City Schs., 1959-60, Santa Clara (Calif.) Unified Sch. Dist., 1960-65, 71-74; asst. prof. Sch. Edn., San Jose (Calif.) State U., 1971; asst. prin. Berryessa Union Sch. Dist., San Jose, Calif., 1974-77, 85-86; ednl. cons. Boston (Mass.) U. Sch. Medicine, 1981-83; asst. prin. Inglewood (Calif.) Unified Sch. Dist., 1986-90; sch. psychologist Clark County Sch. Dist., Las Vegas, 1990-94; contract sch. psychologist Newport News (Va.) Sch. Dist., 1995-96. Med. facility developer Commonwealth Mass., Dept. Mental Health, Boston, 1980-81, ednl. liaison, Roxbury Juvenile Ct., 1979. Author: (with others) The New Our Bodies Ourselves, 1983; prodr.: (video) Individualized Rsch., 1971. Commr. Commn. on the Status of Women, Cambridge, Mass., 1981-83; hostess Ctr. for Internat. Visitors, Boston, 1983-84; pers. recruiter L.A. (Calif.) Olympic Organizing Com., 1984; vol. tutor Las Vegas (Nev.) Libr., 1992. Mem. Am. Ednl. Rsch. Assn., Internat. Assn. Spl. Edn., Coun. for Exceptional Children, Comparative and Internat. Edn. Soc., Phi Delta Kappa, Alpha Kappa Alpha, Kappa Delta Pi. Office: Sch Edn Spl Edn PO Box 8795 Williamsburg VA 23187-8795 E-mail: mhs80@post.harvard.edu.

POLLACK, GERALD ALEXANDER, economist, government official; b. Vienna, Jan. 14, 1929; came to U.S. 1938; s. Stephen J. and Tini (Herschel) P.; m. Patricia E. Sisterson; children: Nora S., Carol A. BA, Swarthmore (Pa.) Coll., 1951; MA, MPA, Princeton U., 1953, PhD, 1958. Corp. economist Leeds & Northrup Co., Phila., 1958-62; officer in charge internat. payments U.S. Dept. State, Washington, 1962-63; internat. economist Joint Econ. Com. of Congress, Washington, 1963-65; chief economist Office Spl. Rep. for Trade Negotiations, 1964; dep. asst. sec. U.S. Dept. Commerce, Washington, 1965-68; v.p. Loeb, Rhoades & Co., N.Y.C., 1968-69, Bendix Corp., Southfield, Mich., 1969-70, Citibank, N.Y.C., 1970-71; internat. economist Exxon Corp., N.Y.C., 1971-86; v.p., chief economist Overseas Shipholding Group, N.Y.C., 1986-89; assoc. prof. fin. Pace U., N.Y.C., 1990-94; assoc. dir. for internat. econs. Bur. Econ. Analysis, U.S. Dept. Commerce, 1994-99. Contbr. articles to profl. jours. Bd. dirs. Jamaica Estates Assn., 1976-80, Oakwood Sch., Poughkeepsie, N.Y., 1979-89; trustee Lindley Murray Fund, 1990-94; mem. Greenwich Dem. Town Com., 1992-94, 2001—; clk. Flushing Monthly Meeting Soc. of Friends, 1990-94; mem. Greenwich Rep. Town Meeting, 1999—. With U.S. Army, 1953-55. Mem.: Violoncello Soc., Coun. on Fgn. Rels., Phi Beta Kappa. Mem. Soc. Of Friends. Avocations: cello, classical music, photography, hiking, bicycling. E-mail: gapollack@hotmail.com.

POLLACK, GERALD LESLIE, physicist, educator; b. Bklyn., July 8, 1933; s. Herman and Jennie (Tenenbaum) P.; m. Antoinette Amparo Velasquez, Dec. 22, 1958; children: Harvey Anton, Samuela Juliet, Margolita Mia, Violet Amata. BS, Bklyn. Coll., 1954; Fulbright scholar, U. Gottingen, 1954-55; MS, Calif. Inst. Tech., 1957, PhD, 1962. Physics student trainee Nat. Bur. Standards, Washington, 1954-58, solid state physicist, 1961-65, cons. Boulder, Colo., 1965-70; assoc. prof. dept. physics Mich. State U., East Lansing, 1965-69, prof., 1969—; cons. NRC, Ill. Dept. Nuclear Safety; physicist Naval Med. Rsch. Inst., Bethesda, Md., summer 1979. Physicist USAF Sch. Aerospace Medicine, San Antonio, Tex., summer 1987. Co-author (with D.R. Stump): Electromagnetism, 2002; contbr. articles to profl. jours. Fellow Am. Phys. Soc.; mem. AAAS, Am. Assn. Physics Tchrs. Office: Mich State U Dept Physics and Astronomy East Lansing MI 48824-1116

POLLACK, HENRY NATHAN, geophysics educator; b. Omaha, July 13, 1936; s. Harold Myron and Sylvia (Chait) P.; m. Lana Beth Schoenberger, Jan. 29, 1963; children: Sara Beth (dec.), John David. AB, Cornell U., 1958; MS, U. Nebr., 1960; PhD, U. Mich., 1963. Lectr. U. Mich., 1962, asst. prof., asso. prof., prof. geophysics, 1964—, assoc. dean for research, 1982-85, chmn. dept. geol. scis., 1988-91. Rsch. fellow Harvard U., 1963-64; sr. lectr. U. Zambia, 1970-71; vis. scientist U. Durham, U. Newcastle-on-Tyne, Eng., 1977-78, U. Western Ont., 1985-86; chmn. Internat. Heat Flow Commn., 1991-95. Author: Uncertain Science...Uncertain World, 2003. Fellow: AAAS, Geol. Soc. Am.; mem.: Am. Geophys. Union. Achievements include research on thermal evolution of the earth, recent climate change. Office: U Mich Dept Geol Scis Ann Arbor MI 48109

POLLACK, ROBERT HARVEY, psychology educator; b. N.Y.C., June 26, 1927; s. Solomon and Bertha (Levy) P.; m. Martha Dee Katz, Aug. 20, 1948; children: Jonathan Keith, Lance Michael, Scott Evan. BS, CCNY, 1948; MS, Clark U., Worcester, Mass., 1950, PhD, 1953. Lectr. U. Sydney, Australia, 1953-61; spl. rsch. fellow Columbia U., N.Y.C., 1960-61; chief div. cognitive devel. Inst. Juvenile Rsch., Chgo., 1961-63, dep. dir. rsch., 1963-69; from clin. asst. prof. to clin. assoc. prof. rsch. U. Ill. Coll. Medicine, Chgo., 1962-67; prof. psychology U. Ga., Athens, 1969-96, chair grad. program. exptl. psychology, 1970-78, chair grad. study com., 1978-86; prof. emeritus, 1996—; chair grad. program in life-span psychology U. Ga., Athens, 1988-96. Editor: The Experimental Psychology of Alfred Binet, 1969; contbr. over 100 articles and chpts. to profl. publs. Cpl. U.S. Army, 1945-46. Grantee Nat. Inst. Child Health and Human Devel., 1965, 67, 72, 78. Fellow AAAS, Am. Psychol. Assn.; mem. Am. Assn. Sex Edn., Counsellors and Therapists, Gerontol. Soc. Am., Australian Psychol. Soc., Soc. for Researching Child Devel., Soc. for Sci. Study Sex, Sigma Xi. Democrat. Avocations: travel, philately, opera, military history. Office: U Ga Dept Psychology Athens GA 30602

POLLAK, BARTH, mathematics educator; b. Chgo., Aug. 14, 1928; s. Samuel and Esther (Hirschberg) P.; m. Helen Charlotte Schiller, Aug. 22, 1954; children: Martin Russell, Eleanor Susan. BS, Ill. Inst. Tech., 1950, MS, 1951; PhD, Princeton U., 1957. Instr. math. Ill. Inst. Tech., Chgo., 1956-58; asst. prof. Syracuse (N.Y.) U., 1958-63; assoc. prof. U. Notre Dame, Ind., 1963-67, prof., 1967-2000, prof. emeritus, 2000—. Office: U Notre Dame Dept Math Notre Dame IN 46556 E-mail: pollak.1@nd.edu.

POLLAK, JOEL MICHAEL, director; b. N.Y.C., May 24, 1947; s. Walter J. and Gladys (Diamond) Pollak; m. Patricia Ansel, Aug. 25, 1968; children: Elyce Pollak Jacobson, Gayle Pollak Harris. BA, SUNY, Buffalo, 1969; MS, St. John's U., Jamaica, N.Y., 1976; EdD, NYU, 1988. Cert. sch. dist. adminstr., N.Y. State Edn. Dept. Tchr. sci. Massapequa (N.Y.) H.S., 1969-76; adminstrv. asst. Nassau BOCES, Westbury, NY, 1976-80, Valley Stream (N.Y.) Union Free Sch. Dist. # 24, 1980-83; asst. supt. Ellenville (N.Y.) Ctrl. Sch. Dist., 1983-87, Eastchester (N.Y.) Union Free Sch. Dist., 1987-95; supt. of schs. Greater Johnstown (N.Y.) Sch. Dist., 1995-98; supt. schs. Marlboro (N.Y.) Ctrl. Sch. Dist., 1998—2001; program dir., Dept. of Curriculum, Instrn. and Dept. of Ednl. Leadership and Adminstrn. Long Island U., Rockland Grad. Campus, 2002—. Adj. asst. prof. NYU, 1992-95; cons., workshop facilitator C. Weeks Assocs., N.Y.C., 1991-95. Trustee, v.p. Yorktown Jewish Ctr., Yorktown Heights, N.Y., 1990-92. Named Educator of Yr., Am. Assn. Jewish Profls., Westchester County, N.Y., 1993; Maurice Osborne scholar Assn. Sch. Bus. Officials, N.Y. State, 1988. Mem. ASCD, Am. Assn. Sch. Adminstrs., Am. Field Svc. (pres. Ellenville chpt. 1983-87), Johnstown Bus. and Profl. Assn., Rotary, Moose. Avocations: golf, reading. Home: 111 Swan Ln Poughkeepsie NY 12603-3534

POLLAK, LOUIS HEILPRIN, judge, educator; b. N.Y.C., Dec. 7, 1922; s. Walter and Marion (Heilprin) P.; m. Katherine Weiss, July 25, 1952; children: Nancy, Elizabeth, Susan, Sarah, Deborah. AB, Harvard U., 1943; LLB, Yale U., 1948; LLD (hon.), Wilkes U., 2002. Bar: N.Y. 1949, Conn. 1956, Pa. 1976. Law clk. to Justice Rutledge U.S. Supreme Ct., 1948-49; with Paul, Weiss, Rifkind, Wharton & Garrison, N.Y.C., 1949-51; spl. asst. to Amb. Philip C. Jessup State Dept., 1951-53; asst. counsel Amalgmated Clothing Workers Am., 1954-55; mem. faculty Yale Law Sch., 1955-74, dean, 1965-70; Greenfield prof. U. Pa., 1974-78, dean Law Sch., 1975-78, lectr., 1980—; judge U.S. Dist Ct (ea. dist.) Pa., Phila., 1978—, now sr. judge. Vis. lectr. Howard U. Sch. Law, 1953; vis. prof. U. Mich. Law Sch., 1961, Columbia Law Sch., 1962 Author: The Constitution and the Supreme Court: A Documentary History, 1966. Mem. New Haven Bd. Edn., 1962-68; chmn. Conn. adv. com. U.S. Civil Rights Commn., 1962-63; mem. bd. NAACP Legal Def. Fund, 1960-78, v.p., 1971-78. Served with AUS, 1943-46. Mem.: ABA (chmn. sect. individual rights 1970—71, Spirit of Excellence award 2003), Am. Law Inst. (coun. 1978—), Am. Acad. Polit. and Social Sci. (bd. dirs. 2001—), Am. Philos. Soc., Am. Acad. Arts and Scis., Assn. Bar City N.Y., Phila. Bar Assn., Fed. Bar Assn. Office: US Dist Ct 16613 US Courthouse 601 Market St Philadelphia PA 19106-1713

POLLARA, BERNARD, immunologist, educator, pediatrician; b. Chgo. s. Joseph and Mamie P. PhB, Northwestern U., 1951, MS, 1954; MD, U. Minn., 1960, PhD, 1963. Intern USPHS Hosp., Seattle, 1960; resident in pediatrics U. Minn. Hosps., 1968-69; rsch. assoc. pediatrics U. Minn., 1960-63, assoc. prof. biochemistry and pediatrics, 1969; prof. pediatrics Albany (N.Y.) Med. Coll., 1969-94, chmn. dept., 1979-93; pediatrician in chief Albany Med. Ctr. Hosp., 1979-93; sabbatical leave, pediatrician Yukon Kuskokwim Regional Hosp., 1992-93; John and Aliese Price prof. pediatrics & adolescent medicine U. South Fla., Tampa, 1994—, head divsn. gen. pediatrics, dept. pediatrics, 1994—, interim chmn. pediats., 1999-2001. V.p. for rsch. affairs Albany Med. Ctr., 1986-89. Dir. N.Y. State Kidney Disease Inst., 1969-79. With USN, 1945-46. Recipient Acad. Laureate award SUNY, Albany, 1991; Arthritis and Rheumatism Found. fellow, 1961-64. Fellow Am. Acad. Pediats.; mem. AAAS, Am. Assn. Immunologists, Am. Pediat. Soc., Am. Soc. Cell Biology, Clin. Immunology Soc., Ambulatory Pediat. Assn., Sigma Xi, Phi Lambda Upsilon, Alpha Omega Alpha. Office: U South Fla Sch Medicine Dept Pediatrics 17 Davis Blvd Ste 308 Tampa FL 33606-3475 E-mail: bpollara@hsc.usf.edu.

POLLARA, JOANNE, learning disabilities educator consultant; b. Hoboken, N.J., Apr. 18, 1954; d. Ralph Frank and Katharine Stark (Cunningham) Pollara; children: Angela, Joshua. BA, St. Joseph Coll., 1976; MA, Montclair State U., 1994. Cert. tchr. elem., spl. edn., L.D.T.C., N.J. 4th grade tchr. Holy Trinity Sch., Hackensack, N.J., 1976-77; tchr. of handicapped Kessler Inst., West Orange, N.J., 1978-86; bedside instructor West Orange Bd. of Edn., 1976-86, spl. edn. inst. aide, 1986-88; tchr. of handicapped Redwood Sch., West Orange, N.J., 1988-97; learning disabled tchr. cons. West Orange Pub. Schs., 1997—. Mem. spl. edn. curriculum com., W. Orange, N.J., 1989, bldg. mgmt. com., 1991-92; spl. edn. rep. reading curriculum com., W. Orange, 1990; PTA faculty rep. Redwood Sch., W. Orange, 1994-95. Religious educator Our Lady of Lourdes Ch., West Orange, N.J., 1984-85, Notre Dame Ch., North Caldwell, N.J., 1991-92; girl scout leader Girl Scouts of U.S., W. Orange, N.J., 1983-84, 86-87. Mem. Coun. for Exceptional Children (learning disabilities divsn.), Coun. for Ednl. Diagnostic Svcs., Assn. Learning Consultants, Phi Kappa Phi. Avocations: reading, music (piano, guitar), swimming. Home: 23 Espy Rd Apt B5 Caldwell NJ 07006-4855 Office: Dept Student Support Svcs 179 Eagle Rock Ave West Orange NJ 07052

POLLARD, DENNIS BERNARD, lawyer, educator; b. Phila., May 12, 1968; BS in Psychology, Pa. State U., 1990; JD, Ohio State U., 1993; postgrad., U. Mich., 1996. Bar: Ohio 1993, U.S. Dist. Ct. (no. dist.) Ohio 1994, U.S. Ct. Appeals (6th cir.) 1994. freelance cons., 1993-. Staff atty. The Legal Aid Soc. Cleve., 1993-95; atty. student affairs, student life Pa. State U., 1995-96; acad. adminstrv. intern U. Mich. Law Sch., Ann Arbor, 1996-97; asst. dean student affairs U. Tenn. Coll. Law, Knoxville, 1997-98; program dir. tenants' rights unit Tenants' Action Group of Phila., 1998-99, dir. devel., 1999—2001. Mem. ABA, Ohio State Bar Assn., Assn. Fundraising Profls., Phi Delta Phi. Avocation: biking. Home: PO Box 41884 Philadelphia PA 19101-1884

POLLARD, JANN DIANN, fine artist, graphic artist, educator; b. Mt. Pleasant, Iowa, Apr. 11, 1942; d. Donald Robert and Mary (Young) Lawrence; m. Gene A. Pollard, Apr. 25, 1970; children: Brittany, Natalie. BFA in interior design, U. Colo., 1963; post grad., Coll. San Mateo, Calif. Interior designer Dohrmann Co., Brisbane, Calif., 1964-68, H. Jander's Design Cons., San Francisco, 1968-70, Jann Pollard Studios, Burlingame, Calif., 1970—; artist The Gallery, Burlingame, 1985—, Cottage Gallery, Carmel, Calif., 1991—2000, Generations Gallery, Calif., 1998, Gallery Americana, Calif., 2000, New Masters Gallery, Carmel, Calif., 2001. One person shows include The Gallery, Burlingame, 1987, 88, 91, 93, 95, 97, 98, 99, 01, 02; Cottage Gallery, Carmel, 1993, 95, 98; SWA Zellerbach Show, San Francisco, 1985 (hon. mention); Soc. Western Artists Ann., 1985, 91; San Diego Internat. Watercolor Show, 1990; artist for bookcovers, Karen Brown Travel Books, 1991-2000. Active Hillsborough Aux. to Family Svc. Agy., 1983-2000; Nat. Kidney Found., 1994—. Mem. Nat. Watercolor Soc. (signature mem.), Am. Soc. Interior Designers (profl.), Calif. Watercolor Soc. (signature mem., Outstanding Achievement award 2000), Soc. Western Artists (signature mem., 2d prize 1973). Avocations: computers, genealogy. Home: 105 La Mesa Dr Burlingame CA 94010-5919 E-mail: jann@jannpollard.com.

POLLEY, MICHAEL GLEN, mathematics educator; b. Mattoon, Ill., Feb. 23, 1964; s. George Warren Polley and Judith Maxine (Yarger) Hull; m. Janet Jorene Gray, June 20, 1987; children: Thias Jorene, Aaron Michael, Jessica Connie, Benjamin Ray. BS, Iowa State U., 1986, M Sch. Math., 1994. Cert. tchr., Tex., Iowa. Tchr. Porter H.S. Brownsville (Tex.) Ind. Sch. Dist., 1986-91; tchr., dept. chair Wapello (Iowa) Comm. Schs. H.S., 1991-97; mem. faculty Southeastern C.C., Burlington, Iowa, 1997—. Adj. tchr. Southeastern C.C., Burlington, Iowa, 1995-97. Author: Geometry: A Lab Approach, 1994. Mem., sound engr., Sunday sch. tchr. Grandview Comm. Bible Ch., 1991-95; mem. Brownsville Bapt. Ch., 1988-91, sound engr., 1989-91; founding mem. Solid Rock Bapt. Ch., 1995—; active Boy Scouts Am., 2998—; coach for youth baseball and football. Evangelical. Avocations: sports, photography, music. Home: 310 S Main St Wapello IA 52653-1544 Office: Southeastern CC 136A 105 S Gear Ave West Burlington IA 52655-1001 E-mail: mpolley@secc.cc.ia.us., mjpolley@louisancom.net.

POLLICK, G. DAVID, academic administrator, philosopher; b. Kansas City, Mo., Oct. 13, 1947; m. Janice Pollick, 1975; 2 children, Dayna, Landon. BA, philosophy, U. San Diego, 1971; Ph.L., philosophy, St. Paul U., Ont., Can., 1973; MA, philosophy, U. Ottawa, Can., 1973, PhD, philosophy, 1981. Lecturer, philosophy U. San Diego, San Diego, 1972-73; tchr.-counselor, neurologically and physically handicapped Aseltine Sch. Neurol. Handicapped, 1972-73; dir. heroin rehab. ctr. Imperial County Diversion Program, El Centro, Calif., 1973-74; tchr.-counselor, emotionally handicapped Finley Elem Sch, Holtville, Calif., 1974-75; lecturer, philosophy U. Ottawa, Ottawa, ON, Canada, 1975-77; asst. prof. philosopy, dept.

chrm., acad. coordinator St. John's U., Collegeville, Minn., 1977-84; assoc. prof., dean coll. arts and scis. Seattle U., 1984-89; provost, v.p. for acad. affairs SUNY, Cortland, 1989-93; acting pres., 1991-93; co-CEO, pres. Art Inst. Chgo., Sch. of Art Inst. of Chgo., 1993—96; pres. Lebanon Valley Coll., Annville, Pa., 1996—. Author: The Work of Roman Ingarden, 1977, (with others) The Aesthetics of Roman Ingarden, 1982; co-editor Supplementary Volume on Aesthetics, 1977. Served with USN. Fellow philosophy and fine arts, Inst. Ecumenical and Culture Rsch., 1976-77; Koscjusko Foundation awd., 1978. Avocations: sculpture, art history, archaeology. Office: Lebanon Valley College 101 N College Ave Annville PA 17003*

POLLIN, BURTON RALPH, English educator; b. Worcester, Mass. s. Louis and Rae (Cohen) P.; m. Alice Pollin, Jan. 30, 1944; children: Diana Claire, Myles Clement. BA, CCNY, 1936; PhD, Columbia U., 1962. Tchr. English N.Y.C. Bd. of Edn., 1936-62, chmn. dept. English, 1956-62; lectr. English CUNY, 1957-62, assoc. prof. to full prof., 1962-73, prof. emeritus, 1973—. Lectr. on Poe N.Y. State Coun. Humanities, 1996—99, 2003—05. Author: Education and Enlightenment in the Works of William Godwin, 1962, Godwin Criticism: A Synoptic Bibliography, 1967, Dictionary of Names and Titles in Poe's Collected Works, 1968, Discoveries in Poe, 1970, Benjamin Constant's Translation of Godwin's Political Justice, 1972, The Music for Shelley's Poems: An Annotated Bibliography of 1309 Compositions, 1974, Poe, Creator of Words, 1974, The Imaginary Voyages, vol. 1 of Collected Writings of...Poe, 1994, Word Index to Poe's Fiction, 1982, The Brevities of Poe, vol. 2 of Collected Writings of Poe, 1985, Poe's Writings in the Broadway Jour., 1986, Insights and Outlooks: Essays on Great Writers, 1986, Images of Poe's Works: A Comprehensive Descriptive Catalogue of Illustrations, 1989, The German Face of Poe (with Thomas Hansen), 1995, Poe's Writings in the Southern Literary Messenger, vol. 5 of Collected Writings of Poe, 1986; adv. bd. editors Poe Studies, 1980—, Poe Rev., 2000—; contbr. over 180 articles to profl. jours. Founder, continuing bd. dirs. Bronxville Beautification Coun., 1980—; active Friends of N.Y. Pub. Libr., Carnegie Hall, Libr. of Bronxville, Eastchester Arts Coun., Columbia U. Libr. Friends, Supporters of Guggenheim Found.; bd. trustees Poe Mus., Richmond, Va. Recipient Poe award, Bronx County Hist. Soc., 2001, Rotary Club award, 2002, Alice and Burton Pollin for effective beautification of Bronxville, 2002; fellow John Hay Whitney, 1947; grantee Am. Philos. Soc., U.S., 1964—65, Am. Philos. Soc., London, 1965, 1968, N.Y. State U. Rsch. Found., 1966, Carl and Lily Pforzheimer, 1966, 1969, SUNY, 1967—73, Am. Coun. Learned Socs., 1968, 1975, 1984, Guggenheim Found., 1973—74, CUNY, 1973, 1980, 1986, NEH, 1983—84, Lectureship on Poe, NY State Humanities Coun., 1996, 2003—05. Mem. MLA (life), Poe Studies Assn., Am. Lit. Assn. Avocations: piano playing, travel, environmentalism. Home: 3 Stoneleigh Plz Apt 4D Bronxville NY 10708

POLLITT, JEROME JORDAN, art history educator; b. Fair Lawn, N.J., Nov. 26, 1934; s. John Kendall and Doris B. (Jordan) P.; m. Susan Baker Matheson, Feb. 10, 1977. BA, Yale U., 1957; PhD, Columbia U., 1963. Instr. history of art Yale U., New Haven, 1962-64, asst. prof., 1964-68, assoc. prof., 1969-73, prof., 1973-98, prof. emeritus, 1998—, chmn. dept. classics, 1975-77, chmn. dept. history of art, 1981-84, dean, 1986-91. Author: Art and Experience in Classical Greece, 1972, The Ancient View of Greek Art, 1975, Art in the Hellenistic Age, 1986, The Art of Greece: Sources and Documents, 1990, Personal Styles in Greek Sculpture, 1996; editor-in-chief: Am. Jour. Archaeology, 1973-77; contbr. articles to profl. jours. Mem. Archaeol. Inst. Am., Coll. Art Assn. Home: 48 Dillon Rd Woodbridge CT 06525-1219 Office: Dept History of Art Yale U PO Box 208272 New Haven CT 06520-8272 E-mail: Jerome.Pollitt@yale.edu.

POLLOCK, BRUCE GODFREY, psychiatrist, educator; b. Toronto, Ont., Can., Aug. 18, 1952; s. Ira Justus and Sheila Joy (Godfrey) P.; m. Judith Arluk, May 18, 1982; children: Debra, Ariel. BS, U. Toronto, 1975, MD, 1979; PhD, U. Pitts., 1987. Chief resident Clarke Inst. Psychiatry, Toronto, 1982-83; fellow U. Pitts., 1983-84, asst. prof. dept. psychiatry, 1984-90, assoc. dir. clin. pharmacology dept. psychiatry, 1987-95, assoc. prof. dept. psychiatry and pharmacology, 1990-96, dir. geriat. psychopharm. dept. psychiatry and pharmacology, 1995—, prof. depts. psychiatry, pharmacology and pharm. scis., 1997—, chief acad. divsn. geriatrics and neuropsychiatry, 2001. Contbr. over 250 articles to profl. jours.; contbg. author books in field. Centennial fellow Med. Rsch. Coun. of Can., Ottawa, 1983, Merck fellow geriatric clin. pharmacology, Am. Fedn. for Aging Rsch., N.Y.C., 1988; recipient Geriat. Mental Health award NIMH, Bethesda, Md., 1992, Ind. Scientist award, 1997, Sr. Investigation Award, Am. Assoc. for Geniatric Psychiatry, Bethesda, Md., 2003. Fellow Royal Coll. Physicians Can., Am. Psychiat. Assn. (disting.). Home: 7032 Meade St Pittsburgh PA 15208-2429 Office: Western Psychiat Inst/Clin 3811 Ohara St Pittsburgh PA 15213-2593 E-mail: pollockbg@upmc.edu.

POLLOCK, LINDA ANNE, history educator; b. London, Oct. 4, 1955; d. Raymond Anthony Willimott and Mary Dodds Norquay; m. Iain Forbes Pollock, July 1, 1978 (div. Feb. 1989); m. Dino Cinel, Oct. 28, 1989; children: Sophia, Cameron. MA, U. St. Andrews, Scotland, 1978, PhD, 1982. Lectr. Churchill Coll., U. Cambridge, Eng., 1987-88; asst. prof. Tulane U., New Orleans, 1988-89, assoc. prof., 1989-93, prof. history, 1993—, chair dept., 1998—, assoc. dean, 2001—. Mem. adv. bd. The Seventeenth Century jour., Durham, Eng., 1989, also History of Edn. Jour. Author: Forgotten Children: Parent-child Relations from 1500 to 1900, 1983, paperback edit., 1983, 85, 87, Japanese edit., 1988, Spanish edit., 1990, 94 (nat. book prize 1984), A Lasting Relationship. Parents and Children over Three Centuries, 1987, paperback edit., 1990, With Faith and Physic: The Life of a Tudor Gentlewoman, Lady Grace Mildmay 1552-1620, 1993, 95; contbr. articles and revs. to profl. publs. Recipient postdoctoral rsch. award Social Sci. Rsch. Coun., 1978-81, 83-86; fellow Churchil Coll., 1983-87, Huntington Libr., 1985, 88, Brit. Acad., 1986-88, Twenty-seven Found. Archive, 1987, Wellcome Found., 1987-88, Folger Shakespeare Libr., 1993; grantee Am. Philos. Soc., 1989, Tulane U., 1991. Mem. Am. Historians Assn., Conf. on Brit. Studies. Democrat. Home: 7513 Hampson St New Orleans LA 70118-5033 Office: Tulane U Dept History St Charles Ave New Orleans LA 70118

POLLOCK, MARC, media fundraising executive, consultant; b. Pitts., Mar. 27, 1945; s. Hyman Sidney and Beatrice (Berman) P.; m. Marjorie Ann Ginsburg, Dec. 16, 1967; 1 child, Brian Seth Ginsburg-Pollock. ABD in Eng., U. Pitts., 1973; BA in Eng. and Chemistry, Washington & Jefferson, 1966; MA in Eng., U. Pitts., 1969. Teaching fellow Eng. U. Pitts., 1968-74; instr. Eng. Chatham Coll., Pitts., 1972-79; exec. asst. to pres. WQED/Pitts., 1979-81, mgr. ednl. project devel., 1981-86; dir. edn. Sta. WQED/Pitts., 1986-93; WQED/Pitts., cons. media and devel., 1993-95, dir. found. and govt. support, 1995—. Lectr., presenter in field. Vol. March of Dimes, Pitts., 1990-92; cons. Am. Heart Assn., 1992-96, Nat. Kidney Assn., 1996, Leukemia Soc., 1999-2002. Recipient Gold Screen award, 2 CINE Golden Eagle awards, 1994. Mem. Acad. of TV Arts and Scis. (Emmy award Info. Series 1986), Modern Lang. Assn., Am. Assn. for Tng. and Devel., Melville Soc., Phi Beta Kappa. Avocations: tennis, skiing. Office: WQED 4802 5th Ave Pittsburgh PA 15213-2957

POLLOCK, MARGARET LANDAU PEGGY, elementary school educator; b. Jefferson City, Mo., Oct. 18, 1936; d. William Wold and Grace Elizabeth (Creamer) Anderson; children by previous marriage: Elizabeth, Charles, Christopher, Jeffrey; m. William Whalen Pollock, Jan. 30, 1993. AA, Stephens Coll., 1956; BS in Elem. Edn., U. Mo., Columbia, 1958; MA in Reading Edn., U. Mo., Kansas City, 1987. Cert. elem. tchr., Mo. Kindergarten tchr. Columbia Schs., 1958-59, Moberly (Mo.) Schs., 1960-62; 1st grade tchr. Kansas City Schs., 1962-63; kindergarten tchr. Independence (Mo.) Schs., 1966-75; chpt. I reading specialist Thomas Hart Benton Elem. Sch., Independence, 1975-93; book reviewer Corpus Christi (Tex.) Caller Times, 1994—; children's libr. Corpus Christi Pub. Libr., 1995-97; dir. Johnson City (Tex.) Libr., 1997—. Cons., presenter in field. Bd. dirs. Boys and Girls Club, Independence, 1990-93; coord. Independence Reading Fair, 1989-93; coord. books and tutoring Salvation Army, Kansas City, 1990-92. Mem. AAUW, Internat. Reading Assn. (People to People del. to USSR 1991, local v.p. 1990-91, pres. 1991-92), Internat. Platform Assn., Austin Writer's League, Archeol. Inst. Am., Tex. Libr. Assn., Earthwatch, Nature Conservancy, Sierra Club, Phi Kappa Phi, Pi Lambda Theta (pres. Beta Upsilon chpt. 1992-93). Avocations: native american history, rights and education, archeology, reading, travel, conservation. Home: PO Box 482 Johnson City TX 78636-0482

POLLOCK, WILLIAM JOHN, secondary school administrator; b. N.Y.C., Nov. 25, 1943; s. Edward and Rose (Favero) P.; m. Jennie Ann Taccetta, Jan. 28, 1967; children: John-Paul, Elizabeth. BSEd, CCNY, 1967; MSEd, Trenton State Coll., 1985; EdD, Nova U., 1993; postgrad., Harvard Graduate Sch., 1992. Tchr. N.Y.C. Pub. Schs., 1967-69; tchr. electronics Howell H.S., Farmingdale, N.J., 1970-85, dept. supr., 1985-89; vice-prin. Monmouth County Vocat. Schs., Middletown, N.J., 1989-90; prin. High Tech. H.S., Brookdale C.C. Campus, Lincroft, N.J., 1990—. Pres. suprs.' assn. Freehold (N.J.) Regional High Sch. Dist., 1988-89; pres. exec. bd. Region V Libr. Coop., Freehold, 1989-92. Treas. Prin. Ctr. for the Garden State, Princeton, 1997-98, v.p., 1998-99; asst. scout master Jackson (N.J.) area Boy Scouts Am., 1987-92; pres. exec. bd. St. Mary Acad., Lakewood, N.J., 1987-89; mem. Ocean County Agrl. Devel. Bd., Toms River, N.J., 1989—. 1st lt. U.S. Army, 1969-70, Vietnam. Decorated Bronze Star; recipient Geraldine R. Dodge Found. "Dodge Fellow principal award, 1993", N.J. Star Sch. award N.J. State Dept. Edn., 1995, Best Practices award N.J. State Dept. Edn., 1995; named N.J. Prin. of Yr. Met/Life, NAASP; U.S. Dept. Edn. Recognized Blue Ribbon Sch. Prin., 1997-98. Mem. ASCD, N.J. ASCD (Outstanding Curriculum award 1995), Nat. Assn. Secondary Sch. Prins., Internat. Tech. Edn. Assn., Am. Vocat. Edn. Assn., Prins. and Suprs. Assn., KC. Avocations: farming, growing christmas trees, photography, pottery, solar energy. Office: High Tech HS PO Box 119 Lincroft NJ 07738-0119

POLOIAN, LYNDA GAMANS, retailing educator; b. Manchester, N.H., Nov. 7, 1943; d. Herbert V. and Rose A. (Hammarbeck) Rauding; children: Kristen Soterion, Erik. BA in Psychology, U. N.H., 1976; MEd, Notre Dame Coll., Manchester, N.H., 1979. Sales promotion dir. A. Machinist, Inc., Manchester, 1966-78; prin. R.G. Cons., Manchester, 1977-89; prof. retailing So. N.H. U. (formerly N.H. Coll.), Manchester, 1975—; pres. Silk Accent, Inc., Manchester, 1991-97. Ptnr. Sylyn Enterprise Senderian Berhad, Alor Setar, Kedah, Malaysia, 1991-93; asst. prof. Lansdown Coll., London, 1985-86; presenter in field. Author: Retailing Principles: A Global Outlook, 2003; Co-author: (textbooks) Fashion: A Marketing Approach, 1983, Retailing: New Perspectives, 1992; (jour.) Nat. Bus. Edn. Assn. Yearbook, 1994. Mem. Miss N.H. Scholarship Program State Com., 1982-89. Mem. Am. Collegiate Retailing Assn. (pres. 2000-2002, mem. exec. bd.). Avocations: art, watercolor and oil painting, designing silk scarves. Office: So NH Univ 2500 N River Rd Manchester NH 03106-1045 E-mail: l.poloian@snhu.edu.

POLON, LINDA BETH, elementary school educator, writer, illustrator; b. Balt., Oct. 7, 1943; d. Harold Bernard and Edith Judith Wolff; m. Marty I. Polon, Dec. 18, 1966 (div. Aug. 1983). BA in History, UCLA, 1966. Elem. tchr. L.A. Bd. Edn., 1967—; writer, illustrator Scott, Foresman Pub. Co., Glenview Ill., 1979—, Frank Schaffer Pub. Co., Torrance, Calif., 1981-82, Learning Works, Santa Barbara, Calif., 1981-82, Harper Row Co.; edtl. reviewer Prentice Hall Pub. Co., Santa Monica, Calif., 1982-83; with Addison Wesley, N.J.; freelance writer, graphic designer, tutor L.A. Writer-illustrator Scott Foresman Pub. Co., Glenview, Ill., 1979—, Frank Schaffer Pub. Co., Torrance, Calif., 1981-82, Learning Works, Santa Barbara, Calif., 1981-82, Harper Row Co.; editorial reviewer Prentice Hall Pub. Co., Santa Monica, Calif., 1982-83. Author: (juvenile-educational books) Creative Teaching Games, 1974, Teaching Games for Fun, 1976, Making Kids Click, 1979, Write Up a Storm, 1979, Stir Up a Story, 1981, Paragraph Production, 1981, Using Words Correctly, 3d-4th grades, 1981, 5th-6th grades, 1981, Whole Earth Holiday Book, 1983, Writing Whirlwind, 1986, Magic Story Starters, 1987, (teacher's resource guides) Just Good Books, 1991, Kids Choice/Libraries, 1991, Write a Story-Grades 4-6, 1977, Story Starters-Grade 4-6, 1999, Grades 1-3 Storywriting, 1999, Grades 4-6 Storywriting, 1999. Mem. Soc. Children's Book Writers. Democrat. Home: 11645 Gorham Ave # 105 Los Angeles CA 90049-4753

POLONSKY, ARTHUR, artist, educator; b. Lynn, Mass., June 6, 1925; s. Benjamin and Celia (Hurwitz) P.; children: Eli, D.L., Gabriel. Diploma with highest honors, Sch. of Mus. Fine Arts, Boston, 1948. Instr. painting dept. Sch. Mus. Fine Arts, Boston, 1950-60; asst. prof. dept. fine arts Brandeis U., 1954-65; assoc. prof. Boston U., 1965-90, prof. emeritus, 1990—. One-man shows include Boris Mirski Gallery, Boston, 1950, 1954, 1956, 1964, Boston Pub. Libr., 1969, 1990, 1993, 1996, 1999, Durlacher Gallery, N.Y.C., 1965, Mickelson Gallery, Washington, 1966, 1974, Boston Ctr. for Arts, 1983, Starr Gallery, Boston, 1987, Fitchburg Art Mus., 1990, Kantar Fine Arts, Newton, Mass., 2002, exhibited in group shows at Met. Mus., N.Y.C., 1950, The Salon Des Jeunes Peintres, Paris, 1950, Stedelijk Mus., Amsterdam, The Netherlands, 1950, Carnegie Internat. Expn., 1951, Inst. Contemporary Art, Boston, 1960, Mus. Fine Arts, 1976, Boston Arts Festival, 1954, 1955, 1985, Expressionism in Boston, Decordova Mus., Lincoln, Mass., 1986, Palais Univ. de Strasbourg, France, 1992, Boston's Honored Artists, Danforth Mus., Framingham, Mass., 1995, Decordova Mus., Lincoln, Mass., 2002, Sagendorph Gallery, Keene State Coll., Keene, N.H., 2003, Represented in permanent collections Mus. Fine Arts, Boston, Fogg Mus., Harvard U., Addison Gallery of Am. Art, Andover, Mass., Stedelijk Mus., Amsterdam, Walker Art Ctr., Mpls., Zimmerli Art Mus., Rutgers U., New Brunswick, N.J., Honolulu Acad. Arts, Decordova Mus., Lincoln, Mass., High Mus. Art, Atlanta. Recipient Louis Comfort Tiffany award for painting, 1951, 1st prize Boston Arts Festival, 1954; European travelling fellow Sch. Mus. Fine Art, Boston, 1948-50 Mem. Artists Equity Assn., Inc. (founding, former dir. New Eng. chpt.). Address: 364 Cabot St Newtonville MA 02460-2252

POLOS, IRIS STEPHANIE, artist, art educator; b. Oakland, Calif., Feb. 14, 1947; d. Theodore C. and Catherine (Pappas) P.; 1 child Apollo Papafrangou. BFA, Calif. Coll. Arts and Crafts, Oakland, 1968, MFA, 1971. Instr. figure drawing Am. Sch. of Art, Athens, Greece, 1969-71 summers; instr. advanced drawing U. Calif. Extension Open Exchange, San Francisco, 1978-79; artist in residence Chabot Elem. Sch., Oakland, Calif., 1986-92, Mus. of Children's Art, Oakland, 1988—96; art tchr. Arrowsmith Acad., Berkeley, 1991—; instr. Oakland children's hosp. MOCHA, 1995—96. Artist: selected exhibitions include: San Francisco Mus. of Modern Art, 1971, Richmond (Calif.) Art Ctr., 1973, Calif. Coll. of Arts and Crafts, Oakland, 1973, Art for Art Sake Gallery, San Francisco, 1977, Jehu Wong Gallery, San Francisco, 1979, Triangle Gallery, San Francisco, 1981, Bond Gallery, N.Y.C., 1985, 86, Berkeley (Calif.) Art Ctr., 1987, 88, Emanuel Radnitzky, San Francisco, 1990 (2 shows), San Francisco Art Commn. Gallery, 1991, Fine Arts Ctr., Irvine, Calif., 1991, Trojanowska Gallery, San Francisco, 1991, Nelson Morales Gallery, San Francisco, 1992, Morphos Gallery, L.A., 1993, 94, Morphos Gallery, San Francisco, 1994, 95, Hotel Triton Art Fair with Morphos Gallery, San Francisco, 1995, Moreau Galeries, Notre Dame, Ind., 1995, Fort Mason Found., San Francisco, 1995, Magic Theater Lobby, San Francisco, 1995, Chgo.-Artspace, Lima, Ohio, 1997, Catherine Clark Gallery, San Francisco, 1997, 98, 99, Circle Elephant Art Galary Los Angeles, 2001, and others; permanent collections include the Oakland Mus., Catharine Clark, Gary Noguera, Helen Salz, Daniel Soto, Caroline Zecca, di Rosa Found., Sonoma County, and others; her works also include book illustration and theatre set design; featured artist in Juxtapoz mag., Fall 1998, Chicago Art Fair with C. Clark Gallery, 2001-02, Mural Proj. with Arrowsmith Acad. at Oakland Zoo. Grantee: Arts in Edn. grant Cultural Arts Divsn., Oakland, 1991-96, Berkeley Repertory Theater, 1995. Democrat. Home: 5801 Broadway Oakland CA 94618-1524 Office: Arrowsmith Acad Art Dept Berkeley CA 94704

POLOSKI, PATRICIA ELIZABETH, elementary school educator; b. Ardmore, Okla., June 30, 1941; d. Anthony Charles and Hazel E. (Colbert) P. AA, St. Joseph Jr. Coll., 1960; BS, Mo. Western U., 1970; MS in Edn., Northwest Mo. State U., 1972, EdS in Adminstrn. and Supervision, 1985. Cert. tchr. elem. tchr., elem. prin., supt. Head tchr. Project Head Start, St. Joseph, Mo., 1965; tchr. St. James Sch., St. Joseph, 1961-70; prin. St. James Parochial Sch., St. Joseph, 1970-77; tchr. St. Joseph Sch. System, 1977-00, mem. 1st curriculum com., 1st instructional math. mgmt. com., sch.-wide discipline com., reading com., libr. skills com. PcD, & com. in charge vols., 1st PDC Com. to Write Career Edn. for Corr., 1991; math. tchr. St. Pat's Parochial Sch., 2000—01; ret., 2001. Instr. bus. dept. evening classes Mo. Western Coll., 1991-94; coord. insvc. program, 1992; mem. Power Positive Students Program. Life mem. PTA St. Joseph Sch. System, 1980—, mem. exec. bd., 1988-93, historian, 1992-93, chair spelling bee, 1997-2000; United Way, 1997-2000. Named Outstanding Young Woman of Am., 1970, Outstanding Young Educator, 1972, Outstanding Young Leader of Am., 1985, 88, 89. Mem. ASCD, NAFE, Mo. State Tchrs. Assn., St. Joseph City Tchrs. Assn. Home: 3501 Sacramento St Saint Joseph MO 64507-1950

POLSBY, NELSON WOOLF, political scientist, educator; b. Norwich, Conn., Oct. 25, 1934; s. Daniel II and Edythe (Woolf) P.; m. Linda Dale Offenbach, Aug. 3, 1958; children: Lisa, Emily, Daniel R. Grad., Pomfret (Conn.) Sch., 1952; AB, Johns Hopkins, 1956; MA, Yale U., 1958, PhD, 1961; LittD, U. Liverpool, 1992; MA, Oxford (England) U., 1997; Dr. h.c. (hon.), Ecole Normale Superieure de Cachan, 2002. Instr. U. Wis., 1960-61; from asst. prof. to prof. Wesleyan U., Middletown, Conn., 1961-68; prof. polit. sci. U. Calif., Berkeley, 1967. Dir. Inst. Govtl. Studies U. Calif., 1989-99; vis. faculty Columbia, 1963, Yale, 1963, 67, 75, Hebrew U., Jerusalem, 1970, Stanford, 1977, Harvard U., 1986-87, Oxford U., 1994, 97-98; com. on pub. engrng. policy Nat. Acad. Engrng., 1973-76; commn. on behavioral and social scis. and edn. NRC, 1983-89. Author: Community Power and Political Theory, 2d edit, 1980, Congress and the Presidency, 4th edit, 1986, (with Aaron Wildavsky) Presidential Elections, 10th edit, 2000, Congress: An Introduction, 1968, Political Promises, 1974, (with Geoffrey Smith) British Government and its Discontents, 1981, Consequences of Party Reform, 1983, Political Innovation in America, 1984; Editor: (with R.A. Dentler and P. Smith) Politics and Social Life, 1963, (with R.L. Peabody) New Perspectives on the House of Representatives, 4th edit, 1993, Congressional Behavior, 1971, Reapportionment in the 1970's, 1971, The Modern Presidency, 1973, (with F.I. Greenstein) Handbook of Political Science, 8 vols., 1975, What If?, 1982, (with G. Orren) Media and Momentum, 1987; book rev. editor: Transaction, 1968-71; mng. editor: Am. Polit. Sci. Rev, 1971-77; editor Ann. Rev. POlit. Sci., 1998; editorial adv. bd. Polit. Sci. Quar., other jours. Mem. commn. on vice presdl. selection Dem. Nat. Com., 1973-74; mem. Yale U. Coun., 1978-2000, pres., 1986-93. Fellow Social Sci. Research Council, 1959, Brookings Instn., 1959-60, Center Advanced Study Behavioral Scis., 1965-66, 85-86, Ford Found., 1970-71, John Simon Guggenheim Found., 1977-78, 85-86, Roosevelt Ctr., 1982-83; recipient Yale U. Wilbur Cross medal, 1985, Yale medal, 1997. Fellow AAAS; mem. Am. Polit. Sci. Assn. (coun. 1971-77, 88-89), Am. Acad. Arts and Scis. (coun. 1993-96), Am. Sociol. Assn., Nat. Acad. Pub. Adminstrn., Coun. on Fgn. Rels., Phi Beta Kappa. Home: 1500 Le Roy Ave Berkeley CA 94708-1914 Office: U Calif Berkeley Inst Govtl Studies Berkeley CA 94720-0001 E-mail: nwpolsby@socrates.berkeley.edu.

POLSELLI, LINDA MARIE, elementary education educator; b. Providence, R.I., June 13, 1958; d. Anthony Natale and Helen Marie (Magnan) P. BS, R.I. Coll., 1982; MEd, Providence Coll., 1986. Spl. edn. educator Wyman Elem., Warwick, R.I., 1986-91; elem. edn. educator Holliman Elem., Warwick, 1991—. Computer software com. Warwick Sch. Dept., mem. math./curriculum revisions com., 1992, report card com., 1995—, tech. adv. bd., 1996—. Adminstr. Warwick Citizens Vol. Assn., Warwick Police Dept., 1983—. Mem. ASCD, Nat. Coun. Tchrs. English, Nat. Coun. Tchrs. Math., Internat. Reading Assn., R.I. Math. Tchrs. Assn., Tchrs. Applying Whole Lang. Roman Catholic. Avocations: travel, guitarist. Home: 128 Cove Ave Warwick RI 02889-8602

POLSTON, BARBARA JEAN, principal, educational psychologist; b. Litchfield, Ill., Oct. 9, 1943; d. Wilbur Lee and Frances (Leitschuh) P.; children: Charles, Beth, Ann. B of Music Edn., Webster Coll., 1965; MA, St. Louis U., 1985. Cert. elem. tchr., cert. prin., Mo., Wash., Oreg. Founding prin. The Franciscan Sch., Raleigh, N.C.; prin. Archdiocese St. Louis, 1986-96, Archdiocese of Portland, Oreg., 1997-99, All Saints Acad., Winter Haven, Fla., 2003—. Archdiocesan coord. alternative sch. practices, sch. calendars, multi media and tech., accelerative learning interventions, Diocesan tech. plans for schs., K-12. Mem. Mo. Lead Program, Nat. Yr. Round Edn., Danforth Found.; assessor SACS. Mem. ASCD, NCEA, Prins. Acad. Mo., Nat. Cath. Prins. Acad., Inst. Responsive Edn., Consortium Responsive Schs.

POLTROCK, NAOMI EUNICE, elementary education educator; b. Elmhurst, Ill., Sept. 12, 1945; d. Herold F. and Leona F. (Reiser) P. BA, Elmhurst Coll., 1967. Cert. tchr,. Ill. 7th and 8th grade social studies tchr. Elmhurst Cmty. Sch. Dist. # 205, 1967—. Recipient Outstanding Tchr. Am. History State of Ill. award Nat. Soc. DAR, 1995. Mem. Nat. Coun. Social Studies. Avocations: reading, aerobics, gardening, travel. Office: Bryan Jr High Sch 111 W Butterfield Rd Elmhurst IL 60126-5096

POLUGA, JUDITH, education educator; b. Budapest, Hungary, Jan. 1, 1952; came to U.S., 1959; d. Laszlo and Irene Takacs; m. Charles Poluga, Dec. 16, 1972; children: Adam Charles, Mia Kyung-Choi, Nathan Lee, Hope Kyung-Choi, David Jonathan, Krystal Kyung-Choi, Danielle Marie (dec.). BS in Edn., Kent State U., 1980, MEd, 1990, postgrad. Cert. tchr., prin. Ohio. Kindergarten tchr. Mother of Sorrows Sch., Ashtabula, Ohio, 1980-85; kindergarten, 4th grade tchr. Ashtabula City Schs., 1985-97; prof. early childhood edn. Kent State U., Ashtabula, 1995—; prin. Kingsville elem. Buckeye Local Schs., Ashtabula, 1997—. Dir. of edn. Intercultural Student Exch., Ashtabula, 1997—. Bd. dirs. Cath. Svc. League, Ashtabula, 1996; mem. Garden Trails Garden Club, Ashtabula, 1987-93. Martha Holden Jennings scholar Martha Holden Jennings Found., 1993. Mem. ASCD, AAUW, Assn. for Childhood Edn. Internat., Comparative and Internat. Edn. Soc., Am. Ednl. Rsch. Assn., Nat. Assn. for the Edn. of Young Children, Phi Delta Kappa. Roman Catholic. Avocations: woodworking, crafts. Home: 4005 W 13th St Ashtabula OH 44004-2109 Office: Buckeye Local Schs Kingsville 5875 Rt 193 Kingsville OH 44048

POLYAK, ROMAN ARONOVICH, mathematics educator; b. Kiev, USSR, Feb. 12, 1937; came to US, 1988; s. Aron W. and Nekhama B. (Sherman) P.; m. Lyuba B. Dergavets, June 29, 1958; children: Bella, Arkady. BS, Ctrl. Econs. Math. Inst., Moscow, 1960, MS, PhD, Ctrl. Econs. Math. Inst., Moscow, 1966. Prof. math. Continuing Edn. Grad. Sch., Kiev, Russia, 1966-88; prof. math. & ops. rsch. George Mason U., Fairfax, Va., 1995—. Vis. scientist dept. math. IBM, T.J. Watson Rsch. Ctr. Yorktown Heights, NY, 1988-92; vis. rsch. prof. George Mason U., 1993-95. Recipient NSF award, 1993, 94, 97, 2003, NASA award, 1993, 95, 98; Fulbright scholar, 2001-02; fellow Internat. Fund for Rsch in Exptl. Econs., 2003. Fellow Internat. Found. for Rsch. on Exptl. Econs.; mem. Mathematical Programming Soc., Soc. for Indsl. and Apply Math., Am. Math. Soc., Inst. for Ops. Rsch. and Mgmt. Sci.(INFORMS), NY Acad. Sci. Home: 4311 Chariot Ct Fairfax VA 22030-7950 Office: George Mason U Univ Dr Fairfax VA 22030

POMERANZ, FELIX, accounting educator; b. Vienna, Mar. 28, 1926; s. Joseph and Irene (Meninger) P.; m. Rita Lewin, June 14, 1953; children: Jeffrey Arthur, Andrew Joseph. BBA, CCNY, 1948; MS, Columbia U., 1949; PhD, U. Birmingham, Eng., 1992. Diplomate Am. Bd. Forensic Acctg.; CPA, N.Y., Va., La., N.C.; cert. computer profl., fraud examiner, govt. fin. mgr. Audit staff Coopers & Lybrand, CPAs, N.Y.C., 1949-56; mgr. Marks, Grey & Shron (now Ernst & Young, CPA's), N.Y.C., 1956-58; asst. chief auditor Am.-Standard, N.Y.C., 1958-62; mgr. systems Westvaco Corp., N.Y.C., 1962-66; dir. operational auditing Coopers & Lybrand, CPAs, N.Y.C., 1966-68, ptnr., 1968-85; disting. lectr./dir. Ctr. for Acctg., Auditing, Tax Studies Fla. Internat. U., Miami, 1985-93, prof. acctg., 1993—2002, assoc. dir. sch. acctg., 1993—99, affil. faculty dept. religious studies, 1996—2002, prof. emeritus, 2003—. Author: Managing Capital Budget Projects, 1984; The Successful Audit: New Ways to Reduce Risk Exposure and Increase Efficiency, 1992; co-author: Pensions-An Accounting and Management Guide, 1976; Auditing in the Public Sector: Efficiency, Economy, and Program Results, 1976; Comparative International Auditing Standards, 1985; contbr. articles to profl. jours. Emeritus trustee Nat. Ctr. for Automated Info. Rsch.; founding mem. Ctr. for Study of Islam and Democracy; mem. bus. sch. adv. bd. Carlos Albizu U.; founder Afghan Inst. Accts. 1st lt. AUS, 1944-46, 51-52. Recipient Spear Safer Harmon faculty fellow Coll. Bus. Adminstrn., 1987, Coll. Bus. Adminstrn., award for outstanding svc., 1998, Matriculation Merit award, 2000. Mem. AICPAs, N.Y. State Soc. CPAs, Assn. Systems Mgmt., Acad. Acctg. Historians, Assn. Govt. Accts., N.Y. Acad. Scis., Am. Acctg. Assn., Inter-Am. Acctg. Assn., Assn. Cert. Fraud Examiners, Beta Gamma Sigma, Beta Alpha Psi (Most Disting. and Most Outstanding Prof. awards 1993, Most Supportive Prof. award 2002), Alpha Kappa Psi (Dr. Felix Pomeranz Faculty of Yr. award, Endless Work award). Home: 250 Jacaranda Dr Apt 406 Fort Lauderdale FL 33324-2532 Office: Fla Internat U Sch Acctg University Park Miami FL 33199-0001 E-mail: pomeranf@fiu.edu.

POMEROY, BENJAMIN SHERWOOD, veterinary medicine educator; b. St. Paul, Apr. 24, 1911; s. Benjamin A. and Florence A. (Sherwood) P.; m. L. Margaret Lyon, June 25, 1938; children: Benjamin A., Sherwood R., Catherine A., Margaret D. D.V.M., Iowa State U., 1933; MS, Cornell U., 1934; PhD, U. Minn., 1944, D. Sci. (hon.), 2001. Diagnostician U. Minn., 1934-38, faculty, 1938-81, prof., 1948-81, prof. emeritus, 1981—, head dept. vet. microbiology and pub. health, 1953-73, assoc. dean, 1970-74, acting dean, 1979-80. Mem. adv. com. FDA; cons. animal scis. divsn. and animal health divsn., meat insp. service, animal health service USDA. Co-author: Diseases and Parasites of Poultry, 1958; contbg. author: Diseases of Poultry, 1972, 78, 84, 91, 97. Republican precinct officer, 1958-60, chmn., 1960-61; chmn. Ramsey County (Minn.) Rep. Com., 1961-65, 4th Congl. Dist., 1961-63, 67-69; mem. Minn. Rep. Central Com., 1961-71; del. Minn. Rep. Conv., 1960-71, 92, 94, 96, Rep. Nat. Conv., 1964. Named Veterinarian of Year in Minn., 1970; recipient Eminent Citizen award St. Anthony Park Legion Post and Aux., 1955, Alumni Merit award, 1975, Stange award, 1977, Disting. Achievement citation, 1981 (all Iowa State U.), Centennial Merit award U. Pa., 1984, Animal Health award USDA, 1986, Siehl Prize for Excellence in Agriculture, U. Minn., 1999; named to Am. Poultry Hall of Fame, 1977, Minn. Livestock Hall of Fame, 1997. Fellow Poultry Sci. Assn.; mem. Nat. Turkey Fedn. (life, Research award 1950), Tex. Poultry Assn. (life), Minn. Turkey Growers Assn. (life), Soc. Exptl. Biology and Medicine, Am. Assn. Avian Pathologists (life), Am. Coll. Vet. Microbiologists, Am. Acad. Microbiology, AVMA (council research 1961-73, Pub. Service award 1980, AVMA award 1999), U.S. Animal Health Assn. (life), Nat. Acad. of Practice, Minn. Vet. Med. Assn. (sec.-treas. 1950-75, pres. 1978-79, Disting. Service award 1980, presdl. award 1992), Sigma Xi, Phi Kappa Phi, Alpha Gamma Rho, Phi Zeta, Gamma Sigma Delta. Presbyterian (elder). Home: 1443 Raymond Ave Saint Paul MN 55108-1430

POMPA, LOUISE ELAINE, secondary school educator; b. Spangler, Pa., Sept. 26, 1958; d. Harry Gregory and Lois Vida Beers; m. David Richard Pompa, Jan. 18, 1985; 1 child, Emilee Louise stepchildren: Angelo, Mary Beth. BS, Pa. State U., 1982; MEd, Ind. U. Pa., 1994. Cert. profl. tchr. Pa. Adult day care provider for mentally handicapped persons Mid-State Intermediate Care Facility for the Mentally Retarded, Altoona, Pa., 1983—84; spl. edn. tchr. Altoona Area Sch. Dist., 1984—86; tchr. Cambria County Children and Youth, Ebensburg, Pa., 1986—87; spl. edn. tchr. Greater Johnstown (Pa.) Vocat.-Tech. Sch., 1987—88, Appalachia Intermediate Unit 8, Ebensburg, 1988—90; spl. edn. tchr., secondary learning support Cambria Heights Sch. Dist., Patton, Pa., 1990—. Author: A Review of the Literature on Motivation and Strategies for Improving Motivation in the Learning Disabled Adolescent: A Comparative Analysis, 1994. Mem.: Kappa Delta Pi, Phi Kappa Phi. Democrat. Roman Catholic. Avocations: health and fitness, gardening, collectibles, quilting. Office: Cambria Heights Sch Dist 426 Glendale Lake Rd Patton PA 16668

POMPER, PHILIP, history educator; b. Chgo., Apr. 18, 1936; s. Solomon and Rebecca (Fenigstein) P.; m. Alice N. Epstein, Aug. 27, 1961 (div.); children: Erica, Stephen, Karen; m. Emily Meyer, June 26, 1994. BA, U. Chgo., 1959, MA, 1961, PhD, 1965. Instr. history Wesleyan U., Middletown, Conn., 1964-65, asst. prof., 1965-71, assoc. prof., 1971-76, prof., 1976—, chmn. dept. history, 1981-84; William F. Armstrong prof. history, 1992—. Author: The Russian Revolutionary Intelligentsia, 1970, 2nd edit., 1993, Peter Lavrov and the Russian Revolutionary Movement, 1972, Sergei Nechaev, 1979 (Choice award 1979), The Structure of Mind in History: Five Major Figures in Psychohistory, 1985, Trotsky's Notebooks, 1933-35: Writings on Lenin, Dialectics and Evolutionism, 1986, Lenin, Trotsky, and Stalin: The Intelligentsia and Power, 1990; assoc. editor History and Theory, 1991—; editor: World History: Ideologies, Structures, and Identities, 1998; co-editor: History and Theory, Contemporary Readings, 1998; co-editor: The Return of Science: Evolution, History and Theory, 2002; contbr. articles on Russian history and theory of history to profl. jours. Fellow, Ford Found., 1963-64, Social Scis. Rsch. Coun., 1968, Hoover Instn., 1987, Wilson Ctr., 1988; Russian Rsch. Ctr. scholar, 1987—. Mem.: Conn. Acad. Arts and Scis. Home: 13 Red Orange Rd Middletown CT 06457-4916 Office: History Dept Wesleyan U Middletown CT 06459-0001 E-mail: ppomper@wesleyan.edu.

POND, BARBARA WELLER, secondary school educator; b. Balt., May 10, 1948; d. Louis Christian and Maria (Mesenbrink) Weller; m. Daniel Chester Pond, Nov. 17, 1973; children: Jennifer, Christopher. BS, Towson State U., 1970; MA, U. Md., 1974, U. Denver, 1981. Math. resource tchr. Montgomery County Schs., Rockville, Md., 1970-78; math. instr. Parker (Colo.) Jr. High, 1978-88; staff devel. specialist Douglas County Schs., Castle Rock, Colo., 1985-86, math. supr., 1988-89; math. educator Castle Rock Jr. High, 1989-91, Cresthill Middle Sch., Highlands Ranch, 1991—; faculty U. Denver, 1992—. Cons. Rocky Mountain Math. Consortium, Littleton, Colo., 1988—; cons., com. mem. New Stds. Project U. Pitts. Editor, author (with others): Process Activities for Math, 1989, (pamphlet) A Bag of Tricks, 1988. Den leader Denver area coun. Boy Scouts Am., 1989-92; elder Our Father Luth. Ch., Littleton, 1986-90, 93-95, lay min., 1996—; field mgr. Youth for Understanding Exch., Denver, 1988-90. Recipient Presdl. Award for Excellence in Math., Colo., 1988. Mem. Nat. Coun. Tchrs. Math., Math. into 21st Century Team, Assn. for Curriculum Devel., New Stds. Project (assessment program 1993-95). Office: Cresthill Mid Sch 9195 S Cresthill Ln Highlands Ranch CO 80130

PONDER, HENRY, educational association administrator; m. Eunice Wilson; children: Cheryl, Anna. BS, Langston U.; MS, Okla. State U.; PhD, Ohio State U. Asst. prof. Va. State Coll., Petersburg, chmn. dept. agri-bus.; chmn. dept. bus. and econs. Ft. Valley (Ga.) State Coll.; v.p. acad. affairs Ala. A&M U., Normal, dean; pres. Benedict Coll., Columbia, S.C., Fisk U., Nashville, Talladega Coll., Ala., Nat. Assn. for Equal Opportunity in Higher Edn., Silver Spring, Md. Cons. Fed. Res. Bank, N.Y., Phila. Nat. Bank, Chase Manhattan Bank, Irving Trust Co., Omaha Nat. Bank; bd. dirs. Fed. Res. Bank of Richmond, Va., chmn. bd. dirs.; bd. dirs. J.P. Stevens & Co., Inc., Suntrust Bank of Nashville, Tenn., SCANA Corp. S.C., C.C. of the Air Force, ETV Endowment S.C. Mem. scholarship fund com. Bishop Desmond Tutu So. African Refugee Assn.; chmn. United Negro College Fund, Inc., Nat. Assn. for Equal Opportunity in Higher Edn.; mem. exec. coun. Commn. on Colls. Mem.: Tenn. Coll. Assn. (pres. 1992), Alpha Phi Alpha (gen. pres.).

PONDER, MARIAN RUTH, retired mathematics educator; b. Waterloo, Iowa, July 12, 1932; d. Lee Roland and Leone Hyacinth (Holdiman) Ridgon; m. Joseph Glen Ponder, June 28, 1953; children: Dwight Lee, David Glen, Dean Joseph. BA (Purple and Gold math. scholar), U. No. Iowa, 1952; MSE, Drake U., 1960; postgrad., U. Wis., 1961—62, San Diego State U., 1980—81, Carleton Coll., 1980—81, U. No. Iowa, 1961—66, Drake U., 1971—75, Chico State U., 1985—86, U. Iowa, 1988, U. Tex., 1990, Des Moines Area C.C., 2003. Tchr. math., sci., Anamosa, Iowa, 1952-53, Monroe, Iowa, 1953-56, Newton, Iowa, 1956-64, 66-92; head dept. math. Newton Schs., 1978-92. Ch. treas. Cmty. Heights Alliance Ch., 1980-82, 83-87, Sunday sch. secretariat, 1966-82, fin. sec., 1993-94, 97-98, women's ministries treas., 1997-2001. Maytag scholar, 1960; Maytag Corp. grantee; Delta Kappa Gamma scholar, 1960, 81, 95, 2002. Mem. NEA, Nat. Coun. Tchrs. Math., Iowa Ret. Sch. Pers. Assn., Iowa Edn. Assn., Newton Cmty. Edn. Assn. (chief negotiator 1985-87, pres. 1985-87), Iowa Coun. Tchrs. Math., Jasper County Hist. Soc., Jasper County Geneaol. Soc., Delta Kappa Gamma (state treas. 1978—, internat. fin. chmn. 1990-92, trustee ednl. found. 1992-98), Jasper County Ret. Sch. Pers. Assn. (treas. 1992-96, v.p. 1996-98, pres. 1998-2000), Kappa Mu Epsilon, Kappa Delta Pi, Lambda Delta Lambda, Delta Kappa Gamma. Republican. Mem. Christian and Missionary Alliance Ch. Home: 3791 Highway F36 W Newton IA 50208-8061

PONDER, WILLIAM STANLEY, university administrator; b. San Diego, Sept. 12, 1949; s. William Bryant and Mary Louise (Parker) P.; m. Deborah Millot, Dec. 22, 1982 (div. 1989); children: Dana Michelle, Jordan Thomas; m. Mary J. Zodrow, Nov. 4, 1993. BA in Music, San Diego State U., 1972, MS in Counseling, 1983. Tchr. San Diego/Riverside Sch. Dist., 1973-77; dir. tng. Twelfth Night Repertory Co., San Diego, 1977-78; counselor Girls Club of Chula Vista, Calif., 1978-79; v.p. Telesis II of Calif., Inc., San Diego, 1979-83; sr. recruitment officer U. Calif.-Riverside, 1983-86, assoc. dir. Office of Admissions, 1986-91; registrar Shoreline Community Coll., Seattle, Wash., 1991-93, Pierce Coll., 1993—. Cons. State of Calif. Health Svc., Sacramento, 1982-83; adj. faculty Riverside Community Coll., 1989—; lectr. Sch. Edn. Calif. State, San Bernardino, 1989-90. Author: Educational Apartheid in a Pluralistic Society, 1995. Commr. City of San Bernardino Bldg. and Safety, 1987-91; mem. planning commn. City of Olympia, Wash., 1996—. Recipient Pub. Svc. award Co. of San Diego, 1984; KPBS TV Svc. award, 1984. Mem. Third World Counselors Assn. (dir. 1983-86), Calif. Articulation Numbering Systems Coun., Western Assn. Coll. Admissions Counselors, Nat. Assn. Coll. Admissions Counselors, Nat. Assn. Coll. Admission Officers (chmn. on minority participation in higher edn.), Am. Assn. Collegiate Registrars and Admissions Officers (profl. access and equity com. 1996-97), Pacific Assn. Collegiate Registrars and Admissions Officers (vice chair Wash. coun. 1996-99, v.p. 1996-97), Rancho Mediterrian Club (Colton, Calif.), Ballys' Pacific West. Democrat. Presbyterian. Avocation: tennis. Home: 1413 20th Ave SE Olympia WA 98501-3095

PON-SALAZAR, FRANCISCO DEMETRIO, diplomat, educator, deacon, counselor; b. Ica, Peru, July 18, 1951; came to U.S., 1982; s. Alejandro Sen Tac and Demetria (Salazar) P. MPhil, Leopold Franzer U., Innsbruck, Austria, 1977; MA in Hispanic Lit. and Lang., St. Louis U., 1985; M of Mgmt., Fontbonne U., 2001. Cert. univ. and coll. tchr., Nat. Coun. Peruvian Univs.; cert. adult literacy tchr.; notary pub., State of Tex. Tchr. San Juan Bautista Sch., Puno, Peru, 1972, Jose Toribio Polo HS, Ica, 1979-82; prof. Catalina Buendia Pecho Coll., Ica, 1980-82; instr. St. Louis U., 1983-85; asst. of the Consul Fgn. Rels. Consulate of Mex., St. Louis, 1988-97; racetrack mgr. The Home Depot. Counselor, tutor Christian Bros. Coll., St. Louis, 1984-85; tchr. St. Gabriel's Hall Reformatory, Audubon, Pa., 1985; mentor Youth Svc. Mo./Pub. and Pvt. Ventures, 1992-93. Participant Internat. Alpach (Tirol, Austria) Forum, 1977; asst. scoutmaster Boy Scouts Am. (Wood badge C-34, 1998), St. Louis, 1990—; vol. State of Mo. Divsn. Youth Svcs. Pub. Pvt. Ventures, 1992-93; mem. adv. bd. Immigration Law Project, Legal Svc. of Ea. Mo., Inc., St. Louis, 1995-97. Mem. Internat. Progress Orgn. of Vienna (Austria), Latin-Am. Soc. of St. Louis U. (v.p. 1983-85), Campus Ministry of Spanish Speaking People, Legal Svc. of Ea. Mo., Inc. (adv. bd. of the Immigration Project, 1995), Sigma Delta Pi, Alpha Sigma Nu. Avocations: jogging, gymnastics, reading, videos, poetry. Home: 417 Old Statium Dr Postal Cluster Box 6206 Port Isabel TX 78578 E-mail: fcopon@hotmail.com.

PONSOT, MARIE, poet; b. N.Y.C., Apr. 6, 1921; d. William Xavier and Marie Candee Birmingham; m. Claude Ponsot, Dec. 16, 1948 (div. Sept. 1970); children: Monique, Denis, Antoine, William, Christopher, Matthew, Gregory. BA, St. Joseph's Coll., 1940; MA, Columbia U., 1941; D (hon), St. Joseph's Coll., 2000. Archivist UNESCO, Paris, 1948-50; prof. English CUNY, N.Y.C., 1966-91. Vis. prof. Beijing U., U. Houston, NYU, Columbia U., 1985—. Author: True Minds, 1958, Admit Impediment, 1982, The Bird Catcher, 1998 (Nat. Book Critics Cir. 1999), SPringing, 2002; co-author: (with Rosemary Dean) Beat Not the Poor Desk, 1981 (Shaughnessy medal 1982). Home: 340 E 93d St New York NY 10128

PONTE, CHARLES DENNIS, pharmacist, educator; b. Waterbury, Conn., Jan. 17, 1953; s. Americo Joseph and Irene (Poirier) P. BSc in Pharmacy, U. Conn., 1975; D Pharmacy, U. Utah, 1980. Diplomate Am. Acad. Pain Mgmt., cert. diabetes edn., bd. cert. pharmacotherapy specialist, bd. cert. advanced diabetes mgmt. Intern Woodbury (Conn.) Drug Co., 1975; hosp. pharmacy resident Yale-New Haven Hosp., 1975-76, ambulatory staff pharmacist, 1976-78; prof. clin. pharmacy, family medicine Robert C. Byrd Health Scis. Ctr. of W.Va. U., Morgantown, 1980—, also dir. PharmD program. Mem. adv. bd. ambulatory care and family practice Annals Pharmacotherapy, Cin., 1985—; mem. steering com. Nat. Diabetes Edn. Program, 1997-2000; mem. adv. panel on family practice U.S. Pharmacopeial Conv., Inc., Rockville, Md., 1990-2000; mem. vis. faculty Upjohn Co., Kalamazoo, 1986; coord. Sch. Pharmacy, Spencer State Tng. Ctr., 1984-88; participant Practical Aspects of Diabetes Care: Conf. for Pharmacy Educators, 1989; chmn. Van Liere Rsch. Convocation for Med. Students, 1990; mem. splty. coun. on nutritional support pharmacy practice Bd. Pharm. Spltys., 1994-99. Editl. adv. bd. Jour. Am. Pharm. Assn., 1999—, Am. Jour. Health-System Pharmacy, 1999—; contbr. to profl. publs. Mem. steering com. Nat. Diabetes Edn. Program, 1997—. Grantee Robert Wood Johnson Found., 1981. Fellow Am. Coll. Clin. Pharmacy, Am. Soc. Health Sys. Pharmacists, Am. Pharm. Assn.; mem. Soc. Tchrs. Family Medicine, Sigma Xi, Phi Kappa Phi, Phi Lambda Sigma, Rho Chi. Roman Catholic. Office: WVa U Robert C Byrd Health Sci Ctr Sch Pharmacy Morgantown WV 26506 E-mail: cdponte@hsc.wvu.edu.

PONTZER, LYNDA MARIE, art educator; b. St. Marys, Pa., Jan. 26, 1947; d. Edward Andrew and Orma Marie (Nicklas) P.; 1 child, Dayna Marie. Student, Pa. State Coll., 1964, Mercyhurst Coll., 1964-65, Cleve. Inst. Art, 1965-68; BFA with distinction, MEd, U. Ariz., 1970; postgrad., Montclair State Coll., 1970-72, U. Ariz. Cert. art tchr., N.J., Pa. Environ. arts tchr. N.J. Pub. Schs., Murray Hill, 1970-72; portrait artist tchr. Sommerset (N.J.) Art Assn., 1972, Denmark Adult Edn., Roskilde, Denmark, 1974-76; social worker Adult Rehab. Network, Copenhagen, 1974-76; English instr. Tehran, Iran, 1976-78; substitute tchr. St. Marys (Pa.) Area Sch. Dist., 1978-83, art tchr., 1990-92; pvt. art instr. Pontzer's Portrait Studio, St. Marys, 1985—. Art guest spkr. Boy Scouts, Secretaries, St. Marys, 1984, 94; art instr. Picture Lady Program, St. Marys, 1986-89; chairperson People's Choice Art Festival, St. Marys, 1987—2001; active Elk County Coun. Arts, 1989—; invited U.S. rep. Biennale Internat. Contemporary Art Show, Florence, Italy, 2003. Founder Mother's Day Healthcare YMCA, Ridgway, Pa., 1987-89, active, 1978—; artist ARC, St. Marys, 1987; chairperson Queen of World Festival, 1985—2001. Mem. Am. Soc. Portrait Artists, Nat. Mus. Women in Arts (charter). Republican. Roman Catholic. Avocations: art, gardening, landscape design, architecture, swimming. Home: 500 Spruce St Saint Marys PA 15857-1767 Office: Pontzer Portrait Studio 500 Spruce St Saint Marys PA 15857-1767

POOL, MARY JANE, writer, lecturer; d. Earl Lee and Dorothy (Matthews) P. Grad., St. de Chantal Acad., 1942; BA in Art with honors, Drury Coll., 1946; LHD (hon.), Drury U., 2002. Mem. staff Vogue mag., N.Y.C., 1946-68, assoc. merchandising editor, 1948-57, promotion dir., 1958-66, exec. editor, 1966-68; editor House and Garden mag., 1969, editor-in-chief, 1970-80. Cons. Baker Furniture Co., 1981-94, Aves Advt., Inc., 1981-94, bd. dirs.; mem. bd. govs. Decorative Arts Trust; past mem. bd. govs. Fashion Group, Inc., N.Y.C. Author: The Gardens of Venice, 1989, The Gardens of Florence, 1992, Gardens in the City-New York in Bloom, 1999; co-author: The Angel Tree, 1984, The Angel Tree—A Christmas Celebration, 1993, The Christmas Story, 2001; editor: 20th Century Decorating, Architecture, Gardens, Billy Baldwin Decorates, 26 Easy Little Gardens. Mem. bus. com. N.Y. Zool. Soc., 1979-86; trustee Drury Coll., 1971— ; bd. dirs. Isabel O'Neil Found., 1978— . Recipient award Nat. Soc. Interior Designers, Disting. Alumni award Drury Coll., 1961, Edith Wharton Women of Achievement award, 1999. Address: 1 E 66th St New York NY 10021-5854

POOL, NANCY ELLEN, school social worker; b. Jersey City, Oct. 16, 1942; d. Frederick John and Anna Catherine (Harbers) Backhaus; m. Michael Furst, Jan. 22, 1967 (div. June 1992); 1 child, Matthew Alan; m. James Lawrence Pool, Jr., Nov. 20, 1992. Grad. in nursing, Paterson (N.J.) Gen. Hosp., 1963; BS, Montclair State Coll., 1978, MA, 1982; postgrad., Rutgers U., 1986—. RN, N.J. Staff nurse Bergen Pines County Hosp., Paramus, N.J., 1963-65, Holy Name Hosp., Teaneck, N.J., 1965-67, Akademische Ziekenhuis, Ghent, Belgium, 1967-70; sch. nurse, tchr. health edn. Bernardsville (N.J.) Bd. Edn., 1978-89, Rockaway Twp. (N.J.) Bd. Edn., 1980-89, social worker, 1989—, curriculum writer, 1975-89. Mem. exec. bd. Parents Exceptional Children, Roxbury, Mass. Mem. Coun. for Exceptional Children, AAUW, Am. Mensa, Eta Sigma Gamma, Phi Kappa Phi. Home: 165 Casterline Rd Denville NJ 07834-3616 Office: Roxbury Twp Spl Svcs 1 Bryant Dr Succasunna NJ 07876-1632

POOLE, RICHARD WILLIAM, economics educator; b. Oklahoma City, Dec. 4, 1927; s. William Robert and Lois (Spicer) P.; m. Bertha Lynn Mehr, July 28, 1950; children: Richard William, Laura Lynne, Mark Stephen. BS, U. Okla., 1951, MBA, 1952; postgrad., George Washington U., 1957-58; PhD, Okla. State U., 1960. Rsch. analyst Okla. Gas & Electric Co., Oklahoma City, 1952- 54; mgr. sci. and mfg. devel. dept. Oklahoma City C. of C., 1954-57; mgr. Office of J.E. Webb, Washington, 1957-58; from instr. to prof. econs. Okla. State U., Stillwater, 1960-65, prof. econs., dean Coll. Bus. Adminstrn., 1965-72, v.p., prof. econs., 1972-88, Regents Disting. Svc. prof., prof. econs., 1988-93, emeritus v.p., dean, Regents Disting. Svc. prof./prof. econ., 1993—. Cons. to adminstr. NASA, Washington, 1961-69; adviser subcom. on govt. rsch. U.S. Senate, 1966-69; lectr. Intermediate Sch. Banking, Ops. Mgmt. Sch., Okla. Bankers Assn., 1968-89; lectr. internat. off-campus programs Okla. City U., 1994-96. Author: (with others) The Oklahoma Economy, 1963, County Building Block Data for Regional Analysis, 1965. Mem. Gov.' Com. on Devel. Ark.-Verdigris Waterway, 1970-71, Gov.'s Five-Yr. Econ. Devel. Plan, 1993; past v.p., bd. dirs., past chmn. Mid-Continent Rsch. and Devel. Coun. 2d lt., arty. U.S. Army, 1946-48. Recipient Delta Sigma Pi Gold Key award Coll. Bus. Adminstrn., U. Okla., 1951, Tchg. award on Am. free enterprise sys. Merrick Found., 1992, Disting. Alumni award Okla. State U., 1995, Henry G. Bennett Distinguished Service Award, 1999; named to Coll. Bus. Adminstrn. Hall of Fame, Okla. State U., 1993, Stillwater Hall of Fame, Payne County Hist. Soc. and Stillwater C. of C., 1996, Okla. Higher Edn. Hall of Fame, 1998. Mem. Southwestern Econ. Assn. (past pres.), Am. Assembly Collegiate Schs. Bus. (past bd. dirs.), Nat. Assn. State Univs. and Land Grant Colls. (past chmn. commn. on edn. for bus. professions), Southwestern Bus. Adminstrn. Assn. (past pres.), Okla. C. of C. (past bd. dirs.), Okla. Heritage Assn. (bd. dirs. 2000—), Santa Fe Trail Assn. (bd. dirs. 2001-02), Stillwater C. of C. (past bd. dirs. and pres.), Beta Gamma Sigma (past bd. dirs.), Phi Kappa Phi, Phi Eta Sigma, Omicron Delta Kappa. Home: 815 S Shumard St Stillwater OK 74074-1136

POOLE, RICHARD WILLIAM, JR., secondary school educator; b. Norman, Okla., Apr. 13, 1951; s. Richrad W. and Lynn (Mehr) P.; m. Sonya Lee, Mar. 20, 1982; 1 child, Amanda Lee. BS in Social Studies, Okla. State U., Stillwater, 1976. Tchr., coach West Jr. H.S., Ponca City, Okla., 1976-80, Ponca City Sr. H.S., 1980-92, Am. history tchr., supr. jr. high athletics, 1992—. Served with USNR, 1969-71, Viet Nam. Mem. Lions Club (tail twister 1992, v.p. 1993, pres. After 5 club 1994), Elks. Democrat. Methodist. Avocations: golf, fishing, country music, reading history books. Home: 2920 Canterbury Ave Ponca City OK 74604-4410

POOLE, ROSEMARY JEAN, art history educator; b. Penang, Malaysia, Nov. 8, 1930; came to U.S., 1964; d. Cecil Stevens and Margaret Nancy (Preece) Sullivan; m. Peter Andrews Poole. BA, George Mason U., 1984; MA, Am. U., 1988. Ofcl. Brit. Fgn. Svc., London, 1951-64; lectr. Nat. Gallery, Washington, 1991-92; adj. prof. art history George Mason U., Fairfax, Va., 1992—. Lectr. Smithsonian Assocs.; lectr. Learning in Retirement George Mason U. Mem. AAUW, Phi Alpha Theta. Avocations: gardening, music, birding, reading.

POOLE, WILLIAM, bank executive; b. Wilmington, Del., June 19, 1937; s. William and Louise (Hiller) P.; m. Mary Lynne Ahroon, June 26, 1960 (div. May 1997); children: William, Lester Allen, Jonathan Carl; m. Geraldine S. Stroud, July 12, 1997. AB, Swarthmore Coll., 1959, LLD (hon.), 1989; MBA, U. Chgo., 1963, PhD, 1966. Asst. prof. polit. economy Johns Hopkins U., Balt., 1963-69; professorial lectr. Am. U., Washington, 1970-71; assoc. professorial lectr. George Washington U., Washington, 1971-73; professorial lectr. Georgetown U., Washington, 1972; vis. lectr. Harvard U., Cambridge, Mass., 1973, MIT, Cambridge, 1974, 77; Bank Mees and Hope vis. prof. econs. Erasmus U. Rotterdam, 1991; prof. econs. Brown U., Providence, 1974-98, dir. ctr. for study fin. markets and insts., 1987-92, chmn. econs. dept., 1981-82, 85-86; economist Bd. Govs. of FRS, Washington, 1964, 69-70, sr. economist, 1970-74; pres., CEO Fed. Res. Bank, St. Louis, 1998—. Adviser Fed. Res. Bank, Boston, 1973-74, cons., 1974-81; vis. economist Res. Bank of Australia, 1980-81; mem. Coun. Econ. Advisers, 1982-85; adj. scholar Cato Inst., 1985-98. Mem. Am. Econ. Assn., Am. Fin. assn. (mem. nominating com. 1979), Western Econ. Assn. (mem. internat. exec. com. 1986-89, mem. nominating com. 1995). Office: Fed Res Bank St Louis 411 Locust St Saint Louis MO 63102-2005

POOLEY, BEVERLEY JOHN, law educator, librarian; b. London, Eng., Apr. 4, 1934; came to U.S., 1957; U.S. citizen, 1993; s. William Vincent and Christine Beatrice (Coleman) P.; m. Patricia Joan Ray, June 8, 1958; children— Christopher Jonathan, Rachel Vanessa BA, Cambridge U., Eng., 1956, LLB, 1957; LLM, U. Mich., Ann Arbor, 1958, SJD, 1961, MLS, 1964. Legis. analyst U. Mich. Law Sch., Ann Arbor, 1958-60; lectr. U. Ghana Law Sch., 1960-62; instr. U. Mich. Law Sch., Ann Arbor, 1962-63, asst. prof., 1963-66, assoc. prof., 1966-70, dir. law library, 1966-84, prof., 1970-98, prof. emeritus, from 1998, assoc. dean law library, 1984-94.

Author: The Evolution of British Planning Legislation, 1960; Planning and Zoning in the United States, 1961 Scholar, King's Coll., Cambridge, Eng., 1956; Blackstone Scholar, Middle Temple, London, 1957 Democrat. Avocations: Acting; musical comedy; food preparation. Home: Ann Arbor, Mich. Died Aug. 23, 2001.

POOR, HAROLD VINCENT, electrical engineering educator; b. Columbus, Ga., Oct. 2, 1951; s. Harold Edgar and Virginia (Hardin) P.; m. Connie Irene Hazelwood, Sept. 1, 1973; children: Kristin Elizabeth, Lauren Alissa. BEE with highest honors, Auburn U., 1972; PhD, Princeton U., 1977. Asst. prof. U. Ill., Urbana, 1977-81, assoc. prof., 1981-84, prof., 1984-90; prof. dept. elec. engring. Princeton (N.J.) U., 1990—. Acad. visitor Imperial Coll. London U., 1985; vis. prof. Newcastle (Australia) U., 1987; sr. visiting fellow Imperial Coll., London U., 1993; cons. and bd. mem. numerous orgns., 1978—. Author: An Introduction to Signal Detection and Estimation, 1988, 2d edit., 1994; co-editor: Wireless Communications: Signal Processing Perspectives, 1998; contbr. numerous articles to profl. jours. Grantee NSF, Office of Naval Rsch., Army Rsch. Office, 1978—; recipient Terman award Am. Soc. Engring. Edn., 1992, Centennial certificate Am. Soc. for Engring. Edn., 1993, NSF Dir.'s award Disting. Teaching scholars; fellow John Simon Guggenheim Meml. Found., 2002—. Fellow IEEE (bd. dirs. 1991-92, Third Millennium medal 2000, grad. tch. award 2001), AAAS, Acoustical Soc. Am., Am. Soc. Engring. Edn., Inst. Math. Stats., Optical Soc. Am.; mem. NAE, Info. Theory Soc. of IEEE (pres. 1990, joint paper award with IEEE Comm. Soc., 2001), IEEE Control Sys. Soc. (Disting. Mem. award 1994), Cosmos Club (Washington). Office: Princeton Univ Dept Elec Engring Princeton NJ 08544-0001

POOS, LAWRENCE RAYMOND, history educator; b. Eaton, Ohio, Feb. 8, 1954; s. Raymond Henry and Edna (Brower) P. AB, Harvard U., 1976; PhD, Cambridge (Eng.) U., 1984. Fellow Fitzwilliam Coll., Cambridge, 1980-83; prof. The Cath. U. of Am., Washington, 1983—; dean sch. of arts and scis. The Catholic U. of Am., Washington, 2002—. Author: A Rural Society After the Black Death, 1991, Lower Ecclesiastical Jurisdiction in Late Medieval England, 2001, (with L. Bonfield) Select Cases in Manorial Courts 1250-1550: Property and Family Law, 1998; editor: Continuity and Change, 1985-00; contbr. articles to scholarly jours. Fellow Royal Hist. Soc. (London). Avocations: exercise, travel, computers. Home: 328 12th St SE Washington DC 20003-2206 Office: The Cath U of Am 620 Michigan Ave NE Washington DC 20064-0001 E-mail: poos@cua.edu.

POPADAK, GERALDINE L. organizational development consultant, educator; b. Warren, Ohio, Sept. 14, 1948; d. John Edward and Leona Margaret (Franko) P. BA, Hiram Coll., 1984; postgrad., The Am. U., 1990; PhD, Union Inst., Cin., 1995. Supr. mfg., gen. supr. mfg., ops. devel. cons. GM Packard Elec. Divsn., Warren, 1966-91; cons. and trainer UAW-GM Human Resource Ctr., Auburn Hills, Mich., 1991-93; cons. GM Vehicle Devel. & Tech. Ops. Group, Warren, Mich., 1993-95, GM Powertrain Group, Pontiac, Mich., 1995—. Vis. lectr. Oakland U. Grad. Sch. Psychology, Rochester, Mich., 1992-93; adj. faculty Hiram (Ohio) Coll., 1995—, U. Phoenix Mich. Campus, Southfield, 1996—; mem. bd. governance Grad. Sch. Mgmt., U. Phoenix, Southfield, 1997. Vol. mediator The Resolution Ctr., Mt. Clemens, Mich., 1995—; mediator U.S. Postal Svc. Mem. APA, AAUW, Assn. Psychol. Type, Nat. Psychology Adv. Bd., Internat. Soc. Gen. Semantics, ODNetwork, Assn. Mgmt. Orgn. Design (bd. dirs. 1995), Inst. Noetic Scis. Democrat. Roman Catholic. Avocations: reading, walking, gardening, spiritual journeys. Home: 303 Baker St Royal Oak MI 48067-2205 Office: General Motors 777 Joslyn Ave Pontiac MI 48340-2925

POPE, DEANNA L. T. music educator; b. Frederick, Md., July 27, 1959; d. Donald Thomas and Nadia Simone (Wheatley) Taylor; m. James Henry Pope; children: Gregory James, Brian Nathaniel, Emily Amanda. BA in Music Edn., Western Md. Coll., 1981, MS in Curriculum and Instrn., 1992. Cert. advanced profl. music tchr. grades 7-12. Tchr. mid. sch. choral & gen. music Middletown (Md.) Mid. Sch., 1982-83; tchr. gen. music Brunswick (Md.) Mid. Sch., 1983, 84; tchr. choral and gen. music Middletown Mid. Sch., 1984, 85-86; tchr. piano Gov. Thomas Johnson H.S., Frederick, 1986—, Visual and Performing Arts Sch., Frederick, 1988-95, instr. adv. musical studies, 1995—; instr. grad. edn. Western Md. Coll./Performance Learning Sys., Inc., Westminster, Md., 1992—. Wellness contact for staff Gov. Thomas Johnson H.S., Frederick, 1989-91, mem. sch. improvement team, 1991-93, staff devel. contact, 1991—. Deacon consistory Christ Reformed Ch., Middletown, 1989-92, mem. missions bd., 1989-92, sec. consistory, 1990-91, dir. children's choirs, 1990—, supr. music summer camp, summer 1992—. Mem. NEA, Md. Music Educators Assn., Music Educators Nat. Conf., Md. State Tchrs. Assn., Assn. for Supr. and Curriculum Devel., Frederick County Tchrs. Assn., Tri-M Music Honor Soc. (life mem., advisor chpt. 2329 1992—, Letter of Commendation 1992). Republican. United Ch. of Christ. Avocations: water exercise, reading, computers, classical music. Office: Gov Thomas Johnson H S 1501 N Market St Frederick MD 21701-4430

POPE, JOHN WILLIAM, judge, law educator; b. San Francisco, Mar. 12, 1947; s. William W. and Florence E. (Kline) P.; m. Linda M. Marsh, Oct. 23, 1970 (div. Dec. 1996); children: Justin, Ana, Lauren. BA, U. N.Mex., 1969, JD, 1973. Bar: N.Mex. 1973, U.S. Dist. Ct. N.Mex. 1973, U.S. Ct. Appeals (10th cir.) 1976. Law clk. N.Mex. Ct. of Appeals, Santa Fe, 1973; assoc. Chavez & Cowper, Belen, N.Mex., 1974; ptnr. Cowper, Bailey & Pope, Belen, 1974-75; pvt. practice law Belen, 1976-80; ptnr. Pope, Apodaca & Conroy, Belen, 1980-85; dir. litigation City of Albuquerque, 1985-87; judge State of N.Mex., Albuquerque, 1987-92, Dist. Ct. (13th jud. dist.), N.Mex., 1992—. Instr. U. N.Mex., Albuquerque, 1983—, prof. law, 1990—; lectr. in field. Mem. state ctrl. com. Dem. Party, N.Mex., 1971-85; state chair Common Cause N.Mex., 1980-83, N.Mex. Legal Aid, 2003; pres. Valencia County Hist. Soc., Belen, 1981-83; active Supreme Ct. Jury (UJI civil instructions com., state bar hist. com., bench and bar com.). Recipient Outstanding Jud. Svc. award N.Mex. State Bar, 1996, Champion of Justice award N.Mex. Legal Aid, 2003; named City of Belen Citizen of Yr. 1995, Excellence in Tchg. award 1998, 2002. Mem. Valencia County Bar, Albuquerque Bar Assn. Avocations: swimming, golf, photography, historical research. Home: 400 Godfrey Ave Belen NM 87002-6313 Office: Valencia County Courthouse PO Box 1089 Los Lunas NM 87031-1089

POPE, MARTIN, chemist, educator; b. N.Y.C., Aug. 22, 1918; s. Philip and Anna (Frimet) P.; m. Lillie Bellin, June 27, 1946; children: Miriam, Deborah Judith. BS, CCNY, 1939; PhD, Poly. Inst. Bklyn., 1950. Asst. rsch. dir. Balco Rsch. Lab., Newark, 1951-56; rsch. scientist NYU, N.Y.C., 1956-60, rsch. assoc. prof. physics, 1960-65, assoc. prof. chemistry, 1965-69, prof., 1969—. Assoc. dir. Radiation and Solid State Lab., 1969-82, dir., 1982-88, hon. festschrift, 1988. Co-author: Electronic Processes in Organic Crystals, transl. into Chinese and Russian, Electronic Processes in Organic Crystals and Polymers Oxford U. Press, 1999; mem. editl. bd. Molecular Crystals, 1965-97; contbr. articles to profl. jours., chpts. to books; patentee in field. Pres. Ezra Jack Keats Found., N.Y.C., 1983. 1st lt. USAAF, 1942-46. Rsch. grantee Dept. Energy, 1958—, NSF, 1960-75. Fellow AAAS, Am. Phys. Soc., N.Y. Acad. Scis.; mem. Am. chem. Soc., Sigma Xi. Avocation; mineralogy. Office: Dept Chemistry NYU New York NY 10003

POPE, SARAH ANN, retired elementary education educator; b. Granite City, Ill., Dec. 4, 1938; d. Vance Guy and Lily Lovinia (Fischer) Morgan; m. Thomas E. Pope; children: Robert, Susan, James, John, William. BS in Edn., So. Ill. U., Edwardsville, 1970, MS in Edn., 1976. Tchr. lang. arts, humanities, sci., English, reading, math. Madison (Ill.) Cmty. Sch. Dist., 1970-99; dist. math. chair K-5, head tchr. Harris Elem. Sch., Madison, 1998-99; ret., 1999. Co-founder libr. Harris Elem. Sch., 1990. Fellow Old Six Mile Hist. Soc.; mem. Am. Hemerocallis Soc. Avocations: reading, growing flowers, visiting historical sites, swimming.

POPOLIZIO, VINCENT, retired secondary education educator; b. Schenectady, N.Y., July 7, 1940; s. Vincent and Jennie (Sifo) P.; m. Marcia Ruth Liebundguth, Aug. 26, 1967; 1 child, Kristin Laurel. AAS, Orange County Community Coll., 1960; BA, Upper Iowa U., 1963; MA, No. Ill. U., 1976; postgrad., Nat. Coll. Edn., 1969-74. Tchr. speech Dist. 129 Aurora (Ill.) Pub. Schs., Franklin Jr. High, 1963-66; tchr. lang. arts, humanities Burnt Hill/Ballston Lake Schs., Burnt Hills, N.Y., 1966-68; tchr. speech Dist. 129 Washington Jr. High, Aurora, 1968-73, Aurora U., 1978-86; lang. arts coord. Dist. 129 Instr. Dept., Aurora, 1988-90, program coord., 1989-90; tchr. English, speech, theater Dist. 129 West High Sch., Aurora, 1973-93, ret., 1992. Part-time instr. Aurora U., 1993-98. Mem. Assn. for Supervision and Curriculum Devel., Nat. Edn. Assn., Ill. Edn. Assn., Aurora Edn. Assn., Moose, Phi Delta Kappa. Home: 1803 Shetland Rd Naperville IL 60565-1788

POPOWSKI, MARY JEAN NANCY, elementary education educator; b. New Brunswick, N.J., Jan. 20, 1952; d. Vincent John and Jean Barbara (Route) Campo; m. Donald Francis Popowski, Dec. 6, 1948; children: Donald, Anthony. BA in Elem. Edn. and English, Georgian Court Coll., 1974. Reading coord./reading tchr. John F. Kennedy Sch., Jamesburg, NJ, 1997—2003; tchr. Helmetta (N.J.) Pub. Sch., 1975-79; English tchr. Spotswood (N.J.) High Sch., 1979-83; tchr. Immaculate Conception Sch., Spotswood, 1991—97; reading specialist John F. Kennedy Sch, Jamesburg, NJ, 2003—. Sci. fair coord. Immaculate Conception, Spotswood, 1991-92, drama club advisor, 1993-95, jr. olympics coord., 1993-95, newspaper advisor, 1994-95. Editor Georgian Court College Yearbook, 1979. Mem. ad hoc com. Bd. of Edn., Jamesburg, N.J., 1990; mem. social com. St. James Ch., Jamesburg, 1994; mem. alumni assn. Georgian Court Coll., Lakewood, 1994. Mem. The Holy Childhood Assn. Roman Catholic. Avocations: skiing, reading, theatre, dance (ballet and jazz), collecting hummels. Home: 2 Deer Path Jamesburg NJ 08831-1905 Office: John F Kennedy Sch Jamesburg NJ 08831-1658

POPP, LILIAN MUSTAKI, writer, educator; b. N.Y.C. d. Peter and Mae Claire (Cary) Mustaki; m. Robert J. Popp. BA, Notre Dame Coll.; postgrad., Columbia U.; MS in Edn., Hunter Coll. Tchr. English McKee Vocat. and Tech. H.S., S.I., N.Y., 1946-63, chmn. acad. studies, 1963-71; prin. William Howard Taft H.S., Bronx, N.Y., 1971-79; adj. prof. Wagner Coll., S.I., 1960-85; instr. Richmond Coll., CUNY, 1968-70; prof. St. John's U., 1991-93. Mem. Cmty. Sch. Bd., 1980—93, chmn., 1989—90, chmn. legis. com., chmn. substance abuse and adolescent issues com., chmn. pupil pers. svcs. com.; chmn. curriculum com.; asst. examiner N.Y.C. Bd. Edn., 1960—85. Author, editor: Journeys in Science Fiction, 1961, Four Complete World Novels, 1961, Gertrude Lawrence as Mrs. A., 1961, Four Complete Modern Novels, 1962, Four Complete Heritage Novels, 1963, Four Complete Novels of Character and Courage, 1964; contbr. articles to profl. jours. Chmn. vols. N.Y.C. Child Abuse Prevention Program, 1984—86; regional dir., mem. exec. bd March of Dimes; book discussion leader Snug Harbor Cultural Ctr., 1981—; pres. Com. for a Nuclear-Free Island, 1986—91; v.p. Staten Islanders Against Nuclear Weapons, 1991—95; pres. Staten Island chpt. Brandeis U. Nat. Women's Com., 1996—99, leader News and Shmews; founder, pres. Coalition of S.I. Women's Orgns., 1996—; mem. edn. com. Staten Island Cmty. TV; mem. Libr. com. Staten Island Hist. Richmond Town; pres. Staten Island Youth Coun.; mem. libr. com. Coll. Staten Island; cmty. outreach chair Women for Women of Sierra Leone, 2001; bd. dirs. Staten Island Mental Health Soc. Recipient Women Helping Women award Soroptimists, 1985, Thomas Wilson award for Substance Abuse Prevention, 1990, S.I. Advance Woman of Achievement award, 1994, Cmty. Hero award S.I. Register, 1996, Woman of Distinction award World of Women, 1998, Paul O'Dwyer Humanitarian award Staten Is. Dem. Assn., 1999; named Outstanding Woman by N.Y. State Sen. Vincent J. Gentile, 1998, Women's History Month award N.Y. City Coun. Spkr. Peter Vallone and Councilmen Jeremiah O'Donovan, Oddo and Fiala, 2001. Mem. AAUW, Belles Lettres Lit. Soc. (pres.), S.I. Hist. soc., N.Y.C. Assn. Tchrs. English (pres. 1967-71), Nat. Coun. Tchrs. English (bd. dirs. 1968-69), Acad. Pub. Edn., McKee Tchrs. Assn. (pres. 1969), H.S. Prins. Assn. (exec. bd.), Coun. Suprs. and Adminstrs., Arista Hon. Soc. (hon.), Delta Kappa Gamma (pres.), Phi Delta Kappa (v.p. 1990-92). Avocations: travel, reading, photography, jewelry making. Home: 40 Flagg Pl Staten Island NY 10304-1119

POPPE, BEVERLY REED, special education educator; b. Cadiz, Ohio, Sept. 23, 1937; d. William Paul and Ruth Lucille (Groves) Reed; children: Barbara, Jill, Kris; m. John Poppe, Sept. 15, 1957 (div. Sept. 1981). BS in Edn., Ohio State U., 1959; MEd, Wright State U., 1983. Cert. Ohio K-8 and K-12 Spl. Edn. Tchr. New Bremen (Ohio) Schs., 1971—. Tutor pvt. practice, New Bremen, 1981—. Choir mem., past treas. St. Paul United Ch. Christ, New Bremen, 1960—; past. pres., mem. Nonprofit Bd. Auglaize Industries, New Bremen, 1980—; pres. Appleseed Ridge Girl Scout Coun. Bd., Lima, Ohio, 1989—; mem. New Bremen Friends Libr. Bd., 1992. Recipient Thanks II Badge Ridge Appleseed ridge Girl Scouts, Lima, Ohio, 1987, 90. Mem. New Bremen Tchrs. Assn. (past pres.), Internat. Reading Assn., Ohio Coun. Tchrs. Lang. Arts, New Bremen Hist. Soc., Assn. Children with Learning Disabilities, Beta Upsilon Chpt. (pres.), Delta Kappa Gamma. Avocations: reading, travel, grandchildren. Office: New Bremen Elem School 210 S Walnut St New Bremen OH 45869-1241

POPPE, DONNA, music educator; b. Newton, Kans., Feb. 25, 1953; d. Louis Gustav and Dorothy Elizabeth (VanDenBrand) P. Student, Hastings Coll., 1970-72; BA in Music Edn., U. North Colo., 1974; cert. Orff-Schulwerk, U. Denver, 1977; MEd in Curriculum, MA in Integrated Arts, Seattle Pacific U., 1990. Band, music, orch. tchr. Weld County Sch. Dist., Greeley, Colo., 1974-79; spl. edn. tchr. Franklin Pierce Sch. Dist., Tacoma, Wash., 1979-84; music tchr. Sumner (Wash.) Sch. Dist., 1984—. Vis. prof. music edn. Pacific Luth. U., 1998-99; cons. Seattle Pacific U., 1982; cons., prof. Fla. State U., Tallahassee, 1985-89, U. Ga., Athens, 1988-89; mem. adj. faculty Pacific Luth. U., Tacoma, 1995—; clinician/presenter U. Nebr., Lincoln, 1991; clinician N.W. Orff Conf., 1994, Orff 100 Conf., Melbourne, Australia, 1995; chair Nat. Orff Conf., Seattle, 1997. Contbr. articles to profl. jours. Mem. Tacoma Symphony, 1983-85; coord. team Wash. State Tchrs. Strike, 1991; chair dist. Valuing Diversity, 1993-95; drama clinician N.W. Orff Conf., 1994; condr. children's performance 20th Anniv. Wash. Orff chpt., 1994, clinician Orff conf., Phoenix, 1999; del. Internat. Soc. Music Edn., Pretoria, South Africa, 1998—. Am. Orff-Schulwerk Assn. grantee, 1991; recipient Wash. State Christa McAuliffe tchg. award. Mem. NEA, Nat. Audubon Soc. (newsletter editor 1974-79, field trip leader Seattle 1992), Am. Orff-Schulwerk Assn. (nat. bd. trustees 1987-90, editorial bd. 1984-87, clinician and presenter Cleve. 1983, Denver, 1990), Music Educators Nat. Conf. (rep. 1983-85, rsch. session Olympia, Wash. 1990), Drum Corps Internat. Democrat. Avocations: music performing ensembles, art movies, theatre-sports, birding. Office: Pacific Lutheran University Music Dept 230 Wood Ave Sumner WA 98390-1279

POPPER, VIRGINIA SOWELL, education educator; b. Macon, Ga., Sept. 10, 1945; d. Clifford E. and Hazel (Lewis) Sowell; m. James Clarence Sikes, June 24, 1967 (div. 1989); children: Zachary Andrew, Cristen Elizabeth; m. Joseph W. Popper, Jr., Dec. 28, 1992. AB, Wesleyan Coll., Macon, 1967; MEd, U. North Fla., 1973; PhD, Ga. State U., 1991. Tchr. 6th grade Jones County Schs., Gray, Ga., 1966-67; tchr. 12th grade Richmond County Schs., Augusta, Ga., 1967-68; guidance counselor Aiken County Schs., North Augusta, S.C., 1968-69, asst. prin., 1969-71; dir. Durham (N.C.) campus Kings Coll., 1974-77; rsch. asst. Ga. Dept. Edn., Atlanta, 1983-85; assoc. prof. Mercer U., Macon, 1989-99, assoc. prof. emeritus, 1999; ptnr. Ednl. Initiatives, Inc., 1999—2003. Tchr. cultural studies exch. program Scinanto Gakuin Coll. of Kitakusha, Japan-Mercer U. Contbg. author: Business in Literature, 1986; contbr. articles, reports to profl. publs. Chmn. Mid. Ga. Regional Libr. System, Macon, 1989-91; bd. dirs. Jr. League Macon, Macon YWCA, Macon Intown, Macon Heritage Found., Bibb County Am. Cancer Soc., March of Dimes, Macon Ballet, Friends of Libr., Gladys Lasky Weller Scholarship Found., Mayor's Lit. Task Force. Mem. ASCD, Assn. Tchr. Educators, Ga. Coun. Social Studies, Ga. Assn. Ind. Coll. Tchr. Edn., Kappa Delta Lambda, Pi Lambda Theta. Republican. Episcopalian. Home: 798 Saint Andrews Dr Macon GA 31210-4769

POPPERS, PAUL JULES, anesthesiologist, educator; b. Enschede, Netherlands, June 30, 1929; came to U.S., 1958; naturalized, 1963; s. Meyer and Minca (Ginsburg) P.; m. Ann Feinberg, June 3, 1969; children: David Matthew, Jeremy Samuel. MD, U. Amsterdam, 1955. Diplomate Am. Bd. Anesthesiology. Instr. anesthesiology Columbia U., N.Y.C., 1962-63, assoc., 1963-65, asst. prof. anesthesiology, 1965-71, assoc. prof. anesthesiology, 1971-74; prof., vice chmn. dept. anesthesiology NYU, 1974-79; prof., chmn. dept. anesthesiology SUNY, Stony Brook, 1979-97, disting. prof., chmn. dept anesthesiology, 1997-2000, disting. prof. emeritus, 2000—. Cons. Brookdale Med. Ctr., Bklyn., 1975-2000, VA Med. Ctr., Northport, N.Y., 1979-2000, The N.Y. Hosp. Med. Ctr. of Queens (formerly Booth Meml. Hosp.), Flushing, N.Y., 1979-98, L.I. Jewish Med. Ctr., New Hyde Park, N.Y., 1980-98, Ea. L.I. Hosp., Greenport, N.Y., 1995-99, Am. Hosp. Paris, 1989-93; cons., lectr. USN, 1968-85 Author: Regional Anesthesia, 1977; editor: Beta Blockade and Anaesthesia, 1979; sect. editor Jour. Clin. Anesthesia, 1990-2000; mem. editl. bd. Internat. Jour. Clin. Monitoring and Computing, 1990-2000, Anaesthesiology Digest, 1991-94, Gynecologic and Obstetric Investigation, 1996-2001; contbr. over 200 articles to profl. jours. Rsch. fellow NIH, 1961; recipient medal Polish Acad. Scis., Poland, 1987, Univ. medal Jagiellonian U., Krakow, Poland, 1987, 1st Sci. award Post-grad. Assembly in Anesthesiology; named Hon. Prof. Anesthesiology, U. Leiden, The Netherlands, 1977. Fellow Am. Coll. Anesthesiology, Am. Coll. Ob-gyns., Royal Soc. Medicine, Post-grad. Assembly in Anesthesiology (hon. chmn. 1989—); mem. Am. Soc. Anesthesiologists, Assn. Univ. Anesthesiologists, Internat. Anesthesia Rsch. Soc., Soc. Obstetric Anesthesia and Perinatology, Am. Soc. Regional Anesthesia, Jerusalem Acad. Medicine, Am. Soc. Pharmacology and Exptl. Therapeutics, Fedn. Am. Soc. Exptl. Biology, Sigma Xi. E-mail: paulpoppers@hotmail.com.

POPPLE, PATRICIA JANE EHLERS, retired principal; b. Chippewa Falls, Wis., July 17, 1939; d. Herbert Herman and Gertrude Caroline (McKinster) Ehlers; m. Melvin Leon Popple, June 16, 1962 (div. Apr. 1982). BS, U. Wis., Eau Claire, 1961, MS, 1970. Tchr. Washington Jr. High Sch., Rice Lake, Wis., 1961-62, Chippewa Falls (Wis.) Area Schs., 1962-66, 67-69; grad. asst. U. Wis., Eau Claire, 1966-67; prin. elem. sch. Chippewa Falls Area Schs., 1967-78, prin. mid. sch., 1978-81, asst. supt., 1981-83; prin. elem. sch. Eau Claire Area Schs., 1983—98, ret., 1998. Bd. dirs. U. Wis. Found., Eau Claire, 1990—, Am. Cancer Soc., pres., 1978-85; bd. trustees Wis. Historical Soc. Recipient Disting. Svc. award U. Wis. Alumni Assn., 1991. Mem. ASCD, Nat. Assn. Elem. Sch. Prins., Assn. Wis. Sch. Adminstrs. (pres., bd. dirs., field rep., Disting. Svc. award 1991), Phi Delta Kappa, Delta Kappa Gamma (local pres. 1978-79, 94-96, chair long range planning com. 1990-99, pres. 1978-80, mem. golden gift fund com. 1990—, state pres. 1999-2001, Disting. Svc. award 1991). Lutheran. Avocations: outdoor activities, reading, volunteer work, animals, travel. Home: 561 Summit Ave Chippewa Falls WI 54729-3520 E-mail: ppopple@execpc.com.

PORRECA, BETTY LOU, education educator; b. Cin., Aug. 8, 1927; d. James Long and Hallie Marie (Jacobs) Hackathorn; m. Charles C. Porreca, Aug. 26, 1949 (widowed 1966); 1 child, Zana Sue Porreca Easley. BA, U. Ariz., 1970, MEd, 1973; PhD, Pacific Western U., 1990. Faculty Cochise Coll., Douglas, Ariz., 1973-83, Pima Community Coll., Tucson, 1983—. Author: (poetry) Selected Poems, 1975; contbr. articles to profl. jours. Chairperson Adult Continuing Christian Edn. Catalina Meth. Ch., Tucson, 1990—; vol. Crisis Pregnancy ctr., Tucson, 1989-91. Mem. MLA, Nat. Coun. Tchrs. English, Pi Lambda Theta, Phi Delta Kappa. Democrat. Methodist. Avocations: reading, hiking, cooking. Office: Pima Community College 1255 N Stone Ave Tucson AZ 85709-3099

PORTA, SIENA GILLANN, sculptor, educator; b. NYC, Nov. 5, 1951; d. Vincent Anthony Porta and Barbara Ann Gill Porta Hutchinson; m. Robert Christopher Dell, May 30, 1986; 1 child, Malcolm Vincent Dell. BS in Studio Arts, Bklyn. Coll., CUNY, 1977; MFA in Sculpture, Pa. State U., 1979. Sci. illustrator Columbia U./Lamont-Doherty Geol. Obs., Palisades, NY, 1980-87; scenic artist Saturday Night Live, NYC, 1986-89, Met. Opera, NYC, 1987-92; master scenic artist numerous Broadway prod., including Frankie and Johnny, Boiler Rm., Sorrows and Rejoicings, 1992—; adj. prof. contemporary arts Ramapo Coll., 2000—; adj. prof. of art St. Thomas Aquinas, Sparkill, NY, 2000—; represented by Noho Gallery, NYC. Adj. prof. Bergen CC, Paramus, NJ, 1984—85; artist-in-residence Brisons Veor, Cornwall, England, 2003. One-woman shows include 14 Sculptors Gallery, NYC, 1984-85, 88, 90, Mid-Hudson Arts and Sci. Ctr., Poughkeepsie, NY, 1992-93, Dominican Coll., Blauvelt, NY, 1980, Noho Gallery, NYC, 2003; group shows at A.B. Condon Gallery, NYC, 1982-83, Terrain Gallery, NYC, 1984, Am. Cultural Ctr., Reykiavik, Iceland, 1988, Notre Dame U., South Bend, Ind., 1990, Lehigh U., Phila., Blue Hill Cult. Ctr., Pearl River, NY, 1995, Eighth Floor Gallery, NYC, 1996, NJ City U., Jersey City, Nassau C.C., Garden City, NY, The Interchurch Ctr., Riverside Dr., NY, 1998, Adelphi U., NY, 2000, St. Thomas Aquinas Coll., Sparkhill, NY, 2000, Galleri Ofeigur, 2001, Noho Gallery, 2001-02, Snaefelsness Regl. Museum, 2002, Hafnarborg Ctr. for Culture, Mus, 2002-03, Regional Mus. of Hornafjorduv, 2003, Rutgers U., 2003, others; represented in collections at Fulbright Commn., Reykjavik, Bergen C.C., Paramus, NJ, 1988, St. Philip R.C. Ch., Norwalk, Conn., Jacob Riis Nat. Park US Embassy, Iceland; subject of video Me and The Mirror, 1990; contbr. articles to popular mag. Pa. State Arts Coun./Hershey Med. Coll. grantee, 1978-79; NY State Coun. on the Arts grantee, 1986; USIA-Ptnrs. of Ams. travel grant to St. Lucia, W.I., 1992, NY Fdn. for the Arts grantee, 2002.; artist resident Brisons Veor, Cornwall, Eng., 2003. Mem. Zen Ctr. of San Diego. Home: PO Box 46 Palisades NY 10964-0046

PORTER, ALAN LESLIE, industrial and systems engineering educator; b. Jersey City, June 22, 1945; s. Leslie Frank and Alice Mae (Kaufman) P.; m. Claudia Loy Ferrey, June 14, 1968; children: Brett, Doug, Lynn. BSChemE, Calif. Inst. Tech., 1967; MS, UCLA, 1968, PhD in Psychology, 1972. Rsch. assoc., asst. prof. program social mgmt. tech. U. Wash., Seattle, 1972-74; asst. prof. indsl. and systems engring. Ga. Inst. Tech., Atlanta, 1975-78, assoc. prof., 1979-85, prof., 1986—, dir. tech. policy and assessment ctr., 1989—2001, prof. pub. policy, 1990—2001, prof. emeritus, 2001—, co-dir. tech policy and assessment ctr., 2002—; dir. rsch. and devel. Search Tech., Inc., Norcross, Ga., 2002—. Cons. Search Tech., IBM, Coca Cola, Rexam, SAIC, SRI. Author, editor: (with others) A Guidebook for Technology Assessment and Impact Analysis, 1980, Interdisciplinarity, 1986, Impact of Office Automation on Clerical Employment, 1985, Forecasting and Management of Technology, 1991, (with Wm. Read) Information Revolution: Present and Future Consequences, 1998, Environmental Methods Review, 1998. NSF grantee, 1974-75, 78-86, 89—, Dept. Transp. grantee, 1977-79. Mem. Internat. Assn. Impact Assessment (co-founder, sec. 1981-87, exec. dir. 1987-90, pres. 1995-96), IEEE Systems Man and Cybernetics Soc. (chmn. tech. forecasting com., Bellcore adv. coun.). Home: 110 Lake Top Ct Roswell GA 30076-3017 Office: Sch Indsl and Systems Engring Ga Tech Atlanta GA 30332-0001 E-mail: alan.porter@isge.gatech.edu.

PORTER, ANDREW CALVIN, academic administrator, psychologist, educator; b. Huntington, Pa., July 10, 1942; s. Rutherford and Grace (Johnson) P.; children: Matthew, Anna, John, Joe, Kate. BS, Ind. State U., 1963; MS, U. Wis., 1965, PhD, 1967. Prof., co-dir. inst. rsch. on teaching Mich. State U., East Lansing, 1967-88; assoc. dir. basic skills group Nat. Inst. Edn., Washington, 1975-76; Anderson-Bascom prof. edn., prof. ednl. psychology, dir. Wis. Ctr. Edn. Rsch. U. Wis., Madison, 1988—2003; Patricia and Rodes Hart prof. ednl. leadership and policy, dir. Learning Sci. Inst., Vanderbilt U., Nashville, 2003—. Vis. asst. prof. Ind. State U., Terre Haute, 1967; mem. adv. bd. Am. Jour. Edn., 1988—; chair bd. Internat. Studies, Nat. Acad. Scis., Nat. Rsch. Coun., 1993-2001; chmn. U.S. Dept. Edn., adv. coun. on edn. stats., 1994-2001. Editor: (with A. Gamoran) Methodological Advances in Cross-National Surveys of Educational Achievement, 2002. Bd. dirs. Madison Urban League, 1992-96. Recipient Disting. Alumni award, Ind. State U., 1994. Mem. Am. Ednl. Rsch. Assn. (pres. 2001), Nat. Coun. Edn. Measurement, Nat. Coun. Tchrs. Math., Nat. Acad. Edn., Phi Delta Kappa (life). Office: Vanderbilt U Learning Scis Inst Box 59 Peabody Sta Nashville TN 37203 E-mail: andy.porter@vanderbilt.edu.

PORTER, BURTON FREDERICK, philosophy educator, writer, dean; b. N.Y.C., June 22, 1936; s. John and Doris (Neloway) P.; m. Susan Jane Porter, May 10, 1966 (div. 1974); 1 child, Anastasia; m. Barbara Taylor Metcalf, Dec. 31, 1980; 1 child, Mark Graham. BA Philosophy cum laude, spl. lit. hons., U. Md., 1959; PhD, St. Andrews U., Scotland, 1968; postgrad., Oxford (Eng.) U. Asst. prof. philosophy U. Md., London, 1966-69; assoc. prof. philosophy King's Coll., Wilkes-Barre, Pa., 1969-71; prof. philosophy, chmn. dept. Russell Sage Coll., Troy, N.Y., 1971-87; prof. philosophy, head dept. humanities-comm. Drexel U., Phila., 1987-91; dean arts and scis. Western New England Coll., Springfield, Mass., 1991-99, prof. philosophy, 1999—. Author: Deity and Morality, 1968, Philosophy, A Literary and Conceptual Approach, 1974, 80, 95, Personal Philosophy: Perspectives on Living, 1976, The Good Life, Alternatives in Ethics, 1980, 91, 94, 2001, Reasons for Living: A Basic Ethics, 1988, Religion and Reason, 1993, The Voice of Reason, 2001, Philosophy Through Fiction and Film, 2003; also articles and book revs. Named Outstanding Educator of Am., NEA, 1975. Mem.: MLA, Am. Philos. Assn. Home: 30 Fearing St Amherst MA 01002-1912 Office: Dept Comm/Humanities Western New Eng Coll Springfield MA 01119

PORTER, DAVID HUGH, pianist, classicist, academic administrator, liberal arts educator; b. N.Y.C., Oct. 29, 1935; s. Hugh B. and Ethel K. (Flentye) P.; m. Laudie Ernestine Dimmette, June 21, 1958 (dec. Nov., 1986); children: Hugh, Everett, Helen, David; m. Helen Louise Nelson, Aug. 24, 1987. BA with highest honors, Swarthmore Coll., 1958; PhD (Danforth Grad. fellow, Woodrow Wilson Grad. fellow), Princeton U., 1962; student, Phila. Conservatory Music, 1955-61. Instr. in classics and music Carleton Coll., Northfield, Minn., 1962-63, asst. prof., 1963-68, assoc. prof., 1968-73, prof., 1973-87, William H. Laird prof. liberal arts, 1974-87, pres. faculty, 1980-82, coll. pres., 1986-87; pres. Skidmore Coll., Saratoga Springs, N.Y., 1987-98, prof. classics, 1987-98. Phi Beta Kappa vis. lectr., 1979-92, vis. scholar, 1994-95; vis. prof. classics Princeton U., 1986; vis. prof. classics Williams Coll., Williamstown, Mass., 1999—; Harry C. Payne vis. prof. liberal arts Williams Coll., 2000—; recitalist, lectr., especially on contemporary music, at colls., univs. throughout U.S., U.K., on radio and TV; chmn. Hudson-Mohawk Assn., 1990-92. Author: Only Connect: Three Studies in Greek Tragedy, 1987, Horace's Poetic Journey: A Reading of Odes I-III, 1987, Virginia Woolf and Logan Pearsall Smith, 2002; editor: Carleton Remembered, 1909-86, 1987, The Not Quite Innocent Bystander: Writings of Edward Steuermann, 1989; contbr. articles on classics, music, twentieth-century lit. and edn. to profl. jours. NEH rsch. fellow, 1969-70, 83-84; Am. Coun. Learned Socs. rsch. fellow, 1976-77. Mem. Am. Philological Assn., Classical Assn. Atlantic States. Democrat. Mem. United Ch. Of Christ. Avocations: hiking, reading, collecting rugs and books. Home: 5 Birch Run Dr Saratoga Springs NY 12866-1023 E-mail: ddodger@skidmore.edu.

PORTER, DOUGLAS TAYLOR, retired athletic administrator; b. Fayetteville, Tenn., Aug. 15, 1928; s. Waudell Phillip and Sophia Mae (Taylor) P.; m. Jean Butcher, Apr. 18, 1953; children: Daria C., Blanche E., Douglas V. BS, Xavier U., 1952; MS, Ind. U., 1960. Asst. football coach St. Augustine High Sch., Memphis, 1955, Xavier U., New Orleans, 1956-60; dir. athletics, head football coach Miss. Vocat. Coll., Itta Bena, Miss., 1960-65; assoc. dir. athletics, coach Grambling (La.) State U., 1966-73; head football coach Howard U., Washington, 1974-78; dir. athletics, head football coach Ft. Valley (Ga.) State Coll., 1979-97; ret., 1997. Pres. Nat. Athletic Steering Com., Ft. Valley, 1990-97. Lt. U.S. Army, 1951-54. Recipient Disting. Am. award Mid. Ga. Chpt. Nat. Football Found., 1997, Citation of Honor for contbns. to football Football Writers Assn. Am., 2000; So. Intra Collegiate Athletic Conf. Hall of Fame, 1997. Mem. Am. Alliance of Health, Phys. Edn. and Dance, Nat. Assn. of Collegiate Dirs. of Athletics (inducted Hall of Fame, 1997), Am. Football Coaches Assn. (life, 35 yr. citation 2003), Sigma Pi Phi, Alpha Phi Alpha (pres. 1983-87), Phi Delta Kappa. Democrat. Roman Catholic. Avocations: reading, listening to jazz. Home: 1415 Martin Luther King Jr Grambling LA 71245-2318 E-mail: ddporter@aol.com.

PORTER, EDITH PRISCILLA, elementary school educator; b. Aberdeen, Wash., Mar. 1, 1941; d. Robert M. and June J. (Crown) Crawford; m. Lawrence A. Porter, June 12, 1963; children: Melanie S., Jeffrey L., Michael A. BA in Edn., Ctrl. Wash. State U., 1963; MA in Edn., Lesley Coll., 1991. Cert. tchr. Wash. 1st grade tchr. Hoquiam (Wash.) Sch. Dist., 1962-63, Oak Harbor (Wash.) Sch. Dist., 1963-66, 3d grade tchr., 1967-68, 90—, 2d grade tchr., 1977-86, 88-90, kindergarten tchr., 1986-88. Co-author, narrator Famous Black Women of Song, 1994. Elder Whidbey Presbyn. Ch., Oak Harbor, 1995—. Recipient 2 May Carvell awards Venture Clubs Am. Mem. NEA, AAUW, Wash. Edn. Assn., Oak Harbor Edn. Assn. (rec. sec. 1994—), Delta Kappa Gamma (chpt. pres. 1977-80, state rec. sec. 1981-83, state area liaison 1983-87, state corr. sec. 1985-87). Democrat. Avocations: computers, hiking, camping, crafts, reading. Home: 904 SE 4th Ave Oak Harbor WA 98277-5219

PORTER, GARY FRANCIS, chemistry educator; b. Jersey City, Nov. 13, 1954; s. Francis Charles Porter and Cynthia (Brown) Porter Alfano; m. Beth T. Miller, Dec. 10, 1983; children: Gary John, Francis Gary. BS, St. Peter's Coll., 1976; MS, Seton Hall U., 1979, PhD, 1985. Lab. asst. Degan Chem. and Oil Co., Jersey City, 1975; teaching asst., then rsch. asst. Seton Hall U., South Orange, N.J., 1977-84; instr. Upsala Coll., East Orange, N.J., 1984-85, asst. prof., 1985-90; asst. prof. chemistry, chair dept. sci. and engring. Passaic County C.C., Paterson, N.J., 1990—; dir. Passaic County Environ. Lab., 1994—. Contbr. articles to profl. jours. Grantee NSF, 1991, 92, 94. Mem. AAUP, Am. Chem. Soc., Nat. Assn. Advisors Health Professions, Two-Yr. Coll. Chemistry Conf., Sigma Xi. Avocations: computers, skiing, sailing. Office: Passaic County CC 1 College Blvd Paterson NJ 07505-1102

PORTER, GERALD JOSEPH, mathematician, educator; b. Elizabeth, N.J., Feb. 27, 1937; s. Fred and Tillie Florence (Friedman) P.; m. Judith Deborah Revitch, June 26, 1960; children: Daniel, Rebecca, Michael. AB, Princeton U., 1958; PhD, Cornell U., 1963; MA (hon.), U. Pa., 1971. Instr. MIT, 1963-65; asst. prof. math. U. Pa., Phila., 1965-69, assoc. prof., 1969-75, prof., 1975—, chmn. undergrad. affairs dept. math., 1971-73, assoc. dean computing Sch. Arts and Scis., 1981-91, dir. Interactive Math. Text Project, 1991-96. Chair-elect faculty senate U. Pa., 1992-93, chair, 1993-94, past chair, 1994-95, 2001-02; prin. investigator NSF MACMATC Grant, 1997-2001. Author: (with D.R. Hill) Interactive Linear Algebra, 1996. Mem. Dem. Com., Haverford Twp., Pa., 1976-82, ward leader, 1980-84, treas., 1984-87. Postdoctoral fellow Office Naval Rsch., 1965-66. Mem. AAUP, AAAS, Am. Math. Soc., Math. Assn. Am. (chmn. com. computers in math. edn. 1983-86, chmn. investment com. 1986-2003, bd. govs. 1980-83, 86-2002, mem. fin. com. 1986-2000, exec. com. 1992-2002, chmn. audit and budget com. 1988-90, 92, treas. 1992-2002, chair com. on profl. devel. 1995-2001, Nat. Assn. Mathematicians. Democrat. Jewish. Home: 161 Whitemarsh Rd Ardmore PA 19003-1698 Office: U Pa 4N69 DRL 209 S 33rd St Philadelphia PA 19104-6395 E-mail: gjporter@math.upenn.edu.

PORTER, JACK, psychologist, educator; b. Phila., Apr. 15; s. Harry and Rose (Solomon) P. BS in Edn., Temple U., 1951, MEd, 1952, DEd, 1959. Diplomate Am. Bd. Sexology; lic. psychologist, Pa., sch. psychologist, Pa. Pvt. practice, Wynnewood, Pa., 1959—. Prof. West Chester (Pa.) U., 1968—. Past pres., bd. dirs. United Synagogue Conservative Judaism, Delaware Valley region; past pres. Bd. Jewish Edn. Fellow Am. Acad. Clin. Sexologists (life); mem. Am. Psychol. Assn., Pa. Psychol. Assn. (past pres.), Pa. Psychol. Found. (founding pres.), Eastern Psychol. Assn., Phila. Soc. Clin. Psychols. (Disting. Svc. award). Home and Office: 1205 Manoa Rd Wynnewood PA 19096-3325

PORTER, JACK RAY, mathematician, educator; b. Oklahoma City, Mar. 31, 1938; s. Joseph Porter and E. Marie (Mills) Hildebrand. BS in Math., U. Okla., 1960; M in Math., N.Mex. State U., 1964, PhD in Math., 1966. Asst. prof. U. Kans., Lawrence, 1966-70, assoc. prof., 1970-77, prof. math., 1977—, Jeffrey S. Balfour teaching prof., 1994—, chair, 1999—. Vis. prof. Va. Poly. Inst., Blacksburg, 1974,83, Messina (Italy) U., 1993. Author: Extensions and Absolutes of Hausdorff Spaces, 1987. Lt. USN, 1960-63. Mem. Math. Assn. Am., Am. Math. Soc., Amateur Radio Club. Home: 4408 W 25th Pl Lawrence KS 66047-9649 Office: U Kans Math Dept 405 Snow Hall Lawrence KS 66045-7504

PORTER, JAMES LOGAN, humanities educator; b. Jesup, Ga., July 24, 1961; s. James William and Shirley Quinelle (Johnson) Porter; m. Miriam Barnard, Aug. 13, 1988; 1 child, Elizabeth. AA in Behavorial Sci., Brewton Parker Coll., 1979-80; BA in Social Sci., History, Tift Coll., 1980-82. Cert. history tchr. Ga. Tchr. Montgomery County High Sch., Mt. Vernon, Ga., 1982-83; buyer Belk-Matthews Co., Vidalia, Ga., 1982-87; tchr., secondary supr. Glennville (Ga.) Christian Acad., 1987-99, Pinewood Christian Acad., Bellville, Ga., 1999—. Mem. edn. adv. bd. Thomas Jefferson's Popular Forest, 2001—, ednl./curriculum cons., 2002—03. Co-chmn. Glennville Tattnall Mus., 1994—95; trustee Tatnall County Libr. Bd., Glennville, 1994—. Named Champion Tchr., CSPAN, 1998—; Taft fellow, Robert A. Taft Inst., 1991, Summer Seminar fellow, NEH, 1992, NEH, VA. Poly. Inst. and State U., 1995, Summer Inst. fellow, 1994. Republican. So. Baptist. Avocations: reading, collecting White House memorabilia, collecting Presidential Christmas cards and prints, researching Thomas Jefferson. Home: 103 W Howard St Glennville GA 30427-1749 Office: Pinewood Christian Acad PO Box 7 Bellville GA 30414

PORTER, JEANNETTE UPTON, elementary education educator; b. Mpls., Mar. 5, 1938; d. Robert Livingston and Ruby Jeannette (Thomas) Upton; divorced; children: Steven, Fritz, Susan Porter Powell. BS, U. Minn., 1960, Mankato State U., 1968; postgrad., St. Thomas U., 1991. Camp dir. St. Paul's Epsicopal Ch., Mpls., 1956-66; tchr. elem. sch. Bloomington (Minn.) Pub. Schs., 1967—, dir. title I, 1975-82, tchr. spl. assignment of rsch. and devel., 1990-91; ednl. adminstrn. Conf. Ctr. Office, Lac du Flambeau, Wis., 1991—. Cons. in ednl. change and innovations The Inst.; team cons. Hillcrest Cmty. Sch., Bloomington, 1990—95; res. tchr. spl. assignment, 1996—; vol. music therapist The Pines Sr. Care, Pine City, Minn., 2001—; edn. cons., 1996—; vol. Nature Conservancy, Avon Park, Fla., 2001—; exchange tchr. Minn./China Tchr., Hangzhou, China, 2002—03; Minn./China exch. tchr., Zhenjiang, China, 2002—03. Tutor Telephone Hot Line Minn. Fedn. Tchrs., Mpls., 1988-92; crisis counselor Neighborhood Improvement Programs, Mpls., 1988-93; adult literacy counselor Right to Read, Mpls., 1987-89; vol. Abbott Northwestern Hosp.; bd. dirs. The Inst. (profl. ednl. think tank, Lac du Flambeau), 1997—. Recipient 1st Bank award Mpls., Red Apple award, Mpls., 1988; named Minn. Tchr. of Excellence, 1988, 89. Mem. Assn. Early Childhood Edn. (treas. 1990-94), Bloomington Edn. Found., Delta Kappa Gamma (1st v.p. 1992-93), PEO (past pres. A.C. chpt.). Avocations: fishing, photography, back packing, global volunteer, music. Home: 4400 W 44th St Minneapolis MN 55424-1064 E-mail: porterfl@strato.net.

PORTER, JOHN WILSON, education executive; b. Ft. Wayne, Ind., Aug. 13, 1931; BA, Albion Coll., 1953; MA, Mich. State U., 1957, PhD, 1962; D in Pub. Adminstrn. (hon.), Albion Coll., 1973; LLD (hon.), Mich. State U., 1977, Cleary Coll., 1987; LHD, Adrian Coll., 1970, U. Detroit, 1979; LLD, Western Mich. U., 1971, Eastern Mich. U., 1975; HHD, Kalamazoo Coll., 1973, Detroit Coll. Bus., 1975, Madonna Coll., Livonia, Mich., 1977; DEd, Detroit Inst. Tech., 1978; AA, Schoolcraft Coll., Livonia, Mich., 1979; DBA, Lawrence Inst. Tech., 1988; LLD, Cleary Coll., 1989. Counselor Lansing (Mich.) Pub. Schs., 1953-58; cons. Mich. Dept. Pub. Instrn., 1958-61; dir. Mich. Higher Edn. Assistance Authority, 1961-65; assoc. supt. for higher edn. Mich. Dept. Edn., 1966-69, state supt. schs., 1969-79; pres. Ea. Mich. U., Ypsilanti, 1979-89; v.p. Nat. Bd. for Profl. Teaching Standards, 1989; gen. supt. Detroit Pub. Schs., 1989-91; CEO Urban Edn. Alliance, Inc., Ypsilanti, Mich., 1991—. Mem. numerous profl. commns. and bds., 1959—, including Commn. on Financing Postsecondary Edn., 1972-74, Commn. for Reform Secondary Edn., Kettering Found., 1972-75, Edn. Commn. of States, 1973-79, Nat. Commn. on Performance-Based Edn., 1974-76, Nat. Commn. on Manpower Policy, 1974-79, Mich. Employment and Tng. Svcs. Coun., 1976-79, Nat. Adv. Coun. on Social Security, 1977-79, Commn. on Ednl. Credit, Am. Coun. on Edn., 1977-80; task panel on mental health of family Commn. on Mental Health, 1977-80; mem. Nat. Coun. for Career Edn. (HEW), 1974-76; pres. bd. dirs. Chief State Sch. Officers, 1974-79; pres. Coun. Chief State Sch. Officers, 1977-78; bd. dirs. Comerica Bank; former chmn. bd. Coll. Entrance Exam. Bd., 1984-86. Trustee Nat. Urban League, 1973-79, Charles Stewart Mott Found., 1981—, Albion Coll., 1989—; bd. dirs. Mich. Internat. Council, 1977—, Mich. Congress Parents and Tchrs.; mem. bd. overseers com. for Grad. Sch., Harvard U., 1980-88; mem. edn. com. NAACP; convener goal 6 Nat. Edn. Goals Panel, 1990—; mem. East Lansing Human Relations Commn.; chmn. Am. Assn. State Colls. and U.'s Task Force on Excellence in Edn.; mem. Mich. Martin Luther King, Jr. Holiday Commn., Gov.'s Blue Ribbon Commn. on Welfare Reform; trustee East Lansing Edgewood United Ch.; mem. Catherine McAuley Health Systems Bd., 1990—. Recipient numerous awards including Disting. Svc. award Mich. Congress Parents and Tchrs., 1963, Disting. Svc. award NAACP, Lansing, 1968; cert. of outstanding achievement Delta Kappa chpt. Phi Beta Sigma, 1970; award for disting. svc. Assn. Ind. Colls. and Univs. Mich., 1974; Disting. Alumni award Coll. Edn., Mich. State U., 1974; award for disting. svc. to edn Mich. State U., 1974; Disting. Alumni award, 1979; award for disting. svc. to edn. in Mich. Mich. Assn. Secondary Sch. Prins., 1974; Pres.'s award as disting. educator Nat. Alliance Black Sch. Educators, 1977; Marcus Foster Disting. Educator award, 1979; recognition award Mich. Ednl. Rsch. Assn., 1978; recognition award Mich. Assn. Secondary Sch. Prins., 1978; recognition award Mich. Assn. Intermediate Sch. Adminstrs., 1979; recognition award Mich. Assn. Sch. Adminstrs., 1979; Mich. Sch. Bus. Ofcls., 1979; resolution Mich. State Legislature, 1978; Anthony Wayne award Coll. Edn., Wayne State U., 1979; Educator of Decade award Mich. Assn. State and Fed. Program Specialists, 1979; Spirit of Detroit award Detroit City Coun., 1981; Disting. Svc. award Ypsilanti Area C. of C., 1988; Philip A. Hart award Mich. Women's Hall of Fame, 1988; Summit award Greater Detroit C. of C., 1991; Mich. State C. of C. award 1991; Olivet Coll. award fr Leadership and Social Responsibility, 2001; inducted Mich. Edn. Hall of Fame, 1992; John W. Porter Disting. Chair endowed at Eastern Mich. U., 1999; Coll. of Edn. bldg. at Eastern Mich. U. named for him, 1999. Mem. Am. Assn. Sch. Adminstrs., Am. Assn. State Colls. and Univs. (president's council, chmn. task force on excellence in edn.), Nat. Measurement Council, NAACP (life), Greater Detroit C. of C. (Summit award 1991), Mich. State C. of C (Disting. Svc. and Leadership award 1991), Tuskeegee Airmen (Disting. Svc. award 1991), Mich. PTA (hon. life), Ea. Mich. U. Alumni Assn. (Disting. Svc. award 1997), Econ. Club (dir. 1979), Sigma Pi Phi, Phi Delta Kappa. Office: Urban Edn Alliance Inc 1547 Fall Creek Ln Ann Arbor MI 48108-9579

PORTER, JOYCE KLOWDEN, theatre educator and director; b. Chgo., Dec. 21, 1949; d. LeRoy and Esther (Siegel) Klowden; m. Paul Wayne Porter, June 8, 1980; 1 child, David Benjamin. BA in Speech Edn., U. Ill., 1971; MA in Theatre, Northwestern U., 1972; postgrad., Northeastern U., Chgo., 1980, 89, 98, Ill. State U., 1985-90. Prof. theatre, play dir. Moraine Valley C.C., Palos Hills, Ill., 1972—2002, emeritus, 2002—, acting theatre coord., 1986-87, theatre coord., 2001—02. Adj. faculty Columbia Coll., 1988—92; text reviewer Harcourt Brace Pub., 1997, Simon & Schuster, 1998, Mayfield, 1999, Martins, 2000—, Pearsons Ednl., 2001—03; actress, Chgo., 1972—. Author: (textbook) Humanities on the Go, 1992, Experiencing the Arts, 2000. Mem. adv. bd. Oak Park (Ill.) Park Dist., 1983; co-chmn. Moraine chpt. Chgo. Area Faculty for nuclear Freeze, Palos Hills, 1985-87; announcer for blind Chgo. Radio Info. Svc., 1982-83; bd. dirs. Festival Theatre, Oak Park, 1989—, sec. 1996-97, pres., 1997-99, v.p. 2002—; mem. play selection com. Village Players of Oak Park, 1992; guest dir. Triton C.C., 2000. Mem. Assn. for Theatre in Higher Edn., U.S. Inst. for Theatre Tech., Ill. Theatre Assn., C.C. Humanities Assn (presenter midwest conf. 1993, presenter & planning com. nat. conf. 1999), Ill. Fedn. Tchrs., Nature Conservancy, Zeta Phi Eta. Avocations: acting, singing, foreign travel, antiquities and antiques. Office: Moraine Valley CC 10900 S 88th Ave Palos Hills IL 60465-2175 E-mail: porter@moraine.valley.edu.

PORTER, LAEL FRANCES, retired communication consultant, educator; b. N.Y.C., July 30, 1932; d. Ronald William Carpenter and Frances Veneranda Fernandez Carpenter; m. Ralph Emmett Porter, June 9, 1954; children: Paula Lee Porter Leggett, Sandra Lynn Porter. BA in Comm. and Theater, U. Colo., Denver, 1982, MA in Comm. and Theater, 1986. Speech instr., Moultrie, Ga., 1954-55; owner, distributor Lael's Cosmetics & Wigs, Alexandria, Va., 1966-69; sales dept. mgr. May D & F, Denver, 1974-80; instr. comm. U. Colo., Denver, 1987-89, Red Rocks C.C., Lakewood, Colo., 1989-97; ret. Mem. coord. com. Nat. Hispana Roundtable, Denver, 1985; mem. diversity coun. and internat. dimensions Red Rocks C.C., Lakewood, Colo., 1994-96. Del. People to People, 1998; mem. adv. bd. cmty. liberal arts and scis. U. Colo., Denver, 1988—93; mem. utility consumers adv. bd. State of Colo., Denver, 1989—91; mem. exec. bd. Friends of Aurora Libr., 1997, v.p.; bd. dirs. Girls Count, Denver, 1991—2001, Colo. Statewide Systemic Initiative, Denver, 1994—98. Recipient Founding Star award Girls Count, 1995, Cert. of Appreciation USAF, 1974, Mack Easton award U. Colo., Denver, 1990. Mem.: AAUW (pub. policy com. 1994—98, state pres. 1992—94, Named Gift award 1991, Br. Named Gift award 1988, Br. Continuing Svc. award 1994), Leadership Lakewood. Episcopalian. Avocations: swimming, writing. Home and Office: 2613 S Wadsworth Cir Lakewood CO 80227-3220

PORTER, MARSHA KAY, language professional and educator; b. Sacramento, Feb. 7, 1954; d. Charles H. and Eileen J. (Miller) P. BA in English and Edn., Calif. State U., Sacramento, 1976, traffic safety credential, 1979, MA in Ednl. Adminstrn., 1982. Cert. lang. devel. specialist, Calif.; cert. first aid instr. ARC. Bookkeeper Chuck's Parts House, Sacramento, 1969-76; substitute tchr. Sacramento City Unified Sch. Dist., 1976-78; coord. Title I, Joaquin Miller Mid. Sch., Sacramento, 1978-81; tchr. ESL and driver's edn. Hiram Johnson H.S., Sacramento, 1981-85, C.K. McClatchy H.S., Sacramento, 1985—. Freelance editor, 1981-87; guest lectr. Nat. U., Sacramento, 1992-93. Co-author film reference book Video Movie Guide, pub. annually; contbr. movie revs., short stories and articles to publs. Vol. instr. CPR and first aid ARC, Sacramento, 1986-92; guest writer United We Stand Calif., Sacramento, 1993-94. Gov.'s scholar State of Calif., 1972. Mem. NEA, Calif. Tchrs. Assn., Calif. Assn. Safety Educators, Calif. Writers, Calif. Writers Assn. (sec. 1987-94, pres. 1996-2000, Jack London award 2000), Delta Kappa Gamma. Roman Catholic. Avocations: swimming, helping wounded and/or abandoned animals, acting.

PORTER, NANCY KAY H. retired secondary school educator; b. Lancaster, S.C., Feb. 1, 1941; d. Quay Charles and Sara Louise (Murphy) Hunter; m. Robert Albert Porter Jr., Mar. 1, 1964; children: Robert Albert III, Sara Alice. BFA, Winthrop Coll., 1962. Cert. tchr., S.C. Math. and sci. tchr. Wray Jr. H.S., Gastonia, N.C., 1962-63; art tchr. Ashley Sr. H.S., Gastonia, N.C., 1963-64; math. tchr. Aiken (S.C.) Jr. H.S., 1964-68, art tchr., 1968-70; math. tchr. South Aiken H.S., 1981—2000; ret., 2000.

PORTER, NANCY LEFGREN, reading recovery educator; b. Council Bluffs, Iowa, Apr. 26, 1945; d. Elvin W. and Verna V. (Hansen) Lefgren; m. Eugene D. Porter, Apr. 3, 1965; children: Theresa McFarland-Porter, M.S., Dr. Tracy K.P. Gregg. BS, U. Iowa, 1976, completed devel. activities program, 1983, MS, 1992. Cert. Reading Recovery trained tchr., reading specialist, 1993. Tchr. Iowa City Sch. Dist., 1976-93, reading recovery Title I tchr., 1993—. Mem. After Sch. Tutoring Program, Iowa City; instr. U. Iowa, 1997. Author (curriculum) Lites and Shadows, 1993, reading curriculum, 1997 (Blue Ribbon award 1997); presenter (cmty. collaboration) NSCI At-Risk, 1994. Precinct chair Dem. Party, Johnson City, Iowa, 1990-96; exec. bd. LWV, 1989-90; WELCA chair Gloria Dei Luth. Ch. Women; mem. corp. bd. Alpha Xi Delta. Grantee K-3 At Risk Grant, 1992, State of Iowa, 1992-97; named Educator of Yr. East Ctrl. Uniserve Unit, 1992. Mem. Iowa State Edn. Assn. (exec. bd. 1993—, Friend of Edn. award 1997, student ISEA), Iowa City Edn. Assn. (pres. 1983-84, 97, govtl. affairs chair 1983—, Educator of Yr. 1992), Delta Kappa Gamma (pres. 1995-96), Pi Delta Kappa (program chair 1994-95). Democrat. Lutheran. Avocations: biking, camping, dancing, reading, enjoying grandchildren. Home: 2519 Potomac Dr Iowa City IA 52245-4827

PORTER, PATRICK KEVIN, secondary education educator, administrator; b. Greenfield, Ind., Jan. 17, 1955; s. Herman Monroe and Juanita Helen (Thomas) P.; m. Bonnie Kay Barkdull, July 3, 1988; children: Andrew, Megan, Sean. BS in Teaching, Ball State U., 1977, MA in Teaching, 1981, EdS in Adminstrn., 1991. Cert. tchr., prin., supt., Ind. Tchr., coach Fayette County Cmty. Sch. Corp., Connersville, Ind., 1977-79, West-Ctrl. Sch. Corp., Anderson, Ind., 1979-87; tchr. Jennings County Sch. Corp., North Vernon, Ind., 1989-90; tchr., coach Bartholomew Consol. Sch. Corp., Columbus, Ind., 1987-89, tchr. sci. and social studies, 1990-94; asst. prin. Richmond (Ind.) H.S., Test, 1994-98; prin. Test Middle Sch., 1997—. Asst. dir. Ball State U. Conf. Office, Muncie, Ind., summer 1985, 86; mgr. Halteman Swim Club, 1987, 88. Chmn. adminstrv. bd. East Columbus United Meth. Ch., Columbus, 1990, chmn. pastor parish com., 1991-93. Named to Outstanding Young Men in Am., 1981. Mem. ASCD, Ind. Profl. Educators Inc., Ind. Basketball Coaches Assn., Ind. High Sch. Athletic Assn. (basketball/volleyball ofcl.), NASSP, Ind. Middle Schs. Assn., Blue Key. Avocations: bowling, hunting, fishing, collecting lapel buttons, tennis. Home: 2708 S G St Richmond IN 47374-6557 Office: Test Middle Sch 33 S 22d St Richmond IN 47374-5398

PORTER, PRISCILLA, elementary education educator; b. Newburgh, N.Y., Jan. 8, 1943; d. Abner M. and Dorothy E. (Hanson) Harper; m. Charles W. Porter, July 12, 1986. BS, SUNY, New Paltz, 1963, MA, 1967; EdD, U. So. Calif., 1990. Elem. sch. tchr. various, New Paltz, 1964-69; supr. curriculum, interns, media ctr. El Camino Real (Calif.) Irvine Sch. Dist., 1969-75; supr. tchr. edn. U. Calif., Irvine, 1973-80; supr. curriculum and staff devel. Venado (Calif.) Irvine Sch. Dist., 1975-76; resource tchr., staff development, intern tchrs. Deerfield Sch., Irvine, Calif., 1976-77, tchr., 1977-78; staff devel. coord. Irvine Sch. Dist., 1978-79, 84-87, tchr. grades 4, 5 and 6, Bonita Canyon Sch., 1979-89, 90-91; assoc. prof. tchr. edn. Calif. State U., Dominguez Hills, 1991-98, prof. emeritus, 1998—; co-dir. Ctr. for History Social Sci. Edn. Editor column Social Studies and the Young Learner; cons. Reagan Presdl. Libr., 2001-03, Bowers Mus. Cultural Art, 2002-03. Author: Harcourt Brace Social Studies, 2000. Recipient Hilda Taba award Calif. Coun. for Social Studies, 2002, Excellence in Edn. award Calif. State U., Dominguez Hills, 2003; named Orange County Tchr. of Yr., 1985. Mem. ASCD, Nat. Coun. Social Studies. Home: 78440 Sunrise Mountain Vw Palm Desert CA 92211-2400 E-mail: prisporter@aol.com.

PORTER, ROBERTA ANN, counselor, educator, school system administrator; b. Oregon City, Oreg., May 28, 1949; d. Charles Paul and Verle Maxine (Zimmerman) Zacur; m. Vernon Louis Porter, Dec. 27, 1975 (div. Dec. 1998). B in Bus. Edn., So. Oreg. Univ., 1971, M in Bus. Edn., 1977; cert. in counseling, Western Oreg. U., 1986; postgrad., Lewis and Clark Coll., 1995. Cert. in leadership Nat. Seminars. Tchr. Klamath Union H.S., Klamath Falls, Oreg., 1971-73, Mazama Mid./H.S., Klamath Falls, 1973-83; instr. Oreg. Inst. Tech., Klamath Falls, Oreg., 1975-92; counselor Mazama H.S., Klamath Falls, 1983-93; vice prin. Bonanza (Oreg.) Schs., 1993-95; counselor Klamath County Sch. Dist., Oreg., 1995—; TAG coordinator Lost River Jr./Sr. H.S., 1995—2002, gender equity team, 1997—. Participant Clinton Cuban-USA Edn. Initiative, Oct. 2000; Blue/Gold Officer USN Acad., 2000—; sch. improvement com. Klamath County Sch. Dist., 2000—; presenter Oreg. and Nat. Assn. Student Coun., 1989-92, Oreg. Sch. Bds. Assn., Sch. Counselor Assn., 1995, state mini workshops counselors/adminstrs., Western Region Br. leadership tng. ACA, 1999, Klamath Youth Summit, 1999; task force for ednl. reform in Oreg., 1993-94; trainer asst. Leadership Devel. Am. Sch. Counselor Assn.; trainer ACA. Mem. editl. bd. Eldorado Wellness, 1996—. Trainer U.S. Army and Marines Recruiters, Portland and Medford, Oreg., 1988-89; master trainer Armed Svcs. Vocat. Aptitude Battery/Career Exploration Program, 1992—; candidate Klamath County Sch. Bd., Klamath Falls; interpreter AMTRAK svc. Klamath Dept. Tourism and Nat. Parks, 1998—; mem. Klamath County Crisis Team. Recipient Promising, Innovative Practices award Oreg. Sch. Counselors, 1990. Mem. NEA, ACA (western region parliamentarian 1999-2001), COSA, ASCD, ASCA, Oreg. Sch. Counseling Assn. (presenter, v.p. h.s. 1988-91, mem. com. 1991-93, pres. 1992-95, pres.'s award), Oreg. Edn. Assn., Oreg. Counseling Assn. (pres. award 1995, parliamentarian 1994-95, area 8 rep. 1995-97, pres.-elect 1997-98, pres. 1998-99, past pres. 1999-2000), Oreg. Assn. Student Couns. (bd. dirs. activity advisors 1989-91), Nat. Assn. Student Couns., Klamath Falls Edn. Assn. (bldg. rep. 1990-93, sec. 1991-92, negotiations team 1992-93), Elks, Delta Kappa Gamma (exec. bd. Alpha chpt. 1985-94, pres. 1990-92, state conv. chmn. 1992, state legis. com. 1991-93, chmn. 1993-95, state expansion com., World Fellowship chair Alpha chpt., scholarship chair 2002—), Elks. Avocations: boating, travel, reading, fishing. Home: 3131 Derby St Klamath Falls OR 97603-7313 Office: Lost River Jr/Sr High Sch 23330 Highway 50 Merrill OR 97633-9706

PORTER, WILLIAM LYMAN, architect, educator; b. Poughkeepsie, N.Y., Feb. 19, 1934; s. William Quincy and Lois (Brown) P.; m. Lynn Rogers Porter; children: Quayny Lyman, Zoe Lynn, Eve Lyman. BA, Yale U., 1955, M.Arch., 1957; PhD, MIT, 1969. Designer, job capt. Louis I. Kahn (architect), Phila., 1960-62; urban designer, asst. chief of design Ciudad Guayana project Joint Center for Urban Studies of Harvard and MIT, Caracas, Venezuela, 1962-64; Mellon fellow dept. urban studies and planning MIT, 1964-65; Samuel Stouffer fellow Joint Center for Urban Studies, Harvard and MIT, 1966-67; asst. prof. urban design, depts. architecture and urban studies and planning MIT, 1968-70, assoc. prof. urban design, 1970-71, prof. architecture and planning, 1971—, Norman B. and Muriel Leventhal prof. architecture and planning, 1988—, head. dept. architecture, 1987-91, dean Sch. Architecture and Planning, 1971-81; co-dir. Aga Khan Program for Islamic Architecture Harvard U.-MIT, 1979-85. Cons. in field; mem. Nat. Archtl. Accrediting Bd., 1978-80, pres., 1979; mem. Mass. Designer Selection Bd., 1978-79, chmn., 1979; mem. steering com. Aga Khan Award for Architecture, 1977-86, mem. master jury, 1989; prin. Four Architecture Inc., Boston, 1994—. Co-author: Excellence by Design: Transforming Workplace and Work Practice, 1999; co-founder, co-editor Places: A Quarterly Jour. Environ. Design, 1982-88, Facilities Engineering and Management Handbook: Commercial, Industrial and Institutional Buildings, 2000, Design Representation, 2003. Trustee Milton (Mass.) Acad., 1989-2001; mem. bd. overseers Coll. Fine Arts, U. Pa., 1984-90, Mus. Fine Arts, Boston, 1992-94. Fellow AIA; mem. Boston Soc. Architects (dir. 1969-73, 77-81) Clubs: Harvard Musical Assn. (Boston). Home: 17 Concord Ave Cambridge MA 02138-2321 Office: MIT Sch Architecture & Planning 77 Massachusetts Ave Cambridge MA 02139-4307

PORTER, WILMA JEAN, educational consultant; b. Sylacauga, Ala., May 30, 1931; d. Harrison Samuel and Blanche Leonard Butcher; m. Douglas Taylor Porter, Apr. 18, 1953; children: Daria Cecile, Blanche Evette, Douglas Vincent. BS, Tuskegee U., 1951; MS, Mich. State U., 1966; PhD, Iowa State U., 1980. Asst. dietitian Miss. State Tb Sanatorium, 1951-52; therapeutic dietitian dept. of hosp. City of N.Y., S.I., 1952-53; libr. asst. Mississippi Valley State Coll., Itta Bena, Miss., 1963-65; asst. prof. Grambling (La.) State U., 1966-75, Howard U., Washington, 1976-80; country dir. U.S. Peace Corps, Tonga, 1980-82; asst. dir. internat. programs Ft. Valley (Ga.) Coll., 1983-84, dir. Inst. Advancement, 1984-88; dir. Sch. Home Econs., Tenn. Technol. U., Cookeville, 1989-96; pvt. ednl. cons. Cookeville, 1996-98. Project dir. Capitol Hill Health and Homemaker, Washington, 1982-83; interim dir. Inst. Advancement Alcorn State U., Lorman, Miss., 1988-89. Author lab. manual for quantity foods, 1977; editor: (cookbook) Some Christmas Foods and Their Origins from Around the World, 1983. Convenor Nat. Issues Forums, Ga. and Tenn., 1985-90; citizen participant Nat. Issues Forums Soviet Dialogue, Newport Beach, Calif., 1988; bd. dirs. Leadership Putnam, Cookeville, 1990-94; chmn. Tenn. Technol. U. campaign United Way, 1989; mem. devel. and planning com. Peach County Ft. Valley, 1985-87; mem. Peach County Heart Fund Dr., 1986-88; participant People to People Citizens Amb. program U.S./China Women's Issues Program, 1995. Title III grantee U.S. Dept. Edn., 1986, 87; Tenn. Dept. Human Svcs. grantee, 1993, 94. Mem. AAUW (program chair 1991-92, pres. Cookeville br. 1993-94), Am. Family and Consumer Scis. Assn., Am. Dietetic Assn., Nat. Coun. Adminstrs. Home Econs., La. Assn. Family and Consumer Scis., La. Dietetic Assn. Democrat. Roman Catholic. Avocations: writing, vegetable and flower gardening. Home: 1415 ML King Jr Ave Grambling LA 71245

PORTERA, ALAN A. religious studies educator, director; b. Buffalo, Jan. 29, 1951; s. Albert Andrew and Adele Beatrice (Pecorella) Portera; m. Marcia Jean Urbaniak, May 16, 1975; 1 child, Alanna Jachelene. BS, State U. Coll. N.Y., Buffalo, 1974; MS in Edn., Niagara U., 1981; postgrad., SUNY, Buffalo, 1984. Cert. nursery sch., kidergarten, grades 1-6, and art grades K-12 N.Y. Tchr. St. Gregory's, Williamsville, NY, 1974-75, St. Mark's, Buffalo, 1975—77, St. James, Depew, NY, 1977-79, St. Teresa's, Niagara Falls, NY, 1979-89; dir. religious edn. St. Joseph's, North Tonawanda, NY, 1978-92, Niagara Falls, 1990-92; ednl. sales cons. Knowledge Nest, Chgo., 1989-90; elem. tchr. Niagara Falls Bd. Edn., 1992-93; religious edn. dept. chair St. John's Acad., Plattsburgh, 1994-96; tchg. asst. North Palm Beach (Fla.) Elem. Sch., 1997-98; ednl. sales cons. Stop, Look and Learn, Palm Beach Gardens, Fla., 1996-97, Get Smart, Palm Beach Gardens, 1998; dir. religious edn. St. Thomas More, Boynton Beach, Fla., 1998—. Religious edn. moderator Region 26, 29, 30 Diocese of Buffalo, 1981—83. Author: (book) Concern for Peace and Justice, 1981, Foundations for Faith Formation, 1989, Fundamental Building Blocks of Faith, 1991. Mem. Nat. Conf. for Catechetical Leadership, 2002—; mem. pastoral formation bd. St. Vincent de Paul Regional Sem., Boynton Beach, Fla., 2001—. Named Religious Educator of the Yr., Diocese of Buffalo, 1979. Mem.: KC, Western N.Y. Assn. Dirs. and Coords. Religious Educators (v.p. 1985—87). Democrat. Home: 903/215 Lake Shore Dr Lake Park FL 33403 E-mail: stm2000@webmail.catholic.org.

PORTERFIELD, DANIEL RYAN, English educator; b. Balt., Aug. 19, 1961; s. H. Gordon Porterfield and Anne M. Butler; m. Karen Anne Herrling, 1990; children: Elizabeth, Caroline. AB, Georgetown U., 1983; BA/MA in English, Oxford U., 1986; PhD in English, CUNY Grad. Ctr., 1995. Various tchg. positions, 1983-91; asst. to the chancellor CUNY, 1991-92; chief speechwriter for the sec. U.S. Dept. Health and Human Svcs., Washington, 1993-95, dep. asst. sec., 1995-96; v.p. comms. and pub. affairs, asst. prof. English Georgetown U., Washington, 1996—, v.p. pub. affairs and strategic devel., 2002—03. Rhodes scholarship, 1984; Mellon fellowship in the humanities Woodrow Wilson Found., 1989. Democrat. Roman Catholic. Home: 5006 34th Rd N Arlington VA 22207-2812

PORTERFIELD, JAMES TEMPLE STARKE, business administration educator; b. Annapolis, Md., July 7, 1920; s. Lewis Broughton and Maud Paxton (Starke) P.; m. Betty Gold, Apr. 23, 1949 (dec. 1985); m. Janet Patricia Gardiner Roggeveen, Oct. 5, 1986. AB, U. Calif., Berkeley, 1942; MBA, Stanford U., 1948, PhD, 1955. From asst. to assoc. prof. Harvard U. Bus. Sch., Boston, 1955-59; prof. fin. Stanford (Calif.) U. Grad. Sch. Bus., 1959-79, James Irvin Miller Prof. fin., 1979-90, prof. emeritus, 1990—; prof. IMEDE Mgmt. Devel. Inst., Lausanne, Switzerland, 1962-63. Author: Life Insurance Stocks as Investments, 1955, Investment Decisions and Capital Costs, 1965; co-author: Case Problems in Finance, 1959. Served as lt. USNR, 1941-46. Recipient Salgo Noren award Stanford U., 1966, Richard W. Lyman award Stanford U. Alumni Assn., 1995. Home: 295 Golden Oak Dr Portola Valley CA 94028-7730 Office: Stanford U Grad Sch Bus Stanford CA 94305

POSCH, MARGARET A. education educator, researcher; b. Detroit, Mich., Nov. 21, 1944; d. James Adam and Gertrude E. (Brown) Kollar; m. Joseph L. Posch, June 15, 1968; children: Joseph III, J. David, Jean Posch Shore, Michael, Christina. PhD, Wayne State U., 1996. Realtor Prudential Grosse Pointe (Mich.) Real Estate, 1990—92; ednl. rschr. Wayne State U., Detroit, 1992—, dir., post-award rsch. dept. Coll. Edn., 1999—2001, prin. investigator, 1999—; v.p., evaluation and rsch. Am. Surg. Ctrs., Inc., 2000—. Dir. career devel. programs, 2000. Contbr. articles to profl. jours. Mem. adv. bd. Detroit Pub. Schs., Office Spl. Svcs./Transition, Detroit, 2000—; LCCE adv. bd. mem. Coun. for Exceptional Children, Divsn. for Career Devel. and Transition, Reston, Va., 2000—; pack 39 leader/adminstr. Boy Scouts Am., Grosse Pointe, Mich., 1978—80; trustee Grosse Pointe Shores (Mich.) Improvement Found., 1993—2002; exec. bd. Friends of Child Abuse Prevention, Mich., 1994—. Named Outstanding Young Woman of Am., Congl. Nomination, 1981; recipient Vol. award, Boy Scouts Am., 1979, State of NH Senate Resolution, City of Detroit Empowerment Zone Devel. Corp. Implementation award, 2000, Best Practice designation in Empowerment Zone/Enterprise Communities, HUD. Mem.: ASCD, Am. Bus. Women's Assn., Am. Ednl. Rsch. Assn., Coun. for Exceptional Children, Am. Statis. Assn. (past pres., pres., v.p., sec. 1997—2002), Detroit Regional C. of C. (Leadership Detroit Class XXIV 1994—), Jr. League Detroit (chair pub. affairs com. 1985—87, chair cmty. rsch. 1987—88). Avocations: performing arts, travel, music.

POSES, ROY MAURICE, physician, educator; b. Bklyn., Apr. 13, 1952; m. June Axelrod, 1978. AB in English magna cum laude, ScB in Engring. magna cum laude, Brown U., 1974, MD, 1978. Diplomate Am. Bd. Internal Medicine, Nat. Bd. Med. Examiners; lic. physician N.J., Va., R.I. Intern in medicine Univ. Hosp-Boston U., 1978-79, resident in medicine, 1979-81; Henry J. Kaiser Family Found. fellow in gen. medicine U. Pa., Phila., 1981-83; asst. prof. medicine U. Medicine and Dentistry of N.J., Rutgers Med. Sch., Camden, 1983-87, Med. Coll. Va.-Va. Commonwealth U., Richmond, 1987-92, dir. rsch. activities divsn. gen. medicine and primary care, 1987-93, assoc. prof. medicine, 1992-94, vice chmn. for rsch. divsn. gen. medicine and primary care, 1993-94; assoc. prof. medicine and cmty. health Brown U. Sch. Medicine, 1994—; dir. rsch. divsn. gen., internal medicine Meml. Hosp. R.I., Pawtucket, 1994-99; dir. gen. internal medicine rsch. Brown U. Ctr. Primary Care and Prevention, 1999—. Dir. med. consultation svc. dept. medicine Cooper Hosp./Univ. Med. Ctr., Camden, 1983-87; adj. asst. prof. medicine U. Pa., Phila., 1985-87; test site coord. Ednl. Commn. for Fgn. Med. Grads., 1987; temp. advisor WHO, Geneva, Switzerland, 1988; cons. Nat. Libr. Medicine, U. Ill., Chgo., 1988, Nat. Heart, Lung and Blood Inst., New Brunswick, N.J., 1990, 92, Ctr. for Clin. Effectiveness, Henry Ford Health System, Detroit, 1992; cons. Nat. Bd. Med. Examiners, 1996-99, 2002—, 2002—; invited participant Forums 2 and 3 Global Forum for Health Rsch., 1998-99; cons. Agy. for Health Care Rsch. and Quality, 2001; presenter in field. Mem. health care tech. study sect. Agy. Health Care Policy and Rsch., 1990-94. Recipient Lange Med. Publs. awards, 1978; Dr. A. Blaine Brower traveling scholar ACP, 1991-92, alternate traveling scholar ACP, 1989. Mem. IEEE, ACP, Soc. Gen. Internal Medicine (ex officio coun. 1990-93, co-chmn. sci. program com. 1999, rsch. subcom. 1990, mem. sci. program 1993), Soc. Med. Decision Making (sec., treas. 1997-99, bd. trustees 1992-94, dir. advanced short courses 1988, sci. program com. 1987, 88, 93, awards com. 1991, chair mem. com. 1994-96, chair annual meeting short courses 1995, chair devel. com. 1999-2002, Eugene Saenger award 2001), Soc. Judgement and Decision Making, Acad. Health, Brunswik Soc. (meeting co-chmn. 1991), Sydenham Soc., Tau Beta Phi, Phi Beta Kappa, Sigma Xi. Office: Meml Hosp RI Ctr for Primary Care and Prevention 111 Brewster St Pawtucket RI 02860 E-mail: roy-poses@brown.edu.

POSEY, CLYDE LEE, business administration and accounting educator; b. Tucumcari, New Mex., Dec. 27, 1940; s. Rollah P. and Opal (Patterson) P.; m. Dora Diane Vassar; children: Amanda Bennett, Julia Forsyth, Rebecca; m. Judith James Jerry, July 31, 1991; stepchildren: David Jerry, Georgia Kenyan. BBA, U. Tex., El Paso, 1963; MBA, U. Tex., 1965; postgrad., U. So. Calif., 1968; PhD, Okla. State U., 1978. Registered investment advisor. Lab. aide FBI, Washington, 1959-60; acct. Lipson, Cox & Colton (now Deloitte & Touche), El Paso, Tex., 1962; auditor Main & Co. (now KPMG), El Paso, 1963; teaching asst. U. Tex., Austin, 1963-65; tax cons. Peat, Marwick, Mitchell & Co. (now KPMG), Dallas, 1965-66; cons. Roberson, Martin, Horg and Ryckman, Fresno, Calif., 1967; pvt. practice acctg., Fresno, Calif., 1966—, Ruston, La., 1966—; registered rep. H.D. Vest & Co., 2003; asst. prof. Calif. State U., Fresno, 1966-76; assoc. prof. La. Tech. U., Ruston, 1978-84, prof., 1984—; investment advisor H.D. Vest & Co. Vis. asst. prof. Ctrl. State U., Edmond, Okla., 1971-72, U. Okla., Norman, 1976-78; cons. J. David Spence Accountancy Corp., Fresno, 1974-76; registered rep. H.D. Vest & Co.; many coms. at La. Tech. U. including acad. senator, new faculty welcoming com., acctg. scholarship chmn.; faculty senate rep.; Faculty Consortium, St. Charles, Ill., 1993; expert witness Superior Ct. Calif. and Dist. Ct., La. Contbr. numerous articles to profl. jours., bus. mags., newspapers, also book reviews; presentations to profl. meetings. Past bd. dirs. Goodwill, Inc., Ctrl. Calif.; ch. deacon and mem. many coms.; pres., treas., state scripture coord. Gideons Internat. Ruston Camp; rep. United Way La. Tech. U., Ruston; deacon 1st Bapt. Ch., Ruston With USCG, 1965. Recipient El Paso CPA's Outstanding Jr. scholarship, Standard Oil scholarship, Price Waterhouse scholarship, Outstanding Educator award Gamma Beta Phi, 1986. Mem. AICPA, Am. Acctg. Assn. (La. membership com. chmn.), Am. Inst. for Decision Scis. (program com. chmn. acctg. track), La. Soc. CPAs, Am. Tax Assn. (internat. tax policy subcom.), Beta Gamma Sigma (pres.), Beta Alpha Psi, Delta Sigma Pi. Baptist. Avocations: triathlons, bicycle racing, golf, tennis, gardening. Home: 2700 Foxxwood Dr Ruston LA 71270-2509 Office: La Tech U Cab 129A Ruston LA 71272-0001 E-mail: posey@cab.latech.edu.

POSKANZER, STEVEN GARY, university administrator, lawyer; b. Cortland, N.Y., Sept. 1, 1958; s. Charles Newton and Joan Rae (Mamolen) P.; m. Jane Anne Nofer; children: Jill Madeline, Craig Robert. BA, Princeton U., 1980; JD, Harvard U., 1983. Assoc. Arent, Fox, Kintner, Plotkin & Kahn, Washington, 1983-85; asst. gen. counsel U. Penn., Philadelphia, Pa., 1985—88; assoc. gen. counsel U. Penn, Philadelphia, Pa., 1988—93; spl. asst. to provost Princeton U., 1991—92; exec. asst. to pres. U. Chgo., 1993-97; assoc. provost SUNY, Albany, 1997—98, interim pres. New Paltz, 2001—03, pres., 2003—. Author: Higher Education Law: The Faculty, 2001. Mem. Phi Beta Kappa, 1980. Office: SUNY New Paltz 75 S Manheim Blvd New Paltz NY 12561*

POSNER, GARY HERBERT, chemist, educator; b. N.Y.C., June 2, 1943; s. Joseph M. and Rose (Klein) P.; children: Joseph, Michael. BA, Brandeis U., 1965; MA, Harvard U., 1965, PhD, 1968. Asst. prof. Johns Hopkins U., Balt., 1969-74, assoc. prof., 1974-79, prof. dept. chemistry, 1979—, Scowe prof. chemistry, 1989—, prof. dept. environ. chemistry, 1982—, chmn. dept. of chemistry, 1987-90. Cons. Batelle Meml. Inst., Columbus, Ohio, 1983, S.W. Rsch. Inst., San Antonio, Nova Pharm. Co., Balt.; mem. Fulbright-Hays Adv. Screening Com. in Chemistry, 1978-81; Fulbright lectr. U. Paris, 1976; Michael vis. prof. Weizmann Inst. Sci., Rehovot, Israel, 1983; leader Round Table discussion Welch Found. Conf. Chem. Rsch., Houston, 1973, 83; Plenary lectr. Nobel Symposium on Asymmetric Synthesis, Sweden, 1984. Author: Introduction to Organic Synthesis Using Organocopper Reagents, 1980; mem. editl. bd. Organic Reactions, 1976-89; exec. editor Tetrahedron Reports, 1996—. Named Chemist of Yr., State of Md., 1987; fellow Japan Soc. for Promotion Sci., 1991; recipient Johns Hopkins U. Disting. Tchng. award, 1994. Mem. AAAS, Am. Chem. Soc., AAUP, NIH (medicinal chemistry study sect. 1986-89), Phi Beta Kappa Office: Johns Hopkins U Dept Chemistry 3300 N Charles St Baltimore MD 21218 E-mail: ghp@jhu.edu.

POST, BARBARA JOAN, elementary school educator; b. Passaic, NJ, June 29, 1930; d. John Ward and Florence Barbara (Barnum) Post; m. Edward Wayne Poppele, Apr. 10, 1954 (dec. Mar. 1978); children: E. Scott Poppele, Sara Elizabeth Poppele, Andrew John Poppele. BSE, William Paterson Coll., 1953; cert. in counseling, Rutgers U., 1981; postgrad., Columbia U., 1983, Northeastern U., 1983. Cert. tchr., N.J. Elem. tchr. Cen. Sch., Glen Ridge, N.J., 1953-55, Middletown (N.J.) Village Sch., 1956, Our Lady of Perpetual Help, Highlands, N.J., 1981-85; reading tchr. Monmouth Reading Ctr., Long Branch, N.J., 1985; tchr. gifted/talented Harmony Sch., Middletown, 1987-88; edn. coord. for Monmouth County Nat. Coun. on Alcoholism, Freehold, N.J., 1988-89; coord. math./sci. consortium Brookdale Community Coll., Lincroft, N.J., 1989-90; tchr., owner Learning Post and Creative Garden of Art for Children, Middletown, 1991—; dir. art Hillel Sch., Ocean, N.J., 1991—. Dir.-owner Learning Post, Middletown, 1986—; art tchr. Art Alliance of Monmouth County, Red Bank, N.J., 1986-88; vol. case mgmt. worker St. Matthews House, Naples, Fla., 1997-98. Author: (poem) The Lift, 1988 (short story) Sarah-Grand, 1984, Hooked on the Classics, 1988; artist (program cover) Country Christmas, 1990, 91. Demonstrator Family Reading Fair, Lincroft, 1989; participant Muscular Dystrophy Telethon, Eatontown, N.J., 1986; tchr. Tower Hill Vacation Bible Sch., Presbyn. ch., Red Bank, N.J., 1998. Mem. AAUW (tchr., mentor for teen women 1989-92, Appreciation award 1989-90), Nat. Soc. DAR (chairperson 1961-62), N.J. Shore Rose Soc. (exhibitor, 2d and 3d prize for roses 1986). Republican. Presbyterian. Avocations: art, swimming, choir, roses, golf. Home: 167 Crown Dr Naples FL 34110 E-mail: post@mymailstation.com.

POST, GAINES, JR., retired history educator, dean, administrator; b. Madison, Wis., Sept. 22, 1937; s. Gaines and Katherine (Rike) P.; m. Jean Wetherbee Bowers, July 19, 1969; children: Katherine Doris, Daniel Lawrence. BA, Cornell U., 1959, Oxford U., 1963; MA, Stanford U., 1964, PhD, 1969. Instr. Stanford U., 1966-69; asst. prof. history U. Tex., Austin, 1969-74, assoc. prof., 1974-83; dean faculty, sr. v.p. Claremont McKenna Coll., Calif., 1983-88, prof., 1998—99, emeritus prof., 1999—. Exec dir. Rockefeller Found. Commn. on Humanities, 1978-81. Author: The Civil Military Fabric of Weimar Foreign Policy, 1973, Dilemmas of Appeasement: British Deterrence and Defense, 1934-37, 1993, Memoirs of a Cold War Son, 2000; co-author The Humanities in American Life, 1980; editor: German Unification: Problems and Prospects, 1992. Mem. exec. com. Forming the Future Project, Austin Ind. Sch. Dist., 1982; mem. Tex. Com. for Humanities, 1981-83; mem. coun. Calif. Congl. Recognition Program, 1984-88, Calif. Coun. Humanities, 1995—. Rhodes scholar, 1961-63; Am. Coun. Learned Socs. fellow, 1982-83; Am. Philos. Soc. grantee, 1974. Office: Claremont McKenna Coll Dept History 850 Columbia Ave Claremont CA 91711-3901

POST, GERALD V. business educator; b. Chippewa Falls, Wis., Nov. 27, 1955; s. Vernon Otto and Doris Post; m. Sarah S. Post, Aug. 14, 1982. BA, U. Wis., Eau Claire, 1978; PhD, Iowa State U., 1983. Asst. prof. Oakland U., Rochester Hills, Mich., 1982-89; prof. Western Ky. U., Bowling Green, 1989-99; prof. dept. bus. U. of the Pacific, Stockton, Calif., 1999—. Cons. analyst/programmer The Wala Group, Arden Hills, Minn., 1985-99. Author: Database Management Systems, 2002, Management Information Systems, 2003; contbr. articles to profl. jours. Office: Univ of the Pacific 3601 Pacific Ave Stockton CA 95211-0197

POST, ROBERT CHARLES, law educator; b. Bklyn., Oct. 17, 1947; s. Ted and Thelma (Feifel) P.; m. Fran Layton, Jan. 22, 1981; children: Alexander, Amelia. AB, Harvard U., 1969, PhD, 1980; JD, Yale U., 1977. Bar: D.C. 1979, Calif. 1983. Law clk. to chief judge U.S. Ct. Appeals (D.C. cir.), 1977-78; law clk. to justice William Brennen Jr. U.S. Supreme Ct. D.C., 1978-79; assoc. Williams & Connelly, Washington, 1980-82; acting prof. law U. Calif., Berkeley, 1983-87, prof. law, 1987-94, Alexander F. and May T. Morrison prof. law, 1994—. Author: Constitutional Domains, 1995; editor: Law and the Order of Culture, 1991, Censorship and Silencing: Practices of Cultural Regulation, 1998; co-editor: Race and Representation: Affirmative Action, 1998, Human Rights in Political Transistions: Gettysburg to Bosnia, 1999, Civil Society and Government, 2001; co-author: Prejudicial Appearances: The Logic of America Antidisaimation Law, 2001. Gen. counsel AAUP, 1992-94. Fellow Guggenheim Found., 1990-91, Am. Coun. Gen. Socs., 1990-91. Mem. AAUP, Am. Acad. Arts and Scis. Office: U Calif Sch Law Boalt Hall Berkeley CA 94720

POST, ROSE ELIZABETH, retired elementary education educator; b. New Kensington, Pa., Aug. 26, 1925; d. Vincent Capo and Josephine Elizabeth (Demio) Capo-Dickson; m. Francis V. Post, Mar. 4, 1947 (dec. Oct. 1982); children: Bradley, David, Claudia Jo, James C., Laura Rose. BS in Edn. cum laude, U. Pitts., 1963, MEd cum laude, 1965. Cert. tchr., metric system specialist. Lectr. Pa. State U., 1966-90; tchr. New Kensington-Arnold Schs., 1967-96. Elem. math. chairperson, head dept. New Kensington, 1978-93. Author Elem. Metric Course of Study, 1978. Mem. Bus. and Profl. Women's Club, New Kensington, 1989—; sec.; mem., del. Quota Club New Kensington, 1987—. Mem. NEA, Pa. State Edn. Assn., New Kensington Edn. Assn., Pi Lamba Theta. Avocations: reading, gardening, writing, decorating, travel.

POSTERARO, CATHERINE HAMMOND, librarian, gerontology educator; b. Hartford, Conn., Nov. 13, 1946; d. Joseph Francis and Elizabeth Claire (Desmond) Hammond; m. Anthony Francis Posteraro, Jr., June 20,

1970; children: Anthony Francis III, Christopher Clarke. AB, Emmanuel Coll., Boston, 1968; MS, Simmons Coll., 1970; MA, St. Joseph Coll., West Hartford, Conn., 1992. Lectr. gerontology St. Joseph Coll., 1991—; clin. libr. St. Francis Hosp. and Med. Ctr., Hartford, Conn., 1999—. Recipient Sister Mary Elizabeth Delice award Inst. Gerontology, St. Joseph Coll., 1992. Mem. ALA, Assn. Coll. and Rsch. Librs., Conn. Libr. Assn., Gerontol. Soc. Am., Med. Libr. Assn., Sigma Phi Omega. Home: 24 Mcdivitt Dr Manchester CT 06040-2240 Office: St Francis Hosp Health Scis Libr 116 Woodland St Hartford CT 06105 E-mail: cposteraro@cox.net., cpostero@stfranciscare.org.

POSTON, IONA, nursing educator; b. Charleston, S.C., 1951; BSN, Med. U. of S.C., 1973; MSN, Med. Coll. of Ga., 1979; PhD, U. Fla., 1988. Instr. Clemson (S.C.) U., 1979-81; asst. prof. U. N.C., Greensboro, 1981-85; assoc. in nursing Fla. State U., Tallahassee, 1989; assoc. prof. East Carolina U., Greenville, N.C., 1989—. Contbr. articles to profl. jours. Alden B. Dow Creativity Ctr. fellow, 1993; HBO & Co. nurse scholar, 1995. Mem.: Soc. Pediat. Nurses, NLN, ANA, AAUP, Sigma Theta TAu.

POSUNKO, BARBARA, retired elementary education educator; b. Newark, July 17, 1938; d. Joseph and Mary (Prystauk) P. BA, Rutgers U., Newark, 1960; MA, Kean U., Union, N.J., 1973; teaching cert., Seton Hall U., Newark, 1966. Cert. elem. tchr., reading specialist, N.J. Social case worker Newark City Hosp., 1960-65; elem. tchr. Plainfield (N.J.) Bd. Edn., 1966; elem., jr. and sr. high sch. tchr. minimum basic skills and reading Sayreville (N.J.) Bd. Edn., 1966-82, tchr. Chpt. I and minimum basic skills, 1982-95, cooperating tchr. to student tchrs., 1983-95, coord. testing, 1984-95; ret., 1995. Sch. coord. for congressionally mandated study of ednl. growth and opportunity, 1991-95; mem. numerous reading coms. Recipient Outstanding Tchr. award N.J. Gov.'s Tchr. Recognition Program, 1988. Mem. NEA, Internat. Reading Assn., N.J. Reading Assn., N.J. Edn. Assn. Home: 17 Drake Rd Mendham NJ 07945-1805

POSUNKO, LINDA MARY, retired elementary education educator; b. Newark, Dec. 24, 1942; d. Joseph and Mary (Prystauk) P. BA, Newark State Coll., Union, N.J., 1964; MA, Kean U., Union, 1974. Cert. permanent elem. tchr., supr., prin., N.J. Elem. tchr. Roselle (N.J.) Bd. Edn., 1964—65; head tchr. 1st grade Garwood (N.J.) Bd. Edn., 1965—76, 1982—95, head tchr., 1974—76, 1979—82, 1984—86, 1987—88, head tchr. 3d grade, 1976—82, acting prin., 1978, lead tchr. early childhood edn., 1993—95; ret., 1995. Cooperating tchr. to student tchrs.; instr. non-English speaking students and children with learning problems; mem. affirmative action, sch. resource coms.; conductor in-svc. workshops on early childhood devel. practices, 1993. Recipient honor cert. Union County Conf. Tchrs. Assn., 1972-73, The Garwood award N.J. Gov.'s Tchr. Recognition Program, 1983, 88, Outstanding Tchr. award N.J. Gov.'s Tchr. Recognition Program, 1988, Tchr. Recognition award Spanish Nat. Honor Soc., 1999, Most Memorable Tchr. Recognition award Spanish Nat. Honor Soc., 1999; nominee N.J. Gov.'s Tchr. Recognition award, 1993-94. Mem. ASCD, NEA, Internat. Reading Assn. (bd. dirs. suburban coun.), N.J. Edn. Assn., Garwood Tchrs. Assn. (sec., v.p., pres.), High/Scope Ednl. Found. Home: 17 Drake Rd Mendham NJ 07945-1805

POTOKER, ELAINE SHARON, international trade services company executive, business educator; b. Bklyn. children: Kristen Aimee, Beth Anne. BA cum laude, SUNY, Potsdam, 1965; MAT in Spanish Lang. and Lit., U. Chgo., 1968; PhD, Ohio State U., 1994. Cert. tchr., Pa., Ill., N.Y. Coord. internat. sales divsn., area mgr. Ctrl. Am. Reed Mfg. Co., Erie, 1978-84; mgr. import-export agy. svcs. Interloqui, Erie, 1984—; chair divsn. bus. Ohio Dominican Coll., Columbus, 1994-95. Judge moot court competition Case Western Reserve U.; lectr. in field; presenter in field; owner Interloqui, Castine, Maine. Asst. editor Comparative Edn. Rev., 1991-93; contbr. articles to profl. jours. Mem. Multicultural Task Force, Ohio State U., Columbus, 1993-94; mem. internat. bus. edn. com. Cleve. World Trade Assn., exec. bd., 1989-91; bd. dirs. Hispanic Coun., Erie, 1985-88; bd. dirs. Ea. Maine chpt. ARC. Mem. Am. Assn. Internat. Execs. in Export Mgmt., Rotary (chair pub. rels. com., sch. liaison 1991-92, internat. trade, exec. bd. Bangor chpt.), Phi Kappa Phi. Office: Loeb Sullivan Sch Internat Bus Divsn of Bus Maine Martime Acad Castine ME 04420-0001

POTTER, ANDREW JAY, mathematics educator; b. Marshall, Tex., Oct. 28, 1964; s. Thomas Preston and Martha Jane (Weaver) P.; m. Jeannette M. Altus, May 16, 1992. BS, Tex. Wesleyan Coll., 1986; MS, U. Ill., 1987; PhD, U. Tex., 1997. Instr. math. Howard Payne U., Brownwood, Tex., 1987-92, asst. prof., 1992-95; asst. prof. math. Hardin-Simmons U., Abilene, Tex., 1995—98, assoc. prof., 1998—. Precinct del. Brown County Republican Party, Brownwood, 1988. Mem. Am. Math. Soc., Math. Assn. Am. (Tex. sect.), Game Theory Soc., Quadrangle Club, Alpha Lamda Delta. Republican. Baptist. Office: Hardin-Simmons U Math Dept PO Box 16060 Abilene TX 79698-0001

POTTER, CHARLOTTE ANN, health education educator, physical education educator; b. Sept. 21, 1943; d. Charles Douglas and Jessie (Lewallen) Faulkner; m. Gary D. Potter, Dec. 24, 1962; 1 child, Bill Douglas. BS in Health and Phys. Edn., Tex. A&M U., 1972, MS in Health and Phys. Edn., 1975. With Westinghouse Corp., 1965; sec. dept. microbiology U. Ky., 1966-67; sec. dept. poultry sci. Tex. A&M U., 1968-69, tchr. dept. phys. edn., 1973; tchr. health and phys. edn. dept. College Station Ind. Schs., A&M Consolidated High Sch., 1973—, dept. head health and phys. edn., coord. intramurals, 1973—, student tchr. supr., 1974—. Guest lectr. Tex. A&M U., College Station, 1993—. Adult leader Equestrian 4-H Club, 1971-83; vol. College Station Little League Baseball, 1971-81; vol. sch. health College Station Ind. Sch. Dist., 1972, com. chmn. PTO South Knoll, 1972-76; cardiopulmonary resuscitation instr. vol., 1972—; vol. Tex. A&M U. Horseman's Assn., 1982—; vol. Phoebe's Home Toy, 1989—. Mem. AAHPER, NEA, Nat. Assn. Secondary Sch. Prins., Am. Heart Assn., Assn. for Advancement Health Edn., Tex. AHPERD, Tex. Edn. Assn., College Station Edn. Assn., Ctrl. Tex. Assn. Student Coun. Sponsors, Tex. Assn. Student Coun. Sponsors, Tex. A&M Assn. Former Students, Am. Sch. Health Assn., Tex. Sch. Health Assn., Ctrl. Tex. Long Ears Assn., Am. Donkey and Mule Assn., S.W. Donkey and Mule Assn., Gulf Coast Donkey and Mule Assn., Delta Psi Kappa, Delta Kappa Gamma. Avocation: training and showing mules in driving events. Home: 5609 Straub Rd College Station TX 77845-6966

POTTER, ELIZABETH STONE, academic administrator; b. Mount Kisco, N.Y., Oct. 18, 1931; d. Ralph Emerson and Elizabeth (Fleming) Stone; m. Harold David Potter, Aug. 1, 1953; children: David Stone, Nicholas Fleming. BA, Wellesley Coll., 1953. Tchr. Spence Sch., N.Y.C., 1960-62; from audiovisual head to asst. to the mid. sch. head Chapin Sch., N.Y.C., 1970-94, sci. tchr., sci. coord., 1970-2000, ret., 2000. Evaluator NYSAIS, N.Y.C., 1994-95. Trustee Leopold Schepp Found., 2000—. Avocations: reading, skiing, tennis, swimming, gardening. Home: 220 Mountain Rd Box 27 Norfolk CT 06058-0027 E-mail: esp1034@cs.com.

POTTER, JANICE BABER, retired school superintendent, educator; b. Roann, Ind., May 15, 1938; d. Matthew and Emma E. (Shillinger) Baber; m. Marcus L. Potter III, Aug. 17, 1957; children: Susan, Julie. MS, No. Ill. U., 1972, CAS, 1976, EdD in Ednl. Adminstrn., 1979. Cert. spl. edn. tchr., chief sch. bus. ofcl., supt., Ill. Tchr. Winfield (Ill.) Pub. Schs., 1969-76; owner, operator Formative Yr. presch., Wheaton, Ill., 1976-79; asst. supr. Bloomingdale (Ill.) Pub. Schs., 1979-81; asst. dir./bus. mgr. So. Met. Assn., Harvey, Ill., 1981-84; supt. Lisbon Grade Sch., 1984-87, 95-97, South Holland Sch. dist., 1987-89; mem. faculty Nat. Coll. Edn., 1970-90, Coll. Du Page, 1972-90. Deacon, Presbyn. Ch. Mem. ASCD, Am. Assn. Sch. Adminst., Ill. Assn. Sch. Bus. Officers, Assn. Children Learning Disabilities, Ill. Women Adminstrs. Home: 28W070 Mack Rd Wheaton IL 60187-6073

POTTER, ROBERT WALLACE, JR., assistant principal, educator; b. Springfield, Mass., Aug. 15, 1947; s. Robert Wallace and Mary Louise (Tilli) P.; m. Betsy Rachael Coleman, Sept. 12, 1981; children: Christopher Coleman, Mary Elizabeth. BA cum laude, St. Anselm Coll., 1969; MEd, Keene State Coll., 1978. Tchr. St. Catherine Sch., Manchester, N.H., 1969-70, St. Patrick Sch., Jaffrey, N.H., 1970-74; tchr. social studies Antrim (N.H.) Mid. Sch., 1974-89, prin., 1978-89, Jaffrey-Rindge Mid. Sch., 1989-92, Athol (Mass.) Mid. Sch., 1992-94, Belmont Mid. Sch., 1994-96; asst. prin. Hawthorne Brook Mid. Sch., Townsend, Mass., 1996-98, Wilton-Lyndeborough Mid./H.S., NH, 1998—. Sec.-treas. Jaffrey War Meml. Com., 1983—; vice chmn. Jaffrey Planning Bd., 1983-84, chmn., 1984-86, vice chmn., 1986-91; mem. bandstand restoration com., Jaffrey, 1986-87, Jaffrey Hist. Dist. Commn., 1986-88; dir. Jaffrey-Gilmore Found., 1985—; incorporator Cathedral of Pines, Rindge, N.H., 1992-96. Mem. NEA, ASCD, New Eng. League Mid. Schs. (recognitions com.), Mass. Tchrs. Assn., N.H. Adminstrs. Assn., N.H. Assn. Secondary Sch. Prins., N.H. Assn. Curriculum and Devel., Contoocook Valley Adminstrs. Orgn. (pres. 1983-86), Jaffrey C. of C. (corr. sec. 1983-85, pres. 1985-86, dir. 1986-88, chmn. edn. com. 1989-92), Jaffrey Tree Farm Com. (sec. 1987-90), Rotary, Thorndike Club (bd. dirs. 1996-2002), Pi Gamma Mu. Republican. Roman Catholic. Home: 10 Wheeler St Jaffrey NH 03452-6566 Office: Wilton-Lyndeborough Mid/H S 56 School Rd Wilton NH 03086 E-mail: pottercole@prodigy.net.

POTTERTON, BARBARA ALICE, artist, educator, illustrator; b. San Francisco, Feb. 17, 1930; d, Dale Howard and Marjorie Louise (Wilson) Drullinger; m. Kenneth Eugene Potterton, May 30, 1948; children: Kathleen Dale Millen, Kenneth Leon. Student, San Francisco Jr. Coll., 1947-48. Exclusive Seascape artist for the following galleries: Mendocino (Calif.) Art Ctr., 1965-73, Gallery Mendocino, 1973-90, Jack London Sq. Gallery, Oakland, Calif., 1978-80, Village Artistry, Carmel, Calif., 1979, Winters Gallery, 1980-83, Calico Whale Gallery, Mendocino, 1991-95, Franki Waters Gallery, Bodega Bay, Calif., 1995-96, Color and Light, Mendocino, 1996-97, Gallery One, Mendocino, 1997-2000; tchr. Gallery Mendocino, Plein Air Class, 1975-85, pvt. studio classes, Rancho Cordova, Calif., 1989—; workshop lectr., demonstrator Lincoln City (Oreg.) Art Ctr., 1979, Golden Valley Art Ctr. Yuba City, Calif., 1983-85. Artist specializing in seascape paintings: over 1500 of her paintings are in private collections throughout the world; illustrator: (childrens' books) Song of the Calico Whale, 1995, Watch Out for Tule Petunia, 1997; (interdisciplinary study unit) Journey to Africa, 1996. Recipient Best of Show awards, Roseville, Calif. Art Ctr. 1970, Stanford Ctr., Palo Alto, Calif., 1975; one-woman show Calif. State U., Sacramento, 1978. Mem. Crocker Art Mus., Soc. Marine Painters (Merit award 1970), Nat. Mus. Women in Arts, N.Y. Met. Mus. of Art (assoc.). Avocations: writing, reading, music, gardening, bird watching. Home: 11150 Trinity River Dr #53 Rancho Cordova CA 95670

POTTHAST, RAY JOSEPH, secondary education educator; b. Highland, Ill., Mar. 15, 1939; s. Raymond W. and Emma (Lunitz) P.; m. Gladys Federer, June 1, 1963. BS, Ill. State U., 1962; MEd, St. Louis U., 1966; postgrad., So. Ill. U., 1973, U. Ill., 1971. Cert. secondary tchr., Ill. Bus. tchr. Carl Sandburg High Sch., Orland Park, Ill., 1962; bus. tchr. and student coun. advisor Roxana (Ill.) High Sch., 1962-70; office occupations coord. Collinsville (Ill.) Area Vocat. Ctr., 1970-87; tchr. acctg. and word processing, bus. dept. chmn. Collinsville High Sch. & Area Vocat. Ctr., 1987—. Mem. adv. coun. bus. edn. Ill. State Bd. Edn., Springfield, 1986-87; advisor secondary Sch. Belleville Area Coll.-Secretarial Studies, 1990—; v.p. Travel One, Inc., Highland, Ill., 1986—. Sec. St. Mary's Elem. Sch. Bd. Edn., Edwardsville, Ill., 1991—. With USAR, 1957-61. Recipient Joseph Cronin Student Svc. award Ill. Office Edn., 1976, Grace E. Sewing Svc. award Kaskaskia Dist. Student Couns., 1978, Ill. award merit Ill. State Bd. Edn., 1990-91, Excellence in Teaching award So. Ill. U., 1990-91. Mem. NEA, Am. Vocat. Assn., Ill. Edn. Assn., Ill. Bus. Edn. Assn., Nat. Bus. Edn. Assn., Collinsville C. of C. (Meritorious Svc. award, 1989), Collinsville Edn. Assn., S.-W. Area Bus. Edn. Assn. Avocations: golf, tennis, sporting events, bicycling, computer operations. Home: 407 Harvard Dr Edwardsville IL 62025-2667

POTTS, GLENDA RUE, music educator; b. Butler, Ala., Nov. 26; d. Jennings Herschel and Erma Rue (Holdridge) Moseley; m. Billy Wayne Blackwell, June 23, 1963 (div. Aug. 1977); children: William Stephen, Melton Jennings; m. Willis Jones Potts, Jr., July 13, 1985; 1 stepchild, Timothy Brendon. BM in Music, Auburn U., 1963. Organist Beverly Meth. Ch., Birmingham, 1964-65; music tchr. grades 3-8 Birmingham Pub. Schs., 1964-65; music tchr. grades 7-9 Chattanooga Pub. Schs., 1965-66; tchr., owner piano/pipe organ studio Kreative Keyboards, Prattville, Ala., 1967-93, Savannah, 1993-99, Rome, Ga., 1999—. Pipe organist 1st Bapt. Ch., Prattville, 1969-85, 87-93, music asst. dir., 1980-85; pianist, dir. children's choirs, asst. organist Bull St. Bapt. Ch., Savannah, 1995-99; sec., mem. chair Savannah Symphony Women's Guild, 1993-99; soprano Savannah Symphony Chorale, 1993-94; mem. chair Savannah Newcomer's, 1994-95; substitute organist and pianist First Baptist Ch., Rome, Ga., 2000-. Honored as one of Top 400 Women Grads. of Centennial of Admission of Women Students, Auburn U., 1992. Mem. Ga. Music Tchrs. Assn. (pres. Savannah chpt. 1997-99, pres. Rome chpt. 2001-03, treas. 2003—), Music Tchrs. Nat. Assn. (nat. and state cert. tchr. and adjudicator), Nat. Guild of Piano Tchrs. (nat. cert. tchr. and adjudicator, established audition ctrs., chmn. Prattville 1967-93, Rome area fall 2001—, Hall of Fame 1990), Am. Coll. Musicians. Republican. Baptist. Home: 2614 Horseleg Creek Rd SW Rome GA 30165-8583 E-mail: glenda@itxmail.net.

POTTS, MARTHA LOU, elementary education educator; b. Enid, Okla., May 30, 1939; d. Hugh David and Luaddie (Williamson) P. BA, Northwestern Okla. U., 1961; postgrad., U. Hawaii, 1966, Phillips U., 1967, 75, Citadel, 1980. Tchr. music pub. schs., Vici, Okla., 1961-62, Enid, 1962-67, Tulsa, 1987-88, Garden City, Kans., 1967-70, Dept. Def., Iwakuni, Japan, 1970-76, pub. schs., Charleston, S.C., 1976-86, Hudson, N.H., 1986-87, San Antonio, 1988—. Mem. tribal coun. Tex. Cherokee and assoc. bands. Vol. Cancer Soc., 1977-87, Dem. Party, Charleston, Enid, San Antonio, 1977-97, Neighborhood Watch, San Antonio, 1990-97; mem. tribal coun. Tex. Cherokees Associated Bands, 1998—. Mem. Am. Assn. Profl. Educators, Music Educators Nat. Conf., Am. String Tchrs. Assn. (People to People award 1997), Tex. Orch. Dirs. Assn., Japanese Am. Cultural Soc., Irish Am. Cultural Soc., Tex. Rangers Assn., Sons and Daus. of Cherokee Strip, Bexar County Geneal. Soc. Civil War Round Table. Roman Catholic. Avocations: traveling, genealogy, civil war. Home: 12647 Sandtrap St San Antonio TX 78217-1822 Office: Connell Middle Sch 400 Hot Wells Blvd San Antonio TX 78223-2602

POTTS, ROBERT LESLIE, academic administrator; b. Jan. 30, 1944; s. Frank Vines and Helen Ruth (Butler) Potts; m. Irene Elisabeth Johansson, Aug. 22, 1965; children: Julia Anna, Robert Leslie. BA, So. Coll., 1966; JD, U. Ala., 1969; LLM, Harvard U., 1971. Law clk. to chief judge U.S. Dist. Ct. (no. dist.) Ala., 1969—70; rschr. Herrick, Smith, Donald, Farley & Ketchum, Boston, 1970—71; lectr. Boston U., 1971, U. Ala., 1973—75, 1988; ptnr. Potts & Young, Florence, Ala., 1971—84; gen. counsel U. Ala. Sys., 1984—89; pres. U. North Ala., 1990—. Mem. Nat. Adv. Com. on Instnl. Quality and Integrity, 1994—2001; com. on colls. So. Assn. Colls. and Schs., 2001—; chmn. Nat. ROTC subcom. for Sec. of Army, 1999—2001; adv. com. rules of civil procedure Ala. Supreme Ct., 1973—88; chmn. Ala. Bd. Bar Examiners, 1983—86, Ala. Coun. Coll. and Univ. Pres., 2001—03, Nat. Conf. Bar Examiners, 1994—95. Contbr. numerous articles to profl. jours., edn. and schs. Trustee Ala. State U., 1976—79, Oakwood Coll., 1978—81; pres. Ala. Higher Edn. Loan Corp., 1988—93. Mem.: ABA (ho. of dels. 2001—), Am. Assn. State Colls. and Univs. (bd. dirs. 2002—), Ala. Bar Assn. (pres. young lawyers sect. 1979—80). Office: U North Ala PO Box 5004 Florence AL 35632-0001 Business E-Mail: rlpotts@una.edu.

POULIOT, ASSUNTA GALLUCCI, retired business school owner and director, consultant; b. West Warwick, R.I., Aug. 14, 1937; d. Michael and Angelina (DeCesare) Gallucci; m. Joseph F. Pouliot Jr., July 4, 1961; children: Brenda, Mark, Jill, Michele. BS, U. R.I., 1959; MS, U. R.I., 1971. Bus. tchr. Cranston High Sch., R.I., 1959-61; bus. dept. chmn. Chariho Regional High Sch., Wood River Junction, R.I., 1961-73; instr. U. R.I., Kingston, 1973-78; founder, dir. Ocean State Bus. Inst., Wakefield, R.I., 1977-95, fin. aid cons., 1995—, ednl. cons., 1996—. Dir. Fleet Nat. Bank, 1985-91; bd. mgrs. Bank of New Eng., 1984-85; commr. Accrediting Coun. Ind. Colls. and Schs., 1995-98, chair accreditation com. team visits, 1998-2001, intermediate rev. com., 2000-01, rev. bd., 2000—; spkr. in field including Glencoe/McGraw-Hill Pub. Co., 1995—. Ednl. author, Glencoe McGraw Hill Pub. Co., 1999-2002. Pres. St. Francis Women's Club, Wakefield, 1975; sec. St. Francis Parish Coun., Wakefield, 1980; mem. Econ. Devel. Commn., Wakefield, 1981-85; mem. South County Hosp. Corp., Wakefield, 1978-97; fin. dir. Bus. and Profl. Women's Club, Wakefield, 1982-84; chmn. Ladies Golf Charity, 1985-91; mem. Computer Info. Systems Com., Chariho Regional Career and Tech. Ctr. Mem. R.I. Bus. Edn. Assn. (newsletter editor 1979-81), New Eng. Bus. Coll. Assn. (sec. 1984-86, pres. 1985-87), R.I. Assn. Career and Tech. Schs. (treas., bd. dirs. 1979-95), Eastern Bus. Edn. Assn. (conf. leader), Nat. Bus. Edn. Assn. (conf. leader), Career Coll. Assn. (conv. speaker, pub. rels. com., govt. rels. com., membership com., key mem., nominating com., evaluator), Assn. Colls. and Schs. (commr. commn. on postsecondary schs. accreditation 1994-98), R.I. Women's Golf Assn., Am. Cancer Soc., U. R.I. Alumni Assn. (Excellence Bus. award 1992), Phi Kappa Phi, Delta Pi Epsilon (pres., newsletter editor). Clubs: Point Judith Country (past ladies golf chmn., R.I. Women's golf rep.). Roman Catholic. Avocations: golfing, gardening. Home and Office: 137 Kenyon Ave Wakefield RI 02879-4242 Office: 15835 Sandy Point Dr Fort Myers FL 33917-5464 E-mail: sjpouliot@aol.com.

POUNCEY, PETER RICHARD, academic administrator, classics educator; b. Tsingtao, Shantung, China, Oct. 1, 1937; came to U.S., 1964; s. Cecil Alan and Eugenie Marde (Lintilhac) P.; m. Bethanne McNally, June 25, 1966; 1 son, Christian; m. Susan Rieger, Mar. 21, 1973; 1 dau., Margaret; m. Katherine Dalsimer, June 9, 1990. Lic. Phil., Heythrop Coll., Eng., 1960; BA, Oxford U., Eng., 1964, MA, 1967; PhD, Columbia U., 1969; AM (hon.), Amherst Coll., 1985; LLD (hon.), Williams Coll., 1985; LHD (hon.), Doshisha U., 1987; LLD (hon.), Wesleyan U., 1989, Amherst (Mass.) Coll., 1995; LHD (hon.), Trinity Coll., 1990. Instr. classics Fordham U., Bronx, N.Y., 1964-67; asst. prof. Columbia U., N.Y.C., 1969-71, dean Columbia Coll., 1972-76, assoc. prof., 1977-83, prof. classics, 1983-84; pres. Amherst (Mass.) Coll., Mass., 1984-94, pres. emeritus, 1994—, prof. classics, 1994—, Fobes prof. Greek, 1995—. Cons. classical lit. Columbia Ency., 1970-73; trustee Columbia Univ. Press, 1972-75 Author: The Necessities of War: A Study of Thucydides' Pessimism, 1980 (Lionel Trilling award 1981). Trustee Brit.-Am. Edn. Found., N.Y.C., 1971-75. Recipient Great Tchr. award Soc. Columbia Grads., 1983 Mem. Am. Philol. Assn., Phi Beta Kappa

POUNDS, JANICE JONES, elementary education educator; b. Palatka, Fla., May 31, 1953; d. Wallace Linwood and Florence (Warwick) Jones; m. Gary Stephen, Sept. 2, 1973; children: G. Stephen, Kathryn, Jonathan. BEd, U. Fla., 1975; MEd, U. North Fla., 1987. Tchr. Putnam County Schs., Palatka, 1975-80, curriculum resource tchr., 1980-92, tchr. on spl. assignment, 1993—95; asst. prin. Palatka (Fla.) H.S., 1995—99; prin. Jenkins Middle Sch., Palatka, 1999—. Cons. for parenting workshops at local chs., various schs., Palatka, 1989—. Sunday sch. tchr. St. Monica's Cath. Ch., Palatka, 1980-93. Named to Outstanding Young Women of Am., 1987. Democrat. Avocations: water skiing, bicycling, travel, reading. Home: PO Box 39 Palatka FL 32178-0039 Office: Jenkins Middle Sch 1100 N 19th St Palatka FL 32177

POWELL, CAROLYN WILKERSON, music educator; b. Hamburg, Ark., Oct. 9, 1920; d. Claude Kelly and Mildred (Hall) Wilkerson; m. Charles Luke Powell, Dec. 12, 1923; children: Charles Luke Jr., James Davis, Mark Wilkerson, Robert Hall. AB, Ctrl. Meth. Coll., Fayette, Mo., 1942; MA in Tchg., U. N.C., 1970. Life tchg. cert., Mo.; cert. tchr., N.C. Choral dir. Maplewood-Richmond Heights Sch., St. Louis, 1943-45; pvt. piano tchr., Greensboro, N.C., 1951-63; organist Presbyn. and Meth. chs., Greensboro, 1950-61; dir. ch. youth choirs, Greensboro, 1958-61; choral and humanities tchr. Page H.S., Greensboro, 1963-67; choral dir. Githens Jr. H.S., Durham, N.C., 1967-80; organist St. Peter's Episcopal Ch., Altavista, Va., 1981-83. Chmn. Dist. Choral Festival N.C. Dist., 1968-78; accompanist and music dir. Altavista Little Theatre Altavista, Va., 1981-83. Sunday and vacation schs. tchr., organist Grace Meth. Ch., Greensboro; den mother Boy Scouts Am., Greensboro, 1951-57; mem. Chapel Hill Preservation Soc., 1985—; vol., chapel organist, pediat. tutor U. N.C. Hosps., Chapel Hill, 1984-89; organist Episcopal ch. svc. Carol Woods Retirement Cmty., Chapel Hill, 1999—; mem. Chapel Hill Hist. Soc. Mem. NEA, AAUW, Music Educators Nat. Conf., Am. Organists Guild, Classroom Tchrs. Assn., Ackland Art Mus. Assn., Chapel Hill Hist. Soc., Nat. Federated Music Club Euterpe, Chapel Hill Country Club, U. Woman's Club, The Carolina Club, Delta Kappa Gamma. Avocations: reading, golf, needlework, gardening, travel and antiques. Home: 750 Weaver Dairy Rd Apt 142 Chapel Hill NC 27514-1440

POWELL, CHRISTA RUTH, educational training executive; b. Dodgeville, Wis., Mar. 3, 1957; d. Robert Franklin and RAchel Jean (Edge) Powell; m. Fred L. Neff, Sept. 10, 1989; 1 child, Rosalena Pauline Neff. BSN, Viterbo Coll., 1979. RN, Minn. Staff nurse Abbott Northwestern Hosp., Mpls., 1979-81, 83-87, asst. head nurse, 1981-83; legal asst. Hyatt Legal Asst., St. Paul, 1981-83, comms. dir. Minn. region, 1983-86; office coord. Neff Law Firm, P.A., Mpls., 1986—; pres., bd. dirs. Profl. Devel. Inst., Bloomington, Minn., 1994—. Cons. A Basic Legal Svc., Bloomington, 1990-94. Editor: Mysterious Persons, 1990, Great Puzzles in History, 1990; co-host TV program Great Puzzles in History, 1989-91. Investigator ethics com. Hennepin County Bar, Mpls., 1989-90; v.p. Endless Fist Soc., Inc. Scholar Gerry Graber Scholarship Com., 1975; State of Wis. honors grantee, 1975. Mem. Edina C. of C. Avocations: reading, sewing, walking, knitting, gardening. Home: 4515 Andover Rd Edina MN 55435-4031 Office: Neff Law Firm PA 7760 France Ave S Bloomington MN 55435-5800

POWELL, KARAN HINMAN, academic administrator; b. Great Lakes, Ill., May 25, 1953; d. David Daniel and Mary Anne (Buretz) Hinman; m. David Leonidas Powell, Feb. 14, 1987; children: Meloni (dec.), Erik. BS, We. Ill. U., 1975; MDiv, B Sacred Theology (hon.), Loyola U., Chgo., 1981; PhD, George Mason U., 1998. Cert. tchr., Ill., Va.; cert. orgn. devel. profl. Tchr. St. Hugh Cath. Sch., Lyons, Ill., 1975-77, Lay Ministry Tng. Program, Chgo., 1980-81, Jackson, Miss., 1981-83; adminstr. Inst. Creation Centered Spirituality Mundelein Coll., Chgo., 1978-79; exec. dir. North Am. Forum Catechumenate, Washington, 1983-88; dir. Profl. Devel. Program, tchr. theol. studies, tng. cons., exec. devel., direct contact tng. Georgetown U., Washington, 1988-94, dir. organization devel. program, 1991-95, mng. acad. dir., 1995, assoc. dean, 1998—, v.p., chief learning officer. Assoc. pastor Annunciation Cath. Ch., Columbus, Miss., 1981-83; cons. dioceses in U.S., Can., 1983—; cons. to fed. govt., profit and non-profit corps.; pres. Powel and Assocs., 1994—; cons. leadership devel. Am. Mgmt. Systems Inc., 1998—; v.p., dir., exec. dir., chief learning officer

AMS U. Author: How to Form a Catechumenate Team, 1985; editor: Breaking Open the Word of God series, 1986-88, The Ninety Days, 1989; contbr. articles Cath. mags.; spkr. in field. Active on Blessed Sacrament RCIA Team, Alexandria, Va., 1984-86; apptd. to Va. State Child Fatality Review Team, 1996-99, 99—. Recipient tchr.'s scholarship State of Ill., 1971-75, cert. recognition KC, Columbus, Miss., 1982; George Mason U. fellow, 1994-97. Mem. ASTD, Orgn. Devel. Inst., Acad. of Mgmt., Assn. Psychol. Type, N.Am. Forum Catechumenate (cons. 1982—), Cath. Edn. Future's Project (mem. com. 1985-88, Va. SIDS Alliance, 1991—, state steering com. 1993-94, bd. dirs., 1993-94, pres. 1994-96), Orgn. Devel. Network (presenter nat. conf. 1996, 97), Internat. Acad. Bus. (reviewer for spirituality and work 1998), Acad. Mgmt. (reviewer mgmt. edn. divsn. 1998). Democrat. Avocations: sailing, music, crafts, travel, foreign exchange student hosting. Office: 4000 Legato Rd Fl 10 Fairfax VA 22033-4055 E-mail: karan_powell@ams.com.

POWELL, KENNETH GRANT, aerospace engineering educator; b. Euclid, Ohio, July 3, 1960; s. Thomas Edward and Mary Catherine (Byrum) P.; m. Susanne Maria Krummel, Aug. 31, 1991; children: Jasmine Tara, Ryan Grant, Nicole Maia. SB in Math., SB in Aeronautics, MIT, 1982, SM in Aeronautics, 1984, ScD in Aeronautics, 1987. Asst. prof. dept. aerospace engrng. U. Mich., Ann Arbor, 1987-93, assoc. prof. dept. aerospace engrng., 1993-2000, prof. dept. aerospace engrng., 2000—. Lectr. Von Karman Inst. for Fluid Dynamics, Brussels, 1990, 96; cons. Ford Motors, Dearborn, Mich., 1992-95; cons. Detroit Edison, 1996-98; exec. dir. Francois-Xavier Bagnoud Prize Bd., 1998—. Named Presdl. Young investigator NSF, 1988; recipient Tchg. Excellence award U. Mich. Coll. Engrng., 1992, Outstanding Tchg. award Tau Beta Pi, 1999, Tchg. Excellence award Sigma Gamma Tau, 1989, 95. Mem. AIAA (sr. mem.), Tau Beta Pi, Sigma Xi, Sigma Gamma Tau. Home: 5531 Spring Hill Dr Ann Arbor MI 48105-9552 Office: U Mich Dept of Aerospace Engring Ann Arbor MI 48109

POWELL, LILLIAN MARIE, retired music educator; b. DeLand, Fla., June 1, 1927; d. Francis Charles and Jessie Agnes (Niven) P.; m. James Armbruster, May 1950 (div. 1957); children: Jeffrey L. Armbruster, Leslie J. Armbruster; m. Dwight M. Liller, Dec. 8, 1957 (div. June 1972). B. Pub. Sch. Music, Capital U., 1950; MA, Ohio State U., 1957. Lic. tchr., N.Y., N.J., Va., Ohio. Vocal and instrumental music tchr. Community Sch., Stoutsville, Ohio, 1949-50, Roosevelt Jr. High Sch., Newark, 1950-51; elem. music tchr. at several schs. Norfolk, Va., 1951-53; music tchr. Naval Base Sch., Guantanomo Bay, Cuba, 1953-55; instr. voice Otterbein Coll., Ohio, 1955-56; music tchr. several elem. and jr. high schs. Lorain, Ohio, 1956-60; music cons. elem. schs. South Orange, N.J., 1960-61; music tchr. elem. schs. Livingston, N.J., 1963-66; music tchr. Roosevelt Jr. high Sch., West Orange, N.J., 1965-72; instr. music lit. County Coll. Morris County, Dover, N.J., 1970-72; elem. sch. tchr. music Pub. Sch. 86, Jamaica Heights, N.Y., 1973-75; tchr. Satellite East Jr. High Sch. for Gifted, Bklyn., 1977-89, Stephen Halsey Jr. High Sch., N.Y.C., 1989-96, ret., 1996. Music theater dir. Children's Theater, Guantanamo Bay, 1953-55; ch. choir dir. Naval Base Chapel, Guantanano Bay, 1953-55; ch. choir dir., soloist Congregational Ch., Lorain, Ohio, 1956-60; ch. soloist, organist Religious Sci. Ch., Morristown, Ohio. CORO assoc. orgn. activities CORO Leadership Found., Manhattan, N.Y., 1985—; vol. vocal/drama coaching Vocal Students for Profl. Goals and Producing Major Musical Prodn., Bklyn., 1977-85. Named Outstanding Woman of State of N.Y., N.Y. State Senate, 1984. Eckankar. Avocations: equestrian activities, astrology, writing, musical composition. Home: 4551 College Ave Ellicott City MD 21043-6817 E-mail: LeeMPowell@aol.com.

POWELL, LINDA, school system administrator; BA in English Edn., Jersey City State Coll., 1968; MS in Secondary Edn., Ind. U., 1980; diploma in Supt. Licensure, Coll. St. Thomas, 1988. Tchr. English No. Valley Regional HS, Old Tappan, NJ; asst. prin. Red Cloud Indian K-8 Sch., Pine Ridge, SD, tchr.; prin. City High Mid. Sch. Grand Rapids (Mich.) Pub. Schs.; asst., interim and supt. schs. Dist. 281, New Hope, Pa.; regional dir. tech. Computer Curriculum Corp.; commr. of edn. Minn. Dept. Edn., 1993—95; supt. schs. Scottsdale, Ariz., 1996—2000, Pocatello, Idaho, 2000—. Cons. in field.*

POWELL, LINDA STERMER, mathematics educator secondary schools; b. Bryan, Tex., Oct. 28, 1949; d. Raymond Andrew and Gladys Frieda (Hoelscher) Stermer; m. James Richard Powell, June 7, 1969; children: Scott Jarvis, Paige Elizabeth. BA, U. Tex., 1971. Cert. tchr., Tex. Tchr. Beckendorf Intermediate Sch., Tomball, Tex., 1980-82, Tomball H.S., 1982-92, Cypress Falls H.S., Cy-Fair Ind. H.S. Dist., Houston, 1992-93, Waller (Tex.) Ind. Sch. Dis, 1993—, chmn. dept. math., 2001—. Team leader Cy-Falls H.S., Houston, 1992-93. 4H Club Mgr., Magnolia, Tex., 1990-92. Nominee for Presidential award for Math. and Sci. Edn., 1994-95. Mem. Nat. Coun. Tchrs. of Math., Coun. for Advancement of Math. Tchrs. Republican. Roman Catholic. Home: 342 Creekwood Dr W Montgomery TX 77356 Office: Waller HS 2402 Waller St Waller TX 77484-8402 E-mail: lpowell@waller.isd.esc4.net.

POWELL, PATRICIA ANN, secondary school educator; b. Covington, Ga., Apr. 6, 1956; d. John Doyle Sr. and Pauline Josephine (Thompson) Dunn; m. Jackie Lee Powell, May 10, 1980; 1 child, Jackie Lee II. BS, Lee U., 1980; MEd in Adminstrn. and Supervision, U. Tenn., 1993. Br. loan officer Am. Nat. Bank and Trust, Chattanooga, 1980—81; tchr. math., bus. edn. Hamilton County Sch. Sys., Chattanooga, 1983-85, tchr. math., 1993-96; customer svc. rep. First Union Nat. Bank, Atlanta, 1986-88; instr. tech. bus., typing DeKalb County Schs., Decatur, Ga., 1989; grad. asst. U. Tenn., Chattanooga, 1991-93; tchr. career tech. Fulton County Sch. Sys., Atlanta, 1996-98, E.X.C.E.L. coord., 1998-99, mid. sch. tchr., 2002—; instr. career tech./bus. DeKalb County Sch. Sys., 2000—02. Instr. English, bus. math. and bus. skills Urban League Bus. Skills Tng. Ctr., Chattanooga; mem. adj. faculty Chattanooga State Tech. CC, 1991—92; joint stds. rep. sch. consolidation, 1995—96; mem. exec. bd. Vocat. Opportunity Clubs Am., 1998—99; active Ga. Home Sch. Edn. Assn., 1999—2000. Co-author: Career Orientation-Grade 8, 1985 (monetary award 1984-85); singer African Americans Against Blood Disorders Benefit, Atlanta, 1994. Singer, Mayor's Office Performing Artists Against Drugs, Atlanta, 1990; vol. Chattanooga Comty. Kitchen, 1990—; tutor, coord. math., reading United Way's Adult Reading Program, Chattanooga, 1991—; instr. aerobics Am. Heart Assn., Chattanooga, 1991—; vol. Warner Park Zoo, Chattanooga; treas. Looking to the Word Ministries, Inc., 1985-94; v.p. parents group 1st Cumberland Child Devel. Ctr., 1992-94; sch. rep. Diversity Com. for Consol., 1996-97. Outstanding Classroom Tchr. nominee, 1993-94; recipient Black Grad. fellowship U. Tenn., Chattanooga, 1992, 93; named Woman of Yr. and Mrs. Congeniality, Mrs. Chattanooga-Am. Pageant, 1990; Endowment scholar, 1977-78. Mem. AAUW, Am. Vocat. Assn., Nat. Bus. Edn. Assn., Hamilton County Edn. Assn. (chmn. minority affairs com. 1995-97), Chattanooga Area Math. Assn. (v.p. mid. schs. 1996-97), Friends of Zoo Preservation Group, Zoo Atlanta, U. Tenn. Alumni Assn., Delta Sigma Theta, Kappa Delta Pi (pres., v.p. 1993-95, contbg. writer substitute handbook). Avocations: singing, jogging, crafts, sewing, stamp collecting, taikwon do (black belt).

POWELL, RAYMOND WILLIAM, financial planner, school administrator; b. Waterbury, Conn., June 17, 1944; s. Don C. and Kathryn (Linhard) P.; m. Janet Yasinski, June 24, 1967; 1 child, Raymond Joseph. BS, So. Conn. State Coll., New Haven, 1966, MS, 1969; postgrad., U. Bridgeport, Conn. CRP; enrolled agt. CEO R.W. Powell Enterprises, Inc., fin. and tax cons., Prospect, Conn., 1972—; dir.-owner Educators Tax Svc., Watertown, 1972—, Powell's Acctg. Svc., 1975—, Powell's Fin. Planning Svc., 1977—; supt. of schs. Winchester, Conn., 1995—. Contbr. articles to profl. jours. Vice chmn. Watertown Town Coun., 1975-76. Mem. Nat. Assn. Enrolled Agts., Internat. Assn. Fin. Planners, Am. Soc. Tax Cons., Conn. Assn. Enrolled Agts. Democrat. Office: PO Box 7077 42 Waterbury Rd Prospect CT 06712-1238 E-mail: powells.financial@snet.net.

POWELL, REBECCA GAETH, education educator; b. Westlake, Ohio, Oct. 23, 1949; d. John Paul and Ione Roxanne (Poad) Gaeth; m. Jerry Wayne Powell, June 14, 1991; children: Justin Matthew(dec.), Ryan Michael 1 stepchild, Michael Carl. B Music Edn., Coll. of Wooster, Ohio, 1971; MEd, U. N.C., 1976; D in Edn., U. Ky., 1989. Cert. curriculum and instrn. Elem. tchr. Rittman (Ohio) Elem., 1971-72; presch. tchr. YWCA, Durham, N.C., 1974-76; spl. reading tchr. Claxton Elem. Sch., Asheville, N.C., 1977; instr. and dir. reading, cert. program Mars Hill (N.C.) Coll., 1977-80; health educator Hot Springs (N.C.) Health Program, 1984-85; asst. prof. Ky. State U., Frankfort, 1989-93; assoc. prof. Georgetown (Ky.) Coll., 1993-99, prof., 1999—, Marjorie Bauer Stafford endowed chair in edn., 2003. Ky. primary sch. rschr. U. Ky. Inst. on Edn. Reform, Lexington, 1993-99; ednl. cons. Jessamine County Schs., Nicholasville, Ky., 1992-93, Dade County Schs., Miami, Fla., 1995, 99, Bethune Inst., 2002—; tchr. educator, trainer, participant pilot project Ky. Tchr. Internship Program, Frankfort, 1990-2000; chmn. Alliance for Multicultural Edn., Ky., 1993-95; coord. Ctrl. Ky. Whole Lang. Network, 1991-93; mem. Ky. Multicultural Edn. Task Force, 1995, Ky. Edn. Equity Task Force, 1998-2001, mem. Minority Student Achievement Task Force, 2000, mem. Commr.'s Edn. Equity Coun., 2001—; instr./site dir. Ky. Reading Project, 1999-2001; rschr. Collaborative Ctr. Literacy Devel., 1999—. Author: Literacy As A Moral Imperative, 1999, Straight Talk: Growing as Multicultural Educators, 2001, Language, Literacy, and the African American Experience, 2004; contbr. articles to profl. jours. Mem. Woodford County Equity Team, 1997-98; bd. dirs Mother-to-Mother, Lexington, Ky., 1998-2001; mem. adv. coun. Underground R.R. Rsch. Inst., 2002—. Dissertation Year fellow U. Ky., Lexington, 1988-89. Mem. Nat. Assn. Multicultural Edn. (pres. Ky. chpt. 1997-99), Nat. Coun. Tchrs. English, Internat. Reading Assn., Ky. Reading Assn., Ky. Assn. Tchr. Educators. Avocation: reading. Office: Georgetown Coll 400 E College St Georgetown KY 40324-1628 E-mail: Rebecca_Powell@georgetowncollege.edu.

POWELL, SHARON JOYCE, retired physical education educator; b. Whitehall, Wis., July 28, 1937; d. Melvin William and Erna Judith (Senty) Luethi; m. Lawrence Ray Powell, July 9, 1961; children: Scott, Jeffrey. BS, U. Wis., 1959, postgrad., 1964—. Phys. edn. tchr. grades 1-12 Boscobel (Wis.) Pub. Schs., 1959-61; phys. edn. tchr. grades 7-12 Oelwein (Iowa) Pub. Schs., 1961-62; phys. edn. tchr. grades 9-12 Jefferson (Wis.) Pub. Schs., 1963-67; phys. edn. tchr. elem. and sr. high Wisconsin Dells (Wis.) Pub. Schs., 1967-69; phys. edn. tchr. sr. high Waunakee (Wis.) Pub. Schs., 1969-72; substitute tchr. Tomah (Wis.) Pub. Schs., 1972-77, phys. edn. tchr. 10-11th grade, 1977—2002; ret., 2002. Coach sr. high tennis, Tomah (Wis.) Pub. Sch., 1977-84, sr. high softball, 1977-86; substitute tchr., 2002— Adminstrv. bd. United Meth. Ch., 1974—; active Monroe County Reps., Sparta, Wis., 1990-93. Mem. NEA, AAUW (sec. 1984-86, v.p. 1988-90, pres. 1990-92), Wis. Edn. Assn., Tomah Edn. Assn. (co-pres. 1994-96, dept. head 1988-2001), Friends of the Libr. Methodist. Avocations: golfing, reading, gardening, cross country skiing, tennis. Home: 23448 Emperor Ave Tomah WI 54660-9728 Office: Tomah Pub Schs Hwy 16 Tomah WI 54660

POWELL, SUSAN LYNN, secondary educator; b. Hayti, Mo., Oct. 26, 1970; d. Lynn Banks III and Nina R. (Sanders) P. BA, Baldwin-Wallace Coll., 1992. Athletic trainer Baldwin-Wallace Coll., Berea, Ohio, 1990-92, women's intercollegiate volleyball coach, 1993-95; tchr. North Olmstead (Ohio) Mid. Sch., 1992-98; varsity bolleyball coach North Olmsted H.S., 1997; tchr. Cardinal Mooney H.S., Sarasota, Fla., 1998—, chair dept. phys. edn., 2003—. Coach varsity track, volleyball and basketball Cardinal Mooney H.S., 1998—, fall sports asst. athletic dir., 2000—, student gov. moderator, chair, phys. edn. dept., 2003—; mem. selection com. Nat. Honor Soc., 2000—. Vol. tchr. cardiopulmonary resuscitation ARC, 1999—. Mem.: Nat. PTA. Roman Catholic. Avocations: sports, travel, boating. Home: 6415 Westward Place University Park FL 34201 Office: Cardinal Mooney HS 4171 Fruitville Rd Sarasota FL 34232-1618

POWELL, WANDA GARNER, librarian; b. Dresden, Tenn., Nov. 16, 1940; d. Lewis C. and Mary (Coleman) Garner; m. William C. Powell, Oct. 26, 1963; children: Gena Rae, Elizabeth Lewis. BS, U. Tenn., Martin, 1971; MA, Murray (Ky.) State U., 1976. Sec. Bay Bee Shoe Co., Dresden, 1958-67; clk. U. Tenn., Martin, 1967-71; tchr., libr. Gleason (Tenn.) High Sch., 1971-76; libr. Dresden High Sch., 1976—. Career ladder evaluator State of Tenn., Nashville, 1984—85, career ladder III, 1986; pres. Women's Missionary Union, 1986—91. Sponsor Beta Club, 1976—; Chair bd. dirs. Weakley County Pub. Libr., 1993—; treas. Oak Grove Ch., 1999—. Mem.: DAR, Tenn. Assoc. Sch. Librs. (TASL) (sec. 2003), United Teaching Profls., Weakley County Edn. Assn. (pres. 1981—82, mem. exec. bd. 1999—, study coun. tchrs. 1999—), Delta Kappa Gamma (pres. Beta Omega chpt. 1990—92), Phi Delta Kappa. Democrat. Baptist. Home: 5646 Greenfield Hwy 54 Dresden TN 38225-1706

POWERS, ALAN WILLIAM, literature educator; b. Springfield, Mass., Nov. 15, 1944; s. Roger Milton and Ida Maxine (Richardson) P.; m. Susan Elizabeth Mohl, June 1, 1944; children: Emily A. Lori, Tess Powers Brau. AB, Amherst Coll., 1966; MA, U. Minn., 1970, PhD, 1976. Tchg. assoc. U. Minn., Mpls., 1966—71; instr. English, Berkshire C.C., Pittsfield, Mass., 1971—73; asst. prof. Bristol C.C., Fall River, Mass., 1974—79, assoc. prof., 1980—86, prof., 1986—, chair dept. English, 1988—92. Author: Birdtalk, 2002, Westport Soundings, 1995, co-author: Acting Funny in Shakespeare, 1994; composer (choral music) Settings to Yeats & Dylan Thomas, 1996; co-scriptwriter: A Loaded Gun, Keats and His Nightingale, 1986; trans. Candelaio, by Giordano Bruno; contbr. articles to profl. jours. Bd. dirs. New Bedford Unitarian Ch., 1992-97, Mass. Found. for Humanities, 1989-95, N.E. Modern Lang. Assn., 1992-95, Creative TV R.I., 1994-96, New Bedford Unitarian Ch., 1991-96. Rsch. fellow Brown U., Providence, 1979-80, Whiting Found. fellow, Milan & London, 1996, NEH fellow, Naples, Italy, 2000,Breadloaf, Vt., 1990, Golger Libr., 1991, Brown, 1992; Nat. Merit scholar, 1962-66. Mem. ASCAP, N.E. MLA (bd. dirs. 1993-95, del.), Assn. Lit. Scholars and Critics, Shakespeare Assn. Am., Renaissance Soc. Am., Acad. Am. Poets. Avocations: jazz trombone, translating, birdwatching. Office: Bristol C C 777 Elsbree St Fall River MA 02720-7307

POWERS, ANTHONY RICHARD, JR., educational sales professional; b. Chgo., June 14, 1942; s. Anthony Richard and Bernadine Rene (Schwenke) P.; m. Marianne Fugiel, Mar. 15, 1980; children: Kathleen Mary, Anthony Richard III. BA, Quincy Coll., 1964; MS, U. Notre Dame, 1974. Cert. tchr., Ill. Sci. tchr. St. Rene Sch., Chgo., 1964-70; sci. coord. Queen of All Saints Sch., Chgo., 1970-76; sci. and math. product mgr. Ideal Sch. Supply Co., Oak Lawn, Ill., 1976-79, customer svc. mgr., 1980-83, Midwest sales mgr., 1983-85; nat. sales mgr. Ednl. Teaching Aids, Vernon Hills, Ill., 1985-89, v.p., 1989-97; accounts mgr. Numerical Algorithms Group, Downers Grove, Ill., 1997-2001; midwest acct. mgr. Freedom Sci., Vernon Hills, Ill., 2001—, midwest regional mgr., 2001—. Lectr., De Lourdes Coll., Des Plaines, Ill., 1970-78; sci. adviser, Archdiocese of Chgo., 1969-76. Author sci. edn. materials. Pres. Orchard Estates Condominium Assn., 1986-87; chmn. Vernon Hills Fire and Police Commn., 1995—. Mem. Northeastern Ill. Sci. Assn. (pres. 1970-75), U.S. Golf Assn., Internat. Brotherhood Magicians, K.C. Roman Catholic. Avocations: magic, music, golf. Home: 241 Tally Ho Dr Vernon Hills IL 60061-2900 Office: Freedom Sci 241 Tally Ho Dr Vernon Hills IL 60061

POWERS, BRUCE RAYMOND, writer, English language educator, consultant; b. Bklyn., Dec. 10, 1927; s. George Osborne and Gertrude Joan (Bangs) P.; m. Dolores Anne Dawson, July 25, 1969; children: Christopher, Patricia. Student, U. Conn., 1947-49; AB, Brown U., 1951, MA (tuition scholar 1961-62), 1965; postgrad., U. Pa., 1961. Announcer, engr. Sta. WNLC, New London, Conn., 1946-47; tng. officer CIA, Dept. Def., 1951-55; TV sales/svc. rep. NBC, 1955; TV news writer and reporter Movietone News, United Press Assns., Inc., 1955-56; asst. to pres. Gotham-Vladimir Advt., Inc., 1956-57; asst. account exec. D'Arcy Advt. Co., 1957-58; asst. campaign dir. Cmty. Counseling Svcs., Inc., 1958-59; fund-raising campaign dir. Tamblyn & Brown, Inc., 1959-60; instr. Brown U., Providence, 1963-65, Ryerson Poly. Inst., Toronto, 1966, Nazareth Coll., Rochester, N.Y., 1966-67; asst. prof. English and comm. studies Niagara U., Lewiston, N.Y., 1967-86, assoc. prof., 1986-92, prof., 1986-92, chmn. permanent curriculum com. English dept., 1970-71; dir. Film Repertory Ctr., 1971-92, dir. comm. studies program, 1973-87. Prodr., mng. dir. Exptl. Film Retrospective, N.Y. State Coun. of the Arts, Buffalo, 1972; narrator (documentary) Niagara: Fading in the Mist, 1996; panelist, judge Artists Com. 2d World Festival of Animated Films, Zagreb, Yugoslavia, 1974; lectr., vis. artist ARTPARK, Lewiston, N.Y., 1975; project dir. Bicentennial Symposium, N.Y. State Am. Revolution Bicentennial Commn., Buffalo, 1975-76; rsch. assoc. Ctr. Culture and Tech., U. Toronto, 1977-81; keynote spkr. Dupont de Nemours & Co. Health and Safety Conf., Buffalo, 1990; ptnr. Moon Island Documentary Group, 1997—. Co-author: (with Marshall McLuhan) The Global Village, Oxford, 1989; editor The Film and Study Guide, 1973-74. Served with Underwater Demolition Teams, USNR, PTO, 1945-46. Recipient Carpenter prize in elocution Brown U., 1951. Mem. MLA, Underwater Demolitions Teams/Seal Assn. Va. Beach, Broadcast Edn. Assn., Soc. Cinema Studies, Am. Soc. Journalism Sch. Adminstrs., Assn. for Edn. in Journalism and Mass. Comm., Internat. Exptl. Film Soc. (founding pres. 1971-73), Ariz. Sr. Acad. U. Ariz. (Tucson), Western N.Y. Audio-Visual Assn., N.Y. Coll. English Assn., Phi Beta Kappa. Roman Catholic. Home: 915 Sun Valley St North Tonawanda NY 14120-1952

POWERS, DAVID RICHARD, educational administrator; b. Cambridge Springs, Pa., Apr. 5, 1939; s. William Herman and Elouise Fancheon (Fink) P.; m. Mary Julia Ferguson, June 11, 1960. Student, Pa. State U., 1957-60; BA, U. Pitts., 1963, MA, 1965, PhD, 1971. Dir. CAS advising ctr. U. Pitts., 1966-68, asst. dean faculty, 1968-70, asst. to chancellor, 1970-76, assoc. provost, 1976-78, vice provost, 1978-79; v.p. for acad. affairs George Mason U., Fairfax, Va., 1979-82; vice chancellor for acad. affairs W.Va. Bd. Regents, Charleston, 1982-88; exec. dir. Minn. Higher Edn. Coord. Bd., St. Paul, 1989-94, Nebr. Coord. Commn. Post-secondary Edn., Lincoln, 1994—. Prin. author: Making Participatory Management Work, 1983, Higher Education in Partnership with Industry, 1988; contbr. articles to Ednl. Record, Adult Learning, Forum for Applied Rsch. on Pub. Policy. Bd. trustees Western Govs. U. Grantee USOE Faculty Seminar, Taiwan, 1967, ARC Ctr. for Edn. & Rsch. with Industry Appalachian Regional Commn., 1983, Republic of China Sino-Am. Seminar, 1985; recipient Award for Acad. Quality W.Va. Coun. Faculty, 1986. Mem. State Higher Edn. Exec. Officers, Western Coop. Ednl. Telecomm., Civil Air Patrol, Pi Sigma Alpha. Avocation: flying. Home: 16017 Middle Island Dr South Bend NE 68058-4311 Office: Nebr Coord Comm Post Secondary Edn PO Box 95005 Lincoln NE 68509-5005

POWERS, EVELYN MAE, education educator; b. Norfolk, Va., Aug. 4, 1946; d. Albert Earl and Dorothy Mae (Weller) P.; m. Curtis Grubb Fitzhugh, June 21, 1969 (div. 1981). BA in Spanish, James Madison U., 1968; MEd in Curriculum & Instrn., Fgn. Langs., U. Va., 1976, PhD in Social Founds. of Edn., 1985. Spanish teacher pub. high schs., Va., 1969-77; grad. instr., instr. U. Va., Charlottesville, 1977-85; adj. and part-time faculty Va. Commonwealth U., Richmond, 1985-88; asst. prof. edn. Lycoming Coll., Williamsport, Pa., 1988-91; asst. prof. social founds. of edn. E. Carolina U., Greenville, N.C., 1991-98. Mem. Am. Ednl. Studies Assn., N.C. Founds. of Edn. Profs., So. Atlantic Philosophy of Edn. Soc. (yearbook editor 1994-98, archivist 1993-96), Phi Delta Kappa. Home: 19085 Sedley Lodge Rd Rapidan VA 22733-9512

POWERS, L. LINDLEY (L. LINDLEY), communication and theatre arts educator; b. Albany, N.Y., Aug. 19, 1926; d. William Tibbits and Winifred Lispenard (Robb) Powers; AB, Smith Coll., 1948; MA in Speech, U. Wis., 1963, MFA in Theatre Directing, 1963, PhD in Theatre and Related Arts (E.B. Fred fellow), 1968; postdoctoral Episcopal Theol. Sch., 1972-74, Weston Coll. Sch. Theology, 1974-75; m. Davis Spencer, Mar. 5, 1949 (div. 1961); children: Eleanor Tibbits Spencer Tupper, Joseph Allen Powers Spencer; m. Gerald E. Fosbroke, Dec. 17, 1976 (div. 1996). Children's libr. N.Y.C. Public Libr., 1948-49; tchr., Racine, Wis., 1959-61; dir. Wis. 4-H Drama Program, also rsch. asst. U. Wis., 1961-64; instr. U. Wis., 1964-65, 66-67, teaching asst. Sch. Music Opera Workshop, 1965-66; asst. prof. drama Bridgewater (Mass.) State Coll., 1968-69; assoc. prof., dir. grad. study theatre edn. Emerson Coll., Boston, 1969-71, assoc. prof. fine arts, 1971-76, prof., 1977-79, founder, adviser creative svc. interdisciplinary program, 1974-79; adjunct prof. Art and Religious Studies The Union Inst., Cin., 1992-96. Condr. community and conv. workshops in theatre arts; lectr. to clergy and parishes on liturgical experience of myth and symbol; also active in ch. renovation and conducting classes for lay lectors and clergy Dioceses of N.J. and Mass. V.p., bd. dirs. Ch. Home Soc., Boston, 1973-84; sec. Iona Community New World Found., 1977-86; founder, sec., trustee Iona Cornerstone Found., Inc., 1981-96, Iona Cornerstone Found. Ltd., 1982-96; mem. Diocesan Ecumenical Commn., 1980-84, sec., 1980-82; mem. Mass. Council Chs. Jewish Community Conn. Dialogues, 1982-84; lay reader, eucharistic min. Episc. Ch. Mem. AAUP, Iona Community (asso.), Soc. St. John the Evangelist (asso.), Dobbs (dir., mem. exec. com. 1949-57, editor Bull., 1949-57), Smith alumnae assns., U. Wis. Alumni Assn., Conservation Law Found. Mem. Ch. of the Messiah. Author: Proclaim the Word, 1980, also drama ednl. materials. Home: 70 Carey Ln 149 Oyster Pond Rd Falmouth MA 02540-1528

POWERS, PATRICIA KENNETT, piano and organ educator; b. Detroit, Feb. 25, 1925; d. Frank and Dorothy (Hurley) Kennett; m. Jack Powers, Jr., June 4, 1948; 1 child, Brian K. BA in Music, Kalamazoo Coll., 1946; MA in Music History, U. Mich., 1947. Instr. music U. Ark., Fayetteville, 1947-49; pvt. tchr. music, Corpus Christi, Tex., 1953-62, 68-72, Beeville, Tex., 1972-99; ret., 2002. Adj. instr. group piano, theory, applied piano and organ music Bee County Coll., Beeville, 1974-89. Pres. Beeville Concert Assn., 1992-94. Mem. MTNA Music Tchr. Nat. Assn. (nat. cert. music tchr. (NCTM), pres. South Ctrl. divsn. 1992-94, bd. dir. 1994-96, South Ctrl. divsn. rep. to ho. of dels. 1996-98), Tex. Music Tchr. Assn. TMTA (sec. and pres.-elect, pres. 1986-88, former cert. chmn., and South Ctrl. divsn. rep. on nat. cert. bd.), Am. Guild Organists, Music Educators Nat. Conf., Tex. Music Educators Conf., Midland Music Tchr. Assn.; ret. from pvt. tchg., June, 2002. Episcopalian. Avocation: music and computers. Home: 113 Abell Hanger Circle Midland TX 79707 E-mail: ppow@swbell.net.

POWERS, STEPHEN, educational consultant, researcher; b. Bakersfield, Calif., June 10, 1936; s. Robert Boyd and Mildred (Irwin) Powers; m. Gail Marguerite Allen, Dec. 28, 1968; children: Rick, Joseph, Rebecca. BS in Edn., No. Ariz. U., 1959; MA, U. Ariz., Tucson, 1970, MEd, 1972, PhD, 1978. Cert. tchr. Calif., tchr., adminstr., jr. coll. tchr. Policeman City of Bakersfield, 1967—69; tchr. Marana (Ariz.) Pub. Schs., 1969—72; dir. Am. Sch. Belo Horizonte, Brazil, 1972—73; tchr. Nogales (Ariz.) Pub. Schs., 1976—94; rsch. specialist Tucson Unified Sch. Dist., 1975—94; prof. U. Ariz., Phoenix, 1990; founder Creative Rsch. Assocs., Tucson, 1991—, now pres. Contbr. articles to profl. jours. Bd. dirs. Manchester Coll., Oxford U.; internat. evaluator USAID, 1991. Grantee, Nat. Inst. Edn., 1980. Mem.: Am. Statis. Assn., Royal Statis. Soc. (U.K. chpt.), Am. Ednl. Rsch. Assn., Bahai. Office: 2030 E Broadway Blvd Ste 221 Tucson AZ 85719-5909

POYNOR, ROBERT ALLEN, JR., retired guidance counselor; b. Franklin, Tenn., Aug. 2, 1939; s. Robert Allen and Agnes Elizabeth (Gillespie) P.; m. Martha Bellah Stark, July 12, 1996; 1 child, Melissa Dawn Hay. BA, Belmont Coll., Nashville, 1967; MEd, Mid. Tenn. State U., 1972, EdS, 1975; postgrad., Tenn. State U. Cert. elem. tchr., elem. sch. counselor, elem. prin.-advanced, Tenn. Teller, mgmt. trainee Third Nat. Bank, Nashville, 1962-67; employment rep. S.S. Bd. of the S.B.C., Nashville, 1967-68; tchr. Sumner County Bd. Edn., Gallatin, Tenn., 1968-69; asst. sec.-treas., br. mgr. Security Fed. Savs. and Loan Assn., Nashville, 1969-71; tchr. Sumner County Bd. Edn., Gallatin, 1971-79, 83-85, prin., 1979-83, guidance counselor, 1985-2000; ret. Mem. textbook adoption com. Sumner County bd. Edn., 1968-69, mem. gifted com., 1980-82. Charter sec. 100 Oaks Sertoma Club, Nashville, 1970; treas. Am. Savs. and Loan Inst., Nashville, 1970. With U.S. Army, 1957-59, France. Mem. Tenn. ACA, Tenn. Assn. Counselor Devel., Mid. Tenn. Assn. for Counselor Devel., United Tchg. Profession, Sumner County Elem. Prins. (past pres. 1982-83), Sumner County Edn. Assn. (past pres. 1978-79), Phi Delta Kappa. United Methodist. Avocations: jogging, reading, yard work, spectator sports, art. Home: 288 Indian Lake Rd Hendersonville TN 37075-4344

POYNTER, JAMES MORRISON, travel educator, travel company executive; b. Kansas City, Mo., July 27, 1939; s. Lewis Alderson and Patricia Connely (Dunn) P.; m. Sorore; children: Lewis, Robert, Michael. BA, George Washington U., 1969, MA, 1975. Cert. travel counselor (honorary). Adminstrv. dir. Inst. Cert. Travel Agents, Arlington, Va., 1967-72; ednl. cons. Saudi Arabian Airlines, Jeddah, 1972-77; specialist employment and tng. Leon County Dept. Human Resources, Tallahassee, 1977-79; pres., CEO Fla. Profl. and Econ. Devel. Corp., Tallahassee, 1979-81; mgr., co-owner The Travel Ctr., Tallahassee, 1979-82, Adventures in Travel, Tallahassee, 1979-82; assoc. prof. travel adminstrn. Met. State Coll. Denver, 1982—; pres. Travel Analysis, Denver, 1988—. Author: Foreign Independent Tours, 1989, Corporate Travel Management, 1990, Travel Agency Accounting Procedures, 1991, Tour Design Marketing and Management, 1992, Travel and Tourism Books in Print, 1992, How to Research and Write A Thesis in Hospitality and Tourism, 1993, Multicultural, Multinational Adjustment and Readjustment, 1995 (with others) Travel Industry Business Management, 1986; compiler editor: Proceedings of the Colloqium on Corporate Travel Curricula Development, 1994, Travel and Tourism Books in Print, 1994, 95. With U.S. Army, 1957-60. Mem. Am. Soc. Travel Agts., Internat. Assn. of Tour Mgrs., Assn. Corp. Travel Execs. (edn. cons. 1988-89, bd govs. 1993-95, v.p. edn. 1994-95, Edn. award 1992, Educator of Yr. award 1993), Soc. Travel and Tourism Educators (bd. dirs. 1989-91, 93-95), Profl. Guides Assn. Am., Rocky Mountain Bus. Travel Assn. (bd. dirs. 1986-87), Rocky Mountain Profl. Guides Assn. (bd. dirs. 1989-90, v.p. 1989-90), Colo. Author's League (treas. 1992). Mem. Am. Soc. Travel Agts., Assn. Corp. Travel Execs. (edn. cons. 1988-89, bd. govs. 1993-95, v.p. edn. 1994-95, Edn. award 1992, Educator of Yr. award 1993), Soc. Travel and Tourism Educators (bd. dirs. 1989-91, 93—), Profl. Guides Assn. Am., Rocky Mountain Bus. Travel Assn. (bd. dirs. 1986-87), Rocky Mountain Profl. Guides Assn. (bd. dirs. 1989-90, v.p. 1989-90), Colo. Author's League (treas. 1992). Republican. Presbyterian. Office: Met State Coll Denver HMTA Dept PO Box 60 Denver CO 80201-0060

POYNTON, JOHN THOMAS, secondary school educator; b. Darby, Pa., Aug. 28, 1947; s. John Thomas and Agnes Penney (Loughlin) P.; m. Catherine H. Schoettler, Aug. 4, 1973; children: Edmund, Patrick, Helen. AB, St. Joseph's U., 1969, MA, 1978. Tchr. Southeast Delco Sch. Dist., Sharon Hill, Pa., 1969—, head coach girls track team, 1995—. Inductee, mentor Southeast Delco Sch. Dist., 1989—. Asst. troop leader Boy Scouts Am., Havertown, Pa., 1980-91. Internat. Studies Inst. fellow, 1970, Pa. Writing Project fellow, West Chester, 1985—. Mem. Southeast Delco Edn. Assn. (newsletter editor 1990—, bd. dirs. 1993—). Democrat. Roman Catholic. Avocations: travel, photography. Office: Acad Park High Sch 300 Calcon Hook Rd Sharon Hill PA 19079-1597 E-mail: Teachjp@aol.com.

POZA, ERNESTO, business consultant, educator; b. Havana, Cuba, Mar. 27, 1950; came to U.S., 1961; s. Hugo Ernesto and Carmen (Valle) P.; m. Karen Elizabeth Saum, Oct. 14, 1978; 1 child, Kali Jennette. BS in Adminstrv. Sci., Yale U., 1972; MS in Mgmt., MIT, 1974. Personnel mgr. rsch. Sherwin Williams Co., Chgo., 1974-75, orgn. specialist Cleve., 1975-77, dir. orgn. planning, 1977-79; pres., sr. mgmt. cons. E.J. Poza Assoc., Cleve., 1979—; prof. Weatherhead Sch. Mgmt. Case Western Res. U., Cleve., 1996—. Advisor Family Firm Inst., 1986; bd. dirs. several privately held firms; vis. lectr. Yale U., U. Chile, MIT, Sloan Sch. Mgmt. Author: Smart Growth: Critical Choices for Business Continuity and Prosperity, 1997, A la Sombra del Roble: La Empresa Privada Familiar y Su Continuidad, 1995, La Empresa Familiar Por Dentro, 1998; contbg. editor Family Bus. Mag.; mem. editl. bd. Family Bus. Rev., 1997—; contbr. articles to profl. jours. Bd. dirs. Neighborhood Health Care, 1980, Family Firm Inst., 1990; program com. United Way, Cleve., 1985, Hispanic Leadership, 1986; founding mem. Family Firm Inst., 1985. Fellow Family Firm Inst. (sr., Richard Beckhard Practice award 1996); mem. Acad. Mgmt. (entrepreneurship div., 1980—, orgn. devel. network, 1975—). Office: Peter B Lewis Bldg 244 Weatherhead Sch Mgmt CWRU 10100 Euclid Ave Cleveland OH 44106-7235 E-mail: Ernesto.Poza@weatherhead.case.edu.

POZO, ANGELICA, ceramic artist, educator; b. Bronx, N.Y., Feb. 17, 1954; d. Ruben and Julia (anglero) P. Student, Moore Coll. Art, 1971-73; BFA, Alfred U., 1976; MFA, U. Mich., 1978. Artist-in-residence Ohio Arts Coun., Columbus, 1987—; minority scholar-in-residence, instr. Pa. State U., State College, 1990; artist-in-residence Manchester Craftsmen's Guild, Pitts., 1995; artist Earthen Angel Ceramics, Cleve., 1990—. Instr. Penland (N.C.) Sch. Crafts, 1994, 97, 99, Cleve. Inst. Art, 1996; meml. artist selection juror Cleve. Fireman's Assn., 1994; selection panelist for individual artist fellowships Mid Atlantic Arts Found., Balt., 1995, Ohio Arts Coun., Columbus, 1995, W.Va. Commn. on Arts, Charleston, 1996; artist-in-residence S.W. Craft Ctr., San Antonio, 1997; mem. selection panelist Oreg. Arts Commn., Salem, 1997. Prin. works displayed in Cleve. Hopkin's Airport, Regional Transit Authority Sta., 1993, Gund Arena, Cleve., 1994, Waxter Ctr. Sr. Citizens, Balt., 1995, E. 9th Regional Transit Authority Sta., Cleve., 1996, Univ. Hosps. Cleve., 1997, Cleveland Marshall Coll. Law Libr., Cleve., 1998, Ohio State U., Columbus, 2002; co-author: The Penland Book of Ceramics: Master Classes in Ceramic Technique, 2003; author: (chpt. in book) Penland Book of Ceramics: Master Classes in Ceramics Technique, 2003. Trustee Performers and Artists for Nuclear Disarmament, Cleve., 1990-93, Cleve. Coun. Cultural Affairs, 1994. NEA regional artist fellow Arts Midwest, 1989-90, individual artist fellow Ohio Arts Coun., 1992-93; recipient Robert Mann award for ceramics Cleve. Mus. Art, 1993. Mem. Nat. Coun. on Edn. of Ceramic Artists, Internat. Sculpture Ctr., Am. Craft Coun. Office: 1193 Holmden Ave Cleveland OH 44109-1877 Fax: 216-861-6566. E-mail: angelicapozo@earthlink.net.

POZZI, DEBRA ELIZABETH, private school art educator; b. New Brunswick, N.J., Nov. 5, 1950; d. Donald Eugene and May Anne (Roche) Boynton; m. Giorgio Pozzi, Jan. 6, 1975 (div. 1984); children: Matthew, Elizabeth. BA summa cum laude, Boston Coll., 1973; MA, U. Del., 1983. Slide curator Boston Coll., Chestnut Hill, Mass., 1973-74; instr. English Istituto Atena British Coll., Varese, Italy, 1975-77; pre-sch. tchr. Fairville (Pa.) Schoolhouse, 1981-82; art instr. The Independence Sch., Newark, Del., 1982—. Art instr. Ctr. for Creative Arts, Yorklyn, Pa., 1985-86 (summers), Newark (Del.) Parks and Recreation, 1992 (summer). Editor: (yearbook) Freedom, 1987-93. Mem. Chester County Rep. Com., Kennett Sq., Pa., 1982. Avocations: painting, pottery, photography, ballet, french, italian. Home: 105 Round Hill Rd Kennett Square PA 19348-2607 Office: Independence Sch 1300 Paper Mill Rd Newark DE 19711-3408

PRABHUDESAI, MUKUND M. pathology educator, laboratory director, researcher, administrator; b. Lolyem, Goa, India, Mar. 17, 1942; came to U.S., 1967; s. Madhav R. and Kusum M. Prabhudesai; m. Sarita Mukund Usha, Feb. 1, 1972; 1 child, Nitin M. MB, BS (MD), G.S. Med., Bombay, 1967, postgrad., 1973-75. Diplomate Am. Bd. Pathology. Asst. pathologist Fordham Hosp., Bronx, N.Y., 1973-74, assoc. pathologist, 1974-76; assoc. dir. clin. pathology Lincoln Med., Bronx, 1976, dep. dir. pathology, 1977-79; chief pathology and lab. medicine svc., coord. R&D VA Med. Ctr., Danville, Ill., 1979—, dir. electron microscopy lab., 1987—. Senator U. Ill. Chgo.; co-investigator U. Ill. Coll. Medicine, Urbana-Champaign, clin. prof. pathology and internal medicine, 1982—. Contbr. articles to Am. Jour. Clin. Nutrition, Jour. AMA, Am. Jour. Clin. Pathology. Member Gifted Student Adv. Bd., Danville, 1984-86; v.p. Am. Cancer Soc. Vermilion County chpt., 1982, pres., 1986-88. VA rsch. grantee, 1980-82, 82-85, 83. Fellow Coll. Am. Pathology (inspector 1981—, Ill. state del. to C.A.P. Ho. Dels. 1992—, mem. reference com. 1993); mem. AAAS, Am. Coll. Physician Execs., Ill. State Soc. Pathologists (bd. dirs. 1990—, chmn. membership com. 1990—). Achievements include development of cancer of bladder following portocarval shunting; research in adverse effects of alcohol on lung structure and metabolism; on effects of soy and bran on cholesterol, endocrine response to soy protein, in induction and reversibility of atherosclerosis in trout, effects of ethanol on Vitamin A, lymphatics in atherosclerosis, iron in atherosclerosis, development of dermofluorometer for detection of P.V.D. Office: VA Med Ctr Pathology and Lab Med Svcs 1900 E Main St Danville IL 61832-5100 E-mail: mukund.prabhudesai@med.va.gov., sarita@soltec.net.

PRADA, GLORIA INES, mathematics and Spanish language educator; b. San Vicente de Chucuri, Colombia, Dec. 2, 1954; came to U.S., 1985; d. Roberto Gomez and Maria Celina (Serrano) Duran; m. Luis Eduardo Prada, June 19, 1975; children: Luis Ricardo, Nicholas. BS in Math., U. Indsl., Santander, Colombia, 1978. Tchr. h.s. math. Santander Sch. Dist., Bucaramanga, 1973-84; tchr. mid. sch. math., mentor tchr. Hayward (Calif.) Unified Sch. Dist., 1989—. Pres. Bilingual Adv. Com., Hayward, 1986-89; mem. Gate Task Force, Hayward, 1990-93, Spanish for Educators Alameda County Office Edn., 1995—. Author: Prada's Spanish Course, 1992, Family Math, 1992, Stations on Probabilities, 1994, (math. replacement unit) Success, 1994. Office: Hayward Unified Dist Winton 119 Winton Ave Hayward CA 94544-1413

PRAGER, SUSAN WESTERBERG, law educator, provost; b. Sacramento, Dec. 14, 1942; d. Percy Foster Westerberg and Aileen M. (McKinley) P.; m. James Martin Prager, Dec. 14, 1973; children: McKinley Ann, Case Mahone. AB, Stanford U., 1964, MA, 1967; JD, UCLA, 1971. Bar: N.C. 1971, Calif. 1972. Atty. Powe, Porter & Alphin, Durham, N.C., 1971-72; acting prof. law UCLA, 1972-77, prof. Sch. Law, 1977—, Arjay and Frances Fearing Miller prof. of law, 1992-99, assoc. dean Sch. Law, 1979-82, dean, 1982-98; provost Dartmouth Coll., Hanover, N.H., 1999—. Bd. dirs. Pacific Mut. Life Holding Co., Newport Beach, Calif. Editor-in-chief, UCLA Law Rev., 1970-71. Trustee Stanford U., 1976-80, 87-97. Mem. ABA (council of sect. on legal edn. and admissions to the bar 1983-85), Assn. Am. Law Schs. (pres. 1986), Order of Coif. Address: Dartmouth College Office of the Provost 6004 Parkhurst Hall Rm 204 Hanover NH 03755-3529

PRAHL-ANDERSEN, BIRTE, orthodontics educator; b. Copenhagen, Apr. 18, 1939; d. Paul and Jessie (Strand) Andersen; m. Soren Prahl; children: Charlotte, Marianne, Kristine. DDS, Royal Dental Coll., Copenhagen, 1962, degree in orthodontics, 1969; PhD, degree in orthodontics, U. Nijmegen, Netherlands, 1968. Dentist Mcpl. Dental Clinic, Copenhagen, 1962-64; with dept. orthodontics U. Nijmegen, 1968-80, project dir. growth study dept. orthodontics, 1970-79, mem. cleft palate team, 1969-80; prof. orthodontics Acad. Ctr. for Dentistry, Amsterdam, The Netherlands, 1980—. Mem. cleft palate team U. Hosp. Vrije Universiteit, Amsterdam, 1980—; cons. cleft palate team U. Hosp. Dijkzigt, Rotterdam, The Netherlands, 1973—. Author: Sutural Growth, 1968, A Mixed Longitudinal Inter-Disciplinary Study of Growth and Development, 1979, (with others) Long-Term Planning of Orthodontic Manpower, 1981, (with others) Peuro-Qual, Towards a Quality Systems for European Orthodontic Professionals, 1997, (with others) Quality of Orthodontic Care, A Concept for Collaboration and Responsibilities, 2002; contbr. numerous articles to profl. jours. Fellow Royal Coll. Surgeons (Edinburgh); mem. Danish Dental Assn., Dutch Assn. Orthodontists, European Orthodontic Soc., Internat. Assn. for Dental Rsch., Am. Cleft Palate Assn. Lutheran. Office: ACTA Dept Orthodontics Louwesweg 1 1066 EA Amsterdam Netherlands

PRAIRIE, CELIA ESTHER FREDA, biochemistry educator; b. Buenos Aires, Sept. 30, 1940; came to U.S., 1963; d. Rafael Emilio A. and Celia Esther (Seijo) Freda; m. James Roland Prairie, Sept. 19, 1970; children: James Roger, Caryn Elizabeth. BS, U. Buenos Aires, 1961, MS, 1963; PhD, U. Pa., 1967. Fellow Nat. Rsch. Inst., Buenos Aires, 1961-63; rsch. assoc. dept. therapeutic rsch. U. Pa., Phila., 1967-70; postdoctoral rsch. assoc. Lab. Molecular Embryology, Arco Felice, Naples, Italy, 1970; lectr. biology and chemistry depts. Holy Family Coll., Phila., 1974-75, asst. prof. biology dept., 1975-80, assoc. prof., 1980-85, prof. biochemistry, 1985—, chmn. dept. natural scis. and math., 1986-88, acting chmn. biology dept., 1982-86. Sr. teaching staff assoc. Marine Biol. Lab., Woods Hole, Mass., 1968-69. Contbr. articles to profl. jours. Bd. dirs. Lower Bucks County Community Ctr., 1970—. Fellow USPHS, 1963-65, U. Pa., 1965-66, Am. Coun. Edn. and Fund for the Improvement of Post Sec. Edn., 1983-84. Mem. AAAS, Nat. Sci. Tchrs. Assn., Am. Inst. Biol. Scis., N.Y. Acad. Scis., Sigma Xi, World Federalist Assn. Democrat. Mem. Religious Soc. of Friends. Avocations: tai chi, yoga, swimming. Home: 31 Full Turn Rd Levittown PA 19056-1924 Office: Holy Family Coll Frankford and Grant Ave Philadelphia PA 19114-2094

PRAKASH, CHANDRA, chemistry educator; b. Delhi, India, Sept. 20, 1952; came to U.S., 1979; s. Deep C. and Ramvati (Goel) Agarwal; m. Usha Goel, June 4, 1979; children: Seema, Sushant. BS, NRCC Coll., 1971; MS, Delhi U., 1973, PhD, 1977. Asst. prof. Delhi U., 1977-79; rsch. asst. prof. Vanderbilt U., Nashville, 1985-90, rsch. assoc. prof., 1990-92; sr. rsch. investigator Pfizer, Inc., Groton, Conn., 1992-95, prin. rsch. investigator, 1996—99, rsch. advisor, 2000—. Faculty Biomed. Rsch. Grant, College Park, 1989. Contbr. articles to profl. jours. Nat. merit scholarship Govt. of India, 1965-71; Md. Cancer grant State of Md., 1982. Home: 4 Friar Tuck Dr Gales Ferry CT 06335-1302 Office: Pfizer Inc Eastern Point Rd Groton CT 06340

PRATER-FIPPS, EUNICE KAY, educational administrator; b. Cleve., Aug. 22, 1949; d. Jesse and Bertha (McCollum) Prater; m. Theodis Fipps, Apr. 13, 1990. BS, Kent State U., 1974; MEd, Cleve. State U., 1978. Cert. tchr., secondary prin., Ohio. Tchr. bus. edn. Cleve. Pub. Schs., 1974-80, adminstrv. intern, 1980-83, asst. prin., 1983—. Mem. ASCD, Ohio Assn. Secondary Sch. Adminstrs., Cleve. Coun. Adminstrs. and Suprs. Avocations: travel, reading, outdoor activities. Home: 565 Cynthia Ct Richmond Heights OH 44143-2949 Office: Cleve Pub Schs 1380 E 6th St Cleveland OH 44114-1606

PRATHER, RHONDA CLIATT, elementary school educator; b. Columbus, Ga., Jan. 18, 1952; d. Charles Patrick and Hazel (McCain) Cliatt; m. Robert L. Prather, Jr., Feb. 18, 1978; children: Jennifer Lynn, Aaron Renee. BS in Phys. Edn., W. Ga. Coll., 1975; MS in Phys. Edn., Auburn U., 1982, ES, 1986. Cert. tchr., Ga. Phys. edn. tchr. Woodbury (Ga.) High Sch., 1975-76; fitness instr. European Health Spa, Columbus, Ga., 1976-78; phys. edn. tchr. Shaw High Sch., Columbus, 1978-84, health instr., 1984-90; phys. edn. tchr. New Mountain Hill Elem. Sch., Fortson, Ga., 1990—. Asst. leader Daisy and Brownie scouts Girl Scouts of U.S., Fortson, Ga., 1990-91; coach Little League Softball, Mountain Hill Little League, Fortson, Ga., 1992. Mem. AAHPERD, GA. Assn. Health, Phys. Edn., Recreation and Dance. Baptist. Avocations: sewing, racquetball, swimming, reading. Home: 130 Layfield Branch Rd Hamilton GA 31811-4021

PRATHER, SOPHIE S. educational administrator; b. Selmer, Tenn., Jan. 23, 1948; d. Argie D. and Doris Prather; 1 child, Kimberly. BEd, Lane Coll., Jackson, Tenn., 1969; MEd, Trevecca U., Nashville, 1987. Cert. ednl. adminstr. K-12, Tenn. Tchr. Milw. Pub. Schs., 1971-72, Juneau Acad., Milw., 1972-76, McNairy County Schs., Selmer, 1977-93; psychiat. tchr. counselor Timber Springs Adolescent Ctr., Bolivar, Tenn., 1993-95, prin., 1995-96, program dir., 1996-98; supr. spl. edn. McNairy County Schs., Selmer, 1998—. Mem. McNairy County Devel. Bd. 1998, McNairy County Health Coun. Adv. Bd., 2001—; mem. bd. trustees Western Mental Health Inst.; mem. adv. coun. S.W. Headstart, McNairy County Family Resource Ctr.; mem. DCS Child Abuse Rev. Team; mem. S.W. Commn. on Children and Youth. Mem. NEA, NAFE, Tenn. Edn. Assn., Phi Delta Kappa, Delta Kappa Gamma. Methodist. Avocations: crafts, embroidery. Office: Spl Edn Ctr 491 High School Rd Selmer TN 38375-3252 E-mail: prathers@k12tn.net.

PRATKANIS, ANTHONY RICHARD, social psychologist, educator; b. Portsmouth, Va., Apr. 2, 1957; s. Tony R. and Rosemarie (Gray) P. BS summa cum laude, Ea. Menonite Coll., 1979; MA, Ohio State U., 1981, PhD, 1984. Rsch. assoc. Ohio State U., Columbus, 1981-83; asst. prof. indsl. adminstrn. & psychology U. Calif., Santa Cruz, 1984-87, asst. prof., then assoc. prof. psychology, 1987-95, prof., 1995—. Expert legal witness; reviewer acad. jours. Co-author: (with E. Aronson) The Age of Propaganda, 1992; co-editor: (with A. Greenwald and S. Breckler) Attitude Structure and Function; contbr. articles to profl. papers, book chpts. Postdoctor fellow Carnegie-Mellon U., Pitts., 1983-84; J.B. Smith scholar Ea. Mennonite Coll., Harristonburg, Va., 1975-79. Fellow APA, Soc. Personality and Social Psychology; mem. Midwestern Psychol. Assn., Soc. Exptl. Social Psychology. Democrat. Research includes attitudes, persuasion, social influence. Home: 166 Montclair Dr Santa Cruz CA 95060-1025 Office: U Calif Bd Psychology Santa Cruz CA 95064 E-mail: peitho@cats.ucsc.edu.

PRATT, ALICE REYNOLDS, retired educational administrator; b. Marietta, Ohio, Mar. 5, 1922; d. Thurman J. and Vera L. (Holdren) Reynolds. BA, U. Okla., 1943. Reporter, high sch. tchr., 1944-50; asst. dir. Houston Office, Inst. Internat. Edn., 1952-58, v.p., 1975-87; ret., 1987. Founding mem. Houston-Galveston/Stavanger Sister City Assn.; past mem. nat. bd. dirs. Sister Cities Internat., Nat. Coun. Internat. Visitors; bd. dirs. Pan Am. Roundtable; bd. dirs. so. regional office Inst. Internat. Edn.; past mem. bd, govs. Houston Forum. Decorated Palmes Academiques (France), Order of Merit (Germany), knight Order of Leopold II (Belgium); named Woman of Yr., Houston Bus. and Profl. Women, 1958; recipient Matrix award Theta Sigma Phi, 1961, Nat. Carnation award Gamma Phi Beta, 1976. Mem. Houston Com. on Fgn. Rels., Japan Am. Soc., Houston Philos. Soc., Houston=Taipei Soc. (founding, pres. 1968-92). Republican. Episcopalian. E-mail: apratt7164@aol.com.

PRATT, CAROLYN KAY, retired language arts/mathematics educator; b. Madison, W.Va., Apr. 30, 1943; d. Lonnie Clifford and Patty (Hicks) Miller; m. Michael Pratt, Dec. 23, 1967 (div. June 1989). BS in Elem. Edn., Concord Coll., Athens, W.Va., 1964; MA in Edn., Salem-Teykyo U., 1995. Cert. elem. educator. Tchr. Boone County Schs., Madison, W.Va., 1964-69; tchr. title I lang. arts/math. Mercer County Schs., Princeton, W.Va., 1969-99; ret., 1999. Presenter W.Va. State Reading Conf., White Sulphur Springs, W.Va., 1991, 93, Nat. Coun. Tchrs. Math. Conf., Charleston, W.Va., 1994, W. Va. State Math. Conf., 1995; adj. prof., supr. student tchrs. Concord Coll., 1999—. Author, editor: (booklet) Math Can Be Fun, 1991; author: (poems) The New American Poetry Anthology, 1991 (cert. of merit 1991), Treasured Poems of America, 1993; contbr. poems to The Coming of Dawn, 1995, Best Poems of 1996, articles to profl. jours. Mem. exec. bd. Read Aloud Mercer County, 1999—, sec., 2000—; active Project Teach; condr. parent involvement programs. Grantee Greater Kanawha Valley Found., 1988, Kellog Co., 1993, 94, Cynthia Lorentz-Cook Found., 1995. Mem. Internat. Reading Assn., Nat. Coun. Tchrs. Math., W.Va. State Reading Coun. (pub. info. com. chair 1989-90, citations and awards com. chair 1991-95, registration com. chair 1996-98, internat. programs com. chair 1998—, mem. exec. bd. 1991—, Eddie C. Kennedy Tchr. of Yr. 1990), W.Va. Coun. Tchrs. Math., Mercer County Reading Coun. (corr. sec. 1987-90, Reading Tchr. of Yr. 1989, recording sec. 1995-96), Mercer County Writer's Workshop, W.Va. Writers', Inc., Delta Kappa Gamma (com. chair Zeta chpt. 1994-96, 2d v.p. 2000-01, 1st v.p. 2002-03, pres. 2000—). Avocations: writing, reading, cross stitch, walking, photography. Home: 124 Valley View St Princeton WV 24740-2314

PRATT, CHRISTINA CARVER, social work and women's studies educator; b. N.Y.C., Dec. 5, 1951; d. Harry S. and Frances Carver (Shaw) P.; 1 child, Cherish Marie. AAS, Rockland U., 1973; BA, Fairleigh Dickinson, 1975; MSW, Columbia U., 1976; D, CUNY. Cons., educator Orange County Cmty. Mental Health, Goshen, NY, 1976-80; prof. social work and gender studies Dominican Coll., Orangeburg, N.Y., 1980—; prof. social work and women's studies NYU, N.Y.C., 1985—98. Exec. dir. Ptnrs. of Ams., Rockland, NY, 1987—97; tng. cons. Govt. of St. Lucia, 1987—93; commr. Coun. on Social Work Edn., Washington, 1990—93; del. NGO Forum-4th World Conf. on Women, 1995; trustee Green Meadow Waldorf Sch., NY, 1996—2000; bd. dirs. Hopf Enterprises, Englewood, NJ. Film maker (video documentaries) India: The Cultural Past, 1985, India: Rural Villages and Urban Villagers, 1986, Tunisia, 1990; editor Jour. Social Devel., 1987—; contbr. articles to profl. jours. Fulbright scholar, India, 1981, Pakistan, 1983; Malone Faculty fellow Nat. Coun. U.S./Arab Rels., Tunisia, 1989, Israel, Syria, Jordan and Palestine, 1991. Mem. NASW, NOW, AAUW, Amnesty Internat., Am. Adoption Congress. Buddhist. Avocations: jazz, opera, hiking, photography, cooking. Office: Dominican Coll 470 Western Hwy Orangeburg NY 10962-1210

PRATT, DIANE ADELE, talented and gifted education educator; b. Battle Creek, Mich., Oct. 24, 1951; d. John Robert and Kathleen Adele (Cooper) Dickert; m. Stephen Howard Pratt, Apr. 29, 1972; children: Eric Stephen, Elizabeth Adele. BS, Western Mich. U., 1972; MS in Edn., Buenta Vista U., 2000. Endorsement K-12 talented and gifted, Iowa. Elem. tchr. Berea (Ohio) Cmty. Schs., 1973-76; tchr. Lemon Tree Nursery Sch., Battle Creek, 1985-88; elem. tchr. Ft. Dodge (Iowa) Cmty. Schs., 1976-78, middle sch. tchr., 1990—, team leader, 1994-97, tchr. talented and gifted, 1997—, advisor talented and gifted for H.S., 2002—. Chearleading coach Ft. Dodge Sr. H.S., 1997-99, 2000-01, Pep Club advisor, 1997-99; advt. exec. Ft. Dodge Today mag., 1989-92; ednl. tutor, Battle Creek, Ft. Dodge, 1986-96; mem. adv. bd. Inst. for Instrn. Svcs., Battle Creek, 1984-88; dir., instr. Battle Creek Presch. Enrichment Program, 1984; chmn. Ft. Dodge Supr.'s Comty. Com. to Study K-8 Curriculum, 1988-89, facilitator K-3 human growth and devel. curriculum, 1989-92; mem. standing com. early childhood needs assessment com. Ft. Dodge Comty. Schs., 1989-95; mem. adv. bd., instr. Kids on Kampus Iowa Ctrl. C.C., Ft. Dodge, 1990-95; trustee Ft. Dodge Comty. Sch. Found. Bd., 1992-97, mem. talented and gifted selection com. Ft. Dodge Comty. Schs., 1993—, mem. promotion taskforce, 1998-99; mem. pub. rels. com. Ft. Dodge Comty. Sch. Dist., 1992-94, mem. ednl. outcomes standing com., 1993-94. Author, editor Headcase and various newsletters. Mem., past chmn. bd. Christian edn. 1st Bapt. Ch., Ft. Dodge, 1978-79, 89-96, music com., 1992-94, dir. children's choirs, 1988-90, mem. bell choir, 1990-91, ch. sch. supt. 1993-96, pastoral rels. com., 1997-99; neighborhood coord. mothers' march March of Dimes, Battle Creek, 1981-83, Ft. Dodge, 1999—; troop leader Lakota coun. Girl Scouts U.S., 1988-90; pres. La Mora Park PTA, 1985-87, Phillips Mid Sch. PTA, Ft. Dodge, 1990-91; bd. dirs. Main Stage Players, jr. theater, Ft. Dodge,

1990-91; sec., pres. Jr. Women's Club, Ft. Dodge, 1977-80; mem. kickoff com. United Way, 1991, Curriculum Instn. Adv. Coun., 2001-, Insvc. Adv. Com., 2000—; tchr. mentor, 2001-; bd. dirs. Nat. Coun. on Youth Leadership, Ft. Dodge, 2002—. Recipient Mem. of Yr. award La Mora Park PTA, l987, Iowa Talented and Gifted Rsch. award, 2000, David Belin Excellence in Tchg. award, 2000. Mem. NEA, ASCD, AAUW (sec., pres. Battle Creek br. 1986-88), PEO (N.J. chpt., Ft. Dodge chpt. 1990-94), Iowa Edn. Assn., Ft. Dodge Edn. Assn., Iowa Assn. Middle Level Educators, Iowa Assn. for Talented and Gifted (bd. dirs. 2001—), Study Club (treas. 1999-2000, pres. 2000-02), Nat. Assn. Gifted Children, Delta Kappa Gamma, Kappa Delta Pi Hon. Soc. Presbyterian. Avocations: educational research, cross-country skiing. Home: 185l 9th Ave N Fort Dodge IA 50501

PRATT, LINDA, reading educator; b. Mass., May 28, 1948; BA, U. Mass., 1970, MEd, 1975, EdD, 1978. Cert. elem. edn., reading specialist, reading supr. Prof., exec. dir. edn. dept. Elmira (N.Y.) Coll.; prof. Gonzaga U., Spokane, Wash.; insvc. tchr. U. Mass., Amherst; reading specialist Southwick (Mass.) Pub. Sch. System. Author: (with J. Beaty) Transcultural Children's Literature, 1999, Early Literacy in Preschools- 2nd Kindergarten, 2003. Mem. IRA, NCTE, Nat. Reading Conf., Kappa Delta Pi, Phi Delta Kappa, Kappa Delta Gamma. Office: Elmira Coll Elmira NY 14901

PRATT, ROSALIE REBOLLO, harpist, educator; b. N.Y.C., Dec. 4, 1933; d. Antonio Ernesto and Eleanor Gertrude (Gibney) Rebollo; m. George H. Mortimer, Esquire, Apr. 22, 1987; children: Francesca Christina Rebollo-Sborgi, Alessandra Maria Pratt Jones. MusB, Manhattanville Coll., 1954; MusM, Pius XII Inst. Fine Arts, Florence, Italy, 1955; EdD, Columbia U., 1976. Prin. harpist N.J. Symphony Orch., 1963-65; soloist Mozart Haydn Festival Avery Fisher Hall, N.Y.C., 1968; tchr. music pub. schs. Bloomfield and Montclair, N.J., 1962-73; mem. faculty Montclair State Coll., 1973-79; prof. Brigham Young U., Provo, Utah, 1984-99, coord. grad. studies dept. music, 1985-87, biofeedback and neurofeedback specialist, 1993—, prof. emeritus, 1999—; dir. R&D Music Health Inst., Provo, 1999—. U.S. chair 1st internat. arts medicine leadership conf., Tokyo Med. Coll., 1993. Author: Hospital Arts, 1997; co-author: Elementary Music for All Learners, 1980; editor Internat. Jour. Arts Medicine, 1991—, (procs.) 2d, 3d, 4th Internat. Symposia Music Edn. for Handicapped, Arts Medicine, 1997; sr. editor Music Medicine 3, 1999, Arts in Healthcare, 2003—; author, sr. editor: The Arts in Healthcare Movement in the U.S., 2003; contbr. articles to profl. jours. Recipient Utah Music Educator of the Yr., Utah Music Educators Assn., 1997; Fulbright grantee, 1979; Myron Taylor scholar, 1954. Mem. Am. Harp Soc. (Outstanding Svc. award 1973), AAUP (co-chmn. legis. rels. com. N.J. 1978-79), Internat. Soc. Music Edn. (chair commn. musicin spl. edn., music therapy, and medicine 1985—), Internat. Soc. Music in Medicine (v.p. 1993—), Internat. Assn. of Music for the Handicapped (co-founder, exec. dir., jour. editor), Coll. Music Soc., Music Educators Nat. Conf., Soc. for Study of Neuronal Regulation, Brigham Young U. Grad. Coun., Phi Kappa Phi, Sigma Alpha Iota. Office: Music Health Inst 3684 Little Rock Ter Provo UT 84604-5291 E-mail: rosalie65_@hotmail.com.

PRAUSNITZ, JOHN MICHAEL, chemical engineer, educator; b. Berlin, Jan. 7, 1928; came to U.S., 1937, naturalized, 1944; s. Paul Georg and Susi Prausnitz; m. Susan Prausnitz, June 10, 1956; children: Stephanie, Mark Robert. B Chem. Engring., Cornell U., 1950; MS, U. Rochester, 1951; PhD, Princeton, 1955; Dr. Ing., U. L'Aquila, 1983, Tech. U. Berlin, 1989; DSc, Princeton U., 1995. Mem. faculty U. Calif., Berkeley, 1955—, prof. chem. engring., 1963—. Cons. to cyrogenic, polymer, petroleum and petrochem. industries; Miller rsch. prof., 1966, 78; sr. investigator Lawrence Berkeley Nat. Lab., Berkeley; Wilhelm lectr. Princeton U., 1980; W.K. Lewis lectr. MIT, 1993; Edward Mason lectr. Brown U., 1999; Danckwerts lectr. Royal Acad. Engring., London, 2000; hon. prof. Tech. U. Shanghai, 2001. Author: (with others) Computer Calculations for Multicomponent Vapor-Liquid Equilibria, 1967, (Computer Calculations for High-Pressure Vapor-Liquid Equilibria, 1968, Molecular Thermodynamics of Fluid-Phase Equilibria, 1969, 2d edit., 1986, 3d edit., 1999, Regular and Related Solutions, 1970, Properties of Gases and Liquids, 3d edit., 1977, 4th edit., 1987, 5th edit., 2000, Computer Calculations for Multicomponent Vapor-Liquid and Liquid-Liquid Equilibria, 1980; contbr. to profl. jours. Recipient Alexander von Humboldt Sr. Scientist award, 1976, Carl von Linde Gold Meml. medal, German Inst. for Cryogenics, 1987, Solvay prize, Solvay Found. for Chem. Scis., 1990, Corcoran award, Am. Soc. for Engring. Edn., 1991, 1999, D.L. Katz award, Gas Processors Assn., 1992, Waterman award, Tech. U. Delft, 1998, Rossini award, Internat. Union of Pure and Applied Chemistry, 2002, others; Guggenheim fellow, 1962, 1973, fellow, Inst. Advanced Study, Berlin, 1985, Christensen fellow, St. Catherine's Coll. Oxford U., 1994, Erskine fellow, U. Canterbury, Christchurch, New Zealand, 1996. Mem. AIChE (Colburn award 1962, Walker award 1967, Inst. Lectr. award 1994), Am. Chem. Soc. (E.V. Murphree award 1979, Petroleum Chemistry Rsch. award 1995), NAE, NAS, Am. Acad. Arts and Scis. Office: U Calif 308 Gilman Hl Berkeley CA 94720-1462 E-mail: prausnit@cchem.berkeley.edu.

PRAZAK, BESSMARIE LILLIAN, science educator; b. Chgo., June 6, 1941; d. William Felix and Bess Blanch (Kostka) Kolar; m. Charles J. Prazak III, June 15, 1963; 1 child, Robin Marie. BS, Rosary U., 1963; MS, Northwestern U., 1965. Rsch. asst. Argonne Nat. Lab., Lemont, Ill., 1965-68; tchr. Morton Coll., Cicero, Ill., 1968-2000, tchr. emeritus, 2000—. Chair curriculum com. Morton Coll., 1984—2000. Author: Laboratory Manual of Anatomy and Physiology, 1997, Laboratory Manual of Microbiology, 1997, Photo Albums of Anatomy and Physiology Histology, 2002. Mem. AAAS, Nat. Assn. Biology Tchrs., Ill. Assn. C.C. Biologists (sec.-treas. 1978), Human Anatomy and Physiology Soc. Avocations: painting, photography.

PREBLE, DUANE, artist, art educator; b. National City, Calif., May 20, 1936; s. Bennett and Mary Salome (Williams) P.; m. Sarah Ann Hamilton, Mar. 13, 1961; children: Jeffrey Hamilton, Malia. BA, UCLA, 1959; MFA, U. Hawaii, Honolulu, 1963. Lectr. U. Hawaii, Honolulu, 1963-64, prof., 1964-91, prof. emeritus art, 1991—. Vis. prof. U. Colo., 1979, 80; advisor to the bd. Honolulu Waldorf Sch., 1993-2000; trustee Honolulu Acad. Arts, 1973—; chair dept. art U. Hawaii, Honolulu, 1985-87; bd. dirs. Hawaii Alliance Arts Edn., 1988-95. Author: (college textbook) Artforms, 7th edit., 2003. Mem., chair City Commn. on Culture & the Arts, Honolulu, 1971-73; bd. Civic Forum for Pub. Edn., 1998-2000. Mem. Author's Guild, Coll. Art Assn., Nat. Art Edn. Assn. Avocations: hiking, swimming, music. Home: 3347 Anoai Pl Honolulu HI 96822-1419

PREDMORE, MICHAEL PENNOCK, Spanish language and literature educator; b. New Brunswick, N.J., Feb. 5, 1938; s. Richard Lionel and Catherine (Pennock) P.; m. Izvara Kleinhempel, Apr. 12, 1969; 1 child, Michael Kleinhempel Predmore. BA, Swarthmore Coll., 1959; MA, U. Wis., 1961, PhD, 1965. Asst. prof. U. Wash., Seattle, 1965-69, assoc. prof., 1969-74, prof., 1974-86, Stanford (Calif.) U., 1986—, chair Spanish and Portuguese, 1987-94. Elected corporator Internat. Inst., Madrid, 1985—; vis. prof. U. Calif., San Diego, 1986; nat. selection com. Am. Coun. Learned Socs., Washington, 1987—. Author: La Obra en prosa de J.R. Jimenez, 1966, La Poesia Hermetica de J.R. Jimenez, 1973, Una España Joven en la Poesia de A. Macnado, 1981; editor: Platero y yo de J.R. Jimenez, 1978, rev. edit., 1995; mem. editl. staff Discurso Literario, 1985—; editor: Diarie de un poeta reciencasado de J.R. Jimenez (1916), 1998, (bilingual edit.) Diary of a Newlywed Poet of J.R. Jimenez, 2003; cons. numerous jours. Fellow Humanities Inst., U. Wis., 1968-69, John Simon Guggenheim Found., U. Wash., 1975-76, NEH, Stanford U., 1990-91, Stanford Humanities Ctr., 1990-91. Mem. MLA (exec. com. divsn. on 20th century Spanish lit. 1981-85, sec. 1983, chair 1984), Am. Assn. of Tchrs. of Spanish and Portuguese. Avocations: tennis, swimming, hiking. Home: 81 Peter Coutts Cir Stanford CA 94305-2512 Office: Stanford U Dept Spanish & Portuguese Bldg 260 Stanford CA 94305

PREECE, JIM, elementary education educator, consultant; b. Keystone, W.Va., Nov. 4, 1951; s. James Albert and Virginia Lee (Leslie) P. AA, Brevard Community Coll., Cocoa, Fla., 1971; BA in Edn., U. Ctrl. Fla., 1973; MEd, Armstrong State Coll., 1991. Cert. middle grades edn., gifted edn. Tchr. grade 6 Moses Jackson Elem. Sch., Savannah, Ga., 1973-79, Francis Bartow Elem. Sch., Savannah, 1979-85; tchr., dept. head DeRenne Middle Sch., Savannah, 1985—. Organist Epworth United Meth. Ch., Savannah, 1978-92; cons. A Scholar Ship/Ednl., Savannah, 1991-92, Chatham/Savannah (Ga.) Bd. Edn., 1986-92. Author: Skills Maintenance, 1989, Making Sense of Manipulatives, 1992; co-author: Learning At Home: A Guide, 1987. Pres. Staff Devel. Coun., Savannah, 1992—. Mem. Nat. Coun. Tchrs. Math. (presentor 1985-92), Ga. Coun. Tchrs. Math., Profl. Assn. Ga. Educators, Am. Guild Organists (dean 1992—). Methodist. Avocations: developing math manipulative materials, trains, hymnody, pipe organs. Home: 31 Brown Rd Senoia GA 30276-1442

PREEDOM, BARRY MASON, physicist, educator; b. Stamford, Conn., Dec. 31, 1940; children: Bonnie Marie, Richard Lawrence. BS, Spring Hill Coll., 1962; MS, U. Tenn., 1964, PhD, 1967. Grad. fellow Oak Ridge (Tenn.) Nat. Lab., 1964-67; rsch. assoc. Mich. State U., East Lansing, 1967-70; asst. prof., then assoc. prof. U. S.C., Columbia, 1970-76, prof. physics, 1976—, Carolina rsch. prof., 1986-95, Carolina Disting. prof., 1995—, assoc. dean for rsch., 2002—. Vis. prof. Swiss Inst. Nuclear Rsch., Villigen, 1976; vis. staff Los Alamos (N.Mex.) Nat. Lab., 1972-91, tech. adv. panel, 1982-85; guest scientist Brookhaven Nat. Lab., Upton, N.Y., 1987—. Contbr. rsch. articles to sci. publs. Sr. teaching fellow Lilly Found., 1994-95; grantee Rsch. Corp., 1971, Office Naval Rsch., 1972-75, NSF, 1975—; recipient Mortar Bd. award for Excellence in Teaching, 1993. Mem. Am. Phys. Soc., Sigma Xi, Alpha Sigma Nu. Achievements include research and study of nuclear reaction mechanisms and nuclear structure, reaction probes including gamma rays, mesons, protons, deuterons and light ions. Office: Univ SC Dept Physics Columbia SC 29208-0001

PREER, JEAN LYON, information science educator; b. Rochester, N.Y., June 25, 1944; d. Henry Gould and Helen Corinne (McTarnaghan) Lyon; m. James Randolph Preer, June 24, 1967; children: Genevieve, Stephen. BA in History with honors, Swarthmore Coll., 1966; MLS, U. Calif., Berkeley, 1967; JD with highest honors, George Washington U., 1974, PhD, 1980. Bar: D.C. 1975. With Henry E. Huntington Libr., San Marino, Calif., 1967-69; Woodrow Wilson Found. teaching intrn Fed. City Coll., Washington, 1969-70; cons. Inst. for Svcs. to Edn., Silver Spring, Md., 1981-82; vol. edn. divsn. Nat. Archives, Washington, 1981-89; adj. prof. U. D.C., 1984-85, Cath. U. Am., Washington, 1985-87, asst. prof. sch. libr. and info. sci., 1987-92, assoc. prof., 1993—, assoc. dean., 1991-93, 94-98, acting dean, 1993-94, 99; adj. assoc. prof. George Washington U., 1985-87. Vis. scholar, U. Wis., Madison, Sch. Libr. and Info. Studies, 2000-01. Contbr. articles to profl. jours. Mem. governing bd. Nat. Cathedral Sch., Washington, 1987—91; bd. dirs. Westmoreland Vol. Corps, 1997—2000; mem. strategic planning com. D.C. Pub. Libr., Washington, 1998—99. Fellow Nat. Acad. Edn., 1984-85; grantee Nat. Endowment for Humanities. Mem. Order of Coif, Beta Phi Mu. Home: 2900 Rittenhouse St NW Washington DC 20015-1524 Office: Cath U Am Sch Libr And Info Sci Washington DC 20064-0001 E-mail: preer@cua.edu.

PREHEIM, JOHN S. secondary education educator; b. Marion, S.D., July 18, 1941; s. Peter P. and Edith (Wenger) P.; m. Jo Ann Doerksen, June 1, 1963; children: Scott, David. BS in Elem. Edn., Bethel Coll., 1963; MS in Elem. Edn., Ind. U., 1968; postgrad., Ind. U., South Bend, 1972-92, U. Notre Dame, 1980, 86. Cert. tchr., Ind., emotionally handicapped tchr., Ind. Dir. indsl. therapy LaRue Carter Hosp., Indpls., 1963-65; 6th grade tchr. Speedway (Ind.) Schs., 1965-72; asst. prin. Allison Elem. Sch., 1968-72; coord treehouse program for emotionally handicapped children Oaklawn Mental Health Ctr./Elkhart (Ind.) Community Schs., 1972-78; 6th grade tchr. Elkhart Community Schs., 1978-81, emotionally handicapped resource tchr., 1981-84, 7th grade math. tchr., 1984—, chmn. math dept., 1987—. Cons. Elkhart Community Day Care Ctr., 1975-78. Bd. pres. Hively Ave Presch., Elkhart, 1978-82; bd. dirs., bd. pres. Camp Friedenswald, Cassopolis, Mich., 1980-86. Named Disting. Vol., Christian Camping Internat., 1986. Mem. NEA, Ind. Tchrs. Assn., Elkhart Tchrs. Assn. (bd. dirs. 1987-91), Nat. Coun. Tchrs. Math. Mennonite. Avocations: visiting state capital buildings, travel, running, genealogy, gardening. Home: 22967 Chestnut Ln Goshen IN 46528-9534 Office: West Side Mid Sch 101 S Nappanee St Elkhart IN 46514-1955

PREISS, MITCHELL PAUL, mathematics educator; b. N.Y.C., Nov. 13, 1956; s. Charles and Lucille Rosalyn (Cohen) P. BS in Math., Cooper Union for Advancement of Sci. and Art, 1977; MS in Indsl. and Applied Math., Poly. Inst. N.Y., 1979, PhD in Ops. Rsch., 1986. Teaching fellow Poly. Inst. N.Y., Bklyn., 1977-79, adj. inst. math., 1978-79; instr. math. St. Peter's Coll., Jersey City, 1979-81; adj. instr. math. Baruch Coll., CUNY, 1979; instr. math. York Coll. CUNY, Jamaica, 1981-82; adj. asst. prof. math. Pace U., N.Y.C., 1978-82, asst. prof., 1982-91, assoc. prof., 1992-97, prof., 1998—. Contbr. articles to profl. jours. Judge N.Y. Met. Math. Fair, 1983—, Jr. Acad. Sci. Rsch. Competition, 1984, 86-88; judge N.Y. Acad. Scis. Sci. and Engring. Event, N.Y.C., 1987—, Polytech. Univ.'s N.Y.C. Sci., Math. and Tech. Fair, Bklyn., 2000-. N.Y. State Regents scholar, 1973. Mem. N.Y. Acad. Scis. (life mem.), Am. Math. Soc., Math. Assn. Am., Pi Mu Epsilon, Kappa Mu Epsilon. Democrat. Avocations: tennis, softball, jogging, reading. Office: Pace U 41 Park Row Rm 701 New York NY 10038-1508 E-mail: mpreiss@pace.edu.

PREISS-HARRIS, PATRICIA, music educator, composer, pianist; b. N.Y.C., May 19, 1950; d. Fredric H. and Madeline (Robbins) P.; m. Eric A. Lerner, Nov. 1970 (div. 1975); m. William H. Harris, Aug. 13, 1995. BA, Harvard U., 1973; MFA, Calif. Inst. Arts, 1987. Performer, bassist Carla Bley Band, Willow, NY, 1977—78; instr. piano, composition The Hall Sch., Pittsfield, Mass., 1983—84; instr. music Santa Monica (Calif.) C.C., 1989; tchr. piano The Hackley Sch., Tarrytown, NY, 1991; tchr. piano and composition Fraioli Sch. of Music, Greenwich, Conn., 1991—2002; accompanist SUNY, Purchase, NY, 1991—95; performer, pianist Gary Wofsey Jazz Orchestra, 1996—, The Jones Factor Big Band, 1999—. Pvt. piano tchr., NY, 1990—, Conn., 1990—, Mass., 1980—84; pianist Greenwich Regency Hyatt Hotel, 1995—; solo and ensemble pianist, 1980—; accompanist Blue Notes vocal ensemble, 2000—; attendee Cummington (Mass.) Cmty. of Arts, 1981. Performer Trust in Love, 1981; composer, pianist Jamaica's Album, 1984; composer Messages (piano & flute), 1980, Invocations (women's choir, medieval instruments), 1981, Complete Enlightenment (woodwinds, spkr.), 1986. Performance grantee Cambridge (Mass.) Arts Coun., 1977, Artists grantee No. Berkshire Coun. on Arts, 1983 Mem.: Schubert Club. Home: 162 Toms Rd Stamford CT 06906-1031 E-mail: patti@pattipreiss.com.

PRELOCK, PATRICIA A. speech pathologist; b. May 31, 1954; BS, Kent State U., 1976, MA, 1977; PhD, U. Pitts., 1983. Cert. clin. speech pathologist, Pa., Ohio, Vt.; bd. recognized child lang. specialist. Lectr. U. Pitts., 1982—83; lang. cons. Children's Hosp. of Pitts., 1983—85; asst. prof. Coll. St. Rose, 1986—87; ind. cons., 1990—; reviewer, cons. Communication Skill Builders, Tucson, 1990—; assoc. prof. U. Vt., 1995—2000, prof., 2000—, chair dept. comm. sci., 2002—. Project dir. U.S. Dept. Edn; editl. cons., assoc. editor Lang., Speech Hearing Svcs. in Schs.; editl. cons. Jour. Edn. and Psychol. Consultation, Am. Jour. Speech Lang. Pathology; project dir. Vt. Rural Autism Project; tng. dir. Vt. Interdisciplinary Leadership Edn. in Neurol. Devel. Disabilities; adj. asst. prof. U. Cin., 1988-90, vis. asst. prof., 1990-93, rsch. asst. prof., 1993-94. Co-author: Meta Magic: Metalinguistic Intervention for Phenological Disorders, 1991, Voice and Articulation: A Workbook for Students, 1991, Communication Science Resource Manual, 1994, Working Across the Classroom Curriculum, 1993; author, co-author numerous articles in field including Mimicry vs. Imitative Modeling: Facilitating Language Production in the Retarded, 1979, The Middle Ground in Evaluating Language Programs, 1981, A Retrospective Examination of Interactional Behaviors Viewed as Experimentally Non-Significant, 1990, The Influence of Processing Mode on the Sentence Productions of LD and Normal Children, 1989, Discourse-Sentence Interaction in the Speech of LD and Normal Children, 1991; prosodic analysis others. Chmn. Pine Ridge Sch., 1999—2003, bd. dirs., 1999—2003. Recipient Pierce Meml. award for Speech, Continuing Edn. award, Friends award Vt. Parent Info. Ctr., 1999, First Autism Excellence in Svc. award Autism Soc. Vt., 2000, Kroepsch-Maurice Excellence in Tchg. award U. Vt., 2000; City of Akron Panhellenic scholar; Univ. scholar U. Vt., 2003. Fellow Am. Speech, Lang. and Hearing Assn. (bd.,coord. 1999, 2001, 2002,); mem. Nat. Com. for Lang. Learning Disabilities, Ohio Speech, Lang. and Hearing Assn. (program com., legis. coun., dist. rep.), Southwestern Ohio Speech, Lang. and Hearing Assn. (ethics com., nominations com., OSHA liaison), Parent to Parent (pres., bd. dirs. 1999-2003), Southwestern Pa. Speech, Lang. and Hearing Assn. (past pres.), Vt. Speech and Hearing Assn., Alpha Lambda Delta, Omicron Delta Kappa. Home: 21 White Lilac Way Colchester VT 05446-3859 Office: Dept Com Sci U VT 489 Main St Burlington VT 05405-1709

PREMUŽIĆ-MCCHESNEY, ARIANNE TAMARA MARIA, elementary education educator; b. Vancouver, B.C., Can., Apr. 30, 1962; d. Eugene Tomislav and Brenda Betty (Leach) P. AA in Liberal Arts/Humanities, Cert. in Word Processing, Suffolk County Community Coll., 1987; BS in Elem. Edn., D'Youville Coll., 1994. Ballet tchr. June Claire Sch. of Dance, Coram, N.Y., 1980-86; asst. mgr. Radio Shack, L.I., N.Y., 1980-86; classical ballerina, soloist Empire State Ballet, Buffalo, 1987-92; ballet tchr. Off Broadway Ctr., East Aurora, NY, 1989—96, Dyan Mulvey Acad., Lockport, 1991—96; dancer Roberta Taylor and Co., Buffalo, 1989—. Extra actor United Artist, Vancouver, 1989. Photographer, dancer (Scholarship Dance Masters award 1978), model, choreographer (2nd Pl. Trophy 1991) in field. Peer counselor West Hampton Beach (N.Y.) High Sch., 1977-80, crisis intervention, 1977-80; tutor D'Youville Coll. Learning Ctr., Buffalo, 1991—. Mem. D'Youville Coll. Tchrs. Assn. (v.p. 1992-94), Dance Masters of Am., (1st and 2nd place competition winner). Home: 2412 Piplar Dr Gwynn Oak MD 21207 Office: St Marks Sch 7501 Adelphi Rd Hyattsville MD 20783

PRENDERGAST, CAROLE LISAK, musician, educator; b. Chgo., Mar. 15, 1949; d. Chester Matt and Emily Julie (Krupa) Lisak; m. Joseph Thomas Prendergast, Oct. 19, 1974; children: Karin, Colin. MusB, DePaul U., 1971; MA in Ch. Music and Liturgy, St. Joseph's Coll., Rensselaer, Ind., 2002. Tchg. cert. K-14, Ill. Substitute organist St. Adalbert Ch., Chgo., 1965-76; music tchr. Chgo. Pub. Schs., 1971-74; music dir. St. Adalbert Ch., 1976-88; freelance musician, 1988—; choir accompanist St. Luke Ch., River Forest, Ill., 1993—, music dir., 2000—. Piano tchr., Chgo., 1970—. Chairperson welcome com. Queen of Martyrs Ch., Evergreen Park, Ill., 1990—. Ill. state scholar, 1968-71, DePaul scholar, 1968. Mem. Am. Guild Organists, Nat. Assn. Pastoral Musicians, Music Tchrs. Nat. Assn., Chgo. Fedn. Musicians, Chgo. Area Suzuki Tchrs., Suzuki Assn. of the Ams. Roman Catholic. Avocations: gardening, travel, antique collecting, cooking. Home: 10417 S Hamlin Ave Chicago IL 60655-3115 Office: St Luke Ch 528 Lathrop River Forest IL 60305

PRENTICE, ANN ETHELYND, university dean; b. Grafton, Vt., July 19, 1933; d. Homer Orville and Helen (Cooke) Hurlbut; divorced; children: David, Melody, Holly, Wayne. AB, U. Rochester, 1954; MLS, SUNY, Albany, 1964; DLS, Columbia U., 1972; LittD (hon.), Keuka Coll., 1979. Lectr. sch. info. sci. and policy SUNY, Albany, 1971-72, asst. prof., 1972-78; prof., dir. grad. sch. library and info. sci. U. Tenn., Knoxville, 1978-88; assoc. v.p. info. resources U. South Fla., Tampa, 1988-93; dean Coll. Info. Studies, U. Md., College Park, 1993—, acting asst. v.p. for info. resources, 1994-98. Y2K compliance coord. U. Md., 1998—. Author: Strategies for Survival, Library Financial Management Today, 1979, The Library Trustee, 1973, Public Library Finance, 1977, Financial Planning for Libraries, 1983, 2d edit., 1996, Professional Ethics for Librarians, 1985; editor Pub. Libr. Quar., 1978-81; co-editor: Info. Sci. in its Disciplinary Context, 1990; assoc. editor Library and Info. Sci. Ann., 1987-90. Cons. long-range planning and pers. Knox County Libr. System, 1980, 85-86, Richland County S.C. Libr. System, 1981, Upper Hudson Libr. Fedn., N.Y., State Libr. Ohio, 1986, Am. U., 1996; trustee Hyde Park (N.Y.) Free Libr., treas., 1973-75, pres., 1976; trustee Mid-Hudson Libr. System, Poughkeepsie, N.Y., 1975-78; trustee adv. bd. Hillsborough County Libr., 1991-93. Recipient Disting. Alumni award SUNY, Albany, 1987, Columbia U., 1991. Mem. ALA, CAUSE, Am. Soc. Info. Sci. (exec. bd. 1986-89, conf. chmn. 1989, pres. 1992-93, chmn. info. policy com. 1994-96), Assn. for Libr. and Info. Sci. Edn. (pres. 1986). Office: Univ Md Coll Libr and Info Svcs 4105 Hornbake Bldg College Park MD 20742-0001

PRENTICE, WILLIAM EDWARD, athletic trainer, physical therapist, educator; b. Nashville, Aug. 23, 1952; s. William Edward and Thelma (Farmer) P.; m. Martena Wootten Prentice, Aug. 11, 1955; children: Brian William, Zachary Robert. BS in Physical Edn., U. Del., 1974, MS, 1976; BS in Physical Therapy, U. N.C., 1984; PhD, U. Va., 1980. Lic. physical therapist, N.C.; cert. athletic trainer. Asst. athletic trainer Temple U., Phila., 1976-78; prof. exercise and sport sci., phys. therapy U. N.C., Chapel Hill, 1980—. Dir. sports medicine edn., Healthsouth Rehab. Corp., 1989-98; Gatorade Bd. Advisors for Sci. and Edn., 1996; athletic trainer, phys. therapist U.S. Olympic Com., Colorado Springs, 1983-88. Author: Get Fit Stay Fit, 2004, Fitness for College and Life, 1999, Therapeutic Modelities for Physical Therapists, 2002, Therapeutic Modalities for Sports Medicine, 2003, Principles of Athletic Training, 2003; contbr. articles to profl. jours. Mem. Nat. Athletic Trainers Assn. Republican. Baptist. Home: 222 Old Forest Creek Dr Chapel Hill NC 27514-5420 Office: U NC Fetzer Gym Chapel Hill NC 27514

PREPARATA, FRANCO PAOLO, computer science and engineering educator; b. Reggio E, Italy, Dec. 29, 1935; came to U.S., 1965, naturalized, 1977; s. Vincenzo and Stefania P.; m. Rosamaria Cupi, Apr. 30, 1964; children: Paola, Claudia. Dr.Ing., U. Rome, 1959; Libera Docenza, Italian U. System, 1969; Doctorate (hon.), U. Padova (Italy), 1997. System analyst, tech. mgr. Univac, Rome, 1960-63; sr. designer Selenia S.p.A., Rome, 1963-65; professorial staff U. Ill., Urbana, 1965-90, prof. elec. engring. and computer sci., 1970-90; An Wang prof. computer sci. Brown U., Providence, 1991—. Author: (with Raymond T. Yeh) Introduction to Discrete Structures, 1972, Introduction to Computer Engineering, 1985, (with M.I. Shamos) Computational Geometry, 1985; assoc. editor: IEEE Trans. on Computers, 1978-82, also 9 other jours.; contbr. articles to profl. jours. Fellow IEEE (Darlington award 1993), Assn. Computing Machinery. Office: 115 Waterman St Providence RI 02912-9016

PRESCOTT, BARBARA LODWICH, educational administrator; b. Chgo., Aug. 15, 1951; d. Edward and Eugenia Lodwich; m. Warren Paul Prescott, Dec. 2, 1979; children: Warren Paul Jr., Ashley Elizabeth. BA, U. Ill., Chgo., 1973, MEd, 1981; MA, U. Wis., 1978; postgrad., Stanford U., 1983-87. Cert. tchr., learning handicapped specialist, cmty. coll. instr., Calif. Grad. rschr. U. Ill., Chgo., 1979-81; learning handicapped specialist St. Paulus Luth. Sch., San Francisco, 1981-83; grad. rsch. asst. Sch. Edn. Stanford (Calif.) U., 1983-87, writing cons. for law students, 1985-86; learning handicapped specialist/lead therapist Gilroy Clinic Speech-Hearing-Learning Ctr., Crippled Children's Soc., Santa Clara, Calif.,

1988-89; ednl. dir. Adolescent Intensive Resdl. Svc. Calif. Pacific Med. Ctr., San Francisco, 1989-95; exec. dir. Learning Profiles, South Lake Tahoe, Calif., 1995—. Instr. evening San Jose City Coll., 1988-92. Contbr. articles to profl. jours.; author: Proceedings of Internat. Congress of Linguistics, 1987; editor: Proceedings - Forum for Research on Language Issues, 1986; author videotape: Making a Difference in Language and Learning, 1989. Recipient Frederick Bork Teaching Trainee award San Francisco State U., 1983; Ill. State scholar, 1973. Mem. Calif. Assn. Pvt. Specialized Edn. and Svcs., Phi Delta Kappa (v.p. 1984-86), Pi Lambda Theta (sec. 1982-83), Phi Kappa Phi, Alpha Lambda Theta.

PRESCOTT, PEGGY COLLINS, higher education administrator; b. Laurens, SC, Mar. 8, 1955; d. Gordon Byron and Mary Hughes (Lanford) Collins; m. Edwin William Prescott II, June 5, 1976; children: Edwin William III, Byron Collins, Tyson Brett. BS, Winthrop Coll., Rock Hill, S.C., 1976, MEd, 1978; EdS, Clemson U., 1984; EdD, S.C. State U., 2001. Cert. tchr., S.C. Tchr. Edgewood Elem. Sch., Rock Hill, 1976-78; tchr., asst. prin. Sanders Elem. Sch., Laurens, 1978-87; asst. prin. Ford Sch., Laurens, 1987-91, prin., 1991-95, E.B. Morse Elem. Sch., Laurens, 1995—; curriculum specialist Workplace Resource Ctr. S.C. State Dept. Edn., 1999—; asst. to v.p. acad. affairs Claflin U., Orangeburg, SC. Dir. children's choir First Bapt. Ch., Laurens, 1992-93. Named Young Career Woman of Yr., Bus. and Profl. Women, 1984. Mem. Kiwanis Club (bd. dirs. 1993-96), Delta Kappa Gamma (treas.). Baptist. Avocations: horseback riding, country-western dancing, reading. Home: 114 Sherwood Frst Laurens SC 29360-2642 Office: Workplace Resource Ctr SC State Dept Edn Laurens SC 29360-2614 E-mail: peggy@scwrc.org.

PRESIDENT, TONI ELIZABETH, counseling administrator, guidance counselor, former elementary educator; b. Charleston, S.C., Aug. 23, 1954; d. Sam and Margaret (Shokes) P.; 1 child, Kayla Javonne. BS cum laude, S.C. State Coll., 1976; MEd, The Citadel, 1984, postgrad., 1996, Coll. of Charleston, 1993. Tchr., grade 5 Berkeley Elem. Sch., Moncks Corner, S.C., 1976-77; tchr., grade 2 Ben Tillman Elem. Sch., Charleston, 1977-85; guidance counselor Ronald E. McNair Elem. Sch., Charleston, 1985-92, Jennie Moore Elem. Sch., Mt. Pleasant, 1992-94, Orange Grove Elem. Sch., Charleston, S.C., 1994-99, DuBose Mid. Sch., Summerville, S.C., 1999—. Mem., ministry to youth dir. Ebenezer A.M.E. Ch., Charleston; mem. Charleston PTA, DuBose Mid. PTSA; active Girl Scouts U.S. Recipient bd. mem. awards Charleston (S.C.) Actors Theatre Soc., 1987, 88, Young Women's Christian Assn., Charleston, 1988; named Best Supporting Actress, Charleston (S.C.) Actors Theatre Soc., 1988. Mem. S.C. Sch. Counselors Assn., Tri-County Counseling Assn., S.C. State U. Alumni Assn., Phi Delta Kappa, Alpha Kappa Alpha. Avocation: reading.

PRESLEY, SUSAN FRANKLIN, secondary school educator, department chairman; b. Columbia, S.C., Sept. 4, 1968; d. Delma Eugene and Beverly Bloodworth Presley. BA, Ga. Coll., 1990; MA, Ga. Southern U., 1992. Cert. learning disabilities tchr. Ga., 1993. Spl. edn. tchr. Savannah (Ga.) H.S., 1993—, dept. head spl. edn., 1998—. Faculty rep. PTA, 2000—01; mem. sch. leadership team, Savannah, Ga., 1999—. Mem.: Profl. Assn. Ga. Educators (sch. rep.). Presbyterian. Avocations: reading, writing, music, walking. Office: Savannah HS 400 Pennsylvania Ave Savannah GA 31404

PRESNALL, BOBBY JOE, retired math educator; b. Olney, Tex., Jan. 11, 1937; s. Charles Haskell and Nora Florence (Jackson) P.; m. Marguerite Mary Watkins, June 7, 1938; children: Jennifer, Jeffrey, John, Joseph. BS, Abilene Christian U., 1959. Chemistry tchr. Cooper Woodrow H.S., Lubbock, Tex., 1960-61, Somersworth (N.H.) H.S., 1961-62, Boling (Tex.) H.S., 1962-64, 65-67; tchr. Throckmorton (Tex.) H.S., 1964-65; tchr. earth sci. Winnacunnet H.S., Hampton, N.H., 1967-72; tchr. math/sci. Goree (Tex.) H.S., 1972—2003. Paraprofl. Boy Scouts Am., Wichita Falls, 1976-79. Pres. Knox County Child Welfare Bd., Goree, 1980-86; city councilman City of Goree, 1982-92; scout master Boy Scouts Am., 1973-78. Mem. NEA, Tex. State Tchrs. Assn., Nat. Sci. Tchrs. Assn., Nat. Coun. of Tchrs. of Math. Democrat. Roman Catholic. Avocation: woodworking. Home: RR 1 Box 4 Goree TX 76363-9702

PRESS, AIDA KABATZNICK, former editor, writer, poet; b. Boston, Nov. 18, 1926; m. Newton Press, June 5, 1947; children: David, Dina Press Weber, Benjamin Presskreischer. BA, Radcliffe Coll., 1948. Reporter Waltham (Mass.) News-Tribune, 1960-63; freelance writer, 1960-63; editl. cons. Mass. Dept. Mental Health, Boston, 1966-72; Waltham/Watertown reporter Boston Herald Traveler, 1963-70; dir. news and publs. Harvard Grad. Sch. Design, Cambridge, Mass., 1972-78; publs. editor Radcliffe Coll., Cambridge, 1978-81, dir., editor of publs., 1981-83, editor Radcliffe Quar., 1971-93, dir. pub. info., 1983-93; cons. editor Regis Coll. Alumnae Mag., Weston, Mass., 1994. Editor emerita Radcliffe Quar., 1993—; contbr. articles to newspapers and mags. Recipient Publs. Distinction award Am. Alumni Coun., 1974, Top 5 coll. Mag., Coun. for Advancement and Support of Edn., 1984, Top 10 Univ Mags., 1991, Gold medal Coll. Mags., 1991, Alumnae Achievement award Radcliffe Coll., 1994, Radcliffe Coll. Presdl. Commendation, 1992. Mem. Phi Beta Kappa. Avocations: hiking, playing recorder.

PRESSEISEN, BARBARA ZEMBOCH, retired educational director, researcher; b. Dayton, Ohio, June 15, 1936; d. William and Ida (Wise) Zemboch; m. Ernst Leopold Presseisen, June 30, 1963; children: Joshua William, Benjamin David. BA, Brandeis U., 1958; MAT, Harvard U., 1959; EdD, Temple U., 1972. Tchr., counselor Sequoia Union High Sch. Dist., East Palo Alto, Calif., 1959-63; lectr. No. Ill. U., De Kalb, 1963-65; teaching assoc. Temple U., Phila., 1967-69; asst. prof. Swarthmore (Pa.) Coll., 1969-71; curriculum coord. Rsch. for Better Schs., Phila., 1971-75, project dir., 1975-80, asst. dir., 1980-85, dir. nat. networking, 1985-99; ret., 1999. V.p. edn. Nobel Learning Communities, Inc., Media, Pa., 1996-99. Author: Unlearned Lessons, 1985; editor and author: At-Risk Students and Thinking, 1988, Teaching for Intelligence, 1999; contbr. editor: (newsletter) Teaching Thinking and Problem Solving, Phila., 1981-96. Bd. trustees Friends Select Sch., Phila., 1987-95. Mem. ASCD (task force 1981—), Am. Ednl. Rsch. Assn., Pi Lambda Theta (editl. bd. 1983—), Nat. Ind. Pvt. Sch. Assn. (bd. dirs. 1998—), Phi Delta Kappa (Ralph D. Owen scholar 1958), Brandeis U. Alumni Assn. (Phila.). Democrat. Office: 1943 Pine St Philadelphia PA 19103-6616

PRESSER, STEPHEN BRUCE, lawyer, educator; b. Chattanooga, Aug. 10, 1946; s. Sidney and Estelle (Shapiro) P.; m. Carole Smith, June 18, 1968 (div. 1987); children: David Carter, Elisabeth Catherine; m. ArLynn Leiber, Dec. 13, 1987; children: Joseph Leiber, Eastman Leiber. AB, Harvard U., 1968, JD, 1971. Bar: Mass. 1971, D.C. 1972. Law clk. to Judge Malcolm Richard Wilkey U.S. Ct. Appeals (D.C. cir.), 1971-72; assoc. Wilmer, Cutler & Pickering, Washington, 1972-74; asst. prof. law Rutgers U., Camden, N.J., 1974-76; vis. assoc. prof. U. Va., 1976-77; prof. Northwestern U., Chgo., 1977—, class 1940 rsch. prof., 1992-93, Raoul Berger prof. legal history, 1992—, assoc. dean acad. affairs Sch. Law, 1982-85. Prof. bus. law Kellogg Sch. Mgmt., Northwestern U., Chgo., 1992—. Author: (with Jamil S. Zainaldin) Law and Jurisprudence in American History, 1980, 5th edit., 2004, Studies in the History of the United States Courts of the Third Circuit, 1983, The Original Misunderstanding: The English, The Americans and the Dialectic of Federalist Jurisprudence, 1991, Piercing the Corporate Veil, 1991, revised ann., (with Ralph Ferrara and Meridith Brown) Takeovers: A Strategist's Manual, 2d edit., 1993, Recapturing the Constitution, 1994, (with Douglas W. Kmiec) The American Constitutional Order: History, Cases, and Philosophy, 1998; assoc. articles editor Guide to American Law, 1985. Trustee Village of Winnetka, Ill., 2000-04; mem. acad. adv. bd. Washington Legal Found. Recipient summer stipend NEH, 1975; Fulbright Sr. scholar Univ. Coll., London Sch. Econs. and Polit. Sci., 1983-84, Inst. Advanced Legal Studies, 1996; Adams fellow Inst. U.S. Studies, London, 1996; assoc. rsch. fellow Inst. U.S. Studies, 1999—. Mem. Am. Soc. Legal History (bd. dirs. 1979-82), Am. Law Inst., Univ. Club Chgo. (bd. dirs. 1997-99, sec. 1999), Legal Club Chgo., Reform Club (London). Office: Northwestern U Law Sch 357 E Chicago Ave Chicago IL 60611-3069 E-mail: s-presser@law.northwestern.edu.

PRESTON, CAROL ANN, special education educator; b. Buffalo, Aug. 11, 1953; m. Robert George Preston, June 7, 1980; children: Nicole, Amy. Student, Keuka Coll., 1971-73; BS, SUNY, Plattsburg, 1975; MS, Russell Sage Coll., 1992. Cert. elem., spl. edn. tchr., N.Y. Program analyst N.Y. State Higher Edn. Svcs. Corp., Albany, 1977-82; tchr. spl. edn. Saratoga Springs (N.Y.) City Sch. System, 1992-94, Schuylerville (N.Y.) Jr./Sr. H.S., 1994-99; CSE chmn. Lansingburgh (N.Y.) Ctrl. Schs., 1999—2002. Daisy Girl Scout leader, 1989-90, Brownie leader Girl Scouts U.S., Clifton Park, N.Y., 1990-93, jr. leader, 1993-94, cadette leader 1997-99; substance abuse chmn. N.Y. State PTA, Albany, 1992-93, spl. edn. chmn., 1993-97, Adirondack Dist. dir. 1997-2000; mem. sch. bd. Shenendehowa Ctrl. Sch. Dist., Clifton Park, 1989-92, coord. student placement, 2002-. Recipient Dist. Svc. award PTA, N.Y., 1998; named Honorary Life mem. Shenendehowa PTA Coun., 1990. Mem. Phi Kappa Phi, Pi Lambda Theta. Home: 15 Turnberry Ln Clifton Park NY 12065-1104

PRESTON, DEBRA SUE, counselor, educator; b. Lansing, Mich., Mar. 28, 1964; d. Thomas Michael and Nancy Jean (Dickenson) P. BSW, East Carolina U., 1986, MA in Edn., 1989; CAGS, Va. Tech., 1994, PhD, 1995. Lic. sch. counselor; lic. profl. counselor; nat. cert. counselor; nat. cert. career counselor; cert. social worker. Sch. counselor Roanoke Rapids Schs., Roanoke, N.C., 1989-91, social worker, 1992-93; pub. rels. specialist Va. Tech., Blacksburg, 1993-95; adj. prof. W.Va. Grad. Sch., Beckley, 1994-95; asst. prof. U. N.C., Pembroke, 1995—. Mem. state tng. team State Occupl. Info. Coordinating Com., Raleigh, N.C., 1995—; pres. NCACES, 1998—. Author monthly letter Counselor's Corner, 1993-95. Mem. ACA, Chi Sigma Iota (pres., sec., faculty advisor). Office: U NC-Pembroke 1 University Rd Pembroke NC 28372-8699

PRESTON, LOYCE ELAINE, retired social work educator; b. Texarkana, Ark., Feb. 25, 1929; d. Harvey Martin and Florence (Whitlock) P.; student Texarkana Jr. Coll., 1946-47; B.S., Henderson State Tchrs. Coll., 1950; certificate in social work La. State U., 1952; M.S.W., Columbia U., 1956. Tchr. pub. schs., Dierks, Ark., 1950-51; child welfare worker Ark. Dept. Public Welfare, Clark and Hot Spring counties, 1951-56, child welfare cons., 1956-58; casework dir. Ruth Sch. Girls, Burien, Wash., 1958-60; asst. prof. spl. edn. La. Poly. Inst., Ruston, 1960-63; asst. prof. Northwestern State Coll., Shreveport, La., 1963-73; asst. prof. La. State U., Shreveport, 1973-79; ret., 1979. Chpt. sec. La. Assn. Mental Health, 1965-67, Gov's. adv. council, 1967-70; mem. Mayor's Com. for Community Improvement, 1972-76. Mem. AAUW (dir. Shreveport br. 1963-69), Acad. Cert. Social Workers, Nat. Assn. Social Workers (del. 1964-65, pres. North La. chpt., state-wide com. 1968-69), La Conf. Social Welfare, La. Fedn. Council Exceptional Children (pres. 1970-71), La. Tchrs. Assn. Home: 4255 Cloud St Shreveport LA 71107-2743

PRESTON, MICHAEL JAMES, English and folklore educator, consultant; b. Wenatchee, Wash., Sept. 5, 1943; s. Jefferson James and Rosamond Catherine (Ward) P.; m. Cathy Lynn Makin, Nov. 13, 1978; children: Theresa Maureen, Stephanie Michele. AB, Gonzaga U., 1965; MA, U. Va., 1967, U. Colo., 1972, PhD, 1975. Instr. English Colo. Women's Coll., Denver, 1967-75; dir. Ctr. Computer Rsch. Humanities U. Colo., Boulder, 1976-90, prof. English, 1990—. Computer panel mem. Nat. Endowment Humanities, Washington, 1980. Author: The Christmas Rhyme Books, 1999; editor: Concordance to the Middle English Shorter Poem, 1975, Urban Folklore from Colorado, 1976, The Other Print Tradition, 1995. Bd. dirs. Denver chpt. Amigos de Las Ams., Denver, 1998-2000. Nat. Endowment Humanities fellow, 1974, rsch. grantee, 1984-86; Am. Coun. Learned Socs. rsch. grantee, N.Y., 1974. Democrat. Roman Catholic. Avocation: home remodeling. Home: 515 S 46th St Boulder CO 80305-6037 Office: U Colo Dept English Boulder CO 80309-0001

PRESTON, PATRICIA ANN, language educator, researcher; b. Milw., Mar. 11, 1933; d. Charles Francis Preston, Dorothy Catherine Engman. BA in Spanish magna cum laude, Bryn Mawr Coll., 1955; MA in Spanish, Cath. U. Am., 1961, PhD in Spanish, 1964. Joined Sch. Sisters of Notre Dame. Prof. Spanish and bilingual edn. Mt. Mary Coll., Milw., 1964—, acad. dean, 1971—76, 1984—92, dir. Ctr. for Assessment, 1998—. Founder, dir. Project Head Start Coun. for the Spanish Speaking, Milw., 1965—71, founder, dir. Guadalupe Ctr., 1966—71; cons., in-svc. trainer Milw. Pub. Schs. Bilingual Program & other local and regional schools and districts, Milw., Waukesha, Kenosha, Wis., 1969—; mem. corp. bd. Mt. Mary Coll., Milw., 1971—96; co-founder, bd. dirs. Milw. Spectrum Alternative H.S., 1972—95; cons., examiner North Ctrl. Assn. Colls., Chgo., 1974—77; co-rschr. Cath. Colls. Milw., 1981; vis. prof. English Notre Dame Women's Coll., Kyoto, 1990. Author: (Book) A Study of Significant Variants in the Poetry of Gabriela Mistral, 1964; contbr. Book Wagering on Transcendence, 1997. Active mem. Coun. on Urban Edn., Milw., 1965—68; apptd. mem. Wis. State Day Care Adv. Bd., Madison, 1967—70; chairperson, bd. dirs. Coun. for the Spanish Speaking, Milw., 1970—74; chairperson Project Head Start Coalition Bd., Milw., 1970—74; bd. dirs. Cath. Social Svcs., Milw., 1971—76; mem. edn. commn. Wis. Cath. Conf., Madison, 1975—79; apptd. mem. Wis. State Adv. Com. on Bilingual-Bicultural Edn., Madison, 1978—82. Recipient Edn.: A Family Affair award of excellence, U. Wis.-Milw., Milw. Pub. Schs., Wis. Dept. Pub. Edn., 1999; fellow, Woodrow Wilson Found., 1960—61, 1963—64, Fellow, Summer Seminar in Spain, Fulbright Found., 1966, Summer Seminar Fellow - Bilingualism, NEH, 1977, Summer Seminar Fellow - European Autobiography, 1993. Mem.: TESOL, Am. Nystagmus Network, Nat. Assn. for Bilingual Edn., Wis. Assn. Fgn. Lang. Tchrs., Am. Assn. for Tchrs. of Spanish and Portuguese. Avocation: active advocate for disabled, mentally ill, poor, under-educated persons, immigrants, children and youth. Office: Mount Mary Coll 2900 Menomonee River Pkwy Milwaukee WI 53222-4597 Home Fax: 414-256-0195; Office Fax: 414-256-0195. Personal E-mail: prestonp@mtmary.edu. Business E-Mail: prestonp@mtmary.edu.

PRESTOPNIK, RICHARD JOHN, electronics and computer educator; b. Little Falls, N.Y., Nov. 23, 1951; s. John William and Frances (Grabowski) P.; m. Jan Sponenberg, June 16, 1973; children: Nathan Richard, Emily Kate, Adam Christopher. AAS in Elec. Tech., Mohawk Valley C.C., 1971; B Engring. Tech. in Elec. Engring., Rochester Inst. Tech., 1974; MSEE in Computer Engring., Syracuse U., 1982. From jr. engr. to sr. assoc. engr. IBM, Endicott, NY, 1974-80; from asst. to assoc. prof. elec. tech. dept. Fulton-Montgomery C.C., Johnstown, NY, 1980-89, prof., 1989-95, acting dean career edn., 1995-96, dean bus. and tech., 1996-99, prof., 2001—; dir. NASA-Fulton-Montgomery C.C. Spatial Info. Tech. Ctr., 2000—01; advisor Spatial Info. Tech. Ctr., 2001—. Coll. rep. on bd. dirs. Fulton-Montgomery, Schoharie Pvt. Industry Coun.; participant long distance learning project Gloversville High Sch.; mem. tech. prep. steering com. Fulton County Econ. Devel. Corp.; v.p. CPT Assocs., Inc., computer and electronic cons., 1983-85; book reviewer Prentice-Hall, Inc. Revision author: The Encyclopedia of Integrated Circuits, 2d edit., 1987; author: The Microprocessor IC Reference Manual, 1989, Digital Electronics: Concepts and Applications for Digital Design, 1990, also lab. manual, 1990; also articles. Faculty grantee SUNY Rsch. Found., 1986, faculty excellence grantee Fulton-Montgomery C.C., 1992, numerous others; NASA/ASEE faculty fellow in aeronautics and space rsch., 1995, 96; recipient V.P. Gore's Nat. Performance Rev. Hammer award, 1997, Chancellor's award for excellence in scholarship and creative activities SUNY, 2003. Mem. IEEE, Am. Soc. Engring. Edn. (Outstanding Educator award St. Lawrence sect. 1990), N.Y. State Engring. Tech. Assn. Avocations: golf, hiking, travel. Office: Fulton-Montgomery CC 2805 State Highway 67 Johnstown NY 12095-3749 E-mail: rprestop@fmcc.suny.edu.

PREVOT, NANCIE LOUISE, middle school educator; b. N.Y.C., May 28, 1957; d. Charles John and Mary Rose (McQuade) Prevot; children: Douglas Charles, Daniel Joseph, Katherine Elizabeth. BA magna cum laude, Mt. St Mary Coll., 1987. Tchr. St. Thomas Elem. Sch., Cornwell-on-Hudson, N.Y., 1988; tchr., acad. advisor Russel O. Brackman Mid. Sch., Barnegat, N.J., 1990—, cheerleading coach, 1991—, mem. mentor program, 1992-94. Coach Barnegat Soccer Club, 1991, Manahawkin So. Regional Pop Warner Football, 1994, track; active PTO, 1991—, Site-Base Mgmt., 1991—; mem. Nat. Junior Honor Soc. Faculty Coun. Recipient Gov.'s Teaching Award. Mem. Alpha Sigma Lambda. Avocations: swimming, walking. Home: 306 Cove Ln Beach Haven NJ 08008-1817

PREYER, NORRIS WATSON, history educator; b. Greensboro, N.C., Feb. 9, 1926; s. William Yost Preyer and Mary Norris Richardson; m. Kathryn Jeanette Cobb, Dec. 15, 1950; children: Norris Watson Jr., Janet McFadyen Nelson. BA, U. N.C., 1947; MA, U. Va., 1950, PhD, 1954. Asst. prof. history Guilford Coll., Greensboro, N.C., 1953-57, Queens Coll., Charlotte, N.C., 1957-58, prof. history, 1958-62, chair dept. history, 1959-90, Dana prof. history, 1962-90, Dana prof. emeritus, 1990—. Bd. dirs. Piedmont Fin. Co. Author: Hezekiah Alexander and the Revolution in the Backcountry, 1987 (Book award N.C. Soc. Historians 1988), The Preyer Boys, 2000; contbr. articles to profl. jours. Bd. dirs. Textile History Soc., 1962-65, Sci. Mus., Inc., Charlotte, 1973-79, Presbyn. Hist. Soc., 1985-91, Mecklenburg Hist. Soc., 1994-2000, cons. Mus. New South, 1990—; mem. adv. com. Spirit Sq. Ctr. for Arts and Edn., 1995-98; bd. dirs. Latta Place, Inc., Charlotte, 1972-75, 85-91, 92-95, 97-2003, pres., 1994-95; elder Myers Park Presbyn. Ch., Charlotte; mem. planning group Charlotte-Mecklenburg Cultural Task Force, 1974-75; bd. visitors Queens Coll., 1997—, Sharon Towers, 1999—; bd. dirs. Charlotte Mus. History, 2002—. Served USNR, 1944-1946. Named Danforth Assoc., Danforth Found., 1962-68; NEH fellow Newberry Libr., Chgo., 1979. Mem. Orgn. Am. Historians, So. Hist. Assn., Soc. for the History of the Early Am. Republic, N.C. Hist. Soc., Mecklenburg Hist. Assn. Democrat. Avocations: tennis, fishing, travel. Home: 960 Cherokee Rd Charlotte NC 28207

PREZIOSI, ROBERT CHARLES, dean, business educator; b. Washington, Feb. 6, 1946; BA in Social Sci., Fla. Atlantic U., 1968, MEd in Ednl. Psychology, 1972; DPA in Mgmt., Nova U., 1977. Pres. Mgmt. Assocs.; assoc. dean, prof. mgmt. edn. Sch. Bus. and Entrepreneurship Nova Southeastern U., Ft. Lauderdale, Fla. Mem. editorial bd. Jour. Rsch. Learning in Workplace, Jour. Leadership Studies; tng. cons. in field. Editor Jour. Applied Mgmt. and Entrepreneurship; mem. editorial bd. Jour. Leadership Studies; past gen. editor Jour. Applied Human Resource Devel.; past productivity editor Sources; contbr. articles to profl. publs.; producer audio and video programs in field. Recipient Torch Leadership award, 1990, Profl. of Yr., 1991. Mem. ASTD (Outstanding Contbn. award 1990). Office: Nova Southeastern Univ Sch Bus 3301 College Ave Fort Lauderdale FL 33314-7796

PRICE, ANNA MARIA, university administrator; b. Dallas, Feb. 17, 1943; d. Lumpkin Calier and Lulu Belle (Smith) Benjamin; m. Hollis Freeman Price Jr., June 22, 1963 (div. Jan. 1981); children: Stacey Ellen (dec.), Hollis Freeman III. BA, Ctrl. State U., 1970; MA, Wright State U., 1971; PhD, U. Miami, 1988. Dir. upward bound U. Miami, Coral Gables, Fla., 1973-88, coord. acad. support athletics, 1988-91, asst. athletic dir., 1991-94, asst. provost, asst. athletic dir., 1994-96, asst. provost, asst. prof., 1996—; dean students Fla. Meml. Coll., Miami, 1983-84. Cons. Nat. Coun. Ednl. Opportunity Assn., Washington, 1986, 87, 96, Western Ky. U. Program Evaluation, Nashville, Tenn., 1988, SAEOPP Tng. Authority, Atlanta, 1987. Contbr. articles to profl. jours. Mayor City of South Miami, Dade County, Fla., 1997, commr., 1996; 1st vice chmn., bd. trustees Hist. Mus. of So. Fla., Dade County, 1997; bd. dirs. Recording for Blind and Dyslexic, 1995—; min., dir. of cmty. missions; mem. Dem. Women's Club, Coral Gables, pres. 1979-80; pres. Hemispheric Congress for Women, 1977. Named Woman of Yr. King of Clubs, 1991, Cmty. Headliner Women in Comms., 1990; recipient Black Achievers award Family Chrisitan Assn. of Am., 1988. Mem. Rotary Club of South Miami, Fla. Sports Found., Omicron Delta Kappa. Democrat. Office: City of South Miami 6130 Sunset Dr South Miami FL 33143-5093

PRICE, BARBARA GILLETTE, college administrator, artist; b. Phila., June 26, 1938; d. Philip and Frances (Bressler) Gillette; 1 child, Michelle Cutler. BFA, U. Ala., Tuscaloosa, 1966, MA, 1968. Acting chair dept. art Judson Coll., Marion, Ala., 1969; faculty Corcoran Sch. of Art, Washington, 1970-78; acad. dean Cranbrook Acad. of Art, Bloomfield Hills, Mich., 1978-82; v.p. acad. affairs Md. Inst. Coll. of Art, Balt., 1982-93; pres. Moore Coll. of Art and Design, Phila., 1994-98; art edn. cons., 1998—. Bd. dirs. AICAD, Washington, Fleisher Art Meml., Phila. One person shows include Cranbrook Acad. Art Mus., Bloomfield Hills, 1980, Robert Kidd Gallery Assocs., Birmingham, Mich., 1980, Ferris State, Big Rapids, Mich., 1981, Schweyer Galdo Galleries, Birmingham, 1982, Md. Inst. Coll. of Art, Balt., 1982, 94, Coll. of Notre Dame of Md., Balt., 1985, Columbia (Md.) Assn. Ctr. for Arts, 1989, Loyola Coll., Balt., 1991, Artshowcase, Balt., 1993; group exhbns. include Gallery 641, Washington, 1975, Washington Women's Art Ctr., 1975, Foundry Gallery, Washington, 1975, 76, Rutgers U., New Brunswick, N.J., 1975, Olympia Internat. Art Ctr., Kingston, Jamaica, 1975, Robert Kidd Gallery Assocs., Birmingham, 1980, Grimaldis Gallery, Balt., 1983, Artscape, Balt., 1986, Md. Inst. Coll. of Art, Balt., 1983, 85, 91, 92, 93, Art in the Bell Tower, Balt., 1988, Morris Mechanic Theatre Gallery, Balt., 1989, Artshowcase, Balt., 1990, 91, 92, 93, Frostburg State U., 1991. Bd. dirs. Friends of Logan Square, Phila., 1994-95, Phila. Vol. Lawyers Arts, Phila., 1994-95. Mem. Nat. Assn. Schs. of Art and Design (bd. dirs., sec. exec. com.), Nat. Coun. Art Adminstrs., Coll. Art Assn. (assoc.), Am. Assn. Higher Edn., Soc. for Coll. and Univ. Planning.*

PRICE, BEVERLY BRUNS, secondary education educator; b. Alamosa, Colo., Feb. 25, 1944; d. Frederick Garnett and Ruth Florence (Remke) Bruns; children: Theresa Lynne, Lawrence Vernon. BEd, Adams State Coll., 1969; MEd, Ariz. State U., 1975. Cert. tchr., Ariz. Tchr. math. Glendale (Ariz.) Union High Sch. Dist., 1970—72, 1973—97, chmn. adv. bd., geometry curriculum guide, 1984; ret., 1997. Tchr. math. div. tech. studies Ind. U.-Purdue U., Ft. Wayne, 1972-73 Mem. Am. Assn. for Nude Recreation (bd. dirs. 1982-85, 88—, pres. 1985-87, Woman of Yr. 1984, 89, 2002, sec. 1988—). Avocations: nude recreation, camping, hiking, boating, travel. Home: 1414 W Wood Dr Phoenix AZ 85029-1750

PRICE, DALIAS ADOLPH, geography educator; b. Newtonville, Ind., June 28, 1913; s. Fred J. and Rose (Gillam) P.; m. Lillian O. Alexander, May 14, 1943; children— David, Curtis, Kent, Roger. BA, U. Ill., 1937, MA, 1938; PhD, U. Wis., 1954. Instr. geography U. Ill., 1938-40; acting head dept. S.W. Mo. State Coll., Springfield, 1940-45; asst. U. Wis., 1945-47; assoc. prof. geography So. Ill. U., 1947-58; prof. geography, head dept. Eastern Ill. U., 1958—. Author articles in field. Mem. Wabash Valley Interstate Commn., 1965— ; Bd. suprs. Coles County, Ill., 1967, chmn., 1971-72; Bd. dirs. Charleston Community Hosp., 1966—, Inst. Urban and Regional Affairs, 1967— . Recipient Distng. Svc. award Nat. Weather Svc., 1988, 90, 95, 97, 2001; hon. fellow U. Wis., 1953. Mem. AAUP (sec.-treas. Ill. conf. 1958-62), Ill. Geog. Soc. (sec. 1950, chmn. 1951,62, distinguished geographer award 1976), Charleston C. of C. (bd. dirs. 1961-64), Assn. Am. Geographers, Gamma Theta Upsilon. Clubs: Rotarian (pres. Charleston 1965). Democrat. Unitarian Universalist. Home: 517 W Coolidge Ave Charleston IL 61920-3860

PRICE, FREDRIC VICTOR, physician, educator, medical researcher; b. Wilmington, Del., Nov. 4, 1957; s. Martin Burton and Mollie (Saline) P.; m. Ellen S. Wilson, Nov. 30, 1985; children: George, Olivia. BA, Yale U., 1980; MD, U. Louisville, 1986. Diplomate Am. Bd. Ob-Gyn.; cert. gynecologic oncologist. Intern, resident in ob-gyn. U. Pitts., 1986-90; fellow in gynecologic oncology Yale U., New Haven, 1990-92; asst. prof. U. Pitts., 1993-98; attending physician Magee-Womens Hosp., Pitts., 1992—; attending physicain Western Pa. Hosp., Pitts., 2000—; pres. Pitts. Gynecol. Oncology, Inc., 1998—; pvt. practice Inc. Med. Practice, 1998—. Peer reviewer Obstetrics and Gynecology, L.A., 1996—, Gynecologic Oncology, San Diego, 1994—; grant reviewer FDA, Rockville, Md., 1995, Calif. Dept. Pub. Health, Sacramento. Contbr. articles to profl. jours. Felix Rutledge fellow M.D. Anderson Cancer Ctr., Houston, 1989; recipient Clin. Oncology award Am. Cancer Soc., 1991, Bristol-Myers Squibb Clin. Rsch. award Bristol-Myers Oncology, 1995, Nat. Faculty Recognition award Com. Resident Edn. in Ob-Gyn., 1997, 2003. Fellow ACS, Am. Coll. Obstetric Gynecology; mem. Am. Soc. Clin. Oncology, Soc. Gynecol. Oncologists, Am. Cancer Soc. (bd. dirs. Southwestern Pa.). Office: 4815 Liberty Ave Ste 127 Pittsburgh PA 15224 E-mail: pitgo@nauticom.net.

PRICE, HELEN (LOIS) BURDON, artist, retired nurse educator; b. St. Louis, Sept. 23, 1926; d. Kenneth Livingston and Estelle Lois (Pemberton) Burdon; m. John Bryan Price, Jr.; children: Diane Price Baker, Jeannette B., John Bryan III. BS, La. State U., 1946; BS, RN, Johns Hopkins U., 1949; postgrad., Boston U., 1951-52. Head nurse in pediatrics Johns Hopkins Hosp., Balt., 1949-51; instr. nursing sch. Boston Children's Hosp., 1951-52; physician's aide, sec. U.S. Army-Osaka (Japan) Hosp., 1952-54; instr. pediat. nursing Holy Name Hosp., Teaneck, N.J., 1965-67; primary nurse Englewood (N.J.) Hosp., 1974-79; dir.- curator Vineyard Theatre Gallery, N.Y.C., 1980-90; bd. mem., coord. pub. lecture series Ward Nasse Gallery, N.Y.C., 1987-92. Program planner, judge, panel participant, curator Salute to Women in the Arts, Bergen County, N.J., 1977-95. Fund raiser Women's Aux., Presbyn. Med. Ctr., N.Y. Hosp. Fund, N.Y.C., 1982-90. Mem. Nat. Assn. Women Artists (past sec., v.p., pres., permanent advisor, Akston Found. award 1987, Blake award 1991, Bronze medal 1995, Kreindler Meml. award 1998, Blum Meml. award 1999). Avocations: bird watching, mycology. Home: 151 Tweed Blvd Nyack NY 10960-4913 Office: Burdon Price Studio 151 Tweed Blvd Nyack NY 10960-4913

PRICE, JOHN RICHARD, lawyer, law educator; b. Indpls., Nov. 28, 1934; s. Carl Lee and Agnes I. P.; m. Suzanne A. Leslie, June 22, 1963; children: John D., Steven V. BA with high honors, U. Fla., 1958; LL.B. with honors, NYU, 1961. Bar: Calif. 1962, Wash. 1977, U.S. Ct. Appeals (9th cir.), U.S. Dist. Ct. (we. dist.) Wash. Assoc. McCutchen, Doyle, Brown & Enersen, San Francisco, 1961-69; prof. law U. Wash., Seattle, 1969-97, dean, 1982-88; of counsel Perkins Coie, Seattle, 1976—. Author: Contemporary Estate Planning, 1983, Price on Contemporary Estate Planning, 1992, 2d edit., 2000, Conflicts, Confidentiality and Other Ethical Issues, 2000. Served with U.S. Army, 1953-55 Root-Tilden fellow NYU Sch. Law, 1958-61 Fellow Am. Coll. Trust and Estate Counsel (former regent); mem. ABA, Am. Law Inst., Order of Coif, Phi Beta Kappa. Congregationalist. Home: 3794 NE 97th St Seattle WA 98115-2564 Office: 1201 3rd Ave Ste 4800 Seattle WA 98101-3029 E-mail: jprice@perkinscole.com.

PRICE, JUDITH, nursing educator; b. N.Y., Feb. 4, 1947; d. Isidore and Evelyn (Simpkins) Price; m. Charles Reed Corn, July 26, 1987. AAS, CUNY, 1966, BA, 1975; BSN, Va. Commonwealth U., 1985; MSN, Barry U., 1993; cert., Fla. Internat. U., 1998. RN, Fla., Calif., Va., N.Y.; CEN; cert. nursing adminstrn.; cert. healthcare quality, cert. psychiatry. Staff nurse, relief charge nurse emergency dept. Mt. Sinai Hosp., N.Y.C.; nurse clinician emergency dept. Med. Coll. Va., Richmond; clin. educator emergency dept. Jackson Meml. Hosp., Miami, Fla.; nursing adminstr. Palmetto Gen. Hosp., Miami; dir. emergency svcs. Cedars Med. Ctr., Miami; QI/IC coord. Columbia Cedars, Miami; asst. prof. Miami-Dade C.C. Adj. faculty Barry U.; psychiat. nurse practitioner Wexvord Health Nurses. Mem. adv. bd. North Dade Health Ctr. Mem. ANA, Fla. Nurses Assn., Emergency Nurses Assn. (past pres. Fla. state, past pres. Dade-Broward chpt., treas. Dade-Broward chpt.), Am. Trauma Soc. (past bd. dirs. Fla. divsn., past v.p. Fla. divsn.), Dade Assn. for Healthcare Quality (past treas., editor newsletter), Sigma Theta Tau. Home: 2525 Marathon Ln Fort Lauderdale FL 33312-4611

PRICE, JUDITH HOLM, educational psychologist; b. Milw, Nov. 6, 1937; d. Paul James and Dorothy Ruth (Munton) Holm; m. Thomas Munro Price, Aug. 8, 1959; children: Scott Michael, Andrea Lynn. BA, Carroll Coll., 1959; MA, U. Iowa, 1973; PhD, U. Wyo., 1980. Nat. cert. sch. psychologist. Tchr. Waukesha Pub. Sch., Wis., 1959, Madison Pub. Sch., 1959-63; preschool assessment specialist Grant Wood Area Edn. Agy. 10, Cedar Rapids, Iowa, 1976-78; Ednl. Resource Ctr. facilitator Albany County Sch. Dist. 1, Laramie, Wyo., 1980-89; dir. spl. svc., 1989-93; acad. dean Brush Ranch Sch., Tererro, N.Mex., 1993—96; hist. home renovator Yerington, Nev., 1997—. Substitute tchr. Melbourne (Australia) Sch., 1978; temporary prof. U. Wyo., Laramie, 1981, 84; mem. computer conf. com. Wyo. Dept. Edn., Casper, 1984-85, com. for devel. spl. edn. database, 1987, task force cert. standards for early childhood spl. edn. tchr., 1988; speaker Wyo. Fedn. CEC, Riverton, 1986, task force on specific learning disability criteria, 1988; conf. mem. Council for Exceptional Children Software Conf., Washington, 1986; provider state-wide inservice Specific Learning Disability Criteria, 1988. Spl. edn. rules and regulations task force Wyo. Dept. Edn., 1990—92; mem. Wyo. gov. Early Intervention Coun., 1990—93; governing bd. mem. South Lyons Health Ctr., Inc., 2003—. Mem. Nat. Assn. Sch. Psychologists (alt. del. 1983), Wyo. Sch. Psychoednl. Assn., Council for Exceptional Children (com. specific learning disability 1987-88, speaker 1988, pres. Frontier chpt. 1989), Assn. Curriculum Devel., N.Mex. Assn. Non-Pub. Sch., Phi Kappa Phi, Phi Delta Kappa, 2003, dir., So. Lyon Hosp. Bd. Avocations: computers, skiing, camping, traveling. Office: The Nordyke House 727 State Route 339 Yerington NV 89447-9553

PRICE, JUSTIN J. mathematics educator; BS, MA, U. Pa., PhD, 1956. Instr. Purdue U., 1963—, now prof. math. Recipient Disting. Tchg. award, Math. Assn. Am., 1993. Office: Purdue U West Lafayette IN 47907*

PRICE, LEROY VERNON, secondary school educator; b. Christiansburg, Va., Apr. 30, 1942; s. Leroy Vernon and Nora Pauline (Grubb) P.; m. Vickie Lee Likens, Mar. 4, 1966; children: Amanda Lee, Alison Denise; 1 child by previous marriage, Paula Renee. BS in Indsl. Arts, Va. Poly. Inst. and State U., 1965. Cert. tchr., Va. Tchr. metals and drafting Warren County High Schs., Front Royal, Va., 1964-65; tchr. woodworking, drafting James River High Sch., Fincastle, Va., 1965-66, Northside High Sch., Salem, Va., 1966-74; tchr. power mechanics, photography, tech. systems Northside Jr. High Sch., Salem, 1974—. Tchr. photography adult edn. program Roanoke County Schs., Salem; tchr. furniture restoration Warren County Schs., Front Royal. Author curriculum materials. Recipient vocat. edn. awards Va. Bd. Edn., 1991. Mem. NEA, Va. Edn. Assn., Roanoke County Edn. Assn., Internat. Tech. Assn., Va. Mid. Sch. Assn., Va. Tech. Edn. Assn. (life), Epsilon Pi Tau. Presbyterian. Avocations: antique car restoration, woodworking, travel, camping. Home: 1580 Richland Hills Dr Salem VA 24153-1612 Office: Northside Jr High Sch 6810 Northside High School Rd Roanoke VA 24019-2830

PRICE, MONA RENITA, music educator, school administrator; b. Kansas City, Mo., Mar. 12, 1958; d. Robert Wayne and Carolyn Sue (Thompson) P.; div. BA in Music Edn., Voice, Avila Coll., 1980; MA in Ednl. Adminstrn., U. Mo., Kansas City, 1985. Cert. music educator, Mo. Tchr. music St. Therese Sch., Parkville, Mo., 1980-83, St. Elizabeth Sch., Kansas City, Mo., 1983-88, St. Stephen's Acad., Kansas City, Mo., 1991-92, Redemptorist Sch., Kansas City, Mo., 1991-92, Guardian Angels Sch., Kansas City, Mo., 1991-92, Our Lady of the Angels Sch., Kansas City, Mo., 1992—, asst. prin., 1994—; pvt. piano tchr. Kansas City, Mo., 1980-91. Big sister Big Bros. and Sisters of Kansas City, 1985-88. Sprint Edn. grantee, 1992, Diocesan Faculty grantee, 1997, Kauffman I.D.E.A. grantee, 2001. Mem. Phi Delta Kappa, Pi Lambda Theta, Phi Kappa Phi. Avocations: photography, bicycling, reading, model railroading, southwest crafts, walking. Office: Our Lady of Angels Sch 211 W Linwood Blvd Kansas City MO 64111-1327

PRICE, PETER WILFRID, ecology educator, researcher; b. London, Apr. 17, 1938; arrived in U.S., 1966; BSc with honors, U. Wales, Bangor, 1958-62; MSc, U. New Brunswick, Fredericton, 1964; PhD, Cornell U., 1970. Asst. prof. U. Ill., Urbana, 1971-75, assoc. prof., 1975-79; research ecologist Mus. No. Ariz., Flagstaff, 1979-80; assoc. prof. No. Ariz. U., Flagstaff, 1980-85, prof. ecology, 1985-94, Regents' prof., 1994—2002, Regents' prof. emeritus, 2002—. Author: Evolutionary Biology of Parasites, 1980, Biological Evolution, 1996, Insect Ecology, 3d edit., 1997, Macroevolutionary Theory on Macroecological Patterns, 2003; editor: A New Ecology, 1984, Evolutionary Strategies of Parasitic Insects, 1975, Plant-Animal Interactions, 1991, Population Dynamics, 1995, Effects of Resource Distribution on Plant-Animal Interactions, 1992, The Ecology and Evolution of Gall-Forming Insects, 1994, Population Dynamics: New Approaches and Synthesis, 1995. Guggenheim fellow, 1977-78; Fulbright Sr. scholar, 1993-94. Fellow Royal Entomol. Soc., NSF (panel mem. 1978-81, 91-93), Ecol. Soc. Am. (bd. editors 1973-76), Brit. Ecol. Soc., Entomol. Soc. Am. (Founders Award, 1993). Office: No Ariz U PO Box 5640 Flagstaff AZ 86011-5640

PRICE, SANDRA HOFFMAN, secondary school educator; b. Emden, Ill., July 24, 1935; d. William Frederick and Grace May Hoffman; m. Arthur Elliott Price, Jr., Dec. 27, 1957; 1 child, Anne Marie Price Powell. BS in Math. Tchg., U. Ill., 1957, MA in Math., 1962. Tchr. Ill. Pub. Schs., 1957-69, Libertyville (Ill.) Pub. Sch. Dist. #70, 1970-98. Adj. staff Coll. Lake County, Grayslake, Ill., 1972-81, Nat.-Louis U., Evanston, Ill., 1996-97; interdisciplinary team leader Highland Sch., Libertyville, 1979-96. Contbr. articles to profl. jours. Pres. Litchfield (Ill.) Women's Club, 1964, Libertyville (Ill.) Edn. Assn., 1979. Univ. scholar-bronze tablet U. Ill., Urbana, 1957; Acad. Yr. fellow NSF, 1961. Mem. Nat. Coun. Tchrs. Math., Phi Beta Kappa, Phi Kappa Phi. Methodist.

PRICE, SUSAN KAY LIND, employment training organization administrator; b. Burley Cassia, Idaho, Apr. 27, 1958; d. Ray Elden and Melba Jean (Koyle) Lind; m. Randy Sam Price, July 18, 1986; 1 child, Jordan Richard. Student, Brigham Young U., 1976-79, U. Utah, 1983-84; BS magna cum laude, Utah State U., 1988, postgrad., 1991-92, So. Calif. U., 1995—. Cert. assertive comm. trainer, Utah State Office Edn.; cert. hypnotist, Am. Coun. Hypnotist Examiners; cert. advanced rapid eye tech. with self discovery processing; cert. core belief therapy. Project coord. single parent/displaced homemaker program Bridgerland Applied Tech. Ctr., Logan; aide, exec. sec., job developer, employment counselor Bear River Assn. of Govt., Logan, Utah. Mem. adv. bd. Cmty.-Family Partnership; mem. social work community adv. com., supr. social work practicum, supr. family and human devel. practicum Utah State U.; part-time transitional therapist. Named Outstanding Job Developer, 1987; recipient Master Tchr. award, 1983. Mem. NAFE, Nat. Displaced Homemaker's Network (Utah rep. 1989-93), Box Elder County Self-Sufficiency Coun., Cache County Interagency Coun., Utah Assn. Adult Cmty. and Continuing Edn. (state bd. 1989-92), Bear River Refugee Coun. (sec. 1986-90), Logan Bus. and Profl. Women (Young Careerist 1991), Soroptimist Internat. Home: 376 E 700 S Logan UT 84321-5532

PRICE, TREVOR ROBERT PRYCE, psychiatrist, educator; b. Concord, N.H., Nov. 29, 1943; BA, Yale U., l965; MD, Columbia U., l969. Diplomate Am. Bd. Psychiatry and Neurology (examiner l985—), Am. Bd. Internal Medicine, Nat. Bd. Med. Examiners. Intern in medicine Med. Ctr. U. Calif., San Francisco, l969-70; resident in internal medicine Med. Ctr. of U. Calif., San Francisco, l972-74; resident in psychiatry Dartmouth Med. Sch., Hanover, N.H., l974-77, asst. prof., assoc. prof. psychiatry and medicine, l977-85; assoc. prof., prof. psychiatry U. Pa. Sch. Medicine, Phila., 1985—88; dir. psychiat. in-patient svcs. Hosp. of U. Pa., 1985-88; prof. psychiatry Med. Coll. Pa., Pitts., l989-90, prof. psychiatry and medicine, 1991-95, 1993—2002; chmn. dept. psychiatry Med. Coll. Pa. and Hahnemann U., Pitts., 1989-95, sr. assoc. dean, 1993-95; pres. Allegheny Neuropsychiat. Inst. Allegheny Neuropsychiat. Inst., Pitts., 1992-94, exec. dir., 1994—; chmn. dept. psychiatry Med. Coll. Pa. Hahnemann Sch. Medicine, Phila., 1995—2002; prof. psychiatry and med. Drexel U. Coll. Med., Phila., 2002—03, chmn. dept. psychiatry, 2002; pvt. practice Bryn Mawr, Pa. Bd. dirs. Coll. Health Consortium, Inc., Phila., Highland Dr. Rsch. and Edn. Found., Yale Club Pitts., Pitts. Psychoanalytic Found., Med. Coll. Pa. Hosp.; mem. blue ribbon bd. Alzheimer's Disease Alliance, Western Pa., 1989-97; mem. governing bd. Med. Coll. of Pa. Hosp., 1999-2002. Mem. editl. bd. Convulsive Therapy, 1984-94, Jour. Neuropsychiatry and Clin. Neurosci., 1992—, Allegheny Gen. Hosp. Jour. Neurosci., 1992-98, Seminars in Neuropsychiatry, 1995—; editl. reviewer 15 psychiat. and med. jours., 1978; contbr. chpts. to books and articles in profl. jours. Mem. N.H. Commn. on Laws Effecting Mental Health, 1974-75; bd. dirs. Advanced Studies Program, Friends of St. Paul's Sch., Concord, N.H., 1983-87. Recipient William C. Menninger award Ctrl. Neuropsychiat. Assn., 1977, Faculty Teaching award dept. psychiatry Dartmouth Med. Sch., 1984, Pres. award for Exceptional Achievement AHERF, 1994, numerous grants. Fellow: Am. Coll. Psychiatrists, Am. Neuropsychiat. Assn. (bd. dirs. 1993—95, exec. dir. 1995), Am. Psychiat. Assn. (disting. fellow); mem.: Assn. Medicine and Psychiatry, Assn. Convulsive Therapy, Assn. Acad. Psychiatry, Am. Assn. Dirs. Psychiat. Residency Tng., Assn. for Acad. Psychiatry, Soc. Biol. Psychiatry, Am. Assn. Chairmen of Depts. Psychiatry, Pa. Psychiat. Assn., H-Y-P Club Pitts., Yale Club Pitts. Avocations: fly fishing, tennis, reading, piano. Office: 950 Haverford Rd Ste 302 Bryn Mawr PA 19010

PRICE, VERLA BLANCHE, elementary education educator; b. Mannington, W.Va., May 13, 1936; d. Paul Byron and Ida Martinia (Newbrough) Stewart; m. Harry Eugene Price, Oct. 20, 1959; 1 child, Dwight Eugene. AA, W.Va. No. C.C., Weirton, 1974; BA, W. Liberty State Coll., 1976; MA, W.Va. U., 1981. Cert. tchr., W.Va. Classroom tchr. Marion County Bd. Edn., Fairmont, W.Va., 1976-84; math. tchr. chpt. 1 Brooke County Bd. Edn., Wellsburg, W.Va., 1984-98. Pianist Free Meth. Ch., Follansbee, W.Va., 1985. Recipient Am. Legion Scholastic award Am. Legion, Mannington, W.Va., 1954. Mem. NEA, Brooke County Edn. Assn. (sec. 1985-87), W.Va. Coun. Tchrs. Math., Phi Theta Kappa. Democrat. Methodist. Avocations: playing piano, gardening, walking, crocheting, knitting. Home: PO Box 208 Follansbee WV 26037-0208 Office: Wellsburg Primary Sch 14th and Main Sts Wellsburg WV 26070

PRICE BODAY, MARY KATHRYN, choreographer, small business owner, educator; b. Fort Bragg, N.C., May 20, 1945; d. Max Edward and Katharine (Jordan) P.; m. Les Boday (div. 1982); children: Shawn Leon Boday, Irmali Ferecho Boday; m. Richard A. Weil, May 1, 1986. BFA, U. Okla., 1968, MFA, 1970; studies with David Howard, 1972-74. Soloist dancer Mary Anthony Dance Co., N.Y.C., 1971-74, Larry Richardson Dance Co., N.Y.C., 1971-73; dancer Pearl Lang Dance Co., N.Y.C., 1971-73, Gaku Dance Theater, N.Y.C., 1972-74; ballet mistress and soloist dancer St. Gallen Ballet, Switzerland, 1974-75; dancer, tchr. Zurich Ballet, Switzerland, 1975-76; asst. prof. U. Ill., Champaign-Urbana, 1976-79; artist-in-residence Cornish Inst., Seattle, 1979-80; pres. The Dance Works, Inc., Seattle, 1981-90; dir. Seahurst Ballet, 1982-84; pres. The Dance Works, Inc., Erie, Pa., 1990-94; dir. dance dept., asst. prof. Mercyhurst Coll., Erie, Pa., 1990-94; dir. Peoria Ballet, 1994-99; asst. prof. Bradley U., Peoria, 1994—; dir. Ill. Ballet (formerly Ctrl. Ill. Ballet), 1999—. Tchr. Harkness Ballet N.Y., Mary Anthony Dance Sch., Zurich Ballet, Nat. Acad. Arts Ill., Jefferson High Sch. Performing Arts Portland, also choreographer; tchr. Summer Dance Lab.; choreographer Mary K. Price Dance Co., U. Ill., Nat. Acad. Arts, Cornish Inst., Seahurst Ballet; tchr. Kneeland Workshops, Port Townsend, Wash., 1988; tchr., co-dir. Kneeland Seminars, Las Vegas, Nev., Port Townsend, summers 1989, 90, Oklahoma City U., summer 1990, Am. Coll. Dance Festival, 1991, 92, 93; tchr. Pa. Gov's. Sch. of the Arts, 1991, 92, 94, David Howard summer seminar Mercyhurst Coll., summer 1992, David Howard Summer Workshop with Tulsa Ballet Theatre, 1993, 94, David Howard workshop Seattle tchrs., 1996, David Howard workshop U. Ill., 1997, David Howard-Western Mich. U., 1999; guest artist, asst. prof. Slippery Rock U., 1994; owner The Dance Works, Peoria, Ill., 1994—; guest artist, Southern Ballet Theatre, summer 2000, 2001, David Howard and Mary Price Boday Summer Intensives, Worcester, summer 2000, 2001, 2002. Choreographer 3 ballets Ballet Co. St. Gallen, 1988, dance concert Mary & Friends, Seattle, 1990, The Nutcracker for Warner Theatre Erie; co-choreographer The Nutcracker Ballet, 1991-93, Coppelia, 1993, The Little Mermaid of Lake Erie at the Warner Theater, 1994; choreographer Peoria Ballet, Nutcracker, Civic Ctr., 1995, 30 Yr. Gala, 1995, Alice in Wonderland, 1996, Little Mermaid of Lake Peoria, 1997; staged Swan Lake, 1999; choreographer Rudolph the Red Nose Reindeer at the Shrine Mosque, 2000; choreographer Rock Ballet and The Lion, Witch, and Wardrobe at the Peoria Civic Ctr. Theatre, 2001, Hansel and Gretel, 2002, Power of Dance, 2002; restaged the ballet Coppelia, 2002. Outstanding Dancer award U. Okla., 1968; named one of Outstanding Young Women of Am., 1977. Address: 719 W Moss Ave Peoria IL 61606-1931

PRICE LEA, PATRICIA JEAN, nurse educator; b. Yanceyville, N.C., May 19, 1950; d. Louis Albert and Mamie Ethel (Graves) Price; m. Wiliam Lea, Oct. 18, 1992. BS in Nursing, Winston Salem State U., 1972; MS in Nursing, U. N.C., 1975; MEd, N.C. Agr. and Tech. State U., 1986; PhD in Nursing, Wayne State U., 1996. Coord. women's health Annie Penn Meml. Hosp., Reidsville, NC, 1972—2003; assoc. prof. nursing N.C. Agr. & Tech. State U., Greensboro, 1975—. Mem. ANA, Nat. League Nursing, N.C. Nurses Assn., Sigma Theta Tau (v.p. 1996-98), Chi Eta Phi. Democrat. Methodist. Avocations: soapmaking, habitat for humanity involvement. Home: PO Box 492 Yanceyville NC 27379-0492 Office: NC Agrl & Tech State U 1601 E Market St Greensboro NC 27401-3209

PRICER, WAYNE FRANCIS, counseling consultant; b. Bogue, Kans., Feb. 11, 1935; s. William C. and Lena I. (Hecke) P.; m. Alice M. Fitzpatrick, July 25, 1964; children: Wayne F. Jr., Elizabeth Anne. AB, Ft. Hays State U., 1957; MEd, U. N.D., 1963; postgrad., Wayne State U. Nat. cert. counselor; nat. cert. career counselor; nat. cert. sch. counselor; lic. prof. counselor Mich.; master career counselor. Tchr. Bogue (Kans.) Grade Sch., 1958-62; counselor Lamphere High Sch., 1963-64, 69-75; asst. prin. Page Jr. High, Madison Heights, Mich., 1964-68, prin., 1968-69; adj. counselor Oakland Community Coll., Bloomfield Hills, Mich., 1969—; dir. guidance Lamphere Schs., Madison Heights, Mich., 1975-99, adj. prof. Oakland C.C., 1969—; counseling cons. Royal Oak, Mich., 1999—. Bd. dirs., 2d v.p., v.p. Haviland Collectors Internat. Ednl. Found. Contbr. articles to prof. jours. Bd. dirs., 2d v.p. Haviland Collectors Internat., 1997—99, Mich. Assn. Retired Sch. Personnel. Named Counselor of Yr. Oakland Counseling Assn., 1999, Lifetime Achievement award MCDA, 1999. Mem. ACA, Am. Mental Health Counselors Assn., Alliance for Ret. Americans, Assn. for Career and Tech. Edn., Assn. for Counselor Edn. and Supervision, Am. Coll. Counselors Assn., Am. Fedn. Tchrs., Am. Sch. Coun. Assn., Am. Vocat. Assn., Assn. for Adult Devel. and Aging, Assn. for Assessment in Counseling, Mich. Assn. for Adult Devel. and Aging, Mich. Assn. Coll. Admission Counselors, Mich. Counseling Assn., Mich. Assn. for Counselor Edn. and Supervision, Mich. Assn. for Measurement and Evaluation in Guidance (pres.), Mich. Assn. Specialists in Group Work, Mich. Career Devel. Assn. (treas. 1994—), Mich. Assn. Ret. Sch. Pers., Mich. Assn. Career and Tech. Edn., Mich. Mental Health Counselors Assn., Mich. Sch. Counselors Assn., Mich. Assn. for Humanistic Edn. and Develop., Mich. Assn. for Multi-Cultural Develop., Nat. Assn. Coll. Admission Counselors, Nat. Career Devel. Assn., Oakland Assn. for Counseling and Devel. (former pres.), Mich. Fedn. Tchrs., Suburban Assn. of Retired Sch. Personnel, Phi Delta Kappa. Office: 719 S Washington Ave Royal Oak MI 48067-3829

PRICHARD, BARBARA ANN, English educator; b. Muskogee, Okla., Jan. 11, 1947; d. Carl Howard Fullbright and Iris Oleta (Staffan) Evans; children: Shelia DeLynn, Katherine Elizabeth, David Warren III. BS, Northeastern Okla. State U., 1976; MEd, U. Okla., 1990. Cert. reading specialist, tchr. nat. bd. Tchr. Muldrow (Okla.) Pub. Schs., 1976-77, Stafford (Mo.) Pub. Schs., 1977-79, Oklahoma City C.C., 1991—, Moore (Okla.) Pub. Schs., 1979—. Sponsor, state pres. Moore West Nat. Jr. Honor Soc.; global classroom dir., chair reading dept. Moore West Sch. Bd. dirs. Moore Parks & Recreation, 1988-89. Mem. NEA, Oklahoma Edn. Assn., Okla. Reading Coun., Okla. Romance Writers Am.)v.p.), Romance Writers Am., Moore Assn. Classroom Tchrs. Avocations: travel, writing, reading, painting, golf. Office: Moore Pub Schs 9400 S Pennsylvania Ave Oklahoma City OK 73159-6903

PRIEST, GEORGE L. law educator; b. 1947; BA, Yale U., 1969; JD, U. Chgo., 1973. Assoc. prof. U. Puget Sound, Tacoma, 1973-75; law and econ. fellow U. Chgo., 1975-77; prof. U. Buffalo, 1977-80, UCLA, 1980-81, Yale U., New Haven, 1981—. Dir. program in civil liability; John M. Olin prof. law and econs., 1986—. Mem. Pres.' Com. on Privatization, 1987-88. Office: PO Box 208215 New Haven CT 06520-8215

PRIETO, CLAUDIO R. academic administrator, lawyer; b. Caguas, P.R., Aug. 17, 1933; s. Claudio Prieto and Carmen (Gutierrez) del Arroyo; m. Myrna Irizarry; children: Claudio, Carmen, Isabel, Rosa, Anna, Alfonso. BS, U. P.R., 1954, JD, 1971. Bar: P.R. Asst. prof. U. P.R., Rio Piedras, 1956-70, coord. student affairs, 1957-59, dir. extension div., 1959-61, assoc. prof. Sch. Law, 1970-71; dir. edn. press Commonwealth of Puerto Rico, Rio Piedras, 1961-65, asst. sec. edn., 1965-67, asst. to gov. San Juan, 1967-68; asst. to dep. commr. Dept. Edn. State of N.Y., Albany, 1977-78, asst. commr., 1978-88; chancellor Turabo U., Gurabo, P.R., 1989-93; exec. dir. office of equity and acccess policy studies N.Y. State Dept. Edn., Albany, 1993-94; dep. asst. sec. for higher edn. programs Dept. Edn., Washington, 1994—. Cons. to chancellor U. P.R., 1969, legal plannning and adminstrn. Tech. Svcs. P.R., 1973-76. Columnist San Juan Star, 1973-76, 1992—Trustee Ewald B. Nyquist Meml. Fund, Albany, 1990—; bd. overseers Regents Coll., 1989-93. Named Edn. Exec. of Yr. Sales and Mktg. Assn., P.R., 1989. Mem. Intercollegiate Athletic League (bd. govs.). Democrat. Roman Catholic.

PRIGMORE, CHARLES SAMUEL, social work educator; b. Lodge, Tenn., Mar. 21, 1919; s. Charles H. and Mary Lou (Raulston) P.; m. Shirley Melaine Buuck, June 7, 1947; 1 child, Philip Brand. AB, U. Chattanooga, 1939; MS, U. Wis., 1947, PhD, 1961; extension grad., Air War Coll., 1967, Indsl. Coll. Armed Forces, 1972. Social caseworker Children's Svc. Soc., Milw., 1947-48; social worker Wis. Sch. Boys, Waukesha, 1948-51; supr. tng. Wis. Bur. Probation and Parole, Madison, 1951-56; supt. Tenn. Vocat. Tng. Sch. for Boys, Nashville, 1956-59; assoc. prof. La. State U., 1959-64; ednl. cons. Coun. Social Work Edn., N.Y., 1962-64; exec. dir. Joint Commn. Correctional Manpower and Tng., Washington, 1964-67; prof. Sch. Social Work, U. Ala., 1967-84, prof. emeritus, from 1984, chmn. com. on Korean relationships, 1980-84. Fulbright lectr., Iran, 1972-73; vis. lectr. U. Sydney, 1976; cons. Iranian Ministry Health and Welfare, 1976-78; frequent lectr., workshop leader. Author: Textbook on Social Problems, 1971, Social Work in Iran Since the White Revolution, 1976, Social Welfare Policy Analysis and Formulation, 1979, 2d edit., 1986; editor 2 books; contbr. articles to profl. jours. Adv. Com. for Former Prisoners of War VA, 1981-83; chmn.

Prisoner of War Bd., State of Ala., 1984-89; state comdr. Am. Ex-Prisoners of War, Ala., 1985-86, nat. legis. officer, 1985—, nat. dir., 1989-92, nat. sr. vice comdr., 1993—, nat comdr., 1994-95; gov.'s liaison U.S. Holocaust Meml. Coun., 1983-89; mem. Ala. Bd. Vets. Affairs, 1986-89, Ala. Bicentennial Commn. on Constn., 1987-90; bd. dirs. Community Svcs. Programs of W. Ala., 1985-89, others in past. Served to 2d lt. USAAF, 1940-45, prisoner of war, Germany, 1944-45; lt. col. Res., ret. Decorated Air medal with oak leaf cluster; recipient Conservation award Woodmen of the World, 1971; Fulbright rsch. fellow Norway, 1979-80. Fellow Am. Sociol. Assn., Royal Soc. Health; mem. Acad. Cert. Social Workers, Nat. Coun. Crime and Delinquency, Tuscaloosa Country Club, Capitol Hill Club, Alpha Kappa Delta, Beta Beta Beta. Home: Alfred, NY. Died Dec. 30, 2000.

PRIGMORE, KATHRYN BRADFORD TYLER, architecture educator, architect; b. St. Albans, N.Y., Nov. 21, 1956; d. Richard Jerome and Shirley Virginia (Neizer) Tyler; m. James Craig Prigmore, June 20, 1986 (div. June 1992); children: Crystal Andrea, Amber Sheriesse. BS in Bldg. Sci., Rensselaer Poly. Inst., 1977, BArch, 1978; MS in Engring., Cath. U. Am., 1981. Registered architect, Va., NCARB. Intern architect VVKR Inc., Alexandria, Va., 1979-82; architect Robert A. Hawthorne, Architects, PC, Washington, 1982; project mgr. Robert Traynham Coles, Architect, PC, Washington, 1982-84; assoc. Segreti Tepper Architects, P.C., Washington, 1984-92; assoc. prof. dept. architecture Howard U., Washington, 1991—2003, assoc. dean Sch. Architecture and Planning, 1992-97, asst. dir. Sch. Architecture and Design, 1997-98, asst. dean Coll. Engring., Arch. and Computer Sci., 1998; sr. assoc. Einhorn Yaffee Prescott, Archs. and Engrs., 1998—2003, HDR Architecture, Inc., Washington, 2003—. Mem. alumni adv. coun. Sch. Architecture, Rensselaer Poly. Inst., 1993—; mem. adv. bd. dept. architecture Hampton U.; guest spkr. in field. Contbr. articles to profl. jours. Mem. adv. coun. No. Va. Urban League, 1980-81. Named to Outstanding Young Women in Am., 1983. Fellow AIA (nat. ethics coun. 2002—); mem. AAUW (mem. selected fellows selection panel 1995—2002), Nat. Orgn. Minority Archs., Black Women in Architecture and Related Professions (faculty advisor Howard U. chpt. 1992—), . Episcopalian. Avocations: writing, gardening. Home: 8911 Union Farm Rd Alexandria VA 22309-3936 Office: Howard U Sch Arch and Design 2366 6th St NW Washington DC 20001-2323 E-mail: kprigmore@eypae.com.

PRINCE, EILEEN SIMKIN, art educator; b. Indpls., July 15, 1947; d. Joseph Solomon and Annette (Marcus) Simkin; m. Irwin Joseph Prince, Apr. 7, 1968; children: Benjamin, Joshua. BS in Edn. cum laude, Butler U., 1970; M in Art Edn. with acad. distinction, Herron/Ind. U., Indpls., 1982. Cert. art specialist K-12, Ind. Art specialist Parrish Country Day Sch., Indpls., 1970-71, Hebrew Acad. Indpls., 1971-75, 79-89; art specialist, dept. head Sycamore Sch., Indpls., 1984—. Mem. tchr. adv. com. Indpls. Mus. Art, 1994—; mem. founding com. Hebrew Acad. Indpls., 1970, mem. personnel and curriculum coms., 1970-95 mem. curriculum and planning coms. Sycamore Sch., 1993—. Author: From Caves to Chateaux, 1987, From Chateaux to Condos, 1988, Art Matters: Strategies, Ideas and Activities to Strengthen Learning Across the Curriculum, 2001; exhibited works in numerous one-woman shows, 1974-87. Mem. founding com., 1st recording sec., pres. Hebrew Acad. Aux., 1970—; bd. dirs. Aux. to Children's Bur. Indpls., 1978-83; mem. edn. com. Ind. Civil Liberties Union, Indpls., 1993-94; bd. dirs., vol. Symphony Women's Group, Civic Theater, Jewish Cmty. Ctr., others; bd. dirs. sisterhood B'nai Torah, 1972-73. Recipient Hai-Life award Hebrew Acad. Indpls., 1985, Maestro award Jr. Group Symphony, Indpls. Women's Group, 1994, 95; named one of Outstanding Young Women Am., 1974, Tchr. of Week Sta. WRTV-Channel 6 and Jon Holden De Haan Found., 1993. Mem. Nat. Art Edn. Assn., Nat. Assn. Gifted Children, Hadassah (bd. dirs. 1971-72). Jewish. Avocations: reading, travel, antique collecting, crossword puzzles. Office: Sycamore Sch 1750 W 64th St Indianapolis IN 46260-4417 E-mail: princee@sycamoreschool.org.

PRINCE, GREGORY SMITH, JR., academic administrator; b. Washington, May 7, 1939; s. Gregory Smith and Margaret (Minor) P.; m. Toni Layton Brewer; children: Tara Wyndom, Gregory S. III. BA, Yale U., 1961, M in Philosophy, 1969, PhD, 1973; cert. in teaching English as a Second Language, Georgetown U., 1961; DHL (hon.), LLD (hon.), Amherst Coll., 1991. Instr. New Asia Coll., Kowloon, Hong Kong, 1961-62, Chinese U., Kowloon, 1962-63, Yale China Assn., Kowloon, 1961-63, Woodberry Forest (Va.) Sch., 1963-65; dean summer programs Dartmouth Coll., Hanover, N.H., 1970-72, asst. dean faculty, 1972-78, assoc. dean faculty, 1978-89; pres. Hampshire Coll., Amherst, Mass., 1989—. Vice chair coun. on racial and ethnic justice ABA; bd. dirs. Mass Ventures. Producer: (film) A Way of Learning, 1988. Trustee Montshire Mus. Sci., Hanover, 1973-89, Washington Campus, 1978—; trustee, chmn. Univ. Press New England, Hanover, 1983-84; trustee, pres. Yale-China Assn., New Haven, 1969-84; bd. dirs. Five Colls., Inc., Amherst, 1989—; bd. dirs. Mass. Internat. Festival for Arts, 1994-98; chmn. bd. dirs. Assn. Ind. Colls. and Univs. Mass., 1994-95; chair commn. on accreditation Am. Coun. Edn.; bd. dirs. Mass. Nature Conservancy, 1996—; bd. dirs. Nat. Assn. Ind. Colls. and Univs., 1999-2001, Friendship House, 2002—. Coe fellow Stanford U., 1965, Woodrow Wilson fellow Yale U., 1966, NDEA fellow, 1967-70. Mem. Internat. Assn. of Chiefs Police Found. (bd. dirs. 1991-95), Nat. Assn. of Ind. Colls. and Univs. Democrat. Episcopalian. Home: 15 Middle St Amherst MA 01002-3009 Office: Hampshire Coll 893 West St Amherst MA 01002-3372

PRINCE, LEAH FANCHON, art educator and research institute administrator; b. Hartford, Conn., Aug. 12, 1939; d. Meyer and Annie (Forman) Berman; m. Herbert N. Prince, Jan. 30, 1955; children: Daniel L., Richard N., Robert G. Student, U. Conn., 1957-59, Rutgers U., Newark, 1962; BFA, Fairleigh Dickinson U., 1970; postgrad., Caldwell Coll. for Women, 1973-75, Parsons Sch. of Design, N.Y.C., 1978. Cert. tchr. art, N.J. Tchr. art Caldwell-West Caldwell (N.J.) Pub. Schs., 1970-75; pres. Britannia Imports Ltd., Fairfield, N.J., 1979-89; tchr. religious studies Bohrer-Kaufman Hebrew Acad., Randolph, N.J., 1981-82; co-founder, corp. sec. Gibraltar Biol. Labs., Inc., Fairfield, 1970—; dir., co-founder Gibraltar Inst. for Rsch. and Tng., Fairfield, 1984—. Cons. Internat. Antiques and Fine Arts Industries, U.K., 1979-89; cons. in art exhibitry Passaic County Coll., Paterson, N.J., 1989-93; art curator Fairleigh Dickinson U., Rutherford, N.J., 1972-74; curator history of design Bloomfield (N.J.) Coll., 1990-91; lectr. Am. Soc. Microbiology, New Orleans, 1989; spkr. in field. Exhibited in group shows at Bloomfield (N.J.) Coll., 1990, Caldwell Women's Club, N.J., 1991, State Fedn. Women's Clubs Ann. Show, 1992 (1st pl. award 1992), Newark Art Mus., 1992, West (N.J.) Essex Art Assn., 1990, Somerset (N.J.) Art Assn., 1994, Mortimer Gallery, Gladstone, N.J., 1994 (1st pl. award 1998), Tewksbury His. Soc. (1st pl. award 1994), Tewksbury Hist. Soc., 2001, 02, Nat. Meeting Am. Pen Women, Calif., 2002; one-woman shows include Passaic County Coll., N.J., 1990, Caldwell Coll., N.J., 1990; author children's stories. Chair ann. juried art awards Arts Coun. of Essex Bd. Trustees, Montclair, N.J., 1984-90; chair fundraising Arts Coun. Essex County, N.J., 1989. Recipient 1st place award, N.J. Tewksbury Hist. Soc., 1994, 1998, Juried Art award, 2001, 2002. Mem. AAUW, Soc. Childrens Book Writers & Illustrators, Somerset Art Assn., Nat. League Am. Pen Women (pres. N.J. br., Juried Art award 2001), Inc., Internat. Platform Assn., Barnegat Light Yacht Club. Republican. Avocations: boating, tennis, opera, painting, travel. Home: 5 Standish Dr Mendham Twp Morristown NJ 07960-3224

PRINGLE, REBECCA, elementary school educator; b. Phila. m. Nathan Pringle; children: Nathan III, Lauren. BS in Elem. Edn., U. Pitts., 1976; EdM, Pa. State U., 1989. Phys. sci. tchr. Susquehanna Twp. Middle Sch., Harrisburg, Pa. Mem. strategic planning com. on diversity Susquehanna Twp. Sch. Dist.; mem. Inst. for Ednl. Leadership Task Force. Named Cmty. Woman of the Yr., Harrisburg Br. AAUW, 2002; recipient award, Pa. Acad. for the Profession of Tchg. Mem.: NEA (mem. exec. com., bd. dirs., mem. women's issues com., dist. learning task force, chair reading task force 1999—2000), Pa. State Edn. Assn. (bd. dirs., chair human and civil rights award com., task force on minority representation, regional chair leadership devel. com.), Nat. Bd. for Profl. Tchg. Stds. (bd. mem.). Office: Susquehanna Twp Middle Sch 801 Wood St Harrisburg PA 17109*

PRINS, ROBERT JACK, retired academic administrator; b. Grand Rapids, Mich., Oct. 12, 1932; s. Jacob and Marie (Vanden Brink) P.; m. Ruth Ellen John, Oct. 10, 1950; children: Linda, Douglas, Debra, Nancy, Eric, Sarah. BA, Hope Coll., 1954; DBA, Coll. Emporia, 1974; DHL, Iowa Wesleyan U., 1999. With Mich. Bell Tel. Co., Detroit area, 1954—64, Chesapeake and Potomac Tel. Co., 1964—66; dir. devel. Bethesda Hosp., Denver, 1966-68; v.p. planning and devel. Park Coll., Parkville, Mo., 1969-70; chief adminstrv. officer Coll. of Emporia, Kans., 1970-75; dir. fin. and devel. The Abbey Sch., Canon City, Colo., 1975-79; dir. devel. Kirksville Coll. Osteo. Medicine, Mo., 1979-84; v.p. devel. McKendree Coll., Lebanon, Ill., 1984-86; pres. Iowa Weslyan Coll., Mt. Pleasant, 1986-99, pres. emeritus, 1999—; exec. dir. Internat. Student Svcs., Canon City, Colo., 1999—. Bd. dirs. Iowa Coll. Found., Iowa Commn. on Vol. Svc.; mem. Iowa Assn. Ind. Colls. and Univs.; former chmn., mem. bd. Potomak Worldwide, Taipei, Taiwan. Mem. Nat. Assn. Ind. Colls. and Univs., Coun. for Advancement and Support Edn.

PRISBELL, KATHLEEN FRANCES, middle education educator, language arts; b. Rahway, N.J., Aug. 9, 1950; d. William Joseph and Helen Frances (Kowaleski) Wolfe; m. Fred Prisbell, Mar. 1, 1973; children: Eric S., Sandra L., Andrew F. BA in English, Kean Coll., 1972. Cert. secondary educator in English, elem. educator, N.J.; cert. Nat. Bd. Tchr. lang. arts Twp. of Ocean (N.J.) Intermediate Sch., 1972-82, Lakewood (N.J.) Middle Sch., 1986-90, Russell O. Brackman Middle Sch., Barnegat, N.J., 1990—. Site-based mgmt. team Lakewood Middle Sch., 1987-90, com. mem. curriculum devel., 1988; site-based mgmt. core team Russell O. Brackman Middle Sch., Barnegat, 1991—, curriculum coun. chair, 1992—. Writer: (curriculums) MAX (Gifted and Talented) Curriculum, 1994, Core Curriculum Stds.-Social Studies. Tchr. Christian Doctrine St. Mary's Cath. Ch., Barnegat, 1989-93. Recipient Governor's Tchr. Recognition award, 1997. Mem. Nat. Coun. Tchrs. English, N.J. Coun. Tchrs. English, Nat. Arbour Day Found. Democrat. Roman Catholic. Avocations: reading, walking. Home: 6 Maplewood Ct Barnegat NJ 08005-2008 E-mail: kprisbell@mail.bts.k12.nj.us.

PRISSEL, BARBARA ANN, paralegal, law educator; b. Plum City, Wis., July 7, 1946; d. John Henry and Mary Ann Louise (Dankers) Seipel; m. Stephen Joseph Prissel, Dec. 16, 1967; children: Angela, Benjamin. Graduate with honors, Mpls. Bus. Coll., 1966; student, Moraine Park Tech. Coll., Wis., 1983—. Cert. interactive TV, adult edn. instr. Legal sec. Mott, Grose, Von Holtum & Hefferan, Mpls., 1966-67, Whelan, Morey & Morey Attys. at Law, Durand, Wis., 1967-70, Murry Law Office, River Falls, Wis., 1968-70, Potter, Wefel & Nettesheim, Wisconsin Rapids, Wis., 1970-71; sec. to adminstr. Moraine Park Tech. Coll., Fond du Lac, Wis., 1971-72; paralegal Kilgore Law Office, Ripon, Wis., 1985—. Chmn. legal adv. com. Moraine Park Tech. Coll., Fond du Lac, Wis., 1996-98, mem. adminstrv. assts. adv. com., 1984-86; mem. legal adv. commn. Moraine Park Tech. Coll., 1984—. Contbr. poems to newspapers. Ch. rep. Ch. Women United, Ripon, Wis., 1984-87; pianist Christian Women's Orgn., Ripon, 1985-95; pianist, organist Our Lady of Lake Ch., Green Lake, Wis., 1987—. Mem.: NAFE, Legal Profls. Assn. (East Ctrl. Wis. pres. 1994—95, sec. 1995—96, chmn. Day-In-Ct. 1999, NALS Fedn. liaison 2000—02, sec. 2001—02, v.p. 2003—, 2003—, state legal ed. task force 2003—, chmn. ednl. liaison com., Legal award of Excellence 1995—96), Wis. Assn. Legal Secs. (state legal ednl. liaison com. 1997—, state legal edn. task force 2003—), Nat. Assn. Legal Secs. Roman Catholic. Avocations: teaching and playing piano, creative writing, cooking, swimming, exercising. Home: 129 Wolverton Ave Ripon WI 54971-1144

PRITCHARD, BETTY JEAN, retired art educator; b. Dana, Ind., Nov. 25, 1934; d. Terrence Ellis and Mary Ethel (Wishard) P. BS in Arts and Crafts, Ind. State U., 1957; MA in Art Edn. and Painting, Purdue U., 1972; postgrad., Ball State U., 1958, 66; postgrad. computer graphics works, Ind. U., Bloomington, 1985. Cert. pub. sch. tchr., supt., Ind., Ky., Ill. Art tchr. 1-12 Sheridan (Ind.) H.S., 1957-60; art tchr. 3-12 Danville (Ind.) City Schs., 1961-62; art tchr. 1-12 Brownsburg (Ind.) Comm. Schs., 1962-64; art tchr. 7-12 Blue River Valley S.C., New Castle, Ind., 1964-67; art tchr. 1-8 Twin Lakes Sch. Corp., Monticello, Ind., 1967-69; art tchr. 1-6 Tippecanoe Sch. Corp., Lafayette, Ind., 1972-75; art tchr., children's art Ctr. Sch., Albuquerque, 1977-78; tutor supr. Albuquerque Pub. Schs., 1977-78, art lab. asst., 1978-79; art tchr. 7-12 Attica (Ind.) Consolid. Schs., 1979-80; art tchr. 1-8 Southwest Parke C.S., Mecca, Ind., 1983-85; painting instr. Danville Area C.C., Ill., 1987-88; substitute tchr. Albuquerque Pub. Schs., 1989-2000; ret., 2000. One-artist and group shows of paintings at Purdue U., Jonson Gallery, U. N.Mex., Union Bldg., U. N.Mex., 1976, 77, 88. One-woman and group shows include Purdue U., Jonson Gallery, U. N.Mex., Union Bldg., U. N.Mex., 1976-78, Arts and Crafts Benefit. Mem. Neighborhood Watch, Bernalillo, N.Mex., 1995—97; mem. animal legal The Nature Conservancy; docent Albuquerque Mus.; vol. greeter Albuquerque Biol. Park; charter mem. WWII Meml. Women's History Mus.; vol. youth exhibit Arts and Crafts Fair. Grantee Wabash Valley Projects, Tippecanoe Arts Fedn. and Nat. Endowment of the Arts, Lafayette, 1987. Mem.: Animal Protection Inst., Sierra Club, Animal Legal Def., Internat. Fund for Animal Welfare, Nat. Wildlife Fedn., Doris Day Animal League, U.S. Defenders of Wildlife, The Wilderness Soc., Mus. of Albuquerque Found., Nat. Resources Def. Coun. Methodist. Avocations: animal rights and environ. issues, music, art. Home: 324 E Avenida Bernalillo Bernalillo NM 87004-9018

PRITCHARD, DAVID EDWARD, physics educator; b. N.Y.C., Oct. 15, 1941; m. Andrea Hasler; children: Orion, Alexander. BS, Calif. Inst. Tech., 1962; PhD, Harvard U., 1968. Postdoctoral fellow MIT, Cambridge, Mass., 1968, instr., 1968-70, asst. prof., 1970-75, assoc. prof., 1975-80, prof., 1980—, Cecil and Ida Chair, 2001—. Vis. scientist Stanford Rsch. Inst., 1975; vis. prof. U. Pais Sud Orsay, 1983; disting. visitor Joint Inst. for Lab., Astrophysics, 1989, 98, mem. subpanel, 1990—94, chmn., 1994; co-chair First Quantum Electronic and Laser Sci. Conf., 1989; chair Internat. Conf. on Atomic Physics, 2002. Div. assoc. editor Phys. Rev. Letters, 1983-88; contbr. articles to profl. jours. Polaroid fellow Harvard U., 1962-63, NSF predoctoral fellow, 1963-68. Fellow: AAAS, Optical Soc. Am., Am. Acad. Arts and Scis., Am. Phys. Soc. (disting. traveling lectr. laser sci. topical group 1992—94, rep. steering com. laser sci. topical group, rep. joint coun. on quantum electronics, Broida prize 1991, Centennial spkr. 1999, Schawlow prize 2003); mem.: NAS, Effective Educational Tech., Inc. (co-founder), Tiverton Yacht Club (R.I.). Avocations: sailing, carpentry. Home: 88 Washington Ave Cambridge MA 02140-2708 Office: MIT Rm 26-241 Dept Physics Cambridge MA 02139 E-mail: dpritch@mit.edu.

PRITCHETT, ROBERT MARVIN, JR., religious organization administrator; b. Centreville, Md., Oct. 15, 1946; s. Robert Marvin Sr. and Bertha (Rozier) P.; m. Christine Emma Jones, June 25, 1966; children: Kaynette Linesha, Dana Marvea. BS, U. Md., 1985; postgrad., Howard U., 1985-87; MA in Religion, Liberty U., 1990. Ordained African Meth. Episcopal Ch.-2d Episcopal Dist., 1979. Pastor Wrights AME Ch., Elkton, Md., 1977-80, St. James AME Ch., Havre De Grace, Md., 1980-85, Adams Chapel AME Ch., Balt., 1985-88; pastor, adminstr. Faith Unity Fellowship, Millington, Md., 1988—. Instr. African M.E. Ch., Balt., 1978-82, Parks and Recreation, Queen Anne's County, Md., 1989-91; dir., instr. Fellowship Biblical & Theol. Inst., Millington, 1993—. Author: (manuals) Christian Education, Retooling for the 21st Century, 1986, Discipline, 1992; editor: Faith Unity Fellowship Ministry Manual, 1992. Mem. Grasonville (Md.) Cmty. Ctr., 1980; advisor, founder Black Bros. for Change, Grasonville, Md., 1988; bd. mem. Commn. Drug & Alcohol, Centreville, 1993. Recipient Cert. of Recognition, U.S. Army, Aberdeen, Md., 1983, Cert. of Recognition, NAACP, Grasonville, 1991. Avocations: fishing, walking, bowling, reading, traveling. Home: 28E Queen Mary Ct Chester MD 21619-2528 Office: 1 Charleswood Ct Baltimore MD 21207-4435

PRITCHETT, SAMUEL TRAVIS, finance and insurance educator, researcher, consultant; b. Emporia, Va., Dec. 18, 1938; s. Harvey Eugene and Mary (Brown) P.; m. Bertha Yates, Feb. 20, 1960; children: John Travis, Meri Katherine. BSBA, Va. Poly. Inst. and State U., 1960, MSBA, 1967; DBA, Ind. U., 1969. CLU, ChFC, CPCU. Claim rep. Equitable Life Assurance Soc., Richmond, Va., 1960-64, asst. div. claim mgr., 1964-65; asst. prof. bus. adminstrn. U. Richmond, 1969-70; asst. prof. ins. Va. Commonwealth U., Richmond, 1970-72, assoc. prof. ins., 1972-73; assoc. prof. fin. and ins. U. S.C., Columbia, 1973-76, prof. fin. and ins., 1976-99, J.H. Fellers prof., 1981-83, W.F. Hipp prof. ins., 1983-2000, program dir., chair banking, fin., ins. and real estate, 1977-83, 99-00, acad. dir. MBA program, 1993-95, disting. prof. finance and ins., 1999-2000, disting. prof. emeritus, 2000—. Vis. prof. ins. Ind. U., Bloomington, 1995-96; chmn. Risk Theory Soc., Columbus, Ohio, 1987-88; acad. dir. internat. exec. devel. program Bamerindus Seguros, Curtiba, Brazil, 1995. Author: Risk Management and Insurance, 7th edit., 1996, Stock Life Insurance Company Profitability, 1986, Individual Annuities as a Source of Retirement Income, 2d edit., 1982, An Economic Analysis of Workers' Compensation in South Carolina, 1994; assoc. editor Jour. Risk and Ins., 1982-86, editor, 1987-91; assoc. editor Fin. Svcs. Rev., 1989-95, 97-99; asst. editor Jour. Am. Soc. CLU and ChFC, 1993-98; mem. acad. rev. bd. Jour. Fin. Planning, 1990-91; mem. editl. bd. Jour. Bus. Rsch., 1976-83, Am. Jour. Small Bus., 1975-79; contbr. articles to profl. jours. Active S.C. Joint Ins. Study Com., 1981-86, 89-95. Mem. Am. Risk and Ins. Assn. (pres. 1980-81), Acad. Fin. Svcs. (pres. 1987-88), So. Risk and Ins. Assn. (pres. 1977-78), Fin. Mgmt. Assn., Profl. Ins. Agts. Found. (named Ins. Educator of Yr. 1989), Beta Gamma Sigma (pres. chpt. 1980-81), Gamma Iota Sigma (nat. trustee 1976-92). Home: 709 Marlin Ln Charleston SC 29412-5039 Office: U SC Moore Sch Bus Columbia SC 29208-0001

PRITZKER, ELISA, painter, sculptor, educator, theater director; b. Rio Cuarto, Cordoba, Argentina, Dec. 10, 1955; came to US, 1993; d. Samuel and Esther (Maladetsky) P.; m. Leonardo Fabio Castria, Sept. 22, 1986 (div. Apr. 1994); 1 child, Jimena Castria; m. Enrique Rob Lunski, June 14, 1994. BA in Ceramic Arts, Sch. of Ceramics, Mar del Plata, Argentina, 1976; student in Theater Direction, Body Expression, Acting, Siembra Group, Mar del Plata, Argentina, 1983; MA in Visual Arts, Superior Inst. Visual Arts, Mar del Plata, Argentina, 1986. Prof. pottery, sculpture Superior Inst. Visual Arts, Mar del Plata, Argentina, 1983-88, prof. drawing, 1987-88; prof. drawing, visual arts Sch. Ceramics, Mar del Plata, Argentina, 1986-88; graphic art designer Alzamora S.A., Palma de Mallorca, Spain, 1991-93; prof. painting, pottery Ulster BOCES, Port Ewen, N.Y., 1995—. Artistic dir. Internat. Club YWCA, Kingston, N.Y.; founder, artistic dir. Highland (N.Y.) Cultural Ctr., curator, juror Nat. Juried Art Exhbn., 1994, juror of selection, 1995, co-chair creation peace park and monument, 1995; organizer, curator Ann. Juried Exhbn. UNISON, New Paltz, N.Y., 1994, prof. ceramics Arts & Learning Ctr.; curator Latin Am. show Latin Am. Studies SUNY, New Paltz, 1994; curator Global Sisters in Peace photography show SUNY, New Paltz, 1995. One woman exhbns. include Agora Art Gallery, Palma de Mallorca, Spain, 1989, Casa Argentina, Jerusalem, 1995, Lynn Prince Gallery, Poughkeepsie, N.Y., 1995; group exhbns. include 28th Pollensa Internat. Festival of Sculpture and Painting, Baleares, Spain, 1989, Colonya Art Gallery, Pollensa, Baleares, Spain, 1990, Es Cafeti, Palma de Mallorca, Spain, 1992, Manzana 50 Art Gallery, Palma de Mallorca, Spain, 1993, Middletown (N.Y.) Art Ctr. Arts Coun. Orange County, 1993, Putnam Arts Coun. Levine Art Ctr., Mahopac, N.Y., 1993-94, Mamaroneck Artists Guild, Inc. Westbeth Gallery, N.Y.C., 1994, Lynn Prince Gallery, Poughkeepsie, N.Y., 1994, Heritage Art Gallery, Poughkeepsie, N.Y., 1994, Fitton Ctr. Creative Arts, Hamilton, Ohio, 1995, Nassau Coliseum, 1995; represented in permanent collections La Pruna Art Gallery, Manzana 50 Art Gallery, La Luna Art Gallery, numerous pub. and pvt. collections; dir. Urban Theater, Palma de Mallorca, Spain, 1990-92. Mem. reflections program com. PTA, Highland, N.Y., 1994-95, 150th Anniversary com. Town of Lloyd, Highland, N.Y., 1995. Recipient Best Original Painting, Ecol. Soc., 1987, First award Galeria Praxis, 1988, award of Excellence Manattan Arts Internat. Cover Arts Competition, 1994, 2nd Place logo contest, Railroad Bridge Co., Inc., 1994, 4th prize ReviewArt Contest Columbia Pacific U., 1994, 1st prize, 1994, 2nd prize 1995. Mem. Nat. Mus. Women in the Arts. Avocations: photography, music, yoga. Office: Highland Cultural Ctr PO Box 851 Highland NY 12528-0851

PRIVALOV, PETER L. biology and biophysics educator; b. Tbilisi, Georgia, Russia, July 25, 1932; came to U.S., 1991; m.; 2 children. M of Physics, U. Tbilisi, 1956; postgrad. fellow in biophysics inst. physics, Gergian Acad. Scis., Tbilisi, 1956-59; PhD, Tbilisi U., 1964; DSc, Inst. Biophysics, Acad. Scis. USSR, 1971. Rsch. scientist inst. physics Georgian Acad. Scis., Tbilisi, 1959-64, sr. rsch. scientist, 1964-66; head lab. thermodynamics inst. protein rsch. Acad. Scis. USSR, Puschino, Moscow Region, 1966-91, prof., 1984, corr. mem., 1984; prof. biology and biophysics Johns Hopkins U., Balt., 1991—. Vis. prof. Reginsburg U., Germany, 1990, dept. biology and inst. biophysical rsch. on macromolecular assemblies Johns Hopkins U., 1991; mem. scientific coun. inst. protein rsch. Acad. Scis. USSR, 1967—, inst. biophysics, 1972-85, scientific coun. molecular biology Moscow State U., 1985-91; internat. lectr. and PhD advisor in field. Mem. adv. bd. Jour. Biophysical Chem.; contbr. numerous articles to profl. jours.; 4 patents in microcalorimetry. Mem. Interunion Comsn. Biothermodynamics, 1976-84, Com. Lenin and State Prizes USSR, 1979-91. Grantee NIH, NSF; recipient State prize USSR, 1978, Alexander Humboldt Rsch. award 1989. Mem. Russian Acad. Scis., Am. Biophysical Soc., Biochemical Soc., Protein Soc. Avocations: gardening, classical music. Office: Johns Hopkins U 3400 N Charles St Baltimore MD 21218-2680

PRIVO, ALEXANDER, finance educator, department chairman; m. Elena Privo. BS, Touro Coll., N.Y.C., 1982; M Profl. Studies, New Sch. for Social Rsch., N.Y.C., 1985; MS in Edn., CUNY, 1988; PhD in Adminstrn. and Mgmt., Walden U., 1991. Cert. govt. fin. mgr.; cert. secondary tchr. math., ESL, social studies, bus., acctg., Russian, N.y. Dir. acctg. and fin. reporting Assoc. Retail Stores Inc., N.Y.C., 1982-85; tchr. acctg. N.Y.C. Bd. Edn., 1985—; prof., dept. bus. and econs. Touro Coll., 1987—; dean CUNY, 1987-90; chmn. dept. bus. econs. Touro Coll., 1991—. Coord. mentoring program CUNY and N.Y.C. Bd. edn., 1985-92; cons. and prof. Russian (former Soviet Union); exec. training program MBA Baruch Coll., CUNY, 1990—; coord. cooperative edn. program NYC BD. Edn./CUNY, 1992—. Curriculum devel. grantee. Mem. ASCD, Am. Acctg. Assn., Assn. Govt. Accts., Nat. Bus. Edn. Assn., Internat. Bus. Edn. Assn., Met. Bus. Edn. Assn., N.Y. Educators (doctorate), Am. Mgmt. Assn., Kappa Delta Pi. Home: 43-33 46th St Apt F15 Sunnyside NY 11104-2036

PROBER, ALEXANDRA JAWORSKI, education educator; b. Nadryb, Poland, Dec. 11, 1907; came to U.S., 1912; d. Leon and Wladyslawa (Bojkowska) Jaworski; m. Theodore Prober (dec. 1961); children: Walter, Martha, Thomas. AA, Pasadena (Calif.) City Coll., 1954, BA, 1957; MA, L.A. State U., 1965. Cert. tchr., Calif. Buyer raw materials Princess Pat Cosmetic Co., Chgo., 1934-39; treas., mgr. AR-EX Cosmetics, Chgo., 1937-43; performer Sta. WIND, Chgo., 1940-42; with counter intelligence U.S. Army, Salt Lake City, Calif., 1943; tchr. Sierra Madre (Calif.) Schs., 1960-61, Pasadena Unified Sch. Dist., 1962-73, L.A. City Coll., 1980-81; reader Nat. Edn. Assn., 1988—. Author: (poetry) Awakened Echoes, 1990;

contbr. articles to profl. jours. Vol. UCLA Hosp., 1981-84; lectr. for various civic groups, 1980; active Friends of Huntington Libr.; mem. Masquers Theatre Group, Chgo., Pacific Asia Mus. Huntington Libr.; performer plays; mem. World Acad. Arts and Culture, 1987—. With U.S. Army, 1944. Recipient 4th prize Nat. Writers Club Article Contest, 1983, 5th prize poetry, 1988, 1st prize for poetry Vega mag., 1983, Golden Poet award World of Poetry, 1985, 87, 88, 89, 90, 91, 92. Mem. AAUW, Internat. Soc. Poets (hon. charter), Nat. League Am. PEN Women, Calif. State U. Alumni Assn., UCLA Alumni Assn., Calif. Tchrs. Assn. (life, Tchr. Edn. and Profl. Standards com. 1938-43, hiring com. 1942), Variety Club Charities (pub. chmn. 1982), Calif. Ret. Tchrs. (life), Sherlock Holmes Club, Pi Lambda Theta. Avocations: gardening, writing poetry and stories, lecturing. Home: 1274 Sonoma Dr Altadena CA 91001-3152

PROBST, CAROL JEAN, mathematics educator; b. Freeburg, Ill., June 13, 1948; d. Lorraine William and Virginia Eloise (Nichols) Baumgarte; m. Dale Elmer Probst, June 6, 1970; children: Jason Dale, Corey Lorraine. EdB, Ea. Ill. U., 1970; MEd, So. Ill. U., 1974, Specialist in Edn., 1994. Math. tchr. Highland (Ill.) Jr. H.S., 1970-76, Highland H.S., 1970—; computer instr. Belleville (Ill.) Area Coll., 1983-89; computer camp instr. So. Ill. U., Edwardsville, 1984-92; dist. math. curriculum chair Highland Cmty. Schs. # 5, 1986—2000; math. dept. chair Highland H.S., 1994—, curriculum dir., chmn. sch. improvement, 2002—. Mem. secondary adv. bd. Greenville Coll., 1990-2000; mem. steering com. strategic planning team Highland Comty. Schs., 1993-98, chmn. Blue Ribbon Schs. Application, 1989, 91, 93; conv. spkr. Ill. Coun. Tchrs. Math.; spkr. Madison County Regional Office Edn. Math. Topics. Contbr.: The Experienced Teacher Handbook, 1993. Recipient Presdl. award Ill. Coun. Tchrs. Math., Those Who Excel award Ill. State Bd. Edn. Mem. ASCD, Nat. Coun. Tchrs. Math. (regional conv. com. 1993-94), Ill. Prins. Assn., Ill. Coun. Tchrs. Math. Home: 702 Peachtree Trl Collinsville IL 62234-5230 Office: Highland Community Schs 1800 Lindenthal St Highland IL 62249-2206 E-mail: jprobst@highland.madison.k12.il.us.

PROCIDANO, MARY ELIZABETH, psychologist, educator; b. New Rochelle, New York, Apr. 1, 1954; d. John D'Arge and Dorothy Diane (Utter) P.; m. Stephen Anthony Buglione, Aug. 9, 1986; children: Daniel Stephen, Katherine Mary, Anne Elizabeth. BS(hon.), Fordham U., 1976; PhD, Ind. U., 1981. Lic. psychologist, N.Y. Assoc. instr. Ind. U., Bloomington, Ind., 1979-80; intern in clin. psychology Inst. of Living, Hartford, Conn., 1980-81; asst. prof. Fordham U., Bronx, NY, 1981-90, asst. chair psychology dept., 1984-87, chair inst. rev. bd. for protection of human subjects, 1986-94, mem. faculty senate, 1992—96, 1998—, mem. coll. coun. and various com., advisor, chair psychology dept., 1996—2002; pvt. practice, clin. psychology Scarsdale, NY, 1992—96; assoc. prof. Fordham U., Bronx, NY, 1990—. Assoc. dean Fordham U. Grad. Sch. of Art's and Sci., 1996. Cons. editor Jour. of Personality and Social Psychology, 1989-92; contbg. articles and chapters to profl. and scholarly journals and books. Mem. Am. Psychol. Assn.; Ea. Psychol. Assn.; Phi Beta Kappa; Sigma Xi; Psi Chi. Roman Catholic. Avocations: gardening, hiking, cooking. Office: Fordham U Dept Psychology Bronx NY 10458

PROCOPIO, MARYLOUISE ELIZABETH, college program director; b. Fountain Hill, Pa., Nov. 30, 1956; d. William Nicholas and Margaret Anastasia (Sekerak) Strobel; m. Thomas Francis Procopio, Aug. 12, 1978 (div. May 1991); children: William Francis, Francesca Ann. BS in Home Econs. Edn., Marywood Coll., 1978; postgrad., Temple U., 1988—. Cert. home economist, nat., cert. TIPS trainer, nat., cert. food exec. Substitute tchr. Salisbury Twp. Sch. Dist., Allentown, Pa., 1979-82, Allentown Sch. Dist., 1979-82; instr. Nat. Edn. Corp.-Allentown Bus. Sch., 1982-87; coord. hosp. edn. Lehigh Carbon C.C., Schnecksville, Pa., 1987—. TIPS trainer HealthComm. Inc., Washington, 1990—; outside agt. Solid Gold Travel Agy., Bethlehem, Pa., 1991—; external auditor Northampton C.C., Bethlehem, 1992; adv. bd. mem. Lehigh County Vo-Tech. Sch., Schnecksville, 1992—. Safety officer Interested Persons Union Terr., Allentown, 1986-87, pres., 1987-90, 94—, advisor, 1990-94; bd. dirs. Union Terr. Athletic Club, Allentown, 1989-90, fin. sec., 1990-91, Big A Booster Club Allen H.S., 1992—, pres., 1993-94; chair bldg. subcom., mem. steering com. Allentown Sch. Dist. Flexible Sch. Calendar Com. Mem. NEA, NAFE, Coun. on Hotel, Restaurant and Instl. Educators, Am. Home Econs. Assn., Pa. State Edn. Assn., Pa. Travel Coun. (edn. com. 1993—), Soc. Travel and Tourism Educators, Pa. Home Econs. Assn. (Mideast dist. treas. 1982-89), Pa. Assn. Two-Yr. Colls. (bd. dirs. 1990-92, v.p. 1992-93, pres. 1993—). Democrat. Roman Catholic. Avocations: reading, tennis, golf, bowling. Office: Lehigh Carbon CC ABE site ABE site 600 Hayden Cir Allentown PA 18109-9353

PROCTOR, RICHARD JEROME, JR., business educator, accountant, expert witness; b. N.Y.C., Oct. 6, 1941; s. Richard Jerome and Edith (Decker) P.; m. Elfriede N. Neundorfer, Aug. 19, 1967; children: Courtney, John, David. BS, Columbia U., 1963, MBA, 1970. CPA, N.Y., Conn.; cert. valuation analyst, cert. govt. fin. mgr.; cert. forensic acct. Am. Bd. Forensic Acctg. Sr. acct. Arthur Andersen, N.Y.C., 1970-72; dir. acctg. N.Y. Stock Exchange, N.Y.C., 1972-75; chief fin. officer Executrans, Greenwich, Conn., 1975-77; dir. planning Irvin Industries, Stamford, Conn., 1977-79; asst. prof. acctg. and taxation U. Hartford (Conn.), 1979-82; prof. and dept. chairperson Ancell Sch. Bus. Western Conn. State U., Danbury, 1983—. Pvt. practice, 1979—; cons., expert witness in field. Author (textbook): Proli Footwear-A Team Based Audit Simulation, 2002. Mem. AICPA, Conn. Soc. CPAs (Disting. Authors award 1983, 92), Nat. Assn. Cert. Valuation Analysts, Inst. Bus. Appraisers, Am. Acctg. Assn., Inst. Mgmt. Accts., Am. Bd. Forensic Acctg. (diplomate). Home: 31 Cooper Hill Rd Ridgefield CT 06877-5903 Office: Western Conn State U 181 White St Danbury CT 06810-6826

PROCTOR, SUSAN DELANEY COBBS, special education educator, consultant; b. Buffalo, N.Y., Sept. 2, 1954; d. Walter Herbert and Jean Graves (Delaney) Cobbs; m. Richard Stephen Proctor, May 1, 1976; children: James, Christopher, Jean. BA, Beloit Coll., 1976; MEd, U. Mich., 1978. Cert. elem. tchr., spl. edn., Ill. Rsch. asst. Ctr. for Human Growth & Devel., Ann Arbor, Mich., 1976-78; learning disabilities tchr. Allegheny Intermediate Unit, Pitts., 1978-84; dir. Collierville (Tenn.) Tutoring Svc., 1989-90; behavior disorder itinerant tchr. Spl. Edn. Dist. of Lake County, Gurnee, Ill., 1991—. Teaching asst. Beloit (Wis.) Coll., 1976; mem. Curriculum Rev. Com., Pitts., 1982; chmn. edn. com. Collierville (Tenn.) Presbyn. Ch., 1988-89. Mem. Com. for Sch. Improvement, Princeton, N.J., 1972; dir. Vol. Tutoring Svc., Beloit, 1973-76; vol. Spl. Olympics, Memphis, 1984, 85. Mem. Internat. Reading Assn., Coun. for Exceptional Children (mental, behavior disorder and learning disability divs.), Coun. for Learning Disabilities, Learning Disability Assn. Avocations: reading, travel, exercise, crafts, early childhood devel. Home: 1518 Forever Ave Libertyville IL 60048-4452 Office: Spl Edn Dist Lake County 4440 Grand Ave Gurnee IL 60031-2620

PROCTOR, WILLIAM LEE, college chancellor; b. Atlanta, Jan. 27, 1933; s. Samuel Cook and Rose Elizabeth (Nottingham) P.; m. Pamela Evans Duke; children: Samuel Matthews (dec.), Priscilla Nottingham. BS, Fla. State U., 1956, MS, 1964, PhD, 1968; DHL honoris causa (hon.), Nova Southeastern U., 2003. Tchr. Seminole County Pub. Schs., Longwood, Fla., 1956-57, 58-62, Orange County Fla. Pub. Schs., Orlando, Fla., 1957-58; athletic coach Fla. State U., Tallahassee, 1962-65, asst. dean men, 1965-67, grad. fellow, 1967-68; supt. of schs. Rock Hill (S.C.) Sch. Dist. #3, 1968-69; dean of men U. Ctrl. Fla., Orlando, 1969-71; pres. Flagler Coll., St. Augustine, Fla., 1971-2001, chancellor, 2001—. Cons. on higher edn. policy Heritage Found., Washington, 1983—, Fla. Bd. Edn., 2001-03, State Bd. Edn., 2003—; mem. Commn. on Colls., So. Assn. Colls. and Schs., 1995-2000; dir. Tchr. Edn. Accreditation Coun. Vice-chmn. Fla. Edn. Stds. Commn., 1995-2001; bd. dirs. Penney Retirement Cmty., chmn., 1991—; bd. dirs. Vicar's Landing Retirement Cmty., chmn., 1992-95, bd., 1990-96; trustee, chmn. Fla. Sch. for Deaf and Blind, St. Augustine, 1984-2001; mem. adv. coun. Salvation Army, St. Johns County; mem. devel. coun. First Coast Work Force, 1998-2001; mem. Bus./Higher Edn. Partnership, 2000-01; chmn. Communities in Schs., St. Johns County, Fla., 2002—. Recipient Disting. Educator award Fla. State U. Coll. Edn., 1989, Phil Carrol award Soc. for Advancement Mgmt., 1990, Disting. Svc. award Fla. Sch. for Deaf and Blind, 1990, Patrick Henry Medallion patriotic achievement Mil. Order of World Wars, 1991, Stetson S Club Achievement award, 1993, Order of the South So. Acad. Letters, Arts, and Scis., Excellence in Mgmt. award Soc. for Advancement of Mgmt., 2000, Lifetime Edn. Achievement award, 2001, Disting. Svc. award Fla. Assn. Colls. and Univs., 2002, Sec. Jim Horne's Life Edn. Leadership award; named to Fla. State U. Athletic Hall of Fame, 1988, Order of La Florida, 2001. Mem. Am. Assn. Pres. of Ind. Colls., State Hist. Assn., Ind. Colls. and Univs. of Fla. (legis. chmn. 1974-77, vice chmn. 1976-77, chmn. 1978-79, Liberty Bell award 2003), Rotary (pres. 1978-79, govs. dist. 697 1988-89). Republican. Presbyterian. Avocations: history, jogging, Karate. Office: Flagler Coll Office of the Chancellor PO Box 1027 Saint Augustine FL 32085-1027 E-mail: proctorw@flagler.edu.

PROFAIZER, JOSEPHINE E. elementary education educator; b. Rock Springs, Wyo., Sept. 2, 1951; d. Joseph and Enrica (Filippi) P. BS, U. Wyo., 1973; MEd, Utah State U., 1983. Cert. tchr., Wyo. Tchr. 3d grade Sweetwater Sch. Dist. 1, Rock Springs, 1973-79, tchr. kindergarten, 1980, tchr. 2d grade, 1980-89, tchr. Title 1 reading and math., 1989—. Bd. dirs. Internat. Tirolean Trentino Orgns. N.Am., 1991-95. Recipient Outstanding Young Educator award Rock Springs Jaycees, 1980, Arch Coal Golden Apple Achievement award, 2003. Mem. NEA, Wyo. Edn. Assn., Sweetwater Edn. Assn. (Tchr. of Yr. 1994-95), Tyrloean Trentini Wyo. (sec. 1986-91, newsletter editor 1989-92, 94-99, pres. 1991-95, v.p. 1999—), Delta Kappa Gamma (sec. 1982-84, v.p. 1990-92, treas. 1994-98), Beta Sigma Phi (sec. 1990-91, v.p. 1993-94, pres. 1996-98, treas. 1999-02). Roman Catholic. Avocations: travel, reading, collecting hummel and anri figurines, gardening.

PROFFITT, DENNIS LEWIS, finance educator; b. St. Louis, Apr. 2, 1949; s. Waldo E. and Madalyn J. (Lewis) P.; m. Judy Carol Laws, Sept. 5, 1970; children: David Gregory, Karen Michelle. BS, Ctrl. Mo. State U., 1971; MBA, Bradley U., 1974; PhD, St. Louis U., 1984. Dir. bus. affairs Mo. Bapt. Coll., St. Louis, 1976-82; asst. prof. Utah State U., Logan, 1982-87; prof. Grand Canyon U., Phoenix, 1987—. Vis. lectr. Russian People's U., Moscow, 1994, Staffordshire U., Stoke-on-Trent, Eng., 1997. Author: Investments, 1991; editor: Financial Management in Transitional Economies, 1993; contbr. 11 articles to profl. jours. Mem. Am. Fin. Assn., Fin. Mgmt. Assn., Christian Bus. Faculty Assn. (dir. 1997-2000, chair 1999-2000), editor newsletter). Avocations: reading, bicycling. Office: Grand Canyon U 3300 W Camelback Rd Phoenix AZ 85017-1097

PROFFITT, JOHN RICHARD, business executive, educator; b. Grand Junction, Colo., Sept. 12, 1930; s. Hillus D. and Joy Elaine (Lindsay) P.; m. Claire Boyer Miller, May 8, 1965 (div. 1992); children: Cameron Lindsay, William Boyer. BA in Edn., U. Ky., 1953, MA in Polit. Sci., 1961; postgrad., U. Mich., 1959-65. Asst. dean of men, instr. polit. sci. dept. U. Ky., Lexington, 1957-59; teaching fellow U. Mich., Ann Arbor, 1961-63, 63-65; asst. dir. Nat. Commn. on Accrediting, Washington, 1966-68; dir. accreditation and eligibility staff U.S. Dept. HEW, Washington, 1968-75; dir. divsn. eligibility and agy. evaluation U.S. Dept. Edn., Washington, 1975-80, dir. divsn. instnl. and state incentive programs, 1980-82; pres. The Clairion Corp., Bethesda, Md., 1982-84, Nat. Asbestos Removal, Inc., Beltsville, Md., 1985-90, Commonwealth Environ. Svcs., Inc., Alexandria, Va., 1987-91, also chmn. bd. dirs.; chmn. Internat. Environ. Engrs., Inc., Alexandria, Va., 1991-92; pres. Canterbury Internat., Vienna, Va., 1992-95; cons., 1995-99; v.p. E-Pass Techs., Inc., McLean, Va., 1999—. Cons. Conn. State Commn. Higher Edn., Hartford, 1967, Am. Coun. Edn., Washington, 1970; cons. U.S. Dept. Hew, 1967, 68; mem. study steering com. Am. Vocat. Assn., Washington, 1968; exec. sec. Nat. Adv. Com. on Accreditation and Instnl. Eligibility, Washington, 1968-80; mem. gen. com. Nat. Study Sch. evaluation, Alexandria, 1970-78; mem. task force Edn. Commn. of the States, Denver, 1972; subcom. chmn. Fed. Interagy. Com. on Edn., Washington, 1974-76; lectr., presenter profl. confs. Co-author: Accreditation and Certification in Relation to Allied Health Manpower, 1971; contbg. author: Health Manpower: Adapting in the Seventies, 1971, Accreditation in Teacher Education, 1975, Transferring Experiential Credit, 1979; contbr. articles to profl. and govtl. agy. publs., 1968-79. V.p., bd. dirs. Nat. Accreditation Coun. for Agys. Serving the Blind, N.Y.C., 1985; pres., chmn. bd. dirs. Found. for Advancement of Quality Svcs. for the Blind, Alexandria, 1988. 1st lt. USAF, 1953-55, Japan and Korea. Higher edn. fellow Univ. Mich., 1959. Mem. Optimist Club (Lexington, Ky.), Club Internat. (Chgo.), Island Club (Hobe Sound, Fla.), Thoroughbred Club Am. (Lexington), Tower Club (Vienna, Va.), Sigma Nu. Democrat. Episcopalian. Avocations: conservation, animal welfare, travel, antiques, art. Home: 515 Beall Ave Rockville MD 20850-2106 E-mail: John.Proffitt@e-pass.com.

PROFICE, ROSENA MAYBERRY, elementary school educator; b. Natchez, Miss., Oct. 8, 1953; d. Alex Jr. and Louise V. (Fuller) Mayberry; m. Willie Lee Profice, Feb. 12, 1977; children: Jamie Martez, Alesha Shermille. BS in History, Jackson State U., 1974, MS in Elem. Edn., 1975, Edn. Splty. in Elem. Edn., 1977. Cert. elem. reading and social studies tchr., Miss. Tchr. reading Ackerman (Miss.) H.S., 1975-76, North Hazlehurst (Miss.) Elem. Sch., 1976-79; tchr. reading and elem. edn. Natchez-Adams Sch. Sys., Natchez, 1979—. Mem. NEA, Miss. Assn. Educators, Nat. Alliance Black Sch. Educators, Natchez Assn. for the Preservation of Afro-Am. Culture, Zion Hill #1 Bapt. Ch. Democrat. Baptist. Avocations: reading, travel, shopping. Home: 11 Elbow Ln Natchez MS 39120-5346 E-mail: rprofice@yahoo.com.

PROFIT, PAMELA ANN, middle school educator; b. N.Y.C., June 25, 1955; d. Louis René and Rita Nellie (Hawkins) P. BA in English Edn., SUNY, Albany, 1977; MS in Reading, CUNY, 1980. Cert. permanent 7-12 English, K-12 reading, N-6 elem. tchr., N.Y. Elem. tchr. Pub. Sch. 103X, Bronx, N.Y., 1982-90; ednl. liaison Bklyn. Borough Office, United Fedn. Tchrs., N.Y.C. Tchr. Ctr. Consortium, 1990-91; tchr. Chpt. I reading Richard R. Green Mid. Sch., Bronx, 1991-92, staff developer, 1994-95; mid. grade tchr. Lincoln Acad., N.Y.C., 1992-94; tchr. ctr. specialist U.F.T./N.Y.C. Tchr. Ctr. Consortium, 1995—; instr. Sch. of New Resources Coll. of New Rochelle, 1992—. Troop leader Girl Scouts U.S.A., 1983-85; tchr. religious instrn. Our Lady of Grace Ch., 1987-91. Mem. Am. Fedn. Tchrs., United Fedn. Tchrs. (exec. bd., ednl. liaison, health com.), Zeta Phi Beta (sec. Delta Mu Zeta chpt. 1988-90, histr. 1992-84, Archonette youth advisor 1982—, Zeta of Yr. award 1990). Avocations: reading, painting, drawing, swimming, travel.

PROKES, JAMES OTTO, special education educator; b. Chgo., Aug. 25, 1941; s. Otto P. and Kayla Ann (Rogal) P.; m. Kim C. Nichols, Sept. 10, 1949; 1 child, James Robert. AA, Wilson Jr. Coll., Chgo., 1963; BS in Edn., Chgo. State U., 1965, MS in Edn., 1969; PhD, U. Chgo., 1972. Cert. edn., guidance and counseling. Tchr. Chgo. (Ill.) Bd. Edn., 1965-66, Sch. Dist. III, Burbank, Ill., 1967-94, Chgo. (Ill.) Assn. for Retarded Citizens, 1993—. Author: Collecting Education, 1969, Railroad Man, 1973. Lt. USMC, 1963-64. Named Tchr. of Yr., PTA, Burbank, Ill., 1969, 73. Mem. Nat. Assn. Timetable Collectors. Republican. Roman Catholic. Home: 7505 W Ute Ln Palos Heights IL 60463-2047 Office: Burbank Cook County Schs 7600 Central Ave Burbank IL 60459-1308

PRONOVOST, STEPHEN H. principal; b. Flushing, N.Y., Aug. 16, 1946; s. Wilbert L. and Margaret N. (Harriman) P.; m. Rose Marie Farrinella, May 20, 1972; children: Jason, Evan. BS, Boston U., 1970, MEd, 1975. Dir. edn. and tng. Paul A. Dever State Sch., Taunton, Mass., 1971-76; extended day coord. Assabet Valley Regional Vocat. H.S., Marlboro, Mass., 1976-84, asst. vocat. chmn., 1984-89, prin., 1989—. Sch. stds. task force Dept. of Edn., Mass., 1993-94, statewide assessment adv. com., 1994—; community edn. adv. coun. Bd. of Edn., 1990-93; asst. dir. Competency Based Vocat. Edn., 1982-83; presenter in field. With U.S. Army, 1966-69. Leadership Acad. fellowship Bd. Edn., 1988-89. Mem. Mass. Secondary Sch. Adminstn. Assn. (vice chair curriculum com. 1990—), Mass. Assn. Vocat. Adminstrn., Mass. Assn. Vocat. Edn. Specialists Needs (pres.). Avocation: model railroading. Office: Assabet Valley Regional Vocat HS 215 Fitchburg St Marlborough MA 01752-1219

PROPHETT, ANDREW LEE, political science educator; b. Lynchburg, Va., Mar. 1, 1948; s. Elisha and Evatna (Gilliam) P. BS in History, Hampton U., 1970; MEd in Social Studies, U. Ill., 1972; postgrad., U. Va., 1986-91. Cert. tchr., N.J. and Va. Tchr. U.S. and African history Camden (N.J.) H.S., 1970-85; tchr. social studies Randolph-Henry H.S., Charlotte Court House, Va., 1986-99, dept. chair social studies, 1992-99; instr. polit. sci. and African-Am. history Southside Va. C.C., Keysville, 1988-99; instr. social studies Chesterfield (Va.) County Pub. Schs., 1999—. Mem. Campbell County (Va.) Sch. Bd., 1992-95; chmn. edn. com. Staunton River Adv. Commn., Randolph, Va., 1994-96; summer participant Armonk Inst. Study Tour of Germany, 1995. Pres. Campbell County NAACP, Rustburg, 1992—; mem. youth adv. bd. Gethsemane Presbyn. Ch., Drakes Branch, Va., 1994—, deacon, 1995-97, elder, 1997—; mem. study tour of Israel, Va. Dept. Edn., 1997; chmn. Task Force on Racism, Presbytery of the Peaks; participant study tour of Spain and Morocco, summer 1997, study tour of Athens and the Greek Islands, summer 1998, study tour of Turkey, summer 1999; lay commr. 211th Gen. Assembly Presbyn. Ch. U.S.A., Ft. Worth, 1999. Recipient Excellence in Tchg. award Southside Va. Cmty. Coll., 1994, Tchr. Recognition award Charlotte County Edn. Found., Inc., 1997, disting. leadership award Campbell County NAACP, 1999, Cmty. Svc. award Lynchburg chpt. Nat. Conf. Cmty. and Justice, 1999. Mem. NEA, Va. Edn. Assn., Va. Geog. Soc., Phi Delta Kappa. Democrat. Presbyterian. Home: 5407 Houndmaster Rd Midlothian VA 23112-6522

PROPST, CATHERINE LAMB, biotechnology company executive; b. Charlotte, N.C., Mar. 10, 1946; d. James Pinckney and Eliza Mayo (Mills) P. BA magna cum laude, Vanderbilt U., 1967; M of Philosophy, Yale U., 1970, PhD, 1973. Head microbiology div. GTE Labs., Waltham, Mass., 1974-77; various mgmt. positions Abbott Labs., North Chgo., Ill., 1977-80; v.p. rsch. and devel. Ayerst Labs., Plainview, N.Y., 1980-83; v.p. rsch. and devel. worldwide Flow Gen. Inc., McLean, Va., 1983-85; pres. and chief exec. officer Affiliated Sci. Inc., Ingleside, Ill., 1985-97; pres., CEO Tex. Biotech. Found., Hempstead, Tex., 1997—. Vis. prof. genetics U. Ill., Chgo., 1989—90; founder, exec. dir. Ctr. for Biotech., Northwestern U., 1990—95; pres. Ill. Biotech. Ctr., 1995—97; bd. dirs. several cos.; bd. dirs., mem. sci. adv. bd. Keystone Symposia on Molecular and Cellular Biology, 1997—2002. Author and editor: Computer-Aided Drug Design, 1989, Nucleic Acid Targeted Drug Design, 1992; contbr. articles to profl. jours. Named to Outstanding Working Women in the U.S., 1982; recipient many sci. and bus. awards. Fellow Soc. Indsl. Microbiology (bd. dirs. 1990-93), Nat. Coun. Biotech Ctrs. (bd. dirs. 1995-97); mem. AAAS, Nat. Wildlife Fedn., Consortium for Plant Biotech. Rsch. (bd. dirs. 1994-99), Phi Beta Kappa, Sigma Xi. Episcopalian. Avocations: horseback riding, skiing, raising Black Angus and Black Brangus cattle. Office: Texas Biotech Found PO Box 17 Hempstead TX 77445-0017 Fax: 979-826-9710.

PROSSER, JOHN MARTIN, architect, educator, urban design consultant; b. Wichita, Kans., Dec. 28, 1932; s. Francis Ware and Harriet Corinne (Osborne) P.; m. Judith Adams, Aug. 28, 1954 (dec. 1982); children: Thomas, Anne, Edward; m. Karen Ann Cleary, Dec. 30, 1983; 1 child, Jennifer. BArch, U. Kans., 1955; MArch, Carnegie Mellon U., 1961. Registered architect, Kans., Colo. Architect Robinson and Hissem, Wichita, 1954-56, Guirey, Srnka, and Arnold, Phoenix, 1961-62, James Sudler Assocs., Denver, 1962-68; ptnr., architect Nuzum, Prosser and Vetter, Boulder, 1969-75; from asst. prof. to prof. U. Colo., Boulder and Denver, 1968—, acting dean, 1980-84, dean, 1984, dir. environ. design Boulder, 1969-72, dir. urban design, 1972-85. Cons. John M. Prosser Assocs., Boulder and Denver, 1974—; vis. prof. urban design Oxford Poly., Eng., 1979; vis. critic Carnegie Mellon U., U. N.Mex., Colo. Coll.; pres. Denver chpt. AIA, 1983; prin. investigator Fitsimmons-U. Colo. Health Scis. City Rsch. Study, 1997-99. Author, narrator: (PBS TV documentary) Cities Are For Kids, Too, 1984; prin. works include (with others) hist. redesign Mus. Western Art, Denver (design honor 1984), Villa Italia, Lakewood, Colo., Denver, Auraria Higher Edn. Ctr., Pueblo C.C. campus plan and new acad. facilities, comprehensive campus plan Denver U., Ft. Lewis Coll., Westminster Golf Course Cmty., Denver Botanic Gardens 20-Yr. Concept Plan, Colo. Coll. Historic Preservation Plan, Buffalo Hills Ranch Golf Course Cmty., Fountain Valley Sch., Urban Design and Campus Planning, Ctrl. Colo. Springs Strategic Urban Design and Planning, 2001—02, Interquest Corp. Park Urban Plan, 1999-2001. Bd. dirs. Denver Parks and Recreation Bd., 1987-93, 96-2003; chmn. design rev. bd. univs. Colo., Boulder, Denver, Aurora, and Colorado Springs, 1981—; archtl. control com. Denver Tech. Ctr., 1984—, Meridian Internat. Bus. Ctr., 1984—, DTC West, 1991—, Denver Internat. Bus. Ctr., 1993—, Nat. Renewable Energy Lab., 1995—; planning cons. Denver Internat. Airport Environs.; Nucleus cofounder U. Colo. Real Estate Ctr., 1989-2000; sr. advisor, dir. campus planning, Endur Enterprise Computing Campuses, 2002-03. Capt. USAF, 1956—59. Co-recipient 2d pl. award Am. Soc. Interior Designers, 1984, Honor award Colo. Soc. Architects, 1984. Mem. Urban Land Inst. (panel adv. svcs. 1990, 2001-02), Denver Country Club (bd. dirs. 1984-88, pres. 1986-87), Beta Theta Pi. Democrat. Avocation: arlberg ski. Home: 390 Emerson St Denver CO 80218 Office: 1512 Larimer St Denver CO 80202-1610 E-mail: jmpros@aol.com.

PROSSER, MICHAEL HUBERT, communications educator; b. Indpls., Mar. 29, 1936; s. Marshall Herbert and Clydia Catharine (O'Dea) P.; m. Carol Mary Hogle, Nov. 27, 1958 (div. 1983); children: Michelle Ann Prosser-Evans, Leo Michael, Louis Mark; m. Joan Ann Kirkeby, Dec. 6, 1986. BA, Ball State U., 1958, MA, 1959; PhD, U. Ill., 1964. Tchr. Latin Urbana (Ill.) Jr. High Sch., 1960-63; asst. prof. speech SUNY, Buffalo, 1963-69; assoc. prof. speech Ind. U., Bloomington, 1969-72; prof. rhetoric and comm. U. Va., Charlottesville, 1972-2001, chair, 1972-77, prof. emeritus, 2001—; William A. Kern prof. in comm. Rochester Inst. Tech., 1994-98. Disting. vis. prof. comm. Rochester Inst. Tech., 1998-2001; adj. prof. SUNY, Brockport, 1998-99; chair AFS Global Awareness Day, U. Va., 1983-90, RIT Global Awareness Day, 1995-98, Intercultural Comm.; confs. at Rochester Inst. Tech., 1995-97, 99, 2000-01; vis. lectr. comm. Queens Coll. CUNY, 1966, 67; vis. assoc. prof. speech Calif. State U., Hayward, 1971; vis. prof. curriculum Meml. U. Newfoundland, St. John's, 1972, St. Paul U. and U. Ottawa (Can.), 1975; cons. intercultural comm. U.S. Info. Agy., Washington, 1977; disting. vis. prof. speech Kent (Ohio) State U., 1978; Fulbright prof. English, U. Swaziland, Kwalusene, 1990-91; fellow New Coll. U. Va., 1990-94; professorial lectr. George Washington Univ., 1994; Gannett lectr. Rochester Inst. Tech., 1995, 2000, Kern lectr., 1995-98; prof. comm. Yangzhou U., China, 2001—. Author: The Cultural Dialogue, 1978 (translated into Japanese 1982); co-author: Diplomatic Discourse: International Conflict at the United Nations: Addresses and Analysis, 1997; editor: An Ethic for Survival: Adlai Stevenson Speaks on International Affairs, 1936-65, 1969, Sow the Wind, Reap the Whirlwind: Heads of State Address the United Nations (2 vols.), 1970, Intercommunication Among Nations and Peoples, 1973; co-editor: Readings in Classical Rhetoric, 1969, Readings in Medieval Rhetoric, 1973, Civic Discourse: Multiculturalism, Cultural Diversity, and Global Communication, 1998, Civic Discourse: Intercultural, International and global Media, 1999; series editor Civic

Discourse for the Third Millennium, 1998— Ablex Pub. Co. Mem. Haiti commn. Cath. Diocese Richmond, 1989-93; bd. dirs., v.p. Assn. Rochester UN, 1996-97, pres., 1997-98; pres. Rochester Area Fulbright Chpt., 1995-97; mem. Spotlight on Scholarship Nat. Comm. Assn., Atlanta, 2001. Recipient Disting. Alumnus award Ball State U., 1978.Prosser-SITARIM award of excellence in internat. comm. theory, 2000. Mem. AAUP, Internat. Soc. for Intercultural Edn., Tng. and Rsch. (pres. 1984-86, Citizen of World 1986, Outstanding Sr. Interculturalist 1990), Internat. Comm. Assn. (v.p., Disting. Svc. award 1978), UN Assn. U.S.A., Fulbright Assn., Nat. Comm. Assn., UN Assn. of Rochester (bd. dirs., v.p., pres.), Am. Field Svc. (pres. intercultural programs 1982-86, Charlottesville), Assn. for Edn. in Journalism and Mass Media. Democrat. Roman Catholic. Avocations: social justice and peace advocacy, youth, travel. Office: Rochester Inst Tech Coll of Liberal Arts 92 Lomb Memorial Dr Rochester NY 14623-5604 Fax: 716-475-7732. E-mail: MHPGPT@rit.edu.

PROSSER, MICHAEL JOSEPH, college librarian; b. Syracuse, N.Y., May 9, 1948; s. Palmer Adelbert and Viola Mary (Clairmont) P. AA, Riverside (Calif.) City Coll., 1971; BA in History, Calif. State Coll., San Bernardino, 1977; MSLS, U. So. Calif., L.A., 1981. Cert. cmty. coll. instr., librarian, Calif. Libr. clk. Riverside C.C., 1968-81, learning resources asst., 1981—. Author: California and the Pacific Plate: A Bibliography, 1979. Tutor, Queen of Angels Ch., Riverside, 1985—, facilitator/patrons, 1985—; photographer. With U.S. Army, 1969-71. Mem. ASCD, Internat. Soc. Poets, Calif. Libr. Assn. Democrat. Roman Catholic. Home: 6800 Palos Dr Riverside CA 92503-1330 Office: Riverside Cmty Coll 4800 Magnolia Ave Riverside CA 92506-1242

PROTHO, JESSIE, educator; d. Duncan and Julia Mae (Edmond) McKenzie; widowed; children: Phyllis Noble, Carl Protho. Diploma, Scientific Beauty Sch., 1947; student, Walker Beauty Coll.; BS in Edn., Indiana U., 1968, MS in Edn., 1971. Lic. vocational dir. Indiana State U., 1979. Cosmetology tchr. Gary (Ind.) Area Career Ctr.; with Johnie's Beauty Shop, 1947-53, Jewelry Tng. Svc., 1948-49, Swartchild and Co., 1949-53; self-employed beauty shop owner, 1953-65; educator Gary (Ind.) Community School Corp., 1965—. Mem. AAUW, NAACP, Ind. U. Alumni Assn., Nat. Cosmetology Assn., Vocat. Indsl. Club, Alpha Phi Omega, Phi Delta Kappa (sec. 1991-92, Tchr. of Yr.). Avocations: bowling, sewing, cooking, creative hair styling. Home: 6710 Adams St Merrillville IN 46410-3407

PROTHRO, MARILYN SMITH, assistant principal; b. Shreveport, La., Aug. 8, 1962; d. Willie Dee Jr. and Carolyn Zulema (Yancey) Smith; m. William Craig Prothro, June 27, 1987; children: Victoria Lynn, Taylor Alyssa, Emory Claire. BS in Elem. Edn., La. State U., Baton Rouge, 1984; MEd in Elem. Adminstrn., Centenary Coll., 1992, postgrad., 1994—, La. State U., Shreveport, 1994—. Cert. elem. tchr., supervision, adminstrn., La. Elem. tchr. Pearl C. Anderson Learning Ctr., Dallas, 1987-88, Herndon Magnet Sch., Caddo Parish Schs., Belcher, La., 1984-87, 88-90, tchr. gifted English, 1988-97, Broadmoor Mid. Lab., 1997-98, Youree Dr. Mid. Sch., 1998-99; asst. prin. C.E. Byrd H.S., 1999—. Guest columnist Leadership mag., 1992-93, 94-95; vol. March of Dimes, 1992; leader Girl Scouts U.S.A., Dallas, 1987-88 Mem. adminstrv. bd. 1st United Meth. Ch., Shreveport, 1989-95, bd. dirs. 1st Beginnings Child Devel. Ctr., 1994-96, mem. nomination com., 1994-96; mem. exec. bd. Herndon Magnet Sch. PTA, 1994-95. Recipient Gifted and Talented Disting. Tchr. award Northwestern State U., Natchitoches, La., 1994, PTA Educators Distinction for La., 1997, 2003. Mem. Nat. Assn. Student Couns., So. Assn. Student Couns., La. Assn. Student Couns. (state v.p. advisor 1993-94), Nat. Assn. Student Activity Advisors, C.E. Byrd H.S. Alumni Assn. (chmn. class of 1980, 1992—), Delta Delta Delta (La. reference chmn. 1985-87, 91—, social advisor La. State U., Shreveport 1984-85, fin. advisor 1985-87, pres. Wish Upon A Star Found. 1991-96), Kappa Delta Epsilon, Phi Delta Kappa (adv. bd. dirs. 1998—). Democrat. Avocations: collecting teddy bears, family and school activities. Home: 574 Spring Lake Dr Shreveport LA 71106-4654 Office: 3201 Line Ave Shreveport LA 71104-4241

PROVENCHER, JEANNE STANSFIELD, secondary education educator; b. Methuen, Mass., June 30, 1948; d. Ernest Daniel and Rita Marie (Vayo) Stansfield; m. Richard Leonard Provencher, Dec. 15, 1978; children: Matthew, Ryan. BA, Newton Coll., 1970; MA, Rivier Coll., Nashua, N.H., 1990. Cert. tchr., Mass.; cert. experienced educator, N.H. Tchr. St. Francis Acad., Nevada, Mo., 1970-71, Salem (NH) H.S., 1971-72, Pelham (NH) Meml. Sch., 1983-87; tchr. English and women's studies Nashua (NH) H.S. North, 1987—. Critical reader Grammar Workshop, 1994; contbg. reader Adventures in Appreciation, 1994; reader/evaluator A.P. Lang. Exams, 2003; presenter in field. Lector St. Kathryn Ch., Hudson, N.H., 1988—. Mem. NOW, N.H. NOW, Nat. Coun. Tchrs. English (state judge for student lit. mags. 1994—), New Eng. Coun. Tchrs. English, N.H. Coun. Tchrs. English. Avocations: reading, gardening, working for equity, bicycling. Office: Nashua HS North 10 Chuck Druding Dr Nashua NH 03063

PROVENGHI, LESA CHRISTINE, educational administrator; b. Sacramento, July 23, 1960; d. Charles Nelson and Erika Nina (Fietz) Germany; m. Arthur S. Provenghi, Dec. 31, 1986; children: Katarina Christine, Michelle Nicole. BA in Math., U. No. Colo., 1982; MA in Ednl. Adminstrn., San Diego State U., 1984; PhD in Ednl. Psychology, U. Okla., 1992. Cert. tchr., adminstr., Tex. Tchr. math. Aurora (Colo.) Pub. Schs., 1983, Thompson R2-J Pub. Schs., Loveland, Colo., 1983-85; ednl. researcher San Diego State U., 1986; math. tchr. Norman (Okla.) Pub. Schs., 1987-88, El Paso (Tex.) Ind. Sch. Dist., 1987, 90-91, evaluator, 1991—. Ednl. cons., Norman, 1987-89; presenter at profl. confs.; evaluator, rschr. Mem. ASCD, Nat. Coun. Tchrs. Math., Assn. Ednl. Communications and Tech., Rocky Mountain Ednl. Rsch. Assn., El Paso Adminstrs. Assn. Democrat. Roman Catholic. Avocations: skiing, swimming, reading, travel. Office: El Paso Ind Sch Dist R&E PO Box 20100 El Paso TX 79998-0100

PROVENZANO, MAUREEN LYNN, secondary school educator; b. Anaheim, Calif., Nov. 25, 1963; d. Andrew Eugene and Maura Ann (McGivern) P. BA in English, Loyola Marymount U., L.A., 1986; teaching credential, Calif. State U., Fullerton, 1991; MA in Teaching English to Speakers of Other Langs., Calif. State U., L.A., 1993; postgrad., Loyola Marymount U. Cert. clear crosscultural, lang. and acad. devel., 1995. Tchr. English, Temple City (Calif.) High Sch., 1991—, supr. Saturday sch., 1991-92; tchr. English lit., intermediate level ESL Temple City Adult Sch., 1994. Mem. adv. bd. Peer Listeners, 1991-92; mem. intercultural com. Temple City Unified Sch. Dist., 1994, sr. class advisor, 1994-98, co-advisor Students Against Drunk Driving, 1993-94. Mem. Nat. Coun. Tchrs. English, Calif. Assn. Tchrs. English, Southland Coun. Tchrs. English, Calif. Tchrs. Assn., Calif. Tchrs. English to Speakers of Other Languages, Calif. Assn. for Counseling and Devel., Calif. Sch. Counselor Assn., Club Europa. Republican. Roman Catholic. Avocations: reading, travel. Office: Temple City High Sch 9501 Lemon Ave Temple City CA 91780-1398

PROVINE, LORRAINE, retired mathematics educator; b. Altus, Okla., Oct. 6, 1944; d. Claud Edward and Emmie Lorraine (Gasper) Allmon; m. Joe A. Provine, Aug. 14, 1966; children: Sharon Kay, John David. BS, U. Okla., 1966; MS, Okla. State U., 1988. Tchr. math. U.S. Grant High Sch., Oklahoma City Schs., 1966-69; tchr. East Jr. High Sch., Ponca City (Okla.) Schs., 1969-70; tchr. Ponca City High Sch., 1978-79, 81-96; lectr. dept. math. Okla. State U., Stillwater, 1996-99. Mem. NEA, Coun. for Exceptional Children, Internat. Soc. Tech. in Edn., Math. Assn. Am., Nat. Coun. Tchrs. Math., Sch. Sci. and Math. Assn., Okla. Edn. Assn., Okla. Coun. Tchrs. Math., Assn. Women in Math., Ponca City Assn. Classroom Tchrs. (treas. 1983-86, 91-96), Okla. Assn. Mothers Clubs (life, state bd. dirs. 1977-87, pres. 1984-85), Delta Kappa Gamma (Delta chpt. treas. 1996-98, Gamma state essay com. 1999-2003, Eta chpt. treas. 2000—). Republican. Baptist. Avocations: reading, knitting, sewing, genealogy. Home: 1019 Greenway Cir Norman OK 73072-6125 E-mail: lorraineprovine@cox.net.

PROVO, WADE ARDEN, foreign language educator; b. Cleve., July 8, 1937; s. Abraham Lincoln and Lillian (Rundle) P.; m. Nesta Mary Williams, Apr. 23, 1962; children: Michele Anne, Ian Victor, Marianne Catherine, Josette Louise. BA, Rollins Coll., 1959; MA, Stanford U., 1964, PhD, 1974. English asst. U. Toulouse, France, 1960-61; English tchr. Lycée Dumont d'Urville, Toulon, France, 1961-62; French tchg. asst. Stanford (Calif.) U., 1962-65; lectr. in French Ind. U., Bloomington, 1965-66; prof. of French Rockford (Ill.) Coll., 1966-98. English tchr. U. Bordeaux, Pau, France, summer, 1961; cons. SOURCE, Rockford, 1995—; translator area bus., Chgo., Rockford, 1970—; cons. Egyptian artifacts Freeport (Ill.) Mus., 1995—. Translator: The Young Calvin, 1987; author: Encyclopedia of World Authors II, 1989; contbr. articles to profl. jours. Tchr., leader LDS Ch., Rockford, 1966—; genealogist, cons. Family History Ctr., Rockford, 1976—; rschr., guide Time Mus., Rockford, 1982-92; humanities advisor Rockford Art Mus.; mem. ednl. rev. bd. Keith Country Day Sch., Rockford, 1975. Fulbright fellow, 1959-61, French Govt. fellow, 1961-62. Mem. MLA, Ill. Coun. on Tchg. of Fgn. Langs. (2d v.p. 1994-97, Lt. Gov.'s award 1992), Am. Assn. Tchrs. French, Ill. Fgn. Lang. Tchrs. Assn., Amis de François Mauriac. Avocations: Egyptian artifacts, German gothic script, family history. Home: 4925 Orchard Ave Rockford IL 61108-4232 Office: Rockford Coll 5050 E State St Rockford IL 61108-2311

PROWN, JULES DAVID, art historian educator; b. Freehold, N.J., Mar. 14, 1930; s. Max and Matilda (Cassileth) P.; m. Shirley Ann Martin, June 23, 1956; children: Elizabeth Anderson, David Martin, Jonathan, Peter Cassileth, Sarah Peiter. AB, Lafayette Coll., 1951, DFA (hon.), 1979; AM, U. Del., 1956, Harvard U., 1953, PhD, 1961. Dir. Hist. Soc. Old Newbury, Newburyport, Mass., 1957-58, Old Gaol Mus., York, Maine, 1958-59; asst. to dir. Harvard U., Fogg Art Mus., Cambridge, Mass., 1959-61; instr. to Paul Mellon prof. history of art Yale U., New Haven, 1961-99, Paul Mellon prof. emeritus history of art, 1999—; curator Am. art Yale U. Art Gallery, New Haven, 1963-68; vis. lectr. Smith Coll., Northampton, Mass., 1966-67; dir. Yale Ctr. for Brit. Art, New Haven, 1968-76, sr. rsch. fellow, 1999—; assoc. dir. Nat. Humanities Inst., New Haven, 1977. Trustee Whitney Mus., N.Y.C., 1975-94; mem. editorial adv. bd. Am. Art-Smithsonian, Washington, 1986-2001, On Common Ground, 1993—; mem. vis. com. Harvard U. Art Museums, 1993-98. Author: John Singleton Copley, 2 Vols., 1966, American Painting from Its Beginnings to the Armory Show, 1969, The Architecture of the Yale Center for British Art, 1977; Art as Evidence: Writings on Art and Material Culture, 2002, (catalogue) American Art from Alumni Collections, 1968; editor (with Kenneth Haltman) American Artifacts: Essays in Material Culture, 2000. Recipient George Washington Kidd award Lafayette Coll., 1986, recipient Iris Found. award for outstanding contbns. to the decorative arts, 2001, Lawrence A. Fleischman award for scholarly excellence in the field of Am. Art History, 2001. Fellow The Athenaeum of Phila. (hon.); mem. Am. Antiquarian Soc., Coll. Art Assn. (Disting. Tchg. of Art History award 1996), Am. Studies Assn., Conn. Acad. Arts & Scis., Walpole Soc., Royal Soc. Arts. Office: Yale Ctr for Brit Art PO Box 208280 New Haven CT 06520-8280 Business E-Mail: jules.prown@yale.edu.

PRUD'HOMME, ROBERT KRAFFT, chemical engineering educator; b. Sacramento, Jan. 28, 1948; s. Earle Sutter and Adele E. (Wilkens) P.; m. Dorothy Bjorklund, Oct. 14, 2000; children: Wendy A., Graham C., Jodie B., Taylor, Robert, Bradley. BSChemE, Stanford U., 1969; Grad. Spl. Studies, Harvard U., 1973; PhD ChemE, U. Wis., 1978. Asst. prof. chem. engring. Princeton (N.J.) U., 1978-84, assoc. prof., 1984-91, prof., 1991—; rsch. engr. AT&T Bell Labs., Murray Hill, N.J., 1984-85. Bd. dirs. Rheometrics Inc., Piscataway, N.J.; McCabe lectr. Dept. Chem. Engring. N.C. State U. Contbr. articles to profl. jours. Deacon Cornerstone Ch., Hopewell, N.J., 1989-92. Capt. U.S. Army, 1969-73. Decorated Bronze Star, Army Commendation Medal; recipient Presdl. Young Investigator award NSF. Mem. Am. Chem. Soc., Am. Inst. Chem. Engrs. (bd. dirs. material sci. and engring. div. 1982-93), U.S. Soc. Rheology (exec. com. 1989-91), Soc. Petroleum Engrs. Achievements include research in areas of polymer fluid mechanics, polymer characterization and transport phenomena. Office: Princeton U Dept Chem Engring Princeton NJ 08544-0001 Address: 31 W Long Dr Lawrenceville NJ 08648 E-mail: prudhomm@princeton.edu.

PRUETT, JAMES WORRELL, librarian, musicologist; b. Mt. Airy, N.C., Dec. 23, 1932; s. Samuel Richard and Gladys Dorne (Worrell) P.; m. Lilian Maria-Irene Pibernik, July 20, 1957; children— Mark, Ellen. BA, U. N.C., Chapel Hill, 1955, MA, 1957, PhD, 1962. Mem. faculty U. N.C., Chapel Hill., 1961-87, prof. music, 1974-87, music librarian, 1961-76, chmn. dept. music, 1976-86; chief music div. Library of Congress, Washington, 1987-95. Vis. prof. U. Toronto, 1976; cons. in music, 1995—. Editor: Studies in the History, Style and Bibliography of Music in Memory of Glen Haydon, 1969; author: Research Guide to Musicology, 1985. Contbr. profl. jours., encys. Newberry Library fellow, summer 1966 Mem. Internat. Musicol. Soc., Am. Musicol. Soc. (chpt. chmn. 1964-66, mem. coun. 1974-77), Music Libr. Assn. (pres. 1973-75, editor jour. 1974-77), Cosmos Club (Washington). Home: 343 Wesley Dr Chapel Hill NC 27516-1520

PRUETT, LINDY NEWTON, special education educator; b. Beaver Dam, Ky., Sept. 16, 1940; d. Godfery Eugene Newton and Virginia Irene Cox Levy; m. David Ross Stigler, Sept. 1958 (div. Nov. 1959); 1 child, Charles Michael; m. Wayne Willard Pruett, Aug. 20, 1965; 1 child, Brenda Michelle Baker. BS, Ind. U., 1971, MS, 1974. Cert. in elem. and spl. edn. Tchr. spl. edn. Indpls. Pub. Schs. Sponsor Brain Game - Acad. Team, Human Resl. Coun. Precinct committeeperson Dem. Com., Indpls., 1982-01. Mem. NEA, Ind. Edn. Assn., Hoosier Sci. Edn. Assn. Ch. of Christ. Avocations: gardening, knitting, restoring dolls. Home: 1421 N Fenton Ave Indianapolis IN 46219-4105 Office: Arsenal Tech High Sch 1500 E Michigan St Indianapolis IN 46201-3098 E-mail: wwpruett@juno.com.

PRUITT, ANNE LORING, academic administrator, education educator; b. Bainbridge, Ga., Sept. 19, 1929; d. Loring Alphonzo and Anne Lee (Ward) Smith; m. Harold G. Logan; children: Leslie; stepchildren: Dianne, Pamela, Sharon, Ralph Pruitt, Jr., Harold, Minda, Andrew Logan. BS, Howard U., Washington, 1949; MA, Columbia U., N.Y.C., 1950, EdD, 1964; HumD hon., Ctrl. State U., Wilberforce, Ohio, 1982. Counsel for women Howard U., 1950-52; tchr., dir. guidance Hutto H.S., Bainbridge, 1952-55; dean students Albany State Coll., Ga., 1955-59, Fisk U., Nashville, 1959-61; prof. edn. Case Western Res. U., Cleve., 1963-79; prof. ednl. policy and leadership Ohio State U., Columbus, 1979-95, prof. emeritus, 1995—; assoc. dean Ohio State U. Grad. Sch., Columbus, 1979-84; assoc. provost Ohio State U., Columbus, 1984-86, dir. Ctr. for Tchg. Excellence, 1986-94; dean in residence Coun. Grad. Schs., Washington, 1994-96, scholar in residence, 1996—2002. Cons. So. Regional Edn. Bd., Atlanta, 1967-78, So. Edn. Found., Atlanta, 1978-87; co-dir. Preparing Future Faculty program, 1994-2002. Author: New Students and Coordinated Counseling, 1973, Black Employees in Traditionally White Institutions in the Adams States 1975-77, 1981, In Pursuit of Equality in Higher Education, 1987; co-author: (with Paul Isaac) Student Services for the Changing Graduate Student Population, 1995, (with Jerry Gaff and Richard Weibl) Building the Faculty We Need: Colleges and Universities Working Together, 2000, (with Jerry Gaff and Joyce Jentoft) Preparing Future Faculty in the Sciences and Mathematics, 2002, (with Jerry Gaff, Leslie Sims and Daniel Denecke) Preparing Future Faculty in the Humanities and Social Sciences: A Guide for Change, 2003. Trustee Urban League, Cleve., 1965-71, Ctrl. State U., 1973-82, Case Western Res. U., 1987-02, Columbus Area Leadership Program, 1988-91; bd. dirs. ARC, Cleve., 1978-79, Am. West Airlines Found., 1992-95; mem. adv. com. USCG Acad., New London, Conn., 1980-83; Ohio State U. rep. to AAUW, 1989-94; univ. co-chairperson United Way, 1990-91; trustee Marburn Acad., 1991-95; mem. Columbus 1992 Edn. Com., 1988-92; mem. edn. subcom. Columbus Found., 1991-94; mem. exec. com. Renaissance League, 1992-94; mem. vis. panel on rsch., Ednl. Testing Svc., 1996-02; mem. Commn. on Future Clemson U., 1997-98; bd. dirs. Black Women's Agenda, Inc., 1997-, pres. 1998-2002; deacon Peoples Congregational United Ch. of Christ, 1998—; mem. B.E.S.T. Expert Panel, 2002—; evaluation external expert NSF Grad. Tchg. Fellows in K-12 Edn. Program, 2002—. Recipient Outstanding Alumnus award Howard U. Alumni Assn., 1975; Am. Council on Edn. fellow, 1977; named one of Am.'s Top 100 Black Bus. and Profl. Women Dollars & Sense Mag., 1986; recipient Disting. Affirmative Action award Ohio State U., 1988; named Sr. Scholar Am. Coll. Personnel Assn., 1989, Woman of Achievement award YMCA, 1993. Mem. NSF (mem. com. on equal opportunities in sci. and engring. 1989-95), Am. Coll. Pers. Assn. (pres. 1976-77), Coun. Grad. Schs. in U.S. (chairperson com. on minority grad. edn. 1980-84), Am. Ednl. Rsch. Assn., Ohio Assn. Counselor Edn. (pres. 1966-67), Links Inc., Cosmos Club, Alpha Kappa Alpha.

PRUITT, FRANCE JULIARD, international educational consultant; b. Brussels, Sept. 27, 1934; d. Andre Louis and Denise (Freedman) Juliard; m. Dean Garner Pruitt, Dec. 26, 1930; children: Andre Juliard, Paul Dudley, Charles Alexander. BA in Biology and French, Swarthmore Coll., 1956; MA in Anthropology, SUNY, Buffalo, 1974; PhD in Sociology with highest hons., La Sorbonne, Paris, 1981. Asst. fgn. student advisor Northwestern U., Evanston, 1960-61; fgn. student advisor U. Del., 1961-66; fgn. student and scholar advisor SUNY, Buffalo, 1966-78; orientation coord. Agy. Internat. Devel., 1978-80; dir. office internat. programs George Mason U., Fairfax, Va., 1980-87; pres. Internat. Edn. Assn., Bethesda, Md., 1987—. Interviewer Japanese Govt. JET program, 1991—; grant reader AID, Dept. Edn., 1993, 94, 99-2003; bd. dirs. NCN Found.; cons. and spkr. in field. Contbr. articles to profl. jours., internat. newspapers. Mem. Fulbright scholarship selection com., 1985, 86; vol. Democratic Party, Buffalo, Bethesda, 1976—. Grantee Agy. Internat. Devel., 1975, U.S. Dept. State, 1976, SUNY, Buffalo; UNESCO fellow, 1974. Fellow Internat. Inst. for Ednl. Planning; mem. Nat. Assn. Fgn. Student Affairs (chair embassy dialogue com., grantee), TESOL. Soc. Internat. Devel., Women Adminstrs. in Higher Edn., Higher Edn. Dinner Group, Va. Com. Internat. Studies and Program Dirs., Rotary Internat. (bd. dirs. 1989—, past chair ambassadorial scholarship), Bethesda/Chevy Chase Club (sec. found., bd. dirs., ambassadorial scholarship com.) Democrat. Mem. Soc. Of Friends. Avocations: music, swimming, cooking, reading, movies. Office: Internat Edn Assocs Inc PO Box 34430 Bethesda MD 20827-0430 E-mail: iea@pruittfamily.com.

PRUITT, GEORGE ALBERT, college president; b. Canton, Miss., July 9, 1946; s. Joseph Henry and Lillie Irene (Carmichael) P.; m. Pamela Young; 1 child, Shayla Nicole. BS, Ill. State U., 1968, MS, 1970, DHL (hon.), 1994; PhD, Union Grad. Sch., Cin., 1974; D Pub. Svc. (hon.), MA (hon.), Bridgewater State Coll., 1990; LLD (hon.), Ill. State U., 1994; DHL (hon.), SUNY Empire State Coll., 1996. Asst. to v.p. for acad. affairs Ill. State U., Normal, 1968-70, dir. high potential students program, 1968-70; dean students Towson State U., 1970-72; v.p., exec. asst. to pres., assoc. prof. urban affairs Morgan State U., 1972-75; v.p., prof. Tenn. State U., 1975-81; exec. v.p. Council for Advancement Experiential Learning, Columbia, Md., 1981-82; pres. Thomas A. Edison State Coll., Trenton, 1982—. Commn. on ednl. credit and credentials, labor/higher edn. coun. Am. Coun. on Edn.; advisor group XII, Nat. Fellowship program W.K. Kellogg Found., 1990-94, advisor group XV, 1995-99; bd. dirs. SEEDCO; nat. adv. com. on instnl. quality and integrity U.S. Dept. Edn., 1994—; bd. dirs. Sun Nat. Bank, Vineland, N.J. Past chair Mercer County Chamber of Commerce; chair Union Inst., Cin., 1989—, Rider U., Lawrenceville, NJ; bd. dirs. N.J. Assn. Colls. and Univs. Recipient Resolution of Commendation Bd., Trustees Morgan State U., 1975, Outstanding Svc. to Edn. award Tenn. State U., 1981, Gubernatorial citation Gov. of Tenn., 1981, Good Guy award George Washington coun. Boy Scouts Am., 1991, Humanitarian award NCCJ, 1992, Educator of Yr. award Black N.J. Mag., 1993, Disting. Alumni award Ill. State U., 1996; apptd. hon. mem. Gen. Assembly Tenn., 1981, hon. mem. U.S. Congress from 5th Tenn. dist., 1981; named ofcr. of the Most Effective Coll. Pres. in U.S., Exxon Edn. Found. Study, 1986; named to Coll. of Edn. Hall of Fame, Ill. State U., 1995; named Mercer Co. N.J. Citizen of Yr., Mercer Co. C. of C., 1997. Mem. Coun. for Advancement Exptl. Learning, Am. Assn. State Colls.and Univs., Coun. for Advancement and Support of Edn., Am. Coun. Edn., Mid. States Assn. Colls. and Schs. (accreditation evaluator commn. on higher edn.), Mercer County C. of C. (chmn.). Office: Thomas Edison Coll 101 W State St Trenton NJ 08608-1101

PRUITT, MELINDA DOUTHAT, elementary school special education educator; b. Warner Robins, Ga., Jan. 24, 1958; d. J.P. and Grace Imogene (Elkins) Douthat; m. Jeffrey Hal Pruitt, Aug. 20, 1983. BS in Phys. Edn., U. Tenn., 1980, MS in Deaf Edn., 1982; doctorate in Ednl. Leadership and Policy Analysis, Tenn. State U. Cert. tchr., Tenn., career ladder III tchr. Elem. tchr. and Title I tchr. math. Ellijay (Ga.) Elem. Sch., Gilmer County Schs.; tchr. spl. edn. Jonesborough (Tenn.) Mid. Sch., Washington County Schs.; tchr. deaf edn. King Springs Elem. Sch., Johnson City (Tenn.) Schs.; tchr. spl. edn., team leader Mosheim (Tenn.) Elem. Sch., Greene County Schs., spl. edn. coord. and asst. prin. spl. programs. Speaker, presenter in field. Cheerleading sponsor coach West Greene H.S.; mem. local PTA; active cmty orgns. and ch. Named Disting. Adminstr., TEA, 2001. Mem. NEA, Tenn. Edn. Assn., Coun. on Edn. of Deaf (cert.), Greene County Edn. Assn. (negotiating team, pres., treas., exec. bd.), Ruritan Club (Midway Vol. chpt.), Pi Lambda Theta. Home: 190 Lonesome Rd Midway TN 37809-4946

PRUITT, NANCY ELIZABETH, social science educator; b. Columbus, Ga., Sept. 17, 1948; d. Richard Connelly and Margaret Wood (Dudley) P.; m. Frank Kalupa, June 1983 (div. 1986). BS in Edn., U. Ga., 1970; MEd, Auburn U., 1971; EdD, U. Ga., 1984. Elem. tchr. DeKalb County Sch. System, Atlanta, 1972-74, Muscogee County Sch. System, Columbus, 1975-77; grad. asst. U. Ga., Athens, 1978-83; asst. prof. U. Ala., Tuscaloosa, 1986-89; asst. prof. dept. instructional leadership and academic instruction U. Olka., Norman, 1989—. Contbr. articles to profl. jours. Mem. ASCD, Assn. for Asian Studies, Nat. Coun. Social Studies, Phi Delta Kappa, Phi Kappa Phi, Kappa Delta Pi. Republican. Methodist. Avocations: raising cockatiels, birding, opera, cooking. Home: 98 Fox Chase Trl Midland GA 31820-5012 Office: U Okla 820 Van Vleet Oval Rm 14 Norman OK 73019-2040

PRUITT, ROSANNE HARKEY, nursing educator, human services researcher; b. Charlotte, N.C., Aug. 3, 1952; d. Martin L., Jr. and Lucille Clark (Wayland) H.; m. John Crayton Pruitt, Aug. 10, 1974; children: Crayton Smith, Martin Curtis. BSN, Emory U., Atlanta, 1974; MN, U. S.C., 1979; PhD, U. Md., 1989. RN, S.C. Family nurse practitioner Nat. Health Svc. Corps, Calhoun Falls, S.C., 1979-81; asst. prof. U. Md., Balt., 1984-89; prof. Clemson (S.C.) U. Sch. Nursing, 1990—. Part-time family nurse practitioner Clemson U. Nursing Ctr., 1990—, Columbia, Md., 1983-87, NIH Occupational Health, Bethesda, Md., 1988-89. Contbr. articles to profl. jours. Recipient grants for rsch. in health promotion. Mem. ANA, Am. Acad. Nurse Practitioners, Nat. Orgn. Nurse Practitioner Faculty (treas, 2002—), S.C. Nurses Assn. (treas.), Sigma Theta Tau (rsch. grantee 1988-89). Home: 117 Carter Hall Dr Anderson SC 29621-1976

PRUITT, STEPHEN WALLACE, finance educator; b. Indpls., Feb. 3, 1957; s. Harry Wallace and Dorothy (Thorp) P.; m. Mary Melinda Settle, Dec. 19, 1981; children: Rebecca Elizabeth, Victoria Barrick. BS in Mgmt.,

Purdue U., 1979; MBA in Fin., Ohio State U., 1980; PhD in Fin., Fla. State U., 1987. Internat. cash mgr. Marathon Oil Co., Findlay, Ohio, 1980-81; fin. analyst Nat. Svc. Industries, Crawfordsville, Ind., 1981-83; asst. prof. fin. U. Miss., Oxford, 1986-88, Ind. U., Bloomington, 1988-93; assoc. prof. fin. U. Memphis, 1993-96, prof. fin., 1996-2000; Arvin Gottlieb/Mo. chair in bus. econs. and fin. U. Mo., Kansas City, 2000—03, Arvin Gottlieb/Mo. chair in bus. econs. and fin., chair dept. fin., info. mgmt. and strategy, 2003—. Cons. in field. Contbr. articles to profl. jours. Bd. dirs. Art Mus. U. Memphis, 1995-2000; founder, pres. Memphis Print Club, 1995-2000. Mem. So. Fin. Assn., Fin. Mgmt. Assn. Republican. Baptist. Avocation: collecting art and antiques. Office: U Mo Henry W Bloch Sch Bus & Pub 5100 Rockhill Rd Kansas City MO 64110-2481 Home: 5316 W 140th St Overland Park KS 66224

PRUSOFF, WILLIAM HERMAN, biochemical pharmacologist, educator; b. N.Y.C., June 25, 1920; s. Samuel and Mary (Metrick) P.; m. Brigitte Auerbach, June 19, 1948 (dec. Apr. 1991); children— Alvin Saul, Laura Ann. BA, U. Miami, Fla., 1941; MA, Columbia U., 1947, PhD, 1949. Research assoc., instr. pharmacology Western Res. U., 1949-53; mem. faculty Yale Med. Sch., 1953—, prof. pharmacology, 1966-90, prof. emeritus. sr. rsch. scientist, 1990—, acting chmn. dept., 1968. Cons. in field, 1965— Mem. Am. Assn. Cancer Rsch., Am. Chem. Soc., Am. Soc. Biol. Chemists, Am. Soc. Pharmacology and Exptl. Therapeutics, Soc. Chinese Bioscientists in Am., Sigma Xi, Internat. Soc. for Antiviral Rsch. Achievements include rsch. in virology, photochemistry, mechanism drug action, synthesis potential drugs; synthesized Idoxuridine; developed (in collaboration with D.T.S. Lin) Stavudine for therapy of AIDS. Home: De Forest Dr Branford CT 06405 Office: Yale U Sch Medicine New Haven CT 06510 E-mail: William.Prusoff@yale.edu.

PRUSSING, JOHN EDWARD, aerospace engineer, educator, researcher; b. Oak Park, Ill., Aug. 19, 1940; s. Milton Carl and Elizabeth (Thompson) P.; m. Laurel Victoria Lunt, May 29, 1965; children: Heidi, Erica, Victoria. BS, MIT, 1962, MS, 1963, ScD, 1967. Lectr. U. Calif., San Diego, 1967-69; asst. prof. aero. and astronautical engring. U. Ill., Urbana, 1969-72, assoc. prof., 1972-81, prof., 1981—, asst. dean engring., 1976-77. Rschr. U.S. Army Rsch. Office, Durham, N.C., 1981-84, NASA Dryden Flight Facility, 1985, NASA Lewis Rsch. Ctr., 1987-90, NASA Jet Propulsion Lab., 1998-99; mem. tech. adv. bd. Space Test, Inc., Houston, 1985-88. Fellow AIAA (chmn. astrodynamics tech. com. 1982-84, Mechanics and Control of Flight award 2002), Am. Astronautical Soc. (Dirk Brouwer award 1994), Am. Soc. Engring. Edn. Office: Univ Ill 104 S Wright St Urbana IL 61801-2935

PRUTZMAN, PENELOPE ELIZABETH, elementary school educator; b. Vancouver, Wash., Apr. 25, 1944; d. Delbert Daniel and Jessie May (Lowry) P. BA in Sociology, CUNY, 1975; diploma, Grand Diplôme Cooking Sch. Tchr. Mt. Carmel-Holy Rosary Sch., N.Y.C., 1968—. Active Vol. Svcs. for Children, N.Y.C., 1980—83; vol. St. Mary's Ch., Manhattanville, 2001—. Recipient 10 Yr. Service to Cath. Schs. of Harlem award Office of Supt. Sch. Archdiocese of N.Y., 1979, 20 Yrs. to Cath. Sch. award Archdiocese of N.Y., 1986; named one of Outstanding Elem. Tchrs. of Am., 1974. Mem.: Nat. Cath. Edn. Assn., Fedn. Cath. Tchrs. (sch. del. 1974—94, exec. coun. 1974—95, negotiating com., Cert. of Honor 1982). Democrat. Episcopalian. Avocations: gourmet cooking, traveling, collecting cookbooks. Home: 35-25 34th St Apt C44 Astoria NY 11106-1953 Office: Mt Carmel-Holy Rosary Sch 371 Pleasant Ave New York NY 10035-3745

PRYBUTOK, VICTOR RONALD, business educator; b. Phila., Sept. 25, 1952; s. Albert and Dorothy (Welt) P.; m. Gayle Linda Trofe, Apr. 11, 1987; children: Alexis Nicole, Sara Kellie. BS, Drexel U., Phila., 1974, MS in BioMath and Environ. Health, 1976, 80, PhD Environ. Analysis and Applied Stats., 1984. Tchr. math. Sch. Dist. Phila., 1976-78; lectr. stats. Drexel U. Coll. Bus. and Adminstrn., 1980-84; sr. biostatistician Campbell Soup Co., Camden, N.J., 1984-85; asst. prof. quantitative methods Drexel U. Coll. Bus. and Adminstrn., 1985-91; dir. Drexel U. Ctr. for Quality and Productivity, 1986-91; assoc. prof. mgmt. sci. U. North Tex., Denton, 1991-96, dir. Ctr. for Quality and Productivity, 1991—, prof. mgmt. sci., 1997—2001, doctoral program dir. Coll. Bus. Adminstrn., 2000—, Regents prof. mgmt. sci., 2001—. Adj. asst. prof. Drexel U., 1984-85, Phila. Coll. Textiles and Sci., 1984-85; cons. Pa. Health Care Cost Containment Coun., Harrisburg, 1987, 88; cons. to dept. rsch. nursing Thomas Jefferson U., Phila., 1989-92. Contbr. more than 60 articles to profl. jours., over 60 conf. procs., presentations and internal reports. Mentor to gifted child Phila. Sch. System, 1988-89. Fellow HEW, 1978-80. Mem. (sr.) Am. Soc. for Quality (cert. quality engr., quality auditor, quality mgr., Phila. sect. exec. bd. 1990-91, Irwin S. Hoffer award), Delaware Valley Partnership for Quality and Productivity (founder). Avocations: running, investments. Office: U North Tex Dept Bus Computer Sys Box 305249 Denton TX 76203-5249 E-mail: prybutok@unt.edu.

PRYOR, DIXIE DARLENE, elementary education educator; b. Anderson, Ind., May 22, 1938; d. Thurman Earle and Alice D. (Watson) Rinker; m. Charles Lee Pryor, Mar. 13, 1958; children: Charles A., Deborah Lee Pryor Evans, Laurinda Ann Pryor Owen. BS, Ball State U., 1967, MEd, 1974. Tchr. Anderson (Ind.) Pub. Schs., 1967-72, Wawasee Cmty. Sch. Corp., Syracuse, Ind., 1972—97, ret. Bd. dirs. Internat. Palace Sports-Scholarship, North Webster, Ind., chair scholarship com., 1996-97, 98-99. Bd. dirs. North Webster Day Care, sec., 1998-2000; bd. dirs. Cardinal Ctr., Inc., Warsaw, Ind., 1996—, sec. bd., 1998; bd. dirs. Kosciusko Co. Found., chmn. scholarship program; trustee Webster United Meth. Ch., chmn. edn. Named Outstanding Mem. Tippkee Reading Coun., 1995, Outstanding Educator Honor Srs., 1995; recipient Ind. State Reading Assn., 1995. Mem.: Ind. Reading Assn. (pres. 1994—95, chair state reading conf. 1996—, Outstanding Mem. award 1996, 2000), Kiwanis (com. chair North Webster 1988—, sec. 1996—97, bd. dirs. 1997—2001). Republican. Methodist. Avocations: travel, reading. Home: 4630 E Armstrong Rd Leesburg IN 46538-9588 Office: PO Box 324 North Webster IN 46555 E-mail: ddpryor@kconline.com.

PRYOR, WILLIAM DANIEL LEE, humanities educator; b. Lakeland, Fla., Oct. 29, 1926; s. Dahl and Lottie Mae (Merchant) P. AB, Fla. So. Coll., 1949; MA, Fla. State U., 1950, PhD, 1959; postgrad., U. N.C., Chapel Hill, 1952—53; pvt. art study with Florence Wilde; pvt. voice study with Colin O'More, Anna Kaskas; pvt. piano study with Waldemar Hille and audited piano master classes of Ernst von Dohnányi. Asst. prof. English, dir. drama Bridgewater (Va.) Coll., 1950-52; grad. tchg. fellow humanities Fla. State U., Tallahassee, 1953-55, 57-58; instr. English U. Houston, University Park, Houston, 1955-59, asst. prof. University Park, 1959-62, assoc. prof., 1962-71, prof., 1971-97, prof. emeritus, 1997. Vis. instr. English, Fla. So. Coll., Lakeland, MacDill Army Air Base, Tampa, Fla., summer 1951, Tex. So. U., 1961-63; vis. instr. humanities, govt. U. Tex. Dental Br., Houston, 1962-63; lectr. The Women's Inst., Houston, 1967-72; lectr. humanities series Jewish Cmty. Ctr., Houston, 1972-73; originator, moderator TV and radio program The Arts in Houston Stas. KUHT-TV and KUHF-FM, 1956-57, 58-63. Contbg. author: National Poetry Anthology, 1952, Panorama das Literaturas das Americas, vol. 2, 1958-60; assoc. editor Forum, 1967, editor, 1967-82; contbr. articles to profl. jours.; dir. Murder in the Cathedral (T.S. Elliot), U. Houston, 1965; performed in opera as Sir Edgar in Der Junge Lord (Henze), Houston Grand Opera Assn., 1967; played the title role in Aella (Chatterton), Am. premiere, U. Houston, 1970. Bd. dirs., founding mem. Contemporary Music Soc., Houston, 1958-63, Houston Shakespeare Soc., 1964-67; bd. dirs., founding mem., program annotator Houston Chamber Orch. Soc., 1964-76; narrator Houston Symphony Orch., Houston Summer Symphony Orch., Houston Chamber Orch., U. Houston Symphony Orch., St. Stephen's Music Festival Symphony Orch., New Harmony, Ind.; narrator world premier of the Bells (Jerry McCathern), 1969, U. Houston Symphony Orch., 1969, Am. premier Symphony No. Seven, Antartica (Vaughn-Williams), Houston Symphony Orch., 1967, L'Histoire du Soldat (Stravinski), U. Houston Symphony Orch., 1957, Am. premier Babar the Elephant (Poulenc-Francais), Houston Chamber Orch., 1967, Le Roi David (Honegger), 1979, Voice of God in opera Noye's Fludde (Britten), St. Stephen's Music Festival, 1981; bd. dirs., program annotator Music Guild, Houston, 1960-67, v.p., 1963-67, adv. bd., 1967-70; mem.-at-large, bd. dirs. Houston Grand Opera Guild, 1966-67; repertory com. Houston Grand Opera Assn., 1967-70; bd. dirs. Houston Grand Opera, 1970-75, adv. bd. 1978-79; cultural adv. com. Jewish Cmty. Ctr., 1960-66; bd. dirs. Houston Friends Pub. Libr., 1962-67, 73-75, 1st v.p., 1963-67; adv. mem. cultural affairs com. Houston C. of C., 1972-75; adv. bd. dirs. The Wilhelm Schole, 1980-98, Buffalo Bayou Support Com., 1985-87, bd. dirs. Moores Sch. Music Soc., 1998—, trustee, 2002—; charter mem. 1927 Soc. U. Houston, 1998—; bd. dirs. U. Houston Retiree Assn., 1999-2001, v.p., 2000-2001.; founding bd. dirs. Internat. Dohna'nyi Rsch. Ctr., Inc., 2002-. Recipient Master Tchg. award Coll. Humanities and Fine Arts U., Houston, 1980, Favorite Prof. award Bapt. Student Union, U. Houston, 1991. Mem. MLA, Coll. English Assn., L'Alliance Francaise, English-Speaking Union, Alumni Assn. Fla. So. Coll., Fla. State U., Am. Assn. U. Profs., South Ctrl. MLA, Conf. Editors Learned Jours., Coll. Conf. Tchrs. English, Nat. Coun. Tchrs. English, Am. Studies Assn., Shepard Soc. Rice U., Nature Conservancy, Nat. Trust for Hist. Preservation, Century Club, Fla. S. Coll., President's Club, James D. Westcott Legacy Soc., Fla. State U., Phi Beta (patron), Phi Mu Alpha Sinfonia, Alpha Psi Omega, Pi Kappa Alpha, Sigma Tau Delta (Outstanding Prof. English U. Houston chpt. 1990), Houston Philos. Soc., Tau Kappa Alpha, Phi Kappa Phi, Caledonian Club (London). Episcopalian. Avocations: tennis, racquetball, swimming, traveling. Home: 2625 Arbuckle St Houston TX 77005-3929 Office: U Houston Dept English U Park 3801 Cullen Blvd Houston TX 77004-2602

PRZYBYZEWSKI, LESLIE CAMILLE, mathematics educator; b. Big Spring, Tex., June 18, 1955; d. Joseph Mac Montgomery and Emily Reese Dann; m. Joseph Stanaslous Przybyzewski, June 20, 1992; children: Jocelyn, Keely, Danny Eagan. AA, Mt. Wachusett C.C., Gardner, Mass., 1980; BS in Math. Edn. magna cum laude, Columbus Coll., 1989; M in Applied Math., Auburn U., 1991, postgrad., 1991-92. Grad. asst. Auburn (Ala.) U., 1991-92; math. instr. Tuskegee (Ala.) U., 1992-96; tutor Sylvan Learning Ctr., 1996-97; instr. math. Ctrl. Ala. C.C., Childersburg, 1997; adj. prof. math. Birmingham (Ala.) So. Coll., 1997-98; instr. math. Montevallo (Ala.) U., 2002—03. Mem. Collegiate Curriculum Reform and Cmty. Action, Greensboro, N.C., 1994-95, 95-96. Recipient scholarship Ga. Bd. Regents, 1975, Columbus Coll., 1987-88, 88-89. Mem. AAUP, MAA, Pi Mu Epsilon, Kappa Delta Pi. Methodist. Avocations: swimming, travel, reading. Home: 106 Juniper Cir Pelham AL 35124-3906 E-mail: lzeski@bellsouth.net.

PSATHAS, GEORGE, sociologist, educator; b. New Haven, Feb. 22, 1929; s. Milton Emanuel and Melpa (Joannides) P.; m. Irma M. Amatruda, Feb. 5, 1951; children: Christine Ann, David George, Anthony Paul. BA, Yale U., 1950; MA, U. Mich., 1951; PhD, Yale U., 1956; diploma, N.E. Sch. Photography, 1979. Instr. to asst. prof. Ind. U., Bloomington, 1955-63; lectr. Harvard U., Cambridge, Mass., 1961-62; assoc. prof. Washington U., St. Louis, 1963-68, rsch. assoc. Social Sci. Inst., 1963-68; program dir. community mental health tng. program NIMH/Washington U., 1966-68; prof. sociology Boston U., 1968—, emeritus, 1997—, acting chair, 1968-69, assoc. chair, 1969-70, 76-78, chair, 1984-85, dir. Ctr. for Applied Social Sci., 1970-73, co-dir. post-doctoral rsch. tng. program in sociology and mental health Nat. Inst. Mental Health, 1976-79; co-dir. Sociology and Health Svcs. Rsch. Tng. Program NCHSR and Boston (Mass.) U., 1970-78. Vis. lectr. MRC Med. Sociology-U. Aberdeen, Scotland, 1974, U. Colo., 1963, U. London, 1973, U. Bologna, 1996; vis. prof. Panteios Sch. Polit. Sci., Athens, 1982, Internat. U. Japan, Yamato-Machi, 1988, Doshisha U., Kyoto, Japan, 1989; Brit. Acad. vis. prof. U. Manchester, Eng., 1996; guest prof. Inst. for Human Scis., Vienna, 1996, 2003; adj. prof. Bentley Coll., 2003; chair Mass. Interdisciplinary Discourse Analysis seminar, 1989-2000; cons. NSF, 1978, 79, 89, 94, 95, Rsch. Coun. Can., 1983-84, Social Sci. Rsch. Coun. Eng., 1981-82; active Ctr. Advanced Rsch. in Phenomenology, 1980—; Alfred Schutz Meml. lectr. Soc. Phenomenology and the Human Scis., 2000; bd. dirs., v.p. Soc. Ret. Faculty and Staff, Boston U., 2001—; presenter 75 presentations at profl. and scholarly socs. Editor: Phenomenological Sociology, 1973, Everyday Language, 1979, Interaction Competence, 1990; co-editor: Situated Order, 1994, Alfred Schutz Collected Papers, IV, 1996; editor-in-chief: Human Studies, Boston, 1978—; assoc. editor Social Problems, 1958-61, Visual Sociology, 1993-2001; hon. bd. mem. Visual Studies, 2000—; internat. editl. bd. Culture and Soc., 2000—; author: Student Nurse in Diploma School of Nursing, 1968, Phenomenology & Sociology, 1989, Conversation Analysis, 1995; cons. editor Temple Univ. Press, Kluwer Academic Pubs., Qualitative Sociology; author 12 book chpts.; contbr. over 60 articles to profl. jours. Cons. Human Rels. Lab., Boston, Bethel, St. Louis, 1967, 69, Sch. for the Blind, Kallithea, Athens, Greece, 1982; tng. dirs. com. Nat. Ctr. for Health Svcs. Rsch., Washington, 1971-73; bd. dirs. Carroll Ctr. for the Blind, Newton, Mass., 1974-79. Named Post-Doctoral fellow NIMH Dept. Social Rels., Harvard U., Cambridge, 1961-62; recipient Sci. Faculty Devel. award NSF, 1978-79, Fulbright grant Fulbright Commn., Greece and Turkey, 1982, Brit Acad. grant, 1996. Mem. AAUP (sec. 1977-79, v.p. Boston U. chpt. 1979-80, pres. 1997—), Am. Sociol. Assn., Ea. Sociol. Assn., Internat. Sociology Assn., Internat. Visual Sociology Assn., Internat. Inst. for Ethnomethodology (chair 1990-2001), Soc. for Phenomenology and Existential Philosophy, Soc. for Phenomenology and Human Scis. (co-chair 1981-85, exec. com. 1993-98), Soc. Study Social Problems (treas., bus. mgr. 1959-61). Home: 150 Mount Vernon St Newton MA 02465-2517 Office: Sociology Dept Boston Univ Boston MA 02215

PSILLOS, SUSAN ROSE, artist, educator; b. Bethpage, N.Y., Feb. 15, 1960; d. Reginald and Gloria Barbara Psillos; 1 child, Jennifer Rose. Student, Alfred U., 1978-80; Tchg. Degree in Art, L.I. U., Southampton, 1996. Substitute tchr. art Shoreham-Wading River Sch. Dist., Shoreham, N.Y., 1992—; tchr. arts and crafts Round-out Shoreham-Wading River Sch., Shoreham, 1995-96; tchr. art Bellport (N.Y.) H.S., 1997-98; art tchr. Raynor Country Day Sch., Speonk, N.Y., 1998—, Plainview-Old Bethpage Sch. Dist., 1999—. Guest spkr. in field. Exhibited sculptures at Smithtown (N.Y.) Mus., 1995, 96-97, Bellemeade Gallery, 1992, Knickerbocker Gallery, N.Y.C., 1997, Studio 88, Hampton Bays, N.Y., 1999, Hampton Bays Pub. Libr.; exhibited paintings at Ambiente Gallery, 1991-92, Smithtown Twsp. Art Mus., 1995, 96, Doweling Coll., 1997. Advisor Partnership for Survival, Smithtown, 1991—; bd. dirs., pub. rels. person Sexual Abuse Survivors, Smithtown,1991—. Recipient Art Judge's award Parrish Art Mus., 1976, Outstanding award Sch. Visual Arts, 1976, Profl. Recognition Day award, 1996, Child Abuse & Neglect Family Violence Vol. award Town of Brookhaven. Mem. NOW, N.Y. Art Tchrs. Assn., Artist Support Group. Avocations: cooking, gardening, fine arts, painting, sculpture.

PSYRIS, THOMAS GEORGE, secondary education educator, consultant; b. Springfield, Mass., Dec. 24, 1957; s. George Peter and Angelina Mary (Lucia) P. AA in Sci., Law Enforcement, Holyoke (Mass.) C.C., 1977; AA in Engring., Sci., Chemistry, Springfield Tech. C.C., Mass., 1986; BS in Chemistry, U. Mass., Amherst, 1988; post baccalaureate tchr. cert., Westfield (Mass.) State Coll., 1994; M Natural Sci., Worcester Poly. Inst., 1998. Cert. tchr., Nat. Bd. Adolescence and Young Adulthood-Sci.; Mass. cert. chemistry, biology, physics, general sci; Conn. cert. chemistry, biology, general sci. With microbiology lab. Baystate Med. Ctr., Springfield, Mass., 1990-93; tchr. chemistry and environ. sci. South Hadley HS, Mass., 1993-94; tchr. chemistry Longmeadow HS, Mass., 1994-97, Holyoke HS, Mass., 1997-98; tchr. chemistry and biology Bristol Ctrl. HS, Conn., 1998-99; tchr. chemistry, biology, phys. sci. and physics West Springfield HS, Mass., 1999—. Cons. Sloan Clinic, Springfield, Mass., 1991-93; proctor Scholastic Aptitude Tests, Westfield and West Springfield, Mass., 1994—; with fast-paced chemistry dept. Hamilton Coll. NY through Johns Hopkins U.; adj. instr. biology Holyoke C.C., Mass., 1998—. Advisor Environ. Club, Longmeadow H.S., 1994-97. Mem. NSTA. Avocations: music, audio/visual equipment, hiking, outdoor activities, motorcycling. Home: 49 Pine St Belchertown MA 01007-9612 E-mail: tpsyris@k12s.phast.umass.edu.

PTACEK, ELAINE VALETTA, special education counselor, consultant; b. Oakley, Kans., Sept. 19, 1952; d. Ralph and Marcella (Ribordy) Albers; m. Ken F. Ptacek, May 26, 1973; children: Scott, Brian. BS in Vocat. Home Edu., Kans. State U., 1973, MS, 1976; cert. in Counseling, Ft. Hays U., Hays, Kans., 1982. Lic. clin. profl. counselor. Secondary tchr. vocat. home econs. Colby (Kans.) Unified Sch. Dist. 315, 1973—90; behavioral disorders counselor N.W. Kans. Ednl. Svc. Ctr., Oakley, 1992—; with Heartland Rural Counseling Svcs., Inc., 1997—. Mem. Unified Sch. 315 Sch. Bd., 1991—; co-leader strategic planning Thomas County, Colby, 1992—; bd. dirs. Kans. High Sch. Action Assn., Topeka, 1992-94. Named Kans. Health Educator of Yr., Kans. Gov.'s Coun. on Fitness, 1988, One of 10 Top Home Econs. Tchrs., Am. Home Econs. Assn., 1990, Tchr. of Yr. award Kans. Home Econs. Assn., 1989, Kans. Vocat. Home Econs. Tchrs. Assn., 1990, Revolutionary Parent Educator, Active Parenting, 1991. Mem. Assn. for Play Therapy, Kans. Assn. for Play Therapy, Kansas Counselors Assn., Kans. Mental Health Counselors Assn. (pres. 2002-03), Phi Delta Kappa (pres. 1985-86, Svc. Key). Avocations: woodworking, bridge, golf, travel, antique dishes. Office: NW Kans Ednl Svc Ctr 702 W 2nd St Oakley KS 67748-1251

PUCCI, ANTHONY J. English language educator; b. Lawrence, Mass. BA, Merrimack Coll., 1971; MS, Elmira Coll., 1979. Cert. tchr. English 7-12. English tchr. assoc. Duquesne U., Pitts., 1971-73; English tchr. Gill/St. Bernard's Upper Sch., Bernardsville, N.J., 1973-74; English tchr./chmn. Notre Dame High Sch., Elmira, N.Y., 1974—. Freelance copywriter, proofreader. Writer poetry, book revs.; developer curriculum in field. Mem. Nat. Coun. Tchrs. English, Friends of Steele Meml. Libr. Avocations: reading, travel, photography. Office: Notre Dame High Sch 1400 Maple Ave Elmira NY 14904-3008

PUCHI, LINDA CAROL, elementary school principal; b. Midland, Tex., Aug. 2, 1944; d. Gonzalo Jr. and Lillian (Grimm) P.; divorced; children: Bianca Michelle Fontes Garcia, Adrian Paulino Fontes. BA in Elem. Edn., Ariz. State U., 1966; MEd in Elem. Edn., U. Ariz., 1972; EdD, No. Ariz. U., 1993. Cert. supt., prin., tchr. elem. edn., bilingual edn., Ariz. Tchr. 1st grade Phoenix Elem. Sch. # 1, 1966-67; teaching prin. Santa Cruz Dist. # 28, Nogales, Ariz., 1967-68; tchr. bilingual elem. edn. Nogales Unified Schs., 1968-74, 76-77, 1978-80, grade level chair, tchr. bilingual elem. edn., 1980-88; tchr. bilingual edn. U. Ariz., Tucson, 1974-76, teaching asst., student tchr., supr., undergrad. advisor, 1977-78; tchr., asst. to pers. dir. Roosevelt Sch. Dist. # 66, Phoenix, 1989, asst. prin., 1989-91, prin., 1991—. Coord. adult edn. Spanish as Second Lang., Nogales, 1968-70; tchr. adult ESL, Pima C.C., Tucson, 1970-72, 87-88, Luth. Social Svcs. Ministry, Phoenix, 1988-90. Scholar Marshall Found. Mem. ASCD, AAUW, Am. Assn. Sch. Adminstrs., Ariz. Sch. Adminstrs., Ariz. Hispanic Sch. Adminstrs. Assn., Nat. Assn. Elem. Sch. Prins., Ariz. AWARE, Phi Delta Kappa. Home: 4225 N 21st St Unit 28 Phoenix AZ 85016-6161 Office: 6401 S 16th St Phoenix AZ 85042-4417

PUCHTLER, HOLDE, histochemist, pathologist, educator; b. Kleinlosnitz, Germany, Jan. 1, 1920; came to U.S., 1955; d. Gottfried and Gunda (Thoma) P. Cand. med., U. Würzburg, 1944; Md, U. Köln, 1949; MD, U. Köln, Germany, 1951. Rsch. assoc. U. Köln, 1949-51, resident in pathology, 1951-55; rsch. fellow Damon Runyon Found., Montreal, Que., Can., 1955-58; rsch. assoc. Med. Coll. Ga., Augusta, 1959-60, asst. rsch. prof., 1960-62, assoc. rsch. prof., 1962-68, prof., 1968-90, prof. emerita, 1990—. Assoc. editor Jour. Histotech., 1982-94; mem. editorial bd. Histochemistry, 1977-90. Honored at Symposium on Connective Tissues in Arterial and Pulmonary Diseases, 1980. Fellow Am. Inst. Chemists, Royal Microscopical Soc.; mem. Royal Soc. Chemistry, Am. Chem. Soc., Histochem. Soc. Gesellschaft Histochemie, Anatomische Gesellschaft, Ga. Soc. Histotech. (hon.). Achievements include development of new techniques for light, polarization, visible and infrared flourescence microscopy based on theoretical and physical chemistry and x-ray diffraction data; demonstration of relations between dye configurations and selective affinity for certain components of human tissues, such as collagens, elastin, myosins, neurofibrils, and amyloids; application of molecular orbital theories to histochemistry. Office: Med Coll Ga Dept Pathology Augusta GA 30912

PUDER, JANICE, special education educator; b. Phila., Apr. 6, 1950; d. Allen Thrasher and Dorothy Ruth (Mathis) P. AA, Pasadena (Calif.) City Coll., 1970; BA, U. Calif., Chico, 1973, postgrad., 1973-74, U. Pacific, 1982; MA in Spl. Edn., Santa Clara U., 1996; postgrad., U. San Diego, 2000. Cert. elem., secondary, and spl. edn. tchr., Calif.; cert. adapted phys. edn. specialist. Tchr. New Covenant Christian H.S., Palo Alto, Calif., 1977-81; spl. edn. tchr. Sunnyvale (Calif.) Christian Jr. and Sr. H.S., 1981-82; adapted phys. edn. and cons. to spl. edn. local plan area 3 Santa Clara County Office Edn., 1983-92, adapted phys. edn. specialist, 1992—. Vol. Christian Counseling. Mem. PEO. Avocations: bible study, reading, sports. E-mail: janp@earthlink.net.

PUGH, JOYE JEFFRIES, educational administrator; b. Ocilla, Ga., Jan. 23, 1957; d. Claude Bert and Stella Elizabeth (Paulk) Jeffries; m. Melville Eugene Pugh, Sept. 21, 1985. AS in Pre-law, S. Ga. Coll., 1978; BS in Edn., Valdosta State Coll., 1980, MEd in Psychology, Guidance and Counseling, 1981; EdD in Adminstrn., Nova U., Ft. Lauderdale, Fla., 1992. Cert. tchr., adminstr., supr., Ga. Pers. adminstr. TRW, Inc., Douglas, Ga., 1981-83; recreation dir. Ocilla (Ga.), Irwin Recreation Dept., 1983-84; exec. dir. Sunny Dale Tng. Ctr., Inc., Ocilla, 1984-96; employment cons. TPS Staffing and Recruiting, Douglas, Ga., 1997-98; mgr. Global Employment Solutions, Inc., 1999—2002; freelance writer, 2002—. Pres. and registered agt. Irwin County Resources, Inc., Ocilla, 1988-97, Camelot Ct., Inc., 1994-97. Author: Antichrist-The Cloned Image of Jesus Christ, 1999; contbr. articles on handicapped achievements to newspapers, mags. (Ga. Spl. Olympics News Media award, 1987, Assn. for Retarded Citizens News Media award, 1988). Mem. adv. bd. Area 12 Spl. Olympics, Douglas, Ga., 1984-88, bd. dirs., 1995-2000; pres. Irwin County Spl. Olympics, 1984-97, mem. adv. task force Spl. Olympics Internat. for 6-7 yr. olds, 1995—97; bd. dirs. Ga. Spl. Olympics, 1995-98, 98-99, mem. comm. and mktg. com., 1995-96, mem. nominations com., 1997-98, outreach and edn. com., 1999-2000; exec. dir., fund raising chmn. Irwin Assn. for Retarded Citizens, Ocilla, 1984-97; arts and crafts chmn. Ga. Sweet Tater Trot 5k/1 Mile Rd. Races, 1993-97; founder, chmn. Joseph Mascolo Celebrity Events, 1985—; vol. Am. Heart Assn., 2000-02. Recipient Spirit of Ga. Spl. Olympics award Ga. Spl. Olymics, Atlanta, 1986, Award of Excellence Ga. Spl. Olympic Bd. Dirs., 2000, Cmty. Svc. award Ga. Assn. for Retarded Citizens, Atlanta, 1987, Govs.' Vol. award Ga. Vol. Awards, Atlanta, 1988, Presdl. Sports award AAU, Indpls., 1988, Humanitarian award Sunny Dale Tng. Ctr., Inc., Ocilla, 1988, Golden Poet award New Am. Poetry Anthology, 1988, Outstanding Coach-Athlete Choice award Sunny Dale Spl. Olympics, Ocilla, 1992, Dist. Coach award, 1993, Outstanding Unified Sports Ptnr. of Yr. award, 1995, Coach of Yr. award, 1996; carried Olympic Torch, Ocilla, Ga., 1996; Ga. Spl. Olympics State Gold medalist Golf Unified Team, 1996, State Silver medalist Unified Table Tennis Team, 1996, State Bronze medalist Master's Unified Softball Team, 1995. Mem. DAR (Author-Educator-Humanitarian award Nathaniel Abney chpt. 2000), Nat. Soc. Daughters Am. Revolution (mem. Nathaniel Abney chpt.), Mut. Unidentified Flying Object Network (Ga. state sect. dir., asst. state dir., cons.

1994—), Ga. State Assn. for Retarded Citizens, Ctrs. Dirs. Ga., Ocilla Rotary Club (program dir. 1995-97, bd. dirs. 1995-97, sec. 1996-97), Sunny Dale Unified Track Club (founder 1991), Sunny Dale Ensemble (founder), Ocilla/Irwin County C. of C., Irwin Assn. Retarded Citizens Inc. Baptist. Avocations: playing musical instruments, jet skiing, weight lifting, dancing, singing. Home and Office: 201 Lakeside Cir Douglas GA 31535-6629 E-mail: drjoye@charter.net.

PUGH, KYLE MITCHELL, JR., musician, retired music educator; b. Spokane, Wash., Jan. 6, 1937; s. Kyle Mitchel, Sr. and Lenore Fae (Johnson) P.; m. Susan Deane Waite, July 16, 1961; children: Jeffray, Kari. BA in Edu., East Wash. U., 1975. Cert. tchr., Wash. Tuba player Spokane Symphony Orch., 1958-63; rec. assoc. Century Records, Spokane, 1965-73; tuba player World's Fair Expo '74, Spokane, 1974; bass player Russ Carlyle Orch., Las Vegas, 1976, Many Sounds of Nine Orch., northwest area, 1969-81; band tchr. Garry Jr. High School, Spokane, 1976-79, Elementary Band Program, Spokane, 1979-96; bass player Doug Scott Cabaret Band, Spokane, 1982-91. Dept. head Elem. Band Dept., Spokane, 1984-89. Editor (newsletter) The Repeater, 1987 (Amateur Radio News Svc. award 1987); extra in movie Always, 1989. Active in communications Lilac Bloomsday Assn., Spokane, 1977. Served to E-5 USNR, 1955-63 Recipient Disting. Service award Wash. State Commn., 1974, Nev. Hollerin' Champ Carl Hayden Scribe, 1979. Mem. Am. Fedn. Musicians (life), Spokane Edn. Assn. (rec. sec. 1987), Music Educator's Nat. Conf., Am. Radio Relay League (asst. dir. 1987), Ea. Wash. Music Educator's Assn. (pres. 1978-79), Dial Twisters Club (pres. 1979-80), VHF Radio Amateurs (dir. 1980-83), Elks. Avocations: ham radio operator, model railroading, photography. Home: 5006 W Houston Ave Spokane WA 99208-3728

PUGH, THOMAS DOERING, architecture educator, educator; b. Jacksonville, Fla., May 27, 1948; s. William Edward Jr. and Lina Lillian (Doering) P.; children: Rachel McRae, Jordan Faith, Nathan Calder. B in Design, U. Fla., 1971, MA in Architecture, 1974. Asst. prof. architecture U. Ark., Fayetteville, 1976-78; pres. Thomas D. Pugh Constrn. Co., Inc., Fayetteville, Ark., 1978-87; assoc. prof. Fla. A&M U. Sch. Architecture, Tallahassee, 1987—; interim dir. Inst. Bldg. Scis. Fla. Argl. and Mech. U., Tallahassee, 1991-93, dir., 1993—. Vis. rsch. fellow Tech. U. Eindhoven, The Netherlands, 1993-94; chmn. radon adv. bd. Fla. State U. Sys., 1988-94; mem. Fla. Coordinating Coun. on Radon Protection; juror Progressive Arch.-AIA Nat. Archtl. Rsch. Awards, 1995; mem. rsch. policy bd. AIA/Assn. Collegiate Schs. of Arch., 1996—; mem. edn. com. Odyssey Sci. Ctr., Tallahassee, 1995—. Bd. dir. Tallahassee Habitat for Humanity, 1987-92; crew leader Habitat for Humanity Internat., Americus, Ga., 1988, 90. Recipient Bronze medal Fla. Assn. AIA, Gainesville, 1975; Named Vol. of Yr. Tallahassee Dem. and Vol. Tallahassee, Inc., 1991. Mem. ASCE (sec. spl. task com. radon mitigation 1990-91), Assn. Collegiate Schs. Architecture (coun. on archtl. rsch. 1994). Democrat. Avocations: sailing, woodworking. Office: Fla A&M Univ Sch Architecture 1936 S Martin Luther King Jr B Tallahassee FL 32307-4200 E-mail: tpugh@famusoa.net.

PUGH-MARZI, SHERRIE, daycare center administrator; b. Atlanta, July 16, 1955; d. Joseph Grey and Mary Elizabeth (Gregory) Pugh; divorced; children: Michael, Mari. BS, Trenton State U., 1977. Cert. early childhood tchr., N.J. Tchr. Beth Torah Nursery Sch., Willingboro, N.J., 1976-79; kindergarten tchr. Fox Learning Ctr., Hainesport, N.J., 1979-84, Indian Mills (N.J.) Preschool, 1984-85; co-dir. Excel Learning Ctr., Marlton, N.J., 1985-87; founder, dir. Day Bear Care Learning Ctr., Medford Lakes, N.J., 1987-97; ednl. dir. Accotink Acad. by the Sea, Ponte Vedra Beach, Fla., 1998; pre-K tchr. The Bolles Sch., Ponte Vedra Beach, 1999-2000; dir. Caimbridge Prep. Sch., Ponte Vedra Beach, 2000—01, La Petite Acad., St. Augustine, Fla., 2001—. Cons. energy program Phila. Electric Co., 1989-90. V.p. recreation Medford Lakes Colony, 1990—; co-chair Medford Lakes Canoe Carnival, 1994, zoning bd., 1993; mem. Medford Lakes Zoning Bd. Adjustment, 1991—; mem. rev. bd. Burlington County Child Placement, 1993-97; active Child Support Recovery, 1992; chair canoe carnival event Mcpl. Alliance Medford Lakes, 1994-97; pres. ADVOCATE (All Deadbeats Violate Our Children And Take from Everyone). Mem. Nat. Assn. for Edn. of Young Children, Medford Lakes Home and Sch. Assn. (exec. bd. 1987-97, pres. 1995, Vol. of Yr. award 1990). Democrat. Baptist. Avocations: cross-stitching, politics.

PUGLIESE, JOANNE GALLAGHER, education educator; b. Glen Ridge, N.J., Dec. 15, 1950; d. Joseph Thomas and Mary (Morrissey) Gallagher; m. Joseph Emil Pugliese, Mar. 8, 1975; children: Kevin Ryan, Patrick Sean. BA, Jersey City State Coll., 1972; postgrad., Montclair (N.J.) State Coll., 1990-93. Whole lang. tchr. Harold Wilson Profl. Devel. Sch., Newark, 1972—. Mentor tchr. Bergen State Sch., 1990—; adj. prof. Montclair State Coll. Mem. Com. for Quality Edn., Nutley, N.J., 1990—, NEC Acad. Task Performance, Newark, 1986-91. A+ for Kids grantee, 1990. Mem. ASCD, N.J. Edn. Assn., N.J. Sci. Tchrs. Conv. (chairperson 1979—), Newark Ednl. Coun., Newark Tchrs. Union. Roman Catholic. Avocations: crafts, reading, drawing. Home: 407 Centre St Nutley NJ 07110-1636

PUI, CHING-HON, hematologist, oncologist, educator; b. Hong Kong, Aug. 20, 1951; came to U.S., 1976; s. Y.T. and Lan Kwan (Ho) Bay-P. MD, Nat. Taiwan U., 1976. Diplomate Am. Bd. Pediat., Am. Bd. Pediatric Hematology and Oncology. Intern St. Louis City Hosp., 1976-77; resident St. Jude Children's Rsch. Hosp., Memphis, Tenn., 1977-79, fellow in pediatric hematology/oncology, 1979-81, rsch. assoc., 1981-82, asst. mem., 1982-86, assoc. mem., 1986-90; assoc. prof. of pediatrics U. Tenn., Memphis, 1986-90, prof. pediatrics, 1990—; mem. depts hematology-oncology, pathology and lab. St. Jude Children's Rsch. Hosp., Memphis, 1990—, dir. lymphoid disease program, vice chmn. dept. hematology and oncology, 1994—, co. dir.dept. hematological malignancies program, 1995—, Fahad Nassai Al-Rashid chair Leukemia Rsch., 1999—. Prin. investigator pediatric onocology group St. Jude, St. Louis, 1990—; reviewer spl. ad hoc rev. com. Nat. Cancer Inst., Bethesd, Md., 1990—. Contbr. articles to profl. jours. Recipient Book Coupon award Nat. Taiwan U., 1971, 74, 75. Fellow Am. Acad. Pediat., Am. Soc. Clin. Oncology, Am. Assn. Cancer Rsch., Am. Soc. Hematology, Soc. Pediatric Rsch., Pediatric Oncology Group, AAAS, Am. Assn. Physicians; mem. Am. Soc. Clin. Investigation, Am. Cancer Soc. (prof. clin. rsch. 2002-). Avocations: music, swimming, bridge, chess, travel. Office: St Jude Childrens Rsch Hosp 332 N Lauderdale St Memphis TN 38105-2729

PULANCO, TONYA BETH, special education educator; b. Portland, Oreg., Apr. 17, 1933; d. Anthony Lorenzo and Adelfa Elizabeth (Dewey) P. BA, San Jose State U., 1955; MA, Columbia U., 1966. Occupl. therapist Langley Porter Hosp., San Francisco, 1958-60; writer ednl. sub-contracts Columbia U., N.Y.C., 1961-64; from tchr. to dir. edn. Gateway Sch. N.Y., N.Y.C., 1965—. Mem. Assn. for Children with Learning Disabilities, Am. Occupl. Therapy Assn., Japanese Am. Citizens League. Avocations: tap dancing, walkathons, silversmithing, jazz, opera. Office: Gateway Sch NY 236 2d Ave New York NY 10003

PULHAMUS, MARLENE LOUISE, retired elementary school educator; b. Paterson, NJ, Sept. 11, 1937; d. David Weeder and Elfrieda (Ehler) Wemmell; m. Aaron R. Pulhamus, Aug. 20, 1960; children: Steven, Thomas, Nancy. Student, Trenton State U., 1957; BS, William Paterson U., 1959; postgrad., Rutgers U., 1992. Cert. elem. tchr., N.J. Kindergarten tchr. Wayne (N.J.) Bd. Edn., 1959-63, Paterson Bd. Edn., 1974-75, 2d grade tchr., 1975-81; basic skills instr. Paterson Pub. Schs., 1981—, tchr. accelerated program 1st grade, 1992—; cons. lang. arts, literacy Kendall Hunt Pegasus, Wayne, N.J. Trainer for insvc. groups of learning ctrs. and math. with manipulatives for local pub. schs., trainer for local pub. schs. Contbr. Lessons 4Mat in Action, 3d edit., 4Mat: A Quest for Wholeness, 1977. Pres. Friends of Eisenhower Libr., Totowa, N.J., 1975-77; coord. ch. sch. Preakness Reformed Ch., Wayne, 1990-93, elder, chair outreach commn. Recipient Gov.'s award for tchg. excellence State of N.J. Commn. Edn., 1991, 4Mation program award, 1994. Mem. ASCD, NEA, AAUW, Nat. Coun. Tchrs. Math., Nat. Assn. for Edn. Young Children, N.J. Edn. Assn., Passaic County Edn. Assn., Paterson Edn. Assn. (mem. exec. bd., 1985-89, legis. chmn. 1986-89). Home and Office: 47 Easedale Rd Wayne NJ 07470-2486

PULLEN, KATHRYN ANN LINK, elementary education educator; b. Rockville Centre, N.Y., Jan. 15, 1958; d. John Andrew and Dorothy Rose (Wohlfarth) Link; m. Edward A. Pullen, Oct. 12, 1980; children: Steven, Kathryn, Kristine, Andrew. AAS in Early Childhood, SUNY, Farmingdale, 1978; BA in Elem. Edn., Dowling Coll., 1980, M of Reading, 1992. Tchr. Headstart Program, Patchoque, N.Y., 1980-83, St. Luke's Early Childhood Edn. Ctr., Farmingdale, N.Y., 1990-92; tchr. 3rd grade Massapequa (N.Y.) Sch. Dist., 1992—. Christian edn. com. mem. St. Luke's, Farmingdale, 1987—, mem. adv. bd. parent rep., 1988—; mem. summer program St. Luke's Ch., Farmingdale, 1991—. Mem. Internat. Reading Assn., Alpha Upsilon Alpha. Republican. Avocations: gardening, swimming, reading. Home: 28 West Dr Massapequa NY 11758-1461

PULLIAM, FREDERICK CAMERON, educational administrator; b. Mesa, Ariz., Jan. 5, 1936; s. Fredrick Posey and Nathana Laura (Cameron) P.; m. Deborah Jean Botts, June 1, 1979; 1 child, Sarah Elizabeth; children by previous marraige: Cameron Dale, Joy Renee. AA, Hannibal LaGrange Coll., 1955; AB, Grand Canyon Coll., 1958; MEd, U. Mo., 1966, EdS, 1976, EdD, 1981. Ordained to ministry So. Bapt. Conv., 1955. Tchr. Centerview (Mo.) Pub. Scsh., 1958-59; min. Bethel Bapt. Ch., Kansas City, Mo., 1959-61; adminstr. Fiti'uta Manu'a Sch., Am. Somoa, 1966-68; cons. in fin. Mo. State Tchrs. Assn., Columbia, 1969-79; supt. schs. Midway Heights C-VII, Columbia, 1979-83; dir. elem. edn. Brentwood (Mo.) Pub. Schs., 1983-90; pres. Life Long Learning Sys. St. Louis, Mt. Vernon, Mo., 1989—; assoc. prof. edn. Mo. So. State Coll., 1990-99, dir. clin. and field experiences in tchr. edn., 1990-99. Pastor Patten Chapel and Miller (Mo.) United Meth. Chs., 1997-2001; assoc. pastor First United Meth. Ch., Mt. Vernon, Mo., 2002-03, Saint Paul's United Meth. Ch., Joplin, Mo., 2003--; founder, coord. Mo. Computer-Using Educators Conf., 1982-84; contbg. writer St. Louis Computing News, 1984-95; adj. asst. profl. ednl. studies U. Mo., St. Louis, 1986-90; adj. assoc. prof. grad. studies S.W. Bapt. U., 1991-98; cons. sch. fin., curriculum improvement. Contbr. articles to profl. jours. Mem. Columbia Am. Revolution Bicentennial Commn.; mem. edn. adv. com. Mo. Gov.'s Transition Team, 1992-93. Inst. Devel. Ednl. Activity fellow, 1969, 78-84. Mem.: ASCD (bd. dirs. 1984—90), Assn. Childhood Edn. Internat., Rotary Internat., Phi Delta Kappa (chpt. advisor). Home: 102 Rocky Cir Carl Junction MO 64834 Office: Saint Paul's United Meth Ch 2423 W 26th St Joplin MO 64804 E-mail: cpulliam66@sbcglobal.net.

PURANDARE, YESHWANT K. chemistry educator, consultant; b. Poona, Purandare, India, Sept. 19, 1934; came to U.S., 1961; s. Kashinath Purandare and Indira Deshpande; m. Margarita Renella, Feb. 8, 1964; children: Sarita, Amar, Jasmine, Ravi. BS with honors, U. Bombay, 1956; MS, U. Poona, 1960, Fordham U., 1964; PhD, NYU, 1981; MD, Spartan Health Sci. U., St. Lucia, B.W.I., 1985. Cert. clin. lab. specialist; cert. lab. dir. Grad. teaching asst. Fergusson Coll., Poona, 1956-60; quality control chemist Sardesai Bros., Bilimora, India, 1960-61; part time clin. chemist Brunswick Hosp., Amityville, N.Y., 1965-81; instr. chemistry Coll. Tech., SUNY, Farmingdale, N.Y., 1964-67, asst. prof., 1967-69, assoc. prof., 1969-74, prof., 1974—2000, chmn. dept. chemistry, 1984—99. Cons. Boat-Life Industries, Old Bethpage, N.Y., 1986—. Author (manuals) Experiments in Physiol. Chemistry, 1985, Lecture Notes on Physiological Chemistry, 1986. Leader Boy Scouts of Am., 1974—. Mem. Am. Chem. Soc., Am. Assn. Clin. Chemistry (cert.), Am. Soc. Clin. Pathologists (cert. chemistry specialist), Rotary (Farmingdale pres. 1989-90, Paul Harris fellow 1992). Office: SUNY Coll Tech Chemistry Dept Lupton Hall Farmingdale NY 11735

PURCELL, KENNETH, psychology educator, university dean; b. N.Y.C., Oct. 21, 1928; s. Herman and Ann (Bulkin) P.; m. Claire Dickson Kepler, Dec. 17, 1949 (div. Dec. 1986); children: Kathleen Ann, Andrew Kepler; m. Marjorie Bayes, Jan. 17, 1987. BA, PhD, U. Nebr. Asst. prof. U. Ky., 1956-58; dir. behavior sci. div. Children's Asthma Research Inst.; asst. prof. U. Colo. Med. Center, 1958-68; prof., dir. clin. tng. psychology U. Mass., 1968-69, chmn. dept. psychology, 1969-70; prof., chmn. psychology U. Denver, 1970—76, dean Coll. Arts and Scis., 1976-84, prof. psychology, 1984—94, prof. emeritus, 1994. Author papers in field. Served to 1st lt. AUS, 1953—56. Fellow Am. Psychol. Assn., Soc. Research Child Devel., AAAS, Colo. Psychol. Assn. (dir. 1962-64) Home: 3254 S Heather Gardens Way Aurora CO 80014-3666 Office: U Denver Coll Arts & Scis Denver CO 80208-0001

PURCELL, MARY HAMILTON, speech educator; b. Ft. Worth; d. Josseph Hants and Letha (Gibson) Hamilton; m. William Paxson Purcell, Jr., Dec. 28, 1950; children: William Paxson III, David Hamilton. BA, Mary Hardin-Baylor Coll., 1947; MA, La. State U., 1948; HHD (hon.), Mary Hardin-Baylor Coll., 1986, U. New England, 2000. Instr. dept speech and dramatic arts Temple U., Phila., 1948-53, 60-61; part-time instr. speech Cushing Jr. Coll., Bryn Mawr, Pa., 1966-78. Pres. Pa. Program for Women and Girl Offend, 1968—73, Nether Providence Parent Tchr. Orgn., 1975—76; treas. Virginia Gildersleeve Internat. Fund U. Women, 1975—81, bd. dirs., 1987—93; mem. U.S. del. UN Commn. on Status of Women, 1996; co-chmn. NGO Com. for UNICEF, 1994—2000, mem. global forum, 2001—; mem. Wallingford-Swarthmore Dist. Sch. Bd., 1977—83; bd. dirs. Ministers and Missionaries Fund Am. Bapt. Conv., 1985—94, pres., 1995—, Internat. Devel. Conf., 1986—; bd. dirs. Nat. Peace Inst. Found., 1983—86; Big Bros./Big Sisters of Am., 1985—90; bd. dirs. Citizens Crime Commn. of Phila., 1976—, Pa. Women's Campaign Fund, 1985—88, 1993—. Named Outstanding Alumna, Mary Hardin-Baylor Coll., 1972, Disting. Dau. Pa., 1982, v.p., 1994—95, pres., 1995—97, Woman of Yr., DECO Women's Conf., 1998; recipient Zeta Phi Eta award excellence in comms., 1983, Eleanor Schnurr award, UNA/USA, 2000. Mem. AAUW (Pa. divsn. pres. 1968-70, v.p. mid. Atlantic region, 1973-77, program v.p. 1979-81, pres. 1981-85, rep. to UN 1985-89), Internat. Fedn. Univ. Women (1st v.p. 1986-89, pres. 1989-92, rep. to UN 1992—; pres. UN Dept. Pub. Info. Non Govt. Orgn. ann. conf. 1993), Speech Assn. Am., Pi Kappa Delta, Pi Gamma Mu, Delta Sigma Rho, Alpha Psi Omega, Alpha Chi. Democrat. Baptist. Home: 9 Oak Knoll Dr Wallingford PA 19086-6315

PURDES, ALICE MARIE, retired adult education educator; b. St. Louis, Jan. 8, 1931; d. Joseph Louis and Angeline Cecilia (Mozier) P. AA, Belleville Area Coll., 1951; BS, Ill. State U., Normal, 1953, MS, 1954; cert., Sorbonne U., Paris, 1964; PhD, Fla. State U., Tallahassee, 1976. Cert. in music edn., elem. edn., secondary edn., adult edn. Tchg. and grad. asst. Ill. State U., 1953-54; music supr. Princeton (Ill.) Pub. Schs., 1954-55; music dir. Venice (Ill.) Pub. Schs., 1955-72, secondary vocal music dir., 1955-72; coord. literacy program Venice-Lincoln Tech. Ctr., 1983-86, chmn. lang. arts dept., 1983-96; ret., 1996. Tchr. in space candidate, 1985. Mem. St. Louis chpt. World Affairs Coun., UN Assn., Nat. Mus. of Women in the Arts, Humane Soc. of Am.; charter mem. St. Louis Sci. Ctr., Harry S. Truman Inst.; contbr. Old Six Mile Mus., 1981, Midland Repertory Players, Alton, Ill., 1991; chair Cystic Fibrosis Spring Bike-A-Thon, Madison, Ill., 1981, Granite City, Ill., 1985. Named to Ill. Sr. Hall of Fame, 2001, Gov's Sr. Hall of Fame, 2001; recipient Gold medal, Nat. Senior Olympics, 1989, Gold medal, more than 400 others, Sr. World Games, 1992, Generations of Success Alumni award, Belleville Area Coll., 1998, several scholarships. Mem.: AAUW, Am. Fedn. Tchrs. (pres. 1957—58), Ill. Adult and Continuing Educators Assn., Am. Choral Dirs. Assn., Ill. Music Educators Assn. (Svc. award 2002), Music Educators Nat. Conf., Ill. State U. Alumni Assn., Slavic and East European Friends (life), Fla. State Alumni Assn., Lovejoy Libr. Friends, Nat. Space Soc., Western Cath. Union, Croation Fraternal Union, St. Louis Numis. Assn., Friends St. Louis Art Mus., Archaeol. Inst. Am., Travelers Abroad (pres. 1966—68, 1989—), Madison Rotary Club (internat. amb., Humanitarian award 1975). Roman Catholic. Avocations: bowling, travel. Home: PO Box 274 Madison IL 62060-0274

PURDY, DENNIS GENE, insurance company executive, education consultant; b. Detroit, June 12, 1946; s. Culver and Tessie (Gillette) P.; m. Ardyce Maxine Wilcox, Aug. 9, 1969; children: Krista Rochelle, Steven Dennis. BS in Edn., Wayne State U., 1969; CLU, Am. Coll., Bryn Mawr, Pa., 1981; ChFC, Am. Coll., 1984. Cert. life underwriter tng. coun. fellow, 1989. Claims adjustor State Farm Ins., Southfield, Mich., 1969-71; pvt. practice Northville, Mich., 1971-73; claims rep. Farmers Ins. Co., Southfield, 1973-76, asst. tng. mgr. Aurora, Ill., 1976-78; life tng. mgr. Ohio State Life Ins., Columbus, 1978-80; sales adminstrn. mgr. Farmers Ins. Co., Columbus, 1980-81, life tng. rep., 1981-86, life mktg. specialist, 1986-94, sr. claims rep., 1994-2000; pvt. practice, 2000—. Continuing edn. coord. for state of Ind., Farmers Ins. Group, Dublin, Ohio, 1990—; mem. pre-lic. adv. bd. State of Ohio, Columbus, 1992, mem. exam. rev. bd., 1992; field faculty mem. Life Underwriters Tng. Coun. Contbr. articles for internal publ., 1980—. Pres. Columbus Barbershop Chorus, 1989-90, v.p., 1991-92. Named Man of Yr. Columbus Barbershop Chorus, 1990. Mem. Nat. Assn. Life Underwriters, Am. Soc. CLUs and ChFCs., Columbus Assn. Life Underwriters. Avocations: music, swimming. Home and Office: 2129 Shirlene Dr Grove City OH 43123-4008

PURDY, LESLIE, community college president; b. Downey, Calif., Aug. 18, 1943; d. Hubert C. and Janice M. (Harker) Noble; m. Ralph Purdy, Aug. 23, 1969; children: Christopher Hugh, George Colin. BA cum laude, Occidental Coll., L.A., 1965; MAT, Oberlin (Ohio) Coll., 1966; EdD, UCLA, 1973. Tchr. Parma (Ohio) Sr. H.S., 1966; ombudsman/instr. social sci. Raymond Coll., U. of Pacific, Stockton, Calif., 1967-69; coord. spl. svcs. ERIC Clearinghouse for C.C.'s, L.A., 1970-74; sr. instrnl. designer Coastline C.C., Fountain Valley, Calif., 1974-84, adminstrv. dean, 1984-94, pres., 1994—. Bd. dirs. Intelecom, Pasadena, Calif.; bd. dirs., pres. Instrnl. Telecom. Coun., Washington, 1987-94; adv. bd. PBS "Going the Distance" program, Washington, 1993-96; cons. Commn. on Innovation, Calif. Colls. Chancellor's Office, 1993-94. Editor: Reaching New Students Through New Technologies, 1983; instrnl. designer Psychology: The Study of Human Behavior, 1989 (Emmy 1990); exec. prodr. (telecourses): Universe: The Infinite Frontier, 1994 (Emmy 1994), Time to Grow, 1992 (Emmy 1992); contbr. articles to profl. jours. Mem. Orange County Forum, 1994—, Ctr. for Studies of Media and Values, L.A., 1990-95, Bread for the World, Washington, 1980—; bd. mem. West County Family YMCA, 1993-2000; bd. mem. Garden Grove Renaissance Found., 1998—; bd. mem. Orange County Nat. Conf. of Cmty. and Justice, 1997—, Orange County Workforce Investment Bd., 2000—; mem. adv. bd. Calif. C.C. Satellite Network, 2001-02. Recipient Emmy awards Am. Acad. TV Arts and Scis., 1987, 90, 92,. 95, Western Region award Instrn. Telecom. Coun., 1995; named one of Women of Distinction City of Garden Grove, 2001. Mem. Assn. of Calif. C.C. Adminstrs., Assn. Ednl. Comms. and Tech., Am. Assn. of Women in C.C.'s, UCLA Alumni Assn. (Doctoral Award in Edn. 1973). Presbyterian. Avocations: backpacking, gardening, conservation, choral singing. Office: Coastline Cmty Coll Office of Pres 11460 Warner Ave Fountain Valley CA 92708 E-mail: lpurdy@cccd.edu.

PURINGTON, DAVID W. elementary education educator; Jr. high sch. tchr. Elm St. Jr. High Sch., Nashua, N.H., 1990—. Recipient Tchr. Excellence award Internat. Tchr. Edn. Assn., 1992. Office: Elm St Jr High Sch 117 Elm St Nashua NH 03060-6473

PURNELL, RONALD JERRY, special education educator; b. Crisfield, Md., July 7, 1957; s. Marvin Jerry and Shirley Virginia (Parks) P.; m. Minnie Kathleen Tyler, July 21, 1979; children: Ronald Jerry II, Melissa Ruth. BS in Elem. Edn., Salisbury State U., 1981; Assocs. Provisional Cert., U. Md., 1986, M in Spl. Edn., 1992. Cert. elem. edn. grades K-8, spl. edn. grades K-12. Media specialist asst. Somerset County Schs., Princess Anne, Md., 1979-80; tchr. grades 2 and 3 Deal Island (Md.) Sch., 1980-81; tchr. spl. edn. Sarah M. Peyton Sch., Marion, Md., 1991-92, Crisfield (Md.) H.S., 1982—. Varsity soccer coach Crisfield (Md.) H.S., 1981—, jr. varsity basketball coach, 1982—, baseball coach, 1984, jr. varsity baseball coach, 1992—. Chmn. Mike Sterlin 10K, Crisfield, 1988—; pres. Crisfield (Md.) Youth Soccer Club, 1991—, Crisfield (Md.) Youth Basketball Club, 1994—; mgr. Crisfield (Md.) Little League, 1992, 93. Named Coach of Yr. 2nd team Bayside Athletic Conf., 1991, Mgr. of Yr., Crisfield (Md.) Little League, 1993. Mem. Coun. for Exceptional Children. Baptist. Avocations: running, boating, collecting indian artifacts, playing basketball. Home: 26546 Asbury Ave Crisfield MD 21817-2216 Office: Crisfield HS 210 N Somerset Ave Crisfield MD 21817 E-mail: RJP@dvm.com.

PURPURA, DOMINICK P. dean, neuroscientist; b. N.Y.C., Apr. 2, 1927; m. Florence Williams, 1948; children: Craig, Kent, Keith, Allyson AB, Columbia U., 1949; MD, Harvard U., 1953. Intern Presbyn Hosp., N.Y.C., 1953-54; asst. resident in neurology Neurol. Inst., N.Y.C., 1954-55; Prof., chmn. dept. anatomy Albert Einstein Coll. Medicine, Yeshiva U., N.Y.C., 1967-74, sci. dir. Kennedy Ctr., 1969-72, dir. Kennedy Ctr., 1972-82, prof., chmn. dept. neurosci., 1974-82, dean, 1984—, Stanford U., Calif., 1982-84. Editor-in-chief Brain Rsch. Revs., 1975—2000, Developmental Brain Rsch., 1981—2000, Molecular Brain Rsch., 1985—2000, Cognitive Brain Rsch., 1991—2000, mem. editl. bd. Brain Rsch., 1965—2000, editor-in-chief, 1975—2000. Served with USAAF, 1945-47 Fellow N.Y. Acad. Scis.; mem. Inst. Medicine of Nat. Acad. Scis., Nat. Acad. Scis., Am. Acad. Neurology, Am. Assn. Anatomists, Am. Assn. Neurol. Surgeons, Am. Epilepsy Soc., Am. Physiol. Soc., Assn. Research in Nervous and Mental Disease, Soc. Neurosci., Sigma Xi Office: Yeshiva U Albert Einstein Coll Medicine 1300 Morris Park Ave Bronx NY 10461-1926

PURVIS, HOYT HUGHES, political scientist, academic administrator, educator; b. Jonesboro, Ark., Nov. 7, 1939; s. Hoyt Somervell and Jane (Hughes) P.; m. Marion M. Purvis; children: Pamela R., Camille C. BJ, U. Tex., 1961, MJ, 1963; postgrad., U. Nancy, France, 1962-63, Vanderbilt U., Nashville, 1963-64. Researcher/writer So. Edn. Reporting Svc., Nashville, 1963-64; reporter Houston Chronicle, 1964-65; press sec., spl. asst. Sen. J.W. Fulbright, Washington, 1967-74; dir. pubs. and lectr. LBJ Sch. Pub. Affairs, U. Tex., Austin, 1974-76; fgn./def. advisor and dep. staff dir. Sen. Majority Leader and Sen. Dem. Policy Com., Washington, 1977-80; sr. rsch. fellow LBJ Sch. Pub. Affairs, U. Tex., 1980-82; dir. and prof. Fulbright Inst. Internat. Rels., U. Ark., Fayetteville, 1982—2000; dir. Internat. Rels., prof. journalism and polit. sci. U. Ark., Fayetteville, 2000—. Author: Interdependence, 1992, Media, Politics and Government, 2001; co-author: Legistling Foreign Policy, 1984, Seoul & Washington, 1993; editor: The Presidency and the Press, 1976, The Press: Free and Responsible?, 1982, Media Issues and Trends, 1998 ; co-editor: Old Myths and New Realities in U.S.-Soviet Relations, 1990; columnist N.W. Ark. Times, 2000—. Mem. adv. coun. Sci. Info. Liaison Office, Ark. Gen. Assembly, Little Rock, 1984-96; chmn. Fayetteville City Cable Bd., 1991-93; apptd. J. Wm. Fulbright Fgn. Scholarship Bd., 1994-2003, vice chair, 1995, chmn., 1996—99. Rotary fellow, 1962-63, others; recipient Fulbright Coll. Master Tchr. award, Disting. Faculty Achievement award U. Ark. Alumni Assn. Mem. Internat. Studies Assn. (regional v.p. 1984-86), Am. Polit. Sci. Assn., Assn. for Edn. in Journalism and Mass Communication, Phi Beta Delta (named Nat. Outstanding Faculty award 2000), Delta Phi Alpha. Methodist. Home: PO Box 1872 Fayetteville AR 72702-1872 Office: University of Ark 116 Kimpel Hall Fayetteville AR 72701

PURVIS, JOHN ANDERSON, lawyer, educator; b. Aug. 31, 1942; s. Virgil J. and Emma Lou (Anderson) P.; m. Charlotte Johnson, Apr. 3, 1976; 1 child, Whitney; children by previous marriage: Jennifer, Matt. BA cum laude, Harvard U., 1965; JD, U. Colo., 1968. Bar: Colo. 1968, U.S. Dist. Ct. Colo. 1968, U.S. Ct. Appeals (10th cir.) 1978. Dep. dist. atty., Boulder, Colo., 1968-69; asst. dir., dir. legal aid U. Colo. Sch. Law, 1969; assoc. Williams, Taussig & Trine, Boulder, 1969; head Boulder office Colo. Pub. Defender Sys., 1970-72; assoc., ptnr. Hutchinson, Black, Hill, Buchanan & Cook, Boulder, 1972-85; ptnr. Purvis, Gray, Schuetze and Gordon, 1985-98, Purvis, Gray & Gordon, LLP, 1999—2001, Purvis Gray LLP, 2001—. Acting Colo. State Pub. Defender, 1978; adj. prof. law U. Colo., 1981, 84-88, 94, others; lectr. in field; chmn. Colo. Pub. Defender Commn., 1979-89; mem. nominating commn. Colo. Supreme Ct., 1984-90; mem. com. on conduct U.S. Dist. Ct., 1991-97, chmn., 1996-97; chmn. Boulder County Criminal Justice Com., 1975-81. Recipient Ames award Harvard U., 1964, Outstanding Young Lawyer award Colo. Bar Assn., 1978, Dist. Achievement award U. Colo. Law Sch. Alumni Assn., 1997. Mem.: ATLA, Am. Bar Found., Colo. Bar Found., Trial Lawyers for Pub. Justice, Colo. Trial Lawyers Assn., Boulder County Bar Assn., Colo. Bar Assn. (chair litigation sect. 1994—95), Am. Coll. Trial Lawyers (state chmn. 1998—2000), Am. Bd. Trial Advs., Internat. Acad. Trial Lawyers, Internat. Soc. Barristers, Faculty of Fed. Advs. (bd. dirs. 1999—2001), Supreme Ct. Hist. Soc. (state chmn. 1998—2002). Democrat. Address: 1050 Walnut St Ste 501 Boulder CO 80302-5144

PURVIS, MARY RUTH MOORE, special education educator; b. Douglas, Ga., July 6, 1932; d. Clifton Franklin and Eva (Burkette) Moore; m. Dillon Morrison, Sept. 18, 1954 (div.); children: Gary Dillon, Belinda Ruth Morrison Baker; m. Gary L. Purvis, Mar. 24, 1989. BS in Edn., Drury Coll., Springfield, Mo., 1974, MEd, 1977. Cert. life elem. tchr., K-12 learning disabilities, educable mentally retarded, socially and emotionally disturbed, remedial reading, Mo.; cert. learning disabilities and elem. tchr., Ga. Payroll clk. Consumers Markets, Springfield, 1955-60; acct. Manpower, Springfield, 1960-66; bookkeeper R.J. Haswell, Springfield, 1966-72; tchr. spl. edn. and learning disabilities Everton (Mo.) Pub. Schs., 1977-79, Spokane (Mo.) High Sch., 1979-83; owner, mgr. Ruth's Square Dance Shoppe, Springfield, 1983-85; substitute tchr. Springfield Pub. Schs., 1985-89; tchr. learning disabilities edn. Coffee County Schs., Douglas, Ga., 1990—. Former instr. Fed. Med. Ctr., Springfield. Mem. Assn. for Children with Learning Disabilities, Ga. Edn. Assn. (rep. 1992—). Democrat. Mem. Ch. of God. Office: Coffee County Schs PO Box 999 Douglas GA 31534-0999

PURYEAR, JAMES BURTON, college administrator; b. Jackson, Miss., Sept. 2, 1938; s. Harry Henton and Doris (Smith) P.; m. Joan Copeland, June 13, 1965; children: John James, Jeffrey Burton, Joel Harry. BS, Miss. State U., 1960, MEd, 1961; PhD, Fla. State U., 1969. Lic. profl. counselor, Ga. Assoc. dir. YMCA Miss. State U., Starkville, 1962-64; dir. YMCA, Starkville, Miss., 1964-65; dir. fin. aid Fla. State U., Tallahassee, 1967-69; asst. dir. student affairs Med. Coll. of Ga., Augusta, 1969-70, dir. student affairs, 1970-86, v.p. student affairs, 1986-2000, v.p. emeritus, student affairs, 2000—. Mem. adv. bd. Ga. Fed. Bank, Augusta, 1978-85; deacon, 1971-, chmn. bd. First Bapt. Ch., Augusta, 1978-80; pres. Learning Disabilities Assn., Augusta, 1987, PTA, 1994, Band Assn.,1996; bd. dirs. Augusta Tng. Shop for Handicapped, 1994-98; mem. exec. bd., v.p. Boy Scouts Am., 1996-02. Yearbook Dedication MCG Student Yearbook, 1975; scholar Med. Coll. Ga., 1988; recipient Svc. to Mankind award Sertoma, 1988. Mem. Nat. Assn. Student Pers. (S.E. regional bd. 1985), Am. Coll. Pers. Assn., So. Assn. Coll. Student Affairs, Rotary (pres. 1978, dist. lt. gov. 1997-99, dist. gov. 2001-02, Paul Harris fellow 1985, Will Watt fellow). Baptist. Avocations: golf, photography, scouting.

PURYEAR, JOAN COPELAND, academic administrator; b. Columbus, Miss., May 10, 1944; d. John Thomas and Mamie (Cunningham) Copeland.; m. James Burton Puryear, June 13, 1965; children: John James, Jeffrey Burton, Joel Harry. BA summa cum laude, Miss. State U., Starkville, 1965; MA, Fla. State U., 1969; EdD, U. Ga., 1987. Instr. English, Fla. State U., Tallahassee, 1965-69, Augusta (Ga.) State U., 1987-88; head English dept. Augusta Tech. Coll., 1989-93, chairperson gen. edn. and devel. studies, 1993-96, mem. dean's coun., mgmt. team, 1994—, dean allied health scis., gen. edn. and devel. studies, 1997—. Chmn. State Exec. Bd. English, Ga., 1990-92, East Ctrl. Consortium English, Ga., 1990-92; facilitator Total Quality Mgmt. Tech. Tng.; mem. exec. steering com. Continous Improvement Coun., 1996-02; mem. and co-chmn. Continuous Improvement Coun., 1996-97. Mem. Cmtys. in Schs., 1996—; trustee Augusta Tech. Inst. Found. Bd., 1996—; mem. founding bd. Junior Achievement, 2001-02; co-pres. Davidson Fine Arts Sch. PTA, 1995, co-pres. bd. assn., 1996; pres. Med. Coll. Spouse's Club, Augusta, 1972; dir. Women's Mission Orgn., First Bapt. Ch., Augusta, 1982, dir. youth Sunday Sch., 1992-98, chmn. 175th Anniversary, 1992, deacon, 1996—, vice moderator, 1998-99, mem. ministerial adv. com., 1992-2001, chair, 2003, vice chmn. scholarship and edn. com., 2002; mem. found. bd. Walton Rehab. Ctr. Mem.: Augusta South Rotary Club (pres. 2002—03), Phi Theta Kappa (advisor 1992—, Horizon regional award for outstanding advisor 1997). Baptist. Avocations: flower arranging, home decorating, reading, traveling. Office: Augusta Tech Coll 3200 Augusta Tech Dr Augusta GA 30906-3375

PUSKARICH, LYNN M(ARY), special education educator; b. Martins Ferry, Ohio, Nov. 25, 1958; d. Michael and Mary Belle (Holliday) Puskarich; children: Catherine Ann White, Malayna Ruth Pelegreen. BS in Spl. Edn., Reading Tchr. Specialist, Ashland U., 1980; MA in Edn. Adminstrn., Franciscan U. Steubenville, 1995. Cert. tchr., supr., Ohio; cert. drug and alcohol advisor, Ohio. Developmentally Handicapped spl. edn. tchr. Harrison Hills City Schs., Hopedale, Ohio, 1980-84; pvt. piano tchr. Hopedale, Ohio, 1985-88; pvt. instrn. and tutoring, 1985-87; remedial math., sci. tchr. Indian Creek Sch. Dist., Wintersville, Ohio, spring 1987; DH spl. edn. tchr. Harrison Hills City Schs., Hopedale, 1987—. Coord. Disability Coll. and Vocat. Career Day, 1998. Pianist Hopedale Meth. Ch., 1988—; mem. Hope Players Theater, Hopedale. Named one of Outstanding Young Women of Am., 1981, Young Community Leaders of Am., 1982, Tchr. of Yr., East Ctrl. Ohio Spl. Edn. Regional Resource Ctr., 1999, Ohio Appalachian Ctr. for Higher Edn., 2001. Mem. ASCD, NEA, Bus. and Profl. Women's Orgn., Internat. Brotherhood of Magicians, Kappa Delta Pi. Republican. Methodist. Avocations: puppets, theater, politics, travel, piano. Home: 622 Kerr Ave Cadiz OH 43907

PUSTILNIK, SEYMOUR W. mathematics and education educator; b. N.Y.C., Apr. 3, 1927; s. Morris and Susan Pustilnik; m. Phyllis Lampert, Apr. 8, 1962; children: Michael, Susan. BA in Math., U. Mich., 1948; MA in Math., Bowling Green State U., 1950. Grad. asst. math. Bowling Green (Ohio) State U., 1948-49; assoc. prof. math. CUNY, 1956-86; asst. prof. math. edn. NYU, N.Y.C., 1988-90; owner SWP Co., Brooklyn, N.Y.; pres. Phylmour, Inc., Fantasy and Reality Pub. Co., Inc. Author: Utopia at Toronto: Three Views of a Harmonious Earth with a Sociologist's Appraisal, 2001; author, editor (pamphlet) Rehabilitation and Redevelopment: A Plan to Rehabilitate the Homeless Men on the Cooper Square Site through Urban Renewal, 1961. Mem. Cmty. Sch. Bd., Dist. 13, Bklyn., 1973-77; chmn. Com. for Coop. of Parents, Tchrs., and Prin., Bklyn., 1973-77, Com. for Kindergarten through 6th Grade P.S. 8, Bklyn., 1972-76. Mem. MLA (presenter), Am. Math. Soc. (presenter), Nat. Coun. Tchrs. Math, Math. Assn. Am. (presenter), Soc. Lit. and Sci. (presenter), Soc. Utopian Studies (presenter), Learning Styles Network, N.Y. State Math. Assn. of 2-Yr. Colls. (presenter), Melus, Soc. for Study of Multi-Ethnic Lit. (presenter), Mid-Atlantic Am. Culture/Popular Culture Assn. (presenter). Avocations: literary criticism, theater, educational games.

PUTNAM, BONNIE COLLEEN, elementary education educator; b. Unionville, Mo., July 29, 1936; d. Randall Lee and Edith Nora (Colton) Pickering; m. Robert Lyle Putnam, Aug. 16, 1953; 1 child, Michael Lee. BA in Edn. cum laude, Wichita State U., 1966; MA in Edn., N.E. Mo. State U., 1971. Cert. elem. edn. Classroom tchr. Liberal (Kans.) Schs., 1966-68, Putnam County R-3 Schs., Unionville, 1968-70, Albia (Iowa) Cmty. Schs., 1970—. Mem. state adv. bd. So. Prairie Area Edn. Agy., Ottumwa, Iowa, 1972-74; instr. Performance Learning Sys., Nevada, Calif., 1983-92. Sec., trustee Albia (Iowa) Pub. Libr., 1975—; co-chair Albia (Iowa) Schs. Fun Walk/Run. Named Woman of Yr., Beta Sigma Phi Sorority, Albia, 1992. Mem. NEA, Internat. Reading Assn., Iowa State Reading Assn., Rathbun Area Reading Coun. (past pres.), Iowa State Edn. Assn. (presenter Mobile Insvc. Tng. Lab. 1977-83), Albia Cmty. Edn. Assn. (treas., Tchr. of Yr. 1974), Delta Kappa Gamma (sec. 1980—), Golden Key Honor Soc. Avocations: gardening, traveling, reading. Home: RR 3 Box 237 Albia IA 52531-9414 Office: Albia Cmty Schs 120 Benton Ave E Albia IA 52531-2035

PUTNAM, MICHAEL COURTNEY JENKINS, classics educator; b. Springfield, Mass., Sept. 20, 1933; s. Roger Lowell and Caroline (Jenkins) P. AB, Harvard U., 1954, AM, 1956, PhD, 1959; LLD (hon.), Lawrence U., 1985. Instr. classics Smith Coll., Northampton, Mass., 1959-60; faculty classics Brown U., Providence, 1960—, prof., 1967—, chmn., 2000-2001, prof. comparative lit., 1980—, MacMillan prof. of classics, 1985—; acting dir. Ctr. for Hellenic Studies, Harvard U., 1961-62, sr. fellow, 1971-86; Townsend prof. classics Cornell U., 1985; Mellon prof.-in-charge Am. Acad. in Rome, 1989-91. Scholar in residence Am. Acad. in Rome, 1969-70, classical jury, 1982-83, trustee, 1991—; assoc. univ. seminar on classical civilization Columbia U., N.Y.C., 1972—; mem. cath. Commn. on Intellectual and Cultural Affairs, 1969—; adv. coun. dept. classics Princeton U., 1981-87, chmn., 1983-87; cons. Am. Coun. Learned Socs., 1987-89; mem. Inst. for Advanced Study, 1987-88; vis. scholar Phi Beta Kappa, 1994-95; councillor Assn. of Lit. Scholars and Critics, 1996-99. Author: The Poetry of the Aeneid, 1965, Virgil's Pastoral Art, 1970, Tibullus: A Commentary, 1973, Virgil's Poem of the Earth, 1979, Essays on Latin Lyric, Elegy and Epic, 1982, Artifices of Eternity: Horace's Fourth Book of Odes, 1986, Virgil's Aeneid: Interpretation and Influence, 1995, Virgil's Epic Designs, 1998, Horace's Carmen Saeculare, 2000; contbr. articles to profl. jours. Trustee Lowell Obs., Flagstaff, Ariz., 1967-87, bd. advisors, 1987—; trustee Bay Chamber Concerts, Camden, Maine, 1972-88, incorporator, 1988-94; mem. bd. cons. Portsmouth Abbey Sch., 1985-89; hon. sec. Keats-Shelley Meml. Assn., Rome, 1989-91. Rome Prize fellow Am. Acad. in Rome, 1963-64; Guggenheim Meml. fellow, 1966-67; sr. fellow NEH, 1973-74, cons. 1974-78, 87-90; Am. Council Learned Socs. fellow, 1983-84. Fellow Am. Acad. Arts and Sci. 1996—; mem. Am. Philol. Assn. (bd. dir. 1972-75, mem. com. on award of merit 1975-78, chmn. 1977-78, 1st v.p. 1981, pres. 1982, del. Am. Coun. Learned Soc. 1984-87, Charles J. Goodwin award of merit 1971, fin. trustee 1997-2004), mem. Am. Philosophical Soc., 1998—; Archaeol. Inst. Am., Classical Assn. New Eng., Medieval Acad. Am., Vergilian Soc. Am. (trustee 1969-73, v.p. 1974-76), Accademia Nazionale Virgiliana, Art Club. Office: Brown U Dept Classics Providence RI 02912-1856 E-mail: michael_putnam@brown.edu.

PUTNAM, RUTH ANNA, philosopher, educator; b. Berlin, Sept. 20, 1927; d. Martin and Marie (Kohn) Hall; m. Hilary W. Putnam, Aug. 11, 1962; children: Samuel, Joshua, Maxima. BS in Chemistry, UCLA, 1954, PhD in Philosophy, 1962. Instr. philosophy UCLA, 1957-59; acting asst. prof. U. Oreg., 1959-62; from lectr. to prof. philosophy Wellesley (Mass.) Coll., 1963-98, chmn. dept., 1979-82, 91-93; ret., 1998. Dir. summer seminar NEH, 1986, 89; mem. extramural grad. fellowships Wellesley Coll., faculty benefits com., com. budget, academic review bd., taskforce on affirmative action, bd. of admissions; presenter in field. Editor: Cambridge Companion to William James, 1997; contbr. chpts. to books, articles to profl. jours., and encys. Mem. Am. Philos. Assn. (program com. ea. divsn. 1977). Jewish. Office: Wellesley Coll 106 Central St Wellesley MA 02481-8268 E-mail: rputnam@wellesley.edu.

PUTNEY, MARY LYNN, bank administrator, educator; b. N.Y.C., Feb. 26, 1948; d. Joseph John Berry and Evelyn Marie (Geoghegan) Schneir; m. Paul Michael McCaffery, May 18, 1968 (div. June 1976); children: Melissa Berry McCaffery, Paul David McCaffery; m. Frederick Bates Putney, May 30, 1992. MBA in Fin., Columbia U., 1982. Various positions Citibank, N.Y.C., 1974-85, v.p. fgn. exch., 1985-88, v.p. leveraged capital, 1988-92, mng. dir. pvt. banking, 1992-95, mng. dir. global equity, 1995—; adj. prof. Columbia Bus. Sch., N.Y.C., 1986—. Dir. Sinter Metal Corp., Cleve.; mem. adv. bd. AIG Millenium Fund, Russia, CVC/Opportunity Ptnrs., Brazil. Contbr. articles to profl. jours. Dir. Project Renewal, N.Y.C., 1995—, Mary Knoll Sch. Theology, Ossining, N.Y., 1994-95. Mem. Emily's List, Women's Campaign Fund, Sleepy Hollow Country Club, Sea Pines Country Club, Beta Gamma Sigma. Avocations: golf, bridge. Office: Citibank NA 153 E 53rd St New York NY 10022-4611

PUTO, ANNE-MARIE, reading specialist; b. Windber, Pa., July 20, 1956; d. John Michael and Ann Theresa (Biel) Puto. BS Elem. Edn., U. Pitts., Johnstown, 1978; EdM in Lang. Comms., U. Pitts., 1981; EdM in Ednl. Psychology, Indiana U. Pa., 1989. Reading specialist Conemaugh Valley Sch. Dist., Johnstown, 1978—79; with Upward Bound Program St. Francis U., Loretto, Pa., 1994—2000; councilor Appalachian Youth Svc., Ebensburg, Pa., 1991—; reading specialist Children's Aid Home, Somerset, Pa., 1999—, Appalachia Intermediate Unit 08, Ebensburg, 1979—. Mem. Cambria Area Reading Coun. Mem.: Cambria Area Reading Council, Keystone State Reading Assn., Pa. Assn. Fed. Program Coords. Avocations: reading, travel, cross country skiing, needlecrafts, theater. Home: 1093 Tener St Johnstown PA 15904

PUTTERMAN, LOUIS G. economics educator; b. N.Y.C., Apr. 27, 1952; s. Milton and Eileen L. (Goldstein) P.; (div.); 1 child, Laura Lee; m. Vivian Tseng, Apr. 5, 1981; children: Serena Rose, Mark Isaac. BA summa cum laude, Columbia U., 1976; MA in Internat. Relations, Yale U., 1978, PhD in Econs., 1980; MA (hon.), Brown U., 1983. From asst. prof. to prof. econs. Brown U., R.I., 1980—; rsch. assoc., Ctr. for East Asian Rsch. Harvard U., Cambridge, Mass., 1987-93. Author: Peasants, Collectives and Choice, 1986, Division of Labor and Welfare, 1990, Continuity and Change in China's Rural Development: Collective and Reform Eras in Perspective, 1993, Dollars and Change: Economics in Context, 2001; co-author: Economics of Cooperation and the Labor-Managed Economy, 1987; editor: The Economic Nature of the Firm, 1986, (with Randall Kroszner) 2d edit., 1996, (with Dietrich Rueschemeyer) State and Market in Development: Synergy or Rivalry, (with Avner Ben-Ner) Economics, Values and Organization, 1998; mem. editl. bd. Modern China, 1990—, Comparative Economic Studies, 1991-93, Annals of Public and Cooperative Economics, 1992—, Jour. Comparative Econs., 1989-91, 97-99, Chine Econ. Rev., 2001—; assoc. editor Pacific Econ. Rev., 1996—. Recipient Sloan Rsch. fellow, Alfred P. Sloan Found., 1983, Fellow in Chinese Studies, Wang Inst., 1986, Am. Coun. Learned Socs., 1997. Mem. Am. Economic Assn., Assn. for Comparative Economic Studies, Phi Beta Kappa. Office: Brown U Dept Econs 64 Waterman St Providence RI 02912-9029

PYERITZ, REED EDWIN, medical geneticist, educator, research director; b. Pitts., Nov. 2, 1947; s. Paul L. and Ida Mae (Meier) P.; m. Jane Ellen Tumpson, May 28, 1972; 2 children. SB in Chemistry, U. Del., 1968; AM, Harvard U., 1971, PhD in Biochemistry, 1972, MD, 1975. Diplomate Am. Bd. Internal Medicine, Am. Bd. Genetics. Intern Peter Bent Brigham Hosp., Boston, 1975-76; resident Peter Bent Bingham Hosp., Boston, 1976-77, Johns Hopkins Hosp., Balt., 1977-78; from instr. to prof. medicine and pediatrics Sch. Medicine, John Hopkins Hosp., Balt., 1977-93, chair dept. human genetics, 1994-00, prof. human genetics, medicine and pediatrics, 1994-01, MCP Hahnemann Sch. Medicine, 1993-00; prof. medicine and genetics U. Pa. Sch. Medicine, Phila., 2001—, chief divsn. med. genetics, 2001—. Dir. Inst. Genetics, Allegheny U. Health Sci., 1993-99; dir. Ctr. for Med. Genetics, Allegheny Gen. Hosp., 1995-2000; chief physician Md. Athletic Commn., Balt., 1978-93; med. adv. bd. Nat. Marfan Found., N.Y.C., 1982—, chmn. 1982-93, clin. care adv. bd., Nat. Neurofibromatosis Found., 1985—; med. adviser Alliance of Genetic Support Groups, 1994-2001; mem. rsch. adv. bd. Nat. Orgn. Rare Disorders, 1989-2000; mem. rsch. adv. com. Am. Heart Assn., 1996-98; mem. genetic adv. bd. Nat. Cancer Inst., 1996-99; mem. med. adv. bd. Can. Marfan Assn., 1999-, chmn., 2003-; mem. sci. adv. bd. Hereditary Hemorrhagic Telangiectasia Found., 2003—, chair med. adv. bd., Canadian Marfan Assn., 2003-. Co-editor Principles and Practice of Medical Genetics, 1992—; mem. editl. bd. New Eng. Jour. Medicine, 1993-96, JAMA, 1997-01; contbr. over 300 articles to profl. publs. NIH grantee. Fellow: ACP, Am. Coll. Med. Genetics (dir. 1992—94, pres.-elect 1995—96, pres. 1997—98, past pres. 1999—2000); mem.: AAAS, AMA, Am. Med. Accred. Program (spl. adv. com. 1998—2000), Assn. Profs. Human Med. Genetics (pres. elect 1998—99, pres. 2000—02), Assn. Am. Physicians, Am. Soc. Clin. Investigation, Am. Fedn. Med. Rsch., Physician Consortium for Performance Improvement, Am. Heart Assn., Am. Soc. Human Genetics (chmn. program com. 1994—95). Office: Divsn Med Genetics Maloney 538 U Pa Sch Medicine 3400 Spruce St Philadelphia PA 19104-4283 E-mail: reed.pyeritz@uphs.upenn.edu.

PYKE, RONALD, mathematics educator; b. Hamilton, Ont., Can., Nov. 24, 1931; s. Harold and Grace Carter (Digby) P.; m. Gladys Mary Davey, Dec. 19, 1953; children: Darlene, Brian, Ronald, Gordon. BA (hon.), McMaster U., 1953; MS, U. Wash., 1955, PhD, 1956. Asst. prof. Stanford U., Calif., 1956-58; asst. prof. Columbia U., N.Y.C., 1958-60; prof. math. U. Wash., Seattle, 1960-98, prof. emeritus, 1998—. Vis. prof. U. Cambridge, Eng., 1964-65, Imperial Coll., London, 1970-71, Colo. State U., Ft. Collins, 1979, Technion, Israel, 1988, 90, 92; pres. Inst. Math. Stats., 1986-87; mem. bd. math. scis. NRC/NAS, 1984-88, chmn. com. applications and theoretical stats., 1985-88. Editor Ann. Prob., 1972-75; contbr. articles to profl. jours. NSF grantee, 1961-91. Fellow Internat. Statis. Inst. (v.p. 1989-91), Am. Statis. Assn., Inst. Math. Stats. (pres. 1986-87); mem. Bernoulli Soc., Statis. Soc. of Can. Office: U Washington PO Box 354350 Seattle WA 98195-4350

PYLE, DAVID, elementary education educator; Elem. tchr. Carson Valley Mid. Sch., Nev., until 1994, vice prin., 1999—; staff trainer Douglas County (Nev.) Sch. Dist., 1994-99. Recipient Tchr. Excellence award Internat. Tech. Edn. Assn., 1992. Office: Carson Valley Middle Sch PO Box 1888 Minden NV 89423-1888

PYLE, WILMA J. retired education educator; b. Red Key, Ind., Feb. 7, 1926; d. William Finley and Mae Ellen Pyle. BS, Ball State U., 1946; MA, Ohio State U., 1950; EdD, Wayne State U., 1964. Cert. tchr. Ind. Tchr. Ft. Wayne (Ind.) Pub. Schs., Battle Creek (Mich.) Pub. Schs.; tchr., prin. Pontiac (Mich.) Pub. Schs.; instr. Wayne State U., Detroit; assoc. prof. Mercy Coll., Detroit; prof., asst. dean SUNY, Fredonia; prof., assoc. dean Fla. Atlantic U., Boca Raton; ret., 1988. Pres. Internat. Reading Assn., Chautauqua County, NY, 1972—74. Author reading series, 1966-1972. Bd. dir. Fla. Bipartisans Civic Affairs Group, Polk County, Fla., 1999—. Named one of Outstanding Women in Fla.; recipient Outstanding Alumni award, Coll. of Edn., Ohio State U., 1979, Outstanding Alumni Achievement award, Ball State U., 1974. Mem.: AAUW (pres. 1996—98, co-pres. 2003—04), Lake Wales Arts Coun. Avocations: painting, reading, walking, gardening.

PYSCH, RICHARD LAWRENCE, principal; b. New Kensington, Pa., Apr. 27, 1950; s. Michael and Mary Louise (Klauscher) P.; m. Carolyn Vargo, Oct. 14, 1978; children: Matthew, Benjamin. BA, U. Pitts., 1972, MEd, 1977, PhD, 1987; MA, Carnegie-Mellon U., 1974. Tchr. The Village Acad., Bethel Park, Pa., 1975-78; program dir. The Bradley Ctr., Dorseyville, Pa., 1978; tchr. Fox Chapel Area Sch. Dist., Pitts., 1979-87; asst. high sch. prin. Pine-Richland Sch. Dist., Pitts., 1987-88, elem. curriculum coord., prin., 1988—. Contbr. articles to profl. jours. Mem. Juvenile Diabetes Found., Pitts., Hampton Athletic Assn., Pitts., Am. Cancer Soc., Pitts. Gateways grantee Pa. Dept. Edn., 1994. Mem. ASCD, Nat. Elem. Sch. Prins. Assn., Pa. Assn. Elem. Prins., Phi Delta Kappa. Avocations: exercising, civil war enthusiast. Home: 3342 Oaknoll Rd Gibsonia PA 15044-8483 Office: Hance Elem Sch 5518 Molnar Dr Gibsonia PA 15044-9308

PYTLINSKI, JERZY TEODOR, physicist, educator, research administrator; b. Warsaw, Apr. 1, 1938; s. Stanislaw and Natalia (Matuszewska) P.; m. Bonnie Laurie Bennett, Dec. 30, 1969; 1 child, Christine Barbara. MS, Tech. U. Warsaw, 1962; PhD in Plasma Physics with distinction, U. Paris, 1967. Program mgr., acting div. head N.Mex. State U., Las Cruces, 1977-80; sr. scientist, div. head U. P.R., Mayaguez, 1981-83, program dir., sr. scientist San Juan, 1983-86, sr. scientist, founding dir. Univ.-Industry Rsch. Ctr. Tampa, Fla., 1986-89; pres. Univ.-Industry Rsch. Ctr., Tampa, Fla., 1989—, prof., 1989—. Mem. adv. bd. on solar energy UNESCO, 1979-85; referee Am. Jour. Physics, 1980—, Solar Energy Jour., 1983-87, 38th Internat. Sci. and Engring. Fair, 1987; mem. U.S. tech. adv. group of ISO TC-180, 1981—. Mem. editl. bd. Internat. Jour. Energy, Environ. Econs., 1990—; co-editor Procs. Internat. Conf. Energy for Ams., 1987; contbr. over 80 articles to profl. jours. and procs. Grantee state and fed. agys., various edn. and rsch.founds.; Postdoctoral fellow U. Liverpool, England, 1968-69; recipient commendation State of Kans., 1977. Mem. Am. Phys. Soc., Nat. Coun. Univ. Rsch. Adminstrs., Soc. Rsch. Adminstrs., Internat. Solar Energy Soc., Internat. Energy Soc. (sci. coun. 1985—), Sigma Phi Sigma. Roman Catholic. Avocations: reading, tennis, travel. Achievements include research in plasma physics and alternative energy sources; managment and administration.

PYTTE, AGNAR, physicist, former university president; b. Kongsberg, Norway, Dec. 23, 1932; arrived in U.S., 1949, naturalized, 1965; s. Ole and Edith (Christiansen) Pytte; m. Anah Currie Loeb, June 18, 1955; children: Anders H., Anthony M., Alyson C. AB, Princeton U., 1953; AM, Harvard U., 1954, PhD, 1958. Faculty Dartmouth Coll., 1958—87, prof. physics, 1967—87, chmn. dept. physics and astronomy, 1971—75, assoc. dean faculty, 1975—78, dean grad. studies, 1975—78, provost, 1982—87; pres. Case Western Res. U., Cleve., 1987—99; adj. prof. physics Dartmouth Coll., 1999—. Rschr. in plasma physics; mem. Project Matterhorn Princeton U., 1959—60, U. Brussels, 1966—67, Princeton U., 1978—79; bd. dirs. Goodyear Tire & Rubber Co., 1988—. Bd. dirs. Accreditation Coun. for Grad. Med. Edn., 2000—, Environ. Careers Orgn., 2003—, Sherman Fairchild Found., Inc., 1987—. Mem.: Am. Phys. Soc., Sigma Xi, Phi Beta Kappa. E-mail: agnar.x.pytte@dartmouth.edu.

PYZOW, SUSAN VICTORIA, artist, educator; b. Bronx, Oct. 27, 1955; d. John and Helen Pyzow; m. Paul Marcus. BFA, Cooper Union, 1976; MFA, Buffalo U., 1978. Instr. painting and drawing Parsons Sch. Design, N.Y.C., 1984—96; tchr. art Ethical Culture Fieldston Sch., 2000—01. One person shows include Caldwell (N.J.) Coll., 1994, Elements of Art Gallery, Columbus, Ohio, 1997; exhibited in group shows N.Y. Pub. Libr., N.Y.C., 1981, P.P.O.W. Gallery, N.Y.C., 1984, The Print Club, Phila., 1987, Mus. Modern Art, N.Y.C., 1988, NY State Mus., Albany, 1990, Spencer Art Mus., Kansas City, 1990, Ann. Juried Exhbn., N.Y.C., 1992, Mus. Contemporary Art, Chgo., 1992, Gallery Three-Zero, N.Y.C., 1993, Butler Inst. Am. Art, Youngstown, Ohio, 1993. Recipient Mervin Honig Meml. award in painting Audubon Artists, Nat. Arts Club, 1992, Ava award for works on paper Assn. for Visual Artists, 1992, Labutis Klue award in painting Am. Artists Profl. League, Salamagundi Club, 1992, Marion de Sola Mendes award Nat. Soc. Painters in Casein and Acrylic, 1996, Fed. Res. Bank of

N.Y. Purchase prize, 2000, 1st place Acrylic prize Joyce Dutka Found., 2002, winner Open Studios Competition, 1997, Anna Hyatt Huntington award Catharine Lorillard Wolfe Art Club, 1998; grantee in oil painting Ludwig Vogelstein Found., 1993, 96, 98.

QADRI, YASMEEN, educational administrator, consultant; b. Hyderabad, India, June 12, 1955; came to U.S., 1979; d. Ghulam and Bilquees Mahmood; m. Najeeb Qadri, Oct. 8, 1978; children: Kamran, Farhan, Sumayya. BA, St. Francis Coll., Hyderabad, 1976; MA in Psychology, Osmania U., Hyderabad, 1978; MA in Social Sci., U. Ctrl. Fla., Orlando, 1991, EdD in Curriculum and Instrn., 1994. Tchr. Indian Embassy Sch. and Minaret-e-Jeddah, Jeddah, Saudi Arabia, 1981-84; asst. adminstr. Muslim Acad. Ctrl. Fla., Orlando, 1991-93, adminstr., 1993—, prin., 1994—. Profl. interaction Trinity Prep. Sch., Orlando, 1993—. Cons. NCCJ, Orlando, 1992—. Recipient Cert. of Appreciation, Orange County Pub. Schs., 1992, Islamic Coun. Calif., 1993. Mem. ASCD, Muslim Women's Assn., Kappa Delta Pi. Moslem. Avocations: counseling, multicultural education, cooking, tourism. Office: Muslim Acad Ctrl Fla 1005 N Goldenrod Rd Orlando FL 32807-8326

QIAN, SHINAN, optical engineer, researcher, educator; b. Hong Kong, June 8, 1939; s. Xiaobo Qian and Lianyin Fung; m. Zhiping Zhang, May 18, 1970; children: Jin, Kun. B in Engring., Beijing Tsinghua U., 1962. Tchg. asst. Beijing Tsinghua U., 1962-71; asst. engr. Inst. Cement Equipment Tangshan, China, 1971-73; engr., group head Inst. Optics Fine Mechics Anhui, Acad. Sinica, Hefei, China, 1973-84; rschr., prof., group head U. Sci. Tech. China, Acad. Sinica, Hefei, 1984-91; rschr., group head Sincrotrone Trieste, Italy, 1991-97; rsch. engr. Brookhaven (N.Y.) Nat. Lab., 1997—. Scientist Brookhaven (N.Y.) Nat. Lab., 1985-87. Recipient People's Rep. China Sci. Tech. Accomplishment award, 1983; R&D 100 award Rsch. and Devel. Mag., 1993. Achievements include patents for surface profiling interferometer, computerized micro-displacement instrument using interference method, inclination beam interferometer for expansion measuring and equipment, quick vacuum actuator. Office: Brookhaven Nat Lab Bldg 535B Upton NY 11973-5000 E-mail: qian@bnl.gov.

QUACKENBUSH, CATHY ELIZABETH, secondary school educator; b. Carthage, N.Y., Sept. 20, 1949; d. James Adrian and Miriam June (Fickes) Seaman; m. Roger E. Quackenbush, March 31, 1973; 1 child, Thomas Bradford. AAS, SUNY, Morrisville, 1969; BS, SUNY, Albany, 1971, MS, 1976; attended, U. Ga., 1978, Cornell U., 1984, U. Calif., 1986, SUNY, Albany, 1986-87. Cert. tchr., N.Y. Tchr., 7th grade sci. Bethlehem Ctrl. Middle Sch., Delmar, N.Y., 1971-92; tchr., biology Bethlehem Ctrl. High Sch., Delmar, N.Y., 1992—. Bd. dirs. Bethlehem Opportunities Unlimited-Corp. for Substance Abuse Prevention, Delmar, 1983-91, 96-98; organizer and co-adv. Bethlehem Ctrl. Leadership Club, 1985-89; chair Middle Sch. Final Assessment Com., 1990-91, Middle Sch. Restructuring Com., 1991-92; organizer and leader Student Ednl. Tours to Kenya, East Africa, 1985, 89, 91, 94, 96, 98; rater and question writer for N.Y. State Regents Competency Exam in Sci., N.Y. State Edn. Dept., Albany, 1990-92; summer participant Cornell Inst. Biology Tchrs., 1996-2000. Sunday sch. tchr. Bethany Reformed Ch., 1988-92. N.Y. State Environ. Coun. and N.Y. State Outdoor Edn. Assn. grantee N.Y. State Outdoor Edn. Inst., 1979, NSF grantee DNA Inst. for Middle Sch. Tchrs., 1990, Human Genetics and Bioethics grantee Greenwall Found., 1993, Molecular Biology for Tchrs. grantee Howard Hughes Med. Inst., 1993, co-inst., 1994-98, 2001. Mem. Delta Kappa Gamma Soc. (sec. 1987-90, 2d v.p. 1990-92). Avocations: traveling, sailing, motorcycling. Home: 25 Robinhood Rd Albany NY 12203-5133 Office: Bethlehem Ctrl High Sch 700 Delaware Ave Delmar NY 12054-2436

QUACKENBUSH, ROGER E. retired secondary school educator; b. Cooperstown, N.Y., Jan. 22, 1940; s. Eugene W. and Marion I. (Clark) Q.; m. Cathy E. Quackenbush, Mar. 31, 1973; children: Michele, Stacey, Thomas. BS, SUNY, Albany, 1961, MS, 1966; PhD, Columbia Pacific U., San Rafael, Calif., 1984; postgrad., numerous univs. Cert. permanent biology and gen. sci. tchr., N.Y. Tchr. gen. sci. and math Troy (N.Y.) Pub. Sch. System, 1961-64; tchr. earth sci. and biology Schuylerville (N.Y.) Cen. H.S., 1964-66; tchr. biology Bethlehem Cen. H.S., Delmar, N.Y., 1966-95; cons. advanced placement biology Niskayuna (N.Y.) H.S., 1995-96; instr. anatomy and physiology lab. Russell Sage Coll., Troy, N.Y., 1996-97. Mentor student tchrs., 1968-90; instr. Tchr. Expectation Student Achievement program, 1985-91; lectr. on marine mammals SUNY, Albany, 1986; instr. DNA Sci. and Tech. for h.s. students SUNY, Albany, 1996; lectr. on whales; workshop leader on use microcomputers in classroom; former mem. Mid States Commn. on Evaluation Local H.S.'s; past mem. adv. bd. Upstate N.Y. Jr. Sci. and Humanities Symposium; test writer Regents biology exams. N.Y. State Dept. Edn.; presenter/cons. N.Y. State Edn. Dept. alt. assessment writer's workshop, 1994; leader, naturalist for whale watch trips and Kenya safaris; presenter for DNA-molecular biology lab. techniques; presenter on use of Tex. Instruments calculator and the Calculator Based Lab. sys. in the sci. classroom; mem Select Seminar on Evaluating Tchrs., 1985; mem. Wells Conf. Regents Biology Syllabus Revision, 1991; faculty cons. AP Biology reading Coll. Bd. Advanced Placement Program, 1997-98; cons. DNA molecular biology technology Greater Capital Region Tchr. Ctr., 1988-2001; instnl. animal care and use com. N.Y. State Health Dept., 1999-2001. Author: Once Upon a Yesterday, 2000, Adrift Upon the Air, 2001, Sketches of the Mind, 2002; editor/writer of alternative assessments for N.Y. State Edn. Dept., 1993-94; contbr. articles to profl. jours.; author: Swahili Phrasebook, 1993. Hon. admisssions liaison officer USAF Acad., 1988. Recipient Eagle award Boy Scouts Am., 1956, Excellence in Tchg. award, 1989, letter of commendation U. Chgo., 1978, MIT, 1985, U.S. Army, 1989, Tufts U., 1990, 94, 97, Tchr. of Yr. award Tufts U., 1985, Golub Tchr.-Scholar award SUNY, 1991, 96; Chpt. II grantee N.Y. State Dept. Edn., 1987, NSF grantee, 1965, 67, 68, 72, 87, 90, Future Directions, 1990, Greenwall Found., 1993, hon. mention Tandy Tech. Scholar award, 1994, Tandy Tech. Scholar prize for excellence in sci. tchg., 1995, Outstanding Tchr. award U. Chgo., 1995; named Hon. Grad. Marshal, 1991, 94, hon. N.Y. State Biology Mentor, 1995. Mem. NEA, Nat. Assn. Biology Tchrs., BALSA, Soc. Marine Mammalogy, Am. Cetacean Soc., Cetacean Soc. Internat., Sci. Tchrs. Assn. N.Y. State (past sect. dir., past state bd. dirs.), NEA of N.Y., Phi Delta Kappa. Home: 25 Robinhood Rd Albany NY 12203-5133 E-mail: rquacken@nycap.rr.com.

QUADE, ROBERT THOMAS, business educator; b. Elizabeth, N.J., Feb. 12, 1929; s. Joseph M. and Myra (Tetter) Q.; m. Rita Elizabeth Kaiser; children: James Ross, Christopher Sean, C. Corey Ian. BA, U. Ozarks, Clarksville, Ark., 1950; MBA, State U. Iowa, 1953; AS (hon.), Churchmans Coll., 2002. Instr. U. Ark., Fayetteville, 1953-54; mktg. rsch. mgr. Am. Type Founders, Elizabeth, N.J., 1954-55, Sinclair & Valentine, N.Y.C., 1955-56, Ethicon, Inc., Somerville, N.J., 1956-64, new products mgr., 1966-70; sales mgr. Arbrook, Inc., Somerville, 1964-66; dir. product devel./evaluation N.Y.C. Health and Hosp. Corp., 1970-87; chair undergrad. bus. Centenary Coll., Hackettstown, NJ, 1987—2002, exec. in residence coord., 1988—, chair grad. bus., 1998—, dir. life learning, 1997—. Adj. instr. Rutgers U., New Brunswick, N.J., Fairleigh Dickinson U., Madison, N.J., 1955-80; coord. Asian Mgmt. Tng. Inst., Hackettstown, 1992; cons. Exxon, C.R. Bard, Quest Internat., French Govt., Port Authority of N.Y./N.J. Patentee (2) in field of medicine. Pres., mem. Bd. of Edn., Bernardsville, N.J., 1963-70; conferee Gov.'s Conf. on Edn., Trenton, N.J., 1968; survey cons. ARC, Girl Scouts U.S., NOW, Mayor of Hackettstown and of Morristown, 1975—, Andover Regional Sch. Dist., 1999, Warren County C. of C., 2000; mem. acad. advising coun. Thomas Edison State Coll., Trenton, 1993—; apptd. nat. adv. bd. Fordham U., N.Y.C.. Recipient Minority Rights Commendation, Mayor Koch of N.Y.C., 1985. Mem. N.J. Collegiate Bus. Adminstrs. Assn. (v.p., pres. 1992-94), Middle-Atlantic Assn. Colls. of Bus. Adminstrn., Alpha Sigma Lambda (advisor 1992-97, sec. mid-Atlantic region Internat. Assembly of Collegiate Bus. Edn., 2002—). Avocations: stamp collecting, coaching college wrestling. Home: 37 Oak Pl Bernardsville NJ 07924-1806 Office: Centenary College 400 Jefferson St Hackettstown NJ 07840-2100 E-mail: profq1@aol.com., rquade@centenarycollege.edu.

QUADER, PATRICIA ANN, elementary education educator; b. Pitts., Sept. 9, 1941; d. Andrew and Julia Supira; m. Walter Anthony Quader, Jan. 15, 1966. BA, Carlow Coll., 1963; MEd, U. Pitts., 1967. Cert. elem. tchr., supt., Pa. Tchr. Diocese of Pitts., 1963-64; tutor Pitts. Tchrs. Tutoring Svc., 1964-65; intern tchr. Burrell Sch. Dist., Lower Burrell, Pa., 1966; tchr. Kiski Area Sch. Dist., Vandergrift, Pa., 1966-91; computer, libr. skills tchr. Vandergrift Elem. Sch., North Washington Elem. Schs., 1991—. Instr. Pa. State U., New Kensington, 1970-72, parent and tchrs. workshops, 1999-2001; in-svc. instr. in computer literacy Kiski Area Sch. Dist., 1985-91, 95-98, edited K-3 computer skills curriculum. Co-author: 4th and 5th grade computer literacy curricula for Kiski Sch. Dist.; editor Kiski Area K-6 Computer Skills Curriculum, 1991—. Chmn. Bell-Avon PTA, Salina, Pa., 1988-91. Recipient scholarship Carlow Coll., 1959. Mem. NEA, ASCD, Pa. State Edn. Assn., Kiski Area Edn. Assn., Phi Delta Kappa. Democrat. Roman Catholic. Avocations: mystery novels, computer games. Office: Vandergrift Elem Sch 420 Franklin Ave Vandergrift PA 15690-1311

QUAIFE, MARJORIE CLIFT, retired nursing educator; b. Syracuse, N.Y., Aug. 21; Diploma in Nursing with honors, Auburn Meml. Hosp; BS, Columbia U., 1962, MA, 1978. Cert. orthopaedic nurse; cert. in nursing continuing edn. and staff devel.; BLS instr. Staff instr. Columbia Presbyn. Hosp., N.Y.C., 1968-97, ret., 1997. Content expert for computer assisted instrn. program-ctrl. venous catheters. Contbr. articles to numerous profl. publs. Mem. ANA, N.Y. State Nurses Assn., Nat. Assn. Orthopaedic Nurses, Nat. Assn. Nursing Staff Devel., Nat. Assn. Vascular Access Networks, Intravenous Nurses Soc., Sigma Theta Tau.

QUAINTANCE, ALICE LYNN, elementary school media specialist; b. Morristown, Tenn., July 20, 1958; d. Celton D. and Mary Lou (Scott) VanCleave; m. David Scott Quaintance, Aug. 2, 1980; children: Jennifer Lee, Allison Marie. BS, East Tenn. State U., 1980. Media specialist Surgoinsville (Tenn.) Elem. Sch., 1980-82, Clearwood Jr. H.S., Slidell, La., 1982-83, 84-86, tchr., 1983-84; media specialist Rose Park Mid. Sch., Nashville, 1987-88, Hermitage (Tenn.) Elem. Sch., 1988—; owner Just Acquaintances. Publicity chairperson Donelson/Hermitage (Tenn.) Neighborhood Assn., 1995-97; parent rep. Nashville Ballet Friends, 1997-99. Recipient Dalcon Arts in Schs. award Nashville Inst. for the Arts, 1992, Merit award Gov. Tenn., 1993, Acts of Excellence award Mayor of Nashville, 1994, Golden Apple award Metro Nashville Pub. Schs., 1996, Vol. of Yr. award Nashville Ballet, 1998, Svc. Above Self Tchr. award Rotary Club, 2003. Mem. NEA, Tenn. Edn. Assn., Met. Nashville Edn. Assn., Delta Kappa Gamma (sec. 1993-97). United Methodist. Avocation: the arts. Home: 3826 Pacifica Dr Hermitage TN 37076-1926

QUALLS, JUNE CAROL, elementary school educator; b. Ft. Worth, June 22, 1954; d. Earl Clayton and Viola Maurine (McFaul) Irvin; m. Richard Eugene Qualls, Apr. 20, 1984. BS, Tarleton State Coll., 1976; MEd, East Tex. State U., 1979, cert. in spl. edn., 1992, cert. in ednl. diagnostics, 1993. Cert. elem. tchr., Tex. Tchr. kindergarten Elisha M. Pease Elem. Sch., Dallas, 1979-80, 87-91, Mt. Auburn Elem. Sch., Dallas, 1983-84; tchr. jr. high sch. Maypearl (Tex.) Ind. Sch. Dist., 1980-83; edn. specialist Alaska Headstart-Rural Cap, Anchorage, 1984-85; multi-level tchr. Tom Thumb Montessori Sch., Anchorage, 1985-87; tchr. 2d grade John Neely Bryan Elem. Sch., Dallas, 1991-92; tchr. kindergarten, chairperson kindergarten John Q. Adams Elem. Sch., Dallas, 1993-94, mentor tchr., 1993-94, tchr. spl. edn. resource/content mastery, 1995-98; ednl. diagnostician Individual Assessment for Dallas Pub. Schs., Dallas, 1998—. Mentor tchr. Elisha M. Pease Elem. Sch., 1989-90; math. coord. Maypearl Jr. H.S., 1980-83. Contbg. writer curriculum materials for gifted edn. Mem. Tex. Diagnostician Assn. Avocations: camping, archaelogical interests, sewing, reading, natural history. Office: Individual Assessment for Dallas Pub Schs South Ervay St Dallas TX 75217 E-mail: jcqualls@wt.net.

QUALLS, SOPHRONIA ANITA, elementary school educator; b. Enfield, N.C., Dec. 31, 1955; d. Waldo and Olympia (Solomon) Q.; m. Charles Wayne Foster, Sept. 30, 1989; 1 child, Sydney. BA, N.C. Ctrl. U., 1978. Cert. tchr., N.C. Tchr. Orange County Schs., Hillsborough, N.C., 1978-92; Kindergarten tchr. Cobb County (Ga.) Schs., Smyrna, 1992—. Dem. judge Durham (N.C.) County Bd. Election; active Cobb-Marietta Jr. League. Mem. NEA, N.C. Ctrl. U. Alumni Assn., Delta Sigma Theta. Avocations: jogging, collecting elephants, decorating, real estate. Home: 3203 Whiteoak Cir Smyrna GA 30082-3363 Office: 3515 Spring Hill Rd SE Smyrna GA 30080-4649

QUALSET, CALVIN O. plant genetics and agronomy educator; b. Newman Grove, Nebr., Apr. 24, 1937; s. Herman Qualset and Adeline (Hanson) Vakoc; m. Kathleen Boehler; children: Douglas, Cheryl, Gary. BS, U. Nebr., 1958; MS, U. Calif., Davis, 1960, PhD, 1964. Asst. prof. U. Tenn., Knoxville, 1964-67; from asst. prof. to assoc. prof. U. Calif., Davis, 1967, prof., 1973-94, prof. emeritus, 1994—, chmn. dept. agronomy and range sci., 1975-81, 91-94, assoc. dean coll. agrl. and environ. sci., 1981-86; dir. Genetic Resources Conservation Program, Davis, 1985—2002. Sci. liaison officer U.S. Agy. Internat. Devel., Washington, 1985-93, rsch. adv. com., 1989-92; nat. plant genetic resources bd. USDA, Washington, 1982-88; bd. trustees Am. Type Culture Collection, 1993-99, Internat. Rice Rsch. Inst., 1999-, Agronomic Sci. Found., 1999—. Contbr. over 200 articles to profl. jours. Bd. dirs. Auksuciai Found., 1999—; contbr. to wheat improvement in Mex. citation, 1988. Fulbright fellow, Australia, 1976, Yugoslavia, 1984; recipient Pub. Plant Breeding award U.S. Coun. Comml. Plant Breeders, 1996, Charles Black award Coun. Agrl. Sci. and Tech., 2002, William L. Brown award Mo. Bot. Garden, 2002, Master Alumni award U. Nebr., 1997. Fellow AAAS (chmn. agr. sect. 1992), Am. Soc. Agronomy (pres. 1994, agronomy honoree Calif. sect. 2001), Crop Sci. Soc. Am. (pres. 1989, editor-in-chief 1980-84); mem. Soc. Conservation Biology, Soc. Econ. Botany, Genetic Soc. Am., Internat. Union Biol. Scis. (mem. U.S. nat. com. 2000—). Achievements include development of more than 15 cultivars of wheat, oat, triticale. Office: U Calif Genetic Res Conserv Prog One Shields Ave Davis CA 95616

QUAM, JON, educational association administrator; b. Glasgow, Mont., May 21, 1949; s. Clifford L. and Kathryn (Lien) Q. MusB, Concordia Coll., 1970. Tchr., music Hysham (Mont.) Pub. Schs., 1970-73; dir., music Cavalier Prodns., Washington, 1973-75; tchr., music Big Timber (Mont.) Pub. Schs., 1975-80; supr., fine arts State of Mont., Helena, 1980-84; grants specialist NEA, Washington, 1984-88; dir. Sch./Coll. Collaboration Project, Washington, 1988-90, Nat. Tchr. of Yr. Programs, Washington, 1989—; dir. arts edn. projects Coun. Chief State Sch Officers, Washington, 1990—. Accompanist, Washington, 1973-75. Recipient NEA Disting. Svc. award, 1986. Avocations: opera, travel.*

QUANDT, RICHARD EMERIC, economics educator; b. Budapest, Hungary, June 1, 1930; came to U.S., 1949, naturalized, 1954; s. Richard F. and Elisabeth (Toth) Q.; m. Jean H. Briggs, Aug. 6, 1955; 1 son, Stephen. BA, Princeton U., 1952; MA, Harvard U., 1955, PhD, 1957; Dr. Econs. (hon.), Budapest U. Econs. Scis., 1991, Kossuth Lajos U., Hungary, 1994, Gödöllő Agrl. U., 1995, Comenius U., Slovakia, 1996; DrLaws (hon.), Queens U., Can., 1996. Mem. faculty Princeton U., 1956-95, prof. econs., 1964-95, prof. emeritus, sr. rsch. economist, 1995—, Hughes-Rogers prof. econs., 1976-95; prof. emeritus, 1995—; chmn. dept. Princeton U., 1968-71, 85-88; dir. Fin. Rsch. Ctr., 1982-95; rsch. prof. Ford Found., 1967-68; prof. emeritus, sr. rsch. economist Princeton U., 1995—. Cons. Alderson Assocs., 1959-61; sr. cons. Mathematica, Inc., 1961-67; cons. Internat. Air Transport Assn., 1974-75, N.Y. Stock Exch., 1976-77, N.Y. State Dept. Edn., 1978; adviser Am.-Hungarian Found., 1977-78; editorial advisor Holt, Rinehart & Winston, 1968-72; fin. adviser Inst. for Rsch. in History, 1986; sr. advisor Andrew W. Mellon Found., 1989—; mem. adv. coun. Budapest U. Econ. Scis., 1992-93; vis. prof. Birkbeck Coll., 1981, U. Leicester, 1989-92; mem. Census Adv. Com., 1983-86; mem. adv. com. Coll. Fin. and Acctg., Budapest, 1993-94; bd. dirs. CERGE-EI Found. Author: (with J. M. Henderson) Microeconomic Theory: A Mathematical Approach, 1958, 2d edit., 1971, 3d edit., 1980, (with W.L. Thorp) The New Inflation, 1959, (with B.G. Malkiel) Strategies and Rational Decisions in the Securities Option Market, 1969; editor: The Demand for Travel: Theory and Measurement, 1970; (with S.M. Goldfeld) Nonlinear Methods in Econometrics, 1972, Studies in Nonlinear Estimation, 1976; (with P. Asch) Racetrack Betting: The Professor's Guide to Strategies, 1986, (with M. Peston) Prices, Competition and Equilibrium, 1986, The Econometrics of Disequilibrium, 1988, (with H.S. Rosen) The Conflict Between Equilibrium and Disequilibrium Theories, 1988, (with R. Ekman) Technology and Scholarly Communication, 1999, The Changing Landscape in Eastern Europe: A Personal Perspective on Philanthropy and Technology Transfer, 2002; mem. editl. bd. Applied Econs., Econs. Planning, Rev. Econ. and Stats., 1980-91; assoc. editor: Econometrica, 1976-80, Jour. Am. Statis. Assn, 1974-80, Bell Jour. Econs., Jour. of Comparative Econs., 1988-91, Empirica, 1988-93; exec. editor Oxford U. Press, 2001—; contbr. articles to profl. jours. Trustee Corvina Found., 1992—. Recipient merit citation Jagiellonian U., Poland, 1991, Gold medal Eötvös Lóránd U., Budapest, 1991, Order of Merit, Govt. of Republic of Hungary, 1997, Medal Merentibus, Jagiellonian U., Poland, 1998; Guggenheim fellow, 1958-59; McCosh fellow, 1964; NSF sr. postdoctoral fellow, 1971-72. Fellow Am. Statis. Assn., Econometric Soc. (mem. coun. 1985-88), Am. Acad. Arts and Scis.; mem. Am. Econ. Assn., Am. Philos. Soc., Hungarian Librs. Assn. (hon.). Home: 162 Springdale Rd Princeton NJ 08540-4948 Office: Princeton U Fin Rsch Ctr Dept Econs Ctr Princeton NJ 08544-1021

QUARCOO, MARILYNNE SMITH, principal; b. Boston, Dec. 11, 1950; d. Ernest Harold and Doris Mae (Jemmotte) S.; m. Gideon Kwame Quarcoo, Mar. 26, 1978; 1 child, Esinam Dede. BA in Elem. Edn., Boston Coll., 1972, M Edn. Edn. Psych., 1974. Reading tchr. K-8 Brookline (Mass.) Pub. Sch., 1974-75, multicultural tchr., 1975-77, tchr. second grade, 1977-87; METCO dir. K-12 Wellesley (Mass.) Pub. Sch., 1987-90; elem. prin. Cabot Sch. Newton (Mass.) Pub. Schs., 1990—. Staff devel. cons. Brookline, 1978-80; curriculum developer Wellesley Pub. Schs., 1990; facilitator Wheelock Coll., Boston, 1992; presenter AERA convention, 1994. Mem. NAACP; trustee Agassiz Village Campe, Waltham, Mass., 1991-94. Recipient award for racial, ethnic and religious harmony, Newton, Mass., 1994, Marion V. Thomas award. Mem. ASCD, AERA, Nat. Alliance Black Sch. Educators, Brookline Sch. Found. Avocations: travel, reading. Office: Cabot Sch 229 Cabot St Newton MA 02460-2018

QUARLES, PEGGY DELORES, secondary school educator; b. Dalton, Ga., July 14, 1947; d. Henry Lemuel and Mae Bradford (Hester) Q. BA, Trevecca Nazarene Coll., 1969; MEd, U. Ga., 1981; EdS, West Ga. Coll., 1987; EdD, Univ. Sarasota, 2001. English tchr. Darlington County Schs., Lamar, S.C., 1969-78, Murray County Schs., Chatsworth, Ga., 1978—. Mem. Shakespeare Inst., NEH, Washington, 1985, Writing Inst., Boulder, Colo., 1988, Italian Renaissance Inst., Del., Ohio and Florence, Italy, 1990, Women in Renaissance Inst., Richmond, Va., 1992; participant Armonk Inst. to Germany, 1998. ARC, 1987—; mem. Dalton Little Theater, 1980—; bd. dirs. Friends of Libr., 1989—92; mem. NW Ga. Humane Soc. Named Teacher of Yr., Murray County Bd. of Edn., 1989, Murray County Schs., 2001—02. Mem. NEA, Nat. Coun. Tchrs. English, Ga. Coun. Tchrs. English (H.S. English Tchr. of Yr. 1994-95), Carpet Capital Running Club (pres. 1980-82, v.p. 1993-94), Lesche Lit. Club (v.p. 2001—). Avocations: running, travel, cooking, reading, attending plays.

QUAST, PEARL ELIZABETH KOLB, retired elementary school educator; b. Omro, Wis., Nov. 21, 1934; d. Frank Kolb and Lavon Opal Buchanan; m. Arthur Roman Quast; children: Arthur R. Jr., Robert F.;1 child, John M. BS in Edn., Edgewood Coll., Madison, Wisconsin, 1956; MA in Edn., Cardinal Stritch Coll., Milw., 1971. Cert. tchr. unlimited 0743, K-3 Wis., remedial reading 42 and 27 (K-12), reading specialist 42 and 27 (K-12). Tchr. grade 2 Deerfield (Ill.) Pub. Schs., 1956—58; tchr. grade 3 Whitefish Bay (Wis.) Pub. Schs., 1958—60; tchr. reading Milw. Pub. Schs., 1969—75; reading specialist Germantown (Wis.) Pub. Schs., 1975—91. Seminar presenter Reading Assn., Milw., 1982—86; vol. coord. The Cath. Ctr., Sun City West, 1998—99; coord. lectors Our Lady of Lourdes Ch., Sun City West, 1996—2003, lector, cantor, choir mem., Sun City West and Phoenix, 1995—2003. Bd. trustees Found. for Sr. Living, Phoenix, 1998—2001; group leader founding com. Cath. Ctr. for Srs.' Needs, Sun City and Sun City West, 1995—2001; coord. lectors Our Lady of Lourdes Ch., 1996—2003, mem.; del. Phoenix Diocesan Synod, 2002—03; Bd. trustees Symphony of the West Valley, Sun City West, 1996—2002. Mem.: AAUW (v.p. membership 1994—96), West Valley Art Mus. (sec. Woman's League 1994—96), Cath. Ctr. (founding officer, v.p. adv. com. 1996—2000, Cert. Appreciation), Found. for Sr. Living, Weavers West Handweaving Guild, Our Lady of Lourdes Church. Roman Catholic. Avocations: handweaving, travel, singing, reading, cultural arts.

QUATAERT, DONALD, history educator; b. Rochester, N.Y., Sept. 10, 1941; s. William Leonard and Norine Louise (Katzenberger) Q.; m. 1963 (div.); 1 child, Laurie; m. Jean H. Grebler, Jan. 24, 1970; 1 child, Eliot. AB, Boston U., 1966; MA, Harvard U., 1968; PhD, UCLA, 1974. Asst. prof. U. Houston, 1974-79, assoc. prof., 1979-87, Binghamton (N.Y.) U., 1988-94, prof., 1994—. Vis. assoc. prof. Binghamton U., 1987-88. Author: Social Disintegration, 1983, Manufacturing and Technology, 1992, Ottoman Manufacturing, 1993; co-editor: An Economic and Social History of the Ottoman Empire, 1300-1914, 1994, The Ottoman Empire 1700-1922, 2000. NEH Sr. fellow, 1985-86, 1999-2000, Social Sci. Rsch. fellow, 1985-86, 1998, Fgn. Area fellow, 1980-81, Guggenheim fellow, 2004—. Mem. Am. Hist. Assn., Mid. East Studies Assn., Turkish Studies Assn. Avocations: tennis, golf, stamp collecting, birdwatching. Home: 4600 Deerfield Pl Vestal NY 13850-3757

QUATE, CALVIN FORREST, engineering educator; b. Baker, Nev., Dec. 7, 1923; s. Graham Shepard and Margie (Lake) Quate; m. Dorothy Marshall, June 28, 1945 (div. 1985); children: Robin, Claudia, Holly, Rhodalee; m. Arnice Streit, Jan. 1987. BS in Elec. Engring, U. Utah, 1944; PhD, Stanford U., 1950. Mem. tech. staff Bell Telephone Labs., Murray Hill, N.J., 1949-58; dir. research Sandia Corp., Albuquerque, 1959-60, v.p. research, 1960-61; prof. dept. applied physics and elec. engring. Stanford (Calif.) U., 1961-95, chmn. applied physics, 1969-72, 78-81, Leland T. Edwards prof. engring., 1986—, assoc. dean Sch. Humanities and Scis., 1972-74, 82-83, rsch. prof. dept. elec. engring., 1995—. Sr. rsch. fellow Xerox Rsch. Ctr., Palo Alto, Calif., 1984—94. Served as lt. (j.g.) USNR, 1944—46. Recipient Rank prize for Opto-electronics, 1982, Pres.'s Nat. medal of Sci., 1992. Fellow: Acoustical Soc., Am. Acad. Arts and Scis., IEEE; mem.: Royal Soc., Royal Microscop. Soc., Am. Phys. Soc., NAS, NAE, Tau Beta Pi, Sigma Xi. Office: Stanford U E L Ginzton Lab Palo Alto CA 94305-4085

QUAY, GREGORY HARRISON, retired secondary school educator; b. Detroit, Dec. 4, 1937; s. Edward H. and Frances J. (Keena) Q. BS in Edn., Wayne State U., 1960, MEd, 1963, MA in Teaching Math., 1966. Cert. math., history and English tchr., Mich. Tchr. Detroit Pub. Schs., 1960-69; cons. Macomb County Intermediate Sch. Dist., Mt. Clemens, Mich., 1969-70; tchr. math. Warren (Mich.) Consol. Schs., 1970-99; ret., 1999—. Activities writer SRA Pub. Co., Chgo., 1970-71, summer assoc. U.S. Army

Tank Automotive Command, Warren, 1986-91, 93-94, 96-97. Author: (manual) Photacoustics and Photoacoustic Spectroscopy, 1986, Thermal Wave Interferometry Applied to Thermally Thick Samples, 1988, A Theoretical Model for Thermal Wave Interferometry Applied to a Two-Layer Coating, 1989, One Dimensional Single Layer Photacoustic Theory, 1991, An Introduction to One Dimensional Dual Layer Thermal Wave/Photoacoustic Theory, 1996; co-author: An Introduction to One Dimensional Single Layer Thermal Wave/Photacoustic Theory, 1994, Use of Advanced Ceramics for Bearings and Engine Wear Applications (An Advanced Technology Assessment Report), 1996, Ceramic and Metal Coatings for Improved Engine Performance (An Advanced Technology Assessment Report), 1997; contbr. articles to profl. jours. Usher Redeemer Bapt. Ch., Warren, 1969-95, asst. treas., fin. sec., 1972-82; usher Bethany Bapt. Ch., Clinton Twp., 1996—; mem. bd. edn. Macomb Christian Schs., 1983-85. Named Tchr. of Yr., Warren Consol. Schs., 1984. Mem. Nat. Coun. Tchrs. Math. (life, editl. referee 1978-99), Mich. Coun. Tchrs. Math., Detroit Area Coun. Math. Tchrs. (life; v.p. 1969-70, treas. 1970-71, pres. 1971-72, co-founder Math. Field Day 1969, co-founder Myriad of Math. Merriment 1972). Avocations: reading, gardening, antique automobiles. Home: 14640 Talbot Dr Warren MI 48088-3825

QUAY, SHARON ROSE, special education educator; b. Pitts., Mar. 3, 1955; d. Joseph James and Caroline Marie (Tira) Gillono; m. Gary Robert Robinson, June 18, 1977 (div. Nov. 1988); children: Brad, Amy; m. A.J. Quay, July 21, 1990. BS in Elem. Edn., Ind. U. Pa., 1977. Cert. tchr., Pa. Tchr. elem. edn. Queen of the Univ. Elem. Sch., Levittown, Pa., 1979-84, Levittown area, 1984-88; tchr. spl. edn. Queen of the Universe Day Ctr., Levittown, 1988—. Piloted DISTAR reading program Queen of Universe Day Ctr., organizer Penn. State"Embryo" project, 1991-93, Meet The Plants project, 1991-93. Puppy raiser for seeing eye program Bucks County 4-H, Richboro, Pa., 1992; active Swan Pointe Civ. Assn., Neshaminy PTO. Mem. Nat. Cath. Edn. Assn., Coun. for Exceptional Children (sec. Bucks County chpt. # 348 1992), Middlestates Assn. for Colls. and Schs. (evaluator 1990—), Sons of Italy Lodge (charter). Democrat. Roman Catholic. Avocations: reading, tennis, dogs, victorian antiques, stained glass. Home: 267 Hidden Spring Ln Langhorne PA 19047-2328 Office: Queen of Universe Day Ctr 2443 Trenton Rd Levittown PA 19056-1424

QUEEN, JOYCE ELLEN, elementary school educator; b. Cleve., Mar. 17, 1945; d. Wilbur Raynor and Mae (Reid) Closterhouse; m. Robert Graham Queen, Mar. 17, 1973. BA in Biology, Macalester Coll., 1966; MS in Conservation and Natural Resource Mgmt., U. Mich., 1968. Cert. tchr. biol. and earth scis., Ohio. Exhibitor, docent, coord. Grand Rapids (Mich.) Pub. Mus., 1967-68; tchr., naturalist Rose Tree-Media (Pa.) Outdoor Edn., 1967, Willoughby-Eastlake (Ohio) Schs., 1969-70, Independence (Ohio) Schs., 1970-78; sci. tchr. grades 1-7, coord. sci. field trip Hathaway Brown Sch., Cleve., 1970—, primary sci. educator, 1970—, primary sci. dept. chair, 1998—2002, prime sci. dept. head, 2003. Designer Courtland Woods nature trail, 1986, designer sci. greenhouse, 1990-92; designer sci. classroom Van Dyke Architects/Hathaway Brown Sch., 1990-92; designer, coord. Dampeer Primary sci. courtyard, 1993, Oliva Herb Garden, 1998, Colini Landscape Design/Hathaway Brown Sch., Shaker Hts., Ohio; mem. ednl. adv. com. William G. Mather Vessel Mus., Cleve., 1992, Holden Arboretum, Kirtland, Ohio, 1992-97; workshop leader Lake Erie Islands Hist. Mus., South Bass Island, Ohio, 1992, H.B. Winter Sci. Symposium Workshop, 1994—; presenter Nat. Assn. Ind. Schs., Columbus, Ohio, 1993; workshop leader for schs. on garden design, sci. labs., and sci. discovery programs; youth divsn. judge Cleve. Botanic Garden Show, 1999, 2000, 2002, NOAA (with Betsy Youngman and Art Traverse) Live From Antarctica, 2003. Contbr. articles to profl. jours. Design cons. Cleve. Bot. Garden and Floral Scape, 1998; active Belize (Ctrl. Am.) Tchrs. Workshop, 1994. Catalyst grantee Hathaway Brown Sch. Gt. Lks. Curriculum, 1991; recipient Environ. Edn. award Ohio Alliance for Environment, 1986, Presdl. Excellence in Elem. Sci. Tchg. award NSF, 1992, Sheldon Exemplary Equipment and Facilities award, 1992; Great Lakes Lighthouse Keepers Assn. scholar; Marine Ecology scholar Marine Resources, Inc., 1989; Internat. Space Sta. Conf. scholar, 2000; Maine Salt Marsh Ecology Curriculum scholar, 2001; Calif. Coastal Wetlands and Desert Study scholar, 2002. Mem. NSTA (recipient Exemplary Environ. and Facilities award with Sheldon Mfg. Co. 1992), Cleve. Regional Coun. Sci. Tchrs., Cleve. Coun. Ind. Schs., Cleve. Natural Hist. Mus., Cleve. Zool. Park, Ind. Sch. Assn. Ctrl. Sts., Internat. Pen Pal Exchange Progam. Presbyterian. Avocations: orchardist, naturalist, horticulturist. Office: Hathaway Brown Sch 19600 N Park Blvd Cleveland OH 44122-1899 E-mail: jqueen@hb.edu.

QUELL, MARGARET ANNE, special education educator; b. Akron, Ohio, Oct. 21, 1942; d. John A and Donna Geraldine (Castello) Quell. BS with hons., Kent (Ohio) State U., 1966; student Inst. des Etrangers, University de Besancon, France, 1962—63; MS in Edn., U. Akron, Ohio, 1976; Grad. studies, U. Aix-Marseille, Aix-en-Provence France, 1968—69; EdD U. Akron, 1982. Cert. Supt. Ariz., Prin. Ariz. Asst. prin., truant officer Wooster (Ohio) City Schs., 1976—80; prin., dir. edn. Apple Creek (Ohio) Devel. Ctr., 1980—81; asst. prin., athletic dir. Mt. Vernon (Ohio) City Schools, 1981—86; cons. child study Columbiana Bd. Edn., Lisbon, Ohio, 1986—87; dir. spl. edn., coord. instrn. Kenston Bd. Edn., Chagrin Falls, Ohio, 1987—90; dir. children's programs Lake County Bd. Mental Retardation/Developmental Disabilities, Mentor, Ohio, 1990—98; dir. spl. edn. Chinle (Ariz.) Unified Sch. Dist., Navajo Nation, 1998—. Mem. adv. bd. Knox County Children's Svcs/, Mt. Vernon, Ohio, 1981—86; exec. dir. Kenston Found., Chagrin Falls, Ohio, 1988—90; mem. exec. coun. Ariz. Sch. for Deaf and Blind, Tucson, 1998—. Author: (Book) Sex Equity in Educational Leadership, 1982; editor: (Book (Hershberger) Amish Life Through a Child's Eyes, 1985. Co-chair silent auction Deepwood Industries, Mentor, Ohio, 1998—98; Lifetime Fellow New Directions Shelter, Mt. Vernon, Ohio, 1984; mem. Proposition 203 Com., Chinle, Ariz., 2000—01. Recipient Innovative Counseling award, John G. Odgers Assn., 1978; fellow Kellogg Fellowship, Kellogg Found. Leadership Program, 1984; grantee Crossage Mentoring, Navajo Workforce Devel., 2000. Mem.: Coun, for Exceptional Children, Nat. Assn. Suprs. Spl. Edn. Programs. Avocations: equine dentistry, music, reading, running, travel. Office: Chinle Unified Sch Dist P O Box 587 Chinle AZ 86503 Office Fax: 928-674-9586. Business E-Mail: mquell@netscape.net.

QUENEAU, PAUL ETIENNE, metallurgical engineer, educator; b. Phila., Mar. 20, 1911; s. Augustin L. and Jean (Blaisdell) Q.; m. Joan Osgood Hodges, May 20, 1939; children: Paul Blaisdell, Josephine Downs (Mrs. George Stanley Patrick). BA, Columbia U., 1931, BSc, 1932, M of Engring., 1933; postgrad., Cambridge (Eng.) U., 1934; DSc, Delft (Netherlands) U. Tech., 1971. With INCO, 1934-69; rsch. supt. Internat. Nickel Co., 1940-41, 46-48, v.p., 1958-69, chief tech. officer, tech. asst. to pres., 1960-66, asst. to chmn., 1967-69; vis. scientist Delft U. Tech., 1970-71; prof. engring. Dartmouth Coll., 1971-87, prof. emeritus, 1987—, Paul and Joan Queneal prof. in environ. design. Cons. engr., 1972—; vis. prof. U. Minn., 1974-75, U. Utah, 1987-91; geographer Perry River Arctic Expdn., 1949; chmn. arctic rsch. adv. com. USN, 1957; gov. Arctic Inst. N.Am., 1957-62; mem. engring. coun. Columbia U., 1965-70; mem. vis. com. MIT, Cambridge, 1967-70; mem. extractive metallurgy and mineral processing panels NAS; pres. Q-S Oxygen Processes Inc., 1974-79, also bd. dirs. Author: (with Hanson) Geography, Birds and Mammals of the Perry River Region, 1956; Cobalt and the Nickeliferous Limonites, 1971; editor: Extractive Metallurgy of Copper, Nickel and Cobalt, 1961; (with Anderson) Pyrometallurgical Processes in Nonferrous Metallurgy, 1965; The Winning of Nickel, 1967; contbr. articles to profl. jours.; patentee 500 internat. patents, 36 U.S. patents including processes and apparatus employed in the pyrometallurgy, hydrometallurgy and vapometallurgy of nickel, copper, cobalt, lead, zinc, iron and steel, extractive metallurgy oxygen tech. including INCO oxygen flash smelting, oxygen top-blown rotary converter, lateritic ore matte smelting, nickel high pressure carbonyl and iron ore recovery processes; co-inventor Lurgi QSL direct lead-making, QSOP direct coppermaking and nickelmaking reactors, Lurgi direct steelmaking reactors, and Dravo oxygen sprinkle smelting copper furnaces. Bd. dirs. Engring. Found., 1966-76, chmn. bd. dirs., 1973-75. With U.S. Army, 1942-45, ETO; col. C.E., USA ret.1971. Decorated Bronze Star, ETO Medal with 5 Battlestars, Army Commendation Medal USAR, 1937-42; Evans Fellow Cambridge U., 1933-34; recipient Egleston Medal Columbia U., 1965, Fletcher Award Dartmouth Coll., 1991, McGraw-Hill Chem. Engring. Award for Personal Achievement in Chem. Engring., 1996. Fellow Metall. Soc. of AIME (dir. 1964, 68-71, pres. 1969, Extractive Metallurgy Lecture award 1977, Paul E. Queneau TMS Internat. Symposium on Extractive Metallurgy of Copper, Nickel and Cobalt 1993); mem. AIME (Douglas Gold medal 1968, v.p. 1970, dir. 1968-71, Henry Krumb lectr. 1984, keynote lectr. ann. meeting 1990, award for personal achievement in chem. engring.), NAE, NSPE, Can. Inst. Mining and Metallurgy, Inst. Mining and Metallurgy U.K. (overseas mem. council 1970-80, Gold medal 1980), Sigma Xi, Tau Beta Pi. Achievements include 36 U.S. patents and 500 foreign patents. Office: Dartmouth Coll Thayer Sch Engring Hanover NH 03755

QUERY, JOY MARVES NEALE, medical sociology educator; b. Worcestershire, Eng. came to U.S., 1952; d. Samuel and Dorree (Oakley) Neale; children: Jonathan, Margo, Evan. AB, Drake U., 1954, MA, 1955; postgrad., U. Syracuse, 1955-56; PhD, U. Ky., 1960. Tchr. secondary schs., Staffordshire, Eng., 1947-52; dep. prin. Smethwich Hall Girls' Sch., Staffordshire, 1948-52; instr. U. Ky., 1956-57, asst. prof., 1960; assoc. prof. sociology Transylvania Coll., Lexington, Ky., 1961-66; assoc. prof. N.D. State U., Fargo, 1966-68, prof. sociology and psychology, 1969-75, also chmn. sociology and psychology depts., 1969-70, chmn. sociology and anthropology dept., 1968-73; prof. div. psychiatry behavioral sci., dept. neurosci. U. N.D. Sch. Medicine, Fargo, 1975-89, prof. emeritus, 1989—; on sabbatical leave Yale U., 1974-75. Coord. AIDS Edn. State Program NIMH, 1989-93. Mem. bd. adv. editors Sociological Inquiry jour., 1987-93; contbr. articles and papers to profl. jours. Field dir. Girl Scouts U.S.A., 1953-55; mem. Lexington Civil Rights Commn., 1960-66; bd. dirs. Fargo-Moorhead Family Service Agy., 1967-70; mem. Mayor's Coordinating Council for Youth, Fargo-Moorhead, 1976—; pres. Hospice of Red River Valley, 1986-87 (Svc. award 1987). Named Profl. Woman of Yr. Fargo-Moorhead YWCA, 1981, Disting. Lectr. of Yr., N.D. State U., 1991, Outstanding Educator U. N.D. Sch. Medicine Class of 1992; recipient Burlington No. award, 1987, Alumni award U. Ky., 1988, Disting. Svc. award Gt. Plains Sociol. Assn., 1988; Joy M. Query scholarship at N.D. State U., U. N.D. Coll. Medicine named in her honor, 1987. Fellow Internat. Assn. Social Psychiatry; mem. AAUP, Am. Sociol. Assn., N.D. Mental Health Assn. (pres. Red River Valley chpt., Heritage award 1987), midwest Sociol. Soc. (dir. 1970-73, 75-78, mem. standards, tng. and employment com. 1988-89), Alpha Kappa Delta. Unitarian Universalist. Home: 1202 Oak St Fargo ND 58102-2707 Office: U ND Sch Medicine 1919 Elm St Fargo ND 58102-2416 also: ND State Univ Dept Sociology Fargo ND 58102

QUESENBERRY, KENNETH HAYS, agronomy educator; b. Springfield, Tenn., Feb. 28, 1947; s. James William and Cora Geneva (Moore) Quesenberry; m. Joyce Ann Kaze; children: James Kenneth, Kendra Joyce. BS, Western Ky. U., 1969; PhD, U. Ky., 1975. D.F. Jones predoctoral fellow U. Ky., Lexington, 1972—75; asst. prof. U. Fla., Gainesville, 1975—80, assoc. prof. agronomy, 1980—86, prof. agronomy, 1986—. Contbr. articles to profl. jours. Served with U.S. Army, 1969—71, Vietnam. Fellow: Crop Sci. Soc. Am. (chair divsn. C-8 1993—94), Am. Soc. Agronomy. Achievements include research in germplasm enhancement of forages with release of four cultivars of tropical grasses and three clovers and genetic transformation of clovers; specialist Trifolium species germplasm. Avocations: sports, antique furniture refinishing. Office: U Fla PO Box 110500 Gainesville FL 32611-0500 E-mail: clover@ifas.ufl.edu.

QUESNEL, ELIZABETH DIMICK, secondary school educator; b. St. Regis Falls, N.Y., Dec. 15, 1934; d. Linus John and Esther Mildred (Hart) D.; m. Lloyd E. Mayville, June 25, 1951 (div. 1972); children: Lloyd A., Deborah E. Mayville Provost; m. Joseph R. Quesnel, Nov. 22, 1972. BA in Edn., Potsdam State Coll., 1974. Cert. tchr., N.Y. Tchr. high sch. English, chmn. dept. Malone (N.Y.) Cen. Sch. System, 1974-94; ret., 1994. Mem. Malone Fedn. Tchrs., N.Y. State Union Tchrs. Republican. Roman Catholic. Office: Franklin Acad High Sch State St Malone NY 12953-2412

QUESTER, GEORGE HERMAN, political science educator; b. Bklyn., July 14, 1936; s. Jacob George and Elizabeth (Mattern) Q.; m. Aline Marie Olson, June 20, 1964; children: Theodore, Amanda. AB, Columbia U., 1958; MA, Harvard U., 1964, PhD, 1965. Instr., then asst. prof. govt. Harvard U., 1965-70; assoc. prof. govt. Cornell U., 1970-73, prof., 1973-82; prof. polit. sci. U. Md., College Park, 1982—. Vis. prof. U.S. Naval Acad., Annapolis, Md., 1991-93. Author: Deterrence Before Hiroshima, 1966, Nuclear Diplomacy, 1970, The Politics of Nuclear Proliferation, 1973, The Continuing Problem of International Relations, 1974, Offense and Defense in the International System, 1977, American Foreign Policy: The Lost Consensus, 1982, The Future of Nuclear Deterrence, 1986, The International Politics of Television, 1990, Nuclear Monopoly, 2000, Before And After The Cold War, 2002. Served with USAF, 1958-61. Fellow Center Advanced Study Behavioral Scis., 1974-75 Mem. Council Fgn. Relations, Inst. Strategic Studies, Am. Polit. Sci. Assn. Home: 5124 37th St N Arlington VA 22207-1862 Office: Univ Md 3140 Tydings College Park MD 20742-0001 E-mail: gqueste@gvpt.umd.edu.

QUICK, BETH NASON, education educator; b. Columbus, Ga., Mar. 2, 1968; d. George W. and Pamelia (Dailey) Nason; m. Jason B. Quick, June 29, 1991. BS in Edn., Samford U., 1989; MEd, Vanderbilt U., 1990, EdD, 1996. Cert. tchr., Tenn. Elem. tchr. Williamson County, Franklin, Tenn., 1990—93; assoc. prof. early childhood edn. Tenn. State U., Nashville, 1998—, Fla. State U., Tallahassee, 1996—98. Avocations: reading, cross-stitching, playing piano. Office: Tenn State U 3500 John Merritt Blvd Box 9598 Nashville TN 37209-1561

QUICK, EDWARD RAYMOND, museum director, educator, curator; b. L.A., Mar. 22, 1943; s. Donald Russell Quick and Gertrude Ruth (Albin) Thornbrough; m. Ruth Ann Lessig; children: Jeannette Lee, Russell Raymond. BA, U. Calif., Santa Barbara, 1970, MA, 1977. Adminstr. supr. Civil Service, Santa Ana, Calif., 1971-75; sr. computer operator Santa Barbara Rsch. Ctr., 1975-77; asst. collections curator Santa Barbara Mus. Art, 1977-78; collections mgr. Montgomery (Ala.) Mus. Fine Arts, 1978-80; asst. dir. Joslyn Art Mus., Omaha, 1980-85; dir. Sheldon Swope Art Mus., Terre Haute, Ind., 1985-95, Berman Mus., Anniston, Ala., 1995-97; mus. curator National Archives, Washington, 1998-2000, William Clinton Presdl. Libr. and Mus., 2000—. Adv. Ind. Arts Commn., Indpls., 1986-91; mem. Arts in Pub. Places Commn., Terre Haute, Ind., 1986-93; pres. Friends Vigo County Pub. Libr., 1988-95, treas., 1990-93. Author: Code of Practice for Couriering Museum Objects, 1985, Gilbert Brown Wilson and Herman Melville's "Moby Dick", 1993, The American West in the Berman Collections, 1997, Cattle Drive, 1997; co-author: Registrars in Record, 1987. Bd. dirs. Vol. Action Ctr., Terre Haute, 1987-90, Terre Haute Cmty. Relief Effort for Environ. and Civic Spirit, 1989. With USAF, 1961-65, Air N.G., 1979-96. Mem. Am. Assn. Mus. (adv. 1994—, mgmt. and long-range planning com. 1994—), Assn. Ind. Mus., Am. Assn. State and Local History, Internat. Coun. Mus., Rotary Internat., Kiwanis Internat., Alpha Gamma Sigma. Avocation: museum administrative research. Office: Clinton Presl Materials Project 1000 La Harpe Blvd Little Rock AR 72201

QUICKEL, KENNETH ELWOOD, JR., physician, medical center executive; b. Harrisburg, Pa., Aug. 20, 1939; s. Kenneth E. and Carolyn (Chick) Q.; m. Mary Wickersham Jennings, July 1, 1961; children: Robert Reid, Mary Elizabeth, David Blake. BA, Dartmouth Coll., 1961, B in Med. Sci., 1962; MD, Johns Hopkins U., 1964. Med. resident Johns Hopkins Hosp., Balt., 1964-66; endocrine fellow Duke U., Durham, N.C., 1966-67, 69-71; staff endocrinologist Geisinger Med. Ctr., Danville, Pa., 1971-84, pres., 1982-84; asst. dean Milton S. Hershey Med. Ctr., Hershey, Pa., 1973-77; pres. Geisinger Med. Mgmt. Corp., Danville, 1978-82, NPW Med. Ctr., Wilkes Barre, Pa., 1979-82; exec. v.p. Geisinger Found., Danville, 1981-84; pres. Ramsey Clinic, St. Paul, 1984-87, Joslin Diabetes Ctr., Boston, 1987-99. Bd. dirs. Controlled Risk Ins. Co., Barbados, 1987—. Contbr. articles to sci. jours. Trustee Deaconess Hosp., Boston, 1987—. Surgeon USPHS, 1967-69. Fellow ACP, Am. Coll. Physician Execs. (disting.); mem. Am. Diabetes Assn., Endocrine Soc., Harvard Club. Republican. Home: 435 Elliott Rd Centerville MA 02632-3666 Office: Joslin Diabetes Ctr 1 Joslin Pl Boston MA 02215-5306

QUIGLEY, JOHN JOSEPH, special education educator; b. Auburn, N.Y., May 28, 1946; s. Thomas Edward and Mary Agnes (Brechue) Q.; m. Nancy Louise Crehan, June 7, 1969 (div. 1979); 1 child, Kris Renae. BS, U. Cen. Mich., 1970; MA, U. No. Colo., 1976. Cert. tchr., spl. edn. tchr., Fla. Tchr. of socially maladjusted Dade County Schs., Miami, Fla., 1970-71, tchr. of trainable mentally handicapped, 1971-74, tchr. profoundly mentally handicapped, 1974-75, tchr. multiply handicapped, hearing impaired, 1975-77, tchr. hearing-impaired total communication, 1977—. Tchr. Habilitation for the Handicapped, Miami, 1972-81; cons. in trainable mentally handicapped curriculum devel., Duval County, Fla., 1973; master tchr. assoc. Gulfstream Elem. Sch., 1984-87; impact tchr. developer Dade Pub. Edn./Nat. Tchr. Network, 1991-92; adj. prof. U. Miami, 1991-92. Mem. Fla. Educators of Hearing Impaired, United Tchrs. Dade, Deaf Svc. Bur. Home: 10776 N Kendall Dr Apt F-1 Miami FL 33176-1426 Office: Gulfstream Elem Sch 20900 SW 97th Ave Miami FL 33189-2399

QUIGLEY, JOHN MICHAEL, economist, educator; b. N.Y.C., Feb. 12, 1942; BS with distinction, U.S. Air Force Acad., 1964; MSc with honors, U. Stockholm, Sweden, 1965; AM, Harvard U., 1971, PhD, 1972. Commd. 2d lt. USAF, 1964, advanced through grades to capt., 1968; asst. prof. econs. Yale U., 1972-74, assoc. prof., 1974-81; prof. pub. policy U. Calif., Berkeley, 1979—, prof. econs., 1981—, Chancellor's prof., 1997—, I. Donald Terner prof., 1999—, chmn. dept. econs., 1992-95; vis. prof. econs. and stats. U. Gothenberg, 1978. Cons. numerous govt. agys. and pvt. firms; econometrician Hdqrs. U.S. Air Force, Pentagon, 1965-68; research assoc. Nat. Bur. Econ. Research, N.Y.C., 1968-78; mem. com. on nat. urban policy NAS, 1985-93. Author, editor, contbr. articles to profl. jours.; editor in chief Reg. Sci. and Urban Econs., 1987-2003; mem. editl. bd. many sci. and scholarly jours. Fulbright scholar, 1964-65; fellow NSF, 1968-69, Woodrow Wilson, 1968-71, Harvard IBM, 1969-71, NDEA, 1969-71, Thord-Gray Am. Scandinavian Found. 1971-72, Social Sci. Research Council, 1971-72. Mem. Am. Econ. Assn., Econometric Soc., Regional Sci. Assn. (bd. dirs. 1986—), Nat. Tax Assn., Assn. for Pub. Policy and Mgmt. (bd. dirs. 1986-89, v.p. 1987-89), Am. Real Estate and Urban Econs. Assn. (bd. dirs. 1987-2001, pres. 1995-97). Home: 875 Hilldale Ave Berkeley CA 94708-1319 Office: U Calif 2607 Hearst Ave Berkeley CA 94720-7305 E-mail: quigley@econ.berkeley.edu.

QUIGNEY, THERESA ANN, special education educator; b. East Cleveland, Ohio, June 19, 1952; d. James and Lenora Mary (McDonald) Q.; m. Joseph Carl Lang, July 23, 1983. BA, Notre Dame Coll., 1974; MEd, Cleve. State U., 1980; PhD, Kent State U., 1992. Cert. tchr. handicapped K-12; cert. ednl. adminstrv. specialist edn. of exceptional pupils; cert. ednl. supr.; cert. elem. prin.; cert. h.s. prin. cert. tchr. French K-12, Ohio. Spl. edn. tchr. Newbury (Ohio) Local Schs., 1974—80; county supr., specific learning disabilities and behavior handicaps Geauga County Bd. Edn., Chardon, Ohio, 1980—86, 1987—88; asst. prof. spl. edn. West Chester (Pa.) U., 1992—93; asst. prof. edn. Heidelberg Coll., Tiffin, Ohio, 1993—94; assoc. prof. spl. edn. Cleve. State U., 1994—, coord. spl. edn. program Coll. Edn., 2000—02. Ednl. rschr.; presenter in field. Contbr. articles to profl. jours. Vol. cons. Tchrs. for Action Rsch. South Euclid/Lyndhurst (Ohio) Sch. Dist., 1996—; past participant issues task force Ohio Coun. for Exceptional Children; presenter, participant Oxford Round Table, Oxford U., England; past bd. mem. Camp Sue Osborne, Lake County, Ohio; mem. steering com. State Improvement Grant (Edn.), 2000—. Grantee Ohio State Supt.'s Task Force on Spl. Edn., 1997, Cleve. State U. Coll. Edn., 1997, Am. Sch. Counselor's Assn.; recipient achievement recognition Assn. for Children and Adults with Learning Disabilities, Ohio, 1980. Mem. CEC, ASCD, Am. Ednl. Rsch. Assn., Learning Disabilities Assn., Mid-We. Ednl. Rsch. Assn., Coun. for Learning Disabilities, Kappa Delta Pi, Phi Delta Kappa, Pi Lambda Theta (vol. cons. Gamma Epsilon chpt. 1996—). Avocations: travel, writing, reading, sketching. Office: Cleveland State Univ Euclid Ave at E 24th St Cleveland OH 44115

QUILLEN, MARY ANN, university administrator, consultant; b. Md., Dec. 10, 1947; 1 child, Jessica. BS, Del. State U., 1977; Cert. Spl. Edn., Pa. State U., 1981; MS in Dynamics of Orgn., U. Pa., 1991. Spl. edn. tchr. Wordsworth Acad., Ft. Washington, Pa., 1979-82; area rep. Pa. State U., King of Prussia, 1983-85; dir. continuing edn. Ea. Montgomery County AVTS, Willow Grove, Pa., 1985-93; mgr. Drexel U., Phila., 1993-97; dir. continuing distance & corp. edn. Harcum Coll., Bryn Mawr, Pa., 1997-2000; regional adminstr. Mid-Atlantic region Women in Cmty. Svc., Phila., 2000—. Cons. in field. Chair Montgomery County Commn. on Women and Families, Norristown, Pa., 1992-2000, created Unsung Heroine award; coord. Domestic Violence Forum for Montgomery County, Norristown, 1994—, creator, chair com. on Coordinated Response to Domestic Violence; apptd. Montgomery County Workforce Investment Bd., 2001. Mem. AAUW, Pa. Assn. for Adult and Continuing Edn., U. Pa. Alumni Assn. (dir. comm. com. 1993—). Avocations: gourmet cooking, flying, gardening, reading. Address: # 206 3 N Columbus Blvd Philadelphia PA 19106-1407

QUILLIGAN, EDWARD JAMES, obstetrician, gynecologist, educator; b. Cleve., June 18, 1925; s. James Joseph and Maude Elvira (Ryan) Q.; m. Betty Jane Cleaton, Dec. 14, 1946; children: Bruce, Jay, Carol, Christopher, Linda, Ted. BA, MD, Ohio State U., 1951; MA (hon.), Yale, 1967. Intern Ohio State U. Hosp., 1951-52, resident, 1952-54, Western Res. U. Hosps., 1954-56; asst. prof. obstetrics and gynecology Western Res. U., 1957-63, prof., 1963-65; prof. obstetrics and gynecology UCLA, 1965-66; prof., chmn. dept. Ob-Gyn Yale U., 1966-69, U. So. Calif., 1969-78, asso. v.p. med. affairs, 1978-79; prof. Ob-Gyn. U. Calif., Irvine, 1980-83, vice chancellor health affairs, dean Sch. Medicine, 1987-89; prof., chmn. ob.-gyn. dept. U. Wis., 1983-85; prof., chmn. Ob-Gyn Davis Med. Ctr. U. Calif., Sacramento, 1985-87, vice chancellor Health Scis., dean Coll. Med. Irvine, 1987-89, prof ob-gyn, 1987-94, prof. emeritus ob-gyn., 1994; exec. dir. med. edn. Long Beach (Calif.) Meml. Health Svcs., 1995—. Contbr. articles to med. jours.; co-editor-in-chief: Am. Jour. Obstetrics and Gynecology. Served to 2d lt. AUS, 1944—46. Recipient Centennial award Ohio State U., 1970 Mem. Soc. Gynecologic Investigation, Am. Gynecol. Soc., Am. Coll. Obstetics and Gynecology, Sigma Xi. Home: 24 Urey Ct Irvine CA 92612-4077 E-mail: equilligan@cox.net.

QUINN, BARBARA ANN, athletics administrator, educator; b. Freehold, N.J., Jan. 13, 1933; d. Walter Stanley and Mary (Craig) Harris. BS in Health and Phys. Edn., Ursinus Coll., 1955; MA, Trenton State Coll., 1968. Dir. phys. edn. for girls Charles Ellis Sch., Newtown Square, Pa., 1956-60; instr. phys. edn. Pennsbury Schs., Yardley, Pa., 1960-63, Exeter Twp. H.S., Reading, Pa., 1963-66, Hartwick Coll., Oneonta, N.Y., 1966-68; asst. prof. phys. and health edn. Madison Coll., Harrisonburg, Va., 1968-71; instr. phys. edn. Whitemarsh Jr. H.S., Plymouth Meeting, Pa., 1971-74; dir.

women's intercollegiate athletics U. Nev., Las Vegas, 1974-76, Simpson Coll., Indianola, Iowa, 1977-78; dir. women's athletics U. N.C., Asheville, 1978-81; dir. women's intercoll. athletics SUNY, Cortland, 1981-84; fitness dir. St. Joseph's Hosp., Asheville, N.C., 1985—. Instr. phys. edn. Asheville-Buncombe C.C., 1989—; activity dir. Emerald Ridge Care and Rehab. Ctr., Asheville, N.C., 1998—; site dir. Western Region, Women's U.S. Olympic Basketball Trials, Las Vegas, 1976, U.S. Volleyball Assn. Coaches Clinic, Simpson Coll., 1977; chmn. selection com. Va. State Lacrosse Tournament, 1970-71; mem. selection com. So. Dist. Lacrosse Tournament, 1970-71; coach So. dist. team U.S. Women's Lacrosse Assn. Nat. Tournament, 1971; mem. women's soccer com. Nat. Collegiate Athletic Assn., 1982-84, chmn. N.E. region; participant 5th Nat. Inst. Girls' Sports Advanced Basketball Coaching, 1969. Mem. AAHPER (sec. coll. divsn. N.Y. state chpt. 1967), Va. Women's Lacrosse Assn. (chmn. nominations com. 1970-71), Nat. Assn. Coll. Athletic Dirs., N.Y. Assn. Intercollegiate Athletics for Women (chair ethics and eligibility com. 1982). Address: 24 Mount Carmel Dr Asheville NC 28806-2117

QUINN, CAROLYN ANNE, special education educator; b. Ft. Bragg, N.C., Oct. 13, 1950; d. John Arthur and Daisy (Brake) Cook; m. Daniel Dennis Quinn, Oct. 27, 1973; 1 child, Patrick Quinn. BS in Edn., Ga. So. U., 1972; MEd, Ga. State U., 1978. Tchr. Gracewood State Sch., Augusta, Ga., 1972-74, Gwinnett County Pub. Schs., Lawrenceville, Ga., 1974-78, instructional lead tchr., 1978—. Bd. dirs. Gwinnett County Spl. Olympics, Lawrenceville (Spirit of Spl. Olympics award 1987); advisor Assn. Persons with Severe Handicaps, Atlanta, 1985—; advisor, bd. dirs. Autistic Group Tng. Home. Co-editor: (video tape) Assessing Severe Students, 1987. Active Leadership Gwinnett. Fellow Gwinnett Assn. Retarded Citizens (past pres. div. mental retardation 1983-85, T.W. Briscoe award 1988); mem. Ga. Coun. Exceptional Children (pres. 1987-90). Avocations: victorian antiques, cooking. Home: 2880 Brookside Run Snellville GA 30078-5943 Office: Suwanee Ctr PO Box 343 Lawrenceville GA 30046-0343

QUINN, CHRISTINE MARIE (JENSEN), elementary education educator; b. Ottawa, Ill., Oct. 5, 1969; d. Laurie Ann (Marta) Clifford; m. Jason R. Quinn. AA, Illinois Valley C.C., Oglesby, Ill., 1989; BS in Edn., We. Ill. U., Macomb, 1992; MS in Edn., Ill. State U., 1995. Tchr. 2nd grade McKinley Grade Sch., Ottawa Elem. Dist. 141, 1992—. Mem. Trinity Luth. Ch. Choir. Lutheran. Avocations: crafts, reading, running, water skiing, weight lifting. Home: 825 Adrienne Ave Ottawa IL 61350-4260 Office: McKinley Grade Sch 1320 State St Ottawa IL 61350-4413

QUINN, ELIZABETH R. elementary education educator; b. Covina, Calif., Oct. 7, 1951; d. John Howard and Rosemary (Branine) Roberts; m. D. Whitney Quinn, July 18, 1980. BA, Ariz. State U., 1973; Marriage, Family and Child Counseling, Azuza Pacific U., 1980; BS, Calif. State U., Fullerton, 1993. Tchr. Saddleback Valley Unified Sch. Dist., Mission Viejo, Calif., 1976—, mentor tchr., 1992—. Cert. life standard elem. credential K-8, Calif. Named Tchr. of Yr. Kiwanis, Mission Viejo, 1992. Mem. Calif. Tchrs. Assn., Saddleback Valley Educators. Avocations: reading, gourmet cooking, weight lifting. Office: Del Lago Elem 27181 Entidad Mission Viejo CA 92691-1099

QUINN, EVELYN SAUL, social work educator; b. Riverside, N.J., Feb. 22, 1952; d. Robert G. and Wanda H. (Zimecki) Saul; m. Thomas Paul Critchett, Dec. 10, 1976 (dec. Dec. 1984); m. Richard Patrick Quinn, Oct. 11, 1985; children: Erin, Ana, Caitlin, Robert. BA, Georgian Ct. Coll., 1974; MA, Seton Hall U., 1978; MSW, Rutgers U., 1983. Income maintenance staff Burlington County Bd. Social Svc., Mt. Holly, N.J., 1974-75; counselor div. vocat. rehab. Dept. Labor, Red Bank and Toms River, N.J., 1975-78; instr. in social work Georgian Ct. Coll., Lakewood, N.J., 1978-80, dir. social work, 1980-90, prof., chair social dept., 1990—. Cons. in stress mgmt. to various orgns., N.J., 1987—. Bd. dirs. Lakewood Sch. Based Program, 1989-91. Mem. NASW, AAUP, Coun. on Social Work Edn., Acad. Cert. Social Workers, N.J. Assn. Social Worker Baccalaureate Dirs., Nat. Assn. Women in Cath. Higher Edn. Roman Catholic. Avocations: sketching, journal writing. Home: 3011 Roosevelt St Wall NJ 07719-4323 Office: Georgian Ct Coll 900 Lakewood Ave Lakewood NJ 08701-2600

QUINN, MARTHA SUE, elementary education educator; b. Great Lakes, Ill., Nov. 15, 1951; d. Calvin Ray and Irma Nell (Burkhalter) Blevins; m. John Micheal Ulakovits Jr., Jan. 16, 1988; children: Sharon Leigh, Sandra Lynn. AA, Hillsborough Coll., 1982; student, Fla. State U., 1982-84; BFA, Miami U., Oxford, Ohio, 1985; postgrad., U. Fla., 1985-93. Cert. elem. tchr., art tchr., Fla. Substitute tchr., artist Hillsborough County, Tampa, Fla., 1984-86; tchr. 5th grade New Orleans Bapt. Sch., Tampa, Fla., 1986-88; tchr. art East Marion Elem. Sch., Ocala, Fla., 1988-89, N.H. Jones Elem. Sch., Ocala, Fla., 1989-91, Fessenden and Sparr Elem. Schs., Ocala and Sparr, Fla., 1991—. Lectr. Marion County Art Educators Insvcs., Ocala, 1990-91. Author: Art and Ecology, 1994; artist pastel portraits. Host, co-organizer Annual County Art & Music Festival, Ocala, 1991-93. Mem. Fla. Art Educators Assn. (del. 1990), Nat. Art Educators Assn., Nat. Art Assn. (panel discussion), Internat. Art Edn. Assn. (asst. dir. for state 1989-90), Fla. Art Assn. (lectr. 1992), Marion County Art Edn. Assn. (pres. elem. divsn. 1989-90). Baptist. Avocation: watching old movies. Home: 4900 SE 102nd Pl Lot 87 Belleview FL 34420-2936

QUINT SEHAT, ARLENE, art history educator, curator, museum administrator; b. Chgo., Sept. 4, 1944; d. Milton and Ruth Quint; m. Kourosh Sehat, July 11, 1938. BA in Art History, U. Calif., 1966, MA in Art History, 1969, PhD in Art History, 1974. Asst. prof. Calif. State U., L.A., 1969-76, assoc. prof., 1976-79; fine arts mgmt. specialist, curator of collections U.S. gen. svcs. adminstrn. Washington, 1980-88; assoc. prof. Coll. Notre Dame, Balt., 1988-90; vis. assoc. prof. Lincoln U., Pa., 1993-95; lectr. in art history Morgan State U., Balt., 1994—. Vis. assoc. prof. HUC Skirball Mus., L.A., 1975-77; cataloger, rschr. NYU, N.Y.C., 1969; rschr. Los Angeles County Mus. Art, 1964-66; chancellor's tchr. fellow U. Calif., 1966-67; adj. prof. Towson U., Balt. Contbr. articles to profl. jours. R & D grantee Coll. Notre Dame, Balt. Mem. Am. Assn. Museums, Internat. Coun. Museums (mem. documentation working group, internat. coord. conservation documentation), Coll. Art Assn., Arts Club Washington (chmn. edn. and scholarship com., admissions and membership com.).

QUIRING, FRANK STANLEY, chemist, educator; b. Goessel, Kans., Sept. 2, 1927; s. Henry and Helen (Lehrman) Q.; m. Evelyn Ruth Wiebe, Aug. 16, 1950; children: Samuel, Sherwood, Natalie, Powell. BA, Bethel Coll., 1950; MA, U. Kans., 1957. Cert. tchr. Kans., Mo. Tchr. sci. Coldwater (Kans.) High Sch., 1950-51, Pretty Prairie (Kans.) High Sch., 1952-55; tchr. chem. Wyandotte High Sch., Kansas City, Kans., 1955-59, Clayton (Mo.) High Sch., 1959-91; lab. dir. NSF Summer Insts. Hope Coll., Holland, Mich., 1964-92; rsch. assoc. Washington U., St. Louis, 1967-68; rsch. chemist Monsanto U., St. Louis, 1976-77, 84-85. Cons. Coll. Bd. Adv. Placement Divsn., Princeton, N.J., 1966—, Ohaus Corp., Florham Park, N.J., 1986-90. Contbr. articles to profl. jours. With USN, 1945-46. Recipient Presdl. award NSF, 1984, Catalyst award Chem. Mfgs. Assn., 1973; Tandy Corp. Tech. scholar, 1990. Mem. NEA (pres. Clayton chpt. 1965-66), Am. Chem. Assn. (pres. St. Louis chpt. 1970-71), Am. Chem. Soc. (Conant award 1969), Nat. Sci. Tchrs. Assn. Mennonite. Avocations: hiking, tennis, church choir. Home: 32 Regal Crescent St North Newton KS 67117-8039 E-mail: fquiring@cox.net.

QUIRKE, LILLIAN MARY, retired art educator; b. West Haven, Conn., Oct. 1, 1928; d. Mortimer Francis and Ellen Louise (Bird) Q. BS, BA, So. Conn. U., 1950; MA, Long Beach State U., 1953; EdD, Columbia U., 1963. Cert. elem. and art tchr., Conn., Calif. Tchr. Long Beach (Calif.) Pub. Schs., 1950-54; jr. high art tchr. Army Dependents Sch., Frankfurt, Germany, 1954-55; art tchr. Navy Dependents Sch., Naples, Italy, 1955-56; art instr. So. Conn. U., New Haven, 1956-64, Foothill C.C., Los Altos, Calif., 1964-67; from art instr. to prof. DeAnza C.C., Cupertino, Calif., 1967-88; adj. prof. Queens (N.Y.) Coll., 1990-91. Author: The Rug Book, 1979; contbr. articles to profl. jours.; mem. editl. bd. Art Edn. mag., 1985-87. Active Dem. and Rep. Ctrl. Coms., San Jose, Calif., 1968-71; mem. arts rev. com. Cupertino Pub. Libr., 1977-81. Title IV grantee, 1967, grantee State of Calif., 1968, NDEA grantee U.S. Office Edn., 1966. Mem. Nat. Art Edn. Assn. (life, sec. Pacific chpt. 1954—, founder higher edn. sect. 1973), Calif. Art Edn. Assn. (rsch. chair 1969-72), Artists and Tech. (bd. dirs. 1984-88), Fla. Shore and Beach Preservation Assn. (founding bd. dirs. St. Johns First Coast chpt. 1996, sec.-treas. 1996-97, sec. 1996-98). Avocations: quilting, boating, cooking, computer graphics. Home: 5916 Rio Royalle Rd Saint Augustine FL 32080-7304 E-mail: liljim@aug.com.

QUIROGA, NINOSKA, university official; b. La Paz, Bolivia, Nov. 29, 1968; came to U.S., 1995; d. Marcelo Quiroga and Sara Loza. B Econs., Cath. U. La Paz, 1991; MBA, S.W. Mo. State U., 1997. Jr. rschr. in projects, cons. Coop. Urban dnr Rural Women, La Paz, 1988-90; tchg. asst. Cath. U. La Paz, 1990-92; freelance writer Hoy, newspaper, La Paz, 1992; hostess, co-prodr. Net Bolivian Network, Red Uno de Bolivia, La Paz, 1992-95; news reporter Sta. KMSU, nat. pub. radio, Springfield, Mo., 1995-96; with distbn. ctr. The News Leader, Springfield, 1996—; grad. asst. to dean Sch. Bus., S.W. Mo. State U., Springfield, 1995—. Tchr. Am.-Bolivian Ctr., La Paz, 1991. Recipient award for exceptional help and effort shown throughout yr. Am.-Bolivian Ctr., 1991; named Miss Bolivia, 1993, Miss La Paz, 1993, Best Friend in Miss Bolivia, 1993, Miss Intelligence and Personality of World and Miss Friendship of Am. in Miss World of Ams. and Caribbean, 1994. Mem. UN of USA, Hispanic Assn. Leaders, Delta Sigma Pi. Avocations: making friends, reading. Office: SW Mo State U Coll Bus Glass Hall 400 901 S National Ave Springfield MO 65804-0027

QUIST, JEANETTE FITZGERALD, television production educator, choreographer; b. Provo, Utah, July 4, 1948; d. Sherman Kirkham and Bula Janet (Anderson) Fitzgerald; m. G. Steven Quist; children: Ryan, Amy, Michelle, Jeremy. Student, U. Redlands, Calif., 1970; BA, Brigham Young U., 1971; postgrad., Calif. State U., Riverside, 1972, Calif. State U., San Bernardino, 1973. Host, co-producer children's show PBS Sta. KBYU-TV, Provo, 1968-69; buyer ready to wear J.C. Penney & Co., Redlands, 1969-71; tchr. spl. reading program Fontana (Calif.) Elem. Sch. Dist., 1971-73; owner, choreographer Jeanette Quist Creative Dance, Tri Cities, Wash., 1975-79; owner, tchr. Dance Studio, Gridley, Calif., 1979-81; producer, instr. Butte Coll., Oroville, Calif., 1986—. Asst. producer Kate Knight Prodn. Co., Chico, Calif., 1987; video producer Gridley Sch. Dist., 1987-88; cmty. svcs. cons. Biggs-Gridley Meml. Hosp., 1999—; workshop presenter 2 yr. small coll. prodn. showcase, Broadcast Edn. Assn., 2003. Prodr., editor promotional video Police Acad., 1986, commls. for Butte Coll., 1987—; prodr., dir. telecourse Interior Designer, 1988—; prodr., hostess TV talk shows Crossroads, 1988—, NVCA Today, BCTV Forum, 1991—; prodr. orientation video Butte Coll., 1989, 90, video series Intro to Telecommunications, video documentary on migrant edn. summer sch., 1994-98, video series on Recycling for Butte Environ. Coun., 1995, Early Alert video for Butte Coll., 1995, promotion video City of Chico, 1995, video Sports Events for Butte Coll., 1995—, video series on Small Bus. Devel. Ctr., 1996, video Work Tng. Ctr., 1996, Project Maestros, 1996, video for bilingual tchrs. recruitment Butte Coll. 1997, video documenting the American Dream: Unity in Diversity, Butte Coll., 1997, Sentencing Video for the Fed. Defs. Office, Ea. Dist. of Calif., 1998; choreographer Kaleidoscope, 1988, South Pacific, 1989, Fantasticks, 1990, Amahl and the Night Visitors, 1990, An Evening of Song and Dance, Butte Coll., 1991, Kiss Me Kate, Butte Coll., 1992, Hello Dolly, Chico Stake, 1992; prodr. videos for Butte Coll. Child Devel. Program, 1999, Multimedia Program, 2001, Radio TV Film Program, 2002, Environ. Hort. Program, 2002, EMT/Paramedics Program, 2002; choreographer Tumbleweeds, Butte Theatre, 1994, Joseph and the Amazing Technicolor Dreamcoat, Gridley H.S., 1999, video for Butte Coll. Tech. Prep. program, 2003. State judge Miss. Am. Contest, Provo, 1968; 1st v.p. Friends of Libr., Gridley, 1988; chmn. Regional Fine Arts Festival Tri Cities, 1978; v.p. Gridley High Sch. Parent Club, 1990; chmn. 3D Expo Fine Arts Festival for Oroville, Gridley, and Butte Coll., 1991; cmty. svcs. cons. Biggs-Gridley Meml. Hosp., 1999—, organizer 50th anniversary celebration, 2000. Recipient Acad. Excellence award Butte Coll., 1993-94, What Would We Do Without You award, Butte Coll., 1998; Mask club scholar Brigham Young U., 1967; Project Maestro grantee, 1994, Svc. Learning grantee Butte Coll., 2002. Mem. AAUW (membership v.p. 1989-91, pres. 1997-99, com. for gender equity for Gridley br., Tech Trek chmn. Gridley br. 2001—), Butte County Arts Coun. (spl. com. 1986), Kaleidoscope Arts Coun., Am. Assn. Women in Cmty. Jr. Colls. Republican., Ch. of Jesus Christ Latter-day Saints. Avocations: family, theatre, music, camping, reading.

QUTUB, CAROL HOTELLING, elementary education educator; b. Portland, Oreg., Jan. 8, 1939; d. Cecil Claire and Mina Alice (Jarrett) Hotelling; m. Ibrahim Qutub, Mar. 1961 (div.); children: Robert, Noelle Schoos, Bilal. BA in Math., U. Oreg., 1960, postgrad., 1992, PhD; MA in Edn., Portland State U., 1968. Math. tchr. Grant Union Sch. Dist., Sacramento, Calif., 1960-61; statistician Aerojet Gen., Sacramento, 1961-67; tchr. Clackamas, Oreg., 1967-93; elem. tchr. math. and computer Portland Pub. Schs., 1967-93, chmn. math. text book com., 1979-80. Contbr. articles to profl. jours. Mem. NEA (rep.), Nat. Coun. Tchrs. Math., Am. Ednl. Rsch. Assn., Internat. Soc. for Tech. in Edn., Phi Lambda Theta. Avocations: piano playing, skiing, boating, traveling. Home: 4610 SW 37th Ave Portland OR 97221-3910 Office: Portland Pub Schs 7452 SW 52nd Ave Portland OR 97219-1315

RAAB, EDWARD LEON, ophthalmologist, educator, lawyer; b. N.Y.C., Jan. 26, 1933; m. Rosanne Brody Raab, Aug. 28, 1955; children: Barbara G., Renee J., Steven B. BA, Columbia U., 1954; MD, NYU, 1958; JD, Fordham U., 1994. Diplomate Am. Bd. Ophthalmology. Intern Montefiore Med. Ctr., N.Y.C., 1958-59; resident Mt. Sinai Hosp., N.Y.C., 1961-64; pvt. practice ophthalmology N.Y.C., 1964-66; prof. ophthalmology, prof. pediats. Mt. Sinai Sch. Medicine, NYU, N.Y.C., 1967—. Cons. ophthalmology USPHS, S.I., N.Y., 1968-81; mem. Am. Orthoptic Coun., 1982—, v.p., 1994-96, pres., 1996-99; advisor Nat. Soc. to Prevent Blindness, N.Y.C., 1974-88, Children's Eye Care Found., Washington, 1973-79. Contbr. articles on ophthalmology to profl. jours., chpts. to books. Capt. U.S. Army, 1959-61. Pediat. Ophthalmology fellow Children's Hosp. Nat. Med. Ctr., Washington, 1966-67. Fellow ACS, Am. Ophthalmol. Soc., Am. Acad. Ophthalmology, Am. Coll. Legal Medicine; mem. ABA, Am. Assn. Pediat. Ophthalmology and Strabismus (bd. dirs. 1996-99), N.Y. Soc. Pediat. Ophthalmology and Strabismus (pres. 1991-92), N.Y. State Bar Assn., Assn. of Bar City of N.Y. Home: 35 E 75th St # 9D New York NY 10021-2761 Office: Mt Sinai Med Ctr Dept Ophthalmology 5 E 98th St Fl 7 New York NY 10029-6501

RAAB, LAWRENCE EDWARD, English educator; b. Pittsfield, Mass., May 8, 1946; s. Edward Louis and Marjorie (Young) R.; m. Judith Ann Michaels, Dec. 29, 1968; 1 child, Jennifer Caroline. BA, Middlebury Coll., 1968; MA, Syracuse U., 1972. Lectr. Am. U., Washington, 1970-71; jr. fellow U. Mich. Soc. Fellows, Ann Arbor, 1973-76; prof. English Williams Coll., Williamstown, Mass., 1976—. Author: (poems) Mysteries of the Horizon, 1972, The Collector of Cold Weather, 1976, Other Children, 1987, What We Don't Know About Each Other, 1993 (National Book award nominee, 1993), The Probable World, 2000, Visible Signs: New and Selected Poems, 2003. Creative Writing fellow Nat. Endowment Arts, 1972, 84; recipient Bess Hokin prize Poetry mag., 1983; residencies at Yaddo, 1979-80, 82, 84, 86-90, 94, MacDowell Colony, 1993, 95. Office: Williams Coll English Dept Williamstown MA 01267

RAABERG, GLORIA GWEN, literature educator; b. Atlanta, Dec. 31, 1932; d. Lawrence Leslie and Gwendolyn Neff (Ewing) Hill; m. Charles B. Raaberg, Jan. 29, 1955 (div. 1983); children: Charlyn L., Ross W., Valerie R. BA, Col. William & Mary, 1954; MA, Calif. State U., 1971; PhD, U. Calif., Irvine, 1978. Instr. lit. UCLA, 1977-78; Mellon fellow lit. Case Western Res. U., Cleve., 1978-79; asst. prof. U. Tex., Dallas, 1979-85, 87-89; vis. prof. U. Calif., Irvine, 1985-86; Fulbright sr. prof. U. Debrecen, Hungary, 1986-87; prof. English, dir. women's studies Western Mich. U., Kalamazoo, 1989—. Fellow Ctr. Humanities U. Calif., 1985-86, U. Va., Charlottesville, 1996; mem. exec. bd. Ctr. Ethics in Soc., Kalamazoo, Mich., 1991—. Author: Toward a Theory of Literary Collage, 1978; co-editor: Surrealism and Women, 1991; contbr. articles to profl. jours. Mem. Women Civic Leaders Network, Kalamazoo, 1989-92. Lilly Found. grantee, 1991-93, NEH grantee, 1983-85. Mem. MLA, Nat. Women's Studies Assn., Am. Studies Assn. Avocations: hiking, art, archaeology. Office: Western Mich U Kalamazoo MI 49008

RAAFLAUB, VERNON ARTHUR, religion educator; b. Magnetawan, Ont., Can., Apr. 30, 1938; s. Arthur Frederick and Olga Elizabeth (Hoerner) R. Diploma in electronics, Radio Electronics TV Schs., North Bay, Ont., 1959; diploma in theology, Concordia Theol. Sem., Springfield, Ill., 1965, BTh, 1972; MDiv, Concordia Theol. Sem., Ft. Wayne, Ind., 1987; addl. theol. studies, Concordia Theol. Sem., Fort Wayne, Ind.; postgrad., Wilfrid Laurier U., Waterloo, Ont., 1974-75; MA in Adminstrn., Briercrest Biblical Sem., Caronport, Sask., 1985; DD (hon.), Concordia Luth. Sem., Edmonton, Alberta, Can., 1998. Ordained to ministry Luth. Ch., 1965. Pastor Nipawin (Sask.) Choiceland Luth. Parish, 1965-76; instr. Can. Luth. Bible Inst., Camrose, Canada, 1976-77, acad. dean, instr., 1977-85, prof. Old Testament studies, acad. dean, 1985—2001; asst. prof. Exeget Theology Concordia Luth. Sem., Edmonton, Canada. Cir. counsellor Luth. Ch. Mo. Synod, Carrot River Cir., 1971—75. Co-editor: The Creation Alternative, 1970; contbr. articles to profl. jours. Chmn. Easter Seal Campaign, Nipawin, 1972; mem. Can. council World Mission Prayer League, 1980-85; bd. dirs. Concordia Coll., Edmonton, Alta., 1975-78. Grantee Luth. Ch. Can., Zion Found., 1975. Mem. Nat. Assn. Profs. Hebrew, Am. Schs. Oriental Rsch., Near East Archeol. Soc., Am. Sci. Affiliation (assoc.), Creation Rsch. Soc. (assoc.), Assn. Psychol. Type, Rotary (pres. Nipawin chpt. 1972-73, bd. dirs. 1968-71). Avocations: electronics, multitrack recording, music, swimming. Office: Concordia Lutheran Seminary 7040 Ada Blvd Edmonton AB Canada T5B 4E3 Home: 114 Howson Cres Edmonton AB Canada T5A 4T8 E-mail: vraaflaubc@yahoo.com., vraaflaub@concordiasem.ab.ca.

RABE, LAURA MAE, mathematician, educator; b. Cin., May 28, 1945; d. Howard Lawrence and Alberta Catherine (Held) R. BS, U. Cin., 1967, MS, 1972, supr. cert., 1982. Tchr. Colerain H.S., Cin., 1967-97, chairperson math. dept., 1980-97; tchr. Mt. St. Joseph Coll., 1997—. Presenter grant writing workshop Miami U., Oxford, Ohio, 1994; pressenter in field. Named Hixon Tchr. of Yr., 1996; grantee GTE, 1994-95, NSF, 1980, Dartmouth Univ., 1995, 96; Tandy Tech. scholar, 1995-96. Mem. NEA, Nat. Coun. Tchrs. Math., Ohio Coun. Tchrs. Math., Greater Cin. Coun. Tchrs. Math. Roman Catholic. Avocations: travel, camping, water skiing, snow skiing, photography.

RABELO, LUIS CARLOS, engineering educator, consultant; b. David, Chiriqui, Panama, Feb. 6, 1960; came to U.S., 1985; s. Luis Carlos and Consuelo (Mendizabal) R. BSEE, BS in Mech. Engring., Tech. U., Panama, 1983; MSEE, Fla. Inst. Tech., 1987; MS in Engring. Mgmt., U. Mo., 1988, PhD in Engring. Mgmt., 1990. Ops. engr. Aeroperlas Airlines subs. Contadora Corp., Panama City, 1982-83; ops. analyst Contadora Corp., Panama City, 1983-84, ops. mgr., 1984-85; grad. rsch. asst. engring. mgmt. dept. U. Mo., Rolla, 1988-90, grad. teaching asst. engring. mgmt. dept., 1989-90, rsch. engr. engring. mgmt. dept. Ctr. for Tech. Transfer, 1990-91; asst. prof. dept. indsl. and sys. engring. Ohio U., Athens, 1991—. Cons. Metalurgia Panama, Panama City, 1982-83, Talema Electronics Inc., Rolla, 1988, S&S Contract Furniture, Inc., Marquand, Mo., 1989, Ohio Tech. Transfer Orgn., Athens, 1993, AMP, Inc., 1992, guest rschr. Automated Mfg. Rsch. Facility Nat. Inst. Standards and Tech., Gaithersburg, Md., 1992-95; lectr. in field. Contbr. articles to profl. jours., chpts. to books.; editor procs. Adaptive Computing Conf., numerous conf. procs. in the areas of neural networks, fuzzy logic, and genetic algorithms. Postdoctoral fellow U. Mo., 1990-91; grantee Ohio Rsch. Challenge Program, 1992-93, 94-95, U.S. NSF, 1994, Nat. Inst. Standards and Tech., 1992, 93, 95—; recipient Disting. Alumni award Tech. U. Panama, 1995. Mem. IEEE, Am. Soc. Engring. Edn., Internat. Neural Networks Soc., Soc. Mfg. Engrs., Inst. Indsl. Engrs., Inst. Ops. Rsch. and Mgmt. Scis., Sigma Xi. Roman Catholic. Avocations: soccer, swimming, chess. Office: Ohio U Dept Indsl & Mfg Sys Engring Athens OH 45701 Home: Apt 2004 1700 Woodbury Rd Orlando FL 32828-6019

RABIDEAU, MARGARET CATHERINE, retired media center director; b. Chgo., Nov. 24, 1930; d. Nicholas and Mary Agnes (Burke) Oberle; m. Gerald Thomas Rabideau, Nov. 27, 1954; children: Mary, Margaret, Michelle, Gregory, Marsha, Grant. BA cum laude, U. Toledo, 1952, MA in Ednl. Media Tech., 1978. Cert. tchr. K-12 media tech., supr. ednl. media, tchr. English and journalism, specialist in edn. Asst. dir. pub. rels. U. Toledo, 1952-55; publicity writer United Way, Toledo, 1974-75; tchr. Toledo Pub. Schs., 1975-80, libr., media specialist, 1980-90; dir. media svcs. Sylvania (Ohio) Schs., 1990—2002, ret., 2002. Task force to evaluate coll. programs Ohio Dept. Edn., 1987; on-site evaluation team, Hiram Coll., Ohio, 1991; north ctrl. evaluation team Northwestern Ohio, 1985—. Citizen task force Toledo/Lucas County Libr., Ohio, 1991, mem. friends of the libr., 1990—; task force Sta. WGTE-TV PBS Sta., Toledo, 1993; mem. tech. com. strategic plan Sylvania Schs., 1997; instr. U. Toledo, 1990— Recipient Disting. Educator for Art Edn. award N.W. Ohio Art Edn. Assn., 1997; nnamed Educator of Yr., Sylvania Schs., 2001. Mem. ALA, U. Toledo Alumni Assn., Ohio Ednl. Libr. Media Assn. (N.W. dir. 1993—, vocat. dir. 1985-89, Libr. Media Specialist of Yr. 1993, disting. educator art edn. 1999), Am. Ednl. Comm. and Tech., Ednl. Leadership Assn. (bd. dirs.), Maumee Valley Computer Assn. (task force), Phi Delta Kappa (Outstanding Newsletter Nat. award 1990, pres. Toledo chpt., svc. key award, 1998). Avocations: running, travelling, cross stitching. Home: 1038 Olson St Toledo OH 43612-2828

RABINO, ISAAC, biology and health science educator, researcher; b. Haifa, Israel, Dec. 2, 1938; came to U.S., 1963; s. Jacob and Natalia (Besser) R.; m. Linda Lurie, June 28, 1970; 1 child, Tahli Jeanne. BS, Hebrew U., Jerusalem, 1962; MS, Cornell U., 1965; PhD, SUNY, Stony Brook, 1976. Asst. prof. St. Peter's Coll., Jersey City, N.J., 1977-81; from assoc. prof. to prof. biol. and health scis. Empire State Coll., SUNY, N.Y.C., 1985—; asst. prof. biol. scis. CUNY, N.Y.C., 1983-85. NSF rsch. assoc. Columbia U., N.Y.C., summers 1978-81. Contbr. numerous articles to profl. jours. Recipient SUNY-Empire State Coll. Found. award for excellence in scholarship, 1996; grantee Lounsbery Found., NSF. Mem. AAAS, Assn. for Politics and the Life Scis., Soc. for Social Studies of Sci., Am. Inst. of Biological Scis. Office: SUNY Empire State Coll 225 Varick St New York NY 10014-4304

RABINOF, SYLVIA, pianist, composer, author, educator; b. N.Y.C., Oct. 10, 1913; d. Morris and Fanny (Edelstein) Smith; m. Benno Rabinof, Sept. 16, 1943 (dec. Apr. 1976); m. Charles Rothenberg, Dec. 22, 1978 (dec. April 1992). Student, 3rd St Music Sch. Settlement, N.Y.C., NYU, Juilliard Sch. Music; MusD (hon.), Lincoln Meml. U., 1947; studied with Marguerite Valentine, Mary Emerson, Rudolph Serkin, Ignace Jan Paderewski, Simon Barere, Georges Enesco, Oscar Ziegler, James Bleeker, Charles Haubiel, Albert Stoessel, Philip James. Tchr. piano, improvisation, ensemble theory Juilliard Sch. Music; mem. faculty Brevard Music. Ctr. N.C. Converse Coll., Spartanburg, S.C., Round Top Music Festival, Tex., SUNY, Fredonia;

lectr. in field. Author: (textbooks) Musicianship Through Improvisation, 1966, The Improviser, 1967, The Improvisers Key Guidebook, 1969; contbr. composers' biographies to NFMC Jr. Keynotes mag., 1971-98; composer: cantata The Deluge, Three Profiles for Piano, Suite for String Orchestra, children's operetta Hamlet the Flea; published piano arrangements for Warner Bros.; piano solo and duo recordings with Benno Rabinof include Beethoven violin and piano sonatas, violin gypsy classics, Vivaldi concerti, others; performances in Vienna, Zurich, London, Phila., Carnegie Hall, N.Y.C., Boston, Chgo., Toronto, Paris, Moscow, Athens, Rome, Milan, others. Mem. ASCAP, Nat. Fedn. Music Clubs (chair improvisation), Musicians Club N.Y. (pres. 1976-79) Home: 8220 Jog Rd Boynton Beach FL 33437-2938

RABINOVITCH, BENTON SEYMOUR, chemist, educator emeritus; b. Montreal, Que., Can., Feb. 19, 1919; came to U.S., 1946; s. Samuel and Rachel (Schachter) R.; m. Marilyn Werby, Sept. 18, 1949; children: Peter Samuel, Ruth Anne, Judith Nancy, Frank Benjamin; m. Flora Reitman, 1980. BSc, McGill U., 1939, PhD, 1942; DSc (hon.), Technion Inst., Haifa, 1991. Postdoctoral fellow Harvard, 1946-48; mem. faculty U. Wash., Seattle, 1948—, prof. chemistry, 1957—, prof. chemistry emeritus, 1985—. Cons. and/or mem. sci. adv. panels, coms. NSF, Nat. Acad. Scis.-NRC; adv. com. phys. chemistry Nat. Bur. Standards. Author Antique Silver Servers, 1991, Contemporary Silver, 2000; former editor: Ann. Rev. Phys. Chemistry; mem. editorial bd.: Internat. Jour. Chem. Kinetics, Rev. of Chem. Intermediates, Jour. Phys. Chemistry, J. Am. Chem. Soc. (assoc. editor). Served to capt. Canadian Army, 1942-46, ETO. Nat. Research Council Can. fellow, 1940-42; Royal Soc. Can. Research fellow, 1946-47; Milton Research fellow Harvard, 1948; Guggenheim fellow, 1961; vis. fellow Trinity Coll., Oxford, 1971; recipient Sigma Xi award for original research, Debye award in phys. chemistry, 1984, Polanyi medal Royal Soc. Chemistry; named hon. liveryman Worshipful Co. of Goldsmiths, London, 2000. Fellow Am. Phys. Soc., Am. Acad. Arts and Scis., Royal Soc. London; mem. Am. Chem. Soc. (past chmn. Puget Sound sect., past chmn. phys. chemistry div., editor jour.), Faraday Soc. Achievements include rsch. in Unimolecular gas phase reaction and history and design of silver implements. Home: 12530 42nd Ave NE Seattle WA 98125-4621 Office: Univ Washington Chemistry Box 351700 Seattle WA 98195 Fax: 206-685-8665.

RABUCK, DONNA FONTANAROSE, English writing educator; b. Edison, N.J., Aug. 2, 1954; d. Arthur Thomas and Shirley Gertrude (Golub) Fontanarose; m. John Frederick Rabuck, July, 28, 1973; 1 child, Miranda Rose. BA in Eng., Rutgers U., 1976, MA in Eng. Lit., 1980, PhD in Eng. Lit., 1990. Prof. writing Pima C. C., Tucson, 1981-86; asst. dir. writing skills program U. Ariz., Tucson, 1983—. Asst. dir. summer inst. writing U. Ariz., Tucson, 1985—, asst. dir. grad. writing inst., 1996—; adj. faculty Pima C. C., Tucson, 1992-95. Author: The Other Side of Silence: Performing Heroinism in the Victorian Novel, 1990, Writing Ctr. Perspectives, 1995; editor: Writing is Thinking: Collected Writings of the Summer Inst., 1985—. Founder, pres. Miles East-West Neighborhood Assn., Tucson, 1983—; dir. Ctr. for Sacred Feminine, Tucson, 1995—; program coord. U. Ariz. Arts and Scis. Minority Retention Program, 1988-93. Rutgers Alumni scholar, 1972-76; Bevier fellow Rutgers U., 1976-78. Mem. Intercollegiate Writing Com. (task force), Commn. Cultural Thinking (task force), Nat. Coun. Tchrs. Eng. Avocations: feminist scholarship, women's rituals, yoga, hiking, meditation. Home: 1115 N Camino Miraflores Tucson AZ 85745-1612 Office: Univ Ariz Writing Skills Program 1201 E Helen St Tucson AZ 85719-4407 E-mail: drabuck@u.arizona.edu.

RACE, GEORGE JUSTICE, pathology educator; b. Everman, Tex., Mar. 2, 1926; s. Claude Ernest and Lila Eunice (Bunch) R.; m. Annette Isabelle Rinker, Dec. 21, 1946; children: George William Daryl, Jonathan Clark, Mark Christopher, Jennifer Anne (dec.), Elizabeth Margaret Rinker. MD, U. Tex., Southwestern Med. Sch., 1947; MS in Pub. Health, U. N.C., 1953; PhD in Ultrastructural Anatomy and Microbiology, Baylor U., 1969. Intern Duke Hosp., 1947-48, asst. resident pathology, 1951-53; intern Boston City Hosp., 1948-49; asst. pathologist Peter Bent Brigham Hosp., Boston, 1953-54; pathologist St. Anthony's Hosp., St. Petersburg, Fla., 1954-55; staff pathologist Children's Med. Center, Dallas, 1955-59; dir. labs. Baylor U. Med. Center, Dallas, 1959-86, chief dept. pathology, 1959-86, vice chmn. exec. com. med. bd., 1970-72; cons. pathologist VA Hosp., Dallas, 1955-71; adj. prof. anthropology and biology So. Meth. U., Dallas, 1969; instr. pathology Duke, 1951-53, Harvard Med. Sch., 1953-54; asst. prof. pathology U. Tex. Southwestern Med. Sch., 1955-58, clin. assoc. prof., 1958-64, clin. prof., 1964-72, prof., 1973-94, prof. emeritus, 1994—, dir. Cancer Center, 1973-76, assoc. dean for continuing edn., 1973-94, emeritus assoc. dean, 1994—. Pathologist-in-chief Baylor U. Med. Ctr., 1959-86, prof. biomed. studies Baylor Grad. sch., 1989-94; chmn. Baylor Rsch. Found., 1986-89; prof. microbiology Baylor Coll. Dentistry, 1962-68, prof. pathology, 1964-68, prof., chmn. dept. pathology 1969-73, dean A. Webb Roberts Continuing Edn., 1973-94; spl. advisor on human and animal diseases to gov. State of Tex., 1979-83. Editor: Laboratory Medicine (4 vols.), 1973, 10th edit., 1983; Contbr. articles to profl. jours., chpts. to textbooks. Pres., Tex. div. Am. Cancer Soc., 1970; chmn. Gov.'s Task Force on Higher Edn., 1981. Served with AUS, 1944-46; flight surgeon USAF, 1948-51, Korea. Decorated Air medal. Fellow AAAS, Coll. Am. Pathologists, Am. Soc. Clin. Pathologists; mem. AMA (chmn. multiple discipline research forum 1969), Am. Assn. Pathologists, Internat. Acad. Pathology, Am. Assn. Med. Colls., Explorers Club (dir., v.p. 1993-2000), Sigma Xi, Alpha Omega Alpha. Home: 3429 Beverly Dr Dallas TX 75205-2928 Fax: 214-526-8607. E-mail: georgejrace@worldnet.att.net.

RACKER, DARLENE KATIE, cardiovascular anatomist and electrophysiologist; b. Chgo., Dec. 8, 1937; d. George Oliver and Katie Venoy (Gibson) Cameron; m. Lester Eugene Racker, Nov. 1, 1959; children: Lester Keith Van Racker, Victoria Venice Racker Finney. Cert. Histologist, U. Chgo., 1962; BSc in Cell Biology, Ill. State U., Chgo., 1976; PhD in Physiology, Chgo. Med. Sch., 1988. Histology technician Northwestern U., Chgo., 1959-60; histology and TEM technician U. Chgo., 1959-60; TEM technologist VA Lakeside Hosp., Chgo., 1965-81; postdoctoral fellow Coll. Phys. & Surgs., Columbia U., N.Y.C., 1988-90; rsch. asst. prof. Northwestern U. Med. Sch., Chgo., 1990—. Presenter in field. Author: Transmission Electron Microscopy Methods of Application, 1983; contbr. articles to profl. jours. APS and Procter & Gamble fellow, 1983-88. Mem. Am. Soc. Clin. Pathology, Am. Physiol. Soc., N.Am. Soc. Pacing and Electrophysiology, Am. Heart Assn. Democrat. Roman Catholic. Achievements include rsch. in seminal demonstrations by TEM of membrane channels, of the sinoventricular conducting system in dog heart, of sinoventricular component tissues and missing links: atrionodal bundles and proximal AV bundle, of the muscular valvular apparatus, transmembrane and extracellular potentials evoked by the sinoventricular conduction sys. and muscular valvular apparatus tissues, of the SAN conduction intervals for the sinoventricular conduction sys. tissues, of the tissues evoling double potentials in electrogram traces of the sanode and AV junction regions; development of new tissue culture techniques for investigation of neuronal development in slice cultures. Home: PO Box 6104 Wilmette IL 60091-6104 Office: Northwestern U Med Sch Medicine Cardiology Dept/CH233 303 E Chicago Ave Chicago IL 60611-3072 E-mail: darkrac@northwestern.edu.

RACKI, JOAN, educational administrator; b. Portland, Oreg., Apr. 15, 1948; d. Elliott Max and Jane (Freidenrich) Flaxman; m. Matthias M. Racki III, June 5, 1970; children: Byron Jason, David Justin. BA, Scripps Coll., 1970; MA, U. Denver, 1973. Admissions and fin. aid officer Inst. of European Studies, Chgo., 1973—77; assoc. dir., budget analyst Ill. Bd. Higher Edn., Springfield, 1978—84; space planner U. Idaho, Moscow, 1984—85; facilities planner Idaho Bd. Edn., Boise, 1985—93; assoc. dir. bus and fin. Iowa Bd. Regents, Des Moines, 1993—. Mem. facilities adv. com. Urbandale Sch. Dist., 2003. Co-author manuscripts: Financing Higher Education Facility Needs in Idaho, 1985, Library Facility Study, 1986. Mem. Parent Adv. Team Local Elem. Sch., Moscow, 1986-93; mem. rev. panel NSF; mem. solid waste adv. com. City Urbandale, Iowa. Edn. Policy fellow, 1980-81. Mem. AAUW (chpt. pres. 1989-90, Edn. Found. program chair 1990-91), LWV (pres. Moscow chpt. 1987-89, treas. Metro Des Moines chpt., 2002—), Idaho League Women Voters (dir. 1989-91, v.p. 1991-93), Iowa League Women Voters (dir. 1995-99), Soc. for Coll. and Univ. Planning (regional communications coord., chair grad. student paper competition 1994, mem. publs. adv. com. 1995—2001), Nat. Working Group on Coll. and Univ. Facilities. Avocations: gardening, exercise, reading. Office: Iowa Bd Regents 11260 Aurora Ave Urbandale IA 50322

RACUSIN, ROBERT JERROLD, psychiatry educator; b. Dayton, Ohio, Mar. 14, 1946; MD cum laude, Georgetown U., 1971. Cert. psychiatry, child psychiatry Am. Bd. Psychiatry and Neurology. Internship in psychiatry Georgetown U. Affiliated Hosp., Washington, 1971-72, resident in psychiatry, 1972-73; child psychiatry fellow Dartmouth Med. Sch., Hanover, N.H., 1973-75, adj. asst. prof. clin. psychiatry, 1976-78, asst. prof., 1978-84, assoc. prof., 1984—, dir. child psychiat. tng., 1988—. Mem. editl. bd. Jour. Am. Acad. Child & Adolescent Psychiatry, 1998—; contbr. articles to profl. jours. Disting. Fellow Am. Psychiat. Assn. (rep. assembly dist. brs. 1981-89), Fellow Am. Acad. Child and Adolescent Psychiatry, Am. Coll. Psychiatrists Office: Dartmouth Hitchcock Med Ctr One Medical Ctr Dr Lebanon NH 03756

RADA, RUTH BYERS, college dean, author; b. Los Angeles, Oct. 3, 1923; d. George and Gerda Marie (Lihm) Byers; children: Kaaren Ruth, Georgene Melanie. AB, U. So. Calif., 1944, MA, 1945; EdD, Nova U., 1976. Asst. dean instrn. and evening East L.A. Coll., 1964-69, dean instrn., 1969-70; dean student personnel L.A. Harbor Coll., 1970-73, East L.A. Coll., 1973-77, L.A. Mission Coll., 1977-83; prof. biol. sci. East L.A. C.C., 1945-69, ret., 1983. Author: Water Biology, 1950, (with others) Human Body in Health and Disease, 1969, Structure and Function of Human Body, 1970, Laboratory Manual for Introductory Microbiology, 1963. Mem. Calif. Cmty. and Jr. Coll. Assn. (area pres. 1973-74), Calif. Woman Adminstrs. Assn., Los Angeles Coll. Adminstrs. Assn. (sec. 1973-74), Phi Beta Kappa, Phi Kappa Phi, Pi Lambda Theta, Phi Sigma. Republican. Mem. Ch. of Religious Sci.

RADAN, GEORGE TIVADAR, art history and archaeology educator; b. Budapest, Hungary, Dec. 31, 1923; came to U.S., 1959; s. Alfred Albert and Jolanda (Odescalchi) R.; m. Maryann Patricia Radan; children: Christopher Byron, Cornelius Alfred. MA, U. Budapest, 1946, PhD, 1948; AEM, Ecole Du Louvre, Paris, 1968. Asst. dir. Nat. Marit Mus. of Israel, Haifa, 1952-58; dir., sr. researcher Wayne State U., Ky. State U., Hist. Inst. Archeology Excavation, Siena, Italy, 1969-84; prof. Dept. Art History Villanova U., Pa., 1967—. Author: Sons of Zebulon, 1980, Archaeology of Roman Pannonic, 1982, The V.U. Art Collection, 1986; contbg. author: Lecceto, Eremi Augustiniani in Terra Siena, 1992, Mediterranean Cities: Historical Perspectives, 1991. Recipient Ancien Eleve Museologie; Rosemont Coll. Connely grantee, 1968; U. Pa. postdoctoral grant in archaeology, 1969; ACLS grantee to Hungarian Acad. Sci., 1972-73; Internat. Rsch. and Exch. grantee to Archaeol. Inst. Hungary, 1975; Friends of the Haifa, Maritime Mus. grantee to Israeli Nat. Maritime Mus., 1985; NEH grantee to Vatican Libr., 1988. Mem. AAUP. Office: Villanova U Dept Art History Villanova PA 19085

RADCLIFF, MELINDA SUE, language arts teacher; b. Weston, W.Va., Jan. 16, 1972; d. Herbert Gary and lela Grace (Beall) R. BEd, Glenville State Coll., 1995. Fin. adi asst. Glenville (W.Va.) State Coll., 1991-94. Pvt. tutor Glenville, 1991, 93. Sec. Gilmer County FFA Alumni, Glenville, 1995-97; project leader Cox's Mill Tailtwisters 4-H Club, W.Va., 1994-95; mem. Mt. Earnest United Meth. Ch., Conings, W.Va., 1994-95. Am. FFA Degree, Nat. FFA Orgn., Kansas City, Mo., 1993. Mem. Kappa Delta Pi. Democrat. Avocations: showing cattle, reading. Home: RR 1 Box 132 New Milton WV 26411-9603

RADCLIFFE, CLARK JEFFREY, mechanical engineering educator; b. Oakland, Calif., June 6, 1947; s. Charles W. and Martha (Clark) R.; m. Arlene Jane Reck, June 9, 1973; children: Nathaniel, Isadora, Eliott. BS of Mech. Engrng., U. Calif., Davis, 1969, MS in Mech. Engrng., 1971; PhD in Mech. Engrng., U. Calif., Berkeley, 1980. Engr. Aerojet Liquid Rocket Co., Sacramento, Calif., 1969-71; engrng. officer USCG Cutter Reliance, Corpus Christi, Tex., 1971-73; engrng. instr. USCG Acad., New London, Conn., 1973-75; rsch. asst. dept. mech. engrng. U. Calif., Berkeley, 1975-80; from asst. prof. to assoc. prof. mech. engrng. Mich. State U., East Lansing, 1980-93, prof. mech. engrng., 1993—. Mgr. ops. A.H. Case Ctr. for Computer-Aided Design, Mich. State U., East Lansing, 1984-86. Editor: Active Control of Noise and Vibration, 1992; contbr. numerous papers to profl. publs. Recipient Wood award Forest Products Rsch. Soc., 1980. Fellow ASME (assoc. editor Jour. Mechanisms, Transmissions and Automation 1985-88, assoc. editor Jour. Dynamic Sys., Measurement and Control 1990-93, editor procs. 1994 ann. meeting); mem. Tau Beta Pi. Avocations: flying, fishing. Office: Mich State U Dept Mech Engrng East Lansing MI 48824

RADELL, CAROL K. elementary school educator; b. Rochester, NY, Feb. 22, 1939; d. Harold LaVerne and Ruth Elinor Kruger; m. Eugene Arthur Radell, Apr. 30, 1971 (dec. Jan. 18, 1998); children: Terry Jean(dec.), Steven Paul, Marcie Ann. Elem. edn., Long Beach (Calif.) City Coll., 1959; chemistry, Rochester Inst. Tech., 1961; BA, Long Beach (Calif.) City Coll., 1961. Lab. technician Eastman Kodak, Rochester, NY, 1959—63; assoc. tchr. Henrietta Sch. Dist., NY, 1969—71, Fairport Bd. Coop. Edn., NY, 1986—99, Fairport Sch. Dist., 1999—, East Rochester Sch. Dist., NY, 1999—2001, Hemet Unified Sch. Dist., Calif., 1999—2002, Riverside County, Calif., 2000—02. Mem. Safe Celebration Com., Fairport, 1989—90. Mem.: MADD. Avocations: rock climbing, fast walking, reading, volunteer work. Home: 87 Eaglesfield Way Fairport NY 14450

RADEMACHER, ANNA MAE, junior high school educator; b. Hillsboro, Ill., Apr. 22, 1947; d. Herbert Reed and Edna Emma (Boettcher) R. BS in Edn., Cen. Mo. State U., 1969, MS in Edn., 1975; postgrad., U. Mo., St. Louis, 1987-88. Cert. elem. tchr., Mo.; cert. in secondary math. and German. 6th grade tchr. Ft. Zumwalt Sch. Dist., O'Fallon, Mo., 1970, 7th grade math. tchr., 1970-74; 8th grade math., 7th grade social studies tchr. Escuela Campo Alegre, Caracas, Venezuela, 1974-76; 7th and 8th grade math. and German tchr. Francis Howell Sch. Dist., St. Charles, Mo., 1976—97, dept. chmn., 1980—93. Author ch. historical book: The First Hundred Years, 1989. Pres., alumni mem. Mo. Internat. 4-H Youth Exch., 1986-89, sec. 1991-93. Mo. Dept. Elem. and Secondary Schs. grantee, 1990, 91. Mem.: Gasconade County Hist. Soc., NEA. Methodist. Avocations: bicycling, german, history. Home: 1535 Northlea Dr Owensville MO 65066-9658

RADER, RHODA CASWELL, academic program director; b. St. Johnsbury, Vt., July 2, 1945; d. Wilbur Forrest and Aline Emma (Langevin) Caswell; m. William Garrett Rader, May 10, 1969; children: Lorelei May, Peter William, Lisa Anne. Diploma with highest honors, Albany Bus. Coll., 1966; AA with highest distinction, Community Coll. Vt., 1987; BSBA summa cum laude, Trinity Coll., 1987. Asst. comptroller Middlebury (Vt.) Coll., 1980-84, budget dir., 1984-89, assoc. comptroller, 1989-96, gift and endowment officer, 1996—. Mem. AAUW, Inst. Mgmt. Accts., Nat. Assn. Coll. and Univ. Bus. Dirs., Nat. Identification Program for Women in Higher Edn. (instl. rep.), Vt. Higher Ednl. Planning Commn., NAFE, DAR. Avocations: reading, cross-country skiing, gourmet cooking, beekeeping. Office: Middlebury Coll Middlebury VT 05753 E-mail: rader@middlebury.edu.

RADER, WILLIAM DONALD, economics educator, university administrator; b. Chgo., July 12, 1929; s. William Joseph Rader and Martha Virginia (Neubauer) Johnson; m. Mary Louise Poss, June 22, 1957; children: Steven, Lucy. BS, No. Ill. U., 1956, MS, 1957; PhD, Purdue U., 1969. Project dir. U. Chgo., 1964-72; asst. prof. Northeastern Ill. U., Chgo., 1968-72; assoc. prof. Fla. State U., Tallahassee, 1972-77; prof. Ohio U., Athens, 1977—, asst. dean, 1980-86, dir. curriculum and instrn., 1986-93; ret., 1999. Author: Economics and Free Enterprise, 1982. With U.S. Army, 1951-53. Recipient George Washington medal, Freedoms Found., 1968. Mem. KC (treas. 1989-91, pres. 1987-88, v.p. 1985-87, sec. 1983-85). Home: 56 Briarwood Dr Athens OH 45701-1301

RADFORD, VIRGINIA RODRIGUEZ, retired secondary education educator, librarian; b. Willcox, Ariz., Nov. 17, 1917; d. Domingo Acosta and Maria Ceveriana (Lopez) Rodriguez; m. John Houston Radford, June 5, 1942; children: Mary Jane, Ann Christine, Patricia Mae. BA, BS, univ. tchrs. diploma, U. Kans., 1940; Librarianship, Benedictine Coll., Atchinson, Kans., 1972-76. Cert. life. tchr. K-12, Kans., master tchr., 1970. Tchr. Spanish, French, English Horton (Kans.) High Schs., 1957-60; 4th and 5th grade tchr. St. Leo's Parochial Sch., Horton, 1961-62; tchr. Spanish, French/librarian Horton High Sch., 1962-82. Translator U.S. War Dept., San Antonio, 1942; past pres. Brown County Ret. Tchrs. Assn., People-to-People (Horton chpt.); commd. lay min. St. Leo's Ch., 1990; pres. bd. dirs. Horton Libr., 1975; bd. dirs. Tri-County Manor, Horton, 2001. Named Outstanding Secondary Educator of Am., 1975; inducted Kans. Tchrs. Hall of Fame, 1984. Mem.: AAUW, Bus. and Profl. Women, Friends of Libr., Horton Hosp. Aux. (life), Horton Sr. Citizens Club, Inc., VFW Aux. Post 3021 (life), Delta Kappa Gamma (pres. Alpha Kappa chpt.). Roman Catholic. Avocations: reading, music, traveling, photography, collecting letter openers. Home: 439 W 8th St Horton KS 66439-1515

RADICE, BEATRICE ROSEMARIE, family nurse practitioner; b. Bklyn., Nov. 6, 1959; d. Anthony and Rosaria (Liosi) R. BSN, Downstate Med. Ctr., 1981; MSN, Pace U., 1993. Cert. family nurse practitioner. Staff RN Brookdale Hosp. Med. Ctr., Bklyn., 1982-83; staff RN surg. ICU/staffing Maimonides Med. Ctr., Bklyn., 1984-86; staff nurse emergency rm. Victory Meml. Hosp., Bklyn., 1986-89; nurse clinician North Shore U. Hosp., Manhasset, N.Y., 1989-92, Elderplan, Inc., Bklyn., 1992-94; FNP Luth. Med. Ctr., Bklyn., 1993; FNP occupl. health svc. The N.Y. Hosp., N.Y.C., 1994; FNP, Heartland Med., S.I., N.Y., 1995, Citibank, N.Y.C., 1995-97; FNP, supr. Health First, N.Y.C., 1997-98; FNP, dir. student health svcs. N.Y.C. Coll. Tech., 1999—. Presenter in field. Mem. Am. Coll. Health Assn., Health Svcs. Assn. So. Calif. (presenter), N.Y. State Nurses Assn. (presenter poster 1991, 92, legis. com. 1993-94), N.Y. State Coalition Nurse Practitioners (presenter poster 1993), N.Y. Acad. Medicine (presenter poster, spkr. 1998). Office: 300 Jay St # P104 Brooklyn NY 11201-1909

RADIE, CHRISTINE JO, middle school educator; b. South Bend, Ind., June 13, 1952; d. Dean E. DeLeury and Rita Lorraine Hall Kroll; children: William, Matthew. BS, Ball State U., 1974; MEd, Kent State U., 1994. Cert. tchr. English and reading, Ohio. Tchr. Marion (Ind.) Pub. Schs., 1974-77, Licking Hts. (Ohio) Schs., 1986-88; tchr. lang. arts Hudson (Ohio) Local Schs., 1991—. Assoc./cons. nat. Writing Project, 1997—; drama advisor Hudson Local Schs., 1994—, asst. varsity softball coach, 1999-2000, content facilitator, 2001—. Contbg. author: Ohio Teachers Write, 1997, Ohio Journal of English Language Art, 1998. Tchr. rep. Hudson PTO, 1997—. Named Outstanding Mid. Sch. English Arts Educator for Ohio, 1999. Mem. Nat. Mid. Sch. Assn., Ohio Coun. Tchrs. English Lang. Arts, Nat. Coun. Tchrs. English. Avocations: writing, roller blading, gardening. Office: Hudson Mid Sch 77 N Oviatt St Hudson OH 44236-3043

RADIN, CHARLES LEWIS, mathematics educator, physicist; b. N.Y.C., Jan. 15, 1945; s. Hy and Matilda (Bourla) R.; m. Diane Fay Sole, June 22, 1969; 1 child, Sarah. BS, CCNY, 1965; PhD, U. Rochester, 1970. Postdoctoral fellow in physics U. Nijmegen, The Netherlands, 1970-71; rsch. assoc. in physics Princeton (N.J.) U., 1971-73; rsch. assoc. in math. Rockefeller U., N.Y.C., 1973-74; instr. in math. U. Pa., Phila., 1974-76; asst. prof. U. Tex., Austin, 1976-80, assoc. prof., 1980-90, prof., 1990—. Contbr. more than 50 articles to profl. jours.; editorial bd. Modern Physics Letters B., Internat. Jour. Modern Physics B. NSF grantee, 1978—. Mem. Am. Math. Soc., Am. Phys. Soc., Internat. Assn. in Mathematical Physics. Office: U Tex Math Dept Austin TX 78712

RADKE, BEVERLY IDA, elementary education educator; b. Sutherland, Iowa, May 17, 1945; d. Henry John and Eleonora Ella (Koehlmoos) Jalas; m. Lee Allen Radke, Aug. 12, 1971. BA, Buena Vista Coll., 1967. Cert. elem. edn. tchr. Kindergarten tchr. Cherokee (Iowa) Schs., 1967-2000, ret., 2000. Mem. NEA, Iowa State Edn. Assn., Cherokee Edn. Assn. (pres., sec. 1988-90), Alpha Delta Kappa (chaplain; state treas. 2000—). Lutheran. Avocations: playing piano and organ, fishing, gardening. Home: 5353 120th St Holstein IA 51025-8134

RADKE, WILLIAM JOHN, biology educator; b. Mankato, Minn., June 8, 1947; s. Gerhard William and Ruth Ida (Stegeman) R.; m. Christine Maria Albasi, Aug. 11, 1984; children: Sarah Catherine, Julia Ruth. BS in Sci., Mankato State U., 1970, MS, 1972; PhD, U. Ariz., 1975. Asst. prof. biology U. Ctrl. Okla., Edmond, 1975-80, assoc. prof. biology, 1980-85, prof. biology, 1985—, assoc. v.p. acad. affairs, 2002—. Co-author: (book/manual) Laboratory Anatomy of the Perch, 1991, Laboratory Anatomy of the Vertebrates, 1992, Laboratory Anatomy of the Cat, 1995, Laboratory Anatomy of the Fetal Pig, 1997, Laboratory Anatomy of the Mink, 1998; author: (book/manual) Human Anatomy for Allied Health Students, 1991, 3d edit., 1995, Laboratory Guide for Human Anatomy, 2002. Mem. Okla. City Audubon Soc., Oklahoma City, 1976. Mem. Okla. Soc. Physiologists (pres.-elect 1993-94), Okla. Ornithological Soc. Bull. (assoc. editor 1987-88), Human Anatomy and Physiology Soc., Sigma Xi (pres.-elect 1993-94). Achievements include research in the control of thyrotropic hormone and aldosterone secretion in the fowl; research in SEM description of pores in plasma membranes of fowl epidermis; development of a technique for collection of stomach contents in birds by emesis. Aging birds using pentosidine cross-linkages. Office: Univ of Ctrl Oklahoma Assoc VP Academic Affairs 100 University Dr Edmond OK 73034

RADMER, MICHAEL JOHN, lawyer, educator; b. Wisconsin Rapids, Wis., Apr. 28, 1945; s. Donald Richard and Thelma Loretta (Donahue) R.; children from previous marriage: Christina Nicole, Ryan Michael; m. Laurie J. Anshus, Dec. 22, 1983; 1 child, Michael John BS, Northwestern U., Evanston, Ill., 1967; JD, Harvard U., 1970. Bar: Minn. 1970. Assoc. Dorsey & Whitney, Mpls., 1970-75, ptnr., 1976—. Lectr. law Hamline U. Law Sch., St. Paul, 1981-84; gen. counsel, rep., sec./asst. sec. 142 federally registered investment cos., Mpls. and St. Paul, 1977—. Contbr. articles to legal jours. Active legal work Hennepin County Legal Advice Clinic, Mpls., 1971—. Mem. ABA, Minn. Bar Assn., Hennepin County Bar Assn. Clubs: Mpls. Athletic. Home: 4329 E Lake Harriet Pky Minneapolis MN 55409-1725 Office: Dorsey & Whitney 50 South 6th St Ste 1500 Minneapolis MN 55402

RADOVICH, DONALD, painter, illustrator, retired art educator; b. Nazareth, Pa, Jan. 3, 1932; s. Zivan and Angeline (Trumich) R.; m. Sheryl Ann Nash; children: Steven Michael, Nicholas Daniel. BFA, U. N.Mex., 1956, MA in Painting, 1960; postgrad., San Miguél Allende, Gto, Mex.,

1970. Instr. of art to prof. of art Western State Coll., Gunnison, Colo., 1964-88, prof. emeritus, 1988—. Illustrator U. N.Mex. Press, 1963, Western State Press, 1980, Reader's Digest Corp., 1990, Phil. Acad. of Sci., 1990, Denver Colo. Sci., 1990, Nat. Wildlife Fedn., 1990, Birds of West Indies, 1998, many others; invitational exhibit Wave Hill Mus., 1982; one person exhibit Nat. Wildlife Fedn., 1988, two person, Tohono Chul Pk. Gallery, Tucson, 2003. With US Army, 1956-58. Avocation: gardening. Home: PO Box 782 Ouray CO 81427-0782

RADTKE, KAREN DOROTHY, school nurse; b. Chgo., Jan. 16, 1951; d. John Mansfield and Dorothy Lena (Kleinau) Byrne; m. Richard F. Radtke, Nov. 18, 1978; children: Erin, Gretchen, R. Eric. BSN, Pacific Luth. U., 1974; AA, Tacoma C.C., 1976; Ma in Human Resource Devel., Redlands U., 1986. RN, Calif.; cert. health svcs., San Diego State U. Patient care liaison St. Josephs Hosp., Tacoma, Wash., 1975-77; educator, interim dir. Mark E. Reed Meml. Hosp., Tacoma, Wash., 1977-78; clin. dir. Home Health Svcs., San Bernardino, Calif., 1979-80; head nurse, orthopaedics Riverside (Calif.) Cmty. Hosp., 1980-85, educator, 1985-89; sch. nurse Riverside County Office Edn., 1989—; adminstrv. liaison Riverside Cmty. Hosp., 1990—. Named Outstanding Achievement Parent Tchr. Assn., Riverside, 1990. Mem.: San Bernardino/Riverside Sch. Nurse Orgn. (pres.-elect 1999—2001, pres. 2001—03), Calif. Sch. Nurse Assn. (spl. edn. rep. 1993, mktg. chmn. 1995, liaison 2001—03), Nat. Assn. Sch. Nurses. Office: Riverside County Office Edn 3939 13th St Riverside CA 92501-3505

RADTKE, PEGGY ANN, physical education educator; b. Owatonna, Minn., Dec. 30, 1953; d. Milton Lowell and Phyllis Ann (Atkinson) Iverson; m. Curtis Lee Radtke, June 19, 1976; children: Brian, Kristin, Scott. BS in Biology, Mankato State U., 1976, B in Teaching Phys. Edn., 1991. Cert. phys. edn., adapted phys. edn. tchr., Minn. Aquatics instr. Mankato State U., Mankato, Minn., 1989-92, health, human performance instr., 1992-93; phys. edn. tchr., asst. boys varsity swim coach Owatonna (Minn.) Pub. Schs., 1993—. Com. mem. Minn. Aquatics Assn., 1990-92. Mem. AAHPERD, Minn. AHPERD. Avocation: scuba diving. Home: 11146 Kenyon Blvd Kenyon MN 55946-2049

RADUN, ARTHUR VORWERK, electrical engineering educator; b. Bristol, Conn., Mar. 14, 1954; s. Albert and Hedwig Anna (Vorwerk) R.; m. Colleen Marie Whalen, Apr. 25, 1981; children: Gregory Arthur, Kathryn Marie. AS in Elec. Technology, Hartford State Tech. Coll., 1974; BSEE, MSEE, MIT, 1978, PhD, 1981. Elec. engr. GE Ordnance System, Pittsfield, Mass., 1981-86, GE Corp. Rsch. & Devel., Schenectady, N.Y., 1986-93; asst. prof. U. Ky., Lexington, 1993-96, assoc. prof., 1996—. Cons. in field. Contbr. articles to profl. jours. Mem. IEEE, Soc. Automotive Engrs. (Arch T. Colwell Merit award 1993, cert. appreciation 1994, 95), N.Y. Acad. Scis. Achievements include patentee in field. Office: U Ky 453 Anderson Hl Lexington KY 40506-0001

RAFFA, JEAN BENEDICT, author, educator; b. Lansing, Mich., Apr. 23, 1943; d. Ernest Raymond and Verna Lois (Borst) Benedict; m. Frederick Anthony Raffa, June 15, 1964; children: Juliette Louise, Matthew Benedict. BS, Fla. State U., 1964, MS, 1968; EdD, U. Fla., 1982. Tchr. Leon County Sch. Sys., Tallahassee, Fla., 1964-69; coord. children's programming WFTV, Orlando, Fla., 1978-80; cons. edn. Tchr. Edn. Ctr. U. Ctrl. Fla., Orlando, 1980-89; writer Orlando, Fla., 1989—; instr. Disney Inst., Orlando, Fla., 1996. Adj. instr. U. Cen. Fla., 1977-85; vis. asst. prof. Stetson U., DeLand, Fla., 1988-89; cons. Lang. Arts Curriculum Com. Orange County Sch. Sys., 1983; CEO Inner World Encounters, Orlando, 1995—, inst. The Jung Center, Winter Park, FL, 1997—. Author: Introduction to Television Literacy, 1989, The Bridge to Wholeness: A Feminine Alternative to the Hero Myth, 1992, Dream Theatres of the Soul: Empowering the Feminine Through Jungian Dreamwork, 1994; contbr. articles to profl. jours., articles and meditations to religious jours. Mistress of ceremonies Young Authors' Conf., Orange and Volusia County Sch. Sys., 1984-85; cons. Young Authors' Conf. Orange and Seminole County Sch. Sys., 1985-89; judge Volusia County Pub. Schs. Poetry Contest, 1983, 84, Seminole County Pub. Schs. Lit. Mag., 1985-89; pres. Maitland (Fla.) Jr. H.S. PTA, 1986-87; pres., bd. dirs. Canterbury Retreat and Conf. Ctr. Episcopal Diocese Ctrl. Fla., 1988-90; chair edn. commn. Episcopal Ch. of the Good Shepherd, 1986-89; sr. warden Vestry of Episcopal Ch. of the Good Shepherd, 1988. Mem. Kappa Delta Pi, Phi Delta Kappa. Democrat. Avocations: antiques, horseback riding, travel, reading. Office: 17 S Osceola Ave Ste 200 Orlando FL 32801-2828

RAFFINI, RENEE KATHLEEN, foreign language professional, educator; b. Racine, Wis., Mar. 10, 1955; d. John Peter and Clara Cecelia (Urli) R.; m. Anthony M. Yezer, Sept. 19, 1984 (div. 1997); children: Claire Eva, Benjamin Anton; m. Mark L. Whipple, June 26, 1999. BA in Econs. and French, U. Wis., 1976; MA in Econs., George Washington U., 1984, MEd, 1996. Cert. secondary edn. tchr. French and social studies, Md. Legis. aide to spkr. Wis. State Assembly, Madison, 1974-78; credit union advisor/auditor U.S. Peace Corps, Bafoussam, Cameroon, 1978-80; exec. aide George Washington U. Med. Faculty Assn., Washington, 1980-84; fin. economist U.S. Securities and Exch. Com., Washington, 1984-89; tchr. of French Bethesda (Md.) - Chevy Chase H.S., 1992-94; history tchr. French Internat. Sch., Bethesda, 1997; tchr. of French Walter Johnson H.S., Bethesda, 1994—. Sponsor Bethesda Comm. Action Team, 1995—; student mentor Walter Johnson H.S., 1994—; advisor U.S. Peace Corps Tchg. Forum, Washington, 1997. Judge of strokes and turns Montgomery County Swim League, Bethesda, 1997; vestry mem. Grace Episcopal Ch., Silver Spring, Md., 1996-97; active mem. Returned Peace Corps Assns., Washington, 1980—. Grantee Youth Rise, State of Md., Annapolis, 1996-97, Neighborhood Empowerment, Rockville, Md., 1996-97. Mem. Am. Coun. Tchrs. of Fgn. Langs., Am. Econs. Assn., Am. Assn. Tchrs. of French, Les Francomeres (founder 1992—), Les Compagnons de la Parole Française, Friends of Cameroon. Democrat. Avocations: sailing, tennis, photography, camping. Office: Walter Johnson HS 6400 Rock Spring Dr Bethesda MD 20814-1913

RAFFO, SUSAN HENNEY, elementary education educator; b. Kendallville, Ind., Feb. 14, 1945; d. Gordon Theron and Sue (Kizer) Henney; m. Lawrence Albert Raffo, Feb. 19, 1977; children: Timothy, Kathleen. BS in Elem. Edn., Ball State U., 1967; M in Spl. Edn., San Francisco State U., 1972. Cert. elem. tchr., Calif. Tchr. East Noble Sch. Corp., Kendallville, Ind., 1967-68, Burlingame (Calif.) Sch. Dist., 1968-2000, Las Lomitas (Calif.) Sch. Dist., 2000—. Master tchr. San Francisco State U., 1970-95, U. Notre Dame de Namur, Belmont, Calif., 1980-95, instr. grad. edn. dept., 1996—. Registrar AYSO, Burlingame, 1987-94; bd. dirs. Burlingame Cmty. Edn. Found., 1989-95, sec., 1992-94. Recipient Svc. award PTA, 1989, J. Russell Kent award for innovative programs San Mateo County Sch. Bds. Assn., 1993; named Tchr. of Yr., Lions Club, 1993. Mem. Calif. Reading Assn., Alpha Delta Kappa, Phi Delta Kappa. Avocations: reading, fabric arts, golf. Office: La Entrada Sch 2200 Sharon Rd Menlo Park CA 94025-6796 E-mail: sraffo@llesd.k12.ca.us., sraffo@email.com.

RAGAN, BETTY SAPP, artist, educator; b. Birmingham, Ala., Mar. 15, 1937; d. Robert William and Emma Mildred (O'Neal) Sapp; m. Thaxton Drew Ragan, Apr. 1958 (div. Aug. 1986); 1 child, Robert McClearan. BA cum laude, Birmingham-So. Coll., 1958; student, Allegheny Coll., 1971-72, Auburn U., 1980-83; MFA, Pratt Inst., 1985. Teachng asst. Pratt Inst., Bklyn., 1985; vis. asst. prof. dept. art Auburn U., 1985-89; asst. prof. dept. art U. Puget Sound, 1989-91, assoc. prof. photography and printmaking, dept. art, 1992—98, prof., 1998—. Panel moderator Soc. for Photo Edn. N.W., Tacoma, 1993; co-curator But Is It Art, Tacoma, 1993. Exhibited photography in solo shows at Maude Kerns Gallery, Eugene, Oreg., 1995, Helen Smith Gallery, Green River C.C., Auburn, Wash., 1996, others; group shows include Hanson Gallery, New Orleans, 1980, Montgomery (Ala.) Mus. Fine Arts, 1981, Ga. State U., Atlanta, 1981, Park Ave Atrium, N.Y.C., 1985, Carnegie Art Ctr., Walla Walla, Wash., 1990, Definitive Image Gallery, Seattle, 1992, Seattle Ctr. Pavilion, 1993, San Diego Art Inst., 1993, Eagle Gallery, Murray, Ky., 1994, B St. Pier Gallery, San Diego, 1995, Camera Club N.Y., 2002, numerous others; artist/photographer various collage series; co-curator But Is It Art?, Tacoma, 1993. Recipient numerous awards for art including Merit award Fine Arts Mus. of the South, Mobile, 1983, Dirk Andrew Phibbs Rsch. award U. Puget Sound, Tacoma, 1994, Disting. Prof. award, 2003. Mem. Soc. for Photog. Edn., Soc. Photog. Edn./N.W. (sec. 1990-93), Artist Trust, Women's Caucus for Art, Coll. Art Assn., Seattle Women's Caucus for Art. Unitarian Universalist. Avocations: entomology, hiking, gardening, existential philosophy. Office: U Puget Sound Dept Art 1500 N Warner St Tacoma WA 98416-0001

RAGANS, ROSALIND DOROTHY, textbook author, retired art educator; b. Bklyn., Feb. 28, 1933; d. Sidney Guy Gordon and Beatrice (Zuckerman) Safier; m. John Franklin Ragans, July 31, 1965; 1 child, John Lee. BFA, CUNY-Hunter Coll., 1955; MEd, Ga. So. Coll., 1967; EdD, U. Ga., 1971. Cert. tchr. art, Ga. Tchr. art Union City (N.J.) Bd. Edn., 1956-62; tchr. 1st grade Chatham Bd. Edn., Savannah, Ga., 1962-64; instr. art Ga. So. U., Statesboro, 1964-69, asst. prof., 1969-76, assoc. prof., 1976-89, prof. emeritus, 1989—. Keynote speaker art edn. confs., Ind., 1987, 88, Ark., Wis., 1989, Md., 1990, others; presenter GA Art Edn. Conf., 1998, 2000, NAEA, 1999. Author: (textbooks) ArtTalk, 1988, 2d edit., 1994, 3d edit., 1999, Introducing Art, 1997, Exploring Art, 1990, 2d edit., 1997, Understanding Art, 1990, 2d edit., 1997, (sr. author) Art Connections K-5, 1997, 2d edit., 2000. Mem. Nat. Assn. Educators (life), Ga. Assn. Educators (life), Nat. Art Edn. Assn. (Southeastern Art Educator of Yr. 1991, Nat. Art Educator of Yr. 1992), Ga. Art Edn. Assn. (Ga. Art Educator of Yr. 1990), Pilot Club Internat. (Ga. dist., Ga. Profl. Handicapped Woman of Yr. 1988). Jewish. Avocation: painting.

RAGHAVAN, DEREK, oncologist, medical researcher and educator; b., Aug. 11, 1949; came to U.S., 1991; m. Patricia Harrison; 2 children. MB, BS with honors, Sydney U., 1974; PhD, London U., 1984. Cert. Royal Australian Coll. Physicians, Fgn. Lic. Exam Coun., Ednl. Coun. Fgn. Med. Grads., Gen. Med. Coun. (U.K.), NSW Med. Bd. (Australia). Resident, registrar Royal Prince Alfred Hosp., Sydney, 1974-77; lectr., sr. registrar Royal Marsden Hosp., London, 1978-80; rsch. fellow Ludwig Inst. Cancer Rsch., London, 1978-80; med. rsch. specialist U. Minn., Mpls., 1980-81; sr. specialist med. oncology Royal Prince Alfred Hosp., Sydney, 1981-91; prof., chief solid tumor oncology and investigational therapeutics Roswell Park Cancer Inst. and SUNY, Buffalo, 1991-97; prof. medicine and urology U. So. Calif., L.A., 1997—, chief divsn. med. oncology, 1997—, assoc. dir. Norris Cancer Ctr., 1997—. Pres. med. staff Roswell Park Cancer Inst., Buffalo, 1995—96; chair VA Merit Rev. Bd. in Oncology, 1996—97; mem. oncology drug adv. com. FDA, 1996—2000; chair cancer clin. investigations review com. Nat. Cancer Inst., 1996—97, mem. cancer ctrs. support rev. com., 2000—; prof. medicine SUNY, Buffalo, 1991—97, prof. urology, 1996—97; chief divsn. med. oncology U. So. Calif., 1997, assoc. dir. U. So. Calif.-Norris Cancer Ctr., 1997—; mem. VA Merit Rev. Bd. for Prostate Cancer, 1998, NIH Support Cancer Ctr. Rev. Com., 2000—; mem. scientific adv. bd. Southwest Oncology Group, 1998—, bd. govs., 1998—, vice chair genitournairy com., 1998; vice chair genitourinary cancer com. Radiation Therapy Oncology Group, 1995—97; mem. sci. adv. com. European Orgn. for Rsch. and Treatment of Cancer, 2000—, mem. external sci. audit com., 2001—; mem. external adv. bd. Comprehensive Cancer Ctr. U. Ala., Birmingham, 2002—; mem. external adv. bd. Ohio State U. James Comprehensive Cancer Ctr., 2002—; mem. clin. trials and awards adv. com. Cancer Rsch. UK, 2002—. Editor: The Management of Bladder Cancer, 1988, Textbook of Uncommon Cancer, 1988, 2d edit. 1999, Principles and Practice of Genitourinary Oncology, 1997, ACS Atlas of Clinical Oncology-Germ Cell Tumors, 2002; assoc. editor Urologic Oncology, 1995—, Clin. Cancer Rsch., 1996—; mem. editl. bd. Jour. Clin. Oncology, 1990-94, European Jour. Cancer, The Prostate, The Breast, Prostate Cancer, Advances in Oncology, Abstracts in Hematology and Oncology, 1998-2000; mem. editl. bd. Oncology; bd. cons. Jour. Urology, 1996—; contbr. numerous articles to profl. jours. Rsch. grantee Nat. Health and Med. Rsch. Coun., Australia, 1983-90; traveling fellow NSW Cancer Coun., Sydney, 1978; named Hospice Physician of Yr., Hospice of Buffalo, 1994. Fellow: ACP (sci. program com. 2000, MKSAP XI com. 1997—98), Royal Australian Coll. Physicians (chair specialist adv. com. in med. oncology 1988—90); mem.: Sydney U. Med. Soc. (pres. 1974), Med. Oncology Group Australia (chmn. 1988—90), Soc. Urologic Oncology, Am. Assn. Cancer Rsch., Am. Soc. Clin. Oncology (chair cancer comms. com. 1998—2000, liaison Am. joint com. on cancer 1995—2000, program com. 1999—2000, chair cancer comms. com. 1998—2000, AJCC liaison 1995—2000, mem. pub. issues com. 2000—). Avocations: tennis, squash. Office: U So Calif-Norris Cancer Ctr 1441 Eastlake Ave Los Angeles CA 90089-0001

RAGLAND, BOB, artist, educator; b. Cleve., Dec. 11, 1938; s. Carey and Violet (English) R. Cert. Completion, Rocky Mount Sch. Art, Denver, 1968. Instr. painting and drawing Denver Pub. Libr., 1969-71, Eastside Action Ctr., Denver, 1969-71; artist-in-residence Model Cities Cultural Arts Ctr. Workshop, 1971-73; artist/tchr. KRMA-TV. Lectr. in field; vis. artist Denver Pub. Sch. for the Arts, 1993-96, Urban Peak Homeless Ctr., Denver, 1996; founding faculty mem. Auraria campus C.C. Denver, 1970-72; lectr. Afro-Am. art of the 60's and 70's; visual arts coord. City Spirit Project, Denver, 1978; instr. Gove Cmty. Sch., 1979-95, Met. State Coll., Denver, Arapahoe C.C., Littleton, Colo.; artist-in-residence Fred N. Thomas Career Edn. Ctr., Denver Pub. Schs., 1997—, Denver Athletic Club, summer 2000; vis. artist Summer Scholars Program, Denver, 1998; founder Non-Starving Artist's Project, Denver, 1996, City Pk. Art Festival, Denver, 2003, Summer Scholars, 2002, Art Students League, 2003; art career coach 1980—; advisor Foothills Art Ctr., 1998; art career coach, 1980—. Exhibited in 16th Ann. Drawing Exhbn., Dallas Mus. Fine Art Traveling Exhbn., 1967, Tubman Gallery, Boston, 1981; one man shows at Cleve. State U., 1968, Denver Nat. Bank, 1980-81, Century Bank Cherry Creek, Denver, 1980-81; works in permanet collections at Denver Pub. Libr., Karamu House, Cleve., Irving St. Ctr. Cultural Arts Program, Denver; group exhbns. include Colo. History Mus., 1993, 94, 95, Savageau Art Gallery, 1995-96, Met. State Coll. Visual Arts Ctr., 1993, The Triumph of the Human Spirit Foothills Art Ctr., Golden, Colo., 1997, 1st Plymouth Congl. Ch., 2000; author: The Artists Survival Handbook or What to do till You're Rich and Famous, 1980; pub.: Colo. Gallery Guide, 1978—; contbr. Black Umbrella/Black Artists Denver. Chmn. Arts and Humanities Com., 1968-69. Inducted in Colo. 100, Denver Post, Colo. Hist. Soc., 1993; recipient Excellence in Arts award Denver Black Arts Festival, 1993, Recognition award KCNC-TV and Denver Ctr. Performing Arts, 1986. Mem. Colo. Black Umbrella. Home: 1723 E 25th Ave Denver CO 80205-5505

RAGLAND, CARROLL ANN, law educator, judicial officer; b. New Orleans, Nov. 28, 1946; d. Herbert Eugene Watson and Mary May (LeCompte) Leathers; children: Robert A. Sinex, Jr., Stacie Bateman, Joy Montgomery. JD, San Francisco Law Sch., 1980. Bar: Calif. 1980, U.S. Supreme Ct. 1993. Pvt. practice, Santa Rosa, Calif., 1980-85; child custody mediator Sonoma County Superior Ct., Santa Rosa, 1985-86; chief dep. county counsel Butte County Counsel, Oroville, Calif., 1986-87; chief dep. dist. atty. Butte County Dist. Atty., Oroville, 1987-95; referee Shasta County Superior Ct., Redding, Calif., 1995-96, commr., 1996—; dean faculty, law prof. Calif. No. Sch. of Law, Chico, 1987—. Instr. Shasta Coll., 1996—. Commr. Yuba County Juvenile Justice and Delinquency Prevention Commn., Marysville, Calif., 1993-94. Fellow Lawyers in Mensa. Avocations: scuba diving, reading, crossword puzzles. Address: 1074 East Ave Ste K3 Chico CA 95926-1052

RAGLAND, INES COLOM, principal; b. Washington, Mar. 12, 1947; d. Jose Luis Sr. and Frances Yerby (Pannill) Colom; m. Benjamin Michael Ragland, Dec. 17, 1977 (div. May 1991); children: Michelle Elizabeth, Rachael Christine. BA in Secondary Edn., Longwood Coll., 1969, MS in Secondary Adminstrn., 1992. Clk. Va. State Water Control Bd., Richmond, 1969; tchr. Spanish Richmond City Pub. Schs., 1969-74; planning supr. Va. State Water Control Bd., 1974-78; asst. prin., tchr., prin. Grove Ave. Bapt. Christian Sch., Richmond, 1978-83; guidance tchr., asst. prin. Victory Christian Acad., Richmond, 1990—. Cons. in field. Mission participant, El Salvador, 1992. Mem. ASCD. Avocations: civil war research, church. Office: Victory Christian Acad 8491 Chamberlayne Rd Richmond VA 23227-1550

RAGLAND, KATHRYN MARIE, dancer, educator; b. Lakewood, Ohio, Nov. 22, 1948; d. Earl Albert and Alice Maxine (Outzs) R.; m. Donald Glen Rubright, Sept. 1, 1973 (div. 1977); m. Jack Victor Rutberg, Mar. 9, 1980 (div. 1988); 1 child, Jessica Erin; m. Johnny Anthony Vergona, Oct. 9, 1988; 1 child, David Sean; stepchildren: Danielle Evelyn Vergona, Jonathan Chaunch Vergona. AA, L.A. Valley Coll., 1971; BFA cum laude, U. Utah, 1973, MFA in Dance, 1975; MA in Marriage, Family and Child Counseling/Clin. Child Devel., Pacific Oaks Coll., 1993; postgrad., Fielding Inst., 2001—. Lic. marriage and family therapist. With Momentum Dance Co., LA, 1975-77; dance spl. pub. sch. LA, 1975-76; instr. Scripps Coll., Claremont, Calif., 1976-77; dir. dance Cypress Coll., Calif., 1978-85, instr. dance, 1978—85, 1986—2002; owner, operator Gymboree, 1985-88. Mem. adj. faculty Antioch U., 1998—; faculty facilitator MA-CEL program Fielding Grad. Inst.; dance instr. Hollywood (Calif.) Little Red Sch. House, 1985-89, sch. coun., 1997—, asst. head of sch., 2000-02, Hollywood Schoullhouse prin., 2002—; dance instr. McGroarty Arts Ctr., 1992-97, bd. dirs., 1991-92, 97-2002; mem. arts assistance team L.A. Supt. Schs.; curriculum coun. LA HS Performing Arts, adv. bd., 1986-88, Dance Resource Ctr., 1991-92; intern Julie Ann Singer Ctr. Therapeutic Sch., 1991-92; coord. infant devel. program Santa Clara Valley Child and Family Devel. Ctr., 1992-93; therapist Julia Ann Singer Ctr. Family Stress Program, 1994-95, Verdugo Mental Health Ctr., 1994—; crisis counselor Verdugo Disaster Recovery Program, 1994-95; trainer Project COPE, 1995-96; co-dir. Verdugo Creative Arts Group, 1995-2002; program coord. Atwater Park Ctr., 1996-97; coach LA Odyssey of the Mind, 1998—, LA regional dir., 2002, bd. dirs., 2002--; bd. dirs. L.A. Basin, 2002—. Author/choreographer Kitty Kats, 1986; choreography work includes Man of La Mancha, 1976-80, Pippin, 1981, Fiddler on the Roof, 1982, Music Man, 1983, Spanish Suite, 1983, A Funny Thing Happened on the Way to the Forum, 1984, Skaters Edge, 1984, Cartoon, 1984, Urban Primitive, 1985, Cabaret, 1985, Healings, 1987, Cloud Reveries, 1988, Guys and Dolls, 1988, The Lottery, 1988, Cabaret, 1989, Atmos, 1990, Damn Yankees, 1990, Conflict of Interest, 1990; author, dir., choreographer We Saved the Day, 1987, The Visit, 1988, Where the Wild Things Are, 1991, Evening's After Image, 1992, Hair, 1992, South Pacific, 1993, Hello Dolly, 1993, In Search of Quieter Times and Places, 1993, Fiddler on the Roof, 1994, Pajama Game, 1994, Nine, 1994, Testosteroni Baloney, 1994, Guys and Dolls, 1995, Into the Woods, 1995, Alice in Wonderland, 1996, Pirates of Penzance, 1997, Rags, 1997; dir. Courage of the Heart, 1998; dir./choreographer Bye Bye Birdie, 1998; choreographer Mikado, 1998, Sweeney Todd, 1999, Funny Thing Happened on the Way to the Forum, 1999, Jesus Christ Superstar, 1999, Oklahoma, 2000, Rocky Horror Show, 2000, Man of La Mancha, 2001, Joseph and the Amazing Technicolor Dreamcoat, 2001, Cabaret, 2002. Mem. So. Calif. steering com. Legis. Action Coalition Arts Edn.; den leader Cub Scouts, 1996-2000. Mem. AAHPERD, ASCD, AARP, Dance Resource Ctr., Calif. Dance Educators Assn. (v.p. 1980-82, legis. rep. 1982-86), Calif. Music Educators (legis. com. 1982-86), L.A. Area Dance Alliance, Faculty Assn. C.C., Calif. Assn. Health, Phys. Edn., Recreation and Dance, Calif. Assn. Marriage and Family Therapists, So. Calif. Assn. Edn. Young Children (bd. dirs. South Bay chpt.), Calif. Confedn. Arts, Calif. Learning Disabilities Assn., Calif. Elem. Edn. Assn., Josephson Inst. Ethics (mem. shared leadership coun. Millikin Middle Sch. 1994-96, mem. learn coun. Apperson Sch. 1994-95), Assn. Ednl. Therapists, Learning Disabilities Assn. L.A., Calif. Elem. Edn. Assn., Assn. Supervision Curriculum Devel. Democrat. E-mail: kaye@hlrsh.com.

RAGLAND, NANCY SIMMONS, physical education educator; b. Glasgow, Ky., July 27, 1950; d. Robert Ellis and Dorothy Maxey (Coleman) Simmons; m. Richard Turner Ragland, Aug. 8, 1970; children: Rae Ann, Wesley Clay. BS with honors, U. So. Miss., 1972; MEd, Murray State U., 1980. Tchr. phys. edn. Blackburn Jr. H.S., Jackson, Miss., 1971-72, McNabb Elem. Sch., Paducah, Ky., 1973-99; thcr. health and phys. edn. Paducah Tilghman H.S., 1999—. Boys golf coach Paducah Tilghman H.S., 1994—; bd. dir. KHSAA Golf Bd. Mem. Jump Rope for Heart program, coord. demo team Am. Heart Assn., Paducah, 1989-95. Named Ky. Coach of the Yr., State of Ky., 2000-02, Boys Varsity Golf-Mideast Region Coach of the Ur., 2000-01. Mem. NEA, AAPHERD, Ky. Assn. Health, Phys. Edn., Recreation and Dance (chair elem. divsn. 1991-92), Ky. Edn. Assn., Paducah Edn. Assn. (McNabb Elem. Sch. rep.) Alumni Assn. Republican. Avocations: golf, gardening, step aerobics, reading. Home: 4445 Maywood Dr Paducah KY 42001-8709 Office: Paducah Tilghman HS 2400 Washing St Paducah KY 42001

RAGNO, NANCY NICKELL, educational writer; b. Phila., Sept. 2, 1938; d. Paul Eugene and Sara Jane (Mensch) Nickell; m. Joseph Diego Ragno, Aug. 25, 1961; 1 child, Michelle Angela. BA, Lebanon Valley Coll., 1960; MA, NYU, 1968. Cert. tchr., N.J. Tchr. N.J. pub. schs., 1961-68; project editor Prentice-Hall, Inc., Englewood Cliffs, N.J., 1968-70, Harcourt Brace Jovanovich, N.Y.C., 1970-72; sr. editor Silver Burdett Co., Morristown, N.J., 1972-76; editor, writer Houghton Mifflin Co., Boston, 1976-77; sr. editor J.B. Lippincott Co., Phila., 1977-79; sr. author Silver Burdett Ginn, Morristown, 1984—. Author: (textbook series) Silver Burdett English, 1984, World of Language, 1992, (sound filmstrip) The City and the Modern Writer, 1970, Buying on the Installment Plan, 1974. Bassoonist Harrisburg (Pa.) Symphony Orch., 1959, Plainfield (N.J.) Symphony Orch., 1976, Somerset (N.J.) County Orch., 1989, Princeton (N.J.) Community Orch., 1992. Mem. ASCD, Nat. Coun. Tchrs. English, Internat. Reading Assn., Am. Soc. Journalists and Authors, Textbook Authors Assn., Authors Guild, U.S. Power Squadron. Democrat. Mem. Ch. of Christ. Avocations: music, writing, boating. Home: 38 Tortoise Ln Tequesta FL 33469-1552

RAGO, DOROTHY ASHTON, retired educator; b. N.Y.C., Oct. 10, 1925; d. Thomas Percy and Isabel (Seddon) Ashton; divorced, 1958; 1 child, Thomas Ashton. BA, Wellesley Coll., 1946; MA, Columbia U., 1964. Cert. early childhood edn. tchr., N.Y. Editor Alford Baby Group mags., N.Y.C., 1948-52; kindergarten tchr. N.Y.C. Bd. Edn., 1964-86, ret., 1986. Mem. vestry Chapel of St. John, Saunderstown, R.I., 1988-91; mem. Human Rights Com., North Kingstown, R.I., 1988-94; treas. Pettaquamscutt Hist. Soc., 1991-98; mem. exec. bd. Friends of Oceanography/GSO-URI, 1997-2001. Mem. South County Mus., Gilbert Stuart Mus., South County Women's Club, Saunderstown Yacht Club, R.I. Wellesley Club. Republican. Episcopalian. Avocations: local history, hand bell ringing.

RAGUSEA, STEPHEN ANTHONY, psychologist, educator; b. N.Y.C., Mar. 26, 1947; s. Anthony S. and Marie (Giampietro) R.; m. Kathleen Fox, Aug. 14, 1971; children: Anthony, Adam. AA, Nassau Coll., Garden City, N.Y., 1967; BS, Bowling Green (Ohio) State U., 1969; D of Psychology, Baylor U., Waco, Tex., 1980. Diplomate Am. Bd. Profl. Psychology in Family Psychology, Am. Bd. Profl. Neuropsychology; lic. psychologist, Pa., Fla. Tchr. Dayton (Ohio) then Cedar Rapids (Iowa) Community Schs., 1969-76; cons. team for local sch. system Waco, Tex., 1976-77; therapist Meth. Home Children's Guidance Ctr., Waco, 1978-79, Heart of Tex. Mental Health/Mental Retardation Ctr., Waco, 1978-79; intern in psychol.

svcs. Norristown (Pa.) State Hosp., 1979-80; cons. Altoona (Pa.) Hosp. Community Mental Health Ctr., 1981-82; interim dir. psychol. svcs. Nittany Valley Rehab. Hosp., Pleasant Gap, Pa., 1983-84; pres., CEO Centre Valley Mgmt., Inc., 1981-85; exec. dir. Psychol. Forensics, P.C., State College, Pa., 1984-2000; clin. dir. The Meadows Psychiat. Ctr., 1984-85; psychologist, dir. ops. Child, Adult, & Family Psychol. Ctr., State College, 1980—. Asst. prof. dept. individual and family studies Pa. State U.; adj. faculty dept. psychology Pa. State U.; cons. psychol. staff The Meadows Psychiat. Ctr.; psychol. staff rep. to med. staff, allied staff Centre Community Hosp.; bd. dirs. Penn PsyPac; presenter in field. Fellow APA, Am. Coll. Forensic Psychology, Cen. Pa. Psychol. Assn. (past-pres., chmn. profl. affairs com.), Pa. Bd. Psychology, Pa. Psychol. Assn. (past-pres. clin. div., chmn. hosp. practice com., fellow and pres. 1993-94), APA (del. from Pa. Coun. Reps. 1994-2000, chair state and provincial caucus 1997-2000); mem. Am. Soc. Clin. Hypnosis, Nat. Acad. Neuropsychologists.

RAHMAN, RAFIQ UR, oncologist, educator; b. Mirali, Pakistan, Mar. 3, 1957; came to U.S., 1985; s. Rakhman and Bibi (Sana) Gul; m. Shamim Ara Bangash; children: Maryam, Hassan, Haider. BS, MB, U. Peshawar, Pakistan, 1980. Bd. cert. internal medicine, med. oncology, hematology; lic. physician Pa., Ala., Ky. House officer in internal medicine Khyber Teaching Hosp.-U. Peshawar, Pakistan, 1980-81, house officer in gen. surgery, 1981, jr. registrar med. ICU, 1983-84; jr. registrar internal medicine Khyber Teaching Hosp., 1981-82; sr. registrar internal medicine Khyber Teaching Hosp.-Lady Reading Hosp. & Postgrad. Inst., Peshawar, 1984-85; Audrey Meyer Mars fellow in med. oncology Roswell Park Cancer Inst., Buffalo, 1985-86; resident in internal medicine SUNY-Buffalo Gen. Hosp.-Erie County Med. Ctr.-VA Med. Ctr., 1986-88; chief resident in internal medicine SUNY-Buffalo-Erie County Med. Ctr., 1988; fellow in hematology and med. oncology SUNY-Buffalo-Roswell Park Cancer Inst., 1989-90; hematologist, med. oncologist Daniel Boone Clinic and Harlan A.R.H., 1991-92; clin. asst. prof. medicine U. Ky., 1991—; attending physician, hematology/med. oncologist Hardin Meml. Hosp., Elizabethtown, 1993—, chief medicine, 1996, pres. elect med. staff, 2001—02, pres. med. staff, 2002—03. Tchr. med. students Med. Sch., SUNY; participant CALGB protocol studies Roswell Park Cancer Inst., investigator. Editor English sect. Cenna mag. Cenna; contbr. articles to profl. jours. Founder Cmty. Uplift Program, Pakistan; founding dir. Pakistan Human Devel. Fund. Mem.: Assn. Pakistan Physicians Ky. and Ind. (pres. 2002—03), Ky. Med. Assn. Avocations: traveling, aeromodeling, swimming, studying political science and history. Home: 400 Briarwood Cir Elizabethtown KY 42701-6915 Office: 1107 Woodland Dr Ste 105 Elizabethtown KY 42701-2789

RAHN, JAMES ROBERT, secondary school educator; b. Orange, N.J., Nov. 11, 1944; s. Edward August and Edna May Rahn; m. Patricia L. Williams, Apr. 11, 1970. Tchr. Gordon Coll., Wenham, Mass., 1968-71, So. Regional H.S., Manahawkin, N.J., 1971—. Contbr. articles to ednl. jours. Recipient Presdl. award for excellence in teaching math. NSF, 1993, Tandy Outstanding Tchr. award, 1996, Max Sobel Outstanding Math. Educator award, 2001, Advanced Placement Recognition award Mid. States Coll. Bd., 2000. Mem. Assn. Math Tchrs. N.J. (outreach programs, v.p., pres., pres. 1994-95). Home: 334 W 5th St Ship Bottom NJ 08008-4702 Office: So Regional H S 90 Cedar Bridge Rd Manahawkin NJ 08050-3022

RAI, KANTI ROOP, hematologist, oncologist, medical educator; b. Jodhpur, Rajasthan, India, May 10, 1932; came to the U.S., 1957; s. Kedar Roop and Chandra Kaur (Mathur) R.; m. Susan Jo Segal, Mar. 31, 1968; children: Samantha, Joshua. MB, BS, Sawai Man Singh Med. Coll., Jaipur, India, 1955. Diplomate Am. Bd. Pediatrics. Rsch. asst. Brookhaven Nat. Lab., Upton, N.Y., 1960-62, 66-70; chief divsn. exptl. medicine Inst. Nuclear Medicine, New Delhi, 1962-66; hematologist, oncologist L.I. Jewish Med. Ctr., New Hyde Park, N.Y., 1970-80, chief divsn. hematology-oncology, 1981—. Assoc. prof. medicine SUNY, Stony Brook, 1972-79, prof. medicine, 1980-89, Albert Einstein Coll. Medicine, Bronx, 1989—. Fellow ACP, Am. Soc. Hematology, Am. Soc. for Clin. Oncology. Office: L I Jewish Med Ctr Divsn Hematology/Oncology New Hyde Park NY 11040

RAICHLE, ELAINE LUCAS, retired art educator; b. Fremont, Nebr., Dec. 14, 1915; d. Arthur Wilson and Lilli Kathryn (Christensen) Lucas; m. Donald Roderick Raichle, Dec. 15, 1942; children: Douglas, Donald, Alan, Lynne. BA, Midland Coll., 1939; MA, Columbia U., 1949, EdD, 1955. Cert. fine arts tchr., Nebr. Elem. tchr. Cedar Bluffs (Nebr.) Sch., 1934-35, Garden City (Nebr.) Sch., 1935-36; primary tchr. Fremont Pub. Schs., 1936-39, supr. art, 1939-42; art tchr. Irvington (N.J.) High Sch., 1951-53; supr. art edn. Irvington Pub. Schs., 1953-87. Dir. fed. grant Performing Arts as Part of Curriculum, 1965-69, Tchg. Reading Through the Arts, 1970-73; N.J. rep. Nat. Innovation Conf., Hawaii, 1964; mem. bd. trustees Classroom Renaissance N.J. Dept. Edn., Trenton, 1968-72; founder, trustee N.J. State Sch. Arts/N.J. State Dept. Edn., Trenton, 1980—; advisor art dept. Kean. Coll. N.J., Union, 1974-98. Co-author: Gifted and Talented in Arts Education, 1983, Art in the Elementary Schools, 1972; co-editor: Art Education Issues, 1989, History of Art Educators of New Jersey, 1990, The Year of Crafts, 1994, Art: A Cultural Connection, 1995, Art History: Our Heritage, 1996; contbr. numerous articles to profl. jours. Founder, pres. Irvington Symphony Orch., 1968-87; founder, trustee Irvington Cultural Com., 1968-87; co-founder Arts Adminstrs., N.J., 1968; designer Teen Arts N.J., 1970. Lt. (s.g.) USN, 1942-44. Named Citizen of Yr. Irvington C. of C., 1988; recipient Art awards Gov. N.J., 1989, 91, 98; Ford Found. grantee, 1971. Fellow N.J. Art Edn. Assn. (pres. 1997, Disting. Fellows of N.J.); mem. Nat. Art Edn. Assn. (N.J. Art Educator of Yr. 1990, Art Adminstr. eastern divsn. 1991), N.J. Congress Parents and Tchrs. (arts chmn. 1966-74, life), Art Educators N.J. (chmn. speakers com. 1988-99, Disting. Art Educator award 1990), Getty Confs. Art Edn., N.J. Coun. on Edn., Ret. Art Educators N.J. (founder), Nat. Ret. Art Educators (treas. 1991-96), Arts Alliance in Edn., Hands and Minds Inst. Avocations: theater, gardening, bridge, opera, travel. Home: Hightstown, NJ. Died Mar. 13, 2002.

RAIDL, MARTHA ANNE, nutrition and dietetics educator, dietitian; b. Chgo., Aug. 28, 1951; d. Frank Karel and Martha (Brodsky) R. BS, U. Ill., 1973, MS, 1983; BS, U. Ill., Chgo., 1975; PhD, Purdue U., 1993. Clin. dietitian Hammersmith Hosp., London, 1975-77; lectr. nutrition Flour Adv. Bur., London, 1977-78; clin. dietitian Loretto Hosp., Chgo., 1978-80; grad. asst. U. Ill., Urbana, 1980-83; clin. dietitian Lakeland (Fla.) Regional Med. Ctr., 1983-85; food technologist Coca-Cola Foods, Plymouth, Fla., 1985-88; grad. asst. Purdue U., West Lafayette, Ind., 1988-93; asst. prof. East Tenn. State U., Johnson City, 1993—. Spkr. weight control classes Franklin Wellness Ctr., Elizabethton, Tenn., 1995; participant radio show WKPT, Kingsport, Tenn., 1995-96. Contbr. articles to profl. jours. including Jour. Am. Dietetics Assn., Nutrition Rsch., Cereal Chemists. Rschr., cons. Jr. League Cookbook, Johnson City, 1995. Mem. Am. Dietetic Assn., Tenn. Dietetic Assn. (planning com. 1994-95), Tri-Cities Dist. Dietetic Assn. (bd. dirs., edn. and rsch. com. 1993-96). Avocations: piano, cello, jogging, swimming. Office: E Tenn State U PO Box 70671 Johnson City TN 37614-1709 Address: 1971 Wood Duck Ln Boise ID 83706-6102

RAIJMAN, ISAAC, gastroenterologist, endoscopist, educator; b. Empalme, Sonora, Mex., July 6, 1959; came to U.S., 1985; s. Jose and Amalia (Langsam) R. MD, Nat. Autonomous U., Mexico City, 1985; postgrad., Nat. U. Houston, U. Wis., 1985. Diplomate Am. Bd. Internal Medicine, Am. Bd. Gastroenterology. Resident in medicine Mt. Sinai Hosp., Milw., 1986-88, chief resident, 1989; clin. fellow in therapeutic endoscopy Wellesley Hosp., Toronto, Ont., Can., 1992-93; rsch. fellow in gastroenterology U. Tex., Houston, 1989-90, clin. fellow, 1990-92, asst. prof. medicine, 1993-97, dir. therapeutic endoscopy, 1993-97, asst. prof. M.D. Anderson Cancer Ctr., 1993—2000, dir. ann. therapeutic endoscopy course, 1995-97; assoc. prof. Med. U. Tex., 2002—; dir. therapeutic endoscopy U. Tex., 2002—. Chair Ann. Therapeutic Endoscopy Meeting; chair gastroenterology and endoscopy sub. com., GI subcom. on endoscopic credentialing and quality assurance Hermann Hosp., Houston. Author: Pancreas, 1993, Bockus Textbook of Gastroenterology, 1993; also numerous articles; reviewer jours. in field. Mem. Am. Coll. Gastroenterology, Am. Gastroenterology Assn., Internat. Assn. Pancreatology, Am. Soc. Gastrointestinal Endoscopy, Am. Soc. Internal Medicine. Avocation: painting. Office: Digestive Assocs 6624 Fannin Ste 1640 Houston TX 77030 E-mail: iraijman@dahpa.com.

RAINER, REX KELLY, civil engineer, educator; b. Montgomery, Ala., July 17, 1924; s. Kelly Kenyon and Pearl (Jones) R.; m. Betty Ann Page, Aug. 28, 1945; children: Rex Kelly, John Kenyon. BS, Auburn (Ala.) U., 1944, MS, 1946; PhD, Okla. State U., 1967. Asst. engr. L. & N. R.R. Co., Cin., 1944-45; design engr. Polglaze & Basenberg, Birmingham, Ala., 1945-51; pres., chmn. Rainer Co., Inc., Orlando, Fla., 1951-62; prof. civil engring. Auburn U., 1962-67, head civil engring. dept., 1967; exec. v.p., 1980; hwy. dir. State of Ala., 1979-80, fin. dir., 1981-82; spl. asst. to gov. of Ala., 1981-82; dir. Office for Advancement Devel. Industry U. Ala., Birmingham, 1982-86; pres., cons. engr. Rex K. Rainer, Inc., 1982-98, ret., 1998. Cons. to ins. cos., constrn. engring. firms; mem. Ala. Bd. Registration Profl. Engrs. and Land Surveyors, 1977-89. Contbr. articles to profl. jours. Mem. Municipal Planning Bd., 1963-65, Indsl. Park Devel. Bd., 1969-71, So. Regional Edn. Bd., 1982-86. Served with AUS, 1943. Fellow ASCE (sec., treas. 1970, pres. Ala. chpt. 1976-77, chmn. Constrn. Rsch. Coun., chmn. hwy. div. publs. com.; Civil Govt. award 1981); mem. Assn. Gen. Contractors Am. (bd. dirs. 1955), Am. Soc. for Engring. Edn. (chmn. constrn. engring. com.), Am. Pub. Works Assn., Phi Kappa Phi, Tau Beta Pi, Chi Epsilon. Home: 2162 Watercrest Dr Auburn AL 36830

RAINES, JUDI BELLE, language educator, historian; b. N.Y.C., July 16, 1955; d. Alfonso Don Raines and Belle Margarite Samuels. BA in Elem. Edn., Adelphi U., 1977, MA in Secondary Edn., 1981; MS in Guidance, St. Johns U., 2000. ESL tchr. Lincoln Farm Camp, Roscoe, NY; project leader Operation Crossroads, Anguilla, B.W.I., 1981; English tchr., sr. activities advisor Andrew Jackson H.S., Jamaica, NY, 1981—83; history and art tchr., step team advisor Magnatech Jr. H.S. 231, Jamaica, NY, 1985—97; English tchr., dorm supr. project Double Discovery Upward Bound, Queens Coll., Columbia Univ. and Queens Coll., 1989—93; English tchr., dean, step team advisor August Martin H.S., Jamaica, NY, 1997—; adj. instr. SAT prep. CUNY, Jamaica, 1999—; guidance counselor Flushing H.S. Step advisor N.Y.C. Bd. End.; adj. instr. Coll. Now, York Coll., 2000—02. Dir. chorus Ctrl. Bklyn. Model Cities, 1976—77. Recipient Marva Collins Award, cmty. award, 2000, Editors Choice award, 2000—03, Project Prize Educator, Flushing HS, 2002, Gear Up (counselor), 2003. Mem.: ACA, Guilder Lehrman Tchrs. Inst. Avocations: poetry, chess, swimming, quilt making, computers. Office: Flushing High Sch 35-01 Union St Flushing NY 11354

RAINEY, JOHN MARK, administrator; b. Laurel, Miss., Mar. 16, 1947; s. Eleanor I. Rainey; children: Trisha, Kelly, Christopher, Heather, Melissa. BFA, U. So. Miss., 1972; M of Ednl. Adminstrn., Ctrl. Mich. U., 1976; postgrad., Western Mich. U., 1994—. Instr. vocat. media, broadcasting, asst. prin. Sch. Dist. of the City of Saginaw, Mich., 1976-77, specialist, media and publ. svcs., 1977-79, prin., coord. of media and printing svcs. Salina elem., 1979-80, coord. media and publ. svcs., 1980-84, supr. Saginaw pub. schs. media ctr., 1984-92; dir. regional ednl. media ctr. and instrn. ctr. Kalamazoo Valley Intermediate Sch. Dist., 1992—. Adj. prof. Ctrl. Mich. U., Mt. Pleasant, 1989—, Western Mich. U., Kalamazoo, 1992—; bd. dirs. TeleCity USA, Kalamazoo, 1994—, Community Cable Access, Kalamazoo, 1994—. Author: (manual) Critical Viewing Skills/Television, Copyright Manual for Educators, HyperCard for the Teacher, Macintosh Basics-Your Recipe for the Macintosh computer. Bd. dirs. Pub. Awareness Com. Saginaw Community Found., 1990-92; commr. Saginaw City Human Rels. Commn., 1990-92. With USAF, 1965-69. Recipient Outstanding Secondary Educator of Am. award, 1974. Mem. AAUW, ASCD, Nat. Staff Devel. Coun., Assn. for Ednl. Comm. and Tech. (pres. 1992-93, Richard B. Lewis Meml. award 1991), Action for Children's TV, Phi Delta Kappa (Leadership award 1991). Office: Kalamazoo Valley Intermed Sch Dist 1819 E Milham Rd Portage MI 49002-3035

RAINEY, KENNETH TYLER, English language educator; b. Memphis, Feb. 27, 1936; s. Andrew Laughlin Jr. and Gracie Ruth (Mullins) R.; m. Elaine Fitts, Jan. 1, 1960; children: Kenneth Tyler Jr., Timothy Andrew, Kevin Laughlin. BA, Miss. Coll., Clinton, 1958; AM, U. Mich., 1959; ThD, New Orleans Bapt. Sem., 1966; PhD, Ohio State U., 1976. Asst. prof. Eng. Miss. Coll., Clinton, 1965-70, Ohio State U., Lima, 1977-83, U. Memphis, 1983-89; prof., chair humanities and tech. comm. So. Poly. State U., Marietta, Ga., 1989—, disting. prof. tchg. and learning, 1997—98. Presenter, cons. in field; vis. prof. Magdeburg, Germany, 1997, 99, Koethen, Germany, 2001-03; proprietor Atlanta ProCom. Woodrow Wilson fellow, 1958-59; Nat. Endowment Humanities grant, 1981-82; Deutsche Akademisches Austansdienst fellow, 1999. Fellow IEEE Profl. Communication Soc., Soc. Tech. Comm. (Jay Gould award for excellence in tchg. tech. comm. 1999, Disting. Chpt. Svc. award 1999, Excellence in Internat. Tech. Pubs. award 1992, 2001), Nat. Coun. Tchrs. English (conf. coll. composition and comm.), Assn. Tchrs. Tech. Writing. Baptist. Avocations: gourmet cooking, traveling in Europe. Home: 1194 Robert Ln Marietta GA 30062-4929 Office: So Poly State U 1100 S Marietta Pkwy SE Marietta GA 30060-2896 E-mail: krainey@spsu.edu.

RAINS, HAZEL GRACE, curriculum director; b. Gainesville, Mar. 27, 1941; d. Clarence Lafayette and Bertie Lucille (Jones) Beeler; m. Alvin Ray Rains, Dec. 22, 1960; children: Shelby Ray, Bradley Myles. BS in Edn., U. N. Tex., 1967; MA in Polit. Sci., Midwestern State U., Wichita Falls, Tex., 1982. Cert. tchr., mid-mgmt. supt., Tex. Elem. tchr. Rad Ware/Callisburg Ind. Sch. Dist., Gainesville, 1967, Henrietta (Tex.) Ind. Sch. Dist., 1967-81; elem., mid. sch. tchr. Pilot Point (Tex.) Ind. Sch. Dist., 1981-86; mid. sch./high sch. tchr. Callisburg Ind. Sch. Dist., Gainesville, 1986-87, elem., mid. sch. and high sch. prin., 1987-92; curriculum dir. Krum (Tex.) Ind. Sch. Dist., 1992—. Adv. com. sch. bd. Henrietta Ind. Sch. Dist., 1979. Mem. Delta Kappa Gamma, Alpha Phi Sigma, Phi Delta Kappa. Democrat. Baptist. Avocations: oil painting, ceramics, crossword puzzles.

RAINS, MURIEL BARNES, retired secondary school educator, real estate agent; b. Atlanta, Feb. 6, 1916; d. George Washington and Nancy Blodgett (Enos) Barnes; m. David Dean Rains (dec.); children: Rose Muriel, David Dean II. BS, Wilberforce (Ohio) U., 1937; MA, Tex. So. U., 1955; postgrad., Temple U., 1956-81. Cert. tchr., N.J., Tex., Del., Pa.; cert. news reporter, Ohio. News reporter Ohio State News, Columbus, 1937-40; tchr. Houston Pub. Schs., 1950-56, Camden (N.J.) Pub. Schs., 1956-63, various schs., Wilmington, Del., 1963-78, Claymont, Del., 1978-81; real estate agt., Phila., 1980—. Former mem. city profl. growth com. Wilmington Pub. Schs., 1963-67; instr. in physics Brandywine Coll., Wilmington; co-author WOMP (Wilmington Occupational Project). Poetry author; contbr. articles to profl. jours. Active Houston Interracial Commn., 1950-56, State Reception Com., Houston, 1949. Mem. AAUW, Am. Assn. Math. Tchrs., Nat. Hist. Soc., Germantown Civic League (rec. sec., 1986-91), Alpha Kappa Alpha (life). Episcopalian. Avocations: tutoring, interior decorating, scene and portrait painting, swimming, poetry. Home and Office: 6909 Boyer St Philadelphia PA 19119-1908

RAISIAN, JOHN, academic administrator, economist; b. Conneaut, Ohio, July 30, 1949; s. Ernest James and Ruby Lee (Owens) Raisian; m. Joyce Ann Klak, Aug. 17, 1984; children: Alison Kathleen, Sarah Elizabeth. BA, Ohio U., 1971; PhD, UCLA, 1978; LLD (hon.), Albertson Coll. Idaho, 1995. Rsch. assoc. Human Resources Rsch. Ctr., U. So. Calif., L.A., 1972—73; cons. Rand Corp., Santa Monica, Calif., 1974—75; vis. asst. prof. econs. U. Wash., Seattle, 1975—76; asst. prof. econs. U. Houston, 1976—80; sr. economist Office Rsch. and Evaluation, U.S. Bur. Labor Stats., Washington, 1980—81; spl. asst. for econ. policy Office Asst. Sc. for Policy, U.S. Dept. Labor, Washington, 1981—83, dir. rsch. and tech. support, 1981—84; pres. Unicon Rsch. Corp., L.A., 1984-86; sr. fellow Hoover Instn., Stanford, Calif., 1986—, assoc. dir., dep. dir., 1986—90, dir., 1990—. Advisor Nat. Coun. on Handicapped, Washington, 1985—86, Nat. Commn. on Employment Policy, Washington, 1987—88; chmn. minimum wage bd. Calif. Indsl. Welfare Commn., 1987; mem. nat. adv. com. Student Fin. Assistance, Washington, 1987—89; corp. mem. Blue Shield Calif., 1994—96; bd. dirs. Sentinel Groups Fund, Inc., 1997—; mem. Pacific Coun. Internat. Policy; nat. adv. bd. City Innovation. Editor (editl. bd.): (jour.) Jour. Labor Rsch., 1983—; contbr. articles to profl. jours. Exec. dir. Presdl. Task Force on Food Assistance, Washington, 1983—84. Recipient Best Publ. of Yr. award, Econ. Inquiry, Western Econ. Assn., 1979, Disting. Tchg. award, U. Houston Coll. Social Scis., 1980, Disting. Svc. award, U.S. Dept. Labor, 1983; fellow predoctoral fellow, Rand Corp., 1976. Mem.: Nat. Assn. Scholars, Coun. on Fgn. Rels., Mont Pelerin Soc., World Affairs Coun., Commonwealth Club of Calif., We. Econs. Assn., Am. Econs. Assn., Phi Beta Kappa. Republican. Avocation: wine collecting, sports enthusiast. Office: Hoover Instn Stanford Univ Museum Way & Lomita Stanford CA 94305*

RAIZEN, SENTA AMON, educational administrator, researcher; b. Vienna, Oct. 28, 1924; came to U.S., 1940; d. John and Helen (Krys) Amon; m. Abraham A. Raizen, Apr. 18, 1948; children: Helen S., Michael B., Daniel J. BS, Guilford Coll., 1944; MA, Bryn Mawr, 1945; Tchr. Cert., U. Va., 1960. Rsch. chemist Sun Oil Co., Norwood, Pa., 1945-48; rsch. asst. NAS, Washington, 1960-62; assoc. program dir. NSF, Washington, 1962-69, spl. asst., 1969-72; sr. researcher The Rand Corp., Washington, 1972-74; assoc. dir. Nat. Inst. Edn., Washington, 1974-78; ind. cons. Washington, 1978-80; study dir. NAS, Washington, 1980-88; dir. Nat. Ctr. for Improving Sci. Edn., Washington, 1988—. Cons. Nat. Ctr. for Edn. Stats., Washington, 1987—, Ednl. Testing Svc., Princeton, N.J., 1988—, Nat. Goals Panel, Washington, 1990-2000, Third Internat. Math. and Sci. Study, Internat. Assn. Evaluation Ednl. Achievement, The Netherlands, 1990—, SRI Internat., 1998—, Orgns. for Econ. Cooperation and Devel., Paris, 1998—. Contbr. articles to profl. jours., encys., books, reports in field. Pres. Cooperative Nursery Sch., Arlington, Va., 1953-57; leader Brownies, Girl Scouts, U.S. and Cub Scouts, Boy Scouts, Am., Arlington, 1958-64. Recipient Disting. Lifetime award WestEd, 2000; grantee NSF, U.S. Dept. Edn., U.S Dept. Energy, pvt. founds., 1988-2000, fellowship for grad. study NSF, 1944-45, Meritorious Svc. award, 1968, The Network Pres.' award, 1991. Fellow AAAS; mem. Am. Chem. Soc., Am. Ednl. Rsch. Assn. Avocations: dancing, swimming, reading, knitting, stitchery, grandchildren. Home: 5513 31st St N Arlington VA 22207-1532 Office: Nat Ctr Improving Sci Edn 1726 M St NW Ste 704 Washington DC 20036-4524

RAJAKARUNA, LALITH ASOKA, civil engineer, land surveyor; b. Pannala, Srilanka, Aug. 25, 1958; came to U.S., 1985; s. Weerathilaka and Padma (Wickramanayaka) R.; m. Janitha Munaweera, Sept. 25, 1985; children: Reginald, Ashley, Keith. BS in Civil Engring., U. Moratuwa, 1984; MS in Civil Engring., Poly. U., N.Y., 1991. Lic. profl. engr., land surveyor, N.Y.; notary pub., N.Y. Civil engr. Colombo Internat. Airport, Srilanka, 1984-85; assoc. of firm, chief engr. Ettlinger & Ettlinger, P.C., Staten Island, N.Y., 1985-93; pres. Rajakaruna & Ettlinger, cons. engrs. and land surveyor, P.C., Staten Island, 1993—; adj. prof. Coll. Staten Island, Staten Island, N.Y., 1992—, Poly. U., Bklyn., 1994—. Dir. profl. engring. rev. course Am. Soc. Civil Engrs., N.Y., 1992—, chmn. edn. com., 1994—. V.p. Asian Am. Coalition of S.I., 1996—. Mem. NSPE. Home: 30 Old Farmers Ln Staten Island NY 10304-1439 Office: Rajakaruna & Ettlinger 49 Englewood Ave Unit 4 Staten Island NY 10309

RAJLICH, VACLAV THOMAS, computer science educator, researcher, consultant; b. Prague, Czech Republic, May 3, 1939; came to U.S., 1980; s. Vaclav and Marie (Janovska) R.; m. Ivana m. Bartova, Aug. 6, 1968; children: Vasik, Paul, John, Luke. MS, Czech Tech. U., Prague, 1962; PhD, Case Western Res. U., 1971. Rsch. engr. Rsch. Inst. for Math. Machines, Prague, 1963-67, scientist, 1971-75, mgr., 1975-79; vis. assoc. prof. computer sci. Calif. State U., Fullerton, 1980-81; assoc. prof. computer and communication sci. U. Mich., Ann Arbor, 1982-85; prof. Wayne State U., Detroit, 1985—, chair dept. computer sci., 1985-90. Vis. scientist Carnegie-Mellon U., Pitts., 1987, Harvard U., Cambridge, Mass., 1988. Contbr. articles to profl. jours. Recipient Chrysler Challenge Fund, 1988. Mem. Computer Soc. of IEEE, Assn. for Computing Machinery. Roman Catholic. Achievements include development of tools for software maintenance, program comprehension, software design methods, parallel grammars, graph rewriting, abstract state machines. Office: Wayne State U Dept Computer Sci Detroit MI 48202 E-mail: rajlich@cs.wayne.edu.

RAJUR, SHARANABASAVA BASAPPA, chemistry educator, researcher; b. Benakanhal, India, June 1, 1956; came to U.S., 1987; s. Basappa and Basamma Rajur; m. Krupa Sharanabasava Mensinkal, June 30, 1990; children, Vinaya S., Naveen S. PhD, Karanatak U., Dharwad, India, 1987. Rsch. asst. Karnatak U., 1984-85; lectr. organic chemistry Kittle Coll., Dharwad, 1985-86; asst. prof. Coll. of Pharmacy, Dharwad, 1986-87; rsch. assoc. U. Tex. Southwestern Med. Ctr., Dallas, 1987-90, Boston Coll., 1990-93; rsch. scientist Millipore Corp., Bedford, Mass., 1993-94; profl. rschr., group leader Boston Coll., 1994-95; instr. Mass. Gen. Hosp., Boston, 1995-97; chmn., CEO Creagen Bioscis., Inc., Woburn, Mass. Adj. assoc. prof. dept. pharmacy Northeastern U., Boston, 1997—. Reviewer Jour. Pharm. Scis., 1990-93; contbr. articles to profl. jours. Recipient grant Dept. Mental Health Clinics, 1988-89. Mem. AAAS, Am. Chem. Soc., Indian Chem. Soc. Hindu. Achievements include patent for developing FMOC protected peptide nucleic acid (PNA) derivatives. Home: 5 Keystone Way Andover MA 01810-5420 Office: Mass Gen Hosp Shriners Burns Inst/Harvard 1400 West One Kendall Sq Cambridge MA 02139 also: Creagan Bioscis Inc Woburn MA 01801

RAJURKAR, KAMLAKAR PURUSHOTTAM, mechanical engineering educator; b. India, Jan. 6, 1942; came to U.S., 1975; s. Purushottam S. and Indira P. Rajurkar; m. Sanjivani K. Natu, Feb. 3, 1972; children: Piyush, Suneela. B.Sc., Vikram U., India, 1962, B.Engring. with honors, 1966; M.S., Mich. Tech. U., 1978, Ph.D., 1982. Lectr. mech. engring. Govt. Poly., Bhopal, India, 1966-75; grad. teaching and research asst. Mich. Tech. U., Houghton, 1975-81, asst. prof., 1981-83; assoc. prof. U. Nebr., Lincoln, 1983-88; Mohr prof. engring. and dir. Nontraditional Mfg. Rsch. Ctr., 1988-2002, disting. prof. engring., 2003—; Contbr. to profl. jours. Fellow ASME (Blackall Machine Tool and Gage award 1995), Soc. Mfg. Engrs.; mem. Internat. Inst. Prodn. Rsch., Tau Beta Pi. Home: 7308 Skyhawk Cir Lincoln NE 68506-4659 Office: University of Nebraska 175 Nebraska Hall Lincoln NE 68588-0158 E-mail: krajurkar1@unl.edu.

RAK, LINDA MARIE, elementary education educator, consultant; b. Dunkirk, NY; d. Felix Joseph and Helen (Dudek) Ruzycki; m. Joseph John Rak, Oct. 11, 1969; children: Joel, Seth. BA in Edn., SUNY, Fredonia, 1969, MS in Edn., 1974; postgrad., SUNY, Brockport, 1980-84, SUNY, Buffalo, 1988-90. Cert. reading and spl. edn. tchr., NY. Tchr. 1st grade Webster Central Sch. Dist., NY, 1969-72; tchr. kindergarten and reading Williamson Central Sch. Dist., 1973-76; instr. in GED Orleans County Job Devel. Agy., Albion, 1979-83; adult basic edn. coord. SUNY, Brockport, 1980-85; tchr. remedial reading, lang. arts coord. Kendall Central Sch. Dist., 1985—, spl. edn. tchr., 1988—. In-svc. presenter Kendall Elem. Sch., NY, 1984—2002; workshop presenter Monroe #2 Orleans BOCES, Spenceport, 1988—91, Genesee Wyoming Bd. of Coop. Ednl. Svcs. (BOCES), 1988—91, NY State Whole Lang. Conf., 1993; reading recovery tchr. Kendall Elem. Sch., 1996—2003; adj. prof. dept. edn. and human devel. SUNY, Brockport, 2001—; early intervention tchr., cons. Kendall Elem. Sch., Kendall, 2003—. Nursery sch. treas. AAUW, Orleans and Niagara Counties, NY,

1977-79; tchr. Sunday sch. St. Joseph's Ch., Lyndonville, NY, 1978-95, mem. parish coun., 1996—. Recipient Cert. of Appreciation, Congressman John J. La False, 1985; named Religious Educator of the Yr., Diocese of Buffalo, 1987. Mem. Internat. Reading Assn., Rochester Area Reading Coordinators (pres. 1992-96), Genesee Valley Devel. Learning Group (satellite rep. 1987-88), Lit. Vols. Orleans County (v.p. 1981-84, Outstanding Leadership award 1984), Somerset Hist. Soc., Reading Recovery Coun. Roman Cath. Avocation: home restoration. Home: 64 N Main St # 329 Lyndonville NY 14098-9672 Office: Kendall Cen Sch Dist 1932 Kendall Rd Kendall NY 14476-9775 E-mail: lrak@kendallcsd.org.

RAKES, RANDI LEE, elementary school educator, test developer; b. Edison, NJ, June 24, 1969; d. Edward Eli and Florence (Yatrofsky) Leviten; children: Allyson B., Randy R. Jr. 1 stepchild, Laura M. BA in Psychology, Rutgers U., 1991; MEd in Spl. Edn., Trenton State Coll., 1998. Cert. spl. edn., elem. edn., N.J. Substitute tchr. Woodbridge (N.J.) Bd. Edn., 1989-91, Pemberton Twp. Schs., Browns Mills, N.J., 1991-92, tchr., 1992-93; test developer N.J. DOP, Trenton, 1993-95; tchr. Pemberton Twp. Schs., Browns Mills, N.J., 1995—. Gov.'s Teaching scholar State of N.J., 1987; Recipient Citation for Outstanding Svc. to Children of Cmty. N.J. Legislature, 1999. Mem. N.J. Edn. Assn., Kappa Delta Phi. Roman Catholic. Avocations: crafts, computers, camping, collecting, hunting. Home: 412 Pardee Blvd Browns Mills NJ 08015-1137 E-mail: rrakes@pemb.org.

RAKOVE, JACK NORMAN, history educator; b. Chgo., June 4, 1947; s. Milton Leon and Shirley (Bloom) R.; m. Helen Scharf, June 22, 1969; children: Robert, Daniel. AB, Haverford Coll., 1968; PhD, Harvard U., 1975. Asst. prof. history Colgate U., Hamilton, N.Y., 1975-80; from asst. to assoc. prof. history Stanford (Calif.) U., 1980-90, prof., 1990—, Coe prof. history and Am. studies, 1996—, prof. polit. sci., 1999—. Author: Beginnings of National Politics, 1979, James Madison and The Creation of the American Republic, 1990, Original Meanings, 1996 (Pulitzer prize for History, 1997), Declaring Rights, 1997; editor: Interpreting the Consitution, 1990, James Madison Writings, 1999, The Unfinished Election of 2000, 2001, The Federalist, 2003. Commr. Calif. Bicentennial Commn., 1986-87. With USAR, 1968-74. NEH fellow, 1985-86, Stanford Humanities Ctr. fellow, 1988-89, 2000-01. Mem. Am. Hist. Assn., Orgn. Am. Historians, Soc. Am. Historians, Am. Polit. Sci. Assn., Am. Acad. Arts & Scis., Am. Antiquarian Soc., Soc. History of Early Am. Rep (pres. 2002). E-mail: rakove@stanford.edu.

RALEIGH, CHERYL ELAINE, academic director, educator; b. Nacogdoches, Tex., Dec. 27, 1949; d. Herman and Charity (Koback) Sweeney; m. Michael Raleigh, May 7, 1988. BA in Comparative Lit., U. Md., 1971; MA in Comparative Lit., Pa. State U., 1975; EdD in Lang., Culture, Rutgers U., 1988; postgrad., Ind. U. Pa. Instr. Ruygers U., New Brunswick, N.J., 1979-85; dir., edn. Nat. Edn. Corp., Bailey's Crossroads, Va., 1985-86, curriculum designer Irvine, Calif., 1986; pres. English Lang. Sch. Voice of Am./Radio Marti, Washington, 1988-90; asst. prof. EFL George Washington U., Washington, 1990-91, dir. acad. svcs. and youth apprenticeships, 1991—. Cadet leader, Civil Air Patrol. IRES grantee. Mem. The Washington Group (Ukrainian Profl. Group), Cen. Jersey Dance Troupe.

RALEY, HOPE MILLER, educational administrator; b. Ft. Walton, Fla., Feb. 9, 1959; d. James Lee and Charlotte Ruth (Troutman) M.; m. Carl Hagood Raley Jr., Aug. 7, 1977 (div. May, 1991); children: Holly Elizabeth, Rex Miller. BS in Elem. Edn., Troy State Coll., 1981; MA in Elem. Edn., Livingston U., 1987; adminstrn. cert., U. S. Ala., 1992. Tchr. 4 yr. old kindergarten Escambia Acad., Atmore, Ala., 1981-83, tchr. 3rd grade, 1983-84; tchr. 1st grade Flomoton (Ala.) Elem. Sch., 1984-86; tchr. 6th and 7th grades math. Flomaton Middle Sch., 1986-88; math. tchr. grades 6-8 Gulf Shores (Ala.) Middle Sch., 1988-89; asst. prin. Gulf Shores Elem. and Middle Schs., 1989-92, Elberta (Ala.) Elem. Sch., 1992—. Workshop presenter Baldwin County (Ala.) Sch. System, 1992—. Mem. Ala. Coun. for Adminstrs. and Supervision, Baldwin County Assn. Profl. Educators, Jr. Women's Club (Gulf Shores). Methodist. Avocations: travel, hiking, canoeing, tennis. Office: Elberta Elem Sch 13355 Main St Elberta AL 36530-2403

RALPH, DAVID CLINTON, communications educator; b. Muskogee, Okla., Jan. 12, 1922; s. Earl Clinton and Rea Jane (Potter) R.; m. Kathryn Juanita Wicklund, Nov. 29, 1947; children: David Randall, Steven Wicklund. AA, Muskogee Jr. Coll., 1941; BS in Theatre, Northwestern U., 1947, MA in Theatre, 1948, PhD in Speech, 1953. Lectr. Ind. U., Hammond, 1947-48; instr. speech U. Mo., Columbia, 1948-53; tchr. debate-forensics summer program for high sch. students Northwestern U., Evanston, Ill., 1949-51; asst. prof. speech Mich. State U., East Lansing, 1953-57, assoc. prof., 1957-64, prof. speech and theatre, 1964-68, prof. communication, 1968-94, prof. emeritus, 1994—, dir. comm. undergrad. program, 1968-88. Cons. on pub. speaking, 1948—. Co-author: Group Discussion, 1954, 2d edit., 1956, Principles of Speaking, 1962, 3d edit., 1975; contbr. articles to profl. jours., chpts. to books. Coach Jr. League Boys' Baseball, Lansing, Mich., 1958-74; mem. civilian aux. to Lansing Fire Dept., 1987—. Lt. USNR, 1942-46, PTO, ETO. Named Hon. State Farmer, Future Farmers Am., 1965; recipient Community Svc. award Mich. State U. Sr. Class Coun., 1979, Outstanding Faculty award, 1987, 91; Teaching Excellence award State of Mich., 1990. Mem. AAUP, Nat. Communication Assn., Cen. States Communication Assn., Golden Key (hon., faculty advisor), Omicron Delta Kappa. Democrat. Methodist. Avocation: model trains and fire engines. Office: Mich State U Dept Communication East Lansing MI 48824

RALPH, DEBORAH MALONE, social services administrator, educator; b. N.Y.C., Aug. 4, 1951; d. Richard Ernest Sr. and Lottie Mae (Richardson) Malone; m. Hilroy Walton Ralph, Aug. 2, 1975; children: Jamaal, Marcus. BS with honors, SUNY, Buffalo, 1972; MSW, Columbia U., 1974; AS in Christian Ednl. Studies, Teamwork Bible Coll. Internat., 2001. Lic. social worker, N.Y. Psychiat. social worker Arthur C. Logan Meml. Hosp., N.Y.C., 1974-77; asst. exec. dir. Community Participation Ednl. Program, N.Y.C., 1976-79; acting social work supr. Bronx Lebanon Hosp., N.Y.C., 1979-84; supr. clin. services Dept. Juvenile Justice City N.Y., 1979—, mem. Com. Women's Concerns, 1985; project mgr. Sch. Social Work, Va. Commonwealth U., Richmond, 1988-90; founder, dir. Rose of Sharon Counseling Svcs., 1993—; cmty. social worker Family LIfeline, 1999—2001; CEO Boundless Potential, LLC, 2002—. Adj. prof. Coll. New Rocheele, N.Y.C., 1979—; adj. mem. faculty CCNY Sophie Davis Sch. Biomed. Edn., 1978-79; vis. prof. Tchr.'s Coll. Inst. Urban Minority Edn. Columbia U., N.Y.C., 1986, guest speaker Sch. Social Work, 1985; mem. field work adv. bd. Sch. Social Work NYU, 1986—; adj. faculty Nat. Video Conf. Sch. Social Work, Va. Commonwealth U., Richmond, 1988-91. Mem. YMCA; site dir. after sch. program Glen Allen Elem. Sch., Richmond, Va., 1990; dir. 13th dist. juvenile and domestic rels. ct. Stepping Stone Group Home, Richmond, 1988. Columbia U. scholar, 1972; recipient Innovations award Dept. Juvenile Justice Ford Found., Boston, 1986. Mem. Nat. Assn. Social Workers (cert.), Assn. Black Social Workers, Nat. Juvenile Detention Assn. Office: Va Commonwealth U Sch 1001 W Franklin St PO Box 2027 Richmond VA 23218-2027

RALSTON, LENORE DALE, academic policy and program analyst; b. Oakland, Calif., Feb. 21, 1949; d. Leonard Earnest and Emily Allison (Hudnut) R. BA in Anthropology, U. Calif., Berkeley, 1971, MPH in Behavioral Sci., 1981; MA in Anthropology, Bryn Mawr Coll., 1973, PhD in Anthropology, 1980. Asst. rschr. anthropology inst. internat. studies U. Calif., Berkeley, 1979-82, rsch. assoc. Latin Am. Study Ctr., 1982-83, acad. asst. to dean Sch. of Optometry, 1990-95, prin. policy analyst, chancellor's office, 1995—; assoc. scientist, rsch. adminstr. Med. Rsch. Inst., San Francisco, 1982-85; cons. health sci. Berkeley, 1986-90. Mem. fin. bd. Med. Rsch. Inst., 1983-84; speaker in field. Co-author: Voluntary Effects in Decentralized Management, 1983; contbr. articles to profl. jours. Commr. Cmty. Health Adv. Com., Berkeley, 1988-90; vice chair, commr. Cmty. Health Commn., Berkeley, 1990-93; mem. bd. safety com. Miles, Inc., Berkeley, 1992-94. Grantee Nat. Rsch. Svc. Award, WHO, NIMH, NSF. Fellow Applied Anthropology Assn.; mem. APHA, Am. Anthropology Assn., Sigma Xi. Home: 1232 Carlotta Ave Berkeley CA 94707-2707 E-mail: ralston@uclink4.berkeley.edu.

RAMAKRISHNAN, VENKATASWAMY, civil engineer, educator; b. Coimbatore, India, Feb. 27, 1929; came to U.S., 1969, naturalized, 1981; s. Venkataswamy and Kondammal (Krishnaswamy) R.; m. Vijayalakshmi Unnava, Nov. 7, 1962; children: Aravind, Anand. B.Engring., U. Madras, 1952, D.S.S., 1953; D.I.C. in Hydropower and Concrete Tech, Imperial Coll., London, 1957; PhD, Univ. Coll., U. London, 1960. From lectr. to prof. civil engring., head dept. P.S.G. Coll. Tech., U. Madras, 1952-69; vis. prof. S.D. Sch. Mines and Tech., Rapid City, 1969-70, prof. civil engring., 1970—, dir. concrete tech. research, 1970-71, head grad. div. structural mechanic and concrete tech., 1971—, program coordinator materials engring. and sci. Ph.D. program, 1985-86, disting. prof., 1996—. Emeritus mem. TRB. Author: Ultimate Strength Design for Structural Concrete, 1969; also over 200 articles. Recipient Outstanding Prof. award S.D. Sch. Mines and Tech., 1980, 1st Rsch. award, 1994; Colombo Plan fellow, 1955-60. Mem. Internat. Assn. Bridge and Structural Engring., ASCE (vice chmn. constrn. div. publs. com. 1974), Am. Concrete Inst. (chmn. subcom. gen. considerations for founds., chmn. com. 214 on evaluation of strength test results, sec.-treas. Dakota chpt. 1974-79, v.p. 1980, pres. 1981, Robert Philio Rsch. Excellence award), Instn. Hwy. Engrs., Transp. Rsch. Bd. (chmn. com. on admixtures and curing, chmn. com. on mech. properties concrete), Am. Soc. Engring. Edn., NSPE, Internat. Coun. Gap-Graded Concrete Rsch. and Application, Sigma Xi. Address: 5260 Autumn Place Rapid City SD 57702 E-mail: vramakri@silver.sdsmt.edu.

RAMALEY, JUDITH AITKEN, former university president, endocrinologist; b. Vincennes, Ind., Jan. 11, 1941; d. Robert Henry and Mary Krebs (McCullough) Aitken; m. Robert Folk Ramaley, Mar. 1966 (div. 1976); children: Alan Aitken, Andrew Folk. BA, Swarthmore Coll., 1963; PhD, UCLA, 1966; postgrad., Ind. U., 1967-69. Rsch. assoc., lectr. Ind. U., Bloomington, 1967-68, asst. prof. dept. anatomy and physiology, 1969-72; asst. prof. dept. physiology and biophysics U. Nebr. Med. Ctr., Omaha, 1972-74, assoc. prof., 1974-78, prof., 1978-82, assoc. dean for rsch. and devel., 1979-81; asst. v.p. for acad. affairs U. Nebr., Lincoln, 1980-82; prof. biol. scis. SUNY, Albany, N.Y., 1982-87, v.p. for acad. affairs, 1982-85, acting pres., 1984, exec. v.p. for acad. affairs, 1985-87; exec. vice chancellor U. Kans., Lawrence, 1987-90; pres. Portland (Oreg.) State U., 1990-97, U. Vt., Burlington, 1997—2001; asst. dir. edn. and human resources NSF, 2001—. Mem. endocrinology study sect. NIH, 1981-84; cons.-evaluator North Cen. Accreditation, 1978-82, 89-90; regulatory panel NSF, 1979-82, bioadv. com., 1994-98; mem. Ill. Commn. Scholars, 1980-90; Vt. tech. coun. Gov.'s Bus. Adv. Coun., Vt. Bus. Roundtable, Com. on Econ. Devel., 1997-2001; presdl. prof. biomed. scis. U. Maine, Orono, 2001—; subcom. on coll. drinking Nat. Inst. Alcohol Abuse & Alcoholism, 1998-01. Co-author: Progesterone Function: Molecular and Biochemical Aspects, 1972; Essentials of Histology, 8th edit., 1979; editor: Covert Discrimination, Women in the Sciences, 1978; contbr. articles to profl. jours. Bd. dirs. Family Svc. of Omaha, 1979-82, Albany Symphony Orch., 1984-87, mem. exec. com., 1986-87, 2d v.p., exec. com., 1986-87, Capital Repertory Co., 1986-89, Assn. Portland Progress, 1990-97, City Club of Portland, 1991-92, Metro Family Svcs., 1993-97, Campbell Inst. for Children, Portland Met. Sports Authority, 1994; vice-chair Ore. Campus Compact, exec. com. 1996-97, nat. adv. coun. Sch.-Work Opportunities, 1996—; bd. dirs. NCAA Pres. Commn., 1991, chair divsn. II subcom., 1994, joint policy bd., 1994; chmn. bd. dirs. Albany Water Fin. Authority, 1987; exec. com. United Way Douglas County, 1989-90; adv. bd. Emily Taylor Women's Resource Ctr., U. Kans., 1988-90; mem. Portland Opera Bd., 1991-92, Portland Leaders Roundtable, 1991-97; bd. devel. com. United Way of Columbia-Willamette, 1991-95; active Ore. Women's Forum, 1991-97, Portland Met. Sports Authority, Greater Burlington Industry Corp., 1998—; progress bd. Portland-Multnomah County, 1993-97; trustee Wilmington Coll. Ohio, 1998—. NSF grantee, 1969-83; fellow Margaret Chase Smith Ctr. for Pub. Policy. Fellow AAAS; mem. Nat. Assn. State Univs. and Land Grant Colls. (exec. com., mem. senate 1986-88, vice-chair commn. urban agenda 1992-94, chair 1995-97), Am. Assn. for Higher Edn. (bd. dirs. 2003—), Assn. Am. Colls. and Univs. (bd. dirs. 1995-98, chair nat. panel on greater expectations 2000-02), ACE (commn. on govt. rels. 1996-2000), Kellogg Commn. on Future of State and Land-Grant Univs., Assn. Governing Bds. Coll. & U. (pres.'s coun. 1998-2000), Endocrine Soc. (chmn. edn. com. 1980-85), Soc. Study Reprodn. (treas. 1983-85), Soc. for Neuroscis., Am. Physiol. Soc., Am. Assn. Schs. and Colls., Am. Coun. on Edn. (chmn. commn. on women in higher edn. 1987-88, commn. on govt rels., bd. dirs. 1999-2001), Assn. Portland Progress (bd. dirs.), Portland C. of C. (bd. dirs. 1995), Western Assn. of Schs. and Colls. (commr. 1994-97). Office: Edn and Human Resources Directorate Nat Sci Found 4201 Wilson Blvd Arlington VA 22230

RAMANA, M. V. director; b. Palakkad, Kerala, India; Undergrad., Indian Inst. Tech., Kanpur, India; PhD in Physics, Boston U. Rsch. staff mem. program on sci. and global security Princeton (N.J.) U., 2002—. Mem. Global Coun. Abolition 2000. Co-editor: Prisoners of the Nuclear Dream, 2003. Fellow, John Simon Guggenheim Meml. Found., 2003, MacArthur Found., Social Scis. Rsch. Coun. Office: Woodrow Wilson Sch Princeton Univ Princeton NJ 08544-1013*

RAMANI, RAJA VENKAT, mining engineering educator; b. Madras, India, Aug. 4, 1938; came to U.S., 1966; s. Natesa and Meenakshi (Srinivasan) Rajaraman; m. Geetha V. Chalam, July 9, 1972; children: Deepak, Gautam. BSc with honors, Indian Sch. Mines, Dhanbad, Bihar, 1962, DSc (hon.), 1997; MS, Pa. State U., 1968, PhD, 1970. Registered profl. engr., Pa., 1971; lic. first class mine mgr., 1965. Mining engr., mgr. Andrew Yule & Co., Asansol, West Bengal, India, 1962-66; grad. asst. Pa. State U., University Park, 1966-70, asst. prof., 1970-74, assoc. prof., 1974-78, prof. mining engring., 1978—, chmn. mineral engring. mgmt. sect., 1974—, head dept. mineral engring., 1987-98, George and Anne Deike chair in mining engring., 1997—. Chmn. com. post-disaster survival/rescue NAS, Washington, 1979-81; mem. health rsch. panel NAS Com. on the Rsch. Programs of the U.S. Bur. of Mines, 1994; mem. NAS Com. on Techs. for the Mineral Industries, 2000-01; mem. NAS Com. on Coal Waste Impoundments, 2001-02; chmn. Gov.'s Commn. on Mine Voids and Mine Safety, Pa., 2002; cons. UN, UN Devel. Program, Dept. Econ. and Social Devel., N.Y.C., 1983-97, World Bank, 1998-99, Nat. Safety Coun., 2003-; cons., expert panels U.S. Dept. Labor, 1979, 92, 96, HHS, 1977, 92, U.S. Dept. State, 1986, 87, U.S. Dept. Interior, 1995, Dept. Environ. Resources, Commonwealth of Pa., 1990, 92; co-dir. Generic Mineral Tech. Ctr. on Respirable Dust, U.S. Bur. Mines, 1983—, Nat. Mines/Land Reclamation Ctr., 1988—, Std. Oil Ctr. of Excellence on Longwall Tech., 1983-89; presenter in field. Sect. editor, author: Computer Methods for the Eighties, 1979, SME Mining Engineering Handbook, 1992; editor State-of-the-Art in Longwall-Shortwall Mining, 1981, Longwall Thick Seam Mining, 1988, Computers in Mineral Industry, 1994, Internat. Mine Ventilation Congress, 1997. Recipient Disting. Alumni award Indian Sch. Mines, Dhanbad, 1978, Ednl. Excellence award Pitts. Coal Mining Inst., 1986, Environ. Conservation award AIME, N.Y.C., 1990, Howard N. Eavenson award SME/AIME, N.Y.C., 1991, Robert Stefanko Best Paper award, 1993, Coal Divsn. Disting. Svc. award, 1993, Howard L. Hartman award, 1997, Percy H. Nicholls award AIME/ASME Joint Soc., 1994, Mineral Industry Edn. award Am. Inst. Mining Engrs., 1999, The Thornton medal Instn. Mining and Metallurgy, 2000; Fulbright scholar to Soviet Union Coun. Internat. Exch. of Scholars, Washington,, 1989-90; Henry Krumb lectr. AIME, 1994. Mem. Internat. Coun. for Application of Computers in the Mineral Industry (chmn. 1984-87, Disting. Achievement award 1989), Soc. Mining, Metall. and Exploration (Disting. Mem. 1989, pres. 1995), Mine Ventillation Soc. South Africa, Inst. for Ops. Rsch. and Mgmt. Scis. Achievements include research in health, safety, environmental and productivity aspects in underground and surface mining engineering. Home: 285 Oakley Dr State College PA 16803-1349 Office: Dept Mineral Engring Pa State U University Park PA 16802 E-mail: RVR@PSU.edu.

RAMAPRASAD, SUBBARAYA, medical educator; b. Mysore, India, May 20, 1954; came to the U.S., 1980, naturalized, 1993; s. Puttaniah and Sharadamma Subbaraya; m. Padma, Sept. 28, 1987; 1 child, Sanjay. PhD, Indian Inst. Sci., 1979. Instr. U. Ark. Med. Scis., Little Rock, 1989-91, asst. prof., 1991-94, assoc. prof., 1995—. Peer rev. breast cancer rsch. Dept. of Def., 1999—2000. Contbr. articles to profl. jours. Recipient Ind. Investigator award Nat. Alliance Rsch. in Schizophrenia and Depression, 1999; grantee NIMH, 1994, Ark. Sci. Tech. Authority, 1991, 95, Dept. of Def., 1999. Mem. Internat. Soc. Magnetic Resonance Medicine, Am. Coll. Radiology, N.Y. Acad. Scis., Soc. Photooptical Instrumentation Engrs., Am. Assn. Diabetes Educators, Nebr. Radiol. Soc., Sigma Xi. Hindu. Avocations: travel, photography, bicycling, gardening. Home: 17626 Jefferson St Omaha NE 68135-3028 Office: U Nebr Med Ctr Dept Radiology Omaha NE 68198-1045 E-mail: sramaprasad@unmc.edu., sramaprasa@aol.com.

RAMBERG, PATRICIA LYNN, college president; b. Melrose Park, Ill., June 15, 1951; d. Roy Andrew and Elsie Elaine (Lossau) Fricke; children: Richard Lynn II, Caitlyn Elizabeth. BS in Bus. Adminstrn. magna cum laude, Elmhurst Coll., 1976; MA in Edn., U. St. Thomas, 1989. Assoc. dir. ops. Bank Mktg. Assn., Chgo., 1972-75; exec. dir. Soc. Tchrs. Family Medicine, Kansas City, Mo., 1975-78, Minn. Assn. Children with Learning Disabilities, St. Paul, 1979-80; sr. instrnl. designer Applied Learning Systems, Mpls., 1989-90; dir. Upper Midwest Conservation Assn., Mpls., 1990-92; account exec. Dean Witter Reynolds, Inc., Bloomington, Minn., 1992-94; investment specialist FBS Investment Svcs., Inc., Mpls., 1994; v.p., dir. profl. devel. US Bank, Mpls., 1994-98; pres., CEO Alfred Adler Grad. Sch., Hopkins, Minn., 1998—. Adj. faculty U. St. Thomas, St. Paul, 1990. Lutheran. Avocations: photography, horses. Home: 7136 W 113th St Bloomington MN 55438-2448 Office: Alfred Adler Grad Sch 1001 Highway 7 Hopkins MN 55305-4723

RAMER, HAL REED, academic administrator; b. Kenton, Tenn., June 8, 1923; s. Claude Orion and Dixie Clayton (Carroll) R. BS, George Peabody Coll., 1947; MSW, U. Tenn., 1952; PhD, Ohio State U., 1963. Asst. dean men Ohio State U., Columbus, 1953-58, dir. internat. house, 1958-60, staff asst. to pres., 1960-62; asst. commr. State Dept. Edn., Nashville, 1963-70; founding pres. Vol. State C.C., Gallatin, Tenn., 1970—2003, pres. emeritus, 2003—. Bd. dirs. Sumner Regional Health Sys., Inc. Com. mem. March of Dimes, Gallatin; Mem. adv. bd. First Union Bank Mid. Tenn., First Union Bank Mid. Tenn., Hendersonville; trustee Nashville United Way, 1970, Hiwassee Coll., 2001; bd. advisors Aquinas Coll., Nashville, 1967—; former chmn. Tenn. Fulbright-Hays Sch. Commn.; YMCA. With U.S. Army Air Corps, 1943—45. Recipient Distinctive Svc. award Devel. Coun. Peabody Coll., Nashville, 1960s, Disting. Svc. award Tenn. Dept. Edn., 1970, Outstanding Leader award Vanderbilt U. chpt. Phi Delta Kappa, 1987, Gov.'s Svc. award State of Tenn., 1993, Sertoma Club Svc. to Mankind award, 1995-96, Disting. Alumnus award Peabody Coll., 1996, Disting. Svc. award Tenn. Bd. Regents, 1997, Svc. award Am. Assn. Cmty. Col., 1999, Otis Floyd Jr. award for excellence Tenn. Coll. Pub. Rels. Assn., 1999, Lifetime Achievement award Peabody Coll. of Vanderbilt U., 2003; named Rotarian of the Yr., 1979; Paul Harris fellow Rotary Internat., 1981. Mem. Am. Legion, Coun. Pres. C.Cs. (chmn. state Tenn. 1988-89), Tenn. Coll. Assn. (pres. 1985-86), Nat. Alumni Assn. Peabody Coll. (pres. 1970-71, trustee), Tenn. Acad. Sci., Tenn. and Sumner County Hist. Socs. (bd. dirs.), English Speaking Union Internat. (Nashville chpt.), So. Assn. Colls. and Schs., Univ. Club Nashville, Gallatin and Hendersonville C. of C., St. Thomas Aquinas Soc., Torch Club, Alpha Tau Omega, Kappa Phi Kappa, Alpha Phi Omega, Phi Delta Kappa. Methodist. Avocations: antiques, antique cars, photography. Home: 120 Abbottsford Nashville TN 37215-2440

RAMEY, PATRICIA ANN, elementary education educator; b. Maries County, Mo., Sept. 5, 1939; d. John Wesely and Ethel Editha (Prewett) Perkins; m. George Grover Ramey, June 7, 1959; children: Jonathan Edward, Steven Wesley. BA in Edn., William Jewell Coll., 1961; MA in Edn., Union Coll., 1981; postgrad., U. Conn., 1985, Purdue U., 1994. Cert. elem. edn. grades 1-8. Tchr. No. Kansas City (Mo.) Pub. Sch. Dist., 1961-63, Jefferson County Pub. Sch. Dist., Louisville, 1963-65; edn. dir. First Bapt. Ch., Williamsburg, Ky., 1974-77; tchr. Williamsburg Ind. Sch. Dist., Williamsburg, 1979—2003; ret., 2003. Ky. tchr. intern program Williamsburg (Ky.) Ind. Sch., 1987-91, leader numerous profl. devel. activities, 1985—; guest lectr., student tchr. supr. Cumberland Coll., 1979—. Mem. rev. panel Sci. and Children, 1997-98, mem. adv. bd., 1998—. Active First Bapt. Ch., Williamsburg, 1968—; den leader Boy Scouts Am., Williamsburg, 1974-82; mem., sec. Laural Lake Camp Bd., Corbin, Ky., 1988-91; active Cultural/Humanitarian Exch., U.S. and Kazakhstan, Almata, Kazakhstan, 1991; bd. dirs. Cleft Rock Retreat Ctr., Mt. Vernon, Ky., 1992—. Recipient State prize Presdl. award for Excellence in Sci. Teaching, 1994. Mem. NEA, Ky. Edn. Assn., Williamsburg Edn. Assn., Nat. Sci. Tchrs. Assn. (presenter nat. meeting 1995-97, 99), Ky. Sci. Tchrs. Assn. (presenter 1995, 97, 97), Nat. Coun. Tchrs. Math. (presenter ctrl. regional conf. 1991), Ky. Coun. Tchrs. Math., Coun. for Elem. Sci. Internat., Ky. Sci. Tchrs. Assn. (bd. dirs. 2002—), Phi Delta Kappa (chpt. v.p.), Delta Kapa Gamma (Alpha Lamda Gamma chpt. sec. 1990-96). Avocations: growing african violets, cooking, archeology, photography. Home: 75 Hemlock St Williamsburg KY 40769-1793 E-mail: pramey@cumberlandcollege.edu.

RAMEY, REBECCA ANN, elementary education educator; b. Dayton, Ohio, Jan. 27, 1948; d. Donald Smith and Margaret Jeanne (Cross) Ingabrand; divorced; 1 child, Joshua David. BS, Miami U., Oxford, Ohio, 1970, MEd in Adminstrn., 1978. Cert. permanent tchr., prin., Ohio. Tchr. social studies and lang. arts Springboro (Ohio) Community Schs., 1970—. Dept. head Clearcreek Elem. Sch., Springboro, 1991—. Choir dir. 1st Bapt. Ch., Franklin, Ohio, 1985—, chmn. bd. Christian edn., 1991-96, 98—; sec. exec. bd. Tamarack Swim Club, Springboro, 1990-96, Springboro Band Boosters Assn., 1992; vol. docent Springboro Area Hist. Mus. Named Worker of Yr., 1st Bapt. Ch., 1992. Mem. NEA, Ohio Edn. Assn., Springboro Edn. Assn., Order Ea. Star (past matron 1973, 84), Ladies Oriental Shrine N.Am. Republican. Avocations: music, reading, needlework. Office: Clearcreek Elem Sch 750 S Main St Springboro OH 45066-1423 Home: Apt B 2155 Sidneywood Dr Dayton OH 45449-2668

RAMIREZ, JANICE L. assistant school superintendent; b. Dodge City, Kans., July 16, 1947; d. Chris William and Lois (Moore) Langvardt; 1 child, Jessica. BS, Emporia State U., 1969, MA, 1970; PhD, Kans. State U., 1982. Div. prin. Highland Park High Sch./Topeka (Kans.) pub. schs.; prin. Topeka pub. schs., Mesa (Ariz.) pub. schs., asst. supt. Mem. mid. level task force Ariz. Dept. Edn. Contbr. articles to profl. jours. Bd. dirs. Maricopa County Sports Commn.; chair merit sys. bd. City of Mesa. Recipient Kamelot award; named one of Top 100 Bus. Women in Ariz., Today's Ariz. Woman Success Mag., 1996—. Mem. Am. Assn. Sch. Pers. Adminstrs., Ariz. Sch. Pers. Adminstrs. Assn., Nat. Assn. Ednl. Negotiators, Ariz. Sch. Adminstrs. Assn., Phi Delta Kappa. Office: 63 E Main St # 101 Mesa AZ 85201-7204

RAMIREZ, LEO ARMANDO, secondary school educator; Math. tchr. McAllen (Tex.) High Sch., 1985—. Named Tex. State Math. Tchr. of Yr., 1993. Office: McAllen High Sch 2021 La Vista Ave Mcallen TX 78501-6130

RAMIREZ, MARIA C(ONCEPCION), retired educational administrator; d. Ines and Carlota (Cruz) R. BA, U. Incarnate Word, San Antonio, 1966; MEd, U. Tex., Austin, 1979; postgrad., S.W. Tex. State U., San Marcos, 1980. Cert. elem. tchr., bilingual tchr., supr. Elem. tchr. regular and bilingual Edgewood Ind. Sch. Dist., San Antonio, 1966-69; elem tchr. regular and bilingual Austin (Tex.) Ind. Sch. Dist., 1969-74, bilingual program coord., 1974-89; instrnl. coord. Austin Ind. Sch. Dist., 1989-91, asst. prin., 1991—96, bilingual instrnl. coord., 1996-97; ret., 1997.

RAMIREZ, MARTIN RUBEN, architect, engineer, educator, cognitive scientist, consultant; b. San Luis Potosi, Mex., Aug. 17, 1962; s. Victorio Niño and Concepcion (Zuñiga) R.; m. Maureen Therese McDermott, July 27, 1991. BS, Northwestern U., 1984, MS, 1986, PhD, 1991. Asst. to v.p. engrng. Perkins & Will, Chgo., 1980-84; cons. engr. Alfred Benesch & Co., Chgo., 1985-86, Teng & Assocs., Chgo.; prof. engrng. Johns Hopkins U., Balt., 1990-94; pres. I.D.E.A.S., Chgo., 1994—99, 5Ps, Chgo., 1999—. Cons. Wiss-Jenney Elstner, Northbrook, Ill., 1985—86, Mitsubishi Heavy Industries, Hunt Valley, Md.; cons. to forune 500 corps., govts., dists. and instns.; founder, dir. program on engrng. Johns Hopkins U., Balt., 1993. Reviewer for several jours.; editor Needs Database. Recipient Fazlur Khan Meml. prize, 1986, Young Investigator award NSF, 1993; Lilly fellow, 1992; NSF grad. fellow, 1985. Mem.: ASME, ASCD, ASCE (assoc.), Am. Acad. Mechanics, IEEE Computer Soc., U.S. Assn. for Computational Mechanics, Am. Soc. Engrng. Edn. (chair Frontiers in Edn. Conf. 1993), Am. Edn. Rsch. Assn., Tau Beta Pi. Achievements include Achievements include major innovations e-business usability, business strategy, learning, integration; orbitz.com, Sprint PCS vision designer. Avocations: bicycling, cars, travel, music. E-mail: martin@5Ps.biz.

RAMIREZ, MARY CATHERINE, retired secondary school educator; b. McLeansboro, Ill., Feb. 16, 1921; d. George Washington and Mary Margaret (Lane) Tousley; m. John Ramirez, Oct. 30, 1948 (dec. 1975). BS, Ctrl. U., Edmond, Okla., 1942; MA, U. Okla., 1945. Tchr. Bradley (Okla.) High Sch., 1942-43, McLeansboro (Ill.) High Sch., 1943-46, No. Okla. Jr. Coll., Tonkawa, Okla., 1946-47, Draughon Bus. Coll., Springfield, Mo., 1947-48, VA Hosp., Springfield, Mo., 1948-52, Madison, Wis., 1952-63, Madison pub. sch., 1963-85. Mem. AAUW (publicity chmn. Madison br. 1954-60)., NEA, Madison Civics Club. Avocations: travel, photography, coin and stamp collecting, needlework. Home: 971 Wellington Ct Nekoosa WI 54457-9040

RAMIREZ, SANDRA LEIGH, ceramic artist, potter, educator; b. Chgo., Aug. 3, 1957; d. J.W. and Elizabeth L. (Smith) Snarr; m. Carlos J. Ramirez, June 7, 1980. BFA, U. S.C., 1979; M of Visual Arts, Ga. State U., 1983. Lic. dispensing optician. Instr. Atlanta Jewish Cmty. Ctrs., 1981-83, Steeple House Arts Ctr., Marietta, Ga., 1990-91; part-time instr. Kennesaw State Coll., Marietta, Ga., 1989—95, Cobb County Pub. Schs., 1995—. Pres. Raku Club, Ga. State U., Atlanta, 1983; art cons. Chamblee (Ga.) H.S., 1991; vis. artist S.C. Arts Coun., Columbia, 1979. One woman shows include Mary Vinson Meml. Libr., 1992; exhibited in group shows at Mus. of Art Columbia, 1979, Cortona, Italy, 1979, U. Ga., 1980, Chattahoochee Nature Ctr., Roswell, Ga., 1982 (Best in Show), Saks Fifth Ave., Atlanta, 1983, Portfolio Gallery, Atlanta, 1983, Praters' Mill Arts Festival, Dalton, Ga., 1984, Merchandise Mart, Atlanta, 1984, Creative Arts Guild of Dalton, 1985, Las Manos, Santurce, P.R., 1988, Kennesaw State Coll., Marietta, 1989, 90, Southern Air, Memphis, 1989, Arts and Crafts Nationwide, Paducah, Ky., 1990, Faculty Exhibition, Kennesaw State Coll, Marietta, Ga., 1990, 92, 93, Taco Bell Corp. Hdqs., Atlanta, 1990, Mountain Valley Fine Arts Exhbn., Guntersville, Ala., 1991, Steeple House Arts Ctr., Marietta, 1991, Atlanta Coll. Art, 1991, Arts Festival of Atlanta, Piedmont Park, Ga., 1991, 92, Aliya Gallery, Atlanta, 1991, Arts Place, Marietta, 1992, Atlanta Apparel Mart, 1992, Trinith Sch., Atlanta, 1992, Governors' Mansion, Atlanta, 1993, Avery Gallery, Marietta, 1993, Auxiliary of the Jewish Home of Atlanta, 1993, 94, Kennesaw Fine Arts Soc., 1993, Arts Place, 1993, Madison-Morgan Cultural Arts Ctr., 1994, Cobb YWCA, 1994, Tucson Arts Coalition, 1994. Vol. Cobb Arts Coun., Marietta, 1990; mem., adv. Nat. Humane Soc., Marietta, 1995—; designer Festival of Trees, Atlanta, Ga., 1998-2000. Recipient Artist in Edn. grant Ga. Arts Coun., 1991. Mem. Nat. Art Edn. Assn., Am. Crafts Coun., Cobb Arts Coun., Ga. Educators Assn., Ga. Artists Registry, Visions. Avocations: painting, water sports, antiques. Home: 170 Club Ridge Drive Marietta GA 30068-4803

RAMLER, SIEGFRIED, educator; b. Vienna, Oct. 30, 1924; s. Lazar and Eugenia Ramler; m. Piilani Andrietta Ahuna, Jan. 27, 1948; children: David K., Dita L., Laurence K., Malia R. Diplôme supérieur, U. Paris, 1958; MA, U. Hawaii, 1961. Interpreter Internat. Mil. Tribunal, Nuremberg, Germany, 1945-46, chief interpreting br., 1946-49; chair fgn. lang. dept. Punahou Sch., Honolulu, 1951-71, dir. instnl. svcs., 1971-91, dir. Wo Internat. Ctr., 1990-95; exec. dir. Found. for Study in Hawaii and Abroad, Honolulu, 1969-90. Sr. adj. fellow East-West Ctr., 1995—; pres. adv. bd. Pacific Basin Consortium, Hawaii, 1997-2002. Contbr. articles to profl. publs. Sec., bd. dirs. crown Prince Akihito Scholarship Found., 1989—; trustee St. Francis Sch., Honolulu, 1996—. Decorated Order of the Palmes Académiques, Ordre National du Mérite (France); Order of the Sacred Treasure (Japan); recipient medal Freedom Found., 1958. Mem. ASCD, Internat./Global Edn. Com. (chair nat. adv. com. 1987-93), Japan-Am. Soc. Hawaii (pres. 1986-87, program chmn. 1975-94, Alliance Française of Hawaii (pres. and founder 1961, bd. dirs. 1992-2001). Avocations: running, travel, swimming. Home: 921 Maunawili Cir Kailua HI 96734-4620 Office: East West Ctr 1777 E West Rd Honolulu HI 96848 Fax: (808) 944-7070. E-mail: sramler@lava.net.

RAMM, ALEXANDER G. mathematics educator; b. Leningrad, U.S.S.R., Jan. 13, 1940; arrived in U.S., 1979; s. Gregory S. and Rose P. (Urinson) Ramm; m. Lubov L. Ramm, Nov. 16, 1988. MS in Maths., Theoretical and Math. Physics., U. Leningrad, 1961; PhD in Maths., U. Moscow, 1964; DSc, Inst. Maths. Acad. Sci., Minsk, U.S.S.R., 1972. Prof. Inst. of Precision Mechanics & Optics, Leningrad, 1962—78, U. Mich., Ann Arbor, 1979—81, Kans. State U., Manhattan, 1981—. Vis. prof. U. Manchester, Eng., 1984, U. London, 1985, U. Bonn, 1985, 89, U. Goteborg, 1983, U. Heidelberg, 1987, U. Uppsala, Sweden, 1987, Indian Inst. Sci., 1987, Acad. Sinica, Taipei, 1986, Concordia U., 1990, U. Stockholm, Sweden, 1991, U. Novosibirsk, Inst. of Math, 1991, Inst. Advanced Study, Istanbul, 1987; Fulbright rsch. prof., Technion, Israel, 1991-92, U. Madrid, 1995, U. Grenoble, 1995, 97, U. Giessen, 1998; cons. SOHIO, Dallas, Dikewood, Albuquerque, Los Alamos Nat. Lab.; prof. Wright-Patterson AFB, 1993, U. Cagliari, 2001, U. Singapore, 1999; rsch. prof. Nat. Ctr. Rsch. Sci. Marseille, 2002; Ctr. Nat. Rsch. Sci. rsch. prof. U. Milano and Palermo, 2002. Author: (monographs) Theory and Applications of Some New Classes of Integral Equations, 1980, Iterative Methods and Wave Scattering by Small Bodies, 1982, Scattering by Obstacles, 1986, Random Fields Estimation Theory, 1990, expanded Russian edit., 1996, Multidimensional Inverse Scattering Problems, 1992, Russian edit., 1994; assoc. editor: Jour. Math. Inequalities and Applications, Jour. Inverse and Ill-Posed Problems, Applicable Analysis, Pan Am. Math. Jour.; editor: (books) The Radon Transform and Local Tomography (with A. Katsevich), 1996, Spectral and Scattering Theory, 1998, Inverse Problems, Tomography and Image Processing, 1998, Operator Theory and Applications, 2000; contbr. more than 460 articles to profl. jours. Mem. Am. Math. Soc., Electromagnetic Acad., N.Y. Acad. Scis., Internat. Soc. Analysis, Applications and Computation (bd. dirs.). Office: Kans State U Math Dept Manhattan KS 66506-2602

RAMMING, MICHAEL ALEXANDER, retired school system administrator; b. St. Louis, Feb. 4, 1940; s. William Alexander and Emily Louise (Reingruber) R.; m. Susan Ray Oliver, July 9, 1962; children: Michael Murray, Todd Alexander. BS, Centenary Coll., 1963; MA, Washington U., St. Louis, 1968. Cert. adminstr. secondary schs., Mo. Teacher and coach Ladue Sch. Dist., St. Louis, 1963-88, adminstr., 1988—2002. Adj. prof. Lindenwood U., 2002—; cons. Ladue Sch. Dist., 2002—. Vol. Sr. Olympics, St. Louis, 1992, 93. Mem. Nat. Assn. Secondary Sch. Prins., Mo. Assn. Secondary Sch. Prins., Nat. Interscholastic Athletic Adminstrs. Assn., Mo. Interscholastic Athletic Adminstrs. Assn. (25 Yr. Svc. award). Avocations: tennis, walking, travel. Home: 18128 Dawns Trail Wildwood MO 63005 Office: Ladue Horton Watkins High Sch 1201 S Warson Rd Saint Louis MO 63124-1266

RAMOS, ROSE MARY, elementary school educator; b. San Antonio, Aug. 8, 1942; d. Henry Barbosa and Bertha Alice (Cuellar) Gonzalez; m. Jesus Ramos Jr., Sept. 11, 1965; children: Rebecca Anne, Veronica Anne. BS in Elem. Edn., Our Lady of Lake U., San Antonio, 1965; MA in Edn., U. Houston, 1992. Cert. elem. educator, kindergarten, reading specialist, bilingual and ESL. Tchr. San Antonio (Tex.) Ind. Sch. Dist., 1965-89, Ft. Bend County Ind. Sch. Dist., 1989-2001, 2002—. Acad. adv. com. Ft. Bend I.S.D., 1996; sales cons. Mary Kay. Mem. Fort Bend Women's Tex. Dem. Party; charter mem., v.p. U.S. Congressman Henry B. Gonzalez Found. Mem. San Antonio Conservation Soc. Democrat. Roman Catholic. Avocations: reading, life sciences, writing. Home: 3614 Belle Grove Ln Sugar Land TX 77479-2257 E-mail: rmramos@houston.rr.com.

RAMOS-CANO, HAZEL BALATERO, caterer, chef, innkeeper, restauranteur, entrepreneur; b. Davao City, Mindanao, Philippines, Sept. 2, 1936; came to U. S., 1960. d. Mauricio C. and Felicidad (Balatero) Ramos; m. William Harold Snyder, Feb. 17, 1964 (div. 1981); children: John Byron, Snyder, Jennifer Ruth; m. Nelson Allen Blue, May 30, 1986 (div. 1990); m. A. Richard Cano, June 25, 1994. BA in Social Work, U. Philippines, Quezon City, 1958; MA in Sociology, Pa. State U., 1963, postgrad., 1966-67. Cert. exec. chef, Am. Culinary Fedn. Faculty, tng. staff Peace Corps Philippine Project, University Park, Pa., 1961-63; sociology instr. Albright Coll., Reading, Pa., 1963-64; rsch. asst. Meth. Ch. U.S.A., State College, Pa., 1965-66; rsch. asst. dept. child devel. & family rels. Pa. State U., University Park, Pa., 1966-67; exec. dir. Presbyn. Urban Coun. Raleigh Halifax Ct. Child Care and Family Svc. Ctr., 1973-79; early childhood educator Learning Together, Inc., Raleigh, 1982-83; loan mortgage specialist Raleigh Savs. & Loan, 1983-84; restaurant owner, mgr. Hazel's on Hargett, Raleigh, 1985-86; admissions coord., social worker Brian Corp. Nursing Home, Raleigh, 1986-88, food svc. dir., 1989-90; regional dir. La Petite Acad., Raleigh, 1989-90; asst. food svc. mgr. Granville Towers, Chapel Hill, N.C., 1990-92; mgr. trainee Child Nutrition Svcs. Wake County Pub. Sch. System, Raleigh, N.C., 1993-94; food svc. dir. S.W. Va. 4-H Ednl. Conf. Ctr., Abingdon, 1994-95; caterer, owner The Eclectic Chef's Catering, 1995—; innkeeper, owner Love House Bed and Breakfast, 1996—; pres. Ramos-Cano Inc., 1996—; owner Withers Hardware Restaurant, Abingdon, Va., 2002—; pres. Ramos-Cano Mgmt. Svcs., LLC, 2002—. Cooking instr. Wake Cmty. Tech. Coll., Raleigh, 1986-92; freelance caterer, 1964-95; chair Internat. Cooking Demonstrations Raleigh Internat. Festival, 1990-93. Pres. Wake County Day Care United Coun., 1974-75, N.C. Assn. Edn. Young Children (Raleigh Chpt.), 1975-76; bd. mem. Project Enlightenment Wake County Pub. Schs., 1976-77; various positions Pines of Carolina Girl Scout Council, 1976-85; chmn. Philippine Health and Medical Aid Com., Phil-Am Assn. Raleigh 1985-88 (publicity chmn.); elder Trinity Presbyn. Ch., Raleigh, 1979-81, bd. deacons, 1993-94; elder, session mem. Sinking Spring Presbyn. Ch., 1997—; treas. Abingdon Newcomers Club, 1997—, Presbyn. Women, Sinking Spring Presbyn. Ch., Abingdon, 1999—; master gardener Va. Tech. Master Gardeners Program, 1998—. Recipient Juliette Low Girl Scout Internat. award, 1953, Rockefeller grant Rockefeller Found., 1958-59, Ramon Magsaysay Presidential award, Philippine Leadership Youth Movement, 1957; Gov.'s Cert. Appreciation State N.C., 1990, Raleigh Mayor's award Quality Childcare Svcs., 1990, Recipient award for keeping hist. Abington beautiful Abington Kiwanis Club, 1997. Mem. Am. Culinary Fedn., Presby. Women, Raleigh, (historian 1975-76), Penn State Dames (pres. 1968-69). Democrat. Office: Victoria & Albert INN 224 Oak Hill St Abingdon VA 24210 also: The Love House Bed and Breakfast 210 E Valley St Abingdon VA 24210 Address: Withers Hardware Restaurant 260 W Main St Abingdon VA 24210 E-mail: v&ainn@naxs.com., lovehouse@naxs.com.

RAMOS-GONZALEZ, CARLOS EDUARDO, law educator, university dean; b. Caguas, P.R., Oct. 10, 1952; BA in Econs., U. P.R., 1974, JD magna cum laude, 1978; Postgrad. Diploma in Social Scis., Stockholm U., 1975; LLM, U. Calif., Berkeley, 1987. Bar: U.S. Dist. Ct. P.R. 1978, Supreme Ct. P.R. 1978, U.S. Ct. Appeals (1st cir.) 1979. Lawyer spl. litigation unit P.R. Legal Svcs., Inc., 1979-80; asst. prof. sch. law Interamerican U. P.R., San Juan, 1980-87, assoc. prof., 1987-93, prof., dean, 1993—2000; prof. Interamerican U., 2000—; dir. clin. edn. program law sch. Interamerican U. P.R., San Juan, 1984-88, assoc. dean acad. affairs law sch., 1988-93; lawyer Santurce (P.R.) Law Offices, 1981, exec. dir., 1984-88. Mem. bd. bar examiners Supreme Ct. P.R., 1987-92, 2001-03, pres. subcom. revise table specifications and matters subject to be examined, 1991-92, mem. various coms.; monitor P.R. Legal Svcs. Program, 1988, 92; lectr. in field. Author: (with others) Derecho Constitucional de Puerto Rico y los Estados Unidos, Volúmen II, 1989; contbr. articles to profl. jours. Active P.R. Law Found., 1984-88; bd. dirs. P.R. Civil Rights Inst., 1985-90. Named Disting. Prof. of Yr., Asociación Nacional de Estudiantes de Derecho, 1982-00. Mem. ABA, Assn. Trial Lawyers Am., Colegio de Abogades de P.R. (bd. dirs. 1989-90, pres. human and constl. rights com. 1991-92, Spl. award 1984), Asociación de Notarios de P.R. Office: Inter Am U PR Sch Law PO Box 70351 San Juan PR 00936-8351

RAMOS MOREAU, IRIS VIOLETA, English educator; b. Santurce, Puerto Rico, Dec. 24, 1948; d. Jose A. and Violeta (Moreau) Ramos; m. Orlando R. Gonzalez Hernandez, June 27, 1970; children: Michelle Marie, Suzanne Elaine, Rebecca Christine. BA in English, U. Puerto Rico, 1970, MA, 1983, postgrad., 1994—. Cert. English tchr., Puerto Rico. English tchr. Tomas C. Ongay Vocat. High Sch., Bayamon, Puerto Rico, 1970-85; asst. prof. bus. English dept. coll. bus. adminstrn. U. Puerto Rico, Rio Piedras, 1985—. English prof. Bayamon Regional Coll., 1984, Interam. U., 1985; curriculum cons. Humacao (P.R.) C.C.; mem. curriculum adv. com. coll. bus. adminstrn. U. P.R., 1988-92, mem. adv. com., 1991-94; mem. pers. com. bus. English dept. U. P.R. Rio Piedras Campus, 1992-94. Mem. adv. bd. ANG Family Program, Isla Verde, Puerto Rico, 1985—, PTA, Guaynabo, Puerto Rico, 1988—, Tintillo's Residents, Guaynabo, 1992—; judge competitions Puerto Rico Forensics, 1994. Mem. Assn. Bus. Communication of Ams. (mem.-at-large, founder, sec. bd. dirs. 1992—, mem. adv. bd. 1992—), ASCD, Puerto Rico TESOL, U.S.A. TESOL, Assn. for Bus. Communication, Nat. Bus. Edn. Assn., Alpha Delta Kappa. Roman Catholic. Avocations: jogging, aerobics, cooking, decorating. Office: U Puerto Rico San Juan PR 00931

RAMPMEYER, KIMBERLY KAY, elementary education educator; b. Clarion, Iowa, June 21, 1959; d. Robert George Wilhelm and Mary Annette (Wicktor) Erickson; m. Robin Jay Rampmeyer, Aug. 11, 1984. B in Phys. Edn., U. Alaska, 1984. Cert. tchr., Alaska. Recreation specialist Municipality of Anchorage, 1980-93; sub. tchr. Anchorage Sch. Dist., 1984-85, tchr., 1985—. Phys. edn. curriculum revision com. Anchorage Sch. Dist., 1995-98; rev. bd. Dept. Health Sch. Plan, Alaska; com. Winning with Stronger Edn., Anchorage, 1991; elem. phys. edn. adv. bd. Anchorage Sch. Dist., 1991-94; exec. com. Coun. Physical Edn. Children, 1998-2001, conv. coord., Cin., 2001. Alaska del. Fitness Exch. Program to People's Republic of China, 1991; sch. site coord. Spl. Olympics World Winter Games, 2001. Recipient Golden Apple award Phi Delta Kappa, 1989, 93; named Alaska Phys. Edn. Tchr. of Yr., 1993, Anchorage Sch. Dist. Tchr. of Yr., 1997, Anchorage Edn. Assn. Tchr. of Yr., 1998. Mem. Alaska AAHPERD (bd. dirs. 1985-93, pres. 1991-92, recognition awards com. 2002-03, Leadership award 1992), N.W. dist. AAHPERD (v.p. phys. edn. 1994-96, pres.'s dist. refunction com. 2002), Nat. Dance Assn., Nat. Assn. Girls and Women in Sports, Nat. Assn Sport and Phys. Edn. (cabinet coun. coord. 2003—, award recognition com. 2001-03, Project Inspiration award 1999), Anchorage Sports Assn. (bd. dirs. 1984-90), Gov.'s Coun. Phys. Fitness and Sports (bd. dirs. 1991-96). Baptist. Avocations: volleyball, softball, reading, hockey, golf. Office: Bowman Elem Sch 11700 Gregory Rd Anchorage AK 99516-1907

RAMSAY, KARIN KINSEY, publisher, educator; b. Brownwood, Tex., Aug. 10, 1930; d. Kirby Luther and Ina Rebecca (Wood) Kinsey; m. Jack Cummins Ramsay Jr., Aug. 31, 1951; children: Annetta Jean, Robin Andrew. BA, Trinity U., 1951. Cert. assoc. ch. edn., 1980. Youth coord. Covenant Presbyn. Ch., Carrollton, Tex., 1961-76; dir. ch. edn. Northminster Presbyn. Ch., Dallas, 1976-80, Univ. Presbyn. Ch., Chapel Hill, N.C., 1987-90, Oak Grove Presbyn. Ch., Bloomington, Minn., 1990-93; coord. ecum. ministry Flood Relief for Iowa, Des Moines, 1993; program coord. 1st Presbyn. Ch., Green Bay, Wis., 1994-95; owner, sole proprietor Hist. Resources Press, Corinth and Denton, Tex., 1994—. Dir. Godspell tour Covenant Presbyn. Ch., 1972-75; mem. Presbytery Candidates Com., Dallas, 1977-82, Presbytery Exams. Com. Dallas, 1979-81; clk. coun. New Hope Presbytery, Rocky Mount, N.C., 1989-90; creator, dir. Thee Holy Fools mime/musical group and This Is Me retreats. Author: Ramsay's Resources, 1983—; pub., editor: Patton's Ill-Fated Raid, 2002; contbr. articles to jours. in field. Design cons. Brookhaven Hosp. Chapel, Dallas, 1977-78; elder Presbyn. Ch. U.S.A., 1982—; coord. Lifeline Emergency Response, Dallas, 1982-84. Mem. Internat. Platform Assn., Small Publisher's Assn. of N. Am.,Pub. Marketing Assoc., Writer's League of Tex.

RAMSEY, ARDETH JANE, retired elementary school educator; b. Sumner, Iowa, Apr. 30, 1933; d. Herbert Carl and Cordella (Griese) Seehase; m. Richard Keith Ramsey, June 5, l955; children: William Robert, Thomas Edward, Patricia Eileen. BA, Upper Iowa U., l965. Cert. tchr., Iowa. Tchr. Arlington (Iowa) Cmty. Schs., l952-55, Rialto (Calif.) Cmty. Schs., l955-56, Bellevue (Iowa) Cmty. Schs., l958-59, Starmont Cmty. Schs., Arlington, l961-68, Oelwein (Iowa) Cmty. Schs., 1970-76, Vinton (Iowa) Cmty. Schs., 1976—94, head reading dept., 1990—94; reading cons. West Elem. Sch., Vinton, 1982—94, reading recovery tchr., 1993—94; ret., 1994. Mem. Vinton Edn. Assn. (sec. 1984-85), P.E.O. (pres. chpt. HG 2001-02), Early Arts Study Club (pres. 2000-01), Alpha Delta Kappa (pres. 1990-92), Delta Kappa Gamma (sec. 1982-84). Republican. Lutheran. Avocations: antiques, children's literature. Home: 1502 Washington Dr Vinton IA 52349-1654

RAMSEY, INEZ LINN, librarian, educator; b. Martins Ferry, Ohio, Mar. 25, 1938; d. George and Leona (Smith) Linn; m. Jackson Eugene Ramsey, Apr. 22, 1961; children: John Earl, James Leonard. BA in History, SUNY, Buffalo, 1971, MLS, 1972; EdD in Audiovisual Edn., U. Va., 1980. Libr. Iroquois Ctrl. H.S., Elma, N.Y., 1971-73, Lucy Simms Elem. Sch., Harrisonburg, Va., 1973-75; instr. James Madison U., Harrisonburg, 1975-80, asst. prof., 1980-85, assoc. prof., 1985-91, prof., 1991-98; ret., 1998. Mem. Va. State Library Bd., Richmond, 1975-80; cons. in field. Author: (with Jackson E. Ramsey) Budgeting Basics, Library Planning and Budgeti;g; contbr. to Ency., articles to profl. jours.; project developer Internet Sch. Libr. Media Ctr.; project dir. Oral (tape) History Black Community in Harrisonburg, 1977-78; storyteller, puppeteer. Recipient Pierian Press's Libr. Hi Tech (periodical) award, 1998; rsch. grantee James Madison U., Harrisonburg, 1981, Commonwealth Ctr. State Va., 1989. Mem. ALA, Am. Assn. Sch. Librs., Assn. Edn. Comm. Tech. (exec. bd. DSMS 1989-98, DSMT Meritorious Svc. award 1998), Va. Ednl. Media Assn. (sec. 1981-83, citation 1983, pres. 1985-86, Educator of Yr. award 1984-85, Meritorious Svc. award 1987-88), Phi Beta Kappa (pres. Shenandoah chpt. 1980-81), Beta Phi Mu, Phi Delta Kappa. Home: 3215 S Torrey Pines Dr Las Vegas NV 89146-6529

RAMSEY, MARL, retired school system administrator; Supt. Osseo Area Schs. # 279, Maple Grove, Minn., ret., 1998. State finalist Nat. Supt. of Yr., 1993. Office: Osseo Area Schs # 279 11200 93rd Ave N Osseo MN 55369-3669

RAMSEY, NANCY LOCKWOOD, nursing educator; b. L.A., Jan. 26, 1943; d. Jack Thanke and Virginia Lee (Slaughter) Lockwood; m. Gordon S. Ramsey, June 24, 1972; children: Douglas Lockwood, Kathryn Anne. BSN, Loma Linda U., 1966; MSN, Duke U., 1969; postgrad., Calif. State U., L.A., 1974. Cert. clin. nurse specialist. Staff nurse various hosps., 1966—82, 1991—92, 1999; clin. instr. Azusa (Calif.)-Pacific U., 1984, 1991; instr. U. N.C., Chapel Hill, 1968—70, Calif. State U., L.A., 1970—74; acting dir. nursing edn. Children's Hosp. L.A., 1974—75; prof. nursing L.A. City Coll., 1974—87, East L.A. Coll., Monterey Park, Calif., 1987—99; instr. lead tchr. Garden Grove, Calif., 2001; staff nurse Hospice Care of Calif., 2001—03. Instr. pediatric nursing State Bd. Rev. Classes, L.A. and San Francisco, 1975-82; instr. statewide nursing program Calif. State U., Dominguez Hills, 1983-84; staff nurse Hospice Care of Calif., 2000-02. Author, editor: Child and Family Concepts of Nursing Practice, 1982, 87; contbr. articles to profl. jours. Mem.: Sigma Theta Tau. Home: 4570 Dopo Ct Las Vegas NV 89135-2542

RAMSEY, RUSSELL WILCOX, national security affairs educator; b. Sandusky, Ohio, May 29, 1935; s. Russell Archibald and Louise (Wilcox) R.; m. Linda Stevens, Apr. 12, 1958 (div. 1976); children: Lyndall Ellen, Sally Ramsey Price, Elizabeth Ramsey Brady; m. Roberta Smith, Sept. 4, 1977; 1 child, Russell Robert. BS, U.S. Mil. Acad., 1957; MA, U. So. Miss., 1963; PhD, U. Fla., 1970. Commd. 2d lt. U.S. Army, 1957, advance through grades to maj., resigned, 1969; rsch. assoc. U. Fla. Ctr. for Latin Am. Studies, Gainesville, 1969-70, adj. prof., 1974-79; prin. Mountain Top Sch., Gainesville, 1970-72, Lincoln Vocat. Ctr., Gainesville, 1972-74, Alternative Sch., Gainesville, 1974-79; dir. Gainesville Job Corps Ctr., Gainesville, 1979-81, Turner Job Corps Ctr., Albany, Ga., 1981-84; author, cons. Albany, 1984-87; prof. nat. security affairs Air command and Staff Coll., Maxwell AFB, Ala., 1987-92; disting. prof. Sch. of the Ams., Ft. Benning, Ga., 1992—. Elected commr. City of Gainesville, 1973-76; adj. prof. Am. U., Ft. Benning, Ga., 1964-65, Nova. U., Ft. Lauderdale, Fla., 1974-80, Cen. Fla. Community Coll., Ocala, 1976-78, Albany (Ga.) State Coll., 1985-87, Troy State U., 1988—, Auburn U., Montgomery, 1989-92, U. Ala., Maxwell AFB, 1990-92; cons. White House, 1970, Superior Ct. Dougherty County, Ga., 1986. Author: Peasant Revolution, 1967, Zarpazo, the Bandit, 1977, Civil Military Relations in Colombia, 1978, Soldiers and Guerrillas, 1982, A Lady, A Champion, 1985, A Lady, A Healer, 1986, God's Joyful Runner, The Biography of Eric H. Liddell, 1987, A Lady, A Peacemaker, 1988, Readings in Latin America Security Issues, 1989, 10 Soviet Sports Stars, 1990, On Law and Country, 1992; contbr. 300 articles and book revs. to profl. jours. Chmn. Action Conf., U. Fla., 1968, Citizen Adv. Bd. for Housing, Gainesville, 1970-73; founder, chmn. Alachua County Juvenile Coun., Gainesville, 1971-79; tenor soloist Montgomery Civic Chorale, 1991, Albany Chorale, 1992—; commd. lay preacher Presbyn. ch., 1994. Lt. col. USAR, 1980-88. Decorated Bronze Star, Air medal, 6 other medals; NEH fellow, 1978; Nat. Record Holder men's age group 55-59 U.S. Masters Swimming. Mem. Am. Assn. Sch. Adminstrs., Res. Officers Assn., Kiwanis, Jaycees (Nat. Fitness Leader award 1988), Phi Alpha Theta, Phi Delta Theta. Home: 6536 Mallard Dr Midland GA 31820-3728 Office: Sch of th Ams Fort Benning GA 31905

RAMSEY, VIRGINIA CAROL MARSHALL, middle school educator; b. Alcoa, Tenn., Aug. 7, 1935; d. Arthur Glenn and Dorothy Alexander (Huff) Marshall; m. David Lawrence Ramsey, July 5, 1957; children: Stephanie Lea, Jennifer Lynne, Thomas Marshall. BA, Maryville Coll., 1957; Ed.M., W. Ga. Coll., 1981; Ed.S., U. Ga., 1984. Cert. tchr. counselor, art supr., data collector, tchr. art. Instr. art Maryville Coll., Tenn., 1957-58; supr. art Alcoa (Tenn.) City Sch. Sys., 1958-59; art instr. Cobb County Pub. Schs., Marietta, Ga., 1972—, Cobb Cmty. Sch., Marietta, 1980-83. Bd. dirs. Student Art Symposium, Athens, Ga.; presenter art shows, confs., 1972, 80, 84, 87. Author: Student Teacher Handbook, 1982. Mem. Kennestone Hosp. Guild, Marietta, 1967—; mem. Cobb PTA, 1967—, treas., 1974-76, pres., 1970-71, 76-77; mem. Sprayberry High Sch. Booster Club, 1972-86; panelist Gov.'s Conf. on Career Devel., Macon, 1972; leader Girl Scouts U.S.A., 1971-72; v.p. Sprayberry Adv. Coun., Marietta, 1981-82, pres., 1982-86; active High Mus. Art, 1969—, Cobb Arts Coun., 1975—, Marietta/Cobb Fine Arts Orgn., 1970—, Kennesaw Fine Arts Orgn. Recipient Middle Sch. Art Tchr. of Yr. award State of Ga., 1997-98. Mem. Nat. Art Edn. Assn., Ga. Art Edn. Assn. (mid. sch. chmn. 1984-87, high sch. chmn. 1977-79, Art Tchr. of Yr. State of Ga. 1988-89), Ga. Assn. Educators, Atlanta Area Art Tchrs. Assn., Cobb County Assn. Educators, Huguenot Soc. (v.p. Tenn. 1974-75), DAR, Bells Ferry Homeowners Assn., Delta Kappa Gamma. Office: Mabry Sch Cobb County Sch System 2700 Jims Rd Marietta GA 30066-1414

RANADA, ROSE MARIE, retired elementary school educator; b. Mc-Clure, Ill., Sept. 21, 1936; d. James F. and Agnes T. (Sullivan) Glaab; m. Anthony Ranada, Oct. 25, 1958; children: James, Thomas. BA, San Jose (Calif.) State U., 1958; MA, U. San Francisco, 1975. Elem. tchr. Alum Rock Sch. Dist., San Jose, Calif., Jefferson Union Sch. Dist., Santa Clara, Calif., Sunnyvale Sch. Dist., Calif. Mentor to student tchrs. Sunnyvale Sch. Dist., Calif., 1963—96. Author: (with J. Rust) Child Care Guidebook for Santa Clara County. Grantee Hewlett Packard Co.

RANALD, MARGARET LOFTUS, English literature educator, author; b. Auckland, N.Z., Sept. 5, 1927; came to U.S., 1952; d. Leonard R. and Geraldine (McGrath) Loftus; m. Ralph Arthur Ranald, Feb. 26, 1955; 1 child, Caroline Margaret. AB, U. N.Z., Wellington, 1949, MA honors, 1951; MA, UCLA, 1954, PhD, 1958. Jr. asst. Dept. Prime Min. Govt. N.Z., Wellington, 1944-52; asst. to sec. Princeton (N.J.) U., 1956-57; from instr. to asst. prof. Temple U., Phila., 1957-61; from asst. prof. to prof. CUNY, N.Y.C., 1961—. Assoc. bibliographer MLA, N.Y.C., 1958—; mem. assoc. faculty, mem. adv. com. Columbia U., N.Y.C., 1976—; vis. prof. UCLA, 1970-85, 98, tchg. asst., 1953-55. Author: The Eugene O'Neill Companion, 1984, Shakespeare and his Social Context, 1987, John Webster, 1989; assoc. editor (book series): International Bibliography of Theatre, 1985—. Fulbright fellow, 1952-54; sr. fellow Folger Shakespeare Libr., 1970-72. Mem. MLA, Am. Soc. Theatre Rsch. (exec. sec., v.p. 1976-83), Eugene O'Neill Soc. (coun., pres. 1996-2000), Shakespeare Soc. Am. (former rsch. asst.), Princeton Club N.Y. Avocations: music, drama, theatrical history, travel. Office: CUNY Dept of Eng 65-30 Kissena Blvd Flushing NY 11367

RANALD, RALPH ARTHUR, former government official, educator; b. N.Y.C., Nov. 25, 1930; s. Josef A. and Pearl R.; m. Margaret Florence Loftus, Feb. 26, 1955; 1 dau., Caroline. AB, UCLA, 1952, MA, 1954; AM, Princeton U., 1958; postgrad. (Carnegie fellow) Law Sch., Harvard U., 1961-62, 76-77, 99-2000; grad., Exec. Program Nat. and Internat. Security, 1978; PhD, Princeton U., 1962; JD, Fordham U., 1997. Bar: N.Y. Teaching asst. UCLA, 1952-54; univ. fellow, rsch. asst. Princeton (N.J.) U., 1956-59; asst. prof. Fordham U. Grad. Sch., N.Y.C., 1959-65; asst. dean acad. affairs, prof. Coll. Arts and Scis. NYU, N.Y.C., 1965-69; prof. CUNY, 1969—; spl. policy asst. HEW, Washington, 1968-69, Office of Mgmt. and Budget, 1976-77; sr. cons. U.S. Dept. Def., 1969-70, 77-78; mem. staffs Dept. Def. and Army Gen. Staff U.S. Govt. Long Com., 1989, U.S. Dept. Def., 1995-96. Vis. prof. and cons. univs. including U. So. Calif., summers 1968-74, Calif. State U., UCLA, summers 1985, 98; vis. scholar Harvard Law Sch., 1999—. Author: Management Development in Government, 1979, George Orwell, 1965; contbr. reports, articles to publs. in law, govt. and edn. Treas. N.Y. State Com. for Pub. Higher Edn., 1975-78, mem. com., 1970—. 1st lt. U.S. Army, 1953-56, to col., 1977-78, res., 1978—. Recipient U.S. Legion of Merit, 1983; sr. fellow Am. Soc. Pub. Adminstrn. (selection com. for fellows, 1970-74); mem. Res. Officers Assn. U.S. (life), Harvard U. Law Sch. Assn., Assn. of Princeton U. Grad. Alumni, U.S. Army War Coll. Alumni Assn., John F. Kennedy Sch. of Govt. Alumni Assn., Princeton Club of N.Y., Army and Navy Club, Phi Beta Kappa. Home and Office: 239 Central Park W New York NY 10024-6038

RANALLI, GEORGE JOSEPH, architect, educator; b. Bronx, Nov. 27, 1946; s. George S. and Kathryn (Heilbron) R.; m. Anne J. Valentino; 1 child. Student, N.Y. Inst. Tech., 1967-68; BArch, Pratt Inst., Bklyn., 1972; MArch, Harvard U., 1974; MA (hon.), Yale U., 1996. Registered architect, N.Y., Conn.; cert. Nat. Coun. Archtl. Registration Bds. Architect Max O. Urbahn and Assocs., N.Y.C., 1973-76; prof. archtl. design Sch. Architecture Yale U., New Haven, 1976-99, William Henry Bishop chair, vis. prof. archtl. design, 1988-89; dean Sch. Artchitecture, Urban Design & Landscape Arch. CCNY, 1999—. Vis. prof. Sch. Architecture, Cooper Union. Author: George Ranalli: Buildings and Projects, 1988, George Ranalli: Bauten und Projekte; Constructions et Projets, 1990; contbr. articles to profl. jours., chpts. to books; one-man shows include U. N.C., Charlotte, 1979, Archtl. Projects, 1980, Artists Space Gallery, N.Y.C., 1997-98, Yale U., 1999; exhibited in group shows at Drawing Ctr. and Cooper-Hewitt Mus., N.Y.C., Otis Art Inst., L.A., 1977, Yale U., 1978, 87, Hudson River Mus., 1979, Cooper-Hewitt Mus., N.Y.C., 1979, New Americans, Rome, 1979, Sperone, Westwater and Fisher Gallery, N.Y.C., 1979, Am. Archtl. Alternatives, Europe, 1979-80, Mus. Contemporary Art, Chgo., 1980, Mus. Finnish Architecture, Helsinki, 1980, Young-Hoffman Gallery, Chgo., 1980, Udine, Italy, 1985, Il Progetto Domestico XVII Milan Triennale, 1986, Centre Pompidou, 1986, AIA, 2988, 89, Deutsches Architekturmuseum, Frankfurt am Main, Germany, 1989, Met. Mus. Art, N.Y.C., 1991, Denver Art Mus., 1992, 96, Mus. Modern Art, N.Y.C., 1994, Can. Ctr. Architecture, Montreal, 1996, Whitney Mus. Art, N.Y.C., 1997, Can. Soc. for Arch., Montreal, 1999; monograph CASAS: George Ranalli, 1998. Recipient artist fellowship in architecture N.Y. Found. for Arts, 1988, design award, citation Progressive Architecture, 1980. Mem. AIA (James Stewardson traveling fellowship 1976, architecture award 1994, projects citations 1995, 96, projects award 1997), N.Y Soc. Architects (Matthew del Gaudio Meml. award, 1972. Office: 150 W 28th St New York NY 10001-6103

RANCK, EDNA RUNNELS, academic administrator, researcher; b. Waterville, Maine, Aug. 24, 1935; d. Everett Elias and Edna May (King) Runnels; m. James Gilmour Ranck, June 30, 1971 (dec. May 1979); children: Matthew, Christopher, Joshua Duggan; m. Martin Fleischer, Apr. 19, 1982; stepchildren: Christina, Laura Ranck. BA cum laude, Fla. State U., Tallahassee, 1957; MDiv magna cum laude, Drew U. Theol. Sch., Madison, N.J., 1971, MEd in Edn. Adminstrn., 1978; EdD in Curriculum and Tchg., Columbia U., N.Y.C., 1986. Dir. Collinsville Child Care Ctr., Morristown, N.J., 1971-78; exec. dir. Children's Svcs. Morris County, Morristown, N.J., 1980-84; co-mgr. N.J. Child Care Clearinghouse, Trenton; coord. N.J. Child Care Adv. Coun., Trenton, 1987-92; dir. N.J. Office Child Care Devel., Trenton, 1992; child care coord. N.J. Dept. Human Svcs., Trenton, 1992-98, Nat. Assn. Child Care Resource & Referral Agys., Washington, 1998—2002, Westover Consultants, Inc., Silver Spring, Md., 2002—. Adj. faculty Kean U. N.J., Union, 1983; dir. Sprout House Preschool, Chatham, N.J., 1984-87; mem. Morris County Human Svcs. Adv. Coun., Morristown, N.J., 1986-87, spkr. in field. Author: Dodge Foundation Project, 1984, Young Children, 1987, Our History, Our Vision: A History of the National Association of Child Care Rsource and Referral Agencies, 1997, monthly Policy Perspectives column, 2000-02; contbr. chapters to books and articles and revs. to profl. jours. Exec. bd. Drew U. Alumni Assn. Theol. Sch., 1986-92; mem. Drew U. Alumni Study Commn., 1993, Non-Govt. Orgn. rep. to UN Internat. Fedn. Educative Cmtys., 1992-99; mem. history/archives panel Nat. Assn. for Edn. of Young Children, 1999-2001; conf. moderator in field. Recipient Volpe Commitment in Child Care award, N.J. Child Care Assn., 1991, Essex C.C. Early Childhood award, 1997, Aletha Wright award for Excellence in Early Edn., 1998. Mem. Internat. Assn. Presch. Edn. N.Am. (bd. dirs.), Child Care Action Campaign Panel, Acad. Child and Youth Care Workers, Nat. Assn. of Regulatory Adminstrn. (bd. dirs. 2000—), World Orgn. Presch. Edn. (bd. dirs. 2000—), Tchrs. Coll. Columbia U. Washington Alumni Assn. (co-chmn.), Phi Beta Kappa, Pi Sigma Alpha. Republican. United Methodist. Avocations: writing, travel, clothing design, art collecting, benefit walks. Home: 4447 MacArthur Blvd NW Washington DC 20007-2564 E-mail: edna.ranck@verizon.net.

RAND, LEON, academic administrator; b. Boston, Oct. 8, 1930; s. Max B. and Ricka (Muscanto) Rakisky; m. Marian L. Newton, Aug. 29, 1959; children: Debra Ruth, Paul Martin, Marta Leah. BS, Northeastern U., 1953; MA, U. Tex., 1956, PhD, 1958. Postdoctoral fellow Purdue U., 1958-59; asst. prof. to prof. U. Detroit, 1959-68; prof., chmn. dept. chemistry Youngstown (Ohio) State U., 1968-74, dean grad. studies and research, 1974-81, acting acad. v.p., 1980; vice chancellor acad. affairs U. NC, Pembroke, 1981—85; chancellor Ind. U.-S.E., New Albany, 1986-96; chancellor emeritus Ind. U., 1996—, prof. emeritus, 1999—; spl. asst. to chancellor IUPUI, 1996-98. Bd. dirs. Jewish Hosp., Louisville, Ky., 1991-96. Bd. dirs., mem. exec. com. Louisville (Ind.) Area chpt. ARC; bd. dirs. Floyd Meml. Hosp., New Albany, 1987-90; docent Indpls. Mus. Art, 1998—. Mem. Am. Chem. Soc., Am. Inst. Chemists, Metroversity (bd. dirs.), Sigma Xi, Phi Kappa Phi. Home: 1785 Arrowwood Dr Carmel IN 46033-9019 E-mail: lrand@iupui.edu.

RAND, SHARON KAY, elementary education educator; b. Carlisle, Pa., Sept. 5, 1947; d. Charles Eugene and Pauline B. (Wheeler) Caldwell; m. David Foster, Jan. 13, 1968; children: Kelly Ann, Neal Patrick (dec.). BSEd, Shippensburg U., 1969, MEd, 1973. Tchr. grade one Big Spring Sch. Dist., Newville, Pa., 1969-79, tchr. grade three, 1979-93, lead tchr. process writing, 1986—, staff developer, 1992—, instrnl. support tchr., 1993—. Mem. Big Spring Area Women's Club, Newville, 1977-95, pres., 1986-88. Recipient Outstanding Tchr. award Shippensburg U. Study Coun., 1993. Mem. NEA, ASCD, Pa. State Edn. Assn., Big Spring Edn. Assn. (pres. 1994-96, v.p. 1996-99), Phi Delta Kappa. Presbyterian. Office: Oakflat Elem/Big Spring Dist 45 Mount Rock Rd Newville PA 17241-9412 E-mail: srand@bigspringk-12.pa.us.

RANDALL, ALAN JOHN, environmental economics educator; b. Parkes, N.S.W., Australia, Mar. 31, 1944; came to U.S. 1967; s. Leonard Wesley and Margaret (Love) Randall; m. Beverley Ann Hathaway, June 20, 1966; children: Glenn, Nicole. BS, U. Sydney, 1965, MS, 1969; PhD, Oreg. State U., 1970; Doctor (hon.), Agrl. U. Norway, 1997. Rsch. economist NSW Dept. Agr., Australia, 1965-67; rsch. fellow Oreg. State U., Corvallis, 1968-70; asst. prof. N.M. State U., Las Cruces, 1970-74; prof. U. Ky., Lexington, 1974-85; vis. prof. U. Chgo., 1981; prof. Ohio State U., Columbus, 1985—, chmn. dept., 1999—. Mem. Environ. Econs. Rsch. Group, Lansing, Mich. Author: Resource Economics, 1981, 2d edit. 1987, Valuation of Wildlands, 1984, Making the Environment Count, 1999; contbr. articles to profl. jours. Chmn. Nat. Rsch. Coun. panel, Washington, 1978-80, mem. panel, 1989-91, 95-99, mem. standing com., 2000-; mem. Coun. on Agrl. Sci. and Tech. Panel, 1988-90. Recipient Rsch. award of merit Gamma Delta Sigma, 1991, Sr. Rschr. award Ohio Agrl. Rsch. Devel. Ctr., 2000; univ. disting. scholar, 1997. Fellow Am. Agrl. Econs. Assn. (pres. Found. 2002-03, awards for excellence 1973, 81, 90); mem. Assn. Environ. and Resource Economists (award for publ. 1991), Am. Econ. Assn. Avocations: horse breeding, training, tennis, travel. Home: 6445 Freeman Rd Westerville OH 43082-8002 Office: Ohio State Univ 2120 Fyffe Rd Columbus OH 43210-1010

RANDALL, HERMINE MARIA, retired power plant engineer; b. Vienna, July 22, 1927; came to U.S., 1948; d. Heinrich Georg Adametz and Maria Antonia (Paul) Safranek; m. May 25, 1948 (div. 1975); children: George Eugene, Dorothy Maria. Lic. 1st class stationary engr., Mass. Shift supr. Stony Brook Generating Sta. Mass. Mcpl. Wholesale Electric Co., Ludlow, 1980-82; chief engr. power plant U. Mass., Amherst, 1982-87, mgr. utility generation and distbn., 1987-90, acting dir. engring., 1990-91; dir. engring., 1991-95; ret., 1995. Recipient spl. achievement award Region I, U.S. Dept. Labor, 1980, Chancellor's Citation U. Mass., 1990, Citation for Outstanding Performance, Commonwealth of Mass., 1990. Mem. Nat. Assn. Power Engrs. (pres. Springfield chpt. 1989-90). Republican. Home: 22 Worthington Dr South Hadley MA 01075-3319

RANDALL, JANET ANN, biology educator, desert biologist; b. Twin Falls, Idaho, July 3, 1943; d. William Franklin and Bertha Silvia Orr; m. Bruce H. MacEvoy. BS, U. Idaho, 1965; MEd, U. Wash., 1969; PhD, Wash. State U., 1977. Postdoctoral fellow U. Texas, Austin, 1977-79; from asst. to assoc. prof. biology Ctrl. Mo. State U., Warrensburg, 1979-87; assoc. prof. biology San Francisco State U., 1987-92, prof., 1992—. Vis. prof. Cornell U., Ithaca, N.Y., 1984-85. Contbr. articles to profl. jours. Rsch. grantee Nat. Geog. Soc., 1982, 86, 94, 96, NSF, 1984, 87, 88-89, 89-91, 91-93, 93-95, 97-00; Civilian R&D Found., 2000, 02. Fellow Calif. Acad. Sci.; mem. Animal Behavior Soc. (mem. at large 1986-89), Am. Soc. Zoologists (program officer), Am. Soc. Mammalogists, Internat. Soc. Behavioral Ecologists, Sigma Xi. Avocations: opera, travel, hiking. Office: San Francisco State U Dept Biology San Francisco CA 94132 Home: 760 Jonive Rd Sebastopol CA 95472-9298

RANDALL, JOHN ALBERT, III, elementary and secondary education educator; b. Great Lakes, Ill., Dec. 2, 1951; s. John Albert Jr. and Barbara Blanche (Coen) R.; m. Jerri Lynn Nesmith, Aug. 10, 1985; 1 child, John Albert IV. BA in Psychology, Loma Linda U., 1974; MA in Edn., Calif. State Poly. U., 1981; MBA, Nat. U., 1982. Cert. tchr. Prof. L.A. City Coll., Fuji, Japan, 1979-80; educator Perris (Calif.) Union High Sch. Dist., 1989-91, Val Verde Unified Sch. Dist., Moreno Valley, Calif., 1991-96, Perris (Calif.) Union H.S. Dist., 1996—. Site rep. Perris Tchr.'s Assn., 1990-91; chairperson Disaster Com., Rancho Verde High Sch., Moreno Valley, 1991-92; mem. emergency preparedness com. Paloma Valley H.S., 1997—, co-chmn. tech. com., 1998—. Author: Motor Developmental Skills, 1981. Mem. Community Action Com., Montclair, Calif., Am. Legion, Boy Scouts Am.; mem. Emergency Preparedness Com., Perris, 1997-98. Lt. Col. USMCR, 1976—, Desert Shield/Desert Storm, 1990-91. Decorated Navy Commendation Medal. Mem. NEA, Calif. Tchr.'s Assn., Nat. Coun. for Social Studies, Calif. Social Studies Coun., Tchrs. of Psychology in Secondary Schs., Marine Corps Res. Officers Assn. (life), Nat. U. Alumni Assn. (life), Eagle Scout Assn. (life). Avocations: family, running, bicycling. Home: 30756 Sky Terrace Dr Temecula CA 92592-3255

RANDALL, LINDA LEA, biochemist, educator; b. Montclair, N.J., Aug. 7, 1946; d. Lowell Neal and Helen (Watts) R.; m. Gerald Lee Hazelbauer, Aug. 29, 1970. BS, Colo. State U., 1968; PhD, U. Wis., 1971. Postdoctoral fellow Inst. Pasteur, Paris, 1971—73; asst. prof. Uppsala (Sweden) U., 1975—81; assoc. prof. Wash. State U., Pullman, 1981—83, prof. biochemistry, 1983—2000; Wurdock prof. biochemistry U. Mo., Columbia, 2000—. Guest scientist Wallenberg Lab., Uppsala U., 1973-75; study section NIH, 1984-88. Mem. edtl. bd. Jour. of Bacteriology, 1982-96; co-editor: Virus Receptors Part I, 1980; contbr. articles to profl. jours. Recipient Eli Lilly Award in Microbiology and Immunology, Am. Soc. Microbiology, Am. Assn. Immunologists, Am. Soc. Exptl. Pathology, 1984, Faculty Excellence Award in Rsch., Washington State U., 1988, Disting. Faculty Address, 1990, Parke-Davis award, 1995. Fellow AAAS, Am. Acad. Microbiology; mem. NAS, Am. Microbiol. Soc., Am. Soc. Biol. Chemists, Protein Soc. Avocation: dancing. Office: Univ Mo Dept Biochemistry 117 Schweitzer Hall Columbia MO 65211

RANDALL, WILLIAM THEODORE, state official; b. Seattle, July 8, 1931; s. Heaton Henry Randall and Mabel Maud (Johnson) Landstrom; m. Barbara Ann Bouffard; children: Julie Randall Waybright, Linda A. Randall Wiggins, Mary Lee Randall Lane. BA in Far Ea. Studies, U. Wash., 1953, BA in Polit. Sci., 1959, MEd in Edn. Adminstrn., 1966; EdD in Edn. Adminstrn., Ariz. State U., 1969. Agt. Aetna Ins. Co., Seattle, 1957-59; tchr. Shoreline Pub. Schs., Seattle, 1959-61, prin., 1961-66, dir. rsch., 1969-70; asst. supt. Wash. Sch. Dist., Phoenix, 1970-73; supt. Scottsdale (Ariz.) Pub. Schs., 1973-80; pres. William Randall Assocs., Phoenix, 1980-83; supt. Creighton Sch. Dist., Phoenix, 1983-88; commr. edn. State of Colo., Denver, 1988—97. Cons. Edge Learning Corp., Tempe, Ariz., 1978-82; edn. advisor Gov. of Ariz., 1985; pres.-elect Ariz. Adminstrs., Inc., 1986-88. Author: Stress Management, 1978; co-author: Role of Teacher, 1979, Management Development, 1980. Chmn. Ariz. Child Care Coalition, Phoenix, 1986; bd. dirs. Colo. Childrens Trust, Denver, 1989—; mem. exec. bd. Communities for Drug Free Colo., Denver, 1988. Sgt. U.S. Army, 1955-57. Named Adminstr. of Yr. Shoreline Edn. Assn., Seattle, 1966, Ariz. Supt. of Yr. Ariz. Sch. Adminstrs., Phoenix, 1988. Avocations: hiking, skiing.*

RANDEL, DON MICHAEL, academic administrator, musicologist; m. Carol Randel; children: Amy Elizabeth Keating, Julia, Emily Catherine Pershing, Sally Randel Eggert. AB magna cum laude, Princeton U., 1962, MFA, 1964, PhD, 1967. With dept. music, dept. chair, vice provost Cornell U., 1968, assoc. dean Coll. Arts and Scis., dean Coll. Arts and Scis., 1991—95, provost, Given Found. prof. musicology, 1995—2000; pres. U. Chgo., 2000—. Editor: New Harvard Dictionary of Music, 1986, Harvard Biographical Dictionary of Music, 1996, Harvard Concise Dictionary of Music and Musicians, 1999. Recipient Fulbright award; Hon. Woodrow Wilson fellow, Danforth Grad. fellow. Fellow: Am. Acad. Arts and Scis.; mem.: Am. Philos. Soc. Office: U Chgo Adminstrn 502 5801 S Ellis Ave Chicago IL 60637-5418

RANDELS, DAVID GEORGE, secondary school educator; b. Bryan, Ohio, Feb. 6, 1943; s. George D. and Doris L. Randels; 1 child, Kellie R. BS in Edn., Bowling Green State U., 1965, MusM, 1971. Instr., counselor Culver (Ind.) Mil. Acad., 1962-67; instr. music Port Clinton (Ohio) City Schs., 1965—. Tchr., drummer various jazz bands, 1960—; drummer Jamie Wight New Orleans Joymakers, 1980—. Musician (drummer): (albums) 6 recordings. Named Outstanding Bandsman, Bowling Green State U., 1965; recipient John Phillips Sousa Band award, Bryan HS, 1961. Mem.: Music Educators Nat. Conf., Port Clinton Fedn. Tchrs. (Lifetime Achievement award 1984), U.S. Capital Hist. Soc., Nat. Sch. Orch. Assn. (Disting. Svc. award 1994), Port Clinton Model R.R. Club (pres. 1965), Elks, Phi Delta Kappa, Kappa Kappa Psi. Democrat. Avocations: model railroading, music, antique cars, camping, fishing. Home: PO Box 182 Port Clinton OH 43452-1901 Office: Port Clinton Mid Sch 110 E 4th St Port Clinton OH 43452-1901 Personal E-mail: drandels@hotmail.com. Business E-Mail: dave_randels@port-clinton.k12.oh.us.

RANDER, JOANN CORPACI, musician, music educator; b. Waterbury, Conn., June 24, 1954; d. Anthony and Victoria Corpaci; m. David Rander, July 22, 1983. MusB Piano magna cum laude, Hartt Coll. Music, 1976, MusM Piano magna cum laude, 1980; studied classical piano with Paul Rutnam, Juilliard Sch., N.Y.C.; studied percussion, with Joe (Skinny) Purcaro, Hollywood, Calif. Musician various org., 1964—; music tchr. Fox Mid. Sch., Hartford, Conn., 1976—77, McDonough Sch., Hartford, 1976—77, Kennelly Sch., Hartford, 1976—77, S. Cath. H.S., Conn., 1977—78, St. Brigid Sch., Elmood, Conn., 1978—80, Wolcott Pub. Sch., Conn., 1980—85; pvt. instr. Zinno Music Studio, Waterbury, Conn., 1985—89. Judge Miss Mattauck Pageant, Conn., 1986, Miss Prospect Pageant, Conn., 1986, Miss Watertown Pageant, Conn., 1986, Miss Cheshire Pageant, Conn., 1987, Music Adjudication Festivals, Hartford, others. Performer: with Buddy Rich Big Band, 1973; performances throughout Fla. including Mar-a-Lago, Gov.'s Club, Four Seasons Hotel, others, conductor, accompanist New Brit. Reperatory Theatre, Miss Conn. and Universe Pageants, 1976—87. Recipient Joseph Summa award; scholar Conn. State scholar, Conn. State Union Barbers Assn. Roman Catholic. Achievements include youngest mem. in musicians union, 1968. Avocations: music performance, piano, percussion, singing, dancing. Home: 2750 Tecumseh Drive West Palm Beach FL 33409-7446

RANDISI, ELAINE MARIE, accountant, educator, writer; b. Racine, Wis., Dec. 19, 1926; d. John Dewey and Alveta Irene (Raffety) Fehd; m. John Paul Randisi, Oct. 12, 1946 (div. July 1972); children: Jeanine Randisi Manson, Martha Randisi Chaney (dec.), Joseph, Paula, Catherine Randisi Carvalho, George, Anthony (dec.); m. John R. Woodfin, June 18, 1994. AA, Pasadena Jr. Coll., 1946; BS cum laude (Giannini scholar), Golden Gate U., 1978. With Raymond Kaiser Engrs., Inc., Oakland, Calif., 1969-75, 77-86, corp. acct., 1978-79, sr. corp. acct., 1979-82, sr. payroll acct., 1983-86; acctg. mgr. Lilli Ann Corp., San Francisco, 1986-89; acting mgr. Crosby, Heafey, Roach & May, Oakland, 1990-98; accounts payable coord. Crosby, Heafy, Roach & May, Oakland, 2003—. Initiated Minority Vendor Purchasing Program for Kaiser Engrs., Inc., 1975-76; corp. buyer Kaiser Industries Corp., Oakland, 1975-77; lectr. on astrology Theosophical Soc., San Francisco, 1979-99; mem. faculty Am. Fedn. Astrologers Internat. Conv., Chgo., 1982, 84. Mem. Speakers Bur., Calif. Assn. for Neurologically Handicapped Children, 1964-70, v.p., 1969; bd. dirs. Ravenwood Homeowners Assn., 1979-82, v.p., 1979-80, sec., 1980-81, mem. organizing com. Minority Bus. Fair, San Francisco, 1976; pres., bd. dirs. Lakewood Condominium Assn., 1984-87; mem. trustee Ch. of Religious Sci., 1992-95; treas. First Ch. Religious Sci., 1994-98, lic. practitioner, pres., 1990-91, sec., 1989-90. Mem. Am. Fedn. Astrologers, Calif. Scholarship Fedn. (life), Alpha Gamma Sigma (life). Home: 742 Wesley Way Apt 1C Oakland CA 94610-2339

RANDLE, ROLINDA CAROL, elementary education educator; b. Fort Worth, Nov. 3, 1959; d. John Arthur and Ann Junette (Jones) Richards; m. Joseph L. Randle, June 12, 1982; children: Joseph Jr., Jennifer Michelle, Ja'Lissa Maurnice. BS in Edn., Tex. Christian U., 1982; postgrad., Tarleton State U. Cert. elem. edn., English, mid-mgmt., Tex. 2d grade tchr. Sunset Valley Elem. Sch., Austin, Tex., 1982-84; 6th grade tchr. Rosemont Middle Sch., Fort Worth, 1985-87; 6th grade tchr., adminstrv. intern Meadowbrook Middle Sch., Fort Worth, 1987—. Mem. site-based decision making team Rosemont Middle Sch., 1985-87, Meadowbrook Middle Sch., 1987-90, mem. leadership team, 1994—, mem. tech. com., 1991—; indsl. tech. trainer Fort Worth Ind. Sch. Dist., 1994—; owner, pres., CEO Triple J Enterprises; exec. distbr. ShapeRite Concepts, Ltd. Fellow Summer Writing Inst; mem. ASCD, NEA, United Educators Assn., Jack-n-Jill of Am. Inc., Ft. Worth Classroom Tchr. Assn., Tex. State Tchr. Assn., Delta Sigma Theta. Mem. Ch. of Christ. Avocations: reading, computers, family activities. Home: 5006 Southpoint Dr Apt 164 Arlington TX 76017-0726

RANDOLPH, BRIAN WALTER, civil engineer, educator; b. Dayton, Ohio, Feb. 23, 1959; s. John Francis and Joan Mary (Botkin) Randolph; m. Clare Ellen Luddy, June 22, 1985; children: Brigid Luddy, Hannah Luddy, Beatrix Luddy. BSCE, U. Cin., 1982, MS, 1983; PhD, Ohio State U., 1989. Registered profl. engr., Ohio. Engr. Woolpert Cons., Dayton, 1979-82; rsch. asst. U. Cin., 1982-83; rsch. assoc. Ohio State U., Columbus, 1983-87; instr. U. Toledo, 1987-89, founding dir. Environ. Geotech. Lab., 1987—, from asst. prof. to assoc. prof., 1989—97, prof., 1997—, dir. under grad. studies, 1994—97, chmn. dept. civil engring., 1997—2002, assoc. dean undergrad.

studies, 2002—. Contbr. articles to profl. jours.; referee Jour. Geotech. and Geoenviron. Engring., 1990—, Jour. Hazardous Materials, 1991—, Jour. Engring. Edn., 1994—; referee: Jour. Profl. Issues Engring. Edn. and Practice, 2003—. Fellow, U. Coll., 2001; grantee, GE, 1986, Ohio Dept. Transp./FWHA, 1989, 1992, 1993, 1994, 1996, Ohio Bd. Regents, 1989, Sokkia Corp., 1992, NSF, 1993, City of Toledo, 2003. Mem.: ASCE (dept. heads coun. 1997—2002, Toledo Young Engr. of the Yr. 1992), Am. Soc. Engring. Edn. (exec. bd. NEE com. 1990—91, Dow Outstanding Young Faculty award 1993), Toastmasters (edn. v.p. 1990—93), Sigma Xi, Tau Beta Pi, Pi Mu Epsilon, Chi Epsilon. Roman Catholic. Achievements include research in reliability analysis of groundwater flow and pavement parameters, permeability of coarse materials, and shear properties of soil and polymer interfaces. Office: Univ Toledo Coll of Engring 2801 W Bancroft St Toledo OH 43606-3390

RANDOLPH, ELIZABETH S. (MRS. JOHN DANIEL RANDOLPH), former educational administrator; b. Farmville, N.C.; d. John Hagans and Pearl (Johnson) Schmoke; A.B., Shaw U., 1936, H.H.D. (hon.), 1979, LHD (hon.); M.A., U. Mich., 1945; postgrad. U. N.C., 1964, DrPub Svc. U. N.C. at Charlotte; m. John Daniel Randolph, June 7, 1950 (dec. Dec. 1963). Tchr., English and French, New Hope High Sch., Rutherfordton, N.C., 1936-37; tchr. librarian DuBois High Sch., Wake Forest, N.C., 1937-43, Jordan Sellars High Sch., Burlington, N.C., 1943-44; tchr. English, adminstrv. asst. W. Charlotte (N.C.) High Sch., 1944-58; prin. University Park Elem. Sch., Charlotte, 1958-68; dir. ESEA activities Charlotte-Mecklenburg Schs., 1968-73, adminstrv. asst. for sch. ops., 1973-76, asst. supt., 1976-77, asso. supt., 1977-82. Mem. bd. trustees Found. for the Carolinas, The Salvation Army; trustee Shaw U., N.C. Agrl. and Tech. State U., Davidson Coll., Queen's Coll., Planned Parenthood Greater Charlotte, Pub. Libr. Charlotte and Mecklenburg County; bd. Christian edn. 1st Bapt. Ch. West; co-chair Friends of Johnson C. Smith U.; bd. dirs. Mus. of the New South, Programs for Accessible Living, Afro-Am. Cultural Ctr., Gethsemane Enrichment Program. Mem. AAUW, NEA (life), ASCD (pres. 1977-78), Nat. Coun. Negro Women, Links, NAACP, Phi Delta Kappa, Delta Kappa Gamma, Alpha Kappa Alpha (Mid-Atlantic regional dir. 1964-68, chmn. standards com., nat. parliamentarian 1974-76). Home: 3420 Shamrock Dr Charlotte NC 28215-3212

RANDOLPH, LINDA JANE, mathematics educator; b. Ypsilanti, Mich., Feb. 25, 1942; d. Roy Lawrence and Sarah (Jefferson) Robinson; m. Jerry F. Basler; children: Deborah L. Bolton, Sandra A. Randolph. BS in Teaching and Math., Ea. Mich. U., 1983, M in Math., 1989, postgrad., 1989—. Math. tutor Ea. Mich. U., Ypsilanti, 1980-82, supr. adult edn., tchr., 1983-94, instr. math.; substitute tchr. Tecumseh (Mich.) Pub. Sch., 1983-91; instr. math., program coord. UAW-FORD/EMU Milan Plastic Plant, 1991-94. Peer-advisor Acad. Svcs. Ctr., Ea. Mich. U., 1979-83; lecturer computer sci. dept. Ea, Mich. U., 1986-89, equity program, 1990-91. Mem. Am. Math. Assn., Mich. Math. Assn., Bus. and Profl. Women (v.p. chpt. 1991-92, sec. 1994-95), Nat. Edn. Computing Conf., Mich. Assn. Computer Users in Learning, Ea. Mich. U. Alumni Assn. (bd. dirs.). Home: 1414 Collegewood St Ypsilanti MI 48197-2022 Office: Ea Mich U 34 N Washington St Ypsilanti MI 48197-2618

RANDOLPH, SARAH ANN BUSH, music supervisor, computer coordinator; b. Oblong, Ill. d. Arthur "Jack" and Anna Fay (Herron) B. B of Music Edn., Ill. Wesleyan U., 1978; MS in Music Adminstrn., U. Ill., 1986. Cert. music specialist, elem. educator, adminstr. Ill. Music supr., computer tchr., coord. Selmaville Sch., Salem, Ill., 1978-97; K-8 music tchr., music tech. coord., choral dir. Lockport (Ill.) Sch. Dist. 91, 1997—; pub. rels., mktg. Raymond Prodns., Inc., Nashville, 1989-93; pres. Am. Prodns., Inc., Salem, 1994—. Prodr. Raymond Prodns., Inc., Nashville, 1989—93, Am. Prodns., Inc., Salem, 1994—; oboist Joliet (Ill) Jr. Coll. band. Chairperson Marion County Talent Show, Salem; music com. 1st Christian Ch., Salem; counselor music and ch. camps. Recipient "Those Who Excel" award Ill. State Bd. Edn., 1989, Award of Excellence in Teaching Fine Arts, So. Ill. U., 1989, 90; named Salem Citizen of the Month, Toastmasters and Salem T-C Paper, 1989, Tchr. of Yr., Joliet Sam's Cub/Wal-Mart; Harmonic Vision grantee, 2003. Mem.: NEA, NAFE, Ill. Music Educators Assn. (state v.p. 1990—96, state chair Music in Our Schs. Month), Selmaville Edn. Assn. (negotiations), Music Educators Nat. Conf. (Soc. Gen. Music state chair 1990—92), S.C. Ill. Cmty. Concert Assn. (bd. dirs. 1978—90), Centralia Cultural Soc. (oboist 1978—88), Sigma Alpha Iota (chorus dir. 1977). Avocations: music, travel, antiques, computers. Home: 1300 Kenmore Ave Joliet IL 60435-3960

RANDRUP, JOY DAVIDSON, college administrator; b. Balt., July 30, 1961; d. Jack Allen and Irene Ellen (Pusey) Davidson; m. Edward Alan Williams, Feb. 29, 1980 (div. June 1987); children: Edward Alan Jr. Williams, Johnathon David Williams; m. David William Efford, Apr. 3, 1993 (div. Oct. 2000); stepchildren: Allison Colleen, Ryan David; m. Anders III Randrup, June 30, 2001; stepchildren: Katherine, Sarah Elizabeth, Anders Nielson. AA in Computer Programming, Wor-Wic C.C., Salisbury, Md., 1985. Mgr. Davidson's Market, Ocean City, Md., 1979-81; office mgr. Internat. Seafood, Inc., Ocean City, 1982-84; sys. analyst S. Lee Smith, Inc., Salisbury, 1984-86; regional account mgr. Delmarva Svcs. Group, Millsboro, Del., 1986; coord. clerical unit Go-Getters, Inc., Salisbury, 1987-89; asst. instr., acad. computer lab. supr. Wor-Wic C.C., Salisbury, 1989-94; owner, cons. Westside Computer Svcs., Nanticoke, Md., 1992—95; network adminstr. Wor-Wic C.C., Salisbury, 1994—99; acad. network adminstr., 1997—; co-owner JA & Assocs., Salisbury, Md., 2000—. Mem. computer program adv. bd. Wor-Wic Computer Club, Salisbury, 1984—97; advisor Wor-Wic Computer Club, Salisbury, 1991—2000; mem. adv. bd. program, 1984—87; cons. Go-Getters, Inc., Salisbury, 1989—96. Active Westside United Meth. Ch., Nanticoke, 1992—98, St. Paul's United Meth. Ch., 2001—. Republican. Avocations: desktop publishing, kneeboarding, water skiing, reading, sewing. Office: Wor-Wic C C 32000 Campus Dr Salisbury MD 21804-1485 E-mail: jrandrup@mail.worwic.cc.md.us.

RANERE, BARBARA PHYLIS, elementary principal; b. Hammonton, N.J., July 12, 1942; d. John J. and Jeanette E. (Testa) R. BS in Secondary Edn., Seton Hall U., South Orange, N.J. Cert. tchr., N.J. Tchr. grade 6 St. Peter Sch., River Edge, N.J., 1962-63; tchr. grades 7-8 Our Lady Queen of Peace, Maywood, N.J., 1963-74; prin. St. Peter Elem. Sch., Merchantville, N.J., 1974-80; formation directress Villa Walsh Mother House of Religious Tchrs. Filippini, Morristown, N.J., 1980-88; tchr. grade 8 St. Joseph Sch., Hammonton, 1988-90, prin., 1990—. Mem. Camden Diocesan Regionalization Bd. Mem. Nat. Cath. Edn. Assn., Nat. Coun. Tchrs. Math., N.J. Prins. and Suprs. Assn. Home: 219 N 3rd St Hammonton NJ 08037-1735 Office: St Joseph Regional Elem Sch 133 N 3rd St Hammonton NJ 08037-1733

RANGE, DENVER HAL, educator; b. Johnson City, Tenn., Oct. 9, 1949; s. Alfred Park and Lois Evangiline (Dickerson) R.; m. Nancy Ann Jones. BS in Indsl. Edn. magna cum laude, East Tenn. State U., 1979, MEd, 1985. Research and devel. technician Pharmaseal Labs., Johnson City, 1972-75; tchr. indsl. arts Johnson City Sch. System, 1979-85; tchr. drafting Washington County Sch. System, Jonesborough, Tenn., 1985—. Treas. East Tenn. Vocat. Indsl. Clubs Am., Johnson City, 1985, 92, sec., 1990—, v.p., 1994, 2000, pres., 1995, 2001, treas., 2003; dir. aerospace workshop East Tenn. State U., Johnson City, 1987-88, instr. tech., summers 1988-89; tchr. East Tenn. State U., 1996—. Chmn. Appalachian Fair, Gray, Tenn., 1987—, bd. dirs., 1995—, v.p., 1998—. With U.S. Army, 1969-72. Mem. Tri-Cities Road Club (sec., reporter 1990—), Vocat. Club Am. (advisor 1985—, 100% award 1986-90). Democrat. Avocations: bicycling, woodworking, model rocketry, computers. Home: 409 S Cherokee St Jonesborough TN 37659-1113 Office: David Crockett High Sch Old State Rd 34 Jonesborough TN 37659-9814

RANIS, GUSTAV, economist, educator; b. Darmstadt, Germany, Oct. 24, 1929; s. Max and Bettina (Goldschmidt) R.; m. Ray Lee Finkelstein, June 15, 1958; children: Michael Bruce, Alan Jonathan, Bettina Suzanne. BA summa cum laude, Brandeis U., 1952, hon. degree, 1982; MA, Yale U., 1953, PhD, 1956. Asst. adminstr. program and policy AID/Dept. of State, 1965-67; dir. Econ. Growth Ctr. Yale U., New Haven, 1967-75, prof. econs., 1964—, Frank Altschul prof. internat. econs., 1981—; dir. Yale Ctr. Internat. and Area Studies, 1996—. Ford Found. vis. prof. U. De Los Andes, Bogota, Colombia, 1976-77; Ford Found. vis. prof. Colegio de Mex., 1971-72; fellow Inst. for Advanced Study, Berlin, 1993-94; cons. World Bank, AID, Ford Found., ILO, FAO, Inter-Am. Devel. Bank. Author: (with John Fei) Development of the Labor Surplus Economy: Theory and Policy, 1964,; (with Fei and Shirley Kuo) Growth with Equity: The Taiwan Case, 1979; (with Keijiro Otsuka and Gary Saxonhouse) Comparative Technology Choice in Development, 1988; (with F. Stewart and E. Angeles-Reyes) Linkages in Developing Economies: A Philippine Study, 1990; (with S.A. Mahmood) Political Economy of Development Policy Change, 1992; (with John C. H. Fei) Growth and Development from an Evolutionary Perspective, 1997; editor: Taiwan: From Developing to Mature Economy, 1992, En Route to Modern Economic Growth: Latin America in the 1990s, 1994, Japan and the U.S. in the Developing World, 1997,; co-editor: The State of Development Economics, 1988, Science and Technology: Lessons for Development Policy, 1990; mem. editl. bd. Jour. of Internat. Devel., 1995—, Oxford Devel. Studies, 1996—. Trustee Brandeis U., 1967-93, chmn. acad. affairs com., 1986-93. Social Sci. Rsch. Coun. fellow, Japan, 1955-56. Mem. Am. Econ. Assn., Coun. Fgn. Rels., Overseas Develop. Coun. (mem. adv. com.). Home: 7 Mulberry Rd Woodbridge CT 06525-1716 Office: Yale Ctr Internat and Area Studies 34 Hillhouse Ave New Haven CT 06511-3704 E-mail: gustav.ranis@yale.edu.

RANKIN, BETTY HILL, retired special education educator; b. Greensboro, N.C., Aug. 28, 1945; d. Wilson Conrad and Elizabeth (Roper) Hill; m. James Whiten Rankin Jr., July 23, 1967; 1 child, John Hunter. BA in History, Winthrop U., 1967; postgrad., U. South Fla., 1971-72, U. Va., 1973-98, George Mason U., 1976-98; MEd, Cambridge Coll., 1999. Tchr. English, history Acad. La Castellana, Caracas, Venezuela, 1967-69; tchr. educable retarded Tampa, Fla., 1970-72; tchr. mentally retarded Loudoun County, Va., 1972—2002; ret., 2002. Lectr. Smithsonian Instn., 1990; presenter N.Am. Conf. Rehab. Internat., Atlanta, 1993; mem. Loudoun County Tech. Steering Com., 1992-93; program dir. Rainbow Ctr. 4-H Therapeutic Equestrian Program, Inc., Manassas, Va., 2001-03; advocate for inclusion and integration of students with mental retardation. Profiled in: (video) The Land of Our Children, Rally Behind the Virginians, Am. Resources Coalition, 1992, (curriculum guide) Reins to Independence, 1999; contbr. articles to mags. Active Contact Endometriosis Assn., Inc., Milw.; treas. N.W. Prince William Citzens Assn., Catharpin, Va., 1986-2002; pres. Save the Battlefield Coalition, Inc., Catharpin, 1988—. Recipient Civic commendation Prince William County Planning Commn., 1987, Peace and Internat. Rels. award Va. Edn. Assn., 1992, Working Women award ABC Ch. 7 News/Washington Toyota Dealers, 2000, Agnes Meyer Outstanding Tchr. award Washington Post, 2001; named Tchr. of Yr., IBM, 1988, Tchr. of Yr., Loudoun County, Va., 2001, Va. Tchr. of the Yr. Region IV, 2002; fellow Internat. Exch. of Experts and Info. in Rehab., U. N.H., 1992; Loudoun Edn. Found. grantee in edn., 1994, 99, 2000; grantee Freddie Mac Found., 2000, 01. Mem. NEA, Assn. Retarded Citizens, Coun. for Exceptional Children (nat. presenter 1989, profl. recognized spl. educator 1997), Tchrs. Internat. Exch. (presenter Japan 1992), N.Am. Riding for Handicapped Assn. (cert. instr.). Avocations: preservation, equestrian activities, swimming, reading. Home: PO Box 14 Catharpin VA 20143-0014

RANKIN, ELIZABETH ANNE DESALVO, nurse, psychotherapist, educator, consultant; b. Wurtzburg, Germany, Sept. 30, 1948; d. William Joseph and Elizabeth Agnes (Faraci) DeSalvo; m. Richard Forrest Rankin, June 5, 1971; children: William Alvin, David Michael. BSN, U. Md., Balt., 1970, MS, 1972; PhD., U. Md., College Park, 1979. Cert. health edn. specialist, specialist stress mgmt. edn., master hypnotherapist, master practitioner neurolinguistic programmer, aquatic fitness instrn., fellow Nat. Bd. Clin. Hypnotherapy. Prof. U. Md., Balt., 1972—97, mem. dept. psychiat. mental health/cmty. health nursing, continuing edn., dir. divsn. bus. and industry Sch. Nursing, adv. Md. Assn. Nursing Students, 1992—97; prof. nursing Hensen Sch. Sci. and Tech. Salisbury U., 1997—, disting. univ. prof., 2001—. Advisor Md. chpt. Nat. Students Nursing Assn., 1987—92, 1998—2000; chair continuing competency com. Md. Bd. Nursing; cons. Ctr. for Alternative Medicine, Pain Mgmt., Women's Health, Rsch. and Evaluation, various publs.; presenter numerous workshops. Author, co-author: books; editor: Network Independent Study, 1993—97; mem. editl. bd. Advana for Nurses, Md. Nurse, Delmarva Found. Newsletter; contbr. chapters to books, articles to profl. jours. Recipient Twila Stinecker Leadership award, 1987, Leadership Excellence award, Md. Assn. Nusring Students, 1990—92, Book of Yr. award, Am. Jour. Nursing, 2001. Mem.: ANA, Capital Area Roundtable on Informatics in Nursing, Aquatic Exercise Assn., Washington Soc. Clin. Hypnosis, Milton H. Erickson Found., Am. Assn. Profl. Hypnotherapists, Nat. Assn. Cert. Health Educators (charter), Coun. Nurse Rschrs., Nat. Coun. Family Rels., Md. Nursing Assn. (bd. dirs., exec. com., 2d v.p. appointments mgr.), Nat. Bd. Cert. Clin. Hypnotherapists, Alpha Xi Delta, Phi Kappa Phi, Phi Epsilon Alpha, Sigma Theta Tau. Office: Salisbury U 1101 Camden Ave Salisbury MD 21801-6837

RANKIN, JACQUELINE ANNETTE, communications expert, educator; b. Omaha, Nebr., May 19, 1925; d. Arthur C. and Virdie (Gillispie) R. BA, Calif. State U., L.A., 1964, MA, 1966; MS in Mgmt., Calif. State U., Fullerton, 1977; EdD, U. LaVerne, Calif., 1981. Tchr. Rowland H.S., La Habra, Calif., 1964-66, Lowell H.S., La Habra, Calif., 1966-69, Pomona (Calif.) H.S., 1969-75; program asst. Pomona Adult Sch., 1975-82; dir. Child Abuse Prevention Program, 1985-86; exec. dir. child abuse prevention Calif. Dept. Pub. Svc., 1985-87; instr. Ind. U., Purdue U., 1993; assoc. prof. speech Ball State U., Muncie, Ind., 1993-94; instr. No. Va. U., 1994—, trainer Loudoun campus, 1996. Faculty evening divsn. Mt. San Antonio C.C., 1966-72; asst. prof. speech Ball State U., Muncie, Ind., 1993; instr. No. Va. U., Alexandria, Annandale, Manassas, Woodbridge, 1995—; assoc. faculty dept. comm. and theatre, Ind. U., Purdue U., Indpls., 1993; trainer internat. convs., sales groups, staffs of hosps., others; spkr., writer, trainer, lectr., cons. in field. Columnist: Jackie's World, Topics Newspapers; author: Body Language: First Impressions, Body Language in Negotiations and Sales, Body Language in Love and Romance, Body Language of the Abused Child, 1999, Using body Language That Kids Trust, Ten Tips for Evaluating Body Language of the Abused Child; contbr. articles to Child Law Practice, ABA and other profl. jours. Mem. Fairfax County Dem. Com.; mem. adv. coun., mem. nat. capital chpt. bd. dirs. ARC. Mem. Internat. Platform Assn., Pi Lambda Theta, Phi Delta Kappa. Home and Office: 7006 Elkton Dr Springfield VA 22152-3330 E-mail: jacki.rankin@cox.net.

RANKIN, MARGARET ANN, retired nursing educator; b. Ames, Iowa, Feb. 1, 1935; d. Meriden Lawrence and Vida Fern (Jorstad) R. BSN, Marycrest Coll., Davenport, Iowa, 1973; MA, U. Iowa, 1975, PhD, 1990. RN, Iowa. Staff nurse Iowa Meth. Mec. Ctr., Des Moines, 1956-57, asst. head nurse, 1957-58, shift med.-surg. supr., 1958-72; instr. med.-surg. nd oncology nursing U. Iowa, Iowa City, 1975-78, asst. prof., 1978-82, tchr. asst., 1982-85, lectr., 1985-98. Co-investigator Nursing-sensitive Outcomes Classification Rsch. Team, 1993—2000; workshop and symposium presenter. Contbr. articles to nursing jours., chpt. to book; co-author video tapes on asepsis, sterile techniques and Accuchek. Recipient nat. rsch. svc. award div. nursing HHS, 1987, Nat. Ctr. for Nursing Rsch., NIH, 1988, 89; rsch. fellow U. Iowa, 1980, grantee, 1989. Mem. ANA, Iowa Nurses Assn., Oncology Nursing Assn., Midwest Nursing Rsch. Soc., Iowa Cancer Pain Relief Initiative, Sigma Theta Tau (rsch. award 1988, Storga award 1991). Methodist. Avocations: reading, sewing. Home: 2227 Russell Dr Iowa City IA 52240-5847

RANKIN, MARTHA MILLER COTTINGHAM (MARTY RANKIN), elementary school educator; b. Bennettsville, S.C., Dec. 24, 1927; d. Colin James and Lily Clarkston (Miller) Cottingham; m. Donald McCray Rankin, Aug. 28, 1949; children: Martha Miller (dec.), Donald McCray Jr., Mary Colin. BS, Queens Coll., 1949; MEd, Francis Marion Coll., 1989. Cert. reading tchr., S.C. Spl. edn. tchr. Marlboro County Bd. Edn., Bennettsville, 1956-58, 1st grade tchr., 1958-59, 5th grade tchr., 1959-67, 81-91, 2d grade tchr., 1969-72, art tchr. K-2, 1991—. Grade 5 rep., advisor social studies curriculum Marlboro County Bd. Edn., 1989-91, observer assessments of performance in teaching, 1991-95. Commr. Marlboro County Parks and Recreation; bd. dirs. Atlanta Area Presbyn. Homes, 1980-90; pres. Pee Dee Presbytery, 1977-79, Women of Ch. Pee Dee Presbytery, 1977-79; elder 1st Presbyn. Ch., Bennettsville, 1983—; reenactor 2d Regiment S.C. Line C. E., Columbia, 1974-81. Mem. Nat. Art Edn. Assn., S.C. Art Edn. Assn., NEA, S.C. Edn. Assn., Marlboro County Edn. Assn. (sec., treas., legis. rep.), Delta Kappa Gamma (pres., v.p., program chmn., sec. 1968—). Avocations: reading, walking, crafts, painting. Home: 1683 Highway 15-401 E Bennettsville SC 29512-7212

RANKIN, RACHEL ANN, retired media specialist; b. High Point, N.C., Mar. 8, 1937; d. Benjamin Carl and Anne Jane Mixson; m. Thomas M. Rankin, July 30, 1961; 1 child, Rachel Roxanne Lineberry. AA, Mars Hill Coll., 1957; BA, Wake Forest U., 1959; MLS, U. S.C., 1977. Caseworker Rockingham County Welfare, Reidsville, N.C., 1959-61, Berlin Am. Sch., 1967-69, Albemarle County Schs., Charlottesville, Va., 1970-72, Lexington County Schs., Ballentine, S.C., 1973-76; tchg. asst., student tchr. supr. Sch. Edn. U. S.C., Columbia, 1976-77; sch. media specialist Montgomery County Schs., Rockville, Md., 1977-99; ret., 1999. Mentor for new librs./media specialists Montgomery Pub. Schs., 2001—03. V.p. Berlin Am. PTA, 1967—68; del. European Conf. PTAs, Garmisch, Germany, 1968; mem. planning com. N.C. Cherry Blossom Ball, Washington, 1983; co-coord. support group Am. Cancer Soc., 1988—89; People to People del. to China, 1998; bd. dirs. Fourth Presbyn. Sch., Potomac, 2001—03. Named Most Outstanding Tchr., Jackson Burley Sch., Charlottesville, 1972; recipient ofcl. citation Ho. of Dels., Md. Gen. Assembly, 1983, 96. Mem. NEA (life), Soc. Sch. Librs. Internat. (del. 1983), Am. Assn. Sch. Librarians (del. Montgomery County 1982, 90, 92, 97), Am. Cancer Soc. (dist. chair crusades 1988-90), Md. Ednl. Media Orgn., Montgomery County Ednl. Media Specialists Assn. (treas. 1981-82, v.p. 1982-83, pres. 1983-84), Montgomery County Edn. Assn., N.C. State Soc. of Washington (bd. govs. 1984-86), Delta Kappa Gamma (sec. Sigma chpt. 1988-91, v.p. 1996-98, pres. 1998-2000). Democrat. Presbyterian. Home: 15219 Red Clover Dr Rockville MD 20853-1645

RANKIN, WILLIAM PARKMAN, educator, former publishing company executive; b. Boston, Feb. 6, 1917; s. George William and Bertha W. (Clowe) R.; m. Ruth E. Gerard, Sept. 12, 1942; children: Douglas W., Joan W. BS, Syracuse U., 1941; MBA, NYU, 1949, PhD, 1979. Sales exec. Redbook mag., N.Y.C., 1945-49, This Week mag., N.Y.C., 1949-55, adminstrv. exec., 1955-60, v.p., 1957-60, v.p., dir. advt. sales, sales devel. dir., 1960-63, exec. v.p., 1963-69; gen. exec. newspaper divsn. Time Inc., N.Y.C., 1969-70; gen. mgr. feature svc. Newsweek Inc., N.Y.C., 1970-74, fin. and ins. advt. mgr., 1974-81; prof., asst. to dir. Walter Cronkite Sch. Journalism & Telecomm., Ariz. State U., Tempe, 1981-98, prof. emeritus, also bd. dirs., 1998—. Lectr. Syracuse U., NYU, Berkeley Sch. Author: Selling Retail Advertising, 1944, The Technique of Selling Magazine Advertising, 1949, Business Management of Consumer Magazines, 1980, 2d edit., 1984, The Practice of Newspaper Management, 1986. Mem. Dutch Treat Club. Home: 2625 E Southern Ave C-18 Tempe AZ 85282-7615 Office: Ariz State U Walter Cronkite Sch Journalism and Mass Communication Tempe AZ 85287-1305

RANKS, ANNE ELIZABETH, retired elementary and secondary education educator; b. Omaha, June 10, 1916; d. Salvatore and Concetta (Turco) Scolla; m. Harold Eugene Ranks, Aug. 20, 1955 (dec.). B in Philosophy, Duchesne Coll., Omaha, 1937; MA, Creighton U., 1947. Tchr. Good Shepherd Parochial H.S., Omaha, 1937-38, St. Benedicts H.S., Omaha, 1938-39, Omaha Pub. Schs., 1939-81. Pres. women's divsn. Dem. Cen. Com., Nebr.; chmn. Gov.'s Profl. Practices Commn. Nebr., 1938-39; vol. Bergan-Mercy Hosp., Omaha, 1980-86, 99—, hosp. mem. aux. bd. dirs., 1985-86; vol. Saddleback Hosp., Laguna Hills, Calif., 1989-91; bd. dirs. Sylvia Tischhauser CRTA divsn. Scholarship Found., 1989-94; mem. bd. dirs. Saddleback Valley Ednl. Found., 1990-92; bd. dirs. Orange County Diocesan Coun. Cath. Women, 1989-90, 2d v.p., 1990-94; vol. Bergan Mercy Hosp., 1998-2001. Mem. AAUW (v.p. Laguna Hills br. 1988-91), Nebr. Edn. Assn. (bd. dirs. 1957-60, pres. dist. II 1960-62), Omaha Edn. Assn. (bd. dirs. 1950-55), Womens Club, Cath. Daus. Regent Omaha Ct. (rec. sec. Lake Forest, Calif. Ct. 1988-90), Coll. Club of Leisure World (v.p. 1990-95), Nat. Ret. Tchrs. Assn., Nebr. Ret. Tchrs. Assn., Local Ret. Tchrs. Assn., Cath. Daus.

RANONE, JOHN LOUIS, school board executive; b. N.Y.C., July 7, 1940; s. Michael Nicholas and Josephine Clara (Iannone) R.; m. Carolyn Margaret Smith, June 13, 1964; children: Michelle Mary, Margaret Anne. AA in data processing, Fairleigh Dickinson, 1960; BA in Elem. Edn., Jersey City State Coll., 1964; AA/Classroom Renaissance, Montclair State Coll., 1969; MA in Adminstrn., Monmouth Coll., 1974. Cert. elem. tchr., adminstr., sex edn., classroom renaissance. Teaching prin. Hollie M. Davis Sch., River Edge, N.J., 1972-77; prin. Lincoln Sch., Ridgefield Park (N.J.) Bd. Edn., 1977-89; dir. curriculum and instruction Ridgefield Park Bd. Edn., 1989—. Cons., lectr., N.J. State Dept. Edn., Trenton, 1974—; chmn. N.J. State Adv. Council, Trenton, 1976—; lectr. Jersey City State Coll., 1979—; rep. U.S. Council for Individually Guided Edn., Atlanta, 1979-87; bd. trustees for teacher edn. Felician Coll. Trustee River Edge Pub. Libr., 1978-85. Recipient Outstanding Svc. award, Cath. Youth Orgn., Newark. 1965, Bergen County Outstanding Tchr. award, PTA, 1971, Child Assault Prevention award, N.J. State Dept. Edn., 1988, Halls Motor Co. scholarship, Jersey City, N.J., 1958-59; named to Edn. at the Met., Met. Opera Co., N.Y.C., Workshop Series I, 1988. Mem. Assn. Supervision and Curriculum Devel., Prins. and Suprs. Assn., River Edge Edn. Assn. (pres. 1974-76, v.p. 1972-74), Ridgefield Park Adminstr. Assn. (treas. 1981-98), River Edge Dem. Club, Friends of the Libr. Roman Catholic. Avocations: travel, reading, ceramic, collector. Home: 5 Oakmont Ln Jackson NJ 08527-3988

RANSFORD, SHERRY, secondary education educator; b. Pitts., June 1, 1948; d. Herbert Earl Jr. and Cora Olive (Kraus) Ransford; m. David K. Frink, Mar. 21, 1970 (div. 1982); children: Jason R., Amanda M.; m. Thomas A. Myers, Dec. 11, 1982 (div. 1996): 1 child, Benjamin J. BA in English, Allegheny Coll., 1970; MA in English, Western Mich. U., 1987. Tutor, manuscript editor Allegheny Coll., Meadville, Pa., 1969-70; asst. buyer Kaufmann's Dept. Store, Pitts., 1970-72; tchr. Baldwin Community United Meth. Ch. Nursery Sch., Pitts., 1978-83; lit. editor, non-traditional instr. Kalamazoo Coll., 1983-87; instr. Western Mich. U., Kalamazoo, 1988—92, 1997; tchr. Kalamazoo Pub. Schs., 1992—, dept. chair, 2003—. Instr. C.C. of Allegheny County, Pitts., 1982-83; instr. Kalamazoo Valley C.C., 1983-90, asst. to dean instrn., 1986-88; instr. Acad. Talented Youth Program, Kalamazoo, 1984—; task force leader Kalamazoo Pub. Schs., 1990-93. Contbr. articles to profl. jours. Chmn. grant com. Arts Coun.

Greater Kalamazoo, 1984-94; v.p., sec., chmn. coms. parent-cmty. adv. coun. Kalamazoo Pub. Schs., 1986-92; mem. adult leadership corps Boy Scouts Am., Kalamazoo, 1987-89; bd. dirs. Civic Theatre, 1992-95; advisor lit. mag., 1991-93; coach Mock Trial Team, 1994-98, 2001; advisor Nat. Honor Soc., 2001—. Recipient Outstanding Educator award, Kalamazoo County, 1987, 1992, 1994—98, 2001—03, Ednl. Ptnr. award, Kalamazoo County Edn. Assn., 2001, Influential Educator award, 2002. Mem.: AAUP, NEA, Mich. Edn. Assn., Internat. Reading Assn. Methodist. Home: 534 Pinehurst Blvd Kalamazoo MI 49006-3050 Office: Kalamazoo Pub Schs 1220 Howard St Kalamazoo MI 49008-1871

RANSIL, BERNARD J(EROME), research physician, methodologist, consultant, educator; b. Pitts., Nov. 15, 1929; s. Raymond Augustine and Louise Mary (Berhalter) R. BS, Duquesne U., 1951; PhD in Phys. Chemistry, Cath. U. Am., 1955; MD, U. Chgo., 1964. NRC-NAS postdoctoral fellow Nat. Bur. Stds., Washington, 1955-56; cons. heat div. thermodynamics sect. Nat. Bur. Standards, Washington, 1956-62; cons. NASA exobiology project, Washington, 1962-68; rsch. assoc. and dir. diatomic molecule project, Lab. Molecular Structure and Spectra, physics dept. U. Chgo., 1956-63; intern Harbor Gen. Hosp., UCLA, Torrance, Calif., 1964-65, Guggenheim fellow, 1965-66; from rsch. assoc. in medicine to assoc. prof. in medicine Harvard Med. Sch., Boston, 1966-96; from rsch. assoc. and clin. fellow to clin. assoc. Harvard II and IV Med. Svcs., 1966-74; core lab. scientist Clin. Rsch. Ctr. Thorndike Meml. Lab Boston City Hosp., Boston, 1966-74; asst. physician Beth Israel Hosp., Boston, 1974-96, sr. physician, 1996—; dir. Core Lab. Clin. Rsch. Ctr., 1974-94, Data Analysis Lab., 1989-94; cons., and mentor, rsch. ops. Beth Israel Hosp., Boston, 1994-96; cons. and mentor, computational stats. dept. neurology Beth Israel Deaconess Med. Ctr., Boston, 1996—. Statis. computing cons. Boston City Hosp. and Beth Israel Hosp., 1966-96; cons. Prophet project NIH, Bethesda, Md., 1971-88, exec. com., 1986-91, Howard Hughes Med. Inst., Boston, 1979-80, Coop. Cataract Rsch. Group, Boston, 1981-83, Mass. Alzheimer's Disease Rsch. Ctr., 1992-94, Peter Bent Brigham Behavioral Neurology Group, 1994-96, depts. of neurology, anesthesiology, gastroenterology, radiology Beth Israel Deaconess Med. Ctr., 1996—; guest lectr. med. ethics Seton Hall U., 1971—; vis. scientist Rockefeller U., 1985, Scripps Rsch. Found., 1986, Calif. State U., 1986, U. Pitts. Med. Sch., 1987. Author: Abortion, 1969, Background to Abortion, 1979; editor: Life of a Scientist: Autobiography of Robert S. Mulliken, 1989, (videocassettes) Elements of Statistics and Data Analysis, 1985; contbr. biography of R.S. Mulliken to Nobel Laureates in Chemistry, 1973; contbr. numerous articles on computational chemistry, med. topics, computational stats. to sci. jours., also book revs. to Boston Globe, other periodicals, essays and poetry to Marsalin Quar. and The Critic. Recipient alumni rsch. award, Cath. U. Am., 1969, Duquesne U. centennial award, 1978, citation for significant contbn. to computational chemistry, 1993, endowment of Vernon F. Gallagher chair for integration of sci., philosophy and theology, Duquesne U., 1999. Mem. numerous profl. socs. Home: 226 Calumet St Boston MA 02120-3303 E-mail: bransil@caregroup.harvard.edu.

RANSOM, EVELYN NAILL, language educator, linguist; b. Memphis, Apr. 20, 1938; d. Charles Rhea and Evelyn (Goodlander) Naill Ransom; m. Gunter Heinz Hiller, June 7, 1960 (div. Mar. 1964). AA, Mt. Vernon Jr. Coll., 1958; BA, Newcomb Coll., 1960; MA, N.Mex. Highlands U., 1965; PhD, U. Ill., 1974. Cert. secondary tchr., N.Mex. Instr. Berlitz Sch. Langs., New Orleans, 1961; tchr. MillerWall Elem. Sch., Harvey, L.A., 1961-62; teaching asst. N.Mex. Highlands U., Las Vegas, 1963-64; instr. U. Wyo., Laramie, 1965-66; teaching asst. U. Ill., Urbana, 1966-70; prof. English lang. Ea. Ill. U., Charleston, 1970-93; vis. prof. in linguistics No. Ariz. U., Flagstaff, 1990-91, adj. faculty, 1993-94, Ariz. State U., Tempe, 1995-98; retired. Referee Pretext: Jour. of Lang. and Lit., Ill., 1981, S.W. Jour. Linguistics, 1999; co-chair roundtable Internat. Congress of Linguistics, 1987; linguistics del. People to People, Moscow, St. Petersburg, Prague, 1993, China, 1998; dissertation reader SUNY, Buffalo, 1982; vis. scholar UCLA, 1977; conductor workshop LSA summer inst. Author: Complementation: Its Meanings and Forms, 1986; contbr. articles to profl. publs. Organizer Prairie Women's Ctr., Champaign, 1981-83. Nat. Def. Fgn. Lang. fellow, 1969; grantee Ea. Ill. U., 1982, 87, 88, NSF, 1988. Mem. Linguistic Soc. Am., Linguistic Assn. S.W. (jour. referee 1999). Avocations: computer applications for the humanities, chess, motorhoming. Home: 201 E Southern Ave # 135 Apache Junction AZ 85219-3740

RANSOM, NANCY ALDERMAN, sociology and women's studies educator, university administrator; b. New Haven, Feb. 25, 1929; d. Samuel Bennett and Florence (Opper) Alderman; m. Harry Howe Ransom, July 6, 1951; children: Jenny Alderman, Katherine Marie, William Henry Howe. BA, Vassar Coll., 1950; postgrad., Columbia U., 1951, U. Leeds, Eng., 1977-78; MA, Vanderbilt U., 1971, EdD, 1988. Lectr. sociology U. Tenn., Nashville, 1971-76; grant writer Vanderbilt U., Nashville, 1976-77, dir. Women's Ctr., 1978-97, instr. sociology, 1972, 74, lectr. sociology and women's studies, 1983, 90-97. Vol. counselor family planning Planned Parent Assn. of Nashville, 1973—77, bd. dirs., 1978—89, mem. adv. coun., 1989—98, v.p., 1981—, pres., 1987—89; bd. dirs. Sr. Citizens, Inc., 1996—, pres., 2001—02, chmn. ann. fund campaign, 2002—03; mem. planning com. ACE/ACE nat. identification program Women in Higher Edn., 1984—92; spkr. at profl. meetings. Recipient Women of Achievement award Middle Tenn. State U., 1996, Mary Jane Werthan award Vanderbilt U., 1998; named to Acad. for Women of Achievement, YWCA, 2000, Molly Todd Cup, 2003; Columbia U. residential fellow, 1951; Vanderbilt U. fellow, 1971. Mem.: LWV, NOW, AAUW, Nat. Women's Polit. Caucus, Cable Club, Phi Beta Kappa (v.p. Alpha of Tenn. 1994—95, pres. 1995—97).

RANSOM, VICTOR HARVEY, engineering educator; b. King Hill, Idaho, Mar. 23, 1932; s. Harvey Edgar and Edna Jessie (Honess) R.; m. Mary Ann Pierce, July 20, 1975 (div. June 1974); children: JoEllen Kay, Vickie Ann, Darin Victor; m. Delrie G. Gridley, July 6, 1974; children: Jessica Delrie, Natasha Lynn. BSChemE, U. Idaho, 1955; PhD, Purdue U., 1970. Registered profl. engr., Calif. Engr. Rocketdyne Divsn., Canoga Park, Calif., 1955-59; rsch. engr. Aerojet Gen. Corp., Sacramento, 1959-73; sci. and engring. fellow Idaho Nat. Engring. Lab., Idaho Falls, 1973-90; head sch. of nuclear engring. Purdue U., West Lafayette, Ind., 1990-98, prof. nuclear engring., 1998—2001; nuclear engr. ISL, Inc., Idaho Falls, 2001—02; mem. adv. com. on reactor safety U.S. Nuclear Regulatory Com., 2002—. Cons. State of Maine, 1996-99, Scientech, 1994-2001, U.S. Nuclear Regulatory Commn., Washington, 1991-2001, Idaho Nat. Engring. Lab., Idaho Falls, 1990-2001, Argonne Nat. Lab., Chgo., 1992-2001. Named to Alumni Hall of Fame U. Idaho, 1991. Fellow Am. Nuclear Soc. (chair T-H divsn. 1988, 1999, tech. achievement award 1999); mem. ASME, ASEE, Sigma Xi, Phi Eta Sigma, Sigma Chi. Achievements include development of the RELAP5 computer code for simulation of the transient response of Nuclear Powerplants under accident conditions. Home: 3035 Hamilton St West Lafayette IN 47906-1155 Office: Purdue U NUCL 112E Lafayette IN 47907 E-mail: ransom@ecn.purdue.edu.

RANSONS, ELLEN FRANCES, high school administrator; b. Orange, Calif., Oct. 2, 1954; d. Kenneth London and Billie Margaret (Jensen) Keith; m. Silvio Theodore Ransons, Apr. 1, 1978; children: Paul, Keith, Amy. BA, Calif. State U., Fullerton, 1977; MEd, Whittier (Calif.) Coll., 1988. Cert. tchr. English, social sci., Calif., Wash.; adminstrv. cert., Calif., Wash. Tchr. Mission H.S., San Gabriel, Calif., 1977-86, Suzanne Mid. Sch., Walnut, Calif., 1986-95; assoc. prin. for acas. Eastside Cath. H.S., 1995-96; asst. prin. student svcs. Lynnwood (Wash.) H.S., 1996-98, prin., 1998—. Mentor tchr. Walnut Valley Unified Sch. Dist., 1994-95. Editor student lit. publs.; author newsletter. Mem. SPARK, Walnut, 1992-94. Mem. NEA, ASCD, Am. Assn. of Sch. Adminstrs., Washington Assn. Sch. Adminstrs., Nat. Assn. Secondary Sch. Prins. Avocations: cooking, reading, writing prose and poetry. Office: Lynnwood HS 3001 184th St SW Lynnwood WA 98037-4701 Home: 10 Kirkland Irvine CA 92602-0119

RANU, HARCHARAN SINGH, biomedical scientist, administrator, orthopaedic biomechanics educator; b. Lyallpur, India; came to U.S., 1976; s. Jodh Singh and Harnam Kaur R. BSc, Leicester Poly., Eng., 1963; MSc, U. Surrey, Guilford, Eng., 1967, Cambridge (Eng.) U., 1972; PhD, Middlesex Hosp. Med. Sch. and Poly. of Cen. London, 1975; diploma, MIT, 1984. Chartered engr., Eng. Med. scientist Nat. Inst. Med. Rsch. of the Med. Rsch. Coun., London, 1967-70; rsch. fellow Middlesex Hosp. Med. Sch. and Poly. of Cen. London, 1971-76; rsch. scientist Plastics Rsch. Assn. of Great Britain, Shawbury, Eng., 1977; asst. prof. Wayne State U., Detroit, 1977-81; prof. biomed. engring./orthopaedic biomechanics biomaterials La. Tech. U., Ruston, 1982—; prof., chmn. dept. biomechanics N.Y. Coll. Osteo. Medicine, Old Westbury, 1989-93; prof., asst. to pres. and dir. doctoral program Life Coll., Marietta, Ga., 1993—; dir. tng. Rehab. Rsch. and Devel. Ctr., 1983-85; mem. La. Tech. U. Libr. Com., 1983-85; chmn. design competition Assn. Biomed. Engrs.; mem. steering com. So. Biomed. Engring. Confs., 1983—; chmn. tech. in health care conf. U. Cambridge, 1985; chmn. Internat. Symposium on Bioengring., Calcutta, India, 1985; dir. orthopaedic biomechanics rsch. labs., staff Nassau County Med. Ctr., Long Island, 1989—; prof., asst. to pres., dir. doctoral program Life Coll., Marietta, Ga., 1993—. Mem. biomed. engring. faculty com. La. Tech. U., faculty com., rsch. awards com., grad. studies com., grad. faculty, acad. bd. dirs; vis. scientist Dryburn Hosp., Durham, Eng., 1985-87, cons., 1988—; vis. prof. U. Istanbul, 1982, Lab. de Recherch Orthopediques, Paris, 1985—, Kings Coll. Med. Sch. U. London, 1989—, Indian Inst. Tech., New Delhi, Postgrad Inst. Med. Edn. and Rsch., Chandigarh, India, 1989—, Inst. Biol. Physics USSR Acad. Sci., Moscow, 1990, Polytech. Ctrl. London, 1991—; adj. prof. Coll. Physicians and Surgeons Columbia U., N.Y.C., 1988—, Inst. Biol. Physics USSR Acad. Sci., Moscow, 1990, N.Y. Coll. Podiatric Medicine, 1991—, CUNY, 1992—; cons. Lincoln Gen. Hosp., Ruston, La., 1982-85, La. State U. Med. Ctr., Shreveport, 1982—, St. Luke's and Roosevelt Hosp. Ctr., N.Y., 1988—, Foot Clinics N.Y., 1991—, Vets. Affairs Med. Ctr., N.Y., 1992—, various biomed. rsch. & legal corps., U.S., U.K.; mem. media resource svc. Inst. Pub. Info., N.Y., 1989—; med. scientist, cons. NATO, 1982—; presenter, lectr., dir. organizer numerous sci. orgns. and nat. & internat. confs.; external examiner for doctoral candidates All India Inst. Med. Scis., New Delhi, Indian Inst. of Tech., New Delhi, Banaras Hindu U., Varanasi, India, 1994—; vis. prof. U. Buenos Aires, Pontific Cath. U. Chile, Fed. U. Rio de Janeiro, numerous others. Author: Rheological Behavior of Articular Cartiliage Under Tensile Loads, 1967, Effects of Ionizing Radiation on the Mechanical Properties of Skin, 1975, Effects of Fractionated Doses of X-irradiation on the Mechanical Properties of Skin--A Long Term Study, 1980, Effects of Ionizing Radiation on the Structure & Physical Properties of the Skin, 1983, 3-D Model of Vertebra for Spinal Surgery, 1985, Application of Carbon Fibers in Orthopaedic Surgery, 1985, Relation Between Metal Corrision & Electrical Polarization, 1989, The Distribution of Stresses in the Human Lumbar Spine, 1989, Medical Devices & Orthopaedic Implants in the United States, 1989, Spinal Surgery by Modeling, 1989, Multipoint Determination of Pressure-Volume Curves in Human Intervertebral Discs, 1993, Evaluation of Volume-Pressure Relationship in Lumbar Discs Using Model and Experimental Studies, 1994, A Mechanism of Laser Nuclectomy, 1994, Microminiaturization in Laser Surgery in Vivo Intradiscal Pressure Measurements in Lumbar Intervertebral Discs, 1994, An Experimental and Mathematical Simulation of Fracture of Human Bone Due to Jumping, 1994; editor The Lower Extremity, 1993—; guest editor IEEE Engring. in Medicine & Biology, 1991; mem. editorial bd. Med. Instrumentation, 1988—, Jour. Biomed. Instrumentation & Tech., 1988—, Jour. Med. Engring. & Tech., 1989—, Jour. Med. Design & Material, 1990—, Jour. Long-Term Effects Med. Implants, 1991—, Biomed. Sci. & Tech., 1991—; reviewer Jour. Biomechanics, 1981—, Clin. Biomechanics, 1984—, Jour. Biomed. Engring., 1981, Phys. Therapy, 1990—, IEEE Biomed. Transactions, 1991—, Jour. Engring. in Medicine, 1989—; contbr. articles to profl. jours. Faculty advisor India Students Assn. Wayne State U., 1980. Recipient Edwin Tate award U. Surrey, 1968, Third Internat. Olympic Com. World Congress On Sprots Scis. award, Atlanta, 1995; numerous rsch. grants. Fellow ASME (bioengring. com. 1990—, award L.I. chpt. 1991), Biol. Engring. Soc. (London) (President's prize 1984), Instn. Mech. Engrs. (chmn. revv. bd. for corp. memberships, James Clayton awards 1974-76); mem. AAAS, Am. Coll. Sports Medicine, Am. Soc. Biomechanics (edn. com. 1990—), Orthopaedic Rsch. Soc., Biomed. Engring. Soc., India Assn., India Assn. North La., Inst. Physics and Engring. in Medicine. Sikh. Achievements include research in microfracture simulation of human vertebrae under compressive loading, laserectomy of the human nucleus pulposus and its effect on the intradiscal pressure, pressure-volume relation in human intervertebral discs, in vitro and in vivo intradiscal pressure measurements before and after laserectomy of the human nucleus pulposus, gait analysis of a diabetic foot, bioengineering in the millennium, bioengineering-building the future of biology and medicine, bioengineering the cutting edge of biology and medicine in the millennium, in vivo micro-fracture simulation in Indian Olympic field hockey players, relief from low-back pain in sports by infusion of saline into the human nucleus pulposus and establishing the pressure-volume relationship, clinical applications of bio-instrumentation for better health, fifth IOC World Congress on sports sciences, micro-fracture simulation in tennis players, human gait analysis normal and pathological, simulation of micro-fracture injury in female gymnasts-an in vivo study, pattern recognition in human gait, identification of ethnicity from human gait; micro-fracture injury simulation in pole-vaulting and female gymnasts; 3-D simulation of drop in intradiscal pressure in spinal discs due to laserectomy. Office: Life Coll Sch Grad Studies Marietta GA 30060 E-mail: drhsranu@yahoo.com.

RANUM, OREST ALLEN, historian, educator; b. Lyle, Minn., Feb. 18, 1933; s. Luther George and Nada (Chaffee) R.; m. Patricia McGroder, July 4, 1955; children— Kristin, Marcus BA, Macalester Coll., St. Paul, 1955; MA, U. Minn., 1957, PhD, 1961. Asst. prof. U. So. Calif., 1960-61; asst. prof. Columbia U., N.Y.C., 1961-63, assoc. prof., 1963-69; prof. history Johns Hopkins U., Balt., 1969-99; ret., 1999. Mem., chmn. GRE Ednl. Testing Service, Princeton, 1973-78 Author: Richelieu and Councilors, 1963, Paris, Age of Absolutism, 1968, revised and expanded edit., 2002, Artisans of Glory, 1981, The Fronde, 1993, Paris in the Age of Absolutism, 2002. Recipient Bronze medal City of Tours, France, 1980. Mem. Am. Hist. Assn., Soc. French Hist. Studies, Inst. de France (corr.), Académie des Sciences Morales et Politiques (Paris; corr. 1989), Société de l'Histoire de France, Collège de France (internat. chair 1994-95). Home: 208 Ridgewood Rd Baltimore MD 21210-2539 Office: History Dept Johns Hopkins U Baltimore MD 21218 E-mail: pranum@compuserve.com.

RAO, CH. V. endocrinologist, educator; b. Bantumelli, India, Dec. 26, 1941; came to U.S., 1964; m. Vijayalakshmi, Oct. 10, 1971; children: Naveen Rao, Satish Rao. B of Vet. Sci., Andhra Vet. Coll., Tirupathi, India, 1964; MS, Wash. State U., 1966, PhD, 1969. Rsch. asst. Wash. State U., Pullman, 1964-69; rsch. assoc. Albert Einstein Coll. Medicine, Bronx, N.Y., 1969-70, Cornell U. Med. Coll., N.Y.C., 1970-72; asst. prof. U. Louisville, 1972-76, assoc. prof., 1976-79, prof., 1979—. Cons. numerous local, nat. and internat. orgns., 1972—. Editl. bd. mem. (several scientific jour.); contbr. articles over 600 and abstracts to profl. jours. Recipient Pres.'s award for Outstanding Scholarship, U. Louisville, 1987, numerous rsch. grants NIH, 1976—. Mem. Am. Soc. Biol. Chemistry and Molecular Biology, Am. Soc. Cell Biology, Am. Fertility Soc., Soc. Study of Reproduction, Soc. Gynecologic Investigation, Endocrine Soc., Am. Physiol. Soc., Sigma Xi. Achievements include pioneering research in molecular reproductive biology and medicine. Office: Univ Louisville Med Dental Rsch 511 S Floyd St Bldg 438 Louisville KY 40202-1825

RAO, MAMIDANNA SESHAGIRI, biostatistics educator, consultant, researcher; b. Kaikalur, India, June 21, 1931; s. Suryanarayana and Satyavatidevi (Banda) Mamidanna; m. Jayasheela Golla Chinna, June 15, 1976; children: Suryasatyasree, Gayatriveena. BSc, Vivekananda Coll., Madras, India, 1951; MA, Punjab U., New Delhi, 1960; MS, U. Pitts., 1968, DSc, 1970. Statistician Safdarjnag Hosp., New Delhi, 1955-62, Indian Coun. Med. Rsch., New Delhi, 1963-67, St. Francis Gen. Hosp., Pitts., 1969-70; asst. prof. U. Tex. Med. Br., Galveston, 1970-71; asst. dir. Montefiore Hosp. and Med. Ctr., Bronx, 1971-72; regional adviser, statistician WHO, Washington, 1972-76; assoc. prof. Howard U., Washington, 1976-88, prof. Coll. Medicine, 1988—. Statistician, liaison USAID/Sudan, Khartoum, 1982-84; cons. OSHA, Dept. Labor, Washington, 1980, Family Health Internat., Raleigh, N.C., 1984, The World Bank, Washington and Sudan, 1988, Bur. of Injuries and Disabilities, Washington, 1994—. Contbr. more than 40 articles to profl. jours. Founding trustee Chinmaya Mission Regional Ctr., Silver Spring, Md., 1988; trustee Hindu Temple of Met. Washington, Adelphi, Md., 1993—, chmn. activities com., 1993-95; chmn. cultural com. Sri Siva Vishnu Temple, Lanham, Md., 1993-94. Fellow WHO, 1967-68; grantee Nat. Cancer Ctr., NIH, D.C. Govt., among others. Mem. APHA, Internat. Biometric Soc., Am. Statis. Assn., Wash. Statis. Soc., Sigma Xi. Avocations: tennis, yoga, classical music, drama, dance. Home: 13005 Buccaneer Rd Silver Spring MD 20904-3313 Office: Howard U Coll Medicine 520 W St NW Rm 2400 Washington DC 20001-2337

RAO, POSINASETTI NAGESWARA, manufacturing engineering educator; b. Palakol, Andhra, India, June 15, 1947; s. Kondaiah and Suramma P.; m. Venkata Rama Lakshmi, Aug. 18, 1976; children: Prasant, Praveen. BSc, The Narsapur (India) Coll., 1967; B of Engring., Govt. Engring. Coll., Anantapur, India, 1970; M of Engring., Birla Inst. Tech. & Sci., Pilani, India, 1973; PhD, Indian Inst. Tech., New Delhi, 1981. Asst. lectr. Birla Inst. Tech. & Sci., Pilani, India, 1973-75; lectr. Indian Inst. Tech., New Delhi, 1975-81, asst. prof., 1981-90, prof., 1990-97; vis. faculty MARA U. Tech., Shah Alam, Malaysia, 1997—2001; assoc. prof. U. No. Iowa, Cedar Falls, Iowa, 2001—. Dir. Rasmi Diecastings Ltd., Hyderabad, India, 1988—; vis. faculty Asian Inst. Tech., Bangkok, Thailand, 1993. Author: Numerical Control and Computer Aided Manufacturing, 1985, Manufacturing Technology Foundry, Forming & Welding, 1987, Computer Aided Manufacturing, 1993, AutoCAD 14 for Engineering Drawing Made Easy, 1999, Manufacturing Technology Metal Cutting and Machine Tools, 2000, CAD/CAM Principles and Application, 2002; editor: Emerging Trends in Manufacturing, 1986; contbr. numerous articles to profl. jours. Mem.: ASME, Nat. Assoc. of Indsl. Tech., Am. Soc. Engring. Edn., Soc. Mfg. Engr., Indian Soc. Mech. Engrs. Home: 319 E St Cedar Falls IA 50613 Office: U No Iowa Dept Indsl Tech Cedar Falls IA 50614-0178 E-mail: rao@uni.edu., pnageswara@hotmail.com.

RAPHAEL, MARY D. physical education educator; b. Marysville, Ga., May 28, 1950; d. Lloyd Cass and Margaret (Nisonger) Dovell; m. David A. Raphael, Aug. 29, 1972; children: Tammy Lynn, Douglas David. AA, Yuba Jr. Coll., 1970; BA, Calif. State U., Long Beach, 1972; MA, U. So. Calif., 1976. Pre-sch. tchr. Sugar Plum Pre-Sch., Los Alimatos, Calif., 1971; elem. tchr. Bellflower (Calif.) Unified Sch. Dist., 1972-73; phys. edn. tchr. middle sch. Bonita Unified Sch. Dist., San Dimas, Calif., 1973-76, phys. edn. tchr. high sch., 1976-80, phys. edn. tchr. middle sch., 1980—. Grievance chair Bonitas Unified Tchrs. Assn., 1990-92, mem. exec. bd. 1990-92. Author: (official contest book) Punt, Pass & Kick Contest Book, 1972. Mem. Am. Assn. Health, Phys. Edn., Recreation & Dance, Phi Kappa Pi. Avocations: water/snow skiing, motorcycling, bicycling, flying. Home: 10356 Park St Bellflower CA 90706-6029

RAPINI, RONALD PETER, dermatology educator; b. Akron, Ohio, Feb. 15, 1954; s. Vincent Thomas and Joann Irene (Tufexis) R.; m. Mary Jo Beigel, June 16, 1979; children: Brianna Marie, Sarina Elizabeth. BS in Biology, U. Akron, 1975; MD, Ohio State U., 1978. Diplomate Am. Bd. Dermatology (bd. dirs. 1996-2004, pres. 2004—), Am. Bd. Dermatopathology. Assoc. prof. U. Tex. Med. Sch., Houston, 1983-93; prof. and chair dermatology dept. Tex. Tech. U., Lubbock, 1994—2002; prof., chair dept. dermatology U. Tex. Med. Sch., Houston, 2002—. Fellow Am. Acad. Dermatology, Am. Soc. Dermatol. Surgery (bd. dirs. 1995-98), Soc. Investigative Dermatology; mem. AMA, Am. Soc. Dermatopathology (pres. 1998-99), Am. Soc. Mohs Surgery (pres. 2003), Internat. Soc. Dermatopathology. Avocations: tennis, entomology, piano, running, bicycling. Office: U TEx Med Sch 6431 Fannin St Houston TX 77030-0001 E-mail: ronrapini@aol.com.

RAPOPORT, FLORENCE ROSENBERG, English language educator; b. N.Y.C., May 1, 1920; d. Samuel and Rebecca (Solomon) Rosenberg; m. Carl A. Rapoport, Sept. 11, 1941; children: Mark S., Miles S. BA magna cum laude, Hunter Coll., 1941; MA, Queens Coll., 1959; Cert. Comm. Theory, Fordham U., 1968. Cert. tchr. secondary English, N.Y. Script writer Emerson Yorke Prodns./Documentary Film Co., N.Y.C., 1941-43; rschr. and speech-writer U.S. Dept. Labor, N.Y.C., 1943-44; econ. analysis and writing U.S. War Labor Bd., N.Y.C., 1944-46; educator Great Neck (N.Y.) Pub. Schs., 1959-78; television talk show producer and host Cable Vision, Great Neck, 1983—; tchr., adminstr. Alternative Sch., Great Neck, 1973-78. Founder, chmn. Task Force on Sexism, Great Neck Pub. Schs., 1974-76; creator/instr. in-svc. course for tchrs., Great Neck, 1975; coord. Title 9, Great NecK Pub. Schs., 1976-78; dir. sr. values seminar program, Great Neck H.S., 1970-74. Founder, faculty sponsor: (literary mag.) Epiphany, 1965-69; founder, editor-in-chief: (literary mag.) More Womanspace, 1981-84; host TV talk show: Focus on Women, 1983—; contbr. articles to profl. publs. Active United Parent-Tchr. Coun., Great Neck, 1952-57; mem. Nat. Speaker's Bur., Women's Am. ORT, Great Neck, 1954-57; campaign chair United Jewish Appeal, Great Neck, 1955-57; co-founder, dir. Womanspace, 1978-85. Named Woman of the Yr., Women on the Job, L.I., 1988, Am. Jewish Congress, L.I., 1990, Crohn's and Colitis Found. of Am., 1994, Women's Honor Roll, Town of North Hempstead, L.I., 1994; inducted Hunter Coll. Hall of Fame, 1996. Mem. Vet. Feminists of Am., Womanspace (dir. emerita), Phi Beta Kappa. Democrat. Jewish. Avocations: writing, reading, theater, travel, family. Home: 1 Hamilton Heights Dr Apt 315 West Hartford CT 06119-1176 Office: Cablevision Long Island 705 Middle Neck Rd Great Neck NY 11023-1216

RAPPAPORT, CAREY MILFORD, electrical engineering educator; b. Tokyo, Jan. 9, 1959; came to U.S., 1964; s. Paul Julian and Evelyn Rappaport; m. Ann Welke Morgenthaler, Nov. 12, 1989; children: Sarah Nason, Brian Hampton. BSEE, BS in Math., MSEE, EngEE, MIT, 1982, PhD, 1987. Asst. prof. elec. and computer engring. Northeastern U., Boston, 1987-93, assoc. prof., 1993-2000, prof., 2000—. Cons. AJ Devaney Assocs., Boston, 1987—; co-founder Berry Rappaport Assocs., Newton, Mass., 1990—, NSF Ctr. for Subsurface Sensing and Imaging Systems. Author: Progress in Electromagnetics Research, Vol. I, 1989; contbr. articles to profl. jours.; patentee in field. Recipient MIT K.T. Compton award, 1985. Mem. IEEE (sr., H.A. Wheeler award 1986), Sigma Xi, Eta Kappa Nu. Avocations: skiing, bridge, backpacking, chess, swimming. Office: Northeastern U 302 Stearns Boston MA 02115 E-mail: rappaport@neu.edu.

RAPPAPORT, MARTIN PAUL, internist, nephrologist, educator; b. Bronx, N.Y., Apr. 25, 1935; s. Joseph and Anne (Kramer) R.; m. Bethany Ann Mitchell; children: Karen, Steven; stepchildren: Aaron Cole, Kevin Cole. BS, Tulane U., 1957, MD, 1960. Diplomate Am. Bd. Internal Medicine, Nat. Bd. Med. Examiners. Intern Charity Hosp. of La., New Orleans, 1960-61, resident in internal medicine, 1961-64; pvt. practice internal medicine and nephrology, Seabrook, Tex., 1968-72, Webster, Tex., 1972-98; internist Univ. Med. Group, Houston, 1998; mem. courtesy staff Mainland Ctr. Hosp. (formerly Galveston County Meml. Hosp.), Texas City,

1968-96, Bapt. Meml. System, 1969-72, 88-98; mem. staff Clear Lake Regional Med. Ctr., 1972-98; cons. staff St. Mary's Hosp., 1973-79; cons. nephrology St. John's Hosp., Nassau Bay, Tex.; fellow in nephrology Northwestern U. Med. Sch., Chgo., 1967—68; clin. asst. prof. in medicine and nephrology U. Tex., Galveston, 1969—; part-time physician dept. family medicine outpatient clinics U. Tex. Med. Br., Galveston, 2000; locum tenens, 2000—. Lectr. emergency med. technician cours e, 1974-76; adviser on respiratory therapy program Alvin (Tex.) Jr. Coll., 1976-82; cons. nephrology USPHS, 1979-80. Served to capt. M.C. U.S. Army, 1961-67. Fellow ACP, Am. Coll. Chest Physicians; mem. Internat., Am. Socs. Nephrology, So. Med. Assn., Tex. Med. Assn., Tex. Soc. Internal Medicine (bd. govs. 1994-96), Am. Soc. Artificial Internal Organs, Tex. Acad. Internal Medicine, Harris County Med. Soc., Am. Geriatrics Soc., Bay Area Heart Assn. (bd. govs. 1969-75), Clear Lake C. of C., Rotary, Phi Delta Epsilon, Alpha Epsilon Pi, Tulane Alumni Assn. Home: 15913 Malibu W Willis TX 77318-6784

RAQUET, MAUREEN GRAHAM, protective services official, educator; b. Seaford, Del., Jan. 28, 1955; d. Robert James and Helen Mary Graham; m. William Jameson Raquet; 1 child, Patrick. BA in Psychology, Lafayette Coll., 1976; MS in Juvenile Justice Adminstrn. and Criminal Justice, Shippensburg U., 1989. Cert. police officer Pa. Police officer Lower Merion Twp. Police Dept., Ardmore, Pa., 1978—80; foster care cons. The Impact Project, Allentown, Pa., 1993—94; juvenile probation officer Montgomery County Juvenile Probation Dept., Norristown, Pa., 1980—92; secure detention coord. Montgomery County Youth Ctr., Norristown, 1992—2000, exec. dir., 2000. Adj. prof. criminal justice West Chester (Pa.) U., 1994—, Montgomery County C.C., Blue Bell, Pa., 1997; mem. adv. bd. Foster Grandparent Program, Norristown, 1998—; bd. dirs. Plays For Living, Norristown, 1995—2000. Recipient Outstanding Scholarship in Juvenile Justice, Pa. Juvenile Ct. Judges' Commn., Ctr. Juvenile Justice Tng. and Rsch., 1989; scholar, Charles A. Dana Found., Lafayette Coll., 1973—76. Mem.: Pa. Assn. Probation, Parole and Corrections, Nat. Coun. Juvenile and Family Ct. Judges, Am. Corrections Assn., Nat. Juvenile Detention Assn., Montgomery County Juvenile Adv. Assn. (v.p. 1991—92), Juvenile Detention Ctrs. Assn. Pa. (mental health adv. bd. 1999—, bd. dirs. tng. commn. 2001—), Alpha Phi Sigma. Office: Montgomery County Youth Ctr 540 Port Indian Rd Norristown PA 19403

RAREWALA, KATHLEEN AGNES BERTI, educational director; b. Bronx, N.Y., Sept. 30, 1949; d. John Woodrow and Josephine May (Calzerano) Berti; m. Jasjit Singh Rarewala, Aug. 13, 1973; 1 child, Kahiksha. Cert, Art Instr. Schs., 1967; BFA, Pratt Inst., 1970, MFA, 1973. Cert. tchr., N.Y. Jewelry designer Design Studio 444, N.Y.C., 1970-78; artist in residence Dakota House-Novak, N.Y.C., 1970-71; sculptor Bellardo's Ltd., N.Y.C., 1974-75; chmn. art Community Sch. P932K, Bklyn., 1970-75; display designer Maimonides Hosp., Bklyn., 1975-76; jewelry designer AIX, L.A., 1978-79; owner, clothing designer Haute Chocolate, Torrance, Calif., 1980-84; sec., treas. Lamborghini of N.Am., Carson, Calif., 1983-87; tchr. gifted Gifted Student Program/Soleado, Palos Verde Estates, Calif., 1987-88; dir., tchr. Children's Acad. of Art, Rolling Hill Estates, Calif., 1988—. Chair, cons. Art at Your Fingertips, Palos Verde, Calif., 1986-88; judge art show PTSA Reflections, Rolling Hills Estates, 1987-90; coord. art show Ridgecrest Sch., Palos Verde, 1989-91, P.V.P. High Schs., Rolling Hills Estates, 1992, coord. PTSA reflections contest, 1993-94, parliamentarian music boosters, 1993-94; chmn. nominating com., 1993-94, directory coord., editor, chmn. art show, 1993-94; 33d dist. coord. Reflections art show PTSA, 1993-94; 5th v.p. PTSA Palos Verdes Peninsula High Sch., 1993-94. Contbg. artist: Designs from Nature: Debrie Taylor, 1971; exhibited in group shows at Soc. Arts and Crafts, 1976, N.Y. Mus. Natural History, 1968, N.Y. Women's Interart Gallery, 1975, N.E. Craftfair Rhinebeck, 1976; one-woman shows include Art Gallery Pratt Inst., 1973. Chair-at-large Athletic Boosters, Rolling Hills Estates, 1991; 3rd v.p. Music Boosters, Rolling Hills Estates, 1992; 4th v.p. PTA, 1986-87, 5th v.p., 1987—, editor newspaper, 1992. Recipient 1st place award for jewelry design Bklyn. Mus. Art Show, 1975, HSA Silver Bar award PTA Calif., 1988, HSA Gold Bar award PTA Calif., 1990, Music Boosters award for continuing svc. Palos Verdes Peninsula H.S., 1994; Pratt fellow, 1971-73. Mem. Nat. Art Edn. Assn. (chair art show 1988—). Home: 49 Seaview Dr S Rolling Hills Estates CA 90274-5777

RASALILANANDA, GURUDEV SRI See MALLETTE, LILA

RASHBA, EMMANUEL IOSIF, physicist, educator; b. Kiev, Ukraine, Oct. 30, 1927; came to U.S., 1991; s. Iosif Ovsei and Rosalia (Mirkine) R.; m. Erna Kelman, July 13, 1957; 1 child, Julia. Diploma with Honor, U. Kiev, Ukraine, 1949; PhD, Ukrainian Acad. Scis., 1956; DSc, Ioffe Inst. Physics and Tech., Leningrad, 1963; Prof. Theoretical and Math. Physics, Acad. Scis. Russia, 1967. Jr. and sr. scientist Inst. Physics, Ukrainian Acad. Scis., Kiev, Ukraine, 1954-60, head theoretical divsn. Inst. Semicondrs., 1960-66; head divsn. of theory of semiconductors, prin. scientist Landau Inst. for Theoretical Physics, Acad. Sci. Russia, Moscow, 1966-97; prof. Moscow Inst. for Physics and Tech., 1967-82; rsch. prof. dept. physics U. Utah, Salt Lake City, 1992—2000, SUNY, Buffalo, 2001—. Vis. scholar CNRS, Grenoble, France, 1987, U. Stuttgart, Germany, 1988, U. Warsaw, Poland, 1989, Inst. for Sci. Interchange, Turin, Italy, 1990, Internat. Ctr. for Theoretical Physics, Trieste, Italy, 1990, Racah Inst. for Physics, Hebrew U., Jerusalem, 1991; adj. prof. Dartmouth Coll., 2000—03. Co-author: Collection of Problems in Physics, Russian edit. 1978, 2d edit., 1987, English edit., 1986, Japanese edit., 1989; Spectroscopy of Molecular Excitons, Russian edit. 1981, English edit. 1985; assoc. editor Jour. Luminescence, 1985—; editl. bd. Letters to the Jour. of Exptl. and Theoretical Physics, 1967-88; contbr. over 210 sci. and rev. articles to profl. jours. Recipient State prize in Sci., Govt. of USSR, 1966, A.F. Ioffe prize Acad. of Scis. of the USSR, 1987, ICL prize Internat. Conf. on Luminescence and Optical Spectroscopy of Condensed Matter, 1999, Alan Berman award Naval Rsch. Lab., 2001. Fellow Am. Phys. Soc. Achievements include research in electron theory of solids, especially prediction of the effect of electric field on electron spin dynamics important for growing field of spintronics; proposed the concepts of giant oscillator strengths of bound excitons and coexistence of free and self-trapped states; initiation of mechanics of growing elastic bodies in civil engineering. Home: 123 Adeline Rd Newton MA 02459-2742 Office: SUNY Dept Physics 239 Fronczak Hall Buffalo NY 14260

RASHID, KAMAL A. university administrator, research educator; b. Sulaimania, Kurdistan, Iraq, Sept. 11, 1944; came to U.S., 1972; s. Ahmad Rashid and Habiba M. Muhiedin; m. Afifa B. Sabir, May 23, 1970; children: Niaz K., Neian K., Suzanne K. BS, U. Baghdad, Iraq, 1965; MS, Pa. State U., 1974, PhD, 1978. Lab. instr. U. Baghdad, Iraq, 1966-72; mem. faculty U. Basrah, Iraq, 1978-80, U. Sulaimania, Iraq, 1980-83; sr. rsch. assoc., vis. prof. Pa. State U., University Park, 1983-86, rsch. assoc. prof. dept. biochemistry and molecular biology, 1992-2000; assoc. dir., prof. biotechnology ctr. Utah State U., Logan, 2000—. Dir. Biotech. Tng. Program program Pa. State U., 1989-2000, dir. summer symposium molecular biology, 1991-92; v.p. Cogenic Inc., State College, Pa., 1989-90; cons., spkr. biotech. tng. program developer. Contbr. articles to profl. jours. Iraqi Ministry Higher Edn. scholar. Mem. AAAS, Soc. for Indsl. Microbiology, Am. Soc. Microbiology, Am. Chem. Soc., Environ. Mutagen Soc., Rotary. Avocations: travel, swimming, reading. Home: 2835 N 2050 E Logan UT 84341-8327

RASMUSSEN, ELLEN L. secondary school educator; b. Clark, S.D., Nov. 25, 1936; d. Lloyd R. and Zella Dollie (Fisk) Acker; m. Donald M. Rasmussen, Aug. 6, 1960; children: LaDonna, Diann, Curtis. BS, S.D. State U., 1963; postgrad., U. Oreg., 1968-72, Portland State U., 1978-89, Fresno Pacific U., 1977, Augustana Coll., 1966. Cert. secondary and elem. edn. tchr., S.D. Educator Strandburg (S.D.) Sch. Dist., 1956-61, Brookings (S.D.) Pub. Sch., 1963, Hurley (S.D.) Sch. Dist., 1963-64, Bridgewater (S.D.) Sch. Dist., 1964-65, Lakeview (Oreg.) High Sch., 1965-66, South Lane Sch. Dist. 45J3, Cottage Grove, Oreg., 1966-95, ret., 1995. Mem. NEA, Nat. Coun. Tchrs. Math., Oreg. Coun. Tchrs. Math., Oreg. Edn. Assn., Lane Unified Bargaining Coun. (sec.-treas. 1988-91), Three Rivers Edn. Coun. (treas. 1991-95), South Lane Edn. Assn. (treas. 1982-95). Lutheran. Avocations: travel, sewing, crafts, gardening, quilting. Home: 1218 W D St Springfield OR 97477-8111 E-mail: erasm@pacinfo.com.

RASMUSSEN, JERRY WILLIAM, secondary school educator; b. Sioux City, Iowa, June 9, 1965; s. John William and Norene Kay (Schott) R.; m. Jean Rachel Richardson, June 6, 1992. BS in Hist. Edn., U. S.D., 1987. Cert. tchr., S.D. Instr. social sci. Dakota Valley H.S. (formerly Jefferson H.S.), North Sioux City, S.D., 1987—. Recipient Outstanding Young Educator award S.D. Jaycees, 1993. Mem. NEA, Nat. Strength and Conditioning Assn., Am. Football Coaches Assn., S.D. Football Coaches Assn. (regional dir. 1992-94), Phi Delta Kappa (Taft fellow 1993), Jefferson Alumni Assn. (pres. 1985). Avocations: weightlifting, hunting, reading, computers. Office: Dakota HS PO Box 1960 North Sioux City SD 57049-1960 Home: 401 Glen Eagle Ct North Sioux City SD 57049-5164

RASOR, DORIS LEE, retired secondary education educator; b. Gonzales, Tex., June 25, 1929; d. Leroy and Ora (Power) DuBose; m. Jimmie E. Rasor, Dec. 27, 1947; children: Jimmy Lewis, Roy Lynn. BS summa cum laude, Abilene (Tex.) Christian U., 1949. Part-time sec. Abilene Christian U., 1946-50; sec. Radford Wholesale Grocery, Abilene, 1950-52; tchr. Odessa (Tex.) High Sch., 1967-98. Author play: The Lost Pearl, 1946. Recipient Am. Legion award, 1946. Mem. AAUW, Classroom Tchrs. Assn., Tex. Tchrs. Assn., NEA, Tex. Bus. Educators Assn., "W" Club for Women, Alpha Delta Kappa (pres. 1976-78), Alpha Chi. Ch. of Christ. Avocations: reading, cooking, camping, fishing. Home: 3882 Kenwood Dr Odessa TX 79762-7018 E-mail: drjrasor@apex2000.net.

RASSAI, RASSA, electrical engineering educator; b. Tehran, Oct. 15, 1951; d. Farjollah and Farideh (Mofakhami) R. BSEE with high honors, U. Md., 1973, MSEE, 1975, PhD, 1985. Sr. engr. Traycor Electronics Co., Arlington, Va., 1975; project engr. Iran Electronics Industry, Tehran, 1977-79; lectr. U. Md., 1980, 81-91, George Washington U., Washington, 1980-82, George Mason U., Fairfax, Va., 1982; rschr. elec. engring. dept. U. md., 1986-92; prof. No. Va. C.C., Annandale, 1986—, program head engring./elec. engring. tranfer program, 1991. Contbr. articles to profl. jours.; patentee remote telephone links. Mem. NOW Democrat. Avocations: reading, philosophy. Home: 6628 Medinah Ln Alexandria VA 22312-3117

RASTLE, MAXINE SHIFLET COLE, retired elementary school educator; b. Glenville, W.Va., Sept. 6, 1937; d. Walter P. and May (Floyd) Shiflet; m. Charles Cole, Dec. 22, 1960 (dec. 1977); children: C.D., Debra Cole Moss; m. Franklin S. Rastle, June 15, 1979. BA, Glenville State Coll., 1958; MA, W.Va. U., 1961, postgrad., 1992. Cert. elem. tchr., W.Va. Tchr. grade 1 and 3 Lathrop Sch., Painesville, Ohio, 1958-59, 59-60; tchr. Putnam Sch., Marietta, Ohio, 1960-61; phys. edn./health tchr. Weston (W.Va.) Jr. High Sch., 1961-66; tchr. grade 1 and 3 Weston Cen. Sch., 1971—2003, ret., 2003. Active Dem. Women, Glenville, 1992—, Farm Bur., Glenville, PTA/Cen. Sch., 1992; sec. Sunday Sch, substitute tchr. Mem. NEA, W.Va. Edn. Assn., Lewis County Edn. Assn., FFA Alumni Assn. (pres. 1991-93), OES (worthy matron 1966-67). Democrat. Baptist. Avocations: cake decorating, cooking, sewing, crafts. Home: 1760 US Hwy 33W Weston WV 26452

RATCHFORD-MERCHANT, BETTY JO, elementary education educator; b. Huntsville, Ala., Feb. 9, 1937; d. Howard Clyde and Margaret (Kyle) Wikle; div.; children: McClellan III, Margaret Lee, Rosalyn Hampton; m. Curtis Marion Merchant, 1992. BS, Auburn U.; MEd, Ala. A&M U., 1998. Cert. tchr. elem. Tchr. elem. Gilbert Sch., Atlanta, Madison County Sch. Sys., Huntsville, Ala., Riverton Elem. Sch., ret., 2003. Mem. NEA, AAUW, Ala. Edn. Assn., Environ. Edn. Assn. Ala., Madison County Edn. Assn. Episcopalian. Avocations: writing poetry, singing, reading, painting, rock climbing. Home: 723 Versailles Dr SE Huntsville AL 35803-1778

RATCLIFFE, BARBARA JEAN, special education educator; BS in Edn., Bridgewater (Mass.) State Coll., 1983; MEd, Eastern Nazarene Coll., Wollaston, Mass., 1988. Cert. elem. tchr., spl. edn. tchr. Asst. tchr., head tchr. Heritage Sch., Inc., Braintree, 1979-82; asst. tchr., supr. summer program South Shore Ctr. for Brain Injured Children, Inc., Braintree, 1982, 85; spl. edn. asst. Blue Hills Collaborative, Canton, Mass., 1983; camp counselor, supr. Heritage Camp, Braintree, 1983; moderate spl. needs tchr. Blue Hills Collaborative, Canton, Mass., 1983-87; spl. needs food svc. instr. Easton (Mass.) Pub. Schs., 1987-92; middle sch. resource tchr., 1992-95; tutor, 1995—; preschool spl. needs tchr. Roland Green Preschool, Mansfield, Mass., 2002—. Co-dir. Jr. High Youth Fellowship; coach Spl. Olympics. Mem. NEA, Bridgewater State Coll. Alumni Assn., Eas. Nazarene Coll. Alumni Assn., Mass. Assn. Vocat. Spl. Needs Personnel, Mass. Tchrs. Assn., (vocat. com., profl. devel. com.), Coun. Exceptional Children (div. career devel. and learning disabilities), Internat. Order Rainbow for Girls (past worthy advisor). Methodist. Home: 19 Erick Rd Mansfield MA 02048-3006 Office: Roland Green Preschool Dean St Mansfield MA 02048

RATHJENS, GEORGE WILLIAM, political scientist, educator; b. Fairbanks, Alaska, June 28, 1925; s. George William and Jennie (Hansen) R.; m. Lucy van Buttingha Wichers, Apr. 5, 1950; children: Jacqueline, Leslie, Peter. BS, Yale U., 1946; PhD, U. Calif., Berkeley, 1951. Instr. chemistry Columbia U., 1950-53; staff weapons systems evaluation group Dept. Def., 1953-58; research fellow Harvard U., 1958-59; staff spl. asst. to Pres. U.S. for sci. and tech., 1959-60; chief scientist Advanced Research Projects Agy., Dept. Def., 1961, dep. dir., 1961-62; dep. asst. dir. U.S. ACDA, 1962-64, spl. asst. to dir., 1964-65; dir. weapons systems evaluation div. Inst. Def. Analyses, 1965-68; prof. dept. polit. sci. MIT, 1968-96, prof. emeritus, 1996—; sec.-gen. Pugwash Confs. on Sci. and World Affairs, 1997—. Fellow Am. Acad. Arts and Scis.; mem. Fedn. Am. Scientists (sponsor), Inst. Strategic Studies. Office: Mass Inst Tech 77 Massachusetts Ave Cambridge MA 02139-4301 also: Pugwash Am Acad Arts/Scis 136 Irving St Cambridge MA 02138-1929 E-mail: pugwash@amacad.org., gwrathje@mit.edu.

RATHKE, BARBARA JOANNE, elementary school educator; b. Carroll, Iowa; d. Wayne Henry and Bernice Marie (Niehaus) Andrews; m. Jerome William Rathke, Aug. 31, 1968; children: Benjamin Jerome, Joseph Andrews. BA, North Ctrl. Coll., 1986. Cert. tchr., Ill. Art tchr. Dist. 68, Edgewood Sch., Woodridge, Ill., 1987—. Program chmn. Faithful Circle Quilters, Downers Grove, Ill., 1986; coord. quilt rsch. days Early Am. Mus., Mahomet, Ill., 1988; mem. PTO, Woodridge, 1971—. Recipient Diane Duvigneaud Sr. Art award North Ctrl. Coll., 1986; named to Pres.'s List for Acad. Achievement, North Ctrl. Coll., 1984, 2003. Mem. NEA, Nat. Art Edn. Assn., Am. Quilters Soc., Ill. Edn. Assn., Woodridge Edn. Assn. Avocations: quiltmaking, gardening with hist. roses and native perennials. Office: Edgewood Sch 7900 Woodridge Dr Woodridge IL 60517-3824

RATHOD, MULCHAND, mechanical engineering educator; b. Pathri, India, Mar. 3, 1945; came to U.S., 1970, naturalized, 1981; s. Shamjibhai Laljibhai and Ramaben Rathod; m. Damayanti Thakor, Aug. 15, 1970; children: Prerana, Falgun, Sejal. BS in Mech. Engring., Sardar Patel U., India, 1970; MS, Miss. State U., 1972, PhD, 1975. Rsch. grad. asst. Miss. State U., 1970-75; cons. engr. Bowron & Butler, Jackson, Miss., 1975-76; asst. prof. Tuskegee Inst., Ala., 1976-78; mem. tech. staff Jet Propulsion Lab., Pasadena, Calif., summer 1980, 81; summer faculty IBM Corp., Endicott, N.Y., 1982-85; assoc. prof., coord. MET program SUNY, Binghamton, 1979-87; dir. engring. tech. divsn. Wayne State U., Detroit, 1987—. Cons. Interpine, Hattiesburg, Miss., 1977-79, Jet Propulsion Lab., 1980-83, IBM Corp., 1982-85; pres. Shiv-Parvati, Inc. 1982—. Contbr. articles to profl. jours.; patentee in field. Den leader Susquahanna coun. Boy Scouts Am., Vestal, N.Y., 1983-84. Recipient award NASA, 1981; grantee SUNY Found., 1984, Dept. Energy, 1978, GM, 1988-92, UAW Chrysler, 1990-91, Hudson-Webber Found., 1991-92, Ford, 1992-93, Kellogg Found., 1993-94, SME Found., 1994, Mich. Dept. Edn., 1994, NSF, 1995—. Fellow: ASME (cert. of appreciation 1991—2001, Dedicated Svc. award 1995, Ben C. Sparks medal 1998, cert. of appreciation 1982—89, BMW award 2001); mem.: ASHRAE, Profl. Order Engring. Tech., N.Y. State Engring. Tech. Assn., Am. Soc. Engring. Edn. (reviewer), India Assn. Miss. State U. (pres. 1972—73), Tau Beta Pi, Tau Alpha Phi (founder, faculty advisor 1989—), Pi Tau Sigma. Home: 1042 Woods Ln Grosse Pointe Woods MI 48236-1157 Office: Wayne State U Div Engring Tech Detroit MI 48202

RATIGAN, HUGH LEWIS, middle school and elementary school educator; b. Rochester, N.Y., Apr. 28, 1946; s. Lewis Bernard and Julia (Berle) R.; m. Norma Ruth Townsend, Aug. 7, 1971; children: Lorrie Ann, Noreen Ruth. BS, SUNY, Brockport, 1968, MS in Zoology, 1973, CAS in Adminstrn., 1977; EdD, U. Sarasota, 1986. Cert. tchr. biology N-12, adminstrn. Sci. tchr. middle sch. Hilton (N.Y.) Cen. Sch. Dist., 1968—. Adj. prof. SUNY, Brockport. Editor, art illustrator Art Corner newsletter Rochester Seneca park Zoo 1 Soc., 1987-90, 92—; contbr. articles to profl. jours.; author booklets. Mem. Rochester Theatre Organ Soc. (v.p. 1986-89, pres. 1989-96). Roman Catholic. Avocations: drawing, painting, playing piano and pipe organ, canoeing, walking. Home: 95 Brook St Hilton NY 14468-1201

RATLIFF, CHARLES EDWARD, JR., economics educator; b. Morven, N.C., Oct. 13, 1926; s. Charles Edward and Mary Katherine (Liles) R.; m. Mary Virginia Heilig, Dec. 8, 1945 (dec. Oct. 2000); children: Alice Ann, Katherine Virginia, John Charles. BS, Davidson Coll., 1947; AM, Duke U., 1951, PhD, 1955; postgrad., U. N.C., Harvard, Columbia. Instr. econs. and bus. Davidson Coll., 1947-48, asst. prof., 1948-49; scholar econs. Duke, 1949-51; faculty Davidson (N.C.) Coll., 1951-60, prof., 1960—, chmn. dept. econs., 1966-83, Charles A. Dana prof., 1967-77, William R. Kenan prof., 1977-92, Kenan prof. emeritus, 1992—; prof. econs. Forman Christian Coll., Lahore, Pakistan, 1963-66, 69-70. Summer vis. prof. U. N.C. at Charlotte, 1958, 60, Appalachian State U., 1962, Punjab U., Pakistan, 1963-64, Kinnaird Coll., Pakistan, 1965, Fin. Svcs. Acad., Pakistan, 1966, NDEA Inst. in Asian History, 1968; lectr. U.S. Cultural Affairs Office, East and West Pakistan, 1969-70. Author: Interstate Apportionment of Business Income for State Income Tax Purposes, 1962, A World Development Fund, 1987, Economics at Davidson: A Sesquicentennial History, 1987; co-author textbooks; contbg. author: Dictionary of the Social Sciences, 1964, Distinguished Teachers on Effective Teaching, 1986, Those Who Teach, 1988, Britain-USA: A Survey in Key Words, 1991; mem. editorial bd. Growth and Change: A Journal of Urban and Regional Policy, 1993-99; contbr. articles to profl. jours. Mem. Mayor's Com. on Affordable Housing, Davidson, 1996-97, Mayor's Com. Comty. Rels., Davidson, 1973-80, chmn., 1973-78; mem. Mecklenburg County Housing and Devel. Commn., 1975-81; mem. exec. com. Mecklenburg Dem. Com., 1967-69, precinct com., 1967-69, 72-74, 89-99, issues com., 1979-99, nat. bd. dirs. Rural Advancement Fund Nat. Sharecroppers Fund, Inc., 1978-94, exec. com., 1981-94, treas., 1981-94; mem. Mecklenburg County Comty. and Rural Devel. Exec. Com., 1981-99; bd. dirs. Bread for the World, Inc., 1983-84, Pines Retirement Comty., 1990-99, Crisis Assistance Ministry, 1992-96, Davidson Coll. Devel. Corp., 1992-95, Our Towns Habitat for Humanity, 1996-98, Davidson Coll. Alumni Assn., 1997-99, Davidson Affordable Housing Coalition, 1997-99; bd. advisors Mecklenburg Ministries, 1992-99, Drs. for Global Health, 1996—; mem. planning com. Fla. Presbyn. Homes, Inc., 2000—, spiritual life com., 2000—, fine arts com, 2001—; holder various local and conf. positions United Meth. Ch. With USN, 1944-46. Rsch. grant Ford Found., 1960-61, Fulbright-Hays grant, 1973; Rsch. fellow Inter-Univ. Com. Econ. Rsch. on South, 1960-61; recipient Thomas Jefferson award Davidson Coll., 1972, Gold medalist Prof. of Yr. award Coun. Advancement and Support of Edn., 1985, Tchg. Excellence and Campus Leadership award Sears Roebuck Found., 1991, Hunter-Hamilton Love of Tchg. award, 1992, Disting. Svc. award Davidson Coll. Alumni, 2002. Mem. AAUP, So. Econ. Assn. (exec. com. 1961-63, v.p. 1975-76, N.C. corr. So. Econ. Jour.), Am. Econ. Assn., So. Fin. Assn. (exec. com. 1966-68), Nat. Tax Assn. (chmn. interstate allocation and apportionment of bus. income com. 1972-74), Assn. Asian Studies, Fulbright Alumni Assn., Old Catawba Soc., Phi Beta Kappa, Omicron Delta Kappa (Teaching award 1991). Methodist. Home: 29 Lake Hunter Dr Lakeland FL 33803-1288 E-mail: ceratliff@msn.com.

RATLIFF, EVA RACHEL, elementary education educator; b. Ada, Mich., Mar. 9, 1944; d. Vernon C. and Edith Rachel (Coffey) Loew; m. Wallace Francis Ratliff, July 27, 1968; children: Ronald, Shelia. BA, Ind. Wesleyan U., 1967; postgrad., East Tenn. State U., 1978, U. Tenn., 1977, 82, 85, 87; MA, Columbia U., 1992. Cert. tchr. music 1-12, classroom 1-9. Tchr. music N. Judson (Ind.)-San Pierre Schs., 1967-68, Mississnewa Community Schs., Gas City, Ind., 1968-69, Mercer County Schs., Harrodsburg, Ky., 1969-73; classroom tchr. Hawkins County Schs., Rogersville, Tenn., 1977-80, Knox County Schs., Knoxville, Tenn., 1980—. Twenty-First Century Classrm. Tchr. of Tenn., 1994—; del. Tenn. Edn. Assn., Nashville, 1989-90. Mem. Knoxville Choral Soc., 1986—. Mem. Knox County Edn. Assn., Rotary Club of Knoxville (Outstanding Tchr. of Yr. 2000). Avocations: doll making, crocheting, church choir, crafts. Home: 8016 Wilnoty Dr Knoxville TN 37931-3453 Office: Sarah Moore Greene Magnet Tech Acad 3001 Brooks Rd Knoxville TN 37914-6270 E-mail: errat.@aol.com.

RATLIFF, GERALD LEE, academic administrator; b. Middletown, Ohio, Oct. 23, 1944; s. Ray and Peggy (Donisi) R. BA magna cum laude, Georgetown (Ky.) Coll., 1967; MA, U. Cin., 1970; PhD, Bowling Green (Ohio) State U., 1975. Area head theatre Glenville State Coll., 1970-72; prof., chair theatre Montclair State U., Upper Montclair, NJ, 1975-92; dean Sch. Fine and Performing Arts Ind.-Purdue U., Ft. Wayne, Ind., 1993-95; dean Coll. Arts and Architecture Mont. State U., Bozeman, Mont., 1995—; assoc. v.p. acad. affairs SUNY, Potsdam, 1997—. Feature writer Lexington (Ky.) Herald-News, 1967-68 Author: Beginning Scene Study: Aristophanes to Albee, 1980, Speech and Drama Club Activities, 1982, Oedipus Trilogy, 1984, Combating Stagefright, 1985, Playscript Interpretation and Production, 1985, (Machiavelli's) The Prince, 1986, (with Suzanne Trauth) Introduction to Musical Theatre, 1986, Playing Scenes: A Sourcebook for Performance, 1993, Playing Contemporary Scenes: A Sourcebook for Performance, 1996, Theatre Audition Handbook, 1998, Introduction to Reader's Theatre, 1999, Millennium Monologues, 2002; contbr. articles and revs. to profl. jours. Exec. coun. mem. Assn. for Commn. Adminstrn., 1995—; bd. dirs. Am. Conf. Acad. Deans. Fulbright scholar, 1989; recipient Nat. Medallion of Honor award Theta Alpha Phi, 1989; Alumni Assn. faculty rsch. grantee, 1980, 83, 86. Mem. Nat. Comm. Assn. (legis. coun. 1987-88, chair theatre divsn. 1986-87), Am. Assn. Theatre in Secondary Edn. (nat. bd. dirs. 1986-87), Secondary Sch. Theatre Assn. (nat. bd. dirs. 1983-86), Internat. Arts Assn. (v.p. 1975-76), Assn. for Commn. Adminstrn. (pres. 2000-02), Ea. Comm. Assn. (exec. sec. 1986-89, 1st v.p. elect 1989, exec. com. 1986—, pres. 1991, Disting. Svc. award 1993, Disting. Svc. Tchg. award 1998), Theta Alpha Phi (nat. pres. 1984-87, nat. coun. 1979-82, 84-87). Avocations: writing, softball. Home: 2 Morningside Dr Potsdam NY 13676-3305 E-mail: ratlifgl@potsdam.edu.

RATLIFF, LOIS L. secondary school educator; b. Anson County, N.C., May 8, 1951; d. Walter A. and Corine S. Ratliff. BS, Bennett Coll., Greensboro, N.C., 1971; MS, N.C. A&T State U., 1974. Cert. tchr., N.C., S.C. Instr. biology Paine Coll., Augusta, Ga., 1976-78, Livingston Coll., Salisbury, N.C., 1979-80; tchr. chemistry Florence (S.C.) Sch. Dist. 1, 1980-85; tchr. phys. sci. Union County Schs., Monroe, N.C., 1985-86; tchr. chemistry Myers Park High Sch., Charlotte, N.C., 1986-89; tchr. phys. sci. Darlington (S.C.) Schs., 1989-96; tchr. chemistry Union County Schs., Monroe, N.C., 1996—. Advisor Jr. Acad. Sci.; mem. evaluation team Nat. Assn. State Dept. Tchr. Edn. Evaluation Com. Mem. NEA, ASCD, NSTA.

RATNER, BUDDY DENNIS, bioengineer, educator; b. Bklyn., Jan. 19, 1947; s. Philip and Ruth Ratner; m. Cheryl Cromer; 1 child, Daniel Martin. BS in Chemistry, Bklyn. Coll., 1967; PhD in Polymer Chemistry, Polytech. Inst. Bklyn., 1972. Fellow U. Wash., Seattle, 1972-73, from rsch. assoc. to assoc. prof., 1973-86, prof., 1986—, Wash. Rsch. Found. Endowed Prof. Bioengring., 2001—. Dir. U. Wash. Engineered Biomaterials NSF Engring. Ctr.; founder Asemblon, Inc. Editor: Surface Characterization of Biomaterials, 1989, Plasmas and Polymers, 1994-99, Biomaterials Science: An Introduction to Materials in Medicine, 1996, Characterization of Polymeric Biomaterials, 1997; mem. editl. bds. 9 jours. and book series; editor Jour. Undergrad. Rsch. in Bioengring., 1998—; contbr. over 300 articles to profl. jours. Recipient Faculty Achievement/Outstanding Rsch. award, Burlington Resources Found., 1990, Perkin Elmer Phys. Electronics award for excellence in surface sci. Fellow Internat. Acad. Med. and Biol. Engring., Am. Inst. Med. Biol. Engring. (founder, pres. 2002-03), Am. Vacuum Soc. (Medard Welsh medal 2002); mem. AAAS, AIChE (C.M.A. Stine award 1998), Nat. Acad. Engring., Am. Chem. Soc., Internat. Soc. Contact Lens Rsch., Materials Rsch. Soc., Soc. for Biomaterials (pres. 1991-92, Clemson award 1989, fellow 1994), Biomed. Engring. Soc. Achievements include 15 patents in field. Office: U Wash Dept Bioengring PO Box 351720 Seattle WA 98195-1720 E-mail: ratner@uweb.engr.washington.edu.

RATNER, DAVID LOUIS, retired law educator; b. London, Sept. 2, 1931; AB magna cum laude, Harvard U., 1952, LLB magna cum laude, 1955. Bar: N.Y. 1955. Assoc. Sullivan & Cromwell, N.Y.C., 1955-64; assoc. prof. Cornell Law Sch., Ithaca, N.Y., 1964-68, prof., 1968-82; prof. law U. San Francisco Law Sch., 1982-99, dean, 1982-89, prof. emeritus, 1999—. Exec. asst. to chmn. SEC, Washington, 1966-68; chief counsel Securities Industry Study, Senate Banking Com., Washington, 1971-73; vis. prof. Stanford (Calif.) U., 1974, Ariz. State U., Tempe, 1974, U. San Francisco, 1980, Georgetown U., Washington, 1989-90, U. Calif., Hastings, San Francisco, 1992; mem. Larkspur (Calif.) Planning Commn., 1992—. Author: Securities Regulation: Cases and Materials, 6th edit., 2002, Securities Regulation in a Nutshell, 7 edit., 2002, Institutional Investors: Teaching Materials, 1978. Fulbright scholar Monash U., Australia, 1981. Mem. Cosmos Club (Washington), Harvard Club of San Francisco (pres. 1999-2000), Phi Beta Kappa. Home and Office: 84 Polhemus Way Larkspur CA 94939-1928 E-mail: dlratner@aol.com.

RATNER, GAYLE, special education educator; b. Bronx, N.Y. BS, SUNY, Plattsburgh, 1991, MS in Edn., 1993. Cert. spl. edn. grades K-12 and elem. edn. grades N-6. Spl. edn. tchr. Chazy (N.Y.) Ctrl. Rural Sch., 1991—. Asst. chief reader N.Y. State Tchr. Cert. Examinations, mem. students with disabilities content adv. com.; instr. N.Y. State United Tchrs. Effective Tchg. Program, 1999—; mem. edn. bias and sensitivity com. for 4th and 8th grade state assessments CTB/McGraw Hill and N.Y. State, 2001—. Mem.: N.Y. State United Tchrs., Chazy Tchrs. Assn. (pres. 1995—), Nat. Bd. for Profl. Tchg. Stds. (bd. mem., spl. edn. and elem. edn. com. 2000—), Phi Delta Kappa. Office: Chazy Ctrl Rural Sch 609 Route 191 Chazy NY 12921*

RATZER, MARY BOYD, secondary education educator, librarian; b. Troy, N.Y., Sept. 6, 1945; d. John Leo and Katherine M. (Van Derpool) Boyd; m. Philip J. Ratzer, July 30, 1972; children: Joseph, David. BA cum laude, Coll. of St. Rose, Albany, N.Y., 1967; MA, SUNY, Albany, 1968, MLS, 1981. Cert. secondary tchr., sch. libr. media specialist, N.Y. Secondary tchr. English, Shenendehowa Cen. Sch., Clifton Park, N.Y., 1968-85; sch. libr. media specialist Shendehowa Cen. Sch., Clifton Park, 1985—2003. Coord., mentor tchr. intern program; lectr. SUNY Grad. Sch. Info. Sci. and Policy, Albany; frequent speaker at state-level confs., 1986—; mem. adv. bd. U. Albany Grad. Sch. Info. Sci. and Policy; advocacy cons. Sch. Libr. Sys. Assn. Contbr.: N.Y. State Teacher Resource Guides for Learning Standards; contbr. articles to profl. jours. Recipient grants. Mem. ALA, N.Y. Libr. Assn., Nat. Coun. Tchrs. English, N.Y. Assn. for Supervision and Curriculum Devel., N.Y. State Acad. for Tchg. and Learning, BIRT, LUERT (past pres.). Home: 433 County Route 68 Saratoga Springs NY 12866-6636

RATZLAFF, JUDITH L. retired secondary school educator; b. Oakland, Calif., May 2, 1937; d. Jack J. Bayard and Billie (Hart) Mills; m. Rulan R. Ratzlaff, Aug. 3, 1957 (dec. May 1991); children: Guy A., Scott A., Elizabeth A. Ratzlaff Locke. Student, Southwestern Jr. Coll., San Diego, 1964-65, U. Md., Rota, Spain, 1968-70; BA in History, Spanish, U. Jacksonville, 1971-74. Cert. secondary tchr. history, Spanish, social studies, state trainer ethics, Fla. Tchr. social studies Clay County Sch. Bd., Orange Park, Fla., 1974-93, tchr. Spanish, 1993—2003, ret., 2003; blueberry farmer, 2003—. Dept. head Clay County Sch. Bd., 1974-77, grade level chairperson, 1977-80, sch. improvement com. 1993-94, 96-98; mem. Edn. Practice Commn., State of Fla., 1985-93, chair, 1991-93; participant First China-Am. Edn. Conf., 1992; co-originator Ethics Workshops for New Tchrs.; ethics trainer State of Fla., 1993; vice chmn. N.E. Fla. Uniserv Coun., 2001-03. Regional dir. Tchrs. Adv. Com., Rep. party State of Fla., 1985—; sec. Clay County Rep. Exec. Com., 1986-93, precinct com., 1983-2000; candidate Fla. State Senate, 1986; sponsor Students Against Drunk Driving, 1982-85; active Rep. Exec. Com.; mem. Sch. Accountability Coun., 1997—, chair, 1998-99. Taft fellow Taft Inst. Polit. Studies Cath. U. Am., 1978, 80, 93. Mem. NEA (del. convs. Miami 1991, Washington 1992, San Francisco 1993, Mpls. 1995, Atlanta, 1997, New Orleans 1998, Orlando 1999, chair legis. com. on Fla. tchg. profession 1985-86, 98—, bd. dirs. 1996-98, 99—), Nat. Coun. Edn. Stds. and Practices Commns. (charter), Clay County Edn. Assn. (pres. 1981-83), N.E. Fla. Univserve Coun. (vice-chair 1990, 2001-03, sec. 1991, 2000-01, chair 1993-95). Baptist. Avocations: scuba diving, swimming, running, knitting. Home: 3211 Doctors Lake Dr Orange Park FL 32073-6927 Office: Orange Park High Sch 2300 Kingsley Ave Orange Park FL 32073-4299

RATZLAFF, RUBEN MENNO, religion educator, minister; b. Burrton, Kans., Jan. 8, 1917; s. Henry and Julia (Foth) R.; m. Frances Irene King, Sept. 7, 1941; children: Keith Lowell, Paul Dennis, Mark Henry, Loren Lee; m. Doris Carr Arneson, Aug. 1, 1992. BA, Johnson Bible Coll., 1940; BD, Butler U., 1955, MA, 1959. Ordained to ministry Chs. of Christ, 1938. Min. Pleasant Hill Christian Ch., Hall, Ind., 1948-50, Christian Ch., Clermont, Ind., 1950-55, Kennard, Ind., 1955-59; prof. San Jose (Calif.) Christian Coll., 1959-98, prof. emeritus, 1998—. Am. vis. lectr. Springdale Coll., Selly Oak Colls., Birmingham, Eng., 1985-97; vis. lectr. Zimbabwe Christian Coll., Harare, 1995, Philippine Coll. Ministry, Baguio City, 1998. Author: Ezra Nehemiah, 1982; contbr. articles to profl. jours. Recipient Hebrew award Hebrew Synagogue, 1950. Mem. Theta Phi. Home: Turner Retirement Homes PO Box 58 5315 Boise St Turner OR 97392-0058

RAU, ALICE MARIE, secondary school mathematics educator; b. Hagerstown, Md., June 2, 1969; d. Glenn Curtis and Martha Sue (Nofsinger) S. BA, Western Md. Coll., 1991, M in Adminstrn., 1993, cert. in Adminstrn., 1994. Math. tchr. Francis Scott Key H.S. Carroll County Bd. Edn., Union Bridge, Md., 1991—. Freshmen basketball coach Francis Scott Key H.S., Union Bridge, 1992-93, jr. varsity, 1993-94, varsity, 1994—, jr. varsity volleyball, 1993-96, varsity volleyball, 1997—. Named Coach of Yr., Balt. Sun, 1995-96, Volleyball Coach of Yr., Balt. Sun, 2000. Mem. Nat. Coun. Tchrs. Math., Md. State Tchrs. Assn., Carroll County Tchrs. Assn. Democrat. Roman Catholic. Office: Francis Scott Key HS Bark Hill Rd Union Bridge MD 21791 Home: 1007 Needle Dr Westminster MD 21158-3625

RAUCCI, FRANCES LUCILLE, secondary education educator; b. Mt. Vernon, N.Y., Aug. 22, 1944; d. Charles G. and Theresa (Pastore) Servidio; m. Basil E. Raucci, Apr. 1, 1966; children: Michael C., Michelle T. BA, SUNY, Albany, 1966; MS, SUNY, New Paltz, 1980, CAS, 1982. Cert. secondary Spanish tchr., sch. dist. adminstr. Spanish tchr. Nanuet H.S., New City, N.Y., 1966-68, Highland (N.Y.) H.S., 1970-96; proprietor Letter Perfect Translation, Hyde Park, 1993—. Curriculum cons. Ulster Boces, New Paltz, 1987; chair Mid-Hudson Regional, New Paltz, 1970-88; moderator, panelist N.Y. State Confs., 1970-88. Editor Modern Lang. Curriculum Guide, 1987. Fund raiser PTA Scholarship Dance. Recipient Leadership award N.Y. State Fgn. Lang. Tchrs., 1985. Mem. Am. Translators Assn., Hyde Park C. of C. Republican. Roman Catholic. Avocations: reading, piano, travel.

RAUCH, CATHERINE KERKES, secondary school educator; b. Ill., Nov. 12, 1951; children: Katie, Elizabeth. BS, Northeastern Ill. U., 1972; MS, U. Ill., Chgo., 1975. Cert. tchr., Ill. Math. tchr. Notre Dame H.S., Chgo., 1973-76, Marillac H.S., Northfield, Ill., 1976-79, Oakton C.C., Des Plaines, Ill., 1979-85; math. tchr., math. team coach Adlai Stevenson H.S., Lincolnshire, Ill., 1985—. Mem. Nat. Coun. Tchrs. Math. (Presdl. Excellence state award 1993, 99, Tandy award for excellence 1988, Edyth Mae Slifte award 2000), Ill. Coun. Tchrs. Math. Office: 1 Stevenson Dr Lincolnshire IL 60069-2824

RAUCH, CHARLES FREDERICK, JR., retired university official and business educator; b. Lancaster, Ohio, Oct. 24, 1925; s. Charles Frederick and Mary Catherine (Getz) R.; m. Diane Matilda Wilcox, Jan. l, l951 (div. July 1974); l child, Frederick Whitman; m. Esther Eleze Nettles, Apr. 25, 1975. BS, U.S. Naval Acad., 1947; MSME, U.S. Naval Postgrad. Sch., Monterey, Calif., l957; MBA, Ohio State U., 1980, PhD, l98l. Commd. ensign USN, 1947, advanced through grades to rear adm., 1972; comdg. officer nuclear submarines, New London, Conn., 1962-66; systems analyst, sr. naval advisor, spl. asst. Office Chief Naval Ops., Washington and Saigon, Vietnam, 1967-71, dir. human resource mgmt. programs Washington, 1971-76; ret., 1976; asst. prof. U. Maine, Orono, 1981-84, dir. fin. mgmt., 1984-92, v.p. bus. and fin., 1992-96, part-time faculty, 1999-2000; acting pres. Am. Univ., Bulgaria, 1992. Cons. to dep. asst. sec. def., Washington, l976; cons. Maine Maritime Acad., Castine, l982-84; bd. dirs. Audubon Expdn. Inst., treas., 1998-; mem. coun. Am. U., Bulgaria, 1997-2000. Contbg. author: Leaders and Managers: International Perspectives on Managerial Behavior and Leaderships, 1984. Bd. dirs. Bangor Symphony Orch., 1999—, pres., 2001—. Decorated D.S.M. with gold star. Mem. Maine Audubon Soc., Greater Bangor C. of C. (chmn. com. on univ.-cmty. rels. 1986-89, bd. dirs. 1988-92), Navy League (pres. Penobscot coun. 1998-2000), Bangor Rotary (treas. 1999—), Phi Kappa Phi, Beta Gamma Sigma. Episcopalian. Avocations: wildlife photography, woodcarving. Home: 102 Stillwater Ave Orono ME 04473-3410 E-mail: CFR@maine.edu.

RAUCH, JANET MELODIE, elementary school educator; b. Mpls., June 17, 1952; d. James Harlan and Myrna Luverne (Prinsen) R. BA, Wheaton Coll., 1974; MA in Tchg., Rockford Coll., 1980; cert. of advanced study, No. Ill. U., 1985. Cert. elem. tchr., spl. edn. tchr., Ill. Elem. sch. tchr. Christian Life Ctr. Sch., Rockford, Ill., 1974-80; remedial reading tchr. Washington Elem. Sch., Belvidere, Ill., 1980-99, Kishwaukee Elem. Sch., Belvidere, 1999—2003, Washington Sch., Belvidere, 2003—. Mem. NEA, Ill. Edn. Assn., Belvidere Edn. Assn. (bldg. rep. 1980-82), No. Ill. Reading Coun., Nat. Assn. Christian Schs., Alpha Delta Kappa (sec. 1994-96, v.p. 1996-98, chaplain 1998-2000). Avocations: church choral singing, flute, violin, guitar, travel. Home: 1112 Fox Chase Ln Rockford IL 61107-6214 E-mail: rauch.janet@mcleodusa.net.

RAUCH, LAWRENCE LEE, aerospace and electrical engineer, educator; b. L.A., May 1, 1919; s. James Lee and Mabel (Thompson) R.; m. Norma Ruth Cable, Dec. 15, 1961; children: Lauren, Maury Rauch. AB, U. So. Calif., 1941; postgrad., Cornell U., 1941; AM, Princeton U., 1948, PhD, 1949. Instr. math. Princeton U., 1943- 49; faculty U. Mich., 1949—, prof. aerospace engring., 1953-79, emeritus, 1979, chmn. instrumentation engring. program, 1952-63, chmn. computer, info. and control engring. program, 1971-76, asso. chmn. dept. elec. and computer engring., 1972-75; chief technologist telecommunication sci. and engring. div. NASA/Calif. Inst. Tech. Jet Propulsion Lab., 1979-85. Vis. prof. Ecole Nationale Supérieure de L'Aéronautique et de l'Espace, Toulouse, France, 1970, Calif. Inst. Tech., Pasadena, 1977-85, U. Tokyo, 1978; cons. govt. and industry, 1946—; chmn. telemetering working group, panel test range instrumentation Research and Devel. Bd. Dept. Def., 1952-53; mem. exec. com. (Nat. Telemetering Conf.), 1959-64; Western Hemisphere program chmn. (1st Internat. Telemetering Conf.), London, 1963, program chmn., U.S.A., 1967; supr. air blast telemetering, Bikini, 1946; mem. project non-linear differential equations Office Naval Research, 1947-49; mem. research adv. com. on communications, instrumentation and data processing NASA, 1963-68. Author: Radio Telemetry, 1956; also numerous sci. articles and papers on radio telemetry. Recipient award for outstanding contbn. to WWII Army and Navy, 1947, award for outstanding contbn. to telemetering field Nat. Telemetering Conf., 1960; Donald P. Eckman award for disting. achievement in edn. Instrument Soc. Am., 1966; Pioneer award Internat. Telemetering Conf./USA, 1985. Fellow IEEE (spl. award contbns. radio telemetry 1957, adminstrv. com. profl. group space electronics and telemetry 1958-64), AAAS, Explorers Club; mem. Am. Math. Soc., AIAA, U. Mich. Research Club, Phi Beta Kappa, Sigma Xi, Phi Eta Sigma, Phi Kappa Phi. Achievements include patent in field; development of first electronic time-division multiplex radio telemetering system, of pre-detection recording; radio telemetry of first U.S. jet aircraft, of air blast over pressure for Operation Crossroads at Bikini Atoll; analysis of optimum demodulation of frequency-modulated signals. Address: 759 N Citrus Ave Los Angeles CA 90038-3401 E-mail: lawrence.l.rauch@jpl.nasa.gov.

RAULERSON, PHOEBE HODGES, school superintendent; b. Cin., Mar. 16, 1939; d. LeRoy Allen and Thelma A. (Stewart) Hodges; m. David Earl Raulerson, Dec. 26, 1959; children: Julie, Lynn, David Earl, Jr., Roy Allen. BA in Edn., U. Fla., 1963, MEd, 1964. Tchr. several schs., Okeechobee, Fla., 1964-79; asst. prin. Okeechobee Jr. H.S., 1979-81, prin., 1983-84; asst. prin. South Elem. Sch., Okeechobee, 1981-82, Okeechobee H.S., 1982-83, prin., 1984-96, asst. supt. for curriculum and instrn., 1996-98, supt., 1998—. Mem. Dept. Edn. Commr.'s Task Force on H.S. Preparation, 1993-94, chair Task Force Tchr. Preparation and Certification, 1995-96, Edn. Practices Commn., 1998-99, Commr.'s Blue Ribbon Com. on Edn., 1999-2000; mem. shared svcs. network Okeechobee County Exec. Roundtable, 1998—; bd. dirs. Small Sch. Dists. Coun. Consortium, 2001—; mem. Treasure Coast adv. bd. Fla. Atlantic U., 2001—. Mem. literacy transition team Gov. Jeb Bush, 2002—03; mem. Pres. Frank Brogan's transitional team Fla. Atlantic U., 2003; bd. dirs. Okeechobee County Farm Bur., 1996—. Recipient Outstanding Citizen award Okeechobee Rotary Club, 1986; week named in her honor, Okeechobee County Commrs., 1990. Mem. Am. Bus. Women's Assn., Fla. Assn. Secondary Sch. Prins. (pres. 1993-94, Fla. Prin. of Yr. award 1990), Fla. Assn. Sch. Adminstrs. (bd. dirs. 1992-95), Fla. Assn. Dist. Sch. Supts. (bd. dirs. 2000—), Small Sch. Dist. Consortium Com. (exec. com. 2000—), Okeechobee Cattlewomen's Assn., Okeechobee C. of C. (bd. dirs. 1995-97), Okeechobee Rotary Club, Okeechobee Exch. Club. Democrat. Episcopalian. Home: 3898 NW 144th Dr Okeechobee FL 34972-0930 Office: Okeechobee County Sch Dist 700 SW 2nd Ave Okeechobee FL 34974-5117

RAUSCHENBERG, DALE EUGENE, music educator; b. Youngstown, Ohio, Jan. 13, 1938; s. Marvin Wilson and Colyn May (Wilhide) R.; m. Theresa Mary Neustupa, June 3, 1964; children: David Edward, Daniel Eric, Catherine Marie. B Music Edn., Youngstown State U., 1960; M Music Performance, Ind. U., 1963. Music dir. Mercer (Pa.) County Schs., 1963-64, Cardinal Mooney High Sch., Youngstown, 1965-66; percussion instr. Youngstown State U., 1965-66; prof. music Towson U., Balt., 1966—. Percussionist Youngstown Philharm., 1957-60, John Devol Orch., Culvermore, N.J., 1960; auxiliary percussionist Balt. Symphony Orch., 1967—; free-lance percussionist Md. Ctr. for Pub. Broadcasting, Balt., 1967—, Balt. Ctr. for Performing Arts, 1967—; prin. percussionist Balt. Opera Orch., 1989—. Composer Discussion, 1963, What?, 1964; arranger Tchaikowsky's Arabian Dance, 1986, Scott Joplin's Solace, 1986, Scott Joplin's Palm Leaf Rag, 1989; contbr. articles to profl. jours. Capt. USAR, 1960-69. Recipient 3d prize, 3d Ann. W.Va. U. Composition Symposium, 1960. Mem. Am. Fedn. Musicians, Percussive Arts Soc. (pres. Md. chpt. 1979—), Nat. Assn. Coll. Wind and Percussion Instrs., Am. Soc. Composers, Authors and Pubs., Phi Mu Alpha Sinfonia (pres. Delta Eta chpt. 1959-60). Avocations: chess, model railroading. Home: 29 Othoridge Rd Lutherville Timonium MD 21093-5412 Office: Towson U Dept Music York Rd Baltimore MD 21252-0001 E-mail: drauschenberg@towson.edu.

RAVELLETTE, BARBARA LYNN, account executive; b. Buffalo, N.Y., Mar. 23, 1954; d. Roy Aaron and Ruth Christine (Steffens) Stewart; m. William Edgar Ravellette Jr., Jan. 17, 1985; 1 child, Jacquelyn Christine. BS, Ind. State U., 1974; MS, Butler U., 1981. Elem. tchr. Clark Pleasant Cmty. Sch., Whiteland, Ind., 1976-81; regional reading cons. Ginn Pub. Co. and Laidlaw Bros., Chgo., 1981-86; so. Ind. sales rep. MacMillian Pub., Greenwood, Ind., 1986-89; mgr. electronic transmission Agy. for Instrnl. Tech., Bloomington, Ind., 1989—. Negotiator rep. Clark Pleasant Sch. Coop., Whiteland, 1976-81; nat. presenter Agy. for Instrnl. Tech., 1989—; pres. Quonset Investment Club, Bloomington, 1991-94; tutor in field. Participant Leadership Bloomington, Ind., 1994. Mem. Assn. Ind. Media Educators, Nat. Coun. Tchrs. Math. Avocations: fitness, reading, public speaking, parenting. Office: PO Box A Bloomington IN 47402-0120

RAVEN, BERTRAM H(ERBERT), psychology educator; b. Youngstown, Ohio, Sept. 26, 1926; s. Morris and Lillian R.; m. Celia Cutler, Jan. 21, 1961; children: Michelle G., Jonathan H. BA, Ohio State U., 1948, MA, 1949; PhD, U. Mich., 1953. Rsch. assoc. Rsch. Ctr. for Group Dynamics, Ann Arbor, Mich., 1952-54; lectr. psychology U. Mich., Ann Arbor, 1953-54; vis. prof. U. Nijmegen, U. Utrecht, The Netherlands, 1954-55; psychologist RAND Corp., Santa Monica, Calif., 1955-56; prof. UCLA, 1956—, chair dept. psychology, 1983-88. Vis. prof. Hebrew U., Jerusalem, 1962-63, U. Wash., Seattle, U. Hawaii, Honolulu, 1968, London Sch. Econs. and Polit. Sci., London, 1969-70; external examiner U. of the W.I., Trinidad and Jamaica, 1980—, rsch. assoc. Psychol. Rsch. Ctr., 1993—; participant Internat. Expert Conf. on Health Psychology, Tilburg, The Netherlands, 1986; cons., expert witness in field, 1979—. Co-dir. Tng. Program in Health Psychology, UCLA, 1979-88; cons. World Health Orgn., Manila, 1985-86; cons., expert witness various Calif. cts., 1978—. Author: (with others) People in Groups, 1976, Discovering Psychology, 1977, Social Psychology, 1983, Social Psychology: People in Groups (Chinese edition), 1994; editor: (with others) Contemporary Health Services, 1982, Policy Studies Rev. Ann., 1980; editor: Jour. Social Issues, 1969-74; mem. editl. bd. Jour. of Criminology and Social Psychology, 2001--; contbr. articles to profl. jours. Guggenheim fellow, Israel, 1962-63; Fulbright scholar The Netherlands, 1954-55, Israel, 1962-63, Britain, 1969-70; recipient Citation from Los Angeles City Council, 1966, Rsch. on Soc. power by Calif. Sch. of profl. psychology, L.A., 1991; NATO sr. fellow, Italy, 1989. Fellow APA (chair bd. social and ethical responsibility 1978-82, ethics com. 2003—), Am. Psychol. Soc., Soc. for Psychol. Study of Social Issues (pres. 1973-74, coun. 1995-97, Kurt Lewin award 1998), Soc. for Personality and Social Psychology; mem. AAAS, Am. Sociol. Assn., Internat. Assn. Applied Psychology, Soc. Exptl. Social Psychology, Assn. Advancement of Psychology (founding, bd. dirs. 1974-81), Internat. Soc. Polit. Psychology (governing coun. 1996-98), Interam. Psychol. Soc., Am. Psychology-Law Soc. Avocations: guitar, travel, international studies. Home: 2212 Camden Ave Los Angeles CA 90064-1906 Office: UCLA Dept Psychology Los Angeles CA 90095-1563 E-mail: raven@ucla.edu.

RAVEN, RONALD JACOB, education educator, researcher, consultant; b. San Francisco, Jan. 7, 1935; s. Jacob and Ella (O'Connor) R.; m. Cynthia Opacinch; children— Michael, Julie. B.S., U. San Francisco, 1952-56; M.A., Calif. State U. at San Francisco, 1960; Ed.D., U. Calif.-Berkeley, 1965. Physics and chemistry tchr. Campbell High Sch., Calif., 1959-62; lectr. in biology Fullerton Coll., Calif., 1962-63; prof. SUNY-Amherst, 1965—96, prof. emeritus, 1996—; vis. prof. U. Calif.-Berkeley, summer 1968, Ontario Inst. for Edn. Studies, summer 1970, U. Iowa, Iowa City, summer 1973, U. Minas Gerais, Belo Horizonte, Brazil, summer 1976; cons. NSF, Nat. Assessment of Ednl. Progress. Author tests: Raven Test of Logical Ops., 1980; Raven Test of Sci. Reasoning, 1982. Mem. editorial bd. Sci. Edn., 1970—93, Jour. Research in Sci. Teaching, 1970-83; sect. editor Sci. Edn., 1972-75. 1st lt. U.S. Army-Armor, 1961-64. Fellow AAAS; mem. Assn. for Edn. Tchrs. Sci. (bd. dirs. 1973-76), Assn. for Research in Sci. Teaching (exec. bd., bd. dirs. 1976-80), Nat. Sci. Tchrs. Assn., Am. Ednl. Research Assn. Roman Catholic. Avocations: piano, tennis. Home: 53 Wellingwood Dr East Amherst NY 14051-1744

RAWSKI, CONRAD H(ENRY), humanities educator, medievalist; b. Vienna, May 25, 1914; came to U.S., 1939, naturalized, 1944; s. Stanislaus and Johanna (Buberl-Maffei) R.; m. Helen Orr, July 5, 1957; children: Thomas George, Judith Ellen Rawski Kleen. MA, U. Vienna, 1936, PhD, 1937; postgrad., Péter Pázmány Egyetem, Budapest, 1938-39, Harvard U., 1939-40; MS in Libr. Sci., Western Res. U., 1957. Lectr. in music U. Louisville, 1940; from asst. prof. to prof. music Ithaca (N.Y.) Coll., 1940-56; dir. grad. studies, dean Ithaca (N.Y.) Coll. Sch. Music, 1951-56; head fine arts dept. Cleve. Public Library, 1957-62; assoc. prof., prof. library sci., coordinator Ph.D. program in info. sci. M.A. Baxter Sch. Info. and Libr. Sci., Case Western Res. U., Cleve., 1957-80, prof., sr. rsch. scholar, 1980-85, prof. emeritus for life, dean emeritus, 1985. Music columnist Boston Evening Transcript, 1939-40, Ithaca Jour., 1943-50; lectr. in musicology, medieval studies, info. sci. Fellow Fund for the Advancement of Edn., Ford Found., 1952-53, Nat. Endowment for Humanities, 1979 Author: Petrarch: Four Dialogues for Scholars, 1967, Toward a Theory of Librarianship, 1973, Petrarch's Latin Prose Works and the Modern Translator, 1977, Introduction to Research in Information Science, 1982; translator, editor: Petrarch's Remedies for Fortune Fair and Foul, 5 vols., 1991, Petrarch to Boccaccio: The Griseldis Letters, 1994, Francisci Petrarchae lectoris Adminiculum: Late Antique and Medieval Latin Words in the Works of Petrarch, 1998; originator: A Petrarch System, 1994-2002; contbr. articles to profl. jours. and encyclopedias. Mem. Renaissance Soc. Am., Medieval Acad. Am., Soc. for Medieval Latin, ALA (nat. Beta Phi Mu award 1979), Rowfant Club of Cleve. Address: 17877 Lost Trl Chagrin Falls OH 44023-5835

RAWSON, CLAUDE JULIEN, English educator; b. Shanghai, Feb. 8, 1935; came to U.S., 1985; m. Judith Ann Hammond, July 14, 1959; children: Hugh, Tim, Mark, Harriet, Annabel. BA, Oxford (Eng.) U., 1955, MA, BLitt, 1959. English lectr. U. Newcastle, Eng., 1957-65; from lectr. to prof., chmn. dept. U. Warwick, Coventry, Eng., 1965-85, hon. prof., 1986—; George Sherburn prof. English U. Ill., Urbana, 1985-86; George M. Bodman prof. English Yale U., New Haven, Conn., 1986-96, Maynard Mack prof. English, 1996—. Vis. prof. U. Pa., Phila., 1973, U. Calif., Berkeley, 1980; chmn. Yale Boswell Papers, 1990—2001; del. for lang. and lit. Oxford U. Press, NY. Author: Henry Fielding and the Augustan Ideal, 1972, 2d edit., 1991, Gulliver and the Gentle Reader, 1973, 2d edit., 1991,

The Charater of Swift's Sahir, 1983, Order from Confusion Sprung, 1985, 2d edit., 1992, (with F.P. Lock) Collected Poems of Thomas Parnell, 1989, Satire and Sentiment 1660-1830, 1994, 2d edit., 2000, (with H. B. Nisbet) Cambridge History of Literary Criticism, vol. 4: The Eighteenth Century, 1997, God, Gulliver, and Genocide, 2001, 2d edit. 2002, Basic Writings of Jonathan Swift, 2002; editor: Modern Lang. Rev. and Yearbook of English Studies, London, 1974-88; gen. editor: Cambridge (Eng.) History of Literary Criticism, 1983—, Unwin Critical Libr., London, 1974—, Blackwell Critical Biographies, 1985—, Cambridge Edition of the Works of Jonathan Swift, 2001—. Recipient Cert. of Merit for Disting. Svc. Conf. of Editors of Learned Jours., 1988; Andrew Mellon fellow Clark and Huntington Libr., 1980, 90, Guggenheim fellow, 1991-92, Sr. Faculty fellow Yale U., 1991-92; NEH grantee, 1991. Fellow Am. Acad. Arts and Scis.; mem. Modern Humanities Rsch. Assn. (life mem., com. mem. 1974-88), Internat. Soc. 18th Century Studies, Am. Soc. for 18th Century Studies, Brit. Soc. for 18th Century Studies (pres. 1973-74), Grolier Club. Office: Yale U Dept English PO Box 208302 New Haven CT 06520-8302

RAY, DENNIS ROBERT, secondary school educator; b. Canton, Ohio, Dec. 12, 1955; s. Robert Earl and Mary Juanita (Smith) R.; divorced. BA, Coll. Wooster, 1978; MEd, Ohio U., 1982. Cert. tchr., Ohio. Math tchr. Chillicothe (Ohio) H.S., 1978—. Mem. Gov. Bob Taft's Tchr. Adv. Bd., 1999—. Martha Holden Jennings scholar Ohio U., 1980-81. Mem. NEA, Ohio Edn. Assn., Chillicothe Edn. Assn. (pres. 1992-93), Nat. Coun. Tchrs. Math., Ohio Coun. Tchr. Math. (Outstanding Tchr. 2000). Avocations: oil painting, sports officiating, reading. Office: Chillicothe High Sch 385 Yoctangee Pky Chillicothe OH 45601-1663

RAY, E. DENISE, assistant principal; b. East Orange, N.J., Aug. 24, 1952; d. Earl David Sr. and Lola (Peebles) Trent; m. Christopher Reynold Ray, Apr. 21, 1979; children: Joshua Sinclair, Alison Marie. BS, Cornell U., 1974; MEd, West Chester U., 1991; EdD, Immaculatu Coll., 1998—2002. Cert. tchr., Pa., prin. cert., Pa. Tchr. Glen Acres Elem. Sch., West Chester, Pa., 1989-91, Sarah K. Starkweather Elem. Sch., West Chester, 1991—2002; diversity trainer Respecting Ethnic and Cultural Hertage, West Chester Sch. Dist., 1995—. Mem. Kappa Delta Pi, Phi Delta Kappa. Baptist. Avocations: piano, singing, reading. Home: 87 Glendale Rd Exton PA 19341-1539 Office: Exton Elem Sch Bartlett Rd West Chester PA 19382-7300

RAY, GEORGE WASHINGTON, III, English language educator; b. Binghamton, N.Y., Dec. 4, 1932; s. George Washington and Margaret (Nicholson) R.; m. Elizabeth DuPree Osborn, Dec. 29, 1956; children—Virginia, George, Melissa, Grace Elizabeth. AB, Wesleyan U., 1954; postgrad., Colgate U., 1957-59; PhD, U. Rochester, 1966. Instr. English U. Rochester, N.Y., 1961-62, U. Va., Charlottesville, 1962-64; instr. English Washington and Lee U., Lexington, Va., 1964-66, asst. prof., 1966-69, assoc. prof., 1969-74, prof., 1974—2001, emeritus prof., 2001—, acting chmn. dept., 1985, 91-92. Vis. fellow Univ. Coll., Oxford (Eng.) U., 1980 Editor: Duke of Byron, 1979, The Chi Psi Story, 1995. Bd. dirs. Rockbridge Concert-Theater Series, 1966-83, Lime Kiln Arts Inc., 1983-86, Rockbridge Area Mental Health Assn., 1975-78. Served as 1st lt. USMC, 1954-57. Recipient various fellowships. Mem. Southeastern Renaissance Conf., Renaissance Soc. Am., Chi Psi (nat. Disting. Svc. award 1985, trustee ednl. trust 1989-95, nat. pres. 1995-2001), Am. Soc. Theatre Rsch., English-Speaking Union (Lexington br. pres. 2001-03, nat. bd. dirs. 2003—). Democrat. Presbyterian (elder 1979-85, 89-91). Home: 13 Sellers Ave Lexington VA 24450-1930

RAY, HELEN VIRGINIA, art educator; b. Safford, Ariz., Mar. 18, 1932; d. Hermon and Vera Maud Ray. BS, North Tex. State U., Denton, 1959; MA, Chapman Coll., Calif., 1974. Cert. counselor 1974. Art, phys. edn. tchr. Clark Jr. H.S., LaCanada, Calif., 1959—65; art, math, phys. edn. tchr. Walton Jr. H.S., Compton, Calif., 1965—67; art tchr. Sonora H.S., Fullerton, Calif., 1967—75, counselor, 1974—75, counselor, psychometrist, 1975—91. Owner H. Ray Fine Arts Studio, Redding, Calif., 1980—; intern in psychology Chapman Coll., Orange, Calif., 1990. Mem. Shasta County Arts Coun., Redding, 1997—, Earthwatch, 2003—, Turtle Bay Mus., Redding, 2000—. With USN, 1951—54. Mem.: AAUW, North Valley Art League, Earthwatch, Audubon Soc., Moose. Republican. Achievements include research in genetic memories through art using subconsious imagery. Avocations: painting, sculpting, scuba diving, tennis. Home and Office: 500 Hilltop Dr #143 Redding CA 96003

RAY, JOHN WALKER, otolaryngologist, educator, broadcast commentator; b. Columbus, Ohio, Jan. 12, 1936; s. Kenneth Clark and Hope (Walker) R.; m. Susanne Gettings, July 15, 1961; children: Nancy Ann, Susan Christy. AB magna cum laude, Marietta Coll., 1956; MD cum laude, Ohio State U., 1960; postgrad., Temple U., 1964, Mt. Sinai Hosp., Columbia U., 1964, 66, Northwestern U., 1967, 71, U. Ill., 1968, U. Ind., 1969, Tulane U., 1969. Diplomate Am. Bd. Otolaryngology. Intern Ohio State U. Hosps., Columbus, 1960-61, clin. rsch. trainee NIH, 1963-65, resident dept. otolaryngology, 1963-65, 66-67, resident dept. surgery, 1965-66, instr. dept. otolaryngology, 1966-67, 70-75, clin. asst. prof., 1975-82, clin. assoc. prof., 1982-92, clin. prof., 1992-2000, clin. prof. emeritus, 2000—; hon. staff, past chief of staff Good Samaritan Hosp., also Bethesda Hosp., Zanesville, Ohio, 1967—. Hon. active staff Meml. Hosp., Marietta, Ohio, 1992—; radio-TV health commentator, 1982—. Contbr. articles to profl. jours.; collaborator with surg. motion picture: Laryngectomy and Neck Dissection, 1964. Past pres. Muskingum chpt. Am. Cancer Soc.; bd. dirs. Zanesville Art Ctr. Capt. USAF, 1961-63. Recipient Barraquer Meml. award, 1965; named to Order of Ky. Col., 1966, Muskingum County Country Music Hall of Fame. Fellow ACS, Am. Soc. Otolaryn. Allergy, Am. Acad. Otolaryngology-Head and Neck Surgery (past gov.), Am. Acad. Facial Plastic and Reconstructive Surgery; mem. AMA, Nat. Assn. Physician Broadcasters, Muskingum County Acad. Medicine (past pres.), Ohio Med. Assn., Columbus Ophthalmol. and Otolaryn. Soc. (past pres.), Ohio Soc. Otolaryngology (past pres.), Am. Soc. Contemporary Medicine and Surgery, Acad. Radio and TV Health Commentators, Fraternal Order of Police Assocs., Internat. Bluegrass Music Assn., Phi Beta Kappa, Alpha Omega Alpha, Beta Beta Beta, Alpha Tau Omega, Alpha Kappa Kappa. Presbyterian. Home: 1245 East Dr Zanesville OH 43701-1445

RAY, REBECCA ANN, elementary school educator; b. Albuquerque, N. Mex., Jan. 7, 1950; d. Thomas Walter and Margaret (Phillips) Dailey; m. Ronnie Leslie Ray, June 30, 1973; children: Ronette Lewise, Lance Micheas. BS in Edn., U. N. Mex., 1977, MA in Elem. Edn., 1998. Tchr's asst. Laguna (N. Mex.) Elem. Sch., 1970-77, classroom tchr., 1977—. Mem. NSTA, Math Sci. Tchrs. (Tribal Coalition), Soc. for Advancement Chicanos and Native Am. in Sci. (edn. com.), Nat. Coun. Tchrs. Math. Democrat. Roman Catholic. Home: PO Box 1406 Paguate NM 87040-1406 Office: Laguna Elem Sch PO Box 191 Laguna NM 87026-0191

RAY, SHIRLEY DODSON, educational administrator, consultant; b. Smithville, Tex., Sept. 20, 1929; d. Pickett James and Marjorie (Dietz) Dodson; m. John Davis Ray, Aug. 12, 1950; children: Ellen Ray Stauffer, Daniel Dodson, John Andrew. BA, Baylor U., 1950; MA, Tex. A&I U., 1964; postgrad., Corpus Christi State U. Cert. supt., mid. mgmt., elem. secondary edn., bus. Tchr., math. cons., coord. elem. instrn. Corpus Christi (Tex.) Ind. Sch. Dist., 1958-73; gen. cons. Ednl. Svcs. Ctr. Region II, Corpus Christi, 1973-78; curriculum dir. Calallen Ind. Sch. Dist., Corpus Christi, 1978-87, asst. supt. instructional svcs., 1987-92; ind. elem. cons. Corpus Christi, 1992—. Cons. Corpus Christi, 1992-2001; adj. prof. Corpus Christi State U., 1983-2001, Tex. A&M U., Kingsville, 1993—; mem. staff NSF, Tex. A&I U., 1973-2001. Author numerous booklets and pamphlets, math. workshops; writer on state com. for EXCET test for suprs. Mem. ASCD, Nat. Coun. Tchrs. Math. (mem. tchr. insvc. com.), Tex. Coun. Tchrs. Math. (past pres.), Tex. Assn. Suprs. Math. (past v.p.), Tex. ASCD (bd. dirs.), Assn. Tex. Profl. Educators, Phi Delta Kappa (Baylor chpt.). E-mail: johnshirleyray@aol.com.

RAYBURN, WENDELL GILBERT, educational association executive; b. Detroit, May 20, 1929; s. Charles Jefferson and Grace Victoria (Winston) R.; m. Gloria Ann Myers, Aug. 19; children: Rhonda Renee, Wendell Gilbert; 1 stepson, Mark K. Williams. BA, Eastern Mich. U., 1951; MA, U. Mich., 1952; Ed.D., Wayne State U., Detroit, 1972. Tchr., adminstr. Detroit public schs., 1954-68; from asst. dir. to dir. spl. projects U. Detroit, 1968-72, asso. dean acad. support programs, 1972-74; dean Univ. Coll., U. Louisville, 1974-80; pres. Savannah (Ga.) State Coll., 1980-88, Lincoln U., Jefferson City, Mo., 1988-97; v.p. fin. Am. Assn. State Colls. and Univs., Washington, 1997—. Chmn. adv. com. Office for Advancement of Pub. Black Colls., 1989-97. Trustee Candler Gen. Hosp., 1982-85, Telfair Acad. Arts, 1980-87; bd. dirs. Candler Health Svcs., 1985-88, YMCA Blue Ridge Assembly, 1986-88, Internat. Food and Agrl. Devel. and Econ. Cooperation, 1988-94, Meml. Cmty. Hosp., Jefferson City, 1988-94, United Way Mo., 1989-97, Mo. Capital Punishment Resource Ctr., 1990-95, Stephens Coll., Columbia, Mo., 1993-97, Capital Regional Med. Ctr., 1994-97; campaign chmn. Jefferson City Area United Way, 1994-95. With AUS, 1952-59. Decorated Commendation medal with pendant; recipient Disting. Alumni award Wayne State U., 1993, Whitney M. Young Jr. award Lincoln Found., 1980, Disting. Citizens award City of Louisville, 1980. Mem. Mo. Bar Assn. (foresight com.), Am. Assn. Higher Edn., Am. Assn. State Colls. and Univs. (bd. dirs. 1988—, chmn. 1992-93), Nat. Assn. State Univs. and Land Grant Colls., Nat. Assn. for Equal Opportunity in Higher Edn., Coun. on Pub. Higher Edn. for Mo. (chmn. 1991-93), Coun. of 1890 Colls. and Univs., Jefferson City C. of C. (bd. dirs. 1988-97), Rotary (bd. dirs. Jefferson City 1989-96, pres. 1994-95), Kappa Alpha Psi, Sigma Pi Phi. Episcopalian. Office: Am Assn State Colls and Univs 1307 New York Ave NW Fl 5 Washington DC 20005-4704

RAYBURN, WILLIAM FRAZIER, obstetrician, gynecologist, educator; b. Lexington, Ky., Aug. 19, 1950; s. Charles Calvin and Charlotte Elizabeth (Ballard) R.; m. Pamela Rae Gilleland, Nov. 27, 1976; children: Lindsay Ann, Britany Beth, Drake Tanner. BS, Hampden Sydney Coll., 1971; MD, U. Ky., 1975. Diplomate Nat. Bd. Med. Examiners, Am. Bd. Ob.-Gyn. (examiner), Divsn. Maternal-Fetal Medicine. Intern family medicine U. Iowa Hosps. and Clinics, Iowa City, Iowa, 1975-76; resident ob.-gyn. U. Ky. Med. Ctr., Lexington, 1976-79; fellow in maternal-fetal medicine dept. ob.-gyn. Ohio State U. Hosps., Columbus, 1979-81; asst. prof. ob.-gyn. U. Mich. Med. Sch., Ann Arbor, 1981-83, assoc. prof. ob.-gyn., 1983-86; assoc. prof. dept. ob.-gyn. and pharmacology U. Nebr. Coll. of Medicine, Omaha, 1985-88, prof. dept. ob-gyn. and pharmacology, 1988-92, U. Okla. Coll. Medicine, Oklahoma City, 1992-98, John W. Records endowed chair, 1992-98; prof. dept. ob/gyn U. N.Mex. Sch. Medicine, Albuquerque, 1998—, chair dept. ob/gyn, 1998—. Prof., ob-gyn dept. chair U. N.Mex. Sch. Medicine, Albuquerque, 1998—,Randolph Seligman endowed prof., 2003--; chief of obstetrics U. Okla. Coll. of Medicine, Okla. City, 1992-98; dir. maternal fetal medicine dept. ob-gyn U. Mich. Med. Ctr., 1981-85, med. edn.; reviewer for Ob and Gyn., Am. Jour. Ob-Gyn., Jour. Reproductive Medicine, Internat. Jour. Gyn. and Ob., New Eng. Jour. Medicine, Jour. Maternal-Fetal Medicine, Jour. Maternal-Fetal Investigation; U. Nebr. Med. Ctr., 1985-92, U. Okla. Health Sci. Ctr., 1992—, Presbyn. Hosp., Okla. City, 1992-98, Univ. Hosp., Albuquerque, 1998—. Author: (books) Obstetrics/Gynecology: Pre Test Self Assessment and Review, 1982; (with others), Every Woman's Pharmacy: A Guide to Safe Drug Use, 1983, Obstetrics for the House Officer, 1984, 2d rev. edition, 1988, Every Woman's Pharmacy, 1984, The Women's Health and Drug Reference, 1993, Oklahoma Notes: Obstetrics and Gynecology, 1994, 2d. rev. edit., 1996, Obstetrics and Gynecology for the House Officer, 1996, 2d rev. edit., 2001; editor: (with F.P. Zuspan) Drug Therapy in Obstetrics and Gynecology, 1982, 3d rev. edit., 1992; symposia editor Diagnosis and Management of the Malformed Fetus, Jour. Reprod. Medicine, 1982, Operative Obstetrics, Clinics in Perinatology, 1983, Controversies in Fetal Drug Therapy, Clin. Obstetrics and Gynecology, 1991, Drugs in Pregnancy, Clinical Obstetrics and Gynecology, 2002, Substance Use Disorders in Women, 2003; reviewer for Ob. and Gyn., Am. Jour. Ob.-Gyn., Jour. Reproductive Medicine, Internat. Jour. Gyn. and Ob., Jour. Maternal-Fetal Medicine, Jour. Maternal-Fetal Investigation; editor-in-chief Jour. Reproductive Medicine, 2002-03; contbr. more than 50 chpts. to books, more than 220 articles to profl. jours., more than 160 abstract papers at sci. meetings. Dir. maternal and infant care programs U. Nebr. Med. Ctr., Omaha, 1986-92; U.S. Pharmacopeia Conv. field reviewer, 1983—. Recipient Residents' prize paper award Ky. Ob.-Gyn. Soc., 1978, 79, Faculty Teaching award for Excellence, 1993, 94, 96, 03, Rsch. Excellence award Soc. Perinatal Obstetricians, 1998. Fellow Am. Coll. Obstetricians and Gynecologists (Ephraim McDowell) prize paper award 2d pl. 1978, 1st pl. 1979, Searle-Donald F. Richardson Prize Paper award 1980, Best Doctors in Am., 1998, 2000); mem. Am. Coll. Obstetricians and Gynecologists, Am. Gynecol. and Obstet. Soc., Coun. Univ. Chairs in Obstet. Gynecol., Soc. Maternal Fetal Medicine, Assn. of Profs. in Gyn.-Ob., Soc. for Gynecol. Investigation, Teratology Soc., Neurobehavioral Teratology Soc., N.Mex. Med. Soc. Achievements include contributions to the knowledge of drug effcts on developing fetus and of principals about induction of labor and to the influence he has had on peers not only through teaching and patient care but through his extensive writing. Office: U New Mex Health Sci Ctr 2211 Lomas Blvd NE # Acc-4 Albuquerque NM 87106-2745 E-mail: wrayburn@salud.unm.edu.

RAYEN, JAMES WILSON, art educator, artist; b. Youngstown, Ohio, Apr. 9, 1935; s. James Wendell and Marjorie (Wilson) R. BA, Yale U., 1957, BFA, 1959, MFA, 1961. Instr. Wellesley (Mass.) Coll., 1961-67, asst. prof., 1967-69, assoc. prof., 1969-76, prof., 1976-80, Elizabeth Christy Kopf prof., 1980—2003; prof. emeritus Wellesley Coll., 2003—. One-man shows include Durlacher Bros., N.Y.C., 1966, Eleanor Rigelhaupt Gallery, Boston, 1968, Brockton (Mass.) Mus., 1973, Chapel Gallery, West Newton, Mass., 1984, Gallery on the Green, Lexington, Mass., 1990, Rice Polak Gallery, 1995, Gallery 79, Boston, 2000, Davis Mus., Wellesley Coll., 2002; paintings commd. by New Eng. Med. Ctr., Boston, Mariott Hotel Corp., Cambridge, Mass., Hyatt Hotel Corp., Washington. Trustee Boston Concert Opera, 1984-88, bd. dirs., 1986-90, pres. Boston Concert League, 1988-90; bd. dirs. Boston Acad. Music, 1991-2002, Boston Opera and Concert Ensemble; trustee, bd. dirs. North Bennet St. Sch. Grantee Italian govt., 1959-60, Ford Found., 1969; recipient Mass. Artists Found. award in printmaking, 1989. Democrat. Episcopalian. Avocation: garden design. Home: 108 Fox Hill St Westwood MA 02090-1120

RAYFORD, PAULA JUDELLE, elementary education educator; b. Holly Springs, Miss., July 12, 1962; d. James T. Sr. and Barbara (Freeman) R. BA in Psychology/Sociology, Rust Coll., 1984; BA in Elem. Edn., U. Miss., 1990. Cert. elem. tchr. Tchr. elem. DeSoto County Schs., Walls, Miss., 1990—. Mem. Miss. Assn. Edn. Roman Catholic. Avocations: walking, reading. Home: 1000 Sutton Pl Apt 1631 Horn Lake MS 38637 Office: DeSoto County Schs 1632 Delta View Rd Walls MS 38680

RAYMAN, PAULA M. economics educator; b. N.Y.C., Feb. 27, 1947; d. Abraham Samuel and Rita (Relkin) R.; m. Robert Russell Read, Apr. 1, 1973; children: Alyssa, Lily. BA, Hunter Coll., 1970; PhD, Boston Coll., 1977. Postdoctoral fellow NIMH, Bethesda, 1982-84; assoc. prof. econs. Wellesley (Mass.) Coll., 1986-94, assoc. prof. sociology, 1990-94, dir. women's sci. program, 1991-94; exec. dir. Radcliff Pub. Policy Inst., Cambridge, Mass., 1994—. Vis. prof. Harvard Med. Sch., Cambridge, 1983-85; mem. faculty Harvard Grad. Sch. Edn., 1995—; disting. vis. scholar Cambridge (Eng.) U., 1992. Editor Temple U. Press, 1983—. Mem. Mass. Jobs Coun., Boston, 1989-98; dir. work-family project Fleet Bank, Boston, 1996-98; bd. dirws. Baumann Found., Washington, 1996—, New England Bd. Higher Edn., 1997—; mem. adv. bd. Working Today, N.Y.C., 1996—. Bunting fellow Radcliffe Coll., 1985-86; grantee NSF, 1985-86; recipient Swedish Bicentennial award, 1990. Mem. Assn. Women Sci. (adv. bd. 1991—), Am. Sociol. Assn. (chair labor sect., Svc. award 1985), Boston Club. Jewish. Avocations: hiking, collage-making. Office: Radcliff Pub Policy Ctr 69 Brattle St Cambridge MA 02138-3442

RAYMO, MAUREEN ELIZABETH, geologist, researcher; b. L.A., Dec. 27, 1959; d. Chester Theodore and Maureen Dorothy (Sterett) R.; m. Chris James Marone, May 24, 1986; children: Victoria Ray, Daniel Chester. ScB, Brown U., 1982; MA, Columbia U., 1985, MPhil, 1988, PhD, 1989. Rsch. asst. Lamont-Doherty Geol. Obs., Palisades, N.Y., 1982-83, adj. assoc. rsch. scientist, 1989—; assoc. scientist dept. geology U. Melbourne, Australia, 1989-90; asst. prof. dept. geology and geophysics U. Calif., Berkeley, 1991-92; asst. prof. dept. earth, atmospheric and planetary scis. MIT, Cambridge, 1992—. Prin. investigator rsch. grants NSF, 1991—; mem. ocean history panel Joint Oceanographic Instns. for Deep Earth Sampling, 1992—. Co-author (with C. Raymo): Written In Stone, 1989; contbr. articles to profl. jours. Named Nat. Young Investigator, NSF, 1992. Mem. AAAS, Am. Geophys. Union, Sigma Xi. Democrat. Office: MIT Earth Atmospheric & Planetary Scis E34-254 Cambridge MA 02139

RAYNOR, EILEEN MARGOLIES, otolaryngologist, educator; b. N.Y.C., Feb. 11, 1965; d. Allan Fred and Noemi (Schmerz) Margolies; m. Dewey Lee Raynor, Jr., Nov. 9, 1991; children: Stephanie Dianne, Logan Foster. AB in Chemistry, Duke U., 1987; MD, U. N.C., 1993. Cert. Am. Bd. Otolaryngology. Resident otolaryngology Med. Coll. Ga., Augusta, 1993—98; asst. prof. otolaryngology U. Fla., Jacksonville, 1998—. Cons. Medimetrics Corp., Jacksonville, Fla., 1999—; med. dir. Pediat. Hearing Program, Jacksonville, 2000—; mem. Cleft Palate Team Childrens Med. Svcs., Jacksonville, 2000—. Contbr. articles to profl. jours., chapters to books. Recipient Nat. Leadership award, 2003; Deafness Rsch. Found. rsch. grantee, 1991. Fellow: Am. Acad. Otolaryngology (cmty., acad. rels. com. 2002—); mem.: AMA, Assn. for Rsch. in Otolaryngology, Triological Soc. (James Harrell award So. sect. 1997), Am. Acad. Facial Plastic Surgery, Duke Alumni Club (bd. dirs. 2000—). Avocations: cooking, skiing, photography, jewelry design. Home: 1031 River Oaks Rd Jacksonville FL 32207 Office: U Fla Jacksonville 655 W 8th St Jacksonville FL 32209 E-mail: eileen.raynor@jax.ufl.edu.

RAYNOR, WANDRA ADAMS, middle school educator; b. Angier, N.C., Oct. 29, 1942; d. Lacoma Eldridge and Edna (Mangum) Adams; m. Donald David Stewart, June 16, 1964 (dec. Dec. 1965); 1 child, Dona Jean Stewart Raynor; m. Ira Kent Raynor, June 28, 1969; children: Richard Kent, Ira Adam. BS in Edn., Campbell Coll., 1971; MA in Early Childhood Edn., Campbell U., 1979; EdS in Adminstrn. Supervision, East Carolina U., 1983. Cert. tchr., advanced adminstr., supr., N.C. Clk. Am. Guaranty Ins. Co., Fayetteville, N.C., 1960-62; sec. Am. Defender Life, Fayetteville, 1962-64; tchr. Gentry Primary Sch., Erwin, N.C., 1971-73; tchr., asst. prin. North Harnett Primary Sch., Angier, 1973-85; tchr. Angier Mid. Sch., 1986—, Harnett Cen. Middle Sch., 1993—, Inst. Children's Lit., 1994—. Mem. Internat. Reading Assn. (pres. Lillington, N.C. 1983-84, treas. Harnett coun. 1992-93, participant state conf. seminars 1992—), N.C. Assn. Educators, Math. Tchrs. Assn., Environ. Educators, N.C. Writers Network, Crepe Myrtle Investors (pres. 1997), Angier C. of C. (Disting. Educator award 1983), Order Ea. Star (worthy matron 1973-75, dist. dep. grand matron 1976-77), Delta Kappa Gamma, Epsilon Phi Beta. Democrat. Baptist. Avocations: golf, reading, snow skiing, writing. Home: 203 Pleasant St Angier NC 27501-9257 Office: Harnett Cen Middle RR 4 Box 293B Angier NC 27501-9543

RAZNOFF, BEVERLY SHULTZ, education educator; b. Ft. Myers, Fla., Apr. 24, 1946; d. John William and Dora Lucille (Galloway) S.; m. Gregory Michael Raznoff, June 8, 1968; children: John Gregory, James William. BA, Fla. So. Coll., 1968; MEd, Fla. Atlantic U., 1974. Elem. educator Pine Grove Elem. Sch., Delray Beach, Fla., 1968-69; secondary educator Pompano Beach (Fla.) High Sch., 1969-70, Deerfield Beach (Fla.) High Sch., 1970-71; prof. Broward C.C., Ft. Lauderdale, 1974-82, Palm Beach C.C., Boca Raton, Fla., 1977-93, Fla. Atlantic U., Boca Raton, Fla., 1984, Truett-McConnell Coll., Cleveland, Ga., 1994—2001; dir. instr. Toccoa (Ga.) Regional Campus, 1994—2001; vocat. rehab. counselor Ga. Dept. Labor Divsn. Rehab. Svcs., Cleveland, 2002—; online practitioner faculty mem. U. Phoenix, 2002—. Advisor Phi Theta Kappa, South campus Palm Beach C.C., 1983—93, Toccoa Regional Campus-TMC, 1994—2001; counselor Ga. Dept. Labor Vocat. Rehab., 2002—. Contbr. articles to profl. jours. Recipient Fred Baker Nat. award Phi Theta Kappa, Outstanding Advisor, Fla. region, 1992, Robert Giles Disting. Advisor award, 1998, Continued Excellence award for Advisors, 2000, Excellence in Counselling, 2003. Mem. Fla. Comm. Assn. (pres. 1990-91, Tchr. of Yr. 1990, Most Disting. Advisor Ga. region 2001), Internat. Listening Assn., So. States Comm. Assn., Ga. Speech Comm. Assn., Ga. Rehabiliation Assn. Avocations: reading, needlework, cooking, mountain living. Home: 307 Old Deer Path Way Cleveland GA 30528-4243 E-mail: 69charger@direcway.com.

REA, DAVID K. geology and oceanography educator; b. Pitts., June 2, 1942; m. Donna M. Harshbarger, Feb. 11, 1967; children: Gregory, Margaret. AB, Princeton U., 1964; MS, U. Ariz., 1967; PhD, Oreg. State U., 1974. Prof. geology & oceanography U. Mich., Ann Arbor, 1975—. Assoc. dir. NSF Climate Dynamics Program, Washington, 1986-87; interim dir. Ctr. for Great Lakes and Aquatic Scis., 1988-89, chmn. dept. geol. scis., 1995-2000. Contbr. more than 300 articles, reports to profl. publs. Recipient numerous NSF rsch. grants, 1976—. Fellow Am. Geophys. Union, Geol. Soc. Am.

REA, PATRICK SHAW, secondary school educator; b. Evansville, Ind., Aug. 30, 1948; s. Ernest Arthur and Mary Carolyn (Steen) R.; m. Linda Joyce Gaisser, Aug. 1, 1970; children: Jason Christopher, Erin Rebecca. BS in Geography, Ind. State U., 1970; MS in Secondary Edn., Ind. U. S.E., 1974, postgrad., 1983. Lic tchr., Ind. Tchr. New Albany (Ind.)-Floyd County Schs., 1970—; mem. adj. faculty Ind. U. S.E., New Albany, 1975-78, 91-92, Jefferson C.C., Louisville, 1983. Mem. state planning com. Geography Awareness Week, Indpls., 1989—; tchr. rep. Project Marco Polo, Nat. Geog. Soc. and USN, 1991; geography test analyst Ind. Dept. Edn., Indpls., 1991. Author: (textbook) Realm of Physical Geography, 1988. Co-pres. New Albany High Sch. Band Boosters, 1992; leader ministry team Northside Christian Ch., New Albany, 1988—. Mem. NEA, Ind. State Tchrs. Assn., Nat. Coun. for Geog. Edn. (Disting. Tchr. award 1993), Geography Educators Network Ind. (tchr. cons., bd. dirs. 1991—, mid. sch. State Geography Tchr. of Yr. 1991), New Albany-Floyd County Edn. Assn. Avocation: travel. Home: 1108 Woodfield Dr New Albany IN 47150-2067 Office: Nathaniel Scribner Jr High 910 Old Vincennes Rd New Albany IN 47150-5401

REA, ROGER UHL, chemistry educator, consultant; b. Newton, Kans., Aug. 26, 1944; s. Harold Hugh and Elinor Lucile (Uhl) R.; m. Elizabeth Agnes Woerdeman. BS, Kans. State U., 1966; MNS, U. S.D., 1973. Cert. tchr., Nebr. Chemistry tchr. Omaha Pub. Schs., 1966—2000. Cons. Kiewit Constrn., Omaha, 1973; planner asst. Waccmaw Planning Ctr., Georgetown, S.C., 1974, driving instr. Dual Driving Sch., Omaha, 1979; computer programmer Merrill Pub. Co., Columbus, Ohio, 1983-89. Reviewer Jour. Chem. Edn., 1984-94; author chemistry and physics software. Pres. Omaha Edn. Assn., 1984-85; v.p. OEA Sr. Citizens Inc., Omaha, 1983-84; del. Douglas County Rep. Conv., Omaha, 1980—; treas. Educators Credit Union, Omaha, 1978-99; vice chmn. of First Nebr. Educators Credit Union, Omaha,1999, trustee Omaha Schs. Employees Retirement System, 1987-94, 2000—, trustee of Nebr. Pub. Employee Retirement Syss.; mem. selection com. Nebr. Christa McAuliffe Prize, Lincoln, 1987—. Recipient

Tchr. of Yr. award Nebr. Dept. Edn., 1989, Cooper Found. Award for Excellence in Teaching, 1981. Mem. NEA (del. 1981—), Am. Chem. Soc. (high sch. exams. com. 1973-91), Nat. Sci. Tchrs. Assn. (Presdl. award for excellence 1985, grantee 1978), Nebr. State Edn. Assn. (chmn. tchr. welfare and svcs. commn. 1988-94, bd. dirs. 1993-99),trustee of Educators Health Alliance BC/BS Group, 1997, Nebr. Acad. Scis., Nebr. Assn. Tchrs. Sci., Omaha Edn. Assn. (pres. 1984-85, trustee 1982-86), Nebr. Profl. Practices Commn. (vice chmn. 1992-93, chmn. 1993-94). Republican. Avocations: piano, gardening, sports car rallies, photography, astronomy. Office: Omaha NW High Sch 8204 Crown Point Ave Omaha NE 68134-1922

READ, SISTER JOEL, academic administrator; BS in Edn., Alverno Coll., 1948; MA in History, Fordham U., 1951; hon. degree, Lakeland Coll., 1972, Wittenburg U., 1976, Marymount Manhattan Coll., 1978, DePaul U., 1985, Northland Coll., 1986, SUNY, 1986, Lawrence U., 1997, Marquette U., 2003. Former prof., dept. chmn. history dept. Alverno Coll., Milw., pres., 1968—2003. Past pres. Am. Assn. for Higher Edn., 1976-77; mem. coun. NEH, 1977-84; bd. dirs. Ednl. Testing Svc., 1987-93, Neylan Commn., 1985-90; past pres. Wis. Assn. Ind. Colls. and Univs.; mem. Commn. on Status of Edn. for Women, 1971-76, Am. Assn. Colls., 1971-77. Bd. dirs. Jr. Achievement, 1991-2003, State of Wis. Coll. Savs. Bd., 2000-03, Greater Milw. Com., Wis. Found. Ind. Colls., 1990-99, Women's Philanthropy Inst., 1997-2000, Wis. Women Higher Edn. Leadership, 1997-2000; bd. dirs. YMCA, 1989-2003, trustee, 2003—; mem. Profl. Dimensions. First recipient Anne Roe award Harvard U. Grad. Sch. Edn., 1980; recipient Morris T. Keaton award, Coun. for Adult and Experiential Learning, 1992; recipient Jean B. Harris award, Rotary; Paul Harris fellow, Rotary. Fellow Am. Acad. Arts and Scis., Wis. Acad. Arts and Scis. Office: Alverno Coll Office of Pres PO Box 343922 Milwaukee WI 53234-3922 E-mail: joel.read@alverno.edu.

READE, KATHLEEN MARGARET, paralegal, author, educator; b. Ft. Worth, Tex., Sept. 6, 1947; d. Ralph S. and Margaret Catherine (Stark) R.; 1 child, Kathryn Michelle Carter. BA in English and Polit. Sci., Tex. Christian U., 1978; student, El Centro Coll.; postgrad., Tex. Christian U., Tex. Tech. Asst. land and legal dept. Am. Quasar Petroleum, Ft. Worth, 1971-74; paralegal and office mgr. Law Offices of George Sims, Ft. Worth, 1974-81; asst. Criminal Cts. #2 and #3 Tarrant County Dist. Atty., Ft. Worth, 1981; ind. paralegal Ft. Worth, 1982-84; paralegal Law Offices of Brent Burford, Ft. Worth, 1982-85; sr. paralegal/litigation Law Offices of Windle Turley, Dallas, 1985-90; major case supr. The Dent Law Firm, Ft. Worth, 1990-96, Whitaker, Chalk, Swindle & Sawyer, LLP, Ft. Worth, 1996—. Cons./instr. paralegal program, U. Tex., Arlington, 1996—; active Tex. Christian U. Writer's Continuous Workshop. Author: Plaintiff's Personal Injury Handbook, 1995; contbg. author: Legal Assistant's Letter Book, 1995; editl. com. Tex. Paralegal Jour.; contbr. articles to profl. jours. Recipient scholarship Tex. Christian U., Ft. Worth. Mem. AAUW, Am. Assn. Paralegal Edn., Assn. Trial Lawyers, State Bar of Tex. (Legal Asst. Divsn.), Nat. Assn. Legal Assts., Nat. Paralegal Assn., Ft. Worth Paralegal Assn., Freelance Writers' Network, Austin Writer's League, Okla. Writers' Fedn., Text and Acad. Authors. Home: PO box 101641 Fort Worth TX 76185-1641 E-mail: kmrparal@aol.com.

REAGAN, LARRY GAY, college vice president; b. Jackson, Tenn., Mar. 30, 1938; d. Larry Alfred and Ann Mabel (Welker) Lane. BA, Union U., 1959; MA, Tulane U., 1961; MS, Ea. Ky. U., 1971; EdD, Vanderbilt U., 1975. Instr. Ill. Coll., Jacksonville, 1961-63, Union Univ., Jackson, Tenn., 1963-64, Chipola Jr. Coll., Marianna, Fla., 1964-67; asst. prof. Campbellsville (Ky.) Coll., 1967-70; divsn. dir. arts and letters, dean acad. affairs Manatee C.C., Bradenton, Fla., 1972—; health educator Tenn. Dept. Pub. Health, Nashville, 1974-75; chair dept. Volunteer State C.C., Gallatin, Tenn., 1975-90, divsn. chair, prof., 1990-92; v.p. Shelby State C.C., Memphis, 1991-92. V.p. Nat. Inst. Leadership Devel., New Coll. Libr. Assn.; lectr. in China, England, and Mexico. Contbr. poems to profl. publs. Bd. dirs. Fla./Colombia Alliance, Marianna, 1964-67; trustee Christian Sr. Housing, Atlanta, 1990—; pres. Tenn. Assn. of Women in C.C.'s, Nashville, 1991-92; mem. Manatee Cultural Alliance, Bradenton, 1993—. Recipient citation award Mex. Sec. of Edn., 1983, award Nat. Inst. Leadership, 1989. Mem. AAUW, AAHPERD, LWV, Am. Assn. Women in C.C.'s (keynote speaker, regional dir., v.p.), Fla. Assn. Women in C.C.'s (bd. dirs. 1993—), Nat. Coun. Instrnl. Adminstrn., Rotary Club, Phi Kappa Iota. Home: 6605 Gulfside Rd Longboat Key FL 34228-1416 Office: Argosy U 5250 17th and Honore Sarasota FL 34235 E-mail: lgreagan@aol.com.

REAM DRAVUS, ANGELA MARIE, elementary education educator; b. Waukesha, Wis., July 27, 1970; d. Kenneth Richard Ream and Kathleen Kay (Meier) Fox. AAS, U. Wis.-Rock County, 1992; BS in Elem. Edn., U. Wis., Whitewater, 1995, MSE, 2002. Baker The Abbey on Lake Geneva, Fontana, Wis., 1986-90; lead tchr. Kids Korner, Evansville, Wis., summer 1990; supr. Pvt. Industry Coun., Janesville, Wis., summer 1992; child care supr. chpt. 1 Washington Elem., Janesville, 1992-95; Title I tchr. Janesville Sch. Dist., 1995—. Supr. YWCA, Janesville, 1990-95, camp counsel, summers 1991-94, instr. early childhood cook class, 1991-92, instr. babysitting clinic, 1991-93, cmty. children's parade, 1993, chaperone for sleep-over, 1993, v.p. fundraiser, fall 1994, accreditation team mem., 1994-95; tchr. summer sch. Ft. Atkinson (Wis.) Sch. Dist., 1995. Author: Personal Portfolio, 1994. Sunday Sch. tchr. K-11, 2002—03. Scholar Grace Alvord, U. Wis., Whitewater, 1993-94, 95. Mem. ASCD, Nat. Assn. for Edn. Young Children, Golden Key Nat. Honors Soc. Avocations: downhill skiing, swimming, bicycling, collecting garfield objects. Home: 1314 Barham Ave Janesville WI 53545-1507

REAMS, BERNARD DINSMORE, JR., lawyer, educator; b. Lynchburg, Va., Aug. 17, 1943; s. Bernard Dinsmore and Martha Eloise (Hickman) Reams; m. Rosemarie Bridget Boyle, Oct. 26, 1968 (dec. Oct. 1996); children: Andrew Dennet, Adriane Bevin; m. Lee Anne Oberhofer, Apr. 19, 2003. BA, Lynchburg Coll., 1965; MS, Drexel U., 1966; JD, U. Kans., 1972; PhD, St. Louis U., 1983. Bar: Kans. 1973, Mo. 1986, N.Y. 1996, Tex. 2002. Instr., asst. librarian Rutgers U., 1966-69; asst. prof. law, librarian U. Kans., Lawrence, 1969-74; mem. faculty law sch. Washington U., St. Louis, 1974-95, prof. law, 1976-95, prof. tech. mgmt., 1990-95, librarian, 1974-76, acting dean univ. libraries, 1987-88; prof. law, assoc. dean, dir. Law Libr. St. John's U. Sch. Law, Jamaica, N.Y., 1995-97, assoc. dean acad. affairs, 1997-98; prof., dir. law libr. and info. tech. St. Mary's U., San Antonio, 2000—03, prof. law, 2000. Vis. fellow Max-Planck Inst., Hamburg, 1995, 97-98, 2001; vis. prof. law Seton Hall U., 1998-2000. Author: Law For The Businessman, 1974, Reader in Law Librarianship, 1976, Federal Price and Wage Control Programs 1917-1979: Legis. Histories and Laws, 1980, Education of the Handicapped: Laws, Legislative Histories, and Administrative Documents, 1983, Internal Revenue Acts of the United States: The Revenue Act of 1954 with Legislative Histories and Congressional Documents, 1983, Congress and the Courts: A Legislative History 1978-1984, 1984, University-Industry Research Partnerships: The Major Issues in Research and Development Agreements, 1986, Deficit Control and the Gramm-Rudman-Hollings Act, 1986, The Semiconductor Chip and the Law: A Legislative History of the Semiconductor Chip Protection Act of 1984, 1986, American International Law Cases, 2d series, 1986, Technology Transfer Law: The Export Administration Acts of the U.S., 1987, Insider Trading and the Law: A Legislative History of the Insider Trading Sanctions Act, 1989, Insider Trading and Securities Fraud, 1989, The Health Care Quality Improvement Act of 1989: A Legislative History of P.L. No. 99-660, 1990, The National Organ Transplant Act of 1984: A Legislative History of P.L. No. 98-507, 1990, A Legislative History of Individuals with Disabilities Education Act, 1994, Federal Legislative Histories: An Annotated Bibliography and Index to Officially Published Sources, 1994, Electronic Contracting Law, 1996, Health Care Reform, 1994, The American Experience: Clinton and Congress, 1997, The Omnibus Anti-Crime Act, 1997, The Law of E-SIGN: A Legislative History of the Electronic Signature in Global and National Commerce Act, 2001; co-author: Segregation and the Fourteenth Amendment in the States, 1975, Historic Preservation Law: An Annotated Bibliography, 1976, Congress and the Courts: A Legislative History 1787-1977, 1978, Federal Consumer Protection Laws, Rules and Regulations, 1979, A Guide and Analytical Index to the Internal Revenue Acts of the U.S., 1909-1950, 1979, The Numerical Lists and Schedule of Volumes of the U.S. Congressional Serial Set: 73d Congress through the 96th Congress, 1984, Human Experimentation: Federal Laws, Legislative Histories, Regulations and Related Documents, 1985, American Legal Literature: A Guide to Selected Legal Resources, 1985, U.S.A. Patriot Act: A Legislative History, 2002. Bd. trustees Quincy Found. for Med. Rsch. Charitable Trust, San Francisco. Fellow Am. Bar Foun.; recipient Thornton award for excellence Lynchburg Coll., 1986, Joseph L. Andrews Bibliog. award, 1995; named to Hon. Order Ky. Cols., 1992. Mem. ABA, Am. Law Inst., ALA, Am. Soc. Law and Medicine, Nat. Health Lawyers Assn., Am. Assn. Higher Edn., Spl. Librs. Assn., Internat. Assn. Law Libr. Coll. and Univ. Attys., Order of Coif, Phi Beta Kappa, Sigma Xi, Beta Phi Mu, Phi Delta Phi, Phi Delta Epsilon, Kappa Delta Pi, Pi Lambda Theta. Office: St Marys U Sch Law One Camino Santa Maria San Antonio TX 78228 E-mail: breams@stmarytx.edu.

REAMS, MAX WARREN, geology educator, researcher; b. Virgil, Kans., Mar. 10, 1938; s. Chester Lyle and Arline (King) R.; m. Carol Ann Cushard, July 28, 1961; children: Brian Scott, Anne Rachelle, Kayla Diane. BA, BS, U. Kans., 1961, MS with grad. honors in geology, 1963; PhD, Washington U., St. Louis, 1968. Prof. geology, chair dept. geology Olivet Nazarene U., Kankakee, Ill., 1967—. Contbr. articles to profl. jours. Cons. local city bds., Ill. Sgt. USAR, 1956-64. Rsch. grantee various pub. and pvt. orgns., 1966-80. Fellow Geol. Soc. Am., Sigma Xi; mem. Am. Quaternary Assn., others. Mem. Church of Nazarene. Achievements include defining the origin of cave sediments, and defining first spring-related stromatolites. Home: 6 Castle Coombe Bourbonnais IL 60914-1828 Office: Olivet Nazarene U Dept Geol Scis Bourbonnais IL 60914 E-mail: mreams@olivet.edu.

REARICK, ANNE, photographer, educator; BA in English with honors, U. Mass., 1982; MFA in Photography with honors, Mass. Coll. Art, 1990. Photographer, instr. photography Cambridge Sch. Weston, 1994—. One-woman shows include Dean's Gallery, MIT, Cambridge, 1997, Salle Buscaillet, Bordeaux, France, 2000, exhibited in group shows at Erector Sq. Gallery, New Haven, 1997, Conant Gallery, Groton, Mass., 1997, 1999, Photographic Resource Ctr., Boston, 1997, Tufts U., Aidekman Arts Ctr., Medford, Mass., 1997, Whistler Mus., Lowell, Mass., 1999, Galerie Vu, Paris, 1999, Boise (Idaho) Art Mus., 1999, S.E. Mus. Photography, Daytona, Fla., 2001, Soc. Contemporary Photography, Kansas City, Mo., 2001, FNAC, Paris, 2002, Photographic Ctr., Skopelos, Greece, 2002, exhibited in group shows, Represented in permanent collections St. Botolph's Club Found. Collection, Boston, S.E. Mus. Photography, Daytona, Rose Art Mus., Brandeis U., Waltham, Mass., Internat. Polaroid Collection, Cambridge, Boise Art Mus., Bibliotheque Nationale, Paris. Recipient Blanche E. Colman award, 1992, Golden Lights award, 1996; fellow, New Eng. Found. for the Arts/Mass. Cultural Coun., 1995, John Simon Guggenheim Meml. Found., 2003; grantee, Polaroid Film, 1990, Somerville Arts Coun., 1990, 1993, 1997, 2003, Janet Wu, 1993, St. Botolph's Club Found., 1995; Fulbright fellow, 1990—91. Office: Cambridge Sch Weston 45 Georgian Rd Weston MA 02493*

REASER, DONALD FREDERICK, retired geology educator; b. Wichita Falls, Tex., Sept. 30, 1931; s. Frederick Summers and Lillian Norene (Wales) R.; m. Bette Jane Forrest, Aug. 2, 1975; 1 child, David Forrest Anderson. BS in Geology, So. Meth. U., Dallas, 1953, MS in Geology, 1958; PhD in Geology, U. Tex., Austin, 1974. Cert. profl. geologist. Tchg. asst. dept. geol. sci. U. Tex., Austin, 1958-61, instr., summer 1960, 63; instr. dept. geology Arlington (Tex.) State Coll., 1961-63; asst. prof. dept. geology West Tex. State U., Canyon, 1964-68; instr. dept. geology U. Tex., Arlington, 1968-70, asst. prof., 1970-74, assoc. prof., 1974-97, prof., 1997—2003. Petroleum geologist Humble Oil and Refining Co. (Exxon), Midland, Tex., 1965-66; cons. Core Labs., Inc. (Western Atlas), Dallas, 1974-78, Halliburton (Gearhart Industries, Inc.), Fort Worth, 1982-84. Author: (Essentials of Earth History, 1996, Geology of the Dallas-Fort Worth Metroplex, 2002. Bd. dirs. Oil Info. Libr. Fort Worth, 1987-90. 1st lt. USAF, 1954-56. Fellow Tex. Acad. Sci.; mem. Masons, Shriners, Scottish Rite, Lambda Chi Alpha (v.p., pres. 1952-53). Republican. Methodist. Avocation: rock and mineral collecting. Home: 200 Rock Springs Ct Waxahachie TX 75165-5302 Office: U Tex Arlington Dept Geology PO Box 19049 Arlington TX 76019-0001

REBAY, LUCIANO, Italian literature educator, literary critic; b. Milan, Apr. 23, 1928; came to U.S., 1955; s. Angelo and Pierina (Doniselli) R.; m. Martha Virginia Krauss, Aug. 2, 1952; children: Alexandra, Ilaria. Maturita classica Liceo Manzoni, Milan, 1946; Licence es lettres, U. Aix-en-Provence, France, 1951; PhD, Columbia U., 1960. Instr. Italian Columbia U., N.Y.C., 1957-60, asst. prof., 1960-63, assoc. prof., 1963-65, prof., 1965-73, Giuseppe Ungaretti prof. Italian lit., 1973—, chmn. Italian Dept., 1970-73; dir. Ctr. Italian Studies, 1985-88. Cons. to scholarly jours.; mem. Nat. Bd. Translators, Columbia U. Transl. Ctr. Author: Le origini della poesia di Giuseppe Ungaretti, 1962, Invitation to Italian Poetry, 1969, Alberto Moravia, 1970, Giuseppe Ungaretti, Gli scritti egiziani, 1909-1912, 1980, Montale, Clizia e l'America, 1982, Montale per amico, 1994, Montale: del dire e del non dire, 1998; editor: Giuseppe Ungaretti, Saggi e interventi, 1974, Jean Paulhan-Giuseppe Ungaretti, Correspondance, 1921-68, 1989. Guggenheim fellow, 1966-67; Am. Council Learned Socs. fellow, 1970-71; NEH fellow, 1980-81; Am. Philos. Soc. research grantee, 1970, 75 Mem. MLA, Am. Assn. Tchrs. of Italian, Associazione Internazionale per gli Studi di Lingua e Letteratura Italiana

REBB, KAREN MARLENE, music educator; b. Columbus, Ga. d. Glen Percival and Vivian Irene (Williams) Loken; 1 child, Michael John-Glen. BS in Music Edn., Elem. Edn., Grand Canyon U., 1981; MA in Music Edn., No. Ariz. U., 1986. Cert. tchr., Ariz.; cert. I, II, III Levels Orff cert. Tchr. Heatherbrae Elem. Sch., Phoenix, 1981-82, Park Meadows Elem. Sch., Phoenix, 1982-95, Arrowhead Elem. Sch., Glendale, Ariz., 1995—. Mem. adj. faculty Ottawa U., 1989—. Author: project Science of Music: Integrating the Arts and Technology, 1995. Mem. 1st Hist. Presbyn. Ch.; mem. site-based mgmt. team Park Meadows Sch., 1994, 95; mem. Dist. Strategic Planning Com., 1994; mem. dist. fine arts coun. writing Fine Arts Curriculum for Dist., Phoenix, 1995, 96. Recipient Ray Maben Scholar award Grand Canyon U., 1980, Ariz.; artist-in-residence grantee, 1989. Mem. NEA, Am. Orff-Schulwerk Assn., Ariz. Edn. Assn., Ariz. Orff-Schulwerk Assn. (sec., bd. dirs. 1990-92), Ariz. Music Educators Assn., Music Educators Nat. Conf. Avocations: playing piano, guitar, singing, reading, writing. Home: 19436 N 83rd Dr Peoria AZ 85382-8790

REBEC, GEORGE VINCENT, neuroscience researcher, educator, administrator; b. Harrisburg, Pa., Apr. 6, 1949; s. George Martin and Nadine (Bosko) R. AB, Villanova U., 1971; MA, U. Colo., 1974, PhD, 1975. Postdoctoral fellow U. Calif., San Diego, 1975-77; asst. prof. Ind. U., Bloomington, 1977-81, assoc. prof., 1981-85, prof. psychology, 1985—, dir. program in neural sci., 1985—, Chancellor's prof., 1999. Mem. rsch. rev. com. NIMH. Author: (with P.M. Groves) Introduction to Biological Psychology, 1988, 92; contbr. articles to profl. jours. Recipient Eli Lilly Tchg. award, 1978, Pres.' award Ind. U., 1990, Ind. U. Tchg. Excellence Recognition award, 1999, 2000; grantee NIDA, 1979—, NSF, 1985-96, NINDS, 1996—. Fellow AAAS, Am. Psychol. Soc.; mem. Soc. for Neurosci. (chmn. Ind. U. chpt.), Internat. Brain Rsch. Orgn., Assn. Neurosci. Depts. and Programs (pres.2003-). Roman Catholic. Avocation: sports. Office: Ind U Program in Neural Sci Dept Psychology Bloomington IN 47405

REBEIZ, CONSTANTIN A. plant physiology educator, laboratory director; b. Beirut, July 11, 1936; came to U.S., 1969, naturalized, 1975; s. Anis C. and Valentine A. (Choueyri) R.; m. Carole Louise Conness, Aug. 18, 1962; children: Paul A., Natalie, Mark J. BS, Am. U., Beirut, 1959; MS, U. Calif. - Davis, 1960, PhD, 1965. Dir. dept. biol. scis. Agrl. Rsch. Inst., Beirut, 1965-69; research assoc. biology U. Calif. - Davis, 1969-71; assoc. prof. plant physiology U. Ill., Urbana-Champaign, 1972-76, prof., 1976—, dir. Lab. Plant Biochemistry and Photobiology, 1999—2002; adj. prof. U. Limerick, Ireland. Adj. prof. U. Limerick, Ireland. Contbr. articles to sci. publs. plant physiology and biochemistry. Named One of 100 Outstanding Innovators, Sci. Digest, 1984—85; recipient Beckman Rsch. award, 1982, 1985, Funk award, 1985, Sr. Rsch. award, U. Ill., 1994, Presdl. Green Chemistry Challenge award, 1999, Sci. Achievement award, Am. U. Beirut Faculty Agrl. and Food Scis., 2002, Faculty of Agr. and Food Scis. Outstanding Sci. Achievement award, Am. U. of Beirut, 2002; grantee John P. Trebellas Rsch. Endowment, 1986, C.A. and C.C. Rebeiz Endowment for basic rsch., 2000. Mem. Am. Soc. Plant Physiologists, Comite Internat. de Photobiologie, Am. Soc. Photobiology, AAAS, Lebanese Assn. Advancement Scis. (exec. com. 1967-69), Sigma Xi. Achievements include research on pathway of chlorophyll biosynthesis, chloroplast devel., bioengring. of photosynthetic reactors; pioneered biosynthesis of chlorophyll in vitro; duplication of greening process of plants in test tube, demonstration of operation of multibranched chlorophyll biosynthetic pathway in nature; formulation and design of laser herbicides, insecticides and cancer chemotherapeutic agents. Home: 301 W Pennsylvania Ave Urbana IL 61801-4918 Office: U Ill 240A Pabl Urbana IL 61801 E-mail: crebeiz@uiuc.edu.

REBEL, AMY LOUISE, elementary education educator; b. Shaker Heights, Ohio, Feb. 26, 1957; d. Paul Vernon Jr. and Louise Alice (Parme) R. BS, No. Ill. U., 1980; postgrad., Nova U., 1992. Cert. tchr., Fla., Ill.; cert. ednl. leadership, Fla.; nat. cert. in water fitness-master level Am. Sport Edn. Program/Nat. Fedn. Interscholastic Coaches Edn. Program instr.; nat. cert. water fitness program coord. Golf coach, mem. support pers. Hinsdale (Ill.) Cen. Twp. High Sch., 1983-85; instructional pers., swimming coach Boca Raton (Fla.) Community Mid. Sch., 1985-86; tchr. phys. edn., swimming coach Boca Raton Community High Sch., 1987; tchr. phys. edn. Whispering Pines Community Elem. Sch., Boca Raton, 1987-88; tchr. phys. and aquatic edn. Sandpiper Shores Cmty. Elem. Sch., Boca Raton, 1989—, ESOL coord., 1991-92; crisis response team Sandpiper Shores Cmty. Elem. Sch., Boca Raton, Fla., 2002—. Personal cons. Water Exercise Programs, Ill. and Fla., 1976—; coach staff swimming Mission Bay Aquatic Tng. Ctr., Boca Raton, 1986-88; co-sponsor Nat. Jr. Beta Honor Soc., 1998-99. Mem. campaign com. Ill. State Rep. 38th dist., 1976; instr. water safety ARC, Fox River Valley, Ill., 1974-90, educator water safety, 1989—. Mem. ASCD, NEA, Palm Beach County Tchrs. Assn., U.S. Water Fitness Assn. Avocations: commercial acting, aquatics, modeling. Home: PO Box 345 Delray Beach FL 33447-0345 Office: Sandpiper Shores Community Elem Sch 11201 Glades Rd Boca Raton FL 33498-6818 E-mail: rebel@rebelemail.palmbeach.k12.fl.us.

REBER, BARBARA LEE, diagnostician, school administrator; b. Ft. Belvoir, Va., June 23, 1947; d. Truman C. and Frances Aurelia (Smith) Goodman; m. Ron Ray Reber, Jan. 25, 1969; children: Stephanie, Amanda. BA, East Tex. State U., 1969; MEd, Tex. Christian U., 1976. Tchr. Dallas Ind. Sch. Dist., 1969, Arlington (Tex.) Ind. Sch. Dist., 1969-78, ednl. diagnostician, 1978-88; asst. prin. Hill Elem. Sch., Arlington, 1988—94, prin., 1994—2000; ret., 2000; interim prin. Arlington Ind. Sch. Dist., 2000—03; prin. Williams Elem. Sch., Arlington, 2003—. Active Council for Exceptional Children; chmn. Accent Arlington, 1984-87; mem. Leadership Arlington, 1985-86. Mem. Tex. Elem. Prins. and Suprs. Assn., Arlington Adminstrs. Assn., Arlington Elem. Adminstrs. Assn., Tex. Ednl. Diagnosticians Assn., Assn. for Children with Learning Disabilities, Tex. Ret. Tchrs. Assn., Delta Kappa Gamma. Republican. Methodist. Home: 901 Kristin Ln Arlington TX 76012-4429 Office: Arlington Ind Schs 4915 Red Birch Dr Arlington TX 76018

REBERG, ROSALIE, principal; m. Larry Alan Reberg, Aug. 16, 1975; children: Camden Ashleigh, Jacob Alan. BA, Holy Names Coll., 1971; MA with distinction, Calif. State U., Stanislaus, 1994. Elem. edn. tchr. Stanislaus Union Sch. Dist., Modesto, Calif., 1974-96; vice prin. Chrysler Elem. Sch., Modesto, Calif., 1996-97; prin. Eisenhut Elem. Sch., Modesto, Calif., 1997-99, Prescott Sr. Elem. Sch., Modesto, 1999-2000, Auberry (Calif.) Elem. Sch., 2000—. Classroom mgmt. mentor tchr., Stanislaus Union Sch. Dist., 1988-89. Mem. Tchrs. English to Spkrs. of Other Langs., Assn. Calif. Sch. Adminstrs. Avocations: reading, computers, languages. Office: Auberry Elem Sch 33367 N Auberry Rd Auberry CA 93602 E-mail: rreberg@sierra.k12.ca.us.

REBOLLEDO, JOSE RAFAEL, pediatrician, educator; b. Popayan, Colombia, Apr. 20, 1933; came to U.S., 1963; s. Jose M. and Enriqueta (Chaux) R.; m. Peggy Joyce Smith, June 11, 1964; children: Michael Anthony, Martha Lucia. MD, U. del Cauca, Popayan, 1961. Diplomate Am. Bd. Pediatrics with subspecialty in pediatric cardiology. Resident in pediatrics U. Tex. Med. Br., Galveston, 1963-65, fellow in pediatric cardiology, 1965-67, instr. pediatrics, 1967-68; clin. prof. U. Tex. Health Sci. Ctr., San Antonio, 1968—, dir. pediatric cardiology clinic, 1995—; chief pediatric cardiology Christus Rosa Children's Hosp., 1998. Chief of staff Santa Rosa Children's Hosp., San Antonio, 1993. Fellow Am. Coll. Cardiology. Avocations: racquetball, snow skiing, travel. Home: 202 Bluffcrest San Antonio TX 78216-1910 Office: 343 W Houston St Ste 811 San Antonio TX 78205-2108

RECASNER, TONY, director; D in Psychology, Tulane U. Staff psychologist Office Acad. Enrichment Loyola U., New Orleans; dir. New Orleans Charter Middle Sch., 1998—. Bd. dirs. S.W. Ednl. Labs., 2002—, chmn. bd. dirs., 2003—. Office: New Orleans Charter Middle Sch 3801 Monroe St New Orleans LA 70118*

RECHTZIGEL, SUE MARIE (SUZANNE RECHTZIGEL), child care center executive; b. St. Paul, May 27, 1947; d. Carl Stinson and Muriel Agnes (Oestrich) Miller; m. Gary Elmer Rechtzigel, Aug. 20, 1968 (div. Feb. 1982); children: Brian Carl, Lori Ann. BA in Psychology, Sociology, Mankato (Minn.) State U., 1969. Lic. in child care, Minn. Rep. ins. State Farm Ins. Co., Albert Lea, Minn., 1969-73; free-lance child caretaker Albert Lea, Minn., 1973-78; owner, dir. Lakeside Day Care, Albert Lea, Minn., 1983—. Asst. Hawthorne Sch. Learning Ctr., Albert Lea, 1978-83. Mem. New Residents and Newcomers Orgn., Albert Lea, 1970—, past. pres.; asst. pre-sch. United Meth. Ch., Albert Lea, 1975-78, tchr. Sunday sch., 1976-80, tchr. Bible sch., 1980-85; active Ascension Luth. Ch., 1976-80. Mem. Freeborn Lic. Day Care Assn. (v.p. 1986, pres. 1987), AAUW (home tour 1977, treas. 1980-81), Bus. and Profl. Women, YMCA, Albert Lea Art Ctr. Clubs: 3M Families. Republican. Avocations: ceramics, calligraphy, painting, art, sewing. Home and Office: 1919 Brookside Dr Albert Lea MN 56007-2142

RECINIELLO, KAREN MARY, language educator; b. Newark, June 20, 1950; d. Michael Nahirny and Helen Petishnok; m. Robert N. Reciniello, Apr. 29, 1972. BA, Montclair State Coll., N.J., 1972, MA, 1982. Tchr. of French Mountain Lakes (N.J.) H.S., 1973; tchr. of Russian Boonton (N.J.)

H.S., 1973; tchr. of French Hopatcong (N.J.) H.S., 1974—. Owner Ivy Rock Acres, Hackettstown, NJ, 1995—. Mem.: Am. Tchrs. French, N.J. Lang. Tchrs. Assn., U.S. Dressage Fed. Avocations: dressage riding, travelling in France.

RECK, ANDREW JOSEPH, retired philosopher, educator; b. New Orleans, Oct. 29, 1927; s. Andrew Gervais and Katie (Mangiaracina) R.; m. Elizabeth Lassiter Torre, June 17, 1987. BA, Tulane U., 1947, MA, 1949; postgrad., U. St. Andrews, Scotland, 1952-53; PhD, Yale U., 1954; student, U. St. Andrews, Scotland, 1952-53, U. Paris, summers 1962, 64. Instr. English U. Conn., 1949-50; instr. philosophy Yale, 1951-52, 55-58; faculty Tulane U., 1958—2003, prof. philosophy, 1964—2003, chmn. dept., 1969-89, dir. Master Liberal Arts program, 1984—2003, ret., 2003. Thomasfest lectr. Xavier U., Cin., 1970; Suarez Lectr. Spring Hill Coll., 1971; Niebuhr lectr. Elmhurst (Ill.) Coll., 1976; vis. prof. Fordham U., 1979; vis. scholar Hastings Ctr. (N.Y.), 1981; Woodruff lectr. Emory U., 1982; Fairchild lectr. U. So. Miss., 1982, 87: Matchette Found. lectr. Cath. U. Am., 1991, 95; Sr. Scholar Inst. Humane Studies, Menlo Park, Calif., 1982; vis. scholar Poynter Ctr., Ind. U., Bloomington, 1983; Tulane U. faculty rep. to bd. adminstrs. Tulane Ednl. Fund., 1988-91. Author: Recent American Philosophy, 1964, Introduction to William James, 1967, New American Philosophers, 1968, Speculative Philosophy, 1972; editor: George Herbert Mead Selected Writings, 1964, 2d edit., 1981, Knowledge and Value, 1972, (with T. Horvath, T. Krittek and S. Grean) American Philosophers' Ideas of Ultimate Reality and Meaning, 1993; co-editor Ultimate Reality and Meaning, Interdisciplinary Studies in the Philosophy of Understanding, 1990-; mem. adv. editl. bd. Internat. Jour. World Peace, Trans. Charles Peirce Soc., Santayana edit. So. Jour. Philosophy, Library of Living Philosophers; editor History of Philosophy Quar., 1993-98. Served with AUS, 1953-55. Howard fellow, 1962-63, Liberty Fund grantee, 1982, Newcomb fellow, 1991-93; Fulbright scholar, 1952-53; Am. Coun. Learned Socs. grantee, 1961-62, Am. Philos. Soc. grantee, 1972, Huntington Libr. grantee, 1973, La. Ednl. Quality State Found. grantee, 1994-96, U.S. Info. Agy. grantee, Brazil, 1993. Mem.: La. Endowment for Humanities (bd. dirs. 1990—96), Internat. Soc. for Study of Human Ideas of Ultimate Reality and Meaning (bd. dirs. 1989—, treas. 2001—03, sec./treas. 2003—), Charles S. Peirce Soc. (sec.-treas. 1985—86, v.p. 1986—87, pres. 1987—88), Soc. Advancement Am. Philosophy (exec. com. 1980—82, pres.-elect 1997—98, pres. 1998—2000, exec. com. 2001—03, chair nominating com. 2002—), Metaphys. Soc. Am. (councillor 1971—75, pres. 1977—78, program com. 1989—90, chair program com. 1995—96), Coun. for Internat. Rsch. Scholars (philosophy screening com. 1974—77), Am. Coun. Learned Socs. (Am. studies adv. com. 1972—76), So. Soc. Philosophy and Psychology (treas. 1968—71, pres. 1976—77), Southwestern Philos. Soc. (exec. com. 1965—69, v.p. 1971—72, pres. 1972—73), Am. Philos. Assn. (program com. ea. divsn. 1969, nominating com. western divsn. 1975—76, 1981—82, mem., chair ad hoc com. on history 1992, adv. com. to program com. ea. divsn. 1994—97, mem., chair ad hoc com. on history 1996—), Tulane U. Emeritus Club (Outstanding Grad. of Class of 1947 award 1997), Omicron Delta Kappa, Alpha Sigma Lambda (hon. Theta chpt. of La.), Phi Beta Kappa (pres. Alpha of La. 1966—67). Home: 6125 Patton St New Orleans LA 70118-5832 E-mail: areck@tulane.edu.

RECKER, ROBERT R. medical educator, internist; b. St. Libory, Nebr., Apr. 5, 1939; s. Robert Libory Recker and Dorothy E. Evers; m. Susan Marie Cody; children: Katherine, Sarah, Robert, Michael. MD, Creighton U., Omaha, 1963. Diplomate Am. Bd. Internal Medicine 1971. Prof. medicine Creighton U., Omaha, 1974—, dir. Osteoporosis Rsch. Ctr., 1974—, divsn. chief endocrinology, 1974—. Flight surgeon USAF, 1965—67. Mem.: Am. Soc. for Bone and Mineral Rsch. (pres. 2001—02). Home: 3309 S 116th St Omaha NE 68144 Office: Creighton Univ 601 N 30th St Omaha NE 68131 Business E-Mail: rrecker@creighton.edu.

RECORD, LINCOLN FREDRICK, speech communications educator, communications consultant; b. Kokomo, Ind., Nov. 12, 1939; s. Fred William Record and Mary Louise (Greene) Pingleton; m. Marlene Jeanette Welly, June 22, 1963; children: Eric, Erin. BA, Ball State U., Muncie, Ind., 1963; MA, St. Francis Coll., Ft. Wayne, Ind., 1973; student, U. Aberdeen, Scotland, 1970. Tchr. Maconaquah Schs., Bunker Hill, Ind., 1963-67; English chairperson Dekalb Schs., Auburn, Ind., 1967-75; speech coord. Ft. Wayne (Ind.) Community Schs., 1975—; assoc. faculty Purdue U., Ft. Wayne, Ind., 1974—. Editor: Dekalb Educator, 1970-74, Educator, 1986-91; author: The Need for Communication in Education. Chmn. Educators for Dick Lugar, Ind., 1977; pres. Parish Coun., Auburn, 1970-72; mem. Auburn Port Authority, 1985-87; councilman Auburn City Coun., 1980-84. Recipient Polit. Action award Ind. State Tchrs., Indpls., 1988; named to Ind. Hall of Fame, 1994. Mem. NEA (local pres. 1966, 68-69), Ind. Forensic Assn., Nat. Forensic League (dist. coun. 1988—, triple diamond award 1993), Ind. Speech Assn., Ind. State Tchrs. Assn. (bd. dirs. 1974-77), KC, Kiwanis. Democrat. Roman Catholic. Avocations: commercial radio announcing, televison voice-overs, speech coaching, volunteer counseling. Home: 908 N Main St Auburn IN 46706-1228

RECORDS, RAYMOND EDWIN, ophthalmologist, medical educator; b. Ft. Morgan, Colo., May 30, 1930; s. George Harvey and Sara Barbara (Louden) R.; 1 child, Lisa Rae. BS in Chemistry, U. Denver, 1956; MD, St. Louis U., 1961. Diplomate Am. Bd. Ophthalmology. Intern St. Louis U. Hosp. Group, 1961-62; resident in ophthalmology U. Colo. Med. Ctr., Denver, 1962-65; instr. ophthalmology, 1965-67, asst. prof., 1967-70; prof. ophthalmology U. Nebr. Coll. Medicine, Omaha, 1970-93, prof. emeritus, 1993, dept. chmn., 1970-89. Author: Physiology of Human Eye (Med. Writers award 1980), 1979. Author, editor: Biomedical Foundations of Ophthalmology, 1982. Med. dir. Nebr. Lions Eye Bank, 1970-81. Fellow Am. Acad. of Ophthalmology (outstanding contbn. award 1978, lifelong edn. award 1995); mem. AMA, Nev. Med. Assn., Clark County Med. Soc., Omaha Ophthal. Soc. (pres. 1981-82), Assn. Rsch. in Vision and Ophthalmology. Home: 1330 Fragrant Spruce Ave Las Vegas NV 89123-5357 Office: 1330 Fragrant Spruce Ave Las Vegas NV 89123-5357

RECTOR, IRENE, retired elementary school educator; b. Vigo County, Ind., June 6, 1917; d. Warren Ray and Nellie (Davis) Rector. BS, Ind. State U., 1940, MS, 1965. Elem. tchr. Brazil City Schs., 1941—44; tchr. Boone County Schs., Thorntown, Ind., 1944—47; tchr. remedial reading Clay Community Schs., Brazil, Ind., 1947—75; elem. tchr. Marshall County Schs., Argos, Ind., 1941—44; tutor speech therapy and remedial reading, Brazil, 1947—64; coord. spl. reading program Boone County Schs., 1971—76, tchr., 1976—77, ret., 1977. Mem. NEA (coord. spl. reading program), Ind. Tchrs. Assn., Clay Community Classroom Tchrs., IRTA, CCRTA (past treas., sec.). Home: 2177 W State Road 340 Brazil IN 47834-7232

RECTOR, ROBERT WAYMAN, mathematics and engineering educator, former association executive; b. San Jose, Calif., Jan. 28, 1916; s. Joseph Jones and Eva (Hembree) R.; m. Margaret Eileen Hayden, Aug. 25, 1940; children: Cleone Rector Black, Robin Rector Krupp, Bruce Hayden. BA, San Jose State U., 1937; MA, Stanford U., 1939; PhD, U. Md., 1956. Instr. Compton (Calif.) Coll., 1939-42; asso. prof. math. U.S. Naval Acad., 1946-56; staff mathematician Space Tech. Labs., Los Angeles, 1956-61; asso. dir. computation center Aerospace Corp., El Segundo, Calif., 1961-65; v.p. Informatics, Inc., Van Nuys, Calif., 1965-70, Cognitive Systems, Inc., Beverly Hills, Calif., 1970-71; asso. dir. continuing edn. engring. and math. UCLA, 1971-73, 81-92; dean Coll. Engring. and Computer Sci. West Cost U., L.A., 1992-96. Exec. dir. Am. Fedn. Info. Processing Socs., Montvale, N.J., 1973-79; spl. asst. White House Conf. Library and Info. Services, 1979; v.p. Conf. and Meeting Assistance Corp., East Greenwich, R.I., 1980— Bd. govs.: Pacific Jour. Math, 1957-92. Mem. Los Angeles Mayor's Space Adv. Com., 1964-73; mem. aviation and space hist. rsch. com. Calif. Mus. Found., 1984-97; mem. aerospace hist. soc. bd. dirs. Mus. of Flying, Santa Monica, Calif., 1997-2001. Served with USNR, 1942-46. Mem. Math. Assn. Am., Assn. Computing Machinery, Naval Res. Assn., Res. Officers Assn., Ret. Officers Assn., Aerospace Hist. Soc. (sec.-treas. 2002—). Home: 10700 Stradella Ct Los Angeles CA 90077-2604

REDD, BETTY, retired elementary school educator; b. Elk City, Okla., Apr. 22, 1943; d. Govie and Johnnie Lois (Crabb) Miller; 1 child, Tana Redd. BA, SW Okla. State U., 1966, MS, 1968. Elem. tchr. Cheyenne Pub. Sch., Okla., 1967—68; tchr. handicapped Sunset-Mesa Sch., Albuquerque, 1970—71; tchr. kindergarten Butler Pub. Sch., Okla., 1975—77, Hammon Pub. Sch., Okla., 1968—70, 1971—72, 1977—90; ret., 1990. Mem. NEA, Okla. Edn. Assn., Hammon Edn. Assn. Home: PO Box 1272 Elk City OK 73648

REDDINGTON, MARY JANE, retired secondary school educator; b. New Rochelle, N.Y., July 21, 1923; d. Gordon William and Katharine Regina (Coleman) Kann; m. John Martin Reddington, Oct. 11, 1947; children: Terence, Martha, Robert. BA cum laude, Coll. New Rochelle, 1945; postgrad., Columbia U., 1947—49; MA, Hunter Coll., 1954; PhD (hon.), Iona Coll., 1996. Tchr. St. Gabriel's H.S., New Rochelle, NY, 1945—51, Albert Leonard Jr. H.S., New Rochelle, NY, 1960—81; dir. devel. The Ursuline Sch., New Rochelle, NY, 1981—88; ret., 1988. Active Bd. Edn., New Rochelle, 1983—, v.p., 1985—87, pres., 1987—89, Colburn Meml. Home; active New Rochelle Pub. Libr. Found. Bd., New Rochelle Cmty. Svcs. Bd.; vol. Sound Shore Med. Ctr.; bd. dirs. United Way New Rochelle, 1972—, pres., 1979—82, campaign chair, 1976—82; trustee Coll. New Rochelle, 1967—73; lector Holy Family Ch.; active Holy Family Ch. Ladies Guild. Recipient Gold Key award, Columbia Scholastic Press Assn., 1976, Ursula Laurus citation, Coll. New Rochelle, 1962, St. Angela Merici medal, 1970, citation, United Way New Rochelle, 1970—82, Spl. Recognition award, 1986, 2001, St. Angela award, The Ursuline Sch., 1977, Nat. Cmty. Svc. award, AARP, 1994, Loyal Svc. and Dedication award, Colburn Home, 1992, Cmty. Salute honoree, New Rochelle Pub. Libr. Found., 1999, Cmty. Svc. award, New Rochelle YMCA, 2001, honoree, Sr. Pers. Placement Bur., 2002, Interreligious Coun. of New Rochelle, 2002, Meals-On-Wheels of New Rochelle, 2003, New Rochelle Found. for Ednl. Excellence, 2004. Mem.: Bus. and Profl. Women's Club New Rochelle (past pres., Woman of Yr. 1979), So. Westchester Ret. Tchrs. Assn. (co-pres.), Coll. New Rochelle Alumnae Assn. (past pres.), Ladies of Charity (past pres.), Cath. Women's Club Westchester (founder, past pres.), Woman's Club New Rochelle (pres.), LWV, Alpha Delta Kappa (past pres.). Roman Catholic. Avocations: travel, reading, antiques, writing, cross country skiing. Home: 56 Wykagyl Terr New Rochelle NY 10804

REDDIX, ROWENA PINKIE, retired elementary school principal; b. New Orleans, Aug. 24, 1930; d. Benjamin James Jr. and Mamie Louise (Mott) R.; m. John David Perry, Oct. 6, 1952 (div. July 1962); children: Barbara Ann, Elston Ricky. BA, Dillard U., 1951; MA, Calif. State U., Hayward, 1978. Cert. tchr., Fla., Calif., La. Tchr. Orleans Parish Sch. Bd., New Orleans, 1951-59, 92—, Richmond (Calif.) Unified Sch. Dist., 1959-78, chpt. I coord., 1978-79, vice prin., 1979-81; prin. Lincoln Unified Sch. Dist., Stockton, Calif., 1981-87, Volusia County Sch. Dist., DeLand, Fla., 1987-91. Pub. speaker chs., librs. and schs., DeLand, 1987-91. Mem. NAESP, PTA (v.p. 1987-91, Svc. award 1982, Continued Svc. award 1987), NAACP, Assn. Calif. Sch. Adminstrs., Coun. for Exceptional Children, Phi Delta Kappa, Pi Lambda Theta. Democrat. Methodist. Avocations: theater, dancing, traveling, walking, shopping. Home: 3104 Audubon St New Orleans LA 70125-2654

REDDY, CHATLA V. RAMANA, internist, cardiologist, educator; b. Vizianagaram, India, 1944; MB, BChir, Andhra (India) U., 1966. Intern St. Lukes Hosp.-Childrens Med. Ctr., Phila., 1968-69; resident internal medicine Misericordia Hosp., 1969-72, fellow cardiology, 1972-74; dir. cardiac cath. lab. SUNY Health Sci. Ctr., Bklyn., 1985-91; chief cardiology, dir. cardiac cath. lab. N.Y. Meth. Hosp., Bklyn., 1991—. Assoc. prof. clin. medicine Weill Med. Coll. of Cornell U. Fellow Am. Coll. Angiology, ACP, Am. Coll. Cardiology, Am. Coll. Chest Physicians, Am. Heart Assn. Home: 506 6th St Brooklyn NY 11215-3609

REDDY, GOPAL BAIREDDY, engineering educator; b. Palwai, India, May 11, 1950; came to U.S., 1974; s. B. Soogi and B. Govindamma Reddy; m. Shanti Baireddy, June 27, 1981; children: Kasthuri, Madhuri, Sumana, Bhargava. BE, Osmania U., Hyderabad, India, 1974; MS, Tex. Tech. U., 1976; PhD, N.C. State U., 1986. Lectr. U. N.C., Charlotte, 1976-78, 81-83; pool officer Coun. Sci. and Indsl. Rsch., Hyderabad, 1980-81; asst. prof. Fairleigh Dickinson U., Teaneck, N.J., 1986-90, Trenton (N.J.) State Coll., 1990-91; assoc. prof., chmn. civil, mech. and related tech. dept. U. Houston, 1991—. Cons. in field. Contbr. articles to Internat. Jour. Heat and Mass Transfer, Internat. Jour. Energy Rsch., Computers in Edn., Internat. Jour. Ambient Energy. Mem. ASME (dir. coll. rels. 1987-90, Outstanding Contribution award 1989), Am. Soc. Engring. Edn. (Outstanding Campus Rep award 1989), Soc. Mfg. Engring., Tau Beta Pi. Home: 35 Fernglen Dr The Woodlands TX 77380-1557 E-mail: greddy@uh.edu.

REDENBACH, SANDRA IRENE, educational consultant; b. Boston, Mass., Nov. 18, 1940; d. David and Celia (Wish) Goldstein; m. Gunter L. Redenbach, Mar. 16, 1963 (div. 1980); 1 child, Cori-Lin; m. Kenneth L. Gelatt, June 25, 1989. BA, U. Calif., Davis, 1972; MEd in Ednl. Leadership, St. Mary's Coll., Moraga, Calif., 1995. Cert. tchr., Calif. Tchr. Solano County Juvenile Hall, Fairfield, Calif., 1968-70, St. Basil's Sch., Vallejo, Calif., 1970-73, St. Philomenes Sch., Sacramento, 1973; tchr., assoc. dean Vet.'s Spl. Edn. Program, U. Calif., Davis, 1973-75, Woodland Jr. HS, Calif., 1973-76, Lee Jr. HS, Woodland, 1976-79, Woodland HS, 1979-87; founder, coord., tchr. Ind. Learning Ctr., Woodland, 1987-94; dir. curriculum and instrn. Dixon Unified Sch. Dist., Calif., 1994—96. Teaching asst., lectr. U. Calif., Davis, 1985-86; pres., cons. Esteem Seminar Programs and Pubs., Davis, 1983—; cons., leader workshop. Author: Self-Esteem: The Necessary Ingredient for Success, 1991; author tng. manual: Self-Esteem: A Training Manual, 1990-91, Innovative Discipline: Managing Your Own Flight Plan, 1994, Curriculum for Autobiography of a Dropout: Dear Diary, 1996-1997, The Roadmap to Consulting: An Educator's Guide, 1998 Active Dem. Club of Davis, 1976-79; human rights chair Capitol Svc. Ctr., Sacramento, 1987-92. Martin Luther King scholar, 1986; Nat. Found. for Improvement of Edn. grantee, 1987-88. Life mem. Assoc. Calif. Sch. Adminstrs., Woodland Edn. Assoc. (pres. 1980-83, Outstanding Educator 1992, 93), Phi Delta Kappa (pres. 1992-93). Jewish. Avocations: singing, acting, dancing, travel, theater. Home: 313 Del Oro Ave Davis CA 95616-0416 Office: Esteem Seminar Programs & Publs 313 Del Oro Ave Davis CA 95616-0416

REDER, ANTHONY THOMAS, neurologist, educator; b. Midland, Mich., Aug. 10, 1952; BS in Psychology and Zoology, U. Mich., 1974, MD, 1978. Resident in neurology U. Minn., Mpls., 1979-82; fellow in neuroimmunology U. Chgo., 1982-84, instr. in neurology, 1984-85, asst. prof. neurology, 1985-92, assoc. prof. neurology, 1992—; intern Hennepin County Med. Ctr., Mpls., 1978-79. Contbr. articles to profl. jours. Mem. Am. Acad. Neurology, Am. Neurol. Assn., Am. Soc. for Neuro. Investigation, Internat. Soc. for Neuroimmunomodulation, AAAS, Am. Assn. Immunology, Chgo. Assn. Immunologists. Office: U Chgo Dept Neurology # MC 2030 5841 S Maryland Ave Chicago IL 60637-1463

REDFIELD, CAROL ANN LUCKHARDT, engineering educator; b. Greencastle, Ind., July 19, 1958; d. Robert Buek and Helen (Brown) K.; m. Josiah Beckley Redfield, Mar. 17, 1990. BS in Edn., U. Mich., Ann Arbor, 1980, MS in Math, MS in Computer & Controls, U. Mich., Ann Arbor, 1982, PhD in Computer Sci. & Engring., 1989. Secondary Teaching Cert. Tchg. asst. U. Mich., Ann Arbor, Mich., 1979-87; rsch. engr. Southwest Rsch. Inst., San Antonio, 1987-94; sr. scientist Mei Tech. Corp., San Antonio, 1995-98; asst. prof. St. Mary's U., San Antonio, 1998—2003, assoc. prof., 2003—. Chair Internat. Space Devel. Conf., San Antonio, 1991. Author: AI and Game Playing, 1986; editor, author: Intelligent Tutoring Systems, 1991, 98; editor: 1991 ISDC Proceedings, 1991, AI in Education, 2001. Seminar leader Landmark Edn.; founder Radiance Acad. West Charter Sch. Mem. AIAA, Nat. Space Soc., San Antonio Space Soc. (pres. 1988—). Avocations: ultimate frisbee, science fiction. Home: 609 Ridge View Dr San Antonio TX 78253-5348 Office: St Marys U 1 Camino Santa Maria St San Antonio TX 78228-8524

REDFIELD, DAVID ALLEN, chemistry educator; b. Grand Junction, Colo., Aug. 26, 1948; s. Donald Lee and Wilda Mae (Bean) R.; m. Sandra Kay Trandem, Dec. 13, 1969; children: Daniel, John, Jessica. BA, Point Loma Nazarene Coll., 1970; PhD, U. Nevada, Reno, 1974. Postdoctoral fellow U. Ill., Urbana, 1974-75; sr. rsch. chemist Olin Corp., New Haven, 1975-80; prof., chair dept. chemistry N.W. Nazarene U., Nampa, Idaho, 1980-99, dean Sch. Health and Sci., 1999—2002; dean math. and sci. Solano C.C., Fairfield, Calif., 2002—. Cons. Nyssa (Oreg.)-Nampa Sugar Beet Growers, 1982-2000, co-dir. Students Investigating Today's Environment. Participant Vallivue Band Parents, Caldwell, Idaho, 1991-99, participant Vallivue Sch. Mission Setting Team, Caldwell, 1994-95; elected Vallivue Sch. Bd., 1998; trustee Vallivue Sch., 1998-2002. Recipient tchr. recognition program Nampa C. of C., 1989. Mem. Am. Chem. Soc., Idaho Acad. Sci. (treas. and pres. 1980-99). Nazarene. Avocations: backpacking, fishing, model trains. Office: 4000 Suisun Valley Rd Fairfield CA 94534-3197 E-mail: dredfiel@solano.cc.ca.us.

REDISH, EDWARD FREDERICK, physicist, educator; b. N.Y.C., Apr. 1, 1942; s. Jules and Sylvia Redish; m. Janice Copen, June 18, 1967; children: A. David, Deborah. AB, Princeton U., 1963; PhD, MIT, 1968. CTP fellow U. Md., College Park, 1968-70, from asst. prof. to assoc. prof., 1970-79, prof., 1979—, chmn. dept. phys. astronomy, 1982-85. Vis. scholar, U. Calif., Berkeley, 1999-00; vis. prof. Ind. U., Bloomington, 1985-86, U. Washington, Seattle, 1992-93; vis. fgn. collaborator CEN, Saclay, France, 1973-74; co-dir. Md. U. Project in Physics and Ednl. Tech., 1983-93, Comprehensive Unified Physics Learning Environment, 1989-96; mem. Nuclear Sci. Adv. Com., Dept. of Energy/NSF, 1987-90; mem. program adv. com. Ind. U. Cyclotron Facility, 1985-89, chmn., 1986-89; mem. Internat. Commn. on Physics Edn., 1993-2002, sec., 1999-2002. Author: Teaching Physics with the Physics Suite, 2003, (textbook) Understanding Physics, 2003, (software) Orbits, 1989, The M.U.P.P.E.T. Utilities, 1994, The Comprehensive Unified Physics Learning Environment, 1994; editor: (conf. procs.) Computers in Physics Instrn., 1990, Internat. Conf. Undergrad. Physics Edn., 1997, Physics Edn. Rsch. Supplement to Am. Jour. Physics., 1999—. Named Sr. Resident Rsch. Assoc., NAS-NRC, 1977-78; recipient Inst. medal Ctrl. Rsch. Inst. for Physics, 1979, Leo Schubert award Wash. Acad. Sci., 1988, Educator award Md. Assn. Higher Edn., 1989, Glover award Dickinson Coll., 1991, Forman award Vanderbilt U., 1996. Fellow AAAS, Am. Phys. Soc., Wash. Acad. Sci.; mem. Am. Assn. Physics Tchrs. (Robert A. Millikan medal 1998). Office: U Md Dept Physics College Park MD 20742-4111

REDLICH, NORMAN, lawyer, educator; b. N.Y.C., Nov. 12, 1925; s. Milton and Pauline (Durst) R.; m. Evelyn Jane Grobow, June 3, 1951; children: Margaret Bonny-Claire, Carrie Ann, Edward Grobow. AB, Williams Coll., 1947, LLD (hon.), 1976; LLB, Yale U., 1950; LLM, NYU, 1955; LLD (hon.), John Marshall Law Sch., 1990. Bar: N.Y. 1951. Practiced in, N.Y.C., 1951-59; assoc. prof. law NYU, 1960-62, prof. law, 1962-74, assoc. dean Sch. Law, 1974-75, dean Sch. Law, 1975-88, dean emeritus, 1992—, Judge Edward Weinfeld prof. law, 1982—; counsel Wachtell, Lipton, Rosen & Katz, N.Y.C., 1988—. Editor-in-chief Tax Law Rev., 1960-66; mem. adv. com. Inst. Fed. Taxation, 1963-68; exec. asst. corp. counsel, N.Y.C., 1966-68, 1st asst. corp. counsel, 1970-72, corp. counsel, 1972-74; asst. counsel Pres. Commn. on Assassination Pres. Kennedy, 1963-64; mem. com. on admissions and grievances U.S. 2d Circuit Ct. Appeals, 1978—, chmn., 1978-87. Author: Professional Responsibility: A Problem Approach, 1976, Constitutional Law, Cases and Materials, 1983, rev. edit., 1996, 2001, Understanding Constitutional Law, 1995, rev. edit., 1999; contbr. articles in field. Chmn. commn. on law and social action Am. Jewish Congress, 1978—, chmn. governing coun., 1996; mem. Borough Pres.'s Planning Bd. Number 2, 1959-70, counsel N.Y. Com. to Abolish Capital Punishment, 1958-77; mem. N.Y.C. Bd. Edn., 1969; mem. bd. overseers Jewish Theol. Sem., 1973—; trustee Law Ctr. Found. of NYU, 1975—, Freedom House, 1976-86, Vt. Law Sch., 1977-99, Practicing Law Inst., 1980-99; trustee Lawyers Com. for Civil Rights Under Law, 1976—, co-chmn., 1979-81; bd. dirs. Legal Aid Soc., 1983-88, NAACP Legal Def. Fund, 1985—, Greenwich House, 1987—. Decorated Combat Infantryman's Badge. Mem. ABA (coun. legal edn. and admissions to bar 1981—, vice chmn. 1987-88, chmn. 1989-90, equal opportunities in legal profession 1986-92, ho. of dels. 1991—), Assn. of Bar of City of N.Y. (exec. com. 1975-79, professionalism com. 1988-92), com. on capital punishment 1998—). Office: 51 W 52nd St Fl 30 New York NY 10019-6119

REDMAN, BARBARA KLUG, nursing educator; b. Mitchell, S.D. d. Harlan Lyle and Darlien Grace (Bock) Klug; m. Robert S. Redman, Sept. 14, 1958; 1 child, Melissa Darlien. BS, S.D. State U., 1958; MEd, U. Minn., 1959, PhD, 1964; LHD (hon.), Georgetown U., 1988; DSc (hon.), U. Colo., 1991. RN. Asst. prof. U. Wash., Seattle, 1964-69; assoc. dean U. Minn., Mpls., 1969-75; dean Sch. Nursing U. Colo., Denver, 1975-78; VA scholar VA Cen. Office, Washington, 1978-81; postdoctoral fellow Johns Hopkins U., Balt., 1982-83; exec. dir. Am. Assn. Colls. Nursing, Washington, 1983-89, ANA, Washington, 1989-93; prof. nursing Johns Hopkins U., Balt., 1993-95; dean, prof. Sch. Nursing U. Conn., Storrs, 1995-98; dean Coll. Nursing Wayne State U., Detroit. Vis. fellow Kennedy Inst. Ethics, Georgetown U., 1993-94; fellow in med. ethics Harvard Med. Sch., 1994-95. Author: Practice of Patient Education, 1968—; contbr. articles to profl. jours. Bd. dirs. Friends of Nat. Libr. of Medicine, Washington, 1987—. Recipient Disting. Alumnus award S.D. State U., 1975, Outstanding Achievement award U. Minn., 1989. Fellow Am. Acad. Nursing. Home: 12425 Bobbink Ct Potomac MD 20854-3005 Office: Wayne State U 5557 Cass Ave Detroit MI 48202-3615

REDMAN-JOYCE, RAMONA LEA, middle school art educator; b. Portsmouth, N.H., May 21, 1962; d. Howard B. and Phyllis C. (Belyea) Redman; m. John J. Joyce, Apr. 30, 1993. BFA, Plymouth (N.H.) State Coll., 1984, BS in Art Edn., 1985, MEd in Middle Level Integrated Arts, 1994. Cert. elem. and secondary art tchr., N.H. Art tchr. Newfound Regional Jr./Sr. H.S., Bristol, N.H., 1985-87; adminstrv. sec. Office of News Svcs., PSC, Plymouth, N.H., 1988; art educator Newfound Meml. Mid. Sch., Bristol, 1989—. Mem. Hood Mus. outreach project Dartmouth Coll., Hanover, N.H., 1992; participant Life Skills Tng., 2000, Prevention Rsch. Inst./Under 21 Tng., 2000. Longview Found. grantee, 1993, grantee Bank Fund for Cmty. Advancement; recipient Recognition of Programmic Contbn., N.H. Assn. Mid. Level Edn., 1993. Mem. Nat. Art Edn. Assn., N.H. Art Edn. Assn. (bd. dirs. 1986, juried mem. 1985-87, N.H. Art Educator 1992. Office: Newfound Meml Mid Sch Lake St Bristol NH 03222

REDMOND, ROBERT, lawyer, educator; b. Astoria, N.Y., June 18, 1934; s. George and Virginia (Greene) R.; m. Georgine Marie Richardson, May 21, 1966; children: Kelly Anne, Kimberly Marie, Christopher Robert. BA, Queens Coll., 1955; MPA, CUNY, 1962; JD, Georgetown U., 1970. Bar: D.C. 1971, Va. 1974, U.S. Supreme Ct. 1974. Commd. 2d lt. USAF, 1955, advanced through grades to lt. col., 1972, ret., 1978; served as spl. investigations officer Korea, Vietnam, W. Germany; adj. prof., acad. dir.

mil. dist. Washington Resident Ctr. Park U., Parkville, Mo., 1977—; pvt. practice Falls Church, Va., 1980—. Precinct capt. Fairfax County Rep. Party, Va., 1981-87; pres. PTO, Falls Church, 1984-86; bd. dirs. Chaconas Home Owners Assn., 1984—, Social Ctr. Psychiat. Rehab., 1987-93. Mem. ATLA, Va. Trial Lawyers Assn., Fairfax Bar Assn., Assn. Former Air Force Office Spl. Investigations Agts. (chpt. pres. 1984-86, nat. membership com. 1986—), Comml. Law League, Delta Theta Phi, K.C. (4th deg.). Roman Catholic. Home: 7802 Antiopi St Annandale VA 22003-1405 Office: Ste 700 2010 Corporate Ridge Mc Lean VA 22102-7838 Address: PO Box 2103 Falls Church VA 22042-0103 E-mail: collectlaw@aol.com.

REDSHAW, PEGGY ANN, molecular biologist, educator; b. Beardstown, Ill., Sept. 4, 1948; d. Francis Benjamin and Margaret Annabel (Lee) R.; m. Jerry Bryan Lincecum, Sept. 28, 1985. BS, Quincy Coll., 1970; PhD, Ill. State U., 1974. Postdoctoral fellow St. Louis U. Med. Sch., 1974-77; asst. prof. Wilson Coll., Chambersburg, Pa., 1977-79; from asst. to prof. Austin (Tex.) Coll., Sherman, 1979—. Leadership com. Project Kaleidoscope, Washington, 1990-96; reviewer NSF. Author: (with J.B. Lincecum and E.H. Phillips) Science on the Texas Frontier, 1997, Gideon Lincecum's Sword, 2001. Mem. AAAS, Am. Soc. Microbiology (undergrad. edn. task area for bd. edn. 1992-95). Avocation: photography. Office: Austin College 900 N Grand Ave Ste 61565 Sherman TX 75090-4400

REDWINE, ROBERT PAGE, physicist, educator; b. Raleigh, N.C., Dec. 3, 1947; s. Robert Word and Hazel Virginia (Green) R.; m. Jacqueline Nina Hewitt, Nov. 22, 1986; children: Keith Hewitt, Jonathan Hewitt. AB, Cornell U., 1969; PhD, Northwestern U., 1973. Rsch. assoc. Los Alamos (N.Mex.) Nat. Lab, 1973-77, staff sci., 1977-79; rsch. assoc. U. Berne, Switzerland, 1974-75; asst. prof. physics MIT, Cambridge, Mass., 1979-82, assoc. prof., 1982-89, prof., 1989—, dir. lab. nuclear sci., 1992-2000, dean for undergrad. edn., 2000—. Contbr. articles to profl. jours. Fellow AAAS, Am. Phys. Soc. Office: MIT Undergrad Edn Bldg 4-110 Cambridge MA 02139

REE, DONNA, social services administrator, educator; b. Pitts., Sept. 28, 1950; d. Anthony Paul and Raphalena (Gatto) Morelli; m. Ronald Ree, June 29, 1974. BA in Edn., Point Park Coll., 1971; MS in Spl. Edn., Duquesne U., 1973; postgrad., No. Ill. U., 1989—. Cert. elem. and spl. edn. tchr., Ill. Head tchr. Turtle Creek Valley Day Care, Pitts., 1971-74; tchr. Chgo. Sch. & Workshop, 1974-76; ednl. cons. Chpt. I, Chgo., 1976-79; dir. curriculum Ada S. McKinley Community Svc., Chgo., 1979-82, dir. adminstrv. svcs., 1982-89, dir. quality assurance, 1989—. Pres. Edn. Resource Ctr., Chgo., 1982-83; sec. Near North Spl. Edn. Ctr., local sch. coun., 1999—. Mem. Am. Assn. on Mental Retardation, Nat. Coun. for Exceptional Children, Chgo. Coun. for Exceptional Children (treas. 1984-86, pres. 1986-87), Ill. Coun. for Exceptional Children (regional dir. 1987-90, pres.-elect 1991, pres. 1992-93, liaison 1997—, convention chair 1999-2000), Ill. Affiliation Pvt. Schs. for Exceptional Children (chmn. membership 1988-97), Chgo. Issues Assn. (chmn. 1990-97), Am. Soc. Quality, Phi Delta Kappa. Avocations: gourmet cooking, skiing, travel. Office: Ada S McKinley Community Svcs 725 S Wells St Chicago IL 60607-4521 E-mail: dree@adasmckinley.org.

REEB, W. SUZANNE, retired middle school educator; b. Glascow, Ky., Jan. 14, 1932; d. Arthur Henry and Wilma (Kolb) R. BA, Asbury Coll., 1955; Assoc. BS, Henry Ford C.C., 1960. Tchr. ctrl. elem. sch. grade 2 Fairborn (Ohio) City Schs., 1960-61, tchr. south elem. grade 5, 1961-65; tchr. social studies Lake Wales (Fla.) H.S., Polk County Sch. Bd., 1965-67; tchr. phys. edn. Avon Park (Fla.) Elem. Sch., Highlands County Sch. Bd., 1967-68, tchr. 5th and 6th grades, 1968-71, tchr. 7th and 8th grade Avon Park Mid. Sch., 1971—2000. Basketball coach Avon Park Mid. Sch., 1973-81, nat. jr. honor soc. peer tutor program, 1990-92, nat. geography bee coach, 1992-95, dept. chmn., team chmn., sch. improvement com. chmn., others, 1966-2000; mem. Polk coun. social studies Polk Edn. Assn., 1964-66. Vol. sch. nurse Avon Park Mid. Sch., 1971-93. Mem. NEA, Nat. Coun. for the Social Studies, Highlands County for the Social Studies, Highlands County Edn. Assn. Home: 2022 N Scenic Hwy Babson Park FL 33827-9798

REECE, GERALDINE MAXINE, elementary education educator; b. L.A., May 13, 1917; d. Charles Kenneth and Bertha (Austin) Ballou; m. Thomas Charles Bauman, Aug. 16, 1942 (div. Oct. 1971); children: Thomas Charles Bauman, Jr., Kathleen Marie Bauman Messenger, Stephen Kenneth Bauman; m. Wilbert Wallingford Reece, Nov. 3, 1973 (dec. 1988). AA, L.A. City Coll., 1942; BA, U. So. Calif., L.A., 1966. Specialist tchr. in reading, elem. edn. Tchr. Archdiocese of L.A., Altadena, Calif., 1962-66; master tchr. Alhambra (Calif.) City and H.S., 1966-79, writer multicultural component early childhood edn. program. Author poetry. Mem. San Gabriel Child Care Task Force, 1984-86; mem. steering com. West San Gabriel Valley Cmty. Awareness Forum, 1985-87; past pres. women's divsn., bd. dirs. San Gabriel C. of C., 1989-90, 98—, publicity chair, 1994-98, incoming pres. women's divsn., 1998—; mem. sch. site and facilities com. Sch. Dist. Unification, San Gabriel, 1992-93; mem. task force Episcopal Parish/Healing Our Cities, San Gabriel, 1992-93; docent San Gabriel Mus., 1989, 92-93; mem. Hearing Our Voice anti-violence com. Episcopal Parish. Recipient Exceptional Svc. awards Am. Heart Assn., West San Gabriel Valley, 1990, 91, 93, 94, 95, Dedicated Svc. award San Gabriel C. of C., 1989, Outstanding and Dedicated Cmty. Svc. award Fedn. Cmty. Coord. Couns., San Gabriel, 1986, 87, 97-98, others, Woman of Yr. award City of San Gabriel, 1994, Diamond Homer trophy Famous Poet Soc., 1995, 96; named Outstanding Older Am., City of San Gabriel, 1999; scholarship named in her honor Divsn. 1 Calif. Ret. Tchrs. Assn. Mem. AAUW (Money Talks sect. chairperson 1981-82, corr. sec.-treas. Alhambra-San Gabriel 1982-85), Calif. Ret. Tchrs. Assn. (pres. 1989-91, Outstanding Svc. plaque 1994, divsn. 1 scholarship named in her honor 1998, bd. dirs. 1999—), DAR (3rd vice regent 1994—, 1st Pl. Poetry award 1996, 3d Pl. Poetry award 1998), Pasadena Women's City Club, St. Francis Guild, San Gabriel Ret. Tchrs. (pres. 1985-89, cmty. rep. 1990-97), San Gabriel Hist. Assn., San Gabriel Cmty. Coord. Coun. (pres. 1986, 1st v.p. 1997-98). Democrat. Episcopalian. Avocations: reading, bridge, writing poetry, stitchery.

REECE, MARILYN KING, college dean; b. Cullman, Ala., July 7, 1949; d. John McCarley and Florence Augusta (Freeman) King; m. John Robert Williamson, Aug. 23, 1970 (div. 1987); children: Joan King, Rachel King; m. David Ronald Reece, Apr. 15, 1995. BA, U. Ala., Tuscaloosa, 1971, MA, 1972. Instr. English, N.E. Ala. C.C., Rainsville, 1973-89, dean extended day, 1989—. Mem. AAUW, MLA, NEA, Nat. Coun. Tchrs. English, Conf. on Coll. Composition and Comm., Ala. Assn. for Women in Edn. Democrat. Office: NE Ala CC PO Box 159 Rainsville AL 35986-0159

REECE-PORTER, SHARON ANN, international human rights educator; b. Cin., Nov. 28, 1953; d. Edward and Claudia (Ownes) Reece; divorced, 1981; children: Erika Lynn, Melanie Joyce. BS in Textiles and Clothing, Edgecliff Coll., 1975; cert. clerical computer, So. Ohio Coll., 1984; MEd in Gen. Edn., SUNY, Buffalo, 1994; PhD in Internat. Human Rights Devel., Brentwick U., London, 2000; EdD in Global Edn. (hon.), Australian Inst. Coordinated Rsch., Victoria, 1995; postgrad. in photojournalism/profl. photography, NY Inst. Photography, 2002—. Cert. tchr., Ohio. Dept. supr., asst. buyer Mabley & Carew, Cin., 1975-76; claims adjuster Allstate Ins. Co., Cin., 1976-78; sales merchandiser Ekco Houseware, Cin., 1979-80; sales rep. Met. Life Inc., Cin., 1981-83; info. processing specialist GPA/Robert Half/Word Source, Cin., Dallas, 1985-87; tchr. adult edn. Princeton City Schs., Cin., 1984-90; with Rainbow Internat. Non-Profit Adult Ednl. Rsch. Ctr., Honolulu, 1990-98, Norfolk, Va., 1998—; edn. specialist rsch. found. SUNY, Buffalo, 1993. Prof. computer sci. So. Ohio Tech. and Bus. Coll., Cin., 1986-90; computer software tng. cons., 1987-89; part-time tchr. adult GED classes Adult Learning Ctr. Buffalo Bd. Edn., 1994-95; participant Am. Forum for Global Edn., Honolulu; lectr. photography N.Y. Inst. Photography, N.Y.C., N.Y., 2002—. Tutor U.S. div. Internat. Laubach Literacy, Clermont County, Ohio, 1984. Fellow Australian Inst. for Coordinated Rsch. (life); mem. NAFE, ASTD, Internat. DOS Users Group, Am. Ednl. Rsch. Assn., Nat. Assn. Women Bus. Owners, UN Assn., World Assn. Women Entrepreneurs, Assn. Baha'i Studies in Australia, Boston Computer Soc., Cin. Orgn. Data Processing Educators and Trainers, Internat. Platform Assn., Cin. C. of C. (cert. minority supplier devel. coun.). Baha'I. Home: 2941 Chilton Pl Virginia Beach VA 23456 Office: Rainbows Global Human Rights Inst 4221-125 Pleasant Valley Rd @ 172 Virginia Beach VA 23464 E-mail: Sharaocean@aol.com., SharonAnHumanRts@aol.com.

REED, ALFRED DOUGLAS, retired academic administrator; b. Bristol, Tenn., July 18, 1928; s. Roy Theodore and Elizabeth Brown (Tuft) R.; m. Emily Joyce Freeman, Mar. 18, 1950; children: Roy Frederick, Robert Douglas, David Clark, Timothy Wayne, Joseph William. AB, Erskine Coll., Due West, S.C., 1949. Reporter Citizen-Times, Asheville, N.C., 1949-51, city editor, 1953-60, mng. editor, 1962-63, assoc. editor, 1963-66, capital corr., 1959-66; asst. editor The Presbyn. Jour., Weaverville, N.C., 1951-52; assoc. editor Shelby (N.C.) Daily Star, 1961-62; dir. pub. info. Western Carolina U., Cullowhee, NC, 1966-96, asst. to the chancellor, 1996—2002. Cons. Devel. Office, East Carolina U., Greenville, 1980; bd. dirs. Wachovia Bank, Sylva, N.C., 1969—. Author: Prologue, 1968, Decade of Development, 1984; exec. editor: Western, The Mag. of Western Carolina University, 1991-96. Mem. Asheville City Bd. Edn., 1958-62; vice chmn. bd. dirs. Sta. WCQS FM, Western N.C. Pub. Radio Inc., Asheville, 1978-88; bd. dirs., mem. exec. com. Cherokee Hist. Assn., 1985—, Western N.C. Assn. Cmtys., 1985-2001, Jackson County Fund of N.C. Cmty. Found., 1991-93; mem. Hunter Libr. Adv. Bd., 1991-98, Pack Place Adv. Coun., Asheville, 1991-95. Recipient Paul A. Reid Disting. Svc. award Western Carolina U., 1980, Disting. Svc. award, 1996. Mem. Pub. Rels. Assn. Western N.C. (bd. dirs. 1988-98, treas. 1966-86), Coll. News Assn. Carolinas (bd. dirs. 1968-71, 80-82), Smoky Mountain Host Assn. (bd. dirs., 1st v.p. 1994-96, pres. 1996-98), Great Smoky Mountains Assn. (bd. dirs. 1998-2002). Democrat. Presbyterian. Avocations: travel, stamps, gardening. Home: 931 University Heights Rd Cullowhee NC 28723-6953

REED, CATHY LORRAINE, elementary education educator; b. Beckley, W.Va., Sept. 23, 1956; d. Clarence and Beulah mae (Perdue) R. AA, Beckley Coll., 1977; BS in Edn., Concord Coll., Athens, W.Va., 1979; MA, Marshall U., 1989. Cert. tchr. elem. edn. 1-6, reading specialist K-12, W.Va. Tchr. Raleigh County Bd. Edn., Beckley, 1979—. Avocations: sewing, reading, travel. Office: Shady Spring Elem PO Box 2009 Shady Spring WV 25918

REED, CHARLES BASS, chief academic administrator; b. Harrisburg, Pa., Sept. 29, 1941; s. Samuel Ross and Elizabeth (Johnson) R.; m. Catherine A. Sayers, Aug. 22, 1964; children: Charles B. Jr., Susan Allison. BS, George Washington U., 1963, MS, 1964, EdD, 1970; postgrad. Summer Inst. for Chief State Sch. Officers, Harvard U. Grad Sch. Edn., 1977; D of Pub. Svc. (hon.), George Washington U., 1987; LLD (hon.), Stetson U., 1987; LHD (hon.), St. Thomas U., 1988; LittD (hon.), Waynesburg Coll., 1990; d of the U. (hon.), British Open U., 2000. From asst. prof. to assoc. prof. George Washington U., Washington, 1963—70; asst. dir. Nat. Performance-Based Tchr. Edn. Project, Am. Assn. Colls. for Tchr. Edn., Washington, 1970—71; assoc. for planning and coordination Fla. Dept. Edn., Tallahassee, 1971—75, dir. Office Ednl. Planning, Budgeting, and Evaluation, 1975—79; edn. policy coord. Exec. Office of Gov., Tallahassee, 1979—80, dir. legis. affairs, 1980—81, dep. chief of staff, 1981—84, chief of staff, 1984—85; chancellor State Univ. System Fla., Tallahassee, 1985—98, Calif. State U. Sys., Long Beach, 1988—. Mem. Nat. Commn. on H.S. Sr. Yr., Pres. Leadership Group, Higher Edn. Ctr. for Alcohol and Other Drug Prevention, Coll. Edn. Nat. Bd., Policy Bd., EdVoice; mem. Rand Edn. Adv. Bd; bd. dirs. Nat. Ctr. for Ednl. Accountability, Mem. Coun. for Advancement and Support of Edn., Coun. on Fgn. Rels., Bus.-Higher Edn. Forum. Disting. fellow,Fullbright Commn. 50th Anniversary, Peru, 1996. Mem. Am. Assn. State Colls. and Univs., Am. Assn. for Higher Edn., Am. Coun. on Edn., Assn. Governing Bds. of Univs. and Colls., Nat. Assn. State Univs. and Land-Grant Colls., Nat. Assn. Sys. Heads, Internat. Assn. Univ. Presidents, Hispanic Assn. Colls. and Univs. Democrat. Roman Catholic. Office: Calif State U Office Chancellor 401 Golden Shore St Fl 6 Long Beach CA 90802-4210 E-mail: creed@calstate.edu.*

REED, ELIZABETH MAY MILLARD, mathematics and computer science educator, publisher; b. Shippensburg, Pa., July 1, 1919; d. Jacob Franklin and Isabelle Bernadine (Dorn) Millard; m. Jesse Floyd Reed, Aug. 5, 1961; 1 child, David Millard. BA, Shepherd Coll., 1941; MA, Columbia U., 1948; postgrad., W.Va. U., U. Hawaii, Columbia U., NSF Summer Insts., Oakland U., 1974-85. Cert. assoc. in tchr. edn., W.Va. Math. tchr. Hedgesville (W.Va.) High Sch., 1941-47, Martinsburg (W.Va.) High Sch., 1948-51, George Washington High Sch. and Territorial Coll. Guam, Agana, 1952-54, Valley Stream (N.Y.) Meml. Jr. High Sch., 1954-55, Rye (N.Y.) High Sch., 1955-57, Elkins (W.Va.) Jr. High Sch., 1971-87; dir. admissions Davis and Elkins Coll., 1957-67, asst. prof. math., 1968-71, adj. prof., 1987—, lectr. geography, 1971-73; pres. Three Reeds Studios, Elkins, 1989—; Vets. Upward Bound, 1989-94. Statis. clk. Lord, Abbett & Co., N.Y.C., 1947-48; customer rep. Kay, Richards & Co., Winchester, Va., 1951-52; mem. adj. grad. faculty W.Va. U., Morgantown, 1984-89; mem. adj. faculty Evans Coll. U. Charleston, W.Va., 1989-90; presenter regional and state computer workshops, W.Va. Author: Computer Literacy at Elkins Junior High School, 1983; project dir. (video) Women: Professionally Speaking, 1988. Dir. pilot project Project Bus., Jr. Achievement, Elkins, 1972-78; organizer Randolph County Math. Field Day, Elkins, 1977; initiator Comprehensive Achievement Monitoring, Elkins, 1980; treas. Humanities Found. W.Va., Charleston, 1983-85, pres., 1985-87; vice-moderator quadrant II Presbytery of W.Va. Recipient Presdl. award for Excellence in Tchg. Math. in W.Va., NSF, 1985. Mem. AAUW (pres. W.Va. divsn. 1977-79, editor 1983—, pres. Elkins br. 1966-68, 88-94, 97-98), W.Va. Coun. Tchrs. of Math., Nat. Coun. Tchrs. of Math., W.Va. Item Writing Workshop-Math. 9-12 (writer 1985-86). Avocations: travel, photography, reading mysteries, sewing, needlepoint. Home and Office: 4 Lincoln Ave Elkins WV 26241-3669

REED, GINA FULTON, mathematics educator; m. Johnny Carl Reed; 1 child, Michael. BS, Appalachian State U., Boone, N.C., 1983, MA, 1985, Pa. State U., 1990. Grad. teaching asst. Appalachian State U., Boone, 1983-85, instr., 1985-86, N.E. Mo. State U., Kirksville, 1986-88; grad. teaching asst. Pa. State U., State College, 1989-90; assoc. prof. math. Gainesville (Ga.) Coll., 1990—. Mem. Math. Assn. Am., Am. Statis. Assn., Am. Math. Assn. of Two Yr. Colls., Pi Mu Epsilon (chpt. pres. 1984). Office: Gainesville College PO Box 1358 Gainesville GA 30503-1358

REED, JACQUELINE K(EMP), educational researcher; b. Newark, June 12, 1947; d. Thomas and Jessie (Bullock) R.; 1 child, Cecil Bernard Brown Jr. BA, U. Ill., Chgo., 1970; MA, Northeastern Ill. U., 1976; PhD, U. Wis., 1978. Rsch. asst. U. Ill., Chgo., 1970-72; zonal coord. Model Cities-Chgo. Com. on Urban Opportunities, Chgo., 1972-73; vocat. specialist Model Cities-CCUO, Chgo., 1973-74, child care tng. coord., 1974-76; program coord. U. Wis., Madison, 1977-79; post-doctoral rsch. fellow Mich. State U., East Lansing, 1979-80; acting asst. dean U. Md., College Park, 1980-81; rsch. assoc. D.C. Pub. Schs., Washington, 1983-85; spl. asst. U. Md., College Park, 1985-89; instructional rsch. coord. Prince George's County Pub. Schs., Upper Marlboro, Md., 1989—. Resource colleague Human Rels. Commn., Evanston, Ill., 1971; reviewer U.S. Dept. Edn., Washington, 1979-81; cons. NEA, Washington, 1982; adv. com. P.G. County Correctional Ctr., Upper Marlboro, 1990—; presenter in field. Contbr. chpt. to book and articles to profl. jours. Exec. bd. Eleanor Roosevelt High Sch. PTSA, Greenbelt, Md., 1980-84; vol. United Communities Against Poverty, Capitol Heights, Md., 1987-89, Md. Higher Edn. Commn., Prince George's County Commn. Women, 1990; bd. dirs. Towns of Kettering, Upper Marlboro, 1992; rep. to NGO Forum on Women, UN 4th World Conf. on Women, Beijing, mem. Prince George's County Commn. for Women, 1997—. Recipient Vol. award United Communities Against Poverty, Capitol Heights, 1989. Mem. AAUW (membership chari Bowie br. 1997), Nat. Assn. Multi-Cultural Edn. (exec. bd. mem. 1990—, editorial bd. mem. 1990—), Am. Ednl. Rsch. Assn., Nat. Coun. Negro Women, Inc., U. Ill. Alumni Assn., U. Wis. Alumni Assn., Md. Choral Soc., Phi Delta Kappa, Pi Lambda Theta (eligibility co-chair 1977-78). Democrat. Office: Prince Georges Pub Sch Divsn Instrn Rm 201F 14201 School Ln Upper Marlboro MD 20772-2866

REED, JOAN-MARIE, special education educator; b. St. Paul, Sept. 8, 1960; d. William Martin Reed and Diana-Marie (Miller) Reed Moss. BA, U. Minn., 1982, BS, 1983; MEd, Tex. Woman's U., 1986. Cert. tchr., Tex. Tchr. emotionally disturbed Birdville Ind. Sch. Dist., Ft. Worth, 1984-86, Goose Creek Ind. Sch. Dist., Baytown, Tex., 1986-92, ctr. leader, 1992-93, dept. chairperson, 1987-91; tchr. emotionally disturbed Conroe (Tex.) Ind. Sch. Dist., 1993-94, Willis (Tex.) Ind. Sch. Dist., 1994-95, Jefferson County Pub. Schs., 1995—. Co-editor: New Teacher Handbook, 1986-87, Behavior Improvement Program Handbook, 1987-88, New Teacher Mentor, 1997—, Student Teacher Supervisor, 1997, 99-2000. Mem. NEA, Coun. for Exceptional Children. Congregationalist. Avocations: reading, cooking, travelling, running. Office: Drake Mid Sch 12550 W 52nd Ave Arvada CO 80002

REED, JOHN HOWARD, school administrator; b. Bloomfield, Mo., July 14, 1934; s. Floyd John and Lena Joyce (Howard) R.; m. Weymuth Heuiser; children: Cathy, David. BS cum laude, SE Mo. State U., 1956; M., U. Mo., 1959; edn. specialist, SE Mo. State U., 1977; PhD, So. Ill. U., 1983. Cert. supt., prin., tchr. Tchr., coach Scott County R-6 Schs., Sikeston, Mo., 1956-63; supr. student tchr. SE Mo. State U., Cape Girardeau, 1963-75; prin. Scott County R-3 Schs., Oran, Mo., 1975-76; supt. schs. Scott County R-2 Schs., Chaffee, Mo., 1976-79; bus. mgr. SE Mo. State U., Cape Girardeau, 1980-83; dean, pres. Sikeston C.C., 1983-86; supt. Marion County Sch. Dist. 1, Centralia, Ill., 1986-88; head New Life Montessori Sch., Shreveport, La., 1989-90, Belleview Schs. and Coll., Westminster, Colo., 1990—. Editor: History of Missouri National Guard, 1963. Bd. dirs., sec. Scott County Bd. Edn., Benton, Mo., 1970-79. Lt. col. U.S. Army, 1960-63. Mem. Rotary (sec. 1976-78), Phi Alpha Theta (pres. 1976-78). Baptist. Avocation: history. Home: 8175 Green Ct Westminster CO 80031-4101 Office: Belleview Schs 3455 W 83rd Ave Westminster CO 80031-4005

REED, JOHN KENNEDY EMANUEL, elementary school teacher; b. Shelby, Tenn., July 9, 1966; s. Robert and Gail Patrick (Caple) R. AA in Tech. and English, Milw. Area Tech. Coll., 1989; student, Clark Atlanta U., 1990. Field agt. Blue Arrow Flexi-Force, Milw., 1988-93; team leader Washington Inventory Svcs., Milw., 1989; tech. paraprofl. tchr. Milw. Pub. Schs. Sys., 1993—2003. Sch. implementor Silver Spring Elem Sch., Milw., 1993, mentor coord., 1993, newspaper sr. editor, 1993-97, tech. coord., 1993-2001. Author and editor (games with books), Star Venture: RPG, 1991, Professor X: RPG, 1996. Mem. Celestial Defender Assn. (founder and CEO 1994—). Home and Office: Celestial Defender Assn 3832 W Nash St Milwaukee WI 53216-3034

REED, JOSEPH RAYMOND, civil engineering educator, academic administrator; b. Pitts., Aug. 15, 1930; s. David Raymond and Mary (O'Neil) R.; m. Mary Morris Leggett, Mar. 19, 1960; children: Michelle Edwards, Stephanie Anne Reed Wilkinson, David Shepard Reed. BS in Civil Engring., Pa. State U., 1952, MS in Civil Engring., 1955; PhD in Civil Engring., Cornell U., 1971. Registered profl. engr., Tex. Asst. engr. George H. McGinness Assocs., Pitts., 1953-55; constrn. liaison officer USAF, Dallas, 1956-59; civil engring. faculty Pa. State U., University Park, 1959-64; rsch. asst. Cornell U., Ithaca, N.Y., 1964-67; prof. civil engring. Pa. State U., 1967-95, prof. emeritus, 1996. Cons. Westvaco, Tyrone, Pa., 1981, Ketron, Inc., Phila., 1982-83, McGraw-Hill Book Co., N.Y.C., 1984-91, MacMillan Pub. Co., N.Y.C., 1987, others; acad. officer dept. civil engring. Pa. State U., 1989-95. Chmn. Stormwater Authority, State College, Pa., 1974-78; coach State College Little League, Teener League (All-Star team state championship 1986) and Am. Legion Baseball, State College, 1978-89. Capt. USAF, 1956-59, USAFR, 1959-71. Sci.-Faculty fellow NSF, 1966-67; recipient Adviser Leadership award Tau Beta Pi Assn., 1986. Mem. ASCE, Internat. Assn. Hydraulic Rsch., Elks, Scottish Rite, Sigma Xi, Tau Beta Pi, Chi Epsilon, Phi Sigma Kappa (v.p. 1952). Presbyterian. Avocations: golf, bowling, youth baseball. Home: 1394 Penfield Rd State College PA 16801-6419 Office: Pa State U Dept Civil Engring 212 Sackett Bldg University Park PA 16802-1408

REED, JOSEPH WAYNE, American studies educator, artist; b. St. Petersburg, Fla., May 31, 1932; s. Joseph Wayne and Gertrude (Cain) R.; m. Kit Craig, Dec. 10, 1955; children: Joseph McKean, John Craig, Katherine Hyde Maruyama. BA, Yale U., 1954, MA, 1958, PhD, 1961. Rsch. asst. Yale Libr., 1956-57; instr. English Wesleyan U., Middletown, Conn., 1960-61, assoc. prof., 1967-71, prof., 1971—, chmn. dept., 1971-73, 75-76, 85-86, prof. English and Am. studies, 1987. Vis. lectr. Yale U., New Haven, 1974; lectr. U.S. dept. State and USIS, Can., India, Nepal, 1974; coord. cultural exch., New Delhi, Bombay, 1992; coord. music and writing workshop U. Va., Georgetown U., others. Author: English Biography in the Early Nineteenth Century, 1801-38, 1966, Faulkner's Narrative, 1973, Three American Originals: John Ford, William Faulkner, Charles Ives, 1984, American Scenarios, 1989; editor: Barbara Bodichon's American Diary, 1972, (with W.S. Lewis) Horace Walpole's Family Correspondence, 1975, (with F.A. Pottle) Boswell, Laird of Auchinleck, 1977, 2d edit., 1994; one-man shows include Portal Gallery, London, 1971, USIS Libr., New Delhi, 1974, 92, Addison/Ripley Gallery, Washington, 1987, 92, 95, 98. Chmn. Wesleyan Sesquicentennial, 1982; chmn. bd. trustees Yale Libr. Assocs., 1984-2000, hon. trustee, 2000—. Lt. (j.g.) USNR, 1954-56. Mem. Elizabethan Club, The Johnsonians (chmn. 1988). Democrat. Episcopalian. Home: 45 Lawn Ave Middletown CT 06457-3135 E-mail: jreed@wesleyan.edu.

REED, LEONARD NEWTON, secondary school educator; b. Alva, Okla., Feb. 27, 1952; s. Leonard S. and Vevian M. (Chew) R. BA, Northwestern Okla. State U., 1970, MA, 1980; postgrad., No. Ariz. U., 1982-89; cert. ESL, U. Phoenix, 1992. Cert. social sci. tchr., Ariz., Okla., ESL, Ariz. Tchr. social sci. Chinle Unified Sch. Dist., Ariz., 1974—, chair dept. social sci., 1982-91, 96—; night staff Diné Coll., 1988—. Student coun. advisor Chinle Unified Sch. Dist., 1975-76, 78-83, 84-93. Mem. com. Apache County (Ariz.) Dem. Party, 1980-88, 93-96, 2001—; state del. Ariz. Dem. Party, 1980; mem. Nat. Gay and Lesbian Task Force, 1976—. NEA (gay and lesbian caucus 1988—, rural and small caucus, 1986—), Ariz. Edn. Assn. (bd. dir. 1984-88, 89-90, human rels. com. 1987-94, 95—, 99-2004, chair human rels. com. 1992-94, 99—, treas. N.E. adv. coun., Bill Hodge award 1989,AEA Human & Civil Rights Award, 2003; first male co-chair gay, lesbian caucus 1995-2001, founder 1995-2003), Ariz. Student Coun. Advisors Assn., Chinle Edn. Assn. (past pres. 1979, 81, treas.). Home: PO Box 1678 Chinle AZ 86503-1678 Office: Chinle Unified Sch Dist # 24 PO Box 587 Chinle AZ 86503-0587 E-mail: lenny727@alva.ok.net.

REED, LESTER JAMES, biochemist, educator; b. New Orleans, Jan. 3, 1925; s. John T. and Sophie (Pastor) R.; m. Janet Louise Gruschow, Aug. 7, 1948; children: Pamela, Sharon, Richard, Robert. BS, Tulane U., 1943; D.Sc. (hon.), 1977; PhD, U. Ill., 1946. Rsch. asst. NDRC, Urbana, Ill.,

1944-46; rsch. assoc. biochemistry Cornell U. Med. Coll., 1946-48; faculty U. Tex., Austin, 1948—, prof. chemistry, 1958—, Ashbel Smith prof., 1984-99, prof. emeritus, 1999—; rsch. sci. Clayton Found. Biochem. Inst., 1949—. Assoc. dir., Clayton Found. Biochem. Inst., 1962-63, dir., 1963-96. Contbr. articles profl. jours. Mem. NAS, Am. Acad. Arts and Scis., Am. Soc. for Biochemistry and Molecular Biology (Merck award 1994), Am. Chem. Soc. (Eli Lilly & Co. award in biol. chemistry 1958), Phi Beta Kappa, Sigma Xi. Home: 3502 Balcones Dr Austin TX 78731-5802 Office: Dept Chem and Biochem 1 Univ Station A5300 Austin TX 78712 E-mail: lreed@mail.utexas.edu.

REED, NANCY BOYD, English language and elementary education educator; b. Lodi, Calif., Oct. 10, 1946; d. Leo H. and Anna Gwen (Coombes) Boyd; m. Maurice Allen Reed, Dec. 22, 1966; 1 child, Scot Alastair. AA Recreational Adminstrn. with honors, Delta Coll., 1974; BA Recreational Adminstrn. with honors, Calif. State U., Sacramento, 1976, MA in Edn., English Lang. Devel., 1988; cert. computers in edn., U. Calif., Davis, 1984. Cert. multiple subject, phys. edn., computers in edn. teaching. Tchr. 4th grade Hagginwood Sch., Sacramento, 1980-81; tchr. 4th/5th grade impacted lang. Noralto Sch., Sacramento, 1981-88, bilingual resource tchr., 1988-91, tchr. English lang. devel., 1991-96, English language resource tchr., 1996-98; mentor tchr. North Sacramento Sch. Dist., Sacramento, 1992-95, bilingual resource tchr., 1996-98, English lang. devel. curriculum assoc., 1997-98, ednl. cons., 1998—; English lang. resource tchr. Woodlake Sch., Sacramento, 2001—. Fellow, tchr./cons. No. Calif. Math. Project, U. Calif., Davis, 1985—. Dir. Jasmine Flower Dancers, Sacramento, 1984-96; comty. rep. Am. Host Found., Sacramento, 1976—. Named Outstanding Educator Capitol Svc. Ctr., 1992, Tchr. of Yr., Noralto Sch., North Sacramento Sch., 1996; scholar Fridtjof-Nansen-Akademie, Ingleheim, Germany, 1993, Adenauer Found., Berlin, 1982, 93. Mem. NEA, Nat. Vis. Tchrs. Assn. (bd. dirs. 1994—), Nat. Assn. Bilingual Edn., Nat. Coun. Tchrs. Math., Calif. Tchrs. Assn. (state coun. rep. 1995-96), North Sacramento Edn. Assn. (sec. 1986-88, v.p. 1988-90, pres. 1990-92, outstanding educator 1992). Avocations: travel, photography, camping. Home: 3665 Halter Ct Sacramento CA 95821-3266 Office: Woodlake Sch North Sacramento Sch Dist 700 Southgate Rd Sacramento CA 95815-1605 E-mail: nancyboydreed@hotmail.com.

REED, NANCY ELLEN, computer science educator; b. Mpls., Aug. 11, 1955; d. Jacob Alen and Mary Emeline (Howser) Lundgren; m. Todd Randall Reed, June 18, 1977. BS in Biology, U. Minn., 1977, MS in Computer Sci., 1988, PhD in Computer Sci., 1995. Rsch. lab. technician gastroenterology rsch. unit Mayo Clinic, Rochester, Minn., 1978-81; phys. sci. technician U.S. Environ. Hygiene Agy., Fitzsimmons Army Med. Ctr., Aurora, Colo., 1982-83; profl. rsch. asst. molecular, cellular, devel. biology dept. U. Colo., Boulder, 1983-84; tchg. asst. U. Minn., 1985-86, rsch. asst., 1985-88; computer programmer Control Data Corp., Arden Hills, Minn., 1986; asst. Artificial Intelligence Lab. Swiss Fed. Inst. Tech., Lausanne, 1989-91; lectr. computer and info. sci. dept. Sonoma State U., Rohnert Park, Calif., 1993-94; lectr. U. Calif., Davis, 1994-95, 96, rschr., 1995, asst. adj. prof. computer sci. dept., 1996—2002; asst. prof. dept. computer and info. sci. Linköping (Sweden) U., 1998—2002; asst. prof. dept. elec. engrs., U. Hawaii, 2002—. Contbr. articles to profl. jours.; presenter in field; spkr. in field; reviewer for Artificial Intelligence in Medicine, Internat. Jour. of Man-Machine Studies, Integrated Computer-Aided Engring. Microelectronic and Info. Scis. Fellowship, 1984-85, Am. Electronics Assn. Fellowship, 1985-89. Mem. IEEE, AAUP, Am. Assn. for Artificial Intelligence (scholarship for travel nat. conf. on artificial intelligence 1992, 94, session chair for spring syposium 1994), Assn. for Computing Machinery, Am. Med. Informatics Assoc., Am. Heart Assoc. Office: Univ Hawaii Dept Elec Engring 2540 Dole St 483 Holmes Hall Honolulu HI 96822

REED, RICHARD JOHN, retired meteorology educator; b. Braintree, Mass., June 18, 1922; s. William Amber and Gertrude Helen (Volk) R.; m. Joan Murray, June 10, 1950; children: Ralph Murray, Richard Cobden, Elizabeth Ann. Student, Boston Coll., 1940-41, Dartmouth Coll., 1943-44; BS, Calif. Inst. Tech., 1945; ScD, MIT, 1949. Research staff mem. MIT, Cambridge, 1950-54; asst. prof. dept. atmospheric scis. U. Wash., Seattle, 1954-58, assoc. prof., 1958-63, prof., 1963-91, prof. emeritus, 1991—. Cons. U.S. Weather Service, Suitland, Md., 1961-62, European Ctr. for Medium Range Weather Forecasts, Reading, Eng., 1985-86; exec. scientist NRC, Washington, 1968-69; trustee Univ. Corp. for Atmospheric Research, Boulder, Colo., 1987-92. Served to lt. (j.g.) USN, 1942-46. Fellow AAAS, Am. Meteorol. Soc. (pres. 1972, Meisinger award 1964, Second Half Century award 1972, Charles Franklin Brooks award 1983, Carl-Gustaf Rossby Rsch. medal 1989, hon. mem. 1999), Royal Meteorol. Soc. (hon. mem. 2000), Am. Geophys. Union; mem. NAS. Democrat. Unitarian Universalist. Office: U Wash Box 351640 Dept Atmospheric Scis Seattle WA 98195-1640 E-mail: richardjreed1@comcast.net.

REED, SHEILA KAYE, academic administrator; b. East Prairie, Mo., Apr. 9, 1950; d. George Allen and Corine Laverne (Tyner) Turner; m. Scott Earl Reed, Oct. 18, 1975; 1 child, Scott Allen Hamilton Reed. BS in Edn., S.E. Mo. State U., 1972; postgrad., N.E. Mo. State U., 1979; MBA, Lindenwood Coll., 1986; cert. adult edn., Ctrl. Mo. State U., 1991. Cert. coord. adult edn., cert. tchr. Tchr. Potosi (Mo.) Elem. Sch., 1972-74, Hazelwood (Mo.) Armstrong Sch., 1974-80; foster care worker Div. Family Svcs., St. Charles, Mo., 1987-89; coord. adult edn. Washington (Mo.) Sch. Dist., 1989-93; coord. admissions and fin. aid Sch. Nursing Mo. Bapt. Med. Ctr., St. Louis, 1993—. Mem. adv. bd. Non-Traditional Careers, Union, Mo., 1991-93; mem. Franklin County Svc. Providers, 1992-93, Practical Nursing Program Adv. Bd., Washington, 1989-93. Bd. mem. Acad. Sacred Heart, St. Charles, Mo., 1989-91; chair Mktg. Com. for centennial celebration Mo. Bapt. Med. Ctr. Sch. Nursing, 1994-95. Recipient Certs. of Appreciation Enactment Com., Washington Sch. Dist./East Ctrl. Coll., 1991, Speaker for Todays Women Seminar, East Ctrl. Coll., 1991. Mem. Am. Vocat. Assn., Mo. Assn. Cmty. and Continuing Educators (bd. mem. for bus. and industry 1991-94, planning com.), Mo. Assn. Customized Trainers, Mo. Vocat. Assn. Avocations: photography, travel, racquetball, horseback riding. Office: Mo Bapt Med Ctr Sch Nursing 3015 N Ballas Rd Saint Louis MO 63131-2329

REED, SUELLEN KINDER, school system administrator; BA in History, Polit. Sci. and Secondary Edn., Hanover Coll., 1967; MA in Elem. Edn. and History, Ball State U., 1970, PhD in Adminstrn. and Supervision; postgrad., Fla. Atlantic U., U. Scranton, Purdue U., Earlham Coll., Ind. U., Ind. State U. Cert. secondary tchr., elem. tchr., gifted and talented tchr., administr., supr., Fla., Ind., supt., Ind. Tchr. 5th and 6th grades Rushville (Ind.) Consol. Sch. Corp., 1967-70, asst. supt., 1987-91, supt., 1991-93; tchr. Shelbyville (Ind.) High Sch., 1970-71; tchr. 6th, 7th and 8th grade social studies, curriculum Broward County (Fla.) Sch. Corp., 1971-76; tchr. Rushville Jr. High Sch., 1976-77; asst. prin. Rushville Elem. Sch., 1977-79; prin. Frazee Elem. Sch., Connersville, Ind., 1979-87; asst. supt. Rushville Consolidated Schs., 1987-90, supt., 1991-93; supt. pub. instrn., chairperson bd. edn., CEO dept. edn. State of Indiana, Indpls., 1993—. Pres.-elect Coun. of Chief State Sch. Officers (CCSSO), pres., 2001—02, v.p., 2002—. Pres. N. Ctrl. Regional Edn. Lab., Oak Brook, Ill.; bd. trustees Hanover Coll., Commn. Drug-Free Ind. Commn. Cmty. Svc., Ind. Higher Edn. Telecom. Sys., Rush County Cmty. Found., Ctr. Agrl. Sci. Heritage; adv. council Ball State U., Sch. Continuing Studies Pub. Svc. (Outstanding Sch. Edn. Alumnus award 1994); bd. dirs. Nat. Children's Film Festival. Recipient Outstanding Svc. Pub. Interest award Ind. Optometric Assn., 1996, Ind. Crime Prevention Coalition award, 1996. Mem. ASCD (nat. and Ind. chpts.), Internat. Reading Assn., Nat. Assn. Elem. Sch. Prins. (assoc.), Ind. Assn. Pub. Sch. Supts., Ind. Assn. Elem. and Mid. Sch. Prins. (assoc.), Ind. Assn., Network Woman Adminstrs., Indpls. Zoo, Indpls. Art Mus., Bus. and Profl. Women of Rushville, Altrusa Club Connersville (chmn. internat. rels. 1979-87), Connersville Area Reading Coun., Smithsonian, Rushville County Players, Rotary (Rushville chpt.), Monday Cir., Delta Kappa Gamma (past pres., Phi Lambda Theta, Phi Delta Kappa (Conner Prairie), K-12 Compact Learning, Citizenship, Edn. Commn. States, Council Chief State Sch. Officers (pres.-elect.) Office: Superintendent Edn Dept 229 State House Indianapolis IN 46204-2798

REED, THOMAS LEE, II, minister, social worker, educator; b. Kansas City, Jan. 9, 1964; s. Thomas Lee and Kathleen E. (Green) R. BA in Preaching, Okla. Christian, 1986; BS in Edn., Mo. Southern State Coll., Joplin, 1994. Cert. elem. edn. Assoc. min Ch. of Christ, Nevada, Mo., 1986-89; music min. Plymouth, Ind., 1989; assoc. min., 1990-98; clin. tchr. 3rd grade Mo. Sch. Dist., Joplin, 1992; practicum tchr. Early Childhood Devel. Ctr. MSSC, Joplin, Mo., 1993; student tchr. 4th grade Web City (Mo.) Sch. Dist., 1994; social worker Pathways Comty. Behavioral Healthcare, El Dorado Springs, Mo., 1999—. Music dir. Ch. of Christ, Nevada, Mo., 1981—89, youth dir., 1990, youth min., 84, dir. religious edn., 1986—. Recipient Key Charitable Fund scholarship, 1993, Selected for Acad. fellowship Mo. So. State Coll., Oxford U., Eng., 1994. Mem.: Phi Eta Sigma. Mem. Churches of Christ. Avocations: music composition, writing, vocal performance, drawing, painting. E-mail: zysogus@hotmail.com.

REED, TIMOTHY MAX, secondary education educator; b. Mar. 16, 1953; BA in Polit. Sci., Calif. State U., 1984; MS in Ednl. Adminstrn., Nat. U., 1994. Activities dir. Culver City (Calif.) H.S., 1990-93, 97-98, restructuring coord., 1992-98; chairperson Accrediting Commn. for Schs., Burlingame, Calif., 1996—2000; advanced placement instr. Govt. and Econ., 2000—. Home: 4203 Gilbert Ave Apt 222 Dallas TX 75219-2953

REED, TRUDY FAYE, elementary school educator; b. Clay Center, Kans., Dec. 30, 1950; children: Daymian, Krystal, Darrin, Kaysie. AA, Cloud County Community Coll., 1970; BS summa cum laude, Kans. State U., Manhattan, 1990. Cert. tchr., Kans. Active in Girl Scouts, 4-H, Faith United Ch., Clifton, Kans., Am. Legion Aux.; elder, Sunday Sch. tchr., dir. Vacation Bible Sch. Recipient Special Presidential award scholarship, 1990, Alumni scholarships, 1989-90, Fenix scholarship, 1989-90, Nat. Communication Edn. Soc. scholarship, Nat. Scholarship award. Mem. Pinnacle, Golden Key Honor Soc., Phi Kappa Phi, Kappa Delta Pi. Presbyterian. Home: 563 28th Rd Clifton KS 66937-9603

REED, VANESSA REGINA, secondary education educator; b. Grenada, Miss., Oct. 4, 1965; d. Willie Mann and Elma Lee (Finley) R. BS in Social Sci. Edn., Miss. Valley State U., 1987; MA in History, Jackson State U., 1988; postgrad., Miss. State U., Meridian, 1991, 92. Cert. tchr. social sci. History tchr. Jackson (Miss.) State U., 1987-88; social studies tchr. Magnolia Mid. Sch., Meridian, 1988-93; U.S. history tchr. Kate Griffin Jr. H.S., Meridian, 1993—. Sunday sch. tchr., dir. children's ch. Mt. Olive Bapt. Ch.; mem. Heroines of Jericho; chmn. Bridge Builders Ministry; mem. adv. bd. Freedom Rock Christian Fellowship Ch. Mem. Am. Fedn. Tchrs., Sigma Gamma Rho. Democrat. Avocations: traveling, geneology, reading. Office: Kate Griffin Jr HS 2814 Davis St Meridian MS 39301-5655

REEDER, CECELIA PAINTER, English educator; b. Tampa, Fla., Oct. 9, 1936; d. William Painter and Cecelia (Bachman) Hendry; children: Susan Reeder Shipp, William J. BEd, U. Miami, 1958; MA in Gifted Edn., U. South Fla., 1983. Cert. elem./gifted-talented tchr., K-12, English 7-9, Fla. Elem. tchr. Dade County Bd. Pub. Inst., Miami, Fla., 1958-70, 83-86, tchr., English, 1986-89; tchr. gifted English and Social Studies 7th and 8th grades Richmond Heights Mid. Sch., Miami, Fla., 1989-94; tchr. 5th grade St. John's Episcopal Day Sch., 1996—. Recipient Assoc. Master Tchr. award State of Fla., 1986. Home: 1520 NW 10th St Homestead FL 33030-3872

REED-WRIGHT, KAREN, school administrator; b. Kingsport, Tenn., Aug. 19, 1950; d. Jack Marion and Sarah Frances (Blessing) Reed; m. James F. Wright, July 15, 1978; 1 child, Peyton Jennings Wright. BS, East Tenn. State U., 1971, MA, 1977, postgrad., 1989—. Cert. tchr. NBPTS. Tchr. Kingsport City Schs., 1972-85, tchr. evaluator, 1985-88, staff devel. coord., 1988—, reading specialist, 2001—. Adj. prof. East Tenn. State U., Johnson City, 1980—; wellness program dir. Kingsport City Schs., 1988—; advisor to commr. edn. State of Tenn., 1987; con. on coop. learning RESA, Whole Lang., Nongraded Schs., 1990—. Chmn. Kingsport Fun Fest, 1990; bd. dirs. Am. Heart Assn., Kingsport, 1989-92; mem. Jr. League of Kingsport, 1981—. Recipient Career Ladder Tchr. award State of Tenn., 1985, Outstanding Tchr. award Kingsport City Schs., 1986, Presidl. Excellence in Tchg. Sci. and Math award, 1999. Mem. ASCD, Kingsport C. of C. (v.p. 1990), Delta Kappa Gamma (rsch. chmn. 1988-90), Kappa Delta Pi. Democrat. Presbyterian. Avocation: travel. Office: 1577 Jessee St Kingsport TN 37664-2463

REEDY, CATHERINE IRENE, elementary school educator; b. Suffolk County, N.Y., Dec. 27, 1953; f. Edward and Catherine (Spindler) Grafenstein. AA, Suffolk C.C., Selden, N.Y., 1980; BA in Social Sci. summa cum laude, Dowling Coll., 1983, MS in Edn., 1986. Tchr. coord. sci. & health, tech. regence earth sci. St. Ignatius Sch., Hicksville, NY, 1983—2002, tchr. tech. grades 6-8, 1983—2002. Contbr. poetry to Beyong the Stars, 1996, Walk Through Paradise, 1995, Best Poems of 1996. Recipient Editor's Choice award Nat. Soc. Poetry, 1996, Nat. Libr. Poetry, 1995. Mem. ASCD, AAUW, N.Y. Acad. Scis., N.Y. Sci. Tchrs. Assn., Nat. Assn. Univ. Women, Nat. Poet Soc., Internat. Poets Soc., Alpha Zeta Nu (1st sec.), Phi Theta Kappa, Phi Alpha Sigma, Jappa DeltaPi (pres. Xi chpt. 1985-87). Home: 15 Nikia Dr Islip NY 11751-2630 Office: St Ignatius Sch 30 E Cherry St Hicksville NY 11801-4396

REES, BRIAN, headmaster; b. Sydney, Australia, Aug. 20, 1929; s. Frederick Thomas and Anne (Keedy) R.; m. Julia Birley, Dec. 17, 1959 (dec. Dec. 1978); children: Robert, Jessica, Philip, Natalia, Camilla; m. Juliet Mary Akehurst, Jan. 3, 1987. BA, Trinity Coll., 1952, MA, 1958. Asst. master Eton Coll., Windsor, Eng., 1952-63, housemaster, 1963-65; headmaster Merchant Taylors' Sch., Northwood, Eng., 1965-73, Charterhouse, Surrey, Eng., 1973-81, Rugby, 1981-84; rsch. asst. Ho. of Commons, Westminster, Eng., 1991. Author: (biography) A Musical Peacemaker, 1987, History and Idealism, 1990, Camille Saint-Saens: A Life, 1999. Home: 52 Spring Lane Flore Northampton NN7 4LS England

REES, NINA SHOKRAII, federal official, writer; b. Iran; BS in Psychology, Va. Polytech and State U., 1989; MS in Internat. Transactions, George Mason U., 1991. Mem. staff Rep. Porter Gross, Washington, 1990—92; dir. outreach programs Inst. for Justice, Washington, 1992—94; policy analyst Ams. for Tax Reform, Washington, 1994—96; chief edn. analyst The Heritage Found., Washington, 1997—2001; aide to v.p. U.S. Govt., Washington, 2001—02. Contbr. commentaries in newspapers, TV, radio on ednl. issues, 1995. Education adviser to Bush Campaign, Phila., 2000; contbr. to Rep. platform in edn. area Rep. Paty, 2000. Recipient Rita Ricardo Campbell award, Heritage Found., 1999. Office: US Dept Edn 400 Maryland Ave SW Washington DC 20202

REES, NORMA S. academic administrator; b. N.Y.C., Dec. 27, 1929; d. Benjamin and Lottie (Schwartz) D.; m. Raymond R. Rees, Mar. 19, 1960; children— Evan Lloyd, Raymond Arthur BA, Queens Coll., 1952; Ma, Bklyn. Coll., 1954; PhD, NYU, 1959; D of Arts and Letters honoris causa, John F. Kennedy U., 2001. Cert. speech-language pathology, audiology. Prof. communicative disorders Hunter Coll., N.Y.C., 1967-72; exec. officer, speech and hearing scis. grad. sch. CUNY, N.Y.C., 1972-74, assoc. dean for grad. studies, 1974-76, dean grad. studies, 1976-82; vice chancellor for acad. affairs U. Wis., Milw., 1982-85, from 1986, acting chancellor, 1985-86; vice chancellor for acad. policy and planning Mass. Bd. Regents for Higher Edn., Boston, 1987-90; pres. Calif. State U., Hayward, 1990—. Chmn. Commn. Recognition of Postsecondary Accreditation, 1994-96; mem. adv. com. quality and integrity U.S. Dept. Edn., commn. on internat. edn. Coun. on Higher Edn. Accreditation, 2003—. Contbr. articles to profl. jours. Trustee Citizens Govtl. Rsch. Bur., Milw., 1985-87; active Task Force on Wis. World Trade Ctr., 1985-87; bd. dirs. Am. Assn. State Colls. and Univs., 1995-97, Coun. of Postsecondary Accreditation, Washington, 1985-94, Greater Boston YWCA, 1987-90; mem. Calif. Sch. to Career Coun.; bd. dir. Econ. Devel. Alliance for Bus., Alameda County, 1995—; sec. edn. Nat. Adv. Com. Institutional Quality and Integrity, 1998-2002; bd. dirs. Bay Area World Trade Ctr., 2001—, Alameda County Health Care Found., 2002-. Fellow Am. Speech-Lang-Hearing Assn. (honors); mem. Am. Coun. Edn. (com. internat. edn. 1991-93), Am. Assn. Colls. and Univs. (chair task force on quality assessment 1991-92), Nat. Assn. State Univs. and Land Grant Colls. (exec. com. divsn. urban affairs 1985-87, com. accreditation 1987-90), Hayward C. of C. (bd. dirs. 1995-98), Oakland C. of C. (bd. dirs. 1997—). Office: Calif State Univ Hayward 25800 Carlos Bee Blvd Hayward CA 94542-3001 E-mail: nrees@csuhayward.edu.

REESE, DOROTHY HARMON, special education educator; b. Fowler, Kans., Feb. 1, 1930; d. Harry Herschel and Edith (Miller) Harmon; m. James Edward Reese, Oct. 4, 1949 (div. 1966); Edie Margolies, Virginia Bryant, Patricia Harrell. BS, Auburn U., 1967; MA, U. South Fla., 1974; EdS, Valdosta State Coll., 1981. Dir. Happy House Sch. for Retarded Children, Albany, Ga., 1963-66; tchr. mentally retarded Silver Sands Sch. for Retarded Children, Ft. Walton Beach, Fla., 1967-70; tchr. physically impaired Chamberlain High Sch./Hillsborough Co., Tampa, Fla., 1970-78, Savannah (Ga.)/Chatham County, 1978-79, Tift County Pub. Schs., Tifton, Ga., 1979-80, Duval County Pub. Schs., Jacksonville, Fla., 1980-87; specialist intellectual disabilities Exceptional Student Edn./Duval County Pub. Schs., Jacksonville, 1987—. Mem. Fla. Devel. Disabilities Adv. Coun., Tallahassee, 1975-78; caseworker Fla. Epilepsy Svcs. Program, Tampa, 1975-78; chairperson Profl. Adv. Bd./Gulf Coast Epilepsy Found., Tampa, 1975-77. Asst. dir. First Fla. Spl. Olympics, Ft. Walton Beach, 1970. Mem. Coun. for Exceptional Children (sec. 1986-87, publicity chmn. 1987-91), Delta Kappa Gamma. Republican. Avocations: writing, wood refinishing, needlework. Office: Duval County Pub Schs 1701 Prudential Dr Jacksonville FL 32207-8152

REESE, KATHERINE ROSE, music educator; b. Mannington, W.Va., July 27, 1937; m. Wallace Reese, July 29, 1955; children: Kyla O'Dell, Ann Landers. BA, W.Va. U., 1986. Cert. profl. music tchr. Artist tchr. of piano Fairmont (W.Va.) State Coll., 1986—. Address: RR 1 Box 122 Mannington WV 26582-9801

REESE, LYMON CLIFTON, civil engineering educator; b. Murfreesboro, Ark., Apr. 27, 1917; s. Samuel Wesley and Nancy Elizabeth (Daniels) R.; m. Eva Lee Jett, May 28, 1948; children: Sally Reese Melant, John, Nancy. BS, U. Tex. at Austin, 1949, MS, 1950; PhD, U. Calif. at Berkeley, 1955. Diplomate: Registered profl. engr., Tex., La. Internat. Boundary Commn., San Benito, Tex., 1939-41; surveyor U.S. Naval Constrn. Bns., U.S., Aleutian Islands, Okinawa, 1942-45; field engr. Assoc. Contractors & Engrs., Houston, 1945; draftsman Phillips Petroleum Co., Austin, 1946-48; research engr. U. Tex., Austin, 1948-50; asst. prof. civil engring. Miss. State Coll., 1950-51, 53-55; asst. prof. U. Tex., Austin, 1955-57, assoc. prof., 1957-64, prof., 1964—, chmn. dept., 1965-72, Taylor prof. engring., 1972-81, assoc. dean engring. for program planning, 1972-79, Nasser I. Al-Rashid Chair, 1981-84; prin. Ensoft, Inc., 1985—, Lymon C. Reese Assocs. Contbr. articles to profl. jours. Served with USNR, 1942-45. Recipient Thomas Middlebrooks award ASCE, 1958; Joe J. King Profl. Engring. Achievement award, 1977, Offshore Tech. Conf. Disting. Achievement award for Individuals, 1985, Disting. grad. Coll. of Engring., U. Tex., Austin., 1985. Mem. ASCE (Karl Terzaghi lectr. 1976 Terzaghi award, 1983, Tex. sect. award of Hon. 1985, hon. mem. 1984—), Nat. Acad. Engring. Baptist (deacon). Office: U Tex Dept Civil Engring Austin TX 78712-1104 Home: 11110 Tom Adams Dr Apt F2 Austin TX 78753-3302 E-mail: lymonreese@aol.com.

REESE, MADGE ELEANOR READ, elementary education educator; b. North Vernon, Ind., Feb. 26, 1917; d. Parley Garfield and Ella Josephine (Smith) Read; m. Harry Boxell Reese, Aug. 12, 1940 (dec. June 1991); children: Paul David, Patricia Ellen, Michele Annette. BEd, Ball State U., 1955, MEd, 1956. Cert. tchr. Tchr. Muncie (Ind.) Cmty. Sch., 1956-76. Author: Sprial of Life, 1996, Humpback Barn, 1997; contbr. articles to profl. jours. Mem. DAR (chaplain 1993-99). Avocations: music, gardening, knitting.

REESE-BROWN, BRENDA, primary education educator; b. Tampa, Fla., Mar. 22, 1948; d. James T. and Mary Reese. AA, Hillsborough C.C., Tampa, 1976; BA, U. South Fla., 1979; M in Early Childhood, Nova U., 1993. Cert. elem. and early childhood tchr., Fla. Tchr. kindergarten Town n County Elem. Sch., Tampa, 1979-80; primary tchr. Temple Terrace Elem. Sch., Tampa, 1980-91, tchr. kindergarten, 1991—, mem. sch. improvement team, 1992-95, math. specialist, 1992—, 1st grade tchr., 1999—. Mem. Zeta Phi Beta, Inc. (grammateus Nu Upsilon Zeta chpt. 1990-92). Avocations: sewing, cooking, reading, listening to gospel music, arts and crafts. Office: Temple Terrace Elem Sch 124 Flotto Ave Tampa FL 33617-5579

REEVE, FRANKLIN D. writer, literature educator; b. Phila., Sept. 18, 1928; m. Laura C. Stevenson, 1997; children: Christopher, Benjamin, Alison, Brock, Mark, Katharine, Margaret. AB, Princeton U., 1950; PhD, Columbia U., 1958; AM (hon.), Wesleyan, 1964. Instr., asst. prof. Columbia U., N.Y.C., 1952-61; assoc. prof. Wesleyan U., Middletown, Conn., 1962-66, adj. prof., 1967-87, prof., 1988—2002, prof. emeritus, 2002—. Founding editor The Poetry Rev., 1982—84; bd. govs., v.p. Poetry Soc. Am., 1976—84; sec. Poets House, NYC, 1985—99; bd. govs. Transl. Ctr., NYC, 1980—94; vis. prof. Oxford (Eng.) U., 1964, Columbia U., 1988, Marlboro Vt. Coll., 1999; bd. dirs. Marlboro Rev.; vis. scholar, Moscow, 1961; vis. lectr. Yale U., New Haven, 1972—84; assoc. fellow Saybrook Coll., 1972—; program scholar Vt. Coun. on Humanities; faculty MFA program in creative writing New Eng. Coll., 2003—; lectr. poetry Ctr., N.Y.C., 1980—84; lectr. USAID, 1999; cons. in field. Author: Aleksandr Blok: Between Image and Idea, 1962, 2d edit., 1981, Robert Frost in Russia, 1964, 2d edit., 2001, The Russian Novel, 1966, The Red Machines, 1968, In the Silent Stones, 1968, Just Over the Border, 1969, The Brother, 1971, The Blue Cat, 1972, White Colors, 1974, The White Monk, 1989; author: (edited with Jay Meek) After the Storm, 1991; author: Concrete Music, 1992; editor: Winged Sprits, 1995, A Few Rounds of Old Maid and Other Stories, 1995, The Moon and Other Failures, 1999, (poetry) A World You Haven't Seen, 2001, The Urban Stampede and Other Poems, 2002; translator: Five Short Novels by Turgenev, 1961, Anthology of Russian Plays, 2 vols., 1961, 1963, 1975, 1991, Contemporary Russian Drama, 1968, The Garden by Bella Akhmadulina, 1990. The Trouble with Reason by Alexander Griboyekov, 1993, The King and the Fool by Alexander Borschagovsky, 2001; mem. editl. bd. Marlboro Rev. Trustee Pettee Meml. Libr. Recipient Lit. award Am. Acad.-Nat. Inst., 1970, Lifetime Golden Rose award New Eng. Poetry Soc., 1994, Binswanger Excellence in Tchg. award Wesleyan U., 2002, May Sarton award, 1999. Mem.: New Eng. Poetry Club (bd. dirs. 1996—). Home: PO Box 14 Wilmington VT 05363-0014

REEVE, THOMAS GILMOUR, physical education educator; b. Memphis, Sept. 23, 1946; s. Paul Goodwin and Dorothy (Bourke) R.; children: Bourke, Spencer. BS in Phys. Edn., Tex. Tech. U., 1969, MEd, 1972; PhD, Tex. A&M U., 1976. Asst. prof. Auburn (Ala.) U., 1977-82, assoc. prof., 1982-87, prof., 1987-91, asst. v.p. for acad. affairs, 1992-93, alumni prof., 1991-95, prof. phys. edn., 1995-98, W.T. Smith Disting. prof., 1998-99; prof., chair Tex. Tech. U., 1999—. Vis. asst. prof. Tex. A&M U., College

Station, 1976-77. Co-editor: Stimulus-Response Compatibility, 1990; sect. editor Rsch. Quar. for Exercise and Sport, 1990-92, editor, 1999—; assoc. editor Jour. Sport Behavior, 1983—. Fellow AAHPERD, Rsch. Consortium, Am. Acad. Kinesiology and Phys. Edn. (pres.-elect 2003—); mem. N.Am. Soc. Psychology of Sport and Phys. Activity (publ. dir. 1985-87, pres. 1991-92). Avocation: masters swimming. Office: Tex Tech U HESS PO Box 43011 Lubbock TX 79409-3011 E-mail: Gilmour.Reeve@ttu.edu.

REEVES, BARBARA, writer, educator; b. Wellington, Tex., Aug. 29, 1931; d. Edward Decatur Reeves and Ruth Caroline Rich; m. Stanley Kolaski, Jan. 15, 1956 (dec. Feb. 1987); children: Anne Marie, Linda Caroline, John Edward. Writing tchr. San Jacinto Coll. Sys., Houston, 1990—. Curriculum cons. San Jacinto Coll. South, Houston, 1998-2000; cons. and mentor in field. Authro: Georgina's Campaign, 1991, The Dangerous Marquis, 1993, The Much Maligned Lord, 1995, My Buffalo Soldier, 2000, Thunder Moon, 2003. Mem. Romance Writers Am. (founder chpt. 30, chairperson, fundraiser for literacy), Bay Area Writer's League (founder, chairperson). Democrat. Roman Catholic. Avocations: social historian, interior design, family history. E-mail: bkwriter@swbell.net.

REEVES, KATHLEEN WALKER, English and French language educator; b. Mt. Pleasant, Mich., Dec. 7, 1950; d. John J. and Gladys M. W.; m. Daniel H. Reeves, Mar. 10, 1972; children: Sheila, Michael. BA, Ctrl. Mich. U., 1973, MA, 1984. Cert. early adolescent English language arts tchr. English and French tchr. Shepherd (Mich.) High Sch., 1973-76, Chippewa Hills High Sch., Remus, Mich., 1978-79, Onekama (Mich.) Pub. Sch., 1983-86; English tchr. Seaholm High Sch., Birmingham, Mich., 1986—. Field test participant Nat. Bd. Profl. Tchg. Stds., Detroit, 1993—; adv. liaison Instrn. and Devel. of Mich. Ednl. Assn., Lansing, 1994—; bd. dirs. Mich. Assn. Tchr. Edn., Lansing, 1996-97. Troop leader Girl Scouts U.S., Dearborn, Mich., 1988-90; asst. gen. Boy Scouts Am., Dearborn, 1990—. Mem. Nat. Coun. Tchrs. of English (pres. 1973), Assn. for Supervision & Curriculum Devel., Mich. Assn. Tchrs. of French, Birmingham Ednl. Assn. (v.p. 1994—, disting. svc. award 1989, 91, 93). Democrat. Roman Catholic. Avocations: gardening, camping, reading, cooking. Home: 1020 N York St Dearborn MI 48128-1754 Office: Seaholm High Sch 2436 W Lincoln St Birmingham MI 48009-1898

REEVES, LUCY MARY, retired school educator; b. Pewamo, Mich., July 2, 1932; d. Lavaldin Edgar and Marian S. (Lee) Hull; m. Walter Emery Reeves, Jan. 21, 1922. BS, Western Mich. U., Kalamazoo, 1965; postgrad., Western Mich. U., 1965-75. Tchr. Country Sch. One Room, Matherton, Mich., 1956-57, Ionia, Mich., 1957-58, Belding, Mich., 1958-62, Saranac, Mich., Belding, Mich., 1965, Belding (Mich.) Area Schs., 1965-89; ret., 1989. Vol. Frederick Meijers Garden, Grand Rapids, Point Man Internat. Ministries, Shiloh Cmty. Ch., United Meml. Health Ctr., Shiloh Cmty. Ch.; vol. United Meml. Health Ctr., Greenville. Mem. NEA, Mich. Edn. Assn., Belding Area Edn., Profl. Businesswomen's Assn. Avocations: computers, reading, travelling, sewing.

REEVES, ROY FRANKLIN, mathematician, engineer, educator; b. Warrensberg, Mo., July 8, 1922; s. Archie R. and Lucie P. (Jahn) R.; m. Priscilla L. LaVanway, Mar. 17, 1951; children: Dennis, James, Terrence, Sandra, Timothy. BEE, U. Colo., 1947; PhD, Iowa State U., 1951. Instr. Iowa State U., Ames, 1948-51; prof. Ohio State U., Columbus, 1951-81, Otterbein Coll., Columbus, 1981—91. Contbr. approximately 20 articles to profl. jours. Mem. Assn. for Computing Machinery, Am. Math. Soc., Math. Assn. Am. Home: 662 Dempsey Rd Westerville OH 43081 Office: Dept Math Sci Otterbein Coll Westerville OH 43081

REFE, SANDRA M. retired elementary school educator; b. Painesville, Ohio, Nov. 24, 1947; d. Anthony and Carla (Schiavelli) R. BS in Edn., Kent State U., 1969, MEd, 1971; postgrad., Cleve. State U., Coll. Mt. St. Joseph. Cert. permanent elem. tchr., Ohio. Tchr. grade 1 Mentor (Ohio) Pub. Schs. Exempted Village, ret. Named Martha Holden Jennings scholar, 1987-88, Mentor Tchr. of Yr., 1988-89; recipient Martha Holden Jennings Master Tchr. award, 1988, Mentor Schs. Excellence in Teaching award. Mem. NEA, ASCD, Ohio Edn. Assn., N.E. Ohio Edn. Assn., Mentor Tchrs. Assn. Home: 934 N State St Painesville OH 44077-4221

REFINSKI, JOSEPH ANTHONY, secondary education educator; b. Orange, N.J., July 7, 1954; s. Chester Walter and Antoinette (DeCarlo) R. BA in History, Seton Hall U., 1976, MA in Secondary Edn., 1978. Cert. tchr. social studies and history, N.J.; supr. cert., N.J. Tchr. Columbia High Sch., Maplewood, N.J., 1977-78; tchr. and coach Edison Jr. High Sch., Westfield, N.J., 1978-85, Verona (N.J.) High Sch., 1985-86, Costley Sch., East Orange, N.J., 1986—. Photographer and cons. N.J. Bicentennial Commn., Mahwah, 1987—; mem. civics consortium E.A. Coleton Inst., Rutgers U. Coord. nat. competition on Constitution and Bill of Rights, Washington, 1988, Nat. Commn. on U.S. Constitution, Calabasas, Calif., 1989; active in local Constitution Day projects, 1987, 88, N.J. Coun. Social Studies, Hands Across Am. State Com., 1986; closing ceremonies staff Liberty Weekend, 1986; tchr. edn. adv. com. Seton Hall U., 1992—; mem. Kodak ProPassport Network, Libr. Congress. Recipient East Orange Sch. Based Program award, 1987, Bicentennial Leadership award Ctr. for Civic Edn., Calabasas, 1989, Alumni Svc. award Seton Hall U., Nat. History Day award Am. Hist. Assn., 1991, N.J. We The People Citation, 1991; Constitution fellow, 1989, Thomas Jefferson fellow, 1991, Woodrow Wilson fellow, 1994, Tcrh. Outreach nat. devel. program (TORCH) presenter, 1995-99, USCHE Bd. Dirs., 1998, Tchr. of the Year, 1995, Excellence in Tchg. award, 1995. Mem.: ASCD, NY Times Learning Network (affiliate), Found. for U.S. Constn. (founding mem.), NJ Dept. Edn. (social studies content stds revision com.), Nat. Coun. for Edn. in Disciplines (history com.), Nat. Bd. for Profl. Tchg. Stds. (assessor, trainer), Fgn. Policy Rsch. Inst., NJ Coun. for History Edn., Am. Hist. Assn., Orgn. Am. Historians, Nat. Coun. Social Studies (del.), Seton Hall U. Alumni Assn. (pres. 1990—92, v.p. 1992—), Athletics Congress (mid. sch. com. NJ State Bar Assn.), Tau Kappa Epsilon, Kappa Delta Pi, Phi Alpha Theta. Roman Catholic. Avocations: photography, piano, guitar, historial celebrations. Home: 2094 Aldene Ave Scotch Plains NJ 07076-4649

REFIOR, EVERETT LEE, labor economist, educator; b. Donnellson, Iowa, Jan. 23, 1919; s. Fred C. and Daisy E. (Gardner) R.; m. Marie Emma Culp, Sept. 12, 1943; children: Gene A., Wendell F., Paul D., Donna M.; m. Betty Pottenger Phelps, Nov. 27, 1993. BA, Iowa Wesleyan Coll., 1942; postgrad., U. Glasgow, 1945; MA, U. Chgo., 1955; PhD, U. Iowa, 1962. Instr. econs. and bus. Iowa Wesleyan Coll., 1947-50; teaching asst. U. Iowa, 1950-51; research asst. Bur. of Labor and Mgmt., 1951-52, instr. mgmt. and social sci., 1954-55; assoc. prof. econs. Simpson Coll., 1952-54; asst. prof. econs. U. Wis. at Whitewater, 1955-62, assoc. prof., 1962-64, prof., 1964-83, prof. emeritus, 1983—, chmn., 1966-75. Lyricist (hymns) Eternal Love, 1980, Divine Order, 1980, Precious Lord Jesus, 1983, If We But Dare, 1984, Humanity, 1989, others. Found. pres. Whitewater chpt. World Federalists Assn., 1960-68, 76-78, 86-92, midwest regional pres., 1969-71, 75-87, nat. bd., 1968-89, 1992-99; del. World Congress, Ottawa, 1970, Brussels, 1972, Paris, 1977, Tokyo, 1980, Phila., 1987, San Francisco, 1995; exec. com. Assn. World Citizens, 1980-96; sec. World Govt. Orgns. Coalition, 1987-96; mem. Gov.'s Commn. on UN, 1971-89, state coord. Campaign for UN Reform, 1984-96, nat. pres., 1996-97; mem. Wis. Conf. bd. Social Concerns, Meth. Ch., 1961-68, 70-76; Dem. precinct com. Whitewater, 1966-96; chmn. Walworth County Dem. Party, 1975-78, Wis. Dem. Platform Com., 1978—; bd. dirs. Alcohol Problems Coun. Wis., 1976-2003. With U.S. Army, 1943-46. Mem. Indsl. Rels. Rsch. Assn. (adv. bd. Wis. chpt. 1964-78, acad. v.p. 1978-83), Peace Action, Population Inst., Fedn. Am. Scientists, South Ctrl. Wis. UN Assn. (pres. 1979-80, v.p. 1995-97), Kiwanis (pres. local club 1987-88), Vets. for Peace. Methodist. Home: 435 W Starin Rd Apt 118AA Whitewater WI 53190-1133

REGA, FRANCES LOUISE, English educator; b. Revere, Mass., July 13, 1950; d. Leo and Marie Frances (Interrante) R. BA in English, Boston Coll., 1972, MEd in Reading, 1977; MEd in Integrated Studies, Cambridge Coll., 1996. Cert. English and Reading Specialist. Tchr. English and reading Abraham Lincoln Sch., Revere, Mass., 1972-90, Beachmont Middle Sch., Revere, Mass., 1990-98; tchr. English Revere H.S., 1998—, lead tchr. English, 2003—. Co-advisor Nat. Jr. Honor Soc., Revere, Mass., 1990-94, co-advisor The Aspirers Club, 1995-98; mem. faculty coun. Nat. Honor Soc., 2002—. Contbr. articles to profl. jours. Mem. NEA, Nat. Coun. Tchrs. English, Internat. Reading Assn., Revere Tchrs. Assn., Mass. Tchrs. Assn., Alpha Upsilon Alpha. Home: 164 Ridge Rd Revere MA 02151-3825 Office: Revere HS 101 School St Revere MA 02151

REGAN, ELLEN FRANCES (MRS. WALSTON SHEPARD BROWN), ophthalmologist, educator; b. Boston, Feb. 1, 1919; d. Edward Francis and Margaret (Moynihan) R.; m. Walston Shepard Brown, Aug. 13, 1955. AB, Wellesley Coll., 1940; MD, Yale U., 1943. Intern Boston City Hosp., 1944; asst. resident, resident Inst. Ophthalmology, Presbyn. Hosp., N.Y.C., 1944-47, asst. ophthalmologist, 1947-56, asst. attending ophthalmologist, 1956-84; instr. ophthalmology Columbia Coll. Physicians and Surgeons, 1947-55, assoc. ophthalmology, 1955-67, asst. clin. prof., 1967-84. Mem. AMA, Am. Ophthal. Soc., Am. Acad. Ophthalmology, N.Y. Acad. Medicine, N.Y. State Med. Soc., Mass. Med. Soc., River Club, Tuxedo Club. Office: PO Box 632 Tuxedo Park NY 10987-0632

REGAN, MARIE CARBONE, retired language educator; b. Massena, N.Y., July 18, 1936; d. Dominick Carbone, Josephine Trimboli; m. Robert John Regan; children: Shawn, Denise, Gavin, Bridget, Stephanie. BA, SUNY, Albany, 1957; MA, SUNY, Potsdam, 1977. Tchr. English Massena H.S., 1957—60; prof. English SUNY, Canton, 1970—97; ret., 1997. Exec. com. faculty senate SUNY, Albany, 1987—93; evaluator curriculum for two-yr. coll. liberal arts offerings N.Y. State Edn. Dept., Albany, 1990—95. Mem. econ. devel. com. Town of Potsdam, 1994—, dep. town supr., 1994—; com. mem. St. Lawrence County Dem.s, 1994—; edn. alumni bd. SUNY, Potsdam, 2000—; dir. St. Lawrence Valley Tchrs. Ctr., Canton, NY, 1989—90; trustee St. Mary's Ch., Potsdam, 1993—95; vol. Alliance for Mcpl. Power, St. Lawrence County, NY, 1996—. Named Disting. Faculty, SUNY-Canton, 1989; recipient Disting. Svc. Prof., SUNY, 1990. Mem.: AAUW (bd. dirs. St. Lawrence County br., chmn. 1999—2001), Inst. for Learning in Retirement (founding mem., v.p. 2000—01). Democrat. Roman Catholic. Avocations: reading, dancing, cooking. Home: 6869 State Hwy 56 Potsdam NY 13676

REGAN, MARIE CHRISTINE, nursing educator; b. Wilmington, Del. d. Jeremiah and Della Agnes (Kelly) R. Diploma in nursing, Wilmington Gen. Hosp., 1959; BSN, U. Md., Balt., 1965; MS in Health Edn., Nova Southeastern U., 1983; cert. Vietnamese langs. culture, U. Hawaii, 1967. RN, Fla.; cert. aerospace medicine, cert. tchr., Fla. Sr. pub. health nurse Balt. City Health Dept.; instr., comty. health nurse Church Home & Hosp. Sch. Nursing, Balt.; advisor to chief of pub. health U.S. Dept. State, Vietnam; nursing instr. Miami-Dade C.C., Miami, Fla.; nursing instr. psychiatry Jackson Meml. Hosp., Miami; nursing supr. Vis. Nurse Assn., Miami; instr. nursing Robert Morgan Inst., Miami; med. crew dir. USAFR, Charleston, S.C. Contbr. articles to med. jours. Bd. dirs. Greater Miami YMCA, Miami, 1973-80. Maj. USAFR, 1972-85. Mem. Nat. League Nursing, Fla. League Nursing, Res. Officers Assn., Fla. Vocat. Assn., Dade Assn. Vocat. Edn., Assn. Nurse Educators of Fla., Exec. Women's GOlf Assn. Roman Catholic. Avocations: golf, assisting at homeless shelter, aerobics. Home: 6516 SW 112th Pl Miami FL 33173-1981

REGAN, ROBERT CHARLES, English language educator; b. Indpls., Mar. 13, 1930; s. Francis Bernard and Alma Ophelia (McBride) R.; m. Katherine Jeanclos, Aug. 11, 1989; children by previous marriage: Christopher, Alison, Amelia. BA, Centenary Coll., 1951; MA, Harvard U., 1952; PhD, U. Calif., Berkeley, 1965. Instr. English, Centenary Coll., 1956-57; asst. prof. English, U. Va., 1963-67; Fulbright-Hays lectr. Am. civilization U. Montpellier, France, 1967-68; assoc. prof. English, U. Pa., Phila., 1968-82, prof., 1982-2000, undergrad. chmn. dept. English, 1978-80, 81-83, 89-90, dir. Penn-in-London program, prof. emeritus, 2000—. Lectr. Internat. Communications Agy., Morocco, Algeria, Jordan, 1980; vis. prof. King's Coll., London, 1983-84 Author: Unpromising Heroes; Mark Twain and His Characters, 1966, Poe: A Collection of Critical Essays, 1967; mng. editor: Am. Quar., 1969-72; mem. editl. bd. Mark Twain Papers, U. Calif., Berkeley, 1997—; contbr. articles to lit. jours. Served with USNR, 1952-56, 61-62. Woodrow Wilson fellow, 1962-63; Am. Philos. Soc. research grantee, 1970 Mem. Univ. Mews Assn. (pres. 1999-2001), Faculty Club U. Pa. (bd. govs. 1997-2001). Democrat. Episcopalian. Office: U Pa Dept English Philadelphia PA 19104

REGAN, SIRI LISA LAMBOURNE, gifted education educator; BA in English Edn., U. New Orleans, 1977, M in Edn. Curriculum and Instrn., 1981, postgrad. Cert. tchr., La. Tchr. Roosevelt Middle Sch., Kenner, La., 1977—. Presenter in field; dir., coord. La. Writing Project Jefferson Parish, 1989-90; co-dir. Greater New Orleans Writing Project Inst., 1990, audio-visual coord., 1992—, comuter project coord., 1995—; coord. Jefferson Dollars for Scholars, 1995—, LEAP Engring. program, 1997—, tech. coord., 1999—. Contbr. articles to profl. jours. Named Tchr. of Yr. for Jefferson Parish, Metairie Jaycees, 1987, Tchr. of the Yr. for State of La., La. Jaycees, 1988, La. Middle Sch. Tchr. of Yr., La. State Dept. Edn., 1989, Tchr. of Yr., Southeastern Regional Middle Sch., 1989; recipient Valley Forge Freedom Found. Educator's medal, 1989-90, Young Careerist award Jefferson Bus. and Profl. Women's Club, Key to City of Kenner, 1989. Mem. Nat. Assn. Bilingual Educators (cert.) Nat. Coun. Tchrs. English (cert.), Nat. Middle Sch. Assn., La. Middle Sch. Assn., Coun. Learning Disabilitis, Coun. Exceptional Children, S.E. La. Profl. Assn. Gifted and Talented, Kappa Delta Phi, Phi Delta Kappa, Alpha Theta Epsilon. Meth. Avocations: reading, needlework, cooking, woodworking, photography. Office: Roosevelt Mid Sch 3315 Maine Ave Kenner LA 70065-3806

REGAN, THOMAS JOSEPH, priest, educator; b. Waltham, Mass., Apr. 13, 1954; s. John C. and Sarah P. (Corbett) R. AB, Boston Col., 1976; AM, Fordham U., 1982, PhD, 1984; M in Divinity, Weston Sch., 1987. Ordained priest Roman Cath. Ch., 1987. Asst. prof. Fairfield (Conn.) U., 1988-93, assoc. prof., chair. Philosophy dept., 1993-2000, assoc. dean Coll. Arts & Scis., 2000—02; co-dir. Ignatian Residential Coll., 2002; provincial superior New Eng. Province Soc. of Jesus, 2003—. Trustee St. Joseph's U., Phila. Mem. Jesuit Philos. Assn. (pres. 1997-98), Alpha Sigma Nu (pres., chmn., nat. bd. dirs. 1991-97). Roman Catholic. Office: 85 School St Watertown MA 02472-4251 E-mail: tjregan@mail.fairfield.edu.

REGAN-GERACI, THERESA ELIZABETH, learning disability educator, consultant; b. Jersey City, Jan. 17, 1947; d. Thomas Edward and Elizabeth Marie (Waleck) Regan; m. Baldassero (Bob) Charles Geraci, June 12, 1987; 1 child, Matthew Regan Geraci. BA, Caldwell Coll., 1968; MA, William Paterson Coll., 1977; postgrad., Boston Coll., 1981. Cert. tchr., prin., N.J. Tchr. art, spl. edn., elem., prin./supr., LDT-C Our Lady of Good Counsel Sch., Pompton Plains, N.J., 1968-75, Little Falls (N.J.) Sch. # 2, 1975-77, Little Falls Schs. # 1 and # 2, 1977-85, Little Falls Sch. # 1, 1985—. Mem. bd. edn. Our Lady of Good Counsel Sch., 1976-77, St. Mary's Sch., Pompton Lakes, 1981-83; instr. Devel. Ctr. Tutoring, Pompton Lakes, 1979-85, cons.; dir. Learning Disability Summer Sch., Bloomingdale, N.J., 1979-80. Tchr. C.C.D. program St. Mary's Sch., 1985—, Project SMART, NJIT 1996—. Mem. Little Falls Edn. Assn. (sec. 1980-83, v.p. 1983-84, pres. 1985-88), Pi Lambda Theta. Democrat. Avocations: reading, painting, ceramics, biking, museums, gardening. Home: 8 Berry Pl Pompton Plains NJ 07444-1001 Office: Little Falls Sch # 1 Stevens Ave Little Falls NJ 07424

REGENAUER, CAROL MCCURDY, elementary education educator, consultant; b. Providence, Oct. 1, 1935; d. Russell Joseph and Margaret Mary (Bresnahan) McCurdy; m. Bernard John Regenauer, Sept. 20, 1958 (dec. Aug. 1988); children: Bernard John Jr., Russell McCurdy, Michael Edward; m. Richard M. Tranfaglia, Nov. 10, 2001. BA, Newton Coll. Sacred Heart, 1957; MS, Lesley Coll., 1991. Cert. tchr. grades 1-8, Mass. Elem. tchr. R.I. Pub. Schs., Providence, 1957-58, Boston (Mass.) Pub. Schs., 1958-60, Hudson (Mass.) Pub. Schs., 1969—2000; prin., owner Academically Speaking, Lexington, Mass., 2000—. Ednl. cons. Sci. Rsch. Assocs., Chgo., 1980-88, IBM, Boca Raton, Fla., 1989-90, CTB Macmillan-McGraw Hill, Monterey, Calif., 1993. Recipient Tchr. of Yr., Local Area Women's Club, Boston, 1985, Grant to Fund Purchase of Books for Cross-Age Program, Digital Corp., Maynard, Mass., 1994. Mem. NEA, Mass. Tchrs. Assn., Hudson Edn. Assn. Avocations: horseback riding, fox hunting, swimming, traveling, reading.

REGIER, ELAINE ROXANNE, elementary school educator, school librarian; b. Oklahoma City, May 12, 1957; d. Dale Gene and Phyllis (Harms) R. BS in Edn., Southwestern Okla. State U., 1980; M in Libr. and Info. Studies, U. Okla., 1999. Cert. libr. media specialist Okla. Tchr. kindergarten Anadarko (Okla.) Pub. Schs., 1980—84, tchr. pre-1st grade, 1984—98, tchr. 1st grade, 1998—99; libr. media specialist Wiley Post Elem. Sch., Oklahoma City, 1999—. Vol. U.S. Olympic Festival, Yukon, Okla., 1989, Anadarko Community Libr., 1990; jmem. ch. choir, Celebration Ringers, 2001—. Recipient Excellence in Aviation Edn. award Gen. Aviation Mfr. Assn., 1992; named Okla. Aerospace Educator of Yr., Okla. Aerospace Edn. Assn., 1994-95. Mem. Assn. Profl. Okla. Educators, Ninety-Nines, Delta Kappa Gamma (sec. 1987-90, 2d v.p. 1990-92), Okla. Pilots Assn. Methodist. Avocations: flying, snow skiing, sewing, reading, computers. Office: Wiley Post Elem Sch 6920 W Britton Rd Oklahoma City OK 73132

REGINA, MARIE ANTOINETTE, parochial school educator; b. Wilkinsburg, Pa., Jan. 10, 1958; d. Albert Edward and Katherine Ann (Mediate) R. BS in Early Childhood/Elem. Edn., California (Pa.) State Coll., 1980; MS in Reading, California U. of Pa., 1986. Cert. tchr. early childhood, elem. and reading. Tchr. grade 3 St. REgis Cath. Sch., Trafford, Pa., 1980-88; early childhood tchr. Little Peoples Ednl. Workshop, Forest Hills, Pa., 1984; Klubmates and early childhood tchr. Kinder Care, North Huntingdon, Pa., 1985-86; tchr. social studies McKeesport (Pa.) Ctrl. Cath. Sch., 1984-88, tchr. grade 6, 1988—. Reading presch. tchr. Happy Home Day Care, North Huntingdon, 1992; dir. for ages 3, 4, 5 YMCA of Penn Hills, Pa., 1993; cons. World Book, North Huntingdon, 1993—; pvt. tutor. Mem. Internat. Reading Assn., Keystone State Reading Assn., Westmoreland Reading Coun., Cath. Alumni Club of Pitts. Roman Catholic. Avocations: volleyball, walking, water aerobics, cooking, arts and crafts. Home: 13327 Dean Dr North Huntingdon PA 15642-1811 Office: McKeesport Ctrl Cath Sch 2412 Versailles Ave Mc Keesport PA 15132-2037

REGIS, NINA, librarian, educator; b. Corinth, Miss., Oct. 19, 1928; d. W.C. and Mary Isabelle (Rushing) Hanner; m. George Regis, Sept. 5, 1949 (dec. Jan. 6, 1990); 1 child, Simonne Marie. BA, Bridgewater (Mass.) State U., 1971, MEd, 1975; MALS, U. South Fla., 1981. tchr., Fla., Mass. Geneal. libr., asst. rschr. to curator New Bedford (Mass.) Pub. Libr., 1963-71; assoc. libr. New England Hist. Geneal. Soc., Boston, 1972-73; media specialist, libr. Brevard County Schs., Port Malabar Elem. Sch., Palm Bay, Fla., 1978-90; libr., faculty Brevard C.C., Palm Bay, 1990-96, Melbourne, Fla., 1996—. Developer and organizer libraries, 1968, 80, 91—. Mem. ALA, Fla. Assn. C.C.s, Libr. Assn. of Brevard County, Phi Kappa Phi, Beta Phi Mu. Avocations: creative writing, genealogical research. Office: Brevard C C Melbourne Campus Libr 3865 N Wickham Rd Melbourne FL 32935-2310

REGISTER, ANNETTE ROWAN, reading educator; b. Doctors Inlet, Fla., Apr. 5, 1931; d. Ernest Ambors and Frances Perlena (Monroe) R.; Henry Ira Register, Oc. 31, 1954; 1 child, Andrew Henry. RN, Grnville Gen.Hosp.Sch.of Nursi, Greenville, 1948-51; BS, Tex. Woman's U., Denton, 1954; MEd, U. Fla., Gainesville, 1959; SEd, Fla. State U., 1983; student, U. West Fla., Okaloosa Walton C.C. Instrn. dir. nursing edn. Alachua Gen. Hosp., Gainesville, Fla., 1955-57; pub. sch. tchr. Okaloosa County, Ft. Walton Beach, Fla., 1966-93. V.p., Internation Training in Communication Ft. Walton Beach, Fla.; active Inst. Sr. Profls. Okaloosa Walton C.C. Pres. Okaloosa Reading Coun., 1976—80; mem. Okaloosa Walton C.C. Symphony Guild, 1998—; pres. United Meth. Women, Ft. Walton Beach, Fla., 1985—87; dist. v.p. Mem. Fla. C. of C. (amb. 1996—), Phi Delta Kappa (1st v.p.). Methodist. Avocations: crafts, painting, sketching, grandmothering, traveling. Office: Okaloosa County Sch Bd 10 Lowery Pl SE Fort Walton Beach FL 32548 E-mail: registerannette@yahoo.com.

REGN FRAHER, BONNIE, special education educator; BA, U. Calif., Santa Cruz, 1978; EdS, Rutgers U., 1982, MA, 1983. Cert. tchr. of the handicapped, cert. elem. tchr. Tchr. Search Day Program, Wanamassa, N.J., 1978-87; v.p. Fin-Addict Charters, Wall, N.J., 1987-93; v.p., dir. fin. William Cook Custom Homes, Wall, 1987-95; v.p. Archtl. Woodworking, 1993-95; tchr. Elmcrest Hosp., 1996—2003; daycare owner Fraher Acad., West Hartford, Conn., 1996—. Mem. Autism Soc. Am., Am. Sailing Assn., Long Branch Ski Club. Avocation: writing.

REHA, ROSE KRIVISKY, retired business educator; b. N.Y.C., Dec. 17, 1920; d. Boris and Freda (Gerstein) Krivisky; m. Rudolph John Reha, Apr. 11, 1941; children; Irene Gale, Phyllis. BS in Bus. and Music Edn., Ind. State U., 1965; MA in Bus. and Psychology, U. Minn., 1967, PhD in Ednl. Psychology and Counseling, 1971. With U.S. and State Civil Svc., 1941-63; tchr. pub. schs., Minn., 1965-66; teaching assoc., instr. U. Minn., Mpls., 1966-68, 68-85; prof. coll. bus. St. Cloud (Minn.) State U., 1968-85, prof. emeritus, 1985—, chmn. bus. edn. & office adminstrn. dept., 1982-83. Advisor Small Bus. Inst., 1972-85, SBA, 1972-85; ct. advocate for women in distress St. Cloud Women's Shelter, 1986-89; adj. prof. profl. and bus. comm. Fla. Atlantic U., Boca Raton, Fla., 1989-90; substitute tchr. Broward County, 1990—; tutor (reading) Lauderdale, Fla., 1990-92; moderator, counselor Posnack Jewish Cmty. Ctr., Davie, Fla.; lectr. in com. Soref Jewish Cmty. Ctr. Continuing Edn. for sr. groups, Sunrise, Fla., 1994—; cons., lectr. in field; small bus. cons. Small Bus. Inst. Coll. Bus. St. Cloud St. U. Minn. Reviewer of bus. comm. and consumer edn. textbooks. Contbr. articles to profl. jours. Camp dir. Girl Scouts U.S., 1960-62; active various cmty. fund drives; sec., mem. relicensure rev. Com. Minn. Bd. Teaching Continuing Edn., 1984-85. Recipient Achievement award St. Cloud State U., 1985, St. Cloud State U. Rsch. and Faculty Improvement grantee, 1973, 78, 83. Mem. Am. Vocat. Assn. (cert.), Am. Counseling Assn. (cert.), Am. Mental Health Counselors Assn. (cert.), Minn. Econ. Assn., Minn. Women of Higher Edn., NEA, Minn. Edn. Assn. (pres. women's caucus 1981-83, award 1983), St. Cloud U. Faculty Assembly (pres. 1975-76), St. Cloud State U. Grad. Coun. (chmn. 1983-85), Fifty-five-plus Sr. Group (moderator North Broward, Ft. Lauderdale moderation counselor for PWP Chptr., 1994-97), Pi Omega Pi (sponsor St. Cloud State U. chpt. 1982-85), Phi Chi Theta, Delta Pi Epsilon, Delta Kappa Gamma. Jewish. Home: Apt 465 3671 Environ Blvd Fort Lauderdale FL 33319-4221 Office: Coll Bus St Cloud State U Saint Cloud MN 56301

REHART, BURTON SCHYLER, journalism educator, freelance writer; b. Pacific Grove, Calif., July 24, 1934; s. Burton Schyler Sr. and Ruth Evelyn (Whitaker) R.; m. Catherine Loverne Morison, Apr. 14, 1962 (div. Aug. 1983); children: William, Anne Marie, Catherine Evelyn; m. Felicia Rose Cousart, June 30, 1984 (div. Aug. 1995); m. Shirlee Jan Mynatt, July 20, 1996. BA in Journalism, Fresno (Calif.) State Coll., 1957; MA in History, Calif. State U., Fresno, 1966; cert., Coro found., 1961, Stanford U., summer 1975. Cert. adult edn. tchr., Calif. Reporter Bakersfield Californian, 1955; reporter, photographer Fresno Bee, 1957, Madera (Calif.) Daily

Tribune, 1960-61, Ventura (Calif.) Free Press, 1961-62; from instr. to prof. journalism Calif. State U., Fresno, 1963—, prof. journalism, 1979—, chmn. dept. journalism, 1992-94, prof. emeritus, 1997—. Author: M. Theo. Kearney-Prince of Fresno, 1988, (with others) Fresno in the 20th Century, 1986; editor, chmn. editorial bd. Fresno City, County Hist. Soc. Jour.; contbr. articles to profl. jours. Asst. foreman Fresno County Grand Jury, 1969. With U.S. Army, 1958-60. Mem. Soc. Profl. Journalists (pres. 1987-89), World Future Soc. (writer), Phi Kappa Phi (pres. 1977-78, Calif. State U. Fresno chpt.), Kappa Tau Alpha. Democrat. Episcopalian. Avocations: model ship building, photography, writing local history, historical romances. Home: 1557 E Roberts Ave Fresno CA 93710-6433 Office: Calif State U Dept Journalism Shaw And Cedar Ave Fresno CA 93740-0001

REHNKE, MARY ANN, academic administrator; b. Faribault, Minn., Jan. 23, 1945; d. Wesley Arthur and Sarah Frances (Smith) Rehnke; m. Charles Orin Willis, Apr. 18, 1924. BA in English, Cornell Coll., 1967; MA in English, U. Chgo., 1968, PhD in Lit., 1974; MS in Ednl Adminstrn., U. Wis., 1975. Head resident Elizabeth Waters Hall, U. Wis., Madison, 1970-73; asst. prof. English No. Ky. U., Highland Heights, 1973-82, acad. adminstr., 1976-77, dir. summer sessions, 1977-80; dir. conf. planning Am. Assn. Higher Edn., Washington, 1980-82; assoc. dean for faculty relations and acad. programs Coll. St. Catherine, St. Paul, 1982-83; assoc. dean of coll. Daemen Coll., Buffalo, N.Y., 1983-85; v.p. ann. programs Council of Ind. Colls., Washington, 1986—. Mem. planning com. nat. identification program Am. Council Edn., Washington, 1978-85; mem. program com. Nat. Conf. Women Student Leaders and Women of Distinction, Washington, 1985-88. Author: Women in Higher Education Administration: A Brief Guide for Conference Planners, 1982, Guide to Spiritual Retreats in the Washington, D.C. Area, 1997; editor: Creating Career Programs in a Liberal Arts Context, 1987; editor newsletter N. Ctrl. Regional Women's Studies, 1978-80; columnist Teaching and Learning, The Independent. Vestry mem Ch. of St. Clement, Alexandria, Va., 1982, vice chair search com., 1986-87. Named one of Outstanding Young Women Am., 1976. Mem. Am. Assn. Higher Edn. (coordinator nat. conf. roundtable 1982-86), Nat. Assn. Women Deans, Adminstrs. and Counselors, N.Am. Assn. Summer Sessions (rsch. chair 1979-80), Soc. for Values in Higher Edn., Jane Austen Soc. N.Am., Phi Beta Kappa, Phi Delta Kappa. Democrat. Episcopalian.

REIBLE, DANNY DAVID, environmental chemical engineer, educator; b. Rantoul, Ill., Dec. 21, 1954; s. George Anthony and Mavis Otilla (Prause) R.; m. Susanne Cecilia Schulte, Mar. 17, 1979; children: Kristin Nicole, Monica Lynn. BS, Lamar U., 1977; MS, Calif. Inst. Tech., 1979, PhD, 1982. Registered profl. engr., La. Asst. prof. La. State U., Baton Rouge, 1981-86, assoc. prof., 1986-92, prof. chem. engring., 1992—, Chevron prof. chem. engring., 1998—, dir. Hazardous Substance Rsch. Ctr., 1995—; Shell prof. environ. engring. U. Sydney, Australia, 1993-95. Vis. rschr. U.S. Army Engr. Waterways Experiment Sta., Vicksburg, Miss., 1990; sr. visitor Cambridge (Eng.) U., 1992; cons. in field. Author: Fundamentals of Environmental Engineering, 1999, Diffusion Models of Environmental Transport, 2000; contbr. articles to profl. publs. Environ. Sci. and Engring. fellow AAAS, 1987. Mem. AIChE (exec. bd. 1990-95, mem. nat. programming com., chair Baton Rouge sect. 2000, L.K. Cecil award 2001), Am. Chem. Soc., Am. Geophys. Union, Am. Soc. Engring. Edn. (New Engring. Educator Excellence award 1985), Coms. Nat. Rsch. Coun., Sigma Xi. Achievements include identification and evaluation of new mechanisms for contaminant release in the environment; further quantitative modeling of fate and transport contaminants in environmental systems. Home: 2112 Oakcliff Dr Baton Rouge LA 70810-1856 Office: La State U HSRC/S&SW 3418 Ceba Baton Rouge LA 70803-0001

REICH, ROSE MARIE, retired art educator; b. Milw., Dec. 24, 1937; d. Valentine John and Mary Jane (Grochowski) Kosmatka; m. Kenneth Pierce Reich, July 13, 1968; 1 stepson, Lance Pierce. BA, Milw. Downer Coll., 1959; MA, U. Wyo., 1967. Art tchr. Oconomowoc (Wis.) Area Schs., 1959-93, ret., 1993. Mem. Oconomowoc Edn. Assn., NEA (life), Wis. Edn. Assn., AAUW (v.p. membership 1989—), Delta Kappa Gamma (past pres.), Oconomowoc Woman's Club. Roman Catholic. Avocations: newfoundland dogs, needlework, designing stationery, polish paper cutting, restoring old church statues and mannequins. Home: 3717 N Golden Lake Rd Oconomowoc WI 53066-4104

REICHELT, SUSAN ANN, educator; b. Wisconsin Rapids, Wis., May 16, 1958; d. Robert Edgar Hamm, Marjorie Theresa Hamm; m. Blane Thomas Reichelt; 1 child, Kellee. BS, U. Wis., Stevens Point, 1980; MS, Fla. Tech., 1994; PhD, Iowa State U., 2001. Asst. prof. Ea. Ky. U., Richmond, 1997—99; supr. Zayed U., Dubai, United Arab Emirates, 1999—2000; asst. prof. Tex. Tech. U., Lubbock, 2000—. Recipient Outstanding Faculty award, Mortar Bd. Soc., 2001, Outstanding Dissertation Award, Am. Assn. of Family and Consumer Sci., 2002. Mem.: Assn. Career and Tech. Educators, Am. Assn. Family and Consumer Scis., Phi Upsilon Omicron. Avocations: travel, reading. Office: East Carolina U 261 Rivers Greenville NC 27858 Office Fax: 806-742-3042. Business E-Mail: sue.reichelt@ttu.edu.

REICHENBACH, DENNIS DALE, physician, pathology educator; b. Billings, Mont., Sept. 14, 1933; s. Ernest A. and Lilli (Stockland) R.; m. Jean Karen Hickey, Feb. 27, 1960; children: Stephen, Laura. BS in Basic Med. Sci., U. Wash., 1955, MD, 1958. Intern King County (Wash.) Hosp., Seattle, 1958-59; resident in pathology U. Wash., Seattle, 1959-63, asst. prof. pathology, 1966-70, assoc. prof., 1970-75, prof., 1975—98, prof. emeritus, 1998—. Dir. pathology residency program, U. Wash., 1981-88; pathologist in chief Harvorview Med. Ctr., Seattle, 1982-98. Contbr. articles to profl. jours. Served with USPHS, 1963-65. Mem. Am. Assn. Pathologists (cert.), Soc. Cardiovascular Pathologists, King County Med. Assn. Home: 80 E Roanoke St #14 Seattle WA 98102 Office: Univ Wash Med Ctr Dept Pathology Box 356100 Seattle WA 98195

REICHENBACH, M. J. GERTRUDE, retired university program director, consultant; b. Heerlen, Limburg, The Netherlands, Aug. 18, 1912; came to U.S., 1946; d. Jan Hubert Emile and M.J. Gertruda (Cardaun) Consten; m. Joseph Winfield, May 7, 1946; children: Paul Joseph, Peter David, Miriam Johanna, Eric Emile, Ingrid Gertrude. MA in English, U. Utrecht, The Netherlands, 1936; postgrad., Post Grad. Sch., The Netherlands, 1942-43; MA in German, U. Pa., 1971. English tchr. St. Clara Coll., Heerlen, The Netherlands, 1940-46; coord., originator Dutch studies U. Pa., Phila., 1969-87, cons. Dutch programs, 1987—, Syracuse (N.Y.) U., 1987—. Co-editor presentations and lectures, 1985. Recipient John Adams medal The Netherlands Govt., 1976; named Officer in the Order of Orange Nassou, The Netherlands Govt., 1986, Officer in the Crown Order of Belgium, Belgian Govt., 1987. Mem. Internat. Assn. Netherlandic Studies, Am. Assn. Netherlandic Studies, Netherlands Soc. Phila. (chmn. lectures, mem. exec. bd. 1988—), Netherland Am. Assn. Delaware Valley (exec. bd. 1988—), Assn. for Advancement Dutch Studies, Can. Assn. English Netherlandic Studies, Am. Translators Assn., Germantown Cricket Club, AAUW. Republican. Roman Catholic. Avocations: swimming, traveling, gardening. Home: 3031 W Coulter St Philadelphia PA 19129-1021

REICHERT, MARLENE JOY, secondary school educator, writer; b. Davao City, Philippines, Nov. 29, 1957; d. Jacob and Lois Marie Bouw; m. David Julius Reichert, June 13, 1981 (June 23, 1991). BA in English, Nyack Coll., 1980; postgrad., St. Thomas Aquinas, 1988; MA in Writing, Manhattanville Coll., 1997. Cert. tchr., N.Y., N.J. Tchr. St. Anne's Sch., Yonkers, N.Y., 1988-89; substitute tchr. Rockland County Pub. Schs., 1989-91; tchr. BOCES Night High Schs., West Nyack, NY, 1989-92, John Peter Tetard Middle Sch. 143, Bronx, NY, 1991—. Tchr. Achieving Success, 1992—94, Project Success, 1997—99, literacy staff developer, 2000—02. Contbr. short stories to lit. mags. Democrat. Episcopalian. Avocation: gardening. Home: 8 Aldine Park Nyack NY 10960-4426 Office: John Peter Tetard Mid Sch 120 W 231st St Bronx NY 10463-5905

REID, GERRY, education minister; b. Carboneer, Newfoundland, Can. m. Cathy Reid; children: Matthew, Lucas. BA, BEd, MPh, Meml. U. Tchr. Coaker Acad., New World Island, Notre Dame Bay; exec. asst. Fisheries Minister, St. John's, 1989—96; elected minister Newfoundland and Labrador, St. John's, Canada, 1996—, appointed parliamentary sec. to Minister of Fisheries and Aquaculture, 2000—01, minister fisheries and aquaculture, 2001—03, minister of edn., 2003—. Govt. whip Newfoundland and Labrador Legis. Assembly, St. John's, 1999—2000. Office: Office of the Minister of Edn PO Box 8700 St John's NL A1B 4J6 Canada

REID, JAMES DOLAN, mathematics educator, researcher; b. Augusta, Ga., June 24, 1930; s. Richard and Katherine (O'Leary) R.; m. Anne Carmody Donohue, Jan. 7, 1959; children: James Jr., Margaret, Gerald. BS, Fordham Coll., 1952, MA, 1954; PhD, U. Wash., 1960; MA (hon.), Wesleyan U., 1972. Asst. prof. Syracuse (N.Y.) U., 1960-61, 1963-65, assoc. prof., 1965-69; research assoc. Yale U., New Haven, 1961-62; asst. prof. Amherst (Mass.) Coll., 1962-63; assoc. prof. math. Wesleyan U., Middletown, Conn., 1969-70, prof., 1970—, chmn. math. dept., 1970-73, 85-88, prof. math., 1980—. Vis. prof. U. Würzburg, Fed. Republic Germany, 1989. Contbr. numerous articles on algebra (Abelian groups) to profl. jours. Mem. Bd. Edn., Regional Sch. Dist. #17, 1983-87. With USN, 1954-56. Mem. Am. Math. Soc., Irish Math. Soc., Math. Assn. of Am. Home: 159 Green Hill Rd Killingworth CT 06419-2218 Office: Wesleyan U Dept Math Middletown CT 06459-0001 E-mail: jreid@wesleyan.edu.

REID, JOHN PHILLIP, law educator; b. Weehawken, N.J., May 17, 1930; s. Thomas Francis and Teresa Elizabeth (Murphy) R. BSS., Georgetown U., 1952; LL.B., Harvard U., 1955; MA, U. N.H., 1957; J.S.D., NYU, 1962. Bar: N.H. 1955. Law clk. U.S. Dist. Ct. N.H., 1956; instr. NYU, N.Y.C., 1960-62, asst. prof. law, 1962-64, assoc. prof., 1964-65, prof. Sch. Law, 1966—. Author: Chief Justice: The Judicial World of Charles Doe, 1967, A Law of Blood: The Primitive Law of the Cherokee Nation, 1970, In a Defiant Stance, 1977, In a Rebellious Spirit, 1979, Law for the Elephant: Property and Social Behavior on the Overland Trail, 1980, In Defiance of the Law, 1981, Constitutional History of the American Revolution: The Authority of Rights, 1986, Constitutional History of the American Revolution: The Authority to Tax, 1987, The Concept of Liberty in the Age of the American Revolution, 1988, The Concept of Representation in the Age of the American Revolution, 1989, Constitutional History of the American Revolution: The Authority to Legislate, 1991, Constitutional History of the American Revolution: The Authority of Law, 1993, Policing the Elephant: Crime, Punishment, and Social Behavior on the Overland Trail, 1997, Patterns of Vengeance: Crosscultural Homicide in the North American Fur Trade, 1999, Contested Empire: Peter Skene Ogden and the Snake River Expeditions, 2002. Fellow Guggenheim Found., 1980, Huntington Library-NEH, 1980, 84; hon. fellow Am. Soc. Legal History, 1986. Fellow Am. Acad. Arts and Scis. Republican. Roman Catholic. Office: NYU Law Sch 40 Washington Sq S New York NY 10012-1099 E-mail: john.reid@nyu.edu.

REID, KATHERINE LOUISE, artist, educator, author; b. Port Arthur, Tex., Mar. 25, 1941; d. Clifton Commodore and Helen Ross (Moore) Reid. BA, Baylor U., 1963; postgrad. in design and illustration, Kans. City Art Inst., 1964; MEd, U. Houston, 1973; cert. supervision, U. Houston-Clear Lake City, 1980; postgrad., San Jacinto Coll., 1982. Litho reprodn. artist Hallmark Cards, Kansas City, Mo., 1963-64; tchr. art high sch. Pasadena (Tex.) Ind. Sch. Dist., 1964-77, supr. art, gifted and talented and photography, 1977-85, supr. art and photography InterAct, 1985-90, instrnl. specialist, 1990-2000, photography and art, 1990-93, instrnl. specialist in art and spl. programs, 1993-96, rsch. planning, data disaggregation, 1996-2000; internet tchr. recruiter, 2001—02; mural artist Old Car Barn, Edna, Tex., 2000—. 4 MAT learning styles trainer DuPont Leadership Devel. Process Trainer, Selective Rsch., Inst., tchr. perceiver specialist, performance quality sys. trainer, coop. learning trainer, outcome based edn. trainer, integrated unit devel. and authentic assessment trainer The Greater Gulf Coast Adminstr. Assessment Project, Assessor, 1990-2000; head crafts, asst. dir., dir. summer, winter discovery program-ski camp Cheley Colo. Camps, Denver, Estes Park, 1967-75; mem. awards com. John Austin Cheley Found., 1990-92; staff artist, media workshop Tex. Edn. Agy., Austin, summer, 1961; art enrichment tchr. Port Arthur Ind. Sch. Dist. (Tex.), summer, 1961; head crafts Camp Waluta, Silsbee, Tex., summer, 1960; mem. Tex. Edn. Agy., Art Leadership Inst., 1989, 90, Tracking Rsch. Com., 1991, Core Strategic Planning Team, 1992-2000, Outcome Based Edn. Dist. Planning Com., 1991-92, Quality Sys. Improvement Team, 1991-92, Outcome Based Edn. Com. Exit Outcomes, 1991; Region IV data disk trainer, 1998-2000, target teach coord., 1993-2000, multiple intelligence trainer, 1997-2000, data disaggregation trainer, 1997-2000, supt.'s rsch. com., 1999. Author: Through Their Eyes, 1989; inventor, patentee Pet Car Seat, U.S.A. and Can. Mem. Friends of Fine Arts-Baylor U., Waco, Tex., 1981—; mem. Scholastic Art awards Regional Bd., Houston, 1978-84, Tex. Edn. Agy.; bd. dirs. Houston Coun. Student Art Awards, Inc., 1984-90. Named Outstanding Secondary Educator of Am., 1975, Tex. Art Educator of Yr., 1985. Mem. ASCD, Tex. ASCD, Tex. Art Edn. Assn. (rep. editor newsletter 1982-85, chmn. supervision divsn. 1982-83, v.p. membership 1978-80, chmn. pub. info. com., regional chmn. youth art month 1980-82; regional chmn. membership com. 1976-78, pres. elect 1986, sec. 1991-93), Tex. Alliance for Arts Edn. (bd. vice chmn. 1984-86, treas. 1988-90), Nat. Art Edn. Assn. (conv. com. 1977, 85), Tex. Assn. Sch. Adminstrs., Houston Art Edn. Assn. (sec. 1969), Tex. Ret. Tchrs. Assn. (Dist. IV historian 2001-03), Pasadena Area Ret. Sch. Employees (parliamentarian 2002--), Delta Kappa Gamma (2d v.p. 1984-86, pres. 2002-2004, state leadership devel. for chpt. pres. com., 2003-2005). Baptist. Home: 106 Ravenhead Dr Houston TX 77034-1520 E-mail: artist@oldcarbarn.com., klreid@mail.esc4.com.

REID, LAURETTA GLASPER, retired principal; b. Balt., Sept. 6, 1931; BS, Coppin State Coll., 1953; MA, Columbia U., 1957; postgrad., Peabody Consevatory of Music, 1962; MS, Johns Hopkins U., 1980. Cert. elem. and middle sch. supr., prin., Md. Asst. prin., edn. specialist, master tchr. Balt. City Pub. Schs., prin. Recipient Senator's Cert. of Merit Tenure; Gov's. Citation. Mem. NAFE, ASCD, Nat. Assn. Elem. Sch. Prins., Md. Assn. Elem. Sch. Prins., Assn. of Tchr. Educators, Phi Delta Kappa. Office: 6405 Laurel Dr Baltimore MD 21207-6326

REID, LORENE FRANCES, middle school educator; b. St. Louis, May 28, 1946; d. Frank Bernard and Marcella Marie (Froechtenigt) Niemeyer; m. Patrick Joseph Reid, Aug. 11, 1967; 1 child, Christina Marie. BA in Spanish, Maryville U., 1968; MED in Secondary Edn., U. Mo., St. Louis, 1990; PhD in Edn., St. Louis U., 1995; MA in English, Southeast Mo. State U., 1996. Cert. Spanish, social studies, ESL tchr., reading specialist K-12, sch. psychologist, Mo.; cert. early adolescence/English lang. arts Nat. Bd. for Profl. Tchg. Stds. Spanish tchr. Rosary H.S., Spanish Lake, Mo., 1968-69, Taylor Sch., Clayton, Mo., 1969-70, Roosevelt H.S., St. Louis, 1988-89, Cleve. Jr. Naval Acad., St. Louis, 1989-90, Thomas Dunn Meml. Adult Edn., St. Louis, 1992-95; social studies tchr. St. Luke's Sch., Richmond Heights, Mo., 1981-88; ESL tchr. Grant Mid. Sch., St. Louis, 1990-92, Fanning Mid. Sch., St. Louis, 1992-98; tchr. leader Mid. Sch. Initiative, 1998-99; Schs. for Thought coord. MEGA Magnet Cluster, St. Louis, 1999-2000; psychol. examiner Student Support Svcs.—Gifted and Talented, St. Louis, 2000—03, sch. psychologist, 2003—; adj. assoc. prof. U. St. Louis, 2000—. Adj. prof. U. Mo.-St. Louis, 2000—; tutor Sylvan Learning Ctr., Crestwood, Mo., 1990-92; mem. St. Louis Ednl. Leadership Inst., 1994-97. Mem. Cmty. Leadership Program for Tchrs., St. Louis, 1993-94. Recipient Emerson Electric Excellence in Teaching award, 1994; named Tchr. of Yr., St. Louis Pub. Schs., 1994-95; named as one of 60 tchrs. recognized by Disney Channel Salutes the Am. Tchr., 1995-96. Mem. ASCD, Tchrs. English to Spkrs. of Other Langs., Nat. Coun. Tchrs. English, Midam. Tchs. English to Spkrs. of Other Langs., Internat. Reading Assn., Nat. Assn. Sch. Psychologists, Mo. Assn. Sch. Psychologists, Phi Delta Kappa. Home: 4400 Lindell Blvd Apt 9A Saint Louis MO 63108-2418 E-mail: lorenereid@aol.com.

REID, PETER LAURENCE DONALD, education educator; b. Edinburgh, Scotland, Jan. 30, 1937; s. Donald William and Dorothy Maud (Moore) R.; m. Kathleen Bentley Sheahan, June 15, 1968; 1 child, James Olivier; m. Heather Anne Johnson, Nov. 25, 1995; 1 child, David Augustus. BA, Cambridge U., 1960, MA, 1964; PhD, UCLA, 1974. Instr. Trinity Coll., Glenalmond, Scotland, 1960-63, Wanganui Collegiate Sch., New Zealand, 1964-66, The Thacher Sch., Ojai, Calif., 1966-70; asst. prof. Tufts U., Medford, Mass., 1973-79, assoc. prof., 1979-99, prof., 1999—. Editor: (2 vols.) Corpus Christianorum: Ratherius, 1976, 84; author: Tenth Century Latinity, 1981, Rather of Verona, 1991. Awarded summer insts. for tchrs., NEH, Tufts U., 1983-85, 87, 90-91, 93-94, 97. Mem. Am. Philol. Assn., Classical Assn. New Eng. Office: Dept Classics Tufts Univ Medford MA 02155 E-mail: peter.reid@tufts.edu.

REID, PIERRE, education minister; Rector Univ Sherbrooke, Canada, 1993—2001; spl. adviser Dep. Minister Econ. Devel., Quebec City, 2001—02; Quebec minister of edn. Quebec City, 2002—. Office: Bldg Marie-Guyart 16th Fl rue De La Chevrotière Québec G1R 5A5 Canada Fax: 418-646-7551. E-mail: ministre@meq.gouv.qc.ca.

REID, SHARON LEA, educational facilitator; b. Wheeler, Tex., Apr. 24, 1949; d. George S. and Arvazine (Deering) Robinson; m. Thomas Michael Reid, July 9, 1989. BS, McMurry Coll., 1970; MEd, Tarleton State U., 1979. Cert. tchr., edn. adminstr., supr., Tex. Tchr. Fleming Elem. Sch., San Antonio, 1971-72, Peebles Elem. Sch., Killeen, Tex., 1972-84, Sugar Loaf Elem. Sch., Killeen, 1984-85, facilitator, 1985-98, campus instructional specialist, 1998-99, Duncan Elem. Sch., Fort Hood, Tex., 1999—; emotional intelligence trainer Killeen ISD, 1999—. Trainer/dist. Marilyn Burns Problem Solving, Killeen, 1982-85, trainer/campus 4 MAT Lesson Design/Excel, Inc., Killeen, 1994-2000. Mem. Heights Concert Band, Harker Heights, Tex. Recipient music scholarship McMurry Coll., Abilene, Tex., 1968. Mem. ASCD, Nat. Read Across Am. Com., Tex. Elem. Prins. and Suprs. Assn., Tex. State Tchrs. Assn., Internat. Reading Assn., Tex. State Reading Assn., Bell County Reading Assn., Phi Delta Kappa. Avocations: instrumental music, bowling, sewing, cross-stitch. Office: Duncan Elem Sch 52400 Muskogee Dr Fort Hood TX 76544-1099

REID FIGUEROA, MARCELLA INEZ, educator, minister; b. Jamaica, N.Y., Mar. 12, 1956; d. Marcellus Emanuel Reid and Elizabeth (Dean) Reid-Joseph; stepfather: Alpha Omega Joseph; m. Steven Figueroa, Oct. 25, 1980. BA in Liberal Arts and Scis., CCNY, 1979; postgrad. Health, Edn., Nursing, Arts., NYU, 1981-82; MDiv, New Brunswick Theol. Sem., 1995. Ordained to ministry, 1996; ministry lic., N.Y., New Jerusalem Bapt. Ch., 1992. Svc. rep. HEW Social Security Adminstrn., Jamaica, N.Y., 1977-78, social ins. rep., 1979-81; dancing tchr. N.Y.C. Bd. Edn., 1983-84; coord., tchr. dance program N.Y.C. Bd. Edn. Aftersch., Jamaica, 1984-85; hosp. chaplain intern N.Y. Hosp. and Med. Ctr., Queens, N.Y., 1994; program design, coord. Assn. Black Seminarians, Queens, 1993-94; minister fine arts New Jerusalem Bapt. Ch., Jamaica, N.Y., 1991—; founder, exec. artistic dir. Dance Explosion Ltd., Laurelton, Queens, N.Y., 1973—; founder, CEO Gethsemane to Paradise Inc., 1996—. Mentor: to coll. student Bernard M. Baruch Coll., Jamaica, 1982, to h.s. student Fiorello La Guardia Middle Coll. H.S., Jamaica, Queens, N.Y., 1983, to handicapped choreographer Deja Vu Dance Theatre, Queens, 1984; dance educator on tour Cultural Exchange Network, USSR, summer, 1991. Contbr. articles to N.J. Bapt. Ch. Messenger, 1994-95; choreographer liturgical dances New Brunswick Theol. Sem. Archives, 1992-95; design coord. Seminars Unity in the Comty. Koinonia, 1992-95 (AOBS 1992-95). Work sponsor Coalition of 100 Black Women & Hunter Coll., Jamaica, 1984, Dept. Employment, Summer Youth Employment, Jamaica 1985; advocate 20's and the 40's Civic Assn., Jamaica, 1994; hdgqtrs. hostess Com. to Re-elect Barbara Clark, N.Y. State Assembly, Jamaica, summer 1993. Recipient Benjamin E. Mays scholarship Fund for Theol. Edn., N.Y.C., 1994-95; grantee for spl. art svcs. N.Y. State Coun. on the Arts, 1978-96. Mem. Sacred Dance Guild, Assn. Black Seminarians (sec. 1992-93 Women in Ministry award 1992), New Brunswick Theol. Sem. Alumni, Democrat. Baptist. Avocations: desktop publ., image cons., singing. Studio: 22401 141st Ave Laurelton NY 11413-2704

REID-MERRITT, PATRICIA ANN, social worker, educator, author, performing artist; b. Phila., Oct. 31, 1950; d. Curtis McDonald Reid and Etrulia Lucille Chapel; m. Ronald C. Bookhart, May 23, 1970 (div.); children: Christina, Brahim; m. William T. Merritt, Jul. 25, 1992; children: Jeffrey, Gregory. BA, Cabrini Coll., 1973; M in Social Work, Temple U., 1975; PhD in Social Work, U. Pa., 1984. Cert. in sch. social work, African-centered social work; cert. Dunham Technique. Psychiat. social worker Phila. Gen. Hosp., 1975-76; prof. Richard Stockton Coll., Pomona, N.J., 1976—. Founder, artistic dir. Afro-One Dance Drama and Drum Theatre, Inc. Recipient NAACP Freedom award, Outstanding Alumni Achievement award Cabrini Coll., Outstanding Alumni Achievement award Temple U. Mem. Nat. Coun. Black Studies (bd. dirs.), Assn. Black Women in Higher Edn., Coun. on Social Work Edn., Assn. Women in Social Work. Avocations: reading, dancing, gardening, cooking. Home: 2 Rosewood Ter Hamilton NJ 08620-9516 E-mail: patreidmer@aol.com.

REID-POLLARD, CHERYL ANN, early childhood education specialist; b. Chgo., Mar. 24, 1948; d. Isiah Akins and Annie Pearl Reid-Akins; m. Renwick Darrell Pollard; 1 child, Donna Luctricia. BS in Elem. Edn., Ga. State U.; MA in Early Childhood Edn., Mercer U.; cert. edn. specialist, West Ga. Coll., 1992. Cert. tchr., Ga. Tchr. East Thomaston (Ga.) Elem. Sch., 1973, Yatesville (Ga.) Elem. Sch., 1973-80; tchr. kindergarten Barnesville (Ga.) Elem. Sch., 1980-87, North Side Elem. Sch., Griffin, Ga., 1987-94; remedial tchr. Jordan Hill Elem. Sch., Griffin, 1994; adult edn., homework tutorial Griffin Tech. Jordan Hill Elem. Sch. Tutor at-risk students; vol. tutor Elbow Learning Lab.; homework tutorial Griffin Tech. Vocat., 1993; lead tchr. Latchkey Program; sch. rep. Am. 2000 Edn. Showcase, Griffin, 1992; participant ednl. workshops, seminars; Remedial Edn. Program Jordan Hill Elem. Sch., Grinnin, Ga., 1994-95; adult edn. Griffin Tech.; cons. in field. Vis. com. mem. for Dekalb County Sch. Sys. So. Assn. Colls. and Schs.; mem. Pres.'s com. Employment of People with Disabilities. Mem. NEA, Ga. Edn. Assn., Ga. Conf. Ministers' Wives, United Meth. Women, Alpha Kappa Alpha. Democrat. Home: 612 E Broad St Griffin GA 30223-3623

REIFF, PATRICIA HOFER, space physicist, educator; b. Oklahoma City, Mar. 14, 1950; d. William Henry and Maxine Ruth (Hoffer) R.; m. Thomas Westfall Hill, July 4, 1976; children: Andrea Hofer Hill, Adam Reiff Hill, Amelia Reiff Hill. Student, Wellesley Coll., 1967-68; BS, Okla. State U., 1971; MS, Rice U., 1974, PhD, 1975. Cert. secondary tchr., Okla., Tex. Resident rsch. assoc. Marshall Space Flight Ctr., Huntsville, Ala., 1975-76; rsch. assoc. space physics and astronomy dept. Rice U., Houston, 1975, asst. prof. space physics and astronomy dept., 1978-81, asst. chmn. space physics and astronomy dept., 1979-85, assoc. rsch. sci., 1981-87, sr. rsch. scientist, 1987-90. Adj. asst. prof. Rice U., 1976-78, disting. faculty fellow, 1990-92, prof. 1992—, chmn. dept. space physics and astronomy, 1996-99, dir. Rice Space Inst., 1999—; mem. sci. team Atmosphere Explorer Mission, Dynamics Explorer Mission; co-investigator Global Geospace Sci. Mission, ESA/Cluster Mission, IMAGE Mission; prin. investigator The Public Connection NASA, Mus. Tchg. Planet Earth; cons. Houston Mus. Natural Sci., 1986—; adv. com. on atmospheric scis. NSF, Washington,

1988-92; mem. stategic implementation study panel NASA, Washington, 1989-91; mem. space sci. adv. com. NASA, 1993-98, mem. space sta. utilization subcom., 1995-98; mem. adv. com. Los Alamos Non-Proliferation Divsn., 1998-2001; univ. rep. U. Space Rsch. Assn., Washington, 1993—, chair Coun. of Instns., 2001—; exec. com. George Observatory, Houston, 1989-92, others. Designer Cockrell Sundial/Solar Telescope, 1989; editor EOS (sci. newspaper), 1986-89; contbr. articles to profl. jours. Trustee, Citizens' Environ. Coalition, Houston, 1978-98, pres. 1980-85, adv. com. 1998-2000; mem. air quality com. Houston/Galveston Area Coun., 1980-83, Green Ribbon Com., City of Houston, 1981-83; active coms. Macedonia United Meth. Ch., 1988—. Named rsch. fellow NAS/NRC., 1975, an Outstanding Young Woman Am., 1977, '80, to Houston's Women on the Move, 1990; named Outstanding Aerospace Educator, Women in Aerospace, 1999; NASA grantee 1993, 94, 95, 98, 99; recipient NASA Group Achievement award. Fellow Am. Geophys. Union (fin. com. 1980-82, editor search com. 1992, pub. edn. com.); mem. Cosmos Club, Wellesley Club, Internat. Union of Geodesy and Geophysics (del. 1975, 81, 83, 89, 91, 93, 95, chair working group 2F, 1991-95). Avocations: organic gardening, beef ranching, scouting. Office: Rice U Dept Physics and Astronomy 6100 S Main St Houston TX 77251 E-mail: reiff@rice.edu.

REILING, HENRY BERNARD, business educator; b. Richmond, Ky., Feb. 5, 1938; s. Henry Bernard and Lucille Frances (Fowler) R.; m. Carol-Lina Maria Schuetz, June 4, 1962; children: Christina Lucille Reiling Breiter, Maria Hays, Carol-Lena Alexis Reiling Lessans. BA, Northwestern U., 1960; MBA, Harvard U., 1962; JD, Columbia U., 1965. Bar: N.Y. 1965. Mem. faculty Columbia U. Bus. Sch., 1965-76, prof., 1974-76; vis. prof. Stanford U. Bus. Sch., 1974-75; vis. asso. prof. Harvard U. Bus. Sch., 1972-73, prof., 1976—, Eli Goldston prof. bus. adminstrn., 1978—. Contbr. articles to profl. jours. Trustee Riverside Ch., NYC, 1976-77; bd. advisors Northwestern U. Coll. Arts and Scis., 1989—, alumni regent, 1997—. Recipient Alumnus Merit award, Northwestern U., 1996, Svc. award, 2002. Mem. ABA, N.Y. Bar Assn., Bar Assn. City N.Y., Am. Fin. Assn., Fin. Mgmt. Assn., Nat. Tax Assn., Tax Inst. Am., Union Club (N.Y.C.), Beta Gamma Sigma (hon.). Home: 28 Meriam St Lexington MA 02420-3618 Office: Harvard U Bus Sch Boston MA 02163

REILLEY, DENNEN, research agency administrator, educator; b. Greenwich, Conn., Mar. 1, 1937; s. Philip Francis and Florence Rita (Junkersfield) R.; m. Margaret Randall, Dougherty, Dec. 26, 1976; children: Philip F., Christopher J., Diane L., Elizabeth S., Katherine M. BSS, Fairfield U., 1959; MEd, U. Hartford, 1965; postgrad., U. Conn., 1965-70, CAGS, 1970. Tchr. New Britain (Conn.) Pub. Schs., 1960-65; tchr., adminstr. West Hartford (Conn.) Pub. Schs., 1965-69, 72-73; mem. faculty Central Conn. State Coll., New Britain, 1969-72; dir. field svcs. Edn. Devel. Ctr., Newton, Mass., 1973-82; sr. assoc., CEO Applied Rsch. Assocs., Sharon, Mass., 1980—. Adj. faculty U. Wyo., U. Minn.; cons. Am. Humane Assn., Edn. Devel. Ctr.; particip. Intl. Wannsee Conf., Berlin, Germany, 2002. Author: Training Program for Animal Care and Control Professionals, Sources: A Resource Guide to Funding Assistance for Parenting Programs, Education for Parenthood Conference Report; the Tri-State Parenting Collaborative, (with Jan Mokros) Summary of Exploring Childhood Evaluation Findings, The Animal Welfare Board of Directors, Total Quality Management: Implications for Animal Care and Control Professionals, Management Perspectives for Animal Care and Control Professionals, Board Perspectives for Nonprofit Organizations, Long Range Planning for Nonprofit Organizations; contbr. articles to profl. jours. Mem. New Britain Rep. town com., 1961-65; conductor mgmt. seminars nationally Not-for-profit orgns., 1982—. Recipient Rosemary Ames award Am. Humane Assn., 1983. Mem. Nat. Coun. Social Studies (conv. spkr. 1963-79, curriculum com. 1974-77, field svcs. bd. 1977-80), Conn. Coun. Social Studies (pres. 1965-66), NEA (life), ASCD, Am. Humane Assn., HSUS (conv. spkr. 1980-94, cons. 1994—). Office: 57 Brook Rd Sharon MA 02067-1415

REILLEY, MARGARET RANDALL, secondary school educator; b. Atlanta, Feb. 7, 1948; d. Guy Randall and Margaret Olivia (Ross) Dougherty; m. Dennen Reilley, Dec. 27, 1975; stepchildren: Philip F., Christopher J., Diane L. Reilley Waitkus, Elizabeth S. Reilley-Matthews, Katherine M. Reilley Lawn. BA in History, Stanford U., 1970; MA in Edn., Tufts U., 1971. Cert. tchr., adminstr., Mass. Tchr. social studies Norwood HS, Mass., 1971—. Founder, chmn. Norwood Law-Related Edn. Adv. Com., 1987-90; vice chmn. law related edn. com. Mass. Bar Assn., Boston, 1989-93; trainer Nat. Inst. for Citizen Edn. in the Law, Washington, 1990—; cons., reviewer Street Law, 4th edit., 1990-91; bd. dirs. Mass. Assn. for Law-Related Edn., 1990-98; mentor for new tchrs., 2000-; particip. Intl. Wannsee Conf., Berlin, Germany, 2002. Contbr. articles to legal jours. Recipient Horace Mann award Norwood Pub. Schs., 1989, Sch.-Cmty. Bar Partnership award ABA, 1990, Law-Related Edn. Tchr. of Yr. award Mass. Assn. for Law-Related Edn., 1990, Excellence in Tchg. award Harriet Goldin Found., 1993, Superior Tchr. of Law-Related Edn. award Norfolk County Bar Assn., 1994, Mass. Team Dist. Team fellow, 1996—, edn./rsch. fellow, JFK Libr. Mem. Nat. Coun. for Social Studies, Mass. Coun. for Social Studies (bd. dirs. 1993-95), South Shore Coun. for Social Studies (pres. 1993-95) Delta Kappa Gamma, Alpha Iota (pres. 1990-92). Avocations: walking, travel, gardening. Office: Norwood Pub Schs Nichols St Norwood MA 02062

REILLY, FRANK KELLY, business educator; b. Chgo., Dec. 30, 1935; s. Clarence Raymond and Mary Josephine (Ruckrigel) R.; m. Therese Adele Bourke, Aug. 2, 1958; children: Frank Kelly III, Clarence Raymond II, Therese B., Edgar B. BBA, U. Notre Dame, 1957; MBA, Northwestern U., 1961, U. Chgo., 1964, PhD, 1968; LLD (hon.), St. Michael's Coll., 1991. CFA. Trader Goldman Sachs & Co., Chgo., 1958-59; security analyst Tech. Fund, Chgo., 1959-62; asst. prof. U. Kans., Lawrence, 1965-68, assoc. prof., 1968-72; prof. bus., assoc. dir. divsn. bus. and econ. rsch. U. Wyo., Laramie, 1972-75; prof. fin. U. Ill., Champaign-Urbana, 1975-81; Bernard J. Hank prof. U. Notre Dame, Ind., 1981—, dean Coll. Bus. Adminstrn., 1981-87. Bd. dirs., chmn. Brinson Funds, Assn. Investment Mgmt. and Rsch.; past chmn. Inst. Chartered Fin. Analysts; past chmn. bd. dirs. NIBCO Corp.; bd. dirs. Internat. Bd. CFPs, Discover Bank, Ft. Dearborn Income Securities, Battery Park High Yield Fund., Morgan Stanley Dean Witter Trust Fed. Savs. Bank (FSB). Author: Investment Analysis and Portfolio Management, 1979, 7th edit., 2003, Investments, 1982, 6th edit., 2003; co-editor: Ethics and the Investment Industry, 1989; editor: Readings and Issues in Investments, 1975, High Yield Bonds: Analysis and Risk Assessment, 1990; assoc. editor Fin. Mgmt., 1977-82, Quar. Rev. Econs. and Bus, 1979-87, Fin. Rev., 1979-87, 92—, Jour. Fin. Edn., 1981—, Jour. Applied Bus. Rsch., 1986—, Fin. Svcs. Rev., 1989-96, Internat. Rev. Econs. and Fin., 1992—, European Jour. Fin., 1994—. Arthur J. Schmidt Found. fellow, 1962-65; U. Chgo. fellow, 1963-65; recipient faculty award U. Notre Dame, 1999. Fellow Fin. Mgmt. Assn. (pres. 1983-84, chmn. 1985-91, bd. dirs.); mem. Midwest Bus. Adminstrn. Assn. (pres. 1974-75), Am. Fin. Assn., Western Fin. Assn. (exec. com. 1973-75), Ea. Fin. Assn. (exec. com. 1979-84, pres. 1982-83), Midwest Fin. Assn. (pres. 1993-94), Fin. Analysts Fedn., Acad. Fin. Svcs. (pres. 1990-91), Inst. Chartered Fin. Analysts (coun. of examiners, rsch. and edn. com., edn. steering com.), Internat. Assoc. Fin. Planners (ednl. resource com., bd. dirs.), Assn. of Investment Mgmt. and Rsch. (C. Stewart Sheppard award 1991, Daniel J. Forrestal III Leadership award for profl. ethics 2001), Investments Analysts Soc. Chgo. (bd. dirs. 1988-89), Beta Gamma Sigma. Roman Catholic. Office: U Notre Dame Mendoza Coll Bus Notre Dame IN 46556-5646 E-mail: reilly.1@nd.edu.

REILLY, JOY HARRIMAN, theatre educator, playwright, actress, director; b. Dublin, May 17, 1942; came to U.S., 1969; d. Rene William and Sybil Mary (MacGowan) Harriman; m. Lawrence W. Kieffer, Dec. 29, 1965 (div. Sept. 1974); m. Richard Reilly, June 23, 1978; 1 child, Patrick Harriman. BFA, Ohio State U., 1977, MA, 1979, PhD, 1984. Intern The Times, London, 1961-62; asst. radio-TV prodn. J. Walter Thompson Advt., Frankfurt and London, 1962-67; copy editor, journalist The Newark (Ohio) Adv., 1970-83, part-time, 1973-80; assoc. prof. Ohio State U., Columbus, 1985—. Founding artistic dir. Grandparents Living Theatre, Columbus, 1984; theatre critic Sta. WOSU Radio, Columbus, 1979—; presenter papers Internat. Found. for Theatre Rsch., Stockholm, 1989, Dublin Eire, 1992, Assn. for Theater in Higher Edn., N.Y.C., 1989, 96, Chgo., 1990, 94, 97, Seattle, 1991, Atlanta, 1992, Phila., 1993, San Francisco, 1995, N.Y.C., 1996, San Antonio, 1998; presenter 1st Internat. Festival Sr. Adult Theater, Cologne, Germany, 1991, 1st Nat. Festival Sr. Theatre, 1993, 95, Disney Inst., Orlando, Fla., 1999, numerous others. Author: (plays) A Grandparent's Scrapbook, 1986, Golden Age is All the Rage, 1989, I Was Young, Now I'm Wonderful!, 1991, A Picket Fence, Two Kids and a Dog Named Spot, 1993, Woman, 1995, I've Almost Got the Hang of It, 1998, (chpt.) Olga Nethersole's Sapho, 1989. Commr. Upper Arlington (Ohio) Arts Coun., 1987. Recipient Ohioana citation Ohioana Libr. Assn., 1989, Columbus Mayor's award for Vol. Svcs. in Arts, 1986, Woman of Achievement award YWCA, 1991, Outstanding Achievement in Theatre award Ohio Theatre Alliance, 1991, Living Faith awards Columbus Met. Area Ch. Coun., 1992, Disting. Teaching award Ohio State U., 1994, Golden Achievement award Drs. Hosp., 1997; Battelle Endowment for Tech. and Human Affairs grantee, 1994. Mem. Am. Theatre Assn., Am. Soc. for Theatre Rsch., Internat. Fedn. for Theatre Rsch., Assn. for Theatre in Higher Edn., Ohio Theatre Alliance. Roman Catholic. Avocations: playwriting, gardening, reading, theatre. Office: Ohio State U Dept Theatre Columbus OH 43210

REILLY, KATHLEEN C. director, retired secondary school educator; b. Bridgeport, Conn., Mar. 24, 1937; d. John J. and Lillian (Higgins) Collins; m. Donald Reilly, Aug. 21, 1988; children: Robert L., John, Maura Williams. BS, Boston U., 1958; MA in Teaching, Manhattanville Coll., Purchase, N.Y., 1973; postgrad., Teachers Coll. Columbia U., 1983; CAS, Wesleyan U., 1985. Cert. permanent-English tchr., grades 7-12, N.Y. English tchr. Sch. of Holy Child, Rye, N.Y., Edgemont High Sch., Scarsdale, NY; ret., 2000; dir. of tng. Tri-State Consortium. Adj. prof. Hofstra U., Hempstead, N.Y., 1991. Grantee Am. Studies Consortium, NEH, SUNY Tchr. Rsch., 1991, Nat. Coun. Tchrs. English, 1990.; recipient Scarsdale-Westchester Phi Beta Kappa award, N.Y. State Educator of Excellence award, 1996; named Edgemont High Sch. Tchr. Yr.; finalist N.Y. State Tchr. of Yr. Mem. Nat. Coun. Tchrs. of English (tchr. researcher grant). Home: 211 Newtown Tpke Wilton CT 06897-4713

REINALDA, DAVID ANTHONY, elementary education educator; b. Lynwood, Calif., May 17, 1966; s. Robert Aarlen and Marie Antoinette (Presicci) R. AA, Riverside (Calif.) City Coll., 1989; BA, Calif. State U., San Bernardino, 1992; cert. elem. tchr., U. Calif., Riverside, 1994. Instrnl. aide Jurupa Unified Sch. Dist., Riverside, 1985, 89-93, substitute tchr., 1993—; day care worker Our Lady of Perpetual Help, 1988-89; substitute tchr. Riverside Unified Sch. Dist., 1996—; adult edn. tchr. Jurupa Unified Sch. Dist., 1999—. Vol. aide Jurupa Unified Sch. Dist., 1989-91; home tutor, 1987-89. Author: ABC, What's at School for Me, 1997; author children's stories Stone Soup, 1981. Little League coach, Riverside, 1980-82, scorekeeper, 1982-84; Sunday sch. tchr., supr. Hope Cmty. Ch., Riverside, 1988-98. Winner 1st pl. Lions Club speech contest, 1984; named Christian Youth of Yr. Kiwanis Club, 1985, Outstanding Young Man Am., 1992, 96. Mem. Phi Lambda Omega. Democrat. Mem. Christian Reformed Ch. Avocations: bowling, dancing, writing, acting.

REINERTSEN, GLORIA MAY, elementary education educator; b. Neptune, N.J., Jan. 28, 1951; d. George Henry and Gloria E. Bennett; m. Bernard Christian Reinertsen, June 17, 1972; children: Erik, Alicia. BA in Elem. Edn., Newark State Coll., Union, N.J., 1973; MA in Reading, Kean Coll., Union, N.J., 1987. Cert. tchr. PreK-12, reading specialist, reading tchr. K-12, English tchr. K-12, supr., N.J. Vol. tchrs. aide, Middletown, N.J., 1972; preshcool aide Morganville Sch., Marlboro Twp., N.J., 1973; mem. unit task force for right to read Morganville & Central Schs., Marlboro Twp., N.J., 1975, intern for learning, 1976, 1st grade tchr., 1973-76; full time sub Title I reading tchr. Central Sch., Marlboro Twp., N.J., 1979; tutor Kean Coll. Reading Clin., Union, N.J., 1986-87; 1st grade tchr. M.F. Atchison Sch., Tinton Falls, N.J., 1987-91, reading specialist, alternative reading tchr., 1991—, basic skills tchr., 1991—. Mem. staff devel. coun., lang. arts curriculum com., elem. sch. consortium, strategic planning com. Tinton Falls Schs. Bldg. goals planning com. Read Across Am. com. Recipient Celebrate Literacy award Internat. Reading Assn., 2000. Mem. ASCD, NEA, Internat. Reading Assn., N.J. Reading Assn., Monmouth County Reading Coun. (rec. sec. 1995-96, treas. 1996-97, v.p. 1997-98, pres. elect 1998-99, pres. 1999-2000, 2002-03), Tinton Falls Edn. Assn., N.J. Edn. Assn., Tinton Falls PTA. Methodist. Avocations: crafts, computers, gardening, reading. E-mail: greinertsen@tfs.k12.nj.us.

REING, ALVIN BARRY, special education educator, psychologist; b. Bklyn., July 10, 1930; s. Louis B. and Sylvia (Weinstein) Reing; m. Barbara R. Reing, Aug. 18, 1957 (dec. June 1992); children: Lynne Laufer, Sheryl Abramson, Naomi, Phyllis Klein; m. Marjorie J. Wortis, Aug. 15, 1998 (dec. May 2001). BA, CUNY, Bklyn., 1952; MA, CUNY, 1955; PhD, NYU, 1969; certs. guidance and sch. psychology, Yeshiva U., 1962. Lic. psychologist, N.Y.; tchr., counselor. Borough guidance coord. Bd. Edn., Bklyn.; prof. edn. CUNY, Bklyn.; pvt. practice. Text author; contbr. articles to profl. jours. Rsch. dir. Corinthian Med. and Health Svcs. Orgn. Fellow Am. Assn. Mental Retardation; mem. APA, NYSPA, CEC, PBK. Home: 579 Johnston Ter Staten Island NY 10309-3954

REINHARDT, ELEANOR HOLLISTER, nursing educator; b. Phila., June 4, 1946; d. Vincent and Eleanor (O'Brien) Hollister; m. Joseph William Reinhardt, Jan. 8, 1972; children: Carolyn, David. Nursing diploma, Jefferson Med. Coll., Phila., 1967; BSN, U. Pa., 1975; MSN, Gwynedd Mercy Coll., 1983. RN, Pa. From staff nurse to head nurse neonatology Jefferson Hosp., Phila., 1967—73, 1993—98; clin. educator Germantown Hosp., Phila., 1975—78, Gwynedd (Pa.) Mercy Coll., 1983, Holy Family Coll., Phila., 1986, Frankford Hosp., Phila., 1986—. Adv. bd. Jeanes Hosp., Phila., 1986—; adj. faculty Pa. State U., Phila., 1988—89, clin. inst., 1988—89; bd. dirs. Jeanes Cmty. Health Care Sys., Phila.; asst. prof. LaSalle Univ. Sch. of Nursing, Phila., 1998—2001. Mem.: ANA, Sigma Theta Tau. Avocations: violin, piano, sketching. Home: 401 Hartel Ave Philadelphia PA 19111-2420 Office: LaSalle Univ 1900 W Olney Ave Philadelphia PA 19141

REINHARDT, UWE ERNST, economist, educator; b. Osnabrueck, Germany, Sept. 24, 1937; came to U.S., 1964; s. Wilhelm and Edeltraut (Kehne) R.; m. Tsung-mei Cheng, May 25, 1968; children— Dirk, Kara, Mark B.Comm. in Econs. with honors, U. Sask., Saskatoon, Can., 1964; MA in Econs., Yale U., 1965, M.Ph. in Econs., 1967, PhD, 1970; DSc (hon.), Med. Coll. of Pa., 1987, CUNY, 1994, SUNY, 1998. Asst. prof. econs. and pub. affairs Princeton (N.J.) U., 1968-74, assoc. prof., 1974-79, prof., 1979—, James Madison prof. polit. economy, prof. econs., 1984—. Bd. dirs. McAllister Holdings; trustee Tchrs. Ins. and Annuity Assn., 1978-93, H&Q Health Fund; cons. Urban Inst., Washington, 1971-75, HEW, 1974—, HHS, Math., Inc., Princeton, 1970-80, AT&T, Basking Ridge, N.J., 1976-82, Nat. Westminster Bank USA, N.Y.C., 1979—, mem. Nat. Leadership Commn. Health Care, 1986—; mem. spl. adv. bd. VA, 1981-85; mem. U.S. Physicians' Payment Rev. Commn., U.S. Congress, 1986—; pres. Assn. for Health Svcs. Rsch., 1989-90, Found. Health Svcs. Rsch., 1990-91; mem. bd. advisors Nat. Inst. Healthcare Mgmt., 1993—, Pew Health Professions Commn., 1997—; mem. Coun. Econ. Impact Health Reform, 1994—; mem. external adv. panel health and nutrition World Bank, 1997—; chair coordinating com. Commonwealth Fund Internat. Program Health Policy, 1998—; commr. Kaiser Commn. Medicaid and Uninsured; trustee Duke U. Health Sys., Triad Hosps., Inc., Medcast/WebMD. Author: Physician Productivity and the Demand for Health Manpower, 1975; mem. editorial bd. Health Affairs, 1982—, New Eng. Jour. Medicine, 1989-92, Health Mgmt. Quar., Health Policy and Edn., Milbank Meml. Quar., Jour. AMA, 1991—; assoc. editor Jour. Health Econs., 1980-85, mem. editorial bd., 1981-83; contbr. articles to profl. jours. Bd. dirs. Nat. Acad. Aging, 1993—. Mem. Nat. Inst. Health Care Mgmt., Inst. Medicine Nat. Acad. Scis. (gov. council 1979-82) Office: Princeton U Woodrow Wilson Sch Prof of Economics & Public Affairs 412 Robertson Hl Princeton NJ 08544-0001

REINHARDT, WILLIAM PARKER, chemical physicist, educator; b. San Francisco, May 22, 1942; s. William Oscar and Elizabeth Ellen (Parker) R.; m. Katrina Hawley Currens, Mar. 14, 1979; children: James William, Alexander Hawley. BS in Basic Chemistry, U. Calif., Berkeley, 1964; AM in Chemistry, Harvard U., 1966, PhD in Chem. Physics, 1968; MA (hon.), U. Pa., 1985. Instr. chemistry Harvard U., 1967-69, asst. prof. chemistry, 1969-72, assoc. prof., 1972-74; prof. U. Colo., Boulder, 1974-84, chmn. dept. chemistry, 1977-80; prof. chemistry U. Pa., Phila., 1984-91, chmn. dept., 1985-88, D. Michael Crow prof., 1987-91; prof. chemistry U.Wash., Seattle, 1991—, assoc. chmn. undergrad. program, 1993-96. Adj. prof. physics U. Wash., Seattle, 1998—; vis. fellow Joint Inst. for Lab. Astrophysics of Nat. Bur. Stds. and U. Colo., 1972, 74, fellow, 1974-84; dir. Telluride Summer Rsch. Ctr., 1986-89, treas., 1989-93; com. on atomic, molecular and optical scis. NRC, 1988-90; sub com. Internat. Union Pure and Applied Physics, Atomic Molecular Physics, 2002—; vis. scientist Nat. Inst. Stds. and Tech., summers 1993—; vis. prof. chemistry U. Melbourne, Australia, 1997, Harvard U., 1998, Davidson Lectr., U. Kans., 2000; Kohler lectr. U. Calif., Riverside, 2002. Mem. editl. bd. Phys. Rev. A., 1979-81, Chem. Physics, 1985-94, Jour. Chem. Physics, 1987-89, Jour. Physics B. (U.K.), 1992—, Internat. Jour. Quantum Chemistry, 1994-2001, Digital Libr. of Math. Functions; rschr. theoretical chem. physics, theoretical atomic and molecular physics for numerous publs. Recipient Camille and Henry Dreyfus Tchr. Scholar award, 1972; Alfred P. Sloan fellow, 1972; J.S. Guggenheim Meml. fellow, 1978; Coun. on Rsch. and Creative Work faculty fellow, 1978; Wilsmore fellow U. Melbourne (Australia), 1997; J.W. Fulbright sr. scholar, Australia, 1997. Fellow AAAS, Am. Phys. Soc., Phi Beta Kappa; mem. Am. Chem. Soc., Sigma Xi (nat. lectr. 1980-82), Phi Lambda Upsilon (Fresenius award 1977), Phi Beta Kappa (vis. scholar 2002-03). Office: U Wash Dept Chemistry Box 351700 Seattle WA 98195-1700 E-mail: rein@chem.washington.edu.

REINHARZ, JEHUDA, academic administrator, history educator; b. Haifa, Israel, Aug. 1, 1944; came to U.S., 1961; s. Fred and Anita (Weigler) R.; m. Shulamit Rothschild, Nov. 26, 1967; children— Yael, Naomi BS, Columbia U., 1967; BRE, Jewish Theol. Sem., 1967; MA, Harvard U., 1968; PhD, Brandeis U., 1972; LHD (hon.), Hebrew Union Coll., 1995; DHL (hon.), Jewish Theol. Soc. Am., 1996, Fairfield U., 1999. Prof. modern Jewish history U. Mich., Ann Arbor, 1972—82; Richard Koret prof. modern Jewish history Brandeis U., Waltham, Mass., 1982—84, dir. Tauber Inst. Study of European Jewry, 1984—94; provost, sr. v.p. for acad. affairs Brandels U., Waltham, Mass., 1992—94; pres. Brandeis U., Waltham, Mass., 1994—. Mem. internat. acad. bd. Annenberg Rsch. Inst., 1986-90; bd. dirs. Yad Chaim Weizmann, 1990-2000, Internat. Editl. Bd. Pardès, 1996—; pres. Israel Prize, 1990, Akiba award, Am.-Jewish Com., 1996. Author: Fatherland or Promised Land: The Dilemma of the German Jew 1893-1914, 1975, Chaim Weizmann: The Making of a Zionist Leader, 1985 (Present Tense Literary award 1985, Kenneth B. Smilen Literary award 1985, Nat. Jewish Book award 1986, Shazar prize in history Israel, 1988), (in Hebrew) Hashomer Hazair in Germany, 1931-39, 1989, Chaim Weizmann: The Making of a Statesman, 1993 (Nat. Jewish Book award 1994); also numerous articles in French, German, Hebrew and English; co-author: Zionism and the Creation of a New Society, 1998, 2d edit., 2000, The Era of Political Zionism, 2000; gen. editor: Studies in Jewish History, 1984, European Jewish History, 1985; co-editor: The Jew in the Modern World, 1980, 2d edit. 1995, Mystics, Philosophers and Politicians, 1982, Israel in the Middle East 1948-83, 1984, The Jewish Response to German Culture, 1985, The Jews of Poland Between Two World Wars, 1989, The Impact of Western Nationalisms, 1992, Zionism and Religion, Hebrew edit., 1994, Essential Papers on Zionism, 1996; editor: The Letters and Papers of Chaim Weizmann, 1918-20, 1977, Dokumente zur Geschichte des deutschen Zionismus, 1882-1933, 1981, Living with Antisemitism, 1987. Bd. govs. United Israel Appeal/Jewish Agy., 1994, 2000; bd. dirs., mem. exec. com. Am. Joint Distbn. Com., 1994-2002; mem. acad. com. U.S. Holocaust Mus., 1990-2003, mem. com. on conscience nat. adv. forum, 1996—; mem. Presdl. Adv. Commn. on Holocaust Assets in U.S., 1998-2000; mem. Commn. on Israel-Diaspora Rels., 1996-97; trustee Am. Hebrew Acad., Greensboro, N.C., 2000—. Recipient Akiba award, Am. Jewish Com., 1996. Fellow Leo Baeck Inst., Royal Hist. Soc., Am. Acad. Jewish Rsch., Am. Acad. Arts and Scis.; mem. Yad Vashem Soc. (adv. bd. 1983), Nat. Coun. Shazar Ctr., Assn. for Jewish Studies (sec. 1986-88, treas./sec., 1988-94), Coun. on Fgn. Rels. Home: 66 Beaumont Ave Newton MA 02460-2331 Office: Office Of The Pres Irving Enclave 113 415 South St # Ms100 Waltham MA 02453-9110 E-mail: jreinharz@brandeis.edu.

REINHOLD, ALLEN KURT, graphic design educator; b. Salt Lake City, Feb. 21, 1936; s. Eric Kurt and Lillian (Hansen) R.; m. Irene Laura Rawlings, May 4, 1962; children: Cindy Anne, David, Alyce, Bryce, Eugene Patrick. BA, Brigham Young U., 1961, MA, 1962. Cert. secondary and post secondary tech. and indsl., Utah, color cons. Freelance artist Allen Reinhold Art & Design Studio, American Fork, Utah, 1962—; tchr. art Emery County High Sch., Castle Dale, Utah, 1962-63; graphic artist Brigham Young U., 1954-56, 63-66; prodn. artist Evans Advt. Agy., Salt Lake City, 1968; dir. ednl. media Olympus High Sch., Salt Lake City, 1966-68; art dir. Telelecture Utah div. Family Svcs., Salt Lake City, 1968-69; art instr. Utah Tech. Coll., Salt Lake City, 1969-85; prof. graphic design Salt Lake Community Coll., 1985-96, prof. emeritus, 1996—. Advisor, coach Vocat. Indsl. Clubs of Am., Salt Lake City, 1978-91. Illustrator: Book of Mormon Stories, 5 vols., 1971-76; exhibited in group shows at Salt Lake Art Festival, 1982, Pageant of the Arts, Am. Fork, 1980-89. Active Boy Scouts Am., American Fork, 1975-90; bd. dirs. art Am. Fork City, 1976-80; team mem. Utah State Bd. for Vocat. Edn. Accreditation, Salt Lake City, 1990; mem. Art Rsch. in Europe, summer 1995; van driver Utah County Foster Grandparents, 2001—. Fellow Delta Phi Kappa (historian 1961-62), Salt Lake Community Coll. Faculty Senate. Republican. Mem. Lds Ch. Avocations: horses, boating, fishing, hunting, gardening. Home: 590 N 200 E American Fork UT 84003-1711 E-mail: reinhold-art@outdrs.net.

REINHORN, ANDREI M. civil structural engineering educator, consultant; b. Bucharest, Romania, Oct. 23, 1945; s. Moritz A. and Dina (Rosenfeld) Reinhorn; m. Tova A. Waldman, Oct. 15, 1968; children: Michael, Gad. BSc, Technion - Israel Inst. Tech., Haifa, 1968, DSc, 1978. Registered profl. engr., N.Y., Israel. Structural engr. Milstein & Singer, Cons. Engrs., Tel Aviv, 1972-73, Haifa, 1973-79, Buffalo, 1980-85, Reinhorn Consulting Engrs., 1990—; vis. asst. prof. U. Buffalo, 1979-81, asst. prof., 1981-86, assoc. prof., 1986-90, prof., 1990—2002; chmn. dept. civil engring. SUNY, Buffalo, 1996-99, eminent prof., 2002—. Assoc. editor: Structures Jour., 2000—, : Spectra Jour., 2002; author: conf. procs.; contbr. chapters to books. Capt. Israel Def. Force, 1968—72. Grantee rsch., NSF, 1983—84, 1986—95, 1994—. Fellow: ASCE (faculty advisor 1981—83, bd. dirs. 1986—96, pres. Buffalo sect. 1993—94, Outstanding Svc. award 1982, 1983); mem.: G.E. Brown Jr. Network Earthquake Engring. Simulation (bd. dirs. 2003—), N.Y. State Profl. Engring. Assn. (Engring. Educator of Yr. award 1991, Hist. Achievement award 1995, Engr. of Yr. 2002), Nat. Ctr. for Earthquake Engring. Rsch. (Outstanding Achievement award L.A. Tall Bldg. Coun. 1995), Earthquake Engring. Rsch. Inst., Am. Concrete Inst. Achievements include invention of press brake deflection compensation structure, automatic diagnostic sys. for elec. cir. breakers; patents for. Avocations: photography, skiing, bicycling, scuba diving. Home: 12 Troy View Ln Buffalo NY 14221-3522 Office: SUNY Buffalo Civil Struct/Environ Engrg 231 Ketter Hall Buffalo NY 14260-4300 E-mail: reinhorn@buffalo.edu.

REINISCH, JUNE MACHOVER, psychologist, educator; b. N.Y.C., Feb. 2, 1943; d. Mann Barnett and Lillian (Machover) R. BS cum laude, NYU, 1966; MA, Columbia U., 1970, PhD with distinction, 1976. Asst. prof. psychology Rutgers U., New Brunswick, N.J., 1975-80, assoc. prof. psychology New Brunswick, N.J., 1980-82, adj. assoc. prof. psychiatry, 1981-82; prof. psychology Ind. U., Bloomington, 1982-93, dir. Kinsey Inst. Rsch. in Sex, Gender, and Reprodn., 1982-93; prof. clin. psychology Sch. Medicine, Indpls., 1983-93; dir. emeritus Kinsey Inst., 1993—. Dir., prin. investigator Prenatal Devel. Projects, Copenhagen, 1976—, sr. rsch. fellow, trustee The Kinsey Inst., 1993—; pres. R2 Sci. Comms., Inc., Ind., N.Y., 1985—; vis. sr. rschr. Inst. of Preventive Medicine, Copenhagen Health Svcs., Kommunehospitalet, Copenhagen, 1994—; cons. SUNY; sci. rsch. cons. Strategic Surveys Internat., N.Y.C. Author: The Kinsey Institute New Report on Sex, 1990, 94, pub. 8 fgn. edits.; editor, contbr. books Kinsey Inst. series; syndicated newspaper columnist: The Kinsey Report; contbr. rsch. reports, revs., articles to profl. jours.; appeared on TV shows including PBS, BBC, ABC and NBC sci. spls., Discovery, ABC Science Specials, 20/20, Oprah Winfrey, Geraldo Rivera, Charles Grodin, Montel Williams, Sally Jessy Rafael, Good Morning Am., Today Show, CBS This Morning; guest host TV shows including CNBC Real Personal, TalkLive, also fgn. appearances. Founders day scholar NYU, 1966; NIMH trainee, 1971-74; NIMH grantee, 1978-80, Ford Found. grantee, 1973-75, Nat. Inst. Edn. grantee, 1973-74, Erikson Ednl. Found. grantee, 1973-74, grantee Nat. Inst. Child Health and Human Devel., 1981-88, Nat. Inst. on Drug Abuse, 1989-95; recipient Morton Prince award Am. Psychopath. Assn., 1976, medal for 9th Dr. S.T. Huang-Chan Meml. Lectr. in anatomy Hong Kong U., 1988, Dr. Richard J. Cross award Robert Wood Johnson Med. Sch., 1991, Award First Internat. Conf. on Orgasm, New Delhi, 1991, Disting. Alumnae award Tchrs. Coll. Columbia U., 1992, award for su contbn. Profl. al Conocimiento dela Sexualidad Humana, Assn. Mexicana de Sexologia, Mexico City, 1996; named Regents lectr. UCLA, 1999. Fellow AAAS, APA, Am. Psychol. Soc., Soc. for Sci. Study Sex; mem. Internat. Acad. Sex Rsch. (charter), Internat. Women's Forum, Women's Forum. Inc., Internat. Soc. Psychoneuroendocrinology, Internat. Soc. Rsch. Aggression, Internat. Soc. Devel. Psychobiology, Am. Assn. Sex. Educators, Counselors and Therapists, Sigma Xi. Office: SUNY HSCB PBL Box 120 450 Clarkson Ave Brooklyn NY 11203-2056 also: The Kinsey Inst Prenatal Devel Project Ind U Bloomington IN 47405

REINKE, DORIS MARIE, retired elementary education educator; b. Racine, Wis., Jan. 12, 1922; d. Otto William Reinke and Louise Amelia Goehring. BS, U. Wis., Milw., 1943; MS, U. Wis., Whitewater, 1967. Tchr. kindergarten Elkhorn (Wis.) Area Sch. Sys., 1943-69, bldg. prin., 1968-70, summer sch. dir., 1974-75, grade 2 tchr., 1970-84, primary dept. chmn., 1971-84, administrv. asst., supervising tchr., 1957-83, student tchr., 1984, ret., 1984; oriented experience tchr. Program Area Sch. Sys., Elkhorn, 1966. Pres. Elkhorn Edn. Assn., 1949-50; rep. dist. State Kindergarten Conf., Oshkosh, Wis., 1966; participant early edn. conf. State Early Edn. Conf., Eagle River, Wis., 1968; tchr. Covenant Harbor Elderhostel, 1997, 98; established Doris M. Reinke Resource Ctr., 2002. Contbr. weekly newspaper column Webster Notes, 1989, weekly newspaper column County Chronicles 1901, weekly newspaper column Bay Times Newspaper, weekly newspaper column Walworth County Diary Monthly column in The Week, 1991, weekly newspaper column County Chronicles weekly column Bay Times and Walworth Times, 2001; author: Doris' Corner newsletter Walworth County Geneal. Soc., 1992—; author: (with Charlotte and William Gates) Guide to Beckwith's History of Walworth County, 2000; contbr. weekly newspaper column Lake Geneva Times, 2001. Chmn. Sch. Centennial, Elkhorn, 1987; mem. Elkhorn Hist. Preservation Com., 1991—; chmn. Sesquicentennial com., 1997—; dir. Webster House Mus., 1991—; mem. Walworth County Sesquicentennial Com., 1997—98; mem. sesquicentennial com. Walworth County Fair, 1998—; archivist Sugar Creek Luth. Ch., 1992—, mem. ch. coun., 2003; choir mem. Luth. Ch., 1995—2001; del. dist. constn. conv. Evang. Luth. Ch. Am., Beloit, Wis., 1987; com. mem. Luth. Ch., Elkhorn, 1987; RSVP Vol. Food Pantry, Elkhorn, 1985—2002, bd. dirs., 1985—88, 1995—. Recipient Wis. Edn. Rsch., West Bend, Wis., 1966, Outstanding Elem. Tchrs., Wash., 1973, Wis. Dept. Edn., Madison, 1980, Local History award State Hist. Soc. Wis., 1993, Outstanding Sr. Citizen award Walworth County Fair, 1999, Cmty. Svc. award, Masons, 2000. Mem.: Walworth County Ret. Tchrs. Assn. (v.p. 1988, pres. 1991), Nat. Ret. Tchrs. Assn., Walworth County Geneal. Soc. (bd. dirs. 1991—92), Walworth County Hist. Soc. (treas. 1985—89, v.p. 1990—91, pres. 1991—96, v.p. 1999—2000, pres. 2000—02), Elkhorn Women's Club (sec. 1999—2000, v.p. 2003), Alpha Delta Kappa (state pres. 1968—70, 1976—78, chpt. pres. 2002). Avocations: reading, baseball, bird watching, traveling. Home: 516 N Wisconsin St Elkhorn WI 53121-1119

REINOLD, CHRISTY DIANE, school counselor, consultant; b. Neodasha, Kans., July 21, 1942; d. Ernest Sherman and Faye Etta (Herbert) Wild; m. Willaim Owen Reinold, Dec. 20, 1964; children: Elizabeth, Rebecca. BA Edn., MA in Edn. and Psychology, Calif. State U., Fresno, 1964. Cert. counselor, Family Wellness instr.; lic. mental health counselor, Fla. Tchr. Clovis (Calif.) Unified Sch. Dist., 1965-66, Santa Clara (Calif.) Unified Sch. Dist., 1966-67, Inst. Internat. Chateaubriand, Cannes, France, 1968-69; tchr., vice prin. Internat. Sch., Sliema, Malta, 1969-70; elem. sch. counselor Duval City Schs., Jacksonville, Fla., 1977-82, Lodi (Calif.) Unified Sch. Dist., 1982—. Cons. Calif. Dept. Edn.; mem. Calif. Commn. on Tchr. Credentialing, Sacramento, 1986—. Co-author: The Best for Our Kids; Counseling in the 21st Century; contbr. articles. Chmn. bd. dirs. Oak Crest Child Care Ctr., Jacksonville, 1979-81. Mem.: AAUW (3rd v.p. 1974, 1st v.p. 1980, by-laws chmn. 1990, chmn. pub. policy 1991—93, pres. 1993), Lodi Pupil Pers. Assn. (pres. 1986—87), Calif. Alliance Pupil Svcs. Orgns. (bd. dirs. 1988—95), Fla. Sch. Counselors Assn., Calif. Assn. Counseling and Devel., Calif. Sch. Counselor Assn. (legis. chmn. 1985—90, pres. 1991), Am. Sch. Counselor Assn. (govt. rels. specialist 1993—94). Republican. Avocations: history, travel, politics. Home: 1180 Northwood Dr Lodi CA 95240-0443

REINSTEIN, TODD RUSSELL, lawyer, educator; b. Chgo., July 30, 1937; s. Paul A. and Estelle R. (Goodkin) R.; m. Anna Reinstein; 1 child, Leif. BS in Acctg., UCLA, 1959, JD, 1962; postgrad., U. So. Calif., 1962-63. CPA, cert. specialist taxation law. Prof. Coll. Bus. Adminstrn. and Econs. Calif. State U., Northridge, 1967—, co-dir. taxation program Grad. Sch. Bus.; CFO, CEO Reinstein & Calkins, L.A., 1968—2003; atty. Valensi, Rose & Magaram, Plc, L.A., 2003—. Contbr. articles to profl. jours. Mem. Calif. Bar Assn., L.A. County Bar Assn., Beverly Hills Bar Assn., Beta Gamma Sigma, Beta Alpha Psi. Office: Valensi Rose and Magaram 2029 Century Park E Ste 2050 Los Angeles CA 90067-3031 Office Fax: 310-277-1706.

REISER, WALTER FREDERICK, athletic director, athletic trainer; b. N.Y., Apr. 8, 1961; s. Edward Eugene and Anne Lorraine (Bassett) R.; m. Kathleen Mary Urbanowicz, July 30, 1988. BS, Springfield Coll., 1983, MEd, 1984; Cert. in Supervision, Georgian Court Coll., 1994. Part-time asst. trainer New Eng. Patriots (NFL), Foxbough, Mass., 1983; asst. athletic trainer Springfield (Mass.) Coll., 1983-84; health-phys. edn. instr./trainer Rumson (N.J.)-Fair Haven Regional H.S., 1984-88, dir. athletics/athletic trainer, 1987—. Mem. Nat. Athletic Trainers Assn., Nat. Interscholastic Athletic Adminstrs., Shore Conf. Athletic Trainers (chairperson 1988-94), Monmouth County Dirs. Athletics (sec. 1992-94, pres.-elect 1994—). Avocations: golf, running, fitness. Home: 28 Sherman Ave West Long Branch NJ 07764-1526 Office: Rumson Fair Haven Regional 74 Ridge Rd Rumson NJ 07760-1851

REISMAN, BERNARD, theology educator; b. N.Y.C., July 15, 1926; s. Herman and Esther Sarah (Kavesh) R.; m. Elaine Betty Sokol, Aug. 26, 1951; children: Joel Ira, Sharon Fay, Eric K., Robin Sue. B in Social Sci, CCNY, 1949; M in Social Sci. and Adminstrn., Western Res. U., 1951; LHD, Hebrew Coll., Boston, 1995; DHL (hon.), Gratz Coll., Phila., 1995; PhD, Brandeis U., 1970; Doctorate (hon.), Hebrew Union Coll., Cin., 2003. Agy. dir. Jewish Cmty. Ctr., Chgo., 1951-67; prof. Brandeis U., Waltham, Mass., 1969—, dir. Hornstein program in Jewish communal svc., 1971-93, Klutznick prof. contemporary Jewish studies, 1993-99, emeritus, 1999—, dir. Adult Learning Inst., 1998—2001. Lectr. in field; vis. prof. Baerwald Sch. Social Work, Hebrew U., Jerusalem, 1978, Ctr. Jewish Edn. in Diaspora, 1978; sr. cons. Josephtal Found., Jerusalem, 1978; cons. European coun. Am. Joint Distbn. Com., 1978, Inst. for Jewish Life, N.Y.C., 1972-76; rsch. assoc. on future of religion Nat. Coun. Chs., 1972-73; Arnulf Pins meml. lectr. Hebrew U., Jerusalem, 1983, 84. Author: Reform Is a Verb, 1972, The Jewish Experiential Book: Quest for Jewish Identity, 1978, The Chavurah: A Contemporary Jewish Experience, 1977, (with Joel I. Reisman) The New Jewish Experiential Book, 2003. Marshal Sklare Awd. Assoc. Soc. Scientific Study Contemporary Jewry, 1998; Brandeis U. honors: Bernard Reisman Grad. Student Lounge, 2001, Bernard Reisman Fund, 2001. Mem. Conf. Jewish Communal Svc., Nat. Jewish Family Ctr., Am. Jewish Com. (1st chmn. acad. adv. com. 1979-82, 75th Anniversary award 1981), Am. Jewish Hist. Soc. (acad. coun. 1979—), Assn. for Jewish Studies. Home: 28 Fairway Dr W Newton MA 02465-1713 Office: Brandeis Univ Adult Learning Inst MS 085 Waltham MA 02454-9110 Fax: (781) 736-2122. E-mail: bali@brandeis.edu.

REISSMAN, ROSE CHERIE, elementary education educator; b. N.Y.C., Nov. 4, 1951; d. Seymour Frank and Sidonia (Blank) R.; m. Steven Feld. Cert. tchr., N.Y. Classroom tchr. various schs., N.Y.C., from 1972; now tchr. specialist for curriculum design Sch. Dist. 25, N.Y.C. Founder, mgr. Writing Inst. Peer Teaching, Forum, and Oral History, 1983—; grant writer, curriculum writer N.Y.C. Bd. Edn.; adj. prof. edn. Manhattanville (N.Y.) Coll., Fordham U., N.Y.C.; mem. tchr. network Cradle Ctr. for Law-Related Edn., Writing Notebook; mem. adv. bd. Giraffe Educator, N.Y. Newsday; v.p. edn. Wedgewood Brandeis Community Group; mem. tchr. adv. coun. Impact II; presenter workshops on grant writing; ednl. liaison project for social and emotional learning, 1998; dir. curriculum Literacy and Learning Project, 1998; rsch. devel. and standards alignment coord. Futurekids Tech. Literacy Ctr., 1998, ednl. cons. Mus. of City N.Y., 1999—, Milennium Mus. City N.Y., 1999—. Author: Newday's 1988 Elections, 1989, Mayoral Curriculum, 1990, Gubernatorial Presidentes Curriculum, 1987, N.Y. Board of Education Infusing Critical Thinking in the Middle Schools with World Processing Software and Picture Disc, 1994, Entrepreneurial Empowerment 6-12 Curriculum Workbook, Rights and Responsibilities, 1992, Mayoral Campaign, 1993, The Evolving Multicultural Classroom, 1995, The Sun's On - It's Your Turn, 1997, Rhythm & Dues, 1997, Anthony Ant and the Grasshopper, Newsday Governor Curriculum, 1999, Newsday Character Education Curriculum, 1999; field editor Learning Mag., 1991—; editor Learning and Leading through Technology Lang. Arts, 1999—. Christa McAuliffe fellow, 1988; grantee Dupont Found., Am. Cancer Heart Assn., 1992; recipient Judy Blume Ctr. award, 1988, Valley Forge Bill of Rights medal, 1992, Newspaper in Edn. Curriculum award, 1996, Md. English Coun. Multicultural award, 1996, Edn. award Mus. of the City of N.Y., 2000; named NYSEC Tchr. of Excellence, 1993; recipient numerous other awards and grants. Mem. Nat. Coun. Tchrs. English (dir. funding), N.Y.C. Assn. Tchrs. English (v.p. 1993, pres. 1994), Nat. Found. Teaching Entrepreneurships (cons., bd. dirs.), Assn. Computers in Edn. (pres.). Office: Writing Inst 110 Seaman Ave Apt 5C New York NY 10034-2808 E-mail: sjm887@yahoo.com.

REITER, DAISY K. retired elementary education educator; b. Lewisburg, Pa., Aug. 25, 1936; d. Clark B. and Maude E. (Bensinger) Zimmerman; m. Edward P. Reiter, June 3, 1978; children: Edward, Amy, Russ, Elizabeth Sieber White, Katheryn Sieber Ellis, Ann Sieber Myers. BS in Elem. Edn., Pa. State U., 1957; postgrad., U. No. Colo., Greeley, Pa. State U. Lic. real estate agt. Tchr. grade 4 Hershey (Pa.) Sch. Dist., 1957-58; tchr. grades 4 and 5 Red Land Sch. Dist., New Cumberland, Pa., 1959-61; kindergarten tchr. Topeka City Schs., 1958-59; tchr. grade 5 Wallaceton-Boggs Elem. Sch. Philipsburg (Pa.)-Osceola Area Sch. Dist., 1975-97, ret., 1997—. Inservice leader transactional analysis and arts in edn.; researcher Civil War, newspapers, animals and habitats, body systems. Writer poetry. Mem. choir lst Luth Ch. Recipient Arts in Edn. grants (4 yrs.). Mem. NEA, Pa. State Edn. Assn., Philipsburg-Osceola Edn. Assn, Toughlove Chpt. (founder). Home: PO Box 704 Philipsburg PA 16866-0704

REITH, LINDA JO, secondary school educator; b. Middlesboro, Ky., Apr. 13, 1950; d. Joseph Hubert and Thelma Elizabeth (Moore) Marcum; m. William Walter Reith II, June 17, 1972; children: Gretchen, Laura, Will. BS and provisional tchg. cert., Union Coll., Barbourville, Ky., 1971; M in Math Edn., U. Va., 1994. Tchr. grade 3 Lee County, Pennington Gap, Va., 1971-72; math tchr. grades 9-12 Orange (Va.) County, 1983—. Co-sponsor Students Against Drunk Driving Club, 1986-94; mem. adj. faculty Piedmont Val C.C., 1997—. Asst. Webelo leader Boy Scouts Am., Gordonville, Va., 1990-92, fund raiser chmn., 1992-93, com. mem., 1992-99. Mem. Nat. Coun. Tchrs. Math., Jefferson Coun. Tchrs. Math. Avocations: reading, needlework-crafts, hiking, dancing. Home: 2007 Carpenters Mill Rd Barboursville VA 22923-8533 Office: Orange County HS Selma Rd Orange VA 22960

REITZ, CURTIS RANDALL, lawyer, educator; b. Reading, Pa. s. Lester S. and Magdalene A. (Crouse) R.; m. Virginia R. Patterson, Dec. 19, 1953 (div.); children— Kevin R., Joanne E., Whitney A.; m. Judith N. Renzulli, Sept. 18, 1983 BA, U. Pa., 1951, LL.B., 1956. Bar: Pa. 1957, U.S. Supreme Ct. 1959. Law clk. to Chief Justice Earl Warren U.S. Supreme Ct., 1956-57; mem. faculty law U. Pa., Phila., 1957—, asst. prof. law, 1957-60, assoc. prof., 1960-63, prof., 1963—, provost, v.p., 1971—73, Algernon Sydney Biddle prof. law, 1985—. Trustee Internat. House Ctr. Phila.; bd. mgrs. Glen Mills Schs., Pa. Served to 1st lt. U.S. Army, 1951-53 Life Mem. Am. Law Inst., Mem., Nat. Conf. Commrs. on Uniform State Laws, Order of Coif Office: U Pa Law Sch 3400 Chestnut St Philadelphia PA 19104-6204 E-mail: creitz@law.upenn.edu.

REKTORIK-SPRINKLE, PATRICIA JEAN, classics consultant, retired Latin language educator; b. Robstown, Tex., Feb. 19, 1941; d. Julius and Elizabeth Lollie (Ermis) Rektorik; m. Edgar Eugene Sprinkle, June 22, 1963; children: Julie Anne, Mark. BA in English and Latin, Our Lady of the Lake Coll., San Antonio, 1963, MA, 1967; doctoral student, Tex. A&M U., 1968-74, U. North Tex., 1987—. Cert. secondary tchr., Tex. Latin and English tchr. Ysleta Independent Sch. Dist., El Paso, Tex., 1963-64, El Paso Independent Sch. Dist., 1964-65; instr. Our Lady of the Lake Coll., 1965-66; rhetoric and composition instr. Tex. A&M U., College Station, 1968-69, 72-74, Harford Community Coll., Bel Aire, Md., 1970-71; Latin tchr. Denton (Tex.) Pub. Schs., 1974—2002. Mem. residents adv. com. Tex. Acad. Math. and Sci., Denton, 1987-88; chmn. Latin reading competition Nat. Jr. Classical League, Miami, Ohio, 1988-93; mem. methodology com. Am. Classical League, 1993-95; dir. Tex. State Jr. Classical League Conv., 1996, 2001; presenter workshops in field; mem. Tex. State Textbook Adv. Com., 1989-90. Costume designer Denton Cmty. Theater, 1984; choir dir. Immaculate Conception Ch., Denton, 1985-87; chmn. costume competition Tex. State Jr. Classical League, 1987-2002, exec. bd. sponsor, 1981-2002. Arthur Patch McKinlay scholar, 1986, 91. Mem. Am. Classical Assn., Classical Assn. of the Mid-West and South, Metroplex Classics Assn. (constl. adv. com. 1988), Classics Assn. Southwestern U.S. (pres. 1987-88), Tex. Classics Assn. (historian 2000—), Tex. Fgn. Lang. Assn. (chmn. hon. mem. 1988-89, chmn. local arrangements 1977). Roman Catholic.

RELDAN, ROBERT RONALD, law educator, psychological consultant, poet; b. Bklyn., June 2, 1942; s. William and Marie (Garis) R.; m. Judith Feldman, Nov. 7, 1971 (div. June 1979); 1 child, Edward. BS, Fairleigh Dickinson U., 1965; MS (hon.), Park Coll., 1975; JD, LaSalle U., St. Louis, 1988. Sales mgr. Pistilli Ford, Oradell, N.J., 1967-69; owner Triple "R" Co., Tenafly, N.J., 1969-75; dir. Legal Ltd., Trenton, N.J., 1975—. Author of poetry. Facilitator in Alternative to Violence program, Trenton. Served with USN, 1965-67. Mem. Nat. Lawyers Guild, Toastmasters Internat. (v.p. Trenton chpt. 1987-88), Am. Entrepreneurs Assn., Aircraft Owners and Pilots Assn. Avocations: flying, skydiving, scuba diving, poetry. Office: ACSU 557463 Bag R Rahway NJ 07065

REMINGTON, PAUL JAMES, mechanical engineer, educator; b. Plainfield, N.J., Mar. 19, 1943; s. Elmer Joseph and Genevieve Leona (Kehoe) R.; m. Lynne Louise Harris, Aug. 21, 1965; children: Christopher, Alexander. BSME, MSME, MIT, 1966, PhD, 1970. Prin. engr. BBN Techs. (Verizon Comm.), Cambridge, Mass., 1969—; adj. prof. mech. engring. Boston U., 1995. Vis. lectr. Tufts U., Medford, Mass., 1979; vis. scientist Tech. U. Berlin, 1990; organizer 3rd Internat. Workshop on Rlwy. and Tracked Transit System Noise, 1981. Contbr. chpts. to: Handbook of Machine Design, 1986, Transportation Noise Reference Book, 1987, Encyclopedia of Acoustics, 1997, Noise and Vibration from High Speed Trains, 2001, also articles to profl. publs. Recipient Cert. of Recognition, NASA, 1976, Excellence in Presentation award Soc. Automotive Engrs., 1984. Fellow Acoustical Soc. Am. (assoc. editor jour. 1982-2001, nominee Biennial award 1977); mem. ASME, Tau Beta Pi, Pi Tau Sigma (pres. 1964-65). Achievements include development of basic understanding of rolling noise generation, development of approaches for controlling wheel/rail noise from trains; 4 patents in field. Office: BBN Technologies 10 Moulton St Cambridge MA 02138-1119 E-mail: premington@bbn.com.

REMLEY, R. DIRK, English educator, consultant; b. Cleve., July 27, 1964; s. Roland E. and Anna Marie Remley. BA, Bowling Green State U., 1986, MA, 1988. Lectr. Kent (Ohio) State U., 1990—; prin. Strategic Market Consulting Group, Ravenna, Ohio, 1994—. Author: The Red Notebook, 1998, Snapshots of Americana, 1999, In Transit, 1999; contbr. articles to profl. jours. Lector Immaculate Conception Ch., Ravenna, 1997—; vol. Meals on Wheels, Chagrin Falls, Ohio, 1996-97; mem. com. Playhouse Square Ptnrs., Cleve., 1992-96. Mem.: MLA, Nat. Coun. Tchrs. English. Office: Kent State U Dept English Kent OH 44242-0001

REMLEY, THEODORE PHANT, JR., counseling educator, lawyer; b. Eustis, Fla., Feb. 7, 1947; s. Theodore Phant Sr. and Era Annie (Forehand) R. BA, U. Fla., 1969, EdS, 1971, PhD, 1980; JD, Catholic U., 1980. Bar: Va. 1981, Fla. 1982; lic. profl. counselor, Va., Miss., La. Exec. dir. Am. Counseling Assn., Alexandria, Va., 1990-94; prof. counseling U. New Orleans, 1994—. Contbr. articles to profl. jours., chpts. to books. Mem. Am. Counseling Assn., Am. Assn. State Counseling Bds. Democrat. Roman Catholic. Home: 3800 Camp St New Orleans LA 70115-2629 Office: Dept Edn Leadership Counseling & Founds Rm 348 U New Orleans New Orleans LA 70148-0001

RENCIS, JOSEPH JOHN, engineering educator, mechanical and civil engineer; b. Denville, N.J., May 19, 1958; s. Joseph John and Leila Jean (Conlin) R.; m. Minerva Vasquez, Sept. 14, 1991; 1 child, Christina. AAS in Archtl. & Bldg. Constrn. Engring., Milw. (Wis.) Sch. Engring., 1978, BS in Archtl. & Bldg. Constrn. Engring., 1980; MS in Theoretical & Applied Mechanics, Northwestern U., 1982; PhD in Engring. Mechanics, Case Western Res. U., 1985. Registered profl. engr., Mass. Engring. technician U.S. Army Armament Rsch., Devel. and Engring. Ctr., Picatinny Arsenal, N.J., summer 1979; instr., grader dept. archtl. & bldg. constrn. engring. tech. Milw. (Wis.) Sch. Engring., 1979-80; rsch. asst. dept. civil engring. Northwestern U., Evanston, Ill., 1980-81; rsch. and tchg. asst. dept. civil engring. Case Western Res. U., Cleve., 1982-85; grad. student rschr. Flight Dynamics Lab. Wright-Patterson AFB, Dayton, Ohio, summer 1984; instr. engring. tech. dept. Cuyahoga C.C., Cleve., 1984; asst. prof. mech. engring. dept. Worcester (Mass.) Poly. Inst., 1985-90, assoc. prof. mech. engring. dept., 1990-2000, assoc. prof., Russel M. Searle disting. instr. mech. engring, 1994-95, Russel M. Searle disting. instr. mech. engring., 1994-95, prof. mech. engring., 2000—. Engring. cons. Brooks Sci., Inc., Cambridge, Mass., 1986-89; ASEE-NASA faculty fellow NASA-Lewis Rsch. Ctr., Cleve., summers 1989, 90; rsch. assoc. Phillips Lab., Geophysics Directorate, Space Sys. Tech. br., Hanscom AFB, Mass., summer 1991; mem. adv. bd. for engring. tech. Sussex County Vocat. Tech. H.S., Sparta, N.J., 1994—; mem. adv. bd. Sussex County Engring. and Design Acad., 1997—. N.J. Coun. of County Vocational Tech. Sch., Successful Grad. Recognition award, 2003. Mem. editl. bd. Boundary Elements Commn., 1989—, Engring. Analysis with Boundary Elements, 1993—; asssoc. editor Advances in Boundary Elements, 1996—; contbr. articles to profl. jours. Recipient Class of 1980 Outstanding Alumni award Milw. (Wis.) Sch. Engring., 1990, Citizen of the Yr. award West Boylston (Mass.) Sch. Sys., 1992, Successful Grad. Recognition award N.J. Coun. County Vocational-Tech. Schs., 2003; Walter P. Murphy fellow Northwestern U., Evanston, 1980-81; Wessex Inst. of Great Britian fellow, 2000. Fellow ASME (sec. Ctrl. Mass. sect. 1988-89, vice-chair 1989-90, chair 1990-92), Wessex Inst. of Gt. Britain; mem. ASCE (structural divsn. com. on electronic computation, subcom. on personal computers and work stas. 1986-91), Internat. Soc. for Boundary Elements (sci. steering com. 1989—), Am. Soc. Engring. Edn. (chair mechanics divsn. 1999-2000 (N.E. sect.), New Eng. Tchr. of Yr. award 2002), Am. Acad. Mechanics, Internat. Assn. for Boundary Element Methods, Pi Tau Sigma, Tau Omega Mu. Roman Catholic. Achievements include pioneering work on error estimation and self-adaptive mesh refinement technique for Boundary Element Method; research on iterative/direct equation solving strategies for Boundary Element Method. Home: 2 Keep Ave Paxton MA 01612-1038 Office: Worcester Poly Inst Mech Engring Dept 100 Institute Rd Worcester MA 01609-2247

RENDA, ROSA A. special education educator; b. Jamaica, N.Y., Nov. 03; d. Liborio and Josephine (Finamore) Lombardo; m. Philip F. Renda, Mar. 30, 1980; children: Felicia-Anne, Philip Jr. BA, Molloy Coll., 1971; MEd, St. John's U., Jamaica, N.Y., 1973; postgrad., L.I. U., 1977. Tchr., asst. prin. St. Rose of Lima, Massapequa, NY, 1967—73, Acad. of St. Joseph, Brentwood, NY, 1973—79; tchr. Sewanhaka H.S., Brentwood, NY, 1979—81, Queen of the Rosary Acad., Amityville, NY, 1981—86, Blessed Trinity, Ocala, Fla., 1987—93, math. coord., 1993—94; S.E.D. tchr. Emerald Ctr., Ocala, Fla., 1994; tchr./children's supr. for the emotionally/mentally disturbed Marion Citrus Mental Health, Ocala, 1994—96; tchr. for autistic children Maplewood Sch., Ocala, 1996—97; tchr. math. Lake Weir H.S., 1997—99; tchr. North Marion Mid. Sch. for Emotionally Handicapped, Citra, Fla., 1999—2001; tchr. math. Webster Coll., Ocala, 2002—03, cmty. tech. and adult edn., 2003; tchr., NovaNet and GED Cmty. Tech. and Adult Edn., 2003—. Author: Teaching Metrics, 1975. Vol. Nassau County Rep. Club, Hempstead, N.Y., 1974-76. Mem. ASCD, NEA, Nat. Coun. Tchrs. Math., Nat. Cath. Edn. Assn., Marion Edn. Assn., Nassau/Suffolk Math. Tchrs., Women of the Moose, Columbiettes, K.C. Aux. Roman Catholic. Avocations: reading, swimming, gourmet cooking. Office: CTAE 1014 SW 7th Rd Ocala FL 34474 E-mail: 3637twofar85@aol.com.

RENDE, TONI LYNN, principal, counselor; b. Alamo, Tenn., Dec. 6, 1957; d. Weldon Simmons and Gladyn Brown; m. Salvatore David Rende, Mar. 7, 1981; children: David, Derek. BS magna cum laude, Union U.,

Jackson, Tenn., 1979; MS, Memphis State U., 1'980; MEd, U. Tenn., 1987. Cert. tchr., guidance counselor, Tenn. Ednl. social worker Alamo Dept. Pub. Health, 1979-80; ednl. rsch. specialist Hamilton County Govt., Chattanooga, 1980-82; guidance counselor Lakeview High Sch., Chattanooga, 1982-84; tchr. spl. edn. Chattanooga City Schs., 1985-86; ednl. diagnostician, now adj. prof. U. Tenn., Chattanooga, 1987—; guidance counselor Hickory Valley Christian Sch., Chattanooga, 1990—, prin., 1991-96. Cons. Attention Deficit Disorder Support Group, Chattanooga, 1990—; mem. Sta. WRCB Children's Panel, Chattanooga, 1990—; network mem. Mid. Tenn. State U. Dyslexic Chair, Chattanooga, 1990; mem. exec. com. Young Author's Conf. Adv. bd. Children's Ctr., U. Tenn., Chattanooga. Mem. Christian Assn. Psychol. Svcs., Coun. Exceptional Children, Alpha Chi, Pi Gamma Mu, Alpha Delta Kappa. Republican. Methodist. Avocations: quilting, reading. Office: Hickory Valley Christian Sch 6605 Shallowford Rd Chattanooga TN 37421-1791

RENDINE, MARIA FARESE, secondary education educator; b. Newark, Apr. 15, 1946; d. Louis Rocco and Angela Maria (Notte) Farese; m. Michael Joseph Rendine, 1967 (div. 1993); children: Renee Danielle, Jon Daniel. BA, Montclair State Coll., 1967; postgrad., Wright State U., Dayton, Ohio, U. Va., Falls Ch., George Mason U. Cert. English, speech, pub. speaking, theatre arts tchr., Va., English, speech tchr., Ohio, English tchr., Fla. Tchr. Bibb County Schs., Macon, Ga.; English, speech tchr., English dept. chair Wayne Township Schs., Dayton, Ohio, 1975; English, drama, speech, photo journalism tchr. Fairfax County Pub. Schs., Va., 1982—2001, chair dept. fine arts, 2001, tchr. mentor, 2001—. Sponsor yearbook Fairfax County Pub. Schs., 1986-94; developed, expanded programs studies of poetry, drama, theatre-goers, film study, Fairfax County Pub. Schs., 1990-95; developed Career I-Search Projects grades 10, 12, 1985-89; critic judge for Fairfax County Short Play Festival, 1988, Va. H.S. League, 2001-03; arts tchr. mentor Fairfax County Theater, 2000-03; curriculum revision team Fairfax County Program Studies, 1998-2001. Author numerous poems. Bd. dirs. The Alliance Theatre, 2001—. Recipient Am. Poetry Assn. grant cert., 1986; named Poet of Merit Am. Poetry Assn., 1989. Mem. Nat. Coun. Tchrs. English, Va. Assn. Tchrs. English, English Tchrs. Assn. No. Va., Ednl. Theatre Assn., Journalism Edn. Assn., Theatre Arts Dirs. Assn. (pres. 2000). Home: 4127 Nomis Dr Fairfax VA 22032-1204

RENEAU, MARVIN BRYAN, military officer, business educator; b. Wharton, Tex., Jan. 22, 1939; s. Marvin Cecil Reneau and Bessie Marie (Petrash) Ward; m. Doris Faye Martin, Jan. 2, 1957; children: Terran Bryan, Kevin Troy, Shannon Lyn. BS, U. Tampa, Fla., 1971; MS, Am. Tech. U., U. Cen. Tex., 1978; MA, Webster Coll., 1979, PhD, 1996, Madison U. Commd. 2d lt. U.S. Army, 1964; advanced through grade to col. USAR, 1990; co. comdr., armor U.S. Army, Vietnam, 1968, engring. ops. mgr., chief, tng. support div., 1989, sr. tng. analyst. Cons. U.S. Army C.E., Ft. Worth, 1978—, Army Rsch. Inst., Boise, Idaho, 1987—, Army Tng. Bd., Ft. Monroe, Va., 1987—; asst. prof. bus. Incarnate Word Coll., San Antonio. Author: Beneath the Canopy, 1978, And Where the Rockets Can't Reach, 1993; contbr. articles to profl. jours. Mem. Army Mut. Aid Fund, Arlington, Va., 1968; acad. advisor Incarnate Word Coll., San Antonio, 1981; vol. counselor DAV, San Antonio, 1980; referral agt. United Way, San Antonio, 1988. Comdr. USAR. Decorated Bronze Star, Purple Heart, 3 Meritorious medals, 2 Air medals (1 for valor), 3 Army Commendation medals, Army Achievement medal, Conbar Infantryman badge, Rep. of Vietnam Cross of Gallantry with palm, Legion of Merit, commd. admiral in Tex. Navy; names to Hon. Order Ky. Cols. Mem. Am. Mktg. Assn., ASTD, Assn. U.S. Army, Mil. Order of Purple Heart, NSW Leagues, Fed. Mgrs. Assn., S.W. Mktg. Assn., Res. Officer Assn., Orders and Medals Soc. Am., Orders and Medals Rsch. of Great Britain, 34th Armor Regiment (disting. mem.), Berlin U.S. Mil. Vets. Assn., 2d Bn. 34th Armor Assn., 25th Inf. Divsn. Assn., Alpha Kappa Psi (sponsor). Methodist. Avocation: researching and collecting historical artifacts. Home: PO Box 39292 San Antonio TX 78218-1292

RENEE, LISABETH MARY, art educator, artist, galley director; b. Bklyn., July 28, 1952; d. Lino P. and Elizabeth M. (Dines) Rivano; m. John S. Witanowski, May 15, 1982. Student, U. Puget Sound, 1972-74; BA in Art, SUNY, Buffalo, 1977; MFA, L.I. U., 1982; EdD, U. Ctrl. Fla., 1996. Cert. art tchr., Fla. Adj. faculty L.I. U., Greenvale, N.Y., 1980-82, Rollins Coll., Winter Park, Fla., 1982; art tchr. Phyllis Wheatley Elem. Sch., Apopka, Fla., 1983-85, McCoy Elem. Sch., Orlando, Fla., 1985-86, Lake Howell H.S., Winter Park, Fla., 1986-93; adj. faculty U. Ctrl. Fla., 1994-95, vis. instr., coord. art edn., 1995-96; gallery dir., prof. West Campus Valencia (Fla.) C.C., 1996-98; owner, designer Nartique, 2002—; dir. Renée Studios, Casselberry, Fla. Adj. faculty Valencia C.C., 1995-96; dir. So. Artists Registry, Winter Park, 1984-87; cons. Fla. Dept. Edn., 1989-90, mem. curriculum writing team for arts edn. program; mem. com. Fla. Bd. Edn. Task Force for Subject Area Subtest of Fla. Tech. Cert. Exam.; visual arts dir. Very Spl. Arts Ctr. Fla. Fest, 1996; presenter at profl. confs. Author: The Phenomenological Significance of Aesthetic Communion, 1996, Co-operative Art, 1991; editor: Children and the Arts in Florida, 1990. Visual arts dir. Very Spl. Arts Ctrl. Fla. Festival, 1995; mem. local Sch. Adv. Coun., Winter Park, 1992. Grantee Found. for Advancement of Cmty. Throught Schs., 1991, Divsn. Blind Svcs. Invision, 1995, Tangelo Park Project, 1995; ACE scholar Arts Leadership Inst., 1993-96; recipient Tchr. Merit award Walt Disney World Co., 1990. Mem. NEA, ASCD, Nat. Art Edn. Assn., Fla. Art Edn. Assn. (regional rep. 1989-94), Seminole County Art Edn. Assn., Coll. Art Assn., Caucus on Social Theory and Art Edn., Women's Caucus for Art, Phi Kappa Phi, Kappa Delta Pi. Home and Office: Nartique Renée Studios 20 Cobblestone Ct Casselberry FL 32707-5410 Office: Nartique Renée Studios at Anclote Harbors Marina 523 Anclote Rd Slip 10 Tarpon Springs FL 34689-6702

RENEGAR, DELILAH A. chiropractor, educator; b. Great Falls, Mont., May 16, 1963; d. Clarence Arthur and Ruth Eloise (Campbell) R. BA in Psychology, U. Ctrl. Fla., 1985; BS in Human Biology, Nat. Coll. Chiropractic, Lombard, Ill., 1986, DC, 1988. Assoc. physician Wymore Chiropractic, Winter Park, Fla., 1989-90; prin. DuPage Chiropractic, Lisle, Ill., 1990—; lectr. chiropractic Nat. Coll. Chiropractic, Lombard, 1993—. Cons. physician Oak Brook Terrace (Ill.) Police, 1992—. Precinct committeeperson Lisle Twp., 1992-94. Mem. NOW (v.p. DuPage County 1992-93), Lisle Jaycees (v.p. 1994—), Rotary Club Lisle, Lisle Women's Club. Avocations: reading, rollerblading. Office: DuPage Chiropractic Assocs 1045 Burlington Ave Lisle IL 60532-1887

RENFREW, MALCOLM MACKENZIE, chemist, educator; b. Spokane, Wash., Oct. 12, 1910; s. Earl Edgar and Elsie Pauline (MacKenzie) R.; m. Carol Joy Campbell, June 26, 1938. BS, U. Idaho, 1932, MS, 1934, D.Sc., 1976; PhD, U. Minn., 1938. Asst. physics U. Idaho, 1932-33, Asst. chemistry, 1933-35, U. Minn., 1935-37, duPont fellow, 1937-38; research chemist plastics dept. duPont Co., 1938-44, supr. process devel., 1944-46, supr. product devel., 1946-49; head chem. research dept., research labs. Gen. Mills, Inc., 1949-52, dir. chem. research, 1952-53, dir. chem. research and devel., 1953-54; dir. research and devel. Spencer Kellogg & Sons, Inc., 1954-58; phys. sci. div. head, prof. chemistry U. Idaho, 1959-73, prof., 1973-76, emeritus, 1976—; dir. U. Idaho (Coll. Chem. Cons. Service), 1969-76. On leave as sr. staff assoc. Adv. Coun. Coll. Chemistry, Stanford, 1967-68; mem. materials adv. bd. Nat. Rsch. Coun.; exec. v.p. Idaho Rsch. Found., 1977-78, patent dir., 1978-88. Editor: Safety in the Chemical Laboratory, Vol. IV, 1981, (with Peter Ashbrook), Safe Laboratories: Principles and Practices for Design and Remodeling, 1991; safety editor: Jour. Chem. Edn, 1977-91; Contbr. to tech. and trade publs. on plastics, coatings, safety, chem. edn. Recipient Excellence in Teaching award Chem. Mfrs. Assn., 1977, Outstanding Achievement award U. Minn., 1977; named to U. Idaho Hall of Fame, 1977, Idaho Hall of Fame, 1996. Fellow AAAS, Am. Inst. Chemists; mem. Am. Chem. Soc. (councilor 1948, 59, 67-89, chmn. paint varnish and plastics div. 1949, chmn. chem. mktg. and econs. div. 1958-59, chmn. chem. health and safety div. 1982, James Flack Norris award 1976, Chem. Health and Safety award 1985, Mosher award 1986), Am. Inst. Chem. Engrs., Soc. Chem. Industry, Phi Beta Kappa, Sigma Xi, Phi Kappa Phi, Sigma Pi Sigma, Phi Gamma Delta (disting. Fiji 1986). Presbyterian. Home: 1271 Walenta Dr Moscow ID 83843-2426 Office: U Idaho Coll Sci Dept Chemistry PO Box 442343 Moscow ID 83844-2343

RENFRO, ANNA STURGIS, principal; b. Gastonia, N.C., Mar. 30, 1957; d. Harry L. and Iris (Fouché) Sturgis; m. Don Hugh Renfro Jr., July 19, 1980. MusB, Mars. Hill Coll., 1979; math. cert., Wingate Coll., 1984; MEd, Queens Coll., Charlotte, N.C., 1990; adminstrn. cert., U. N.C., Charlotte, 1991. Choral dir. T.C. Roberson H.S., Skyland, N.C., 1979-80; primary reading asst. Alderman Elem. Sch., Wilmington, N.C., 1980-81; Chpt. I reading asst. Parkwood Mid. Sch., Monroe, N.C., 1981-82; 5th grade tchr. Southview Acad., Wadesboro, N.C., 1984-85; math. tchr. Anson Jr. H.S., Wadesboro, 1985-87; math. tchr., dept. chmn. Highland Jr. H.S., Gastonia, N.C., 1987-92; asst. prin. Cramerton (N.C.) Jr. High Sch., 1992-93, 1993-94, Springfield Elem. Sch., Stanley, N.C., 1993-94; prin. Cramerton Mid. Sch., 1994—. Editl. advisor Scholastic MATH Mag., 1986-90. Recipient awards NASA, NSTA, NCTM, Kennedy Space Ctr., 1989. Mem. ASCD, NEA, N.C. Assn. Educators, Nat. Coun. Tchrs. Math., N.C. Coun. Tchrs. Math., Delta Omicron. Avocation: golf. Home: 2212 Monticello Dr Gastonia NC 28056-6568 Office: Cramerton Mid Sch 601 Cramer Mountain Rd Cramerton NC 28032-1662

RENGARAJAN, SEMBIAM RAJAGOPAL, electrical engineering educator, researcher, consultant; b. Mannargudi, Tamil Nadu, India, Dec. 12, 1948; came to U.S., 1980; s. Srinivasan and Rajalakshmi (Renganathan) Rajagopalan; m. Kalyani Srinivasan, June 24, 1982; children: Michelle, Sophie. BE with honors, U. Madras, India, 1971; MTech, Indian Inst. Tech., Kharagpur, 1974; PhD in Elec. Engring., U. N.B., Fredericton, Can., 1980. Tech. staff Jet Propulsion Lab., Pasadena, Calif., 1983-84; asst. prof. elec. engring. Calif. State U., Northridge, 1980-83, assoc. prof., 1984-87, prof., 1987—. Vis. rschr. UCLA, 1984-93, vis. prof., 1987-88; vis. prof. U. de Santiago de Compastela, Spain, 1996, U. Pretoria, South Africa, 1997, Tech. U. Denmark, 1999; cons. Hughes Aircraft Co., Canoga Park, Calif., 1982-87, NASA-Jet Propulsion Lab., Pasadena, 1987-90, 92-94, 96—, Ericsson Radar Electronics, Sweden, 1990-92, Martin Mariette, 1995-96; guest rschr. Chalmers U., Sweden, 1990, UN Devel. Program, 1993, Rome Lab., USAF, summer 1995, Naval Rsch. Lab., Washington, summer 1995, guest prof. Technical U. Denmark, 1999. Contbr. articles to profl. jours. Recipient Outstanding Faculty award Calif. State U., Northridge, 1985, Disting. Engring. Educator of Yr. award Engrs. Coun., L.A., 1995, Meritorious Performance and Profl. Promise award, 1986, 88, Merit award San Fernando Valley Engrs., Coun., 1989, Cert. of Recognition NASA, 1991-92; Nat. Merit scholar Govt. India, 1965-71. Fellow Inst. Advancement Engrs., IEEE (L.A. chpt. sec., treas. antennas and propagation soc. 1981-82, vice-chmn. 1982-83, chmn. 1983-84), Internat. Union Radio Sci. (U.S. nat. com.), The Electromagnetics Acad. Avocations: swimming, camping, jogging, tennis. Office: Calif State U 18111 Nordhoff St Northridge CA 91330-0001

RENGER, MARILYN HANSON, elementary education educator; b. Shelly, Idaho, July 17, 1949; d. Merril H. and Betty Jean (Hendricksen) Hanson; m. Robert Carl Renger, Sept. 11, 1971; children: Katherine, James. BA in History, U. Calif., Santa Barbara, 1971; postgrad., Calif. Luth. U., 1973-74. Tchr. Ventura (Calif.) Unified Schs., 1974-79, 85-98, asst. prin., 1998—. Cons. State of Calif., 1989-93. Recipient Disting. Tchr. K-12 award Nat. Coun. for Geog. Edn., 1992. Mem. Nat. Coun. Geographic Edn. (Nat. Disting. Teaching award 1992), Calif. Geographic Soc. (steering com. 1989-93, co-dir. summer inst. 1992), Nat. Coun. Social Studies. Office: Balboa Mid Sch 247 S Hill Rd Ventura CA 93003-4401

RENKA, ROBERT JOSEPH, computer science educator, consultant; b. Summit, N.J., Dec. 28, 1947; s. John and Elizabeth (Pierce) R. BA in Computer Sci., BS in Math., U. Tex., 1976, MA in Math., 1979, PhD in Computer Sci., 1981. Numerical analyst Oak Ridge (Tenn.) Nat. Lab., 1981-84; asst. prof. computer sci. U. North Tex., Denton, 1984-89, assoc. prof. computer sci., 1989-99, prof. computer sci., 1999—. Cons. in scientific computing. Contbr. articles to profl. jours. With USN, 1967-69, Vietnam. Rsch. grantee U. North Tex., 1984-89, NSF, 1990-93, Nat. Security Agy., 1999—. Mem. Assn. for Computing Machinery (algorithms editor 1988-94, editor-in-chief 1989-94), Soc. Indsl. and Applied Math. Avocations: racquetball, rock climbing. Home: 1700 Kendolph Dr Denton TX 76205-6931 Office: U North Tex Dept Computer Scis PO Box 311366 Denton TX 76203-1366

RENO, LEE CURTIS, school system administrator, consultant; b. Port Jefferson, Ohio, Dec. 5, 1949; s. John Paul and Viola Jane (Gooden) R.; m. Melanie Jean King, Nov. 27, 1970; children: L. Curtis, Jennifer, Maggie. BA, Cedarville Coll., 1971; MEd, Wright State U., 1979; postgrad., U. Dayton, 1980—; Wright State U., 1981—. Tchr., coach Dayton (Ohio) Christian Schs., 1971-74, head social studies dept., 1975-77, high sch. prin., 1978-92, asst. supt., 1992—. Mem. Mid.-Am. accreditation commn. Assn. Christian Schs. Internat., 1978-90, chmn. 1989, 90. Author: (with others) Sowing for Excellence, 1988. Elder, Sunday Sch. tchr. Hillside Chapel, Dayton, 1980—. Mem. ASCD, Nat. Assn. Secondary Sch. Prins., Phi Delta Kappa. Mem. Christian and Missionary Alliance. Office: Dayton Christian Schs 325 Homewood Ave Dayton OH 45405-4397

RENOUX, ANDRÉ, physicist, educator; b. Courbevoie, France, Oct. 27, 1937; s. Robert and Jeanne (Noël) R.; divorced; children: Vincent, Nathalie. Lic. Sci., Faculty Scis. Paris, 1958, Dr 3rd cycle, 1961, Drs, 1965. Asst. Faculty Scis., Paris, 1959-61, master asst., 1961-66; prof. faculty of scis. U. Tunis, Tunisia, 1966—69, U. Brest, France, 1969-80; prof. U. Paris, 1980—2003, dir. lab. phys. aérosols et transfert des contaminations, 1980—, dir. DESS (3d cycle) sci. des aerosols-génie de l'Aérocontamination, 1981—2003, prof. emeritus, 2003—. Gen. conf. chmn. European Aerosol Conf., Blois, France, 1994; del. Internat. Coun. for Engring. and Tech., UNESCO, 2000—. Author: (with D. Boulaud, Lavoisier, Ed.) Les Aérosols, Physique et Métrologie, 1998; mem. editl. bd. Idojaras, 1979—, Pollution Atmospherique, 1979—, Aerosol Sci. & Tech., 1992-2000, Revue Salles Propres, 2000-02; contbr. over 300 articles to profl. jours. Gen. sec. Syndicat d'initiative, Brest, 1973-77; mem. Cons. Com. Univs., France, 1973-77. Mem. AAAS, N.Y. Acad. Scis., Com. Regional Anti-Pollution Brest (pres. 1973-80), Soc. France for Nuclear Energy idFNE (pres. 1987-91), Am. Assn. Aerosol Rsch., Gesellschaft Aerosolforschung, Hungarian Meteorol. soc. (hon.), French Aerosol. Rsch. Assn. (pres. 1983-2000, hon. pres. 2000—), European Aerosol Assembly (co-founder, pres. 1998-2000), Office Professionnel de qualification des Entreprises de l'Ultrapropreté (pres. 1995—), Chevalier des Dames du vin et de la Table, Ordre de l'Echarpe. Avocations: tennis, opera, photography. Home: 11 Sq de L'eau Vive 94000 Créteil France Office: U Paris XII Lab Phys Aerosols Ave Gal de Gaulle 94000 Creteil France E-mail: renoux@univ-paris12.fr.

RENSHAW, JOHN HUBERT, retired secondary education educator; b. Hazleton, Pa., July 9, 1936; s. Charles William and Mary (Drobeck) R.; m. Dorothy Sharon Montgomery, June 20, 1964; children: John Michael, Rebecca Lynn. BS in Edn., East Stroudsburg State U., 1961; MA in History, U. Del., 1965. Cert. tchr., Del. 10th and 12th grade social studies tchr. Pocomoke City (Md.) High Sch., 1961-64; 7th and 8th grade social studies tchr. Forwood Jr. High Sch., Wilmington, Del., 1965-78; 8th grade U.S. govt. and U.S. history tchr. Springer Jr. High Sch., Wilmington, 1978-81; 8th grade U.S. history tchr. Hanby Middle Sch., Wilmington, 1981-96, ret., 1996. Audiovisual dir., equipment maintenenace Hanby Jr. High Sch. and Brandywine Sch. Dist., 1981-94; curriculum leader social studies dept. Hanby Jr. High Sch., 1988—, chmn. social studies dept., 1994—; coach baseball, girl's softball teams Forwood Jr. High Sch., 1973-78, Springer Jr. High Sch., 1979-81, Hanby High Sch., 1982-86. Cpl. USMC, 1954-57. Mem. Nat. Coun. Social Studies, Del. Edn. Assn., Brandywine and New Castle County Edn. Assn. (rep. 1978-81). Republican. Methodist. Avocations: jogging, reading, mind-body readings and projects, baseball card collecting, sports watching and participation. Home: 2506 Bona Rd Wilmington DE 19810-2220 E-mail: emrjhr@aol.com.

RENSINK, JACQUELINE BIDDIX, secondary school educator; b. Spruce Pine, N.C., May 17, 1954; d. Joe and Virginia Dare (Glenn) Biddix; m. Michael Lynn Rensink, Apr. 2, 1988; 1 child, Sarah Jane Buchanan. MusB, Appalachian State U., 1976, MA, 1983, specialist in mid. grades edn., 1990. Cert. level A music, N.C., level G middle grades edn., N.C. Band dir. Mitchell County Sch. System, Bakersville, N.C., 1977, tchr., 1981—. Mem. supt. adv. coun. Mitchell County Sch. System, 1986-88, site-based mgmt. team Harris Mid. Sch., Spruce Pine, 1992-93; student-tchr. supr. Harris Mid. Sch., 1988, 89, 90; coord. World Day Festival Harris Mid. Sch, 1988—. Organist Cen. Bapt. Ch., Spruce Pine, 1990—; bd. dirs. Winterstar-Fairway Assn., Burnsville, N.C., 1992-93. Named Tchr. of Yr., Harris Mid. Sch., 1992, 94. Mem. NEA, Nat. Coun. Social Studies, N.C. Assn. Educators (treas. 1987-88, 91-92, assn. rep. 1992-93), N.C./Nat. Geographic Alliance, N.C. Coun. Social Studies, Delta Kappa Gamma. Republican. Baptist. Avocations: reading, hiking, piano. Home: 185 Laurel Acres Rd Burnsville NC 28714 Office: Harris Middle Sch 121 Harris St Spruce Pine NC 28777-3119 E-mail: jrensink@mitchell.main.nc.us.

RENT, CLYDA STOKES, academic administrator; b. Jacksonville, Fla., Mar. 1, 1942; d. Clyde Parker Stokes Sr. and Edna Mae (Edwards) Shuemake; m. George Seymour Rent, Aug. 12, 1966; 1 child, Cason Rent Lynley. BA, Fla. State U., 1964, MA, 1966, PhD, 1968; LHD (hon.), Judson Coll., 1993. Asst. prof. Western Carolina U., Cullowhee, N.C., 1968-70, Queens Coll., Charlotte, N.C., 1972-74, dept. chair, 1974-78, dean Grad. Sch. and New Coll., 1979-84, v.p. for Grad. Sch. and New Coll., 1984-85, v.p. acad. affairs, 1985-87, v.p. cmty. affairs, 1987-89; pres. Miss. U. for Women, Columbus, 1989—. Mem. adv. bd. Nat. Women's Hall of Fame; cons. Coll. Eb. N.Y.C., 1983-89; sci. cons. N.C. Alcohol Rsch. Authority, Chapel Hill, 1976-89; bd. mem. So. Growth Policies Bd., 1992-94; adv. bd. Nat. Women's Hall of Fame, Trustmark Nat. Bank, 1991-97; rotating chair Miss. Instns. Higher Learning Pres. Coun., 1990-91; commn. govtl. rels. Am. Coun. Edn., 1990-93; mem. adv. bd. Entergy/Miss., 1994-97, Freedom Forum 1st Amendment Ctr., 1996-2001; mem. Miss. adv. bd. Trustmark Nat. Bank, 1991-97; mem. Mary Baker Eddy Adv. Group, 2000—; mem. Rhodes Scholar selection com. of Miss., 1996-98; mem. Free Sprit Awards selection com., 1996—; mem. ACE Commn. on Women in Higher Edn., 1999—. Mem. editl. bd. Planning for Higher Education, 1995; contbr. articles to profl. jours.; speeches pub. in Vital Speeches; mem. editl. bds. acad. jours. Trustee N.C. Performing Arts Ctr., Charlotte, 1988-89, Charlotte County Day Sch., 1987-89; bd. visitors Johnson C. Smith U., Charlotte, 1985-89; exec. com. bd. dirs. United Way Allocations and Rev., Charlotte, 1982-88; bd. advisors Charlotte Mecklenburg Hosp. Authority, 1985-89; bd. dirs. Jr. Achievement, Charlotte, 1983-89, Miss. Humanities Coun., Miss. Inst. Arts and Letters, Miss. Symphony, Miss. Econ. Coun.; chair Leadership Miss. and Collegiate Miss.; chmn. bd. dirs. Charlotte/Mecklenburg Arts and Sci. Coun., 1987-88; Danforth assoc. Danforth Found., St. Louis, 1976-88, Leadership Am., 1989; mem. golden triangle adv. bd. Bapt. Meml. Hosp., 1999—; pres. So. Univs. Conf., 1994-95; mem. commn. govt. rels. Am. Coun. Edn., 1990-93; mem. alumni bd. First United Meth. Ch., 1996—. Recipient Grad. Made Good award Fla. State U., 1990, medal of excellence Miss. U. for Women, 1995, Women Who Make a Difference award IWF, 2000; named Prof. of Yr., Queens Coll., 1979, One of 10 Most Admired Women Mgrs. in Am., Working Women mag., 1993, One of 1000 Women of the 90's, Mirabella mag., 1994; Ford Found. grantee, 1981; Paul Harris fellow, 1992; OWHE fellow, 1999—. Mem. Am. Assn. State Colls. and Univs. (bd. dirs. 1994-96, 99), Sociol. Soc., So. Assn. Colls. and Schs. (mem. commn. on colls. 1996-98), N.C. Assn. Colls. and Univs. (exec. com. 1988-89), N.C. Assn. Acad. Officers (sec.-treas. 1987-88), Soc. Internat. Bus. Fellows, Miss. Assn. Colls. (pres. 1992), Newcomen Soc. U.S., Internat. Women's Forum, Univ. Club, Rotary. Achievements include 1st female pres. of Miss. U. for Women (1st pub. coll. for women in Am.). Office: Miss State U Social Scis Rsch Ctr PO Box 5287 Mississippi State MS 39762

RENZULLI, MARY ANN, parochial education educator; b. Bklyn., June 6, 1937; d. Frederick M. and Carmela (Giustra) Palumbo; m. Vincent Richard Renzulli, Apr. 23, 1960; children: Richard, Barbara, Ann Mary, Peter, Linda. BA, Montclair State Coll., 1959. Tchr. Union Hill High Sch., Union City, N.J., 1959-62; substitute tchr. Edison (N.J.) Bd. Edn., 1981-87, part-time English tchr., 1987-88; tchr. St. Francis Cathedral Sch., Metuchen, N.J., 1988-90, St. Mary of the Assumption, Elizabeth, N.J., 1990—. Sr. class advisor Union Hill High Sch., yearbook advisor; key club advisor Edison Bd. Edn., 1980-87; asst. dir. sch. play St. Francis Cathedral Sch., 1990; asst. prodr.-dir. sch. play St. Mary of the Assumption, 1992, freshmen class advisor, 1990—. Roman Catholic. Avocations: needlework, reading, cooking, sewing. Home: 20 Montclair Ave Edison NJ 08820-2039

REOCK, ERNEST C., JR., retired government services educator, academic director; b. Belleville, N.J., Oct. 13, 1924; s. Ernest C. and Helen Rutan (Evans) R.; m. Jeanne Elizabeth Thomason, Jan. 25, 1953; children: Michael, Thomas, Kathleen. BS, Swarthmore Coll., 1945; AB, Rutgers U., 1948, MA, 1950, PhD, 1959. Rsch. assoc. bur. govt. rsch. Rutgers U., New Brunswick, N.J., 1950-59, asst. prof., dir., 1960-63, assoc. prof., dir., 1963-68, prof., dir., 1968-92. Cons. N.J. Constnl. Conv., New Brunswick, 1966, N.J. State and Local Revenue and Expenditure Commns., 1986-88. Author: Handbook for New Jersey Assessors, 1962, School Budget Caps in New Jersey, 1981 (Govtl. Rsch. Assn. award, 1983), Unfinished Business: The New Jersey Constitutional Conv. of 1966, 2003; editor: New Jersey Legislative District Data Book, 1972—92. Chmn. Middlesex County Charter Study Commn., New Brunswick, 1973—74; cons. State Apportionment Commn., 1981, 1991, 2001, various mcpl. charter commns., 1965—2003. Lt. USN, 1943—46, 1 USN, 1951—53. Recipient Gov.'s award for Pub. Svc., 1997. Mem. Am. Soc. Pub. Adminstrn. (Pub. Adminstr. of Yr. 1982), Am. Ednl. Fin. Assn. Avocations: sailing, swimming. Home: 7 Kendall Rd Kendall Park NJ 08824-1010 Office: Rutgers U Ctr Govt Svcs 33 Livingston Ave New Brunswick NJ 08901-1900

REPASKE, DAVID ROY, pediatric endocrinologist, educator; b. Madison, Wisconsin, Oct. 11, 1951; s. Roy and Anne Christine R.; m. Mary Gaile (Christian), June 19, 1976; children: Elizabeth Christina and Daniel David. AB in biol. sci., Cornell U., 1973; PhD in biochemistry, U. Wis., 1980; MD, Vanderbilt Univ., 1985. Diplomate Am. Bd. Pediat.; Am. Bd. Pediat. Endocrinology. Postdoctoral fellow dept. physiology Vanderbilt U., Nashville, 1982-83; postdoctoral fellow in pediat. and genetics Vanderbilt Univ., Nashville, 1985-86; resident in internal medicine and pediat. U. N.C., Chapel Hill, 1986-88, fellow in pediatric endocrinology, 1989-92; asst. prof. pediat. U. Cin., Cin., 1992—99, assoc. prof., 1999—. Office: Childrens Hosp Med Ctr 3333 Burnet Ave Cincinnati OH 45229-3026

REPPERT, JAMES EUGENE, mass communications educator; b. Paxton, Ill, Sept. 24, 1958; s. Everett and Berdine Anita (Nelson) R.; m. Rita Jane Glennon, Aug. 1, 1987. Cert., Brown Coll., 1977; B Univ. Studies, N.D. State U., 1981; MA, U. Nev., Las Vegas, 1985. Lic. 1st class FCC. Vis. instr. Purdue U. Calumet, Hammond, Ind., 1985-86; instr. Southeastern La. Univ., Hammond, La., 1986-87, So. Ark. Univ., Magnolia, 1987-93, asst. prof., 1993-2001, assoc. prof., 2001—, dir. broadcast journalism, 1987—, exec. prodr. radio news and TV interview programs, 1987—, exec. prodr. audio webcasts, 1999—, faculty senator, 2000—. Co-anchor WRTL-AM,

Rantoul, Ill., 1973-76, KFME-TV, Fargo, ND, 1981; assoc. dir. forensics, tchg. asst. U. Nev., Las Vegas, 1983-85; news intern WJLA-TV, Washington, 1984; textbook reviewer Focal Press, 1994, Wadsworth, 1991, 94, Houghton Mifflin, 1993, 96, Longman, 1999, Harcourt, 2001, Allyn & Bacon, 2001-03; mem. selection com. MBC Radio Hall of Fame, Chgo., 1994; faculty seminar del. C-SPAN, 1993, 95, Acad. TV Arts and Sci., 1989, Internat. Emmy Nominee Festival, 1999; presenter at more than 90 confs.; cons. in field. Contbg. author: Video Rating Guide for Libraries, 1990-95, C-SPAN Campaign '96: A Resource Guide for Professors, 1995, College Broadcaster, 1993, The Ency. of Television News, 1998, Resources in Ed.: ERIC Document Reproduction Svc., 1996—; mem. editl. adv. bd. Roxbury Pub., 1990-91, Collegiate Press, 1992-93. Recipient Landmark award Ark. Com. State Lands Office, 1998; named Ky. Comm. Assn. Scholar of Yr., 1997-98; grantee Tangipahoa Parish, Amite, La., 1987, C-SPAN, 1993, 95, So. Ark. U., 2003; Faculty fellow Nat. Assn. TV Program Exec., 1999, Radio and TV News Dir. Found., 2002. Mem. Nat. Comm. Assn., So. States Comm. Assn., So. Forensics Assn. (divsn. chair 1998-99), Internat. Radio TV Soc. Found. (faculty seminar del. 1993, 95, 97, 99, 2002, 03, Stephen H. Coltrin award 1999), Ark. Broadcast Edn. Assn., Ark. State Comm. Assn., Ky. Comm. Assn. (Tchr. of Yr. 2000-01), Phi Kappa Phi. Home: PO Box 2149 Magnolia AR 71754-7149 Office: So Ark Univ PO Box 9229 Magnolia AR 71754-9229 E-mail: jereppert@saumag.edu., jereppert@usa.net.

REPPUCCI, NICHOLAS DICKON, psychologist, educator; b. Boston, May 1, 1941; s. Nicholas Ralph and Bertha Elizabeth (Williams) R.; m. Christine Marlow Onufrock, Sept. 10, 1967; children: Nicholas Jason, Jonathan Dickon, Anna Jin Marlow Chapman. BA with honors, U. N.C., 1962; MA, Harvard U., 1964, PhD, 1968. Lectr., rsch. assoc. Harvard U., Cambridge, Mass., 1967-68; from asst. prof. to assoc prof. Yale U., New Haven, 1968-76; prof. psychology U. Va., Charlottesville, 1976—, dir. grad. studies in psychology, 1984-95, 97-98. Originator biennial conf. on community rsch. and action, 1986. Author: (with J. Haugaard) Sexual Abuse of Children, 1988; (with P. Britner and J. Woolard) Preventing Child Abuse and Neglect Through Parent Education, 1997; editor: (with J. Haugaard) Prevention in Community Mental Health Practice; (with E. Mulvey, L. Weithorn and J. Monahan) Mental Health, Law and Children, 1984; assoc. editor Law and Human Behavior, 1986-96, mem. editl. bd., 1996—; mem. editl. bd. Am. Jour. Cmty. Psychology, 1974-83, 88-91; contbr. articles to profl. jours., chpts. in books. Adv. bd. on prevention Va. Dept. Mental Health, Mental Retardation and Substance Abuse Svcs., Richmond, 1986-92. Recipient Disting. Scholar in psychology award Va. Assn. Social Sci., 1991. Fellow APA (chmn. task force on pub. policy 1980-84), Am. Psychol. Soc., Soc. for Cmty. Rsch. and Action (pres. 1986, Disting. Contbn. award in theory and rsch. 1998, Inaugural award for ednl. mentoring 1999), Phi Beta Kappa. Office: U Va Dept Psychology PO Box 400400 Charlottesville VA 22904-4400 E-mail: ndr@virginia.edu.

REPS, DAVID NATHAN, finance educator; b. N.Y.C., July 30, 1926; s. Samuel and Fannie (Ginsberg) R.; m. Helene Shifrin, Aug. 10, 1958; children: Tamara, Aaron, Steven, Jennifer. BSEE, Columbia U., 1948; MSEE, U. Pitts., 1953, PhD, 1966. Elec. utility systems engr. Westinghouse Elec. Corp., Pitts., 1950-63, corp. planner, 1963-67; prin. mgmt. svcs. Ernst & Young, N.Y.C., 1967-75; prof., chmn. bus. econs., fin., pub. policy L.I. Univ., N.Y.C., 1975-78; prof. fin. Pace U., Pleasantville, N.Y., 1978—; v.p. Video Frame Store, Inc., N.Y.C., 1983—, The Photoboard Group, N.Y.C., 1989-92; v.p. and treas. Digital Video Photo Imaging, Inc., N.Y.C., 1992—. Bd. dirs. The Storyboard Group, Inc., N.Y.C.; exec. v.p. Video Frame Imaging, Inc., N.Y.C., 1994—. Contbr. articles to profl. jours. With USN, 1944-46. Home: 98 Soundview Ave White Plains NY 10606-3617 Office: Pace U Bedford Rd Pleasantville NY 10570

RESCH, MARY LOUISE, town agency administrator; b. David City, Nebr., Oct. 26, 1956; d. Ernest John and Mary Jean (Roelandts) Cermak. BS in Psychology, SUNY, Albany, 1984; MS in Counseling and Edn. with high honors, U. Wis., Platteville, 1986. Enlisted U.S. Army, 1974, advance through ranks to sgt., 1982, bomb disposal tech., 1977-79, bomb disposal instr. Indian Head, Md., 1979-80, resigned, 1985; instr., intern family advocacy Army Community Svc., U.S. Army, Ft. Belvoir, 1986; sr. counselor, child therapist Community Crisis and Referral Ctr., Inc., Waldorf, Md., 1986-87; adminstr. Walter Reed Army Med. Ctr. USDA Grad. Sch., Washington, 1987-88, contract mgr. Ft. Jackson, S.C., 1988-91; pres. Athena Cons., Columbia, S.C., 1991-93; dir. spl. programs Newberry (S.C.) Commn. on Alcohol and Drug Abuse, 1993-95; resource devel. coord. Cities in Schs.-SC, Inc., Columbia, 1995-97; exec. dir. S.C. Ctr. for Family Policy, Columbia, 1997—2001; pub. rels. dir. Xpress Group, Inc., 2001—02; resource devel. specialist Town of Lexington, SC, 2002—. Human svcs. cons., Washington, 1986-87; adj. instr. Coker Coll., Ft. Jackson, 1989-95. Active Govs. Juvenile Justice Adv. Coun., Govs. Substance Abuse Prevention Coun. Mem. S.C. Assn. Prevention Profls. and Advs., State Assn. Crime Prevention Officers, Nat. Contract Mgmt. Assn. (fellow, former pres., mentor). Republican. Lutheran. Avocations: needlepoint, racquetball, reading, bowling, jewelry making. Home: 312 Edgewater Ln West Columbia SC 29169-6957 Office: Town of Lexington 111 Maiden Lane Lexington SC 29072

RESCH, RITA MARIE, music educator; b. Minot, N.D., Dec. 26, 1936; d. Clement Charles and Magdalena Marie (Zeltinger) Resch. BS in Edn., Minot State U., 1957; MM in Music Lit., Eastman Sch. Music, Rochester, N.Y., 1960; MA in English Lit., U. N.D., 1967; MFA in Voice, U. Iowa, 1973, DMA in Piano Chamber Music/Accompanying, 1974. Music tchr. (vocal) Biwabik (Minn.) Sch. Dist., 1957—58, S. Redford Twp., Detroit, 1958—59; instr. music Fontbonne Coll., St. Louis, 1960—63; asst. prof. music Wis. State U., Stevens Point, 1965—68, Ctrl. Mo. State U., Warrensburg, 1974—, assoc. prof., 1979, full prof., 1989—. Adjudicator for vocal music Mo. State High Sch. Activities Assn., Columbia, Kans. State High Sch. Activities Assn., Topeka, other orgns., 1976—. Author (with Judith E. Carman, William K. Gaeddert, Gordon Myers): Art Song in the United States: An Annotated Bibliography, 1976, 3rd edit., 2001. Assoc. organist Sacred Heart Cath. Ch., Warrensburg, 1980—. Mem.: Mo. Music Tchrs. Assn. (v.p. auditions 1995—98), Music Tchrs. Nat. Assn., Nat. Assn. Tchrs. Singing. Office: Ctrl Mo State U Dept Music Warrensburg MO 64093 E-mail: resch@cmsul.cmsu.edu.

RESCHLY, DANIEL J. education educator, psychologist, educator; b. Wayland, Iowa, Dec. 30, 1943; married; 3 children. BS, Iowa State U., 1966; MA, U. Iowa, 1968; PhD, U. Oreg., 1971. Lic. sch. psychologist Iowa, Oreg., Ariz.; nat. cert. sch. psychologist, cert. secondary edn. educator Iowa. Sch. psychologist Louisa County Schs., Wapello, Iowa, 1967—69; dir. summer head start program Louisa County, Iowa, 1969; sch. psychology intern Albina Youth Opportunity Ctr. and Portland (Oreg.) Pub. Schs., 1970—71; asst. prof. U. Ariz., Tucson, 1971—75; assoc. prof., prof., disting. prof., dir. Sch. Psychology Program Iowa State U., 1975—98, interim assoc. dean Coll. Edn., 1996—98, dir. Rsch. Inst. for Studies in Edn., 1996—98; prof. edn. and psychology, chair dept. spl. edn. Vanderbilt U., Nashville, 1998—. Presenter in field. Contbr. chapters to books, articles to profl. jours. Fellow: APA, Am. Psychol. Soc.; mem.: Tenn. Assn. Sch. Psychologists, Internat. Sch. Psychology Assn., Am. Assn. Applied and Preventive Psychology, Coun. for Exceptional Children, Am. Assn. on Mental Retardation, Am. Ednl. Rsch. Assn., Iowa Acad. Edn. (charter), Nat. Assn. Sch. Psychologists (pres., editor Sch. Psychology Rev., chair grad. program approval, Lifetime Achievement award, three Disting. Svc. awards). Office: Vanderbilt Univ Box 328 Peabody Coll Nashville TN 37203-5701*

RESIDES, DIANE LOUISE, academic administrator; b. Bellefonte, Pa., June 24, 1959; d. George Clair and Evelyn Louise (Immel) R. BS, Penn State U., 1981, MEd, 1989, DEd in Adult Edn., 1997. Cert. rehab. counselor, Pa. Program mgr. Skills of Ctrl. Pa. Inc., Bellefonte, 1983-85; coord. student svcs. Ctr. Bus. Sch., Inc., State College, Pa., 1985-86; tng. coord. Pvt. Industry Coun. of Center Co., Pleasant Gap, Pa., 1986; coord. residence halls Penn State U., University Park, 1986-90, counselor Ctr. Adult Learner Svcs., 1990-96, interim dir. Office for Disability Svcs., 1996-97, dir. assistance and info., 1997—2002; assoc. dean for student devel. svcs., assoc. v.p. for student devel. Harford C.C., Bel Air, Md., 2002—. Mem. Phi Delta Kappa, Pi Lambda Theta, Phi Kappa Phi Home: 632 N Bend Rd Baltimore MD 21229-2210

RESING, MARYLORETTO RACHEL, guidance counseling administrator, elementary school educator, pastoral counselor; b. Covington, Ky., Jan. 27, 1949; d. Raymond Anthony and Carole Mary (Glover) Seifert; m. John Joseph Resing, Sept. 6, 1969; children: Jayne Carole, Matthew Raymond-Albert, Markus John, Joseph Thomas. BA, Thomas More Coll., Crestview Hills, Ky., 1984; MEd, Xavier U., Cin., 1989; M of Religious Studies, Athenaeum, Cin., 1994. Cert. elem. tchr. Ky., elem. and secondary guidance counselor Ky., Nat. Cert. Counselors, Nat. Cert. Counselor 2002. Tchr. St. Joseph Sch. Diocese of Covington, Crescent Springs, Ky., 1969-70, tchr. St. Cecelia Sch. Independence, Ky., 1984-85, tchr. Covington Cath. H.S. Park Hills, Ky., 1985-90, dir. religious edn. St. Therese Parish Southgate, Ky., 1990-95; guidance counselor Kenton County Sch., Erlanger, Ky., 1995-96; dir. religious edn. St. Agnes Parish Diocese of Covington, Park Hills, 1995-96; tchr., dir. alternative coop. edn. program Covington Ind. Sch., 1997-99; counselor Holmes Jr. H.S., 2000—. Mem. Covington Diocesan Family Life Bd., Erlanger, Ky., 1994-96; initiator, chair Religious Edn. Group, Erlanger, 1991-96. Contbr. to mag. and diocesan newspaper. Active Boy Scouts Am., Independence, Ky., 1983—; bd. dirs. YMCA, Independence, 1986-92; mem. Greater Cin. NCCJ, 1985-90; chair St. Cecilia Sch. Bd., Independence, 1985-89; mem. La Leche League No. Ky., 1970-80, leader, 1976-80; bd. dirs. Nat. Assn. Parish Coords. and Dirs. of Religious Edn., 1997. Mem.: No. Ky. Counseling Assn. (v.p. and pres.-elect 2002—03, pres. 2003—), Am. Counseling Assn., Ky. Edn. Assn. (rep.), Dirs. of Religious Edn. Support Group, Phi Delta Kappa. Roman Catholic. Avocations: antiques, gardening, reading.

RESKA-HADDEN, MARCIA ANN, special education educator, educator; b. LacKawanna, N.Y., Mar. 16, 1952; d. Edward Walter and Harriet Theresa (Kozlowski) Reska; m. Dennis Lynn Hadden; 1 child, Dennis Edward. BA in History, Canisius Coll., 1974, MS in Edn., 1979; MAT in History, Niagara U., 1974-76; mentally impaired student, Eastern Mich. U., 1988-90. Tchr. Spl. Edn., N.Y., Mich. Jr. high sch. tchr. St. Barbara's Sch., Lackawanna, N.Y., 1974-75; 5th grade tchr. St. Ambrose Sch., Buffalo, N.Y., 1975-76; jr. high sch. tchr. The Cathedral Sch., Buffalo, N.Y., 1976-79, St. Mary's of the Lake Sch., Hamburg, N.Y., 1979-83, Our Lady of Victory Sch., Lackawanna, N.Y., 1983-85; substitute tchr. Lakeville (Mich.) Sch. Dist., 1986-87, Genesee Intermediate Sch. Dist., Flint, Mich., 1986-88, spl. edn. tchr., 1988—. Mem. Coun. for Exceptional Children, Reston, Va., 1988—; speaker, presentor Functional Curriculum for a SMI Student, 1991. Co-author: Functional Curriculum GISD Secondary Functional Curriculum, 1989-90. Mem. Polish Union Am., Canisus Coll. Alumnae Assn., Genesee County Hist. Soc., Mich. Edn. Assn., Genesee Intermediate Ednl. Assn., Beta Sigma Phi. Home: 7211 Timberwood Dr Davison MI 48423-9522 Office: Genesee Intermediate Sch Dist 2413 W Maple Ave Flint MI 48507-3429

RESSETAR, NANCY, foreign language educator; b. Paterson, N.J., Dec. 19, 1947; d. Marino Angelo and Florence Mae (Patterson) DeMattia; m. Michael Ressetar, Jr., Aug. 15, 1981; 1 child, Tatyana Marina. BA, Montclair State U., 1970. Cert. tchr., N.J. Model various agencies, 1953-84; tchr. Spanish Clifton (N.J.) Sch. Sys., 1970—. Sponsor Spanish Club, Clifton, 1981—, Student Leadership, Clifton, 1988—, Travel to Spain, Clifton, 1982-96; campaign worker Dem. Party, Clifton, 1968-72. Recipient Gov.'s award for excellence in tchg. State of N.J., 1996. Mem. NEA, N.J. Edn. Assn., Passaic County Edn. Assn., Clifton Tchrs. Assn. (sec. 1973-75), Fgn. Lang. Tchrs. N.J., Am. Assn. Tchrs. Spanish and Portuguese. Democrat. Lutheran. Avocations: travel, theatre, doll collecting, classic hollywood, tutoring. Home: 20 Robin Hood Rd Clifton NJ 07013-3112

RESWEBER, ELLEN CAMPBELL, retired secondary education educator; b. Scott, La., June 21, 1930; d. Milton George and Louise (Mouton) Campbell; m. Francis Thomas Resweber, Dec. 27, 1954; children: Paul Adolphe, Henrietta Louise, Milton George, Louis Joseph, Peter John. BS, U. Southwestern La., 1951; MEd, La. State U., 1957. Math. tchr. Youngsville (La.) High Sch., 1950-52, Lafayette (La.) High Sch., 1952-55, Northside High Sch., Lafayette, 1970-91; ret., 1991. Head math. dept. Northside High Sch., 1986-91. Mem. Nat. Coun. Tchrs. Math., La. Ret. Tchrs. Assn., Lafayette Ret. Tchrs. Assn. (v.p. 1993). Roman Catholic. Avocations: reading, needlework. Home: 1010 Roper Dr Scott LA 70583-4702

RETHEMEYER, KAY LYNN, secondary school educator; b. Nevada, Mo., Oct. 27, 1946; d. John Albert and Wanda Lee (Hill) Kinnamon; m. Robert J. Rethemeyer, Aug. 22, 1971; children: Robin, Rustin. BS in Edn., Ctrl. Mo. State U., Warrensburg, 1968, MA in History, 1971. Tchr. Lee's Summit (Mo.) Jr. High, 1968-73, Longview C.C., Lee's Summit, 1984-88, Pleasant Lea Jr. High, Lee's Summit, 1988-89, Lee's Summit H.S., 1989—. Mem. R-7 Adv. Com. Mem. NEA, Nat. Coun. Social Studies, Delta Kappa Gamma. Home: 1026 SE Timbercreek Ln Lees Summit MO 64081-3003 Office: Lees Summit HS 400 SE 8th St Lees Summit MO 64063-4214

RETHEMEYER, ROBERT JOHN, social studies educator; b. St. Louis, Jan. 20, 1948; s. John Henry and Olivia Antonia (Fallbeck) R.; m. Kay Lynn Jones, Aug. 22, 1971; children: Robin Lynn, Rustin John. BS in Edn., Cen. Mo. State Coll., 1970; M in Sch. Adminstrn., Cen. Mo. State U., 1973, EdS in Supt., 1985. Tchr. 7th grade social studies Smith-Hale Jr. HS, Kans. City, Mo., 1970-78, asst. prin., 1978-80, tchr. 7th and 8th grade social studies, 1980-2000. Chmn. bldg. dept. Cons. Sch. Dist. 1, Kansas City, 1982-2000, alt. sch. com., 1993-94, summer sch. prin., 1981-97, summer sch. coord., 1998, ret., 2000; part-time profl. staff Hickman Mills C-1 Sch., 2000-02; supr. U. Mo.-Kansas City student tchrs.; adj. istruct. Edn. for Ctrl. Mo. State U., Warrensburg, Mo. Mem. NEA, Nat. Coun. for Social Studies, Phi Delta Kappa. Home: 1026 SE Timbercreek Ln Lees Summit MO 64081-3003

RETTON, SANDRA JO, physical education educator, coach; b. Fairmont, W.Va., June 1, 1956; d. Frank Richard and Shirley Jean (Martin) R. BA in Edn., Fairmont State Coll., 1978; AS in Data Processing, North Ctrl. Tech. Coll., Mansfield, Ohio, 1985; MS in Phys. Edn., Ohio U., 1991. Cert. profl. tchr., Ohio. Tchr. W.Va. Career Coll., Fairmont, 1979-80; tchr., coach Crestview High Sch., Ashland, Ohio, 1980-81; coal miner Consol. Coal Co., Mannington, W.Va., 1982-83; tchr., coach Morgan High Sch., McConnelsville, Ohio, 1986—. Named Muskingum Valley League Track Coach of Yr., 1993, 95, Ea. Dist. Divsn. I Girls Track Coach of Yr. Ohio, 1993, 95, Dist. # 8 Girls Track Coach of Yr. Mem. NEA, Ohio Edn. Assn., AAHPERD, Ohio Assn. Health, Phys. Edn., Recreation and Dance, Nat. Fedn. Interscholastic Coaches and Officials Assn., Ohio Assn. Track and Cross Country Coaches. Avocations: walking, hiking, collecting glass mugs. Home: 60 N 9th St Mc Connelsville OH 43756-1106 Office: Morgan High Sch 800 Raider Dr Mc Connelsville OH 43756-9633

RETZER, KENNETH ALBERT, mathematics educator, entrepreneur; b. Jacksonville, Ill., Nov. 6, 1933; s. Samuel Stark and Cora Edith (Martin) R.; m. Dorcas Anne Schroeder, Apr. 18, 1953 (dec. Aug. 4, 1990); children: Martin Wayne, Kent Arnold, Sheryl Kaye; m. Wei Dong, Feb. 14, 1991; 1 child, Roger Dong Retzer. AB, Ill. Coll., 1954; MEd, U. Ill., 1957, PhD, 1969. Cert. tchr., Ill., 1954-57; cert. sch. adminstrn., Ill., 1957—. Tchr. Saunemin (Ill.) Twp. High Sch., 1954-58, asst. supt., 1955-58; prof. math. Ill. State U., Normal, 1959-89, Abilene (Tex.) Christian U., 1989—97; v.p., bd. dirs. DR Global Enterprises, DBA Cafe China, DBA DR Gifts and Accessories, 1995—2000; v.p., bd. dir. WD Mgmt. LLC, DBA Gary's Pizza, 2002—. Asst. chmn. math. dept. Ill. State U., Normal, 1969-71; vis. prof. U. Ga., Athens, 1973, Tex. A&M U., College Station, 1984, U. Hawaii-Maui, Kahului, 1990, 91; cons. Arabian Am. Oil Co., Dhahran, Saudi Arabia, 1984, Ill. State Bd. Edn., Springfield, 1983-88; rsch. fellow U. Western Sydney, Australia, 1993; lectr. Zhejiang U., Hangzhou, China, Northwest Normal U., Lanzhou, China, Gansu Edn. U., Lanzhou, Lanzhou Normal U., Zhangye Normal U., China, summer 1994. Contbr. articles to profl. jours. in the U.S., Can., China. Mem. NEA, AAUP, Nat. Coun. Tchrs. Math., Sch. Sci. and Math. Assn., Math. Assn. Am., Rsch. Coun. on Diagnostic and Prescriptive Math., Ill. Coun. Tchrs. Math. (Max Beberman award 1988), Tex. Coun. Tchrs. Math., Big County Coun. Tchrs. Math., Ill. Assn. Higher Edn., Pi Mu Epsilon, Phi Delta Kappa. Mem. Church of Christ. Avocations: travel, photography, hiking, reading, Christian studies. Home: 31 Rue Maison St Abilene TX 79605-4710 E-mail: ken.retzer@math.acu.edu.

REUBISH, GARY RICHARD, English language educator; b. Breckenridge, Minn., Jan. 6, 1946; s. Irving Earl and Genevieve Loretta (Miller) R. AA, N.D. State Coll. Sci., Wahpeton, 1969; BS, Valley City State Coll., 1971. Cert. tchr., N.D. Tchr. English Wolford (N.D.) Pub. Sch., 1971-72, Lake Benton (Minn.) Pub. Sch., 1972-76, Wahpeton (N.D.) Pub. Sch., 1976—. With USAF, 1965-71. Mem. NEA, N.D. Edn. Assn., Wahpeton Edn. Assn. Office: Wahpeton Mid Sch 1209 Loy Ave Wahpeton ND 58075-5038 Address: PO Box 181 Wahpeton ND 58074-0181

REUTER, JEANETTE MILLER, psychologist, educator; b. Sheboygan, Wis., Sept. 9, 1921; d. Arthur Herbert and Evangeline Miller; m. Louis Frederick Reuter, Feb. 1, 1943; children: Louis Frederick IV, Katherine Evan, James Arthur. BS, U. Wis., 1944; MS, Case Western Res. U., 1959, PhD, 1962. Diplomate Am. Bd. Profl. Psychology, Am. Bd. Profl. Neuropsychology; lic. psychologist, Ohio. Lectr. U. Md., Heidelberg, Fed. Republic of Germany, 1962; clin. psychologist USAF Hosp., Weisbaden, Fed. Republic of Germany, 1962-63; psychologist IV Sagamore Hills (Ohio) Children's Psychiat. Hosp., 1964-65; asst. prof. psychology Kent (Ohio) State U., 1965-70, assoc. prof. psychology, 1970-75, prof. psychology, 1975-88; prof. emerita, 1988—; pres. Kent (Ohio) Devel. Metrics, 1982—2002. Cons. psychologist Hattie Larlham Found., Mantua, Ohio, 1974—; prin. investigator handicapped children's early edn. program U.S. Dept. Edn., 1974-82; rsch. cons. U. Barcelona (Spain), V.I. Clinic-Saint Joan de Déu, 1985—, Free U. Amsterdam, The Netherlands, 1988—, Early Intervention Inst., St. Petersburg, 1993—, Szombatheley Krankenhaus, Hungary, 1993—, Maternal and Child Health, Prague, Czech Republic, 1994—; apptd. by gov. Ohio Interagy. Early Intervention Coun., 1987-89. Prin. author Kent Infant Devel. Scale, 1982, Kent Inventory of Devel. Skills, 1999; contbr. articles to profl. jours. Bd. dirs., v.p. Ardmore, Inc., Akron, Ohio, 1986-95. Recipient Lifetime Achievement award, Ohio Women in Psychology, 1990. Mem. Am. Psychol. Assn., Soc. Behavioral Pediat., Soc. for Rsch. in Child Devel. Democrat. Home: 43 Laurel Lake Dr Hudson OH 44236

REUTER, JOAN COPSON, retired program director; b. London, July 7, 1919; came to US, 1921; d. Denis and Florence (Copson) Soucy; widowed; children: David, Robert N., Joan Ellen Swanson, Alan, Ronald (dec.). AA, Asnuntuck C.C., 1975; BS, N.H. Coll., 1982. Dir. women's ctr. Asnuntuck C.C., Enfield, Conn., 1975—98, ret., 1998. Adj. faculty Asnuntuck C.C., 1984-95, dir. childcare ctr., 1974—; bd. dir. Mentor Program, Town Enfield, After Sch. Program. Bd. dir. Enfield Bd. Edn., 1979-91; justice of peace Town of Enfield, 1980—; sec. Enfield Loan Rev. Com., 1957—. Mem. Women's Club Enfield (sec., bd. dir. 1957—), Asnuntuck Alumni Assn. (v.p., pres.). Republican. Episcopalian. Avocations: reading, walking, gardening. Home: 9 Homestead Dr Enfield CT 06082-4639

REUTER, STEWART RALSTON, retired radiologist, lawyer, educator; b. Detroit, Feb. 14, 1934; s. Carl H. and Grace M. R.; m. Marianne Ahfeldt, June 6, 1966. BA, Ohio Wesleyan U., 1955; MD, Case Western Res. U., 1959; JD, U. San Francisco, 1980. Diplomate: Am. Bd. Radiology, Am. Bd. Legal Medicine. Bar: Tex. 1981. Intern U. Calif., San Francisco, 1959-60, resident in radiology, 1960-63; instr. radiology Stanford (Calif.) U., 1963-64; asst. prof. U. Mich., Ann Arbor, 1966-69, prof., 1972-76; assoc. prof. U. Calif., San Diego, 1969-72, prof. San Francisco and Davis, 1976-80; prof., chmn. dept. radiology Health Scis. Ctr., U. Tex., San Antonio, 1980-2001, prof. emeritus, 2001. Co-author: Gastrointestinal Radiology, 3d edit., 1986; mem. editorial bd. Am. Jour. Roentgenology, 1975-91, Iatrogenics, 1990-93; contbr. articles to profl. jours. Picker fellow, 1964-66 Fellow: Soc. Interventional Radiologists (pres. 1978, Gold medal 2004), Am. Coll. Legal Medicine (pres. 1996, bd. govs. 1985—91, 1992—94, sec. 1994, pres.-elect 1995), Am. Heart Assn., Am. Coll. Radiology (councillor 1996—99, fellow emeritus); mem.: AMA, Soc. Gastrointestinal Radiologists, Tex. Radiol. Assn. (trustee 1989—92, pres. 1994, trustee 1995—98, Gold medal 2000), Am. Roentgen Ray Soc., Assn. Univ. Radiologists, Am. Bd. Legal Medicine, Tex. Bar Assn. Home: 3923 Morgans Creek San Antonio TX 78230-1945 Office: U Tex Health Sci Ctr Dept Radiology 7703 Floyd Curl Dr San Antonio TX 78284-6200 E-mail: reuter@uthscsa.edu.

REUTHINGER, GEORGEANNE, special education educator; b. Laredo, Tex., Mar. 10, 1952; d. George and Maria Josefina (Elizondo) Ramon; m. David Lawrence Reuthinger, Apr. 5, 1952; 1 child, David L. Jr. AA in Music and Drama, Laredo Jr. Coll., 1972; BS in Speech and Drama Edn., Tex. A&I U., 1974, MS in Edn., 1978; postgrad., Tes. A&M Internat. U. Lic. speech therapist, Tex.; cert. speech therapist, ednl. diagnostician, profl. supervision. Speech and drama tchr. Laredo ISD Martin High Sch., 1974; supr., diagnostician spl. edn. program Laredo ISD Martin H.S., 1992-96, Cigarra H.S., Nixon H.S., 1998—; speech therapist Laredo ISD, 1974-78, ednl. diagnostician, 1978-92; sales assoc. Country Wide Real Estate, Laredo, 1997—; cons. in spl. edn. United Ind. and Laredo Ind. Sch. Dists., 1997-98. Founding mem., lead actress in bilingual theatrical touring co. Tex. A&I U., 1974. Active in fundraising for charities Women's City Club, Boy Scouts Am.; judge UIL Acad. & Fine Arts events, Spl. Olympics. Scholar Art League, 1970, Tex. A&I Alumni, 1972-74; recipient awards U.S. Army, 1973, USO Shows, 1973-74. Mem. Tex. Speech and Hearing Assn. (legis. network 1992-97), Coun. for Exceptional Children (lobbyist 1995, sec. Laredo chpt. 1975), Valley Coun. Adminstrs. and Suprs. in Spl. Edn., ASCD, Tex. Coun. Adminstrs. and Suprs. in Spl. Edn., Delta Kappa Gamma (sec. Alpha Nu chpt. 1977-78). Avocations: directing and acting in theatrical productions, singing in community choirs, special olympics volunteering and judging. Home: 206 Granada Dr Laredo TX 78041-2615 Office: Country Wide Real Estate 1303 Calle Del Norte Ste 6 Laredo TX 78041-6041 also: Laredo Ind Sch Dist 1702 Houston St Laredo TX 78040-4906

REUTTER, EBERHARD EDMUND, JR., education and law educator; b. Balt., May 28, 1924; s. Eberhard Edmund and Irene Louise (Loewer) R.; m. Bettie Marie Lytle, Aug. 16, 1947; 1 son, Mark Douglas. BA, Johns Hopkins U., 1944; MA, Columbia U., 1948, PhD, 1950. Dir., Tokyo Army Edn. Program Sch., 1945-47; head math. dept. Barnard Sch., N.Y.C., 1947-49; mem. faculty Tchrs. Coll., Columbia U., 1950—, prof., 1957-96, prof. emeritus, 1996—. Vis. prof. U. Alaska, 1960, 66, U. P.R., 1954, U. So. Calif., 1960; speaker, cons. Coordinator spl. edn. projects NAACP Legal Def. Fund, 1965-68 Author: The School Administrator and Subversive

Activities, 1951, Schools and the Law, 5th edit., 1981, (with W.S. Elsbree) Staff Personnel in the Public Schools, 1954, (with R.R. Hamilton) Legal Aspects of School Board Operation, 1958, (with W.S. Elsbree) Principles of Staff Personnel Administration in Public Schools, 1959, (with L.O. Garber) The Yearbook of School Law, 1967, 68, 69, 70, Legal Aspects of Control of Student Activities by Public School Authorities, 1970, The Law of Public Education, 4th edit., 1994, The Courts and Student Conduct, 1975, The Supreme Court's Impact on Public Education, 1982; also articles, chpts. in books. Chmn. citizens adv. com. Emerson (N.J.) Bd. Edn., 1954-57. Served from pvt. to 1st lt. inf. AUS, 1943-46. Recipient Marion A. McGhehey award for outstanding service in field edn. law, 1986. Mem. Nat. Orgn. Legal Problems of Edn. (pres. 1967), AAUP, Am. Assn. Sch. Adminstrs., NEA, Am. Assn. Sch. Personnel Adminstrs., Internat. Personnel Mgmt. Assn., Phi Beta Kappa, Kappa Delta Pi, Phi Delta Kappa. Home: 316 Grand Blvd Emerson NJ 07630-1157 Office: Columbia Univ Tchrs Coll New York NY 10027

REVAK, JOANN, special education educator; b. Tucson, Jan. 21, 1943; d. Jack Charles and Irene Ruby (Zumwalt) Stubblefield; m. John James Revak, May 8, 1965; children: Elizabeth L., Elson L. BA in Edn., U. Ariz., 1965; MA in Edn., Ariz. State U., 1969. Cert. tchr. elem. and spl. edn., Ariz. Tchr. 1st grade Murphy Sch. Dist., Phoenix, 1965-67; spl. edn. resource tchr. Sierra Vista (Ariz.) Pub. Schs., 1980-81, tchr. spl. edn., 1981—. Leader Girl Scouts Am., Sierra Vista, 1976-78; coach Spl. Olympics, Sierra Vista, 1981-84; den mother Boy Scouts Am., 1981; v.p. Coun. for Exceptional Children, 1993—. Mem. NEA, Coun. for Exceptional Children (chair libr. com. 190-93), Autism Soc. Am. Democrat. Eastern Orthodox. Avocations: hiking, reading, camping, traveling, gardening with house plants. Home: 2064 E Sonoita Dr Sierra Vista AZ 85635-2104 Office: Sierra Vista Pub Schs 3555 E Fry Blvd Sierra Vista AZ 85635-2972

REVEL, JEAN-PAUL, biology educator; b. Strasbourg, France, Dec. 7, 1930; came to U.S., 1953; s. Gaston Benjamin and Suzanne (Neher) R.; m. Helen Ruth Bowser, July 27, 1957 (div. 1986); children: David, Daniel Neher, Steven Robert; m. Galina Avdeeva Moller, Dec. 24, 1986; 1 stepchild, Karen. BS, U. Strasbourg, 1949; PhD, Harvard U., 1957. Rsch. fellow Cornell U. Med. Sch., N.Y.C., 1958-59; from instr. to prof. Harvard Med. Sch., Boston, 1959-71; prof. Calif. Inst. Tech., Pasadena, 1971—, AB Ruddock chair in biology, 1978—, dean of students, 1996—. Mem. sch. advisors bd. Nat. Insts. Aging, Balt., 1977-80; mem. ad hoc adv. biology NSF, Washington, 1982-83; mem. Nat. High Voltage Microscopy Adv. Group, Bethesda, Md., 1983, Nat. Rsch. Resources Adv. Coun., 1986-90. Author: (with E.D. Hay) Fine Structure of Developing Avian Cornea, 1969; editor: Cell Shape and Surface Architecture, 1977, Science of Biological Specimen Preparation, 1986; mem. editl. bd. Jour. Cell Biology, 1969-72, Internat. Rev. Cytology, 1970, Cell and Tissue Rsch., 1979—, Molecular and Cell Biology, 1983-91; editor in chief Jour. Microscopy Soc. Am., 1994-96. Fellow AAAS (leader biol. scis. sect. 1991-92, Gordon conf. cell adhesion); mem. Am. Soc. Cell Biology (pres. 1972-73), Electron Micros. Soc. Am. (pres. 1988, Disting. Scientist award 1993), Soc. Devel. Biology. Avocations: watercolors, photography. Office: Calif Inst Tech # 156-29 Pasadena CA 91125-0001 E-mail: revelj@caltech.edu.

REVELEY, WALTER TAYLOR, III, dean; b. Churchville, Va., Jan. 6, 1943; s. Walter Taylor and Marie (Eason) R.; m. Helen Bond, Dec. 18, 1971; children: Walter Taylor, George Everett Bond, Nelson Martin Eason, Helen Lanier. AB, Princeton U., 1965; JD, U. Va., 1968. Bar: Va. 1970, D.C. 1976. Asst. prof. law U. Ala., 1968-69; law clk. to Justice Brennan U.S. Supreme Ct., Washington, 1969-70; fellow Woodrow Wilson Internat. Ctr. for Scholars, 1972-73; internat. affairs fellow Coun. on Fgn. Rels., N.Y.C., 1972-73; assoc. Hunton & Williams, Richmond, Va., 1970-76, ptnr., 1976-98, mng. ptnr., 1982-91, cons., 1998—; dean William and Mary Law Sch., 1998—. Lectr. Coll. William and Mary Law Sch., 1978-80; cons. in field. Author: War Powers of the President and Congress: Who Holds the Arrows and Olive Branch, 1981; mem. editl. bd. Va. Law Rev., 1966-68; contbr. articles to profl. jours. Trustee Princeton U., 1986-90, 91-2001, Presbyn. Ch. (U.S.A.) Found., 1991-97, Va. Hist. Soc., 1991-96, 2003—, Union Theol. Sem., 1992-2000, Andrew W. Mellon Found., 1994—, JSTOR, 1995—, Va. Mus. Fine Arts, 1995—, pres. 1996-99, St. Christopher's Sch., 1996-01, Carnegie Endowment for Internat. Peace, 1999—; bd. dirs. Fan Dist. Assn., Richmond, Inc., 1976-80, pres., 1979-80; bd. dirs. Richmond Symphony, 1980-92, pres., 1988-90, pres. symphony coun., 1994-99; bd. dirs. Presbyn. Outlook Found., 1985-2003, pres., 1992-95; bd. dirs. Va. Mus. Found., 1990-99; elder Grace Covenant Presbyn. Ch.; bd. dirs. New Covenant Trust Co., 1997-99, Va. Found. Humanities, 2001-. Mem. ABA, Va. Bar Assn., D.C. Bar Assn., Am. Bar Found., Va. Bar Found., Princeton Assn. Va. (bd. dirs. 1981—, pres. 1983-85), Va. State Bar (edn. Lawyers sect. bd. govs. 1992—, chmn. 1992-95), Raven Soc., Phi Beta Kappa, Omicron Delta Kappa. Home: 2314 Monument Ave Richmond VA 23220-2604 Office: William and Mary Law Sch PO Box 8795 Williamsburg VA 23187-8795 E-mail: Taylor@wm.edu.

REVES, JOSEPH GERALD, dean, anesthesiology educator; b. Charleston, S.C., Aug. 14, 1943; s. George Everett and Frances (Masterson) R.; m. Virginia Cathcart, Jan. 05, 1945; children: Virginia Masterson, Christine Frances, Elizabeth Cathcart. BA, Vanderbilt U., 1965; MD, Medical Coll. S.C., 1969; MS, U. Ala., Birmingham, 1973. Lic. anesthesiologist S.C., Ala., Md., N.C.; Diplomate Am. Coll. Anesthesiology, Am. Bd. Anesthesiology. Rsch. asst., dept. pharmacology Med. Coll. S.C., 1965, 66 (summers); intern U. Ala. Hosp. and Clinics, Birmingham, Ala., 1969-70, resident in anesthesiology, 1970-72; post-doctoral, dept. anesthesia and physiology U. Ala. Med. Sch., 1972; instr., dept anesthesiology U. Ala. Hosp. and Clinics, 1973; dept. tng. staff, anesthesiology Nat. Naval Med. Ctr., Bethesda, Md., 1973-75; clin. instr., dept. anesthesiology George Washington U. Sch. Med., Washington, 1973-75; assoc. prof., dept. anesthesiology U. Ala. Hosp. and Clinics, 1975-78; dir., div. anesthesiology rsch. U. Ala., 1977-84, prof. anesthesiology, 1978-84; clin. anesthesia coord. UAB Cardiac Transplant Program, Birmingham, 1982-84; prof. anesthesiology, dir. cardiothoracic anesthesia Duke U. Med. Ctr., Durham, N.C., 1984-1991; dir., Duke Heart Ctr., Duke Med. Ctr., Durham, N.C., 1987-97; interim chmn., dept. anesthesiology Duke U. Med. Ctr., 1990-91, prof. and chmn., dept. anesthesiology, 1991—2001; dean, v.p. for medical affairs U. of South Carolina Sch. of Med., 2001—. Cons. Hoffman-LaRoche, Somatogen, Abbott/Oximetric. Contbr. to numerous profl. jours., refereed jours., chpts. in books, published scientific reviews, selected abstracts, editorials, films, audio visual presentations, letters, positions and background papers; author: Acute Revascularization of the Infracted Heart, 1987, Common Problems in Cardiac Anesthesia, 1987, Intravenous Anesthesia and Analgesia, 1988, Anesthesiology Clinics of North America, 1988, Anesthesia, 1990, International Anesthesiology Clinics, 1991; Cardiac Anesthesia, Privileges and Practice, 1994; editor: Anesthesia and Analgesia, 1984—, cardiovascular sect. editor 1991—; editorial bd. Society Cardiovascular Anesthesia Monograph Series (chmn. 1986-89), Current Opinion in Anaesthesia 1987—, American Antec Newsletter 1989—; co-editor in chief: Current Opinion in Anaesthesiology 1990—. Dir. Clairmont Ave Hist. Preservation Com. 1976-78; Am. Heart Assn. (Durham chpt. pres. 1988-90, com. mem. anesthesiology, radiology and surgery rsch. study com. 1988-91). Grantee NIH 1991—, Janssen Pharmaceutica 1991-93, Anaquest 1989-92, Diprivan Ednl. grant ICI Pharmaceuticals Group 1991-92. Fellow Am. Coll. Cardiology; mem. AMA, Durham County Medical Soc., Internat. Soc. on Oxygen Transport to Tissue, N.C. Soc. Anesthesiologist (edn. com. 1992—), N.C. State Medical Soc., Birmingham Vanderbilt Club (bd. dirs. 1975-80, 1st v.p. 1979, pres. 1980), Southern Med. Assn. (chmn. elect. anesthesiology sect. 1976-77, chmn. 1977-78, chmn. 1988-89), Southern Soc. Anesthesiologists (v.p. 1978-79, pres. elect 1979-80, pres. 1980-81), Soc. Cardiovascular Anesthesiologists (pres. 1979-80), Assn. Univ. Anesthetists (elected to mem. 1980), Assn. Cardiac Anesthesiologists (elected to mem. 1982, pres. 1990), Soc. for Neuroleptanalgesia (bd. dirs. 1988), U. Ala. Birmingham Nat. Alumni Soc. (dist. dir., bd. dirs. 1991-93), Internat. Anesthesia Rsch. Soc. (bd. Trustees 1992—), Am. Soc. Anesthesiologists (com. sub-specialty representation 1980—, subcommittee on clin. circulation 1992—, com. geriatric anesthesia 1992—), Sigma Xi, Alpha Omega Alpha. Achievements include research on effects of age on neurologic response to cardiopulmonary bypass; cerebral blood flow and metabolism during cardiac surgery; automated delivery system of intravenous anesthetic drugs; pathophysiology of cardiopulmonary bypass. Office: U of South Carolina PO Box 250617 96 Jonathan Lucas St, Ste 601 Charleston SC 29425

REVIE, JEAN E. science educator; b. Davenport, Iowa; d. Lloyd E. and Margaret V. Bentley; m. Steven T. Revie, May 26, 1972; children: Jonathan, Brian, Kevin, Alanna, Lindsey, Mikel, Carin. BA, U. Northern Colo., 1970, MA, 1973. Sci. tchr. Banner County H.S., Harrisburg, Nebr., 1970-71; life and earth sci. tchr. Kyrene Jr. H.S., Tempe, Ariz., 1983-85; biology instr. Northland Pioneer Coll., Winslow, Ariz., 1997-2000, South Mountain C.C., Phoenix, 2000—. Adj. instr. Minot State U., N.D., 1995-97, N.D. State Coll. Sci., Minot AFB, 1994-97; soil conservationist Natural Resource Conservation Svc., Turtle Lake, N.D., 1992-93; mus. aid Theodore Roosevelt Nat. Park, Medora, N.D., 1992. Field exec. Sakakawea Girl Scout Coun., Bismarck, N.D., 1991-92. Recipient Great Ideas scholarship Great Books, 1966, Acad. scholarship U. Northern Colo. 1966-70. Mem. Lds Ch. Avocations: family and nature activities, reading, cross stitch, music. Office: 7050 S 24th St Phoenix AZ 85042-5806 Fax: 602-243-8080. E-mail: jean.revie@smcmail.maricopa.edu.

REVOR, BARBARA KAY, secondary school educator; b. Mt. Vernon, Ill., June 16, 1948; d. Russell Harold and Mary Alice (Byars) Page; m. Bryan J. Revor, Dec. 19, 1981; children: Rachel, Joshua, Jacob. BA, Okla. Bapt. U., 1971; MS in Edn., Nat. Louis U., 1991. Tchr., chair English dept. North Palos Sch. Dist. 117, Hickory Hills, Ill., 1971—. Author: Immanuel, a collection of poems and inspirational stories, 2002. Mem. Nat. Coun. Tchrs. of English, Ill. Assn. Tchrs. of English, Romance Writers Am., Windy City Romance Writers.

REX, JOHN WILLIAMS, assurance company executive; Pres. Am. Fidelity Assurance Co., Oklahoma City, 1992—. Mem. adv. bd. Cmty. Coun. Ctrl. Okla.; bd. mem. United Way Met. Oklahoma City, 1992—, chmn., 1998; bd. mem. Okla. Commn. for Tchr. Preparation, Edn. Policy Bd. of the Okla. Bus. and Edn. Coalition. Named Friend of End., Okla. Edn. Assn., 2001; recipient Richard H. Clements Lifetime Achievement award, United Way, 2001, Meritorious Svc. award, U. Okla. Coll. Edn., 2002. Mem.: Nat. Children's Reading Found., Nat. Bd. for Profl. Tchg. Stds. (bd. mem., nat. bd. mem.). Office: Am Fidelity Assurance Co 2000 Classen Blvd PO Box 25523 Oklahoma City OK 73125-0523*

REXROAT, VICKI LYNN, occupational child development educator; b. Oklahoma City, Okla., June 12, 1957; d. Troy Bill and Opal Pauline (Flinn) Miller; m. David Edward Rexroat, Sept. 6, 1980; children: Jamie Lynn, Amber Donn, Emily Sue. BS, U. of Sci. and Arts, 1991; MS, U. Ctrl. Okla., 1997. Presch. tchr. Caddo-Kiowa Vocat. Sch., Fort Cobb, Okla., 1981-84, child devel. dir., 1984-89, child devel. instr., 1989—. Rep., advisor Child Devel. Assoc., Washington, 1989—; mem. curriculum team Okla. Dept. of Vocat. Edn., Stillwater, Okla., 1991—; adv. bd. Child Care Careers, Oklahoma City, 1992—. Contbr. articles to profl. jours. Co-chair Reach Out, Inc. Homeless Shelter, Anadarko, Okla., 1995—; founder, vol. Caddo County Welfare Vols., 1989—; friends for life mem. Fort Cobb Sr. Citizens, 1990—; mem. Fort Cobb Booster Club, 1989—. Named Friend of Children Okla. Inst. of Child Advocacy, 1993, New Tchr. of Yr. Okla. Vocat. Assn., 1993. Mem. Friends in the Okla. Early Childhood Assn. (pres. 1989—), So. Early Childhood Assn., Okla. Assn. for the Edn. of Young Children, Nat. Assn. for the Edn. of Young Children, Am. Vocat. Assn. (dist. v.p. 1989—, New Tchr. of Yr. 1994). Democrat. Bapt. Avocations: basketball games, fishing, boating, student organizations. Office: Caddo-Kiowa Vocat Sch North 7th Fort Cobb OK 73038

REX TON, SHEILA WARD, elementary school educator; b. Ft. Ord, Calif., Apr. 14, 1954; d. James F. Rex and Elizabeth L. Ward Carroll; m. Steven E. Ton, June 20, 1987; children: Pamela Eileen, Garrett Edward. BA in Edn. and Liberal Studies, Loyola Marymount U., L.A., 1975, M.Reading, 1982. Tchr. 1st grade St. Catherine LaBoure Sch., Torrance, Calif.; tchr. 3d grade Notre Dame Acad., L.A.; tchr. 4th grade Holy Trinity Sch., San Pedro, Calif., 1985-92; tchr. 5th grade, 1992—. Mem. Internat. Reading Assn., Torrance Reading Assn., Calif. Reading Assn., nat. Coun. Tchrs. English. Home: 21313 Talisman St Torrance CA 90503-5405

REYES, EDWARD, pharmacology educator; b. Albuquerque, May 5, 1944; s. Salvador and Faustina (Gabaldon) R.; m. Shirley Ann Trott, Aug. 15, 1970; children: David Joshua, Elizabeth Ann, Steven Mark. BS in Pharmacy, U. N.Mex., 1968; MS in Pharmacology, U. Colo., 1970, PhD in Pharmacology, 1974. Asst. prof. pharmacy U. Wyo. Sch. of Pharmacy, Laramie, 1974-75; asst. prof. pharmacology Dept. Pharmacology, U. N.Mex., Albuquerque, 1976-85, assoc. prof. pharmacology, 1985-97, assoc. prof. biochemistry and molecular biology, assoc. prof. pharmacy, 1997-2000; dir. minority biomed. rsch. support program U. N.Mex. Sch. of Medicine, Albuquerque, 1994-97, co-coord. MBRS program, 1998—; prof. emeritus U. N.Mex., 2000—. Referee Pharmacology Biochemistry Behavior, San Antonio, 1986—; adv. com. mem. NIMH Minority Neuro Sci. Fellowship, Washington, 1991—; cons. alcohol pharmacokinetics and breath alcohol testing. Author: (with others) Alcohol and Drug Abuse Review, 1991; contbr. articles to profl. jours. Scoutmaster Boy Scouts Am., Albuquerque, 1986-94, dist. camping com. chair, 1994—, Silver Beaver, 1996; vis. scientist N.Mex. Acad. Sci., Las Vegas, 1988—; youth preacher Rio Grande Bapt. Ch., Albuquerque, 1980—. Grantee Nat. Inst. of Alcohol Abuse and Alcoholism, NSF. Mem. Rsch. Soc. on Alcoholism, Western Pharmacology Soc., Soc. for Neurosci. (chair minority edn. tng. and profl. adv. 1987-94), Soc. for Advancement of Chicanos and Native Ams. in Sci., UNM/MBRS (co-dir. program). Achievements include rsch. that the in utero adminstration of alcohol produces an increase in liver and brain Y-glutamyl transpeptidase activity; isolated-GTP from brain of rats, in utero adminstration of alcohol lowers GSH in liver and brain.

REYES, SHIRLEY NORFLIN, computer learning center educator; b. New Orleans, Aug. 5, 1949; d. William Jr. and Annie (Stephens) Norflin; m. Vide Manuel Reyes, Oct. 2, 1972 (div. 1979); 1 child, Drew Haynes Reyes. BS, U. New Orleans, 1975, MA, 1990. Elem. tchr. Caddo Parish Pub. Sch. Sys., Shreveport, La., 1975-78; 4th grade tchr. St. Charles Parish Sch. Sys., Luling, La., 1979-80; elem. tchr. Jefferson Parish Sch. Sys., Gretna, La., 1980—; GED tchr. St. Bernard Cmty. Bapt. Ch., New Orleans, 1991—; kindergarten tchr. Bridge City (La.) Elem. Sch., 1995—. Coord. sch. tutoring program Bridge City Elem. Sch., 1996—; ranking tchr. Live Oak Manor Elem. Sch., Westwego, La., 1991—, dir. child care site, 1992-94, coord. testing and La. Edn. Assessment Program, 1992-94, La. Assessor for Intern Tchrs.: Field Test and Pilot, 1993-94; chmn. drug free schs. Jefferson Parish Pub. Sch. Sys., also instrnl. TV chmn.; pres. Edn. Network Agy., Inc.; writer program 2001 CLP with Black Arts Nat. Diaspora, Inc. Writer/storyteller children's books and songs; writer gospel songs; producer, writer learning aids for children. Edn. program writer The Reading Literacy Project, 1991—, A Pathway to Learning Program; coord. reading literacy project St. Bernard Cmty. Bapt. Ch., 1991—; den mother Boy Scouts Am., 1991—. Recipient Parent Adv. award Waggaman Kindergarten Ctr., 1985-86, New Music writer Gospel Music Workshop of Am., 1989. Mem. AAUW (chmn. community interest), Jefferson Fedn. of Tchrs., La. Edn. Assn., U. New Orleans Alumni Assn. Democrat. Avocations: storyteller, singer. Home and Office: 131 Prairieview Ct Westwego LA 70094-2541

REY-HERNANDEZ, CESAR A. school system administrator; BA in Polit. Sci. and Internat. Rels., MA Polit Sc. and Internat. Rels., PhD in Sociology, NA U. Mex. Sec. edn. PR Dept. Edn., San Juan, 2001—. Office: Puerto Rico Dept Edn PO Box 190759 San Juan PR 00919-0759*

REYNOLDS, ANNE MARIE, mathematics educator; b. Townsville, Queensland, Australia, Dec. 20, 1946; came to U.S., 1990; d. Owen Charles and Mary Carmelia (Rooney) R. BEd, James Cook U., Townsville, 1979; MEd, James Cook U., 1987; PhD, Fla. State U., 1993. Cert. math. tchr., Fla. Elem. and secondary sch. tchr. Cath. Edn. Office, Townsville, 1971-75, resource tchr., 1976-85, adminstr., 1986-87, secondary sch. tchr., 1988-90; tchr., rschr. Fla. State U., Tallahassee, 1990-93; assoc. prof. math. edn. U. Okla., Norman, 1993—. Author: Shape, 1991, Coming to Know Number, 1999, also conf. procs. in field; contbr. articles to profl. jours. Mem. Nat. Coun. Tchrs. Math. (editor rsch. into practice sect. Tchg. Children Math. 1998-2000), Math. Assn. Am., Internat. Group for Psychology of Math. Edn., Am. Edn. Rsch. Assn., Rsch. on Math. Learning (sec. 2000-03), Phi Delta Kappa (rsch. rep. 1993-97). Office: U Okla 820 Van Vleet Oval Norman OK 73019-2040 E-mail: areynolds@ou.edu.

REYNOLDS, ANNETTE, secondary school educator; Master degree, Ind. U., 1973. 7th and 8th grade physical edn. health tchr. Grissom Mid. Sch., Mishawaka, Ind.; 10th-12th grades physical edn. tchr. Penn HS, Mishawaka, Ind., Tipton HS, Ind.; 9th-12th grades physical edn. tchr. Northridge HS, Middlebury, Ind.; 10th-12th grades dance tchr., gymnastics coach, cheerleader sponsor Richardson HS, Tex. Vol. Iron Kids Triathalon, Am. Heart Assn. Mem. Nat. Assn. Student Activity Advisors, Richardson Edn. Assn., Delta Kappa Gamma (chmn., dir. Flip For Sight fundraiser). Home: 9554 Atherton Dr Dallas TX 75243-6134*

REYNOLDS, BETTY ANN, elementary education educator; b. Plattsburgh, N.Y., Nov. 16, 1942; d. Morton Jay and Thelma Gladys (Baxter) R. BS in Edn., SUNY, Plattsburgh, 1964; MS in Edn., SUNY, Potsdam, 1973. Tchr. 1st grade Ogdensburg (N.Y.) Ctrl. Schs., 1964-65, Massena (N.Y.) Ctrl Schs., 1965-68, 69—; tchr. 2d grade Ft. Richardson (Alaska) On-Base Sch., 1968-69, Ctrl. Schs., Massena, 1969-98—. Mem. N.Y. State Reading Assn. Avocations: reading, cross-county skiing, walking, travel, crafts.

REYNOLDS, CAROLYN MARY, elementary education educator; b. Bklyn., May 17, 1936; d. Wesley and Christine (Cardieri) Russo; m. Richard Martin Reynolds, Apr. 12, 1958; children: Donna Marie Reynolds Dewey, Richard Edward. BS, Adelphi U., 1968; MA, SUNY, Stony Brook, 1971. Cert. tchr., N.Y. Tchr. Rocky Point (N.Y.) Sch., 1956-57, Little Flower Sch., Wading River, N.Y., 1957-59, Shoreham (N.Y.)-Wading River Sch. Dist., 1969—. Mem. sch. consolidation task force Shoreham-Wading River Sch. Dist., 1992-93, mem. supt. search com., 1995, mem. dist. shared decision making team, 1995-96; supervising tchr. St. Joseph Coll., 1991, 95, 96, Dowling Coll., Oakdale, N.Y., 1992, C.W. Post Coll., Southampton, N.Y., SUNY, Stonybrook; coord. constructivist course Briarcliff Sch., Shoreham, N.Y., 1990-93. Editor tchr. union publ. VOX, 1989-90 (award 1990). Leader Girl Scouts U.S., Rocky Point, N.Y., 1956. Noyes Found. fellow; NSF grantee. Mem. ASCD, Nat. Coun. Tchrs. English, N.Y. State United Tchrs., Shoreham-Wading River Tchrs. Assn. (co-pres., sec., negotiator tchrs. contract 1996-97), United Fedn. Tchrs. (10 Yr. pin for leadership), Internat. Reading Assn. (coun. pres. 1980—). Home: 50 Highland Down Shoreham NY 11786-1122

REYNOLDS, CLARK WINTON, economist, educator; b. Chgo., Mar. 13, 1934; m. Nydia O'Connor Viales; children: Rebecca, C. Winton III, Matthew, Camila. AB, Claremont (Calif.) Men's Coll., 1956; student, MIT, 1956-57, 58; student divinity sch., Harvard U., 1957-58; MA, U. Calif., Berkeley, 1961, PhD in Econs., 1962. Asst. prof. Occidental Coll., L.A., 1961-62; from asst. to assoc. prof. dept. edn. and econ. growth Yale U., New Haven, 1962-67; sr. fellow The Brookings Inst., Washington, 1975-76; prof. econs., prin. investigator, founding dir. Americas program Stanford (Calif.) U., prof. emeritus econs., 1996—. Vis. prof. Nat. U. Mex., Chapingo, 1966, El Colegio de Mex., Mexico City, 1964, 65, 79, Hopkins-Nanjing Ctr. for Chinese and Am. Studies, Nanjing, China, 1999-2002, China Europe Internat. Bus. Sch., Shanghai, 2002, 03; vis. lectr. in econs. Stockholm U. Econs., 1968; fellow St. Antony's Coll., Oxford, 1975; vis. rsch. scholar Internat. Inst. for Applied Systems Analysis, Laxenburg, Austria, 1978; Fulbright chair in internat. econs. U. Viterbo, Italy, 2001. Author: The Mexican Economy, 1970; co-author: Essays on the Chilean Economy, 1965, (with C. Tello) U.S.-Mexican Relations: Economic and Social Aspects, Las Relaciones Mexico Estados Unidos, 1983, Dynamics of North American Trade, 1991, North American Labor Market Interdependence, 1992, Open Regionalism in the Andes, 1996. Dir. Monticello West Found., 1980-2003. Woodrow Wilson Found. fellow, 1956-57, Rockefeller Found. fellow, 1957-58, Doherty Found. fellow, 1960-61, Inst. Internat. Studies fellow Stanford U., 1990-2000; grantee Social Sci. Rsch. Coun., Ford Found., Hewlett Found., Rockefeller Found., Mellon Found., MacArthur Found., Tinker Found. Mem. Am. Econ. Assn.

REYNOLDS, GENEVA B. special education educator; b. Saginaw, Mich., Nov. 2, 1953; d. Roger and Alrine (Braddock) Rucker; m. Montie Reynolds, Aug. 1, 1981; children: Monte, Marcus. BS, Chgo. State U., 1992, MA in Gen. Adminstrn., 2000. Cert. educable mental handicap and learning disability, social/emotional disturbed. Adminstrv. specialist USAF, 1973-77, command and control specialist, 1977-81; info. supt. USAFR, Chgo., 1981—; prin. South Ctrl. Cmty. Svcs., Chgo., 1986—. SM sgt. USAF, 1973-81, USAFR, 1981—. Mem. Coun. for Exceptional Children, Kappa Delta Pi. Democrat. Baptist. Avocations: reading, computers, going to plays.

REYNOLDS, GERALD A.(JERRY), assistant secretary of education for civil rights, lawyer; BA, CUNY York Coll.; JD, Boston U. Assoc. Schatz & Schatz, Ribicoff & Kotkin, Hartford, Conn.; legal analyst Ctr. for Equal Opportunity, Washington; pres. Ctr. for New Black Leadership, Washington, 1997—98; sr. regulatory counsel KCPL, Kansas City, Mo., 1998—2002; asst. sec. edn. for civil rights U.S. Dept. Edn., Washington, 2002—. (mem. editl. bd.) Am. Jour. Law and Medicine. Office: US Dept Edn 400 Maryland Ave SW Washington DC 20202 E-mail: gerald.reynolds@ed.gov.

REYNOLDS, GLENDA CAROL, elementary school educator; b. Cheyenne, Wyo., Dec. 7, 1947; d. Charlie Clyde and Mary Payton (Clatterbuck) Kidd; m. James Francis Reynolds, June 6, 1970; children: Todd, Craig. BA, U. Wyo., 1970; MA, U. No. Colo., 1997. 2d grade tchr. San Felipe Sch. Dist., Del Rio, Tex., 1970-71; elem. tchr. Laramie County Sch. Dist., Cheyenne, 1971—. Computer facilitator Laramie County Sch. Dist., 1986—, math. mentor tchr., 1990—; math. mentor tchr. U. Wyo., Laramie. Cub scout leader Boy Scouts Am., Cheyenne, 1988-92; vacation Bible sch. dir. Meadowbrooke Bapt. Ch., Cheyenne, 1987—; trainer, Family Math. Wyoming, 1990—. Recipient Presdl. award for Excellence Elem. Math. Teaching, NSF, 1991. Mem. NEA, Wyo. Edn. Assn., Cheyenne Tchrs. Edn. Assn., Wyo. Coun. Tchrs. Math. (state finalist 1991), Delta Kappa Gamma (state pres. 1991-93, grad. leadership/mgnt. seminar U. Tex., 1991). Democrat. Avocations: bridge, spectator sports. Home: 5149 Mccue Dr Cheyenne WY 82009-4814

REYNOLDS, HERBERT HAL, academic administrator; b. Frankston, Tex., Mar. 20, 1930; s. Herbert Joseph and Ava Nell (Taylor) R.; m. Joy Myrla Copeland, June 17, 1950; children: Kevin Hal, Kent Andrew, Rhonda Sheryl. BS, Trinity U., 1952; MS, Baylor U., 1958, PhD, 1961; ScD (hon.), Seinan Gakuin U., Japan, 1990, Baylor Coll. Dentistry, 1993, Yonok Coll., Thailand, 2000. Entered USAF, 1948, advanced through grades to col., 1966; dir. research (Aeromed. Lab.), Alamogordo, N.Mex., 1961—68; comdr., dir. of plans Air Force Human Resources Lab., San Antonio, 1968; ret., 1968; exec. v.p. Baylor U., Waco, Tex., 1969—81, pres., 1981—95, chancellor, 1995—2000, pres. emeritus, 2000—. Vis. fellow, scholar Cambridge U., 1994-97. Contbr. articles to profl. jours. Mem.: Sigma Xi, Phi Beta Kappa, Omicron Delta Kappa, Alpha Chi. Office: Baylor U Office of Pres Emeritus Waco TX 76798 E-mail: president_emeritus@baylor.edu.

REYNOLDS, KASANDRA MASSINGILL, nursing educator; b. Miss., Sept. 11, 1950; d. Samuel Aubrey and Mary Overy (Askew) Massingill; m. Anse Harold Reynolds, Jan. 28, 1967; children: John, Kristy. AA, Meridian Community Coll., 1973; BSN, U. So. Miss., Hattiesburg, 1978; MSN, U. Miss., Jackson, 1980; postgrad., Miss. State U., Meridian, 1982-87. Faculty mem., coord. Matty Hersee Sch. Nursing, Meridian; staff and charge nurse intensive care unit Rush Found. Hosp., Meridian; faculty mem. Meridian Community Coll. Mem. OAADN, MCC (patron), Phi Theta Kappa, Kappa of Miss.

REYNOLDS, LINDA KAY, librarian; b. Moberly, Mo., Sept. 6, 1947; d. Homer Lee and Lura Frances (Alverson) Nichols; m. Leonard Rae Reynolds, Jr., Aug. 3, 1969 (wid. Mar. 1990); children: Christopher Alan, Leslie Ann. Gen. Edn. degree, Moberly Jr. Coll., 1967; BSEd., Northeast Mo. State U., 1969, MA, 1985. Cert. tchr. English, libr. sci. Lang. arts tchr. Moberly Pub. Schs., 1969-71, 72-73, libr./jr. high sch., 1973—76, 1977—2003. Tchr. faculty workshops on computers Moberly Pub. Schs., 1987-88, 2999-03, St. Pius Cath. Sch., Moberly, 1988. Adv. bd. Am. Cancer Soc., Moberly, 1990-91; mem. Trinity United Meth. Ch., Moberly, 1986-03, West Park Meth. Ch., Moberly, 1950-86. Named to Outstanding Young Women of Am., 1972. Mem. Mo. Assn. Sch. Librs., Mo. State Tchrs. Assn., Mo. Edn. Assn., NEA, Moberly Edn. Assn. (sec. 1980-82, treas. 1982-83, v.p. 1983-84), Mo. Nat. Edn. Assn. Democrat. Avocations: travel, sewing, reading, walking. Office: Moberly Middle Sch 920 Kwix Rd Moberly MO 65270-3813

REYNOLDS, LYNNE WARREN, special education educator, speech pathologist; b. Richmond, Va., June 6, 1940; d. Edward Paul Jr. and Margie (Meads) Warren; m. Thomas Grover Reynolds III, June 23, 1962; children: Thomas G. IV, Marguerite Agee. BS, U. Va., 1962, postgrad., 1963-65; MEd, R.I. Coll., 1973; EdD, Heed U., 1985. Cert. tchr., spl. edn. tchr., N.Y., Mass., R.I., Va.; lic. speech and lang. pathologist, N.Y. Tchr. spl. edn. Nelson County Pub. Schs., Lovingston, Va., 1962-63, Albemarle County Pub. Schs., Charlottesville, Va., 1963-66; tchr. spl. edn., program coord. Plainville (Mass.) Pub. Schs., 1967-73; pvt. practice speech-lang. pathology, edn. cons. Kingston, N.Y., 1973-85; edn. cons. Edn. for Relocation, Neunen and Eindhoven, Netherlands, 1986-91; tchr. spl. edn. W.S. Hart Union High Sch. Dist., Santa Clara, Calif., 1991-92; ind. edn. cons. Smyrna, Ga., 1992—. Sec., chmn. mental health and mental retardation com. Ulster County Community Svcs. Bd., Kingston, 1978-85; mem. N.Y. State com. UN Yr. of Child, 1983-84; mem. community svcs. adv. bd. Spl. Edn. Svcs. Santa Clarita, Calif., 1991-92; mem. People to People citizen amb. del. on learning disabilities to Russia & Estonia; presenter seminars to parent, educator and profl. groups; presenter tng. workshops. Author classroom tchrs.' handbook: HELP, 1969. Mem. Chaminade Singers, 1966-73; sec., chmn. Indsl. Devel. Commn., Town of Plainville, 1969-73, mental health svcs. coord., 1970-73; dir. nautographer ann. synchronized swimming show Zena Recreation Park, N.Y., 1975-84; mem. learnint disabilities delegation to Russia and Estonia: People to People Citizen Amb. Program, 1993; active Internat. Women's Club Eindhoven, 1985-90; guest performer Alliance Theatre Christmas House, 1993-95, Atlanta Symphony Open House; vol. Sci. Trek Sci. Mus., 1992-94; mem. E. Cobb Quilters Guild, 1993—, sec. 1994, 1st v.p. 1995—, pres. 1996; vol. Alliance Children's Theatre of Atlanta, 1993—, Georgia Olympic Quilt Project, 1993—. Recipient Profl. Svc. Recognition award Girl Scouts U.S., Plainville, 1971, Recognition award Girl Scouts U.S., Plainville, 1971, Recognition of Svc. award Ulster County Mental Health Assn., 1983, 84, Award for Svc. Ulster County Cmty. Svcs. Bd., 1985, Vol. of Yr. Sci. Trek Sci. Mus., 1993, Outstanding Me. Alliance Childrens Theatre, 1994. Mem. Coun. Exceptional Children (div. communication disorders, div. learning disabilities, coun. ednl. diagnostic svcs., coun. behavioral disorders), Orton Dyslexia Soc., Assn. for Citizens with Learning Disabilities (chpt. bd. dirs. 1976-85, state bd. dirs. 1978-84, chair memberships com.), N.Y. Speech, Lang. and Hearing Assn., Assn. Ednl. and Psychol. Cons., Assn. Ednl. Therapists, Zeta Tau Alpha. Avocations: music, theater, reading, quilting, needlework.

REYNOLDS, MEGAN BEAHM, primary and elementary education educator; b. Lima, Ohio, Aug. 29, 1955; d. Walter Clarence and Jo Ann (Wood) Beahm; m. Dale Myron Reynolds, Aug. 28, 1976 (div. July 1983); 1 child, Emily Jo Reynolds. BS, Tenn. Wesleyan Coll., 1977; postgrad., U. Tenn., 1986-88. Cert. elem. and early edn. tchr., Tenn. Tchr. adult basic edn. Athens (Tenn.) City Schs., 1977-78; asst. dir. Child Shelter Home, Cleveland, Tenn., 1978; tchr. kindergarten First Bapt. Presch./Kindergarten, Cleveland, 1978-80; teller, bookkeeper C & C Bank Monroe County, Sweetwater, Tenn., 1982-83; substitute elem. tchr. Knox County Schs., Knoxville, Tenn., 1983-85, elem. tchr., 1985-87, tchr. kindergarten, 1987—, career ladder III, 1993. Mem. adv. bd., grade-level chairperson Norwood Elem. Sch., Knox County Schs., 1990-93, mem. adopt a sch. com., 1992-93, S team rep., 1991-92. Editor Norwood Elem. Yearbook, 1989-90. Parent helper Girl Scouts U.S., 1986-90; neighborhood collector Am. Heart Assn., 1987—; v.p. Norwood Elem./Knox County Schs. PTO, 1991-92; Norwood rep. Ft. Kid, 1990-91; youth counselor Middlebrook Pike Meth. Ch., mem. Costa Rica missions team; active participant Vols. of Am. Mem. NEA, Tenn. Edn. Assn., Knox County Edn. Assn., Knox County Assn. Young Children, Children and Adults with Attention Deficit Disorder (pre-sch. Summer intervention program, parent/sch. comms. program 1995—). Methodist. Avocations: reading, outdoor activities, travel, family activities, church and community volunteering. Home: 8525 Savannah Ct Knoxville TN 37923-6341 Office: Norwood Elem Sch 1909 Merchants Dr Knoxville TN 37912-4700

REYNOLDS, ROGER LEE, composer, educator; b. Detroit, July 18, 1934; s. George Arthur and Katherine Adelaide (Butler) Reynolds; m. Karen Jeanne Hill, Apr. 11, 1964; children: Erika Lynn, Wendy Claire. BSE in Physics, U. Mich., 1957, MusB in Music Lit., 1960, MusM in Composition, 1961. Assoc. prof. U. Calif. San Diego, La Jolla, 1969—73, founding dir. Ctr. Music Expt. and Related Rsch., 1972—77, prof., 1973—; George Miller prof. U. Ill., 1971—. Vis. prof. Yale U., New Haven, 1981; sr. rsch. fellow ISAM Bklyn. Coll., 1985; Valentine prof. Amherst (Mass.) Coll., 1988; Rothschild composer in residence Peabody Conservatory of Music, 1992—93; pub. Peters Music Pubs.; mgr. Graham Hayter, Contemporary Music Promotions. Author: MIND MODELS: New Forms of Musical Experience, 1975, A Searcher's Path: A Composer's Ways, 1987, A Jostled Silence: Contemporary Japanese Musical Thought, 1992—93, Form and Method: Composing Music, 2002; first Dolby Digital 5.1 DVD release of custom-designed, multichannel classical compositions: WATERSHED, Mode Records, 1998; contbr. numerous articles and revs. to profl. jours. Mem. bd. govs. Inst. Current World Affairs; co-founder ONCE festivals, 1960; bd. dirs. Am. Music Ctr., Meet the Composer; bd. dirs. Fromm Found. Harvard U. Named sr. fellow, Inst. Studies in Am. Music, 1985, fellow, Inst. Current World Affairs, Rockefeller Found., Guggenheim Found., Fulbright scholar; recipient Koussevitzky Internat. Rec. award, 1970, Nat. Inst. Arts and Letters award, 1971, NEA awards, 1975, 1978, 1979, 1986, Pulitzer prize for music, 1989. Office: U Calif San Diego Dept Music 0326 La Jolla CA 92093 E-mail: rlr@rogerreynolds.com.

REYNOLDS, SCOTT WALTON, academic administrator; b. Summit, N.J., July 15, 1941; s. Clark Leonard and Shirley (Hill) R.; m. Margaret Ann Johnson, July 5, 1969; children: Jane, Amy, David. BA, Trinity Coll., Hartford, Conn., 1963; MBA, Harvard U., 1965. Mng. dir. corp. staff Bankers Trust Co., N.Y.C., 1967-94; asst. to the pres. St. Peter's Coll., Jersey City, 1994-96, Trinity Coll., Hartford, Conn., 1996-98, sec., 1998—. Chmn. fund campaign Montclair (N.J.) ARC, 1974; chmn. bus. and fraternal group Montclair Bicentennial Com., 1976; bd. fellows Trinity Coll., 1982-88, trustee, 1992-96, sec., exec. com., 1993-96. 1st lt. U.S. Army, 1965-67. Recipient 150th Anniversary award Trinity Coll., 1978, Alumni medal for Excellence, 1988, Pres.' Leadership medal, 1993. Mem. Montclair Jaycees (treas. 1973), Trinity Coll. Alumni Assn. N.Y. (pres. 1972-73) Clubs: Harvard (N.Y.C.). Episcopalian. Office: Trinity Coll Office of Pres 300 Summit St Hartford CT 06106-3100

REYNOLDS, TERRY SCOTT, social science educator; b. Sioux Falls, S.D., Jan. 15, 1946; s. Ira Ebenezer and Therasea Anne (Janzen) R.; m. Linda Gail Rainwater, June 4, 1967; children: Trent Aaron, Dane Adrian, Brandon Vincent, Derek Vinson. BS, So. State Coll., 1966; MA, U. Kans., 1968, PhD, 1973. Asst. prof. U. Wis., Madison, 1973-79, assoc. prof., 1979-83; dir. program in sci., tech. and soc. Mich. Technol. U., Houghton, 1983-87, prof., 1987—, head dept. social scis., 1990—2002. Adv. editor History of Technology, Encyclopedia Americana, 1980-92; adv. bd. St. Martin's Press Great Engrs. Project, 1980-84. Author: Sault Ste marie: The Hydroelectric Plant's History, 1982, Stronger Than a Hundred Men, 1983, History of American Institute of Chemical Engineers, 1983, The Engineer in America, 1991; co-editor: Technology and American History, 1998, Technology and The West, 1998; assoc. editor IA: Jour. of Soc. for Indsl. Archaeology, 1994—. Mem. Soc. for the History Tech. (chair awards com. 1988-89, v.p. 1998-98, pres. 1999-2000), Soc. for Indsl. Archeology (Norton prize 1985, 98). Methodist. Office: Mich Technol Univ Dept Social Scis 1400 Townsend Dr Houghton MI 49931-1200

REYNOLDS, TOMMY, secondary school educator; b. Dec. 23, 1956; BSE ind. tech., CMSU, 1979, MS ind. voc. tech. edu., 1983. Secondary tchr. Lee's Summit (Mo.) North High Sch., 1979; tchr. PLJH, 1979-80, Lee's Summit High Sch., 1980—, Lee's Summit North High Sch., 1995-98; ind. tech. dept. coord., 1992-96. Recipient Tchr. Excellence award Internat. Tech. Edn. Assn., 1992. Office: Lee's Summit North High Sch 901 NE Douglas St Lees Summit MO 64086-4505

REYNOLDS, WILLIAM CRAIG, mechanical engineer, educator; b. Berkeley, Calif., Mar. 16, 1933; s. Merrill and Patricia Pope (Galt) R.; m. Janice Erma Reynolds, Sept. 18, 1953; children: Russell, Peter, Margery. BS in Mech. Engring., Stanford U., 1954, MS in Mech. Engring., 1955, PhD in Mech. Engring., 1957; D in Engring. (hon.), UMIST, U.K., 2000. Faculty mech. engring. Stanford U., 1957—, chmn. dept. mech. engring., 1972-82, 89-93, Donald Whittier prof. mech. engring., 1986—, chmn. Inst. for Energy Studies, 1974-81; staff scientist NASA/Ames Rsch. Ctr., 1987—; dir. Ctr. for Integrated Turbulence Simulations, 1997—2003. Author: books, including Engineering Thermodynamics, 2d edit, 1976; contbr. numerous articles to profl. jours. NSF sr. scientist fellow Eng., 1964, Otto Laporte awd., Am. Physical Soc., 1992. Fellow: ASME (Fluids Engring. award 1989), Am. Phys. Soc.; mem.: AIAA (Fluid Dynamic award), Am. Acad. Arts & Scis., Nat. Acad. Engrs., Stanford Integrated Mfg. Assn. (co-chmn. 1990—94, dir. Stanford Ctr. Integrated Turbulence Simulation), Tau Beta Pi. Achievements include research in fluid mechanics and applied thermodynamics. Office: Stanford U Dept Mech Engring Stanford CA 94305-3030

REYNOLDS, W(YNETKA) ANN, academic administrator, educator; b. Coffeyville, Kans., Nov. 3, 1937; d. John Ethelbert and Glennie (Beanland) King; m. Thomas H. Kirschbaum; children— Rachel Rebecca, Rex King. BS in Biology-Chemistry, Kans. State Tchrs. Coll., Emporia, 1958; MS in Zoology, U. Iowa, Iowa City, 1960, PhD, 1962; DSc (hon.), Ind. State U., Evansville, 1980; LHD (hon.), McKendree Coll., 1984, U. N.C., Charlotte, 1988, U. Judaism, L.A., 1989, U. Nebr., Kearney, 1992; DSc (hon.), Ball State U., Muncie, Ind., 1985, Emporia (Kans.) State U., 1987; PhD (hon.), Fu Jen Cath. U., Republic of China, 1987; LHD (hon.), U. Nebr., Kearney, 1992, Colgate U., 1993; LHD, No. Mich. U., 1995. Asst. prof. biology Ball State U., Muncie, Ind., 1962-65; asst. prof. anatomy U. Ill. Coll. Medicine, Chgo., 1965-68, assoc. prof. anatomy, 1968-73, rsch. prof. ob-gyn, 1973—, prof. anatomy, 1973—, acting assoc. dean acad. affairs Coll. Medicine, 1977, assoc. vice chancellor, dean grad. coll., 1977-79; provost, v.p. for acad. affairs, prof. ob-gyn. and anatomy Ohio State U., Columbus, 1979-82; chancellor Calif. State Univ. system, Long Beach, 1982-90, prof. biology, 1982-90; chancellor CUNY, 1990-97; pres. U. Ala., Birmingham, 1997—2002. Bd. dirs. Abbott Labs., Maytag, Owens-Corning, Humana, Inc., News-Gasette, Champaign, Ill.; clin. prof. ob-gyn. UCLA, 1985-90; mem. Nat. Rsch. Coun. Com. Undergrad Si. Edn., 1993-97; co-chair Fed. Task Force on Women, Minorities and Handicapped in Sci. and Tech., 1987-90, Pacesetter Program Reform for Secondary Sch. Coll. Bd., 1992-96. Contbr. chpts. to books, articles to profl. jours; assoc. editor Am. Biology Tchr., 1964-67. Active activities involving edn. and the arts; nat. adv. bd. Inst. Am. Indian Arts, 1992-97; bd. dirs. Lincoln Ctr. Inst., 1993—; trustee Internat. Life Scis. Inst.-Nutrition Found., 1987-2001, Southwest Mus. Recipient Disting. Alumni award Kans. State Tchrs. Coll., 1972, Calif. Gov.'s Award for the Arts for an Outstanding Individual in Arts in Edn., 1989, Prize award Cen. Assn. Obstetricians and Gynecologists, 1968; NSF Predoctoral fellow, 1958-62, Woodrow Wilson Hon. fellow, 1958. Fellow ACOG; mem. AAAS, Perinatal Rsch. Soc., Soc. Gynecol. Investigation (sec./treas. 1980-83, pres. 1992-93), Nat. Assn. Systems Heads (pres. 1987-88), Sigma Xi. Office: Ctr for Cmty Outreach Devel Univ Ala 933 19th St S Birmingham AL 35294-2041

REYNOLDS-SAKOWSKI, DANA RENEE, science educator; b. Centralia, Ill., June 28, 1968; d. David Lavern and Betty Lou (Shelton) Reynolds; m. Jason Bielas Sakowski, Oct. 8, 1994. BS in Edn., U. No. Colo., 1991, MEd in Middle Sch. Edn., 1996. Tchr. life sci. and math. Ken Caryl Mid. Sch., Littleton, Colo., 1991-92; tchr. sci. Moore Mid. Sch., Arvada, Colo., 1992-93, tchr. life sci., 1993—. Mem. Nat. Wildlife Fedn., Colo. Assn. Sci. Tchrs., Colo. Biology Tchrs. Assn., Sierra Club, World Wildlife Fund, Nat. Parks and Conservation Assn., Natural Resources Def. Coun., Audubon Soc., Nature Conservancy. Avocations: camping, writing poetry, hiking, singing. Office: Moore Mid Sch 8455 W 88th Ave Arvada CO 80005-1620

REZABEK, CHRISTINA JOANN, adult education educator; b. Piedmont, Ohio, Sept. 29, 1930; d. Joseph and Mildred (Burger) R.; m. Richard B. Gargulinski (div.); children: Christine Fox, Richard, William. AA, Ohio U., 1982, BA, 1985; MA, Wayne State U., 1988, specialist cert., 1992. Mgr., asst. curator Heritage Lace & Textile Mus., Belmont, Ohio, 1981-85; computer lab asst. Ohio U. Learning Ctr., St. Clairsville, Ohio, 1984-85; tchr., cons. adult edn. Detroit (Mich.) Pub. Schs., 1985—. Part time tchr. East Detroit (Mich.) Pub. Schs., 1986-92; cons., pres. EZ Instrnl. Systems Tech., Mount Clemens, Mich., 1989-92; dir. Adult Career and Ednl. Support Found., Detroit, 1992. Peer counselor Ohio U., St. Clairsville, 1984-85; facilitator adult edn. Detroit (Mich.) Pub. Schs., 1988. Mem. ASCD, Mich. Coun. on Learning Adults, Educators Network of Andragogy for Bldg. Learning Excellence (rsch. com. 1992—), Women of Wayne (bd. dirs. 1990-92), Wayne State U. Alumni Assn., Kappa Delta Pi, Pi Lambda Theta (pres. Alpha Pi chpt. 1991-92). Methodist. Avocations: travel, photograhy, artist, outdoor activities, stamp collecting. Home: 5706 Chene St Detroit MI 48211-2751 Office: Detroit Pub Schs Adult Edn 3700 Pulford St Detroit MI 48207-2328

REZAC, DEBRA DOWELL, bilingual educator; b. Modesto, Calif., Feb. 20, 1952; d. Charles Hubert and Peggy Sue (Hittle) Dowell; divorced; children: Aaron Vincent, Amanda Lael; m. Stephan R. Rezac, Feb. 2, 2002. Cert. tchr., Calif. State U., Fresno, 1986, BS, 1994; M Lang. Devel., Pacific Coll., 1995; cert. reading recovery tchr. leader, Calif. State U., Fresno, 2000. Cert. lang. devel. specialist, Calif., cert. reading recovery tchr., recover tchr. leader; cert. reading specialist Calif. Dept. Edn.; cert. equity trainer, character counts trainer. Bilingual tchr. Selma (Calif.) Unified Sch. Dist., 1986—, mentor tchr. drug prevention edn., 1989-93, mentor tchr. health edn., 1993—, mentor tchr. lang. devel. and early literacy, 1996—, staff developer, 1996-97, tchr. spl. assignment reading recovery tchr., 2000-01. Project Drug Alcohol and Tobacco Edn. coord. Selma Unified Sch. Dist., 1989—, chair Healthy Kids Healty Calif. task force, 1990—, parent educator, 1992—; mem. adv. bd. Gang Task Force, Selma, 1993—; mem. English Lang. Arts Curriculum Com., 1990—, Health Curriculum Com., 1993—; mentor tchr. Early Literacy, 1996-97; mem. coordinating com. Gifted and Talented Edn., 1996, 97-98, mem. adv. bd., 1996; instr. 2nd grade literacy group, mentor tchr. Beginning Tchr. Mentor Program, 1998—, adult literacy/ESL Selma High Adult Sch.; mentor Beginning Tchr. Support Adv., 1998—; mem. CalStat TEACH Learning Support faculty Calif. State U., Fresno, 2000-01. Author: Mostly Magnets, 1990, Supplemental Guide to HLAY 200, 1995, other curriculum materials; co-author: Gang Curriculum 1993. Mem. El Concilio, Fresno, 1993-94, Fresno Zool. Soc., 1980—, Selma Pub. Edn. Found. Grantee Selma Unified Sch. Dist., 1987, Selma Pub. Edn. Found., 1994, S. USD Pub. Edn. Found., 1996. Mem. NEA, Calif. Tchrs. Assn., Nat. Coun. Tchrs. Edn., C.U.E. Democrat. Methodist. Avocations: snow skiing, snow boarding, ice skating, running, swimming. Home: 2051 Oak St Selma CA 93662-2443

REZNIK, ALAN A. petroleum engineering educator; b. Pitts., Sept. 25, 1939; s. Lawrence S. and Rose R.; m. Marion Bergstein, Sept. 8, 1963; children: Amy Jean, Robert I.S. BS, U. Pitts., 1963, MS, 1964, PhD, 1971. Research scientist Continental Oil Co., Ponca City, Okla., 1964-66; instr. chem. and petroleum engring. dept. U. Pitts., 1966-67; instr. dept. civil engring. Technion-Israel Inst. Tech., Haifa, 1967-68; sr. research assoc. Calgon Corp., Pitts., 1969; engring. supr. U.S. Bur. Mines, Pitts., 1973-75; assoc. prof. chem. and petroleum engring. U. Pitts., 1975—, dir. petroleum engring. program, 1981-92 ; cons. and lectr. in field. Assoc. editor Jour. Petroleum Sci. and Engring., 1986-93 . Contbr. articles to profl. jours. Recipient Continental Oil Co. fellowship, 1961, Socony Mobil Internat. fellowship, 1962, U. Pitts. Outstanding Sr. award, 1963; U.S. Dept. Energy grantee, 1976-78, Gulf Oil Found. grantee, 1979, U.S. Dept. Energy grantee, 1978-79, 80-82, 85-86. Mem. Soc. Petroleum Engrs. of AIME, Am. Chem. Soc. (sec.-treas. 1975-76), Sigma Xi, Sigma Tau, Sigma Gamma Epsilon. Achievements include research in flow in porous media enhanced petroleum recovery and methane production from coals, tensor analysis. Office: U Pitts Chem & Petroleum Engring Dept 1249 Benedum Hall Pittsburgh PA 15261-2212

RHEAMS, ANNIE ELIZABETH, education educator; b. Lake Providence, La. d. Curtis Kleinpeter Sr. and Annie Augusta (Webb) Kleinpeter; 1 child, Darryl Jemall Rheams. BA, Grambling (La.) U., 1971; MS, Ala. A&M U., 1975; PhD, U. Wis., Milw., 1989. Cert. tchr. in exceptional edn., adminstrn. Tchr. Ala. A&M U., Normal, 1971-79, adminstr., 1977-79; acad. specialist U. Wis., Milw., 1979-82, Parkside, 1982-84; tchr. diagnostician, adminstr. Milw. Schs., 1984-89; asst. prof. dept. edn. Marquette U., Milw., 1989-96; asst. prin. North Divsn. H.S., Milw., 1996—, Marshall H.S., Milw., 1997—99, tchr. exceptional edn. cognitively disabled, consumer math., 1999—, adminstr., asst. prin., 1999. Career counselor Madison County Career Counseling Svcs., Huntsville, 1975; adj. prof. Oakwood (Ala.) SDA Coll., 1975-78; tchr. Gateway to Engring. Program, Milw., 1984-88; cons. pub. schs./Wee Care Day Care, Milw., 1992-96; condr. workshops in field. Author: P.A.C.E.: A Thematic Approach to Developing Essential Experiences, 1996. Voter registrar/poll watcher NAACP, Lake Providence, 1966; v.p. Work for Wis., Inc., Milw., 1993-94, Messmer H.S. Bd., Milw., 1990-94; com. chmn. Citizen's Rev. Bd., Milw., 1980-82, Met. Milw. Alliance Black Sch. Educators, 1994-95. Assoc. fellow Ctr. for Great Plains Studies, U. Nebr.-Lincoln, 1995; named Outstanding Tchr. Educator, Am. Assn. for Coll. Tchr. Educators Directory, 1995. Mem. Zonta Internat., Alpha Kappa Alpha, Phi Delta Kappa. Avocations: tennis, sewing, ceramics, horseback riding, biking. Home: PO Box 90681 Milwaukee WI 53209-0611 Fax: 414-902-8315. E-mail: rheams@mailandnews.com.

RHETT, HASKELL EMERY SMITH, educator; b. Evanston, Ill., Aug. 29, 1936; s. Haskell Smith and Eunice Campbell (Emery) R.; m. Roberta Teel Oliver, Sept. 9, 1961 (div. 1973); children: Kathryn Emery, Cecily Coffin; m. Anita Leone, May 30, 1983 (div. 1993); m. Janet Lee Rollings, Nov. 15, 1997. Diploma, Gov. Dummer Acad., 1954; AB, Hamilton Coll., 1958; MA, Cornell U., 1967, PhD, 1968. Asst. to the pres. Hamilton Coll., Clinton, N.Y., 1961-64; rsch. asst. Cornell U., Ithaca, N.Y., 1964-66; rsch. assoc. U. London, 1966-67; dir. program devel. Ednl. Testing Svc., Princeton, N.J., 1967-73; asst. chancellor N.J. Dept. Higher Edn., Trenton, 1973-85; v.p. The Coll. Bd., N.Y.C., 1985-90; pres. The Woodrow Wilson Nat. Fellowship Found., Princeton, 1990-97, pres. emeritus, 1997—. Author: Going to College in New Jersey, 1978; contbg. author: Government's Role in Supporting College Savings, 1990. Commr. N.J. Pub. Broadcasting Authority, Trenton, 1983-85; mem. Nat. Task Force on Student Aid Problems, Washington, 1974-75; mem. Gov.'s Adv. Panel on Higher Edn. Restructuring, State of N.J., 1994; trustee Dominican U. of Calif., San Rafael, Calif., 1990-99, 2001—, William Alexander Procter Found., 1998-2002; del. Dem. Nat. Conv., Miami, 1972; sr. warden Trinity Episcopal Ch., Princeton, 1988-92, vestryman, 1979-82, 87-88, 2001—; dep. Gen. Conv., Detroit, 1988, Phoenix, 1991; mem. standing com. Episcopal Diocese of N.J., 1992-97; trustee The Coll. of N.J., 1992-97, vice-chmn., 1995-97, chmn., 1997; trustee Gov. Dummer Acad., Mass., 1993—, Heartland Edn. Cmty., Ohio, 1992-97, Forums Inst. for Pub. Policy, N.J., 1999—, treas., 2000—; bd. dirs. Reach the World, Inc., N.Y.C., 1998-2000, Trenton After Sch. Program, 2001—. Lt. USNR, 1958—61, Heavy Attack Squadron 5 (VAH-5), USS Forrestal. Nat. Def. fellow U.S. Govt., 1966-67, Eliot-Winant fellow Brit.-Am. Assocs., 1982, Harvard U. fellow, 1985, faculty fellow Wilson Coll., Princeton U., 1993-97. Mem. Nat. Assn. State Scholarship and Grant Programs (pres. 1976-78), Princeton Officers Soc., English-Speaking Union, Springdale Golf Club. Avocations: travel, tennis, golf, sailing, classic automobiles. Home: 80 Province Line Rd Skillman NJ 08558-1102 E-mail: hrhett@patmedia.net.

RHINELANDER, ESTHER RICHARD, secondary school educator; b. Honolulu, Aug. 31, 1940; d. William Wise and Elizabeth (Chilton) Richard; m. Harvey James Rhinelander, July 24, 1965; 1 child, Lori. BEd, U. Hawaii, 1963, profl. cert., 1964. Tchr. music Kamehameha Sch., Honolulu, 1965—, Kamehameha Sch. for Girls, Honolulu, 1964, Waianae High and Intermediate Sch., Honolulu, 1965. Dir. Waiokeola Ch. Choir, Honolulu, 1964-67, Kawaiahao Ch. Choir, Honolulu, 1980-87; judge song contest Kamehameha Schs., 1972, 88; judge choral composition contest Hawaii Found. on Culture and Arts, Honolulu, 1984, 85; pianist Kahikuonalani Ch., Honolulu, 1987—, Ch. Choral Ensemble, 1987—; tchr. Sunday Sch., 1988—. Mem., asst. accompanist Honolulu Opera Guild, 1955-59. Mem. Am. Choral Dirs. Assn., Soc. Gen. Music Tchrs. (sec. 1989-90), Music Educators Nat. Conf., Hawaii Music Educators Assn. Democrat. Mem. United Ch. of Christ. Avocations: reading, gardening, baking. Office: Highlands Child Care Ctr 757 Hoomalu St Pearl City HI 96782-2711

RHOADES, EVA YVONNE, retired elementary school educator; b. Henderson, Tex., Sept. 27, 1935; d. Cecil Milton Andrus and Olga Mae Maddox; m. Samuel Jeffery Rhoades (dec. Jan. 1994). BS in Elem. Edn., U. Tex., 1958; ME in Spl. Edn., U. Tex., Tyler, 1982. Tchr. I.W. Popham Elem. Sch., Austin, 1958—62, Kelso Elem. Sch., Houston, 1962—72; tchr. spl. edn. jr. high West Rusk Ind. Sch. Dist., New London, Tex., 1980—94. Mem.: ATPT, Coun. for Exceptional Children, Anna B. Kelso Elem. PTA (life), Rusk County Poetry Soc., Ex-Students U. Tex. (life). Home: 1900 Castlegate Henderson TX 75654

RHODA, RICHARD G. educational administrator; BA, Vanderbilt U., 1972, MA, 1974, PhD, 1985. Asst. to chancellor Tenn. Bd. Regents, Nashville, 1973-85; exec. dir. Higher Edn. Commn., Nashville, 1998—; v.p. adminstrn. Tenn. Bd. Regents, Nashville, 1985-90, vice chancellor, 1990-94; rsch. prof. Vanderbilt U., Nashville, 1995-96; sr. vice chancellor Tenn. Bd. Regents, Nashville, 1997-98. Office: Higher Edn Commn Office of Exec Dir Ste 1900 404 James Robertson Pkwy Nashville TN 37219-1505

RHODE, DEBORAH LYNN, law educator; b. Jan. 29, 1952; BA, Yale U., 1974, JD, 1977. Bar: D.C. 1977, Calif. 1981. Law clk. to judge U.S. Ct. Appeals (2d cir.), N.Y.C., 1977-78; law clk. to Hon. Justice Thurgood Marshall U.S. Supreme Ct., D.C., 1978-79; asst. prof. law Stanford (Calif.) U., 1979-82, assoc. prof., 1982-85, prof., 1985—; dir. Inst. for Rsch. on Women and Gender, 1986-90, Keck Ctr. of Legal Ethics and The Legal Profession, 1994—; sr. counsel jud. com. Ho. of Reps., Washington, 1998. Trustee Yale U., 1983-89; pres. Assn. Am. Law Schs., 1998; Ernest W. McFarland prof. Stanford Law Sch., 1997—; sr. counsel com. on the jud. U.S. Ho. of Reps., 1998; dir. Stanford Ctr. on Ethics. Author: Justice and Gender, 1989, (with Geoffrey Hazard) the Legal Profession: Responsibility and Regulation, 3d edit., 1993, (with Annette Lawson) The Politics of Pregnancy: Adolescent Sexuality and Public Policy, 1993, (with David Luban) Legal Ethics, 2001, (with Barbara Allen Babcock, Ann E. Freedman, Susan Deller Ross, Wendy Webster Williams, Rhonda Copelon, and Nadine H. Taub) Sex Discrimination and the Law, 1997, Speaking of Sex, 1997, Professional Responsibility: Ethics by the Pervasive Method, 1998, In the Interests of Justice, 2000 (with Geoffrey Hazard, Jr.) Professional Responsibility and Regulation, 2002; editor: Theoretical Perspectives on Sexual Difference, 1990, Ethics in Practice, 2000, The Difference Difference Makes: Women and Leadership, 2002 ; contbr. articles to profl. jours. Mem.: ABA (chmn. commn. on women 2000—02). Office: Stanford U Law Sch Crown Quadrangle Stanford CA 94305

RHODEN, MARY NORRIS, educational center director; b. Greenville, S.C., Jan. 3, 1943; d. Tony and Carrie Thelma (Rueben) Norris; 1 adopted child, Scottie Brooks-Rhoden. BS in Biology, Allen U., Columbia, S.C., 1966; postgrad., Atlanta U., 1967-68. Dir., tchr. MSR Learning Ctr., Riverdale, Ga., 1989—. Author poetry. Vol. Buffalo Soldiers Monument Commn., Ft. Leavenworth, Kans., 1991—; developed letters for nat. campaign to petition Congress, Postmaster Gen. to issue Buffalo Soldiers Stamp. Recipient Cert. Appreciation NAACP, Greenville, S.C., 1979, Wheat St. Bapt. Ch., Atlanta, 1989. Mem. Alpha Kappa Alpha, Alpha Kappa Delta. Democrat. African Meth. Episcopal Ch. Avocations: jogging, writing, swimming, skating, skiing. Office: PO Box 742442 Riverdale GA 30274-1343

RHODES, ANN FRANCES BLOODWORTH, artist, art history lecturer; b. Gadsden, Ala., Jan. 30, 1940; d. Frederick Allen and Mildred (Chunn) Bloodworth; m. Thomas Willard Rhodes, May 31, 1975; children: Mildred Ruth, Andrew James Howard. BA, Queens Coll., Charlotte, N.C., 1962; MA, Ga. State U., 1972. Computer programmer 1st Nat. Bank, Atlanta, 1962-63; child welfare aide Fulton County Dept. Family and Children Svcs., Atlanta, 1963; tchr. Brandon Hall, Atlanta, 1964-66; lectr. art history Atlanta Coll. Art, 1973-77, mem. adj. faculty, 1987-90; lectr. art history DeKalb C.C., Atlanta, 1975. Vis. prof. Ga. State U., Atlanta, 1985; lectr. DAR, Atlanta, 1997. One-woman show Vines Bot. Garden, Loganville, Ga., 1998; exhibited in group shows Art South, Avondale Estates, Ga., 1995, Level II Gallery, Atlanta, 1996, Creative Arts Guild, Dalton, Ga., 1996, 97, Atelier, Atlanta, 1996 (award of merit), Atlanta Bot. Garden, 1996, Art Sta., Stone Mountain, Ga., 1996, 98, Chateau Elan, Ga., 1997, Quinlan Art Ctr., Gainesville, Ga., 1997, Opus One Gallery, Atlantz, 1997, Madison (Ga.)-Morgan Cultural Ctr., 1998 (award of merit), Roswell (Ga.) Visual Arts Ctr., 1998; represented in collections: Frameworks Gallery, Lynne Farris Gallery, Vermilion Gallery, Atlanta, Gallery One, St. Simon's Island, Ga. Chmn. St. Helena chpt. of women All Saints Ch., Atlanta, 1980, 81, 83, 98, lectr. art history, 1991—, participant numerous on-going outreach programs; chmn. Twigs svc. club Egleston Children's Hosp., Atlanta, 1985; chmn. Party with Purpose, Am. Cancer Soc., Atlanta, 1987. Recipient numerous awards for paintings. Mem. Fine Art Folio, Ansley Park Garden Club (sec. 1993-95, parliamentarian 1995-97). Democrat. Episcopalian. Avocations: reading, swimming, photography, walking, gardening. Studio: Tula K-1 75 Bennett St NW Atlanta GA 30309-5206

RHODES, ANNA MARGARET, retired elementary school educator and school system administrator; b. Roanoke, Va., Dec. 6, 1933; d. Chester Arthur and Ruth (Tate) Young; m. Donald H. Rhodes, Mar. 17, 1933; children: Donald H. Jr., Chester C. BS, Madison Coll., 1955; MEd, U. Va., 1960; Edn. specialist, George Washington U., 1986. Elem. tchr. Roanoke City Pub. Schs., Roanoke, Va., 1955-59; elem. tchr. Charlottesville Pub. Schs., Charlottesville, Va., 1959-61, Norfolk City Pub. Schs., Norfolk, Va., 1961-63, Virginia Beach City Pub. Schs., Virginia Beach, Va., 1963-67, elem. prin., 1968-74, curriculum asst., 1974-84, instrnl. specialist, 1984—93. Former pres., mem. W. Ghent Circle King's Daughters & Sons, Norfolk, 1962—, Virginia Beach Br. AAUW; former membership v.p., recording sec. Va. div. AAUW; bd. dirs. Order of Cape Henry 1607, Tidewater, Va.; bd. dirs. Norfolk City Union of the King's Daus., 1993-2002, mem., leader Princess Anne Cir., 2001-03. Named Tchr. of Yr. State Va. State Bd. Edn. Mem.: DAR (sec. Lynnhaven Parish 1993—), Alpha Sigma Tau (former nat. panhellenic del., chmn. bd. trustees). Methodist. Avocations: reading, bridge, sports.

RHODES, BETTY MOORE, elementary education educator; b. Suffolk, Va., Aug. 23, 1963; d. Albert Eugene and Phyllis Imogene (Byrum) Moore; m. Robert Joseph Rhodes, Dec. 29, 1985. BA in Elem. Edn., Coll. William and Mary, 1985. Cert. tchr. 5th grade tchr. Virginia Beach (Va.) City Pub. Schs., 1985—; aerobics instr. Chesapeake (Va.) Gen. Hosp., 1987—. Mem. Suffolk Bus. and Profl. Women, 1990-92; chmn. women's fellowship Suffolk Christian Ch., 1993-95; chair Bd. Christian Edn., 1999, fin. bd., 2000—. Mem. NEA, Va. Edn. Assn., Virginia Beach Edn. Assn., Virginia Beach Reading Coun. Avocations: aerobics, reading. Home: 109 Meeting Rd Suffolk VA 23435-1765 Office: Kempsville Elem Sch Kempsville Rd Virginia Beach VA 23464

RHODES, DAVID J. academic administrator; Pres. Sch. Visual Arts, 1980—. Office: Sch Visual Arts Office of Pres 209 E 23rd St New York NY 10010-3994*

RHODES, EDDIE, JR., medical technologist, phlebotomy technician, educator; b. Memphis, Apr. 14, 1955; s. Eddie Sr. and Mabel (Payne) R. AS, Shelby State C.C., Memphis, 1979; BS, Memphis State U., 1981. Cert. med. technologist. Rsch. technologist St. Jude's Children Rsch. Hosp., Memphis, 1980-81; med. lab. asst. Roche Biomedical Lab., Tucker, Ga., 1991-92; med. technologist Damon / MetPath Clin. Lab., Smyrna, Ga., 1992-93, ARC, Norcross, Ga., 1993-95, Ga. Bapt. Med. Ctr., Atlanta, 1994—; instr. microbiology Atlanta Area Tech., 1995-96, adv. bd. mem., 1995—; blood donor specialist Civitan Regl. Blood Sys., Atlanta, 1996—; med. lab./phlebotomy program coord. W. Ga. Tech., LaGrange, 1996—. Named one of the Outstanding Young Men of Am., Atlanta, 1989. Mem.: Am. Med. Technologists (cert.), Am. Soc. of Phlebotomy Technicians, Am. Soc. Microbiology. Avocations: cycling, basketball, chess. Home: 410 Park Pl Lagrange GA 30240-1747 Office: West Ga Technical 303 Fort Dr Lagrange GA 30240-5901

RHODES, GERALDINE BRYAN, secondary school administrator; b. Asheville, N.C., Dec. 7, 1941; d. Robert Gerald and Myrtle (Bartlett) B.; m. Gayle Dean Rhodes, May 27, 1967; children: Jennifer, Rebecca. BM, So. Meth. U., 1967; MA, Columbia U., 1987, MEd, 1988, postgrad., 1988—. Permanent tchr. cert., N.Y. Music tchr. Dallas Ind. Sch. Dist., 1967-69, Yamaha Music Sch., Poughkeepsie, N.Y., 1971-75, Hudson Valley Philharmonic Music Sch., Poughkeepsie, 1986-88, Poughkeepsie Day Sch., 1987-90, dir. music edn., 1990-92; tchr. fine arts Ctrl. Tex. Coll., Youngsan U.S. Army Base, Seoul, 1992-94; music tchr. Arlington Ctrl Schs, Poughkeepsie, NY, 95—. Tchr., cons. Dutchess Arts Camp, Poughkeepsie, 1986-92, Hollingworth Pre-sch., Columbia U., N.Y.C., 1987-88; tchr., dir. Inter-generation Chorus N.Y. State Coun. Arts, Poughkeepsie, 1988-92. Bd. dirs. Children's Home Poughkeepsie. Mem. Music Educators Nat. Congress, N.Y. State Sch. Music Assn., Am. Orff Schulwerk Assn. Republican. Episcopalian. Office: Arlington Ctrl Schs 120 Dutchess Tpke Poughkeepsie NY 12603-6426

RHODES, JUDITH KAY, elementary education educator; b. Memphis, Feb. 4, 1947; d. Claude Louis and Virginia (McQuiston) Ferguson; m. Alfred Stephen McDaniel, June 3, 1967 (div. Jan. 1987); children: John Stephen, Michael Allen; m. Joe Rhodes, Mar. 16, 1991; stepchildren: Greg Rhodes, Robyn Wallace. BSEd, U. Memphis, 1985. Cert. elem. tchr., K-8, Tenn. Bookkeeper Signature Fin. Co., Memphis, 1967-71; salesperson Brownlee's Bric-A-Brac, Memphis, 1972-73; tchr. Shelby County Bd. Edn., Memphis, 1986—. Pres. Sunday Sch. class Bellevue Bapt. Ch., Memphis. Grantee for purchase of microscopes for classsrooms, Carrier Corp., Memphis, 1992. Mem. NEA, Tenn. Edn. Assn., Shelby County Edn. Assn. (assn. rep. 1992-94), Nat. Coun. Tchrs. Math., Tenn. Reading Assn. Avocations: watercolor painting, reading, arts and crafts, tchg.

RHODES, RHODA ELLEN, gifted education educator; b. Chgo., Aug. 20, 1941; d. Nathan and Pearl (Wald) Krichilsky; m. Mitchell Lee Rhodes, Aug. 4, 1963; children: Steven, Dana, Jeffrey. BEd, Chgo. Tchrs. Coll., 1963; MEd in Curriculum and Instrn., Nat. Louis U., Evanston, Ill., 1989. Tchr. Harvey (Ill.) Sch. Dist. 152, 1963-66; tchr., curr. developer Indpls. Hebrew Congregation, 1982-84; tchr. gifted primary pilot program Indpls. Pub. Schs., 1984; coord./tchr. gifted edn. Highland Park-Highwood (Ill.) Sch. Dist. 111, Ill., 1986-89; project discovery tchr. gifted edn. Waukegan (Ill.) Community Sch. Dist. 60, 1989-90; gifted edn. tchr. Kildeer Countryside Sch. Dist. 96, Buffalo Grove, Ill., 1990—2002, mentor tchr., 1999-2001; freelance cons. Northbrook, Ill., 2003—. Mem. Lake County Adv. Bd. Gifted Edn., Grayslake, Ill., 1992-96; profl. adv. bd. Sycamore Sch. for Gifted, Indpls., 1984-85; lectr. Barat Coll., Ill., 1995; adj. instr. Carthage Coll., 2003. Plan comm. mem. Washington Twp. Pub. Schs., Indpls., 1984-85; bd. dir. Bur. Jewish Edn., Indpls., 1979-81. Mem.: ASCD, Ill. Assn. Gifted. Avocations: reading, interior design. E-mail: mitchellrhodes@attbi.com.

RHODIN, JOHANNES ARNE GÖSTA, medical educator; b. Lund, Sweden, Sept. 30, 1922; s. Johannes and Alma Rhodin; m. Gunvor Thorstenson, Aug. 9, 1947 (div. July 1, 1980); children: Anders, Erik; m. Judith Rae Laurent, May 21, 1994. BA, Hvitfeldtska Gymnasium, Göteborg, Sweden, 1942; MD, Karolinska Inst., Stockholm, 1950; PhD in Anatomy, Karolinska Inst., 1954. Lic. gen. med. practitioner Sweden. Prof. anatomy NYU, 1958—64; chmn. dept. anatomy N.Y. Med. Coll., Valhalla, 1964—74, U. Mich., Ann Arbor, 1974—77, Karolinska Inst., 1977—79, U. South Fla., Tampa, 1979—98, prof. anatomy, 1998—. Mem. Nobel Assembly, Karolinska Inst., 1977—79; mem. adv. panel Edn. Commn. for Fgn. Med. Grads., Washington, 1995—97. Author: An Atlas of Ultrastructure, 1964, Histology: A Text and Atlas, 1974, An Atlas of Histology, 1975. Served with Swedish Army, 1942—43. Recipient Landis Rsch. award, Microcirculatory Soc. of USA, 1970, Freshman Class Outstanding Instruct., 1996, Most Outstanding Pre-Clin. Prof., 1997, USF Prof. Excellence Award, 1998. Mem.: Tampa Yacht and Country Club. Home: 5101 Tollbridge Ct Tampa FL 33647 Office: Dept Anatomy Coll Medicine U South Fla 12901 Bruce B Downs Blvd Tampa FL 33612

RHOE, WILHELMINA ROBINSON, retired science educator; b. Columbia, S.C., Nov. 21, 1936; d. William Howard Taft Robinson, Jessie M. Robinson Howard; m. Reginald Mussolini Rhoe, Nov. 28, 1959; children: Chantaine Rhoe-Bulluck, Reginald M., Jandrette, William O. BS in Biology, Benedict Coll., 1958; MS in Sci. Edn., Clemson U., 1980. Tchr. sci. Ruffin H.S., Ruffin, SC, 1958—59; tchr. biology Sterling H.S., Greenville, SC, 1959—60; tchr. sci. Westside H.S., Anderson, SC, 1961—62; tchr. biology, chemistry, physics, math. New Deal H.S., Starr, SC, 1964—68; chemist, statistician Dow-Badische Co., Anderson, 1968—70; tchr. biology, chemistry, physics, math. McDuffie H.S., Anderson, 1971—92; ret., 1992. Bd. dirs. Anderson Civic Ctr., Anderson, SC, 1992—98; del. Dem. Nat. Conv., Chgo., 1996, L.A., 2000; rules committeeperson S.C. Dem., Columbia, 1994—. Mem.: Anderson County Ret. Tchrs., Order Ea. Star (sec. Thomasena chpt. #206 1984—86). Avocations: reading, sewing, travel. Home: 105 Rhoe Cir Anderson SC 29621

RHONE, DOUGLAS PIERCE, pathologist, educator; b. Bloomsburg, Pa., Mar. 27, 1940; s. Wilbur Clayton and Marian Faye (Shaffer) R.; m. Leta Daiva Budelskis, Sept. 27, 1969; children: Jennifer Ann, Todd Brader. BS, Ill. Benedictine U., 1965; MD, MS in Pathology, U. Ill., 1969. Diplomate Am. Bd. Pathology. Attending pathologist Ill. Masonic Med. Ctr., Chgo., 1976, chmn. dept. pathology, 1976—, dir. residency pathology, 1976—90; asst. prof. pathology U. Ill. Coll. Medicine, Chgo., 1976—80, assoc. prof. pathology, 1980—98; prof. pathology, 1998—; dir. residency pathology U. Ill. Met. Hosps., Chgo., 1990—; assoc. dir. med. affairs Ill. Masonic Med. Ctr., Chgo., 1992—95; pres. Ill. Masonic Med. Ctr. Pathologists, S.C., Chgo., 1977—, Lab. Cons., Ltd., Chgo., 1977—2001. Contbr. articles to profl. jours. Maj. U.S. Army, 1974-76. Recipient Raymond B. Allen award U. Ill. Coll. Medicine, 1979, 80, 95, 97, 98, 2000, C. Thomas Bombeck award, 1991, 2002. Fellow: Coll. Am. Pathologists, Am. Soc. Clin. Pathologists (Sheard-Sanford Rsch. award 1969); mem.: Ill. Soc. Pathologists, Chgo. Pathology Soc., Alpha Omega Alpha. Roman Catholic. Avocations: antiquities, gardening, oil painting, classical music and opera, russian history and culture. Home: 222 S Spring Ave La Grange IL 60525-2243 Office: Ill Masonic Med Ctr Dept Pathology 836 W Wellington Ave Chicago IL 60657-9224

RHOTON, ALBERT LOREN, JR., neurological surgery educator; b. Nov. 18, 1932; s. Albert Loren and Hazel Arnette (Van Cleve) R.; m. Joyce L. Moldenhauer, June 23, 1957; children: Eric L., Albert J., Alice S., Laural A. BS, Ohio State U., 1954; MD cum laude, Washington U., St. Louis, 1959. Diplomate Am. Bd. Neurol. Surgery (bd dirs. 1985-91, vice-chmn. 1991). Intern Columbia Presbyn. Med. Ctr., N.Y.C., 1959; resident in neurol. surgery Barnes Hosp., St. Louis, 1961-65; cons. neurol. surgery Mayo Clinic, Rochester, Minn., 1965-72; chief divsn. neurol. surgery U. Fla., Gainesville, 1972-80, R.D. Keene prof., 1980—, chmn. dept. neurol. surgery, 1980-2000, chmn. emeritus, 2000—. Developer microsurg. tng. ctr.; guest lectr. Neurol. Socs. Switzerland, Japan, Venezuela, France, Colombia, Costa Rica, Uruguay, Korea, Australia, Egypt, Argentina, Hong Kong, U.K., Turkey, Thailand, Latin Am., Portugal, Peru, S. Africa, China, Taiwan, Middle East, Peru, Brazil, Chile, Taiwan, Portugal; invited faculty, guest lectr. Harvard U., Washington U., Emory U., UCLA, U. Calif., San Francisco, Stanford U., U. Miami, U. Okla., U. So. Calif., U. Mich., Northwestern U., U. Chgo., U. Pa., Johns Hopkins U., Ohio State U., Temple U., Duke U., Cornell U., NYU, Mt. Sinai, N.Y.C., U. Cin., Tulane U., Vanderbilt U., U. Minn., U. Md., U. Pa., Albany Med. Coll., Cleve. Clin. Found., St. Louis U., Henry Ford Med. Found., Med. Coll. N.Y., Jefferson Med. Coll., Hahnemann Med. Coll., U. P.R., U. Calif., Irvine, U. Hong Kong, La. State U., U. Ky., U Tenn., Memphis, U. Louisville, Singapore Nat. U., U. Adalaide, U. Sydney, U. Western Australia, Walter Reed Army Med. Ctr., Beijing Capital U., China, Sinshu U., Japan, Kitasato Univ., 2002, Mt. Sinai Coll. Medicine, U. Western Australia, Perth, Driscoll Found., England; Olivecorona lectr. Stockholm, Krayenbuhl lectr. Switzerland; Elsberg lectr. N.Y. Neurol. Soc., 2003. Author: The Orbit and Sellar Region: Microsurgical Anatomy and Operative Approaches, 1996, Millenium issue Neurosurgery, 25th Anniversary issue; designed more than 200 microsurgery instruments; mem. editl. bd. Neurosurgery, Jour. Microsurgery, Surg. Neurology, Jour. Fla. Med. Assn., Am. Jour. Otology, Skull Base Surgery; contbr. articles to profl. jours. Bd. dirs. Neurosurgery Edn. and Rsch. Found. Recipient Disting. Faculty award, U. Fla., 1981, Alumni Achievement award, Washington U. Sch. Medicine, 1985, Jones award for outstanding spl. med. exhibit of yr., Am. Assn. med. Illustrators, 1969, Jameison medal, Neurosurg. soc. Australasia, 1997, Outstanding Achievement award, World Congress of Skull Base Surgery, 2000, medal of honor, World Fedn. Neurosurg. Socs., 2001, medal, Neurosurg. Soc. Am., 2001, endowed professorship named in his honor, U. Fla., Lifetime Achievement award, Wall of Fame Honoree, Honorary Alumnus award, 2001, medal of honor, Neurosurg. Soc. of Am., 2001, Bucy award, Univ. Chgo., 2002; grantee NIH, VA, Am. Heart Assn. Mem. ACS (bd. govs. 1978-84), AMA (Billings Bronze medal 1969), Congress Neurol. Surgeons (pres. 1978, honored guest 1993), Nat. Found. Brain Rsch. (bd. dirs. 1990-94), Nat. Coalition for Rsch. in Neurol. Disorders (bd. dirs. 1990-94), Neurol. Soc. Am. (medal 2001), Internat. Congress Meningiomas (hon. pres. 2000), Neurosurg. Soc. Brazil (hon.), Neurosurg. Soc. Japan (hon., Honored guest 2002), Neurosurg. Soc. Mex. (hon.), Neurosurg. Soc. Can. (hon.), Neurosurg. Soc. Uruguay (hon.), Neurosurg. Soc. Venezuela (hon.), Neurosurg. Soc. Turkey (hon.), Neurosurg. Soc. Tex. (hon.), Neurosurg. Soc. Okla. (hon.), Neurosurg. Soc. Wis. (hon.), Neurosurg. Soc. Ga. (hon.), Neurosurg. Soc. Rocky Mountain (hon.), Neurosurg. Soc. China (hon.), Neurosurg Soc. Argentina (hon.), Fla. Neurosurg. Soc. (pres. 1978), Am. Assn. Neurol. Surgeons (chmn. vascular sect., treas. 1983-86, v.p. 1987-88, pres. 1989-90, exec. com. 1993, Cushing medal 1998), Soc. Neurol. Surgeons (treas. 1975-81, pres. 1993), So. Neurol. Soc. (v.p. 1976), Alachua County Med. Soc. (exec. com. 1978), Fla. Med. Assn., Am. Surg. Assn., Soc. Univ. Neurosurgeons, Am. Heart Assn. (stroke coun., Outstanding Achievement award 1971), N.Am. Skull Base Soc. (pres. 1993-94, honored guest 2001), Am. Acad. Neurol. Surgery, Acoustic Neuroma Assn. (med. adv. bd. 1983-2000, chmn. 1992-2001, chmn. emeritus 2001--), Trigeminal Neurol. Assn. (med. advisor bd. 1992—), Hemifacial Spasm Assn. (med. adv. bd. 2002--), Internat. Interdisciplinary Congress on Craniofacial and Skull Base Surgery (pres. 1996-97), Internat. Soc. Neurosurg. Tech. and Instrument Invention (pres. 1997—), Japanese Skull Base Soc. (hon. pres. 2000), Internat. Soc. for Microsurgery Anatomy (hon. pres. 2002). Home: 2505 NW 22d Ave Gainesville FL 32605-3819 Office: U Fla Shands Hosp Gainesville FL 32610

RHYAN, JEANETTE DELORES, physical education educator; b. Clarinda, Iowa, June 26, 1952; d. Warren DeLos and Delores Elenore (Goecker) Renander; m. James William Rhyan, Aug. 5, 1978. BS, Dana Coll., 1974. Cert. secondary tchr., Ariz. Tchr. phys. edn. and sci. Moe (Victoria) High Sch., Australia, 1974-76; tchr. phys. edn. and health and social studies Holbrook (Ariz.) Jr. High Sch., 1977—. Mem. AAHPERD, Ariz. Assn. Jr. High Student Couns. (sec. 1984-85, v.p. 1985-86, pres. 1986-87), Order Ea. Star, Delta Kappa Gamma. Republican. Lutheran. Avocations: travel, crafts, music, collecting reindeers. Office: Holbrook Sch Dist 3 PO Box 640 1001 N 8th Ave Holbrook AZ 86025-2331

RHYNE, THERESA-MARIE, computer graphics and university executive; b. Denver, Sept. 20, 1954; d. Jimmie Lee and Marie Baker (Britt) R. BSCE, Stanford U., 1976, MS, 1977, MS, 1981. Engr. Stanford (Calif.) U., 1979, systems analyst Ctr. for Info. Tech., 1981-82, long range planner, 1982-83, budget and planning officer, 1983-85; fine artist, cons. Stanford, 1986—; sr. systems requirements analyst Unisys Corp., Research Triangle Park, N.C., 1987-90, tech. leader U.S. EPA sci. visualization lab., 1990-92; lead-sci. visualization rschr. USA EPA Sci. Vis. Lab. Lockheed Martin Svcs. Group, Research Triangle Park, N.C., 1993-2000; multimedia and visualization expert, learning tech. svcs. N.C. State U., Raleigh, 2001—03, coord. spl. tech. projects, 2003—. Teaching fellow English for fgn. students Stanford (Calif.) U., summers 1977-81; artist-in-residence Wake County Arts Coun., N.C., 1987-89; lectr. Meredith Coll., 1990; instr. N.C. Mus. of Art, 1992; keynote spkr. Eurographics, 1994; invited spkr. Interface, 1995, Assn. Computing Machinery Siggraph Panels chair, 1996; Siggraph exec. com., dir.-at-large, 1996-2000; lead co-chair IEEE Visualization 98. One woman shows include Old Uncle Gaylord's Expresso and Ice Cream Parlor, Palo Alto, Calif., 1981, numerous others U.S. and abroad; author video procs. ACM/SIGGRAPH, IEEE Visualization, 1993; mem. editl. bd. IEEE Computer Graphics and Applications Mag., 1998—, Jour. Game Devel., 2003—. Mem. Accessibility Cons. Team for Physically Handicapped, Stanford, 1978-80; coord. Celebration '85 Palo Alto Celebrates the Arts, 1985; program co-chair Eurographics 2001. Mem. AAAS, NAFE, IEEE (sr.), Coun. Arts of Palo Alto (membership chmn. bd. dirs. 1985-86, pres. 1986-87), Assn. for Computing Machinery (chair SIGGRAPH panel visualizing environ. data sets 1993, SIGGRAPH panels com. 1995, SIGGRAPH panels chair 1996, SIGGRAPH conf. adv. group 1999-2000, SIGGRAPH Ednl. Resource grantee 1986, keynote spkr. Eurographics '94), Western Art Dirs. Club, Am. Craft Coun., Nat. Art Edn. Assn., Nat. Mus. Women in Arts (charter), Pacific Art League, Menlo Art League, San Jose Art League, USEPA/RTP Macintosh Users' Group (founder-leader 1987—), Am. Math. Assn., IEEE Computer Soc. (organizer visualization tutorial process visualizing environ. scis. data 1993, chair IEEE/Visualization panel on visualization and beyond 1993, co-chair demonstrations IEEE/Visualization 1993, co-chair publicity 1994, co-chair panels 1995, IEEE/Visualization, 1996, chair panels, 1996, program co-chair, 1997, past co-chair 1999—, IEEE/Visualization program com. 2000, IEEE tech. com. on Visualization and Graphics, 1997—, conf. dir. internat. environ. scis. visualization symposium 1993, 94, 95, Internat. Cartographic Assn.'s Commn. on Visualization, organizer supercomputing tutorial on visualizing and examining large sci. data sets Assn. Computing Machinery/IEEE Super Computing '95), Air and Waste Mgmt. Assn., Artspace (Raleigh, N.C.), Durham Art Guild, Internat. Application Visualization Sys. Users' Group (chair earth scis. track 2d ann. internat. conf. 1993, 94, 95). Avocations: mountain and rock climbing, jazz music, fashion design. Office: Learning Tech Svcs NC State U Campus Venture III Ste 267 Box 7113 Raleigh NC 27695-7113

RIASANOVSKY, NICHOLAS VALENTINE, retired historian, educator; b. Harbin, China, Dec. 21, 1923; came to U.S., 1938, naturalized, 1943; m. Arlene Ruth Schlegel, Feb. 15, 1955; children— John, Nicholas, Maria. BA, U. Oreg., 1942; AM, Harvard U., 1947; DPhil, Oxford (Eng.) U., 1949. Mem. faculty U. Iowa, 1949-57, U. Calif., Berkeley, 1957—, prof. history, 1961—. Sidney Hellman Ehrman prof. European history, 1969—2003, ret., 2003; trustee Nat. Council Soviet and E. European Research, 1978-82; mem. Kennan Inst. Acad. Council, 1986-89. Vis. research prof. USSR Acad. Scis., Moscow, 1969, Moscow and Leningrad, 1974, 79 Author: Russia and the West in the Teaching of the Slavophiles: A Study of Romantic Ideology, 1952, Nicholas I and Official Nationality in Russia, 1825-1855, 1959, A History of Russia, 1963, 6th edit., 1999, The Teaching of Charles Fourier, 1969, A Parting of Ways: Government and the Educated Public in Russia, 1801-1855, 1976, The Image of Peter the Great in Russian History and Thought, 1985, The Emergence of Romanticism, 1992, Collected Writings 1947-94, 1993; co-editor: California Slavic Studies, 1960—; editl. bd.

Russian rev., Zarubezhnaia Periodicheskaia Pechat' na Russkom Iazyke, Simvol; contbr. articles to profl. jours. 2d lt. AUS, 1943—46. Decorated Bronze Star; recipient Silver medal Commonwealth Club Calif., 1964; Rhodes scholar, 1947-49; Fulbright grantee, 1954-55, 74, 79; Guggenheim fellow, 1969; sr. fellow Nat. Endowment Humanities, 1975; Fulbright sr. scholar, sr. fellow Ctr. Advanced Studies in Behavioral Scis., 1984-85; sr. fellow Woodrow Wilson Internat. Ctr. for Scholars, 1989-90. Mem. Am. Assn. Advancement Slavic Studies (pres. 1973-76, Disting. Contbr. award 1993), Am. Hist. Assn. (award for Scholarly Distinction 1995), Am. Acad. Arts and Scis.

RIBA, NETTA EILEEN, retired secondary school educator; b. Bronx, N.Y., Apr. 6, 1944; d. Jack and Anne (Parnes) Browner; m. Benjamin Riba, July 22, 1975; children: Rebecca, Joseph. BS, Queens Coll., 1965, MS, 1968. Cert. tchr., N.Y. Math. tchr. Bayside (N.Y.) H.S., 1965-68, Flushing (N.Y.) H.S., 1968-75, Harry S Truman H.S., Bronx, 1975-95, Christopher Columbus H.S., Bronx, 1996-2001, SUNY Rockland Country C.C., Suffern, 2001—. Vol. guide N.Y. Zool. Soc., Bronx, 1973-75; leader Rockland County Coun. Girl Scouts USA, 1985-88. Mem. Nat. Coun. Tchrs. Math. Jewish. Avocations: animal behavior, sewing. Office: SUNY Rockland County CC 145 College Rd Suffern NY 10901

RIBARY, URS, neuroscientist, researcher, educator; b. Lucerne, Switzerland, Nov. 24, 1955; came to U.S., 1988; s. Max and Hilde (Brunner) Ribary; m. Evelyne Dahinden, July 11, 1986; 1 child, Samanta R. MS, U. Tech., Zurich, Switzerland, 1981, DSc, 1985. Rsch. asst. prof. NYU Med. Ctr., N.Y.C., 1988-93, dir. ctr. for neuromagnetism, 1989—, assoc. prof., 1993—. Vis. asst. prof. Simon Fraser U., Can., 1986-88. Cons. (Time Life series) The Brain, 1990; contbr. articles to profl. jours. Co-founder, chmn. Samanta S. Ribary Found. Inc. Mem. AAAS, Am. Soc. Neurosci., N.Y. Acad. Scis., European Neurosci. Assn., Soc. Cognitive Neuroscience. Achievements include work on using functional brain imaging techniques, especially magneto encephalography (MEG) to study coherent thalamo-cortical activity in humans during normal cognitive processing, and its alterations in neurological and neuropsychiatric patients. Office: Dept Physiology and Neurosci NYU Med Ctr 550 1st Ave New York NY 10016-6402 E-mail: urs.ribary@med.nyu.edu.

RIBBANS, GEOFFREY WILFRID, Spanish educator; b. London, Apr. 15, 1927; came to U.S. 1978; s. Wilfrid Henry and Rose Matilda (Burton)R.; m. Magdalena Willmann, Apr. 21, 1956; children: Madeleine Elizabeth, Helen Margaret, Peter John. BA with 1st class hons., Kings Coll., U. London, 1948, MA, 1953. Asst. lectr. U. Sheffield, Eng., 1954-56, lectr., 1956-61, sr. lectr. Spanish, 1961-63; Gilmour prof. Spanish U. Liverpool, Eng., 1963-78; vis. Mellon prof. Spanish U. Pitts., 1970-71; Wm. R. Kenan Jr. U. prof. Spanish Brown U., Providence, 1978-99, chmn. dept., 1981-84, prof. emeritus, 1999—. Editor Bull. Hispanic Studies, 1964-78; vis. prof. U. Salamanca, Spain, 1995. Author: Catalunya i Valencia al Segle XVIII, 1955, 2d edit., 1993, Niebla y Soledad: Aspectos de Unamuno y Machado, 1971, Galdós: Fortunata y Jacinta, 1977 (Spanish transl. 1988); editor: Antonio Machado, Soledades, Galerias, Otros Poemas, 1984, revised 16th edit., 2000, Campos de Castilla, 1989, 9th edit., 1999, History and Fiction in Galdós's Narratives, 1993, 2d edit., 1995, Conflicts and Conciliations: The Evolution of Galdós's "Fortunata y Jacinta", 1997. Decorated La Encomienda de la Orden de Isabel la Catolica Spain; recipient prize for excellence in Galdos studies, Las Palmas, 1997, Batista i Roca prize, Barcelona, 2000; Hispanic studies in his honour, Liverpool, 1992, Symposium on Modernism and Modernity in his honor, Brown U., 1998. Mem. MLA, Internat. Assn. Hispanists (v.p. 1974-80), Internat. Assn. Galdós Scholars (pres. 1988-89), N.Am. Catalan Soc. (hon.). Office: Brown U Dept Hispanic Studies PO Box 1961 Providence RI 02912-1961

RIBBLE, RONALD GEORGE, retired psychologist, educator, writer; b. West Reading, Pa., May 7, 1937; s. Jeremiah George and Mildred Sarah (Folk) Ribble; m. Catalina Valenzuela Torres, Sept. 30, 1961; children: Christina, Timothy, Kenneth. BSEE cum laude, U. Mo., 1968, MSEE, 1969, MA, 1985, PhD, 1986. Bd. cert. forensic examiner, diplomate Am. Bd. Psychol. Specialities, Am. Coll. Forensic Examiners. Enlisted man USAF, 1956-60, advance through grades to lt. col., 1976; rsch. dir. Coping Resources, Inc., Columbia, Mo., 1986; pres., co-owner Towers and Rushing Ltd. (Pubs. and Psychol. Cons., Troubadour 1997-2001), San Antonio, 1986—; referral devel. Laughlin Pavilion Psychiat. Hosp., Kirksville, Mo., 1987; program dir. Psychiat. Insts. of Am., Iowa Falls, Iowa, 1987-88; lead psychotherapist Gasconade County Counseling Ctr., Hermann, Mo., 1988; sr. lectr. U. Tex., San Antonio, 1989—2002; lectr. Trinity U., San Antonio, 1995-96; assessment clinician Afton Oaks Psychiat. Hosp., San Antonio, 1989-91; ret. from tchg., 2002. Faculty cons. Edn. Testing Svc., 1997; psychologist Olmos Psychol. Svcs., Inc., San Antonio, 1991—93; vol. assessor Holmgreen Children's Shelter, San Antonio, 1992—93; founder Ruth Bohn Weissman Scholarship in Creative Writing U. Tex., San Antonio, 1994; cosponor Lyric Recovery Festival, Carnegie Hall, 2000; condr. seminars, revs. for maj. publs. Author: (book) Apples, Weeds, and Doggie Poo, 1995, Dont' Eat the Snake!; contbr. essays to psychol. refernce books, poetry to anthologies periodicals, lyrics to popular music; interviewer: celebrities in performing and lit. arts, 1995—, columnist: Feelings, 1993—97; pub. access TV appearances, 1991—. Founding cabinet mem. World Peace and Diplomacy Forum; vol. announcer pub. radio sta., Colombia, 1993; vol. Cath. Family and Children's Svc., San Antonio, 1989—91; chpt. advisor Rational Recovery Program for Alcoholics, San Antonio, 1991—92; mem. Pres. Leadership Cir., 1994—2002; contbg. mem. Dem. Nat. Com., 1983—, Presdl. Congl. Task Force, 1994; del. Boone County (Mo.) Dem. Conv., 1984. Nominee Pushcart award, 1999, 2001; recipient Roberts Meml. prize in Poetry, 1995, Internat. Peace prize, United Cultural Conv., U.S.A., 2002. Master: APA; fellow: Am. Coll. Forensic Examiners; mem.: ACLU, AAUP, NEA, La Société Des Sages (founder 2002), Physicians for Social Responsibility (leadership cir.), So. Poverty Law Ctr. (leadership coun. for tchg. tolerance), Poetry Soc. Am., Soc. Profl. Journalists, Interfaith Alliance, Mil. Officers Assn., Air Force Assn., Internat. Platform Assn. (Poetry award 1995), World Peace and Diplomacy Forum (founding mem. 2003). Deist. Avocations: running and fitness, poetry, singing, public speaking. Home: 14023 N Hills Village Dr San Antonio TX 78249-2534 also: Towers and Rushing Ltd San Antonio TX 78249 E-mail: rgrib@stic.net.

RICAPITO, JOSEPH VIRGIL (GIUSEPPE RICAPITO), Spanish, Italian and comparative literature educator; b. Giovinazzo, Bari, Italy, Oct. 30, 1933; came to U.S., 1935; s. Frank and Filomena (Cervone) R.; m. Carolyn Sue Kitchen, Apr. 7, 1958; children: Frank Peyton, Maria Avadna. BA, CUNY, Bklyn., 1955; MA, U. Iowa, 1956; PhD in Romance Langs., U. Calif., L.A., 1966. From instr. to asst. prof. Pomona Coll., Claremont, Calif., 1962-70; from assoc. prof. to prof. Ind. U., Bloomington, Ind., 1970-80; prof. La. State U., Baton Rouge, 1980—, chmn. dept., 1980-85, Joseph Yenni disting. prof. Italian studies, 1999. Author: Bibliografia Razonada y anotada, 1980; editor: La Vida de Laz de Tormes, 1976; translator: Dialogue of Mercury and Charon, 1986, Cervantes's Novelas ejemplares: Between History and Creativity, 1996. Pres. Greater Baton Rouge Am.-Italian Assn., 1984-85. With U.S. Army, 1957-59. Grantee NEH, 1981; named Knight Order of Merit, Republic of Italy, 1988, Knight Order of Queen Isabel, Govt. of Spain, 1990; named Disting. Rsch. Master La. State U., 2001. Mem. MLA, Renaissance Soc. Am., Am. Comparative Lit. Assn., Am. Assn. Tchrs. Spanish and Portuguese, Cervantes Soc. Am. Avocations: music, photography, films. Office: La State U 309 Hodges Hall Baton Rouge LA 70803-0001 E-mail: ricapito@lsu.edu.

RICCA, ROSELINDA FRANCES, mathematics educator; b. Bklyn., Sept. 22, 1956; d. Dominic and Nancy (Renno) Schimmenti; m. Ronald Reich, Mar. 25, 1979 (div. Sept. 1984); 1 child, Nancy; m. Robert Ricca, Dec. 27, 1998. BA, Queens Coll., 1978, MS, 1987; Cert. Adminstrn., Hofstra U., 1995. Math. tchr., dist. math. chmn. Malverne (N.Y.) Sch. Dist. Named All Star Tchr., Scope, 2000, Malverne Tchr. of Yr., 1993. Mem. Assn. Suprs., Nassau County Math. Tchrs. Assn. (bd. dirs. 1992—, Math. Tchr. of Yr. 1993), Nat. Coun. Tchrs. of Math. Roman Catholic. Avocations: travel, music.

RICCARDS, MICHAEL PATRICK, academic administrator; b. Hillside, N.J., Oct. 2, 1944; s. Patrick and Margaret (Finelli) Riccards; m. Barbara Dunlop, June 6, 1970; children: Patrick, Catherine, Abigail. BA, Rutgers U., 1966, MA, 1967, MPhil, 1969, PhD, 1970. Spl. asst. to chancellor Dept. Higher Edn., Trenton, NJ, 1969-70; from asst. prof. to assoc. prof. SUNY, Buffalo, 1970-77; dean U. Mass., Boston, 1977-82; provost, prof. Hunter Coll. CUNY, 1982-86; pres. St. John's Coll., Santa Fe, 1986-89, Shepherd Coll., Shepherdstown, W.Va., 1989-95, Fitchburg (Mass.) State Coll., 1995—2002; pub. policy scholar-in-residence Coll. Bd., Washington, 2002—. Mem. joint commn. tchr. preparation, 1999—2000. Author: (book) The Making of the American Citizenry, 1973, If You Can Keep It, 1987, The Ferocious Engine of Democracy, 2 vols., 1995, 2002, Vicars of Christ, 1998, The Presidency and the Middle Kingdom, 2000, The Odes of DiMaggio, 2001, The Papacy and the Early Christendom, 2003; co-editor: Relfections on American Political Thought, 1973. Chmn. N.Mex. Endowment Humanities, 1989; trustee Albuquerque Acad.; mem. Coun. Humanities W.Va., Nat. Skills Stds. Bd., 1993—98; mem. nat. adv. com. Ctr. Study Presidency, 1987—89. Fulbright fellow, 1973, Huntington Libr. fellow, 1974, NEH fellow, Princeton U., 1976—77. Home: 3319 14th St NE Washington DC 20017 Office: Coll Bd 1233 20th St NW Washington DC 20036

RICCIO-SAUER, JOYCE, art educator; b. Jersey City, Nov. 19, 1950; d. Frank and Jennie (Giuliano) Riccio; children: Jessica, Joshua; m. Peter Edmund Sauer, Aug. 8, 1992. BA, William Paterson Coll., 1972, MA, 1981. Cert. elem. tchr., art tchr., N.J., supr. cert., 1997. Elem. art tchr. West Milford (N.J.) Bd. Edn., 1972-74; art tchr. Bridgewater Raritan Bd. of Edn., Raritan, N.J., 1974-81, tchr. 4th grade, 1975-76, tchr. 6th grade, 1981-82; tchr. reading, social studies 7th and 8th grade Wood-Ridge (N.J.) Bd. Edn., 1985-86; secondary tchr. visual arts, computer coord. Ridgewood (N.J.) High Sch., 1986—. Cons. Grove Pubs., Teaneck, N.J., 1992. Mem. NEA, N.J. Edn. Assn., Nat. Art Edn. Assn., Art Educators of N.J. (conf. speaker), Ridgewood Edn. Assn. (rep. 1991—), Internat. Platform Assn. Avocations: ceramics, canoeing, travel, silver smith, webmaster. Office: Ridgewood High Sch 627 E Ridgewood Ave Ridgewood NJ 07450-3394

RICE, CARRIE SOTTILE, public relation director, retired principal; b. Phila., Nov. 2, 1927; d. Gaetano and Lucia Francesca (Domanico) Sottile; children: William Thomas, Steven Malin. BA in Edn., Chestnut Hill. Coll., Phila., 1948; postgrad., U. Pa., Phila., 1948—50; Prin. Cert., Temple U., Phila., 1974; MEd, Beaver Coll., Glenside, Pa., 1974. Fashion model, Phila., 1957—64; tchr. Sch. Dist. Phila., 1948—54, human rels. coord., 1957—72, 1972—76; tchr. Antilles Consolidated Sch. USN, San Juan, PR, 1954—56; prin. Kennedy-Crossan Sch., Phila., 1976—91; ednl. cons., fundraiser Phila. Children's Network, Phila., 1992—94; dir. pub. rels. and alumae affairs Nazareth Acad. High Sch., Phila., 1995—. Adj. prof. Chestnut Hill Coll., Phila., 1982—85, Beaver Coll. (now Arcadia U.), Glenside, Pa., 1993—98; supr. teenage br. Frankford br. Free Lib. Phila., Phila., 1947—48; tv model Channels 3, 6, 10, Phila., 1949—54; guest lectr. Spkr.'s Showcase Assocs., Phila., 1968—79; lectr. Holy Family Coll., Phila., 1978—79; tchr. Phila. Modeling and Charm Sch., Phila., 1957—62; apptd. commr. by Gov. Tom Ridge to Jud. Adv. Commn. Phila. County, Commonwealth of Phila., 1995—; pres. Phila. Coun. Adminstrv. Women in Edn., 1983—89; alternate rep. Phila. Orgn. Sch. Adminstrs., 1976—91. Served on merit selection panels Fed. Ct., 2001; vol. Overbrook Sch. Blind, 1972—74, March of Dimes, Am. Red Cross; edn. chmn. N.E. divsn. Am. Cancer Soc., 1981—88, vol.; mem. N.E. divsn. Human Rels.Coun., 1972—78; mem. choir Presentation Cath. Ch., 1980—83; bd. dirs. The Bridge Drug Rehab. Ctr. Phila., 1972—78; sec. women's bd. Arcadia U., 1994—; chairperson 80th Ann. Frankford High Sch., Phila., 1990, 85th Ann. Frankford High Sch., Phila., 1995; state chairperson Cooley's Anemia, 1986—89; mem. pres.'s coun. Manor Jr. Coll., 1989—. Named Woman of the Yr., Columbus Ednl. Forum, 1985; recipient award, Vocat. Indsl. Clubs. Am., 1980, Achievement award for volunteerism, YWCA N.E. divsn., 1981, award, Chapel fo the Four Chaplains, 1982, Adminstrv. Ednl. award, City Coun. Phila., 1985, Disting. Svc. award, N.E. High Sch., 1985, Award of Excellence in Cmty. Svc., Lawncrest, 1985, Pioneer award for achievement, Frankford H.S., 1989, Paul Harris Fellow award, 2003. Mem.: AAUW (v.p. 1990), Women for Gtr. Phila., Sons of Italy (v.p. commn. social justice 1983—89, nat. sec. commn. social justice 1986—91, pres. commn. social justice 1989—90, Judge F.J. Montemuro Lodge), Phi Delta Kappa. Avocations: modeling, reading, singing, public speaking. Home: 802 Knorr St Philadelphia PA 19112 Office: Nazareth Acad 4001 Grant Ave Philadelphia PA 19114

RICE, CATHY SUE HARRISON, educational administrator; b. Vidalia, Ga., Oct. 8, 1951; d. Charles Curtis and Bonnie Faye (Smith) Harrison; m. Jerry Clifford Rice, Nov. 23, 1983; 1 child, James West Page. BS in Elem. Edn., Ga. So. U., 1972, MEd in Elem. Edn., 1980, EdS in Early Childhood Edn., 1993. Cert. L-5 adminstrn. and supervision. Tchr. Claxton (Ga.) Elem. Sch., 1973-74, Brooklet (Ga.) Elem. Sch., 1974-76, Dearing (Ga.) Elem. Sch., 1976-78, Glyndale Elem. Sch., Brunswick, Ga., 1978-94; instrnl. specialist Burroughs-Mollette Elem. Sch., Brunswick, 1994—. Speaker S.E. Regional Math. Conf., 1993, Ga. At Risk Conf., 1994; presider Ga. Math. Conf., 1993. Pres. Brunswick Exchangettes, 1986, v.p., 1992, sec., 1994. Mem. ASCD, Delta Kappa Gamma (program chmn. 1993—), Phi Delta Kappa. Baptist. Avocations: reading, camping, boating, playing golf, fishing. Home: 119 Regal Rd Brunswick GA 31523-6281 Office: Burroughs Molette Elem Sch 1900 Lee St Brunswick GA 31520-6340

RICE, DAVID LEE, university president emeritus; b. New Market, Ind., Apr. 1, 1929; s. Elmer J. and Katie (Tate) R.; m. Betty Jane Fordice, Sept. 10, 1950; children: Patricia Denise Rice Dawson, Michael Alan. BS, Purdue U., 1951, MS, 1956, PhD, 1958; degree (hon.), U. Evansville, 1994, U. So. Ind., 1995; LHD, U. Evansville, 1994; LLD, U. So. Ind., 1995. Dir. prof. research Ball State U., Muncie, Ind., 1958-66; v.p. Coop. Ednl. Research Lab., Inc., Indpls., 1965-67; research coordinator, bur. research HEW, Washington; dean campus Ind. State U., Evansville, 1967-71, pres. campus, 1971-85; pres. U. So. Ind., Evansville, 1985-94, pres. emeritus, 1994—. Adminstrv. asst. Gov.'s Com. on Post High Sch. Orgn. Contbr. articles to profl. jours. Past mem. State Citizens Adv. Bd. Title XX Social Security Act; bd. dirs., past pres. bd. commrs. Evansville Housing Auth.; pres. Leadership Evansville, 1978-79; bd. dirs., past pres. S.W. Ind. Pub. TV, 1972—; chair Indian Pub. Broadcasting Sts., 1990-93; bd. dirs. Villages Inc.; mem. Buffalo Trace Coun. Boy Scouts Am., 1963—, New Harmony Commn., 1989-94; chair So. Ind. Rural Devel. Project., Inc.; bd. trustees Rapp Granary-Owen Found.; bd. dirs. So. Ind. Higher Edn. Inc., U. So. Ind. Found. With inf. U.S. Army, 1951-53. Decorated Bronze Star, Combat Infantryman's Badge; recipient Svc. to Others award Salvation Army, 1974, Citizen of Yr. award Westside Civitan Club, 1972, Boss of Yr. award Am. Bus. Women's Assn., 1976, Disting. Citizen of Yr. award Ivy Tech State Coll., 1994; David L. Rice Libr./U. So. Ind. named in his honor, 1994. Mem. DAR (medal of honor for cmty. svc. 1998), Am. Assn. Higher Edn., Am. Ednl. Rsch. Assn., Am. Assn. State Colls. and Univs., Nat. Soc. Study Edn., Met. Evansville C. of C. (dir.), Evansville Kennel Club, Rotary (civic award Evansville club 1985, life), Alpha Kappa Psi, Alpha Zeta, Phi Delta Kappa. Methodist. Home: 1223 S Main St New Harmony IN 47631 Office: Neef Lesueur House 404 Church St New Harmony IN 47631

RICE, EARL CLIFTON, retired mathematics educator; b. Edmond, Okla., Aug. 28, 1915; s. Ernest Clifton and Bertha Tillie (Rieckhoff) R.; m. Alyce Loree McConnell; children: Margaret Earlene, Loren Lynwood. BA in Math., Ctrl. State Tchrs. Coll., 1937; MA, George Peabody Coll. Tchrs., 1948, PhD, 1957. Math. and Spanish tchr. Dustin (Okla.) Pub. Schs., 1937-39, Marlow (Okla.) Pub. Schs., 1940-42, 45-46; math. instr. Peabody Coll., Nashville, 1948-49; asst. prof. math. Ark. A&M Coll., Monticello, 1952-53; prof. math. U. Ctrl. Okla., Edmond, 1953-81, math. lectr., 1981-94. Dir. NSF Insts. in Math. and Sci. for Tchrs. U. Ctrl. Okla., 1959-63, chmn. dept. math., statistics and computing, 1970-71. Author: Test of Generalizing Ability, 1956. Sgt. U.S. Army, 1942-45. Mem. Math. Assn. Am., Nat. Coun. Tchrs. Math., Okla. Edn. Assn., NEA, Am. Legion, Rotary (pres. Edmond chpt. 1972-73), Kappa Delta Pi (pres. 1948), Phi Delta Kappa. Avocations: fishing, ping pong, hunting. Home: 808 Myrtle Dr Edmond OK 73034-4639

RICE, EMILY JOY, retired secondary school and adult educator; b. Terrell, Tex., Aug. 30, 1928; d. Martin Alexander Joy Jr. and Susan Martha (Helen) Ruth Joy; m. LeRoy Noonon Rice Jr., May 30, 1951; children: Edna Anne Rice-Padhi, Margaret Elizabeth (dec.). BS, Tex. Woman's U.; postgrad., U. Tex., Tex. A&I U. Tchr. adult Bible studies First United Meth. Ch., Harlingen and Austin, Tex., Bellaire United Meth. Ch., Houston; instr. Austin C.C., 1982-90; tchr. Austin Ind. Sch. Dist., 1982-92; writer, lectr. Vol. Meth. Hosp., Houston, 1993-2001; mem. scholarship com. U. Tex. Mem. Current Study Club Houston (pres. 2000-2002), Tex. Woman's Univ. Nat. Alumnae Assn. (pres. 2001-2002 Houston chpt.), Delta Kappa Gamma. Home: 5220 Weslayan St # 201 Houston TX 77005-1095 E-mail: emilyjrice@aol.com.

RICE, GARY RUSSELL, special education educator; b. Franklin, Pa., Oct. 11, 1951; s. Robert Russell and Della Elizabeth Rice. Grad. cum laude, Cleve. State U., 1973. Cert. polit. sci. tchr., learning disabilities, behavioral disorders, Ohio. Substitute tchr. Lakewood, Rocky River, Westlake (Ohio) Schs., 1973-77; instr. West Side Inst. Tech., Cleve., 1977-78; spl. edn. tchr. Parma (Ohio) City Sch. Dist., 1978—. Learning disabilities tutor, Lakewood, 1974-75; guitar cons. Rock and Roll Hall of Fame and Mus., Cleve. Asst. scoutmaster, leader Boy Scouts Am., Cleve.; former Sunday sch. tchr. local chs., Lakewood; spkr. to various groups on Exceptional Children, the Holocaust and Native Americans; charter mem. U.S. Holocaust Meml. Mus. Recipient Outstanding Spl. Educator award Parma PTA Spl. Edn. com., 1985, Thanks to Tchrs. award Sta. TV-8 WJW, Cleve., 1994, dist. award of merit Boy Scouts Am., 1997. Mem. Parma Edn. Assn., Cleve. Fedn. Musicians, DeMolay (active Legion of Honor 1996), Masons, Shriners. Avocations: music, photography.

RICE, JAMES ROBERT, engineering scientist, geophysicist; b. Frederick, Md., Dec. 3, 1940; s. Donald Blessing and Mary Celia (Santangelo) R.; m. Renata Dmowska, Feb. 28, 1981; children by previous marriage: Douglas, Jonathan. BS, Lehigh U., 1962, Sc.M., 1963, PhD, 1964; DSc (hon.), Northwestern U., Evanston, Ill., 1996, Brown U., 1997. Postdoctoral fellow Brown U., Providence, 1964-65, asst. prof. engring., 1965-68, assoc. prof., 1968-70, prof., 1970-81, Ballou prof. theoretical and applied mechanics, 1973-81; McKay prof. engring. sci. and geophysics Harvard U., Cambridge, Mass., 1981—. Recipient awards for sci. publs. ASME, awards for sci. publs. ASTM, awards for sci. publs. U.S. Nat. Com. Rock Mechanics, Timoshenko medal Am. Soc of Mechanical Engineers, 1994, Francis J. Clamer medal Franklin Institute, 1996, Arpad L. Nadai award, 1996. Fellow ASME, AAAS; mem. NAS, NAE, ASCE, Am. Geophys. Union, Fgn. Mem. Royal Soc. Achievements include research contbns. to solid mechanics, materials sci. and geophysics. Office: Harvard U Divsn Engring Applied Sci Cambridge MA 02138

RICE, JOHN RISCHARD, computer scientist, researcher, educator; b. Tulsa, June 6, 1934; s. John Coykendal Kirk and Margaret Lucille (Rischard) R.; m. Nancy Ann Bradfield, Dec. 19, 1954; children: Amy Lynn, Jenna Margaret. BS, Okla. State U., 1954, MS, 1956; PhD, Calif. Inst. Tech., 1959. Postdoctoral fellow Nat. Bur. Standards, Washington, 1959-60; rsch. mathematician GM Rsch. Labs., Warren, Mich., 1960-64; prof. Purdue U., West Lafayette, Ind., 1964-89, head dept. computer sci., 1983-96, disting. prof., 1989—. Editor-in-chief ACM Trans. Math. Software, N.Y.C., 1975-93; chmn. ACM-Signum, N.Y.C., 1977-79; dir. Computing Rsch. Bd., Washington, 1987-94; chair Computing Rsch. Assn., Washington, 1991-93. Author: The Approximation of Functions, 1964, Vol. 2, 1969, Numerical Methods, Software and Analysis, 1983; author and editor: Mathematical Software, 1971; editor: Intelligent Scientific Software Systems, 1991. Fellow AAAS, ACM (George Forsythe Meml. lectr. 1975); mem. IFIP (working group 2.5, vice chmn. 1977-91), Soc. Indsl. and Applied Math., Nat. Acad. Engring., Phi Kappa Phi. Home: 112 E Navajo St West Lafayette IN 47906-2153 Office: Purdue U Computer Sci Dept West Lafayette IN 47907

RICE, JOY KATHARINE, psychologist, educational policy studies and women's studies educator; b. Oak Park, Ill., Mar. 26, 1939; d. Joseph Theodore and Margaret Sophia (Bednarik) Straka; m. David Gordon Rice, Sept. 1, 1962; children: Scott Alan, Andrew David. B.F.A. with high honors, U. Ill., Urbana, 1960; MS, U. Wis., Madison, 1962, MS, 1964, PhD, 1967. Lic. clin. psychologist. USPHS predoctoral fellow dept. psychiatry Med. Sch. U. Wis., Madison, 1964-65, asst. dir. Counseling Ctr., 1966-74, dir. Office Continuing Edn. Svcs., 1972-78, prof. ednl. policy studies and women's studies, 1974-95, clin. prof. psychiatry, 1995—; pvt. practice psychology Psychiat. Svcs., S.C., Madison, 1967—. Mem. State Wis. Ednl. Approval Bd., Madison, 1972-73; mem. Adult Edn. Commn., U.S. Office Career Edn., Washington, 1978 Author: Living Through Divorce, A Developmental Approach to Divorce Therapy, 1985, 2d edit., 1989; edit. bd. Lifelong Learning, 1979-86; cons. editor Psychology of Women Quar., 1986-88, assoc. editor, 1989-94; cons. editor Handbook of Adult and Continuing Education, 1989, Encyclopedia of Women and Gender, 2001; contbr. articles to profl. jours. Knapp fellow U. Wis.-Madison, 1960-62, teaching fellow, 1962-63; recipient Disting. Achievement award Ednl. Press Assn. Am., 1992. Fellow APA (exec. bd. psychology of women divsn. 1994—, internat. psychology divsn. 1998—, chair internat. com. for women 2000-02, exec. bd. 1998—, Disting. Leadership award 2000-02); mem. Nat. Assn. Women in Edn. (editl. bd. jour. 1984-88, cons. editor Initiatives 1988-91), Internat. Coun. Psychologists (sec. 2000—, bd. dirs. 2003—), Am. Assn. Continuing and Adult Edn. (meritorious svc. award 1978-80, 82), TEMPO Internat. (bd. dirs., sec. 2000—), Big Bros. Big Sisters of Dane County (pres. 2002, bd. dirs. 1995—), Rotary Internat., Phi Delta Kappa. Avocations: interior design, collecting art, gardening, travel. Home: 4230 Waban Hl Madison WI 53711-3711 Office: 2727 Marshall Ct Madison WI 53705-2255 E-mail: jkrice@facstaff.wisc.edu.

RICE, KENNETH LLOYD, environmental services executive, educator; b. St. Paul, June 17, 1937; m. Elizabeth Lyman VanKat, May 11, 1963 (dec. 1992); children: Anne Louise, Ken neth L. Jr., Elizabeth Ellen, Stephen James. BBA, U. Wis., 1959; postgrad., N.Y. Inst. Finance, 1960-64; completed 71st Advanced Mgmt. Program, Harvard U., 1975. Trainee, asst. br. mgr. JW Sparks & Co., St. Paul, 1959-64, mgr. corp. fin., 1964-70; mgr. corp. finance The Milw. Co., St. Paul, 1969-70; dir. finance Cedar Riverside Assocs. Inc., Mpls., 1970-71; prin. Kenneth L. Rice & Assocs., St. Paul, 1971-88; investment banking chmn., CEO Allegro Tech. Corp., St. Paul, 1988-92; prof. mgmt. and environ. econs. Budapest (Hungary) U. Econs. Scis., from 1992; chmn., edtl. bd. New Horizons Magazine, Hungary, from 1995. Minn. del. World Trade Ctrs. Assn., Budapest, Hungary, 1987; dir. Hungarian U.S. Fulbright, 1995-97. Founder Chimera Theatre, St. Paul, 1969; pres. Liberty Pla. Non-Profit Housing Project, St. Paul, 1975-77; judge Leadership Fellows Bush Found., St. Paul, 1985-90; co-chmn. Parents Fund, Macalester Coll., St. Paul, 1985-87; Hungary hon. rep. State of Minn. Trade Office, 1992-99. Bush Leadership fellow, 1974. Mem. Harvard Bus. Club Minn.(local bd. dirs. 1978-83), Harvard Club of Hungary (v.p. 1994—), Am. C. of C. in Hungary (dir. 1995-97, v.p. 1997), Masons, KT, Shriners. Home: Budapest, Hungary. Died May 24, 2001.

RICE, LINDA ANGEL, music educator; b. New Philadelphia, Ohio, July 23, 1939; d. Leonard Leroy and Anna Mary (Fackler) Angel; m. James Kinsey Rice, June 9, 1963; children: Deborah Lynn, Diane Rice Sequra. BS in Music Edn., Muskingum Coll., 1961. Organist, choir dir., Ohio, 1957-63; organist, 1963-70; tchr. music Jr. High and Elem. Schs., Ohio, 1962-63, Elem. Sch., Calif., 1963-67; organist Albuquerque, 1970—; pvt. practice pvt. practice, Albuquerque, 1970—; founder Albuquerque Girl Choir, 1991—. Pres. N.Mex. Symphony Chorus, Albuquerque, 1991-92, bd. dirs., 1991-95, pres., 1988-89. Mem. Am. Choral Condrs. Guild, Am. Guild Organists (exec. bd. 1967), Sigma Alpha Iota. Avocations: knitting, travel, gardening. Home: 12428 Chelwood Trl NE Albuquerque NM 87112-4628 Office: Albuquerque Girl Choir PO Box 23037 Albuquerque NM 87192-1037

RICE, MARGARET LUCILLE, computer technology educator; b. Saginaw, Mich., May 18, 1958; d. Richard Joseph Glowacki and Carolyn Ann (Roberts) Hajos. BS in Edn., Ctrl. Mich. U., 1980; MA, U. Ala., 1986, PhD, 1991. Instr. U. Ala., Tuscaloosa, 1990-92, asst. rsch. ednl. psychologist, 1988-91, assoc. rsch. ednl. psychologist, 1991-93, assoc. rsch. computer technologist, 1993-94, asst. prof. instnl. computer tech., 1994—. Cons. Tuscaloosa City Schs., 1993-94. Prodn. editor Rsch. in the Schs., 1993-94. Mem. Internat. Reading Assn., Am. Ednl. Rsch. Assn., Mid-South Ednl. Rsch. Assn. (mem. program com. 1993-94, Disting. Dissertation award 1991), Phi Delta Kappa, Mu Sigma Rho. Avocations: reading, creative writing. Home: 2308 Lane Cir Mountain Brook AL 35223-1714 Office: U Ala Box 870302 204 Wilson Hall Tuscaloosa AL 35487

RICE, MARVIN ELWOOD, dentist; b. Mexico, Mo., Nov. 18, 1951; s. Marvin Everett and Una Belle (Hogan) R.; m. Elizabeth Kay Pearl, Mar. 3, 1977; children: Nicole Josephine, Megan Elizabeth, Laura Ellen, Marvin Elliott. BS in Biology, Cen. Mo. State U., 1975; med. asst., Coll. Med. and Dental Assts., 1976; MBA, Cen. Mo. State U., 1978; DDS, U. Mo., 1982. Gen. practice dentistry, Mexico, Mo., 1982—. Commr. TIF commn. City of Mex., 1995. Bd. dirs. Mo. Dental Found., 1992-99; mem. Cmty. Betterment Com., Mexico, 1984-92, PTA, Mexico, 1986; mem. state legis. com. Mo. Sch. Bd. Assn., 1989-97, regional exec. com., 1989, pres., 1995-97, bd. dirs., 1995-97; mem. fed. rels. network Nat. Sch. Bd. Assn., 1992-97; bd. dirs. Mexico Sch. Bd., 1987-2000, v.p. 1989-91, 97-98, treas., 1999-2000, v.p. Choir Boosters, 1999-2000, co-pres. 1999-2000; co-pres. McMillian PTA, Mexico Dixie Gray Band, 1997-98; chmn. Christian edn. com., Sunday Sch. tchr., deacon First Presbyn. Ch., elder, 1999—. Recipient Resolution for Dedicated Svc. for Pub. Edn., Mo. Senate, 1987-2000. Fellow Am. Coll. Dentists, Internat. Coll. Dentists; mem. ADA (Mo. del. 1988-92, pol. action com. 1997—), Mo. Dental Assn. (comms. com. 1983-88, peer rev. com. 1987—, coun. dental health 1987, alt. to ho. of dels. 1983-86, del. 1987-88, chmn. peer rev. com. 1989-90, chmn. use tax com. 1990-91, sec. treas. 1992-99, bd. dirs. 1992-99, found. bd. 1994-99, Disting. Svc. award 1999), Columbia Dental Soc., Cen. Dental Soc. (v.p., pres.-elect 1987-88, pres. 1988-89), Mo. Dental Mgmt. Svcs. (bd. dirs. 1995—, treas.), Mo. Dental Ins. Svcs. (bd. dirs. 1993—, sec.-treas. 1999—), Mexico Area C. of C. (chmn. edn. com. 1995, 96, 97-98), Kiwanis (treas. Mex. 1983, v.p. 1984, pres. 1986—, chmn. youth svcs. com. 2002-03, Disting. Svc. award 1993), Sigma Tau Gamma (Outstanding Alumnus 1977, bd. dirs., treas. 1983-89). Republican. Avocations: gardening, art, canoeing, fishing, drummer ultrasound group. Home: 11340 Audrain Road 9907 Mexico MO 65265-7213 Office: 703 Medical Park Dr Mexico MO 65265-3727

RICE, PATRICIA OPPENHEIM LEVIN, special education educator, consultant; b. Detroit, Apr. 5, 1932; d. Royal A. and Elsa (Freeman) Oppenheim; m. Charles L. Levin, Feb. 21, 1956 (div. Dec. 1981); children: Arthur David, Amy Ragen, Fredrick Stuart; m. Howard T. Rice, Dec. 16, 1990 (div. Apr. 1994). AB in History, U. Mich., 1954, PhD, 1981; MEd, Marygrove Coll., 1973. Cert. elem. tchr., Mich. Tchr. reading and learning disabled, cons., Detroit Pub. Schs., 1967-76; assoc. prof., coord. spl. edn., Marygrove Coll., 1976-86; adj. prof. Oakland U., 1987-90, U. Miami, 1989-95; edn. curriculum cons. Lady Elizabeth Sch., Jávea (Alicante) Spain, 1988-91; v.p. Machpelah Cemetary Bd., Ferndale, Mich., 1978-87, co-pres., 1987—; adv. bd. Eton Acad., Birmingham, Mich., 1991-93; workshop presenter Dade City Schs., 1992-97; presenter in field. Mem. Mich. regional bd. ORT, 1965-68; mil. affairs and youth svcs. S.E. Mich. chpt. ARC Bd., 1973-79; v.p. exec. bd. Women's Aux. Children's Hosp. Mich., 1968-73; bd. dirs. women's com. United Cmty. Svcs., 1968-73; judge Dade County Schs. for Tchr. Grants, 1996—; bd. dirs. Detroit Grand Opera Assn., 1970-75; com. chair morning of music benefits Detroit Symphony Orch.; torch drive area chmn. United Found., 1967-70; benefactor Fla. Grand Opera, 1990-2001, grand benefactor, 2002—, guild exec. bd., 1992-, v.p., 1998-99, co-pres. 2000-02, chair, found. bd. dirs., 2000-01; guild exec. bd. Miami City Ballet, 1996-2000, Choreographers Cir., 1990-; chair Lincoln Rd. Walk, 1996, co-chair All Star Luncheon, 1996, Ball Com., 1992; active Diabetes Rsch. Inst. & Found. Love & Hope Com., Fla. Concert Assn. Cresendo Soc., 1993-97, Villa Maria Angel, 1996—, v.p. angel bd. 1998—, found. bd. dirs. 2000—; panel judge Dada County Cultural Affairs Coun., 2002—. Mem. NAACP (life), Navy League, Greater Miami Social Register, Citizens Interested in the Arts (charter, grant chair, exec. bd. 1997—), Williams Island Club, Turnberry Isle Golf Club (signature), Miami Shores Country Club, Surf Club, Phi Delta Kappa, Pi Lambda Theta. E-mail: oceania32@msn.com.

RICE, PAUL JACKSON, lawyer, educator; b. East St. Louis, Ill., July 15, 1938; s. Ray Jackson and Mary Margaret (Campbell) Rice; m. Carole Jeanne Valentine, June 6, 1959; children: Rebecca Jeanne Ross, Melissa Ann Hansen, Paul Jackson Jr. BA, U. Mo., 1960, JD, 1962; LLM, Northwestern U., 1970; student, Command and Gen. Staff Coll., 1974-75, Army War Coll., 1982-83. Bar: Mo. 1962, Ill. 1969, U.S. Dist. Ct. (no. dist.) Ill. 1970, U.S. Supreme Ct. 1972, U.S. Ct. Appeals (DC cir.) 1991, DC 1993, U.S. Dist. Ct. DC 2000. Commd. 1st lt. U.S. Army, 1962, advanced through grades to col., 1980; asst. judge advocate 4th Armored Div., Goeppingen, Germany, 1966-69; dep. staff judge advocate 1st Cavalry Div., Vietnam, 1970-71; inst., prof. Judge Adv. Gen. Sch., Charlottesville, Va., 1971-74, commdt., dean, 1985-88; br. chief Gen. Law Br., Pentagon, 1975-78; chief adminstrv. law div. Office Judge Adv. Gen., Pentagon, Washington, 1978-79; staff judge adv. 1st Inf. Div., Ft. Riley, Kans., 1979-82, V Corps U.S. Army, Frankfurt, Germany, 1983-85, USACAC, Ft. Leavenworth, Kans., 1989-90; faculty Indsl. Coll. Armed Forces, 1988-89; chief counsel Nat. Hwy. Traffic Safety Adminstrn., Washington, 1990-93; ptnr. Arent Fox Kintner Plotkin & Kahn, Washington, 1993—. Contbr. articles to profl. jours. Recipient Granted Legal Svc. award, State of Hessen, Germany, 1985, cert. of merit, U. Mo. Alumni Assn., 1987. Mem.: Ctr. Law and Nat. Security, Mo. Bar Assn., Lion Tamers, Phi Delta Phi. Methodist. Avocations: writing, reading, golf. Home: 7835 Vervain Ct Springfield VA 22152-3107 Office: Arent Fox Kintner Plotkin & Kahn 1050 Connecticut Ave NW Washington DC 20036-5339 E-mail: ricepj@arentfox.com.

RICE, ROBERT ARNOT, school administrator; b. San Francisco, Apr. 4, 1911; s. Abraham Lincoln and Mary Eugenia (Arnot) R.; m. Frances Von Dorsten, Aug. 15, 1936 (dec. sept. 1986); m. Esther Roossink Railton, July 11, 1989. BA, U. Calif., Berkeley, 1934, MA, 1947; postgrad., Columbia U., 1948. Various ednl. positions, 1935-61; supr. sci. and math. Berkeley Unified Sch. Dist., 1961-64; adminstr. NSF Summer Insts. for Sci. Tchr., U. Calif., Berkeley, 1957-65; dir. On Target Sch., Berkeley Unified Sch. Dist., 1971-73; coord. pub. programs Lawrence Hall of Sci., 1964-70; work experience edn. coord. Berkeley Unified Sch. Dist., 1973-75; exec. dir. Calif. Sci. Tchr. Assn., 1964-90; dir. No. Calif.-Western Nev. Jr. Sci. and Humanities Symposium, 1962-93. Cons. Berkley Unified Sch. Dist., 1964-70; bd. dirs. San Francisco Bay Area Sci. Fair, 1960—; mem. steering com. Chem. Study, 1960-75; coord. Industry Initiatives for Sci. and Math. Edn. Program, 1985-86; dir. Industry Initiatives for Sci. and Math. Edn. Acad., 1987; mem. Internat. Sci. and Engring. Fair Coun., Sci. Svc., Inc., 1959-68; dir. 18th Internat. Sci. and Engring. Fair, San Francisco, 1967; exec. dir. San Francisco Bay Area Sci. Fair, 1954-59; resource cons. Calif. Farm Bur. Fedn.-Youth Power Conf., Asilomar, 1966; judging chair Nat. Jr. Sci. and Humanities Symposium, 1993-97. Contbr. articles to profl. publs. Bd. dirs. Calif. Heart Assn., 1966-71, Alameda County Heart Assn., 1966-71; mem. Cen. Calif. Sci. Com., 1965-70; mem. rsch. com. Alameda County TB and Health Assn., 1965-69, mem. adv. com., 1965-69. Named to Berkeley H.S. Hall of Fame, 1994; recipient Benjamin Ide Wheeler medal, 1985, San Francisco Bay Area Sci. Fair award, Calif. Acad. Sci., 1970, Armed Forces Chem. Assn. award for outstanding chemistry tchr. in San Francisco Bay Area, 1965, Robert Rice award, No. Calif. JSHS Competition, 1996, 50-yr. award for starting the San Francisco Bay Area Sci. Fair, 2003. Mem. NEA, Nat. Sci. Tchrs. Assn. (pres. 1960-61, region VIII dir. 1955-57, Calif. state dir. 1949-56, mem. chemistry com. 1956-60, Disting. Svc. to Sci. Edn. award 1986), No. Calif. Com. on Problem Solving in Sci., Calif. Sci. Tchrs. Assn. (pres. no. sect. 1949-50, Disting. Svc. to Sci. Tchg. award 1981, Lifetime Achievement award 1999), Calif. Tchrs. Assn., N.C. Sci. Specialists, Berkeley Kiwanis Club, Phi Delta Kappa (pres. Lambda chpt. 1942-43). Office: U Calif Berkeley Lawrence Hall Of Sci Berkeley CA 94720-0001

RICE, STEPHEN LANDON, university official; b. Oakland, Calif., Nov. 23, 1941; s. Landon Frederick and E. Genevieve (Hunt) R.; m. Penny Louise Baum, Dec. 29, 1965; children: Andrew Landon, Katherine Grace Hall. BS, U. Calif., Berkeley, 1964, MEngring., 1969, PhD, 1972. Registered profl. engr., Fla. Design engr. Lawrence Berkeley Lab., 1964-69; asst. prof. U. Conn., Storrs, 1972-77, assoc. prof., 1977-82, prof., 1982-83; prof., chmn. U. Ctrl. Fla., Orlando, 1983-88, assoc. dean, rsch. dir., 1988-96, interim asst. v.p. acad. affairs, 1995-96; assoc. provost for rsch. U. Nev., Las Vegas, 1996—2001, vice provost for rsch., 2001—03, assoc. v.p. rsch. and econ. devel., 2003—. Program evaluator ASME/ABET, N.Y.C., 1988-93; NASA predoctoral fellow, 1969-72; U.S. del. to Internat. Rsch. Group, Orgn. for Econ. Cmty. Devel., 1993-98. Inventor impact wear apparatus, 1975. Named Outstanding Young Faculty Dow/ASEE, 1975, Eminent Engr., Tau Beta Pi, 1988; Fulbright rsch. scholar U. South Pacific, 1978-79; participant Fulbright exch. program for adminstrs. in internat. edn., Germany, 1995. Fellow ASME; mem. Am. Soc. Engring. Edn., Theta Delta Chi. Avocations: sailing, tennis, hiking. Office: U Nev Box 451046 4505 S Maryland Pkwy Las Vegas NV 89154-1046

RICE, SUE ANN, dean, industrial and organizational psychologist; b. Ponca City, Okla., Sept. 17, 1934; d. Alfred and Helen (Revard) R. BS in Edn., U. Okla., 1956; MA, Cath. U., 1979, PhD, 1988. Ensign USN, 1956, advanced through grades to comdr., 1973; ednl. svcs. officer 9th Naval Dist., Great Lakes, Ill., 1956-58; adminstr., asst. staff, comdr. in-chief Pacific Fleet, Honolulu, 1958-61; head edn. div. Naval Air Sta., Lemoore, Calif., 1961-63; instr., acad. dir. Women Officers' Sch., Newport, R.I., 1963-66; head. tng. div. Naval Command Systems Support Activity, Washington, 1966-70; head, ops. support sec., comdr.-in-chief Lant, Norfolk, Va., 1970-74; sr. U.S. rep. NATO, subgroup 5 orgn. JCS, Washington, 1974-77; ret. USN, 1977; head vocation office Archdiocese of Washington, 1977-78; cons. Notre Dame Inst., Arlington, Va., 1989-97, dean of students, 1990-95. Lectr. Cath. U. Am., Washington, 1983-84; bd. dirs. Villa Cortona Apostolic Ctr., Bethesda, 1984-94. Tech. reviewer Personnel Administration, 1964; editor (newsletter) Vocation News, 1978. Conoco scholarship Continental Oil Co., 1952-56; recipient Meritorious Svc. medal Pres. of U.S., 1977, rsch. grant Cath. U., Sigma Xi, 1986. Mem.: Lay Women's Assn. (internat. v.p., internat. mem. fin. com., nat. v.p.), Cath. War Vets. (nat. membership task force com., nat. youth act com., vets. affairs com.), Gamma Phi Beta, Kappa Delta Pi. Roman Catholic. Avocations: travel, music, gardening, woodworking. Home: PO Box 2742 Ponca City OK 74604-2742

RICE-DIETRICH, THERESE ANN, elementary education educator; b. Washington, June 27, 1954; d. Harry Woodrow and Catherine Frances (Hefinger) Rice; m. Robert Lynn Dietrich, Aug. 21, 1979; children: Tasha Marie, Robin Michael, Christopher Lee, Dana Jeffrey. BS in Music Edn., U. Ala., Tuscaloosa, 1976; M. Music in Music Therapy, Fla. State U., 1978. Cert. tchr., Nev. Music therapist Washoe County Sch. Dist., Reno, Nev., 1978-86, spl. edn. tchr., 1986-89, elem. edn. tchr., 1989—. Mem. Nat. Assn. Tchrs. of Math., Nat. Coun. Tchrs. of English, Washoe County Tchrs.' Assn. (Disting. Performance award 1988), Nev. State Edn. Assn., Phi Kappa Phi, Internat. Reading Assn.

RICH, CYNTHIA GAY, elementary education educator; b. Jamestown, N.Y., Feb. 16, 1945; d. Alpheus T. and Gloria (Adler) Gable; m. David G. Rich, Aug. 26, 1967. BA in Elem. Edn., SUNY, Fredonia, 1967, MS in Elem. Edn. and Remedial Reading, 1971; EdD in Elem. Edn., Gifted and Talented Edn., Remedial Reading and Early Childhood, SUNY, Buffalo, 1989. Cert. tchr. elem., remedial reading, N.Y. Tchr. Ft. Carson (Colo.) Sch., 1967-68, Frewsburg (N.Y.) Cen. Sch., 1968-2000; ret., 2000. Cheerleading advisor Frewsburg (N.Y.) Cen. Sch., 1977-79; coun. for Spl. Edn., 1990-2000, student adv. bd., 1990-2000, chmn. early literacy com., 1998-2000, Reading coun., 1991-2000; dance instr. Heron's Glen, Ft. Myers, Fla., 2002—, Pine Lakes, Ft. Myers, Fla., 2002—; presenter in field. Vol. Am. Cancer Soc., Am. Heart Assn., Mental Health Assn.; mem. Parent, Student and Tchr. Assn., 1968-2000, Chautauqua County Humane Soc., 1990—; mem. ednl. commn. First United Meth. Ch., Jamestown, N.Y., mem. parish commn., also Altar Guild, United Meth. Women; mem. ednl. commn. Good Shepherd Meth. Ch. of N. Fort Myers, Fla., 2000—; patron Little Theater of Jamestown, 1968—, Repertory Theater of Ft. Myers, 2000—, Royal Palm Theater of Ft. Myers, 2000—; mem. Herons Glen Choral Soc., Ft. Myers. Mem. AAUW (rec. sec., chairperson numerous programs, conv. del., v.p. 1994—), Bus. and Profl. Women (chairperson New Careerist), Internat. Reading Assn. (presenter New Orleans conf. 1989, Phila. conf. 1986), Green Thumb Garden Club, Order Ea. Star, Shriners Aux., Consistory Aux., Soc. for Prevention Cruelty Animals, Kiwanis (Disting. Kiwanian 1989-92, pres. 1991-93, Disting. Pres. Southwestern N.Y. 1991-92), Kiwanis Wives (pres.), Phi Delta Kappa (life, rec. sec., historian 1980—, Educator of Yr. 1988, Researcher of Yr. 1988).

RICH, DOROTHY KOVITZ, writer, educational administrator; BA in Journalism and Psychology, Wayne U.; MA, Columbia U.; EdD, Catholic U. Founder, pres. The Home and Sch. Inst., Inc., Washington, 1964—. Adv. coun. Nat. Health Edn. Consortium; adv. com. Ctr. for Workplace Prep. and Quality Edn., U.S. C. of C.; mem. readiness to learn task force U.S. Dept. Edn., urban edn. team Coun. Gt. City Schs.; legislative nat. initiatives including work on Family/Sch. Partnership Act, 1989, Improving America's Edn. Act, 1994; formulator New Partnerships for Student Achievement program, 1987; creator MegaSkills Edn. Ctr. The Home and Sch. Inst. Inc., 1990; designer MegaSkills Leader Tng. for Parent Workshops, 1988, MegaSkills Essentials for the Classroom, 1991, Learning and Working program for sch.-to-work initiatives, 1996, Career Megaskills, 1999, New MegaSkills Bond Tchr./Parent Partnership, 1994, Career MegaSkills materials and tng., 1998, Adult MegaSkills for Profl. Growth, 1999, MegaSkills Behavior Mgmt. Kit, 2002; developer NEA/MegaSkills nat. mentor tng. initiative, 2000—, MegaSkills for the Job, 2002, Adult MegaSkills and MegaSkills for Teachers, 2002., MegaSkills for Teachers Video Programs, 2003. Author: MegaSkills in School in Life: The Best Gift You Can Give Your Child, 1988, rev. edit., 1992, What Do We Say? What Do We Do? Vital Solutions for Children's Educationsl Success, 1997, MegaSkills, 3d edit., 1997, 18 tng. books, MegaSkills: Building Children's Achievement for the Information Age, new and expanced edit., 1998, Improving Student Teaching through MegaSkills; TV appearances include The Learning Channel, NBC Today Show, Good Morning Am.; subject of videos nat. ednl. programs in Thailand and China: Families and Schools: Teaming for Success, Survival Guide for Today's Parents. Recipient Am. Woman Leader award, Citation U.S. Dept. Edn., Nat. Gov.'s Assn., Alumni Achievement award in edn. Cath. U., 1992, Golden Apple award for MegaSkills Tchrs. Coll., Columbia U., 1996; grantee John D. and Catherine T. MacArthur Found.; named Washingtonian of Yr. Mem. Nat. Press Club. Office: MegaSkills Edn Ctr Home and Sch Inst Inc 1500 Massachusetts Ave NW Washington DC 20005-1821 E-mail: edstaff@megaskillshsi.com.

RICH, GRETCHEN GARNET, English educator; b. Yankton, S.D., Nov. 28, 1947; d. Harry Lawrence and Winifred Dorothy (Hubler) Speece; children: Lisa Leann Roberts Arhart, Joy Jeannette Roberts. BA in Speech and Theatre, Yankton Coll., 1977; MA in Am. Lit., U. S.D., 1981. Instr. English and speech St. Mary's Sch./Indian Girls, Springfield, S.D., 1977-79; teaching asst. English U. S.D., Vermillion, 1979-81; interim instr. English Wayne (Nebr.) State Coll., 1981-83; instr. English, speech comms., ESL Si Tanka U. at Huron, SD, 1983—. Mem. MLA, Tchrs. of English as Second or Other Lang. Lutheran. Avocations: poetry writing and reading, knitting, movies, music, cross stitchery. Home: 804 Frank Ave SE Huron SD 57350-2949 Office: Si Tanka U 333 9th St SW Huron SD 57350-2798 E-mail: grich@sitanka.edu.

RICH, LAURIE M. federal official, educator; b. Dallas, Tex. Grad., U. N. Tex., Denton. Tchr. Dallas Pub. H.S.; spl. asst. and sr. legis. asst. Sen. Phil Gramm, Washington, 1985—93; acting adminstrv. asst. Sen, Kay Bailey Hutcison, Washington, 1993—95; exec. dir. Tex. Office of State-Fed. Rels., Dallas, 1995—2001; asst. sec. for intergovt. and interagy. affairs U.S. Dept. Edn., Washington, 2001—. Dir. of coalitions Bush/Quayle Campaign, Washington, 1992. Office: US Dept Edn 400 Maryland Ave SW Washington DC 20202

RICH, LONNIE KEVEN, art educator, artist; b. Savannah, Tenn., May 21, 1955; s. Emry Seaman and Mary Kathrine Rich; m. Eva Lillian Doss, Mar. 22, 1993. BFA, Austin Peay State U., 1978; MA, U. Ala., Tuscaloosa, 1985. Tchg. cert. Ala. State Bd. Edn. Chmn. fine arts, art instr. Jefferson County Bd. Edn., Birmingham, Ala., 1978-84; grad. asst. U. Ala., Tuscaloosa, 1984-85; visual merchandising staff Parisian Dept. Stores, Birmingham, 1986-87; chmn. art program, art instr. Lurleen B. Wallace C.C., Andalusia, Ala., 1987—. Discipline com. State Ala. Articulation and Ala. State Bd. Edn., Montgomery, 1996-98; childrens workshop instr., 1998, mem. Cultural Diversity Com., Lurleen B. Wallace Coll.; presenter in field. Recipient Merit award Tennessee Valley Art Ctr., Tuscumbia, Ala., 1996, Resolution for Achievement, Ala. State Bd. Edn., Montgomery, 1997. Mem.: Montgomery Art Guild, Montgomery Mus. Art, Ala. Edn. Assn. Democrat. Avocations: botany, landscaping, cooking. Office: Lurleen B Wallace Cmty Coll Art Program PO Box 1418 Andalusia AL 36420-1418 Fax: 334-222-6567.

RICH, ROBERT F. law and political science educator; married; 3 children. BA in Govt. with honors, Oberlin Coll., 1971; student, Free U. of Berlin, 1971-72; MA in Polit. Scis., U. Chgo., 1973, PhD in Polit. Scis., 1975. Project dir., asst. rsch. scientist Ctr. for Rsch. on Utilization Sci. Knowledge, Inst. Social Rsch., U. Mich., lectr. dept. polit. sci., 1975-76; asst. prof. politics and pub. affairs Princeton U., 1976-82, coord. domestic and urban policy field Woodrow Wilson Sch., 1976-82; assoc. prof. polit. sci., pub. policy and mgmt. Sch. Urban and Pub. Affairs, Carnegie-Mellon U., 1982-86; prof. polit. sci. law, health resources mgmt., med. humanities and social svcs., cmty. health, prof. Inst. Environ. Studies U. Ill., Urbana, 1986—2003, dir. Inst. Govt. and Publ. Affairs, 1986-97, acting head med. humanities and social scis. program Urbana-Champaign, 1988-90, prof. law and polit. sci., health resources mgmt., 1996—, prof. law; fellow Johns Hopkins U. Ctr. for Study of Am. Govt., Washington, 1993-95; Mercator prof. Humboldt U., Berlin, 2002—03. Cons. U.S. Dept. Health and Human Svcs., Carnegie-Mellon U., 1986—, MacArthur Found., NIMH, 1988-89, Food, Drug and Law Inst., HHS, 1989, Am. Career Soc., 1996-97; disting. lectr. German Marshall Fund, Hamburg, Germany, 1997. Author: Social Science Information and Public Policy Making: The Interaction Between Bureaucratic Politics and the Use of Survey Data, 1981; co-author: Government Information Management: A Counter-Report of the Commission on Federal Paperwork, 1980; editor: Translating Evaluation into Policy, 1979, The Knowledge Cycle, 1981, Knowledge, Creation, Diffusion, Utilization, 1979-88, 88-91; co-editor: Competitive Approaches to Health Policy Reform, 1993, Health Policy, Federalism and the Role of the American States, 1996; assoc. editor Society, 1984-88, Evaluation Rev., 1985-89; mem. editl. bd. Policy Studies Rev. Series, 1980-83, Evaluation and Change, 1979-82, Law and Human Behavior, 1983-87; contbr. articles to profl. jours., book chpts. Recipient Emil Limbach Teaching award Carnegie-Mellon U., Sch. Urban and Pub. Affairs, 1985; fellow German Acad. Exch. Program, Fed. Republic Germany, 1971-72, Nat. Opinion Rsch. Ctr. fellow, 1972-73, German Govt. fellow, 1974, Russel Sage Found. Rsch. fellow, 1974-75; vis. scholar Hastings Ctr. for Society, Ethics and Life Scis., 1982. Mem. APA (task force on victims of crime and violence 1982-84), Soc. for Traumatic Stress Studies (bd. dirs. 1980—), World Fedn. for Mental Health (chmn. com. on mental health needs of victims 1985—, vice chmn. 1981-83, Robert F. Rich rsch. ann. award established in his honor, sci. com. on mental health needs of victims 1983), Howard R. Davis Soc. for Knowledge Utilization and Planned Change (pres. 1986-89), Polit. Sci. 400, Policy Studies Assn. (Aaron Wildausky award 1994), Phi Beta Kappa, Sigma Xi, Phi Kappa Phi. Office: U Ill Inst Govt & Pub Affairs 1007 W Nevada St # 204 Urbana IL 61801-3812 also: 815 W Van Buren St Chicago IL 60607-3506

RICHARD, ELAINE, educational therapist; b. N.Y.C., Apr. 24, 1930; d. Jacob Michael and Mildred (Levenstein) Simon; m. Jack Richard, Apr. 11, 1954; children: Mark Steven, Susan Richard Weiller. BA, St. Lawrence U., 1950; MA, Columbia U., 1981. Cert. spl. edn. tchr N.Y. Psychiat. social worker Ralph S. Banay, M.D., N.Y.C., 1950-54, 61-66; asst. to headmaster Dalton Sch., N.Y.C., 1967-70; asst. to prin. Horace Mann Elem. Sch., N.Y.C., 1970-72; dir. admissions Calhoun Sch., N.Y.C., 1972-80; ednl. cons. Ethical Culture Schs., N.Y.C., 1980-81; pvt. practice as ednl. therapist N.Y.C., 1981—. Bd. dirs. Ind. Schs. Admissions Assn. Greater N.Y., 1974-80. Creator "bright ideas" learning games for children, 2000. Mem. Internat. Reading Assn., Nat. Coun. Tchrs. Math., Assn. for Children with Learning Disabilities, N.Y. Orton-Dyslexia Soc. Achievements include development of "bright ideas" learning games for children. Avocations: theater, golf, travel. Home and Office: 501 E 79th St New York NY 10021-0735

RICHARD, PETER WAYNE, math educator; b. Torrington, Conn., June 27, 1961; AS, Northwestern Conn. C.C., 1981; BS, Ctrl. Conn. State U., 1982; MSEd, U. New Eng. Retail sales The Quality Shop, Torrington, Conn., 1977-81; internat. acct. exec. Value Vacations, Winsted, Conn., 1982-84; sales engr. Gavlick Machinery, Bristol, Conn., 1984-86; sales supr., acct. exec. WSNG - Consumer Svc. Radio, Inc., Torrington, 1985-86; mortgage originator Winsted Savs. Bank, 1986-90; tchr. math. Weaver H.S., Hartford, Conn., 1991-94; tchr. honors algebra, pre-algebra Quirk Mid. Sch., Hartford, Conn., 1994-98; tchr. math. Wilby H.S., Waterbury, Conn., 1998—2000; instr. math So. Adirondack Edn. Ctr., Hudson Falls, NY, 2000—. Recipient Chopin Piano award, 1977, Outstanding Senator award, 1982, Lead Learner Leadership award, 1998. Mem. Nat. Assn. Curriculum & Devel. (assoc.). Independent. Avocations: music, hiking. Home: 1237 County Route 47 Argyle NY 12809-3014 Office: So Adirondack Edn Ctr Dix Ave Hudson Falls NY 12839

RICHARDS, AMY KATHLEEN BURR, secondary school educator; b. St. Louis, Mar. 4, 1961; d. Richard Henry Jr. and Marian Ladeen (Sanders) Burr; m. Curt Raymond Richards, Jan. 22, 1983; children: Curtis James, Kyle Mason. BS in Edn., S.W. Mo. State U., Springfield, 1982; MAT in French, Ind. U., 1988. French tchr. Notre Dame HS, St. Louis, 1982-84, Sperreng Mid. Sch., Lindbergh Sch. Dist., St. Louis, 1984-95, Adult Edn. Night Sch., St. Louis, 1983-86; drug awareness coord. Sperreng Mid. Sch., Lindbergh Sch. Dist., St. Louis, 1987—; coord. Lindbergh HS, Dist. Character Edn., St. Louis, 1992—; 3d grade tchr. Kennerly Elem. Sch., Lindbergh Sch. Dist., St. Louis, 1995—2003; French tchr. Lindbergh HS, St. Louis, 2000—. Exec. bd. dirs. Early Childhood Edn. Found., St. Louis, 1994; mem. Drug-Free Schs. Adv. Bd., St. Louis, 1990—. Author action rsch. study A Call for Character, 1994. Coord. Bingo Buddy program Greenpark Nursing Home, 1990—; mem. aux. St. Anthony's Hosp., St. Louis. Named Tchr. of Yr., Lindbergh Sch. Dist., 1994. Mem. Mo. State Tchrs. Assn. (sec., v.p., pres.), Mo. Mid. Sch. Assn., Character Edn. Partnership, Fgn. Lang. Tchrs. Assn., Am. Club for Tchrs. of Fgn. Langs., Advocates of Lang. Learning, Delta Kappa Gamma. Avocation: travel with family. Office: Kennerly Elem Sch 10025 Kennerly Rd Saint Louis MO 63128-2105

RICHARDS, ANN, actress, poet; b. Sydney; came to U.S., 1942; d. Mortimer Delaforce and Marion Bradshaw (Dive) Richards; m. Edmond J. Angelo, Feb. 4, 1949 (dec. Mar. 1983); children: Christopher E., Mark R., Juliet M.; m. Paul M. Kramer, Feb. 14, 1987 (dec. Aug. 1996). Student, Stotts Coll., 1936-37, Studio Sch. of Drama, 1936-38. Actress Cinesound Studio, Australia, 1936-42, Metro-Goldwyn Mayer, 1942-45, Hall Wallis-Paramount, 1945-47, R.K.O., 1947, Eagle-Lion Studios, 1947-48, Edmond Angelo Prodns., 1953, Anthony Buckley Prodns., Australia, 1995. Poetry reader with Robert Pinsky's nat. program Lib. of Congress Bicentennial Project, 1999. Author: The Grieving Senses, 1971, Odyssey for Edmond, 1996, New Poems-Old Themes, 1997; contbr. poetry to anthology Poetry From the Art, 1999; actress films including An American Romance, Love Letters, The Searching Wind, Badman's Territory, Sorry, Wrong Number, Lost Honeymoon, Breakdown, Don't Call Me Girlie, Celluloid Heroes, 1994-95; appearances TV program, film, and tape maker Australia, Time Life Assocs., 1977. Vice pres. Tchr. Rememberance Day Found., 1952—; internat. chmn. Apple of Gold Edn. awards, 1953—. Recipient meritorious svc. citation Govs. of Great Britain, U.S., New Zealand, Australia, 1939-46, Star Pattern award Inst. Profl. Direction, 1951, Cert. of Appreciation award Literacy is Reading Program, 1997, Edward Dean Mus., 1996. Mem. AAUW, Nat. Mus. Women in Arts, San Gorgonio Poets Soc., San Gorgonio Artists Soc., Zeta Phi Eta (v.p. nat. coun. 1970-73).

RICHARDS, BILL ARTHUR, artist, educator; b. Bklyn., Sept. 19, 1944; s. Donald F. and Mildred (Pedersen) R.; m. Judith Fonda Olch, May 2, 1971. BFA, Pratt Inst., 1966; MA, U. Iowa, 1968; MFA, U. N.Mex., 1970. Instr. Sch Visual Arts, N.Y.C., 1977-79, Parsons Sch. Design, N.Y.C., 1986—. Ad. asst. prof. art SUNY, Purchase, 1977—78; vis. asst. prof. fine arts Pratt Inst., Bklyn., 1999—. One-man shows include Irwin Tuttie Gallery, Dallas, 1973, Nancy Hoffman Gallery, N.Y.C., 1980, 85, 89, 96, 2003, Allen R. Hite Inst., U. Louisville, 1983, Moravian Coll., Pa., 1985, Union County Coll., Cranford, N.J., 1986, Fellow NEA, 1977-78, Creative Artists Pub. Svc. Program, 1975-76. Home: Apt 2B 575 Avenue Of The Americas New York NY 10011-2029

RICHARDS, CARMELEETE A. computer training executive, network administrator, consultant; b. Springport, Ind., Feb. 8, 1948; d. Gordon K. and Virginia Christine (New) Brown; 1 child, Annasheril. AA in Elem. Edn., No. Okla. Coll., 1969; BS in Edn., Southwestern State Coll., Weatherford, Okla., 1971; postgrad., Ashland (Ohio) Coll., 1981—; postgrad. in Edn., U. Phoenix, 1994—; postgrad., MEd, AIU. Cert. tchr., Ohio. 6th grade tchr., Scott City, Kans., 1971; salesperson, customer svc. Jafra Cosmetics, 1979-81; br. asst. mgr. Barclays Am. Fin., Columbus, 1981-84; tng. mgr., ednl. dir. Computer Depot, Columbus, Ohio, 1984-85; corp. trainer, exec. sales Litel Telecommunications, Worthington, Ohio, 1985-87; communications cons. Telemarketing Communications of Columbus, Ohio, 1988-89; corp. computer tng. O/E Learning, Troy, Mich., 1989-98; corp. computer trainer ETOP Cols., Ohio, 1989—; dist. asst. network adminstr. Bexley Sch. Dist., 1998-99; dir. tech., computer instr. MCS, 2001—02; info. tech. specialist, trainer Franklin County Common Pleas Ct., 2002—. Pres. PTA, 1981-82. Recipient Outstanding Participation award Dorothy Carnegie Pub. Speaking; winner Ms. Ohio Beauties of Am. Pageant, 1991. Mem. IEEE, NAFE, Am. Soc. for Tng. and Devel., Columbus Computer Soc., Kappa Delta Pi. Baptist. Avocations: western square dancing, bowling, boating, reading, hiking.

RICHARDS, CONSTANCE ELLEN, nursing school administrator, consultant; b. Exeter, N.H., June 21, 1941; d. Edward Nowell and Mary Isabel (Bean) R. BSN, U. Cin., 1971, MA in Pub. Adminstrn., MS in Comprehensive Health Planning, U. Cin., 1973. RN, Mass. Nurse ICU/Opening CCU Syracuse (N.Y.) Meml. Hosp., 1964; instr. ICU and CCU Crouse-Irving Meml. Hosp., Syracuse, 1967-72; instr. cardiovascular, orthopedic and surg. The Christ Hosp., Cin., 1973-78; instr. med.-surg. nursing Md. Gen. Hosp., Balt., 1978-80; night supr. Manor Care Ruxton, Towson, Md., 1980-82; adult health svcs. mgr. Exeter Vis. Nurses Assn., 1982-83; dir. insvc. edn. Bethany Hosp., Framingham, Mass., 1983-85; assoc. prof. nursing Mass. Bay C.C., 1985-86; instr. insvc. edn. Brockton-West Roxbury (Mass.) VA Hosp., 1986-87; staff nurse Charles River Hosp., Wellesley, Mass., 1987-88; night supr. Blair House, Milford, Mass., 1988-89; staff nurse psychogeriatrics Worcester State Hosp., 1989-90; with Agys. Internat. Health Talent Tree, Olsten Health Care Svcs., 1990-92; with indsl. svcs. program, CNA tng. program Northampton State Hosp., 1992; nursing asst., state tester ARC, 1992-93; pres. Caring Hands, Inc., 1993—; DON Excel Health Svcs., Inc., 1993—. Instr. LPN evening program Greater Lowell Regional Vocat. Tech. Sch., 1992-94; adv. bd. Excel Health Svcs., Tewksbury, Mass., 1993-94; pres. Splitap Arts, Lowell, Mass., 1993-94. Author: Freddie the Foot, 1982. Mem. Lowell Hist. Soc., 1994, Women's Network, Lowell, 1994, Crime Watch Group Edn. Component, Lowell, 1994. Recipient academic honors. Mem. ANA, Mass. Nurses Assn., Nat. League Nurses. Democrat. Roman Catholic. Avocations: writing, poetry, miniature dollhouses, painting, church group. Home: 130 South St Apt 57 Lowell MA 01852-3382

RICHARDS, DAVID GLEYRE, German language educator; b. July 27, 1935; s. Oliver L. and Lilian Marie (Powell) R.; m. Annegret Horn, Sept. 3, 1959 (div. 1992); 1 child, Stephanie Suzanne; m. Friederike Hensler, Oct. 11, 1997. BA, U. Utah, 1960; MA, 1961; PhD, U. Calif.-Berkeley, 1968. Asst. prof. German SUNY, Buffalo, 1968-74; assoc. prof., 1974-84; prof., 1984-99; prof. emeritus, 1999—. Author: Georg Buchners Woyzeck, 1975, George Buchner and the Birth of the Modern Drama, 1976, The Hero's Quest for the Self: An Archetypal Approach to Hesse's Demian and other Novels, 1987; editor: (with H. Schulte) Crisis and Culture in Post-Enlightenment Germany: Essays in Honor of Peter Heller, 1993, Exploring the Divided Self: Hermann Hesse's Steppenwolf and its Critics, 1996, Georg Buchner's Woyzeck: A History of Its Criticism, 2001. SUNY grantee, 1973; NEH grantee, 1977-78, Fulbright Commn. grantee, 1980. Rsch. Found. of SUNY fellow, 1982. Democrat. Avocation: photography. E-mail: dgrich1@cs.com.

RICHARDS, HUGH TAYLOR, physics educator; b. Baca County, Colo., Nov. 7, 1918; s. Dean Willard and Kate Bell (Taylor) R.; m. Mildred Elizabeth Paddock, Feb. 11, 1944; children: David Taylor, Thomas Martin, John Willard, Margaret Paddock, Elizabeth Nicholls, Robert Dean. BA, Park Coll., 1939; MA, Rice U., 1940, PhD, 1942. Research assoc. Rice U., Houston, 1942; scientist U. Minn., Mpls., 1942-43, U. Calif. Sci. Labs., Los Alamos, N.Mex., 1943-46; research assoc. U. Wis., Madison, 1946-47, mem. faculty, 1947-52, prof., 1952-88, prof. emeritus, 1988—, physics dept. chairperson, 1960-63, 66-69, 85-88. Assoc. dean Coll. Letters and Sci., U. Wis, 1963-66. Author: Through Los Alamos 1945: Memoirs of a Nuclear Physicist, 1993; contbr. articles to profl. jours. Fellow Am. Phys. Soc.; mem. Am. Assn. Physics Tchrs. Unitarian-Universalist. Achievements include neutron measurements first A-Bomb test; fission neutron (and other) spectra by new photo-emulsion techniques; mock fission neutron source; spherical electrostatic analyzer for precise reaction energy measurements; negative ion sources for accelerators (He ALPHATROSS, SNICS); accurate proton, deuteron, and alpha particle scattering and reaction cross sections; systematics mirror nuclei; isospin violations in nuclear reactions. Home: 1320 12th Ave E Apt # 115 Menomonie WI 54751

RICHARDS, JODY, state legislator, journalism educator, small business owner; b. Columbia, Ky., Feb. 20, 1939; m. Neva Richards; 1 child, Roger. BA in English, Ky. Wesleyan Coll., Owensboro; MA in Journalism, U. Mo., 1962. Mem. faculty in journalism Western Ky. U., from 1962; owner Superior Books, Bowling Green, Ky.; mem. Ky. Ho. of Reps., 1976—, speaker, 1995—; vice chair So. Legislative Conf., 1998—. Mem. adv. bd. dirs. Republic Savs. Bank. Pres. bd. dirs. So. Ky. Fair; bd. dirs. Bowling Green Girls Club, United Way, Warren County (Ky.) Drug Abuse Task Force. Recipient Disting. Svc. award Nat. Art Edn. Assn., 1992. Mem. Bowling Green C. of C., Bowling Green Noon Rotary Club. Office: Ky Ho of Reps State Capitol Frankfort KY 40601

RICHARDS, MARK ANTHONY, special education educator; b. Ft. Payne, Ala., Aug. 18, 1957; s. Marvin C. and Martha Lois (Rice) R.; m. Deborah Ganje-Richards, Mar. 28, 1992. BA, Jacksonville State U., 1983, MS in Edn., 1992. Cert. tchr., Ala., Tex., Ga. Machine operator Republic Steel, Rainsville, Ala., 1976-82; carpenter Bailey Constrn., Midland, Tex., 1982-85; ticket agt. S.W. Airlines, Midland, 1985-86; tchr. Stanton (Tex.) Ind. Sch. Dist., 1986-88; case mgr. Cherokee/Etowah/DeKalb Mental Health, Ft. Payne, 1988-91; tchr. Ft. Payne City Schs., 1990-91, Polk County, Cedartown, Ga., 1992—. Baptist. Avocations: woodworking, vegetable and fruit gardening, writing poetry. Home: PO Box 354 Rainsville AL 35986-0354

RICHARDS, PATRICIA FAE, elementary education educator; b. St. Louis, Mich., June 30, 1950; d. Paul Gerald and Ellen Elizabeth (Anderson) Flowers; m. David Joseph Richards, Apr. 15, 1988; children: Mark David, Emily Elizabeth. BA, Cen. Mich. U., 1971, MA in Gen. Edn., 1978. Elem. tchr. Carson City (Mich.) Elem., 1971-88, chpt. I tchr., 1988—. Union sec. Carson City, 1973-74, region 9 del., 1974-75; rep. Young Author's Conf., Montcalm County, Mich., 1980. Fellow Am. Legion Aux., Womens Club of Carson City. Avocations: camping, photography, gardening. Home: 9484 Mount Hope Rd Carson City MI 48811-9724 Office: Carson City Crystal Schs 115 E Main St Carson City MI 48811-9728

RICHARDS, PAUL LINFORD, physics educator, researcher; b. Ithaca, N.Y., June 4, 1934; s. Lorenzo Adolph and Zilla (Linford) R.; m. Audrey Jarratt, Aug. 24, 1965; children: Elizabeth Anne, Mary-Ann. AB, Harvard U., 1956; PhD, U. Calif., Berkeley, 1960. Postdoctoral fellow U. Cambridge (Eng.), 1959-60; mem. tech. staff Bell Telephone Labs., Murray Hill, N.J., 1960-66; prof. physics U. Calif., Berkeley, 1966—. Faculty sr. scientist Lawrence Berkeley Lab., 1966-2001; advisor NASA, 1975-92, 98—; hon. prof. Miller Inst. Rsch. in Phys. Scis., Berkeley, 1969-70, 87-88, 2001; vis. prof. Ecole Normale Superieure, Paris, 1984, 92; vis. astronomer Paris Obs., 1984. Contbr. over 300 articles to profl. jours. Guggenheim Meml. Found. fellow, Cambridge, Eng., 1973-74; named Calif. Scientist of Yr. Mus. Sci., L.A., 1981; recipient sr. scientist award Alexander von Humboldt Found., Stuttgart, Fed. Republic Germany, 1982, Button medal, 1997; Berkeley Faculty Rsch. lectr. 1991. Mem. NAS; fellow Am. Phys. Soc. (Isakson prize 2000), Am. Acad. Arts and Scis. Avocations: vineyardist, wine making.

RICHARDS-KORTUM, REBECCA RAE, biomedical engineering educator; b. Grand Island, Nebr., Apr. 14, 1964; d. Larry Alan and Linda Mae (Hohnstein) Richards; m. Philip Ted Kortum, May 12, 1985; children: Alexander Scott, Maxwell James, Zachary Alan. BS, U. Nebr., 1985; MS, MIT, 1987, PhD, 1990. Assoc. U. Tex., Austin, 1990—. Named Presdl. Young Investigator NSF, Washington, 1991; NSF presdl. faculty fellow, Washington, 1992; recipient Career Achievement award Assn. Advancement Med. Instrumentation, 1992, Dow Outstanding Young Faculty awd., Am. Soc. for Engineering Education, 1992. Mem. AAAS, Am. Soc. Engrng. Edn. (Outstanding Young Faculty award 1992), Optical Soc. Am., Am. Soc. Photobiology. Achievements include research in photochemistry, photobiology, applied optics and bioengring. Office: U Tex Dept Elec & Computer Engring Austin TX 78712

RICHARDSON, BETTY KEHL, nursing educator, administrator, counselor, researcher; b. Jacksonville, Ill., Mar. 24, 1938; d. Alfred Jason and Hilda (Emmons) Kehl; m. Joseph Richardson, June 27, 1959 (div. 1980); children: Mark Joseph, Stephanie Elaine. BA in Nursing, Sangamon State U., 1975, MA in Adminstrn., 1977; MSN, Med. Coll. Ga., 1980; PhD in Nursing, U. Tex., 1985. Cert. advanced nursing adminstrn., clin. specialist child and adolescent psychiat. nursing ANCC; lic. profl. counselor, marriage and family counselor. Instr. nursing Lincoln Land Community Coll., Springfield, Ill., 1978-79; acting dir. nursing MacMurray Coll., Jacksonville, Ill., 1979-81; asst. prof. Sangamon State U., Springfield, 1981-82; adminstr. children and adolescent programs Shoal Creek Hosp., Austin, 1989-90; nursing dir. Austin State Hosp., 1983-89; therapist San Marcos (Tex.) Treatment Ctr., 1989-90; instr. Austin C.C., 1990—. Pvt. practice psychotherapy, Austin, 1990—. Advising editor: Austin Parent jour.; contbr. articles to profl. jours. Pres. PTA, 1968. Named Outstanding Nurse, Passavant Hosp., 1958, Nurse of Yr., Tex. Nurses Assn., 1994-95; recipient Plaque for Outstanding Leadership, Austin State Hosp., 1989, plaque for svc. to the poor people of Mexico and C.Am. Internat. Good Neighbor Coun. (Austin chpt.) and U. Area Rotary Club, 1995, tchg. excellence award NISOD, 1997; inducted into Rotary Hall of Fame, 1999. Mem. ANA, DAR, Sigma Theta Tau, Phi Kappa Phi. Avocations: swimming, tennis, genealogy, writing. Home: 5207 Doe Valley Ln Austin TX 78759-7103 Office: Austin C C 1020 Grove Blvd Austin TX 78741-3337 E-mail: richb@austin.cc.tx.us.

RICHARDSON, DANIEL PUTNAM, director, educator; b. Boston, Sept. 17, 1941; s. Frederick Leopold William Jr. and Helen (Warren) R.; m. Patricia Randle, Apr. 6, 1962; children: Daniel P. Jr., Randle Bayard, Mary Elizabeth. BA in Econs. and History, U. Denver, 1965; MEd, Harvard U., 1982. Tchr., dir. ops. Woodstock (Vt.) Country Sch., 1970-73; tchr., asst. headmaster Barlow Sch., Amenia, N.Y., 1975-76; tchr., head of sch. Wykham Rise Sch., Washington, Conn., 1976-80; interim head of sch. St. Michael's Sch., Newport, R.I., 1980-81; tchr., head of upper sch. Tatnall Sch., Wilmington, Del., 1982-87, dir. athletics, 1985-86; tchr., head of sch. Cape Henry Collegiate Sch., Virginia Beach, Va., 1987—. Mgr. Gillette Co., 1965-70; pres. Real Estate and Contrn. Co., 1973-75. Treas., bd. dirs. Urban League, Hampton Road, Va., 1990—; treas. Chesapeake Bay Acad. Mem. Nat. Assn. Ind. Schs., AIS (Mid-Atlantic bd. dirs.), Nat. Assn. Prins. Schs. for Girls, Va. Assn. Ind. Schs. (pres.-elect), Two Dans Discussion Group (co-founder 1991-98). Office: Cape Henry Collegiate Sch 1320 Mill Dam Rd Virginia Beach VA 23454-2306

RICHARDSON, EARL STANFORD, university president; b. Westover, Md., Sept. 25, 1943; m. Sheila Bunting; 1 child, Eric. BA, U. Md., Eastern Shore, 1965; MA, U. Pa., 1973, EdD, 1976. Lectr. edn. dept. U. Md., Eastern Shore, 1975-82, acting dir. admissions, 1971-72, dir. career planning and placement, 1974-75, exec. asst. to chancellor, 1975-82; grad. asst. U. Pa., Phila., 1973-74; asst. to pres., Cen. Adminstrn. U. Md., Adelphi, 1982-84; pres. Morgan State U., Balt., 1984—. Mem. segmental adv. com. Md. State Bd. Higher Edn., 1984—. Mem. Policy Com. Greater Balt., 1982—; bd. dirs. Goldseker Found., Balt., 1985—, Balt. Symphony Orch., 1984—. Ford Found. fellow, 1972, Kellogg Found. fellow, 1980. Mem. Phi Kappa Phi. Office: Morgan State U 1700 E Cold Spring Ln Baltimore MD 21251-0002*

RICHARDSON, EARL WILSON, elementary education educator, retired; b. Emporia, Kans., June 4, 1942; s. Clarence Earl and Dorothy Ann (Draper) R.; m. Mariann Hirsig, July 31, 1965; 1 child, Rachelle Ranae. BS in Elem. Edn., Emporia (Kans.) State U., 1964; MEd in Elem. Edn., U. Wyo., 1971. Tchr. 5th-6th grades Alta Vista Elem. Sch., Cheyenne, Wyo., 1964-68, eco-lab. and sci. tchr. 5th-6th grades, 1972-74, 83-84; tchr. 5th-6th grades Bain Elem. Sch., Cheyenne, 1968-97, ret., 1997. Recipient Presdl. award NSF, 1990. Mem. NEA, Wyo. Edn. Assn., Wyo. Sci. Tchrs. Assn. (Excellence in Sci. Teaching award 1984), Phi Delta Kappa. Home: 708 Arapaho St Cheyenne WY 82009-4216

RICHARDSON, EDWARD R. school system administrator; b. Pensacola, Fla., Jan. 24, 1939; s. Edward H. and Doria (Parker) R.; m. Nell C.; children: Merit Lynn Richardson Smith, Laura Leigh. BS, Auburn U., 1962, MEd, 1967, EdD, 1972. Sci. tchr. Montgomery Pub. Schs., Montgomery, Ala., 1962-64, prin., 1967-70, Andalusia High Sch., Andalusia, Ala., 1972-80; asst. prof. Auburn U., Montgomery, 1980-82; supt. Auburn City Schs., Auburn, Ala., 1982-95, state of Ala., Montgomery, 1995—. Bd. mem. So. Regional Edn. Bd., Atlanta, 1989—; co-dir. Ala. Mgmt. Inst. Sch. Leaders, Montgomery, 1980-82. Ednl. advisor Gov. Guy Hunt, Montgomery, 1987—; active Landmarks Found., Montgomery, 1968-69. Named Supt. of Yr., State PTA, Montgomery, 1986-87, Educator of Yr., Andalusia Jaycees, 1973-74. Mem. Ala. Assn. Secondary Sch. Adminstrs. (pres. 1978-79), Ala. Assn. Sch. Adminstrs. (pres. 1986-87), Rotary (Auburn chpt. pres. 1987-88), Capitol Lions Club (pres. 1968-69), Phi Delta Kappa (Auburn U. chpt. pres. 1971-72). Republican. Methodist. Avocations: tennis, reading, gardening. Office: Ala Dept of Edn 50 Ridley St Rm 5114 PO Box 302101 Montgomery AL 36130-2101*

RICHARDSON, EVERETT VERN, hydraulic engineer, educator, administrator, consultant; b. Scottsbluff, Nebr, Jan. 5, 1924; s. Thomas Otis and Jean Marie (Everett) R.; m. Billie Ann Kleckner, June 23, 1948; children: Gail Lee, Thomas Everett, Jerry Ray BS, Colo. State U., 1949, MS, 1960, PhD, 1965. Registered profl. engr., Colo. Hydraulic engr. US Geol. Survey, Wyo., 1949-52, 1953-56, rsch. hydraulic engr., 1956-63, project chief, 1963-68; prof. civil engring. Colo. State U., Ft. Collins, Colo., 1968—88, prof. civil engring., adminstr. engring. rsch. ctr., 1968—88, dir. Egypt water use project, 1977-84, prof. in charge of hydraulic program, 1982-88, dir. hydraulic lab. engring. rsch. ctr., 1982-88, prof. emeritus, 1988—, dir. Egypt irrigation improvement project, 1985-90; dir. Egypt Water Rsch. Ctr. Project, Ft. Collins, Colo., 1988-89; sr. assoc. Ayers Assocs. Inc. (formerly Resource Cons./Engr., Inc.), Ft. Collins, 1989—. Dir. Consortium for Internat. Devel., Tucson, Ariz., 1972-87; developer stream stability and scour at hwy. bridges course for State Dept. Transps. for NHI, FHWA; investigator for NTSB 1987 I-90 bridge failure, NY, 1997, railroad bridge failure, Ariz., CALTRAN of 1995 I-5 bridge failure; cons. in field; lectr. in field. Sr. author: Highways in the River Environment: Hydraulic and Environmental Considerations, FHWA, 1975, 1990, Evaluating Scour at Bridge, FHWA, 1991, 1993, 1995, 2001, FHWA Hydr. Design Series No. 6: River Engineering for Highway Encroachments, 2001; contbr. papers TRB 9th Internat. Bridge Mgmt. Conf., 2003, to Engring. and Civil Engring. Handbook, 1995, Handbook of Fluid Dynamics and Fluid Machinery, 1996, Water Resources-Environmental Planning, Management and Development, 1996, articles to profl. jours., chapters to books. Mem. Ft. Collins Water Bd., 1969-84; mem. NY State Bridge Safety Assurance Task Force, 1988-91. Decorated Bronze Star, Purple Heart, Combat Infantry Badge; U.S. Govt. fellow MIT, 1962-63. Fellow: ASCE (chair task com., bridge scour rsch. 1990—96, vice chair 1997—2002, editor Compendium of Stream Stability and Scour Papers 1991—98, J.S. Stevens award 1961, hydraulics divsn. task com. excellence award 1993, Hans Albert Einstein award 1996); mem.: Internat. Congress for Irrigation and Drainage (bd. dirs.), Sigma Xi, Sigma Tau, Chi Epsilon. Home: 824 Gregory Rd Fort Collins CO 80524-1504 Office: Ayres Assocs PO Box 270460 Fort Collins CO 80527-0460

RICHARDSON, IRENE M. management consultant; m. Joseph Richardson, Dec. 27, 1960; children: Pamela, Joseph, John, Karen. BS, Ramapo Coll., Mahwah, N.J., 1981; MBA, Farleigh Dickinson U., 1987; nursing diploma summa cum laude, St. Thomas Sch. Nursing, Nashville, 1959. RN, N.J.; cert. sr. profl. in human resources. Clin. instr. St. Thomas Hosp., Nashville; coord. edn., staff nurse St. Clare's Hosp., Denville, N.J.; pres. Cygnus Assocs., Inc., Kinnelon, N.J., 1986—; dir. edn. and tng. Northwest Covenant Med. Ctr. (formerly St. Clares Riverside), Denville, N.J., 1981-97; pvt. practice mgmt. cons. Kinnelon, N.J., 1997—. Author: RN Job Satisfaction, 1987. U.S. Pub. Health Svc. scholar. Mem. Soc. Human Resource Mgmt., Soc. for Health Care Edn. and Tng. N.J. (bd. dirs.), Women's Svc. Orgn. (pres. 1995-96, 2002—, sec. 1998—). Home: 65 Fayson Lake Rd Kinnelon NJ 07405-3129

RICHARDSON, JOHN THOMAS, academic administrator, clergyman; b. Dallas, Dec. 20, 1923; s. Patrick and Mary (Walsh) R. BA, St. Mary's Sem., Perryville, Mo., 1946; S.T.D., Angelicum U., Rome, Italy, 1951; MA, St. Louis U., 1954. Prof. theology, dean studies Kenrick Sem., St. Louis, 1951-54; lectr. Webster Coll., 1954; dean Grad. Sch. DePaul U., Chgo., 1954-60, exec. v.p., dean faculties, 1960-81, pres., 1981-93; prof. DePaul U. Coll. Law, Chgo., 1955; chancellor DePaul U., Chgo., 1993—. Vis. mem. theology faculty Christ the King Major Sem., Nyeri, Kenya, East Africa, 1997—. Trustee DePaul U., Chgo., 1954-93, life trustee, 1993—.—. Office: De Paul U 1 E Jackson Blvd Chicago IL 60604-2287

RICHARDSON, JOSEPH BLANCET, retired science educator, educational consultant; b. Louisville, Nov. 12, 1936; m. Mary Irene Murphy, Dec. 27, 1960; children: Pamela, Joseph Blancet Jr., John, Karen. BSCE, The Citadel, 1958; BA in Zoology with high honors, Rutgers U., 1973, PhD in Zoology, 1979; MS in Anatomy, N.Y. Med. Coll., 1975; cert. in work life ministry, Immaculate Conception Sem., 2001. Ordained deacon Roman Cath. Ch., 1995. Design engr. Ky. Hwy. Dept., 1958-59; tech. rep. Shell Oil Co., Balt., 1968-72; asst. prof. biology Ramapo Coll., Mahwah, NJ, 1976-80, from program coord. biology to dir. campus planning, 1979-86; pres. Richardson Recreational Svcs., Inc., Kinnelon, NJ, 1981-88, Whitehall Assocs., Inc., Kinnelon, 1986—. Dir. recreational water testing programs Kinnelon Environ. Commn., 1977—82; trustee Kinnelon Bd. Edn., 1989—94; pres. Morris County Ednl. Svcs. Commn., 1991—92; deacon Our Lady of Mt. Carmel Roman Cath. Ch., Boonton, NJ, 2001; coord. Work Life Ministry Diocese of Paterson, NJ, 1997—; bd. dirs. St. Ephrem Found., Inc., 1998—. Capt. U.S. Army, 1959—68, Vietnam. Mem.: Coun. Ednl. Facilities Planners, N.Y. Acad. Sci., Soc. Am. Mil. Engrs., N.J. Assn. Sch. Bus. Ofcls., N.J. Assn. Sch. Bus. Adminstrs., N.J. Sch. Bds. Assn., N.Y. Med. Coll. Alumni Assn., Rutgers U. Alumni Assn., Citadel Alumni Assn., Sigma Xi. Republican. Home and Office: 65 Fayson Lake Rd Kinnelon NJ 07405-7823 E-mail: whitehall6@msn.com.

RICHARDSON, JOSEPH HILL, physician, medical educator; b. Rensselaer, Ind., June 16, 1928; s. William Clark and Vera (Hill) R.; m. Joan Grace Meininger, July 8, 1950; children: Lois N., Ellen M., James K. MS in Medicine, Northwestern U., 1950, MD, 1953. Diplomate Am. Bd. Internal Medicine. Intern U.S. Naval Hosp., Great Lakes, Ill., 1953-54; physician internal medicine, hematology pvt. practice, Marion, Ind., 1959-67, Ft. Wayne, Ind., 1967—. Assoc. clin. prof. medicine Ind. U. Sch.

Medicine, 1993—; founding mem. The Reviewing Physician Group, 2001—. Contbr. articles to profl. jours. Fellow in medicine Cleve. Clinic, 1956-59. Fellow ACP, AAAS; mem. AMA, Masons. Home and Office: 8726 Fortuna Way Fort Wayne IN 46815-5725

RICHARDSON, ROBERT ALLEN, retired lawyer, educator; b. Cleve., Feb. 15, 1939; s. Allen B. and Margaret C. (Thomas) R.; m. Carolyn Eck Richardson, Dec. 9, 1968. BA, Ohio Wesleyan U., 1961; LLB, Harvard U., 1964. Bar: Ohio 1964, Hawaii 1990. Ptnr. Caffee, Halter & Griswold, Cleve., 1968-89; counsel Mancini, Rowland & Welch (formerly Case & Lynch), Maui, Hawaii, 1990—2001; lectr., affirmative action officer, atty., exec. com. Maui (Hawaii) C.C., 1989—2001; ret., 2001. Chmn. gov. fin. dept., chmn. cmty. svc. com., mem. oper. com. Caffee, Halter & Griswold; past lectr. Sch. Law Cleve. State U.; counsel Maui C. of C., Kahului, 1994-98. Pres. trustee Big Bros., Big Sisters of Maui, 1990-94; v.p., trustee, pres. Ka Hole A Ke Ole Homeless Resource Ctr., 1990—; trustee Maui Acad. Performing Arts, 1990-97, Maul Counseling Svc., 1990-96, Kapalua Music Festival, Friends of Children Advocate Ctr., Legal Aid Soc. Hawaii, pres., 1998-88; v.p., trustee, chmn. devel. com. Cleve. Playhouse, 1984-89; trustee, mem. exec. com., program chmn. Cleve. Coun. World Affairs, 1970-89; past model UN chmn. Cleve. Com. on Fgn. Rels.; trustee, mem. exec. com., budget chmn. Neighborhood Ctrs. Assn., 1980-89; trustee Maui Symphony, 1995-98, v.p., 1999—. Recipient T.S. Shinn award Maui C. of C., 2000. Mem. Rotary Club of Maui, Maui Country Club, Roufant Club (adv.), Cleve. Skating Club. Home: 1365 Lower Kula Rd Kula HI 96790-9724

RICHARDSON, RUDY JAMES, toxicology and neurosciences educator; b. May 13, 1945; BS magna cum laude, Wichita State U., 1967; Sc.M., Harvard U., 1973, Sc.D., 1974. Diplomate Am. Bd. Toxicology. Rsch. geochemist Columbia U., N.Y.C., summer 1966; NASA trainee SUNY, Stony Brook, 1967-70; rsch. biochemist Med. Research Council, Carshalton, England, 1974-75; asst. prof. U. Mich., Ann Arbor, 1975-79, assoc. prof., 1979-84, prof. toxicology, 1984—, assoc. prof. neurotoxicology neurology dept., 1987—, Dow prof. toxicology, 1998—, acting dir. toxicology program, 1993, dir., 1994-99, dir. toxicology tng. program, 2003—. Vis. scientist Warner-Lambert Co., Ann Arbor, 1982-83; vis. prof. U. Padua, Italy, 1991; cons. NAS, Washington, 1978-79, 84, Office Tech. Assessment U.S. Congress, 1988-90, Nat. Toxic Substance Disease Registry, 1990—; mem. sci. adv. panel on neurotoxicology EPA, 1987-89; chmn. work group on neurotoxicity guidelines Orgn. for Econ. Coop. and Devel., 1990, Nat. Inst. Orgnl. Safety and Health, 1990, 94; mem. acute cholinesterase risk assessement expert panel Internat. Life Scis. Inst., 1996; mem. steering com., working group Risk Sci. Inst., 1997; presenter sci. adv. panel U.S. EPA, 1998-99, WHO, Geneva, 1998; chair expert panel on dichlorvos neurotoxicity and cholinesterase inhibition SRA Internat., Washington, 1998-99, guest panel mem. Mich. Environ. Sci. Bd., 2003—; invited spkr. in field. Mem. editorial bd. Neurotoxicology, 1980—, Toxicology and Indsl. Health, 1986—, Toxicology and Applied Pharmacology, 1989-97, Jour. Toxicology and Environ. Health, 1997—; contbr. articles to profl. jours., chpts. to books. Mem. Mich. Lupus Found., Ann Arbor, 1979— Grantee NIH, 1977-86, 95—, EPA, 1977-86, U.S. Civilian R & D Found., 1996—, U.S. Army Rsch. Office, 2002—. Mem. AAAS, Am. Coll. Toxicology, Soc. Toxicology (pres. neurotoxicology sect. 1987-88, councillor 1988-89, co-recipient Best Paper award 2003), Soc. for Neurosci., Am. Diabetes Assn., Am. Chem. Soc., Internat. Soc. Neurochemistry, Internat. Brain Rsch. Orgn. Achievements include co-discoverer (with B.R. Dudek) of lymphocyte neuropathy target esterase (NTE); development of lymphocyte NTE as biomarker of exposure to neuropathic organophosphates; refinement of NTE assay for use in neurotoxicity testing; use of protein mass spectrometry in mechanistic toxicology and sensor development. Office: U Mich Toxicology Program M 7525 Sph # 2 Ann Arbor MI 48109 E-mail: rjrich@umich.edu.

RICHARDSON, RUTH DELENE, retired business educator; b. May 27, 1942; d. Daniel Edgar and Allie Myrtle (Skinner) R.; 1 child, John Daniel. BS, Mars Hill Coll., 1965; MS, U. Tenn., Knoxville, 1968, EdD (EPDA fellow), 1974. Cert. profl. sec., 1986. Tchr. LaFollette (Tenn.) High Sch., 1965-66; instr. Clinch Valley Coll., Wise, Va., 1967-68, U. S.C., Union, 1968-69, Tenn. Wesleyan Coll., Athens, 1969-71, Roane State C.C., Harriman, Tenn., 1971-73; assoc. prof., chmn. dept. bus. edn. and office adminstrn. Ala. State U., Montgomery, 1974-75; assoc. prof. U. South Ala., Mobile, 1975-80; assoc. prof. adminstrv. sys. mgmt. U. North Ala., Florence, 1980-92, prof., 1992—99, retired, 1999. Cons. career edn.; employment tester. Contbr. articles to profl. jours. Lutheran. Home: 230 Woodcrest Dr Florence AL 35630-6672

RICHARDSON, SANDRA LORRAINE, retired elementary school educator; b. Ypsilanti, Mich., Feb. 5, 1947; d. Alfred Jack and Marianna (Boersema) O'Key; m. Frank Raymond Richardson, Dec. 27, 1969; 1 child, Elaine Ellen. BS, Eastern Mich. U., 1969. Tchr. Eaton Rapids (Mich.) Schs., 1969-70, Salinas (Calif.) Schs., 1970-71, Paso Robles (Calif.) Elementary Schs., 1971-72, San Luis Coastal Schs., San Luis Obispo, Calif., 1972—2002, mentor tchr., 1985—88, 1992—2003, coord. gifted and talented edn., 1988-89, dept. chmn., 1988—2003; ret., 2002. Adj. prof. Calif. Poly. State U., San Luis Obispo, 1988-90; cons. self-esteem workshops, San Luis Obispo, 1988—. Author: Touch and Feel ABC, 1974; contbr. articles to profl. jours. and mags., poetry to Nat. Poetry Press. Pres. Coun. for Exceptional Children, San Luis Obispo, 1973-74; life mem. Friends of the Libr., San Luis Obispo; founder San Luis Obispo Womenade, 2002. Recipient award San Luis Obispo br. Calif. Reading Assn., 1985, Tchr. of Yr. award San Luis Coastal Schs., 1991, San Luis Obispo County, 1991. Mem. AAUW (pres. San Luis Obispo, Calif. 1981-82, honored with scholarship in her name 1989), NEA, Nat. Coun. Tchrs. of English, Calif. Tchrs. Assn., San Luis Coastal Tchrs. Assn., Calif. Assn. Tchrs. English, founder San Luis Obispo Womenade-Direct Charity for Essential Needs, Alpha Phi (founding chpt. advisor Calif. Polytechnic U.).

RICHARDSON, THOMAS ANDREW, business executive, educator; b. Providence, Aug. 31, 1955; s. Edward Ferris and Olive Elizabeth (Lynaugh) R.; m. Patricia Ann Mundie, Dec. 30, 1982; children: Michael Edward, Lauren Elizabeth, Kristen Mundie. AS in Oceanography, Fla. Inst. Tech., 1977, BS in Environ. Sci., 1979, MBA, 1985; EdD, Nova Southeastern U., 2003. Asst. prof., div. head sch. marine and environ. tech. Fla. Inst. Tech., Jensen Beach, 1979-85; tng. mgr. PADI Internat., Santa Ana, Calif., 1985-88, dir. tng. and edn., 1988-90, sr. v.p., 1991—2003, pres., 2003—; v.p. Capital Investment Ventures Corp., 1991—2003; pres., COO Emergency First Response Corp., 2003—; pres. Current Pub., 2003—. Dir. lakefront City of Evanston, Ill., 1980-82; bd. dirs. CIVCO; chmn. bd. dirs. Project AWARE Found., Santa Ana; pres. DSAT Inc., Santa Ana, 1989—, DSAT Worldwide, 2003—; pres., CEO, Emergency First Responce Corp., 2003—; guest faculty Duke Med. Sch. continuing edn., Durham, N.C., 1992. Editor in chief: Open Water Diver Manual, 1988, Rescue Diver Manual, 1988, Divemaster Manual, 1990, Undersea Journal, 1987, Adventures in Diving; Open Water Diving video, Adventures in Diving video, Peak Performance video; contbr. articles to profl. jours. CPR and first aid instr. Martin County Sch. Dist., Stuart, Fla., 1982-83. Recipient Diver of Yr. award Divers Alert Network/Rolex, Inc., 1992, Craig Hoffman Meml. award for diving safety, Undersea and Hyerbaric Med. Soc., 2000; scholar Nova Southeastern U., 1998. Mem. Am. Mgmt. Assn., Am. Soc. Training and Devel., Am. Soc. Assn. Exec., Undersea and Hyperbaric Med. Soc., South Pacific Undersea Med. Soc., Sierra Club, Nat. Audubon Soc., Emergency Med. Planning Inc., Am. Acad. Underwater Scis., Nat. Assn. Search and Rescue, PADI Diving Soc. (pres. 1998—). Avocations: photography, music, woodworking, family activities, scuba diving. E-mail: drewr@padi.com.

RICHARDSON, VANESSA, education educator; b. Camp Lejeune, N.C., Aug. 31, 1960; d. Matthew and Margaret Ethel (Cox) R. Cert. in traffic mgmt., U.S. Army Transp. Sch., Ft. Eustis, Va., 1985; BS in Urban and Regional Planning, East Carolina U., 1988; MS in Safety and Driver Edn., N.C. Agrl. and Tech. State U., 1990, MS in Reading Edn., 1992; PhD, U. N.C., Greensboro, 1998. Cert. G grad. level tchr., N.C. Planning intern Pitt County Econ. Devel. Commn., Greenville, N.C., summer 1987; grad. intern in transp. planning City of Greensboro, 1989; transp. adminstrn. mgmt. clk. USMCR, Greensboro, 1985-90; planning/grants coord. City of Fayetteville, N.C., 1990-91; rsch. asst. Sch. Bus. and Econs. N.C. Agrl. and Tech. State U., Greensboro, 1988, grad. asst. Sch. Tech., 1989-90, tutor coord., 1991-92, instr. Upward Bound program, 1992-93, instr., tech. assoc., 1992-94; grad. tchg. asst. U. N.C., Greensboro, 1993-97; cmty. rels. coord. Sch. Tech., N.C. A&T State U, Greensboro, 1997—. Co-author: New Teacher Handbook for Trade and Industrial Educators, 1993, Research on Teaming: Insights from Selected Studies; also author articles. Vol. Greater Greensboro Cities in Schs., 1991-92; coord. Fayetteville Area Sys. Transit campaign United Way. With USMCR. Mem. NEA, ASCD, N.C. Assn. Educators, Internat. Reading Assn., Soc. Tech. Comm., Assn. Grad. Students (v.p.), Am. Planning Assn., N.C. Pub. Transp. Assn., N.C. Driver and Traffic Safety Edn. Assn., Gamma Theta Upsilon, Epsilon Pi Tau, Delta Nu Alpha. Avocations: physical fitness, health, travel. Home: 1504 Cedar Ln Kinston NC 28501-5844

RICHARDSON, WILLIAM CHASE, foundation executive; b. Passaic, N.J., May 11, 1940; s. Henry Burtt and Frances (Chase) R.; m. Nancy Freeland, June 18, 1966; children: Elizabeth, Jennifer. BA, Trinity Coll., 1962; MBA, U. Chgo., 1964, PhD, 1971. Rsch. assoc., instr. U. Chgo., 1967-70; asst. prof. health services U. Wash., 1971-73, assoc. prof., 1973-76, prof., 1976-84, chmn. dept. health services, 1973-76, assoc. dean Sch. Pub. Health, 1976-81, acting dean, 1977, 78, dean Grad. Sch., vice provost, 1981-84; exec. v.p., provost, prof. dept. family and community medicine Pa. State U., 1984-90; pres. Johns Hopkins U., Balt., 1990-95, pres., prof. emeritus, 1995, prof. dept. health policy, mgmt., 1990-95, prof. emeritus, 1995—; pres., CEO W.K. Kellogg Found, Battle Creek, Mich., 1995—. Cons. in field; bd. dirs. Kellogg Co., CSX Corp., Mercantile Bankshares Corp., Mercantile-Safe Deposit & Trust Co., Coun. on Founds. Author: books, including Ambulatory Use of Physicians Services, 1971, Health Program Evaluation, 1978; contbr. articles to profl. jours. Mem. external adv. com. Fred Hutchinson Cancer Rsch. Ctr. Kellogg fellow, 1965-67 Fellow Am. Public Health Assn.; mem. Inst. Medicine, Nat. Acad. Scis. Office: WK Kellogg Found One Michigan Ave E Battle Creek MI 49017*

RICHARDSON-MELECH, JOYCE SUZANNE, music educator, singer; b. Perth Amboy, N.J., Nov. 15, 1957; d. Herbert Nathaniel and Fannie Elaine (Franklin) Richardson; m. Gerald Melech, July 28, 1990. MusB, Westminster Choir Coll., 1979, MusM, 1981; postgrad., Rutgers U., 1999—. Cert. music tchr. N.J., supr. N.J. Musical play dir. Perth Amboy H.S., 1989-92, asst. band dir., 1984-94; music tchr. Perth Amboy Bd. Edn., 1981—, gifted and talented music tchr., 1992-96; vocal soloist N.Y.C. Vocal soloist N.Y. Philharm. and Westminster Symphonic Choir, 1977, United Moravian Ch., N.Y.C., 1980-81, Ctrl. Jersey Concert Orch., Perth Amboy, 1994-96; mezzo-soprano soloist in The Messiah, John Hus Moravian Ch., Bklyn., 1998; master tchrs. collaborative with N.J. Symphony Orch., 2000-01, 03. Contbg. author: Teacher's Resource Book, 2000, 2001, 2003. Participant Perth Amboy Adult Cmty. Theatre, 1983. Recipient award for excellence in tchg., NJ Symphony Orch., 2000, 2001, 2003. Mem. NAACP, Am. Fedn. Tchrs., Am. Fedn. Musicians (local 204-373), Music Educators Nat. Conf., Internat. Platform Assn., Am. Mus. Natural History (assoc.), Alliance for Arts Edn. N.J., Ctrl. Jersey Music Educators, N.J. Music Educators Assn., Alpha Phi Omega. Democrat. Mem. African Meth. Episcopal Zion Ch. Avocations: needlepoint, cross-stitch, knitting, sewing, crocheting. Home: 148 Carson Ct Somerset NJ 08873-4790 Office: Samuel Shull Sch 380 Hall Ave Perth Amboy NJ 08861-3205 E-mail: joycrichardson@paps.net.

RICHBART, CAROLYN MAE, mathematics educator; b. Catskill, N.Y., Aug. 12, 1945; d. George R. and Frances (Reynolds) Eden; m. Lynn A. Richbart, Aug. 15, 1987. BS, SUNY, Geneseo, 1967, MEd, 1982; PhD, U. Albany, 1992. Cert. math. tchr., elem. tchr., N.Y. Tchr. Wolcott St. Sch., Le Roy, N.Y., 1967-69; math. tchr. Le Roy Cen. High Sch., 1969-72, Attica (N.Y.) Mid. Sch., 1978-84; assoc. prof. Genesee C.C., Batavia, N.Y., 1984-87; grad. asst. U. Albany, 1987-90; asst. prof. Russell Sage Coll., Troy, N.Y., 1990-92, SUNY, New Paltz, 1992-97; assoc. in math. edn. N.Y. State Edn. Dept., 1997-2000; adj. prof. Charleston So. U., 2001—02. Project dir. grades kindergarten through 8, 1994-97, N.Y. State Math. Mentor Network, 1999-2000; facilitator Network of Urban Math. Edn. Leaders. Contbr. articles to profl. jours. Mem. Nat. Coun. Tchrs. Math. (speaker), Assn. Math. Tchrs. N.Y. State (rec. sec. 1988-89, corr. sec. 1991-92, pres. 1995-96, chair workshop 1992, chair program 1989, chair Wyoming County sect. 1985-88), N.Y. State Assn. Two-Yr. Colls. (exec. bd. 1986-90, legis. chair 1986-89, curriculum chair 1989-90). Home and Office: 2419 Racquet Club Dr Johns Island SC 29455

RICHBURG, TERRI SCROGGINS, English educator; b. Tallassee, Ala., Oct. 18, 1951; d. James Douglas and Adna Meadows Scroggins; m. William R. Richburg, Aug. 29, 1970 (div. Dec. 1979); 1 child, Manderley Tara. BA, Auburn U., 1973, EdM, 1987, EdS, 1999; NBCT Nat. Bd. Cert. Tchr., 2002. Nat. bd. cert. tchr. Social worker Dept. Human Resources, Montgomery, Ala., 1973-79; coord. Family Ct., Montgomery, Ala., 1979-81; instr. English U. Ala., Tuscaloosa, 1981-85, Lee H.S., Montgomery, 1989—, Auburn U., Montgomery, 1995—. Instr. creative writing Cmty. Edn., Montgomery, 1991-96. Author: Red Mountain Rendevous, 1995, Fan, 1996. Pub. chair Montgomery County Edn. Assn., 1999; newspaper, literary mag. advisor Lee H.S., 1993-99. Recipient Hackney Fiction award Hackney Corp./So. Writers, Birmingham, 1994, Ala. Poet Designation Birmingham Pub. Librs., 1997; South Ctrl. Bell grantee, Birmingham, 1995, Ala. Coun. Arts grantee, Montgomery, 1994-95. Mem. Am. Pen Women (judge fiction/poetry 1994), Ala. Poetry Soc. (sr. leader fiction writing 1994). Avocations: creative writing, fishing, camping, canoeing, hiking,. Home: 3517 N Georgetown Dr Montgomery AL 36109-2203 Office: Lee High Sch 225 Ann St Montgomery AL 36107-2599

RICHBURG, W. EDWARD, nurse educator; b. New Orleans, Jan. 18, 1948; m. Kathryn S. Richburg, June 24, 1972; children: Bill, Kate. BA, U. Miss., 1970; BSN, U. Miss., Jackson, 1973; MEd, Memphis State U., 1977; MSN, Med. U. of S.C., 1991. RN, Fla., S.C.; cert. nursing adminstrn. advance, continuing edn. and staff devel. Commd. ensign USN, 1971, advanced through grades to comdr.; instr. hosp. corps Naval Sch. of Health Sci., San Diego, 1978-81; head nurse U.S. Naval Hosp.; dir. nursing svcs. Branch Med. Clinic, Mayport, Fla., 1983-87; head staff edn. and tng. U.S. Naval Hosp., Charleston, S.C., 1987-92, asst. dir. nursing Yokosuka, Japan, 1992-95; head Command Edn. Dept., 1995—; head command edn. dept. U.S. Naval Hosp., Yokosuka, Japan, 1995-96, performance improvement coord. Charleston, S.C., 1996-98; instr. nursing Trident Tech. Coll., Charleston, 1998—. Recipient Excellence in Nursing Education award Trident Nurses' Assn., 1991, S. C. Nurses' Assn., 1992. Mem. ANA (cert.), S.C. Nurses Assn. (pres. 1999—, chair continuing edn. com., treas. dist. chpt., pres. 1999—, Excellence in Nursing Edn. award 1992), Navy Nurse Corps Assn. (treas. Palmetto chpt. 1998—), Trident Nurses Assn. (pres.-elect 1997-98, pres. 1998—, Excellence in Nursing Edn. award 1991), Continuing Edn. Coun. (chair), Sigma Theta Tau.

RICHENS, MURIEL WHITTAKER, marriage and family therapist, educator; b. Prineville, Oreg. d. John Reginald and Victoria Cecilia (Pascale) Whittaker; children: Karen, John, Candice, Stephanie, Rebecca. BS, Oreg. State U.; MA, San Francisco State U., 1962; postgrad., U. Calif., Berkeley, 1967-69, U. Birmingham, Eng., 1973, U. Soria, Spain, 1981. Lic. sch. adminstr., tchr. 7-12, pupil pers. specialist, Calif.; lic. marriage and family therapist, Calif. Tchr. Springfield (Oreg.) High Sch.; instr. San Francisco State U.; instr., counselor Coll. San Mateo, Calif., San Mateo High Sch. Dist., 1963-86; therapist AIDS Health Project U. Calif., San Francisco, 1988—; marriage and family therapist, pvt. practice San Mateo. Guest West German-European Acad. seminar, Berlin, 1975. Lifeguard, ARC. Postgrad. student Ctr. for Human Communications, Los Gatos, Calif., 1974, U. P.R., 1977, U. Guadalajara (Mex.), 1978, U. Durango (Mex.), 1980, U. Guanajuato (Mex.) 1982. Mem. U. Calif. Berkeley Alumni Assn., Am. Contract Bridge League (Diamond Life Master, cert. instr., cert. dir.), Women in Comm., Computer-Using Educators, Commonwealth Club, Pi Lambda Theta, Delta Pi Epsilon. Republican. Roman Catholic. Home and Office: 847 N Humboldt St Condo 309 San Mateo CA 94401-1451

RICHERSON, HAL BATES, physician, internist, allergist, immunologist, educator; b. Phoenix, Feb. 16, 1929; s. George Edward and Eva Louise (Steere) R.; m. Julia Suzanne Bradley (dec. 1996), Sept. 5, 1953; children: Anne, George, Miriam, Julia, Susan. BS with distinction, U. Ariz., 1950; MD, Northwestern U., 1954. Diplomate Am. Bd. Internal Medicine, Am. Bd. Allergy and Immunology, Bd. Diagnostic Lab. Immunology; lic. physician, Iowa. Intern Kansas City (Mo.) Gen. Hosp., 1954-55; resident in pathology St. Luke's Hosp., Kansas City, 1955-56; trainee in neuropsychiatry Brooke Army Hosp., San Antonio, 1956; resident in medicine U. Iowa Hosps., Iowa City, 1961-64, fellow in allergy and immunology, 1964-66; fellow in immunology Mass. Gen. Hosp., Boston, 1968-69; instr. internal medicine U. Iowa Coll. Medicine, Iowa City, 1964-66, asst. prof., 1966-70, assoc. prof., 1970-74, prof., 1974-98, prof. emeritus, 1998—; acting dir. divsn. allergy/applied immunology U. Iowa Hosps. and Clinics, Iowa City, 1970-72, dir. allergy and clin. immunology sect., 1972-78, dir. divsn. allergy and immunology, 1978-91; gen. practice, asst. to Gen. Surgeon Ukiah, Calif., 1958; gen. practice medicine Holbrook, Ariz., 1958-61. Vis. lectr. medicine Harvard U. Sch. Medicine, Boston, 1968-69; vis. prof., rsch. scientist U. London and Brompton Hosp., 1984; prin. investigator Nat. Heart, Lung and Blood Inst., 1971-94, mem. pulmonary diseases adv. com., 1983-87; prin. investigator Nat. Inst. Allergy and Infectious Diseases, 1983-94; dir. Nat. Inst. Allergy and Infectious Diseases' Asthma and Allergic Diseases Ctr., U. Iowa, 1983-94; mem. VA Merit Rev. Bd. in Respiration, 1981-84; mem. com. NIH Gen. Clin. Rsch. Ctrs., 1989-93; mem. rev. reserve NIH, 1993-98; mem. bd. sci. advisors Merck Inst., 1990-94; presenter lectures, seminars, continuing edn. courses; mem. numerous univ., coll. and hosp. coms., 1970—; cons. Merck Manual, 1982, 87, 92, 96-97. Contbr. numerous articles and revs. to profl. jours., chpts. to books; reviewer Sci., Jour. Immunology, Jour. Allergy and Clin. Immunology, Am. Rev. Respiratory Disease, New Eng. Jour. Medicine, Ann. Internal Medicine. Served to capt. U.S. Army, 1956-58. NIH fellow 1968-69. Fellow ACP (Laureate award 1996), Am. Acad. Allergy Asthma & Immunology (Disting. Clinician award 1998); mem. AMA (mem. residency and rev. com. for allergy and immunology; mem. accreditation coun. for grad. med. edn. 1980-85, vice-chmn. 1984-85), AAAS, Iowa Med. Soc., Iowa Thoracic Soc. (chmn. program com. 1964-65, 69-71, pres. 1972-73, mem. exec. com. 1972-74), Am. Thoracic Soc. (bd. dirs. 1981-82, councilor assembly on allergy and immunology 1980-81, mem. nominating com. 1988-90), Iowa Clin. Med. Soc., Am. Fedn. Clin. Rsch., Am. Assn. Immunologists, Ctrl. Soc. Clin. Rsch. (chmn. sect. on allergy-immunology 1980-81, mem. coun. 1981-84), Alpha Omega Alpha. Avocations: reading, trombonist, swimming, scuba diving. Home: 331 Lucon Dr Iowa City IA 52246-3300 Office: U Iowa Health Care Dept Internal Medicine 200 Hawkins Dr Iowa City IA 52242-1009 E-mail: richersonh@mchsi.com., hal-richerson@uiowa.edu.

RICHEY, EVERETT ELDON, religious studies educator; b. Claremont, Ill., Nov. 1, 1923; s. Hugh Arthur and Elosia Emma (Longnecker) R.; m. Mary Elizabeth Reynolds, Apr. 9, 1944; children: Eldon Arthur, Clive Everett, Loretta Arlene, Charles Estel. ThB, Anderson U., 1946; MDiv, Sch. Theology, Anderson, Ind., 1956; ThD, Iliff Sch. of Theology, Denver, 1960. Pastor Ch. of God, Bremen, Ind., 1946-47, Laurel, Miss., 1947-48, First Ch. of God, Fordyce, Ark., 1948-52; prof. Arlington Coll., Long Beach, Calif., 1961-68; pastor Cherry Ave. Ch. of God, Long Beach, 1964-68; prof. Azusa (Calif.) Pacific U., 1968-93. Chmn. Commn. on Christian Higher Edn./Ch. of God, 1982-93; pres. Ch. Growth Investors, Inc., 1981-2003, v.p. 2003-. Author: ednl. manual Church Periodical--Curriculum, 1971-83, 97. Mem.: Christian Ministries Tng. Assn., Assn. Profs. and Rschrs. Religious Edn. Republican. Avocation: gardening. Home and Office: 413 N Valencia St Glendora CA 91741-2418 E-mail: eerichey@juno.com.

RICHGELS, GLEN WILLIAM, mathematics educator; b. Madison, Wis., Aug. 5, 1949; s. Marion Urban and Eudelma Rosena (Bomkamp) R.; m. Sharon Rae Hart, Aug. 14, 1976; children: Amber Rae, Erin Ellen, Erik Glen. BA, U. Wis., 1971, MA, 1976, PhD. Cert. tchr. math./computer sci. Tchr. math. Woodstock (Ill.) Cmty. H.S., 1973-76; tchr. math. and computer sci. Beloit (Wis.) Pub. Schs., 1976-82, Baraboo (Wis.) Pub. Schs., 1982-93; prof. math. Bemidji (Minn.) State U., 1993—, dir. summer math. insts., 1993—. Computer cons. Custom Data Svcs., Baraboo, 1984—. Author: Individualized Planning Program, 1990. Named Regional Basketball Coach of Yr., Wis. Basketball Coaches Assn., 1984, Basketball MVP, U. Wis.-Madison, 1971. Mem. Nat. Coun. Tchrs. Math., Math. Assn. Am., Wis. Math. Coun. Avocations: computer programming, fishing, basketball, football. E-mail: grichgels@bemidjistate.edu.

RICHMAN, HAROLD ALAN, social welfare policy educator; b. Chgo., May 15, 1937; s. Leon H. and Rebecca (Klieman) R.; m. Marlene M. Forland, Apr. 25, 1965; children: Andrew, Robert. AB, Harvard U., 1959; MA, U. Chgo., 1961, PhD, 1969. Asst. prof., dir. Ctr. for Study Welfare Policy, Sch. Social Svc., U. Chgo., 1967-69, dean, prof. social welfare policy, 1969-78, Hermon Dunlap Smith prof., 1978—, dir. of ctr., 1978-81, dir. Children's Policy Rsch. Project, 1978-84, dir. Chapin Hall Ctr. for Children, 1985—2002, faculty assoc. Chapin Hall Ctr. for Children, 2002—, chmn. univ. com. on pub. policy studies, 1974-77. Chmn. Univ. Lab. Schs., 1985-88; cons. to gov. State of Ill., Edna McConnell Clark Found., 1984-95, Lilly Endowment, 1987-90, Ford Found., 1987-89; co-chair Aspen roundtable on comprehensive cmty. initiatives, 1993—. Chmn. editorial bd. Social Svcs. Rev., 1970-79; contbr. articles to profl. jours. Bd. dirs. Chgo. Com. Fgn. and Domestic Policy, 1969-78, S.E. Chgo. Commn., 1970—, Jewish Fedn. Met. Chgo., 1970-75, Ill. Facilities Fund, 1989-94, Welfare Coun. Met. Chgo., 1970-72, Erikson Inst. Early Childhood Edn., 1972-79, Nat. Urban Coalition, 1975-86, Family Focus, 1980-89, Jewish Coun. Urban Affairs, 1982-87, Ctr. for Study Social Policy, 1983-92, chmn., 2003—; bd. dirs. Nat. Family Resource Coalition, 1990-93, Pub./Pvt. Ventures, 1992-98, Benton Found., 1994—; bd. dirs. Israel Ctr. on Children, chmn., 1995—; bd. dirs. Jordan Children's Rsch. Ctr., 2001—, Michael Reese Health Trust, 2002--; bd. dirs. U. Capetown Childen's Inst., dep. chair, 2002—. White House fellow, Washington, 1965-66; recipient Disting. Svc. citation U.S. Dept. Health, Edn. & Welfare, 1970, Quantrell award U. Chgo., 1990. Mem. White House Fellows Assn. (v.p. 1976-77), Am. Pub. Welfare Assn. (bd. dirs. 1989-92). Home: 5715 S Dorchester Ave Chicago IL 60637-1726 Office: U Chgo Chapin Hall Ctr for Children 1313 E 60th St Chicago IL 60637-2830 Business E-Mail: richman-harold@chmail.spc.uchicago.edu.

RICHMAN, MARC HERBERT, forensic engineer, educator; b. Boston, Oct. 14, 1936; s. Samuel and Janet (Gordon) R.; m. Ann Raeshel Yoffa, Aug. 31, 1963 BS, MIT, 1957, ScD, 1963; MA, Brown U., 1967. Registered profl. engr., Conn., Mass., R.I.; cert. forensic examiner. Cons. engr., 1957—; engr. shipbldg. div. Bethlehem Steel Corp., Quincy, Mass., 1957; instr. metallurgy MIT, Cambridge, 1957-60, research asst. dept. metallurgy, 1960-63; instr. metallurgy div. univ. extension Commonwealth of Mass.,

1958-62; asst. prof. engring. Brown U., Providence, 1963-67, assoc. prof., 1967-70, prof., 1970-98, dir. central electron microscopy facility Materials Research program, 1971-86, dir. undergrad. program in engring., 1991-98; prof. emeritus, 1998—; pres. Ednl. Aids of Newton Inc., Providence, 1968-71, Marc H. Richman Inc., Providence, 1981—. Guest scientist Franklin Inst., Phila., 1959; vis. prof. U. R.I., Kingston, 1970-71; biophysicist dept. medicine Miriam Hosp., Providence, 1974-87; biogengr. dept. orthopaedics R.I. Hosp., 1979-93; prof. emeritus Brown U., Providence, 1998—. Author: Introduction to Science of Metals, 1967; also articles; editor Soviet Physics: Crystallography, 1970-94; mem. editorial adv. bd. Materials Characterization, 1970—; mem. editorial adv. bd. Jour. Forensic Engring., 1985-88. Maj. Ordnance Corps, U.S. Army, 1963. Served to maj. Ordnance Corps, U.S. Army, 1963 Recipient Engr. of Yr. award R.I. Soc. Profl. Engrs., 1993. Fellow Nat. Acad. Forensic Engrs. (cert.), Am. Coll. Forensic Examiners (cert.), Am. Inst. Chemists, Inst. Materials (U.K.); mem. ASCE, AIME, NSPE, ASEE (Outstanding Young Faculty award 1969), NAFE (bd. cert. diplomate in forensic engring.), Am. Acad. Forensic Scis., Am. Soc. Metals (sec.-treas. 1965-68, chmn. R.I. chpt. 1968-69, Albert Sauveur Meml. award 1968, 69), Providence Engring. Soc. (pres. 1991-92, Freeman award for engring. achievement 1989), B'nai B'rith, Sigma Xi, Tau Beta Pi. Home: 291 Cole Ave Providence RI 02906-3452 Office: One Richmond Sq Providence RI 02906 E-mail: MHRichman@aol.com.

RICHMOND, ALLEN MARTIN, speech pathologist, educator; b. N.Y.C., July 24, 1936; m. Deborah Moll (dec.). BS, SUNY, Geneseo, 1958; MEd, Pa. State U., 1961; PhD, Ohio U., 1965. Instr. N.Y. State Pub. Schs., 1958-60, Penn. Rehab. Ctr., 1960-62, Buffalo Hearing and Speech Ctr., 1969-88; clin. instr. dept. otolaryngology SUNY Med. Sch., 2002—03; adj. asst. prof. dept. comms. SUNY, Buffalo, 1994—; lectr. Buffalo State Coll., 2002—03. Vis. prof. U. Md., 1968; adj. asst. prof. comm. disorders dept., 1989—; advisor New Voice Club of Niagara Frontier, Buffalo, 1975—2002; cons. Bry-Lin Hosp, Buffalo, 1989—95; faculty SUNY, Fredonia, 2002, Buffalo State Coll., 2002—03. Contbr. atlas of head and neck surgery 4th edit. Participant Very Spl. Arts, Niagara, 1990—. Mem.: Am. Speech-Lang.-Hearing Assn. Avocations: running, baseball, reading, travel. Home: 423 Walton Dr Cheektowaga NY 14225-1005

RICHMOND, LEE JOYCE, psychologist, educator; b. Balt., May 31, 1934; d. Alexander J. and Anne (Morganstern) Blank; m. Aug. 9, 1953 (div. 1983); children: Ruth, Stephen, Sharon, Jessica. BS, Loyola Coll., 1961; MEd, Johns Hopkins U., 1968; PhD, U. Md., 1972. Licensed psychologist. Prof. psychology Dundalk Community Coll., Balt., 1971-75; prof. edn. Johns Hopkins U., Balt., 1975-86, Loyola Coll., Balt., 1986—; pvt. practice Balt., 1974—. Author of numerous articles and books; co-author: Soulwork: Finding the Work You Love-Loving the Work You Have, 1998, What Brings You to Life?, 2001, To Promote Good Will; co-editor: Connections Between Spirit and Work, 1997. Recipient Outstanding Contbn. to Psychology award Md. Psychol. Assn., 1986, Disting. Svc. award Nat. Vocat. Guidance Assn., 1984, Eminent Career award Nat. Career Devel. Assn., 2002. Mem. Coun. for the Accreditation of Coun. and Ednl. Related Programs (bd. dirs. 1999-2000), ACA (gov.'s coun. 1988-90, pres. 1992, mem. ins. trust 1994-99, chair 1998-99, Appreciation cert. 1990), Nat. Career Devel. Assn. (pres. 1988-89, Past Pres. award 1990, chmn. profl. stds. com. 2003-), Balt. Psychol. Assn. (pres. 1998-99), MD Assn. Coun. and Devel. (pres. 2003-). Home: 8907 Greylock Rd Baltimore MD 21208-1004 Office: Loyola Coll Grad Ctr 2034 Greenspring Ave Lutherville Timonium MD 21093

RICHMOND, PAUL, JR., educational consultant; b. Newark, N.J., Feb. 10, 1938; BA magna cum laude, Minot State Tchrs. Coll., 1962; MA, Mich. State U., 1971. Engl. tchr. Minot Pub. Schs., ND, 1961—74; exec. dir. Meriks Corp., Helena, Mont., 1975—. Mem.: Mont. Reading Assn. Office: Meriks Corp 1215 Beaverhead Dr Helena MT 59602-7602

RICHMOND, SAMUEL BERNARD, management educator; b. Boston, Oct. 14, 1919; s. David E. and Freda (Braman) R.; m. Evelyn Ruth Kravitz, Nov. 26, 1944; children: Phyllis Gail, Douglas Emerson, Clifford Owen. AB cum laude, Harvard U., 1940; MBA, Columbia U., 1948, PhD, 1951. Mem. faculty Columbia U., 1946-76, assoc. prof., 1957-60, prof. econ. and statistics, 1960-76; assoc. dean Grad. Sch. Bus. Columbia U., 1971-72, acting dean, 1972-73; dean prof. mgmt. Owen Grad. Sch. Mgmt. Vanderbilt U., Nashville, 1976—86, Ralph Owen prof. mgmt., 1984—88, Ralph Owen prof. mgmt. emeritus, dean emeritus, 1988—, adj. prof., 1988—96. Vis. prof. U. Sherbrooke, Que., 1967, U. Buenos Aires, Argentina, 1964, 65, Case Inst. Tech., Cleve., 1958-59, Fordham U., N.Y.C., 1952-53; dir. IMS Internat. Inc., N.Y.C., 1978-88, 1st Am. Corp., Nashville, 1981-86, Winners Corp., Nashville, 1983-89, Corbin Ltd., N.Y.C., 1970-85, Ingram Industries Inc., Nashville, 1981-92; cons. to maj. comml., ednl., profl. and govtl. orgns. Author: Operations Research for Management Decisions, 1968, Statistical Analysis, 1957, 2d edit., 1964, 3d edit., 1997, Regulation and Competition in Air Transportation, 1961; talk show host Nashville Bus. Edit., WDCN-TV, 1984-86. Trustee Ramapo Coll., N.J., 1975-76; bd. dirs. Jewish Fedn. Nashville and Mid. Tenn., Temple Ohabai Shalom, Nashville; trustee Endowment Fund Jewish Fedn. Nashville and Mid. Tenn. 1st lt. USAAF, 1943-45. Recipient Honor award CAB, 1971, Alumni award for outstanding svc. Grad. Sch. Bus., Columbia U., 1973 Mem. Am. Statis. Assn. (chmn. adv. com. rsch. to CAB 1966-74, dir. 1965-67), Am. Econ. Assn., Inst. Mgmt. Sci., Ops. Rsch. Soc. Am., Beta Gamma Sigma. Home: 5404 Camelot Rd Brentwood TN 37027-4113 Office: Vanderbilt U Owen Grad Sch Mgmt Nashville TN 37203 E-mail: samuel.b.richmond@vanderbilt.edu.

RICHTER, VIRGINIA ANN, special education educator; b. Galion, Ohio, June 4, 1945; d. Russel Ira Coulter and Reva Bessie Cook; m. Donald Frederick Richter, June 20, 1970; children: Darrel Russel, Roger Ray. BA of Edn., Ashland Coll., 1967; MA of Edn., Ohio State U., 1970; cert. spl. edn., Bowling Green State U., 1993. Cert. permanent kindergarten, elem. and elem. music tchr., provisional spl. edn. kindergarten through h.s. Kindergarten tchr. Marion (Ohio) City Schs., summer 1967, 3d grade tchr., 1967-70, Gibsonburg (Ohio) Schs., 1970-72, substitute tchr., 1978-88, Woodmore Schs., Woodville, Ohio, 1988-90, tutor learning disabled, 1989-90; tchr. multiple handicapped Sandusky County Schs., Woodville, 1990—. Mem. tchr. com. Woodmore and Sandusky County Schs. Mem. Sandusky County Farm Bur.; past pres. Zion Luth. Ch. Women. Named one of Outstanding Young Women of Am., 1973. Mem. NEA, Ohio Edn. Assn., Sandusky County Edn. Assn., Woodmore Acad. Boosters, Kappa Delta Pi. Republican. Avocations: reading, music, family. Office: Sandusky County Schs 500 W State St Fremont OH 43420-2534

RICHTER, WILLIAM LOUIS, social sciences educator; b. Covina, Calif., Apr. 9, 1939; s. Louis Ernest and Gwendolyn Marguerite (Hughes) R.; m. Linda Kay Clark, Aug. 29, 1964; children: Mark William, Robert Clark. BA, Willamette U., 1961; MA, U. Chgo., 1963, PhD, 1968. Instr. Ill. Inst. Tech., Chgo., 1964, U. Hawaii, Honolulu, 1964-66; asst. prof. Kans. State U., Manhattan, 1966-73, assoc. prof., 1973-81, prof., 1981—, dept. head, 1984-93, asst. provost, 1991-96, assoc. provost for internat. programs, 1996—2002. Vis. Fulbright lectr. Panjab U., Chandigarh, India, 1969-70; faculty rsch. fellow Am. Inst. Indian Studies, New Delhi, India, 1972-73, 1985; faculty rsch. fellow Am. Inst. Pakistan Studies, Lahore, Pakistan, 1976-77; cons. USAID, NDI, 1990—. Co-editor: (books) The Landon Lectures, 1987, Combating Corruption/Encouraging Ethics, 1990. Mem. Rotary (Rotarian of Yr., 1993). Home: 2383 Grandview Ter Manhattan KS 66502-3729 Office: Kans State U Dept Polit Sci 226 Waters Hall Manhattan KS 66506-4030 E-mail: wrichter@ksu.edu.

RICKARD, CAROLYN LUCILLE, retired elementary school educator; b. Colorado Spg., Colo., Aug. 26, 1937; d. Irving Edwin and Viola Esther (Essman) Sims; m. Kenneth Allan Rickard, Sept. 2, 1961 (div. 1977); children: Kenneth Allan, Keith Andrew. BS, Iowa State U., 1959; MA, Colo. Coll., 1986. Kindergarten tchr. Colorado Springs Sch. Dist. #11, 1960-66, 1st grade tchr., 1966-82, 2nd grade tchr., 1982-86, 4th grade tchr., 1986-91; ret.; curriculum writer Colo. State Kindergarten Guide Colo. Springs Sch. Dist. #11. Dist #11 chair Penrose Quality Cir., 1990-91; neighborhood leader El Paso County Rep. Party, Colorado Springs, 1968, office vol., 1978. Mem. Kindergarten Tchrs. Assn., Palmer Alumni Assn. (sec. 1996-2002, pres. 2002—), Phi Kappa Phi, Psi Chi, Omicron Nu, Delta Kappa Gamma. Republican. Congregationalist.

RICKARD, RUTH ANN (TONI RICKARD), secondary school educator; b. Waukesha, Wis., Dec. 10, 1945; d. Herbert Henry and Georgia May (Stark) Zietlow; m. James Ivan Miklovich, Aug. 24, 1968; m. Robert Burney Rickard, Mar. 4, 1981. AA in Biology, Pensacola Jr. Coll., 1972; BA in Elem. Edn. summa cum laude, BA in Studio Art summa cum laude, U. West Fla., 1973, BA in Art Edn. magna cum laude, 1974. Head rsch. asst. dept. genetics Cambridge (Eng.) U., 1968-70; tchr. art, chmn. art dept. Pensacola (Fla.) Cath. High Sch., 1973-80; sales mgr., asst. buyer R.H. Macy Corp., Atlanta, 1981-84; tchr. art, team leader Cobb County Pub. Schs., Marietta, Ga., 1984—, curriculum coord. Teaching cons. U. West Fla., Pensacola, 1976-78; presenter Mid. Sch. Ednl. Conf., Marietta, 1992; cooperating staff mem. Ga. State U., 1995. Sculpture displayed Fla. Craftsmen Traveling Show, Fla. Crafts Coun., Gainesville, 1972. Vis. artist Clarkesville Pottery, Austin, Tex., 1978; grantee Cobb County Jr. League, 1989. Mem. Nat. Art Edn. Assn., Ga. Art Edn. Assn. (area rep.), ASCD. Democrat. Episcopalian. Avocations: travel, reading, clothing design, jewelry design. Home: 855 Woodlawn Dr Marietta GA 30068-4256 Office: Dickerson Mid Sch 855 Woodlawn Dr NE Marietta GA 30068-4267

RICKARD, RUTH DAVID, retired history and political science educator; b. Fed. Republic Germany, Feb. 20, 1926; came to U.S., 1940; d. Carl and Alice (Koch) David; m. Robert M. Yaffe, Oct. 1949 (dec. 1959); children: David, Steven; m. Norman G. Rickard, June 1968 (dec. 1988); 1 stepson, Douglas. BS cum laude, Northwestern U., 1947, MA, 1948. Law editor Commerce Clearing House, Chgo., 1948; instr. history U. Ill., Chgo., 1949-51, instr. extension program Waukegan, 1960-67; instr. history Waukegan Schs., 1960-69; original faculty, prof. western civilization, polit. sci. Coll. of Lake County, Grayslake, Ill., 1969-92. Mem. Inter-Univ. Seminar on Armed Forces and Soc.; mem. Hospitality Info. Svc. for Diplomatic Residents and Families affiliate Meridian Internat. Ctr.; spkr. in field. Author: History of College of Lake County, 1987 (honored by city of Waukegan 1987), (poem) I Lost My Wings, 1989, Au Revoir from Emeritusdom, 1993, Where are the Safety Zones, 1994; contbg. author: History of National Press Club: Reliable Sources, 1997; contbr. articles to profl. jours. Mem. Econ. Devel. Com., Waukegan, 1992-93; working with homeless through Samaritans of Greater Washington area, 2000—. Scholar Freedoms Found. Am. Legion, Valley Forge, Pa., 1967. Mem. AAUW (pres. Waukegan chpt. 1955-57, scholarship named for her 1985, program co-chair McLean chpt. 1997-2000), LWV (charter, v.p. Waukegan chpt.), Nat. Press Club D.C., Northwestern U. Alumni Washington (bd. dirs.). Avocations: writing, travel, lecturing, reading, theater.

RICKEL, ANNETTE URSO, psychology and psychiatry researcher, educator; b. Phila. d. Ralph Francis and Marguerite (Calcaterra) Urso; 1 child, John Ralph Rickel. BA, Mich. State U., 1963; MA, U. Mich., 1965, PhD, 1972, MD, 1972. Lic. psychologist, Mich. Faculty early childhood edn. Merrill-Palmer Inst., Detroit, 1967-69; adj. faculty U. Mich., Ann Arbor, 1969-75; asst. dir. N.E. Guidance Ctr., Detroit, 1972-75; asst. prof. psychology Wayne State U., Detroit, 1975-81; vis. assoc. prof. Columbia U., N.Y.C., 1982-83; assoc. prof. psychology Wayne State U., 1981-87, asst. provost, 1989-91, prof. psychology, 1987-95; Am. Coun. on Edn. fellow Princeton and Rutgers Univs., 1990-91. AAAS and APA Congl. Sci. fellow on Senate Fin. Subcom. on Health and Pres.'s Nat. Health Care Reform Task Force, 1992—93; dir. mental health and devel. Nat. Com. for Quality Asurance, Washington, 1995—96; clin. prof. dept. psychiatry Georgetown U., Washington, 1995—2000; program officer The Rockefeller Found., 2000—. Cons. editor Jour. of Cmty. Psychology, Jour. Primary Prevention; co-author: Social and Psychological Problems of Women, 1984, Preventing Maladjustment..., 1987; author: Teenage Pregnancy and Parenting, 1989, Keeping Children From Harm's Way, 1997, Understanding Managed Care, 2000; contbr. articles to profl. jours Mem. Pres.'s Task Force on Nat. Health Care Reform, 1993; bd. dirs. Children's Ctr. of Wayne County, Mich., The Epilepsy Ctr. of Mich., Reading is Fundamental, Nat. Symphony Orch., Chamber Music Soc. of Lincoln Ctr., Soc. Meml. Sloan Kettering Cancer Ctr., The Kellogg Found., 1996-97, The John D. and Catherine T. MacArthur Found., 1998-99. Grantee NIMH, 1976-86, Eloise and Richard Webber Found., 1977-80, McGregor Fund, 1977-78, 82, David M. Whitney Fund, 1982, Katherine Tuck Fund, 1985-90, NIH, 2000; recipient Career Devel. Chair award, 1985-86. Fellow APA (div. pres. 1984-85); mem. Internat. Women's Forum, Soc. for Rsch. in Child Devel., Soc. for Rsch. in Child and Adolescent Psychopathology, Internat. Assn. of Applied Psychologists, Sigma Xi, Psi Chi. Roman Catholic. E-mail: arickel@rbf.org.

RICKERT, ROBERT RICHARD, pathologist, educator; b. Harrisburg, Pa., Oct. 19, 1936; s. Alton G. and Henrietta (Gey) R.; m. Sonja Murray Hansen, Aug. 26, 1961; children: Kristin, Robin, Anne. AB, U. Mich., 1958; MD, John Hopkins U., 1962. Diplomat Am. Bd. of Pathology. Intern Yale-New Haven (Conn.) Med. Ctr., 1962-63, resident in pathology, 1963-64, 66-67; rsch. assoc. Atomic Bomb Casulty Commn., Hiroshima, Japan, 1964-66; asst. prof. pathology Yale U. Sch. Med., New Haven, 1968-70; attending pathologist Yale New Haven Med. Ctr., 1968-70; dir. surg. pathology U. Med. and Dentistry N.J.-N.J. Med. Sch., Newark, 1970-73, assoc. prof. pathology, 1970-73; clin. prof. pathology U. of Med. and Dentistry N.J.-N.J. Med. Sch., Newark, 1985—; co-chmn. dept. pathology St. Barnabas Med. Ctr., Livingston, N.J., 1973-2000, chmn. dept. pathology, 2000—. Adj. assoc. prof. pathology Columbia U. Coll. Physicians & Surgeons, N.Y.C., 1974-89. Contbr. chpts. to med. textbooks and articles to profl. jours. Chmn. med. com. Am. Cancer Soc., N.J., 1989-91, v.p. 1991-93, pres. elect 1993-94, pres. 1995-97 (Physician of Yr., N.J. Divsn., 1998), chief med. spokesperson, bd. dirs. Ea. divsn., 1998-2000. Fellow Coll. Am. Pathologists (vice-chmn., internat. regional commr. commn. on lab. accreditation, Pathologist of Yr. 2001), Am. Soc. Clin. Pathologists, U.S.-Can. Acad. Pathology; mem. AMA, N.J. Soc. Pathologists (pres. 1980-82), Gastrointestinal Pathology Soc. (pres. 1988-89), Med. Soc. N.J., Acad. Medicine N.J. (trustee 1988—, treas. 1994-95, v.p. 1995-97, pres. 1998), Am. Soc. Cytopathology, Short Hills Club, Phi Beta Kappa, Alpha Omega Alpha. Republican. Congregationalist. Avocations: antiques, wine collecting, art. Office: St Barnabas Med Ctr Dept Pathology Livingston NJ 07039

RICKETT, CAROLYN KAYE MASTER, artist, criminologist; b. Ft. Worth, Apr. 24, 1941; d. Lester Buford and Dorothy Minerva (Whittington) Master; m. David Franklin Rickett, May 3, 1981; 1 child, Julia Beth Allen. BFA, Tex. Christian U., 1993; MFA, Tex. Woman's U., 1997; M in Criminology, U. Tex., Arlington, 2001, postgrad. in Econs., 2002—. Artist, owner StarMaster Graphic Design and Fine Art, Ft. Worth, 1988—; represented by Downstairs Gallery, Dallas, Kincannon Fine Arts Gallery. Presenter in field. Represented in permanent collections Jasper Mus., Nat. Women's Caucus Arts Archives, also pvt. collections, one-woman shows include Jasper Mus., Alta., Can., 1994, Downstairs Gallery, Jasper, 1994, Del Bello Gallery, Toronto, Ont., Can., 1996, exhibitions include Tex. Christian U., Ft. Worth, 1991, Greater Denton Coun. Arts., Tex., 1994—96, Tex. Christian U., 1995, 1997, UN 4th Conf. Women, Beijing, 1995, Bass Mus., Miami Broward C.C., Davie, Fla., 1996, San Jacinto Coll., Houston, 1996, Aisling Studio, Durango, Colo, 1996, U. Tex., Arlington, 1998, World Trade Ctr., Dallas, 1998, (traveling show) Beijing and Beyong, N.Y., 1998—2000, others. Grantee, Tex. Christian U., 1990—93; scholar, 1991—93, Ray and Bertha Lakey Meml., 1994—96. Mem.: Am. Soc. Crime, Tex. Art Educators Assn., Nat. Trust for Hist. Preservation, Mus. Women in Arts, Am. Soc. Criminology, Am. Criminal Justice Scis. Home: 5816 Broadway Ave Fort Worth TX 76117-3305

RICKS, DAVID ARTEL, business educator, editor; b. Washington, July 21, 1942; s. Artel and Focha (Black) R. BS, Brigham Young U., 1966; MBA, Ind. U., 1968, PhD, 1970. Asst. prof. Ohio State U., 1970-75, assoc. prof., 1975-81; prof. internat. bus. U. S.C., Columbia, 1981-92; v.p. acad. affairs Thunderbird-the Am. Grad. Sch. Internat. mgmt., 1992-94, disting. prof., 1992-99, U. Mo., St. Louis, 1999—2002, curators' prof., 2002—. Author books, articles in field, including Directory of Foreign Manufactures in the U.S. (Best Reference Book 1974 ALA, 1975); editor Kent Pub. Co., Boston, 1978—; editor-in-chief Jour. of Internat. Bus. Studies, 1984-92, Jour. Internat. Mgmt., 1994-97. Mem. Acad. internat. Bus. (treas. 1981-82), Acad. Mgmt. (chmn. internat. divsn. 1988-89). Home: 7445 Byron Pl Clayton MO 63105-2967 Office: 8001 Natural Bridge Rd Saint Louis MO 63121-4401

RICKS, MAE LOIS, secondary education educator; b. Tyler, Tex., Apr. 21, 1929; d. Roy and Athrea (Thomas) McCauley; m. Robert Earl Ricks, Sept. 12, 1965 (div. July 1977). BS, Tex. Coll., 1951; MS, Windsor U., 1975, Pepperdine U., 1985. English tchr. Plano H.S., Tex., 1952-55; subsitute tchr. San Diego Unified Sch. Dist., 1960-61; tchr. third grade Palo Verde Sch. Dist., Blythe, Calif., 1964-67; tchr. kindergarten Baldwin Park Sch. Dist., Calif., 1967-70; tchr. L.A. Unified Sch. Dist., Calif., 1973-83, Compton Unified Sch. Dist., Calif., 1992-96; substitute tchr. Dallas Pub. Schs., 1997—. Author (poetry) There Is No Care In The World, Poetry Parade, 1967, Fellowship in Prayer, 1967, The Lonely Desert, The Guild, 1968, The Loneliness I Choose, It Is Good to Be, Children. Mem. Am. Assn. U. Women, sec., 1994-96, Plano Cmty Forum, sec. 1996—; fundraiser L.A. County Rep. Party, 1983-95. Mem. Luth. Women's Missionary League (pres. 1983-85), Assistance League of Stovall Found. (sec. 1979-82), West Side Republican Women (sec.), Tex. Coll. Alumni Assn. (sec.), Delta Sigma Theta Sorority, Inc. Avocations: writing, volunteering, teaching, sewing, painting.

RICKS, MARY F(RANCES), archaeologist, anthropologist, consultant; b. Portland, Oreg., July 6, 1939; d. Leo and Frances Helen (Corcoran) Samuel; m. Robert Stanley Ricks, Jan. 7, 1961; children: Michael Stanley, Allen Gilbert. BA, Whitman Coll., 1961; MA, Portland State U., 1977, MPA, 1981, PhD, 1995. Asst. to dir. auxiliary services Portland State U., 1975-79, instnl. researcher, 1979-85, dir. instnl. research and planning, 1985-97, rsch. assoc. prof., 1994-97, rsch. assoc. prof. emerita, 1997—. Presenter in field. Contbr. articles to profl. jours. Vol. archeologist BLM-USDI, Lakeview, Oreg., 1975—. Fellow Soc. Applied Anthropology; mem. Soc. Am. Archaeology, Pacific N.W. Assn. Instnl. Rsch. and Planning (pres. 1990-91), Assn. Oreg. Archaeologists (v.p. 1988-90), Assn. Instl. Rsch., Sigma Xi. Home: 8106 SW 187th Ave Beaverton OR 97007-5697 E-mail: ricksm@pdx.edu.

RICKS, THOMAS MILLER, Middle East historian, university administrator; b. Lafayette, Ind, Oct. 15, 1938; s. Michael T. and Veronica C. (Jordan) R.; m. Janice D. Grasso, Aug. 26, 1967; children: Cynthia C., Laila M. BA, U. Notre Dame, 1961; MA, Ind. U., 1968, PhD, 1975. Tchr. history Tehran Internat. Sch., 1972-73; instr. history Macalester Coll., St. Paul, 1974-75; asst. prof. history Georgetown U., Washington, 1975-83; asst. dir. Ctr. for Arab and Islamic Studies Villanova U., Pa., 1985-91, dir. internat. studies, 1991-2002; adj. assoc. prof. history U. Pa., 2002—. Adj. assoc. prof. history Ctr. for Arab and Islamic Studies, Villanova U., 1985-2002; bd. dirs. Palestine CAssn. Cultural Exch., Ramallah, Palestine, 1998—; vis. asst. prof. history Birzeit U., Palestine, 1983-85; mem. Am. Friends Svc. Com., Mid. East Panel, 1996—. Editor, compiler, author: (bibliography) Persian Studies: A Bibliography, 1970, Iran: Contemporary Persian Literature, 1974, Critical Perspectives on Persian Literature, 1976; co-author: (textbook) Middle East: Past and Present, 1986; co-founder, co-editor: (jour.) Rev. of Iranian Polit. Economy and History, 1976-80, Birzeit Rsch. Rev., 1985-90, Frontiers: An Interdisciplinary Jour. of Study Abroad, 1994—. Vol. Iran III program Peace Corps, Mashhad and Mahabad, Iran, 1964-66. Asian scholar, Ind. U., 1966-67, Gert. Scholar, Haverford Coll., 2003; Jerusalem scholar Birzeit U., 1983-84, Fulbright sr. scholar, 1993, 94, 95; Nat. Def. Edn. Act grantee US Dept. Edn., 1967-70, Fulbright-Hays doctoral dissertation grantee, 1971-72, NEH grantee, 1976, 91, Social Sci. Rsch. Coun. grantee, 1977, US Dept. Edn. grantee, 1988-90, Pa. Dept. Edn. grantee, 1990-94; Palestinian Am. Rsch. Ctr. grantee, 2003. Mem. Coun. for Internat. Ednl. Exch. (bd. dirs. 1997-2000), Coun. for Internat. Exch. of Scholars (bd. dirs. 1996—), Pa. Coun. for Internat. Edn. (bd. dirs. 1994—, pres. 1994-99), Mid. East Studies Assn. (co-editor jour. 1980-82), Ctr. for Iranian Rsch. and Analysis (bd. dirs. 1997-2000), Soc. for Iranian Studies, Mid. East Inst., Am. Hist. Assn., Oral History Assn., Hist. Soc. Pa., Presbyn. Hist. Soc., Sons of Civil War Vets., Palestinian Am. Rsch. Ctr. Democrat. Roman Catholic. Avocations: civil war living history/reenactment, musician. Office: U Pa Dept History Rm 208 College Hall Philadelphia PA 19104-3335 E-mail: tmricks@sas.upenn.edu.

RICORDI, CAMILLO, surgeon, transplant and diabetes researcher; b. N.Y.C., Apr. 1, 1957; m. Valerie A. Grace, Aug. 8, 1986; children: M. Caterina, Eliana G., Carlo A. MD, U. Milan (Italy) Sch. Medicine, 1982. Trainee in gen. surgery San Raffaele Inst., Milan, 1982-85; NIH trainee Washington U. Sch. Medicine, St. Louis, 1985-88; attending surgeon San Raffaele Inst., Milan, 1988-89; asst. prof. to assoc. prof. surgery U. Pitts., Pa., 1989-93; prof. surgery and medicine, pathology, microbiology and immunology, chief divsn. cellular transpl. Diabetes Rsch. Inst., U. Miami, Fla., 1993—, sci. dir., chief acad. officer, 1996—, Stacy Joy Goodman chair in Diabetes Rsch., 1998—. Reviewer of applications for grants Can. and Am. Diabetes Assns., Juvenile Diabetes Found., NIH; chmn. First and Third Internat. Congresses of Cell Transplant Soc., Pitts., 1992, Miami, 1996, 5th Internat. Congress on Pancreas and Islet Transplantation, Miami, 1995, others; mem. editl. bd. Transplantation, Cell Transplantation, Transplantation Procs., Jour. Tissue Engring. Editor: Pancreatic Islet Cell Transplantation, 1992, Methods in Cell Transplantaion, 1995; co-editor-in-chief Cell Transplantation, Graft; contbr. numerous chpts. to books and articles to jours. including Immunology Today, Jour. Clin. Investigation, New Eng. Jour. Medicine, Hepatology, Diabetes, Transplantation, Endocrinology, Procs. NAS, USA, Am. Jour. Physiology, Surgery, Nature, Nature Genetics, Lancet. Grantee Juvenile Diabetes Found. Internat., 1988—, NIH, 1993—; recipient NIH trainee award, 1986-88, Nessim Habif World prize of surgery, 2001. Mem. AAAS, Cell Transplant Soc. (founder, pres. 1992-94), Am. Soc. Transplant Surgeons, Internat. Pancreas and Islet Transplant Assn. (v.p. 1979-99, pres. 1999—), The Transplantation Soc., Am. Diabetes Assn. (Rsch. award 1996, Outstanding Achievement award 2002), Am. Fedn. Clin. Rsch., Nat. Diabetes Coalition (co-founder 1994—, chmn. 1997—). Achievements include patent for Automated Method for Cell Separation. Office: U Miami Diabetes Rsch Inst 1450 NW 10th Ave Miami FL 33136-1011

RICOTTA, JOHN JOSEPH, vascular surgeon, educator; b. Buffalo, N.Y., Sept. 13, 1949; s. Joseph J. and Joan (Tarantino) R.; m. Gloria DeSantis, July 25, 1970; children: Joseph, Genna, Lise. BA, Yale Coll., 1969; MD, Johns Hopkins U., 1973. Diplomate Am. Bd. Surgery with spl. certification in vascular surgery. Intern, resident Johns Hopkins Hosp., 1973-79; instr. surgery Johns Hopkins U., Balt., 1979-80; asst. prof. surgery U. Rochester, N.Y., 1980-85, assoc. prof. surgery, 1985-88; prof. surgery, dir. vascular surgery SUNY, Buffalo, 1988-97, prof., chmn. dept. surgery Stony Brook, 1997—. Fellow ACS; mem. Soc. Vascular Surgery, Soc. Univ. Surgeons, Ctrl. Surg. Assn., Ea. Vascular Soc. (recorder 1992—, sec. 1996—, pres.

2001), Soc. Clin. Vascular Surgery (pres. 2001), Am. Surg. Assn.,Am. Assn. Vascular Surgery. Office: U Med Ctr Hsc T 19 Rm 020 Stony Brook NY 11794-0001 E-mail: JRicotta@notes.cc.sunysb.edu.

RIDDELL, ALICE MARY, educator; b. N.Y.C., Aug. 12, 1928; d. Arthur Edward and Alice Mary (McAuliffe) Robertson; B.A., Queens Coll., 1963, M.S., 1966; profl. diploma, St. John's U., 1973; m. Robert Lawrence Riddell, Jan. 17, 1948; 1 son, Jeffrey Lawrence. Tchr. and narcotics coordinator N.Y.C. Bd. Edn., Queens, 1963-70; dist. narcotics coordinator Community Sch. Dist. 25, Flushing, N.Y., 1970-71, dir. Project 25, 1971-89; dir. program svcs. drug abuse prevention program Archdiocese of N.Y., 1990—; asst. adj. prof. Queens Coll., Flushing, 1970-92. Mem. N.Y. State Adv. Council on Substance Abuse, 1978-83; mem. Borough Pres.' Adv. Council on Substance Abuse, 1970-89; co-chmn. Greater Flushing Substance Abuse Conf., 1980, Women in Crisis Conf., Drug Abuse Task Force, 1981; bd. trustees and bd. govs. Daytop Village, Inc., 1972—; bd. dirs. College Point Sports Assn., 1981—; mem. N.Y. State Bd. Regents Com. for Profl. Assistance, 1986—; parish facilitator Roman Cath. Ch. Recipient Merit cert. Flushing Drug Alert Com., 1972, Frank DeSilva Meml. award N.Y. State, 1982, N.Y. State award for Excellence in Prevention, 1986; named Educator of Yr., N.Y.C. Bd. Edn., 1985, Cath. Tchrs. Assn. Bklyn. and Queens, 1985. Mem. N.Y. State Assn. Substance Abuse Programs (dir.), N.Y.C. Coalition Dirs. Sch.-Based Drug Prevention Programs, N.Y. State Assn. Sch.-Based Prevention Profls. (pres., award for Excellence in Prevention Programming 1986), Assn. Curriculum and Supervision, N.Y.C. Adminstrv. Women in Edn., Chancellor's Task Force for Sch.-Based Drug Programs, Internat. Platform Assn., Ladies of Charity, Phi Delta Kappa. Democrat. Author: (with others) NCCJ Handbook for School Staffs Re: Alcohol & Drugs, 1981; contbr. articles to profl. jours.; editor Quar., 1981—. Home: 65-25 160th St Flushing NY 11365-2567 Office: ADAPP 2789 Schurz Ave Bronx NY 10465-3247

RIDDIFORD, LYNN MOORHEAD, zoologist, educator; b. Knoxville, Tenn., Oct. 18, 1936; d. James Eli and Virginia Amalia (Berry) Moorhead; m. Alan William Riddiford, June 20, 1959 (div. Jan. 1966); m. James William Truman, July 28, 1970. AB magna cum laude, Radcliffe Coll., 1958; PhD, Cornell U., 1961. Rsch. fellow in biology Harvard U., Cambridge, Mass., 1961-63, 65-66, asst. prof. biology, 1966-71, assoc. prof., 1971-73; instr. biology Wellesley (Mass.) Coll., 1963-65; from assoc. prof. zoology to prof. biology U. Wash., Seattle, 1972—2003, prof. biology, 2003—. Mem. study sect. tropical medicine and parasitology NIH, Bethesda, Md., 1974—78, Bethesda, 1997; mem. Competitive Grants panel USDA, Arlington, Va., 1979, Arlington, 89, Arlington, 95; mem. regulatory biology panel NSF, Washington, 1984—88; mem. governing coun. Internat. Ctr. for Insect Physiology and Ecology, 1985—91, chmn. program com., 1989—91; chmn. adv. com. SeriBiotech, Bangalore, India, 1989; mem. biol. adv. com. NSF, 1992—95. Contbr. articles to profl. jours. Bd. dirs. Entomol. Found., 1998—2001, Whitney Lab., 2000—. Recipient Gregor J. Mendel award, Czech Republic Acad. Scis., 1998; fellow, NSF, 1958—63, John S. Guggenheim Found., 1979—90, NIH, 1986—87; grantee, NSF, 1964—, NIH, 1975—, Rockefeller Found., 1970—79, USDA, 1978—82, 1989—. Fellow: AAAS, Entomol. Soc. Am. (Recognition award in insect physiology, biochemistry and toxicology), Royal Entomol. Soc., Am. Acad. Arts and Sci.; mem.: Soc. Devel. Biology, Am. Soc. Cell Biology, Am. Soc. Biochem. and Molecular Biology, Soc. Integrative and Comparative Biology (pres. 1991). Methodist. Home: 16324 51st Ave SE Bothell WA 98012-6138 Office: U Wash Dept Biology PO Box 351800 Seattle WA 98195-1800 E-mail: lmr@u.washington.edu.

RIDDLE, DONALD RAY, SR., retired art educator; b. Brookfield, Mo., Sept. 20, 1943; m. Mary K. Streett, Aug. 7, 1965; children: Michele, Donald Ray. BS, N.E. Mo. State U., 1966, MA, 1979. Cert. tchr. art, K-12, Mo. Art tchr. Brunswick (Mo.) RII, 1966-96, ret., 1996. Scout master, dist. com. mem. Boy Scouts Am., Brunswick, 1967-94; elder, Brunswick Christian Ch.; mem. Manitou Bluffs Mid.-Mo. chpt. Lewis & Clark Trail Heritage Found., Inc. Mem. Nat. Art Edn. Assn., Mo. Art Edn. Assn., Ret. Tchrs. Assn. Mo., Phi Delta Kappa. Home: 709 W Broadway St Brunswick MO 65236-1132 E-mail: riddler@mcmsys.com.

RIDDLE, JAMES DOUGLASS, retired academic administrator; b. Austin, Tex., Oct. 8, 1933; s. Prebble Elmer and Jewel Lee (Nalley) R.; m. Marilyn Brown Moore, Sept. 8, 1956; children: Mary Elizabeth, Margaret Allison, Charles Douglass. BA in History and Govt., Southwestern U., 1958; MDiv in Theology and Social Ethics, Boston U. Sch. Theology, 1962; postgrad., Boston U., 1962-65; D Ministry, San Francisco Theol. Sem., 1991. Ordained to ministry Meth. Ch., 1963, transferred to United Ch. of Christ, 1966. Co-pastor The First Parish Ch., Lincoln, Mass., 1963-67; sr. pastor The Community Ch., Chapel Hill, N.C., 1967-80, Historic First Ch. of Christ Congl. United Ch. of Christ, Springfield, Mass., 1980-89; v.p. devel. Am. Internat. Coll., Springfield, 1989-97; prin. The River Group, Springfield. Tchg. fellow, lectr. in human rels. Boston U. Sch. Bus., 1960-64; mem. Chapel Hill-Carrboro Bd. Edn., Chapel Hill, 1975-80. Mem. governing bd. Nat. Coun. Chs., 1969-72, commn. on faith and order, 1969-72, com. on future ecumenical study and svc. United Ch. of Christ, 1969-75, del. gen. synod, mem. exec. coun., 1969-75; pres. N.C. Legal Def. Fund, 1969-80, Orange-Chatham Counties Cmty. Action Agy., 1970-76, Chapel Hill-Carrboro Inter-Ch. Coun. Housing Corp., 1969-77; mem. bd. Cmty. Care Mental Health Ctr., 1980-90, chair, 1985-88; chair Downtown Ministry Project, 1981-84; mem. governing bd. Greater Springfield Coun. Chs., 1980-86, Downtown Econ. Devel. Corp., Springfield Ctr., 1981-95, StageWest Regional Theatre Co., 1982-92, Springfield YMCA, 1982-87, City of Springfield 350th Anniversary, 1984-87, Springfield Adult Edn. Coun., 1984—; corporator Zone Arts Ctr., 1986-94; mem., chmn. Hampden Assn. Ch. & Ministry Com. United Ch. of Christ, 1990—. Named Person of Yr. NOW, 1987; recipient 350th Anniversary Medallion, City of Springfield, 1986. Mem. ACLU, Coun. for Advancement and Support of Edn., Nat. Soc. Fund Raising Execs. (Cert. Fund Raising Exec.), Estate Planning Coun. Hampden County, New Eng. Devel. Rsch. Assn., Acad. Religion and Mental Health, Congl. Christian Hist. Soc. (mem. bd. 1987-95), Assn. Humanistic Psychology, Common Cause, The Reality Club of Springfield, Springfield Rotary, The Paul Harris Fellowship. Democrat. Avocations: backpacking, sailing, travel, cooking.

RIDDLE, KATHARINE PARKER, nutrition educator; b. Mussoorie, Uttar Pradesh, India, May 21, 1919; (parents Am. citizens); d. Allen Ellsworth and Irene (Glasgow) Parker; m. Charles W. Riddle, Sept. 2, 1941 (div. Oct. 1976); children: Dorothy Irene, William Parker, Patricia Karen. BA with honors, Park Coll., 1940; MSc in Nutrition, U. Chgo., 1942; cert. Chinese lang. and culture, Yale U., 1946; PhD, Union Grad. Sch., Yellow Springs, Ohio, 1974. Nutritionist Elizabeth McCormick Meml. Fund, Chgo., 1942-44; missionary United Presbyn. Ch., Peiping, China and Punjab, India, 1944-65; assoc. dir., home economist Agrl. Missions Div. Overseas Ministry Nat. Coun. Chs., N.Y.C., 1965-69; rsch. cons. Morehead (Ky.) State U., 1970-74; asst. prof. nutrition Pa. State. U., State Coll., 1974-76; dir. Nourishing Space for Women, Vail, Ariz., 1976-78; adj. prof., researcher Dept. Family and Community Medicine, Coll. Medicine U. Ariz., Tucson, 1978-81; nutrition specialist, officer women in devel. Coop. Extension Internat. Programs U. Nebr., Lincoln, 1981-86, prof. emerita, 1986—. Cons. Ch. Women United, N.Y.C., 1966-69, others; vis. scholar Coll. Bus. Adminstrn., U. Nebr., 1988. Author: Food with Dignity, 1977, Women and the Development of the World, 1983, (with C.M. Taylor) International Bibliography of Nutrition Education, 1971; editor: The Landour Book of International Recipes, 1965. Mem. Task Force on Voluntary Action by Women, White House Conf. Food, Nutrition, and Health, Washington, 1970, Gov.'s Commn. on Elderly, Ky., 1972; pres. bd. dirs. Internat. Ctr., Lincoln, 1986-88; researcher, program dir. Papago Breast Feeding Project, Sells, Ariz., 1979-81; project dir. Nebr. in the World, Lincoln, 1983-88; bd. dirs. Doté Found., San Antonio, Tex., 1989—; founder (with USDA, USAID, UNICEF, World Hunger Orgn., Food and Agrl. Orgn.) Task Force on Women's Participation in Rural Devel. Recipient Svc. award Agrl. Missions Inc., 1969, Disting. Alumna award Park Coll., 1977, Tribute to Women award YWCA, 1987. Mem. Am. Home Econs. Assn., Internat. Fedn. Home Econs., Soc. Nutrition Edn., Assn. Women in Devel. (founder 1982). Democrat. Home and Office: 13603 Forest Walk San Antonio TX 78231-1810

RIDDLE, MATTHEW C(ASEY), physician, educator; b. Portland, Oreg., Dec. 9, 1938; s. Matthew Casey and Katharine Hope (Kerr) R.; children from previous marriage: Matthew Casey III, Ann E., James K., Sarah A. BA in English magna cum laude, Yale U., 1960; MD, Harvard U., 1964. Diplomate Am. Bd. Internal Medicine. Resident in medicine Rush-Presbyn. St. Luke Hosp., Chgo., 1964—66, 1968, fellow endocrinology, 1969—71, U. Wash., Seattle, 1971—73; asst. prof. medicine Oreg. Health Scis. U., Portland, 1973-82, assoc. prof. medicine, 1982-96, head diabetes sect., 1975—, prof. medicine, 1996—. Mem. editl. bd.: Diabetes Care, Diabetes Therapeutics and Tech., Jour. Clin. Entocrinology and Metabolism; contbr. articles to profl. jours. Capt. U.S. Army, 1966-68, Vietnam. Mem. Am. Diabetes Assn. (bd. dirs., pres., chmn. bd. Oreg. affiliate), Am. Fedn. Clin. Rsch., Endocrine Soc., Am. Assn. Clin. Endocrinologists. Office: Oreg Health and Sci U L-345 3181 SW Sam Jackson Park Rd Portland OR 97201-3011

RIDDLESWORTH, JUDITH HIMES, elementary and secondary education educator; b. Hammond, Ind., Feb. 2, 1954; d. James Bernerd and Jane (Hall) Himes; m. Kim A. Riddlesworth, July 30, 1977; children: Sara, Becky. BS, Ill. State U., Normal, 1976; MA, No. Ariz. U., 1981. Cert. elem., spl. edn. tchr., Ariz. With Safford (Ariz.) Sch. Dist., 1976—, middle sch. tchr. spl. edn., 1987—, grade level chmn., 1989-93. Tech. team mem., peer evaluator, staff devel. mem., inservice facilatator Safford Sch. Dist.; Career Ladder participant. Mem. AAUW, Delta Kappa gamma. Avocations: horseback riding, cross-country skiing, cooking, aerobics, crafts. Office: Safford Unified Sch Dist 734 W 11th St Safford AZ 85546-2967

RIDENOUR, JAMES FRANKLIN, fund raising consultant; b. Peoria, Ill., Aug. 2, 1932; s. Arthur S. and Ruth (Ohlzen) R.; m. Doris K. Maxeiner, June 21, 1958; children: James Franklin Jr., David Arthur, Eric Carl, Anne Catherine. BS, Ill. Wesleyan U., 1954; MS, Ill. State U., 1970. Mktg. rep. Armstrong Cork Co., 1955-67; assoc. dir. devel. Ill. Wesleyan U., 1967-73; v.p. devel. Western Md. Coll., Westminster, 1973-84, Berry Coll., Rome, Ga., 1984-88; Marts and Lundy Inc., Lyndhurst, N.J., 1988, sr. cons., 1989—. Cons. Nikken Wellness, 2003—. Co-author: Handbook of Institutional Advancement, 1986. Chmn. Carroll County Tourism Coun., 1976-79, Families of Evenglow, 1979—; active Boy Scouts Am.; bd. dirs. YMCA, 1976-79, Kanuga Conf. Ctr., 1994—, Ill. Wesleyan U., 1996—, Church Club; chmn. mem. Diocesan Devel. Com., 1989—, chair, 1998—. Mem. Coun. Advancement and Support of Edn. (com. gift standards 1977-84, campaign reporting 1989-94), Pine Ridge Sr. Golf Club (pres.), Crozier Soc. (bd. dirs.), Six Napoleons, Rotary, Pi Gamma Mu, Gamma Upsilon. Republican. Episcopalian. Home: 648 Regester Ave Baltimore MD 21212-1917 Office: Marts & Lundy Inc 1200 Wall St W Lyndhurst NJ 07071-3680 E-mail: james.ridenour@verizon.net.

RIDER, SHERRI EILEEN, critical care nurse, educator; b. Wichita, Kans., Feb. 26, 1954; d. Bernard James Malone and Judy Ann (Jones) Hoffman; m. Terry Kendall Rider, Nov. 19, 1977; 1 child, Stephanie Marie. BSN, Wichita State U., 1986, M of Health Sci., 1992. RN, Kans.; cert. BLS instr., Kans., ACLS instr., Kans. Charge nurse emergency rm. Osteopathic Hosp., Wichita, 1977; charge nurse, relief charge nurse ICU, critical care unit Osteopathic Hosp. (name changed to Riverside Hosp.), Wichita, 1977—; cardiac rehab. coord. Riverside Hosp., Wichita, 1983-84, 87-89, orientation coord., 1989, continuing edn. facilitator, 1984—; patient care coord. ICU/critical care unit Riverside Health Sys., Wichita, 1993—. Clin. instr. Kans. Newman Coll., Wichita, fall 1993, 94. Severe weather spotter Nat. Weather Svc., Wichita, 1993-95. Mem. AACCN (vols. in participation 1993, treas. local chpt. 1993-94), Kans. Health Care Edn. Coun., Midwest Nursing Rsch. Soc., Kans. Assn. Nursing Continuing Edn. Providers, Alpha Eta. Lutheran. Avocations: climatology, astronomy, railroading, crochet, cross-stitch. Office: Riverside Health System 2622 W Central Ave Wichita KS 67203-4999

RIDGLEY, FRANCES AROC, principal; b. Manila, Jan. 29, 1936; came to U.S., 1966; d. Celestino Pascual and Urbana Ortaliza (Velasco) Aroc; m. Ignacio Flores Rilloraza, Aug. 1, 1958 (div. July 1970); children: Ignacio Aroc Rilloraza II, Joel A. Rilloraza; m. Charles Delbert Ridgley, Jan. 29, 1983. BS, Philippine Normal Coll., 1964; MS in Edn., Ind. State U., 1967; EdD, U. Pacific, 1980. Tchr. Cubao Elem. Sch., Quezon City, Philippines, 1955-61; unit chief GSIS, Manila, 1961-66; grad. asst. Ind. State U. Sch. Edn., Terre Haute, 1966-67; tchr. elem. sch. Vijo County Sch. Corp., Terre Haute, 1967-68; team leader, tchr. tng. supr. Tchr. Corps New Careers, Stockton, Calif., 1968-74; coord., sch. dist. cons. Stockton Unified Sch. Dist., 1974-80; tchr. intern supr., instr. U.O.P., Stockton, 1976-80; tchr. intern supr., instr., mem. basic edn. coun. Sch. Edn. U. Pacific, 1980-82; tchr. Alum Rock Union Elem. Sch. Dist., San Jose, 1982-85, coord., vice prin., 1985-93, prin., 1993—2000. Guest lectr. U.O.P. Sch. Edn., 1974-80; cons. in field. Vol. ARC, San Jose, 1988; participant, mem. Poco Way Redevel. Project, San Jose, 1993—; mem. Filipino Affirmative Action, Oakland, Calif., 1995—; commr. sister cities City of Milpitas; region commr. St Clara County & Moscow. Recipient Disting. Educator award I.D.E.A. Program for Sch. Adminstrs., Columbia., Mo., 1981, 82; Math. and Tech. grantee Santa Clara Office Edn., 1984, Global Edn. grantee Stanford U., 1978-80; Bilingual Edn. Doctoral fellow, 1976; I.D.E.A. fellow Kettering Found., 1981, 82; P.E.O. Internat. scholar, 1967. Mem. Filipino Am. Movement in Edn. (pres. 1986-88, LEadership award 1988), Filipino Am. Educators Assn. Calif. (v.p. 1987-89), Assn. Calif. Sch. Adminstrs. (pres. Capitol Charter chpt. 1994-95), Calif. Sch. Leadership Acad. (sr. assoc.), Phi Delta Kappa, Delta Kappa Gamma. Avocations: travel, golf, fitness exercise, reading, gardening. Home: 755 Tramway Dr Milpitas CA 95035-3606 Office: Alum Rock Union Elem Sch 2930 Gay Ave San Jose CA 95127-2322

RIDILL, WINIFRED MARIE MEYERS, retired English educator; b. Brownsville, Pa., July 11, 1949; d. George William and Sarah Winifred (Murray) Meyers; m. Jack Richard Ridill, Mar. 13, 1972. BA, Cleve. State U., 1971; MA, Old Dominion U., 1990. English tchr. Bay H.S., Bay Village, Ohio, 1972-81, Wando H.S., Mt. Pleasant, S.C., 1981-82, Bay H.S., 1982-83, First Colonial H.S., Virginia Beach, Va., 1983—2000; ret., 2000. Vol. emergency rm. Va. Beach Gen. Hosp., 1986-2000; vol. reading tutor Lit. Coun. of Tidewater, Portsmouth, Va., 1994-2000. Mem. Virginia Beach Assn. Tchrs. English (sec. 1989-90, English Tchr. of Yr. 1992-93). Roman Catholic. Avocations: travel, gardening. E-mail: wmridill@att.net.

RIDLEY, CAROLYN FLUDD, retired social studies educator; b. Nashville, Jan. 21, 1942; d. Quitman Daniel and Glennora Elizabeth (Cannon) F.; m. Raymond Bennett, June 23, 1962 (div. 1984); 1 child, Karen Elizabeth Bennett Moore; m. Cornelius Theodore Ridley, July 16, 1988; stepchildren: Constance Maria Ridley Smith, William Keith. BA, CUNY, 1973; MEd, Tenn. State U., 1985. Cert. tchr., prin., Tenn., N.Y. Tchr. N.Y.C. Bd. Edn., 1973-75, Dickson (Tenn.) County Bd. Edn., 1976-77, Hickman County Bd. Edn., Centerville, Tenn., 1977-86, Met. Nashville Bd. Edn., 1986—2003; ret, 2003. Dir. Hickman County Career Day, 1982-83; bd. dirs. Assn. Retarded Citizens, Centerville, 1982-86; adv. com. Hickman County Bicentennial Com., Centerville, 1984-86, initiator commemorative quilt; participant NEH lectr. Author: A Black History of Hickman County, 1985. Campaign worker Met. Nashville Bd. Edn., 1991; campaigner Met. Nashville Edn., Assn., 1992; attendant Dem. Socialization Meeting, Nashville, 1992; participant Nat. Endowment for the Humanities Summer Inst. Furman U., Greenville, Tenn., 1995. Grantee Mid. Tenn. State U., Murfreesboro, 1990, Tenn. State U., Nashville, 1992; James R. Stokeley Inst. fellow U. Tenn., 1993; participant NEH Summer Inst. at Furman U., Greenville, Tenn., 1995; named Tchr. of Yr., 1997, 2002-03. Fellow Taft Inst. (cert. 1992, tchr. of yr. 1997, 2002-03); mem. AAUW, NEA, NASA Space Inst. (cert. 1990), Met. Nashville Edn. Assn. (campaign worker and assn. rep.), Smithsonian Instn., Internat. Platform Assn., Nat. Historic Preservation Soc., Nat. Geographic Soc., Nat. Coun. Social Studies, Internat. Platform Assn., Holocaust Meml. Mus. (charter mem.). Democrat. Mem. Ch. of Christ. Avocations: travel, reading, music, studying quilting folk art. Home: 4348 Setters Rd Nashville TN 37218-1839 Office: Haynes Mid Sch 510 W Trinity Ln Nashville TN 37207-4944

RIDLEY, DENNIS RAYMOND, university director; b. Portland, Oreg., Apr. 13, 1942; s. Glenn Arthur and Naomi Esther (Tobie) R.; m. Liane Gale Fink, Sept. 16, 1973; children: Daniela Kimberly, Janna Gabriela. AB in Psychology cum laude, Amherst Coll., 1965; MA, U. Calif., Santa Barbara, 1968, PhD, 1972. C.C. tchg. credential, Calif. Prof. psychology Houghton (N.Y.) Coll., 1974-76, 78-79, SUNY, Geneseo, 1976-78; rsch. assoc. Inst. for Occupl. Edn. Cornell U., Ithaca, N.Y., 1979-84, rsch. specialist com. on edn. in the cmty., 1984, rsch. assoc. dept. human svcs., 1984-85, vis. fellow dept. edn., 1983; asst. provost Christopher Newport U., Newport News, Va., 1985-90, dir. assessment and evaluation, 1990-99, prof., 1996-99; dir. instnl. rsch. and planning Va. Wesleyan Coll., 1999—. Chmn. working com. on internat. studies State Coun. Higher Edn. for Va., Richmond, 1989-90; bd. dirs. Hampton Roads Rsch. Partnership; mem. vis. teams Mil. Installation Vol. Edn. Rev., Yuma, Ariz., 2000, Seoul, 2001, Ft. Eustis, 2003; mem. Ed. Adv. Bd., Rsch, Post Compulsory Ed., 2003. Author: (monograph) Assessing Student Learning in Light of How Students Learn, 1988; also numerous articles. Mem., officer Neighborhood Civic League, Virginia Beach, Va., 1985-87. A.P. Sloan Found. fellow Amherst Coll., 1960, Regents' and Blaney fellow U. Calif., 1967-69. Mem. Am. Ednl. Rsch. Assn. (Disting. Paper award 1997), Assn. Study Higher Edn., Va. Assn. for Mgmt. Analysis and Planning, Assn. for Instnl. Rsch., Va. Assessment Group (sec.-treas. 1993-94, v.p. 2002-2003). Avocation: writing fiction and nonfiction. Home: 4117 Marblehead Dr Virginia Beach VA 23456-5304 Office: Va Wesleyan Coll 1584 Wesleyan Dr Norfolk VA 23502-5599 E-mail: dridley@vwc.edu.

RIDNER, KATHLEEN RADER, elementary education educator; b. Manchester, Ky., Feb. 11, 1949; d. Herman Ralph Sr. and Beatrice (Benge) Rader; m. Daniel Lewis Ridner, Oct. 4, 1969; 1 child, Mark Fredrick. BS, Cumberland Coll., 1980; M in Bus., Ea. Ky. U., 1982. Cert. tchr., Ky. Tchr. Belmont Jr. High Sch., Winchester, Ky., 1982-83; tchr. math. McKee (Ky.) Elem. Sch., 1985-86; tchr. lang. arts North Laurel Mid. Sch., London, Ky., 1986—. Republican. Baptist. Avocations: reading, cross-stitch, travel. Home: 60 Cypress Way London KY 40741-8250 Office: North Laurel Mid Sch 101 Johnson Rd London KY 40741-9500

RIECK, JANET RAE, special education educator; b. Atchison, Kans., Oct. 24, 1948; d. Clinton Everett and Bernice Marie (Schreurs) Wendland; m. Arthur Wyman Hand, Mar. 1970 (div. Feb. 1977); m. Doyle Elmer Rieck, Sept. 21, 1986. B in Music Edn., Otterbein Coll., 1970; MA, U. No. Colo., 1980; MS, No. Ill. U., 1989. Cert. tchr. Nebr. Music tchr. Blanchester (Ohio) Schs., 1970-74; tchr. aide N.Mex. Sch. for Visually Handicapped, Alamogordo, 1976-78; tchr. visually impaired Edn. Svc. Unit 7, Columbus, Nebr., 1979—. Piano tchr., Cin., 1975-76, Alamogordo, 1976-78. Mem. NEA, Coun. Exceptional Children, Assn. for Edn. and Rehab. of Blind and Visually Impaired (Nebr. pres. elect 1990-92, pres. 1992-94, cert. orientation and mobility specialist). Lutheran. Avocations: piano, sewing, horseback riding, swimming. Office: Ednl Svc Unit 7 2657 44th Ave Columbus NE 68601-8537

RIECK, WILLIAM ALBERT, secondary school educator and administrator, professor; b. Hackensack, N.J., Jan. 15, 1942; s. William Emanual and Grace Adeline (Bormann) R.; m. Judith Ann Klindt, Apr. 18, 1965; children: Melissa, William Albert Jr. BA, Jersey City State Coll., 1963; MA, Montclair (N.J.) State Coll., 1966; DEd, Loyola U., Chgo., 1976. Asst. prof. Trenton State Coll., NJ, 1966-69; area mgr. Dupont Chem., Chgo., 1969-72; chemistry tchr. Lockport H.S., 1972-74; asst. prin. Oak Forest H.S., Ill., 1974-75; prin. Evanston Twp. H.S., Ill., 1975-76, Rock Island H.S., Ill., 1975-77, Fallsburg H.S., NY, 1977-80, Hicksville H.S., NY, 1980-90, Nottingham H.S., Trenton, 1982-90; prof. edn./dir. tchr. cadet corps U. La., Lafayette, 1991—, prof., dir. grad. studies edn., 1991—. Contbr. articles to profl. jours. Mem. Hamilton (N.J.) Say No to Drugs Com., 1987—, Hamilton Citizens for Edn., 1989—; advisor DeMolay chpt., Hamilton Sq., N.J., 1987—; trustee First Presbyn. Ch., Levittown, N.Y., 1981-84. Recipient Disting. Alumnu award Jersey City State Coll., 1983, Citation, N.J. Gen. Assembly, 1983, Cert. of Appreciation, N.Y. Congress Parents and Tchrs., 1982; NSF grantee, 1968, 1994-95. Mem. Nat. Assn. Secondary Sch. Prins. (Svc. award 1989), N.J. Prins. and Suprs. Assn. (exec. coun. 1985—, Svc. award 1989), Assn. for Supervision and Curriculum Devel., Mercer County Prins. and Suprs. Assn. (sec. 1988—), Masons, Shriners (youth com. chmn. 1975-80). Presbyterian. Home: 108 Shadowbrush Bnd Lafayette LA 70506-7852 Office: U La Foster Hall 221 PO Box 42051 Lafayette LA 70504-0001 E-mail: wrieck@louisiana.edu.

RIECKEN, ELLNORA ALMA, retired music educator; b. Delaware, Ohio, Mar. 21, 1934; d. William Emil and Alma Ellanora (Gollner) R. BA cum laude, Millsaps Coll., 1955; M in Music, Fla. State U., 1957; grad., U. Miami, 1986-87. Tchr. Filer Jr. High, Hialeah, Fla., 1956-72; choral dir. H. Mann Jr. High, Miami, Fla., 1972-74; music tchr. Olympia Heights Elem., Miami, 1974-80; music. tchr. Melrose Elem., Miami, ret., 1996. Tour mem. Kjelson Summer Chorale, Miami, 1970; performing mem. Civic Chorale of Greater Miami, 1970--; dept. rep. Melrose Faculty Council, Miami, 1984-87. Composer: 5 Incidental Songs for Christmas All Over the Place by J. Martin, 1986, 6 songs to go with the story The Elves and the Shoemaker, 1991, 3 songs to go with children's story Santa Has the Sniffles by Diane Stortz, 1994, elem. chorus arrangement of the spiritual Trampin with strings, melody, bells and pianicas. Panel speaker Soroptomist Club Regional Conv., Atlanta, 1960; credentials chmn. Venture Club Nat. Conv., Miami, 1964; team lay speaker Sunshine Via De Cristo Retreat, Miami, 1984; Sunday sch. class rec. sec. 1st United Meth. Ch. Coral Gables, Fla., 1984-85, v.p., 1998-99, pres., 1999-2000. Named Tchr. of Yr., 1989. Mem. Music Educators Nat. Conf., Fla. Music Educators Assn., Dade County Music Educators Assn., Am. Choral Dirs. Assn., Fla. Elem. Music Educators Assn., United Tchrs. of Dade County, Hibiscus Fine Arts Guild Miami Springs, United Meth. Women (circle vice chmn. 1987-89). Democrat. Avocations: bowling, sewing, travel, plants, artwork, landscape painting. Home: PO Box 660177 Miami FL 33266-0177

RIEDINGER, EDWARD ANTHONY (TED RIEDINGER), international educator, Brazilianist; b. Cin., Mar. 26, 1944; s. Charles Anthony and Ida Gertrude (Winter) R. Student, Latin Sch. Indpls., 1962; BA cum laude, Butler U., 1967; MA, U. Chgo., 1969, PhD, 1978; MLIS, U. Calif., Berkeley, 1989; postgrad., Harvard U., 1969, U. Oxford, 1970, U. Cambridge, 1986. Pvt. sec. to ex-Pres. Brazil Juscelino Kubitschek, 1972-76; asst. prof. Pontifical Cath. U., Rio de Janeiro, 1976-77, U. Ams., Puebla, Mex., 1978; ednl. adv. officer Fulbright Commn. U.S. Consulate, Rio de Janeiro, 1979-88; founder Overseas Ednl. Advisers Profl. Edn. Group Nat. Assn. for Fgn. Student Affairs, 1985, Latin Am. rep., 1988; acting bibliographer L.Am., Spain, Portugal U. Calif., Berkeley, 1990; lectr. Brazilian history San Francisco State U., 1990; prof., head Latin Am. Libr. Ohio State U., 1991—. Mem. organizing exec. com. Brazilian Studies Assn., 1993, sec., 1994-96; founder, adminstr. Overseas Ednl. Advisers

Profl. Net, 1992-95; cons. on Brazil and internatl ednl. advising for U.S. and internat. orgns. and agys.; adj. prof. Dept. History, Spanish and Portuguese, Ohio State U.; adj. prof. Ohio U., Athens, Ohio, 1998—; cons. in field. Author: Brief View of American Literature, 1976, Como Se Faz Um Presidente, a Campanha de J.K., 1988, Procs. of 1st BRASA conf., 1994, Procs. of 2d BRASA conf., 1995, Turned on Advising, 1995, Where in the World to Learn, 1995, Bibliography of Rise of West, 2002; contbr. numerous articles to profl. and scholarly jours. and reference books; mem. editl. bd. Phi Beta Delta Internat. Rev., 1992-96, Manguinhos, 1994—. Ford Found. fellow, 1968-72; travel grantee NEH, 1992, OSU/Tinker Found. field rsch. grantee 1992, 96; Fulbright-Hays scholar, 1996, Fulbright Sr. Specialist, 2001-06; recipient commendations Brazilian Army Corps of Engrs., 1982, U.S. Info. Svc., 1984, Brazilian War Coll., 1985, Fulbright Commn., 1988, 2001—, U.S. amb. to Brazil, 1988, Berkeley City Commons, 1990, Instituto Brasil-Estados Unidos, Rio de Janeiro, 1995. Office: Ohio State U Librs 1858 Neil Ave Rm 312 Columbus OH 43210 E-mail: riedinger.4@osu.edu.

RIEDL, JOHN ORTH, university dean; b. Milw., Dec. 9, 1937; s. John O. and Clare C. (Quirk) R.; m. Mary Lucille Priestap, Feb. 4, 1961; children: John T., Ann E., James W., Steven E., Daniel J. BS in Math. magna cum laude, Marquette U., Milw., 1958; MS in Math., U. Notre Dame, 1960, PhD in Math., 1963; postgrad., Northwestern U., 1963. Asst. prof. math. Ohio State U., Columbus, 1966-70, assoc. prof., 1970—2003, asst. dean Coll. Math. and Phys. Sci., 1969-74, assoc. dean, 1974-87, acting dean, 1984-86, spl. asst. to provost, 1987—2003, dean, dir. Mansfield (Ohio) Campus, 1988—2003, exec. dean regional campus, 1988—2003, assoc. prof. emeritus, 2003—. Panelist sci. edn. NSF, 1980-91; cons. Ohio Dept. Edn., 1989, Ohio bd. regents subsidy cons., 1991, 95, 97, 99, 2001, 03; bd. dirs. U. and Coll. Access Network. Pres., v.p. exec. com. Univ. Cmty. Assn., Columbus, 1970-78; mem. edn. commn. St. Peter's Schs., Mansfield, 1989-95; trustee Rehab. Svc. N. Ctrl. Ohio, Mansfield, 1990-99, v.p., 1993-94, pres., 1995-97; pres. Ohio Assn. Regional Campuses, 1993-94; co-chair capital campaign St. Peter's Schs., 1998. NSF grad. fellow, 1960, 61, 62; recipient Faculty Svc. award Nat. U. Continuing Edn. Assn., 1988, Creative Programming award, 1988. Mem. Math. Assn. Am. (chair com. on minicourse 1981-87), Downs Am. Chestnut Found. of Ohio (bd. dirs. 2001-), Rotary Internat. (bd. dirs., pres.-elect, pres.) C. of C. (bd. dirs.). bd. dirs., Richland County U. and Coll. Access Network, 2002-. Democrat. Roman Catholic. Avocations: fishing, woodworking, handball, gardening. Home: 745 Clifton Blvd Mansfield OH 44907-2284 Office: Ohio State U 1680 University Dr Mansfield OH 44906-1547 E-mail: riedl.1@osu.edu.

RIEF, SANDRA FAYE, special education educator, consultant; b. Chgo., Oct. 21, 1951; d. Jack H. and Edith Fisdel; m. Itzik Rief, Dec. 17, 1972. BA in Elem. Edn., U. Ill., Chgo., 1973; MEd, U. Ill., Urbana, 1976. Cert. tchr. elem. and spl. edn., Calif. Learning disabilities tchr. Peotone (Ill.) Sch. Dist., 1973, Beecher (Ill.) Sch. Dist., 1974; spl. edn. tchr., resource specialist San Diego Unified Sch. Dist., 1980-2001; instr. Bur. Edn. and Rsch., San Diego, 1998—. Cons. on tchr. tng.; lectr. in field; mentor tchr. San Diego Unified Schs., 1988-91. Author: How to Reach and Teach ADD/ADHD Children, 1993, How to Reach and Teach All Children in the Inclusive Classroom, 1996, Systematic Phonics, 1986, Simply Phonics (curriculum), 1994, The ADD/ADHD Checklist, 1998, Ready...Start...School, 2001; co-author: Alphabet Learning Center Activities Kit, 2000; developer/presenter video: ADHD: Inclusive Instruction and Collaborative Practices, 1994, How to Help Your Child Succeed in School, 1996, The ADHD Book of Lists, 2003, Successful Schools: How to Raise Achievement and Support for At-Risk Students, 1999, Successful Classrooms: Effective Teaching Strategies for Raising Achievement in Reading and Writing, 1999, ADHD: Powerful Strategies and Accommodations, 2003. Mem. profl. adv. bd. Children and Adults with Attention Deficit Disorders, 1995-98. Recipient EXCEL award Corp. for Excellence in Pub. Edn., San Diego County, 1993. Mem. Coun. for Exceptional Children, Children and Adults with Attention Deficit Disorder, Calif. Assn. for Resource Specialists (Calif. Resource Specialist of Yr. 1995), Learning Disabilities Assn., Phi Kappa Phi. Democrat. Address: PO Box 19207 San Diego CA 92159-0207

RIEGER, BIN HONG, secondary school educator; b. Kota Bharu, Kelantan, Malaysia, Oct. 6, 1948; came to U.S., 1974; d. Kee Teong and Leng Yean (Tan) Teo; m. Paul Leonhard Rieger, Aug. 1, 1979; 1 child, Natasha Irina. BA, Ambassador Coll., 1978; MA, Calif. State U., L.A., 1982. Cert. tchr., Calif.; cert. lang. devel. specialist. Temporary tchr. Zainab Secondary Sch., Kota Bharu, 1971, Islah Nat. Primary Sch., Kota Bharu, 1972-74; contract tchr. L.A. Unified Sch. Dist., 1979—, presenter dance workshop, 1988. Presenter workshop fair L.A. Ednl. Partnership, 1987-89, presenter emergency immigrant edn. assistance program, 1989-90, 92-2001; participant Korean Bilingual Staff Devel. Project, Seoul, 1992, English Edn. Curriculum, Inc. Explore Korea Program, 2001, 02; numerous presentations in field. Presenter folk dance 14th Ann. Citywide Elem. Tchrs. Staff Devel., 1987, LA City Elem. Schs. Music Assn., Inc. Staff Devel., 2001, 8th Annual Title VII Conf. for LA Unified Sch. Dist., 2002; Fun Day coord. Pacific Asia Mus., Pasadena, Calif., 1988. Nominee 17th Annual BRAVO award, Music Ctr. Edn., LA, 1999; recipient Outstanding Tchr. of Yr. award, Wilshire Rotary Club of LA, 1996; Grant, LA Ednl. Partnership, 1986, 1989. Avocations: folk dancing, swimming. Home: 4906 Viro Rd La Canada Flintridge CA 91011-3746

RIEGER, PHILIP HENRI, chemistry educator, researcher; b. Portland, Oreg., June 24, 1935; s. Otto Harry and Carla (Oertli) R.; m. Anne Bioren Lloyd, June 18, 1957; 1 child, Christine Lloyd BA, Reed Coll., 1956; PhD, Columbia U., 1962. Prof. chemistry Brown U., Providence, 1962—, ret., 2002, prof. emeritus chemistry, 2002—. Rschr. in field. Contbr. articles to profl. jours. Mem. Am. Chem. Soc. (chmn. R.I. sect. 1978), Royal Soc. Chemistry, New Eng. Assn. Chemistry Tchrs. Epscopalian. Home: 36 Anawan Rd Pawtucket RI 02861 Office: Brown U Dept Chemistry Box H Providence RI 02912 E-mail: philip_rieger@brown.edu.

RIEHL, JANE ELLEN, education educator; b. New Albany, Ind., Oct. 17, 1942; d. Henry Gabbart Jr. and Mary Elizabeth Willham; m. Richard Emil Riehl, June 15, 1968; 1 child, Mary Ellen. BA in Elem. Edn., U. Evansville, 1964; MS, Ind. U., Bloomington, 1966; postgrad., Spalding U., 1979, Ind. U. S.E., New Albany, 1991—2002. Cert. 1-8 and kindergarten tchr., Ind.; lic. profl. elem adminstrn., reading minor kindergarten tchr., Ind. Elem. tchr. Clarksville (Ind.) Cmty. Sch., 1964-68, 70-75, 81-82, tchr. kindergarten, 1975-81; elem. tchr. Chapelwood Sch. Wayne Twp., Indpls., 1968-70; lectr. edn. Ind. U. S.E., 1988-97, dir. tchg. and rsch. project, 1990-91, 92-93, dir. field and career placement, cert./lic. grad advisor, 1998, coord. elem./spl. edn. field and career placement, license and grad. advisor, 1998—. Cons. Riehl Assocs., Jeffersonville, Ind., 1995—. Co-author: An Integrated Language Arts Teacher Education Program, 1990, The Reading Professor, 1992, Multimedia: HyperStudio and Language Education, 1996, Technology: Hypermedia and Communications, 1997, others; author procs. Parent vol. Girl Scouts U.S.A., Jeffersonville, 1988-95; mem. adminstrtv. bd. Wall Street United Meth. Ch., Jeffersonville, 1993-95; mem. women's health adv. coun. Clark Meml. Hosp., Jeffersonville, 1995—; bd. dirs. Clark Meml. Hosp. Found., vice chair, 1999, chair 2000, sec. 2002-03; team mem. People to People Citizen Amb. Program, 1993, 95, 96; chair internat. bylaws Altrusa Internat., Inc., 2001—. Named Young Career Woman of Yr. Bus. and Profl. Women New Albany and Dist. 13 Ind., 1966; tchg. and rsch. grantee Ind. U. S.E., 1990, 94, 95, 96, 97, 2000; recipient Disting. Tchg. award Ind. U. S.E., 1997, Tchg. Excellence Recognition award, 1997. Mem. Nat. Coun. Tchrs. English, Profs. Reading Tchr. Edn., Ind. State Med. Assn. Alliance (v.p. so. area 1999-2000), Clark County Med. Soc. Alliance (pres.-elect 1997-98, pres. 1998-99), Altrusa Internat. Inc. (internat. bd. 1993-95, dist. gov. 1993-95, svc. award 1995), Phi Delta Kappa (v.p. 1991-92, pres. 1997—, svc. award 1991), Kappa Kappa Kappa (pres. Jeffersonville 1975-76, 90-91, Outstanding Mem. award 1987). Avocations: travel, reading, crafts, decorating. Home: 1610 Fox Run Trl Jeffersonville IN 47130-8204 Office: Ind U SE 4201 Grant Line Rd New Albany IN 47150-2158

RIENDEAU, DIANE, secondary school educator; Teacher Barrington (Ill.) H.S., Barrington, Ill., 1985—. Recipient Innovative Teaching Grants Program, Am. Assn. of Physics Teachers, 1992. Home: 310 James St Barrington IL 60010-3329 Office: Barrington HS 616 W Main St Barrington IL 60010-3015

RIESS, GEORGE FEBIGER, lawyer, educator; b. New Orleans, Oct. 22, 1943; s. Frank and Jane (Kelleher) R.; m. June 22, 1968 (div. June 1976); 1 child, Katherine Cody; m. Maida Magee, Aug. 23, 1980; children: Frank Henry, Carson Magee, Maida Jean. BA, Tulane U., 1965; JD, La. State U., 1969. Bar: La. 1969, Mich. 1972, U.S. Dist. Ct. (ea., we. and mid. dists.) La. 1970. Mng. ptnr. Johnson & Riess Law Firm, New Orleans, 1970-76; ptnr. Monroe & Lemann Law Firm, New Orleans, 1976-96, Polack, Rosenberg, Endom & Riess, L.L.P., New Orleans, 1996—. Bd. dirs. Plaquemines Oil and Devel. Corp., New Orleans; adj. prof. law Tulane U. Law Sch., New Orleans, 1987-94. Sec. of vestry St. Martin Episcopal Ch., Metairie, La., 1992—. Recipient Ford Found. grant, 1969. Fellow La. State Bar Found.; mem. ABA, Am. Judicature Soc., Fed. Bar Assn., La. Assn. Def. Counsel, La. State Bar Assn., New Orleans Assn. Def. Counsel, So. Yacht Club, New Orleans Lawn Tennis Club. Office: Polack Rosenberg Edom & Riess LLP 938 Lafayette St Ste 100 New Orleans LA 70113-1067

RIESZ, WANDA WALLACE, educational consultant; b. Lafayette, Ind., July 13, 1942; d. George Murdock and Byrdena Maude (McDill) Wallace; m. William H. Riesz, July 28, 1963 (div. 1972); children: James W. (Jay) (dec.), Nicole Elies. Student, Purdue U., 1960-61, U. Md., Madrid, 1962; AB in Spanish, Ind. U., 1962, BS in Edn., 1963, MS in Edn., 1965, D in Cultural Studies, 1972; cert., U. Madrid, 1962; student, Berlitz Lang. Sch., Freiburg, Germany, 1966, Internat. U. Menendez Pelayo, Santander, Spain, 1967, Alliance Francaise, Paris, 1967. Lic. superintendent adminstr. K-12, tchr. Spanish K-9, elem. tchr., Ind.; lic. K-12 elem. sch., Spanish K-12, Va.; lic. real estate sales, broker, Ind. Tchr. elem. sch., French Fairfax (Va.) County Schs., 1963-65; dir. GED drop-out program U.S. Army, Kaiserslautern, Germany, 1965-66; assoc. prof. SUNY, Stony Brook, 1968-70; lectr. sch. edn. Ind. U., Purdue U., Columbus, Bloomington, Ind., 1970-78; founder, prin. Pub. Alternative H.S., Bloomington, 1970-80; legis. aide Ind. Ho. of Reps., Indpls., 1988-96, edn. policy analyst, family & social svcs. specialist, 1996-97. Cons. edn., legis., polit., drunk driving, vets.' affairs Hampton Inst.,Appalachia, Cleve., Lexington, Ky., L.A., Cleveland, Tenn., Grand Rapids, Mich., 1970—; grant writer Fed. Law Enforcement Agy., Ind., Washington, 1970—; dir. alternative edn. programs Indpls. Pub. Schs., 1997—; spkr. in field. Contbr. articles to profl. jours.; co-developer: (video and board game) Peer Supervision, 1976. Rep. Ind. Baccalaureate Edn. Sys. Trust Ind. Ho. of Reps. Dem. Caucus; cons. Vietnam and Korean War Meml. Commn., 1990—, Goals 2000, 1990—, U.S. Sec. Edn., 1990—, Coalition Essential Schs., 1990—; bd. dirs. Luggage for Foster Kids, State of Ind., 1990—, Middle Way Shelter for Battered Women, Bloomington, 1984, State Juvenile Justice Task Force, 1982, Big Brothers/Big Sisters; bd. dirs., pres. Jay Riesz Found. to Prevent Drunk Driving, Women for Better Govt., Greater Indpls., 1994-96; legis. liaison State Mothers Against Drunk Driving; vol. Habitat for Humanity, Indpls., 1995; pres. Dem. Woman's Club, 1994—; founding mem. Ind. Victims of Violent Crimes, 1995—; elected del. Ind. Dem. State Conv., 1988, 92, 96; mem. youth adv. bd., New Directions Com. St. Paul's Episc. Ch., 1994—; pres. Ind. State Alternative Learning Options, Ind. Sagamore of the Wabash, 1997. Named Ky. Col., 1995; recipient State POW/MIA award DAV, Spl. Merit Recognition award State of Ind. Dept. Vets. Affairs, 1995, Spl. Legis. award Mothers Against Drunk Driving, State of Ind., 1990, Outstanding Cmty. award Indpsl. Boys and Girls' Club, 1998. Mem. Edn. Commn. of the States, NOW, Indpls. Athletic Club, Culver Mil. Acad. Club (Indpls.), Am. Legion Aux. (life), Metro. Indpls. Bd. Realtors, Studebaker Drivers Club, Mustang Owners Club, Maxinkuckee Yacht Club, Inpls. Ski Club, Phi Sigma Iota (treas. 1972), Pi Lambda Theta (sec. 1971), Psi Iota Xi. Avocations: swimming, skiing, vintage cars. Office: Indpls Pub Schs Edn Svc Ctr 501E Indianapolis IN 46204 Home: 9804 Gulfstream Dr Fishers IN 46038-9726

RIFE, RONALD EUGENE, elementary education educator; b. Iowa City, Oct. 18, 1936; s. Charles Raymond and Helen Imogene (Tone) R.; m. Dolores Fay, Oct. 3, 1959; children: Knute Arthur, Kirsten Anne. BA, U. Iowa, 1971, postgrad., 1971-72; MEd, U. Nebr., 1981. Cert. tchr., elem. adminstr., Iowa, Nebr. Farmer, Lone Tree, Iowa, 1956-62; clk. Lincoln Mut. Ins. Assn., Lone Tree, 1962-64; real estate salesman Poots-Freed Assn., Iowa City, 1964-65; newspaper reporter, advt. salesman Lone Tree Reporter, 1965-69; tchr. elem. social studies Meridian Pub. Sch., Daykin, Nebr., 1972-95; substitute tchr., ednl. cons., 1995—. Contbr. columns to newspapers. Precinct chmn. Lone Tree Rep. Com., 1962-72; del. Johnson County Rep. Conv., Iowa City, 1968, 70, 72, Iowa Rep. Conv., Des Moines, 1972; mem. troop com., scoutmaster, merit badge counselor Boy Scouts Am., 1950—; actor community theater, Lincoln, Nebr., 1980, Fairbury, Nebr., 1984, 89. Mem. NEA, Nebr. Edn. Assn., Meridian Edn. Assn. (pres. 1973, 79, 83), Nat. Wrestling Coaches Assn., Masons (master Lone Tree 1964, Hebron, Nebr. 1984). Presbyterian. Avocations: golf, bridge, reading, traveling, stamp collecting. Home: 5695 Highway 22 SE Lone Tree IA 52755-9329 Office: Meridian Pub Sch PO Box 190 Daykin NE 68338-0190

RIFFE, STACY CHRISTINE, secondary school educator; b. Beckley, W.Va., Aug. 16, 1970; d. Clinton Gilbert and Frances Loise (Martin) Forren; m. Vincent Rodger Riffe, Apr. 17, 1993. Student, So. W.Va. C.C., Pineville; BA in Edn., Glenville State Coll., 1993; M in Curriculum and Instrn., Coppin State Coll. Cert. tchr., W.Va., 2002. Waitress Pineville (W.Va.) Restaurant, 1988; teller Bank of Oceana, W.Va., 1988-90; substitute tchr. Fayette County Bd. Edn., Fayetteville, W.Va., 1993; teller 1st State Bank and Trust, Rainelle, W.Va., 1993; tchr. math. Jackson County Bd. Edn., Ripley, W.Va., 1993—. Presenter Ctr. for Profl. Devel., Charleston, 1993—; tech. specialist Jackson County Bd. Edn., Ripley, 1995-97; cheerleading coach Ripley H.S., 1996-97. Sponsor Young Christians Club, Ripley, 1993—; pianist West Ripley Bapt. Ch., 1993—; pianist, alto Hill Top Quartet, Ripley, 1995-97. Mem. NEA, W.Va. Edn. Assn., Jackson County Tchr. Assn. Avocations: music, arts and crafts, reading. Home: 229 Simmons Dr Ripley WV 25271-1336 Office: Ripley HS # 2 School St Ripley WV 25271

RIFKIN, GARY D. physician, educator; b. N.Y.C., Feb. 24, 1946; s. Ira and Ruth (Mann) R.; m. Thelma Freeman, Nov. 22, 1969; children: Jay, Scott, Lori. BA, Rutgers U., 1967; MD, Albert Einstein Coll. Medicine, 1971. Diplomate Am. Bd. Infectious Diseases, Am. Bd. Internal Medicine. Physician epidemiologist St. Anthony Med. Ctr., Rockford, Ill., 1981—; cons. Rockford Infectious Disease Cons., Rockford, 1981—; assoc. prof. of medicine U. Ill. Coll. Medicine, Rockford, 1983—, acting chmn. dept. medicine, 2001—03. Pres. Rockford Infectious Disease Cons., 1981—. Pres. No. Ill. AIDS Resource Ctr., Rockford, 1989-2000; chmn. Mayors Task Force on Harm Reduction, Rockford, 1995-96; v.p. No. Ill. HIV/MDS Network, Rockford, 2000-01. Maj. U.S. Army, 1973-75. Fellow ACP, Infectious Diseases Soc. Am. Avocations: tennis, reading, golf. Office: Univ Ill Coll Medicine 1601 Parkview Ave Rockford IL 61107-1822 also: Rockford Infectious Disease Consultants 129 Phelps # 508 Rockford IL 61108 E-mail: grifkin@uic.edu.

RIFMAN, EILEEN, music educator; b. Bklyn., June 10, 1944; m. Samuel Sholom Rifman, Aug. 12, 1972; children: Edward, Aimee. MusB, Manhattan Sch. Music, 1966, M Music Edn., 1967; MusM, Ind. U., 1970; cert., Fontainebleau, France, 1967. Music specialist N.Y.C. Pub. Sch. System, 1966-67; instr. Long Beach (Calif.) City Coll., 1970-72, Immaculate Heart Coll., Hollywood, Calif., 1971-74, U. Judaism, Hollywood, 1973-74; co-coord. Community Sch. Performing Arts, L.A., 1974-82, instr., 1973-83; pvt. piano tchr. Manhattan Beach, Calif., 1963—; tchr. gifted and talented edn. program GATE, Manhattan Beach, Calif., 1990-91. Tchr. Etz Jacob Hebrew Acad., L.A., 1991-95, Ohr Eliyahu Acad., Culver City, 1995-96; peer counselor Beach Cities Health Dist., 1997—. Performer Pratt Inst., Clinton Hill Symphony, N.Y.C., 1962, Sta. WNYC-FM, 1964. Chair Cultural Arts Com., Manhattan Beach, 1985-86; bd. dirs. Hermosa Beach (Calif.) Community Ctr., 1990-91. Mem. Nat. Fedn. Music Clubs (adjudicator 1970). E-mail: eileenrifman@hotmail.com.

RIGAS, ANTHONY LEON, university department director; b. Andros, Greece, May 3, 1931; s. Leon Anthony and Katina (Sarris) R.; m. Harriett B. Rigas, Feb. 14, 1959 (dec. 1989); 1 child, Marc Leonard; m. Mary Dunham, Dec. 29, 1990. BSEE, U. Kans., 1958, MSEE, 1962; postgrad., Stanford U., 1965; PhD in Engring., U. Beverly Hills, 1978. Elec. engr. Naval Missile Ctr., Point Mugu, Calif., 1958-61; engring. analyst Mpls. Honeywell Co., 1962; instr. elec. engring. U. Kans., Lawrence, 1962-63; sr. rsch. engr. aerospace systems Lockheed Missile and Space Co., Sunnyvale, Calif., 1963-65, Dalmo-Victor Co., Belmont, Calif., 1965-66; asst. prof. elec. engring. San Jose (Calif.) State U., 1963-65; asst. prof., assoc. prof., then prof. elec. engring. U. Idaho, Moscow, 1966-84, dir. instrnl. media svcs., 1983-84; prof. elec. and computer engring. Naval Postgrad. Sch., Monterey, Calif., 1984-87; dir. engring. lifelong edn. Mich. State U., East Lansing, 1987-92; prof. elec. engring., dir. engring outreach emeritus U. Idaho, 1994—. Presenter at profl. confs.; prof. elec. engring., dir. engring. outreach emeritus U. Idaho, 1994—. Contbr. to profl. publs. Grantee NSF, 1971-75, 71-76, 1979-82, HEW, 1979-80, Kellogg Found., 1977-80. Fellow IEEE; mem. Am. Soc. Engring. Edn., Nat. Soc. Profl. Engrs., Nat. Univ. Continuing Edn. Assn., Sigma Xi, Sigma Tau, Tau Beta Pi. Home: 300 Hidden Harbor Ln Sandpoint ID 83864-7488

RIGGS, DONALD EUGENE, librarian, university official; b. Middlebourne, W.Va., May 11, 1942; m. Jane Vasbinder, Sept. 25, 1964; children: Janna Jennifer, Krista Dyonis. BA, Glenville State Coll., 1964; MA, W.Va. U., 1966; MLS, U. Pitts., 1968; EdD, Va. Poly. Inst. and State U., 1975. Head librarian, tchr. sci. Warwood (W.Va.) High Sch., 1964-65; head librarian, audiovisual dir. Wheeling (W.Va.) High Sch., 1965-67; sci. and econs. librarian California State Coll. of Pa., 1968-70; dir. library and learning center Bluefield State Coll., 1970-72; dir. libraries and media services Bluefield State Coll., Concord Coll., Greenbrier Community Coll., and So. campus W.Va. Coll. of Grad. Studies, 1972-76; dir. libraries U. Colo., Denver, Met. State Coll., and Community Col. of Denver— Auraria Campus, 1976-79; univ. librarian Ariz. State U., 1979-88, dean univ. libraries, 1988-90; prof. info. and libr. sci., dean univ. libr. U. Mich., Ann Arbor, 1991-97; prof., v.p. for info. svcs., univ. libr. Nova Southeastern U., Ft. Lauderdale, Fla., 1997—. Adj. prof. Calif. State Coll., 1968-70, W.Va. U., 1970-72, U. Colo., 1977-79, U. Ariz., 1985, Emporia State U., 1996—, U. South Fla., 1997—; fed. rels. coord. Am. and W.Va. Libr. Assns., 1970-75; chmn. bd. dirs. Ctrl. Colo. Libr. Sys., 1976-79; chmn. Colo. Coun. Acad. Librs., 1977-78; mem. exec. bd. Colo. Alliance Rsch. Librs., 1978-79; cons. to librs.; fgn. assignments in Xi'an, China, 1988, Guadalajara, Mex., 1990, Budapest, Hungary, 1991, 95, Hong Kong, 1992, 94, San Juan, P.R., 1993, Melbourne, Australia, 1994, Eupatory, Republic Crimea, Ukraine, 1995, London, 1996, Prague, Czech Republic, 1996, Beijing, China, 1996, 98, Pretoria, South Africa, 1996, others; del. Users Coun. Online Computer Libr. Ctr., Dublin, Ohio, 1987-91, pres.-elect, 1990-91, chair artificial intelligence and expert systems nat. group, 1987-88; bd. govs. Rsch. Librs. Group, Inc., Mountain View, Calif., 1991-92; vice chmn. mgmt. com. William L. Clements Libr., 1991-97. Editor: W.Va. Librs., 1973-75, Libr. Hi Tech, 1993-96, Coll. & Rsch. Librs., 1996-2002; founding editor: Libr. Adminstrn. and Mgmt., 1987-89; assoc. editor: Southeastern Libr., 1973-75; contbg. editor: Libraries in the Political Process, 1980, Options for the 80's, 1982, Library and Information Technology: At the Crossroads, 1984; contbg. author, editor: Library Leadership: Visualizing the Future, 1982; author: Strategic Planning for Library Managers, 1984, (with Helen Gothberg) Time Management in Academic Libraries, 1986, (with Gordon Sabine) Libraries in the 90's: What the Leaders Expect, 1988, Creativity, Innovation and Entrepreneurship in Libraries, 1989, Library Communication: The Language of Leadership, 1991, (with Rao Aluri) Expert Systems in Libraries, 1990, Cultural Diversity in Libraries, 1994; editl. bd. Am. Librs., 1987-89, Jour. Libr. Adminstrn., 1987-97, Coll. and Rsch. Librs., 1990-96, Coll. and Rsch. Librs. News, 1996-2002. Trustee Mesa (Ariz.) Pub. Library, 1980-86, chmn., 1985-86; mem. Ariz. State Library Adv. Council, 1981-84; bd. dirs. Documentation Abstracts, Inc., 1986-90. Recipient Alumnus of Yr. award Glenville State Coll., 1992; named Outstanding Young Educator, Ohio County Schs., 1966; Coun. on Libr. Resources grantee, 1985; sr. fellow UCLA, 1989. Mem. ALA (councilor-at-large 1982-86, 89-93, chmn. coun.'s resolutions com. 1985-86, pub. com. 1988-92, Hugh Atkinson award 1991), Ariz. Libr. Assn. (pres. coll. and univ. divsn. 1981-82, pres. 1983-84, Spl. Svc. award 1986, Disting. Svc. award 1990), Colo. Libr. Assn. (pres. 1978-79), W.Va. Libr. Assn. (pres. 1975-76), Assn. Coll. and Rsch. Librs. (pres. Tri-State chpt. 1972-74, pres. Ariz. chpt. 1981-82), So. Libr. Assn. (chmn. coll. and univ. sect. 1982-83), Assn. Rsch. Librs. (100th meeting planning com. 1982, mgmt. of rsch. libr. resources com. 1990-93, rsch. collections com. 1993-96), AMIGOS Bibliograph Coun. (trustee 1986-90, chmn. bd. trustees 1988-89), Libr. Adminstrn. and Mgmt. Assn. (bd. dirs. 1987-89, pres.-elect 1993-94, pres. 1994-95), Libr. Info. and Tech. Assn. (bd. dirs. 1989-93), Ctr. for Rsch. Librs. (councilor 1979-97), Fla. Libr. Assn. (chair leadership devel. com. 2003—), Mountain Plains Libr. Assn. (bd. dirs. 1987-90, pres.-elect 1990-91), S.E. Fla. Libr. Info. Network (exec. com., bd. dirs. 1997—, pres. 1998-99), Beta Phi Mu, Chi Beta Phi, Phi Delta Kappa, Phi Kappa Phi. Office: Nova Southeastern U Libr Rsch & Info Tech Ctr Ray Ferrero Jr Blvd Fort Lauderdale FL 33314-7721 E-mail: driggs@nova.edu.

RIGGS, HENRY EARLE, academic administrator, engineering educator; b. Chgo., Feb. 25, 1935; s. Joseph Agnew and Gretchen (Walser) Riggs; m. Gayle Carson, May 17, 1958; children: Elizabeth, Peter, Catharine. BS, Stanford U., 1957; MBA, Harvard U., 1960. Indsl. economist SRI Internat., Menlo Park, Calif., 1960—63; v.p. Icore Industries, Sunnyvale, Calif., 1963—67, pres., 1967—70; v.p. fin. Measurex Corp., Cupertino, Calif., 1970—74; prof. engring. mgmt. Stanford U., Calif., 1974—88, Ford prof., 1986—88, Ford prof. emeritus, 1990, v.p. for devel., 1983—88; pres. Harvey Mudd Coll., Claremont, Calif., 1988—97, pres. emeritus, 1997; pres. Keck Grad. Inst., Claremont, 1997—2003, chmn. bd., pres. emeritus, 2003—. Bd. dirs. Capital Rsch. Group. Author: Accounting: A Survey, 1981, Managing High-Tech Companies, 1983, Financial and Cost Analysis, 1994, 2d edit., 2003; contbr. articles to profl. jours. Recipient Gores Tchg. award, Stanford U., 1980; scholar Baker scholarship, Harvard Bus. Sch., 1959. Mem.: Stanford U. Alumni Assn. (bd. dirs. 1990—94, chmn. 1993), Sunset Club, Calif. Club, Tau Beta Pi, Phi Beta Kappa. Congregationalist. Office: Keck Grad Inst 535 Watson Dr Claremont CA 91711-4817 Home: 24 Peter Coutts Circle Stanford CA 94305 E-mail: henry_riggs@kgi.edu.

RIGGS, JACKI PIERACCI, educational consultant; b. San Jose, May 13, 1954; d. Leo A. Pieracci and Laura B. Petersen LaRue; m. Joseph N. Riggs III, Aug. 27, 1978; children: Joseph N. IV, Amanda Marie, Austin Spenser. BS in Child Devel., Brigham Young U., 1981; MA in Spl. Edn., U. N.Mex., 1983, PhD in Spl. Edn., 1992. Treatment liaison ATASC Project, Albuquerque, 1976-79; dir. alcohol edn. program Juvenile Ct., Albuquerque, 1978-79; tchr. Children's Psychiat. Hosp., Albuquerque, 1985-88; div. dir. Juvenile Facilities N.Mex. Corrections Dept., Santa Fe, N.Mex., 1988-89; cabinet sec. N.Mex. Youth Authority, Santa Fe, 1989-90; pvt. practice cons.

Albuquerque, 1990—; dir. admissions Bosqee Prep. Sch., 1995-96. Mem. Gov. Johnson's Transitional Team Children, Youth and Families Dept., 1994; apptd. by Gov. Johnson as commr. Edn. Commn. of States, 1997—. Commr. Youth Authority Commn., Santa Fe, 1988; mem. Gov.'s Substance Abuse Adv. Coun., 1989; mem. Community Corrections Panel, 1988; vol. Bosque Prep.; pres., CEO N.Mex. Found. for Ednl. Excellence, 1999—. U. N.Mex. fellow, 1986-87, 87-88, 91-92. Mem. NAFE, Coun. for Exceptional Children, Women Execs. in State Govt., Nat. Assn. Juvenile Correctional Adminstrs., Univ. Women. Avocations: writing, photography, travel.

RIGGS, ROBERT DALE, plant pathology and nematology educator, researcher; b. Pocahontas, Ark., June 15, 1932; s. Rosa MacDowell and Grace (Million) R.; m. Jennie Lee Willis, June 6, 1954; children: Rebecca Dawn, Deborah Lee, Robert Dale Jr., James Michael. BS in Agr., U. Ark., 1954, MS in Plant Pathology, 1956; PhD in Plant Pathology, N.C. State U., 1958. Grad. asst. U. Ark., Fayetteville, 1954-55, asst. prof., 1958-62, assoc. prof., 1962-68, prof., 1968-92, univ. prof., 1992—; grad. asst. N.C. State U., Raleigh, 1955-58. Chair of faculty Coll. Agrl., Food and Life Scis., 1999. Editor: Nematology in the Southern United States, 1982; co-editor: Biology and Management of the Soybean Cyst Nematode, 1992; contbr. articles to profl. jours.; inventor fungal control of nematodes. Recipient John W. White award Coll. Agr. and Home Econs., 1989, Honor award for Rsch. in Environ. Protection USDA, 1994, Outstanding Rschr. award Ark. Agrl. Extension Specialists, 2000, Spitze Land Grant Univ. Faculty award, 2001, Meritorious Svc. award United Soybean Bd., 2002. Fellow Soc. of Nematologists (v.p. 1991-92, pres.-elect 1992-93, pres. 1993-94, editor-in-chief jour. 1987-90), Am. Phytopath. Soc. (Outstanding plant pathologist in so. region 1994); mem. So. Soybean Disease Workers (Disting. Svc. award 1987), U. Ark. Alumni Assn. (Dist. Faculty Achievement award 1993), Orgn. of Nematologists of Tropical Am., Sigma Xi, Gamma Sigma Delta. Democrat. Baptist. Home: 1840 Woolsey Ave Fayetteville AR 72703-2557 Office: U Ark 217 Plant Sci Fayetteville AR 72701 E-mail: rdriggs@mail.uark.edu.

RIGGS, SONYA WOICINSKI, elementary school educator; b. Newhall, Calif., Oct. 9, 1935; d. Jack Lewis Woicinski and Mittie Mozelle (Bennett) Gillett; m. Eugene Garland Riggs, Dec. 21, 1956; children: Georgia Ann, Madeline Sue, Dana Eugene. BS in Elem. Edn., U. Tex., 1970; MEd in Reading Edn., S.W. Tex. State U., 1980. Cert. elem. tchr., Tex.; cert. reading specialist K-12. Sec. state govts., Nebr./Tex., 1955-57; piano instr. Elgin, Tex., 1961-66; tchr. 1st grade Elgin Elem. Sch., Elgin, 1967-69, tchr. Music 3rd/4th grades, 1971-72, tchr. 4th grade, 1972-73; pres. El Tesoro internacionale, 1973-74; sec. region office Planned Parenthood/World Population, Austin, 1975-76; tchr. 8th-12th grades Giddings (Tex.) State Sch., 1976-78; tchr. 4th/5th grades Thorndale (Tex.) Ind. Sch. Dist., 1979-80; tchr. remedial reading Brazosport Ind. Sch. Dist., Freeport, Tex., 1980-81; tchr. 6th grade reading and chpt. I Bastrop (Tex.) Mid. Sch., 1981-94, Bastrop Intermediate, 1994-99. Developer Enrichment Ctr., Bastrop Intermediate, 1995—2000, Cedar Creek Elem. Enrichment, 2000—01; mem. 12th ann. Highlights Found. Writers Workshop at Chautauqua Instn., NY, 1996; adj. instr. reading Austin C.C., 2000—; puppy cons. Contbr. articles to Shih Tzu Reporter, 1993 French Bulldog Ann., French Bullytin, Boston Quar., Golden Retriever World; contbr. poetry to anthologies Garden of Life, 1996, Best Poems of 1996, Of Sunshine and Daydreams, 1996, A View from Afar, 1997. Mem. Elgin Band Boosters, 1970-83, sec., 1976. Mem. Assn. Tex. Profl. Educators (campus rep. 1996-97, state del. 1997, sec. 1997-98), Austin Kennel Club (bd. dirs. 1990-91, 95-97, sec. 1996-97), Am. Shih Tzu Club (edn. and rescue com. mem. south ctrl. regional hearing com.), French Bulldog Club Am. (rescue com.), Mission City Ring Stewards Assn., Internat. Soc. Poets, Tex. Writers League, Greater Austin Doberman Pinscher Club. Avocations: exhibiting dogs to Am. Kennel Club confirmation and obedience championships, writing poetry, playing piano, painting, drawing.

RIGGSBY, ERNEST DUWARD, science educator, educational development executive; b. Nashville, June 12, 1925; s. James Thomas and Anna Pearl (Turner) R.; m. Dutchie Sellers, Aug. 25, 1964; 1 child, Lyn-Dee. BS, Tenn. Polytech. Inst., 1948; BA, George Peabody Coll. Tchrs., 1952, BA, 1953, MA, 1956, EdS, 1961, EdD, 1964. Vis. grad. prof. U. P.R., Rio Piedras, George Peabody Coll., 1963-64; prof. Auburn (Ala.) U., Troy (Ala.) State U., Columbus (Ga.) Coll.; pres. Ednl. Developers, Inc., Columbus, Ga. Vis. grad. prof. George Peabody Coll., 1963-64; vis. lectr. Fla. Inst. Tech., summers 1967-77. Contbr. articles to profl. jours. Col., USAF, 1944-85. Named to Aerospace Crown Cir., 1984; elected to Aerospace Edn. Hall of Fame, 1982. Fellow AAAS; mem. Nat. Sci. Tchrs. Assn., World Aerospace Edn. Assn. (v.p. for the Ams.). Office: Columbus State U Columbus GA 31907-5645

RIGHTMIRE, GEORGE PHILIP, anthropology educator; b. Boston, Sept. 15, 1942; s. Brandon Garner and Marcia (Ham) R.; m. Berit Johansson, Aug. 20, 1966; children: Anna Marcia, Eric Philip. AB, Harvard U., 1964; MS, U. Wis., 1966, PhD, 1969. Asst. prof. SUNY, Binghamton, 1969-73, assoc. prof., 1973-82, prof., 1982—2002, chmn., 1976-78, disting. prof., 2002—. Vis. in archaeology U. Cape Town, South Africa, 1975-76; rsch. fellow in osteology U. Stockholm, Sweden, 1973. Author: The Evolution of Homo erectus, 1990; contbr. articles to Am Jour. Phys. Anthropology, Sci., Nature, Ency. Britannica, Jour. Human Evolution. Fellow Nat. Inst. Gen. Med. Scis., 1973; rsch. grantee NSF, 1975—, Nat. Geographic Soc., 1978-79, L.S.B. Leakey Found., 1990-91, 1992-93, 1995-96, 98-99. 2001-2003. Fellow AAAS; mem. Am. Assn. Phys. Anthropologists, Human Biology Assn., Sigma Xi. Achievements include rsch. in skeletal biology and human paleontology, fossil evidence for hominid evolution examined in East Africa, South Africa, Europe, the Near East and Southeast Asia. Home: 4004 Fuller Hollow Rd Vestal NY 13850-5542 Office: SUNY Dept Anthropology PO Box 6000 Binghamton NY 13902-6000

RIGOLOT, FRANÇOIS, French literature educator, literary critic; b. Château-du-Loir, Sarthe, France, May 21, 1939; s. Paul and Madeleine (Overnoy) R.; m. Carol Nolan, Sept. 5, 1970; children— Sophie, Stephanie Diplôme, Hautes Etudes Commerciales, Paris, 1961; MA in Econs., Northwestern U., 1963; PhD in French, U. Wis.-Madison, 1969. Asst. prof. U. Mich, Ann Arbor, 1969-74; bicentennial preceptor Princeton U., N.J., 1974-77, assoc. prof. dept. romance langs. and lits., 1977-79, prof., 1979-81, Meredith Howland Pyne prof. French lit., chmn. dept., 1984-91, 96-99, chair Renaissance studies, 1993—. Prof. French Middlebury (Vt.) Coll., 1973; dir. NEH seminar for coll. tchrs., Princeton, 1981, 84, 86, 88, 90; vis. prof. Johns Hopkins U., 1981; vis. mem. Inst. for Advanced Study, Princeton, 1982-83, 1999-2000; dir. seminar The Folger Inst., Washington, 1987; prof. Inst. d'Etudes Françaises, Avignon, 1989, 95; ofcl. lectr. Alliance Française, 1994-95. Author: Les Langages de Rabelais, 1972, reprint, 1996, Poétique et Onomastique, 1977, Le Texte de la Renaissance, 1982 (Gilbert Chinard Lit. prize 1984), Les Métamorphoses de Montaigne, 1988, Louise Labé ou La Renaissance au féminin, 1997; editor: Complete Works of Louise Labé, 1986, Jour. de Voyage of Montaigne, 1992; co-editor: A New History of French Literature, 1989 (MLA James Russell Lowell prize 1990), De la Littérature Française, 1993; collaborator: Sémantique de La Poèsie, 1979, L'Erreur de la Renaissance, 2002, Posie et Renaissance, 2003. Recipient Médaille de la ville de Bordeaux, Médaille de la ville de Tours, 1992, Officier des Palmes Académiques, 1993, Howard T. Behrman award for Disting. Achievement in the Humanities, 1993; Chevalier dans l'Ordre Nat. du Mérite, 2002, NEH fellow, 1979-80, Guggenheim Found. fellow, 1982-83. Mem. Acad. Literary Studies, Am. Assn. Tchrs. French, Renaissance Soc. Am., MLA, Assn. Internat. des Etudes Françaises. Home: 81 Pretty Brook Rd Princeton NJ 08540-7537 Office: Princeton U East Pyne Dept French and Italian Princeton NJ 08544-5264 E-mail: rigolot@princeton.edu.

RIGSBY, CAROLYN ERWIN, music educator; b. Franklinton, La., Apr. 11, 1936; d. Sheldon Aubrey and Edna Marie (Fussell) Erwin; m. Michael Hall Rigsby, May 30, 1959; 1 child, Laura Elaine Rigsby Boyd. B in Music Edn., Northwestern State U., La., 1958; MEd, Nicholls State U., 1970. Cert. vocal music tchr. k-12. Music tchr. Terrebonne Parish Sch., Houma, La., 1958-81, 81-83, music coord., 1983-84; music tchr. Pasadena (Tex.) Ind. Sch. Dist., 1988—. Mem. Tex. Music Educators Assn., Packard Autombile Classics, Lone Star Packard Club, Delta Kappa Gamma (pres. 1988-90). Republican. Methodist. Avocations: bay area chorus, golf, gardening. Home: 16014 Mill Point Dr Houston TX 77059-5216

RIKARD, YVONNE H. elementary educator; b. Blakely, Ga., Nov. 23, 1955; d. Connie C. and Merle W. (Welch) Hodges; m. Dan Edwards Pridgen Jr., Mar. 18 (div. Sept. 1979); 1 child, Dan Edwards III; m. Donald Myrick Rikard, May 1, 1981. AS, Enterprise State Jr. Coll., 1978; BS in Edn., Troy State U., 1986; MS in Edn., Troy State U., Dothan, Ala., 1991; MS in Ednl. Leadership, Troy State U., 1997. Cert. tchr., Ala. 1st and 2d grade tchr. Enterprise (Ala.) City Schs., 1986—; instr. coll. reading Enterprise State Jr. Coll., 1991—. Curriculum cons. Auburn (Ala.) U., 1989—, Troy State U., 1987-97; presenter in field. Finalist Albert Einstein Fellowships, 2003; recipient Outstanding Ala. Reading Tchr. award Ala. Reading Assn., 1996—97, Special Svc. Tchr., Ala. State Dept of Edn., 2001; Wiregrass Writing Project fellow, 1994, Ala. Reading Assn. scholar, 1997, Fulbright Meml. Fund Scholar, 2002. Mem. Ala. Reading Assn., Internat. Reading Assn., Boll Weevil Reading Coun. (pres. 1986-97, award 1997), Nat. Bd. Cert. Tchr., Delta Kappa Gamma (Annie Merts scholar 1997), Kappa Delta Pi. Home: PO Box 310636 Enterprise AL 36331-0636 Office: Enterprise City Schs Watts Ave Enterprise AL 36330

RILEY, BARBARA POLK, retired librarian; b. Roselle, N.J., Nov. 21, 1928; d. Charles Carrington and Olive Bond P.; AB, Howard U., 1950; BS, N.J. Coll. Women, 1951; MS, Columbia U., 1955; m. George Emerson Riley, Feb. 23, 1957 (dec.); children: George E., Glenn C., Karen O.; m. William I. Scott, Oct. 6, 1990 (div. 1998). Asst. librarian, Fla. A&M U., 1951-53; with Morgan State Coll., 1955; with Dept. Def., 1955-57, S.C. State Coll., 1957-59, U.Wis., 1958-59; asst. librarian Atlanta U., 1960-68; asst. dir. Union County Anti Poverty Council, 1968; librarian Union County Tech. Inst., Scotch Plains, N.J., 1968-82, Plainfield campus Union County Coll., 1982-95; ret., 1995. Mem. Roselle Bd. Edn., 1976-78; bd. dirs. Union County Anti Poverty Council, 1969-72; mem. Roselle Human Relations Commn., 1971-73, Plainfield Sci. Center, 1974-76, Union County Psychiat. Clinic, 1980-83, Pinewood Sr. Citizens Council, 1981-85; bd. dirs. Project, Women of N.J., 1985-93, Pinewood Sr. Citizen Housing, 1981-85, Black Women's History Conf., 1985-92, pres., 1989-91. Mem. N.J. Library Assn., Council Library Tech., ALA (Black caucas), N.J. Coalition of 100 Black Women, African Am. Women's Polit. Caucus, N.J. Black Librarians Network (bd. dirs.), Links, Inc. (North Jersey chpt.), Black Women's History Conf., Alpha Kappa Alpha. Mem. A.M.E. Ch. Club: Just-A-Mere Lit. Home: 114 E 7th Ave Roselle NJ 07203-2028

RILEY, DAWN C. educational philosopher, researcher; b. Rochester, N.Y., Mar. 18, 1954; d. John Joseph Jr. and June Carol (Cleveland) R. BA in Edn., Polit. Sci., SUNY, 1976; MEd, in Special Edn., summa cum laude, U. Ariz., 1980; PhD, Univ. Calif., Berkeley, 1994. Cert. multiple subject credential (K-Coll.), specialist credential (K-12), Calif., coun. of educators for deaf; elem. permanent credential, N.Y. Elem. sch. tchr., 4th grade Escola Americana do Rio de Janeiro, Brazil, 1975; pvt. practice, comml. artist Rochester, 1972-80; elem. tchr. Rochester City Sch. Dist., 1976-78; rsch. asst., summer vestibule program The Nat. Tech. Inst. for Deaf, 1976-79; tchr. English, 7th-12th grades The Calif. Sch. for Deaf, 1980-94; rsch. asst. to Dr. Richard J. Morris The Univ. Ariz., 1978-80; rsch. asst., Calif. new tchr. support project The Far West Lab. for Ednl. R & D., San Francisco, 1989; chair high sch. English dept. The Calif. Sch. for Deaf, 1990-96; prin. Calif. Sch. for the Deaf, Fremont, 1996-97; asst. prof. edn. founds. So. Ill. U., 1998—2003; with ednl. founds. Skidmore Coll., 2003—. Coord. & devel. Practical Lang. in Applied Settings Program, 1981-82; chair Computer Curriculum Com., 1982-84, Critical and Creative Thinking Skills Com., 1983-84; coord. Gifted and Talented Program, 1983— Recipient Kate Navin O'Neill Grad. scholar Univ. of Calif., Berkeley, 1989; University fellow, 1978-80, Evelyn Lois Corey fellow, 1990; Recipient Sustained Superior Accomplishment award Calif. Dept. Edn., 1991. Mem. AAUW, Nat. Coun. Tchrs. English, Far Western Philosophy of Edn. Soc., Am. Ednl. Rsch. Assn., Am. Assn. Colls. for Tchr. Edn., Philosophy of Edn. Soc., John Dewey Soc., Soc. Profs. Edn. (bd. dirs. 2001-03)m Phi Beta Kappa (Berkeley chpt.). Home: 1205 Oakland Ave Edwardsville IL 62025-2452 Office: Skidmore Coll Edn Dept Saratoga Springs NY 12866 E-mail: driley@skidmore.edu.

RILEY, HARRIS DEWITT, JR., pediatrician, medical educator; b. Clarksdale, Miss., Nov. 12, 1924; s. Harris DeWitt and Louise (Allen) R.; m. Margaret Barry, Sept. 16, 1950; children: Steven Allen, Mark Barry, Margaret Ruth. BA, Vanderbilt U., 1945, MD, 1948. Intern Balt. City Hosps., Johns Hopkins Hosp., 1948-49; resident in pediatrics Babies and Children's Hosp., Case Western Res. U., Cleve., 1949-50, Vanderbilt U. Hosp., 1950-51; instr., fellow in pediatrics and infectious diseases Vanderbilt U. Med. Sch., 1953-57; prof. pediatrics, chmn. dept. U. Okla. Med. Sch., 1958—; med. dir. Children's Meml. Hosp., 1972—; disting. prof. pediatrics U. Okla., 1976; prof. pediatrics Vanderbilt U. Sch. of Medicine, Nashville, 1991—. Served as capt. M.C. USAF, 1951-53. Office: Vanderbilt Children Hosp Vanderbilt U Med Ctr Nashville TN 37232-0001 E-mail: harris.riley@mcmail.vanderbilt.edu.

RILEY, RICHARD WILSON, lawyer, former federal official; b. Greenville, S.C., Jan. 2, 1933; s. Edward Patterson and Martha Elizabeth (Dixon) Riley; m. Ann Osteen Yarborough, Aug. 23, 1957; children: Richard Wilson, Anne Y., Hubert D., Theodore D. BA, Furman U., 1954; JD, U. S.C., 1959. Bar: S.C. 1960. Ptnr. Riley & Riley, Greenville, 1959—78, Nelson, Mullins, Riley & Scarborough, Greenville and Columbia, 1987—93, Greenville, 2001—; gov. State of S.C., 1979—87; sec. U.S. Dept. Edn., Washington, 1993—2001; disting. univ. prof. U. S.C., Columbia, 2001—. Spl. asst. to subcom. U.S. Senate Jud. Com., 1960; mem. S.C. Ho. of Reps., 1963—66, S.C. Senate senate form Greenville-Laurens Dist., 1966—76. Lt. (j.g.) USNR, 1954—56. Recipient Dist. Svc. award, Coun. Chief State Sch. Officers, 1994, James Bryant Conant award, Edn. Commn. of the States, 1995, T.H. Bell award for outstanding edn. advocacy, Com. for Edn. Funding, 1996, Dist. Svc. award, Am. Coun. on Edn., 1998. Mem.: Greenville Bar Assn., S.C. Bar Assn., Furman U. Alumni Assn. (pres. 1968—69), Rotary, Phi Beta Kappa. Office: Nelson Mullins Riley & Scarborough Poinsett Plaza Ste 900 104 S Main St Greenville SC 29601 E-mail: rwr@nmrs.com.

RILEY, ROBERT, governor; b. Ala. m. Patsy Adams; children: Rob, Jenice, Minda, Krisalyn. Degree in bus. administrn., U. Ala. Past poultry and egg bus. co-owner, Ala.; past owner automobile dealership, Ala.; owner trucking co., Ala.; past owner grocery store and local pharmacy, Ala.; mem. Ho. of Reps. from 3d Ala. dist., 1996—2002, asst. whip, mem. house armed svcs. com., mem. house banking and fin. svcs. com., mem. house agr. com., house-senate conferee on FY 1998 Def. Authorization bill, 1997, mem. ho. agrl. com.; gov. State of Ala., 2003—. Past chmn. fin. com. Clay County Hosp.; mem. First Baptist Ch., men's Sunday sch. tchr., past chmn. bd. trustees; pres., Ala. State Bd. Edn, 2003-. Mem. Masons, Shriners, Jaycees (past pres. Ashland chpt.). Office: Office of the Governor State Capitol 600 Dexter Ave Montgomery AL 36130*

RILLING, JOHN ROBERT, history educator; b. Wausau, Wis., Apr. 28, 1932; s. John Peter and Esther Laura (Wittig) R.; m. Joanne Marilyn McCrory, Dec. 21, 1953; children: Geoffrey Alan, Andrew Peter. BA summa cum laude, U. Minn., 1953; AM, Harvard U., 1957, PhD, 1959. Asst. prof. history U. Richmond, Va., 1959-62, assoc. prof. history, 1962-68, prof. history, 1968-99, prof. English history emeritus, 1999—, chmn. dept. history, 1977-83, Westhampton Coll., 1965-71. Pres. Faculty Senate of Va., 1975-77. Contbr. articles to profl. jours. Elder, Ginter Park Presbyn. Ch., 1973-83. Served with U.S. Army, 1953-55. Recipient U. Richmond Disting. Educator award, 1975, 76, 77, 80, 87, Prof. of Yr. finalist Coun. for Advancement and Support of Edn., 1981. Woodrow Wilson fellow, 1955-59; Harvard U. travelling fellow, 1958; Coolidge fellow, 1955-56; Folger Libr. fellow, 1960. Mem. Am. Hist. Assn., Econ. History Soc., Agecroft Assn. (bd. dirs.), Conf. Brit. Studies, Phi Beta Kappa, Omicron Delta Kappa (Prof. of Yr. 1995). Avocations: hiking, bicycling, enology. Home: 1507 Wilmington Ave Richmond VA 23227-4429 Office: U Richmond Dept History Richmond VA 23173 Business E-Mail: jrilling@richmond.edu.

RINDONE, JOSEPH PATRICK, clinical pharmacist, educator; b. Santa Fe, Oct. 4, 1954; s. Guido Salvatore and Elizabeth Ann (Murphy) R.; m. Diane Marie Rollins, June 23, 1991; children: Jacqueline, Alexandra. BS, U. Nebr., 1977; PharmD, Creighton U., 1978. Lic. pharmacist, Nebr., Calif. Staff pharmacist Bergan Mercy Hosp., Omaha, 1978, Phoenix (Ariz.) VA Med. Ctr., 1978-81, clin. resident, 1981; clin. pharmacist Tucson VA Med. Ctr., 1982-93; assoc. prof. U. Ariz., Tucson, 1982—; clin. pharmacist Prescott (Ariz.) VA Med. Ctr., 1993—, rsch. coord., 1994—. Author: Therapeutic Monitoring of Antibiotics, 1991; contbr. articles to Arch. Internal Medicine, Pharmacotherapy, Clin. Therapeutics, Am. Jour. Cardiology, Am. Jour. Therapeutics, Chest, West Jour. Medicine, Am. Jour. Health Sys. Pharm., Fereral Practioner, Jour. AMA. Regents scholar U. Nebr., 1976. Avocations: sports, photography, bridge, astronomy. E-mail: JosephRindone@med.va.gov.

RING, JAMES WALTER, physics educator; b. Worcester, NY, Feb. 24, 1929; s. Carlyle Conwell and Lois (Tooley) R.; m. Agnes Elizabeth Muir, July 18, 1959; 1 son, Andrew James. AB, Hamilton Coll., 1951; PhD (Root fellow), U. Rochester, 1958. Asst. prof. physics Hamilton Coll., Clinton, NY, 1957—62, assoc. prof., 1962—69, prof., 1969—75, Winslow prof., 1975—2003, chmn. dept. physics, 1968—80, 1987—88, 1991—92, radiation safety officer, 1964—84, engring. liaison officer, 1969—2002, prof. emeritus, 2003—. Attached physicist Atomic Energy Rsch. Establishment, Harwell, Eng., 1965-66; vis. physicist Phys. Chemistry Lab., Oxford (Eng.) U., 1973; vis. fellow Ctr. for Energy and Environ. Studies, Princeton U., 1981; vis. scientist Lab. for Heating and Air Conditioning, Danish Tech. U., Copenhagen, 1987. Contbr. articles to profl. jour. and books in physics, chemistry, solar energy, environ. sci., health physics, archaeology, and engring. Recipient prize Acad. Edn./Devel., 1980; NSF grantee, 1959-66; NSF sci. faculty fellow, 1965-66 Mem. AAUP (chpt. pres. 1987-92), Am. Phys. Soc., Am. Assn. Physics Tchrs., Phi Beta Kappa, Sigma Xi. Achievements include solar house design and testing; indoor air studies in radon dangers and thermal comfort; study of the use of solar energy by the Romans during the Roman Empire; analysis of experimental evidence for the validity of continuous spontaneous localization theory as an alternative to standard quantum mechanics; detection of Pb210 gamma radiation to establish geochronology for sediment core samples taken in antarctic peninsula bay and straits; to study global warming. Office: Hamilton Coll Dept Physics Clinton NY 13323

RINGEL, KAREN ELAINE (KILLIAN), elementary education educator; b. Detroit, Aug. 4, 1942; d. Frederick C. and Olga (Ravas) Killian; m. Larry H. Ringel, Dec. 28, 1963; children: Jonathan, Steven, Elizabeth. BS in Edn., Concordia Tchs. Coll., Seward, Nebr., 1963; MS in Edn., Kans. State U., 1967; instr. Cert. tchr., Kans., Mo. Tchr. St. John's Luth. Sch., Alma, Kans., 1963-65; tchr. grade 8 Unified Sch. Dist. 329 Alta Vista (Kans.) Sch., 1965-67; counselor grades 7-9 Unified Sch. Dist., Geary County Schs., Junction City, Kans., 1967-69; instr. St. Mary Coll., Leavenworth, Kans., 1981; elem. tchr. Piper Elem. Sch., Kansas City, Kans., 1986-93; tchr. Piper Middle Sch., Kansas City, Kans., 1993—2000. Ednl. tour guide Agrl. Hall of Fame, 1982-86; participant Nat. Inst., KCPT-TV, Kansas City, Mo., 1992, Sci. Grasp, Upjohn/Delta Edn., Kalamazoo, Mich., 1992—. Author: (edn. game) Historic Lawrence, 1983. Recipient Kans. Econ. Edn. award Kans. Bankers Assn., 1983. Mem. NEA, Kans. Edn. Assn., Nat. Coun. State Garden Clubs (accredited flower show judge 1982), Bonner Springs Garden Club, Kansas City Garden Club, Kansas City Judges Coun. Republican. Lutheran. Home: 14683 158th St Bonner Springs KS 66012-7794

RINGKAMP, STEPHEN H. lawyer, educator; b. St. Louis, Nov. 14, 1949; s. Aloysius G. and Melba Ann (Finke) Ringkamp; m. Patricia Sue Fuse, July 5, 1971; children: Christa, Angela, Laura, Stephen M., Kara. BSEE, St. Louis U., 1971, JD cum laude, 1974. Bar: Mo. 1974, U.S. Dist. Ct. (ea. dist.) Mo. 1974, U.S. Ct. Appeals (8th cir.) 1974, U.S. Supreme Ct. 1990. Law clk. 22d Jud. Cir. Mo., St. Louis, 1974-75; mng. prin. The Hullverson Law Firm, St. Louis, 1976—. Chmn., mem. com. on civil instrns. Mo. Supreme Ct., 1981— ; adj. prof. law St. Louis U., 1983— ; mem. faculty Mo. Jud. Coll., 1993-2003; lectr. legal seminars. Contbr. articles to legal jours. Recipient Trial Lawyer award Mo. Bar Found. 1983, Smithson award for Excellence, 1996. Mem. ABA, ATLA, Mo. Bar Assn. (vice chmn. civil practice com. 1983-84), Mo. Assn. Trial Attys. (pres. 1991), Bar Assn. Met. St. Louis, Lawyers Assn. St. Louis. Office: The Hullverson Law Firm 1010 Market St Ste 1550 Saint Louis MO 63101-2091 E-mail: sringkamp@hullverson.com.

RINGSTROM, JAMES RODNEY, retired secondary school educator; b. Devils Lake, N.D., Nov. 3, 1938; s. Marlin Paul and Edytha (Kain) R.; m. Rosalie Mae LeClerc, Aug. 20, 1961; children: Paul Jason, Conni Jo, David Jay. BS, Jamestown (N.D.) Coll., 1960. Tchr. Fessendon (N.D.) H.S., 1960-61, Jamestown (N.D.) Jr. H.S., 1961-62, Benjamin Franklin Jr. H.S., Fargo, N.D., 1963-65; tchr. math. San Diegnito H.S., Encinitas, Calif., 1966-96, La Costa Canyon H.S., 1996-2000; ret., 2000. NSF fellow, 1965-66; named Tchr. of the Yr., San Diegnito Union H.S. Dist., 1973. Mem. Nat. Coun. Tchrs. Math. Republican. Lutheran. Home: 1440 Valleda Ln Encinitas CA 92024-2410

RINSKY, JUDITH SUE LYNN, foundation administrator, educator consultant; b. Sept. 12, 1941; d. Allan A. and Sophie (Schwartz) Lynn; m. Joel C. Rinsky, Jan. 29, 1963; children: Heidi Mae Schnapp, Heather Star Maxon, Jason Wayne. BA in Home Econs., Montclair State U., 1963. Notary pub., N.J. Tchr. home econs. Florence Ave. Sch., Irvington, N.J., 1963-66; substitute tchr. Millburn-Short Hills Sch. System, Millburn Twp., N.J., 1978-82, 90-98, sr. citizen coord., 1982-87; respite care coord. Essex County Divsn. on Aging, East Orange, N.J., 1988-90; pvt. practice educator Short Hills, NJ, 1990—98; tchr. basic skills Millburn (N.J.) H.S., 1998—. Bd. mem. adv. com. gerontology Seton Hall U., 1984—90; coord. Mayor's Adv. Bd. Sr. Citizens, Millburn-Short Hills, 1982—87; home instrn. Millburn-Short Hills Sch. Sys., 1997—98; tchr. adv. Millburn H.S. Interart Club, 2000—. Pres. Deerfield Sch. PTA, 1979-80, Millburn H.S. PTA, 1983-85; co-chmn. dinner dance Charles T. King Student Loan Fund, 1981; active Handicapped Access Study Com., 1983-85; bd. dirs. Coun. on Health and Human Svcs., 1985-90, 94-97; acting dir. B'nai Israel Nursery Sch., 1994. Mem. Lake Naomi Assn. (chmn. sailing com. 1981), N.J. Home Econs. Assn., Am. Home Econs. Assn., Rotary (hon. mem., pres. Millburn-Short Hills club 1992-93, bd. dirs. 1992-2000, advisor Millburn interact club 1987-98, 2000—, chmn. internat. interact dist. 7470 1993-95, advisor 1995-98). Home and Office: 87 Sullivan Dr West Orange NJ 07052-2262 E-mail: jsr_07041@yahoo.com., rinsky@millburn.org.

RINSLAND, ROLAND DELANO, retired university official; b. Apr. 11, 1933; s. Charles henry and Lottie Rinsland. AB with distinction, Va. State U.; AM, profl. diploma, EdD, Columbia U. Asst. to dean of men Va. State

Coll., Petersburg; asst. purchasing agt. Glyco Products Co., Inc., N.Y.C.; asst. office registrar Tchrs. Coll. Columbia U., N.Y.C., tchr. cert. advisor, registrar, 1966-71, asst. dean student affairs, registrar, dir. doctoral studies, 1971-95; ret., 1995. Mem. Tchrs. Coll. Devel. Coun.; rep., presenter degrees Tchrs. Coll., Japan, 1989, 91, 93, 94. 1st lt. AUS, 1954-56. Mem. AAAS, NEA (Leah B. Sykes award for life mem.), Am. Coll. Pers. Assn., Nat. Soc. Study Edn., Am. Ednl. Rsch. Assn., Assn. Collegiate Registrars and Admission Officers (inter-assn. rep. to state edn. depts. tchr. cert. 1973-74, mem. com. orgn. and adminstrn. registrars activities 1973, 74-76), Assn. Records Execs. and Adminstrs. (charter mem., by-laws and program chmn. 1969), Am. Acad. Polit. and Social Sci., Am. Assn. Higher Edn., Assn. Instl. Rsch., Internat. Assn. Applied Psychology, Soc. Applied Anthropology, Am. Assn. Counseling and Devel., Assn. Study Higher Edn., Mid. States Assn. Collegiate Registrars and Officers of Admission., N.Y. State Pers. and Guidance Assn., N.Y. Acad. Scis., Scabbard and Blade, Kappa Phi Kappa, Kappa Delta Pi, Phi Delta Kappa (emeritus).

RIOS, DIEGO MARCIAL, artist, educator; b. Frenso, Calif., Jan. 28, 1962; s. Herminio and Rosa (Aredondo) R. BA, U. Calif., Berkeley, 1985; MA, U. Wis., 1987, MFA, 1989; Cert. Paralegal, U. San Francisco, 1993. Instr. art Nat. Art Inst. and Disabilities, Richmond, Calif., 1989—, Mission Cultural Ctr., San Francisco, 1989, Richmond (Calif.) Art Ctr., 1992, Via Skills Ctr., Richmond, Calif., 1992; artist in residence Fresno (Calif.) Art Mus., 1991, Armory Ctr. Arts, Pasadena, Calif., 1992. Mem. art dept. Just Publ., Berkeley, Calif., 1978-80; head art illustrator V.I.D.A. Internat., San Francisco, 1992. Exhibited in group shows at The Machine Shop Gallery, Washington, Mo., 2003, Woodcuts, Berkeley, 2003, Surrealist View, Nappa (Calif.) C.C. Art Gallery, 2003, Glory Be!, Johnson-Humrich Mus. Art, Coschocton, Ohio, 2002, Political Art, San Juaquin Delta Coll. Art Gallery, Stockton, Calif., 2002, Religion and Art, U. Wyo. Art Gallery, 2002, Calif. Works, Juried Show, Calif. State Fair, Sacramento, 2002, Spirit of Hope, Phila., 2002, Diego M. Rios Graphics, Cedar Lake, Ill., 2002, Spiritual Art, Period Gallery, Omaha, Nebr., 2002, Artists in Print, Chemeka Gallery, Oreg., 2002, D.M. Rios Graphics, Pima Coll. Art Gallery, Tucson, Ariz., 2002, Gallery 76, Salem, Oreg., 2002. Active United Farmworkers, 1968—79. Recipient Purchase award Madison (Wis.) Print Club, 1988, Phelan award Phelan Soc., 1989, Purchase award, Nat. Works on Paper/Mo., 1991; named Best in Polit. Show of 80s U. Wyo. Art Mus., 1989. Mem. L.A. Printmakers, Calif. Etching Soc., Coll. Art Assn., U. Calif. Libr. Soc., San Francisco Bar Assn. Home: 3010 Carey St Antioch CA 94509-5012 Fax: 925-753-1156. E-mail: horios@msn.com.

RIPLEY, JOHN WALTER, academic administrator; b. Welch, W.Va., June 29, 1939; m. Molin B. Ripley, May 9, 1964; children: Stephen B., Mary D., Thomas H., John M. BSEE, U.S. Naval Acad., 1962; MS, Am. U., 1976. Commd. 2d lt. USMC, 1962, advanced through grades to col., 1984, ret., 1992; polit./mil. planner Office of Joint Chiefs of Staff, Washington; asst. prof. history Oreg. State U., Corvallis, 1972-75; dir. divsn. English and history U.S. Naval Acad., Annapolis, Md., 1984-87; commanding officer Naval ROTC unit Va. Mil. Inst., Lexington, 1990-92; pres. So. Va. Coll., Buena Vista, 1992-96, chancellor, 1996-97; pres. Hargrave Mil. Acad., Chatham, Va., 1997—. Lectr. in field. Decorated Navy Cross, Legion of Merit (2), Silver Star, Bronze Star (2), Purple Heart. Mem. Phi Alpha Theta. Office: Hargrave Mil Acad 200 Military Dr Chatham VA 24531-4658

RIPPY, FRANCES MARGUERITE MAYHEW, English language educator; b. Ft. Worth, Sept. 16, 1929; d. Henry Grady and Marguerite Christine (O'Neill) Mayhew; m. Noble Merrill Rippy, Aug. 29, 1955 (dec. Sept. 1980); children: Felix O'Neill, Conrad Mayhew, Marguerite Hailey. BA, Tex. Christian U., 1949; MA, Vanderbilt U., 1951, PhD, 1957; postgrad., U. London, 1952-53. Instr. Tex. Christian U., 1953-55; instr. to asst. prof. Lamar State U., 1955-59; asst. prof. English Ball State U., Muncie, Ind., 1959-64; assoc. prof. English, Ball State U., 1964-68, prof., 1968—, dir. grad. studies in English, 1966-87; editor Ball State U. Forum, 1960-89. Vis. asst. prof. Sam Houston State U., 1957; vis. lectr., prof. U. P.R., summers 1959, 60, 61; exch. prof. Westminster Coll., Oxford, Eng., 1988; cons.-evaluator North Cen. Assn. Colls. and Schs., 1973—, commn.-at-large, 1987-91; cons.-evaluator New Eng. Assn. Schs. and Colls., 1983. Author: Matthew Prior, 1986; contbr. articles to profl. jours., encys., ref. guides, chpts. to anthology; contbr. to Dictionary of Literary Biography. Recipient McClintock award, 1966; Danforth grantee, 1964, Ball State U. Rsch. grantee, 1960, 62, 70, 73, 76, 87, 88, 89, 90, 92, 93, 95, 96, 98, Lilly Libr. Rsch., 1978; Fulbright scholar U. London, 1952-53; recipient Outstanding Faculty award Ball State U., 1992, Ind. Coll. Tchr./Scholar of 1994, Ind. Coll. English Assn., 1994. Mem. MLA, AAUP, Coll. English Assn, Nat. Coun. Tchrs. English, Am. Soc. 18th Century Studies, Am. Fedn. Tchrs., Ind. Coll. English Assn. (pres. 1984-85) Johnson Soc. Midwest (sec. 1961-62). Home: 1205 S Main St Georgetown TX 78626-6726

RISDEN, NANCY DIKA, mathematics educator; b. Englewood, N.J., Sept. 14, 1948; d. John and Dorothy Louise (Eisberg) Macris; m. Dennis Richard Risden, Apr. 6, 1974; children: Jeannine, Steven, David. BS, Ursinus Coll., Collegeville, Pa., 1970; MA, Montclair State Coll., Upper Montclair, N.J., 1976. Cert. postgrad. prof. tchr. secondary math., Va., N.J. Tchr. math. West Essex Regional Mid. Sch., North Caldwell, N.J., 1970-71, South Jr. H.S., Bloomfield, N.J., 1971-79; substitute tchr. Oldham County Mid. Sch., Oldham County, Ky., 1981-82; instr. math. Watterson Coll., Louisville, 1984; tchr. math. Duke U. Hosp. Sch., Durham, N.C., 1988-90; substitute tchr. York County Pub. Schs., Yorktown, Va., 1991-93; tchr. math. Tabb Mid. Sch., Yorktown, 1993—. Treas. Mangum Primary Sch. PTA, Durham County, 1988-89; cookie chmn. Girl Scouts U.S., Durham County, 1989; den leader cub scouts Boy Scouts Am., Durham County, 1988-91, com. chairperson pack 104, Yorktown, Va., 1991-95, advancement chair Troop 201, 1994-2003. Mem. NEA, Va. Edn. Assn., York County Edn. Assn., Nat. Coun. Tchrs. Math., Va. Mid. Sch. Assn., Order Ea. Star N.J. (Worth Matron 1975-76, Grand Adah 1976-77). Presbyterian. Avocations: needlework, church choir. Home: 113 Daphne Dr Yorktown VA 23692-3220 Office: Tabb Middle School 300 Yorktown Rd Yorktown VA 23693-3504

RISHEL, KENN CHARLES, school superintendent; b. Utica, N.Y., Nov. 19, 1946; s. Lester and Lois (Keehle) R.; m. Leslie Ann Syposs, Dec. 30, 1967; children: Samantha D., Andrea L. BS, SUNY, Oneonta, 1968; MS in Edn., SUNY, Cortland, 1973, Cert. Advanced Study/Adminstrn., 1985. Elem. tchr. Holland Patent (N.Y.) Ctrl. Sch., 1968-81, math coord., 1977-81; cons. CIMS program Oneida/Madison BOCES, New Hartford, N.Y., 1977-81; asst. supt. for bus. Carthage (N.Y.) Ctrl. Sch., 1981-87, supt., 1987-96; supervising adminstrn., CEO Carthage Area Hosp., 1994-98; cons. Sch. Constrn. & Collective Bargaining Radio Broadcaster, Lowille, N.Y., 1998-99; supt. S.A.U. #30, Laconia, NH, 1999—2001. Excelsion examiner N.Y. State Award for Quality, Albany, 1992—94; adj. prof. SUNY-Oswego, Watertown, 1994, SUNY, Oneonta, 2001—; notary pub. N.Y. State. Author: Be True to Your School-Reality and the School Superintendency. Recipient Pathfinder award NYSAWA, 1995. Mem. N.Y. Coun. Sch. Supts. (mem. ethics com. 1991-95, Black River Coun. Sch. Supts., Am. Assn. Sch. Adminstrs., Assn. U.S. Army, Rotary (v.p., pres. 1981-86), Lions, Elks. Home: 1006 Trackside Dr Marcy NY 13403 E-mail: mgtcon1@aol.com.

RISINGER, C. FREDERICK, social studies educator; b. Paducah, Ky., July 15, 1939; s. Charles Morris and Mary Neal (Barfield) R.; m. Margaret M. Marker, July 4, 1994; children: Donna Lyne, Alyson, Laura, John. BS in Edn., So. Ill. U., 1961; MA in History, No. Ill. U., 1968. Newscaster, disc jockey WMOK Radio, Metropolis, Ill., 1955-61; tchr., adminstr., coach Lake Park H.S., Roselle, Ill., 1962-73; coord. sch. social studies Ind. U., Bloomington, 1973-86, assoc. dir. social studies devel. ctr., 1986-90, dir. nat. clearinghouse for U.S.-Japan studies, 1990—, assoc. dir. tchr. edn., 1995-97, dir. profl. devel., sch. svcs. and summer sessions, 1997—. Mem. adv. bd. Learning Mag., Boston, 1988—; pres. Nat. Coun. for the Social Studies, 1990-91. Co-author: America! America!, 1974, America's Past and Promise, 1997, Creating America, 2000, Scott Foresman Social Studies K-6 Series, 2003; editor jour. News and Notes on the Social Sciences, 1973-86. Pres. Social Studies Suprs. Assn., Washington, 1985-86; exec. dir. Ind. Coun. for Social Studies, Bloomington, 1975-87. Recipient numerous pub. and pvt. ednl. grants; named Tchr. of Yr. DuPage County Edn. Assn., 1973. Mem. ASCD, Nat. Coun. for Social Studies, Ind. Assn. Historians, Phi Delta Kappa. Democrat. Home: 7039 E State Rd 45 Bloomington IN 47408-9580 E-mail: risinger@indiana.edu.

RISKO, VICTORIA J. language educator; BS, U. Pitts., 1966; MS, W.Va. U., 1969, EdD, 1971; postgrad., U. London, 1975. Fellow Learning Disabilities Inst. W.Va. U., 1969—70; tchr. Johnstown (Pa.) Pub. Sch. Sys., 1967—68; tchr. remedial reading Johnstown (Pa.) Pub. Sch. Dist., 1967; instr. home econs. W.Va. U., 1968—69, instr., supr. reading clinic, 1969; rschr.-tchr. Robert F. Kennedy Youth Ctr., Morgantown, W.Va., 1969—70; tchr.-cons. inservice edn. of tchrs. Belair-Manchester Schs. of Mandeville, Jamaica, 1974—75; instr., asst. prof., assoc. prof., dir. reading clinic programs, mem. grad. faculty SUNY, Fredonia, 1970—75; rsch. scientist Learning Tech. Ctr., mem. faculty interdisciplinary team Child Study Ctr., Kennedy Ctr. Peabody Coll., Vanderbilt U., Nashville, 1978—89, assoc. prof., 1975—94, prof. lang. and learning, 1994—. Vis. prof. reading W.Va. U., 1971. Recipient Disting. Svc. and Leadership award, Coll. Reading Assn., 1995, Disting. Rsch. in Tchr.'s Edn. award, Assn. Tchr. Educators Conf., 1992. Office: Vanderbilt U Peabody Coll Box 330 Nashville TN 37203*

RISNER, ANITA JANE, vocational school educator; b. Durant, Okla., Nov. 10, 1946; d. Forrest W. and Jane J. (Nelms) Carter; m. Curt Risner, Jan. 21, 1968; children: Patrick, Brandon. AS, Eastern Okla. Jr. Coll., 1967; BS, Okla. State U., 1971; MEd, Northeastern State U., 1981. Hospitality careers tchr. Pryor (Okla.) Pub. Schs., 1971-73, N.E. Area Vo-Tech, Pryor, 1973-75; child devel. tchr. Tulsa Tech. Ctr., 1976-81, counselor, 1981-89; staff devel. specialist Okla. Dept. of Vo-Tech Edn., Stillwater, Okla., 1989-94; instrnl. coord. Indian Capital Area Vo-Tech Sch., Muskogee, Okla., 1994—; regional career devel. specialist Okla. Dept. Vocat. Tech. Edn., 1994-97; asst. supt. Tri-County Tech. Ctr., Bartlesville, Okla., 1997-99, dep. supt., 1999—. Advisor Vocat. Student Orgns., Tulsa, 1976-89; career adv. com. mem. Bixby (Okla.) Pub. Schs., 1992—; participant Craftmanship 2000 program, Tulsa; presenter in local, state, nat. confs. Editor: (curriculum guide) Integrating Career Days, 1992, Integrating OK Career Search, 1993; editor (newsletter) Classworks, 1995. Mem. ASCD, Am. Vocat. Assn. (Region IV Outstanding Vocat. Educator of Yr. 1994, Outstanding Vocat. Educator of Yr. award 1995), Okla. Vocat. Assn. (Educator of Yr.-Guidance 1993), Okla. Assn. for Supervision and Curriculum Devel., Phi Delta Kappa. Democrat. Avocations: reading, flower gardening. Address: 1729 Melrose Dr Bartlesville OK 74006-7025 Office: Tri-County Tech Ctr 6101 Nowata Rd Bartlesville OK 74006-6029

RISOLI, ALLISON LEE, secondary school educator; b. Peekskill, NY, Apr. 24, 1960; d. Alexander J. and Barbara M. (Chefalo) R. BA in Polit. Sci., Manhattanville Coll., Purchase, NY, 1982; MS in Ednl. Psychology, Fordham U., 1986; continuing ed. baking and pastry arts, Inst. for Culinary Ed., 2002. Cert. secondary social studies tchr., N.Y. Tchr. St. Mary's Sch., Yonkers, NY, 1985-87, Sacred Heart Middle Sch., Bronx, NY, 1987-88; tchr./counselor The Hartsdale Sch., Tuchahoe, NY, 1988-91; tchr. social studies Peekskill HS, 1991—. Peekskill: vol. Historic Hudson Valley, Tarrytown, NY, 1991, Ctrl. Westchester Humane Soc., Elmsford NY, 1987; mem. City of Peekskill Human Rels. Comm. Hudson River Tchrs. Ctr. grantee, 1993. Mem. Westchester Coun. for Social Studies, N.Y. State Coun. for Social Studies, Nat. Coun. for Social Studies. Democrat. Roman Catholic. Avocations: animal rights activist, gardening, baking. Home: 1670 Westchester Ave Peekskill NY 10566-3007

RISPETTOSO, GEORGE ALPHONSE, vocational educator, diesel technology consultant; b. Arlington, Mass., Feb. 21, 1941; s. Samuel and Marie (Valeriano) R.; m. Mary Ann C. Tempesta, Oct. 11, 1987. BS in Edn., Fitchburg (Mass.) State Coll., 1984, MS in Edn., 1988. Cert. tchr., supt. and dir. vocat. tech. high sch., Mass. Tchr. Blue Hills Regional Vocat. Tech. High Sch., Canton, Mass., 1978-85; asst. prof. Massasoit C.C., Canton, 1985-88; industry instr. Caterpillar Corp., Hopkinton, Mass., 1988; tchr. diesel tech. Southeastern Regional Tech. High Sch., Easton, Mass., 1988—. Cons. Diesel Tech. Mgmt. Inc., Kingston, Mass., 1982—. Curriculum writer. Charter mem. Rep. Presdl. Task Force, Washington, 1982—. With USAF, 1962-66. Mem. Masons (3d and 32d degrees), Shriners (mem. Shriners Burn Ctr. Motorcycle Drill Team). Roman Catholic. Avocations: cars, boating, motorcycling. Home: 4 Bay View Ave Kingston MA 02364-1712

RISSER, JAMES VAULX, JR., journalist, educator; b. Lincoln, Nebr., May 8, 1938; s. James Vaulx and Ella Caroline (Schacht) R.; m. Sandra Elizabeth Laaker, June 10, 1961; children: David James, John Daniel. BA, U. Nebr., 1959, cert. in journalism, 1964; JD, U. San Francisco, 1962. Bar: Nebr. 1962. Pvt. practice law, Lincoln, 1962-64; reporter Des Moines Register and Tribune, 1964-85, Washington corr., 1969-85, bur. chief, 1976-85; dir. John S. Knight fellowships for profl. journalists, prof. communication Stanford U., 1985-2000. Lectr. Wells Coll., 1981; mem. com. on agrl. edn. in secondary schs. Nat. Acad. Scis., 1985-88. Trustee Reuter Found., 1989-2000, Am. Conservatory Theater, 2000-2003, Oreg. Shakespear Fest., 2003—; mem. Pulitzer Prize Bd., 1990-99; mem. journalism adv. com. Knight Found., 2000—. Profl. Journalism fellow Stanford U., 1973-74; recipient award for disting. reporting public affairs Am. Polit. Sci. Assn., 1969; Thomas L. Stokes award for environ. reporting Washington Journalism Center, 1971, 79; Pulitzer prize for nat. reporting, 1976, 79; Worth Bingham Found. prize for investigative reporting, 1976; Raymond Clapper Meml. Assn. award for Washington reporting, 1976, 78; Edward J. Meeman award for Conservation Reporting, 1985. Mem. Soc. Environ. Journalists, Soc. Profl. Journalists (Disting. Svc. award 1976), Investigative Reporters and Editors Assn., Com. Concerned Journalists, Gridiron Club. Clubs: Gridiron. Home: 1111 Bay St # 404 San Francisco CA 94123 E-mail: jimrisser@earthlink.net.

RISSER, PAUL GILLAN, academic administrator, botanist; b. Blackwell, Okla., Sept. 14, 1939; s. Paul Crane and Jean (McCluskey) R.; children: David, Mark, Stephen, Scott. BA, Grinnell Coll., 1961; MS in Botany, U. Wis., 1965, PhD in Botany and Soils, 1967. From asst. prof. to prof. botany U. Okla., 1967-81, also asst. dir. biol. sta., chmn. dept. botany and microbiology, 1977-81; dir. Okla. Biol. Survey, 1971-77; chief Ill. Natural History Survey, 1981-86; program dir., ecosystem studies NSF; provost and v.p. acad. affairs U. N.Mex., 1989-92; former pres. Miami U., Oxford, Ohio; pres. Oreg. State U., 1996—. Author: (with Kathy Cornelison) Man and the Biosphere, 1979, (with others) The True Prairie Ecosystem, 1981; research, numerous publs. in field. Trustee Pioneer Multi-County Library Bd. Mem. Am. Acad. Arts and Scis., Ecol. Soc. Am. (pres.), Brit. Ecol. Soc., Soc. Range Mgmt., Southwestern Assn. Naturalists (pres.), Am. Inst. Biol. Sci. (pres.), Torrey Bot. Club. Presbyterian. Office: Oregon State U Kerr Adminstrn Bldg Office of the Pres Corvallis OR 97331-8507

RISSONE, DONNA, educator, financial executive; b. Stamford, Conn., July 13, 1943; d. Thomas and Carmela (Sabato) Galasso; m. Robert Rissone, Aug. 21, 1965; children: Robert, Jeannine. AB in Classics, Rosemont (Pa.) Coll., 1965; MSEd, Nazareth Coll., 1975. Cert. elem. secondary fgn. lang. tchr., N.Y. Tour escort various, Europe; fgn. lang. tchr. W. Irondequoit H.S., Rochester, N.Y., 1973—; treas. Door and Hardware Systems, Rochester, 1972—. Named Activity Advisor of Yr. N.Y. State Advisors/Student Assn., 1996. Avocation: travel. Home: 305 Harbor Hill Dr Rochester NY 14617-1469 Office: W Irondequoit High Sch 260 Cooper Rd Rochester NY 14617-3095

RISTOW, GAIL ROSS, art educator, paralegal, children's rights advocate; b. Carmel, Calif., Oct. 18, 1949; d. Kenneth E. and Lula Mae (Craft) Ross; m. Steven Craig Ristow, Sept. 15, 1971. BS in Biochemistry, Calif. Polytech State U., San Luis Obispo, 1972; MEd, Ariz. State U., 1980. Cert. tchr., Calif. Asst. instr. Calif. State Polytech U., Pomona, 1972; grad. asst. Calif. Polytech State U., Pomona, 1973-74; tchr. Mt. Carmel High Sch., L.A., 1974-76, Cartwright Sch. Dist., Phoenix, 1976-80; pres., owner Handmade With Love, Bay City, Tex., 1984-88; tchr. art Aiken, S.C., 1989-96. Tchr. Community Edn., Bay City, 1986-88, Palacios, Tex., 1987. Sec. Chukker Creek Homeowners, Aiken, S.C., 1989-96; mem. S.C. Foster Care Rev. Bd., 1991-96; vol. tchr. elem. schs., Korea. Mem. AAUW, Am. Chem. Soc., Nat. Soc. Tole and Decorative Painters, Aiken Newcomer's Club (sec. 1989-91), Aiken Lioness Club (pres. 1991-94), Aiken Lions Club, Alpha Delta Kappa (v.p. 1986-87). Avocations: painting, woodworking, sewing, reading, children's rights advocacy. Home: 396 Lombardy Ln Richland WA 99352

RISTOW, THELMA FRANCES, elementary educator; b. Plymouth, Wis., Sept. 9, 1938; d. Ambrose J. and Marie A. (Lauby) Enders; m. William A. Ristow, Nov. 7, 1964; children: James, Lora, Kim Marie, Robert, Donald. BS, U. Wis., Oshkosh, 1960, MS in Edn., 1995. Cert. elem. tchr. Tchr. Webster Stanley Elem., Wis., 1995—; peer coach Oshkosh Area Sch. Dist. Contbr. chapters to books; co-author (with Dr. Ava McCall): Teaching State History: A Guide to Developing a Multicultural Curriculum. Mem. ASCD, Internat. Reading Assn. (coord.), Wis. State Reading Assn., Ctrl. Wis. Reading Coun., Mid-East Reading Coun., Wolf River Reading Coun., Fox Valley Reading Coun., Delta Kappa Gamma, Phi Delta Gamma, Kappa Delta Pi. Home: 1600 Northpoint St Oshkosh WI 54901-3119 Office: Webster Stanley Elem 915 Hazel St Oshkosh WI 54901-4057

RITCHIE, ANNE, educational administrator; b. Grants Pass, Oreg., July 1, 1944; d. William Riley Jr. and Allie Brown (Clark) R.; m. Charles James Cooper, Sept. 4, 1968 (div. 1985); children: Holly Anne, Wendy Nicole. BA in Edn. with honors, Calif. State U., Sacramento, 1981. Cert. elem. tchr., Calif. CEO El Rancho Schs., Inc., Carmichael, Calif., 1981—. Citizen amb. del. People to People Internat., Russia, Lithuania, Hungary, 1993, China, 1994. Active Crocker Art Mus.; mem. Rep. Senatorial Inner Circle, Washington, 1999. Mem. AAUW, Nat. Assn. Edn. for Young Children, Profl. Assn. Childhood Educators, Nat. Child Care Assn. Episcopalian. Avocations: traveling, skiing, reading.

RITCHIE, DANIEL LEE, academic administrator; b. Springfield, Ill., Sept. 19, 1931; s. Daniel Felix and Jessie Dee (Binney) R. BA, Harvard U., 1954, MBA, 1956. Exec. v.p., CFO MCA, Inc., LA, 1962—70; pres. Archon Pure Products Co., Los Angeles, 1970-73; exec. v.p. Westinghouse Electric Corp., Pitts., 1975-78; pres. corp. staff and strategic planning Westinghouse Broadcasting Co., 1978-79, pres., chief exec. officer, 1979-81, chmn., chief exec. officer, Westinghouse Broadcasting & Cable, Inc., 1981-87; owner Rancho Cielo, Montecito, Calif., 1977—; chancellor U. Denver, 1989—. With U.S. Army, 1956-58. Office: U Denver Office of Chancellor University Park Denver CO 80208-0001 E-mail: dritchie@du.edu.*

RITCHIE, J. MURDOCH, pharmacologist, educator; b. Aberdeen, Scotland, June 10, 1925; came to U.S. 1956; s. Alexander Farquharson and Agnes Jane (Bremner) R.; m. Brenda Rachel Bigland; children: Alasdair J., A. Jocelyn. BSc, Aberdeen (Scotland) U., 1944, U. Coll. London, 1949, PhD, 1952, DSc, 1960; MA, Yale U., 1968; DSc, Aberdeen U., 1987. Lectr. physiology U. Coll. London, 1949-51; sci. staff Nat. Inst. Med. Rsch., London, 1951-55; asst. prof. to prof. Albert Einstein Coll. Medicine, N.Y.C., 1954-63, prof. pharmacology, 1963-68; prof. and chmn. pharmacology Yale U., New Haven, 1968-74, dir. biol. scis., 1975-78, prof. pharmacology, 1968—. Contbr. articles to profl. jours.; editor sci. books and jours. Fellow Royal Soc., Univ. Coll. London, Inst. Physics London. Home: 47 Deepwood Dr Hamden CT 06517-3414 Office: Yale Univ Sch Medicine 333 Cedar St New Haven CT 06510-3206 E-mail: murdoch.ritchie@yale.edu.

RITCHIE, ROBERT OLIVER, materials science educator; b. Plymouth, Devon, U.K., Jan. 2, 1948; came to U.S., 1974; s. Kenneth Ian and Kathleen Joyce (Sims) R.; m. Connie Olesen (div. 1978); 1 child, James Oliver; m. HaiYing Song, 1991. BA with honors, U. Cambridge, Eng., 1969, MA, PhD, 1973, ScD, 1990. Cert. engr., U.K. Goldsmith's rsch. fellow Churchill Coll. U. Cambridge, 1972-74; Miller fellow in basic rsch. sci. U. Calif., Berkeley, 1974-76; assoc. prof. mech. engring. MIT, Cambridge, 1977-81; prof. U. Calif., Berkeley, 1981—; dep. dir. Materials Scis. Divsn. Lawrence Berkeley Nat. Lab., Cambridge, 1990-94, dir. Ctr. for Advanced Materials, 1987-95, head Structural Materials Dept., Materials Scis. Divsn., 1995—. Cons. Alcan, Allison, Applied Materials, Boeing, Chevron, Cordis, Exxon, GE, GM, Grumman, Guidant, Instron, Northrop, Rockwell, Westinghouse, Baxter, Carbomedics, Med. Inc., Shiley, St. Jude Med.; Van Horn Disting. lectr. Case Western U., 1997. Editor: 15 books; contbr. more than 450 articles to profl. jours. Recipient Curtis W. McGraw Rsch. award Am. Soc. Engring. Educators, 1987, Rosenhain medal Inst. Materials London, 1992, G.R. Irwin medal ASTM, 1985, Mathewson gold medal TMS-AME, 1985, Van Horn Disting. Lectr. award Case Western Res. U., 1997; named one of Top 100 Scientists, Sci. Digest mag., 1984. Fellow: Royal Acad. Engring. (London), Minerals, Materials and Metals Soc. (Mathewson Gold medal 1985, Disting. Structural Materials Scientist/Engr. award 1996), Internat. Congress on Fracture (pres. 1997—2001), Am. Soc. Metals Internat., Inst. Materials (London); mem.: NAE, ASME, Materials Rsch. Soc., Am. Soc. Materials. Avocations: skiing, antiques, orchids, tennis. Home: 590 Grizzly Peak Blvd Berkeley CA 94708-1238 Office: U Calif Dept Materials Sci and Engring Berkeley CA 94720-1760 E-mail: RORitchie@LBL.gov.

RITTEL, KATHLEEN ANN MAURER, former assistant principal and school system administrator, middle school educator; d. William Michael and Ann Marilyn; m. Donald Russell Rittel; 1 child, Sophia Anndrina Maria. BA in English and Edn., Queens Coll., 1972, MS in Edn., 1977; postgrad., SUNY, Albany, 1978, Brigham Young U., 1978, McPherson Coll., 1978; PhD in Adminstrn. and Supervision, St. John's U., Jamaica, NY, 1982; postgrad., Adelphi U., 1983, U. Mont., 1986, U. N.Mex., 1999, L.I. U., 2000, Coll. St. Rose, 2000, Ind. Wesleyan U., 2003, Endicott Coll., 2003. Cert. tchr., adminstr., supr., N.Y. Tchr. Elijah Clark Jr. H.S., South Bronx, N.Y., 1972-75, Intermediate Sch. 291, Bklyn., 1975; tchr., dean, asst. prin. Jean Nuzzi Jr. H.S., Queens Village, N.Y., 1975-83; asst. prin. William Cowper Intermediate Sch., Maspeth, N.Y., 1983-93; asst. prin.-in-charge I.S. 73 Annex, Elmhurst, N.Y., 1994-97; adminstr.-in-charge 51st Ave. Annex for P.S. 7 and P.S. 71, Elmhurst, N.Y., 1997-99; adminstr.-in charge 51st Ave. Annex for P.S. 7 and I.S. 5, Elmhurst, 1999—2003; tchr. Jericho (N.Y.) Middle Sch., 2003—. Doctoral fellow Hofstra U., 1990. Mem. Nat. Coun. Tchrs. English, Internat. Reading Assn. Roman Catholic. Avocations: playing piano, roller skating, ice skating, dancing, traveling. E-mail: superprofessor@yahoo.com.

RITTER, ELIZABETH CARROLL, elementary education educator; b. Augusta, Ga., June 22, 1953; d. Hugh Oscar and Margaret Elizabeth (Carroll) Queen; m. Robert Hilton Ritter, June 21, 1975; 1 child, Robert Hilton Jr. MusB, Meredith Coll., 1975; M in Music Edn., U. N.C., Greensboro, 1991. Cert. music edn. grades K-12, N.C. Music educator Richmond County Schs., Hamlet, N.C., 1975-92. Bd. mem., past v.p. Richmond County Arts Coun., Rockingham, N.C., 1978-89; ch. choir dir.

First Presbyn. Ch. of Hamlet, N.C., 1989-92; bd. mem. Richmond County Community Concerts, Rockingham, 1991-92. Mem. NCAE, MENC, Delta Kappa Gamma. Democrat. Baptist. Avocations: reading, singing. Home: 331 Main St Hamlet NC 28345-3339

RITTER, FREDERICK EDMOND, plastic surgeon, educator; b. Cin., Aug. 21, 1959; s. Edmond J. and Alexandra (Engel) R.; m. Christina Weltz, Aug. 2, 1993. BS, U. Cin., 1980; MD, Washington U., St. Louis, 1984. Intern, resident U. Medicine and Dentistry N.J., 1984-90; resident in plastic and reconstructive surgery U. Calif., San Francisco, 1990-92; asst. prof. surgery Duke U., Durham, N.C., 1992—. Contbr. chpts. in books and articles to profl. jours. Republican. Achievements include reducing thrombogenicity biomaterials in contact with blood, innovations in reconstructive and asthetic surgery, tissue bioengineering.

RITTMER, ELAINE HENEKE, retired library media specialist; b. Maquoketa, Iowa, Feb. 4, 1931; d. Herman John and Clara (Luett) Heneke; m. Sheldon Lowell Rittmer, June 11, 1950; children: Kenneth, Lynnette, Robyn (dec.), infant son (dec.). BA, Marycrest Coll., 1973; MS, Western Ill. U., 1980. Permanent teaching cert. K-14, Iowa; cert. libr. media specialist K-14, Iowa. Sch. libr. Calamus-Wheatland (Iowa) Community Schs., 1970-74; high sch. libr. media specialist, libr. coord. Camanche (Iowa) Community Sch., 1974-96; legis. asst. State Senate, Des Moines, 1997—2002; ret., 2002. Mem. Iowa Edn. Media Assn., Iowa State Edn. Assn., Camanche Edn. Assn., Camanche Cmty. Schs. Tech. Com., Media Tech. Cons. Republican. Avocations: reading, walking, education, political activities, technology developments. Home: 3539 230th St De Witt IA 52742-9208 E-mail: shelaine@netins.net.

RITTNER, CARL FREDERICK, educational administrator; b. Boston, Feb. 28, 1914; s. Philip and Augusta (Beich) R.; m. Eunice Carin, 1940; 1 child, Stephen. BS in Edn., Boston U., 1936, EdM, 1937. Ednl. cons., Boston, 1940's; founder, dir. Rittners Floral Sch., Boston, 1947—. Co-author: Flowers for the Modern Bride, 1965, Arrangements for All Occasions, 1966, Flowers for the Modern Bride (In Living Color), 1968, Rittner's Silver Anniversary Book, 1972, Dried Arrangements, 1978, Rittners Guide to Permanent Flower Arranging, 1978, Vase Arrangements for the Professional Florist, 1979, Christmas Designs, 1979, Flowers for Funerals, 1980, Manual of Wedding Design Styles, 1980, Contemporary Floral Designs, 1983, Floral Designs for That Special Occasion, 1985, Inexpensive Bread & Butter Designs, 1986. Mem. Soc. Am. Florists, Florist Transworld Delivery Svc., Phi Delta Kappa. Office: 345 Marlborough St Boston MA 02115-1713

RITTNER, STEPHEN LEE, academic administrator; b. Boston, Oct. 31, 1952; s. Carl Frederick and Eunice (Carin) R. BS in Biology, BA in Religion, Tufts U., 1974, EdM, 1977; EdD, Boston U., 1981. Assoc. dir. Rittners Floral Sch., Boston, 1974—. Producer videotapes on floral design. Author: Window Display for the Retail Florist, A Philosophy of Floral Designing, 1989, Introductory Floral Designing, 1992, A Bibliography of Floral Design Books for Teachers of Floral Designing, 1992; co-author: Vase Arrangements for the Professional Florist, 1979, Dried Arrangements, 1978, Christmas Designs, 1979, A Manual of Wedding Design Styles, 1980, Contemporary Floral Designs, 1983, Floral Designs for that Special Occasion, 1985, Inexpensive Bread and Butter Designs, 1986. Mem. Soc. Am. Florists, Assn. Ednl. Comms. and Tech., Florists Transworld Dslivery Svc., Redbook, Phi Beta Kappa, Phi Delta Kappa, Pi Lambda Theta. Office: Rittners Floral Sch 345 Marlborough St Boston MA 02115-1713 E-mail: stevrt@tiac.net.

RITVO, ROGER ALAN, vice chancellor, health management-policy educator; b. Cambridge, Mass., Aug. 12, 1944; s. Meyer and Miriam R.S. (Meyers) R.; m. Lynn Lieberman; children: Roberta, Eric. BA, Western Res. U., 1967; MBA, George Washington U., 1970; PhD, Case Western Res. U., 1976. Asst. adminstr. N.Y. Mental Health System, 1968-70; asst. prof., asst. dean Sch. Applied Social Scis. Case Western Res. U., Cleve., 1976-79, assoc. prof., 1981-83; assoc. prof., founding dir. Grad. Program in Health Adminstrn. Cleve. State U., 1983-87; prof. health mgmt. and policy, dean Sch. Health and Human Svcs. U. N.H., Durham, 1987-97; sr. health policy analyst to sec. DHHS, Washington, 1980-81; vice chancellor acad. and student affairs Auburn U. Montgomery, Ala., 1997—. Vis. rsch. scholar WHO, Copenhagen, 1978; vis. prof. Am. U., Washington, 1980-81, U. W.I., 1993; chair Ala. Coun. Chief Acad. Officers, 1998-2000; vis. scholar U. Sheffield, Eng., 1985; cons. to numerous orgns. on profit and non-profit strategic planning. Editor, author 5 books, including Managing in the Age of Change, 1994, Improving Governing Board Effectiveness, 1996, Sisters in Sorrow Voices of Care in the Holocaust, 1998; mem. cmty. editl. bd. Montgomery Advertiser newspaper, 1999; contbr. articles to profl. jours. Trustee Hosp. Sisters of Charity, Cleve., 1980-85, Greater Seacoast United Way, 1991-93; chmn. health care adv. com. Ohio Senate, 1983-85; bd. mem. Fairmount Temple, Beachwood, Ohio, 1980-85; trustee Leadership Seacoast, 1991-93, bd. dirs., 1992-95; bd. dirs. N.H. chpt. United Way, 1992-95, Higher Edn. Leadership Partnership, 1998-2000. Recipient Outstanding Adminstr. award, 1992, Cert. of Merit U. N.H. Pres.'s Commn. on Women, 1994; Govt. fellow Am. Coun. Edn., 1980-81. Mem. Nat. Tng. Labs. Inst. (bd. dirs. 1981-85, 92-96), Cert. Cons. Internat., Jewish Philatelic, Hist. Soc. N.Y.C. Avocations: collecting flat irons and masks, philatelist, white water rafting. Office: Auburn U Montgomery 7300 University Dr Montgomery AL 36117-3596

RITZ, JOHN MICHAEL, education educator; b. Latrobe, Pa., Oct. 31, 1948; s. John Edward and Catharine May (Mills) R.; m. Sally Louise Ward, July 18, 1970; 1 child, Molly. BS, Purdue U., 1970; MS, U. Wis., Stout, 1974; EdD, W.Va. U., 1977. Tech. tchr. Nova High Sch., Ft. Lauderdale, Fla., 1970-72; faculty asst. U. Wis.-Stout, Menomonie, 1973-74; tng. assoc. W.Va. U., Morgantown, 1974-77; prof., chmn. Old Dominion U., Norfolk, Va., 1977—. Bd. dirs. Tidewater Tech. Assocs., Virginia Beach, Va. Author: Exploring Communication, 1996, 4th edit., 2002, Exploring Production Systems, 1990, Standards for Technological Literacy: The Role of Teacher Education, 2002. With U.S. Army, 1971-73, Fed. Republic of Germany. Recipient Tonelson award Old Dominion U., 1982 Mem. Internat. Tech. Edn. Assn. (bd. dirs. 2000—, Disting. Tech. Educator 1986, Meritorious Svc. award 1990, Acad. Fellows award, 1997, Ednl. Exhibitions Assn., Hall of Fame, 2003), Coun. on Tech. Tchr. Edn. (treas. 1981-85, pres. 1996-2000, Tech. Tchr. Educator of Yr. 1993), Va. Tech. Edn. Assn. (pres. 1983), Acad. of Scholars, Tech. Found. Am. (Honor Roll 2000). Avocations: salt water fishing, writing. Office: Old Dominion U 4600 Hampton Blvd Norfolk VA 23529

RITZHEIMER, ROBERT ALAN, educational publishing executive; b. Trenton, Ill., Dec. 29, 1931; s. Leslie H. and Hilda M. (Fochtmann) R.; m. Shirley Ann Wharrie, Sept. 11, 1954; children: Kim E. Ritzheimer Chase, Gina C. Ritzheimer Hartle, Scott D., Susan L. Ritzheimer Kelly. BS in Edn., Ill. State Normal U., 1953, MS in Edn., 1960; postgrad., Columbia U., 1955. Cert. tchr., supr., k-12, Ill. Tchr. Bloomington (Ill.) Pub. Schs., 1955-57; prin., elem. and jr. high sch. Wesclin Community Unit #3, New Baden, Ill., 1957-62; ednl. sales rep. Scott Foresman Co., Bradford Woods, Pa., 1962-81, field sales mgr. Sunnyvale, Calif., 1981-91, mgr. sales support, 1992-93; ret., 1993. Guest lectr. Stanford U., Palo Alto, Calif., 1983, Santa Clara (Calif.) U., 1992. Treas. Little League, New Baden, Ill., 1958-62; pres. Ill. Edn. Assn., Kaskaskia Div., E. St. Louis, 1961. With U.S. Army, 1953-55. Mem. ASCD, NEA (life), Calif.Sci. Teachers Assn. Republican. Avocations: travel, golf, plate collecting, oil painting. Home: 2083 Mataro Way San Jose CA 95135-1254

RIVERA, JANE MARKEY, special education educator, educator; b. Frederick, Md., Feb. 26, 1954; d. Willard Hanshew and Mary Leone (Palmer) Markey; m. Edric Rafael Rivera, Mar. 7, 1981; children: Edric Rafael Jr., Julian Rafael, Marisa Leona. BA, Wittenberg U., 1976; M in Spl. Edn., Antioch U., 1980. Remedial reading tchr. Cen. Bucks Sch. Dist., Doylestown, Pa., 1976-78; chpt. 1 reading tchr. Pennridge Sch. Dist., Perkasie, Pa., 1978-93, spl. edn. tchr., 1993—. Student assistance team mem. Pennridge Sch. Dist., Perkasie, 1992—; youth aid panel Hilltown (Pa.) Police Dept., 1986—. Bd. mem. Deep Run. Valley Sports Assn., Hilltown, 1993—. Mem. St. Andrew's Ch. Handbell Choir. Avocations: gardening, reading, traveling, piano. Home: 408 Longleaf Dr Perkasie PA 18944-5413 Office: Pennridge Cen Jr High Sch 1500 N 5th St Perkasie PA 18944-2207

RIVERA, RUTH ELLEN, special services director; b. Auburn, N.Y., Aug. 1, 1944; d. Robert James and Edna Louise Stebbins; m. Edward L. Malec, Sept. 2, 1967 (div. Oct. 1977); children: Edward L., Amy Beth; m. Carlos A. Rivera, July 18, 1999. B, Houghton (N.Y.) Coll., 1966; student, Ohio U., 1966-67; M, Montclair State Coll., 1970; EdD, Nova Southeastern U., 1999. Tchr. Newark Pub. Schs., N.J., 1967-69; social worker Passaic County Bd. Soc. Svcs., Paterson, N.J., 1970-72, Boonton Pub. Schs., N.J., 1979-88; dir. spl. edn. Sch. Union 44, Sabattus, Maine, 1988-90; dir. spl. svcs. Kinnelon Pub. Schs., N.J., 1990-93, Linden (N.J.) Pub. Schs., NJ, 1993—2000, Bloomfield Pub. Schs., NJ, 2000—. Women's ministry Jacksonville Chapel, Lincoln Park, N.J. Mem. ASCD, N.J. Dept. Edn. Prof. Svcs. Coun., N.J. Assn. Sch. Social Workers (v.p. 1985-87, pres. 1987-88), N.J. Assn. for Pupil Svcs. Adminstrs., N.J. Prins. and Suprs. Assn., N.E. Coalition of Ednl. Leaders, Union County Assn. of Dirs. of Spl. Svcs., Morris County Assn. Dirs. Spl. Edn., Knnelon Women's Svc. Orgn. Avocations: reading, music. Home: 35 Cliff Trl Kinnelon NJ 07405-3107 Office: Bloomfield Pub Schs 155 Broad St Bloomfield NJ 07003-2638

RIVERA-MARTINEZ, SOCORRO, retired elementary school educator, assitant principal; b. Mayagüez, P.R., Apr. 19, 1942; d. Sotero R. and Rafaela Martinez; m. Carmelo Torres, Dec. 26, 1965; 1 child, Yolivette. AEd., Catholic U., 1963, BA in Elem. Edn., 1980. Cert. tchr., mentor tchr. Tchr. 1-6 grades P.R. Dept. Edn., Mayagüez, 1962-93; auxilliary adminstr. Colegio San Agustin, Cabo Rojo, P.R., 1993-94, asst. principal, 1994-98. Tchr. in charge Rio Hondo Sch. Mayagüez, 1964-70, 73-93, gifted children club, 1990-91, dir.'s resource for tng., 1985-93; math and sci. counselor Rio Hondo, Sch., Castillo Sch., 1971-93. Co-leader troop 384 Girl Scouts Am., Rio Hondo Sch., Mayagüez, P.R., 1975-79; vol. leader Catholic Ch. Summer camp, Cabo Rojo, P.R., 1990-92. Recipient Presidential award Excellence in Sci. and Math. Tchg. The White House, 1993, State award Excellence in Math. Nat. Coun. Math. Tchrs., 1993, Excellence in Math. award Dept. Edn., 1993; named Tchr. of the Year Dept. Edn., 1975, 82. Mem. Educadores Puertorriqueños en Acción, Coun. Elem. Sci. Internat., Coun. Presidential Awardees. Roman Catholic. Avocations: reading, poetry, writing, wire craft, gardening. Home: L22 Calle 3 Borinquen Cabo Rojo PR 00623-3324 Office: Colegio San Agustin Cabo Rojo PR 00623

RIVERA-RAMIREZ, ANA ROSA, secondary school educator; b. Bronx, Sept. 5, 1950; d. Marcelino and Ana Maria (Reyes) Rivera; m. Jose Antonio Ramirez, July 11, 1986; 1 child, Marisol Helena Feijoo. Bachelors, Hunter Coll., 1973, Masters, 1986; postgrad., NYU, 1990—. Cert. ESL tchr., N.Y. Tchr. bilingual Bethel Bapt. Day Care Ctr., Bklyn., 1974-75, Pequeños Souls Day Care Ctr., N.Y.C., 1975-76; tchr. Sacred Heart Sch., Carvin Sch., Santurce, P.R., 1977-79; tchr. adult edn. Mobicentrics Bus. Inst., Bronx, 1979-85; tchr. spl. edn. CJ High Sch. 145, Bronx, 1986-88, tchr. English, 1988—; tchr. ESL Clinton High Sch., Bronx, 1989-90. Con. ESL curriculum Clinton High Sch., Bronx, 1988-89, cons., writer ESL curriculum Mobicentrics Bus. Inst., Bronx, 1984-85. Participant Constitution Works Program, N.Y.C., 1992. Recipient Bronx Rookie Tchr. award Bd. Edn., 1987. Mem. ASCD, AAUW, Phi Delta Kappa (NYU chpt.). Avocations: writing poetry, reading.

RIVERA-URRUTIA, BEATRIZ DALILA, psychology and rehabilitation counseling educator; b. Bayamón, P.R., Jan. 16, 1951; d. José and Carmen B. (Urrutia) Rivera; m. Julio C. Ribera, July 1, 1978; 1 child, Alejandra B. Ribera. BA, U. P.R., 1972, MA, 1975; PhD, Temple U., 1982. Cert. rehab. counselor Commn. Rehab. Counselor Cert., lic. pscyhologist P.R. Staff pscyhologist Learning Plus, Inc., Phila., 1979-80; cons. Hispanic Mental Health Inst., Phila., 1981-82; staff psychologist J.F. Kennedy Community Mental Health Ctr., Phila., 1982-83; prof. U. P.R., Rio Piedras, 1983—. Cons. Jewish Employment & Vocat. Svcs., Phila., 1980; staff psychologist San Juan VA Hosp., Rio Piedras, 1990—; coord. grad. program Rehab. Counseling Grad. Sch., 2000—; prof., Rehab. Counseling Grad. Sch., 1995. Contbr. articles to profl. jours. Vol. Parroquia San Juan Apóstol y Evangelista, Caguas, PR, 1988—90, ARC, San Juan, 1990. Grantee Faculty Instnl. Rsch., U. P.R., 1986—87. Mem.: P.R. Lic. Bd. Psychologists (pres. ethics com. 1991—92), P.R. Psychol. Assn. (bd. editors jour. 1984—89, bd. dirs. 1989—91). Avocations: walking, theater. Home and Office: PO Box 22724 San Juan PR 00931-2724 E-mail: ribera@prtc.net.

RIVERS, WILGA MARIE, foreign language educator; b. Melbourne, Australia, Apr. 13, 1919; came to U.S., 1970; d. Harry and Nina Diamond (Burston) R. Diploma in edn, U. Melbourne, 1940, BA (hon.), 1939, MA, 1948; Licence es L., U. Montpellier, France, 1952; PhD, U. Ill., 1962; MA (hon.), Harvard U., 1974; PhD languages (hon.), Middlebury Coll., 1989. HS tchr., Victoria, Australia, 1940-48; asst. in English lang., 1949-52; tchr. prep. schs., 1953-58; asst. prof. French No. Ill. U., DeKalb, 1963-64; assoc. prof. Monash U., Australia, 1964-69; vis. prof. Columbia U., 1970-71; prof. French U. Ill., Urbana-Champaign, 1971-74; prof. Romance langs. and lit., coord. lang. instrn. Harvard U., 1974-89, prof. emerita, 1989—. Cons. NEH, Ford Found., Rockefeller Found., others; lectr 44 countries and throughout U.S.; mem. adv. bd. Modern Lang. Ctr., Ont. Inst. for Studies in Edn., Nat. Fgn. Lang. Ctr., Lang. Acquire Rsch. Ctr., San Diego. Author: The Psychologist and the Foreign-Language Teacher, 1964, Teaching Foreign-Language Skills, 1968, 2d edit., 1981, Speaking in Many Tongues, 1972, 3d edit., 1983, A Practical Guide to the Teaching of French, 1975, 2d edit., 1988,3rd edit., 2001 (on Web), Opportunities for Careers in Foreign Languages, 1993; co-author: A Practical Guide to the Teaching of German, 1975, 2d edit., 1988, A Practical Guide to the Teaching of Spanish, 1976, 2d edit., 1988, 3rd edit., 2003 (on Web), A Practical Guide to the Teaching of English as a Second or Foreign Language, 1978, Communicating Naturally in a Second Language, 1983, Teaching Hebrew: A Practical Guide, 1989, others; editor, contbr. Interactive Language Teaching, 1978, Teaching Languages in College: Curriculum and Content, 1992, Down Under/Up Top: Creating a Life, 2003; writing translated into 11 langs.; editl. bd. Studies in Second Language Acquisition, Applied Linguistics, Language Learning, Mosaic, System; adv. com. Can. Modern Lang. Rev.; contbr. articles to profl. jours. Recipient Nat. Disting. Fgn. Lang. Leadership award N.Y. State Assn. Fgn. Lang. Tchrs., 1974. Decorated Chevalier des Palmes Académiques, 1995; recipient Disting. Alumni award U. Ill., 1999. Mem. MLA, Am. Assn. Applied Linguistics (charter pres.), Am. Coun. on Teaching Fgn. Langs. (Florence Steiner award 1977, Anthony Papalia award 1988), Mass. Fgn. Lang. Assn. (Disting. Svc. award 1983), Tchrs. of English to Speakers of other Langs., Am. Assn. Tchrs. French, Linguistic Soc. Am., Am. Assn. Univ. Suprs. and Coords. Fgn. Lang. Programs Northeast Conf. (Nelson Brooks award 1983), Internat. Assn. Applied Psycholinguistics (v.p. 1983-89), Japan Assn. Coll. English Tchrs. (hon.), Am. Assn. Tchrs. German (hon.), Internat. Assn. Lang. Labs. (hon.). Episcopalian. Home and Office: 84 Garfield St Watertown MA 02472-4916

RIZZI, MARGUERITE CLAIRE, music educator; b. New York, NY, Aug. 4, 1955; d. Joan Henderson, Norman Henderson (Stepfather), John N. Rizzi; life ptnr. Brenda June Mottram. BA, Clark U., 1976; MusM, New Eng. Conservatory, 1991; EdD, Boston U., 2000. Cert. std. tchr. cert. music, spl. edn. tchr. Coord. guitar program Boston U., Boston, 1993—99; tchr. Beacon H.S., Brookline, Mass., 1993—2001. Musician (recording): Sympatico, 1999 (listed for grammy nomination, 1999). Capt. sailing vessels. Mem.: Boston Women's Jazz Coalition, Am. Profl. Capt.'s Assn., Internat. Assn. Jazz Edn., Music Educators Nat. Conf. Democrat. Avocations: sailing, bicycling, reading. Office: 74 Green St Brookline MA 02446-3305 Personal E-mail: mottriz@attbi.com.

RIZZO, GARY EDWARD, academic administrator; b. Erie, Pa., Mar. 28, 1944; s. Carl Joseph and Marie Grace (Manuele) R.; children: Brian, Gary, Thomas. BS, Gannon U., Erie, Pa., 1967; MS, Case Western Res. U., Cleve., 1969; PhD, U. Pitts., 1974. Nat. cert. counselor. Counselor Cuyahoga C.C., Cleve., 1969-71, Westmoreland County C.C., Youngwood, Pa., 1972-82; dir. counseling Montgomery C.C., Blue Bell, Pa., 1982-84, assoc. dean lifelong learning, 1984-89, assoc. acad. dean, 1989—, assoc. v.p., 2003—. Cons. in field. Chairperson, bd. dirs. Harmony Theater, 1997—; ednl. rep. Montgomery County Fire Academy, 1994—. Am. Coun. on Edn. fellow, 1984-85, Inst. for Ednl. Leadership/Ednl. Policy fellow, 2001-2002; named Outstanding Faculty Mem., Westmoreland Community Coll., Greensburg, Pa., 1974. Fellow Am. Coun. on Edn.; mem. Pa. Coll. Personnel Assn. (bd. dirs. 1984-88, Outstanding Contbr. 1988), Am. Coll. Personnel Assn., Montgomery County Counselors Assn. (cons.), Pa. Counseling Assn. (dir. Outstanding Counseling Ctr. 1982). Fellow Inst. Ednl. Leadership, 2001-02. Fellow Edn. Policy Fellows Program Penn., 2001-02. Avocations: skiing, camping, travel, model trains, nascar racing. Home: 705 Karens Ct North Wales PA 19454-2039 Office: Montgomery County CC 340 Dekalb Pike Blue Bell PA 19422-1412

RIZZOLO, LOUIS B. M. artist, educator; b. Ferndale, Mich., Oct. 8, 1933; s. Louis and Bella (Bronson) R.; m. Patricia Ann, June 30, 1956 (div. 1982); children: Connie Lucille, Louis Matthew, Marc Angelo; m. Linda Talbot, Dec. 3, 1982; stepchildren: Heather MacIntyre, Cameron Smith, Jennifer Talbot, Meghan Smith. BS in Art, Western Mich. U., 1956; MA in Fine Art, U. Iowa, 1960; postgrad., U. Ga., 1969. Tchr. art Petoskey (Mich.) Pub. Schs., 1956-64; tchr. art history, art studio North Ctrl. Mich. Coll., Petoskey, 1959-64; grad. teaching asst. U. Iowa, Iowa CIty, 1958-60; tchr. painting Kalamazoo Inst. Art, 1970-85; prof. art Western Mich. U., Kalamazoo, 1964—. Tchr. painting, drawing, interdisciplinary/multi media, installation/performance/exhbn. juror, lectr. and tchr. internat. workshops, Switzerlan, Austria, Can., France, Scotland, Hawaii, Norway, 1989—; artistic and gen. dir. Rizzolo and Assocs.: Inflatale Light Workshop Collaborative, Kalamazoo, 1980-92; co-dir. rsch. Creative Learning Program, Kalamazoo, 1986-92; R.W.S. London Watercolor del. Rep. of China (Best of Watercolor Book 1995). Capt. AUS, 1958-68. Grantee Ford Found., Dow Corning, Du Pont, Upjohn, Mich. Coun. Arts, Mich. Millenium Project, 1995-2000, Mich. Found. Arts, 1996, Edn. for the Arts, W.K. Kellogg, Kalamazoo Arts Cóun., Nat. Exhbn./Collections: Western Mich. U. fellow. Mem. Internat. Soc. Art & Tech., Mich. Watercolor Soc., World Forum of Acoustic Ecology. Independent. Home: PO Box 62 Glenn MI 49416-0062

RIZZONI, GIORGIO, engineering educator; b. Bologna, Italy, Oct. 8, 1958; s. Ivan and Rosa (Campanella) R.; m. Kathryn Klaus, June 30, 1992; children: Alessandro Ivan, Maria Caterina, Michael Giorgio. BSEE, U. Mich., 1980, MSEE, 1982, PhD, 1986. Asst. dir. Vehicular Electronics Lab. U. Mich., 1986-90, rsch. fellow, asst. rsch. scientist, 1986-90; asst. prof. dept. mech. engring. Ohio State U., 1990-95, assoc. prof., 1995-99, prof. elec. engring., 2000—, Ford Motor Co. chair in electromech. sys., 2002—, dir. Ctr. Automotive Rsch., 1999—. Scientific advisor Nat. Rsch. Coun. Italy, 1999—; chair IFAC Tech. Com. Automotive Control, 1998-2002. Assoc. editor: ASME Jour. of Dynamic Systems, Measurements and Control, 1993-99, IEEE Transactions on Vehicular Technology, 1988-98; guest editor/contbr. articles in field; author: A Practical Introduction to Electronic Instrumentation, 1989, Principles and Applications of Electrical Engineering, 1993, 4th edit., 2002; patentee in field. Recipient Presdl. Young Investigator award NSF, 1991; grantee NSF, Ford Motor C., IBM, others. Mem. ASME, IEEE, Am. Soc. Engring. Edn., Soc. Automotive Engrs. (Ralph R. Teetor Ednl. award 1992), Tau Beta Pi, Eta Kappa Nu. Avocations: racquetball, golf, wine collecting, cooking. Office: Ohio State U Ctr Automotive Rsch 930 Kinnear Rd Columbus OH 43212 E-mail: rizzoni.1@osu.edu.

ROACH, JAMES RICHARD, university president; b. Lynn, Mass., July 29, 1932; married. BS in Edn. cum laude, Boston Coll., 1957; postgrad., St. John's Coll., Brighton, Mass., 1963; certificat d'etude, U. Geneva, Switzerland, 1969; PhD in World Religions, Boston U., 1972; postgrad., Harvard U. Inst. Ednl. Mgmt., summer 1978. Tchr. Annotto Bay Coll., Jamaica, West Indies, 1957-58, Coll. Ctr., Salem State Coll., 1965-69; tchr. grad. sch. St. John's and Boston Univs., 1970-72; tchr. divsn. grad. studies Salem State Coll., 1972-73, North Adams State Coll., 1974-75, tchr. dept. philosophy, 1973-76, dir. acad. counseling svcs., 1973-76, acad. dean, 1976-78, v.p. acad. affairs, 1978-86, acting pres., 1984; interim vice chancellor acad. affairs Mass. Bd. Regents, 1980-81; pres. U.Maine, Presque Isle, 1986-92, Western Conn. State U., Danbury, 1992—. Bd. dirs. Savs. Bank Danbury; state rep. Am. Assn. State Colls. and Univs., chair com. acad. affairs, 1991-92, mem. task force on bldg. polit. support, 1991-92; chmn. reaccreditation vis. com. Castleton (Vt.) State Coll., 1991; mem Trustee Task Force on Rsch. and Grad. Edn.; mem. State of Maine Legislature's Spl. Commn. to Study and Evaluate the Status of Edn. Reform in Maine, 1990; mem. Univ. Sys./State Govt. Partnership Policy Group, 1989—, Mass.Bd. Regents Design Team for Collective Bargaining, 1983, Gov.'s Edn. Task Force, 1982-86, Mass. Bd. Regents Adv. Task Force on Program Rev., 1982-86; mem. Mass. State Coll. Sys. Task Force for Devel. Skills, 1977, Task Force for Profl. Devel., 1978, Pers. Mgmt. Adv. Com., 1979; dir. Maine Devel. Found., 1989-92; pres. Maine Higher Edn.Coun., 1989-92; chmn. bd. dirs. Maine Rsch. and Productivity Ctr., 1988-92; coord.-tchr. Monroe Ednl. Release Program, 1973-77; chmn. Mass. State Coll. Ad Hoc Com., 1979; corporator North Adams State Coll. Found., 1981-86; dir. acad. program evaluation project North Adams State Coll., 1977-82; cons. Wang Inst. Grad. Studies, 1983; state rep. Am. Assn. State Colls. and Univs. Acad. Affairs Resource Ctr. Assocs., 1982-86; presenter papers, spkr. various orgns. and confs. Bd. trustees United Way of No. Fairfield County, Inc.; mem. exec. bd. dirs. No. Maine Regional Planning Commn./Econ. Devel. Dist., 1987—; bd. dirs. Maine/Loring Assn., 1986—; bd. dirs. Croissant Club No. Berkshire County, 1984-86. With USN, 1952-53. Mem. Danbury C. of C. (bd. dirs.), Am. Acad. Religion, Am. Assn. Higher Edn.,Am. Assn. Colls. Tchr. Edn., Assn. Am. Colls., Internat. Assn. Univ. Pres., Pi Lamba Theta. Home: 177 Lake Pl S Danbury CT 06810-7264 Office: Western Conn State Univ 181 White St Danbury CT 06810-6826

ROACH, MAUREEN S. primary school educator; Bachelors Degree, Boston U.; Masters Degree, U. Mass. Primary sch. educator Lyndon Pilot Sch., West Roxbury, Mass. Presenter Nat. Bd. Insts. Mem.: Nat. Bd. for Profl. Tchg. Stds. (bd. mem.). Avocations: cross country skiing, reading. Office: Lyndon Pilot Sch 140 Russett Rd West Roxbury MA 02132*

ROACH-REEVES, CATHARYN PETITT, librarian, educator; b. Houston, Sept. 25, 1950; d. Robert Duane and Nelma Belle Petitt; m. Paul Alton Roach, Aug. 21, 1971 (div. Aug. 1982); m. Gary L. Reeves, Nov. 27, 1991. BS in Elem. Edn., Dallas Bapt. Coll., 1974; MLS, North Tex. State U., 1976; PhD in Libr. Sci., U. North Tex., 1989. Cert. elem. tchr., Tex.; cert. libr., Tex. Tchr., libr. White Hall Sch., Cedar Hill, Tex., 1976-78; libr. Patton Elem. Sch., Dallas, 1978-83, Macmillan Elem. Sch., Dallas, 1981-82, George Washington Carver Elem. Sch., Dallas, 1982-86, Arlington Pk. Elem. Sch., Dallas, 1982-86, W.L. Cabell Elem. Sch., Dallas, 1986-90, Dan

D. Rogers Elem. Sch., Dallas, 1990—. Presenter various workshops; cons. (video) In Search of a Libr. Adventure, 1995. Author: Teaching Library Skills in Grades K-6, 1993; co-editor Libr. Media Program Handbook, 1991. Troop leader Girl Scouts AM., 1982-88, coun. trainer, 1987-88; instr. Dallas Mus. Natural History, Summer Ednl. Program, 1984-87; hon. life mem. PTA, 1990, 93. Recipient Green Angel award Girl Scouts USA, 1985. Mem. Tex. Libr. Assn., Tex. Assn. Sch. Librs., Dallas Assn. Sch. Librs. (v.p., pres. elect. 1991-92, pres. 1992-93, Elem. Libr. of Yr. 1992-93, Positive Parents of Dallas Libr. Apple award 1992-93), Delta Kappa Gamma, Alpha Chi, Lambda Sigma Alpha, Phi Lambda Theta. Republican. Avocations: rubber stamp art, doll collecting, cake/cookie decorating, needlework, collecting beatrix potter and laura ingalls wilder books and memorabilia. Home: 10106 Deermont Trl Dallas TX 75243-2523 Office: Dan D Rogers Elem Sch 5314 Abrams Rd Dallas TX 75214-2001

ROADS, JANE ELIZABETH MCNATT, mathematics educator; b. Bklyn., Aug. 8, 1948; d. William John and Elizabeth McNatt; m. Charles Andrew Roads, Dec. 23, 1971; children: Sarah Elizabeth, Ariel Susan. BS in English, Ill. State U., 1970; MEd in Math. Edn., U. Mo., 1994. Cert. tchr. secondary math., English. Tchr. English Balt. City Pub. Schs., 1970-74, Rutland (Vt.) City Schs., 1974-76; dir. Christian edn. Presbyn. Ch., Moberly, Mo., 1983-86; curriculum specialist Moberly Area C.C., 1986-87, math./sci. divsn. chair, math. faculty, Learning Ctr. supr., 1987—. Mem. Presbytery sr. high ministry com. Presbyn. Ch., 1992-99, nurture com. moderator, 1993, mem. older adult ministry com., 1990-95; treas. Little Dixie Concern Assn., 1985-87. Presbyterian. Avocations: reading, cross-stitch, singing. Office: Moberly Area CC 101 College Ave Moberly MO 65270-1304 E-mail: JaneRoads@macc.edu.

ROARK, EDITH HUMPHREYS, private school language arts educator, reading specialist; b. Raleigh, N.C., Jan. 26, 1943; d. Sidney Frederick and Jennie Mildred (Swain) Humphreys; m. Larry Alden Roark, Nov. 27, 1964; children: Jonathan Laurance, Nancy Elaine, Naomi Elizabeth. BS, Appalachian State U., 1965; MA, East Tenn. State U., 1980, postgrad., 1986-88. Cert. elem. tchr., Tenn. Tchr. Memphis City Schs., 1966, Wake County Schs., Garner, N.C., 1967, Dover (N.J.) Twp. Schs., 1968, Kingsport (Tenn.) Christian Sch., 1974-77, Tri-Cities Christian Sch., Kingsport, 1983-84, reading tutor, 1980-84, Ashley Acad., Johnson City, Tenn., 1984-87, tchr., 1987—. Ofcl. judge Odyssey of the Mind, Tenn., coach, 1992, regional judge, 1991-96, state judge, 1994-96; leader Gt. Books, Johnson City, 1988; participant NIE Playshop, Kingsport, summers 1989-95, Slingerland Multisensory Reading Tchr. Tng. Mem. Internat. Reading Assn., Orton Dyslexia Soc., Kappa Delta Pi, Delta Kappa Gamma (chair literacy com. 1991—, corr. sec. 1994-96). Baptist. Avocations: reading, collecting newspaper trivia, gardening, decorating, teaching sunday school. Home: 222 Norwood Dr Johnson City TN 37615-3858 Office: Ashley Acad 1502 Knob Creek Rd Johnson City TN 37604-3775

ROARK, PEGGY JEAN, business educator, academic specialist, consultant; b. Hazard, Ky., Oct. 18, 1950; d. John R. and Emma Lou (Fowler) R. AA, Hazard Community Coll., 1972; BA, Morehead (Ky.) State U., 1972, M in Bus. Edn., 1985; postgrad. in Ednl. Policies and Evaluation, U. Ky. Cert. bus. edn. tchr., Ky. Acct., office mgr. Mellott & Adams, P.C., Hazard, 1972-76, Red Fox Coal Co., Isom, Ky., 1977-85; counselor Morehead State U., 1984-85; instr. So. W.Va. Community Coll., Logan, 1985-87; dean bus. affairs Hazard Community Coll., 1987-89; bus. mgr. So. State Community Coll., Hillsboro, Ky., 1989—, assoc. prof., 1990—. Cons. So. State Community Coll., 1989. Mem. Nat. Assn. Bus. Officers, So. Assn. Coll. and Univ. Bus. Officers, Nat. Assn. Coll. Aux. Svcs. Avocations: travel, tennis, cooking, reading. Office: So State Community Coll 100 Hobart Rd Hillsboro OH 45133-9406

ROBAK, ROSTYSLAW WSEWOLOD, psychologist, educator; b. Passau, Germany, Nov. 15, 1948; s. Bohdan and Maria R.; m. Loretta J. Tallon; children: Marika, Boyan. BA, Seton Hall U., 1970; MA, Fairleigh Dickinson U., 1973; PhD, Hofstra U., 1976. Lic. psychologist N.Y., Pa., Mass. Prof. Pace U., Pleasantville, N.Y., 1988—, dir. M.S. program in substance abuse counseling, 1992—. Adj. prof. Orange County Community Coll., Middletown, N.Y. 1985-88; founding faculty advisor Pace U. chpt. Psi Chi Nat. Honor Soc., 1991—. Author: A Primer for Today's Substance Abuse Counselor, 1991. Mem. APA, Am. Orthopsychiat. Assn., Nat. Register Health Svc. Providers in Psychology, Assn. Death Edn. and Counseling. Office: Pace Univ Dir Substance Abuse Counseling Prog Pleasantville NY 10570

ROBARDS, BOURNE ROGERS, elementary education educator; b. Milw., Jan. 5, 1950; s. William Simpson and Janet (Cross) R.; m. Martha Jane Snider, Oct. 29, 1977; children: Jonathan Matthew, Sara Elizabeth. BS, U. Mo., 1971; MAT, Webster U., St. Louis, 1989. Cert. elem. tchr., Mo. Classroom tchr. 4th and 6th grades Hazelwood Sch. Dist., Florissant, Mo., 1971-73; classroom tchr. 4th grade Jennings (Mo.) Sch. Dist., 1986—. Troop leader Boy Scouts Am., St. Louis, 1972-73; ch. leader St. Mark's Episcopal Ch., St. Louis, 1977—. Mem. Omicron Delta Kappa. Avocations: travel, reading, swimming, bicycling, music, photography. Home: 6320 Monterey Dr Saint Louis MO 63123-1510 Office: Northview Elem Sch Jennings Sch Dist 8920 Cozens Ave Jennings MO 63136-3996

ROBARDS, SHIRLEY JEAN NEEDS, education educator; b. Marietta, Ohio, Feb. 11, 1939; d. Lloyd Thomas and Wilma Imogene (Ballard) Needs; m. Frank Henry Robards, June 26, 1959; 1 child, Linda Renee Robards-Bull. BA, Ky. Wesleyan Coll., Owensboro, 1964; MA, Western. Ky. U., 1965; EdD, Ind. U., 1972. Cert. tchr. Ind., Ky., Okla. Tchr. Webster County Ky. Schs., Slaughters, Ky., 1959-64, Hopkins County Ky. Schs., Madisonville, Ky., 1964-66, Tell City (Ind.) Pub. Schs., 1966-68; assoc. instr. Ind. U., Bloomington, 1971-72; dept. chair, dir. field svcs. U. Tulsa, 1972—. Author: (monograph) Webster's Baby Interpreting Research in Language Arts, 1971; contbr. articles to profl. jours. Recipient Integrating Math. & Sci. award, 1992, Integrating Math., Sci. and Lang. Arts award, 1993, Integrating Core Disciplines with Aerospace award, 1994, Using Cmty. Resources to Integrate Sci. and Math. award, 1996, Reflective Sci. and Math. for Mentors award, 1996, Two-Tiered Model for Sci. and Math. Tchrs. award, 1998; Gaining Early Awareness and Readiness for Undergraduate Programs grantee, 1999—. Mem.: Assn. Tchr. Educators (pres. 1989—92), Kappa Delta Pi (counselor 1993—), Phi Delta Kappa (v.p. 1989—95, co-dir. edn. seminar Russia 1990). Methodist. Avocations: reading, cooking, travel. Office: U Tulsa 600 S College Ave Tulsa OK 74104-3126 E-mail: shirley-robards@utulsa.edu.

ROBB, BABETTE, retired elementary school educator; b. St. Paul, Minn., Jan. 25, 1923; d. Roy F and Eda Johnson; m. David L Robb, July 23, 1945; children: Deborah G. Jankura, Pamela W. BA, So. Meth. U., Dallas, 1945; Elem. Educator, U. Wis., River Falls, 1948. Asst. to county auditor Washington County, Stillwater, Minn., 1945—46, county sch. tchr. Stillwater, 1947—53; elem. sch. tchr. Stillwater (Minn.) Dist. 834, 1953—81. Author: (elem.sch. text) St. Croix Valley Story, 1970; contbr. articles Childrens Mags., 1979. Chmn. Washington County Young Reps., Stillwater, 1946—50; mem. bd. dirs. Family Svc., Stillwater, Minn.; Grand Marshall of 4th of July Parade Afton (Minn.) Hist. Soc., 1973. Recipient Drama award, Minn. Regional Speech Contest, 1940; chosen to christen army troup transport shop as President's plane, U.S. Maritime Commn. Mem.: AAUW (life; Founder local chpt. 1946), Minn. Ednl. Assn. (sec. local br. 1953—), Delta Kappa Gamma (Sec. 1972—). Methodist. Achievements include first to introduce Spanish to Elementary Students in 1958. Avocations: modeling, photography, swimming, writing, water biking. Home (Winter): Apt 407 3500 S Ocean Blvd Palm Beach FL 33480 Home (Summer): 2803 S St Croix Tr Afton MN 55001 Home Fax: 561-588-0226.

ROBB, JAMES WILLIS, Romance languages educator; b. Jamaica, N.Y., June 27, 1918; s. Stewart Everts and Clara Johanna (Mohrmann) R.; m. Cecilia Uribe-Noguera, 1972. Student, Inst. de Touraine, Sorbonne, 1937-38; BA cum laude, Colgate U., 1939; postgrad., U. Nacional de Mex., 1948; MA, Middlebury Coll., 1950; PhD, Cath. U. Am., 1958. Instr. romance langs. Norwich U., 1946-50; from asst. prof. to prof. romance langs. George Washington U., Washington, 1950-88, prof. emeritus, 1988—. Corr. mem. Academia Mexicana de la Lengua, 1998. Author: El Estilo de Alfonso Reyes, 1965, 78, Repertorio Bibliográfico de Alfonso Reyes, 1974, Prosa y Poesía de Alfonso Reyes, 1975, 84, Estudios sobre Alfonso Reyes, 1976, Por los Caminos de Alfonso Reyes, 1981, Imágenes de América en Alfonso Reyes y en Germán Arciniegas, 1990, Más Páginas Sobre Alfonso Reyes, 1996-97; contbr. articles to profl. jours. With USNR, 1942—44, Brazil, with USNR, 1944—46, PTO. Recipient Alfonso Reyes Internat. Lit. prize, 1978; Lit. Diploma of Merit, State of Nuevo León and City of Monterrey, Mex., 1979; OAS grantee, 1964; Am. Philos. Soc. grantee, 1977 Mem. MLA, Internat. Assn. Ibero-Am. Lit., Am. Assn. Tchrs. Spanish and Portuguese, Assn. Colombianistas, Phi Beta Kappa. Office: George Washington U Romance Langs Dept Washington DC 20052-0001

ROBBERT, LOUISE BUENGER, retired historian; b. St. Paul, Aug. 18, 1925; d. Albert and Myrtle (Rubbert) Buenger; m. George S. Robbert, Sept. 17, 1960; 1 child, George Harold. BA, Carleton Coll., 1947; MA, U. Cin., 1948, B. Edn., 1949; PhD, U. Wis., 1955. Instr. history Smith Coll., Northampton, Mass., 1954-55, Hunter Coll., N.Y.C., 1957-60; asst. prof. history Tex. Tech U., Lubbock, 1962-63, assoc. prof. history, 1964-75; vis. assoc. prof. history U. Mo., St. Louis, 1978-79, assoc. prof. history, 1979-91, prof. history, 1991—2000, ret., 2001. Author: Venetian Money Market in: Studi Veneziani, 1971, Venice and the Crusades in: The Crusades V., 1985, Il sistema monetario in: Storia di Venezia, II l'eta del comune, 1995. Officer Wednesday Club, St. Louis, 1981-83, 87-90, 94-96, v.p., 1997—99, pres., 1999-2001. Scholar Fulbright Commn., 1955-57; grantee A.C.L.S., 1960, Gladys Krieble Delmas Found., 1983, 87. Mem. Medieval Acad. Am., Soc. for Study of Crusades & the Latin East, Midwest Medieval History Conf. (pres.). Lutheran. Home: 709 S Skinker Blvd Apt 701 Saint Louis MO 63105-3259 Office: U Mo St Louis Dept History 8001 Natural Bridge Rd Saint Louis MO 63121-4401

ROBBINS, ALLEN BISHOP, physics educator; b. New Brunswick, N.J., Mar. 31, 1930; s. William Rei and Helen Grace (Bishop) R.; m. Shirley Mae Gernert, June 14, 1952 (div. 1978); children: Catherine Jean, Marilyn Elizabeth, Carol Ann, Melanie Barbara; m. Alice Harriet Ayars, Jan. 1, 1979. Student, Oberlin Coll., 1948-49; BS, Rutgers U., 1952; MS, Yale U., 1953, PhD, 1956. Research fellow U. Birmingham (Eng.), 1957-58, lectr., 1960-61; instr. physics Rutgers U., New Brunswick, N.J., 1956-57, asst. prof. physics, 1957-60, assoc. prof., 1960-68, prof., 1968-97, prof. emeritus, 1997—, chmn. dept. physics and astronomy, 1979-95. Contbr. articles on nuclear physics to profl. jours. Recipient Lindbach Christian and Mary F. Lindbach Found., Rutgers U., 1975 Fellow Am. Phys. Soc.; mem. Am. Assn. Physics Tchrs., AAAS, Phi Beta Kappa, Sigma Xi Office: Rutgers U Dept Physics and Astronomy 136 Frelinghuysen Rd Piscataway NJ 08854-8019 E-mail: robbins@physics.rutgers.edu.

ROBBINS, ARLENE AGNES, elementary education educator; b. Pa. d. Raymond and Rose Goff; m. Carle B. Robbins Jr.; children: Carle III, Lauri. BS, So. Conn. State Coll; MEE, State of Pa., 1987. Tchr. instrl. support Palisades Sch. Dist., Kintnersville, Pa.; tchr. elem. Trumbull (Conn.) Sch. Dist.; tchr. math. Palisades Mid. Sch., Kintnersville, tchr. gifted. Mem. Nat. Pa. Edn. Assn., Pa. State Edn. Assn., Assn. Gifted Edn., Nat. Coun. Tchrs. English, Nat. Reading Assn., Buck County Tchrs. Reading. Office: Palisades Mid Sch 425 Hilltop Rd Riegelsville PA 18077-9727 E-mail: arobbins@nni.com.

ROBBINS, BRENDA SUE, early childhood educator; b. Langdale, Ala., June 28, 1950; d. Richard Cecil and Audrey Millicent (Smallwood) R. Student, Mich. State U., 1968-72; BS in Edn., Auburn U., 1974, MS in Edn., 1977. Title 1 reading, math tchr. Muscogee Co. Sch. Dist., Columbus, Ga., 1977-78, fed. preschool tchr., 1978-80, tchr. grade 1, 1980-81, 1984-85, tchr. kindergarten, 1981-84, 1985—. Staff devel. instr. Muscogee County Sch. Dist., Columbus, Ga., 1994; presenter in field. Mem. Georgia Assn. Educators, Nat. Edn. Assn. Avocations: snorkeling, whitewater rafting, traveling, reading. Office: Saint Marys Elem Sch 4408 Saint Marys Rd Columbus GA 31907-6286

ROBBINS, CARRIE F(ISHBEIN), costume designer, educator; b. Balt., Feb. 7, 1943; d. Sidney W. and Bettye A. (Berman) Fishbein; m. Richard D. Robbins, Feb. 15, 1969. BS, BA, Pa. State U., 1964; MFA, Yale Drama Sch., 1967. Over 30 Broadway shows, N.Y.C., 1968-2001, A Class Act at the Ambassador Theatre, 2001—, Grease (Tony nomination best costumes), Over Here (Tony nomination best costumes), Secret Affairs of Mildred Wilde, Yentl, Cyrano, Iceman Cometh, Octette Bridge Club, Look to the Lillies, Sweet Bird of Youth, Agnes of God, Boys of Winter, The First, Frankenstein, Shadow Box, Samson et Dalila, San Francisco Opera, 1980, L.A. Opera, 1999, Houston Grand Opera, 2002, Rigoletto, Russlan et Ludmilla, Taverner, Bernstein's Mass, Opera Co. of Boston, 1975-76, 86, 89, Hamburg State Opera (W.Ger.), 1979, Washington Opera Soc., 1975, designed for N.Y. Shakespeare Festival, Jules Irving's Lincoln Ctr. Repertory Theatre, Tyrone Guthrie Theatre, Mpls. (including Hamlet, Julius Caesar and Three Penny Opera), various shows Mark Taper Forum, L.A. (including The Tempest with Anthony Hopkins, Fashion Inst. Tech. Surface Design award, Flea in Her Ear (Dramalogue Critics award), others including The Wedding Banquet, 2003, Williamstown, Chelsea Theatre Ctr., Bklyn., John Houseman's City Ctr. Acting Co., Juilliard Sch., N.Y.C, WNET and cable TV, off-broadway theatres, N.Y.C., including High Infidelity, Promenade Theatre, It's Only a Play, Big Potato (by Arthur Laurents), Women's Project's Exact Center of the Universe, Two-Headed, Westport Country Playhouse Bench's in the Sun, Arclite Theatre Tennessee Williams Remembered, Paper Mill Playhouse Rags, designer sets and costumes Tallulah Hallelujah (by Ed Dixon); tchr. Henry Le Tang Profl. Sch. Tap Dance, 1989-91; vis. guest lectr. costume design U. Ill., UCLA, Oberlin Coll., Pa. State U., others; master tchr. costume design NYU, over 30 yrs.; costume designer Saturday Night Live-NBC, 1985-86, The Rita Show (CBS pilot), (feature film) In the Spirit, 1987; designer apparel Rainbow Room, Rockefeller Ctr., 1987-97, Aurora Grill, 1988, Empress Ct., Caesar's Palace, Las Vegas, 1988, Windows on the World Restaurant Complex, 1996 (Image of the Yr. award Nat. Assn. Uniform Mfrs. and Distbrs. 1997); recent regional theatre includes Berkshire Theatre, Mass., Toys in the Attic (directed by John Tillinger), Fla. Stage It's Only a Play (by Terrance McNally). One-woman show Cen. Falls Gallery, N.Y.C., 1980; exhibited in group shows at Cooper Hewitt Mus., Pa. State U., Wright-Hepburn Gallery, N.Y.C., Scottsdale, Ariz., Cen. Falls Gallery, 1983; illustrations and calligraphy pub. ann. calendar Soc. of Scribes competition, Ms. mag.; work chosen to hang in juried show Salmagundi Club (Fine Arts Soc.), 1983-84; original costume work photographed in books; Costume Design, 1983, Fabric Painting and Dying for the Theatre, 1982; original drawing reproduced Time-Life Series: The Ency. of Collectibles; profiled in Costume Design-Techniques of Modern Masters, 1996, Contemporary Designers, 1990, 97; designer loft conversions, comml. lobby space, studios, others; contbr. articles to Theatre Crafts International, Theatre Design & Tech., Theatre Designers & Computers; illustrator: Who Was Wolfgang Amadeus Mozart?", 2003; contbr. to profl. jours. Named Disting. Alumna, Pa. State U., 1979; recipient Antoinette Perry nominations for Best Costumes for a Broadway Show, 1971-72, 73-74, Drama Desk award, Am. Theatre Wing, N.Y.C., 1971, 72, Maharam award for design, Joseph Maharam Found., N.Y.C., 1975, nomination, 1984, Juror's Choice award for surface design, Fashion Inst. of Tech., 1980, Dramalogue Critics' award for Outstanding Achievement in Theatre Costume Design, L.A., 1982, Silver Medal, 6th Triennial of Theatre Design, Novisad, Yugoslavia, 1981, Diplome L'Honneur, 1990, Audelco nomination, 1990, Henry Hewes nomination, 1999, League N.Y. Theatres, N.Y.C., 1971-72, 73-74. Mem. League Profl. Theatre Tng. Programs (steering com.), League Profl. Theatre Women (bd. dirs. 2001—), Graphic Artists Guild, Soc. Scribes, Am. Soc. Interior Designers, United Scenic Artists Local 829; adv. com. The Costume Collection of Theatre Devel. Fund. Home and Office: 11 W 30th St 15th Fl New York NY 10001 E-mail: crobb10001@aol.com.

ROBBINS, CHRISTOPHER MARK, English educator; b. Albany, Ga., May 12, 1965; s. DAvid Allen and Rhonda (Goodman) R.; m. Rachel DeAnn Denton, Dec. 19, 1992. BS in Edn., U. Ga., 1988, MEd, 1990. Cert. lang. arts tchr., Ga. English instr. Terrell County High Sch., Dawson, Ga., 1991—. Adj. prof. comm. Meadows Coll., Albany, 1992-94; pilot applied comm. course Terrell Bd. Edn., Dawson, 1992—; trainer Applied Comm. Tchrs. for Ga. Tech. Prep. Consortium; adj. English tchr. Darton Coll., 1993—; v.p. Applied Comm. Consortium, Inc. Contbr. poems to mags. Chair subcaucus Dem. Party, 10th Congl. Dist., Ga., 1988. Ga. Coun. of Tchrs. of English Merit award, 1990. Mem. ASCD, Profl. Assn. Ga. Educators, Nat. Coun. Tchrs. English, Lions. Methodist. Office: Terell County High Sch 1001 5th Ave Albany GA 31701-1739

ROBBINS, DICK LAMSON, internist, educator; b. Boston, May 13, 1941; married; 3 children. BA, Lawrence U., 1963; MD, U. Vt., 1967. Diplomate Am. Bd. Internal Medicine, Nat. Bd. Med. Examiners, Am. Bd. Rheumatology. Intern Good Samaritan Hosp., Phoenix, 1967-68; resident in internal medicine U. Oreg. Med. Sch., Portland, 1968-71; research fellow rheumatology Scripps Clinic and Research Found., La Jolla, Calif., 1973-76, U. Calif., Davis, 1976-82, assoc. prof., 1982-88, prof., 1988—, VA North Calif. Health Care Sys., 1994—2003. Program chmn. Soc. Fellows Scripps Clinic and Rsch. Found., 1974-75, pres., 1975-76; adminstrn. coms. held at U. Calif. Med. Ctr. include med. records 1976-78, patient care 1978-79, capital equipment 1979-80, quality assurance outpatient rev. subcom. 1985-86, med. staff exec. com.; chmn. patient care 1979-81; coms. held with dept. Internal Medicine include internship-residency selection 1979-80, residency rev. 1980-82, internal medicine research 1984-86, internal medicine quality assurance rev. 1984-86, 89-93, chmn. 1982-84, internal medicine fin. coun., 1990-97, acad. senate rep., 1991-93, capitation com., 1994-96, internal medicine residency program dir., 1998-2000, clin. competence, 1998-2000; coms. held with Sch. Medicine include grad. group immunology 1977—, comparative pathology group 1977—, faculty affairs 1977-78, faculty exec. 1984-85; exec. com. grad. group in immunology 1985-86; grade change 1979-81, chmn. 1981-85, Sch. Medicine faculty exec. com., 1989-92, vice chair acad. senate, 1989-90, chair promotions bd., 1989-90, chair acad. senate, 1990-91, sch. pers. com., 1991-94, student progress com., 2002—; coms. held with U. Davis include gen. edn. ad hoc 1981-82; chmn. grad. research awards 1983-84, exec. coun. acad. senate, 1990-1991, 1997-1998, biotech. adv. com., 1991-1993, acad. senate rep., 1994-1996, lab. animal medicine program advisor, 1995-1998, faculty welfare com., 1995-1997, com. acad. pers., 1995-1998, chair, 1997-1998, provost's acad. leadership adv. com., 1997-1998, recruitment adv. com. univ. provost, 1997-1998, acad. adv. com. Sch. Medicine, 1997-1998, adminstrv. rev. com. office univ. provost acad. pers., 1999-2000; coms. held Div. Rheumatology/Allergy and Clin. Immunology include dir. postgrad. fellowship program 1977—, dir. rheumatology-orthopedics combined clinics 1978-81, acting chmn. 1985-86; cons. San Joaquin Gen. Hosp., Stockton, Calif., 1976—, Calif. Crippled Children Services, Sacramento, 1976—, Kaiser Hosp., Sacramento, 1979—, VA Hosp., Martinez, Calif., 1979—, Woodland (Calif.) Meml. Hosp., 1979-81, David Grant Meml. Hosp., Travis AFB, Calif., 1980—; internal medicine continuous quality ins. review com., 1989-93; internal med. fin. coun., 1990—. Editor: (with M.E. Gershwin) Musculoskeletal Diseases of Children, 1983; mem. rev. bd. Revs. in Contemporary Pharmacotherapy; contbr. more than 60 articles to profl. jours. Recipient Earle C. Anthony award 1976-77, Faculty Rsch. award 1976-81; New Eng. Bd. Higher Edn. scholar 1963-67; NIH fellow 1974-76; rsch. grantee NIH, 1976-83, Calif. Lung Assn., 1977-79, NIH, 1978-81, Am. Heart Assn., 1980-81, NIH, 1983-87, 91-95. Fellow Am. Coll. Rheumatology (coun. we. region 1977-94, co-chair programs we. region), Am. Rheumatism Assn.; mem. AMA, AAAS, Am. Heart Assn. (no. Calif. affiliate rsch. peer review com. 1991-92)Am. Rheumatism Assn. (mem. western region coun. 1988-1990), Am. Soc. Zoologists (comparative immunology sect.), Western Soc. Naturalists, Internat. Soc. Devel. and Comparative Immunology. E-mail: dlrobbins@ucdavis.edu.

ROBBINS, DOROTHY ANN, foreign language educator; b. Little Rock, Mar. 17, 1947; d. W.E. and Ina (Spencer) R. BA in Sociology, U. Ark., 1971; cert., U. Heidelberg, Germany, 1975; PhD, U. Frankfurt, Germany, 1981. Cert. state translator, Germany. Prof. Ctrl. Mo. State U., Warrensburg, 1999—. Faculty advisor Alpha Mu Gamma, 1998—. Author: (introduction) Collected Works of L. S. Vygotsky, 1999, Vygotsky's Psychology-Philosophy: A Metaphor for Language Theory and Learning, 2001, Voices within Vygotskian Non-Classical Psychology: Past, Present and Future, 2002, L.S. Vygotsky's and A.A. Leontiev's Russian Educational Semiotics and Psycholinguistics: Applications for Second Language Theory, 2003; contbr. articles to profl. jours. Fulbright-Hays Travel fellow to Russia, 1994, sr. level Fulbright fellow to Moscow, 1999. Mem. Am. Assn. Applied Linguistics, Phi Beta Delta (campus pres. 1994-95). Avocations: travel to russia, russian language and literature, writing prose, trips to the sea, candlelight meals. Office: Ctrl Mo State U Martin 236 Warrensburg MO 64093 E-mail: drobbins@cmsu1.cmsu.edu.

ROBBINS, ELLEN SUE, lawyer, educator; b. Chgo., Mar. 15, 1967; d. Sheldon Neal and Barbara Lynn (Corenman) R. BS in Bus. Adminstrn. summa cum laude, U. Ill., 1988; JD magna cum laude, Harvard U., 1991. Bar: Ill. 1991. Jud. clk. to Judge Charles Kocoras U.S. Dist. Ct., Chgo., 1991-92; ptnr. Sidley & Austin, Chgo., 1992—. Adj. prof. law DePaul Coll. Law, Chgo., 1997—. Mem. ABA, Chgo. Bar Assn. Avocations: jogging, golf, sports. Office: Sidley & Austin One First Nat Plz Chicago IL 60603-2003 E-mail: erobbins@sidley.com.

ROBBINS, FRANCES ELAINE, educational administrator; b. Prescott, Mich., Oct. 27, 1928; d. Arlington Clifford and Anna Maria (Melrose) Osborne; m. Robert Allen Robbins, July 29, 1950 (dec. Feb. 1992); children: Gloria Jean, Reginald David, Eric Lynn. Student, Cen. Mich. U., 1948; BS, No. Mich. U., 1967, MA, 1974. Cert. elem. tchr., prin., Mich. Tchr. kindergarten Rose City (Mich.) Elem. Sch., 1948-51; tchr. Rudyard (Mich.) Elem. Sch., 1961-62, Pickford (Mich.) Elem. Sch., 1962-64, Skandia (Mich.) Elem. Sch., 1964-66; tchr. kindergarten Brimley (Mich.) Elem. Sch., 1966-69, tchr., coord., 1969-70, prin., 1970-95. Mem. Ea. Upper Peninsula Substance Abuse Adv. Bd., Sault Ste. Marie, Mich., 1975-77; owner Robbins Refinishing and Repair, Brimley, 1985-95; adj. prof. Mich. State U., 1997—; supr. intern tchrs. Mich. State U. and Lake Superior State U., 1997—. Dir. choir, Sunday sch. tchr. Brimley Congl. Ch., 1970—; vol. Superior Twp. Ambulance Corp., Brimley, 1972-91. Recipient Celebrate Literacy award Internat. Reading Assn., 1986. Mem. NAESP, MARSP (life), Mich. Elem. and Mid. Sch. Prins. Assn., Ea. Upper Peninsula Reading Assn., Ea. Upper Peninsula Elem. Prins. Assn. (pres. 1990-91), Brimley Hist. Soc., Delta Kappa Gamma (state rec. sec. 1989-91, Woman of Distinction award Alpha Tau chpt. 1988), Chippewa Mackinaw Area Ret. Sch. Pers. Avocations: knitting, travel, grandchildren.

ROBBINS, JANE BORSCH, library science educator, information science educator; b. Chgo., Sept. 13, 1939; d. Reuben August and Pearl Irene (Houk) Borsch; married; 1 child, Molly Warren. BA, Wells Coll., 1961; MLS, Western Mich. U., 1966; PhD, U. Md., 1972. Asst. prof. library and info. sci. U. Pitts., 1972-73; assoc. prof. Emory U., Atlanta, 1973-74; cons. to bd. Wyo. State Libr., 1974-77; assoc. prof. La. State U., Baton Rouge,

1977-79; dean La. State U. Sch. Library and Info. Sci., 1979-81; prof., dir. Sch. Library and Info. Studies U. Wis., Madison, 1981-94; dean, prof. Fla. State U. Sch. Info. Studies, Tallahassee, 1994—. Author: Public Library Policy and Citizen Participation, 1975, Public Librarianship: A Reader, 1982, Are We There Yet?, 1988, Libraries: Partners in Adult Literacy, 1990, Keeping the Books: Public Library Financial Practices, 1992, Balancing the Books: Financing American Public Library Services, 1993, Evaluating Library Programs and Services: A Manual and Sourcebook, 1994, Tell It! The Complete Manual of Library Evaluation, 1996; editor Libr. and Info. Sci. Rsch., 1982-92; contbr. articles to profl. jours. Bd. dirs. Freedom to Read Found., 1997-99. Mem.: ALA (councilor 1976—80, 1991—95), Fla. Libr. Assn. (bd. dirs. 1997—99), Wis. Libr. Assn. (pres. 1986), Assn. for Libr. and Info. Sci. Edn. (dir. 1979—81, pres. 1984), Am. Soc. Info. Sci., Beta Phi Mu (exec. dir. 2000—). Democrat. Episcopalian. Office: Fla State U Sch Info Studies Louis Shores Bldg Tallahassee FL 32306-2100 E-mail: robbins@lis.fsu.edu.

ROBBINS, JANE LEWIS, elementary school educator; b. New Iberia, La., Dec. 14, 1942; d. William Lewis and Maurine (James) R. BS, U. Okla., 1965; ME, So. Meth. U., 1972; postgrad., Tex. Women's U., 1981, 83, 85; cert. in edn. adminstrn., Tex A&M U. Commerce, 1991. Tchr. Lone Grove Ind. Sch. Dist., Okla., 1964-65, Concord-Carlisle (Mass.) Regional Sch. Dist., 1966-67, Newton (Mass.) Pub. Schs., 1967-68, Highland Park Ind. Sch. Dist., Dallas, 1968—, instrnl. specialist, dist. appraiser, coord. dist. gifted and talented, coord. student tchrs., mentor new tchrs., coord. instrnl. leadership program, interim elem. prin., 1990-93; asst. prin. McCulloch Intermediate Sch., Dallas. Instr. reading clinic So. Meth. U., 1972-75, Sch. Edn., summer 1978, adj. prof. Div. Ednl. Studies; chmn. English dept. McCulloch Middle Sch.; regional coordinator Tex. Acad. Pentathlon, 1985-89. Mem. ASCD, Tex. Assn. Improvement Reading, Tex. Assn. Gifted and Talented, Assn. Children with Learning Disabilities, Internat. Reading Assn. (North Tex. Coun.), Tex. Elem. Prins. and Suprs. Assn. (Acad. III), Nat. Coun. Tchrs. of English, Tex. Mid. Sch. Assn., Mid. Sch. Consortium, Tex. Assn. Secondary Sch. Prins., Pi Beta Phi, Delta Kappa Gamma. Republican. Episcopalian. Office: McCulloch Intermediate 3555 Granada Ave Dallas TX 75205-2235

ROBBINS, JEFFREY HOWARD, media consultant, research writer, educator; b. N.Y.C., Mar. 29, 1941; s. Stanley Samuel and Miriam (Cooper) R.; m. Marsha Sue Rimler, Nov. 3, 1984 (div. Dec. 1996); 1 child, Nina Camille. BSME, Carnegie Mellon U., 1962; MS in Physics, U. N.Mex., 1966, ABD in Physics, 1967; postgrad., U. Calif., Berkeley and L.A., 1963-64. Summer rsch. assoc. Linde Co., Tonawanda, N.Y., 1961; rsch. engr. N.Am. Aviation (Rockwell), Downey, Calif., 1962-64; summer rsch. assoc. Los Alamos (N.Mex.) Nat. Lab., 1965; sr. engr. Radio Engring. Labs., L.I., N.Y., 1968-70; engring. cons. PRD Electronics, Syosset, N.Y., 1972-73; sr. cons. Bendix Corp., Teterboro, N.J., 1974-76; sr. engr. Giordano Assocs., Franklin Lakes, N.J., 1977-81; sr. applications engr. Racal-Redak, Mahwah, N.J., 1981-83; tech. media cons. Allied Signal Corp., Teterboro, 1983-92, U.S. Army, Picatinny Arsenal, N.J., 1992; tech. cons. Ford Motor Co., Lansdale, Pa., 1992-98, Visteon Automotive Electronics, Markham, Canada, 1998; adj. prof. Rutgers U., New Brunswick, NJ, 2002—. Cons. Tyco Internat., Clark, N.J., 1998-2002; tech. cons., rsch. writer media literacy programs Packer Collegiate Inst., Bklyn., N.Y.C., 1992-93, On TV, Inc., N.Y.C., 1992; initiator, moderator Media Literacy Forum, 1995; evening sch. instr. New Sch. for Social Rsch., N.Y.C., 1979-85; presenter in field. Author: On Balance and Higher Education, 1970; contbr. articles to profl. jours. Organizer, co-moderator Future Impact of Artificial Intelligence, Robotics Forum, 1984. Recipient 1st prize for essay The World and I Mag., 1990; nominee Grawemeyer award in Edn., 1988; NDEA fellow, 1966-67, others; feature essay premier issue Plain mag., 1994. Mem. IEEE (presenter Internat. Symposium in Tech. and Soc. 1993, 96, 98, Internat. Soc. Sys. Scis. Conf. 1993, 95, 97, 99, 2000, 02, initiator, moderator, media literacy forum Packer Collegiate Inst. 1995, presenter World Order Conf., Toronto 1999, 2001), N.Y. Acad. Scis., Sigma Xi, Phi Kappa Phi, Pi Tau Sigma. Home and Office: PO Box 335 Long Beach NY 11561-0335 E-mail: jhrobbins@erols.com.

ROBBINS, MARJORIE JEAN GILMARTIN, elementary education educator; b. Newton, Mass., Sept. 19, 1940; d. John and Helen (Arbuckle) Gilmartin; m. Maurice Edward Robbins, Aug. 1, 1962; children: John Scott, Gregory Dale, Kris Eric. BS in Edn., Gordon Coll., 1962; postgrad., U. Maine, Augusta, 1976, U. Maine, Orono, 1986, U. Maine, Portland, 1987. Cert. tchr. Tchr. Ctr. St. Sch., Hampton, N.H., 1962-64, Claflin Sch., Newton, 1965-66, Israel Loring Sch., Sudbury, Mass., 1966-67, Cheney Sch., Orange, Mass., 1967-69, Palermo (Maine) Consolidated Sch., 1975—, head tchr., 1997—. Founder, tchr. Primary Edn. Program, Palmero, 1990—; dir., author Child Sexual Abuse Program, Palmero, 1988—; mem. Title I Com., 1995—, Health Curriculum Com., 1995—, health grant coord., 1997—. Mem. bd. Christian edn., mem. wellness team, facilitator for Skillful Tchr. course Winter St. Bapt. Ch., Gardiner, Maine, 1993—, mem. bd. missions, 1993-94; bd. dirs. Hillside Christian Nursery Sch., 1994—; coord. student assistance team Maine Sch. Union #51, 1993—, bd. dirs. United Team, 1993—, mem. publicity com., 1991-92; coord. Nursing Home Ministry, Gardiner; invited by Commr. of Edn. to help develop State of Maine Assessment, 2001-03. Mem. NEA, Maine Tchrs. Assn., Palermo Tchrs. Assn. (pres. 1984-86, 96-98), Maine Educators of the Gifted and Talented, Maine Sch. Union 51 (sec. certification steering com. 1988—, rep. gifted-talented com. 1976—), Palermo Tchrs. Assn. (treas. 1998—), Palermo Sch. Club (exec. bd. 19 85-88. Avocations: travel, swimming, camping, basketball. Home: 99 S Dondero Rd Robbins Ln Chelsea ME 04330 Office: Palermo Consolidated Sch RR 3 Palermo ME 04354

ROBBINS, MARY ANN, secondary school educator; b. Vincennes, Ind., Oct. 2, 1944; d. Cecil D. and Mary E. (Kaufman) R. AS, Vincennes U., 1964; BS, Ind. State U., Terre Haute, 1966, MS, 1972. Cert. tchr. secondary math., Ind. Tchr. math. Northside Mid.Sch., Bartholomew Consol. Sch. Corp., Columbus, Ind., 1966—. Math. tchr. TV program Mathworks, Columbus, 1985, 1989—92. Mem. NEA (life), Nat. Coun. Tchrs. Math., Ind. Coun. Tchrs. Math, Ind. State Tchrs. Assn., Columbus Educators Assn., Nat. Mid. Sch. Assn., Delta Kappa Gamma Soc. Internat.(treas. 1973-92). Democrat. Roman Catholic. Avocations: reading, travel. Home: 611 Willow Ln Columbus IN 47203-1533 Office: Northside Mid Sch 1400 27th St Columbus IN 47201-3107 E-mail: robbinsm@bosc.k12.in.us.

ROBBINS-WILF, MARCIA, educational consultant; b. Newark, Mar. 22, 1949; d. Saul and Ruth (Fern) Robbins; 1 child, Orin. Student, Emerson Coll., 1967-69, Seton Hall U., 1969, Fairleigh Dickinson U., 1970; BA, George Washington U., 1971; MA, NYU, 1975; postgrad., St. Peter's Coll., Jersey City, 1979, Fordham U., 1980; MS, Yeshiva U., 1981, EdD, 1986; postgrad., Monmouth Coll., 1986. Cert. elem. tchr., N.Y., N.J., reading specialist, N.J., prin., supr., N.J., adminstr., supr., N.Y. Tchr. Sleepy Hollow Elem. Sch., Falls Church, Va., 1971-72, Yeshiva Konvitz, N.Y.C., 1972-73; intern Wee Folk Nursery Sch., Short Hills, N.J., 1978-81, dir. day camp, 1980-81, tchr., dir., owner, 1980-81; adj. prof. reading Seton Hall U., South Orange, N.J., 1987, Middlesex County Coll., Edison, N.J., 1987-88; asst. adj. prof. L.I. U., Bklyn., 1988, Pace U., N.Y.C., 1988—. Ednl. cons. Cranford High Sch., 1988; presenter numerous workshops; founding bd. dirs. Stern Coll. Women Yeshiva U., N.Y.C., 1987; adj. vis. lectr. Rutgers U., New Brunswick, N.J., 1988. Chairperson Jewish Book Festival, YM-YWHA, West Orange, N.J., 1986-87, mem. early childhood com., 1986—, bd. dirs., 1986—; vice chairperson dinner com. Nat. Leadership Conf. Christians and Jews, 1986; mem. Hadassah, Valerie Children's Fund, Women's League Conservative Judaism, City of Hope; assoc. bd. bus. and women's profl. divsn. United Jewish Appeal, 1979; vol. reader Goddard Riverside Day Care Ctr., N.Y.C., 1973; friend N.Y.C. Pub. Libr., 1980—; life friend Millburn (N.J.) Pub. Libr.; pres. Seton-Essex Reading Coun., 1991-94. Co-recipient Am. Heritage award, Essex County, 1985; recipient Award Appreciation City of Hope, 1984, Profl. Improvement awards Seton-Essex Reading Council, 1984-86, Cert. Attendance award Seton-Essex Reading Counci, 1987. Mem. N.Y. Acad. Scis. (life), N.J. Council Tchrs. English, Nat. Council Tchrs. English, Am. Ednl. Research Assn., Coll. Reading Assn. (life), Assn. Supervision and Curriculun Devel., N.Y. State Reading Assn. (council Manhattan), N.J. Reading Assn. (council Seton-Essex), Internat. Reading Assn., Nat. Assn. for Edn. of Young Children (life N.J. chpt., Kenyon group), Nat. Council Jewish Women (vice chairperson membership com. evening br. N.Y. sect. 1974-75), George Washington U. Alumni Club, Emerson Coll. Alumni Club, NYU Alumni Club, Phi Delta Kappa (life), Kappa Gamma Chi (historian). Clubs: Greenbrook Country (Caldwell, N.J.); George Washington Univ. Avocations: reading, theatre. Home: 242 Hartshorn Dr Short Hills NJ 07078-1914 E-mail: dr.mrw349@aol.com.

ROBBOY, HOWARD ALAN, sociologist, educator; b. Phila., June 16, 1945; s. Benjamin and Irma Helen (Lee) R.; m. Candace Clark, July 7, 1977 (div. Dec. 1989). BA, Temple U., 1967; AM, Rutgers U., 1972, PhD, 1976. Asst. prof. Beaver Coll., Glenside, Pa., 1972—73, Trenton (N.J.) State Coll., 1976-82, assoc. prof., 1983—, chmn., 1988-94. Vis. asst. prof. U. Miss., 1977-81, 2001-02. Co-editor: Social Interaction, 1974, 83, 88, 4th edit., 1992. Mem. Am. Sociol. Assn., Soc. for Study of Social Problems, Soc. for Study of Symbolic Interaction, So. Sociol. Soc. Democrat. Avocation: oriental rugs. Home: 1600 Riverside Dr Trenton NJ 08618-5837 Office: Coll NJ Library Ct PO Box 7718 Ewing NJ 08628-0718 E-mail: robboy98@yahoo.com.

ROBECK, MILDRED COEN, education educator, writer; b. Walum, N.D., July 29, 1915; d. Archie Blain and Mary Henrietta (Hoffman) Coen; m. Martin Julius Robeck, Jr., June 2, 1936; children: Martin Jay Robeck, Donna Jayne Robeck Thompson, Bruce Wayne Robeck. BS, U. Wash., 1950, MEd, 1954, PhD, 1958. Ordnance foreman Sherman Williams, U.S. Navy, Bremerton, Wash., 1942-45; demonstration tchr. Seattle Pub. Schs., 1946-57; reading clinic dir. U. Calif., Santa Barbara, 1957-64; rsch. cons. State Dept. Edn., Sacramento, Calif., 1964-67; prof., head early childhood edn. U. Oreg., Eugene, Oreg., 1967-86; vis. scholar West Australia Inst. Tech., Perth, 1985; v.p. acad. affairs U. Santa Barbara, Calif., 1987-95. Vis. prof. Victoria Coll., B.C. Can., summer 1958, Dalhousie U., Halifax, summer 1964; trainer evaluator U.S. Office of Edn. Head Start, Follow Thru, 1967-72; cons., evaluator Native Am. Edn. Programs, Sioux, Navajo, 1967-81; cons. on gifted Oreg. Task Force on Talented and Gifted, Salem, 1974-76; evaluator Early Childhood Edn., Bi-Ling. program, Petroleum and Minerology, Dhahran, Saudi Arabia, 1985. Author: Materials KELP: Kgn. Evaluation Learning Pot, 1967, Infants and Children, 1978, Psychology of Reading, 1990, Oscar: His Story, 1997, 2nd edit., 2000; contbr. articles to profl. jours. Evaluation cons. Rosenburg Found. Project, Santa Barbara, 1966-67; faculty advisor Pi Lambda Theta, Eugene, Oreg, 1969-74; guest columnist Oreg. Assn. Gifted and Talented, Salem, Oreg., 1979-81; editorial review bd. ERQ, U.S. Calif., L.A., 1981-91. Recipient Nat. Dairy award 4-H Clubs, Wis., 1934, scholarships NYA and U. Wis., Madison, 1934-35, faculty rsch. grants U. Calif., Santa barbara, 1958-64, NDEA Fellowship Retraining U.S. Office Edn., U. Oreg., 1967-70. Mem. APA, Am. Ednl. Rsch. Assn., Internat. Reading Assn., Phi Beta Kappa, Pi Lambda Theta. Democrat. Avocations: dyslexia research, historical research, duplicate bridge, writing. Home: 95999 Highway 101 S Yachats OR 97498-9714 E-mail: mrobeck@casco.net.

ROBERSON, CAROLYN A. elementary school counselor; b. McComb, Miss., Jan. 12, 1950; d. Vernon and Christine (Alexander) Williams; m. Sylvester Roberson, June 17, 1975; 1 child, Carol Syleste. BS, Abilene Christian U., 1972; MS with honors, Chgo. State U., 1978, MS in Guidance and Counseling, 1987; PhD, Loyola U., Chgo., 1993. Cert. spl. educator, bus. eucator, phys. edn. instr., elem. counselor Ill. Tchr. phys. edn. and health Waukegan (Ill.) Sch. Dist., 1972—75; phys. edn. coord., asst. activities dir. Hamlin House, Chgo., 1975—76; mental health therapist Ridgeway Hosp., Chgo., 1976—77; adaptive phys. tchr. phys. therapy dept. Spalding H.S., Chgo., 1977—78; tchr. emotionally and mentally handicapped Blue Island (Ill.) Sch. Dist., 1978—79; tchr. emotionally disturbed Ray Graham Assn., Des Plaines, Ill., 1980; tchr. EMH, TMH, phys. edn., health Spalding H.S., Chgo., 1980—, learning disability dept. chair, 1997—2000, acting asst. prin. in charge of discipline, 1983—84, discipline counselor, 1984—85, sch. disciplinarian, Phys. Edn. dept., 1985—86; tchr. handicapped Chgo. Bd. Edn., 1985—90, learning devel. resource tchr., 1990—, discipline counselor, 1990—93, supr. tchr. aides, instr., behavior disorder tchr., disciplinarian, 1991—92, learning disabilities resource, 1993—94, mem. Profl. Pers. Adv. Coun., Profl. Problem Com., Ill. Staff Devel. Coun. Grantee tchg. sci. to handicapped, U. Chgo., 1984—85. Mem.: NAACP, Ill. Assn. Health, Phys. Edn. and Recreation, Coun. Exceptional Children, Am. Assn. Counseling and Devel., Coun. Basic Edn., Assn. Supervision and Curriculum Devel., Phi Delta Kappa. Church Of Christ. Home: PO Box 289268 Chicago IL 60628-9268 Office: Spalding High Sch 1628 W Washington Blvd Chicago IL 60612-2613 E-mail: doccal@hotmail.com.

ROBERSON, CAROLYN REA, elementary school educator; b. Coffeyville, Kans., Oct. 5, 1950; d. Claud A. and Helen Pauline (Hardy) McMichael; m. Freddie Lee Frederick, June 16, 1973 (div. 1977); m. Ellis Howard Roberson, Nov. 7, 1980; 1 stepchild, Tom Roberson. AA, Coffeyville Community Coll., 1970; BS in Elem. Edn., Kans. State Coll., 1972; MS, Pittsburg (Kans.) State U., 1985. Tchr. 6th grade Garfield Sch., Coffeyville, 1973-77, tchr. 5th grade, 1977-88, tchr. 2d grade, 1988—. Mem. NEA (del. nat. conv. 1999, 2000), Ky. Nat. Edn. Assn. (treas. 1978-81, bldg. rep., local pres. 1999-2001, Uniserv del. 2000, profl. negotiation commr.), Dist. Profl. Devel. Coun., Delta Kappa Gamma. Republican. Methodist. Avocations: walking, reading, baking, music, gardening. Home: 312 N Parkview St Coffeyville KS 67337-1225 Office: Garfield Sch 701 W 4th St Coffeyville KS 67337-3999

ROBERSON, DEBORAH KAY, secondary school educator; b. Crane, Tex., Jan. 15, 1955; d. David B. and Virginia L. (King) Cole; m. Larry M. Roberson; children: Justin, Jenai, Julie. BS in Secondary Edn., Coll. S.W., 1981; MA in Sch. Adminstrn., Sul Ross State U., 1991. Cert. biology and history tchr., mid-mgmt. cert., supt. cert., Tex., biology and history tchr., secondary prin., supt., Okla. Sci. and social studies tchr. Andrews (Tex.) Ind. Sch. Dist., 1987-95; forum tchr. gifted social studies program, social studies dept. chair Ctrl. Mid. Sch., Broken Arrow, Okla., 1995—99; asst. prin. Ctrl. Middle Sch., Broken Arrow, Okla., 1999—2001; sci. tchr. 6th grade Jamison Mid. Sch., Pearland, Tex., 2001—02; asst. prin. Alvin Jr. HS, 2002—. 7th grade history curriculum com. Andrews Ind. Sch. Dist., 1988, outdoor classroom com., 1989-90, chair sci. curriculum com., 1989-90, chair health curriculum com., 1990-91, Tex. pub. schs. open house com., 1989-90, 92-93, dist. textbook com., 1990-91; secondary edn. rep. Ptnrs. in Parliament, Berlin, 1993; site-based com. Broken Arrow Pub. Schs., 1995—, B.A.S.I.S. com., 1995—, nat. history day coord. Ctrl. Middle Sch., 1995, geography bee coord., 1995—, tech. com., 1996—, discipline com., 1996, remediation com., 1996—, Tools for Tomorrow Conf. com., 1996—, others; state geography com. Okla. State Dept. Edn., 1997. Prodr., dir.: Real History Radio, Broken Arrow Hist. Soc., 1997. Livestock leader Andrews County 4-H Program, 1985-89; vol. Am. Heart Assn., Andrews, 1988; vol., team mother Little League, Andrews, 1990; vol., treas. Mustang Booster Club, Andrews, 1993-95. Recipient Appreciation awards Mustang Booster Club, 1993, 94, VFW Ladies Aux. Post 10887 award, Broken Arrow, 1996—, Tchr. of Today award Masons, Broken Arrow, 1997, Nat. History Day Outstanding Tchr. award Tulsa C.C., 1997, Best Mentored Tchr. award Nat. Jr. Cotillion, 1999; Tchr. Program scholar Fulbright Meml. Fund, Japan, 1998. Mem. AAUW, Nat. Assn. Secondary Sch. Prins., Nat. Staff Devel. Coun., Assn. Tex. Profl. Educators (pres. local unit 1992-93, mem. resolutions com. 1994-95, Appreciation award 1993, sec. region 1993-94, v.p. region 1994-95), ASCD, Tex. Assn. Supervision and Curriculum Devel., Tex. Network for Continuous Quality Improvement, Nat. Coun. Social Studies, Okla. Assn. Supervision and Curriculum Devel., Okla. Alliance Geographic Edn., Okla. Assn. Secondary Sch. Prins., Coop. Orgn. Okla. Secondary Adminstrs., Redskins Booster Club (sec. 1996-97). Avocations: meeting people, travel, golf, rafting, hiking. Office: Alvin Jr HS 2301 W South St Alvin TX 77511 Home: 9402 Sunperch Ct Pearland TX 77584-2886

ROBERSON, KELLEY CLEVE, health care administrator; b. McAlester, Okla., July 11, 1950; s. Cleo Connie and Helen Frances (Sewell) R.; m. Georgia Lee Brown, Jan. 15, 1970; children: Kevin Christopher, Matthew Guy. BBA, Tex. Christian U., 1973; postgrad., U. Md., 1983-88, U. So. Calif., 1991-93. Cert. govt. fin. mgr. Commd. 2d lt. U.S. Army, 1973, advanced through grades to lt. col., 1992; exec. officer Med. Co., Ft. Carson, Colo., 1974; aviation sect. leader 377th Med. Co., Republic of Korea, 1975-76; ops. officer Aeromed. Evacuation Unit, Ft. Stewart, Ga., 1976-79, exec. officer Grafenwoehr, Germany, 1980-81; comdr. Med. Co. 2nd Armored Evacuation Unit, Garlstedt, Germany, 1981-83; compt. Walter Reed Army Inst. Rsch., Washington, 1983-88; comdr. Aeromed. Evacuation Unit, Hickam AFB, Hawaii, 1988-90; chief manpower Tripler Army Med. Ctr., Honolulu, 1990-92; chief resource mgmt., dep. comdr. adminstrn. Letterman U.S. Army Hosp. and Health Clinic, San Francisco, 1992-94; chief resource mgmt. Tripler Army Med. Ctr., Honolulu, 1994-97; chief program and budget U.S. Army Med. Dept., 1997-98; ret. U.S. Army, 1998; v.p., CFO Hawaii Health Sys. Corp., Honolulu, 1998-2000. COO/CFO Hawaii Health Sys. Corp., Honolulu, 2000—; dir. Hawaii Prescription Care Pres. Parents Club Damien Meml. High Sch., Honolulu, 1990-91; dir. Hawaii Health Sys. Found., 1999—, Hawaii Health Info. Corp., 1999—; bd. dirs. Alii Cmty. Care. Mem. Assn. Govt. Accts. (cert. govt. fin. mgr.), Am. Acad. of Med. Admintrs., Order Mil. Med. Merit, Am. Soc. Mil. Comptrs. (pres. Golden Gate chpt. 1992-93), Assn. U.S. Army, Mil. Officers of Am. Assn.. United Methodist. Avocations: writing, golf, reading. Home: 1414 Hoakoa Pl Honolulu HI 96821 Office: Hawaii Health Sys Corp 3675 Kilauea Ave Honolulu HI 96816-2333 E-mail: kroberson@hhsc.org., kelleyroberson@hawaii.rr.com.

ROBERSON, MARK ALLEN, physicist, educator; b. Lufkin, Tex., Nov. 12, 1961; s. Roy and Thelma (Weist) R. AAS, Angelina County Jr. Coll., 1982; BSEE, Tex. A&M U., 1984; MS, Stephen F. Austin State U., 1989; PhD, Tex. Tech. U., 1994. From rsch. asst. to instr. Tex. Tech. U., Lubbock, 1990-95; instr. Vernon (Tex.) Regional Jr. Coll., 1995—. Robert A. Welch Found. fellow, 1991-94. Mem. AAAS, Am. Phys. Soc., Sigma Pi Sigma. Avocation: books. Office: Vernon Regl Jr Coll Vernon TX 76384-4092

ROBERSON, PATT FOSTER, mass communications educator; b. Middletown, N.Y., Dec. 3, 1934; d. Gilbert Charles and Mildred Elizabeth (O'Neal) Foster; m. Murray Ralph Roberson Jr., May 10, 1963 (dec. 1968). AA, Canal Zone Jr. Coll., 1954; BA in Journalism, La. State U., 1957, MA in Journalism, 1973; MA in Media, So. U., Baton Rouge, 1981; PhD in Mass Communication, U. So. Miss., 1985. Exec. sec. Lionel H. Abshire and Assocs., AIA, Architects, Baton Rouge, 1958-60, Murrell and Callari, AIA, Architects, Baton Rouge, 1960-63; bus. mgr. So. Rev. La. State U., Baton Rouge, 1963-69; free-lance researcher, ind. contractor Baton Rouge, 1969-74; rep. dept. info. State of La., Baton Rouge, 1974-75; asst. prof. mass. comm. So. U., 1976-86, assoc. prof. mass comm., 1986-93, prof. mass comm., 1993-96, prof. emeritus, 1996—. Printed program, advt., & editl. cons. Baton Rouge performing arts org., 1971; reviewer Random House Pubs., N.Y.C., 1981; profl. devel. intern Baton Rouge Morning Advocate, 1991, Baker Observer, 1991-92; reporter-photographer Canal Record, Seminole, Fla., 1967—; biographer of Edward Livermore Burlingame, John H. Johnson, Daniel Kimball Whitaker, (book) American mag. journalists series, Dictionary Literary Biography, Detroit, 1986-87; tutor Operation Upgrade, 1978-82; vol. reporter, photographer, proofreader The Platinum Record, Baton Rouge, 1996-99; cons. in field. Co-editor: La. State U. cookbook Tiger Bait, 1976; biographer Frank E. Gannett in Biographical Dictionary of American Journalism, 1987; freelance writer/editl. cons.; editl. bd. Am. Journalism, 1986-87; reviewer Longman Publs. 1991-92; contbr. articles to profl. jours. Mem. poll commn. East Baton Rouge Parish Govt., 1978-95; pres. Our Lady Lake Regional Med. Ctr., 1971-72; bd. dirs. Dist. Atty.'s Rape Crisis Commn., 1976-79, Plan Govt. Study Commn., 1973-76, Selective Svc. System Bd. 8, Baton Rouge, 1986-98, 2002—; docent Greater Baton Rouge Zoo, 1974-77, 2002-; vol. ARC, 1989-99, Capital Area Ct.-Apptd. Spl. Adv., 1997-99; mem. East Baton Rouge Parish Commn. on Govtl. Ethics, 1992-93; council appointee Baher Strategic Planning Com., 2003-; mayoral appointee Baker Mobile Home Rev. Bd., 1990—; v.p. Baker Hist. and Cultural Found., 1990-93; mem. Baker Interclub Coun., 1990-91; organizer human-animal therapy svc. Baker Manor Nursing Home, 1994; mem. 1st class Citizens Basic Police Tng. Acad., Baton Rouge Police Dept., 1994; chairpub. rels., bd. dirs. Panama Canal Mus., 1998-2001. Mem. AAUP (sec.-treas. La. conf. 1988-89, sec. 1992-93, chmn. pub. rels. 1994-95), Assn. Edn. Journalism and Mass Comm., Am. Newspapers Pubs. Assn. (nat. coop. com. on edn. in journalism 1989-92), Women in Comm. (pres. Baton Rouge chpt. 1982, nat. judge Clarion awards 1987), Pub. Rels. Assn. La., La. State U. Journalism Alumni Assn. (pres. 1977), Soc. Profl. Journalists (pres. S.E. La. chpt. 1982), Am. Journalism Historians Assn., Oral History Assn., La. State U. Alumni Assn. (pres. East Baton Rouge Parish chpt. 1978-80), Popular Culture Assn., Investigative Reporters and Editors Assn., Baker C. of C., Toasmasters (adminstrv. v.p. Baton Rouge 1977), Pilot Club of Baker. Home: 2801 Allen Ct Baker LA 70714-2253

ROBERTS, ALICE NOREEN, educational administrator; b. Los Lunas, N.Mex., July 1, 1947; d. Earnest Lee and Lora Mae (Leatherman) Mayo; m. David Ivan Roberts, Apr. 18, 1975; children: Debra, Danielle, David II, Diana, Earnest. BA, Brescia Coll., 1970; MA, U. N.Mex., 1974. Cert. elem. tchr., adminstr., Calif. 5th and 6th grade tchr. St. John's Parochial Sch., Plattsmouth, Nebr., 1970-71; 5th grade tchr. Sacred Heart Parochial Sch., Farmington, N.Mex., 1971-72; 4th-6th grade tchr. Our Lady of Assumption Sch., Albuquerque, 1972-75; 6th grade tchr. St. Catherine's Parochial Sch., Martinez, Calif., 1981—82; correctional officer Calif. Dept. Corrections, San Quentin, 1975-82, adult edn. tchr. Soledad, 1983-86, San Luis Obispo, 1984, supr. acad. instrn. Norco, 1986-90, supr. correctional edn. programs Corcoran, 1990—, ltd. term correctional adminstr., 1996. Mem. curriculum adv. com. Calif. Dept. Corrections, Sacramento, 1984—86, mem. computer adv. com., 1984—88, mem. literacy adv. com., 1990—94; adj. prof. criminology Porterville (Calif.) Jr. Coll., 1996—98. Candidate for King City (Calif.) Bd. Edn., 1985; vol. Youth for Understanding rep., Hanford, 1994-96. Mem.: ASCD, Calif. Coun. for Adult Edn., Calif. Literacy Inc., Correctional Edn. Assn. (treas. region VII 1999—2001), Am. Vocat. Assn., Hanford Emblem Club (rec. sec. 1994—99, 1st v.p. 1999—2000, pres. 2000—). Roman Catholic. Avocations: computers, pencil puzzles, video games, crocheting. Office: Calif State Prison Visions Adult Sch PO Box 8800 Corcoran CA 93212-8800 Personal E-mail: anroberts@iwon.com.

ROBERTS, ALIDA JAYNE, elementary school educator; b. Bristol, Conn., Aug. 11, 1967; d. James and Barbara Mae (Carlson) R. BA in Elem. Edn., Anna Maria Coll., Paxton, Mass., 1990; MS in Reading and Lang. Arts, Calif. State U., Fullerton, 1992; adminstrn. and supervision cert., U. Hartford, 1997, postgrad., 1999—. Cert. tchr., Conn., Mass. Elem. tchr. Rowland Unified Sch. Dist., Rowland Heights, Calif., 1990-94, Edgewood Elem. Sch., Bristol, Conn., 1994-95, Clara T. O'Connell Elem. Sch., Bristol, Conn., 1995-96, Edgewood Elem. Sch., Bristol, 1995-98, Chippers Hill Mid. Sch., Bristol, 1998—, softball coach, 1999—, asst. to prin., 2000—01. Tchr. Gifted and Talented Edn. After Sch. Program, West

Covina, Calif., 1993-94, Chpt. 1 After Sch. Program, West Covina, 1993-94; intramural coach After Sch. Program Edgewood Elem. Sch., Bristol, Conn., 1994-95. Tchr. advisor PTA, La Puente, 1992-92, Clara T. O'Connell PTA, 1995-96. Bristol Fedn. Tchrs. scholar, 1986; Anna Maria Coll. grantee, 1986-90. Mem. NEA, ASCD, Internat. Reading Assn., Bristol Fedn. Tchrs., Nat. Coun. Tchrs. English, Conn. Coun. Tchrs. English, New Eng. League Middle Schs., Kappa Delta Pi. Avocations: reading, physical fitness. Home: 291 Morris Ave Bristol CT 06010-4418

ROBERTS, ANTONETTE, retired special education educator; b. San Francisco, Nov. 14, 1940; d. Anthony Francis and Lois Wilma (Litton) Jacklevich; m. Raymond Daly Roberts, Feb. 1, 1964; children: Shirley Lois Roberts Murphy, Alice Evelyn, Daniel Anthony. BA, U. Calif., Davis, 1962; MS, U. Nebr., 1971. Cert. elem. and spl. edn. tchr., Iowa. Elem. educator Esparto (Calif.) Unified Sch. Dist., 1962-66; itinerant resource educator Pottawattamie County Schs., Council Bluffs, Iowa, 1972-75; multi-categorical resource educator Lewis Ctrl. Cmty. Sch. Dist., Council Bluffs, 1975—2003, ret., 2003. Mem. parent educator connection Lewis Ctrl. Cmty. Schs., 2001—03, Area Edn. Agy. XIII, 2001—03. Mem. tchr. cadre U. No. Iowa, Cedar Falls and Lewis Ctrl. Cmty. Schs., Council Bluffs, 1990—2003; sponsor Lakeview Sch. Student Coun., Council Bluffs, 1990-92; mem. Lewis Ctrl. Instructional Coun., 1992-96, Lakeview Sch. Bldg. Cadre, 1994-95; mem. Lakeview Grant Writing Com., 1997-98; establishing mem., facilitator Parent Lending Libr. Com., 1998-99; mem. Lewis Ctrl. Mid. Sch. Bldg. Cadre, 2000-2001; facilitator Read Across Am., Lakeview Sch., 1998-99, mid. sch., 2000-03. Mem. NEA, Iowa State Edn. Assn., Lewis Cen. Edn. Assn., Coun. for Exceptional Children, Iowa Coun. Tchrs. of English, Phi Delta Kappa. Avocations: reading, writing, swimming, sewing, pottery. E-mail: Roberts@Novia.Net.

ROBERTS, CHRIS, strategy and finance educator, researcher; b. New Castle, Pa., July 16, 1954; s. Samuel Bruce and Jan Roberts, Della V. Roberts (Stepmother), Sheldon S. Smith (Stepfather). BS in Mgmt., U. Utah, 1975, BS in Fin., 1981; MBA, U. Phoenix, Salt Lake City, 1986; PhD in Mgmt., U. Mass., 1995. Supr. Holiday Inns Reservation Ctr., Memphis, Utah, 1972—78; product mgr. Mountain Bell/Qwest Comms., Salt Lake City, 1978—89; assoc. prof. Isenberg Sch. Mgmt. U. Mass., Amherst, 1993—, assoc. dept. head dept. Isenberg Sch. Mgmt., 2001—. Contbr. articles to profl. jours.; editor: Jour. Hospitality and Tourism Edn. Mem.: Acad. Mgmt., Strategic Mgmt. Soc., Coun. Hotel, Restaurant & Instnl. Edn. (chair symposium com. 1998—2002, Outstanding Peer Reviewer 1999), Beta Gamma Sigma. Avocations: contract bridge, international travel. Home: PO Box 521895 Salt Lake City UT 84152-1895 Office: U Mass Flint 206 90 Campus Center Way Amherst MA 01003-9247 Office Fax: 413-545-1235. Personal E-mail: Q@qutah.com. Business E-Mail: Q@ht.umass.edu.

ROBERTS, DAVID LOWELL, journalist, educator; b. Lusk, Wyo., Jan. 12, 1954; s. Leslie James and LaVerne Elizabeth (Johns) R. BA, U. Ariz., 1979; MA, U. Nebr., 1997. Founder, editor, publisher Medicine Bow (Wyo.) Post, 1977-88; journalism instr. U. Wyo., Laramie, 1987-92; adviser U. Wyo. Student Publs., Laramie, 1987-92; gen. mgr. Student Media Corp U No. Colo., Greeley, 1995-98; founder, publisher Hanna Herald, Wyo., 1979-80; asst. prof. mass comm. Missouri Valley Coll., Marshall, Mo., 2001—. Exch. reporter The Washington Post, 1982; freelance reporter Casper (Wyo.) Star-Tribune, 1978-83, various publs.; freelancer, 1977—. Co-author: (book) The Wyoming Almanac, 1988, 90, 94, 96, 2001; author: (book) Sage Street, 1991; columnist Sage Street, 1989-92. Chmn. Medicine Bow Film Commn., 1984; treas. Friends of the Medicine Bow Mus., 1984-88; pres. Medicine Bow Area C. of C., 1984; dir. Habitat for Humanity of Albany County, Laramie, 1991-92. Recipient Nat. Newspaper Assn. awards, over 40 Wyo. Press. Assn. awards, Five Editorial awards U. Wyo., Citizen of Yr. award People of Medicine Bow, 1986, Student Publs. awards U. Wyo., 1990, 92. Mem. Friends of Medicine Bow Mus. Mem. Green Party. Methodist. Avocations: writing, golf, visiting museums, photography. Home: 221 E Rosehill Marshall MO 65340

ROBERTS, DONALD FRANK, JR., communications educator; b. Seattle, Mar. 30, 1939; s. Donald Frank Sr. and Ruth Amalia (Geiger) R.; m. Karlene Hahn, 1963 (div. 1981): 1 child, Donald Brett; m. Wendy G. Roberts, Aug. 26, 1983; stepchildren: Richard L., David L., Katherine M. AB, Columbia U., 1961; MA, U. Calif., Berkeley, 1963; PhD, Stanford U., 1968. Instr., dept. English U. Hawaii, Honolulu, 1963-64; asst. dir. ednl. svc. bur. The Wall Street Jour., Princeton, N.J., 1964-65; asst. prof., rsch. assoc. dept. Comm., Inst. Comm. Rsch. Stanford (Calif.) U., 1970-76, assoc. prof., 1976-84, prof. Comm., 1984—, dir. Inst. Comm. Rsch., 1985-90, chmn. dept. Comm., 1990-96, Thomas More Storke Prof., 1991—. Cons. NIMH, 1970—71, Rand Corp., 1972—74, Sta. KQED-TV, 1975—77, Far West Lab. Ednl. Rsch. and Devel., 1978—79, FTC, 1978—80, Westinghouse Broadcasting, 1983—86, Soc. Nutrition Edn., 1984—86, The Disney Channel, 1986—87, WHO, 1988—89, SRI Internat., 1988—89, Carnegie Coun. Adolescence, 1989—90, NBC, 1992, Ctr. Disease Control, 1992, Children Now, 1992—, Software Pubs. Assn., 1994, Nickelodeon, 1994, JP Kids, 1995—97, MGM Animation, 1996—98, DIC Entertainment, 1997—, Planet Lingo, 1997—2001, Sunbow Entertainment, 1999—2000, ABC/Disney TV Animation, 2000—02, Disney Online, 2000—02, Nelvana, Ltd., 2000—01; bd. advisors Media Scope, 1992—94; proposal reviewer NIMH, NSF, U.S. Agy. Internat. Devel., Can. Coun., John and Mary R. Markle Found., W.T. Grant Found.; spkr. numerous seminars, confs., symposia. Co-author: Process and Effects of Mass Communication, 1971, Television and Human Behavior, 1978, It's not ONLY Rock and Roll, 1998, Kids and Media at the New Millennium, 1999, Kids and Media in America, 2003; mem. editl. bd. Jour. Broadcasting, 1980—88, Pub. Opinion Quarterly, 1981—86, Communicare, 1986—, editl. reviewer Commn. Rsch., —, Comm. Monograph, Comm. Yearbook, Human Comm. Rsch., Jour. Comm., Jour. Quarterly, Child Devel., Jour. Applied Psychology, Jour. Ednl. Psychology, Psychology Bull., Jour. Adolescent Health; contbr. articles, chapters to books. Fellow Human Scis. Rsch. Coun., Pretoria. South Africa, 1985, 1987, Fullbright Teaching fellow Inst. for Unterrichtstechnologie Und Medienpadagogic, Austria, 1987. Mem. APA, Internat. Comm. Assn., Assn. Edn. in Journalism and Mass Comm., Soc. Rsch. Child Devel., Soc. Personality and Soc. Psychology. Office: Stanford U Dept Comm McClatchy Hall Stanford CA 94305-2050 E-mail: droberts@stanford.edu.

ROBERTS, DONALD JOHN, economics and business educator, consultant; b. Winnipeg, Man., Can., Feb. 11, 1945; came to U.S., 1967; s. Donald Victor and Margaret Mabel (Riddell) R.; m. Kathleen Eleanor Taylor, Aug. 26, 1967. BA with honors, U. Man., 1967; PhD, U. Minn., 1972. Instr. dept. managerial econs. and decision scis. J.L. Kellogg Grad. Sch. Mgmt., Northwestern U., Evanston, Ill., 1971—72, asst. prof., 1972—74; assoc. prof. J. L. Kellogg Grad. Sch. Mgmt., Northwestern U., Evanston, Ill., 1974—77; prof. J.L. Kellogg Grad. Sch. Mgmt., Northwestern U., Evanston, Ill., 1977—80, Grad. Sch. Bus., Stanford (Calif.) U., 1980, Jonathan B. Lovelace prof., 1980—2001, assoc. dean, dir. rsch., 1987—90, dir. exec. program in strategy and orgn., 1992—, dir. global mgmt. program, 1994—, sr. assoc. dean, 2000—, John H. and Irene S. Scully prof., 2001—; co-dir. Ctr. for Global Bus. and the Economy, 2003. Prof. (by courtesy) dept. econs. Stanford U., 1986—; vis. rsch. faculty U. Catholique de Louvain, Belgium, 1974-75; inaugural Clarendon lectr. mgmt. studies Oxford U., 1997; cons. bus., econs. and antitrust, 1976—; vis. fellow All Souls Coll., Oxford U., 1995, Nuffield Coll., Oxford U., 1999-00; vis. acad. fellow in leadership and orgn. McKinsey & Co., London, 1999-00. Co-author: Economics, Organization and Management, 1992;; assoc. editor Jour. Econ. Theory, 1977-92, Econometrica, 1985-87, Games and Economics Behavior, 1988—; mem. editl. bd. Am. Econ. Rev., 1991-95, Jour. Econs. and Mgmt. Strategy, 1991-98, Orgns. and Markets Abstracts, 1996—; contbr. articles to profl. jours. NSF grantee, 1973-93; rsch. fellow Ctr. Ops. Rsch. and Econometrics, Heverlee, Belgium, 1974, fellow Ctr. for Advanced Study in the Behavioral Scis., 1991-92. Fellow Econometric Soc. (coun. 1994-96); mem. Am. Econ. Assn., Beta Gamma Sigma. Home: 835 Santa Fe Ave Stanford CA 94305-1022 E-mail: roberts_john@gsb.stanford.edu.

ROBERTS, E. F. lawyer, educator; b. 1930; m. Alice A. Dunn, July 4, 1955; children: Martha, Ernest III, Michael, Marianne. BA, Northeastern U., Boston, 1952; LL.B., Boston Coll., 1954. Bar: Mass. 1954. Asst. prof. law Villanova U., Pa., 1957-59, assoc. prof. law, 1959-60, prof. law, 1960-64, Cornell U., Ithaca, N.Y., 1964-96, Edwin H. Woodruff prof. law, emeritus prof., 1996. Vis. prof. Nottingham U., Eng., 1962-63, Harvard U., 1983; mem. edn. panel Environ. Law Reporter, 1971-80; cons. in field. Author: Public Regulation of Title Insurance, 1960, Land Use Planning, 2d edit., 1975, Law and the Preservation of Agricultural Land, 1982, (with Strong et al) McCormick on Evidence, 5th edit., 1999. Mem. Am. Law Inst. (life). Office: Cornell U Sch Law Ithaca NY 14853 E-mail: e-f-roberts@postoffice.law.cornell.edu.

ROBERTS, EDWARD BAER, technology management educator; b. Chelsea, Mass., Nov. 18, 1935; s. Nathan and Edna (Podradchik) Roberts; m. Nancy Helen Rosenthal, July 14, 1959; children: Valerie Jo Friedman, Mitchell Jonathan, Andrea Lynne. BSEE, MSEE, MIT, 1958, MS in Mgmt., 1960, PhD in Econs., 1962. Founding mem. system dynamics program MIT, 1958-84, instr., 1959-61, asst. prof., 1961-65, assoc. prof., 1965-70, prof., 1970—, David Sarnoff prof. mgmt. of tech., 1974—, assoc. dir. research program on mgmt. of sci. and tech., 1963-73, chmn. tech. and health mgmt. group, 1973-88, chmn. mgmt. of tech. and innovation, 1988-99, founder, chmn. ctr. for entrepreneurship, 1992—94, 1997—, co-dir. internat. ctr. rsch. mgmt. tech., 1993-2000, dir. mgmt. of tech. program, 1980-89, co-chmn., 1989-99, chmn. mgmt. tech. innovation and entrepreneurship, 1999—. Co-founder, dir. Med. Info. Tech., Inc., Westwood, Mass., 1969—; co-founder, gen. ptnr. Zero Stage Capital Group, 1981—99; co-founder, dir. SOHU.com, Inc., Beijing, 1996—; bd. dirs. Advanced Magnetics, Inc., Cambridge, Pegasystems, Inc., Cambridge, PR Restaurants, LLC, Andover, Mass., OrgSupply, Inc., Cambridge. Author: (book) The Dynamics of Research and Development, 1964, Systems Simulation for Regional Analysis, 1969, The Persistent Poppy, 1975, The Dynamics of Human Service Delivery, 1976, Entrepreneurs in High Technology, 1991; prin. author, editor: book Managerial Applications of System Dynamics, 1978; editor (with others): Biomedical Innovation, 1981; editor: Generating Technological Innovation, 1987, Innovation, 2002; mem. editl. bd. IEEE Trans. on Engring. Mgmt., Indsl. Mktg. Mgmt., Jour. Engring. and Tech. Mgmt., Jour. Product Innovation Mgmt., Sloan Mgmt. Rev., Tech. Forecasting and Social Change, Internat. Jour. Entrepreneurship and Innovation, Internat. Jour. Product Devel., Internat. Jour. Tech. Mgmt. Mem.: IEEE, Tau Kappa Alpha, Eta Kappa Nu, Tau Beta Pi, Sigma Xi. Home: 300 Boylston St Apt 1102 Boston MA 02116-3940 Office: MIT 50 Memorial Dr Cambridge MA 02142-1347

ROBERTS, FRANCIS JOSEPH, retired army officer, retired educational administrator, global economic advisor; b. Holyoke, Mass., July 26, 1918; s. Francis Raymond and Mary (Curry) R.; m. Mary Murray Prickett, May 30, 1942; children: Murray Francine Roberts Mux, Laurel Virginia Roberts Manning, Randall Curry, Phillip Raymond. BS, U.S. Mil. Acad., 1942; postgrad., George Washington U., 1960, Harvard U., 1964. Commd. 2d lt. U.S. Army, 1942, advanced through grades to brig. gen., 1966; comdg. officer (B Battery, 358th F.A.), 1942-43; ops. and tgn. staff 358th F.A., 1943-45; ops. and tng. staff officer (Hdqrs. III Corps), 1946; instr. tactics (U.S. Mil. Acad.), 1946, instr. academics, 1950-53, grad. mgr. athletics, dir. athletics, 1956-59; intelligence staff officer, plans officer (Amphibious Force U.S. Atlantic Fleet), 1946-48; pers. staff officer (Hdqrs. 101st Airborne Div.), 1948; dep. chief of staff 101th Airborne Divsn., 1948-49; plans and ops. staff officer (Hdqs. I Corps), Korea, 1953-54; comdg. officer (159th F.A.), Korea, 1954; plans and policy staff officer (J-3, Hdqs. Far East Command), Japan, 1954-55; chief pers. services div. (Office Asst. Chief of Staff for Pers.), Washington, 1960-61; mil. asst. to dep. sec. def. Washington, 1961-64; comdg. officer (4th Inf. Div. Arty.), 1964-66; chief war plans (SHAPE), 1966, chief strategic plans br., 1966-68; chief of staff (Alaskan Command), 1968-69; comdg. gen. (II Field Force Arty. Vietnam), 1969-70; chief of staff (Hdqs. II Field Force), Vietnam, 1970-71; chief (Europe-Middle East-Africa Div. Orgn. Joint Chiefs Staff), 1971-72, ret., 1972; dean of cadets N.Y. Mil. Acad., 1972, supt., 1972-82. Bd. dirs. Global Econ. Action Inst., 1980-93, Am. Child Guidance Found., 1966-74; v.p. AMP 45, Harvard; bd. dirs., mem. exec. com. U.S. Olympic Com.; mem. exec. com. Ea. Collegiate Athletic Conf.; mem. Western Alaska coun. Boy Scouts Am.; mem. nat. bd. trustees Boys and Girls Clubs Am.; mem. panel Golf Digest. Decorated D.S.M., D.F.C., Silver Star, Legion of Merit with 3 oak leaf clusters, 10 Air medals, Croix de Guerre avec Etoile de Argent, French Legion of Honor, Army Disting. Order 1st Class medal Vietnam, Vietnam Gallantry Cross with Palm, Nat. Honor medal Vietnam, Royal Army Aiguillette Thailand, others; first inductee Nat. Alumni Hall of Fame, Boys and Girls Clubs Am. Mem. Assn. Grad. West Point, Harvard Alumni Assn., Grads. Nat. War Coll., U.S. Golf Assn. (sectional affairs com.), U.S. Srs. Golf Assn. (bd. govs., sec. internat. golf team), Internat. Srs. Amateur Golf Soc., Assn. U.S. Army (chpt. pres., chmn. nat. resolution com., bd. advisors), Ret. Officers Assn.(bd. dirs., exec. com.), So. Srs. Golf Assn., N.C. Srs. Golf Assn., Global Econ. Action Inst. (bd. dirs.), Can. Sr. Golf Assn. (hon.). Clubs: Army-Navy Country (Washington); Pinehurst (N.C.) Country; Union League (N.Y.C.); Harvard-Radcliffe of Hudson Valley (pres. 1976-80), Touchdown of Am. (dir.), Ambs. Club-Duke U., Can. Srs. Golf Assn. (hon., 1st Am. mem.). Address: PO Box 2017 Pinehurst NC 28370-2017

ROBERTS, GINNY BARKLEY, middle school language arts educator; b. Gainesville, Tex., Sept. 15, 1945; d. Edward Phillip and Myra Ruth (Durham) B.; m. Dennis LeRoy Roberts, Dec. 8, 1967 (div. May 1989); children: Danny Roberts, Ward Roberts, Seth Roberts. BA, U. North Tex., 1967, MEd, 1993. Cert. tchr., Tex.; cert. all level reading specialist. Traffic dir., newswriter Sta. KVET Radio, Austin, 1967-68; traffic/continuity dir. Sta. KOKE Radio, Austin, 1968-69, Sta. WINQ Radio, Tampa, 1969-71; title I reading aide Hedrick Middle Sch., Lewisville, Tex., 1986-89; radio-TV tchr. Griffin Middle Sch., The Colony, Tex., 1993-94, speech and drama tchr., 1993-94, 6th and 7th reading improvement tchr., 1993-94, 6th grade lang. arts tchr., 1989-94, 7th grade lang. arts tchr., 1994—. Reading dept. chairperson Griffin Middle Sch., 1992—, mem. supt. adv. com., 1994-97, mem. faculty adv. com., 1996-97, mem. bldg. leadership team, 1999-2001. Pres. Lewisville H.S. Cross Country/Track Booster Club, 1986-87, bd. dirs. 1986-90; charter mem. Lewisville H.S. Choir Booster Club, 1989-95; mem. Lewisville Football Booster Club, 1993-95. Mem. Internat. Reading Assn., Phi Kappa Phi. Baptist. Avocations: reading, computer word processing. Home: 417 Hardwicke Ln Little Elm TX 75068 Office: Griffin Middle Sch 5105 N Colony Blvd The Colony TX 75056-1219

ROBERTS, GLENN DALE, microbiologist, educator; b. Gilmer, Tex., Apr. 9, 1943; s. B. C. and Mary Fern (Baker) R.; m. Kathleen Louise Brackin, Oct. 13, 1973; children: Michael Glenn, Heather Michelle, Megan Louise. BS, North Tex. State U., 1967; MS, U. Okla., 1969, PhD, 1972. Diplomate Am. Bd. Med. Microbiology. Fellow dept. community medicine Coll. Medicine U. Ky., Lexington, 1971-72; dir. clin. mycology and mycobacteriology labs. Mayo Clinic, Rochester, Minn., 1972—; prof. Mayo Med. Sch., Rochester, 1986—. Advisor Nat. Com. for Clin. Lab. Standards, Villanova, Pa., 1985-90; found. lectr. Am. Soc. Microbiology, 1993; pres. Med. Mycological Soc. for Ams., 1999—. Co-author: Practical Laboratory Mycology, 1985. Recipient Meridian award for Clin. Mycology, Med. Mycol. Soc. of Ams., 1988, Pasteur award Ill. Soc. Microbiology, 1999. Fellow Am. Acad. Microbiology; mem. Am. Soc. Microbiology, Am. Soc. Clin. Pathologists, Internat. Soc. Human and Animal Mycology. Lutheran. Achievements include development of pronase method to eliminate interference factors from body fluids prior to testing for cryptococcal antigen, new methods for identification of clinically important yeasts, and molecular detection and identification of mycobacterial and fungal infections. Home: 1751 Walden Ln SW Rochester MN 55902-0901 Office: Mayo Clinic 200 1st St SW Rochester MN 55905-0002

ROBERTS, JO ANN WOODEN, school system administrator; b. Chgo., June 24, 1948; d. Tilmon and Annie Mae (Wardlaw) Wooden; m. Edward Allen Roberts Sr. (div.); children: Edward Allen Jr., Hillary Ann. BS, Wayne State U., 1970, MS, 1971; PhD, Northwestern U., 1977. Speech, lang. pathologist Chgo. Bd. Edn., 1971—78, adminstr., 1987—88; dir. spl. svcs. Rock Island (Ill.) Pub. Schs., 1988—90; supt. Muskegon Hts. (Mich.) Pub. Schs., 1990—93; dep. supr. Chgo. Pub. Schs., 1993—96; supt. of schs. Hazel Crest (Ill.) Sch. Dist. #152 1/2, 1996—98; cons. Chgo. Pub. Schs., 1998—2000, dep. accountability svcs., 1999—, InterVention officer, 2000—01, chief troubleshooter, 2001—. Instr. Chgo City C.C., 1976-77; chief troubleshooter Chog. Pub. Schs., 2001—; project dir. Ednl. Testing Svc., Evanston, Ill., 1976-77; exec. dir. Nat. Speech, Lang. and Hearing Assn., Chgo., 1984-86; hon. guest lectr. Govs. State U., University Park, Ill., 1983-86; cons. in field. Author: Learning to Talk, 1974. Trustee Muskegon County Libr. Bd., 1990, Mercy Hosp. Bd., Muskegon, 1990, St. Mark's Sch. Bd. Dirs., Southborough, Mass., 1989, United Way Bd., Muskegon, 1990; mem. Mich. State Bd. Edn. Systematic Initiative in Math and Sci., 1991, Gov. John Engler Mich. 2000 Task Force, 1991, Chpt. II Adv. Commn., 1991. Recipient Leadership award Boy Scouts Am., 1990; named finalist Outstanding Young Working Women, Glamour Mag., 1984, Outstanding Educator, Blacks in Govt., 1990. Mem. Am. Assn. Sch. Adminstrs., Nat. Alliance Black Sch. Educators, Mich. Assn. Sch. Adminstrs., Assn. Supervision & Curriculum Devel., Phi Delta Kappa. Avocations: creative writing, peotry, modern dance, theater, drawing. Address: Chgo Pub Schs 125 S Clark St Chicago IL 60603-5200

ROBERTS, JUDITH MARIE, librarian, educator; b. Bluefield, W.Va., Aug. 5, 1939; d. Charles Bowen Lowder and Frances Marie (Bourne) Lowder Alberts; m. Craig Currence Johnson, July 1, 1957 (div. 1962); 1 child, Craig Jr.; m. Milton Rinehart Roberts, Aug. 13, 1966 (div. 1987). BS, Concord State Tchrs. Coll., 1965. Libr. Cape Henlopen Sch. Dist., Lewes, Del., 1965—91; with Lily's Gift Shop, St. Petersburg, Fla., 1991—. Pres. Friends of Lewes Pub. Libr., 1986—90; chmn. exhibits Govs. Conf. Librs. and Info. Svcs., Dover, Del., 1978; mem. Gov.'s State Libr. Adv. Coun., 1987—91. Mem.: NEA, ALA, Del. Learning Resources Assn. (pres. 1976—77), Del. Library Assn. (pres. 1982—83), Sussex Help Orgn. for Resources Exch. (pres. 1984—85), Del. State Edn. Assn. Methodist. Business E-Mail: judyoffice2003@yahoo.com. E-mail: robertsjud@aol.com.

ROBERTS, KATHLEEN JOY DOTY, secondary education educator; b. Jamaica, N.Y., Apr. 19, 1951; d. Alfred Arthur and Helen Caroline (Sohl) Doty; m. Robert Louis Roberts, Nov. 24, 1974; children: Robert Louis, Michael Sean, Kathleen Meagan. BA in Edn., CUNY, 1972, MS in Spl. Edn., 1974; cert. advanced study in ednl. adminstrn., Hofstra U., 1982; Ednl. Specialist in Computing Tech. in Edn., Nova Southeastern U., 2003. Cert. sch. adminstrn., tchr. math., N.Y.; cert. N.Y. Dept. Mental Hygiene; lic. spl. edn. supr., ednl. dminstr., N.Y. Tchr. health conservation Woodside (N.Y.) Jr. H.S., 1973-77; coord. spl. edn. dept. Ridgewood (N.Y.) Jr. H.S., 1977-81; adminstrv. asst., health, compliance and mainstream coord. Grover Cleveland H.S., Ridgewood, 1981—, also coord. transition linkage, resource tchr. mentor, 1981—. Grant writer. Author: Closed Circuit Television and Other Devices for the Partially Sighted. 1971, National Society Colonial Daughters of the Seventeenth Century Lineage Book (Centennial Remembrance edit.), 1999, Universal Design in Online Learning Environments (Society for Information Technology and Teacher Education), 2002. Legis. chmn. Fairfield Jr. and Sr. H.S. PTA and Massapequa coun., 1987-92. Mem.: ACM, DAR, NEA, Internat. Soc. Tech. in Edn., N.Y. State Tchrs. Assn., Colonial Dames of the XVII Century, Colonial Daus. of the XVII Century (pres. 1985—91, nat. chmn. hist. activities com. 1988—91, registrar, historian Founders chpt. 1991—94, nat. councillor, publicity chmn. 1991—94, centennial com. 1994—96, registrar gen. nat. soc. 1997—2000, pres. 2000—), Pilgrim Edward Doty Soc. Republican. Home: 52 Hicksville Rd Massapequa NY 11758-5843 Office: Grover Cleveland HS 2127 Himrod St Flushing NY 11385-1299

ROBERTS, KATHLEEN MARY, school system administrator, retired; b. Syracuse, N.Y., Apr. 15, 1947; d. Casimer and Lorrayne Arletta (Molloy) Piegdon; m. James C. Roberts, June 29, 1968 (div. Sept. 1988). BA, Cen. State U., Edmond, Okla., 1968, MEd, 1971; PhD, U. Okla., 1977. Cert. tchr., prin., supt., Okla.; cert. supt., N.Y. Tchr. Putnam City Schs., Oklahoma City, 1960-72; reading specialist Moore (Okla.) Pub. Schs., 1973-74, Crooked Oak Pub. Schs., Oklahoma City, 1974-77, supt., 1990-95; rsch. assoc. Oklahoma City Pub. Schs., 1977-80; supt. Okla. Dept. Corrections, Oklahoma City, 1980-86, Healdton (Okla.) Pub. Schs., 1986-90, Piedmont (Okla.) Pub. Schs., 1995-98, ret., 1998; registered investment advisor McDonald & Assocs., 1998—. Contbr. articles to profl. publs. Bd. dirs. United Meth. Prism Ministry, Oklahoma City, 1986—, Children's Shelter, Ardmore, Okla., 1989-90; mem. State Vocat. Edn. Coun., Oklahoma City, 1980-85. Recipient citation Okla. State Senate, 1986. Mem. ASCD, Internat. Reading Assn., Am. Assn. Sch. Adminstrs., Okla. Assn. Sch. Adminstrs., Piedmont C. of C. (v.p. 1997—), Phi Delta Kappa, Alpha Chi, Kappa Delta Phi. Democrat. Roman Catholic. Avocations: furniture refinishing, reading, gardening.

ROBERTS, KEVIN LEE, township recreation administrator; b. Tampa, Fla., June 26, 1959; s. Horace E. Roberts and Helen M. (Novak) Amy; m. Kathy Ann Daugherty, May 6, 1990; children: Kevin Lee Jr., Kegan Dennis. BS, Wingate Coll., 1990; MS, Middle Tenn. State U., 1992. Landscape bus. owner Kevin Roberts, Inc., Largo, Fla., 1983-88; asst. football coach Wingate (N.C.) Coll., 1988-90; grad. teaching asst. Middle Tenn. State U., Murfreesboro, 1990-92; recreation supt. Cheltenham Twp. Parks and Recreation, Elkins Park, Pa., 1994. Guest editor: Tenn. Recreation and Pks. Assn., 1991. Recipient Presdl. Merit scholarship Wingate (N.C.) Coll., 1988, Morgan scholarship Wingate (N.C.) Coll., 1989. Mem. Am. Football Coaches Assn., Nat. Recreation and Parks Assn., Nat. Youth Sports Coaches Assn., Sports Sci. Inst., Pa. Recreation and Parks Soc. Republican. Baptist. Avocations: softball, golf, racquetball, football, coaching sports. Home: 3021 Raymond Ave Roslyn PA 19001-3507

ROBERTS, LINDA SUE MCCALLISTER, gifted and talented education educator; b. Huntington, W.Va., Aug. 1, 1947; d. Clifford Paul and Ruth Eloise (Triplett) McCallister; m. Harvey Monrce Roberts Jr., Aug. 28, 1965; children: Tiffany Ann Roberts Absten, Harvey Paul, Lorinda Sue. AB in Edn., Glenville (W.Va.) State Coll., 1968; MA in Home Econs. Edn., Marshall U., Huntington, 1976; cert. in gifted edn., Coll. Grad. Studies, Institute, W.Va., 1981. Tchr., dir. Cross Lanes (W.Va.) United Meth. Ch. Nursery Sch., 1976-78; tchr. of gifted Kanawha County Schs., Charleston, W.Va., 1978—. Coord. acad. decathlon U. Charleston, 1986-89; coord. state quiz bowl W.Va. State Coll., 1987-88; coord. county quiz bowl Kanawha County Schs., 1986—; judge county and state social studies fairs, 1990-92; evaluator W.Va. Future Problem Solving Program, 1987-92; U.S. del for edn. gifted children, 1991. Editor: Gifted Gazette, 1984-91. Day camp coord. Girl Scouts Am., Cross Lanes, 1976-78; cheerleading coord. Midget League Football, Nitro, W.Va., 1977-81. Named Alumni of Week, Glenville State Coll., 1991. Mem. Soviet Union Assn. for Edn. Gifted Children, World Coun. for Gifted and Talented Children, Fedn. Acad. Coaches and Team Sponsors, W.Va. Gifted Edn. Assn., W.Va. Acad. Coaches Assn. (v.p.

1993). Methodist. Avocations: cooking, travel, sewing, teaching about party foods, sponsoring cheerleaders. Home: 5337 Westbrook Dr Charleston WV 25313-1745 Office: Capital High Sch 1500 Greenbrier St Charleston WV 25311-1098

ROBERTS, LINDA TAYLOR, reading specialist; b. Stillwater, Okla., Dec. 19, 1954; d. Wayne Lewis and Peggy Jane (Radcliff) Taylor; 1 child, Taylor Zachary Roberts. BS in Elem. Edn., Okla. State U., 1977, M of Curriculum, 1979, Elem. Prin. Cert., 1993. Cert. std. elem. prin. K-8, std. reading specialist K-12, elem. edn. K-8, Okla., Nat. Bd. cert early childhood specialist. Reading specialist Ator Heights Elem./Owasso (Okla.) Pub. Schs., 1979—. Lit. reviewer Scholastic Pub. Co., 1993-94, mem. tchr. adv. bd. reading program, 1994-95. Contbr. articles to profl. publs. Active States Nat. Young Readers' Day celebration com., 1994-95; pres. Tulsa County Reading Coun. Young Authors' Com., 1994-95; invited by Citizen Ambassador Program as a reading edn. delegate to work with Russian Educators in Russia, 1993-94; mem. phonics task force com. Okla. State Dept. Edn., 1998-99. Mem. ASCD, Tulsa County Reading Coun., Okla. Reading Assn. (bd. dirs., chair Adminstr.'s award 1994-95, treas. 1995-96, v.p. elect 1996-97, v.p. 1997-98, state pres. 1998-99), Internat. Reading Assn. (subcom. to select outstanding tchr. educator), Assn. of Children and Learning Disabilities, Okla. Edn. Assn., Kappa Kappa Iota, Gamma Phi Beta. Avocations: painting, reading, promoting children's lit. Office: Owasso Pub Schs 1500 N Ash St Owasso OK 74055-4919 Home: 12312 E 81st St N Owasso OK 74055-3546

ROBERTS, LYNN ERNEST, theoretical physicist, educator; b. N.Y.C., Aug. 10, 1948; s. Lynn Ernest Roberts and Dorothy Elizabeth (Johnson) Woods; m. Brenda Joyce James, Aug. 1985; children: Natasha, Timothy, Lynn, Brendan, Ashleigh. BS in Physics, SUNY, Stony Brook, 1972; MS in Physics, Adelphi U., 1976, PhD in High Energy Theory, 1981. Teaching asst. Adelphi U., Garden City, N.Y., 1973-77, rsch. fellow, 1977-79, Ford Found., Atlanta, 1977-79; rsch. collaborator Brookhaven Nat. Lab., Upton, N.Y., 1979-81, rsch. assoc., 1981-83, physicist, 1983-85; assoc. prof. physics Lincoln U., Lincoln University, Pa., 1985-90, prof., 1991—, acting chair, 1992-94; chair, 1995—. Vis. rsch. scientist Argonne (Ill.) Nat. Lab., 1986-88; rschr. NSF, Washington, 1989-92, proposal reviewer, 1990, 93; specializing in lattice gauge theory, ultra-relativistic heavy ion collisions, phenomenology, relativistic field theory, math. physics, phase transitions and compositeness. Contbr. articles to sci. jours. Mem. Rotary (pres. Oxford, Pa. 1990), Inst. Advanced Sci. Studies (founding mem. and prin. officer). Home: 2501 Baynard Blvd Wilmington DE 19802-2961 Office: Lincoln U Dept Physics Wright Hall Lincoln University PA 19352

ROBERTS, MARGARET REYNOLDS, art educator; b. Nashville, Oct. 10, 1914; d. Elijah and Margaret (Sanders) Brugh; m. Morgan Boaz Reynolds, June 3, 1937 (dec. Mar. 1976); children: Margaret, Susanne, Morgan, Brugh, Liza, Elaine; m. William Clyde Roberts, Apr. 23, 1977. Student, Ward-Belmont Jr. Coll., Nashville, 1934; BA, Vanderbilt U., 1936; postgrad., William and Mary Coll., 1937-38, U. Wis. Tchr. decorating Watkins Inst., Nashville, 1965-70; tchr. Cheekwood, Nashville, 1973-74; tchr. period furniture Belle Meade Club, Nashville, 1994, 1994. One-woman exhibits include Vanderbilt U., 1986, 88, 94, 2001, Belmont U., 1989, Barnes & Noble, The French Shoppe, Belle Meade Plantation, 2002. Mem. Tenn. Art League, Le Petit Salon Literary Club (pres. 1979-80), Marsh Creek County Club, Centennial Club, Belle Meade Club, Kappa Alpha Theta. Roman Catholic. Avocations: tennis, golf, painter. Home and Office: 5100 Boxcroft Pl Nashville TN 37205-3702

ROBERTS, MAURA M. retired secondary school educator; b. Washington, Mar. 2, 1944; d. John E. and Mary M. (McCann) Martin; m. Charles D. Roberts, Aug. 15, 1987; 1 child, Caragh M. McLaughlin. AB, U. Mass. at Lowell, 1965; MAT, Salem State Coll., 1973. Cert. tchr. English, Mass. Tchr. English Hilton Head (S.C.) Prep Sch.; with Concord (Mass.)-Carlisle Sch. Dist.; tchr. English, instr. understanding learning course Concord-Carlisle Sch. Dist.; ret., 2002. Adj. instr. Fitchburg State Coll. Mem. edn. adv. bd. Orchard House Mus., Concord, 1994—.

ROBERTS, PATRICIA LEE, education educator; b. Coffeyville, Kans. d. Philip Lee Brighton and Lois Ethel Wortham; m. James E. Roberts, Oct. 5, 1953; children: James Michael, Jill Frances. BA, Calif. State U., Fresno, 1953, MA, 1964; EdD, U. Pacific, 1975. Lifetime tchg. diploma; sch. adminstrn. cert. Prof. edn. Calif. State U., Sacramento, 1969—. Cons. in field. Author (textbooks): Alphabet: A Handbook of ABC Books and Book Extensions for the Elementary Classroom, 2d edit., 1994, Integrating Language Arts and Social Studies for Kindergarten and Primary Children, 1996, Literature-Based History Activities for Children, Grades 4-8, 1997, Taking Humor Seriously in Children's Literature, 1997, Multicultural Friendship Stories and Activities for Children Ages 5-14, 1997, Literature-Based History Activities for Children, Grades 1-3, 1998, Family Values Through Children's Literature, Grades K-3, 1999, A Resource Guide for Elementary School Teaching, 5th edit., 2000, Family Values Through Children's Literature, Grades 4-6, 2003, A Guide for Developing an Interdisciplinary Thematic Unit, 3d edit., 2003, Language Arts and Environmental Awareness, 1998. Named Disting. Alumnae of Yr., U. Pacific, 1975-76. Mem. Internat. Reading Assn., Nat. Coun. Rsch. on English.

ROBERTS, PETER ALLEN, physical education educator; b. Buffalo, Feb. 20, 1943; s. Hobart Vosburgh and Bertha Jane (Ash) R.; m. Sherri Ann Olson, Sept. 12, 1986; 1 child, Sarah Jane. BS, Mich. State U., 1966, MA, 1970. Cert. tchr., Mich.; cert. water safety instr. trainer, lifeguard instr. trainer, CPR instr. trainer, standard first aid instr.-trainer. Educator Alpena (Mich.) Pub. Sch., 1966-69; prof. Wayne State U., Detroit, 1970—. Head coach swimming Wayne State U., Detroit, 1969-84; cons. in field. Bd. dirs. ARC, Detroit, chair aquatic com., 1972—, mem. aquatic enhancement adv. com., 1993; staff mem. Mich. Aquatic Sch., 1968—. Recipient Outstanding Svc. medal ARC, 1981, Fifteen Yrs. Outstanding Svc. award, 1985, Joan B. Warren award ARC, 1986, 30 Yr. Svc. Pin, ARC, 1992. Mem. AAHPERD, Mich. AHPERD, Coll. Swimming Coaches Assn., Phi Epsilon Kappa. Democrat. Methodist. Avocations: golf, swimming, racquetball, boating. Home: 23055 Beck Rd Novi MI 48374-3622 Office: Wayne State U 264 Matthaei Bldg Detroit MI 48202

ROBERTS, RANDOLPH WILSON, health and science educator; b. Scranton, Pa., Oct. 8, 1946; s. S. Tracy and Alecia Francis (Sullivan) R.; m. Martha Jeanne Burnite, July 12, 1969 (div. Dec. 1985); children: Gwendolyn Suzanne, Ryan Weylin; m. Ava Elaine Brown, June 17, 1989. AB in Biology, Franklin & Marshall Coll., 1968, MA in Geoscis., 1974; MS in Sci. Teaching, Am. U., 1977; MS in Counseling, Western Md. Coll., 1990; CHES, Towson State U., 1993; postgrad., U. Md., Johns Hopkins U., Loyola Coll., Md. Cert. tchr., counselor, health educator, health edn. specialist (CHES), tax cons. Tchr. Woodlawn Jr. High Sch., Balt., 1968-73, Deer Park Jr. High/Mid. Sch., Randallstown, Md., 1973-87, Franklin Mid. Sch., Reisterstown, Md., 1987-89; counselor and chmn. health/sci. dept. Balt. County Home & Hosp. Ctr., 1989—. Math and sci. tchr. Loyola H.S., Towson, Md., 1981-86, Talmudical Acad., Pikesville, Md., 1983-86; health educator Loyola Coll., Md., 1994; ednl. cons. Scott Fetzer Co., Chgo., 1981-86; founder, pres. Tax Assistance, Ltd., Owings Mills, Md., 1981—; curriculum cons. Balt. County Bd. Edn., Towson, 1977, 78, 93, 95, 96; founder Building Children, 1982—; photographer Am. Sch. Pictures, 1993-98. Author: Earth Sciences Workbook, 1979. Mem. Glyndon (Md.) Meth. Ch., 1993—, scholarship com. chmn., handbell choir mem., Christian edn. com., liturgist, mem. adminstrv. coun.; treas. Boy Scouts Am. Pack 315, Reis, Md., 1986-90, Webelos Den leader, 1987-90, advancement chmn., com. mem. Troop 315, 1990-93; founding ptnr. Bare Hills Investment Group, 1994—; founder, pres. Wellth Quest, Inc., 2002—. Mem.: AAHPERD, ACA, NEA, Am. Assn. Health Edn., Chesapeake Bay Found., Nature Conservancy, Balt. Rd. Runners, Eta Sigma Gamma, Mu Upsilon Sigma, Phi Delta Kappa. Avocations: travel, gardening, running, investing. Home: 9 Indian Pony Ct Owings Mills MD 21117-1210 Office: Home and Hosp Ctr 6229 Falls Rd Baltimore MD 21209-2120

ROBERTS, RICHARD, mechanical engineering educator; b. Atlantic City, N.J., Feb. 16, 1938; s. Harold and Marion (Hofman) R.; m. Rochelle S. Perelman, Oct. 2, 1960; children: Lori, Lisa, Scott. BSME, Drexel U., 1961; MSME, Lehigh U., 1962, PhD in Mech. Engring., 1964. Asst. prof. mech. engring. Lehigh U., Bethlehem, Pa., 1964-68, assoc. prof., 1968-75, prof., 1975—. Editor: Proceedings of the Thirteenth Nat. Symposium on Fracture Mechanics, 1980, ASME PVP Division's Design Handbook, Materials and Fabrication, Vol. III. Recipient W. Sparagen award Am. Welding Soc., 1972, Adams Meml. award, 1981. Home: 317 Bierys Bridge Rd Bethlehem PA 18017-1142 Office: Lehigh Univ MSE/200 W Packer Bethlehem PA 18015

ROBERTS, ROBERT CHARLES, secondary school educator; b. Passaic, N.J., June 2, 1940; s. Frank Douglas and Johanna (Cornelisse) Ungemah; Marian Elizabeth Spittel, Nov. 17, 1962 (widowed Oct. 1985); children: Donn, Lynn; m. Jane Francis Purdy, Apr. 5, 1986; children: Christopher, Dustin, B.J. BS, Montclair State U., N.J., 1963, MA, 1967. Cert. phys. edn. and health educator N.J.; supr., N.J., prin., N.J. Tchr. Clifton (N.J.) Bd. Edn., 1963-79, football coach, 1964-78, basketball coach, 1963-73, lacrosse coach, 1975-79, dir. phys. edn. health and athletics, 1979—. Exec. sec. No. N.J. Interscholastic League, 1984—; pres. N.J. Interscholastic Hockey League, 1982-83, N.J. lacrosse League, 1983-84. Lay Leader United Meth. Ch., Franklin Lakes, N.J., 1986-90. Mem. Nat. Interscholastic Athletic Adminstrn. Assn., AAHPERD, N.J. Prin. and Suprs. Assn., N.J. Edn. Assn., N.J. Assn. for Health, Phys. Edn., Recreation and Dance. Republican. Methodist. Avocation: golf. Office: Clifton High School 333 Colfax Ave Clifton NJ 07013-1701

ROBERTS, RUTH W. retired elementary school educator; b. Reading, Pa., Jan. 24, 1936; d. Jason W. and Margaret J. (Smith) White; m. James B. Steffy, Dec. 23, 1956 (div. Aug. 1974) ; m. George R. Roberts, Sept. 8, 1995; children: James M., John W., Susan E. BS in Elem. Edn., West Chester (Pa.) U., 1956; MA, Commonwealth of Pa., 1985. Tchr. Selinsgrove (Pa.) Area Schs., 1965-66, Lewisburg (Pa.) Area Sch. Dist., 1966—99. Curriculum cluster leader Lewisburg Area Sch. Dist., 1984—. Mem. NEA, Pa. Edn. Assn., MENSA, PASR (Union County chpt. v.p.). Avocations: cross stitch, reading, traveling. Home: 156 Redtail Ln Lewisburg PA 17837-9615

ROBERTS, SAMUEL ALDEN, secondary school educator; b. Kansas City, Kans., Oct. 30, 1930; s. Elester and Sadie Lillian (Lewis) R.; m. Sallie Senora, Aug. 26, 1962; children: Sadie, Alden, Samuel Jr., William, Tyrone AB, Knoxville Coll., 1954; MDiv, Interdenominational Theol. Ctr, 1960; MS, Ind. State U., 1974; DMin, Chgo. Theol. Sem., 1981; EdS, Ind. State U., 1986. Cert. secondary English tchr., secondary prin. Supt. Lott Carey Bapt. Mission Sch., Haiti, 1964-68, Hardy Jr. High Sch., Chattanooga; tchr. Wirt High Sch., Gary, Ind.; asst. prin. Elston Jr. High Sch., Michigan City, Ind., athletic dir., 1976-80; tchr. Rogers High Sch., Michigan City; lang. arts tchr. Bailly M. Sch., Gary, Ind. Bible tchr., lectr. Mem. Fedn. Block Units of Urban League N.W. Ind. (past pres.), Fedn. Block Clubs, Nat. Trust, U.S. Holocaust Mus., Smithsonian Instn., Phi Delta Kappa (pres.), Alpha Phi Alpha. Home: 2721 W 65th Pl Merrillville IN 46410-2872

ROBERTS, SANDRA MILLER, middle school language arts educator; b. Owensboro, Ky., Apr. 30, 1947; d. Everett E. and Virginia Frances (Oldham) Miller; m. John Clayton Roberts, Nov. 20, 1941; children: Jason Eric, Ryan Alan, Gavin Clayton, Gretchen Elizabeth. BS in Spanish, French and English, Ky. Wesleyan U., 1969; postgrad., Western Ky. U., 1988, 92. 8th grade Spanish and French tchr. So. Jr. H.S., Owensboro, 1969-71; 8th grade lang. arts tchr. Daviess County Mid. Sch., Owensboro, 1988—, portfolio cluster leader, 1991-92, lang. arts curriculum coord., 1993-95; tchr. 6th grade lang. arts Coll. View Mid. Sch., Owensboro, 1995—. Mem. Christian Ch. (Disciples Of Christ). Avocations: travel, cooking, church, family. Home: 8328 State Route 815 Owensboro KY 42301-9429

ROBERTS, SCOTT OWEN, exercise physiologist, educator; b. San Anselmo, Calif., June 3, 1958; s. William O. and Patricia M. (Swall) R.; m. Julia M. Westman, July 28, 1984; children: Andrew Owen, Daniel James. BA, Calif. State U., Chico, 1986; MS, Calif. State U., Sacramento, 1988; postgrad., U. N.Mex., 1991—. Fitness dir. Willow Creek and Rollingwood Tennis and Fitness Ctrs., Sacramento, 1986-88; program dir. Roseville (Calif.) Hosp., 1988-90; gen. mgr. Chart Sports Medicine Clinic, Sacramento, 1990-91; teaching asst., rsch. asst. U. N.Mex., Albuquerque, 1991-92; clin. exercise physiologist Lovelace Med. Ctr., Albuquerque, 1992—; pres. Scott O. Roberts Enterprises, Ltd., 1992—. Vis. instr. Calif. State U., Chico, Sacramento, U. N.Mex.; fitness cons. Author: Developing Strength in Children, 1993. Bd. dirs. Am. Heart Assn., Sacramento, 1990-91; program com. N.Mex. Am. Heart Assn., 1992—. Grantee Nat. Assn. Sport and Phys. Edn., 1992, Lovelace Found., 1993. Mem. Am. Coll. Sports Medicine (cert. exercise program dir., exercise specialist, exercise test technologist, ad hoc youth clinics in sports medicine com. 1992—), Nat. Strength and Conditioning Assn. Avocations: staying fit, writing. Office: Lovelace Med Ctr Dept Cardiology 5400 Gibson Blvd SE Dept Albuquerque NM 87108-4763 Home: 68 Plumwood Ct Chico CA 95928-4024 Address: 68 Plumwood Ct Chico CA 95928-4024

ROBERTS, SYLVIA DALE, elementary school educator; b. Stockton, Calif., Sept. 18, 1956; d. Wayne LeRoy and Katherine Adelia (von Glahn) Bonham; m. Robin Michael Roberts, Aug. 5, 1978; children: Terra Lynn, Tamara Lee. AA, San Joaquin Community Coll., 1976; BA in Psychology with high honors, Fresno Pacific Coll., 1977, MA in Edn., 1981. Classroom tchr. Hanford Elem. Sch. Dist., Calif., 1978—99, acting asst. prin., mentor tchr., 1991—94, literacy coach, 1999—. Adj. faculty Fresno (Calif.) Coll., 1989-91. Republican. Baptist. Home: 2786 Chestnut St Hanford CA 93230-1201 Office: Hanford Elem Sch Dist PO Box G-1067 Hanford CA 93232

ROBERTS, WILLIAM WOODRUFF, JR., applied mathematics educator, researcher; b. Huntington, W.Va., Oct. 8, 1942; s. William Woodruff Sr. and Sarah Louise (Huddleston) R.; m. Linda Louise Nelson, June 17, 1967; children: William Woodruff III, David Christopher. SB, MIT, 1964, PhD, 1969. Asst. prof. Sch. Engring. and Applied Sci. U. Va., Charlottesville, 1969-74, assoc. prof. Sch. Engring. and Applied Sci., 1974-82, prof. Sch. Engring. and Applied Sci., 1982-92, dir. math.-computational modeling lab., 1990—, Commonwealth prof. engring. and applied sci., 1992—. Vis. scientist Kapteyn Astron. Inst., U. Groningen, The Netherlands, 1974; NORDITA guest prof. Stockholms Observatorium, Saltsjabaden, Sweden, 1974-75; pres. Computational Modeling Technologies, Inc., 1991—. Contbr. over 100 papers to profl. jours.; author 5 books. Mem. AAAS, AIAA, Am. Astron. Soc., Am. Inst. Physics, Am. Men and Women Sci. (div. dynamical astronomy), Fiber Soc., Internat. Astron. Union, Soc. Indsl. and Applied Math., Va. Acad. Scis., Sigma Xi. Office: U Va Dept Mech & Aerospace Engring Charlottesville VA 22904-4746

ROBERTS-DEMPSEY, PATRICIA E. secondary school educator; Tchr. Challenger High Sch., Spanaway, Wash., 1969—. Recipient Wash. State Tchr. of Yr. award, 1991-91. Office: Challenger HS 18020 B St E Spanaway WA 98387-8316

ROBERTS-HARVEY, BONITA, elementary education educator; b. Detroit, June 24, 1947; d. Walter James and Mattie Louise Hall; father, Dolphus Hall Sr.; 1 child, Paula Renee. BA, Grand Valley State U., 1974; cert. in continuing edn., Western Mich. U., 1987; MA in Edn. Leadership, Mich. State U., 1998. Art specialist Jenison (Mich.) Pub. Schs., 1974—, JEA pub. rels. rep., 1994—. Visual/performing artist Summer at Arts Place-Grand Rapids C.C., 1980-92; cons. art edn. Detroit Inst. Art, 1988; adj. instr. Grand Rapids C.C., 2000-. Bd. dirs., performing artist Robeson Players, Grand Rapids, Mich., 1973-94, Cmty. Cir. Theatre, Grand Rapids, 1981-84, 97—, Coun. Performing Arts for Children, Grand Rapids, 1981-88, Grand Rapids Art Mus., 1997; active First Cmty. African Meth. Episc. Ch., NAACP. Mem. ASCD, NEA (del., regional rep.), Nat. Fine Arts Caucus, Nat. Art Edn. Assn., Mich. Art Edn. Assn., Mich. Edn. Assn. (tri-county pub. rels. 1994-95, regional del.), Mich. Alliance Arts Edn., Nat. Mus. Women in Arts, Jenison Edn. Assn. (pub. rels. 1993—), Delta Sigma Theta, Delta Kappa Gamma. Avocation: performing/visual arts advocate. Office: Jenison Pub Schs 8375 20th Ave Jenison MI 49428-9230

ROBERTSON, JACK CLARK, accounting educator; b. Marlin, Tex., Apr. 27, 1943; s. Rupert Cook and Lois Lucille (Rose) R.; m. Caroline Susan Hughes, Oct. 23, 1965; children: Sara Ellen, Elizabeth Hughes. Student, Rice U., 1961-63; BBA with honors, U. Tex., Austin, 1965, M in Profl. Acctg., 1967; PhD, U. N.C., 1970. CPA, Tex. Tax acct. Humble Oil and Refining Co., Houston, 1964-65; auditor Peat, Marwick, Mitchell & Co., Houston, 1965-66; acct. Wade, Barton, Marsh CPAs, Austin, Tex., 1966-67; from asst. prof. to prof. emeritus U. Tex., Austin, 1970—2003, prof. emeritus, 2003—. Acad. assoc. Coopers & Lybrand, N.Y.C., 1975-76; acad. fellow U.S. Securities and Exchange Commn. Office of the Chief Acct., Washington, 1982-83; Erskine fellow U. Canterbury, Christchurch, New Zealand, 1988; tng. the trainers instr. Vilnius, Lithuania, 1993; lectr. in field. Contbr. articles to profl. jours. Lay reader St. Matthews Episcopal Ch., Austin, 1972-75, mem. vestry, 1973-75, 77-79, 84-86, treas., 1974-75, 77-96, chmn. bldg. fund, 1976-87, chmn. everymen. canvass, 1980, sr. warden, 1986; del. Diocese of Tex. Coun., 1993-95; Trompetista El Grupo Valor Latino, lector laico, 2000—, Miembro comite del obispo Iglesia San Francisco de Asis, 2000—03, treas., 2002-03. Mem. AICPA, Am. Acctg. Assn. (sec.-treas. auditing sect. 1976-77, v.p. auditing sect. 1977-78, pres. auditing sect. 1978-79, chmn. auditing stds. com. 1980-81, chmn. SEC liaison com. 1983-84, historian auditing sect. 1999-2001), Tex. Soc. CPAs (vice-chmn., profl. ethics com. 1986-94, 95-97, Presdl. citation 1994), Assn. Cert. Fraud Examiners (regent emeritus, cert.), Phi Kappa Phi, Beta Gamma Sigma, Beta Alpha Psi. E-mail: jrobertson5@austin.rr.com.

ROBERTSON, LINDA F. educational adminstrator; b. Powell, Wyo., July 15, 1946; d. Lee and Dorothy W. (Schweighart) Brunk; m. Darrell G. Robertson II, July 2, 1965; 1 child, Michelle. BA in elem. edn., U. Wyo., 1968; MA in edn. adminstrn., U. Akron, 1978; postgrad., Kent State U. Cert. supt., elem. prin., secondary prin., Ohio. Elem. prin. Aurora (Ohio) City Schs., asst. supt., high sch. prin.; dir. Ctr. for Internat. and Intercultural Edn., Kent State U. Named Ohio Prin. of Yr., 1992. Mem.: Kappa Delta Pi, Phi Delta Kappa. Home: 8220 Timber Trl Chagrin Falls OH 44023-5071

ROBERTSON, MARY VIRGINIA, retired elementary education educator; b. Lincoln, Nebr., Oct. 1, 1925; d. Dean Leroy and Anna Charlotte (Boge) R. AB in Philosophy and Psychology, U. Nebr., Lincoln, 1949, BS in Elem. Edn., 1953; postgrad., U. Toronto, Ont., Can., 1949. Cert. elem. tchr., Nebr. Country sch. tchr. Lancaster County schs., Nebr., 1943-44, Otoe County schs., Palmyra, Nebr., 1944-45; 3d-5th grade tchr. Palmyra Schs., 1945-46; 3d grade tchr. Valley (Nebr.) Schs., 1953-57, Lincoln Pub. Schs., 1957-81; ret. Leader workshop in field; math. coord. Riley Elem. Sch., Lincoln, 1970-71. Author pamphlet A Letter for You, 1954. Mem. NEA, AAUW, Nebr. State Edn. Assn., Nat. Coun. Math. Tchrs., Am. Child Edn. Internat., Belmont PTA (life), Eastern Star, Lincoln Women's Club. Methodist. Avocations: reading, cats, rocks, bridge, writing children's stories.

ROBERTSON, PATRICIA AILEEN, adult and geriatric nurse practitioner; b. Washington, Dec. 15, 1950; d. John Thomas and Virginia Aileen (Parker) Dickmeyer; m. Lee Eiden; children: Jason Earle, Alyssa Michelle. BS, U. Mass., 1973; BSN with honors, George Mason U., 1982, MSN, 1999. RN, Va.; cert. adult and geriatric nurse practitioner; ARNP Va., Wash. Staff nurse, perdiem intravenous therapist Inova Fairfax Hosp., St. Joseph's Hosp., Tacoma Gen. Hosp., Tacoma; pediatric nurse, health educator Western Clinic, Tacoma; nurse cons., intravenous therapy educator Pharmacy Corp. Am., Seattle; developer, dir. Careline health adv. and case mgmt. program Weyerhaeuser, Tacoma; cons. Home IV Therapy Agys.; cons. UR Case Mgmt. Olympic Counseling Svcs., Tacoma; program developer Coord. Adolescent Assessment Ctr.; adult and geriatric nurse practitioner Arlington (Va.) Free Clinic, Fairfax County Pub. Safety Occupl. Health Clinic; staff nurse vascular access team INOVA Fairfax (Va.) Hosp. Adult and geriatric nurse practitioner Chest Pain Observation Unit INOVA Fairfax Hosp.; developer, AIDS edn. program for high sch. students and corp. employee, 1990; cons. alzheimer's dementia unit Weatherly Inn, 1992; speaker in field. Vol. NP Arlington Free Clin. Named Pierce County Nurse of Yr. nominee, 1986. Mem. ANA, Am. Coll. Nurse Practitioners (task force on End of Life/palliative care), Am. Coll. Nurse Practitioners in Women's Health, Am. Acad. Pain Mgmt., Nat. League Nursing, Nat. Assn. Vascular Access Networks, Wash. State Nurses Assn., Intravenous Nurses Soc., South Sound AIDS Network, Healthcare Providers Coun. Wash., Va. Coun. Nurse Practitioners, Sigma Theta Tau. Achievements include design and development of peripheral and central venous access device charts for teaching to patients and staff; designed and coordinated first national conference on caring for AIDS patients in the long term care setting. Home and Office: 8621 Cherry Dr Fairfax VA 22031-2136 E-mail: proberts@cco.net.

ROBERTSON, PIEDAD F. college president; BA, MA, U. Miami. Pres. Bunker Hill C.C., 1988-91; sec. edn. State of Mass., Boston, 1991-95; pres., supt. Santa Monica (Calif.) Coll., 1995—. Named Woman of Yr. Santa Monica YMCA, 1999. Office: Santa Monica Coll Office of President 1900 Pico Blvd Santa Monica CA 90405-1628*

ROBERTSON, SAMUEL HARRY, III, transportation safety research engineer, educator; b. Phoenix, Oct. 2, 1934; s. Samuel Harry and Doris Bryle (Duffield) R.; m. Nancy Jean Bradford, 1954 (div. 1989); children: David Lyle, Pamela Louise; m. Linda Faye O'Neill, 1999. BS, Ariz. State U., 1956; D in Aviation Tech. (hon.), Embry-Riddle Aero. U., 1972. Registered profl. engr.; cert. comml. pilot--fixed wing, rotary wing, glider and balloon. Chief hazards divsn. Aviation Safety Engring. and Rsch., Phoenix, 1960-70; pres. Robertson Rsch. Engrs., 1960-70; rsch. prof., dir. Safety Ctr. Coll. Engring. and Applied Scis., Ariz State U., Tempe, 1970-79; pres. Robertson Rsch. Inc., 1970-86, Robertson Aviation Inc., 1977-86, Internat. Ctr. for Safety Edn., 1982-96; pres., CEO Robertson Rsch. Group, Inc., Tempe, 1986—, Robertson Aviation, LLC, Tempe, 1995—. Airplane design and accident investigator, 1961—; instr. aircrash investigation Internat. Ctr. Safety Edn., 1960—, inst. aerospace safety U. So. Calif., 1962-70, Armed Forces Inst. Pathology, 1970-90, Dept. Transp. Safety Inst., 1970-89; pres. Pine Springs Ranch, Inc, 1976—; adv. bd. Rio Salado Bank, Tempe, 1985-94; mem. adv. coun. Ctr. Aerospace Safety Edn., Embry-Riddle Aero. U., Daytona Beach, Fla., 1986—, trustee, 1992—; pres. Devil Dog Rsch., Inc., 1990—, Robertson Land & Cattle Inc., 1990—; comml. pilot, 1957—. Contbr. over 85 articles to profl. jours.; patentee applying plastic to paper, fuel system safety check valves, crash resitant fuel system, safety aircraft seats; holder FAA STC's various fuel systems, fuel system components; designer, developer, mfr. crash resistant fuel systems for airplanes, helicopters, championship racing cars. Pilot USAF, 1956-60, Ariz. Army NG 1960-61, 70-74, Ariz. Air NG, 1961-69. Recipient Contbns.

Automotive Racing Safety award CNA, 1976, Adm. Luis De Florez Internat. Flying Safety award, 1969, Cert. Commendation Nat. Safety Coun., 1969, Gen. W. Spruance award for safety edn., SAFE Soc., 1982; holder Nat. Speed Record for one class of drag racing car, 1955-62, 5 nat. records for flying model aircraft, 1950-56; named to Ariz. Aviation Hall of Fame, 1996, OX5 Aviation Pioneers Hall of Fame, 1996, U.S. Army Aviation Hall of Fame, 2001, Army Aviation Assn. Am. Hall of Fame, 2001. Mem. AIAA, Internat. Soc. Air Safety Investigators (Jerome Lederer Aircraft Accident Investigation award, 1981), Aerospace Med. Assn., Exptl. Aircraft Assn., Soc. Automotive Engrs., Soc. Exptl. Test Pilots, Am. Helicopter Soc., Nat. Fire Protection Assn., Aircraft Owners and Pilots Assn., U.S. Automobile Club (tech. com.). Home: PO Box 58 Pine Springs Ranch Williams AZ 86046 Office: 1024 E Vista Del Cerro Dr Tempe AZ 85281-5709

ROBERTSON, SAMUEL LUTHER, JR., special education educator, therapist, researcher; b. Houston, Apr. 28, 1940; s. Sam L. and Portia Louise (Burns) R.; children: Samuel Luther IV, Sean Lee (dec.), Ryan William, Susan Elizabeth (dec.), Henry Philmore. BS, McMurry U., 1969; MA, Hardin-Simmons U., 1973; PhD, U. Tex., 1993. Cert. tchr., adminstr., counselor, prevention specialist, Tex.; lic. chem. dependency counselor, lic. clin. mental health counselor, advanced addiction counselor., Tex. Instr., coach, athletic dir. Tex. and La. schs., 1969-94; social worker, supr. Children's Protective Svcs., Abilene, Tex., 1978-79; instr., adminstr. Harlandale Sch. Dist., San Antonio, 1980-84, 87-90; adminstr. night sch. Harlandale Ind. Sch. Dist., San Antonio, 1988-89; instr. Edgewood Ind. Sch. Dist., San Antonio, 1985-87; developer, instr., integrated unit program San Antonio, 1990—; CEO The Educative Inst., San Antonio, 1992—. CEO Educative Therapeutic Processes, 1972—; co-founder, dir. Inst. Organizational Personal Devel.; adj. prof. San Antonio Coll.; lectr. U. Tex. at San Antonio. Author: (play) The Challenged, 1965, Dream Poems, 1998; (poem) Trains in the Night, 1969; (screenplay) Tom & Jane, 2000; dir. (film) Tom & Jane, 2003. State co-chmn. Youth for Kennedy-Johnson, Tex., 1960; mem. W. Tex. Dem. Steering Com., Abilene, 1962-63; founding dir. Way Off Broadway Cmty. Theater, Eagle Pass, Tex., 1971-72; founding bd. dirs. Battered Women's Shelter, Abilene, 1978-79; v.p. bd. dirs. Mental Health Assn., San Antonio, 1980-83, bd. dirs Palmer Drug Abuse Program, San Antonio, 1985-87; pres., bd. dir. Alcoholic Rehab. Ctr., 1985-86, 1987-92; vice-chmn. Civilian and Mil. Addictive Programs, San Antonio, 1991-92; author, implementer Cmty. Vitalization Program, 1994—; mem. vestry St. George Episcopal Ch., mem. sch. bd., St. George Sch.1999—02; mem. standards chair Tex. Certification Bd. of Addiction Profls.; chmn. 1999—01. Named Tchr. of Yr. Southside Ind. Sch. Dist., San Antonio, 1970-71, Harlandale Alternative Ctr., San Antonio, 1987-88; Vol. of Yr., Mental Health Assn., San Antonio, 1982, Alcoholic Rehab. Ctr., San Antonio, 1992-93. Mem. ACA, NEA, Am. Mental Health Counseling Assn., Tex. State Tchrs. Assn., Am. Ednl. Rsch. Assn., Am. Assn. Sch. Adminstrs. Internat. Consortium Reciprocity Commn. Nat. Alcoholism and Drug Abuse Counselors, N.Mex. Mental Health Counselors Assn., N.Mex. Profl. Counselors Assn., Phi Kappa Phi, Kappa Delta Pi. Episcopalian. Avocations: reading, writing, travel, theater, sports. Office: Educative Therapeutic Processes 339 E Hildebrand Ave San Antonio TX 78212-2412

ROBERTSON, SUSAN JOYCE COE, special education educator; b. Pinedale, Wyo., May 22, 1954; d. Cecil James and Geraldine Ada (Greene) Coe; children: Jamie Michelle, Mark David. BS in Edn., Chadron (Nebr.) State Coll., 1976, MS in Counseling and Guidance, 1977; specialist in emotionally disturbed, U. No. Colo., 1982. Cert. crisis prevention intervention master trainer, peer mediation facilitator. Elem. tchr. pub. schs., Alliance, Nebr., 1976-77; social worker Community Action, Cheyenne, Wyo., 1978-79; Chpt. 1 tchr. Laramie County Sch. Dist. 1, Cheyenne, 1979-81, elem. tchr., 1981-84, tchr. severely emotionally disturbed, 1984-89, cons., specialist for severely emotionally disturbed, 1989-92, behavior intervention team specialist, 1992-95, tchr. learning disabled, 1995-97, tchr. behavior lab., 1997—. Mem. Dist. Placement Com., 1981-92. Mem. Cmty. Commn., Cheyenne, 1981—92; basketball coach YMCA, 1994; competitive soccer asst., 1999—2001; elder Presbyn. Ch., 1996—97. Mem.: PEO, NEA, Cheyenne Tchr. Edn. Assn., Wyo. Edn. Assn., Coun. Exceptional Children (faculty advisor 1991), Am. Guidance and Counseling Assn. Methodist. Avocations: reading, swimming, racquetball, music. Home: 5425 Gateway Dr Cheyenne WY 82009-4035 Office: 6000 Education Dr Cheyenne WY 82009-3991

ROBERTSON, SUZANNE MARIE, primary education educator; b. Canton, Ohio, Nov. 21, 1944; d. Jules Michael and Emma Louise (Olmar) Franzen; m. William K. Robertson, June 30, 1973 (dec. 1979). BS in Early Childhood Edn., Kent State U., 1966; M in Early Childhood Edn., So. Conn. U., 1976; postgrad., Fairfield U. and U. Bridgeport, 1981-82. Kindergarten tchr. Ridgefield (Conn.) Bd. Edn., 1966-97, Internat. Sch. Basel, Switzerland, 1993-94; kindergarten post The Am. Internat. Sch. of Vilnius, Lithuania, 2000—. Children's gymnastics instr. Ridgefield (Conn.) YMCA, 1982-83, Sherman Parks and Recreation, Conn., 1983-85; com. mem., facilitator Young Writer's Conf., Ridgefield, Conn., 1996; storyteller for two-yr.-olds Danbury (Conn.) Jr. Libr., 2000; presenter in field. Toy designer. Campaign vol. Cancer Fund of Am., Sherman, 1980-81. Recipient Honorable mention Learning Mag., 1989, Profl. Best Teaching awards. Mem. NEA, Tchrs. Assn. Supporting Children (chmn. 1986-89, Fairfield County pub. rels. com. 1986-89), Conn. Edn. Assn., Internat. Platform Assn., Sherman Hist. Soc., Phi Delta Kappa (historian 1989-90, rsch. rep. 1990-91). Avocations: collecting children's books, water color painting, photography, winter skiing. Address: care Am Embassy Vilnius Akmenu g 6 2600 Vilnius Lithuania Fax: (370) (2) 22 10 31.

ROBERTSON, SYLVIA DOUGLAS, middle school educator; b. Lynchburg, Va., June 25, 1952; d. Alfred Lynch and Rena (Irvin) Douglas; m. Lawrence Edward Robertson, Apr. 26, 1975 (div. May 1985); 1 child, Lawrence Edward Jr. BA, Cedar Crest Coll., 1974; MEd, Lynchburg Coll., 1990. Cert. tchr., Va. Tchr. 7th grade Big Island (Va.) Elem. Sch., 1974-89; tchr., team leader 7th grade Bedford (Va.) Mid. Sch., 1989—, tchr., grade level chairperson 7th grade, 1993-94. Facilitator Police, Pub. Educators and Peer Counselors Utilizing the Leadership of Students at Risk, Bedford, Va., 1991-92; vol. Free Clinic Ctrl. Va., Inc., Lynchburg, Va., 1993. Mem. Nat. Coun. Tchrs. Math., Nat. Sci. Tchrs. Assn., Nat. Energy Edn. Devel. Project, Bedford County Edn. Assn., Va. State Reading Assn., Va. Mid. Sch. Assn., Piedmont Area Reading Coun., Kappa Delta Pi, Phi Delta Kappa, Alpha Delta Kappa (corr. sec. 1993—), Alpha Kappa Alpha. Avocations: reading, drawing, walking. Home: Rte 7 Box 122 Arbor Ct Madison Heights VA 24572 Office: Bedford Mid Sch 503 Longwood Ave Bedford VA 24523-3401

ROBERTSON, WANDA SUE, secondary school educator; b. Martin, Tenn., Jan. 24, 1949; d. Charles Eugene and Ruby Velma (Edwards) Bailey; m. Gene Revelle Robertson, June 13, 1970 (div. Jan. 1984); 1 child, Alecia Revelle. BS in Edn., U. Tenn., Martin, 1970, MS in Math. Edn., 1974. Cert. secondary math. tchr., Tenn. Computer operator U. Tenn., 1969-72, instr. math., 1981-88; tchr. math. Milan (Tenn.) High Sch., 1972-81, Dyersburg (Tenn.) High Sch., 1988—. Newsletter editor Parents without Ptnrs., 1988—. Named Outstanding H.S. Tchr., U. Tenn., Martin. Mem. Nat. Coun. Tchrs. Math., Tenn. Edn. Assn., Delta Kappa Gamma. Democrat. Baptist. Avocations: travel, reading, bicycling, granddaughter. Home: 2502 Stoneville St Dyersburg TN 38024-5230 Office: Dyersburg High Sch Hwy 51 By-Pass Dyersburg TN 38024

ROBERTSON, WYNDHAM GAY, university official, journalist; b. Salisbury, N.C., Sept. 25, 1937; d. Julian Hart and Blanche Williamson (Spencer) R. AB in Econs., Hollins Coll., Roanoke, Va., 1958. Rsch. asst. Standard Oil Co., N.Y.C., 1958-61; rschr. Fortune Mag., N.Y.C., 1961-67, assoc. editor, 1968-74, bd. of editors, 1974-81, asst. mng. editor, 1981-86; bus. editor Time Mag., N.Y.C., 1982-83; v.p. comm. U. N.C., Chapel Hill, 1986-96. Bd. dirs. Media Gen. Inc. Contbr. numerous articles to Fortune Mag. Trustee Thomas S. Kenan Inst. for the Arts, U. NC Health Care Sys., Hollins U. Recipient Gerald M. Loeb Achievement award, U. of Conn., 1972. Mem. Phi Beta Kappa. Episcopalian.

ROBERTSON-THORN, KAREN, middle school educator; b. Morgantown, W.Va., Nov. 18, 1954; d. Frederick Grey and Deloris Jean (Burnside) Robertson; m. Martin Albert Thorn, Apr. 15, 1978. BA in Psychology, W.Va. U., 1976, MA in Spl. Edn., 1981, postgrad., 1994. Learning disabilities tchr. Morgantown (W.Va.) H.S., 1981-86, Cheat Lake Jr. H.S., Morgantown, 1986-90; educator dual diagnosis unit Chestnut Ridge Psychiat. Hosp., Morgantown, 1990; reading educator Cheat Lake Jr. H.S., Suncrest Jr. H.S., Morgantown, 1990-92; learning disabilities tchr. Univ. H.S., Morgantown, 1992; reading educator South Jr. H.S., Morgantown, 1992—. Mem. local sch. improvement coun. South Jr. H.S., Morgantown, 1994—, sch. based assistance team, 1994, v.p. faculty senate, 1994-95, curriculum com., 1994-95. Aerobics instr. Monongalia County Cmty. Schs., Cheat Lake Sch., 1989-92; mem. United We Stand Am., Morgantown, 1992—. Named Monongalia County Tchr. of Yr., Morgantown, 1985-86. Mem. W.Va. State Reading Coun., Internat. Reading Assn., Psi Chi, Alpha Delta Kappa (Julia Kovach Meml. scholar 1985), Phi Delta Kappa (Monongalia County Tchr. of Month 1995). Avocations: aerobics, basketball, showing persian cats. Office: South Jr HS 500 E Parkway Dr Morgantown WV 26501-6839

ROBERTS-PARAST, ANN TALBOT, English and foreign language educator; b. Roanoke, Va. d. David Charles and Audrey Louise (Cassell) Roberts; m. Rudy M. Parast, Feb. 22, 1980; 1 child, Layla Ann. BA in French, Tulane U.; BA in Fgn. Lang. Edn., U. New Orleans; degree in translating and interpreting, profl. diploma, U. Paris; M English, U. Paris VIII; MA in French, ABD in Comparative Lit., U. Wash. Freelance translator, interpreter, English instr., Paris, 1968-72; French/English instr. pub. and pvt. schs., New Orleans, 1972-78; translator, adminstrv. asst. Ivory Coast Embassy, Washington, 1974-75; tchg. asst. in French U. Wash., Seattle, 1978-83; French tchr. Marine Mil. Acad., Harlingen, Tex., 1983-84, Harlingen H.S., 1984-89; English instr. Tex. State Tech. Coll., 1989—. Freelance translator, interpreter, New Orleans and Seattle, 1975—; French/English interpreter, 1994—; placement of fgn. exch. students, 1990—; mgr., writer Profl. Resume and Writing Svc., Harlingen, 1989—. Contbr. articles to profl. publs. Former bd. dirs. Jr. Peacemaker Club, Harlingen; former bd. dirs. Tex. French Symposium. French Govt. scholar, Vichy, France, 1983. Mem. DAR (chair good citizens com. 1997—), Tex. C.C. Tchrs. Assn., Alliance Française of Lower Rio Grande, Nat. Coun. Tchrs. English. Mem. Baha'i Faith. Home: 2402 E Adams Ave Harlingen TX 78550-2723 Office: Tex State Tech Coll Dept English Harlingen TX 78550 E-mail: eroberts@tstu.edu.

ROBEY, SHERIE GAY SOUTHALL GORDON, secondary education educator, consultant; b. Washington, July 7, 1954; d. James Edward and Gene Elizabeth (Gray) Southall; children: m. Robert Jean Claude Robey; children: Michael Aaron Gordon, Robert Eugene Robey, Jamie Lea Robey. BS, U. Md., 1976; MA in Edn. and Human Devel., George Washington U., 1988. Tchr. Esperanza Mid. Sch., Hollywood, Md., 1980-84, Chopticon High Sch., Morganza, Md., 1984—. Coach Odyssey of the Mind, 1985-95; sponsor Future Tchrs. Am., Morganza, 1990-2002, S.H.O.P./S.A.D.D., Morganza, 1990-2002; cons. Ednl. Cosn., Waldorf, 1980—; pres. BNA Swim Team, 1990-2002; driver edn. classroom and lab instr. Greg's Driving Sch., 1996—. Parish com. Good Shepherd United Meth. St. Church, 1999. Mem. Ednl. Rep. Assn. St. Mary's County, Lighthouse Hist. Soc. Methodist. Avocations: swimming, writing, visiting lighthouses, collection miniature lighthouses. Home and Office: 11181 Carroll Dr Waldorf MD 20601-2656 Business E-Mail: rrobey@olg.com. E-mail: lightbeacon2@yahoo.com.

ROBIN, CLARA NELL (CLAIRE ROBIN), English language educator; b. Harrisonburg, Va., Feb. 19, 1945; d. Robert Franklin and Marguerite Ausherman (Long) Wampler; m. Phil Camden Branner, June 10, 1967 (div. May 1984); m. John Charles Robin, Nov. 22, 1984 (div. Dec. 1990). BA in English, Mary Washington Coll., 1967; MA in English, James Madison U., 1974; postgrad., Jesus Coll., Cambridge, Eng., 1982, Princeton U., 1985-86, Auburn U., 1988, U. No. Tex., 1990-91. Cert. tchr. English, French, master cert., Tex. Tchr. 7th grade John C. Myers Intermediate Sch., Broadway, Va., 1967-68; tchr. 10th grade Waynesville (Mo.) H.S., 1968-70; tchr. 6th, 7th, 8th grades Mary Mount Jr. Sch., Santa Barbara, Calif., 1970-72; tchr. 9th grade Forest Meadow Jr. H.S. Richardson (Tex.) Ind. Sch. Dist., 1972-78, tchr. 10th grade Lake Highlands H.S., 1972-84; tchr. 11th, 12th grades Burleson HS, Burleson (Tex.) Ind. Sch. Dist., 1986—2003; tchr. 9th and 10th grade English Ft. Worth Country Day Sch., 2003—. Instr. composition Hill Coll., 1989-90. Contbg. author: (book revs.) English Journal, 1989-94, (lit. criticism) Eric, 1993. Vol. Dallas Theater Cir., 1990—96; active Kimbell Art Mus., Ft. Worth, 1990—, Modern Art Mus., Ft. Worth, 1992—, KERA Pub. TV, Dallas, 1990—, Amon Carter Mus., Ft. Worth, 2001—; mem. MOMA, N.Y.C., 1995—2003, Whitney Art Mus., 2002—03. Fellow NEH, 1988, 89, 92, 95, Fulbright-Hays Summer Seminar, 1991; ind. study grantee Coun. Basic Edn., 1990; recipient Chpt. Achievement award Epsilon Nu Delta Kappa Gamma, 1993, Honorable Mention Tex. Outstanding Tchg. of the Humanities award, 1995, Burlesson Independent Sch. Dist., Campus Ednl. Improvement Com., 1997-2000, Dist. Ednl. Improvement Com., 1998-2001. Mem.: United Educators Assn., Nat. Coun. Tchrs. English (spring conf. presenter 2000, 2002), Acad. Am. Poets, Epsilon Nu of Delta Kappa Gamma (1st v.p. 1988—94, v.p. 1992—94, profl. affairs com. 1996—98, comms. chair 1998—). Avocations: bicycling, travel, reading, writing, landscaping. Home: 4009 W 6th St Fort Worth TX 76107-1619 Office: Ft Worth County Day Sch 4200 Country Day Ln Fort Worth TX 76109-4299 E-mail: crobin@fwcds.org.

ROBINSON, AGNES CLAFLIN, educational administrator; b. N.Y.C., Oct. 2, 1918; d. Crittenden Hull and Agnes Sanger (Claflin) Adams; m. Albert Lewis Robinson (div.); children: Nicholas Adams, John Claflin, Hugh Wesley, James Allen, Lewis Stewart. AB, Barnard Coll., 1941; MS, NYU, 1949. Tech. asst. BEll Telephone Labs., Whippany, N.J., 1943-44; v.p. Family Service Assn., Morristown, N.J., 1946-48; bd. dirs. Adult and Child Guidance Clinic, San Jose, Calif., 1955-58; v.p. Palo Alto (Calif.) Mental Health Soc., 1959-63; pres. PTA, Palo Alto, 1961-63; trustee Palo Alto Unified Sch. Dist., 1963-73, pres., 1965-67. Chmn. Drug Abuse Bd., Palo Alto, 1971-74; mem. adv. bd. Nairobi Day Schs., East Palo Alto, 1969-72; mem. adv. bd. Child Care Now, 1972-73; mem. Calif. Post-Secondary Edn. Commn., 1974-80, chmn., 1978-80; advisor to pub. affairs com. YWCA, 1974-2002; mem. Mid-Peninsula Com. for Integrated Edn., 1974-80; bd. dirs. Addiction Research Found., 1974-78, pres., 1974-77; bd. dirs. Mid-Peninsula Learning Ctr. 1980-83; pres. New Ways to Work, 1976-79; mem. spl. legis. com. Calif. Student Fin. Aid Study Group, 1979; mem. Palo Alto Human Rels. Commn., 1981-82; bd. govs. Calif. Cmty. Colls., 1982—, pres., 1986-87; mem. accreditation coms. Western Assn. Schs. and Colls., 1989-97; co-chair Palo Alto com. Study Circles for Racial Understanding, 1998-2002. Author: (with Ruth McAneny Loud) New York, New York! A Knickerbocker Holiday for You and Your Children, 1946. Mem. NAACP (life), PTA (life), Sierra Club (life), Radcliffe Club of Mid-Peninsula. Democrat. Home: 1765 Fulton St Palo Alto CA 94303-2943 E-mail: acr1765@aol.com.

ROBINSON, ALICE HELENE, English language educator, administrative assistant; b. Cleve., Oct. 16, 1946; d. Alford B. and Willie Helena (Knuckles) R. BA, Cleve. State U., 1968, MA, 1992; postgrad., John Carroll U. Cert. tchr. English, Ohio. English language educator Cleve. Bd. Edn., Ohio. Presenter 1st Celtic Conf. Cleve. State U., 1993. Cleve. Edn. Fund scholar, 1991. Mem.: Cleve. Mus. Art. Episcopalian. Avocations: collecting stamps, plates, and artifacts, word puzzles, logic problems. Home: 3344 E 142nd St Cleveland OH 44120-4009 Office: Cleve Bd Edn 1380 E 6th St Cleveland OH 44114-1606

ROBINSON, ALICE JEAN MCDONNELL, retired drama and speech educator; b. St. Joseph, Mo., Nov. 17, 1922; d. John Francis and Della M. (Mavity) McDonnell; m. James Eugene Robinson, Apr. 21, 1956 (dec. 1983). BA, U. Kans., 1944, MA, 1947; PhD, Stanford U., 1965. Tchr. Garden City (Kans.) High Sch., 1944-46; asst. prof. Emporia (Kans.) State U., 1947-52; dir. live programs Sta. KTVH-TV, Hutchinson-Wichita, Kans., 1953-55; assoc. prof. drama and speech U. Md. Baltimore County, Balt., 1966-99, rsch. theatre history. Author: The American Theatre: A History in Slides, 1992, Betty Comden and Adolph Green: A Bio-Bibliography, 1993; co-editor: Notable Women in the American Theatre, 1989; appeared in plays, including Landscape, 1983, Tartuffe, 1985, Rockaby, 1990. Mem. Am. Soc. Theatre Rsch., Assn. Theatre Higher Edn., Phi Beta Kappa. Republican. Avocations: travel, reading, acting, directing. Home: 111 N Main St Caldwell KS 67022-1535

ROBINSON, CHRISTINE MARIE, mathematics educator; b. Savannah, Ga. d. Aaron Sr. and Lucille (Jones) Williams; m. Amos Robinson, Aug. 2, 1953; children: Michael Anthony, Pamela Michele. BS in Math. magna cum laude, Savannah State U., 1951; MA, U. Mich., 1965. Instr. in math. Chatham County Bd. of Instruction, Savannah, 1951-64, Duval County Bd. of Instruction, Jacksonville, Fla., 1964-71, master and resource tchr., 1971-76; prof. math. Fla. C.C., Jacksonville, 1976-99, ret., 1999. Mem. faculty task force Fla. Dept. Edn./Fla. Assn. C.C., Tallahassee, 1979-81; on-site coord. Fla. Devel. Edn. Assn. Conv., Jacksonville, 1986; chmn. Fla. C.C. EA/EO Com., Jacksonville, 1988, 89. Mem. YWCA, Jacksonville, 1989—; vol. driver Wheels for Cancer-AKA Sorority, Jacksonville, 1986; chmn. United Way, Jacksonville, 1987. Recipient Outstanding Faculty Mem. award Fla. Community Coll., 1987, Teaching Excellence award U. Tex., 1988; scholar U. Mich., U. Ill.; grantee NSF. Mem. Am. Math. Assn. Two-Yr. Colls., Fla. Devel. Edn. Assn. (bd. dirs. Jacksonville chpt. 1983-86), Fla. Assn. C.C., Math. Assn. Am., So. Assn. Colls. and Schs. (Fla. com.), LWV, Alpha Kappa Alpha. Democrat. Roman Catholic. Avocations: reading, piano, dancing, bicycling. Home: 7426 Simms Dr Jacksonville FL 32209-1023

ROBINSON, CUMMIE ADAMS, librarian, consultant; b. Mansfield, La., Sept. 27, 1945; d. Roosevelt and Annie B. Adams; m. Johnnie Robinson Jr.; children: Jared, Cynara, Cynecia. BS, So. U., Baton Rouge, 1967; MSLS, U. So. Calif., 1972; PhD, Walden U., 1992. Cert. tchr., La. Tchr. Compton (Calif.) Unified Schs., 1970-73; libr. Xavier U., New Orleans, 1973-75, Nicholls H.S., New Orleans, 1989—. Tchr. Delgado C.C., 1992; adj. faculty So. U., New Orleans, 1994—. Block coord. Nat. Leukemia Soc., New Orleans, 1992—, March of Dimes, New Orleans, 1992—, Muscular Dystrophy Assn., New Orleans, 1988—. Mem. Nat. Coun. Negro Women, Delta Sigma Theta. United Methodist. Avocations: exercising, collecting crystal glasses and mugs, reading. Home: 10701 Sabo Rd Apt 1604 Houston TX 77089-1639 Office: 3820 Saint Claude Ave New Orleans LA 70117-5736

ROBINSON, DANIEL N. psychology and philosophy educator; b. N.Y., Mar. 9, 1937; s. Henry S. and Margaret R.; children: Tracey, Kimberly; m. Francine Malasko, 1967. BA, Colgate U., 1958; MA, Hofstra U., 1960; PhD, CUNY, 1965. Rsch. psychologist, electronics rsch. labs. Columbia U., 1960-65, asst. dir. sci. honors program electronics rsch. labs., 1964-68, sr. rsch. psychologist, electronics rsch. labs., 1965-68, asst. dir. of life scis. electronics rsch. labs., 1967-68; asst. prof. dept. psychology Amherst Coll., 1968-70, assoc. prof., 1970-71; dir. grad. program dept. psychology Georgetown Univ., 1981-83, chmn. dept. psychology, 1973-76, 85-91, assoc. prof., 1971-74, prof., 1974—, adj. prof. philosophy, 1996—, disting. rsch. prof. and prof. psychology, 1998—2001, disting. prof. emeritus, 2002—. Vis. lectr. psychology Princeton U., 1965-68; vis. prof. Folger Shakespeare Inst., 1977; vis. sr. mem. Linacre Coll., vis. lectr. philosophy Oxford (Eng.) U., 1991—, faculty fellow, 1999—, philos. faculty, 2002—; vis. prof. Princeton U., 2001; adj. prof. Columbia U., 2002—; cons. NIH, 1967-70, NSF, 1965-75, PBS, 1978-84, 1985-88, MacArthur Found., 1985, Atty. Gen's. Task Force on Crime, 1980, HHS, NIH, 1988. Author: Psychology: A Study of Its Origins and Principles, 1972, The Enlightened Machine: An Anlytical Introduction to Neuropsychology, 1973, 80, Psychology: Traditions and Perspectives, 1976, An Intellectual History of Psychology, 1976, The Mind Unfolded: Essay's on Psychology's Historic Texts, 1978, Systems of Modern Psychology: A Critical Sketch, 1979, Psychology and Law: Can Justice Survive the Social Sciences?, 1980, An Intellectual History of Psychology-Revised Edition, 1981, 3rd edit., 1995, Toward A Science of Human Nature: Essays on the Psychologies of Hegel, Mill, Wundt, and James, 1982, Philosophy of Psychology, 1985, Aristotle's Psychology, 1989, (with William R. Uttal) Foundations of Psychobiology, 1983, (with Sir John Eccles) The Wonder of Being Human: Our Mind and Our Brain, 1984; editor Heredity and Achievement, 1970, Readings in the Origins and Principles of Psychology, 1972, Significant Contributions to the History of Psychology, 1977-78, Annals of Theoretical Psychology, 1990, Social Discourse and Moral Judgment, 1992, Wild Beasts and Idle Humours: Legal Insanity from Antiquity to the Present, 1996; editor Jour. Theoretical and Philosophical Psychology, 1997-2002; contbr. chpts. to books, reference books, articles to profl. jours. Recipient Inst. for Advanced Study in the Humanities fellow, U. Edinburgh, 1986-87; Pres's. medal Colgate U., 1986, Pub. Svc. award Gen. Svcs. Adminstrn., 1986. Fellow APA (past pres. divsns. 24 and 26, Lifetime Achievement award Divsn. History of Psychology 2001, Disting. Contbn. award Divsn. Theoretical and Philos. Psychology 2001), Brit. Psychol. Soc.; mem. Sigma Xi, Psi Chi. Home: 300 E Main St Middletown MD 21769 Office: Columbia U Dept Psychology New York NY 10027

ROBINSON, DIXIE FAYE, elementary and secondary school educator; b. Lexington, Ky., Feb. 7, 1944; d. John David and Betty Lou (Taylor) Moore; m. Jim Darrell Robinson, June 25, 1978. BA, Georgetown (Ky.) Coll., 1966; MA in Edn., Ball State U., 1972; postgrad., Miami U., Oxford, Ohio, 1989—, Ind. U., 1990-92. Cert. tchr., Ind. Tchr. Richmond (Ind.) Community Schs., 1966-91, adminstr., 1991-97, alt. sch. tchr., 1997—. Team leader Richmond Community schs., 1983-90, mentor tchr., 1989-91, coop. learning staff devel. mem., 1989-91, coord. ptnrship in edn., 1990-91, site-base convenor, 1990-91; v.p. Richmond Area Reading Coun., 1984. Pres. Historic Richmond, Inc., 1982; tour guide Richmond-Wayne County Tourism Bur., 1986-87; vice-chmn. Richmond Area Rose Festival, 1988-89; adv. bd. Palladium Item, Richmond, 1990. Recipient Hoosier Meritorious award Ind. Sec. of State, 1986, Nat. Energy Edn. Devel. award, Washington, 1991, Exemplary Program award for alternative schs. State of Ind., 2001; grantee Newspapers in Edn., 1986. Mem. NEA, NAFE, ASCD, Nat. Mid. Sch. Assn., Assn. Tchr. Educators, Nat. Assn. Secondary Sch. Prins., Nat. Coun. Tchrs. English (Ctr. of Excellence award 1988-91), Ind. Coun. Tchrs. of English (Hoosier Tchr. English 1991), Ind. Middle Level Inst., Richmond Area Reading Coun., Kappa Delta Gamma, Phi Delta Kappa. Avocations: historic preservation, antiques, community affairs, reading, travel. Home: 100 NW 8th St Richmond IN 47374-4055

ROBINSON, DONALD LEE, clergyman, educator; b. Pleasant Hill, Ohio, Nov. 29, 1929; s. John Amos and Nora Edna (Minnich) R.; m. Eleanor Jane Judy, June 7, 1952; children: John Raymond, Jane Diane, James Edward. BA, Juniata Coll., 1951; MDiv, Bethany Theol. Sem., 1954; DMinistry, Lancaster Theol. Sem., 1986. Ordained to ministry, Ch. of Brethren, 1951. Pastor Wilmington (Del.) Ch. of Brethren, 1954-57; dir. fin. Ch. Fedn. Greater Dayton, Ohio, 1957-61; pastor First Ch. of Brethren, Reading, Pa.,

1961-92. Cons., Carr & Assocs., North Manchester, Ind., 1956-59, Ch. of Brethren, Elgin, Ill., 1965—; mem. faculty, Reading Area Community Coll., 1974-90, Pace Inst., Reading, 1972—; pres. Family Guidance Ctr., Reading, 1978-86. Pres. HELP crisis intervention ctr., Reading, 1972-80; mem. White House Conf. on Problems of Youth in Am., 1974; cons. various sch. dists., Phila., Washington and Reading, 1978—, Reading Domestic Rels. Ct., 1982—, Concept Mgmt., 2001—. Mem. Rotary. Republican. Home: 107 Hawthorne Ct Reading PA 19610-1028 Office: First Ch Brethren 2200 Bern Rd Reading PA 19610-1904

ROBINSON, EDWARD LEE, retired physics educator, consultant; b. Clanton, Ala., Nov. 6, 1933; s. Alonzo Lee and Ollie Sarah (Mims) R.; m. Shirley Anne Burnett (div. Sept. 1972); children: Edward Lee Jr., James Allan, Paul David; m. Linda G. Moon, 1990. AB with honors, Samford U., 1954; MS, Purdue U., 1958, PhD, 1962. Dir. Cyclotron Lab. Samford U., Birmingham, Ala., 1961-67, asst. prof. physics, chmn. dept., 1961-62, assoc. prof., chmn. dept., 1962-66, prof., chmn. dept., 1966-67; assoc. prof. U. Ala., Birmingham, 1967-77, co-radiation safety officer, 1967-85, dir. Van de Graaff Accelerator Lab., 1970-91, acting chmn. dept., 1973-74, prof. physics, 1977-91, adj. prof. forensic sci., 1983-91, cons. in applied physics and accident reconstrn., 1991—; prin., owner Robinson & Assocs., LLC, 1998—. Cons. Hayes Internat. Corp., Birmingham, 1963-68, So. Rsch. Inst., Birmingham, 1968-69; rschr. Oak Ridge (Tenn.) Nat. Lab., 1968, 74-75, 82, U. Md., College Park, 1966, 67; bd. overseers Samford U., 1999—. Active Birmingham YMCA; mem. at large nat. coun., chmn. sci. adv. com. for explorer scouting Boy Scouts Am., 1999—2002. Mem. Am. Phys. Soc., Soc. Automotive Engrs., AAAS, Ala. Acad. Sci. (life, v.p. 1964-65), Tex. Assn. Accident Reconstrn. Specialists (bd. dirs.), numerous other nat. and internat. profl. assns. Baptist. Achievements include discovery, co-discovery of six radioisotopes. Home: 233 Oakmont Rd Birmingham AL 35244-3264 E-mail: elrobinson@charter.net.

ROBINSON, EFFIE, social worker, educator; b. Healdsburg, Calif., Jan. 7, 1920; d. Jessie C. Robinson and Elzora Emily Harper Robinson. AB, San Francisco State U., 1943; MSW, U. Calif., Berkeley, 1945. From case worker to acting dir. San Francisco Family Svc. Agy., San Francisco, 1945—63, dir. sr. program, 1964—87; ret., 1987. Devel. sr. housing San Francisco Housing Authority; chmn. edn. com. UN Assn. of San Francisco, 1994—, bd. dir.; devel. U.N. Program Tchr. Tng. Co-author (with David Christenson): Social Activity and Housing Environment of the Elderly, 1975. Life mem. NAACP; founder San Francisco Housing Authority Program Centuries 2002, San Francisco, 1972; founding mem. Internat. Mus. of Women, 2002. Named in Ladies Home Jour. Mag., 1975; recipient Wave award, Lifeprint, 2000, Koshland award, San Francisco Found., 1974. Mem.: AAUW, Calif. Women's Agenda, Am. Women Internat. Understanding, AKA. Democrat. Protestant. Avocations: ballet, opera, symphony, book club. Home: 1999 Green St 102 San Francisco CA 94123

ROBINSON, ELLA SCALES, language educator; b. Wedowee, Ala., Apr. 16, 1943; d. Leslie S. and Mary Ella (Mcpherson) Scales; m. John W. Robinson (dec. Feb. 1986); 1 child, John W. BS, Ala. State U., 1965; MA, U. Nebr., 1970, PhD, 1976. Tchr. English Selma (Ala.) Pub. Schs., 1965-69; rsch. asst. English dept. U. Nebr., Lincoln, 1969-70, tchr. asst. English dept., 1971-75, asst. prof. English, 1981-91; asst. prof. English, dir. freshman English U. Ill., 1975-78; asst. prof. English Atlanta U., 1978-80; assoc. prof. English Tuskegee (Ala.) U., 1994-2001; head humanities and fine arts dept. Concordia Coll., Selma, Ala., 2001—, head English dept., 2000—. Author: (poetry) Selected Poems, 1995, To Know Heaven, 1996, Love, The Seasons and Death, 1996, Poems: Angels in the Sun, 1996, Heritage: Tuskegee Poems a Celebration, 1997. Mem. NCTE, NAACP (life), MLA, Coll. Lang. Assn., African Lit. Assn., Lincoln Nebr. Chaparral Poets. Democrat. Methodist. Avocations: poetry, gardening, cooking, painting. Home: 6607 Luxembourg Cir Montgomery AL 36117-3447

ROBINSON, EMMA HAIRSTON, artist, educator; b. Lexington, N.C., Sept. 13, 1942; d. Cardell and Martha Ann (McCarter) Hairston; m. Daniel Louis Robinson, Dec. 26, 1963; 1 child, Gardell Lewis. BFA, Howard U., 1990, MFA, 1992; PhD, Ohio Univ., Athens, Ohio, 1994; DSc, Robert Morris Coll., Moon Twp., Pa., 2001; graduate, Strayer Univ., Washington, 2001—. Sec. Dept. Navy, Washington, 1968-70, NSF, Washington, 1970-81; artist, tchr., lectr. Arts for Aging, Bethesda, Md., 1990—. CEO Impace, 1997; office mgr., cons. Nat. Assn. Minority Contractors, Washington, 1993—94; art instr. Thomas House, Washington, 2000—, Md. Nat. Capital Pk. and Planning Commn., Oxen Hill, Md., 2000. Exhibitions include Dept. of Commerce, Dept. of the Navy, Nat. Sci. Found., Howard Univ., Atonement Episc. Ch., The World Bank, DC Commn. on the Arts, Martin King Libr., The Dist. Bldg., Dept. of State, many others. Lucy E. Moten fellow, 1989; Spl. Talent scholar, 1988-92. Mem. Nat. Conf. Artists, New D.C. Collage Soc., Nat. Coun. Negro Women, Washington Area Lawyers for Arts, Golden Key Nat. Honor Soc., Order of Ea. Star, Zeta Phi Beta. Democrat. Avocations: music, linguistics, travel, gardening. Home: 1523 Church St NW Washington DC 20005-1905

ROBINSON, ESTHER MARTIN, secondary school educator; b. Buffalo, N.Y., Sept. 19, 1956; d. Douglas Charles and Esther (Hagen) Martin; m. Stephen Mark Robinson, May 6, 1978; children: Rachel Anne, Sarah Elizabeth. BA, Oral Roberts U., 1978; MA, U. Tulsa, 1983. Tchr. secondary sch. history Tulsa Pub. Schs., 1978-80, Jenks (Okla.) High Sch., 1980-92, chair dept. social studies, 1990-92; tchr. world history, advanced placement U.S. history Langham Creek High Sch., Houston, 1992-97; tchr. advanced placement U.S. history and econs. Ridgefield (Conn.) H.S., 1997-2000, Langham Creek H.S., Tex., 2000—, chair dept. social studies, 2001—. Adj. prof. U.S. history Houston C.C., 1995-97, Cy Fair Coll., 2001—; presenter in field. Mem. Nat. Coun. Social Studies, Tex. Coun. Social Studies, Conn. Coun. for Social Studies, Cypress Fairbanks Coun. for Social Studies, Tex. Assn. Gifted and Talented, Orgn. Am. Historians, Nat. Coun. History Edn., Coll. Bd. Advanced Placement Reader, Assn. Supr. and Curriculum Devel. Home: 7518 Rivendell Dr Spring TX 77379-7046 Office: Langham Creek HS 17610 FM 529 Houston TX 77095

ROBINSON, EVELYN EDNA, educator; b. St. John, Maine, Feb. 23, 1911; d. Registe Jalbert and Olive Michaud; m. Carl Robinson, July 19, 1939; children: Robert, James. BA in Math., U. Maine, 1934; MS, U. N.H., 1963; MEd, Hillyer Coll. U., 1960. Tchr. English and math. Ft. Kent (Maine) H.S., 1934; tchr. English and math., coach girls basketball Madewaska (Maine) H.S., 1935-55; tchr. math. Stamford (Conn.) H.S., 1955-56; tchr. math and English, Bristol (Conn.) H.S., 1956-63; prof. math. Worcester (Mass.) State Coll., 1963-77, chmn. dept., 1970-77. Coord. cmty. bus. Worcester State Coll., 1970-77, class advisor, 1968-72, salary equity bd., 1971-73. Vol. libr. Madawaska Pub. Libr., 1936-55; lector Christ the King, Worcester, 1974-2000. Mem. Delta Kappa Gamma. Republican. Roman Catholic. Avocations: decorating, flower arrangements, ceramics, tailoring. Home: 12 Brookside Ave Worcester MA 01602

ROBINSON, GARY DAVID, principal; b. Altoona, Pa., Oct. 6, 1953; s. Donald R. and Theada (Brooks) R.; m. Nancy L., Aug. 15, 1981; children: Melissa, Brooke, David. BS, Pa. State U., 1975, MEd, 1979; EdD, Temple U., 1991. Grad. instr. Pa. State U., Altoona, 1978-83; math. tchr. Altoona Area Sch. Dist., 1975-83; asst. prin. Downingtown (Pa.) Area Sr. High Sch., 1983-88, athletic dir., 1983-86; high sch. prin. Octorara Area High Sch., Parkesburg, Pa., 1988-90, Hollidaysburg (Pa.) Area Sr. High Sch., 1990—. Vocat. adv. com. Pa. Dept. Edn., 1991-96, prins. adv. com. 1987-91; pres. Prins. Adv. to Ctr. Arts/Tech, Brandywine Campus, 1988-90. Active Jail and Bail project Am. Cancer Soc., Chester County, 1988; vol. Pa. State Sen. and Ho. of Reps., AAU Jr. Olympics, 1982; active student coun. activities, Hollidaysburg Area Sch. Dist., 1982; bd. dirs. Am. Heart Assn., Altoona, 1992; established Heart of Tiger Found. for Hollidaysburg Area Sch. in cooperation with area alumni assn., 1991-92; pres. Blair County chpt. Am. Heart Assn., 1993—; numerous community activities. Mem. ASCD, Pa. Assn. Supervision and Curriculum Devel., nat. Assn. Secondary Sch. Prins., Pa. Assn. Secondary Sch. Prins. (mem. com. 1986-90), Pa. Sch. Bd. Assn., Chester County Prins. Orgn. (chmn. 1989-90), Phi Delta Kappa. Avocations: staff devel., sch. climate and culture, student employment and self-esteem. Home: 211 Bristol Ln Hollidaysburg PA 16648-2937 Office: Hollidaysburg Area Sr High 1510 N Montgomery St Hollidaysburg PA 16648-1909

ROBINSON, GENE EZIA, biologist, educator; b. Buffalo, N.Y., Jan. 9, 1955; s. Jack and Sonja (Rubin) R.; m. Julia O. Robinson, Aug. 29, 1982; children: Aaron, Daniel, Sol. BS, Cornell U., 1977, MS, 1982, PhD, 1986. Postdoctoral assoc. Ohio State U., Columbus, 1986-89; asst. prof. biology U. Ill., Urbana, 1989-93, assoc. prof. biology, 1993-98, prof. biology, 1998—. Fulbright Sr. Rsch. fellow, Hebrew U., 1995-96. Fellow AAAS; mem. Animal Behavior Soc., Entomol. Soc. Am., Internat. Soc. Neuroethology, Soc. Neurosci., Internat. Union Study of Social Insects, Sigma Xi. Achievements include discovery of hormone, neural and genetic factors that regulate behavioral plasticity and division of labor in honeybee colonies. Office: U Ill Entomology Dept 505 S Goodwin Ave Urbana IL 61801-3707

ROBINSON, HELENE M. retired music educator; b. Eugene, Oreg., May 30, 1912; d. Kirkman K. and Emily A. Robinson. BA in Music, U. Oreg., 1935; MusM, Northwestern U., Evanston, Ill., 1945. Piano tchr. No. Ariz. U., Flagstaff, 1952—60, Calif. State U., Fullerton, 1960—61, U. Calif., Santa Barbara, 1961—62, Ariz. State U., Tempe, 1963—77. Author: Basic Piano for Adults, vol. I and II, 1964, Intermediate Piano for Adults, vols. I and II, 1970; author: (with others) Teaching Piano in Classroom and Studio; contbr. articles to profl. jours. Mem.: Music Tchrs. Nat. Assn. (spkr. convs. 1974—76), Phi Beta. Avocation: piano. Home: 1300 NE 16th Ave # 315 Portland OR 97232

ROBINSON, HERBERT HENRY, III, educator, psychotherapist; b. Leavenworth, Wash., Mar. 31, 1933; s. Herbert Henry II and Alberta (Sperber) R.; m. Georgia Murial Jones, Nov. 24, 1954 (div. 1974); children: Cheri Dean Asbury, David Keith, Peri Elizabeth Layton, Tanda Rene Graff, Gaila Daire. Grad. of Theology, Bapt. Bible Coll., 1959; BA in Philosophy/Greek, Whitworth Coll., 1968; MA in Coll. Teaching, Ea. Wash. U., 1976; PhD, Gonzaga U., 2002. Cert. psychotherapist, perpetrator treatment program supervision; nat. bd. cert. counselor. Choir dir. Twin City Bapt. Temple, Mishawaka, Ind., 1959-61; min. Inland Empire Bapt. Ch., Spokane, Wash., 1961-73; tchr. philosophy Spokane C.C., 1969-72; dir. Alternatives to Violence, Women in Crisis, Fairbanks, Alaska, 1985-87; tchr. pub. rels. U. Alaska, Fairbanks, 1986-87; dir. Alternatives to Violence Men Inc., Juneau, 1988-89; tchr. leadership mgmt. U. Alaska S.E., Juneau, 1988-89; min. Sci. of Mind Ctr., Sandpoint, Idaho, 1989-92; dir., therapist Tapio Counseling Ctr., Spokane, 1991—; cert. psychotherapist, supr. perpetrator treatment program Wash. Cons. Lilac Blind/Alpha Inc./Marshall Coll., Spokane, 1975-85, Alaska Placer Mining Co., Fairbanks, 1987; tchr. Spokane Falls C.C., Spokane, 1979-85; seminar, presenter Human Resource Devel., Spokane and Seattle, Wash., Pa., 1980; guest trainer United Way/Kellogg Found. Inst. for Volunteerism, Spokane, 1983. 1st trombone San Diego Marine Band, 1953-56, Spokane Symphony, 1961; bd. dirs. Tanani Learning Ctr., Fairbanks, 1987; mem. consensus bldg. team Sci. of Mind Ctr., Sandpoint, 1989-92. Cpl. USMC, 1953-56. Mem. ACA, Assn. for Humanistic Edn. and Devel., Assn. for Religious Values in Counseling, Internat. Assn. Addictions and Offender Counselors, Internat. Assn. Marriage and Family Counselors, Am. Assn. Profl. Hypnotherapists, Masterson Inst. Office: Tapio Counseling 5325 E Sprague Ave Spokane WA 99212-0820

ROBINSON, JAMES LAWRENCE, biochemistry educator, researcher; b. Boston, Feb. 23, 1942; s. Lawrence Hanny and Carolyn Ruth (Conklin) R.; m. Janet Lynn Thorpe, Feb. 23, 1963; children: Mark, Marjorie, Glen. BS in Chemistry, U. Redlands, 1964; PhD in Biochemistry, UCLA, 1968. Postdoctoral rschr. Inst. Cancer Rsch., Phila., 1968-70; asst. prof. U. Ill., Urbana, 1970-76, assoc. prof., 1976-85, prof., 1985—2002, prof. emeritus, 2002—. Vis. scientist Inst. Nat. Recherche Agrom, Jouy-en Josas, France, 1978-79; vis. scientist dept. biochemistry U. Nijmegen, The Netherlands, 1986-87, Macarthur Agrl. Inst., Camden, NSW, Australia, 1993-94. Mem. Am. Soc. Biochem. Molecular Biology, Am. Dairy Sci. Assn., Am. Soc. Nutritional Sci. Democrat. Methodist. Avocations: camping, hiking, bicycling, gardening. Home: 902 E Mumford Dr Urbana IL 61801-6327 Office: U Ill Dept Animal Sci 1207 W Gregory Dr Urbana IL 61801-4733 E-mail: jlrobins@uiuc.edu.

ROBINSON, JAMES LEROY, architect, educator, developer; b. July 12, 1940; s. Willie LeRoy and Ruby Nell Robinson; m. Martha Robinson; children: James LeRoy II, Kerstin Gunilla, Maria Theresa Narvaez, Jasmin Marisol, Ruby Nell, Kenneth Arne. BArch, So. U., 1964; MCP, Pratt Inst., 1972. Arch. Pt. of N.Y. Authority, 1964; arch., store planner W.T. Grant, 1964; with Herbst & Rusciano, AIA, 1965; arch. Carson, Lundin & Shaw, N.Y.C., 1966, Kennerly, Slomanson & Smith, N.Y.C., 1967-69, arch.-on-bus., 1969; pres. Robinson Archs., P.C., N.Y.C., 1969—. V.p. J&K Constrn. Cons., Inc.; vis. prof. CUNY; adj. prof. Pratt Inst. Prin. works include Stuyvesant Heights Christian Ch., David Chavis House, Fulton Ct. Houses, Sinclair Houses, Hamilton Heights Terr., Eliot Graham Houses, Sojourner Truth Houses, Nehemiah Plan, Casas Theresa, N.Y.C. Postal Data Ctr., Mt. Carmel Bapt. Ch., Consol. Edison Collection Ctr., Jasmin Houses, City-Homes CD&E, The Promenade, Gore Residence & Tse Residence. Bd. dirs. Boys Club Am. With U.S. Army, 1966. Decorated knight Order of St. John, Knight of Malta; recipient AIA Design award, 1976; Martin Luther King fellow Pratt Inst., 1972. Mem. Am. Arbitrators Assn. (arbitrator). Democrat. Address: 55C DeLancey St New York NY 10002-2804 E-mail: jackrabbit85@hotmail.com.

ROBINSON, JANIE MONETTE, education educator; b. Merkel, Tex., Oct. 20, 1941; d. Orvin Leon and Velma Cleone (Rutledge) R.; div.; children: Gregory Blake Keller, Karel Blynn Keller. BS, Howard Payne U., 1963; MEd, U. Nev., Las Vegas, 1990; postgrad., U. Nev., Reno, 1991-92, Brigham Young U., 1990-91. Cert. tchr., Tex., N.Mex. Tchr., coach Eula Rural Sch., Clyde, Tex., 1961-63; tchr. Grand Lake High Sch., Lake Charles, La., 1964; instr. history Colo. Bapt. Coll., Denver, 1977-78; tchr. Lincoln County Sch. Dist., Caliente, Nev., 1978-86, Abilene (Tex.) Ind. Sch. Dist., 1986-87, Lander County Sch. Dist., Battle Mountain, Nev., 1990-93, Raton (N.Mex.) Mcpl. Sch. Dist., 1993—; instr. edn. Trinidad Jr. Coll., 1995. Dir. day care A Child's World, North Las Vegas, Nev., 1988-89; dir. girls' group home Regina Hall, Henderson, Nev., 1989-90. [e]m. NEA, ASCD, Coun. for Exceptional Children. Baptist. Avocations: quilting, camping, reading. Home: HC 62 Box 111 Raton NM 87740-9705 Office: Raton High Sch 1535 Tiger Cir Raton NM 87740-4360

ROBINSON, JOAN, education educator; b. White Plains, N.Y., Aug. 28, 1963; d. Joseph Franklin and Mattie Ann (Chapman) R.; children: Jovan R., Derrick C., Gian D. BS, Mercy Coll., 1987. Respite counselor Westchester Ass. for Retarded Citizens, White Plains, 1986-87; educ. cons. sales Early Learning Ctr., White Plains, 1987; crisis counselor Children's Village, Dobbs Ferry, N.Y., 1986-87, sociotherapist; psych. counselor Med. Ctr. of Cen. Ga., Macon, 1987-88; career agt. Prudential Co., Ryebrook, N.Y.; dir. KIDS daycare and afterschool enrichment program WMJ. Edn. cons. Discovery Toys, White Plains, 1985-87; proprietor Heavens Little Creations, White Plains, Juana Prodns., Scarsdale; cons. Mary Kay Beauty; dir. WMJ's Kids Daycare and Afterschool. Mem. Mt. Vernon Community Choir, Calvary Bapt. Ch.; vol. Union Child Day Care Ctr., Victim Info. Bur.'s Children's Village Program, Exch. Club Child Abuse Prevention Program. Mem. NAFE, Entrepreneurs Am., Cen. Westchester Audubon Soc., Westchester Assn. Women Bus. Owners. Republican. Avocations: photography, aerobic exercise, modeling, singing, acting. Home: 60 Gibson Ave White Plains NY 10607-2003

ROBINSON, JOE SAM, neurosurgeon, educator; b. Atlanta, Ga., July 21, 1945; s. Joe Sam and Nell (Mixon) R.; m. Elizabeth Ann Moate, Apr. 3, 1982; children: Joe Sam III, Edward Richard, Thomas McRae. AB cum laude, Harvard Coll., 1967; MD, U. Va., 1971; MS, Northwestern U., 1975. Surg. intern Emory U., 1971-72, resident in surgery, 1972-73; resident in neurosurgery Northwestern U., 1973-78; instr. U. Ill., 1978-79, Yale U., 1979-81; pres. Ga. Neurosurg. Inst. P.A., Macon, 1981—. Prof., chief neurosurgery Mercer U. Sch. Medicine, Macon, 1986; chief surgery Med. Ctr. Ctrl. Ga., Macon, 1989—, vice chmn. surgery, 1991-97, chmn. dept. surgery, 1996—; vis. neurosurgeon China, 1992, Konaus Acad. Neurosurgery Inst., Lithuania, 1992; clin. prof. Med. Coll. Ga., 2002. Lt. col. USANG, 1972-95. Fellow Internat. Coll. Surgeons (vice regent 1983-93); mem. Am. Assn. Neurol. Surgeons, Congress Neurol. Surgeons, AAAS, Ga. Neurosurg. Soc., Alpha Omega Alpha. Republican. Methodist. Office: Ga Neurosurg Inst PA 840 Pine St Ste 880 Macon GA 31201-7525

ROBINSON, JOHN HAYES, law educator; b. Providence, Apr. 4, 1943; s. William Philip and Dorothy Frances (Hayes) R.; m. Deborah Ann Deery, Aug. 15, 1981; children: Gena, John. BA, Boston Coll., 1967; MA, Notre Dame U., 1972, PhD, 1975; JD, U. Calif.-Berkeley, 1979. Bar: R.I. 1980. Asst. prof. U. San Francisco, 1973-76; instr. law U. Miami, Coral Gables, Fla., 1979-80; jud. clk. U.S. Dist. Ct., Hartford, Conn., 1980-81; asst. prof. law and philosophy U. Notre Dame (Ind.), 1981-96, assoc. prof. law, 1996—, assoc. dean for acad. affairs, 2002—. Office: U Notre Dame Law Sch Notre Dame IN 46556

ROBINSON, LINDA SCHULTZ, art educator, artist; b. Oakland, Calif., Mar. 15, 1949; d. James Richie Schultz and Dorothy Louise Koster-Schultz; m. Steven R. Robinson, Aug. 10, 1980; children: Laura Anne, Chelsea Marie, Emily Louise. AA in Art, Mauna Olu Coll., 1970; BA in Criminal Justice, Calif. State U., Sacramento, 1979. Cert.: Calif. (paralegal). Legal typist U.S. Govt., Concord, Calif., 1975—79; paralegal Alternative Legal Choices, Pleasant Hill, Calif., 1985—87; spl. edn. para-profl. Acad. Sch. Dist., Colorado Springs, Colo., 1995—96; pvt. art instr. to spl. needs individuals Colorado Springs, 1999—. Art therapist Meml. Hosp., Colorado Springs, 2001—. Exhibitions include Colorado Springs Art Guild, 2001. Bd. dirs. Interfaith Hospitality Network, Colorado Springs, 1995—99; vol. art tchr. Acad. Dist. 20 Schs., Colorado Springs, 2001—. Avocations: guitar, reading, crafts.

ROBINSON, NANCY DIANE, secondary school educator; b. Altoona, Pa., Apr. 14, 1950; d. Earl Clifford and Helen Frances (Weamer) R. BS, Juniata Coll., 1972; MEd, Indiana U. Pa., 1976. Tchr. math. Altoona Area Sch. Dist., 1973—. Mem. Allegheny Chorale, Tyrone, Pa., 1988—; admissions vol. Juniata Coll., Huntingdon, Pa., 1989—; vol. Mathcounts, Altoona, 1989—. Mem. NEA, Pa. Edn. Assn., Nat. Coun. Tchrs. Math., Pa. Coun. Tchrs. Math., Altoona Area Edn. Assn., Altoona Bus. and Profl. Women, Delta Kappa Gamma. Republican. Mem. Ch. of Brethren. Avocations: counted cross-stitch, piano, violin, guitar, singing.

ROBINSON, NAOMI JEAN, educational training systems educator; b. Storm Lake, Iowa, Oct. 10, 1951; d. Wendell and Norma (Wright) Robinson. BA, Buena Vista Coll., 1973; MAEd., George Washington U., 1978. Tchr. elem. sch., Storm Lake, Iowa, 1973—75; edn. specialist intern US Army, Ft. Monroe, Va., 1976—78, edn. and test specialist Ft. Eustis, Va., 1978—79; tng. systems analyst U.S. Army, White Sands Missile Range, N.Mex., 1979—82; tng. effectiveness analysis study coord. US Army, White Sands Missile Range, 1983—85, analyst ops. rsch. and tng. systems, 1985—87, edn. specialist, dir. tng. tech. field Advanced Concepts Team Ft. Huachuca, Ariz., 1987—88, edn. specialist, dir. tng. lab. for Tng. Devel. and Analysis Directorate, NJ N.G. High Tech. Tng. Ctr. Ft. Dix, NJ, 1988—90, program mgr., COR Tng. Devel. and Analysis Directorate for TRADOC tng. mission support contract, 1990—94, chief spl. projects team, 1990—91, acting divsn. chief tng. rsch and studies divsn., 1992—96; chief TRADOC tng. Mission Support Contract Br., Ft. Monroe, 1991—94; chmn. Tng. Devel. Revitalization Joint Task Force Pentagon, Washington, 1994—96; dir. ops. support divsn. and exec. officer tng. devel. analysis activity Ft. Monroe, Va., 1996—97; asst. dep. chief of staff Tng. Hdqs. 5th Army, Ft. Sam Houston, Tex., 1997—2000; chief ADCST and Chief Resource Support Div., 2000—02; asst. dep. chief of staff G3-TNG, HQ Fifth Army, 2002—. Author: Guidelines for Development of Skill Qualification Tests, 1977, Standard Operating Procedure for TRADOC Training Mission Support Contract, 1991, 1992. V.p. Young Reps., 1972—73. Mem.: NAFE, Iowa Edn. Assn., Human Factors Soc., Federally Employed Women (1st v.p. chpt. 1982—83, 1984—85), Bus. and Profl. Women Club. Republican. Presbyterian. Home: 13999 Old Blanco Rd Apt 3311 San Antonio TX 78216-7790 Office: Hdqs 5th US Army Ste 146 Bldg 16 Rm 110 1400 E Grayson St Fort Sam Houston TX 78234-7000 Business E-Mail: naomi.robinson@us.army.mil.

ROBINSON, NICHOLAS ADAMS, lawyer, educator; b. NYC, Jan. 20, 1945; s. Albert Lewis and Agnes Claflin (Adams) R.; m. Shelley Miner, Jan. 5, 1969; children: Cynthia M., Lucy A. BA cum laude, Brown U., 1967; JD cum laude, Columbia U., 1970. Bar: N.Y. 1971, U.S. Dist. Ct. (so. and ea. dists.) N.Y. 1972, U.S. Supreme Ct. 1974, U.S. Ct. Appeals (2d and 7th cirs.) 1972. Law clk. to U.S. dist. judge So. Dist. Ct., N.Y., 1970-72; assoc. Marshall, Bratter, Greene, Allison & Tucker, N.Y.C., 1972-78, counsel, 1978-82; assoc. prof. Pace U. Sch. Law, White Plains, N.Y., 1978-81, prof., 1981-99, Gilbert and Sarah Kerlin Disting. prof. environ. law, 1999—; counsel Winer, Neuburger & Sive, N.Y.C., 1982-83; dep. commr., gen. counsel N.Y. State Dept. Environ. Conservation, Albany, 1983-85; counsel Sive, Paget & Reisel, 1985-92, Sidley & Austin, N.Y., London, 1992-96; legal advisor Internat. Union Conservation of Nature and Natural Resources, 1996—. Co-dir. Ctr. for Environ. Legal Studies, Pace U., 1982—; dir. IUCN Acad. Environ. Law, 2003—; del. U.S.A. environ. law meetings with USSR, 1974-92; chmn. Environ. Adv. Bd. to Gov. Mario Cuomo, 1985-94. Contbr. articles to profl. jours. Nat. bd. dirs. UN Assn. U.S.A., 1966-76, 79-84, U.S. Com. for UNICEF, 1970-80, World Environment Ctr., 1981—, chmn., 1993-96; bd. dirs. Westchester County Soil and Water Conservation Dist., 1976-83; chmn. N.Y. State Freshwater Wetlands Appeals Bd., 1976-83; chmn. planning bd. Village of Sleepy Hollow, N.Y., 1999—; bd. edn. Union Free Sch. Dist., Tarrytown, 1981-83, 85. Recipient N.Y. State Gov.'s Citation for Hist. Preservation, 1983, Eliz Haub prize in environ. law Free U., Brussels, 1992, Nat. Environ. Quality award Natural Resources Coun. Am., 2002. Fellow Am. Bar Found.; mem. Internat. Coun. Environ. Law (gov. 1993—), Commn. Environ. Law (chmn. 1996-2004), Am. Soc. Internat. Law, ABA, ALI, N.Y. State Bar Assn. (chmn. environ. law sect. 1979-80, Environ. Law award 1981), Assn. Am. Law Schs. (chair sect. on postgrad. legal edn. 1999-2000, chair sect. environ. law 1987-88), Assn. Bar City N.Y. (chmn. environ. law com. 1977-78, internat. law com. 1985-88, internat. environ. law com. 1990-92, Russian law com. 1992-95), Westchester County Bar Assn., Sierra Club (nat. bd. dirs. 1979-83), Phi Beta Kappa. Democrat. Unitarian Universalist. Home: 258 Kelbourne Ave Sleepy Hollow NY 10591-1322 Office: Pace U Sch Law 78 N Broadway White Plains NY 10603-3710 E-mail: nrobinson@law.pace.edu.

ROBINSON, PREZELL RUSSELL, academic administrator; b. Batesburg, SC, Aug. 25, 1922; s. Clarence and Annie (Folks) R.; m. Lulu Harris, Apr. 9, 1950; 1 dau. AB in Econs. and Social Sci., St. Augustine's Coll., 1946, hon. degree; MA in Sociology and Econs., Cornell U., 1951, Ed.D. in Sociology-Ednl. Adminstrn., 1956; D.C.L. (hon.), U. of the South, 1970; L.H.D., hon. degree, Cuttington U. Coll., Monrovia, Liberia; L.H.D., Voorhees Coll., 1981, hon. degree; L.H.D., Episcopal Theol. Sem., 1982;

LL.D. (hon.), Bishop Coll., 1979; D.C.L., Columbia U., 1980, hon. degree; DHL (hon.), Kenyon Coll., 1988; hon. degree, Va. Theology Sem., Alexandria, Barton Coll., Campbell U., N.C. State U., Shaw U. Tchr. social sci., French Bettis Jr. Coll., Trenton, S.C., 1946-48; sucessively registrar, tchr., acting prin. high sch., acting dean jr. coll., instr., dir. adult edn. Voorhees Jr. Coll., Denmark, S.C., 1948-56; prof. sociology, dean coll. St. Augustine's Coll., Raleigh, N.C., 1956-64, exec. dean, 1964-66, acting pres., 1966-67, pres., 1967-95, pres. emeritus, 1995—. Pres. United Negro Coll. Fund, Inc., 1978-81, Nat. Assn. Equal Opportunity Higher Edn., 1981-84, N.C. Assn. Coll. & U., Cooperating Raleigh Colls., 1981, 86—; bd. dirs. Learning Inst. N.C.; scholar-in-residence Nairobi (Kenya) U., 1973; vis. lectr. Dept. State del. to African nations, 1971, 73, 78; dir. Wachovia Bank & Trust Co.; vice chmn. N.C. State Bd. Edn., mem., 1973-99, vice-chmn., 1994-99. Contbr. articles to profl. publs. Exec. com. N.C. Edn. Com. on Tchr. Edn.; active N.C. Bd. Edn.; chmn. bd. Assn. Episcopal Colls.; mem. Mayor's Community Relations Com.; vice-chmn. Wake County divsn. Occoneechee coun. Boy Scouts Am., 1959-67; chmn. Wake Occoneechee coun., 1963-66, exec. com., 1965—; vice-chmn. Wake County chpt. ARC; chmn. edn. divsn. United Fund of Raleigh, budget com., 1965— ; exec. com. Wake County Libraries.; trustee Voorhees Coll. Fulbright fellow to India, 1965; appointed US alt. rep. or public mem. amb. Gen. Assembly UN, by Pres. George Bush, 1992, by Pres. Clinton, 1996. Served with AUS, 1942. Recipient Distinguished Alumni award Voorhees Coll., 1967, Silver Anniversary award N.C. Community System, 1989; decorated Star of Africia Liberia; recipient numerous service awards and citations; named one of the most effective coll. pres.s in U.S. Coun. for Advancement and Support of Edn., Washington, 1986; Univ. fellow Cornell U., 1954, rsch. fellow, 1955-56; Fulbright fellow, 1965. Mem. AAAS, Nat. Assn. Collegiate Deans and Registrars, Am. Acad. Polit. and Social Sci., Am. Sociol. Soc., N.C. Sociol. Soc. (exec. com.), Ctrl. Intercollegiate Athletic Assn. (exec. com.), N.C. Assn. Ind. Colls. and Univs. (dir.), Raleigh C. of C. (A.E. Finley Disting. Svc. award 1989), So. Sociol. Assn., Am. Acad. Polit. Sci., N.C. Lit. and Hist. Soc., N.C. Hist. Soc., Delta Mu Delta, Phi Delta Kappa, Phi Kappa Phi, Alpha Kappa Mu, Phi Beta Lambda. Protestant Episcopalian (lay reader). Home: 821 Glascock St Raleigh NC 27604-2317 Office: St Augustine's Coll 1315 Oakwood Ave Raleigh NC 27610-2247

ROBINSON, RUTH HARRIS, elementary education educator; b. Washington, Mar. 6, 1937; d. Joseph Fountain and Anozella (Tutty) Harris; children: Jose T. Harris, Lisa G. Robinson. BA, Howard U., 1953; MA, George Washington U., 1963. Tchr. reading St. Augustine Sch., Washington, 19173-80; elem. tchr. D.C. Pub. Schs., Washington, 1961-63, reading specialist, 1963-73, computer assisted instrn. reading and math., 1980-95; retired, 1995. Vol. Washington Hosp. Ctr., 1984-92, So Others Might Eat, 1993; mem. youth coun. ARC, Washington, 1992; mem. Assn. Community Of Reform Now, 1990—. Named Tchr. of Yr. Am. Red Cross, 1990. Mem. Nat. Reading Assn., Nat. Math. Assn., D.C. Math. Assn., D.C. Reading Assn. Democrat. Roman Catholic. Home: 632 Irving St NW Washington DC 20010-2906 Office: 415 12th St NW Washington DC 20004-1905

ROBINSON, SHARON PORTER, professional society administrator; b. Louisville; B in Edn., English and Psychology, U. Ky., 1966, M in Edn., Curriculum and Instrn., 1976, D in Edn. Adminstrn. and Supervision, 1979. Tchr., Lexington, Ky., U.S. AFB, Bitburg, Germany; assoc. dir. Jefferson County Edn. Consortium, Ky., late 1970's; dir. instrn. and profl. devel. NEA, 1980-89, dir. R & D arm Nat. Ctr. Innovation, 1989-93; asst. sec. ednl. rsch. and improvement U.S. Dept. Edn., 1993—96; v.p. State and Fed. Regulations EPS, Washington, 1997—98, sr. v.p., COO, 1998—. Cons. Nat. Bd. Profl. Teaching Standards; head tchr. edn. initiative Nat. Ctr. Innovation. Office: EPS 1800 K St NW Washington DC 20006*

ROBINSON, TERENCE VACHEL, secondary education educator; b. Yakima, Wash., Dec. 13, 1943; s. Claude Vachel and Sibyl Lucille (Terry) R.; m. Nancy Ann Main, June 27, 1965; children: Teri Suzanne, Andrew Tai, Melissa Kay, Gregory Scott, Nicholas Aaron. BS, Calif. State U., Fullerton, 1972; MEd, U. La Verne, 1991. Cert. elem. tchr. Tchr. ABC Unified Sch. Dist., Cerritos, Calif., 1972—. Bd. dirs. La Mirada Little League, La Mirada, Calif., 1985; deacon Ch. of Christ, Norwalk, Calif., 1987-90. With U.S. Army, 1962-65. Mem. ASCD, Assn. Calif. Sch. Adminstrs., Nat. Coun. Social Studies. Republican. Avocations: fishing, golf, R.V. camping, travel, heavy duty truck driving. Home: 15224 San Ardo Dr La Mirada CA 90638-5724 Office: Haskell Jr High Sch 11525 Del Amo Blvd Cerritos CA 90703-7404

ROBISON, CAROLYN LOVE, retired librarian; b. Orlinda, Tenn., Aug. 9, 1940; d. Fount Love and Martha Desha (Jones) R. BA, Denison U., 1962; MLS, Emory U., 1965; PhD, Ga. State U., 1982. Tchr. Dag Hammarshjold Jr. H.S., Wallingford, Conn., 1962-64; asst. libr., lectr. Architecture Libr., Ga. Inst. Tech., Atlanta, 1965-67; head circulation Ga. State U., Atlanta, 1967-71, asst. prof., then assoc. prof., asst. libr., 1971-75, prof., assoc. libr., 1975-98, prof. emeritus, 1998. Active Friends of Atlanta-Fulton County Pub. Libr., 1981—98. Recipient Woman of Achievement award YWCA, 1989. Mem. ALA, AAUP, Ga. Libr. Assn., Delta Kappa Gamma, Phi Kappa Phi, Kappa Delta Pi. Republican. Presbyterian. Home: 1057 Capital Club Cir NE Atlanta GA 30319-2662 E-mail: clrobison@mindspring.com.

ROBLES, ROSALIE MIRANDA, elementary education educator; b. LA, Calif., Oct. 30, 1942; d. Richard and Carmen (Garcia) Miranda; m. Ralph Rex Robles, July 12, 1986; children: Gregory, Eric, Karen Cassandra. BA, Calif. State Coll., L.A., 1964; postgrad., Northridge State Coll. Playground supr. L.A. City Schs., 1961-64; elem. tchr. Montebello (Calif.) Unified Schs., 1964—. Rep. Montebello Credit Union, 1973-75, Bilingual Com., 1983-88; mem. Sch. Site Coun., 1989-92, chmn. 1980-83. Chmn. Monterey Park Christmas Food Baskets, 1973-91; boys coord. Am. Youth Soccer, 1993-94, girls coord.; chmn. Boy Scouts Am., 1980-85; exec. bd. PTA, 1978, 80, 85, 87, 92—, pres. 1990-92; sec. St. Paul Parent Group, 1992-93, Palimentarian, 1993—; rep. Cost Containment Com., 1994-96; Eucharistic minister Roman Cath. Ch. Recipient Hon. Svc. award PTA, 1979, Hon. Svc. Continuing award, 1982, Golden Oak award, 1995. Mem. AAUW (pres. 2001-2003, v.p. program 2003—, cultural chair), Montebello Tchrs. Assn., Delta Kappa Gamma (sec.-pres., recording sec.). Roman Catholic.

ROBOLD, ALICE ILENE, retired mathematician, educator; b. Delaware County, Ind., Feb. 7, 1928; d. Earl G. and Margaret Rebecca (Summers) Hensley; m. Virgil G. Robold, Aug. 21, 1955; 1 son, Edward Lynn. BS, Ball State U., 1955, MA, 1960, EdD, 1965. Substitute elem. tchr. Am. Elem. Sch., Augsburg, Germany, 1955-56; instr. Ball State U., Muncie, Ind., 1960-61, tchg. fellow, 1961-64, asst. prof. math. scis., 1964-69, assoc. prof., 1969-76, prof., 1976-98; ret., 1998. Mem. Nat. Coun. Tchrs. Math., Ind. Coun. Tchrs. Math. Mem. Ch. of God.

ROBOTIN, BARBARA ZIELINSKI, elementary school educator; b. Trenton, N.J., Apr. 20, 1951; d. Edward John and Mary Zielinski; m. Robert John Robotin, July 22, 1972. BS, Trenton State Coll., 1972. 1st grade tchr. Holy Cross Sch., Trenton, 1973-95, sec. adv. bd., 1992. Named Outstanding Educator of Cath. Schs., Diocese of Trenton, N.J., 1994. Mem. Cath. War Vets. Aux.

ROBSMAN, MARY LOUISE, education educator; b. Galena, Ill., June 19, 1943; d. Wilbur Henry and Stella Loretta (Bussan) Timpe; m. Igor Victor Robsman, Dec. 29, 1987. BS in Edn. and Math., No. Ill. U., 1964; MA in Edn. and Gifted Edn., U. Cen. Fla., 1981, EdD in Curriculum Instr. and Psychology, 1991. Cert. tchr. K-9. Tchr. math grades 7-8, grade 5 Dist. 300, Dundee, Ill., 1964-67; tchr. grade 5 Dept. Def. Overseas Schs., Frankfurt, Germany, 1967-69, Dist. 120, Galena, Ill., 1969-70; tchr. grades 5-6 Franklin-McKinley Dist., San Jose, Calif., 1970-72; tchr. math. grades 7-8 Dept. Def. Overseas Schs., Spangdahlem, Germany, 1972-74, tchr. grades 5-6, 1975, Dubuque (Iowa) Comty. Schs., 1976-80, tchr. learning resource K-6, 1981-87; instr. edn. dept. U. Cen. Fla., Orlando, 1988-91, Rollins Coll., Cocoa, Fla., 1991-93, prof. Melbourne, Fla., 1993-1998. Recipient Recognition of Svc. award Omicron Lambda, 1992, Appreciation award Kappa Delta Pi, 1994; Critchfield rsch. study grantee, 1994; Christa McAuliffe Tchg. award, 1998. Mem. ASCD, Nat. Coun. Tchrs. of Math., Omicron Lambda-Kappa Delta Pi. Republican. Roman Catholic. Avocations: international travel, creative writing. Home: 1578 Omega St NE Palm Bay FL 32907-2305 Office: Rollins Coll 475 S John Rodes Blvd West Melbourne FL 32904-1009

ROBSON, BARBARA S. elementary education educator; b. Phila., July 4, 1938; d. Robert John and Gladys Blodwyn (Williams) Smith; m. William John Robson, Oct.. 1, 1960; children: William Charles, Robin Lynne, Robert Bruce. BS, West Chester U., 1960; postgrad., Pa. State U., Millersville U., Fla. State U. Cert. elem. edn. Tchr. Lansdowne (Pa.) Aldan Sch. Dist., No. Lebanon Sch. Dist., Fredericksburg, Pa., Ea. Lebanon County Sch. Dist., Myerstown, Pa. Cooperating tchr., mentor Lebanon Valley Coll., curriculum coord. grade K-1. Delta Kappa Gamma scholar. Mem. NEA, Internat. Reading Assn., Assn. Supervision and Curriculum Devel., Pa. Edn. Assn., Ea. Lebanon County Edn. Assn., Lebanon County Ednl. Honor Soc., Delta Kappa Gamma. Home: RR 2 Box 240 Myerstown PA 17067-2704

ROBY, PAMELA ANN, sociology educator; b. Milw., Nov. 17, 1942; d. Clark Dearborn and Marianna (Gilman) R.; m. James Peter Mulherin, July 15, 1977 (div. 1987). BA, U. Denver, 1963; MA, Syracuse U., 1966; PhD, NYU, 1971. Instrn. ednl. sociology NYU, 1966; asst. prof. George Washington U., Washington, 1970-71; asst. prof. sociology and social welfare Brandeis U., Waltham, Mass., 1971-73; chair cmty. studies bd. U. Calif., Santa Cruz, 1974-76, 79, assoc. prof., 1973-77, prof. sociology and women's studies, 1977—, dir. sociology doctoral program, 1988-91, chair sociology dept., 1998-2001. Vis. scholar U. Wash., Seattle, 1991-92; mem. anthropology, linguistics and sociology panel NSF, Washington, 1993; mem. sociology program rev. com. Northeastern U., Boston, 1990; assessor Social Scis. and Humanities Rsch. Coun. Can., Toronto, 1993; cons. James Irvine Found., San Francisco, 1986; vice chair Nat. Commn. on Working Women, Washington, 1977-80; mem. social sci. rsch. rev. com. NIMH, Washington, 1976-78; Re-evaluation Counseling (coll. and U. faculty reference person), 1980—. Author: Women in the Workplace, 1981; editor: The Poverty Establishment, 1974, Child Care: Who Cares? Foreign and Domestic Infant and Early Childhood Development Policies, 1973-75; co-author: The Future of Inequality, 1970; adv. editor: Sociol. Quar., 1990-93, Gender and Society, 1986-89. Andrew W. Mellon sr. scholar Wellesley Coll., 1978-79; vis. fellow Indian Coun. Social Sci. Rsch., 1979. Mem. Soc. for Study Social Problems (pres. 1996-97), Sociologists for Women in Soc. (pres. 1978-80), Am. Sociol. Assn. (chair sect. on sex and gender 1974-78, exec. coun. mem.-at-large 1975-78), Internat. Sociol. Assn. (rsch. coun. mem.-at-large 1978-82), Pacific Sociol. Assn. (v.p. 1996-97), Ea. Sociol. Assn. (exec. coun. mem.-at-large 1973-74), Re-evaluation Counseling (internat. ref. person for coll. and univ. faculty), Phi Beta Kappa, Alpha Kappa Delta. Avocations: camping, hiking, painting, swimming, pen and ink drawing. Office: U Calif Dept Sociology C8 Santa Cruz CA 95064

ROCHA, OSBELIA MARIA JUAREZ, librarian, assistant principal; b. Odessa, Tex., Aug. 3, 1950; d. Tomas R. and Maria Socorro (Garcia) Juarez; m. Ricardo Rocha, July 8, 1972; children: Nidia Selina, René Ricardo. AA, Odessa Coll., 1970; BA, Sul Ross State U., 1972; MA, Tex. A&I U., 1977; MLS, Tex. Woman's U., 1991; Mid-Mgmt. Cert., U. Tex. of the Permian Basin, 1999. Cert. life provisional reading specialist, learning res. tchr., secondary english, math., Tex.; cert. mid-mgmt. adminstr. Math. tchr. Del Rio (Tex.) Jr. High Sch., 1972-78; reading tchr. Del Rio High Sch., 1978-79; math. tchr. Ector High Sch., Odessa, 1979-81, Permian High Sch., Odessa, 1981-88; libr. Blackshear Elem. Magnet Sch., Odessa, 1988-93, Bowie Jr. H.S., Odessa, 1993-95, Ector Jr. H.S., Odessa, 1995-96, Permian H.S., Odessa, 1996-2000; asst. prin. Big Spring H.S., Tex., 2000—02; prin./curriculum dir. Weimar HS I.S.D., 2002—. Reviewer of children's and adolescents' books for MultiCultural Rev.; author articles. Mem. ASCD, Tex. Assn. Secondary Sch. Prins., Tex. Assn. Bilingual Edn., Tex. Reading Assn., Tex. Libr. Assn., Tex. Elem. Prins. and Suprs. Assn., Tex. Coun. Women Sch. Execs., Beta Phi Mu, Delta Kappa Gamma. Roman Catholic. Avocations: reading, needlework, collecting realia from various cultures. Home: PO Box 279 Weimar TX 78962-0279 Office: Weimar HS 506 S Main St Weimar TX 78962 E-mail: osbeliar@yahoo.com., orocha@esc3.net.

ROCHA, PEDRO, JR., academic administrator, educator; b. Indé, México, Dec. 25, 1939; came to U.S., 1955; s. Pedro Sr. and Maria (Hernández) R.; m. Maria-Cruz Molina, Dec. 6, 1969; children: Diana-Marie, Delma-Irene, Pedro-Hugo. BA in History, U. Tex., El Paso, 1967, MA in Spanish, 1969; PhD in Edn. Adminstrn., U. Tex., 1981. Cert. secondary tchr., supr., adminstr., supt., Tex. Textbook adminstr. Ysleta Jr. High Sch., El Paso, 1976; secondary tchr. Ysleta Ind. Sch. Dist., El Paso, 1969-77; grad. student asst. U. Tex., El Paso, 1976-77, rsch. assoc. Austin, 1979-80; adminstrv. intern Austin (Tex.) C.C., 1978, substitute assoc. dean, 1981-83; rsch. intern S.W. Ednl. Devel. Lab., Austin, 1980-81; tax examiner div. clk. IRS, Austin, 1982; dir., coord. Cook Community Sch., Austin, 1982-85; from ESL instr. to dir., coord. Brooke Community Sch., Austin, 1985-86; dean Mesabi C.C., Virginia, Minn., 1987-92; v.p. for instrn. Trinidad (Colo.) State Jr. Coll., 1992-96; provost Union County Coll., Elizabeth, N.J., 1996—; instr. Spanish Kean U., Union, N.J., 1997—. Instr. Spanish Vermilion C.C., Ely, Minn., 1990; adj. instr. Spanish Trinidad State Jr. coll., 1995, 96, Union County Coll., N.J., 1997—; cons.-evaluator for Commn. on Instns. of Higher Edn. of North Ctrl. Assn. Colls. and Schs.; cons. Raton (N.Mex.) Arts and Humanities Coun., 1993, U. Tex., Austin, 1982-86, Tex. Assn. Chicanos in Higher Edn., Denton, 1982, Mexican Am. Legal Def. & Edn. Fund, San Antonio, 1982, Intercultural Rsch., Inc., El Paso, 1981. Author: Staff Orientation Program: Welcoming the Employee to Our Team, (calendar) Historic Trinidad 1996: Hispanic Contributions to Las Animas County. Active mem., bd. dirs. So. Colo. Coal Miners Meml. and Scholarship Fund, 1994; pres. Marquette Sch. Bd., Virginia, 1991-92; active San Juan Coun. Cmty. Agencies, Farmington, 1986-87; leader Quarterly Dates Group, Farmington, 1986-87; adv. bd. Austin Cmty. Gardens, 1985-86. With USAF, 1961-65. Richardson fellow U. Tex., 1977-79; nominated and selected for Nat. Cmty. Coll. Hispanic Coun. Leadership Tng. Program for Hispanic C.C. Adminstrs., 1994. Mem. Am. Assn. for Higher Edn., Am. Assn. Cmty./Jr. Coll., Genealogical Soc. Hispanis Am., Minn. Chief Acad. Adminstrs., Colo. Coun. Acad. Deans and Vice Pres., Colo. Ednl. Svcs. Coun., Kiwanis Club (first v.p. Trinidad 1995), Hispanic C. of C. (bd. dirs. Trinidad-Las Animas County Hispanic C. of C., pres. 1995-96), Elizabeth C. of C., K.C. (mem. coun. 1072, 1995—), Rotary, Kappa Delta Pi, Sigma Delta Pi. Democrat. Roman Catholic. Avocations: bowling, basketball, walking, travel. Home: 330 Jerusalem Rd Scotch Plains NJ 07076-1437 Office: Union County Coll 12 W Jersey St Elizabeth NJ 07201-2314

ROCHE, JOHN EDWARD, educator, human resources consultant; b. St. Albans, N.Y., Nov. 11, 1946; s. John F. and Carolyn C. (Miller) R.; m. Valerie Vastola; children: Christopher B., Danielle, Ryan J., Jennifer M. BA, Marist Coll., 1968, MBA, 1975; MS in Edn., SUNY, New Paltz, 1974; EdD, Nova Southeastern U., 1998. Tchr. Kingston (N.Y.) City Schs., 1968-76; employment supr. ACLI Internat. Inc., N.Y.C., 1976-78; dir. pers. Balfour MacLaine Internat., N.Y.C., 1978-80; mgr. employee rels. Harcourt Brace Jovanovich, N.Y.C., 1980-82; nat. dir. pers. Hayt, Hayt & Landau, Great Neck, N.Y., 1982-86; pres. Pers. Mgmt. Svcs., Great Neck, N.Y., 1983-86, Martin-Roche Assocs., Inc., Levittown, N.Y., 1986-94; prof. instrnl. tech. N.Y. Inst. Tech., Old Westbury, 1989-2000, chair Sch. Edn. Manhattan Campus, 1997-2000, acting dir. Ctr. Labor & Indls. Rels., 2000; dean Sch. Continuing Studies L.I. U., Bklyn., 2000—; pres. Human Resources Dept. Inc., Syosset, NY, 1994—2002, L.I. Bus. Network, Inc., 1994-2000. Pres. Martin-Roche Internat. Ltd., Plainview, N.Y., 1992-94. Exec. dir. Jr. Achievement, Kingston, 1972-76, coach Syosset Baseball Assn., Syosset Youth Athletic Commn., CYO Basketball Assn.; human resource com. mem. Adults and Children with Learning and Devel. Disabilities, 1990-2000; mem. Long Island U. Coun. Deans, Middle States Com. Mem. ASTD, WorldatWork (cert. compensation profl.), Soc. for Human Resource Mgmt. (cert. sr. profl. in human resources), KC (grand knight 1967-68). Republican. Roman Catholic. Avocations: astronomy, photography, painting. Home: 17 Meadow Ln Syosset NY 11791-4126 Office: L I Univ Sch Continuing Studies Brooklyn NY 11201 E-mail: jeroche@juno.com., jroche@liu.edu.

ROCHELEAU, JAMES ROMIG, retired university president; b. Anchorage, Mar. 21, 1940; s. James Albert and Sophia (Rivord) R.; m. Margaret Anne Sheehan, Nov. 28, 1981; children from previous marriage: Renee, Tanya, Andrea. BA, U. Idaho, 1968, MA, 1969; PhD, Wash. State U., Pullman, 1975. Account exec. Spokesman Rev., Spokane, Wash., 1963; sales rep. RJR Nabisco, Inc., Spokane, 1963-66; grad. asst. U. Idaho, Moscow and Wash. State U., Pullman, 1967-70; instr. history Wash. State U., 1970-71; asst. prof. history Buena Vista Coll., Storm Lake, Iowa, 1971-76, dir., 1976-81, dean continuing edn., 1981-84; pres. Upper Iowa U., Fayette, 1984-94, pres. emeritus, 1994—. Cons. North Ctrl. Assn., Chgo., 1981—, Kellogg Found., 1994-99, Univ. Pres., 1994—. Active N.E.-Midwest Leadership Coun. Served with U.S. Army, 1958-61. Mem. Nat. Assn. Ind. Colls. and Univs., Iowa Assn. Ind. Colls. Univs., Coun. Ind. Colls., Iowa Coordinating Coun. for Post-High Sch. Edn., C. of C.*

ROCHELLE, LUGENIA, academic administrator; b. Maple Hill, N.C., July 14, 1943; d. John Edward and Ruby Lee (Holmes) R. BA, St. Augustine's Coll., 1965; MS, N.C. A & T State U., 1969; D of Pedagogy, Barbar-Scotia Coll., 1993. Cert. tchr., N.C. Tchr. French, English Butler High Sch., Barnwell, S.C., 1965-67; instr. English N.C. A & T State U., Greensboro, 1970-77, St. Augustine's Coll., Raleigh, N.C., 1977-86, dir. freshman studies program, 1986-91, dean lower coll., 1991-95, asst. to v.p. acad. affairs, 1991-92; dir. gen. studies, asst. prof. English Voorhees Coll., Denmark, S.C., 1996-98, spl. asst. to pres. external affairs, 1999—2002, dir. Hons. Coll., 1999—, dean, Coll. of General Studies, 2002—. Dir. Mellon program St. Augustine's Coll., Raleigh, 1980-83; adv. bd. cooperating Raleigh Colls., 1986—, Off to Coll., Montgomery, Ala., 1993—; mem. profl. practices commn. N.C. Dept. Pub. Instrn., 1994-96; coord. Title III, 1999-00, coord. Bd. Trustees Rels., 1999-02; dir. Ctr. Excellence in Humanities, Vorhees Coll., April 2000-02; Hostess for Radio Talk Show, Views and News from Voorhees Coll., Sept. 2001-03. Author: English Manual of Writing, 1980, (with others) Off to College, 1997, 98, reprinted, 1999, 2000, 01; editor: Can't Nobody Do You Like Jesus, 1998. Judge oratorical contests, Optimist Club, Raleigh, 1985-93; chair pro tem Raleigh Bicentennial Hist. Com., Raleigh, 1991-92; initiated, effected chartering of Phi Eta Sigma St. Augustine's Coll., 1995; bd. dirs. Garner Rd. YMCA, Raleigh, 1994-1996; coord. Honda Campus All-Star Challenge, 1996—; lay min., sec. vestry St. Philip's Episcopal Ch., 1997—; instnl. rep. S.C. Women in Higher Edn., Voorhees Coll., 1998—. Nat. teaching fellow N.C. A & T State U., Greensboro, 1968-70. NCTE Fellow Nat. Coun. Tchrs. English; mem. ASCD (assoc.), Am. Assn. U. Women (pres. Denmark Br.), Cardinal Club. Avocations: reading, collecting antique birds, travel. E-mail: rochelle@voorhees.edu.

ROCHOWICZ, JOHN ANTHONY, JR., mathematician, mathematics and physics educator; b. Reading, Pa., Mar. 20, 1950; s. John Anthony and Sara Jane (Binckley) R. BS in Math., Albright Coll., 1972; MS in Math., Lehigh U., 1974; secondary edn. cert. math., Albright Coll., 1975; EdD in Ednl. Tech., Lehigh U., 1993. Cert. secondary teaching, Pa. Math. tchr. Bethlehem (Pa.) Cath. High Sch., 1980-81; instr. math. Pa. State U.-Berks, Reading, 1982-84, Kutztown (Pa.) U., 1983-84, Lehigh County C.C., Schnecksville, Pa., 1984, Alvernia Coll., Reading, 1984, Reading (Pa.) Area C.C., 1984-86; prof. math. Alvernia Coll., 1985—. Recipient Alumni Educator award Albright Coll., Reading, 1987. Mem. AAUP, Math. Assn. Am., Assn. for the Advancement Computing in Edn., Assn. for Ednl. Communications and Tech., Nat. Coun. Tchrs. Math.; contbr. articles to scientific jours. Democrat. Roman Catholic. Avocations: collecting music, computers, calculators, billiards, swimming. Home: 41 Columbia Ave SCM Reading PA 19606-1316 Office: Alvernia College 400 Saint Bernardine St Reading PA 19607-1799

ROCKART, JOHN FRALICK, information systems researcher; b. N.Y.C., June 20, 1931; s. John Rachac and Janet (Ross) R.; m. Elise Jean Feldmann, Sept. 16, 1961; children: Elise B. Liesl, Scott F. AB, Princeton U., 1953; MBA, Harvard U., 1958; PhD, MIT, 1968. Sales rep. IBM, 1958-61, dist. med. rep., 1961-62, fellow in Africa, 1962-64; instr. MIT, Cambridge, Mass., 1966-67; asst. prof. IBM, Cambridge, Mass., 1967-70, assoc. prof., 1970-74, sr. lectr., 1974—; dir. MIT, Cambridge, 1976—. Bd. dirs. Keane, Inc., Boston, Comshare, Inc., Ann Arbor, Mich., Selective Ins. Group, Branchburg, NJ. Co-author: Computers & Learning Process, 1974, Rise of Managerial Computing, 1986, Executive Support Systems, 1988 (Computer Press Assn. 1989); contbr. articles to profl. jours. Trustee New Eng. Med. Ctr., Boston. Lt. USN, 1953-56. Mem. Assn. for Computing Machinery, Inst. for Mgmt. Sci., Soc. for Info. Mgmt. (bd. dirs. mem. at large 1989-94), Weston (Mass.) Golf Club, Lake Sunapee Country Club (New London, N.H.). Republican. Unitarian Universalist. Home: 150 Cherry Brook Rd Weston MA 02493-1308 Office: CISR MIT Sloan Sch Mgmt 3 Cambridge Ctr NE20-336 Cambridge MA 02142

ROCKENSIES, KENNETH JULES, physicist, educator; b. N.Y.C., June 10, 1938; s. John William and Wilma (Mercz) R.; m. Eileen Regina Dros, June 6, 1970; children: Kevin John, Patricia Ann, Regina Marie. BS in Physics, Polytech. U. Bklyn., 1960, MS in Physics, 1962; postgrad., NYU, 1965-67, Adelphi U., 1969-75, Nova U., 1992—. Physicist We. Union Telegraph, N.Y.C., 1962-63; prof. CUNY, Bklyn., 1963-93, Coll. Misericordia, Dallas, Pa., 1993—. Author: The Rotational Interferometer, 1962, The Effect of Class Size on Achievement in College Physics, 1995. Mem. NSTA, Am. Assn. Physics Tchrs., Soc. Coll. Sci. Tchrs., Optical Soc. Am. Achievements include rsch. in interferometry, relativistic optics, electrostatic data storage, electrosensitive recording papers and statis. studies in edn. Office: College Misericordia 301 Lake St Dallas PA 18612-1090

ROCKOFF, SHEILA G. nursing and health facility administrator, nursing and health occupations educator; b. Chgo., Mar. 15, 1945; d. Herbert Irwin and Marilyn (Victor) R.; divorced. ADN, Long Beach City Coll., 1966; BSN, San Francisco State U., 1970; MSN, Calif. State U., L.A., 1976; EDD, South Ea. Nova U., 1993. RN, pub. health nurse, nursing instr., prof., health facility supr., Calif. Staff nurse Meml. Hosp., Long Beach, Calif., 1966-67, Mt. Zion Med. Ctr., San Francisco, 1967-69; instr. nursing Hollywood Presbyn. Med. Ctr., L.A., 1970-74; nursing supr. Orthop. Hosp., L.A., 1974-76; instr. nursing Ariz. State U., Tempe, 1976-78; nurse supr. Hoag Meml. Hosp., Newport Beach, Calif., 1977-78; nurse educator U. Calif., Irvine and Orange, 1978-80; nursing prof. Rancho Santiago Coll., Calif., 1980-89, dir. health svcs., 1989-95, dir., chair Health Occupations, 1995—; nursing prof. Rancho Santiago C.C., Santa Ana Campus; nurse cons. Home Health Care Agy., Irvine, 1983; educator, cons. Parenting Resources, Tustin, Calif., 1985-89. Contbr. articles to profl. jours. Mem. Nat. Assn. Student Personal Adminstrs., Am. Coll. Health Assn., Calif. Nurses Assn. (chmn. com. 1970-73), Assoc. of Calif. C.C. Administr., Calif

C.C. Health Occpl. Educators, Assn. (bd. dirs.), Pacific Coast Coll. Health Assn., Soroptomist Internat., Phi Kappa Phi. Democrat. Jewish. Office: Rancho Santiago CC 1530 W 17th St Santa Ana CA 92706-3398

ROCKWELL, KAY ANNE, elementary education educator; b. Brighton, Mich., Feb. 12, 1952; d. Philip Oscar and Patricia Irene (Bennett) Newton; m. Lawrence Edward Rockwell, Aug. 23, 1975. BA in Social Sci. & Elem. Edn. cum laude, Spring Arbor Coll., 1974; MA in Early Childhood Edn., Ea. Mich. U., 1981. Dir. child care St. Luke's Luth. Day Care Ctr., Ann Arbor, Mich., 1980-82; tchr. 3d grade Colo. Christian Sch., Denver, 1982-94; tchr. 1st grade Front Range Christian Sch., Littleton, Colo., 1994—. Chmn. Nat. Children's Book Week Colo. Christian Sch., 1993-94, chmn. ACSI spelling bee, 1991-94, 95-98, chmn. ACSI speech meet, 1985-86; mem. Bible curriculum com., chmn. reading curriculum com. Front Range Christian Sch., 1999-2000, mem. edn. com., 1999-2001. Spring Arbor Coll. scholar, 1972-74. Office: Front Range Christian Sch 4001 S Wadsworth Blvd Littleton CO 80123-1358

RODDEN, JOHN GALLAGHER, communications educator, writer; b. Phila., Oct. 18, 1956; s. John and Rose Gallagher Rodden. BA, LaSalle U., Pa., 1978; MA, U. Va., 1982, PhD, 1987. Asst. prof. U. Va., 1983-89, U. Tex., 1989-93. Author: the Politics of Lit. Reputation, 1989, Performing the Lit. Interview, 2001, Repainting the Little Red Schoolhouse: A History of East Germany, 2002, Orwell: The Politics of Reputation, 2001, Reunification through American Eyes and German Voices, 2003, Scenes from An Afterlife: the Legacy of George Orwell, 2003, Irving Howe and the Critics, 2003; editor: Lionel Trilling, 1999, Conversations With Isabel Allende, 1999, Understanding George Orwell's Animal Farm, 2000. Recipient dissertation award Nat. Comm. Assn., 1988, 1st place book award Nat. Communication Assn., 1990, Nat. Champion in persuasive speaking, Nat. forensic Assn., 1978. Roman Catholic. Avocation: running. Home: 2502 Nueces St Apt 212 Austin TX 78705-4835

RODEN, CAROL LOONEY, retired language educator; b. Boston, Mass., Jan. 10, 1939; d. William Vincent and Margaret Carey Delaney; m. Vincent James Looney, Feb. 11, 1961 (div. Nov. 1995); children: Vincent J. III Looney, Kara A. Putnam, Douglas B. Looney, John W. Looney; m. Thomas Edward Roden, July 7, 1997. BA, Emmanuel Coll., 1960; postgrad., SUNY, Albany, 1974. Spanish tchr. Hingham (Mass.) H.S., 1960—61, Kennedy H.S., Utica, NY, 1974—80, Waterville (N.Y.) Cen. Sch., 1983—94, Archbishop Carroll H.S., Wayne, Pa., 1995—96; ret., 1996. Author (numerous poems) ; photographer. Pres. PTA, Whitesboro, NY, 1971; v.p. Newcomers Group, Utica, NY, 1970; vol. Puerto Rican Cmty. House, Boston, 1959. Fellow, U. Kans., 1960; scholar Gov. Furcolo scholar, State of Mass., 1956. Mem.: AAUW (v.p. membership 1995—99, Gift honoree 1999, Outstanding Woman of Yr. 2000), Alpha Mu Gamma. Democrat. Roman Catholic. Home: 119 Sawgrass Dr Blue Bell PA 19422

RODENBERG, ANITA JO, academic administrator; b. Dodge City, Kans., Jan. 27, 1956; d. Albert Milton and Anita Marileen (O'Bleness) Kidder; m. Leland Leroy Lambert, Nov. 25, 1972 (div. July 1991); children: Justin, Mason, Vanessa; m. Lindell Vern Rodenberg, Mar. 10, 1994; children: Dawn, Elaina, Lynell. AS in Bus. Adminstrn., Seward County C.C., 1995; BS in Human Resource Mgmt., Friends U., 1996; MS in Edn. Adminstrn., Fort Hays State U., 1999. Cert. devel. edn. specialist Appalachian State U. Co-owner LA Inc., Liberal, Kans., 1980-90; accts. payable clk. Seward County C.C., Liberal, 1990-93, asst. dir. bus. and industry, 1993-95, peer tutor coord., 1995—, coord. devel. edn., 1996—, dir. acad. achievement ctr., 1996—. Mem. adult learning ctr. adv. bd. Seward County C.C., 1996—, mem. continuous quality coun., 1996—. Mem. Liberal Transition Coun., 1996—. Mem. Nat. Assn. for Devel. Edn., Midwest Regional Assn. for Devel. Edn., Coll. Reading and Learning Assn., Seward County C.C. Profl. Employee Assn., Liberal C. of C. (edn. com. 1996—). Home: 2164 N Carlton Ave Liberal KS 67901-2127 Office: Seward County CC 1801 N Kansas Ave PO Box 1137 Liberal KS 67905-1137

RODENSCHMIT, HELEN JULIANA, elementary education educator; b. Cross Plains, Wis., Jan. 8, 1932; d. Frank William and Juliana Helen (Schmelzer) R. BS in Edn., Alverno Coll., 1962; MS in Edn., U. Wis., Whitewater, 1988. Cert. elem. tchr., reading tchr., bilingual tchr., Wis., elem. tchr., Costa Rica; lifetime elem. tchr., N.Y. Tchr. primary St. Bernardine Sch., Forest Pk., Ill., 1951-58, St. Cyprian Sch., River Grove, Ill., 1958-59; tchr. elem. St. Monical Sch., N.Y.C., 1959-64, Holy Spirit Sch., Milw., 1964-66, St. Joseph Sch., Phlox, Wis., 1966-67; tchr. sci. and art St. Clare Collegio, Moravia, Costa Rica, 1968; tchr. elem. St. Joseph Primary, Moravia, Costa Rica, 1969-80; tchr. Kindergarten St. Francis Colegio, Moravia, Costa Rica, 1981-84; elem. libr. Lincoln Colegio, Moravia, Costa Rica, 1985-86; tchr. migrant and bilingual Marshall (Wis.) Pub. Sch., 1988-94; ESL tchr. Westside Elem. Sch., Sun Prairie, Wis., 1994-95, Mauston (Wis.) Elem. Sch., 1995—. Rsch. project tchr. U. Minn., 1964-66; tchr. tng. ESL, St. Joseph Pirmary, St. Francis Colegio, Moravia, Costa Rica, elem. coord. ESL, 1981-84; home tutor, Costa Rica, 1975-86. Mem. St. Vincent DePaul Project, Barrio Corazon de Jesus, Moravia, Costa Rica, 1970-73. Mem. Assn. Childhood Internat., Tchrs. English as Second Lang., Nat. Assn. Bilingual Edn., Sch. Sisters of St. Francis. Avocations: fgn. travel, gardening. Home: 4517 County Trunk Hwy P Cross Plains WI 53528

RODGERS, BERNARD FRANCIS, JR., academic administrator, dean; b. Hazleton, Pa., Mar. 21, 1947; s. Bernard F. and Anna V. (Gulla) R.; m. Patricia Hick, Dec. 6, 1969 (div. June, 1982); m. Jane Powell, Oct. 27, 1984. BS in English and Edn., Mt. St. Mary's Coll., 1969; MA in English, U. Bridgeport, 1972; PhD in English with honors, U. Chgo., 1975. Tchr. Eng., dir. drama Somers Ctrl. High Sch., Lincolndale, N.Y., 1969-72; seminar coord. Shakespeare Inst. U. Bridgeport, 1972; lectr. Am. Lit. U. Chgo. Extension, 1975; instr., asst. prof. lit. and humanities City Colls. Chgo., 1975-82, spl. asst. to chancellor, 1984-85; faculty Eng. Simon's Rock Coll. of Bard, Great Barrington, Mass., 1985—, dean acad. affairs, 1985-87, v.p., dean, 1987—. Chair lit. and humanities sect. coll. accreditaiton program Chgo. City-Wide Coll., 1977—78, chair coll. acceleration program, 1977—78, mem. adminstrv. coun., 1980—81; bd. overseers Simon's Rock Coll. of Bard, 1987—; evaluator NEH Summer Insts. H.S. English Tchrs., 1985, 86; proposal evaluator Fund for Improvement Postsecondary Edn., 1984; mem. planning com. humanists Write On, Chgo., 1982—83; mem. nom. com. Eisenhower Fellowship Am. Embassy, Warsaw, 1980; mem. writing panel artists-in-residence program Chgo. Coun. Fine Arts, 1978; spkr. in field. Author: Philip Roth: A Bibliography, 1974, 2nd edit., 1984, Philip Roth, 1978, Contemporary American Fictoin 1944-79: A Chronology, 1980, Voices and Visions: Selected Essays, 2001; essayist, reviewer in field; contbr. articles; assoc. prodr. TV talk show U. Chgo., 1974—75; prodr.: TV talk show U. Chgo., 1975—76; prodr., host interview program City Colls. Chgo., 1981—82. Bd. dirs. Fairview Hosp., Great Barrington, 1988-94, Mass. Found. for Humanities, chair, 1992-94, vice chair, 1991-92, chair program com., 1990-92, pres., 1992-94, Friends of Chgo. Pub. Libr., 1982; mem. South County cabinet Berkshires United Way, 1988, mem. planning com. humanists Read Ill., 1984-85, ad hoc com. excellence Ill. C.C. Trustees Assn., 1984-85. U. Chgo. fellow, 1973, Ford Found. fellow, 1974-75, Fulbright-Hays sr. lectr. to Poland, 1979-80, Chgo. Pub. Libr. assoc. scholar, 1976-78. Mem. So. Berkshire C. of C. (bd. dirs. 1987-90), New Eng. Assn. Schs. and Colls. (evaluation team chair commn. instns. higher edn. 1986—), North Ctrl. Assn. Colls. and Schs. (asst. dir. commn. instns. higher edn 1982-84), Soc. Midland Authors (chair fiction award com. 1985), Lambda Iota Tau, Pi Delta Epsilon, Delta Epsilon Sigma. Home: PO Box 778 Great Barrington MA 01230-0778 Office: Simon's Rock Coll of Bard 84 Alford Rd Great Barrington MA 01230-1559

RODGERS, BETH L. nursing educator, researcher; ASN, Floyd Jr. Coll., 1977; BS, Ga. State U., 1982; MSN, U. Va., 1983, PhD, 1987. RN Ala. Staff nurse U. Ala. Med. Ctr., Birmingham, 1977-78; staff, charge nurse Piedmont Hosp., Atlanta, 1978-82; tchg. asst. U. Va., Charlottesville, 1982-85, grad. rsch. asst., 1983-86; instr. U. Wis., Milw., 1986, asst. prof., 1987-91, assoc. prof., 1991—99, prof., 2000—, dir. PhD program, 2002—. Rsch. facilitator Trinity Meml. Hosp., Cudahy, Wis., 1992-99. Author: Concept Development in Nursing, 1993, 2d edit., 2000; contbr. articles to profl. jours. Dupont fellow U. Va., 1985, others. Fellow Am. Acad. of Nursing; mem. ANA, Wis. Nurses Assn. (commn. ethics 1989-94, polit. action com. 1990-92), Midwest Nursing Rsch. Soc., Midwest Sociol. Soc., Sigma Theta Tau, Phi Kappa Phi. Office: U Wis-Milw Coll Nursing 1921 E Hartford Ave Milwaukee WI 53211-3060

RODGERS, DANIEL TRACY, history educator; b. Darby, Pa., Sept. 29, 1942; s. Oliver Eliot and Dorothy (Welch) R.; m. Irene Wylie, 1971; children: Peter Samuel, Dwight Oliver. AB, BS in Engring., Brown U., 1965; PhD in History, Yale U., 1973. Instr. history U. Wis., Madison, 1971-73, asst. prof., 1973-78, assoc. prof., 1978-80; assoc. prof. history Princeton (N.J.) U., 1980-86, prof., 1986-98, Henry Charles Lea prof. history, 1998—, chair, 1988-95, 97-98. Fulbright lectr., Frankfurt, Fed. Republic Germany, 1983-84; Pitt prof., Cambridge Univ., 2003-04. Author: The Work Ethic in Industrial America, 1860-1920 (Frederick Jackson Turner award 1978), 1978, Contested Truths: Keywords in American Politics since Independence, 1987, Atlantic Crossings: Social Politics in a Progressive Age, 1998 (Ellis W. Hawley award 1979, George Louis Beer prize 1979). Recipient Chancellor's award U. Wis., Madison, 1978, Am. Coun. Learned Socs. fellow, 1976, NEH fellow, 1987-88, Ctr. for Advanced Study in Behavioral Scis. fellow, 1991-92; Woodrow Wilson Ctr. fellow, 1999-2000. Office: Princeton U Dept History Princeton NJ 08544-0001 E-mail: drodgers@princeton.edu.

RODGERS, DIANNA SUE, private school educator; b. Mineral Wells, Tex., Feb. 18, 1953; d. William Floyd and Nellie Rose (Frazier) R. Student, Glassboro State Coll., 1971-73; BA, Southeastern Coll. Assemblies of God, 1975; postgrad., Rollins Coll., 1976-77. Cert. tchr., N.J. 6th grade tchr. First Christian Assembly Acad., Memphis, 1975-81; kindergarten tchr. Ambassador Christian Acad., Glassboro, N.J., 1981-85; dir. Children's Edn. Ctr., Upland, Pa., 1985-86; 7th and 8th grade tchr. Ambassador Christian Acad., Glassboro, 1986-87, presch. tchr., 1987-88; 3d-6th grade tchr. Cen. Jersey Christian Sch., Asbury Park, N.J., 1988-94, elem. prin., 1989-93; tchr. 2d grade Calvary Acad., Lakewood, NJ, 1994—2000, elem. prin., 2000—. Asst. Brownie leader Girl Scouts Am., Glassboro, 1971-72; dir., organizer Vacation Bible Sch., Calvary Hill Assembly of God, Glassboro, 1988, Children's Ch. leader, 1981-88; tchr. Vacation Bible Sch., First Assembly of God, Shrewsbury, N.J., 1991, 92, 93, sec., bd. dirs., 1991-96, toddler ch. tchr., 1989-98, Sunday sch. supt., 1999-2002; Sunday Sch. tchr. First Christian Assembly, Memphis, 1975-81. Mem.: Internat. Assn. Christian Sch. Adminstrs. Avocations: reading, arts and crafts, volleyball, cooking. Home: 54 Belshaw Ave Eatontown NJ 07724-2930 Office: Calvary Acad 1133 E County Line Rd Lakewood NJ 08701-2115

RODGERS, GERALDINE ELLEN, retired elementary school educator; b. Newark, Dec. 20, 1925; d. Charles Joseph and Katharine Geraldine (Murtha) Rodgers. BS in Elem. Edn. magna cum laude, Fairleigh Dickinson U., 1963; MA in Nat. History, William Paterson Coll., 1967. Elem. tchr. Wayne (N.J.) Twp. Schs., 1963-85; ret., 1985. Sabbatical leave to observe and test the tchg. of beginning reading, United States, Netherlands, Sweden, Germany, Austria, France, 1977—78; rschr. in field, 1978—; spkr. in field. Author: (book) Why Jacques, Johann and Jan Can Read, 1979, The Case of the Prosecution in the Trial of Silent Reading Comprehension Tests, 1981, The Wary Reader's Guide to Psycholinguistics: Subjective vs. Objective Readers, 1982, The Flat Earth of American Reading Instruction, 1983, A Counter-Report on the Report of the Commission on Reading, 1985, The History of Beginning Reading: From Teaching by "Sound" to Teaching by "Meaning", 1995, The History of Beginning Reading: From Teaching by "Sound" to Teaching by "Meaning", 2d edit., 2001, The Hidden Story, 1998; contbr. articles to profl. jours. Vol. Lyndhurst Twp. Schs., 1998—2003. Republican. Roman Catholic. Avocations: gardening, travel, classical music, natural history.

RODGERS, GRACE ANNE, university official; b. South Bend, Ind., Apr. 19, 1936; d. Morris and Barbara Mae (Hamm) Morrow; m. Eugene M. Rodgers, July 7, 1956; children: Craig Eugene, Kimberly Sue. BS, Ind. State U., 1981; pub. mgmt. cert., Ind. U., South Bend, 1991, MPA, 1993. Dir. spl. programs Ivy Tech. State Coll., South Bend, 1990-94, mktg. cons., 1994; mem. assoc. faculty dept. pub. affairs--non-profit marketing and environ. Ind. U., 1994—, dir. internships-student svcs. Sch. Pub.-Environ. Affairs, 1994—, dir. cmty. links, 1997—. Author: (manuals) Resume and Beyond, 1990, Strategic Marketing Plan, 1994. Mem. Youth Svcs. Bur., South Bend Recipient Indiana U. South Bend Student Gov. Lifetime Achievement award. Mem. Ind. U. Sch. Pub. end Environ. Affairs Alumni Assn. (adv. coun. 1993—), Ind. U.-South Bend Alumni Assn., Ind. State U. Alumni Assn., Phi Theta Kappa (hon., award for outstanding svc. 1993), Pi Alpha Alpha (sec. 1996—). Republican. Methodist. Avocations: travel, reading, classical music. Home: 17120 Killarney Ct Granger IN 46530-9771 Office: Ind U 1800 Mishawaka Ave South Bend IN 46615-1621 E-mail: profgrac@aol.com.

RODGERS, JOHN JOSEPH, III, educational administration consultant, educator; b. Jamaica, N.Y., Oct. 13, 1941; s. John Joseph Rodgers, Edith (McInerney) Rodgers; m. Iris Rodgers; children: Janet, John Joseph IV, Yvette. BS, Fordham U., 1962; Profl. diploma, St. Johns U., 1970, EdD, 1979; postgrad., CUNY, Flushing. Asst. prin. N.Y.C. Bd. Edn., 1972-82; prin. Howard T. Herber Sch., Malverne, N.Y., 1982-85, Norman Thomas H.S., N.Y.C., 1988-96, Matawan Regional H.S., Aberdeen, N.J., 1996-97; cons. on ednl. adminstrn. Valley Stream, NY, 1999—; prof. math. Farleigh Dickinson U., Madison, N.J., 1999-2001; prof. ednl. adminstrn. Coll. New Rochelle, N.Y., 2000-01; dean acad. affairs Five Towns Coll., Dix Hills, NY, 2001—02; acad. dean Bus. Informatics Ctr., The Coll. for Bus., Valley Stream, NY, 2002—. Mem. ASCD, Am. Assn. Sch. Adminstrs., Math. Assn. Am., Nat. Assn. Secondary Sch. Prins. Home: 350-34 N Corona Ave Valley Stream NY 11580-3403 E-mail: jrodgers@thecollegeforbusiness.com., pelicula419@hotmail.com.

RODGERS, LOIS EVE, secondary school educator; BA, U. So. Miss.; MEd, William Carey Coll.; student, Bread Loaf Sch. English. Tchr. Hattiesburg (Miss.) High Sch. Named Miss. State English Tchr. of Yr., 1993.*

RODGERS, MARILYN CAROL, special education educator; b. Derby, Conn., May 20, 1951; d. Stanley and Mary Irene (Wojiski) Slowik; m. Billy John Rodgers, Oct. 25, 1940; children: David Warner, Merlenna, Jai, Daniel. BA in Psychology, U. Conn., 1973; AMS Cert., Montessori Western Tchr. Prog., Los Alamitos, Calif., 1975; MA in Spl. Edn., U. Hawaii, Manoa, 1998. Tchr. Hans Christian Anderson Montessori Sch., Tolland, Conn., 1974-76; breath therapist Rebirth America, San Francisco, 1977-80; singer Allright Family Band, 1980-94; spl. edn. tchr. Pahoa Elem. Sch., 1994-98; tchr. Family Treatment Ctr. Queens Med. Ctr., Honolulu, 1998—2001; spl. edn. tchr. Lanikai Elem. PUb. Charter Sch., 2001—. Cameraperson Buck Rodgers Hawaiian Beat TV Show and Public Access; founder Hawaii Island for Inclusive Vocat. Experiences, 1996—; lectr. in field. Contbr. articles to profl. jours. Jehovah'S Witness. Home: 354 Keolu Dr Kailua HI 96734-4264 E-mail: fordavid@hawaii.rr.com.

RODGERS, MARY COLUMBRO, literature educator, writer, academic administrator; b. Aurora, Ohio, Apr. 17, 1925; d. Nicola and Nancy (DeNicola) Columbro; m. Daniel Richard Rodgers, July 24, 1965; children: Robert, Patricia, Kristine. AB, Notre Dame Coll., 1957; MA, Western Res. U., 1962; PhD, Ohio State U., 1964; postgrad., U. Rome, 1964-65; EdD, Calif. Nat. Open U., 1975, DLitt, 1978. Tchr. English Cleve. elem. schs., 1945-52, Cleve. secondary schs., 1952-62; supr. English student tchrs. Ohio State U., 1962-64; asst. prof. English U. Md., 1965-66; assoc. prof. Trinity Coll., 1967-68; prof. English D.C. Tchrs. Coll. U. D.C., 1968—2000; pres. Md. Nat. U., 1972—; chancellor Open U. Am., 1965—; dean Am. Open U. Acad.; ret., 2000; ind. rschr., writer, 2000—. Author: A Short Course in English Composition, 1976, Chapbook of Children's Literature, 1977, Comprehensive Catalogue: The Open University of America System, 1978-80, Open University of America System Source Book, V, VII, VII, 1978, Essays and Poems on Life and Literature, 1979, Modes and Models: Four Lessons for Young Writers, 1981, Open University Structures and Adult Learning, 1982, Papers in Applied English Linguistics, 1982, Twelve Lectures on the American Open University, 1982, English Pedagogy in the American Open University, 1983, Design for Personalized English Graduate Degrees in the Urban University, 1984, Open University English Teaching, 1945-85: Conceptual History and Rationale, 1985, Claims and Counterclaims Regarding Instruction Given in Personalized Degree Residency Programs Completed by Graduates of California National Open University, 1986, The American Open University, 1965 to 1985: History and Sourcebook, 1986, New Design II: English Pedagogy in the American Open University, 1987, The American Open University, 1965 to 1985: A Research Report, 1987, The American Open University and Other Open Universities: A Comparative Study Report, 1988, Poet and Pedagogue in Moscow and Leningrad: A Travel Report, 1989, Foundations of English Scholarship in the American Open University, 1989, Twelve Lectures in Literary Analysis, 1990, Ten Lectures in Literary Production, 1990, Analyzing Fact and Fiction, 1991, Analyzing Poetry and Drama, 1991, Some Successful Literary Research Papers: An Inventory of Titles and Theses, 1991, Catalogue for the Mary Columbro Rodgers Literary Trust, 1992, A Chapbook of Poetry and Drama Analysis, 1992, Convent Poems, 1943-1961, 1992, Catholic Marriage Poems 1962, 1979, 1993, Catholic Widow with Children Poems 1979-1993, 1994, First Access List to the Mary Columbro Rodgers Trust by Year, 1994, Nicola Columbro: A Brief Biography, 3d edit., 1994, Biographical Sourcebook I: Mary Columbro Rodgers 1969-1995, 1995, Catholic Teacher Poems, 1945-1995, 1995, Fables and Farm Stories for Fiction Analysis, 1995, Second Access List to the Mary Columbro Rodgers Literary Trust by Alphabet, 1995, Third Access List to the Mary Columbro Rodgers Literary Trust by Subject, 1996, Fourth Access List to the Mary Columbro Rodgers Literary Trust for K-PhD, Open Learning-Open University Methods with Data Batches Delineated, 2002, Journals: Reflections and Resolves 1992-2002, 14 vols., 2002; contbr. articles to profl. jours. Fulbright scholar U. Rome, 1964-65. Fellow Cath. Scholars; mem. U.S. Distance Learning Assn., Poetry Soc. Am., Nat. Coun. Tchrs. English, Am. Ednl. Rsch. Assn., Am. Acad. Poets, Pi Lambda Theta. Home and Office: Coll Heights Estates 3916 Commander Dr Hyattsville MD 20782-1027 E-mail: openuniv@aol.com.

RODGERS, SHERRY HOVIOUS, elementary education educator; b. Louisville, Oct. 8, 1947; d. Buell and Frona (Humphress) Hovious; m. Alex Rodgers, Aug. 26, 1966; children: A. Matthew, R. Jeremy. BS in Edn., U. Louisville, 1988; postgrad., Spalding U. Cert. elem. tchr. Tchr. elem. Cobb County Pub. Schs., Cobb County, Ga., 1989—95, Jefferson County Pub. Schs., Louisville, 1995—2003, Belmont Hills Elem. Sch., Smyrna, Ga., 2003—. Mem. NEA, Ky. Edn. Assn., Jefferson County Tchrs. Assn. Republican. Methodist. Avocations: reading, baking, music. Home: 1813 Mount Berry Dr Douglasville GA 30135-1191 E-mail: shrgram@yahoo.com.

RODIN, JUDITH SEITZ, academic administrator, psychology educator; b. Phila., Sept. 9, 1944; d. Morris and Sally R. (Winson) Seitz. AB, U. Pa., 1966; PhD, U. Columbia, 1970. Asst. prof. psychology NYU, 1970—72; assoc. prof. Yale U., 1975—79, prof., dir. grad. studies, 1982—89, Philip R. Allen prof. psychology, medicine and psychiatry, 1984—94, chmn. dept. psychology, 1989—91, dean Grad. Sch., 1991—92, provost, 1992—94; pres. U. Pa., Phila., 1994—, prof. psychology, medicine and psychiatry, 1994—. Chmn. John D. and Catherine T. MacArthur Found. Rsch. Network on Determinants and Consequences of Health-Promoting and Health-Damaging Behavior, 1983-93; vice chair coun. press. U. Rsch. Assn., 1994-95, chair, 1995-96; mem. Ind. Panel to Review Safety Procedures at The White House, 1994-95; chair adv. com. Robert Wood Johnson Found., 1994—; mem. Pres. Clinton's Com. Advisors Sci. and Tech., 1994—; mem. Coun. Competitiveness, 1997—; mem. nominating com. N.Y. Stock Exch., 1998—; bd. dirs. Aetna, Electronic Data Sys., AMR. Author: (with S. Schachter) Obese Humans and Rats, 1978, Exploding the Weight Myths, 1982, Body Traps, 1992; chief editor Appetite Jour., 1979-92; contbr. articles to profl. jours. Mem. Pa. Task Force on Higher Edn. Funding, 1994; bd. dirs. Catalyst, N.Y.C., 1994—; trustee Brookings Inst., 1995—; pres. steering com. Am. Reads, 1997—. Fellow Woodrow Wilson Found., 1966-67, John Simon Guggenheim Found., 1986-87; grantee NSF, 1973-82, NIH, 1981—. Fellow AAAS, APA (bd. sci. affairs 1979-82, pres. divsn. 38 health psychology 1982-83, Outstanding Contbn. award 1980, Disting. Sci. award 1977), Am. Acad. Arts and Scis., Soc. Behavioral Medicicine; mem. AAUW (mem. exec. com. 1996—), Am. Philosophical Soc., Inst. Medicine of NAS, Acad. Behavioral Medicine Rsch., Ea. Psychol. Assn. (exec. bd. 1980-82), Phi Beta Kappa, Sigma Xi (pres. Yale chpt. 1986-87). Office: U Pa Office of the Pres 100 College Hall Philadelphia PA 19104-6380 also: University of Pennsylvania 3451 Walnut Philadelphia PA 19104

RODKEY, FRANCES THERESA, elementary school educator; b. Germantown, Pa., Sept. 3, 1952; d. Joseph Milton and Elizabeth Jane Parsons; m. Glenn Leroy Rodkey, May 1, 1976; children: Jennifer, Rachel. Student, Immaculata Coll., 1970—72; BS in Elem. Edn., Bloomsburg U., 1975. Cert. emergency edn. Pa., 1986. Substitute tchr. Coatesville Sch. Dist., Pa., 1984—89, tchr. 6th grade, 1989—, head dept. social studies, 2000. Mem.: NEA, Pa. State Edn. Assn. Republican. Roman Catholic. Avocations: reading, camping, hiking. Home: 1111 Oak St Coatesville PA 19320 Office: Coatesville Sch Dist 1515 E Lincoln Hwy Coatesville PA 19320

RODMAN, JAMES PURCELL, astrophysicist, educator; b. Alliance, Ohio, Nov. 11, 1926; s. Clarence James and Hazel (Purcell) R.; m. Margaret Jane Kinsey, Aug. 14, 1950; children: William James, Jeffrey Kinsey, David Lawrence, Gretchen. BS in Physics, Chemistry and Math, Mt. Union Coll., 1949; MA in Nuclear Physics, Washington U., St. Louis, 1951; PhD in Astrophysics, Yale U., 1963. Sec. Alliance Ware, Inc., 1954-55, Alliance Machine Co., 1959-69; v.p., treas. Alliance Tool Co., 1951-54, pres., 1954-59; instr. dept. physics and math. Mt. Union Coll., Alliance, 1951-59, assoc. prof. physics, 1962-66, prof., 1966-92, head dept. physics, 1963-65, head dept. physics and astronomy, 1965-74, 77-85, staff astronomer, 1992—2002; dir. Clarke Obs., 1953—2002, Computer Center, 1967-74, 77; coll. marshal, 1990-92; prof. emeritus, 1993. Rsch. assoc. astronomy Yale U., 1963-68, rsch. fellow, 1982; cons. astrophys. engr. astron. instrumentation, 1962—; chief engr., owner Rodman Rsch., 1986—; v.p. and chmn. bd. Westmont Inc., 1988-2001. Author books; also contbr. articles to profl. jours.; leader JR4 Musical Combo, 1962—. Mem. Alliance Bd. Edn., 1957-59, pres., 1959; exec. com. Buckeye coun. Boy Scouts Am., 1963-77, mem. nat. scouting com., 1973-77; dept. sheriff Stark County, 1972-73; spl. police officer Alliance Police Dept., 1974-90, tech. insp., 1976-90; exec. com. Stark County Disaster Svcs., 1976-78, chmn., 1979; trustee Western Res. Acad., 1969-92, Alliance Cmty. Hosp., Inc., 1980-87, pres., 1986; mem. Cape May Cottagers Assn. Inc., 1967—; grand marshal Carnation City Parade, 1986. With USNR, 1944-45. Recipient Gt. Tchr. award, 1976, Alliance Mayor's Award as outstanding citizen, 1978 Fellow AAAS, Royal

Astron. Soc.; mem. Am. Phys. Soc., Am. Astron. Soc., Astron. Soc. Pacific, Am. Assn. Physics tchrs., Optical Soc. Am., Nantucket Maria Mitchell Assn. (pres. 1974), Masons (32 degree), Shriners, Corinthian Yacht Club, Beach Cape May Club, Alliance Country Club, Wranglers Club (pres. 1986-2000), Sigma Xi. Home: 1125 Fernwood Blvd Alliance OH 44601-3764 also: 1613 Beach Dr Cape May NJ 08204-3608

RODMAN, LEIBA, mathematician; b. Riga, Latvia, June 9, 1949; came to U.S., 1985; s. Zalman and Haya Rodman; m. Ella Levitan, Feb. 2, 1983; children: Daniel, Ruth, Benjamin, Naomi. Diploma in maths., Latvian State U., 1971; MA in Statis., Tel Aviv (Israel) U., 1976, PhD in Maths., 1978. Instr. Tel Aviv U., 1976-78, sr. lectr., 1981-83, assoc. prof., 1983-85; postdoctoral fellow U. Calgary, Can., 1978-80; from assoc. to full prof. Ariz. State U., Tempe, 1985-87; prof. math. Coll. William and Mary, Williamsburg, Va., 1987—. Author: Introduction to Operator Polynomials, 1989, (with others) Matrix Polynomials, 1982, Matrices and Indefinite Scalar Products, 1983, Invariant Subspaces of Matrices with Applications, 1986, Interpolation of Rational Matrix Functions, 1990, Algebraic Riccati Equations, 1995; co-editor: Contributions to Operator Theory and Its Applications, 1988. Mem. IEEE, Am. Math. Soc., Math. Assn. Am., Internat. Linear-Algebra Soc., Soc. Indsl. and Applied Maths. Office: Coll of William & Mary Dept Math PO Box 8795 Williamsburg VA 23187-8795 E-mail: lxrodm@math.wm.edu.

RODNUNSKY, SIDNEY, lawyer, educator; b. Edmonton, Alta., Can., Feb. 3, 1946; s. B. and I. Rodnunsky; m. Teresita Asuncion; children: Naomi, Shawna, Rachel, Tevie, Claire, Donna, Sidney Jr. BEd, U. Alberta, 1966, LLB, 1973; MEd, U. Calgary, 1969, grad. diploma, 1990; BS, U. of State of N.Y., 1988; MBA, Greenwich U., 1990. Served as regional counsel to Her Majesty the Queen in Right of the Dominion of Can.; former gov. Grande Prairie Regional Coll.; now prin. legal counsel Can. Nat. exec., Alta. coord. for gifted children, ombudsman, SIG coord. Mensa Can.; past pres. Grande Prairie and Dist. Bar Assn., Alta Tchrs. Assn., Aspenview. Author: Breathalyzer Casebook; editor: The Children Speak. Decorated knight Grand Cross Sovereign and Royal Order of Piast, knight Grand Cross Order of St. John the Baptist; knight Hospitaller Order St. John of Jerusalem; Prince of Kiev, Prince of Trabzon, Prince and Duke of Rodari, Duke of Chernigov, Count of Riga, Count of St. John of Alexandria; named to Honorable Order of Ky. Colonels; named adm. State of Tex.; recipient Presdl. Legion of Merit. Mem. Law Soc. Alta., Law Soc. Sask., Can. Bar Assn., Inst. Can. Mgmt., Phi Delta Kappa. Address: PO Box 92 Whale Cove NU Canada X0C 0J0 E-mail: wonderfulschool@hotmail.com.

RODOS, JOSEPH JERRY, osteopathic physician, educator; b. Phila., July 7, 1933; s. Harry and Lisa (Perlman) R.; m. Bobbi Golden, Apr. 6, 1957 (div. 1974); m. Joyce L. Pennington, Sept. 26, 1981; children: Adam Justin, Nicole Ann. BS, Franklin and Marshall Coll., 1955; DO, Kirksville Coll. Medicine, Mo., 1959; DSc in Pub. Health, Somerset U., 1993. Diploamte Am. Bd. Family Medicine, Am. Osteo. Bd. Pub. Health and Preventive Medicine, Bd. Neuropsychiatry, Am. Bd. Pain MGmt., Am. Bd. Correctional Health Care, Am. Bd. Forensic Medicine; lic. Am. Kennel Club judge. Intern Grandview Hosp., Dayton, Ohio, 1959-60; NIMH fellow in psychiatry Brown U./Butler Hosp., Providence, 1966-68; gen. practice medicine Cranston, R.I., 1960-78; exec. sec. R.I. Soc. Osteo Physicians and Surgeons, Cranston, 1960-78; assoc. exec. dir. Am. Osteo. Assn., 1978-79; dean New Eng. Coll. Osteo. Medicine, Biddeford, Maine, 1979-82; acting dean Chgo. Coll. Osteo. Medicine, 1982-88; spl. ast. to pres. Chgo. Osteo. Health Sys., 1987-95; chief exec. officer Still Behavioral Medicine Group; chair dept. psychiatry, prof. family medicine and psychiatry Midwestern U., spl. asst. to pres., interim chair dept. psychiatry. Adj. prof. med. edn. U. Ill. Sch. Medicine; adj. prof. Sch. Medicine, Ohio State U.; cons. to dir. Nat. Health Svc. Corps, HHS; Disting. practitioner Nat. Acad.Practitioners; fellow Int. of Medicine, Chgo., 1990; clin. dir. Dept. Mental Health, Providence, 1973-78; med. dir. Dept. Corrections, Providence, 1976-78; sr. cons. medicine Pub. Sector Cons., Lansing, Mich., 1980—; prin. health cons. Rhodes Group, 1989—; lectr. in field. Assoc. editor am. Jour. Clin. Medicine, Jour. Osteo. Annals, 1982. Bd. dirs. Cranston Red Cross, R.I. Camps, Inc., Dial Dictation, Inc., Cranston Mental Health Clinic; lectr. premarital confs. Cath. Diocese of Proficence. Named Pioneer in Osteopathy, U. New England, 2003; recipient Disting. Svc. award, U.S. Surgeon Gen., 2002. Fellow Am. Acad. Osteo. Specialists, Am. Coll. Forensic Examiners, Am. Coll. Gen. Practice, Acad. Psychosomatic Medicine, Royal Soc. Health (Eng.), Acad. Osteo. Neurology and Psychiatry; mem. Am. Assn. Osteo. Specialists, Am. Coll. Osteo. Ob-Gyn., Acad. Clin. and Exptl. Hypnosis, Internat. Platform Assn., ACLU. Avocation: breeding and showing saint bernards and scottish terriers. Home: 5204 Lawn Ave Western Springs IL 60558-1844 Office: Transitions 20320 Crawford Ave Matteson IL 60443-1732

RODRIGUES-PAVAO, ANTONIO, vocal music teacher; b. Fall River, Mass., Dec. 13, 1943; s. Joseph Rodrigues and Maria Teresa (Braga) Pavao; children: Aaron, Stephen; m. Nora Macins, July 7, 1984. BMusic, MMusic, U. Mass., 1970, U. Ill., 1974. Cert. secondary music tchr., Mass., Ill., Wis. Vocal music tchr. William Horlick H.S., Racine, Wis., 1977-2000; voice tchr. Carroll Coll., Waukesha, Wis. Artistic dir. Elizabethan High Renaissance Feaste, Racine, 1977-2000. Composer various choral pieces, pieces for voice and piano; bass-baritone solo profl. performances; dir. numerous profl. and amateur musicals; dir. choirs touring U.K., Denmark, Czech Republic, Austria, Slovakia, Bulgana, Carnegie Hall, 27 states. Served with USAF, 1961-65. Mem. Nat. Assn. Tchrs. of Singing (chpt. corr. sec. 1992-98, exec. v.p. 1998-2001), Am. Choral Dirs. Assn. Avocations: racquetball, home design and remodeling. Home: 1239 N Osborne Blvd Racine WI 53405-1719

RODRIGUEZ, CARMEN VILA, artist, art educator, art historian; b. N.Y.C., July 16, 1927; d. Manuel and Julia (Lopez) Vila; m. Sabino Rodriquez Jr., Aug. 22, 1948; children: Sabino III, Manuel. BA in Art, Hunter Coll., 1948; studied with muralist Raul Anguiano, U. Mexico, 1966; student in advanced Ceramics and Jewelry, Calif. Coll. Arts and Crafts, 1966; student, U. Madrid, Spain, 1968; MA in Art and Art History, Columbia U., 1969, EdD in Art and Art Edn., 1977; postgrad., Fairfield U., 1982-93. Cert. in adminstrn. and supervision, Conn., art tchr., Conn., N.Y. Art tchr. Yorkville Vocat. H.S., N.Y.C., 1951-52; art history lectr. Instituto de Bellas Artes, Caracas, Venezuela, 1953-55; art tchr., dept. chmn. Eastchester (N.Y.) Sch. Dist. 1, 1958-92; cons., pres. VILA, Inc., Visual Instrnl. Libr. Art, Inc., 1981—; art edn. leader, lectr. art history Discovery Mus., Bridgeport, Conn., 1992—, Mus. Arts and Scis., Daytona Beach, Fla., 1997—; co-chair ednl. programs Lockwood-Mathews Manor Mus., Norwalk, Conn., 1992-94. Adj. faculty Daytona Beach C.C., 1993—, Norwalk (Conn.) Cmty. Tech. Coll., 1996—; art instr. Norwalk Sr. Citizen Ctr., 1992—, New Canaan (Conn.) Sr. Ctr., 1993—; art counsellor Girl Scouts USA, Norwalk, 1990-93; instr. history of western art Sacred Heart U., Stamford, Conn., 1990—. Author: Tracy Loves Picasso, 1993; one-woman shows include Picture This Gallery, Westport, Conn., 1995-98, 1st Fidelity Bank, Norwalk, 1995, Sun Trust Bank, Daytona Beach, Fla., Sun Trust Bank, Daytona Beach, Fla., 1996, First Union Bank, Daytona Beach, 1997, 98, Daytona Beach Shores Ctr., 1998; group shows include Rowayton (Conn.) Arts Ctr., 1994, 96 (ribbon 1994), Bonnie Blair Country Club, Scarsdale, N.Y., 1962, N.Y. Gallery, 1970, Scarsdale Pub. Libr., 1975, Portland Gallery, Norwalk, Conn., 1996, Sun Trust Bank, 1996, Artist Workshop Inc., New Smyrna, Fla., 1997; editor J. Walter Thompson Advt., N.Y.C., 1970; editor, head stylist Trimble Studios, N.Y.C., 1949-53; contbr. articles to profl. jours. Art instr. Norwalk (N.Y.) Sr. Citizen Ctr., 1992—, Girl Scouts USA, Norwalk, Conn., 1990-93; instr. History of Western Art, Stetson U.-Elder Hostel programs, 1998—. Recipient Painting award Eastchester Womens Club, 1964, Premio Major de Arte U. Mex., 1961, Painting award Brush and Palette Club, 2001, 03. Mem. NEA, AAUW, NOW, Nat. Art Edn. Assn., Rowayton Art Assn., Art League Daytona Beach, Port Orange Art Assn., Artists Workshop Inc. Avocations: painting, travel, sculpture, writing, art history. Home: Gran Coquina-1801 3333 S Atlantic Ave Daytona Beach FL 32118-6306

RODRIGUEZ, DAVID GONZALEZ, JR., priest, art and religion educator; b. San Antonio, Tex., June 9, 1947; s. David Campos and Maria Beatrice (Gonzalez) R. BFA, Coll. St Francis, 1979; M in pastoral studies, Loyola U., 1984; M in divinity, Cath. Theo. Union, 1988; M in arts inter-discipline, Columbia Coll., 1993; MFA, Md. Inst. Coll. Art, 1995. Cert. elem. tchr., art tchr., Ill. Clk. USAF, 1968-72; tchr. St. Ann's Cath. Sch., Great Falls, Mont., 1969-72; sales & design Gen. Men's Wear, San Antonio, 1972-73; tchr. art and religon St. Jude's Cath. Sch., New Lenox, Ill., 1974-79; tchr. cont. edn. Joliet Jr. Coll., New Lenox, 1976-77; tchr., chair fine arts Providence H.S., New Lenox, 1979-84; tchr., chair arts & religion Hales Franciscan H.S., Chgo., 1984—; priest Chgo. and Joliet Dioc., Chgo., 1989—; chaplain Cruise Lines, Fla., 1989—. Art teach core mem. Chgo. Cath. H.S., 1989—; art dept. evaluator Ill. North Cen., Chgo., 1990—; curriculum staff and evaluator Hales Franciscan H.S., 1990—; adj. faculty art edn. dept. The Sch. of Art Inst. Chgo., 1994—, apprentice tchr. supr., 1995—. One-man show Courtyard Gallery, Chgo., 1997; exhbns. include Fox Gallery, Balt., 1999, Alex Gallery, Washington, 1999, South Shore Cultural Ctr., Chgo., 2000; represented in permanent collections at Mus. Sci. & Industry, Chgo., Sco. of Art Inst. Chgo., Columbia Coll., Chgo. Juror fine arts Art Reach, Chgo., 1990—; mem. Arts Basics, Art. Inst. Chgo., 1990—; mem. Gt. Falls Symphony Chorus. With USAF, 1968-72. Coca-Cola fellow Md. Inst. Coll. Art, 1991-95. Mem. Nat. Cath. Edn. Assn., Nat. Art Edn. Assn., Cath. Edn. Archdiocese of Chgo., Facets Cinema, Art Inst. Chgo., Mex. Fine Arts Mus. Roman Catholic. Avocations: dance, remodeling design, floral design, cooking, choreography, painting. Home: 5225 S Greenwood St Chicago IL 60615-2623 Office: Hales Franciscan HS Province 4930 S Cottage Grove Ave Chicago IL 60615-2623

RODRIGUEZ, GLADYS MONTALVO, elementary education educator; b. Chgo., Feb. 11, 1951; d. Santos and Gloria Elena (Jackson) Montalvo; m. Ernesto Jose Rodriquez Archilla, June 3, 1979; children: Glorimir, Ernesto J. BA, U. Ill., 1974; student, Northeastern Ill. U., 1975-76, Nova U., 1993—; MA, Norwich U., 1990. Cert. elem. tchr., P.R. Tchr. Antilles Mil. Acad., Trujillo Alto, P.R., 1976-82, Antilles Consolidated Sch. System, Ft. Buchanan, P.R., 1982—. Mem. budget com., staff devel. com., assertive discipline com.; chairperson grade level. Author: (pamphlet) Stay Informed this Summer 1985. Recipient Superior Performance award. Mem. NEA, ASCD, Am. Ednl. Rsch. Assn., Overseas Edn. Assn., Antilles Consolidated Edn. Assn. Home: L-4 Via Del Parque La Vista Rio Piedras PR 00924 Office: Antilles Elem Sch Ft Buchanan San Juan PR 00934

RODRIGUEZ, KATHLEEN MOORE, art educator; b. Wynnewood, Pa., Mar. 16, 1971; d. John Francis and Mary Louise (McCahon) N.; married, May 18, 2002. BS, Kutztown U., 1993. Art educator Villa Maria Acad., Malvern, Pa., 1994—, cons. fine arts ctr., 1995-97, dept. chair visual arts, 1996-97; mem. faculty precoll. programs U. of Arts, 2000—. Art tchr. summer enrichment program Archbishop John Carroll H.S., Radnor, Pa., summers 1996, 97; spl. recreation camp counselor, summers 2001–. Bd. dirs. Archdiocesan Curriculum Com. for Fine Arts, Phila., 1996—; vol. tchr. aide GED course Ardmore Libr., 1995. Recipient Connelly Art Connection award Connelly Found., Mus. Am. Art, 1997. Mem. NEA, Nat. Art Edn. Assn., Pa. Art Edn. Assn., Am. Crafts Coun., Phila. Mus. Art, Main Line Art Ctr. Roman Catholic. Avocation: coaching field hockey and basketball. Home: 316 E Athens Ave Ardmore PA 19003-3108

RODRIGUEZ, LINDA TAKAHASHI, secondary school educator, administrator; b. L.A., June 22, 1941; d. Edward S. and Mary Takahashi; divorced; children: Regina Marie, Marla Sari. AA, Trinidad (Colo.) Jr. Coll., 1961; BA, We. State Coll., Gunnison, Colo., 1963; MA, U. Colo., Denver, 1991. Cert. tchr., adminstr., Colo. Tchr. Stratton (Colo.) Jr./Sr. High Sch., 1964-65, Pikes Peak Elem. Sch., Colorado Springs, 1966-68, Prince Sch., Tucson, 1968-70, Ipava (Ill.) Grade Sch., 1970-72, Macomb (Ill.) Schs., 1972-74, Colchester (Ill.) Jr./Sr. High Schs., 1979-83, Hazel Park (Mich.) Alternative Sch., 1984-85; tchr. 8th grade lang. arts and social studies Denver Pub. Schs., 1986-95, chair lang. dept., 1987-96, tchr. reading resource, 1987-92; asst. prin. Martin Luther King Jr. Efficacy Acad.-Middle Sch. Creator, dir. Reading Summer Sch., 1987-95; presenter insvcs. Denver Pub. Schs., 1987-94; mentor Alternative Tchr. Cert. Program; mem. bd. dirs. Asian Cultural Ctr. Advisor Asian Edn. Adv. Bd., Denver, 1989-95; bd. dirs. Colo. Youth-at-Risk, Denver, 1992-93, Colo. Aids Project. Mem. Landmark Edn. Forum, Highland Park Optimists, Delta Kappa Gamma. Avocations: reading, skiing, personal growth, swimming, socializing. Home: 1617 Daphne St Broomfield CO 80020-1155

RODRIGUEZ, LOUIS JOSEPH, academic administrator, economist, educator; b. Newark, Mar. 13, 1933; m. Ramona Dougherty, May 31, 1969; children: Susan, Michael, Scott. BA, Rutgers U., 1955; MA, La. State U., 1957, PhD, 1963. Dean, Coll. Bus. Adminstrn., Alcee Fortier Disting. prof. Nichols State U., Thibodaux, La., 1958-71; dean Coll. Bus. U. Tex.-San Antonio, 1971-72, v.p. acad. affairs, dean faculty, 1972-73; dean Sch. Profl. Studies U. Houston-Clear Lake City, 1973-75, vice-chancellor, provost, 1975-80; pres. Midwestern State U., Wichita Falls, Tex., 1981—2000; ret., 2000; Hardin Found. prof. Midwestern State U., Wichita Falls, Tex., 1994—. Vice chmn. Coun. Tex. Pub. Univ. Pres. and Chancellors, 1992-93; mem. formula and health professions edn. adv. coms. Tex. Higher Edn. Coordinating Bd. Author 4 books; contbr. over 50 articles to profl. jours. Chmn. bd. Tex. Council on Econ. Edn., Houston, 1981-83; bd. dirs. Joint Council on Econ. Edn., N.Y.C., 1981-83, Goodwill Industries Am., Washington, 1976-82, Robert Priddy Found., 1993-96, Wichita Falls Met. Y.M.C.A., 1999-2000, 4A Economic Devel. Bd., 2000-2003, Wichita Falls Area Cmty. Found., 1999-2001; pres. Wichita Falls Bd. Commerce and Industry, 1988-89, Clear Lake City Devel. Found., Houston, 1976-77, Goals for Wichita Falls, Inc., 1983; mem. internat. adv. com. Tex. Higher Edn. Coordinating Bd.; pres. United Way Greater Wichita Falls, 1998-99. Recipient Tchr. Edn. Supportive Pres. award Am. Assn. Colls. Tchr. Edn., 1991, Disting. Citizen award N.W. coun. Boy Scouts Am., 1998; named Wichitan of the Yr., 1987; Ford Found. grantee, 1964; Fulbright fellow, 1976 Mem. Am. Assn. State Colls. and Univs. (bd. dirs.), So. Assn. Colls. and Schs. (Commn. on Colls.), Assn. Tex. Colls. and Univs. (pres. 1988-89), Rotary (pres. Downtown Wichita Falls club 1990-91). Mem. Ch. of Christ. Home: 2403 N Elmwood Cir Wichita Falls TX 76308-3813

RODRIGUEZ, TERESA IDA, elementary education educator, educational consultant; b. Levittown, N.Y., Oct. 10, 1951; d. George Arthur and Frieda (Diaz) R. BA in Secondary Edn., Hofstra U., 1973, MA in Bilingual Edn., 1978; profl. diploma in multicultural leadership, L.I. U., 1990. Cert. permanent nursery, kindergarten, elem. Spanish 7-12, bilingual K-6, ESL tchr., sch. dist. adminstr., sch. adminstr., supr., N.Y. Bilingual elem. tchr. Long Beach (N.Y.) Pub. Schs., 1973-76, Hempstead (N.Y.) Pub. Schs., 1976-79; account exec. Adelante Advt., N.Y.C., 1979-81; adminstrv. asst. Assocs. and Nadel, N.Y.C., 1981-84; freelance outside prop and set decorator for TV commls. N.Y.C., 1984-88; tchr. ESL Central Islip (N.Y.) Pub. Schs., 1988-92; ednl. cons. Houghton Mifflin Co., Princeton, N.J., 1992-95; tchr. 5th grade Central Islip (N.Y.) Pub. Schs., 1995—. Cons. on tchr. tng. Staff Devel. Ctr. Islips, Central Islip, 1989—; cons. on staff devel. Nassau Bd. Coop. Ednl. Svcs., Westbury, N.Y., 1990—, edn. instrn. specialist IBM, 1991; presenter confs., workshops, seminars; cons. and grant writer, N.Y.C. and suburbs. Exhibited in group shows for photography, also one-woman show, 1999. Grantee N.Y. State Div. Bilingual Edn., 1988-90, Staff Devel. Ctr. Islips, 1988, Suffolk Bd. Coop. Ednl. Svcs., 1989; WLIW Pub. TV mini grantee; Pres.'s fellow L.I.U., 1989-90. Mem. ASCD, Internat. Reading Assn. (presenter nat. conf. 1992, 93), N.Y. State ASCD, Suffolk Reading Coun., Smithtown Township Arts Coun. Avocations: tennis, photography, bicycling, swimming. Home: 30 Wheelwright Ln Levittown NY 11756-5233 Office: 545 Clayton St Central Islip NY 11722-3021

RODRIGUEZ-ACEVEDO, FELIX MANUEL, secondary school educator; b. Guaynabo, P.R., Mar. 16, 1958; s. Felix and Dolores (Acevedo) Rodriguez. BA in Secondary Edn., U. P.R., Rio Piedras, 1981; cert. in philosophy, St. Alphonsus Coll., Suffield, Conn., 1982; MS in Adminstrn./Supervision, Ctrl. Conn. State U., 1988; MA in Theology, Holy Apostles Coll., Cromwell, Conn., 1992; PhD in Curriculum and Instrn., U. Conn., 1992. Tchr. sci. Dept. Edn., San Juan, P.R., 1980-81; religious edn. tchr. Sagrados Corzaones Cath. Sch., Guaynabo, 1984-85; tchr. math. Hartford (Conn.) Bd. Edn., 1985-94, tchr. Spanish lang. arts, 1985-90, tchr. sci., 1994—. Cons. U.S. Dept. Edn., Washington, 1993; vis. instr. Spanish Holy Apostles Coll., 1991-92; guest spkr. U. Hartford, 1992-94; panel moderator U. Conn., Hartford, 1989-93. Cultural advisor Am. Sch. for the Deaf, West Hartford, Conn., 1994; guest spkr. outreach New England Assn. Supts., Middletown, Conn., 1993. Mem. Am. Ednl. Rsch. Assn., Nat. Assn. Bilingual Edn., Conn. Assn. Bilingual-Bicultural Edn. Roman Catholic. Avocations: dancing, roller skating, travel, reading. Home: 285 Elm St Apt A6 Windsor Locks CT 06096-2228 Office: Hartford Pub HS 55 Forest St Hartford CT 06105-3243

RODRIGUEZ-CAMILLONI, HUMBERTO LEONARDO, architect, historian, educator; b. Lima, Peru, May 30, 1945; came to U.S., 1963; s. Alfonso and Elda (Camilloni) R.; m. Mary Ann Alexanderson, July 1, 1972; children: Elizabeth Marie, William Howard. BA magna cum laude, Yale U., 1967, MArch, 1971, MPhil, 1973, PhD, 1981. Rsch. asst. Sch. Architecture Yale U., 1964-70, teaching fellow dept. history art, 1971-72, 74-75; chmn. research dept. Centro de Investigacion y Restauracion de Bienes Monumentales Instituto Nacional de Cultura, Lima, 1973; restoration architect OAS, Washington, 1976—; prof. Sch. Architecture Tulane U., New Orleans, 1975-82; prof., dir. Henry H. Wiss Ctr. Theory and History of Art and Architecture, Coll. Architecture and Urban Studies Va. Poly. Inst. and State U., Blacksburg, 1983—, dir. Ctr. for Preservation and Rehab. Tech., Coll. Architecture, 1986—. Vis. prof. U. Ill., Chgo., 1982-83; reviewer, cons. Choice, 1975—; mem. interim bd. dirs. Ctr. Planning Handbook Latin-Am. Art, 1978-87; cons., adviser Internat. Exhbn. and Symposium Latin-Am. Baroque Art and Architecture, 1980; mem. adv. bd. Mountain Lake Symposium on Art and Architecture Criticism, 1985—, Internat. Symposium Luis Barragan, 1990; coord., advisor exhbn. Tradition and Innovation: Painting, Architecture and Music in Brazil, Mex. and Venezuela between 1950-80, 1991, Internat. Art History Colloquium, 1993, 48th Internat. Congress of Americanists, 1994, Congress Internat. Union Architects, 1996, 49th Internat. Congress Americanists, 1997, 2nd European Assn. for Archtl. Edn./Archtl. Rsch. Ctrs. Consortium Conf., 2000; coord., adv. exhbn. Frank Lloyd Wright: An Architect in America, 1995, The Jesuits, Conf. II: Cultures, Scis. and the Arts, 1540-1773, 2002, 1st Internat. Congress on Constrn. History, 2003. Author: (with Walter D. Harris) The Growth of Latin American Cities, 1971; (with Charles Seymour, Jr.) Italian Primitives, The Case History of a Collection and its Conservation, 1972, Religious Architecture in Lima of the Seventeenth and Eighteenth Centuries: The Monastic Complex of San Francisco el Grande, 1984; contbg. editor Handbook of Latin American Studies, 1987—, The Retablo Facade as Transparency: A Study of the Frontispiece of San Francisco, Lima, 1991, Tradición e Innovación en la Arquitectura del Virreinato del Perú, Constantino de Vasconcelos y la Invención de la Arquitectura de Quincha en Lima Durante el Siglo XVII, 1994, (with Graziano Gasparini) Arquitectura Iberoamericana, 1997, Manuel de Amat y Junyent y la Navona de Lima: un ejemplo de diseño urbano barroco del siglo XVIII en el virreinato del Perú, 1999, (with Mehdi Setareh) Monticello's Dome: Development of an Integrated Resource for the Study of Thomas Jefferson's Architecture, 2000, Quincha Architecture: The Development of an Antiseismic Structural System in Seventeenth Century Lima, 2003; contbg. editor: The Dictionary of Art, 1991-96, Encyclopedia of Twentieth Century Architecture, 1999. Named Ellen Battell Eldridge fellow, 1970-72, Robert C. Bates Jr. fellow Jonathan Edwards Coll., Yale U., 1970-71, Social Sci. Rsch. Coun. fellow, 1972-74, Yale Concilium Internat. Studies fellow, 1972-73, Giles Whiting fellow, 1974-75, NEH fellow Columbia U., 1983, Hobart and William Smith Colls. fellow, 1987, U. Ill. fellow, 1990, Edilia De Montequin fellow, 1991, NEH fellow U. N.Mex., 1992. Mem. Internat. Archive of Women in Architecture (treas. 1999—), Soc. Archtl. Historians (bd. dir. 1977-80, past pres., past sec. South Gulf chpt.) SE sect. Soc. Archtl. Historians, Coll. Art Assn. Am., SE Coll. Art Conf., Latin Am. Studies Assn., Assn. Latin Am. Art, Assn. Preservation Va. Antiquities, New River Valley Preservation League (bd. dir. 1987—), Nat. Trust Historic Preservation, Save our Cemeteries (past dir.), Preservation Resource Ctr. (past bd. dir.), Assn. for Preservation Tech., Blacksburg Regional Art Assn. (bd. dir), Inter-Am. Inst. Advanced Studies in Cultural History (bd. dirs. 1996—), KC, Tau Sigma Delta, Phi Beta Delta. Roman Catholic. Office: Va Poly Inst and State U Coll Architecture & Urban Studies Blacksburg VA 24061-0205 E-mail: hcami@vt.edu.

RODRIGUEZ-FLORIDO, JORGE JULIO, language educator, mathematics educator; b. Manzanillo, Cuba, Mar. 15, 1943; came to U.S., 1962; s. Julio Cesar and Josefa Lidia (Rodes) R.-F. BA in Math. and Spanish, U. Miami, 1966; MA in Spanish, U. Wis., 1967, PhD in Spanish, 1975; MS in Math., U. Ill., Chgo., 1979. Cert. secondary edn., cert. bus. computing. Instr. math. Banes (Cuba) H.S., 1960-62; instr. Spanish U. Wis., Sheboygan, 1967-68; instr. Spanish, asst. prof. U. Ill., Chgo., 1970-78; asst. prof. Chgo. State U., 1978-81, assoc. prof., 1981-87, prof., 1987-2000; lectr. math. Roosevelt U., Chgo., 2000—. Supr. Chgo. Consortium of Colls. and Univs., summers 1989-93, oral proficiency examiner Ill. Bd. of Edn., Chgo., 1989-90; affirmative action officer Chgo. State U., 1987-88; census enumerator U.S. Dept. of Labor, Chgo., 1980. Author: El Lenguaje en la Obra Literaria, 1977, Visiones de Ventana, 1986, Por Dentro, 1991; editor: Diaspora, So. Ark. U., Magnolia, 1992-94. Campus liaison Campus Compact, Chgo., 1987-88; reader theatre contest Northeastern Ill. U., 1988; judge Ill. Regional Math. Contest, Chgo., 1988. Faculty enrichment grantee Chgo. State U., 1992, 93, 96-98. Mem. Am. Assn. Tchrs. Spanish and Portuguese, Circulo De Cultura Pan Americano, Nat. Assn. Cuban Am. Educators, The Math. Assn. of Am. Office: Roosevelt U Sch Sci and Math 430 S Michigan Ave Chicago IL 60605-1394 E-mail: j-florido@csu.edu.

RODRIGUEZ-ROIG, AIDA IVELISSE, school system administrator; b. Humacao, P.R., June 22, 1958; d. René and Aida L. (Roig) Rodriguez. BA cum laude, U. P.R., Humacao, 1979; MEd, Pa. State U., 1983, EdD, 1989. Elem. sch. social worker P.R. Dept. Edn., Humacao, 1981-82, exec. dir. Positive Action for Sch. Safety Hato Rey, 1983-85; admissions counselor Pa. State U., University Park, 1987-88; asst. rschr. Office of Planning U. P.R., Humacao, 1988-89; program dir. Office of Vice Pres./Vice Provost, Pa. State U., University Park, 1989-90; asst. v.p. for info., promotion and mktg. Inter Am. U. P.R., San Juan, 1990-93. Part-time prof. div. behavioral scis. and professions Inter Am. U., Hato Rey, 1992-93; asst. sec. edn., San Juan, 1992-93, asst. sec. edn. planning and edn. devel., 1993—. Contbr. articles to profl. jours. Bd. dirs. Women's Counseling Svcs. of Berks County, Inc., Reading Pa., 1989-90, Berks Teen Inst., Reading, 1989-90; mem. adv. bd. Community Outreach com. Meridian Bank, Reading, 1989-90. Recipient awards and scholarships, including U.S. Office of Edn. fellowship, 1985-87. Mem. Am. Assn. Higher Edn., Nat. Assn. Bilingual Edn., Nat. puerto Rican Coalition, Nat. Ctr. Community Edn., ASCD, Phi Delta Kappa.

RODRIGUEZ-SAMALOT, JOSÉ ANGEL, vocational education administrator; b. Santurce, P.R., May 15, 1955; s. Pedro J. Rodríguez and Estilita Samalot. BS in Edn., Temple U., 1977; MA in Religious Studies, St. Charles Borromeo Sem., Overbrook, Pa., 1988; cert. internat. travel svcs., Travel

Cen., Inc., Seattle, 1982; postgrad., U. del Sagrado Corazón, Santurce, P.R., 1992. Career counselor Camden (N.J.) County Coll., 1978-80; bilingual tchr., guidance counselor Woodrow Wilson High Sch., Camden, 1978-80; mgr. shore excursions Royal Caribbean Cruise Lines, Miami, Fla., 1980-82; tour mgr. E.F. MacDonald Co., Dayton, Ohio, 1983-85; ednl. cons. Fairleigh Dickinson U., Camden, 1985-86; translator, tchr. conversational Spanish Camden City Schs., 1984-88, adminstrv. asst. curriculum and instrn., 1988-89; editor, asst. to pres. Periódico la Estrella de Puerto Rico, Puerto Nuevo, 1989-91; coord. religious studies Colegio Nuestra Señora de Belén, Rio Piedras, P.R., 1990-91; dir. edn. Liceo de Arte y Tecnología, Hato Rey, P.R., 1991—. Multilingual edn. cons. Merit Ctr., Temple U., Phila., 1977-79; adj. instr. basic skills Camden campus Glassboro State Coll., 1979; tchr. conversational Spanish to adults Gloucester Twp. Pub. Schs., Blackwood, N.J., 1984-89. Social svcs. counselor Christian Community Svcs., Luth. Ch., Miami, 1982-83; Sunday sch. tchr., coord. St. Vincent Pallotti Cath. Ch., Haddon Heights, N.J., 1984-89. Mem. ASCD, Am. Vocat. Assn., Career Coll. Assn., Assn. Escuelas Privadas de P.R., Assn. Orquesta Sinfónica P.R. Mem. Popular Democratic Party. Roman Catholic. Avocations: reading, travel, nature walks, music, swimming. Home: Central Plz # 586 San Juan PR 00920-5402 Office: Liceo de Arte y Tecnologia 405 Ave Ponce De Leon San Juan PR 00901-2221

RODRIGUEZ-WALLING, MATILDE BARCELO, special education educator; b. Santiago, Cuba, Aug. 15, 1950; d. Humberto Jacinto and Matilde Amelia (Cuervo) Barcelo; m. Luis Alfredo Rodriguez-Walling, June 29, 1973; 1 child, Alfredo Luis. BA, U. Miami, Fla., 1972; MS in Diagnostic Tchg., Fla. Internat. U., 1981; EdS, Barry U., 1988. Cert. ednl. specialist computer edn., Fla. Tchr., chair fgn. lang. dept. Notre Dame Acad., Miami, Fla., 1972-80; tchr., coord. English as 2d lang. adult edn. program Dade County Pub. Schs., Miami, elem. sch. tchr., tchr. middle sch. spl. edn. Homestead, Fla., elem. spl. edn. tchr. Miami, 1986—, behavior mgmt. specialist, exceptional edn. dept. chair; tchr. on spl. assignment Fla. Dept. of Edn., 1994—. Mem. spkrs. bur. Nat. Clearinghouse for Professions in Spl. Edn.; sch. adv. chairperson Blueprint 2000; presenter and spkr. at state and nat. profl. confs.; coord. Fla. Spkrs. Bur.; mem. Fla. Edn. Stds. Commn. Commr. Fla. Edn. Stds. Commn.; mem. State Adv. Com.; mem. Commrs. Blue Ribbon Panel Edn. Governance; co-chair Nat Commn. Improve Spl. Edn. Teaching & Learning. Recipient Gran Orden Martiana, Cuban Lyceum, Miami, 1976. Mem. Coun. Exceptional Children (sec. 1989, v.p. 1990, pres. 1991-92, multicultural chair 1992-93, Mainstreaming Tchr. of Yr. 1983, region finalist Dade County Tchr. of Yr. 1991, Fla. Tchr. of Yr.), Fla. Fedn. Coun. for Exceptional Children (pres. 1997-98, past pres. 1998-99), Coun. Children with Behavior Disorders, Nat. Bd. for Profl. Tchg. Stds. (exceptional needs com.), Internat. Coun. for Exceptional Children (Tchr. of Yr. 1994), Delta Kappa Gamma (Epsilon chpt.). Roman Catholic. Avocations: travel, guitar. Office: Miami-Dade County Pub Schs 1500 Biscayne Blvd Ste 409G Miami FL 33132-1400

ROE, ENID ADRIAN TALTON, retired elementary and special education educator; b. Eldorado, Ark., Dec. 11, 1921; d. Adolphus Wiltz and Ileta Dennett (Frank) Talton; m. Joseph Benjamin Roe Sr., Aug. 31, 1942; children: Joseph Benjamin Jr., Phyllis C., Rebecca Louise (dec.), Deborah Elizabeth. AA, Hendrix Coll., 1941; BSEd, Northwestern U., 1946; MEd, U. Nebr., 1973. Cert. elem. tchr., Nebr., Kans.; cert. spl. edn. tchr., learning disabilities and educable mentally handicapped tchr., Kans. Tchr. Pooler Sch. Dist. #273, Sheridan, Ill., 1943-44; tchr., dir. student svcs. Hawthorne Pub. Sch., Lincoln, Nebr., 1975-76; tchr. Shelton (Nebr.) Pub. Sch., 1976-79; resource tchr. Cambridge Pub. Sch. K-12, Cambridge, Nebr., 1980-81; spl. edn. resource tchr., learning disabled and handicapped Norton (Kans.) Pub. Sch., 1981-91; diaconal minister United Meth. Ch., Nebr., Ks., 1983-91. Cert. lay speaker United Meth. Ch., 1988. Sec. First United Meth. Ch., Ainsworth, Nebr., 1959, vacation ch. tchr., 1958-64, ch. libr., 1964-66, vacation ch. sch. tchr., Big Springs, Nebr., 1955-56, Elmwood, Nebr., 1966-70, St. Marks-Lincoln, Nebr., 1964-68, tchr. trainer lab. schs., Elmwood, 1964-68, tchr. study sessions with jr. choir, 1966-70, jr. high youth camp counelor, Fremont, Nebr., 1966, mem. United Meth. women and circle 4, Norton, Kans., 1985—, worship commn., 1988-91, tchr. after sch. program, 1991—; cub scout den mother Boy Scouts Am., 1956-58; asst. scout leader Girl Scouts Am., 1967-79; dialysis nurse trainee Mayo Clinic, 1973; tchr. Laubach Literacy Tutor in Reading, 1974-75; pres. Mother's Club Internat. Order Job's Daughters of Lincoln, 1974-75; mem. Norton Arts Coun., 1989— Consecrated diaconal minister United Meth. Ch., 1983; presented monetary gift in honor of Enid. Kans. to Spl Olympics Program, 1983; recipient bronze trophy for dedication Spl. Olympics, 1985, coach's cert., 1986. Mem. AAUW, NEA, Kans. Nat. Edn. Assn., Norton Tchrs. Assn., Philanthropic Ednl. Orgn. Sisterhood (chpt. CE 1983-85, chpt. AA 1985—), Delta Kappa Gamma, Kappa Kappa Iota (Alpha conclave 1974-76). Democrat. Methodist. Avocations: music, traveling, sewing. Home: 502 N 1st Ave Norton KS 67654-1304

ROE, GERALD BRUCE, director, writer; b. Cushing, Wis., June 16, 1940; s. Fred Walter and Maybell Meranda (Swenson) R.; m. Laurel A. Nagel, Sept. 12, 1964 (dec. Feb. 1990); children: Stephen, David. BA, U. Minn., 1964, postgrad., 1969-71; MA, Coll. St. Thomas, 1967. Tchr. St. Anthony Padua H.S., Mpls., 1965-68, Ctrl. H.S., St. Paul, 1968-69; asst. to dir. bur. recommendations U. Minn., Mpls., 1973; assoc. dir. ednl. placement U. Iowa, Iowa City, 1974—. Co-author: (with Rebecca Anthony) Over 40 and Looking for Work, 1991, The Curriculum Vitae Handbook, 1994, 3d edit., 2003, 101 Grade A Resumés for Teachers, 1994, 3d edit., 2003; contbr. articles to profl. jours. Bd. dirs. Iowa City Cmty. Theatre, 1994-98. Mem. Phi Delta Kappa (chpt. 0005, v.p. 1990-94, pres. 1994-97). Avocation: theatre. Office: Univ Iowa Ednl Placement 302 Lindquist Ctr N Iowa City IA 52242-1529 E-mail: gerald-roe@uiowa.edu.

ROE, LESLIE EILEEN, elementary education educator; b. St. Louis, Apr. 18, 1960; d. Lloyd Jr. and Miriam Eileen (Greene) R. BA, U. Evansville, 1983; postgrad., Wash. U., St. Louis, 1985; MEd, U. Mo., St. Louis, 1990. Cert. tchr., Mo., N.J., Minn. Resource tchr. Clayton (Mo.) Sch. Dist., 1984-87, tchr. 2d grade, 1987—95, Internat. Sch. of Minn., 1995—98; resource tchr. 4th-6th grade St. Louis Pk. Sch., 1998—2003, tchr., 2003—. Mem. Regional Consortium Ednl. Tech. Inst., 1992-93. Vol. tutor program New Providence Presbyn. Ch., 1983-84, polo tournament Kidney Found., St. Louis, 1986, Kinderfair Lakeland Children's Arts Program, Minocqua, Wis., 1990, 92, 93, YMCA Camp Manito-Wish, Boulder Junction, Wis., 1999-2002. Mem. ASCD, NEA, P.E.O. (corr. sec. 1990-92, 97-99), Children Cancer Rsch. Fund Club Butterfly, Chi Omega. Avocations: traveling, golf, crafts, reading, camping. Office: Susan Lindgran Intermediate Ctr 4801 West 41st St Minneapolis MN 55416-2220

ROE, MARK J. law educator; b. N.Y.C., Aug. 8, 1951; m. Helen Hsu, Aug. 12, 1974; children: Andrea Hsu, Jessica Hsu. BA, Columbia U., 1972; JD, Harvard U., 1975. Bar: N.Y. 1976. Atty. Fed. Res. Bank, N.Y.C., 1975-77; assoc. Cahill Gordon & Reindel, N.Y.C., 1977-80; prof. Rutgers U. Law Sch., Newark, 1980-86, U. Pa. Law Sch., 1986-88, Columbia U. Law Sch., N.Y.C., 1988-2001, Harvard Law Sch., Cambridge, Mass., 2001—. Author: (book) Strong Managers, Weak Owners: The Political Roots of Amercian Corporate Finance, 1994, Corporate Reorganization and Bankruptcy, 2000, Political Determinants of Corporate Governance, 2003. E-mail: mroe@law.harvard.edu.

ROEBUCK, JUDITH LYNN, retired secondary school educator; b. Huntington, W.Va., Jan. 1, 1946; d. Russell Vance and Janice Lee (Adams) Dickey; m. William Benjamine Roebuck Jr., Mar. 28, 1970; children: Lisa, Paul. AB, Marshall U., 1968; MA, W.Va. U., 1973; postgrad., Marshall U., 1973—, W.Va. U., 1973—. Cert. tchr., adminstr., W.Va. Tchr. art, English Vinson High Sch., Huntington, 1967-68; tchr. art Wayne (W.Va.) and Crockett Elem. Sch., 1968-69; tchr. art, speech Ona (W.Va.) Jr. High/Mid. Sch., 1969-91; tchr. speech, debate Huntington H.S., 1991-92; tchr. art Barboursville (W.Va.) H.S., 1992-94, Cabell Midland H.S., Ona, W.Va., 1994—96, ret., 1996; chair related arts team Ona Mid. Sch., 1988-91, sch. improvement team, 1990-91; ret., 1996. Adv. bd. Teen Inst., Huntington, 1990—, W.Va. Teen Inst., 1995, leader, 1990—; mem. drama and debate program, Huntington, 1991-92, Invitationalism Coun., Huntington, 1990—, Cabell County Curriculum Coun., Huntington, 1991-92, Cabell County Reading Coun., 1991-92, Cabell County Tchrs. Acad., Tchr. Expectancy Student Achievement, W.Va. Health Schs. Program; mediator, trainer Healping Improve Peace, 1994; mentor, tchr. Impact. Contbr. articles to profl. jours. Counselor, Coll. Scouts Program, 1994—; vol. nat. disaster ARC, 1996—, human rels. liaison asst. officer, 1996—. Mem. NEA, DAR (sec. 1988—), Nat. Art Edn. Assn. (curriculum coun., art chair 1993-96, county del. 1994), W.Va. Edn. Assn., Cabell Edn. Assn. (membership chair 1989-91), Horizons, Phi Delta Kappa (pres. 1998—). Avocations: crafts, sewing, reading, diet and health, walking. Home: 30 Chris Ln Rt 2 Milton WV 25541

ROEDER, CHARLES WILLIAM, structural engineering educator; b. Hershey, Pa., Oct. 12, 1942; s. Francis William and Myrtle Marie (Garrison) R.; m. Nancy Lee Newman, June 14, 1969; 1 child, Michael Thomas. BSCE, U. Colo., 1969; MSCE, U. Ill., 1971; PhD, U. Calif., Berkeley, 1977. Mem. gen. constrn. crew Shaffer and Son, Palmyra, Pa., 1960-66; structural engr. J. Ray McDermott, New Orleans, 1971-74; prof. of civil engr. U. Wash., Seattle, 1977—. Cons. in field; team leader on connection performance for SAC Steel Project, 1995-2001; bd. dirs. Consortium of Univs. in Earthquake Engring., 2003—; mem. instnl. bd. Pacific Earthquake Engring. Rsch. Ctr. Editor: Composite and Mixed Construction, 1985; contbr. articles to profl. publs. With U.S. Army, 1964-66, Vietnam. Mem. ASCE (mem. steering com., chmn. 4 tech. coms., J. James R. Croes medal 1979, Raymond C. Reese Rsch. prize 1984), Earthquake Engring. Rsch. Inst., Structural Engrs. Assn. Wash. (Puget Sound Engring. Coun. Acad. Engrs. of 2002), Wilderness Soc., Sierra Club. Avocation: hiking. Home: 5300 NE 67th St Seattle WA 98115-7755 Office: U Wash Box 352700 PO Box Fx-10 Seattle WA 98195-2700

ROEDER, ROBERT GAYLE, biochemist, educator; b. Boonville, Ind., June 3, 1942; s. Frederick John and Helene (Bredenkamp) Roeder; m. Suzanne Himsel, July 11, 1964 (div. 1981); children: Kimberly, Michael; m. Cun Jing Hong, June 2, 1990; 1 child, Maxine. BA summa cum laude (Gilbert scholar), Wabash Coll., 1964, DSc (hon.), 1990; MS, U. Ill., 1965; PhD (USPHS fellow), U. Wash., 1969. Am. Cancer Soc. fellow dept. embryology Carnegie Instn. Washington, Balt., 1969-71; asst. prof. biol. chemistry Washington U., St. Louis, 1971-75, assoc. prof., 1975-76, prof., 1976-82, prof. genetics, 1978-82, James S. McDonnell prof. biochem. genetics, 1979-82; prof. lab. biochemistry and molecular biology Rockefeller U., N.Y.C., 1982—, Arnold O. and Mabel S. Beckmann prof. molecular biology and biochemistry, 1985—. Cons. USPHS, 1975-79, Am. Cancer Soc., 1983-86. Recipient Dreyfus Tchr.-Scholar award Dreyfus Found., 1976, molecular biology award NAS-U.S. Steel Found., 1986, outstanding investigator award Nat. Cancer Inst., 1986-2002, Dickson prize in medicine, 2001. Albert Lasker award for basic med. rsch., 2003; co-recipient Lewis S. Rosenstiel award for disting. work in basic med. scis. Brandeis U., 1995, Passano award Passano Found., Inc., 1995, Alfred P. Sloan prize GM Cancer Rsch. Found., 1999, ASBMB-Merck Award, 2002, Albert Lasker Basic Med. Rsch. award, 2003; grantee NIH, 1972—, NSF, 1975-79, Am. Cancer Soc., 1979-85; co-recipient Louisa Gross Horowitz award Columbia U., 1999, Gairdner Found. Internat. award, 2000. Fellow AAAS, Am. Acad. Arts and Scis., Am. Acad. Microbiology, N.Y. Acad. Scis.; mem. NAS, Am. Chem. Soc. (Eli Lilly award 1977), Am. Soc. Biol. Chemists, Am. Soc. Microbiologists, Harvey Soc. (pres. 1994), Phi Beta Kappa. Office: Rockefeller U 1230 York Ave New York NY 10021-6399 E-mail: roeder@mail.rockefeller.edu.

ROEHL, NANCY LEARY, marketing professional, educator; b. Natick, Mass., Mar. 25, 1952; d. Norman Leslie and Dorothy (Holmquist) Pidgeon; m. Patrick J. Leary, Sept. 17, 1977 (div. May 1984); m. Patrick F. Roehl, July 2, 1995. AA, Mass Bay Coll., Wellesley, Mass., 1979; BS, Lesley Coll., Cambridge, Mass., 1988; MA in Edn./Arts and Scis., U. South Fla., 1992. Cert. tchr., Fla. Sec. GTE Corp., Needham, Mass., 1973-78; coord. edn. Cullinet Software Inc., Westwood, Mass., 1983-84, adminstrv. asst., 1984-85, mgr. adminstrn., 1985-86; specialist product mktg. Cullinet Co., Westwood, Mass., 1986-88; v.p. mktg. and adminstrn. Jonathan's Landscaping, Bradenton Beach, Fla., 1988-89; tech. support staff A Plus Tax Product Group, Arthur Andersen, Inc., Sarasota, Fla., 1989-90; cons. Palmetto, Fla., 1990—; tchr. Manatee County, 1992—, corp. shopper, 2000—. Contbr. articles to profl. jours. Mem.: AAUW, Fla. Cmty. Assn. Mgrs., Nat. Trust for Hist. Preservation, Phi Kappa Phi. Office: 305 17th Street E Palmetto FL 34221

ROEHRICH, CHERYL BRINKLEY, elementary education educator; b. Nashville, May 29, 1954; d. Edgar William and Effie Virginia (Williams) Brinkley; m. Thomas Kevin Roehrich, Aug. 14, 1992; 1 child, Benjamin Marcus. BS in Edn., Mid. Tenn. State U., 1976. Cert. tchr., Ga., Tenn.; cert. career ladder I, Tenn. Tchr. Antioch Elem. Sch. Whitfield County Schs., Dalton, Ga., 1976-79; substitute tchr. Met. Nashville Schs., 1979-80; tchr. East Cheatham Elem. Sch. Cheatham County Schs., Ashland City, Tenn., 1986—. Tutor reading and math. East Cheatham Schs., Ashland City, 1992-93, Slingerland tchr., 1989—. Author: Alternative 3-Heroes, 1977. Treas. East Cheatham Athletic Assn., EAst Cheatham Sch., 1990—, scholastic advisor Jr. Pro Basketball, 1991—. Mem. NEA, Nat. Coun. Social Studies, Nat. Geog. Soc., Slingerland Inst., Tenn. Edn. Assn., Mid. Tenn. Math. and Sci. Assn., Cheatham County Edn. Assn. Mem. Ch. of Christ. Avocations: motorcycle riding, drag racing. Home: 1013 Eastside Rd Ashland City TN 37015-3801 Office: East Cheatham Sch 3201 Bearwallow Rd Ashland City TN 37015-4553

ROELSE, LORI ANN, elementary school educator; b. Sheboygan, Wis., Nov. 11, 1963; d. Eugene and LaVerne Betty (Handrow) Maeuser; m. William James Roelse, Oct. 22, 1988; children: Matthew, Andrew, Nathan. BS, Silver Lake Coll., 1986; MA, Cardinal Stritch U., 1998. Spl. edn. tchr. Sheboygan Area Schs., 1986-90, 5th grade tchr., 1990-98, 2d grade tchr., 1998-99, reading specialist, 1999—. Vacation Bible sch. tchr. St. Mark's United Ch. of Christ, Cleveland, Wis., 1980—. Mem. Internat. Reading Assn., Wis. State Reading Assn., Interlake Reading Coun. (pres. 1994-95), Nat. Coun. Tchrs. English. Avocations: sewing, reading. Home: 14530 Center Rd Cleveland WI 53015 Office: Madison Elem Sch 2302 David Ave Sheboygan WI 53081 E-mail: lroelse@sheboygan.k12.wi.us.

ROER, ROBERT DAVID, physiologist, educator; b. N.Y.C., Oct. 15, 1952; s. Edwin Marvin and Dorothy Barbara (Blaymore) R.; m. Marjorie Elizabeth Smith, May 29, 1976; 1 child, Sara Elizabeth. BS, Brown U., 1974; PhD, Duke U., 1979. Asst. prof. U. N.C., Wilmington, 1979-85, assoc. prof., 1985-90, prof., 1990—, dean Grad. Sch., 2002—. Contbr. articles to various jours. and publs. Grantee NSF, NASA, N.C. Biotech. Ctr., N.C. Sea Grant. Mem. AAUP, Am. Physiol. Soc., Soc. Integrative & Comparative Biology, Crustacean Soc., Sigma Xi, Phi Kappa Phi. Office: Univ North Carolina 601 S College Rd Wilmington NC 28403-5955 E-mail: roer@uncw.edu.

ROESELER, WOLFGANG GUENTHER JOACHIM, city planner; b. Berlin, Mar. 30, 1925; s. Karl Ludwig and Therese (Guenther) R.; m. Eva Maria Jante, Mar. 12, 1947; children: Marion, Joanie, Karl. PhD, Philipps State U. of Hesse, Marburg, Germany, 1949; LLB, Blackstone Sch. Law, Chgo., 1958. Assoc. planner Kansas City (Mo.) Planning Commn., 1950-52; city planning dir. City of Palm Springs, Calif., 1952-54; sr. city planner Kansas City, 1954-56; prin. assoc. Ladislas Segoe & Assocs., Cin., 1956-64; dir. urban and regional planning Howard, Needles, Tammen & Bergendoff, cons., Kansas City and N.Y.C., 1964-68; owner W.G. Roeseler, Cons. City Planner and Transp. Specialist, Bryan, Tex., 1969—90. Head dept. urban and regional planning Tex. A&M U., 1975-81, 85-88, prof., 1975-90, dir. Tex A&M Ctr. Urban Affairs, 1984-88, exec. officer for edn. Coll. of Architecture, 1987-88, prof. emeritus, 1990—. Author: Successful American Urban Plans, 1982; author tech. reports; contbr. articles to profl. jours. Fellow Am. Inst. Cert. Planners; mem. Am. Planning Assn., Transport Planners Coun., Urban Land Inst. Address: 5945 W 199th St Stilwell KS 66085-9032

ROFMAN, ETHAN SAMUEL, psychiatrist, educator; b. NYC, July 26, 1940; s. Joseph and Clara (Ginzberg) R.; m. Barbara Elaine Johnson, July 29, 1972; children: Amy J., Julie A. AB, Columbia U., 1961, MD, 1965. Diplomate Nat. Bd. Med. Examiners. Psychiatrist Mental Health Clin. Utapao AFB, Thailand, 1969-70; psychiatrist Mental Health Clinic, Westover AFB, Mass., 1970-71; assisting physician Boston City Hosp., 1971-75, chief psychiat. cons. svc., 1971-76; chief psychiat. svc. E.N. Rogers Meml. Vets. Hosp., Bedford, Mass., 1976-80; med. dir. Charles River Hosp., Wellesley, Mass., 1980-85; dir. human svcs. New Eng. Meml. Hosp., Stoneham, Mass., 1985-89; chmn. psychiat. dept. Framingham (Mass.) Union Hosp., 1989-93; dir. cmty. psychiatry Metrowest Med. Ctr., Natick, Mass., 1993—, chmn. psychiat dept., 1995-96; med. dir. Mass. Behavioral Health Partnership, Boston, 1996—99; svc. line dir. for mental health VA New Eng. Healthcare Sys., 1999—. Assoc. prof. psychiatry Boston U., 1976—; lectr. psychiatry Harvard U., Cambridge, Mass., 1986-90, 95-96. Author: chpt. Emergency Psychiatry, 1977, 2d edit., 1983, Programs for Chronic Patients, 1981. Bd. dirs. Alternative Homes, Newton, Mass., 1983-85, Metrowest Mental Health Assn., 1991-95. Fellow Am. Psychiat. Assn.; mem. Mass. Med. Soc. (Pride in Medicine award 1989). Avocations: golf, accordion, ice skating.

ROGAN, ROBERT WILLIAM, management educator, consultant, osteopath, psychiatrist; b. Buffalo; BA, MBA, SUNY, Buffalo; cert. in data processing, Cornell U.; DO, W.Va. Sch. Osteo. Medicine, 1983; postgrad., Virginia Beach, 1986-88; JD, Regent U., 1990. Bar: Pa. 1992; diplomate Nat. Bd Examiners for Osteo. Medicine and Surgery, Am. Bd. Psychiatry; cert. data processor, data educator. Assoc. prof. bus. West Liberty (W.Va.) State Coll., 1976-79; chief intern Metro Health Ctr., Erie, Pa., 1983-84; asst. prof. computer sci. Gannon U., Erie, Pa., 1984-85; asst. prof. mgmt. Slippery Rock (Pa.) U., 1985-86; practice medicine specializing in osteopathy Harborcreek Family Practice, Erie, Pa., 1985; resident physician Univ. Med. Ctr.-East Carolina U., Greenville, N.C., 1992-96; med. officer Miv Anastasis, 1988—89. Temp. physician Oceana (W.Va.) Med. Ctr., 1992-95; rschr., tchr. law Inst. Fine Mechanics and Optics, St. Petersburg, Russia, 1993, Poland, 1994; part-time radio announcer Sta. WGHB, Farmville, N.C., 1993-96; psychiat. and mgmt. cons., critical incident stress debriefer, 1996—; asst. prof. W.Va. U. Sch. Medicine, 1999—; chmn. ethics com. William R. Sharpe Hosp., 2000—; med. officer M/V Doulos, 2003. Counselor Contact Crisis Care, Lewisburg, W.Va., 1980—81; constrn. vol. various locations internationally, 1991; mem. Hist. Preservation Commn., City of Greenville, 1995—96, disaster vol., 2001—; med. vol. various orgns., Jamaica, 1988—. Scholar U. Buffalo, N.Y. State Bd. Regents; grantee NSF, Cornell U.; Group for Advancement of Psychiatry fellow, 1995-96. Mem. Am. Osteo. Assn., N.C. Psychiat. Assn. (psychiatry and law rep. 1994-96, mem. econ. affairs com. 1995-96, mem. exec. coun. 1994-96, candidate Raleigh city coun., 2003). Avocations: travel, sports, volunteering. E-mail: nagor36@hotmail.com.

ROGAN, THOMAS PAUL, physical education educator; b. Ellenville, NY, May 23, 1945; s. Kevin Patrick and Antoinett Rene (Sass) R.; m. Susan Beth McDonald, Jan. 27, 1967; children: Thomas, Paul, Kathleen. BS in Phys. Edn., Cortland State U., 1967; MA in Phys. Edn., Ball State U., 1968. Instr. phys. edn. Hudson Valley C.C., Troy, N.Y., 1968-72, dept. chair, 1972-74, assoc. prof., 1974-83, prof. phys. edn., coach, 1968—. Pvt. tennis tchr., Troy, 1975—. Dir., coach Spl. Olympics, N.Y., 1985—; dir., coach youth sports orgns., Troy, 1975—. Recipient various Coach of Yr. and Excellence in Tchg. awards, Chancellor's award SUNY, 1996. Mem. AAHPERD, N.Y. State Assn. Health, Phys. Edn. and Recreation, Nat. Soccer Coaches Assn., Nat. Track and Field Coaches Assn. Roman Catholic. Avocations: gardening, snow sports, racquet sports, triathlons, bridge. Home: 9 Petticoat Ln Troy NY 12180-7240 Business E-Mail: rogantho@hvcc.edu.

ROGER, JERRY LEE, academic administrator; b. Chase, Kans., Mar. 11, 1945; s. LeRoy J. and Lottie E. (Maphet) R.; m. Tucky Saint Smith, 1995. BS, U. Tulsa, 1966, MA, 1969, EdD, 1975. Cert. tchr., supt., Okla. Math. tchr. Kansas City (Mo.) Pub. Schs., 1966-67, Shawnee Mission (Kans.) Pub. Schs., 1967-71; rsch. asst. Tulsa Pub. Schs., 1972-73, rsch. coord., 1973-81, adminstrv. asst., 1981-90, rsch. dir., 1990-95, dir. planning and assessment, 1995-2000; chmn. U. Phoenix Sch. Gen. Studies, Tulsa, 2000; dir. acad. affairs U. Phoenix, Tulsa, 2001—. Adj. instr. Tulsa Jr. Coll., 1975-88; adj. asst. prof. U. Tulsa, 1980-85; sr. faculty U. Phoenix, Tulsa campus, 1998-2000. Contbr. book revs. to Tulsa Sunday World, 1990-92. Paul Harris fellow; Rotary benefactor. Mem. NEA, Am. Ednl. Res. Assn., Nat. Book Critics Cir., Nature Conservancy, Nat. Conf. for Cmty. and Justice, Phi Delta Kappa. Home: 3504 N Narcissus Ave Broken Arrow OK 74012 Office: U Phoenix 10810 E 45th St Tulsa OK 74146-3818 E-mail: Jerry.Roger@phoenix.edu.

ROGERS, AILENE KANE, retired secondary school educator; b. Jamaica, N.Y., Jan. 17, 1938; d. Daniel H. and Helen (Shirkey) Kane; m. Edward Lee Rogers, Nov. 18, 1961 (dec. Mar. 1998); children: Ruth, John, Helen, Daniel (dec.). BA, Middlebury Coll., 1959; MS, Am. U., 1963; MS in Environ. Sci., George Mason U., 1998. Asst. dir. program Student Conservation Assn., Charlestown, N.H., 1959-60, dir., 1960; teaching asst. Am. U., Washington, 1961-62; naturalist Nat. Park Svc., 1966-68; tchr. sci. Hauppauge (N.Y.) Middle Sch., 1972-73, Oak Grove Coburn Sch., Vassalboro, Maine, 1974-75, head sci. dept., 1976-79; tchr. sci. lower sch. Nat. Cathedral Sch., Washington, 1979-82, tchr. sci. upper sch., 1982-2000, head sci. dept., 1989-93, 94-95; ret., 2000; educator Marine Program Cornell Coop. Ext. Suffolk County, 2003—. Counselor Sci. Camp, The Potomac Sch., McLean, Va., summers 1982-88, 90, dir. sci. camp, 1986-88, co-dir., 1991; cons. Nat. Geographic Soc. Edn. Programs, 1982-92, Nat. Geographic Soc., 1980-92, Greenhouse Crisis Found., 1991; tchr., cons. Nat. Assn. Biology Teachers, 1993; lectr. Young Assoc. Program Smithsonian Inst., Jan., Feb., 1988, 89; facilitator Com. for Math. and Sci., Washington, 1993-95. Founder Setauket Environ. Ctr., 1970, bd. govs., 1970-72; bd. dirs. Student Conservation Program, 1970-79; cons. Sch. Wide Environ. Edn. Program, N.Y.C., 1978, Population Reference Bur., 1995; chmn. Pittston (Maine) Conservation Commn., 1975-78; co-pres. McLean High Sch. Student-Parent-Tchr. Assn., 1982-84; mem. State Team D.C., Mid-Atlantic Consortium Math. and Sci. Edn.-Dwight D. Eisenhower Nat. Program Math. and Sci. Edn., 1989-94; marine sci. tchr. Oceans Program Phillips Acad., Andover, Mass., 1996. Chopinsky fellow for Ukrainian Ednl. Exch., 1994; NSF grantee, 1962. Mem. Nat. Parks and Conservation Assn., Student Conservation Assn., Nature Conservancy (dir. Maine chpt. 1976-78). Home: 91 Little Neck Rd Centerport NY 11721-1615

ROGERS, BRENDA GAYLE, educational administrator, educator, consultant; b. Atlanta, July 27, 1949; d. Claude Thomas and Louise (Williams) Todd; m. Emanuel Julius Jones Jr., Dec. 17, 1978; children: Lavelle, Brandon, Albre Jede, Briana Adanne. BA, Spelman Coll., 1970; MA, Atlanta U., 1971, EdS, 1972; PhD, Ohio State U., 1975; postgrad., Howard U., 1980, Emory U., 1986. Program devel. specialist HEW, Atlanta, 1972; rsch. assoc. Ohio State U., Columbus, 1973-75; asst. prof. spl. edn. Atlanta U., 1975-78, program adminstr., 1978—, CIT project dir., 1977-91, exec.

dir. Impact project, 1992—. Tech. cons. Dept. Edn., Washington, 1978-93, 96, 97-98, cons. Head Start, 1990-91; cons. Princeton Testing Svcs., 1996—; due process regional hearing officer Ga. State Dept. Edn., Atlanta, 1978-84, adv. bd., 1980-84; regional cons. Access project, 1995—; mem. parent adv. coun. APS, 1988—; cons. program devel. Ga. Respite Care, Inc., 1988-89; mem. exec. bd., pres. PTA Stone Mountain elem. Sch., 1989-92; mem. test verification panel Edn. Testing Svcs., Princeton, N.J., 1995-96; cons. So. Assn. Colls. & Univs., 1998. Mem. Ga. Assessment Project com. Atlanta Pub. Schs. Adv. Coun., 1986—; bd. dirs. Mountain Pines Civic Assn., 1988—; mem. Grady Meml. Hosp. Cmty. Action Network, Atlanta, 1982-83; exec. bd. PTA Shadow Rock Elem. Sch., 1992-94. Recipient disting. svc. award Atlanta Bur. Pub. Safety, 1982, Mountain Sch. PTA, 1995, award Atlanta Pub. Sch. Sys., 1980, 82, 83, 89-90, Disting. Svc. award CAU, 1998; fellow Ohio State U., 1972-74, Howard U., 1980. Mem. NAFE, Assn. for Retarded Citizens, Coun. for Exceptional Children, So. Assn. Colls. and Univs. (cons. com. 1998—), Nat. Assn. Learning Disabilites, Phi Delta Kappa, Phi Lambda Theta. Democrat. Roman Catholic. Avocation: gourmet cooking. Office: Clark Atlanta U James P Brawley Atlanta GA 30314-3913 E-mail: dr.brenda.rogers@mediaone.net.

ROGERS, CHARLES EDWIN, physical chemistry educator; b. Rochester, N.Y., Dec. 29, 1929; s. Charles Harold and Maybelle (Johnson) R.; m. Barbara June Depuy, June 12, 1954; children: Gregory Newton, Linda Frances, Diana Suzanne. BS in Chemistry, Syracuse U., 1954; PhD in Phys. Chemistry, SUNY at Syracuse U., 1957. Rsch. assoc. dept. chemistry Princeton U., 1957-59, Goodyear fellow, 1957-59; mem. tech. staff Bell Telephone Labs., Murray Hill, N.J., 1959-65; assoc. prof. macromolecular sci. Case Western Res. U., Cleve., 1965-74, prof., 1974-98, prof. emeritus, 1998—. Sr. vis. fellow Imperial Coll., U. London, 1971; assoc. dir. Ctr. for Adhesives Sealants Coatings, Case Western Res. U., 1984-88, dir., 1988-91; co-dir. Edison Polymer Innovation Corp., Ctr. for Adhesives, Sealants and Coatings, 1991-97; cons. to polymer and chem. industries; devel. overseas ednl. instns. Editor: Permselective Membranes, 1971, Structure and Properties of Block Copolymers, 1977; contbr. numerous articles to profl. jours.; patentee in field. Mem.: The Adhesion Soc., N.Am. Membrane Soc., Am. Phys. Soc., Am. Chem. Soc. Home: 8400 Rockspring Dr Chagrin Falls OH 44023-4645 Office: Case Western Reserve U Dept Macromolecular Sc Cleveland OH 44106-7202 E-mail: cer@po.cwru.edu.

ROGERS, DAVID ANTHONY, electrical engineer, educator, researcher; b. San Francisco, Dec. 21, 1939; s. Justin Anthony and Alice Jane (Vessey) R.; m. Darlene Olive Hicks, Feb. 20, 1965; 1 child, Stephen Arthur. BSEE cum laude, U. Wash., 1961, PhD in Elec. Engring., 1971; MSEE, Ill. Inst. Tech., 1964; MDiv cum laude, Trinity Evang. Div. Sch., Deerfield, Ill., 1966. Registered profl. engr., Wash. Assoc. engr. Ford Aero., Newport Beach, Calif., 1961; tech. asst. IIT Rsch. Inst., Chgo., 1963, grad. fellow, 1963-64; predoctoral lectr. U. Wash., Seattle, 1964-65, 66-71, acting asst. prof., 1971-72; asst. prof. State U. of Campinas, Brazil, 1972-77, assoc. prof., 1977-80; assoc. prof. elec. engring. N.D. State U., Fargo, 1980-86, prof., 1986—2000, prof. elec. and computer engring., 2000—. External MS thesis examiner Poly. Sch. U. Sao Paulo, Brazil, 1974; external PhD thesis examiner Inst. Tech., Banaras Hindu U., India, 1989, 91, 95; rschr. microwaves, fiber optics, electromagnetics, profl. and rsch. ethics, tech. and soc., engring. edn.; faculty seminar (interdisciplinary, multi-cultural and internat. studies 1991-94) N.D. State U.-Bush Found.; presenter N.D. State U.-Bush Found. Industry-Ethics Inst., 1995-96. Co-author: Fiber Optics, 1984; mem. editl. rev. bd. IEEE Transactions Microwave Theory and Techniques, 1987-97; contbr. articles to profl. publs. including IEEE Transactions on Antennas and Propagation, Transactions on Edn., Transactions on Microwave Theory and Techniques, Jour. Quantum Electronics, Electronics Letters, Radio Sci., Engring. Edn., Computers in Edn. Jour. Mem. rev. panel NSF, Quantum Electronics Waves and Beams program, 1989; mem. tech. paper rev. com. Internat. Symposium on Recent Advances in Microwave Tech., China, 1989, 97, Reno, 1991, India, 1993, Ukraine, 1995, Spain, 1999; reviewer procs. ASEE/IEEE Frontiers in Edn. Conf., Phoenix, 1998, San Juan, P.R., 1999, Kansas City, 2000, others; judge N.D. Sci. Olympiad, 1987-95, S.E. N.D. Regional Sci. and Engring. Fair, 1993, 95-96; reviewer SBMO/IEEE MTT-S Internat. Microwave and Optoelectronics Conf., Natal, Brazil, 1997, Belem, Brazil, 2001; vol. examiner FCC Amateur Radio Exams thru Am. Radio Relay League. 2d lt. Signal Corps, U.S. Army, 1961-62. NSF Summer fellow, 1965; grantee Ford Found., 1969-70, TELEBRAS (Brazil), 1973-80, NSF, 2001-03. Mem. IEEE, IEEE Antennas and Propagation Soc., Am. Soc. Engring. Edn. (internat. and other divsn., grantee summer 1984), N.D. Acad. Sci., Am. Geophys. Union, Applied Computational Electromagnetics Soc., Am. Sci. Affiliation, Am. Radio Relay League (life), Order of Engr., IEEE Edn. Soc., Microwave Theory and Techniques Soc., Sigma Xi, Tau Beta Pi, Eta Kappa Nu. Evangelical. Office: ND State U Elec Computer Engring Dept Fargo ND 58105

ROGERS, DEBRA LYNN, secondary school educator, artist; b. Camden, N.J., Sept. 7, 1954; d. William Edward and Elizabeth Jane (Money) MacDermott; 1 child, Devon Elizabeth Eastlack; m. Mark D. Rogers, Apr. 14, 2001. BFA, Temple U., 1976; postgrad., Pa. State U., 1981-82, Rowan U., 1985-89, U. of the Arts, Phila., 1996—2002. Art educator primary sch. Cinnaminson (N.J.) Bd. Edn., 1979-80, Somerdale (N.J.) Bd. Edn., 1980-89; tchr. art h.s. and adult edn. Mainland Regional Bd. Edn., Linwood, NJ, 1989—. Instr. Airbrush Action, Inc., Lakewood, NJ, 1995—2000, Thayer & Chandler, Inc., Medford, 1997—98. Contbg. editor: Airbrush Action, 1995—2002. Recipient Vargas award for excellence in airbrush edn., Airbrush Action Mag., 1996, 1st pl. award, Campbell's Soup Co., 1997; grantee, Geraldine Dodge Found., 1996. Mem.: Mainland Regional Edn. Assn., N.J. Edn. Assn., Nat. Art Edn. Assn., Internat. Fedn. Airbrush Artists (bd. dirs.). Avocations: photography, gardening. Office: Mainland Regional HS 1301 Oak Ave Linwood NJ 08221-1653 Home: 878 Central Ave Hammonton NJ 08037-1115

ROGERS, DOUGLAS W. education educator; BS in Secondary Edn. magna cum laude, Baylor U., 1978; MLS, East Tex. State U., 1982, EdD in Ednl. Media and Tech., 1987. English and speech tchr. E. M. Pease Mid. Sch., San Antonio, 1978-80; speech and drama tchr. W. W. Jackson Mid. Sch., San Antonio, 1980-81; grad. asst. dept. ednl. media and tech. East Tex. State U., 1981-82, asst. instr. libr./info. sci. dept. ednl. media and tech., 1982-83, asst. instr. instnl. systems lab. dept. computer sci., 1983-84; dir. learning resource svcs., asst. prof. Wayland Bapt. U., 1984-87; dir. instnl. tech Baylor U., Waco, Tex., 1987—, asst. prof. curriculum and instrn., 1987-90, assoc. prof. curriculum and instrn., 1990—. Chair faculty senate Baylor U., 1993-94, dir. Ctr. Ednl. Tech., 1993—; presenter in field; state leve. ptnr. S.W. Ednl. Devel. Lab., 1988-90; manuscript revewer Boyd and Fraser Pub. Co. Co-author: Technology and Media: Instructional Applications, 1994; contbr. articles to profl. publs. Mem. ASCD, Assn. Ednl. Comm. and Tech. (bd. dirs. div. instnl. systems and computers 1992—, assembly rep. 1990, 92, state hose com. nat. conv. 1989, leadership devel. com. 1983-84), Tex. Assn. Ednl. Tech. (editorial and publ. com. 1983-84, univ. co-chair membership com. 1988-89, bd. dirs. 1991—, pres.-elect 1992-93, pres. 1993-94), Cen. Tex. Ctr. for Improvement of Tchr. Edn. (bd. dirs. 1989-92), Tex. ASCD (steering com. 1991-92, bd. dirs. 1993-94), Tex. Libr. Assn., Phi Delta Kappa. (pres. Baylor chpt. 1991-92), others. Office: Baylor U PO Box 97314 Waco TX 76798-7314

ROGERS, EVELYN M. retired speech and language pathologist; b. Binghamton, N.Y., Sept. 21, 1951; d. Llewellyn L. and Mildred E. (Hodge) R. AA, Cazenovia Coll., 1971; BS, SUNY, Fredonia, 1974; MS, SUNY, Albany, 1976. Cert. tchr., N.Y.; cert. clin. competence. Speech therapist Mary Imogene Bassett Hosp., Cooperstown, N.Y., 1974-76; speech pathologist No. Catskills Bd. Cooperative Ednl. Svcs., Stamford, N.Y., 1977-90, Cooperstown (N.Y.) Ctrl. Sch., 1990—2002; ret., 2002. Named Pres.'s coun. award Am. Speech, Lang., Hearing Assn., 1992. Mem. Delta Kappa Gamma, Order Ea. Star. Republican. Methodist. Avocations: traveling, gardening, reading, naturalist, birder. Home: 251 Lake Shore Dr N Maryland NY 12116-1921

ROGERS, FRANCES EVELYN, author, retired educator and librarian; b. Mobile, Ala., Aug. 30, 1935; d. James Richard Graves and Jessie Reynolds (Butler) Lay; m. Jay Dee Rogers, Mar. 22, 1957; children: Laura, Larry. BA, North Tex. State U., 1957; MSLS, Our Lady of the Lake U., San Antonio, 1975. Cert. tchr., libr., Tex. Tchr. Ector County Ind. Sch. Dist., Odessa, Tex., 1958-59; social dir. svc. club Lackland AFB, San Antonio, 1960-61; tchr. San Antonio Ind. Sch. Dist., San Antonio, 1965-70; tchr., libr. Northside Ind. Sch. Dist., San Antonio, 1970-90, ret., 1990. Author: (hist. novels under name Keller Graves) Brazen Embrace, 1987, Rapture's Gamble, 1987, Desire's Fury, 1988, Velvet Vixen, 1988, Lawman's Lady, 1988, (hist. novels) Tex. Sins, 1989, Midnight Sins, 1989, Wanton Slave, 1990, Surrender to the Night, 1991, A Love So Wild, 1991, Sweet Texas Magic, 1992, Desert Fire, 1992, Desert Heat, 1993, Flame, 1994, Raven, 1995, (contemporary novels) Second Opinion, 1999, (hist. novels) Angel, 1995, Wicked, 1996, The Forever Bride, 1997, Betrayal, 1997, Hot Temper, 1997, Crown of Glory, 1998, Lone Star, 1999, (contemporary novels) Golden Man, 1999, (hist. novels) Longhorn, 2000, Devil in the Dark, 2001, The Loner, 2001, The Grotto, 2002, The Ghost of Carnal Cove, 2002, Dark of the Moon, 2003. Sec., vol. Opera Guild San Antonio, 1980—; pres. San Antonio Romance Authors, 1997. Recipient Spirit of Romance award Rom Con, 1996, Prism Award Romance Writers Am., 1997, Tex. Gold award East Tex. Romance Writers Am., 1998. Mem. Nat. Soc. Arts and Letters. Home: 2722 Belvoir Dr San Antonio TX 78230-4507

ROGERS, FRANCES NICHOLS, assistant principal; b. Fontana Dam, N.C., July 25, 1944; d. Fred Edward and Violet Bernice (Slagle) Nichols; m. Terry William Rogers, July 3, 1970. BA in English, Berea Coll., 1966; MA in Elem. Edn., U. Ky., 1968; postgrad., U. N.C., 1992. Tchr. intern Breathitt County Schs., Jackson, Ky., 1966-68; tchr. elem. sch. Haywood County Schs., Waynesville, N.C., 1968-72, resource program developer, 1972-75, 77-83, asst. prin., 1983-89, 92-98, prin., 1989-92. Pres. Haywood County Chpt. N.C. Edn. Assn., 1969-70. Author: Mount Zion United Methodist Church: A History 1850-1982, 1982; author of poems; contbr. articles to profl. jours. Mem. Youth for Christ, Waynesville, 1980—. Named Outstanding Young Educator Waynesville Jaycees, 1968-69, Leader of Am. Elem. Edn., 1971. Mem. N.C. Ret. Sch. Pers., NEA, N.C. Edn. Assn. Methodist. Avocations: travel, reading, gardening. Home: 138 Mayapple Trail Clyde NC 28721-9718

ROGERS, JACK DAVID, plant pathologist, educator; b. Point Pleasant, W.Va., Sept. 3, 1937; s. Jack and Thelma Grace R.; m. Belle C. Spencer, June 7, 1958. BS in Biology, Davis and Elkins Coll., 1960; MF, Duke U., 1960; PhD, U. Wis., 1963. From asst. prof. to prof. Wash. State U., Pullman, 1963-72, chmn. dept. plant pathology, 1986-99. Contbr. articles to profl. jours. Recipient William H. Weston Teaching Excellence award Mycological Soc. Am., 1992. Mem. Mycological Soc. of Am. (pres., 1977-78), Am. Phytopathol. Soc., Botanical Soc. Am., British Mycological Soc.

ROGERS, JAMES GARDINER, accountant, educator; b. St. Louis, May 6, 1952; s. Gardiner and Virginia Joy (Goodbar) R.; m. Barbara May Baird, Feb. 14, 1976; children Andrew Baird, Benjamin Baird, Samuel Baird. BA, Washington and Lee U., 1973; MBA, Am. U., 1975. CPA, Pa. Credit officer loan workout div. Phila. Nat. Bank, Phila., 1975-78; mgr. cash and banking Gen. Waterworks Corp., Phila., 1978-81, asst. treas., 1981-85; v.p. fin., treas. Phila. Presbyn. Homes, Inc., Phila., 1985-88; exec. dir. devel. Eastern U., St. Davids, Pa., 1988—. Ptnr., bd. dirs. PC Mgmt. Enterprises, Inc., Bryn Mawr, Pa.. Treas. Lower Merion Bapt. Ch., Bryn Mawr, 1978-85; v.p. Lupus Foundn. of Am., Inc., Washington, 1985-87, asst. v.p., 1982-85, bd. dirs., 1977—; pres., bd. dirs. Pa. Lupus Foundn., Wayne, 1973—, bd. dirs.; elder Proclamation Presbyn. Ch., 1996—. Mem. Mensa. Clubs: Merion Cricket (Haverford, Pa.). Republican. Avocations: reading, microcomputers, tennis, skiing. Home: 8 Paul Rd Saint Davids PA 19087-3627 Office: Eastern Univ Saint Davids PA 19087 E-mail: jrogers@eastern.edu., jgrogers.cpa@verizon.net.

ROGERS, KAREN BECKSTEAD, gifted studies educator, researcher, consultant; b. L.A., Nov. 28, 1943; d. Maurice Webster and Helen Dorothy (Nalty) Beckstead; m. William Geoffrey Rogers, Sept. 11, 1965; children: Jeanne Elizabeth Rogers Armstrong, Jennifer Lynn Rogers Hasbrouck, William Carey. BA in Humanities, U. Calif., Berkeley, 1965; MA in Spl. Edn., San Diego State U., 1969; MA in Ednl. Psychology, U. Minn., 1983, PhD in Curriculum and Instrn. Sys., 1991. Cert. elem. tchr., Calif. Pace project coord. West Jr. Paul Schs., 1975-77; Omnibus project dir. Jr. League of Mpls., 1978-83; instr. U. Minn., Mpls., 1985—95; gifted studies instr. U. St. Thomas, Mpls., 1984-87, asst. prof. gifted studies, 1987-93, assoc. prof. gifted studies, 1993-98, prof., 1999—. Cons., Burnsville, Minn., 1978—. Author: Ability Grouping and Gifted Learners, 1991 (Early Scholar award, 1991), Talent Development, Re-Forming Gifted Education; contbg. editor Roeper Rev., 1994—, contbg. reviewer Jour. Secondary Gifted Edn., 1994—, Jour. for the Edn. of the Gifted, 1994—, Gifted Edn. Internat., 1998—, Gifted Child Quarterly, 1997—; contbr. 90 articles to profl. jours., 12 chpts. to books. Docent Mpls. Inst. Arts, 1975—. Recipient Lifetime Achievement award Minn. Coun. for Gifted and Talented, 1989. Mem. Coun. for Exceptional Children (pres. The Assn. for the Gifted 1994-96), Nat. Assn. for Gifted Children, Am. Ednl. Rsch. Assn. Democrat. Avocations: art collecting, art history, music appreciation, writing, reading. Home: 14004 Whiterock Rd Burnsville MN 55337-4717 Office: U St Thomas MOH 217 1000 Lasalle Ave Minneapolis MN 55403-2025 E-mail: kbrogers@stthomas.edu.

ROGERS, KATE ELLEN, interior design educator; b. Nashville, Dec. 13, 1920; d. Raymond Lewis and Louise (Gruver) R.; diploma Ward-Belmont Jr. Coll., 1940; BA in Fine Arts, George Peabody Coll., 1946, MA in Fine Arts, 1947; EdD in Fine Arts and Fine Arts Edn., Columbia U., 1956. Instr., Tex. Tech. Coll., Lubbock, 1947-53; co-owner, v.p. Design Today, Inc., Lubbock, 1951-54; student asst. Am. House, N.Y.C., 1953-54; asst. prof. housing and interior design U. Mo., Columbia, 1954-56, assoc. prof., 1956-66, prof., 1966-85, emeritus, 1985—, chmn. dept. housing and interior design, 1973-85; mem. accreditation com. Found. for Interior Design Edn. Rsch., 1975-76, chmn. stds. com., 1976-82, chmn. rsch., 1982-85. Mem. 1st Bapt. Ch., Columbia, Mo.; bd. dirs. Meals on Wheels, 1989-91. Nat. Endowment for Arts rsch. grantee, 1981-82. Fellow Interior Design Educators Coun. (pres. 1971-73, chmn. bd. 1974-76, chmn. rsch. com. 1977-78); mem. Am. Soc. Interior Designers, (hon., medal of honor 1975), Am. Home Econs. Assn., Columbia Art League (adv. bd. 1988-93), Pi Lambda Theta, Kappa Delta Pi, Phi Kappa Phi (hon.), Gamma Sigma Delta, Delta Delta Delta (Phi Eta chpt.), Phi Upsilon Omicron, Omicron Nu (hon.). Democrat. Author: The Modern House, USA, 1962; editor Jour. Interior Design Edn. and Research, 1975-78.

ROGERS, LAVANCHA JAYNE, elementary school educator; b. Sunbury, Pa., Sept. 3, 1948; d. Daniel Woodrow and Gladys (Brennan) Rohrbaugh; m. Samuel Harry Rogers Jr., Apr. 6, 1974 (dec. Oct. 2000); children: Jeremy, Jonathan. BS in Elem. Edn., Lock Haven U., 1970; MSLS, Villanova U., 1975; postgrad., Trenton State U., Pa. State U. Cert. tchr., Pa. Mem. summer playground staff Shikellamy Sch. Dist., Sunbury, 1967-70; libr. aid Lock Haven (Pa.) U., 1968-70; tchr. 2d grade Pennsbury Sch. Dist., Fallsington, Pa., 1970-83, transitional first tchr., 1983—. Mem. handbell choir First United Meth. Ch., Bristol, Pa., 1985-2000, mem. vocal choir, 1987-94, v.p. Ladies Aux. Auditorium Ushers, Ocean Grove, N.J., 1983—, trustee, mem. worship/music com.; vol. ticket office Ocean Grove (N.J.) Camp Meeting Assocs., 1989—. Mem. NEA, Pennsbury Edn. Assn. (past bldg. rep.), Pa. Edn. Assn. Avocations: reading, crafts, traveling, gardening, family. Home: 10 Red Berry Rd Levittown PA 19056-2306 E-mail: rogerslvt@aol.com.

ROGERS, LINDA GAIL, educator, consultant; b. Beaumont, Tex., July 12, 1957; d. Silas McCray and Audrey Lee (Jones) R. AA, Tyler (Tex.) Jr. Coll., 1978; B of Applied Arts and Sci., Lamar U., Beaumont, 1992; Cert., John Robert Powers Modeling, Dallas, 1981. Fashion salesperson Palais Royal Dept. Store, Beaumont, 1978-80; file clk. Mobil Oil Fed. Credit Union, Beaumont, 1978-80; pers. sec. Merc. Ctr., Dallas, 1980-83; mail clk. Fed. Res. Bank, Dallas, 1980-83; energetics instr. North Park Racket Club, Dallas, 1981-83; makeup and fragrance artist, makeup cons. Dallas, 1983; aerobics instr. Spa Lady, Dallas, 1983-84; sec. JMB Porperty Mgmt., Dallas, 1984-85; adminstrv. asst. NRM Oil & Gas Corp., Dallas, 1984-85; legal asst. Granoff Law Office, Dallas, 1985-86; substitute tchr. Beaumont Ind. Sch., 1989-95; instr. Delta Career Sch., Beaumont, 1995—. Sr. cons. Mary Kay, Beaumont, 1996-97. Mem. NAFE, AAUW. Home: 3461 Westmoreland St Beaumont TX 77705-1252

ROGERS, OLIVIA JOHNSON, elementary school counselor; b. Hays, Kans., Nov. 23, 1947; d. Norman Bruce and La Rene (Miller) Johnson; m. John E. Rogers, Mar. 23, 1991. BS in Edn., Emporia State U., 1971; MS in Edn., Kans. State U., 1976; EdS in Counseling, Wichita State U., 1990. Lic. profl. counselor; nat. cert. counselor. Elem. sch. tchr. Topeka Pub. Schs., 1972-82; spl. edn. tchr. Wichita Pub. Schs., 1982-87, elem. sch. counselor, 1987-91; counselor Diabetes Ctr. at St. Joseph-Via Christi Med. Ctr., Wichita, 1987-91; counselor, clinician CPC Gt. Plains Hosp., Wichita, 1987-91; elem. sch. counselor Salina (Kans.) Pub. Schs., 1991—. Counselor, Child Abuse Prevention Svcs., Salina, 1997—, Rogers Counseling Svcs., Salina, 1997—. Ednl. cons. Topeka Girls Club, 1980-81. Mem. Am. Counseling Assn., Am. Sch. Counselor Assn., Kans. Sch. Counselor Assn., Kans. Mental Health Assn.

ROGERS, PAULA ANN, secondary school educator; b. Springfield, Ill., July 21, 1954; d. Paul I. and Pearl L. (Montgomery) R.; m. Ron Klass. BS in Math. Edn., Ill. State U., 1976; postgrad., Murray State, 1977; MS in Animal Sci., U. Ill., 1981. Cert. math. tchr., Ill. Math. tchr. Griffin High Sch., Springfield, Ill., 1976-78; adult educator Urbana, Ill., 1981-83; math. tchr. Danville (Ill.) High Sch., 1983-85, Urbana High Sch., 1985—. Tutor Urbana Sch. Dist., 1985—; Job Tng. Partnership Act summer youth worksite coord. Urbana Adult Edn., 1983-99; coach math. team competitions Urbana H.S., 1985—, booster pal participant, 1992-93. Contbr. articles to profl. jours. Mem. Math. Assn. Am., Ill. Coun. Tchrs. Math., Delta Kappa Gamma. Methodist. Avocations: horseback riding, piano playing, reading, biking. Office: Urbana High Sch 1002 S Race St Urbana IL 61801-4998

ROGERS, PETER PHILLIPS, environmental engineering educator, city planner; b. Liverpool., England, Apr. 30, 1937; arrived in U.S., 1960, naturalized, 1970; s. Edward Joseph and Ellen (Duggan) R.; m. Suzanne Ogden, Oct. 24, 1998; children: Christopher, Justin. B in Engring., Liverpool U., 1958; MS, Northwestern U., 1961; PhD, Harvard U., 1966. Asst. engr. Sir Alfred McAlpine & Sons Ltd., Cheshire, Eng., 1958-60; mem. faculty Harvard U., 1966—, Gordon McKay prof. environ. engring., 1974—, prof. city planning, 1974—. Mem. Center Population Studies, Harvard U. Sch. Pub. Health, 1974—; cons. World Bank, UN, U.S. Agy. for Internat. Devel., Govt. India, Govt. Pakistan, Govt. Bangladesh, Govt. Nepal, Govt. Italy, Govt. Costa Rica, Commonwealth P.R. Co-author: Urbanization and Change, 1970, Land Use and The Pipe: Planning for Sewerage, 1975, Resource Inventory and Baseline Study Methods for Developing Countries, 1983, Systems Analysis for River Basin Management, 1985, Evaluacion de Projectos de Desarrollo, 1990, America's Waters, 1993, Water in the Arab World, 1994, Measuring Environmental Quality in Asia, 1997, Science with a Human Face, 1997. Mem. World Commn. for Water in 21st Century. Gordon McKay tchg. fellow 1961; Radley rsch. student, 1962-64; doctoral dissertation fellow Resources for Future 1964-65; recipient Clemens Herschel prize Harvard U., 1964; Guggenheim fellow, 1973, 20th Century Found. fellowship, 1989, Maass-White fellow U.S. Army C.E., 2003. Mem. Third World Acad. Scis. (corr.), Indian Inst. Agrl. Engring. (life), Cosmos Club (Washington), Cambridge Tennis Club, Sigma Xi. Home: 20 Berkeley St Cambridge MA 02138 Office: Harvard U 116 Pierce Hall Cambridge MA 02138 E-mail: rogers@deas.harvard.edu.

ROGERS, RICHARD LEE, educator; b. N.Y.C., Sept. 17, 1949; s. Leonard J. and Beverly (Simon) R.; m. Susan Jane Thornton, Aug. 14, 1976; children: Caroline, Meredith. BA, Yale U., 1971, MA in Religion, 1973; postgrad., U. Chgo., 1977-80; MS in Edn., Bank St. Coll. Edn., N.Y.C., 1989. Tchr. Foote Sch., New Haven, 1974-77; devel. assoc. U. Chgo., 1980-81; spl. asst. to v.p. planning, 1981-82; spl. asst. to pres. New Sch. Social Rsch., N.Y.C., 1982-83, sec. of corp., then v.p., sec., 1983-94; pres. Coll. for Creative Studies, Detroit, 1994—. Office: Coll for Creative Studies 201 E Kirby St Detroit MI 48202-4048 E-mail: rrogers@ccscad.edu.

ROGERS, ROY STEELE, III, dermatology educator, dean; b. Hillsboro, Ohio, Mar. 3, 1940; s. Roy S. Jr. and Anna Mary (Murray) R.; m. Susan Camille Hudson, Aug. 22, 1964; children: Roy Steele IV, Katherine Hudson. BA, Denison U., 1962; MD, Ohio State U., 1966; MS, U. Minn., 1974. Cert. dermatologist, dermatopathologist and immunodermatologist. Intern Strong Meml. Hosp., Rochester, NY, 1966—67; resident Duke U. Med. Ctr., Durham, NC, 1969—71, Mayo Clinic, Rochester, Minn., 1972—73, cons., 1973—, prof. dermatology, 1983—, dean Sch. Health Related Scis., 1991—99. Adv. coun. Rochester Community Coll., 1991-2000. Contbr. over 250 sci. articles to publs. Capt. USAF, 1967-69. Recipient Alumni Achievement award Ohio State U. Coll. of Medicine, 1991, Alumni citation Denison U., 1993, Faculty Svc. award Mayo Med. Sch., 1993, Gold medal 2d Med. Sch., Charles U., Prague, 2002. Mem. Am. Acad. Dermatology (bd. dirs. 1987-91, v.p.-elect 1998, v.p. 1999), Am. Soc. Dermatologic Allergy and Immunology (sec.-treas. 1988-2000), Am. Dermatologic Assn. (v.p. 2002-03), Soc. Investigative Dermatology, Assn. Schs. Allied Health Professions, Dermatology Found. Avocations: travel, family, reading, walking. Office: Mayo Clinic 200 1st St SW Rochester MN 55905-0002 Home: 1924 Greenfield Lane SW # 204 Rochester MN 55902-1083

ROGERS, SHEILA WOOD, elementary and secondary school educator; b. Louisville, May 10, 1949; d. John Cornelius and Gladys Virginia (Moody) Wood; m. Franklin Don Rogers, Mar. 23, 1969; children: Pamela, Rachel. BA in Math., Christopher Newport Coll., 1974; MEd in Computer Edn., Hampton U., 1986. Tchr. Hampton (Va.) City Schs., 1974-86; instructional specialist York County Pub. Schs., Yorktown, Va., 1986-91; tchr. York County (Va.) Schs., 1991—. Math. cons. Nat Diffusion Network, Washington, 1988-90; York County rep. Consortium for Interactive Instrn., Norfolk, Va., 1986-91; facilitator Star Schs. Tech. Edn. Rsch. Ctrs., U. Va., Boston, Charlottesville, 1989-91; coord. computer contest U. Wis., Peninsula Coun. of Math. of Va., Hampton, Newport News, 1980-86. Pres. PTA, R. E. Lee Elem. Sch., Hampton, 1987-89, C. A. Lindsay Middle Sch., Hampton, 1989-91; pres. on coun. Hampton Coun. of PTAs, 1990-91, 1st v.p., 1991-93; dir. preschool choirs West Hampton Bapt. Ch., Hampton, 1988—. Mem. NEA, Va. Edn. Assn., York County Edn. Assn. (sec. 1996-2002, v.p. 2002—), Colonial Uniserv (sec. 2002-03, chair 2003—), Va. Coun. Tchrs. Math., Peninsula Coun. Tchrs. Math., Greater Peninsula Swimming Assn. (rep. 1989-96), Delta Kappa Gamma. Baptist. Avocations: music, reading, handcrafts. Home: 109 Prince James Dr Hampton VA 23669-3609 Office: Grafton HS Yorktown VA 23693-0530

ROGOFF, JAY, poet, educator; b. N.Y.C., Feb. 21, 1954; s. Herbert Walter and Diane Pearl (Wolf) R.; m. Annis Faith Grover, June 17, 1978 (div. 1987); m. Penny Beth Howell Jolly, June 16, 1994; stepchildren: Jennifer Jolly, Joseph Jolly. BA, U. Pa., Phila., 1975; MA, Syracuse (N.Y.) U., 1978, DA, 1981. Tchg. asst. Syracuse U., 1975-80; asst. prof. English LeMoyne Coll., Syracuse, 1980-85; acad. advisor Skidmore U. Without Walls, Saratoga Springs, N.Y., 1985-95; lectr.English and liberal studies Skidmore Coll., Saratoga Springs, 1993—. Poetry workshop dir.l Lake George (N.Y.) Arts Project, 1996, Saratoga Springs, 1997; writer in residence Corp. of Yaddo, Saratoga Springs, 1989, 94, 96, 98, 2001, 02, 03, Sloan/Solomon writer in residence, 1991; spkr. N.Y. Coun. Humanities, 1997—. Author: (poetry) The Cutoff, 1995 (Washington prize 1994), First Hand, 1997, How We Came to Stand on That Shore, 2003; contbr. poetry to profl. jours. Com. mem. Dem. Party, Saratoga Springs, 1996—. Recipient fellowship MacDowell Colony, Peterborough, N.H., 1989, 97, 2nd prize Dorfman Poetry Competition, Rome (N.Y.) Art and Cmty. Ctr., 1996, grantee Saratoga Cty Prog. for Arts Funding Artist, N.Y. State Coun. of the Arts Decentralization Program, 1999. Mem. Poets and Writers Inc., Poetry Soc. Am. (John Masefield Meml. award 1982), Acad. Am. Poets, Nat. Book Critics Cir. Avocations: attending ballet, visiting museums, travel, softball. Home: 35 Pinewood Ave Saratoga Springs NY 12866-2622 Office: Skidmore Coll Liberal Studies Program Saratoga Springs NY 12866-1632

ROGOFF, KENNETH SAUL, economics educator; b. Rochester, N.Y., Mar. 22, 1953; s. Stanley Miron and June Beatrice (Goldman) R.; m. Evelyn Jane Brody, Aug. 18, 1979 (div. 1989); m. Natasha Lance, June 25, 1995; children: Gabriel, Juliana. BA/MA in Econs., Yale U., 1975; PhD in Econs., MIT, 1980. Economist Internat. Monetary Fund, Washington, 1983; economist, sect. chief Internat. Fin. divsn., Bd. Govs. of the Fed. Res. Sys., Washington, 1979-84; assoc. prof. econs. U. Wis., Madison, 1985-89; prof. econs. U. Calif., Berkeley, 1989-92; prof. econs. and internat. affairs Princeton (N.J.) U., 1992—; Charles and Marie Robertson prof. of internat. affairs Princeton U., 1995-98; prof. econs. Harvard U., 1999—, dir. Ctr. for Internat. Devel., 2003—; econ. counselor, dir. rsch. IMF, 2001—03; dir. Ctr. Internat. Devel. Harvard U., 2003—. Vis. scholar San Francisco Fed. Res., 1990-92, World Bank, Washington, 1989, IMF, Washington, 1988-94. Author books and contbr. articles to profl. jours. Alfred P. Sloan Rsch. fellow, 1986-87, Hoover Instn. Nat. fellow, 1986-87, NSF fellow, 1985—, John Simon Guggenheim fellow, 1998. Fellow World Econ. Forum, Econometric Soc., Am. Acad. Arts and Scis., World Econ. Forum; mem. Am. Econ. Assn.(mem. trilateral commn.), Internat. Grandmaster Chess. Office: Harvard U Econs Dept Littauer Ctr Cambridge MA 02138-3001 E-mail: krogoff@harvard.edu.

ROGOFF, PAULA DRIMMER, English and foreign language educator; b. N.Y.C. d. George and Florence (Levine) Drimmer; m. Arnold Stevan Rogoff; children: Jeffrey Scott, Eric Todd, Brian Craig. BA cum laude, Hunter Coll., 1961; MEd summa cum laude, William Paterson Coll., 1979. Cert. elem. tchr., ESL tchr., supr., N.J. Tchr. handicapped Herricks Bd. Edn., Williston Park, N.J.; tchr. reading compensatory edn. Oakland (N.J.) Bd. Edn.; tchr., coord. gifted-talented program N. Haldeon (N.J.) Bd. Edn.; ESL adult tchr., h. s. students Passaic County Tech. Inst., Wayne, N.J. Presenter Children's Libr. programs. Named Tchr. of Yr., Passaic County Tech. Inst., 1999-2000. Mem. ASCD, NEA, TESOL, Internat. Platform Assn., N.J. Edn. Assn., Phi Beta Kappa, Phi Lambda Theta, Kappa Delta Pi. Home: 11 Furman Dr Wayne NJ 07470-5304 Office: Passaic County Tech Inst 45 Reinhardt Rd Wayne NJ 07470

ROHAN, VIRGINIA BARTHOLOME, college development director; b. Helena, Mont., Apr. 19, 1939; d. William Franklin and Virginia Marie (Gibson) Bartholome; m. William Patrick Rohan, Dec. 29, 1962; children: Virginia Marion, William Patrick Jr., Christopher James. AB summa cum laude, St. Teresa's Coll., 1960; MA in Am. Lit., Cath. U. Am., 1961; postgrad., Kans. U., 1961-62; PhD in English, U. Mass., 1974. Instr. western civilization program Kans. U., Lawrence, 1961-62; instr. English St. Joseph Coll., Emmitsburg, Md., 1962-63; lectr. English U. Mass., Amherst, 1975-76; research assoc. Smith Coll. Devel. Office, Northampton, Mass., 1976-77, asst. dir. for founds., 1977-80, dir. devel. svcs., 1980-89; asst. v.p. devel. U. Vt., Burlington, 1989-90, interim v.p. for devel. and alumni rels., 1990-92; dir. devel. Hampshire Coll., Amherst, 1992—98; contbg. editor Cornell Yeats Series Deirdre vol. Cornell U. Press, 1999—. Lectr. English Holyoke (Mass.) C.C., 1976-77, Mt. Holyoke Coll., South Hadley, Mass., 1977-78; mem. faculty, mgmt. Inst. for Women in Higher Edn., Wellesley, Mass., 1983, 93; pres. Investments Unltd. Inc., Northampton, 1983-84. Author: (play) The Happy Prince, 1959; contbr. articles to profl. jours. Treas., bd. dirs. Friends WFCR (pub. radio), Amherst, 1983-85. Fellow Woodrow Wilson Found., 1960-61. Mem. Women in Devel. Western Mass. (co-founder, chairperson 1983-85), Coun. for Advancement and Support of Edn. (mem. faculty, panelist, chairperson roundtable, discussant 1979-94), Kappa Gamma Pi, Pi Beta Phi.

ROHLOFF, LORI LUANNE, artist, former special education educator; b. Calgary, Alberta, Can., June 23, 1961; came to U.S., 1977; d. Robert John and Catherine Anne (Sled) R.; m. Leon A. Peek, 1993. BS in Psychology, U. N. Tex., 1984; BA in Edn., Tex. Women's U., 1991. Cert. tchr. spl. edn., Tex.; cert. art edn. 1-12, Tex. Spl. edn. art educator Jane Marshall Elem., Middle Sch., Denton, Tex., 199-91; spl. edn. educator high sch. Sanger (Tex.) Ind. Sch. Dist., 1991—; tchr. secondary art Sanger High Sch., 1994—. One-woman shows include Connectivity, 1992, E. Gallery, 1998; exhibited in group shows at North Tex. Area Arts League, 1993 (Best of Show), 95, Martha Robbins Ann. Exhb., 1997, Dallas Visual Art Ctr., 1997, Tex. Womans U. Gallery, 1997., Mem. Mortarboard. Democrat. Episcopalian. Avocations: photography, jogging, gardening.

ROHNER, RALPH JOHN, lawyer, educator, university dean; b. East Orange, N.J., Aug. 10, 1938; AB, Cath. U. Am., 1960, JD, 1963. Bar: Md. 1964. Teaching fellow Stanford (Calif.) U., 1963-64; atty. pub. health div. HEW, 1964-65; prof. law Cath. U. Am. Sch. Law, Washington, 1965—, acting dean, 1968-69, assoc. dean, 1969-71, dean, 1987-95; staff counsel consumer affairs subcom. U.S. Senate Banking Com., 1975-76; cons. Fed. Res. Bd., 1976-83, chmn. consumer adv. council, 1981; cons. FDIC, 1978-80; spl. counsel Consumer Bankers Assn., 1984—. Cons. U.S. Regulatory Coun., 1979-80. Co-author: Consumer Law: Cases and Materials, 1979, 2d edit., 1991; co-author, editor The Law of Truth in Lending, 1984, republished, 2000. Bd. dirs. Migrant Legal Action Program, Inc., Washington, Automobile Owners Action Coun., Washington, Credit Rsch. Ctr., Georgetown U., Am. Fin. Svcs. Assn. Edn. Found. Conf. on Consumer Fin. Law. Mem. ABA, Am. Law Inst., Coll. of Consumer Fin. Svcs. Lawyers. Home: 10909 Forestgate Pl Glenn Dale MD 20769-2047 Office: Cath U Sch Law 620 Michigan Ave NE Washington DC 20064-0001 E-mail: rohner@law.edu.

ROHR, BRENDA ANN, band and vocal director; b. Hays, Kans., Dec. 10, 1962; d. Gilbert Julius and Edna Marie (Wasinger) R. B of Music Edn., Fort Hays State U., 1986. Cert. music educator, Kans. Band dir. Lincoln (Kans.) Unified Sch. Dist. 298, 1986-88; band dir., vocal tchr. Claflin (Kans.) Unified Sch. Dist. 354, 1988-91, Atwood (Kans.) Unified Sch. Dist. 318, 1991-92, Macksville (Kans.) Unified Sch. Dist. 351, 1992—. Tenor sax player Jay Bennet Band, Great Bend, Kans., 1988; bass clarinet, clarinet player Kans. Winds, Hutchinson, 1988—; lead tenor sax player Pawnee County Big Band, Larned, Kans. Mem. Olde Tyme Towne Bd., 1999—. Mem. Nat. Assn. Student Council Advisors, Kans. Bandmasters Assn. (sec. 1990-92), Kans. Music Educators Assn. (small sch. rep. 2003—), Kans. Nat. Educators Assn., Phi Beta Mu. Republican. Avocations: photography, bowling, golf, bicycle riding, collecting pig figurines. Home: 226 N Colyer PO Box 16 Macksville KS 67557-0016 Office: Macksville High Sch PO Box 307 Macksville KS 67557-0307

ROHR, KAROLYN KANAVAS, school system administrator; b. Chgo., Dec. 10, 1947; d. John George and Lorraine Marian (Erickson) Kanavas; m. Stephen Mitchell Rohr, Oct. 8, 1983; stepchildren: Susan Anne, John S. BA, Conn. Coll., 1969, MAT, 1971. Cert. adminstrn. and supervision, secondary prin., supr., tchr., Md.; cert. assessor Md. State Dept. Edn. and Nat. Assn. Secondary Sch. Prins. Tchr. Norwich (Conn.) Free Acad., 1971-72; tchr., acting dept. chair Fairport (N.Y.) Ctrl. Schs., 1972-74; tchr. Montgomery County Pub. Schs., Rockville, Md., 1975-78, specialist gifted and talented edn., area office, 1978-79, specialist leadership tng. dept. staff devel., 1979-81, coord. adminstrv. programs, 1981-92, coord. systemwide tng. Office Pers. Svcs., 1992—. Insvc. course instr. Montgomery County Pub. Schs., Rockville, 1979-83; sr. faculty assoc. Johns Hopkins U., Balt., 1991—; cons. on leadership and prins. tng., assessment, Mich., Fla., Md. Sch. Systems, 1980—. Author: (with others) Principal Selection Guide, 1987 Dir. Ijamsville (Md.) Community Assn., 1989-92. Recipient Showcase of Excellence Program award Nat. Coun. of States on In-Svc. Edn., 1988, Exemplary Leadership Devel. Program award Am. Assn. Sch. Adminstrs., 1988, Outstanding Achievement in Profl. Devel. award Am. Assn. Sch. Adminstrs. and Nat. Staff Devel. Coun., 1990. Mem. NAESP, ASCD, Nat. Staff Devel. Coun., Nat. Assn. Secondary Sch. Prins., Md. Coun. Staff Developers. Avocations: equine business, architectural design, travel. Office: Montgomery County Pub Schs 850 Hungerford Dr Rockville MD 20850-1718

ROHRER, JANE CAROLYN, retired gifted education specialist, academic administrator, poet, consultant; b. Faribault, Minn., July 17, 1940; d. Christian A. and Lydia G. (Hilleboe) R.; children: Paula Eisenrich, Lisa Eisenrich, Peter Eisenrich. BS in English, U. Minn., 1962, MA in English, 1964; MA in Edn., Boise (Idaho) State U., 1976; PhD in Spl. Edn./Gifted, Kent State U., 1992; student, Seabury We. Theol. Sem. Tchr. English Lompoc (Calif.) High Sch., 1962-63; gifted and talented facilitator Boise Sch. Dist., 1976-84, spl. edn. cons. tchr., 1984-89, spl. edn. adminstrv. intern, 1989-90; faculty Kent (Ohio) State U., 1991-92; dir. Tchr. Edn. Program Sierra Nev. Coll., Incline Village, Nev., 1993-1996, dean acad. programs, 1995-1996, dean faculty, 1997-99, v.p. acad. affairs, 1999—2002, acting pres., 2001, ret., 2002. Mem. Nev. Statewide Task Force on Tchr. Edn., Nev. State English Framework Commn.; numerous publs. and conf. presentations. Choir dir., La., Japan, Idaho, Ohio, Nev., 1966-98. Whittenberger fellow Boise State U., 1975-76. Mem. Ch. Women United (state pres. 1980), Coun. Exceptional Children (state bd. dirs. 1987-88), Nat. Assn. Gifted Children, S.W. Regional Spl. Edn. Adv. Bd., Idaho Talented and Gifted Assn. (state pres. 1988-89), Nev. Assn. Colls. of Tchr. Edn. (sec.-treas.), Mortar Bd., Phi Beta Kappa, Eta Sigma Upsilon, Pi Lambda Theta, Phi Delta Kappa. Avocations: reading, music, swimming, hiking, writing.

ROHRER, RICHARD JEFFREY, surgeon, educator; b. Columbus, Mar. 14, 1950; s. James William and Nancy Lenore (Acheson) R.; m. Jill Ellen Stein, Nov. 29, 1981; children: Benjamin, Noah. BS, Yale U., 1973; MD, Columbia U., 1977. Surgeon New England Deaconess and Harvard Med. Sch., Boston, 1984-87; surgeon, chief transplantation New Eng. Med. Ctr., Boston, 1988—; assoc. prof. surgery Tufts Sch. Medicine, Boston, 1988—. Trustee New Eng. Organ Bank, Boston, 1988—, chmn. bd. dirs., 1999—; councillor United Network for Organ Sharing, 1996—, sec., 2000—. Fellow ACS; mem. Am. Soc. Transplaant Surgeons, Transplantation Soc., Physicians for Social Responsibility, Assn. for Acad. Surgery, Assn. for Surg. Edn., Soc. Critical Care Medicine. Office: New England Med Ctr Box 40 750 Washington St Boston MA 02111-1526

ROHRER, SUSAN JANE, mayor; b. Springfield, Ill., Apr. 30, 1945; d. Russell Shriver and Margaret (Shumaker) Rohrer. AB, MacMurray Coll., 1967; MS, U. Ill., 1971, PhD, 1973. Cert. tchr. spl. K-14, H.S., Gen. Adminstr. K-12, Ill. Instr., Virden Jr. H.S., Ill., 1967-69; asst. to dean U. Ill. Coll. Medicine-Urbana, 1974-75, adminstrv. assoc., 1975-80; asst. prin. Virden Jr. and Sr. H.S., 1983-84, prin., 1984-87; sports writer News Gazette Newspaper, Champaign, Ill., 1973-74; owner Home Care Svcs., Inc., 1990—; co-owner Capitol Foods, Inc., Springfield, Ill., 1992-96. Dir. Dana Thomas Found., Springfield, Ill., 1989, Virden Unit 4 Sch. Bd.; sec. Virden Sch. Bd., 1992-93, v.p., 1993-94; mayor Virden. Ill., 1993—. Methodist. Home: 121 W Hill St Virden IL 62690-1232

ROHRICH, RODNEY JAMES, plastic surgeon, educator; b. Eureka, S.D., Aug. 5, 1953; s. Claude and Katie (Schumacher) R.; m. Diane Louise Gibby, July 3, 1990; children: Taylor Rodney, Rachel Nicole. BA summa cum laude, N.D. State U., 1975; MD with honors, Baylor Coll., 1979. Diplomate Am. Bd. Plastic Surgery, Nat. Bd. Med. Examiners. Instr. surgery Harvard Med. Sch. Mass. Gen. Hosp., Boston, 1985-86; asst. prof. U. Tex. Southwestern Med. Ctr., Dallas, 1986-89, assoc. prof., 1989-91; chief plastic surgery Parkland/Zale Univ. Med. Ctr., Dallas, 1989-99; prof., chmn. dept. plastic surgery U. Tex. Southwestern Med. Ctr., Dallas, 1991—, Betty and Warren Woodward chair in plastic surgery, 1999. Pres., faculty senate U. Tex., crystal charity ball disting. chair in plastic surgery. Mem. editl. bd. Selected Readings in Plastic Surgery, The Cleft Palate and Craniofacial Jour.; co-editor Plastic and Reconstructive Surgery Jour., 1998—; contbr. articles to med. jours. Bd. dirs. Save-the-Children Found., Dallas, March of Dimes, Dallas, Dallas for Children; class mem. Leadership Dallas, 1989-90; mem. Adopt-A-Sch., Dallas Summer Mus. Guild, Dallas Mus. Art, Dallas Symphony Assn., Tex. Health Found., Youth Leadership Dallas. Grantee Urban Rsch. Fund, 1982, United Kingdom Ltd. Ednl. Rsch. Fund, 1983, Oxford Cleft Palate Found., 1983, Am. Assn. Plastic Surgeons, 1985, Plastic Surgery Ednl. Found., 1985, 89, 90, U. Tex. Health Sci. Ctr. Dept. Surgery, 1986, Howmedica, 1989, ConvaTec-Squibb, 1989, 91, ConvaTec, 1991; recipient Disting Svc. award Plastic Surg. Ednl. Found., 1997, Alumni Achievement award, N.D. State U., 1997. Mem. AAAS, ACS, AMA (Thomas Cronin award 1988, 90, Clifford C. Snyder award 1990), Am. Assn. Hand Surgery, Am. Burn Assn., Am. Cleft Palate Assn., Am. Soc. Law and Medicine, Am. Soc. Maxillofacial Surgeons, Am. Soc. for Surgery the Hand, Am. Soc. Plastic and Reconstructive Surgeons, Am. Trauma Soc., British Med. Assn., Nat. Vascular Malformations Found. Inc. (med. and sci. adv. bd.) Tex. Med. Assn., Tex. Soc. Plastic Surgeons, Mass. Gen. Hosp. Hand Club, Dallas County Med. Soc., Assn. Acad. Chmn. Plastic Surgery, Dallas Soc. Plastic Surgeons, Harvard Med. Sch. Alumni Assn., Inst. for Study of Profl. Risk, Plastic Surgery Rsch. Coun., Reed O. Dingman Soc. Plastic Surgeons, So. Med. Assn., Am. Soc. Plastic Surgeons (pres. elect 2003). Republican. Roman Catholic. Office: U Tex Southwestern Med Ctr Dept of Plastic Surgery 5323 Harry Hines Blvd Dallas TX 75390-9132 E-mail: Rod.Rohrich@UTSouthwestern.edu.

ROHWER, WILLIAM D., JR., university dean; b. Denver, Oct. 2, 1937; AB, Harvard U., 1959; PhD, U. Calif., Berkeley, 1964. Asst. prof. education U. Calif., Berkeley, 1964-68, assoc. prof., 1968-70, prof., 1970-95, acting assoc. dean grad. div., 1969-70, assoc. dean, 1970, acting dir. Inst. Human Learning, 1971, chmn. div. ednl. psychology, vice-chmn. dept. edn., 1982, assoc. dean edn., 1983-86, acting dean, 1989-90, dean, 1990-95, prof. emeritus, dean emeritus, 1996—; acting dir. Inst. Human Devel., Berkeley, 1996-98. Vis. lectr. psychology U. Wis., Madison, 1967; rsch. psychologist U.S. Naval Pers. Rsch. Activity, San Diego, 1964. Contbr. articles to profl. jours.; ad hoc reviewer Child Develop., Devel. Psychology, Jour. Ednl. Psychology, Jour. Exptl. Child Psychology, Psychol. Rev., Sci. Recipient Palmer O. Johnson Meml. award Am. Ednl. Rsch. Assn., 1972; fellow Van Leer Jerusalem Found., 1974-75, Ctr. Advanced Study Behavioral Scis. Stanford U., 1979-80; scientific adviser Bernard Van Leer Found., 1974-75; grantee U.S. Office Edn., OEO, NSF, Nat. Inst. Child Health and Human Devel. E-mail: wdr@socrates.berkeley.edu.

ROISMAN, HANNA MASLOVSKI, classics educator; b. Wroclaw, Poland; d. Leon and Eugenia (Shlager-Katz) Maslovski; m. Joseph Roisman, Aug. 5, 1971; children: Elad L., Shalev G. BA in Classics, MA in Classics, Tel Aviv U., Ramat Aviv, Israel, 1977; PhD in Classics, U. Wash., 1981. Lectr. classics Tel Aviv U., 1981-87, sr. lectr. classics, 1987-90; assoc. prof. classics Colby Coll., Waterville, Maine, 1990-94, prof., 1994—. Vis. scholar U. Wash., Seattle, 1983; jr. fellow Ctr. Hellenic Studies, Washington, 1985—86; vis. assoc. prof. (summers) Cornell U., 1986—94; sec. Israel Soc. for Promotion of Classical Studies, 1987—89; vis. scholar Cornell U., Ithaca, NY, 1989, Ithaca, 1995—96, vis. prof. (summers), 1995—97, 2000—03, vis. scholar, 2001—02. Author: Loyalty in Early Greek Epic and Tragedy, 1984, Nothing is as it Seems: The Tragedy of Implicit in Euripides' Hippolytus, 1999; co-author: The Odyssey Re-Formed, 1996; co-editor: Essays on Homeric Epic, 1993, Studies in Roman Epic, 1994, Essays on the Drama of Euripides, 1997, Essays on Homeric Epic, 2 vols., 2002, Text and Presentation, Jour. Comparative Drama Conf., 1999—2000; contbr. articles to profl. jours. AAUW fellow, 1980-81. Office: Colby Coll Mayflower Hill Waterville ME 04901 E-mail: hroisman@colby.edu.

ROJAS, VICTOR HUGO MACEDO, retired vocational education educator; b. Mollendo, Peru, Jan. 11, 1923; came to U.S., 1944; s. Mariano A. and Maria Santos (Macedo) R.; m. Mary Emily Bush, Apr. 28, 1945 (dec. 1984). AA, Miami-Dade C.C., 1982; BS in Vocat. Edn., Fla. Internat. U., 1986. Cert. tchr., Fla. Automotive mechanic various Ford dealerships, Miami, Fla., 1945-60; automotive technician East Tenn. Motors, Knoxville, 1960-63, Tally-Embry Ford, Inc., Miami, 1964-66, shop foreman, then mgr., 1966-75, master technician, automotive instr., 1973-75; instr. automotive tech. Dade County Pub. Schs., Miami, 1975-91; ret., 1991. Adviser, sponsor Vocat.-Indsl. Clubs Am., Miami, 1988-91. Contbr. articles to newspapers. With Armada Peruana, 1940-44, USN, 1945. Recipient Cert. of Achievement Motor Age mag., 1961, 62, St. Mary's Cathedral, Miami, 1988, Automotive Svc. Excellence award Nat. Inst. Automotive Svc., 1975. Mem. Am. Legion (historian 1989), Elks. Democrat. Roman Catholic. Avocations: music, ballroom dancing, reading, writing, photography. Home: 2365 Ainsworth Ave Spring Hill FL 34609-4402

ROJER, OLGA ELAINE, German studies educator, translator; b. Curaçao, Netherlands Antilles, Mar. 29, 1953; came to U.S., 1972; BA cum laude, Mt. Holyoke Coll., 1976; MA with distinction, The Am. U., 1978; PhD, U. Md., 1985. Vis. asst. prof. German and Spanish St. Mary's Coll. Md., St. Mary's City, 1986-87; asst. prof. German Studies The Am. U., Washington, 1987—. Translator Nat. Geog. Soc., Washington, 1985—. Author: Exile in Argentina 1933-1945, 1990; contbr. chpts. to books. Mem. MLA, South Atlantic MLA, Am. Assn. Tchrs. German, Soc. for Exile Studies, Women in German, Mid. Atlantic Coun. Latin Am. Studies, Am. Translators Assn. Office: Am U Dept Lang & Fgn Studies 4400 Massachusetts Ave NW Washington DC 20016-8003

ROKOSZ, GREGORY JOSEPH, emergency medicine physician, lawyer, educator; b. Passaic, N.J., Mar. 27, 1955; s. Ferdinand and Stella D. (Wirkowski) R.; m. Christine M. Muller, Oct. 1, 1983; 1 child, Stefanie Lee. BA in Biol. Scis. with honors, Rutgers U., 1977; DO, Des Moines U., 1980; JD magna cum laude, Seton Hall U., 1999. Diplomate Am. Bd. Emergency Medicine, Am. Bd. Osteo. Emergency Medicine, Am. Osteo. Bd. Family Physicians. Intern Met. Hosp., Phila., 1980-81; resident in family practice Union (N.J.) Hosp., 1981-82, emergency dept. physician, 1982-94, 98, dir. med. edn., 1993-2001, v.p. med. affairs, 1994-2000, sr. v.p. med. and acad. affairs, 2001—, dir. transitional yr. residency program, 2000—02, v.p. med. edn., 2000—; med. dir. N.J. Paramedic Registry Exam., 1990-94; mobile ICU insp. N.J. Dept. Health, Office EMS, Newark, 1990-94; med. dir. St. Barnabas Outpatient Ctrs., 2003—; assoc. dean Mt. Sinai Sch. Medicine for St. Barnabas Health Care Sys., 2003—. Mem. N.J. Bd. Med. Examiners, Trenton, 1994—, v.p., 1997—99, pres., 1999—2001; clin. instr. dept. emergency medicine U. Medicine and Dentistry Sch. Osteo. Medicine, Stratford, 1992—93, asst. clin. prof., 1993—; asst. prof. emergency medicine N.Y. Coll. Osteo. Medicine/N.Y. Inst. Tech., Old Westbury, 1994—96, assoc. prof., 1996—, clin. asst. dean, 1997—; assoc. prof. dept. medicine St. George's U. Sch. Medicine, 2001—; assoc. mem. PRO of N.J., 1991—; dir. emergency medicine residency program Newark (N.J.) Beth Israel Med. Ctr., 1998—99; expert witness in emergency medicine; vice-chmn. N.Y. Coll. Osteo. Medicine Ednl. Consortium, 1999—; mem. accreditation rev. com. Accreditation Coun. for Continuing Med. Edn., 2000—, chair, 2004—. Contbg. author: Continuous Quality Improvement for Emergency Departments, 1994; mem. Seton Hall Law Rev., 1997-99. Fellow Am. Coll. Emergency Physicians, Am. Coll. Osteo. Emergency Physicians; mem. ABA, Am. Osteo. Assn., Am. Coll. Osteo. Family Physicians, Assn. Osteo. Dirs. and Med. Educators, Am. Coll. Physician Execs., Assn. for Hosp. Med. Edn., Grad. Med. Edn. Coun. N.J. (mem. adv. bd. 1997—). Republican. Roman Catholic. Avocations: skiing, sports, cultural events, music, family activities. Home: 8 Wildlife Run Boonton NJ 07005-9043 Office: St Barnabas Med Ctr 95 Old Short Hills Rd Livingston NJ 07039

ROLLE, MYRA MOSS See MOSS, MYRA

ROLLER HALL, GAYLE ALINE, gifted and talented education educator; b. L.A., Dec. 3, 1959; d. Willard E. and Ruby A. (Meek) Roller; m. Samuel Hall, May 20, 1995. BA in Elem. Edn., Hendrix Coll., 1982; M in Elem. Edn., Ark. Tech. U., 1985, MS in Edn. Gifted and Talented, 1992. Cert. elem. edn., gifted K-12. Substitute tchr. Ft. Smith (Ark.) Pub. Schs., 1982-84; grad. asst. Ark. Tech. U., Russelville, 1984-85; gifted and talented tchr. Russellville (Ark.) Schs., 1985-86; gifted and talented adminstr., coord., tchr. Hartford (Ark.) Sch., 1986—. Vis. lectr. Ark. Tech. U., Russellville, 1987-89; conf. presenter, 2000. Mem. Circle K Svc. Orgn., Conway, Ark., 1978-82, Big Sister Youth Svcs., Conway, 1978-81; asst. leader 4-H Hartford, 1988-93, main leader, 1993-94. Baptist. Avocations: needle crafts, reading, working with children and plants. Office: Hartford Sch PO Box 489 Hartford AR 72938-0489 Home: 40249 Round Mountai Howe OK 74940-7439

ROLLE-RISSETTO, SILVIA, foreign languages educator, writer, artist; d. Dante and Gladys Rolle. BA in Spanish, BA in French and Italian, Calif. State U., Long Beach, 1987, MA in Spanish, 1990; PhD in Spanish, U. Calif., Riverside, 1996. Assoc. prof. Spanish, grad. coord. and fgn. lang. assessor of Spanish and Italian, dept. world langs. and lit. Calif. State U., San Marcos, 1996—. Participant numerous confs. Author: La Obra de Ana Maria Fagundo: Una Poetica Fememino-Feminista, 1997, Plazas: un lugar de encuentropara la hispanidad (lab manual); contbr. articles to profl. jours.; translator. Recipient Patrons of Italian scholarship U. degli Studi di Siena, 1987. Mem. MLA, Nat. Hispanic Soc., Asociacion de Literatura Fememina Hispanica, Hispanic Assn. of the Humanties, Letra Femeninas, Mairena, Assn. Internat. Hispanistas. Office: Calif State U San Marcos World Langs & Hispanic Lit 333 S Twin Oaks Valley Rd San Marcos CA 92096-0001

ROLLINGER, MARY ELIZABETH, school counselor; b. Jamestown, N.Y., May 12, 1950; d. Ernest Robert and June Armina (Carlson) Furlow. BS, Edinboro U., 1974; MEd, St. Bonaventure U., 1994. Cert. secondary edn. and elem. edn., N.Y., adv. cert. in counseling, 1996; advanced tng. in critical incident stress debriefing, 1996. English tchr. Bemus Point (N.Y.) Ctrl. Sch., 1974—2000; part-time clothing buyer Good Morning Farm, Stow, N.Y., 1976-84; part-time GED instr. Erie 2 BOCES, Fredonia, N.Y., 1979-84; sch. counselor Bemus Point Ctrl. Sch. Dist., 2000—. Creative writing tchr. Chautauqua County Sch. Bd., Fredonia, 1986—; adj. prof. SUNY, Fredonia, 1994-96; turnkey trainer for N.Y. State syllabus N.Y. State Dept. Edn., Albany, 1985. Vol. Reg Lenna Civic Ctr., Jamestown, 1992; tchr. rep. Parent/Tchr./Student Assn., Bemus Point, 1980-94; bd. dirs.

Amicae-Hotline for Rape/Battering/Abuse, Jamestown, 1986-88, Mutuus Mime Theater, Jamestown, 1982-86. Mem. Am. Counseling Assn., Am. Sch. Guidance Counselors Assn., Chautauqua County Counselors Assn., NY State Sch. Counselors Assn., Delta Kappa Gamma (publicity chair 1985-90). Avocations: photography, reading, hiking, cross stitching, travel. Home: PO Box 551 Bemus Point NY 14712-0551 Office: Bemus Point Ctrl Sch Dutch Hollow Rd Bemus Point NY 14712

ROLLINGS, MARTHA ANDERSON, retired school system administrator; b. Andersonville, Va., Sept. 3, 1929; d. Herbert Greenway and Alma Virginia (Abernathy) Anderson; m. Norman Gregory Rollings, Aug. 11, 1951 (dec. Feb. 1969); 1 child,Alma Faye Rollings-Carter. BA with honors, Longwood Coll., 1948; MEd, Coll. William and Mary, 1967. Cert. postgrad. profl. Tchr. English/Spanish Culpeper (Va.) County H.S., 1948-49, Surry (Va.) County H.S., 1949-53, Wakefield (Va.) H.S., 1959-64, Waverly (Va.) H.S., 1964-70; tchr., counselor, headmistress Surry (Va.) County Acad., 1970-75; tchr. English/Spanish Surry County H.S., Dendron, Va., 1975-78, asst. prin., assoc. prin., 1978-80; dir. instrn. Surry County Schs., 1989-91, asst. supt., 1991—95. Sec. bd. dirs. Am. Heart Assn., Surry, 1993-94; treas. Dendron United Meth. Ch., 1968-94; treas. Surry County Hist. Soc.; charter mem. Dendron County Hist. Soc. Named Adminstr. of Yr. SCAEOP, Surry, 1992, 94; recipient Alumni Achievement award Longwood Coll., Farmville, Va., 1994. Mem. ASCD, Va. ASCD, AASA, Surry C. of C., Delta Kappa Gamma (sec. 1986-88, 2nd v.p. 1988-90, 1st v.p. 1990-92, pres. 1992-94). Avocations: reading, travel, working crossword puzzles. Office: Surry County Pub Schs School St Govt Ctr Surry VA 23883

ROLLINS, DIANN E. nurse, primary school educator; b. Newark, Dec. 13, 1943; d. Lewis Paul and Letitia Lavinia Rollins. RN, Meth. Hosp. Sch. Nursing, Phila., 1964; postgrad., Howard U., 1966, Milton Coll., 1969—72, West Chester State Coll., 1972—79; cert. bldg. maintenance, John F. Kennedy Vocat. Tech., 1992; BSN, Thomas Jefferson U., 2000. RN, Pa., N.J. Nurse Meth. Hosp., Phila., 1964—66, 1967—69, Mercy Hosp., Janesville, Wis., 1969—72, Chester County Hosp., West Chester, Pa., 1972—74, Cheyney U., Pa., 1974—75, Embreville State Hosp., coatesville, 1976—78; agy. nurse Morristown, 1978—86, Medox, Olsten, Kimberly, Phila., 1985-86; RN supr. New Ralston House, Phila., 1986-87, 88-89; agy. nurse Kimberly, Quality Care, Olsten, Medox, others, Phila., 1987-89; info. and referral specialist Nat. Mental Health Consumer Self Help Clearing House, Phila., 1992-93; intern ACT NOW Southeastern Mental Health Program, Phila., 1993-94; nursery sch. tchr. Bambino Gesu Child Devel. Ctr., Phila., 1994-99; primary instr. nursing assts. ARC, 2000—01, Clin. Pathways Educators Ins., 2001—02; supplemental staff nurse Breslin Learning Ctr., 2002—, LPN instr., 2003—; staff nurse Bayada Nurses, 2002—. Vol. instr. program Franklin Inst., Phila., 1973-74; vol. multimedia first aide instr. ARC, Wilmington, Del., 1975-83; vol. plan II nurse blood mobiles ARC, S.E. Pa., 1982-85. Mem. Alumnae Meth. Hosp. Sch. Nursing, Four Chaplains Legion of Honor. Avocations: reading, writing, walking. Home: 308 S 10th St Philadelphia PA 19107-6134

ROLLINS, JUNE ELIZABETH, elementary education educator; b. Turin, N.Y., June 24, 1929; d. Jay Elihue and Mildred (Evans) Hoskins; m. Clair Austin Rollins, June 28, 1952; children: Timothy, Teri June, Scott, Tracy. BS in Music, Fredonia (N.Y.) State U., 1950. Cert. tchr. nursery, kindergarten, elem. edn., music, N.Y. Tchr. instrumental and vocal music Greenwood (N.Y.) Ctrl. H.S., 1968-71, Greenwood Ctrl. Sch., 1950-58, 59-68, Whitesville Ctrl., 1958-59; tchr. kindergarten Greenwood Ctrl. Sch., 1965-68, tchr. 3rd grade, 1971-97, tchr. pre-K, 1997—2001, tchr. music, 2001—. Tchr. piano. Organist, Greenwood Meth. Ch., 1972—; organist Andover Meth. Ch., 1995—; dir. Greenwood Cmty. Band, 1999—2000. Recipient Spl. Mission Recognition award Meth. Ch. for Music, 1981, Spl. Recognition award Music Dean Dist. United Meth. Houghton Coll., 1992, Gen. Douglas MacArthur Youth award Grand Lodge of State of N.Y., 1994, Outstanding Educator award Twin Tiers of N.Y. and Pa., 1995; named Outstanding Citizen West Greenwood Grange, 1992; featured in Evening Tribune, Hornell, N.Y., 1990. Mem. Delta Kappa Gamma (publicity chair 1989—, sec. 1994-97). Methodist. Avocations: flower gardening, crafts, needlework, quilling. Home: 2671 Main St Greenwood NY 14839 Office: Greenwood Ctrl Sch PO Box 936 Greenwood NY 14839-0936

ROLLMAN, CHARLOTTE, artist, educator; b. Harrisburgh, Ill., Oct. 15, 1947; d. Joseph and Beulah (Overton) R.; m. Edward H. Shay, 1971 (div. 1982); m. William B. Holland, 1987; 1 child, Danielle Suzanne Holland. BFA, Murray State U., 1969; MFA, U. Ill., 1971. Instr. art Ball State U., Muncie, Ind., 1971-75; supr. hand-painted silk garments Nicole, Ltd., Chgo., 1980-84; textile designer, stylist Thybony Wallcovering, Chgo., 1983-88; prof. art No. Ill. U., DeKalb, 1987—. Exhibitions include New Harmony (Ind.) Gallery Art, Charlotte Brauer, Munster, Ind., Jan Cicero, Chgo., Roy Boyd, Chgo, Locus, St. Louis, Suzanne Brown, Scottsdale, Ariz, Nestle's Corp., DeKalb, Capitol State Bank, St. Louis, others; illustrator New Internat. Dictionary Music, 1991; AV coord. Women's Caucus Art, Beijing, 1995. Grad. Sch. Rsch. grantee No. Ill. U., 1993, Faculty Enhancement grantee, 1995, Undergrad. Improvement grantee No. Ill. U., 1996. Mem. AAUW, Women's Caucus Art, Nat. Mus. Women Arts, Chgo. Area Women's Studies, DeKalb Area Women's Ctr. Office: No Ill U Sch Art Dekalb IL 60115

ROLLO, F. DAVID, hospital management company executive, health care educator; b. Endicott, N.Y., Apr. 15, 1939; s. Frank C. and Augustine L. (Dumont) R.; m. Linda Wood, June 1, 1991; children : Mindee, Alex. BA, Harpur Coll., 1959; MS, U. Miami, 1965; PhD, Johns Hopkins U., 1968; MD, Upstate Med. Ctr., Syracuse, N.Y., 1972. Diplomate Am. Bd. Nuclear Medicine. Asst. chief nuclear medicine services VA Hosp., San Francisco, 1974-77, chief nuclear medicine Nashville, 1977-79; sr. v.p. med. affairs Humana Inc., Louisville, 1980-92; dir. nuclear medicine div. Vanderbilt U. Med. Ctr., Nashville, 1977-81; prof. radiology Vanderbilt U., Nashville, 1979—; pres., CEO Metricor Inc., Louisville, 1992-95; sr. v.p. med. affairs HCIA, Louisville, 1995-96; sr. v.p. med. affairs, med. dir. Raytel Med. Corp., San Mateo, Calif., 1996-99; chief med. officer ADAC Labs., Milpitas, Calif., 1999—. Mem. med. adv. com. IBT, Washington, 1984—; mem. pvt. sector liaison panel Inst. of Medicine, Washington, 1983—; bd. dirs. ADAC Labs. Editor: Nuclear Medicine Physics, Instruments and Agents, 1977; co-editor: Physical Basis of Medical Imaging, 1980, Digital Radiology: Focus on Clinical Utility, 1982, Nuclear Medicine Resonance Imaging, 1983; mem. editorial adv. bd. ECRI, 1981—. Pres. bd. dirs. Youth Performing Arts Coun., Louisville, 1984-85; bd. dirs. Louisville-Jefferson County Youth Orch., 1983-85; sr. v.p., exec. com. USA Internat. Harp Competition, 1992-94, chmn., 1994—. Fellow Am. Coll. Cardiology, Am. Coll. Nuclear Physicians (profl. Am. Coll. Radiology com. 1982-84, chmn. 1984); mem. AMA, Soc. Nuclear Medicine (trustee 1979-83, 84—, Cassen Meml. lectr. western region 1980, 84), Radiol. Soc. N.Am., Am. Coll. Radiology, Ky. Sci. Tech. Coun. (exec. bd. 1987—), Advancement Med. Instrumentation (bd. dirs. 1986—), Louisville C. of C. (chmn. MIC com. 1987—). Avocations: racquetball, squash, golf. Home: 15735 Peach Hill Rd Saratoga CA 95070-6447

ROLLO, MARY-JO VIVIAN, special education educator; b. Port Chester, N.Y., Aug. 16, 1938; d. Salvatore James and Vivian (Cusamano) R.; children: Vivian, Phyllis, Cynthia, Mary-Jo, Salvatore, Joseph. BA, Pace U., 1968; MA, Western Conn. U., 1973; MS, Nova U., 1992, postgrad. Cert. tchr., N.Y., Fla. Tchr. Mahopac (N.Y.) Mid. Schs., 1968-71; tchr., spl. edn. specialist Karafin Schs., Mt. Kisco, N.Y., 1971-76; remedial reading specialist Lincoln Hall, Lincolndale, N.Y., 1976-78; tchr., specialist in emotionally handicapped students Orange County Schs., Orlando, Fla., 1978-93; owner, dir. SAT Prep. Ctr., Maitland, Fla., 1993—. Contbr. articles to profl. publs. De. Seminole Dem. Com., Seminole County, Fla., 1988. Mem. NEA (sec.), Fla. Tchrs Profession (sec. 1984-86), Classroom Tchrs. Assn. (sec. 1984-86, coord. coun. 1984-86), Coun. Exceptional Children, Nat. Coun. Tchrs. English. Roman Catholic. Avocations: reading, fishing, sports, cooking, travel.

ROLLS, BARBARA JEAN, nutritionist, educator, director; b. Washington, Jan. 5, 1945; d. Howard Julian and Patricia Jane (Pratt) Simons; m. Edmund Thomson Rolls, Sept. 6, 1969 (div. Jan. 1983); children: Melissa May, Juliet Helen. BA, U. Pa., 1966; PhD, Cambridge (Eng.) U., 1970; MA (hon.), Oxford (Eng.) U., 1970. Mary Somerville rsch. fellow Oxford U., 1969—72, IBM rsch. fellow, 1972—74, jr. rsch. fellow Wolfson Coll., 1974—75, E.P. Abraham rsch. fellow Green Coll., 1979—82, fellow in nutrition, 1983—84; assoc. prof. psychiatry Johns Hopkins U. Sch. Medicine, Balt., 1984-91, prof., 1991-92, dir. Lab. for Study Human Ingestive Behavior, 1984—; Jean Phillips Shibley prof. biobehavioral health Pa. State U., State College, 1992-94, prof., Helen A. Guthrie chair nutrition, 1994—. Mem. Nat. Diabetes and Digestive and Kidney Diseases Adv. Coun., 1994—98; cons. in field. Author: (book) Thirst, 1982, Carbohydrates and Weight Management, 1998, Volumetrics: Feel Full on Fewer Calories, 2000; mem. editl. bd. Am. Jour. Physiology, 1985—99, Trends Food Sci. and Tech., 1991—93, Am. Jour. Clin. Nutrition, 1992—98, Obesity Rsch., 1992—, Nutrition Rev., 1993—97; contbr. articles to profl. jours. Recipient Merit award, NIH, 1997—, Internat. award for Modern Nutrition, 2001; grantee, NIH, 1987—, Med. Rsch. Coun. U.K., 1969—84; Thouron scholar, Cambridge U., 1966—69. Mem.: Am. Soc. Clin. Nutrition, Am. Soc. Nutritional Scis. (award in human nutrition 1995), N.Am. Assn. Study Obesity (coun. 1991—93, v.p. 1994—95, pres.-elect 1995—96, pres. 1996—97), Soc. Study Ingestive Behavior (bd. dirs. 1986—90, pres.-elect 1990—91, pres. 1991—92), Am. Physiol. Soc., Am. Dietetic Assn. (hon.). Office: Pa State U 226 Henderson Bldg University Park PA 16802-6501

ROLSTON, HOLMES, III, theologian, educator, philosopher; b. Staunton, Va., Nov. 19, 1932; s. Holmes and Mary Winifred (Long) R.; m. Jane Irving Wilson, June 1, 1956; children: Shonny Hunter, Giles Campbell. BS, Davidson Coll., 1953; BD, Union Theol. Sem., Richmond, Va., 1956; MA in Philosophy of Sci., U. Pitts., 1968; PhD in Theology, U. Edinburgh, Scotland, 1958. Ordained to ministry Presbyn. Ch. (USA), 1956. Asst. prof. philosophy Colo. State U., Ft. Collins, 1968-71, assoc. prof., 1971-76, prof., 1976—. Vis. scholar Ctr. Study of World Religions, Harvard U., 1974-75; official observer UNCED, Rio de Janiero, 1992. Author: Religious Inquiry: Participation and Detachment, 1985, Philosophy Gone Wild, 1986, Science and Religion: A Critical Survey, 1987, Environmental Ethics, 1988, Conserving Natural Value, 1994, Genes, Genesis and God, 1999; assoc. editor Environ. Ethics, 1979—; mem. editorial bd. Oxford Series in Environ. Philosophy and Pub. Policy, Zygon: Jour. of Religion and Sci.; contbr. chpts. to books, articles to profl. jours. Recipient Oliver P. Penock Disting. Svc. award Colo. State U., 1983, Coll. award for Excellence, 1991, Univ. Disting. Prof., 1992; Disting. Russell fellow Grad. Theol. Union, 1991, Disting. Lectr., Chinese Acad. of Social Scis., 1991, Disting. Lectr., Nobel Conf. XXVII, Gifford Lectr., U. Edinburgh, 1997; featured in Fifty Key Thinkers on the Environment, 2001, Templeton prize in Religion, 2003. Mem. AAAS, Am. Acad. Religion, Soc. Bibl. Lit. (pres. Rocky Mountain-Gt. Plains region), Am. Philos. Assn., Internat. Soc. for Environ. Ethics (pres. 1989-94), Phi Beta Kappa. Avocation: bryology. Home: 1712 Concord Dr Fort Collins CO 80526-1602 Office: Colo State U Dept Philosophy Fort Collins CO 80523-0001

ROMAGUERA, ENRIQUE, foreign language educator, corporate interpreter; b. Mayaguez, P.R., June 2, 1942; s. José Mariano Jr. and Aminta Marina (Martinez) R. BA, U. Dayton, Ohio, 1965; MA, Ohio U., 1966; cert., McGill U., Montreal, 1966, U. Leningrad, USSR, 1967; postgrad., U. Ariz., 1970. Cert. oral proficiency tester in French for Am. Coun. for Teaching of Fgn. Lang. and Ednl. Testing Svcs., 1988-90. Instr. in langs. U. Dayton, 1969-73, asst. prof. langs., 1973-85, tenured prof. langs., 1976, assoc. prof. langs., 1985—; acad. assoc. Avraham Y. Goldratt Inst., 1991—. Part-time instr. Wilberforce (Ohio) U., summer 1971; interpreter, Nat. Cash Register, Dayton, 1973, Reynolds & Reynolds, Dayton, 1986; translator Delco Moraine/GM, Dayton, 1974, Congress of Astrol. Orgns., N.Y.C., 1978, Philips Industries, Dayton, 1980, WAMCO Products, Centerville, Ohio, 1991, Internat. Marian Rsch. Inst., Dayton, 1991, PMI Food Equipment Group, Troy, Ohio, 1993; translator, voice recorder in French and Spanish, Dayco Corp., Dayton, 1979, L/E/O Systems, Dayton, 1982, 83, AV Tech, Dayton, 1982, 94, Monarch Marking, Dayton, 1990, Bergamo Ctr., Dayton, 1991; translator, cons. Oracle Corp., Dayton, 1990; cert. yoga therapist Phoenix Rising, Housatonic, Mass., 1993—. Mem., composer, dir., tenor, percussion sect. Queen of Apostles Community Choir, Dayton, 1970—; vol. Yoga tchr. Greenewood Manor, Xenia, Ohio, 1978-88; marianist Assisted Living Ctr., Dayton, Ohio, 1989; workshop leader wellness program U. Dayton, 1986—; bd. dirs. Yoga Fellowship of Dayton, 1978—; Midwest regional coord. Kripalu Internat. Network, Kripalu Ctr. for Yoga and Health, Lenox, Mass., 1988—; cert. yoga therapist Phoenix Rising Housatonic, Mass., 1993—. Mem. Am. Assn. Tchrs. of French, Modern Lang. Assn., Internat. Soc. for Astrological Rsch., Ohio Fgn. Lang. Assn., Midwest Modern Lang. Assn. Roman Catholic. Avocations: theatre, cinema, music. Office: U Dayton Dept Langs 300 College Park Ave Dayton OH 45469-0001

ROMAN, STANFORD AUGUSTUS, JR., medical educator, dean; b. N.Y.C. s. Stanford Augustas and Ivy L. (White) D.; m. Norma Dabney Roman; children: Mawiyah Lythcott, Jane E. Roman-Brown. AB, Dartmouth Coll., 1964, MA (hon.), 1992; MD, Columbia U., 1968; MPH, U. Mich., 1975. Diplomate Nat. Bd. of Med. Examiners. Intern Columbia U.-Harlem Hosp. Ctr., N.Y.C., 1966—69, resident in medicine, 1969—71, chief resident in medicine, 1971—73; 1972assoc. dir. ambulatory care Columbia U. Harlem Hosp., 1972—73; instr. medicine Columbia U., N.Y.C., 1972—73; asst. physician Presbyn. Hosp., 1972—73; clin. dir. Healthco, Inc., Soul City, NC, 1973—74; dir. ambulatory care, asst. prof. medicine/sociomed. scis. Boston City Hosp., Boston, 1974—78; asst. prof. medicine U. N.C., Chapel Hill, 1973—74; asst. dean Boston U. Sch. Medicine, 1974—78; med. dir. D.C. Gen. Hosp., Washington, 1978—81; from assoc. dean acad. affairs to dep. dean Dartmouth Med. Sch., Hanover, NH, 1981—87, assoc. prof., 1981—87, dep. dean, 1986—87; dean, v.p., prof. medicine Morehouse Sch. Med., Atlanta, 1987—89; sr. v.p., med. and profl. affairs Health and Hosps. Corp., N.Y.C., 1989—90; dean med. sch., prof. cmty. health and social medicine CUNY, 1990—; interim pres. CCNY, 1999—2001. Dir. Boston Comprehensive Sickle Cell Ctr., 1975—78; bd. dirs. Winifred Masterson Burke Rehab. Hosp., White Plains, NY, 1993—94; mem. Dartmouth Hitchcock Med. Ctr. Bd. of Medicine, NY, 1993—98; trustee Dartmouth Coll., Hanover, NH, 1992—2002. Contbr. to book chpts. and profl. jours. and editls. Fellow N.Y. Acad. Medicine; mem. AMA, APHA, Nat. Med. Assn., N.Y. State Coun. Grad. Med. Edn., N.Y. State Dept. Edn. Bd. Medicine. Democrat. Episcopalian. Avocations: photography, travel, music.

ROMANO, DONNA MARIE, secondary school educator; b. Boston, Dec. 17, 1941; d. Adolph F. and Edna M. (Brill) DeSalvo; m. Nunzio Romano, June 24, 1961; children: Salvatore, William A. A Bus. Sci., Cardinal Cushing Coll., Brookline, Mass., 1961; BA in Social Studies, South Mass. U., 1974; MEd in Computer in Edn., Leslie Coll., 1991. Cert. English, bus., social studies, computer tchr., Mass. Tchr. bus. edn. New Bedford (Mass.) H.S., 1974—, tchr. tech. preparation program, 1991, tchr. computer workshop, 1992. Mem. adv. bd. for occupl. Edn., New Bedford, 1990. Author, editor: Word Perfect 5.1 for the Classroom, 1992. Mem. ASCD, NEA, AAUW, Mass. Tchrs. Assn., Mass. Bus. Edn. Assn.,. New Bedford Educators Assn. (sec. 1989-90), Bristol County Edn. Assn. Avocations: travel, gourmet cooking, collecting pairpoint glass. Home: 749 Pine Hill Dr New Bedford MA 02745-1932 Office: New Bedford HS 230 Hathaway Blvd New Bedford MA 02740-2818

ROMANO, MENA N. artist, educator; b. Bronx, N.Y., Oct. 16, 1943; d. Gerardo and Paulina (Sciurba) DeSanctis; m. Nicholas Romano, Nov. 23, 1963; children: Dina Marie Girola, Nicholas Carmine, Jr.(dec.). AS in Fine Arts, Suffolk County C. C., Selden, N.Y., 1983; BFA summa cum laude, Long Is. U., 1986, MFA, 1988. Mem. faculty, coord. art internships Nassau C.C., Garden City, NY, prof. art, 1996—; adj. asst. prof. art Suffolk County C. C., Selden, NY, 1988—. Vis. artist B.O.C.E.S. Art in Edn. program, 1992-; curator art, exhbns. Chess Collectors Internat., 1990; lectr. in field. Exhbns. include Islip Art Mus., S.W. Tex. State U. Gallery, Fine Art Mus. Long Island, The Pen and Brush Club N.Y.; permanent installations Meditation Garden, Garden City, 13th St. Garden Portals, Chgo. Grantee Artist Space, N.Y., 1990, others. Mem. Nat. Drawing Assn. (chair membership 1990-91), Long Island Craft Guild (pres. 1994-95), Phi Theta, Pi Alpha Sigma. Avocations: travel, gardening.

ROMANOFF, MARJORIE REINWALD, retired education educator; b. Chgo., Sept. 29, 1923; d. David Edward and Gertrude (Rosenfield) Reinwald; m. Milford M. Romanoff, Nov. 6, 1945; children: Bennett Sanford, Lawrence Michael, Janet Beth (dec.). Student, Northwestern U., 1941-42, 43-45, Chgo. Coll. Jewish Studies, 1942-43; BEd, U. Toledo, 1947, MEd, 1968, EdD, 1976. Tchr. Old Orchard Elem. Sch., Toledo, 1946-47, McKinley Sch., Toledo, 1964-65; substitute tchr. Toledo, 1964-68; instr. Mary Manse Coll., Toledo, 1974; instr. children's lit. Sylvania (Ohio) Bd. Edn., 1977; supr. student tchrs. U. Toledo, 1968—73, 1985—2001, instr. advanced comms., 1977, rschr., 1973-74; instr. Am. Lang. Inst., 1978—2002. Part-time asst. prof. elem. edn. Bowling Green (Ohio) State U., 1978—88; chair rsch. com. Am. Lang. Inst., U. Toledo, 1985—94, asst. prof. elem. edn. in lang. arts, 1985—87, part time asst. prof. elem. edn., ESL specialist, 1978—2002; presenter numerous workshops and demonstrations in children's lit. and analysis of tchr. behavior, 1976—99. Author: Language and Study Skills: For Learners of English, Prentice Hall Regents, 1991. Trustee Children's Svcs. Bd., 1974-76; pres. bd. Cummings Treatment Ctr. for Adolescents, 1978-80; mem. Crosby Gardens Adv. Bd., 1976-82, Cmty. Planning Coun., 1980-84, Citizens Rev. Bd. of Juv. Ct., 1979—; allocations com. Mental Health and Retardation Bd., 1980-81; active Bd. Jewish Edn., 1976—, pres., 1982-84; active Jewish Family Svc., 1978-85, v.p., 1980-85; allocations com. Jewish Welfare Fedn., 1980, 89-91; bd. dirs. Family Life Edn. Coun., 1984-90, sec., 1988-90; budget and allocations com. Jewish Fedn., 1989-93; bd. dirs. Friends Toledo-Lucas County Librs., 1991—, bd. pres., 1991-93; program chair U. Toledo Women's Commn., 1991-93; bd. dirs. Ohio Friends of Pub. Librs., 1992-94; presenter ann. conf. N.W. Ohio Libr. Assn., 1993, Bowling Green State U., 1997; condr. workshop Internat. Conf./Teaching Langs., U. Cin., 1996. Named One of Ten Women of Yr., St. Vincent's Hosp., Guild, 1984, Outstanding Instructional Staff Woman, U. Toledo, 1990, Excellence award Citizen's Rev. Bd., 2003. Mem. Tchrs. English to Speakers Other Langs. (presenter 1986, presenter Internat. TESOL Atlanta 1993), Toledo Libr. Legacy Found., Orgn. Rehab. and Tng. (named Outstanding Woman in Cmty. Svc. 1987), Hadassah (chpt. pres. regional bd. 1961-64), Northwestern U. Alumni Assn., Phi Kappa Phi, Phi Delta Kappa, Kappa Delta Pi (pres./faculty adv. 1971-75, Point of Excellence award 1992), Pi Lambda Theta (chpt. pres. 1978-80, nat. com. 1979-84). Home: 4343 W Bancroft Apt 4B Toledo OH 43615 E-mail: MRR1923@aol.com.

ROMANO-MAGNER, PATRICIA R. English studies educator, researcher; b. N.Y.C., Mar. 22, 1928; d. Al and Nicole (Siriani) Romano; m. Ralpha M. Magner, Dec. 24, 1954. AA, BA, L.A. City Coll.; MA, Calif. State U., L.A.; D (hon.), Stanford U., Cambridge (Eng.) U., Queens Coll. Master tchr. Burbank (Calif.) Unified Sch. Dist., L.A. City Schs., Stanford (Calif.) U. Sch. for the Gifted; prof. Calif. State U., L.A., curriculum lab. asst. LA. Mem. AAUW, AAUP (award 2000), Am. Legion Aux., Sierra Club, Natural Resources Def. Coun., The Friends of the William J. Clinton Presdl. Libr. (founding mem.), Scholarship Soc. of Calif. State U. L.A. Republican. Avocation: horseback riding. Home: 5975 N Odell Ave Chicago IL 60631-2358

ROMANOWSKI, SYLVIE, French literature educator; b. Paris, May 12, 1940; BA, Carleton U., Ottawa, Can., 1962; MA, Harvard U., 1963; PhD, Yale U., 1969. Lectr. York U., Toronto, Canada, 1968-69; asst. prof. U. Wis. at Milw., 1969-71, Northwestern U., Evanston, Ill., 1971-76, assoc. prof., 1976—. Dir. Women's Studies Program, Northwestern U., Evanston, 1986-87. Author: L'illusion chez Descartes, 1974; contbr. articles to profl. jours. Mem. MLA, North Am. Assn. for French Seventeenth Century Lit., Am. Soc. for Eighteenth Century Studies, Internat. Assn. for Philosophy and Lit., Midwest MLA, Midwest Am. Soc. for Eighteenth Century Studies. Address: Northwestern U Dept French & Italian Evanston IL 60208-2206

ROMANOWSKI, THOMAS ANDREW, physics educator; b. Warsaw, Apr. 17, 1925; came to U.S., 1946, naturalized, 1949; s. Bohdan and Alina (Sumowski) R.; m. Carmen des Rochers, Nov. 15, 1952; children: Alina, Dominique. BS, Mass. Inst. Tech., 1952; MS, Case Inst. Tech., 1956, PhD, 1957. Rsch. assoc. physics Carnegie Inst. Tech., 1956-60; asst. physicist high energy physics Argonne Nat. Lab., Ill., 1960-63, assoc. physicist, 1963-72, physicist, 1972-78; prof. physics Ohio State U., Columbus, 1964-92, prof. emeritus, 1992-98; sr. scientist Argonne Nat. Lab., 1992; physicist U.S. Dept. Energy, Washington, 1992-98; cons. in pvt. practice, 1998—. Contbr. articles to profl. jours. and, papers to sci. meetings, seminars and workshops. With high energy program U.S. Dept. Energy, 1993-98. Served with C.E. AUS, 1946-47. Fellow Am. Phys. Soc., AAAS; mem. Lambda Chi Alpha. Achievements include research in nuclear and high energy physics. Home: 319 Tano Rd Santa Fe NM 87506-8823 E-mail: romanowski@santafe-newmexico.com.

ROMBOUTS, JEAN JACQUES, orthopaedic surgery educator, dean; b. Anvers, Belgium, Dec. 6, 1941; s. René and Emilie (Pigneur) R.; m. Christiane Lindemans (dec. July 1983); m. Veronique Godin, Aug. 1, 1985; children: Marie-Eve, François-Xavier, Jean-Sebastien. MD, Catholic U. of Louvain, Belgium, 1966. Specialist in orthopedic surgery. Orthopedic surgeon Cliniques U. St.-Luc, Brussels, 1976—2002, head, chmn. dept. orthopaedic surgery, 1996—; prof. orthopedic surgery Cath. U. Louvain Med. Sch., Brussels, 1988—; chief, chmn. Dept. Orthopedic Surgery U. St. Luc, Brussels, 1996—; dean faculty medicine Cath. U. Louvain, 2002—. Invited prof. U. Geneva, Switzerland, 1991-92. Maj. Belgian Army Res. Mem. Belgian Hand Group (gen. sec. 1972-82), Belgian Orthopedic Assn. (gen. sec. 1981-89, pres.-elect 1996-97, pres. 1998-99). Avocations: jogging, mountain climbing. Home: Ave des Ducs 160 B 1970 Wezembeek-Oppem Belgium Office: Cliniques Univ Saint-Luc 1200 Brussels Belgium

ROMEO, CHRISTINA IOANNIDES, speech language pathologist; b. Livingston, N.J., Oct. 19, 1968; d. Paul M. and Carol J. (Mancuso) Ioannides; m. Michael J. Romeo, Mar. 26, 1994; children: Tia C., Michael N. BS, Trenton State Coll., 1990; MA, Kean Coll. N.J., 1992. Grad. asst., asst. tchr. comm. handicapped class Kean Coll. N.J., Union, 1990-92; speech lang. specialist Old Bridge (N.J.) Twp. Bd. Edn., 1992—. Fundraiser Am. Cancer Soc., Edison, N.J.; cmty. svc. vol. Local Vets. Orgn., Iselin, N.J. Mem. NEA, N.J. Edn. Assn., Old Bridge Edn. Assn., Am. Speech Lang. Hearing Assn. (cert. clin. competence), N.J. Speech Lang. Hearing Assn., Jonas Salk Middle Sch. PTA, McDivitt Sch. PTA, Shore Athletic Club. Avocation: race walking. Home: 593 S Laurel Ave Hazlet NJ 07730-2682 Office: Old Bridge Twp Bd Edn Jonas Salk Middle Sch 370 W Greystone Rd Old Bridge NJ 08857-4029

ROMEO, JOANNE JOSEFA MARINO, mathematics educator; b. Youngstown, Ohio, Nov. 21, 1943; d. Joseph James and Ann Marie (Bonamase) Marino; m. John Homer Romeo, Aug. 14, 1965; children: Christopher, Chrisanne, Jonathan. BS, Ohio State U., 1965; postgrad., Youngstown State U., 1969-70; MS, Purdue U., 1974; postgrad. in computer sci., U. Tenn., Knoxville, 1982-91. Substitute tchr., Columbus, Ohio, 1964-65; tchr. geometry, math. and French Hamilton Sch. Dist., Columbus, Ohio, 1965-66; tchr. gifted children Bluegrass Elem. Sch., Knoxville, Tenn., 1976-77; tchr. math. and sci. Webb Sch., Knoxville, 1977-85, also developer computer sci. program, 1977-85; headmistress Greenbrier Acad., Sevierville, Tenn., 1985-86; instr. math. Pellissippi State Tech. Community Coll., Knoxville, Tenn., 1986—; dir. religious edn. Sacred Heart Parish, Knoxville, Tenn., 1987—2001; tchr. advanced math. Knox County Sch., Knoxville, Tenn., 2000—. Delegate to go to Russia and Lithuania Ministries of Edn., NCEA. Vol dir. religious edn. Sacred Heart Parish, Knoxville, 1979-87, lay pastoral minister, 1988—. Mem. Nat. Council Tchrs. Math., Nat. Cath. Edn. Assn., Nat. Council Parish and Religious Coordinators and Dirs., Nat. Sci. Tchrs. Assn., Nat. Assn. Exec. Females, Ohio State U. Alumni Assn., Tenn. Assn. Dirs. Religious Edn., Purdue U. Alumni Assn., Alpha Gamma Delta. Republican. Home: 1708 Capistrano Dr Knoxville TN 37922-6302

ROMEO, WILLIAM JOSEPH, middle school educator; b. Cleve., Mar. 4, 1952; s. Joseph A. and Frances L. (Wetzel) R.; m. June Ann Hart, June 21, 1975. BS in Edn., Kent (Ohio) State U., 1975; MA in English, Cleve. State U., 1981; PhD in Edn., Kent State U., 1997. Cert. tchr., Ohio. Tchr. English Valley Forge H.S., Parma, Ohio, 1975-78, Greenbriar Mid. Sch., Parma, 1978—, head dept. English, 1979—96. Instr. tchr. edn. Kent State U., 1991, 93, 96, 97, 98, student tchr. preceptor, 1990, 93; student tchr. preceptor Baldwin Wallace Coll., Berea, Ohio, 1988; conf. spkr., presenter in field. Contbr. articles, book revs. to profl. jours. NEH fellow Folger Shakespeare Libr., 1994. Mem. Nat. Coun. Tchrs. English, Internat. Reading Assn., Ohio Coun. Tchrs. English Lang. Arts, Ohio Coun. Internat. Reading Assn., Phi Delta Kappa, Kappa Delta Pi. Office: Greenbriar Middle Sch 11810 Huffman Rd Parma OH 44130-2298 E-mail: wjromeo@hotmail.com.

ROMER, DANIEL, university official, psychologist, educator; b. Caracas, Venezuela, Apr. 19, 1947; arrived in U.S., 1948; s. Adolf and Eleanor (Rittermann) R.; m. Lauren B. Alloy, Jan. 4, 1985; 1 child, Adrienne. AB, Dartmouth Coll., 1969; PhD, U. Ill., Chgo., 1974. Rsch. fellow Dept Mental Health, Chgo., 1976-79; vis. asst. prof. Northwestern U., Evanston, Ill., 1979-81; adj. assoc. prof. U. Ill., 1981-89; assoc. rsch. dir. Leo Burnett Co., Chgo., 1982-89; sr. rschr. Annenberg Sch. for Comm., U. Pa., Phila., 1990—2000, sr. fellow Ctr. for Cmty. Partnerships, 1996—, rsch. dir. Inst. for Adolescent Risk Comm., 2001—. Mem. nat. expert panel on adolescent STD prevention Ctr. for Disease Control and Prevention, Atlanta, 2000-01; mem. rev. panels NIH, Washington, 1994-97, 98—. Mem. editl. bd. Jour. Exptl. Social Psychology, 1988-91, Youth and Society, 2001—; contbr. over 60 articles to psychol. and pub. health jours., chpts. to books. Grantee NIMH, 1992—, Ford Found., 1994. Mem. APA, APHA. Office: Annenberg Pub Policy Ctr 3620 Walnut St Philadelphia PA 19104 E-mail: dromer@asc.upenn.edu.

ROMERO, JORGE ANTONIO, neurologist, educator; b. Bayamon, P.R., Apr. 15, 1948; s. Calixto Antonio Romero-Barcelo and Antonia (de Juan) R.; m. Helen Mella, June 20, 1970 (div. 1983); children: Sofia, Jorge, Alfredo, Isabel; m. Cheryl Raps, Aug. 1994; 1 child, Jessica. SB, MIT, 1968; MD, Harvard U., 1972. Diplomate Am. Bd. Psychiatry and Neurology. Intern U. Chgo. Hosp. and Clinics, 1972-73; resident Mass. Gen. Hosp., Boston, 1975-78; rsch. fellow in pharmacology NIMH, Bethesda, Md., 1973-75; asst. prof. neurology Harvard Med. Sch., Boston, 1979-92; mem. staff VA Med. Ctr., Brockton, Mass., 1979-92; assoc. physician Brigham and Women's Hosp., Boston, 1980-92; chmn. dept. neurology Ochsner Clin. Baton Rouge, 1993-97; assoc. clin. prof. neurology La. State U. Sch. Medicine, 1996-97; attending physician Baylor U. Med. Ctr., Dallas, 2002—. Cons. Mass. Mental Health Ctr., Boston, 1987-92. With USPHS, 1973-75. Recipient Career Devel. award VA, 1979. Mem. Am. Acad. Neurology. Office: 3600 Gaston Ave Dallas TX 75246

ROMICK, JOYCE TRUDEAU, elementary school educator; b. Plattsburgh, N.Y., Jan. 23, 1939; d. Norman Samuel and Lurena (Flemming) Trudeau; m. Ronald Virgil Romick, Jan. 3, 1959; children: Cynthia Lynne, Norman Charles. BS in Early Childhood Edn., SUNY, Plattsburgh, 1959, MS in Elem. Edn., 1964; EdS in Reading Edn., Ariz. State U., 1970. Cert. tchr., elem. prin., elem. supr., Ariz., Wash. 1st grade tchr. Heartwood Elem. Sch., Tacoma, 1960-62, Tolleson (Ariz.) Grammar Sch., 1963; tchr. 2nd grade Cartwright Elem. Sch., Phoenix, 1963-72, tchr. 6th grade, 1973-92. Intermediate rep. for lang. arts curriculum Consortium Sch. Dists., Phoenix, 1974-77; mem. cadre corps Ariz. Dept. Edn., 1977-79. Contbr. articles to Boston Bull., 1982-83. Mem. fin. com. Shepherd of the Valley United Meth. Ch., Phoenix, 1985-90, mem. choir, 1963-93, mem. adminstrv. bd., 1965-68, mem. stewardship com., 1990-98; assoc. mem. worship com. Calvary United Meth. Ch., Lake Worth, Fla., 2001—, adult Sunday sch. tchr., 2002—. Mem. NEA (life), Alpha Delta Kappa (life, state historian 1984-86, Nu chpt. historian 1990-92, state treas. 1988-90, 90-92, state ways and means chmn. 1992-94, ctrl. dist. co-chmn. 1997-98, silver sister), Daughters of Nile, Nefertiti Club (v.p. 1999-2000), Phi Delta Kappa, Ladies Oriental Shrine of N.Am. Republican. Avocations: travel, showing boston terriers, theater, music, reading.

ROMINE, DONNA MAE, gifted and talented program educator; b. Moreauville, La., Feb. 18, 1949; d. Marvin Peter and Ethel Mae (Young) Bordelon; m. James Rufus Romine, Dec. 4, 1946 (dec. 1999); children: Michael, Shelia, Larry. BA, McNeese State U., 1969; M in Gifted Edn., U. La., 2002. Cert. elem. tchr., La. Tchr. 6th grade Acadia Parish Schs., Rayne, La., 1969-71; tchr. jr. high Basile (La.) High Sch., 1972-77; tchr. 4th and 6th grades Hathaway High Sch., Jennings, La., 1980-82; elgibility worker Acadia Parish Office Family Security, Crowley, La., 1982-87; tchr. Church Point (La.) Mid. Sch., 1987-99; tchr. gifted program Jeff Davis Parish Schs., Jennings, La., 1999—. Leader 4-H, Church Point, 1988—98. Mem.: La. Fedn. Tchrs., Assn. for Gifted and Talented. Democrat. Roman Catholic. Avocations: reading, science fiction films, jeopardy. Home: 223 Violet Ln Iota LA 70543-4320 Office: Jeff Davis Parish Schs 203 E Plaquemine St Jennings LA 70546-5853

ROMNEY-MANOOKIN, ELAINE CLIVE, music educator, composer; b. Salt Lake City, July 11, 1922; d. Joseph Campbell Clive and Katie Winifred Gilroy; m. Eldon Brigham Romney, May 5, 1941 (dec. May 1998); children: Ruth Romney Powell, Frederic Clive Romney, Clive Jay Romney, Stanley Clive Romney, Eldon Clive Romney, Roslyn Kay Romney Reynolds, Rae Lynne Romney Johnson, Vincent Clive Romney; m. Stuart Midgley Manookin. Studied piano, violin and cello, Clive Music Studios, Salt Lake City, 1938; cert., U. Utah, 1941; studied organ, U. S.C., 1954; studied piano with Frederic Dixon, McCune Sch., 1938—42; studied paino with Alton O'Steen, Juilliard, 1936. Musician: Assembly Hall with McCune Symphony, 1941, author organ book for beginning organists; composer: (sch. song) South H.S., 1939, Skyline H.S., 1962, Wasatch Jr. H.S., 1964; organist Grandview Second Ward, 2001—; organist: Columbia (S.C.) Stake Ctr., 1953—54, East Millcreek Stake, 1956—, Monument Pk. Stake, 1955—56. Bd. dirs. Utah Hemophlia Found., Salt Lake City, 1965—99; vol. specialist Welfare Employment; vice chmn. dist. Rep. Party, Salt Lake City, 1970—90. Recipient Dedicated Svc. award, Hemophilia Found., 1991. Mem.: Alpha Dorian Fine Arts Soc. (past pres.), AXO Luncheon Club (pres.), Agalia Mu (past pres.). Avocations: traveling, writing, volunteering. Address: 2987 Hartford St Salt Lake City UT 84106-3468

ROMO, RICARDO, academic administrator, history educator; b. San Antonio, June 23, 1943; s. Henry and Alice (Saenz) R.; m. Harriett Durr, July 1, 1967; children: Anadelia, Carlos. BS, U. Tex., 1967; MA in History, Loyola U., L.A., 1970; PhD in History, UCLA, 1975. Tchr. Franklin H.S., L.A., 1967-70; asst. prof. Chicano studies Calif. State U., Northridge, 1970-73; asst. prof. history U. Calif., San Diego, 1974-80; assoc. prof. history U. Tex., Austin, 1980-99, vice provost, 1993-99, pres. San Antonio, 1999—; v.p., dir. Tomas Rivera Ctr., San Antonio, 1987-93. Expert witness in field; Chancellor's disting. lectr. U. Calif., Berkeley, 1985. Author: East Los Angeles: History of A Barrio, 1983; co-author: The Mexican American Experience: An Interdisciplinary Anthology, 1985; editl. bd. Social Sci. Quar. Mem. Men's Athletic Coun., Nat. Coun. of La Raza, 1999—; bd. dirs. Smithsonian Nat. Bd.for Latino Initiatives, 1999—, Greater San Antonio C. of C., 1999—. Fellow Ctr. for Advanced Studies in Behavioral Studies, Stanford U., 1989-90; named to Longhorn Hall of Honor. Mem. San Antonio Med. Found. (trustee 1999—), Tex. Rsch. Park Found. (bd. trustees 1999—). Roman Catholic. Avocations: hiking, photography. Office: U Tex Pres office 6900 N Loop 1604 W San Antonio TX 78249-1130 E-mail: president@utsa.edu.

ROMZEK, BARBARA S(UE), public administration educator; b. Mt. Clemens, Mich., Aug. 3, 1948; d. Lawrence John and Theresa Agnes (Kociba) R.; m. David Alan Greenamyre, May 19, 1984; children: Wallis Greenamyre Romzek, Spencer Romzek Greenamyre. BA, Oakland U., 1970; MA, Western Mich. U., 1972; PhD, U. Tex., Austin, 1979. Asst. instr. U. Tex., Austin, 1977-79; asst. prof. polit. sci. U. Kans., Lawrence, 1979-85, rsch. assoc. Ctr. for Pub. Affairs, 1981-84, assoc. prof. pub. adminstrn., 1985-95, chairperson Dept. Pub. Adminstrn., 1988-93, prof. pub. adminstrn., 1995—, assoc. dean Coll. Liberal Arts and Scis., 2000—. Cons. pub. affairs various local, state, nat. and internat. orgns., 1980—; interim dir. human resources Bd. Pub. Utilities, Kansas City, Kans., 1986; guest scholar Brookings Instn., 1995. Co-author: American Public Administration: Politics and the Management of Expectations, 1991, New Governance for Rural America: Creating Intergovernmental Partnerships, 1996; co-editor: New Paradigms for Government: Issues for the Changing Public Service, 1994; mem. editorial bd. Pub. Adminstrn. Rev., 1987-90, Adminstrn. and Soc., 1990—, Jour. Pub. Adminstrn. Rsch. and Theory, 1990-93, Am. Jour. Polit. Sci., 1994-97, Jour. Pub. Adminstrn. Edn., 1994-97, Jour. Politics, 2001--; contbr. articles to profl. jours. Fellow, AAUW, 1978—79. Fellow Nat. Acad. Pub. Adminstrn.; mem. Am. Polit. Sci. Assn. (pub. adminstrn. sect. chairperson 1988-89, mem. pub. adminstrn. sect. exec. coun. 1986-91, mem. Gaus award com. 1989, mem. White award com. 2000-01, mem. Kaufman award com. 2002-03, nat. coun. 1992-94, chair com. organized sects. 1993-97, Kaufman award, 2002), Am. Soc. Pub. Adminstrn. (governing bd. Kans. chpt. 1983-84, Brownlow award com. 1987, Mosher award com. 1988, chair Levine award com. 1993-95, vice chair task force confs. 1994-95, Webb award com. 1996-97, Waldo award com. 2001-03), Acad. Mgmt. (Levine award com. 1989, exec. com. pub. sector div. 1989-95, Mosher award 1988), Nat. Assn. Schs. of Pub. Affairs and Adminstrn. (exec. coun. 1990-93, dissertation award com. 1988-89, com. chair 1989, commn. on peer rev. and accreditation 1989-92, rsch. com. 1987-90, joint task force on local govt. edn. with Internat. City Mgmt. Assn. 1987-90, task force on edn. for state and local pub. svc. 1991-93, Staats award com. 1994-95, com. chair 1994-95, nominating com. 1996, constn. com. 1996-97, stds. com. 1999-2002), Internat. City Mgmt. Assn. (task force on continuing edn. and profl. devel. 1991-93, bd. regents ICMA U. 1996-99), League Kans. Mcpls. (spl. com. on future 1989), Pi Alpha Alpha (nat. coun. 1989-93). Avocations: reading, travel, walking. Office: Coll Liberal Arts & Scis 200 Strong Hall 1450 Jayhawk Blvd Lawrence KS 66045-7535

RONAYNE, MICHAEL RICHARD, JR., academic dean; b. Boston, Apr. 29, 1937; s. Michael Richard and Margaret (Fahey) R.; m. Joanne Maria, Aug. 7, 1971; 1 child, Michelle Eileen. BS, Boston Coll., 1958; PhD, U. Notre Dame, 1962. Instr. chemistry Providence Coll., 1962-63, asst. prof. chemistry, 1963-64; rsch. chemist Panametrics, Inc., Waltham, Mass., 1964-66; asst. prof. chemistry Suffolk U., Boston, 1966-67, assoc. prof., 1967-70, prof., chmn. dept. chemistry, 1970-72, dean Coll. Arts and Sci., 1972—. Reaccreditation vis. team mem. New Eng. Assn. Schs. and Colls., Winchester, Mass., 1974-80, Mass. Dept. Edn., Boston, 1975; mem. acad. adv. com. Mass. Bd. Higher Edn., Boston, 1977. Contbr. articles to sci. jours., profl. publs. Mem. Winchester Sch. Com., 1983-92, chmn., 1984-85, 86-87; mem. Winchester Town Meeting, 1983-98, mem. town capital planning com., 1983-84, town coun. on youth, 1987-88, 89-90; mem. exec. com., bd. dirs. Mass. Bay Marine Studies Consortium, 1985-87; project dir. U.S. Dept. of Edn. Title III Grants. Shell Oil Corp. fellow, 1958-59, AEC fellow 1959-62; recipient Contbns. in Sci. and Edn. citation New Eng. Sch. Art and Design, Boston, 1991; named to Matignon High Sch. Alumni Achievement Hall of Fame, 1997. Mem. AAAS, Am. Chem. Soc., Am. Conf. Acad. Deans, Coun. for Liberal Learning, Am. Assn. for Higher Edn., Sigma Xi, Phi Alpha Theta, Phi Gamma Mu, Sigma Tau Delta, Omicron Delta Epsilon, Sigma Zeta, Pi Sigma Alpha. Office: Suffolk U Beacon Hill Boston MA 02114 E-mail: mronayne@suffolk.edu.

RONCO, WILMA LILLEY, chief operating officer; b. Pottstown, Pa., Oct. 9, 1948; d. William Arthur and Anna May (Lines) Lilley; m. Arthur C. Smith, Aug. 15, 1992; children: William Matthew, Daniel Christopher. BS, Boston U., 1975; MBA, Northeastern U., 1987. Cert. spl. edn. tchr. Spl. needs tchr. Ipswich (Mass.) Pub. Schs., 1975-77; 2nd grade tchr. Acton (Mass.) Pub. Schs., 1977-78; nursery sch. tchr. Community Nursery Sch., Lexington, Mass., 1979-80; dir. early intervention program Marlboro Early Intervention, 1988-2000; chief program officer Thom Child and Family Svcs., 2000—. Pres. Community Nursery Sch., Lexington, 1987-88. Chair fin. com. Follen Cmty. Ch., Lexington, 1990-95, pres. bd., 2000-01; mem. appropriations com. Town of Lexington, 1988-90. Mem. Pi Lambda Theta, Beta Gamma Sigma. Democrat. Unitarian Universalist. Avocations: skiing, world travel, scuba diving.

RONDESTVEDT, KAREN ANNE, librarian, educator; b. Ann Arbor, Mich., Mar. 30, 1948; d. Christian S. Jr. and Estelle S. Rondestvedt; m. Matias G. Aranda, Nov. 26, 1988. BA, Oberlin Coll., 1972; MA, PhD, U. Chgo., 1986. Slavic libr. asst. U. Chgo., 1972-85; Slavic bibliographer librs. U. Pitts., 1985-2000; curator for Slavic and East European collections Stanford (Calif.) U., 2001—. Editor (jour.) Slavic East European Information Resources, 2000—, (book series) Slavic & East European Librarianship, 2000—. Mem. Am. Assn. for Advancement of Slavic Studies (chair bibliography and documentation com. 1996-98), Polish Inst. Arts & Scis. of Am. Democrat. Unitarian Universalist. Avocations: cooking, travel. Office: Green Libr ASRG 3rd Flr Stanford Univ Stanford CA 94305-6004

RONDINELLI, DENNIS A(UGUST), business administration educator, researcher; b. Trenton, N.J., Mar. 30, 1943; s. August P. and Vincentia Rondinelli; m. Soonyoung Chang, Dec. 19, 1976; children: Linda, Lisa. BA, Rutgers U., 1965; PhD, Cornell U., 1969. Asst. prof. urban affairs U. Wis., Milw., 1971-73; assoc. prof. grad. sch. of mgmt. Vanderbilt U., Nashville, 1973-76; assoc. prof. planning Maxwell Sch. of Citizenship and Pub. Affairs Syracuse U., N.Y., 1976-79, prof. social scis., 1979-86; prin. scientist and sr. policy analyst Office for Internat. Programs, Research Triangle Inst., Research Triangle Park, N.C., 1986-90; Glaxo Disting. Internat. Prof. Mgmt. Kenan-Flagler Bus. Sch. Cons. World Bank, U.S. Dept. State, UN Devel. Program, Govts. of Colombia, South Korea, Can., Indonesia, Philippines, China, India, mem. com. of experts on pub. adminstrn., United Nations Econ. and Social Coun., 2002—. Author: Decentralization and Development: Policy Implementation in Developing Countries, 1983, Applied Methods of Regional Analysis: The Spatial Dimensions of Development Policy, 1985, Development Administration and U.S. Foreign Aid Policy, 1987, Urban Services in Developing Countries: Public and Private Roles in Urban Development, 1988, Planning Education Reforms in Developing Countries, 1990, Development Projects as Policy Experiments, 1993, Privatization and Economic Reform in Central Europe, 1994, Expanding Sino-American Business and Trade: China's Economic Transition, 1994, Great Policies: Strategic Innovations in Asia and the Pacific, 1995, Policies and Institutions for Managing Privatization, 1996, Market Reform in Vietnam, 1999, Reinventing Government for the 21st Century, 2003; mem. editl. adv. bd. Leadership Rev., Jour. Internat. Bus. Edn., Jour. Internat. Devel. Planning; contbr. articles to Jours. Mem. expert com. pub. admin. unecon. and social coun. UN, 2002—. Capt. U.S. Army, 1965—72. Decorated Julio Lieras Order of Merit (Colombia), 1988; recipient Rural Devel. medal Republic of Vietnam, 1971, Ethnic Minorities Devel. medal, 1971, W. Bloomberg award for excellence in futures studies, 1997, Weatherspoon Disting. Rsch. award, 1997; East-West Ctr. sr. fellow, 1975-76, Pacific Basin Rsch. Ctr./Soka U. of Am./Harvard U. rsch. fellow, 1991-92. Avocations: gardening, writing nonfiction. Office: Kenan-Flagler Bus Sch U NC CB #3490 Chapel Hill NC 27599-3490 E-mail: dennis_rondinelli@unc.edu.

RONN, AVIGDOR MEIR, chemical physics educator, consultant, researcher; b. Tel Aviv, Nov. 17, 1938; came to U.S., 1959; m. Linda Ann Tenney, Aug. 25, 1963; children: David A., Karin J. BS in Chemistry, U. Calif., Berkeley, 1963; AM in Phys. Chemistry, Harvard U., 1964, PhD in Phys. Chemistry, 1966. Rsch. asst. Nat. Bur. Standards, 1966-68; from asst. prof. to assoc. prof. chemistry Poly. Inst. Bklyn., 1968-73; prof. chemistry Bklyn. Coll. CUNY, 1973-2000, Broeklundian prof. Bklyn. Coll., 1987-90, dir. Laser Inst., 1987—; sr. rsch. fellow Long Island Jewish Med. ctr, 1992—, Albert Enstein Med. Coll., 1992—; pres. PhoDyne Technologies, Inc., Great Neck, N.Y., 1995—. Exec. officer PhD program in chemistry CUNY, Manhattan, 1984-90, exec. dir. Applied Sci. Inst., Bklyn., 1987-90; vis. prof. U. Tel Aviv, 1971-72; Fulbright Sr. scholar U. Sao Paulo, Brazil, 1983-84; v.p., gen. mgr. Lic Industries, Inc., Suffern, N.Y., 1979-80. Author: (with others) Advances in Chemical Physics, 1980, Techniques of Chemistry, 1981. Pres. Towne House 27, Inc., Great Neck, 1984—. 1st sgt. Israeli Army, 1956-58. Alfred P. Sloan Found. fellow, 1971-73, OAS fellow, U. Sao Paulo, Brazil, 1973. Mem. Israel Chem. Soc., Am. Phys. Soc., Am. Chem. Soc., SPIE, Am. Assn. Laser Medical & Surgery, Phi Beta Kapp. Achievements include 6 patents for Laser Initiated Chain Reactions for Producing a Sintered Product, Method for Forming Patterns on Substrate or Support, Production of Chain Reaction by Laser Chemistry, Preparation of Metal Containing Polymeric Materials via Laser Chemistry, Method of Molecular Species Alteration by Nonresonant Laser Induced Dielectric Breakdown, Plasma Assay Spectrometer; 2 patents on method for assaying photosentizing drug in whole blood; 1 patent on assaying photosentizing drug in plasma; 1 patent on optical cable assembly; 1 patent on assaying photosensitizing drug in tissue. Address: LI Jewish Med Ctr New Hyde Park NY 10040 E-mail: aronn@lij.edu.

ROODIN, PAUL A. psychology educator; b. Brookline, Mass., June 1, 1943; s. Harry and Blossom (Sugarman) R.; m. Marlene Linda Lubarsky, Aug. 27, 1967; children: Neal D., Pamela L. AB, Boston U., 1965; MS, Purdue U., 1968, PhD, 1970. Asst. prof. psychology SUNY, Oswego, 1969-75, assoc. prof., 1975-81, prof., 1981—, assoc. dean, 1989-91, assoc. provost, 1991-95, dir. experience-based edn., 1996—. Co-author: Developmental Psychology, 1980, Adult Cognition and Aging, 1986, Adult Development and Aging, 1991, 3d edit., 1995, 5th edit., 2003; contbr. articles on devel. psychology to profl. jours. Jewish. Avocations: cooking, golf, tennis, running. Home: 122 Stanwood Ln Manlius NY 13104-1412 Office: SUNY Coll at Oswego Oswego NY 13126

ROOKER, LEROY S. federal agency administrator; Dir., family compliance off. US Dept. Edn., Innovation and Improvement, Wash., 1988—; spec. asst. dep. sec. for mgmt. US Dept. Edn. Office: US Dept Edn Off Innovation and Improvement 400 Maryland Ave SW FOB-6 Rm 2W103 Washington DC 20202 E-mail: leroy.rooker@ed.gov.*

ROOMKIN, MYRON J. management educator, arbitrator, consultant; b. N.Y.C., July 16, 1945; s. William and Jennie (Maninsky) R.; m. Janice Johnson, Feb. 12, 1946. BS, Cornell U., 1967; MS, U. Wis., 1970, PhD, 1971. Asst. prof. U. Chgo. Grad. Sch. Bus., 1971-75; assoc. prof. Case Western Res. U. Sch. Mgmt., Cleve., 1975-76; prof. Northwestern U. Kellogg Grad. Sch. Mgmt., Evanston, Ill., 1976-98; Arlene and Robert Kogod Fund dean, prof. human resources Am. U. Kogod Sch. Bus., Washington, 1998—. Arbitrator Fed. Mediation and Conciliation Svc., Washington, 1972—. Editor: The Shrinking Perimeter, 1979, Managers as Employees, 1990, Managerial Compensation and Incentives in For-Profit and Nonprofit Hospitals, 1999, Models of International Labor Standards, 2001; mem. editl. bd. several jours.; contbr. numerous articles to profl. jours. Trustee Profit Sharing Rsch. Found., Chgo., 1989-93, Greater Washington Initiative; dir. Greater Washington Bd. Trade. Father William Kelly scholar Cornell U., 1963-67; Manpower Devel. and Tng. Act fellow U.S. Dept. Labor, 1970-71. Mem. Indsl. Rels. Rsch. Assn., Strategic Human Resources Mgmt. Soc., Econ. Club Washington. Avocations: sculpture, tennis. Office: Am Univ Kogod Sch Bus 4400 Massachusetts Ave NW Washington DC 20016-8044 E-mail: bizdean@american.edu.

ROOP, KAREN DANSTEDT, elementary and secondary school educator; b. Worcester, Mass., Feb. 20, 1947; d. Robert Spencer and Lucille (Rice) Danstedt; m. William Reed Roop, Sept. 17, 1988; stepchildren; Kim, Matthew. BFA, Boston U., 1969, MFA, 1975; pvt. studies with, Patricia Forrester, 1994-95, George Nick, 1996. Tchr. art Braintree (Mass.) Pub. Schs., 1970—. Mem. state frameworks com. for edn. reform, Braintree, 1995-97, art curriculum revision com. Exhibitor in numerous one-woman and group shows, 1975—; commd. paintings for pub. and pvt. orgns. Reader tapes for the blind Talking Info. Ctr., Marshfield, Mass., 1985-96. Mem. NEA, Nat. Art Edn. Assn., Concord Art Assn., Spenbrook Conservation Assn. (prin. 1995-96). Avocations: local theater set designs, tennis, yoga, boating, travel.

ROOS, SYBIL FRIEDENTHAL, retired elementary school educator; b. L.A., Jan. 29, 1924; d. Charles G. and Besse (Weixel) Friedenthal; m. Henry Kahn Roos, May 8, 1949 (dec. Dec. 1989); children: Catherine Alane Cook, Elizabeth Anne Garlinger, Virginia Ann Bertrand. BA in Music, Centenary Coll., 1948; MEd, Northwestern State U., 1973. Cert. elem. edn. tchr., spl. edn. tchr. Tchr. Caddo Parish Schs., Shreveport, 1968-75, Spring Branch Ind. Schs., Houston, 1975-85; vol. Houston Grand Opera/Guild, 1979—, Houston Mus. of Fine Arts/Guild, 1990—, Houston Symphony Soc./Guild, 1997—. Author tchrs. guides. Pres. Nat. Coun. Jewish Women, Shreveport, 1958; bd. dirs. Mus. Fine Arts; area coord. Spl. Olympics, Shreveport, 1974-75; bd. dirs. U. Houston Moore Sch. Music. With USN, 1944-46. Mem. AAUW (pres. Spring Valley Houston chpt. 1985-87), Houston Grand Opera Guild (pres. 1991), Houston Symphony League, Houston Ballet Guild, Mus. of Fine Arts Guild (bd. dirs.), U. Houston Sch. of Music (bd. dirs.) Am. Needlepoint Guild, Delta Kappa Gamma (bd. dirs., treas. 1987-89), Phi Mu. Republican. Avocations: music, tennis, needlepoint, volunteering. Home: 10220 Memorial Dr Apt 78 Houston TX 77024-3227 E-mail: s.roos@worldnet.att.net.

ROOT, EDWARD LAKIN, education educator, university administrator; b. Cumberland, Md., Dec. 5, 1940; s. Lakin and Edna Grace (Adams) R. BS, Frostburg (Md.) State Coll., 1962, MEd, 1966; EdD, U. Md., 1970. Cert. tchr., Md. Tchr. Allegany County Bd. of Edn., Cumberland, 1962-66; grad. fellow U. Md., College Park, 1966-67, fellow, 1967-69; with Frostburg State U., 1969-99, prof., head edn. dept., 1980-87, dean, 1987-95, prof., head MEd. adminstrn., 1995-99. Gubernatorial appointee to Md. State Bd. Edn., 1999—, pres. 2003—; mem. Profl. Stds. Bd. Md., Balt., 1980-87, 95-99, Cert. Rev. Bd. Md., Balt., 1987-90, Md. Task Force Adminstrn., Balt., 1985-88, Md. Task Force: Essentials in Tchr. Edn., 1995, Md. Task

Force: Prisoners of Time and Response; task force tchr. assessment, 1995-97, Md. Task Force on Tchr. Quality, 2002-03, Md. Task Force on Disadvantaged but Capable Students, 2000-02; chmn. Md. Tchr. Quality Task Group, 2002-03. Mem. Allegany County (Md.) Planning and Zoning Bd. Appeals, 1995-96. Mem. ASCD, Nat. Assn. Secondary Sch. Prins., Nat. Soc. for the Study of Edn., Mensa, Elks, Shriners, Masons, Phi Delta Kappa. Democrat. Methodist. Avocation: photography. Home: 100 Pennsylvania Ave Cumberland MD 21502-4236 Office: Frostburg State U College Ave Frostburg MD 21532-1724

ROOT, ELAINE HARPER, elementary education educator; b. Weatherford, Tex., June 8, 1952; d. H.D. and Claire (Timbes) Harper; m. Richard Alexis Root, Dec. 26, 1970 (div. Dec. 1998); children: Jennifer, Donovan. BS, MEd, U. North Tex., 1990. Cert. tchr., Tex.; cert. ESL tchr. Asst. tchr. Meadowbrook Montessori, Dallas, 1972-74, Terrell (Tex.) State Hosp., 1974-76; asst. dir. Nat. Child Care Ctr., Dallas, 1976-78; dir. Daybridge Learning Ctr., Dallas, 1978-85; dir. edn. Children's World Learning Ctr., Dallas, 1986-89; dir. St. Mark Presbyn. Ch., Dallas, 1988-90; tchr. Happiness House Pvt. Sch., Dallas, 1985-90, Routh Roach Elem. Sch., Garland, Tex., 1990-92, Paul L. Dunbar Learning Ctr., Dallas, 1992-95, Julius Dorsey Elem., 1995-99; specialist III Sch. to Careers Ctr. Dallas Ind. Sch. Dist., 1999—2003; asst. dir. Best Christian Acad., 2003; instr. Poetry Cmty. Christian Sch. Contbg. author The Giant Encyclopedia, 1992. Democrat. Methodist. Avocations: reading, sewing, home repairs. Office: 1004 E Moore Ave Terrell TX 75160 E-mail: clairelaine@juno.com.

ROOT, JANET GREENBERG, private school educator; b. Atlantic City, N.J., May 16, 1936; d. Louis and Edith (Shapiro) Greenberg; m. Allen W. Root, June 15, 1958; children: Jonathan, Jennifer, Michael. BS, U. Md., 1958. Tchr. Bd. Edn., Brighton, N.Y., 1958-60; dir. music/art parent program, chmn. dept. arts-humanities Shorecrest Prep. Sch., St. Petersburg, Fla., 1989—. Trustee Shorecrest Prep. Sch., 1980—86, 1990—96, 1998—, dir. cultural enrichment program, 1978—; mem. edni. bd. Bayfront Ctr., 1993—2000; mem. art com. Tampa Bay Holocaust Mus., mem. edn. com., 2003—; trustee Salvador Dali Mus., 1998—, chmn. edn. com., mem. long range bldg. com., mem. exec. com.; trustee Order of Salvador, 1999—. Named Honoree, Nat. Philanthropy Day. E-mail: jroot@shorecrest.org.

ROOT, WILLIAM LUCAS, electrical engineering educator; b. Des Moines, Oct. 6, 1919; s. Frank Stephenson and Helen (Lucas) R.; m. Harriett Jean Johnson, Dec. 10, 1918; children: William Lucas Jr., Wendy Elizabeth Root Cate. BEE, Iowa State U., 1940; MEE, MIT, 1943, PhD in Math., 1952. Staff mem. MIT Lincoln Lab., Lexington, Mass., 1952-61, group leader, 1959-61; lectr. Harvard U., Cambridge, Mass., 1958-59; visitor U. Wis., Madison, 1963-64; vis. prof. Mich. State U., East Lansing, 1966, 68, U. Calif., Berkeley, 1966-67; prof. aerospace engrng. U. Mich., Ann Arbor, 1961-87, prof. emeritus, 1988—. Visitor U. Cambridge (Eng.), 1970; mem. U.S. Army Sci. Bd., 1979-82. Co-author: Random Signals and Noise, 1958 (Russian and Japanese transls.); assoc. editor: (IEEE) Information Theory Transactions, 1977-79; Soc. Indsl. and Applied Math. Jour. Applied Mathematics, 1962-72; contbr. 65 articles to profl. jours., book chpts. and conf. procs. Served to lt. USMCR, 1943—45. NSF Sr. postdoctoral fellow, 1970, vis. fellow Cambridge Clare Hall, 1970; recipient Claude E. Shannon award IEEE Info. Theory Soc., 1986, Career Achievement award ComCon Conf. Bd., 1987. Life fellow IEEE (vice chmn. adminstrv. com. info. theory group 1965-66); mem. Am. Math. Soc. Home: PO Box 3785 Ann Arbor MI 48106-3785 Office: Univ Mich Dept Aerospace Engring Ann Arbor MI 48109

ROOT, WILLIAM PITT, poet, educator; b. Austin, Minn., Dec. 28, 1941; s. William Pitt and Bonita Joy (Hilbert) R.; m. Judith Carol Bechtold, 1965 (div. 1970); 1 dau., Jennifer Lorca; m. Pamela Uschuk, 1987. BA, U. Wash., 1964; MFA, U. N.C. at Greensboro, 1967; postgrad., Stanford, 1968-69. Asst. prof. Mich. State U., 1967-68; tchr. writing Mid-peninsula Free U., 1969; writer-in-residence Amherst Coll., U. Southwestern La., 1976, U. Mont., 1978, 80, 83-84; with poet-in-schs. program state art councils Oreg., Miss., Idaho, Ariz., Vt., Mont., Wyo., Wash., Tex., 1971—; Distinguished writer-in-residence Wichita State U., 1976; vis. writer in residence U. Mont., 1978, 80, 83-86, Hunter Coll., N.Y.C., 1986—; vis. writer NYU, 1986. Vis. writer Westside Young Men's Hebrew Assn., N.Y.C., 1988, Pacific Lutheran U., 1990. Author: The Storm and Other Poems, 1969, Striking the Dark Air for Music, 1973, The Port of Galveston, 1974, Coot and Other Characters, 1977, 7 Mendocino Songs, 1977, A Journey South, 1977, Fireclock, 1981, Reasons for Going It on Foot, 1981, In the World's Common Grasses, 1981, The Unbroken Diamond: Nightletter to the Mujahideen, 1983, Invisible Guests, 1984, Faultdancing, 1986, Trace Elements from a Recurring Kingdom, 1994; collaborated (with filmmaker Ray Rice) on poetry films Song of the Woman and the Butterflyman (Orpheus award 1st Internat. Poetry Film Festival 1975), 7 For a Magician, 1976, Faces, 1981. Rockefeller Found. grantee, 1969-70; Guggenheim Found. grantee, 1970-71; Nat. Endowment for Arts grantee, 1973-74; U.S./U.K. Bicentennial Exchange Artist, 1978-79, Wallace Stegner creative writing fellow Stanford U., 1968-69; recipient 1st prize univ. poetry contest Acad. Am. Poets, 1966, Atlantic Young Poet award, 1967, Stanley Kunitz Poetry award, 1981, Guy Owen Poetry Prize, 1982, Pushcart Prize (Poetry), 1977, 1980, 1985; named Poet Laureate of Tucson, 1997-2002. Address: CUNY Hunter Coll Dept Eng 695 Park Ave New York NY 10021-5024

ROPER, BERYL CAIN, writer, publisher, retired library director; b. Long Beach, Calif., Mar. 1, 1931; d. Albert Verne and Ollie Fern (Collins) Cain; m. Max H. Young, Aug. 22, 1947 (div. 1958); children: Howard, Wade, Debra, Kevin, John R., Christopher; m. George Albert Roper, Mar. 24, 1962 (dec. July 1978); children: Ellen, Georgianne; m. Jack T. Hughes, Sept. 21, 1993 (dec. May 2001). BA, West Tex. State U., 1986; MA, Tex. Womans U., 1989. Libr. clk. Cornette Libr., West Tex. State U., Canyon, 1981-87; dir. Clarendon (Tex.) Coll. Libr., 1988-96. Lectr. in history and archaeology; owner Aquamarine Publs. Editor, pub.: In the Light of Past Experience, 1989, Transactions of the Southwest Federation of Archaeological Societies, 1993, Greenbelt Site, 1996, Presbyterian Mission Work in New Mexico: Memoirs of Alice Blake, 1997; author, pub.: Trementina, 1990, Trementina Revisited, 1994, Seekers After Truth, 1998; author articles on women and history. Mem.: Internat. Soc. for Archeology and the Bible, Archeology Conservancy, Panhandle Archaeol. Soc., Phi Alpha Theta, Alpha Chi, Beta Phi Mu, Pi Gamma Mu. Republican. Mem. Lds Ch. Avocations: music, gardening, decorating, remodeling old houses, genealogy. Office: Aquamarine Publs 8001 Cattle Dr Canyon TX 79015 E-mail: beryl0l@sprynet.com.

ROPER, BIRDIE ALEXANDER, social sciences educator; b. New Orleans; d. Earl and Ethel (Charmer) Alexander; m. Morris F. Roper; 1 child, Andree Marie Driskell. BS, U. Dayton, 1949; MA, Azusa Pacific U., 1971, Claremont Grad. Sch., 1978, PhD, 1980. DON Flint Goodridge Hosp., New Orleans, 1954, 55; sch. nurse, health educator, classroom tchr. L.A. Unified Sch. Dist., 1963-91; extended day prof. social scis. dept. Pasadena City Coll., 1972—; clin. instr. dept. nursing Calif. State U., San Bernardino, 1993—. Researcher, author, cons. in gerontology. Editor: (newsletter Calif. Nurses Assn.) Vital Signs. Mem. ANA, Am. Soc. Univ. Profs., Am. Soc. on Aging, Inst. for Rsch. on Aging, Nat. Coun. on Aging, Nat. Gerontol. Nursing Assn., Nat. Assn. Profl. Geriatric Care Mgrs., Phi Delta Kappa (bd. mem. San Antonio chpt. 1981-92), Alpha Kappa Alpha. Home and Office: 1700 Heritage Park Rd Charleston SC 29407-5839

ROPER, WILLIAM LEE, dean, physician; b. Birmingham, Ala., July 6, 1948; s. Richard Barnard and Jean (Fyfe) R.; m. Maryann Roper, Jan. 14, 1978 AA, Fla. Coll., 1968; BS, U. Ala, 1970, MD, 1974, M.P.H., 1981. Diplomate Am. Bd. Pediatrics, Am. Bd. Preventive Medicine. Intern, resident in pediatrics U. Colo. Med. Ctr., Denver, 1974-77; health officer Jefferson County Dept. Health, Birmingham, 1977-82, 83; White House fellow Washington, 1982-83; spl. asst. to Pres. for health policy, 1983-86; adminstr., Health Care Finance Adminstrn. HHS, Washington, 1986-89; dep. asst. to pres. for domestic policy The White House, Washington, 1989-90; adminstr. Agy. for Toxic Substances and Disease Registry and dir. Ctrs. for Disease Control and Prevention, Atlanta, 1990-93; sr. v.p. Prudential Health Care, Roseland, NJ, 1994-97; pres. Prudential Ctr. for Health Care Rsch., Atlanta, 1993-95; dean sch. pub. health U. N.C., Chapel Hill, 1997—. Mem. Inst. Medicine of NAS, Phi Beta Kappa, Alpha Omega Alpha Republican. Home: 10424 Stone Chapel Hill NC 27517-8549 Office: U NC 170 Rosenau Hall Campus Box 7400 Chapel Hill NC 27599-7400

ROPPA, KATHLEEN MARIE, educational administrator; b. Sewickley, Pa., Jan. 24, 1957; d. Joseph and Josephine (Budimir) R. BA in Health and Phys. Edn., Slippery Rock State Coll., 1977, MS in Sci., 1982; EdD in Adminstrv. Policies, U. Pitts., 1992. Cert. prin., Pa. Educator Quaker Valley Sch. Dist., Sewickley, Pa., 1978-90; adminstr. North Allegheny Sch. Dist., Pitts., 1990—. Cons. Beaver (Pa.) Battered Womens Shelter, 1978-79, Allegheny Intermediate Unit, Pitts., 1981; dir., coord. Slippery Rock (Pa.) Coll. Soccer Camp, 1979-80; bus. leader Loan Office, Anaheim, Calif., 1987-90. Author: Developmental Disability Prevention, 1981. Sponsor Student Community Volunteerism, Pitts., 1990—; facilitator North Allegheny Community Wellness, Pitts., 1992-93. Recipient award of recognition Middle States of Colls. and Schs., Harrisburg, Pa., 1985, Tribute of Time award Quaker Valley Sch. Dist., North Allegheny Sch. Dist., 1987-91, Outstanding Health Curriculum, Davis & Wilkens Coll., W.Va., 1991. Mem. ASCD, NEA, Pa. State Edn. Assn., Nat. Assn. Secondary Prins., North Allegheny Assn. Secondary Sch. Prins., Pa. Sch. Bd. Assn., Am. Red Cross (award of recognition 1980-89). Avocations: football, baseball, golf, tennis, gymnastics. Office: North Allegheny Sch Dist 350 Cumberland Rd Pittsburgh PA 15237-5410

RORER, LEONARD GEORGE, psychologist, writer; b. Dixon, Ill., Dec. 24, 1932; s. Leonard Gleason and Marion Emma (Geyer) R.; m. Gail Evans, Apr. 30, 1958 (div. May 11, 1964); children: Liat, Eric Evans; m. Nancy McKimens, Jan, 9, 1969 (div. Jan. 19, 1976); 1 child, Mya Noelani. BA, Swarthmore Coll., 1954; PhD, U. Minn., 1963 . Rsch. assoc., then assoc. dir. Oreg. Rsch. Inst., Eugene, 1963-75; prof. psychology Miami U., Oxford, Ohio, 1975-93, dir. clin. psychology tng. program, 1976-86; pres. Oreg. Psychol. Assn., 1973-75. NIMH spl. rsch. fellow U. Calif., Berkeley, 1967-68; fellow Netherlands Inst. Advanced Study, 1971-72; postdoctoral fellow Inst. for Rational-Emotive Therapy, 1982-83. Fellow APA (coun. reps. 1968-72), Am. Psychol. Soc. (charter), We. Psychol. Assn.; mem. Midwestern Psychol. Assn., Assn. Advancement Behavior Therapy, Soc. Multivariate Exptl. Psychology. Author articles in field, mem. editorial bds. profl. jours. Home: 407 High St Santa Cruz CA 95060-2613

RORICK, WILLIAM CALVIN, librarian, educator, portrait artist; b. Elyria, Ohio, June 23, 1941; s. Harold R. and Edythe E. (Harris) R.; m. Anne L. Sherbondy, Aug. 21, 1971. BA in Econs. and Bus. Adminstrn., Ohio Wesleyan U., 1963; MusB in Music History and Lit., U. Utah, 1968; MusM in Music History and Lit., Northwestern U., 1970; MLS, Pratt Inst., 1974; MA in Musicology, NYU, 1982; trainee in portraiture, various art schs., workshops. Curator orchestral-choral libr., reference asst., office mgr. Manhattan Sch. Music Libr., NYC, 1970-74; music reference libr. CUNY Queens Coll. Music Libr., Flushing, 1974-96, instr., 1974-79, asst. prof., 1979-96, asst. prof. emeritus, 1996—, mem. senate nominating com., del.-at-large arts divsn., 1984-86. Contbr. articles and revs. to profl. jour. Bd. deacons South Britain (Conn.) Congl. Ch., 1998—2001, historian, 2002. Grantee Rsch. Found. CUNY, 1981-84; recipient regional and nat. art awards including Best in Show Conn. Classic Arts Assn. Mem. Am. Musicological Soc., Am. Printing History Assn., Assn. for Recorded Sound Collections, Internat. Assn. Music Libr., Libr. Assn. CUNY (chmn. grants com. 1978-80, mem. publ. com. 1979-81, editor Directory 1980-81, del. 1983-85), Music Libr. Assn. (program chmn. Greater NY chpt. 1977-79, sec.-treas. 1979-81, chpt. chmn. 1983-85, mem. nat. subcom. on basic music collection 1977-79, chmn. nat. membership com. 1979-82, mem. Music Pub. Assn. joint com. 1986-88), Am. Soc. Portrait Artists, Sonneck Soc., Conn. Classic Arts, Inc. (publicity chmn. 1996-99), Soc. Creative Artists of Newtown (corr. sec. 1999-2002), Portrait Soc. of Am., Inc., Portrait Soc. Atlanta, Conn. Soc. Portrait Artists, N.Y. Soc. Portrait Artists (mem. leadership team 2001—02), Portrait Clubs Am. (cert. leader-instr. 2003—), Kent Art Assn. (elected artist 2003), Beta Phi Mu. Home: 63 Beacon Hill Dr Southbury CT 06488-1914

RORIE, NANCY CATHERINE, retired elementary and secondary school educator; b. Union County, NC, May 31, 1940; d. Carl Evander and Mary Mildred (Pressley) Rorie. BA, Woman's Coll. U. N.C., 1962; MEd, U. N.C., 1967; EdD, Duke U., 1977. Cert. curriculum and instrnl. specialist, social studies tchr. for middle and secondary levels, English tchr., N.C. Social studies and English tchr. Guilford County Schs., Greensboro, NC, 1962—67; social studies instr. Lees-McRae Coll., Banner Elk, NC, 1967—76; social studies and English tchr. Monroe (NC) City Schs., 1977—93, Union County Schs., Monroe, 1993—2002; ret., 2002. Mem.: Kappa Delta Pi, Phi Alpha Theta. Democrat. Southern Missionary Baptist. Home: 2401 Old Pageland Monroe Rd Monroe NC 28112-8163

RORISON, MARGARET LIPPITT, reading consultant; b. Wilmington, N.C., Feb. 6, 1925; d. Harmon Chadbourn and Margaret Devereux (Lippitt) Rorison. AB, Hollins Coll., 1946; MA, Columbia U., 1956; Diplôme in Lang., L'Alliance Française, Paris, 1966; postgrad., U. S.C., 1967-70, 81—. Market and editorial researcher Time, Inc., N.Y.C., 1949-55; classroom and corrective reading tchr. N.Y.C. public schs., 1956-65; TV instr. ETV-WNDT, Channel 13, N.Y.C., 1962-63; grad. asst., TV instr. U. S.C., Columbia, 1967-70; instrnl. specialist in reading S.C. Office Instrnl. TV and Radio, S.C. Dept. Edn., Columbia, 1971-81; reading cons. S.C. Office Instrnl. Tech., Columbia, 1982—. Author instrnl. TV series: Getting the Word (So. Ednl. Communications Assn. award 1972, Ohio State award 1973, S.C. Scholastic Broadcasters award 1973), Getting the Message, 1981. Episcopalian. Home: 460 S 23rd St Wilmington NC 28403-0200

ROSA, EUGENE ANTHONY, sociologist, environmental scientist, educator; b. Canandaigua, NY, Sept. 20, 1941; s. Louis Gastaldo and Flora Louise (Brevette) R.; m. Jody Ross, Sept. 7, 1985 (div. 1993). BS, Rochester Inst. Tech., 1967; MA, Syracuse U., 1975, PhD, 1976. Research assoc., instr. Stanford U., 1976-78; from asst. to prof. Wash. State U., Pullman, 1978—, prof., 1993—. Cons. Brookhaven Nat. Lab., Upton, N.Y., 1978—, Nuclear Regulatory Commn., Washington, 1978—; vis. prof. London Sch. Econs., 1988, U. Klagenfurt, 1996, 99; chmn. dept., 1996-2001, Edward R. Meyer Disting. prof. natural resources and environ. policy Wash. State U., Pullman, 1996—. Co-author: Risk, Uncertainity and Rational Actioneditor: Public Reactions to Nuclear Power, 1984, Pub. Reactions to Nuclear Waste, 1993; bd. dirs. several profl. jours.; contbr. articles to profl. jours. Mem. nuclear waste adv. coun. Wash. State, 1987-92; mem. Nat. Bd. on Radioactive Waste Mgmt., 2002—. Mem. Am. Sociol. Assn. (Disting. Contbn. award), AAAS, NAS (bd. on radioactive waste mgmt.), Sociol. Rsch. Assn., Internat. Soc. Assn., Soc. for Human Ecology, Soc. Risk Analysis, Sigma Xi. Avocations: conceptual art constrns., skiing, collecting native masks, gardening, collection fine art. Home: 510 East C St Moscow ID 83843 Office: Wash State U Dept Sociology Pullman WA 99164-4020

ROSADO, ELIZABETH SCHAAR, elementary bilingual and ESL program coordinator; b. Mpls., Aug. 5, 1961; d. Merton Arnold and Mardelle Anne (Lindborg) Schaar; children: Kristina, Alexander. BA, U. Minn., 1985; MEd, Houston Bapt. U., 1990; postgrad., U. Houston, 1993—. Cert. bilingual, ESL, reading recovery, Descubriendo la lectura, early childhood tchr., Tex. Tchr. Harlandale Ind. Sch. Dist., San Antonio, 1986-87; coord. elem. bilingual and ESL programs Spring Branch Ind. Sch. Dist., Houston, 1987—. Fed. grant reader, 1996. Title VII scholar Houston Bapt. U., 1988-90, U. Houston, 1992; Title 7 fellow, 1994, 97. Mem. ASCD, Internat. Reading Assn., Phi Delta Kappa, Kappa Delta Pi. Roman Catholic.

ROSADO, RODOLFO JOSE, psychologist, educator; b. N.Y.C., Jan. 9, 1959; s. Rodolfo Jose and Maria (Gonzalez) R.; m. Ruth Laura Morrison, June 11, 1982; children: Emily Hope, Adam Philip. BS in Psychology, Fordham U., Bronx, N.Y., 1979, MA in Clin. Psychology, 1986, PhD in Clin. Psychology, 1992. Diplomate in clin. psychology and child psychology Am. Bd. Psychol. Specialties; lic. psychologist, N.Y., Conn. Psychology tng. fellow N.Y. Med. Coll., Valhalla, 1979-81; clin. psychology intern Hall-Brooke Hosp., Westport, Conn., 1982-83; therapist Child Guidance Ctr., Bridgeport, Conn., 1983-85, office coord., 1985-90, program dir., 1990-93; asst. prof. Fairfield (Conn.) U., 1993-97, program dir. coll. access, 1995-96; pvt. practice specializing in psychol. evaluations Norwalk, Conn., 1993—. Initial Rev. Group profl. reviewer USPHS, Rockville, Md., 1990-95; regional adv. com. Dept. Children & Families, Bridgeport, 1995—; oversight collaborative Bridgeport Futures, 1994-95; faculty co-sponsor SALSA Hispanic Students Assn., Fairfield U., 1995-97; bd. dirs., clin. cons. R.E.A.C.H. Program, Riverside, Conn.; bd. dirs. Side by Side Charter Sch., Norwalk, Conn., 2002--. Author, moderator TV show Conversation in Edn., 1994; co-author proposal Empowerment Zone Grant, 1994; author proposal Comprehensive Child & Adolescent Svc., 1993. Mem. Youth Svc. Bur., City of Bridgeport, 1991-93; family preservation initiative Conn. Dept. Children & Families, Bridgeport, 1995-2000; coach Little League Baseball, 2000-02; asst. coach Biddy Basketball Youth Program, Norwalk, 2001-02; vice chmn. bd. dirs. Side by Side Charter Sch., Norwalk, Conn., 2002—. Recipient N.Y. Regents scholarship, 1975-79, scholarship Fordham U., Bronx, 1975-79, Appreciation award for collaborative support State of Conn. Dept. Children & Families, 1995, Outstanding Contbns. to Latino Cmty. Recognition award Puerto Rican/Latino employees of Human Resources Adminstrn. and Affiliated Agys., Dept. Homeless Svcs. and Adminstrn. for Children's Svcs., 1999. Mem. APA, Am. Coll. Forensic Examiners, Hispanic Assn. Mental Health and Allied Professions (exec. com., treas. 1988-92), Conn. Coalition for Children of Alcoholics (steering com. 1986-87), Sigma Xi. Avocations: racquetball, hiking. Office: 71 East Ave Ste U Norwalk CT 06851

ROSALDO, RENATO IGNACIO, JR., cultural anthropology educator; b. Champaign, Ill., Apr. 15, 1941; s. Renato Ignacio and Mary Elizabeth (Potter) R.; m. Michelle Sharon Zimbalist, June 12, 1966 (dec. Oct. 1981); children: Samuel Mario, Manuel Zimbalist; m. Mary Louise Pratt, Nov. 26, 1983; 1 child, Olivia Emilia Rosaldo-Pratt. AB, Harvard U., 1963, PhD, 1971. Asst. prof. cultural anthropology Stanford (Calif.) U., 1970-76, assoc. prof., 1976-85, prof., 1985—, Mellon prof. interdisciplinary studies, 1987-90, dir. Ctr. for Chicano Rsch., 1985-90, chair anthropology, 1994-96, Lucie Stern prof. social scis., 1993—. Author: Ilongot Headhunting 1883-1974, 1980, Culture and Truth, 1989. Recipient Harry Benda prize Assn. for Asian Studies, 1983; Guggenheim fellow, 1993. Fellow Am. Acad. Arts and Scis. Avocations: poetry, swimming, drawing, dancing. Home: 2520 Cowper St Palo Alto CA 94301-4218 Office: Stanford U Dept Cultural and Social Anthropology Palo Alto CA 94305-2145

ROSALES, SANDRA JOHNSON, school system administrator; b. Riverside, Calif., June 21, 1944; d. William Emory Johnson and Mildred Alice (Alford) Wimer; m. Wynn Neal Huffman, Feb., 1962 (div. May 1967); 1 child, Kristen Lee; m. Steven Jack Herrera, June, 1985 (div. Dec. 1997); m. Mario Rosales, Sept. 22, 2000. AS in Purchasing Mgmt., Fullerton Coll., 1983; BSBA, U. Redlands, 1985, MA in Mgmt., 1988. Sr. purchasing clk Fullerton (Calif.) Union High Sch. Dist., 1969-77, buyer, 1977-79, coord. budgets and fiscal affairs, 1979-83; asst. dir. fin. svcs. Downey (Calif.) Unified Sch. Dist., 1983-85; dir. acctg. Whittier (Calif.) Union High Sch. Dist., 1985-89; asst. supt. bus. Whittier City Sch. Dist., 1989-91, Oxnard Elem. Sch. Dist., 1991—. Cons. Heritage Dental Lab., El Toro, Calif, 1981-97. Spl. dep. sheriff Santa Barbara (Calif.) County Sheriff's Mounted Posse, 1986-90; spl. dep. marshal U.S. Marshals Posse, LA, 1987-95. Mem. Calif. Assn. Sch. Bus. Ofcls. (treas. S.E. sect. 1985, mem. acct. R & D com. 1983-89, chief bus. ofcls. com. 1989-92), So. Calif. Paraders Assn. (exec. sec. 1976-97), Calif. State Horsemens Assn. (regional v.p. 1986-87, sec. 1988), Alpha Gamma Sigma. Avocations: horseback riding, golf, reading, micro-computers, model trains. Office: Oxnard Elem Sch Dist 1051 S A St Oxnard CA 93036-7442 Home: 1900 Muirfield Dr Oxnard CA 93036-7736

ROSAR, VIRGINIA WILEY, librarian; b. Cleve., Nov. 22, 1926; d. John Egbert and Kathryn Coe (Snyder) Wiley; m. Michael Thorpe Rosar, April 8, 1950 (div. Feb. 1968); children: Bruce Wiley, Keith Michael, James Wilfred. Attended, Oberlin Coll., 1944-46; BA, U. Puget Sound, 1948; MS, C.W. Post Coll., L.I.U., Greenvale, N.Y., 1971. Cert. elem. and music tchr., N.Y.; cert. sch. library media specialist, N.Y. Music programmer Station WFAS, White Plains, N.Y., 1948; prodn. asst. NBC-TV, N.Y.C., 1948-50; tchr. Portledge Sch., Locust Valley, N.Y., 1967-70; librarian Syosset (N.Y.) Schs., 1970-71, Smithtown (N.Y.) Schs., 1971-92; ret., 1992; pres. World of Realia, Woodbury, N.Y., 1969-86; founder Cygnus Pub., Woodbury, 1985-87. Active local chpt. ARC, 1960-63, Community Concert Assn., 1960-66, Leukemia Soc. Am., 1978—. Mem. AAAS, N.Y. Acad. Scis., L.I. Alumnae Club of Pi Beta Phi (pres. 1964-66). Republican. Presbyterian. Avocations: music, sewing, gardening, writing. Home: 101 Ripley Ct Cary NC 27513-5121

ROSATO, LAURA MARIE, toxicologist, educator; b. Pitts., Jan. 13, 1958; d. William A. and Mary (Wachter) R. BS, U. Pitts., 1981, MS, 1985, PhD, 1990. Grad. student rschr. U. Pitts., 1983-85, rsch. asst. III, 1982-83, coord. & lectr., 1987-89, grad. student rschr., 1985-90; divsnl. toxicologist Procter & Gamble Co., Cin., 1990-92; prin. toxicologist Millennium Petrochem. Inc. (formerly Quantum Chem. Corp.), Cin., 1992-94, sr. prin. toxicologist, 1994-97; sr. dir. pub. health policy and rsch. programs Chem. Mfrs. Assn., Arlington, Va., 1998; sr. assoc. Karch & Assocs. Inc., Washington, 1998-2000; mgr. occupl. health rsch. Brush Wellman, Inc., 2000—. Adj. prof., cons. toxicologist U. Cin., 1995—; ind. cons. Pitts., 1985-90; provider internat. toxicity estimates for risk peer review bd., 1997—. Contbr. numerous articles to sci. jours. Bd. dirs. Great Rivers coun. Girl Scouts Am., 1997—. Recipient Student Leadership award U. Pitts., 1989, Leading Women in Cin. award for rsch. and tech., 1997, Great Rivers Girl Scout Coun. Woman of Distinction award, 1997. Mem. Ohio Valley Soc. Toxicology, Greater Cin. Women's Network (bd. dirs. 1996—, chair awards and recognition com. adv. coun., co-chair leading women corp. sponsorship com. 1997, co-chair Cin./No. Ky. United Way mgmt. cabinet for cmty. outreach 1997), Internat. Soc. Regulatory Toxicology and Pharmacology, Nat. Capitol Area Soc. Toxicology, Ohio Valley Soc. Environ. Toxicology and Chemistry, Soc. Toxicology, Vinyl Acetate Toxicology Group (v.p. and treas. 1994-97), Diethyl Ether Prodrs. Assn. (chair 1995-97), Chem. Mfrs. Assn. (Olefin panel and ethylene/propylene toxicology rsch. task group 1996-97), Chem. Industry Inst. Toxicology (devel. & mem. coms. 1994-97), Toastmasters Internat. (sec.), Leading Women, Inc. (trustee, pres.-elect exec. com. 1997—). Avocations: reading, walking, teaching, mentoring. Office: Brush Wellman 14710 West Portage River South Rd Elmore OH 43416 Home: 3820 Pier St Pittsburgh PA 15213-4024 E-mail: LRASSOCIAT@aol.com.

ROSBERG, MERILEE ANN, education educator; b. Oak Park, Ill., June 1, 1942; d. Andrew Clark and Martha (Kester) Adamson; m. William H. Rosberg, Aug. 17, 1963; children: Peter E., Trent W. AB, Augustana Coll., 1963; MA, U. Iowa, 1971, PhD, 1985. Tchr. Cedar Rapids (Iowa) Pub. Schs., 1963-65, Internat. Sch. Kuwait, 1965-67, N. Winnisheik Cmty. Schs., Decorah, Iowa, 1967-69, St. Mark's Luth. Ch. Presch., Cedar Rapids, 1969-71; staff tng. specialist Linn County Day Care Svcs., Cedar Rapids,

1971-76; dir. early childhood program Jane Boyd Comty. House, Cedar Rapids, 1976-86; prof., divsn. chair Mt. Mercy Coll., Cedar Rapids, 1986—. Vis. prof. U. Sts. Cyril & Methodius, Veliko Turnovo, Bulgaria, 1992, Czech Tech. U., Prague, Czech Rep., 1990. Fulbright scholar U. Brunei Darusalam, 1994-95. Mem. Nat. Assn. Early Childhood Edn., Nat. Coun. Tchrs. English, Internat. Readign Assn. (Reading Adminstr. of Yr., Cedar Rapids 2002, Iowa 2002), Orgn. Mondiale Pour L'Education Prescolaire (U.S. nat. com.). Avocations: reading, travel. Home: 1900 Bever Ave SE Cedar Rapids IA 52403-2715 Office: Mt Mercy Coll 1330 Elmhurst Dr NE Cedar Rapids IA 52402-4763 E-mail: merilee@mmc.mtmercy.edu.

ROSBOTTOM, RONALD CARLISLE, French, arts and humanities educator; b. New Orleans, July 15, 1942; s. Albert Carlisle and Marjorie Catherine (Chavez) R.; m. Betty Elane Griffin, Sept. 5, 1964; 1 child, Michael K. BA, Tulane U., 1964; MA, Princeton U., 1966, PhD, 1969; MA (hon.), Amherst Coll., 1990. Instr. U. Pa., Phila., 1967-69, asst. prof., 1969-73; assoc. prof. Ohio State U., Columbus, 1973-78, prof. French lit., 1978-89, chmn. Romance langs., 1982-88; dean of faculty Amherst (Mass.) Coll., 1989-95, prof. French lit. and European studies, 1989—, Winifred L. Arms prof. arts and humanities, 1996—, chair European Studies program, 1996—. Author: Marivaux's Novels, 1974, Choderlos de Laclos, 1979 (Havens prize 1980); editor: Studies in 18th Century Culture, 1975, 76, Essays in the French Enlightenment, 1991; mem. editorial bds. Eighteenth Century: Theory & Interpretation, Romance Quarterly Decorated Ordre des Palmes Académiques; Woodrow Wilson Found. fellow, 1964-65, 66-67; Am. Council Learned Socs. summer fellow, 1970 Mem. MLA, Internat. Soc. 18th Century Studies (exec. com. 1978-83), Am. Soc. 18th Century Studies (exec. sec. 1978-83, 2d v.p. 1992-93, 1st v.p. 1993-94, pres. 1994-95), Am. Assn. Tchrs. French, Phi Beta Kappa. Democrat. Home: 326 Shays St Amherst MA 01002-2943 Office: Amherst Coll PO Box 2255 Amherst MA 01004-2255

ROSE, ANITA CARROLL, retired educator; b. New Bedford, Mass., Oct. 14, 1922; d. Louis Arthur and Aline (Chicoine) Carroll; m. Anthony E. Rose, Sept. 24, 1955 (dec.); children: Anthony David, Stephen Arthur. BA, U. Mass., Dartmouth, 1971; MAT, R.I. Coll., 1975. Exec. sec. Berkshire-Hathaway, Inc., New Bedford, 1941—55, New Bedford Cancer Soc., 1956-59; tchr. French and English New Bedford Pub. Schs., 1971-88; ret., 1988. Clk. Friends of Coastline Elderly Svcs., Inc., 1991-93; bd. dirs. Our Lady's Haven, 1995—. Pres. New Bedford Jr. Women's Club, 1950-51, Fairhaven Mothers' Club, 1967-69, book chmn., 1989-91, sunshine chmn., 1991-93, nominating com. chmn., 1993—; v.p. Cath. Women's Club, 1957-59, del. Coun. of Women's Orgns., 1989-91; active Fairhaven Town Mtg., Mass., 1965—; trustee Millicent Libr., Fairhaven, 1980—; rec. sec. Fairhaven Improvement Assn., 1982-99; sec. Fairhaven Rep. Town Com., 1980—; bd. dirs. St. Anne Credit Union, New Bedford, 1988—, asst. treas., investment com. 1991-93, pres., chmn. bd., 1993—; adv. coun. Coastline Elderly Svc. Inc., 1988-92; del. Mass. Rep. Conv., 1974, 82, 86, 90, 94, 98; mem Old Dartmouth Hist. Assn., Friends of the Zeiterion Theatre, Friends New Bedford Festival Theatre. Testimonial dinner in her honor for years of cmty. svc. Fairhaven Improvement Assn., 1997. Mem. AAUW (pres. Coll. Club New Bedford 1983-85, 1st v.p. 1989-91, del. nat. conv. 1981, 83, 85, 93, chmn. nominating com. Mass. divsn. 1988-90, chmn. art study group 1992—, honored Mass. chpt. 1986), Tri-County Music Assn. (pres. 1992-95, bd. dirs. 1988—), R.I. Coll. Alumni Assn., U. Mass.-Dartmouth Alumni Assn., Southeastern Mass. Assn. Social Studies, Libr. Assocs. U. Mass.-Dartmouth, Ret. Officers Assn., Am. Ex-Prisoners of War, St. Joseph's Couples Club (pres. 1987-88, 2001-02), Fairhaven Colonial Club (2d v.p. 1988-89), MONETA Assocs. Investment Club (chmn. 1998-99), Republican Club Southeastern Mass., Greater New Bedford Garden Club, Friends of Buttonwood Park Zoo. Avocations: travel, music, theater. Home: 49 Laurel St Fairhaven MA 02719-2817 E-mail: fairhavenacr@msn.com.

ROSE, DONNA MARIE, secondary school educator, farmer; b. Rochester, N.Y., May 11, 1951; d. Robert James and Dorothy Lorraine (Shortsleeve) Weagley; m. Francis Ernest Rose, Aug. 18, 1973; children: Daniel Richard, William Michael. Student, SUNY, Albany, 1969-70; BS in Math./Edn., Nazareth Coll., Pittsford, N.Y., 1973, 76; MA in Edn./Spl. Edn., U. Rochester, 1991, postgrad., 1991—94. Tchr. math. and bus. East Irondequoit Schs., Irondequoit, N.Y., 1973-78; tchr. math. Greece (N.Y.) Arcadia H.S., 1978, Rush Henrietta (N.Y.) Schs., 1978-79; tchr. math./computers East Rochester (N.Y.) Schs., 1979-82, Palmyra-Macedon H.S., N.Y., 1982—, K-12 math. curriculum coord., 1996—2002. Pres., sec., county meet coord. Monroe County Math. League, Rochester, 1973—2000, state meet coord.; math. team coach, advisor Pal-Mac Math. Team, Palmyra, 1982—. Cantor, flutist St. Louis Ch. folk Group-Choir, Pittsford, N.Y., 1980—2001, mem. choir, 2001—; mgr. Fairport (N.Y) Farmer's Market, 1976—. Mem. Nat. Coun. Tchrs. Math. (life), Assn. Math. Tchrs. N.Y. State, Nat. Arbor Day Found., N.Y. State Assn. Math. Suprs., Women's Internat. Bowling Congress, Ontario County Farm Bur. Roman Catholic. Avocations: sewing, reading, baking, gardening, collecting stamps, dolls, spoons and coins. Home: 7335 Valentown Rd Victor NY 14564-9714 Office: Palmyra-Macedon HS 151 Hyde Pky Palmyra NY 14522-1235 E-mail: drose1@rochester.rr.com.

ROSE, HUGH, retired economics educator; b. London, July 20, 1920; came to U.S., 1960, naturalized, 1977; s. William and Ann (Ogus) R. Student, Oxford (England) U., England, 1939-40, 45-47, Nuffield Coll., 1950-52. Lectr. in econs. Rhodes U., South Africa, 1947-50, lectr., 1952-53; lectr. in econs. Exeter U., England, 1954-60; assoc. prof. econs. U. Rochester, N.Y., 1961-63, prof., 1965-70; assoc. prof. econs. U. Toronto, Can., 1963-65; hon. rsch. assoc. Harvard U., Cambridge, Mass., 1969-70; prof. econs. Johns Hopkins U., Balt., 1970-91. Author: Macroeconomic Dynamics, 1991; contbr. articles to profl. jours. With British Army, 1940-45. Home: 112 Cross Keys Rd Apt D Baltimore MD 21210-1536 Office: Johns Hopkins U Dept Econs 3400 N Charles St Dept Econs Baltimore MD 21218-2680 E-mail: hrose@charm.net.

ROSE, KATHY LERNER, artist; b. N.Y.C., Nov. 20, 1949; d. Ben and Miriam (Burden) R. BFA, Phila. Coll. Art, 1971; MFA, Calif. Inst. of Arts, 1974. Vis. lectr. Harvard U., Cambridge, Mass., 1979-80; self-employed artist N.Y.C., 1976—. Dir., animator (animated films) 10, 1972-78; dir., performer 11 performance pieces (combining film with live performance); numerous articles about this pioneering work appeared in : Print, Dance Mags.; N.Y. Times, Boston Globe, Phila. Inquier, Washington Post and others. Grantee: NEA, 1981, 83, 84, 85, 86, 87, N.Y. Found. for Arts, 1984, 91; N.Y. State Coun. for the Arts, 1985, 86, Am. Filmmakers Inst., 1976.

ROSE, KIM MATTHEW, lawyer, educator; b. Gallipolis, Ohio, Mar. 21, 1956; s. Dave and Lois Ann R.; m. Pamela Carol Sims, Aug. 11, 1990. Student, USMA, 1974—76; BBA, Ohio U., 1977; JD, Capital U. Law, 1981; MBA, Ashland Coll., 1988. Bar: Ohio 1981, U.S. Dist. Ct. (so. dist.) Ohio 1981, U.S. Ct. Appeals (6th cir.) 1987, U.S. Supreme Ct. 1988. Asst. prosecutor Knox County Prosecutor, Mt. Vernon, Ohio, 1982-90; with Critchfield, Critchfield & Johnston, Mt. Vernon, 1982—. Adj. prof. Mt. Vernon Nazarene Coll., 1982-2002. Active Met. Housing Authority, Knox County, 1990-2002; adv. bd. Salvation Army, Mt. Vernon, 1991—; bd. dirs. Knox Cmty. Hosp., Mt. Vernon, Ohio, 2000. Maj. USAR, 1974-95. Mem. Ohio State Bar Assn., Knox County Bar Assn. (past pres.), Mt. Vernon Nazarene Coll. Found. (rec. sec. bd. 1995—), Mt. Vernon-Knox County C. of C., Masons. Avocations: flying, skiing, fishing, golfing, biking. Home: 1413 Greenbrier Dr Mount Vernon OH 43050-9101 Office: Critchfield Critchfield & Johnston 10 S Gay St Mount Vernon OH 43050-3546 E-mail: rose@core.com., kimr@ccj.com.

ROSE, MARIANNE HUNT, business educator; b. Portsmouth, Ohio, Nov. 6, 1940; d. Harry Duke and B. Marie (Craycraft) Hunt; m. W. Craig Rose, Aug. 9, 1958 (dec. 1988); children: W. Stuart, Deirdre Anne. BS in Edn., Ohio U., 1962; postgrad., U. Va., James Madison U., George Mason U. Cert. tchr., Va., Ohio. Asst. editor Morehead (Ky.) News, 1962-63; mgr. Birthday Calendar Co., Morehead, 1963-64; bus. tchr. Clay Twp. Schs., Portsmouth, 1964-65, Prince William County Adult Edn., Woodbridge, Va., 1977-80, Prince William County Schs., Woodbridge, 1973—95; ret., 1995. Co-sponsor Future Bus. Leaders Am., Gar-Field Sr. H.S., Woodbridge, mentor TLC program, 1990-95; team mem. Tech.-Prep. Consortium, No. Va. C.C., Woodbridge, 1992-95. Mem. Dale City Civic Assn., Woodbridge; elder, deacon 1st United Presbyn. Ch., Dale City, 1972—. Recipient Professionalism award Tchr. Recognition Com./Gar-Field, 1993. Mem. NEA, AAUW, Va. Edn. Assn., Va. Bus. Edn. Assn., Prince William Edn. Assn. (bldg. rep.). Avocations: reading, music, dancing. Home: 14415 Fairview Ln Woodbridge VA 22193-2045

ROSE, MARK ALLEN, humanities educator, educator; b. New York, Aug. 4, 1939; s. Sydney Aaron and Rose (Shapiro) R.; m. Ann (Bermingham); 1 son, Edward Gordon. AB(hon.), Princeton, 1961; LittB, Merton Coll., Oxford, Eng., 1963; PhD, Harvard Univ., 1967. Instr. to assoc. prof. in English Yale U., 1967-74; prof. English U. Ill., 1974-77; prof. U. Calif., Santa Barbara, 1977—, chmn. dept. English, 1987-89; dir. U. Calif., Humanities Rsch. Inst., Santa Barbara, 1989-94, chmn. dept. English, 1997—2001, assoc. vice chancellor, 2002—. Author: Heroic Love, 1968; (fiction) Golding's Tale, 1972; Shakespearean Design, 1972; Spenser's Art, 1975; Alien Encounters, 1981; Authors and Owners, 1993; editor: Twentieth Century Views of Science Fiction, 1976; Twentieth Century Interpretations of Antony and Cleopatra, 1977, (with Slusser and Guffey); Bridges to Science Fiction, 1980; Shakespeare's Early Tragedies, 1994; (CD-ROM) Norton Shakespeare Workshops. Woodrow Wilson Fellow, 1961; Henry Fellow, 1961-62; Dexter Fellow, 1966; Morse Fellow, 1970-71; NEH Fellow, 1979-80, 90-91. Mem. MLA, Renaissance Soc. Am., Shakespeare Soc. Am., Phi Beta Kappa. Office: U Calif English Dept Santa Barbara CA 93106

ROSE, MARY CATHERINE, elementary educator; b. Pomeroy, Ohio, Mar. 17, 1949; d. Lawrence Walter and Ruth Agnes (Curtis) Francis; m. Thomas L. Rose Jr., Sept. 28, 1973. BA, Marshall U., 1971, MA, 1980; postgrad., Ohio U., 1974; Ednl. Leadership Cert., U. Ctrl. Fla., 1994. Kindergarten tchr. Meigs Local Sch., Middleport, Ohio, 1971-83, Orange County Pub. Sch., Orlando, Fla., 1983-91, 4th grade tchr., 1991—. Nat. cons. in field. Author: 10 Easy Lessons That Get Kids Ready for Writing Assessments, 15 Easy LessonsThat Build Basic Writing Skills in Grades K-2, Week by Week Homework for Building Reading Comprehension and Fluency. Mem. Internat. Reading Assn., NEA, Nat. Coun. Tchr. Math., Nat. Sci. Tchr. Assn., Fla. Assn. Sci. Tchr., Classroom Tchr. Assn., Fla. Reading Coun., Nature Conservancy. Home: 118 Sheridan Ave Longwood FL 32750-3930 Office: Lake Sybelia Elem Sch 600 Sandspur Rd Maitland FL 32751-4781

ROSE, MARY MABEL, elementary school educator; b. Monticello, Iowa, Dec. 16, 1940; d. Ralph Richard and Flora Birdena (Hawkins) Ganfield; m. Paul Roger Rose, Dec. 30, 1961 (dec. Oct. 1979); children: Lynn Marie, Carol Ann. BA, Upper Iowa U., 1962; postgrad., U. No. Iowa, 1990—. Cert. profl. tchr., Iowa. Elem. tchr. North Fayette County Cmty. Schs., West Union, Iowa, 1962-67, Marion Ind. Schs., Iowa, 1963-64; instr. adult edn. Marion Ind. Schs., Iowa, 1967; substitute tchr. Bremer County Schs., Waverly, Iowa, 1974-84; tchr. Waverly-Shell Rock Schs., Iowa, 1984—, mem. early childhood adv. bd., 1990-91. Mem. edn. com. Waverly Trinity Meth. Ch., 1979-84, trustee, 1984-86, mem. fin. com., 1989-92, staff parish relationship com., 1999-2001; vol. Waverly Hosp. Aux., 1984-86. Mem. ASCD, Nat. Assn. for Edn. Young Children, Shell Rock Music Assn. (bd. dirs. 1995-98). Home: 107 S Ridge Dr Waverly IA 50677-3908

ROSE, MARY PHILOMENA, business educator; b. Detroit, Sept. 27, 1943; d. Henry Joseph and Marie Frances (Wilt) Mueller; m. Robert Henry Rose, June 24, 1966; children: Christopher, Jennifer, Matthew. BS, U. Detroit, 1966; MA in Tchg., Oakland U., 1992. Cert. secondary tchr., Mich.; adminstrv. cert. Vocat. tchr. Detroit Public Schs., 1966-70; tchr. presch. Utica Cmty. Schs., Sterling Heights, Mich., 1980-82, tchr. computers, 1982-92, tchr. in charge, computers adult edn., acad. adv., 1992-97, coord. bus. partnership programs, 1992-94; instr. Lotus Macomb Intermediate Sch. Dist., Clinton Twp., Mich., 1988-90. Adj. faculty Oakland Cmty. Coll., Auburn Hills, Mich., 1991; co-chair UCS Adult Edn. Sch. Improvement team, Sterling Heights, Mich., 1992—96; coord. Skills Enhancement Ctr. Ford Mich. Proving Grounds (Romeo Cmty. Schs.), 1996—98; bldg. adminstr., adult, alternative and cmty. edn. Van Dyke Pub. Schs., Center Line, Mich., 1998—. Mem. Utica Cmty. Schs. Citizen's adv. com., Sterling Heights, Mich., 1975-85; pres. PTO, Shelby Twp., Mich., 1980-83. Mem. Mich. Assn. Acad. Adv. Adult and Cmty. Edn. (pres. 1994-95), Grtr. Detroit Employment Opportunity Assn., Macomb County Assn. Placement Personnel, Mich. Assn. Cmty. and Adult Edn., Nat. Ctr. Cmty. Edn. Avocations: reading, dancing, walking, traveling. Office: Kramer Ctr 8830 E Ten Mile Center Line MI 48015

ROSE, PEGGY JANE, artist, art educator, gifted education advocate; b. Plainfield, N.J., Oct. 4, 1947; d. Kenneth Earl and Mary Elizabeth (Taylor) R.; m. Byram Soli Daruwala, July 30, 1988; 1 child, Mathew Byram Daruwala. BA magna cum laude, U. Tex., Austin, 1971; BFA with distinction, Acad. of Art Coll., San Francisco, 1980; student of, Burton Silverman. With curriculum devel. com. Calif. Coll. Arts and Crafts, Oakland, 1985-86; with Walnut Creek (Calif.) Civic Arts, 1985-95; with faculty exec. com. Acad. of Art Coll., 1983-97; solo show Dragon Gallery, Mill Valley, Calif., 1987; Brenda Hall Gallery, San Francisco, 1993; featured artist Sausalito (Calif.) Art Festival, 1986; group shows U.S. Art, San Francisco, 1994; Marin open studios Marin Arts Coun., San Rafael, Calif., 1996. Art exhbn. juror, No. Calif., 1994-97; instr. painting, drawing. Editor: Resource Notebook for Teaching Gifted Children; artist (exhibitions) Mercer County Ann. Exhibit, 2003 (Juror's Choice award, West Windsor Arts Coun. award, 2003), Acad. Art Faculty Exhibits, City of Walnut Creek, 1994—97, Carmel Gallery, 1990; prin. works include include portrait and landscape paintings and commns.; author: Whistler's Pastels in Venice. Founder advocacy group Raising Exceptionally Able Children; co-chmn. G&T Resource Com., West Windsor-Plainsboro Regional Sch. Dist.; advocate gifted edn. Recipient Parent of Yr. award, NJ Assn. Gifted Children, 2002, Nat. Assn. Gifted Children. Mem.: Alamo Danville Artists Soc. (Best of Show Gold Medallion 1984), San Francisco Women Artists Gallery (Merit award 1987), N.Y. Soc. Illustrators (Lila Atcheson Wallace award), San Francisco Acad. Art Coll., Marin Soc. Artists (Grumbacher Gold Medallion awards), Arts Coun. Princeton, Audubon Artists, Pastel Soc. West Coast (signature mem., Best of Show 1996, Handell award 1996, Ferrari Color award 1997), Pastel Soc. Am. (Sauter-Miggins award 1998, Bd. Dirs. award 2003), Internat. Assn. Pastel Socs., Allied Artists Am. (signature mem., Gold Medal of Honor 2002), Calif. Art Club, Arts Coun. Princeton (Juror's Choice awards 2001, 2002), Portrait Soc. Am., Catherine Lorillard Wolf Art Club (Gold Medal of Honor 2002). Avocations: music, gifted education advocacy. Studio: 12 Perry Dr Princeton Junction NJ 08550-2803 E-mail: prose47@comcast.net.

ROSE, ROBERT HENRY, arts education administrator; b. Butler, Pa., Sept. 10, 1948; s. Robert C. and Olga (Matzko) R.; m. Melanie Sue McKamish, Sept. 12, 1987; children: Aaron, Joseph, Julie. BS, Geneva Coll., Beaver Falls, Pa., 1991; MEd, Pa. State U., 1993. Cert. in environ. protection CDC; cert. in human resource devel. With Armco Steel Corp., Butler, Pa., 1978-83; commd. U.S. Army, 1983, advanced through grades to master sgt., 1992; ret., 1995; dir. Oakbridge Acad. Arts, 1995—, Newport Bus. Inst., 1995—. Decorated Purple Heart; Vets. grantee PHEAA, 1990. Mem. New Kensington C. of C. (exec. bd. dirs.), Masons, Elks (lecturing knight 1983-84), Strategic Planning Com. Plum Boro Sch. Dist., Pi Lambda Theta. Avocations: running, writing, golf, tennis. Home: 155 Shearer Rd New Kensington PA 15068-9320 Office: 1309 Greensburg Rd Lower Burrell PA 15068-3843

ROSE, ROBERT MICHAEL, materials science and engineering educator; b. N.Y.C., Apr. 15, 1937; s. Lawrence Lapidus and Lillian (Rosen) R.; m. Martha Gibbs, Oct. 15, 1961; children: Cynthia J., James L., Joshua S. S.B., MIT, 1958, Sc.D., 1961. Registered profl. engr., Mass. Asst. prof. materials sci. and engring MIT, Cambridge, 1961-66, assoc. prof., 1966-72, prof., 1972—; dir. MIT Concourse program, 1988—; prof. health scis. and tech. Harvard Med. Sch.- MIT, 1978-90; prof. emeritus MIT, 2003—; dir. Cryoelectro Assocs., Wenham, Mass., 1978-90. Author: Structure and Properties of Materials, 1964, Practical Biomechanics for the Orthopedic Surgeon, 1979, 92, The Chicken From Minsk, 1995. Recipient Kappa Delta prize Am. Acad. Orthopedic Surgeons, 1973 Mem. Am. Soc. Metals (vice chmn. 1971-72, Bradley Stoughton prize, chmn. 1972-73), Metal Soc. AIME, Boston Yacht Club. Jewish. Home: 18 Morgan St Wenham MA 01984-1114 Office: Room 4-132 MIT 77 Massachusetts Ave Cambridge MA 02139-4301

ROSE, SARA MARGARET, English as a second language educator; b. Johnstown, Pa., Sept. 22, 1950; d. William S. and Mary Margaret (Leberknight) R.; m. Akbar Ahamadian (common law, separated); 1 child, Meryem Rose. Student, U. Copenhagen, Denmark, 1971-73; MEd, Blagard Tchrs. Seminarium, Copenhagen, 1981. Cert. tchr., Denmark. Lang. tchr. and cons. Adult Edn., Hillerød, Denmark, 1981-90; cons. on immigrant and refugee issues Danish Dept. Welfare, Hillerød, 1983-88; ESL instr. Balt. City C.C., 1991-94, Catonsville C.C., Balt., 1992-96, Balt. Hebrew U., 1993-95, Balt. County Adult Edn., 1990-96, ESL facilitator, adminstr., 1994-96; dir. English Lang. Inst. Coll. Notre Dame of Md., Balt., 1996-99; ESL instr. U. Md., Baltimore County, 2000—. Cmty. coord. Au Pair Care, Balt., 1991-98. Lectr. on Immigrant and Refugee Issues, AOF Hillerød, 1983-90; founder, adminstr. Fgn. Women's Social Club, Hillerød, 1985-87; mem. People's Movement Against Racial Hatred and Discrimination, Denmark, 1983-90. Recipient Study Tour to Turkey, Danish Ministry of Edn., 1986, Cert. of Appreciation Balt. City C.C., 1993. Mem. TESOL, Md. TESOL (pres. 1999-2000, past pres. 2000—), Amnesty Internat., Greenpeace. Methodist. Avocations: reading, travel, music, theater, time with daughter. Home: 3905 Darleigh Rd Apt 2H Baltimore MD 21236-5808

ROSE, VIRGINIA SHOTTENHAMER, secondary school educator; b. San Jose, Calif., Feb. 3, 1924; d. Leo E. and Mae E. (Slavich) Shottenhamer; m. Paul V. Rose, June 21, 1947; children: Paul V. Jr., David P., Alan P. AB, W. Calif., San Jose, 1945, MA, 1972. Tchr. grades 5-6 Evergreen Sch. Dist., San Jose, 1945-47; 6th grade tchr. Washington Sch., San Jose, 1947-57; elem. tchr. San Jose Unified Sch. Dist., 1967-82, reading specialist, tchr. grades 6-8, 1982-92; ret., 1992. Cons. in field; mem. project literacy San Jose Unified Schs., 1987-91; mem. instrnl. materials evaluation panel Calif. State Edpt. Edn., Sacramento, 1988; master tchr. U. Calif., San Jose, 1991. Co-author: Handbook for Teachers' Aides, 1967. Active Alexian Bros. Hosp. League, San Jose, 1965, bd. dirs., chair libr. cart, 1966-76; vol. San Jose Hist. Mus., 1992—. Mem. AAUW (com. chair 1978-81), Internat. Reading Assn., Calif. Reading Assn. (Margaret Lynch award for Outstanding Contbn. to Reading 1999), Santa Clara County Reading Coun. (pres. 1986-87, Asilomar conf. chair 1991, IRA honor coun. pres. club 1987, bd. dirs.), Santa Clara U. Calala Club (bd. dirs. 1994-96), Soroptimist Internat. (sec. 1993-94), Pi Epsilon Tau (pres. 1944-45), Kappa Delta Pi (pres. 1943-45), Pi Lambda Theta (pres. San Jose chpt. 1987-89, auditor 1980, sec. 1985-86, Biennium award 1987). Avocations: reading, hiking, biking, gardening, cooking. Office: Willow Glen Ed Park S 2001 Cottle Ave San Jose CA 95125-3502

ROSE-ACKERMAN, SUSAN, law and political economy educator; b. Mineola, N.Y., Apr. 23, 1942; d. R. William and Rosalie Rose; m. Bruce A. Ackerman, May 29, 1967; children: Sybil, John BA, Wellesley Coll., 1964; PhD, Yale U., 1970. Asst. prof. U. Pa., Phila, 1970-74; lectr. Yale U., New Haven, Conn., 1974-75, asst. prof., 1975-78, assoc. prof., 1978-82; prof. law and polit. economy Columbia U., N.Y.C., 1982-87; Ely prof. of law and polit. econ. Yale U., New Haven, 1987-92, co-dir. Ctr. Law, Econ. and Pub. Policy, 1988—, Luce prof. jurisprudence law and polit. sci., 1992—. Panelist Am. studies program Am. Coun. Learned Socs., 1987-90; review panelist, faculty Fulbright Commn., 1993-96; vis. rsch. fellow World Bank, 1995-96. Author: (with Ackerman, Sawyer and Henderson) Uncertain Search for Environmental Quality, 1974 (Henderson prize 1982); Corruption: A Study in Political Economy, 1978; (with E. James) The Nonprofit Enterprise in Market Economies, 1986; editor: The Economics of Nonprofit Institutions, 1986; (with J. Coffee and L. Lowenstein) Knights, Raiders, and Targets: The Impact of the Hostile Takeover, 1988, Rethinking the Progressive Agenda: The Reform of the American Regulatory State, 1992, Controlling Environmental Policy: The Limits of Public Law in Germany and the United States, 1995, Corruption and Government: Causes, Consequences and Reform, 1999 (Levine Prize 2000); contbr. articles to profl. jours.; bd. editors: Jour. Law, Econs. and Orgn., 1984—, Internat. Rev. Law and Econs., 1986—, Jour. Policy Analysis and Mgmt., 1989—, Polit. Sci. Quar., 1988—. Guggenheim fellow 1991-92, Fulbright fellow, Free U. Berlin, 1991-92; fellow Ctr. for Advanced Study in the Behavioral Scis., Stanford, Calif., 2002, Collegium Budapest, 2002. Mem. Am. Law and Econs. Assn. (bd. dirs. 1993-96, 2002-), Am. Econ. Assn. (mem. exec. com. 1990-93), Am. Polit. Sci. Assn., Assn. Am. Law Schs., Assn. Pub. Policy and Mgmt. (policy coun. 1984-88, treas. 1998-2000). Democrat. Office: Yale U Law Sch PO Box 208215 New Haven CT 06520-8215

ROSEHNAL, MARY ANN, educational administrator; b. Bklyn., July 25, 1943; d. Frank Joseph and Mary Anna (Corso) R.; 1 child, Scott Stoddart. BA in Sociology, San Francisco State U., 1968; M in Sch. Bus. Adminstrn., No. Ariz. U., 1985. Lic. substitute tchr., Ariz.; lic. vocat. nurse, Calif.; Ariz. Delinquency Counselor, Calif., 1969-73. Office mgr. Nurses Cen. Registry, Sun City, Ariz., 1973-75; bus. mgr. Nadaburg Sch. Dist., Wittmann, Ariz., 1975-78, Morristown (Ariz.) Sch. Dist., 1978—; served on 1st Assessment Handbook editing task force Fair Employment Practices Handbook Task Force, 1979-80. Mem. tech. adv. com. Ariz. Dept. Tech. adv. com. Ariz. Dept. Edn., 1993-94; mem. adv. com. Ariz. Auditor Gen. Uniform Sys. Fin. Records, Auditor, 1993-99. Columnist Wickenburg Sun, 1975—. Clk. Morristown sch. bd., 1974-76; pres. Morristown PTA, 1977-78; sec. Wickenburg area bd., 1979; bd. dirs. Future Frontiers, 1979-81; rep. HUD block grant adv. com., 1979-85; active Wickenburg Friends of Music, 1984—, bd. dirs. 1986—, sec. bd. dirs., 1986-92, 96; sec. Wickenburg Regional Health Care Found., 1989-92, trustee, 1988-94; mem. com. Wickenburg Scenic Corridor, 1990-92. Named to Ariz. Sch. Bd. Assn. Honor Roll, 1976; named Morristown Area Vol. of Yr., 1988. Mem. AAUW, Ariz. Assn. Sch. Bus. Ofcls. (fin. dir., bd. dirs. 1985-91, v.p. 1991, pres.-elect 1992-93, pres. 1993-94, immediate past pres. 1994-95, Gold award 1986-88, 90-95, 96, Silver award 1989, 97, 99, cert. award 1998), Assn. Sch. Bus. Ofcls. Internat. (mem. pres.'s adv. coun. 1993-94, election com. 1994-95), Morristown Federated Women's Club (charter mem., edn. chmn. com. 1990-97), Ariz. Theatre Guild, Wickenberg C. of C. (assoc. 1993-95). Office: PO Box 98 Morristown AZ 85342-0098

ROSELL, SHARON LYNN, physics and chemistry educator, researcher; b. Wichita, Kans., Jan. 6, 1948; d. John E. and Mildred C. (Binder) Rosell. BA, Loretto Heights Coll., 1970; postgrad., Marshall U., 1973; MS in Edn., Ind. U., 1977; MS, U. Wash., 1988. Cert. profl. educator, Wash. Assoc. instr. Ind. U., Bloomington, 1973-74; instr. Pierce Coll. (name formerly Ft. Steilacoom (Wash.) Community Coll.), 1976-79, 82, Olympic Coll., Bremerton, Wash., 1977-78; instr. physics, math. and chemistry Tacoma (Wash.) Community Coll., 1979-89; instr. physics and chemistry Green

River Community Coll., Auburn, Wash., 1983-86; researcher Nuclear Physics Lab., U. Wash., Seattle, 1986-88; asst. prof. physics Cen. Wash. U., Ellensburg, 1989—. Faculty senate Ctrl. Washington U., 1992-98. Lector and dir. Rite of Christian Initiation of Adults, St. Andrew's Ch., Ellensburg, Wash., 1993—, mem. parish coun., 1995-2000. Mem. Am. Phys. Soc., Am. Assn. Physics Tchrs. (rep. com. on physics for 2-yr. colls. Wash. chpt. 1986-87, v.p. 1987-88, 94-95, pres. 1988-89, 95-96, past pres. 1996-97), Am. Chem. Soc., Internat. Union Pure and Applied Chemistry (affiliate), Pacific Northwest Assn. Coll. Physics (bd. dirs. 1997-99, 2001-03, treas. 2002—), Soc. Physics Students (councilor zone 17 1998—). Democrat. Roman Catholic. Avocations: leading scripture discussion groups, reading, writing poetry, needlework. Home: 1100 N B St Apt 2 Ellensburg WA 98926-2570 Office: Ctrl Wash U Physics Dept Ellensburg WA 98926 E-mail: rosells@cwu.edu.

ROSELLE, CATHY COLMAN, kindergarten education, educational consultant; b. Riverside, Calif., Dec. 2, 1946; d. Carl Eugene and Elma (Skinner) Colman; m. Charles Perry Roselle, Sept. 1, 1968; children: Robert Andrew, Charles Eugene, Scott Perry. BSEE, N.Mex. State U., Las Cruces, 1977; MA, Hood Coll, 1990. Cert. tchr., reading specialist, Ariz., bilingual & ESL endorsements. Bilingual kindergarten tchr. P.T. Coe Sch., Phoenix, 1977-80; bilingual 1st grade tchr. Alta Loma Sch., Phoenix, 1981-83; Chpt. I reading tchr. Carpenter Mid. Sch., Nogales, Ariz., 1990; Chpt. I bilingual kindergarten tchr. A.J. Mitchell, Nogales, 1991-97; bilingual ESL tchr. K-2 Clark County, 1997—; ESL instr. So. Nev. C.C. Ednl. specialist S.W. Internat. Tech., Rio Rico, Ariz., 1994—; team leader Ariz. Student Assessment Profile, Nogales, 1992; mem. curriculum com. Project Wellhead, 1993-95. Co-author: Chapter I Handbook for Nogales School District, 1990. Campaign mgr. Sch. Bd Election Charles P. Roselle, Rio Rico, 1994. Mem. NEA, Ariz. Edn. Assn., Ariz. Assn. for Edn. of Young Children, Interventional Reading Assn. Avocations: reading, Scrabble, hiking, computer techonology in education. Office: 2501 Sunrise Ave Las Vegas NV 89101-4639 E-mail: swianc@worldnet.att.net.

ROSELLE, DAVID PAUL, university president, mathematics educator; b. Vandergrift, Pa., May 30, 1939; s. William John and Esther Suzanne (Clever) R.; m. Louise Helen Dowling, June 19, 1967; children— Arthur Charles, Cynthia Dowling BS, West Chester State Coll., 1961; PhD, Duke U., 1965; LLD, West Chester U., 1994; hon. degree, Westchester U., Soha U., Japan. Asst. prof. math. U. Md., College Park, 1965-68; assoc. prof. math. La. State U., Baton Rouge, 1968-73, prof., 1973-74, Va. Poly. Inst. and State U., Blacksburg, 1974-87, dean grad. sch., 1979-81, dean research and grad. studies, 1981-83, provost, 1983-87, chmn. Commn. on Rsch., 1981-83, chmn. Commn. on Grad. Studies, 1983-87; prof. U. Ky., 1987-90, pres., 1987-90; prof. math., pres. U. Del., 1990—. Pres. COMAP, Inc., Lexington, Mass., 1986-95; bd. dirs. Wilmington Trust Corp., VTLS, Inc. Editor: Proc. of the First Louisiana Conf. on Combinatorics, Graph Theory and Computing, 1970, Proc. of the Second Louisiana Conf. on Combinatorics, Graph Theory and Computing, 1971; mem. editorial bd. The Bicentennial Tribute to American Mathematics, 1977; contbr. numerous research articles to profl. jours. Mem. Del. Roundtable, 1990—, Bus.and Pub. Edn. Coun., 1990—; trustee Winterthur Mus., 1991—; bd. dirs. Del. Acad. Medicine, 1991—, Med. Ctr. Del., 1991—; mem. USAID adv. com. vol. fgn. aid, 2000—. Named Outstanding Alumnus West Chester State Coll., 1979; Westinghouse Coop. scholar, 1957; NSF grantee, 1965-75; Teaching Excellence Cert., 1978; Digital Equipment grant, 1984; Nat. Coun. Tchrs. Math. Cert. of Appreciation, 1984; founding fellow of Inst. for Combinatorics and Its Applications, 1990; numerous invited addresses at univs. and profl. soc. meetings. Mem. Am. Math. Soc., Math. Assn. Am. (sec., fin. com., exec. com., com. on publs. 1975-84; com. on spl. funds 1985—; chmn. com. on accreditation 1985; numerous other coms.). Home: 47 Kent Way Newark DE 19711-5201 Office: U Del Rm 104 Hullihen Hall Newark DE 19716-0099 E-mail: roselle@udel.edu.

ROSEMAN, SAUL, biochemist, educator; b. Bklyn., Mar. 9, 1921; s. Emil and Rose (Markowitz) R.; m. Martha Ozrowitz, Sept. 9, 1941; children: Mark Alan, Dorinda Ann, Cynthia Bernice. BS, CCNY, 1941; MS, U. Wis., 1944, PhD, 1947; MD (hon.), U. Lund, Sweden, 1984. From instr. to asst. prof. U. Chgo., 1948-53; from asst. prof. to prof. biol. chemistry, also Rackham Arthritis Research Unit, U. Mich., 1953-65; Ralph S. O'Connor prof. biology Johns Hopkins U., Balt., 1965—, chmn. dept., 1969-73; dir. McCollum-Pratt Inst., 1969-73, chmn. dept. biology, dir., 1988-90. Cons. NIH, NSF, Am. Cancer Soc., Hosp. for Sick Children, Toronto; sci. counselor Nat. Cancer Inst.; Lynch lectr. U. Notre Dame, 1989; Van Niel lectr. Stanford U., 1992. Author articles on metabolism of complex molecules containing carbohydrates and on solute transport.; former mem. editorial bd.: Biochemistry, Jour. Biol. Chemistry. Served with AUS, 1944-46. Recipient Sesquicentennial award U. Mich., 1967, T. Duckett Jones Meml. award Helen Hay Whitney Found., 1973, Rosenstiehl award Brandeis U., 1974, Internat. award Gairdner Found. award, 1981, Townsend Harris award CUNY, 1987, Spl. award 11th Internat. Symposium on Glycoconjugates, 1991, Karl Meyer award Soc. Glycobiology, 1993. Fellow Am. Acad. Microbiology; mem. Am. Soc. Biol. Chemists, Am. Soc. Cell Biology, Am. Acad. Arts and Scis., Nat. Acad. Scis., Am. Chem. Soc., Am. Soc. Microbiologists, Biochem. Soc. Japan (hon.). Office: Johns Hopkins U 34th Charles St Baltimore MD 21218

ROSEN, ADRIENNE, artist, educator; b. St. Louis, Dec. 18, 1940; d. Charles and Rena Gallop; m. Alex Paul Tucker, June 21, 1961 (dec. June 1965); children: Michele Lori Tucker, Valerie Joy Tucker, Alex Paul II Tucker; m. Martin M. Rosen, Dec. 1967; 1 child, Marissa Angele. BFA, Washington U., St. Louis, 1972. Illustrator, designer Internat. Shoe Co., St. Louis, 1961; owner, illustrator, graphic designer A.R. Art Studio, St. Louis, 1961—; painter portraits of people and pets St. Louis, 1995—. Art tchr. St. Louis Artist Guild; art tchr. Coll. for Kids program Meramec C.C.; pvt. instr. Designer, illustrator (dolls) Bethany Farms Inc., 1990—. Vol. artist Leukemia Soc. Am., St. Louis, 1999, Animal Aid, St. Louis, 1975, Am. Med. Ctr., St. Louis, Cystic Fibrosis Found.; vol. St. Louis Showstoppers for Breast Cancer Rsch. Recipient 2d pl. award, Jewish Cmty. Ctrs. Assn., St. Louis, 1997, University City Art Assn., St. Louis, 1999, award of mention, South County Art Assn., St. Louis, 1998, Recognition award, Art Happening, 2001—02, 1st pl. award profl. watercolor, Jewish Cmty. Ctrs. Assn., 2002, 2003. Mem.: Greater St. Louis Art Assn. (publicity dir. 1994—99, sec. 1995—98, v.p. 1998—2000, pres. 2000—02, exhibits chair 2002—03), St. Louis Watercolor Soc., St. Louis Artist Guild (bd. dirs. 1993—94), Art World Art Assn. Avocations: running races, dancing, photography, marathon running. Office: A R Art Studio 1717 Seven Pines Dr Saint Louis MO 63146-3713

ROSEN, BONNIE, elementary school principal, consultant; b. Sellersville, Pa., Nov. 23, 1950; d. Willard Miller and Anna Agnes (Dugard) Berthold; m. Robert G. Rosen. BS in Elem. Edn. with high honors, Kutztown State U., Pa., 1972; MS in Edn. with disting. recognition, Temple U., 1975; Prin.'s cert., U. Pa., 1978. Elem. sch. tchr. Reading Sch. Dist., Pa., 1972-79, summer sch. instr., 1972—, curriculum developer, 1974-79, adminstv. inter, 1977-79; owner, adminstr. Wooly Bear Day Care Sch., Lansdale, Pa., 1979-94; asst. prof. Montgomery County C.C., Blue Bell, Pa., 1985—; 2d grade tchr. No. Penn. Sch. Dist., 1995-98; instr. Montgomery County Intermediate Unit, 1995-98; sch. prin. Bridle Path Elem. Sch., Lansdale, Pa., 1998—. Cons. in field; presenter in field. Bd. dirs. No. Penn Boys and Girls Club. Recipient Outstanding Tchrs. Am. award Bd. of Advisors, 1975; named Tchr. of Yr. Reading/Berks County C. of C., 1976; George B. Hancher scholar Kutztown State U., 1971. Mem.: Delaware Valley Child Care Coun. (sec.), Small Bus. Coun. (presenter), Pa. Assn. Child Care Adminstrs., Montgomery/Bucks Assn. for Edn. of Young Children (pres. 1982—84, bd. dirs. 1993—), Pa. Assn. for Edn. of Young Children, Nat. Assn. for Edn. of Young Children, North Penn C. of C. (small bus. coun.). Republican. Lutheran. Avocations: piano, water sports, reading, constructing and designing learning materials. Home: 106 Holly Dr Lansdale PA 19446-1617 Office: Bridle Path Elem Sch 200 Bridle Path Rd Lansdale PA 19446-1567

ROSEN, DAVID MATTHEW, education educator; b. Hagerstown, Md., Dec. 29, 1948; s. Norman and Lois (Barbanell) R.; m. Kara Kennedy, June 14, 1997; children: Louis Wardlaw, Samuel Barbanell, Jesse James Robertson, Gabriel Alan. BA in English, Haverford Coll., 1971; MA, John Hopkins U., 1974, PhD, 1979. Prof. English and drama, chair divsn. arts and letters U. Maine, Machias, 1994—2001, co-chair divsn. scis., 1994—95, v.p. acad. affairs, 2001—03, acting pres., 2003; sr. v.p., v.p. acad. affairs Woodbury U., Burbank, Calif., 2003—. Author: Changing Fictions of Masculinity, 1993, Embodying Masculinity, 1994. Founder, exec. dir. Maine Youth Summer Theater Inst.; mem. exec. bd. Acadia Annex Repertory. Mem. MLA, Nat. Coun. Tchrs. English, Maine Humanities Coun. (chair exec. bd.). Office: Univ Maine Machias ME 04654 Home: 5 Court St Machias ME 04654-1118

ROSEN, DAVID MICHAEL, public relations administrator, public affairs consultant; b. Cambridge, Mass., Mar. 26, 1945; s. Maynard S. and Irma (Leavitt) R.; m. Nina J. Glick, Apr. 8, 1967; children: Michelle, Elisabeth. BA, Boston U., 1967, MS, 1977. Reporter The Day, New London, Conn., 1968-69, Boston Herald, 1969-73; polit. writer UPI, Boston, 1973-76, State House bur. chief, 1976-77; polit. commentator WGBH-TV, Boston, 1975-77; pub. affairs cons. Boston, 1977-79; pub. info. dir. U.S. Commodity Futures Trading Commn., Washington, 1979-80; dir. pub. rels. Harvard U., Cambridge, Mass., 1980-84, assoc. v.p., 1984-85, U. Chgo., 1986-88; v.p. Nicolazzo Assocs., Boston, 1988; chief of staff Office of Lt. Gov., Boston, 1988-89; v.p. Brandeis U., Waltham, Mass., 1989-93; cons. David Rosen Assocs., Boston, 1993; dir. pub. rels. Yeshiva U., N.Y.C., 1993-99; assoc. v.p. pub. affairs Emerson Coll., Boston, 2000—. Cons. U.S. GAO, Washington, 1977-79, Mass. Ins. Divsn., Boston, 1977-78, Harvard U., 1977-80, Radcliffe Coll., 1993, New Eng. Bd. Higher Edn., 1993, Clark U., 1993, Pilgrim Health Care, 1993; substitute tchr. Boston Pub. Schs., 1967-68. Author: Protest Songs in America, 1977. Avocations: piano, running. Home: 157 Bishops Forest Dr Waltham MA 02452-8800 Office: Emerson Coll Pub Affairs 120 Boylston St Boston MA 02116-4624 E-mail: david_rosen@comcast.net., david_rosen@emerson.edu.

ROSEN, GEORGE, economist, educator; b. St. Petersburg, Russia, Feb. 7, 1920; s. Leon and Rebecca (Rosenoer) R.; m. Sylvia Vatuk; 1 son, Mark. BA, Bklyn. Coll., 1940; MA, Princeton U., 1942, PhD, 1949. Prof. econs. Bard Coll., Annandale-on-Hudson, N.Y., 1946-50; economist Dept. State, Washington, 1951-54, Council Econ. Indsl. Research, Washington, 1954-55, MIT, CENIS, Cambridge, 1955-59, UN, N.Y.C., 1959-60, Ford Found., N.Y.C., Nepal and India, 1960-62, Rand Corp., Santa Monica, Calif., 1962-67; chief economist Asian Devel. Bank, Manila, Philippines, 1967-71; prof. econs. U. Ill.-Chgo., 1972-85, prof. econs. emeritus, 1985—, head dept., 1972-77; fellow Woodrow Wilson Internat. Ctr., Washington, 1989-90. Adj. prof. Johns Hopkins U.-Nanjing U. Ctr. Chinese-Am. Studies, 1986-87; cons. USAID, Egypt, 1994; book rev. editor Econ. Devel. and Cultural Change, 1988-2001; treas. Am. Com. for Asian Econ. Studies, 1990-98; Golden Jubilee spkr. Dept. Commerce Osmania U., Hyderabad, India, 1999; disting. spkr. Ctr. for Advanced Study of Internat. Devel., Mich. State U., East Lansing, 1999. Author: Industrial Change in India, 1958, Some Aspects of Industrial Finance in India, 1962, Democracy and Economic Change in India, 1966, 67, Peasant Society in a Changing Economy, 1975, Decision-Making Chicago-Style, 1980, Western Economists and Eastern Societies, 1985, Industrial Change in India 1970-2000, 1988, Contrasting Styles of Industrial Reform: China and India in the 1980s, 1992, Economic Development in Asia, 1996; contbr. The India Handbook, 1997. Ford Found. fellow NYU, 1971-72; grantee U. Ill., 1977-78, Social Sci. Research Council and Am. Inst. Indian Studies, 1980-81, Am. Inst. Indian Studies, 1983-84, 87-88, Rockefeller Found. Bellagio Study Ctr., 1984. Office: U Ill Dept Econs M/C 144 601 S Morgan St Chicago IL 60607-7121 Home: 5830 S Stony Island Ave 11A Chicago IL 60637

ROSEN, HARRIET R. elementary school educator; m. Neil C. Rosen, Dec. 26, 1959; children: Cindy, Jody, Sherry. BS, Pa. State U.; postgrad., U. Pa., Mercer U., Fau-Fla. Atlantic U. Cert. middle grades 4-8. Tchr. Gwinnett County Schs., Lawrenceville, Ga., Lower Merion Sch. Dist., Ardmore, Pa., Temple Beth Israel, Sunrise, Fla., Beth Tfiloh Sch., Pikesville, Md., Am. Heritage Sch., Delray Beach, Fla. Mem. Nat. Coun. Tchrs. English, Nat. Assn. Preservation Storytellers, Nat. Jr. H.S., Profl. Assn. Gifted Educators, So. Order Storytellers (profl. storyteller). Home: 8597 Chevy Chase Dr Boca Raton FL 33433-1803

ROSEN, HARVEY SHELDON, economics educator; b. Chgo., Mar. 29, 1949; s. Edward and Eleanor (Altman) R.; m. Marsha E. Novick, June 20, 1976; children: Lynne, Jonathan. AB, U. Mich., 1970; AM, Harvard U., 1972, PhD, 1974. Dep. asst. sec., tax analysis US Dept. Treasury, Washington, 1989-91; asst. prof. econs. Princeton (N.J.) U., 1974-80, assoc. prof., 1980-84, prof., 1984—, chmn. dept. econs., 1993—96, John L. Weinberg prof. econs. and bus. policy, 1995—, co-dir. Ctr. for Econ. Policy Studies, 1991—. Vis. fellow Inst. Advanced Studies, Hebrew U., Jerusalem, 1978; vis. scholar Hoover Intsn., Stanford, Calif., 1981. Fellow Econometric Soc.; mem. Phi Beta Kappa, Council Econ. Advisors, Exec. Office of the Pres. 2003-.. Office: Princeton U Dept Econs Princeton NJ 08544-0001

ROSEN, JACQUELINE I. flutist, music educator; b. Los Angeles, Sept. 28, 1952; d. Samuel Morris and Blanche (Seigel) R.; m. James Andrew Meckel, July 14, 1979; children: Sean Aaron, Eric Rosen. Student, Music Acad. of the West, Santa Barbara, Calif., 1973-74; BS in Music, UCLA, 1974; studies with Julius Baker, James Galway, Jean-Pierre Rampal, 1974-80. Freelance musician, Los Angeles, San Francisco and Monterey, Calif., 1974—; mem. Laurel Wind Quintet, 1977-80, Allegra Trio, 1980—, Farrell/Rosen Duo, Carmel, Calif., 1978-87, Terrence Farrell Consort, Carmel, 1980—. Instr. flute pvt. studio, Monterey, 1976—, Monterey Peninsula Coll., 1981-85; instr. Hidden Valley music seminars, Cazadero Music Camp; prin. flutist Hidden Valley Opera, Carmel Valley, Calif., 1976—; condr. master classes numerous Calif. colls., 1982—; music specialist Salinas City Sch. Dist. Premiere performance (flute-guitar duo) Sonatine for Flute and Guitar, 1981; rec. artist (with Terrence Farrell) Alla Romanza, Merry Christmas; appearances with San Francisco Spring Opera, 1979, Cabrillo Music Festival, 1978-84, Carmel Bach Festival, 1996, 98, 99, Camerata Singers; flutist Michael Culver Trio; editor CTBF/Macmillan-McGraw-Hill; radio broadcasts, 1977—. Recipient Southwestern Music Conf. award, 1972; Leonard Bernstein fellow, Tanglewood, 1977. Mem.: Calif. Music Educators Assn., Music Educators Nat. Conf. Avocations: playing jazz, gourmet cooking. Home: 15 Paseo Primero Salinas CA 93908-9110 E-mail: jjmeckel@pacbell.net.

ROSEN, RICHARD DAVID, lawyer; b. Pitts., June 24, 1940; s. Benjamin H. and Bertha B. (Broff) R.; m. Ellaine H. Heller, June 23, 1963; children: Deborah H. Fidel, Jaime M. Cohen. BA, Yale U., 1962; JD, Harvard U., 1965. Bar: Pa. 1966, Fla. 1979. Mgr. Bachrach, Sanderbeck & Co., Pitts., 1965-70; mng. ptnr. Grant Thornton, Pitts., 1970-76; chmn. tax dept. Baskin & Sears, Pitts., 1977-78; pres. Gas Transmission, Inc., Pitts., 1979—2000; dir., shareholder Cohen & Grigsby, Pitts., 1989—. Dir. UPMC Presbyn./UPMC Shadyside Hosps., 2003—. Contbr. articles to profl. jours. Trustee Jewish Healthcare Found., 1995—, chmn. investment com., 2001—. Fellow: Am. Coll. Trust and Estate Counsel; mem.: ABA, Pa. Bar Assn. (mem. estate planning com. 1996—, com.chmn. 1998—2000), Westmoreland Country Club, United Jewish Fedn. Greater Pitts. (chmn. profl. adv. com. 1997—). Avocations: golf, tennis. Home: 1198 Beechwood Ct Pittsburgh PA 15206-4522 Office: Cohen & Grigsby PC 11 Stanwix St 15 Fl Pittsburgh PA 15222-1312 E-mail: rrosen@cohenlaw.com.

ROSEN, ROBERT STEPHEN, humanities, theatre arts, TV and English educator; b. N.Y.C., Mar. 20, 1947; s. George Bernard and Elaine Lucille (Lavinsky) R.; m. Mary Patricia Bush; 1 child, David Michael. BA, U. Pitts., 1969, PhD in secondary edn., 1987; MA, California U. of Pa., 1980. Cert. secondary edn. tchr. in English and Speech, N.Y., secondary sch. prin., Pa. Studio dir. WQED-TV, Pitts., 1968-69; tchr. The Village Acad., Bethel Park, Pa., 1969-71; tchr. communication skills, humanities, theatre arts, TV and English Mt. Lebanon (Pa.) Sch. Dist., 1976—. Instr. edn. U. Pitts., 1986-89; mem. steering com. for arts Commonwealth of Pa., Pa. State U., 1988; mem. steering coun. Arts Edn. Collaborative, 2000-03. Contbr. articles to compendium on schs. and the arts. Presenter Pitts. Assn. for Edn. of Young Children at Carnegie-Mellon U., 1988-90, Kennedy Ctr. for Performing Arts, AATE Think Tank on the Future of Theatre and Education, 1990, U. Pitts. Literacy Conf. 1991; mem. steering coun. Arts Edn. Collaborative, 2000-03, profl. devel. taskforce and search com., 2000-01; contbr. 21st Century Visual Arts Curriculum Project K-12, Hillman Visual Arts Curriculum, 2001; mem; mem. adv. com. Pa. Gov.'s Inst. in Humanities, 2001; pres. fine arts divsn. South Hills Area Sch. Dist. Assn., 2000-02. Recipient Gift of Time Tributes, Am. Family Inst., 1989, 1990, 1st pl. award for creativity and excellence for directing Romeo and Juliet, Nat. H.S. Theatre Contest, 1992, Mt. Lebanon PTSA Outstanding Svc. award, 1997, Tchr. Excellence Found. award, 2000, Robert F. Wolf Tchr. of the Year, Tchr. Excellence Found., 2002. Mem.: AFTRA, NEA, ASCD (conf. presenter 1993), Pa. Assn. Supervision and Curriculum Devel. (conf. presenter 1991), Pa. Ednl. Rsch. Assn., Inst. Ednl. Rsch. (spl. merit award 1989), Am. Ednl. Rsch. Assn., Am. Alliance Theatre and Edn. (secondary sch. chairperson for U.S. 1989—91, rsch. award 1989), Southwestern Pa. Tchrs. of Distinction (sec. 2003—), Phi Delta Kappa. Avocations: swimming, writing. Home: 552 Oxford Blvd Pittsburgh PA 15243-1562 Office: Mt Lebanon Sch Dist 155 Cochran Rd Pittsburgh PA 15228-1360

ROSEN, ROBERTA, philosophy educator; b. Madawaska, Maine, Aug. 9, 1935; d. Bernard and Dolores (Bourgoin) Dionee; m. Frank Rosen, June 8, 1963; children: Ruth, Rachael, David, Sarah. BA, Gov. State U., University Park, Ill., 1975, MA, 1976; PhD, Walden U., 1977; postdoctoral, K.A.M.I.I. Temple. Free-lance writer, Chgo.; dir. religious edn. ASFU, Chgo.; minister All Souls 1st Universalist Soc., Chgo., 1975—95; prof. philosophy Prairie State Coll., Chicago Heights, Ill., 1976—89. Leader seminars on prevention of child abuse, 1976-1999. Author: (novel) Call Her Dolores, (children's) Johnny Linny's Nightmare; contbr. articles to religious jours. Bd. trustees Gov. State U., Unitarian-Universalist Women's Fedn. Recipient Humanitarian award, Humane Soc. award; named Best Tchr. Mem. Unitarian-Universalist Women's Assn. (life). Address: 2444 Madison Rd Apt 1004 Cincinnati OH 45208-1269

ROSEN, SARAH ANN, elementary education educator; b. South Bend, Ind., Feb. 25, 1946; d. William Elroy and Mary Frances (Samide) Richardson; m. Charles J. Falcone, Mar. 2, 1973 (dec. 1973); m. Michael Martin Rosen, Feb. 27, 1979. BS, U. Ariz., 1968. Cert. tchr., Ariz. Tchr. Sierra Vista (Ariz.) Pub. Schs., 1969-78, 79—, Dept. Def. Schs., Stuttgart, Germany, 1978-79. Chair Citizens for Excellence in Edn. and Govt., Phoenix, 1988; mem. Ariz. Citizens for Edn., Phoenix, 1988—. Mem. NEA, Ariz. Edn. Assn. (bd. dirs. 1986—), Sierra Vista Classroom Tchrs. Assn. (pres. 1977-78), U. Ariz. Alumni Club (bd. dirs. 1989—), Alpha Delta Kappa (pres. 1992—), Phi Delta Kappa. Democrat. Avocations: theater, fitness, collecting. Office: Bella Vista Elem Sch 5200 Garden Loop Sierra Vista AZ 85635

ROSENAU, RUTH ELIZABETH, retired elementary and secondary school educator; b. Dupree, S.D., June 3, 1919; d. William and Wilhelmina (Picker) R. BS, BHSU, 1969. Tchr. various schs., Ziebach, S.D., 1939-41, Perkins, S.D., 1941-43, Lind Sch., Dewey, SD, 1943-44, Akaska Sch., Walworth, S.D., 1944-45, various schs., Perkins, S.D., 1945-60, 62-72, 73—, Carson, SD, 1960-62, Redig Sch., Harding, S.D., 1972-73; ret., 1995. Mem. Internat. Reading Assn. Home: 19053 Rolling Hills Rd Meadow SD 57644

ROSENBERG, CHARLES ERNEST, historian, educator; b. N.Y.C., Nov. 11, 1936; s. Bernard and Marion (Roberts) R.; m. Carroll Ann Smith, June 22, 1961 (div. 1977); 1 child, Leah; m. Drew Gilpin Faust, June 7, 1980; 1 child, Jessica. BA, U. Wis., 1956; MA, Columbia U., 1957, PhD, 1961; DHL, U. Wis., 1997. Fellow Johns Hopkins U., Balt., 1960-61; asst. prof. U. Wis., 1961-63; assoc. prof. U. Pa., Phila., 1965-68, prof. history, 1968—, chmn. dept., 1974-75, 79-83; prof. history of sci. Harvard U., 2001—, chmn. Dept. History of Sci., 2003—. Bd. dirs. Mental Health Assn. Southeastern Pa., 1973-76, Library Co. of Phila., 1980—, Ctr. Advanced Study Behavioral Scis., 1999—. Author: The Cholera Years: The United States in 1832, 1849 and 1866, 1962, The Trial of the Assassin Guiteau: Psychiatry and Law in the Gilded Age, 1968, No Other Gods: On Science and Social Thought in America, 1976, The Care of Strangers: The Rise of America's Hospital System, 1987, Explaining Epidemics and Other Studies in the History of Medicine, 1992; editor Isis, 1986-89. Nat. Inst. Health Research grantee, 1964-70; Guggenheim Found. fellow, 1965-66, 89-90; Nat. Endowment Humanities fellow, 1972-73; Rockefeller Found. humanities fellow, 1975-76; fellow Inst. Advanced Study, 1979-80, Ctr. Advanced Study in Behavioral Scis., 1982-83. Fellow Am. Acad. Arts and Scis., Am. Philos. Soc.; mem. Inst. Medicine of NAS, Am. Assn. History of Medicine (William H. Welch medal 1969, coun. 1974-76, pres. 1992-94), History of Sci. Soc. (George Sarton medal 1995, coun. 1972-75), Soc. Social History of Medicine (pres. 1981), Orgn. Am. Historians (exec. bd. 1985-88). Home: 76 Brattle Cambridge MA 02138 Office: Harvard U Dept History of Sci Cambridge MA 02138 E-mail: rosenb3@fas.harvard.edu.

ROSENBERG, CHARLES MICHAEL, art historian, educator; b. Chgo., Aug. 3, 1945; s. Sandor and Laura (Fried) R.; m. Carol Ann Weiss, June 25, 1967; children: Jessica Rachel, Jasper Matthew. BA, Swarthmore Coll., 1967; MA, U. Mich., 1969, PhD, 1974. Asst. prof. SUNY, Brockport, 1973-80; assoc. prof. U. Notre Dame, Ind., 1980-96, prof., 1996—. Author: 15th Century North Italian Painting and Drawing: Bibliography, 1986, Art and Politics in Late Medieval and Early Renaissance Italy, 1990, Este Monuments and Urban Development in Renaissance Ferrara, 1997; contbr. articles to Art Bull., Renaissance Quar., others. Kress Found. fellow Kunsthistorisches Inst., Florence, Italy, 1971-73, Am. Coun. Learned Socs. fellow, 1977-78, NEH fellow, Brown U., 1979-80, Villa i Tatti, Florence, 1985-86, Rome prize Am. Acad. Rome, 2000-01. Mem. Coll. Art Assn., Renaissance Soc. Am., Centro di Studi Europa Della Corti, Italian Art Soc. Office: Notre Dame U Dept Art History & Design Notre Dame IN 46556 E-mail: rosenberg.1@nd.edu.

ROSENBERG, DALE NORMAN, retired psychology educator; b. St. Ansgar, Iowa, Dec. 12, 1928; s. Eddie Herman and Ella (Kirchgatter) R.; BS, Mankato State Coll., 1956; M.Ed., U. S.D., 1959; postgrad. Ball State Tchrs. Coll., 1962, U. Nebr., 1961, Colo. State Coll., 1963-67; D.Arts, U. Central Ariz., 1978; m. Delrose Ann Hermanson, Sept. 10, 1950; children—Jean Marie, James Norman, Julie Ann, Lisa Jo. Tchr. public schs., Holstein, Iowa, 1956-60; prin., guidance dir., Crystal Lake, Iowa, 1960-62; prin. Grafton (Iowa) Jr. High Sch., 1962-66; psychol. tester Dept. Rehab., State of Iowa, 1960-66; prof. psychology North Iowa Area Community Coll., Mason City, 1966-97 ; vis. lectr. Buena Vista Coll., Storm Lake, Iowa, 1984; invited speaker Inst. Advanced Philosophic Research, 1984-85. Served with USAF, 1949-53. Mem. NEA, Iowa Edn. Assn., Kappa Delta Pi, Phi Delta Kappa. Lutheran. Author multi-media curriculum for teaching disadvantaged introductory welding; author textbook-workbook, 1985. Recipient Golden Apple award Iowa TV Channel 3, 1994. Home: 100 Brook Ter Mason City IA 50401-1710

ROSENBERG, FRED ALLAN, microbiology educator; b. Berlin, Mar. 19, 1932; came to U.S., 1939; s. Adolf and Lotte (Bieber) R.; m. Liane Balter, June 9, 1957; 1 child, Alysa Gail. AB, NYU, 1953; PhD, Rutgers U., 1960. Rsch. assoc. U. Pitts. Grad. Sch. Pub. Health, 1960-61; asst. to full prof. Northeastern U., Boston, 1961—99; prof. microbiology Calif. Luth. U., Thousand Oaks, Calif.; lectr. microbiology. Vis. rsch. prof. U. Hannover, Germany, 1985, 87-88, 91, 92, 94-95; cons. Ford Found., 1962-63, Foods Rsch. Labs., Boston, 1963-91; adv. com. Bioxy Internat., Ltd., Ft. Worth, 1991—. Contbr. articles to profl. jours. Mem. Mass. Dept. Pub. Health Com. on Water Quality Standards, Boston, 1987-89; U.S. House Reps. subcom. on Bottled Water Standards. With U.S. Army, 1954-56. Recipient rsch. grant Dept. Health & Human Svcs., Sigma Xi, USPHS, 1957-60. Fellow Am. Acad. Microbiology, APHA; mem. Am. Soc. Microbiology (pres. northeast br. 1971), Boston Bacteriological Club (dir. 1969-81), Sigma Xi. Office: Calif Luth Univ 60 W Olsen Rd Thousand Oaks CA 91360

ROSENBERG, JOHN DAVID, English educator, literary critic; b. N.Y.C., Apr. 17, 1929; s. David and Dorothy Lilian (Shatz) R.; m. Barbara E. Hatch, 1952 (div. 1969); m. Maurine Ann Hellner, June 11, 1972; 1 child, Matthew John. BA, Columbia U., 1950, MA, 1951, PhD, 1960; BA, Clare Coll., Cambridge U., 1953, MA, 1958. Editor-in-chief Columbia Rev., 1949-50; lectr. English Columbia U., N.Y.C., 1953-54, asst. prof., 1962-65, assoc. prof., 1966-67, prof. English, 1967—, William Peterfield Trent prof., 1994—; instr. CCNY, 1954-62; chmn. Columbia Coll. humanities program, 1970-73, dir. grad. studies in English, 1986-89. Vis. prof. English Harvard U., 1968, U. B.C., 1970, Princeton U., 1978; vis. fellow Clare Hall Cambridge U., England, 1969; guest lectr. U.S. Mil. Acad., Cambridge U., Lancaster U. Author: The Darkening Glass: A Portrait of Ruskin's Genius, 1961, The Fall of Camelot: A Study of Tennyson's Idylls of the King, 1973, Carlyle and the Burden of History, 1985; editor: The Genius of John Ruskin, 1963, 2nd edit., 98, Mayhew, 1968, Swinburne: Selected Poetry and Prose, 1968, The Poems of Alfred, Lord Tennyson, 1975; contbr. essays and reviews on English lit. to N.Y. Times Book Rev., N.Y. Rev. Books, Harper's mag., Hudson Rev. and profl. jours. Recipient Clarke F. Ansley award Columbia U., 1960, Disting. Svc. award Columbian Coll. Core Curriculum, 1997; Coun. for Rsch. in Humanities grant-in-aid, 1965; Euretta J. Kellett fellow Cambridge U., 1951-53, Edward Coe fellow, 1956-57, Samuel S. Fels fellow, 1959-60, Am. Coun. Learned Soc. fellow, 1965-66, 70, Lawrence H. Chamberlain fellow, 1965-66, Guggenheim fellow, 1968-69, NEH fellow, 1982-83. Mem. MLA (chmn. exec. com. Victorian divsn. 1970, exec. com. 1979-83), Tennyson Soc., Ruskin Assn., Camp Rising Sun Alumni Assn., Columbia Coll. Alumni Assn. (dir. 1980-82, Alexander Hamilton medal 1994), Phi Beta Kappa. Office: Columbia U Dept English 1150 Amsterdam Ave New York NY 10027-7051

ROSENBERG, JUDITH LYNNE, middle school educator; b. Bklyn., Nov. 1, 1944; d. Benjamin and Rose (Delbaum) Jackler; m. Joel Barry Rosenberg, Aug. 26, 1965; children: Jeffrey Alan, Marc David. BA in Edn., Queens Coll., Flushing, N.Y., 1966, MS in Edn., 1972. Lic. advanced profl. elem. and mid. sch. math., Md., elem. edn., N.Y. Elem. tchr., N.Y.C. and Cranston, R.I., 1966-68; tchr. math. Earl B. Wood Mid. Sch., Rockville, Md., 1981-82, Walt Whitman High Sch., Bethesda, Md., 1982-83, Robert Frost Mid. Sch., Rockville, Md., 1983-89; math. and interdisciplinary resource Julius West Mid. Sch., Rockville, 1989—. Mem. NEA, Nat. Coun. Tchrs. Math., Md. State Tchrs. Assn. Home: 16 Flameleaf Ct Gaithersburg MD 20878-5216 Office: Julius West Mid Sch Great Falls Rd Rockville MD 20850

ROSENBERG, RAYMOND DAVID, special education educator, consultant; b. Jersey City, Apr. 25, 1951; s. Fabulous Sam and Arlene (White) R.; m. JoAnn Gabriella Simchera, June 10, 1984; 1 child, Anna Teresa. BA, Boston U., 1974; MEd, William Paterson Coll., 1989, MEd in Sch. Adminstrn., 1994. Cert. tchr., N.J. Tchr. Lodi (N.J.) Boy's and Girl's Club Preschool, 1979-80; tchr. reading Passaic County Tech. Vocat. High Sch., Wayne, NJ, 1980-82; specialist learning disabilities North Jersey Devel. Ctr., Totowa, 1983-84, adaptive switch tchr., 1986-87; ednl. specialist Div. Devel. Disabilities, Totowa, NJ, 1984-85, tchr. profoundly retarded students, 1987-89, tchr. medically frail, 1990-91; tchr. mildly retarded, emotionally disturbed students North Jersey Devel. Ctr., Totowa, NJ, 1992-93; learning disabilities tchr. Office of Edn., NJ, 1993-96; cons. youth consultation svcs. George Washington Sch. Annex, Hackensack, NJ, 1993-96; learning cons. child study team North Bergen (N.J.) H.S., 1996-98; GED tchr. Bergen C.C. Computer Learning Ctr., Paramus, 1998—. Learning disabilities tchr., cons., 1997-2000; pres. Ednl. Assessment Svcs., Inc., 2002—; mem. child study team and behavioral intervention team West N.Y. Early Childhood Sch., 2002-. Editor: Jour. Learning Cons., 1996. With ABA discrete trial learning with PDD autistic students, 1995. Recipient Eagle Scout award Boy Scouts Am., Ridgefield, N.J., 1968, 7 tchg. certs., 1978-89. Mem. Nat. Eagle Scout Assn., Pi Lambda Theta (Beta Chi chpt.). Episcopal. Lodge: Order of Arrow. Office: 5204 Hudson Ave West New York NJ 07093

ROSENBERG, ROBERT ALLEN, psychologist, educator, optometrist; b. Phila., July 31, 1935; s. Theodore Samuel and Dorothy (Bailes) R.; m. Geraldine Bella Tishler, Sept. 3, 1961; children: Lawrence David, Ronald Joseph. BA, Temple U., 1957, MA, 1964; BS, Pa. Coll. Optometry, 1960, OD, 1961. Lic. optometrist, psychologist, Pa. Instr. Pa. Coll. Optometry, Phila., 1962-65, asst. prof., 1965-67; asst. prof. psychology Community Coll. Phila., 1967-76, assoc. prof., 1976—. Pvt. practice optometry, Roslyn, Pa., 1965-95; assoc. in practice optometry, Huntingdon Valley, Pa., 1995-98. Contbr. articles to profl. jours. Named Humanitarian Chapel of Four Chaplains Bapt. Temple, 1980. Fellow Am. Acad. Optometry; mem. Am. Optometric Assn., Pa. Optometric Assn., Bucks-Montgomery Optometric Assn., Alumni Assn. Pa. Coll. Optometry (v.p. 1992-98, sec. 1991—). Avocations: singing, acting, photography, writing, public speaking. Home: 970 Corn Crib Dr Huntingdon Valley PA 19006-3304 Office: Community Coll Phila 1700 Spring Garden St Philadelphia PA 19130-3991

ROSENBERG, SHEILA RAE, secondary education educator; b. L.A., Mar. 6, 1936; d. David A. and Jean I. (Milstien) Winston; m. Herbert Rosenberg, Apr. 14, 1957 (div. 1977); children: Zachary, Daniel, Jordana. AA, U. Calif., L.A., 1956, BS, 1960, MA, Calif. State U., 1980. Cert. secondary tchr. and adminstr., Calif. Recereation leader Juvenile Hall, L.A., 1957-59; tchr. phys. edn. and sci. Los Palmas Sch. for Girls, L.A., 1960-63; tchr. phys. edn. social sci. Sequoia Intermediate Sch., Thousand Oaks, Calif., 1977—, dept. chair social sci. Newbury Park, Calif., 1989—, gate coord., 1990—. Pres. Applause, The Music Ctr., L.A., 1992—; mem. social action com. Stephen S. Wise Temple, L.A., 1989—, co-chair social action com., 1993. Recipient Vol. Svc. award Nat. Coun. Jewish Women; Calif. Dept. Edn. grantee, 1986. Mem. NEA, Calif. Tchrs. Assn., Nat. Coun. for Social Studies, United Tchrs. L.A., So. Calif. Jewish Hist. Soc. (docent 1989—). Democrat. Jewish. Home: 21520 Burbank Blvd Apt 317 Woodland Hills CA 91367-7054 Office: Sequoia Intermediate Sch 2855 Borchard Rd Thousand Oaks CA 91320-3898

ROSENBERG, VICTOR I. plastic surgeon, educator; b. N.Y.C., Nov. 15, 1936; s. Leonard C. and Sarah G. (Berger) R.; m. Deborah Iskoe, Jan. 2, 1966; children: Spencer, Ria. AB, NYU, 1957; MD, Chgo. Med. Sch., 1961. Diplomate Am. Bd. Plastic Surgery. Intern Beth Israel Hosp., N.Y.C., 1961-62, resident, 1962-63, 64-66, Beekman Downtown Hosp., 1963-64, Bronx Mcpl. Hosp., 1966-67, Mt. Sinai Hosp., N.Y.C., 1967-68; pvt. practice in plastic surgery N.Y.C., 1968—. Assoc. attending surgeon Beth Isreal Hosp., 1968—; assoc. attending surgeon Beekman Downtown Hosp., 1968—, chief plastic surgery, 1976-80; attending surgeon N.Y. Infirmary-Beekman Downtown Hosp., 1980-98, dir. cosmetic surgery, 1984-97; asst. attending surgeon Mt. Sinai Hosp., N.Y.C., 1968—; asst. clin. prof. Mt. Sinai Sch. Medicine CUNY. Comdr. USN, 1968-70. Fellow ACS, Internat. Coll. Surgeons; mem. Am., N.Y. Regional socs. plastic and reconstructive surgeons, Am. Soc. Aesthetic Plastic Surgery, AMA, Am. Cleft Palate Assn., N.Y. Acad. Medicine, N.Y. State, N.Y. County Med. Socs., Pan Am. Med. Assn. (diplomate sect. plastic surgery), Friars Club. Office: 4 Sutton Pl New York NY 10022-3056

ROSENBERGER, MARGARET ADALINE, retired elementary school educator, writer; b. Micanopy, Fla., Oct. 30; d. Eugene David and Lillian Adeline (Bauknight) Rosenberger. Student, Stetson U., 1946—48; BA in Edn., U. Fla., 1949, MEd, 1952. Drama sec. Nat. Youth Adminstrn., Gainesville, Fla., 1939—40; civil svc. clk. U.S. Army, Camp Blanding, Fla., 1940—46; tchr. J.J. Finley, Gainesville, 1949—52; prin., tchr. Micanopy Jr. H.S., 1952—55; gen. supr. Alachua County Schs., Gainesville, 1955—57, elem. supr., 1958—59; tchr. U.S. Army Dependents' Sch., Heidelberg, Germany, 1957—58; prin. Littlewood Elem. Sch., Gainesville, 1959—73, Prairie View Elem. Sch., Gainesville, 1973—82, ret., 1982; owner Rose Hill Publs. Mem. sch. adv. com. Prairie View Elem. Sch., 1975—82. Co-author: Reflections of Light, 1995; author: My God of Love, Mercy, Miracles and Angels, 1996, Secrets and Songs of Payne's Prairie, 1998, A Teacher's Odyssey, 2001, My Pets and I, 1999, Poems for Children, 2001, My Angels and I, 2001, Spiritual Interpretations of God's Truths, 2002, The Birth and Growth of the Village, 2003; author, composer: St. Augustine Song; contbr. articles to The Gainesville Sun, to WLUS Radio Talk Show, 1992-95, poems to mags. & papers. Pres. Children's Commn., Gainesville, 1956—57; dir. The Village Chorus, Gainesville, 1987—; mem. Gainesville Schs. PTA, 1959—82; mem. PTA Micanopy, 1952—55; Dem. candidate Fla. House Rep., 1974; pianist/organist The Village Vespers on Sunday Evenings, 1990—; bd. dir. Foster Grandparents, Gainesville, 1974—76; chmn. bd. dir. No. Fla. Retirement Village, Inc., Gainesville, Fla., 1982—86, bd. rep. to residents, 1986—, v.p. bd. dir., 1981—82. Mem.: Internat. Soc. Poets, Am. Soc. Composers, Authors & Pub., Micanopy Hist. Soc., Altrusa Internat. Club Gainesville (chmn. internat. com., chmn. newsletter, spkr. for programs), Order of Eastern Star, Delta Kappa Gamma (internat. soc. 1959—). Democrat. Baptist. Avocations: stamp collecting, coin collecting, book collecting, post card collecting, creative writing. Home: 410 SW Wacahoota Rd Micanopy FL 32667 Mailing: 8015 NW 28th Pl B 110 Gainesville FL 32606

ROSENBLATT, JASON PHILIP, English language educator; b. Balt., July 3, 1941; s. Morris D. and Esther (Friedlander) R.; m. Zipporah Marton, June 2, 1964; children: Noah David, Raphael Mark. BA, Yeshiva U., 1963; MA, Brown U., 1966, PhD, 1969. Asst. prof. English U. Pa., Phila., 1968-74, Georgetown U., Washington, 1974-76, assoc. prof., 1976-83, prof. English, 1983—. Vis. lectr. English lit. Swarthmore (Pa.) Coll., 1972-73; cen. exec. com. Folger Inst./Folger Shakespeare Libr., Washington, 1976-88. Author: Torah and Law in "Paradise Lost", 1994; co-editor: Not in Heaven: Coherence and Complexity in Biblical Narrative, 1991; mem. editl. bd. Milton Studies, 1992—; contbr. articles to scholarly publs. Recipient Virginia Graham Healey award, 1998-99; Guggenheim Found. fellow, 1977-78, NEH fellow, 1990-91, Folger Shakespeare Libr./NEH fellow, 1999-2000. Mem. MLA (del. assembly 1989-91, exec. com. div. religion and lit. 1982-86, exec. com. 17th century Eng. lit. 2002—), Milton Soc. Am. (exec. com. 1977-80, James Holly Hanford award 1989, v.p. 1998, pres. 1999), Milton Seminar, Phi Beta Kappa. Democrat. Jewish. Avocations: talmud study, music, swimming. Office: Dept English Georgetown Univ PO Box 571131 Washington DC 20057-1131 E-mail: rosenblj@georgetown.edu.

ROSENBLUM, JOHN WILLIAM, finance educator; b. Houston, Jan. 1, 1944; s. H. William and Susan (Ullmann) R.; m. Carolyn Edith Jones, Sept. 12, 1964; children: J. Christopher, Kathryn, Nicholas. AB, Brown U., 1965; MBA, Harvard U., 1967, DBA, 1972. Instr. Harvard U. Bus. Sch., Boston, 1969-72, asst. prof., 1972-75, assoc. prof., 1975-79; prof. Darden Grad. Sch. Bus. Adminstrn., U. Va., Charlottesville, 1979-80, assoc. dean, 1980-82, dean, 1982-93, Tayloe Murphy prof., 1993—; dean Jepson Sch. Leadership Studies, U. Richmond, Va., 1996-2000. Bd. dirs. Chesapeake Corp., Cone Mills Corp., The Providence Jour. Co., Grantham, Mayo, Van Otterloo, Thomas Rutherford, Inc. Co-author: Strategy and Organization, 1973, (2d edit.), 1977, Cases in Political Economy-Japan, 1980. Bd. dirs. Landmark Vols., Tredeger Nat. Civil War Ctr., Jamestown-Yorktown Found., Inc., Atlantic Challenge Found. Mem. Phi Beta Kappa, Omicron Delta Kappa. Home: 854 Crozet Ave Crozet VA 22932-9803

ROSENBLUTH, GWEN SOCOL, secondary educator; b. Breckenridge, Tex., Oct. 11, 1940; d. Jake and Rae (Zola) Socol; m. Sidney Alan Rosenbluth, June 3, 1962; children: Kirby Wade, Brady Warren. BA, U. Tex., Austin, 1962; MEd, Memphis State U., 1968; EdD, W.Va. U., 1990. Tchr. English Univ. Jr. High/Austin Sch., 1962-66; tchr. English, guidance counselor Auburndale Sch., Memphis, 1976-81; tchr. English Morgantown (W.Va.) High Sch., 1981—2000; ret. Co-dir. W.Va. U. Writing Project, Morgantown, 1990-2000. Program coord. Sat. Sch. for Gifted, Morgantown, 1981-84. Mem. NEA, W.Va. Edn. Assn., Nat. Coun. Tchrs. English, Phi Delta Kappa, Kappa Delta Pi. Jewish. Home: 141 Poplar Dr Morgantown WV 26505-2540 Office: Morgantown High Sch 109 Wilson Ave Morgantown WV 26501-7521

ROSENBLUTH, MARION, educator, consultant, psychotherapist; b. Chgo., Apr. 4, 1928; d. Edwin William and Louise (Sulzberger) Eisendrath; m. Paul Richard Rosenbluth, June 16, 1950 (dec. Nov. 1972); children: Daniel, Jane Baldwin, Thomas, James, Catherine Rothschild. BA, Harvard U., 1949; MSW, Cath. U. of Am., 1951; PhD, U. Ill., 1986. Lic. clin. social worker, Ill. Clin. therapist Chgo. Dept. of Health; pvt. practice Chgo., 1980—; prof. Loyola U., Chgo., 1986—; cons. Inst. for Clin. Social Work, Chgo., 1988—. Cons. student health Loyola U., 1978-80; assoc. Yale U. Child Study Ctr.; mem. women's bd. dirs. U. Chgo., 1978—. Mem. NASW, Coun. on Social Work Edn., Bd. Examiners Clin. Social Work (diplomate), Ill. Soc. Clin. Social Work, Arts Club of Chgo., Cliff Dwellers, Friday Club. Office: 676 N St Clair St Chicago IL 60611-2927 E-mail: mers03@aol.com.

ROSENDALE, SUZANNE MOORE, library media specialist; b. Utica, N.Y., July 12, 1942; d. Clark Wilbur and Lynda Louise (Hokerk) Moore; m. Walter R. Rosendale Jr., June 18, 1966; children: Kristen, Jennifer. AA, Penn Hall Jr. Coll., Chambersburg, Pa., 1962; BS in Elem. Edn. and BS in English 7-12, SUNY, Oswego, 1980; MLS, Syracuse U., 1986. Cert. elem. edn. tchr., N.Y. English tchr. VVS Middle Sch., Verona, N.Y., 1980-85, libr. media specialist, 1986—. Co-author: Creative Mathematics, 1980. Bd. dirs. Sherrill-Kenwood Community Chest, Sherrill, N.Y., 1980-84; trustee/regent Sherrill-Kenwood Free Libr., 1992—, chmn. pers. com. 1992-94; mem. beautification com. City of Sherrill, 1992. Named 1st runner-up Vol. Yr. Oneida (N.Y.) Daily Dispatch, 1970. Mem. ASCD, Cen. N.Y. State Libr. Assn., Sherrill, N.Y. Garden Club (sec., treas. 90-93). Republican. Methodist. Avocations: fishing, gardening, antiquing, boating, refinishing. Home: 177 Willow Pl Sherrill NY 13461-1056

ROSENFELD, HERB, educational consultant; b. N.Y.C., Feb. 13, 1931; s. David and Bertha (Kutler) R.; m. Esther Halfon, Dec. 25, 1957; children: Michele Eve, Seth Zvi, Amy Lynn. BA in Math. and Physics, CUNY, 1960; MS in Math. Edn., Yeshiva U., 1963; postgrad., Pa. State U., 1963, Columbia U., 1964, Fordham U., 1965-67. Tchr. math. Walton High Sch., N.Y.C., 1960-63, New Rochelle (N.Y.) High Sch., 1963-64; tchr. math., dean students, dir. discovery program Bronx (N.Y.) High Sch. Sci., 1964-82, founder, dir. outreach program, 1964-82; mem. planning com., then chmn. math. dept. Manhattan Ctr. for Sci. and Math., N.Y.C., 1982-84; co-founder, asst. dir. Central Park East Secondary Sch., N.Y.C., 1984-89; founder, cons. Eastside Community High Sch., Wooster (Mass.) and Boston Sch. Dists., I.S. 184, N.Y.C., 1990—. Cons. Panasonic Found., Coalition Essential Schs., Bank Street Coll., Lyndhurst (N.J.) Sch. Dist.; project dir. N.Y.C. Dist. 1 Secondary Sch. Project. Contbg. author: Teaching Advanced Skills to Educationally Disadvantaged Students; You Must Have a Dream to Create a School, 1993. Home and Office: 711 Amsterdam Ave Apt 17L New York NY 10025-6925

ROSENFELD, SANDRA KAYE, elementary school educator; b. Portland, Oreg., Aug. 6, 1953; d. Howard Wayne and Ruth Eileen (Russell) Darling; m. Stephen Barry Rosenfeld, June 25, 1983; 1 child, Austin Harrison. BS in Edn., Portland State U., 1975, MS in Edn., 1983. Ticket agt. Meml. Coliseum, Portland, 1971-93, Civic Stadium, Portland, 1975—; early childhood educator Portland Pub. Schs., 1975—; mem. parent involvement com., sabbatical leave com., dislocated workers com., Portland Pub. Sch. System, 1992—; mem. consortium Concordia Coll., 1992—; mem. site visit com. Oreg. Tchrs. Standards and Practice Commn. Dir. youth and edn. Congregation Neveh Shalom, 1987-94. Mem. NEA, Oreg. Edn. Assn. (mem. jud. panel), Portland Assn. Tchrs. (mem. contract maintenance com., sec. exec. bd., co-chair Impact II, mem. instrnl. profl. devel. com., head bldg. rep., chair site coun.), Theatrical Employees Union Local B-20 (bus. agt., past pres.), Women's League for Conservative Judaism (regional chmn., past pres.), Coalition of Alternatives in Jewish Edn., Hadassah. Home: 6837 SW 11th Dr Portland OR 97219-2149 Office: Chapman Elementary Sch 1445 NW 46th Portland OR 97210

ROSENKRANTZ, DANIEL J. computer science educator; b. Bklyn., Mar. 5, 1943; s. Harry and Ruth (Sirota) R.; m. Carole Jaffee, Aug. 2, 1969; children: Holly, Sherry, Jody, Andrew. BS, Columbia U., 1963, MS, 1964, PhD, 1967. With Bell Telephone Labs., Murray Hill, N.J., 1966-67; info. scientist GE Co. R & D Ctr., Schenectady, N.Y., 1967-77; prof. dept. computer sci. U. Albany-SUNY, 1977—, dept. chair, 1993-99; prin. computer scientist Phoenix Data Systems, Albany, 1983-85. Author: (with P.M. Lewis II and R.E. Stearns) Compiler Design Theory, 1976. Fellow ACM (editor-in-chief jour. 1986-91, area editor for formal langs. and models of computation 1981-86, mem. spl. interest group on mgmt. of data, mem. numerous conf. coms., Sigmod Contbns. award 2001); mem. IEEE Computer Soc., ACM Spl. Interest Group on Automata and Computability Theory (sec. 1977-79). Home: 1261 Cranbrook Ct Niskayuna NY 12309-1203 Office: U at Albany SUNY Dept Computer Sci Albany NY 12222-0001 E-mail: djr@cs.albany.edu.

ROSENMANN, DANIEL, physicist, educator; b. Lima, Peru, Sept. 6, 1959; came to U.S., 1991; s. Lothar and Eva (Roiter) R.; m. Patricia Edith Alvarado, Jan. 21, 1989. BS in Physics, U. Nac. Mayor de San Marcos, Lima, Peru, 1986; postgrad., No. Ill. U., 1991-93. Instr. U. Nacional Mayor de San Marcos, Lima, 1982-91; tchr. Coll. Leon Pinelo, Lima, 1986-91; teaching asst. No. Ill. U., DeKalb, 1991-93, grad. rsch. asst., 1993; lab. grad. participantship Argonne (Ill.) Nat. Lab., 1993-96; rsch. lab. mgr. physics dept. No. Ill. U., DeKalb, 1994-96; sci. assoc. Argonne Nat. Lab., 1996—. Author: Lab. guide book, 1988, 89. Scholar, fellow Argonne Nat. Lab. 1993-96. Mem. AAAS, Am. Phys. Soc., N.Y. Acad. Scis., Nat. Geographic Soc., Sigma Xi, Sigma Pi Sigma. Home: Apt 101 812 Beaumont Dr Naperville IL 60540-1830

ROSENN, KEITH SAMUEL, lawyer, educator; b. Wilkes-Barre, Pa., Dec. 9, 1938; s. Max and Tillie R. (Hershkowitz) R.; m. Nan Raker, June 21, 1960; 1 child, Eva; m. Silvia R. Rudge, Mar. 21, 1968; children: Jonathan, Marcos. AB, Amherst Coll., 1960; LLB, Yale U., 1963. Bar: Pa. 1964, U.S. Ct. Appeals (3rd cir.) 1979, Fla. 1981, U.S. Ct. Appeals (11th cir.) 1982. Law clk. to Judge Smith U.S. Ct. Appeals (2nd cir.), 1963-64; asst. prof. law Ohio State U. Coll. Law, 1965-68, assoc. prof., 1968-70, prof., 1970-79; project assoc. Ford Found., Rio de Janeiro, 1966-68; assoc. Escritorio Augusto Nobre, Rio de Janeiro, 1979-80; prof. law U. Miami, Fla., 1979—; project coord. Olin Fellowship Program Law and Econs. Ctr., U. Miami, Fla., 1980-81, assoc. dean Law Sch., 1982-83, chmn. fgn. grad. law program, 1985—. Cons. Hudson Inst., 1977, U.S. State Dept., 1981-82, World Bank, 1988-90; Fulbright lectr. Argentina, 1987, 88. Author: (with Karst) Law and Development in Latin America, 1975; Law and Inflation, 1982, Foreign Investment in Brazil, 1991; co-editor: A Panorama of Brazilian Law, 1992, Corruption and Political Reform in Brazil, 1999; advisor InterAm. Law Rev.; contbr. articles to law jours. Recipient Order of Democracy award Congress of Republic of Colombia, 1987, Lawyer of the Ams. award, 1989, Inter-Am. Jurisprudence prize, 1998, Order of Congress award Republic of Colombia, 2000; grantee Social Sci. Rsch. Coun., 1970, Dana Found., 1982. Mem. ABA, Am. Law Inst., Inter-Am. Bar Assn., Fla. Bar, Am. Soc. Comparative Law (bd. dirs.). Jewish. Office: U Miami Law Sch PO Box 248087 Coral Gables FL 33124-8087

ROSENSAFT, JEAN BLOCH, university administrator; b. N.Y.C., Jan. 6, 1952; d. Sam E. and Lilly Bloch; m. Menachem Rosensaft, Jan. 13, 1974; 1 child, Joana Deborah. BA in Art History, Barnard Coll., 1973; postgrad., NYU, 1978. Gallery lectr. in spl. exhbns. Mus. of Modern Art, N.Y.C., 1977-80; NEA lectr. on collections Modern Art Edn. Dept., 1979-80, spl. asst. for ind. sch. program, 1980-83, spl. asst. for publs., 1983-84; coord. pub. programs The Jewish Mus., N.Y.C., 1984-86, asst. dir. of edn., 1986-89; sr. nat. dir. for pub. affairs and institutional planning Hebrew Union Coll.-Jewish Inst. of Religion, N.Y.C., 1989—, exhbns. dir., 1994—2000, dir., 2000—. Author: Chagall and the Bible, 1987. Mem. collections and acquisitions com. U.S. Holocaust Meml. Mus., Washington, 1980—; mem. steering com. Coun. of Am. Jewish Mus., N.Y.C., 1995—; chair task force on the arts UJA/Fedn. Women's Task Force, N.Y.C., 1995—; v.p. Internat. Network of Children of Jewish Holocaust Survivors, N.Y.C., 1987—; chair Park Ave Synagogue H.S. Parents Assn., N.Y.C., 1993-96, sch. bd., 1993—, adv. bd. 1996—. George Welwood Murray fellow Barnard Coll., 1973. Home: 179 E 70th St New York NY 10021-5109 Office: Hebrew Union Coll-Jewish Inst Religion 1 W 4th St New York NY 10012-1105

ROSENSTEIN, BEVERLY BELLA, speech and language pathologist; b. N.Y.C., Aug. 8, 1921; d. George Solomon and Gretchen (Drucker) Gutterman; m. Solomon Nathan Rosenstein, Dec. 19, 1943; children: Roger, Dwight, Frederick, Elliott. BA, Hunter Coll., N.Y.C., 1943; postgrad., Cornell U., 1948, Montclair State U., 1966, 70, Patterson Coll., 1969. Lic. speech-lang. pathologist, N.J.; cert. tchr. English, speech arts and dramatics, N.J. On-call speech therapist Pascack Valley Hosp., Westwood, N.J., 1970-75; tchr. English, speech N.Y.C. Pub. Schs., 1947-49; tchr. speech Hunter Coll., N.Y.C., 1949; speech therapist in pvt. practice Hillsdale, N.J., 1956-66; speech pathologist No. Valley Parochial/Pub. Schs., N.J., 1966-68; speech-lang. pathologist River Dell Regional Sch. Dist., Oradell, N.J., 1968-93, Passaic County Career Ctr., Clifton, N.J., 1994-95, Norman A. Bleshman Regional Day Sch., 2000—. Advisor lit. mag. River Dell Sr. H.S., Oradell, 1980-90, girls' varsity tennis coach, 1971-93. Dir. Pascack Players, Hillsdale, 1980-84; dir., actress Bergen County Players, Oradell, 1957—; town chmn. Girl Scouts U.S., Hillsdale, 1955-59; town chmn. Citizens for Eisenhower, Hillsdale, 1953; mem. debutante cotillion com. Project HOPE, N.Y.C., 1963, 64; pres. George G. White Sch. PTA, Hillsdale, 1966-67; mem., chmn. Columia Coll. Parents Coun., 1971—. 1st lt. WAC, U.S. Army, 1943-46. Recipient Svc. to Youth award YMCA of Greater Bergen County, 1992, Cert. of Commendation Bergen County Bd. of Chosen Freeholders, 1993; inducted to Hall of Fame N.J. Scholastic Coaches Assn., 1996, Hall of Fame Alumni Assn. Hunter Coll., 1998. Mem. Am. Speech-

Lang.-Hearing Assn. (cert. Clin. competence in Speech, Lang., Pathology, 1969), Bergen County Speech-Lang.-Hearing Assn. Avocations: tennis, swimming, travel, acting, directing. Home: 32 Saddlewood Dr Hillsdale NJ 07642-1336

ROSENTHAL, EDWARD LEONARD, secondary school educator; b. Chgo., June 15, 1948; s. Irving H. and Nina (Kritchevsky) R.; m. Hilary Rosenberg, June 29, 1969; children: Rachel, Rebecca. BS in Sci. and Letters, U. Ill., 1969; MEd in Earth Sci., Northern Ill. U., 1972. Tchr. St. Joseph Sch., Dyer, Ind., 1969-70; tchr., golf coach Joliet (Ill.) Cath. High Sch., 1970-77; tchr., girls golf coach Naperville (Ill.) N. High Sch., 1977—. Chmn. United Multi Family Homeowners, Bolingbrook, Ill., 1974-75; v.p. Ill. Jr. Miss Program, Bolingbrook, 1985-87; trustee Village of Bolingbrook, 1975-81, mayor, 1981-85; bd. dirs. West Suburban Temple Har Zion, 1988-92. Named one of Outstanding Young men Am., 1975, 82, Ill. Girls' Golf Coach of Yr., 1988-89; elected to Ill. Golf Coaches Hall of Fame, 1995; recipient Disting. Svc. award, 1974. Mem. NEA, (bd. dirs. 1999—) Ill. Edn. Assn. (bd. dirs., 1992—, exec. com. 1994-98, 2001—, chmn. legis. com. 1987-90), Ill. Earth Sci. Assn., Nat. Sci. Tchrs. Assn., Ill. Girls' Golf Coaches Assn. (pres. 1985-88), Naperville Unit Edn. Assn. (1st v.p. 1990-95), Cmty. Assn. Inst. Ill. (bd. dirs. 1980-83), Ill. Jr. Golf Assn. (bd. dirs.). Jewish. Avocation: golf. Home: 508 Clover Ln Bolingbrook IL 60440-1416 Office: Naperville N High Sch 899 N Mill St Naperville IL 60563-2909 E-mail: edrosenthal@hotmail.com.

ROSENTHAL, ELEANOR, psycho-physical therapist, educator; b. N.Y.C. d. Benjamin and Jeannette Miriam (Pasachoff) R. BA in Philosophy with distinction, U. Mich.; student, Harvard U., 1961-62; JD cum laude, Columbia U., 1964; cert. in psycho-phys. therapy, Am. Ctr. Alexander Technique, 1975. Bar: N.Y. 1964, Calif. 1970. Editorial researcher NBC, N.Y.C., U.S. Steel Hour, N.Y.C.; assoc. Winthrop, Stimson, Putnam & Roberts, N.Y.C., 1964-66, Hays, Sklar & Herzberg, N.Y.C., 1966-70; atty. Bay Area Rapid Transit Dist., San Francisco, 1970-73; ind. instr. Alexander technique psycho-phys. therapy San Francisco, 1975—. Contbr. articles to profl. publs. Bd. dirs. Integrative Ctr. Culture and Healing, 1998-99. Mem. Am. Ctr. for Alexander Technique (bd. dirs. 1982-85, pres. 1982-84), Am. Soc. for Alexander Technique. Home and Office: 530 Presidio Ave San Francisco CA 94115-2423

ROSENTHAL, HILARY, secondary school educator; b. Chgo., July 10, 1948; d. Aaron Leo and Mildred Estelle (Levin) Rosenberg; m. Edward Leonard Rosenthal, June 29, 1969; children: Rachel Irene, Rebecca Stacy. BA, U. Ill., 1970; MEd, Nat.-Louis U., Evanston, Ill., 1985. Cert. tchr. social studies and English Ill. Tchr. Kahler Mid. Sch., Dyer, Ind., 1970-71, Lockport (Ill.) HS, 1971-73, 77, Downers Grove (Ill.) South HS, 1985-88; tchr., chair dept. Ill. Math. and Sci. Acad., Aurora, 1988-94; tchr. Glenbrook South HS, Glenview, Ill., 1994—. Co-dir. Glenbrook Acad. Internat. Studies; project coord. sr. project pilot program Glenbrook South HS, Glenview; mem. curriculum devel. Ill. Math. and Sci. Acad., Aurora, 1988—94, mem. strategic plan team, 1992—94; psychology exam. reader advanced placement, 1997, 2000, 01. Co-author: (pamphlet) Pub. Libr. Stds., 1987. Trustee, bd. pres. Fountaindale Pub. Libr. Dist., Bolingbrook/Romeoville, Ill., 1976—2001; chair Bolingbrook Arts Fair, 1984, 1985. Hitachi Corp. grantee, 1991, Ill. Math. and Sci. Acad. grantee, 1991, NSF Psychology Study grantee, 1994, Stratford Hall Seminar on Slavery grantee, 1997, Freeman Found. grantee, 1999. Mem.: APA, Ill. Libr. Assn., Tchg. Psychology, Ill. Coun. Social Studies (pres. 2003), Nat. Coun. Social Studies, Phi Beta Kappa. Jewish. Avocations: art collecting, travel. Home: 508 Clover Ln Bolingbrook IL 60440-1416 Office: Glenbrook South HS Glenview IL 60025 E-mail: psycho@imsa.edu.

ROSENTHAL, LEE, electrical engineer, educator; b. Bklyn., Nov. 28, 1937; s. Louis Julius and Ida (Stern) R. BSEE, Poly. Inst. N.Y., 1958, PhD in Electrical Engring., 1967; MSEE, Calif. Inst. Tech., 1959. Asst. prof. Stevens Inst. Tech., Hoboken, N.J., 1966-70, Hofstra U., Hempstead, N.Y., 1970-72; prof. Fairleigh Dickinson U., Teaneck, N.Y., 1972—. Recipient Dow Outstanding Young Faculty award Am. Soc. Engring. Edn., 1973. Home: 1185 Hoagerburgh Rd Wallkill NY 12589-3431

ROSENTHAL, MARILYN, school librarian, educator; b. Cambridge, Mass., Oct. 8, 1941; d. Edward and Helen Ruth Goldman; m. Stephen Alan Rosenthal, Apr. 11, 1964; children: Diane Wood, David. AB, Vassar Coll., 1963; MA in French, NYU, 1965; MS in Libr. Sci., Palmer Sch. Libr. and Info. Sci., 1979. Reference trainee Post Ctr. for Bus. Rsch., Brookville, NY, 1978—79; adj. reference librarian North Bellmore (N.Y.) Pub. Libr., 1979—83; adj. librarian Nassau C.C. Libr., Garden City, NY, 1983—88, instr., 1988—93, asst. prof., 1993—98, assoc. prof., reference libr., 1998—. Mem. interlibr. loan com. L.I. Libr. Coun., 1988—, chmn., 1989—95; presenter in field.; mem. adv. panel on info. literacy Mid. States Commn. on Higher Edn., 2002—; v.chmn. academic senate Nassau C.C., 1997—2001. Contbr. chapters to books, articles, revs. to profl. publs. Del. SUNY Librs. Assn. Coun., 1990—2001. Mem.: Assn. Coll. Rsch. Librs. (symposium planning com.), Assn. Coll. and Rsch. Librs. (vice chmn. L.I. sect. 1992, membership sec. 1994—2000, v.p. 2000, mem. chpts. coun. 2000—02, pres. 2001, past pres. 2002, L.I. sec. 2003), Women's Faculty Assn. Nassau C.C. (membership sec. 1993—96, pres. 1996—2000, past pres. 2000—02, recording sec. 2003—). Home: 4 Northwood Ct Woodbury NY 11797

ROSENTHAL, MICHAEL ROSS, academic administrator, consultant; b. Youngstown, Ohio, Dec. 2, 1939; s. Samuel Herman and Frances Vance (Schlesinger) R.; m. Linda Gabler, Sept. 6, 1963; children: Heidi, Erika, Nicolas Gabler. AB, Case Western Res. U., 1961; MS, U. Ill., 1963, PhD, 1965. Asst. prof. chemistry Bard Coll., Annandale, N.Y., 1965-68, assoc. prof. chemistry, 1968-73, prof. chemistry, 1973-84, assoc. dean acad. affairs, 1980-84; v.p. acad. affairs St. Mary's Coll. of Md., St. Mary's City, 1984-89; provost, dean faculty, prof. chemistry Southwestern U., Georgetown, Tex., 1989-96; dep. sec. Md. Higher Edn. Commn., Annapolis, 1996—99; spl. asst. to provost McDaniel Coll., Westminster, Md., 1999—. Acad. cons., ind. and as rep. of Assn. Am. Colls. Author or co-author of numerous articles in jours. of inorganic chemistry and chem. edn. Chmn. Environ. Mgmt. Coun., Dutchess County, N.Y., 1978-84; founding chmn. Heritage Task Force for Hudson River Valley, 1980-84; pres., bd. dirs. Hudson River Heritage, N.Y., 1978-84; bd. dirs. Hudson River Rsch. Coun., 1976-84; teaching assoc. Danforth Found., 1980. Recipient Outstanding Community Svc. award, Dutchess County (N.Y.) Legislature, 1980. Mem. Am. Chem. Soc., The Royal Society (Chemistry, London), Hudson River Environ. Soc., Sigma Xi, Phi Beta Kappa, Phi Lambda Upsilon Democrat. Office: McDaniel Coll 2 College Hill Westminster MD 21157 Business E-Mail: mrosenth@mcdaniel.edu.

ROSENTHAL, ROBERT, psychology educator; b. Giessen, Germany, Mar. 2, 1933; came to U.S., 1940, naturalized, 1946; s. Julius and Hermine (Kahn) R.; m. Mary Lu Clayton, Apr. 20, 1951; children: Roberta, David C., Virginia. AB, UCLA, 1953, PhD, 1956. Diplomate: clin. psychology Am. Bd. Examiners Profl. Psychology. Clin. psychology trainee Los Angeles Area VA, 1954-57; lectr. U. So. Calif., 1956-57; acting instr. UCLA, 1957; from asst. to assoc. prof., coordinator clin. tng. U. N.D., 1957-62; vis. assoc. prof. Ohio State U., 1960-61; lectr. Boston U., 1965-66; lectr. clin. psychology Harvard U., Cambridge, Mass., 1962-67, prof. social psychology, 1967-95, chmn. dept. psychology, 1992-95, Edgar Pierce prof. psychology, 1995-99, Edgar Pierce prof. emeritus, 1999—; disting. prof. U. Calif., Riverside, 1999—. Author: Experimenter Effects in Behavioral Research, 1966, enlarged edit., 1976; (with Lenore Jacobson) Pygmalion in the Classroom, 1968, expanded edit., 1992, Meta-analytic Procedures for Social Research, 1984, rev. edit., 1991, Judgment Studies, 1987; (with others) New Directions in Psychology 4, 1970, Sensitivity to Nonverbal Communication: The Pons Test, 1979; (with Ralph L. Rosnow) The Volunteer Subject, 1975, Primer of Methods for the Behavioral Sciences, 1975, Essentials of Behavioral Research, 1984, 2d edit., 1991, Understanding Behavioral Science, 1984, Contrast Analysis, 1985, Beginning Behavioral Research, 1993, 4th edit., 2002, People Studying People: Artifact and Ethics in Behavioral Research, 1997, (with Ralph L. Rosnow and Donald B. Rubin) Contrasts and Effect Sizes in Behavioral Research: A Correlational Approach, 2000; (with Brian Mullen) BASIC Meta-analysis, 1985; editor: (with Ralph L. Rosnow) Artifact in Behavioral Research, 1969, Skill in Nonverbal Communication, 1979, Quantitative Assessment of Research Domains, 1980, (with Thomas A. Sebeok) The Clever Hans Phenomenon: Communication With Horses, Whales, Apes and People, 1981; (with Blanck and Buck) Nonverbal Communication in the Clinical Context, 1986; (with Gheorghiu, Netter and Eysenck) Suggestion and Suggestibility: Theory and Research, 1989. Recipient Donald Campbell award Soc. for Personality and Social Psychology, 1988, James McKeen Cattell Sabbatical award, 1995-96; co-recipient Golden Anniversary Monograph award Speech Comm. Assn., 1996; named Watson lectr. U. N.H., Lanzetta Meml. lectr. Dartmouth Coll., Bayer lectr. Yale Sch. Medicine, Foa lectr. Temple U., Disting. Alumni lectr. UCLA; Guggenheim fellow, 1973-74, fellow Ctr. for Advanced Study in Behavioral Scis., 1988-89; sr. Fulbright scholar, 1972; recipient Gold Medal for Life Achievement in Sci. of Psychology Am. Psychol. Found., 2003. Fellow AAAS (co-recipient Sociopsychol. prize 1960, co-recipient Behavioral Sci. Rsch. prize 1993), APA (divsn. evaluation, measurement, and stats., co-recipient Cattell Fund award 1967, co-chmn. Task Force on Statis. Inference, Disting. Sci. award for applications of psychology, 2002, Disting. Sci. Contbns. award, 2002, divsn. evaluation, measurement and stats., others), Am. Psychol. Soc. (charter, James McKeen Cattell award 2001); mem. Soc. Exptl. Social Psychology (Disting. Scientist award 1996), Ea. Psychol. Assn. (Disting. lectr. 1989), Mid-we. Psychol. Assn., Mass. Psychol. Assn. (Disting. Career Contbn. award 1979), Soc. Projective Techniques (past treas.), Phi Beta Kappa, Sigma Xi. Home: 6985 Withers Rd Riverside CA 92506-5621 Office: U Calif LS-p Riverside CA 92521-0001

ROSENZWEIG, NORMAN, psychiatry educator administrator; b. NYC, Feb. 28, 1924; s. Jacob Arthur and Edna (Braman) R.; m. Carol Treleaven, Sept. 20, 1945; 1 child, Elizabeth Ann. MB, Chgo. Med. Sch., 1947, MD, 1948; MS, U. Mich., 1954. Diplomate Am. Bd. Psychiatry and Neurology. Asst. prof. psychiatry U. Mich., Ann Arbor, 1957-61; chmn. dept. psychiat. Sinai Hosp., Detroit, 1961-90; asst. prof. Wayne State U., Detroit, 1961—66, assoc. prof., 1967-73, prof., 1973-98, chmn. dept. psychiat. Sch. Medicine, 1987-90, prof. emeritus, 1998—. Spl. cons., profl. advisor Oakland County Community Mental Health Services Bd., 1964-65; mem. protem med. adv. panel Herman Kiefer Hosp., Detroit, 1970, psychiat. task force N.W. Quadrangle Hosps., Detroit, 1971-78, planning com. mental health adv. council Dept. Mental Health State of Mich., Lansing, 1984-90, tech. adv.rsch. com., 1978-82; psychiat. bed need task force Office Health and Med. Affairs State of Mich., 1980-84; bd. dirs. Alliance for Mental Health, Farmington Hills, Mich., 1986-94; chief psychiatry svc. USAF Hosp.; speaker in field. Author: Community Mental Health Programs in England: An American View, 1975; co-editor: Psychopharmacology and Psychotherapy-Synthesis or Antithesis?, 1978, Sex Education for the Health Professional: A Curriculum Guide, 1978; contbr. articles to profl. jours. and chpts. to books. Mem. profl. adv. bd. The Orchards, Livonia, Mich., 1963. Served as capt. USAF, 1955-57. Recipient Appreciation and Merit cert. Mich. Soc. Psychiatry and Neurology, 1970-71, Career Svc. award Assn. Mental Health in Mich., 1994. Fellow Am. Coll. Mental Health Adminstrn., Am. Coll. Psychiatrists (emeritus; hon. membership com., com. on regional ednl. programs, liaison officer to Royal Australian and New Zealand Coll. Psychiatrists 1984-88), Am. Psychiat. Assn. (disting. life fellow, coun. on internat. affairs 1970-79, chmn. 1973-76, assembly liaison to coun. on internat. affairs 1979-80, 82-84, reference com. 1973-76, nominating com. 1978-79, internat. affairs survey team 1973-74, assoc. rep. to Inter-Am. Coun. Psychiat. Assns. 1973-75, chair com. to organize 2nd Pacific Congress Psychiatry, 1978-80, treas. APA lifers 1991-94, v.p. 1994-95, pres. 1995-96, com. on sr. psychiatrists 1993-98, others, Rush Gold Medal award 1974, cert. Commendation, 1973-76, 78-80, Warren Williams award 1986); mem. AAUP, AMA (Physician's Recognition award 1971, 74, 77, 80-81, 84, 87, 90, 92), Am. Assn. Dirs. Psychiat. Residency Tng. (nominating com. 1972-74, task force on core curriculum 1972-74), Am. Assn. Gen. Hosp. Psychiatry, Puerto Rico Med. Assn. (hon., Presdl. award 1981), Am. Hosp. Assn. (governing coun. psychiat. svcs. sect. 1977-79, ad hoc com. on uniform mental health definitions, chmn. task force on psychiat. coverage under Nat. Health Ins. 1977-79, others), Brit. Soc. Clin. Psychiatrists (task force on gen. hosp. psychiatry 1969-74), Can. Psychiat. Assn., Mich. Assn. Professions, Mich. Hosp. Assn. (psychiat. and mental health svcs. com. 1979-81), Mich. Psychiat. Soc. (com. on ins. 1965-69, chmn. com. on cmty. mental health svcs. 1967-68, chmn. com. on nominations of fellows 1972-73, 94-98, com. on budget 1973-74, task force on pornography 1973-74, chmn. commn. on health professions and groups 1974-75, pres. elect 1974-75, pres. 1975-76, chmn. com. on liaison with hosp. assns. 1979-81, chmn. subcom. on liaison with Am. Hosp. Assn. 1979-81, others, Past Pres. plaque, 1978, cert. Recognition, 1980, Disting. Svc. award 1986), Mich. State Med. Soc. (vice-chmn. sect. psychiatry 1972-73, chmn. sect. psychiatry 1974-75, mem. com. to improve membership 1977-78, alt. del for Mich. Psychiat. Soc. to Ho. of Dels. 1978-79, del. from Wayne County Med. Soc. to Mich. Med. Soc. Ho. of Dels. 1982-88), NY Acad. Scis., Pan Am. Med. Assn., Wayne County Med. Soc. (com. on hosp. and prof. rels., 1983-84, com. on child health advocacy 1983-87, med. edn. com. 1983-87, mental health com. 1983-87), Royal Australian and New Zealand Coll. Psychiatrists (hon.), Indian Psychiat. Soc. (hon. corr.), World Psychiat. Assn., World Jewish Congress (pres.'s coun.) Avocations: music, films, reading. Home: 1234 Cedarholm Ln Bloomfield Hills MI 48302-0902 Office: 1234 Cedarholm Ln Bloomfield Hills MI 48302-0902

ROSETT, ANN DOYLE, librarian; b. Valdosta, Ga., Jan. 9, 1955; d. David Spencer Doyle and Lois Annette Gray; m. Robert Allen Richardson, Aug. 1, 1976 (div. June 1981); children: Caitlin Ann, Brendan Wesley; m. John David Rosett, Aug. 6, 1983. Student, Kenyon Coll., 1972-75, U. Dayton, 1974, U. Ala., Birmingham, 1978; BA, Shepherd Coll., 1982; MLS, U. Wash., 1988. Cert. profl. libr., Wash. College libr. Northwest Coll., Kirkland, Wash., 1988—. Mem. ALA, Assn. Christian Librs. (dir.-at-large 1992-93), Assn. Coll. and Rsch. Librs., Am. Theol. Lib. Assn., N.W. Assn. Christian Librs. (treas. 1989-91, pres. 1991-93). Democrat. Office: NW Coll DV Hurst Libr PO Box 579 5520 108th Ave NE Kirkland WA 98033-7523

ROSETT, ARTHUR IRWIN, lawyer, educator; b. N.Y.C., July 5, 1934; s. Milton B. and Bertha (Werner) R.; m. Rhonda K. Lawrence; children: David Benjamin, Martha Jean, Daniel Joseph. AB, Columbia U., 1955, LL.B., 1959. Bar: Calif. 1968, N.Y. State 1960, U.S. Supreme Ct. 1963. Law clk. U.S. Supreme Ct., 1959-60; asst. U.S. atty. So. Dist. N.Y., 1960-63; practice law N.Y.C., 1963-65; assoc. dir. Pres.'s Commn. on Law Enforcement and Adminstrn. Justice, 1965-67; acting prof. law UCLA, 1967-70, prof., 1970—. Author: Contract Law and Its Application, 1971, 6th edit. (with D.J. Bussell), 1999, (with D. Cressey) Justice by Consent, 1976, (with E. Dorff) A Living Tree, 1987. Served with USN, 1956-58. Mem. Am. Law Inst. Home: 641 S Saltair Ave Los Angeles CA 90049-4134 Office: UCLA Law Sch 405 Hilgard Ave Los Angeles CA 90095-1476

ROSHONG, DEE ANN DANIELS, dean, educator; b. Kansas City, Mo., Nov. 22, 1936; d. Vernon Edmund and Doradell (Kellogg) Daniels; m. Richard Lee Roshong, Aug. 27, 1960 (div.). BMusEd., U. Kans., 1958; MA in Counseling and Guidance, Stanford U., 1960; postgrad., Fresno State U., U. Calif.; EdD, U. San Francisco, 1980. Counselor, psychometrist Fresno City Coll., 1961-65; counselor, instr. psychology Chabot Coll., Hayward, Calif., 1965-75, coord. counseling svcs. Livermore, Calif., 1975-81, asst. dir. student pers. svcs., 1981-89, Las Positas Coll., Livermore, Calif., 1989-91, assoc. dean student svcs., 1991-94, dean student svcs., 1991—, life coach, 2000—. Writer, coord. I, A Woman Symposium, 1974, Feeling Free to Be You and Me symposium, 1975, All for the Family Symposium, 1976, I Celebrate Myself Symposium, 1978, Person to Person in Love and Work Symposium, 1978, The Healty Person in Mind and Spirit Symposium, 1980, Change Symposium, 1981, Sources of Strength Symposium, 1982, Love and Friendship Symposium, 1983, Self Esteem Symposium, 1984, Trust Symposium, 1985, Prime Time: Making the Most of This Time in Your Life Symposium, 1986, Symposium in Healing, 1987, How to Live in the World and Still Be Happy Symposium, 1988, Student Success is a Team Effort, Sound Mind, Sound Body Symposium, 1989, Creating Life's Best Symposium, 1990, Choices Symposium, 1991, Minding the Body, Mending the Mind Symposium, 1992, Healing through Love and Laughter Symposium, 1993, Healing Ourselves Changing the World Symposium, 1994, Finding Your Path Symposium, 1995, Build the Life You Want Symposium, 1996, Making Peace With Yourself and Your Relationships Symposium, 1997, Everyday Sacred Symposium, 1998, Wisdom of the Heart Symposium, 1999, Inner Wisdom Symposium, 2000, Second Half of Life Symposium, 2001, A Celebration of Life Symposium, 2003, others; mem. cast TV prodns. Eve and Co., Best of Our Times, Cowboy; chmn. Falling Awake Symposium, 2002, Celebration of Life Symposium, 2003, Calif. C.C. Chancellor's Task Force on Counseling, Statewide Regional Counseling Facilitators, 1993-95, Statewide Conf. Emotionally Disturbed Students in Calif. C.C.s, 1982—, Conf. on the Under Represented Student in Calif. C.C.s, 1986, Conf. on High Risk Students, 1989. Author: Counseling Needs of Comunity College Students, 1980. Bd. dirs. Teleios Sinetar Ctr., Ctr. for Cmty. Dispute Resolution, 1998—, Pleasanton Youth Collaborative Bd., 1997—, Pleasanton Youth Master Plan Bd., 1998—; choir dir., 1996-99; pres. Tri-Valley Unity Ch. bd., 1998, Tri-Valley Haven bd., 2000—, Calif. State U. at Hayward Inst. of Mental Illness and Wellness Edn. bd., 2000—, Ellis Life Coach Tng., 1999—; title III activity dir. Las Positas Coll., 1995-99, dir. pace program, 1999—, dir. quest program, 2000—. Mem.: Calif C.C. Counselors Assn. (svc. award 1986—87, award for Outstanding and Disting. Svc. 1986—87, Pleasanton Mayor's award 2000—01, 2002), Calif. Assn. C. C. (chmn. commn. on students svcs. 1979—84), Assn. Counseling and Devel., Nat. Assn. Women Deans and Counselors, Western Psychol. Assn., Assn. Humanistic Psychologists. Home: 1856 Harvest Rd Pleasanton CA 94566-5456 Office: 3033 Collier Canyon Rd Livermore CA 94550-9797 E-mail: deeroshong@comcast.net.

ROSKENS, RONALD WILLIAM, international business consultant; b. Spencer, Iowa, Dec. 11, 1932; s. William E. and Delores A.L. (Beving) R.; m. Lois Grace Lister, Aug. 22, 1954; children: Elizabeth, Barbara, Brenda, William. BA, U. No. Iowa, 1953, MA, 1955, LHD (hon.), 1985; PhD, U. Iowa, 1958; LLD (hon.), Creighton U., 1978, Huston-Tillotson Coll., 1981, Midland Luth. Coll., 1984, Hastings Coll., 1981; LittD (hon.), Nebr. Wesleyan U., 1981; PhD (hon.), Ataturk U., Turkey, 1987; LHD (hon.), U. Akron, 1987; DSc (hon.), Jayewardenepura U., Sri Lanka, 1991; LHD (hon.), Am. Coll. of Greece, Athens, 1994. Lic. min. United Ch. of Christ (Congl. and E&R). Tchr. Minburn (Iowa) High Sch., 1954, Woodward (Iowa) State Hosp., summer 1954; asst. counselor to men State U. Iowa, 1956-59; dean of men, asst. prof. spl. edn. Kent (Ohio) State U., 1959-63, assoc. prof., then prof., 1963-72, asst. to pres., 1963-66, dean for adminstrn., 1968-71, exec. v.p., prof. ednl. adminstrn., 1971-72; chancellor, prof. ednl. adminstrn. U. Nebr., Omaha, 1972-76; pres. U. Nebr. System, 1977-89, pres. emeritus, 1989; hon. prof. East China Normal U., Shanghai, 1985; adminstr. USAID, Washington, 1990-92; pres. Action Internat., Inc., Omaha, 1993-96, Global Connections, Inc., Omaha, 1996—. Interim exec. officer Omaha Pub. Libr., 1996-98; mem. Bus.-Higher Edn. Forum, 1979-89, exec. com., 1984-87; mem. govtl. relations com. Am. Council Edn., 1979-83, bd. dirs., 1981-86, vice chair, 1983-84, chair, 1984-85; chmn. com. on financing higher edn. Nat. Assn. State Univs. and Land Grant Colls., 1978-83, vice chmn. com. on financing higher edn., 1983-84, chmn. com. on fed. student fin. assistance, 1981-87; mem. nat. adv. com. on accreditation and instl. eligibility U.S. Dept. Edn., 1983-86, chmn., bd. dirs., 1986; exec. bd. North Cen. Assn., 1979-84, chmn. exec. bd., 1982-84, pres., 1989-90; active Environ. Ams. Bd., 1991-92, Strategic Command Consultation Commn., 1993-96, Nat. Exec. Res. Corps, Fed. Office Emergency Preparedness, 1968-88; chmn. Omaha/Douglas Pub. Bldg. Commn., 1996—. Co-editor: Paradox, Process and Progress, 1968; contbr. articles profl. jours. Mem. Kent City Planning Commn., 1962-66; bd. dirs. United Ch. of Christ Bd. Homeland Ministries, 1968-74, Met. YMCA, Omaha, 1973-77, Mid-Am. council Boy Scouts Am., 1973-77, Midlands United Community Services, 1972-77, NCCJ, 1974-77, Omaha Rotary Club, 1974-77, 93—, Found. Study Presdl. and Congl. Terms, 1977-89, First Plymouth Congl. Ch., 1989-90, Midland Luth. Coll., 1993—, Coun. Aid to Edn., 1985-89, ConAgra Foods, Inc., 1993—, Russian Farm Cmty. Project, Capitol Fed. Found., Topeka, Kans., 1999—; trustee Huston Tillotson Coll., Austin, Tex., 1968-81, chmn., 1976-78, Joslyn Art Mus., 1973-77, Nebr. Meth. Hosp., 1974-77, 1st Ctrl. Congregational Ch., Brownell-Talbott Sch., 1974-77, Harry S. Truman Inst., 1977-89, Willa Cather Pioneer Meml. and Ednl. Found., 1979-87; pres. Kent Area C. of C., 1966; mem. Met. Commn. Coll. Found., 1993-96; min.-in-residence Countryside Cmty. United Ch. Christ, Omaha, 2003—. Decorated comdr.'s cross Order of Merit (Germany); recipient Disting. Svc. award for community svc., Kent, Ohio, 1967, Brotherhood award NCCJ, 1977, Americanism citation B'nai B'rith, 1978, Legion of Honor, Order of DeMolay, 1980, gold medal Nat. Interfrat. Coun., 1987, Agri award Triumph Agr. Expn., Omaha, 1989; named Nat. 4-H Alumnus, 1967, Outstanding Alumnus, U. No. Iowa, 1974, Midlander of Yr., Omaha World Herald, 1977, King Ak-Sar-Ben LXXXVI, 1980; named to DeMolay Hall of Fame, 1993; named Hon. Consul Gen. of Japan, 1999. Mem. AAAS, APA, AAUP, Am. Coll. Pers. Assn., Assn. Urban Univs. (pres. 1976-77), Am. Ednl. Rsch. Assn., Coun. on Fgn. Rels., Chief Execs. Orgn., Young Pres. Orgn., Scottish Rite (bd. dirs. Omaha coun. 1999-), Lincoln C. of C. (bd. dirs. 1989-90), Masons (33 deg.), Rotary (bd. dirs. Omaha 1974-77, pres. Kent, Ohio chpt., 1970-71), Phi Delta Kappa, Phi Eta Sigma, Sigma Tau Gamma (pres. grand coun. 1968-70, Disting. Achievement award 1980, Disting. scholar 1981), Omicron Delta Kappa (nat. pres. 1986-90, Found. pres. 1986-96). Home: 10849 N 58th Plz Omaha NE 68152

ROSNER, ANTHONY LEOPOLD, research director, biochemist; b. Greensboro, N.C., Nov. 13, 1943; s. Albert Aaron and Elsie Augustine (Lincoln) R.; m. Ruth Francis Marks, June 19, 1966; 1 child, Rachael. BS, Haverford Coll., 1966; PhD, Harvard U., 1972; LLD, Nat. U. Health Scis., 2002. Staff fellow NIH-NINDS, Bethesda, Md., 1972-74; gen. dir. Receptor Lab. Beth Israel Hosp., Boston, 1976-83, tech. dir. Chem. Lab., 1981-83; tech. dir. New Eng. Pathology Svcs., Wilmington, Mass., 1983-86, cons., 1986-96; dept. adminstr. Brandeis U., Waltham, Mass., 1986-91; rsch. ops. mgr. in newborn medicine Children's Hosp., 1991-92; dir. rsch. and edn. Found. for Chiropractic Edn. and Rsch., Brookline, Mass., 1992—; cons. Ctr. for Alternative Medicine Beth Israel Hosp., Boston, 1996—. Vis. fellow Lab. Molecular Biology, CNRS, Gif-sur-Yvette, France, 1973. Assoc. editor: Jour. Manipulative and Physiol. Therapeutics, mem. editl. bd.:, 1993—, assoc. editor: Jour. Neuromusculoskeletal Sys., —, sect. editor:, 1993—, mem. adv. bd.: Alternative Therapies in Health and Medicine, 1994—; contbr. numerous articles to profl. jours., papers on status of chiropractic rsch. and efficacy, design and interpretive problems in clin. rsch., spontaneous dissection and structure of vertebral arteries. Testified before various fed. agencies and state legis. regarding status of chiropractic rsch. and efficacy of treatment. Harvard U. fellow, 1966; recipient Humanitarian of Yr. award Am. Chiropractic Assn., 2000. Mem. AAAS, APHA, Am. Chem. Soc. (auditor N.E. chpt. 1990—), Internat. Assn. for Study of Pain, Am. Assn. Integrative Medicine, N.Y. Acad. Scis., Clin. Ligand Assay Soc., Am. Back Soc. Democrat. Jewish. Achievements include identification of meso-diaminopimelic acid for the first time in any organism as an allosteric feedback inhibitor (affecting aspartokinase activity); development of new radioligand assay for measuring estrogen receptor, about 10 times more sensitive and rapid than other methodologies; provision of evidence showing negative cooperativity of binding to estrogen receptor; convening of international workshops to develop a chiropractic research agenda; initiation and coordination of research efforts pertaining to chiropractic science and healthcare worldwide; review of misinterpretations, misuses, and abuses of randomized clinical trials. Home: 1443 Beacon St Apt 201 Brookline MA 02446-4709 Office: Found for Chiropractic Edn and Rsch 1330 Beacon St Ste 315 Brookline MA 02446-3202 E-mail: rosnerfcer@aol.com.

ROSNER, DIANE A. academic administrator; b. New Haven, July 21, 1949; d. William A. and Clarice (Podheiser) Alderman; (div. May 1990); children: Jason E., Matthew L. BA, Clark U., 1970; MS, So. Conn. State U., 1984, profl. diploma, 1989. Lic. counselor, Conn. Asst. dir. coll. achievement program So. Conn. State U., New Haven, 1982-83, dir. coll. achievement program, 1983-86, coord. ednl. and summer ednl. opportunity program, 1986—, asst. dir. student support svcs., 1986—. Mem. univ. retention com. So. Conn. State U., 1983-84, mem. task force on racism, 1989, coord. stress opposition series, 1990-91, univ. assessment com., 1991—, chairperson subcom. on retention, 1991—. Author: (handbook) Surviving! A Handbook for College Survival, 1985. Mem. PTA. Mem. Am. Coll. Pers. Assn., Am. Counseling Assn., Nat. Coun. Ednl. Opportunity Assns., Conn. Assn. Ednl. Opportunity Programs, Conn. Coll. Pers. Assn., Nat. Acad. Advising Assn., New Eng. Assn. Ednl. Opportunity Program Pers. Avocations: painting, drawing, music. Home: 1008 Rainbow Trl Orange CT 06477-1041 Office: So Conn State U 501 Crescent St New Haven CT 06515-1330

ROSOF, PATRICIA J.F. retired secondary education educator; b. N.Y.C., May 19, 1949; d. Sylvan D. and Charlotte (Fischer) Freeman; m. Alan H. Rosof, Sept. 13, 1970; children: Jeremy, Simon, Ali. BA, NYU, 1970, MA, 1971, PhD, 1978. Cert. tchr. social studies, N.Y. Instr. history Iona Coll., New Rochelle, N.Y., 1978-81; tchr. social studies Profl. Children's Sch., N.Y.C., 1981-82, Hunter Coll. H.S., N.Y.C., 1984—2003; ret., 2003. European history reader Advanced Placement Ednl. Testing Svcs.; adj. asst. prof. Sch. Edn., Pace U., 2003. Co-editor Trends in History, 1978-84, Hunter Outreach, 1988-92; contbr. articles to profl. jours. Internat. Cultural Soc. Korea fellow, 1989; CUNY Women's Rsch. and Devel. Fund grantee, 1993-95. Mem. Am. Hist. Assn., Orgn. History Tchrs. Avocations: tennis, attending concerts, shows and dance performances.

ROSOFF, BARBARA LEE, religious education administrator; b. Chgo., Apr. 14, 1936; d. Ben Zion and Ruth Gwendolyn (Daniels) Ginsburg; m. Jack Rosoff, June 18, 1957; children: Ranana, Aviva, Joshua. AB cum laude, Brandeis U., 1957; MA in Teaching summa cum laude, Monmouth Coll., 1977; EdD, Rutgers U., 1990. Lic. early childhood-nursery sch. tchr., elem. tchr., N.J.; lic. tchr. and rpin. Nat. Bd. Lic. of Jewish Edn. Svc. N.Am. Supr. Congregation B'nai Israel Religious Sch., Rumson, N.J., 1965-78, dir. edn., 1978—. Condr. seminars and workshops in field; mem. Jewish Educators' Assembly, United Synagogue Commn. on Jewish Edn.; ednl cons. Behrman House Pub. Co., West Orange, N.J., 1985—; instr. religious edn. Monmouth Coll. Grad. Sch. Edn., West Long Branch, N.J., 1976-77; prin., tchr. trainer Solomon Schecter Sch., Marlboro, N.J., 1979-81; mem. part-time faculty Rutgers U., New Brunswick, N.J., 1986-92, Fairleigh Dickinson U., Teaneck, N.J., 1991; instr., lectr. United Synagogue Tchr. Tng., N.Y.C., 1991—. Editor Coalition for the Advancement of Jewsih Education jour., 1994—; contbr. articles to profl. pubs. Guiding mem. Interfaith Cmty. Coun., Rumson, 1992—. Mem. Phi Delta Kappa, Kappa Delta Pi. Avocations: swimming, yoga. Office: Congregation B'nai Israel Rumson NJ 07760 Home: 36 Kentucky Way Freehold NJ 07728-4637

ROSS, ANN DUNBAR, secondary school educator; b. Longview, Tex., Jan. 21, 1945; d. Louie and Myra Lee (Fanning) Dunbar; m. John Reuben Ross, Sept. 9, 1967; children: Jennifer Ann, John Byron. BA in Math., U. Tex., 1968; M in Liberal Arts, So. Meth. U., 1974; Endorsement in Gifted Edn., U. North Tex., 1992. Tchr. math., Dallas, 1968-72, Duncanville (Tex.) High Sch., 1979-89; tchr. math., dept. chairperson Duncanville Ninth Grade Sch., 1989—. Vertical team mem. Math. Dept. Duncanville High Sch., 1993—; site based mgmt. mem. Duncanville Ninth Grade Sch., 1993; presenter in field at math. conf. Mem. Tex. Fedn. Tchrs. Avocation: ceramics.

ROSS, BRENDA MARIE, elementary school educator; b. New Orleans, May 5, 1944; d. Leslie Carl and Dorothy Marie (McElroy) R. BS, La. State U., 1968, cert. in gifted teaching, 1985. With Orleans Parish Schs., New Orleans, 1968-70, 1970—. Mem. Internat. Reading Assn., Nat. Acad. Games, Assn. for Gifted and Talented Students, New Orleans Acad. Games League, Greater New Orleans Tchrs. of Math., La. Assn. Tchrs. of Math., Delta Kappa Gamma (Pi chpt.). Republican. Episcopalian. Office: Claiborne Sch 4617 Mirabeau Ave New Orleans LA 70126-3540

ROSS, CONNIE L. music educator; b. Pratt, Ks., Nov. 5, 1952; d. Eugene Haile and Alta Ross. BA, Mid-Am. Nazarene U., 1975; MusM in Edn., Fort Hays State U., 2003. Vocal music tchr. USD 483, 1975—82; elem. vocal music tchr. USD 443, Dodge City, Kans., 1982—2003. Pvt. piano tchr. Ch. pianist & accompanist. Mem.: NEA, Music Edn. Nat. Conf., Delta Kappa Gamma (co-chmn. music com.). Home: 2805 Buffalo Dr Dodge City KS 67801

ROSS, DONALD, JR., English language educator, university administrator; b. N.Y.C., Oct. 18, 1941; s. Donald and Lea (Meyer) R.; m. Sylvia Berger (div.); 1 child, Jessica; m. 2d, Diane Redfern, Aug. 27, 1971; children— Owen, Gillian BA, Lehigh U., 1963, MA, 1964; PhD, U. Mich., 1967. Asst. prof. English U. Pa., Phila., 1967—70; prof. English U. Minn., Mpls., 1970—, dir. composition program, 1982—86, 2002—03, dir. Univ. Coll., 1984—89. Author: American History and Culture from the Explorers to Cable TV, 2000; co-author: Word Processor and Writing Process, 1984, Revising Mythologies: The Composition of Thoreau's Major Works, 1988; co-editor, contbr.: American Travel Writers, 1776-1865, 1997, American Travel Writers, 1850-1915, 1998; contbr. articles to profl. jours. Grantee Am. Coun. Learned Socs., 1976, 90, NSF, 1974, Fund for Improvement of Postsecondary Edn., 1982-85; recipient Disting. Teaching award U. Minn., 1992. Mem. MLA, Assn. for Computers and Humanities (exec. sec. 1978-88), Internat. Soc. for Travel Writing (exec. sec. 2001—). Office: U Minn Dept English 207 Lind Hall 207 Church St SE Minneapolis MN 55455-0152 E-mail: rossj001@umn.edu.

ROSS, DONNA FAYE, educational administrator; b. Wabash, Ark., Oct. 19, 1958; d. Wash Ross and Rosie Lee (Wallace) Williams. BS in Edn., U. Ark., 1980, MEd, 1982. Cert. prin. Ark. 1990. Tchr. Pine Bluff (Ark.) Schs., 1980-82, United World LEarning Ctr., L.A., 1982-84, Lakeview (Ark.) Elem. Sch., 1984-85; tchr. West Side Elem. Sch., 1985-91, vice prin., 1991-93, asst. prin., adminstrv. asst. to supt. for elem. programs, 1993—, assoc. dir. RISE/MOVE program, summer 1988. Tchr. adult edn. Phillips County C.C., Helena, Ark., 1987-89; coord. teen pregnancy intervention program, Pine Bluff, 1980-82; mem. pers. policy com. Helena-West Helena Schs., 1988-91, adv. com. West Side Sch., 1987-93, multicultural com., 1990-92, equity com., 1990-92. Co-author: Multicultural Curriculum Guide, 1982. Active Drug Awareness-Teens Coaching Kids, summer 1990. Recipient Sports Illustrated for Kids-5 Year award, West Side Sch., 1993; grantee Ea. Ark. Private Industry Coun., Inc., 1988. Mem. NEA, ASCD, Ark. Edn. Assn. (election com. 1992-93), Ark. Assn. Edn. Adminstrs., Classroom Tchrs. Assn., APPLE Program (lang. component 1984-85), Alpha Kappa Alpha. Democrat. Baptist. Avocations: reading, tutoring kids, travel. Home: Rt 1 Box 558-E Helena AR 72342 Office: West Side Sch 339 S Ashlar St West Helena AR 72390-3401

ROSS, DOUGLAS, lawyer; b. L.A., July 12, 1948; s. Mathew and Brenda Butler (Boynton) R.; m. Lynne Rose Maidman, June 14, 1970. AB cum laude, Tufts U., 1970; JD with honors, George Washington U., 1973. Bar: Ohio 1973, D.C. 1980, U.S. Supreme Ct. 1976. Asst. atty. gen., antitrust sect. Office of Ohio Atty. Gen., Columbus, 1973-74; spl. asst. U.S. atty. Ea. Dist. Va., Alexandria, 1977; trial atty. antitrust divsn. U.S. Dept. Justice, Washington, 1975-82; atty. advisor Office of Legis. Affairs, 1984-86, Office of Legal Policy, 1987-89, Office Policy Devel., 1989-92; Supreme Ct. counsel Nat. Assn. Attys. Gen., 1982-91. Ran advocacy project for states to enhance their effectiveness before Supreme Ct., 1982—91; operated clearinghouse on state constl. law, 1987—91; civil divsn. Appellate Staff U.S. Dept. Justice, Washington, 1992—94, Office of Consumer Litigation, 1994—2000, spl. counsel for agr. antitrust divsn., 2000—. Recipient Meritorious award Dept. Justice, 1979, Spl. Achievement award, 1984, 96, 97. Mem. Supreme Ct. Hist. Soc., D.C. Bar Assn., Supreme Ct. Opinion Network (bd. dirs. 1989-91), Arlington County Sports Commn. (chair subcom. on swimming pools 1995—). Jewish. Home: 3153 19th St N Arlington VA 22201-5103 Office: US Dept Justice 601 D St NW Washington DC 20530-0001

ROSS, ELGENIA RUTH SNIPES, art educator; b. Winston-Salem, N.C., July 3, 1940; d. Carl Homer and Elsie Beatrice (Berry) Snipes; m. James Asbury Ross, Jr., Oct. 10, 1965; children: Kimberly McCall, Molly Shannon. BA, Furman U., 1962; MS, Parson's Sch. Design/Bank St. Coll., 1991. Cert. art specialist, art supr. Tchr. North Charleston (S.C.) High Sch., 1963-65, Monticello (Ark.) High Sch., 1979-94. Regional bd. dirs. Mus. Women in Arts, 1991; adj. instr. U. Ark., Monticello, 1993; mem. panel tchr. licensure task force Ark. Dept. Edn., Little Rock, 1994, fine arts framework com., 1994. Exhibited in group shows including Pine Art Show, Monticello, 1989-94, Mus. Women in Arts, 1990, U. Ark., Monticello, 1993. Bd. dirs. Ark. Endowment Humanities, 1980-83; founding mem., bd. dirs. Ark. Women's History Inst., Little Rock, 1983-86. Mem. Nat. Art Educators Assn., Ark. Art Educators Assn. (sec. exec. bd. coun. 1992-94, membership chmn. 1994-96, pres.-elect 1996-98, pres. 1998-2000, Secondary Educator of Yr. 1994, Ark. Art Educator of Yr. 1998), S.E. Ark. Concert Assn. (bd. dirs. 1973-76, 89-94), Monticello Women's Investment Club (sec. 1992-94, pres. 2000-2002), Monticello Art League (founder, pres. 1989), Delta Kappa Gamma. Home: 267 Mason Hill Rd Monticello AR 71657-0209 Address: PO Box 209 Monticello AR 71657

ROSS, JAMES ROBERT, physical education educator; b. Franklin, N.H., June 10, 1961; s. Robert John and Doria A. (Bilodeau) R.; m. Theresa Quinn, June 26, 1987; children: Gregory Robert, Brian James. BS in Phys. Edn. cum laude, Springfield (Mass.) Coll., 1983, MS, 1992. Tchr. phys. edn. Cobleskill (N.Y.) Pub. Schs., 1983-87, Ridgewood (N.J.) Pub. Schs., 1988—. Football, basketball, baseball and soccer coach, Cobleskill, 1983—87; asst. dir. Lake George (N.Y.) Youth Commn. Summer Recreation Program, 1983—93; conf. coord. Lake Conf. for K-8 Phys. Edn., NJ, 1990—2000; workshop presenter in field. Contbr. articles to profl. jours. Coord. Orchard Sch. Fundraiser, 1994—, Save Your Head Day, 1989—94, Jump Rope for Heart, 1986—87, 1991—; clinician, program cons. Ridgewood Soccer Assn., Ridgewood Biddy Basketball, Ridgewood Spl. Needs Basketball; commr. Cobleskill Flag Football League; umpire Lake George Youth Commn. Softball/Baseball, 1983—93; Jingle Bell Program, 1995—. Mem.: NEA, AAHPERD-EDA (Elem. Phys. Edn. Tchr. of Yr. 1995), Bergen County Women's Coaches Assn. (Basketball Coach of Yr. 1998), N.J. Edn. Assn., Bergen County Coaches Assn., N.J. Alliance for Health, Phys. Edn., Recreation and Dance (v.p. phys. edn. 1992—94, program chair 1991—94, Elem. Tchr. of Yr. 1993, Presdl. citation for oustanding svc. 1991—92, 1994, Outstanding Tchr. award 1993). Avocations: swimming, hiking, golf, music, basketball. Home: 49 Saratoga Dr Oakland NJ 07436-2209 Office: Orchard Sch 230 Demarest St Ridgewood NJ 07450-4298

ROSS, JAMES ULRIC, lawyer, accountant, educator; b. Del Rio, Tex., Sept. 14, 1941; s. Stephen Mabrey and Beatrice Jessie (Hyslop) R.; m. Janet S. Calabro, Dec. 28, 1986; children: James Ulric Jr., Ashley Meredith. BA, U. Tex., 1963, JD, 1965. Bar: Tex. 1965, U.S. Tax Ct. 1969; CPA, Tex. Estate tax examiner IRS, Houston, 1965-66; tax acct. Holmes, Raquet, Harris & Shaw, San Antonio, 1966-67; pvt. practice law and acctg. Del Rio and San Antonio, Tex., 1968—. Instr. St. Mary's U., San Antonio, 1973-75; assoc. prof. U. Tex., San Antonio, 1975-99, ret. Contbr. articles on U.S. and Internat. Estate Planning and Taxation to legal and profl. jours. Active Am. Cancer Soc., Residential Mgmt., Inc., Am. Heart Assn. Mem. ABA, Tex. Bar Assn., Tex. Soc. CPAs, San Antonion Bar Assn., San Antonio Estate Planners Coun. Home: 3047 Orchard Hl San Antonio TX 78230-3078 Office: 760 Tex Commerce Bank Bldg 7550 IH 10 W San Antonio TX 78229-5803

ROSS, JANE ARLENE, music educator; b. Uniontown, Pa., July 19, 1945; d. Earl Frank Diamond and Iva Jane Gower; m. Orval Jones Ross, June 17, 1967; 1 child, Elizabeth Jane. BS in Music Edn., Indiana U. of Pa., 1967; MusM in Music Edn., U. Akron, 1985, postgrad., Oberlin Coll., Ashland U. Music tchr. - elem. Fairview Park (Ohio) City Schs., 1967—70; music tchr.-jr. h.s. Medina (Ohio) City Schs., 1970—76, music tchr. - elem., 1979—2000; adj. prof. Ashland (Ohio) U., 2001—. Handbell choir cons. various area chs., Medina, 1994—99; guest clinician U. Akron, Ohio, 1986, Medina Coutny Schs., 1990; curriculum writer Medina City Schs., 1973. Contbr. articles to profl. jours. Organist, choir dir. United Ch. of Christ, Congl., Medina, 1972—79, Mt. Zwingli United Ch. of Christ, Wadsworth, Ohio, 1983—93; dir. music ministries First Christian Ch., Wadsworth, 2001—. Grantee, Rockefeller Bros. Fund, N.Y.C., 1984; scholar, Martha Holden Jennings Found., Cleve., 1988. Mem.: Am. Guild Organists, Am. Guild English Handbell Ringers, Music Educators Nat. Conf., Medina County Ret. Tchrs. Assn. (life), Ohio Ret. Tchrs. Assn. (life), Kappa Delta Pi, Delta Omicron (life). Democrat. Avocations: reading, collecting bells, old hymnals and music boxes, needlework, travel. Office: First Christian Ch 116 E Boyer St Wadsworth OH 44281 Fax: 330-336-2099. E-mail: jross@neo.rr.com.

ROSS, JANINE, elementary education educator; b. Detroit, June 5, 1945; d. Peter J. and Evelyn (Stowell) Jensen; m. Michael F. Ross, Apr. 7, 1973; children: Neil, Daniel. BSEd, U. Nebr., 1967; MSEd, Wayne State U., Detroit, 1973; postgrad., U. Nev., Las Vegas. Tchr. 2nd and 4th grades Cherry Hill Sch., Inkster, Mich., 1967-78; literacy Specialist William K. Moore Elem. Sch., Las Vegas, Nev., 1978—. V.p. RIP Coun. Clark County; mem. Las Vegas (Nev.) Reading Coun. Mem. Internat. Reading Assn.(Las Vegas coun.), Nev. Reading Edn. Assn. (grantee), Delta Omicron, Sigma Kappa (alumnae), Phi Delta Kappa. Office: Moore Elementary School 491 N Lamb Blvd Las Vegas NV 89110

ROSS, JEAN LOUISE, physical education educator; b. Lebanon, Pa., June 20, 1951; d. Jonas John and Eloise Mary (Miller) Walmer; m. Edward Richard Ross, Nov. 10, 1978; 1 child, Aaron Edward. BS in Health and Phys. Edn., West Chester U., 1973; MS in Phys. Edn., Pa. State U., 1979; MSEd in Counseling Psychology, St. Bonaventure U., 1992. Health and phys. edn. tchr. Lower Dauphin Sch. dist., Hummelstown, Pa., 1973-78; health and phys. edn. tchr., mentor tchr. Bradford Area Sch. Dist., Pa., 1978-80, health and phys. edn. tchr., 1986—; in-home edn. specialist SCAN/PEP Program, The Guidance Ctr., Bradford, 1985-86. Recipient mini-grants Rotary Club of Bradford, 1984, 86-88, 93, 95, 97. Mem. NEA, AAHPERD, Pa. State Edn. Assn., Bradford Area Edn. Assn., Pa. State Alliance Health, Phys. Edn., Recreation and Dance. Democrat. Avocations: recreational activities, sewing, knitting, rollerblading, mountain biking. Office: Fretz Middle Sch 140 Lorana Ave Bradford PA 16701-1831

ROSS, JOAN STUART, artist, art educator; b. Boston, Sept. 21, 1942; d. John Stuart and Lulu Margery (Nelson) Ross. BA, Conn. Coll., 1964; postgrad., Yale U., 1964-65; MA, U. Iowa, 1967, MFA, 1968; Advanced Cert. in Poetry, U. Wash., 1996. Cert. tchr., Wash. Instr. painting, printmaking Seattle Art Mus., 1992, Edmonds (Wash.) C.C., 1992-96, Pratt Fine Arts Ctr., Seattle, 1992-96, North Seattle C.C., 1996—. Mem. artist in city program Seattle Arts Commn., 1979-81, New Proposals program King County Arts Commn., 1977, 80. One-person shows include Seattle (Wash.) Art Mus., 1981, 82, Karl Bornstein Gallery, Santa Monica, 1982, Surrey (B.C., Can.) Art Gallery, 1982, Seattle Art Mus., 1981, 82, Lawrence Gallery, Portland, Oreg., 1987, 88, Foster/White Gallery, Seattle, 1981, 83, 85, 87, 89, 90, Skagit Valley Coll., Mt. Vernon, Wash., 1990, Green River C.C., Auburn, Wash., 1985, 90, 1004 Gallery, Port Townsend, Wash., 1993, Grover/Thurston Gallery, Seattle, 1991, 93, 95, Friesen Gallery, Seattle, 1997, also others; exhibited in more than 200 group and juried shows. Mem. Bumbershoot Festival Commn., Seattle, 1985-91; mem. Seattle Arts Commn., 1981-85; bd. dirs. Northwest Women's Caucus for Arts. Recipient Betty Bowen award Seattle Art Mus., 1981. Mem. N.W. Print Coun. (charter), Seattle Print Arts, Book Arts Guild, N.W. Inst. for Architecture and Urban Studies in Italy (Rome fellow 1993).

ROSS, JOHN, JR., cardiologist, educator; b. N.Y.C., Dec. 1, 1928; s. John and Janet (Moulder) R.; children: Sydnie, John, Duncan; m. Lola Romanucci, Aug. 26, 1972; children: Adan, Deborah Lee. AB, Dartmouth Coll., 1951; MD, Cornell U., 1955. Intern Johns Hopkins Hosp., 1955—56; resident Columbia-Presbyn. Med. Center, N.Y.C., 1960—61, N.Y. Hosp.-Cornell U. Med. center, 1961—62; chief sect. cardiovascular diagnosis cardiology br. Nat. Heart Inst., Bethesda, Md., 1962—68; prof. medicine U. Calif., San Diego, 1968—2000, also dir. cardiovascular div., 1968—91, rsch. prof. medicine, 2000—; prof. cardiovascular research Am. Heart Assn. San Diego Co. Affiliate, San Diego, 1986—99. Mem. cardiology adv. com. Nat. Heart, Lung and Blood Inst., 1975-78, task force on arteriosclerosis, 1978-80, adv. council, 1980-84; bd. dirs. San Diego Heart Assn.; vis. prof. Brit. Heart Assn., 1990. Author: Mechanisms of Contraction of the Normal and Failing Heart, 1968, 76, Understanding the Heart and Its Diseases, 1976; mem. editorial bd. Circulation, 1967-75, 80-88, editor in chief 1988-93, Circulation Research, 1971-75, Am. Jour. Physiology, 1968-73, Annals of Internal Medicine, 1974-78, Am. Jour. Cardiology, 1974-79, 83-88, JOur. Clin. Investigation, 1992-97, Italian Heart Jour., 1999—, JOur. Cardiac Failure, 2000—, Circulation JOur. Japan, 2000—; cons. editor Circulation, 1993—; contbr. chpts. to books, sci. articles to profl. jours. Served as surgeon USPHS, 1956-63. Recipient Ing. Enzo Ferrari prize for Enzo Ferrari, Modena, Italy, 1989, James B. Herrick award Coun. Clin. Cardiology Am. Heart Assn., 1990, Grande Ufficiale Order of Merit Republic of Italy, 1998. Fellow Am. Coll. Cardiology (master 1998—, v.p. trustee, pres. 1986-87, Disting. Scientist award 1990), ACP; mem. Am. Soc. Clin. Investigation (councillor), Am. Physiol. Soc., Assn. Am. Physicians, Cardiac Muscle Soc., Assn. Univ. Cardiologists, Assn. West. Physicians (councillor). Home: 8599 Prestwick Dr La Jolla CA 92037-2025 Office: U Calif Dept Med M # 0613B San Diego CA 92093

ROSS, JOHN, physical chemist, educator; b. Vienna, Oct. 2, 1926; arrived in U.S., 1940; s. Mark and Anna (Krecmar) Ross; m. Virginia Franklin (div.); children: Elizabeth A., Robert K.; m. Eva Madarasz. BS, Queens Coll., 1948; PhD, MIT, 1951; D (hon.), Weizmann Inst. Sci., Rehovot, Israel, 1984, Queens Coll., SUNY, 1987, U. Bordeaux, France, 1987. Prof. chemistry Brown U., Providence, 1953—66, MIT, Cambridge, 1966—80, chmn. dept., 1966—71, chmn. faculty of Inst., 1975—77; prof. Stanford (Calif.) U., 1980—2001, chmn. dept., 1983—89, prof. emeritus, 2001—. Cons. to industries; mem. emeritus bd. govs. Weizmann Inst., 1971—. Author: Physical Chemistry, 1980, Physical Chemistry, 2d edit., 2000; editor: Molecular Beams, 1966; contbr. articles to profl. jours. 2nd lt. U.S. Army, 1944—46. Recipient medal, Coll. de France, Paris, Presdl. Nat. Medal of Sci., 1999, Austrian Cross of Honor for Sci. and Art, 1st class, 2002. Fellow: AAAS, Am. Phys. Soc.; mem.: NAS, Am. Chem. Soc. (Irving Langmuir Chem. Physics prize 1992, Peter Debye award in phys. chemistry 2001), Am. Acad. Arts and Sci. Home: 738 Mayfield Ave Palo Alto CA 94305-1044 Office: Stanford U Dept Chemistry Stanford CA 94305-5080 E-mail: john.ross@stanford.edu.

ROSS, JOSEPH COMER, physician, educator, academic administrator; b. Tompkinsville, Ky., June 16, 1927; s. Joseph M. and Annie (Pinckley) R.; m. Isabelle Nevins, June 15, 1952; children: Laura Ann, Sharon Lynn, Jennifer Jo, Mary Martha, Jefferson Arthur. BS, U. Ky., 1950; MD, Vanderbilt U., 1954. Diplomate Am. Bd. Internal Medicine (bd. govs. 1975-81), with added qualifications in pulmonary disease. Intern Vanderbilt U. Hosp., Nashville, 1954-55; resident Duke U. Hosp., Durham, N.C., 1955-57, rsch. fellow, 1957-58; from instr. medicine to prof. Ind. U. Sch. Medicine, Indpls., 1958-70; prof., chmn. dept. medicine Med. U. of S.C., Charleston, 1970-80; vis. prof. Vanderbilt U. Sch. Medicine, Nashville, 1979-80, prof. medicine, 1981-99, prof. medicine emeritus, 1999—, assoc. vice chancellor for health affairs, 1982-99, assoc. vice chancellor for health affairs emeritus, 1999—. Mem. cardiovascular study sect. NIH, 1966-70, program project com., 1971-75; mem. adv. coun. Nat. Heart, Lung and Blood Inst., 1982-86; mem. ad hoc coms. NAS, 1966, 67; mem. Pres.'s Nat. Adv. Panel on Heart Disease, 1972; mem. merit rev. bd. in respiration VA Rsch. Svc., 1972-76, chmn., 1974-76. Mem. editorial bd. Jour. Lab. and Clin. Medicine, 1964-70, Chest, 1968-73, Jour. Applied Physiology,1968-73, Archives of Internal Medicine, 1976-82, Heart and Lung, 1977-86; contbr. articles to profl. jours. Bd. dirs. Nashville Ronald McDonald Ho., past pres.; bd. dirs. Agape, Leadership Nashville, v.p.; mem. adv. com. Davidson County Cmty. Health Agy.; active Tenn. Lung Assn.; elder Ch. of Christ. With U.S. Army, 1945—47. Fellow: ACP, Am. Coll. Cardiology, Am. Coll. Chest Physicians (gov. S.C. 1970—76, chmn. sci. program com. 1973, vice chmn. bd. govs. 1974—75, exec. coun. 1974—80, chmn. bd. govs. 1975—76, pres.-elect 1976—77, pres. 1977—78, chmn. by-laws com. 2002—04, bd. regents 2002—04); mem.: AMA (sect. on med. schs.), Am. Soc. Internal Medicine, So. Soc. Clin. Rsch., Am. Thoracic Soc. (nat. councillor 1972—76), S.C. Med. Soc., Ctr. Social Clin. Rsch., Assn. Profs. Medicine, Assn. Am. Physicians, Am. Soc. Clin. Investigatrion, Am. Physiol. Soc., Am. Fedn. Clin. Rsch. (chmn. Midwest sect.), S.C. Lung Assn. (v.p. 1974—75), Phi Beta Kappa, Alpha Omega Alpha. Office: Vanderbilt U Med Ctr Oxford House Ste 212 Nashville TN 37232-0001 E-mail: joseph.ross@comcast.net., joseph.ross@vanderbiltmcmail.edu.

ROSS, KATHLEEN, elementary and secondary school educator, author; b. New Orleans, July 5, 1948; d. William H. and Marilyn (Shoop) R.; m. Thomas Warren, Nov. 10, 1979. BS, U. New Orleans, 1971; MST, Loyola U., New Orleans, 1973. Cert. math. tchr., prin., adminstr., supr., supr. student tchrs. Math. cons. Jefferson Parish Pub. Sch. Sys., Harvey, 1971—91; cons. Digi-Block, LLD, 2000—. Instr. La. systemic initiative project program Loyola U., 1991-97; cons., author Scott-Foresman Pub., 1991-98. Mem. ASCD, Nat. Coun. Tchrs. Math., Nat. Coun. Suprs. Math., La. Tchrs. Math., Greater New Orleans Tchrs. Math., Textbook Authors Assn., Tex. Tchrs. Math., Oreg. Tchrs. Math., La. Coun. Suprs. Math., Phi Delta Kappa. Home: 3900 S Inwood Ave New Orleans LA 70131-8456

ROSS, KATHLEEN ANNE, college president; b. Palo Alto, Calif., July 1, 1941; d. William Andrew and Mary Alberta (Wilburn) Ross. BA, Ft. Wright Coll., 1964; MA, Georgetown U., 1971; PhD, Claremont Grad. U., 1979; LLD (hon.), Alverno Coll. Milw., 1990, Dartmouth Coll., 1991, Seattle U., 1992; LHD (hon.), Whitworth Coll., 1992; LLD (hon.), Pomona Coll., 1993; LHD (hon.), Coll. of New Rochelle, 1998; LLD (hon.), U. Notre Dame, 1999, Gonzaga U., 1999; LHD (hon.), Carroll Coll., 2003. Cert.

tchr., Wash. Secondary tchr. Holy Names Acad., Spokane, Wash., 1964-70; dir. rsch. and planning Province Holy Names, Wash. State, 1972-73; v.p. acads. Ft. Wright Coll., Spokane, 1973-81; rsch. asst. to dean Claremont Grad. Sch., Calif., 1977-78; assoc. faculty mem. Harvard U., Cambridge, Mass., 1981; pres. Heritage Coll., Toppenish, Wash., 1981—. Cons. Wash. State Holy Names Schs., 1971-73; coll. accrediting assn. evaluator N.W. Assn. Schs. and Colls., Seattle, 1975—; dir. Holy Names Coll., Oakland, Calif., 1979—; cons. Yakama Indian Nation, Toppenish, 1975—; speaker, cons. in field. Author: (with others) Multicultural Pre-School Curriculum, 1977, A Crucial Agenda: Improving Minority Student Success, 1989; Cultural Factors in Success of American Indian Students in Higher Education, 1978. Chmn. Internat. 5-Yr. Convocation of Sisters of Holy Names, Montreal, 1981, 96; TV Talk show host Spokane Coun. of Chs., 1974-76; mem. Nat. Congl. Adv. Com. on Student Fin. Assistance, 2002—. Named Yakima Herald Rep. Person of Yr., 1987, MacArthur fellow, 1997; recipient E.K. and Lillian F. Bishop Founds. Youth Leader of Yr. award, 1986, Disting. Citizenship Alumna award, Claremont Grad. Sch., 1986, Golden Aztec award, Wash. Human Devel., 1989, Harold W. McGraw Edn. prize, 1989, John Carroll awrd, Georgetown U., 1991, Holy Names medal, Ft. Wright Coll., 1981, Pres.'s medal, Estern Wash. U., 1994, First Ann. Leadership award, Region VIII Coun. Advancement and Support Edn., 1993, Wash. State Medal of Merit, 1995, Lifetime Achievement award, Yakima YWCA, 2001, numerous grants for projects in multicultural higher edn., 1974—. Mem. Nat. Assn. Ind. Colls. and Univs., Soc. Intercultural Edn., Tng. and Rsch., Sisters of Holy Names of Jesus and Mary-SNJM. Roman Catholic. Office: Heritage Coll Office of Pres 3240 Fort Rd Toppenish WA 98948-9562

ROSS, KATHLEEN MARIE AMATO, retired secondary school educator; b. Rochester, N.Y., June 14, 1947; d. Walter Charles Poff and Margaret Lorraine (Cummings-Amato) Herkimer; m. William Anthony Ross, Apr. 4, 1970; children: Jay William, Daniel Clark. BA in History, Nazareth Coll., Rochester, 1969; postgrad., SUNY, Brockport, 1970-72, SUNY, Oswego, 1972-75, U. Rochester, 1979-81. Cert. secondary social studies tchr., N.Y. Tchr. social studies Webster Ctrl. Sch. Dist., NY, 1969—2003, ret., 2003—. Home: 2757 Lake Rd Williamson NY 14589-9517

ROSS, MARY CASLIN, medical researcher; b. N.Y.C., Oct. 15, 1953; d. Michael John and Mary Rose (Harkins) Caslin; m. Alexander Barker Ross, Mar. 21, 1992. BA, St. John's U., 1975; MA, Manhattanville Coll., 1986; Doctorate (hon.), Marymount U., 1990. Exec. dir. The Fund for Am. Studies, Washington, 1976-77; library researcher Interbank Card Assn., N.Y.C., 1977-78; devel. cons. Martin J. Moran Co., N.Y.C., 1978-80; dir. devel. Internat. Ctr. for Disabled, N.Y.C., 1980-83; trustee, v.p. bd. ICD Internat. Ctr. for the Disabled, N.Y.C., 1984—; exec. dir. The Bodman/Achelis Found., N.Y.C., 1983-94; dir. programs Econ. Sci. Lab. U. Ariz., Tucson, 1994—2000; rsch. fellow Claremont Inst., 1994—98; mem. grants com. Barker Welfare Found., 1996—; v.p., dir. Internat. Found. for Rsch. in Exptl. Econs., 1998—2002; exec. cons. Dreman Found., 2000—02; rsch. fellow Claremont Inst., 2002—. Cons. Nat. Ctr. for Policy Analysis, 1995—; mem. grants com. Barker Welfare Found., 1996—; trustee JM Found., N.Y.C., 1984—, Goldwater Inst., 1996—; bd. dirs. Philanthropy Roundtable, Indpls. and N.Y.C., 1988—94; mem. adv. bd. A Different Sept. Found., 1992; advisor Gilder Lehrman Inst., 1998—. Recipient Pres.'s medal, St. John's U., Jamaica, N.Y., 1975. Republican. Roman Catholic. Office: Claremont Inst 250 W First St # 330 Claremont CA 91711

ROSS, MATHEW, medical educator; b. Boston, July 29, 1917; s. Abraham and Frances (Lampke) R.; m. Brenda Boynton, Dec. 24, 1946; children: Douglas Ross, Gail Ross, Craig Ross, Bruce Ross. BS, Tufts U., 1938, MD, 1942. Diplomate Am. Bd. Psychiatry and Neurology. Intern Kings County Hosp., N.Y.C., 1942-43; resident VA Med. Ctr., L.A., 1946-48, L.A. Psychoanalytic Inst., 1949-53; prof. Sch. Medicine UCLA, 1953-58, George Washington U., Washington, 1958-73; psychiat. adminstrn. U. Chgo., 1959; prof. Sch. Medicine Harvard U., Boston, 1963-73, Brown U., Providence, 1964-65, R.I. U., Providence, 1964-65, U. Calif., Irvine, 1974—; fellow Sch. Alcoholism U. Utah, 1977. Fulbright prof., rsch. scholar U. Gronigen and U. Amsterdam, The Netherlands, 1962-63; med. dir. Am. Psychiat. Assn., Washington, 1958-62. Editor: Newsletter Am. Psychiat. Assn., 1958-62, Mental Hosp. & Community Psychiatry, 1958-62, PDE Scientific Journal, 1975-90. Sr. legislator State of Calif., 1985-86, sr. senator, 2002—; mem. Newport Beach (Calif.) Arts Commn., 1989-95; pres. Med. Soc. of Leisure World. Maj. U.S. Army, 1943-46, ETO. Fellow ACP (life), Am. Psychiat. Assn. (life), Am. Assn. Psychiatrists, Am. Pub. Health Assn., So. Calif. Psychiat. Soc. (founding pres. 1953-60); hon. fellow Australia-New Zealand Coll. Psychiatrists. Home: Unit 1162 24055 Paseo Del Lago Laguna Woods CA 92653-2675 E-mail: matross@att.net.

ROSS, MELANIE ANN, education specialist; b. Harvey, Ill., Nov. 19, 1957; d. John Bennett and Nola (Santi) R.; m. Kirk Franklin McIntosh, Oct. 8, 1978 (div. 2000); children: Jackson Ross McIntosh, Daniel Ross McIntosh. BA, Austin Coll., 1978, MA, 1979; postgrad., Tex. Tech U., 1981-83, U. Tex., 1985. Tchr. early childhood spl. edn. Floydada (Tex.) Ind. Sch. Dist., 1981-83, Eanes Ind. Sch. Dist., Austin, Tex., 1983—99; rsch. assoc. U. Tex. at Austin Ctr. for Reading and Lang. Arts, 1999—2002; edn. specialist in reading and lang. arts Region IV Edn. Svc. Ctr., Houston, 2002—. Vol. Humane Soc. for Travis County, Austin, 1990, Four Seasons Retirement Ctr., Austin, 1990, Interfaith Hospitality Network, Covenant Presbyn. Ch., Austin, 1994-99, Interfaith AIDS Care Team, 1994-99. Mem. Coun. for Exceptional Children, Nat. Assn. for the Edn. of Young Children, Internat. Reading Assn. Office: 7145 W Tidwell Houston TX 77092-2096

ROSS, PATTI JAYNE, obstetrics and gynecology educator; b. Nov. 17, 1946; d. James J. and Mary N. Ross; B.S., DePauw U., 1968; M.D., Tulane, U., 1972; m. Allan Robert Katz, May 23, 1976. Asst. prof. U. Tex. Med. Sch., Houston, 1976-82, assoc. prof., 1982-98, prof., 1998—, dir. adolescent ob-gyn., 1976—, also dir. student edn., dir. devel. dept. ob-gyn.; cons. OrthoMcNeil and Wyeth-Pharm., 3M; speaker in field. Bd. dirs. Am. Diabetes Assn., 1982—; mem. Rape Coun. Diplomate Am. Bd. Ob-Gyn, Children's Miracle Network Hermann's Children's Hosp; Olympic torch relay carrier, 1996; founder Women's Med. Rsch. Fund, U. Tex. Med. Sch., Houston; bd. mem. Susan Komen Found. Appeared on Lifetime TV network. Mem. Tex. Med. Assn., Harris County Med. Soc., Houston Ob-Gyn. Soc., Assn. Profs. Ob-Gyn., Soc. Adolescent Medicine, AAAS, Am. Women's Med. Assn., Orgn. Women in Sci., Sigma Xi. Roman Catholic. Clubs: River Oak Breakfast, Profl. Women Execs. Contbr. articles to profl. jours. Office: 6431 Fannin St #3278 Houston TX 77030-1501

ROSS, RICHARD STARR, medical school dean emeritus, cardiologist; b. Richmond, Ind., Jan. 18, 1924; s. Louis Francisco and Margaret (Starr) Ross; m. Elizabeth McCracken, July 1, 1950; children: Deborah Starr, Margaret Casad, Richard McCracken. Student, Harvard U., 1942—44, MD cum laude, 1947; ScD (hon.), Ind. U., 1981; LHD (hon.), Johns Hopkins U., 1994. Diplomate Nat. Bd. Med. Examiners, Am. Bd. Internal Medicine (subsplty. bd. cardiovasc. disease). Successively intern, asst. resident, chief resident Osler Med. Service, Johns Hopkins Hosp., 1947—54; research fellow physiology Harvard Med. Sch., 1952—53; instr. medicine Johns Hopkins Med. Sch., 1954—56, asst. prof. medicine, 1956—59, assoc. prof., 1959—65, assoc. prof. radiology, 1960—71, prof. medicine, 1965—, Clayton prof. cardiovascular disease, 1969—75; dir. Wellcome Research Lab., Johns Hopkins; physician Johns Hopkins Hosp.; dir. cardiovascular div. dept. medicine, adult cardiac clinic Johns Hopkins Sch. Medicine and Hosp., dir. myocardial infarction research unit, 1967—75; dean med. faculty, v.p. medicine Johns Hopkins U., 1975—90, dean emeritus, 1990—. Sir Thomas Lewis lectr. Brit. Cardiac Soc., 1969; John Kent Lewis lectr. Stanford U., 1972; bd. dirs. emeritus Johns Hopkins Hosp., Francis Scott Key Med. Ctr.; mem. cardiovasc. study sect. Nat. Heart and Lung Inst., 1965—69, chmn. cardiovasc. study sect., 1966—69, mem. tng. grant com., 1971—73, chmn. heart panel, 1972—73, adv. coun., 1974—78; mem. Inst. Medicine, 1976—; chmn. vis. com. Harvard Med. and Dental Sch., 1979—86; bd. overseers Harvard U., 1980—86. Editor: Modern Concepts Cardiovascular Disease, 1961—65, The Principles and Practice of Medicine, 17th-22nd edits., 1968—88; mem. editl. bd.: Circulation, 1968—74, mem. editl. com.: Jour. Clin. Investigation, 1969—73; contbr. numerous articles to profl. jours. Capt. M.C. U.S. Army, 1949—51. Named hon. fellow, UMDS, Guy's and St. Thomas's Hosps., London, 1996; recipient Flexner award, Assn. Am. Med. Coll., 1994. Master: ACP; fellow: Am. Coll. Cardiology (Convocation medal 1990); mem.: Heart Assn. Md. (pres. 1967—68), Am. Heart Assn. (chmn. sci. sessions program com. 1965—67, chmn. publs. com. 1970—73, pres. 1973—74, dir. 1974—77, Gold Heart award 1976, Connor lectr. 1979, James B. Herrick award 1982), Assn. Univ. Cardiologists (councillor 1972—75), Am. Clin. and Climatol. Assn. (pres. 1978—79, councillor 1979—83, Metzger lecture 1986), Am. Soc. Clin. Investigation (councillor 1967—69), Sociedad Peruana de Cardiologie (corr.), Brit. Cardiac Soc. (corr.), Cardiac Soc. Australia and New Zealand (corr.), Assn. Am. Physicians, Am. Physiol. Soc., Am. Fedn. Clin. Rsch., Boylston Med. Soc., Elkridge Club, Interurban Club (pres. 1978), Peripatetic Club, Alpha Omega Alpha, Sigma Xi. Home: 830 W 40th St # 851 Baltimore MD 21211-2181 Office: Johns Hopkins U 1830 E Monument St Baltimore MD 21287 E-mail: rross@jhmi.edu.

ROSS, ROBINETTE DAVIS, publisher; b. London, May 16, 1952; d. Raymond Lawrence and Pearl A. (Robinette) Davis; m. William Bradford Ross, III, Mar. 16, 1979; children: Nellie Tayloe, William Bradford IV. Student, Am. U., 1977-78. Asst. to editor The Chronicle of Higher Edn., Washington, 1978, advt. mgr., 1978-82, advt. dir., 1983-88, assoc. pub., 1988-94, The Chronicle of Philanthropy, 1988-94; publ. The Chronicle of Higher Edn., Washington, 1994—; pub. The Chronicle of Philanthropy, Washington, 1994—. Mem. Am. News Women's Club, City Tavern Club, Mt. Vernon Club. Episcopalian. Office: The Chronicle of Higher Edn 1255 23rd St NW Ste 700 Washington DC 20037-1146

ROSS, THERESA MAE, secondary school educator; m. H. Richard Ross; 1 child, Gwendolyn Denise. BS, Eastern Mich. U., 1967, MS, 1970; PhD, U. Mich., 1981. Tchr. Jackson (Mich.) Pub. Schs., 1967—68, Ann Arbor (Mich.) Pub. Schs., 1968—69, 1971—; grad. intern Inkster (Mich.) Child Devel. Ctr., 1968—70. HEW Early Childhood fellow, 1969—70. Mem.: NEA, Internat. Platform Assn., Am. Bus. Women's Assn., Assn. Curriuclum and Supervision (curriculum cons.), World Orgn. Early Childhood Edn., Mich. Edn. Assn., Ann Arbor Edn. Assn. (lang. arts rep., multicultural coord., motivational spkr., life coach), Delta Kappa Gamma, Beta Sigma Phi, Phi Delta Kappa. Home: 1835 N Franklin Ct Ann Arbor MI 48103-2444

ROSS, WALTER BEGHTOL, music educator, composer; b. Lincoln, Nebr., Oct. 3, 1936; s. Robert Thurber and Barbara Adeline (Ellis) R.; m. Marion Helen Wright, July 22, 1960; 1 child, Douglas Campbell. BA, U. Nebr., 1960, MusM, 1962; student, Inst. Torcuato Di Tella, Buenos Aires, 1965-66; D of Mus. Arts, Cornell U., 1966. Asst. prof. music CUNY, Cortland, 1966-67; prof. U. Va., Charlottesville, 1967—. Mem. judging panel symphonic awards ASCAP, 1978, Internat. Biennial Composition Contest, P.R., 1981, Va. chpt. Coll. Band Dir.'s Nat. Assn. Nat. Band Composition Contest, 1982, 88; bass Blue Ridge Chamber Orch., Charlottesville, 1992—. Composer over 100 works, including compositions for symphony orch., symphonic band, brass, chamber music, piano, voice, opera, theatre, and film; recs. include Clarinet Concerto for Piano and Orch., Wind Quintet, Nos. 2 and 3, Harlequinade for piano and wind quintet, Escher's Sketches, Concerto for Wind Quintet and String Orch., Piano Concerto, also others. Nominee Pulitzer Prize, 1973; recipient ASCAP award, 1974—, 1st prize Internat. Trombone Assn., 1982; grantee Am. Music Ctr., 1983; fellow Presser Found., 1958, 59, Orgn. Am. States, 1965, NEA, 1975. Democrat. Avocations: chess, cooking, amateur astronomy. Office: U Va Dept Music Charlottesville VA 22903 E-mail: wbr@virginia.edu.

ROSSBACHER, LISA ANN, university president, geology educator, writer; b. Fredericksburg, Va., Oct. 10, 1952; d. Richard Irwin and Jean Mary (Dearing) R.; m. Dallas D. Rhodes, Aug. 4, 1978. BS, Dickinson Coll., 1975; MA, SUNY, Binghamton, 1978, Princeton U., 1979, PhD, 1983. Cons. Republic Geothermal, Santa Fe Springs, Calif., 1979-81; asst. prof. geology Whittier (Calif.) Coll., 1982-84, Calif. State Poly. U., Pomona, 1984-86, assoc. prof. geol. sci., 1986-91, assoc. v.p. acad. affairs, 1987-93, prof. geol. sci., 1991-93; v.p. acad. affairs, dean faculty Whittier (Calif.) Coll., 1993-95; dean of coll., prof. geology Dickinson Coll., Carlisle, Pa., 1995-98; pres. So. Poly. State U., Marietta, Ga., 1998—. Vis. researcher U. Uppsala, Sweden, 1984. Author: Career Opportunities in Geology and the Earth Sciences, 1983, Recent Revolutions in Geology, 1986; (with Rex Buchanan) Geomedia, 1988; columnist Geotimes, 1988—; contbr. articles to profl. jours. Recipient scholarship Ministry Edn. of Finland, Helsinki, 1984; grantee NASA, 1983-94. Fellow mem. AAAS (geol. nominating com. 1984-87, chair-elect geology and geography sect. 1997-98, chair 1998-99, past chair 1999-2000); mem. Geol. Soc. Am., Sigma Xi (grantee 1976). Office: So Poly State U 1100 S Marietta Pkwy SE Marietta GA 30060-2855

ROSSE, THERESE MARIE, reading and special education educator, curriculum, school improvement and instruction consultant; b. Orleans, Nebr., Dec. 23, 1936; d. Ford Huston and Bertha Therese (Flamming) McCoy; m. John A. Rosse, Apr. 19, 1958 (div. 1979); children: Michelle, John, Robert, David. BS, Coll. St. Mary, Omaha, 1972; MS, U. Nebr., Omaha, 1973; PhD, U. Nebr., Lincoln, 1994. Cert. tchr. reading, spo. edn., history, elem. Tchr., reading clinician Omaha Pub. and Parochial Schs., 1958-72; grad. asst. U. Nebr., Omaha, 1972-73; reading cons. Ralston (Nebr.) Pub. Schs., 1973-75; reading and spl. edn. cons. Area Edn. Agy. 13, Council Bluffs, Iowa, 1975—. Adj. prof. Buena Vista Coll., Storm Lake, Iowa, 1976-79, U. Nebr. Omaha, 1978-79, Marycrest Coll., Danveport, Iowa, 1985—, N.W. Mo. State U., Maryville, 1985—, Met. Cmty. Coll., Omaha, 1990—; tester Ednl. Testing Svcs., Princeton, N.J., 1972-73; cons. Creative Cons., Muncie, Ind., 1973-75, Midlands Ednl. Cons., Omaha, 1974-75; rschr. Iowa Dept. Pub. Instrn., Dept. Edn., Des Moines, 1980-82, advisor, 1987-89; text reviewer Scott Foresman, Glenview, Ill., 1980-82, Zepher Press, Tucson, Ariz.; evaluation team North Ctrl. Accredidation Assn., 1980-82. Author: Viewing Reading Comprehension as a Problem Solving Skill: Approaches to Developing Comprehensive Strategies, 1982, Breaking the Language Barrier of Mathematical Thought Problems, 1982, A Grounded Theory of An Organizaed Learner; A Balanced Ecological System, 1994. Advisor Mayor's Commn. on Status of Women Edn. Divsn., Omaha, 1973-75; trustee Links-for-the-Future. Mem. ASCD, Internat. Reading Assn. (state bd. sec. 1973-75, v.p. local chpt., state co-chairperson, reading chairperson), Am. Ednl. Rsch. Assn. (sec.), The Brain and Edn., Coun. Exceptional Children, Phi Delta Kappa, Phi Delta Gamma (pres. local chpt. 1979-80, mem. nat. bd. 1980-82), Phi Alpha Theta. Avocations: travel, reading, classical music and art, writing/research, tennis. Home: 817 N 131st Plz Omaha NE 68154-4037

ROSSELL, CHRISTINE HAMILTON, political science educator; b. Bklyn., Jan. 22, 1945; d. Robert Hamilton and Ann (Bezold) R.; 1 child, Elise. AB, UCLA, 1967; MA, Calif. State U., Northridge, 1969; PhD, U. So. Calif., 1974. Asst. prof. Pitzer Coll., Claremont, Calif., 1973-74; rsch. assoc. U. Md., College Park, 1974-75; asst. prof. Boston U., 1975-82, assoc. prof., 1982-89, prof., 1989—, chair dept. polit. sci., 1992-95. Vis. asst. prof. Duke U., Durham, N.C., 1977-78, U. Calif., Berkeley, 1981; vis. lectr. Canberra (Australia) Coll., 1985; vis. fellow Pub. Policy Inst. Calif., 1999. Author: (with others) Strategies for Effective Desegregation, 1983, Carrot or Stick for School Desegregation, 1990, Bilingual Education in Massachusetts: The Emperor Has No Clothes, 1996;; co-editor: Consequences of School Desegregation, 1983, Sch. Desegreation in the 21st Century, 2002. Mem. Citywide Coord. Coun., Boston, 1976-77. Home: 44 High St Brookline MA 02445-7707 Office: Boston U Dept Polit Sci 232 Bay State Rd Boston MA 02215-1403 E-mail: crossell@bu.edu.

ROSSER, JAMES MILTON, academic administrator; b. East St. Louis, Ill., Apr. 16, 1939; s. William M. and Mary E. (Bass) R.; 1 child, Terrence. BA, So. Ill. U., 1962, MA, 1963, PhD, 1969. Diagnostic bacteriologist Holden Hosp., Carbondale, Ill., 1961-63; rsch. bacteriologist Eli Lilly & Co., Indpls., 1963-66; coordinator Black Am. studies, instr. health edn. So. Ill. U., Carbondale, 1968-69, asst. prof. Black Am. studies dir., 1969-70, asst. to chancellor, 1970; assoc. vice chancellor for acad. affairs U. Kans., Lawrence, 1970-74, assoc. prof. edn., pharmacology and toxicology, 1971-74; vice chancellor dept. higher edn. State of N.J., Trenton, 1974-79, acting chancellor, 1977; pres., prof. health care mgmt. Calif. State U., Los Angeles, 1979—. Mem. tech. resource panel Ctr. for R&D in Higher Edn., U. Calif., Berkeley, 1974-76; mem. health maintenance orgn. com. Health Planning Coun., State of N.J., 1975-79; mem. standing com. on R&D bd. trustees Ednl. Testing Service, 1976-77; mem. steering com. and task force on retention of minorities in engring. Assembly of Engring. NRC, 1975-78; mem. Bd. Med. Examiners, State of N.J., 1978-79; vis. faculty Inst. Mgmt. of Lifelong Edn., Grad. Sch. Edn., Harvard U., 1979; mem. Calif. State U. Trustees Spl. Long Range Fin. Planning Com., 1982-87; mem. Am. Coun. on Edn., 1979—, AFL/CIO Labor Higher Edn. Coun., 1983—, Nat. Commn. Higher Edn. Issues, 1981-82; mem. The Calif. Achievement Coun., 1983-89, strategic adv. counc. Coll. and Univs. Systems Exch., 1988-91; bd. dirs. Am. Humanities Coun., So. Calif. Am. Humanics, Inc. Coun., United Calif. Bank, Edison Internat., Fedco, Inc.; task force on equality and fairness Texaco, 1999-2002. Author: An Analysis of Health Care Delivery, 1977. Mem. exec. bd., chmn. varsity scouting program L.A. area coun. Boy Scouts Am., 1980—; bd. dirs. Hispanic Urban Ctr., L.A., 1979—, L.A. Urban League, 1982-95, Cmty. TV of So. Calif., Sta. KCET, 1980-89, 98—, United Way, L.A., 1980-91, Orthopaedic Hosp., 1983-86, L.A. Philharm. Assn., 1986-99, Nat. Health Found., 1990-98; mem. Citizen's Adv. Coun. Congl. Caucus Sci. and Tech., 1983—; mem. performing arts coun./edn. coun. Music Ctr., 1984—; minority bus. task force Pacific Bell, 1985-86; bd. govs. Nat. ARC, 1986-91, Mayor's Blue Ribbon Task Force on Drugs, City of L.A., 1988, L.A. Annenberg Met. Project, 1994-2001; Nat. Adv. Coun. on Aging, 1989-93; trustee Woodrow Wilson Nat. Fellowship Found., 1993—; bd. advisors Historically Black Colls. and Univs. and Minority Insts., Dept. Air Force, 1997-2001; bd. dirs. Ams. for the Arts, 1991—; mem. L.A. Adv. Alliance, Pasadena Tournament of Roses, 2000—; mem. Action Forum on Diversity in the Engring. Workforce, Nat. Acad. Engring., 2000—; mem. Calif. Coun. on Sci. and Tech., 1999--; mem. campaign adv. com. The Audubon Ctr. L.A., 2001--. NSF fellow, 1961; NDEA fellow, 1967-68; recipient award of recognition in Edn. Involvement for Young Achievers, 1981, Pioneer of Black Hist. Achievement award Brotherhood Crusade, 1981, Alumni Achievement award So. Ill. U., 1982, Friend of Youth award Am. Humanics, Inc., 1985, Leadership award Dept. Higher Edn. Ednl. Equal Opportunity Fund Program, 1989, Medal of Excellence Gold State Minority Found., 1990, Take Charge of Learning Success award Inst. for Redesign of Learning. Mem. Calif. C. of C. (bd. dirs. 1993—), Alhambra C. of C. (bd. dirs. 1979—), Los Angeles C. of C. (bd. dirs. 1985-90), Am. Assn. State Colls. and Univs., Kappa Delta Pi, Phi Kappa Phi. Roman Catholic. Office: Calif State U LA Office of Pres 5151 State University Dr Los Angeles CA 90032-4226

ROSSETTI, LINDA ELAINE, special education educator; b. Boston, Sept. 17, 1946; d. Bert A. and Angela (Calliontzis) Badavas; m. John Peter Rossetti, Dec. 26, 1969; children: Lisa, Nicholas. BA in Sociology, U. Mass., Amherst, 1969; MA in Spl. Edn., W.Va. U., 1972. Cert. tchr., Md. Program dir. Zia Sch. for Children, Alamogordo, N.Mex., 1972-73; tchr., prescriptive specialist Alamogordo Ctr. for Exceptional Students, 1973-78; head tchr. Golden Hills Acad., Auburn, Calif., 1978-79; resource tchr., team leader Bushy Park Elem. Sch., Glenwood, Md., 1986—. Mem. tchr. interview team Howard County Pub. Schs., Ellicott City, Md., 1990—; initiator and coord. Spl. Olympics, Alamogordo Pub. Schs., 1973-78; coord. Working on Wellness team Bushy Park Elem. Sch., 1990-92; presenter in field. Bd. dirs. Otero County Assn. Retarded Citizens, Alamogordo, 1973-77; rep. Howard County Leadership Com., 1998-2000, lead tchr. rep., 2000. Nominee for Md. Tchr. of Yr. Mem. Coun. for Exceptional Children (pres. 1973-77), Howard County Ednl. Assn., Phi Delta Kappa. Office: Bushy Park Elem Sch 2670 State Route 97 Glenwood MD 21738-9799

ROSSI, FAUST F. lawyer, educator; b. 1932; BA, U. Tornoto, 1953; JD, Cornell U., 1960. Bar: N.Y. 1960. Tax trialy atty. Dept. Justice, Washington, 1960-61; sole practice Rochester, N.Y., 1961-66; assoc. prof. Cornell U., Ithaca, N.Y., 1966-69, prof., 1970—, assoc. dean, 1973-75, Samuel S. Leibowitz prof. trial techniques, 1982—. Vis. prof. Emory U., 1990; cons. report of fed. class actions Am. Coll. of Trial Lawyers, 1971-72; cons. com. on proposed fed. rules of evidence N.Y. Trial Lawyers Assn., 1970; cons., instr. annual seminar N.Y. State Trial Judges, 1970-78; cons., instr. Nat. Inst. for Trial Advocacy, 1974-75, 80-84, 88; cons. N.Y. Law Revision Commn. Project for N.Y. Code of Evidence, 1978-80. Author: Study of the Proposed Federal Rules of Evidence, 1979, Report on Rule 23 Class Actions, 1972, The Federal Rules of Evidence, 1970, Expert Witnesses, 1991; co-author: New York Evidence, 1997; contbr. articles to profl. jours. Lt. j.g. USN. Recipient Jacobsen prize for tchg. trail advocacy, 1992. Mem. Order of Coif. Office: Cornell U Law Sch Myron Taylor Hall Ithaca NY 14853 E-mail: ffr1@cornell.edu.

ROSSI, MIRIAM, chemistry educator, researcher; b. Asti, Italy, Mar. 8, 1952; arrived in U.S., 1956. d. Antonio and Aldegonda R. BA, Hunter Coll., 1974; PhD, John Hopkins U., 1979. Post doctoral fellow, Fox Chase Cancer Ctr., Phila., 1979-82; asst. prof. chemistry Vassar Coll., Poughkeepsie, NY, 1982-89, assoc. prof., 1989—, chair dept., chemistry, 1990-95, prof., 2000—. Author: (with J.P. Glusker and M. Lewis) Crystal Structure Analysis for Chemists and Biologists, 1994; editor: Patterson and Pattersons, 1988. Recipient Texaco Rsch. Award, Mid-Hudson Am. Chem. Soc., 1993. Office: Vassar Coll PO Box 484 Poughkeepsie NY 12604-0001

ROSSMANN, ANTONIO, lawyer, educator; b. San Francisco, Apr. 25, 1941; s. Herbert Edward and Yolanda (Sonsini) R.; m. Kathryn A. Burns, Oct. 6, 1991; children: Alice Sonsini, Maria McHale. Grad., Harvard Coll., 1963, JD, 1971. Bar: Calif. 1972, D.C. 1979, N.Y. 1980, U.S. Supreme Ct. 1980. Law clk. to Justice Mathew Tobriner Calif. Supreme Ct., 1971-72; assoc. Tuttle & Taylor, L.A., 1972-75; pub. advisor Calif. Energy Commn., 1975-76; sole practice San Francisco, 1976-82, 85—; exec. dir. Nat. Ctr. for Preservation Law, 1979-80; mem. McCutchen, Doyle, Brown & Enersen, San Francisco, 1982—85. Adj. prof. law Hastings Coll. Law, 1981-84; vis. prof. UCLA Sch. Law, 1985-87; Fulbright lectr. U. Tokyo, 1987-88; adj. prof. Stanford Law Sch., 1989-90, U. Calif. Sch. Law, Boalt Hall, 1991—. Editor Harvard Law Rev., 1969-71; contbr. articles to legal jours. Bd. dirs. Planning and Conservation League, 1984—, Calif. Water Protection Coun., 1982-83, San Francisco Marathon, 1982-90; pres. Western State Endurance Run, 1991-96, counselor, 1996—; pres., bd. dirs. Toward Utility Rate Normalization, 1976-79. Served to lt. comdr. USN, 1963-68. Mem. Calif. State Bar (chmn. com. on environment 1978-82), U.S. Rowing Assn., U.S. Soccer Fedn. (state referee) L.A. Athletic Club, Harvard Club (San Francisco, N.Y.C.), Harvard Law Sch. Assn. No. Calif. (pres. 1997-2002). Office: 380 Hayes St San Francisco CA 94102-4421 E-mail: ar@landwater.com.

ROSSMANN, MICHAEL GEORGE, biochemist, educator; b. Frankfurt, Germany, July 30, 1930; s. Alexander and Nelly (Schwabacher) R.; m. Audrey Pearson, July 24, 1954; children— Martin, Alice, Heather. BSC with honors, Polytechnic, London, 1951, MSc in Physics, 1953; PhD in Chemistry, U. Glasgow, 1956; PhD (hon.), U. Uppsala (Sweden), 1983, U. Strasbourg (France), 1984, Vrije U. Brussel, 1990, U. Glasgow (Scotland), 1993, U. York (England), 1994, U. Quebec (Can.), 1998. Fulbright scholar U. Minn., 1956-58; research scientist MRC Lab. Molecular Biology, Cambridge, Eng., 1958-64; assoc. prof. biol. scis. Purdue U., West Lafayette, Ind., 1964-67, prof., 1967-78, Hanley Disting. prof. biol. scis., 1978—, prof. biochemistry, 1975—. Editor: The Molecular Replacement Method, 1972; contbr. more than 400 articles to profl. jours. Grantee NIH, NSF; recipient Fankuchen award Am. Crystallographc Assn., 1986, Horwitz prize Columbia U., 1990, Gregori Arminoff prize Royal Swedish Acad. Sci., 1994, Stein & Moore award Protein Soc., 1994, Ewald prize Internat. Union Crystallography, 1996, Cole award Biophysical Soc., 1998, Elion award Internat. Soc. for Antiviral Rsch., 2000, Ehrlich and Darmstaedter prize Paul Erhlich-Fedn., 2001. Mem. Am. Soc. Biol. Chemists, Am. Chem. Soc., Biophys. Soc. (Cole award 1998), Am. Crystallographic Assn. (Fankuchen award 1986), Brit. Biophys. Soc., Inst. Physics., Chem. Soc. (U.K.), AAAS, NAS, Indian Nat. Sci. Acad., Royal Soc., Nat. Sci. Bd., Lafayette Sailing Club. Democrat. Home: 1208 Wiley Dr West Lafayette IN 47906-2434 Office: Purdue U Dept Biol Scis 915 W State St West Lafayette IN 47907-2054 E-mail: mgr@indiana.bio.purdue.edu.

ROSSOF, ARTHUR HAROLD, internal medicine educator; b. Chgo., Dec. 12, 1943; s. Jack and Libby (Gordon) R.; m. Rebecca Ann, Aug. 11, 1967 (div. 1983); children: Jacob Earl, Lizabeth Eva; m. Kristine Ann, Feb. 14, 1985. Student, Bradley U., 1961-64; MD, U. Ill., 1968. Diplomate Nat. Bd. Med. Examiners, Am. Bd. Internal Medicine, Am. Bd. Oncology, Am. Bd. Hematology. Fellow sect. neurobiology dept. neurology Presbyn.-St. Luke's Hosp., Chgo., 1965-68, intern straight medicine, 1968-69, resident dept. medicine, 1969-71, Eastern Coop. Oncology Group fellow sect. oncology, dept. medicine, 1971-72, asst. attending physician dept. internal medicine, 1976-80, assoc. attending physician, dept. internal medicine, 1980-82, sr. attending physician dept. internal medicine, 1982-90; med. dir. MacNeal Cancer Ctr., Berwyn, Ill., 1985-99; asst. medicine U. Ill. Coll. Medicine, 1969-71; clin. asst. prof. medicine U. Tex. health Sci. Ctr., San Antonio, 1973-76; instr. medicine Rush Med. Coll., 1971-72, asst. prof. medicine, 1976-81, assoc. prof. medicine, 1981-90, Loyola U. Med. Ctr., Chgo., 1990-91, attending physician, 1990-97, prof., 1991-97. Mem. resident selection com. Rush-Presbyn.-St. Luke's Med. Ctr., 1976-88, mem. ethics conf. planning group, 1981-90, tumor com., 1981-90; chmn. med. edn. com., continuing med. edn. subcom., 1982-90; mem. pharmacy and therapeutics com., chmn. instnl. rev. bd., chmn. cancer com. MacNeal Hosp.. chmn. med. edn. com., continuing med. edn. subcom., 1993-97; cons. Cancer Info. Svcv., Ill. Cancer Coun., mem. clin. trials com. 1978-92, credentials rev. com.; mem. adv. com. Lincoln Park Zoo, 1978-2000; med. advisor Y-ME sci. adv. bd. Chgo. chpt. Israel Cancer Rsch. Found. Author: Lithium Effects on Granulopoiesis and Immune Function, 1980; contbr. articles in field to profl. jours.; patentee in field. Mem. exec. com. prevention com. Cancer Incidence and End Results com. Am. Cancer Soc.; mem. profl. adv. bd. Wellness House, Y-ME, Israel Cancer Rsch. Found. Fellow ACP; mem. AAAS, Internat. Soc. Exptl. Hematology, Am. Soc. Clin. Oncology, Am. Assn. Cancer Research, Am. Soc. Hematology, N.Y. Acad. Scis., Soc. Air Force Physicians, Soc. Med. History Chgo., Chgo. Soc. Internal Medicine, Assn. Community Cancer Ctrs., Sigma Xi, Phi Eta Sigma, Alpha Omega Alpha. Republican. Jewish. Avocation: tennis. Office: Hematology/Oncology Assocs Ill 610 S Maple 5400 Oak Park IL 60304 Fax: 708-445-3157. E-mail: krisart@rcnchicago.com., arthur.rossof@usoncology.com.

ROTBERG, IRIS COMENS, social scientist; b. Phila., Dec. 16, 1932; d. Samuel Nathaniel and Golda (Shuman) Comens; m. Eugene H. Rotberg, Aug. 29, 1954; children: Diana Golda, Pamela Lynn. BA, U. Pa., 1954, MA, 1955; PhD, Johns Hopkins U., Balt., 1958. Research psychologist Pres.'s Commn. on Income Maintenance Programs, Washington, 1968-69, Office Planning, Research and Evaluation, Office Econ. Opportunity, Washington, 1970-73; dep. dir. compensatory edn. study Nat. Inst. Edn., Washington, 1974-77, dir. Office Planning and Program Devel., 1978-82; program dir. NSF, Arlington, Va., 1985-87, 89-91, 1993-96; tech. policy fellow Com. on Sci., Space and Tech., U.S. Ho. of Reps., Washington, 1987-89; sr. social scientist RAND, Washington, 1991-93; rsch. prof. edn. policy Grad. Sch. Edn. and Human Devel. George Washington U., Washington, 1996—. NSF fellow, 1956-58. Home: 7211 Brickyard Rd Potomac MD 20854-4808 E-mail: irotberg@gwu.edu.

ROTBERG, ROBERT IRWIN, historian, political economist, educator, editor; b. Newark, Apr. 11, 1935; s. Louis and Mildred S. R.; m. Joanna H. Henshaw, June 17, 1961; children: Rebecca T.H., Nicola S.D., Fiona J.Y. AB, Oberlin Coll., 1955; MPA, Princeton U., 1957; DPhil, U. Oxford, 1960. Asst. prof. history, rsch. assoc. Ctr. for Internat. Affairs Harvard U., 1961-68, rsch. assoc. Ctr. for Internat. Affairs, 1968-95; rsch. dir. Twentieth Century Fund, 1968-71; prof. polit. sci. and history MIT, 1968-87; acad. v.p. for Arts, Scis. and Tech. Tufts U., Medford, Mass., 1987-90; pres. Lafayette Coll., Easton, Pa., 1990-93, World Peace Found., Cambridge, 1993—; coord. Inst. for Internat. Devel. Harvard U., 1993-99, dir. program on intrastate conflict Kennedy Sch., 1999—. Adj. prof. Kennedy Sch. Govt., Harvard U., 1993—; mem. coun. NEH, 1993-99; cons. Dept. State, 1968-78, Commrs. of Middlesex County, Mass., 1976-77. Author: A Political History of Tropical Africa, 1965, The Rise of Nationalism in Central Africa, 1965, Protest and Power in Black Africa, 1970, Joseph Thomson and the Exploration of Africa, 1971, Haiti: The Politics of Squalor, 1971, Africa and Its Explorers, 1971, The Black Homelands of South Africa, 1977, Black Heart: Gore-Browne and the Politics of Multiracial Zambia, 1978, Conflict and Compromise in South Africa, 1980, Suffer the Future: Policy Choices in Southern Africa, 1980, Imperialism, Colonialism and Hunger, 1982, Namibia: Economic and Political Prospects, 1983, South Africa and its Neighbors, 1985, The Founder: Cecil Rhodes and the Pursuit of Power, 1988, rev. edit. 2002, Africa in the 1990s and Beyond: Policy Opportunities and Choices, 1988, From Massacres to Genocide: The Media, Public Policy, and Humanitarian Crises, 1996, Vigilance and Vengeance: NGOs Preventing Ethnic Conflict in Divided Societies, 1996, Haiti Renewed: Political and Economic Prospects, 1997, Burma: Prospects for a Democratic Future, 1998, War and Peace in Southern Africa, 1998, Creating Peace in Sri Lanka, 1999, Peacekeeping and Peace Enforcement in Africa, 2000, Truth v. Justice, 2000, Patterns of Social Capital, 2001, Ending Autocracy, Enabling Democracy, 2002, State Failure and State Weakness in a Time of Terror, 2003; editor Jour. Interdisciplinary History, 1970—. Chmn. Middlesex County Govtl. Rev. Task Force, 1972; v.p. Cambridge Civic Assn., 1969-72; mem. Lexington Town Meeting, 1973-90, 94—, Lexington Sch. Com., 1974-77; mem. Ciskel Commn., 1979-80; trustee World Peace Found., 1980—, Oberlin Coll., 1983—, Coun. Internat. Exch. Scholars, 1991-95. Rhodes scholar U. Oxford, 1960; Guggenheim fellow, 1970-71; Hazen Found. fellow, 1976-77. Fellow Royal Geog. Soc.; mem. Am. Hist. Assn., African Studies Assn., Coun. on Fgn. Rels., Oberlin Coll. Alumni Assn. (pres. 1981-82). Office: World Peace Found Belfer Ctr 79 John F Kennedy St Cambridge MA 02138-5758 E-mail: robert_rotberg@harvard.edu.

ROTH, ALEDA VENDER, business educator; b. Cleve., Oct. 8, 1945; d. Joseph Patrick and Beatrice Vender; m. G. Douglas Roth, Sept. 26, 1970; children: G. Brian, Lauren Carter. BS in Psychology with honors, Ohio State U., 1968; MSPH in Biostats., U. N.C., 1970; PhD in Ops. Mgmt., Ohio State U., 1986. Chief statistician Ark. Children's Colony Ark. State Dept. Human Svcs., 1968-69; rsch. assoc., epidemiologist Epidemiologic Field Sta. Greater Kansas City Mental Health Found., 1970-72, statis. cons. Epidemiologic Field Sta., 1972-74; nat. dir. stats. dept. ANA, 1972-79; grad. teaching and rsch. assoc. faculty mgmt. sci. Ohio State U., 1979-83, grad. teaching and rsch. assoc. acctg. dept., 1983, instr. computer and info. sys. Coll. Engring., 1983-84, instr. faculty mgmt. sci. Coll. Adminstrv. Sci., 1984-85; asst. prof. Boston U. Sch. Mgmt., 1985-89, prin. investigator retail banking futures project, 1986-94; co-investigator mfg.'s future rsch. Boston U., 1985-89, prin. co-investigator rsch. DTT-UNC gloal vision in mfg., 1989—2001, rsch. assoc. ctr. health rsch. and edn., 1989-93; assoc. prof. dept. health administrn. Duke U. Med. Ctr., Durham, 1989-91; assoc. prof. bus. Duke U., Durham, N.C., 1989-93; Disting. Mary Farley Ames Lee prof., chair Global Supply Chain Concentration U.N.C, dept. Tech. and Innovation Mgmt., Chapel Hill, 1993—. Prin. rsch. co-investigator Internat. Svc. Study, 1996—; vis. scholar London Business Sch., 2000; Vis. prof. WHU Vallender Germany, 2001; adj. faculty mem. Sch. Pub. Health, U. N.C., Chapel Hill, 1972-74; mem. Coop. Health Stats. Sys. Adv. Com., Nat. Ctr. Health Stats., DHHS, 1974-76; membership svcs. com. Nat. Decision Scis. Inst., 1989-90; adj. rsch. faculty Boston U. Mfg. Roundtable, 1985-90; rsch. adv. com. U. N.C. Ctr. for Mfg. Excellence, 1989-94; exec. com. U. N.C. Cato Ctr. Applied Bus. Rsch., 1994-97, rsch. com. 1997-99. Author (with M. van der Velde): The Future of Retail Banking Delivery Systems, 1988; author: Retail Banking Strategies: Opportunities for the 1990s, 1990, World Class Banking: Benchmarking the Market Leaders, 1992; author: (with C. Giffi and G. Seal) Competing in World Class Manufacturing: America's 21st Century Challenge, 1990; editor: Facts About Nursing, 1972-73 edit., 1974, 1974-75 edit., 1976, 1980-81 edit., 1981; editor: (with J. Jaeger and A. Kaluzny) The Management of Continuous Improvement: Cases in Health Administration, 1993; dep. editor: Manufacturing and Service Operations Management, 1996—, assoc. editor: Decision Sciences, 1993—2002, Jour. Ops. Mgmt., 1993—2001, 2001—, mem. editl. rev. bd.:, 1998—, area editor: Prodn. and Ops. Mgmt. Jour., 1993—, mem. editl. adv. bd.:, 1991—93, assoc. editor: OM Review, 1992—94, Benchmarking for Quality and Tech. Mgmt., 1993—, mem. editl. bd.: Internat. Jour. Prodn. and Ops. Mgmt., 1995—99, Jour. Svc. Rsch., 1998—, ad hoc referee: Mgmt. Sci., Jour. Ops. Mgmt., Decisions on Scis., Prodn. and Ops. Mgmt. Jour., IEEE Trans.; contbr. articles to profl. jours., chpts. to books. Recipient Book award of excellence Soc. for Tech. Comm., 1992, Kenan Inst. Faculty Rsch. award, 1994, Outstanding Paper award Literati Club, London, 1995, Kenan-Flagler Bus. Sch. Disting. Rsch. award 1996, Best Paper award Acad. Mgmt., 1996, 2000, Best Paper award XXII Brazilian Assn. Post Grad. Courses in Adminstrn., 1998, 99; winner Decision Scis. Inst.'s Interdisciplinary Paper award, 1996, Best Theoretical/Empirical Rsch. Paper award 1985, Doctoral Dissertation award 1985; Anna Dice scholar Ohio State U., 1985; grantee Performance Excellence Coun. of the Conf. Bd., 1991—; NIMH fellow, 1969-70, U. N.C. Cato Ctr. fellow, 1995, Kenan Inst. fellow, 1995-96, Dalton L. McMichael Sr. Rsch. fellow, 1998; Disting. O'Herron Faculty scholar, 1996. Mem. Prodn. and Ops. Mgmt. Assn. (sec. 1988-91, bd. dirs. 1988-94, planning com. ann. conf. 1990-91, session chair ann. mtg. 1991, pres.-elect 2000-02, pres. 2002—), Decision Scis. Inst. (bd. dirs. 1996-98), Phi Kappa Phi, Delta Omega. Office: U NC Kenan-Flagler Bus Sch Chapel Hill NC 27599-3490

ROTH, BERNARD, mechanical engineering educator, researcher; b. N.Y.C., May 28, 1933; s. Morris Michael and Sara (Goldfarb) R.; m. Ruth Ochs, June 24, 1954; children: Steven Howard, Elliot Marc. BS, CCNY, 1956; MS, Columbia U., 1958, PhD, 1962. Engr. Ford Instrument Co., L.I., N.Y., 1955, Lockheed Aircraft Co., Van Nuys, Calif., 1956, Atlantic Design Co., Newark, 1958; lectr. CCNY, 1956-59; rsch. asst. Columbia U., N.Y.C., 1959-62; prof. Stanford (Calif.) U., 1962—. Guest prof. U. Paris, 1988-90; expert, team leader UN Devel. Orgn., Vienna, Austria, 1986-88; mem. tech. adv. bd. Adept Tech., Inc., San Jose, Calif., 1983—; mem. adv. bd. Ctr. for Econ. Conversion, Mountain View, Calif., 1988—98; bd. dirs. Peace Rev. Jour., Palo Alto., Calif., 1988-93. Co-author: Theoretical Kinematics, 1979, 2d edit., 1990; contbr. numerous articles on kinematics, robotics and design to profl. jours. Recipient Joseph F. Engelberger award Robotics Industries Assn., 1986. Fellow ASME (Melville medal 1967, Best Papers award mechanism conf. 1978, 80, 82, 92, 94, chair design engring. divsn. 1981-82, Mechanisms Coms. award 1982, Machine Design award 1984, Outstanding Design Educator award 2000), Japanese Soc. for Promotion Sci., IEEE (Pioneer in Robotics award 2000), Internat. Fedn. for Theory of Machines and Mechanisms (pres. 1980-83, hon. chmn. 7th World Congress 1987). Office: Stanford U Dept Mech Engring Stanford CA 94305

ROTH, CAROLYN LOUISE, art educator; b. Buffalo, June 17, 1944; d. Charles Mack and Elizabeth Mary (Hassel) R.; m. Charles Turner Barber, Aug. 4, 1991. Student, Art Student's League N.Y., 1965, Instituto Allende, San Miguel de Allende, Mex., 1966; BFA, Herron Sch. Art, 1967; MFA, Fla. State U., 1969. Asst. prof. art U. Tenn., Chattanooga, 1969-72; lectr. art So. Ill. U., Carbondale, 1973-75; asst. prof. art U. Evansville, Ind., 1975-80; lectr. art U. So. Ind., Evansville, 1984—. Exhbn. coord., gallery dir. Krannert Gallery, U. Evansville, 1977-79; exhbn. coord., conf. advisor Ind. Women in Arts Conf., Ind. Arts Commn., Evansville, 1978; reviewer in field. One-woman shows include Wabash Valley Coll., Mt. Carmel, Ill., 1994, So. Ind. Ctr. for Arts, Seymour, Ind., 1996, Zionsville (Ind.) Muncie Art Ctr., 1997, Oakland City (Ind.) U., 1998; exhibited in group shows Liberty Gallery, Louisville, 1992, Artlink Contemporary Art Gallery, Ft. Wayne, Ind., 1994, S.E. Mo. Coun. on Arts, Cape Girardeau, 1994, Lexington (Ky.) Art League, 1996, Mills Pond Horse Gallery, St. James, N.Y., 1996, SOHO Gallery, Pensacola, Fla., 1996, Indpls. Art Ctr., 1996, Artemesia Gallery, Chgo., 1997, DelMar Coll., Corpus Christi, Tex., 1998, La. State U., Baton Rouge, 1998, Woman Made Gallery, Chgo., 2002; works appeared in various publs.; represented by Gallery Hertz, Louisville. Malone fellow visitor to Morocco and Tunisia, 1996. Mem. Nat. Mus. Women in Arts, Met. Mus. Art, Evansville Mus. Arts and Sci., New Harmony Gallery of Contemporary Art, Golden Key Honor Soc. (hon.). Democrat. Mem. Unity Ch. Avocation: travel to study art works in museums and galleries in europe and mex. Home: 10801 S Woodside Dr Evansville IN 47712-8422 Office: U So Ind 8600 University Blvd Evansville IN 47712-3534

ROTH, EVELYN AUSTIN, retired elementary school educator; b. Coronado, Calif., May 31, 1942; d. Robert Emmett and Marjorie Eastman (Rice) Austin; m. John King Roth, June 25, 1964; children: Andrew Lee, Sarah Austin. BA, San Diego State U., 1964; MA, U. of LaVerne, Calif., 1984; postgrad., U. Calif., Riverside, 1985. Cert. elem. tchr., Calif. Elem. tchr. Poway (Calif.) Unified Schs., 1964, Wallingford (Conn.) Unified Schs., 1964-66, Ontario (Calif.) Montclair Sch. Dist., 1982-88, Claremont (Calif.) Unified Schs., 1966-67, 83-93, Foothill Country Day Sch., Claremont, 1993-97; ret., 1997. Pres., bd. trustees Friends of Stone Libr., Claremont, 1993-94. Mem. AAUW, NEA, Calif. Tchrs. Assn., Internat. Reading Assn. (treas. Foothill Reading Coun. 1985-86), Delta Kappa Gamma (v.p. 1991-92). Republican. Presbyterian. Avocations: travel, reading, gardening.

ROTH, JAY BRIAN, mathematics educator; b. Columbus, Ohio, June 5, 1969; s. Geoffrey Jay Roth and Sharon Lynn (Kirchhoff) Dykes. BS in Edn., S.E. Mo. State U., 1991. Cert. math. educator, Mo. Tchr. math. Iron County C-4, Viburnum, Mo., 1992-94, Willard (Mo.) R-2, 1994—, head math. dept., 2003—. Mem. Springfield (Mo.) Cmty. Band, 1994-2002. Mem. Nat. Coun. Tchrs. Math., Mo. State Tchrs. Assn., Mo. Acad. Coaches Assn. (sec., treas. 1999-2001), Huna Rsch., Inc. (sec. bd. 1992-2002). Home: 829 Mark St Willard MO 65781-9489 E-mail: jroth@willard.k12.mo.us.

ROTH, LANE, communications educator; b. N.Y.C., Apr. 10; BA with nat. honors in German, NYU; MA, Fla. State U., 1974, PhD in Mass Comm., 1976. Camera operator Sta. WFSU-TV, Tallahassee, 1973-74; broadcast engr., producer-creator, writer, performer Sta. WFSU-FM, Tallahassee, 1974-76; co-host Sta. WNIN-TV, Evansville, Ind., 1976-77; asst. prof. radio-TV-film U. Evansville, 1976-78; asst. prof. comm. Lamar U., Beaumont, Tex., 1978-82, assoc. prof., 1982—. Bd. dirs. Mental Health Assn. of Jefferson County, pres., 1997, 98; writer, performer fund-raising promos, Sta. KVLU-FM, Beaumont, 1995—. Author: Film Semiotics, Metz, and Leone's Trilogy, 1983; contbr. articles to profl. mags., jours.; contbr. to acad. books. Bd. dirs. Mental Health Assoc. of Jefferson Co., 1993—. Recipient Regents Merit award for excellence in tchg., 1980, Mental Health Assn. award for dedicated leadership, 1999. Mem. Internat. Assn. for the Fantastic in the Arts, World Comm. Assn. Roman Catholic. Avocations: Jungian psychology, analysis of popular film and tv, singer-impressionist-songwriter. Office: Lamar U Dept Communications Beaumont TX 77710

ROTH, MARJORY JOAN JARBOE, special education educator; b. Ranger, Tex., May 24, 1934; d. James Aloysius and Dorothy Knight (Taggart) Jarboe; m. Thomas Mosser Roth, Jr., Dec. 22, 1959; children: Thomas Mosser III, James Jarboe. BA in English, Rice U., 1957; MEd in Ednl. Adminstrn., U. N.C., Greensboro, 1981. Cert. tchr.-specific learning disabilities, middle grades lang. arts and social studies, intermediate grades, adminstr.-prin., N.C. Tchr. 4th grade Houston Ind. Sch. Dist., 1957-60; specific lang. disabilities instr. Forsyth Tech. C.C., Winston-Salem, N.C., 1976-77; specific learning disabilities tchr. Forsyth Country Day Sch., Winston-Salem, 1977-80; tchr. 5th grade Winston-Salem/Forsyth County Schs., 1982-83, specific learning disabilities tchr. Mt. Tabor High Sch., 1983-86; part time instr. English and Learning Disabilities Forsyth Tech. C.C., 1986-90; founding pres., prin. Greenhills Sch., Winston-Salem, 1990—. Co-author, co-editor booklets. Sunday Sch. dir., tchr. Galloway Meml. Episcopal Ch., 1960-70, pres., treas., sec. Churchwomen, 1963-74; treas. Elkin Jr. Woman's Club, 1962; chmn. Elkin Heart Fund Drive, 1968; bd. dirs. Hugh Chatham Hosp. Auxillary, 1968, Friends of the Elkin Pub. Libr., 1968-74, chmn., 1970-72, chmn., exhibits chmn. summer reading program; pres. South Surry Heart Assn., 1969; mem. Churchwomen of St. Paul's Episcopal Ch., Winston-Salem, 1982—, Fiddle and Bow Folk Music Soc., Winston-Salem, 1992—. Recipient June Lyday Orton award for outstanding svc. in the field of dyslexia, 1997; Forsyth fellow NEH, 1985; grantee in field. Fellow Acad. Orton-Gillingham Practitioners and Educators; mem. ASCD, Children with Attention Deficit Disorder (profl. adv. bd. N.C. Triad chpt. 1990-96), Learning Disability Assn. N.C. (sec., bd. dirs. 1981-86), Internat. Dyslexia Assn. (sec., bd. dirs. Carolinas br. 1981-85, founding pres. N.C. br. 1987-91, bd. dirs. 1987-96, nat. nominating com. 1992-94), Internat. Multisensory Structured Lang. Edn. Coun., Inc. (bd.dirs. 2000-). Republican. Avocations: tennis, hiking, folk music. Home: 940 Fox Hall Dr Winston Salem NC 27106-4431 Office: Greenhills Sch 1360 Lyndale Dr Winston Salem NC 27106-9739

ROTH, MICHELLE LYNN, computer educator; b. Lousville, Feb. 21, 1967; d. Walter James and Helen Louise (Gofourth) R. BA, Alice Loyd Coll., 1990; MA, Morehead State U., 1996. Cert. tchr. mid. sch., Ky. Computer instr., tech. coord. James D. Adams Mid. Sch., Prestonsburg, Ky., 1992—. Ky. instnl. tech. leader 21st Century Tchr. Network. Mem. NEA, ASCD, Nat. Mid. Sch. Assn., Ky. Edn. Assn. (program participant), Floyd County Edn. Assn. (sec. 1993-94). Democrat. Southern Baptist. Avocations: music, academic competition.

ROTH, SHARON A. elementary school educator, consultant; b. Watervliet, N.Y., Feb. 9, 1954; d. Patrick John Donlon Sr. and Elmina Helen (Wickware) McQuire; m. Richard L. Roth, June 16, 1973; children: Issac Jacob, SerahRose Gillett. AS, Norwalk C.C., 1984; BA, Goddard Coll., 1986, MA, 1988; postgrad., U. Mass. Tchr., adminstr. Learning Comty., Westport, Conn., 1980-86; tchr. Mead Sch., Greenwich, Conn., 1988-90; adminstr. Inst. for Children's Lit., Redding, Conn., 1990-92, Saugatuck Child Care Svcs., Inc., Westport, 1992-96; cons. Hampshire Ednl. Collaborative, Northampton, Mass., 1997-99; faculty Greenfield (Mass.) C.C., 1999—. Author: (student anthology) Goddard College Collection, 1987, 88; cons. editor Young Children, 2001—. Mem. AAUW (bull. editor 1994-95), Nat. Assn. for Edn. of Young Children. Avocations: sewing, quilting, walking. E-mail: roth@gcc.mass.edu.

ROTHBERGER, SUE ELLEN, language educator; b. NY, Feb. 29, 1944; d. Irving Harry and Jean Dorothy (Seider) Weitz; m. Louis, June 30, 1972 (dec. Aug. 1976). BA, Bklyn. Coll., 1964, MA, 1968; Cert. in Bus. Adminstrn., L.I. U., 1980. Cert. tchr., NY. Tchr. NYC Bd. of Edn., 1964-70, Greenburgh Ctrl. #7, Hartsdale, NY, 1970—99. Adj. lectr. Spanish John Jay Coll. Criminal Justice; pres. Greenburgh Tchr. Fedn., Hartsdale, 1986-99; policy bd. Westchester Tchr. Ctr., Hartsdale, 1986-93; presenter Summer Inst. John Jay Coll., NYC, 1988. Recipient Tchr. Incentive Project Westchester Tchr. Ctr., Hartsdale, 1987. Mem. NY State Assn. of Fgn. Lang. Tchr. (presenter 1988), Am. Assn. of Tchr. of Spanish & Portuguese, NY State United Tchr., Kiwanis. Home: 5800 Arlington Ave Apt 16U Bronx NY 10471-1418 Office: John Jay Coll Criminal Justice 445 W 59th St New York NY 10019

ROTHENBERG, HARVEY DAVID, educational administrator; b. May 31, 1937; s. Max and Cecelia Rothenberg; m. Audrey Darlynne Roseman, July 5, 1964; children: David Michael, Mark Daniel. BBA, State U. Iowa, 1960; MA, U. No. Colo., 1961; postgrad., Harris Tchrs. Coll., 1962-63; PhD, Colo. State U., 1972. Distributive edn. tchr. Roosevelt H.S., St. Louis, 1961-63, Proviso West H.S., Hillside, Ill., 1963-64, Longmont (Colo.) Sr. H.S., 1964-69, 70-71; supr. rsch. and spl. programs St. Vrain Valley Sch. Dist., Longmont, 1971-72; chmn. bus. divsn. Arapahoe C.C., Littleton, Colo., 1972-75; dir. vocat., career and adult edn. Arapahoe County Sch. Dist. 6, Littleton, 1975-96; part-time instr. Met. State Coll., Denver, 1975-85, Arapahoe C.C., Littleton, 1975-80, Regis U., 1980—. Dir. faculty, curriculum Sch. Profl. Studies, Regis U., 1996-98, instr., facilitator, 1998—; owner HDR Bus. and Ednl. Consulting, 1988—; owner Shreveport Bombers Indoor Football Team of Indoor Profl. Football League, 1999-2001; vis. prof. U . Ala., Tuscaloosa, summer 1972; dir. Chatfield Bank, Littleton, 1974-83, Yaak River Mines Ltd., Amusement Personified Inc.; pres. Kuytia Inc., Littleton, 1975—; co-owner Albuquerque Lasers. Author: Conducting Successful Business Research, 1996. Mem. City of Longmont Long-Range Planning Commn., 1971-72, pres. Homeowners Bd., 1978-80; mem. Denver Union Sta. renovation com., 2002—; mem. Jefferson County Cmty. Devel. Com., 2003—. Recipient Outstanding Young Educator award St. Vrain Valley Sch. Dist., 1967, Outstanding Vocat. Educator, Colo., 1992, Western Region U.S., 1993. Mem. Am. Vocat. Assn., Nat. Assn. Local Sch. Adminstrs., Colo. Vocat. Assn. (mem. exec. com. 1966-68, treas. 1972-73), Littleton C. of C., Colo. Assn. Vocat. Adminstrs., Colo. Educators for and About Bus., Elks, Masons, Delta Sigma Pi, Delta Pi Epsilon. Home: 7461 S Sheridan Ct Littleton CO 80128-7084 E-mail: rothenbergs@msn.com.

ROTHENBERG, JEROME, author, visual arts and literary educator; b. N.Y.C., Dec. 11, 1931; s. Morris and Estelle (Lichtenstein) R.; m. Diane Brodatz, Dec. 25, 1952; 1 son, Matthew. BA, CCNY, 1952; MA, U. Mich., 1953; LittD (hon.), SUNY, Oneonta, 1997. With Mannes Coll. Music, N.Y.C., 1961-70. Vis. prof. U. Calif., San Diego, 1971, 77-84, U. Wis.-Milw., 1974-75, San Diego State U., 1976-77, U. Calif., Riverside, 1980, U. Okla., Norman, 1984; vis. Aerol Arnold prof. English U.So. Calif., 1983; vis. writer in residence SUNY, Albany, 1986, prof. English SUNY, Binghamton, 1986-88; prof. visual arts and lit. U. Calif., San Diego, 1989—, chmn. visual arts, 1990-93; head, creative writing, 1994-95. Poet, freelance writer, 1956—; author: numerous books of poetry and prose including Between, 1967, Technicians of the Sacred, 1968, Poems for the Game of Silence, 1971, Shaking the Pumpkin, 1972, America a Prophecy, 1973, Revolution of the Word, 1974, Poland/1931, 1974, A Big Jewish Book, 1978, A Seneca Journal, 1978, Vienna Blood, 1980, Pre-Faces, 1981, Symposium of the Whole, 1983, That Dada Strain, 1983, New Selected Poems, 1986, Khurbn, 1989, Exiled in the Word, 1989, The Lorca Variations I-VIII, 1990, Apres le jeu de silence, 1991, The Lorca Variations (complete), 1993, Gematria, 1994, An Oracle for Delfi, 1995, Poems for

The Millennium, vol. 1, 1995, Seedings, 1996, The Book, Spiritual Instrument, 1996, Poems for the Millennium, Vol. 2, 1998, A Paradise of Poets, 1999, A Book of The Book, 2000, The Case for Memory, 2001, Livre de Temoignage, 2002, A Book of Witness, 2003, María Sabina, 2003; editor, pub. Hawk's Well Press., N.Y.C., 1958-65, Some/Thing mag., 1966-69, Alcheringa: Ethnopoetics, 1970-76, New Wilderness Letter, 1976-86. Served with AUS, 1953-55. Recipient award in poetry Longview Found., 1960, Am. Book award, 1982, PEN Ctr. USA West award, 1994, 2002, PEN Oakland Josephine Miles award, 1994, 96; Wenner-Gren Found. grantee-in-aide for rsch. in Am. Indian poetry, 1968; Guggenheim fellow in creative writing, 1974; NEA poetry grantee, 1976. Mem. P.E.N. Am. Center, New Wilderness Found., World Poetry Acad. Office: care New Directions 80 8th Ave New York NY 10011-5126 E-mail: jrothenb@ucsd.edu.

ROTHENBERG, MARC ELLIOT, pediatrics educator; b. N.Y.C., Jan. 17, 1961; s. Leonard Martin and Helen Ava (Weissman) R.; m. Joy Hannah Malka, Aug. 26, 1990; children: Eliana Nitza, Danielle Shoshana, Joelle Adina, Mayer Ethan. BA, Brandeis U., 1983; MD, Harvard U., 1990, PhD. Diplomate Am. Bd. Pediatrics. Intern Children's Hosp., Boston, 1990-91, resident, 1991-92, fellow, 1992-95; instr. Harvard Med. Sch., Boston, 1995-96; assoc. prof., sect. chief Children's Hosp. - U. Cin., 1996—; prof. pediatrics, chief divsn. allergy & immunology clin. childrens Hosp. Med. Ctr. Physician Harvard Med. Sch., Boston, 1990-96, scientist, 1990-96; physician U. Cin., 1996, asst. prof., 1996, assoc. prof., 1999, dir. allergy-immunology, 2001, prof., 2002. Contbr. articles to profl. jours. Recipient Physician Scientist award Howard Hughes Med. Inst., 1994-96, Damon-Runyon Walton Winchell Cancer Inst. award, N.Y., 1993, NIH-NIAID awards, 1997, 99, Pharmacia Internat. Rsch. Found. award, 1998, Human Frontiers Sci. Program award, 1999. Mem. Am. Acad. Allergy and Immunology (scholar 1993), Am. Acad. of Pediatrics, Am. Assn. Immunology, Am. Soc. Clin. Investigation. Jewish. Achievements include development of first culture system for human eosinophils. Office: Childrens Hosp Med Ctr 3333 Burnet Ave Cincinnati OH 45229-3026 E-mail: rothenberg@chmcc.org.

ROTHERMICH, GAYLA, music educator, director; b. Denver, May 5, 1946; d. C. Stanley and Bessey Welsh; children: Stefan, Candace. B in Music Edn., Wichita State U., s, 1968; MusM, So. Ill. U., Edwardsville, 1973; student, Hamburg Musickhochschule, Germany, 1973—75. Cert. instrumental/vocal K-12. Dir. Rothermich Studio for violin and viola, Ballwin, Mo., 1976—, St. Louis Suzuki Edn. Program, 1976—81; dir. strings, Suzuki specialist Parkway Sch. Dist./Barretts, Manchester, 1983—; program dir. Barretts Voyage to Mars, Manchester, Mo., 1999—. Freelance spkr. Parkway Sch. Dist., St. Louis, 1997—, Barretts Voyage to Mars, 1999—2000, musician website design, 1999—, prodr. integrated arts and scis. program, 1999—. Named All-State Award winner, Nat. Federated Music Club, 1964. Mem.: NEA (workshop leader Mo. state convention 2001), Music Educators Nat. Conf. (curriculum coun.), Am. String Tchrs. Assn., Social Concerns Com. Presbyterian. Avocations: computer technology/graphic design, gardening, travel, research, exploring. Office: Barretts Elem Sch 1780 Carman Rd Ballwin MO 63021 Office Fax: 314-415-6012. Personal E-mail: GRothermic@aol.com. Business E-Mail: grothermich@pkwy.k12.mo.us.

ROTHKOPF, ARTHUR J. college president; b. N.Y.C., May 24, 1935; s. Abraham and Sarah (Mehlman) Rothkopf; m. Barbara Sarnoff, Dec. 25, 1958; children: Jennifer, Katherine. AB, Lafayette Coll., 1955; JD, Harvard U., 1958. Bar: N.Y. 1959, D.C. 1967. Atty. U.S. Dept. Treasury, N.Y.C., 1958—60, SEC, Washington, 1960—63; assoc. tax legis. counsel U.S. Dept. Treasury, Washington, 1963—66; ptnr. Hogan & Hartson, Washington, 1967—91; gen. counsel U.S. Dept. Transp., Washington, 1991—92, dep. sec., 1992—93; pres. Lafayette Coll., Easton, Pa., 1993—. Bd. dirs. Lehigh Valley Econ. Devel. Corp., Ins. Svcs. Office, Inc., Jersey City, Lehigh Valley Partnerships. Trustee Fed. City Coun., Washington, 1983—91, Lehigh Valley Hosp.; chair bd. dirs. Coun. Higher Edn. Accreditation; bd. dirs., past chmn. Assn. Ind. Colls. and Univs. Pa. Mem.: The Pa. Soc. (treas.), Harvard Club of N.Y.C., Chevy Chase Club, Met. Club of Washington. Jewish. Home: 515 College Ave Easton PA 18042-7623 Office: Lafayette Coll 316 Markle Hall Easton PA 18042

ROTHMAN, DAVID J. history and medical educator; b. N.Y.C., Apr. 30, 1937; s. Murray and Anne (Beier) R.; m. Sheila Miller, June 26, 1960; children: Matthew, Micol. BA, Columbia U., 1958; MA, Harvard U., 1959, PhD, 1964. Asst. prof. history Columbia U., N.Y.C., 1964-67, assoc. prof., 1967-71, prof., 1971—, Bernard Schoenberg prof. social medicine, dir. Ctr. for Study of Society and Medicine. Fulbright-Hayes prof. Hebrew U., Jerusalem, 1968-69, India, 1982; vis. Pinkerton Prof. Sch. Criminal Justice, State U. N.Y., at Albany, 1973-74; Samuel Paley lectr. Hebrew U., Jerusalem, 1977; Mem. Com. for Study of Incarceration, 1971-74; co-dir. Project on Community Alternatives, 1978-82; chmn. adv. bd. on criminal justice Clark Found., 1978-82; mem. bd. advisors The Project on Death in Am., Open Soc. Inst., 1995-2000, trustee; mem. bd. trustees Open Soc. Inst., 1996—, pres. Inst. on Medicine as a Profession, 2003—. Author: Politics and Power, 1966, The Discovery of the Asylum, 1971; co-author: Doing Good, 1978, Conscience and Convenience: The Asylum and its Alternatives in Progressive America, 1980; (with Sheila M. Rothman) The Willowbrook Wars, 1984; Strangers at the Bedside, 1991, Beginings Count: The Technological Imperative in American Health Care, 1997; editor: The World of the Adams Chronicles, 1976, (with Sheila M. Rothman) On Their Own: The Poor in Modern America, 1972, The Sources of American Social Tradition, 1975, (with Stanton Wheeler) Social History and Social Policy, 1981, (with Norval Morris) The Oxford History of the Prison, 1995, (with Steven Marcus and Stephanie Kiceluk) Medicine and Western Civilization, 1995, (with Sheila M. Rothman) The Pursuit of Perfection, 2003. Recipient Albert J. Beveridge prize Am. Hist. Assn., 1971. Mem. Am. Hist. Assn., N.Y. Acad. Medicine, Phi Beta Kappa. Office: Columbia U Coll Physicians and Surgeons Ctr Study Soc and Medicine 630 W 168th St New York NY 10032-3702

ROTHMAN, FRANK GEORGE, biology educator, biochemical genetics researcher; b. Budapest, Hungary, Feb. 2, 1930; came to U.S., 1938; s. Stephen and Irene Elizabeth (Manheim) R.; m. Joan Therese Kiernan, Aug.22, 1953; children: Michael, Jean, Stephen, Maria. BA, U. Chgo., 1948, MS, 1951; PhD, Harvard U., 1955. Postdoctoral fellow NSF, U. Wis., MIT, 1956-58, Am. Cancer Soc., MIT, Cambridge, 1958-59; postdoctoral assoc. MIT, Cambridge, 1957-61; asst. prof. Brown U., Providence, 1961-65, assoc. prof., 1965-70, prof., 1970-97, dean of biology, 1984-90, provost, 1990-95, prof. emeritus, 1997—. Sr. advisor, Project Kaleidoscope, 1999—. Contbr. articles to profl. jours. Served with U.S. Army, 1954-56. Spl. fellow USPHS, U. Sussex, Eng., 1967-68; NSF grantee, 1961-84. Fellow AAAS; mem. Genetics Soc. Am. E-mail: frank_rothman@brown.edu.

ROTHMAN, JULIET CASSUTO, social work educator, writer; b. Chgo., Jan. 29, 1942; m. Leonard A. Rothman; children: Susan R. Kolko, Deborah M. Rothman, Daniel M. (dec.). BA, Tufts U., 1962; MSW, CUNY, 1973; MA, St. John's Coll., Annapolis, Md., 1988; PhD, Am. U., 1990. Cert. social worker Md. Geriat. cons. Chesapeake Manor Extended Care Annapolis Convalescent Ctr., 1974-90; tri-county social svcs. coord. Nat. Multiple Sclerosis Soc., Balt., 1980-82; lectr. sch. social welfare U. Calif., Berkeley, 1998—, UCB/UCSF Joint Medkel Program, 2002—; prof. devel. faculty NASW, 1998—. Tutor Italian, Annapolis, 1974—88; chair ethics com. Chesapeake Manor, Annapolis, 1986—90, chair adv. bd., 1987—90; lectr. Anne Arundel C.C., Arnold, Md., 1988—90; vis. asst. prof. Nat. Cath. Sch. Social Svc., Cath. U., Washington, 1990—98; mem. ethics com. Hospice Chesapeake, 1992—97. Author: Saying Goodby to Daniel, 1994, A Birthday Present for Daniel, 1995 (award Parent Coun. 1997), The Bereaved Parent's Survival Guide, 1997, German edit., Dutch edit., From the Front Lines: Student Cases in Social Work Ethics, 1998, Contracting in Clinical Social Work, 1998, The Self-Awareness Workbook for Social Workers, 1999, Stepping Out into the Field: A Field Work Manual for Social Workers, 2000, Social Work Practice Across Disability, 2002; contbr. articles to jours. in field; series editor Internat. Healthcare, Bern, Switzerland, 1990-2000. Judge Bd . of Elections, Anne Arundel County, Md., 1985-90; sec. Anne Arundel County Cmty. Svcs. Coalition, Annapolis, 1992-93; pres. Friends of Annapolis Chorale, 1992-94; mem. San Francisco City Chorus; docent Nat. Park Svc., Calif. Acad. Sci., 2003-; inspector Bd. Elections San Francisco City and County, 2003-. Mem. NASW, Am. Philos. Assn. Avocations: travel, music, photography, arts and crafts, outdoor activities.

ROTHSCHILD, JENNIFER ANN, artist, educator; b. Mesa, Ariz., Aug. 16, 1948; d. Joe Dean and Frances Ann (McFarland) Johnston; m. Harry Ronald Rothschild, Feb. 14, 1981. Diploma, El Camino Jr. Coll., 1968; BA in Art Edn., Calif. State U., 1970. Cert. secondary sch. tchr., Calif. Arts and crafts specialist City of Hawthorne (Calif.) Parks and Recreation, 1966-67; portrait artist Disneyland, Anaheim, Calif., 1970-74; secondary sch. art tchr. Orange (Calif.) Unified Schs., 1972-80; freelance custom apparel designer Honolulu, 1982-94; sculptor, artist, 1994—. One woman show at Roy's Honolulu, 2001, Art Centre Gallery, Honolulu, 1997; corp. artist Arts of Paradise Gallery, Honolulu, 1997—; exhibited in show at City of Manhattan Beach, Calif., 1966, Assn. of Hawaii Artists, 1996—, in book Encyclopedia of Living Artists, 10th edit., 1997. Bd. dirs. Hawaii Tennis Patrons, Honolulu, 1996—, Assn. of Hawaii Artists Show chairwoman, 2002. Recipient scholarship Chouinard Sch. Art Inst., 1965-66, 1st Place Stamp Design award Easter Seals, 1995-96, Hokele Artists award Hawaiian Airlines, 1996, Most Unique Art award Assn. of Hawaii Artists Aloha Show, 1997. Fellow Nat. Mus. Women in Arts; mem. AAUW, Honolulu Art Acad., Assn. Hawaii Artists (v.p. 1996-97, pres. 1999-2000), Hawaiian Pacific Tennis Assn. (rules chmn. 1997), mem. Windward Art Guild, 2002, Nat. League of Am. Pen Women, Hon., chapter, Alpha Omicron Pi. Republican. Presbyterian. Avocations: tennis, reading, writing, painting, sculpting.

ROTHSCHILD, MAX FREDERICK, animal science educator; b. Highland Park, Mich., May 26, 1952; s. Bill F. and Gertrude (Rosenberg) R.; m. Denise J. Rothschild, June 22, 1975; children: Louise, Daniel. BS, U. Calif., Davis, 1974; MS, U. Wis., 1975; PhD, Cornell U., 1978. Asst. prof. animal sci. U. Md., College Park, 1978-80, Iowa State U., Ames, 1980-83, assoc. prof. animal sci., 1983-87, prof. animal sci., 1987-99, Charles F. Curtiss disting. prof. agr., 1999—. U.S. pig genome coord. USDA-Coop. State Rsch. Edn. and Econ. Svc., 1994—; cons. to industry. Contbr. over 190 refereed articles, 400 other articles to profl. jours., chpts to 11 books; mem. several editl. bds. profl. jours. Bd. dirs. Boy Scouts Am.; mem. several charity bds. Recipient Young Rschr. award Midwest Am. Soc. Animal Sci., 1990, Am. Soc. Breeding and Genetics Award, 1998, Iowa Inventor of the Yr., 2002. Mem. AAAS, Am. Soc. Animal Sci. (Animal Breeding award 1995), Internat. Soc. Animal Genetics. Achievements include 5 patents on genetic tests to improve litter size in pigs, several research projects leading to industry acceptance. Home: 511 Oliver Cir Ames IA 50014-3569 Office: Iowa State U Dept Animal Sci Ames IA 50011-0001

ROTHSTEIN, ANNE LOUISE, education educator, college official; b. Bklyn., Feb. 15, 1943; d. William and Rose Mary (Smith) R. BS, Bklyn. Coll., 1963; MA, Tchrs. Coll. Columbia, N.Y.C., 1965, EdD, 1970. Tchr. Erasmus Hall High Sch., Bklyn., 1963-64, Fort Hamilton High Sch., Bklyn., 1964-64; lectr. Hunter Coll. in the Bronx, N.Y., 1965-68; instr., prof. Lehman Coll., Bronx, 1968—, dept. chair, 1980-83, assoc. dean, 1983-93, assoc. provost/dir. for sponsored program devel., 1993-98. Dir. Lehman Ctr. for Sch./Coll. Collaboratives, Bronx, 1988—; grant specialist for sch./coll. programs, 1985--; small sch. developer, 1999--. Editor, pub. (jour.) Motor Skills: Theory into Practice, 1976-87; chair editorial bd. (jour.) Strategies, 1986-92; author: Research and Statistics, 1985, Motor Learning: Basic Stuff, 1987. Grantee in field. Fellow Rsch. Consortium Am. Alliance, Am. Alliance for Health, Physical Edn., Recreation and Dance; mem. Nat. Assn. for Sport and Physical Edn., Nat. Assn. for Girls and Women in Sport, Assn. for Supervision and Curriculum Devel., Am. Ednl. Rsch. Assn. Avocations: computers, grants consulting. Home: PO Box 3007 Newtown CT 06470-3007 Office: Lehman Coll Bedford Park Blvd W Bronx NY 10468 E-mail: anner@lehman.cuny.edu., arothstein@aol.com.

ROTITHOR, HEMANT GOVIND, electrical engineer, educator; b. Patan, India, July 5, 1958; came to U.S., 1985; s. Govind Hari and Suman (Govind) R.; m. Shubhada Hemant, Sept. 1, 1987; children: Sagar, Jaydeep. PhD in Elec. Engring., U. Ky., 1989. Devel. engr. ORG Systems, Baroda, India, 1981-82, Philips India, 1982-85; asst. prof. Worcester (Mass.) Poly. Inst., 1990-95; prin. engr. Digital Equipment Corp., Nashua, N.H., 1995-98; prin. engr. Performance Microprocessor Divsn. Intel Corp., Hillsboro, Oreg., 1998—. Mem. steering com. 3d Internat. Symposium on personal, indoor, mobile, radio comm., 1992; program com. Internat. Conf. on Parallel & Distributed Computing, 1998. Contbr. articles to profl. jours. Grantee Worcester Poly. Inst., 1990, NSF, 1992, 94, 95, Nynex Corp. Mem. IEEE (sr.), Assn. for Computing Machinery, Sigma Xi, Tau Beta Pi, Eta Kappa Nu. Achievements include research in instrumentation measurement, computer architecture and distributed computers, compilers, and performance management; research in microprocessor function and performance validation. Home: 399 NE Autumn Rose Way Apt D Hillsboro OR 97124-5329 Office: Intel Corp RA2-302 2501 NW 229th Ave Hillsboro OR 97124-5503

ROTMAN, JOSEPH JONAH, mathematician, educator; b. Chgo., May 26, 1934; s. Ely and Rose (Wolf) R.; m. Marganit Weinberger, Aug. 25, 1978; children: Ella Rose, Daniel Adam. BA, U. Chgo., 1954, MA, 1956, PhD, 1959. Rsch. assoc. U. Ill., Urbana, 1959-61, asst. prof., 1961-63, assoc. prof., 1963-68, prof., 1968—. Vis. prof. Queen Mary Coll., London, 1965-66, 1985-86, Hebrew U., Jerusalem, 1970; Lady Davis prof. Technion, Haifa, Israel, 1977-78, Hebrew U., Jerusalem, 1977-78, Tel Aviv U., Israel, 1984, Oxford U., Eng., 1990. Author: Theory of Groups, 1965, 2d edit., 1973, 3d edit., 1984, 4th edit., 1995; Homological Algebra, 1970, 2d edit., 1979, Algebraic Topology, 1988, Galois Theory, 1990, 2d edit., 1998, Abstract Algebra, 1997, 2d edit., 2000, Journey into Mathematics, 1998, Advanced Modern Algebra, 2002; editor: Proc. AMS, 1970, 1971, mng. editor, Proc. AMS, 1972, 1973. Mem. Am. Math. Soc., Math. Assn. Am., London Math. Soc. Office: Dept Math 1409 W Green St Urbana IL 61801-2943

ROTTIER, KATHLEEN LOUISE, secondary education educator; b. Cheverly, Md., Nov. 10, 1950; d. Walter Raymond and Ann Louise (Baicar) Smith; m. Dennis Michael Farley, June 28, 1975 (dec. Sept. 1987); m. Jay Arthur Rottier, Oct. 12, 1990. BA, U. Md., 1972; MA in Edn., George Washington U., 1982; PhD, U. Md., 1993. Cert. tchr., Md. Tchr. social studies Prince George's County (Md.) Schs., 1972—, chair dept., 1979-83, tchr., coord., 1983-85. Tchr. trainer in coordination with Bowie (Md.) State U., 1992; computer trainer Md. Nat. Capital Parks and Planning Commn., Bowie, 1987-88; cons. Div. Instrn., Prince George's County Schs., Upper Marlboro, 1988-90; evaluator Middle States Assn. Colls. and Schs., 1989. Author, researcher Psychology of Learning, 1989—. Lay Eucharistic min. St. Paul's Episcopal Ch., Waldorf, Md., 1989—; sch. coord. VFW Voice of Democracy Contest, Prince George's County, 1992. Recipietn Cert. of Recognition Am. Hist. Assn., 1989, award citation VFW Voice of Democracy, 1980; named to Outstanding Young Women of Am., 1983. Mem. APA, ASCD, NEA, U.S. Captiol Hist. Assn. (hon. life). Avocations: golf, hiking, skiing, Karate. Office: 13800 Brandywine Rd Brandywine MD 20613-5802

ROUGH, MARIANNE CHRISTINA, librarian, educator; b. Glen Cove, N.Y., June 27, 1941; d. Michael Anthony Scarangello, Ann Nancy (Kulka) Scarangello; m. Allan Conrad Rough; 1 child, William Johnson. AAS, SUNY, Farmingdale, 1976; BA, SUNY, Old Westbury, 1977; MLS, L.I. U., 1978; cert. in advanced librarianship, Columbia U., 1985. Art dir. Technamation, Inc., Port Washington, NY, 1962—68; dir. new product design Queens Lithography, Inc., L.I., NY, 1968—70; tech. specialist SUNY, Coll.at Farmingdale, 1970—78; dir. Libr. Learning Resources Ctr. SUNY, Coll. Old Westbury, 1978—82; prof., libr. Prince George's C.C., Largo, Md., 1983—. Mem. C.C. adv. group OCLC Online Computer Libr. Ctr., Inc., Dublin, 2001—. Contbr. chapters to books. Regional publicity coord. Audubon Soc., L.I., 1978—79; coordinating team mem. Sierra Club, Annual C&O Canal Hike, Washington, 1991—95; bd. dirs. Friends Pub. Libr., Port Washington, NY, 1980—81. Recipient award of merit, Md. Assn. Higher Edn., 1987; grantee Pathfinder grants, Prince George's C.C., 1999, 2001. Mem.: Assn. Coll. and Rsch. Librs. of ALA (sec. cmty. and jr. coll. sect. 2001—02, vice-chmn., chmn.-elect, past chmn. 2002—), Assn. Libr. Collections and Tech. Svcs. of ALA (sec. coun. regional groups 1999—2001, Md. rep. Potomac Tech. Processing Librs.). Methodist. Avocations: fine art, art history, history, historical preservation. Home: 1015 Danbury Dr Bowie MD 20721-3202 Office: Prince Georges CC 301 Largo Rd Upper Marlboro MD 20774-2199 Home Fax: 301-390-7824; Office Fax: 301-808-8847. Personal E-mail: mrough@pgcc.edu.

ROUMM, PHYLLIS EVELYN GENSBIGLER, retired literature educator, writer; b. New Alexandria, Pa., Jan. 1, 1927; d. Theodore Roosevelt and Daisy Isabelle (Patterson) Gensbigler; m. Milton Leonard Roumm, Nov. 23, 1946; children: David Lynn, Nikolyn, Dennis Eric, Janna Leigh. BS in English Edn., Indiana U. of Pa., 1945, MEd, 1963; postgrad., Ohio U., 1964, 65; PhD, Kent State U., 1977. Tchr. English Elders Ridge (Pa.) Joint HS, 1945-46, Apollo (Pa.) HS, 1946-47; tchr. English, speech Indiana (Pa.) Area Jr.-Sr. HS, 1959-67; tchg. fellow Kent (Ohio) State U., 1970-71; prof. English Indiana U. Pa., 1967-85, prof. emeritus, 1985—. Freelance writer, 1985—; mem. strategic planning steering com. Indiana Area Sch. Dist. Bd. dirs. Hist. and Geneal. Soc. Indiana County, 1984, Indiana Free Libr., 1988—91; mem. health promotion com. Aging Svcs., Inc., Indiana; mem. Last Stand, Key West, Fla., Friends of Libr., Key West. Mem.: AAUW, Indiana Wordsmiths, So. Humanities Conf., Ligonier Valley Writers Assn., Coll. English Assn. (life), Assn. Pa. State Coll. and Univ. Ret. Faculty (bd. dirs. 1998—), Hadassah (life), Derry Hist. Soc. (life), Kent State Alumni Assn. (life), Pa. Ret. State Employees (v.p. Indico chpt. 1996—97, pres. 1997—98, bd. dirs. 1998—), Am. Assn. Ret. People, New Century Club, Alpha Delta Kappa (pres. 1968—70, Silver Sister award 1991), Phi Delta Kappa. Avocations: reading, reviewing books, walking, writing. Home: 310 Poplar Ave Indiana PA 15701-3024

ROUND, ALICE FAYE BRUCE, school psychologist; b. Ironton, Ohio, July 19, 1934; d. Wade Hamilton and Martha Matilda (Toops) Bruce; children: Leonard Bruce, Christopher Frederick. BA, Asbury Coll., 1956; MS in Sch. Psychology, Miami U., Oxford, Ohio, 1975. Cert. tchr., sch. psychologist, supr., Ohio; cert. tchr., Calif. Tchr. Madison County (Ohio) Schs., 1956-58, Columbus (Ohio) Pub. Schs., 1958, San Diego Pub. Schs., 1958-60, Poway (Calif.) Unified Sch. Dist., 1960-64; substitute tchr. Princeton City Schs., Cin., 1969-75; sch. psychologist, intern Greenhills/Forest Park City Schs., Cin., 1975-76; sch. psychologist Fulton County Schs., Wauseon, Ohio, 1976-77, Sandusky (Ohio) pub. and Cath. schs., 1977-96, Eric County Ednl. Svc. Ctr., 1996-98; pre-sch. psychologist Huron County Bd. Edn., Norwalk, Ohio, 1998—. Tchr. art cmty. group and pvt. lessons, Sandusky, 1962, Springdale, Ohio, 1962-69; mem. Youth Svcs. Bd., Sandusky, 1978-88; bd. dirs., cons. Sandusky Sch. Practical Nursing, 1983-91; presenter suicide prevention seminars for mental health orgns.; speaker at ch., civic and youth orgns., local radio and TV programs; cons. on teen pregnancy to various schs., health depts. Mem. Huron (Ohio) Boosters Club, 1978-92, Vols. in Action, Sandusky, 1987—. Mem. NAACP, NEA, Nat. Sch. Psychologist Assn., Ohio Sch. Psychologist Assn., Maumee Valley Sch. Psychologist Assn., Ohio Edn. Assn., Sandusky Edn. Assn., Phi Delta Kappa (historian 1984-88, Most Innovative Preservation of History award 1988). Home: 821 Seneca Ave Huron OH 44839-1842 Office: Huron City Schs Cleveland Ave Huron OH 44839 E-mail: AFRound@aol.com.

ROUNTREE, PATRICIA ANN, youth organization administrator; b. Rochester, N.Y., Apr. 2, 1942; d. Robert James and Myrtle Margaret (Cuthbertson) R. AA, Cazenovia Coll., 1961; BA, Parsons Coll., 1965. Gen. clk. Eastman Kodak, Rochester, 1961-63; 6th grade tchr. Wayland (N.Y.) Ctrl. Sch., 1965-67; field dir. Seven Lakes Coun. Girl Scouts U.S.A., Phelps, N.Y., 1967-73, program dir. Palm Glades Coun. Lake Worth, Fla., 1973-76, asst. exec. dir. Seven Lakes Coun., 1976-86, exec. dir. Mich. Trails Coun., 1986-89, exec. dir. Ctrl. N.Y. Coun. Syracuse, 1989—. Pres., bd. dirs. Planned Parenthood of Fingerlakes, Geneva, N.Y., 1982-86. Mem. Rotary Syracuse. Presbyterian. Avocations: needlework, reading, travel. Home: 4 Robinson Dr Baldwinsville NY 13027-2807 Office: Ctrl NY Girl Scout Coun 6724 Thompson Rd # 482 Syracuse NY 13211-2122

ROUSE, ELAINE BURDETT, retired secondary school educator; b. Point Pleasant, W.Va., Feb. 4, 1915; d. John Wallace and Edna Ada (Johnson) Burdett; m. Douglas Philip Rouse, Sept. 27, 1943 (dec. June 1971); 1 child, Julia Ann. BA, W.Va. U., 1938, MA in Econs., 1953; MA in Pub. Svc. (hon.), U. Rio Grande, 1990. Cert. secondary tchr., W.Va., Ohio. H.S. tchr. Mason County Schs., Point Pleasant, 1938-40, 46-53, 64-77, Pomeroy (Ohio) Schs., 1953-64; sec. field office FBI, Huntington, W.Va., 1940-43; part-time tchr. Rio Grande (Ohio) Coll., 1960-65, Point Pleasant br. Marshall U., 1978-83. Author: John W. Gard and the Gard Families of the Mid-Ohio River Valley, 1992, William Burdett of Monroe County, West Virginia, and His Descendants, 1755-1997, 98. Chmn. bd. trustees Rio Grande C.C., 1993-95, Gallia County Bd. Elections, Gallipolis, Ohio, 1994-98; mem. Gallia County Dem. Exec. Com., 1985-99. Recipient 1st pl. econs. edn. in W.Va. award Pub. Utilities of the Virginias, 1971. Mem. NEA, Gen. Fedn. Women's Clubs (pres. Riverside Study Club 1990-92). Presbyterian. Avocations: travel, genealogy.

ROUSE, LEGRAND ARIAIL, II, retired lawyer, educator; b. Spartanburg, S.C., June 11, 1933; s. LeGrand and Hilda Virginia (Ariail) R.; m. Patricia Adelle White, Aug. 23, 1958; children: LeGrand A. III, Laurie Adelle Rouse-Hazel, Daniel Morris. AB in History and Polit. Sci., Wofford Coll., 1954; LLB, U. S.C., 1959, JD, 1970; MA in Govt., Am. U., 1969. Bar: S.C. 1959, U.S. Dist. Ct. S.C. 1959, U.S. Ct. Appeals (4th cir.) 1964, U.S. Supreme Ct. 1963. Sole practice, Spartanburg, 1959-63, 68-69; assoc. counsel, jud. improvements subcom. U.S. Senate Judiciary Com., Washington, 1963; profl. staff mem. U.S. Senate P.O. and Civil Svc. Com., Washington, 1964-68; instructional specialist Office of Instrnl. TV, S.C. Dept. Edn., Columbia, 1970-73; social studies cons. curriculum devel. S.C. Dept. Edn., 1973-79, spl. asst. legal and legis. affairs to State Supt. Edn., 1979-91; spl. asst. to sr. exec. asst. Policy, Rsch. and Leadership, Columbia, 1991. Cons. S.C. Council for Social Studies, Columbia, 1973-78; dir. S.C. Council Econ. Edn., Columbia. Author: Government-Politics-Citizenship, tchr. lesson guide, 1971-72; creator, on-camera instr. Government-Politics-Citizenship TV series, 1970-72; project dir. econs. edn. kit for tchrs. grades 1-12: People, Production, Profits, 1977. Mem. S.C. Ho. of Reps., Columbia, 1961-64; alt. del. Nat. Dem. Conv., 1964. Served to 1st lt. USAR, 1955-57. Recipient Schoolmens' medal Freedoms Found. at Valley Forge, 1974. Mem. S.C. Bar Assn., S.C. State Employees' Assn. (pres. 1980-82), Masons, Nat. Sojourners (past pres. chpt. 184). Methodist. Home: 1021 Milton Ln Columbia SC 29209-2321

ROUSE, ROSCOE, JR., librarian, educator; b. Valdosta, Ga., Nov. 26, 1919; s. Roscoe and Minnie Estelle (Corbett) R.; m. Charlie Lou Miller, June 23, 1945; children: Charles Richard, Robin Lou. BA, U. Okla., 1948,

MA, 1952; MALS, U. Mich., 1958, PhD, 1962; student (Grolier Soc. scholar), Rutgers U., 1956. Bookkeeper C & S Nat. Bank, Valdosta, Ga., 1937-41; draftsman R.K. Rouse Co. (heating engrs.), Greenville, S.C., 1941-42; student asst. U. Okla. and Rice U., 1947-48; asst. librarian Northeastern State Coll., Tahlequah, Okla., 1948-49, acting librarian, instr. library sci., 1949-51; circulation librarian Baylor U., 1952-53, acting univ. librarian, 1953-54, univ. librarian, prof., 1954-63, chmn. dept. library sci., 1956-63; dir. libraries State U. N.Y. at Stony Brook, L.I., 1963-67; dean libr. svcs., prof. Okla. State U., Stillwater, 1967-87, univ. libr. historian, 1987-92, chmn. dept. libr. edn., 1967-74. Vis. prof. U. Okla. Sch. Library Sci., summer 1962, N. Tex. State U., summer 1965; acad. library cons.; mem. AIA-Am. Library Assn. Library Bldg. Awards Jury, 1976; bd. dirs. Fellowship Christian Libr. and Info. Specialists. Author: A History of the Baylor University Library, 1845-1919, 1962; editor: Okla. Librarian, 1951-52; co-author: Organization Charts of Selected Libraries, 1973; A History of the Okla. State U. Library, 1992; contbr. articles, book revs., chpts. to publs. in field. Bd. dirs. Okla. Dept. Librs., 1989-92, chmn., 1990-92. 1st lt. USAAF, 1942-45. Decorated Air medal with 4 oak leaf clusters; recipient citation Okla. State Senate, 1987, Rotary Outstanding Achievement award, 1996; named in 150 Prominent Individuals in Baylor's History. Mem. ALA (life, mem. coun. 1971-72, 76-80, 83-84, 84-88, chmn. libr. orgn. and mgmt. sect. 1973-75, planning and budget assembly 1978-79, coun. com. on coms. 1979-80, bldgs. and equipment sect. exec. bd. 1979-80, chmn. bldgs. for coll. and univ. librs. com. 1983-85, chmn. nominating com. libr. history roundtable 1993-94), AARP, (sec. local chpt. 1998-2000), Okla. Libr. Assn. (life, pres. 1971-72, ALA coun. rep. 1976-80, 83-84, OLA Disting. Svc. award 1979, Spl. Merit award 1987), S.W. Libr. Assn. (chmn. coll. and univ. div. 1958-60, chmn. scholarship com. 1968-70), Internat. Fedn. Libr. Assns. (standing com. on libr. bldgs. and equipment 1976-88), Assn. Coll. and Rsch. Librs. (chmn. univ. librs. sect. 1969-70, mem. exec. bd. and rep. to ALA Coun., 1971-72), U. Mich. Sch. Libr. Sci. Alumni Soc. (pres. 1979-80, Alumni Recognition award 1988), mem. Alumni Found. Com., 1992-94, Payne County Ret. Educators Assn. (v.p., pres. elect 1991-92, pres. 1992-93), Okla. State U. Emeriti Assn. (pres. 2000-01), Okla. Hist. Soc. (com. on Okla. Higher Edn. mus. 1985—), Stillwater Rotary Club (pres. 1980-81, Rotarian of Yr. 1999, editor Rotary Weekly bulletin, vol. contbr. local daily newspaper), Beta Phi Mu. Baptist (chmn. bd. deacons 1973). Clubs: Archons of Colophon, Stillwater Rotary (dir. 1978-82, pres. 1980-81).

ROUSH, DOROTHY EVELYN, medical laboratory educator, consultant; b. Flatwoods, Ky., July 16, 1930; d. William Arch and Mary Jane (Frasure) Salyers; m. Gilbert Riley Dush, Aug. 26, 1951 (div. 1972); m. Virgil Bernard Roush, Nov. 18, 1972. Med. tech. degree, Clin. Lab., Mt. Vernon, Ohio, 1953; student, Ohio State U., 1967-72. Registered med. tech. Med. tech. Hosp. & Tb Hosp., Newark, Ohio, 1953-60; office nurse various physicians, Newark and Columbus, Ohio and Seattle, 1960-93; nursing home coord. Med. Lab., Seattle, 1980-89; sr. phlebotomist Roche BioMed. Lab., Burlington, N.C., 1990-95. Nurse, phlebotomist ARC Blood Program, Columbus, Ohio, 1961-72; instr. in field; cons. in field. Contbr. articles to profl. jours. Vol. ARC, 1957-72, Boulder (Colo.) County Foster Parents, 1976, Cath. Shared Missions, Seattle, 1987. Recipient Appreciation award Gt. Brit. Red Cross Nursing Svc., 1969, Internat. Cancer Congress, 1982. Mem. Am. Assn. Med. Assts., Am. Med. Techs. (chairperson com., sci. chairperson Ariz. chpt., expert adhoc rev. com. 1994-95, Disting. Achievement award 1991), Wash. State Soc. Am. Tech. (sec., v.p., Tech. of Yr. 1989, 90), Am. Legion Aux. (pres.). Roman Catholic. Avocations: reading, writing poetry, travelling, golfing, tennis. Home and Office: 18002 N Hyacinth Dr Sun City West AZ 85375-5348

ROUSH, JOHN A, academic administrator; b. Wisconsin; B in English summa cum laude, Ohio U.; M, M, D, Miami U. Exec. asst. to pres. U. of Richmond, 1982—90, v.p. planning, 1990—98; exec. asst. to pres. Miami U.; pres. Centre Coll., 1998—. Contbr. articles to profl. jours. Capt. U.S. Army. Office: Centre Coll 600 W Walnut St Danville KY 40422

ROUSSEY, ROBERT STANLEY, accountant, educator; b. N.Y.C., July 20, 1935; m. Jeanne Archer, May 8, 1965; children: Robert Scott, John Stephen. BS, Fordham U., 1957. CPA, N.Y., Japan. Staff acct. Arthur Andersen & Co., N.Y.C., 1957-63, mgr. N.Y.C. and Tokyo, 1964-69, ptnr. N.Y.C. and Chgo., 1969-92, dir. auditing procedures, 1977-92; prof. acctg. U. So. Calif., L.A., 1992—. Adj. prof. auditing Northwestern U. Kellogg Grad. Sch. Mgmt., 1990, 91; mem. coll. bus. adminstrn. adv. bd. Fordham U., 1999—. Edit. cons. Handbook of Corporate Finance, 1986, Handbook of Financial Markets and Institutions, 1987; mem. editl. bd. Advances in Accounting, 1987—, Jour. Internat. Acctg. Auditing and Taxation, 1991—, Auditing: A Journal of Theory and Practice, 1994—; mem. adv. bd. Internat. Jour. Acctg., 1998—; contbr. articles to profl. jours. Treas., bd. dirs. Kenilworth (Ill.) Community House, 1979-81, Troop 13 Boy Scouts Am., Kenilworth, 1978-80, St. Joseph's Ch. Men's Club, Bronxville, N.Y., 1971-73. With U.S. Army, 1958, 61-62. Mem. AICPA (chmn. EDP auditing stds. com. 1978-81, auditing stds. bd. 1986-90, MAS practice stds. and adminstrn. com. 1990-93, internat. spl. strategy com. 1997-98, internat. auditing stds. subcom. 1998-2002, internat. strategy com. 1998—), Am. Acctg. Assn. (v.p. auditing sect. 1987-90, pubs. com. 1993-96), Info. Systems Audit and Control Assn. (stds. bd. 1986-96, v.p., mem. internat. bd. dirs. 1996-2001, mem. audit com. 2000-01, internat. pres. 2001—), Info. Tech. Governance Inst. (internat. pres. 2001—), Ill. State Soc. CPAs, N.Y. State Soc. CPAs, Inst. Internal Auditors (bd. rsch. advisors 1986-99), Internat. Fedn. Accts. (internat. auditing practices com. 1990-2000, chmn. 1995-2000, EDP audit com. 1980-88), Met. Club (gov. 1977-78), Tokyo-Am. Club (life), Beaver Creek Club, Beta Alpha Psi, Beta Gamma Sigma. Republican. Roman Catholic. Avocations: skiing, sailing, tennis, Karate. Office: U So Calif Dept Acctg Los Angeles CA 90089-0441

ROUTSON, SUSAN HUTCHINS, secondary school educator, consultant, peer counseling specialist; b. Cin., May 13, 1943; d. Ralph Pearson and Sarah Minabelle (Abbott) Hutchins; m. Ronald Irving Routson, Oct. 7, 1967; children: Sarah Mary, David Patrick. BS in Math. and Biology, Purdue U., 1965; MS in Microbiology/Clin. Pathology, Mich. State U., 1967. Cert. secondary math. and biology tchr., Ind.; cert. non-profit bd. trainer; cert. peer program educator; cert. trainer, Nat. Peer Helpers Assn., 2003. Researcher Miami U., Oxford, Ohio, 1968; apt. mgr. Miami U. Student Housing, Oxford, 1969-74; substitute tchr. Richmond (Ind.) Community Schs., 1976—, coord. vol. tutors, 1978-80; bus. mgr. Richmond Cotillion, 1983-87; dir. Peer Info. Ctrs. for Teens, 1986—; trainer Planning Programs for Young Adolescents, 1989—. Trainer Living with 10-15 Yr. Old, 1989—; adult educator Girl Scouts U.S.A., 1978—, svc. unit mgr., 1983—87; program dir. Richmond YMCA, 1986—95; state bd. dirs. Ind. Youth Adv. Program, 1989—2000, pres., 1992—2000; bd. dirs. Nat. Youth Adv. Program, 1989—2000; mem. state dept. of edn. svc. learning com. Mem. Nat. Peer Helper Assn., 1992—, Richmond Sch. Supt.'s Adv. Com., 1975—88, Greater Richmond Progress Com. Edn., Child Care, Teen Pregnancy and Substance Abuse Task Forces, 1986—91; mem. agy. dirs. coun. United Way, 1995—, pres., 1998—2001; mem. Ind. Coun. on Adolescent Pregnancy, bd. dirs., 1991—, v.p., 1993—96; mem. exec. bd. Treaty Line Girl Scouts U.S.A., Richmond, 1976—88, pres., 1990—96. Named Vol. of Yr., Whitewater Valley United Way, 1986, Pres. Bush Vol. Action Leader, 1991, Exemplary Youth Orgn. Creator, Lilly Endowment, 1988, leadership assoc., 1992; recipient Thanks badge, Treaty Line Girl Scouts U.S.A., 1984, Peer Program of Yr., Nat. Peer Helpers Assn., 2002, first cert. Peer Program, 2002. Children's Def. Fund, So. Poverty Law Ctr., Nature Conservancy, Internat. Altrusa (scholarship chair 1996—, Woman of Achievement 2002), Delta Kappa Gamma (pres. 1996-2002), Alpha Phi (pres. Richmond chpt. 1985-90). Republican. Roman Catholic. Home: 4566 Smyrna Rd Richmond IN 47374-9659 Office: Richmond High Sch 380 Hub Etchison Pkwy Richmond IN 47374-5398

ROUX, MILDRED ANNA, retired secondary school educator; b. New Castle, Pa., June 1, 1914; d. Louis Henri and Frances Amanda (Gillespie) R. BA, Westminster Coll., 1936, MS in Edn., 1951. Tchr. Farrell (Pa.) Sch. Dist., 1939-55; tchr. Latin, English New Castle (Pa.) Sch. Dist., 1956-76; ret., 1976. Chmn. sr. H.S. fgn. lang. dept. New Castle Sch. Dist., 1968-76, faculty sponsor sch. fgn. lang. newspapers, 1960-76, Jr. Classical League, 1958-76. Mem. Lawrence County Hist. Soc., Am. Classical League, 1958-76. Mem. AAUW (chmn. publicity, chmn. program com. Lawrence County chpt. 1992-96), Am. Assn. Ret. Persons, Nat. Ret. Tchrs. Assn., Pa. Assn. Sch. Retirees (chmn. cmty. participation com. Lawrence County br. 1976-81, telephone com. Lawrence County br. 1990-98), Coll. Club New Castle (chmn. sunshine com. 1989-91, mem. social com. 1991-92), Woman's Club New Castle (chmn. pub. affairs com. 1988-90, internat. affairs com. 1990-92, program com. 1990-92, telephone com. 1992-99). Republican. Roman Catholic. Avocations: church choir, reading, civic interests. Home: 6 E Moody Ave New Castle PA 16101-2356

ROVELSTAD, MATHILDE V(ERNER), library science educator; b. Germany, 1920; came to U.S., 1951. m. Howard Rovelstad, 1970. PhD, U. Tubingen, 1953; MS in L.S, Catholic U. Am., 1960. Prof. libr. sci. Cath. U. Am., 1960-90, prof. emeritus, 1990—. Vis. prof. U. Montreal, 1969 Author: Bibliotheken in den Vereinigten Staaten, 1974; translator Bibliographia, an Inquiry into its Definition and Designations (R. Blum), 1980, Bibliotheken in den Vereinigten Staaten von Amerika und in Kanada, 1988; contbr. articles to profl. jours. Research grantee German Acad. Exch. Svc., 1969, Herzog August Bibliothek Wolfenbüttel, Germany, 1995. Mem. Internat. Fedn. Libr. Assns. and Instns. (standing adv. com. on libr. schs. 1975-81), Assn. for Libr. and Info. Sci. Edn. Home: Apt HR-T35 719 Maiden Choice Ln Catonsville MD 21228-6231 Office: Cath U Am Sch Libr & Info Sci Washington DC 20064-0001

ROVERE, ROBERT JOHN, secondary school language educator; b. N.Y.C., Jan. 4, 1943; s. Emilio and Clelia (Garlasco) R. BA, Seton Hall U., 1964; MA, NYU, 1968. Cert. nursery, elem., secondary tchr., ednl. adminstr. and supr., N.J. French tchr. St. Mary H.S., Jersey City, 1964-67; French and Italian tchr. North Bergen (N.J.) H.S., 1967-94, chair dept. langs., 1994—. Mem. Nat. Honor Soc. selection com. North Bergen H.S., 1988—; mem. staff devel. com., 1990—, fundraiser project graduation com., 1992—. V.p. North Bergen Fedn. Tchrs., 1974-75; draft counselor Peace and Freedom House, Jersey City, 1968-69; rep. to United Farm Workers, AFL-CIO, North Bergen, 1971-72; bioregional connector Creation Spirituality Mag., Oakland, Calif., 1988-90. Mem. NEA, ASCD, Am. Coun. of Tchr. Fgn. Langs., Am. Assn. Tchrs. of French, Am. Assn. Tchrs. Italian, Fgn. Lang. Educators N.J. Democrat. Avocations: creation spirituality, shamanism, birding, cross-country skiing. Office: North Bergen HS 7417 Kennedy Blvd North Bergen NJ 07047-4080

ROVNER, LEONARD IRVING, education educator; b. Phila. s. Harry and Fay (Rosenberg) R.; m. Nov. 21, 1970; children: Alisha, Allison. BS in Edn., Temple U., 1953, MS in Edn., 1957; PhD, Tianjin Coll. (China) and U., 1999. Cert. sch. adminstr., supt. schs., prin./supr., N.J.; cert. prin., supt. schs., Pa. Instr. psychology Temple U., Phila., 1960-65; mus. tchr. Acad. Natural Scis., Phila., 1960-65; tchr. Sch. Dist. of Phila., 1953-60, prin. at large, 1965-70, asst. to supt., 1970-74; prin. McCall Sch., Phila., 1974-94; adj. prof. edn. Coll. Edn., coord. Sch. Bus. and Mgmt. Temple U., Phila., 1994—, prof. edn. Exec. dir., bd. dirs., Phila. chmn. Prins. Ctr., 1991—93; advisor Kasetsart U., Bangkok; guest prof. fine arts Tianjin; sr. advisor Chinese Am. C. of C.; pres. Asiaquest Internat., LLC. Mem. editl. bd. Reflections--Jour. of Nat. Network of Prin. Ctrs. at Harvard. Mem. Police Adv. Com., Phila., 1991-95; mem Prins.' Ctr. and Nat. Network of Prins.' Ctrs. at Harvard; mem. Mayor's Adv. Coun., Cherry Hill, N.J., 1989-94; chmn. Cherry Hill Hist. Commn., 1989-92, 94, mem., 1995; Sino-Am. Ambassador of Friendship, Tianjin. Citation recipient Phila. City Coun., 1989; recipient Rose Lindenbaum Prin. of Yr. award, 1971, Letter of Commendation, Pres. George H.W. Bush, Washington, 1989; named Hon. Headmaster, Hon. Chancellor of Edn., Hon. Prof., Tianjin. Mem.: ASCD, Phila. Assn. Sch. Administrn., Ednl. Dynamics Cons. Orgn. (pres.), Phi Delta Kappa. Avocations: photography, skiing, scuba diving, history, travel. Home: 26 Greensward Ct Cherry Hill NJ 08002-4702 E-mail: proflenr@aol.com.

ROWAN, JO, ballerina, educator; d. Joseph T. and Nona (Meyer) R.; m. John Richard Bedford. Student ballet, Cin. Sch. Am. Ballet, N.Y.C. Ballet Theatre Sch.; BFA, MA in Dance, U. Cin.; student ballet, Bolshoi Sch., Moscow. Ballet mistress Dallas Ballet; dancer Cin. Ballet, Dallas Ballet, Garden State Ballet; soloist Met. Opera, Phila. Opera, Dallas Civic Opera, Cin. Summer Opera, Tulsa Civic Opera. Ballet soloist, guest artist Kans. City Philharm., Balt. Symphony Orch., Cin. Symphony Orch.; lectr. history Am. Dance; founder, dir. Am. Spirit Dancers, Oklahoma City U.; founder Oklahoma City U. Liturgical Dancers; guest tchr. Okla. Dance Masters Assn., St. Louis Dance Tchrs. Assn., Dance Troup, Dance Makers, Tex. Assn. Tchrs. Dance, Am. Dance Assn., Miami Valley Assn. Dance Tchrs.; dance dept. chmn., prof. Oklahoma City U., artist-in-residence U. Wyo., Laramie; dir., writer, choreographer Oklahoma City Philharm. Yuletide Festival; guest artist U. Nebr., Lincoln; guest artist, artist-in-residence Cin. Sch. Creative and Performing Arts; toured nationally Dance Caravan Red, Dance Olympus; faculty Nilo Toledo's Summer Fine Arts Camp, Tampa, Fla., Dance Camp Am.; guest lectr. on dance injuries Am. Acad. Orthopedic Surgeons; adjudicator N.Am. Ballet Festival, Boston, State of Tenn. Individual Artists Fellowship; spkr. in field. Prodr. dance instrn. records, tapes, CDs and videos. Recipient Preservationist award, Tap Heritage, 2001. Home: 745 Jenkins Ave Norman OK 73069-4951 Office: Oklahoma City U Sch Am Dance & Arts Mgmt 2501 N Blackwelder Ave Oklahoma City OK 73106-1493

ROWAN, RICHARD G. academic administrator; BS, Furman U.; MEd, EdS, Ga. State U.; D of Design (hon.), Nottingham Trent U., Eng. Pres., co-founder Savannah (Ga.) Coll. Art and Design, 1979—. Mem. Savannah adv. bd. Bank of Am. Recipient Oglethorpe award, Freedom award NAACP; named to Hon. Order Ky. Cols. Mem. Savannah C. of C. (pres., bd. dirs.). Office: Savannah Coll Art & Design Office of the Chancellor PO Box 3146 Savannah GA 31402-3146

ROWAN, RICHARD LAMAR, business management educator; b. Guntersville, Ala., July 10, 1931; s. Leon Virgle and Mae (Williamson) R.; m. Marilyn Walker, Aug. 3, 1963; children: John Richard, Jennifer Walker. AB, Birmingham-So. Coll., 1953; postgrad., Auburn U., 1956-57; PhD, U. N.C., 1961. Instr. Auburn (Ala.) U., 1956-57, U. N.C., Chapel Hill, 1958-59, 60-61; lectr. U. Pa., Phila., 1961-62, asst. prof., 1962-66, asso. prof. industry, 1966-73, prof. industry, 1973—. Dir. indsl. research unit, 1989-91; co-dir. Ctr. for Human Resources, 1991—; visitor to Faculty Econs. and Politics Cambridge (Eng.) U., 1972; pvt. sector advisor U.S. State Dept. Com. on Internat. Investment and Multinational Enterprises, OECD, 1982-89; chmn. Labor Relations Council, 1985— . Author: (with H.R. Northrup) The Negro and Employment Opportunity, 1965, Readings in Labor Economics and Labor Relations, 5th edit., 1984, The Negro in the Steel Industry, 1969, The Negro in the Textile Industry, 1970, (with others) Studies of Negro Employment, 1970, Educating the Employed Disadvantaged for Upgrading, 1972, Collective Bargaining: Survival in the 1970's, 1972, Opening the Skilled Construction Trades to Blacks, 1972, The Impact of Government Manpower Programs, 1975, International Enforcement of Union Standards in Ocean Transport, 1977, The Impact of OSHA, 1978, Multinational Bargaining Attempts: The Record, the Cases, and the Prospects, 1980; (with H.R. Northrup) Employee Relations and Regulations in the 80s, 1982; (with others) Multinational Union Organizations in the Manufacturing Industries, (with D.C. Campbell) The Multinational Enterprises and the OECD Industrial Relations Guidelines, 1984, Trade Union Clout Erodes, But For How Long?, 1985, Employee Relations Trends and Practices in the Textile Industry, 1986; contbr. articles to profl. jours. Mem. personnel com. Del. Valley Settlement Alliance, 1966-68. Served with Transp. Corps U.S. Army, 1953-56. Recipient Disting. Alumni award, Birmingham-So. Coll., 2000. Mem. Indsl. Rels. Rsch. Assn. (sec. Phila. 1964-65), Acad. Internat. Bus.. Democrat. Episcopalian. Home: 113 Blackthorn Rd Wallingford PA 19086-6046 Office: U Pa Wharton Sch 3733 Spruce St Philadelphia PA 19104-6301

ROWAN, WILLIAM HAMILTON, JR., computer science educator; b. Nashville, Tenn., May 8, 1933; s. William Hamilton and Elizabeth (Lowry) R.; m. Sarah Conley, June 9, 1973; children: Elizabeth, Bill. BE, Vanderbilt U., 1955; PhD, N.C. State U., 1965. Registered profl. engr., Tenn. Jr. engr. Boeing Airplane Co., Seattle, 1955-57; instr. of mechanics Vanderbilt U., Nashville, Tenn., 1959-60; electronics engr. Tenn. State Hwy. Dept., Nashville, 1960-61; grad. student civil engring. N.C. State U., Raleigh, N.C., 1961-64; asst. prof. math. Vanderbilt U., Nashville, 1964-67, assoc. prof. and chmn. computer sci. dept., 1967-71, prof. computer sci., 1971-95, prof. computer sci. emeritus, 1996—. Staff couns. AVCO Corp. aerostructures divsn., Nashville, 1965-70; pres., CEO, On-Line Computing, Inc., Nashville; bd. dirs. On-Line Data, Inc., Nashville, 1974-85. Co-editor: (book) Application of Finite Element Methods in Civil Engineering, 1969; co-author: (book) Computer Methods of Structural Analysis, 1970. 1st lt. U.S. Army, 1957-59. Recipient fellowship grant Ford Found., N.C. State U., Raleigh, 1961-64. Mem. IEEE, Am. Soc. for Engring. Edn., Assn. for Computing Machinery, Phi Kappa Phi, Tau Beta Pi. Avocation: golf. Home: 604 Summerwind Cir Nashville TN 37215-6125 Office: Vanderbilt Univ Box 1679 Sta B Nashville TN 37235

ROWE, BOBBY LOUISE, art educator; b. Montgomery, Ala., Feb. 15, 1930; d. Herbert and Louise (Barbaree) R. AB, Montevallo U., 1950; MA, Columbia U., 1959; PhD, Fla. State U., 1974. Cert. tchr. K-12 and jr. coll., Fla. Supr. student tchrs. U. Fla. Coll. Edn., Gainesville; assoc. prof. art edn. Mid. Tenn. State U., Murfreesboro; art edn. dir. Cleve. State U.; art curriculum specialist Palm Beach County Sch. Bd., West Palm Beach, Fla. Fiber artist, computer imagist, digital photographer, writer; lectr., presenter in field. Contbr. articles to profl. jours. Mem. Nat. Art Edn. Assn., Am. Edn. Rsch. Assn., Alpha Delta Kappa. E-mail: artrowe711@aol.com.

ROWE, DEVONA POWELL, guidance counselor, social worker; b. Bethesda, Md., Jan. 28, 1951; d. Julius Devon and Martha Ann (Molnar) Powell; m. Ralph Leon Rowe, June 11, 1971; children: Adam Powell, Reagan Powell. BA in History and Libr. Sci. magna cum laude, Fla. State U., 1971; MA in Edn. summa cum laude, U. North Fla., 1982; EdS in Counselor Edn., U. Fla., 1990; EdD, U. North Fla., 1999. Cert. counselor, Nat. Bd. Cert. Counselors; cert. media specialist and guidance and adminstrn. tchr., Fla.; lic. mental health counselor. Sch. libr. Most Holy Redeemer Sch., Tampa, Fla., 1972-74; asst. dir. N.E. Fla./S.E. Ga. divsn. Nat. Health Svcs., Palatka, Fla., 1981-83; guidance counselor St. Joseph Acad., St. Augustine, Fla., 1983-85; tchr. 8th grade social studies Putnam County Sch. System, 1985-86; county svcs. coord. Child Abuse Prevention Project, Palatka, 1986-92; guidance counselor E.H. Miller/Dist. Opportunity Ctr., Palatka, 1992-94; social worker Palatka H.S., 1994—99, tchr., 1999—. Mem. Health Edn. Coun., 1986—, v.p., 1986, pres., 1987; workshop presenter in field. Crucillo coord. St. Mark's Episcopal Ch., 1977-80; mem. Putnam Children's Task force, Children's Home Soc.; rep. Dist. Juvenile Justice Bd. Dept. Health and Rehab. Svcs. Dist. III, rep. State Coun. on Juvenile Justice; mem. Local Juvenile Justice Bd., Putnam County, 1993. Named Women Involved Today winner Palatka Daily News, 1988; grantee in field; Fla. Regent scholar. Mem. Am. Assn. Counseling and Devel., Nat. Com. Prevent Child Abuse, Fla. Ctr. Children and Youth, Fla. Com. Prevent Child Abuse, Child Welfare League, Adv. Network Severely Emotionally Disturbed Children, Jr. Woman's Club Palatka (hon., state jr. project chair 1975, leadership chair 1976, 1st v.p. 1977, pres. 1979, Outstanding Clubwoman 1978), Woman's Club Palatka (edn. chair 1988), Beta Sigma Phi (program chair 1987, cultural chair 1988), Chi Sigma Iota, Kappa Delta Pi. Democrat. Avocations: reading, duplicate bridge, doll making. Office: Palatka HS 302 Mellon Rd Palatka FL 32177-4018 E-mail: devonaprowe@yahoo.com.

ROWE, JOSEPH CHARLES, elementary school educator, principal; b. Cheyenne, Wyo., June 8, 1953; s. Clyde Joseph and Brunhild W. C. (Bielinski) Rowe. BS, U. Md., 1976; MEd, George Mason U., 1981. Cert. adminstr., supr., elem. tchr., spl. edn. tchr., mid. sch. tchr., jr. gt. books trainer. Case mgr. intermediate EI program Lakewood Elem. Sch., Brown Sta. Elem. Sch.; tchr., dir. wellness program Watkins Mill Elem. Sch.; prin. Stedwick Elem. Sch.; asst. prin. Gaithersburg Elem. Sch. Outreach coord. Families of the 90s; chmn., humna rels., prin.'s adv., discipline, mainstreaming, homework and cmty. action team against substance and alcohol abuse PTA, sch. assessment team coord., v.p., quality mgmt. coun. facilitator, comprehensive behavior coord., reading initiative coord. Coord. adult/child programs Reading USA, gifted & talented coord., testing coord., vol. coord.; prin. Extended Learning Opportunities "Adventures in Learning". Mem.: ASCD, NEA, Montgomery County Adminstrs. Assn. Elem. Prins., Md. State Tchrs. Assn., Phi Delta Kappa. Home: 2117 Bordly Dr Brookeville MD 20833-2124 E-mail: Heidelbger@aol.com., Joseph_Rowe@fc.mcps.k12.md.us.

ROWE, MARIELI DOROTHY, media literacy education consultant, organization executive; b. Bonn, Germany, Aug. 13; came to U.S., 1939; m. John Westel Rowe; children: Peter Willoughby, William Westel, Michael Delano. BA, Swarthmore Coll.; postgrad., U. Colo., 1990; MA, Edgewood Coll., 1990. Interim exec. dir. Friends of Sta. WHA-TV, Madison, Wis., 1976; exec. dir. Nat. Telemedia Coun., Madison, 1978—. Project assoc. Loyola U., Chgo., 1989-92; bd. dirs. Sta. WYOU, Madison. Co-prodr., author TV documentary Kids Meet Across Space, 1983; editor Telemedium, Jour. of Media Literacy, 1980—. Co-founder, bd. dirs., pres. Friends of Pub. Stas. WHA-TV, radio, Madison, 1968-78; v.p. bd. Nat. Friends of Pub. Broadcasting, N.Y. and Washington, 1970-76; pres., v.p. bd. Wis. Coun. and Am. Coun. for Better Broadcasts, Madison, 1963-75; commr. Gov.'s Blue Ribbon Commn. on Cable Communications, Wis., 1971-73; bd. dirs. Broadband Telecommunications Regulatory Bd., Madison, 1978-81. Recipient Spl. Recognition award Am. Coun. Better Broadcasts, 1981, Spl. award Joint Congress and World Meeting on Media Literacy, Spain, 1995, Meritorious Svc. award Alliance for Media Literate Am., 2003. Mem. Soc. Satellite Profls. Internat. (charter), Internat. Visual Literacy Assn., Zeta Phi Eta (1st v.p. 1992, pres. 1993, Marguerite Garden Jones award 1989). Unitarian Universalist. Avocations: skiing, mountain hiking, travel, music. Home: 1001 Tumalo Trl Madison WI 53711-3024 E-mail: NTelemedia@aol.com.

ROWE, MARY P. organizational ombudsman, management educator; b. Chgo., Feb. 18, 1936; married; children: Katherine, Susannah, Timothy. BA in History, Swarthmore Coll., 1957; PhD in Econs., Columbia U., 1971; LLD (hon.), Regis Coll., 1975. With World Council of Chs./Office of UN High Commr. for Refugees, Salzburg and Vienna, Austria, 1957-58; research asst. Nat. Bur. Econ. Research, N.Y.C., 1961; economist planning bd. Office of Gov., V.I., 1962-63; free-lance cons. Nigeria, 1963-66, 1967-69; cons., sr. economist with Ctr. for Ednl. Policy Research, Harvard U. Harvard U., Cambridge, Mass., 1970, cons., sr. economist with Abt Assocs., 1970, tech. dir. early edn. project, 1971-72, cons. economist with Abt Assocs., 1971; dir. Carnegie Corp. Grant Radcliffe Inst., Cambridge, 1972; spl. asst. to pres., ombudsperson MIT, Cambridge, 1973—, adj. prof. Sloan Sch. Mgmt., 1985—. Mem. steering com., program on negotiations Harvard U., 1995—. Mem. editorial bd. Negotiation Jour., 1985—, Alternative Dispute Resolution Report, 1987-90; contbr. articles to profl. jours. Trustee Cambridge Friends Sch., 1969-75; mem. bd. advisors Brookline

Children's Ctr., 1971-76; mem. Cambridge Friends Meeting and Com. on Clearness, 1971-78, New Eng. Concerns Com., 1973—, Mass. Policy Adv. Com. on Child Abuse/Neglect, 1977-79, Mass. State Youth Council, 1978-83; mem. Mass. State Employment and Tng. Council, 1975-83, chair, 1980-83; mem. nat. adv. Com. Black Women's Ednl. Policy and Research Network Project/Wellesley Coll. Ctr. for Research on Women, 1980-83; bd. dirs. Bay State Skills Commn., 1980-81, Wellesley Women's Research Ctr., 1984-87; sec. bd. dirs. Bay State Skills Corp., 1981-90; mem. panel on employment disputes Ctr. for Pub. Resources, 1986—. Recipient Meritorious Civilian Svc. award Dept. of Navy, 1993. Mem. Am. Econs. Assn., Soc. Profls. in Dispute Resolution (chair com. on ombudspersons 1982-92, com. law and pub. policy in employment disputes), Calif. Caucus Coll. and Univ. Ombudsmen, Univ. and Coll. Ombudsman Assn., Ombudsman Assn. (pres. 1985-87, program on negotiation steering com. 1995—, Disting. Neutral Ctr. for Pub. Resources 1990—, covenor, presenter confs. 1982, 84, 85, 88, 89, 90-2003). Office: MIT 10-213 77 Massachusetts Ave Cambridge MA 02139

ROWE, SHERYL ANN, librarian; b. Stephenville, Tex., Sept. 29, 1946; d. Horace Milton and Letha Faye (Hensley) Hughes; m. Darrell Vanoy Rowe, Nov. 27, 1969; children: Jason Burt, Shelley Jean. BA in English, Tarleton State U., Stephenville, 1967; MS in Libr. Sci., Tex. Women's U., Denton, 1986. Cert. tchr. secondary edn. Tchr. Lake Worth (Tex.) H.S., 1967-69, Aledo (Tex.) H.S., 1967-73, 78-84, libr., 1984—. Mem. ALA, Tex. Libr. Assn., Region XI Librs. Assn. (treas. 1984—). Office: Aledo HS 1000 Bailey Ranch Rd Aledo TX 76008-4407 E-mail: srowe@aledo.k-12.tx.us.

ROWE, VICKIE CALDWELL, reading resource educator; b. Roanoke, Va., Dec. 18, 1951; d. Charles Ray and Della Alice Caldwell; m. Howard William Rowe Jr., June 16, 1974; 1 child, Scott Allen. BS, Longwood Coll., 1974; M of Liberal Studies, Hollins Coll., 1978. Tchr. Roanoke City Schs., 1974—, tchr., team leader, 1982-87, 95—, tchr., relief prin., 1987-89, reading resource tchr., 1989-94. Dir. Vacation Bible Sch., Fairview United Meth. Ch., Roanoke, 1979, 80, 92, asst. dir. Vacation Bible Sch., 1990, 91, 93, chairperson Coun. on Ministries, 1991, 92, chairperson PPR, 1993, 94, 95. Roanoke City Schs. grantee, 1990-91, 91-92, others. Mem. NEA, Va. Edn. Assn., Roanoke Edn. Assn., Roanoke Valley Reading Assn., Internat. Reading Assn. Home: 2412 Olde Salem Dr Salem VA 24153-6667 Office: Grandin Court Elem Sch 2815 Spessard Ave SW Roanoke VA 24015-4215

ROWELL, BARBARA CABALLERO, retired academic administrator; b. New Orleans, Sept. 5, 1922; d. Albert Henry Wischnewske (stepfather) and Antoinette (Angelo) Caballero; m. J.C. Rowell, Dec. 17, 1941; children: Jerrie Carlene, Kerry Gene, Ricky Ray. AA in Bus. Adminstrn., Okaloosa Walton Jr. Coll., Niceville, Fla., 1973; BA in Social Scis., U. West Fla., 1987. Exec. sec. Bishop Enterprises, Ft. Walton Beach; office mgr. and real estate property mgr. Fred Cooke Real Estate, Ft. Walton Beach, Fla.; adminstrv. sec. to v.p. Okaloosa Walton Jr. Coll., Niceville. Leader brownie scouts Girl Scouts U.S., 1954-56, cub scouts Boy Scouts Am., 1957-59; bd. dirs., mem. curriculum com. U. West Fla. Ctr. for Life Long Learning; chair univ svc. com., pres., began Writing Lab; originator, implementor U. West Fla. Tutor Program, Career Fair, started scholarship program, Proctor Program; mem. curriculum com. U. West Fla.Ctr. for Lifelong Learning, presenter S.E. Conf. Insts. of Learning in Retirement, Charleston, S.C.; gov.'s campaign vol.; state legislature campaign vol.; mem. Sr. Ctr. Life Long Learning, U. West Fla. Mem. AAUW, DAV Aux., Order of Ea. Star (past matron). Avocations: education, travel, reading, gardening, dancing, volunteering.

ROWEN, BETTY J. (ROSE), adult education educator; b. Bklyn., May 22, 1920; d. Louis C. and Amelia (Kuh) Rose; children: Lois Winter, Richard K. BA, Bklyn. Coll., 1941; MA, Adelphi U., 1958; EdD, Columbia U., 1966. Elem. tchr. Merrick (N.Y.) Pub. Schs., 1960-65; instr. Peabody Coll., Nashville, 1965-66, Kean Coll., Union, N.J., 1966-69; prof. U. Miami, Coral Gables, Fla., 1969-85. Author: Learning Through Movement, 1963, The Children We See, 1973, The Learning Match, 1980, Dance and Grow, 1994, (video tape), 1995. Home: 1951 Sagewood Ln Apt 105 Reston VA 20191-5411 E-mail: bettyrowen@webtv.net.

ROWEN, RUTH HALLE, musicologist, educator; b. N.Y.C., Apr. 5, 1918; d. Louis and Ethel (Fried) Halle; m. Seymour M. Rowen, Oct. 13, 1940; children: Mary Helen Rowen, Louis Halle Rowen. BA, Barnard Coll., 1939; MA, Columbia U., 1941, PhD, 1948. Mgmt. ednl. dept. Carl Fischer, Inc., N.Y.C., 1954-63; assoc. prof. musicology CUNY, 1967-72, prof., 1972—, mem. doctoral faculty in musicology, 1967—. Author: Early Chamber Music, 1948, reprinted, 1974; (with Adele T. Katz) Hearing-Gateway to Music, 1959, (with William Simon) Jolly Come Sing and Play, 1956, Music Through Sources and Documents, 1979, (with Mary Rowen) Instant Piano, 1979, 80, 83, Symphonic and Chamber Music Score and Parts Bank, 1996; contbr. articles to profl. jours. Mem. ASCAP, Am. Musicol. Soc., Music Library Assn., Coll. Music Soc., Nat. Fedn. Music Clubs (nat. musicianship chmn. 1962-74, nat. young artist auditions com. 1964-74, N.Y. state chmn. Young Artist Auditions 1981, dist. coord. 1983, nat. bd. dirs. 1989-2000, rep. UN 1991-2000), N.Y. Fedn. Music Clubs (pres.), Phi Beta Kappa Home: 115 Central Park West At 25D New York NY 10023-4153

ROWLAND, DAVID JACK, academic administrator; b. Columbus, Ohio, June 17, 1921; s. David Henry and Ethel (Ryan) R.; m. Mary Ellen Stinson, Apr. 8, 1944; children: David Allen, Ryan Stinson, Sue Ellen Rowland Summers. BS, Ohio U., 1949; MA, U. Ala., 1951; LittD (hon.), Athens State Coll., 1967; LLD (hon.), Jacksonville State U., 1969. Pres. Walker Coll., Jasper, Ala., 1956-88, chancellor, 1988-95; interim pres. U. Ala./Walker Coll., 1995-96. Bd. dirs. First Nat. Bank, Jasper, first Comml. Bancshares, Birmingham, Ala.; chmn. Ala. ACT Bd., Tuscaloosa, 1968—; real estate developer. Wildlife columnist and illustrator. Chmn. Jasper Indsl. Bd., 1987—; commr. Ala. Mining commn., Jasper, 1976—; mem. Ala. Employer Guard Res. commn., Birmingham, 1988—; trustee Walker Coll.; chmn. adv. bd. Jasper Salvation Army. Col. U.S. Army, 1942-46, ATO. Decorated Legion of Merit; recipient Silver Beaver award Boy Scouts Am., 1972. Mem. Res. Officers Assn. (pres. Jasper chpt.), Summit Club, Met. Dinner Club, Rotary (pres. Jasper 1967-68, Paul Harris fellow), Masons, Ala. Silver Hair Legislature. Avocations: tree farmer, growing christmas trees, wildfowl carver. Home: 1000 Valley Rd Jasper AL 35501-4925

ROWLAND, HOWARD RAY, mass communications educator; b. Eddy County, N.Mex., Sept. 9, 1929; s. Lewis Marion and Ursula Lorene (Hunt) R.; m. Meredith June Lee, Apr. 19, 1951; children: Runay Ilene Olson, Rhonda Lee Fisher. B in Journalism, U. Mo., 1950; MS in Journalism, So. Ill. U., 1959; PhD, Mich. State U., 1969. Feature writer Springfield (Mo.) Newspapers, Inc., 1954; newspaper editor Monett (Mo.) Times, 1954-55; editl. writer So. Ill. U., Carbondale, 1955-59; pub. rels. dir. St. Cloud (Minn.) State U., 1959-86, asst. dean, 1986-87, 88-90; dir. Ctr. for British Studies, Alnwick, Eng., 1987-88, 90-91. Emeritus prof. St. Cloud State U., 1991—; cons. Conf. of Campus Ombudsmen, Berkeley, 1971; recorder Seminar on Fund Raising, Washington, 1985; bibliographer Higher Edn. Bibliography Yearbook, 1987. Author: American Students in Alnwick Castle, 1990, St. Cloud State University—125 Years, 1994, Big War, Small Town, 2003; editor: Effective Community Relations, 1980; sect. editor: Handbook of Institutional Advancement, 1986; author book revs. Chair All-Am. City Com., St. Cloud, 1973-74. With U.S. Army, 1951-53. NDEA doctoral fellow Mich. State U., 1967-69; recipient Appreciation award Mayor of St. Cloud, 1974, Disting Svc. award Coun. for Advancement and Support Edn., 1985. Mem. Soc. of Profl. Journalists (Minn. chpt. pres. 1963-64, dep. dir. 1965-67), Coun. for Advancement and Support of Edn. (dist. 5 chair 1977-79, Leadership award 1979), Phi Delta Kappa (Mich. State U. chpt. pres. 1968-69, St. Cloud State Univ. chpt. pres. 1978-79). Presbyterian. Avocations: writing, fishing, travel, photography, antiques. Home: 29467 Kraemer Lake Rd Saint Joseph MN 56374-9646 E-mail: rjrowland@mymailstation.com.

ROWLAND, PAUL MCDONALD, education educator; b. Waverly, N.Y., Oct. 27, 1948; s. Donald Victor and Edith Irene (McDonald) R.; m. Ann G. Batchelder. BA, Rutgers U., 1970, MS, 1979; PhD, N.Mex. State U., 1988. Sci. tchr. South Jefferson Ctrl. Schs., Adams, N.Y., 1973-80; edn. specialist N.Mex. Solar Energy Inst., Las Cruces, 1983-86; asst. prof. sci. edn. East Carolina U., Greenville, N.C., 1988-89; prof. curriculum and instrn., environ. scis. No. Ariz. U., Flagstaff, 1989—. Dir. office acad. assessment No. Ariz. U., Flagstaff, 2002—03; dir. No. Ariz. Environ. Edn. Resources Ctr., Flagstaff, 1994—2003; bd. dirs. Global Network Environ. Edn. Ctrs., Knoxville; dean sch. edn. U. Mont., 2003—. Contbr. articles, chapters to books. Dir. Environ. Scis. Day Camp, Flagstaff; bd. dirs. Arboretum at Flagstaff. Mem.: Am. Ednl. Rsch. Assn., N.Am. Assn. Environ. Edn., Phi Kappa Phi, Sigma Xi. Avocations: sea kayaking, landscape design, photography. Home: 6686 E Eagle Crest Dr Flagstaff AZ 86004-7141 Office: Sch Edn U Montana Missoula MT 59812 E-mail: paul.rowland@nau.edu.

ROWLAND, THEODORE JUSTIN, physicist, educator; b. Cleve., May 15, 1927; s. Thurston Justin and Lillian (Nesser) R.; m. Janet Claire Millar, June 28, 1952 (div. 1967); children: Theodore Justin, Dawson Ann, Claire Millar; m. Patsy Marie Beard, Aug. 21, 1968. BS, Western Res. U., 1948; MA, Harvard U., 1949, PhD, 1954. Rsch. physicist Union Carbide Metals Co., Niagara Falls, N.Y., 1954-61; prof. phys. metallurgy U. Ill., 1961-92, asst. dean Coll. Engring., acting assoc. dean Grad. Coll., 1990-91, prof. emeritus, 1992—; pres., dir. Materials Cons., Inc. Cons. physicist, 1961—; cons. metallurgist, 1976—. Editor 2 books; author monograph; contbr. articles to profl. jours. Fellow Am. Phys. Soc.; mem. AIME, AAAS, AAUP, Phi Beta Kappa, Sigma Xi. Achievements include initial verification of charge density waves in dilute alloys; original contributions to theory and experiment in nuclear magnetic resonance in metals. Home: 805 Park Lane Dr Champaign IL 61820-7613 Office: U Ill Dept Materials Sci and Engring 1304 W Green St Urbana IL 61801-2920 E-mail: trowland@uiuc.edu.

ROWLAND-RAYBOLD, ROBERTA, insurance agent, music educator; b. Utica, N.Y., Apr. 15, 1938; d. Robert Stanley and Mildred Celia (Easton) Rowland; children: Betsy Ross Raybold, Paul Robert Raybold. Bus. student, King's Coll., Briarcliff Manor, N.Y., 1957; student, Wittenberg U., Springfield, Ohio, 1998—. Organist Ch. of God, Moundsville, W. Va., 1969-71, Presbyn. Ch., Natrona Heights, Pa, Univ. Bapt. Ch., State College, Pa., 1981-98; sales rep. Am. Ch. Dirs., Havertown, Pa., 1972-76; ins. agt. Equitable of N.Y., State College, 1976-83, Allstate Ins. Co., State Collete, 1983-91; piano instr. pvt. practice, State College, 1987—97; ins. staff assoc. State Farm Ins., State College, 1997-98; dir. music U. Bapt. Ch., State College, 1981-98; music dir. Meml. United Presbyn. Ch., Xenia, Ohio, 1998—. Bd. dirs. Ctr. County Life Underwriters, State College, 1978—80; interim dir., staff piano instr. Ctr. for Musical Devel., Wittenberg U., 2001—. Composer-arranger music. various hymns, 1983—. Pres. Interfaith Singles, State College, Pa., 1982-86; active Nittany Valley Handbell Festival, Am. Cancer Soc., State College, 1994-98. Mem.: Suzuki Assn. Am., Music Tchrs. Nat. Assn., Palatine Hist. Soc. N.Y., Organ Historic Soc. U.S., Am. Guild of Organists (dean, pres. State College chpt. 1985—87, 1996—98, Svc. Organist status 1989). Republican. United Methodist. Home: 1420 Saint Paris Pike Apt C Springfield OH 45504-1651

ROWLETT, JEANNETTE GAIL, elementary education educator; b. London, Ky., Jan. 1, 1950; d. Paul William and Hazel (Sowder) Cornett; m. Harold James Rowlett, May 15, 1971. AA, Sue Bennett Coll., London, Ky., 1969; BA, Ea. Ky. U., 1971, MA, 1974, cert. adminstrn., supr., 1979. Cert. tchr., Ky. Tchr. Madison County Schs., Richmond, Ky., 1971-93, prin., 1993—. Adv. coun. mem. Ky. Effective Schs., Frankfort, 1991—, trainer 1991—, sec. 1993. Named to Honorable Order of Ky. Colonels. Mem. NEA, ASCD, Ky. ASCD, Nat. Reading Assn. (Ky. chpt.), Ky. Edn. Assn., Ky. Assn. Sch. Adminstrs., Madison County Edn. Assn. Republican. Baptist. Avocations: reading, travel, crafting. Home: 104 Glades St Berea KY 40403-1248 Office: Daniel Boone Elem 710 N 2nd St Richmond KY 40475-1260

ROWLEY, CHARLENE MARIE, educational administrator; b. Chgo., May 27, 1943; d. Edward Joseph Flis and Mary Irene (Radosevic) Hoyt; m. Douglas Allen Rowley, Nov. 6, 1987; children: Tammy, Shannon, Chris, Kevin, Jon, Rebecca. AA, Glen Oaks Community Coll., 1978; BS, We. Mich. U., 1980, M in Edl. Leadership, 1984, EdS, 1988. cert. adminstr., tchr, vocat. Bus. educator Burr Oak (Mich.) Pub. Schs., 1981-83, Constantine (Mich.) Pub. Schs., 1983-84; asst. supt. Watervliet (Mich.) Pub. Schs., 1984-87, Comstock Park (Mich.) Pub. Schs., 1987—. Trustee Rist Mgmt. Trust, Grand Rapids, Mich., 1990—, Comstock Park Ednl. Found., 1988—; dir. North Kent Community Edn. Consortium, Comstock Park, 1987—; chmn. leg. com. Kent County Community Edn. Assn., Grand Rapids, 1989-91. Co-author: A Typing Simulation, 1984, Document Processing, 1989; author, speaker, presentor in field. Chmn. Watervliet Econ. Devel. Corp., 1987; trustee Berrien County Econ. Commn., Bridgeport, Mich., 1987; mem. allocations com. Kent County United Way, Grand Rapids, 1989. Mem. Mich. Sch. Bus. Ofcls., Mich. Assn. Sch. Adminstrs., Kent Negotiators Assn. (v.p.), Kent Regional Community Edn. Assn. (exec. bd. 1987), Grand Valley Sch. Bus. Ofcls., West Mich. Risk Mgmt. Trust, West Mich. Workers Compensation Fund (v.p.), Watervliet C. of C. (pres., svc. recognition award 1989). Republican. Avocations: ballroom dancing, golfing, reading.

ROY, ASIM, business educator; b. Calcutta, India, May 5, 1948; arrived in U.S., 1975; s. Samarendra Nath and Chhaya (Mukherjee) R.; m. Suchandra Mukherjee, Feb. 10, 1974; 1 child, Sion Roy. BE, Calcutta U., 1971; MS (scholar), Case Western Res. U., 1977; PhD, U. Tex., 1979. Foreman, supr. Guest, Keen, Williams, Calcutta, 1972—74; mgr. optimization group Execucom Systems Corp., Austin, 1980-82; asst. prof. U. Nebr., Omaha, 1983, Ariz. State U., Tempe, 1983-89, assoc. prof., 1989-99, prof., 1999—. Vis. prof. Stanford (Calif.) U., 1991; cons. Mid-Am. Steel Corp., 1976-77, Fabri-Centre, Inc., Cleve., 1976; pres., CEO Decision Support Software, Inc., 1984-98, Autolearn, Inc., 2003—. Author: (software) IFPS/Optimum and Maxima, Autolearn; contbr. articles to profl. jours. Calcutta U. Merit scholar, 1967, U. Tex. Rsch. scholar, 1978-80; grantee NSF. Mem. IEEE, Inst. Mgmt. Sci. (program chmn. 1990), Ops. Rsch. Soc. Am. (gen. chmn. 1993), Internat. Neural Network Soc. Hindu. Achievements include patents in field. Home: 5771 W Gail Dr Chandler AZ 85226-1232 Office: Ariz State U Sch of Business Tempe AZ 85287

ROY, JOHNNY BERNARD, urologist; b. Baghdad, Iraq, Jan. 21, 1938; s. Bernard Benedict and Regina V. (Saka) R.; came to U.S., 1965, naturalized, 1976; M.D., U. Baghdad, 1962; m. Sandy L. Gaede, Sept. 23, 1978; children— Jennifer Anne, John II, Geoffrey Benedict. Diplomate Am. Bd. Urology. Chief resident in urology U. Ky. Hosp., 1969-70; NIH research fellow U. Okla. Med. Center, 1970-71; chief urology Kaiser Found. Hosps. Hawaii, 1972-75; chief urology VA Med. Center, Oklahoma City, also prof. urology U. Okla. Med. Center, 1981-96. Contbr. articles to med. jours. Mem. AMA (Physicians Recognition award 1970—), Am. Urol. Assn. (South ctrl. sect.), ACS, Am. Fertility Soc., Soc. Univ. Urologists, Okla. Med. Assn., Okla. County Med. Soc. (pres. 1999), Okla. County Med. Assn., Okla. Kidney Found. (pres. 1979-80), Okla. Urol. Assn. (exec. sec., pres. 1980-81), Soc. Mil. Surgeons, Sigma Xi. Republican. Roman Catholic. Office: U Okla Health Scis Ctr 105 S Bryant Ave Edmond OK 73034-6399 Home: 2625 W Sierra Springs Edmond OK 73003

ROY, KENNETH RUSSELL, school system administrator, educator; b. Hartford, Conn., Mar. 29, 1946; s. Russell George and Irene Mary (Birkowski) R.; m. Marisa Anne Russo, Jan. 27, 1968; children: Lisa Marie, Louise Irene. BS, Ctrl. Conn. State Coll., New Britain, 1968, MS, 1974, PhD, 1985. Tchr. sci. Rocky Hill (Conn.) H.S., 1968-73, N.W. Cath. H.S., West Hartford, Conn., 1973-74; coord. math. and sci. Bolton (Conn.) H.S., 1974-78; chmn. scis. Bacon Acad., Colchester, Conn., 1978-81; dir. K-12, dir. sci. and safety Glastonbury (Conn.) Pub. Schs., 1981—. Pres. Nat. Safety Cons., Vernon, Conn., 1996—; pres. Roy Ednl. Cons.; mem. adj. faculty manchester C.C., 1976-90, Tunxis C.C., 1975-90; instr. U. Conn. Coop. Program, 1974-78; cons./adv. Project Rise, 1978-81; lectr., sci. curriculum cons.various Conn. sch. dists.; nat. dir. Nat. Sci. Suprs. Assn., 1988-91, exec. dir.Leadership Inst. Cen. Conn. State U., New Britain, 1989-91; exec. dir. Nat. Sci. Suprs. Assn., 1992-95; bd. dirs. Lab. Safety Workshop Nat. Ctr., 1995—, Conn. United for Rsch. Excellence, 1995-98; authorized OSHA instr., 1996—. Co-editor Conn. Jour. Sci. Edn., 1984-88; editor Sci. Leadership Trend Notes, 1989-91; contbr. articles to profl. jours. Mem. St. Christopher Sch. Bd., 1982-83. Recipient Disting. Educator's and Conn. Educator's awards Milken Family Found., 1989, Nat. Sci. Supr. of the Yr. award Nat. Sci. Edn. Leadership Assn., 2003; named Tchr. of Yr. Colchester, 1980; grantee NSF, 1968, staff devel. 1979, 80, Nat. Sci. Supr. Leadership Conf., 1980. Mem. ASCD, AAAS, Am. Indsl. Hygiene Assn., Am. Soc. Safety Engrs., Nat. Sci. Tchrs. Assn., Nat. Sci. Suprs. Assn. (pres.-elect 1986-87, pres. 1987-88), Conn. Sci. Tchrs. Assn., Conn. Sci. Suprs. Assn. (pres. 1985-86, Sci. Supr. of the Yr. award 2002), Conn. Assn. Profl. Devel., Conn. Assn. Supervision and Curriculum Devel., Glastonbury Adminstrs. and Suprs. Assn., Nat. Ctr. Improvement Sci. Tchg. and Learning (mem. adv. bd. 1988-91), Internat. Coun. Assn. Sci. Edn. (nat. rep. 1987-88, N.Am. region rep. and exec. com. mem. 1989—), Phi Delta Kappa. Roman Catholic. Office: Glastonbury Pub Schs Glastonbury CT 06033

ROY, PAUL EMILE, JR., county official; b. Sumter, S.C., Dec. 18, 1942; s. Paul Emile and Harriette Orvilla (Sorenson) R.; m. Patricia Jane Stariha, July 2, 1977; 1 child, Jennifer Jo. AA, Grand Rapids Jr. Coll., 1963; student, Universidad de las Americas, Mexico City, 1963-64, Instituto Mexicano-Norteamericano de Relaciones Culturales, 1964-65; BA, Aquinas Coll., Grand Rapids, 1967; MA, U. Americas Escuela de Graduados, Mexico City, 1968; postgrad., U. Mich., 1977-79; MBA, Calif. Coast U., 1994. Asst. prin., instr. Spanish Muskegon (Mich.) Cath. Cen. High Sch., 1971-75; govt. offcl. County of Muskegon, 1975—, dir. employment and tng. Muskegon/Oceana Consortium, 1975-87, dir. employment and tng., 1988-95, dir. employment and tng. and facilities mgmt., 1995—, dir. pub. facilities, 2003—. Mem. Mich. Com. for Devel. of Romance Lang. Performance Objectives; adult edn. adv. com. Muskegon Pub. Schs.; appointee Mich. Youth Employment Coun.; v.p. regional adv. coun. U.S. Dept. Labor, 1981; mem. City of Muskegon Local Devel. Funding Authority, 1988—, Downtown Devel. Authority, 1988—, City of Whitehall (Mich.) Local Devel. Funding Authority, 1988—, Muskegon Econ. Growth Alliance Edn. Com.; bd. dirs. United Way, 1998—, YMCA, 1999-01; cons. U.S. Dept. Labor, Washington, Mich. Dept. Labor, Lansing, Gov.'s Office Manpower, Ind., U. Mich., Ann Arbor, various pvt. cos., non-profit orgns. Campaign chmn. Muskegon County United Way, 1986-88, Pacesetter award, 1987; bd. dirs. United Way, 1998—, YMCA, 1999-2001. Mem. Am. Assn. Tchrs. Spanish and Portuguese, Mich. Assn. Tchrs. English as Second Lang., Mich. Assn. Employment and Tng. Dirs. (pres. 1980-81), Mich. Employment and Tng. Inst. (founding bd. dirs. 1980-81), Nat. Assn. Counties (employment steering com.), Nat. Assn. County Employment and Tng. Adminstrs. (nat. bd. dirs. 1979-80, nat. chmn. organizational resources com. 1981). Avocations: golf, travel, reading, theater. Office: Muskegon Cty Dept Employment & Tng 1611 Oak Ave Muskegon MI 49442-2405

ROYAL, NANCY B. primary school educator; b. Newnan, Ga., Mar. 27, 1949; d. Harold C. and Jewell (Stephens) Batchelor; m. Mayo H. Royal Jr., Aug. 15, 1970; children: Amanda Elizabeth, Molly Cole. BSEd, Ga. Coll., 1971; MEd, Ga. State U., 1978; EdS, West Ga. Coll., 1986. Cert. early childhood edn. Second grade tchr. Jo Wells Elem. Sch., Hapeville, Ga., 1970-71; kindergarten tchr. Columbia Drive Bapt. Sch., Decatur, Ga., 1972-75, Indian Creek Bapt. Sch., Stone Mountain, Ga., 1975-77, Meml. Drive Presbyterian Sch., Stone Mountain, 1978-80; first grade tchr. Elm St. Elem. Sch., Newnan, Ga., 1980-83, kindergarten tchr., 1980-96, prin., 1999. Active State Reading Textbook Adoption Com., 21st Century Consortium Edn.; presenter edn. workshops. Treas. Newnan Jr. Svc. League, chairperson selection com. christmas program; pre-sch. Sunday sch. tchr. Newnan First Bapt. Ch., 1980—, children's choir dir., mem. stewardship com., chair weekday ministries com. Recipient Presdl. Excellence in Math. award 1992, Disting. Alumni award Ga. State U., 1993; named Atlanta Jour.-Constitution's Honor Tchr., 1989, Ga. Tchr. of Yr., 1993, Nat. Educator award Milken Family Found., 1995. Mem. Alpha Delta Kappa, Phi Kappa Phi, Phi Delta Kappa, Ga. Coun. Tchrs. Math. Home: 6 Summit Ln Newnan GA 30263-5531 Office: Ruth Hill Elem Sch 57 Sunset Ln Newnan GA 30263-2836

ROYCE, BARRIE SAUNDERS HART, physicist, educator; b. Eng., Jan. 10, 1933; came to U.S., 1957, naturalized, 1978; s. Vincent Pateman Hart and Kathlene (Saunders) R.; m. Dominique J.M. Vallee, May 7, 1964; children: Vincent Rene Hart, Marc Edward Hart. BSc in Physics, King's Coll., U. London, 1954, PhD, 1957. Rsch. assoc. Carnegie Inst. Tech., 1957-60, Princeton U., 1960-61, mem. faculty, 1961—2003, prof. applied physics and materials scis., 1978—2003, prof. emeritus, 2003—; master of Dean Mathey Coll. Dean Mathey Coll., 1986-94. Editorial adv. bd. Jour. Photoacoustics, to 1984. Mem. Princeton Borough Zoning Bd. Adjustment, 1980-93, chair, 1993—. Grantee NSF; Grantee Air Force Office Sci. and Rsch.; Grantee Army Rsch. Office. Mem. Am. Phys. Soc., Sigma Xi. Office: Princeton U D416 Duffield Hall Eq Princeton NJ 08544-0001

ROYER, RONALD ALAN, entomologist, educator; b. Des Moines, Feb. 27, 1945; s. Charles Melvin and Sylvia Edith (Noe) R.; children from previous marriages: Jon Michael, Lara Lanai, Jesse Alan, Adam Joseph; m. Margaret Ruth (Tavis), Nov. 27, 1982; children: Daniel Grant, Emily Ann, Noah Michael. BS, Iowa State U., 1972; PhD, U. N.D., 1984. Rsch. asst. Iowa State U., 1972-73; tchg. asst. Bemidji State U., Minn., 1973-74; instr. coord. Long Lake Conservation Ctr., Palisade, Minn., 1977-82; tchg. asst. U. N.D., 1983—84; asst. prof. sci. edn. U. Minn., Morris, Minn., 1984-85; prof. sci. Minot State U., ND, 1985—; dir. honors program Minot State U., ND, 1989-95. Artist, cover illustration, Jour. of the Lepidopterists' Soc., 1988; author: book, Butterflies of North Dakota, an Atlas and Guide, 1988, second edition, 2003; contbg. articles to profl. jour. Mem. The Lepidopterists' Soc., Great plains coord. 1988—, The Xerces Soc., N.D. Natural Sci. Soc., N.D. Acad. Sci., Sigma Xi. Achievements include discovery of numerous range extensions and distribution records for North Am. butterflies; substantial work on endangered butterfly species, and biogeography for public lands in northern Gt. Plains. Office: Minot State U 500 University Ave W Minot ND 58707-0002

ROYSE, SUE MARION, special education educator; b. Ironton, Ohio, Oct. 28, 1944; d. Paul Hurt and Clyda (Forson) Marion; m. David T. Royse, May 20, 1972. BS in Edn., Concord Coll., Athens, W.Va., 1971; MS in Edn., Ind. U., 1977. Tchr. Greater Clark County Schs., Jeffersonville, Ind., 1977-88, Phoenix (Ariz.) Union Dist. 210, 1989-91, Warren Achievement Ctr., 1991-93, State of Ill. Dept., Corrections Hill Correction Ctr., 1993-94, Ind. Sch. Dist. # 196, Rosemount, Minn., 1994-96, Knox County Sch. Transition Program, 1996—98, Karns H.S. Resource Program, 1998—. Recipient Olin Davis award State of Ind., 1982. Mem. Coun. for Exceptional Children, Correction Edn. Assn., Beta Sigma Phi. Home: 2700 Ed Stallings Ln Knoxville TN 37931-4135

ROYSTER, DAVID CALVIN, computer educator, mathematics educator, researcher; b. Lexington, Ky., Feb. 16, 1952; s. Wimberly Calvin and Betty Jo (Barnett) R.; m. Norma Portalatin, Aug. 14, 1976; children: Thomas Wilkins, Robert Benjamin. BA, U. of the South, 1973; PhD, La. State U., 1978. Vis. asst. prof. U. Va., Charlottesville, 1978-79; rsch. lectr. U. Tex., Austin, 1979-82; asst. prof. U. N.C., Charlotte, 1982-88, assoc. prof., 1988—, dir. ctr. math. sci. tech. edn., 2000—. Computer cons. math. dept. U. N.C., 1986-2000. Contbr. articles to profl. jours. Mem. Assn. Math. Tchr. Educators, Nat. Coun. Tchrs. Math., N.C. Coun. Tchrs. Math., Am. Math. Soc., Math. Assn. Am., Phi Beta Kappa, Phi Kappa Phi (pres. 1984-87). Democrat. Methodist. Avocations: raising rhododendrons and azaleas, golf, computer, calligraphy. Office: U NC CMSTE Dept Math Charlotte NC 28223

ROYSTON, LLOYD LEONARD, educational marketing consultant; children: Sharon, William, Jayston. AB, Talladega Coll., 1958; MEd, Tuskegee Inst., 1971; EdD, U. Ala., 1980. Cert. tchr., counselor. Tchr. Ala. State Bd. Edn., Dadeville, 1959-63; social caseworker N.Y.C. Social Svcs., 1963-65; continuing edn. Tuskegee Inst., Ala., 1965-77, dir. human resources, 1980; faculty devel. coord. U. Ala. U., 1977-80; dean continuing edn. Pensacola Jr. Coll., Fla., 1982-86; sr. assoc. Ednl. Transactions Assocs., 1986—. Spl. cons. Ala. A&M U., 1988, assoc. dean Sch. Grad. Studies, 1988-89; head staff and program devel., Tuskegee U., 1990-93; asst. to dir. mktg. rels. Auburn U. Coop. Ext. Sys., 1993-98; cons. AID, 1976-78, Multi-Racial Corp., New Orleans, 1970-72. Author: Methods of Teaching Adults, 1968, Planning Practices at Predominantly Black Institutions, 1980. Bd. dirs. PUSH, Pensacola, 1983, Wedgewood Homeowners Assn., Pensacola, 1982, Fla. Inst. Govt., U. West Fla., 1982-86, Pvt. Industry Coun., Pensacola, 1984-86; mem. Gannett Found. Scholarship Com., 1984. Recipient Svc. award Dept. Social Svc., N.Y.C., 1964, Outstanding Svc. award Ala. Migrant Coun., 1974, Youth Svcs. award Tuskegee Inst., 1977, Svc. award Equal Opportunity Commn., Pensacola, 1985. Mem. Am. Coun. on Edn., Am. Assn. Adult and Continuing Edn., Talladega Alumni Assn. (v.p. 1984-86), Kappa Delta Pi. Baptist. Avocations: fishing, camping, swimming, specialty cooking. E-mail: jlroywal@bellsouth.net.

ROZANSKI, MORDECHAI, historian, university dean; b. Lodz, Poland, July 4, 1946; came to U.S., 1968; s. Louis and Bertha R.; m. Bonnie Gail Asher, May 30, 1970; 1 child, Daniel K. BA, McGill U., 1968; postgrad. Columbia U., 1970, New Asia Coll., 1971-72; PhD, U. Pa., 1974. Instr. history U. Pa., Phila., 1969-71; assoc. prof. Asian history Berry Coll., Rome, Ga., 1974-76; asst. prof. Asian history, dir. Office of Internat. Edn. and fgn. area studies program Pacific Luth. U., Tacoma, 1976-82; assoc. dean for internat. studies Adelphi U., Garden City, N.Y., 1982-84, assoc. provost, 1984-86; dean Coll. Liberal Arts, Fairleigh Dickinson U., Teaneck, N.J., 1986-89, v.p. for academic affairs, 1989-1991, provost, Wagner Coll., Staten Island, 1991-1993, pres. Univ. of Guelph, Ontario, 1993-2003, pres., Rider Univ., Lawrenceville, 2003- ; dir. programs Nat. Council on Fgn. Langs. and Internat. Studies, 1983-86. Trustee, World Affairs Council, Seattle, 1978-81; vice chmn. Nat. Com. on Internat. Studies and Program Adminstrs., 1979-80; chmn. Pacific N.W. Internat./Intercultural Edn. Consortium, 1979-82. Que. Province fellow, 1967; Wilson Meml. scholar, 1968; U. Pa. fellow, 1968-71; Am. Hist. Assn. Am.-East Asian Relations fellow, Columbia U., 1970; Can. Council doctoral fellow, 1971-73; U.S. Office of Edn. research grantee, 1977; Lilly Found. fellow Stanford U., summer 1978. Author: Manual of World History, 1975; Guide to U.S. State Papers on China, 1979; editor-in-chief Am.-East Asian Relations Newsletter, 1980-83; contbr. articles to profl. publs. Office: Rider Univ 2083 Lawrence Rd Lawrenceville NJ 08648-3099*

ROZARIE, VERA JEAN, school district administrator; b. Kansas City, Kans., Jan. 23, 1937; d. James Lee and H. Eola (Londea) Kazee; m. Edward C. Rozarie, Jan. 28, 1955 (dec. Nov. 1983); chldren: Gwenann B. Eaton, Edwina L. Lucenius, Dirk L. Rozarie, Carla J. Rozarie. BS, Sacred Heart U., Fairfield, Conn., 1973; MLS, So. Conn. State U., New Haven, 1976, postgrad., 1978. Cert. tchr., adminstr., supr., Conn. Pub. librarian City of Bridgeport, Conn., 1962-73; tchr. social studies Stratford (Conn.) Bd. Edn., 1973-80, coord. libr. svcs., 1980-85, supr. media svcs., 1985-88, asst. prin., 1988-90, media specialsit, 1990-91, supr. media K-8, 1991—. Adj. instr. Conn. Bd. Edn., Bridgeport, 1976-80, mem. standards and rev., 1985-90, trainer/assessor, 1988-90, assessor, 1989. Lay min. St. James' Parish, Stratford, 1989—; elections moderator Democratic Party, Stratford, 1980-87; organizing v.p. Friends of Stratford Libr., 1980-84. Recipient Human Rels. award Conn. Edn. Assn., 1982; E.E.A. fellow Conn. Bd. Edn., 1988-89. Fellow Inst. Devel. of Ednl. Activities (named to Women of Distinction 1993); mem. ALA, Conn. Edn. Talent Pool, Phi Delta Kappa. Roman Catholic. Avocations: reading, theater, travel, storytelling. Home: 27 Selleck Pl Stratford CT 06615-5824 Office: Stratford Bd Edn 1000 E Broadway Stratford CT 06615-5911

ROZMAN, GILBERT FRIEDELL, sociologist, educator; b. Mpls., Feb. 18, 1943; s. David and Celia (Friedell) R.; m. Masha Dwosh, Jan. 25, 1945; children: Thea Dwosh, Noah Dwosh. BA, Carleton Coll., Northfield, Minn., 1965; PhD (Woodrow Wilson fellow 1965-66), Princeton U., 1971. Mem. faculty Princeton U., 1970—, prof. sociology, 1979—, Musgrave prof. sociology, 1992—. Mem. com. studies Chinese civilization Am. Council Learned Socs., 1975-80; mem. U.S.-USSR Bi-Nat. Commn. Humanities and Social Scis., 1978-86, IREX Univ. Coun., 1998-2001. Author: Urban Networks in Ch'ing China and Tokugawa Japan, 1973, Urban Networks in Russia, 1750-1800, and Premodern Periodization, 1976, Population and Marketing Settlements in Ch'ing China, 1982, A Mirror for Socialism: Soviet Criticisms of China, 1985, The Chinese Debate About Soviet Socialism 1978-85, 1987, Japan's Response to the Gorbachev Era, 1985-1991: A Rising Superpower Views a Declining One, 1992; co-author: The Modernization of Japan and Russia, 1975; editor: The Modernization of China, 1981, Soviet Studies of Premodern China: Assessments of Recent Scholarship, 1984, Japan in Transition: From Tokugawa to Meiji, 1986, The East Asian Region: Confucian Heritage and Its Modern Adaptation, 1991, Dismantling Communism: Common Causes and Regional Variations, 1992, Russia and East Asia: The 21st Century Security Environment, 1999, Japan and Russia: The Tortuous Path to Normalization, 1949-1999, 2000. Guggenheim fellow, 1979-80; grantee NSF, NEH, Social Sci. Rsch. Coun., Nat. Coun. for Soviet and E. European Studies, U.S. Inst. Peace, Woodrow Wilson Internat. Ctr. Mem. Assn. Asian Studies, Am. Sociol. Assn., Am. Assn. Advancement Slavic Studies, Internat. Studies Assn. Home: 20 Springwood Dr Trenton NJ 08648-1048 Office: Princeton U 149 Wallace Hill Princeton NJ 08544-0001 E-mail: grozman@princeton.edu.

ROZMAN, KEVIN MICHAEL, middle school arts educator; b. Mpls., May 30, 1949; s. Joseph Daniel and Frances Margaret (Chernivetz) R.; 1 child, Robert Joseph Regent-Rozman. BA, St. Mary's Coll. Minn., 1971; MA, Marquette U., 1991, PhD, 1996. Cert. mid. and secondary English, drama, speech tchr., mid., secondary and dist. adminstr. Dir. religious edn. Ch. of St. Kevin, Mpls., 1972-75; tchr., dept. chair St. John Cath. H.S., Milw., 1975-76; tchr., dir. religious activities St. Catherine H.S., Racine, Wis., 1977-79; dir. Christian formation St. Eugene Parish, Fox Point, Wis., 1984-86; tchr. Milw. Pub. Schs., 1986—; artistic dir. Lincoln Center Mid. Sch. Arts, Milw., 1995—2001; drama tchr. Lincoln Ctr. of the Arts, Milw., 2001—. Instr. Concordia Internat. U., Porto Alegre, Brazil, 1994-2002; pres.-elect Wis. Alliance for Arts Edn., 2000—. Recipient Tchr. Recognition award Wis. Bell/Ameritech, 1990, Spl. Commendation, Learning Mag., 1991, Excellence in End. award Milw. Bd. Sch. Dirs., 2001. Mem. ASCD, Nat. Coun. Tchrs. English, Wis. Assn. for Mid. Level Edn., Wis. Alliance for Arts Edn. (pres. 2001-02), Phi Delta Kappa (rsch. rep. 1992). Home: 4208 N 16th St Milwaukee WI 53209-6923 E-mail: drkevin@execpc.com.

ROZYCKI, EDWARD GEORGE, education educator; b. Phila., June 30, 1943; s. Edward George and Marguerite Marie (Zuschmidt) R.; m. Carole Jean Carpey, Apr. 21, 1964; children: Sara Beth, David Michael. AB in Philosophy, U. Pa., 1964; MEd, Temple U., 1971, EdD, 1974. Cert. German and math. tchr., prin., fgn. lang. supr., Pa. Counselor Coll. Settlement Camps, Horsham, Pa., 1961-63; substitute tchr. math. Sch. Dist. of Phila., 1964-66, tchr. ESL J.P. Jones Jr. H.S., 1972-86, tchr. ESL Cooke Mid. Sch., 1987-92; German tchr. George Washington H.S., Phila., 1966-71; headmaster Swarthmore (Pa.) Acad., 1986-87; assoc. prof. edn. Widener U., Chester, Pa., 1992—. Adj. prof. German Phila. Coll. Art, 1968-72; adj. prof. philosophy of edn. Temple U., Phila., 1977-83. Pres., treas. Germantown Children's Cmty., Phila., 1974-76; bd. dirs. Phila. Consumer's Coop., Phila., 1967-69. Fellow Philosophy of Edn. Soc. (pres. Mid. Atlantic States chpt. 1991-93); mem. AAUP, Ea. Pa. Assn. Tchrs. English to Spkrs. Other Langs. (founder 1980, pres. 1983), Pi Lambda Theta (pres. Phila. chpt. 1993-94), Phi Delta Kappa (McComb award 1973). Home: 534 General Patterson Dr Glenside PA 19038-3202 Office: Widener U Ctr for Edn Chester PA 19013

RUANE, JOSEPH WILLIAM, sociologist, educator; b. Lansdowne, Pa., Feb. 23, 1933; s. Joseph William and F. Viola (Davis) R.; m. Nancy Di Pasquale, Nov. 25, 1971; 1 child, Krista. Student, St. Joseph's U., 1951-53, 68-69; BA in Philosophy, St. Charles Sem., 1958; MA in Sociology, Temple U., 1971; PhD in Sociology, U. Del., 1978. Ordained priest Roman Catholic Ch., 1962. Asst. pastor, priest Archiocese Phila., 1962-68; tchr. social studies Sch. Dist. of Phila., 1968-71; asst. prof. sociology Phila. Coll. Pharmacy and Sci., 1971-77, assoc. prof., 1977-99; prof. U. Scis. in Phila., 1999—, prof. health policy, 2001—. Mem. adj. faculty Gt. Lakes Colls. Assn., Phila., 1983-90; interim chmn. dept. humanities and social scis. Phila. Coll. Pharmacy and Sci., 1984-86, chair dept. social sci,, 1986-96; dean religious studies Global Ministries U., 2001--; dir. West Phila. Mental Health Consortium, 1985-86, Health Svcs. Group, Inc., 1986—; vice chair, 1987—; dir. West Phila. C. of C., 1993—2000, ARC, West Phila., 1990-98; dir., exec. com., chmn. urban com. West Phila. Partnership, 1975—, chair, 1999—2003. Contbr. articles to profl. jours.; co-author, co-editor Pub. Edn. Platrofm of W. Wilson Goode, 1983; co-author Handbook of Home Healthcare Administration, 1997. Founding dir. West Phila. Cmty. Fed. Credit Union, 1980-88, pres., 1982-88; bd. dirs. University City Clean, Phila., 1981-87, Friends of Clark Park, Phila., 1982-86; dir. Green to Green, 1995-97, Spruce Hill Cmty. Assn., 1995-99, pres., 1997-99, Univ. City Cmty. Coun., 1997-99. Decorated Legion of Honor Chapel of Four Chaplains, 1967; Lilly fellow, 1980. Mem. AAUP, Am. Sociol. Assn., Ea. Sociol. Soc., Pa. Sociol. Soc. (chmn. long range planning com. 1982-86, pres. 1989-90, exec. com. 1987—), Nat. Coun. State and Regional Soc. Assocs. (pres. 1999-2000), global Edn. Assn., Fedn. Christian Ministries (v.p. Mid. Atlantic 1981-84, pres. 1988-92, chmn. bd. dirs. 1992-96, 99), Corps of Res. Priests U.S. (regional coord. 1984—), Westwood Club, Sigma Xi. Democrat. Avocations: basketball, attending theater, travel. Home: 4226 Regent Sq Philadelphia PA 19104-4439 Office: Univ of Scis in Phila 600 S 43d St Philadelphia PA 19104

RUBACH, JIMMY DALE, vocational services educator; b. Campbell Hill, Ill., Jan. 23, 1946; s. Adolph and Ida (Casten) R.; m. Marlene Susan Bookman, Oct. 25, 1968; children: Jamie Rene, Candace Rose. BS in Occupational Edn., SW Tex. State U., 1977; MS in Adminstrn., Tex. A&I U., 1979, Cert. in Mid-Mgmt., 1986, Cert. profl. vocat. supr., 1990. Tchr. auto mechanics Kingsville (Tex.) Ind. Sch. Dist., 1973-79; instr. curriculum dept. TEX. A&M U., College Station, 1979; tchr. auto mechanics Dickinson (Tex.) Ind. Sch. Dist., 1979-86, asst. prin. vocat. services, 1986—99, dir. career and tech., 1994—97; owner, operator R&B Glass Tinting, Dickinson, 1985, Rubach Enterprizes, network mktg., Dickinson; dir. ops. Dickerson Ind. Sch. Dist., 2000—. Trustee Gulf Coast Educators Fed. Credit Union, membership chmn., v.p., 1991, chmn. bd. dirs., 1999-2000. Coun. mem., fin. sec. Faith Luth. Ch., 1984-85. Mem. Tex. Assn. Secondary Sch. Prins., Tex. Vocat. Adminstrs. and Suprs. Assn., Gulf Coast Vocat. Adminstrs. and Suprs. Assn., Optimists (bd. dirs. Dickinson chpt. 1986-87). Home: 5409 Sycamore Dr Dickinson TX 77539-6711

RUBBA, PETER ANTHONY, JR., science educator; b. Vineland, N.J., Oct. 10, 1947; s. Peter Anthony and Henryetta (Layer) R.; m. Susan Joyce Stauffer, Aug. 23, 1969; children: Jane Erin, David Matthew. B.S., Ashland Coll., Ohio, 1969; M.A., Ind. U., 1974, Ed.D., 1977. Sci. tchr. Hillsdale High Sch., Jeromesville, Ohio, 1969-71; grad. asst. Ind. U., Bloomington, 1973-76; instr. So. Ill. U.-Carbondale, 1976-77, asst. prof., 1977-81, assoc. prof., 1981-84; assoc. prof. Pa. State U., University Park, Pa., 1984—85, dir. Pa. State Ctr. Edn. in Sci. Tech. and Soc., University Park, Pa., 1985-88, prof.-in-charge sci. edn., 1988-92, continuing edn. fellow Coll. Edn., 1993-95, head Dept. Curriculum and Instrn. Coll. Edn., 1994-2000, dir. Academic Programs Penn State World Campus, 2000—; coordinator region 8 Ill. Jr. Acad. Sci., Carbondale, 1977-80; former mem. Nat. Bd. Profl. Tchg. Standards, early adolescence sci. standards com. Contbr. numerous articles to profl. pubs. Recipient numerous grants for tchr. training, 1978—. Mem. Nat. Sci. Tchrs. Assn. (former bd. dirs.), Assn. for Edn. of Tchrs. in Sci. (founder annual mtg. proceedings, lead editor, 1996-2002, former bd. dirs., pres. 1994-95, Innovation in Tchg. Sci. Tchrs. award 1992), Nat. Assn. Research Sci. Teaching, Pa. Sci. Tchrs. Assn., Sch. Sci. and Math. Assn., Am. Distance Edn. Assn. (commonwealth of courses com.), Phi Delta Kappa, Sigma Chi. Avocations: swimming; carpentry. Home: 728 Sunset Rd State College PA 16803-3451*

RUBENSTEIN, ALBERT HAROLD, industrial engineering and management sciences educator; b. Phila., Nov. 11, 1923; s. Leo and Jean (Kaplan) R.; m. Hildette Grossman, Sept. 11, 1949; children: Michael Stephen, Lisa Joan. BS in Indsl. Engring. magna cum laude (Sr. prize econs.), Lehigh U., 1949; MS in Indsl. Engring, Columbia, 1950, PhD in Indsl. Engring. and Mgmt, 1954; DEng (hon.), Lehigh U., 1993. Asst. to pres. Perry Equipment Corp., 1940-43; rsch. assoc. Columbia U., 1950-53; asst. prof. indsl. mgmt. MIT, 1954-59; prof. indsl. engring. and mgmt. scis. Northwestern U., 1959-97; emeritus prof., 1997—; Walter P. Murphy prof. Northwestern U., 1986—, dir. Ctr. for Info. Tech., 1986-97; pres. Internat. Applied Sci. and Tech. Assos., 1977—; vis. prof. U. Calif., Berkeley; pres. Sr. Strategy Group, 1995—. Adj. prof. U. Calif., San Diego, 1997—; cons. to govt. and industry. Dir. Narragansett Capital Corp. Author books and articles in field. Served with inf. AUS, World War II. Decorated Purple Heart, Combat Inf. badge.; Recipient Lincoln Arc Welding Found. prize paper, 1948, Pioneer in Innovation Mgmt. award Ctr. Innovation Mgmt., 1992; Omicron Delta Kappa annual fellow, 1949-50; Fulbright research fellow, 1955 Fellow IEEE (editor trans. 1959—, Engring. Mgr. of Yr. award 1992), Soc. Applied Anthropology; mem. AAAS (chmn. indsl. sci. and tech. sect. 1997—), Inst. Mgmt. Scis. (sr. mem., dir. studies for coll. on R & D 1960—, v.p. rsch. and edn. 1966-68) Home and Office: 1630 Chicago Ave Apt 2010 Evanston IL 60201-6025

RUBENSTEIN, ARTHUR HAROLD, medical school official, physician; b. Johannesburg, Dec. 28, 1937; came to U.S., 1967; s. Montague and Isabel (Nathanson) R.; m. Denise Hack, Aug. 19, 1962; children: Jeffrey Lawrence, Errol Charles. MB BCh, U. Witwatersrand, 1960, MD, 2001; DSc in Medicine (hon.), 2002. Diplomate Am. Bd. Internal Medicine. Intern, then resident Johannesburg Gen. Hosp., 1961, 63-65, 66-67; fellow in endocrinology Postgrad. Med. Sch., London, 1965-66; fellow in medicine U. Chgo., 1967-68, from asst. prof. to assoc. prof., 1968-74, prof., 1974-97, Lowell T. Coggeshall prof. med. sci., 1981-97, assoc. chmn. dept. medicine, 1975-81, chmn., 1981-97; attending physician Mitchell Hosp., U. Chgo., 1968-97; dean, CEO, Gustave L. Levy disting. prof. Mt. Sinai Sch. Medicine, N.Y.C., 1997—2001; exec. v.p., dean U. of Penn. Health System, School of Med., Phila., 2001—. Mem. study sect. NIH, 1973-77, Hadassah Med. Adv. Bd., 1986-95, adv. council Nat. Inst. Arthritis, Metabolism and Digestive Diseases, 1978-80; chmn. Nat. Diabetes Adv. Bd., 1982, mem., 1981-83. Mem. editorial bd. Diabetes, 1973-77, Endocrinology, 1973-77, Jour. Clin. Investigation, 1976-81, Am. Jour. Medicine, 1978-81, Diabetologia, 1982-86, Diabetes Medicine, 1987-91, Annals of Internal Medicine, 1991-96, Medicine, 1992—; contbr. articles to profl. jours. Mem. Gov.'s Sci. Adv. Coun. State of Ill., 1989-96. Recipient David Rumbough Meml. award Juvenile Diabetes Found., 1978 Master ACP (John Phillips Meml. award 1995); fellow South African Coll. Physicians, Royal Coll. Physicians (London), N.Y. Acad. Medicine; mem. Am. Soc. for Clin. Investigation, Am. Diabetes Assn. (Eli Lilly award 1973, Banting medal 1983, Solomon Berson Meml. lectr. 1985), Brit. Diabetes Assn. (Banting lectr. 1987), Endocrine Soc., Am. Fedn. Clin. Rsch., Ctrl. Soc. Clin. Rsch. (v.p. 1988, pres. 1989), Assn. Am. Physicians (treas. 1984-89, councillor 1989-94, v.p. 1994-95, pres. 1995-96), Am. Bd. Internal Medicine (bd. govs. 1985-93, exec. com. 1990-93, chmn. 1992-93), Residency Rev. Com., Am. Acad. Arts and Scis., Inst. Medicine (coun. 1991-96), Assn. Profs. Medicine (councillor 1991-94, v.p. 1994-95, pres. 1995-96, Robert Williams award 1997), Assn. Am. Med. Colls. (mem. coun. of deans adminstrv. bd. 2002—). Office: U of Penn School of Med 295 John Morgan Bldg, 3620 Hamilton Walk Philadelphia PA 19104

RUBENSTEIN, DANIEL IAN, biology educator; b. N.Y.C., June 19, 1950; s. Ira Saul and Babette Hannah (Wattel) R.; m. Nancy Gail Finkelstein, May 7, 1972; children: Dustin, Alison. BS, U. Mich., 1972; PhD, Duke U., 1977; MA, Cambridge (Eng.) U., 1978. Asst. prof. Princeton (N.J.) U., 1980-86, assoc. prof., 1986-90, prof., 1990—. Eastman prof. Oxford (Eng.) U., 2003. Author, editor: Current Problems in Sociology, 1982, Ecological Aspects of Social Evolution, 1986. Mem., pres. Hopewell Valley Bd. Edn., 1985-91; trustee Friends of Hopewell Valley Open Space, 1990—. Named Presdl. Young Investigator, NSF, 1985; jr. rsch. fellow King's Coll., 1977, NSF-NATO postdoctoral fellow, 1977, Japan Promotion of Sci. fellow. Fellow Animal Behavior Soc.; mem. Ecol. Soc. Am., Brit. Ecol. Soc., Soc. Conservation Biology, Soc. Am. Naturalists, Soc. for Study of Evolution, Soc. Behavioral Ecology. Office: Princeton U Dept Ecology and Evol Biol Princeton NJ 08544-1003 E-mail: dir@princeton.edu.

RUBIN, ARTHUR HERMAN, retired university official, consultant; b. N.Y.C., Aug. 14, 1927; s. Samuel and Bessie (Moritt) R.; m. Janice Levy, Apr. 9, 1950 (div. 1965); children: Renee Ellen, Linda Joy; m. Audrey M. Schmidt, July 1, 1973. BS, NYU, 1950, MA, 1951. Adminstrv. asst. to asst. dean Sch. Edn. NYU, 1947-54, lab. asst. bus. edn. dept., 1950-54, instr., 1954-56, program dir. grad. students orgn., 1954-63, dir. tours, 1955-58, coord. summer sessions activities, 1959-64, dir. Bur. Pub. Occasions, 1963-74, asst. v.p. pub. occasions, 1974-75, dir. extramural affairs Coll. Dentistry, 1976, assoc. dean adminstrn., 1976-80, adj. asst. prof. behavioral scis. and cmty. health, 1976-80, dir. alumni rels. Sch. of Med., 1980-95, dir. spl. events med. ctr., 1988-95; cons. to Office Alumni Rels. NYU Sch. Medicine, 1995-2000; cons. to Office Spl. Events, NYU Med. Ctr., 1995-2000; ret., 2000. Tchr. Patrick Henry Jr. High Sch., N.Y.C., 1949-58; acting asst. prin. Robert F. Wagner Jr. High Sch., N.Y.C., 1958-63; cons. in field. Trustee Agnew Found., 1967—. Recipient NYU Presdl. citation, 1971, GSO award, 1980, Ernest O. Melby award Sch. Edn. Alumni Assn., 1976, citation Bus. Edn. Assn. Met. N.Y., 1976, Sesquicentennial award NYU Alumni Fedn., 1982, Meritorious Svc. award, 1985, dir. Emeritus citation, 1992. Mem. Ea. Bus. Tchrs. Assn. (chmn. exhibits 1953-74, exec. bd. 1969-71, pres. 1972-73, award 1974), Bus. Edn. Assn. Met. N.Y. (exec. bd. 1962-83), Nat. Bus. Edn. Assn. (exec. bd. 1972-74, conv. mgr. 1974-92, Disting. Svc. award 1992, Cert. of Appreciation 1992), N.Y. Acad. Pub. Edn. (bd. dirs. 1979-98, pres. 1992-94), NYU Edn. Alumni Assn. (v.p. 1961-62, 64-67), NYU Club (bd. govs. 1972-78, 79-89, v.p. 1983-86, chmn. bd. 1986-87), Princeton Club N.Y., Delta Pi Epsilon Rsch. Found. Inc. (bd. dirs. 1990-92), Delta Pi Epsilon (Svc. awards Alpha chpt. 1971, 81). Home: 2605 Houghton Lean Macungie PA 18062-9506

RUBIN, DAVID LEE, humanities educator, publisher; b. Indpls., Sept. 30, 1939; s. Ira Bertram and Jeanne Iva (Gamso) R.; m. Carolyn Dettman, June 12, 1965; 1 child, Timothy Craig. BA, U. Tenn., 1962; cert., U. Paris, 1963; MA, U. Ill., 1964, PhD, 1967. Instr. French U. Ill., Urbana, 1966-67; asst. prof. U. Chgo., 1967-69, U. Va., Charlottesville, 1969-74, assoc. prof., 1974-82, prof. French, 1982-2001, mem. com. on comparative lit., 1997-2001, prof. emeritus, assoc. univ. seminar program, 2001—; seminar dir. Folger Inst., 1989. Assoc. ctr. advanced studies U. Va., 1979, 80-81, 87, 93, 99-2000; founder Rookwood Press, 1992—; cons. Can. Coun., Etudes littéraires françaises, NEH, numerous univ. presses; lectr., spkr. in field. Author: Higher Hidden Order, 1972, The Knot of Artifice, 1981, A Pact with Silence, 1991; editor: The Selected Poetry and Prose of John T. Napier, 1972, La poésie française du premier 17e siècle, 1986, Sun King, 1991; co-editor: La Cohérence Intérieure, 1977, Convergences, 1989, The Ladder of High Designs, 1991, The Fulbright Difference, 1993; founding editor Continuum, 1989-93, EMF: Studies in Early Modern France, 1994-2002, EMF Critiques, 1994-2002, Rookwood Texts, 1997—, Rookwood Reprints, 2002—; mem. editl. bd. Purdue Studies in Romance Literatures, 1975-2001, Oeuvres et Critiques, 1976-2001, French Rev., 1986-94; Am. corr. Cahiers Maynard, 1973-2001, Cahiers Tristan L'Hermite, 1989-2001; contbr. articles to profl. jours., chpts. to books. U.S. State Dept. Fulbright fellow, 1963—64, fellow, Woodrow Wilson Found., 1963—64, Guggenheim Found., 1980—81, Hewlett fellow, summer, 1997, The Shape of Change: Studies in Honor of David Lee Rubin, 2002. Mem. MLA, ACLU, Farmington Club, Boar's Head Club, Phi Beta Kappa. Avocations: reading, travel, fitness. Home: 520 Rookwood Pl Charlottesville VA 22903-4734

RUBIN, DAVID M. dean, educator; BA in Am. History, Columbia U.; MA in Comm., Stanford U., PhD in Comm., 1972. Mem. faculty and chair dept. journalism NYU; prof. Syracuse U., dean Newhouse Sch. Pub. Comm., 1990—. Juror Pulitzer Prize, journalism, 1998, 99. Contbr. articles to profl. jours. Mem. adv. bd. Syracuse Opera. Avocations: dogs, music. Office: Syracuse U 215 University Pl Syracuse NY 13244-0001*

RUBIN, DONALD BRUCE, statistician, educator, research company executive; b. Washington, Dec. 22, 1943; s. Allan A. and Harriet Rubin; m. Kathryn M. Kazarow; children: Scott Wilk, Paul Stuart. AB magna cum laude, Princeton U., 1965; MS, Harvard U., 1966, PhD, 1970. Rsch. statistician Ednl. Testing Svc., Princeton, N.J., 1971-75, chmn. stats., 1975-79, sr. statis. advisor, 1979-81; pres. Datamatrics Rsch. Inc., Waban, Mass., 1981—; prof. U. Chgo., 1982-84, Harvard U., Cambridge, Mass., 1984—, chmn. stats., 1985-94, 2000—, John L. Loeb Prof. Stats., 2002—. Author: Handling Nonresponse in Sample Surveys by Multiple Imputation, 1980, Multiple Imputation for Nonresponse in Surveys, 1987; author: (with others) Incomplete Data in Sample Surveys (Vol. 2): Theory and Bibliography, 1983; co-author: (with R.J.A. Little) Statistical Analysis With Missing Data, 1987, 2d edit., 2002, (with A. Gelman, J. Carlin. H. Stern) Bayasian Data Analysis, 1995, (with R. Rosenthal and R. Rosnow) Contrasts and Effect Sites in Behavioral Research: A Correlational Approach, 2000; co-editor: (with P.W. Holland) Test Equating, 1982; contbr. over 300 articles to profl. jours. Recipient Parzen prize for statis. innovation, 1996; Woodrow Wilson Grad. fellow, 1965; NSF Grad. fellow, 1965, 68, John Simon Guggenheim fellow, 1977-78. Fellow AAAS (chmn. stats. 1992), Am. Statis. Assn. (editor jour. 1980-82, dir. 1980-82, statistician of yr. Boston chpt. 1995, Chgo. chpt. 2000, S.S. Wilks medal 1995), Inst. Math. Stats. (coun. mem. 1990-92, 99-2001); mem. NAS (com. on nat. stats. 1989-92, mem. panel on confidentiality data 1989-92, panel on bilingual edn. 1990-92, working group on statis. analysis of com. on basic rsch. in behavioral and social scis. 1985-86, panel statis. in 21st century 1995, other coms.), AAAS, Am. Acad. Arts and Sci., Biometric Soc., Internat. Assn. Survey Statisticians, Internat. Stats. Inst., Psychometric Soc., Royal Statis. Soc. Office: Harvard U Dept Statistics Cambridge MA 02138 E-mail: rubin@stat.harvard.edu.

RUBIN, GERALD MAYER, molecular biologist, biochemistry educator; b. Boston, Mar. 31, 1950; s. Benjamin H. and Edith (Weisberg) R.; m. Lynn S. Mastalir, May 7, 1978; 1 child, Alan F. BS, MIT, 1971; PhD, Cambridge (Eng.) U., 1974, ScD, 2002. Helen Hay Whitney Found. fellow Stanford U. Sch. Medicine, Calif., 1974-76; asst. prof. biol. chemistry Sidney Farber Cancer Inst.-Harvard U. Med. Sch., Boston, 1977-80; staff mem. Carnegie Instn. of Washington, Balt., 1980-83; John D. MacArthur prof. genetics U. Calif., Berkeley, 1983—. Investigator Howard Hughes Med. Inst., 1987—, v.p. biomed. rsch., 2000-01, v.p., dir. planning Janelia Farm Campus, 2001-03, v.p., dir. Janelia Farm Rsch. Campus, 2003—. Recipient Young Scientist award Passano Found., 1983, U.S. Steel Found. award Nat. Acad. Scis., 1985, Eli Lilly award in biochemistry Am. Chem. Soc., 1985, Genetics Soc. Am. medal, 1986. Mem. NAS, Inst. of Medicine, Am. Acad. Arts and Scis. Office: Howard Hughes Med Inst 4000 Jones Bridge Rd Bethesda MD 20815-6789 E-mail: rubing@hhmi.org.

RUBIN, MELVIN LYNNE, ophthalmologist, educator; b. San Francisco, May 10, 1932; s. Morris and May (Gelman) R.; m. Lorna Isen, June 21, 1953; children: Gabrielle, Daniel, Michael. AA, U. Calif., Berkeley, 1951, BS, 1953; MD, U. Calif., San Francisco, 1957; MS, State U. Iowa, 1961. Diplomate Am. Bd. Ophthalmology (bd. dirs. 1977-83, chmn. 1984). Intern U. Calif. Hosp., San Francisco, 1957-58; resident in ophthalmology State U. Iowa, 1958-61; attending surgeon Georgetown U., Washington, 1961-63; asst. prof. surgery U. Fla. Med. Sch., Gainesville, 1963-66, assoc. prof. ophthalmology, 1966-67, prof. ophthalmology, 1967—, chmn. dept. ophthalmology, 1978-95, eminent scholar, 1989-97, eminent scholar emeritus, 1997. Author: Studies in Physiological Optics, 1965, Fundamentals of Visual Science, 1969, Optics for Clinicians, 1971, 2d edit., 1974, 25th ann. edit., 1995, The Fine Art of Prescribing Glasses, 1978, 3d edit., 2004; editor: Dictionary of Eye Terminology, 1984, 4th edit., 2001, Eye Care Notes, 1989, revised edit., 2001, Taking Care of Your Eyes, 2003; cons. editl. bd. Survey Ophthalmology; contbr. more than 100 articles to profl. jours. Co-founder Gainesville Assn. Creative Arts, Citizens for Pub. Schs., Inc., ProArteMusica Gainesville, Inc., 1969, pres., 1971-73; mem. Thomas Ctr. Adv. Bd. for the Arts, 1978-84, nat. sci. adv. bd. Helen Keller Eye Rsch. Found., 1989-96; bd. dirs. Hippodrome State Theater, 1981-87; Friends of Photography Ansel Adams Ctr., 1991-97; trustee U. Fla. Performing Arts Ctr., 1995—. With USPHS, 1961-63. Recipient Best Med. Book for 1978 award Am. Med. Writers Assn., 1979, Shaler Richardson award for svc. to medicine Fla. Soc. Ophthalmology, 1995; M.L. Rubin Ann. Lectureship established in his honor by Fla. Soc. of Ophthalmology, 1993. Fellow ACS, Am. Acad. Ophthalmology (sec., dir. 1978-92, pres. 1988, Sr. Honor award 1987. Guest of Honor 1992), Found. Am. Acad. Ophthalmology (bd. trustees, 1988-95, chmn., 1992-94), Joint Commn. on Allied Health Pers. in Ophthalmology (Statesman of Yr. award 1987); mem. Assn. Rsch. in Vision and Ophthalmology (trustee 1973-78, pres. 1979), Retina Soc., Macula Soc., Club Jules Gonin, N.Y. Acad. Sci., Fla. Soc. Ophthalmology, Am. Ophthal. Soc. (coun. 1998-2002), Pan Am. Soc. Ophthalmology, Ophthalmic Photographers Soc., Alachua County Med. Soc., Fla. Med. Assn., AMA (editorial bd. Archives of Ophthalmology 1975-85), Sigma Xi, Alpha Omega Alpha., Phi Kappa Phi. Office: U Fla Med Ctr PO Box 100284 Gainesville FL 32610-0284 E-mail: mrubin@eye.ufl.edu.

RUBIN, PHYLLIS GETZ, health association executive; b. N.Y.C., Aug. 6, 1937; d. Joseph and Sylvia (Rosenberg) Getz; m. James Milton Rubin, Oct. 28, 1961; children: Felicia Sue, Andrea Faith. BA, Syracuse U., 1959; MA, Columbia U., 1961, Adelphi U., 1975. Physical edn. tchr. Hicksville (N.Y.) Pub. Schs., 1959-93; bd. dirs., pres. Assoc. Am. Acad. Allergy, Asthma and Immunology. Producer: (video) Aerobic Dancercise for Children, 1987. Bd. dirs. COPAY, Great Neck, N.Y., 1986-91; v.p., sec. Pierpont Condominium Bd., 1986-90. Recipient Founder's Day award PTA, 1986. Mem.: N.Y. State Alliance for Health, Phys. Edn., REcreation and Dance (program spkr. 1984, 85, 93, v.p. Nassau zone 1987—2000, Zone Svc. award 1993). Avocations: tennis, reading, meditation, golf.

RUBIN, STEPHEN CURTIS, gynecologic oncologist, educator; b. Phila., May 24, 1951; s. Alan and Helen (Metz) R.; m. Anne Loughran, May 30, 1985; children: Michael, Elisabeth. BS, Franklin & Marshall U., 1972; MD, U. Pa., 1976. Diplomate Am. Bd. Ob-Gyn. (mem. divsn. gynecol. oncology 1997-2003), Nat. Bd. Med. Examiners. Intern in ob.-gyn. Hosp. of Univ. of Pa., Phila., 1976-77, residency in ob.-gyn., 1977-80, fellow in gynecologic oncology, 1980-82; asst. prof. of ob-gyn Med. Coll. of Pa., Phila., 1982-85, dir. surg. gynecology, 1982-85, chief gynecol. oncology, 1984-85; asst. mem. gynecol. staff Meml. Sloan-Kettering Hosp., N.Y.C., 1985-90, assoc. mem., 1990-93; asst. prof. ob-gyn Cornell U. Med. Coll., N.Y.C., 1985-90, assoc. prof., 1990-93; prof. ob-gyn., dir. gynecologic oncology U. Pa., Phila., 1993—. Editor: Ovarian Cancer, Cervical Cancer, Chemotherapy of Gynecologic Cancer, Uterine Cancer; contbr. over 250 articles to profl. publs. Recipient Career Devel. award Am. Cancer Soc., 1987, Boyer award Meml. Sloan-Kettering; grantee Nat. Cancer Inst., 1991, 96, 98, 99. Mem. ACS, ACOG, Am. Soc. Clin. Oncology, Soc. Gynecol. Oncologists (Pres.'s award 1993), Am. Gyn. and Obstet. Soc., Soc. Gynecologic Investigation, Soc. Pelvic Surgeons, Gynecol. Cancer Found. (Karin Smith award 1996). Office: U Pa Med Ctr 3400 Spruce St Philadelphia PA 19104-4206

RUBIN, STUART HARVEY, computer science educator, researcher; b. N.Y.C., Mar. 18, 1954; s. Jack and Rhoda Rochelle Rubin. BS, U. R.I., 1975; MS in Indsl. and Systems Engring., Ohio U., 1977; MS, Rutgers U., 1980; PhD, Lehigh U., 1988. Lectr. U. Cin., 1977-78; electronic engr. U.S. Army Rsch. Labs., Ft. Monmouth, N.J., 1980-83; assoc. prof. computer sci. Ctrl. Mich. U., Mt. Pleasant, 1988—2002, assoc. prof., 1996—, founder, dir. Ctr. for Intelligent Systems, 1990—2002. Tech. cons. RCA, Princeton, N.J., 1982-83, Babcock and Wilcox Corp., Alliance, Ohio, 1990, Booz-Allen and Hamilton, Inc., San Diego, 1990-91, Adept Tech., San Jose, Calif., 1990-91; mem. rsch. coun. Scripps Clin.; cons. USAF, 1995. Contbr. articles to profl. jours.; inventor in field. Agt. United Fund Isabella County, Mt. Pleasant, 1988; supporting coach Mich. Spl. Olympics, Mt. Pleasant, 1990; event capt. San Diego Regional Sci. Olympic Competition, 1990, 92; judge 37th, 38th, 39th, 40th, 41st, 42nd, 43d, 44th, 45th, 46th, 47th, 48th, Ann. Greater San Diego Sci. and Engring. Fair, 1991-2003. Recipient Am. Chem. Soc. award, 1972, U.S. Govt. Cert. of Merit, Washington, 1987, Letter of Appreciation, Gen. Charles C. McDonald, 1990; grantee NSF, Office Naval Tech., State of Mich., others, 1988—. Mem. IEEE (sr.), Am. Assn. Artificial Intelligence, Am. Soc. Engring. Edn. (ONT postdoctoral fellow 1990-93), N.Y. Acad. Scis., Internat. Assn. Knowledge Engrs., Assn. for Computer Machinery. Avocations: boating, skiing, hiking and nature. Home: 1542 La Playa Ave # 4-208 San Diego CA 92109-6328 Office Fax: 619-553-1130. E-mail: srubin@spawar.navy.mil., stuart.rubin@navy.mil.

RUBINS, ALEX, physical education educator; b. Cleve., Feb. 26, 1926; s. Harry and Nellie (Cutler) R.; m. Betty Buller, May 19, 1946; children: Ira Marc, Jan Merl, Brett Cory. BS in Phys. Edn. and Math., Case Western Res. U., 1949, MA in Ednl. Adminstrn., 1950, PhD in Ednl. Adminstrn., 1971. Tchr. math., athletic dir. Cleve. Pub. Schs., 1950-58, tchr. math. and adult edn., 1966; prof. phys. and health edn. and math. Cuyahoga Community Coll., Cleve., 1966—; pres. Keystone Mortgage Corp. and CCC Ins. Agy. Cleve., 1958-63; broker Realty Mortgage Svc., 1958-63; regional mgr. World Book Ency., 1963-66. Football and basketball ofcl., 1946; adminstr. religious sch. Fairmount Temple, Cleve., 1978-91; tchr. Sunday sch. Park Synagogue, 1991; dir. Red Wing Day Camp, summers 1950--58; visitor, evaluator community colls., Calif., 1978. Author: Programmed Learning Activities for Fencing, 1973. Tchr. religious sch. Park Synagogue, Heights Temple, Community Temple, Cleve., 1946-78; coach Little League Baseball, Cleveland Heights, Ohio, 1962-67; tchr. Cleve. Soc. for Blind, 1971—, County Jail, Cleve., 1981-85; reader Cleve. Soc. for Blind, 1971—; pub. speaker to community orgns., 1967—; lectr. Coun. Gardans Retirement Home, Cleve., 1985—; program dir. Elders Hostel, 1980—; div. head Jewish Welfare Fund, Cleve., 1970—. Master sgt. AUS, 1944-46, CBI. Named Advisor of Yr., Cuyahoga Community Coll., 1971; named to Founders wall as ofcl. Basketball Hall of Fame, 1974. Mem. AAUP, AAHPER and Dance, Midwest Alliance Health, Phys. Edn., Recreation and Dance, Ohio Assn. Health, Phys. Edn., Recreation and Dance (bd. dirs. 1980-85, Mentoring award 1990), Internat. Assn. Approved Basketball Ofcls., Ohio High Sch. Athletic Assn., Ohio Assn. 2-Yr. Colls. (past pres., bd. dirs.), Greater Cleve. Football Ofcls. Assn. (pres., bd. dirs., Outstanding Football Ofcl. award 1985), Jewish War Vets., B'nai B'rith. Avocations: bridge, crossword puzzles, jogging, writing pooetry, sketching. Home: 1112 Rutherford Rd Cleveland OH 44112-3654 Office: Cuyahoga Community Coll 2900 Community College Ave Cleveland OH 44115-3123

RUBINSTEIN, ARYE, pediatrician, microbiologist, educator, immunologist, educator; b. Tel Aviv, Oct. 02; came to U.S., 1971; s. Reuven and Kathe (Samson) R.; m. Orna Eisenstein, Dec. 7, 1965 (div. 1982); children: Ran, Yair, Avner, Noam; m. Charline Nezri, Dec. 27, 1983; children: Reuven, Rena, Rachel. MD, U. Berne, Switzerland, 1962. Diplomate Am. Bd. Pediatrics; bd. cert. in pediatrics, Israel, Switzerland; Am. Bd. Allergy and Immunology cert. in allergy and immunology. Intern, pediatrics resident, fellow U. Tel Aviv, 1962-67; rsch. assoc. divsn. immunology Med. Sch. Harvard Coll., 1971-73; dir. divsn. immunology and bone marrow transplantation U. Berne, 1969-71; asst. prof. cell biology Albert Einstein Coll. Medicine, Bronx, 1973-80, asst. prof. pediatrics, 1973-77, assoc. prof., 1977-82, assoc. prof. microbiology and immunology, 1981-85, prof. pediatrics, 1982—, prof. microbiology and immunology, 1985—. Dir. divsn. clin. allergy and immunology Albert Einstein Coll. Medicine, dir. tng. program for allergy and immunology; dir. divsn. clin. allergy and immunology Albert Einstein Coll. Medicine, Montefiore Med. Ctr.; attending pediatrician Bronx Mcpl. Med. Ctr., Hosp. Albert Einstein Coll. Medicine; mem. study sect. on AIDS rsch. NIH; dir Focis affiliated Clin. Immunology Ctr. Albert Einstein Coll. Medicine Montegiare Med. Ctr. Mem. editl. bd. Annals of Allergy; reviewer New England Jour. Medicine, Jour. for Clin. Investigation, Jour. Pediatrics, Jour. Clin. Allergy and Immunology; contbr. over 175 articles to profl. publs. Lt. armed svcs., Israel, 1955-57. Recipient Lifetime award in Immunology, Humanitarian award DIFFA, Birch Svcs. for Children, Annual award U.S. Asst. Sec. of Health for excellence in AIDS rsch. and treatment, 1990, Bela Shick award for Pediatric Rsch., 1993, Ackerman award for Sci. and Humanity, 1995, Heroes in Medicine Internat. award, 2000; AIDS Rsch. Program grantee NIH, Bronx. Fellow Am. Acad. Allergy and Immunology, Am. Coll. Allergy & Immunology; mem. N.Y. Acad. Scis., Soc. Pediatric Rsch., The Harvey Soc., Am. Coll. Allergy, Clin. Immunology Soc., Clin. Immunology Soc. Office: Albert Einstein Coll Medicine 1625 Blondell Ave Bronx NY 10461-1926

RUBINSTEIN, JOSEPH HARRIS, education educator; b. N.Y.C., Oct. 5, 1936; s. Morris M. and Anne (Roslofsky) R.; m. Heike Buechler, Aug. 12, 1968; children: Mark Philip, Sara Erika. AB, N.Y.U., 1960, MS, 1964, PhD, 1969. Assoc. rsch. scientist N.Y.U., 1969-71, asst. prof., biology, 1971-72; dir. maths. and sci. curriculum Open Court Publ. Co., La Salle, Ill., 1972-79, cons., 1979-84; prof. Coker Coll., Hartsville, S.C., 1984—, chmn. dept. edn., 1984-99. Author: Realmath, 1975, 2d edit. 1989, 3d edit. 1991, Math Explorations and Applications, 1998, 2d edit., 2003, Real Science, 1999. With U.S. Army, 1955-58. Mem. Nat. Coun. Tchrs. Math., Nat. Sci. Tchrs. Assn., N.Y. Acad. Scis., S.C. Assn. Coll. Tchr. Edn., Sigma Xi. Jewish. Home: 414 Laurel Oak St Hartsville SC 29550-3712 Office: Coll Ave Coker College Hartsville SC 29550-3797 E-mail: jrubinstein@coker.edu.

RUBINSTEIN, ROBIN LEVINE, secondary school educator; b. N.Y.C., June 16, 1956; d. Alvin Benjamin and Eileen (Levy) Levine. BA, Am. U., 1976; MA, Kean Coll. of N.J., 1981. Cert. secondary math. tchr., Nev. Math. tchr. Bergen County (N.J.) Schs., 1977-82, L.A., 1982-90, Clark County (Nev.) Sch, 1990—, Green Valley High Sch., Henderson, Nev., 1991—. Insvc. edn. instr. Clark County Sch. Dist., Las Vegas, 1991—, Shoreline (Wash.) Sch. Dist., 1996—; mem. NSF Transit Team Ohio State U.; math. cons. McDougal, Littel Pub. Co., Evanston, Ill., 1993—; nat. instr. Tex. Instruments Graphing Calculator. Recipient State Presdl. award for Excellence in Math. Teaching NSF, 1991, 92, 93, Nat. Presdl. Excellence in Math. award, 1993, Tandy Tech. scholar, 1996-97. Mem. So. Nev. Math. Coun. (mem. exec. bd., rec. sec. 1992—, co-chair conf. 1991-92), Nat. Coun. Tchrs. Math (mem. exec. bd., rec. sec. 1992-93, co-chair conf. 1991-92, membership chair 1993-94). Avocations: travel, skiing, knitting. Office: Shorewood HS 17300 Fremont Ave N Shoreline WA 98133-5249

RUBLE, RONALD MERLIN, humanities and theater communications educator; b. Shelby, Ohio, July 4, 1940; s. Eldred Roy and Dessie Cedelia (Shaw) Briner; m. Nancy Kay Dillon, Aug. 29, 1970 (div. Apr. 1976); children: Eric Douglas, Kristofer Philip. BA, Otterbein Coll., 1962; MA, Bowling Green State U., 1966, PhD, 1975. Site coord. Arts Unltd. Firelands Coll. of Bowling Green U., Huron, Ohio, 1989-92, instr. speech and theater, 1970-75, program dir. speech and theater, 1970—98, asst. prof. speech and theater, 1976-79, chmn. dept. humanities, 1976-80, assoc. prof. humanities and theater, 1979-98, tchg. artist Arts Unltd., 1987-89, assoc. prof. emeritus humanities, 1998—; bus. mgr., play dir. Huron Playhouse Bowling Green U., 1966-78, 2002—03; artistic dir. Caryl Crane Children's Theatre, Huron, 1990—. Co-chmn. Arts in the Parks Festival, North Ctrl. Ohio Arts Coun., Sandusky, 1976-78, v.p. bd. dirs., 1977-78; theater cons. Caryl Crane Children's Theatre, Sandusky, 1984-90. Dir. play The Gingerbread lady, 1978 (1st place N.W. region Ohio Cmty. Theatre Assn. 1978); contbr. poems, short story to profl. publs; playwright. Unit commr. Erie dist. of Firelands coun. Boy Scouts Am., Huron, 1984-87, mem. troop rev. bd., 1985-96, merit badge counselor Firelands dist. Heart of Ohio coun., Vermilion, Ohio, 1984—; elder 1st Presbyn. Ch., Huron, 1988-90, 95-97. Recipient Outstanding Educator in Arts award Ohio Ho. of Reps., 1975, Outstanding Young Man of Am. award Nat. Jaycees, 1977, Outstanding Cmty. Svc. award Huron C. of C., 1983, 84, 85, Outstanding Leader award Firelands Area Coun. Boy Scouts Am., 1988, Scouter's Key award, 1987, Scouter of the Yr. award Troop 31, 1985, Marcellus F. Cowdery Educator of Yr. award Erie County C. of C., 1998. Mem. Am. Alliance Theatre Edn., Drama League, Ohio Theatre Alliance, Am. Film Inst., Ohio Humanities Coun., Internat. Soc. of Poets (disting.), Nat. Authors Registry, Poets Guild, Acad. of Am. Poets. Avocations: creative writing, concerts, plays, yardwork. Home: 729 Taylor Ave Huron OH 44839-2522 Office: Bowling Green State U Firelands Coll 1 University Dr Huron OH 44839-9719

RUBY, RALPH, JR., vocational business educator; b. Newburgh, N.Y., Apr. 11, 1944; m. Dorothy Nelle Privette; children: Laconya Dannet, Ralph III, Vanessa Rae. AAS, Orange County C.C., 1968; BS, U. Tenn., Knoxville, 1969, MS in Bus. Edn., 1972; EdD, U. Mo., Columbia, 1975. Cert. tchr., adminstr., N.Y. Tchr. keyboarding, bus. law Valley Ctrl. High Sch., Montgomery, N.Y., 1969-76, chair bus. dept., 1974-75; asst. prof. vocat. bus. edn. U. Ark., Fayetteville, 1976-79; from asst. prof. to prof. bus. edn., coord. vocat. bus. edn. Ark. State U., State University, 1979—. Mem. ednl. adv. com. 26th Congl. Dist., N.Y.; vis. prof. McGill U., Montreal, Que., Can., 1977; acctg. author Gregg divsn. McGraw-Hill Book Co., 1978—; presenter workshops, tngs. programs. Author: Rough Draft Typing Practice, 1980, Target Type!: Improving Speed and Accuracy, 1987, Word Processing and Editing Techniques, 1988, Real Life Keyboarding Applications: (Word Processor, Data Base, Spreadsheet), 1990, Top Row Target Type, 1991, Starship Speller, 1991, Number Pad Tutor, 1991, Lotus in Your Classroom, 1991, WordPerfect in Your Classroom, 1992, Microsoft Works in Your Classroom, 1993, The Big Board Stock Market (simulation), 1993, PageMaker in Your Classroom, 1993, MS-DOS Made Easy, 1993, WordPerfect for Desktop Publications, 1993, Microsoft Windows in Your Classroom, 1994, Mystery at Laser Age Hardware, 1994, The Class Works, 1994, WordPerfect in Your Classroom Using the MacIntosh, 1994, PageMaker in Your Classroom for Windows, 1996, WordPerfect for Desktop Publishing, 1996, Quattro Pro in Your Classroom, 1996, Espionage at International Electronics, 1996, Microsoft Works for Windows in Your Classroom, 1996, Ami Pro For Windows in Your Classroom, 1996, System 7 in Your Classroom, 1997, Excel in Your Classroom, 1997, Microsoft Word 97, 1998, Microsoft Word 97 Economy Pack, 1998; editor Jour. Edn. for Bus., 1980—, also others; contbr. articles to profl. jours. Mem. Am. Vocat. Assn. (life), Nat. Bus. Edn. Assn., So. Bus. Edn. Assn., Nat. Assn. Tchr. Edn. for Bus. and Office Edn. (life), Delta Pi Epsilon, Kappa Delta Pi, Phi Delta Kappa (life). Office: Ark State U Coll Bus State University AR 72467

RUCH, CHARLES P. academic administrator; b. Longbranch, N.J., Mar. 25, 1938; s. Claud C. and Marcella (Pierce) R.; m. Sally Joan Brandenburg, June 18, 1960; children: Cheryl, Charles, Christopher, Cathleen. BA, Coll. of Wooster, 1959; MA, Northwestern U., 1960, PhD, 1966. Counselor, tchr. Evanston (Ill.) Twp. High Sch., 1960-66; asst. prof. U. Pitts., 1966-70, assoc. prof., dept. chmn., 1970-74; assoc. dean sch. edn. Va. Commonwealth U., Richmond, 1974-76, dean sch. edn., 1976-85, interim provost, v.p., 1985-86, provost, v.p., 1986-93; pres. Boise (Idaho) State U., 1993—. Cons. various univs., govtl. agys., ednl. founds. Author or co-author over 50 articles, revs., tech. reports. Mem. Am. Psychol. Assn., Am. Ednl. Research Assn., Phi Delta Kappa. Office: Boise State U 1910 University Dr Boise ID 83725-0399 E-mail: cruch@boisestate.edu.

RUCH, MARCELLA JOYCE, retired elementary school educator, biographer; b. Brutus, Mich., Sept. 20, 1937; d. Virgil Murray and Grace Milbry (Collier) Wallace; m. Robert Kirkman McMain, Aug. 29, 1956 (div. Aug. 1970); children: Melodie McMain, Kirk McMain, Nancy Hedges, Elizabeth Curran; m. Peter Jerome Ruch, Dec. 22, 1973; children: David, Dan, Michael and Justin Moore Ruch. BS, Western Mich. U., 1964; MA, U. Colo., Colorado Springs, 1973; PhD, U. Colo., Boulder, 1980. Cert. tchr., prin., counselor, Colo. Tchr. Colorado Springs Pub. Schs., 1964-69; supr. child care El Paso County Social Svcs., Colorado Springs, 1970-73; exec. dir. Antlers Day Care Ctr., Colorado Springs, 1973-77, Green Shade Schs., Colorado Springs, 1977-81, Pueblo (Colo.) Toddler Ctr., 1981-83; tchr. Penrose (Colo.) Elem. Sch., 1983-86; adminstrv. intern Cottonwood Elem. Sch., Denver, 1986-87; elem. prin. Simla (Colo.) Pub. Schs., 1987-89; tchr. Colorado Springs Pub. Schs., 1989-97. Adv. bd. for early childhood edn. Pikes Peak C.C., Colorado Springs, 1970-75; child care specialist Cmty. Agencies Working Together, Colorado Springs, 1970-75; humanitarian and med. aid mission trips to Russia with United Meth. Ch. Author: The Gang of One, 1998, Pablita Velarde: Painting Her People, 2001, Just Doing My Job, 2002. Founder Green Shade Schs., 1977; campaign chair United Way, Canon City, Colo., 1983—84, pres., 1984—85; chair adult edn. St. Paul's United Meth. Ch., 1994—96, participant mission trips to Russia, 1997, 1999; lay evangelist. Mem. Delta Kappa Gamma (v.p. membership 1994-96), Phi Delta Kappa. Methodist. Avocations: gardening, hiking, reading, camping. Home and Office: 1111 Modes St Colorado Springs CO 80904-3242

RUCKER, KENNETH LAMAR, law enforcement officer, educator, military officer; b. Atlanta, July 16, 1961; s. Jack Lamar and Priscilla Anne (Anderson) R.; m. Kerri Lynn Hairston; children: Kenneth Lamar II, Kerbi Lynn. BSBA, Brenau U., 1991; MPA in Pub. Mgmt., Ga. State U., 1993; postgrad., U. Ga., 1993—. Cert. peace officer, supr., Ga., field tng. officer, law enforcement exec.; cert. supply corps, Navy Supply Corps Sch., 1997. Law enforcement officer Met. Atlanta Rapid Transit Authority, 1984-93; sch. resource officer Fulton County Bd. Edn., Atlanta, 1993-95; field facilitator Cmtys. in Schs. of Ga., Inc., Atlanta, 1995-97, field facilitator Cross Roads program, 1995-97; chief of police Fulton County Schs. Police Dept., 1997—. Bd. dirs. Benefactors of Edn., Inc., Atlanta; cons. pub. security Fulton County Bd. Edn., Atlanta, 1993-95; supply corps officer Navy Supply Corps Sch. USNR, Athens, 1997; bd. advisors Fulton County Pub. Safety Tng. Ctr., 2000—; tng. cons. Internat. Assn. of Chiefs of Police, 2000—. Sunday sch. tchr., deacon Simpson St. Ch. of Christ, Atlanta, 1991—; youth motivator Atlanta Pub. Schs., 1988—. Commd. officer Supply Corps, USNR, 1995—. Doctoral fellow U. Ga. Mem. Am. Soc. Pub. Adminstrn., Internat. Assn. Chiefs of Police, Nat. Orgn. Black Law Enforcement Execs., Nat. Forum Black Pub. Adminstrs., Ga. Assn. Chiefs of Police, Benefactors of Edn., Inc. (bd. dirs. 1996-99), Brenau U. Alumni Club (bd. dirs. 1999—), Ga. State U. Alumni Club, U.S. Naval Inst., Naval Res. Assn., Res. Officer's Assn., Navy Supply Corps Assn., Fulton County Pub. Safety Tng. Ctr. (Bd. of advisors 1999—, v. chmn., 2003—); Pi Alpha Alpha, Pi Sigma Alpha, Omicron Delta Kappa (cir. pres. 1992-93). Avocations: computer tech., reading, photography, classical music, fitness. Home: 1835 Jenny Ln Lithia Springs GA 30122-2857 Office: Fulton County Schs Police Fulton County Bd Education 786 Cleveland Ave SW Atlanta GA 30315-7239 E-mail: rucker@fulton k12.ga.us.

RUCKER-HUGHES, WAUDIEUR ELIZABETH, educator; b. Washington, July 30, 1947; d. Jeter and Jeannette Belle (Toomer) Rucker; B.S., D.C. Tchrs. Coll., 1969; M.A. in Edn. Admin., U. Redlands, 1974; 1 child, Teliece E.M. Tchr. history J.W. North High Sch.. Riverside, Calif., 1969-76, dean students, 1976-79; lectr. Afro-Am. history Riverside City Coll., 1972-74; exec. dir. Inland Area Opportunities Industrialization Center, Riverside, 1979-90; tchr., coord. steps of success program RUSD, 1990-92; asst. prin. J.W. North High Sch., 1992—; cons. in field. Commr. Community relations City of Riverside, 1972-76; sec. State Inter-Group Relations Educators, 1976-77; pres. Coalition of Urban Peoples, 1978-80; lay mem. Riverside County Jud. Selection Com., 1978-84; Calif. State Bar ct. referee, 1979-84. NSF fellow, 1970-71; Center for Leadership Edn. grantee, 1978. Mem. NAACP, Urban League, Riverside Women's Polit. Caucus, Nat. Women's Polit. Caucus, Exec. Dirs. Assn. (sec. 1983-84, nat. historian), Officers In Charge Am. (community devel. adv. com.), Nat. Council Negro Women, Delta Kappa Gamma, Hunter Pk. C. of C. (treas., pres.), Delta Kappa Gamma. Mem. C.M.E. Ch. Club: The Thurs. Group, Phi Delta Kappa. Author: Canine Capers, 1976; A Book to Match our Diversity, 1980. Office: 1550 3rd St Riverside CA 92507-3404

RUCKERT, RITA E. retired elementary education educator; b. Monett, Mo., Feb. 15, 1947; d. Wesley Swearengin and Eva Anna Harriet (Spradling) R. BS in Edn., U. Mo., 1969. Cert. tchr., Mo. Jr. high sch. tchr. Milw. (Wis.) Pub. Schs., 1969-70; high sch. tchr. Houston (Mo.) Schs., 1970-79, elem. tchr., 1979-95; ret., 1997. Volleyball ofcl. Mo. State High Sch. Activities Assn., Columbia, 1980-93, volleyball rules interpreter, 1983-93. Election judge Tex. County Clk.'s Office, Houston, 1987-95; mem. Houston (Mo.) Pk. Bd., 1988-92, pres., 1991-92. Recipient Fitness Ctr. grant Wells Fargo Bank, Calif., 1990; named Volleyball Outstanding Ofcl., Nat. Fedn. Interscholastic Ofcls. Assn., 1991. Mem. NEA (v.p. 1994-95, pres.-elect 1995-96, pres. 1996-97), AAHPERD, Mo. Assn. Health, Phys. Edn., Recreation and Dance (Dist. Elem. Phys. Educator of Yr. 1990, quality phys. edn. com. 1991-93), Optimist Internat., Delta Kappa Gamma. Republican. Methodist. Avocations: stained glass, cross-stitch, reading, gardening. Home: 505 Hawthorn St Houston MO 65483-1721 Office: Houston Elem Sch 423 W Pine St Houston MO 65483-1147

RUDAN, VINCENT THADDEUS, nursing educator, administrator; b. N.Y.C., June 19, 1955; s. Vincent and Elvira (Palma) R. BSN, SUNY, Stony Brook, 1977; MA, NYU, 1979; postgrad., Villanova U., 1984-85; EdD, Columbia U., 1998. RN, N.Y., N.J.; CNAA. Instr. Rutgers U., Newark, 1980-83; asst. DON, Manhattan Eye, Ear and Throat Hosp., N.Y.C., 1983-84, assoc. DON, 1984-94, DON/patient care svcs., 1994-97; asst. prof. nursing Lehman Coll., CUNY, N.Y.C., 1998—2002; adj. asst. prof. Tchrs. Coll., Columbia U., N.Y.C., 1999—. Mem. ANA, Ea. Nursing Rsch. Soc., Am. Orgn. Nurse Execs., Sigma Theta Tau, Kappa Delta Pi. Avocations: tennis, jogging, reading, travel. E-mail: prof157@aol.com.

RUDCZYNSKI, ANDREW B. academic administrator, medical researcher; b. Nottingham, England, Sept. 7, 1947; came to U.S., 1951; s. Richard B. and Krystyna Z. R.; m. Andrea Skalny, Oct. 16, 1976 (div. Oct. 1990); children: Christina, Thomas. BSc in Biology/Biochemistry, McGill U., 1969; PhD in Immunology, Syracuse U., 1974; MBA in Adminstrn., So. Ill. U., 1984. Prin. investigator scrub typhus project divsn. Rickettsiology U.S. Army Med. Rsch. Infectious Diseases, Ft. Detrick, Md., 1974-76; rsch. assoc. dept. biology Mich. Cancer Found., Detroit, 1976-77, rsch. scientist dept. immunology, unit chef immunology unit Breast Cancer Prognostic Study, 1977-80; asst. dir. Office Rsch. and Grants U. Md. Ea. Shore, Princess Anne, 1980-83; extramural assoc. Office Extramural Rsch. and Tng., Office of Dir. NIH, 1981-82; asst. dir. Office Rsch. & Sponsored Programs Rutgers U., Piscataway, N.J., 1983-84, dir., 1984-99, asst. v.p. rsch. adminstrn., 1985-93, assoc. v.p. rsch. policy and adminstrn., 1993-99; assoc. v.p. fin., exec. dir. rsch. svcs. U. Pa., Phila., 1999—. Field reader strengthening devel. instns. program U.S. Dept. Edn., 1990; mem. Chancellor's task force instrn. and rsch. infrastructure support N.J. Dept. Higher Edn., 1992. Contbr. articles, abstracts to profl. jours. Capt. U.S. Army Med. Svc. Corps, 1974-76. Recipient traineeship award NSF, 1969-71; predoctoral fellow NIH, 1973-74. Mem. AAAS, Nat. Coun. Univ. Rsch. Adminstrs. (profl. devel. com. 1988-90, region II program com. 1989-90, chmn. region II 1990-92, nat. program com. 1994-95), Coun. Govtl. Rels. (fed. mgmt. devel. com. 1989-90, bd. dirs. 1998-2003, tech. transfer and ethics com. 1998-99, chair rsch. compliance and adminstrn. com. 1999-2003), Beta Gamma Sigma, Sigma Xi. Roman Catholic. Home: 2033 Rodman St Philadelphia PA 19146-1359 Office: Univ Pa Office Rsch Svcs 3451 Walnut St Ste P-221 Philadelphia PA 19104-6205

RUDD, DARCIE KAY, elementary education educator; b. Wichita, Kans., Sept. 27, 1956; d. William Dean and Donna Lee (Pinon) Wise; children: Courtney Lynn, Grant David. BA in Elementary Edn., Wichita (Kans.) State U., 1978, MA in Elementary Edn., 1984. Tchr. Unified Sch. Dist. 259, Wichita. Dist. in-svc. leader for writing process in elem. schs. Recipient 2d place Kansas Film Festival, 1986, recognition for Learn Not to Burn project, Wichita Fire Dept. Home: 6350 Danbury St Wichita KS 67220-3821

RUDDEN, JANE FRANCES, education educator; b. St. Louis, Apr. 22, 1945; d. Francis Edward and Julia Margaret (Chartrand) R. BA, Fontbonne Coll., 1968; MA, W.Va. U., 1992, EdD, 1994. Cert. reading specialist, K-12 multi-subject tchr., 7th-8th grade remedial reading tchr. 5th-8th grade lang. arts tchr. Our Lady of the Ams., Kansas City, Mo., 1968-71; 7th-8th grade lang. arts tchr. St. Anthony's Jr.-Sr. H.S., Wailuku Maui, Hawaii, 1971-75; 7th-8th lang. arts tchr. St. Margaret of Scotland, St. Louis, 1977-78; unit supr., 3d-4th grade tchr. St. Joseph's Child Care Ctr., Chgo., 1975-77; dir. meetings and convs. Smith, Bucklin and Assocs., Washington, 1978-80; mgr. data processing tng. Riggs Nat. Bank, Washington, 1980-82; edn. cons., mktg. rep. Deltak, Inc., Fairfax, Va., 1982-89; 8th grade lang arts tchr. Berkeley Springs (W.Va.) Jr.-Sr. H.S., 1990-92; asst. prof. elem. edn. Millersville (Pa.) U., 1995—; adj. prof. reading W.Va. U., Morgantown, 1995. Guest lectr., cons. W.Va. Writing Project, Morgantown, 1993-94; mem. pedagogy team W.Va. U., 1993-94; liaison to pub. sch. Benudum Project, Morgantown, 1994; grad. asst. W.Va. U., 1992-94; presenter in field. Accreditation coord. Nat. Coun. Accreditation Tchr. Edn., 1999—, Millersville U., 1999—. Recipient Golden Apple Achiever award Ashland Oil Corp., 1991; W.Va. U. Fellow, 1992-94, Millersville U. Sch. Edn. fellow, 1999—; W.Va. U. grantee, 1993-94. Mem. Coll. Reading Assn. (session chair 1994), Pa. Reading Tchr. Edn., Coll. Reading Improvement (treas., mem. chair), Internat. Reading Assn., Lancaster Lebanon Reading Coun. (co-chair), Keystone State Reading Assn., Phi Delta Kappa, Phi Delta Phi. Avocations: writing children's books, reading, stitchery, gardening. E-mail: jane.rudden@millersville.edu.

RUDDER, ROBERT SWEEN, Spanish language educator; b. Long Beach, Calif., Aug. 9, 1937; s. George Walter and Nora Geneva (Sween) R.; m. Karen Elizabeth Foshee; children: Lisa Carty, Christopher Michael. BA, U. Redlands, 1959; MA, PhD, U. Minn., 1968; postgrad., U. So. Calif., 1977-78. Instr. U. Minn., Mpls., 1963-68; asst. prof. UCLA, 1968-76; computer lab. coord. L.A. Unified Sch. Dist., 1977-2000. Lectr. Calif. State U., Pomona, 1976-79, L.A., 1991—; cons. NEH, Washington, 1977; adv. bd. Explicacion de Textos, Sacramento, 1973-76. Author: Literature of Spain in English, 1975; editor, translator: Magic Realism in Cervantes, 1970, Lazarillo of Tormes, 1973, The Orgy, 1974, City of Kings, 1993, Nazarin, 1997, Medicine Man, 2000, Solitaire of Love, 2000. With USN, 1960-62. Recipient Writing award NEA, 1993, Writing award Ministerio de Cultura of Spain, 1997. Mem. Nat. Coun. Tchrs. Math. Avocations: tennis, sailing. Home: 1556 Lafayette Rd Claremont CA 91711-3413 E-mail: rsrudder@aol.com.

RUDE, PHYLLIS AILEEN, retired secondary school educator; b. Jacksonville, Ill., Oct. 2, 1943; d. Chester Raymond and Thelma Grace (Pahlmann) Stewart; m. Gary Rude, Sept. 11, 1966; children: Richard Gary, Meredith Arlene. BA, Ill. State U., 1964; AM, U. Chgo., 1967. Cert. tchr. Alaska. Tchr. Farmington (Ill.) H.S., 1963-65, Wheeling (Ill.) H.S., 1965-67, Mears Jr. H.S., Anchorage, 1967-74, lang. arts dept. chair, 1984—2003, ret., 2003. Recipient scholarship Carnegie Found., 1966. Mem. Nat. Coun. Tchrs. English, Alaska Coun. Tchrs. English (Honor award 1987), Anchorage Coun. Tchrs. English. Lutheran. Home: 2567 Arlington Dr Anchorage AK 99517-1304 Office: Mears Jr HS 2700 W 100th Ave Anchorage AK 99515-2214

RUDENSTINE, NEIL LEON, former academic administrator, educator; b. Ossining, NY, Jan. 21, 1935; s. Harry and Mae (Esperito) R.; m. Angelica Zander, Aug. 27, 1960; children: Antonia Margaret, Nicholas David, Sonya. BA, Princeton U., 1956; BA (Rhodes Scholar), Oxford U., 1959, MA, 1963; PhD, Harvard U., 1964. Instr. dept. English Harvard U., Cambridge, Mass., 1964-66, asst. prof., 1966-68; assoc. prof. English Princeton (N.J.) U., 1968-73, prof. English, 1973-88, dean of students, 1968-72, dean of Coll., 1972-77, provost, 1977-88, provost emeritus, 1988—; exec. v.p. Andrew W. Mellon Found., N.Y.C., 1988-91; pres. Harvard U., Cambridge, Mass., 1991-2001, prof. English, 1991-2001, pres. emeritus, 2001—. Chair bd. ArtStor, A.W. Mellon Found., 2001—. Author: Sidney's Poetic Development, 1967, Pointing Our Thoughts, 2001; (with George Rousseau) English Poetic Satire, 1972; (with William Bowen) In Pursuit of the PhD, 1992. Trustee Princeton U., N.Y. Pub. Libr., Courtauld Inst. Art, London, Goldman Sachs Found. 1st lt. arty. U.S. Army, 1959—60. Hon. fellow New Coll./Oxford U., Emmanuel Coll./Cambridge U., 1991. Fellow Am. Acad. Arts and Scis.; mem. Am. Philos. Soc., Coun. on Fgn. Rels., Com. for Econ. Devel. Office: AW Mellon Found 140 E 62d St New York NY 10021

RUDER, DAVID STURTEVANT, lawyer, educator, government official; b. Wausau, Wis., May 25, 1929; s. George Louis and Josephine (Sturtevant) R.; m. Susan M. Small; children: Victoria Chesley, Julia Larson, David Sturtevant II, John Coulter; m stepchildren: Elizabeth Frankel, Rebecca Wilkinson. BA cum laude, Williams Coll., 1951; JD with honors, U. Wis., 1957, LLD, 2002. Bar: Wis. 1957, Ill. 1962. Of counsel Schiff Hardin & Waite, Chgo., 1971-76; assoc. Quarles & Brady, Milw., 1957-61; asst. prof. law Northwestern U., Chgo., 1961-63, assoc. prof., 1963-65, prof., 1965—, William W. Gurley meml. prof. of law, 1994—, assoc. dean Law Sch., 1965-66, dean Law Sch., 1977-85; chmn. Securities and Exch. Commn., Washington, 1987-89; ptnr. Baker & McKenzie, Chgo., 1990-94, sr. counsel, 1994-99. Cons. Am. Law Inst. Fed. Securities Code; planning dir. Corp. Counsel Inst., 1962-66, 76-77, com. mem., 1962-87, 90—; adv. bd. Ray Garrett Jr. Corp. and Securities Law Inst., 1980-87, 90—; vis. lectr. U. de Liege, 1967; vis. prof. law U. Pa., Phila., 1971; faculty Salzburg Seminar, 1976; mem. legal adv. com. bd. dirs. N.Y. Stock Exch., 1978-82; mem. com. profl. responsibility Ill. Supreme Ct., 1978-87; adv. bd. Securities Regulation Inst., 1978—, chmn., 1994-97; bd. govs. Nat. Assn. Securities Dealers, 1990-93, chmn. Legal Adv. Bd., 1993-96, Arbitration Policy Task Force, 1994-97; trustee Fin. Acctg. Found., 1996-2002, Internat. Acctg. Stds. Com. Found., 2000—; mem. Internat. Acctg. Stds. Com. Strategy Working Party, 1997-99; chmn. Securities and Exch. Commn. Hist. Soc., 1999—; chmn. Mut. Fund Dirs. Forum, 1999—. Editor-in-chief: Williams Coll. Record, 1950-51, U. Wis. Law Rev, 1957; editor: Proc. Corp. Counsel Inst, 1962-66; contbr. articles to legal periodicals. 1st lt. AUS, 1951-54. Fellow Am. Bar Found.; ABA (sec. bus. law 1970—, coun. 1970-94, com. chmn., mem. various coms.), Chgo. Bar Assn., Wis. Bar Assn., Am. Law Inst., Order of Coif, Comml. Club of Chgo., Lawyers Club Chgo., Gargoyle Soc., Phi Beta Kappa, Phi Delta Pi, Zeta Psi. Home: 325 Orchard Ln Highland Park IL 60035-1939 E-mail: d-ruder@law.northwestern.edu.

RUDIBAUGH, MELINDA CAMPBELL, mathematics educator; b. Indiana, Pa., Feb. 25, 1948; d. Steele Evans and Kathryn Norine (Grater) C.; m. Jerry Rudibaugh, Dec. 5, 1970; children: Amy, Evan. BS in Edn., Indiana (Pa.) U., 1970; M Natural Sci., Arizona State U., 1981, postgrad., No. Arizona U., Ariz. State U. Tchr. sci., math. Western Christian High, Phoenix, Ariz., 1979-80, Phoenix Hebrew Sch., 1980-81; instr. math. Arizona State U., Tempe, 1980-84, Maricopa C.C., Phoenix, 1981-89, Chandler-Gilbert C.C., Chandler, Ariz., 1989—, chair sci. & math. divsn., advisor Christians in Action, 1998—. Instr. Ottawa U. Vol. March of Dimes, 1988—, Am. Cancer Soc., 1989—; advisor Phi Theta Kappa, Chandler-Gilbert C.C., 1993. 2d lt. USAF, 1970-71. Mem. ASCD, Nat. Coun. Tchrs. Math., Math. Assn. Am., Am. Math. Assn. Two-Yr. Colls., Am. Assn. Higher Edn., Ariz. Assn. Supervision and Curriculum Devel., Phi Delta Kappa, Phi Kappa Phi. Republican. Avocations: jogging, hiking, swimming. Office: Chandler Gilbert C C 2626 E Pecos Rd Chandler AZ 85225-2413 Home: 480 E Canyon Creek Ct Gilbert AZ 85296-5967

RUDIG, STEPHANIE SCOTT, gifted and talented education educator; b. Sacramento, Feb. 22, 1951; d. Norman Marks and Eleanor (Holmes) R.; m. Charles Henry Rudig, Apr. 15, 1972; children: Matthew Scott, Nathan Oehme. BA in Psychology, Calif. State U., Sacramento, 1975, MA in Math. Edn., 1983. Substitute tchr. San Juan Unified Sch. Dist., Sacramento, 1975-76, elem. tchr., 1976-77, 82-85, tchr., Chpt. I math. specialist, 1978-82; rxhe. K-6 gifted and talented edn. Fairbanks (Alaska) North Star Borough Sch. Dist., 1985—, judge, dist. sci. fair, 1991—. Follow-up presenter, instr. Ctr. for Innovation in Edn., Campbell, Calif., 1991-94, presenter Fairbanks NorthStar Borough Sch. Dist., 1986—; mem. adv. bd. Alaska Sci. Consortium, Fairbanks, 1991, 95-96; coord., tchr. trainer Alaska EQUALS/Family Math., Fairbanks, 1993—. Author: Math and Money Management, 1995; contbr. articles to profl. jours. Recipient Presdl. award for excellence in tchg. math. NSTA, 1990, Phoebe Apperson Hearst Tchr. award, 1995; fellow Calif. Math. Project, 1984—; sch. improvement in astronomy grantee Alaska Dept. Edn., 1994; named Tchr. of Excellence, British Petroleum, 2001. Mem. NEA, Fairbanks Edn. Assn. (rep. bargaining support com. Fairbanks 1987, 89, 91). Democrat. Presbyterian. Avocations: quilting, drawing, painting, textile arts, dance. Office: Fairbanks North Star Borough Sch Dist 520 5th Ave Fairbanks AK 99701-4718

RUDIGER, LANCE WADE, secondary school educator; b. Bklyn., Mar. 27, 1948; s. H.F. and Muriel Marie (Staudermann) R.; 1 child, Heidi. BS in Chemistry, SUNY, Albany, 1976; MEd, St. Lawrence U., 1982. Cert. tchr., N.Y. Tchr. chemistry Potsdam H.S., 1982—, chmn. dept. sci., 1992—. Adj. prof. Canton (N.Y.) Coll. Tech., Mater Dei Coll., Ogdensburg, N.Y., Empire Coll., Albany, 1986—; tchr. Inst. Chem. Edn.-Sci. demonstration; bd. dirs., treas. St. Lawrence Valley Tchrs. Learning Ctr., Canton; sci. coord. Upward Bound St. Lawrence U.; program com., bd. dirs. N.Y. Assn. State Computers & Tech. in Edn.; writer for N.Y. State Regents chemistry core curriculum; mem. N.Y. State Part D Performance Regents Test Devel. Com.; mem. SED Regents Benchmark Commn.; item writer NYS Chem. Regents; mem. NYSED-McGraw Hill Chemistry Regents Anchor Com. Co-author: Chemistry Environment, 1990. Bd. dirs. March of Dimes N.Y. State, Syracuse, N.Y. State chemistry regional and state coord. mentor; mem. environ. mgmt. bd. St. Lawrence County, 1997-, edn. com. chair, 1999-, vice chair, 2003-; mem. bd. examiners Nat. Coun. Accreditation Tchr. Edn., 2001—. Recipient Newmast award NASA, 1987, Dreyfus Master Tchr. award, 1989, Fulbright Symposium award Australia, 2002; grantee NSTA-FDA, 2003, Am. Chem Soc., Woodrow Wilson Found., Binghamtom U. Step Program, St. Lawrence Valley Tchrs. Ctr., 1991-98, Sweetwater Found., Miami U. (Ohio), 1995, Johns Hopkins Space Grant Consortium, Wright Ctr. for Aerospace and Space Engring., Reynolds Metals Excellence in Edn., 1990-94, Cornell U. Sci. Workshop, IRIS; named solar sys. amb. Jet Propulsion Lab., NASA. Mem. Nat. Sci. Tchrs. Assn. (local leader, manuscript review adv. panel The Sci. Tchr., sci. safety com. 2000, webwatchers 2001, Exxon BaP key leader and North Country liaison), Nat. Radio Astronomy Obs. (assoc., mentor astronomy workshop), Am. Astron. Soc. (tchr. resource agent 1996-98, Leadership Workshop award 1998), Sci. Tchrs. Assn. N.Y. State (bd. dirs. 1990—, chmn. sect. 1992—, fin. com. 2000—, grant com. chair, presenter at convs. 1988—, hospitality chair ann. conf. NYSC & TE 1996, 98, 2000), North Country Conservation Edn. Assn. (life), USCG Acad. Nat. Parents Assn. (bd. dirs. 1997-98), Canton Club, Lions (past pres. Waddington, N.Y., Pres.'s award, bd. dirs. Canton, pres. 1997-98, treas. 1998-99, dir. 1999-2003), Potsdam Kiwanis (charter, bd. dirs. 1989-91), Phi Delta Kappa (rsch. dir., v.p. program 1999, v.p. membership, pres. 2001—). Home: 54 Court St Canton NY 13617-1159 Office: Potsdam High School Leroy St Potsdam NY 13676-1798

RUDOLPH, ANDREW HENRY, dermatologist, educator; b. Detroit, Jan. 30, 1943; s. John J. and Mary M. Rudolph; children: Kristen Ann, Kevin Andrew. MD cum laude, U. Mich., 1966. Diplomate Am. Bd. Dermatology. Intern Univ. Hosp., U. Mich. Med. Ctr., Ann Arbor, 1966-67, resident dept. dermatology, 1967-70; pvt. practice medicine specializing in dermatology, 1972—. Asst. prof. dermatology Baylor Coll. Medicine, Houston, 1972-75, assoc. prof., 1975-83, clin. prof., 1983—; chief dermatology svc. VA Hosp., Houston, 1977-82; mem. staff Meth. Hosp., Tex. Children's Hosp., St. Luke's Episcopal Hosp. Mem. editl. bd. Jour. Sexually Transmitted Diseases, 1977-85; contbr. to med. publs. Served as surgeon USPHS, 1970-72. Regent's scholar U. Mich., 1966. Fellow Am. Acad. Dermatology; mem. AMA, Am. Dermatol. Assn., So. Med. Assn., Tex. Med. Assn., Harris County Med. Soc., Houston Dermatol. Soc. (past pres.), Tex. Dermatol. Soc., Internat. Soc. Tropical Dermatology, Dermatology Found., Skin Cancre Found., Am. Venereal Disease Assn. (past pres.), Am. Soc. Dermatol. Surgery, Soc. Investigative Dermatology, S. Ctrl. Dermatol. Congress, Mich. Alumni Assn. (life), Alpha Omega Alpha, Phi Kappa Phi, Phi Rho Sigma, Theta Xi. Office: 6560 Fannin St Ste 724 Houston TX 77030-2768

RUDOLPH, FREDERICK BYRON, biochemistry educator; b. St. Joseph, Mo., Oct. 17, 1944; s. John Max and Maxine Leah (Wood) R.; m. Glenda M. Myers, June 18, 1971; children: Anna Dorine, William K. BS in Chemistry, U. Mo., Rolla, 1966; PhD in Biochemistry, Iowa State U., 1971. Prof. biochemistry Rice U., Houston, 1972—, chair biochemistry and cell biology, 1995—2003, dir. Lab. for Biochem. and Genetic Engring., 1986—, exec. dir. Inst. Biosci. and Bioengring., 1993—2003; dir. Inst. Biosci. and Bioengring., Houston, 2003—. Cons. World Book, Chgo., 1972—; mem. biochemistry study sect. NIH, Bethesda, Md., 1983-87; bd. dirs. Coun. Biotech. Ctrs., Tex. Healthcare & Bioscis. Inst. Contbr. over 160 articles to profl. jours. including Jour. Biol. Chemistry, Biochemistry, Transplantation, Exptl. Hematology, Jour. Parenteral and Enteral Nutrition, Jour. Molecular Biology, Applied and Environ. Microbiology, Life Scis., Archives Biochem. Biophysics, Critical Care Medicine, Archives Surgery, Sci.; also chpts. in books. Recipient Disting. Alumnus award Iowa State U., 1980, 99, 2000. Fellow AAAS; mem. Am. Chem. Soc., Am. Soc. for Biochemistry and Molecular Biology, Am. Soc. Nutritional Scis. Achievements include research on dietary requirements for immune function, new enteral feeding formulas and infant formulas, new techniques for protein purification, new methods for kinetic analysis of enzymes, structure and function of various enzymes. Office: Rice U Dept Biochemistry and Cell Biology MS 140 6100 Main St Houston TX 77005-1827

RUDOLPH, ROBERT NORMAN, secondary school educator, adult education educator; b. Ft. Worth, Nov. 2, 1956; s. Robert John and Lenabel (Thurman) R.; m. Cynthia Ann Williams, Oct. 20, 1979; 1 child, Renee Megan Rudolph. BSE, Millersville U., 1978, MEd in Tech. Edn., 1983, supervisory cert., 1992. Cert. profl. tchr., program specialist, Pa. Project engr. Frankel Engring., Reading, Pa., 1978; tech. edn. tchr. Cumberland Valley Sch. Dist., Mechanicsburg, 1978—, chmn. tech. edn. dept., 1993—, adult edn. tchr., 1979—; carpenter R.G. Lunger Industries, Mechanicsburg, Pa., 1979-82; landscape designer Country Market Nursery, Mechanicsburg, 1983-90. Advisor Tech. Student Assn., Mechanicsburg, 1991—, Am. Tech. Honor Soc., 1996—; cons. Calif. (Pa.) U. Dept. Industry and Tech., 1990; evaluator Mid. Atlantic States Accrediting Assn. for Secondary Schs., 1995; cons. Tech. for All Americans Project, 1998; ednl. exhibits mgr. 1998 Nat. Tech Student Assn. Conf. Creator display of calligraphy at Am. Indsl. Arts Assn. conv., 1979. Recipient Certs. of Merit Indsl. Arts Assn. of Pa., 1985, Tech. Edn. Assn. Pa., 1996, Nevin Andre Meml. award for outstanding jour. article Tech. Edn. Assn. Pa., 1996. Mem. NEA, Future Farmers Am. (hon.), Internat. Tech. Edn. Assn., Nat. Air and Space Mus., Soc. Mfg. Engrs., Robotics Internat., Tech. Edn. Assn. of Pa. (supr.'s coun.), Pa. Nurseryman Assn. (accredited nurseryman), Epsilon Pi Tau. Avocations: reading, triathlons. Office: Cumberland Valley High Sch 6746 Carlisle Pike Mechanicsburg PA 17050-1711

RUDOWSKI, MICHAEL HENRY, secondary school educator; b. Jersey City, Aug. 7, 1950; s. Henry Joseph and Violet (KosoBucki) R.; m. Elena Eloise Testa, Aug. 2, 1980; 1 child, David Michael. BA, Rutgers U., 1972; MA, Jersey City State Coll., 1974. Cert. secondary sch. tchr., N.J. Tchr. comm. arts St. Aloysius H.S., Jersey City, 1975-76; tchr. lang. arts Jersey City Bd. Edn., Jersey City, 1977—. Mem. NEA, Jersey City Edn. Assn. (bd. dirs. 1982—). Democrat. Avocations: raquetball, golf, photography, programming, stamp collecting.

RUDY, DAVID ROBERT, physician, educator; b. Columbus, Ohio, Oct. 19, 1934; s. Robert Sale and Lois May (Arthur) R.; m. Rose Mary Sims; children by previous marriage: Douglas D., Steven W., Katharine L. Rudy Hoffer, Hunter A. Elam. BSc, Ohio State U., 1956, MD, 1960; MPH, Med. Coll. Wis., 1995. Diplomate Am. Bd. Family Practice, Am. Bd. Preventive Medicine. Intern Northwestern Meml. Hosp., Chgo., 1960-61; resident in internal medicine Ohio State U. Hosp., 1963-64; resident in pediatrics Children's Hosp., Columbus, Ohio, 1964; pvt. family practice Columbus, 1964-75; dir. residency program Riverside Meth. Hosp., Columbus, 1975-85; dir. family practice residency Monsour Med. Ctr., Jeannette, Pa., 1985-88; dir. residency Bon Secours Hosp., Grosse Pointe, Mich., 1988-91; prof., chmn. Finch U. Health Scis., Chgo. Med. Sch., Dept. Family Preventive Medicine, 1991-95, 97—; prof. Pomerene chair family medicine Ohio State U., 1995-97. Editor, contbr. (textbook) Family Medicine for the House Officer; author: Family Medicine Q & A: NMS Series; contbr. articles to profl. jours. Capt. flight surgeon MC. USAF, 1961—63; col. USAFR (ret.). Recipient USAF Commendation medal. Fellow Am. Acad. Family Physicians; mem. AMA, Ill. State Med. Assn. Republican. Office: Chgo Med Sch Finch U Clinic 3333 Green Bay Rd North Chicago IL 60064-3037

RUDY, LINDA MAE, secondary school educator; b. York, Maine, Mar. 26, 1948; d. Maynard Everett and Frances Irene (Cross) Fuller; m. Jacob William Rudy, Sept. 27, 1980. BS, U. So. Maine, 1971, postgrad., 1978-81, George Washington U., 1983-86. Cert. tchr., Md. Math tchr. Cape Elizabeth (Maine) Middle Sch., 1971-78, Meml. Jr. High Sch., South Portland, Maine, 1978-79, York (Maine) High Sch., 1979-81, LaPlata (Md.) High Sch., 1983—, chmn. Md. student assistance program, 1988-94. Math tchr. Md. Tomorrow Program, LaPlata, 1988, Certificate of Appreciation, 1988. Co-author: (teaching program) Challenging Choices, 1989. Mem. Cobb Island Citizens Assn., 1983—; treas. Cobb Island Bapt. Ch., 1989-94. Recipient Certificate of Recognition, Charles County Bd. Edn., LaPlata, 1988, Certificate of Appreciation, 1990, Certificate of Instructional Leadership, Md. State Dept. of Edn., Annapolis, Md., 1989. Mem. NEA, Nat. Coun. Tchrs. Math., Edn. Assn. Charles County (bldg. rep. 1988-89), Md. State Tchrs. Assn., Md. Coun. Tchrs. Math. Baptist. Avocations: needlework, sailing, aerobics. Home: 12048 Neale Sound Dr Cobb Island MD 20625 E-mail: lrudy@ccboe.com.

RUDY, YORAM, biomedical engineer, biophysicist, educator; b. Tel Aviv, Feb. 12, 1946; arrived in U.S., 1973; s. Nahum and Yaffa (Krinkin) R. BSc, Technion/Israel Inst. Tech., Haifa, 1971, MSc in Physics, 1973; PhD in Biomed. Engring., Case Western Res. U., 1978. Asst. prof. dept. biomed. engring. Case Western Res. U., Cleve., 1981-86, assoc. prof., 1986-89, prof., 1989—, prof. dept. of physiology and biophysics, 1991—, prof. dept. medicine, 1992—. Dir. cardiac bioelectricity rsch. and tng. ctr., vis. prof. Technion/Israel Inst. Tech., 1982-83, U. Parma, Italy, 1986, 87, U. Utah, Salt Lake City, 1990, Tel-Aviv (Israel) U., 1991, Russian Acad. of Scis., St. Petersburg, 1997, U. Berne, Switzerland, 1998; mem. cardiovascular and pulmonary study sect. NIH, 1984-88; Rijlant disting. lectr. Internat. Congress on Electrocardiology, 2000; Ueda Meml. lectr. Japanese Soc. Electrocardiology, 2002. Mem. editl. bd. Jour. Electrocardiology, Jour. Cardiovasc. Electrophysiology, Cardiovasc. Rsch., Cardiac Electrophysiology Rev.; contbr. articles to profl. jours. Grantee NIH, 1985—, Am. Heart Assn., 1990-95, NSF, 1987-94; recipient Gordon K. Moe Prof. award, 1997, NIH-Nat. Heart, Lung and Blood Inst. Merit award, 1998. Fellow IEEE, Am. Physiol. Soc., Am. Inst. Med. and Biol. Engring.; mem. NAE, Am. Heart Assn., Biophys. Soc., Biomed. Engring. Soc. (sr., Disting. Lectr. award 2001). Achievements include development of a novel imaging modality for non-invasive imaging of cardiac electrical events from electrical potentials measured on the body surface (electrocardiographic imaging, ECGI), of theoretical models of cardiac excitation at the cellular, sub-cellular and tissue levels; elucidation of the cellular mechanisms of cardiac arrhythmias and the role of tissue architecture in arrhythmogenesis. Office: Case Western Res U Dept Biomed Engring Cleveland OH 44106-7207

RUEBNER, BORIS HENRY, pathologist, educator; b. Düsseldorf, Germany, Aug. 30, 1923; came to U.S., 1959, naturalized, 1965; s. Fred and Martha (Klein) R.; m. Susan Mautner, Sept. 20, 1957; children: Sally, Anthony. MB, Edinburgh (Scotland) U., 1946, MD, 1956. Diplomate Am. Bd. Anatomic Pathology, Am. Bd. Clin Pathology. Intern Royal Infirmary, Edinburgh, 1946-47; resident Royal Bristol (Eng.) Infirmary, 1947—50, Hammersmith Hosp., London, 1950-56; asst. prof. pathology Dalhousie U., Halifax, N.S., Can., 1957-59; assoc. prof. Johns Hopkins U., Balt., 1959-68; prof. U. Calif., Davis, 1968—94, prof. emeritus, 1994—. Author: Diagnostic Pathology of the Liver, 1982, 2d edit., 1991, The Gastrointestinal System, 1983. Served to capt. M.C., Brit. Army, 1947-49. Recipient Career Devel. award NIH, 1962-68. Fellow Coll. Am. Pathologists; mem. Assn. Am. Pathologists, Internat. Acad. Pathologists. Office: U Calif Sch Medicine Dept Med Pathology Davis CA 95616

RUECKER, MARTHA ENGELS, retired special education educator; b. South Gate, Calif., Sept. 22, 1931; d. Eugene and Minna (Wilhelm) Engels; m. Geert Frank Ruecker, Aug. 10, 1959 (div. 1964); 1 child, Ann. MusB, U. So. Calif., 1954, Calif. tchr. credential, 1955. Cert. tchr. for non-English speaking students, Calif. Tchr. educationally handicapped Downey (Calif.) Unified Schs., 1964-92; tchr. 2d grade Lynwood (Calif.) Unified Schs.,

1992-97, 1997—2001. Recipient award for work with mentally gifted Johns Hopkins U., 1992; South Gate Kiwanis scholar U. So. Calif., 1949-54. Mem. NEA (life), Los Angeles County Art Mus. Republican. Methodist. Avocations: interior design, gardening, music, travel. Home: PO Box 630 Downey CA 90241-0630

RUECKERT, ROLAND RUDYARD, retired virologist, educator; b. Rhinelander, Wis., Nov. 24, 1931; s. George Leonard and Monica Amelia (Seiberlich) R.; m. Ruth Helen Ullrich, Sept. 5, 1959; 1 child, Wanda Lynne. BS in Chemistry, U. Wis., 1953, PhD in Oncology, 1960. Fellow Max Planck Inst. for Biochemistry, Munich, 1960-61, Tübingen, Fed. Republic Germany, 1961-62; asst. rsch. virologist virus lab. U. Calif., Berkeley, 1962-65; asst. prof. biophysics lab. U. Wis., Madison, 1965-69, assoc. prof. biophysics lab., 1969-73; prof. Inst. for Molecular Virology, Madison, 1973-85, dist. rsch. prof., 1985-96, prof. emeritus, 1996-97. Mem. viology study sect. NIH, Bethesda, Md., 1981-85; pres. Am. Soc. Virology, 1989-90. With U.S. Army, 1953-55. Recipient William D. Stovall award, U. Wis., 1953, Marie Christine Kohler award U, Oneida County Tree Farmer of the Yr., 2001. Achievements include research in dodecahedral model for picornavirus structure and assembly, molecular biology of picornaviruses (polio 8 common cold), structure 8 biology of small insect viruses, mechanism of neutralization by antibodies and antivirals. Home: 2234 W Lawn Ave Madison WI 53711-1952 E-mail: rrruecke@facstaff.wisc.edu.

RUEGER, DANIEL SCOTT, horticulture educator; b. Flint, Mich., May 16, 1957; s. William John and Barbara Jane (Ledford) R.; m. Michel Sharon Holzbach, July 22, 1989; children: Danielle Sharon, Christina Anne, Michael Scott. BS in Agr., MS in Agr. Edn., Ohio State U., 1980. Cert. profl. vocational, horticulture teacher, Ohio. Mgr. Idle R's Farms, Plain City, Ohio, 1973-77; research services worker O.M. Scott & Sons Co., Marysville, Ohio, 1977; tng. counselor Cen. Ohio Rural Consortium, Delaware, 1978; supt. parks grounds City of Delaware, 1979; tchr. horticulture Ashland (Ohio) City Schs., 1980—. Co-author: Success Handbook, 1980. Sustaining mem. Rep. Nat. Com., 1980-92; lay leader Emmanuel Meth. Ch., 1988-94; chmn. adminstrv. bd., 1990-91, 2003. Named Citizen of Yr. Citizens Commn. for the Right to Keep and Bear Arms, 1986, 87, 88, Disting. Patriot Concil for Inter-Am. Security. Mem. NEA, Nat. Assn. Agrl. Educators, Inc., Ohio Edn. Assn. (state coun. ednl. polit. action com. 1988-91, profl. devel. com. 1990-98), North Cen. Ohio Edn. Assn. (exec. com. 1986—), Ohio Assn. Agrl. Educators (hort. state chmn. 1988-92, Outstanding Agrl. Edn. Program 1992), Assn. for Career and Tech. Edn., Ohio Assn. for Career and Tech. Edn., Ashland City Tchrs. Assn. (pres. 1988-89), Ohio State U. Alumni Assn., Air Force Assn., Future Farmers Am. Alumni Assn., Orgn. for Secondary Students Enrolled in Agrl. Edn., Ohio Forestry Assn., Bass Angler Sportsmen Assn., Gamma Sigma Delta, Phi Delta Kappa. Avocations: reading, aviation, swimming, fishing, philately. Office: Ashland High Sch 1440 King Rd Ashland OH 44805-3635 E-mail: darueger@ashland-city.k12.oh.us.

RUEGSEGGER, DONALD RAY, JR., radiological physicist, educator; b. Detroit, May 29, 1942; s. Donald Ray and Margaret Arlene (Elliot) R.; m. Judith Ann Merrill, Aug. 20, 1965 (div.); children: Steven, Susan, Mark, Ann; m. Patricia Ann Mitchell, Oct. 16, 1999. BS, Wheaton Coll., 1964; MS, Ariz. State U., 1966, PhD (NDEA fellow), 1969. Diplomate Am. Bd. Radiology. Radiol. physicist Miami Valley Hosp., Dayton, Ohio, 1969—, chief med. physics sect., 1983—. Physics cons. X-ray dept. VA Hosp., Dayton, 1970—; adj. asst. prof. physics Wright State U., Fairborn, Ohio, 1973—, clin. asst. prof. radiology, 1976-81, clin. assoc. prof. radiology, 1981—, group leader in med. physics, dept. radiol. scis. Med. Sch., 1978—. Mem. AAAS, Am. Assn. Physicists in Medicine (pres. Ohio River Valley chpt. 1982-83, co-chmn. local summer sch. arrangements com. 1986), Am. Coll. Radiology, Am. Coll. Med. Physics (founding chancellor), Am. Phys. Soc., Ohio Radiol. Soc., Health Physics Soc. Baptist. Home: 6252 Donnybrook Dr Centerville OH 45459-1837 Office: Radiation Therapy Miami Valley Hosp 1 Wyoming St Dayton OH 45409-2722

RUEHLE, DIANNE MARIE, retired elementary education educator; b. Detroit, Aug. 14, 1943; d. Richard Francis and Luella Mary (Kopp) R. BS, Ea. Mich. U., 1966, MA, 1971, adminstrv. cert., 1990, renewed adminstrv. cert., 1995. Cert. tchr., adminstr., Mich. Tchr. Cherry Hill Sch. Dist., Inkster, Mich., 1966-85; tchr. elem. sch. Wayne-Westland (Mich.) Community Schs., 1985-95; retired. Dist. com. Pub. Act 25 for State of Mich., Westland, 1990-93, chair bldg., 1991-95. Improvement Instrn. grantee Wayne Westland Found., 1992-94. Mem. ASCD, NEA, Mich. Edn. Assn. Avocations: reading, golf, photography, travel. Home: 13385 N Heritage Gateway Ave Marana AZ 85653-4013

RUFENACHT, ROGER ALLEN, accounting educator; b. Waldron, Mich., Dec. 17, 1933; s. Alphus Leroy and Frieda (Aschliman) R.; m. Carol Carnahan, June 13, 1965; children: Jeffrey, Jonathan. BS, Mich. State U., 1959, MS, 1965. Cert. tchr., Fla. Tchr. Madison High Sch., Adrian, Mich., 1959-61; bus. edn. instr. Charlotte High Sch., Rochester, N.Y., 1961-62, Edgewater High Sch., Orlando, Fla., 1962-68, chmn. bus. dept., 1965-68; instr. in acctg. Orlando Vo Tech. Ctr. (formerly Orlando Vocat. Sch.), 1968-94, chmn. bus. dept., 1980-85; ret., 1994. Bd. dirs., v.p. Winter Park Jaycees, 1963-68; asst. coach, scorekeeper N.W. Little League; chmn. adv. com. local PTA, 1973-83; pres. Bandboosters 1985-86; cub scout den leader, com. chmn., mem. dist. com., mem. coms. Boy Scouts Am.; adminstrv. bd. local Meth. Ch., 1965—. Recipient Scouters Tng. award, Fifteen Yr. Vet. award Boy Scouts Am., 1996. Mem. NEA, Am. Vocat. Assn., Fla. Vocat. Assn. (registration com. ann. conf., pres.'s reception planning com.), Orange County Classroom Tchrs. Assn. (bd. dirs., bldg. rep.), Orange County Credit Union (rep.), Orange County Vocat. Assn. (bd. dirs., Pres.'s award 1988-89, Outstanding Vocat. Educator Bus. Edn. award 1988-89), Fla. Bus. Edn. Assn. (chmn., mem. various coms.), Orange County Bus. Edn. Assn. (pres. 1968, 76, chmn., mem. various coms.). Republican. Avocations: reading, gardening, golf, swimming. Home: 9510 Bear Lake Rd Apopka FL 32703-1917

RUFF, DAN GEORGE, academic administrator; b. Columbia, S.C., June 16, 1950; s. Dan George and Marguerite (Johnson) R.; m. Shirley Paul, Nov. 20, 1977; children: Jennifer, Jessica. AB in Polit. Sci., Newberry (S.C.) Coll., 1972; MA in Govt., U. S.C., 1975, MPA, 1980, postgrad., 1990—. Planner cmty. devel. divsn. S.C. Gov.'s Office, Columbia, 1975-76, planner employment/tng. divsn., 1976-83; dir. planning and analysis Midlands Tech. Coll., Columbia, 1983-85; trainee, intern and cons. Am. Campaign Acad., Arlington, Va., 1986-87; dir. instnl. planning and rsch. U. S.C.-Salkehatchie, Allendale, 1987—. Adj. prof. U. S.C., Allendale and Walterboro, 1987—, Golden Gate U., Shaw AFB Campus, Sumter, S.C., 1985; cons. St. Andrews Middle Sch., Columbia, 1985, S.C. Regional Housing Authority #3, Barnwell, 1994; lectr. in field. Contbr. articles to profl. jours. Bd. dirs. Citizens for the Advancement of Physically Handicapped. Mem. Assn. for Instnl. Rsch., So. Assn. for Instnl. Rsch., Southeastern Assn. for Cmty. Coll. Rsch., Soc. for Coll. and Univ. Planning, Southeastern Employment and Tng. Assn., Am. Soc. for Pub. Adminstrn., Am. Polit. Sci. Assn., So. Polit. Sci. Assn., S.C. Polit. Sci. Assn., Ga. Polit. Sci. Assn., World Future Soc. (S.C. chpt. steering com. on employment and edn.), Cayce-West Columbia Kiwanis (bd. dirs.). Methodist. Home: 3418 Heyward St Columbia SC 29205-2756

RUFFING, JANET KATHRYN, spirituality educator; b. Spokane, Wash., July 17, 1945; d. George Benjamin and Dorothy Edith (Folsom) R. BA, Russell Coll., 1968; M of Applied Spirituality, U. San Francisco, 1978; lic. in Sacred Theology, Jesuit Sch. Theology, 1984; PhD in Christian Spirituality, Grad. Theol. Union, 1986. Joined Sisters of Mercy Congregation, Roman Cath. Ch., 1963. Tchr. reading and English Mercy High Sch., Burlingame, Calif., 1968-72, 75-77, San Francisco, 1972-75; tchr., dept. head Marian High Sch., San Diego, 1978-80; faculty and originating team mem. Fully Alive, Burlingame, 1980-86; faculty, facilitator Permanent Diaconate Formation Program, Oakland, Calif., 1984-86; faculty Internship in Art of Spiritual Direction, Burlingame, 1984, 85, 87; prof. spirituality and spiritual direction Fordham U., Bronx, NY, 1986—, prof., 2000—. Spkr. Villanova Theol. Inst., 1995, Roger Williams Symposium, Pullman, Wash., 1985; vis. faculty Australian Cath. U., Brisbane, summer 1994, San Francisco Theol. Sem., summer 1993, U. San Francisco, summer 1991, St. Michael's Coll., Vt., summer 1990, Fordham at Limerick, Ireland, 1996-97, Colston Symposium, Bristol, Eng., 2000, San Francisco Theol. Sem., 2001, Gettysburg Luth. Sem., 2001, Inner Sabbath, Leuven, Belgium, 2002; Holy Wisdom lectr. Washington Theol. Union, 2003; presenter in field. Author: Uncovering Stories of Faith, 1989, Spiritual Direction: Beyond the Beginnings, 2000; contbg. author, editor: Mysticism and Social Transformation, 2001; assoc. editor The Way; contbr. articles to profl. jours. Mem. Cath. Theol. Soc. Am. (seminar moderator 1987-90), Am. Acad. Religion (chairperson mysticism group 1994-98), Mercy Assn. in Scripture and Theology (treas. 1987-96, mem. editorial bd. MAST jour.), Spiritual Dirs. Internat. (founding coord. com. mem. 1990-93, coord. of regions 1990-93), Women's Ordination Conf. Democrat. Avocations: cooking, hiking, swimming. Office: Fordham U Grad Sch Religion and Religious Bronx NY 10458

RUFOLO, ANTHONY MICHAEL, economics educator; b. Newark, Aug. 9, 1948; s. Philip and Marie Antoinette (Petrillo) R.; m. Patricia Jeanne Lickorai, Aug. 29, 1970; children: Amy, Laura, Christine. BS in Econs., MIT, 1970; PhD in Econs., UCLA, 1975. Cons. Appraisal Rsch. Assocs., Thousand Oaks, Calif., 1971-72; adj. asst. prof. Temple U., Phila., 1976-79; economist Fed. Res. Bank Phila., 1974-78, sr. economist, 1978-80; adj. assoc. prof. U. Pa., Phila., 1978-80; assoc. prof. Portland (Oreg.) State U., 1980-85, prof. urban studies and planning, 1985—. Vis. prof. Jilin U. Tech., People's Republic of China, 1984, UCLA, 1984, 85, 88. Co-author: Public Finance and Expenditure In A Federal System, 1990; co-editor: Economics of Municipal Labor, 1983. Mem. Pub. Works Adv. Coun., Washington County, Oreg., 1981-84; mem. budget com. City of Beaverton, Oreg., 1989-95, chair, 1992-94; mem. Gov.'s Coun. Econ. Adv., Oreg., 1983-94; mem. Citizen's Adv. Coun. on Budget, Tri-Met, 1991-95, chair, 1994-95; mem. investment adv. coun. City of Portland, 1992—. Rsch. grantee Urban Mass Transp. Adminstrn., 1984, 86, Portland State U., 1986, 87, Ford Found., 1988, U.S. Dept. Transp., 1991, 92, 94, Oreg. Dept. Transp., 1994, 96, 98, 2001, 02. Mem. Am. Econ. Assn., Nat. Tax Assn. Avocations: racquetball, bridge, reading. Home: 13255 SW Saratoga Ln Beaverton OR 97008-7607 Office: Portland State U PO Box 751 Portland OR 97207-0751

RUGARI, SUSAN MARIE, medical/surgical nurse, nursing educator; b. Amarillo, Tex., July 10, 1964; BSN, Stephen F. Austin State U., 1986; MSN, U. Tex., Arlington, 1991; PhD, Tex. Woman's U., 1999. RN, Tex. Staff nurse Meth. Hosp.-Charlton, Dallas, 1989-91; diabetes nurse educator Baylor U. Med. Ctr., Dallas, 1987-89, clin. nurse I, 1987-2000, rsch. facilitator, 1991—97; assoc. clin. prof. U. Tex. Nursing Faculty, Arlington, 1991—, dir. Nursing Learning Resources Ctr., 1996-99; rsch. facilitator St. Paul U. Hosp., Dallas, 2001—02. Mem.: Soc. Gastroenterology Nurses and Assocs., Inc., Tex. Nurses Assn., Sigma Theta Tau (chpt. sec., scholar). Office: U Tex Arlington PO Box 19407 Arlington TX 76019-0001 E-mail: rugari@uta.edu.

RUGGIERI, CATHERINE JOSEPHINE, management educator; b. Bklyn., Dec. 28, 1951; d. Joseph A. and Elvira E. Ruggieri; m. Ken Joseph; children: Christian, Alexis. BA, St. John's U., N.Y.C., 1973, MBA, 1979; postgrad., CUNY, 1993-94; JD, Bklyn. Law Sch., 1998. Asst. to dean St. Vincent's Coll. of St. John's U., N.Y.C., 1973-77, asst. dean acad. advisement, 1977-79, asst. dean, 1979-80, acting dean, 1980-81, dean, 1981-86, asst. v.p., dean, 1986-87, assoc. v.p., dean, 1987-93, univ. dir. study abroad, 1987-92, prof. mgmt., dean emerita, 1993—. Chair St. John's Telecomm. Inst. for Non-Profit Video Prodns., N.Y.C., 1987-93. Recipient Hon. Citation Ministry of Edn. Hungary, Budapest, 1986, Bklyn. Bar Assn. Women's Leadership award, 1998. Mem. AAUW, ASCD, AAUP, Am. Assn. Higher Edn.; student mem. ABA, N.Y. State Bar Assn., N.Y. County Lawyers Assn., N.J. Bar Assn., Conn. Bar Assn. Roman Catholic. Avocations: travel, reading. Office: St Johns U 8000 Utopia Pkwy Jamaica NY 11432-1343 E-mail: ruggierc@stjohns.edu.

RUGGLES, BARBARA ANN, elementary education educator; b. Chgo., Mar. 19, 1943; d. Ernest Leonard and Nigel Marie Hvale; 1 child, David M. BS in Edn., Kans. U., 1965; MA in Social Scis., Gov.'s State U., 1984. Tchr. Sch. Dist. 163, Park Forest, Ill. Bd. dirs. Employee's Fed. Credit Union. Legis. Adv. Coun. State Ill. 80th House Dist. Mem. ASCD, Devel. Am. Women in Sci., Nat. Women's History Project, Intermediate Svc. Ctr. #4 (governing bd.), Am. Fedn. Tchrs. Local 604 (v.p.), Tchrs. Fedn. Park Forest (pres.), Am. Fedn. Tchrs. Edn. Rsch. and Dissemination (local site coord.). Home: 21426 S Hillside Rd Frankfort IL 60423-9195

RUIZ, VICKI LYNN, history educator; b. Atlanta, May 21, 1955; d. Robert Paul and Erminia Pablita (Ruiz) Mercer; m. Jerry Joseph Ruiz, Sept. 1, 1979 (div. Jan. 1990); children: Miguel, Daniel; m. Victor Becerra, Aug. 14, 1992. AS in Social Studies, Gulf Coast Community Coll., 1975; BA in Social Sci., Fla. State, 1977; MA in History, Stanford U., 1978, PhD in History, 1982. Asst. prof. U. Tex., El Paso, 1982-85, U. Calif., Davis, 1985-87, assoc. prof., 1987-92; Andrew W. Mellon prof. Claremont (Calif.) Grad. Sch., 1992-95, chmn. history dept., 1993-95; prof. history Ariz. State U., Tempe, 1995—, chair dept. Chicano studies, 1997—. Dir. Inst. of Oral History, U. Tex., El Paso, 1983-85, minority undergrad. rsch. program U. Calif., Davis, 1988-92. Author: Cannery Women, Cannery Lives, 1987, From Out of the Shadows, 1998 (Choice Outstanding Book of 1998); editor: Chicana Politics of Work and Family, 2000; co-editor: Women on U.S.-Mexican Border, 1987, Western Women, 1988, Unequal Sisters, 1990, 3d edit., 1999. Mem. Calif. Coun. for Humanities, 1990-94, vice chmn., 1991-93. Fellow Univ. Calif. Davis Humanities Inst., 1990-91, Am. Coun. of Learned Socs., 1986, Danforth Found., 1977. Mem. Orgn. Am. Historians (chmn. com. on status of minority history 1989-91, nominating com. 1987-88, exec. bd. 1995-98), Immigration History Soc. (exec. bd. 1989-91), Am. Hist. Assn. (nat. coun. 1999—), Am. Studies Assn. (nominating bd. 1992-94, nat. coun. 1996-99), Western History (nominating bd. 1993-95). Democrat. Roman Catholic. Avocations: walking, needlework. Office: Ariz State U History Dept Tempe AZ 85287

RULLKOETTER, JILL E. museum education administrator; b. St. Louis, Oct. 2, 1953; d. Robert Carl Rullkoetter and Evelyn K. (Herrman) Stacy; m. William L. Hurley, Jr., Sept. 1, 1985; 1 child, Nicholas Rullkoetter Hurley. BA in Art History, U. Mo., 1976; MA, U. Wash., 1984. Rsch. asst. Mus. Art & Archaeology U. Mo., Columbia, 1975-76; curatorial asst. Henry Art Gallery U. Wash., Seattle, 1978-79, teaching asst. dept. art history, 1979-80; coord. edn. program Seattle Art Mus., 1982-85, head edn., 1986-98, dir. edn. and pub. programs, 1998—. Staff liason architect selection com. Seattle Mus. Art; speaker and panelist in field. Author (guide booklet) Treasures from the National Museum of American Art: A Family Guide, 1986. Trustee Seattle Archtl. Found., 1990-92. Mem. Am. Assn. Mus. (chmn. edn. com. western region 1985-87, bd. dirs. 1994-95), Wash. Mus. Assn., Western Mus. Assn. (bd. dirs., sec. 1988-92, 2d v.p. 1992-94, pres. 1994-96), N.W. Inst. Architecture and Urban Studies in Italy (bd. dirs. 1981-91, 2d v.p. 1987-88). Office: Seattle Art Mus PO Box 22000 Seattle WA 98122-9700

RUMBLER, SANDRA LYNN, special education educator; b. Chgo., July 11, 1946; d. Albert and Ida (Barrett) Panken; m. Michael R. Lefkow, Apr. 27, 1969 (div. Apr. 1987); children: Mark and David (twins), Susan; m. William R. Rumbler, Dec. 14, 1991. BA, Mundelein Coll., 1968; MSEd in Early Childhood Spl. Edn., Ill. State U., 1992; postgrad. in Administrn. and Supervision, Loyola U., Chgo., 1992—. Cert. tchr. early childhood, bilingual (Spanish), spl. edn., Ill. Tchr. grade 2 Komensky Sch., 1972-73; ESL tchr. Universidad Popular, 1974-75; bilingual team tchr. Greeley Sch., 1975-76; bilingual tchr. primary grades Brennemann Sch., 1976-80; bilinual and multilingual kindergarten tchr. Community Consolidated Sch. Dist. 21, 1981-82; mktg. and editor McDougla Pub. Co., 1983-89; tchr. ESL Amnisty and Oakton Coll. MONACEP programs, 1988-89; bilingual tchr.primary grades Cooper Sch., 1986-91; early childhood spl. edn. tchr. LeMoyne Elem. Sch., Chgo., 1991-92, bilingual early childhood spl. edn. tchr., 1992—. Mem. core planning team canal project Cooper Sch., Chgo., 1988-90; chair integration com. Courtney Sch., Chgo., 1991; mem. Profl. Problems Adv. Com. LeMoyne Sch., Chgo., 1992. Bilingal early childhood spl. edn. tuition grantee U.S. Govt., 1990. Mem. Coun. Exceptional Children (exceptional learners), Ill. Divsn. Culturally and Linguistically Diverse (exec. bd.), Phi Delta Kappa. Jewish and Unitarian. Avocations: cooking, running, sewing, reading, travel. Home: 1532 W Jackson Blvd Chicago IL 60607-5304

RUMER, RALPH RAYMOND, JR., civil engineer, educator; b. Ocean City, N.J., June 22, 1931; s. Ralph Raymond and Anna (Hibbard) R.; m. Shirley Louise Haynes, Nov. 30, 1953 (dec. 1995); children: Sherri, Sue, Sandra, Sarah; m. Sallie Anne Wallace Kornegay, 1997. BS. in Civil Engring, Duke U., 1953; MS, Rutgers U., 1959; Sc.D. (ASCE research fellow), M.I.T., 1962. Lic. prof. engr., N.Y. With Lukens Steel Co., Coatesville, Pa., 1953-54; instr. dept. civil engring. Rutgers U., New Brunswick, N.J., 1956-59; civil engr. U.S. Dept. Agr., New Brunswick, summer 1957-59; research asst. Hydrodynamics lab. M.I.T., Boston, 1961-62, asst. prof. dept. civil engring., 1962-63; assoc. prof. dept. civil engring. SUNY, Buffalo, 1963-69, prof., 1969-76, 78-97, acting head, 1966-67, chmn., 1967-73, 84-87; dir. SUNY (Gt. Lakes Program), 1986-90, acting provost engring. and applied scis., 1974-75; prof., chmn. dept. civil engring. U. Del., Newark, 1976-78; dir. N.Y. Ctr. Hazardous Waste Mgmt., 1987-95. Vis. prof. Duke U., Durham, N.C., 1997-2000; tech. cons. to govt. and industry in hydraulics, water resources and environ. engring.; mem. water resources rsch. com. Nat. Acad. Sci., 1985-86; mem. water mgmt. adv. com. N.Y. State Dept. Environ. Conservation, 1988-93; chmn. sci. adv. com. EPA regions 1 & 2 Hazardous Substance Rsch. Ctr., N.J. Inst. Tech., 1989-2000; mem. sci. adv. com. Gulf Coast States Hazardous Substance Rsch. Ctr., Lamar U., Tex., 1991-97. Contbr. research articles in field to profl. jours. Served with U.S. Army, 1954-56. Recipient Educator of Yr. award Erie-Niagara chpt. N.Y. State Soc. Profl. Engrs., 1989, Excellence award N.Y. State/United Univ. Professions, 1990; Ford fellow, 1962-63; sr. rsch. fellow Calif. Inst. Tech., 1970-71. Fellow ASCE (dir. Buffalo sect., pres. Buffalo sect. 1984-85); mem. Internat. Assn., Hydraulic Rsch., Am. Geophys. Union, Internat. Assn. Gt. Lakes Rsch., Sigma Xi, Tau Beta Pi, Chi Epsilon. Home: PO Box 184 Pilot Mountain NC 27041-0184

RUMORE, MARTHA MARY, pharmacist, educator; b. N.Y.C., Feb. 29, 1956; d. Barney B. and Frieda A. (Sinacore) R. BS in Pharmacy, St. John's U., Jamaica, N.Y., 1978, PharmD, 1980; JD, Thomas Jefferson Coll., L.A., 1986; MS in Drug Info., Arnold & Marie Schwartz Coll., 1990. Registered pharmacist, N.Y., Fla., Conn.; cert. in drug regulatory affairs. Lab. asst. St. John's U., 1973-77; pharmacy intern Queens Hosp. Ctr., Jamaica, 1977-78; sr. info. scientist Richardson-Vicks, Inc., Shelton, Conn., 1981-84; assoc. dir. profl. svcs. Sterling Drug Inc., N.Y.C., 1984-90; assoc. prof. pharmacy adminstrn. Arnold & Marie Schwartz Coll. Pharmacy, Bklyn., 1990-97, regulatory cons., 1997—. Clin. pharmacist Lenox Hill Hosp., N.Y.C., 1990-93, Beth Israel Hosp.-North, 1993—; cons., lectr., presenter in field. Contbr. over 70 articles to profl. jours. Pharmacoepidemiology, Drug Info., Pharmacy Law, Drug Regulatory Affairs, Pharmacotherapeutics; mem. several jour. editl. adv. bds. Recipient Hosp. Pharmacy Achievement award L.I. Soc. Hosp. Pharmacists, 1978, Vis. Scientist award Pharm. Mfrs. Assn., 1990-91, Larry Simonsmeier Legal Writing award, 1999; named Outstanding Young Women Am., 1988. Fellow Am. Pharm. Assn. (trustee, ho. of dels. 1988-97, vice chmn. publs. 1988-89, polit. action com. 1990-97, policy com. on sci. affairs), Acad. Pharm. Practice and Mgmt. (bd. of pharm. specialties, mem. specialty coun. on nuclear pharmacy, 1993—), Am. Soc. Pharmacy Law (bd. dirs. 1996-98); mem. Drug Info. Assn., Regulatory Affairs Profls. Soc., Pharm. Soc. of State of N.Y., Am. Inst. on History of Pharmacy, Am. Assn. Colls. of Pharmacy. Republican. Roman Catholic. Office: Beth Israel Med Ctr North Divsn 170 E End Ave New York NY 10128-7603

RUMPELTES, SHERRIE JAN, primary school educator, pre-school educator; b. Weiser, Ida., Jan. 23, 1952; d. Louis Kinji and Hide (Sako) Ishino; m. Craig Robert Rumpeltes, Aug. 21, 1976; stepchildren: Justin James, Brittan. BA, Boise State U., 1974. Std. teaching cert., Idaho. Tchr. Sch. Dist. #393, Wallace, Idaho, 1974-75, Zion Luth. Preschool, Corvallis, Oreg., 1984-90; tchr. kindergarten Good Shepherd Luth. Sch., Boise, Idaho, 1990—98; tchr. Ind. Sch. Dist. Boise, Idaho, 1999—. Mem.: NEA, Boise Edn. Assn. Lutheran. Avocations: sewing, bicycling. Home: 712 E Bridgewater Ct Boise ID 83706-6424 Office: Ind Sch Dist of Boise 8169 W Victory Rd Boise ID 83709

RUNDELL, ORVIS HERMAN, JR., psychologist, educator; b. Oklahoma City, June 16, 1940; s. Orvis Herman and Virginia Reid (George) R.; m. Jane Shannon Brians, June 25, 1966; children: Leslie Jane, Anne Reid. BS, U. Okla., 1962, MS, 1972, PhD, 1976. Lab. mgr. Okla. Ctr. Alcohol and Drug-Related Studies, Oklahoma City, 1969-76, staff scientist, 1974—. Asst. prof. psychiatry and behavioral scis. U. Okla. Health Sci. Center, 1976—; dir. clin. physiology and sleep disorders ctr. Columbia Presbyterian Hosp., Oklahoma City, 1982-2001; clin. dir. Diagnostic Sleep Ctr. of Dallas, 1989-93; ptnr. Sleep Medicine Assocs., 1994—, Sleep Assocs., 2000—, Sleep Remedies, LLC, 2002—; dir. Columbia Sleep Ptnrs. Program, 1996-2001; clin. dir. The Sleep Clinic, Oklahoma City, 2000—, Sleep Labs PRN, 2001—; cons. in field; instl. rev. bd. U. Okla. Health Sci. Ctr., 1989-2001. Contbr. articles to profl. jours., chpts. in books; asst. editor Alcohol Tech. Reports, 1976-90; cons. editor Psychophysiology, 1974-2001. Bd. dirs. Hist. Preservation, Inc., Oklahoma City, 1978-90. With USAR, 1963-69. Grantee, Nat. Inst. Drug Abuse, Nat. Inst. Alcohol Abuse and Alcoholism. Fellow Am. Acad. of Sleep Medicine; mem. N.Y. Acad. Scis., Psi Chi, Phi Gamma Delta. Home: 431 NW 20th St Oklahoma City OK 73103-1918 Office: 5530 N Francis Oklahoma City OK 73118 Fax: 405-879-2476. E-mail: zzzs@cox.net.

RUNION, KATHERINE GOETZ, special education educator; b. Mattoon, Ill., Dec. 30, 1950; d. Elmer Franklin and Helen Virginia (Lawrence) G.; m. Roy Arthur Runion, July 28, 1984 (dec. June 2002); 1 child, Maureen Katherine. BS in Edn., Ill. State U., 1972; grad. sch., U. Iowa, 1975-76. Cons., tchr. Dubuque (Iowa) County Bd. Edn., 1972-75, Keystone Iowa, Dubuque, 1975-78; mgmt. program J.C. Penney's, Oklahoma City, 1978-80; visually impaired educator Buchanan Elem., 1980—94; intermediate tchr. Okla. City Schs., 1994—98; tchr. Northeast Acad. Middle and H.S. Elem. tchr. Piney Woods (Miss.) Country Life Sch., summer, 1973; staff devel. trainer Oklahoma City Pub. Schs., 1991—; NASA Edn. Program Okla. State U., Stillwater, 1987; tchr./tng. cert. program Okla. State U.-Oklahoma City Pub. Schs., 1991; computer sch. mgr. Network System of Buchanan. Presenter, trainer Multi-Cultural, 1992, Parental Involvement, 1992, Styles and Environment of Learning, 1994. Bd. mem. Cedar Lakes Estates, Oklahoma City, 1979; adminstrv. bd. May Ave. Meth., Oklahoma City, 1991, 92; awards and program chmn. Epsilon Sigma Alpha, Oklahoma City, 1991, 92, 93; interpretive guide Harm Homestead, Oklahoma City, 1989-92; leader Girl Scouts U.S., 1992—, svc. unit team mem., troop organizer. Mem. Phi Delta Kappa (v.p. membership, 1993—), Delta Kappa

Gamma. Republican. Methodist. Avocations: early american and oklahoma history, travel, golf, tap dancing. Home: 2733 NW 25th St Oklahoma City OK 73107-2225 Office: Northeast Acad 3100 N Kelly Oklahoma City OK 73111

RUNNION, CINDIE J. elementary school educator; b. Knoxville, Tenn., Mar. 8, 1958; d. James B. and Josephine Marie (Sykes) Runnion. BS, East Tenn. State U., 1979, MEd, 1989; postgrad., U. Madrid. Sec. Runnion Ent., Newport, Tenn.; tchr. 3rd grade Cocke County Bd. Edn., Newport, 1980—. First Bapt. Ch. meml. scholar. Mem. NEA, ASCD, Tenn. Edn. Assn., Cocke County Edn. Assn. (faculty rep., v.p. 1991-92, accreditation com. for sch.). Home: 146 New Cave Church Rd Newport TN 37821-7404 E-mail: runnionj@planetc.com.

RUNO, MICHAEL JOSEPH, psychologist, school system administrator; b. Cleve., Oct. 6, 1952; s. Raymond George and Audrey Marie (Schwartz) R.; m. Karen Marie Esgro, Sept. 2, 1972. BA, U. Fla., 1974; MEd, Fla. Atlantic U., 1976; PsyD, Nova U., 1985. Mental health asst. Hollywood (Fla.) Pavilion Hosp., 1975-76; psychotherapist Inst. Human Rels., Miami, Fla., 1976-80; team leader mental health Cedars Med. Ctr., Miami, 1980-83; psychotherapist Hollywood Treatment Ctr., 1980-83; clin. intern U.S. Dept. Justice, Fed. Correction Inst., Butner, N.C., 1983-84; program dir. Fair Oaks Hosp., Delray Beach, Fla., 1985-88; cons. psychologist Univ. Pavilion Hosp., Tamarac, Fla., 1990-92; pvt. practice Coral Springs, Fla., 1988—; coord. family counseling Sch. Bd. Broward County, Ft. Lauderdale, Fla., 1988-94; chief psychol. svcs. Cir. Ct. of Broward County, Fla., 1994—. Adv. bd. Broward Commn. Substance Abuse, 1985-86; mem. ADHD task force Sch. Bd. Broward County, 1990. Mem. APA, So. Psychol. Assn., Am. Counseling Assn. Democrat. Roman Catholic. Avocations: golf, skiing, photography, reading, sports. Office: Sch Bd Broward County 540 SE 3rd Ave Fort Lauderdale FL 33301-2937

RUNYON, STEVEN CROWELL, university administrator, communications educator; b. San Rafael, Calif., June 20, 1946; s. Charles A. and Katherine C. (Pease) R.; m. Lynna Lim, Mar. 9, 1974; 1 child, Wendy Victoria. BA in Econs., U. San Francisco, 1971, postgrad., 1978; MA in Radio and TV, San Francisco State U., 1976. Lic. gen. class radiotelephone operator FCC. Radio producer Sta. KGO, San Francisco, 1965-68; engr., announcer Stas. KSFR, KSAN, San Francisco, 1966-68; publicist Kolmar Assocs./Chuck Barris Prodns., San Francisco, 1970; instructional media technician U. San Francisco, 1968-72; technician, archivist, mgr. Wurster, Bernardi & Emmons, San Francisco, 1972-73; projectionist So. Pacific R.R., San Francisco, 1974; broadcast ops. engr. Stas. KPEN, KIOI, KIQI, San Francisco, 1968-74, pub. and cmty. affairs program prodr., 1971-74, AM transmitter engr., 1974; lectr. comm. arts, gen. mgr. Sta KUSF-FM U. San Francisco, 1974—, dir. mass media studies program, 1975-98, acting chmn. comm. arts dept., 1976. TV historian; prodr., engr., cons. radio and TV programs; comm. and audiovisual cons. Author: Educational Broadcast Management Bibliography, 1974, A Study of the Don Lee Broadcasting Sys.' TV Activities, 1930-41, 1976; author: (with others) Television in America, 1996; author: The Ency. of Television, 1997, Historical Dictionary of American Radio, 1998, Indelible Images: Women of Local Television, 2001; contbr. articles. Grantee Calif. Coun. Humanities in Public Policy, Rockefeller Found., Father Spieler Meml. Trust, NSF; recipient cert. of merit for documentary radio series Peninsula Press Club, 1979, Diploma of Honor, Internat. Robert Stolz Soc., 1981, Fr. Dunne award U. San Francisco, 1986, Coll. Svc. award Coll. Arts and Scis. U. San Francisco, 1988. Mem. Soc. Broadcast Engrs., Broadcast Edn. Assn. (Divsnl. First Place award Refereed Paper Competition 1996), Assn. for Edn. in Journalism and Mass Comm., Assn. Recorded Sound Collections, Assn. Moving Image Archivists, Diamond Circle of U. San Francisco, Internat. Comm. Assn. Office: U San Francisco 2130 Fulton St San Francisco CA 94117-1080 E-mail: runyon@usfca.edu.

RUOFF, A. LAVONNE BROWN, English language educator; b. Charleston, Illinois, Apr. 10, 1930; d. Oscar and Laura Alice (Witters) Brown; m. Milford Anthony Prasher, Aug. 19, 1950 (div. 1964); m. Gene W. Ruoff, Jan. 10, 1967; children: Stephen Charles, Sharon Louise(dec.). Student, U. Ill., 1948—50; BS in Edn., Northwestern U., Ill., 1953, MA in English, 1954, PhD in English, 1966. Instr. to asst. prof. Roosevelt U., Chgo., 1961—66; asst. prof. English U. Ill., Chgo., 1966—69, assoc. prof., 1969—81, prof., 1981—94, prof. emeritus, 1994. Interim dir. D'Arcy McNickle Ctr. for Am. Indian History, Newberry Libr., 1999-2000; editor Am. Indian Lives series U. Nebr. Press, Lincoln, 1985—; mem. Am. lit. com. Internat. Exch. of Scholars, Washington, 1987-90, chair, 1989-90; NEH dir. Summer Seminars for Coll. Tchr. on Am. Indian Lit., 1979, 83, 89, 94. Author: American Indian Lit., 1990; Lit. of the Am. Indian, 1990; editor: The Moccasin Maker, 1987, 2d edit., 1998; Wynema, 1997; From the Deep Woods to Civilization and Indian Boyhood, 2001; (with Jerry W. Ward, Jr.) Redefining Am. Lit. History, 1990; (with Donald Smith) Life, Letters and Speeches of George Copway, 1997. Bd. dir. Am. Indian Coun. Fire Chgo., 1980-88. Recipient Lifetime Achievement Award Before Columbus Found., 1998, Lit., MLA and Assn. for Study of Am. Indian Lits. Award for Outstanding Contbn., 1993; MELUS Award for Outstanding Contbn. to Multiethnic Lit., 1986; named Writer of Yr. for Annotation/Bibliography, Wordcraft Circle of Native Writers and Storytellers, 1999; Writer of Yr. for Series Editing Am. Indian Lives; Svc. Award Wordcraft Cir. of Native Writers, 2002; NEH fellow, 1992-93, U. Ill. Chgo. Inst. for Humanities fellow, 1990-91; NEH Rsch. Divsn. grantee, 1981. Mem.: MLA (chair discussion group Am. Indian lit., co-chair lit. of people of color com. 2000—01, exec. coun. 2002—, award for lifetime scholarly achievement 2002), Assn. for Study of Am. Indian Lits., Multi-ethnic Lit. in the U.S., Am. Studies Assn. E-mail: lruoff@uic.edu.

RUOFF, CYNTHIA OSOWIEC, foreign language educator; b. Chgo., Mar. 1, 1943; d. Stephen R. and Estelle (Wozniak) O.; m. Gary Edward Ruoff, June 5, 1965; children: Gary S., Laura A. AB, Loyola U., 1965; MA, Western Mich. U., 1973; PhD in French Lang. and Lit., Mich. State U., 1992. Tchr. Kalamazoo (Mic.) Pub. Schs., 1965-68; asst. prof. Western Mich. U., Kalamazoo, 1980—. Asst. prof. Western Mich. U.; spkr. in field. Contbr. articles to profl. jours. Mem. MLA, N.Am. Soc. Seventeenth-Century French Lit., Am. Assn. Tchrs. French, Am. Soc. Phenomenology and Aesthetics, L'Alliance Française, Soc. Interdisciplinary French Seventeenth-Century Studies, Phi Sigma Iota, Pi Delta Phi. Avocations: piano, skiing. Office: Dept Fgn Langs & Lit Western Mich Univ Kalamazoo MI 49008

RUPERT, DANIEL LEO, education and educational technology consultant; b. Waynoka, Okla., Nov. 12, 1953; s. Robert Anthony and Georgia Yvonne (Lewis) R.; m. Emily Carol Lummus, June 12, 1977; 1 child, Joshua Daniel. AA, Miss. County C.C., 1979; BA in Social Psychology, Park Coll., 1981; MDiv, New Orleans Bapt. Theol. Sem., 1985; EdS, Miss. State U., Starkville, 1991. Chaplain East Miss. State Hosp., Meridian, 1985-87; dir. of rsch. Am. Family Assn., Tupelo, Miss., 1988-89; cons. Rupert & Assocs., Tupelo, 1989-93; guidance counselor Okolona (Miss.) Elem. Sch., 1993-94, guidance counselor, asst. prin., chpt. 1 coord., 1994-96, prin., 1996-97; edn. and ednl. tech. cons. Rupert Cons., 1997—. Computer cons. Lee County Schs., Tupelo, 1990. Author: Selected Poems by Author, 1990; co-author: (state core objectives) Health Education Core Objectives for the State of Mississippi, 1991. Prt-time pastor Koinonia Bapt. Mission, Mooreville, Miss., 1992-96; mem. Christian Bus. Men's Com., Tupelo, 1989-94. With USAF, 1976-82; capt. USAFR, 1983-91, ret., 1995. Mem. ASCD, Am. Assn. Christian Counselors, United Am. Karate Assn., Christian Martial Arts Instrs. Assn. (bd. dirs.), Miss. Counseling Assn. (bd. dirs.), Miss. Spiritual, Ethical and Religious Values in Counseling (pres.), Tupelo Martial Arts Acad., Luncheon Civitan Club, Chi Sigma Iota. Republican. Southern Baptist. Avocations: Karate, writing, singing, playing guitar, spending time with family. Home: 1931 E Main St PO Box 495 Tupelo MS 38802-0495 Office: 1933 E Main St Tupelo MS 38804-2972

RUPERT, WILLIAM ALPHONSE, secondary school educator, counselor; b. Delphos, Ohio, Feb. 7, 1953; s. George Arthur and Genevieve Elizabeth (Markward) R.; m. Christina Joan Albu, Apr. 10, 1976; children: Douglas James, Timothy John. BS in Edn., Ohio State U., 1975; MS in Edn., Youngstown (Ohio) State U., 1980. Cert. comprehensive sci., math. and vocat. edn.tchr., counselor, Ohio. Tchr. chemistry Liberty Local Schs., Youngstown, 1976—94, head track coach, 1977-84, cross-country coach, 1977-89, vocat. edn., 1994—98, counselor, 1998—. Recipient Coach of Yr. award Ohio Assn. Track and Cross-Country Coaches, 1986, 88. Mem. NEA, Ohio Edn. Assn., NE Ohio Edn. Assn., Liberty Assn. of Sch. Employees (treas. 1979—). Democrat. Roman Catholic. Avocations: bicycling, swimming, electronics, basketball, running. Home: 581 N Rhodes Ave Niles OH 44446-3825 Office: Liberty High Sch 1 Leopard Way Youngstown OH 44505-1399

RUPP, GEORGE ERIK, not-for-profit administrator; b. Summit, NJ, Sept. 22, 1942; s. Gustav Wilhelm and Erika (Braunoehler) R.; m. Nancy Katherine Farrar, Aug. 22, 1964; children: Katherine Heather, Stephanie Karin. Student, Ludwig Maximilians U., Munich, Germany, 1962-63; AB, Princeton U., 1964; BD, Yale U., 1967; post grad., U. Sri Lanka, Peradeniya, 1969-70; PhD, Harvard U., 1972. Ordained to ministry Presbyn. Ch. USA, 1971; faculty fellow in religion, vice chancellor Johnston Coll., U. Redlands, Redlands, Calif., 1971-74; asst. prof. Harvard Div. Sch., Harvard U., Cambridge, Mass., 1974-76, assoc. prof., 1976-77, prof., dean, 1979-85; prof., dean acad. affairs U. Wis., Green Bay, 1977-79; prof., pres. Rice U., Houston, 1985-93, Columbia U., NYC, 1993—2002; pres. Int. Rescue Comm., NY, 2002—. Bd. dir. Com. for Econ. Devel., Inst. Internat. Edn., InterAction. Author: Christologies and Cultures: Toward a Typology of Religious Worldviews, 1974, Culture Protestantism: German Liberal Theology at the Turn of the Twentieth Century, 1977, Beyond Existentialism and Zen: Religion in a Pluralistic World, 1979, Commitment and Community, 1989; contbr. articles to profl. jour. Danforth Grad. fellow, 1964-71 Mem.: AAAS, Soc. Values in Higher Edn., Coun. Fgn. Rels., Am. Acad. Religion. Office: International Rescue Committee 122 East 42nd Street New York NY 10168

RUPPERT, MARY FRANCES, management consultant, school counselor; b. Flushing, N.Y., May 14; d. Raymond Edward and Mary Josephine (Reilly) R.; m. Donald Francis O'Brien (div.); children: Donald Francis O'Brien III, Kevin Raymond O'Brien; m. Patrick J. Falzone, July 31, 1993. BA in English, Loyola Coll.; MS in Psychology, Counseling, Queens Coll., 1965. Counselor Plainview (N.Y.)-Old Bethpage Schs., 1965—; trainer, cons. stress mgmt., time mgmt., comm., pres. Productivity Programs, Huntington, N.Y., 1975—. Contbr. articles in field; author audiotapes on stress mgmt., 1975—; appearances radio and TV. Mem. ASTD (pres. 1988, chmn. bd. dirs. 1989-95), AAUW, N.Y. State Counselors Assn., Nassau Counselors Assn., Huntington Camera Club (treas. 1996-97, sec. 1997—). Avocations: photography (awards), tennis, golf, reading, wine tasting. Office: 20 Richard Ln Huntington NY 11743-2354

RUPPRECHT, NANCY ELLEN, historian, educator; b. Coeur d'Alene, Idaho, Sept. 23, 1948; d. George John and Nancy Berneeda (Baird) R. BA with honors, U. Mo., 1967, MA, 1969; PhD, U. Mich., 1982. Acad. dir. pilot program U. Mich., Ann Arbor, 1971-73, lectr. in women studies, 1973-75; vis. lectr. history U. Mo., St. Louis, 1976-77; vis. instr. of history Wash. U., St. Louis, 1977-79, Grinnell (Iowa) Coll., 1979-81; asst. prof. Oakland U., Rochester, Mich., 1981-83; asst. prof. of history Mid. Tenn. State U., Murfreesboro, 1985-91, assoc. prof., 1991-97, prof. history, 1997—. Dir. women's studies program Middle Tenn. State U., 1988—, publicity dir. women's history month, 1989-92, mem. faculty senate, 1992-95; bd. dir. Remember the Women. Mem. editl. bd. German Studies Rev., 1999—; contbr. articles to profl. jours. Bd. dirs. Remember the Women Found. Mem.: NOW, AAUW, AAUP (chpt. v.p. 1988—89, pres. 1989—93), Remember the Women (bd. mem.), Assn. Faculty and Adminstrv. Women (chpt. pres. 1995—), Concerned Faculty and Adminstrv. Women (chpt. v.p. 1993—95, chpt. pres. 1995—96), Women in Higher Edn. in Tenn., German Studies Assn., Mid Tenn. Women's Studies Assn., Holocaust Studies Assn., So. Humanities Assn., So. Hist. Assn. (chair nominating com. European divsn. 1996—97, mem. exec. com. 1996—, mem. program com. 1997—, chmn. program com. 2001—02, vice chair European divsn. 2002—, chair European divsn. 2003—), S.E. Women's Studies Assn., Am. Hist. Assn. Home: 1106 Jones Blvd Murfreesboro TN 37129-2310 Office: Middle Tenn State U 275 Peck Hall Murfreesboro TN 37132-0001

RUSCH, PAMELA JEAN, middle school educator; b. Berwyn, Ill., Mar. 1, 1949; d. James M. and Arlene A. (Meyer) Sanders; m. Steven Paul Rusch, Dec. 23, 1973; children: Matthew, Christiana. BFA with honors, U. Denver, 1971; MA, Lesley Coll., Cambridge, Mass., 1983. Art tchr. Jefferson County Pub. Schs., Lakewood, Colo., 1971—. Area coord. Lesley Coll. Outreach Program, Denver, 1981-84; cons. Standard Based Edn., Jefferson County, 1993—; writing team mem. Jefferson County Art Stds., 1995—, mem. mentoring program, 1997—, dist. facilitator, 1998—, author curricula; cons. Middle Sch. Resource Team, 1990—. Mem. ASCD, Nat. Mid. Sch. Assn., Colo. Art Edn. Assn. Lutheran. Avocations: flower arranging, skiing, water sports, painting, travel. Home: 7037 Robb St Arvada CO 80004-1360

RUSCIANO, FRANK LOUIS, political science educator, consultant; b. Elizabeth, N.J., Oct. 4, 1954; s. Francis Joseph and Philomena (Martucci) R.; m. Roberta Louise Fiske, Sept. 8, 1979; 1 child, Francesco Fiske Rusciano. BA, Cornell U., 1976; MA, U. Chgo., 1978, PhD, 1983. Rsch. asst. Nat. Opinion Rsch. Ctr., Chgo., 1978-80; rsch. assoc. Upsala Coll., East Orange, N.J., 1980-82; asst. prof. Rider Coll., Lawrenceville, N.J., 1982-89; methodology cons. Total Rsch. Corp., Lawrenceville, N.J., 1995—; prof. polit. sci. Rider U., 1996—, chair polit. sci. dept., 1998—. Guest lectr. Columbia U., N.Y.C., 1984; vis. prof. U. Mainz, Germany, 1985-86; cons. Ednl. Testing Svc., 1995, Total Rsch. Corp. Author: Isolation and Paradox: Defining the Public in Modern Political Analysis, 1989, World Opinion and the Emerging International Order, 1998; contbr. Magill's History of Europe, 1991, Great Events from History: Human Rights, 1992, Media and the Persian Gulf War, 1993, Ready Reference: Ethics, 1994, Cyberimperialism, Framing Terrorism, 2003, Encyclopedia of Public Opinion, 2003; editor Adminstrn. and Policy Jour., 1983-85. Survey cons. Planned Parenthood Assn., 1990. NSF grantee, 1980-82; Alexander von Humboldt Found. fellow, 1985-86, 87, 95, 99. Mem. Am. Polit. Sci. Assn., Am. Assn. for Pub. Opinion Rsch., Phi Beta Kappa. Avocation: running. Office: Rider U Polit Sci Dept 2083 Lawrenceville Rd Trenton NJ 08648-3099 E-mail: rusciano@rider.edu.

RUSH, MARY BETH, elementary education educator; b. Columbus, Ohio, Apr. 3, 1952; d. Forrest Alvin and Mildred Lucille (Francis) Becker; m. Ronald Thomas Lech, Apr. 6, 1974 (div. June 1986); children: Heather, April, Ryan; m. Tom Edward Rush, Mar. 24, 1990. BA, Capital U., 1974; postgrad., Ashland U., Columbus, 1979-91, Ohio State U., 1981-92, MA in Ednl. Tech. and Design, 1997. Cert. tchr., Ohio. Title I tchr. reading Northridge Local Schs., Johnstown, Ohio, 1974-75; learning disabilities tchr. Columbus Pub. Schs., Ohio, 1975-77; elem. tchr. Gahanna (Ohio)-Jefferson Schs., 1977-92, head tchr., 1993—. Bldg. chmn. Dist. Tech. Com., Gahanna, 1986-92; mem. Dist. Drug Awareness Com., 1987-90; Ohio State Dept. of Edn., Praxis, 1997-; Ohio First, 2001. Lobbyist Columbus Young Reps., 1974-77; mem. women's aux. Children's Hosp. Columbus 162, 1978-86; music, edn. coms. Grace Luth. Ch., Columbus, 1980—, elder 1992-94; deacon, Peace Luth. Ch. Gahanna, Ohio, 1994-. Mem. NEA, Ohio Edn. Assn., Gahanna-Jefferson Edn. Assn. (pres. 1982-83, bd. dirs. 1987-91), Nat. History Acad. Avocations: reading, swimming, softball, gardening, crafts. Home: 254 Caswell Dr Columbus OH 43230-6224 Office: Gahanna-Jefferson Schs 136 Carpenter Rd Gahanna OH 43230-2669

RUSH, RICHARD R. academic administrator; Pres. Calif. State U. Channel Islands, Camarillo. Office: Calif State U Channel Islands 1 University Dr Camarillo CA 93012 Fax: 805-437-8414. E-mail: richard.rush@csuci.edu.

RUSHFORTH, CRAIG K. electrical engineering educator, researcher; b. Ogden, Utah, Sept. 4, 1937; s. Knewel H. and June (Nelson) R.; m. Martha Hollist, June 19, 1958; children— Kevin, Kim, Alan, Rebecca, Brett. B.S. in E.E., Stanford U., 1958, M.S., 1960, Ph.D., 1962. Asst. prof. elec. engring. Utah State U., Logan, 1962-66; staff mem. Inst. for Def. Analyses, Arlington, Va., 1967-68; prof. Mont. State U., Bozeman, 1966-73; prof. elec. engring. U. Utah, Salt Lake City, 1974—97, assoc. dean Coll. Engring., 1995—97, prof. emeritus, 1997; cons. Unisys Corp., Salt Lake City. Contbr. articles to profl. jours. Bell Labs. fellow, 1960-61, NSF fellow, 1961-62. Mem. IEEE (sr.), Phi Beta Kappa, Tau Beta Pi. Democrat. Mormon. Home: 1152 Sherwood Dr Kaysville UT 84037-1349

RUSKAUP, CALVIN, therapist, history professor; b. St. Louis, Feb. 5, 1939; s. Henry and Viola (Vogt) R.; m. Chandricka Maharaj, Apr. 1, 1991. BSc, U. Mo., St. Louis, 1967; PhD, Ohio State U., 1979. Diplomate Am. Psychotherapy Assn., Am. Assn. Integrative Medicine. Co-founder Cmty. Broadcasting-Sta. WFAC, Columbus, Ohio, 1975-77; lectr. Ohio State U., 1975-79; designer Trimobile Safety Car, Aspen, Colo., 1980-81; pastoral counselor United Luth. Ch., Knoxville, Tenn., 1982—85, pres. Hilo, Hawaii, 1986—. Spkr. World Parliament Scientists, 2000. Chmn. Commn. to Stop Violence, 1999-2000; editor Patriot Press, 1997-98; Patriot and Libertarian parties U.S. presdl. candidate, 1996. Mem. AAAS Sr. Scientists Engrs. (emeritus), Am. Anthropol. Assn., Acad. Polit. Sci., Orgn. Am. Historians, Assn. Transpersonal Psychology, N.Y. Acad. Scis., Am. Psychoanalytic Assn., Pub. Rels. Soc. Am., Nat. Press Club, Circumnavigators Club.

RUSSELL, ALAN JAMES, chemical engineering and biotechnology educator; b. Salford, Lancashire, Eng., Aug. 8, 1962; came to U.S., 1987; s. Francis Anthony and Yvonne (Heilbrunn) R.; m. Janice Elaine Quoresimo, Sept. 19, 1987; children: Hannah Justine Serena, Vincent Anthony Alexander, Christian Sebastian, Trevor Alan James, Emily Christine Samantha. BSc with honors, U. Manchester, U.K., 1984; PhD, Imperial Coll., London, 1987. NATO rsch. fellow MIT, Cambridge, 1987-89; chmn., Nickolas DeCecco prof. dept. chem. engring. U. Pitts., 1989-2001, assoc. dir. Ctr. for Biotech., 1991-2001, dir. program in advanced biomaterials, prof. surgery; dir. McGowan Inst. for Regenerative Medicine. Prof. biochemistry and molecular genetics U. Pitts. Med. Ctr.; exec. dir. Pitts. Tissue Engring. Initiative; founder Alerhan Techs., Inc., Agentase, LLC; cons. to chem. and pharm. industries, 1988—. Contbr. articles to profl. jours. Recipient Presdl. Young Investigator award NSF, 1990, Chancellor's Disting. Rsch. award U. Pitts., 1993; NATO fellow, 1988, Am. Inst. Med. and Biol. Engrs. fellow, 1998. Mem. Am. Chem. Soc. (session chmn. 1990-91, awards 1989, 93), Biochemistry Soc., Am. Inst. Chem. Engrs., Tissue Engring. Soc. N.Am. (pres.). Lutheran. Achievements include pioneering use of protein engineering to alter rationally the pH dependence of enzymes; discovery of the phenomenon of enzyme memory in organic solvents, biotechnological destruction of chemical weapons. Office: McGowan Inst 401 Scaife Pittsburgh PA 15261

RUSSELL, CHARLES E. secondary school educator; b. Indpls., Apr. 15, 1935; s. Charles M. and Frances A. (Stoll) R. AB, Butler U., 1957; MA, Ind. U., 1960. Cert. secondary tchr., Ind. Tchr. Arsenal Tech. High Sch., Indpls., 1957-63, North Ctr. High Sch., Indpls., 1963-79, chmn. sci. dept., 1979—. Adj. instr. zoology Butler U., Indpls., 1960-90. Mem. Nat. Assn. Sci. Tchrs., Nat. Assn. Biology Tchrs., Am. Ornithologist's Union, Am. Soc. Herpetologists and Ichtyologists, Ind. Acad. Scis., Hoosier Assn. Sci. Tchrs., Wilson Soc. Methodist. Avocation: conchology. Home: 10602 Jordan Rd Carmel IN 46032-4066 Office: 1801 E 86th St Indianapolis IN 46240-2345

RUSSELL, CYNTHIA PINCUS, social worker, educator; b. N.Y.C., May 30, 1935; BA magna cum laude, Radcliffe Coll., 1957; MSW, Columbia U., 1959; postgrad., Hebrew U., Jerusalem, 1974-75; PhD, Union Rsch. Inst., 1978. Med. social worker Neurol. Inst.-Columbia-Presbyn. Med. Ctr., N.Y.C., 1958; caseworker Edwin Gould found. for Children, N.Y.C., 1958-61; med. social worker Yale-New Haven Hosp., 1961, instr., 1961-62; rsch. asst. Yale Child Study Ctr. Nursery Sch., 1962-65; psychiat. social worker, rsch. asst. Regional Ctr. for Mental Retardation U. Conn. Sch. Social Work, 1966; psychiat. social worker Clifford Beers Guild Guidance Clinic, New Haven, 1966; dir. Info. and Counseling Svc. for Women Yale U., 1969-77, asst. clin. prof. dept. psychiatry, 1969—; mem. dept. student counseling Hebrew U., Jerusalem, 1974-75; pvt. practice New Haven and Stratford, Conn., 1977—. Lectr. Albertus Magnus Coll., 1975; supr. social and counseling U. Bridgeport, So. Conn. State U., 1975—77; psychosynthesis trainer Temenos Inst., Westport, 1987; founder Conn. Inst. for Psychosynthesis, 1990, trainer, supr., 1990—; adj. prof. Union Doctoral Program, 1990; supr. Yale Dept. Clin. Psychiatry; cons. Davenport Residence, Hamden, Conn., 2002—. Author: Double Duties, 1978 (Book of Yr. New Haven Pub. Libr., Woman Today Book Club); author: (with others) At Grandmother's Table, 2000; editor: Psychosynthesis Lifeline, 1984—; contbr. chapters to books, articles to profl. jours. Nat. adv. bd. Vital Active Life After Trauma, Cambridge, Mass., 1990—99; mem. regional manpower coun. New Haven, 1975—76; mem. New Haven YWCA Women in Leadership, 1977—78, 1989—91; pres. Except. Cancer Patients, 1990—91, health profl. trainer, 1995—98; mem. Mayor's com. on volunteerism, 1975—76; bd. dirs. Connection for Health, 1990. Mem. NASW, Acad. Cert. Social Workers (diplomate), Address: PO Box 1183 Stratford CT 06615-8683 also: 2225 Main St Stratford CT 06615-5920

RUSSELL, JOYCE WEBER, principal; b. Detroit, Feb. 21, 1948; d. Ronald Robert and Eleanor Treva (Burns) Weber; m. James Edward Russell, Mar. 25, 1970; 1 child, Jennifer Eileen. AA, Palm Beach C.C., Lake Worth, Fla., 1968; BA, Fla. Atlantic U., 1970, MA, 1975. Cert. tchr., prin. Tchr. Palm Beach County Sch. Bd., West Palm Beach, Fla., 1970-79, staff devel. specialist, 1979-84; asst. prin. Allamanda Elem., 1984-88; prin. Addison Mizner Elem., Boca Raton, Fla., 1988-90, South Olive Elem., West Palm Beach, 1990-95; mem. dist. ESOL support team dept. multicultural edn. Sch. Bd. Palm Beach County, 1996—2001, coord. Dept. Multicultural Edn., 1999—. Adminstr. Safe Schs. AFTER Sch. Programs, Sch. Police, 1995-96. Rebus Work Sampling Sys. authentic assessment trainer, 1997-2000, chair Vision 2000 Good Shepherd Meth. Ch., West Palm Beach, 1990-99, chancel choir, sec. pastor parrish com., 1996-98; mem. Leadership Palm Beach County, 1990-2003; vol. funding distbn. United Way Palm Beach County. Mem.: ASCD, Forum Club of the Palm Beaches (sec. 2000—01, v.p. 2001—02, pres. 2003—, bd. dirs.), Palm Beach County Adminstrn. Assn., Phi Kappa Phi, Phi Delta Kappa (treas., sec.). Avocations: water sports, genealogy, mother goose character reader for literacy, writing poetry. Office: Sch Bd Palm County Ste 204A 3330 Forest Hill Blvd West Palm Beach FL 33406-5869

RUSSELL, JUDY ELAINE, consumer science and health educator; b. Ohio County, Ky., Apr. 14, 1950; d. Ralph and Ruby Jean (Nabours) R. BS, Western Ky. U., 1972, MA in Edn., 1974. Home econs. tchr. Ohio County Schs., Hartford, Ky., 1972-73, 74-75; child care svcs. instr. Meade County Vocat., Brandenburg, Ky., 1975-78, 85-88; home econs. curriculum specialist U. Ky., Lexington, 1978-79, Ky. Dept. of Edn., Frankfort, 1979-85; home econs. tchr. Franklin County Schs., Frankfort, 1988-91; head start tchr. Audubon Area Community Svc., Fordsville, Ky., 1992; life skills tchr. Ohio County Schs., Hartford, 1992—. Freelance writer Nat. Instructional Media Co.; resource tchr. Ky. Tchr. Internship Program, 1999—. Mem. Ohio County Cmty. Edn. Bd., 1990-2002, Youth Svcs. Ctr. Adv. Coun., Hartford, 1992-95, Ky. Jaeger Mills Std. Setting for Test Items, 2000, Practical Living Skills Acad., 2001-02; babysitting instr. Ohio County ARC, Hartford, 1992-94. Recipient Golden Apple award Ashland Oil Co., 1994. Mem. NEA, ASCD, Am. Vocat. Assn., Ky. Vocat. Assn., Nat. Vocat. Assn., Ohio County Edn. Assn., Ky. Edn. Assn., Alpha Delta Kappa (Pi chpt., v.p. 1994-96), Phi Delta Kappa (rep. Edn. Found. 1995-96, v.p. leadership 1996-97, sec. 1997-99). Democrat. Mem. Lds Ch. Avocations: reading, folk dancing, ballroom dancing, gardening.

RUSSELL, KENNETH CALVIN, metallurgical engineer, educator; b. Greeley, Colo., Feb. 4, 1936; s. Doyle James and Jennie Frances (Smith) R.; m. Charlotte Louise Wolf, Apr. 13, 1963 (div. 1978); children: David Allan, Doyle John. Met.E., Colo. Sch. Mines, 1959; PhD, Carnegie Inst. Tec., 1963. Engr. Westinghouse Rsch. and Devel. Ctr., 1959-61; NSF postdoctoral fellow Physics Inst., U. Oslo, 1963-64; asst. prof. metallurgy M.I.T., Cambridge, 1964-69, assoc. prof., 1969-78, prof. metallurgy, 1978—, prof. nuc. engring., 1979—. Contbr. articles to profl. publs. Served as 2d lt. U.S. Army, 1959-60. DuPont fellow, 1961-62; NSF fellow, 1962-63 Mem.: Metallurgical Soc. Am. Inst. Mining, Metallurgical and Petroleum Engrs., Am. Phys. Soc. Office: MIT Rm 13-5050 Cambridge MA 02139

RUSSELL, LEONIA LAVERN, mathematics educator; b. Norfolk, Va., June 7, 1964; d. Clarence Vernie and Leonia (Jackson) R. BS in Electronics Engring., Norfolk State U., 1987, endorsement in math., 1988, MA in Urban Edn., 1992. Math. tchr. Chesapeake (Va.) Pub. Schs., 1988—. Mem. NEA, ASCD, Chesapeake Edn. Assn., Nat. Coun. Tchrs. Maths., Local Coun. Tchrs. Maths., Optimist Club Internat. (sponsor Chesapeake chpt.). Baptist. Avocations: playing the piano and organ, reading, singing, bowling. Home: 4029 Cedar Grove Cres Chesapeake VA 23321-3107

RUSSELL, LOUISE, education educator, folklorist; b. Stratford, Okla., Aug. 9, 1931; d. Virgel Wylie and Louise J. (Hayden) R. BA magna cum laude, Oklahoma City U., 1953; MA, Northwestern U., 1955; PhD, Ind. U., 1977; postgrad., Colo. State U., 1981-82. Tchr. pub. schs., Sterling, Colo., 1958-59, Washington-Lee H.S., Arlington, Va., 1959-62, John Handley H.S., Winchester, Va., 1962-63, Weld Sch. Dist. No. 6, Greeley, Colo., 1963-68, 72-87, Colegio Internat., Valencia, Venezuela, 1968-69, Holmdel Schs., N.J., 1971-72; chmn. staff devel. team, English and basic skills Northland Pioneer Coll., Holbrook, Ariz., 1987-91, also subject specialist, 1987-91; instr. English humanitiea Ea. N.Mex. U., 1992-93; grant dir. Title V Indian edn. Dulce Ind. Sch. Dist., 1994-96; chmn. English dept. Santa Rosa Consol Schs., 1996-98. Adj. faculty Otero Jr. Coll., La Junta, Colo., 1999—. Author: Understanding Folklore, 1975, Understanding Folk Music, 1977; also articles. Named Tchr. of Yr., Masons. Mem. MLA, Am. Anthrop. Assn., Am. Folklore Soc., Nat. Coun. Tchrs. English, Phi Delta Kappa.

RUSSELL, LOUISE BERNICE, instructional designer; b. San Diego, Apr. 14, 1949; d. Donald J. and Caroline J. (Jasper) Boyd. BA in Social Sci., San Diego State U., 1972, MA in Ednl. Tech., 1993. Cert. multiple subject tchr., Calif. Tchr. Victorian Edn. Dept., Melbourne, Australia, 1973-78, 81-84, lang. arts and social studies curriculum cons., 1979-80; tchr. Cajon Valley Union Sch. Dist., El Cajon, Calif., 1985-91; lead instrnl. designer MediaShare Corp., Carlsbad, Calif., 1991-93; lead instrnl. designer multimedia elem. math curriculum Jostens Learning, San Diego, 1993—. Co-author Mus. Photographic Arts' edn. packet Manuel Alvarez Brazo, 1990 (award of distinction Am. Assn. Mus. 1991), Sebastio Selgado, 1991. Chair edn. com. Mus. Photographic Arts. Grantee Cajon Valley Union Sch. Bd., 1987, 90. Mem. Nat. Coun. Tchrs. Math., Computer Using Educators, Assn. for Ednl. Comm. and Tech., Nat. Soc. for Performance and Instrn., Internat. Interactive Comm. Soc., Soc. Photographic Edn. Avocations: photography, art, tennis. Home: 3407 Mississippi St San Diego CA 92104-4026

RUSSELL, MARGARET JONES (PEG RUSSELL), secondary school educator, retired writer; b. Durham, N.C., Apr. 25, 1938; d. Roderic O. and Margaret (Moore) Jones; m. Michael Morgan Russell; children: Lauren Skinner, Carol Martin, Seth Russell, Jay Russell. BA, Muskingum Coll., 1961. Ordained deacon Presbyn. Ch., 1970. Tchr. Sarasota (Fla.) County Sch. Bd., 1962-97, Sarasota H.S., 1982-96, ret., 1997. Sponsor literary mag. Quest, 1988—. Editor: (newsletter) The Mainsail, 1992-95; contbr. poems to profl. pubs. ARC vol. Sarasota Meml. Hosp., 1966-83, aux. vol., 1994—; reader Fla. Studio Theatre, Sarasota, 1980—. Sarasota Herald Tribune scholar, 1993; Fla. Writing Project fellow, 1990. Mem. Nat. Coun. Tchrs. English, Fla. Coun. Tchrs. English, Light Verse Workshop (co-chair 1995, chair 1998—), Sarasota Fiction Writers, Selby Poets, Sarasota Genealogical Soc., Alpha Gamma Delta. Republican. Presbyterian. Home: 1150 Willis Ave Sarasota FL 34232-2148

RUSSELL, MARY ANN, secondary school educator; b. Murray, Ky., Oct. 12, 1932; d. Elginn Newton Underwood and Mary Louise Orr Underwood; m. Allen Wells Russell, Aug. 6, 1953; children: Mark Allen, Lisa Louise. BA, Murray State U., 1954, MA, 1956; cert. Rank 1, U. Colo., 1958; PhD, Vanderbilt U., 1970. Cert. Tchr. Ky. Dept. Edn., 1955. Tchr. English Murray City Sch., Murray, Ky., 1955—65, Paducah C.C., Paducah, Ky., 1965—66, Martin Jr. Coll., Pulaski, Tenn., 1968, Murray H.S., Murray, 1970—95; ret., 1995. Com. mem. Cmty. Edn., Murray, 1999—2000, Calloway 2020, Murray, 1999—2002, Cmty. United Benevolance Svc., Murray, 2001—02. Recipient Ky. Shakespeare Tchr. of Yr. award, State Shakespeare Festival, 1987, Golden Tchr. award, Ashland Oil, 1992, Tchr. of Yr. award, Kiwanis Club, 1992. Mem.: Calloway County Tchrs., Ky. Retired Tchrs., Murray Women's Club (pres. 1999—2002, Outstanding Clubwoman award 2001). Republican. Baptist. Avocations: reading, bridge, travel, cooking. Home: 1503 Sycamore Street Murray KY 42071

RUSSELL, NEDRA JOAN BIBBY, secondary school educator; b. May, Tex., Mar. 19, 1942; d. Samuel Ross Bibby and Velva (Osburn) Bibby Bowden; m. James L. Russell, Aug. 27, 1960; children: Pettye Russell Arrington, Jamie Len Russell Trammell, Joan Lee Russell Dela Rosa. BS, Howard Payne U., 1967; postgrad., Hardin Simmons U., summer 1968; MA in Teaching, Angelo State U., 1976; vocat. office cert., North Tex. State U., 1986. Cert. tchr. secondary gen., bus., provisional lang./learning disabilities, Tex. Tchr. bus. and vocat. courses to at-risk students Coleman (Tex.) Ind. Sch. Dist. Alternative H.S., 1967—. Instr. keyboarding technique Brain Damaged Children Conf., Angelo State U. and San Angelo Sch. Sys.; participant profl. workshops and confs., including State Vocat. Office Conf., 1985—, Trade and Indsl. Arts State Conf., 1990, Tex. Commn. on Ednl. Tech. Conf., summer 1992. Named Bus. Tchr. of Yr. for Dist. XV, 1993. Mem. NEA, ASCD, Tex. Bus. Edn. Assn. (dist. chmn. 1977, state historian 1980-81,, state treas. 1997-99, mem. ednl. adv. com. to dist. 15 rep.), Tex. State Tchrs. Assn. (treas. Coleman County unit, dist. del., membership chairperson), Nat. Bus. Edn. Assn., Vocat. Office Edn. Assn., Tex. Computer Edn. Assn., Mountain-Plains Bus. Edn. Assn. Home: RR 2 Box 199 Coleman TX 76834-9518 Office: CAP High Sch RR 1 Box 43 Talpa TX 76882-9608

RUSSELL, PEGGY TAYLOR, soprano, educator; b. Newton, N.C., Apr. 5, 1927; d. William G. and Sue B. (Cordell) Taylor; m. John B. Russell, Feb. 23, 1953; children: John Spotswood, Susan Bryce. MusB in Voice, Salem Coll., 1948; MusM, Columbia U., 1950; postgrad., U. N.C., Greensboro, 1977; student, Am. Inst. Music Studies, Austria, 1972, student, 1978; student of Clifford Bair, Nell Starr (hon.), Salem Coll., Winston-Salem, N.C.; student of Edgar Schofield, Chloe Owen, N.Y.C.; student operadramatics, Boris Goldovsky, Southwestern Opera Inst.; student of Ande Andersen, Max Lehner, Graz, Austria. Mem. faculty dept. voice Guilford Coll., Greensboro, NC, 1952—53, Greensboro Coll., 1971—72; pvt. tchr. voice Greensboro, 1963—. Co-founder, v.p. sales, mktg. Russell Textiles, Inc., Greensboro, 1988; vis. instr. in voice U. N.C., Chapel Hill, 1973—77; founding artistic dir., gen. mgr. Young Artists Opera Theatre, Greensboro, 1983, staged and produced 18 operatic prodns., 1983—91; gues lectr. opera workshop U. N.C., Greensboro, 1990—91; lectr. opera Friends of Weymouth, Southern Pines, NC, 1994; lectr. on music history and opera, High Point, NC, Ctr. Creative Leadership, Greensboro, 1979—80, 1st Presbyn. Ch., 1982. Singer: debut in light opera as Gretchen in The Red Mill, 1947; singer: (debuts) Rosalinda in Die Fledermaus, 1949, Lola in Cavalleria Rusticana, 1951, Violetta in La Traviata, 1953, Fiordiligi in Cosi fan Tutte, 1956; singer: Marguerite in Faust, 1967, First Lady in The Magic Flute, 1972, mem. Greensboro Orotario Soc., 1955—59; singer: (soprano soloist) The Messiah, 1952, 1958, The Creation, 1955, Solomon, 1958, Presbyn. Ch. of the Covenant, 1958—71; singer: guest appearances Sta. WFMY-TV, 1958—62; singer: (soprano soloist) Greensboro Symphony Orch., 1964, 1980, Ea. Music Festival Orch., 1965, Greensboro Civic Orch., 1980; singer: (soloist in numerous recitals). Judge Charlotte Opera Guild Auditions, 1994; mem. Friendship Force of Guilford County, Netherlands, 1985, 1987; bd. dirs. Music Theater Assocs., Greensboro Friends of Music, N.C. Lyric Opera, Piedmont Opera Theatre. Grantee N.C. Arts Coun. and NEA, 1991. Mem.: Piedmont Triad Coun. Internat. Vis. (Appreciation award Nat. Coun. Internat. Visitors 1994), N.C. Symphony Soc., Civic Music Assn. (chmn. 1963—64), Atlanta Opera Guild, Broadway Theater League (chmn. 1961—63), Symphony Guild (dir. 1977—78), Greensboro Music Tchrs. Assn. (pres. 1966—67), Music Educators Nat. Conf., N.C. Fedn. Music Clubs (dir. 1956—58), Nat. Assn. Tchrs. of Singing (state gov. 1976—82, coord. Regional Artist Contest 1982—84), Ctrl. Opera Svc., Nat. Opera Assn. (chmn. regional opera cos. com. 1985—91, judge vocal competition auditions 1991, 1992, 1994, chmn. trustees Cofield Endowment 1991), Weatherspoon Art Mus. Guild, English Speaking Union (bd. dirs. Greensboro chpt., chmn. Shakespeare competition 1995), Guilford County Planning/Devel. Office (Forecast 2015 com.), Greensboro Preservation Soc., Greensboro City Club. Home: 3012 W Cornwallis Dr Greensboro NC 27408-6730

RUSSELL, RHONDA CHERYL, piano educator, recording artist; b. Ada, Okla., May 19, 1947; d. Joe Roy and Vina Olive (McEntire) Sammons; m. James Michael Davis, June 1, 1973 (div. Mar. 1986); m. Joel Reed Russell, Apr. 2, 1989; 1 child, Christopher Nathaniel. BFA in Music, U. Okla., 1969, postgrad., 1970-71; M of Ch. Music, Performance, Golden Gate Bapt. Theol. Sem., 1984; postgrad., U. Ariz., 1986. Piano tchr., various states, 1969—; music evangelist So. Bapt. Conv., nationwide, 1969—; asst. choral dept. Elk City (Okla.) H.S. Elk City Pub. Schs., 1975-78; supr. banking ops. Alaska Statebank, Anchorage, 1978-82; tchg. asst. to piano prof. Golden Gate Bapt. Theol. Sem., Mill Valley, Calif., 1982-83, mem. adj. faculty, 1984-85, mem. music adv. coun., 1998-01; touring accompanist, ednl. tutor Tucson Ariz. Boys Chorus, 1985; choral dir., program founder fine arts dept. Buckingham Charter Sch., Vacaville, Calif., 1994-2001; rec. artist, 2002. State music cons. Calif. Bapt. Conv., Fresno, 1984-01; music dir., artistic dir. Solano Childrens Chorus, Fairfield, Calif., 1993-94; music dir. Playground Prodns. Theatre, Vacaville, 1994-96; music conf. clinician Nev. Bapt. Conv., Reno and Las Vegas, 1995, 96; con. pianist N.Am. Mission Bd., So. Bapt. Conv., Santa Clara, Calif., 1995; accompanist Anchorage Civic Opera, 1979-81, So. Ariz. Light Opera Co., 1985; minister of music Internat. Bapt. Ch., 1999-2000, Garland Rd. Bapt. Ch., Enid, Okla., 2001-. Contbr. poetry to anthologies, 4 original songs to CD You're Not Alone, 2003. Pres. Decent Lit. Coun., Ponca City, Okla., 1977-78; campaign office helper Dem. Party of Okla., Oklahoma City, 1968; music dir. nursing home; beauty pageant coach, cons. Miss Am. Pageant Scholarships, Okla. and Calif., 1969—. Scholar Calif. Singing Churchwomen and Calif. Bapt. Conv., 1983. Mem. Nat. Guild Piano Tchrs., Music Ednl. Nat. Conf., Music Tchr. Assn. of Calif. (past treas. 1987-89), Calif. Profl. Music Tchrs. Assn. (program chair 1996), Tau Beta Sigma (life mem., treas., v.p., pres. 1965-69, Outstanding Mem. 1965). Democrat. Southern Baptist. Avocations: writing, composing, traveling, reading. Home and Office: 3012 Bluebird Ln Enid OK 73703-1555

RUSSELL, S. G., III, (JACKY RUSSELL), principal; b. Merkel, Tex., May 16, 1939; m. S.G. and Anna May (Harris) Russell; m. Marty Bunch, July 22, 1961; children: Shelly Gwynn, Chrystal Ann. BS, North Tex. State U., 1961, MEd, 1965. Cert. sch. adminstrn., Tex. Tchr. math., coach Lake Highland Jr./Sr. High Sch., Richardson, Tex., 1961-76; asst. prin. Richardson High Sch., 1976-80; prin. Westwood Jr. High Sch., Richardson, 1980—. Coord. Crime Watch, Richardson, 1990-93. Mem. Richardson assn. Sch. Prins. (pres. 1982-83), Nat. Assn. Secondary Sch. Prins., Tex. Assn. Secondary Sch. Prins., Dallas County Assn. of Sch. Adminstrs., North Tex. Sch. Masters Assn., Tex. Exchange Clubs (pres. 1986-87), Phi Delta Kappa (pres. 1987-88). Methodist. Avocations: racquetball, snow skiing, water skiing, track official. Office: Westwood Jr High Sch 7630 Arapaho Rd Dallas TX 75248-4498

RUSSELL, SHANNON FERGUSON DARLING, special education educator; b. Spokane, Wash., Feb. 25, 1968; d. Carl Frederick Jr. and Roberta Ernestine (Phelps) Ferguson; m. Timothy Russell, Aug. 1999. BA in Elem. and Spl. Edn., La. State U., Shreveport, 1991. Cert. tchr., spl. edn. tchr., La., respite caregiver for handicapped foster children. Tchr. autistic spl. edn. Meadowview Elem. Sch., Bossier City, La., 1991—. Spl. edn. com. to develop spl. edn. alternative program curriculum Bossier Parish, 1994-95, spl. edn. adv. coun., 1994-97, sec., 1994-97, coun. exceptional children, 1988-95. Vol. Com. for Spl. Arts Festival and Sports Day, 1993-94; vol. tutor Bossier Parish, 1992—; asst. dir. Camp Rainman: Autistic Camp, 1994-99; vol. Alternat. Family Care Foster Svcs., 1985—, Caddo-Bossier Assn. Retarded Citizens, 1980-85; active Meadowview PTA, 1991—. Recipient Spl. Edn. Tchr. of Yr., Bossier Parish, 1994, PTA Educator of Distinction award, 1998; grantee Optimist Club, summer 1992, 93, 95, Isle of Capri Casino, summer 1994, 96, Nightmares: Charity Fundraising Com., fall 1995, Horseshoe Casino, summer 1996, Quota Club, winter 1996, PTA Educator of Distinction award, 1998, Bossier Dist. PTA, 1998, State PTA, 1998; named Meadowview Elem. Tchr. of Yr., 2000. Mem. Autism Soc. Am. (rep. to bd. dirs. mtgs. 1994-2000, mem. La. State Autism chpt. 1994—, sec. 1997-2000, mem. N.W. La. Autism chpt. 1994—, sec. 1994-96, pres. 1996-2000). Methodist. Office: Meadowview Elem Sch 4315 Shed Rd Bossier City LA 71111-5299 Home: 2516 Douglas Dr Bossier City LA 71111-3450

RUSSELL, SUSAN WEBB, elementary and middle school education educator; b. Richmond, Va., Feb. 18, 1948; d. William Camper and Isabel McLeod (Smith) Webb; m. Russell Christian Proctor, III, Dec. 30, 1972 (div. 1981); 1 child, Alexander Christian Proctor; m. Walter William Russell, III, July 16, 1988; stepchildren: Walter William IV, Brian Earl. AB in English, Fine Arts, and Edn., Randolph-Macon Woman's Coll., 1970. Cert. tchr., Va. Customer svc. rep. Xerox Corp., Richmond, 1970-72; tchr. English grades 7, 8, 9 Am. Internat. Sch., Lagos, Nigeria, West Africa, 1973-75; group travel counselor Dynasty World Travel, Richmond, 1980-81; sec. to dir. athletics and receptionist The Collegiate Schs., Richmond, 1982-84, tchr. English and reading grades 6, 7, 9, 1984-88, tchr. word processing grade 5, 1984-86; tchr. social studies Norfolk (Va.) Acad., 1988-91, tchr. English and reading, 1991—. Forensics coach Norfolk Acad., 1991—, 6th grad. chmn. 1995—. Editor Bulldog News, 1988-90; advisor Bullpup News, 1990-95. Mem. Norfolk Reading Coun., Va. Beach Reading Coun. Methodist. Avocations: travel, collecting art, theatre, music, movies. Office: Norfolk Acad 1585 Wesleyan Dr Norfolk VA 23502-5591

RUSSELL, WILLIAM JOSEPH, educational association administrator; b. Boston, Sept. 23, 1941; s. Stanley Whiteside and Helen Rita R.; m. Frances Marie Chapdelaine, June 25, 1967; 1 son, Scott David. BS, Boston Coll., 1963; M.Ed., Northeastern U., 1966; PhD, U. Calif., Berkeley, 1971. Head math. dept. Oceana, Pacifica, Calif., 1966-71; asst. for fed. and profl. affairs Am. Ednl. Research Assn., Washington, 1971-73, dep. exec. dir., 1973-74, exec. dir., 1974—2002. Adv. bd. Edn. Resource Info. Center Ednl. Testing Center, Princeton, N.J., 1975-87; exec. officer Nat. Council on Measurement in Edn., Internat. Assn. Computing in Edn., 1987-89. Editor: Ednl. Researcher, 1979-90. Mem. Am. Ednl. Research Assn., Phi Delta Kappa. Roman Catholic. Home: 1443 Creekside Ct Vienna VA 22182-1701 Office: AERA 1230 17th St NW Washington DC 20036-3078

RUSSELL-RADER, KATHLEEN, secondary school educator; b. Dayton, Ohio, Jan. 23, 1954; d. Reid Jerome and Margie (Miller) Russell; m. Donald Mark Rader, July 9, 1977. BS, Bowling Green (Ohio) State U., 1975; MS, U. Dayton, 1987. Cert. tchr., Ohio. English tchr. Fairborn (Ohio) City Schs., 1976—, Sinclair C. C., Dayton, 1991—. Dir., choreographer Fairborn High Sch. Flyerette Dance Corps, 1976-81; adv. Nat. Jr. Honor Soc., Fairborn, 1985—, student leadership, 1990—, mem. acad. coun., 1988—; adv./dir. Drama Club, Fairborn, 1991—; coach Power of the Pen Writing Team, Fairborn, 1987—. Recipient Golden Apple Tchr. Achiever award Ashland Oil Corp., 1996, Howard L Post Excellence in ed. award, 1997-2001, Disney State teacher Nominee, 1995; named Tchr. of Yr. Fairborn City Schs., 1989-90, Tchr. Honor Roll, Ohio Interscholastic Writing League, Cleve., 1990; Vera Schneider Teaching grantee Fairborn City Schs., 1988-92. Mem. Nat. Coun. Tchrs. English (judge Promising Young Writers Program 1991-97), Western Ohio Coun. Tchrs. English, Ohio Coun. Tchrs. English, Ohio Coun. English and Lang. Arts (judge writing contest 1989-97), Dayton Area Coun. Internat. Reading Assn. (pres. 1991-92), Ohio Coun. Internat. Reading Assn., Internat. Reading Assn., Nat. Assn. Student Activity Advisers, Phi Delta Kappa. Republican. Roman Catholic. Avocations: dancing, travel. Home: 1701 Provincetown Rd Centerville OH 45459-3452 Office: Fairborn City Schs 200 Lincoln Dr Fairborn OH 45324-5349

RUSSELL-WOOD, ANTHONY JOHN R. history educator; b. Corbridge-on-Tyne, Northumberland, Eng., Oct. 11, 1939; came to U.S., 1971; s. James and Ethel Kate (Roberts) R.-W.; m. Hannelore Elisabeth Schmidt, May 19, 1972; children: Christopher James Owen, Karsten Anthony Alexander. Diploma in Portuguese studies, Lisbon U., Portugal, 1960; BA with honors, Oxford (Eng.) U., 1963, MA, DPhil., 1967. Lectr. Portuguese lang. and lit. Oxford U., 1963-64; rsch. fellow St. Antony's Coll., Oxford, 1967-70; vis. assoc. prof. Johns Hopkins U., Balt., 1971-72, assoc. prof., 1972-76, prof., 1976—, chmn. dept. history, 1984-90, 96-99, chmn. dept. Hispanic and Italian studies, 1996-97, Herbert Baxter Adams prof., 2001—. Disting. vis. prof. U. Mass.-Dartmouth, 2000; vis. prof. Portuguese and Brazilian studies and history Brown U., 2001. Author: Manuel Francisco Lisboa: A Craftsman of the Golden Age of Brazil, 1968, Fidalgos and Philanthropists: The Santa Casa da Misericordia of Bahia, 1550-1755, 1968, The Black Man in Slavery and Freedom in Colonial Brazil, 1982, Society and Government in Colonial Brazil, 1500-1822, 1992, A World on the Move: The Portuguese in Africa, Asia and America 1415-1808, 1992, Portugal and the Sea: A World Embraced, 1997, The Portuguese Empire, 1415-1808, 1998; Slavery and Freedom in Colonial Brazil, 2002; co-author: From Colony to Nation: Essays on the Independence of Brazil, 1975; editor: Local Government in European Overseas Empires, 1450-1800, 1999, Government and Governance of Empires, 1415-1800, 2000; sr. editor: The Americas, 2002—; gen. editor: An Expanding World: The European Impact on World History, 1450-1800, 1995-2000; mem. editl. bd. L.Am. Studies, Tsukuba, Japan, 1989—. Chmn. CLAH Columbus Quincentennial Com., 1987-90, Md. State Humanities Coun., 1980-82; mem. Md. Heritage Com., 1982-85, Balt. County Commn. Arts and Scis., 1982-84. Decorated comendador Order of Prince Henry (Portugal), Order of Rio Branco (Brazil); recipient Bolton Meml. prize Conf. Latin Am. Hist., 1969, Whitaker prize Middle-Atlantic Coun. Latin Am. Studies, 1983, Dom João de Castro prize Portuguese Nat. Commn. for Commemoration of Discoveries, 1993, Benemérito, Santa Casa da Misericordia, Bahia, 1999, comdr. Internat. Order of Merit of Misericórdias, 2000. Fellow: European Acad. Scis. & Arts, Royal Hist. Soc., Academia de Letras da Bahia (corr.), Instituto Geografico e Historico da Bahia (corr.), Royal Geog. Soc. (life), Instituto Historico e Geografico Brasileiro (corr.); mem.: Conf. on Latin Am. History, Forum on European Expansion and Global Interaction. Avocations: hiking, cycling. Home: 113 Belmore Rd Lutherville Timonium MD 21093-6111 Office: Johns Hopkins Univ Dept Of History Baltimore MD 21218

RUSSETT, BRUCE MARTIN, political science educator; b. North Adams, Mass., Jan. 26, 1935; s. Raymond Edgar and Ruth Marian (Martin) R.; m. Cynthia Margaret Eagle, June 18, 1960; children: Margaret Ellen, Mark David, Lucia Elizabeth, Daniel Alden. BA magna cum laude, Williams Coll., 1956; diploma in econs., Cambridge (Eng.) U., 1957; MA, Yale U., 1958, PhD, 1961, Uppsala U., 2002. Instr. MIT, Cambridge, 1961-62; asst. prof., then assoc. prof. Yale U., New Haven, 1961-68, prof., 1968—, Dean Acheson prof. internat. rels. and polit. sci., 1985—, chair dept. polit. sci., 1990-96, dir. UN studies, 1993—. Vis. prof. Columbia U., 1965, U. Mich., 1965-66, U. Libre Brussels, 1969-70, U. N.C., 1979-80, Richardson Inst., London, 1973-74, Netherlands Inst. Advanced Study, 1984, Tel Aviv U., 1989, U. Tokyo, 1996, Harvard U., 2001; prin. cons. pastoral letter on peace Nat. Conf. Cath. Bishops, Washington, 1981-83; co-dir., secretariat ind. working group Future of the UN, 1993-96. Author: World Handbook of Political and Social Indicators, 1964, What Price Vigilance?, 1970 (Kammerer award Am. Polit. Sci. Assn. 1971), Interest and Ideology (with E. Hanson), 1975, Controlling the Sword, 1990, Grasping the Democratic Peace, 1993, The Once and Future Security Council, 1997, (with John Oneal) Triangulating Peace, 2001, others; editor: Jour. Conflict Resolution, 1972—; contbr. articles to profl. jours. Grantee NSF, 1964, 65, 69, 77, 79, 85, 88, 89, 90, 95, 98, Ford Found., 1993, 94, 97, John and Catherine MacArthur Found., 1988, 91; Fulbright-Hays fellow, Belgium and Israel, 1969, 89; John Simon Guggenheim Found. fellow, 1969, 77; German Marshall Fund fellow, 1977. Fellow Am. Acad. Arts and Scis.; mem. AAUP, Am. Polit. Sci. Assn. (coun. 1984-86), Internat. Studies Assn. (pres. 1983-84), Peace Sci. Soc. Internat. (pres. 1977-79). Avocations: tennis, classical music, hiking. Home: 70 Martin Ter Hamden CT 06517-2333 Office: Yale U Dept Polit Sci PO Box 208301 New Haven CT 06520-8301 E-mail: bruce.russett@yale.edu.

RUSSI, JOHN JOSEPH, priest, educational administrator; b. San Francisco, Oct. 27, 1939; s. Frank John and Catherine Mary (Carroll) R. BA, Chaminade U., 1962; STL, U. Fribourg, Switzerland, 1967; MA, U. San Francisco, 1978; PhD, Kennedy We. U., 1993. Cert. secondary tchr., jr. coll. tchr., marriage, family, child counselor, Calif. Tchr. St. Louis Sch., Honolulu, 1961-62, pres., 1988—; tchr. Riordan High Sch., San Francisco, 1962-63; tchr., counselor, prin., pres. Archbishop Mitty High Sch., San Jose, Calif., 1967-88; pres. St. Louis Sch., 1988-97. Regent Archbishop Mitty High Sch., 1990-97, Chaminade U., Honolulu, 1988—; bd. dirs. St. Anthony Sch., Wailuku, Hawaii, 1989-97. Pres. Provincial of the Marianists Province of the Pacific, 1997—; chmn. region 6 Conf. Major Superior Men; chancellor chaminade U. Hawaii, 2000—. Mem. Elks Club, Pacific Club. Democrat. Roman Catholic. Office: Box 1775 Cupertino CA 95015-1775

RUSSO, ANGELA BROWN, assistant principal; b. Balt., Apr. 21, 1948; d. Johnny Jeff and Lavonia Vernette (Davis) Royster; m. James Elton Brown, Oct. 5, 1975 (div. Aug. 1993); 1 child, Tiffany Lavonne; m. John Russo, Nov. 26, 1993. BS in Health Edn., Morgan State U., Balt., 1971; MS in Adult Edn., Kans. State U., 1977; postgrad., Charles County C.C., LaPlata, Md., 1983. Tchr. Harlem Park Jr. H.S., Balt., 1972-73, St. Maur's Internat.

Sch., Yokohama, Japan, 1973-74, Herring Run Jr. H.S., Balt., 1974-75; Homebound tchr. Geary County Unified Schs., Junction City, Kans., 1975-77; counselor/head counseling dept. Dededo (Guam) Jr. H.S., 1977-79; tchr. Walker Mill Jr. H.S., Capitol Heights, Md., 1979-82; asst. dir./instr. pre-employment tng. program Charles County C.C., LaPlata, 1982-84; ednl. dir., counselor Odyssey Alternative Sch. Utah State Employment, Salt Lake City/Clearfield, 1984-85; tchr. North Davis Jr. H.S., Ogden, Utah, 1985-87; prin. Island Paradise Sch., Honolulu, 1989-90; asst. prin. C.W. Woodbury Mid. Sch., Las Vegas, 1994—. Tchr. Mahlon Brown Jr. H.S., Las Vegas, Nev., 1990-91; adminstrv. dean Green Valley H.S., Las Vegas, 1992-93, asst. prin., 1994—; asst. prin. Becker Mid. Sch., Las Vegas, 1993-94; part-time coord./counselor Sinajaha (Guam) Adult Basic Edn. Program, 1978. Foster parent; vol. Juvenile Ct. Recipient Pub. Svc. Commendation, U.S. Dept. Commerce. Mem. AAUW, ASCD, Phi Delta Gamma, Alpha Kappa Alpha, Phi Delta Kappa. Avocations: travel, community choir. Office: CW Woodbury Mid Sch 6500 E Sahara Ave Las Vegas NV 89142-2800 Address: 3105 La Entrada St Henderson NV 89014-3606 Home: 7502 Milligan Ln Clinton MD 20735-3018

RUSSO, GILBERTO, engineering educator; b. Rome, Aug. 23, 1954; s. Guido and Maria (Mazzoni) R. Laurea, Poly. Inst. Turin, Italy, 1975; ScD, MIT, 1980; MD, U. Chgo. Pritaker Sch. of Medicine. Pres. Studio Russo, Inc. Engring. Cons., Turin, 1970; asst. prof. Poly. Inst. Turin, 1975-80; lectr. MIT, Cambridge, Mass., 1985-91; dr. dept. plastic and reconstructive surgery U. Chgo., 1992-95; mem. dept. surgery U. Calif., San Francisco, 1995—. Mem. designer selection bd. State of Mass., Boston, 1989. Contbr. articles to profl. publs., chpts. to books. Pres. Dante Alisheri Soc., Cambridge, 1986-88; treas. MIT/Poly. Alumni Assn., Turin, 1970. Fulbright fellow, 1978. Fellow Nat. Coun. Engring. Examiners; mem. Mass. Soc. Profl. Engrs. (v.p. 1991—), Tau Beta Pi (chpt. advisor 1985, Eminent Engr. 1985). Achievements include patents in solar energy collectors, development of computer aided therodynamics, computer methods for engineering, optimization of non-steady-state systems, compressible fluid flow with heat transfer, thermal dynamics models, diagnostics and surgical repair of electric/burn injuries. Address: Dept Surgery LIJ Med Ctr New Hyde Park NY 11004 Office: U Chgo Dept Plastic-Reconstrv Surg Chicago IL 60637 also: U Calif Dept Surgery Rm S-343 Box 0470 513 Parnassus Ave San Francisco CA 94122-2722

RUSSO, JOAN MILDRED, special education educator; b. New Haven, Aug. 23, 1933; d. Stanley Alfred and Mildred Mary (Burns) Marcotte; div.; children: David C., Thomas E., Mary Russo Herrmann, Elizabeth Russo Sant, Robert J., James E. Goeth. AA, Coll. DuPage, 1975; BS in Edn., No. Ill. U., 1977; MEd, Lewis U., Evanston, Ill., 1985. Cert. K-12 educable mentally handicapped, K-12 learning disabilities, K-12 Trainable mentally handicapped, K-9 elem tchg., Ill. Tchrs. aid Pioneer Sch., West Chgo., 1977-78; pvt. practice Wheaton, Ill., 1978—. Co-editor: Yes, You Can, 1994. Active Dem. political campaigns, Ill., 1960—; sec. Winfield Libr. Assn., 1963-68; bd. dirs. Orton Dyslexia Soc., Ill., 1980-81, sec., 1981-82. Mem. LWV (con-con com., 1972), Orton Dyslexia Soc. (bd. dirs. 1980-81, sec. 1981-82), Nat. Assn. Learning Disabilities, Nat. Ctr. Learning Disabilities. Avocations: music, theater, reading, art, travel. Home and Office: 10 Old Blue Point Rd Scarborough ME 04074-7600

RUSSO, PEGGY ANNE, English language educator; b. Sturgis, Mich., Sept. 7, 1940; d. Dale Miller and Virginia (Rifenburg) B.; m. Jerry Russo (dec.); children: Daniel Carleton, Christopher Sanford. AA with honors, Jackson C.C., 1967; BA in English Lang. and Lit., U. Mich., 1972, MA in English Lang. and Lit., 1979, PhD in English Lang. and Lit., 1988. Teaching asst. English dept. U. Mich., Ann Arbor, 1979-83; lectr. Pa. State U., University Park, 1985-88, asst. prof. English Mont Alto, 1988—. Part-time instr. Jackson (Mich.) C.C., 1979; adj. instr. Wayne C.C., Detroit, 1979-83; adj. lectr. U. Mich., 1984-85; participant workshops in field; presenter in field. Sr. editor: The Adelphi Theater Calendar, Part II, 1993; asst. editor RaJah, 1981-83; contbr. articles to profl. jours. Recipient Avery Hopwood award in drama U. Mich., 1979; Roy W. Cowden Meml. fellow U. Mich., 1983, Rackham Thesis grantee, 1982, Dorothy Guies McGuigan scholar, 1983; Cranbrook Writers Conf. scholar Cranbrook Acad., 1979, 80. Mem. MLA, Am. Soc. Theatre Rsch., Internat. Fedn. Theatre Rsch., Pa. Coll. English Assn., Shakespeare Assn. Am. Office: Pa State U Dept English Mont Alto PA 17237 E-mail: u7k@psu.edu.

RUSSO, THOMAS ANTHONY, lawyer; b. N.Y.C., Nov. 6, 1943; s. Lucio F. and Tina (Iarossi) R.: m. Nancy Felipe, June 18, 1966 (div. 1974); m. Janice Davis, June 10, 1977 (div. 1979); m. Marcy C. Appelbaum, June 16, 1985; children: Morgan Danielle and Alexa Anne (twins), Tyler James. BA, Fordham U., 1965; MBA, JD, Cornell U., 1969. Bar: N.Y., 1970, U.S. Ct. Appeals (2d cir.) 1971, U.S. Dist. Ct. (so. and ea. dists.) N.Y. 1971, U.S. Ct. Appeals (7th cir.) 1982. Staff atty. SEC, Washington, 1969-71; assoc. Cadwalader, Wickersham & Taft, N.Y.C., 1971-75; dir. divsn. trading and markets Commodity Futures Trading Commn., Washington, 1975—77; ptnr., mem. mgmt. com. Cadwalader, Wickersham & Taft, N.Y.C., 1977-92; vice chmn., chief legal officer, mng. dir. Lehman Bros., N.Y.C., 1993—. Vice chmn. bd. trustees, mem. exec. com. Inst. for Fin. Markets; bd. dirs. Rev. Securities and Commodities Regulation, N.Y.C.; trustee, chmn. exec. com., chmn. devel. com. Inst. Internat. Edn.; trustee NYU Downtown Hosp.; mem. adv. com. SEC Hist. Soc.; mem. nat. bd. trustees, exec. com. and nominating com., chmn. pension investments com., vice chmn. fin. and audit com. March of Dimes; mem. monitoring com. The Group of Thirty; mem. U.S. Coun. for Internat. Bus. Author: Regulation of the Commodities Futures and Options Markets; co-author: Regulation of Brokers, Dealers and Securities Markets, Supplement Markets; editorial bd. mem. Internat. Jour. Regulatory Law and Practice; practitioner bd. advisors Stanford Jour. of Law.; mem. editl. bd. Futures and Derivatives Law Report. Mem. ABA (mem. subcom. on exec. coun., fed. regulation of securities, derivative instruments subcom., regulation of futures and derivative instruments), Assn. of Bar of City of N.Y. (chmn. internat. law sub com. of the com. on commodities regulation 1984-85, chmn. com. commodities regulations 1981-82), D.C. Bar Assn., Fgn. Policy Assn., Econ. Club N.Y. Office: Lehman Bros Inc 745 7th Ave 31st Fl New York NY 10019-6801 E-mail: trusso1@lehman.com.

RUSSO, VINCENT BARNEY, music educator; b. Carmel, Calif., Oct. 19, 1944; s. Salvatore Dody and Betty Lou (Posey) R. BA, San Francisco State U., 1967, MA, 1969; lic. de concert, Ecole Normale de Musique, Paris, 1973; PhD, U. Calif., San Diego, 1978. Assoc. in voice U.S. Internat. U., San Diego, 1976-83; assoc. in music Internat. U., London, 1979-80; adj. prof. Tex. Christian U., Ft. Worth, 1986-88, asst. prof. vocal performance pedagogy, 1988-95; faculty Coll of the Redwoods, Mendocino, Calif., 1996—. Apprentice artist Santa Fe Opera Co., 1971; tching. asst., rsch. asst. U. Calif., San Diego, 1974-78; baritone San Diego Opera Co., 1976-82; asst. editor, editor Jour. Rsch. in Singing, Ft. Worth, 1978-95; music coach, dir. Inst. Vocal Studies, Ft. Worth, 1981-88. Baritone soloist French Radio TV, 1971; performer The Merry Widow, PBS, 1977; editor: Jour. Rsch. in Singing and Applied Vocal Pedagog, 1987-95; vocal dir. Gloriana Opera Co., 1995—, Opera Fresca, 1996—; appeared at Mendocino Music Festival, 1996, 97, 98, 99, 2000, 01, 02, 03. Recipient Alexander Saunderson award Met. Opera San Francisco, 1969, Young Artist award Nat. Fedn. Music Clubs, 1969, 77, Harriet H. Wooley and Frank Huntington Beebe award, 1972, 73, William M. Sullivan Music Found. award for European audition, 1974. Mem. Internat. Assn. Rsch. in Singing (gen. sec. 1987-95), Nat. Assn. Tchrs. Singing (Singing Artist award 1971), Coll. Music Soc. Avocations: bicycling, hiking, movies, theater.

RUSSO-RUMORE, NANCY, retired secondary education educator; b. N.Y.C., July 6, 1948; d. Matteo and Rose A. Russo; m. Victor M. Rumore, Sept. 15, 1938. BA, Queens Coll., 1969; MS in Edn., St. John's U., Hillcrest, N.Y., 1974; postgrad., L.I. U., Greenvale, N.Y., 1966. Cert. tchr. Spanish 7-12, N.Y. Spanish tchr. South H.S., Valley Stream, NY, 1969—2003, dept. head, L.O.T.E. dept., 1991—2003; adj. prof. dept. European lang., coord. student tchg. SUNY, Stony Brook, 2003—. Mem. ASCD, L.I. Lang. Tchrs. (2nd v.p. 2001-02, 1st v.p. 2002-), N.Y. State Assn. Lang. Tchrs., Fgn. Lang. Assn. Chairpersons and Suprs., Phi Delta Kappa. Avocations: travel, boating, hand crafts, collecting depression glass.

RUST, FRANCES O'CONNELL, education educator, department chairman; b. Laguna Beach, Calif., Oct. 10, 1944; d. Walter Francis and Pauline Peyton (Forney) O'Connell; m. Langbourne Williams Rust, June 4, 1966; children: Edgar Forney Rust, Susanne Lancaster Rust. BA in English Lit., Manhattanville Coll., 1966, MA in Teaching, 1970; MEd, Columbia U., 1982, EdD, 1984. Asst. tchr. Bede Sch., Englewood, N.J., 1966-67; tchr., trainer, supr. Am. Montessori Soc., Fairleigh Dickinson U., Tenafly, N.J., 1967-68; tchr. Acorn Sch., N.Y.C., 1967-68; lectr. in edn. Briarcliff Coll., Briarcliff, N.Y., 1968-70; founder, dir., head tchr. Hudson Community Sch., Briarcliff, 1970-71; dir., head tchr. Woodland Sch., Chappaqua, N.Y., 1975-81; assoc. dir., asst. prof. preservice program Tchr.'s Coll. Columbia U., N.Y.C., 1983-85; assoc. prof., dir. dept. edn. Manhattanville Coll., Purchase, N.Y., 1985-89; assoc. prof., chair dept. of curriculum and teaching Hofstra U., Hempstead, N.Y., 1989-91; assoc. prof., dir. undergrad. early childhood/elem. edn. NYU, 1991—. Mem. editl. bd. Ency. of Early Childhood, 1988-92; mem. adv. bd. Great Potential Westchester, Purchase, 1989; cons. on early childhood Metro Ctr. of NYU, N.Y.C., 1986—. New Rochelle (N.Y.) Pub. Schs., 1989-90; bd. dirs. N.Y. Assn. Coll. of Tchr. Edn., Nat. Assn. Early Childhood Tchr. Educators. Author: Changing Teaching; Changing Schools: Bringing Early Childhood into Public Education, 1993; editor: Care & Education of Young Children, 1989. Chair Region 2 Resource Team of Episcopal Diocese of N.Y., Westchester County, 1980-88; bd. dirs. alumni coun. Columbia U. Tchr.'s Coll., N.Y.C., 1987-97; pres., 1994-97; bd. dirs. Westchester County Jr. Achievement, 1988-89. Mem. Am. Ednl. Rsch. Assn. (pres. instrnl. supervision Spl. Interest Group 1995—, Nat. Soc. for Study of Edn., Assn. for Supervision and Curriculum Devel., Nat. Assn. for Edn. of Young Children, Soc. for Rsch. in Child Devel. Democrat. Episcopalian. Avocations: sailing, running. Home: 96 Round Hill Dr Briarcliff Manor NY 10510-1929 Office: NYU Dept of Teaching and Learning 239 Greene St New York NY 10003-6674

RUSTCHENKO, ELENA, geneticist, educator; b. Kharkiv, Ukraine; came to U.S., 1985; d. Petro and Larysa (Tytarenko) R.; m. Aurel Bulgac, Sept. 23, 1977 (div. 1993); m. Fred Sherman, May 5, 2001. MS, Kharkiv State U., 1971; PhD, Leningrad (USSR) State U., 1975. Asst. rsch. scientist Inst. of Endocrinology and Hormone Chemistry, Kharkiv, 1976-78; staff mem. Inst. Biol. Scis., Bucharest, Romania, 1979-85; rsch. assoc. Scripps Clinic and Rsch. Found., La Jolla, Calif., 1986-87, U. Rochester, N.Y., 1987-89, scientist, 1989-95, rsch. asst. prof. genetics, 1995-97, rsch. assoc. prof., 1997—. Contbr. articles to profl. jours. Brit. Council grantee, 1982. Mem. Ukrainian Autocephalous Orthodox Ch. Achievements include discovery of chromosomal rearrangements in a pathogen Candida albicans, which coltrol vital physiological functions, for example, utilization of different nutrilites or resistance to antibiotics; established a new principle of gene regulation by reduction of chromosomal copy number; discovered rDNA plasmids in Candida. Home: 69 Westminster Rd Rochester NY 14607-2223 Office: Univ of Rochester Dept of Biochemistry PO Box 712 Rochester NY 14642-0001 E-mail: elena_bulgac@urmc.rochester.edu.

RUSTGI, ANIL K (UMAR), gastroenterologist, educator; b. New Haven, Jan. 31, 1959; s. Moti Lal and Kamla (Rohatgi) R.; m. Poonam Sehgal Rustgi, July 27, 1991. BS summa cum laude, Yale U., 1980; MD, Duke U., 1984. Diplomate Am. Bd. Internal Medicine, Am. Bd. Gastroenterology. Intern Beth Israel Hosp., Sch. Medicine Harvard U., Boston, 1984-85, resident, 1985-87; fellow in gestroenterology Mass. Gen. Hosp., Sch. Medicine Harvard U., Boston, 1987-90, instr. medicine, 1990-92, asst. prof. medicine, 1992-98, assoc. prof. medicine, 1998, physician, scientist, 1987—; chief of gastroenterology U. Pa., Phila., 1998—, T. Grier Miller assoc. prof. medicine and genetics, 1998—2002. Editl. bd. Gastroenterology, GI Cancer. Editor textbook: GI Cancers: Biology, Diagnosis and Therapy, 1995; contbr. numerous articles to sci. and profl. jours. Grantee NIH, 1990—, Am. Cancer Soc., 1988—. Mem. Am. Gastroenterol. Assn., Am. Assn. Study of Liver Diseases, Am. Assn. Cancer Rsch. Achievements include work related to molecular genetics of GI cancers. Office: U Pa GI Divsn 600 CRB 415 Curie Blvd Philadelphia PA 19104-4218

RUSTIFO, PHYLLIS MARIE WEHR, special education educator; b. Salem, Ohio, June 5, 1956; d. Glenn L. and Lille A. (Jackson) Wehr; m. Charles E. Rustifo, July 25, 1981 (dec. 1995); children: Kyle R., Anna M. BA in edn., Malone Coll., Canton, Ohio, 1978; cert. in moderate, severe, and profoundly retarded, Walsh Coll., North Canton, Ohio, 1979; M in early childhood edn. for handicapped., 1995, M in supervision, 2002. Instr. Stark County Ednl. Svc. Ctr., Canton, Ohio, 1978-88; tchr. Stark County Bd. Edn., Canton, 1988—. V.p. Stark County Educators Assn. for Retarded Citizens, Canton, 1980-85. Recipient Profl. of Yr., Assn. for Retarded Citizens, 2003. Avocations: quilts, herbs, antiques. Home: 8036 Kent Ave NE Canton OH 44721-1324

RUTFORD, ROBERT HOXIE, geologist, educator; b. Duluth, Minn., Jan. 26, 1933; s. Skuli and Ruth (Hoxie) R.; m. Marjorie Ann, June 19, 1954; children: Gregory, Kristian, Barbara. BA, U. Minn., 1954, MA, 1963, PhD, 1969; DSc (hon.), St Petersburg State Tech U., Russia, 1994. Football and track coach Hamline U., 1958-62; rsch. fellow U. Minn., 1963-66; asst. prof. geology U. S.D., 1967-70, assoc. prof., 1970-72, chmn. dept. geology, 1968-72, chmn. dept. physics, 1971-72; dir. Ross Ice Shelf Project U. Nebr., Lincoln, 1972-75; dir. divsn. Polar Programs NSF, Washington, 1975-77; vice chancellor for research and grad. studies, prof. geology U. Nebr., 1977-82, interim chancellor, 1980-81; pres., prof. geoscis. U. Tex., Dallas, 1982-94, Excellence in Edn. Found. prof. of geoscis., 1994—. U.S. del. to Sci. Com. on Antarctic Rsch., 1986-2002, v.p., 1996-98, pres., 1998-2002, mem. exec. com., 2002--; chmn. NRC Polar Rsch. Bd., 1991-95. Mem. editl. bd. Issues in Sci. and Tech., 1991-94. Trustee Baylor Coll. Dentistry, 1989—96. 1st lt. U.S. Army, 1954-56. Recipient Antarctic Svc. medal, 1964, Disting. Svc. award NSF, 1977, Ernie Gunderson award for svc. to amateur athletics S.D. AAU, 1972, Outstanding Achievement award U. Minn., 1993, "M" Club Lifetime Achievement award, 1995. Fellow Geol. Soc. Am.; mem. Antarctican Soc. (pres. 1988-90), Arctic Inst. N.Am., Explorers Club, Am. Polar Soc. (hon.), Philos. Soc. Tex., St. Petersburg Acad. Engring. (Russia), Tex. Acad. Sci., Nebr. Acad. Scis., Cosmos Club, Sigma Xi. Lutheran. Home: 1882 Quail Ln Richardson TX 75080-3456 Office: Univ Tex Dallas Geosciences Program Richardson TX 75083-0688

RUTH, BETTY MUSE, school system administrator; b. Florence, Ala., Oct. 24, 1943; d. Paul and Mary Lucille (Gresham) Muse; m. Thomas Gary Ruth, Dec. 17, 1965 (div. Sept. 1979); 1 child, Thomas Paul; m. Charles Larry Oliver, Jr., Mar. 10, 1990. BSBA, Athens State Coll., 1982; MBA, U. N.Ala., 1986. Sec., bookkeeper Anderson News Co., Florence, 1963-65; acct. receivable bookkeeper McConnell AFB, Wichita, Kans., 1967-68; legal sec. Reynolds Law Firm, Selmer, Tenn., 1973-74; subs. tchr. Athens (Ala.) City Schs., 1974-78, dir. RSVP, 1978—. Del. White House Conf. on Aging, 1995; mem. Nat. Coun. on Aging, 1985—. Active United Way, Athens, 1990-94; sec. Gov.'s Commn. Nat. and Comty. Svc., Ala, 1994, v.p., 1990—, pres. 1998-2000, chair., 1998—; vice chair Tenn. Valley Exhibit Commn., Ala., 1984-96; past pres. Athens-Limstone County Beautification Bd., 1991-94; People-to-People internat. del. to People's Republic of China, 1994; bd. dirs. Ala. Dept. Senior Svcs., 2003—. Named outstanding project dir. Action, Atlanta, 1985, outstanding woman of Ala., 1989. Mem. NEA, Ala. Edn. Assn., Nat. Assn. RSVP Dirs. (v.p., treas., del. 1985—, pres. 1999—, svc. award 1993), Region IV Assn. RSVP dirs. (pres., v.p., treas. 1979—, svc. ard 1989), So. States Assn., Ala. Assn. RSVP Dirs. (v.p., sec., treas. 1978—, Citizens award 1991), Athens State Coll. Alumni Assn. (bd. dirs. 1993—). Mem. Ch. of Christ. Avocations: reading, traveling, volunteerism. Home: 15705 Kings Dr Athens AL 35611-5667 Office: PO Box 852 Athens AL 35612-0852

RUTH, EDWARD B. supervisor; b. Lancaster, Pa., Aug. 23, 1943; s. Edward B. and Jeanne L. (Schaeffer) R.; m. Betsy A. Lorenz, Aug. 28, 1965; 1 child, Heather L. BS in Biology, Lebanon Valley Coll., Annville, Pa., 1965; MEd, Millersville (Pa.) U., 1970; cert. secondary prin., Temple U., 1990. Cert. secondary prin., secondary tchr. gen. sci., biology. Sci. tchr. Milton Hershey (Pa.) Sch., 1965-87, mid. sch. asst. prin., 1987-92, mid. sch. prin., 1992-99, coord. pre-svc. and in-svc. tng., 1999—2003, asst. athletic dir., 1983-87; master educator Whitaker Ctr. for Sci. and the Arts, Harrisburg, Pa., 2003—. Recreation supr. Milton Hershey Sch.; mgr. Palmyra Swimming Pool; evaluation team Pa. Assn. Pvt. Acad. Schs., 1991; planning com. Pa. Commonwealth Partnership, F&M Coll., Lancaster, Pa., 1987; biol. safety and recombinant DNA com. Hershey Med. Ctr., 1987—; union negotiations team Milton Hershey Sch., 1994, 2002; judge regional and state meetings Pa. Jr. Acad. Sci., Capital Area Sci. and Engring. Fairs, Pa. Coll. Energy Debates; bd. dirs. Pa. Staff Devel. Coun.; mem. Nat. Staff Devel. Coun. Author, editor: Energy Teaching Units Energy Concepts, 1982; tech. writer Harrisburg Energy Edn. Adv. Coun.; author: (flow chart) Summary: Modern Interpretation of the Central Dogma (Watson & Crick's DNA Model), 1983; reviewer pre-publ. articles, books, audio-visual materials Am. Biology Tchr. Mem. camping program com. Keystone Area Boy Scouts, Harrisburg, Pa., 1994; chmn. Derry Twp. Environ. Adv. Coun., Hershey, Pa., 1993-94. Mem. Nat. Assn. Biology Tchrs. (Outstanding Pa. Biology Tchr. 1984), Nat. Assn. Secondary Sch. Prins., Pa. Assn. Secondary Sch. Prins., Nat. Eagle Scout Assn., Lancaster County Conservancy. Avocation: walking. Home: 356 William Dr Hershey PA 17033-1859 Office: Milton Hershey Sch PO Box 830 Hershey PA 17033-0830 E-mail: eruthe@whitakercenter.org.

RUTH, SHIELA GRANT, music educator; b. Sagamiono, Japan, May 12, 1955; came to U.S., 1957; d. Allan Francis and Eiko (Nagasawa) Grant; m. Terrence Allan Ruth, Sept. 8, 1979. BA, Frostburg State Coll., 1977. Health care asst. Deaton Med. Ctr., Balt., summer 1974, 75, Nursing Staff, Annapolis, Md., 1977; sub. tchr. Anne Arundel County Schs., Md., 1977-78; tchr. piano/organ Jordan Kitts, Glen Burnie, Md., 1978-79; music asst. Lindale Jr. H.S., Ferndale, Md., 1986-90, Harundale Presbyn. Ch., Glen Burnie, 1990—; tchr. piano/organ Severn, Md., 1977—. Mem. Md. State Music Tchrs. Assn., Music Tchrs. Nat. Assn., Anne Arundel Music Tchrs. Assn. (corr. sec. 1997—), Delta Omicron (warden 1975-77), Sigma Delta Pi. Republican. Presbyterian. Avocations: playing piano, touring civil war battlefields, ice skating. Home: 753 Rosewood Rd Severn MD 21144-2069 Office: Harundale Presbyn Ch 1020 Eastway Glen Burnie MD 21060-7303

RUTHERFOORD, REBECCA HUDSON, computer science educator; b. Elkhart, Ind., Feb. 24, 1948; d. Charles Melvin Hudson and Eunice Klaire (Lund) Edmonds; m. James Kincanon Rutherfoord, Aug. 31, 1968; children: James Kincanon Jr., Charles Penn. BS, Ind. State U., 1971, MS, 1972, EdD, 1975; MS in Computer Sci., So. Poly State U., Marietta, Ga., 1995. Cert. data processor. Staff asst. Ind. State U., Terre Haute, 1969-71; vocal music tchr. S.W. Parke Schs., Rockville, Ind., 1971-73; fellowship asst. Ind. State U., Terre Haute, 1974-75; vocal music tchr. Slidell (La.) H.S., 1977-78; programmer, analyst La. State U., Baton Rouge, 1978-79, dir. computer rehab. program, 1979-80; programmer, analyst Hanes Corp., Atlanta, 1980-81; asst. prof. Devry Inst., Atlanta, 1981-83; acting dept. chair So. Poly. State U., Marietta, Ga., 1989-92, prof. computer sci., 1983—, computer sci. grad. program coord., 1996-97, asst. to pres., 1997-98, interim dean arts and scis., 1998-99, chair MSIT program, 1999—, acting head dept. computer sci., 2000-01, dept. chair, info. tech., 2001—. Cons. The Assocs. Group, Inc., Roswell, Ga., 1986-88, Crawford Comm., Atlanta, 1987; adj. prof. Cobb County Bd. Edn., Marietta, 1985-87, Joseph T. Walker Sch., Marietta, 1985-86; vis. prof. Leicester (U.K.) Poly., 1990. Choir dir. St. Peter and Paul Episcopal Ch., Marietta, 1981—85, choir mem., 1992—2001, bd. dirs., 1998—2001; Christian edn. dir. St. Francis Episcopal Ch., Denham Springs, La., 1978—80; choir mem. St. David's Episcopal Ch., Roswell, 1985—92; choir dir. Ch. of the Messiah, 2001—; bd. dirs., mem. Cherokee Cmty. Habitat for Humanity, 1994—98. Mem. Data Processing Mgmt. Assn., Assn. Computing Machinery, Nat. Assn. Women in Edn., Computer Sci. Edn. (spl. interest group), Nat. Assn. Women Edn., Delta Kappa Gamma, Sigma Alpha Iota. Republican. Avocations: boating, reading. Office: So Poly State Univ 1100 S Marietta Pky Marietta GA 30060-2855

RUTHERFORD, MARY JEAN, laboratory administrator, science educator; b. Webb City, Mo., Apr. 23, 1935; d. John Edward and Martha Rose (Hare) R. AA, Joplin Jr. Coll., 1955; BS, Northwestern U., 1957; MEd, Drury Coll., 1984. Cert. med. technologist, specialist in chemistry. Med. technologist Northwestern U., Chgo., 1957-60; lab. supr., instr. St. Louis U. Hosp.-Med. Tech., 1961-67; supr. in chemistry, instr. U. Ill. Rsch. and Edn. Hosp., Chgo., 1967-68; teaching supr. in chemistry L.E. Cox Med. Ctr. Sch. of Med. Tech., Springfield, Mo., 1968-86; asst. prof., mem. faculty Ark. State U., Jonesboro, 1986-90, program dir. clin. lab. scis., asst. prof., 1990-98, assoc. prof., 1998—, chmn. faculty senate, 1999-2000. Mem. adv. bd. Springhouse (Pa.) Pub., 1992—; mem. rev. com. Nat. Accrediting Agy. for Clin. Lab. Scis., Chgo., 1993-94, 95-2003. Author: Inorganic Chemistry-Applied Science Review, 1992. Pres. LWV, Jonesboro, 1991-92. Mem. Am. Soc. Clin. Lab. Scis., Ark. Soc. Clin. Lab. Scis. (editor 1997-99, bd. dirs. 1996-99, pres. 2001-03), Ark. Clin. Lab. Educator's Forum (chair 1993-94), Ark. Coalition of Lab. Profls. (treas. 1992—), Ark. State U. Faculty Assn. (pres. 1999-2000). Avocations: travel, photography, needlecrafts. Office: Ark State U PO Box 910 State University AR 72467-0910 E-mail: mjruth@astate.edu.

RUTHERFORD, VICKY LYNN, special education educator; b. Florence, S.C., Sept. 12, 1947; BS, Hampton U., 1969, MA, 1971; PhD, Mich. State U., 1991. Cert. tchr. French, spl. edn., reading specialist, Va., tchr. spl. edn., S.C. Social worker day care Hampton (Va.) Dept. Social Svc., 1970-72; reading therapist, asst. dir., dir. Bayberry Reading Clinic, Hampton, 1973-77; tchr. reading, English, counselor York County Schs., Yorktown, Va., 1977-85; staff advisor, asst. to course coord. Mich. State U., East Lansing, 1985-90; tchr. autism Florence (S.C.) Dist. 1 Sch. Sys., 1992-96, tchr. emotionally impaired, 1996—. Instrnl. designer: Addiction Severity Index #1, 1987, #2, 1988, Managing a Diverse Workforce, 1990; designer, trainer: Project Teach, 1991; designer, developer: (video) Camp Takona Summer Experience, 1992. Bass guitarist, Sun. sch. sec., youth worker, Sun. sch. supt. Progressive Ch. of Jesus, Florence, 1992-98, Greater Zion Tabernacle Apostolic Ch., Florence, 1998—. Fellow Mich. Dept. Edn., 1987-89. Mem. Internat. Reading Assn. Office: Delmae Heights Elem Sch 1211 S Cashua Dr Florence SC 29501-6399 E-mail: v_rutherford@fsdl.org.

RUTIGLIANO, ANTONIO, secondary school and college educator; b. Bari, Italy, Sept. 11, 1951; came to U.S., 1963; s. Giacomo and Anna (DeMarco) R.; m. Josephine DeCaro, June 27, 1981; children: Annabella, Mariangela, Bianca-Erminia. BA, Davis and Elkins Coll., Elkins, W.Va., 1974; MAT, Fordham U., 1976; MA, NYU, 1981, PhD, 1989. Asst. prof. W.Va. U., Morgantown, 1975-76; tchr. social studies Franklin D. Roosevelt H.S., Bklyn., 1976—. Adj. assoc. prof. NYU, N.Y.C., 1991—, advisor, 1994—, weekend program coord., 1992-98; adj. assoc. prof. Kingsborough/CUNY, Bklyn., 1992—. Author: In Search of a Saint: Chiara, 1995, Lorenzetti's Golden Mean, 1999; contbr. articles to profl. jours. W.Va. U. assistantship, 1974-75; Fordham U. fellow, 1975-76; NYU scholar,

1979-80. Mem. Am. Hist. Assn., Renaissance Soc. Am. Avocations: chess, soccer, book collecting, pergolesi and bach, searching for the noumenon. Office: New York University SCE 225 Shim Kin Hall New York NY 10012-1165

RUTLAND-AMAGLIANI, CAROL ELAINE, music director, educator; b. Memphis, Aug. 11, 1952; d. Charles Wesson and Evelyn (Matthew) Rutland; m. Malcolm Brown Futhey (div. Mar. 1986); children: Malcolm Brown III, Meredith Elaine; m. Michael Lewis Amagliani, July 1993; 1 child, Christopher Ian Amagliani. Cert. in theory teaching/piano pedagogy, St. Louis Inst. Music, 1970, 71; BS in Edn., Memphis State U., 1989. Cert. in theory and piano, Tenn. Pvt. tchr. piano, voice and keyboard, Memphis, 1970—; lower sch. music coord. Evangelical Christian Sch., Memphis, 1983—. Judge piano competitions, drama tchr. and choreographer; fgn. study culture and music and missions trip, Papua, New Guinea, 1990. Keyboard accompanist, voice tchr. various chs., Memphis; mem. King's Daughter Women's Fellowship. Mem. Tenn. Counseling Assn., Women's Fellowship, Kings Daus., Pi Mu Beta. Avocations: gardening, music groups.

RUTLEDGE, BARBARA JEAN, special education educator; b. Detroit, Nov. 6, 1946; d. Bertram Underwood and Emma Lou (Fluellen) Williams; m. Walter Rutledge, Sept. 14, 1968 (div. Feb. 1979); 1 child, Maurice LaMarr. BS in Edn., U. Detroit, 1978; MEd, Wayne State U., 1980, cert. in edn., 1991, ednl. specialist cert., 1993. Cert. tchr., Mich.; cert. in elem. adminstrn., mid. sch. adminstrn., Mich.; spl. edn. supr.'s approval, spl. edn. dir.'s approval, ctrl. office cert., Mich. Tchr. Detroit Pub. Schs., 1978-84; tchr. adult edn. Highland (Mich.) Park Pub. Schs., 1985; tchr. learning disabled Detroit Pub. Sch., 1986-89, tchr. spl. edn. resource rm., 1989—. Clin. tchr. Mich. Dept. Mental Health, Pontiac, 1984-86, program writer, supr., 1986-88; speaker and cons. in field. Contbr. articles to profl. jours. Del. Dem. Com., Oak Park, Mich., 1979-81; founder, pres. Rutledge Tutoring Svc., Oak Park, 1980-83; co-pres. PTA, Oak Park, 1986-87; v.p. Kentucky Homeless Shelter, Detroit, 1992—. Grantee Salvation Army, 1992, Dept. Social Svcs., 1992, Mich. State Housing Devel. Authority, 1992. Mem. Am. Fedn. Tchrs., Mich. Assn. Emotionally Disturbed Children, Detroit Fedn. Tchrs., Farmington Assn. Children and Adults with Learning Disability, Wayne State U. Assn. in Edn., Pi Lambda Theta. Democrat. Mem. Ch. of Christ. Avocations: debates, mystery stories, gospel music, plays, charity work. Home: 19525 Suffolk Dr Detroit MI 48203-1471 Office: Ky Homeless Shelter Inc 16135 Kentucky St Detroit MI 48221-2905

RUTLEDGE, CHARLES OZWIN, pharmacologist, educator; b. Topeka, Oct. 1, 1937; s. Charles Ozwin and Alta (Seaman) R.; m. Jane Ellen Crow, Aug. 13, 1961; children: David Ozwin, Susan Harriett, Elizabeth Jane, Karen Ann. BS in Pharmacy, U. Kans., 1959, MS in Pharmacology, 1961; PhD in Pharmacology, Harvard U., 1966. NATO postdoctoral fellow Gothenburg (Sweden) U., 1966-67; asst. prof. U. Colo. Med. Ctr., Denver, 1967-74, assoc. prof., 1974-75; prof., chmn. dept. pharmacology U. Kans., Lawrence, 1975-87; dean, prof. pharmacology Purdue U., West Lafayette, Ind., 1987—2002, exec. dir. Discovery Park, 2001—, interim vice provost rsch., 2002—. Contbr. articles on neuropharmacology to profl. jours. Grantee NIH, 1970-87. Mem. AAAS, Am. Soc. Pharmacology and Exptl. Therapeutics (councillor 1982 84, sec.-treas. 1990-93, pres. 1996-97), Am. Assn. Coll. Pharmacy (chmn. biol. scis. sect. 1983-84, chmn. coun. faculties 1986-87, chmn. coun. deans 1993-94, com. implement change pharm. edn. 1989-92, pres. 1996-97), Soc. for Neurosci., Am. Pharm. Assn. Avocations: gardening, skiing. Home: 40 Brynteg Est West Lafayette IN 47906-5643 Office: Purdue U Hovde Hall Rm 313 610 Purdue Mall West Lafayette IN 47907-2040 E-mail: chipr@purdue.edu.

RUTLEDGE, DEBORAH JEAN, secondary school educator, music educator; b. St. Louis, Mar. 13, 1954; d. George Roosevelt and Morie Louise Albin; m. Mark H. Rutledge, Mar. 12, 1978 (div. July 28, 1997); children: Mary-Esther, Martha-Ann, Joanna-Ruth, Susanna-Rachel, Sarah-Naomi. MusB, So. Meth. U., 1976. Cert. tchr. reading, elem., ESL, music, English lang., arts and English Tex. Reading tchr.'s aide Sam Houston Mid. Sch., Irving, Tex., 1994—95; reading tchr. Irving H.S., 1995—2002; reading and ESL tchr. Lorenzo de Zawala Mid. Sch., Irving, 2002—. Reading tutor, Irving; piano tchr., Irving. Pianist The Ch. in Oklahoma City, 1976—81. Grantee, Irving Schs. Found., Tex. Pub. Edn., U. North Tex. Mem.: Irving Music Tchrs. Assn., Internat. Reading Assn., Assn. Tex. Profl. Educators, Tex. Counselling Assn., Tex. Music Tchrs. Assn., Nat. Guild Piano Tchrs., Nat. Music Tchrs. Assn., Phi Delta Kappa. Home: 2008 Addington St Irving TX 75062

RUTLEDGE, MARIAN SUE, middle school language arts and social studies educator; b. New Albany, Ind., Feb. 21, 1946; d. Harold Berry Colvin and Wilma Louise (Kingsley) Abel; m. Mark Alan Rutledge, Nov. 30, 1974 (div. Sept. 1985); 1 child, Krista. BS in Elem. Edn., Ind. U., 1968, MS in Elem. Edn., 1971. Cert. tchr. elem. edn., mid. sch. lang. arts, social studies. Tchr. grades 4, 5, 6 Rogers Elem. Monroe County Comty. Sch. Corp., Bloomington, Ind., 1968-75; tchr. grades 3, 5 Ind. State U. Lab. Sch., Terre Haute, 1975-79; tchr. grades 3 and 6 Union Elem. Sch., Zionsville Cmty. Schs., Ind., 1979-88, tchr. lang. arts and social studies Zionsville Mid. Sch., 1988—. Math. club sponsor, 1984-94, 97—; future problem solving coach, 1984—, cheerleading coach, 1991-95; mem. adv. bd. Ind. Future Problem Solving, Indpls., 1991—. Mem. NEA, Ind. State Tchrs. Assn., Ind. Gifted Edn., Zionsville Edn. Assn. (v.p., pres. 1979—), Kappa Kappa Kappa (v.p., pres. 1977—). Republican. Methodist. Office: Zionsville Mid Sch 900 N Ford Rd Zionsville IN 46077-1199 Home: 11633 Buttonwood Dr Carmel IN 46033-3284

RUTTER, JEREMY BENTHAM, archaeologist, educator; b. Boston, Mass., June 23, 1946; s. Peter and Nancy Kendall (Comstock) R.; m. Sarah Robbins Herndon, Jan. 31, 1970; children: Benjamin Ryerson, Nicholas Kendall. BA Classics with honors, Haverford Coll., 1967; PhD Classical Archaeology, U. Pa., 1974; MA, Dartmouth Coll., 1993. Vis. asst. prof. dept. classics UCLA, 1975-76, from asst. prof. to prof. dept. classics, 1976—, prof. humanities, 2001—, chmn. dept. classics, 1992-98, 2003—. Participant excavations West Germany, 1966, Italy, 1968-69, Greece, 1972, 73-74, 75, 77, 78, 80-81, 84-86, 88-89, 91—; mem. numerous coms. Am. Sch. Classical Studies, Athens. Author: Lerna III: The Pottery of Lerna IV, 1995; exec. com. Am. Sch. Classical Studies at Athens; contbr. numerous articles, reviews to profl. jours. With U.S. Army, 1969-71, Vietnam. Woodrow Wilson fellow, 1967-68; NDEA fellow U. Pa., 1968-69, 71-73; Olivia James Traveling fellow Archeol. Inst. Am., 1974-75; NEH rsch. grantee, 1979-81; travel grantee Am. Coun. Learned Socs., 1982; sr. faculty grantee, 1985-86, 91-92, 2001-02. Mem. Am. Schs. Oriental Rsch., Archaeol. Inst. Am. (numerous coms.), Classical Assn. New England, Phi Beta Kappa. Home: 47 Eagle Rdg Lebanon NH 03766-1900 Office: Dept Classics Dartmouth College Hanover NH 03755-3506 E-mail: jeremy.rutter@dartmouth.edu.

RUTZ, MIRIAM EASTON, landscape architecture educator; b. Anaheim, Calif., June 12, 1943; d. George Carr and Jane (van Booven) Easton; m. Earl William Rutz; children: Kristi, Carrie, Mari. B in Landscape Architecture, U. Calif., Berkeley, 1965, cert. in edn., 1967; MS Renewable Natural Resources, U. Ariz., Tucson, 1973. Landscape arch., 1967; primary sch. tchr., art specialist, 1968—69; primary sch. tchr., 1st and 2d grade, 1968—71; asst. prof. architecture U. Ariz., Tucson, 1973—76; prof. urban and regional planning and landscape architecture with a specialization, historic preservation planning, women's studies Mich. State U., East Lansing, 1977—2002. Vis. faculty U. We. Australia, Technion Inst. Tech., Haifa, Israel, U. Dortmund (Germany); cons., cmty. design Southwest Detroit; cons., historic preservation Iron County, Mich., Small Towns, Mich.; cons. Mich. Bur. History, 1985—2001, Nat. Park Svc., Historic Landscape Initiative, 1990—2001. Author: Art Today and Everyday, 1973, Public Gardens of Michigan, 2002; contbr. chapters to books. Mem.: Mich. Women's Studies Assn., Coun. Educators in Landscape Architecture (past bd. mem., treas., pres.), Am. Soc. Landscape Architects (pres. Mich. chpt.), Am. Soc. Land Architecture Recognition, Honor Soc. Land Architecture Educators. Avocation: gardening. Home: PO 1337 Pauma Valley CA 92061 E-mail: earlrutz@aol.com.

RUUD, JAY WESLEY, dean; b. Racine, Wis., Nov. 3, 1950; s. Wesley J. and Alyce; m. Cynthia Lee Kristopeit, Sept. 4, 1971 (div. Nov. 29, 1993); m. Stacey Margaret Jones, Mar. 2, 2001. BA, U. Wis.-Parkside, Kenosha, Wis., 1972; MA, U. Wis.-Milw., 1974, PhD, 1981. Instr. English U. Wis.-Parkside, Kenosha, 1978-83, testing coord., 1983-84; instr. English U. Wis.-Marathon County, Wausau, Wis., 1984-85; prof. English Northern State U., Aberdeen, S.D., 1985-96, asst. dean coll. arts and scis., 1996-97, dean coll. arts and scis., 1997—. Dir. NEH Inst. on Lit. of Plains Indians, Aberdeen, S.D., 1994, NEH Inst. on Chaucer's Canterbury Tales, Aberdeen, S.D., 1989. Author: Many a Song and Many a Leccherous Lay: Tradition and Individuality in Chaucer's Lyric Poetry, 1992; editor: Proceedings of the First Dakotas Conference on Earlier British Literature, 1992, Proceedings of the Seventh Northern Plains Conference on Early British, 1999; contbr. articles to profl. jours. Named Outstanding Faculty Mem. Northern State U., 1989; recipient Burlington Northern Faculty Achievement award and Northern State U., 1989. Mem. New Chaucer Soc., Medieval Assn. of the Midwest. Avocation: acting. Office: Northern State U 1200 S Jay St Aberdeen SD 57401-7155 Fax: 605-626-2635. E-mail: ruudj@northern.edu.

RUVOLO, BARBARA, elementary education educator; b. S.I., July 19, 1953; d. John Lawrence and Ann Marie (Mullaney) Rice; m. John Thomas Ruvolo, Aug. 23, 1975; children: John, James, Anne Marie. BS in Elem. Edn./BA in History cum laude, St. John's U., 1975; MS in Spl. Edn., Coll. S.I., 1978. Cert. tchr., N.Y. Tchr. Our Lady Star of the Sea, S.I., 1975-78, Pub. Sch. 38, S.I., 1985-86, Pub. Sch. 4, S.I., 1986-91, Pub. Sch. 32, S.I., 1991—; supr. for student tchrs. P.S. 32, S.I., 1992—. Adj. prof. L.I. U., N.Y.C., 1988—, Coll. of S.I., N.Y., 1988—, Coll. of St. Rose; design facilitator grad. course N.Y. State United Tchrs., Albany, 1992; mem. design team for Pub. Sch. 32, New Am. Sch. for Yr. 2000, S.I., 1991—. Contbr. articles to profl. jours. Mem. United Fedn. Tchrs., N.Y. State United Tchrs. Home: 1124 Central Ave Westfield NJ 07090-2233

RUZICKA, CHARLES EDWARD, music educator, director; b. Grafton, N.D., Mar. 15, 1941; m. Barbara Jean Finney, Oct. 8, 1945; children: Todd, Tami, Amy. MA in Vocal Music, U. N.D., 1974; D in Choral Conducting and Choral Conducting, U. Iowa, 1983. Music tchr. pub. and parochial sch., N.D., Minn., and Iowa, 1963—76; choral music dir. Dakota Wesleyan U., SD, 1979—80, Bemidji (Minn.) State U., 1980—83, Mayville (N.D.) State University, 1983—92; dir. choral activities Minn. State U., Moorhead, 1992—. Singer, chorister: Norman Luboff Choir, 1967; composer: (choral arrangement) Swing Low, Sweet Chariot-SSATB, 1987, Bound For The Promised Land-SATB, 1989, Alleluia! Sing To Jesus-SATB/piano/flute, 1988, Loch Lomond-SATB, 1992, Numerous arrangements for the Catholic Church Service, (songs) Come To Me and Rest-SATB, 1996, Flow Gently, Sweet Afton-TTBB, 2003, (choral edit.) Te Deum in C, 1994. Mem.: N.D. Am. Choral Dirs. Assn. (pres. 1990—91), Nat. Assn. Tchrs. Singing, Music Educators Nat. Conf., Am. Choral Dirs. Assn., Pi Kappa Lambda. Avocations: photography, choral music composing and arranging. Home: 2855 Edgewood Dr Fargo ND 58102 Office: Minn State U Moorhead 1104 7th Ave S Moorhead MN 56563 Office Fax: 218-236-4097. Personal E-mail: ruzicka@mnstate.edu. Business E-Mail: ruzicka@mnstate.edu.

RYAN, BONNIE MAE, business office technology educator; b. Wooster, Ohio, May 26, 1953; d. Clarence Roger and Dorothy Mae Reynolds; m. Richard Dean Ryan, May 4, 1974; children: Sean Patrick Ryan, Heather Marie Ryan. AS, Sauk Valley C.C., Dixon, Ill., 1979; BA, Western Ill. U., 1980; MS in Bus. Edn., So. Ill. U., 1982. Sec. to dir. of admissions Sauk Valley C.C., 1973-74, sec. to dean of students, 1974-76, ednl. specialist, 1976-84; office tech. instr. Highland C.C., Freeport, Ill., 1984—. Adv. bd. Stephenson Area Career Ctr., Freeport, 1984-86. Religion tchr. St. Patrick's Cath. Ch., Dixon, 1986; v.p. Al Morrison Baseball Ladies Aux., Dixon, 1986. Mem. ASCD, AFT, Nat. Bus. Edn. Assn., Ill. Bus. Edn. Assn., Ill. Vocat. Assn., No. Ill. Bus. Edn. Assn. (pres. 1991-92, v.p. 1990-91, sec. 1988-90), Profl. Secs. Internat., Delta Pi Epsilon (2d v.p. 1994-95). Roman Catholic. Avocations: reading, swimming, refinishing furniture. Home: 711 E Chamberlin St Dixon IL 61021-2225 Office: Highland C C 2998 W Pearl City Rd Freeport IL 61032-9338

RYAN, BRYAN, college administrator, language educator, writer, editor; b. Mt. Vernon, Ohio, Oct. 5, 1959; s. Dwight Otis and Janetta Bell (Hains) R.; m. Susan Joy Herriman, Oct. 13, 1985; children: Samantha Joy, Sydney Marie. BA in English, Kalamazoo Coll., 1982; MA in Tchg. ESL, Eastern Mich. U., 1990. Editor Gale Rsch. Inc., Detroit, 1984-90; instr. ESL Wake Tech. C.C., Raleigh, N.C., 1991-98, dept. head, 1998—2002, dean of math. and sci. divsn., 2002—. Editor: (reference books) Hispanic Writers, 1990, Major 20th Century Writers, 1990; co-editor: (reference books) Hispanic American Almanac, 1995, Hispanic American Chronology, 1996. Office: Wake Tech CC 9101 Fayetteville Rd Raleigh NC 27603-5655

RYAN, DABERATH, chemistry educator; b. Sacramento, May 3, 1946; d. Clarence Arthur and Ernestine H. (Croy) Kouts; divorced. BS in Chemistry, So. Oreg. U., 1968; MS in Chemistry, Oreg. State U., 1971, MS in Food Sci. and Tech., 1987. Instr. So. Oreg. U., Ashland, 1971-72; prof., dept. chair Rogue Community Coll., Grants Pass, Oreg., 1971-76; chemist State of Alaska, Juneau, 1978; chem. cons. Appleby Sailplanes, Albuquerque, 1978-79; prof. U. Alaska-S.E., Juneau, 1981-82, Mt. Hood Community Coll., Graham, Oreg., 1987, Coll. of Siskiyous, Weed, Calif., 1987—. Mem. Am. Chem. Soc., Coll. of Siskiyous Faculty Assn, Two Yr. Coll. Chemistry Conf., Calif. Tchrs. Assn., Calif. Sci. Tchrs., No. Calif. Sci. Tchrs., Oreg. State U. Alumni Assn., So. Oreg. U. Alumni Assn. Avocations: outdoor recreation, fishing, camping, hunting. Home: PO Box 381 Montague CA 96064-0381 Office: Coll of the Siskiyous 800 College Ave Weed CA 96094-2806 E-mail: ryan@siskiyous.edu.

RYAN, ELLEN MARIE, elementary education and gifted education educator; b. Flushing, N.Y. d. Francis and June Marie Ryan. BA in Elem. Edn., Queens Coll., 1971; MA in Edn., Adelphi U., 1974; MEd in Adminstrn., Stetson U., 1982; postgrad., Fla. Tech., 1988—. Cert. tchr. N.Y.C.; profl. cert. N.Y., Pa., Fla.; cert. tchr., elem. edn. adminstr., early childhood, gifted tchr.; cert. sch. site trainer in tech. Miami Mus. Sci. Tchr. grade 3 Park View Elem Kings Park (N.Y.) Sch. Dist., 1971-75; tchr. grade 6 So. Lehig Sch. Dist., Center Valley, Pa., 1975-77; resource tchr. grades K-6 North Penn Sch. Dist., Lansdale, Pa., 1977-79; tchr. grade 1 Holland Elem., Brevard County Schs., Satellite Beach, Fla., 1979-81; tchr. gifted student program Surfside Elem., Satellite Beach; tchr. grades K-6 Brevard County Schs., 1981—; asst. prin. Callahan Mid. Sch., 2002—; asst. prin. Fla. Nassau Co. Schs., 2002—. Grant writer, reviewer Grantsmanship Cadre, Brevard Schs., Fla., 1992—; cons. multimedia presentation NSF, State Systemic Initiative, Surfside Elem., Fla. Tech., Melbourne, 1994; cons., trainer, spkr. Surfside Elem., Satellite Beach, 1994, 95; presenter in field. Dir., prodr., photographer various prodns., 1992. Treas. Melbourne (Fla.) Panhellenic, 1987, yearbook chairperson, 1988, installation banquet chair, 1989; publicity chair Holy Name of Jesus Fall Festival, Indialantic, Fla., 1991. Fla. Instrnl. Tech. grantee Fla. Tech., 1991-93, Creative Tchg. grantee Brevard Schs. Found., Fla. Found., Melbourne, 1993, Tchrs. and Tech.-NSF grantee, 1993-95, Multimedia Life Sci. mini grantee Fla. Assn. for Gifted, 1994, Tech. Apprentice Program grantee Bell South Found., 1994—. Mem. Fla. Assn. Computer Educators (integrating tech. into the curriculum 1994—), Fla. Edn. Tech. Conf. (workshop presenter 1994), Fla. Assn. Sch. Adminstrs., Nat. Assn. Secondary Sch. Prins., Delta Kappa Gamma (Beta Sigma chpt. yearbook chairperson, membership chair 1994—), Phi Delta Kappa (Creative Tchg. grants Cape Kennedy chpt. 1993), Delta Kappa (chaplain).

RYAN, HALFORD ROSS, speech educator; b. Anderson, Ind., Dec. 29, 1943; AB, Wabash Coll., 1966; MA, U. Ill., 1968, PhD, 1972. Prof. Washington and Lee U., Lexington, Va., 1970—. Author: FDR's Rhetorical Presidency, 1988, Harry Emerson Fosdick, 1989, Henry Ward Beecher, 1990, Classical Communication for the Contemporary Communicator, 1992, Harry S. Truman, 1993; editor: Oratorial Encounters, 1988, Inaugural Addresses of Twentieth-Century American Presidents, 1993, U.S. Presidents as Orators, 1995; also articles. Recipient awards Eleanor Roosevelt Inst., 1979, Herbert Hoover Inst., 1986, Maurice Mednick Found., 1991; Rockefeller Theol. fellow, 1967. Mem. Speech Communication Assn. Office: Washington and Lee U Robinson Hall Lexington VA 24450

RYAN, JOHN WILLIAM, association executive; b. Manchester, N.H., Sept. 16, 1937; s. William Charles and Mary Ann (Marcoux) R.; m. Carol Jean Battaglia, Sept. 17, 1960; children: James, Kathleen, John, Michael. AB, St. Anselm Coll., 1959; MA, Niagara U., 1960; PhD, St. John's U., 1965. Asst. prof. history Gannon U:, Erie, Pa., 1965-66; edn. specialist, div. grad. programs U.S. Office Edn., Washington, 1966-68, regional coordinator, grad. acad. programs, 1968-70; dir. univ. programs Univ. Assos., Inc., Washington, 1970-72; asst. to pres., sec. Council of Grad. Schs. in U.S., Washington, 1972-80; exec. v.p. Renewables Research Inst., Annandale, Va., 1980-81; exec. dir. Worcester (Mass.) Consortium Higher Edn., 1981-89, N.H. Coll. and Univ. Coun., Manchester, 1989-93; cons.; exec. dir. Mass. Vet. Med. Assn., Marlborough, Mass., 1995-98; cons., 1998—. Contbr. articles to profl. jours. Bd. dirs. No. Va. C.C., 1999—, Loudoun Healthcare, Inc., 2000—, Loudoun County Econ. Devel. Commn., 2000.

RYAN, KENNETH JOHN, physician, educator; b. N.Y.C., Aug. 26, 1926; s. Joseph M. Ryan; m. Marion Elizabeth Kinney, June 8, 1948; children: Alison Leigh, Kenneth John, Christopher Elliot. Student, Northwestern U., 1946—48; MD, Harvard U., 1952. Diplomate Am. Bd. Ob-Gyn. Intern, then resident internal medicine Mass. Gen. Hosp., Boston, also Columbia-Presbyn. Med. Center, N.Y.C., 1952—54, Mass. Gen. Hosp., N.Y.C., 1956—57; resident in ob-gyn. Boston Lying-in Hosp., also Free Hosp. for Women, Brookline, Mass., 1957—60; prof. ob-gyn., dir. dept. Med. Sch. Western Res. U., 1961—70; prof. reproductive biology, dept. ob-gyn. U. Calif. San Diego, La Jolla, 1970—73; chief of staff Boston Hosp. for Women, 1973—80; chmn. dept. ob-gyn. Brigham Women's Hosp., Boston, 1980—93; instr. ob-gyn. Harvard U., also dir. Fearing Rsch. Lab., 1960—61, Kate Macy Ladd prof., chmn. dept. ob-gyn. Med. Sch., 1973—93, dir. Lab. Human Reprodn. and Reproductive Biology, 1974—93, Disting. prof., 1993—96, prof. emeritus, from 1996; chief staff Boston Hosp. for Women, 1973—80; chmn. dept. ob-gyn. Brigham Women's Hosp., Boston, 1980—93; now chmn. ethic com. Chmn. Nat. Commn. for Protection of Human Subjects Biomed. and Behavioral Rsch., 1974—78. Recipient Schering award, Harvard Med. Sch., 1951, Soma Weis award, 1952, Bordon award, 1952, Ernst Oppenheimer award, 1964, Max Weinstein award, 1970; fellow, Mass. Gen. Hosp., 1954—56. Fellow: Am. Cancer Soc.; mem.: Mass. Med. Soc., Am. Soc. Clin. Investigation, Am. Gynecol. Soc., Soc. Gynecol. Investigation, Endocrine Soc., Am. Soc. Biol. Chemists, ACOG, Alpha Omega Alpha. Died Jan. 5, 2002.

RYAN, KEVIN WILLIAM, virologist, researcher, science educator, clinical research administrator; b. Ft. Dodge, Iowa, Dec. 8, 1952; s. Joseph Michael Ryan and Etoile Evelyn Werth; m. Mary Ellen Lyman, June 1, 1974; children: Matthew Lyman, Mark Joseph. BS, U. Iowa, 1978; PhD, U. Mich., 1984. Staff fellow Nat. Inst. Allergy and Infectious Diseases, NIH, Bethesda, Md., 1984-86; rsch. asst. dept. virology and molecular biology St. Jude Children's Rsch. Hosp., Memphis, 1986-89, asst. mem., 1989-98; asst. prof. pathology U. Tenn. Coll. Medicine, Memphis, 1994-98; sci. rev. adminstr. Nat. Inst. Allergy and Infectious Diseases, NIH, Rockville, Md., 1998-2000; program officer virology vaccine and prevention rsch. prog. divsn. AIDS, Nat. Inst. Allergy and Infectious Diseases, NIH, Bethesda, Md., 2000—; deputy chief Prevention Scis. Br., 2001—02, chief, 2002—, mem. Prevention Leadership Group, 2002; lead program ofcl. HIV Prevention Trials Network, 2002—; mem. working group NIAID, comprehensive Internat. Program for Rsch. in AIDS (CIPRA), 2001—. Prin. investigator Nat. Inst. Allergy and Infectious Diseases, 1992—98; lead program officer HIV prevention trials network HPTN, 2002—; NIAID Rep. HPTN Prevention Leadership Group, 2000—. Contbr. articles to profl. jours., chpts. to tech. manuals. Fellow postdoctoral Mich. Cancer Rsch. Inst., U. Mich., 1982. Mem.: Am. Soc. for Microbiology. Roman Catholic. Avocations: woodworking, golf. Office: Nat Inst Allergy and Infectious Diseases Divsn AIDS 6700-b Rockledge Dr Bethesda MD 20892-0001

RYAN, LEO VINCENT, business educator; b. Waukon, Iowa, Apr. 6, 1927; s. John Joseph and Mary Irene (O'Brien) Ryan. BS, Marquette U., 1949; MBA, DePaul U., 1954; PhD, St. Louis U., 1958; postgrad., Catholic U. Am., 1951-52, Bradley U., 1952-54, Northwestern U., 1950; LLD, Seton Hall U., 1988; DHL, Ill. Benedictine U., 1997. Joined Order Clerics of St. Viator, Roman Cath. Ch., 1950. Faculty Marquette U., Milw., 1957-65, dir. continuing edn. summer sessions, coord. evening divsns., 1959-65, prof. indsl. mgmt., 1964; prof., chmn. dept. mgmt. Loyola U., Chgo., 1965-66; dep. dir. Peace Corps, Lagos, Nigeria, 1966-67, dir. Western Nigeria Ibadan, 1967-68; asst. superior gen. and treas. gen. Clerics of St. Viator, Rome, 1968-69, dir. edn. Am. province Arlington Heights, Ill., 1969-74; pres. St. Viator H.S., 1972-74; dean, prof. mgmt. U. Notre Dame Coll. Bus. Adminstrn., Ind., 1975-80; dean DePaul U. Coll. Commerce, 1980-88, prof. mgmt., 1980-99; Wicklander prof. ethics DePaul U., 1993-94; prof. emeritus, 1999. Dir. Peace Corps tng. programs Marquette U., 1962-65; adj. prof. human devel. St. Mary's Coll., Winona, Minn., 1972-74; mem. sch. bd. Archdiocese Chgo., 1972-75, vice-chmn., 1973-75, nat. edn. com. U.S. Cath. Conf., 1971-75, exec. com., 1973-75; nat. adv. bd. Benedictine Sisters of Nauvoo, 1973-83; nat. adv. coun. SBA, 1982-85, vice-chmn. minority bus., 1982-85, exec. com. Chgo. chpt., 1982-84; vis. prof. U. Ife, Ibadan, 1967-68,; chmn. trust audit com. First Bank-Milw., 1980-85, chmn. audit and examination com., 1985-90, adv. coun., 1991-93; bd. dirs. Henricksen & Co., Inc., 1978—; fin. commn. Clerics of St. Viator, 1978-, provincial chpt., 1985-97, 2001-, devel. adv. bd. 1996-2001, new foundations com. 1996-98, alt. mem., 1997-2001, provincial coun., 2001—, coord. comprehensive devel., U.S., Belize, Columbia, 2001—; Fulbright prof. Adam Mickiewicz U., Poland, 1993-95; vis. prof. Helsinki Sch. Econs., 1992-2002, Polish-Am. Ctr., U. Lodz, 1998, Poznan Acad. Econs., 1991, 1999—; co-chair bus. and profl. com. Archdiocese of Chgo. Sesquetennial Com. Out Reach Divsn. Ctrl. Planning Group, 1993-94; vis. prof. Notre Dame, 2000, Helsinki Sch. Econs., 2000; adv. bd. Sch. of Bus. Univ. Kiev, Ukraine, 2001. Author: Human Action in Business, 1996, Etyka Biznesu, 1997, 4th edit., 2000, From Autarcy to Market: Polish Economics and Politics, 1945-1995, 1998, 2d edit., 1999, Students Focus on Business Ethics, 2000, Praxiology and Pragmatism, 2002; mem. editl. bd. Internat. Jour. Value Based Mgmt., European Bus. Jour., 1990-2002, Bus. Ethics Quar., Mid Atlantic Jour. of Bus., 1990-2002. Mem. Pres.'s Com. on Employment Handicapped, 1959-65, Wis. Gov.'s Com. on Employment Handicapped, 1959-65, Wis. Gov.'s Com. on UN, 1961-64, Burnham Park Planning Commn., 1982-88; bd. dirs. Ctr. Pastoral Liturgy U. Notre Dame, 1976-79; trustee Lake Forest Grad. Sch. Mgmt., 1989-91, St. Mary of Woods Coll., 1978-81, Cath. Theol. Union, U. Chgo., 1992-95, Divine Word Coll., 1997—; regent Seton Hall U., 1981-87, mem. acad. affairs com., 1981-87, chmn., 1983-87; dir. Ctr. for Enterprise Devel., 1992-95; elected fellow St. Edmonds Coll. Cambridge U., 1992—; mem. Cath. Commn. Intellectual and Cultural Affairs, 1992—, Cath. Campaign for Am., 1994-98; bd. dirs.

Internat. Bus. Ethics Inst., Am. Grad. Sch. Internat. Mgmt., 1995-97; mem. adv. com. Mgmt. Edn. in Poland, U. Md., College Park, 1995-2000. Recipient Freedom award Berlin Commn., 1961, chieftancy title Asoju Atoaja of Oshogbo Oba Adenle I, Yorubaland, Nigeria, 1967, B'nai B'rith Interfaith award, Milw., 1963, Disting. Alumnus award Marquette U., 1974, DePaul U., 1976, Tchr. of Yr. award Beta Alpha Psi, 1980, Centennial Alumni Achievement award Marquette U., 1981, Boland Meml. Disting. Alumni award, St. Louis, 1989, Disting. Alumni and Bicentennial awards Jesuit Bus. Schs., 1989, Pres.' award St. Viator H.S., 1992, Medal of Merit Adam Mickiewicz U., 1995, Excellence in Tchg. award Adam Mickiewicz U., 1997, Ill. Ernst and Young Entrepreneur Supporter award, 1999, Vincentian U. Ethics Scholar award, 2000, Centennial award Dominican U. for lifetime leadership and bus. ethics Dominican U. Sch. Bus., 2002; Brother Leo V. Ryan award named in his honor Cath. Bus. Edn. Assn., 1962; Ryan Scholars in Mgmt. established in his honor DePaul U., 1989, Outstanding Svc. award, 1991-93, Commerce Alumni award of merit, 1997; DePaul Creativity Ctr. named in his honor, 1997, trustee; named hon. life chmn. Nat. Adv. Com., Ryan Creativity Ctr., Creative Cutting Edge award, 1999; Ryan Scholarship named in his honor St. Viator H.S., 1992, Lion award, 1997, trustee, 2000-01, gov., 2001-; named Man of Yr. Jr. C. of C., Milw., 1959, Marquette U. Bus. Adminstrn. Alumni Man of Yr., 1974; named Disting. Vis. Term Prof. Seton Hall U., 2001; Milw. Bd. Realtors traveling fellow, 1964, Nat. Assn. Purchasing Agts. faculty fellow, 1958, German Am. Acad. Exch. Coun. fellow, summer 1983, Presdl. fellow Am. Grad. Sch. Internat. Mgmt., 1989, vis. scholar, 1995, Malone fellow in Islamic studies, 1990, fellow Kosciuszko Found. Adam Mickiewicz U., 1990; scholar-in-residence Mgmt. Sch. Imperial Coll. Sci. and Tech. U. London, 1988; vis. scholar U. Calif., Berkeley, 1989; USIA Acad. Specialists grantee, Poland, 1991-93; fellow St. Edmund's Coll. Cambridge U., 1992; named vis. rsch. fellow Von Hugel Inst., 1992-93; scholar-in-residence Am. Grad. Sch. Internat. Mgmt., 1995; guest scholar Kellogg Inst. Internat. Studies U. Notre Dame, 1997. Mem. Cath. Bus. Edn. Assn. (nat. pres. 1960-62, nat. exec. bd. 1960-64), Assn. Sch. Bus. Ofcls. (nat. com. chmn. 1965-67), Am. Assembly Collegiate Schs. Bus. (com. internat. affairs 1977-84, chmn. 1981-84, bd. dirs. 1981-87, program chmn. 1979-80, exec. com., chmn. projects/svc. mgmt. com. 1984-86), Am. Fgn. Svc. Assn., Am. Assn. Profl. Ethics (bd. dirs. 1996-98), Allamakee County Hist. Soc. (charter life), Acad. Internat. Bus., Acad. Mgmt. (social issues div., chmn. membership com. 1990-91), Ancient Order of Hibernians, Nat. Returned Peace Corps Assn., Atomic Vets. Assn., August Derleth Soc., Chgo. Area Return Peace Corps Vols., Econ. Club Chgo., Chgo. Coun. Fgn. Rels., Coun. Fgn. Rels. (Chgo. com., diplomat cir. 1998), European Bus. Ethics Network Poland (hon. 1998), Soc. Bus. Ethics (mem. exec. com. 1991—, pres. 1993-94, adv. bd. 1995-97), Assn. Social Econs. (life), Assn. Christian Economists, Dubuque County Hist. Soc., Iowa Hist. Soc., Iowa Postal History Soc., Fulbright Assn. (life), Internat. Assn. for Bus. and Soc. (founder), Internat. Soc. for Bus., Econs. and Ethics (charter), Internat. Trade and Fin. Assn. (founder, bd. dirs. 1989-92, 96-98, v.p. membership 1991-92, 96-97), Internat. Learned Soc. Praxiology, (hon. life, internat. adv. bd. praxiology ann.), Polish Inst. Arts and Scis. in Am., DePaul Inst. Bus. and Profl. Ethics (founder 1984, adv. bd. 1984-94, Founders award 1999), USS Mt. McKinley Reunion Assn. (hon. chaplain AGC-7 1989-96, Disting. Svc. award 1991, 96), Alpha Sigma Nu, Alpha Kappa Psi (bd. dirs. found. 1985-91, vice-chmn. 1987-91, chmn. scholarship com. 1987-91, chmn. devel. com. 1987, exec. com. 1990-91, Bronze Disting. Svc. award 1949, Silver Disting. Svc. award 1958, Recognition medal, 2001), Beta Alpha Psi, Beta Gamma Sigma (co-chair 75th Anniversary com. Ill., faculty advisor DePaul chpt. 1986-92), Century Travel Club (Silver award), Delta Mu Delta, Pi Gamma Mu, Tau Kappa Epsilon. E-mail: LeovRyan@aol.com.

RYAN, NANCY MARIE, Spanish-English educator; b. Johnson City, N.Y., Mar. 13, 1938; d. Edward P. and Margie E. (Devine) R. BA, N.Y. State Coll. for Tchrs., 1960, MA, 1966. Cert. Spanish-English tchr., N.Y. Spanish-English tchr. Weedsport (N.Y.) Cen. High Sch., 1960-64; English tchr. Universidad de la Frontera, Temuco, Chile, 1964-65; Spanish-English tchr. Guilderland (N.Y.) Cen. High Sch., 1966—. Advisor Open Door Student Exch., 1968-84; tchr. coll. Spanish LaSalette Sem., Altamont, N.Y., 1966-73. Author: Shades of Green and Darkness, 1981, Islands in a Bay, 1989, Past Green Edges of Realities, 1990, A Soft Feathering into Silence, 2001, Mountains Anticipating Footsteps, 2001, Swirling Winds of Change, 2002, The Condor's Message to the World, 2002, Spiraling Beyond Clouds, 2002, An Everywhere of Trees, 2002, When Earth Lingers on the Tip of Spring, 2003, numerous poems; contbr. chpts. to books. Vol. Albany (N.Y.) Ronald McDonald House, 1984—; Papal vol. Roman Cath. Ch., Temuco, Chile, 1964-65; vol. mem. Friends of The Lakota People, 1996—. Recipient Vol. Svc. award Guilderland Elks Lodge, 1988. Mem. Guilderland Tchrs. Assn. (rep. coun.), High Sch. Faculty Assn. (sec.). Avocations: writing, crafts, gardening. Home: 111 Beverwyck Dr Guilderland NY 12084-9306

RYAN, RANDA CATHERINE, university administrator, business owner; b. Austin, Tex., Jan. 25, 1955; d. James Prewitt and Susan Farrington Holt; m. Steve Klepfer; children: Seth, Rhett, Kasey, Shea. BA, Schreiner Coll., Kerrville, Tex., 1984; MA, U. Tex., 1989, PhD, 1996. Asst. to nat. team swim coach U.S. Swim, Colorado Springs, Colo., 1984-88; asst. swim coach U. Tex., Austin, 1984-88, performance team dir., 1988-92, asst. athletic dir., 1992—. Meet dir. Olympic trials-swimming U. Tex., 1988. Writer Performance Team Newsletter, 1988-91; contbr. chpt. to book, articles to profl. jours. Mem. AAUW, Am. Coll. Sports Medicine, Am. Assn. Phys. Edn., Nat. Assn. Coll. Athletic Dirs. Office: Women's Athletics 718 Belmont Hall Austin TX 78712-1201

RYAN, RAY DARL, JR., academic administrator; b. Joliet, Ill., Dec. 2, 1945; s. Ray D. and Oral Ada (Smiley) R.; m. Marianne Rossetto, Aug. 28, 1965; children: Kimberley, Kristin, Matthew. BS, U. Wis., Menomonie, 1970; MEd, U. Mo., 1973, EdD, 1975; Doctorate (hon.), Tomsk (Siberia) Poly. U., 1992. Cert. vocat./tech. tchr., adminstr., chief sch. officer. Dep. supt. pub. instrn. Nev. Dept. Edn., Carson City; dep. supt. spl. programs Ariz. Dept. Edn., Phoenix, state dir., vocat. educator; exec. dir. Ctr. Edn. and Tng. for Employment Ohio State U., Columbus, assoc. dean rsch., internat. affairs. Bd. dirs., vice-chair Coun. Ednl. Devel. and Rsch.; pres., CEO Nat. Occup. Testing Inst., 1999—. Mem. OTT, ASTD, Phi Delta Kappa, Epsilon Pi Tau, Omicron Tau Theta. Home: 20738 Walnut Dr Reed City MI 49677-8055 Office: NOCTI 500 N Bronson Ave Big Rapids MI 49307

RYAN, SARAH (SALLY RYAN), retired secondary education educator; b. Cornwall, N.Y., Apr. 8, 1938; d. Benjamin Marco and Sarah Loretta (McEvilly) Santoro; m. Leo Joseph Ryan, Aug. 12, 1961 (dec. July 1988); children: Sean, Ada, Sarah, Caithlin. BA in English, Coll. New Rochelle, 1959; MS in Edn. and Reading, SUNY, New Paltz, 1985; cert. reading recovery, NYU, 1991. Cert. elem. tchr., N.Y.; cert. English 7-12 grade. 3rd grade tchr. Willow Ave. Sch., Cornwall, 1959-64; jr. high English tchr. Cornwall H.S., 1964-70; from 6th-4th grade tchr. Temple Hill Sch., New Windsor, N.Y., 1970-80, title I reading tchr., 1990—97; acad. specialist Temple Hill Acad., Newburgh, NY, 1992-95, reading tchr., 1980-90, 1990-95, tchr. third grade, 1995-97; ret., 1997; supr. student tchrs. Mt. St. Mary Coll., 2000—, ednl. cons., 2003—. Jr. league trainer Vol. Career Devel., 1978-82; cons. student leadership Cornwall H.S., 1985-86. Pres. Jr. League Orange County, 1972-73, sustainer rep., 1988-90, 1999-2001; v.p. Hudson Valley Philharmonic, 1974-76; bd. dirs., v.p. Orange County YWCA, New Windsor, N.Y., 1988-94, vol., 1994—; vol. Mus. Hudson Highlands, Cornwall, 1994—; trustee, 2001—; trustee Sands Ring Homestead, Cornwall, 2003—; docent Storm King Art Ctr., Mountainville, N.Y., 2001—. Mem. Newburgh Tchrs. Assn. (del. 1986-92), N.Y. State United Tchrs., Reading Recovery Inst. Democrat. Roman Catholic. Avocations: antiques, gardening, reading, interior decorating. Home: 61 Clinton St Cornwall NY 12518-1561

RYAN, STEPHEN JOSEPH, JR., ophthalmology educator, university dean; b. Honolulu, Mar. 20, 1940; s. S.J. and Mildred Elizabeth (Farrer) Ryan; m. Anne Christine Mullady, Sept. 25, 1965; 1 child, Patricia Anne. AB, Providence Coll., 1961; MD, Johns Hopkins U., 1965. Intern Bellevue Hosp., N.Y.C., 1965—66; resident Wilmer Inst. Ophthalmology, Johns Hopkins Hosp., Balt., 1966—69, chief resident, 1969—70; fellow Armed Force Inst. Pathology, Washington, 1970—71; instr. ophthalmology Johns Hopkins U., Balt., 1970—71, asst. prof., 1971—72, assoc. prof., 1972—74; prof. ophthalmology Keck Sch. Medicine, U. So. Calif., L.A., 1974—, chmn. dept. ophthalmology, 1974—95, dean, 1991—, sr. v.p. for med. care, 1993—; acting head ophthalmology div., dept. surgery Children's Hosp., L.A., 1975—77; med. dir. Doheny Eye Inst. (formerly Estelle Doheny Eye Found.), L.A., 1977—86; chief of staff Doheny Eye Hosp., L.A., 1985—88. Mem. adv. panel Calif. Med. Assn., 1975—. Editor (with M.D. Andrews): A Survey of Ophthalmology--Manual for Medical Students, 1970; editor: (with R.E. Smith) Selected Topics on the Eye in Systemic Disease, 1974; editor: (with Dawson and Little) Retinal Diseases, 1985; editor: (with others) Retina, 1989; exec. prodr.(with others): Retina, 2000; assoc. editor: Ophthalmol. Surgery, 1974—85, mem. editl. bd.: Am. Jour. Ophthalmology, 1981—, Internat. Ophthalmology, 1982—, Retina, 1983—, Graefes Archives, 1984—; contbr. articles to med. jours. Recipient cert. of merit, AMA, 1971, Louis B. Mayer Scholar award, Rsch. to Prevent Blindness, 1973, Rear Adm. William Campbell Chambliss USN award, 1982. Mem.: AMA, Jules Gonin Club, Rsch. Study Club, Nat. Eye Care Project, Retina Soc., Macula Soc., Pan-Am. Assn. Microsurgery, L.A. Acad. Medicine, Pacific Coast Oto-Ophthal. Soc., Los Angeles County Med. Assn., Calif. Med. Assn., L.A. Soc. Ophthalmology, Assn. Univ. Profs. of Ophthalmology, Pan-Am. Assn. Ophthalmology, Am. Ophthal. Soc., Am. Acad. Ophthalmology and Otolaryngology (award of Merit 1975), Wilmer Ophthal. Inst. Residents Assn., Soc. Scholars of Johns Hopkins U. (life). Office: 1450 San Pablo St Los Angeles CA 90033

RYAN, SUZANNE IRENE, nursing educator; b. Yonkers, NY, Mar. 13, 1939; d. Edward Vincent and Winifred E. (Goemann) R. BA in Biology, Mt. St. Agnes Coll., Balt., 1962; BSN, Columbia U., 1967, MA in Nursing Svc., 1973, MEd in Nursing Edn., 1975, MS in Oncology, 1982, EdD in Nursing Edn., 1997. RN, N.Y.; cert. AIDS educator, N.Y. Prof. nursing Molloy Coll., Rockville Centre, N.Y., 1970—, co-dir. health svcs., dir. ednl. programs, 1987-94, dir. health svcs., 1994—, health educator, 1992—, co-dir. mobile health van, adminstr. health edn., 1992—; pres., CEO SIR Enterprises, Inc., 1982—; photographer Molloy Coll. Pubs., 1991—. Photographic dir. Bali-Art, Inc., 1992—; mem. N.Y. State AIDS Coun., 1987—, L.I. Alcohol Consortium, 1987—; educator Nassau County Dept. Sr. Citizens Health, 1991—; photographer-in-residence Molloy Coll., 1992—; lectr. on landscape, wildlife and flower photography, L.I., N.H., Can., 1993—. Represented in permanent collections in photographic galleries in Carmel, Calif., Laconia, Wolfboro and Moultonboro, N.H., 1963—; one-woman shows include Mollay Coll., Rockville Ctr. Library; photographer 4 books on Monterey Peninulsa, New Eng. and N.H.; writer, editor Health News Letter Molloy Coll., 1990—. Health educator Nassau County Dept. of Sr. Citizens Outreach Program, Molloy Coll., AIDS educator, 1991—; adminstr., chief AIDS counselor Interaction AIDS Counseling, Babylon, N.Y., 1992—; lic. AIDS educator N.Y. Metro Area; chairperson of grants com. in higher edn. Nassau U.; dir. AIDS Outreach Program, Episcopal Diocese of L.I., 1997—; dir. photography Visual Graphics N.H., 1997—; co-chair AIDS Outreach Cathedral of the Incarnation, 1998—. USPHS fellow, 1962, Nat. Cancer Inst. fellow, 1981-82. Mem. AAUP, AAUW, Nat. Congress Oncology Nurses, N.Y. State Fedn. Health Educators, Inc., Nurses Assn. Counties L.I. Dist. 14, N.Y. State Nurses Assn., World Wildlife Orgn., Audubon Soc., Internat. Ctr. Photography, Nature Conservancy, Sierra Club, Cathedral Womens Club, Alter Guild, Sigma Theta Tau (Epsilon Kappa chpt., rsch. grantee 1985, 87), Zeta Epsilon Gamma. Episcopalian. Avocations: writing, photography. Home: 16 Walker St Malverne NY 11565

RYAN, WILLIAM JOSEPH, multimedia and distance education designer, information technology executive; b. Amsterdam, N.Y., Aug. 12, 1958; s. William John and Joann Gail (Birmingham) R.; m. Amy Diane Friedberg, Aug. 31, 1997; children: Rachel Erin, Haley Ann. BS, SUNY, Brockport, 1979; MS, Ithaca Coll., 1987; PhD, Nova Southeastern U., 2001. Prodn. coord., disc jockey WWBK, Brockport, N.Y., 1979; video prodn. asst. Nat. Tech. Inst for Deaf at Rochester Inst. of Tech., Rochester, N.Y., 1979-80; media specialist Coll. of St. Rose, Albany, 1980-85; video developer Sci. Rsch. Assocs., Chgo., 1987-89; sr. tng. comms. specialist Westinghouse Savannah River Co., Aiken, S.C., 1989-97; dir. instrnl. techs. Lakeland C.C., Kirtland, Ohio, 1997—, v.p. tech., 1998—2003. Mem. adv. com. on tng. and learning Educause, 2002—; cons. Infocomm, Internat. Comms. Industries Assn., Internat. TV Assn. Transition Team, 1991-94; mem. nat. stds. com. for. curriculum devel. for multimedia developers and producers/dirs; bd. dirs. Nat. Adv. Com. Women Tech. Online Project. Contbr. articles to profl. jours.; presenter at tng. and ednl. workshops. Recipient Total Quality Achievement award Environ. Safety, Health and Quality Assurance divsn. Westinghouse Savannah River Co., 1991; grantee Am. Speech-Hearing Assn. and Dept. Edn., 1986; multiple tech. grant Ohio Bd. of Regents, 1997-2001. Mem. Internat. TV Assn. (chair electronic com. commn. 1995-96, bd. dirs. Augusta chpt. 1990-97, chmn. tech. support svcs. 1989-95, judge and panel host ann. video festival interactive category, 1991-99, Nat. Svc. award 1993, 95), Assn. for Applied Interactive Multimedia (bd. dirs. 1993-95), Soc. Motion Picture and TV Engrs., U.S. Sailing Assn., Phi Kappa Phi. Avocations: sailing, music, computers, skiing. Home: 1325 Avondale Rd South Euclid OH 44121-2527 Office: Lakeland CC Tech Divsn 7700 Clocktower Dr Kirtland OH 44094-5198 E-mail: WJRyan@lakelandcc.edu.

RYANS, REGINALD VERNON, music education educator, special education educator; b. Easton, Md., Oct. 12, 1955; s. Alfred Sr. and Alfreda Elizabeth (Thomas) R. AA, Chesapeake Coll., 1975; BS, Morgan State U., 1980; postgrad., Liberty U., Faith Biblical Theol. Inst.; MA, Coll. Notre Dame of Md., 2002. Cert. tchr., Md. Tchr. music Balt. City Pub. Schs., 1980-82; minister of music Faith Unity Fellowship Ch., Millington, Md., 1987-92; tchr. spl. edn. inclusion Balt. City Pub. Sch. Sys., 1997-99; spl. edn. tchr. Anne Arundel County Pub. Sch. Sys., 1999—. Guest musician various chs., Queen Anne's County, Md., 1970—; European tour to Switzerland, Belgium, France, Germany, The Whosoever Will Choir of Balt., Md., 1995. Mng. editor (news publ.) In Touch, 1992. Mem. NAACP. Recipient Svc. award St. James Male Chorus, 1990, Cert. of Appreciation Faith Unity Fellowship Ministries, 1992; ordained elder Faith Unity Ministries, 1992; scholar Raskob Found., 1975, Md. State Senate. Avocations: photography, traveling. Home: 121 Rustic Acres Ln Queenstown MD 21658-1270

RYBAK, JAMES PATRICK, engineering educator; b. Cleve., Mar. 16, 1941; s. John Anthony and Irene Marcella (Kovar) R.; m. Linda Louise Watkins, Oct. 12, 1968. BSEE, Case Western Res. U., 1963; MS, U. N.Mex., 1965; PhD, Colo. State U., 1970. Registered profl. engr., Colo. Mem. tech. staff Sandia Nat. Labs., Albuquerque, 1963-66; rsch. asst., NDEA fellow Colo. State U., Ft. Collins, 1966-70, postdoctoral fellow, 1970-72; prof. engring. and math. Mesa State Coll., Grand Junction, Colo., 1972—, asst. v.p. acad. affairs, 1986-88, v.p. acad. affairs, 1988-98. Contbr. articles to profl. publs. including IEEE Transactions, Engring. Edn., Popular Electronics, Elektrosvyaz (Russia), Radio (Russia). Mem. adv. bd. Grand Mesa Youth Svcs., Grand Junction, 1986-88; bd. dirs. Hilltop Rehab. Hosp., Grand Junction, 1989-93, Salvation Army, Grand Junction, 1993—. NEDA fellow, 1968-70, THEMIS fellow, 1970-72. Mem. IEEE, Am. Soc. Engring. Edn. (vice chmn. Rocky Mountain sect. 1974-75, chmn. 1975-76). Avocation: amateur radio. Home: 314 Quail Dr Grand Junction CO 81503-2527 Office: Mesa State Coll 1175 Texas Ave Grand Junction CO 81501-7605

RYDER, GEORGIA ATKINS, university dean, educator; b. Newport News, Va., Jan. 30, 1924; d. Benjamin Franklin and Mary Lou (Carter) Atkins; m. Noah Francis Ryder, Sept. 16, 1947; children: Olive Diana, Malcolm Eliot, Aleta Renee. BS, Hampton (Va.) Inst., 1944; MusM, U. Mich., 1946; PhD, NYU, 1970. Resource music tchr., Alexandria, Va., 1945-48; faculty music dept. Norfolk State U., 1948—, prof., 1970—, head dept., 1969-79, dean Sch. Arts and Letters, 1979-86. Contbr. chpts. to books and articles to profl. jours. Trustee Va. Symphony, Va. Wesleyan Coll.; bd. dirs. Black Music Rsch. Ctr., Columbia Coll., Chgo., Nat. Assn. Negro Musicians, Southeastern Va. Arts Assn.; Va. Adv. Com. Young Audiences, Va. Coalition for Mus. Edn., Virginians for the Arts. Recipeint Norfolk Com. Improvement Edn. award, 1974, People's Acad. of Arts award, 1985, City of Norfolk award, 1989, Nat. Assn. Negro Musicians award, 1989, NCCJ award, 1990, Va. Laureate in Music award, 1992, Cultural Alliance award Greater Hampton Roads, 1992, Disting. Alumni award Hampton U., 1993, Norfolk State U. Alumni award, 1994, Maude Ellen Coats Armstrong Found. award, 1995; grantee So. Fellowship Fund, 1967-69, Consortium Rsch. Tng., 1973. Mem. Music Educators Nat. Conf., Coll. Music Soc., Intercoll. Music Assn., Va. Music Educators Assn., Delta Sigma Theta.

RYDER, HARL EDGAR, economist, educator; b. Mt. Vernon, Ill., July 11, 1938; s. Harl Edgar and Pearl (Kirkpatrick) R.; m. Mary Irene Kingsolver, June 30, 1970; children— Jonathan Harl, David Eugene, Benjamin James AA, Mt. Vernon Community Coll., 1958; BA, U. Ill., 1960, MS, 1961; PhD, Stanford U., 1967. Asst. prof. econs. Brown U., Providence, 1965-69, assoc. prof., 1969-73, prof., 1973—, chmn. dept. econs., 1974-81. Mem. Am. Econ. Assn., Econometric Soc. Office: Brown Univ Dept Econs 79 Waterman St Providence RI 02912-9079

RYERSON, MARJORIE GILMOUR, journalist, educator, poet, photographer; b. Germantown, Pa., Mar. 28, 1943; d. William Newton and Jean (Hamilton) R.; children: Nicholas, Emily. BA, Beloit Coll., 1965; MFA, U. Iowa, 1976. Assoc. editor, reporter, photographer White River Valley Herald, Randolph, Vt., 1981-85; dir. pub. rels. and fund devel. Gifford Meml. Hosp., Randolph, 1986; editor Country Courier mag., Barre, Vt., 1986-90; features editor Burlington (Vt.) Free Press, 1990; asst. prof. English dept. Johnson (Vt.) State Coll., 1990-91; prof. Comm. Dept. Castleton (Vt.) State Coll., 1991—, chair Comm. Dept., 1996-98. New Eng. Young Writers Conf. faculty, Middlebury Coll., 1991—; dir. Vt. Network Cmty. Newspapers, 1996—; journalism tchr. Dorothy Canfield Fisher Writing Conf., Burlington, 1993; mem. faculty Vt. Coun. on Arts, 1992, lit. advisor; mem. state poet adv. com. for Vt.; faculty fellow Vt. State Colls., 2000-2001; creator, dir. Global Water Music Project, 2002—. Author: Water Music, 2003. Selectman, Town of Randolph, 1995; mem. Randolph Cmty. Devel. Corp. Bd.; corporator Gifford Meml. Hosp.; justice of the peace County of Orange; bd. dirs. Vt. Mozart Festival; vol. Big Bros./Big Sisters Program. Mem. Am. Med. Writers Assn., Image Co-op (pres. bd. dirs.), Vt. League of Writers (hon.), Physicians for Social Responsibility. Avocations: saxophone, piano, voice, hiking, canoeing. Home: 36 Randolph Ave Randolph VT 05060

RYLEE, GLORIA GENELLE, music educator; b. Commerce, Ga., Nov. 26, 1947; d. John Otis Sr. and Genelle Byrd Rylee. BS in Edn., Ga. So. Coll., 1969; MusM, Southwestern Bapt. Theol. Sem., 1973. Tchr. Banks County Bd. Edn., Homer, Ga., 1969-71; piano tchr. Ft. Worth, 1972-73; min. music, ch. sec. Mt. Olive Bapt. Ch., Commerce, Ga., 1974-81; sec. Ga. Bapt. Conv., Atlanta, 1981-86; parapro Banks County Bd. Edn., Homer, 1986-87, tchr. music, 1987—. Tchr. piano, Homer, 1975-81, 89-96; staff mem. Youth II Music Camp, Norman Park, Ga., 1996-98. Pianist Webbs Creek Bapt. Ch., Commerce, 1991—. Active Grassroots Arts Coun., Gainesville, Ga., 1994—, State Bapt. Women's Choral Group, 1979-86, 1996-2001, Messiah Singers, Khabarovsk, Russia, 2003; team mem. Vol. Missions-Ga. Bapt. Conv., Seoul, Korea, 1998-2000; mem. Messiah singers Kahbarovsk, Russia, 2003. Mem. Nat. Mus. Educators Assn., Music. Tchrs. Nat. Assn., Ga. Music Educators Assn., Profl. Assn. Ga. Educators. Home: 1785 Wilson Bridge Rd Homer GA 30547-2911 Office: Banks County Elem Sch 335 Evans St Homer GA 30547

RYMAN, RUTH (STACIE) MARIE, primary education educator; b. Moline, Ill., July 22, 1952; d. Henry Joseph and Gladys Julia (Campbell) DeKeyzer; m. Phillip DeForrest Ryman, Aug. 14, 1976; children: Michelle, Daniel, Jennifer. BA, Augustana Coll., 1974; MA, U. Denver, 1988. Cert. tchr. Resource tchr. Notre Dame Sch., Denver, 1986-91, 2nd grade tchr., 1991—. Cons. Notre Dame Sch., Denver, 1991—. Mem. Nat. Cath. Edn. Assn., Nat. Coun. Tchrs. Math. Office: Notre Dame Sch 2165 S Zenobia St Denver CO 80219-5058

RYMER, ILONA SUTO, artist, retired art educator; b. N.Y.C., Dec. 1, 1921; d. Alexander and Elizabeth (Komaromy) Suto; m. Robert Hamilton Rymer, Mar. 27, 1944 (dec. Dec. 1999); children: Thomas Parker, Shelley Ilona. BA, Long Beach State U., 1953, MA, 1954. Tchr., cons. Long Beach (Calif.) Sch. Dist., 1953-56; tchr. Orange (Calif.) Sch. Dist., 1956-58; tchr., cons. Brea (Calif.)-Olinda Sch. Dist., 1958-80; ind. artist, designer Graphic Ho. Studio, Santa Ynez, Calif., 1980—, Stampa-Barbara, Santa Barbara, Calif., 1990—. Lectr. folk art Brea Sch. Dist., 1975—80. Author: (instrn. book) Folk Art U.S.A., 1975 (Proclamation City of Brea, 1975); art editor, feature writer, illustrator: Arabian Conneciton mag., 1985—86; needlepoint designer Backstitch Store, Solvang, Calif., 1982—83; one-woman shows include Liberty Bell Race Track, Pa., exhibited in group shows, 1970—, exhibitions include Dennas Mus. Ctr., Northwestern Mich. Coll., 2001, exhibited in group shows at Nat. Exhbn. Am. Watercolor, 2002, Adirondack's Nat. Exhbn. of Am. Watercolors, Old Forge, N.Y., 2002—, commission, Pres. Regan's portrait on his stallion, Reagran Libr., Simi Valley, Calif., Khemosabi and Ruth, 1995. Co-founder, mem. Gallery Los Olivos, pres., 1993—. Recipient 1st pl. Seminar award, Rex Brandt, 1961, Affiliate award, Laguna Art Mus., 1967, Best of Watercolor award, Orange County Fair, 1969, Bicentennial trip to France, Air France, 1975, Proclamation for Tchg., City of Brea, 1980, Theme award, Santa Barbara County Fair, 1991. Mem.: Artist Guild Santa Ynez Valley, Ctrl. Coast Art Assn., Santa Barbara ARt Assn., Calif. Gold Coast Watercolor Soc. (signature). Presbyterian. Studio: PO Box 822 Santa Ynez CA 93460-0822 E-mail: ilonarymer@aol.com.

RYMER, WILLIAM ZEV, research scientist, administrator; b. Melbourne, Victoria, Australia, June 3, 1939; came to U.S., 1971; s. Jacob and Luba Rymer; m. Helena Bardas, Apr. 10, 1961 (div. 1975); children: Michael Morris, Melissa Anne; m. Linda Marie Faller, Sept. 5, 1977; 1 child, Daniel Jacob. MBBS, Melbourne U., 1962; PhD, Monash U., Victoria, 1971. Resident med. officer dept. medicine Monash U., Victoria, 1964-66; Fogarty internat. fellow NIH, Bethesda, Md., 1971-74; rsch. assoc. Johns Hopkins U. Med. Sch., Balt., 1975-76; asst. prof. SUNY, Syracuse, 1976-78, Northwestern U., Chgo., 1978-81, assoc. prof., 1981-87, prof., 1987—; rsch. dir. Rehab. Inst. Chgo., 1989—. Contbr. articles to profl. jours. Grantee NIH, VA, Dept. of Def., Nat. Inst. Disability Rehab. Rsch., pvt. founds. Fellow Royal Australian Coll. Physicians; mem. Soc. Neurosci., Am. Soc. Biomechanics. Democrat. Avocations: tennis, racquetball. Office: Rehab Inst Chgo 345 E Superior St Chicago IL 60611-4805

RYNEARSON, PATRICIA HEAVISIDE, elementary school educator; b. Balt., Dec. 19, 1951; d. William and Evelyn (Davis) Heaviside; m. Leo E. Rynearson, Jr., Aug. 6, 1977; children: Courtney, Cliff. BS, U. Del., 1973; MA, U. N. Mex., 1979. Cert. tchr. multiple subjects and reading, Calif. Tchr. Lavaland Sch., Albuquerque, N. Mex., 1977-78, Santo Domingo Sch., Albuquerque, 1978-79, Chapparal Sch., Albuquerque, 1979-80, Liberty Sch., Buckeye, Ariz., 1980-86, Royal Palm Sch., Phoenix, 1986-87, Juniper Sch., Fontana, Calif., 1987-89, Almeria Middle Sch., Fontana, 1989-90, Redwood Sch., Fontana, 1990-98, Truman Mid. Sch., Fontana, 1998—.

Mem. planning com. Environ. EXPO Calif. State Univ., San Bernardino, Calif., 1995-96. Named Inland Empire Environ. Educator of Yr., Calif. State U., San Bernardino, 1996, Conservation Tchr. of Yr., Inland Empire West Resource Conservation Dist., 1997; recipient Eleanor Roosevelt Tchg. fellowship AAUW, 1996; NORCAL model sch. grantee, 1998. Home: 2233 Drummond St Riverside CA 92506-1533 Office: Truman Mid Sch 16224 Mallory Dr Fontana CA 92335-7844

SAADA, ADEL SELIM, civil engineer, educator; b. Heliopolis, Egypt, Oct. 24, 1934; came to U.S., 1959, naturalized, 1965; s. Selim N. and Marie (Chahyne) S.; m. Nancy Helen Hernan, June 5, 1960; children: Christiane Mona, Richard Adel. Ingénieur des Arts et Manufactures, École Centrale, Paris, 1958; MS, U. Grenoble, France, 1959; PhD in Civil Enging, Princeton U., 1961. Registered profl. engr., Ohio. Engr. Société Dumez, Paris, 1959; research assoc. dept. civil enging. Princeton (N.J.) U., 1961-62; asst. prof. civil enging. Case Western Reserve U., Cleve., 1962-67, asso. prof., 1967-72, prof., 1973—, chmn. dept. civil enging., 1978-98, Frank H. Neff prof. civil enging., 1987. R.J. Carroll Meml. lectr. Johns Hopkins U., 1990; cons., lectr. soil testing and properties Waterways Expt. Sta. (C.E.), Vicksburg, Miss., 1974-79; cons. to various firms, 1962—. Author: Elasticity Theory and Applications, 1974, 2d edit., 1993; contbr. numerous articles on soil mechanics and foundation enging. to profl. jours. Recipient Telford Prize Instn. of Civil Engrs., U.K., 1995, Disting. Leadership award Cleve. Tech. Socs., 2001. Fellow ASCE (named Outstanding Civil Engr. of Yr. Cleve. sect. 1992); mem. Internat. Soc. Soil Mechanics, ASTM, One Two One Athletic Club. Achievements include invention of pneumatic analog computer and loading frame. Home: 3342 Braemar Rd Shaker Heights OH 44120-3332 Office: Case Western Res U Dept Civil Engring Case Sch Engring Cleveland OH 44106 E-mail: axs31@po.cwru.edu.

SABAJ, NANCY J. secondary school educator; b. Chgo., Mar. 23, 1969; d. Eugene A. and Florence M. Sabaj. BS in Music Edn., U. Ill., 1992; M in Music Edn., Vander Cook Coll. Music, Chgo., 1997. Cert. tchr. Ill. Band dir. St. John Luth. Sch., Champaign, Ill., 1992—94, Iuka (Ill.) Cmty. Consolidated Dist. 7, 1994—96, Odin (Ill.) Pub. Schs., 1997—2000, Roxana (Ill.) Cmty. Unit Sch. Dist. 1, 2000—. Mem.: Madison County Band Dirs. Assn., Ill. Music Educators Assn., Music Educators Nat. Conf. Avocations: church, fitness, sports. Home: 608 Hillside Bethalto IL 62010

SABATELLA, ELIZABETH MARIA, clinical therapist, educator, mental health facility administrator; b. Mineola, N.Y., Nov. 9, 1940; d. D. F. and Blanche M. (Schmetzle) S; 1 child, Kevin Woog. BS, SUNY, Brockport, 1961; MA, SUNY, Stony Brook, 1971, MSW, 1983; postgrad., Univ. Calif., San Diego, 1999. Lic. social worker N.Y., N.Mex., Oreg.; tchr., sch. counselor Oreg., N.Y., cert. pupil pers. credential, sch. counselor, registered clin. social worker Calif., Oreg. Tchr. physical edn. Comsegogue Sch. Dist., Port Jefferson, N.Y., 1968-73, 84-87, 88-91; sch. counselor, 1975—84; clin. therapist Cibola Counseling Svcs., Grants, N.Mex., 1991-95, regional dir., 1993-95; clin. therapist Family Growth Counseling Ctr., Encinitos, Calif., 1995-96; clin. social worker Family Advocacy, San Diego, 1995-99; sch. counselor San Diego, 1999-2000; counselor Navy Coll., 2000—01; sch. counselor Redmond (Oreg.) Sch. Dist., 2001—, 2001—. Therapist for abused children Farmingville Mental Health Clinic; therapist for adolescents Comsewogue Sch. Dist.; therapist for alcoholics Lighthouse Ctr.; mem. Family Systems Network for Continuing Edn., Calif., Colo., 1978-80; mem. biofeedback and mediation com. McLean Hosp., Boston, 1978; mem. therapeutic touch team East and West Ctr., N.Y.C., 1980-84, sexual abuse treatment coord., 1992-95. Art and photographs exhibited at group show N.Mex. Art League, 1991; author: Stop Before You Blow Your Top, 1998, We Want You To Stop. Children Who Witness Domestic Violence, 1998, Children at Play: Tales of Gang Boys in Treatment, 1999; contbr. poetry and children's story to various publs. Recipient Editor's Choice award and Best New Poet award Nat. Libr. Poetry, 1988, Merit award and Place Winner for Poetry, Iliad Press, 1993. Mem.: NASW, Oregon Ed. Assn., Writers Assn., Oreg. Tchrs. Assn., Acad. Cert. Social Workers, N.Y. State United Tchrs., Sierra Club. Avocations: travel, cycling, yoga, dance, photography. Home: 826 NE Providence Dr Bend OR 97701 E-mail: LIZSABOR@MSN.com.

SABAT-RIVERS, GEORGINA, Latin American literature educator; b. Santiago, Oriente, Cuba; came to U.S., 1962; d. José and Balbina (Mercadé) Sabat; m. Armando A. Guernica (div.); children: Armando A., Antonio J., Rodolfo M., Georgina M.; m. Elias L. Rivers, Sept. 19, 1969. MA in Romance Langs., Johns Hopkins U., 1967, PhD in Romance Langs., 1969. Instr. U. Oriente, Santiago de Cuba, 1956-61; asst. prof. Georgetown Visitation Coll., Washington, 1962-63, Western Md. Coll., Westminster, 1963-69, assoc. prof., 1969-73, prof., 1973-78, chair dept., 1974-78; assoc. prof. SUNY, Stony Brook, 1978-86, prof., 1986—, chair dept., 1981-84. Vis. prof. U. Calif., Irvine, 1989, U. Iowa, Iowa City, 1994, UNAM, Mexico City. Author: El Sueño de Sor Juana Inés de la Cruz: tradiciones literarias y originalidad, 1976, Sor Juana Inés de la Cruz Inundación castálida, 1982, Literatura Femenina conventual: Sor Marcela de San Félix Hija de Lope, 1992, others; mem. editl. bd. Colonial L.Am. Rev., 1990—, Calíope, En busca de Sor Juana, 1998, others; contbr. articles to profl. jours. Fellow NEH, 1984-85, Fulbright, 1987; Soviet Union Internat. Rsch. and Exch. Bd. grantee, 1986, Summer seminar grantee NEH, 1995. Fellow Am. Philos. Soc.; mem. MLA (del. 1988-93), AAUW, Inst. Internat. Revista Iberoamericana Lit. (editl. bd. 1987-90).

SABBAGHA, RUDY E. obstetrician, gynecologist, educator; b. Oct. 29, 1931; arrived in U.S., 1965, naturalized; s. Elias C. and Sonia B.S.; m. Asma E. Sahyouny, Oct. 5, 1957; children: Elias, Randa. BA, Am. U., Beirut, 1952, MD, 1958. Diplomate Am. Bd. Ob-Gyn. Sr. physician Tapline, Saudi Arabia, 1958-64, ob-gyn specialist, 1969-70; tchg. fellow U. Pitts./Magee Women's Hosp., 1965-68; fellow diagnostic ultrasound U. Glasgow, Scotland, 1970; asst. prof. ob-gyn U. Pitts., 1970-75; prof. Northwestern U., Chgo., 1975-94; med. dir. Obstet. and Gynecol. Ultrasound S.C., 1994—; clin. prof. U. Chgo. Pritzker Sch. Medicine, 1995-2000; prof. emeritus Northwestern U., Ill., 1995—. Obstetrician, gynecologist Prentice Women's Hosp., Chgo., 1975—. Editor: Ultrasound Applied to Obstetrics and Gynecology, 1980, 3d edit., 1994; co-editor: Fetal Anomalies: Ultrasound Diagnosis and Postnatal Management, 2001; contbr. articles to profl.jours. Fellow Am. Coll. Obstetricians and Gynecologists, Am. Inst. Ultrasound in Medicine; mem. Soc. Gynecol. Investigation, Am. Gynecol. and Obstet. Soc., Ctrl. Assn. Obstetricians and Gynecologists. Research on diagnostic ultrasound, obstetrics and gynecology. Office: 680 N Lake Shore Dr Ste 1430 Chicago IL 60611-8702 Fax: 312-656-9202.

SABEY, J(OHN) WAYNE, academic administrator, consultant; b. Murray, Utah, Dec. 10, 1939; s. Alfred John and Bertha (Lind) Sabey; m. Marie Bringhurst, Sept. 10, 1964; children: Clark Wayne, Colleen, Carolyn, Natasha Lynne. BA in Asian Studies, Brigham Young U., 1964, MA in Asian History, 1965; PhD in E. Asian History, U. Mich., 1972. Tchg. asst. Brigham Young U., Provo, Utah, 1964-65, rsch. asst., 1965, adj. prof. history, 1988-89, 2002—; rsch. asst. U. Mich., Ann Arbor, 1966; from instr. to asst. prof. history U. Utah, Salt Lake City, 1970-80; v.p. Western Am. Lang. Inst., Salt Lake City, 1980-84, dir., 1984-86, pres., 1986—; exec. v.p. Pacific Rim Bus. Coords., Salt Lake City, 1993—, also bd. dirs., 1993—; dir. Japan Ops. E'OLA Products, Inc., St. George, Utah, 1996-99; MBA program dir. Walden U., Mpls., 1999—2001. Assoc. dir. exch. program U. Utah and Nagoya Broadcasting Network Japan, 1973—79; lectr. in field. Contbr. articles to ency. Sec. to bd. trustees We. Am. Lang. Inst., 1980—86, chmn. bd. trustees, 1986—, Found. Internat. Understanding, 1982—; internat. adv. coun. Salt Lake CC, 1988—94; bd. advisors Consortium Internat. Edn., 1972—77. Recipient Superior award in extemporaneous speaking, 1956; U.S. Nat. Def. Fgn. Lang. fellow, 1965—68, Fulbright-Hays Rsch. fellow, Japan, 1968—69, Horace H. Rackham Sch. Grad. Studies fellow, 1969—70. Mem.: Assn. Asian Studies (gen. chairperson, chairperson arrangementw we. conf. 1970—72), Phi Kappa Phi. Avocations: piano, hiking, basketball, stamp collecting, tennis. Home and Office: 8710 Oakwood Park Cir Sandy UT 84094-1800 E-mail: wmnsabey@aros.net.

SABHARWAL, CHAMAN LAL, computer science educator; b. Ludhiana, Panjab, India, Aug. 15, 1937; came to U.S., 1963; s. Milkhi Ram and Tara Vanti (Kaura) S.; m. Chander Lekha Khosla, July 12, 1968 (div. Sept. 2001); children: Anup K., Aman D. MS, U. Ill., 1966, PhD, 1967. Asst. prof. St. Louis U., 1967-71, assoc. prof., 1971-75, prof., 1975-83; sr. systems analyst McDonnell Douglas Co., St. Louis, 1980-81, specialist, 1981-82, lead engr., 1984-85, sr. specialist, 1985-86; prof. computer sci. U. Mo.-Rolla, St. Louis, 1986—. Cons. McDonnell Douglas Co., St. Louis, 1986-90. Home: 5892 Chrisbrook Dr Saint Louis MO 63128-4413 Office: U Mo-Rolla 1870 Miner Cir Rolla MO 65409

SABIK, JOSEPH ANDREW, psychometrist, counselor; b. Uniontown, Pa., Dec. 28, 1943; s. Joseph Andrew and Dorothy G. (Maycheck) S. AB in Philosophy, St. Vincent Coll., 1966; MDiv, St. Vincent Sem., 1969; postgrad., John Carroll U., 1982-84, MA in Counseling and Human Svcs., 1991. Ordained priest Roman Cath. Ch., 1970; profl. clin. counselor, Ohio. Assoc. pastor, Pa., 1970-80, St. Paul Parish, Euclid, Ohio, 1982, St. Peter & Paul Parish, Garfield Heights, Ohio, 1982-85; psychometrist John Carroll U., Cleve., 1986-91; cons. Cleve., 1991—; counselor family svcs. dept. Cleve. Christian Home, 1998—. Counselor CAEL/Ohio Bell, Cleve., 1989-91; instr. John Carroll U., 1989, 92. Mem. ACA, Assn. for Religious Values in Counseling, Assn. for Assessment in Counseling. Roman Catholic. Avocations: sculpting, ukrainian easter eggs, computers. Home: 19508 Meadowlark Ln Cleveland OH 44128-2743 Office: Cleve Christian Home Family Svcs Dept 1700 Denison Ave Ste 205 Cleveland OH 44109-2926 E-mail: jsabik@cchome.org.

SABINI, BARBARA DOROTHY, art educator, artist; b. Bklyn., June 11, 1939; d. Joseph and Fannie (Ciazzia) Gugliucci; m. John Sabini Jr., June 22, 1957 (div. 1982); children: Michael, John, Gerald, Barbara-Jo. AAS in Psychology, Orange County C.C., Middletown, N.Y., 1979; BFA in Painting, SUNY, New Paltz, 1984, MFA in Painting, 1988. Cert. tchr. art edn. Tchg. asst. drawing and design SUNY, New Paltz, 1986; art tchr. Newburgh (N.Y.) Free Acad. H.S., 1987—. Lectr. freshman drawing SUNY, NW Paltz, 1990; painting instr. Orange County C.C., 1991; instr. collage Coll. New Rochelle, N.Y., 2001; faculty supr. teen art projects Newburgh Free Acad. H.S., 1990-99; instr. Kosciuszko Found./UNESCO, Poland, 1995, 96, 97; mem. China Study Tour, 1998; lead tchr. Travel & Tourism Acad., 1999. One-woman shows include White Herron Lounge, Virginia Beach, Va., 1986, Ave. A Cafe, N.Y.C., 1987, Pumpkin Eater, N.Y.C., 1989, Painters Tavern, Cornwall-on-Hudson, N.Y., 1992; exhibited in group shows including Hammerquist Gallery, N.Y.C., 1984, Ariel Gallery, N.Y.C., 1985, James Callahan Gallery, Palm Springs, Calif., 1985, The Real Gallery, Cornwall, N.Y., 1986, Cork Gallery, Lincoln Ctr., N.Y.C., 1986, Mid Hudson Arts and Sci. Ctr., Poughkeepsie, N.Y., 1986, Ledo Gallery, N.Y.C., 1987, Outer Space Gallery, N.Y.C., 1989, 91, Wall Gallery, N.Y.C., 1989, 90, Women in the Arts Found. Gallery, N.Y.C., Ledger DeMain Gallery, N.Y.C., China Phoenix Gallery Store, Albuquerque, 1995. Recipient Appreciation cert. N.Y. State Art Tchrs. Assn., 1st pl. award Most Creative Olympics of Visual Arts. Mem. Nat. Art Tchrs. Assn., N.Y. State Tchrs. Assn., N.Y. State Art Tchrs. Assn. Avocations: travel, cross country skiing, reading, arts. Home: 27 Manor Dr Cornwall NY 12518-1474 Office: Newburgh Free Acad 201 Fullerton Ave Newburgh NY 12550-3798

SABLAN, RITA ALDAN, state agency administrator; b. Saipan, No. Mariana Islands, Oct. 24, 1956; d. Ignacio C. and Merced A. Deleon (Guerrero) Aldan; m. Francisco C. Sablan, June 2, 1979; children: Sonnie, Lela. BS, Coll. St. Mary, Omaha, 1978; MA, San Jose State U., 1983. Classroom tchr. Mt. Carmel Sch., Chalan Kanoa, Saipan; classroom tchr. Garapan (Saipan) Elem. Sch., prin.; vice prin. Dept. Edn. Commonwealth No. Mariana Islands, Garapan, asst. dep. commr. for instrn., 1991—. Chair exec. com. Edn. Week, Commonwealth No. Mariana Islands, 1992, chair ORA com. sch. restructuring, 1992; chair pacific region Healthy Children Ready to Learn Conf., 1993. Rsch. A Study on Pre-Sch. Edn. on Saipan. Vol. Hotline/ Crisis 1989—; Exec. Mem. Spl. Sports Championship, 1990; leader Boy Scouts Am. Grantee Prin.'s Inst. Peabody Coll. Vanderbilt U. Mem. ASCD, Nat. Coun. Social Studies, Leaders Ednl. Adminstrn. Devel. (adv. com.). Home: PO Box 1548 Saipan MP 96950-1548

SABO, MARY JANE, secondary school educator; b. Perth Amboy, N.J., Apr. 16, 1953; d. John William and Mary (Toth) S. AA, Middlesex County Coll., Edison, N.J., 1973; BA, Kean Coll. of N.J., 1976, MA, 1982. Cert. tchr., adminstr., N.J. reading specialist, English. Tchr. English, reading Woodbridge (N.J.) H.S., 1977—; tchr.-in-charge 3 program sites after-care program Woodbridge Twp. Schs., 1995—. Cons. Holistic Scoring, N.J., 1984—; participant Woodbridge-Rutgers project, 1988; mem. student rev. assessment com. Woodbridge Twp. Schs., 1994. Com. rels. dir. Mayor's Adv. Com., Woodbridge Twp., 1988-92, cons. to News Letter editor Blinded Vets. Assn., 1987-89. Mem. Woodbridge Twp. Edn. Assn. (bldg. rep.) Democrat. Roman Catholic. Home: 265 East Rd Belford NJ 07718-1608 Office: Woodbridge HS Rt 35 Woodbridge NJ 07095

SABOTA, CATHERINE MARIE, horticulturist, educator; b. Bridgeton, N.J., Sept. 9, 1949; d. John Robert Sabota and Colleen Catherine Schultz. BS, Tex. Tech. U., 1973, MS, 1975; PhD, U. Ill., 1983. Rsch. asst. Tex. Tech. U., Lubbock, 1973-75, rsch. assoc., 1975-76; asst. horticulturist U. Ill., Dixon Springs, 1978-80, rsch. assoc. Champaign, 1980-83; horticulturist, asst. prof. Ala. A&M Normal U., Normal, 1983-88, horticulturist, assoc. prof., 1988-95, prof., 1995—. Advisor Ala.-Tenn. Fruit and Vegetable Assn., Elora, Tenn., 1986-90. Contbr. articles to profl. jours. Recipient award of excellence coop. ext. program Ala. A&M U., 1989, 93; Tex. State scholar, 1971-73; grantee Coop. State Rsch. Ext. Edn. Svc.-USDA, 1986, 93—, Soil Conservation Svc., 1986, U. Ala.-TVA Consortium, 1987. Mem. Am. Soc. Hort. Sci. (Continuing Edn. Aids award 1994, ext. div. award 1995), Ala. Fruit and Vegetable Growers, So. Region Soc. Hort. Sci. (chmn. awards com. 1990, chmn. ext. div. 1994). Achievements include research of shiitake mushrooms, sustainable agriculture and evening primrose. Office: Ala A&M Univ PO Box 69 Normal AL 35762-0069

SACCOMAN, STEFANIE ANN, science educator; b. San Francisco, Dec. 13, 1953; d. Frank and Jacqueline (Collier) S. BS in Biology, Calif. Poly. U., 1976, MA in Edn., 1980; postgrad., Calif. State U., L.A., 1994; MS in Psychology, Calif. Coast U., 1996, PhD in Psychology, 1998. Environ. scientist Engring.-Sci. Inc., Arcadia, Calif., 1978-83; sci. tchr. Pasadena (Calif.) H.S., 1983-90; sci. and math curriculum specialist Pomona (Calif.) Unified Sch. Dist., 1990-95; project dir. Sci. Inst. for Modern Pedagogy & Creative Tchg. Coll. Sci. Calif. Poly. U., 1995—. Instr. sci. edn. for secondary tchrs. La. State U., Baton Rouge, summer 1990, 91. Contbr. (lab. manual) Cal Poly University Institute for Cellular and Molecular Biology Experiments for Science Teachers, 1985. Spkr. on math curriculum Rotary Club, Pomona, 1993; spkr. on sci. instrn. and student self esteem Human Rights Conf., Pomona, 1994. Recipient Calif. Congress of Parents, Tchrs., Students Svc. award PTA, Pasadena, 1987, Disting. Tchr. award Verdugo Hills Hosp., Glendale, 1988, Bautzer award for university advancement, 1999; named Outstanding Young Woman of Am., 1981. Mem. ASCD, Nat. Coun. Tchrs. Math., Nat. Assn. Biology Tchrs., N.Y. Acad. Sci. Avocations: travel, gardening, nature study. Office: Calif Poly U 3801 W Temple Ave Pomona CA 91768-2557 E-mail: sasaccoman@csupomona.edu.

SACHA, ROBERT FRANK, osteopathic physician; b. East Chicago, Ind., Dec. 29, 1946; s. S. Frank John and Ann Theresa S.; m. Linda T. LePage, 1988; children: Joshua Jude, Josiah Gerard, Anastasia Levon, Jonah Bradley. BS, Purdue U., 1969; DO, Chgo. Coll. Osteo. Medicine, 1975. Diplomate Am. Bd. Pediatrics, Am. Bd. Allery and Immunology. Pharmacist, asst. mgr. Walgreens Drug Store, East Chicago, Ind., 1969-75; intern David Grant Med. Ctr., San Francisco, 1975-76, resident in pediatrics, 1976-78; fellow in allergy and immunology Wilford Hall Med. Ctr., 1978-80; staff pediatrician, allergist Scott AFB (Ill.), 1980-83; practice medicine specializing in allergy and immunology Cape Girardeau, Mo., 1983—. Assoc. clin. instr. St. Louis U., 1980—; clin. instr. Purdue U., 1971-72, Pepperdine U., 1975-76, U. Tex.-San Antonio, 1978-80, assoc. clin. instr. So. Ill. U. Pres., Parent Tchrs. League; bd. gov. Chgo. Coll. Osteopathic Medicine. Maj. M.C. USAF, 1975-83, comdr. USNR. Named one of Top Pediatricians 2002-2003, Pediatric Allergy, Immunology. Fellow Am. Coll. Allergy, Am. Coll. Chest Physicians, Am. Acad. Pediatrics, Am. Acad. Allergy-Immunology, Am. Assn. Cert. Allergists; mem. ACP, AMA, Am. Acad. Allergy, Assn. Mil. Allergists, Am. Coll. Emergency Physicians, Mil. Surgeons and Physicians. Republican. Lutheran. E-mail: bsacha@charter.net.

SACHDEV, SUBIR, education educator; b. New Delhi, Dec. 2, 1961; BSc, Mass. Inst. Tech., 1982; MA, Harvard U., 1984, PhD, 1985; MA (hon.), Yale U., 1995. Prof. physics and applied physics Yale U., 1987—; postdoctoral mem. of tech. staff AT & T Bell Lab., Murray Hill, NJ, 1985—87; asst. prof. Yale U., New Haven, 1987—89, assoc. prof. (term), 1987—89, assoc. prof. (tenured), 1992—95, prof., 1995—. Vis. scientist IBM Thomas J. Watson Rsch. Ctr., 1988, AT&T Bell Lab., 1987—89; vis. prof. U. de Paris VII, 1993, U. Joseph Fourier, 1997, Inst. Henri Poincare, 1999, U. of Fribourg, 2000, Harvard U., 2001. Recipient Creativity award, Nat. Sci. Found., 1998, Presdl. Young Investigator, 1988—93, LeRoy Apker award for outstanding achievement in physics by an undergraduate, Am. Phys. Soc., 1983; fellowship, John Simon Guggenheim Meml. Found., 2003, Alfred P. Sloan fellow, 1989. Fellow: Am. Phys. Soc. Office: Dept Physics Yale U PO Box 208120 New Haven CT 06520

SACHITANO, SHEILA MARIE, secondary school educator, small business owner; b. Austin, Tex., July 25, 1948; d. Marvin Valery and Dorthy Marie (Gunn) Louviere; m. Bennett Meigs Jenkins, Jr. June, 1973 (div. Sept. 1975); m. Fred Clarke Sachitano, May 8, 1979; 1 child, Derek Alexander. BA, U. Tex., 1970, MA, Lamar U., 1975. Cert. tchr., supr., Tex. Tchr. Anahuac (Tex.) H.S., 1970-75; sales mgr. Jarad's Inc., Beaumont, Tex., 1976—78; tchr. Hamshire (Tex.) Fannett H.S., 1978—2002; ret., 2002. Mng. agt. Young Estate Farm, Port Arthur, Tex., 1987-2003; sec. campus site base Hamshire Fannett H.S., 1994-96, 98-99; pres. dist. site base, Hamshire-Fannet Ind. Sch. Dist., 1996-2000; presenter New Tchr. Orientation, Hamshire-Fannett H.S., 1994—, UIL coord., 1999-2002, chair dept. English, 1999-2002; owner Modern Electric Co. of Beaumont, Inc., 1988-2003. Compiler Genealogical Books: The D'Amours de Louvieres in France, Canada, Louisiana, (3 vols.). Pres. Twin County Babe Ruth League, Winnie, Tex., 1994, 95; team organizer Twin County Baseball, Sour Lake, Tex., 1996-97. Recipient UIL Sponsor Excellence award, 2000—01. Mem NEA, Am. Assn. Tchrs. French (v.p. East Tex. chpt. 1998-2000), Nat. Coun. Tchrs. of English, Tex. State Tchrs. Assn. (pres. 1986-88), Pi Delta Phi. Roman Catholic. E-mail: fscaesar@aol.com.

SACHS, DAVID HOWARD, surgery and immunology educator, researcher; b. N.Y.C., Jan. 10, 1942; s. Elliot and Elsie (Hurvitz) S.; m. Kristina Olsson, Mar. 15, 1969; children: Michelle, Jessica, Karin, Teviah. AB, Harvard U., 1963; DES, U. Paris, 1964; MD, Harvard U., Boston, 1968. Intern in surgery Mass. Gen. Hosp., Boston, 1968-69, resident in surgery, 1969-70, dir. transplantation biology rsch. ctr. surgery dept., 1991—; chief immunology br. Nat. Cancer Inst., Bethesda, Md., 1982-90; prof. surgery and immunology Harvard U. Med. Sch., 1991—. Capt. PHS, 1970-91. Avocations: gardening, fishing, windsurfing, skiing. Office: Mass Gen Hosp East Bldg 149-9019 13th St Boston MA 02129

SACKETT, GLENN CHARLES, theology studies educator; b. Caldwell, Idaho; s. Glenn Clarence and Iva Blanche (Bonde) S.; m. Gail L., Aug. 23, 1970; children: Michelle, Amy, Jill. BA, Boise Bible Coll., 1972; MDiv, Lincoln Christian Sem., 1982; D of Ministry, Trinity Evang. Divinity Sch., 1989. Minister Garibaldi (Oreg.) Ch. of Christ, 1972-77, Pontoon Beach Ch. of Christ, Granite City, Ill., 1977-83; prof. Christian ministries Lincoln (Ill.) Christian Coll., 1983—2003; preaching min. Madison Park Christian Ch., Quincy, Ill., 1999—; prof. preaching Lincoln Christian Sem., 2003—. Interim ministry 1st Christian Ch., Moweagua, Ill., 1995-96, 2d Ch. of Christ, Danville, Ill., 1989-90. Bd. dirs. YMCA, Lincoln, 1992-2000, Boise Bible Coll., 1974-77, Bond Christian Svc. Camp, Greenville, Ill., 1979-82; pres. Lady Railers Booster Club, Lincoln, 1988-89. Recipient Disting. Svc. award Boise Bible Coll., 1987. Mem. Am. Acad. Ministry, Acad. Homiletics, Evangelical Homiletics Soc. Avocation: marathon running. Office: Lincoln Christian Sem 100 Campus View Dr Lincoln IL 62656-2111 E-mail: csackett@lccs.edu.

SACKIN, CLAIRE, retired social work educator; b. N.Y.C., Oct. 1, 1925; d. Harry and Diana (Mednick) Gershfeld; m. Milton Sackin, Feb. 4, 1955; children: William, Daniel, David. BA, Hunter Coll., 1946; MEd, U. Pitts., 1968, MSW, 1972, PhD, 1976. Tenured tchr. jr. high sch., Bronx, N.Y., 1947-57; rsch. asst. U. Pitts., 1973, instr. dept. urban mgmt., 1974; rsch. assoc. U. Pitts. Sch. of Social Work, 1975-76, Health & Welfare Planning Assn., 1974; prof. social work, dir. social work program St. Francis U., Loretto, Pa., 1976-97, prof. emerita, 1997—. Registered trainer alcoholism specialists cert. program; mem. adv. bd. Cedar Manor Treatment Ctr., Cresson, Pa., 1994-95; mem. Pa. Gov.'s Coun. Alcoholism, 1980, Nat. Assn. People with AIDS; presenter in field. Contbr. articles to jours. Mem. NASW (social action com. Pa. chpt. 1983-85, mem. Del. Assembly 1984, eastern regional coalition liaison 1984), Coun. on Social Work Edn., Amyotrophic Lateral Sclerosis Assn., Alpha Delta Mu (nat. bd. dirs.). Avocations: reading, crossword puzzles, opera, gardening, travel. Home: 531 Sandrae Dr Pittsburgh PA 15243-1727 Office: St Francis U Loretto PA 15940 E-mail: sackin@worldnet.att.net.

SACKS, SUSAN BENDERSKY, mental health clinical specialist, educator; b. San Antonio, June 1, 1957; d. Gordon and Renée (Freedman) Bendersky; m. Stephen Sacks, Sept. 18, 1988. BSN, U. Pa., 1981, MS in Nursing. Cert. psychiat. clin. nurse specialist, cognitive behavioral hypnotherapist and trauma response clinician. Faculty U. Pa. Sch. Nursing, Phila.; pvt. practice hypnosis and psychotherapy and cons. Spkr. in field. Home: 650 Malin Rd Newtown Square PA 19073-2613 E-mail: sacksfamily@yahoo.com.

SACKSTEIN, ROSALINA GUERRERO, music educator, consultant; b. Camaguey, Cuba, Mar. 5, 1923; came to U.S., 1948; d. Luis and Rosalina (Santana) Guerrero; m. Louis Aguirre, Jan. 1, 1939 (div. June 1946); 1 child, Louis Aguirre Jr.; m. Harold C. Sackstein, Apr. 19, 1952; children: Rosalin R., Robert. B in Arts and Scis., Inst. Camaguey, 1941; prof. piano, violin theory, solfege, Conservatory of Music, Camaguey, 1944; D in Pedagogy, U. Havana, Cuba, 1947; M in Secondary Edn., U. Miami, Coral Gables, 1964. Music tchr. Abraham Lincoln Jr. H.S., Havana, 1944-47; psychology of music tchr. Tchrs. Coll., Havana, 1953-59; tchr. music theory, ear tng., solfege U. Miami Sch. Music, Coral Gables, 1963-65, asst. prof. to assoc. prof., 1963-78, prof. music, 1978—. Faculty advisor Sigma Chi chpt. U. Miami, 1970-90; founding mem. women's adv. com. acad. affairs, U. Miami, 1972—. Concert pianist, Cuba, 1944-48, U.S., 1952—; various solo recitals and orch. solos, U.S. and abroad; also appearances on radio and T.V. Chair of judges, Fla. Fedn. Music Clubs, Royal Poinciana, 1980—; mem. bd. Chopin Found. Miami, 1998. Recipient Gold medal, concerto competition, Havana, 1947; recipient Baldwin Keyboard award, 1977-78, 83-84; recipient Cmty. Svc. award B'nai B'rith, 1992. Mem. Am. Coll. Musicians (judge 1964—), Nat. Music Tchrs. Assn., Fla. State Music Tchrs. Assn. (pres. dist. 6 1969-71, pub. sch. liaison dist. 1971-73), Miami Music Tchrs. Assn. (pres. 1991-93, bd. dirs. 1993—), Young Performers Music Club (advisor 1970—), Miami Civic Music Assn. (v.p. 1981-83, pres. 1983—), Sigma Alpha Iota (advisor, v.p. 1964—, sword of honor 1975), Pi Kappa Lambda. Avocations: sports, games. Office: U Miami Sch Music PO Box 248165 Coral Gables FL 33124-8165

SACKTON, FRANK JOSEPH, public affairs educator; b. Chgo., Aug. 11, 1912; m. June Dorothy Raymond, Sept. 21, 1940. Student, Northwestern U., 1936, Yale, 1946, U. Md., 1951-52, BS, 1970; grad., Army Inf. Sch., 1941, Command and Gen. Staff Coll., 1942, Armed Forces Staff Coll., 1949, Nat. War Coll., 1954; MPA, Ariz. State U., 1976, DHL (hon.), 1996. Mem. 131st Inf. Regt., Ill. N.G., 1929-40; commd. 2d lt. U.S. Army, 1934, advanced through grades to lt. gen., 1967; brigade plans and ops. officer (33d Inf. Div.), 1941, PTO, 1943-45; div. signal officer, 1942-43; div. intelligence officer, 1944; div. plans and ops. officer, 1945; sec. to gen. staff for Gen. MacArthur, 1947-48; bn. comdr. 30th Inf. Regt., 1949-50; mem. spl. staff Dept. Army, 1951; plans and ops. officer Joint Task Force 132, PTO, 1952; comdr. Joint Task Force 7, Marshall Islands, 1953; mem. gen. staff Dept. Army, 1954-55; with Office Sec. Def., 1956; comdr. 18th Inf. Regt., 1957-58; chief staff 1st Inf. Div., 1959; chief army Mil. Mission to Turkey, 1960-62; comdr. XIV Army Corps, 1963; dep. dir. plans Joint Chiefs Staff, 1964-66; army general staff mil. ops., 1966-67; comptroller of the army, 1967-70; ret., 1970; spl. asst. for fed./state relations Gov. Ariz., 1971-75; chmn. Ariz. Programming and Coordinating Com. for Fed. Programs, 1971-75; lectr. Am. Grad. Sch. Internat. Mgmt., 1973-77; vis. asst. prof., lectr. public affairs Ariz. State U., Tempe, 1976-78; founding dean Ariz. State U. Coll. Public Programs, 1979-80; prof. public affairs Ariz. State U., 1980—, finance educator, v.p. bus. affairs, 1981-83, dep. dir. intercollegiate athletics, 1984-85, dir. strategic planning, 1987-88. Contbr. articles to public affairs and mil. jours. Mem. Ariz. Steering Com. for Restoration of the State Capitol, 1974-75, Ariz. State Personnel Bd., 1978-83, Ariz. Regulatory Coun., 1981-93. Decorated D.S.M., Silver Star, also Legion of Merit with 4 oak leaf clusters, Bronze Star with 2 oak leaf clusters, Air medal, Army Commendation medal with 1 oak leaf cluster, Combat Inf. badge. Mem. Ariz. Acad. Public Adminstrn., Pi Alpha Alpha (pres. chpt. 1976-82) Clubs: Army-Navy (Washington); Arizona Country (Phoenix). Home: 12000 N 90th St Unit 3072 Scottsdale AZ 85260-8643 Office: Ariz State U Sch Pub Affairs Tempe AZ 85287-0603 E-mail: frank.sackton@asu.edu.

SADE, DONALD STONE, anthropology educator; b. Charleston, W.Va., July 17, 1937; s. Samuel and Charlotte Tracy (Stone) S.; m. Bonita Diane Chepko, Dec. 24, 1971 (div. Feb. 1994); children: Irony Cuervo del Norte, Omen Ondatra; m. Kerry L. Knox, Nov. 24, 1994. Grad., N.Y. State Ranger Sch., 1957; student, Hamilton Coll., 1957-60; AB, U. Calif., Berkeley, 1963, PhD, 1966. Instr. anthropology Northwestern U., Evanston, Ill., 1965-66, asst. prof., 1966-70, assoc. prof., 1970-75, prof., 1975-95, sr. lectr., 1995—97; scientist-in-charge Cayo Santiago, U. P.R., 1970-77; prof. emeritus Northwestern U., 1997—. Founder, pres. North Country Inst. for Natural Philosophy, Inc., Mexico, N.Y., 1980— Sr. author: Basic Demographic Observations on Free-Ranging Rhesus Monkeys, 3 vols., 1985; editor: The North Country Naturalist, Vol. 1, 1987. Recipient Merit cert., Eastman Sch. Music., 2002; grantee, NSF, 1967—. Mem. Animal Behavior Soc., Guild Am. Luthiers, The Nature Conservancy, The Adirondack Mountain Club, The Adirondack Coun. Office: North Country Inst for Natural Philosophy Inc 18 Emery Rd Mexico NY 13114-3311

SADEGHI-NEJAD, ABDOLLAH, pediatrician, educator; b. Meshed, Iran, Apr. 29, 1938; s. Abdolhossein and Azizeh (Jabbari) S.-N.; m. Marion M. Marquardt, Jan. 26, 1974; children; Nathan R., Adrienne R. BA, Beloit Coll., 1960; MS in Pathology, MD, U. Chgo., 1964. Diplomate Am. Bd. Pediatrics. Intern then resident U. Chgo., 1964-67; fellow pediatric endocrinology Tufts-New Eng. Med. Ctr., Boston, 1967-69, U. Calif., San Francisco, 1969-70; from asst. prof. to prof. pediatrics Tufts-New Eng. U., Boston, 1970—; chief pediatric endocrinology and metabolism divsn. New Eng. Med. Ctr., Boston, 1989—. Author and co-author books and articles. Mem. town meeting Town of Brookline, Mass., 1987-2001, mem. adv. com., 1993-99; founder, mem. Friends of Lost Pond. Fellow Am. Acad. Pediatrics; mem. Am. Pediatric Soc., Am. Diabetes Assn., Endocrine Soc., European Soc. Pediatric Rsch., Lawson Wilkins Pediat. Endocrine Soc., Soc. Pediat. Rsch. Office: Tufts-New Eng Med Ctr 750 Washington St Boston MA 02111-1526

SADLER, CHARLOTTE BROOKS, special education educator; b. Freemont, Ohio, Feb. 17, 1956; d. Lewis Watson and Jane Brooks (Buehler) S. BS in Recreation Adminstrn., Slippery Rock State Coll., 1979; MA in Spl. Edn., W.Va. U., 1982, postgrad., 1983-84. Cert. spl. edn. tchr., N.J., Pa., Va., W.Va., Md. Grad. teaching asst. reading lab. W.Va. U., Morgantown, 1983-84; learning disabilities resource educator Stafford (Va.) County Schs., 1984-85; spl. edn. educator grades 9-12 resource room Berkeley Springs (W.Va.) High Sch., 1985-87; spl. edn. tchr. grades 9-12 Middle Twp. High Sch., Cape May Court House, N.J., 1987—. Home bound instr., Mid. Twp. High Sch., 1987—, summer sch. tchr., 1988-91, tutor, 1992—. Mem. NEA, N.J. Edn. Assn., Mid. Twp. Edn. Assn., Coun. for Exceptional Children. Avocations: genealogy, film, leisure reading. Home: 8404 Pacific Ave Wildwood Crest NJ 08260-3512 Office: Mid Twp High Sch 212 Bayberry Dr Cape May Court House NJ 08210-2433

SADOSKI, MARK CHRISTIAN, education educator; b. Bristol, Conn., June 2, 1945; s. Waldmyr John Sadoski and Ruth Elaine (Gustafson) Kantorski; m. Carol Ann Bove, June 28, 1969; 1 child, Thomas Christian. BS, So. Conn. State U., 1968, MS, 1973; PhD, U. Conn., 1981. Cert. reading, English, social studies tchr. Tchr., reading cons. Milford (Conn.) Pub. Schs., 1968-81; assoc. faculty So. Conn. State U., New Haven, 1978-81; prof. edn. Tex. A&M Univ., College Station, 1981—. Author: (with Allan Paivio) Imagery and Text: A Dual Coding Theory of Reading and Writing, 2001; mem. editl. bd. Reading Rsch. Quar., 1989—, Jour. Reading Behavior, 1990-95, Reading Psychology, 1990—, Jour. Literacy Rsch., 1995—, Document Design, 1998—, Reading and Writing, 2001—; contbr. over 75 articles to profl. jours. and books. Accident prevention counselor S.W. region FAA, 1989-91. Recipient Disting. Alumnus award So. Conn. State U., 1994. Mem. Internat. Reading Assn. (outstanding dissertation award com. 1983-85, finalist Outstanding Dissertation award 1982), Nat. Reading Conf. (Outstanding Book award com. 1994-99), Am. Ednl. Rsch. Assn. (outstanding book award com. 1994-2000), Soc. for Sci. Study of Reading (chair pubs. com. 1996-97), Phi Kappa Phi. Avocations: reading, cinema. Office: Tex A&M Univ Dept TLAC College Station TX 77843-4232 E-mail: msadoski@tamu.edu.

SADOWAY, DONALD ROBERT, materials science educator; b. Toronto, Mar. 7, 1950; s. Donald Anthony and Irene Mary (Romanko) S.; m. Sandra Lynn Mary Babij, Sept. 8, 1973 (div. Sept. 1996); children: Steven, Laryssa, Andrew; m. Anne Marie Mayes, Jan. 4, 1997. BASc, U. Toronto, 1972, MASc, 1973, PhD, 1977. Cert. in chem. metallurgy. Asst. prof. materials engring. MIT, Cambridge, 1978-82, assoc. prof., 1982-92, prof. materials chemistry, 1992—, MacVicar faculty fellow, 1995—, John F. Elliott prof. of chem. metallurgy, 1999—. Assoc. editor Jour. Materials Rsch., 1995—; contbr. over 100 articles on electro and phys. chemistry to profl. jours.; patentee in field, U.S., Can., and Europe. Recipient Grad. Student Coun. Tchg. award MIT, 1982, 84, 87, 88, 93, Prof. T.B. King Meml. award dept. materials sci. and engring. undergrad. students MIT, 1986, Bose award, 1997; NATO postdoctoral fellow Nat. Rsch. Coun. Can., 1977, AT&T Faculty fellow in indsl. ecology, 1993-95, MacVicar Faculty fellow, 1995—. Mem. AAAS, Minerals, Metals and Materials Soc., Electrochem. Soc., Internat. Soc. Electrochemistry, Materials Rsch. Soc. Home: 75 Trapelo Rd Waltham MA 02452-6303 Office: MIT # 8-109 77 Massachusetts Ave Cambridge MA 02139-4307

SAFAAI-JAZI, AHMAD, electrical engineering educator, researcher; b. Isfahan, Iran, Nov. 18, 1948; came to U.S., 1986; s. Ali and Talaat (Niroomand) S.-J.; m. Zohreh Azargoshasb, Mar. 1, 1983; children: Rokhsana, Amir-Arsalan. BSc, Sharif U. Tech., Tehran, Iran, 1971; MASc, U. B.C., Vancouver, Can., 1974; PhD, McGill U., Montreal, Que., Can., 1978. Asst. prof. dept. elec. and computer engring. Isfahan U. Tech., 1978-84; rsch. assoc. dept. elec. engring. McGill U., 1984-86; prof. Va. Poly. Inst. and State U., Blacksburg, 1986—. Contbr. articles to IEEE Trans. on Microwave Theory and Tech., IEEE Trans. on Ultrasonics, Ferroelectrics and Frequency Control, Optical Soc. Am. Jour., Jour. Lightwave Tech., IEEE Trans. Antennas and Propogation, Radio Sci., Electronic Letters, Optics Letters, Acoustic Soc. Am. Jour., Applied Optics, Laser Tech., IEE Procs., IEEE Jour. Quantum Electronics, Jour. Modern Optics, Microwave and Optical Technology Letters. Recipient Best Application Paper award Va. Tech. Propogation Experiment, IEEE Antennas and Propagation Soc., 1995, Dean Engring. award Excellence in Tchg., 2002. Mem. IEEE (sr., treas.-sec. Va. Mountain sect. 1989-90, vice chmn. 1990-91, chmn. 1991-92, exec. com. 1992-93), Optical Soc. Am. Achievements include patent for narrowband fiberoptic spectral filter formed from fibers having a refractive index with a W-profile and a step profile, longitudinal mode fiber acoustic waveguide with solid core and solid cladding, birefringent single-mode acoustic fiber, session chair at 1996 internat. symposium on antennas and propagation, Chiba, Japan, 1997 progress in electromagnetic rsch. symposium, Cambridge, Mass., and 1998 internat. conf. on fiber optics and photonics, New Delhi, India, also others. Office: Va Poly Inst and State U Bradley Dept Elec Engr Blacksburg VA 24061

SAFFER, AMY BETH, foreign language educator; b. N.Y.C., Apr. 19, 1950; d. William and Evelyn (Yankowitz) S. BA, Fairleigh Dickinson U., 1972, MA, 1983; postgrad., Jersey City State Coll., 1983-84. Cert. tchr. Spanish K-12, N.J. Tchr. Madison (N.J.) High Sch., 1973, Livingston (N.J.) High Sch., 1973—. Mem. faculty and dist. coms. Livingston Sch. Dist., 1975—; advisor to class of 1977, Livingston High Sch., 1975-77, chair mid. states subcom., 1990; tchr. mentor. Inducted Livington H.S. Alumni Hall of Fame, trained tchr. mentor, 1993. Mem. NEA, Am. Assn. Tchrs. of Spanish and Portuguese, N.J. Edn. Assn., Fgn. Lang. Educators of N.J., Livingston Edn. Assn. (negotiations rep. 1980—), Essex County Edn. Assn. Office: Livingston High Sch Livingston NJ 07039

SAFRIT, MARGARET, physical education educator; Chair dept. phys. edn. U. Wis., Madison; chair dept. health and fitness Am. Univ., Washington, prof. emeritus. Presenter in field. Author several books; editor Rsch. Quarterly. Mem. AAHPERD (chair measurment and evaluation coun., Gulick award 1994), Am. Acad. Phys. Edn. Higher Edn. (pres.), Internat. Soc. Measurement and Evaluation (founder, pres.).*

SAGAFI-NEJAD, TAGI, business educator; b. Bainabaj, Khorasan, Iran, Dec. 19, 1941; arrived in U.S., 1968; m. Nancy Gail Black Sagafi-nejad, Nov. 22, 1967; children: Jahan Crawford Reza, David Joseph Hossein. MA, U. Pa., 1971, PhD, 1979. Lectr. U. Pa., Phila., 1974-76; asst. prof. U. Wash., Seattle, 1976-80, U. Tex., Austin, 1980-84; assoc. prof. Loyola Coll., Balt., 1984-93, prof., 1993—, dept. chair, 1995-96, prof. emeritus, 2002—; Keating-Crawford chair in internat. bus. Stillman Sch. Bus., Seton Hall U., 2002—03; Killam Disting. prof., dir. PhD program in internat. bus. Tex. A&M Internat. U., 2003—. Cons. UN Indsl. Devel. Orgn., 1982—84, UN Ctr. on Transnat. Corp., 1993—, U.S. Congress, 1983—84; lectr., spkr. in field. Author: Technology Transfer Trilogy, 1980, 1981, The United Nations and Transnational Corporations, 2004; editl. bd. Transnational Corp., 1993—. Recipient Best Paper award Acad. of Mgmt., 1994, Pacific Asia Mgmt. Inst., U. Hawaii, 1988. Mem. Acad. of Internat. Bus. (chair N.E. chpt. 1988-93), Iranian Scholars Assn. (founding mem., v.p. 1989-90), Middle East Studies Assn., Middle East Inst., Strategic Mgmt. Soc. Democrat. Avocations: gardening, golf, painting, walking. E-mail: Tagi.Sagafi@tamiu.edu.

SAGER, CLIFFORD J. psychiatrist, educator; b. N.Y.C. s. Max and Lena (Lipman) S.; m. Anne Scheinman; children by previous marriage: Barbara L., Philip T., Rebecca J., Anthony F. BS, Pa. State U., 1937; MD, NYU, 1941; cert. in psychoanalysis, N.Y. Med. Coll., 1949. Diplomate: Am. Bd. Psychiatry and Neurology. Rotating intern Montefiore Hosp., N.Y.C., 1941-42; AUS Capt.,chief neurologist 312th and 42nd Psychiatry Hosp., 1942—46; sr. special resident in psychiatry Bellevue Hosp., N.Y.C., 1946—48; practice medicine specializing in psychiatry N.Y.C. and East Hampton, N.Y., 1946—; dir. therapeutic services, assoc. dean, dir. tng. Postgrad. Ctr. Mental Health, 1948-60; vis. psychiatrist, med. bd. Flower and Fifth Ave Hosp., 1960-71, Met. Hosp., 1960-71; dir. psychiat. tng. and edn. N.Y. Med. Coll., 1960-71; attending psychiatrist Bird S. Coler Hosp., 1960-71; clin. dir. N.Y. Med. Coll., 1960-63, assoc. prof. psychiatry, 1960-65, prof., 1966-71, dir. partial hosp. programs and family treatment and study unit, 1964-71; clin. prof. psychiatry Mt. Sinai Sch. Medicine, 1971-80; assoc. dir. psychiatry Beth Israel Hosp. for Family and Mental Therapy; chief of psychiatry Gov. Hosp., 1970-74; dir. family therapy Mt. Sinai Sch. Medicine, 1974-80; prof. clin. psychiatry N.Y. Hosp.-Cornell Univ. Med. Ctr., 1980—; attending psychiatrist N.Y. Hosp.-Payne Whitney Clinic, 1980—2002; dir. marital and family clinic N.Y. Hosp., 1991—2000; prof. emeritus Cornell U. Coll. Medicine, 2000—. Attending psychiatrist Mt. Sinai Hosp., 1971-80; chief behavioral scis. Gouverneur Hosp.; chief family treatment unit Beth Israel Med. Ctr., 1970-74, assoc. dir. psychiatry family and group therapy, 1971-74; psychiat. dir. Jewish Family Svc., 1974-77; dir. family psychiatry Jewish Bd. Family and Childrens Svcs., 1978-90; dir. Remarried Consultation Svc., 1976-90; dir. Tng. and Sex Therapy Clinic, 1974-90; psychiat. dir. Employee Consultation and Corp. Health Programs, 1980-83; faculty, supr. Contemporary Ctr. Advanced Psychoanalytic Studies; chief neuropsychiatry 42d and 312th Gen. Hosp.; psychiat. cons. Employee Consultation Svc. and Corp. Health Svcs., 1983-1992. Author: Marriage Contracts and Couple Therapy, 1976, Intimate Partners, 1979, Treating the Remarried Family, 1983; 4 other books; mem. editorial bd. Am. Jour. Orthopsychiatry, 1960-69, Internat. Jour. Group Psychotherapy, 1968—, Family Process, 1969-92, Divorce and Remarriage, 1977—, Comprehensive Rev. Jour. Family and Marriage, 1978—; cons. Sexual Medicine, 1974-82; co-editor, founder Jour. Sex and Marital Therapy, 1974—; mem. editorial bd.: Jour. Marriage and Family Counseling, 1977—, Internat. Jour. Family Counseling, 1977—; author or contbr. some 100 sci. articles to jours. Capt. M.C. U.S. Army, 1942—46, with M.C. U.S. Army, 1942—46. Recipient Am. Family Therapy Assn. award for Outstanding Contribution to Family Therapy 1983, Assn. Marriage and Family Therapists award for Outstanding Contributions to the field of Marital and Family Therapy, 1984. Fellow Am. Psychiat. Assn. (life), Am. Orthopsychiat. Assn. (life), Acad. Psychoanalysis (charter), Am. Group Psychotherapy Assn. (pres. 1968-70, dir. 1962-74), Soc. Med. Psychoanalysts (pres. 1960-61, dir. 1958-62, pres.-elect 1997-99), Am. Assn. Marital and Famiy Therapists; mem. AMA (life), Am. Soc. Advancement Psychotherapy (dir. 1954-67), N.Y. Soc. Clin. Psychiatry, Soc. for Sex Therapy and Rsch. (pres. 1976-77, bd. dirs. 1953-58) PAIRS Found. (bd. dirs. 1985—). Home and Office: 35 East 75th St New York NY 10021-2761

SAGGINARIO, JOAN THERESA VETERE, elementary and secondary education educator; b. Bklyn., Dec. 30, 1953; d. Frank Alfred and Louise (Martinelli) Vetere; (div.); 1 child, Tara Michelle. BA in Elem. Edn. and Spanish, Hofstra U., 1976, MA in Bilinguialism and Elem. Edn., 1977. Cert. Spanish tchr. 7-12, elem. edn. N-6, bilingual elem. edn., N.Y., permanent cert. N.Y. Bilingual kindergarten and 1st grade tchr. Harry Daniels Primary Ctr., Roosevelt Pub. Schs., 1977-78; ESL teaching asst. Meadow Sch., Baldwin (N.Y.) Pub. Schs., 1978-79; tchr. bilingual ESL 1st and 2d grades Martin Luther King Sch., Wyandanch, N.Y., 1979-88; ESL, bilingual tchr. 1st grade Park Ave. Sch., Westbury, N.Y., 1988-97; tchr. Spanish, William Fleming H.S., Roanoke, Va., 1997-99; 1st grade tchr. Forest Park Elem. Sch., Roanoke, Va., 1999—; tchr. ESL adult edn. Roanoke City Schs., 2001—, tchr. Spanish adult edn., 2002—. ESL tchr. adult edn. New Horizons Program, Oceanside, N.Y., 1990-97. Bilingual fellow, 1976-77. Mem. State Assn. Bilingual Educators, Am. Assn. Spanish and Portuguese Tchrs. (treas. 1988-90, pres. L.I. chpt. 1990-92), Va. Edn. Assn., Roanoke Edn. Assn. Roman Catholic.

SAGO, JANIS LYNN, photography educator; b. St. Louis, Nov. 27, 1948; d. Bernard William and Eunice Alberta (Henry) Osthof; m. William Leo Sago Jr., Feb. 18, 1967 (dec. Mar. 1989); children: Brian William, Shelley Lynn, Carrie Renee. AA, St. Louis C.C., 1990; BA cum laude, Webster U., 1993. Office mgr. C.B. Smith Co., St. Louis, 1989—; free-lance photographer St. Louis, 1990—; adj. faculty photography St. Louis C.C., 1993—, St. Charles County C.C., 1998—. Interim staff photographer St. Louis C.C., 1990; gallery asst. Webster U., St. Louis, 1993; adj. faculty photography St. Louis C.C., 1993—, St. Charles County C.C., 1998—; photography instr. Mo. Bot. Gardens, 1999—. Photographer The Webster Jour., 1992-93; photo's exhibited at May Gallery, 1993, Campus Gallery, 1996—, Martin Schweig Gallery, 1996, St. Charles County C.C., 1998—, St. Peters Cultural Art Ctr., 2002—. Mem. St. Louis Art Mus., 1994—, St. Louis Sci. Ctr., 1996-97, Mo. Bot. Gardens, 1997—; officer, asst. chief YMCA Indian Guides, St. Louis, 1989-97; vol./chair Mothers' Club, Lindbergh Schs., St. Louis, 1974-90, PTO, 1974-90. Mem. AAUW, Greater St. Louis Orchid Soc., Phi Theta Kappa. Avocations: gardening, reading, travel, music. Office: St Louis C C 11333 Big Bend Rd Saint Louis MO 63122-5720

SAH, RAAJ, economist, advisor, educator; b. Muzaffarpur, Bihar, India, Oct. 18, 1952; arrived in U.S., 1976; m. Cynthia Serina Tabios, June 22, 1983; 1 child, Jaya T. MBA, Indian Inst. Mgmt., Ahmedabad, India, 1975; PhD in Econs., U. Pa., 1980. Ford asst. prof. MIT, Cambridge, 1980—82; vis. asst. prof. U. Pa., Phila., 1982—84; from asst. to assoc. prof. Yale U., New Haven, 1984—92; prof. U. Chgo., 1992—. John M. Olin vis. prof. Princeton (N.J.) U., 1987-88; vis. assoc. prof. U. Chgo., 1989-90; advisor to numerous corps., fin. instns. and govts. Contbr. numerous articles in field to scholarly and profl. jours. Office: U Chicago 1155 E 60th St Rm 141 Chicago IL 60637-2745

SAHAI, HARDEO, medical statistics educator; b. Bahraich, India, Jan. 10, 1942; m. Lillian Sahai, Dec. 28, 1973; 3 children. BS in Math., Stats. and Physics, Lucknow U., India, 1962; MS in Math., Banaras U., Varanasi, India, 1964; MS in Math. Stats., U. Chgo., 1968; PhD in Stats., U. Ky., 1971. Lectr. in math. and stats. Banaras U., Varanasi, India, 1964-65; asst. stats. officer Durgapur Steel Plant, Durgapur West Bengal, India, 1965; statistician Rsch. and Planning div. Blue Cross Assn., Chgo., 1966; statis. programmer Cleft Palate Ctr., U. Ill., 1967, Chgo. Health Rsch. Found., 1968; mgmt. scientist Mgmt. Systems Devel. Dept. Burroughs Corp., Detroit, 1971-72; from asst. prof. to prof. dept. math. U. P.R., Mayaguez, 1972-82; vis. research prof. Dept. Stats. and Applied Math. Fed. U. of Ceara, Brazil, 1978-79; sr. research statistician Travenol Labs., Inc., Round Lake, Ill., 1982-83; chief statistician U.S. Army Hqrs., Ft. Sheridan, Ill., 1983-84; sr. math. statistician U.S. Bur. of Census Dept. of Commerce, Washington, 1984-85; sr. ops. rsch. analyst Def. Logistics Agy. Dept. Def., Chgo., 1985-86; prof. Dept. Biostats. and Epidemiology U. P.R. Med. Scis., San Juan, 1986—. Cons. P.R. Univ Cons., P.R. Driving Safety Evaluation Project, Water Resources Rsch. Inst., Travenol Labs., Campo Rico, P.R., U.S. Bur. Census, Washington, Lawrence Livermore Nat. Lab., Calif., others; vis. prof. U. Granada, Spain, U. Veracruzana, Mex., patrimonial prof. stats., 1997—; vis. prof. U. Nacional de Colombia, U. Nacional de Trujillo, Peru, 1993-94, hon. prof. stats., 1994—; adj. prof. dept. math. U. P.R. Natural Scis. Faculty, 1995—; Patrimonial prof. stafs U. Veracruzana, 1997—. Author: Statistics and Probability: Learning Module, 1984; author: (with Jose Berrios) A Dictionary of Statistical Scientific and Technical Terms: English-Spanish and Spanish-English, 1981, (with Wilfredo Martinez) Statistical Tables and Formulas for the Biological Social and Physical Sciences, 1996, (with Anwer Khurshid) Statistics in Epidemiology: Methods, Techniques and Applications, 1996, (with Satish C. Misra and Michael Graham) Quotations on Probability and Statistics with Illustrations, 2000, (with Anwer Khurshid) A Pocket Dictionary of Statistics, 2000, (with Mohammad I. Ageel) The Analysis of Variance: Fixed, Random and Mixed Models, 2000, (with Wilfredo Martnez) Statistical Glossary: English-Spanish, 2000, (with Lucas López Segovia and Hector W. Colón-Rosa) A Glossary of Medical Epidemiologic and Demographic Statistics: English-Spanish, 2002, (with Mario M. Ojeda) Un Manual de Distribuciones t, x2y F Centrales Y No Centrales, 2000, (with Mario M. Ojeda) A Glossary of Computer and Management Terms: English/Spanish, 2000, (with Mario M. Ojeda) Comparisons of Approximations to the Percentiles of Noncentral t, x2 and F Distributions, 2001, (with A. Khurshid) Pocket Dictionary of Statistics, 2001, Noncentral t, x2y and F Distributions, 1998, Analysis of Variance for Random Models, Vol. 1: Balanced Data and Vol. 2: Unbalanced Data, 2002; mem. editl. bd. Sociedad Colombiana de Matematicas, P.R. Health Scis. Jour.; contbr. editor Current Index to Stats.; reviewer Collegiate Microcomputer, Comm. in Statistics, Indian Jour. Stats., Jour. Royal Statis. Soc. (series D, The Statistician), New Zealand Statistician, Biometrics, Can. Jour. Stats., Technometrics, Problems, Resources and Issues in Math. Undergrad. Studies; contbr. more than 150 articles and papers to profl. and sci. jours., numerous articles to tech. mags. Active Dept. Consumer Affairs Svcs. Commonwealth of P.R., San Juan, Dept. Anti-Addiction Svcs., Commonwealth of P.R., San Juan., Inst. of AIDS, Municipality of San Juan, VA Med. Ctr. of San Juan, Caribbean Primate Rsch. Ctr., Ctr. Addiction Studies Caribbean Ctrl. U. Recipient Dept. Army Cert. Achievement award, 1984, U. Ky. Outstanding Alumnus award, 1993, medal of honor U. Granada, 1994, plaque of honor U. Nacional de Trujillo, 1994; fellow Coun. Sci. and Indsl. Rsch., 1964-65, U. Chgo., 1965-68, Harvard U., 1979, Fulbright Found., 1982; U.P. Bd. Merit scholar, 1957-59, Govt. India Merit scholar, 1959-64; grantee NSF, 1974-77, NIMH, 1987-90, 91—, NIDA, 1991—. Fellow AAAS, Am. Coll. Epidemiology, Inst. Statisticians (charter statistician), Inst. Math. and Its Applications (charter mathematician), N.Y. Acad. Scis., Royal Statis. Soc.; mem. Internat. Statis. Inst., Internat. Assn. Tchg. Stats., Soc. Epidemiol. Rsch., Inst. Math. Stats., Bernouilli Soc. for Math. Stats. and Probability, Internat. Biometric Soc., Am. Soc. for Quality Control, Am. Stats. Assn., Japan Stats. Soc., Can. Statis. Soc., Inter-Am. Statis. Inst., Internat. Assn. Statis. Computing, Sch. Sci. and Math. Assn., Sigma Xi. Avocations: religious studies, philosophy, reading, gardening. Home: Urb Mayaguez Terrace 7083 Calle B Gaudier Texidor Mayaguez PR 00682-6617 E-mail: hsahai@centennialpr.net.

SAHS, MAJORIE JANE, art educator; b. Altadena, Calif., Aug. 27, 1926; d. Grayson Michael and Janie Belle (Aaron) McCarty; m. Eugene Otto Sahs, July 21, 1949; children: Victoria, Stephen, Jeffry. Student, Art Ctr. of L.A., 1943-45, Emerson Coll., Boston, 1945; BA, Sacramento State U., 1970; MA in Art Edn., Calif. State U., Sacramento, 1972, postgrad., 1973-79. Cert. cmty. coll. tchr., secondary tchr., Calif. Tchr. art Sacramento County Schs., 1971-80; cons. Whole Brain Learning Modes, Sacramento, 1980-84; tng. specialist Art Media, Sacramento, Calif., 1983—. Instr. Found. for Continuing Med. Edn., Calif., 1985; presenter Nat. Art Edn. Conf., Chgo., 1992, 93, Asian Pacific Conf. on Arts Edn., Franklin, Australia, Internat. Conf., Montreal, Can., 1993; cons., lectr. in field; judge Calif. State Fair Art Show, 1989, 95, Fed. Treasury Poster Contest, 1994, 95, 96, 97, 99. Prodr., writer guide and video Gesture Painting Through T'ai Chi, 1992; editor, pub. Calif.'s state newspaper for art edn., 1987-90; editor: Crocker Mus. Docent Guide, 1990; mem. editl. bd. Jour. for Nat. Art Edn. Assn., 1980-97; editor: (newsletter) U.S. Soc. for Edn. Through Art,

1994-97; designer of ltd. edits. scarves and cards for Nat. Breast Cancer Rsch. Fund, Exploration Inspiration '95; works publ. in The Best in Silk Painting, 1997; exhibited paintings in art gallery showings. Del. Calif. Arts Leadership Symposium for Arts Edn., 1979, Legis. Coalition Through The Arts, Calif., 1989, 95; organizer and host art show and fundraiser for women candidates, 1992; co-founder Visual Arts for Youth, Sacramento, 1998; bd. chair Visual Arts for Youth Greater Sacramento, 1998-99; co-organizer Non-Profit Visual Arts for Youth, 1998—, 6 Women of Mettle, 2003. Recipient Patriotic Svc. award Fed. Treasury Dept., 1996, 97, 99, State award of Merit. Mem. Internat. Assn. Edn. through Art, U.S. Soc. Edn. through Art (editor newsletter 1994-97), Nat. Art Edn. Assn. (mem. editl. bd. jour. 1990—, Nat. Outstanding Newspaper Editor award 1988, 89), Calif. Art Edn. Assn. (mem. state coun., mem. area coun., editor state paper, State Award of Merit), Calif. Children's Homes Soc. (pres. Camellia chpt. 1990-91), Asian Pacific Arts Educators Assn., Creative Arts League Sacramento, Emerson Coll. Alumni, Art Ctr. L.A. Alumni. Avocations: writing, designing jewelry, designing greeting cards, painting, art. Home and Office: 1836 Walnut Ave Carmichael CA 95608-5417 Fax: 916-359-8809.

SAHU, ATMA RAM, mathematics educator, university administrator, consultant, researcher; m. Kusum Sahu; children: Anurag Sahu, Shelley Sahu. MS in Applied Math., Roorkee (India) U., 1971, PhD in Applied Math., 1973; MEd in Math., U. Md., 1982, PhD in Math. Edn., 1984, cert. in Computer Sys. Mgmt., 1991. Math. lectr. Nat. Coun. Ednl. Rsch. and Tng. Ctr., New Delhi, India, 1975-80; grad. asst. math. dept. U. Md., College Park, 1980-84; asst. prof. math. and computer sci. U. Md. East Shore, Princess Anne, 1984-88; math. specialist U. Md., College Park, 1988-90; assoc. prof. Coppin State Coll., Balt., 1990—. Asst. editor: Arithmetic for Middle School, 1979; contbr. articles to profl. jours. Mem. ASCD, Math. Assn. Am., Am. Math. Soc., Am. Ednl. Rsch. Assn., Nat. Coun. Tchrs. of Math., Md. Coun. Tchr. of Math. Avocations: swimming, gymnastics. Home: 7416 Lake Glen Dr Glenn Dale MD 20769-2000 E-mail: asahu@coppin.edu.

SAIA, DIANE PLEVOCK DIPIERO, nutritionist, educator, legal administrator; b. Oct. 2, 1941; d. Charles and Monica (Alexandravich) Plevock; married; 1 child, David. BS, Framingham (Mass.) State Coll., 1962; MS, Simmons Coll., Boston, 1969; doctoral candidate, U. Mass., 1974—75. Field nutritionist Mass. Dept. Edn., Boston, 1962—64; sch. program coord. New Eng. Dairy and Food Coun., Boston, 1964—67, sr. staff Springfield, Mass., 1970—83; tchr. Weymouth (Mass.) Schs., 1967—70; adj. prof. Springfield Coll., 1970—80. Nutrition tchr. Baystate Med. Ctr., Springfield; adj. faculty Western New Eng. Coll., 1982—84; legal adminstr. SAIA Law Offices, 1984—; host radio show Law Talk, 1997—; prodr. TV shows, radio and consumer edn. programs. Fund raiser Am. Heart Assn., 2000—02. Mem.: ATLA, Assn. Legal Adminstrs., Sales and Mktg. Execs., Assn. Family and Consumer Econs. (exec. bd. 1972—, pres. 1978—79), New Eng. Pub. Health Assn., Mass. Bar Assn., Valley Press Club (assoc. dir. 1976—79, chmn. scholarship ball 1977—79). Roman Catholic. Home: 502 Frank Smith Rd Longmeadow MA 01106-2928 Office: 106 State St Springfield MA 01103-2034

SAID, PHYLLIS DIANNE, elementary school educator; b. Muncie, Ind., Aug. 21, 1942; d. Russel Philip and Edna Ann (Kiracofe) Donhauser; m. William Lee Said, Aug. 24, 1963; children: Denise Janine, Douglas James. BS, Ball State U., Muncie, Ind., 1970, MA in Edn., 1976. Kindergarten tchr. Delaware Cmty. Schs., Eaton, Ind., 1970-76, tchr. 1st grade, 1976—. Author/prodr.: (video prodn.) Prime Time - Indiana Dept. of Edn., 1986, 87, 89. Vol. Minnetrista Cultural Ctr., Muncie, Delaware County Coalition for Literacy, Muncie. Lilly Endowment Tchr. Creativity fellow, Indpls., 1992; Ind. Dept. Edn. Tchr. Tech. grantee, 1988, 90, Energy Edn. grantee, 1990, Bell grantee, 1995, Ctrl. Bur. Eng. Enhancement grant, 1996; recipient Fulbright Tchr. Exch. award, Eng., 1995—, Eisenhower Sci. and Math. award, 1995, Ind. Wildlife Fedn. Conservation Educator of Yr., 1995, Nila Purvis Animal Helper of Yr., 1994. Mem. Internat. Reading Assn., Ind. Wildlife Assn., Audubon Soc., Muncie Area Reading Coun., Hoosier Mgrs. (pres. 1993-94), Alpha Delta Kappa (treas. 1992-94). Republican. Methodist. Avocations: reading, herb gardening, quilting, travel.

SAINE, CHRISTY WATSON, special education educator; b. Atlanta, Nov. 29, 1955; d. Louis H. and Carlene (Sisk) Watson; m. James L. Saine III, Mar. 3, 1980; children: Carey, Matthew. BA in English, N. Ga. Coll., Dahlonega, Ga., 1977; MEd, N. Ga. Coll., 1981; Secondary Cert., Piedmont Coll., Demorest, Ga., 1978. English tchr. Stephens County Schs., Toccoa, Ga., 1978-79; tchr. Jefferson City (Ga.) Schs., 1980-81; 5th and 6th grade SLD resource tchr. Okeechobee (Fla.) County Schs., 1982-90; tchr. Cen. Elem. Sch., Okeechobee, 1990-95, North Elem. Sch., Okeechobee, 1995—. Mentor tchr., yearbook sponsor Tech. Grant Team. Active Girl Scouts U.S.A. Mem. ASCD, Coun. for Exceptional Children, Nat. Coun. Learning Disabilities, PEER, First United Meth. Ch. (v.p. trustees, United Meth. Women Com.). Office: 3000 NW 10th Ter Okeechobee FL 34972-1859

SAINT-AMAND, PIERRE NEMOURS, humanities educator; b. Port-Au-Prince, Haiti, Feb. 22, 1957; came to U.S., 1978; s. Nemours and Carmen (Clerveaux) Saint-A. BA, U. Montreal, 1978; MA, Johns Hopkins U., 1980, PhD, 1981. Asst. prof. Yale U., New Haven, 1981-82, Stanford (Calif.) U., 1982-86; assoc. prof. Brown U., Providence, 1986-90, prof., 1990—, Francis Wayland prof., 1996—. Vis. prof. Harvard U., Cambridge, Mass., 1992, U. Iowa, Iowa City, 2001. Author: Diderot, Le Labyrinthe de La Relation, 1984, Séduire Ou La Passion des Lumières, 1986, Les Lois de L'Hostilité, 1992, The Libertine's Progress, 1994, The Laws of Hostility, 1996; editor: Diderot, 1984, Le Roman au Dix-huitième siécle, 1987, Autonomy in the Age of the Enlightenment, 1993, Thérèse philosophe, 2000. Fellow Stanford Humanities Ctr., 1985-86, John Simon Guggenheim Meml. Found., 1989; decorated chevalier dans l'Ordre des Palmes académiques, 2001. Office: Brown U PO Box 1961 Providence RI 02912-1961

ST. ANTOINE, THEODORE JOSEPH, retired law educator, arbitrator; b. St. Albans, Vt., May 29, 1929; s. Arthur Joseph and Mary Beatrice (Callery) S.; m. Elizabeth Lloyd Frier, Jan. 2, 1960; children: Arthur, Claire, Paul, Sara. AB, Fordham Coll., 1951; JD, U. Mich., 1954; postgrad., U. London, 1957-58. Bar: Mich. 1954, Ohio 1954, D.C. 1959. Assoc. Squire, Sanders & Dempsey, Cleve., 1954; assoc., ptnr. Woll, Mayer & St. Antoine, Washington, 1958-65; assoc. prof. law U. Mich. Law Sch., Ann Arbor, 1965-69, prof., 1969—, Degan prof., 1981-98, Degan prof. emeritus, 1998—, dean, 1971-78. Pres. Nat. Resource Ctr. for Consumers of Legal Svcs., 1974—78; mem. pub. rev. bd. UAW, 1973—, chmn., 2000—, UAW-GM Legal Svcs. Plan, 1983—95; spl. counselor on workers' compensation Gov. of Mich., 1983—85; reporter Uniform Law Commrs., 1987—92; mem. Mich. Atty. Discipline Bd., 1999—, vice-chmn., 2000—02, chmn., 2002—; life mem. Clare Hall, Cambridge (Eng.) U. Co-author: (with R. Smith, L. Merrifield and C. Craver) Labor Relations Law: Cases and Materials, 4th edit., 1968, 10th edit., 1999; editor: The Common Law of the Workplace: The Views of Arbitrators, 1998; contbr. articles to profl. jours. 1st lt. JAGC U.S. Army, 1955—57. Fulbright grantee U. London, 1957-58. Mem. ABA (past sec. labor law sect., coun. 1984-92), Am. Bar Found., State Bar Mich. (chmn. labor rels. law sect. 1979-80), Nat. Acad. Arbitrators (bd. govs. 1985-88, v.p. 1994-96, pres. 1999-2000), Internat. Soc. Labor Law and Social Security (U.S. br. exec. bd. 1983—, vice chmn. 1989-95), Am. Arbitration Assn. (bd. dirs. 2000—), Indsl. Rels. Rsch. Assn., Coll. Labor and Employment Lawyers, Order of Coif (life). Democrat. Roman Catholic. Home: 1421 Roxbury Rd Ann Arbor MI 48104-4047 Office: U Mich Law Sch 625 S State St Ann Arbor MI 48109-1215 E-mail: tstanton@umich.edu.

ST. CLAIR, PHILIP ROLAND, humanities educator, poet; b. Warren, Ohio, Apr. 30, 1944; s. Harvey Lee St. Clair and Ruth A. Sutton; m. Christina St. Clair, Aug. 24, 1996. BA, Kent State U., 1970, MA, 1972, MLS, 1974; MFA in Poetry, Bowling Green State U., 1985. Instr. Bowling Green (Ohio) State U., 1985-86; lectr. So. Ill. U., Carbondale, 1986-91; prof. composition and creative writing Ashland (Ky.) C.C., 1991—, chair humanities divsn., 1998—. Dir. Jesse Stuart Writers' Conf., Ashland, 1992-2002. Author (books of poetry): In the Thirty-Nine Steps, 1980, At the Tent of Heaven, 1984, Little-Dog-of-Iron, 1985, Acid Creek, 1997, Greatest Hits, 1982-2002, 2003. With USAF, 1961-65. NEA Creative Writing fellow, 1994, Al Smith fellow, Ky. Arts Coun., 1999; recipient Hellen Bullis prize, Poetry Northwest Mag., 1986. Mem. Christian Ch. (Disciples Of Christ). Avocations: travel, philately, postal history. Office: Ashland Cmty Coll 1400 College Dr Ashland KY 41101 E-mail: philip.stclair@kctcs.edu.

ST. CLAIR, ROBERT NEAL, English language and linguistics educator; b. Honolulu, Apr. 24, 1934; divorced; 1 child, Tiffany Neal. BA, U. Hawaii, 1964; MA, U. Wash., 1966, U. Calif., La Jolla, 1970; PhD, U. Kans., 1973. Asst. prof. Calif. State U., L.A., 1966-67; asst. prof. English and linguistics U. Louisville, 1974-75, assoc. prof., 1975-76, prof., 1978—, disting. prof. rsch., 1995—. Chmn. Forum for Interdisciplinary Rsch., Cancun, Mex., 1976, Curacao, Antilles, 1978; disting. vis. prof. N.Mex. State U., Las Cruces, 1978, Internat. Christian U., Tokyo, 1979, Josai Internat. U., Chiba, Japan, 1996. Author: Language and Social Psychology, 1976, Social Metaphors, 1990, Languages of the World, 1990, numerous others; editor Lektos, 1974-78; contbr. over 400 articles and revs. to profl. jours. Sgt. U.S. Army, 1957-60. Grantee Philips Found., 1974, NEH, 1975-77, U.S. Office Edn., 1977-79. Mem. MLA, Nat. Coun. Tchrs. English, Coll. Composition Comm. Conf. Office: 9431 Westport Rd Ste 343 Louisville KY 40241-2219

ST. LAURENT, PATRICIA ROSE, secondary parochial school educator; b. Rockville, Conn., Dec. 28, 1958; d. Paul Edward and N. Christine (Crawford) Boland; m. Richard Arthur St. Laurent, Feb. 16, 1986; 1 child, Meghan Theresa. BS, Lyndon State Coll., 1981. Cert. tchr., Vt. Tchr., athletic dir. Blessed Sacrament Sch., Holyoke, Mass., 1981-86; tchr. phys. edn. and sci. Our Lady of Sacred Heart Sch., Springfield, Mass., 1988-90; tchr. phys. edn. and environ. sci. Cathedral High Sch., Springfield, 1990—. Coach girls jr. varsity basketball Cathedral High Sch., 1990—, mem. accreditation com., 1991-92. Vol. winter/spring Spl. Olympics, Lyndonville, Vt., 1980-81; vol. coach softball Holyoke Pk. Dept., 1985; vol. St. Patrick's Bingo, Chicopee, Mass., 1992, Childrens Miracle Network, Springfield, 1991. Mem. AAHPERD, Nat. Assn. Sport and Phys. Edn., Nat. Assn. Girls' and Women's Sports, Am. Sch. Health Assn., Women's Basketball Coaches Assn., Am. Turner Soc., Mass. Assn. Sci. Tchrs., Sigma Psi. Democrat. Avocations: volleyball, tennis, bowling, reading, coaching. Office: Cathedral High Sch 260 Surrey Rd Springfield MA 01118-1199

ST. LOUIS, PAUL MICHAEL, foreign language educator; b. Vernon, Conn., Aug. 30, 1946; s. Wilfred Henry and Alice Agnes (Brennan) St. L. Spl. cert. Jr. Yr. Abroad program, U. Louvain, Belgium, 1967; BA, Boston Coll., 1968; MA, Trinity Coll., 1975. Cert. tchr. secondary French, Conn. Tchr. French East Hartford (Conn.) H.S., 1968-96, head dept. fgn. lang., 1984-85; retired, 1996. Advisor to French club East Hartford H.S., 1969-85, jr. class advisor, 1985, 87, 89-90, 92, sr. class advisor, 1986, 88, 90-92, bus. mgr. grades 9-12, 1993—. Vis. com. New England Assn. Schs. and Colls., Milford, Conn., 1980, steering com. for sch. evaluation, 1978, 88. Mem. Am. Coun. Tchg. of Fgn. Lang., Mass. Fgn. Lang. Assn., Conn. Coun. Lang. Tchrs. (treas. bd. dirs. 1992—, chairperson registration fall conf. 1989—, co-chairperson fall conf. 1991, cons. poetry recitation contest 1992—, Disting. Svc. award 1999), Am. Assn. Tchrs. of French (cons. regional conf. 1990), Mass. Fgn. Lang. Assn., East Hartford Edn. Assn. Avocation: computer technology. Home and Office: 275 Cedar Swamp Rd Monson MA 01057-9303

ST. ONGE, BARBARA S. media services coordinator, educator; b. Hartford, Conn., Dec. 3, 1949; d. Bruno P. and Marguerite C. (Wunsch) Skaroupski; m. Robert J. St. Onge; children: Bethany, Bryan. BS in Elem. Edn., Cen. Conn. State U., New Britain, 1971; M in ELem. Edn., Cen. Conn. State Coll., New Britain, 1977, postgrad., 1990; cert. libr. media specialist K-12, U. Conn., Storrs, 1992. Cert. intermediate adminstr. and supr. Tchr. 2d grade Bristol (Conn.) Bd. Edn., 1971-73, chpt. I instr., 1977-81, tchr. 3d grade, 1981-82, tchr. reading and lang. arts, 1982-85, instr. chpt I, 1985-90, coord. media svcs., 1990—. Mem. bd. dirs. Bristol Pub. Library, 1991-92, Conn. Edn. Media Assn., 1993-94, Conn. Educators Computer Assn., 1995—; mem. adv. bd. TCI Cable TV, 1995—. Contbr. articles to profl. jours. Chair craft show Bristol Mum Festival, 1990; pres. Women's Coll. Club, 1990-91; assoc. bd. mem. New England Carousel Mus., Bristol, 1993; bd. dirs. Family Ctr. Girl and Boys, 1996—. Recipient PLUS (Providing Leadership and Unselfish Svc.) award for outstanding woman honoree 1990, Woman of Yr. award Bus. and Profl. Women's Orgn., 1996; Danforth Found. scholar U. Conn., 1993. Mem. ASCD, Internat. Reading Assn., Am. Assn. Sch. Librs., Conn. Assn. for Supervision and Curriculum Devel., Conn. Reading Assn., Info. Literacy Network, Pi Lambda Theta. Avocations: shaker communities and furniture, herb horticulture, antiques. Home: 592 East Rd Bristol CT 06010-6845

ST. PIERRE, CHERYL ANN, retired art educator; b. Buffalo, Apr. 26, 1945; d. Guy Thomas and Madeline (Duncan) St. P. BS in Art Edn., SUNY, Buffalo, 1967, MS in Art Edn., 1970; MA in Italian, Middlebury Coll., 1976; PhD in Humanities, NYU, 1992. K-12 art tchr. Kenmore-Town of Tonawanda (N.Y.) Union Free Sch. Dist., 1967-2000; mentor to new tchrs., 1995-98. Cooperating tchr. for art student tchrs. SUNY, Buffalo, 1972-2000; advisor on original multi-media prodn. N.Y. State Coun. for Arts, Tonawanda, 1990-95; coord., tchr. Parents As Reading Ptnrs. Artwork, Tonawanda, 1990-98; grad. asst. NYU, N.Y.C., 1987-88, adj. prof. grad. sch., Medaille Coll., 1999-2000; coll. supr. for student tchrs. in art SUNY Coll. Buffalo, 2000-02; sr. ptnr. for the arts N.Y. State Acad. Tchg. and Learning, 2000-01. Illustrator jour. Italian Americana, 1971-81; designer greeting cards for State of N.Y. and Maine, Am. Lung Assn., 1978-79. Earthwatch vol. Identity through Native Costume, Macedonia, 1995. Mem.: AAUW, ASCD, Kenmore Tchrs.' Assn., Am. Fedn. Tchrs., N.Y. State Art Tchrs. Assn. (Outstanding Svc. award 2001), N.Y. State Tchrs. Assn., Nat. Art Edn. Assn., N.Y. State United Tchrs., Internat. Mentor Assn., Alpha Delta Kappa. Avocations: travel, photography, film studies, animal rights, reading. Home: 3881 N Bailey Ave Buffalo NY 14226-3202 E-mail: cherstpier@aol.com.

SAITO-FURUKAWA, JANET CHIYO, primary school educator; b. L.A., June 29, 1951; d. Shin and Nobuko Ann (Seki) Saito; m. Neil Yasuhiko Furukawa, June 30, 1990. BS, U. So. Calif., 1973; MA, Mt. St. Mary's Coll., L.A., 1990. Cert. elem. tchr. K-8, adminstrn. 1st tier, lang. devel. specialist, Calif. Tchr. grades four through six Rosemont Elem. Sch., L.A., 1973-80, psychomotor specialist, 1979-80; tchr. mid. sch. lang. arts Virgil, Parkman Mid. Schs., L.A./Woodland Hills, Calif., 1980-87, 87-90, dept. chairperson, 1974-77, 80-84, 1989-90; drama tchr. Virgil Mid. Sch., L.A., 1980-81, dance tchr., 1984-87; mid. sch. advisor L.A. Unified Sch. Dist., Encino, Calif., 1990-91, practitioner facilitator, 1990-97. Young authors chairperson Parkman Mid. Sch., Woodland Hills, 1988-90; multicultural performance educator, Great Leap, L.A., 1988-93; mentor tchr. L.A. Unified Sch. dist., 1980-90; trainer dist. standards project, 1996—; presenter/cons. in field. Tchr./leader Psychomotor Grant, 1979; writer Level II Teamin' and Theme-in, 1994. Recipient Nancy McHugh English award English Coun. L.A., Woodland Hills, 1987, 88, 91, Outstanding Reading and Lang. Tchr. award L.A. Reading Assn., Woodland Hills, 1991, Apple award L.A. Mayor's Office, 1990, Tchr. of the Month award Phi Delta Kappa, San Fernando, Calif., 1989. Mem. ASCD, Nat. Mid. Schs. Assn. (presenter, diverse cultures com. 1996—), Nat. Coun. Tchrs. Math., Calif. Sci. Tchrs. Assn., Nat. Coun. Tchrs. English, The Learning Collaborative. Lutheran. Avocations: volleyball, fishing, reading, skiing. Office: Practitioner Ctr LA Unified Sch Dist 3010 Estara Ave Los Angeles CA 90065-2205

SAKSON, SHARON R(OSE), journalist, writer, educator; b. Trenton, N.J., June 6, 1952; d. John Andrew and Helen Hope (Haggerty) S. BA, Georgetown U., 1974. Desk asst. ABC News, Washington, 1972-73, prodn. asst., 1973-74; TV news field prodr. ABC-TV News, London and Miami, Fla., 1979-85; news producer Sta. WBAL-TV, Balt., 1974-75; news prodr. Stas. ABC-TV/CBS-TV, Chgo., 1976-77; exec. producer Sta. KPIX-TV (Westinghouse), San Francisco, 1977-79; freelance writer Lawrenceville, N.J., 1985—; tchr. Oxbridge Acads., Paris, 1990-94; exec. dir. Oxbridge Academics, 1994-97; owner Paris Prodns., 1997—. AKC lic. dog show judge, 1996—; pvt. practice speech and presentation skills instrn., 1992—. Author: (short stories) 2d Gazette Fiction Collection, 1987, Streetsongs, 1990, (book) Miami, 1990, Florida, 1991. Recipient Katherine Ann Porter prize for fiction, 1989, Nimrod Lit. prize, 1989; grantee Commonwealth of Pa., 1989. Mem. Am. Whippet Club (Top Breeder of Whippet Champions 1994, 95), Dog Writers Assn. Am., Trenton Kennel Club. Roman Catholic. Avocation: dog shows. Home: 3375 Brunswick Ave # 273 Lawrenceville NJ 08648-2414

SALACUSE, JESWALD WILLIAM, lawyer, educator; b. Niagara Falls, N.Y., Jan. 28, 1938; s. William L. and Bessie B. (Buzzelli) S.; m. Donna Booth, Oct. 1, 1966; children: William, Maria. Diploma, U. Paris, 1959; AB, Hamilton Coll., 1960; JD, Harvard U., 1963. Bar: N.Y. 1965, Tex. 1980. Lectr. law Ahmadu Bello U., Nigeria, 1963-65; assoc. Conboy, Hewitt, O'Brien & Boardman, N.Y.C., 1965-67; assoc. dir. African Law Ctr., Columbia U., N.Y.C., 1967-68; prof., dir. Rsch. Ctr., Nat. Sch. Adminstrn., Zaire, 1968-71; Mid. East regional advisor on law and devel. Ford Found., Beirut, 1971-74, rep. in Sudan, 1974-77; vis. prof. U. Khartoum, Sudan, 1974-77; vis. scholar Harvard Law Sch., 1977-78; prof. law So. Meth. U., Dallas, 1978-86, dean, 1980-86; dean, prof. internat. law Fletcher Sch. Law and Diplomacy, Tufts U., Medford, Mass., 1986-94, Henry J. Braker prof. comml. law, 1994—. Fellow Inst. Advanced Legal Studies, U. London, 1995; vis. prof. Ecole Nat. Ponts et Chaussées, Paris, 1990-95, Inst. Empressa, Madrid, 1995, U. Bristol, U. London Sch. Oriental and African Studies, 1995—; cons. Ford Found., 1978-82, 93, U.S. Dept. State, 1978-80, UN Ctr. on Transnat. Corps., 1988—, Harvard Inst. Internat. Devel., 1990—, Asia Found., 1992, Harvard Law Sch./World Bank Laos Project, 1991-93; with Sri Lanka fin. sector project ISTI/U.S. AID, 1993-94; lectr. Georgetown U. Internat. Law Inst., 1978-94, Panam. U., Mexico City, 1981; chmn. com. on Mid. Ea. law Social Sci. Rsch. Coun., 1978-84; chmn. Coun. Internat. Exch. Scholars, 1987-91; bd. dirs. Boston World Affairs Coun., 1988-95, Emerging Markets Income Funds. I & II, Inc., Global Ptnrs. Income Fund, Inc., Salomon Bros. Worldwide Income Fund, Inc., Asia Tigers Fund, Inc., India Fund, Inc., Emerging Markets Floating Rate Fund, Inc., Mcpl. Ptnrs. Funds I & II, Salomon Bros. High Income Funds I & II, Salomon Bros. 2008 Worldwide Dollar Govt. Term Trust, Mcpl. Ptnrs. Funds I & II; trustee Southwestern Legal Found., 1992—, Am. U. Paris, 1993-97; pres. Internat. Third World Legal Studies Assn., 1987-91; chmn. Inst. Transnat. Arbitration, 1991-93; pres. Assn. Profl. Schs. Internat. Affairs, 1988-89; Fulbright disting. chair in comparative law, Italy, 2000. Author: (with Kasunmu) Nigerian Family Law, 1966, An Introduction to Law in French-Speaking Africa, Vol. I, 1969, Vol. II, 1976, (with Steng) International Business Planning, 1982, Making Global Deals-Negotiating in the International Marketplace, 1991, The Art of Advice, 1994, (video course) Negotiating in Today's World, 1995, The Wise Advisor, 2000, The Global Negotiator, 2003; contbr. articles to profl. jours. Mem. ABA, Dallas Bar Found. (trustee 1983-86), Coun. on Fgn. Rels., Am. Law Inst., Am. Soc. Internat. Law, Cosmos Club (Washington). Home: 220 Stone Root Ln Concord MA 01742-4755 Office: Tufts U Fletcher Sch Law-Diplomacy Medford MA 02155 E-mail: jeswald.salacuse@tufts.edu.

SALAGI, DORIS, educational administrator, retired; b. Perth Amboy, N.J., July 30, 1947; d. Joseph William and Anna Salagi. BA, Trenton State Coll. (name now Coll. of N.J.), 1969, MA, 1973. Cert. elem. sch. tchr., supr., tchr. of the handicapped. 3d grade tchr. Willingboro (N.J.) Bd. Edn., 1969-79, basic skills math. tchr., 1979-83, resource rm. tchr., 1983-87, tchr. of the handicapped, 1987-92, 95-98, individualized ednl. plan facilitator, 1992-95; Homebound instr. Woodbridge (N.J.) Twp. Sch. Dist., 1999—. Curriculum writer Willingboro Bd. Edn., 1973, 77, 79-83, 88-89, 98. Co-author: (curriculum) The Care and Handling of Compositions, 1973. Vol. Rancocas Hosp., Willingboro, 1978-98. Named for Outstanding Achievement in Edn., Trenton State Coll. Alumni Assn., 1991. Mem.: NEA, Burlington County Edn. Assn., N.J. Ret. Educators Assn., Willingboro Edn. Assn. (rep. 1974—76), Burlington County Ret. Edn. Assn., N.J. Educators Assn., Rancocas Hosp. Aux. (scholarship chair 1978—81, bazaar chair 1981—85, rec. sec. 1983—87, pres. 1987—89), Alpha Zeta (rec. sec. 1995—99, chmn. social 1997—2001, chmn. nominations 1999—2001, chmn. rsch. 2001—03, chmn. World Fellowship Eta chpt. 1985—87, 1st v.p. 1988—90, pres. 1990—92, treas. 1992—), Delta Kappa Gamma Soc. Internat. (internat. rep. to UN dept. pub. info. 1998—2000). Avocations: reading, travel, walking, theatre, gardening.

SALAMANCA, MERLINA ESPIRITU, secondary education educator; b. Abra, Philippines, Feb. 6, 1940; came to U.S., 1970; d. Santiago and Luisa (Panday) Espiritu; m. Manuel Valdez Salamanca; children: Merilyn Elaine, Michael Edward. LLB, Manuel L. Quezon U., Manila, 1963; BA, Columbus (Ga.) Coll., 1980, MEd, 1987; EdS, Troy State U., 1992. Legal researcher Paredes & Poblador Law Offices, Manila, 1965-69; title searcher Lawyer Title Ins., Inc., Ohio, 1970-72; acct. clk. St. Vincent Charity Hosp., Cleve., 1975-77; tchr. St. Patrick Sch., Phenix City, Ala., 1983-84, Adult Edn. Urban League, Columbus, Ga., 1984-85; tchr., behavior disorder therapist Woodall Psychoednl. Program, Columbus, 1985—. Contbr. articles to various publs. Mem. AAUW (pres. 1989—). Avocations: reading, cooking. Office: Woodall Psychoednl Program 4312 Harrison Ave Columbus GA 31904-6634

SALAMON, LINDA BRADLEY, English literature educator; b. Elmira, N.Y., Nov. 20, 1941; d. Grant Ellsworth and Evelyn E. (Ward) Bradley; divorced; children: Michael Lawrence, Timothy Martin. BA, Radcliffe Coll., 1963; MA, Bryn Mawr Coll., 1964, PhD, 1971; Advanced Mgmt. Cert., Harvard U. Bus. Sch., 1978; D.H.L., St. Louis Coll. Pharmacy, 1993. Lectr., adj. asst. prof. Eng., Dartmouth Coll., Hanover, N.H., 1967-72; mem. faculty lit. Bennington Coll., Vt., 1974-75; dean students Wells Coll., Aurora, N.Y., 1975-77; exec. asst. to pres. U. Pa., Phila., 1977-79; assoc. prof. English, Washington U., St. Louis, 1979-88, prof., 1988-92, dean Coll. Arts and Scis., 1979-92; prof. English, George Washington U., Washington, 1992—; dean Columbia Coll. Arts and Sci., Washington, 1992-95; interim v.p. for acad. affairs George Washington U., Washington, 1995-96. Mem. faculty Bryn Mawr Summer Inst. for Women, 1979-99. Author, co-editor: Nicholas Hilliard's Art of Limning, 1983; co-author: Integrity in the College Curriculum, 1985; contbr. numerous articles to literary and ednl. jours. Bd. dirs. Assn. Am. Colls., vice chmn., 1985, chmn., 1986; bd. dirs. Greater St. Louis council Girl Scouts U.S.A.; trustee Coll. Bd., St. Louis Coll. Pharmacy. Fellow Radcliffe Inst., 1973-74, Ringler, Fulbright Fellow Taiwan, 2003; Am. Philos. Soc. Penrose grantee, 1974; fellow Folger Shakespeare Libr., 1986, NEH Montaigne Inst., 1988, Fulbright Scholar, 2003; Riugler Fellow, Houtington Libr., 2004. Mem. MLA, Renaissance Soc. Am., Cosmos Club, Phi Beta Kappa. Office: George Washington U Dept of Eng Rome Hall 760 801 22D St NW Washington DC 20052-0001

SALAMON, MIKLOS DEZSO GYORGY, mining engineer, educator; b. Balkany, Hungary, May 20, 1933; came to U.S., 1986; naturalized, 1993; s. Miklos and Sarolta (Obetko) S.; m. Agota Maria Meszaros, July 11, 1953; children: Miklos, Gabor. Diploma in Engring., Polytech U., Sopron,

Hungary, 1956; PhD, U. Durham, Newcastle, England, 1962; doctorem honoris causa, U. Miskolc, Hungary, 1990. Rsch. asst. dept. mining engring. U. Durham, 1959-63; dir. rsch. Coal Mining Rsch. Controlling Coun., Johannesburg, South Africa, 1963-66; dir. collieries rsch. lab. Chamber of Mines of South Africa, Johannesburg, 1966-74, dir. gen. rsch. orgn., 1974-86; disting. prof. Colo. Sch. Mines, Golden, 1986-98, disting. prof. emeritus, 1998—, head dept. mining engring., 1986-90; dir. Colo. Mining and Mineral Resources Rsch. Inst., 1990-94; pres. Salamon Cons. Inc., Arvada, Colo., 1995—. 22d Sir Julius Wernher Meml. lectr., 1988; hon. prof. U. Witwatersrand, Johannesburg, 1979-86; vis. prof. U. Minn., Mpls., 1981, U. Tex., Austin, 1982, U. NSW, Sydney, Australia, 1990, 91-96; mem. Presdl. Commn. of Inquiry into Safety and Health in South African Mining Industry, 1994-95. Co-author: Rock Mechanics Applied to the Study of Rockbursts, 1966, Rock Mechanics in Coal Mining, 1976; contbr. articles to profl. jours. Mem. Pres.'s Sci. Adv. Council, Cape Town, South Africa, 1984-86, Nat. Sci. Priorities Com., Pretoria, South Africa, 1984-86. Recipient Nat. award Assn. Scis. and Tech. Socs., South Africa, 1971. Fellow South African Inst. Mining and Metallurgy (hon. life, v.p. 1974-76, pres. 1976-77, gold medal 1964, 85, Stokes award 1986, silver medal 1991, 99), Inst. Mining and Metallurgy (London), Hungarian Acad. Scis. (external), 1998; mem. AIME, Internat. Soc. Rock Mechanics. Roman Catholic. E-mail: mdg_salamon@msn.com.

SALAMON, MYRON BEN, physicist, educator, dean; b. Pitts., June 4, 1939; s. Victor William and Helen (Sanders) S.; m. Sonya Maxine Blank, June 12, 1960; children— David, Aaron. BS, Carnegie-Mellon U., 1961; PhD, U. Calif., Berkeley, 1966. Asst. prof. physics U. Ill., Urbana, 1966-72, assoc. prof., 1972-74, prof., 1974—, program dir. Materials Research Lab., 1984-91, assoc. dean. Coll. Engring., 2000—. Vis. scientist U. Tokyo, 1966, 71, Tech. U. Munich, Fed. Republic Germany, 1974-75; cons. NSF; Disting. Vis. Prof. Tsukuba (Japan) U., 1995-96. Editor: Physics of Superionic Conductors, 1979; co-editor: Modulated Structures, 1979; divisional assoc. editor: Phys. Rev. Letters, 1992-96; contbr. sci. papers to profl. jours. Recipient Alexander von Humboldt Sr. U.S. Scientist award, 1974-75; NSF coop. fellow, 1964-66; postdoctoral fellow, 1966; A.P. Sloan fellow, 1972-73; Berndt Matthias scholar Los Alamos Nat. Lab., 1995-96; visiting scientist CNRS and Inst. Laue-Langevin Grenoble, France, 1981-82. Fellow Am. Phys. Soc. Office: U Ill Coll Engring 1308 W Green St Urbana IL 61801-9013

SALAMONE, JOHN DOMINIC, neuroscientist, educator; b. Bay Shore, N.Y., Oct. 21, 1956; s. Joseph Anthony and Margaret (Silvis) S.; m. Donna Nicholson, Dec. 21, 1983 (div. Apr. 1988); m. Alexandria Roe; 1 child, Isabella Marie. BA, Rockhurst Coll., 1978; MA, Emory U., 1978, PhD, 1982. Rsch. fellow U. Cambridge, Eng., 1982-83; rsch. pharmacolgist Merck, Sharp & Dohme, Harlow, Eng., 1983-86; rsch. fellow U. Pitts., 1986-88; asst. prof. to prof. U. Conn., Storrs, 1988—, head behavioral neurosci. divsn., psychology dept. Editl. bd. mem. Behavioral Brain Rsch., 1995; contbr. articles to profl. jours. NATO fellow NSF, 1982. Mem. AAAS, Soc. Neurosci., N.Y. Acad. Scis. Democrat. Roman Catholic. Achievements include rsch. in brain mechanisms involved in Parkinson's disease and motivation. Home: 31 Laurel St Manchester CT 06040-5126 Office: U Conn Dept Psychology 406 Babbidge Rd Storrs Mansfield CT 06269-9025

SALAMONE, JOSEPH CHARLES, polymer chemistry educator; b. Bklyn., Dec. 27, 1939; s. Joseph John and Angela (Barbagallo) S.; children: Robert, Alicia, Christopher. BS in Chemistry, Hofstra U., 1961; PhD in Chemistry, Poly. Inst. N.Y., 1967. NIH postdoctoral fellow U. Liverpool, Eng., 1966-67; rsch. assoc., Horace H. Rackham postdoctoral fellow U. Mich., Ann Arbor, 1967-70, adminstrv. sec., 1968-70; asst. prof., then assoc. prof. chemistry U. Mass., Lowell, 1970-76, prof., 1976-90, prof. emeritus, 1990—, dean Coll Sci., 1978-84, Disting. Rsch. fellow, 1984-90, chmn. dept. chemistry, 1975-78. Pres. Optimers Inc., Lowell, 1985-99; bd. dirs. Rochal Industries, Inc., Boca Raton, Fla.; cons. editor CRC Press, Inc., Boca Raton, 1992-97; v.p. chem. rsch. Bausch and Lomb, 1997-2000, v.p. rsch., 2000—. Author 2 books, 2 encys.; mem. editl. bd. Polymer, 1976-94, Jour. Macromolecular Sci.-Chemistry, 1985-2003, Progress of Polymer Sci., 1987-2002, ChemTech, 1995-99; adv. bd. Jour. Polymer Sci., 1974—; editor-in-chief Polymeric Materials Ency., 1993-97; contbr. over 170 articles to profl. jours.; holder 27 U.S. and internat. patents. Recipient Disting Alumnus award, Poly. Inst. N.Y., 1984. Mem. Am. Chem. Soc. (chmn. div. polymer chemistry 1982), Polymer Sci., Am. Acad. Ophthalmology (assoc.), Pacific Polymer Fedn. (sec., treas. 1988-90, dep. v.p. 1991-92, v.p., 1993, pres. 1994-95). Office: Bausch & Lomb 1400 N Goodman St PO Box 30450 Rochester NY 14603-0450 E-mail: joe_salamone@bausch.com.

SALAND, DEBORAH, psychotherapist, educator; b. Val Dosta, Ga., July 25, 1954; d. Charles and Audrey (Horan) Gianniny. B in Profl. Studies, Barry U., 1990, MSW, 1992; D in Psychology, So. Calif. Sch. Profl. Studies, 1996. Lic. clin. social worker, Fla. Substance abuse counselor Spectrum Programs, Ft. Lauderdale, Fla., 1974-79; owner Obsession in Time, Miami, Fla., 1984-88; asst. clin. dir. Interphase Recovery, Miami, 1988-89; substance abuse counselor Transitions Recovery, Miami, 1989-91; clin. dir. level II Pathways Treatment, Miami; pvt. practice Inst. Human Potential, Miami, 1993—; founder Eating Disorder Tex. Program, 1997—. Lectr. Addiction Traingin Inst. U. Miami, 1992, mem. faculty, 1993—; clin. supr. Transitions Recovery, Miami, 1993—, Treatment Resources, Miami, 1993-94; adj. faculty N.Y. Inst. Tech., Boca Raton, Fla., 1997—; dir. Am. Family Eating Disorder Tract, 1997-98. Contbr. articles to profl. jours. Named Spl. Alumni Barry U., 1996. Mem. NASW, APA, Am. Group Psychotherapy Assn. (clin.), Med. Psychotherapist Am. (assoc. clin.) Nat. Bd. Cert. Counselors (counselor), Broward County Mental Health Assn. Office: Inst Human Potential 19501 NE 10th Ave Ste 305 Miami FL 33179-3502

SALAVERRIA, HELENA CLARA, retired language educator; b. May 19, 1923; d. Blas Saturnino and Eugenia Irene (Loyarte) S. AB, U. Calif., Berkeley, 1945, secondary tchg. cert., 1946; MA, Stanford U., 1962. H.S. tchr., 1946-57; asst. prof. Luther Coll., Decorah, Iowa, 1959-60; prof. Spanish Bakersfield (Calif.) Coll., 1961-84, chmn. dept., 1973-80; ret., 1984. Mem. srs. adv. group edn. Cuesta Coll. Cmty. Svcs. Mem. AAUW (edn. com.), NEA, Calif. Fgn. Lang. Tchrs. Assn. (dir. 1976-77), Kern County Fgn. Lang. Tchrs. Assn. (pres. 1975-77), Union Concerned Scientists, Natural Resources Def. Coun., Calif. Tchrs. Assn. (chpt. sec. 1951-52), Yolo County Coun. Retarded, Soc. Basque Studies in Am., RSVP, Amnesty Internat., Common Cause, Sierra Club, Prytanean Alumnae, U. Women of Cambria, U. Calif. Alumni Assn., Stanford U. Alumni Assn., Friends of the Cambria Libr. Democrat. Home: PO Box 63 Cambria CA 93428-0063

SALAZAR, GUMERCINDO PRUDENCIO, mathematics educator; b. Santa Fe, Apr. 11, 1950; s. Jose Prudencio and Sibila Erminda S. BS, N.Mex. Highlands U., 1973; MST, N.Mex. Tech., 1979; adminstrv. cert., N.Mex. Highlands U., 1992. Math. tchr. Dulce (N.Mex.) Ind. Schs., 1973-76, Chama Valley Schs., Tierra Amerilla, N.Mex., 1976—. Budget com. Chama Valley Schs., Tierra Amarilla, N.Mex., 1980-92; sci. adv. State N.Mex., Santa Fe, 1980-84; mem. Nat. Coun. Tchrs. Math., N.Mex. Tchrs. Math., Albuquerque, 1973—. Vice chmn. Ganados Del Valle, Los Ojos, N.Mex., 1983-92. Recipient Exemplary Svc. to N.Mex. Schs., State Bd. Edn., Santa Fe, 1985, Number Sense Trainer award Math Learning System, N.Mex., 1986, Cert. Profl. Growth N.Mex. Prin. Ctr., Las Vegas, 1992. Mem. Knights Columbus, Chama Valley Fedn. United Sch. Employees. Democrat. Roman Catholic. Avocations: ranching, hunting, camping, weight lifting. Home: 3601 Majesta St Farmington NM 87402-4674

SALAZAR, OMAR MAURICIO, radiation oncologist, educator; b. Havana, Cuba, Sept. 22, 1942; came to U.S., 1959; naturalized, 1970; s. Aramis Victor and Nelida Raquel (Acosta) S.; m. Margarita Cristina Pedraza, July 7, 1979; children: Omar M.II, Sofia M. BS in Biology, Georgetown U., 1965; MD, U. P.R., 1969; MS, U. Rochester, 1974. Diplomate Am. Bd. Radiology. Intern U. Hosp. U. P.R., Rio Piedras, 1969—70, radiotherapy resident, 1970—73, chief resident, 1972-73; instr., fellow U. Rochester, NY, 1973-74, asst. prof., 1974-78, assoc. prof., 1978-81; prof., chmn. dept. radiation oncology U. Md., Balt., 1981-95; dir. radiation oncology La. State U. Med. Ctr., New Orleans, 1995-99; dir. dept. radiation oncology, dir. Cancer Ctr. Excellence Oakwood Health Sys., Dearborn, Mich., 1999—; pres. Assoc. in Radiation Oncology, PC, 2000—. Mem. CCIRC Nat. Cancer Inst., Bethesda, Md., 1980-84; prof. clin. oncology Am. Cancer Soc., 1989-1993; coord. USA, Circulo Radioterapeutas Ibero-Latino-Americanos-L.Am. Assn. Radiation Therapy, 1981-98, v.p., 1998-2000, pres. elect, 2000-2002, pres. 2002-; expert cons. internat. Atomic Energy Agy., Vienna, Austria, 1996—; examiner Am. Bd. Radiology, Phila., 1983-93; chmn. site cancer visit Nat. Cancer Inst., Bethesda, 1983, site visitor, 1982; co-investigator Whitaker Found., 1983; prof. clin. oncology Am. Cancer Soc., 1989-94. Author: Moments of Decision/Primary Brain Tumors, 1979, Bronchogenic Carcinoma, 1981, Unveiling Mysteries to Create Miracles, 2002; contbr. articles to profl. jours. Arthur A. Ward Trust grantee, 1981; Am. Cancer Clin. Fellowship award, 1984-86. Fellow: Am. Coll. Radiation Oncology (past pres., past chmn. bd. dirs., chancellor, Gold medal), Am. Coll. Radiology; mem.: AMA, Am. Assn. Cancer Edn., Am. Radiol. Soc., Radiol. Soc. Am., Md. Radiol. Soc., Med. Chirurgical Soc., Tex. Radiol. Soc., Ea. Coop. Oncology Group (chmn. brain and lung com. 1979—80), Radiation Therapy Oncology Group, Mask and Bauble Dramatic Soc., Big Five Club. Roman Catholic. E-mail: salazaro@oakwood.org.

SALAZAR, PAMELA SUE, secondary education educator; b. Pensacola, Fla., Aug. 24, 1951; d. Raymond Earl and Mary JoAnn (Lister) Cummins; m. George Watson (div. Sept. 1975); 1 child, Jason Watson; m. Thomas Joseph Salazar, Mar. 26, 1980; children: cortney Diann, Cresen Denise. BS, U. Nev., Las Vegas, 1975; MS in Physics and Edn., U. Nev., 1980, EdD in Ednl. Leadership, 2001. Tchr. sci. and math. Woodbury Jr. H.S., Las Vegas, 1975-78; tchr. physics Basic H.S., Henderson, Nev., 1978-90, Green Valley H.S., Henderson, 1990-96; asst. prin. Western H.S., Las Vegas, 1996—99; prin. Basic H.S., Henderson, 1999—2002; prins. on spl. assignment, prof. U. Nev., Las Vegas, 2002—. Assoc.dir. Nev. Inst. for Gifted and Talented, U. Nev., Las Vegas, 1991—; project dir. Dept. Energy MST Grant, 1994—. Author: (lab. experiments) Mesur-NASA, 1992. Asst. coord. pub. events So. Nev. Muscular Dystrophy, Las Vegas, 1990-93; race dir. sporting events Multiple Sclerosis Soc., Las Vegas, 1986-92. Named Tandy Tech. Techr., 1992. Mem. Am. Assn. Physics Tchrs., Nat. Sci. Tchrs. Assn. (Presdl. award in sci. 1993), Nat. Assn. Secondary Sch. Prins. (nat. task force prin. preparation, co-editor jour.). Democrat. Roman Catholic. Avocations: triathlons, half-marathons, mountain bike riding, tandem cross-country touring. Home: 7145 W Le Baron Ave Las Vegas NV 89124 Office: Ednl Leadership U Nev Las Vegas NV 89154

SALAZAR-CARRILLO, JORGE, economics educator; b. Jan. 17, 1938; came to U.S., 1960; s. Jose Salazar and Ana Maria Carrillo; m. Maria Eugenia Winthrop, Aug. 30, 1959; children: Jorge, Manning, Mario, Maria Eugenia. BBA, U. Miami, 1958; MA in Econs., U. Calif., Berkeley, 1964; cert. in econ. planning, U. Calif., 1964, PhD in Econs., 1967. Sr. fellow, non-resident staff mem. Brookings Instn., Washington, 1965—. Dir., mission chief UN, Rio de Janeiro, 1974—80; prof. econs. Fla. Internat. U., Miami, 1980—, chmn. dept. econs., 1980—89; dir. Ctr. Econ. Rsch. & Edn.; former mem. coun. econ. advisors State of Fla.; advisor USIA; former advisor, contbg. editor Libr. of Congress, Washington; chmn. program com. Hispanic Profs. of Econs. and Bus.; cons. econs. AID, Washington, 1979—; former coun. mem. Internat. Assn. Housing, Vienna, 1981—; former exec. bd. Cuban Am. Nat. Coun., Miami, 1982—; bd. dirs., pres. Fla. chpt. Insts. of Econ. and Social Rsch. of Caribbean Basin, 1983—, U.S.-Chile Coun., Miami, 1984—, Fla.-Brazil Inst. Co-author: Trade, Debt and Growth in Latin America, 1984, Prices for Estimation in Cuba, 1985, The Foreign Debt and Latin America, 1983, External Debt and Strategy of Development in Latin America, 1985, The Brazilian Economy in the Eighties, 1987, Foreign Investment, Debt and Growth in Latin America, 1988, World Comparisons of Incomes, Prices and Product, 1988, Comparisons of Prices and Real Products in Latin America, 1990, The Latin American Debt, 1992, International Comparisons of Prices, Output and Productivity, 1996, Capital Markets, Growth and Economic Policy in Latin America, 1999, Growth in Latin America in the 1990s, 2000, Macroeconomics, 2001, Social Christian Doctrine and Econ. Devel., 2002; author: Wage Structure in Latin America, 1982, Oil and Development of Venezuela During the Twentieth Century, 1994. Fellow Brit. Coun., London, 1960, Georgetown U., Washington, 1961-62, OAS, Washington, 1962-64, Brookings Instn., Washington, 1964-65. Mem.: Collegium of Cuban Economists (1st v.p.), Cuban Banking Study Group (dir.), Assn. for Study Cuban Economy (former mem. exec. com.), Nat. Assn. Forensic Economists, Internat. Assn. Energy Economists, Nat. Assn. Cuban Am. Educators (exec. com.), N.Am. Econs. and Fin. Assn., Econometric Soc. Latin Am., Am. Econ. Assn., Knights of Malta. Roman Catholic. Home: 1105 Almeria Ave Coral Gables FL 33134-5503 Office: Fla Internat U Tamiami Campus Dm 319-B Miami FL 33199-0001 E-mail: salazar@fiu.edu.

SALCEDO-DOVI, HECTOR EDUARDO, anatomist, educator, surgeon; b. Cordoba, Argentina, Nov. 9, 1958; s. Domingo and Rosa (Dovi) Salcedo; m. Adriana Gomez, Apr. 3, 1993; children: Camila, Marianna. MD, U. Nat. Cordoba, 1984; DO, N.Y. Coll. Osteopathic Medicine, 1995. Asst. prof. anatomy, histology N.Y. Coll. Osteo. Medicine, Old Westbury, 1990—93, prof. anatomy, physiology, 1993; chief intern Good Samaritan Hosp., 1996—, chief resident surgery, 2000. Fellow critical care/trauma, 2001—03. Mem.: ACS, Soc. CCM, Am. Coll. Chest Physicians, Am. Osteopathic Assn., Am. Med. Student Assn. Roman Catholic. Avocations: soccer, bicycling, tennis. Home: 2 Manchester Rd Huntington NY 11743-5532

SALE, TOM S., III, financial economist; b. Haynesville, La., July 27, 1942; s. Thomas and Mary Belle (Fagg) S.; divorced; children: Jennifer Elizabeth, Sarah Elaine. BA, Tulane U., 1964; MA, Duke U., 1965; PhD, La. State U., 1972. CFA. Faculty La. Tech. U., Ruston, 1965-75, prof. econs., 1975-98, ret., 1998. Head dept. econs. and fin. La. Tech. U., 1974-86, 90-95, dir. grad. studies Coll. Adminstrn and Bus., 1988-89; fin. cons. Contbr. articles to profl. jours. Mem. Southwestern Fin. Assn. (pres. 1985-86), Assn. Investment Mgmt. and Rsch. (exam. com. 1983-92, curriculum com. 1993—), SW Fedn. Adminstrv. Disciplines (v.p. 1988-89, pres. 1989-90), Dallas Assn. Fin. Analysts, Omicron Delta Kappa, Omicron Delta Epsilon. Episcopalian. Home: PO Box 1365 Ruston LA 71273-1365 E-mail: tomsale3@tcainternet.com.

SALEH, BAHAA E. A. electrical engineering educator; b. Cairo, Sept. 30, 1944; came to U.S., 1977. BS, Cairo U., 1966; PhD, Johns Hopkins U., 1971. Lectr. Johns Hopkins U., Balt., 1969-71; asst. prof. U. Santa Catarina, Brazil, 1971-74; rsch. assoc. Max Planck Inst., Göttingen, Germany, 1974-76; asst. prof. elec. engring. U. Wis., Madison, 1977-79, assoc. prof., 1979-81, prof., 1981-94, chmn. dept. elec. and computer engring., 1990-94; prof., chmn. dept. elec. and computer engring Boston U., 1994—. Author: Photoelectron Statistics, 1978, Fundamentals of Photonics, 1991; also over 200 articles on optics and image processing. Romnes faculty fellow U. Wis., 1981, Guggenheim fellow, 1984. Fellow IEEE, Optical Soc. Am. (editor-in-chief jour.); mem. Phi Beta Kappa, Sigma Xi. Office: Eight St Mary's St Boston MA 02215-2421

SALEH, FARIDA YOUSRY, chemistry educator; b. Cairo, June 17, 1939; came to U.S., 1968; d. Michael Yousry and Fakiha Yousef (Badawy) Wassif; m. Hosny Gabra Saleh, Oct. 8, 1959; children: Magda, Nagwa. BS, Ain Shams U., 1959; MS, Alexandrial U., Egypt, 1967; PhD, U. Tex., 1976. Postdoctoral rsch. assoc. Tex. A&M U., College Station, 1977-78; rsch. scientist II U. North Tex., Denton, 1978-83, asst. prof. chemistry, 1980-83, assoc. prof., 1985-94, prof., 1994—. Cons. Stanford Rsch. Inst., Menlo Park, Calif., 1983-84, Allied Chems. Co., Hackettstown, N.J., 1985-86, Am. Chrome Chems., Corpus Christi, Tex., 1988-89, USEPA Rev. Panel, Washington, 1986—. Contbg. author book chpts. in field; contbr. more than 60 articles to profl. jours. Recipient Svc. award U.S. EPA, Washington, 1993; recipient numerous grants in field. Mem. Am. Chem. Soc., Internat. Union of Pure and Applied Chemistry, Internat. Humic Substances Soc., Assn. Women in Sci. Avocations: music, swimming, tennis. Office: Univ North Tex PO Box 310559 Denton TX 76203-0559 E-mail: saleh@unt.edu.

SALEM, DOROTHY CARLSON, social science and history educator; b. Dayton, Ohio, Jan. 29, 1946; d. Donald R. and Ethel (Carlson) Meyer; m. Thomas Coopland (dec. 1967); m. Thomas Gregory Salem, Oct. 21, 1932; children: Kelle Ann, Beth Marie, Jennifer Lynn. AS, Cuyahoga Community Coll., Cleve., 1969; BA, Cleve. State U., 1971, MA, 1972; PhD, Kent State U., 1985, cert. in instrnl. design, 2001. Teaching asst. history Cleve. State U., 1971-72, adj. prof. history, 1985—; lectr. Cuyahoga Community Coll., Cleve., 1972-75, from asst. prof. to prof. social sci. women's studies, 1975-85, prof. social sci. and history, 1985—, dir. Inst. on Human Rels., 1985-89. Cons. multicultural curriculum and women's studies Cleve. Pub. Schs., 1987—. Author: To Better Our World, 1990; editor: African American Women: A Biographical Dictionary, 1992, The Journey, 1997; contbr. articles to profl. jours. Mem. adv. bd. Displaced Homemakers Networks, Cleve., 1987—. Recipient Besse award for tchg. excellence Cuyahoga C.C. Found., 1985, Nat. Teaching Excellence award Nat. Inst. Staff and Orgn. Devel., 1989, Disting. Alumnae award Cleve. State U., 1990, Ohio Prof. of Yr., Carnegie Found., 2002, Women of Profl. Excellence award YWCA, 2003; NEH summer study grantee, 1992. Mem. Am. Assn. Cmty. and Jr. Colls. (Inst. for Leadership), AAUW (Am. fellow), Am. Hist. Assn., Nat. Women's Studies Assn., Ohio Acad. History, So. Assn. Women Historians. Democrat. Lutheran. Avocations: walking, gardening. Office: Cuyahoga Community Coll 2900 Community College Ave Cleveland OH 44115-3123

SALEMI, JOSEPH SALVATORE, classics and humanities educator, poet, writer; b. N.Y.C., Feb. 1, 1948; s. Salvatore Joseph and Liberty Luce (Previti) S.; m. Helen Louise Palma, June 1, 1991. BA, Fordham U., 1968; MA, NYU, 1970, PhD, 1986. Permanent cert. English tchr., N.Y. Prof. composition and lit. Pace U., N.Y.C., 1977-84; prof. English, Nassau C.C., Westbury, N.Y., 1984-86, Fordham U., Bronx, N.Y., 1988-89; prof. classics Bklyn. Coll., CUNY, 1993-2000, Hunter Coll., CUNY, N.Y.C., 1989—; prof. humanities NYU, N.Y.C., 1983—. Author: Formal Complaints, 1997, Nonsense Couplets, 1999, Masquerade, 2003; poems and translations published in over seventy jours.:, book reviewer, essayist: Expansive Poetry and Music Online, assoc. editor: Iambs and Trochees; contbr. Expasive Poetry and Music On-Line. Recipient award Classical and Modern Lit. Jour., 1993; Musurillo scholar CUNY Grad. Ctr., 1975; sr. fellow NEH, 1982, Lane Cooper fellow NYU, 1983-84. Mem. Nat. Assn. Scholars, Am. Lit. Translators Assn., Renaissance Soc. Am. Roman Catholic. Avocation: military research. Home: 220 9th St Brooklyn NY 11215 Office: CUNY Hunter Coll Classics Dept 695 Park Ave New York NY 10021

SALERNO, SISTER MARIA, nursing educator, adult and gerontological nurse; b. Syracuse, N.Y. d. Joseph and Josephine (Ostrowski) S. Diploma in nursing, St. Joseph's Hosp., Syracuse, 1962; BSN summa cum laude, Cath. U. Am., 1974, MS in Nursing, 1976, D of Nursing Sci., 1981; cert. nurse practitioner, U. Rochester, 1984. RN, N.Y., Md., Washington; cert. adult, geriatric nurse practitioner ANCC; joined Sisters of Third Franciscan Order, Roman Cath. Ch., 1963. Staff nurse St. Joseph Hosp. Health Ctr., Syracuse, 1962-63; sr. charge nurse ICU, gen. med. and surg. units St. Elizabeth Hosp., Utica, N.Y., 1965-66, head nurse pediatrics unit, 1966-69; head nurse ECF Loretto Geriatric Ctr., Syracuse, 1969-72; lectr. Cath. U. Am., Washington, 1977—81, asst. prof. nursing, 1978-79, 81-92, assoc. prof., 1992—, dir. primary care adult/geriatric nurse practitioner programs, 1984—, co-dir. FNP program, 1994-97. Contbr. chpts. to books; contbr. articles to profl. jours. Vol. nurse practitioner Cmty. of Hope, Washington; instl. animal care and use com. George Washington U., 1996—; scholarship com. Franciscan Found. for the Holy Land, 1996—. Grantee NIH, 1984-89, Cath. U. Am., 1989-90. Mem.: AAUP, ANA, D.C. League for Nursing (bd. dirs. 1995—97, 1999—), D.C. Nurse Practitioners Assn., N.Y. Acad. Scis., Nat. League for Nursing, Nat. Orgn. Nurse Practitioner Facilities, Nat. Gerontol. Nurses Assn., Am. Coll. Nurse Practitioners, Am. Acad. Nurse Practitioners, Am. Assn. for History of Nursing, Cath. U. Am. Nursing Alumni Assn. (pres. 1986—87, chpt. exec. bd. 1992—, treas. 1998—2003), Nat. Italian Am. Found. (assoc.), Sigma Theta Tau (grad. counselor Kappa chpt. 1985—87, eligibility com. 1985—87, awards com. 1987—89, grad. counselor Kappa chpt. 1991—97, eligibility com. 1991—97, 2003—). Fax: 202-319-6485. E-mail: salerno@cua.edu.

SALERNO, TOMAS ANTONIO, cardiothoracic surgeon, educator; b. Cassia, Minas, Brazil, Jan. 17, 1944; s. Jose and Silveria (Ferreira) Salerno; m. Helen Salerno; m. Michele Salerno (div.); children: Mark, Kim. BSc, McGill U., Can., 1964; MD, McGill U., 1971, MSc, 1973; Dr. h.c. (hon.), U. Chiety, Italy, 1997. Diplomate Am. Bd. Thoracic Surgeons. Asst. prof. surgery Queen's U., Canada, 1971—75; assoc. prof.. surgery McGill U., Canada, 1975—81; assoc. prof. to prof. surgery U. Toronto, Canada, 1981—93; prof. surgery SUNY, Buffalo, 1993—98, U. Miami, Fla., 1999—. Chief cardiothoracic surgery Jackson Meml. Hosp., Miami, 1999—. Editor: (book) Warm Heart Surgery; co-editor: Beating Heart Surgery, 2001, Secrets of Thoracic Surgery, 2001, Secrets of Cardiac Surgery, 2001; mem. editl. bd. Annals of Thoracic Surgery, 2002—. Office: Univ of Miami 1611 NW 12th Ave ET3072 Miami FL 33136 E-mail: tsalerno@med.miami.edu.

SALESMAN, JANET FAY, speech language pathologist; b. Sullivan, Ind., Nov. 29, 1951; d. Howard N. and Margaret F. (Aaron) Lee; m. Jerry L. Salesman, June 1, 1975; 1 child, Elizabeth A. BS, Ind. State U., 1975, MS, 1977. Speech, lang. pathologist Bloomfield (Ind.) Sch. Dist., 1974-85, Met. Sch. Dist. of Shakamak, Jasonville, Ind., 1985—. Mem. tech. com. Met. Sch. Dist. of Shakamak, Jasonville, 1993-94. Pres. Shakamak Jr. Sr. High Choir Boosters, Jasonville, Ind., 1994-95. Mem. VFW Aux., Delta Kappa Gamma. Home: PO Box 127 Coalmont IN 47845-0127 E-mail: jsalesman@shakamak.k12.in.us.

SALGADO, MARIA ANTONIA, education educator; b. Puerto de la Cruz, Tenerife, Canary Island, Spain, Jan. 15, 1933; came to U.S., 1951; d. Felipe Antonio Lopez-González and Juliana Rafela (Garcia) de Lopez; m. Daniel E. Salgado, June 12, 1954; children: M. Liane, Danny. BA cum laude, Fla. State U., 1958; MA, U. N.C., 1960; PhD, U. Md., 1966. Asst. prof. U. N.C., Chapel Hill, 1967-72, assoc. prof., 1972-77, prof., 1977—. Author: Las caricaturas de J.R.J., 1969, Hablemos!, 1976, Rafael Arevalo Martinez, 1979; contbr. articles to profl. publs. Democrat. Roman Catholic. Office: U NC Rom Langs Clb # 3170 Chapel Hill NC 27599-0001

SALGANICOFF, LEON, pharmacology educator; b. Buenos Aires, Sept. 11, 1924; came to U.S., 1964; s. Marcos Salganicoff and Ana Rosa Zelicson; m. Matilde Saffier, Dec. 11, 1957; children, Alina, Marcos. MSc in Pharmacy, U. Buenos Aires, 1948, DSc in Biochemistry, 1955; D honoris causa, U. Sapienza, Rome, 2001. Instr. U. Buenos Aires, 1947-49; chief clin. pathologist Hosp. Mil. Cen., Buenos Aires, 1955-59; chief lab. Conicet, Buenos Aires, 1959-64; rsch. assoc. Nat. Coun. Investigation, Buenos Aires, 1959-64; rsch. fellow Johnson Found., U. Pa., Phila., 1965-68, Nat. Multiple Sclerosis Soc., 1968-71; assoc. prof. pharmacology Temple U., Phila., 1972-84, sect. leader, 1971—, prof. pharmacology Med.

Sch., 1979—94, prof. emeritus, 1995—. Vis. prof. U. Rome la Sapienza, 1976—, NATO vis. prof., 1992; dir. rsch. Barnett Found. for Mitochondrial Diseases; ajd. prof. neurology St. Christopher's Hosp. for Children. Grantee NIH, 1972-87, WW Smith, 1987-92, R Schwab, 1992—; recipient W.W. Smith Charitable Trust award, 1992. Mem. AAAS, Fedn. Am. Socs. Exptl. Biology, Sigma Xi. Avocation: piano music. Home: 556 N 23rd St Philadelphia PA 19130-3117 Office: Temple U Sch Medicine 3400 N Broad St Philadelphia PA 19140-5104 E-mail: ls23529@astro.temple.edu.

SALINAS, SONIA, elementary school educator; b. Corpus Christi, Tex., Nov. 20, 1955; BA, St. Mary's U., 1978; postgrad., Incarnate Word Coll., 1983-87, Tex. A & I U., 1983-87; bilingual edn. certificate, Corpus Christi State U., 1993. Provisional teaching cert., Tex. Tchr. migrant program grades 1,2,3,4,5 Ind. Sch. Dist., Corpus Christi, 1978-79, tchr. grade 1, 1979-90, after-sch. tutorial program grades 1 and 2, 1983-86, tchr. grade 2, 1990-92, tchr. grade 3, 1992—. Sect. leader Garcia Elem. Primary Module I, Corpus Christi, 1986-88, Garcia Elem. Bldg. Leadership Team, 1988-92, Garcia Elem. Primary Module II, 1990-92, Garcia Elem. Site Base Mgmt. Decision Making Team, 1990-92; tchr. young readers summertime reading program Lulac Ednl. Svc. Ctr., Corpus Christi, 1991; chmn. Garciafest Coronation Pageant, Corpus Christi, 1991-92; officer standing com. PTA, Corpus Christi, 1992-93. Roman Catholic. Avocations: reading, painting. Home: 2925 Morris St Corpus Christi TX 78405-2235

SALISBURY, MARGARET MARY, retired public school educator; b. LaGrange, Tex., Oct. 23, 1932; d. Charles Frederick and Hedwig Mary (Fajkus) Meyer; m. Harrison Bryan Salisbury, Jan. 8, 1955; children: Elaine, Kathleen, David, Stephen, Mark, Margaret II. BA, Our Lady of the Lake, San Antonio, 1954; MA, U. Tex., San Antonio, 1975. Lic. elem., secondary edn., English and sch. adminstrn. Tchr. h.s. St. Joseph's Sch. for Girls, El Paso, Tex., 1954-55; tchr. 1st grade St. Patricks Cathedral Sch., El Paso, 1955; tchr. 2nd grade S.W. Ind. Sch. Dist., San Antonio, 1971-74, tchr. 6th grade, 1974-75, supr. testing, reading, 1974-81, prin. jr. h.s., 1981-82; reading supr., 1982-86; dir. alternative sch. S.W. Ind. Sch. Dist., San Antonio, 1986-87, tchr. 3rd grade, 1987-96, ret., 1996. Pres. Cooperating Tchr./Student Tchr. U. at Tex., San Antonio, 1986-87. Mem. pastoral coun. Resurrection of the Lord, 1997—2002. Mem. AAUW (chairperson pub. policy com. 1995-98, co-chairperson book fair), Internat. Reading Assn., Tex. State Reading Assn., Alamo Reading Coun., Reading Improvement, Pres. Club (San Antonio coun. corr. sec. 2001—), San Antonio Ret. Tchrs. Assn. Republican. Roman Catholic. Avocations: gardening, reading, travel, photography. Home: 126 Meadow Trail Dr San Antonio TX 78227-1639

SALKIND, ALVIN J. electrochemical engineer, biomedical engineer, educator, dean; b. N.Y.C. s. Samuel M. and Florence (Zins) S.; m. Marion Ruth Koenig, Nov. 7, 1965; children: Susanne, James. B.Ch.E., Poly. Inst. N.Y., 1949, M.Ch.E., 1952, D.Ch.E., 1958; postgrad. and mgmt. courses, Pa. State U., 1965, Harvard U., 1976. Registered profl. engr., N.Y., N.J. Chem. engr. U.S. Electric Mfg. Co., N.Y.C., 1952-54; sr. scientist Sonotone Corp., Elmsford, NY, 1954-56; research assoc. Poly. Inst. N.Y., 1956-58, adj. prof. chem. engring., 1960-70; with ESB-Ray OVAC Co., Yardley, Pa., 1958-79, dir. tech., 1971-72, v.p. tech., 1972-79; pres. ESB Tech. Co., 1978-79; prof., chief bioengring. divsn., dept. surgery UMDNJ-Robert Wood Johnson Med. Sch., Piscataway, NJ, 1970—; prof. biomed. engring. and chem. and biochem. engring Rutgers U., Piscataway, NJ, 1985—2002, assoc. dean Coll. Engring., 1989—2001, vis. prof., 2002—, U. Miami, 2002—. Vis. prof. and exec. officer Case Ctr. for Electrochem. Sci., 1981-82, U. Miami, 2003-04; bd. dirs., cons. various cos., rsch. instns. and govt. orgns.; mem. rev. panels Nat. Rsch. Coun., NIH. Author: (with S.U. Falk) Alkaline Storage Batteries, 1969, (with Herbert T. Silverman and Irving F. Miller) Electrochemical Bioscience and Bioengineering, 1973; editor: (with E. Yeager) Techniques of Electrochemistry, 1971, vol. 2, 1973, vol. 3, 1978, History of Battery Technology, 1987, (with F. McLarnon and V. Bogatzky) Rechargeable Zinc Electrodes, 1996; contbr. articles to profl. jours. Served with USNR, 1945-46. Recipient Alumnus citation Poly. Inst. N.Y., 1975, award Internat. Tech. Exch. Soc., 1992, Frank Booth award Internat. Power Sources Symposium Eng., 1999; Case Centennial scholar Case-Western Res. U., 1980. Fellow Acad. Medicine of N.J., Am. Coll. Cardiology, AAAS; mem. Electrochem. Soc. (past chmn. new tech. com., past chmn. battery div.), Assn. Advancement Med. Instrumentation, Indsl. Rsch. Inst. (emeritus 1979), N.Y. Acad. Scis., Sigma Xi, Phi Lambda Upsilon. Home: 51 Adams Dr Princeton NJ 08540-5401 also: UMDNJ-Robert Wood Johnson Med Sch 675 Hoes Ln Piscataway NJ 08854-5627 E-mail: salkinaj@umdnj.edu., asalkind@miami.edu.

SALKIND, MICHAEL JAY, technology administrator; b. N.Y.C, Oct. 1, 1938; s. Milton and Esther (Jaffe) S.; m. Miriam E. Schwartz, Aug. 16, 1959 (div. 1979); children: Michael Jay, Elizabeth Jane, Jonathan Hillson, Joshua Isaac; m. Carol T. Gill, Dec. 23, 1990. B in Metall. Engring., Rensselaer Polytech. Inst., 1959, PhD, 1962. Chief advanced metallurgy United Techs. Rsch. Labs., East Hartford, 1964-68; chief structures and materials Sikorsky Aircraft div. United Techs. Corp., 1968-75; dir. product devel. Avco Systems div., 1975-76; mgr. structures NASA, 1976-80; dir. aerospace scis. Air Force Office of Sci. Rsch., 1980-89; pres. Ohio Aerospace Inst., 1990—2003, Business Tech Network, 2003—. Adj. faculty metallurgy Trinity Coll., Hartford; adj. faculty aerospace U. Md., 1982-85; adj. faculty materials Johns Hopkins U., 1985-89; chair Ohio Math. and Sci. Coalition. Cons. editor Internat. Jour. Fibre Sci. and Tech.; editor Applications Composite Materials, 1973; contbr. to profl. jours. and textbooks. Evaluator Accreditation Bd. Engring. and Tech., 1989—; mem. Daniel Guggenheim Medal Bd. Awards, 1984-90; mem. Spirit of St. Louis Medal Bd., 1984-89; mem. bd. Citizens' Acad. Charter Sch., Cleve. Internat. Program; mem. bd. NCCJ. Capt. U.S. Army, 1962-64. Recipient Disting. Leadership award, Cleve. Tech. Socs. Coun., 2002. Fellow AAAS, AIAA (assoc.), ASM Internat.; mem. ASME (Disting. lectr. 1989-93), ASTM (chmn. com. D-30 on high modulous fibers and their composites 1968-74), Am. Helicopter Soc., AIME, Brit. Inst. Metals, Rsch. Soc. Am., Plansee Soc., India Ohio C. of C., Cosmos Club, Union Club, 50 Club, Leadership Cleve., Sigma Xi, Alpha Sigma Mu. E-mail: michaelsalkind@adelphia.net.

SALLOWAY, JOSEPHINE PLOVNICK, psychologist, marriage and family therapist, mental health counselor, psychology educator, college counselor; b. Brookline, Mass., July 30, 1944; d. Isadore B. and Gladys J. (Press) Plovnick; m. Richard B. Salloway, July 4, 1967; 1 child, Matthew. AB in History, Boston U., 1965, EdM in Counseling, 1966; cert. in human resource mgmt., Bentley Coll., 1980. Cert. sch. psychologist, sch. adjustment counselor, history and social studies tchr.; clinically cert. forensic counselor, domestic violence counselor; lic. mental health counselor, marriage and family therapist; cert. psychologist. Counselor Boston Pub. Schs., 1966-78; counselor, psychologist ednl. enrichment program Milton (Mass.) Acad., 1970-71; psychologist Braintree (Mass.) Pub. Schs., 1983-89; psychologist, adjustment counselor Norwood Pub. Schs., 1990-92; sch. adjustment counselor Stoughton, Mass., 1993-94; cons. psychologist Waltham (Mass.) Schs., 1997—2000; pvt. practice Braintree, 1997—. Faculty psychology and child devel. Quincy (Mass.) Coll., 1997—, head counselor student support advisor, 1997-2003; faculty psychology and early childhood edn. and devel., faculty advisor Massassoit C.C., 1999—; faculty Program for Advancement of Learning Curry Coll., 1999, faculty psychology, 2000—, diagnostic tchr. Edn. and Diagnostic Ctr., 1999-00; field supr. dept. counselor edn. Harvard U., Cambridge, Mass., Northeastern U., Boston; del. Coastline Coun. for Children, Mass., 1985-2000, del. Mass. Soc. for Prevention of Cruelty to Children, 1998—; psychometrist Mass. Gen. Hosp., Boston; asst. coord. Boston U. Counseling Clinic; diagnostic tchr. Braintree, Mass., 1999—, Mass. Edn. Reform, Tutor, Canton Pub. Schs., 2000; mem. edn. reform Mass. Comprehensive Assessment Sys., 2000; commn. on child advocacy and domestic violence Dist. Atty.'s Office, 2000-02; lectr., presenter in field. Pub. dir. Curtain Call Theatre, 1997; contbg. editor Gazette newsletter, 1996— Class agt. Boston U. Alumni Assn., 1996—; ednl. dir. House of Worship, Braintree, 1994—; del. Braintree Fair Housing Commn., 1994-2000, Braintree Multicultural Com., 1994-2000; pres., bd. chmn. Cmty. Friends for Human Svcs., Inc., Boston, 1995—, chmn. edn. bd.; vol. Genesis Fund Telethon. Recipient Presdl. award Cmty. Friends for Human Svcs., Inc., 1996-97, 2001, Svc. award, 1998, 99, 2001, 03, Senatorial award, 1998; award for contbn. to svcs. for children Mass. Soc. for Prevention Cruelty to Children, 1998, 99, Senatorial award for outstanding contbn. to mental health Mass. Senate, 1998, award for contrbn. to Adult and Family Edn., 2003, Award for Contbr. Edn. N.E. Educators Assn., 2003. Mem. APA, AAUP, ACA (clin.), NASP, NAMP, Nat. Assn. Cert. Forensic Counselors, Am. Assn. Marriage and Family Therapists (clin.), N.E. Assn. Coll. Educators, Mass. Assn. Sch. Adjustment Counselors, Mass. Assn. Marriage and Family Therapists, Mass. Assn. Mental Health Counselors, Mass. Tchrs. Assn., Pi Lambda Theta, Scarlet Key. Avocations: antique collecting, reading, travel, volunteer work, theater. Home: 57 Cochato Rd Braintree MA 02184-4628 E-mail: jsalloway@aol.com.

SALLS, JENNIFER JO, secondary school educator, consultant; b. Reno, May 8, 1952; d. Edmund Allenby and Georgia Theresa (Mullison) Naphan; m. Mitchell Aaron Marshall, Dec. 18, 1971; children: Kevin Alexander, Christopher Allen, Brian Andrew. BS, U. Nev., 1974, MEd, 1985. Cert. math., lang. and computer tchr., Nev. Tchr. Reno High sch., 1977-82; chair math. dept., tchr. McQueen High Sch., Reno, 1982-90; edn. cons. Nev. Dept. of Edn., Carson City, 1990-91; secondary math./computer coord. Washoe County Sch. Dist., Reno, 1991-94, K-12 math. coord., 1994-2000; tchr. Sparks (Nev.) H.S., 2000—, math dept. leader, 2003. In-svc. instr. Washoe County Sch. Dist., Reno, 1980—; cons. U. Nev., Reno, 1986-87; referee Math. Tchr., Reston, Va., 1988—, mem. editl. bd., 1990-94. Co-author: Turtle Geometry, 1986; contbr.: (video course) Teaching Mathematics with Manipulatives Grades 7-12, 1995. NSF grantee, 1984. Mem. Nat. Coun. Tchrs. Math. (program com. annual meeting 1999, meeting the needs of beginning tchrs. com. 2000—, local arrangements com. ann. meeting 2002), Nat. Coun. Suprs. Math., Assn. State Suprs. Math., Calif. Math. Coun., Oreg. Coun. Tchrs. Math., No. Nev. Math. Coun. (pres. 1984-85, 87-88, treas. 2000-01), Nat. State Tchrs. Yr., Coun. Presdl. Awardees of Math. Democrat. Mem. Lds Ch. Avocations: needlework, tennis. Office: Sparks HS 820 15th St Sparks NV 89431 E-mail: jsalls@washoe.k12.nv.us.

SALMON, PHYLLIS WARD, early education educator; b. Dallas, Aug. 10, 1948; d. Clinton David and Reba (Gilbert) Ward; m. James Y. Barbo, Dec. 12, 1970 (div. Jan. 1975); m. William Wellington Salmon, Jan. 21, 1977; 1 child, Megan Alyssa. BS in Edn., Stephen F. Austin U., 1971; A in Acctg., Richland Coll., 1977. Cert. tchr. secondary edn. Tex. Cost acct. Jackson-Shaw, Dallas, 1975—79, Dal-Mac Devel., Dallas, 1979—81; store mgr. Shepard & Vick, Dallas, 1983—84; mktg. coord. Tex. Instruments, Dallas, 1984—85; pres. Computer Expertise, Richardson, Tex., 1985—91, TI's Only, 1986—91, TechnaServe, 1987—91; early edn. tchr. The da Vinci Sch., Dallas, 1992—94; mgr. Kids Town, 1994—96; tchr. kindergarten Parish Episc. Ch., Dallas, 1997—. Mem.: NAFE, Dallas Needlework and Textile Guild, Tex. Computer Dealers Assn. (organizing mem.), St. Clare's Guild Club (bd. dirs. 1980—81, Dallas). Republican. Episcopalian. Avocations: needlepoint, photography, travel.

SALONER, GARTH, management educator; b. Johannesburg, Jan. 18, 1955; came to U.S. 1978; s. Max and Rachel (Aronowitz) S.; m. Marlene Shoolman, Dec. 26, 1978; children: Amber, Romy, Kim. BCom, U. Witwatersrand, 1976, MBA, 1977; MS in Stats., Stanford U., 1981, MA in Econs., PhD, 1982. Asst. lectr. U. Witwatersrand, 1977-78; asst. prof. econs. MIT, Cambridge, 1982-86, assoc. prof. econs. and mgmt., 1986-89, prof., 1990; vis. assoc. prof. bus. adminstrn. Harvard Bus. Sch., Boston, 1989-90; vis. asst. prof. Stanford (Calif.) U., 1986-87, prof. strategic mgmt. and econs. Grad. Sch. Bus., 1990—, Robert A Magowan prof., 1993-99, dir. rsch. and curriculum devel., 1993-96, assoc. dean for acad. affairs, 1994-96, co-dir. Ctr. Elec. Bus. & Commerce, 1999—, Jeffrey S. Skoll prof., 2000—. Bd. dirs., chmn. Quick Response Svcs., Inc.; chmn. Synthean, Aplia, Covisint; rsch. assoc. Nat. Bur. Econ. Rsch., 1991—; mem. adv. bd. eOneGlobal, Spoke Software, Fiber Tower, It's The Content. Author: Strategic Management, 2001, Creating and Capturing Value, 2001; assoc. editor Rand Jour. Econs., 1986-88, co-editor, 1988-95; assoc. editor Internat. Jour. Indsl. Orgn., 1988-95, Econs. of Innovation and New Tech., 1988-95, Strategic Mgmt. Jour., 1991-94; contbr. articles to profl. jours. Nat. fellow, Hoover Inst., 1986-87, Sloan fellow, 1987-89; grantee, NSF, 1982, 85, 88. Mem. Am. Econ. Assn., Acad. Mgmt. Jewish. Avocations: bicycling, photography. Home: 4151 Amaranta Ave Palo Alto CA 94306-3903 Office: Stanford U Grad Sch Bus Stanford CA 94305

SALOPEK, JENNIFER JACKSON, private/parochial school administrator; b. Charleston, S.C., July 11, 1965; d. Charles Alvan Jr. and Sarah Jeannette (Bergstrom) Jackson; m. Richard Stuart Salopek, Mar. 11, 1989. BA in English, U. Va., 1987. Tech. writer Orkand Co., Silver Spring, Md., 1987-88; mktg. assoc. Viar and Co., Alexandria, Va., 1988-89; coord. mktg. Wisnewski Blair and Assocs, Alexandria, 1989; editorial asst. Architecture Mag., Washington, 1990; dir. mktg. and communications Madeira Sch., McLean, Va., 1990—. Adv. bd. Nat. Coalition Girls' Schs., Concord, Mass., 1991—. Mem. Jr. League Washington, 1988-91. Recipient Gold medal Univ. and Coll. Designers Assn., 1992. Mem. AAUW, Coun. Advancement and Support Edn. (Gold medal 1991, 92). Avocations: reading, walking, travel, crafts. Office: Madeira Sch 8328 Georgetown Pike Mc Lean VA 22102-1200

SALTEN, DAVID GEORGE, b. N.Y.C., Aug. 23, 1913; s. Max Elias and Gertrude (Brauer) S.; m. Frances Claire Brown (div. 1983); children: Phoebe, Cynthia, Melissa; m. Adrienne O'Brien, 1989. ScB, Washington Sq. Coll., N.Y.C., 1933; AM, Columbia U., 1939; PhD, NYU, 1944; LLD (hon.), Lynn U., 1976; L.H.D., Nova U., Ft. Lauderdale, Fla., 1983; Sc.D. (hon.), N.Y. Inst. Tech., 1984; LHD (hon.), Hofstra U., 1996. Registered psychologist, N.Y. Chemist Almay Cosmetics, 1934-35, City of New York, 1938-40; tchr., chmn. dept., high sch. prin. N.Y.C. Bd. Edn., 1940-50; assoc. prof. Hunter Coll. Grad. Program, 1947-63; supt. of schs. City of Long Beach, N.Y., 1950-62, City of New Rochelle, N.Y., 1962-65; exec. v.p. Fedn. of Jewish Philanthropies, N.Y.C., 1965-69; exec. v.p., provost N.Y. Inst. Tech., Old Westbury, 1969-90; chmn. Nassau County Indsl. Devel. Agy., Mineola, NY, 1985—2002; exec. dir. Nassau County Tax Relief Commn., 1990-93. Mem. White House Conf. on Edn., 1955, White House Conf. on Youth, 1960; U.S. resource person on edn. World Mental Health Congress, Paris, 1961; mem. Bd. Edn., Hawthorne, Cedar Knolls, N.Y., 1963-65; mem. adv. council Columbia U. Sch. of Social Work, 1967-69; chmn. adv. council NYU Sch. Edn., 1963-65; chmn. adv. council to Select Com. on Higher Edn. N.Y. Legislature, 1971-73. Author: Mathematics: A Basic Course, 1957. Editor instructional software. Contbr. articles on edn. and ednl. adminstrn. to profl. publs. Vice chmn. N.Y. State Mental Health Council, Albany, 1965-72; pres. N.Y. State Citizens Council, 1957; pres. Nat. Council on Aging, Washington, 1975-77; chmn. Nassau County Local Devel. Agy., 1982—, Nassau County Local Devel. Corp., N.Y., 1982—, pres., 1992—; chmn. Nassau County Cultural Devel. Bd., 1980—94; bd. dirs. NAACP Legal Def. Fund, 1964-74; chmn. bd. trustees The Hewlett Sch., 1991—. Recipient citation U.S. Navy, 1947, Mental Health Assn., Nassau County, N.Y., 1955, Long Beach Edn. Assn., N.Y., 1962, Council of City of New Rochelle, N.Y., 1965, Council of Town of Islip, N.Y., 1982. Fellow AAAS, Am. Orthopsychiat. Assn.; mem. Princeton Club (N.Y.C.). Avocations: opera, ballet, international travel, photography. Office: Office of the President Hoffstra University Hempstead NY 11549

SALTER, CHRISTOPHER LORD, geography educator; BA, Oberlin Coll., 1961; MA, U. Calif. Berkeley, 1968, PhD, 1970. Tchr. Tunghai U., Taiwan, 1961; prof. Dept. Geography UCLA, 1968—87; coord. Alliance Network Nat. Geog. Alliance, 1987—89; prof. geography U. Mo., Columbia, Mo., 1989—2002, chmn. Dept. Geography, 1989—2002, prof. emeritus, 2002—. Founder Calif. Geog. Alliance, 1983—87. Editor: The China Geographer, 1975—78; author: Social Studies for the 21st Century; editor; author (and editor): over 20 books. Recipient George J. Miller award Nat. Coun. for Geog. Edn., 1992, Disting. Geography Educator award Nat. Geog. Soc., 1990, Disting. Tchg. Achievement award Nat. Coun. for Geog. Edn., 1999, Disting. Faculty award U. Mo. Alumni Assn., 1999. Mem.: Mo. Geog. Alliance, Geography Edn. Proram, Nat. Geog. Soc., Nat. Coun. Geog. Edn. (pres. Calif. chpt. 1975—76, Outstanding Educator award Calif. chpt. 1981), Am. Geog. Soc., Assn. Am. Geographers. Office: Univ Mo Dept Geography Dept Geography 3 Stewart Hall Columbia MO 65211-6170*

SALTER, DAVID WYATT, secondary school educator; b. Augusta, Ga., Aug. 10, 1950; s. Wyatt Jackson and Annie Lee (Coleman) S.; m. Dorothy Mikell Fishburne, Aug. 11, 1973; 1 child, Caroline Elizabeth. BS, U. S.C., 1973, MEd, 1977, postgrad., 1982-92, Clemson U., 1985. Cert. tchr., S.C. Tchr. biology Aiken (S.C.) High Sch., 1973—, chair dept. biology, 1985—. Curriculum assoc. for h.s. sci., Sch. Dist. of Aiken County, 1994—, adult edn. tchr., 1976-85, mem. h.s. sci. curriculum revision com., 1997; bd. dirs. S.C. Jr. Acad. Sci., 1984-97; mem. adult edn. curriculum com. S.C. Dept. Edn., 1984; mem. state textbook com., 1989, 92, 2002; mem. biology test rev. com., S.C. Dept. Edn., 2003. Organist Warrenville (S.C.) United Meth. Ch., 1963-91, 93—, St. John United Meth. Ch., Graniteville, S.C., 1998—; dir. men's choir St. John's United Meth. Ch., Aiken, S.C., 1997—; spkr. Prayer Breakfast for H.S. Srs. St. John's United Meth. Ch., Aiken, 1984; mem. commn. on worship S.C. Ann. Conf. United Meth. Ch.; mem. ednl. adv. com. Aiken County Human Rels. Commn., 1993-95. Recipient Svc. award to S.C. Jr. Acad. Sci., 1994; named Outstanding Tchr. in Math. and Sci., Am. Nuclear Soc. Savannah River Sect., 1991-92, Midlands Sci. Tchr. of Yr., U. S.C. chpt. Sigma Xi, 1994, Sci. Tchr. of Yr., 1998, S.C. Acad. Sci. award Excellence in Sci. or Math. Teaching, 1995. Mem. NEA, Nat. Biology Tchrs. Assn., S.C. Edn. Assn., Aiken County Edn. Assn., S.C. Acad. Sci., S.C. Assn. Biology Tchrs. (2d v.p. 1993-94, 1st v.p. 1994-95, pres. 1996-97), S.C. Suprs. Assn., S.C. Sci. Coun., Nat. Sci. Tchrs. Assn., Am. Guild Organists (sub-dean Augusta chpt. 1993-94, dean 1994-96, treas. 2001--), Phi Delta Kappa. Methodist. Avocations: piano and organ music, fishing, travel. Home: PO Box 904 52 Sunnyside Ln Aiken SC 29803-9420 Office: Aiken High Sch 449 Rutland Dr NE Aiken SC 29801-4098 E-mail: dsalter@aiken.k12.sc.us., salterdav@aol.com.

SALTUS, PHYLLIS BORZELLIERE, music educator; b. Rochester, N.Y., Jan. 17, 1931; d. Nicholas and Sadie Veronica (Leone) Borzelliere; m. William Thomas Saltus, Aug. 21, 1965 (div. Apr. 1991); children: Julie Marie Nicole, William Nicholas. AA, Burlington County Coll., Pemberton, N.J., 1987; MEd in Measurement and Guidance, U. Maine, Orono, 1963; BS in Music Edn., SUNY, 1953, MS, 1957. Cert. student personnel svcs., music and guidance, N.J., N.Y., Me. Music tchr., choral dir. Rochester Pub. Schs., 1953-56, 62-63, 1969-70, high sch. guidance counselor, 1963-65; asst. prof. music edn. SUNY, Geneseo and Fredonia, 1956-62; music tchr, choral dir. Concord (Mass.) Pub. Schs., 1965-66; owner, dir. Saltus Music Studio, Medford, N.J., 1982-94. Music tchr., choral dir. Delanco (N.J.) Pub. Schs., 1984-86; prof. voice N.J.Dept. Edn. Sch. Arts, Rowan Univ., Glassboro (N.J.) State Coll., 1987-89; sr. adj. prof. & coordn., piano lab Burlington County Coll., Pemberton, N.J and Ft. Dix Mil. Post, Cmty. Coll. of the Air Force at McGuire AFB, 1989—, Interactive Classroom Program, 1995—, Power Package Accelerated Program, 1995—, Telecourse for Distance Learners Program WBZC, 1995—; music coord., dist. tchr. for gifted and talented program Mt. Laurel (N.J.) Pub. Schs., 1989-94; music dir., founding mem. Triple Threat Prodns., Cherry Hill, N.J., 1991—, Burlington County Cmty. Chorus, N.J., 1995—, Kosciusko Boys Choir, Rochester, 1959-60, Young Adults Cath. Youth Orgn. Choir, Dunkirk, N.Y., 1960-62; faculty adv. N.Y. Province of Newman Clubs Fedn. SUNY, 1957-62, lectr., researcher in field. Artist: The Fredonia Main Street Diner, 1952-53, Clarence Welcome Wagon Gourmet Cook Book, N.Y., 1973; contbr. poems to various publs.; soloist Rochester Philharm. Orch. Concert Series, Songsters, Inc., 1953-59. Choir dir., organist, soloist St. Philip Neri R.C. Ch., Rochester, 1949-65, St. Peter's Episc. Ch., Medford, 1989-90; choir dir., accompanist Thessalonia Baptist Ch. Sr. and Jr. Choirs, Willingboro, N.J., 1990-91; vocal dir., accompanist Pineland Players of South Jersey Community Theatre, Medford, 1987-89, Cherry Hill East High Sch., N.J., 1991—; team capt. United Way, Rochester, 1953-56; membership chair Rochester Community Theater, 1955-56; founding mem. Sta. WCVF, 1952-58; bd. dirs., founding mem. Rochester Chamber Orch., 1964-65, Medford (N.J.) Newcomers Club, 1977—; vol. Cmty. Companions of Erie County Office of the Aging, N.Y., 1972-76, Medford PTO, 1976-85; judge preliminary Miss Am. contest Jr. C. of C., Jamestown, N.Y., 1962, vocal dir., accompanist Miss Dunkirk (N.Y.) pageant, 1962, vocal coach Miss Burlington County Pageant, Jr. C. of C., 1989,97-99; active Welcome Wagon, Inc., Clarence, N.Y., pres., 1974, historian, 1981; chair Medford (N.J.) Evening Book Review Group, 1978-80; mem. Medford Morning Book Review Group, 1980—; active Meml. Health Alliance, Burlington County Women's Health Network. NDEA grantee, 1964; EEOC scholar, 1986-87; recipient Jr. County Rifle Championship award Monroe County Dept. Health and Recreation, 1948, Womens Student Table Tennis Championship award SUNY, 1952, Outstanding Scholarship award Charlotte Putnam Landers Outstanding Scholarship award SUNY, 1953. Mem. AAUP (treas. 1960-62, state del. 1961), Music Educators Nat. Conf., Am. Personnel and Guidance Assn., South Jersey Music Tchrs. Assn., Meml. Health Alliance, Women's Health Network, AARP Medford chpt. of Deborah heart & lung hosp. foudn.,Red Lion wildlife Refuge, Vincetown, N.J., Cedar Run Wildlife Refuge, Medford, N.J., Order Sons of Italy in Am., Kappa Delta Pi (del. Barnard Coll., N.Y., 1952, state del., Atlantic City, N.J., 1953). Roman Catholic. Avocations: reading and research, creative writing, golf, painting, crossword puzzles, gourmet cooking. Home: 112 Pine Valley Dr Medford NJ 08055-9214

SALTZER, JEROME HOWARD, computer science educator; b. Nampa, Idaho, Oct. 9, 1939; s. Joseph and Helene (Scheuermann) S.; m. Marlys Anne Hughes, June 16, 1961; children— Rebecca, Sarah, Mark. BS, MIT, 1961, MS, 1963, Sc.D., 1966. Faculty dept. elec. engring. and computer sci. MIT, Cambridge, Mass., 1966—, now prof. emeritus and sr. lectr.; tech. dir. Project Athena, Cambridge, Mass., 1984-88. Cons. Chem. Abstracts Svc., 1968-88, IBM Corp., 1970-84. Mem. Mayor's Telecomms. Adv. Bd., Newton, Mass., 1984—. Fellow AAAS, IEEE; mem. NRC (computer sci. and telecom. bd. 1991-93), NAE, Assn. for Computing Machinery (mem. com. on computers and pub. policy 1984—), Eta Kappa Nu, Tau Beta Pi. Home: 54 Gammons Rd Waban MA 02468-1216 Office: MIT Lab Computer Sci 545 Technology Sq Cambridge MA 02139-3539 E-mail: saltzer@mit.edu.

SALTZMAN, CHARLES MCKINLEY, educational consultant; b. N.Y.C., Apr. 6, 1937; s. Charles Eskridge Saltzman and Gertrude (Lamont) Saltzman Rockwood; m. Cornelia Metz Biddle, Sept. 3, 1965; children: Cornelia Biddle Saltzman Tierney, Charles Eskridge. AB, Harvard Coll., 1959, MA in Teaching, 1962. Cert. prin. and supr., La. Tchr., coach, dorm head St. Albans Sch., Washington, 1962-66, 67-73; tchr., coach Athenian Sch., Danville, Calif., 1966-67; headmaster Hannah More Acad., Reisterstown, Md., 1973-74, Metairie (La.) Park Country Day Sch., 1974-81, Madeira Sch., McLean, Va., 1981-88; cons. Ind. Ednl. Svcs., Princeton, N.J., 1988-95. Adj. instr. Gettysburg (Pa.) Coll., 1988—; dir. Upper Adams Sch. Dist., Biglerville, Pa., 1991-95, 96-97; cons. Search Assocs., 1996—.

Capt. U.S. Army, 1959-61. Mem. Country Day Sch. Headmasters Assn. Episcopalian. Avocations: farming, gardening, tennis. Home and Office: 622 Chestnut Hill Rd Aspers PA 17304-9425 E-mail: csaltzman@supernet.com.

SALUSSO, CAROL JOY, apparel design educator, consultant; b. Butte, Mont., Dec. 25, 1950; d. George B. and Ruth M. (Richards) S.; (div.); children: Ryan R. and Daron A. Deonier. BS, Mont. State U., 1975; MS, U. Minn., St. Paul, 1977, PhD, 1983. Grad. asst. U. Minn., St. Paul, 1975-81; asst. prof. Iowa State U., Ames, 1981-86; assoc. prof. Mont. State U., Bozeman, 1986-94, Wash. State U., Pullman, 1994—99, chair, 1999—2002. Cons. product devel., Bozeman, Mont., 1986-94. Author: (handbook) Users Guide to Fabrics, 1993. Challenge grantee USDA, Faculty grantee Sunbury Textiles. Mem.: Internat. Textiles and Apparel Assn. (chair spl. events 1986—88, chair electronic comm. 1993—95, book rev. editor 1995—98, media rev. editor 1988—2001, co-author World Wide Web ITAA server 1995—). Avocation: apparel product devel. Office: Wash State U Dept Apparel Merch Int Design 51 Kruegel Hall Pullman WA 99164-0001

SALVATIERRA, OSCAR, JR., transplant surgeon, urologist, educator; b. Phoenix, Apr. 15, 1935; s. Oscar and Josefine S.; m. Pamela Moss; children: Mark, Lisa Marie. BS, Georgetown U., 1957; MD, U. So. Calif., 1961. Intern, resident in surgery and urology U. So. Calif.-Los Angeles County Med. Ctr., 1961-66; practice medicine Pomona, Calif., 1968-72; chief staff Casa Colina Hosp., 1972; post doctoral fellow in transplantation U. Calif.-San Francisco, 1972-73, asst. prof. surgery and urology, 1973-75, assoc. prof., 1975-81, prof., 1981-91, chmn. transplant service, 1974-91; attending surgeon and urologist Moffitt Hosp., 1973—; exec. dir. Pacific Transplant Inst., 1991-94; prof. surgery/pediatrics, dir. pediat. renal transplantation Stanford U. Med. Ctr., 1994—, attending surgeon, urologist and pediat. Chair faculty senate Stanford U. Sch. Medicine, 2002—; study sect. NIH, 1981-85, nat. adv. bd., 1986-92, chmn. nat. adv. bd. 1990-92, chmn. spl. study sect., 1997, 99. Contbr. over 250 articles and chpts. to med. lit.; mem. editl. bd. Transplantation and Immunology, 1984—, Transplantation, 1987—, Transplantation Procs., 1990—, Pediat. Transplantation, 1998—; assoc. editor Am. Jour. Kidney Diseases, 1987-89. Nat. bd. advisors Agent Orange Class Assistance Program, 1988-96. With M.C., U.S. Army, Vietnam, 1966-68. Decorated Army Commendation medal, Grand Ufficiale of Italian Rep. with title His Excellency award; named Oscar Salvatierra Transplantation Fellows Symposium in his honor, 2001; recipient Chancellor's award for pub. svc., U. Calif., 1986, Commendation resolution, Calif. State Legislature, 1990, Presdl. medal and Diploma of Honor, Argentina, 1999, Rambar-Mark award, Stanford U., 1999, Franklin Ebaugh award, 2003; grantee, NIH, 1974—76, 1980—83, 1988—90, 2003—, USPHS, 1986—89. Fellow ACS (bd. govs. 1986-92); mem. Am. Surg. Assn., Am. Soc. Transplant Surgeons (bd. dirs. 1977-85, pres. 1983-84, chmn. adv. com. on issues 1984-87), Soc. Univ. Surgeons, Soc. Univ. Urologists, N.Y. Acad. Scis., Am. Soc. Nephrology, Internat. Transplantation Soc. (bd. dirs. 1984—, pres.-elect 1996-98, pres., 1998-2000), Soc. Pediatric Urology, Am. Urol. Assn., Nat. Kidney Found., Renal Physicians Assn. (bd. dirs. 1984-87), Pacific Coast Surg. Assn., San Francisco Surg. Soc., United Network Organ Sharing (bd. dirs. 1984-88, pres. 1985-86), Internat. Soc. for Organ Sharing (bd. dirs. 1991—, pres. 1993-95), Am. Soc. for Minority Health and Transplant Profls. (pres. 1992-94), Nafziger Surg. Soc. Achievements include being the principle lay figure in passage and enactment of National Organ Transplant Act, 1984; introduction of Pope John Paul II to the 18th International Transplantation Congress for Encyclical on Organ Transplantation, 2000. Office: Stanford U Med Ctr 703 Welch Rd Ste H2 Palo Alto CA 94304-1708 E-mail: oscar.salvatierra@medcenter.stanford.edu.

SALVUCCI, RICHARD JOSEPH, economics educator; b. Upper Darby, Pa., Apr. 9, 1951; s. Louis Richard and Madeline Joan (Villari) S.; m. Linda Helen Kerrigan, Aug. 25, 1973; children: Martin, Rosemary. AB, Villanova (Pa.) U., 1973; AM, Princeton U., 1976, PhD, 1981. Instr. econs. Villanova U., 1978-80; asst. prof. history U. Calif., Berkeley, 1981-87, assoc. prof., 1987-90; assoc. prof. econs. Trinity U., San Antonio, 1990-93, prof., 1993—. Author: Textiles and Capitalism in Mexico, 1987. Mem. alumni schs. com. Princeton U., San Antonio, 1993—. Doherty Found. fellow, 1976, Social Sci. Rsch. Coun. fellow, 1988, NEH fellow, 1990; Am. Philos. Soc. sabbatical fellow. Mem. Econ. History Assn., Conf. on Latin Am. History. Home: 120 Alta Ave San Antonio TX 78209-4509 Office: Trinity U 715 Stadium Dr San Antonio TX 78212-7200 E-mail: richard.salvucci@trinity.edu.

SALZER, JACQUELINE ANN, anesthesiologist, educator; b. Queens, N.Y., Oct. 29, 1952; d. Victor Cornelius and Pearl (Kramer) S. BA in Math., CUNY, Flushing, 1972; MD, SUNY, Downstate, 1978. Intern Maimonides Med. Ctr., Bklyn., 1978-79; resident in anesthesiology N.Y. Hosp.-Cornell Med. Ctr., N.Y.C., 1979-81, fellow in anesthesiology, 1981-82; anesthesiologist Beth Israel Med. Ctr., N.Y.C., 1982—. Clin. instr. anesthesiology Albert Einstein Coll. Medicine. Mem. AMA, Soc. for Ambulatory Anesthesia, Am. Soc. Anesthesiologists, N.Y. State Soc. Anesthesiologists (del.). Jewish. Office: Beth Israel Med Ctr Dept Anesthesiology 16th St and 1st Ave New York NY 10003

SALZMAN, JOANNA MICHELE, special education educator; b. N.Y.C., May 15, 1969; d. Robert and Janet Miriam (Weiler) S. BS, James Madison U., 1991; MA, Am. U., Washington, 1992; cert. edn. specialist, George Washington U., 1997. Cert. elementary tchr., K-12 learning disabled tchr. Sub. tchr. The Lab. Sch. Washington, 1991-92; spl. edn. resource tchr. Prince Georges County Pub. Schs., Mt. Rainier, Md., 1992-96, spl. edn. self-contained tchr. Takoma Park, Md., 1996-98. Camp counselor Lane Robbins II, Newton, N.J., summers 1989-91; pvt. tutor The Lab. Sch., 1993—; chmn. social com. Mt. Rainier Elem. Sch., 1995-96. Campaign mgr. Bd. Edn., Somerset, 1981; vol. Sean Williard Liver Transplant Fund, Somerset, 1983, Salvation Army, Somerset, 1985. Recipient Acad. grant George Washington U., 1995. Mem. Prince George's County Edn. Assn., Coun. Exceptional Children. Jewish. Avocations: working out at the gym, movies, reading, exploring the internet, spending time with friends. Home: 5701 Chapman Mill Dr Apt 350 North Bethesda MD 20852-5559 Office: Twinbrook Elem Sch 5911 Ridgeway Ave Rockville MD 20851-1931

SAM, DAVID FIIFI, political economist, educator; b. Winneba, Ghana, Sept. 9, 1957; came to U.S., 1975; s. Alfred Sam and Christiana Impraim; m. Juliana Sam, Jan. 3, 1987; children: Michelle Ann Tabirwaa, David Charles Impraim. BA, Ill. State U., 1981; MBA, Northwestern U., 1987; MAL.D., Tufts U., 1984, PhD, 1990. Tchg. asst. in polit. sci. Tufts U., Medford, Mass., 1982-84, adminstr. Fletcher Sch., 1983-84; fin. asst. Arthur Andersen & Co., Chgo., 1984-86; assoc. dir. City Colls. of Chgo., 1986-88; asst. prof., coord. Coll. of DuPage, Glen Elyn, Ill., 1988-90; dean natural and social scis. Mott C.C., Flint, Mich., 1990-92, acting exec. v.p., 1992-93; v.p., prof. Harrisburg (Pa.) Area C.C., 1993-96; dean, prof. social sci. U. Akron, 1996—. Cons. internat. bus. and edn., 1989—. Co-editor: International Business: Designing Effective Programs for Community Colleges, 1988. Bd. dirs. Flint Internat. Inst., 1992-93, Am. Coun. Internat./Intercultural Edn., 1994—, Ill. Consortium for Internat. Studies and Programs, 1987-90. Recipient Martin Luther King Svc. award Ill. State U., 1981. Avocations: reading, travel, sports. Office: U Akron Akron OH 44325-0001 Home: 802 Hancock Glen Ln Spring TX 77373-8214

SAM, JOSEPH, retired university dean; b. Gary, Ind., Aug. 15, 1923; s. Andrew and Flora (Toma) S.; m. Frances Adickes, Sept. 11, 1945; children— Sherrie, Joseph A., Suzanne F. Student, Drake U., 1942-43; BS, U. S.C., 1948; PhD, Kans. U., 1951. Sr. research chemist McNeil Labs., Phila., 1951-54; research group leader Bristol Labs., Syracuse, N.Y., 1955-57; sr. scientist E.I. duPont de Nemours & Co., Inc., 1957-59; faculty U. Miss., 1959-86, prof. pharm. chemistry, 1961-68, chmn. dept., 1963-68, dir. univ. research, 1968-81, asso. vice chancellor research, 1981-86; dean U. Miss. (Grad. Sch.), 1968-86. Fulbright lectr. Cairo U., 1965-66 Mem. Am. Pharm. Assn. (found. research achievement award in pharm. and medicinal chemistry 1968), Rho Chi, Phi Lambda Upsilon, Phi Kappa Phi. Home: PO Box 351 University MS 38677-0351

SAMA, JOY LYN, mathematics educator; b. Canton, Ohio, Apr. 24, 1971; d. Vincent A. and Lois A. Sama. BS in Math. and Computer Sci., Walsh U., North Canton, Ohio, 1993; MEd in Adminstrn., Ashland U., 1998. Cert. tchr. secondary math. Math. tchr. Marion (Ohio) City Schs., 1993-95; math. tchr. and transition program Cuyahoga Falls (Ohio) City Schs., 1995-96; math. tchr. Lake H.S., Uniontown, Ohio, 1996—. Part-time faculty Marion Tech. Coll., 1993—; adj. instr. Walsh U., 1997—. Vol. United Way, Marion, 1994. Mem. NEA, Ohio Edn. Assn., Marion Edn. Assn., Ctrl. Ohio Tchrs. Assn., Nat. Coun. Tchrs. Math., DAR. Democrat. Roman Catholic. Avocations: reading, aerobics, piano, hiking. Home: 2955 Blake Ave NW Canton OH 44718-3417 Office: Lake H S 1025 Lake Center St NW Uniontown OH 44685-9466

SAMANIEGO, JULIA ROSE, elementary educator; b. El Paso, Tex., Aug. 19, 1930; d. Josefino and Josefina (Gomez) Bencomo; m. Henry Samaniego, June 24, 1950; children: Sylvia Mae Howell, Robert Edward, Cynthia R. Heitzman. BA, U. Tex., 1949. Cert. elem. tchr., N.Mex., Tex. Tchr. El Paso Ind. Schs., 1949-50, 52-58, 71-93, parent and cmty. liaison, 1993-94; tchr. Dallas Ind. Sch. Dist., 1950-52, Farmington (N.Mex.) Mcpl. Schs., 1968-71; kindergarten tchr. Gadsden Ind. Sch. Dist., Anthony, N.Mex., 1995-97, tchr., 1997—. Pres. El Paso Ind. Sch. Dist. PTA, 1986-87, 93-95; v.p. Tex. State PTA, 1995-96; active U. Tex. Womens Aux., El Paso, 1966—; active womens dept. El Paso C. of C., 1992-96; tchr. St. Patricks Confraternity of Christian Doctrine, El Paso, 1958-68, Queen of Peace Cath. Ch., El Paso, 1974-94. Named Outstanding Tchr., El Paso Pilot Club, 1966, Tchr. of Yr., Mesita Sch., El Paso, 1967, one of Outstanding Elem. Tchrs. Am. El Paso Ind. Sch. Dist., 1974; Tchr. scholar Delta Kappa Gamma, 1969; recipient Extended Svc. award Tex. State PTA, 1992, Outstanding Achievement award Chaparral Sch., 1995. Mem. AAUW (pres. 1985-86), Assn. for Childhood Edn. (pres. 1967-68), El Paso Tchrs. Assn. (pres. 1977-78), Delta Kappa Gamma (pres. 1966-68, Outstanding Achievement award 1986). Roman Catholic. Avocations: travel, swimming, dancing, children, grandchildren. Home: 1205 Cerrito Alegre Ln El Paso TX 79912-2041

SAMETZ, LYNN, educator; b. NYC, Mar. 29, 1951; d. Leo Jacob and Barbara Weil Sametz; m. Victor Lee Streib, Feb. 25, 1978; children: Noah, Jessi. BA, Johns Hopkins U., 1973; MA, U. Conn., 1974; PhD, Ind. U., 1979. Learning disabilities tchr. Bloomfield (Conn.) Schs., 1974-76; instr. Lesley Coll., Cambridge, 1978-80, Kent (Ohio) State U., 1980-82; sr. rsch. and planning assoc. Fedn. for Cmty. Planning, Cleve., 1985-96; sch. to work coord. Ohio State U., Lima, 1996-98, edn. outreach dir., 1998—. Cons. Case Western Res. U., Cleve., 1995—98; adj. asst. prof. Cleve. State U., 1981—87. Editor: Educators, Children and the Law, 1985; contbr. articles to profl. jours. Trustee Ohio Juvenile Justice Coalition, 1996—, GRADS adv. bd., Lima, 1998—; active Lima/Allen County Edn. Com., 1996—. Grantee Ohio Environ. Edn. Fund, 1999-2000, Ohio Dept. Agr., Martha Holden Jennings, 1998-99, Sch. to Work, 1997-2000, EPA, 2002. Mem. Ohio No. Women's Assn. (treas. 1997-98), Phi Delta Kappa. Office: Ohio State Univ 4240 Campus Dr Lima OH 45804-3576

SAMMONS, JEFFREY LEONARD, foreign language educator; b. Cleve., Nov. 9, 1936; s. Harold Leonard and Therese (Herrmann) S.; m. Kathryn Josephine Stella, July 1958 (div. 1962); 1 child, Rebecca Kathryn Serabrini; m. Christa Ann Smith, Oct. 20, 1967; children: Charles Leonard, Harold Hawthorne, Benjamin Gardner. BA, Yale U., 1958, PhD, 1962. Instr., asst. prof. Brown U., Providence, 1961-64; asst. prof. German, Yale U., 1964-67, assoc. prof., 1967-69, prof., 1969—2001, Leavenworth prof. German, 1979—2001; Craig vis. prof. German, Rutgers U.2003. Author: Heinrich Heine: The Elusive Poet, 1969, Six Essays on the Young German Novel, 1972, Literary Sociology and Practical Criticism, 1977, Heinrich Heine: A Modern Biography, 1979, Wilhelm Raabe: The Fiction of the Alternative Community, 1987, The Shifting Fortunes of Wilhelm Raabe, 1992, Ideology, Mimesis, Fantasy: Charles Sealsfield, Friedrich Gerstacker, Karl May and Other German Novelists of America, 1998. Guggenheim fellow, 1972-73, Am. Coun. Learned Socs. fellow, 1977-78, Travel grantee, 1983; Duke August Libr., Wolfenbuttel Ger. adoptive stipend, 1983. Mem. MLA, Am. Assn. Tchrs. German, Goethe Soc. N.Am., Conn. Acad. Arts and Scis., N.Am. Heine Soc. Home: 211 Highland St New Haven CT 06511-2001 Business E-Mail: jeffrey.sammons@yale.edu.

SAMPLE, STEVEN BROWNING, university executive; b. St. Louis, Nov. 29, 1940; s. Howard and Dorothy (Cunningham) Sample; m. Kathryn Brunkow, Jan. 28, 1961; children: Michelle Sample Smith, Elizabeth Ann. BS, U. Ill., 1962, MS, 1963, PhD, 1965; DHL (hon.), Canisius Coll., 1989; LLD (hon.), U. Sheffield, Eng., 1991; EdD (hon.), Purdue U., 1994; DHL (hon.), Hebrew Union Coll., 1994; DL (hon.), U. Nebr., 1995. Sr. scientist Melpar Inc., Falls Ch., Va., 1965—66; assoc. prof. elec. engring. Purdue U., Lafayette, Ind., 1966—73; dep. dir. Ill. Bd. Higher Edn., Springfield, 1971—74; exec. v.p. acad. affairs, dean Grad. Coll., prof. elec. engring. U. Nebr., Lincoln, 1974—82; prof. elec. and computer engring. SUNY, Buffalo, 1982—91; pres. U. So. Calif., LA, 1991—, prof. elec. engring., 1991—, Robert C. Packard pres.'s chair, 1995—. Bd. dirs. Santa Catalina Id. Co., UNOVA, William Wrigley Jr. Co., Advanced Bionics, AMCAP/Am. Mut. Fund, Inc., Keck Sch. Medicine; vice-chmn. Western NY Tech. Devel. Ctr., Buffalo, 1982—91; chmn. bd. dirs. Calspan-UB Rsch. Ctr., Inc., Buffalo, 1983—91; mem. Calif. Coun. Sci. and Tech., Irvine, Calif., L.A. Bus. Advisors, Nat. Acad. of Engring., 1998—; cons. in field; chmn. Pacific-10 Conf., 1997—; bd. dirs. Galaxy Inst. Edn., 1991—94; mem. Knight Commn. on Intercoll. Athletics, 2003—. Author: Contrarian's Guide to Leadership, 2001; contbr. articles to profl. jour. Timpanist St. Louis Philharm. Orch., 1955—58; chmn. Western NY Regional Econ. Devel. Coun., 1984—91; trustee U. at Buffalo Found., 1982—91, Studio Arena Theatre, Buffalo, 1983—91, Western NY Pub. Broadcasting Assn., 1985—91; chmn. Gov.'s Conf. on Sci. and Engring. Edn., Rsch. and Devel, 1989—91; sr. warden Ch. of Our Savior, 1996—98; mem. Calif. Bus.-Higher Edn. Forum (CBHEF), 1995—97; trustee LEARN, 1991—; mem. bd. dir. 1st Interstate Bancorp, 1991—96, Galaxy Inst. Edn., 1991—94, Niagara Mohawk Power Corp., 1988—91; vestry Ch. of Our Savior, 1996—2001; mem. bd. gov. LA Annenberg Met. Project (LAAMP), 1994—2000; mem. bd. dir. Western Atlas, Inc., 1994—97, The Presley Co., 1991—; bd. dir. Buffalo Philharm. Orch., 1982—91, Regenstrief Med. Found., Indpls., 1982—, Rsch. Found. SUNY, 1987—91; bd. dir. LA chpt. World Affairs Coun., Hughes Galaxy Inst. Edn., Calif., 1991—94; bd. dir. Rebuild LA Com., Coalition of 100 Club, L.A.; mem. bd. dir. Dunlop Tire Corp., 1987—91, Greater Buffalo C. of C., 1985—91, United Way Buffalo and Erie County, 1985—91; bd. dir. U. So. Calif. Keck Sch. Medicine. Named Engr. of Yr., NY State Soc. Profl. Engrs., 1985; recipient Disting. Alumnus award, U. Ill., 1980, Alumni Honor award, U. Ill. Coll. Engring., 1985, citation award, Buffalo Coun. on World Affairs, 1986, Outstanding Elec. Engr. award, Purdue U., 1993, Humanitarian award, Nat. Conf. Christians and Jews, 1994, Hollzer Meml. award, Jewish Fedn. Coun. Greater L.A., 1994, Eddy award, LA County Econ. Devel. Corp., 2000; fellow, Sloan Found., 1962—63, Grad. fellow, NSF, 1963—65, Am. Coun. Edn. fellow, Purdue U., 1970—71. Mem.: NAE, IEEE (Outstanding Paper award 1976), Knight Commn. on Intercollegiate Athletics, Am. Acad. Arts and Sci., Assn. Pacific Rim Univ. (co-founder, chmn. 1997—2002), Coun. on Fgn. Rels., Nat. Assn. State Univ. and Land-Grant Coll. (ednl. telecomms. com. 1982—83, chmn. coun. of pres. 1985—86, edn. and tech. com. 1986—87, exec. com. 1987—89), Assn. Am. Univ. (exec. com. 1995—2000, vice-chmn. 1997—98, tenure com. 1997—2001, chmn. 1998—99, assessing quality of univ. edn. and rsch. com. 2000—, co-chair task force on rsch. accountability 2001—02, internationalization com. 2002—). Episcopalian. Achievements include patents in field. Office: U So Calif Office of Pres University Park Adm 110 Los Angeles CA 90089-0012

SAMPLE, TRAVIS LAMAR, business educator; b. Shelbyville, Tex., Sept. 15, 1940; m. Barbara Lee Neely; children: Andrew, Jessica. BS in Sociology, U. Houston, 1964; grad. diploma, Def. Intelligence Coll., 1969; MS, So. Ill. U., 1974; grad. diploma, Indsl. Coll. Armed Forces, 1982; MPA, DPA, U. So. Calif., L.A., 1987. Commd. 2d lt. USAF, 1964, advanced through grades to col., 1984, ret., 1990; sr. mktg. mgr. GE Corp., Arlington, Va., 1976-81; dir. reserve forces Def. Intelligence Coll., Washington, 1985-90, prof. strategic intelligence, 1985-90; prof. bus. and pub. adminstrn. Shenandoah U., Winchester, Va., 1990—; founder, prin. Travis Sample Seminars, Leesburg, Va. Cons. and presenter in field. Author: Humanizing Change, 2002. Parishioner, former vestry mem. St. James Episcopal Ch., Leesburg; former pres. Loudoun County Pub. Libr. Found., Va. Mus.-Loudoun chpt.; active Vietnam Meml. Com. Loudoun County, Waterford Found., Commn. on the Western By-Pass; former mem., bd. dirs., head coach Loudoun County Ctrl. Little League; former mem. Oatlands Historic Property Found., Econ. Devel. Commn. Town of Leesburg; former bd. mem. Loudoun Symphony Orch., Loudoun County Small Bus. Devel. Ctr., Leadership Loudoun, Loudoun Symphony; bd. mem. Loudoun Edn. Found., Loudoun Health Partnership; mem. Dulles dist. Loudoun County Bd. Suprs.; chmn. Oatlands Conversations. Decorated Legion of Merit, Air medal with 2 oak leaf clusters. Mem. ASPA, Air Force Assn. (life), ICAF Assn. (life), Res. Officers Assn. (life), Vietnam Vets. Assn. (life), Nat. Trust for Hist. Preservation, Keep Loudoun Beautiful, Joseph Inst. for the Advancement of Ethics, Am. Legion, Shrine Club Leesburg, USAF Acad. Officers Club, Johns Hopkins Faculty Club, Sigma Beta Delta. Home: 41121 Bryn Bach Ln Leesburg VA 20175-8747 Office: Shenandoah Univ 1460 University Dr Winchester VA 22601-5195 Fax: 540-665-5437. E-mail: tsample@su.edu.

SAMPLES, RITA KARMELIN, special education educator; b. Queens, N.Y., Aug. 2, 1958; d. Leonard Joseph and Sheila (Seulowitz) Karmelin; m. Randall Wiley Samples, Sept. 1, 1979; children: Justin Elliott, Alexander Nathan. BS, Ga. State U., 1980, MEd, 1983. Cert. tchr. Ga. Tchr. spl. edn. Gwinnett County Pub. Schs., Lawrenceville, Ga., 1980—. Mem. NEA, Coun. Exceptional Children, Ga. Assn. Educators, Gwinnett County Edn. Assn.

SAMPSON, BONITA LIPPARD, health occupations educator; b. Lane, Tenn., Apr. 3, 1934; d. Clayton Ivie and Maurine Evelyn (Roddy) Lippard; m. William Franklin Sampson, Dec. 22, 1957; children: William Franklin Jr., James Edward (dec.), Dennis Wayne, David Allen. BSN, Columbia Union Coll., Takoma Park, Md., 1956; MPH, Loma Linda U., 1980. RN, Fla.; cert. tchr., Fla. Emergency rm. nurse Washington Adventist Hosp., Takoma Park, 1956-57; insvc. edn. dir., asst. dir. nursing Ft. Pierce (Fla.) Meml. Hosp., 1958-69; office mgr. Sampson Bros. Bldrs., 1970-76; insvc. edn. dir., asst. dir. nursing Sunrise Manor Care Ctr., 1976-79; tchr. Westwood High Sch., Ft. Pierce, 1979-92; tech. prep. coord. Ft. Pierce Cen. High Sch., 1992—. Disaster nurse ARC, Ft. Pierce, 1979-91; sec. St. Lucie County Health Occupations Adv. Bd., Ft. Pierce, 1983-92; pres. Upper Gold Coast Fed. Community Svc. of Fla., 1970-77; peer counseling com. St. Lucie County Health Dept., 1986-88. Named Tchr. of the Yr. Westwood High Sch., 1988, 89, St. Lucie County Schs., 1989. Mem. Am. Vocat. Assn., Fla. Vocat. Assn., Health Occupations Edn. Assn. Fla., Occupational Spl. Guidance Assn. Fla., Health Occupations Students of Am. (bd. dirs. 1985-90, regional advisor 1985-90). Avocations: crochet, camping, biking, walking, sewing. Home: 500 W Melvin Hill Rd Columbus NC 28722-8568 Office: Ft Pierce Cen High Sch 1101 Edwards Rd Fort Pierce FL 34982-4314

SAMPSON, EARLDINE ROBISON, education educator; b. Russell, Iowa, June 18, 1923; d. Lawrence Earl and Mildred Mona (Judy) Robison; m. Wesley Claude Sampson, Nov. 25, 1953; children: Ann Elizabeth, Lisa Ellen. Diploma, Iowa State Tchrs. Coll., 1943, BA, 1950; MS in Edn., Drake U., 1954; postgrad., No. Ill. U., Iowa State U., 1965-66, 74. Cert. tchr., guidance counselor, Iowa. Tchr. elem. sch. various pub. sch. sys., 1943-48; cons. speech and hearing Iowa Dept. Pub. Instrn., Des Moines, 1950-52; speech therapist Des Moines Pub. Schs., 1952-54, 55; lectr. spl. edn. No. Ill. U., DeKalb, 1964-65; tchr. of homebound Cedar Falls (Iowa) Pub. Schs., 1967-68; asst. prof. edn. U. No. Iowa, Cedar Falls, 1968; asst. prof., counselor Wartburg Coll., Waverly, Iowa, 1968-70; instr. elem. edn., then head of advising elem. edn. Iowa State U., Ames, 1972-82; field supr. elem. edn. U. Toledo, 1988, 89; ind. cons. Sylvania, Ohio, 1989—. Cons. Des Moines Speech and Hearing Ctr., 1958-59, bd. dirs., 1962, 63; cons. Sartori Hosp., Cedar Falls, 1967-69; bd. dirs. Story County Mental Health Ctr., Ames, 1972-74. NDEA fellow, 1965. Methodist. Avocations: public speaking on preservation of prose and poetry, reading, music, photography. Home: 4047 Newcastle Dr Sylvania OH 43560-3450

SAMPSON, EDWARD COOLIDGE, humanities educator; b. Ithaca, N.Y., Dec. 20, 1920; s. Martin W. and Julia (Pattison) S.; m. Frances P. Hanford, Oct. 26, 1946 (div. 1968); children: Susan S. Wilt, Edward H.; m. Cynthia R. Clark, 1968. BA, Cornell U., 1942, PhD, 1957; MA, Columbia U., 1949. Instr. Hofstra Coll., Hempstead, N.Y., 1946-49; teaching fellow Cornell U., Ithaca, 1949-52; with faculty Clarkson Coll. Tech., Potsdam, N.Y., 1952-69, assoc. prof. humanities, 1957-61, prof., 1961-69, SUNY, Oneonta, 1969-82, ret., 1982. Author: Hemingway's The Killers, 1952, Afterword, The House of the Seven Gables, 1961, Some Sights and Sounds, 1970, E.B. White, 1974, Thomas Hardy, Justice of Peace, 1977, E.B. White: Dictionary of Literary Biography, 1982,. Capt. USAAF, 1942-46. Decorated Bronze Star medal; Fulbright prof. U. Panjab, 1959-60. Fellow Am. Coun. Learned Socs.; mem. MLA. Home: 89 Hemlock Dr Killingworth CT 06419-2225 E-mail: esampson1@comcast.net.

SAMPSON, ROGER, education commissioner; Prin., sch. adminstr. Annette Island Sch. Dist., Metlakatia, Alaska, 1970—84; prin. Kenai Peninsula Borough Sch. Dist., Alaska, 1984—94; supt. Chugach Sch. Dist., Alaska, 1994—2000; commr. edn. and early devel. State of Alaska, 2003—. Mem. standards based edn. com. State of Alaska. Named Alaska Prin. of Yr., 1987, Nat. Rural Supt. of Yr., 1997. Office: Dept Edn & Early Devel 801 W 10th St Ste 200 Juneau AK 99801 Office Fax: 907-465-3452.

SAMSON, FREDERICK EUGENE, JR., neuroscientist, educator; b. Medford, Mass., Aug. 16, 1918; s. Frederick Eugene and Annie Bell (Pratt) S.; m. Camila Albert; children Cecile Samson Folkerts, Julie Samson Thompson, Renée. DO, Mass. Coll. Osteopathy, 1940; PhD, U. Chgo., 1952. Asst. prof. U. Kans., Lawrence, 1952-57, prof. physiology, 1962-73, chmn., prof. dept. physiology and cell biology, 1968-73; prof. physiology U. Kans. Med. Ctr., Kansas City, 1973-89, prof. emeritus, 1989—; dir. Ralph L. Smith Rsch. Ctr. U. Kans., Kansas City, 1973-89. Staff scientist neuroscis. rsch. program MIT, Cambridge, Mass., 1968-82, cons., 1982-91; vis. prof. neurobiology U. Catolica de Chile, Santiago, 1972; prof. Inst. de Investigaciones Citologicas, Valenica, Spain, 1981-89; hon. lectr. Mid-Am. State Univs. Assn., 1987. Editor: (with George Adelman) The Neurosciences: Paths of Discovery, II, 1992, (with Merrill Tarr) Oxygen Free Radicals in Tissue Damage, 1993; contbr. articles to profl. publs. Scientist, U.S.A., Spain Friendship Treaty, Madrid and Valencia, 1981. Staff sgt. U.S. Army, 1941-45, PTO. Recipient Rsch. Recognition award U. Kans. Med. Ctr., Kansas City, 1984; Van Liere fellow U. Chgo., 1948; Rawson fellow U. Chgo., 1949-51; USPHS fellow MIT, 1965 Fellow AAAS; mem. Am.

Soc. Neurochemistry (chmn. program com. 1980), Am. Soc. Cell Biology (local host com. 1984), Am. Physiol. Soc. (emeritus 1990), Soc. Neurosci. (program com. 1972-73), The Oxygen Soc., N.Y. Acad. Sci., U. Chgo. Kansas City Club (chmn. alumni fund bd. 1975-82, pres. 1979-81), Sigma Xi (regional lectr. 1974-75, pres. Kansas City chpt. 1977-78, pres. neurosci. chpt. 1978). Avocations: writing, hand balancing. Home: 171 Lakeshore Dr S Lake Quivira KS 66217-8516 Office: U Kans Med Ctr Ralph L Smith Rsch Ctr Bldg 37 Kansas City KS 66160-0001

SAMSON, GORDON EDGAR, educator, consultant; b. Waterville, Que., Can., Oct. 25, 1923; came to U.S., 1952; s. Edgar John Knox and Ethel May (Holyon) S. BSc, Bishop's U., 1942, MEd, 1948; PhD, U. Chgo., 1955. Cert. tchr. h.s., 1943. Tchr., prin. various sch. sys., Que., 1943-52; rsch. asst. U. Chgo., 1952-54; exec. asst. Ednl. Policies Commn., NEA, Washington, 1954-57; chmn. dept. edn. Fenn Coll., Cleve., 1957-65; assoc. prof. Cleve. State U., 1965-85, acting dean, 1965-67, prof. emeritus, 1985—2001. Vis. scholar Brock U., St. Catharines, Ont., summer 1986, 87, external examiner, 1988. Contbr. articles to profl. jours. Mem. NEA (life), Am. Ednl. Rsch. Assn., Nat. Soc. for Study of Edn., Phi Delta Kappa. Avocations: genealogy, reading. Home: Cleveland, Ohio. Died Dec. 14, 2001.

SAMSON, LINDA FORREST, nursing educator and administrator; b. Miami, Dec. 7, 1949; d. Alvin S. and Grace (Kanner) Forrest; m. Mark I. Samson, Jan. 29, 1972; children: Amy, Josh. BSN, Emory U., 1972, MN, 1973; PhD, U. Pa., 1989. RN, Fla., Ga., N.J., Pa. Nursing instr. Ga. State U., Atlanta, 1974-78; neonatal intensive care nurse Northside Hosp., Atlanta, 1976-78; perinatal clin. specialist Our Lady of Lourdes Med. Ctr., Camden, N.J., 1978-82, per diem staff nurse, ICU nursery, labor and delivery, 1982-88; asst. prof., nursing Kennesaw Coll., Marietta, Ga., 1988-89; asst. prof. Clayton Coll. and State U., Morrow, Ga., 1989-92, assoc. prof., 1992-98, prof., 1998—, head baccalaureate nursing dept., 1991-94, acting dean Sch. Health Scis., 1992-94, dean Sch. Health Scis., 1994—2002; dean Coll. Health Professions, Govs. State U., University Park, Ill., 2002—. Adj. faculty Gloucester County Coll., 1981-83; adj. clin. preceptor U. Pa. Sch. Nursing, 1981-83, lectr. in perinatal nursing, 1983-88; nursing dir. So. N.J. Perinatal Coop., 1982-84; researcher and lectr. in field. Mem. editorial rev. bds.; contbr. chpts. to textbooks, articles to profl. jours. Bd. dirs., chmn. profl. adv. com. South Jersey chpt. March of Dimes, 1980-85. Named Nurse of Yr. N.J. State Nurses Assn., 1985; recipient Network Edn. grant N.J. State Dept. Health, 1982-84, numerous grants for rsch., 1983-89, Outstanding Svc. award March of Dimes, 1983, Disting. Leadership award March of Dimes, 1984; grantee Fuld Inst. Post Secondary Edn., 1997—. Mem. ANA (cert. advanced nursing adminstrn., RNC high risk perinatal nursing), AACN (program com. 1987-88, rsch. com. 1988-89, project devel. task force 1989, strategic planning com. 1989, bd. dirs. 1987-90, bd. dirs. certification corp. 1987-90, chair neonatal and pediatric appeal panels 1992), Am. Orgn. Nurse Execs. (planning com. 1994-95), Nat. Assn. Neonatal Nurses (pub. policy and legis. com. 1994-96), Assn. Women's Health, Obstetrics and Neonatal Nurses, Nat. Perinatal Assn. (program planning com. 1983-85, resolutions com. 1984-88, stds. devel. com. spl. interest group task force 1985-88, bd. dirs. 1985-89, chmn. resolutions com. 1988, fin. com. 1989, pub. health policy com.), Ga. Nurses Assn., Ga. Perinatal Assn. N.J. (pres. 1982-86), Sigma Theta Tau (bylaws com.). Home: 11644 Anise Dr Frankfort IL 60423 Office: Govs State U Coll Health Professions 1 University Pkwy University Park IL 60466-0975

SAMSON, VALERIE J. elementary education educator; b. Mar. 28, 1948; EdB, U. Mont., 1986; EdM, Mont. State U., 1995. Nat. bd. cert. tchr. 2001. Facilitator Project WET Mont., Bozeman, 1994—2001; elem. sch. tchr. Kalispell Sch. Dist. # 5, Mont., 1986—2001; edn. cons., 2002—. Cons. Ensley Elem. Sch., Pensacola, 2003—. Mem.: ASCD, NEA (State Presdl. award for excellence in sci. and math. tchg. 1999, Nat. Presdl. award for excellence in sci. and math. tchg. 2000), Nat. Assn. Edn. Young Children, Nat. Sci. Tchrs. Assn., Nat. Coun. Tchrs. Math., Phi Delta Kappa (pres. Pensacola (Fla.) chpt. 2003—, exec. bd. sec. 2003). Home: 412 Cornwall Cir Pensacola FL 32514

SAMSON, WANDA KAY, secondary school educator, consultant; b. Shenandoah, Iowa, July 1, 1950; d. Carl Frederick and Margaret Ann (Vette) Sickman. BA, Midland Luth Coll., Fremont, Nebr., 1972; MA in Bus. Edn., U. Nebr., 1983. Cert. tchr., Nebr. Tchr. bus. edn. Fremont (Nebr.) H.S., 1972—. Cons. Cortez Peters Keyboarding, 1991—. Bd. dirs., coord. bloodmobile ARC of Dodge County, Fremont, 1990—. Recipient Belong Excel Study Travel award Nebr. Dept. Edn., 1991—. Mem. NEA, Internat. Soc. Bus. Edn., Am. Vocat. Assn., Nat. Assn. Classroom Educators Bus. Edn., Nebr. Edn. Assn., Fremont Edn. Assn., Nat. Bus. Edn. Assn., Mountain-Plains Bus. Edn. Assn. (legis. chmn. 1997-2002, treas. 2003—), Nebr. Bus. Edn. Assn. (met. rep. 1990-91, pres.-elect 1993-94, pres. 1994-95, past pres. 1995-96, sec. 1999-2002, treas. 1999-2003), Delta Pi Epsilon (rec. sec., newsletter editor). Lutheran. Avocations: working on computer, reading, counted cross-stitch. Office: Fremont HS 1750 N Lincoln Ave Fremont NE 68025-3206

SAMUELS, ANGELLA V. academic administrator; b. Jamaica, Jan. 14, 1961; came to U.S., 1980; d. Solomon and Victoria (Godfrey) S.; m. Everald Mendis, Aug. 28, 1986; children: Dirk Smith, Glenese Smith. BA, Marymount Manhattan, 1987; MSc, Coll. New Rochelle, 1990; AA, Borough Manhattan C.C., 1996. Sec. United Jewish Appeal, N.Y.C., 1982-84; adminstrv. asst. Travelers Ins., N.Y.C., 1985-87; asst. to editor-in-chief Am. Inst. Physics, N.Y.C., 1987-90; exec. asst. SUNY, N.Y.C., 1990-93, asst. dir. pub. rels., 1993—. Mem. employee adv. Am. Inst., N.Y.C., 1989; sch. vol. tchr. N.Y.C. Sch. Vol. Program; mem. strategic planning com. Women in Comm., Va., 1993-94. Mem. N.Y. State Assn. Coll. Admission, N.Y. Women in Comm. Mem. Ch. of God. Avocations: reading, writing, jogging. Home: 724 E 231st St Bronx NY 10466-4106

SAMUELSON, CECIL O. academic administrator; b. 1942; BS, MS, MD, U. Utah. V.p. health scis. U. Utah, Salt Lake City, 1970-90; sr. v.p. Intermountain Health Care, Inc., Salt Lake City, 1990—; dean IHC Hosps. Inc., Salt Lake City, 1990—; pres. BYU, Provo, Utah, 2003—. Office: Office of the Pres Brigham Young U Provo UT 84602*

SAMUELSON, RITA MICHELLE, speech language pathologist; b. Chgo., July 15, 1954; d. Mike Dabetic and Rita Lorraine (Stasny) Dabertin; m. K. Alan Samuelson, May 7, 1977; children: Amber Michelle, April Claire. BS, Ind. U., 1976, MA in Teaching, 1977. Speech lang. therapist East Maine Dist. 63, Des Plaines, Ill., 1977-80, Cmty. Cons. Dist. 59, Elk Grove, Ill., 1980-83, Fenton High Sch. Dist. 100, Bensenville, Ill., 1988-93, Addison (Ill.) Dist. 4, 1993-94, Elgin (Ill.) Dist. U-46, 1994—. Author: Sound Strategist, 1989, The Birthday Party Adventure, 1991, The Lizard Princess Adventure, 1991; contbr. chpt.: Yuletide Reverie, 1993. Mem. Am. Speech Lang. Hearing Assn., DuPage County Speech Hearing Lang. Assn. (v.p. bd. dirs. 1995—), Ill. Speech Lang. Hearing Assn., Villagers Club Bloomingdale, Writer's Workshop of Bloomingdale (steering com. rep.). Roman Catholic. Avocations: singing in church choir, lectr. in children and humor, doll collecting, antiquing. Home: 156 Longridge Dr Bloomingdale IL 60108-1416 Office: Oakhill Elementary Sch 502 S Oltendorf Rd Streamwood IL 60107-1575

SAN, NGUYEN DUY, psychiatrist, educator; b. Langson, Vietnam, Sept. 25, 1932; arrived in Can., 1971, naturalized, 1977; s. Nguyen Duy and Tran Tuyet, Quyen (Trang) San; m. Eddie Jean Ciesielski, Aug. 24, 1971; children: Thuan Le, Megan Thuloan, Muriel Mylinh, Claire Kimlan, Robin Xuanlan, Baodan Edward. MD, U. Saigon, 1960; postgrad, U. Mich., 1970. Intern Cho Ray Hosp., Saigon, 1957—58; resident Univ. Hosp., Ann Arbor, Mich., 1968—70, Lafayette Clinic, Detroit, 1970—71, Clarke Inst. Psychiatry, Toronto, Canada, 1971—72; chief of psychiatry S. Vietnamese Army, 1964—68; sr. psychiatrist Queen St. Mental Health Ctr., Toronto, 1972—74; unit dir. Homewood San., Guelph, 1974—80; cons. psychiatrist Guelph Gen. Hosp., Guelph, 1974—80, St. Joseph's Hosp., Guelph; practice medicine specializing in psychiatry Guelph, 1974—80; unit dir. inpatient svc. Royal Ottawa Hosp., Canada, 1980—84, dir. psychiat. rehab. program, 1985—87; asst. prof. psychiatry U. Ottawa Med. Sch., 1980—85; assoc. prof. psychiatry, 1985—87; bd. dir. Hong Fook Mental Health Svc., Toronto, 1987—; dir. East-West Mental Health Ctr., Toronto, 1987—; chmn., bd. dir. Access Alliance Multicultural Health Ctr., Toronto, 1988—; cons. UN High Commr. for Refugees, 1987—. Author: (novels) Etude du Tetanos au Vietnam, 1960; co-author The Psychology and Physiology of Stress, 1969; author Psycholsomatic Medicine: Theoretical, Clinical, and Transcultural Aspects, 1983, Uprooting, Loss and Adaptation, 1984—87, S.E. Asian Mental Health, 1985, Ten Years Later: Indochinese Communities in Can., 1988, Refugee Resettlement and Well-Being, 1989. Served, 1953—68, Army Republic of Vietnam. Mem.: NY Acad. Sci., Internat. Soc. Hypnosis, Am. Soc. Clin. Hypnosis, Am. Psychiat. Assn., Can. Psychiat. Assn., Can. Med. Assn. Buddhist. Office: 2238 Dundas St W Ste 306 Toronto ON Canada M6R 3A9

SANAZARO, LEONARD ROCCO, language educator, writer; b. Chgo., Oct. 29, 1949; BA, Lewis U., 1971; MA, U. Nev., 1979. Tchr. St. John the Bapt. Sch., Harvey, Ill., 1972-74; tchr. U. Nev., Reno, 1982-86, City Coll. San Francisco, 1986—. Author: (critical essays) Sylvia Plath: A Reconsideration, 1982; contbr. poetry to Antioch Rev., Seattle Rev., Denver Quar., Art and Understanding. Mem. Nat. Coun. Tchrs. English (com. mem. 1996-98), Acad. Am. Poets. Democrat. Office: City Coll San Francisco 50 Phelan Ave San Francisco CA 94112-1821

SANBORN, MARIE LOUISE, special education educator; b. Cass Lake, Minn., May 19, 1941; d. Orion A. and I. Luella (Johnson) Anderson; children: Timothy Eugene, Diane Marie, Linda Kay, Susan Renee. BA, Augustana Coll., 1963; postgrad., U. Minn., 1968, U. Wis., Eau Claire, 1974, U. Wis., Superior, 1978, 82. Cert. elem. edn. tchr. Tchr. hearing impaired Minn. Sch. for Deaf, Faribault, 1963-68, Nebr. Sch. for the Deaf, Omaha, 1968-73, CESA #11, Turtle Lake, Wis., 1974—; instr. in sign lang. WITC, New Richmond, Wis., 1975—. Mem. NEA, NUE, Wis. Edn. Assn. Home: 1507 Augusta St Rice Lake WI 54868-1818

SANCAKTAR, EROL, engineering educator; b. Ankara, Turkey, July 13, 1952; came to U.S., 1974; s. Mehmet Ali and Ulker Mualla (Elveren) S.; m. Teresa Sue Sancaktar, Feb. 16, 1979; children: Orhan Ali, Errol Alan. BS in Mech. Engring., Robert Coll., Istanbul, Turkey, 1974; MS in Mech. Engring., Va. Poly. Inst. and State U., 1975, PhD, 1979. Tchg. asst. Robert Coll., Istanbul, 1972-74; instr. Va. Poly. Inst. and State U., Blacksburg, Va., 1977-78; vis. scholar Kendall Co., Boston, 1985-86; assoc. prof. Clarkson U., Potsdam, N.Y., 1984-95; prof. U. Akron (Ohio), 1996—. Cons. to the UN Devel. Programme, 1987, ALCOA, 1990-91, U.S. Army Benet Labs., 1991. Mem. editl. adv. bd. Jour. Adhesion Sci. Tech., 1993—; assoc. tech. editor Transactions of the ASME, Jour. of Mech. Design, 1995-98, 2003—; contbr. articles to profl. jours.; patentee in field. Recipient various rsch. grants awarded by NSF, NASA, U.S. Army, N.Y., Grumman Corp., Kendall Co., GE, IBM. Fellow ASME (assoc. tech. editor transactions of ASME Jour. of Mech. Design 1995-1998, 2003—, editor Reliability, Stress Analysis and Failure Prevention: Aspects of Composite and Active Materials, Issues in Fastening & Joining, Composite & Smart Structures, Numerical & FEA Methods, Risk Minimization, elected chair RSAFP tech. steering com.). Home: 465 Evergreen Dr Tallmadge OH 44278-1356 Office: Univ Akron Dept Polymer Engring Akron OH 44325-0001

SANCHEZ, FRANK PEREZ, elementary education educator; b. Artesia, N.Mex., June 25, 1957; s. Dolores R. and Delia R. (Perez) S.; m. Angi Lynn Rowland, Sept. 24, 1977; children: Jessica Lynn, Joshua Andrew, Jeremy Franklin; 1 foster child, Tiffiny Maree Robinson; 1 adopted child, Christina Yvette Sanchez. AA, N.Mex. State U., Carlsbad, 1989; BS, Ea. N.Mex. U., Portales, 1991. Cert. tchr., N.Mex. Adult basic edn. tchr. N.Mex. State U., Carlsbad, 1991-92; tchr. math., social studies Artesia (N.Mex.) Pub. Schs., 1992—. Roman Catholic. Avocations: camping, guitar, sports, woodworking. Home: PO Box 103 Loco Hills NM 88255-0103

SANCHEZ, JANICE PATTERSON, psychotherapist, educator; b. Indpls., Nov. 5, 1948; d. Jack Downey and Elizabeth (Evard) Patterson; m. Adel Sanchez, Sept. 20, 1972; children: Christina, Alison. BS in Edn., Ind. U., 1970; MSW, Cath. U. Am., 1983; grad. adv. psychotherapy tng. prog., Washington Sch. Psychiatry, 1988-91, grad. nat. group psychotherapy tng., 1994-96. Lic. clin. social worker, Va., Washington. Tchr. Fairfax County Pub. Schs., McLean, Va., 1970-76; psychotherapist D.C. Inst. Mental Hygiene, Washington, 1984-89; pvt. practice Arlington, Va., 1989—. Vol. tchr. Jr. Gt. Books, Taylor Elem. Sch., Arlington, Va., 1987-89; mem. Nat. Presbyn. Ch.; vol. chaplain Alexandria (Va.) Hosp., 1998-99; bd. trustees Korean Bapt. Sem., Falls Church, Va., 1994-99. Mem. Am. Group Psychotherapy Assn., Inst. Contemporary Psychotherapy, Greater Washington Soc. for Clin. Social Workers. Office: Ste 14 3801 Fairfax Dr Arlington VA 22203-1762

SANCHEZ, MARY ANNE, retired secondary school educator; b. Galesburg, Ill., Aug. 4, 1939; d. Stephen Mingare and M. Margaret Kennedy; m. J. Manuel Sanchez, Dec. 26, 1980. BS in Edn., Western Ill. U., 1961; MA, Ill. State U., 1970. Tchr., Stanford, Ill., 1962-64, Titusville, Fla., 1964-66, Montgomery County Bd. Edn., Chevy Chase, Md., 1969-72, Hillsborough County Bd. Edn., Tampa, Fla., 1972-96; ret., 1996. Mary Anne Sanchez Young Woman scholarship named in her honor by Social Studies Dept. Leto Comprehensive H.S., 1999. Mem. Nat. Coun. for Social Studies, Fla. Coun. for Social Studies, Adult Edn. Assn. Home: 2715 W Ivy St Tampa FL 33607-1922

SANCHEZ, MIGUEL RAMON, dermatologist, educator; b. Havana, Cuba, May 5, 1950; came to the U.S., 1962; s. Rodolfo and Maria Sanchez. BS, CCNY, 1971; MD, Albert Einstein Coll. Medicine, 1974. Instr. Montefiore Dept. Family Medicine, Bronx, N.Y., 1978-79; sr. med. specialist Kingsborough Psychiat. Ctr., Bklyn., 1979-80; med. dir. Ten Communities Health Ctr., Tulare, Calif., 1980-82; assoc. prof. clin. dermatology NYU, N.Y.C., 1982-83; assoc. dir. Dept. Dermatology Bellevue Hosp. Ctr, N.Y.C., 1983—. Mem. Tulare County Mental Health Bd., 1980-81; mem. med. bd. Bellevue Hosp., 1990—. Contbr. articles to profl. jours. and chpts. to books; editor: (software) Derm-Rx, 1986-90, (book) Dermatology Educational Review Manual, 1993. Bd. dirs. Community Health Project, N.Y.C., 1993; mem. patient care com. community bd. Bellevue Hosp., 1990-93; co-founder, pres. Assn. Latino Faculty and Students. Recipient Testimonial of Appreciation So. Tulare County, 1981, 1st Place award Scientific Forum N.Y. Acad. Dermatology, 1985. Mem. Am. Acad. Dermatology, Acad. for Advancement Sci., Dermatologic Found. Democrat. Roman Catholic. Achievements include development of clinics for tropical dermatology, HIV skin disease, disorders of keratinization, connective tissue disease, and phototherapy; research in infectious diseases, dermatopharmacology and cutaneous manifestation of HIV infection. Office: NYU Dept Dermatology 562 1st Ave New York NY 10016-6402

SANCHEZ, PAULINE STELLA, artist; MFA, UCLA. Artist and mem. faculty Art Ctr. Coll. of Design, 1989—. One-woman shows include Rosamund Felsen Gallery, Angeles Gallery, ACME, Ace Gallery, Marc Jancou Galerie, Zurich, Froment y Putman Galerie, Paris, exhibited in group shows at MOCA, Santa Monica Mus., The Drawing Ctr., N.Y., Galerie Krinzinger, Vienna, Monash U. Gallery, Australia, Kulturzentrum bein den Minoriten, Austria, New Langton Arts, San Francisco, Fotouhi Cramer Gallery, N.Y., Auckland Art Mus., New Zealand, Los Angeles Contemporary Exhibitions, Museu de Arte de Sao Paulo, Brazil. Recipient Credac Artist award, France-Europe;, John Simon Guggenheim Meml. Found. fellow, 2003, Foundation Cartier pour l'Art fellow, Nat. Endowment of Arts fellow. Office: Art Ctr Coll of Design 1700 Lida St Pasadena CA 91103

SAND, GREGORY WILLIAM, history educator, researcher; b. Newark, N.J., Oct. 22, 1935; s. John Ferdinand and Marie Catherine (Gallagher) S.; m. Mary Jane Arnold, Aug. 11, 1962; children: Christopher, Rachel, Thomas. BA, Seton Hall U., 1959; MA in History, Creighton U., 1963; PhD in Am.-Modern European History, St. Louis U., 1973. Instr. history Duchesne Coll., Omaha, 1965-66, Mt. Marty Coll., Yankton, S.D., 1966-67, So. Ill. U., 1969-70; grad. fellow in history St. Louis U., 1968-69; adj. prof. internat. rels. Webster U., St. Louis, 1986-90; adj. prof. history East Ctrl. Coll., Union, Mo., 1993, Concordia U. Wis. St. Louis Ctr., 1994—. Vis. lectr. history U. Mo., Kansas City, 1982; ednl. sales rep. Concordia Pub. House, St. Louis, 1994-96, fund-raising assoc., 1996—. Author: Soviet Aims in Central America, 1989, Truman in Retirement, 1993; editor, reviewer for hist. accuracy part II: Nobility and Analogous Traditional Elites, 1993. Fund-raising assoc. St. Louis Zoo, 1986, Repertory Theatre of St. Louis, 1987-96; devel., exec. dir., Big River Assn., St. Louis, 1985-86. Asia fellow Hamline U., 1966, archives by-fellow Churchill Coll., Cambridge (Eng.) U., 1999-2000, fellow Earhart Found., 1999-2000; travel grantee Fritz Thyssen Found., 1981, gen. edn. grantee Marguerite Eyer Wilbur Found., 1986, rsch. grantee Truman Libr. Inst., 1989-90. Mem. Nat. Assn. Scholars, Phi Alpha Theta. Roman Catholic. Avocations: reading, theatre, travel. Home: 28 Jeanette Dr Granite City IL 62040-6511 Office: Concordia Pub House 3558 S Jefferson Ave Saint Louis MO 63118-3910

SAND, PHYLLIS SUE NEWNAM (PHYLLIS SUE NEWNAM), retired special education educator; b. Epworth, N.D., Feb. 12, 1931; d. Zelnoe Jackson and Susie Ella (Lindley) Newnam; m. Shirley Sylvester Sand, Aug. 24, 1952; children: Thomas Richard, James Waldow, Catherine Roberta, Constance Renae. AA, Minot State Tchrs. Coll., 1952; BS in Edn., U. N.D., 1970, MEd, 1971. Cert. profl. educator, N.D., tchr., Minn. Tchr. various rural schs., Ward/Cavalier Counties, N.D., 1950-53; cons., tchr. Griggs, Steele, & Trail Spl. Edn. Unit, N.D., 1976-78; diagnostician, tchr. learning disabled Larimore (N.D.) Elem., 1978-92. Mem. NEA (life), N.D. Edn. Assn. (life), Coun. for Exceptional Children, N.D. Ret. Tchrs. Assn., Greater Grand Forks Sr. Citizens Assn., DAV Aux., North Star Quilters Guild (charter), Minnkota Geneal. Soc., Delta Kappa Gamma (pres. Rho chpt., 1990-92, program chmn.). United Methodist. Avocations: writing poetry, sewing, reading, quilting, travel.

SANDAGE-MUSSEY, ELIZABETH ANTHEA, retired market research executive; b. Larned, Kans., Oct. 13, 1930; d. Curtis Carl and Beulah Pauline (Knupp) Smith; m. Charles Harold Sandage, July 18, 1971; children by previous marriage: Dianna Louise Danner Wilson, David Alan Danner; m. Robert D. Mussey, Oct. 21, 2000. BS, U. Colo., 1967, MA, 1970; PhD in Comms., U. Ill., 1983. Pub. rels. rep., editor Martin News Martin Marietta Corp., Denver, 1960-63, 65-67; retail advt. salesperson Denver Post, 1967-70; instr. advt. U. Ill., 1970-71, vis. lectr. advt., 1977-84; v.p., corp. sec., dir. Farm Rsch. Inst., Urbana, Ill., 1984-95; ret., 1995. Editor: Advertising as a Social Force: Selected Speeches and Essays by Charles H. Sandage, 1998, Occasional Papers in Advertising, 1971, The Sandage Family Cookbook, 1976, 3d edit., 2002, The Inkling (Carle Hosp. Aux. Newsletter), 1975-76. Bd. dirs. U. Ill. Libr. Friends, 1991-95; exec. dir. Sandage Charitable Trust, 1986—. Mem. U. Ill. Alumni Assn. (pres.'s coun.), Champaign Social Sci. Club, The Book Club, Moneymakers Investment Club, Kappa Tau Alpha.

SANDBERG, MARILYN LEE, special education educator; b. Indpls., May 7, 1936; d. Chester Lee and Florence A. (Wilkens) Hughes; m. Donald Lawrence Sandberg, June 14, 1958; children: Robert Lawrence, Gregory Lee, Steven Lawrence. BS, Butler U., 1958; MS, Ind. U., 1971; endorsement learning disabilities edn., Indpls. U., 1985; endorsement mentally handicapped edn., Butler U., 1987. Tchr. elem. edn. Klondike (Ind.) Schs., 1958, Indpls. Pub. Schs., 1959; tchr. 1st grade M.S.D. Warren Twp. Schs., Indpls., 1971-74, tchr. kindergarten, 1974-85, tchr. spl. edn., 1985—96. With Reach Out and Read Wischard Hosp. Primary Care children. Mem. Alpha Delta Kappa (chaplain 1991-93, historian 1995-97). Avocations: antiques, stained glass, craft work, church work. Home: 2540 Andrews Ct Indianapolis IN 46203-5619 E-mail: dsandb@mibor.com.

SANDEFUR, JAMES TANDY, mathematics educator; b. Madison, Ind., Apr. 25, 1947; s. James Tandy and Evelyn (Gayle) S.; m. Mary Elizabeth Epes, Sept. 6, 1969 (div. 1982); m. Helen Moriarty, Apr. 14, 1984; 1 child, Scott David. BA, Vanderbilt U., 1969; MA, U. Denver, 1971; PhD, Tulane U., 1974. Prof. math. Georgetown U., Washington, 1974—, chair honor coun.; faculty chair Georgetown Honor Coun., 2000—. Vis. assoc. prof. Ctr. for Applied Math., Cornell U., Ithaca, N.Y., 1981-82; vis. prof. U. Iowa, Iowa City, 1988-89; math. cons. It's Academic TV show, Altman Prodns., Washington, 1985—; prin. investigator, dir. math. modelling workshop NSF, Washington, 1988-91; visitor Freudenthal Inst., Utrecht, The Netherlands, 1996; writing team Principles and Stds. for Sch. Math., 2000; mem. adv. bd. Exploratorium's Math Explorer Project; cons. Cerebellum Corp. Author: Discrete Dynamical Systems: Theory and Applications, 1990, Discrete Dynamical Modeling, 1993, Elementary Mathematical Modeling, 2002; adv. bd. to Annenberg/CPB math. and sci. project's Guide to Math and Science Reform; contbr. articles to math. jours. Program dir. in Instrl. Materials Devel. for Div. of Materials, Devel., Rsch. and Informal Sci. Edn.; directorate for Edn. and Human Resources NSF. NSF grantee, prin. investigator Tchr. Leadership Inst., 1993—. Mem.: Nat. Coun. Teachers Math. (adv. panel Yearbook Discrete Math., mem. writing team for standards 2000, ed. panel Math. Teacher), Nat. Faculty, Math. Asn. Am. (former chmn. minicourse com.), Am. Contract Bridge League (chap. bd. dir. 1983-85) (life). Democrat. Avocations: bridge, tennis, skiing. Office: Georgetown U Dept Math Washington DC 20057-0001

SANDER, FRANK ERNEST ARNOLD, law educator; b. Stuttgart, Germany, July 22, 1927; came to U.S., 1940, naturalized, 1946; s. Rudolf and Alice (Epstein) S.; m. Emily Bishop Jones, Apr. 26, 1958; children: Alison Bishop, Thomas Harvey, Ernest Ridgway Sander. AB in Math. magna cum laude, Harvard U., 1949, LLB magna cum laude, 1952. Bar: Mass. 1952, US Supreme Ct. 1952. Law clk. to Chief Judge Magruder U.S. Ct. Appeals, 1st Cir., 1952-53; law clk. to Justice Frankfurter, U.S. Supreme Ct., 1953-54; atty. tax divsn. Dept. Justice, 1954-56; with firm Hill & Barlow, Boston, 1956-59; mem. faculty Harvard Law Sch., 1959—, prof. law, 1962—, Bussey prof., 1981—, assoc. dean, 1987-2000. Spl. fields fed. taxation, family law, welfare law, dispute resolution; chmn. Coun. on Role of Cts.; mem. panels Am. Arbitration Assn., Fed. Mediation and Conciliation Svc.; chmn. Coun. on Legal Edn. Opportunity, 1968—70; cons. Dept. Treasury, 1968; treas. Harvard Law Rev., 1951—52; mem. dispute resolution standing com. Mass. Supreme Jud. Ct., 1994—; drafting com. Uniform Mediation Act, 1998—2001. Author: (with Westfall and McIntyre) Readings in Federal Taxation, 2d edit., 1983, (with Foote and Levy) Cases and Materials on Family Law, 3d edit., 1985, (with Gutman) Tax Aspects of Divorce and Separation, 4th edit., 1985, (with Goldberg, Rogers and Cole) Dispute Resolution, 4th edit., 2003. Mem. tax mission Internat. Program Taxation to Republic of Colombia, 1959; mem. com. on civil and polit. rights President's Commn. on Status of Women, 1962-63; trustee Buckingham Browne and Nichols Sch., 1969-75; chmn. Mass. Welfare Adv. Bd., 1975-79. With AUS, 1945-46. Recipient Whitney North Seymour medal Am. Arbitration Assn., 1988, spl. award for disting. svc. to dispute resolution Ctr. for Pub. Resources Inst. for Dispute Resolution, 1990. Mem.

ABA (chmn. standing com. dispute resolution 1986-89, Kutak medal 1993, D'Alemberte-Raven award 1999), Boston Bar Assn., Phi Beta Kappa. Home: 74 Buckingham St Cambridge MA 02138-2229 Office: Harvard U Sch of Law Cambridge MA 02138

SANDERS, ADRIAN LIONEL, educational consultant; b. Paragould, Ark., Aug. 3, 1938; s. Herbert Charles and Florence Theresa (Becherer) S.; m. Molly Jean Zecher, Dec. 20, 1961. AA, Bakersfield Coll., 1959; BA, San Francisco State U., 1961; MA, San Jose State U., 1967. 7th grade tchr. Sharp Park Sch., Pacifica, Calif., 1961-62; 5th grade tchr. Mowry Sch., Fremont, Calif., 1962-64; sci. tchr. Blacow Sch., Fremont, Calif., 1964-76; 5th grade tchr. Warm Springs Sch., Fremont, 1977-87, 5th grade gifted and talented edn. tchr., 1987-94; edn. cons., 1994—. Mem. San Diego Hist. Soc., 1999, Alzheimer's Family Relief Program, Rockville, Md., 1986; vol. 7 km. Race for Alzheimer's Disease Willow Glen Founders Day, San Jose, 1988-92. Named Outstanding Young Educator, Jr. C. of C., Fremont, Calif., 1965. Mem. Zoolog. Soc. San Diego, Calif. Ctr. for the Arts (Escondido). Avocations: photography, travelling, visiting presidents' birthplaces, collecting license plates, collecting matchbooks worldwide. Home and Office: 1437 Stoneridge Cir Escondido CA 92029-5514

SANDERS, BARBARA FAYNE, artist, educator; b. Draper, N.C., Apr. 20, 1936; d. Elwood Oris and Gladys (Martin) Fayne; m. Joseph J. Sanders, June 11, 1960; children: J. Gregory, Kimberly Ann. Student ., Rockingham C.C., Wentworth, N.C., 1970—92. Jr. designer Design Dept., Karastan Rug Mill, Eden, NC, 1954—60; art instr. Rockingham C.C., Wentworth, 1985—2000; pvt. instr./condr. workshops, 1985—. Art coord. Eden Pub. Libr., 1985—90, Eden City Hall, 1995—. One-woman shows include Eden (N.C.) Pub. Libr., Eden City Hall Gallery, Rockingham County Govtl. Ctr., Wentworth, N.C., Forum VI, Greensboro, N.C., Stokes County Arts Coun. Gallery, Danbury, N.C., Chinqua Penn Plantation, Reidsville, N.C., Women's Club Gallery, Reidsville, Mt. Airy (N.C.) Art Guild, others, exhibited in group shows at Rockingham County Fine Arts Festival, Wentworth, Arts Davidson County Mus., Lexington, N.C., Carolina Craftsmen, Greensboro, Southeastern Artists Assn., Benton Conv. Ctr., Winston-Salem, N.C., Sawtooth Gallery, Winston-Salem, Art in the Pk., Blowing Rock, N.C., High Point (N.C.) Theatre Art Galleries, Carolina St. Scene, Winston-Salem, Arts Coun. Gallery, Cary, N.C., Piedmont Arts Assn. Gallery, Martinsville, Va., Danville Mus. History and Art, Capt.'s Ho. Gallery, others, Represented in permanent collections NationsBank, Wachovia Bank, First Nat. Bank, Home Savs. Bank., Miller Brewing Co., RJR Nabisco, Gem Dandy, Inc., Rockingham Arts Coun., Rockingham CC, Rockingham County Pub. Libr., Morehead Meml. Hosp., Steamway Internat., Gov. James Martin, N.C. U.S. area dir. Y's Menettes YMCA, Geneva, 1995—96, regional dir. Kannapolis, NC, 1993—95; pres. Draper Y's Menettes, Eden, 1978—2001. Named Y's Menette of the Yr., Draper Y's Menettes, 1984; recipient Vis.'s Favorite award, Fine Arts Festival Rockingham County, 1975, Best in Show, Rockingham County Fine Arts Festival, 1980, 1st pl., Sr. Art Expo, 1996, award of distinction, Danville Artists League, 1998, Piedmont Arts Assn., 2000, 2001, others. Mem.: Studio Group of Rockingham County (pres. 1996—97), High Point Art Guild (RECEPTION COORD. 1992—), Watercolor Soc. N.C. Avocations: reading, music, writing poetry and stories. Home: 135 River Ridge Rd Eden NC 27288-8004

SANDERS, CATHARINE DOWNER, retired adult educator, historical researcher; b. Reno, Aug. 6, 1935; d. Robert Carpenter and Alice Marie (Gottschalk) Downer; m. Archable O'Neill Sanders, May 1, 1955; children: Christopher O'Neill, Eric Downer, Scott Carpenter. BA in Elem. Edn., U. Nev., 1975, MEd in Edn. Adminstrn. and Higher Edn., 1984. Cert. elem. tchr. grades K-8, Nev. Dir. ind. study by correspondence U. Nev., Reno, 1984-95; ret., 1995. Mem. Nat. Univ. Continuing Edn. Assn. (emeritus, Devoted Svc. award 1996), Nev. Adult Edn. Assn. (pres. 1989-90, Commendation award 1991), Nev. Women's History Project (no. Nev. vice chair 1996-98, state bd. chair 1997-98, co-chair conf. 1997, 98), Mountain Plains Adult Edn. Assn. (emeritus, co-editor newsletter 1994-96, award of merit 1996). Democrat. Presbyterian. Avocations: hiking, skiing, reading, music, traveling.

SANDERS, DOUGLAS CHARLES, horticulturist, researcher, educator; b. Lansing, Mich., May 21, 1942; s. Charles S. and Dorthy Sanders; m. Ellen Joyce, Apr. 26, 1965. BS, Mich. State U., 1965; MS, U. Minn., 1969, PhD, 1970. From rsch. asst. to rsch. assoc. U. Minn., St. Paul, 1965-70; from asst. prof. N.C. State U., Raleigh, 1970-75, assoc. prof., 1975-82, prof., 1982—. Cons. Orgn. of Am. States, others. Contbr. over 185 articles to profl. jours. Recipient Outstanding Ext. award N.C. State U., 1993, Outstanding Ext. Specialist award Epsilon Sigma Phi, 1993; named Covington Outstanding Ext. Educator, 1999. Fellow Am. Soc. Hort. Sci. (Outstanding Extention Educator award, 1993); mem. Am. Soc. Agronomy, Crop Sci. Soc. Am. Achievements include development of drip fertigation systems for vegetables, of cultural systems for vegetables; investigation of integrated aquaculture and vegetable production system, and of nutrient cycling in vegetables; development of new cropping systems for asparagus, carrots, lettuce and onions. Office: NC State U Dept Horticultural Sci PO Box 7609 Raleigh NC 27695-0001 E-mail: Doug_Sanders@ncsa.edu.

SANDERS, GEORGIA ELIZABETH, secondary school educator; b. Holmwood, La., July 14, 1933; d. Frederick Rudolph and Susie W. (Hackett) S. Student, La. Coll., 1951-53, La. State U., 1959-60; BS, then MS in Microbiology, U. Southwestern La., 1970; MS in Math., U. So. Miss., 1983. Instr. dept. biology U. New Orleans, 1976-79, instr. dept. math., 1983-86; tchr. East Baton Rouge Parish Schs., 1988-89; tchr. math. St. Tammany Parish, La., 1990—. Mem. NEA, Am. Math. Soc., Math. Assn. Am., Nat. Coun. Tchrs. Math. Home: PO Box 968 Slidell LA 70459-0968 E-mail: gsan863722@aol.com.

SANDERS, GLADYS NEALOUS, retired secondary school educator; b. Appling, Ga., June 27, 1937; d. Rile Harrison and Rebecca (Luke) Nealous; m. Robert B. Sanders, Dec. 23, 1961; children: Sylvia Lynne, William Nealous. BA, Paine Coll., 1959. Math. tchr. Blanchard Consol. Schs., Appling, 1959-61, Richmond County Pub. Schs., Augusta, Ga., 1961-62, Lawrence (Kans.) Pub. Schs., 1973-88, 91—, math. supr., 1988-91, 93—; math. cons. Macmillan/McGraw-Hill, 1991, ret., 1998. Chair, writing team Kans. Math. Standards, 1989—; mem. Kans. Math. Assessment, 1990-91; cons. Scott, Foresman, Glenview, Ill., 1989-90; trainer Kans. Math. Acad., Olathe, summer 1990; mem. subcom. interstate new tchr. assessment and support consortium on math, chief state sch. officers, 1993—. Mem. ASCD, Nat. Bd. Profl. Teaching Standards (vice chair mid. childhood and early adolescence math. com. 1992—), Kans. Assn. Tchrs. Maths., Nat. Coun. Tchrs. Maths., Nat. Coun. Suprs. Maths. Democrat. Methodist. Avocations: cooking, sewing, gardening, cross-stitch, reading.

SANDERS, HELEN CARAVAS, art educator; b. Cepholonia, Greece, Feb. 2, 1938; came to U.S., 1948; d. James and Stella (Doriza) Caravas; m. Earl Cook Sanders, June 10, 1962; children: Timothy, Dwayne. BS in Edn., Art, English, James Madison, 1961; MA in Edn., Va. Commonwealth U., 1974. Cert. tchr., Va. Tchr. art Monroe Jr. High Sch., Roanoke, Va., 1961-62, George Wythe High Sch., Richmond, Va., 1962-68, Elem. Art Cons., Chesterfield, Va., 1973-75, Cloverhill High Sch., Chesterfield, 1975-76, Thomas Dale High Sch., Chesterfield, 1977-78, L C Bird High Sch., Chesterfield, 1978—. Supr. student tchr. Longwood Coll., Va. Commonwealth U., Va. State U., Richmond and Chesterfield, 1962—; mem. state art evaluation com. Pulaski High Sch., Annandale High Sch., Cox High Sch., Colonial High Sch., 1982-84, 91; adjudicator Gov.'s Sch., State Dept., Chesterfield, 1992; com. chair state publ. Standards of Learning Com., 1983-84. Recipient Presdl. citation Gov.'s Sch. for Gifted and Talented, 1991; Mellon fellow in the Humanities, State Va., 1966; grantee Chesterfield Edn. Assn., 1975. Fellow Ctrl. Va. Art. Edn. Assn. (REB award Excellence in Teaching, 1992); mem. Nat. Art Edn. Assn. (Southeastern High Sch. Art Tchr. of Yr. 1986), Va. Art Edn. Assn. (v.p. 1979-81, editor newsletter 1979-81, Sr. High Sch. Art Tchr. of Yr. 1984), James River Art League. Avocations: gardening, bicycling, hiking, scuba diving, traveling. Home: 4207 Winterberry Ct Midlothian VA 23112-4957

SANDERS, JACQUELYN SEEVAK, psychologist, educator; b. Boston, Apr. 26, 1931; d. Edward Ezral and Dora (Zoken) Seevak; 1 child, Seth. BA, Radcliffe Coll., 1952; MA, U. Chgo., 1964; PhD, UCLA, 1972. Counselor, asst. prin. Orthogenic Sch., Chgo., 1952—65; rsch. assoc. UCLA, 1965—68; asst. prof. Ctr. for Early Edn., L.A., 1969—72; assoc. dir.. Sonia Shankman Orthogenic Sch., U. Chgo., 1972—73, dir., 1973—93, dir. emeritus, 1993—; curriculum cons. day care ctrs. L.A. Dept. Social Welfare, 1970—72; instr. Calif. State Coll., L.A., 1972; lectr. dept. edn. U. Chgo., 1972—80, sr. lectr., 1980—93, clin. assoc. prof. dept. psychiatry, 1990—93, emeritus, 1993—; instr. edn. program Inst. Psychoanalysis, Chgo., 1979—82. Cons. Osawatomie State Hosp. (Kans.), 1965—68; reading cons. Foreman H.S., Chgo.; treas. Chgo. Inst. Psychoanalysis, 2003—. Author: Greenhouse for the Mind, 1989; editor (with Barry L. Childress): Psychoanalytic Approaches to the Very Troubled Child: Therapeutic Practice Innovations in Residential & Educational Settings, 1989; editor: Severely Disturbed Children and the Parental Alliance, 1992; editor: (with Jerome M. Goldsmith) Milieu Therapy: Significant Issues and Innovative Applications, 1993; editor: The Seevak Family, The Zoken Family; contbr. articles to profl. jours. Mem. vis. com. univ. sch. rels. U. Chgo.; bd. dirs. KAM Isaiah Israel Congregation, 1997—2001, Chgo. Inst. for Psychoanalysis. Recipient Alumna award, Girls' Latin Sch., Boston, Bettelheim award, Am. Assn. Children's Residential Ctrs., Disting. Svc. award, Radcliffe Assn., 2002; scholar Radcliffe Coll. scholar, 1948—52; Univ. fellow, UCLA, 1966—68. Mem.: Chgo. Inst. for Psychoanalysis, Assn. Children's Residential Ctrs. (past pres.), Harvard Club (bd. dirs. 1986—2001, Chgo.), Radcliffe Club (sec.-treas. 1986—87, pres. 1987—89, Chgo.). Home: 5842 S Stony Island Ave Apt 2G Chicago IL 60637-2033 E-mail: jsand09@attglobal.net.

SANDERS, JOHN LASSITER, retired academic administrator; b. Four Oaks, NC, June 30, 1927; s. David Hardy and Louie Jane (Lassiter) S.; m. Ann Beal, Aug. 14, 1954; children— Tracy Elizabeth Sanders Justus, Jane Nesbit, William Hardy. AB, U. N.C., 1950, JD, 1954. Bar: N.C. 1955. Law clk. to judge U.S. Ct. Appeals, 1954-55; pvt. practice Raleigh, NC, 1955-56; mem. faculty Inst. Govt., UNC, Chapel Hill, 1956-94, dir., 1962-73, 79-92, v.p. planning at Univ., 1973-78. Served with USNR, 1945-46. Recipient NC award State of NC, 1996. Democrat. Baptist. Home: 1107 Sourwood Dr Chapel Hill NC 27517-4914 Office: 205 Providence Rd Chapel Hill NC 27514

SANDERS, MARLENE, anchor, journalism educator; b. Cleve., Jan. 10, 1931; d. Mac and Evelyn (Menitoff) Sanders; m. Jerome Toobin, May 27, 1958 (dec. Jan. 1984); children: Jeff, Mark. Student, Ohio State U., 1948-49. Writer, prodr. Sta. WNEW-TV, N.Y.C., 1955-60, P.M. program Westinghouse Broadcasting Co., N.Y.C., 1961-62; asst. dir. news and public affairs Sta. WNEW, N.Y.C., 1962-64; anchor, news program ABC News, N.Y.C., 1964-68, corr., 1968-72, documentary prodr., writer, anchor, 1972-76, v.p., dir. TV documentaries, 1976-78; corr. CBS News, N.Y.C., 1978-87; host Currents Sta. WNET-TV, N.Y.C., 1987-88; host Met. Week in Review, 1988-90; host Thirteen Live Sta. WNET-TV, 1990-91; prof. dept. journalism NYU, N.Y.C., 1991-93; adj. prof. journalism, adminstr. Columbia U. Grad. Sch. Journalism, N.Y.C., 1994-95; adj. prof. journalism NYU, 1996—. Profl.-in-residence Freedom Forum Media Studies Ctr., 1997-2000; freelance broadcaster, narrator; chmn. bd. womensenews.org, chair RSVP, Inc., 1997—. Co-author: Waiting for Prime Time: The Women of Television News, 1988. Mem. N.Y.C. Commn. on Women's Issues, NY, 2003—. Recipient award N.Y. State Broadcasters Assn., 1976, award Nat. Press Club, 1976, Emmy awards, 1980, 81, others. Mem. Am. Women in Radio and TV (Woman of Yr. award 1975, Silver Satellite award 1977), Women in Comm. (past pres.), Coun. Fgn. Rels.; chair bd. womensenews.org. E-mail: sanders110@aol.com.

SANDERS, RICHARD L. academic administrator; b. Clintonville, Wis., Jan. 2, 1937; s. Claude H. and Lucille B. (Wedde) S.; m. Janice Miles, Aug. 30, 1958; children: Scott, Jennifer, Todd, Zachary, Nicole. BS, U. Wis., Eau Claire, 1959; MS, U. Wis., Milw., 1966; EdD, Marquette U., 1971. Tchr. music Milw. Pub. Schs., 1959-62, rsch. assoc., 1966-67; tchr. music West Allis (Wis.) Pub. Schs., 1962-66; registrar, asst. prof. Lakeland Coll., Sheboygan, Wis., 1967-71; dean Lakewood C.C., St. Paul, 1971-81; pres. Lincoln Trail Coll., Robinson, Ill., 1981-84, Mattatuck C.C., Waterbury, Conn., 1984-92, Naugatuck Valley C.C., Waterbury, Conn., 1992—; sec. Naugatuck Valley C.C. Founds., Inc., Waterbury, Conn. Mem. United Way Bd. of Greater Waterbury. Disting. Svc. award Charter Oak State U., 1993. Mem. Am. Assn. C.C., Conn. Coun. of Higher Edn., New Eng.Cmty.-Tech. Coun. (editor The Collegian 1992-94), Alliance for C.C. Innovation, Am. Assn. Higher Edn., Am. Assn. Univ. adminstrs., Am. Coun. Edn., C.C. Humanities Assn., Nat. Coun. Occupl. Edn., Nat. Coun. Instrl. Adminstrss., New Eng. Assn. Schs. and Colls., New Eng. Coll. Coun., Conn. Cmty.-Tech. Coll. Coun. Pres., Conn. Assn. Latin Am. in Higher Edn., Greater Danbury C. of C., Greater Valley C. of C., Greater Waterbury C. of C., Waterbury Found., Waterbury Exec. Educators Roundtable, Waterbury Hosp. Health Network, Inc., Phi Delta Kappa (cert. outstanding membership 1990). Avocations: music, tennis, public speaking. Office: Naugatuck Valley CC 750 Chase Pkwy Waterbury CT 06708-3011

SANDERS, ROBERT B. biochemistry educator, administrator; b. Augusta, Ga., Dec. 9, 1938; s. Robert and Lois (Jones) S.; m. Gladys Nealous, Dec. 23, 1961; children: Sylvia Lynne, William Nealous. BS, Paine Coll., 1959; MS, U. Mich., 1961, PhD, 1964; postdoctoral, U. Wis., 1964-66. Vis. scientist Battelle Meml. Inst., Richland, Wash., 1970-71; vis. assoc. prof. U. Tex. Med. Sch., Houston, 1974-75; program dir. NSF, Washington, 1978-79; from asst prof. to prof. U. Kans., Lawrence, 1966-86, prof. biochemistry, 1986—, assoc. dean Grad. Sch., 1987-96, assoc. vice chancellor, 1989-96. Cons. NSF, Washington, 1983-92; cons. Dept. Edn., Washington, 1983-96 and 2003, NIH, Washington, 1982, Interx Rsch. Corp., Lawrence, 1972-80, NRC, Washington, 1973-93, Ednl. Testing Svc., NJ, 2001-03; v.p. Nat. Phys. Sci. Consortium, 1994-96; reviewer biology texts, McGraw Hill, 2000-02. Contbr. over 60 articles to profl. jour. Bd. dir. United Child Devel. Ctr., Lawrence, Kans., 1968-93; mem. bd. high edn. United Meth. Ch., 1976-80. With USAR, 1955-62. Paine Coll. Alumni Assn. scholar, 1958; U. Mich. grad. fellow, 1959-64; NIH postdoctoral fellow, 1974-75, Am. Cancer Soc. fellow, 1964-66, Battelle Meml. Inst. fellow, 1970-71; recipient numerous rsch. grants. Mem. AAUP, Am. Soc. Biochemistry and Molecular Biology, Sigma Xi. Office: U Kans Dept Molecular Bioscis Lawrence KS 66045-0001

SANDERS, ROBERTA MAE, secondary school educator; b. Albuquerque, Dec. 30, 1954; d. Joseph Najeeb and Cecilia Mae (Reid) Rockos; m. George Wayne Sanders. BS in Vocat. Home Econs., Edn., U. N.Mex., 1977, cert. in health edn., 1987. Cert. home econs. tchr., N.Mex. Instr., demonstrator Amana Corp., Albuquerque, 1976-77; tchr. home econs. Moriarty (N.Mex.) Mcpl. Schs., 1977-79, Harrison Mid. Sch., 1979-92, West Mesa High Sch., 1992—. Mem. prin. selection com. Albuquerque Pub. Schs., 1992, mem. textbook evaluation com., 1989-90; com. mem. N.Mex. Mid. Sch. Curriculum Guide for Home Econs. Edn., 1987-88. Recipient Focus on Excellence award Albuquerque ASCD, 1990, tchr. enrichment awards N.Mex. Dept. Edn., 1988-90. Mem. NEA, Am. Vocat. Assn., Am. Home Econs. Assn., N.Mex. Home Econs. Assn. (planning com., exhibit chmn. ann. meeting 1979-81), N.Mex. Vocat. Assn., N.Mex. Vocat. Home Econs. Tchrs. Assn. (conf. exhibit com. 1987-92), Home Econs. Edn. Assn. Roman Catholic. Avocations: gourmet cooking, crafts, raising orchids, volunteering, nature. Office: West Mesa High Sch 6701 Fortuna Rd NW Albuquerque NM 87121-1399

SANDERS, TED, educational association administrator; Tchr. Mountain Home, Idaho, Bur. Indian Affairs pub. sch. sys.; with N.Mex. Dept. Edn.; Nev. state supt. of edn., 1979—85; Ill. state supt. of edn., 1985—89; dep. U.S. sec. of edn., 1989—91; acting U.S. sec. of edn., 1990—91; Ohio supt. pub. instrn., 1991—95; pres. So. Ill. U., 1995—2000, Edn. Commn. of the States, 2000—. Office: ECS 700 Broadway 1200 Denver CO 80203-3460*

SANDERS, TRISHA LYNN, middle school educator; b. Chowchilla, Calif., June 7, 1965; d. Kenneth L. and Karen L. (Lobo) S.; 1 child, Craig. BA in Social Sci., Calif. State U., Stanislaus, 1987; MA in Ednl. Adminstrn., MA in Curriculum and Instrn., Chapman U., 1992. Cert. tchr., Calif. 6th grade tchr. lang. arts and math. Merced (Calif.) City Sch. Dist., 1988-91, 6th grade tchr. sci. and math., 1991-94, 8th grade sci. tchr., 1994-95; 7th grade tchr. Cruickshank Mid. Sch., Merced, Calif., 1995—. Mentor tchr. Merced City Schs., 1993-95, sci. cadre, 1992-95; mem. steering com. Merced High Sch., 1992-95. Mem. ASCD, CUE, Phi Delta Kappa.

SANDERSON, ARTHUR CLARK, engineering educator; b. Providence, Oct. 23, 1946; s. Robert Leroy and Julia Ayer (Oldham) S.; m. Susan Rita Walsh, Aug. 14, 1971; children: Angeline Mirada, Andrew McWain. BS, Brown U., 1968; MS, Carnegie-Mellon U., 1970, PhD, 1972. Rsch. engr. Westinghouse Electric Corp., Pitts., 1968-70; vis. rsch. scientist Delft (The Netherlands) U. Tech., 1972-73; prof. Carnegie-Mellon U., Pitts., 1973-87, co-dir. robotics inst., 1981-87; rsch. dir. Philips Rsch. Labs., Briarcliff Manor, N.Y., 1985-87; prof., dept. chmn. Rensselaer Poly. Inst., Troy, N.Y., 1987—; divsn. dir. elec. & comm. systems NSF, Arlington, Va., 1998-2000; v.p. rsch. Rensselaer Poly. Inst., 2000—. Vis. prof. Univ. Iberoamericana, Mexico City, 1975-77, Inst. Info. Sci. & Elecs., U. Tsukuba, Japan, 1996-97. Contbr. 3 books, over 250 articles to profl. jours. Fellow AAAS, IEEE (pres. robotics and automation soc. 1989, 90); mem. AIAA (mem. space automation and robotics tech. com.), Am. Assn. Artificial Intelligence, Soc. Mfg. Engrs. Home: 26 Riverwalk Way Cohoes NY 12047-3335 Office: Rensselaer Poly Inst 110 8th St Troy NY 12180-3522 E-mail: sandea@rpi.edu.

SANDERSON, DEBORAH SHIRLEY, elementary education educator, writer; b. New Britain, Conn., Feb. 3, 1958; d. Leland S. and Colleen Margaret (Payton) B.; m. Frederick Lee Sanderson, Nov. 25, 1995. BSE, Clarion U. of Pa., 1980, postgrad., 1995—. Cert. tchr., Pa. Substitute tchr. Cambria Hts. Sch. Dist., Patton, Pa., 1981-84, Purchase Line Sch. Dist., Commodore, Pa., 1981-84, Harmony Sch. Dist., Westover, Pa., 1981-84; tchr. Bradford (Pa.) Area Christian Acad., 1984-85, Riverside Christian Acad., Johnstown, Pa., 1985-86, Lindley Ave Bapt. Day Sch., Tarzana, Calif., 1986-88; sec.-treas. Liberty Twp., McKean Co., Port Allegany, Pa., 1988-92; elem. sch. tchr. Elfers Christian Sch., New Port Richey, Fla., 1992-95; dir., tchr. Coryville Ch. Faith Presch., Eldred, Pa., 1995-97; tchr. Bradford (Pa.) Area Christian Acad., 1997—, asst. prin., 1999-2000, acting prin., 2000—01. Daycare worker Happy Days Child Care Ctr., New Port Richey, summers 1993-94. Contbg. author: (poetry) Whispers in the Wind, 1990, Down Peaceful Paths, 1991, Celebrate! Poets Speak Out, 2003, In Celebration of Poetry, 2003; photographer Pa. Mag., 1991, Classical Moments, The Internat. Libr. Photography, 2001. Auditor Burnside (Pa.) Borough, 1981-82, pollster, 1983; organizer of fundraiser Cystic Fibrosis Found., Cherry Tree, Pa., 1981-82; EMT, Indiana County EMT Svc., Ind., Pa., 1981; head counselor Assn. Evang. Chs., East Smethport Christian Ch., 1989-92; dir. children's choir 1st Bapt. Ch. of Elfers, 1992-95. Republican. Avocations: reading, writing, crafts, trivia games. Office: Bradford Area Christian Acad PO Box 399 365 Bolivar Dr Bradford PA 16701-0399

SANDERSON, KENNETH CHAPMAN, horticulture educator, consultant, researcher; b. Woodbury, N.J., Jan. 9, 1933; s. Christopher John and Mary Aden (Powell) S.; m. Barbara Joan Hoffman, Jan. 28, 1961; children: Lesley Mary, Kenneth Hoffman. BS, Cornell U., 1955; MS, U. Md., 1958, PhD, 1965. Teaching asst. U. Md., College Park, 1955-57, mgr. greenhouse, 1960-65; florist C.J. Sanderson, Woodbury, 1958-60; asst. prof. La. State U., Baton Rouge, 1965-66; asst. prof., assoc. prof. horticulture Auburn (Ala.) U., 1966-76, prof., 1976-94, prof. emeritus, 1994—. Lectr. Calif. Poly. State U., San Luis Obispo, 1975-76, 85-86. Assoc. editor Hort. Sci., Jour. Am. Soc. Hort. Sci., 1976-80; contbr. over 50 articles to sci. jours. and 150 articles to popular publs. Pres. Dean Road Sch. PTA, Auburn, 1971, Auburn Civitan Club, 1971; precinct worker San Luis Obispo Dem. Com., 1976. With U.S. Army, 1957-58. Recipient Outstanding Rsch. award So. Nurseryman's Assn., 1975, McGreen Wisdom Environ. award, 1991, hon. degree Future Farmers Am., 1989. Fellow Am. Soc. Hort. Scis. (environ. com. 1980-84, chmn. floriculture com. 1991—); mem. SigmaXi, Pi Alpha Xi (sec.-treas. 1987-89, pres. 1989-90), Gamma Sigma Delta. Presbyterian. Achievements include pioneering use of growth retardants and other chemicals on florist crops; demonstrating the use of municipal waste as a growing medium; expert on snapdragon culture and identification culture and use of interior plants. Home: 2329 Appaloosa Cir Sarasota FL 34240-8572

SANDFORD, MARY ANN, Spanish language educator; b. Lackawanna, N.Y., May 2, 1947; d. Raymond George and Irene Emma (Beebe) Hubbs; m. Paul B. Sandford, Dec. 20, 1975; children: Paul Nathan, Sarah Kathryn, Daniel Raymond. BA, Am. U., 1969; MEd, SUNY, Buffalo, 1973. Cert. secondary edn. fgn. lang. Tchr. Spanish West Seneca (N.Y.) Schs., 1969-75; instr. Spanish N.Mex. State U., Carlsbad, 1976—; tchr. Spanish Carlsbad Mcpl. Schs., 1988—2003. Dept. chair West Seneca Schs., 1970-75, Carlsbad Mcpl. Schs., 1989-1999. Pres. Child Conservation, Carlsbad, 1987-88. Recipient James D. Allen Dept. award N.Y. State, 1974. Mem. AAUW (v.p. 1983, 2001—, pres. 1998-2000), Am. Assn. for Tchrs. of Spanish and Portuguese, N.Mex. Orgn. Lang. Educators, Delta Kappa Gamma (v.p. 1993-94, 2000—). Democrat. Methodist. Avocations: collecting antiques, china, glassware, furniture. Home: 1724 Sandy Ln Carlsbad NM 88220-8821

SANDFORD, VIRGINIA ADELE, motivational speaker, writer; b. Tacoma, Nov. 29, 1926; d. Fred John and Lucille Lillian (Skok) Wepfer; m. Calvert H. Sandford, Sept. 16, 1949 (div. 1970); children: Susan L., Kaye E., James C. Student, U. Wash., 1946-49. Tchr. stringed instruments dept. music Puyallup (Wash.) Sch. Dist., 1944-46; sec. Fife (Wash.) Sch. Dist., 1969-72; exec. sec. Tacoma (Wash.) Sch. Dist., 1972-75; tchr. ednl. sec. program Clover Park Vocat. Tech. Inst., Tacoma, 1975-82; profl. spkr., seminar prodr. Virginia Sandford & Assocs., Tacoma, 1982—. Author: You Can't Smell the Roses When You're Pushing Up Daisies, 2001. Violinist, Tacoma Symphony, 1972-75. Mem. Am. Vocat. Assn., Wash. Vocat. Assn., Ednl. Office Personnel, Nat. Spkrs. Assn., Pacific N.W. Spkrs. Assn., Alpha Chi Omega. E-mail: vsandford@nventure.com.

SANDIDGE, JUNE CAROL, retired physical education educator; b. Lynchburg, Va., Mar. 16, 1936; d. Fred Brown and Sarah Elizabeth (Cocks) S. BS, Longwood Coll., Farmville, Va., 1959; MEd, U. Va., 1967; cert. advanced grad. studies, Va. Tech. Inst., 1981. Tchr. Roanoke (Va.) City Schs., 1959-65; prof. phys. edn. and recreation Ferrum (Va.) Coll., 1965-2001, mem. emeritus faculty, 2003—. Asst. dir. YWCA Camp-on-Craig, Roanoke, 1965-83, dir., 1984-85; interim dir. Henry Forks Svc. Ctr., United Meth. Ch., Rocky Mount, Va., 1986-87, chair bd., 1989-91, cons. ARC, Roanoke, 1986-90, chair S.W. Va. territory, 1988-91, chair Va./D.C. field svc., 1992-95. Recipient Disting. Service Alumni award Longwood Coll., 1984, Honor award for vol. svc. ARC, 1982, Sl. Citation II for exceptional vol. svc. Roanoke Valley chpt. ARC, 2003; inductee Ferrum Coll. Sports Hall of Fame, 2002. Mem. AAUW, AAHPERD, Va. Assn. Health, Phys. Edn., Recreation and Dance (rep. aquatic coun. so. dist. 1991-93), Coun. Nat. Coop. Aquatics, Phi Delta Kappa. Baptist. Home: 437 Hedgelawn Ave Roanoke VA 24019

SANDLER, JULIA ANN, special education educator; b. Passaic, N.J., May 21, 1955; d. Elio and Beatrice Lee (Bernstein) Cohen; m. David Mark Sandler, June 8, 1980; children: Danielle, Scott, Sarah. BS tchr. handicapped (K-12), Trenton State Coll., 1977; cert. nursery sch., Kean Coll., 1979. Tchr. Berkeley Heights (N.J.) Pub. Schs., 1978-79; tchr. pre-sch. Summit (N.J.) Child Care Ctr., 1979; tchr. spl. edn. Cerebral Palsy Assn., Edison, N.J., 1979-86; day care dir. Discovery Time Day Care Ctr., Bensalem, Pa., 1987; resource rm. tchr., spl. edn. coord. Abrams Hebrew Acad., Yardley, Pa., 1990-97; resource ctr. tchr./coord. Trenton (N.J.) Comty. Charter Sch., 1997—. Summer program coord. Cerebral Palsy Assn., Edison, 1981; family day care provider, Newtown, Pa., 1988-91; ednl. v.p. Strausfogel Religious Sch. for Ahavath Israel Congregation, Trenton, 1992-93. Avocations: local travel, reading, baking, creative writing. Home: 302 Wexley Dr Newtown PA 18940-1661

SANDLER, ROSS, law educator; b. Milw., Jan. 31, 1939; s. Theodore T. and Laurette (Simons) S.; m. Alice R. Mintzer, Sept. 15, 1968; children: Josephine, Jenny, Dorothy. AB, Dartmouth Coll., 1961; LLB, NYU, 1965. Bar: N.Y. 1965, Fla. 1965. Assoc. atty. Cahill Gordon Reindel & Ohl, N.Y.C., 1965-68; asst. U.S. atty. So. Dist. N.Y., 1968-72; assoc. atty. Trubin Sillcocks Edelman & Knapp, N.Y.C., 1972-75; sr. staff atty. Natural Resources Def. Coun., N.Y.C., 1975-81, 83-86; spl. advisor to mayor City of N.Y., 1981-82; exec. dir. Hudson River Found., N.Y.C., 1983-86; commr. N.Y.C. Dept. Transp., 1986-90; ptnr. Jones Day Reavis & Pogue, N.Y.C., 1991-93; law prof. N.Y. Law Sch., 1993—, dir. Ctr. for N.Y.C. law, 1993—; pres. N.Y. Legis. Svc., 1998—. Mem. N.Y.C. Procurement Policy Bd., 1994—; vis. lectr. Yale Law Sch., New Haven, 1977; adj. prof. law NYU Law Sch., 1976-94; chair, mem. N.Y.C. Taxi and Limousine Commn., 1980-90. Co-author: A New Direction in Transit, 1978, Democracy by Decree, 2003; columnist Environ. Mag., 1976—80; editor: (jour.) City Law; contbr. chapters to books, articles. Trustee Woods Hole (Mass.) Rsch. Ctr., 1983—; mem. exec. com. Hudson River Found., 1986-96; mem. adv. coun. Ctr. Biodiversity and Conservation Am. Mus. Nat. History, 1996—. Recipient Pub. Interest award NYU Law Alumni, 1987, Louis J. Lefkowitz award Fordham Law Sch. Urban Law Jour., 1989, Lifetime Achievement award N.Y. State Bar Assn., 1998. Mem. City Club of N.Y. (chair 1992-93, trustee). Office: NY Law Sch 57 Worth St New York NY 10013-2959

SANDLER, STANLEY IRVING, chemical engineering educator; b. N.Y.C., June 10, 1940; s. Murray C. and Celia M. (Kamenetsky) S.; m. Judith Katherine Ungar, June 17, 1962; children: Catherine Julietta, Joel Abraham, Michael Howard. BChemE, CCNY, 1962; PhD, U. Minn., 1966. NSF postdoctoral fellow Inst. Molecular Physics, U. Md., College Park, 1966-67; successively asst. prof., assoc. prof., prof. dept. chem. engring. U. Del., Newark, 1967-82, H.B. du Pont prof., 1982-2000, chmn. dept., 1982-86, dir. Ctr. for Molecular and Engring. Thermodynamics, 1992—, interim dean Coll. of Engring., 1992, H.B. duPont chair, 2000—. Vis. prof. Imperial Coll., London, 1973—74, U. Nat. del Sur, Bahia Blanca, Argentina, 1985, Tech. U., Berlin, 1981, Berlin, 1988—89, U. Queensland, Brisbane, Australia, 1989, Brisbane, 96, U. Calif., Berkeley, 1995, U. Melbourne, Australia, 2003; cons. maj. oil and chem. cos. Author: Chemical and Engineering Thermodynamics, 1977, 3d rev. edit., 1998, Modeling Vapor-Liquid Equilibrium, 1998; editor: Fluid Properties and Phase Equilibria, 1977, Chemical Engineering Education in a Changing Environment, 1989, Kinetic and Thermodynamic Lumping of Multicomponent Mixtures, 1991, Models for Thermodynamic and Phase Equilibria Calculations, 1993, AI Chem E. Jour., 2000—; mem. adv. bd. Jour. Chem. Engring. Data, Chem. Engring. Edn., Indsl. Engring. Chem. Rsch., Indian Chem. Engr., Engring. Sci. and Tech. (Malaysia); also numerous articles. Mem. adv. bd. chem. engring. La. State U., Carnegie-Mellon U., Princeton U. Recipient U.S. sr. Scientist award Alexander von Humboldt Found., 1988, Francis Alison award U. Del., 1993, Ashton Cary award Ga. Tech. U., 1994, Phillips Lecture award Okla. State U., 1993, Rossini Lectureship award Internat. Union Pure Applied Chemistry, 1998; Miegunyah fellowship, U. Melbourne, Australia, 2003. Mem. AIChE (jour. adv. bd., editor 2000—, Profl. Progress award 1984, Warren K. Lewis award 1996, Del. Soc. award 1998), U.S. Nat. Acad. Engring., Am. Chem. Soc. (award Del. sect. 1989, E.V. Murphree award 1997), Am. Soc. Engring. Edn. (lectr. chem. engring. div. 1988), Cosmos Club (Washington). Jewish. Avocations: jogging, philately. Home: 202 Sypherd Dr Newark DE 19711-3627 Office: U Del Dept Chem Engring Newark DE 19716 E-mail: sandler@udel.edu.

SANDLER, TODD MICHAEL, economist, educator, political scientist, educator; b. Mt. Kisco, N.Y., Dec. 16, 1946; s. Louis and Susie Sandler; m. Jean Marie Murdock, June 28, 1985; 1 child, Tristan Jon. BA, SUNY, Binghamton, 1968, MA, 1969, PhD, 1971. Asst. prof. Ariz. State U., Tempe, 1971-76; assoc. prof. U. Wyo., Laramie, 1976-79, prof., 1979-85, U. S.C., Columbia, 1985-86; prof. econs. and polit. sci. Iowa State U., Ames, 1986-2000, Disting. prof., 1995—2001; Dockson prof. U. So. Calif., L.A., 2000—. Author: Collective Action: Theory and Applications, 1992, Global Challenges, 1997, Economic Concepts for the Social Sciences, 2001; co-author: The Theory of Externalities, Public Goods and Club Goods, 1986, The Economics of Defense, 1995, (book) The Theory of Externalities, Public Goods and Club Goods, 2d edit., 1996, International Terrorism in 1980s, 1989, The Political Economy of NATO, 1999, The Future of Development Assistance: Common Pools and International Public Goods, 1999, Regional Public Goods: Typologies, Provision, Financing, and Development Assistance, 2002; co-editor: Defense Economics, 1989—94, Handbook of Defense Economics, 1995; assoc. editor: Jour. Environ. Econs. and Mgmt., 1988—89, Jour. Pub. Econ. Theory, 1999—, mem. editl. bd.: Social Sci. Quar., Pub. Fin. Rev., Fiscal Studies, Bull. Econ. Rsch., Internat. Studies Quar., spl. adv. editor: Def. and Peace Econs., 2000—. Co-recipient Rsch. Related to Prevention of Nuc. War award, Nat. Acad. of Scis., 2003; fellow NATO postdoctoral, 1977, 1998—2000, Australian Nat. U., 1981, 1994, Sr., Inst. Policy Reform, 1990—91, 1992—94, Hon., U. Wis.-Madison, 1990; grantee NSF, 1989, 1993. Mem.: Pub. Choice Soc., So. Econ. Assn., Assn. Environ. and Resource Econs. (editl. bd.), Royal Econ. Soc., Am. Econ. Assn., Internat. Def. Econs. Assn. (exec. bd.). Office: U So Calif Sch Internat Rels Los Angeles CA 90089 E-mail: tsandler@usc.edu.

SANDMAN, PETER M. risk communication consultant, speaker; b. N.Y.C., Apr. 18, 1945; s. Howard Edwin and Gertrude Leah (Orgel) S.; m. Susan Marie Goertzel, June 18, 1967 (div. 1975); m. Jody Sue Lanard, June 10, 1990; children: Alison, Jennifer; 1 stepchild, James Sachs. BA in Psychology, Princeton U., 1967; MA in Comm., Stanford U., 1968, PhD, 1971. Reporter Toronto (Ont.) Star, Can., 1966; stringer Time, 1966-67; instr. comm. Stanford (Calif.) U., 1968-70; instr. journalism Calif. State Coll., Hayward, 1970; sr. editor The Magazine, 1970; asst. prof. Ohio State U., Columbus, 1971-72; asst. prof. natural resources, journalism U. Mich., Ann Arbor, 1972-75, assoc. prof. natural resources, 1975-77; assoc. prof. comm., coord. Cook Coll. comm. program Rutgers U., New Brunswick, N.J., 1977-83, prof. journalism, 1983-94, prof. dept. human ecology, 1992-94; adj. prof., 1994—. Adj. prof. TV, radio Ithaca (N.Y.) Coll., 1976, grad. program in pub. health Rutgers U., 1986—, dept. environ. and cmty. medicine Robert Wood Johnson Med. Sch., Rutgers U., 1987—; adv. com. environ./occupl. health info. program 1984-89; founder, dir. environ. comm. rsch. program N.J. Agrl. Exptl. Sta., Rutgers U., 1986-92; vis. scholar urban and environ. policy Tufts U., Medford, Mass., 1990-91; rsch. prof. George Perkins Marsh Inst., Clark U.; comm. coun. Environ. Def. Fund, 1985—; bd. advisors grad. program in tech. and sci. comm. Drexel U., Phila., 1988—; cons. on comm. ACP, 1976-79, The Cousteau Soc., 1977-79, Pres. Com. on the Accident at Three Mile Island; specialist in comm. coop. ext. svc. U.S. Dept. Agr., 1977-86; cons. risk commn. office policy analysis EPA, 1986-88; exec. com. Sci. Writing Educators Group, 1978-81; cons. ARCO Chem., Boise Cascade, Chevron, Ciba-Geigy, Consumers Power, Dow, Du Pont, Johnson and Johnson, Johnson Wax, Procter and Gamble, Union Carbide, others. Cons. editor Random House, 1982-89, McGraw-Hill, 1989-94, Holt, Rinehart and Winston, 1978-81; contbg. editor Apt. Life, 1971-75; freelance writer, 1966—; editl. bd. Pub. Rels. Rsch. Ann., 1981-91, Jour. Pub. Rels. Rsch., 1991-94; editl. adv. bd. Environ. and Behavior, 1976-86; contbr. articles to profl. jours. Bd. dirs. N.J. Environ. Lobby, 1984-90, Nuclear Dialogue Project, 1985-90, pres. 1986-90; pub. info. com. N.J. chpt., Am. Cancer Soc., 1981-86, vice-chmn., 1983-86; comm. coord. N.J. Campaign for a Nuclear Weapons Freeze, 1982-85; socioeconomic subcom., com. on biotechnology agr. divsn. Nat. Assn. State Univs. and Land Grant Colls., 1988-90; bd. advisors Environ. Scientists for Global Survival, 1988-91; sci. review panel, radium/radon adv. bd. N.J. Dept. Environ. Protection, 1987-88; com. to survey the health effects mustard gas and lewisite Inst. Medicine, NAS, 1992. Mem. AAUP, ACLU (bd. dirs. N.J. chpt. 1984-87), Environ. Def. Fund, Nat. Assn. Profl. Environ. Communicators, Sci. Writing Educators Group, Soc. for Risk Analysis, Soc. Environ. Journalists, Internat. Assn. Pub. Participation Practitioners, Sigma Delta Chi. Home: 59 Ridgeview Rd Princeton NJ 08540-7601 Fax: 609 683-0566. E-mail: peter@psandman.com.

SANDONATO, ERNEST R. English language educator; b. Elizabethtown, N.J., Apr. 6, 1962; s. Ernest R. and Barbara A. (Eigner) S.; m. Diane Doran, Mar. 30, 1990. BA, NYU, 1984, postgrad., 1991—. Cert. tchr., N.J. Tchr. English Delbarton Sch., Morristown, N.J., 1984—, head soccer coach, 1989-92. Soccer clinician Tournament of Champions, Spl. Olympics, Somerset County, N.J., 1989-92. Named Morris County Coach of Yr. Star Ledger newspaper, Newark, 1989. Mem. Nat. Coun. Tchrs. English, N.J. State Coaches Assn., Morris Soccer Coaches Assn. (sec. 1992—). Democrat. Roman Catholic. Avocations: fishing, music, cooking, running, travel. Home: 103 Mills St Morristown NJ 07960-3723

SANDOVAL, ISABELLE MEDINA, education educator; b. Laramie, Wyo., Sept. 30, 1948; d. John Ben and Ida Medina Sandoval; 1 child, Tomas Andres Duran. BA, U. N.Mex., 1970; MA, U. Mo., 1976; EdD, U. Wyo., 1982. Cert. Spanish, reading, English, adminstrn. Tchr. Spanish and English Menaul Sch., Albuquerque, 1971-73; tchr. bilingual edn. and reading Kansas City, Mo., 1973-78; tchr. title I Sch. Dist. #60, Pueblo, Colo., 1978-83, adminstr., 1983-88, Acad. Dist. 20, Colorado Springs, Colo., 1988-95; human resources coord. Harrison Dist. 2, Colorado Springs, 1995-98; prof. education Coll. of Santa Fe, N.Mex. V.p. Hispano Crypto Jewish Resource Ctr., Denver. Author numerous poems. Pres. South Holman Domestic Water Assn. Mem. Geneal. Soc. Hispanic Am., Hispanic Geneal. Rsch. Ctr. N.Mex., Mana del Norte, Olibama Lopez Tushar Hispanic Legacy Rsch. Ctr., N.M. Jewish Hist. Soc. (bd. dirs.), N.Mex. Acequia Assn., N.Mex. Land Grant Forum, Soc. for Crypto Judaic Studies, Nat. Assn. Sephardic Artists, Writers and Intellectuals, LaSallian Leadership (bd. dirs.), Phi Kappa Phi, Kappa Delta Phi, Phi Delta Kappa. Jewish. Avocations: writing poetry, researching family history and hispano jewish materials. Home: 4358 Lost Feather Santa Fe NM 87507-2580 Office: Coll of Santa Fe 1600 Saint Michaels Dr Santa Fe NM 87505-7615

SANDOVAL, MONA LISA, daycare provider, educator; b. Wilmington, Calif., Aug. 2, 1965; d. Alfred Rudy and Lita Candelaria (Machado) S. AA, Trinidad State Jr. Coll., 1992, 1993. Tchr. asst. Trinidad (Colo.) State Jr. Coll., 1992-93; infant/toddler tchr. Alta Vista Preschool, Trinidad, 1993; preschool tchr. Headstart, Trinidad, 1994—. Mem. Child Daycare Task Force, Trinidad, 1992-93; participant Workshop in Early Child Devel., Trinidad, 1993. Editor: (newspaper) Trojan Tribune, 1993, cartoonist, 1992-93. Rep. State Supervisory Adv., Denver, 1993, State Bd. for C.C.s, Denver, 1992-93. Recipient scholarship in edn., Delta Kappa Gamma, 1991, sign lang. tng., Amy Martin, Trinidad State, 1994. Mem. ASCD, Colo. Assn. for Edn. Young Children. Democrat. Roman Catholic. Avocations: sign language, spl. edn., children's book writer. Office: Headstart PO Box 42 Trinidad CO 81082-0042

SANDRY, KARLA KAY FOREMAN, industrial engineering educator; b. Davenport, Iowa, Apr. 2, 1961; d. Donald Glen and Greta Geniveve (VanderMaten) Foreman; m. William James Sandry, Oct. 12, 1985; children: Zachary Quinn, Skyler David, Andrew Trey. BS in Indsl. Engring., Iowa State U., 1983; MBA, U. Iowa, 1992. Quality control supr., indsl. engr. Baxter Travenol Labs, Hays, Kans., 1983-84; indsl. engr. HQ Amccom, Rock Island, Ill., 1984-86; mgmt. engr. St. Lukes Hosp., Davenport, 1986-90. Adj. instr. engring. St. Ambrose U., Davenport, 1990—; chair space allocations St. Luke's Hosp., Davenport, 1987-90; pres. employee rels. coun. HQ Amccom, Rock Island, 1986, chair savings bonds, 1985; speaker in field. Vol., past counselor Fellowship Christian Athletes Ctrl. H.S., Davenport, 1984-87, vol., adult chpt., 1988-90; counselor Explorer Scout Troop, Davenport, 1984-85; leader, counselor ch. youth group, 1985-89; v.p., bd. dirs. Crisis Pregnancy Ctr., 1996-98, pres. bd. dirs., 1998, co-chmn. walkathon, 1996, pres. ch. choir, 1992, 95-96, bible study fellowship, 1996—, discussion leader bible study fellowship 2000—, orch. ch., 1994-2000, fin. com. 1995, 97-98, dream team, 1996, security com. 1996, prayer com., 1995, 97, co-lead moms group, 1992-97, choir ch. 1984—. Mem. Healthcare Info. & Mgmt. Systems Soc. (recognition & comms. com. 1988), Soc. for Health Systems (founding mem.), Found. for Christian Living, Iowa State U. Alumni Assn., U. Iowa Alumni Assn., Positive Thinkers Club, Beta Gamma Sigma. Avocations: vocalist, tennis, golf, violinist, playing with sons.

SANDS, AMY CATHERINE, nursing administrator, educator; b. Rochester, Minn., Mar. 16, 1968; d. Byron James and Lorraine Ann (Volmer) Reha; m. Todd Michael Sands, June 22, 1991; children: Jessica, Emily. BA in Nursing, Luther Coll., 1990. RN, Minn. Pediatric nurse, RN United Med. Ctr., Moline, Ill., 1990-92; pediatric home care RN Kimberly Quality Care, Moline, 1990-92; asst. DON Samaritan Bethany Home Health Svcs., Rochester, 1992—; program coord. 25 Hour Home Health Aide Tng. Program, 1995—. Home health aide instr. Riverland Tech. Coll., Rochester, 1992—, alt. adv. bd., 1993—, cert. nursing asst., home health aide state examiner, 1994—; asst. dir. tng., program coord., cons. Samaritan Bethany Home Health Svcs., 1994—; program coord. home health aide-nurse asst. tng. program Minn. Home Care Agy. Program, 1994—; instr., coord. care giver classes to Rochester Cmty. Fellowship vol. Zumbro Luth. Ch., Rochester, 1993—. Recipient Small Bus. award Rochester C. of C., 1994. Mem. Minn. Home Care Assn. Avocations: crafts, hiking, traveling, movies. Home: 1401 48th St NW Rochester MN 55901-0490

SANDS, MIRIAM LINDA, special education educator; b. Claxton, Ga., June 12, 1954; d. Luther and Juanita (Clark) Morris; m. Carson Sands Jr., Mar. 27, 1971; children: Sallie, Charles, Sarah. BS in Edn. magna cum laude, Ga. So. U., 1994. Cert. tchr., Ga. Tchr. Meth. Ch., Claxton, 1978-83, Presch. Intervention Program, Collins, Ga., 1989-94; spl. edn. tchr. Claxton Elem. Sch., 1994—. Fellow Coun. for Exceptional Children, Ga. Assn. Educators, Phi Kappa Phi. Republican. Baptist. Avocation: writing short stories. Home: PO Box 26 Daisy GA 30423-0026

SANDT, JOHN JOSEPH, psychiatrist, educator; b. N.Y.C., June 29, 1925; s. John Jacob and Victoria Theodora Sandt; m. Mary Cummings Evans, Sept. 14, 1946; children: Christine, Karen, John K., Kurt, Colin, Carol; m. Mary W. Griswold, July 10, 1992 (dec. Dec. 1998). BA, Vanderbilt U., 1948; MA, Yale U., 1951; MD, Vanderbilt U., 1957. Instr. English Vanderbilt U., Nashville, 1951-52, Syracuse (N.Y.) U. Coll., 1960-61; intern SUNY Upstate Med. Ctr., Syracuse, 1957-58, resident, 1958-61; instr. psychiatry Southwestern Med. Sch., Dallas, 1961-63; chief psychiatry VA Med. Ctr., Dallas, 1961-63; chief outpatient clinic Dept. Mental Health, Springfield, Mass., 1963-66; asst. prof. psychiatry U. Rochester (N.Y.) Med. Sch., 1966-75, clin. assoc. prof. psychiatry, 1975-98; chief psychiatry Clifton Springs (N.Y.) Hosp., 1985-88, VA Med. Ctr., Bath, N.Y., 1988-96; pvt. practice Hammondsport, N.Y., 1996—. Cons. psychiatry VA Med. Ctr., Northampton, Mass., 1965-66, Springfield Coll., 1964-66, Brockport (N.Y.) State Coll., 1966-75, Fairport (N.Y.) Bapt. Home, 1966-88; asst. dir. ind. study program U. Rochester Med. Sch., 1971-75. Author: Clinical Supervision of Psychiatric Resident, 1972; contbr. articles to profl. jours. Vestryman All Saints Episcopal Ch., South Hadley, Mass., 1963-66. With USNR 1944-46, PTO. Nathaniel Currier fellow Yale Grad. Sch., 1948-49. Mem. AAAS, Am. Psychiat. Assn.

SANDWEISS, JACK, physicist, educator; b. Chgo., Aug. 19, 1930; s. Charles Ray and Florence (Hymovitz) S.; m. Letha Ann Boeck, Jan. 16, 1956; children: Daniel Howard, Anne Florence, Benjamin Lewis. Student, UCLA, 1948-50; BS, U. Calif., Berkeley, 1952, PhD, 1957. Research assoc. Radiation Lab., U. Calif., Berkeley, 1957; instr. Yale U., New Haven, 1957-59, asst. prof., 1959-62, assoc. prof., 1962-64, prof. physics, 1964—, Donner prof. physics, 1980—, former chmn. dept. physics. Cons. Brookhaven Nat. Lab., Fermi Nat. Accelerator Lab.; chmn. high energy physics adv. panel Dept. Energy-NSF, 1982-86. Editor Phys. Rev. Letters, 1988—; contbr. articles to profl. jours. Fellow Am. Phys. Soc. (chmn. div. particles and fields 1980); mem. NAS, AAAS. Home: 248 Ogden St New Haven CT 06511-1221 Office: Yale Univ Physics Dept Sloane Physics Lab PO Box 2081-21 New Haven CT 06520-8121 E-mail: sandweiss@hepmail.physics.yale.edu.

SANDWELL, KRISTIN ANN, special education educator; b. Topeka, Kans., Jan. 13, 1955; d. Edwin C. and E. Maxine (Nelson) Henry; m. Steve Sandwell, Dec. 27, 1997; children: Dustin Grimm, Chris Creek, Brandon Grimm, Sarah Sandwell, Paul Sandwell. AA, Hutchinson (Kans.) C.C., 1986; BS, McPherson (Kans.) Coll., 1989; MEd, Wichita State U., 1992. Cert. tchr. elem., gifted. Math/parenting tchr. Flint Hills Job Corps Ctr., Manhattan, Kans., 1992; gifted facilitator Unified Sch. Dist. 353, Wellington, Kans., 1993-94, Unified Sch. Dist. 260, Derby, Kans., 1995-97; tchr. City of Wichita Summer Youth Employment Program-Edn., 1997—98; gifted facilitator Unified Sch. Dist. 259, 1998—. Head injury counselor, life skills trainer Three Rivers Ind. Living Ctr., Wamego, Kans., 1992; facilitator Summer Youth Employment Edn. Program, 1997-98. Epiphany Festival prodr. Trinity Luth. Ch., McPherson, 1991, 93; CASA organizer McPherson Coll., 1988-89; vol. Coun. on Violence Against Persons, McPherson, 1990-92. Mem. ASCD. Avocations: reading, travel, working with disability issues. E-mail: ksandwell@yahoo.com., ksandwell@usd259.net.

SANDY, STEPHEN, writer, educator; b. Aug. 2, 1934; s. Alan Francis and Evelyn Brown (Martin) S.; m. Virginia Scoville, 1969; children: Nathaniel Merrill, Clare Scoville. AB, Yale U., 1955; AM, Harvard U., 1958, PhD, 1963. Instr. Harvard U., 1963-67; vis. prof. U. Tokyo, 1967-68; asst. prof. Brown U., Providence, 1968-69; mem. faculty Bennington (Vt.) Coll., 1969—2002; McGee prof. writing Davidson (N.C.) Coll., 1994. Lectr. U. R.I., 1969; prof. Summer Sch. Harvard U., 1986, 87, 88; poetry workshop dir. Chautauqua Instn., 1975, 77, Johnson (Vt.) State Coll., 1976, 77, Bennington Coll., 1978-80, 89, Bennington Writing Seminars Program, 1994-96, Wesleyan Writers Conf., 1981. Author: Stresses in the Peaceable Kingdom, 1967, Roofs, 1971, End of the Picaro, 1977, The Hawthorne Effect, 1980, The Raveling of the Novel: Studies in Romantic Fiction from Walpole to Scott, 1980, Riding to Greylock, 1983, To a Mantis, 1987, Man in the Open Air, 1988, The Epoch, 1990, Thanksgiving Over the Water, 1992; translator: Seneca's Hercules Oetaeus, 1995, Vale of Academe A Prose Poem for Bernard Malamud, 1996, Marrow Spoon, 1997, Aeschylus's Seven Against Thebes, 1998, The Thread, New and Selected Poems, 1998, Black Box, 1999, Surface Impressions:A Poem, 2002. Councillor English Harvard Grad. Soc. Coun., 1969-74. With U.S. Army, 1955-57. Recipient Fulbright postdoctoral award, 1967-68; Dexter fellow, 1961, Yaddo fellow, 1963-68, 76, 93, 97, 98, 00, 02, Invited Poetry fellow Breadloaf Writers Conf., 1968, Ingram Merrill Found. fellow, 1985, MacDowell Colony fellow, 1986, 93, Blue Mt. Ctr. fellow, 1985, 88, Creative Writing fellow Nat. Endowment Arts, 1988, Vt. Coun. Arts fellow, 1988—, Sr. fellow Provincetown Fine Arts Work Ctr., 1998, Rockefeller Found. residency Bellagio Study and conf. ctr., 2001, Huber Found. grantee, 1973, Vt. Coun. Arts grantee, 1974; nominee for Pulitzer Prize, 1971; named Phi Beta Kappa Poet, Brown U., 1959, Yale U., 2003. Mem. Signet Soc., Elizabethan Club.

SANFORD, DELORES MAE, retired elementary school educator, assistant principal; b. Hull, Iowa, Feb. 18, 1931; d. Elmer Richard and Martha Marie (De Smet) Remmerde (div.); children: Bonnie Senescall, Debra Blackburn, Donn Bosler; m. Dayton Sanford, June 16, 1979 (dec. Feb. 26, 1997); m. Madison Walker, July 10, 1999. BS in Elem. Edn., Augustana Coll., Sioux Falls, SD, 1967; MS in Elem. Adminstrn., SD State U., 1973. K-8 tchr. Alvord Lyon County Rural Schs., Rock Rapids, 1950-58; elem. tchr. Cen. Lyon Sch. Dist., Rock Rapids, 1960-62; elem. tchr., asst. prin. Brandon Valley Schs., Valley Springs, SD, 1966-90, ret., 1990. Developer workshop for tchrs., 1990. Mem. Am. Bus. Women's Assn. (pres. Sioux Falls 1985-86, Woman of Yr. award 1986), Augustana Coll. (auxilliary 1992—) Democrat. Roman Cath. Avocations: sewing, cake decorating. Home: 1404 S Snowberry Trl Sioux Falls SD 57106-3346

SANFORD, WILBUR LEE, retired elementary education educator; b. Lexington, Ky., Aug. 2, 1935; s. Lloyd Daniel and Catherine (Kirtley) S.; m. Dorothy Moore; children: James, Venessa. BA, Ky. State Coll., 1958; MA in Adminstrn., Xavier U., 1969, cert. elem. counselor, 1973. Cert. elem. counselor, Ohio; cert. elem. tchr. and prin., Ohio. Elem. tchr. North Coll. Hill (Ohio) Sch., 1960-65, Cin. Pub. Schs., 1965-73, St. Joseph Elem. Sch., Cin., 1993—; adminstrv. intern Cin. Pub. Schs., 1983-85, asst. prin., 1975-80, elem. prin., 1980-92; ret. Cons. PTA, Cin., 1989-92, GED program, Cin., 1990-91; prin./instrnl. leader Windsor Sch. Meritorious Achievement, Cin., 1985-86; dir. After Sch. Evening Tutorial, Cin., 1988-92. Leader 4-H Club, Cin., 1991-92, Boy Scouts Am., Cin., 1985-89; mem. Walnut Hills Victory Community Coun., Cin., 1985-89, Avondale Community Coun., Cin., 1990-92; mem. Sinai Temple. Recipient Notable Recognition award Youth Crime Intervention, Cin., 1991, Community Svc. award So. Bapt. Ch., Cin., 1991, Outstanding Svc. award Cincinnatians Active to Support Edn., 1989. Mem. Ohio Assn. Elem. Sch. Adminstrs. (Exemplary Svc. award 1987), Cin. Assn. Adminstrs. and Suprs., Cin. Assn. Elem. Prins. Democrat. Methodist. Avocations: music, reading, dancing, gardening, traveling. Home: 6748 Stoll Ln Cincinnati OH 45236-4039

SANFTNER, TAMMY JEAN, secondary school educator; b. Fridley, Minn., July 28, 1977; d. Sanftner Leo Vernon, Jean Burg. BA, U. No. Iowa, 1999. Lic. sec. lang. arts tchr., CPR Red Cross, cert. lifeguard, water safety instr. Camp counselor Des Moines YMCA Camp, Boone, Iowa, 1992—99; life guard, swimming instr. Black Hawk YMCA, Waterloo, Iowa, 1997—99; tchr. Dallas Ctr. Grimes Schs., 2000—02; waitress Vieux Carre, Des Moines, 2001—; tchr. Guamani Pvt. Sch., Guayama, PR, 2002—. Substitute tchr. Waukee Cmty. Schs., 1999—2000; swimming instr. YMCA, Waukee, 2001—. Roman Catholic. Avocations: travel, swimming, bicycling, rollerblading, hiking. Home and Office: Guamani Pvt Sch PO Box 3000 Guayama PR 00785 Home: 4328 98th St Urbandale IA 50322

SANKARAN, HARIKUMAR, finance educator; b. Madras, Tamilnadu, India, July 20, 1959; s. Narayanaswamy and Vasantha Sankaran; m. Jayashree Krishnan, July 4, 1988; 1 child, Sanjiv. BA in econ., Madras U., 1975—78; MBA, Xavier Labour Rels. Inst., Jamshedpur, India, 1978—80;

PhD, U. Houston, 1982—87. Cert. Online Instr. The Walden Inst., 2000. Fin. officer Assoc. Cement Cos., Bombay, 1980—82; asst. prof. fin. U. Miami, Coral Gables, 1987—91; prof. fin. U. Alaska - Fairbanks, 1991—2001; assoc. prof. fin. N.Mex State U., Las Cruces, 2002—. MBA dir. U. Alaska - Fairbanks, 1998—2000. Contbr. articles to profl. jours. Mem.: Am. Fin. Assn. Home: 2224 47th St Los Alamos NM 87544

SANKOVITZ, JAMES LEO, retired development director, lobbyist; b. St. Paul, July 3, 1934; s. John L. and Mabel A. (Hanrahan) S.; m. Margaret E. Mathews, Aug. 3, 1957; children: Richard, Therese, Patrick, Margaret, Katherine. BS in Journalism, Marquette U., 1956; MA in Speech, U. Denver, 1963. Dir. pub. rels. Coll. of St. Mary of the Wasatch, Salt Lake City, 1956-57; dir. pub. info. Colo. Sch. of Mines, Golden, 1957-63; assoc. dir. devel. Marquette U., Milw., 1963-66, dir. alumni fund, 1966-67, dir. alumni rels., 1967-69, asst. v.p. univ. rels., 1969-70, v.p. univ. rels., 1970-78, v.p. govtl. rels., 1978-86, v.p. govtl. and community affairs, 1986-97; ret., 1997. Contbr. articles to profl. jours. Founding dir. Univ. Nat. Bank, Milw., 1971-74; bd. dirs. St. Coletta Sch., Jefferson, Wis., 1970-76, 86-93, chair, 1974-76. Mem. Nat. Assn. for Ind. Colls. and Univs. (bd. dirs. Washington 1986-90), Disting. Svc. award 1986), Assn. Jesuit Colls. and Univs. (fed. affairs cons. Washington 1974-90), Assn. Cath. Colls. and Univs. (fed. affairs cons. Washington 1974-85, Blue Key, Alpha Sigma Nu. Roman Catholic. Avocations: woodworking, reading. Home: 4057 N Prospect Ave Milwaukee WI 53211-2121 E-mail: jsankovitz@wi.rr.com.

SANNEH, LAMIN, religion educator; married; 2 children. MA in Arabic and Islamic Studies, U. Birmingham, Eng., 1968; postgrad., Near East Sch. Theology, Beirut, 1968-69; PhD in African Islamic History, U. London, 1974. Resident tutor Ctr. for Study of Islam and Christianity, Ibadan, Nigeria, 1969-71; vis. scholar U. Sierra Leone, Freetown, 1974-75; lectr. U. Ghana, Legon, 1975-78, U. Aberdeen, Scotland, 1978-81; from asst. prof. to assoc. prof. history of religion Harvard U., Cambridge, Mass., 1981-89; prof., chmn. Coun. on African Studies Yale U., New Haven, 1989—. Cons. World Coun. Chs., 1974-79, The Africans TV series, PBS, 1986, Program on Christian-Muslim Rels. in Africa, 1988—, Prof. Lamin Sanneh Found., Banjul, The Gambia; instr. San Francisco Theol. Sem., San Anselmo, Calif., 1987, Iliff Sch. Theology, Denver, 1988, lectr. Mennonite Brethern Bible Coll., 1988, Princeton (N.J.) Theol. Sem., 1988; guest lectr. Haverford (Pa.) Coll., 1988; Mars lectr. Northwestern U., 1988, Spriggs lectr. Protestant Episcopal Theol. Sem., Alexandria, Va., 1990; Cullum lectr. Augusta Coll., U. Ga., 1990; mem. Clare Hall, Cambridge (Eng.) U., 1995; Sprunt lectr. Va. Union. Theol. Sem., 1999. Author: West African Christianity: The Religious Impact, 1983, Translating the Message: The Missionary Impact on Culture, 1989, The Jakhanke Muslim Clerics: A Religious and Historical Study of Islam in Senegambia (c. 1250-1905), 1990, Encountering the West: Christianity and the Global Cultural Process, 1993, The Crown and the Turban, 1997, Piety and Power: Muslims and Christians in West Africa, 1996, Faith and Power: Christianity and Islam in "Secular" Britain, 1998, Abolitionists Abroad: American Blacks and the Making of Modern West Africa, 1999, Whose Religion is Christianity, 2003, also articles; co-editor Jour. Religion in Africa, 1979-84; mem. adv. bd. Studies in Interreligious Dialogue; editor-at-large The Christian Century; contbg. editor Internat. Bull. Missionary Rsch. Mem. Coun. of 100 Leaders of the World Econ. Forum, Davos, Switzerland. Decorated comdr. de l'Ordre Nat. du Lion (Senegal); recipient award Theol. Edn. Fund, 1971-74, award U. London, 1972, Carnegie Truste of Univs. of Scotland, 1980. Mem. Am. Theol. Soc., African Theologians (exec. com.), Royal African Soc. Home: 47 Morris St Hamden CT 06517-3426 Office: Yale U Div Sch 409 Prospect St New Haven CT 06511-2167

SANNITO, JUDITH ANN, elementary education educator; b. Moline, Ill., Sept. 1, 1945; d. Milton Conrad and Alice Marie (Baker) Johnson; m. Eugene Herbert Sannito, Aug. 12, 1967 (dec. Feb. 1992); children: Heather, Matthew. BA, Clarke Coll., Dubuque, Iowa, 1967; MA, Western Ill. U., 1977. Lic. tchr., Ill. Tchr., Kirkland, Ill., 1967-68, East Moline, Ill., 1968—2003. Roman Catholic. Avocations: reading, golf.

SANOK, GLORIA, mathematics educator, author; b. Irvington, N.J., Sept. 3, 1928; d. Joseph Roland and Amelia (Campana) Senopole; m. Michael Sanok, Dec. 12, 1953; children: Michael Jr., Leslie Orndorff. AB, Montclair State, 1949; MA, William Paterson Coll., 1969; postgrad., Columbia U., 1970-71, 77-79, U. So. Calif., 1972; PhD, Pacific State U.-Brunel U., London, 1977. Tchr. Union (N.J.) Pub. Schs., 1949-59; tchr. conversational Spanish Union Adult Sch., 1958-66; instr. Secondary Sch. Math. Curriculum Improvement Study Drexel U., Phila., 1974; adj. prof. William Paterson Coll., Wayne, N.J., 1977-80; instr. math. Trinity Coll., Washington, 1980; math. specialist Montclair State, Upper Montclair, 1980-81, 84; instr. math. Inst. for New Tchrs., Rutgers U., New Brunswick, N.J., 1987, 88; tchr. gifted-talented Wayne (N.J.) Pub. Schs., 1982—, tchr. secondary math., Spanish, 1962—, in-svc. instr., 1970—. Cons. N.J. Dept. Edn., Trenton, 1975-85, Nat. Assessment Ednl. Progress, 1990, 92; lectr., tchr., South Africa, Peru, Mex. Recipient Christa McAuliffe award U.S. Dept. Edn., 1987, N.J. Presdl. award for excellence in teaching math., 1987, Gov.'s Tchr.'s Recognition award, 1987, Business Week award, 1992. Mem. Assn. Math. Tchrs. N.J., Nat. Coun. Tchrs. Math. (editorial panel 1978-81), Nat. Coun. Suprs. Math., Pi Lambda Theta. Avocations: studying, writing, traveling, piano. Home: 66 Holiday Dr West Caldwell NJ 07006-7417 Office: Wayne Pub Schs Packanack Sch 190 Oakwood Dr Wayne NJ 07470-5652

SANQUIST, NANCY JOHNSON, facitliy management executive; b. Muncie, Ind., Aug. 31, 1947; d. Charles Elof and Pauline Lydia (Murphy) S.; m. James M. Johnson, Dec. 1988. BA, UCLA, 1970; MA, Bryn Mawr Coll., 1973; MS, Columbia U., 1978. Cert. facilities mgr. Instr. Lafayette Coll., Easton, Pa., 1973-74, Muhlenberg Coll., Bethlehem, Pa., 1974-75, Northampton Area Community Coll., Bethlehem, 1974-75; dir. Preservation Office City of Easton, 1977-78; cons. El Pueblo de Los Angeles State Historic Park, 1978-79; dir. restoration Bixby Ranch Co., Long Beach, Calif., 1979-82; mgr. computer applications Cannel-Heumann & Assoc., Los Angeles, 1982-84; dir. Computer-Aided Design Group, Marina del Rey, Calif., 1984-93; v.p. PAE Facility Mgmt. Svcs., L.A., 1993—97, Vanderweil Facility Advisors, Boston, 1997—99; dir. strategic initiatives Peregrine Sys., San Diego, 1999—2002; strategic asset mgmt. adv. Autadesk, San Rafael, Calif., 2003—. Adj. instr. UCLA, 1979-86, Grad Sch. Calif. State U., Dominguez Hills, 1981. Author numerous tech. articles and manuals. Bd. dirs. Historic Easton, Inc., 1977-78, Simon Rodia's Towers in Watts, Los Angeles, 1979-81, Los Angeles Conservancy, 1982-86, Friends of Schindler House, West Hollywood, Calif., 1978—, pres., 1982-85. Recipient Outstanding Contbn. award Nat. Computer Graphics Assn., 1987. Fellow Internat. Facility Mgmt. Assn. (seminar leader, lectr. N.Am., Asia, Australia, Europe and Mid. East 1987—); mem. AIA (assoc.). Avocations: travel, art and architecture, photography.

SANSONE, ROSEMARY MARGARET, retired gifted and talented education educator; b. Medina, N.Y., Sept. 19, 1947; d. Leonard Joseph and Mary Elizabeth (Slattery) Matusak; m. James Joseph, Nov. 29, 1969; 1 child, Samantha Ellen. BS in Elem. Edn., SUNY, Brockport, 1969; MS in Elem. Edn., SUNY Coll. at Buffalo, Buffalo, 1973, cert. creative studies, 1987; PhD in Elem. Edn., SUNY, Buffalo, 1994. Elem. tchr. Lockport (N.Y.) Sch. Dist., 1969-81, enrichment tchr., 1987; rsch. asst. early childhood rsch. dept. SUNY, Buffalo, 1987-88; tchr. gifted/talented Lockport (N.Y.) Sch. Dist., 1988—2003. Facilitator lang. arts curriculum devel. Nat. Javits Found., 1991. Contbr. articles on gifted edn. and emerging literacy to profl. jours. Mem. Lockport Cath. Sch. Bd., 1987, Krull Olcott Devel. Com., 2000—; chair Olcott Beach Carousel Park, Inc., 2000—. Tchr. fellow N.Y. State PTA, 1992-93; Internation Women's Decade II honoree, 1995, N.Y. State Senate's Women of Distinction Nominee, 1998. Mem.: Olcott Beach Carousel Pk. Assn. (chmn. 2001—), Advocacy for Gifted and Talented Edn., Elem. Tchrs., Assn. Gifted, Coun. Exceptional Children, Nat. Assn. Gifted Children, Olcott Beach Cmty. Assn. (co-sec. 2001—). Roman Catholic. Avocations: writing, aerobics, boating, reading, researching local history. Home: PO Box 308 5853 Ontario St Olcott NY 14126

SANSTEAD, WAYNE GODFREY, school system administrator; b. Hot Springs, Ark., Apr. 16, 1935; s. Godfrey A. and Clara (Buen) S.; m. Mary Jane Bober, June 16, 1957; children: Timothy, Jonathan. BA in Speech and Polit. Sci, St. Olaf Coll., 1957; MA in Pub. Address, Northwestern U., 1966; Ed.D., U. N.D., 1974. Tchr., Luverne, Minn., 1959-60; dir. forensics Minot (N.D.) High Sch., 1960-71, tchr. social sci., 1960-78; mem. N.D. Ho. of Reps., 1965-70, 83-85, N.D. Senate, 1971-73; lt. gov. N.D. Bismarck, 1973-81; supt. pub. instrn. N.D., Bismarck, 1985—. Served with AUS, 1957-59. Recipient Disting. Alumnus award St. Olaf Coll., 1991; named Outstanding Freshman Senator A.P., 1971, Outstanding Young Educator, N.D. Jr. C. of C., 1967, Outstanding Young Man, Minot Jr. C. of C., 1964; Coe Family Found. scholar, 1963, Eagleton scholar Rutgers U., 1969. Mem. N.D. Edn. Assn., NEA (legis. com. 1969—), Central States Speech Assn., Am. Forensic Assn., Jr. C. of C., Sons of Norway, Elks, Toastmasters. Democrat. Lutheran (Chmn. We. Nd Rsch. And Social Action Com 1962-68). Home: 1120 Columbia Dr Bismarck ND 58504-6514 Office: Dept Pub Instrn 600 E Boulevard Ave Dept 201 Fl 9,10,11 Bismarck ND 58505-0660*

SANTA-COLOMA, BERNARDO, secondary school educator, counselor; b. N.Y.C., May 31, 1934; s. Bernardo Santa-Coloma Sr. and Belma Remotti; m. Sofia A. Santa-Coloma, Dec. 22, 1981; childen: Ananda, Anita. BA in Humanistic Psychology, U. Calif., Santa Cruz, 1973; MA in Integral Counseling Psychology, Calif. Inst. Integral Studies, San Francisco, 1976; MEd in Secondary Edn., U. Nev., Las Vegas, 1979; 3 level cert., Feuerstein's Instrumental, Enrichment Program; postgrad., U. Sarasota and U. Houston. Cert. secondary edn. tchr. ESL, history, English Tex., guidance counselor Tex. Edn. Agy., nat. counselor, lic. marriage and family therapist Tex., profl. counselor Tex. Mem. tchr. corps., vol. VISTA, Las Vegas, Nev., 1976-79; family counselor, English tutor Diocese of Matamoros and Valle Hermoso Tamps, Mexico, Cath. Family Svcs. and Vol. Ednl. and Social Svcs., Amarillo, Tex., 1980-82; grad. asst. Pan Am. U., Brownsville, Tex., 1983-84; at-risk program, low-level reading instr. Brownsville Ind. Sch. Dist., 1984-94; basic skills instr. James Pace High Sch., Brownsville; pres. Alternative Edn. Ctr./Brownsville Ind. Sch. Dist., 1994—. Counselor and psychotherapist Family Effectiveness and Devel. Program, Kids in Crisis, Teenage Crisis Hotline, La Casa Esperanza Home for Boys; basic adult reading instr. Southmost Coll.; ESL, lang. arts tchr. Alternative Ctr.; at-risk tchr., pvt. practice counselor, Brownsville Ind. Sch. Dist. Family Ctrs., 1994—; part-time counselor Holistic Mind and Health Inst., Brownsville, 1998; counselor, psychotherapist, contract worker, counselor supr., chem. dependency counselor Recovery Ctr., Cameron County Housing Authority, 1999-2001, Citadel Group, 2000—; medicaid provider, approved supr. LPC interns, LMFT assocs.; supr. Weslaco, Deer Oaks Mental Health Assocs., 2002—. Contbr. articles to profl. jours. in U.S. and Mex. including Integracion Integral, Journey in Matamoros. Vol. VISTA, 1976-79, VISTA Tchr. Corps, Las Vegas, Peace Corps, Thailand, 1979, Vol. Edn./Soc. Svc., Tex., Mex., 1980-82. With USN, 1952-56, medic neuropsychiatric wards San Diego and Guam. Recipient scholarship U. Calif.-Santa Cruz, 1971-73, U. Nev. tchr. corps scholar, 1977-79; named grad. asst. Calif. Inst. Integral Studies, 1974-76. Home: PO Box 3941 Brownsville TX 78523-3941 also: Country Club 2009 Madero Dr Brownsville TX 78526-1734 Fax: 956-982-2868. E-mail: bsantacoloma@rgv.rr.com.

SANTIAGO, JUAN JOSE, secondary school president; b. San Juan, P.R., July 8, 1931; s. Juan Jose and Mercedes (Asenjo) S. BA and BS, Colegio de Belen, Habana, Cuba, 1957; licensee in philosophy, Cath. U., Quito, Ecuador, 1958; licensee in theology, Woodstock Coll., 1965; D in Missiology, Gregorian U., Rome, 1988. Prof. Interdiocesan Seminary, Aibonito, P.R., 1958-59, Colegio San Ignacio, Rio Piedras, P.R., 1959-61; spiritual dir. Interdiocesan Seminary, Aibonito, 1966-67, Major Seminary, Ponce, P.R., 1967-68; vocation dir. Soc. of Jesus, San Juan, 1969-74; pres. Colegio San Ignacio, Rio Piedras, 1972-78, 88—, prof., 1983-84, prin., 1984-88. Pres. adv. bd. P.R. Symphony Orch., 1986-92. Author: Frutos de Soledad, 1978, Y el rio sigue fluyendo, 1989; contbr. articles to profl. jours. Mem. Am. Soc. for Psychical Rsch., Soc. for Psychical Rsch. (assoc.), Acad. Cath. Hispanic Theologians of the U.S., Cath. Theol. Soc. Am., Internat. Yoga Tchrs. Assn. (Australia). Roman Catholic. Avocations: reading, music, photography, writing. Home and Office: Urb Santa Maria 1940 Calle Sauco San Juan PR 00927-6718

SANTIAGO, THERESA MARIE, special education educator; b. Bronx, N.Y., Dec. 30, 1970; d. Louis C. and Maria M. (Rodriguez) Berrios; m. Mark C. Santiago, Aug. 19, 1995; 1 child, Louis Anthony. BS, St. John's U., 1992, MS, 1996. Cert. elem. tchr., tchr. of handicapped, N.Y. Elem. tchr. Leif Ericson Day Sch., Bklyn., 1992-93; tchr. handicapped Perth Amboy (N.J.) Pub. Schs., 1993—. Contbr. articles to profl. jours. Vol. Multicultural Fun Day, Perth Amboy, 1994—. Recipient Prin.'s award, Humane Educator of Yr. N.J. Humane Edn. Soc., 1996, Good Neighbor award Farmers Ins., others; subject of mag. articles for work in tchg. field. Mem. Coun. Exceptional Children, Alliance N.J. Environ. Educators (Educator of Yr. 1998). Democrat. Roman Catholic. Avocations: travel, computers, golf, arts and crafts. Home: 13 Kirschman Dr Matawan NJ 07747-6667 Office: Perth Amboy Pub Schs 178 Barracks St Perth Amboy NJ 08861-3402

SANTNER, THOMAS, statistician, educator; b. St. Louis, Aug. 29, 1947; s. Joseph Frank and Margaret Ann (Dolak) S.; m. Gail DeFord, Aug. 29, 1970; children: Emily, Matthew, Abigail, Dominick. BS, U. Dayton, 1969; MS, Purdue U., 1971, PhD, 1973. Asst. prof. Cornell U., Ithaca, N.Y., 1973-80, assoc. prof., 1980-86, prof., 1986-89, dir. stats. ctr., 1982-86; prof. Ohio State U., 1990—, chair dept. stats., 1992—2000. Cons. Hosp. for Spl. Surgery, N.Y.C., 1983—. Co-author: The Statistical Analysis of Discrete Data, 1989, Design and Analysis of Experiments for Statistical Selection, Screening and Multiple Comparasons, 1995, Design and Analysis of Computer Experiments, 2003; co-editor: Design of Experiments: Ranking and Selection, 1984; contbr. articles to profl. jours. NSF, ASA and IMS fellow, Fulbright fellow; numerous grants. Mem. Inst. Math. Stats., Biometric Soc., Am. Statis. Assn. Home: 1042 Putney Dr Columbus OH 43085-2903 Office: Ohio State U Dept Stats Columbus OH 43210 E-mail: santner.1@osu.edu.

SANTOMERO, ANTHONY M. bank executive, public policymaker; b. N.Y.C., Sept. 29, 1946; s. Camillo and Jean (Oddo) S.; m. Marlena Belviso, Aug. 21, 1971; children: Jill Renee, Marc Anthony. AB, Fordham U., 1968; PhD, Brown U., 1971; EDhe (hon.), Stockholm Sch. Econs., 1992; LHC, U. Rome, 2003. Successively asst. prof., assoc. prof., prof. fin. Wharton Sch., U. Pa., Phila., 1972-84, R.K. Mellon prof. fin., 1984—2002, R.K. Mellon prof. emeritus of fin., 2002—, vice dean, dir. grad. div., 1984-87, dep. dean, 1990-94; dir. Wharton Fin. Instns. Ctr., 1995-2000; pres. Fed. Reserve Bank, Phila., 2000—. Asst. prof. econs. Baruch Coll., CUNY, 1971-72; vis. prof. European Inst. Advanced Studies in Mgmt., Brussels, 1977-78, Stockholm Sch. Econs., 1989-90, U. Rome, Tor Vergata, 1994-97, Ecole Superieure des Sciences Economiques and Commerciales, France, 1977-78. Author: Financial Markets, Instruments and Institutions, 1997, 2001, Challenges for Modern Central Banking, 2001; adv. editor Jour. Banking and Fin., 1978—, assoc. editor Jour. Money, Credit and Banking, 1980—2002, Jour. Fin. Svc. Rsch., 2000—, bd. editors Jour. Econs. and Bus., 1979—, European Fin. Mgmt., 1996—, Advances in Internat. Banking and Fin., 1993—, founding co-editor Brookings-Wharton Papers on Fin. Svcs., 1997—2000, adv. bd. European Banking Report, 1994—, Jour. Internat. Econ. Law, 1997—, editl. bd. Open Econs. Rev., 1990—, mem. faculty adv. bd. Jour. Internat. Econ. Law, 1997—, mem. bd. advisory editors Advances in Fin., Investment and Banking, 1992, editl. adv. bd. Jour. Fin. Stability, 2003—; contbr. articles to profl. jours. Mem.: Am. Econs. Assn., Am. Fin. Assn. Roman Catholic. Home: 310 Keithwood Rd Wynnewood PA 19096-1224 Office: Fed Reserve Bank Phila Ten Independence Mall Philadelphia PA 19106-1574 E-mail: santomero@phil.frb.org.

SANTONI, RONALD ERNEST, philosophy educator; b. Arvida, Que., Can., Dec. 19, 1931; s. Fred Albert and Phyllis (Tremaine) S.; m. Marguerite Ada Kiene, June 25, 1955; children: Christina, Marcia, Andrea, Juanita, Jonathan, Sondra. BA, Bishop's U., Lennoxville, Que., 1952; MA, Brown U., 1954; PhD, Boston U., 1961; postgrad., U. Paris-Sorbonne, 1956-57. Asst. prof. philosophy U. Pacific, Stockton, Calif., 1958-61; postdoctoral rsch. fellow Yale U., New Haven, 1961-62; asst. prof. philosophy Wabash Coll., Crawfordsville, Ind., 1962-64; faculty Denison U., Granville, Ohio, 1964—, prof. philosophy, 1968—2002, chmn. dept., 1971-73, 82-84, 92, Maria Theresa Barney chair in philosophy, 1978—, prof. emeritus, 2002—. Peace lectr. Bethel Coll., 1985; vis. scholar in philosophy Cambridge U., Eng., 1986, 90, 94, 97, 99, 2001, vis. lectr. in philosophy, 1990; vis. fellow Clare Hall, Cambridge U., 1986; vis. fellow in philosophy Yale U., 1975, 81, 93-94, 97; keynote speaker 2d Internat. Conf. on Nuclear Free Zones, Cordoba, Spain, 1985; Internat. Studies Assn., London, 1989, speaker and U.S.A. co-chair Internat. conf. Internat. Philosophers for Prevention of Nuclear Omnicide, Moscow, 1990; del. and raporteur UN meeting of Peace Messenger Orgns., Dagomys, Sochi, USSR, 1991; invited participant Colloquium on Technological Risks to Environment, Montreal, 1993; spkr. in field. Contbg. author: Current Philosophical Issues: Essays in Honor of C.J. Ducasse, 1966, Towards an Understanding and Prevention of Genocide, 1984, Nuclear War: Philosophical Perspectives, 1985, Genocide: A Critical Bibliographic Review, 1988, Just War, Nonviolence and Nuclear Deterrence: Philosophers on War and Peace, 1992, The Institution of War, 1991, Violence and Human Co-Existence, 1994, Hiroshima's Shadows, 1998, The Encyclopedia of Genocide, 1999, Human Coexistence and Sustainable Development, 2001, Das Sein und das Nichts, 2003; author: Bad Faith, Good Faith and Authenticity in Sartre's Early Philosophy, 1995, Sartre on Violence: Curiously Ambivalent, 2003; editor, contbr. Religious Language and the Problem of Religious Knowledge, 1968; co-editor Social and Political Philosophy, 1963; contbg. editor Internet on the Holocaust and Genocide; mem. editl. bd. Jour. Peace and Justice Studies; contbr. over 130 articles to profl. jours. V.p. NAACP, Licking County, 1967; co-organizer Crawfordsville (Ind.) Human Rels. Coun., 1962-64; nat. exec. com. Episcopal Peace Fellowship, 1968-78; internat. coun. Internat. Inst. on the Holocaust and Genocide, 1985—; nat. coun. Fellowship of Reconciliation, 1988-89; trustee Margaret Hall Sch., Versailles, Ky., 1972-74; nat. bd. dirs. Promoting Enduring Peace, 1982—. Canadian Govt. Overseas fellow Royal Soc. Can., 1956-57; Church Soc. for Coll. Work faculty fellow, 1961-62; Yale postdoctoral rsch. fellow, 1961-62; Danforth assoc., 1963-64; Soc. for Religion in Higher Edn. postdoctoral fellow, 1972—; Yale rsch. fellow, 1975; guest fellow Berkeley Coll., Yale U., 1975, 81, 93-94, 97, elected assoc. fellow, 1994—; vis. fellow in philosophy Yale U., 1981, 93-94, 97; Robert C. Good faculty fellow Denison U., 1985-86, 2000-01, Robert C. Good Faculty Rsch. fellow, 1993-94 elected life mem. Clare Hall, Cambridge (Eng.) U., 1986; elected mem. High Table, King's Coll., Cambridge U., 1999; recipient Mellon award for disting. faculty Denison U., 1972, Crossed Keys Faculty of Yr. award Denison U., 1986-87; Philosophy, Freedom and Action Conf. held in his honor, 2002. Mem. Am. Philos. Assn., Ch. Soc. for Coll. Work, Soc. for Phenomenology and Existential Philosophy, Internat. Philosophers for Peace (v.p. 1983-85, v.p. cen. div. 1990-91, internat. pres. 1991-96, internat. exec. com. 1996—), Sartre Soc. of N.Am. (exec. com. 1994—), Sartre Circle (coord. 1997—), le groupe d'Etudes Sartriennes, Gandhi-King Soc., Union of Bi-Nat. Profls. Against Omnicide (v.p. 1978—), Concerned Philosophers for Peace (founding 1980—, pres. 1996-97), Fellowship of Reconciliation. Episcopalian. Home: 500 Burg St Granville OH 43023-1005 E-mail: santoni@denison.edu.

SANTOPOLO, BETH FRANKLIN, elementary education educator; b. Bklyn., Mar. 13, 1955; d. Lawrence Howard and Beverly Florence (Weiss) Franklin; m. John Lucian Santopolo, July 22, 1979; children: Jill Lauren, Alison Brooke, Suzanne Heather. BA in Elementary Edn./Speech Arts magna cum laude, Hofstra U., 1976, MS in Edn./Reading, 1978. Cert. reading tchr. Classroom tchr. grades 1 and 2 Hewlett (N.Y.) Elem., 1976-81, reading support svc. grades 1 and 2, 1984-86, reading tchr. grades 1-3, 1986-87, classroom tchr. grade 1, 1990-94, classroom tchr. grade 2 & 3, 1994—99; early childhood libr. Franklin Early Childhood Ctr., Hewlett, 1987-89, reading recovery tchr., 2000—, Eng. lang. arts lead tchr., 2003—. Com. mem. Sci. Curriculum Work, Hewlett, 1991-93, Crisis Intervention Team, Hewlett, 1994-99. Past com. mem. Peninsula Counseling Ctr. Aux. Bd., Woodmere, NY; pres. Temple Sinai of L.I., 2002. Mem.: Reading Recovery Coun. N.Am., Nat. Coun. Tchrs. Math., Kappa Delta Pi. Avocations: reading, boating, skiing, baking. Office: Franklin Early Childhood Ctr Hewlett NY 11557 E-mail: bsantopolo@hewlett-woodmere.net.

SANTORA, OLGA MARIE, retired education educator; b. Paterson, N.J., Dec. 17, 1915; d. Joseph and Mary (Mondon) S. Tchg. cert., SUNY, Oneonta, 1935; BS in Elem. Edn., Columbia U., 1942; MS in Elem. Edn., Harvard U., 1952; EdD in Elem. Edn., SUNY, Albany, 1972. 1-8 grade tchr. one rm. sch., East Peacham, Vt., 1935—37; 1-4 grade tchr. Barnet (Vt.) Schs., 1937—42; 1-6 grade tchr. one rm. sch., Carlisle, N.Y., 1942-43; 4th grade tchr. Waterville (N.Y.) Schs., 1943-47; 2d grade tchr. Schenectady (N.Y.) Schs., 1947-53; prin. K-6 sch. Coxsackie (N.Y.) Schs., 1953-60; prin. 1-6 sch. U.S. Dependent Schs., Wiesbaden, Germany, 1960-63; prof. directed grad. reading SUNY, New Paltz, 1963-85, prof. intensive tchr. tng., summers 1957-60; ret., 1985. Spkr., presenter workshops in field; organizer Children's Lit. Festival SUNY, New Paltz, organizer, dir. master's reading program and reading clinic. Mem. planning com. Columbia Greene C.C., Hudson; mem., sec. Mid Hudson Libr. Svc., Poughkeepsie, N.Y.; v.p./pres. Greene County Hist. Soc., Coxsackie; bd. dirs. Greene County Hist. Soc.; bd. govs. Thomas E. Cole Cedar Grove. Honored by Columbia Greene C.C. 25th Yr. Reception; recipient Ann. Svc. award VFW, 1997. Mem. Columbia-Greene Reading Coun. (pres., charter mem.), Bus. and Profl. Women (pres., Woman of Yr.), Ulster County Reading Coun. (founder, advisor, Literacy award, found. rep.), Phi Delta Kappa (advisor), Kappa Delta Pi (counselor). Home: 69 Ely St Coxsackie NY 12051-1415

SANTOS, KAREY MICHALE, elementary school educator; b. Paramus, N.J., Oct. 3, 1956; d. Donald James Keeney and Barbara Jean (Wilson) Alderman; m. Joseph Karl Santos, Aug. 28, 1976; children; Sonya Rae, Donald Wesley. BA, U. S.C., Aiken, 1989, Interdisciplinary MA in Natural Sci., 1995. Math./sci. specialist Millbrook Elem. Sch., Aiken, SC, 1989—. Tchr., sponsor math. and sci. acad. teams, 1992—; mem. State Curriculum Standards Revision Team and Assessment Coms., 1999—. Recipient Sci. Scope award NASCO, 1992, Palmetto Cablevision Tchr. of Yr., 1992, Am. Nuclear Soc. Achievement award, Nat. Presdl. award for excellence in math. and sci. tchg., 2000; grantee Westinghouse, 1992-2002 EIA, So. Bell, Project Wild, Bryan Foods, Am. Chem. Soc. Mem. NSTA (Optical Data Corp. Videoisk award 1992, 93), S.C. Coun. Tchrs. Math., Soc. Elem. Pres. Awardees, S.C. Marine Edn. Assn., Environ. Edn. Assn. S.C. Home: 13 Normandy Ln Aiken SC 29801-2852 Office: Millbrook Elem Sch 225 E Pine Log Rd Aiken SC 29803-7613

SANTOS, ROBERT DAVID, health and fitness educator, consultant; b. Chalan, Pago, Guam, Jan. 1, 1952; s. Joaquin L. G. and Carmen I. (Pinaula) S.; m. Elaine Marie Pudwill, Sept. 1, 1975; children: Zane, Deylene, Makao, Shane. AAS in Gen. Studies, Pierce County C.C., Wash., 1973; EdB in Physical Edn., Ctrl. Wash. U., 1975; MPE, U. Oreg., 1979; PhD in Higher Edn. Administrn. and Adult Edn., U. North Tex., 1990; ABD in Adminstrn.

in Kinesiology, Tex. Woman's U. Cert. tchr. Physical edn. tchr. George Washington H.S., Guam, 1975-76, John F. Kennedy H.S., Guam, 1978-80; math, physical edn., health tchr. Battle Mt. H.S., Battle Mt., Nev., 1981-82; math. tchr. E.C. Best Jr. H.S., Fallon, Nev., 1982-83; rsch. cons. Sitterly Mgmt. and Cons. Firm, Ft. Worth, Tex., 1986-87; health tchr. S. Sanchez H.S., Guam, 1989-91; dir., mem. gov.'s cabinet Guam Health Planning and Devel. Agy., 1991-93; lectr. divsn. health, physical edn. and athletics Western Oreg. State Coll., Monmouth, from 1993; instr. dept. physical edn. and health Linn-Benton C.C., Albany, Oreg., from 1994; pvt. personal fitness instr., 1992-95. Dir. fundraiser Sports Medicine Design by Guam--A Wholistic Approach, 1992; dir. 1st Ann. Gov.'s Health Task Forces' Forum, 1992; rsch. dir. Gov.'s 21st Century Health Work Force Survey, 1991-93; wellness cons. Clark Hatch Health and Fitness Ctr., 1992-93; fitness cons. Gold's Gym, 1992-93; coaches' lectr., cons. athletic injuries Oreg. H.S., 1977-79; student teaching asst. supr. U. Nev.-Reno, 1981; wellness instr. U. North Tex., 1986-90, adj. prof. kinesiol. studies, 1986-90 Co-author: (with John Eddy) Circle of Excellence: Basketball, 1986; contbr. articles to profl. jours. Clinic dir. Albany Boys and Girls Club, 1993; mem. fellowship com. WHO; hon. amb.-at-large Gov. Joe Ada, Guam, 1991. Recipient Coat of Arms, Mayor of Rutherford, Eng., 1991. Mem. AAHPERD, Internat. Coun. for Health, Phys. Edn., Recreation, Sport and Dance (dir. philosophy edn. and sport commn.), Am. Assn. for Wellness Edn., Counseling & Rsch., Oreg. Athletic Trainer's Soc., Nat. Athletic Trainers Assn. (cert.). Roman Catholic. Home: Albany, Oreg. Deceased.

SANTOSO, MICHELLE JO, music educator, pianist; b. Surabaya, Indonesia, Sept. 8, 1968; arrived in U.S., 1993; d. Kim Man Jo and Kiem Ing Tio; m. Peter Santoso, July 10, 1994; children: Hillary Lin, Herbert Lin. BA cum laude, IKIP, Jakarta, Indonesia, 1992; MA, Calif. State U., L.A., 1998. Music dir. Yip's Children Choir, San Marino, Calif., 1994—96; dir., tchr. piano Master Artists Piano Performing Studio, Alhambra, 1996—. Performer: Chopin's Nocturne, 1992 (Best Performance and Interpretation award, 1992), Bratislava Chamber Orch., Austria, 2001, Internat. Chamber Music Festival, Italy, 2002, Internat. Chamber Music Festival, Prague, 2003. Vol. Tiu Chi Orgn. Recipient prize, Yamaha Piano Competition, 1992, L.A. Liszt Piano Competition, 2000; scholar Inez Schubert scholarship, Calif. State U., L.A., 1996. Mem.: Southwestern Youth Music Festival, Nat. Guild Piano Tchrs., Calif. Assn. Profl. Music Tchrs., Music Tchrs. Assn. Calif., Nat. Fedn. Music Clubs. Home: 1475 Rubio Dr San Marino CA 91108

SANTSCHI, PETER HANS, marine sciences educator; b. Bern, Switzerland, Jan. 3, 1943; came to U.S., 1976; s. Hans and Gertrud (Joss) S.; m. Chana Hoida, Mar. 28, 1972; children: Rama Aviva, Ariel Tal. BS, Gymnasium, Bern, 1963; MS, U. Bern, 1971, PhD summa cum laude, 1975; Privatdozent, Swiss Fed. Inst. Tech., Zurich, Switzerland, 1984. Lectr. chemistry Humboltianum Gymnasium, Bern, 1968-70; teaching rsch. asst. U. Bern, 1970-75; rsch. scientist Lamont-Doherty Geol. Obs., Columbia U., Palisades, N.Y., 1976-77; rsch. assoc. Lamont-Doherty Geol. Obs. Columbia U., Palisades, N.Y., 1977-81; sr. rsch. scientist Lamont-Doherty Geol. Obs., Columbia U., Palisades, N.Y., 1981-82, Swiss Inst. Pollution Control, Zurich-Duebendorf, Switzerland, 1982-88; prof. oceanography Tex. A&M U., College Station, 1988—, prof. marine scis. Galveston, Tex., 1988—, sect. head chem. oceanography dept. oceanography College Station, 1990—. Head isotope geochemistry and radiology sect. Swiss Inst. Water Resources and Water Pollution Control, Zurich, 1983-88; mem. rev. panel on chem. oceanography NSF, 1990-91. Contbr. articles to profl. jours. Cpl. Swiss Army, 1964-65. Mem. AAAS, Am. Chem. Soc., Am. Geophys. Union, Oceanography Soc., Am. Soc. Limnology and Oceanography. Avocation: swimming. Office: Tex A&M U Oceanography Dept Galveston TX 77553-1675 E-mail: santschi@tamug.tamu.edu.

SAPIRMAN, NADINE KADELL, university official; b. Nov. 15, 1969; BA, SUNY, Geneseo, 1990; MPA, Rutgers U., Newark, 1994. Dir. residence hall Rutgers U., Newark, 1994-95, program coord. Ctr. for Govt. Svcs., New Brunswick, NJ, 1995—99, assoc. program specialist, 2000—. Office: Rutgers U 33 Livingston Ave Ste 200 New Brunswick NJ 08901-1979 E-mail: sapirman@rci.rutgers.edu.

SAPORTA, JACK, psychologist, educator; b. N.Y.C., Oct. 21, 1927; s. David and Victoria (Fils) S.; m. Judith Hammond, May 28, 1967 (div. 1979); children: David J., Victoria Johnson. AB cum laude, Adelphi U., 1951; PhD, U. Chgo., 1962. Diplomate Am. Bd. Profl. Psychology; lic. clin. psychologist. Pvt. practice, 1962-99; supt. Tinley Park (Ill.) Mental Health Ctr., 1975-78; chief manpower tng. and devel. Ill. Dept. Mental Health, Chgo., 1978-82; dean, prof. Forest Inst. Profl. Psychology, Des Plaines, Ill., 1982-85; coord. studies Fielding Grad. Inst., Santa Barbara, Calif., 1984—; prof. Ill. Sch. Profl. Psychology, Chgo., 1985-97. Mem. adj. faculty psychology Lake Forest Grad. Sch. Mgmt., 1987-97; mem. Ill. State Clin. Psychology Lic. and Disciplinary Com., Springfield, 1984-93; profl. staff Forest Hosp., Des Plaines, 1977-96; mem. attending doctoral profl. staff Luth. Gen. Hosp., Park Ridge, Ill., 1986-2000, emeritus, 2000—. Served with U.S. Army, 1946-47, Germany. Named Educator of Yr., Forest Inst., 1982, Outstanding Faculty Mem. Lake Forest Grad. Sch. Mgmt. Fellow Acad. Clin. Psychology, NTL-Inst. (faculty); mem. APA (accreditation site vis. team), Ill. Psychol. Assn., Chgo. Psychol. Assn. (cert. recognition 1999, mem. exec. bd.). Avocations: tennis, computers, do-it-yourself home projects. Home: 13077 Stone Creek Court Huntley IL 60142

SAPOUGH, ROY SUMNER, JR., educational administrator; b. Rock Hill, S.C., Nov. 13, 1951; s. Roy Sumner and Janie Lee (Price) S.; m. Bonne Barmore, June 17, 1978; children: William Sumner, Blaksley Rhett. BS in Edn., Ga. So. U., 1976, MEd, 1986, EdS, 1988. Cert. tchr., adminstr., Ga. Tchr. Wayne County Jr. High Sch., Jesup, Ga., 1976-77, Claxton (Ga.) High Sch., 1977-79, Taliaferro County Sch., Crawfordville, Ga., 1980-81, Thomson (Ga.) High Sch., 1981-85; purchasing agt. Hatteras Yacht, High Point, N.C., 1979-80; prin. Glascock County Schs., Gibson, Ga., 1985-87, Norris Mid. Sch., Thomson, 1987-93, Thomson Mid. Sch., 1993—. Mem. ASCD, Nat. Assn. Secondary Sch. Prins., Ga. Assn. Mid. Sch. Prins., Ga. Assn. Ednl. Leaders, Belle Meade Country Club, Kiwanis, Phi Delta Kappa. Republican. Methodist. Avocation: hunting. Home: 1835 Folly Lake Dr Thomson GA 30824-4708 Office: Thomson Mid Sch PO Box 1140 Main St Thomson GA 30824

SAPP, NANCY L. educational administrator; b. Joplin, Mo., July 22, 1951; d. Jim L. and Leah (Smith) Hayes; children: Michael A., Julie D. B in Music Edn., Pittsburg (Kans.) State U., 1973; MEd in Psychology, Wichita State U.; cert. in elem./secondary sch. adminstrn., Emporia State U., 1994. Cert. elem./secondary vocal/instrumental music tchr., learning disabled tchr., behavior disorder tchr., adminstr., dist. level adminstrn. dir. spl. edn. Vocal and instrumental music instr., Cherokee, Kans., 1973-75, Holy Cross Grade Sch., Hutchinson, Kans., 1980-85, Trinity H.S., Hutchinson, 1980-82; learning disabilities tchr. Unified Sch. Dist. # 308, Hutchinson, 1987-89, behavior disorder tchr., 1989-95, behavior cons., 1990-95; asst. sch. prin. Unified Sch. Dist. 308, Hutchinson, 1995-97; prin., coord. student svcs. Unified Sch. Dist. 443, Dodge City, Kans., 1997-99; asst. dir. spl. edn. Southwest Kans. Area Coop. Dist., Dodge City, 1999—. Prin. second violin Hutchinson Symphony, 1991-97; pres. exec. bd. Hutchinson Regional Youth Symphony, 1994-95; bd. dirs. Reno Choral Soc., Kans. Youth Soc. Grantee Southwestern Bell Tel., Hutchinson, 1992. Mem. Internat. Reading Assn., NEA, Kans. NEA, Kans. Reading Assn., Hutchinson NEA (bldg. rep. 1992-94), Ark Valley Reading Assn. (pres. 1994-95), Phi Delta Kappa. Republican. Methodist. Avocations: theater, music, cross stitch, quilting. Home: 108 La Vista Blvd Dodge City KS 67801-2848

SAPPINGTON, SHARON ANNE, retired school librarian; b. West Palm Beach, Fla., Sept. 15, 1944; d. A.D. and Laura G. (Jackson) Chambless; m. Andrew Arnold Sappington III, June 11, 1966; children: Andrew Arnold IV, Kevin Sean. Student, Fla. So. coll., 1962-64; BA in Edn., U. Fla., 1966; media specialist, U. Ala., 1980. 5th grade tchr. Tates Creek Elem., Lexington, Ky., 1966-68; 4th grade tchr. Sadieville (Ky.) Elem., 1968-69; libr. media specialist A.H. Watwood Elem., Childersburg, Ala., 1980-98; ret. Guest storyteller Young Author's Conf., Winterboro, Lincoln, Sylacauga, and Fayetteville, Ala., 1982-94; vis. com. mem. Southeastern Accreditation Assn.; program presenter Internat. Reading Assn., Birmingham, Ala., 1983; guest speaker rare children's books "By the Way" TV talk show, 1983; pres. Tale Tellers of St. Augustine, 2003—; chmn. RSVP Read Aloud Program, 2002—. Creator, presenter: (slide presentation) Tellers of Tales and Sketchers of Dreams, 1983, (multimedia programs) Dinosaurs, Teddy Bears, and Wild Things, 1990, Shanghaied in the Beijing Airport, 1994. Circle chmn., Sunday tchr. Grace United Meth. Ch., Birmingham, 1973, 92-95; delivery mem. Meals on Wheels, Birmingham, 1975-76; radio reader for the blind WBHM Pub. Broadcasting, Birmingham, 1980; guest speaker, program presenter Jaycees, Kiwanis, and C. of C., Childersburg, 1993-94; chmn. Nat. Librl Week Ala, 1993-94. Title I grantee, 1991, Stutz Bearcat grantee, 1992. Mem. AAUW, ALA, Internat. Platform Assn., Am. Assn. Sch. Librs., Ala. Libr. Assn. (children's and sch. divsn. publicity chmn. 1991-93, chmn. Nat. Libr. Week in Ala. 1993-94, Outstanding Youth Svcs. award 1989), People to People Internat. (libr. del. to China 1993), Kappa Delta Pi, Internat. Platform Assoc., 1997-98. Democrat. Methodist. Avocation: collector of 19th century illustrated children's literature. Home: 5131 Shore Dr Saint Augustine FL 32086-6473

SARANGAPANI, JAGANNATHAN, embedded systems and networking engineer, educator; b. Madurai, India, June 14, 1965; s. Jagannathan and Janaki (Ramaswamy) S.; m. Sandhya (Srinivasan), June 16, 1997; 1 child, Sadhika. BS, Anna U., Madras, 1987; MS, U. Sask., Can., 1989; PhD, U. Tex., Arlington, 1994. Engr. Engr. India Ltd., New Delhi, 1986-87; rsch. asst. U. Sask., Saskatoon, 1987-89; rsch. assoc. U. Man., Winnipeg, Can., 1990-91; rsch. asst. Automation and Robotics Rsch. Inst., Ft. Worth, 1992-94; cons., rsch. Caterpillar, Inc., Peoria, Ill., 1994-98; asst. prof. elec. engring. and computer engring., dir. embedded sys. and networking lab. U. Tex., San Antonio, 1998—2001; assoc. prof. elect. and computer engring. U. Mo., Rolla, 2001—. Cons., collaborator Adv. Sensors and Controls Group, Ft. Worth, 1994-98; cons. Caterpillar Inc., 1994-98. Co-author: Neural Network Control of Robot and Nonlinear systems, 1999; contbr. chpts. to books, over 90 articles to profl. jours. Recipient Presdl. award for Rsch. Excellence, 2001, rsch. award of excellence Caterpillar, 2001, also several gold medals and scholarships; U. Tex. fellow, 1992-94; Sigma Xi doctoral rsch. awardee, 1994; NSF career awardee, 2000. Mem. IEEE (sr.; program chmn. Illinois Valley sect. 1994, program com. symposium on int. control, fin. chair symposium on intelligent control, conf. on recisions finance chair in control, 2004), Sigma Xi, Tau Beta Pi, Eta Kappa Nu. Achievements include 17 patents and 8 patents pending; development of novel neural network methods for control and relaxation of certainty equivalence assumption, linearity in the paramaters and persistence of excitation; novel prognostic algorithms. Avocations: tennis, jogging, walking, chess, biking. Office: Dept Elec and Computer Engring 133 Emerson Electric Hall Rolla MO 65409 E-mail: sarangap@umr.edu.

SARASOHN, EVELYN LOIS LIPMAN, principal; b. Charleston, S.C., Sept. 17, 1937; d. Hyman Isaac and Gittel (Ingberman) Lipman; m. Nachum Hershel Sarasohn, Aug. 14, 1960; children: Michele Beth, Hyman Isaac, Jeffrey Steven, Jonah Mendel, Jenny Tzipporah. BS in English, Coll. of Charleston, 1959; MEd in Supervision and Adminstrn., The Citadel, 1974. Elem. tchr. Addlestone Hebrew Acad., Charleston, 1959-64, 1964-68, middle sch. math. and sci. tchr., 1968-80, asst. prin. early childhood, 1968-80, computer coord., 1980-81, asst. prin., 1981-90, prin., 1990-99. Test supr. Ednl. Testing Svc., Princeton, N.J., 1971-99. Author: Aleph-Bet Readiness, 1980, also video tape. Co-leader parenting group B'rith Shalom Beth Israel Synagogue, 1986-94; mem. Mayor's Task Force on Aging; vol. Low Country Sr. Ctr.; bd. dirs. Porter Gaud Sch., 2000—; mem. mayor's coun. on aging, 2001—; vol. Low Co. Sr. Ctr., 2002—. Mem.: Palmetto Assn. Ind. Schs. (hon.; past pres.). Jewish. Avocations: reading, walking, cooking. Home: 131 Chadwick Dr Charleston SC 29407-7472

SARATH, CAROL ANN, library/media coordinator; b. Ossining, N.Y., Apr. 2, 1952; d. Edward Noah and Florence Louise (Cafarelli) S.; m. Karl Burton Lohmann, July 9, 1986; children: Maria Estella, Patrick Noah. BS in Early Childhood Edn., So. Conn. State U., 1974; MLS, U. Ariz., 1980. Tchr. Gallup (N.Mex.) McKinley County Schs., 1975-79, libr./media coord., 1982—; rschr. Fenn Galleries, Santa Fe, N.Mex., 1980-82. Chair libr. br. Octavia Fellin Pub. Libr., Gallup, 1990—; mem. libr. adv. coun. State of N.Mex., Santa Fe, 1992-2000; co-chair N.Mex. Task Force on Sch. Librs., 1999—. Contbr.: Exploring the Southwest Through Childrens Literature, 1994. Bd. mem. Red Rock Balloon Rally Assocs., Gallup, 1983—. Mem. ALA, Am. Assn. Sch. Librs., N.Mex. Libr. Assn. Avocations: hot air ballooning, gardening. Office: Gallup McKinley County Schs PO Box 1318 Gallup NM 87305 E-mail: csarath@gmcs.k12.nm.us.

SARAVANJA-FABRIS, NEDA, mechanical engineering educator; b. Sarajevo, Yugoslavia, Aug. 2, 1942; came to U.S., 1970; d. Zarko and Olga Maria (Majstorovic) Saravanja; m. Gracio Fabris, Nov. 4, 1967; children: Drazen Fabris, Nicole. Diploma in mech. engring., U. Sarajevo, 1965; MSME, Ill. Inst. Tech., 1972, PhD in Mech. Engring., 1976. Lectr. in mech. engring. U. Sarajevo, 1965-70; teaching asst. Ill. Inst. Tech., Chgo., 1970-76; lectr. U. Ill., Chgo., 1974-75; mem. tech. staff Bell Telephone Lab., Naperville, Ill., 1976-79; prof. mech. engring. Calif. State U., L.A., 1979—, chair mech. engring. dept., 1989-92. Assoc. researcher Lab. for Machine Tools, Aachen, Fed. Republic Germany, 1966-67; cons. Northrop Corp., L.A., 1984; COO FAS Engring. Inc., Burbank, Calif., 1993—. Contbr. articles to profl. publs. Grantee NSF, 1986, Brown & Sharpe Co., 1989; German Acad. Exch. fellow DAAD, 1966-67, Amelia Earhart fellow Zonta Internat., 1973-74, 75-76; recipient Engring. Merit award San Fernando Valley Engring. Coun., 1990, Disting. Chair award sch. of engring. and tech. Calif. State U., L.A., 1993. Mem. AAUW, Soc. for Engring. Edn. (dir. at large mfg. divsn.), Soc. Women Engrs. (sr.), Soc. Mfg. Engrs. (sr., chpt. chmn. 1997). Home: 2039 Dublin Dr Glendale CA 91206-1006 Office: Calif State U 5151 State University Dr Los Angeles CA 90032-4226

SARDI, ELAINE MARIE, special education educator; b. Shippenville, Pa., Dec. 2, 1952; d. Willis Henry and Genevieve Evelyn (Hanby) Etzel; m. Michael James Sardi, Dec. 28, 1974; children: Jason Michael, Justin James. BS in Spl. Edn., Clarion State Coll., 1974; MEd in Reading, Clarion U., 1991. Tchr. spl. edn. North Clarion Sch. Dist., Leeper, Pa., 1974-75, Riverview Intermediate Unit, Shippenville, 1986-92; tchr. learning support Keystone H.S., Knox, Pa., 1992-97; lead tchr. Riverview Intermediate Unit, Shippenville, 1991-92; cross-categorical tchr. Louisburg (N.C.) H.S. Franklin County Sch. Sys., 1998; learning disabilities specialist Wake Tech. C.C., Raleigh, N.C., 1998—. Clin. field supr. Clarion (Pa.) U., 1988-97; Lamaze instr. Clarion Orgn. Parent Edn., 1976-83; mentor tchr. Keystone Sch. Dist., 1993-94. Sunday sch. tchr. 1st United Meth. Ch., Clarion, 1977-86; treas. Clarion County Spl. Olympics, 1986-93. Mem. DAR, Nat. Coun. Tchrs. English, Coun. Exceptional Children, Internat. Reading Assn., Learning Disabilities Assn. Wake County, Daus. Union Vets., Kappa Delta Pi, Delta Kappa Gamma. Republican. Avocations: reading, cooking, travel. Home: 8812 Valley Springs Pl Raleigh NC 27615-8120 E-mail: emsardi@mindspring.com.

SARFO, KWASI, history and political science educator; b. Acherensua, Ghana, June 2, 1955; arrived in U.S., 1980; m. Monica Sarfo; children: Ama, Akua, Abena. BA with honors, U. Ghana, Accra, 1979; MPA, SUNY, Albany, 1981, PhD, 1985. Lectr. SUNY, Albany, 1985-92; asst. prof. history and political sci. York Coll. of Pa., 1992—. Field faculty adv. Vt. grad. program Norwich U., Montpelier, 1986; adj. lectr. Coll. Saint Rose, Albany, 1988-89, Russell Sage Coll., Troy, N.Y., 1988-90; cons., external examiner degrees and exams program Regents Coll., Albany, 1988, 91. Author: Life in the Third World, 1988, Issues in Modern African Politics, 1991, Politics and Government in the 3rd World, 1992, History of Africa, 1993, 95; author 3 other books; contbr. articles to profl. jours. Rsch. and publ. grantee York Coll. Pa., 1993, 95. Mem. Internat. Studies Assn., Am. Polit. Sci. Assn., Am. Soc. Pub. Adminstrn., African Studies Assn., Acad. Polit. Sci. Home: 41 Fox Run Dr York PA 17403-4931 Office: York Coll Pa History Dept Country Club Rd York PA 17405-7199

SARGENT, LYMAN TOWER, political science educator, academic administrator; b. Rehoboth, Mass., Feb. 9, 1940; s. Stanley Morse and Doris Ellen (Tower) S.; m. Patricia M. McGinnis Wilhelm (div.); 1 child, Evan C. Sargent; m. Mary T. Weiler (div.). BA, Macalester Coll., 1961; MA, U. Minn., 1962, PhD, 1965. Asst. prof. polit. sci. U. Mo., St. Louis, 1965-70, dir. polit. sci. lab., 1968-69, assoc. prof., 1970-75, dir. undergrad. studies, 1972-75, 84-85, prof., 1975—, chair dept. polit. sci., 75-78, 92-97. Vis. prof. U. Exeter, Eng., 1978-79, 83-84, London Sch. Econs., 1985-86, Victoria U., New Zealand, 1995-96, 2000-01, U. East Anglia, Eng., 1998-99; mem. sch. of hist. studies, Inst. for Advanced Studies, Princeton, N.J., 1981-82; hon. curator Utopia Collection, Thomas Jefferson Libr., U. Mo., St. Louis, 1986-2002. Author: New Left Thought, 1972, British and American Utopian Literature, 1516-1985, 1988, Contemporary Political Ideologies, 12th edit., 2003, Extremism in America, 1995; editor Utopian Studies, 1990—; editor: Political Thought in the United States, 1997; co-editor: The Utopia Reader, 1999; co-editor: Utopia: The Quest for the Ideal Society in the Western World, 2000. Fellow NEH, Inst. for Advanced Study, 1981; travel grantee Am. Coun. Learned Socs., 1983, 88. Mem. Soc. for Utopian Studies (chmn. 1986-90), Communal Studies Assn. (bd. dirs. 1989-92), Conf. for Study Polit. Thought (at-large). Office: U Mo St Louis Dept Polit Sci 8001 Natural Bridge Rd Saint Louis MO 63121-4401 E-mail: lyman.sargent@umsl.edu.

SARMIENTO, SISTER MARY KATHLEEN, principal; b. Tamuning, Guam, May 20, 1958; d. Jose Babauta and Maria (Cepeda) S. BA magna cum laude, U. Guam, Mangilao, 1986; postgrad., U. San Francisco, 1992—. Joined Sisters of Mercy, 1978. Clk. St. Anthony Sch., Tamuning, 1977-78, tchr., student coun. advisor, 1989-91, vice prin., 1989-91, prin., 1991—; tchr., student body advisor Acad. of Our Lady, Agana, Guam, 1981-84, 86-87; tchr., student coun. advisor, vice-prin., tchr. Bishop Baumgartner Sch., Sinajana, Guam, 1987-89, cafeteria mgr., 1987-89. Co-founder, bd. mem. I acha'ot Guahan Siha, Agana, 1989—. Youth min. Archdiocesan Youth Ministry, Agna, 1984-87, music min., 1986-87; bd. mem. v.p. Inter-Faith, Agana, 1988-90; coord., presentor Archdiocese Summer Youth Tng., Agana, 1989: mem. Historic Preservation, Agana, 1989; advisor Cath. Youth in Active Ministry, 1989-90; govt. apptd. mem. Krista McCulliffe Found. bd., 1994. Recipient Certs. of Appreciation Govt. Dept. Youth Affairs, Agana, 1986, 87, 91, Spl. Olympics, Agana, 1990; Svc. awards Govt. Guam, Agana, 1989, 90, Inter-Faith, Agana, 1990. Mem. Nat. Cath. Edn. Assn., Nat. Assn. Secondary Sch. Prins., Mercy Elem. Edn. Network. Roman Catholic. Office: 529 Chalan San Antonio Tamuning GU 96913-3600

SARNECKI, THOMAS GEORGE, special education educator; b. Wilkes-Barre, Pa., Mar. 24, 1932; s. John Andrew and Anna (Selepak) S.; m. Christine C. Serafin, June 9, 1956; children: Karen, Kristine, Nancy, John. BA, King's Coll., Wilkes-Barre, Pa., 1957; MEd, Wayne State U., 1969, Edn. Specialist, 1974; EdD, Nova U., 1992. Adj. instr. psychology Henry Ford C.C., Dearborn, Mich., 1976-86; tchr. Detroit Pub. Schs., 1957-72, sch. psychologist, 1973-86; tchr. severely emotionally disturbed Pasco County Pub. Schs., Land O'Lakes, Fla., 1986—. Union rep. Detroit psychologists Detroit Pub. Schs., 1974-76. Author: Practicum-Improving Multi-Disciplinary Team Effectiveness in High School, 1991, Practicum-Organizational Guidelines for Establishing Alcohol/Drug Prevention Intervention Team in a High School, 1992. With USCG, 1949-52. Mem. Coun. Exceptional Children. Roman Catholic. Home: 15253 Eastwood Trl Brooksville FL 34604-8182

SARNI, CAROL A. school psychologist; b. Bklyn., Sept. 16, 1948; d. Charles and Anna V. (Curry) Kleis; m. Costantino G. Sarni, Mar. 19, 1966; children: David, Erin Ann. BA in Psychology, Bklyn. Coll., 1987, sch. psychology PD, 1987-89; ednl. adminstrn. and supervision, Fordham U., 1990—. Cert. sch. psychologist, N.Y., sch. dist. adminstr. Sch. counselor Kennedy Assocs., Bklyn., 1989—; sch. psychologist The Child Study Ctr., Bklyn., 1989—; ednl. adminstrn. and supervision Fordham U., 1990-93. Mem. ASCD, Nat. Assn. Sch. Psychologists, N.Y. League for Hard of Hearing, Alexander Bell Assn., Kappa Delta Phi, Phi Delta Kappa. Office: 1845 85th St Brooklyn NY 11214-3112

SARNO, MARTHA TAYLOR, speech and language pathologist, educator; b. N.Y.C., Nov. 25, 1927; d. Edward and Milagros Abril-Lamarque; m. John Ernest Sarno, Jan. 8, 1967; 1 child, Christina. BA, Mich. State U., 1949; MA, NYU, 1954; D in medicine honoris causa, U. Goteborg, Sweden, 1982. Cert. Am. Bd. Neurogenic Comm. Disorders in Adults and Children. Speech-lang. pathologist Goldwater Meml. Hosp., N.Y.C., 1949-50; dir. speech-lang. pathology dept. Rusk Inst. Rehab. Medicine, N.Y.C., 1950—; instr. prof. dept. rehab. medicine NYU Sch. Medicine, 1957-65, asst. prof. dept. rehab. medicine, 1965-78, assoc. prof., 1978-90, prof., 1990—; asst. prof. dept. speech-lang. pathology NYU Sch. Edn., 1964-73. Faculty Kurt Goldstein Inst. Neuropsychology, Straubing, Germany, 1995—; chmn. tech. adv. speech and lang. disorder Dept. Health, N.Y.C., 1967-77; mem. task force to study ethics in rehab. medicine Hastings Ctr., Garrison, N.Y., 1985-88; cons. editor jour. Comm. Disorders, 1967-91. Co-author: Stroke: The Condition and The Patient, 1979; editor: Acquired Aphasia, 1981, 3rd edit., 1999; editor: Topics in Stroke Rehabilitation, 1995. Founder, pres. Nat. Aphasia Assn., 1987—; charter mem. Acad. Aphasia, 1962—, bd. govs., 1979-83, 90-96. Recipient Outstanding Alumni award Mich. State U., 1976, Rusk award Howard A. Rusk Inst. Rehab. Medicine, 1985, Frank Kleffner Lifetime Career Achievement award Speech Found. Am., 1998. Fellow Am. Speech-Lang.-Hearing Assn. (Honors of the Assn. award 1999); mem. Am. Congress Rehab. Medicine (Gold Key award 1974), Acad. Aphasia (chmn. sci. program com. 1969-72), Acad. Neurologic Comm. Disorders and Scis. (bd. cert.), Daily Points of Light award 2001). Office: New York Univ Sch Medicine Dept Rehab Medicine 400 E 34th St New York NY 10016-4901

SARNO, PATRICIA ANN, biology educator; b. Ashland, Pa.; d. John Thomas and Anna (Harvest) S. BS, Pa. State U., 1966, MEd, 1971; postgrad. Bucknell U., 1967, Bloomsburg U., 1970. Programmer planetarium, tchr. sci. Pottsville (Pa.) High Sch., 1967; tchr. biology Schuylkill Haven (Pa.) Area High Sch., 1967-91, sci. chmn., coord. dist., 1973-91; lead tchr. sci. Pa. Acad. Suprs. and Curriculum Devel. Dist. Pa. Sch., 1991—; cons. Contbr. to profl. jours. Pa. Edn. Dept., career program Pottsville Hosp. Dow Chem. Co. grantee, 1971. Mem. AAAS, AAUW, NEA, Pa. Edn. Assn. (exec. bd.), Nat. Assn. Biology Tchrs., Nat. Tchrs. Assn., Pa. Assn. Supervision and Curriculum Devel., N.Y. Acad. Scis., Pa. Tchrs. Assn., Am. Inst. Biol. Scis., Pa. Acad. Scis., Pa. State U. Alumni Assn., Schuylkill Haven Edn. Assn., Phi Sigma, Delta Kappa Gamma. Discoverer spider species Atypus snetzingeri, 1973. Home: 49 S Balliet St Frackville PA 17931-1703 Office: Schuylkill Haven HS Schuylkill Haven PA 17972

SAROJINI, GURUGUNTLA VENKATRAMAN, special education educator; b. Berbera, Somalialand, Nov. 27, 1931; came to U.S., 1979; d. G.V. and Vimala Devi (Yogin) Raman. BA in Hindi, Dakshin Bharat Hindi Prachar Sabha, Madras, India, 1948, BEd in Hindi, MA in Hindi, 1954;

student, Queen Mary's Coll., Madras, 1962-64; Sanskrit Kovit diploma, Bharathiya Vidya Bhavan, Madras, 1967; BA, Delhi U., 1972; diploma in geography, Madras U., 1976; BEd, St. Mary's Tng. Coll., Shillong, India, 1979; MA in Educating Physically Handicapped, Columbia U., 1984; postgrad., CUNY, 1985; post grad. diploma, KOVID. Cert. tchr. spl. edn., social studies 7-12, bilingual edn., N.Y. Tchr. Govt. Girls H.S., Salem, Madras, India, 1949-51; tchr. Hindi lang. Vidyodaya Girls H.S., Madras, 1954-66, Padma Seshadri Higher Secondary Sch., Madras, 1966-67; tchr. humanities Ctrl. Schs., Madras and Shillong, 1966—78; tchr. spl. edn. N.Y.C. Pub. Schs., 1980—97. Author: (children's story) Hindi Prachar, 1954, poems in English; contbr. articles to profl. jours. Vol. North Bronx Hosp. Ctr., 1997-2000. Mem. United Fedn. Tchrs., Am. Fedn. Tchrs. Avocations: travel, reading, writing, singing. Home: 5700 Arlington Ave Apt 17 L Bronx NY 10471-1519 Office: NYC Bd Edn CES 73 X 1020 Anderson Ave Bronx NY 10452-5302

SARPY, SUE ANN CORELL, environmental health sciences educator; b. Roanoke, Va., June 24, 1965; d. Gaylord Stafford and Betty Frances (Spangler) Corell; m. Christopher Alexis Sarpy, Feb. 18, 1995. BA in Psychology, U. Richmond, 1987; MS in Indsl. and Orgnl. Psychology, Tulane U., 1990, PhD in Indsl. and Orgnl. Psychology, 1996. Tchg. asst. dept. psychology Grad. Sch., Tulane U., New Orleans, 1988-94, rsch. assoc. Hammer rsch. project, 1995-96, tng. evaluation coord., 1996—, rsch. asst. A.B. Freeman Sch. Bus., 1989-90, rsch. asst. dept. psychology, 1992, tutor, 1993-94; clin. asst. prof. dept. environ. health scis. Tulane U. Med. Ctr., 1996—. Psychometrician Test Devel. and Validation Unit, New Orleans, 1990-92; asst. prof. Loyola U. Coll. Bus. Adminstrn., New Orleans, part-time 1994095 Advocate New Orleans Mus. Art, 1994—; mem. Heritage Club, Preservation Resource Ctr. New Orleans, 1996—. Scholar Tulane U., 1987. Mem. APA, ASTD, Soc. Indsl. and Orgnl. Psychologists, Audubon Inst. (charter), Psi Chi. Avocations: skiing, walking, photography, classical music. Home: One River Pl 244 Arlington Dr Metairie LA 70001-5510 Office: Tulane U Med Ctr Environ Health Edn-Tng Proj 1440 Canal St Ste 800 New Orleans LA 70112-2793

SARRAF, SHIRLEY A. secondary school educator; BA in polit. sci., U. Calif., Davis, 1968; MEd, Idaho State U., 1976, postgrad., 1976—. Cert. Educator Nat. Bd. Edn., 2001. Asst. psychometrist U. Wash., 1969-72; asst. prof. dept. fgn. lang. Farah Pahlavi U., Teheran-Vanek, Iran, 1978-79; tchr. presch. program T.L.C. Child Care Ctr., Pocatello, Idaho, 1980-82; dir. of curriculum for English as a second lang. Idaho State U., Pocatello, Idaho, 1982-85; tchr. English, Math, History, Computers Highland High Sch. Sch. Dist. 25, Pocatello, Idaho, 1986—2001; tchr. English Folsom H.S., Folsom, Calif., 2001—. Infant and child stimulation workshops Idaho State U. Pocatello, Idaho, adj. prof. U. Teheran, Iran, 1978-79. Recipient Tchr. of the Year award State of Idaho, 1994-95. Home: PO Box 6001 Folsom CA 95763-6001

SARSFIELD, LUKE ALOYSIUS, school system administrator; b. Luzerne, Pa., July 29, 1925; s. Luke Aloysius and Margaret Ann (Conahan) S.; m. Nancy Ann Chiavacci, Aug. 19, 1961; 1 child, Luke Aloysius III. BA, King's Coll., Wilkes-Barre, Pa., 1952; MA, Montclair (N.J) State Coll., 1962; PhD, NYU, 1973. Diplomate Ednl. Adminstrn. Tchr. Ogdensburg (N.J) Pub. Schs., 1953-55, Luzerne Pub. Schs., 1955-60, Rutherford (N.J.) Pub. Schs., 1960-70, adminstrv. asst. to supt., 1970-72, supt. schs., 1972—. Trustee Rutherford Pub. Libr., 1972—, v.p.; trustee Williams Inst. Inc., Rutherford, 1986—, treas.; trustee Bergen County Tenn Arts, 1989—; pres. Jack Frost Jr. Racing Found., White Haven, Pa., 1987-93, South Bergen Jointure Com. With USN, 1943-46. Mem. Am. Assn. Sch. Adminstrs., N.J. Assn. Sch. Adminstrs., Bergen County Supts. Assn. (past pres.), Bergen County Assn. Sch. Adminstrs., Bergen County Audio-Visual Com., King's Coll. Alumni Assn. (past pres.), Rotary (past pres.), Phi Delta Kappa. Roman Catholic. Office: Rutherford Pub Schs 176 Park Ave Rutherford NJ 07070-2310

SARTORIUS, GREGG STEVEN, educational administrator; b. St. Louis, June 7, 1957; s. Carl Robert and Ruth Joan S.; m. Paula Ann Sartourus, Nov. 25, 1978; children: Andrea Theresa, Michael Steven, Nicole Christine. BFA in Graphic Design, S.W. Mo. State U., 1982; B Elem. Edn., U. Mo., St. Louis, 1988; MEd, Maryville U., 1991; EdS in Ednl. Adminstrn., St. Louis U., 1994, EdD in Ednl. Adminstrn., 1996; grad. art-craft of prin. fellow's prog., Harvard U., 1996; grad. Leadership Acad., Mo. Dept. Elem. and Secondary Edn., 1996. Cert. elem. and secondary edn. tchr., advanced elem. and secondary prin., Mo. Mgr. Red Lobster, Inc., St. Louis, 1979-83; salesman Reliable Ins. Co., St. Louis, 1983-84; kitchen mgr. Tippin's Pie & Pantry, St. Louis, 1984-85; mgr. Internat. House of Pancakes, St. Louis, 1985-86; server Casa Gallardo, St. Louis, 1986-88; elem. tchr. Hazelwood Sch. Dist., Florissant, Mo., 1988-94; asst. elem. prin. Rockwood Sch. Dist., Eureka, Mo., 1994—2000, presenter dist. sci. fair, 1995—; prin. Ft. Zumwalt Sch. Dist., Eureka, Mo., 2000—. Facilitator strategic planning Babler Elem. Sch., St. Louis, 1995-97; adj. prof., Lindenwood U., 2001—. Pres. Cultural Arts Adv. Bd., St. Peters, Mo., 1996—2000; mem. Eagle Scout Rev. Bd., N. Star Dist., Boy Scouts Am., 1990-93, focus group St. Louis 2004, 1997-98; host family for three fgn. exchange students from Germany and Italy, 1998-00; chmn. Millennium Commn., St. Peters, 1999—2000; mem. adv. bd. St. Peters Pks. Recreation and Arts, 2000-03. Grantee Hazelwood Sch. Dist., 1994; scholar Mo. Dept. Elem. and Secondary Edn., 1996, Costa Rica Aloré T-shirt Co., 1997, Costa Rica Ednl. Symposium, 1997. Mem. NAESP, Mo. Assn. Elem. Sch. Prins., St. Louis Suburban Elem. Prins. Assn., Phi Delta Kappa. Avocations: family activities, visual arts, history, studying other cultures.

SARUBBI, JUDITH ALICE CLEARWATER, guidance counselor; b. Engelwood, N.J., Oct. 5, 1956; d. Jasper and Mary (Fadden) Clearwater; m. Edward J. Sarubbi, July 7, 1979; children: Brian, Alyssa, Christopher. BA, William Paterson Coll., 1978; MA, Kean Coll. N.J., 1983. Cert. tchr., spl. edn. tchr., reading specialist, guidance and counseling, N.J. Tchr. Bergen County Bd. Spl. Svcs., Paramus, N.J., 1978-82; asst. dir. Day Camp Oratam, Harriman State Park, N.Y., 1980-82; co-dir. Skyland Learning and Guidance Assocs., Ringwood, N.J., 1985--89; guidance counselor Wharton (N.J.) Borough Pub. Schs., 1992—. Cons. Embossography, Paramus, 1979-81. Steering com. Alliance of Wanaque (N.J.) and Ringwood for Edn. and Substance Abuse Prevention, 1989-92. Mem. ASCD, ACA, Pi Lambda Theta. Roman Catholic. Avocations: reading, collecting farm antiques, skiing, crafts, computers. Office: Alfred C MacKinnon Mid Sch 137 E Central Ave Wharton NJ 07885-2431

SARVELA, PAUL D. health facility administrator, educator; BA in Psychology, U. Mich., 1981, MS in Ednl. Psychology, 1983, PhD in Health Edn., 1984. With Ford Aerospace and Comms. Corp., 1984—86; from asst. prof. to prof. health edn., family and cmty. medicine U. Ill., Carbondale, Ill., 1986—92, prof. health edn., family and cmty. medicine, 1992—, chmn. dept. Health Care Professions, 1999—, interim dean Coll. Applied Scis. and Arts, 2002—. Dir. Ctr. Rural Health and Social Svc. Devel., 1993—2000; cons. in field. Contbr. numerou articles to jours. in field. Mem.: Am. Coun. Edn., Am. Coll. Healthcare Execs., Am. Acad. Health Behavior. Office: So Ill Univ Coll Applied Scis and Arts Carbondale IL 62901-6604 Office Fax: 618-453-7286. E-mail: psarvela@siu.edu.*

SARVER, KATHRYN MARGARET, elementary education educator; b. Spring Valley, Ill., Jan. 28, 1965; d. Hubert Eugene and Camilla Ann (Rumsavich) S. BA, Western Ill. U., 1989. Cert. tchr., Ill. Tchr. music, choir dir., mus. dir. Brookwood Jr. High Sch., Glenwood, Ill., 1989-90; tchr. music, choir dir. Spring Valley Elem. Schs., 1990—; dir. swing choir Ill. Valley C.C., Oglesby, 1991—; pvt. tchr. vocal music, keyboards Peru, Ill., 1991—. J.F.K. swing choir dir. Spring Valley Elem. Schs., 1990—, sponsor Wildcatette, 1993—. Performer, dir. theater dept. Ill. Valley C.C., 1986—; performer Summer Stage Playhouse, Spring Valley, 1988, 89, 92; dir., prodr. (music book and tape) Ladybug, 1992; performer, music dir. Stage 212, LaSalle, Ill., 1993 Vocal presenter Meml. Day Peru Amvets, 1988-93; nat. anthem vocalist Ill. Little Leage Assn., Peru, 1987. Scholar Newcomers, 1988. Mem. Ill. Music Educators Assn., Ill. Grade Sch. Music Assn., Music Educators Nat. Conf., Mu Phi Epsilon, Delta Psi Omega (hon., co-sponsor). Roman Catholic. Avocations: acting, playing piano, reading, sports. Home: 1816 Green St Peru IL 61354-1639

SARVER, VERNON THOMAS, JR., gifted education educator; b. Bluefield, W.Va., Dec. 17, 1943; s. Vernon Thomas Sr. and Dorothea Dora (Ellis) S.; m. Mary Ellen Duran, June 13, 1970; children: Laura Edythe, Anne Marie. BA, Fla. State U., Tallahassee, 1966; MDiv, Tufts U., 1969; STM, Boston U., 1971; MA, Ohio State U., 1976; PhD, U. Fla., Gainesville, 1994. Cert. tchr., Fla. Tchr. drafting Boston Pub. Schs., 1972-74; substitute tchr. Licking County Schs., Johnstown, Ohio, 1976-78; tchr. of gifted Nassau County Schs., Fernandina Beach, Fla., 1978-81, Alachua County Schs., Gainesville, Fla., 1981-82; grad. rsch. asst. U. Fla., Gainesville, 1982-85; tchr. emotionally handicapped Bradford County Schs., Starke, Fla., 1985-86; tchr. of gifted Marion County Schs., Ocala, Fla., 1986—. Adj. instr. Fla. Jr. Coll., Jacksonville, 1978-81, Lake City (Fla.) C.C., 1981-83, adj prof. St. Leo U., Ocala, Fla., 1994—2000; fellow Ctr. for Social and Polit. Thought, U. South Fla., 2001—. Referee: Jour. Value Inquiry, 1997—; contbr. articles to profl. jours. Treas. Loblolly Learning Community, Gainesville, 1984-86. Recipient Disting. Svc. award Marion County Schs., Ocala, 1993, Cert. of Recognition for Excellence in Edn. award, 1990. Mem. Am. Philos. Assn. (Rockefeller prize 1996), Gainesville Chess Club (pres. 1985-89), U.S. Chess Fedn. (life cert. expert). Avocations: chess, recreational mathematics. Home: PO Box 605 Archer FL 32618-0605 E-mail: sarverv@marion.k12.fl.us.

SARVIS, ELAINE MAGANN, retired assistant principal; b. Conway, S.C., May 11, 1947; d. John Thomas and Gloria (Winkler) Duckett; m. John Wesley Magann, Aug. 2, 1969 (dec. Nov. 1975); children: Christiane, James Wesley; m. Francis Mack Sarvis, Dec. 18, 1982. BA in Elem. Edn., U. S.C., 1969, MEd in Early Childhood, 1976, postgrad., 1990. Cert. elem. adminstrn. tchr., S.C. Tchr. Southside Elem. Sch., Augusta, Ga., 1969-70, Homewood Elem. Sch., Conway, 1970-71, Timmerman Sch., Columbia, S.C., 1972-73, South Conway Elem. Sch., Conway, 1973-74, 1975-76, instructional specialist, 1976-80, tchr., 1980-90, Horry County Gifted and Talented Program, Conway, 1990-91. Mem. com. Horry County Tchr. Incentive Program, Conway, 1989-91; bd. dirs. Horry County Sick Leave Bank Program, 1990-92. Mem. First Bapt. Ch., Conway, 1958-99, Ocean Dr. Presbyn. Ch., 1999—, North Myrtle Beach High Parent Tchr. Orgn., 1990; neighborhood chmn. Am. Heart Assn., Conway, 1978. Named Tchr. of Yr. County of Horry, 1990. Republican. Baptist. Avocations: reading, decorating, gardening, movies, travel. Office: 4317 Turtle Ln Little River SC 29566 E-mail: emsarvis@yahoo.com.

SARWAR, BARBARA DUCE, education consultant; b. Mpls., Aug. 9, 1938; d. Harold Taylor and Barbara (Thayer) Duce; m. Mohammad Sarwar, Dec. 28, 1972; 1 child, Barbara Sarah Franklin. BS, U. Colo., 1972; M Spl. Edn., Ea. N.Mex. U., 1975, Edn. Specialist, 1979. Cert. tchr., adminstr., N.Mex. Tchr. 2d grade, English as 2d lang. Lake Arthur (N.Mex.) Mcpl. Schs., 1972-74; tchr. spl. edn. Artesia (N.Mex.) Pub. Schs., 1974-79, ednl. diagnostician, 1979-88, dir. spl. edn., 1988-97; cons. Edn. Diagnosis, Artesia, 1998—; owner Barbara's Diagnostic Svcs., Artesia, 1998—. Contbr. to profl. publs. Pres. Altrusa Club Artesia, 1981-82, 86-87, The Arc of Artesia, 1990-92; bd. dirs. Zia Girl Scout Coun., 2002—. Named Employee of Yr. Arc of N.Mex., 1994. Mem.: Coun. for Exceptional Children (professionally recognized spl. educator in ednl. diagnosis), Nat. Assn. Sch. Psychologists, Internat. Reading Assn. (pres. Pecos Valley chpt. 1975—76, sec. N.Mex. unit 1977—78), Artesia Edn. Assn. (pres. 1978—79), Phi Delta Kappa, Phi Kappa Phi. Avocations: reading, sewing, golf. Home and Office: PO Box 1493 Artesia NM 88211-1493 E-mail: bsarwar@bulldogs.org.

SARWER-FONER, GERALD JACOB, physician, educator; b. Volkovsk, Grodno, Poland, Dec. 6, 1924; arrived in Can., 1932, naturalized, 1935; s. Michael and Ronia Sarwer-F.; m. Ethel Sheinfeld, May 28, 1950; children: Michael, Gladys, Janice, Henry, Brian. BA, Loyola Coll. U., Montreal, 1945, MD magna cum laude, 1951; DPsychiatry, McGill U., 1955. Diplomate: Am. Bd. Psychiatry and Neurology. Intern. Univ. Hosps. U. Montreal Sch. Medicine, 1950-51; resident Butler Hosp., Providence, 1951-52, Hosps. Western Res. U., Cleve., 1952-53, Queen Mary Vets. Hosp., Montreal, 1953-55; cons. psychiatry, dir. psychiatric rsch., 1955-61; lectr. psychiatry U. Montreal, 1953-55; lectr., asst. prof., assoc. prof. McGill U., 1955—70; dir. dept psychiatry Queen Elizabeth's Hosp, Montreal, 1964-71; prof. psychiatry U. Ottawa, Ont., 1971-89, prof., chmn. psychiatry, 1974-86, prof., 1989—; dir. dept. psychiatry Ottawa Gen. Hosp., 1971-87; dir. Lafayette Clinic, Detroit, 1989-92; prof. psychiatry and behavioral Neurosciences Wayne State U., Detroit, 1989—. Cons. in psychiatry Ottawa Gen. Hosp., Royal Ottawa Hosp., Children's Hosp. of Eastern Ont., Ottawa, Windsor (Ont.) Western Hosp. Ctr., Ottawa Sch. Bd.; Z. Lebensohn lectr. Silbey Meml. Hosp. Cosmos Club, Washington, 1991; disting. lectr. XI World Congress Psychiatry, Hamburg, 1999, XII World Congress Psychiatry, Yokohama, Japan, 2002; mem. test com. Nat. Bd. Med. Examiners, 1975-81; pres. Que. Psychiat. Assn., 1966-68; mem. adv. panel on psychiatry Def. Rsch. Bd. Can., Dept. Nat. Def., 1958-62. Editor: Dynamics of Psychiatric Drug Therapy, 1960, Research Conference on the Depressive Group of Illnesses, 1966, Psychiatric Crossroads-the Seventies, Research Aspects, 1972, Social Psychiatry in the Late 20th Century, 1993; editor in chief Psychiat. Jour. U. Ottawa, 1976-90, emeritus editor in chief, 1990—; mem. editorial bds. of numerous internat. and nat. profl. jours.; editor numerous audio-video tapes; contbr. to more than 200 articles to profl. jours. Bd. govs. Queen Elizabeth Hosp., Montreal, 1966-71; life gov. Queen Elizabeth Hosp. Found.; cons. Protestant Sch. Bd., Westmount, Que., 1966-71; advisor Com. on Health, City of Westmount, 1969-71. Served to lt. col. Royal Can. A Med. Corps, 1949-62. Fulbright fellow, 1951-53; recipient Sigmund Freud award Am. assn. Psychoanalytic Physicians, 1982, William V. Silverberg Meml. award Am. Acad. Psychoanalysis, 1990, Poca award Assn. Psychiat. Out Patient Ctrs. Am., 1990; Simon Bolivar lectr. Am. Psychiat. Assn., New Orleans, 1981; Can. Decoration, Knight of Malta. Fellow: AAAS, Am. Assn. Social Psychiatry (v.p. 1987—89, pres.-elect 1990, pres. 1992—94), World Psychiat. Assn. (v.p. sect. on edn. 1989—, mem. internat. adv. com. 9th World Congress Rio de Janeiro 1993, disting. lectr. 1996, XI World Congress Hamburg 1999, organizing com. sci. com. X World Congress in Madrid, mem. nominating com.), Benjamin Rush Soc. (founding mem., councillor), Am. Coll. Psychiatrists (bd. regents 1978—80, pres. com. long range planning and policy 1986—89, emeritus), Am. Psychopath. Assn., Collegium Internat. Neuropsychopharmacology, Internat. Psychoanalytical Assn. (mem. program com. 31st congress NY 1979), Royal Coll. Psychiatry (Found. fellow), Can. Psychiat. Assn. (life; bd. dirs. 1958—62, founder, chair com., sect. psychotherapy 1962—64), Am. Acad. Psychiatry and the Law (sr.; pres. 1977, Silver Apple award), Am. Coll. Neuropsychopharmacology (life), Can. Coll. Neuropsychopharmacology (life; hon. found. 1958—), Am. Psychiat. Assn. (life; chair sci. program com., VI World Congress of Psychiatry, Honolulu 1974—77, chair com. psychiatry, law 1975—77, chair task force model commitment code 1976—80, disting. mem., VI World Congress of Psychiatry Honolulu 1974—77), Am. Coll. Psychoanalysts (life; pres.-elect 1983, pres. 1984—85, chair by-laws and constn. com. 1994—2001, Henry Laughlin award 1986), Am. Coll. Mental Health Adminstrn. (life), Royal Coll. Physicians and Surgeons (exec. sec. test psychiat. com. 1987—89), Internat. Coll. Psychosomatic Medicine (sec.-gen. 1979—83); mem.: Am. Psychoanalytic Assn. (mem. program com. 1972—76), Alliance for Mental Health Svcs. (pres. 1999—2000), Mich. Psychoanalytic Soc., Soc. Biol. Psychiatry (sr.; pres. 1983—84, H. Azina Meml. lectr. 1963, George M. Thompson award 1997), Can. Assn. Profs. Psychiatry (pres. 1976—77, 1982—86), Can. Psychoanalytic Soc. (pres. 1979—81), Royal Can. Mil. Inst. Club, Cosmos Club. Home and Office: 3220 Bloomfield Shr Dr West Bloomfield MI 48323-3300 Fax: 248 855-8321. E-mail: sarwfon@aol.com.

SASEK, GLORIA BURNS, English language and literature educator; b. Springfield, Mass., Jan. 20, 1926; d. Frederick Charles and Minnie Delia (White) Burns; m. Lawrence Anton Sasek, Sept. 5, 1960. BA, Mary Washington Coll. of U. Va., 1947; student, U. Paris, 1953, U. Stranieri, Perugia, Italy, 1955; MA, Radcliffe Coll., 1954; EdM, Springfield Coll., 1955. Tchr., head dept. jr. and sr. hs English, Pub. Schs., Somers, Conn., 1947—59; tchr. English, Winchester (Mass.) Pub. Schs., 1959—60; mem. faculty La. State U., Baton Rouge, 1961—, asst. prof. English, 1971-96, chmn. freshman English, 1969-70. Named La. State U. Yearbook Favorite Prof., 1978; recipient George H. Deer Disting. Tchg. award, La. State U., 1977, Disting. Undergrad. Tchg. award, Amoco Found., 1994, commendation, La. Ho. of Reps., 1996. Mem. MLA, AAUP (chpt. v.p. 1981-84), South Ctrl. MLA, South Ctrl. Renaissance Soc., South Ctrl. Conf. on Christianity and Lit. Office: Dept English La State U Baton Rouge LA 70803 E-mail: glsasek@worldnet.att.net.

SASLOW, GEORGE, psychiatrist, educator; b. N.Y.C., Dec. 5, 1906; s. Abram and Becky (Zinkoff) S.; m. Julia Amy Ipcar, July 28, 1928; children: Michael G., Rondi, Steven, Marguerite. ScB magna cum laude, Washington Sq. Coll. NYU, 1926; postgrad., U. Rochester, 1926-28; PhD in Physiology, NYU, 1931; MD cum laude, Harvard U., 1940. Instr., asst. prof. biology N.Y. U., 1928-37; vis. research asso. physiology Cornell Med. Coll., 1935-36, U. Rochester Sch. Medicine, 1936-37; research asso. physiology Harvard Sch. Pub. Health, 1937-40; neurology-neurosurgery intern Boston City Hosp., 1940-41; resident Worcester State Hosp., 1941-42; chief resident psychiatry Mass. Gen. Hosp., Boston, 1942-43, staff, 1955-57; instr., successively asst., asso. prof., prof. pychiatry Washington U. Sch. Medicine, 1943-55; staff Barnes Hosp., St. Louis, 1943-55; practice of psychiatry, 1943—; clin. prof. psychiatry Harvard, 1955-57; prof. psychiatry U. Oreg. Med. Sch., Portland, 1957-74, head dept., 1957-73, prof. emeritus, 1979—. Chief mental health and behavioral sci. edn., chief psychiatry service VA Hosp., Sepulveda, Calif., 1974-79; prof. psychiatry in residence UCLA, 1974-79; mem. Psychiat. Security Rev. Bd., 1983— Nat. Tng. Labs. fellow. Fellow Am. Psychiat. Assn. (disting. life; mem. task force on nomenclature and stats.), Am. Coll. Psychiatrists (charter); mem. AMA, Assn. for Advancment of Behavioral Therapy, Delta Soc. (bd. dirs. 1986-89). Home: 02403 SW Greenwood Rd Portland OR 97219-8394

SASMOR, JAMES CECIL, publishing representative, educator; b. N.Y.C., July 29, 1920; s. Louis and Cecilia (Mockler) S.; 1 child from previous marriage, Elizabeth Lynn; m. Jeannette L. Fuchs, May 30, 1965. BS, Columbia U., 1942; MBA, Calif. Western U., 1977, PhD, 1979. Fellow, Diplomate Am. Bd. Med. Psychotherapists, Am. Assn. Sex Educators, Counselors and Therapists; lic. healthcare risk mgr., Am. Inst. Med. Law; diplomate Am. Bd. Sexology, Am. Bd. Disability Analysts (sr. analyst); cert. tchr. health scis.. Registered rep. Nat. Assn. Security Dealers, 1956-57; founder, owner J.C. Sasmor Assocs., Pub.'s Reps., N.Y.C., 1959-89; co-founder, pres., dir. adminstrn. Continuing Edn. Cons., Inc., 1976—. Pub. cons., 1959—; clin. assoc. U. So. Fla. Coll. Medicine, 1987-89, mem. adj. faculty Coll. Nursing, 1980-89; dir. Ednl. Counseling Comprehensive Breast Cancer Ctr., U. So. Fla. Med. Ctr., 1984-89, client librn. mental health inst., 1979-89; lectr. divsn. allied health nursing and pub. svc. Yavapi Coll. Author: Economics of Structured Continuing Education in Selected Professional Journals, Perception May Be Reality Vols. I and II; contbr. chpts. to Childbirth Education: A Nursing Perspective; contbr. articles to profl. jours. Team tchr. childbirth edn. Am. Soc. Childbirth Educators; bd. dirs. Tampa chpt. ARC; pres. Sedona (Ariz.) unit Am. Cancer Soc., 1995—, co-chmn. adult edn. com., founder Am. Cancer Soc. edn. dept. Sedona Med. Ctr.; bd. dirs. Ariz. divsn., mem. pub. edn. com.; county nursing ednl. cons. ARC, chmn. instrnl. com. on nursing and health, 1979-85; founding mem. coun. trustees Ariz. Nurses Found., 1998. With USN, 1942-58, PTO; lt. USNR ret. Recipient cert. of appreciation ARC, 1979, Am. Fgn. Svc. Assn., 1988, Dept. Health and Rehab. Svcs. award for Fla. Mental Health Inst. Svc., 1980; Internat. Coun. Sex Edn. and Parenthood fellow Am. U., 1981, Accomplished Elder award Ariz. Coun. of Govts. Mem. NAACOG (bd. dirs. Tampa chpt.), Nat. Assn. Pubs. Reps. (pres. 1965-66), Am. Soc. Psychoprophylaxis in Obstetrics (dir. 1970-71), Am. Soc. Childbirth Educators (co-founder, dir. 1972—), Internat. Coun. Women's Health Issues (chmn. resources com.), Health Edn. Media Assn., Nursing Educators Assn. Tampa, Lions (bd. dirs. Found. Ariz. 1991-2000, past pres. Sedona club, chair sight, hearing, and scholarship coms.), Phi Theta Kappa (hon., advisor Beta Gamma Pi chpt.), Honors Scholar,, 2000-2002. Home: 235 Arrowhead Dr Sedona AZ 86351-8900 Office: PO Box 2282 Sedona AZ 86339-2282 E-mail: jsasmor@iglide.net.

SASS, ARTHUR HAROLD, educational executive; b. N.Y.C., Nov. 22, 1928; s. Maxwell Sigmund and Alice May (McGillick) S.; m. Eleanore G. Schmidt, Dec. 31, 1949; children: Nancy, Arlene, Susan, Eric. BS, Oswego (N.Y.) State Coll., 1949; EdM, Rutgers U., 1959, postgrad., 1960-68. Cert. chief sch. adminstr. Tchr. Millsboro (Del.) Pub. Sch. System, 1949-51, Eatontown (N.J.) Pub. Sch. System, 1955-66; coord. coop. indsl. edn. Monmouth Regional High Sch., Tinton Falls, N.J., 1966-68; prin. Mt. Holly (N.J.) Pub. Sch. System, 1968-71; supt. schs. Lumberton Twp. (N.J.) Pub. Sch. System, 1971-72, Lacey Twp. (N.J.) Pub. Sch. System, 1972-74; analyst mil. pers. Naval Sea Systems Command, Washington, 1975-79; head employee devel. Naval Rsch. Lab., Washington, 1979-83, 85-90; acad. dir. Naval Res. Engring. Duty Officer Sch., Leesburg, Va., 1983-85. Pres. DEVPRO, Inc., Warrenton, Va., 1985—; prin. founder Dept. Def. Sci. and Engring. Apprentice Program; established nation's first fed. svc. high sch. coop. indsl. edn. program, 1967. Author: Guide to the Naval Ammunition Depot, 1967; editor: (brochure) Commodore John Barry-Father of the U.S. Navy, 1976. Chmn. Shade Tree Commn., Little Silver, N.J., 1968-75, Rapidan/Rappahannock (Va.) Cmty. Mental Health Ctrs., 1980-81; deacon Warrenton Ch. of Christ, 1985, elder, 1995-99; mem. Va. Gov.'s Adv. Bd. for Emergency Med. Svcs., 1994-96, Shade Tree Commn., Monmouth Coutny, N.J., 1969-75. With USN, 1952-55; capt. USNR, 1952-88. Recipient Tng. Officers' Conf. Disting. Svc. award, 1988, Outstanding Contbn. to Engring. Edn. and Rsch award George Washington U., 1991. Mem. Am. Soc. Tng. and Devel., Res. Officers Assn. (v.p. Va. chpt. 1982-83), Naval Res. Assn. (Plimsoll Mark award 1975), Am. Soc. Naval Engrs., Navy League, Wash. Acad. Scis., Tng. Dirs. Forum. Republican. Avocation: outdoor activities. Home and Office: 604 Dam Lake Ct Williamsburg VA 23185-2796

SASSAMAN, PAULA, reading specialist; b. Harrisburg, Pa., Nov. 2, 1943; d. Charles and R. Pauline Huggins; m. James H. Sassaman, Apr. 8, 1967; children: Craig, David, Joseph. BS in Elem. Edn., Millersville (Pa.) U., 1966; MEd, Shippensburg (Pa.) U., 1969. Cert. elem. tchr., reading specalist and supr., reading recovery tchr., Pa. Elem. tchr. Susquenita Sch. Dist., Duncannon, Pa., 1966-69, reading specialist, 1969-71, West Perry Sch. Dist., Elliottsburg, Pa., 1987—, reading recovery tchr., 1993—. Presenter in field. Sunday sch. thcr., historian Otterbein United Meth. Ch., Duncannon; booster Susquenita H.S. Band, Duncannon, 1988; mem. cmty. liaison adv. com. to Susquenita Sch. Bd.; vol. Alliance for Acid Rain Monitoring, 1986—. Recipient lead tchr. award South Ctrl. Pa. Lead Tchr. Ctr., 1992. Mem. ASCD, NEA, Pa. Edn. Assn., West Perry Edn. Assn., Internat. Reading Assn., Audubon Soc., Perry Historians. Avocations: genealogy, gardening, nature appreciation, reading. Office: Blain Elem Sch Box 38 Main St Blain PA 17006

SASSER, ELLIS A. gifted and talented education educator; b. Norfolk, Va., June 14, 1946; d. Haywood Ellis and Jessie (Johnson) S.; m. R. Wayne Kitsteiner, June 11, 1983. BA, Emory and Henry Coll., 1968; MA, Va. Commonwealth U., 1976; cert. creative problem solving, cert. advanced creative problem solving, Ctr. for Creative Learning, Honeoye, N.Y., 1990. Primary tchr. Henrico County Pub. Schs., Richmond, Va., 1968-76, tchr. gifted, 1976—, tchr. humanities Three Chopt Gifted Ctr. Gifted adv. bd. Henrico County Programs for the Gifted, Richmond, 1990—. Recipient R.E.B. award for teaching excellence Greater Richmond Community Found., 1989. Mem. AAUW, NEA, Va. Edn. Assn., Henrico Edn. Assn., Coun. for Exceptional Children, Va. Assn. for Gifted Edn., Va. Hist. Soc., Richmond Area Friends of the Gifted, Richmond Symphony Chorus, 1973-94, West of the Blvd. Civic Assn., Delta Kappa Gamma Soc. Internat. (pres. Gamma Chi chpt. 1994-96). Avocations: travel, drawing and painting, reading, photography. Home: 3223 Floyd Ave Richmond VA 23221-2903 Office: Henrico County Pub Schs Three Chopt Elem Sch 1600 Skipwith Rd Richmond VA 23229-5205

SASSOON, JANET, ballerina, educator; b. Sorabaya, Indonesia, Sept. 2, 1936; came to U.S., 1937; d. Edward and Flora (Bar) S.; m. John Roland Upton Jr., Aug. 7, 1983. Began training with Christensen brothers, Ruby Asquith, and Gisella Caccialanza, San Francisco; Studied with Leo Staats, Lubov Egorova, Olga Preobrajenska, Mathilde Kshessinskaya, Paris, 1951. Dancer Grand Ballet du Marquis de Cuevas, Paris, 1952-55, Chgo., Utah and San Francisco Ballets, 1955; prima ballerina Berlin Ballet, 1956; dir. Acad. of Ballet, San Francisco, 1974-89, assoc. dir., 1989-97. Coach master classes in ballet, profl. dancers including Natalia Makarova, Karen Averty, Wes Chapman, Jean Charles Gil, others. Avocations: cooking, gardening, writing. Home: 1112 Pine St Calistoga CA 94515-1734

SATAUA, SILI K. school system administrator; BS in Elem. Edn., Northeast Mo. State U.; MA, U. Hawaii; PhD, Brigham Young U. Dir. Am. Samoa Dept. Edn., Pago Pago. Office: Am Samoa Dept Edn Education Bldg PO Box 186 Pago Pago AS 96799*

SATIN, JOSEPH, language professional, university administrator; b. Phila., Dec. 16, 1920; s. Reuben Philip and Harriet (Price) Satin; m. Selma Rosen (dec. 1978); children: Mark, Diane; m. Barbara Jeanne Dodson (dec. 1987); m. Terrye Sagan, 1992. BA, Temple U., 1946; AM, Columbia U., 1948, PhD, 1952. Instr. integrated studies W.Va. U., Morgantown, 1952-54; prof. English and Comparative Lit. Moorhead (Minn.) State U., 1954-63; chmn. dept. English and Journalism Midwestern U., Wichita Falls, Tex., 1963-73; dean Sch. Arts and Humanities Calif. State U., Fresno, 1973-89. Mgr concert series Moorhead State Univ, 1956—61; mem nat bd consult NEH, Washington, 1979—; dir London semester Calif State Univ, Fresno, 1982—92; dir Frank Lloyd Wright Auditorium Project. Author: (book) Ideas in Context, 1958, The 1950's: America's "Placid" Decade, 1960, Reading Non-Fiction Prose, 1964, Reading Prose Fiction, 1964, Shakespeare and His Sources, 1966, Reading Literature, 1968, The Humanities Handbook (2 vols), 1969, (poems) The Journey Upward, 1999, Poems on the Internet (www.Poetry.com), 2000; editor: (book) Frank Lloyd Wright-Letters to Apprentices, 1982, Letters to Architects, 1984, Letters to Clients, 1986, Treasures of Taliesin, 1985, The Guggenheim Correspondence, 1986, Frank Lloyd Wright: His Living Voice, 1987, Frank Lloyd Wright, The Crowning Decade, 1989; translator: Federico Fellini, Comments on Film, 1987; contbr. Encyclopedia Int Educ, 1978; dir: Univ Press, Calif State Univ, 1982—92. With U.S. Army, 1943—46, ETO. Named Nat Grand Prize Winner, Nat Library Poetry N Am Ann Poetry Contest, 1998. Jewish. Avocations: creative writing, music. Home: 65 Maywood Dr San Francisco CA 94127-2007 E-mail: terryellen1965@hotmail.com.

SATTERTHWAITE, CAMERON B. physics educator; b. Salem, Ohio, July 26, 1920; s. William David and Mabel (Cameron) S.; m. Helen Elizabeth Foster, Dec. 23, 1950 (div. July 31, 1979); children: Mark Cameron, Tod Foster, Tracy Lynn, Keith Alan, Craig Evan (dec.). BA, Coll. Wooster, 1942; postgrad., Ohio State U., 1942-44; PhD, U. Pitts., 1951. Chemist Manhattan dist. project Monsanto Chem. Co., Dayton, Ohio, 1944-47; research chemist DuPont, Wilmington, Del., 1950-53; researcher, adv. physicist Westinghouse, Pitts., 1953-61; asso. prof. physics U. Ill., Urbana, 1961-63, prof., 1963-79, prof. emeritus, 1979—; prof. physics Va. Commonwealth U., Richmond, 1979-85, prof. emeritus, 1985—, chmn. dept. physics, 1979-82. Program dir. NSF, 1975-76; field sec. Friends Com. on Nat. Legis., 1988-90. Contbr. articles to profl. jours.; patentee in field. Sch. dir., Monroeville, Pa., 1959-61; trustee, mem. fin. com. Southeastern Univs. Research Assn., 1980-85; Democratic nominee for U.S. Congress, 1966; del. to Dem. Nat. Conv., 1968, 72, 2000; sec. Urbana Free Libr. Found., 1998—. Fellow Am. Phys. Soc.; mem. Fedn. Am. Scientists (chmn. 1968). Home: 308 E Colorado Ave Urbana IL 61801-5918 E-mail: csattert@uiuc.edu.

SATTERTHWAITE, FRANKLIN BACHE, JR., management educator, executive coach, author; b. Mt. Holly, N.J., Apr. 30, 1943; s. Franklin Bache and Emily Vaux (Cresson) S.; m. Antonia Mitchell, Oct. 6, 1987 (div. Oct. 1992); m. Martha Werenfels, May 21, 1994; children: Peter Franklin, Thomas Peabody. AB, Princeton U., 1965; M in Urban Studies, Yale U., 1968, MPhil, 1972, PhD, 1975. Sci. faculty Escola Americiana, Rio Janeiro, Brazil, 1965-66; planner Nat. Inst. Mental Health, Chevy Chase, Md., 1968-70; cons. Battelle Meml. Inst., Columbus, Ohio, 1971-72; touring squash pro W.P.S.A., N.Am., 1976-84; sr. cons. Brown Cronson Assocs., N.Y.C., 1981-87; prin. Frank Satterthwaite, N.Y.C., 1982—, 1995—; asst. prof. Johnson & Wales U., Providence, 1993-97, assoc. prof., 1997—; prin. Dimensional Leadership L.L.C., 1999—, dir. Grad. Ctr. for Bus., 1999—2001. Cons. Cost of Living Coun., Washington, 1972-73; dir. Grad. Ctr. for Global Enterprise Leadership, 1999-2001, Johnson and Wales U., 1999—; prin. Career P.E.A.K.S., LLC, 2001—. Author: The Three-Wall Nick and Other Angles, 1979; co-author (with Gary D'Orsi): The Career Portfolio Workbook, 2003. Lt. USPHS, 1968-70. Mem. Acad. Mgmt. Avocations: squash (World Profl. Vets. Squash Champion 1984), tennis, golf, piano, travel. Home: 107 Shaw Ave Cranston RI 02905-3828 Office: Johnson and Wales U 8 Abbott Park Pl Providence RI 02903-3775

SATTINGER, MICHAEL JACK, economics educator, researcher; b. Toledo, Aug. 23, 1943; s. Irvin J. and Barbara R. (Lowenthal) S.; m. Ulla M. Jensen, Oct. 25, 1969; children: Graham, Andrew, Nicholas. BS, U. Mich., 1965; MS, Carnegie-Mellon U., 1969, PhD, 1973. Asst. prof. economics SUNY, Stony Brook, N.Y., 1970-77; assoc. prof. Miami U., Oxford, Ohio, 1977-81; assoc. prof. econs. SUNY, Albany, 1981-91, prof. econs., 1991—. Adj. lectr. Aarhus U., Denmark, 1974-75, lectr., 1982-83. Author: Capital and the Distribution of Labor Earnings, 1980, Unemployment, Choice and Inequality, 1985; contbr. articles to profl. jours. Grantee N.Y. Dept. Social Svcs., 1989-90. Avocation: cycling. Home: 271 Mccormick Rd Slingerlands NY 12159-9320 Office: SUNY 1400 Washington Ave Albany NY 12222-1000

SATURNELLI, ANNETTE MIELE, school system administrator; b. Newburgh, N.Y., Dec. 1, 1937; d. William Vito and Anna (Marso) M.; m. Carlo F. Saturnelli, Oct. 15, 1960; children: Anne, Karen, Carla. BA, Vassar Coll., 1959; MS, SUNY, New Platz, 1978; EdD, NYU, N.Y.C., 1993. Rsch. chemist Lederle Labs/Am. Cyanamid, Pearl River, N.Y., 1959-64; sci. coord. Marlboro (N.Y.) Cen. Sch. Dist., 1974-84; state sci. supr. N.Y. State Dept. Edn., Albany, 1984-86; dir. sci. edn. Newburgh (N.Y.) City Sch. Dist., 1986-98, exec. dir. funded programs, 1998—2001; dep. supt. of schs. Newburgh Enlarged City Sch. Dist., NY, 2001—. Project dir., proposal reviewer NSF, Washington, 1984—; state coord. N.Y. State Sci. Olympiad, 1985-86; mem. Gov. Cuomo's Task Force on Improving Sci. Edn., Albany, N.Y., 1989—; mem. adv. bd. N.Y. State Systemic Initiative, 1993—, N.Y. State Tech. Edn. Network, 1993— Author: Focus on Physical Science, 1981, 87; editor: Transforming Testing in New York State--A Collection of Past, Present and Future Assessment Practices, 1994. Project dir. Goals 2000: Educate America Act, 1996, 97, 98, 99. Recipient Presdl. award Excellence in Sci. Tchg., Washington, 1983, Pillars of the Cmty. award, City of Newburgh Family Health Ctr., 2001, Orange County Women of Achievement award, 2002; NSF 3-yr. summer sci. camp grantee, 1995, 96, 97, N.Y. State Edn. Dept. Workforce Preparation grantee, 1993-94, N.Y. State Edn. Dept. Sch.-to-Work grantee, 1995-96, 96-97, NSF Comprehensive Partnership for Math. and Sci. Achievement grantee, 1996—, Goals 2000 Educate Am. Act grantee, 1996, 97, 98, 99, Obey-Porter Comprehensive Sch. Reform Demonstration Programs grantee, 1998-99, 99-2000, 21st Century Comty. Learning Ctrs. grantee, 1999—, U.S. Dept. Edn. Small Learning Cmtys. grantee, 2000—. Mem. ASCD, Nat. Sci. Tchrs. Assn. (Exemplary Sci. Tchrs. award 1982), N.Y. State Sci. Suprs. (bd. dirs., pres. 1991, Mid Hudson Sch. Study Coun. Excellence in Adminstrn. award 1993), Sci. Tchrs. Assn. N.Y. State (pres. 1993, Outstanding Sci. Tchrs. award 1983, N.Y. State Outstanding Sci. Supr. award 1988, Fellows award 1990), Phi Delta Kappa, Delta Kappa Gamma. Home: 3 Taft Pl Cornwall On Hudson NY 12520-1713 Office: Newburgh Enlarged City Sch Dist Bd Edn 124 Grand St Newburgh NY 12550-4615

SAUCERMAN, ALVERA ADELINE, secondary school educator; b. Colorado Springs, Nov. 29, 1932; d. Alva Arthur and Delpha Adeline (Cole) Gieck; m. James Ray Saucerman; 1 child, James Randall. Student, Stephens Bus. Sch., Denver, 1950-51; AA, Scottsbluff Coll., 1961; BEd, NW Mo. State U., 1965, MEd, 1971. Cert. French, reading specialization and learning disabilities tchr. Tchr. Lake Alice (Nebr.) Sch., 1961-62, West Nodaway Sch., Clearmont, Mo., 1965-67; remedial reading tchr. Maryville (Mo.) R II, 1968-74, dir. learning lab., 1975-88, tchr. learning disabilities, 1974-97; ret. Lectr. spl. edn. N.W. Mo. State U., Maryville, 1978-97. Mem. Maryville State Tchrs. Assn. (sec. 1978-79), AAUW (life, pres. 1981-83 Maryville Br.), Mo. State Tchrs. Assn. (life), Delta Kappa Gamma, Kappa Delta Pi (life). Avocations: travel, photography, reading, dancing. Home: 1331 NW 107th Ter Gainesville FL 32606-5489

SAUDEK, MARTHA FOLSOM, artist, educator; b. Palo Alto, Calif., Nov. 27, 1923; d. David Morrill and Clinton Erwin (Stone) Folsom; m. William Morrison Kingsley, Dec. 3, 1943 (div. 1971); 1 child, Lucy Clinton Kingsley; m. Victor Mead Saudek, Aug. 18, 1973. BA, Pomona Coll., 1947. Tchr. Concord (Calif.) Sch. Dist., 1949-51, Hermosa Beach (Calif.) City Schs., 1966-76, adminstrv. asst. to supt., 1977-81. Contbg. artist: (books) Painting With Passion, 1994, How to Paint Trees, Flowers, and Foliage, 1995, How to Paint Water, 1996. Sch. bd. dirs. Manhattan Beach (Calif.) Sch. Dist., 1964-72, pres., 1965. Named to Top 100, Arts for the Parks, 1994, 96, Region III winner, 2001, One of Nat. Gold Winners, Grumbacher Hall of Fame, 1995. Fellow Am. Artists' Profl. League, Calif. Art Club (signature mem.), Oil Painters of Am. (signature). Democrat. Avocations: photography, cooking, reading, gardening. Home: 5556B Rayo Del Sol Laguna Woods CA 92653-6903 E-mail: msaudek@aol.com.

SAUER, HAROLD JOHN, physician, educator; b. Detroit, Dec. 1, 1953; s. Peter and Hildegard (Muehlmann) S.; m. Kathleen Ann Iorio, Sept. 4, 1982; children: Angela Karin Ferrante, Peter Rolf Jan Muehlmann, Josef Andrew John Iorio. BS, U. Mich., 1975; MD, Wayne State U., 1979. Diplomate Am. Bd. Ob-Gyn. Resident in ob-gyn William Beaumont Hosp., Royal Oak, Mich., 1979-83, fellow in reproductive endocrinology and infertility, 1983-85; asst. prof. dept. ob-gyn and reproductive biology Mich. State U., East Lansing, 1985-91, assoc. prof. ob.-gyn, 1991—, chmn. group practice clinicians coun., 1995—, interim chmn., 1996-98, 2002—, dept. vice chair, 1998—. Mem. staff St. Lawrence Hosp., Lansing, Mich., 1985—98, Sparrow Hosp., Lansing, 1985—; cons. Mich. Dept. Social Svcs., Lansing, 1985—; mem. Mich. Bd. Medicine, 1992—2000, chmn., 1994—97, mem., 2003—; bd. dirs. Fedn. State Med. Bds.; examer Am. Bd. Ob-gyn., 1998—; mem. Bd. of Medicine, 2003—. Fellow Am. Coll. Ob.-Gyn. (sec. Mich. sect. 1990-96, treas. 1996-99, vice-chmn. 1999-2002, chmn. 2002—); mem. AMA, Ingham County Med. Soc., Lansing Ob-Gyn. Soc., Am. Soc. Reproductive Medicine, Am. Assn. Gynecol. Laparoscopists, Wayne State U. Med. Alumni Assn., Mich. Soc. Reproductive Endocrinology (sec.-treas. 1991-93). Roman Catholic. Avocations: classical piano, microcomputers, skiing. Home: 2601 Creekstone Trl Okemos MI 48864-2455 Office: Mich State U Dept Ob-Gyn Reproductive Biology 1200 E Michigan Ave Ste 730 Lansing MI 48912-1895 E-mail: sauerh@msu.edu.

SAUER, HARRY JOHN, JR., mechanical engineering educator, university administrator; b. St. Joseph, Mo., Jan. 27, 1935; s. Harry John and Marie Margaret (Witt) S.; m. Patricia Ann Zbierski, June 9, 1956; children: Harry John, Elizabeth Ann, Carl Andrew, Robert Mark, Katherine Anne, Deborah Elaine, Victoria Lynn, Valerie Joan, Joseph Gerard. BS, U. Mo., Rolla, 1956, MS, 1958; PhD, Kans. State U., 1963. Instr. mech. engring. Kans. State U., Manhattan, 1960-62; sr. engr., cons. Midwest Rsch. Inst., Kansas City, Mo., 1963-70; mem. faculty dept. mech. and aerospace engring. U. Mo., Rolla, 1957—, prof., 1966—, assoc. chmn., 1980-84, dean grad. study, 1984-92. Cons. in field; mem. Gov.'s Commn. on Energy Conservation, 1977; mem. Mo. Solar Energy Resource Panel, 1979-83; mem. Accreditation Bd. for Engring. and Tech. Co-author: Environmental Control Principles, 1975, 4th edit., 1985, Thermodynamics, 1981, Heat Pump Systems, 1983, Engineering Thermodynamics, 1985, Principles of Heating, Ventilating and Air Conditioning, 1991, 4th edit., 2001; contbr. articles to profl. jours. Pres. St. Patrick's Sch. Bd., 1970-72, St. Patrick's Parish Council, 1975-76. Recipient Ralph R. Teetor award Soc. Automotive Engrs., 1968; Hermann F. Spoehrer Meml. award St. Louis chpt. ASHRAE, 1979; also E. K. Campbell award of merit, 1983; Louise and Bill Holladay disting. fellow, 1999. Mem. ASME, ASHRAE (disting. svc. award 1981, exceptional svc. award 2001), NSPE, Soc. Automotive Engrs., Am. Soc. Engring. Edn., Mo. Soc. Profl. Engrs., Mo. Acad. Sci. (Most Disting. Scientist award 2003), Sigma Xi. Roman Catholic. Home: 10355 College Hills Dr Rolla MO 65401-7726 Office: Dept of Mech Engring U Mo Rolla MO 65401 E-mail: sauer@umr.edu.

SAUER, JANE GOTTLIEB, artist, educator; b. St. Louis, Sept. 16, 1937; d. Leo and Sally (Walpert) Gottlieb; m. Martin Rosen, June 6, 1959 (div. 1967); children: Julie, Leo, Rachel; m. Donald Carl Sauer, Oct. 31, 1972; children: Jeffrey, Diane. BFA, Washington U., St. Louis, 1960; pvt. study with Leslie Laskey, 1976-78. Artist in residence New City Sch., St. Louis, 1976-78; artist in schs. Mo. Arts Council, St. Louis, 1979; studio artist St. Louis, 1979—. Tchr. Craft Alliance Art Ctr., St. Louis, 1979-82; juror, lectr., artistic dir. Thirteen Moons Gallery, Santa Fe, 2001—; cons. Harris Stowe Tchrs. Coll., St. Louis, 1980-84; lectr. and workshop leader various orgns. throughout country, also Australia, 1979—. Represented in collections Wash. U., Joseph & Emily Rauh Pulitzer, St. Louis, Nordenfjeldske Kunstindustrimuseum, Trondheim, Norway, Vera Mott U. Mo., Columbia, Prudential Ins. Co. Am., Dallas, Erie (Pa.) Art Mus., St. Louis Art Mus., Mus. of Nanjing, Republic of China, Mus. of Suwa, Japan, Wadsworth Atheneum Mus., Hartford, Conn., Jack Lenor Larsen, N.Y.C., Am. Craft Mus., Ark.Art Mus., Detroit Inst. of Art. M. H. De Young Mus., San Francisco, Phila. Mus. of Art, Racine (Wis.) Mus. of Art, Smithsonian Mus. Am. Art, St. Louis Art Mus., others; one and two person exhibits Craft Alliance Gallery, St. Louis, 1981, The Hand and the Spirit Gallery, Scottsdale, Ariz., 1982, 85, Am. Craft Mus., N.Y.C., 1986, Miller Brown Gallery, San Francisco, 1987, Delaware Ctr. for Contemporary Art, Johnson Mus. Art, Ithaca, N.Y., Chgo. Cultural Arts Ctr., Grand Rapids (Mich.) Art Mus., Ella Sharp Mus., Jackson, Mich., B.Z. Wagman Gallery, St. Louis, St. Louis Art Mus., 1988, Bellas Artes Gallery, Santa Fe, 1989, The Works Gallery, Phila., 1989, Folk & Craft Art Mus., San Francisco, 1989; numerous selected exhbns. U. Nebr., 2001, Ark. Art Mus., 2000, Mint Mus. of Craft and Design, 2000, R. Duane Reed Gallery, 2000, 02, Mus. Fine Arts, Santa Fe, 2003; contbr. articles to profl. publs. Mem. Sch. of Fine Arts Nat. Coun., Washington U., St. Louis; trustee New Mex. Mus. Found., 2002. Recipient Critic's Choice award, Christmas Exhibit Craft Alliance Gallery, 1979—80, Vera Mott Purchase award, 1981, Disting. Alumni award, Washington U., St. Louis, 2000, Disting. Citizen award, Arts and Edn. Coun. St. Louis, 1999; grantee, Nat. Endowment for Visual Arts, 1984, 1990, Mo. Arts Coun., 1986. Fellow: Am. Craft Coun. (hon.; bd. trustees 1992—2000, chair 1997—2000); mem.: N.Mex. Mus. Found. (trustee 2002—), St. Louis Weavers Guild, Area Coordinating Coun. (sec 1984—86, past bd. dirs.). Home: 652 Canyon Rd Santa Fe NM 87501-6108 Office: 652 Canyon Rd Santa Fe NM 87501-6108

SAUERACKER, EDWARD, academic administrator; b. Bethpage, N.Y., Apr. 20, 1956; s. William Francis and Carol Veronica (Schuyler) S. BS magna cum laude, Hofstra U., 1978; MPh in Econs., CUNY, 1982, PhD in Econs., 1984. Rsch. asst. CUNY Grad. Ctr., 1978-82; asst. prof. econs. and fin. Baruch Coll., CUNY, 1984-86, asst. dir. Ctr. for Study of Bus. and Govt., 1982-86; asst. dean for assessment SUNY Empire State Coll., Old Westbury, N.Y., 1986—, asst. prof. econs., 1990—; asst. dean for assessment Harry Van Arsdale Jr. Sch. Labor Studies SUNY-ESC, N.Y.C., 1994—. Adj. instr. dept. econs. and geography Hofstra U., 1979-84, adj. asst. prof., 1987—; editor Baruch Prospectus, Baruch Coll., CUNY, 1984; cons. in field. Author articles and column. N.Y. state rep. Coun. for Adult and Exptl. Learning, 1993-95; founder, mem. steering com. The Learning Collaborative, 1992—; bd. dirs. Help-Aid-Direction, Inc., 1991; sec. Met. Econ. Assn., 1988-91; trustee Hicksville Pub. Libr., 1994—. Unied Hosp. Fund grantee, 1985-86; CUNY fellow, Hofstra scholar, Danforth nominee; named to Outstanding Young Men of Am.; recipient Excellence in Profl. Svc. award SUNY Emprie State Coll. Mem. Kiwanis (pres. 1994-96, divsn. circle-K chair 1994—), Phi Beta Kappa, Omicron Kappa Epsilon. Home: 43 Jay St Hicksville NY 11801-5855 Office: SUNY Empire State Coll Long Island Ctr PO Box 130 Old Westbury NY 11568-0130

SAUL, BARBARA ANN, English studies educator; b. Vincennes, Ind., Feb. 20, 1940; d. Charles Dudley and Essie Faye (York) Green; children: Beth Suzanne, Becca Lynn, Brian William. BA with honors, So. Ill. U., Carbondale, 1961; MS with honors, So. Ill. U., Edwardsville, 1988. Cert. secondary English tchr., spl. reading K-12 tchr., Mo.; cert. lang. arts specialist, K-12, English 6-12, Ill. English tchr. James Island High Sch., Charleston, S.C., 1961-63, Waterloo (Ill.) High Sch., 1963-65; instr. rhetoric and composition Belleville Area Coll., 1966-67; homebound tchr. Belleville Twp. High Sch., 1966-73; Title I reading tchr. Freeburg (Ill.) Community High Sch., 1973-80; grad. asst. So. Ill. U., Edwardsville, 1986-87; reading specialist Hazelwood Schs., St. Louis, 1987-92; tchr. English, East Richland H.S., Olney, Ill., 1995—. Instr. Lion's Quest, 1988-91; team mem. Write-On project Highland (Ill.) Cmty. Schs., 1980-83; clinician Edwardsville Adult Literacy Prescription Project, 1986-88; presenter Mo/IRA State Conv., 1991; coordinating tchr. Intergenerational Oral History Gateway Writing Project, 1991-92; securities rep. Equitable Assurance Co. Bd. dirs. presch. 1st Presbyn. Ch., Belleville, 1969-73; mem. coun., conf. del. Evang. United Ch. of Christ, Highland, 1979-85, mem. choir, 1985-87; mem. Jr. High Reading Curriculum Revision Com.; mem. choir and libr. bd. First United Meth. Ch., Olney, Ill. Mem. Sigma Kappa, Phi Kappa Phi, Kappa Delta Pi, Beta Sigma Phi. Avocations: traveling, reading, cooking, music. Home and Office: PO Box 306 Olney IL 62450-0306

SAUL, MARK E. mathematics educator, consultant; b. N.Y.C., June 17, 1948; s. Sidney and Shura Saul; m. Carol Portnoy, June 26, 1968; children: Susanna, Michael, Peter. BA, Columbia U., 1969; MS, Courant Inst. Math. Scis., NYU, 1975; PhD, NYU, 1987. Tchr. math. and computer sci. Bronx High Sch. Sci., NY, 1969—85; tchg. fellow Adm. Hyman H. Rickover Found., 1985; tchr. Bronxville Schs., NY, 1985—; project dir. NSF, 2003—; dir. for curriculum rsch. and innovation Gateway Project, CUNY Rsch. Found., 2003—. Dir. Rsch. Sci. Inst. Ctr. Excellence in Edn., McLean, Va., 1987, San Diego, 90, Cambridge, Mass., 1992—99; cons. computer graphics 1984 Olympics ABC-TV, N.Y.C., 1983—84; pres. N.Y.C. Interscholastic Math. League, N.Y.C., 1979—89, Am. Regions Math. League, 1989—2000; dir. ARML-Soviet Student Exch., 1991—96; cons. Ednl. Testing Svc., Princeton, NJ, 1980—82; panelist/cons. LaGuardia HS Performing Art, N.Y.C., 1977—86; tchr. trainer N.Y.C. Bd. Edn., 1981; tchr.-coord. computer sci. Hollingworth Ctr. for Gifted, Tchrs. Coll., Columbia U., 1984; instr. Lehman Coll., 1984—92, Johns Hopkins U. Ctr. Talented Youth, 1986, Sophie Davis Biomed. Ctr. CCNY, 1986—94, Sarah Lawrence Coll., 1987—94; mem. U.S. del. to Internat. Congress Math. Educators, Budapest, 1988, Quebec, 92, Seville, 96, Tokyo, 2000. Co-author: Science/Mathematics Research Programs in the High School, 1982, The New York City Problem Book, 1986, Read the Question: A Thinking Student's Guide to the SAT's, 1992; co-author: (with I.M. Gelfand) Trigonometry, 2001; author: Enrichment Problems in Leadership Manual for High School Supervisors in Mathematics, 1982; assoc. editor edn. Notices of Am. Math. Soc., 1996—, contbr. Jour. N.Y. State Assn. Computers and Tech. in Edn., math. field editor Quantum, 1991—2001, mem. editl. bd. Mathematics and Informatics Jour., 1991—, Math. Horizons Jour., 1992—96, mem. editl. panel MAA Anneli Lax New Math. Libr., 1996—. Judge Internat. Math. Olympiad, Washington, 1981, chief guide, 2001; author contest questions Mass. Math. League Ann. Contest, 1981; mem. authors' com. Educating Teachers of Science, Mathematics, and Technology: New Practices for the New Millennium, 1998—2000. Recipient Presdl. award for Excellence in Teaching Math., NSF, 1984, Paul Erdos award, World Fedn. Nat. Math. Competitions, 1998; Tandy Tech. scholar, 1994, Gabriela and Paul Rosenbaum Found. fellow, 1995. Mem.: Nat. Coun. Tchrs. Math. (bd. dirs. 2001—04), Am. Math. Soc., Math. Assn. Am. (mem. com. on high sch. contests 1981—92), Assn. Tchrs. Math. (exec. bd. mem. 1980—85). Avocation: chamber music. Home: 711 Amsterdam Ave Apt 27K New York NY 10025-6929

SAULMON, SHARON ANN, college librarian; b. Blackwell, Okla., June 13, 1947; d. Ellis Gordon and Willa Mae Overman; 1 child, John Henry. AA, No. Okla. Coll., 1967; BA, Ctrl. State U., 1969, MBA, 1987; MLS, U. Okla., 1974; postgrad., Okla. State U., 1982. Children's libr. Met. Libr. Sys., Oklahoma City, 1969-74, coord. pub. svcs., 1974-77, asst. chief ext. svcs., 1977-80; reference/special projects libr. Rose State Coll., Midwest City, Okla., 1980-91, head libr., 1991—. Adj. faculty Rose State Coll., 1983—; program chair Global Okla. Multi-Cultural Festival, 1993; mem. Nat. Adv. Panel for Assessment of Sch. and Pub. Librs. in Support of Nat. Edn. Goals, 1995—96, project dir. internet tng., 1997, chair website com., 1996—98, v.p. profl./adminstrv. staff, 1998—99, pres., 1999—2000; vice chair Okla. Coun. Acad. Libr. Dirs., 2001—03, chair, 2003—; spkr. in field. Contbr. articles to profl. jours. Bd. dirs. Areawide Aging Agy., 1974-77; chair Met. Libr. Commn., 1990-98, disbursing agt., chair fin. com., 1986-88, long-range planning com., 1985-87; chair bd. dirs. Met. Librs. Network Ctrl. Okla., 1989-90, chair alternative funding com., 1990-98, newsletter editor, 1987-89, chair electronic media com., 1987-89, chair bd. dirs., 1997-98, Webmaster, 1997-2000. Recipient Outstanding Contbn. award Met. Libr. Sys., Friends of the Libr., 1990, Disting. Svc. award Okla. Libr. Assn., 1995, OLA/SIRS Intellectual Freedom award 1999. Mem. ALA (mem. legis. com. 1996-98, adv. bd. 1996-98, Cited Trustee award 1999), Am. Libr. Trustee Assn. (bd. dirs. 1997-98, 2000-03, pres. 1994-95, 1st v.p., pres. elect 1993-94, newsletter editor 1989-93, 99-2003, chair publs. com. 1987-92, regional v.p. 1985-88, chair speakers bur. com. 1991-92, chair awards com. 1998-99, chair pres. program com. 2000-03), Assn. Coll. and Rsch. Librs. (Cmty. and Jr. Coll. sect.), Pub. Libr. Assn., Okla. Libr. Assn. (conf. preview editor 1990-91, chair trustees divsn. 1989-90, com. mem., disting. svc. award 1995, chair divsn. univ. colls. 1996-97, chair program com. 1998-99, v.p. 1999-2000, pres. 2000-01, budget com. chair 2001-02, navigating info. chair 2002-03, career recruit, ret. chair 2003—), Am. Guild Organists. Democrat. Methodist. Office: Rose State Coll Libr 6420 SE 15th St Midwest City OK 73110-2704 E-mail: ssaulmon@yahoo.com.

SAUNDERS, DORIS EVANS, editor, educator, business executive; b. Chgo., Aug. 8, 1921; d. Alvesta Stewart and Thelma (Rice) Evans; m. Vincent E. Saunders Jr., Oct. 28, 1950 (div. 1963); children: Ann Camille, Vincent E. III. BA, Roosevelt U., 1951; MS, MA, Boston U., 1977; postgrad., Vanderbilt U., 1984. Sr. libr. asst. Chgo. Pub. Libr., 1942-46, prin. reference libr., 1946-49; libr. Johnson Pub. Co., 1949-66, dir. book divsn., 1961-66, 73-77; prof., coord. print journalism Jackson (Miss.) State U., 1977-96, acting chair dept. mass comm., 1990-91, chair, 1991-96, ret., 1996; Disting. minority lectr. U. Miss., Oxford, 1986-88; cons. book editor Kith and Kin Newsletter, 2000—. Pres. Ancestor Hunting, Chgo., 1982—; dir. cmty. rels. Chgo. State Cl., 1968-70; acting dir. instnl. devel. and cmty. rels Chgo. State Coll., 1969-70; columnist Chgo. Daily Defender, 1966-70, Chgo. Courier, 1970-73; staff assoc. Office of Chancellor, U. Ill. at Chgo. Circle, 1970-73; cons. book editor book divsn. Johnson Pub. Co., Inc., 1997-2000. Host: (radio) The Think Tank, 1971-72; writer, producer: (TV) Our People, 1968-70; producer, host: Faculty Review Forum, Sta. WJSU, 1987-93; author: Black Society, 1976; assoc. editor: Negro Digest mag, 1962-66; editor: The Day They Marched, 1963, The Kennedy Years and the Negro, 1964, DuBois: A Pictorial Biography, 1979, Wouldn't Take Nothin' for My Journey (L. Berry), 1981; compiler, editor: The Negro Handbook, 1966, The Ebony Handbook, 1974, Special Moments in African-American History: The Photographs, 1955-96, 1998; pub. Kith and Kin; contbr. to profl. jours., mags. Bd. dirs. Arts Alliance, Jackson-Hinds County, Miss., 1993, 97; mem. com. on racial reconciliation Diocese of Miss., 1982-97. Mem. NAACP. Democrat. Episcopalian. Home: 6223 Whitestone Rd Jackson MI 39206

SAUNDERS, JOANNE HINES, elementary educator; b. Yonkers, N.Y., Mar. 5, 1952; d. Bernard L. and Jean (Filippone) Hines; m. Earl Duston Saunders, June 2, 1973. BA, Marymount Coll., 1973; EdM, Boston U., 1981; cert. in gifted edn., Coll. New Rochelle, 1990. Cert. tchr., N.Y., Ky., N.J.; cert. in gifted edn., N.Y. Tchr. Marshall Elem. Sch., Ft. Campbell, Ky., 1974-77; adult tchr. Dept. of Def. Schs., Vicenza, Italy, 1978-81; elem. tchr. Little Britain Sch., Newburgh, N.Y., 1982—. Co-author: Beyond the Book, 1997; appearances include (TV) Good Morning America, 1996; contbr. articles to profl. jours. Recipient Excellence in Teaching award Springhouse Corp., 1990. Mem. Nat. Assn. Gifted Children, Cath. Women of Chapel, Nat. Honor Soc. Avocations: reading, racquetball, tennis, cross-stitch, drawing, photography, fitness. Office: Little Britain Sch 1160 Little Britain Rd New Windsor NY 12553-5906

SAUNDERS, KAREN ESTELLE, secondary school educator; b. San Carlos, Ariz., June 13, 1941; d. Walter Carl and Irma Marie (Gallmeyer) Sorgatz; m. John Richard Saunders, Dec. 27, 1962 (div. Nov. 1981). BA, Ariz. State U., 1964, MA, 1968, postgrad., 1982—. Tchr., chair art dept. McClintock H.S., Tempe, Ariz., 1964-77; tchr. Corona del Sol H.S., Tempe, 1977-98, chair art dept., 1977-87, adminstv. counc., 1977-97, chair fine arts dept., 1987-97. Coord. artists-in-schs. program Tempe Union H.S. Dist., 1975-80, program adminstr. travel/study program, 1976-78, 80, Corona del Sol H.S., 1994-95; Arizona North Central Assn. Evaluation Vis. Teams, 1969-89, program chair Four Corners Art Educators Conf., Scottsdale, Ariz., 1982; co-chair S.W. Indian Art Collectibles Exhbn., Carefree, Ariz., 1982, also editor, designer catalogue; adv. editorial bd. Sch. Arts Mag., 1989-96; artist-in-schs. coord. Corona del Sol High Sch., 1994-95; strategic planning team Tempe Union H.S. Dist., 1993-96; mem. occupational edn. adv. com. Tempe Union H.S. Dist., 1995-98; East Valley Sch.-To-Work-Equity Team liason to Corona Del Sol H.S., 1996-98; editor Connections to Career Pathways newsletter Union H.S. Dist. Sch.-to-Work Liason Team, 1997-98 Editorial bd. Jour. Art Edn., 1982-85; dir. mural project Corona Del Sol H.S., 1994-95. Mem. State Art Guide Com., Tempe, 1975-77; mem. planning com. Sheldon Lab. Systems Facilities, 1980-83; chmn. Tempe Sculpture Competition, Fine Arts Ctr., 1983; mem. Ariz. Scholastic Art Adv. Bd., Phoenix, 1983-87; judge Mill Ave. Arts Festival, Tempe, 1989, 1991-94; bd. dirs. Hackett House, 1998—, Tempe Sister Cities, 1999—. Recipient Vincent Van Gogh award Colo. Alliance for Arts Edn., 1978, Ariz. Art Educator of Yr. award Ariz. Art Edn. Assn., 1979, Leadership award Four Corners Art Educators Conf., 1982, Lehrer Mel. award Ariz. State U. Sch. Art, 1986, Tempe Diablos Ednl. Excellence awards, 1991; Ariz. State U. fellow, 1967-68. Mem. NEA, Nat. Art Edn. Assn. (v.p., bd. dirs. 1980-82, chmn. leadership workshop 1979, Nat. Assn. Gender Diversity Tng. (mem. profl. counsel com. 1998), Pacific Secondary Art Educator of Yr. award 1985, co-chair Pres.' Day 1992-95 Conv.), Assn. Secondary Curriculum Devel., Ariz. Alliance for Arts Edn. (bd. dirs. 1976-81, co-chmn. western regional conf. 1978), Tempe Secondary Edn. Assn., Ariz. Art Edn. Assn. (pres. 1976-78), Tempe Sister Cities Orgn. (bd. mem., exch. tchr. Regensburg, Germany 1992, Tchr. Exchange Core Team, 1997-2003, chmn. young artist program 1997-2003, Hackett House bd.), Mortar Bd., Phi Delta Kappa, Alpha Phi. Avocations: art, photography, flying, travel.

SAUNDERS, MAUDERIE HANCOCK, psychology educator; b. Bartlesville, Okla. d. Allen Alonzo and Maud (Giddings) Hancock; m. Leonard I. Saunders, July 4, 1950 (div.); children: Cheryle Saunders Crawford, Leonard Anthony. BS, Langston (Okla.) U., 1949; MS, U. Okla., 1950, PhD, 1961. Psychol. cons. W. Va. State Mental Health, Charleston, 1966-70; vis. counselor psychology Oklahoma City Pub. Schs., 1951-59; assoc. prof. spl. edn., dir. mental retardation So. U., Baton Rouge, 1960-62; prof. psychology and spl. edn. Minot (N.D.) State U., 1963-66; prof. human devel. W. Va. State Coll., Institute, 1966-70; prof. psychology Ea. Ill. U., Charleston, 1970-73; prof. psychoednl. studies Howard U., Washington, 1973—. Contbr. articles to profl. jours. Pres. Florigia Club of Metro. AME Ch., Washington, 1988-90; mem. com. on cert. Washington Pub. Schs., 1991. Mem. Coun. for Exceptional Children (advisor of student chpt. 1975—), Am. Psychol. Assn., Alpha Kappa Alpha, Delta Kappa Gamma (chmn. legis. com. 1990—). Home: 8148 Eastern Ave NW Washington DC 20012-1312

SAUNDERS-SMITH, GAIL ANN, educational administrator, consultant; b. Pitts., Nov. 23, 1952; d. John E. and Ruth L. Saunders; m. Charles D. Smith, June 21, 1975. BS in Early Childhood Edn., Kent State U., 1974, MA in Early Childhood Edn., 1977; MS in Adminstrn. and Supervision, Youngstown State U., 1981; PhD in Elem. Edn., U. Akron, 1994. Classroom tchr. Youngstown Diocese, Warren, Ohio, 1974-76; cooperating tchr. Kent (Ohio) State U. Lab. Sch., 1976-77; classroom tchr. Maplewood Bd. Edn., Cortland, Ohio, 1977-85; reading/lang. arts supr. Summit County Bd. Edn., Akron, Ohio, 1985-90, reading recovery tchr. leader, 1986-89, coord. state and fed. programs, 1990-94; mgr. cons. svcs. Rigby, Chgo., 1994-96, mgr. content devel. for profl. devel. dept., 1996—. Part-time faculty Kent (Ohio) State U., 1986-89; bd. mem. Stark, Summit, U. of Akron (Ohio) Tchrs. Applying Whole Lang. Group, 1987-96, Ohio Coun. Tchrs. English Lang. Arts, Columbus, Ohio, 1989-92; bd. mem. edn. com. Akron Symphony Orch., 1993-94. Author: (children's books) Giant's Breakfast, 1993, Half for You, Half for Me, 1993, Worms, 1993, How Dogs and Man Became Friends, 1993, Laughing Giraffes, 1991. Mem. Internat. Reading Assn., AAUW, Nat. Staff Devel. Coun., Phi Delta Kappa, Kappa Delta Pi, Pi Lambda Theta.

SAUTER, GAIL LOUISE, speech pathologist; b. Williamsport, Pa., Mar. 14, 1951; d. Irvin Lamont and Mary Christine (Gephart) Guthrie; m. Gary Lee Sauter, Apr. 1974; children: Amberlynn Marie, Steven James. BS in Edn., Calif. State Coll., 1974; M of Communicative Disorders, Brigham Young U., 1985. Cert. clin. speech/lang. pathologist, resource tchr. Asst. dir., dir. rehab. Summer Camp for Handicapped Children, Amherst, Ohio, 1976-77; speech/lang. pathologist Easter Seal Summer Clinic, Lorain, Ohio, 1978, Vermilion (Ohio) Sch. System, 1975-80, Alpine Sch. Dist., Orem, Utah, 1980-86, spl. edn. tchr., 1986—. Mentor Alpine Sch. Dist.; ednl. cons. Accelerated Learning Ctr., also mem. adv. bd. Pres. No. Ohio Speech & Lang. Assn., 1978-79. Mem. Am. Speech/Lang. Hearing Assn., Utah Speech/Lang. Assn., Learning Disabilities Assn. Utah. Republican. Home: 920 N 840 E Orem UT 84097-3437 Office: Orchard Elem Sch 1035 N 800 E Orem UT 84097-3462

SAUTER, MARSHA JEANNE, elementary school educator; b. Ft. Wayne, Ind., Apr. 13, 1951; d. Donald Paul and Juanita Mae (Foltz) Harsch; m. Michael Charles Sauter, Dec. 11, 1971; 1 child, Paul Michael. Student, Ball State U., 1969-71; BS in Edn. summa cum laude, U. Cin., 1974. Cert. tchr., Ohio, Okla. 6th grade tchr. Norwood (Ohio) Schs., 1974-75, 1st grade tchr., 1975-77; kindergarten tchr. Mason (Ohio) Schs., 1979-81; 1st grade tchr. Oak Park Elem. Sch. Bartlesville (Okla.) Schs., 1988—, primary curriculum coord., 1992-96, edn. com., 1991, English/math. textbook selection com., 1992, 93. Jr. H.S. youth advisor Good Shepherd Presbyn. Ch. Bartlesville, 1982-85, Sr. H.S. youth advisor, 1991-92, elder on session, 1985-88, 96—; mem. sunshine squad-crisis line Women Children in Crisis, Bartlesville, 1993—; sec. Bartlesville Cmty. Singers. Grantee Bartlesville Sch. Found., 1992, 94-96. Mem. NEA, Nat. Coun. Tchrs. Math., Tchrs. Assn. of Whole Lang., Nat. Reading Assn., Okla. Reading Assn., Soc. for Prevention of Cruelty to Animals, Okla. Edn. Assn., Toastmasters (Competent Toastmaster award 1993, sec.-treas. 1994-95, v.p. membership 1995-96), Alpha Delta Kappa. Avocations: singing, church, traveling. Home: 365 Turkey Creek Rd Bartlesville OK 74006-8116 Office: Bartlesville Pub Schs Oak Park Elem 200 Forest Park Rd Bartlesville OK 74003-1503

SAVAGE, JAY MATHERS, biology educator; b. Santa Monica, Calif., Aug. 26, 1928; s. Jesse Mathers and Mary Louise (Bird) S.; m. Ruth Louise Byrnes, June 28, 1952 (div. Feb. 1978); children: Nancy Diane, Charles Richard; m. Rebbeca E. Papendick, June 30, 1981. AB, Stanford U., 1950, MA, 1954, PhD, 1955. Asst. prof. biology Pomona Coll., Claremont, Calif., 1954-56, U. So. Calif., L.A., 1957-59, instr. biology, 1956-57, assoc. prof. biology, 1959-64, prof. biology, 1965—82; chair biology U. Miami, Coral Gables, Fla., 1982-86; prof. emeritus U. So. Calif., L.A., 1999—; prof. biology U. Miami, Coral Gables, Fla., 1982—99. Assoc. dir. Allan Hancock Found., U. So. Calif., L.A., 1964-82; rsch. dir. Evolution and Ecological Biology Sect., L.A., 1977-82; chmn. NAS com. biol. humid tropics, Washington, 1980-82; commr. Internat. Commn. Zoology, London, 1982-2000; adj. prof. biology San Diego State U., 1999—. Author: Evolution, 3d edit., 1977, Ecological Aspects of Development in the Humid Tropics, 1982, Introduction to the Herpetofauna of Costa Rica, 1986, The Amphibians and Reptiles of Costa Rica, 2002. Grants: Nat. Sci. Found, Nat. Inst., Nat. Acad.of Sci., U.S. Agency for Internat. Devel.; Guggenheim Found. fellow, 1963-64, The Explorers Club fellow, 1978; recipient Individual Achievements award Skull and Dagger, U. So. Calif., 1978, Archie F. Carr medal, 2001, Fitch award for excellence in herpetology, 2000. Mem. Am. Soc. Ichth and Herpetologists (pres. 1982), Orgn. Tropical Studies (bd. dirs. 1963—, pres. 1973-80), So. Calif. Acad. Scis. (pres. 1966-68), Soc. Sys. Biol. (pres. 1995-96), Univ. Nat. Oceaneographic Lab Sys. (vice chair 1971-73). Office: Rana Dorada Enterprises Ste A 3401 Adams Ave San Diego CA 92116-2490

SAVAGE, MARSHA KAY, education educator; b. Linden, Tex., Mar. 22, 1947; d. William Travis and Jewel Marie (Craver) Bowden; m. Tom Verner Savage, May 28, 1988; stepchildren: Greg, Steve. BS, Sam Houston State U., 1968; MEd, Tex. A&M U., 1985, PhD, 1989. Cert. tchr. secondary schs., Tex. Tchr. English A&M Consolidated High Sch., College Station, Tex., 1968-85; lectr. Tex. A&M U., College Station, 1985-88; chmn. dept edn. Calif. Bapt. Coll., Riverside, 1989-91, chmn. div. profl. svcs., 1991—. Contbr. articles to profl. jours. Mem. ASCD, Nat. Coun. Tchrs. of English, Am. Ednl. Rsch. Assn., Internat. Reading Assn., Phi Delta Kappa, Phi Kappa Phi, Kappa Delta Pi. Office: Calif Bapt Coll 8432 Magnolia Ave Riverside CA 92504-3206

SAVAGE, MICHAEL PAUL, medicine educator, interventional cardiologist; b. Wilkes-Barre, Pa., Jan. 25, 1955; s. Peter J. and Olga J. (Sekerchak) S.; m. Kathleen A. Gallagher, June 1989; children: Katherine, Andrew. BA, Wesleyan U., Middletown, Conn., 1976; MD, Jefferson Med. Coll., 1980. Diplomate Am. Bd. Internal Medicine, Am. Bd. Cardiovascular Disease Interventional Cardiology, Nat. Bd. Med. Examiners. Intern, then resident New Eng. Deaconess Hosp.-Harvard U. Med. Sch., Boston, 1980-83; fellow Jefferson Med. Coll., Phila., 1983-86, asst. prof. medicine, 1986-91, assoc. prof., 1991—, dir. cardiac catheterization, 1990—, dir. interventional cardiology sect., 1996—. Cons. Johnson & Johnson Interventional Sys. Co., Warren, N.J., Scimed/Boston Scientific, Maple Grove, Minn., GlaxoSmith-Kline, Phila.; lectr. coronary angioplasty and cardiac catheterization. Contbr. articles to profl. jours. including New Eng. Jour. Medicine, Circulation, Am. Jour. Cardiology, Jour. Am. Coll. Cardiology, JAMA, Lancet, chpts. to books. Fellow Am. Coll. Cardiology, Soc. Cardiac Angiography and Interventions, Pa. Med. Soc., Am. Heart Assn., Am. Fedn. for Clin. Rsch. Roman Catholic. Achievements include rsch. in interventional cardiology concerning new techniques in treatment of coronary artery disease, culminating in international, prospective trials demonstrating superiority of implantable coronary stents over conventional balloon angioplasty. Office: Jefferson Heart Inst 925 Chestnut St Philadelphia PA 19107-5001

SAVAGE, SANDRA HOPE SKEEN, mathematics educator, curriculum writer; b. Charleston, W.Va., Apr. 4, 1938; d. Raymond and Freda (Burgess) Skeen; m. Steven William Savage, Aug. 17, 1963; 1 child, Samantha. BS in Secondary Edn. Math and English, Bob Jones U., 1960; MS in Math., Ill. Inst. Tech., 1966; EdD in Math. Edn., Columbia U., 1976. Cert. tchr., Calif., N.Y., Ill., Fla., W.Va., Minn. Math. tchr. S. Charleston Jr. High Sch., 1960-61, Citrus Grove Jr. High Sch., Miami, Fla., 1961-62, Skiles Jr. High Sch., Evanston, Ill., 1962-65, Evanston Twp. High Sch., 1965-67, White Plains (N.Y.) High Sch., 1967-68; chmn. math. dept. The Scarborough Sch., Scarborough-on-Hudson, N.Y., 1968-71; math. tchr. Alexander Ramsey High Sch., Roseville, Minn., 1971-72, Minnehaha Acad., Mnpls., 1971-72; lectr. math. Pace U., Westchester County, N.Y., 1972-73; team leader, math. tchr. Fox Lane Mid. Sch., Bedford, N.Y., 1973-74; prof. math. Orange Coast Coll., Costa Mesa, Calif., 1977—. Lectr. math. edn. North Park Coll., Chgo., 1965; judge Odyssey of the Mind Competition, 1995; math. media cons. Annenberg Found., Washington, 1991; cons Business Link, Costa Mesa, 1990—. Designer/developer Mathematics Video Series, 1996-97, CD-ROM Design/Development, 1997. Speaker Expanding Your Horizons Women's Conf., Irvine, Calif., 1984-87; guild mem. Orange County Performing Arts Ctr., Costa Mesa, 1985-87; asst. troop leader Girl Scouts Am., Laguna Niguel, Calif., 1985-87; active Geneva Presbyn. Ch., Laguna Hills, Calif., 1983—. Recipient Cert. Merit, Nat. Merit Scholarship Corp., 1956, Tchr. of Yr. award Orange County Tchrs., 1994, Nat. Inst. for Staff and Orgn. Devel. awrd U. Tex., 1993, U.S.A. Today Teaching Excellence award, 1993; Dept. Edn. Nat. Workplace Literacy Program grantee, 1995. Fellow NSF (grantee 1983); mem. AAUW, Am. Math. Assn. Two Yr. Colls., Math. Assn. Am., Assn. for Women in Sci., Calif. Math. Coun., Orange County Math. Assn. (sec. 1982-83), Phi Delta Kappa (pres. Trabuco chpt. 1986-87, 95-96). Democrat. Avocations: music, computer graphics, multimedia/cd-rom design, poetry. Office: Orange Coast Coll PO Box 5005 2701 Fairview Rd Costa Mesa CA 92626-5563 Home: Apt P 24832 Hidden Hills Rd Laguna Niguel CA 92677-8857

SAVANNAH, MILDRED THORNHILL, public school educator; b. Lynchburg, Va., Aug. 10, 1951; d. Norman Nemrod and Ruby (Brown) Thornhill; m. Ronald L. Savannah, June 17, 2000. BS in Intermediate Edn., Elizabeth City State U., 1973; postgrad., U. Va., 1974—82, U. Tex., 1986—87; M in Ednl. Adminstr., U. North Tex., 1994. Cert. tchr., Va., Tex. Tchr. Campbell County Pub. Sch., Rustburg, Va., 1973-84; leader recreation City Lynchburg, Va., 1976-77; tchr. Dallas Ind. Sch. Dist., 1984—99, instrnl. specialist for mid. schs. math. dept., 1999—. Dir. Dealey After Sch. Tutoring Program; mem. cert. com. grades 4-8 math., 4-8 math./sci., 4-8 gen. studies, master math. tchr. Tex. State Bd. Educators, 2000; mem. assessment com. for 8th grade Tex. Assessment of Knowledge and Skills Tex. Edn. Agy., 2000—. Adult leader Campbell County 4-H Clubs, 1973—83; officer NAACP, Campbell County, Va., 1980—84; sch. coord. March of Dimes; mem. Task Force Excellence in Edn., Richmond, 1982—84; charter mem. leadership edn. com. S.W. Edn. Devel. Labs., Austin, 1985—86; appointee Tex. Edn. Agy. Grant Reader Rev. Com., Tex.; amb. to People's Republic of China People to People, 2001; dir. youth dept. devel. programs Bethany Bapt. Ch., 1974—83; chaplain, tchr. Missionary Soc.-1st Bapt. Ch., Hamilton Park; v.p. mission 2, deaconess South Oak Cliff Bapt. Ch. Named Outstanding Young Woman Am., 1981. Mem.: NEA, Tex. State Tchrs. Assn. (cert. trainer for profl. staff devel. 1984—, campus coord. Project Early Options, chair, regional rep. to state instrnl. advocacy com., bd. dirs. 1999—2002, pres. Region 19 bd. dirs.), Campbell County Edn. Assn. (pres. 1982—83), Va. Edn. Assn., Classroom Tchrs. Dallas (minority affairs chair, Black caucus chair, instrnl. and profl. devel. chair, v.p. region 19 exec. bd.), Nat. Coun. Supr. Math., Nat. Coun. Tchrs. Math., Nat. Mid. Sch. Assn., Elks, Phi Delta Kappa, Zeta Phi Beta (chair, 3d v.p. Kappa Zeta chpt., Kappa Zeta chpt. Zeta amicae 1998—). Baptist. Home: 1207 Shady Ln Lancaster TX 75146 Office: PO Box 77 3700 Ross Ave Dallas TX 75204 E-mail: msavannah@dallasisd.org.

SAVARD, CHRISTINE ELIZABETH, music educator; b. Boston, Apr. 25, 1940; d. Albert Eugene and Catherine Marie (Lusk) Lloyd; m. Emile Joseph Savard, June 27, 1964; children: Peter Joseph, Paul Eugene, Elizabeth Jane. BS, New Eng. Conservatory of Music, 1964; MM in Arts Edn., Spring Arbor U., 2002. Music tchr. Glen Cove (Maine) Christian Acad., 1962-63, The Pub. Schs., Malden, Mass., 1964-65, Vestal (N.Y.) Ctrl. Schs., 1965-68, Johnson City (N.Y.) Ctrl. Sch. Dist., 1969, Ctrl. Bapt. Christian Acad., Binghamton, NY, 1975-78, Ross Corners Christian Acad., Vestal, 1978-82, Tamworth (N.H.) Sch. Dist., 1987-90, Rogers City (Mich.) Area Schs., 1991-96; elem. music supr., tchr. Onaway Area Cmty. Schs., 1996-97; music tchr. Richardson Elem. Sch., Oscoda, Mich., 2002—03, Cedar Lake Elem. Sch., Oscoda, 1999—2002, 2003—. Music tchr. Freedom & Madison (N.H.) Sch. Dists., 1988-89. Profl. entertainer, singing and playing 8 instruments at each performance. Competition judge N.Y. State Talents for Christ, 1977-85; choir dir. First Baptist Ch., N. Conway, N.H., 1970-74; organist Mich. Home Health Care Hospice, Indian River, Mich., 1993. Mem. No. Mich. Gen. Assn. Regular Baptist Chs. (pres., spkr. ladies group 1991-96). Home: 7768 E County Line Rd South Branch MI 48761-9645

SAVAS, EMANUEL S. public management and public policy educator; b. N.Y.C., June 8, 1931; s. John and Olga (Limbos) S.; m. Helen Andrew, Dec. 25, 1955; children: Jonathan, Stephen. BA, U. Chgo., 1951, BS, 1953; MA, Columbia U., 1956, PhD, 1960; PhD (hon.), U. Piraeus, Greece, 2000. Control systems cons. IBM, Yorktown Heights and White Plains, N.Y., 1959-65; urban systems mgr. N.Y.C., 1966-67; 1st dep. city adminstr. Office of Mayor of N.Y.C., 1967-72; chmn. Mayor's Urban Action Task Force, 1969-72; prof. pub. mgmt. Columbia U., N.Y.C., 1972-83, dir. Center for Govt. Studies, 1973-83, assoc. dir. Center for Policy Rsch., 1973-81; asst. sec. for policy devel. and rsch. HUD, Washington, 1981-83; prof. mgmt. Baruch Coll., CUNY, 1981-94, prof. public policy, 1994—, dir. public policy program, 1994-97, chm. dept. mgmt., 1986-93; dir. Privatization Rsch. Orgn., 1986—. Cons. NSF, HUD, Dept. Transp., Dept. Energy, World Bank, AID, U.S. Dept. State, Pres.'s Commn. on Privatization, UN, UN Devel. Program, ILO, UNIDO, USIA, also others; mem. voting bd. Blue Cross and Blue Shield Greater N.Y., 1976-79, bd. dirs., 1979-81; mem. Pres.-Elect's Urban Affairs Task Force, 1980, N.Y. State Senate Adv. Commn. on Privatization, 1990-95; mem. Gov. Pataki privatization coun., N.Y., 1995-2000; dir. U.S.-USSR Joint Project on Mgmt. of Large Cities, 1973-81; advisor on privatization Govt. Poland, 1990-92, Govt. Lesotho, 1992, Govt. Ukraine, 1993, N.Y.C. mayor, 1994-98, Govt. South Africa, 1996, Govt. Botswana, 1996, Govt. Philippines, 1997, others. Author: Computer Control of Industrial Processes, 1965, Organization and Efficiency of Solid Waste Collection, 1977, Privatizing the Public Sector, 1982, Moscow's City Government, 1985, Privatization, 1987, Privatization and Public-Private Partnerships, 2000, 17 fgn. edits., others; editor: Alternatives for Delivering Public Services, 1977, Privatization for New York, 1992; co-author The New Public Management, 2002; mem. editorial bd. Urban Affairs Quar., Privatization Report, Privatization Watch, State and Local Govt. Rev.; contbr. 115 articles to profl. jours. Mem. N.Y.C. Mayor-elect Giuliani transition team, 1993, N.Y. Gov.-elect Pataki transition team, 1994; mem. Tenafly (N.J.) Borough Coun., 1996. With U.S. Army, 1953-54, Korea. Recipient Systems Sci. and Cybernetics award IEEE, 1968, Louis Brownlow award Am. Soc. Public Adminstrn., 1970, Honor award Templeton Found., 1989, Leadership award Nat. Coun. Pub.-Private Partnerships, 1993, Outstanding Acad. award Am. Soc. Pub. Adminstrn., 1996. Mem. Sigma Xi, Psi Upsilon. Clubs: City of N.Y. (trustee 1974-77, Richard Childs award 1979). Greek Orthodox. Office: CUNY Baruch Coll Box C-305 17 Lexington Ave New York NY 10010-5518 E-mail: prisect@aol.com.

SAVERCOOL, SUSAN ELISABETH, elementary school educator; b. La Grande, Oreg., Aug. 1, 1947; d. Edwin Gilbert and Francis Gwynne Kirby; m. Niles Seymour Duncan, June 21, 1971 (div. Sept. 1976); m. Lawrence Yeldham Savercool, Aug. 6, 1983; 1 child, David R. BA in Theater/English, Calif. State U., Northridge, 1969; MA in Elem. Edn., No. Ariz. U., 1988. Cert. elem. tchr. Calif., Ariz. Elem. tchr. St. Catherine of Siena Sch., Reseda, Calif., 1969—71; presch. tchr. La Palma E. Preschool, Anaheim, Calif., 1973—74; elem. tchr. Egremont Sch., Encino, Calif., 1977—80, Ganado Intermediate, Ariz., 1980—84, Blue Ridge Elem., Lakeside, Ariz., 1986—98; freelance writer Penn Yan, NY, 2000—. Presenter poetry for tchrs. workshop Blue Ridge Elem., Lakeside, 1991—96; instr. elem. lang. arts No. Ariz. U., Flagstaff, 1992; creatorArs Poetica. Editor: (books) Mountains of Time, vols. 1-5, 1992—97, Saint Bobo and Other Contemporary Short Stories, 1994; Ars Poetica. Actress, make-up head Theater Mountain, Lakeside, 1993—97; contbg. author Oliver House Mus., Penn Yan, 2000—. Scholar, Arts Coun., 1968. Mem.: Nat. Acad. Songwriters, Nat. Homer Poet Famoun Poets Soc., Loyal Order Moose, Phi Kappa Phi. Democrat. Roman Catholic. Achievements include development of Ars Poetica gift line. Avocations: reading, fishing, community chorus, community theater.

SAVERY, C(LYDE) WILLIAM, mechanical engineering educator; b. White Plains, N.Y., Jan. 3, 1935; s. Clyde William S. and Jean Abigale (Fisher) Taylor; m. Meredith Gore, July 25, 1958; children: Caitlin, Benjamin. BS, U. Ill., 1957; MS, U. Wash., 1960; PhD, U. Wis., 1969.·R&D assoc. Gen. Atomic, San Diego, 1960-66; from asst. prof. to prof. Drexel U., Phila., 1969-80; prof. of mech. engring., chair Portland (Oreg.) State U., 1980-89, vice provost for grad. studies and rsch., 1989-92, prof., tech. transfer officer, 1992—. Vis. prof. Katholiche U. Leuven, Belgium, 1977, U. Maribor, Slovenia, 1988; mem. vis. faculty Battelle Pacific N.W. Labs., Richland, Wash., 1992; cons. Gilbert Commonwealth Assn., Reading, Pa., 1972-80; mem. adv. bd. Advanced Sci. and Tech. Inst., Eugene, Oreg., 1991-93; bd. dirs. N.W. Acad. Computing Consortium, Seattle, 1990-92. Contbr. numerous articles to profl. jours. Bd. dirs. Friends of Chamber Music, Portland, 1994-2000. Lt. j.g. USN, 1957-59. Sr. rsch. fellow Fulbright Commn., 1988, Norcus fellow Battelle Pacific N.W. Labs., 1992. Mem. SAE (Teetor award 1972), Sigma Xi, Tau Beta Pi. Democrat. Episcopalian. Avocations: mountain climbing, skiing, travel. Office: Portland State U PO Box 751 Portland OR 97207-0751 E-mail: saveryw@comcast.com.

SAVIGNAC, AMY LYNN NORRIS, special education educator; b. Richmond, Va., Sept. 10, 1969; d. Bruce Charles Norris and Trude Newman Young; m. Kevin R. Savignac, Oct. 1, 1994. BS, Longwood U., 1991, MS, 1992. Cert. spl. edn. tchr. for emotionally disturbed, mentally retarded, learning disabled, Va. Learning disabled resource tchr. Stonewall Jackson Middle Sch., Hanover, Va., 1992-93; learning disabled self contained, resource tchr. Richard C. Haydon Elem. Sch., Manassas, Va., 1993-94, tchr. educable retarded, self contained, 1994—. Mem. NEA, Coun. for Exceptional Children. Home: 4146 Rectortown Rd Marshall VA 20115-3216

SAVINELL, ROBERT FRANCIS, engineering educator; b. Cleve., May 26, 1950; s. Robert D. and Lotte R. Savinell; m. Coletta A. Savinell, Aug. 23, 1974; children: Teresa, Robert, Mark. BSChemE, Cleve. State U., 1973; MS, U. Pitts., 1974, PhD, 1977. Registered profl. engr., Ohio. Rsch. engr. Diamond Shamrock Corp., Painesville, Ohio, 1977-79; assoc. prof. U. Akron, Ohio, 1979-86; prof. Case Western Reserve U., Cleve., 1986—, dir. Ernest B. Yeager Ctr. for Electrochem. Scis., 1991—, assoc. dean engring., 1998—, interim dean of engring., 2000, dean engring., 2001. Divsn. editor Jour. Electrochem. Soc., 1988-91; N.Am. editor Jour. Applied Electrochemistry, 1991-97; contbr. articles to profl. jours. Named Presdl. Young Investigator, NSF, Washington, 1984-89, Outstanding Engring. Alumnus, Cleve. State U., 1984. Fellow Electrochem. Soc.; mem. AIChE (program chmn. 1986-92), Electrochem. Soc. (divsn. officer 1992—), Internat. Soc. Electrochemistry (v.p. 1995-98). Avocations: sailing, skiing. Office: Case Western Reserve U AW Smith Bldg Dept Chem Eng 10900 Euclid Ave Cleveland OH 44106-4901 E-mail: Rfs2@PO.cwru.edu.

SAVIO, FRANCES MARGARET CAMMAROTTA, music educator; b. Phila., Oct. 2, 1936; d. Frank Cammarotta and Margaret Eleanor Cammarotta Parilla; m. Savio, Sept. 12, 1959; 1 child, Margaret Mary. B Music Edn., Immaculata Coll., 1958; M Music Edn., Trenton State U., 1976. Music and English tchr. East Lansdowne (Pa.) schs., 1958—59; music tchr. Mary Calcott Elem. Sch., Norfolk, Va., 1959—61; music and English tchr. Northside Jr. High, Va., 1961—63; kindergarten tchr. Bar H. Crocker Country Day Sch., Oceanside, NY, 1965—68; gen. music tchr. K-8, drama dir. St. Bartholomew Sch., NJ, 1968—. Leader Girl Scouts U.S.A.; music dir., counselor, music coord. summer camps, Pa., N.J., Va.; organist, pastoral musician St. Bartholomew Ch., East Brunswick, 1968—90; mem. curriculum com. Diocese of Trenton, 1977; organist adult choir, dir. folk group St. Bartholomew Ch., East Brunswick, NJ; mem. profl. day com., mem. com. for outstanding Cath. educator Metuchen Diocese; mem. Altar Rosary Soc. Named Tchr. of Excellence, Diocese of Metuchen, 1995. Mem.: Nat. Music Honor Soc., Pi Kappa Lambda. Home: 14 Hershey Rd East Brunswick NJ 08816

SAVISTE, TAMI RAE, early childhood educational specialist; b. Springfield, Ill., Sept. 1, 1964; AS in Early Childhood Edn., Northwest Conn. Community Coll, 1988. Nursery mgr. Courthouse One and Fitness Ctr., Simsbury, Conn., 1984-87; head tchr. pre-sch. Kinder Care Learning Ctr., Simsbury, 1987-89; ednl. program coord. Children's Discovery Ctr., East Granby, Conn., 1989-92; pre-kindergarten head tchr. Children's World Learning Ctr., Antioch, Tenn., 1992—. Mem. ASCD, Assn. for Childhood Edn. Internat., Nat. Assn. Edn. Young Children, Tenn. Assn. on Young Children, So. Assn. for Children Under Six. Avocations: aerobics, tennis, racquetball, gardening, latchwork. Office: Children's World Learning Ctr 592 Bell Rd Antioch TN 37013-2014 Address: PO Box 140652 Nashville TN 37214-0652

SAVIT, ROBERT STEVEN, physics educator, consultant; b. Chgo., Aug. 21, 1947; BA with honors, U. Chgo., 1969; MS in Physics, Stanford U., 1970, PhD in Physics, 1973. Vis. scientist CERN, Geneva, 1974-75; physicist Fermi Nat. Accelerator Lab., Batavia, Ill., 1975-78; asst. rsch. scientist U. Mich., Ann Arbor, 1978-83, assoc. prof. physics, 1983-90, prof., 1990—, dir. program for study complex sys., 1994—2000; dir. Alaska Summer Inst. in Complex Sys., 2003—. Vis. rsch. scientist Inst. Theoretical Physics, Santa Barbara, Calif., 1981-82; vis. prof. Racah Inst. Physics, Hebrew U., Jerusalem, 1986; rsch. fellow Columbia Futures Ctr., Columbia U., N.Y.C., 1988; cons. Powers Rsch., Jersey City, 1987-88, various fin. instns., non-profit instns., govt. agys., 1988—; mem. fin. strategies group Merrill-Lynch, N.Y.C., 1988. NDEA grad. fellow Stanford U., 1969-71, postdoctoral fellow NATO, Geneva, 1974-75, fellow Am. Swiss Found., 1974-75, rsch. fellow A.P. Sloan Found., 1981-85. Office: U Mich Physics Dept Ann Arbor MI 48109

SAVOIE, RONALD E. secondary educator; b. Northampton, Mass., Oct. 11, 1948; s. Emery Joseph and Marguerite (Provost) S.; m. Linda Jean Popielarczyk, Oct. 17, 1970; children: Kelly Irene, Ronelle Erin. BA in U.S. History, Assumption Coll., Worcester, Mass., 1970; MEd in History, Westfield (Mass.) State Coll., 1979. Cert. history, social studies, English tchr., Mass., Conn. Tchr. U.S. history, intramural dir., jr. varsity baseball coach St. Michael's High Sch., Northampton, 1970-76; tchr. U.S. history, jr. varsity baseball coach West Springfield (Mass.) High Sch., 1976-77; tchr. U.S. history, intramural dir. Cowing Jr. High Sch., West Springfield, 1977-81; tchr. U.S. history and geography McAlister Mid. Sch., Suffield, Conn., 1981—, coord. social studies dept., 1989-91. Mem. Suffield Social Studies Curriculum Bd., coord. 1950's and 1960's interdisciplinary unit; jr. varsity and varsity baseball coach Suffield High Sch., 1984-91. Mem., coach Southampton (Mass.) Youth Athletic Assn., 1979-91; pres. Hampshire Regional Jr.-Sr. High Sch. Booster Club, Westhampton, Mass., 1992—. Mem. NEA, Nat. Coun. for Social Studies, Conn. Coun. for Social Studies, Orgn. Am. Historians, Conn. Edn. Assn., Suffield Edn. Assn. Roman Catholic. Avocations: coaching baseball and softball, reading, golf, listening to 1950-60's music. Home: 81 Hillcrest Cir Westfield MA 01085-1872 Office: McAlister Mid Sch 260 Mountain Rd Suffield CT 06078-2086

SAVUKINAS, ROBERT STEVEN, education educator, director; b. Washington, June 2, 1971; s. John and Margaret Savukinas. BA in Spanish and Politics, Duquesne U., 1993; MA in Spanish Lit., Cath. U. Am., 1997; postgrad., George Washington U., 1998—. Staff asst. U.S. Ho. of Reps., Washington, 1993-94; instr. in Spanish Cath. U. Am., Washington, 1995-97; instr. Acad. of Holy Cross, Kensington, Md., 1997-99; grad. asst. George Washington U., Washington, 1999—2001; dir. info. mgmt. HEATH Resource Ctr., Washington, 2000—. Contbr. articles in English and Spanish to profl. jours. Capt. USAR, 1993—. Army ROTC scholar Dept. Def., 1990. Mem. Am. Assn. Tchrs. Spanish and Portuguese, Am. Translators Assn., Am. Assn. CCs. Republican. Roman Catholic. Avocations: car racing, boating. Home: 1600 N Oak St Arlington VA 22209 Office: Heath Resource Ctr 2121 K St NW Ste 220 Washington DC 20037 E-mail: rss@gwu.edu.

SAWAI, DAHLEEN EMI, language educator; b. Honolulu, Mar. 13, 1954; d. Kiyoto and Aiko Sawai. BA, U. Hawaii, Manoa, 1975, diploma in elem. edn., 1977, diploma in secondary edn., 1981, MEd, 1984. Cert. tchr. Hawaii. English tchr. Tokyo Family Court, 1977—78; Japanese tchr. Kailua H.S., Honolulu, 1978—80; English tchr. Family Ct. Probation Officer Tng. Sch., Tokyo, 1983—84; Japanese tchr. W. R. Farrington H.S., Honolulu, 1985—; educator Consortium for Tchg. Asia and the Pacific in the Schs., Honolulu, 1989—95; tchr. Family Court Probation Officer Training Sch., Tokyo. Instr. Sch. Cmty. Based Mgmt., Honolulu, 2000—; interpreter Star Tanjo, 1976; chmn. Dept. World Langs. W.R. Farrington H.S., Honolulu, 2001—. Dir. Moanalua Gardens Cmty. Assn., Honolulu, 1976—77, sec., 1978—80. Scholar, Keio Gijuku Daigaku, 1982—84. Mem.: Farrington Alumni and Cmty. Found., Japanese Cultural Ctr. of Hawaii, Temari Ctr. for Asian and Pacific Arts, Alliance for Drama Edn., Pi Lambda Theta.

SAWYER, CHERYL LYNNE, foundation administrator, educator, consultant; b. Balt., Mar. 8, 1954; d. Carolyn (Brooks) Bulcken; m. Gary W. Sawyer, July 16, 1976; children: Jesse, Stacy. BA in English, Sam Houston State U., 1976; MA in Behavioral Scis., U. Houston, Clear Lake, 1984; EdD in Adminstrn. and Supervision, U. Houston, University Park, 1993. Lic. psychol. assoc., Tex.; cert. trauma cons.; cert. English, history, psychology, learning disabilities tchr., Tex.; cert. diagnostician, counselor, spl. edn. counselor, assoc. sch. psychologist, Tex.; lic. specialist sch. psychology. Tchr. Alvin (Tex.) Ind. Sch. Dist., 1976-84, LaMarque (Tex.) Ind. Sch. Dist., 1985-90; ednl. cons. Dickinson, Tex., 1992—; from vis. asst. prof. to adj. prof. U. Houston, 1990—99; dir. acute children's programs Devereux Found., League City, Tex., 1994-97; counselor LaMarque (Tex.) Ind. Sch. Dist., 1997-98; tchr. Dickinson Ind. Sch. Dist., 1998—2000; asst. prof. counselor edn. U. Houston, Clear Lake, 2000—, coord. counselor edn., 2000—. Mem. adv. bd. spl. edn. Santa Fe Sch. Dist., 1993, 94, 95; mem. adv. bd. drug and alcohol prevention LaMarque Sch. Dist., 1989, 90, 91, 92; spkr. child-related psychol. issues; presenter in field. Contbr. articles to profl. jours. Mem. Am. Counseling Assn., Tex. Counseling Assn., Nat. Assn. for Gifted, Coun. for Exceptional Children, Dickinson Civic Assn. (bd. dirs. 1996-99, 2002—), Beta Sigma Phi, Phi Delta Kappa, Chi Sigma Iota. Home: 12308 Marion Ln Dickinson TX 77539-9224

SAWYER, THOMAS HARRISON, health, physical education and recreation director; b. Apr. 5, 1946; s. Harrison Donald and M. Daughn (Geer) Sawyer; m. Kathleen Ann Daly, July 5, 1969; children: Shawn Thomas, Meghan Daly. BS, Springfield Coll., 1968, MPE, 1971; EdD, Va. Polytech Inst., 1977. Instr. health, phys. edn., recreation Va. Mil. Inst., Lexington, 1969—72, asst. prof., 1972—75, assoc. prof., 1975—79; dir. recreation ctr. U. Bridgeport, 1979—81; assoc. prof. head dept. Mont. Tech. Inst., Butte, 1981—84; prof., chmn. phys. edn. dept. Ind. State U., Terre Haute, 1984—89, prof., 1984—, coord. sport mgmt. programs, 1984—. Cons. Mont. Fitness, Butte, 1981—84, ARC, Mont., 1981—83, Wellness-Pillsbury Co.; pres. Ind. Ctr. Sport Edn., Inc., 1995—. Mem. editl. bd.: Jour. Employee Health and Fitness, Mag. Health Mgrs., 1984—89; contbr. articles to profl. jours. Bd. dirs. YMCA, Butte, 1981—84; mem. Sch. Bd. Dist. 1, Butte, 1982—84; bd. dirs. Vocation Edn. Coun. Mont., 1983—84; chair Task Force for Encouragement of Quality, Daily Phys. Edn. Programs for Ind. Pub. Schs., 1987—88, Phys. Edn. Adv. Task Force, 1988—91; dir. Ctr. Coaching Edn., 1988—94, Ind. PACE, 1984—99, Ind. LANCE, 1999—. Recipient Founder's award, Alcohol Svcs., Buena Vista, Va., 1979, Red Triangle, YMCA, Butte, 1982; scholar, NDEA, 1968; N.Am. fellow, Health, Phys. Edn., Recreation, Sport, and Dance, 2000. Mem.: ARC (bd. dirs. Terre Haute chpt. 1985—87, 1988—94, state svc. coun. 1993—99, chair 1994—97, bd. dirs. Terre Haute chpt. 1996—2000, 2002—, state svc. coun. 2002—, Vol. Safety award 1981), Soc. Study of Legal Aspects of Sport and Phys. Activity (treas. 1994—96, exec. dir. 1997—2001, editor Jour. Legal Aspects of Sports 1995—2000, Hon. award 2003), Coun. Facilites and Equipment (chair 1995—97, Prof. Recognition award 2002, Hon. award 2002), Am. Assn. Active Lifestyles and Fitness (pres.-elect 1996—97, pres. 1997—2000, Hon. award 2003), Employee Svcs. Mgmt. Assn., Assn. Fitness in Bus., Nat. Assn. Sports Offcls., Ind. Assn. Phys. Edn., Recreation and Dance (editor jour and newsletter 1987—, conv. coord. 1992—2000), Am. Alliance for Health, Phys. Edn., Recreation and Dance (editl. bd. 1991—95, chair 1993—95). Office: Acad Partnership Terre Haute IN 47809-0001

SAWYER, WILLIAM DALE, physician, educator, university dean, foundation administrator; b. Roodhouse, Ill., Dec. 28, 1929; s. Cloyd Howard and Eva Collier (Dale) S.; m. Jane Ann Stewart, Aug. 25, 1951; children—Dale Stewart, Carole Ann. Student, U. Ill., 1947-50; MD cum laude, Washington U., St. Louis, 1954; ScD (hon.), Mahidol U., Bangkok, 1988; DPH (hon.), Chiang Mai U., Thailand, 1993, Chulalongkorn U., 1998. Intern Washington U.-Barnes Hosp., 1954-55, resident, 1957-58, fellow, 1958-60; asst. prof. microbiology Johns Hopkins U., Balt., 1964-67; prof., chmn. dept. microbiology Rockefeller Found.-Mahidol U., Bangkok, 1967-73, Ind. U. Sch. Medicine, Indpls., 1973-80; prof. depts. medicine, microbiology and immunology Wright State U., Dayton, Ohio, 1981-87, dean Sch. Medicine, 1981-87; pres. China Med. Bd. N.Y., Inc., 1987-97. Adj. prof. biology Ball State U., Muncie, Ind., 1978-80; hon. prof. microbiology Sun Yat Sen U. Med. Sci., 1987; hon. prof. Peking Union Med. Coll., 1989; hon. advisor Beijing Med. U.; cons. U.S. Army Med. R & D Command, WHO Immunology Ctr., Singapore, 1969-73; mem. bd. sci. advisers Armed Forces Inst. Pathology, 1975-80, chmn., 1979-80; adj. prof. medicine and microbiology and immunology N.Y. Med. Coll., Valhalla, 1990-96; hon. prof. China Med. U., 1995, West China U. Med. Sci., 1995, Zhejiang Med. U., 1995, Jiujang Med. Coll., 1995, Hunan Med. U., 1996, Xian Med. U., 1996, Shanghai Med. U., 1996. Contbr. numerous articles to profl. jours. Mem. Lobund adv. bd. U. Notre Dame; dir. Georgetown Area Cmty. Found., 1998-2002, pres. 1999. Served to maj. M.C., USA, 1955-64. Recipient Gold medal of merit Airlangga U., Indonesia, 1992, Pub. Health Recognition award Asia-Pacific Acad. Consortium Pub. Health, 1993, China Health medal, 1996, White Magnolia award, 1996. Fellow ACP; mem. AAAS, Am. Soc. Microbiology (br. pres. 1976), Sci. Rsch. Soc. Am., Am. Fedn. Clin. Rsch., Ctrl. Soc. Clin. Rsch., Infectious Diseases Soc. Am., Soc. Exptl. Biology and Medicine, Am. Acad. Microbiology, Am. Assn. Pathologists, Assn. Am. Med. Colls. (coun. deans 1980-87), Phi Beta Kappa, Sigma Xi, Alpha Omega Alpha. Home: 124 Poppy Hills Cv S Georgetown TX 78628-1179 E-mail: wllmsawyer@aol.com.

SAX, BORIA, intellectual history studies educator, writer; b. NYC, Mar. 31, 1949; s. Saville and Susan Sax; m. Linda Jean Wooh, Apr. 16, 1977. BA, U. Chgo., 1972; MA in German, SUNY, Buffalo, 1978, PhD in German and History, 1981. Adj. full prof. Pace U., White Plains, N.Y., 1982-91; adj. prof. Mercy Coll., Dobbs Ferry, N.Y., 1986—, dir. online acad. svcs., 2000—; instr. N.Y. Bot. Garden, 1998—, Audrey Cohen Coll., N.Y., 2000-01. Cons. Ammesty Internat., N.Y.C., 1988-89, Eastern Europe coord., 1981-90; pres. Nature in Legend and Story, White Plains, 1992—. Author: (nonfiction) The Frog King, 1990, The Parliament of Animals, 1992, The Serpent and the Swan, 1998, Animals in the Third Reich, 2000, The Mythological Zoo, 2001, The Crow, 2003, (poetry) Rheinland Market, 1987. Recipient Online Learning Effectiveness award The Sloan Consortium, 2002; grantee Modern German Studies, 1979, Pace U., 1985-90, N.Y. Coun. Humanities, 1993, 96, 98, AT&T, 2003. Mem.: Internat. Soc. Anthrozoology, Nature In Legend and Story. Avocations: jewelry making, miniature sculptures, hiking, history. Home: 25 Franklin Ave Apt 2F White Plains NY 10601-3819 Office: Mercy Coll 555 Broadway Dobbs Ferry NY 10522 E-mail: vogelgreif@aol.com.

SAX, DANIEL SAUL, neurologist, educator; b. Balt., Jan. 27, 1935; s. Benjamin and Miriam (Helfgott) S.; m. Joan Atherton Bond, Mar. 25, 1962; children: Karen Bond, John Derek, Diana Atherton. AB, Johns Hopkins U., 1955; MD, U. Md., 1959. Diplomate Am. Bd. Psychiatry and Neurology. Intern Boston City Hosp., 1959—60, resident in neurology and neuropathology neurologic unit, 1961—64; resident in neurology N.E. Med. Ctr., Boston, 1961; asst. prof. neurology Northwestern U., Chgo., 1966-67; assoc. prof. neurology Albert Einstein Med. Sch., N.Y.C., 1967-69, Boston U. Sch. Med., 1969-76, prof. neurology, 1976-2000, prof. emeritus neurology, 2000—. Chief neurology svcs. Boston VA Outpatient Clinic, 1974-90; EEG lab. dir., cons. Gifford Med. Ctr., Randolph, Vt., 1977—, neurologist, 1977—; cons. neurology Boston VA Med. Ctr., 1991-2000, hon. staff, 2002. Clin. adv. com. Vt. divsn. Nat. MS Soc., 2001, clin. adv. com. ctrl. N.E. chpt., 1977—. Lt. comdr. USNR, 1964-66. Fellow: Am. Acad. Neurology; mem.: AMA, Internat. Soc. Women Health and Sexuality, Huntington's Study Group, Huntington's Dx Soc. (mem. adv. bd. Mass. chpt. 1980—2000, clin. adv. bd. 2001—), Multiple Sclerosis Soc. (clin. adv. bd. 1977—), Boston Soc. Neurology and Psychiatry (pres. 1982—83, exec. com. 1985—, Vt. bd. med. practice 2002—), Mass. Med. Soc., Am. Soc. Neuroimaging, Am. Assn. for Study of Headache, Am. Neurol. Assn. Avocations: tree farmer, oenology, music. Office: Gifford Med Ctr Neurology 44 S Main St Randolph VT 05060 also: 258 W Cummings Park Woburn MA 01801 E-mail: dsax@giffordmed.org., dssax@adelphia.net.

SAX, JOSEPH LAWRENCE, lawyer, educator; b. Chgo., Feb. 3, 1936; s. Benjamin Harry and Mary (Silverman) S.; m. Eleanor Charlotte Gettes, June 17, 1958; children: Katherine Elaine Dennett, Valerie Beth, Amber Sax Rosen. AB, Harvard U., 1957; JD, U. Chgo., 1959; LLD (hon.), Ill. Inst. Tech., 1992. Bar: D.C. 1960, Mich., 1966, U.S. Supreme Ct. 1969. Atty. U.S. Dept. Justice, Washington, 1959-60; pvt. practice law Washington, 1960-62; prof. U. Colo., 1962-65, U. Mich., Ann Arbor, 1966-86; dep. asst. sec. and counselor U.S. Sec. Interior, Washington, 1994-96; prof. U. Calif. Law Sch., Berkeley, 1986—. Fellow Ctr. Advanced Study in Behavioral Scis., 1977-78. Author: Waters and Water Rights, 1967, Water Law, Planning and Policy, 1968, Defending the Environment, 1971, Mountains Without Handrails, 1980, Legal Control of Water Resources, 3rd edit., 2001, Playing Darts with a Rembrandt, 1999. Fellow: AAAS. E-mail: saxj@law.berkeley.edu.

SAXE, THELMA RICHARDS, secondary school educator, consultant; b. Ogdensburg, N.J., Apr. 21, 1941; d. George Francis and Evelyn May (Howell) Richards; m. Kenneth Elwood Meeker, Jr., June 22, 1957 (div. 1965); children: Sylvia Lorraine Meeker Hill, Michelle Louise Meeker Aromando, David Sean (dec.); m. Frederick Ely Saxe, Feb. 18, 1983; stepchildren: Jonathan Kent, Holly Harding Schenker. BA, William Paterson Coll., Wayne, N.J., 1972, MEd, 1975, postgrad., 1983-84; Dyslexia cert., Fairleigh Dickinson U., 1994; organ student, Rick Roberts; voice student, Dr. Roberta Moger; studied organ with, Rick Roberts. Cert. paralegal. Tchr. handicapped Sussex (N.J.)-Wantage Regional Sch. Dist., 1972-75; resource rm. tchr. Sussex County Vo-Tech Sch., Sparta, N.J., 1975-77, learning cons., 1977-83; learning specialist Bennington-Rutland Supervisory Union, Manchester, Vt., 1986-87; learning cons. Stillwater (N.J.) Twp. Sch., 1987-88, Independence Twp. Cen. Sch., Great Meadows, N.J., 1989; learning cons., tutor in pvt. practice specializing dyslexia Sparta, 1986-97; asst. prin. Harmony Twp. Sch., Harmony, N.J., 1989-92; learning cons. Montague (N.J.) Elem. Sch., 1996-98; coord. gifted/talented Sussex Vo-Tech, 1980-83; coord. child study team Stillwater Twp. Sch., 1987-88, Montague Twp. Sch., 1996-98; ret., 1998; learning cons. Sandyston-Walpack Consolidated Sch., 1997-98. Soprano mem. Nature Coast Festival Singers, Spring Hill, Fla. Mem.: Kappa Delta Pi. Democrat. Presbyterian. Avocations: piano, organ, travel. Home: 3029 N Annapolis Ave Hernando FL 34442-4718

SAXTON, MARY JANE, management educator; b. Syracuse, N.Y., Mar. 3, 1953; d. John Cook and Florence (Cooper) S.; m. Paul Hood. BA, SUNY, Cortland, 1975; MBA, U. Pitts., 1979, PhD, 1987. Counselor Methadone Mgmt. Svcs., Inc., N.Y.C., 1975-76; resident mgr. Crossroads Svcs., Inc., Jackson, Miss., 1976; outreach worker Jackson Mental Health Ctr., 1977-78; cons. Organizational Design Cons., Inc., Pitts., 1982-83, mktg. dir., 1984-86; asst. prof. mgmt. U. Houston, 1988-93; lectr. mgmt. U. Colo., Denver, 1994-97, U. Denver, 1994-96, Colo. Christian Coll., Denver, 1996; lectr. Met. State Coll., Denver, 1996-97; vis. assoc. prof. in strategy Norwegian Sch. Mgmt., Oslo, 1997-98, vis assoc. prof. in knowledge mgmt., 1999; orgnl. cons. Internat. Petroleum Cons. Assn., Inc., Evergreen, Colo., 1999—; vis. instr. U. Colo., Denver, 2000. Sabbatical researching Arab culture, Abu Dhabi, United Arab Emirates, 2001—01; cons. Wessex, Ctr. for Creative Comm., Kodak, Children's Hosp., Pullman Swindell, Westinghouse Elec. Corp., IPCA, Inc., Bergen, Norway, 2002—03; lectr. in field. Co-editor: Gaining Control of the Corporate Culture, 1985; co-author: The Kilmann-Saxton Culture-Gap Survey, 1983; contbr. articles to profl. jours. Active Greater Houston Women's Found., 1991-93. U.S.-Soviet Joint Ventures grantee U. Houston, 1990. Mem. ASTD, Acad. of Mgmt., Inst. Ops. Rsch. and Mgmt. Svcs. Avocations: flying, sailing, reading, biking, movies. Home and Office: PO Box 1657 Evergreen CO 80437-1657 E-mail: ipcainc@attglobal.net.

SAYAVEDRA, LEO, academic administrator; Formerly Tex. A&M Internat. U., Laredo; now vice chmn. acad. and student affairs The Tex. Univ. Sys., College Station. Office: The Tex Univ System 301 Tarrow College Station TX 77840-7896

SAYER, COLETTA KEENAN, gifted education educator; b. Cleve., July 4, 1950; d. Nicholas Charles and Coletta (Kuonen) Yawarsky; m. Mark Andrew Sayer, June 3, 1978; 1 child, Mark Martin. BA, St. Mary of the Wood Coll., 1972. Classroom tchr. Cath. Diocese of Cleve., 1972-76; learning disabilities specialist Brunswick (Ohio) Bd. Edn., 1976-77; classroom tchr. of gifted Houston Bd. Edn., 1988-91; tchr. ESL Benbrook Elem. Sch. Houston Ind. Sch. Dist., 1991-96; coord. gifted and talented Benbrook Elem. Sch., 1998—. Peer coord. Houston Ind. Sch. Dist., Algebra Initiative Fifth Grade. Houston Bus. Com. for Excellence in Edn. grantee, 1989. Mem. ASCD, Houston Classroom Tchrs. Assn. (pres. 1996—). Roman Catholic. Avocation: drama. Office: Benbrook Elem Sch 4026 Bolin Rd Houston TX 77092-4711 E-mail: csayer@houstonisd.org., teachers@mail.evl.net.

SAYLES, SANDRA, nursing educator; b. Chicago; d. Timothy Sayles, Lessie Sayles. PhD, U. Tex., 1989. RN 1972. Asst. prof. DePaul U., Chgo., 1976—88; assoc. prof., asst. dean St. Xavier U., Chgo., 1989—92; dir., spl. asst. to pres. U. Tex.-Tyler, 1992—99; prof. Northwestern State U., Shreveport, La., 1999—. Mem.: Consortium Drs., Black Nurses Assn., Assn. Cmty. Health Nurse Educators, Assn. Black Nursing Faculty, Sigma Theta Tau. Office: Northwestern State U 1800 Line Ave Shreveport LA 71101 Office Fax: 419-791-7680. Business E-Mail: sayless@nsula.edu.

SAYLOR, ROSELLEN BETH, special education educator; b. Johnstown, Pa., May 21, 1954; d. Wilford R. and Elizabeth (Weaver) S. BS in Education, Otterbein Coll., 1976; MA in Counseling, Ind. U., 1998. Cert. tchr. Pa. Jr. h.s. tchr. remedial reading, math. and English, Johnstown Christian Sch., Hollsopple, Pa., 1976-77, elem. tchr., 1977-86; tchr. Petersburg Elem. Sch., Pageland, S.C., 1986-87; elem. tchr. Johnstown Christian Sch., Hollsopple, Pa., 1987-93, ednl. therapist, 1993—. Mennonite. Avocations: swimming, writing poetry, reading, farming, travel. Office: Johnstown Christian Sch RR 2 Box 166 Hollsopple PA 15935-9802

SAYRE, KENNETH MALCOLM, philosophy educator; b. Scottsbluff, Nebr., Aug. 13, 1928; s. Harry Malcolm and Mildred Florence (Potts) S.; m. Lucille Margaret Shea, Aug. 19, 1958 (dec. Apr. 1980); children: Gregory, Christopher, Jeffrey; m. Patricia Ann White, Apr. 4, 1983; 1 child, Michael. AB, Grinnell Coll., Iowa, 1952; MA, Harvard U., 1954, PhD, 1958. Asst. dean Grad. Sch. Arts and Letters Harvard U., Cambridge, Mass., 1953-56; systems analyst MIT, Cambridge, Mass., 1956-58; from instr. to prof. philosophy U. Notre Dame, Ind., 1958—, dir. Philosophic Inst., 1966—. Author: Recognition, 1965, Consciousness, 1969, Plato's Analytic Method, 1969, Cybernetics and the Philosophy of Mind, 1976, Moonflight, 1977, Starburst, 1977, Plato's Late Ontology, 1983, Plato's Literary Garden, 1995, Parmenides' Lesson, 1996, Belief and Knowledge, 1997. Served with USN, 1946-48 NSF grantee, 1962-79; NEH fellow, 1995-96. Mem. Am. Philos. Assn., Phi Beta Kappa Home: 910 Weber Sq South Bend IN 46617-1850 Office: Univ Notre Dame Dept Philosophy Notre Dame IN 46556

SBUTTONI, KAREN RYAN, reading specialist; b. Albany, Sept. 9, 1953; d. Patrick Frederick and Virginia Mary Ryan; m. Michael James Sbuttoni, Aug. 9, 1975; children: Michael Louis, Ashley Ryan. BS in Bus. Edn., Buffalo State Coll., 1979; MS in Bus. Edn., SUNY, Albany, 1983, MS in

Reading, 1991, cert. advanced study in reading, 1994. Cert. reading specialist K-12 and bus. edn. 7-12, N.Y. Tchr. Williamsville East H.S., Buffalo, N.Y., spring 1979, East Irondequoit H.S., Rochester, N.Y., 1979-81; reading specialist Albany Acad., 1992—. Tchg. asst. SUNY, Albany, 1992; mem. admissions com., curriculum com., 1999. Religious edn. tchr. St. Pius X Ch., Loudonville, N.Y., 1982-84. Mem. ASCD, Internat. Reading Assn., Nat. Coun. Tchrs. English. Avocations: skiing, walking, reading, cross-stitching.

SCAFFIDI, JUDITH ANN, academic administrator; b. Bklyn., Aug. 2, 1950; d. Anthony William and Rose Virginia (Nocera) S. BA, SUNY, Plattsburg, 1972, MS, 1973; postgrad., Einstein Coll. Medicine, 1983; PhD (hon.), Internat. U. Bombay, 1993; HHD (hon.), London Inst. Applied Rsch., 1993. Cert. secondary edn. English. VISTA mem. ACTION, N.Y.C., 1976-77; coord. cultural resources Learning Leaders, N.Y.C., 1977-80, tng. splst. in Bklyn., 1980—. Field supr., adj. faculty Coll. for Human Svcs., N.Y.C., 1984-86; adv. coun. chair Ret. Sr. Vol. Program in Bklyn., 1983-86; adv. bd. Ret. Sr. Vol. Program in N.Y.C., 1983-86. Acvive Am. Friends Svc. Com., 1994—. Recipient award for svcs. in promotion literacy Internat. Reading Assn. and Bklyn. Reading Coun., 1986, award for outstanding leadership Ret. Sr. Vol. Program, 1986, cert. of appreciation Mayor City of N.Y., 1991, cert. of appreciation for exceptional support and encouragement of volunteerism, 1998. Mem. NAFE, Cath. Tchrs. Assn. Bklyn. (del. sch. dist. 18, 1982-91), Internat. Platform Assn., World Found. Successful Women, Am. Biog. Inst. (rsch. bd. advisors 1992-93), Am. Biog. Inst. Rsch. Assn. (bd. govs. 1992—), Internat. Parliament for Safety and Peace (dep. mem. and diplomatic passport), Maisson Internat. de Intellectuels (Acad. MIDI), Cath. Alumni Club N.Y., Amnesty Internat. Roman Catholic. Avocations: foreign and domestic travel, reading, walking. Home: 2330 Ocean Ave Apt 3H Brooklyn NY 11229-3036 Office: Learning Leaders 352 Park Ave S Fl 13 New York NY 10010-1709

SCAFFIDI-WILHELM, GLORIA ANGELAMARIE, elementary education educator; b. Vineland, N.J., June 3, 1960; d. Joseph J. and Gloria Scaffidi; m. Andrew H. Wilhelm, Nov. 7, 1992; 1 child, Joseph Nicholas. BA summa cum laude, Glassboro State Coll., 1982. Cert. tchr. elem. edn., N.J. Tchr. 3rd grade St. Nicholas Sch., Egg Harbor City, NJ, 1982—85; 4th grade tchr. Charles L. Spragg Sch., Egg Harbor City, NJ, 1986—2002. Advisor cheerleading club Egg Harbor City Schs., 1988-91, journalism club, 1989-93, staff mem. yearbook com., 1990-94, 96-97, editor sch. newspaper, 1989-94, 96-97, advisor pub. rels. sch. activities, 1989-94, 96-97. Named Tchr. of Yr., Egg Harbor City Schs., 1989-90. Mem. N.J. Edn. Assn., Kappa Delta Pi. Roman Catholic.

SCALA, JOHN CHARLES, secondary education educator, astronomer; b. Summit, N.J., Mar. 20, 1958; s. John Michael and Lola Ann (Bevilacque) S.; m. Virginia Anne Ronen, Oct. 11, 1980; children: Aubrey Lyn, Valerie Anne. BA in Astronomy, Lycoming Coll., 1980. Tchr. Stetson Mid. Sch., West Chester, Pa., 1980-82, Mendham (N.J.) H.S., 1982-83, Hopatcong (N.J.) Mid. Sch., 1983; shipment insp. Ciba-Geigy Pharms., Summit, 1983-87; tchr., dir. planetarium Lenape Valley H.S., Stanhope, N.J., 1987—. Adj. prof. astronomy County Coll. Morris, Randolph, N.J., 1983-89, Sussex County C.C., Newton, N.J., 1989—; resource tchr. Am. Astron. Soc., Austin, Tex., 1994—; people to people citizen amb., China, 1997. Merit badge counsellor Morris-Sussex coun. Boy Scouts Am., 1988—. Recipient Gov.'s Recognition award N.J. Dept. Edn., 1991, award A-Plus for Kids Network, 1993; named Tchr. of Yr., Lenape Valley H.S., 1995, Air Force Assn. High Point chpt., 1999, N.J. Air Force Assn., 1999; Geraldine R. Dodge Found. grantee, summer 1993. Mem. NSTA, Internat. Planetarium Soc., Mid. Atlantic Planetarium Soc., Garden State Planetarium Resource Assn. Avocations: photography, reading, camping. Office: Lenape Valley HS Planetarium Sparta Rd Stanhope NJ 07874

SCALA, MARILYN CAMPBELL, literacy and inclusion consultant, writer; b. Lansing, Mich., June 25, 1942; d. Coral Edward and Eloise Campbell; children: Nicholas, Anne. BS Edn., U. Mich., 1964; MA Spl. Edn., Columbia U., 1967. Cert. elem. edn., spl. edn. tchr., N.Y. Tchr. physically handicapped Multi-Age, Port Chester, N.Y., 1964-66; tchr. spl. edn. PS 199, N.Y.C., 1966-69, Manhattan Sch. for Seriously Disturbed, N.Y.C., 1969-70; tchr. regular and spl. edn. Munsey Park Sch., Manhasset, N.Y., 1970-99. Cons. in field. Co-author: Three Voices: An Invitation to Poetry Across the Curriculum, 1995; author: Working Together: Reading and Writing in Inclusive Classrooms, 2001; contbr. articles to profl. jours. Avocations: reading, writing, travel, museum visits.

SCALETTA, PHILLIP JASPER, lawyer, educator; b. Sioux City, Iowa, Aug. 20, 1925; s. Phillip and Louise (Pelmulder) S.; m. Helen M. Beedle; children: Phillip R., Cheryl D. Kesler. BS, Morningside Coll., Sioux City, Iowa, 1948; JD, U. Iowa, 1950. Bar: Iowa 1950, U.S. Dist. Ct. Iowa 1950, Ind. 1966, U.S. Supreme Ct. 1968. Ptnr. McKnight and Scaletta, Sioux City, 1950-51; field rep. Farmers Ins. Group, Sioux City, 1951-54, sr. liability examiner, Aurora, Ill., 1954-60; br. claims mgr., Ft. Wayne, Ind., 1960-66; prof. law Purdue U., West Lafayette, Ind., 1966—; dir. profl. masters programs of the Krannet Grad. Sch. of Mgmt. Purdue U., 1987-90; of counsel with Mayfield & Brooks Attys. at Law, 1967—; arbitrator Panel of Arbitrators Am. Arbitration Assn. Co-author: Business Law and Regulatory Environments, 5th edit., 1996, Business Law Workbook, 5th edit., 1996, Foundations of Business Law and Legal Environment, 1986, 4th edit., 1997, Student Workbook and Study Guide, 1986, 4th edit., 1997; contbr. numerous articles to profl. jours. Mem. Ind. Gov's Commn. Individual Privacy, 1975. Recipient Best Tchr. of Yr. award Standard Oil Ind. Found., 1972, Outstanding Tchr. award Purdue U. Alumni Assn., 1974, Most Effective Tchr. award Krannert Grad. Sch. Mgmt. Purdue U., 1991. Mem. Am. Bus. Law Assn. (pres., Sr. Faculty Excellence award 1989), Tippecanoe County Bar Assn., Tri State Bus Law Assn. (past pres.), Midwest Bus. Adminstrn. Assn., Beta Gamma Sigma (bd. govs.). Office: Purdue U 511 Krannert Bldg West Lafayette IN 47907

SCALISE, FRANCIS ALLEN, administrator, consultant; b. Rochester, N.Y., Dec. 16, 1930; s. Sam and Margaret Rose (Seran) Scalise; children: Allen, Stephen. BS in Elem. Edn., SUNY, Brockport, 1952; MEd in Ednl. Adminstrn., U. Rochester, 1956. Tchr. Virgil I. Grissom Sch. 7, Rochester, 1955-60, acting prin., 1960-61; prin. Gen. Elwell S. Otis Sch. 30, Rochester, 1962-67, Susan B. Anthony Sch. 27, Rochester, 1967-71, Dr. Louis A. Cerulli Sch. 34, Rochester, 1971-90; ret., 1990. Supr. student tchr. satellite sch., SUNY, Brockport, 1976-90; workshop presenter Wayne County Schs., Goldsboro, N.C., 1988. Team capt. new bldg. drive YMCA, Rochester, 1983; vol. ptnr. Compeer Psychiat. Program, Rochester, 1988; vol. Monroe County Dem. Com., Rochester, 1986, 89, 90. Recipient Community Svc. awards Neighborhood Hope, 1990, Rochester Police Dept., 1990. Mem. Sch. Adminstrs. Assn. N.Y. State, Adminstrs. and Suprs. Assn. Rochester, Phi Delta Kappa. Roman Catholic. Avocations: racquetball, world travel, photography. Home: 1000 East Ave Apt 508 Rochester NY 14607-2247

SCALZO, ROBERT EDWARD, middle school mathematics educator; b. Danbury, Conn., Aug. 13, 1941; s. John and Teresa (Falvo) S; m. Cynthia A. Watts, Aug. 9, 1997; children by previous marriage; Laura L., William D., Robert M. BS, W.Va. State Coll., 1966; MA, Fairfield U., 1970, Cert. of Advanced Study, 1979. Cert. 7-12 history tchr., adminstr., supr. 4th-6th grade tchr. Mill Ridge Intermediate Sch., Danbury, 1966-79; 7th grade math. tchr. Rogers Park Mid. Sch., Danbury, 1980—, math. specialist, 1996—. Vol. fireman Phoenix Hose Co. # 8, Danbury, 1960—, rec. sec., 1973—, pres., chief, 1997—. Recipient 25 Yr. Longevity award Phoenix Hose Co. # 8, 1985, Appreciation award Phoenix Hose Co. # 8, 1986, Appreciation award Danbury Vol. Firemen's Coun., 1987. Mem. NEA (grievance chairperson 1992-95, Danbury bldg. chairperson 1986-90), Conn. Edn. Assn. (retirement commn. 1988—), Phi Delta Kappa (former rec. sec.). Democrat. Roman Catholic. Avocations: golf, biking, furniture refinishing, gardening. Home: 3 Ford Ln Danbury CT 06811-4614

SCANDARY, E. JANE, special education educator, consultant; b. Saginaw, Mich., Sept. 12, 1923; d. Leonard William and Reva Charlotte (Smith) Leipprandt; m. Theodore John Scandary; children: John S., Robert G. BA, Mich. State U., East Lansing, 1945, EdS, 1963, PhD, 1968; MEd, Wayne State U., 1951. Cert. secondary and spl. edn. tchr., Mich. Therapist speech and lang. Ann J. Kellogg Sch., Battle Creek, Mich., 1945-47; supr. speech therapy programs Wayne County Schs., Detroit, 1948-52; supr. programs for phys., hearing and visually impaired Ingham Intermediate Schs., Mason, Mich., 1960-78; spl. edn. cons. Mich. Dept. of Edn., Lansing, 1978-87, Livingston Intermediate Schs., Howell, Mich., 1987—. Rsch. assoc. Mich. State U., East Lansing, 1965-66, adj. prof., 1969-75, 81-82; mem. adv. com. China-U.S. Sci. Exchange Program Spl. Edn.; guest lectr. seminars spl. edn. Australia, Eng., Iran, Israel, Aruba, Germany, Scotland. Editor Chronicles newsletter, 1987—; contbr. articles to profl. jours. Vol. Mich. Hist. Mus., 1995—, Meals-on-Wheels, 1998-2001, Salvation Army, 2000—; chair futures com. Mich. Dept. Edn., 1992, editor, chair Task Force Futuresin Spl. Edn. 2000 AD and Beyond, 1992; bd. dirs. Delta Dist. Libr., 1998—. 1st Chance Early Childhood grantee, 1972-78; recipient Resolution of Tribute Mich. State Senate, 1986, 3d Pl. award Mid-Mich. Spring Art Show, 1998; Scandary award for outstanding contbrs. early childhood edn. established in her name, 1990. Mem. Nat. Coun. Exceptional Children (field editor 1976-86, pres. div. physically handicapped 1982-83), Mid-Mich. Art Guild, World Future Soc., Capitol Area Quilt Guild. Avocations: painting, writing, reading, creative sewing.

SCANDARY, ROBERT GLENN, administrator; b. Lansing, Mich., Mar. 12, 1954; s. Theodore John and Emma Jane (Leipprandt) S.; m. Teresa Louise Neal, July 31, 1982; children: Kristin Nicole, Laura Terese. BS, Cen. Mich. U., 1977; MEd, U. Ariz., 1986. Cert. elem. edn. adminstrn., N.Mex., Wyo, Mich., spl. edn., N.Mex., Wyo. Mich. Tchr., spl. edn. Muskegon (Mich.) Area Learning Programs, 1977-79, Orchard View Pub. Schs., Muskegon, 1979-80, Sweetwater County Sch. Dist. #1, Rock Springs, Wyo., 1980-89; dir. spl. svcs., edn. Bloomfield (N.Mex.) Mcpl. Schs., 1989-94; vice prin. Aztec (N.Mex.) Mcpl. Schs., 1994—. Mem. Coun. Exceptional Children, Assn. Supervision Curriculum Devel. Office: Koogler Middle Sch 455 N Light Plant Rd Aztec NM 87410-1517

SCANLAN, THOMAS JOSEPH, college president, educator; b. NYC, Mar. 5, 1945; s. Thomas Joseph and Anna Marie (Schmitt) S. BA in Physics, Cath. U. Am., 1967; MA in Math., NYU, 1972; PhD in Bus. Adminstrn., Columbia U., 1978. Prin. Queen of Peace HS, North Arlington, NJ, 1972-75; dir. fin., edn. NY Province, Bros. of Christian Sch., Lincroft, NJ, 1978-81; vice chancellor Bethlehem U., Israel, 1981-87; pres. Manhattan Coll., Bronx, NY, 1987—. Bd. dirs. Am. Coun. on Edn. Trustee Commn. on Ind. Colls. and Univs., 2002, Assn. Cath. Colls. and Univs., 1994—. Recipient Pro Ecclesia et Pontifice medal, Pope John Paul II, Vatican City, 1986. Mem. Bros. of Christian Schs., Am. Coun. Edn., Assn. Cath. Colls. and Univs. (trustee 1994—), Assn. Am. Colls., Nat. Cath. Edn. Assn., Nat. Asns. Ind. Colls. and Univs., Nat. Collegiate Athletic Assn. (exec. com. & divsn. 1), Metro Atlantic Athletic Assn., Equestrian Order of the Holy Sepulchre of Jerusalem, Phi Beta Kappa, Beta Gamma Sigma. Avocations: golf, reading, movies. Office: Manhattan Coll Office of Pres Manhattan Coll Pky Bronx NY 10471-3913

SCANLON, DOROTHY THERESE, history educator; b. Bridgeport, Conn., Oct. 7, 1928; d. George F. and Mazie (Reardon) Scanlon. AB, U. Pa., 1948, MA, 1949, Boston Coll., 1953; PhD, Boston U., 1956; postdoctoral scholar, Harvard U., 1962—64, postdoctoral scholar, 1972. Tchr. history and Latin Marycliff Acad., Winchester, Mass., 1950—52; tchr. history Girls Latin Sch., Boston, 1952—57; prof. Boston State Coll., 1957—82, Mass. Coll. Art, Boston, 1982—95, prof. emerita, 1995—; lectr. Cape Mus. Fine Arts, Dennis, Mass., 1997—. Author: Instructor's Manual to Accompany Lewis Hanke, Latin America: A Historical REader, 1974; contbr. Biographical Dictionary of Social Welfare, 1986. Recipient Disting. Svc. award, Boston State Coll., 1979, Faculty award of excellence, Mass. Coll. Art, 1985, Faculty Disting. Svc. award, 1987. Mem.: AAUW, AAUP, History of Sci. Soc., Am. Assn. History of Medicine., Am. Studies Assn., Orgn. Am. Historians, Am. Hist. Assn., L.Am. Studies Assn., Pan-Am. Soc., Delta Kappa Gamma, Phi Alpha Theta. Home: 23 Mooring Ln Dennis MA 02638-2321 Office: Mass Coll Art Dept History 621 Huntington Ave Boston MA 02115-5801

SCANLON, PATRICK LEE, special education educator; b. Greenville, Pa., Oct. 9, 1959; s. Eugene Francis and Shirley Louise (Hoover) S.; m. Donna Kathleen Hoare, Aug. 29, 1981; children: Justine M., Kalynne K., Ryan D. BS in Edn., Indiana U. Pa., 1984. Cert. instr., Pa. Learning support tchr. Purchase Line Sch. Dist., Commodore, Pa., 1989-93, instrnl. support tchr., 1993—. Mem. ARC, Coun. Exceptional Children, Pa. State Edn. Assn., Purchase Line Edn. Assn. Home: RR 1 Box 75K Penn Run PA 15765-9801

SCANLON, PETER JOSEPH, priest; b. Worcester, Mass., Sept. 2, 1931; s. Peter and Julia (O'Sullivan) Scanlon. AB, STB, St. Mary's Sem. and U., 1953, licentiate in sacred theology, 1957. Ordained priest Roman Cath. Ch., 1957, cert. campus minister. Asst. pastor St. Mary's Parish, Southbridge, Mass., 1957-58; adminstr. St. Patrick's Parish, Rutland, 1958-61; Cath. chaplain Worcester Poly. Inst., 1961—; Bishop's vicar for coll. Roman Cath. Diocese Worcester, 1969—; fire chaplain City of Worcester Fire Dept., 1971—. Diocesan bd. edn. Roman Cath. Diocese Worcester, 1969—; trustee Becker Coll., Worcester, 1971—2002, Aquinas Assn. Phi Kappa Theta, Worcester, 1975—2000. Recipient award to hon. alumnus, Worcester Poly. Inst., 1985, award, Becker Coll., 1990. Mem.: Cath. Campus Ministry Assn., Nat. Assn. Diocesan Dirs. Campus Ministry. Home: 44 Westwood Rd Shrewsbury MA 01545 Office: Campus Ministry Diocese Worcester PO Box 903 Worcester MA 01613-0903 E-mail: priest@wpi.edu.

SCANNELL, ANN ELIZABETH, nurse, educator; b. Evanston, Ill., Sept. 23, 1953; BSN, Villanova U., 1975; MS in Community Health, Cath. U., 1977; ND, Case Western Reserve U., 1996. Staff nurse emergency rm. Rahway (N.J.) Hosp., 1975-76; staff nurse med. ICU Georgetown U. Med. Ctr., Boston, 1977-78; continuing care nurse Mass. Rehab. Hosp., Boston, 1977-78; skills coord. dept. nursing Coll. Health Professions U. Lowell, Mass., 1978-79; clin. supr. Melrose (Mass.) Vis. Nurse Svc., 1979-80, exec. dir., 1980-87; dir. coords. and continuing care VNA of Greater Lowell, 1988-89; child and adolescent psychiat. nurse Brookside Hosp., Nashua, N.H., 1989-93; instr. community health nursing St. Anselm Coll., Manchester, N.H., 1991-96; asst. prof., comm. health nurse Fitchburg State Coll., Fitchburg, Mass., 1996—. Mem. ANA (cert. community health, home health and nursing adminstrn.), Sigma Theta Tau (treas. Eta Omega chpt.). Home: 271 Sanders Ave Lowell MA 01851-3418 Office: Dept Nursing Fitchburg State Coll 160 Pearl St Fitchburg MA 01420-2631 E-mail: ascannell@fsc.edu.

SCARBOROUGH, ANN BARLOW, secondary school educator; Tchr. sci. Farmville (N.C.) Mid. Sch., South Ctrl. HS, Winterville, NC. Recipient Outstanding Earth Sci. Tchr. award, 1992. Mem.: N.C. Sci. Tchrs. Assn. (pres. 2003).*

SCARF, HERBERT ELI, economics educator; b. July 25, 1930; s. Louis H. and Lena (Elkman) W.; m. Margaret Klein, June 28, 1953; children: Martha Anne Samuelson, Elizabeth Joan Stone, Susan Margaret Merrell. AB, Temple U., 1951; MA, Princeton U., 1952, PhD, 1954; LHD (hon.), U. Chgo., 1978. With RAND Corp., Santa Monica, Calif., 1954-57; asst. assoc. prof. stats. Stanford (Calif.) U., 1957-63; prof. econs. Yale U., New Haven, 1963-70, Stanley Resor prof. econs., 1970-78, Sterling prof. econs., 1979—. Vis. assoc. prof. Yale U., New Haven, 1959-60; dir. Cowles Found. Rsch. in Econs., Yale U., 1967-71, 1981-84, divsn. social sciences, 1971-72, 1973-74. Author: Studies in the Mathematical Theory of Inventory and Production, 1958, Computation of Economic Equilibria, 1973; editor: Applied General Equilibrium Analysis, 1984. Recipient Lanchester prize Ops. Rsch. Soc. Am., 1974, Von Neumann medal, 1983; named Disting. fellow Am. Econ. Assn., 1991. Fellow: INFORMS, Econometric Soc. (pres. 1983); mem.: NAS, Am. Philos. Soc., Am. Acad. Arts and Scis. Democrat. Jewish. Office: Yale U Cowles Found Rsch Econs PO Box 208281 New Haven CT 06520-8281 E-mail: herbert.scarf@yale.edu.

SCARLETT, NOVLIN ROSE, public health nurse, educator; b. Jamaica, West Indies, Jan. 11, 1938; d. Cyrus Freeman and Sylvia Belafonte; m. Sherlock Anthony Scarlett, Dec. 19, 1964 (dec. Jan. 8, 1970); children: Douglas, Anne. Nursing degree, Queensboro C.C., 1978, York Coll., 1984. RN N.Y. Staff nurse City Hosp., Elmhurst, NY, 1978—82; asst. head nurse Margaret Tietz, NY, 1982—86, head nurse, 1986—97; public health nurse City of N.Y., 1997—.

SCAROLA, JOHN MICHAEL, dentist, educator; b. N.Y.C., Nov. 18, 1934; s. Michael Fidelis and Filomena Mary (Turso) S.; m. Theodora Mary Marty, June 15, 1963; children: Michael A., John P., Stephen A., Robert M., Mary E. BS, Fordham Coll., 1956; DDS, Columbia U., 1960. Instr. Columbia Dental Sch., N.Y.C., 1962-68, asst. clin. prof., 1969-72, course dir. fixed partial dentures, 1969-72, assoc. clin. prof., 1973-86, course dir. prosthodontic elective, 1977-91, clin. prof., 1986—. Lectr., clin. prof. postgrad. prostodontics Columbia U., N.Y.C., 1986—, AEGD-Columbia U., N.Y.C., 1990-92, Luth. Med. Ctr., Bklyn., 1993—; cons. in prosthodontics Northport VA Hosp., East Northport, N.Y., 1970-91. Scoutmaster Boy Scouts Am., Port Washington, N.Y., 1976-78; chmn. spl. gifts Bishop's Annual Appeal, St. Peter's-Port Washington, 1977-78; Cath. Youth Orgn. sports coach St. Paul The Apostle, Brookville, N.Y., 1980-83; fundraising com. The Yard, Martha's Vineyard, Mass., 1990; concert com. Musician's Emergency Fund, N.Y.C., 1992. Lt. USNR, 1960-62. Fellow Am. Coll. Dentists (chmn. N.Y. sect. 1994, regent of Regency 1), N.Y. Acad. Dentistry (pres. 1989-90), Greater N.Y. Acad. Prosthodontics (dir. 1993-97); mem. Greater N.Y. Acad. Prosthodontics Found. (dir., pres. 1989-97), N.Y. Acad. Dentistry Endowment Fund (dir., pres. 1992-93). Republican. Roman Catholic. Avocations: golf, opera, classical music, gardening. Home: 83 Fruitledge Rd Glen Head NY 11545-3317 Office: 501 Madison Ave New York NY 10022-5602

SCARPELLI, VITO, adult education educator, administrator; b. Passaic, N.J., July 17, 1946; s. Peter and Celia (Pignataro) S.; m. JoAnn Motti, Aug. 23, 1970; children: Anthony, Michele. BA in Acctg. and Edn., Montclair State Coll., 1968; MA, Kean Coll., 1984; postgrad., St. Peters, Jersey City State U., Seton Hall U., Kans. State U. Prin. Roselle Park Mid. Sch., 1996—; supr. P. Scarpelli & Sons, Nutley, N.J., 1968-84; bus. adminstr. John J. Baum, Inc., Wayne, N.J.; salesman Realty World-Monaco Realty, Nutley, 1980—; asst. track coach, tchr. jr. H.S. Belleville Bd. Edn., 1968-69; dir. adult edn. and summer programs Roselle Park (N.J.) Bd. Edn., 1984-96. Dir. Union County Summer Youth Employment and Tng., Roselle Park, 1986, asst. curriculum coord., 1992-96, dir. tech., 1993-96; adj. prof. Jersey City State Coll., 1993-96. Pres. Nutley Am. Little League, 1987-97; v.p. Nutley Basketball Assn.; past pres. Lincoln Sch. PTA. Mem. N.J. Prins. and Supr. Assn., Nas. Assn. Secondary Sch. Prins., N.J. Bus. Edn. Assn., N.J. Edn. Assn., Roselle Park Edn. Assn., LERN, KC (grand knight 1976). Independent. Roman Catholic. Avocation: fishing. Home: 81 Milton Ave Nutley NJ 07110-3017 Office: Roselle Park Bd Edn 510 Chestnut St Roselle Park NJ 07204-1928

SCARPITTI, FRANK ROLAND, sociology educator; b. Butler, Pa., Nov. 12, 1936; s. Frank and Geneva (Costanza) S.; m. Ellen Louise Canfield, Sept. 5, 1959; children: Susan, Jeffrey. BA, Cleve. State U., 1958; MA, Ohio State U., 1959, PhD, 1962. Research asso. Ohio State U. Psychiat. Inst., Columbus, 1961-63; asst. prof. Rutgers U., 1963-67; asso. prof. sociology U. Del., 1967-69, prof., 1969—2000, chmn. dept., 1969-80, 88-94, Edward and Elizabeth Rosenberg prof., 2000—. Cons. state and fed. govts.; Bd. dirs. Joint Commn. on Criminology and Criminal Justice Edn. and Standards, 1977-81 Author: Schizophrenics in the Community, 1967, Combatting Social Problems, 1967, Youth and Drugs, 1970, Group Interactions as Therapy, 1974, Social Problems, 1974, 77, 80, Deviance: Action, Reaction, Interaction, 1975, Women, Crime and Justice, 1980, The Young Drug User, 1980, Poisoning for Profit, 1985, Social Problems, 1989, 92, 97, Social Problems: The Search for Solutions, 1994, Crime and Criminals, 1999; contbr. articles to profl. jours. Recipient Hofheimer prize for research Am. Psychiat. Assn., 1967; mem. Danforth Found. asso. program. Mem. Am. Sociol. Assn., Am. Soc. Criminology (v.p. 1978-79, pres.-elect 1979-80, pres. 1980-81), AAUP, Alpha Kappa Delta, Phi Kappa Phi, Omicron Delta Kappa. Home: 104 Radcliffe Dr Newark DE 19711-3147

SCARTELLI, JOSEPH PAUL, music therapy educator, dean; b. Scranton, Pa., May 4, 1952; s. Joseph Anthony and Angela Rose Scartelli; m. Frances Marie DiMaggio, June 15, 1974; children: Nicole, Joseph. BS in Music, Mansfield U., 1974; MusM in Music Therapy, U. Miami, Fla., 1977, PhD in Music Edn., 1981. Cert. music therapist. Tchr. Dade County Pub. Schs., South Miami, Fla., 1976-77; grad. tchg. fellow U. Miami, 1979-80, instr. music therapy, 1980-81; asst. prof. music Radford (Va.) U., 1981-87, assoc. prof. music, 1987-89, prof. music, 1989—, dean Coll. Visual and Performing Arts, 1988—. Mem. editl. bd. Jour. Music Therapy, 1996—, Arts in Psychotherapy, 1984—. Author monograph: Music and Self-Management, 1989; contbr. articles to profl. jours., chpts. to book. Bd. dirs. Radford U. Found., 1990—; bd. commrs. renovation project Dumas Music Ctr., Roanoke, Va., 1998—; bd. dirs. Va. Arts, Richmond, Va., 1992—; mem. City of Radford Arts and Events Commn., 1996—. Recipient Outstanding Young Alumni award Mansfiled U., 1986, Music Alum Honor Roll, 1990, Resolution of Recognition, Va. State Bd. Edn., 1999, Educator of Yr. award Radford C. of C., 2001. Mem. Am. Music Therapy Assn. (award of merit 1998), Assn. Performing Arts presenters, Internat. Coun. Fine Arts Deans. Avocations: music performance, golf, martial arts, tennis, carpentry. Home: 501 Randolph St Radford VA 24141 Office: Radford U Coll Visual/Performing Arts Radford VA 24142 E-mail: jscartel@radford.edu.

SCEDROV, ANDRE, mathematics and computer science researcher, educator; b. Zagreb, Croatia, Aug. 1, 1955; came to U.S., 1977, naturalized, 1987; s. Oleg and Mira (Petric) S.; m. Bonnie Carol Hoke, July 23, 1983. BA, U. Zagreb, 1977; MA, SUNY, Buffalo, 1979, PhD in Math., 1981. T.H. Hildebrandt asst. prof. rsch. U. Mich., Ann Arbor, 1981-82; asst. prof. U. Pa., Phila., 1982-88, assoc. prof., 1988-92, prof., 1992—. Vis. scholar U. Milan, 1982, McGill U., Montreal, 1985, U. Sydney, Australia, 1986, U. Catholique de Louvain, Louvain-La-Neuve, Belgium, 1988, U. Paris 7, 1992, Rijksuniv Utrecht, The Netherlands, 1993, CNRS Lab. de Math. Discretes, Marseille, France, 1995, Stanford U., 1995, Isaac Newton Inst. for Math. Scis., Cambridge, Eng., 1995, IST, Lisbon, Portugal, 2002; vis. scientist Math. Scis. Inst. Cornell U., Ithaca, N.Y., 1987; vis. fellow SRI Internat., Menlo Park, Calif., 1995, Mittag-Leffler Inst. Stockholm, 2001; vis. assoc. prof. Stanford U., 1989-90; cons. Odyssey Rsch. Assocs., Ithaca, 1987, HP Labs., Palo Alto, 1990; vis. prof. Keio U., Tokyo, 1997; program chair IEEE Symposium on Logic in Computer Sci., Santa Cruz, Calif., 1992, mem. organizing com., 1992-97, mem. adv. bd., 1997—, mem. program com. Phila., 1990, Copenhagen, 2002, program co-chair Math. Founds. Programming Semantics, New Orleans, 1999, mem. program com., 2001; mem. program com. Logical Found. Computer Sci., Tver, Russia, 1992, St. Petersburg, Russia, 1994, Linear Logic Tokyo '96, 1996,

Computer Sci. Logic '98, Brno, Czech Republic, 1998, Typed Lambda Calculi and Applications L'Aquila, Italy, 1999, Category Theory in Computer Sci., Edinburgh, Scotland, 1999, Theoretical Aspects of Computer Software, Japan, 2001, IEEE Computer Security Found. Workshop, N.S., Can., 2001, Asilomar, Calif., 2003; plenary spkr. 2d Croatian Math. Congress, Zagreb, 2000; invited spkr. Math. Founds. Programming Semantics, Oxford (Eng.) U., 1992, U. Colo., Boulder, 1996, Computer Sci. Logic, San Miniato, Italy, 1992, Internat. Summer Sch. Logic Computer Sci., Chambery, France, 1993, Proof and Computation, Marktoberdorf, Germany, 1993, Logic and Computer Sci. CIRM, Marseille-Luminy, France, 1994, Winter Sch. on Linear Logic and Applications, Lisbon, Portugal, 1995, 10th Internat. Congress on Logic, Philosophy and Methodology of Sci., Florence Italy, 1995, Linear Logic Meeting and Spring Sch., Tokyo, 1996, Linear Logic Workshop CIRM, Marseille-Luminy, France, 1998, Constructivism in Mathematics and Computing, The Netherlands, 1999, EEF summer sch. logical methods BRICS, Aarhus, Denmark, 2001, First Joint Meeting between Am. Math Soc and Soc. Math de France, Lyon, 2001; Second Internat. Workshop on Secure and Survivable Systems, Tokyo, 2001, Internat. Symposium on Software Security, Tokyo, 2001, Logic and Interaction Programme, CIRM, Marseille-Luminy, 2002, CONCUR 2003, Concurrency Theory, Marseille, France, 2003. Author: (with P. Freyd) Categories, Allegories; editor Math. Structures in Computer Sci., 1989—, Annals Pure Applied Logic, 1993—, Perspectives in Mathematical Logic book series, 1997—; contbr. articles and rsch. papers to profl. publs. Recipient Young Faculty award Nat. Scis. Assn. U. Pa., 1987; Rsch. grantee NSF, 1985—, Office Naval Rsch., 1988—. Fellow Japan Soc. for Promotion Sci. (sr.); mem. AAAS, Am. Math. Soc. (Centennial rsch. fellow 1993-94, mem. 1st joint internat. meeting with Soc. Math of France, Lyon, 2001), Assn. for Symbolic Logic (editor jours. 1988-93, chair nominating com. 1993, program com. 1988-90, coun. 1990-96, coordinating editor jours. 1994-96 exec. com. 1998-2001, program chair ann. meeting 2001), Assn. for Computing Machinery, Math. Assn. Am. Office: U Pa Dept Math 209 S 33rd St Dept Math Philadelphia PA 19104-6317 E-mail: scedrov@cis.upenn.edu.

SCHAAP, MARCIA, special education educator; b. Grand Rapids, Mich., May 21, 1938; d. William Jr. and Margaret D. (Dekker) Hertel; m. Richard A. Schaap, June 16, 1962; children: Sandra, Linda, Kathy, Esther. AB in Edn., Calvin Coll., 1962; MS in Spl. Edn., Chgo. State U., 1984. Cert. tchr., Mich. 2d grade tchr. West Side Christian Sch., Grand Rapids, 1960-62, Roseland Christian Sch., Chgo., 1963, with remedial reading dept., 1984-85, with chpt. I remedial computers dept., 1986, learning disabilities resource, author, dir., 1987-92; tutor St. Paul Luth. Sch., Dolton, Ill., 1992—, Salem Luth. Sch., Blue Island, Ill., 1992—. Owner, dir. Marcia's Music and Tutoring, South Holland, Ill.; mem. ABLE. Mem. Nat. Learning Disabilities Assn., Ill. Learning Disabilities Assn., Chgo. Learning Disabilities Assn., Orland C.H.I.L.D. Assn., Nat. Music Tchrs. Assn., South Suburban Music Tchrs. Assn., Orton Dyslexia Soc., Advocates Behind Legal Edn., Nat. Piano Tchrs. Orgn., Ill. State Music Tchrs. Profl. Orgn., Christian Educators Assn. Home and Office: 643 E 162nd Pl South Holland IL 60473-2302

SCHABELMAN, SERGIO EDUARDO, cardiologist, educator; b. San Juan, Argentina, Mar. 7, 1951; came to U.S., 1977; s. Moises and Dora (Roitman) S.; m. Florencia Iris Levinton, Nov. 9, 1974; children: Esteban, Andres. MD, Buenos Aires Nat. U., 1973. Diplomate Am. Bd. Internal Medicine, 1980, Am. Bd. Cardiovascular Diseases, 1983, cert. Am. Bd. Interventional Cardiology, 2002. Internal medicine trainee Marcial Quiroga San Juan Hosp., San Juan, 1973-74; resident in cardiology Buenos Aires Argerich Hosp., 1974-77; fellow cardiology dept. Cardiovascular Rsch. Inst. U. Calif., San Francisco, 1977; fellow cardiovascular radiology Loma Linda (Calif.) U. Med. Ctr., 1978, instr. internal medicine, 1979; asst. prof. medicine cardiology sect., head invasive lab. La. State U., New Orleans, 1979-82; asst. to dir. Charity Hosp. Heart Sta., New Orleans, 1979-82; clin. asst. prof. cardiology La. State U., 1982—. Spkr. in field; contbr. articles to profl. jours. Fellow ACP, Am. Coll. of Cardiology; mem. Argentine Soc. Cardiology (assoc.; sec. Am. chpt. 1994-96), La. State Med. Soc., Orleans Parish Med. Soc. (emergency med. svcs. com. 1988—), N.Am. Soc. Pacing and Electrophysiology, Hispanic Am. Med. Assn. La. (sec. 1991-93, v.p. 1993-95), Ind. Physician Assn. New Orleans (bd. dirs. 1994-95), Hispanic Ind. Physician Assn. La. (bd. dirs. 1994-95). Office: 3715 Prytania St Ste 203 New Orleans LA 70115-3766

SCHACHMAN, HOWARD KAPNEK, molecular biologist, educator; b. Phila., Dec. 5, 1918; s. Morris H. and Rose (Kapnek) S.; m. Ethel H. Lazarus, Oct. 20, 1945; children— Marc, David. BSChemE, Mass. Inst. Tech., 1939; PhD in Phys. Chemistry, Princeton, 1948; DSc (hon.), Northwestern U., 1974; MD (hon.), U. Naples, 1990. Fellow NIH, 1946-48; from instr. to asst. prof. U. Calif., Berkeley, 1948-54, assoc. prof. biochemistry, 1954-59, prof. biochemistry and molecular biology, 1959-91, chmn. dept. molecular biology, dir. virus lab., 1969-76, prof. emeritus, dept. molecular and cell biology, 1991-94, prof. grad. sch., 1994—. Mem. sci. coun. and sci. adv. bd. Stazione Zoologica, Naples, Italy, 1988—; cons. bd. sci. Meml. Sloan-Kettering Cancer Ctr., 1988—97; mem. sci. adv. com. Rsch. ! Am., 1990—; William Lloyd Evans lectr. Ohio State U., 1988; Carl and Gerty Cori lectr. Washington U. Sch. Medicine, 1993; faculty rsch. lectr. U. Calif., Berkeley, 1994; Alta. Heritage Found. for Med. Rsch. vis. prof. U. Alta., 1996; Wellcome vis. prof. in basic med. scis., 1999—2000; Walter C. MacKenzie lectr. Sch. Medicine U. Alta., Edmonton, Canada, 2001. Author: Ultracentrifugation in Biochemistry, 1959. Mem. bd. sci. counselors Cancer Biology and Diagnosis divsn. Nat. Cancer Inst., 1989-92; ombudsman in basic scis. NIH, 1994—2002. Lt. USNR, 1945-47. Recipient John Scott award, 1964, Warren Triennial prize Mass. Gen. Hosp., 1965, Alexander von Humboldt award, 1990, Berkeley citation for disting. achievement and notable svc. U. Calif., 1993, Theodor Svedberg award, 1998; Guggenheim Meml. fellow, 1956. Mem.: NAS (chmn. biochemistry sect. 1990—93, panelist sci. responsibility and conduct of rsch. 1990—92), AAAS (mem. com. on sci. freedom and responsibility 1998—, Sci. Freedom and Responsibility award 2000), Acad. Nat. Dei Lincei (fgn. mem.), Fedn. Am. Socs. for Exptl. Biology (pres. 1988—89, pub. affairs exec. com. 1989—, pub. svc. award 1994), Am. Soc. Biochemistry and Molecular Biology (pres. 1987—88, chmn. pub. affairs com. 1989—2000, Merck award 1986, Herbert A. Sober award 1994, pub. svc. award established in his name 2001 2001), Am. Chem. Soc. (Calif. sect. award 1958, award in chem. instrumentation 1962). Achievements include development of the ultracentrifuge as a tool for studying macromolecules of biological interest; studies on structure and function of a regulatory enzyme: Aspartate transcarbamylase. Office: U Calif Berkeley Dept Molecular Cell Bio 229 Stanley Hall # 3206 Berkeley CA 94720-3206

SCHACHT, RUTH ELAINE, nursing educator; b. Milw., Nov. 3, 1935; d. Paul Henry and Mavelle V. (Van de Kamp) Nickchen; m. Leonard L.Schacht, Nov. 17, 1962; children: Lisa, Lynette, Lori, Renee Terese. BSN, Marquette U., 1957, MSN, 1962. RN, Wis. Surg. head nurse Oconomowoc (Wis.) Meml. Hosp., 1957-60, day supr. staff nurse, 1970-86, staff pool nurse, 1986-96; mem. nursing faculty Marquette U., Milw., 1961-70, Cardinal Strich U., Milw., 1986-88, Waukesha County Tech. Coll., Pewaukee, Wis., 1988-98; ret., 1998. Cons., mem. nursing faculty Excelsior Coll., Albany, N.Y., 1988—. Mem. ANA, Waukesha Dist. Nurses Assn. (past pres., bd. mem.), Nat. League for Nursing, Wis. Nurses Assn. (past sec., mem. continuing edn. approval program com.). Home: 731 Browning Cir Oconomowoc WI 53066-4309

SCHACHTEL, BARBARA HARRIET LEVIN, epidemiologist, educator; b. May 27, 1921; d. Lester and Ethel (Neiman) Levin; m. Hyman Judah Schachtel, Oct. 15, 1941 (dec. Jan. 1990); m. Louis H. Green, Feb. 26, 1995; children: Bernard, Ann Mollie. Student, Wellesley Coll., 1939-41; BS, U. Houston, 1951, MA in Psychology, 1967; PhD, U. Tex., Houston, 1979. Psychol. examiner Meyer Ctr. for Devel. Pediats., Tex. Children's Hosp., Houston, 1967-81; instr. dept. pediats. Baylor Coll. Medicine, Houston, 1967-81, asst. prof. dept. medicine, 1982—. Asst. dir. biometry and epidemiology Sid W. Richardson Inst. for Preventive Medicine, Meth. Hosp., Houston, 1981-88, dir. quality assurance, 1988-93; ret., 1993; mem. instl. rev. bd. for human rsch. Baylor Coll. Medicine, Houston, 1981-87, 97—; mem. devel. bd. U. Tex. Health Sci. Ctr., Houston, 1987-97; mem. dean's adv. bd. Sch. Arch., U. Houston, 1987-89. Contbr. articles to profl. jours. V.p., bd. dirs. Houston-Harris County Mental Health Assn., 1966—67; vice-chmn. bd. mgrs. Harris County Hosp. Dist., Houston, 1974—90, chmn., 1990—92, bd. dirs., 1970—93; trustee Inst. Religion in Tex. Med. Ctr., 1990—, vice chmn., 2000—; sec. Bo Harris County Hosp. Dist. Found. Bd., 1993—; bd. dirs. Congregation Beth Israel, 1993—95, Planned Parenthood of Houston, Inc., 1994—2000, Houston Ind. Sch. Dist. Found., 1993—2001, Crisis Intervention, 1994—96. Named Great Texan of Yr., Nat. Found. for Ilietis and Colitis, Houston, 1982, Outstanding Citizen, Houston-Harris County Mental Health Assn., 1985; recipient Good Heart award B'nai Brith Women, 1984, Women of Prominence award Am. Jewish Com., 1991, Mayor's award for outstanding vol. svc., 1994. Mem. APA, APHA, Wellesley Club of Houston (pres. 1968-70). Avocations: golf, tennis, books. Home: 2527 Glen Haven Blvd Houston TX 77030-3511

SCHACHTER, JULIUS, epidemiology educator; b. N.Y.C., June 1, 1936; s. Samuel Isidore and Mary (Kudisch) S.; m. Joyce Ann Poynter (dec. 1990); children— Marc, Sara, Alexander. B.A. in Chemistry, Columbia Coll., 1957; M.A. in Physiology, Hunter Coll., 1960; Ph.D. in Bacteriology, U. Calif.-Berkeley, 1965. Assoc. prof. epidemiology U. Calif.-San Francisco, 1971-75, asst. dir. G.W. Hooper Found., 1972-77, acting dir., 1977-79, prof. epidemiology, 1975-80, prof. lab. medicine, 1980—; dir. WHO Collaborating Centre, San Francisco, 1978—; mem. expert panel on trachoma WHO, 1974-2002, expert com. on venereal diseases and treponematoses, 1982—. Co-author: Human Chlamydial Infections, 1978; editor: Sexually Transmitted Disease, 1989—; contbr. numerous articles to sci. jours. Mem. Am. Soc. Microbiology, Am. Venereal Disease Assn. (bd. dirs. 1983), Infectious Diseases Soc. Am., Am. Epidemiol. Soc., Am. Acad. Microbiology (bd. govs. 1989-97), Am. Sexually Transmitted Disease Assn. (pres. 1996-2002). Home: 17 Channel Dr Corte Madera CA 94925-1845 Office: U Calif Dept Lab Medicine 1001 Potrero Ave Rm 41 San Francisco CA 94110-3518

SCHADE, CHARLENE JOANNE, adult and early childhood education educator; b. San Bernardino, Calif., June 26, 1935; d. Clarence George Linde and Helen Anita (Sunny) Hardesty; m. William Joseph Jr., Apr. 12, 1958 (div., 1978); children: Sabrina, Eric, Camela, Cynthia; m. Thomas Byron Killens, Sept. 25, 1983. BS, UCLA, 1959. Tchr. dance and phys. edn. L.A. Unified Secondary Schs., Calif., 1959-63; dir., instr. (Kindergym) La Jolla YMCA, Calif., 1972-76; instr. older adults San Diego Cmty. Colls., 1977—, assoc. prof. continuing edn., 1997—; artist in residence Wolf Trap/Headstart, 1984-85. Workshop leader S.W. Dance, Movement and Acro-Sports Workshop, prime-time adult activities coord., 1988—, Am. Heart Assn., Arthritis Found., Am. Lung Assn., AAHPERD, S.W. Dist. AHPERD, Calif. Assn. Health, Phys. Edn., Recreation and Dance, Head Start, San Diego Assn. Young Children, Calif. Assn. Edn. Young Child, Calif. Kindergarten Assn., So. Calif. Kindergarten Assn., 1997, Assn. Childhood Edn. Internat., Nat. Pediat. Support Svcs., 1999, Calif. Dance Educators, 1999, IDEA Internat. Assn. Fitness Profls., San Diego C.C., Am. Soc. on Aging, Fourth Internat. Congress Phys. Activity, Aging and Sports, 1996, others; cons. to Calif. Gov.'s Coun. on Phys. Fitness and Sports, 1993—; feature guest Sta. KFMB and KPBS TV shows, San Diego, 1980-88; assoc. prof. San Diego C.C. Continuing Edn., 1997—; spl. advisor San Diego Coun. on Phys. Fitness and Sports, 1998—. Author: Move With Me From A to Z, 1982, Move With Me, One, Two, Three, 1988; co-author: Prime Time Aerobics, 1982, Muevete Conmigo, uno, dos, tres, 1990; co-writer: Guide for Physical Fitness Instructors of Older Adults, Grant Project, 1990, The Empowering Teacher, 1990, Handbook for Instructors of Older Adults, 1994. Bd. dirs. We Care Found., San Diego, 1977-79, Meet the Author programs San Diego County Schs., 1988—; founder SOLO, San Diego, 1981-83; adminstr., v.p. ODEM chpt. Toastmasters, San Diego, 1982; chmn. People with Arthritis Can Exercise com. San Diego chpt. Arthritis Found., 1994-95; trainer PACE instrs. Nat. Arthritis Found., 1995—. Grantee Video Showcase of Exercises for Older Adults, 1992-93. Mem. AAPHERD (workshop leader), Calif. Assn. Health, Phys. Edn., Recreation and Dance (workshop leader). Avocations: hiking, dancing, travel. Office: Exer Fun/Prime Time Aerobic 3089C Clairemont Dr #130 San Diego CA 92117-6802 E-mail: cschade@sdccd.cc.ca.us.

SCHADE, STANLEY GREINERT, JR., hematologist, educator; b. Pitts., Dec. 21, 1933; s. Stanley G. and Charlotte (Marks) S.; m. Sylvia Zottu, Mar. 24, 1966; children: David Stanley, Robert Edward. BA in English, Hamilton Coll., 1955; MD, Yale U., 1961. Diplomate Am. Bd. Internal Medicine, Am. Bd. Hematology, Am. Bd. Oncology. Intern, resident, hematology fellow U. Wis., Madison, 1962-66; chief hematology Westside VA Hosp., Chgo., 1971-77; prof. medicine, chief hematology U. Ill., Chgo., 1978—97. Contbr. articles to profl. jour. Served to maj. US Army, 1967-69. Fulbright fellow Tubingen, Fed. Republic of Germany, 1956. Fellow Am. Coll. Physicians; mem. Am. Soc. Hematology. Presbyterian. Avocation: medical ethics. Home: 189 N Delaplaine Rd Riverside IL 60546-2060 Office: Westside VA Med Ctr Dept Medicine MP111 820 S Damen Ave Chicago IL 60612-3728

SCHADE, WILBERT CURTIS, education administrator; b. St. Louis, Jan. 4, 1945; s. Wilbert Curtis and Florence Mary (Allen) S.; m. Jacqueline Siewert, May 14, 1977; children: Benjamin Allen Siewert, Timothy Knorr Siewert. BA, U. Pa., 1967; AM, Washington U., St. Louis, 1970; PhD, Ind. U., 1986. Tchg. asst. dept. romance lang. Washington U., St. Louis, 1967-68; tchr. French St. Louis Priory Sch., 1970-71; assoc. instr. dept. French and Italian Ind. U., Bloomington, 1972-74, 76-80; tchr. French Webster Groves (Mo.) H.S., 1975-76; asst. dir. admissions Beloit (Wis.) Coll., 1980-83, assoc. dir. admissions, 1983-84; dir. coll. placement and dir. admissions Westover Sch., Middlebury, Conn., 1984-90; head upper sch. The Key Sch., Annapolis, Md., 1990-94, interim dir. devel., 1994-95; tchr. French, head lang. dept. Wasatch Acad., Mt. Pleasant, Utah, 1995-96, asst. headmaster for acad. affairs, 1996-2000; tchr., dir. of studies Internat. Seminar Series, Paris, 1999—. Lectr. in field. Co-editor: African Literature in its Social and Political Dimensions, 1983; mem. edtl. bd. Jour. Coll. Admission, 2000—; contbr. articles to profl. jours. including World Lit. Written in English, Studies in 20th Century Lit. Active Anne Arundel County (Md.) Task Force on Year Round Edn., 1994-95, Utah State Office of Edn.'s Fgn. Lang. Instrl. Materials and Texbook Adv. Com., 1996-98. NEH Summer Inst. on African Am. Lit. and Film grant, 1994. Mem. Nat. Assn. Coll. Admission Counseling (presenter nat. conf. 1985), Rocky Mountain Assn. for Coll. Admission Counseling (exec. bd., chief assembly del. to Nat. Assn.), African Lit. Assn. (exec. com. 1979), Phi Delta Kappa. Mem. Soc. Of Friends. Avocation: tennis. Home: PO Box 3549 20 Malheur Ln Sunriver OR 97707

SCHAEFER, JOSEPH ALBERT, physics and engineering educator, consultant; b. Bellevue, Iowa, Dec. 24, 1940; s. Albert Francis and Eileen Clara (Schilling) S.; m. Carol Ruth Deppe, Nov. 20, 1965; children: Sarah Ellen, Amy Marie. BS, Loras Coll., 1962; MS, U. Toledo, 1964; PhD, Northwestern U., 1972. Profl. engr., Iowa. Physicist Inst. Gas Tech., Chgo., 1963, U.S. Naval Ordnance Lab., Silver Spring, Md., 1964; prof. physics & engring. sci. Loras Coll., Dubuque, Iowa, 1964—99; lectr. Aero. Engring. Iowa State U., Ames, 1999—. Team mem. U.S. AID Team in India/Tchrs. Coll. Columbia U., Agra, India, 1966; cons. applied mechs. group John Deere, Dubuque, 1980; assoc. rsch. scientist Iowa Inst. Hydraulic Rsch., Iowa City, 1985-91; cons., evaluator North Cen. Assn., Chgo., 1990—; reviewer NSF, Washington, 1981—; mem. organizing com. 8th Internat. Ice Conf., Iowa City, 1986; NASA/Am. Soc. for Engring. Edn. faculty fellow Lewis Rsch. Ctr., summer 1997. Author: Study Guide for Physics of Everyday Phenomena, 1992; contbr. articles to profl. jours.; author, reviewer Wm. C. Brown Pubs., Dubuque, McGraw-Hill, 1988—. Chmn. equity adv. com. Dubuque Sch. Bd., 1991-99; bd. dirs. Area Residential Care, Dubuque, 1977-96; v.p. Dubuque Tchrs. Credit Union, 1987-99; mem. team for systemic reform of sci. curriculum Dubuque Cmty. Schs., 1995-99. Named Iowa Prof. of Yr. Coun. for Advancement & Support of Edn., 1989; recipient Teaching Excellence & Campus Leadership award Sears-Roebuck Found., 1990; Danforth assoc. Danforth Found.; sci. faculty fellow NSF, 1968, 70; grantee NSF, 1981, 90, Shining Moment award Dubuque Human Rights Commn., 1998. Democrat. Roman Catholic. Achievements include patent for Bulk Polycrystalline Switching Materials for Threshold and/or Memory Switching; anomalies in induced torque in potassium. Home: 306 NW 27th St Ankeny IA 50021-9082 E-mail: jschaefr@iastate.edu.

SCHAEFER, NANCY TURNER, artist, educator; b. Hamilton, Ohio, July 4, 1940; d. Edward and Leota (Taylor) Turner; m. Richard Burton Price, June 16, 1967 (div. July 1970); m. Donald Raymond Schaefer, July 6, 1970 (dec. Nov. 1990). BA in English and Art, Ea. Ky. U., 1965; postgrad., Cin. Art Acad., 1995—. Cert. tchr., Ky., Ohio, Va. Tchr. Boone County Bd. Edn., Florence, Ky., 1965-67, Rockingham County Bd. Edn., Harrisonburg, Va., 1967-69, Hamilton County Bd. Edn., Cin. and Greenhills, Ohio, 1969-86; pvt. tchr. art, instr. cmty. colls., Sarasota and Bradenton, Fla., 1986—. Demonstrator Palm Aire Artists Orgn., Sarasota, 1995; bd. dirs. Art League Manatee County. Works exhibited in two woman show Longboat Key (Fla.) Edn. Ctr., 1996, four woman show Art League of Manatee County, 1995 (Equal Merit award 1995), group shows Hilton Leech Studio, Sarasota, Fla., 1995 (1st honorable mention for mixed media 1995); represented in permanent collections Art League of Manatee County and many pvt. collections. Recipient numerous awards for paintings. Mem. Fla. Suncoast Watercolor Soc., Art League Manatee County (demonstrator 1995), Nat. Mus. Women in Arts (assoc.). Avocations: piano, gourmet cooking, calligraphy, cats, interior decorating.

SCHAEFER, PATRICIA ANN, retired librarian; b. Lebanon, Ohio, Jan. 22, 1933; d. Riley Ray and Louise Collette (Fraher) Freeze; m. William H. Schaefer, Aug. 11, 1956; childen: Susan P., Nancy A., William H. III (dec.). BS, Miami U., Oxford, Ohio, 1954. Med. technologist Mercy Hosp., Hamilton, Ohio, 1954-58, Middletown (Ohio) Hosp., 1958-62; libr. Middletown City Schs., 1979-93; intermediate libr. McKinley Sch., 1982-93; ret., 1993. Active YMCA, pres., 1977-79; bd. dirs. Middletown Symphony, 1974-78, Arts in Middletown, 1983—, Middletown Symphony Women, 1992—, mem. exec. bd., 1995—, co-chmn. Luncheon Style Show, 1998-2003; hon. bd. dirs. Am. Cancer Soc., 1961—; chmn. legis. City Charter Rev. Com., 1970, charter revision com., 1989; residential chmn. United Way, 1976, residential-retiree chmn., 1990; chmn. Sch. Tax Levy, 1978; mem. Middletown City Commn., 1983-88; mem. exec. com. Ohio-Ky.-Ind. Regional Coun., 1986-88; mem. Bicentennial Com., Middletown; mem. Citizen's Adv. Com. for Miami U.; pres. Middletown Needy Youth Bd.; mem. adv. bd. Manchester Tech. Ctr., Drug Task Force Bd., Middletown Schs.; bd. dirs. Citizens Adv. Bd. Manchester Tech., 1991—, Middletown Fine Arts, 1993—, Dental Emergency Fund Area Children, 1994—; mem. Leadership Middletown Exec. Bd., Adminstrv. Bd. Meth. Ch.; sec. bd. dirs. Care View Home Health, 2000, now pres.; mem. fin. com., sec. bd. trustees First United Meth. Ch., 1999—; mem. exec. bd. United Meth. Women; co-chmn. Mary Alice Mack City Golf Tournament, 1998. Recipient Stuart Ives Service to Youth award, 1980; named Outstanding Woman of Butler County, 1997, hon. chmn. 1998 Charity Ball, Woman of Distinction, Soroptomists Internat., 2000. Mem. LWV (pres. 1962-63), PEO (pres. 1995—, co-chair state conv. 1997), Am. Soc. Clin. Pathologists, Registry Med. Technologists, Am. Bus. Women's Assn. (pres. 1961-62, Middletown C. of C., Browns Run Country Club, Sigma Sigma Sigma. Methodist. Home: 1909 Antrim Ct Middletown OH 45042-2901

SCHAEFER, RHODA PESNER, elementary school educator; b. Bronx, N.Y., Mar. 15, 1947; d. Herman Pesner; m. Alan Jacob Schaefer, Sept. 23, 1967; children: Ira Marc, Melissa Anne. BA, Dominican Coll., Orangeburg, N.Y., 1980; MA in Edn., SUNY, New Paltz, 1987; MA in Supervision and Adminstrn., Coll. New Rochelle, 1999. Cert. tchr., N.Y. Tchg. asst. East Ramapo Ctrl. Sch. Dist., Spring Valley, NY, 1984—87, tchr., 1987—; supr., dist. adminstr. Elmwood Elem. Sch., Monsey, NY, 2000—. Instr. East Ramapo Tchrs.' Ctr., 1988—, instrnl. facilitator, 2000—; adj. prof. L.I. U., 1989—, SUNY, New Paltz, 1994—, Coll. of New Rochelle, N.Y.; mem. Hudson Valley Portfolio Project, 1993-96. Pres., officer PTA, Spring Valley, 1972—. Mem. ASCD, Internat. Reading Assn., N.Y. Reading Assn., Rockland Reading Coun., N.Y. Assn. for Computers and Tech. Edn., Nat. Coun. English Tchrs., Nat. Coun. for Social Studies, Delta Kappa Gamma. Office: Elmwood Elem Sch Robert Pitt Dr Monsey NY 10952

SCHAEFER, SANDRA ELLEN, secondary education educator; b. Troy, Ohio, Oct. 19, 1945; d. Charles Donald and Maribelle (Morrin) Brown; m. James J. Wagner, Aug. 12, 1967 (div. 1975); m. Kenneth Lee Schaefer, Feb. 27, 1976; 1 child, Kenneth Charles. BS in Edn., Miami U., Oxford, Ohio, 1967, MEd in Ednl. Adminstrn., postgrad., Miami U., Oxford, Ohio, 1974, Wright State U., 1976-82. Cert. tchr., Ohio. Tchr. College Corner (Ohio) Schs., 1967-68, West Milton (Ohio) Pub. Schs., 1968-69, Smith Jr. High Sch., Vandalia, Ohio, 1969-73; math. coord. intermediate unit McGuffey Lab. Sch., Oxford, Ohio, 1973-74; math. coord. Vandalia-Butler City Schs., 1976-77; tchr. math., algebra Smith Jr. High Sch., Vandalia, Ohio, 1974-86; tchr. algebra and precalculus Butler High Sch., Vandalia, 1986—. Participant profl. confs.; presenter workshops. Contbr. to profl. publs. Mem. fundraising com. Miami Montessori Sch., Troy, 1989-94; curriculum coordinating coun. Vandalia-Butler City Schs., 1985—; coach Mathcounts, 1983-87, Butler H.S. Acad. Challenge Team, 1990—; treas. GMVC Acad. Challenge League, 1992—. Mem. NEA, Am. Montessori Soc., Ohio Edn. Assn., Western Ohio Edn. Assn., Vandalia-Butler Edn. Assn., Assn. Supervision and Curriculum Devel., Sch. Sci. and Math. Assn., Nat. Coun. Tchrs. Math., Ohio Coun. Tchrs. Math. (Outstanding Math. Classroom Tchr. award 1986), Wright State U. Area Coun. Tchrs. Math. Avocations: swimming, travel. Home: 2610 Greenlawn Dr Troy OH 45373-4363 Office: Butler High Sch 600 S Dixie Dr Vandalia OH 45377-2594

SCHAEFER-WICKE, ELIZABETH, reading consultant, educator; b. Bridgeport, Conn., Mar. 30, 1941; d. William Joseph and Loretta Schaefer; m. Frederick Paul wicke, July 3, 1976. BS, U. Conn., 1963; MA, Columbia U., 1966; 6th yr. profl. diploma, U. Bridgeport, 1975. Cert. reading cons. Elem. sch. tchr. Miles Ave. Sch., Huntington Park, Calif., 1963-64, Eli Whitney Sch., Meriden, Conn., 1966-68; supr. student tchg. interns Tracey Sch., Norwalk, Conn., 1968-70; reading splst. Wolfpit Sch., Norwalk, 1970-81; remedial reading and math tchr., cons. Rowayton (Conn.) Sch., 1981—2003. Mentor tng. program BEST, 1987-94, tchr. reading recovery, 1994-2003. Grantee Norwalk Fund for Excellence, 1986-87. Mem. Norwalk Fedn. Tchrs. (bldg. steward 1981-2003), Internat. Reading Assn., Reading Recovery Coun. Am., Delta Kappa Gamma, Phi Delta Kappa, Pi Beta Phi. Democrat. Roman Catholic. Avocations: writing short stories, worldwide enll. rsch., photography, scuba diving. Home: 41 Lakeview Dr Norwalk CT 06850-2003 also: 535 Broad Ave S Naples FL 34102-7159

SCHAEFFER, BRENDA MAE, psychologist, author; b. Duluth, Minn. d. Ralph J. Bernice M. (Johnson) Furtman; children: Heidi, Gordon III. BA in Sociology, Psychology and English cum laude. U. Minn., 1962; MA in Human Devel., St. Mary's Coll., Winona, Minn., 1976; D of Ministry, U. Creation Spirituality, Oakland, Calif., 2000. Lic. psychologist, Minn.; cert.

addictions specialist. Mem. faculty Coll. St. Scholastica, Duluth, 1976—; trainer, therapist, communications cons. Transactional Analysis Inst., Mpls., 1984-88; owner, clin. dir. Brenda M. Schaeffer and Assocs., Inc., 1985—, Healthy Relationships, Inc., 1991—; continued edn. instr. St. Thomas U., 1995—. Vis. prof. U. Minn., Duluth, 1976—; guest lectr. dep. counseling U. Wis., Superior, 1980—81; founder, bd. dirs. Inst. for Indigenous Healing Practice, Inc.; nat. and internat. lectr. in field. Author: Is It Love or Is It Addiction, 1987, 97, Loving Me, Loving You, 1991, Signs of Healthy Love, Signs of Addictive Love, Power Plays, Addictive Love, Help Yourself Out, Loves Way, 2001; mem. editorial bd. Transactional Analysis Jour.; editor Healthy Relationships newsletter. Planner Lake Superior Task Force, Duluth, 1980-83; bd. dirs., sec. Nat. Coun. Sexual Addictions/Compulsions, 1992—, sec. 1994-95; v.p. H. Milton Erickson Inst. Minn., 1992-93. Mem. Internat. Transactional Analysis Assn. (1975), Transactional Anaylsis Inst. Minn. (founder, pres. 1984-86), U.S. Assn. Transactional Analysis, Northeast Minn. Transactional Analysis Seminar (founder and chairperson 1977-83). Office: 6542 Regency Ln Ste 207 Eden Prairie MN 55344-7848

SCHAFER, PATRICIA DAY, physical education educator; b. Terre Haute, Ind., July 27, 1937; d. Charles Loran and Dorothy Pearl (McCool) Day; m. Dennis Meyer, Oct. 16, 1964 (div. Mar. 1975); children: Jennifer Jo Heerdink, Amy Kay Meyer. BS, Ind. State U., 1959, MS, 1964, MS, 1994, PhD, 1998. Cert. tchr. health, physical edn., recreation. Tchr. Flora High Sch., Ill., 1959-63; graduate asst. Ind. State U., Terre Haute, 1963-64; tchr. Speedway High Sch., Ind., 1964-65; asst. prof. Oakland City U., Ind., 1965-74, asst. prof./chairperson, 1984—; tchr. Pike County Schs., Petersburg, Ind., 1974-84. Instr. Am. Red Cross, 1957—. Leader 4-H Club, Princeton, Ind. 1985-88; umpire Summer League Softball, Oakland City, Ind., 1980-83; supr. Special Olympics, Oakland City, 1987-90 Recipient Realizing the Dream award Ind. Colls. and Univs. Ind., Inc., 1991. Mem. Am. Alliance Health, Physical Edn., Recreation and Dance, Ind. Assn. Health, Physical Edn., Recreation and Dance, Am. Assn. Tchr. Edn., ASCD, NAIA (voting delegate 1986, workshop leader 1986—), NCAA, DAR, Am. Quarter Horse Assn. (horseshow judge 1960—), Alpha Delta Kappa, Sigma Kappa. Meth. Avocations: raising, breeding and training registered quarter horses, swimming, camping, travelling. Home: RR 3 Box 259 Oakland City IN 47660-9371 Office: Oakland City University Lucretia St Oakland City IN 47660

SCHAFER, RUTH ERMA, artist, educator; b. Thompson, Mo., Nov. 23, 1923; d. Lewis Maxwell and Ethel (Keller) Johnson; m. Paul Linzy Starlin (dec. Jan. 1987); children: Barbara Ann White, Larry David Starlin, Stephen Pual Starlin, Paula Lynn Norris, Randal Lee Starlin. Student, Art Sch. of Ft. Wayne, Ind. Bus. mgr. Chevrolet Dealership, Portland, Ind. Tchr. Portland Art Sch., 1964—68. Oil paintings, portraits, sea scapes, landscapes, still life, exhibitions include, Atlanta, Chgo., N.Y.C., Inpls., Ft. Wayne, Brown Country Art Guild. Leader Girl Scouts U.S., Boy Scouts Am., 4-H Club; head art booths Jay County Fairs; selected by Gov. Bowen of Ind. to serve as Ind. Arts Commn. cultural rep., 1967; tchr. Sunday sch. Ch. of Christ. Named Mother of the Yr., C. of C. Portland, 1957; recipient honored by Sen. Birch Bayh as one of the Ind. Artists, Washington, 1965. Mem.: Hoosier Salon, Nat. Endowment Arts (charter), Ind. Fedn. Art Clubs (pres. 1975—77, treas. 1971—75).

SCHAFFER, EUGENE CARL, education educator; b. Phila., May 10, 1944; BA, Temple U., 1968, EdD, 1976. Dir. field experience Valparaiso U., Valparaiso, Ind., 1974-76; prof. curriculum and instrn. U. N.C., Charlotte, 1976-2000, chair dept. mid., secondary and K-12 edn., 1996-2000, chair curriculum and instrn. dept., 1994-96; prof., chair dept. edn. U. Md., Balt., 2000—03. Co-author: Recent Advances in School Effects Research, 1994, World Class Schools, 2002. Recipient Fulbright scholarship, Japan rsch. fellowship. Mem. Am. Edn. Rsch. Assn. E-mail: schaffer@umbc.edu.

SCHAFFLER, MITCHELL BARRY, research scientist, anatomist, educator; b. Bronx, N.Y., Apr. 10, 1957; s. Walter and Shirley (Balter) S. BS, SUNY, Stony Brook, 1978; PhD, W.Va. U., 1985. Rsch. fellow in radiobiology U. Utah, Salt Lake City, 1985-87; asst. prof. surgery and anatomy U. Calif., San Diego, 1987-90; assoc. prof. orthopaedics, head anatomy Bone and Joint Ctr. Henry Ford Health Scis. Ctr., Detroit, 1990-98; assoc. prof. arthopaedics, head anatomy Bone and Joint Ctr. Case Western Res. U., 1990-98; prof. orthop., cell biology and anatomy, dir. orthop. rsch. Mt. Sinai Sch. Medicine, N.Y.C., 1998—. Adj. prof. Anatomy U. Mich., Ann Arbor, 1990-98. Mem. editl. bd. Bone, Jour. Orthop. Rsch.; contbr. articles to profl. jours. Grantee Whitaker Found., 1988, NIH, 1991—, NASA, 1996—. Mem. Am. Assn. Anatomists, Am. Assn. Phys. Anthropology, Am. Soc. Bone Mineral Rsch., Orthop. Rsch. Soc., Sigma Xi, Phi Kappa Phi. Achievements include rsch. in skeletal biology, osteoporosis, osteoarthritis, and biomechanics. Office: Mt Sinai Sch Medicine Dept Orthop Box 1188 1 Gustave L Levy Pl Dept Orthop New York NY 10029-6500

SCHAFFNER, CYNTHIA VAN ALLEN, writer, curator, lecturer; b. Washington, Jan. 28, 1947; d. James Alfred and Abigail Fifthian (Halsey) Van Allen; m. Robert Todd Schaffner, June 11, 1972; 1 child, Hilary Van Allen. BA, Western Coll., 1969; MAT, Simmons Coll., 1971; MA in History of Decorative Arts, Cooper Hewitt Smithsonian Instn., N.Y.C., 1999. Editor Mademoiselle mag., N.Y.C., 1972-79; dir. devel. Am. Acad. in Rome, N.Y.C., 1987-89; curator Phila. Antiques Show, 1997-98; rsch. asst. Metropolitan Mus. Art, New York, 1999—; curator Halsey House, Southampton, N.Y., 1999—. Author: Discovering American Folk Art, 1991; co-author: Folk Hearts, 1984, American Painted Furniture, 1997; contbr. articles to popular mags. Co-chair Fall Antiques Show, N.Y.C., 1979-93; trustee Mus. Am. Folk Art, N.Y.C., 1980-95. Lisa Taylor fellow, 1995-96; Smithsonian Instn. Grad. Student fellow, 1998. Mem. Coll. Art Assn., Decorative Arts Soc., Cosmopolitan Club, Victorian Soc., Lenox Hill Hosp. Aux., Southampton Hist. Mus. (trustee 1996-2002). Avocations: canoeing, gardening, antiquing. Home: 850 Park Ave New York NY 10021-1845 E-mail: cvanschaf@aol.com.

SCHAFFNER, LINDA CAROL, biological oceanography educator; b. Freeport, N.Y., Dec. 8, 1954; d. John Charles Schaffner and Shirley Garnet Voges Sanders; m. Stephen Marshall Bennett, Apr. 7, 1979; 1 child, William Schaffner. BA, Drew U., 1976; MA, Coll. of William and Mary, 1981, PhD, 1987. Asst. prof. Va. Inst. Marine Sci., Coll. of William and Mary, Gloucester Point, 1988—. Vis scientist Swedish Environ. Protection Bd., 1988. Contbr. articles to profl. jours. Scholar Drew U., 1975-76, Houston Underwater Club, 1981, U. Wash., 1983; grantee NOAA, 1987-91, U.S. Fish and Wildlife Svc., 1991, NOAA-EPA, 1991-93, 93—, Office of Naval Rsch., 1993—. Mem. Assn. of Women in Sci., Atlantic Estuarine Rsch. Soc. (treas. 1988-90), Estuarine Rsch. Fedn., Am. Soc. Limnology and Oceanography. Office: Sch Marine Sci RR 8 Gloucester Point VA 23062

SCHAGH, CATHERINE, federal agency administrator; Dir. impact aid program US Dept. Edn., Off Elem. Secondary Edn., Wash., DC, 1995—; analyst US Dept. Edn., Budget Off., divsn. dir. to program dir. Team leader US Dept. Edn., Class-Size Reduction Program, 1998—2000; co-pres. Annandale Bus. and Profl. Women, Va. Mem.: Annandale Bus. and Profl. Women Investment Club (treas.). Office: US Dept Edn Elem Secondary Edn 400 Maryland Ave SW FB-6 Rm 3E105 Washington DC 20202*

SCHAIBERGER, GEORGE ELMER, microbiologist educator; Prof. microbiology U. Miami, Coral Gables, Fla., also dir. undergrad. microbiology immunology dept. Recipient Disting. Tchr. award Carski Found., 1992. Office: Univ Miami Cox Sci Bldg 251 1301 Memorial Dr Coral Gables FL 33124

SCHAIE, K(LAUS) WARNER, human development and psychology educator; b. Stettin, Germany (now Poland), Feb. 1, 1928; came to U.S., 1947, naturalized, 1953; s. Sally and Lottie Luise (Gabriel) S.; m. Coloma J. Harrison, Aug. 9, 1953 (div. 1973); 1 child, Stephan; m. Sherry L. Willis, Nov. 20, 1981. AA, City Coll., San Francisco, 1951; BA, U. Calif., Berkeley, 1952; MS, U. Wash., 1953, PhD, 1956; DPhil (hon.), Friedrich-Schiller U., Jena, Germany, 1997; ScD (hon.), W.Va. U., 2002; PhD (hon.), U. Wash. Lic. psychologist, Calif., Pa. Fellow Washington U., St. Louis, 1956-57; asst. prof. psychology U. Nebr., Lincoln, Nebr., 1957-64, assoc. prof., 1964-68; prof. chmn. dept. psychology W.Va. U., Morgantown, W.Va., 1964-73; prof. psychology, dir. Gerontology Rsch. Inst., U. So. Calif., 1973-81; Evan Pugh prof. human devel. and psychology Gerontology Ctr., Pa. State U., University Park, Pa., 1981—, dir., 1985—2003. Devel. behavior study sect. NIH, Bethesda, Md., 1970-72, chmn., 1972-74, chmn. human devel. and aging study sect., 1979-84, mem. expert panel in comml. airline pilot retirement, 1981, data and safety bd. shep project, 1984-91. Author: Developmental Psychology; A Life Span Approach, 1981, Adult Development and Aging, 1982, 5th rev. edit., 2002, Chinese and Spanish edits., 2003, Intellectual Development in Adulthood: The Seattle Longitudinal Study, 1996; editor: Handbook of Psychology of Aging, 1977, 5th rev. edit., 2001, Longitudinal Studies of Adult Development, 1983, Cognitive Functioning and Social Structure over the Life Course, 1987, Methodological Issues in Research on Aging, 1988, Social Structure and Aging: Psychological Processes, 1989, Age Structuring in Comparative Perspective, 1989, The Course of Later Life, 1989, Self-Directedness: Cause and Effects Throughout the Life Course, 1990, Aging, Health Behaviors and Health Outcomes, 1992, Caregiving Systems: Formal and Informal Helpers, 1993, Societal Impact on Aging: Historical Perspectives, 1993, Adult Intergenerational Relations: Effects of Societal Change, 1995, Older Adults Decision Making and the Law, 1996, Impact of Social Structures on Decision Making in the Elderly, 1997, Impact of the Workplace on Older Persons, 1998, Handbook of Theories of Aging, 1999, Mobility and Aging, 2000, Evolution of the Aging Self, 2000, Effective Health Behavior in the Elderly, 2002, Mastery and Control in the Edlerly, 2002, Influence of Technology on Successful Aging, 2003; Independent Aging: Living Arrangements and Mobility, 2003; editor Ann. Rev. Gerontology and Geriat., vol. 7, 1987, vol. 11, 1991, vol. 17, 1997; contbr. articles to profl. jours. Recipient Lifetime Achievment award, Mensa, 2000. Fellow APA (coun. reps. 1976-79, 83-86, Disting. Contbn. award, 1992), Gerontol. Soc. (Kleemeier award 1987, Disting. Mentorship award 1996),Lifetime cancer award, Mensa Society, 2000. Am. Psychol. Assn.; mem. Psychometric Soc., Internat. Soc. Study Behavioral Devel. Unitarian Universalist. Avocations: hiking, stamps. Home: 425 Windmere Dr Apt 3A State College PA 16801-7670 Office: Pa State U Gerontology Ctr 135 E Nittany Ave Ste 405 State College PA 16802 E-mail: kws@psu.edu.

SCHAKE, LOWELL MARTIN, animal science educator; b. Marthasville, Mo., June 6, 1938; s. Martin Charles and Flora Olinda (Rocklage) S.; m. Wendy Anne Walkinshaw, Sept. 11, 1959; children: Sheryl Anne, Lowell Scott. BS, U. Mo., 1960, MS, 1962; PhD, Tex. A&M U., 1967. Asst. prof. Tex. A&M U., College Station, 1965-67, assoc. prof., 1969-72, prof., 1972-84, asst. prof., area livestock specialist Lubbock, 1967-69; prof., head animal sci. dept. U. Conn., Storrs, 1984-92; prof., chmn. animal sci. dept. Tex. Tech. U., Lubbock, 1992-95. Developer applied animal ethology program Tex. A&M U., 1970, New Eng. Biotech Conf. series, 1990, S.W. Beef Forum, 1993; chmn. Am. Registry of Profl. Animal Scientist Com. on Profl. Stds., 1988; chmn. Nat. Com. Exec. Officers of Animal Vet., Dairy and Poultry Sci. Depts., 1992; cons. Alpart, Kingston, Jamaica, 1975, U.S. Feeds Grain Coun., 1970-73, A.O. Smith Products Inc., 1968-92, Humphrey Land & Cattle Co., Dallas, 1980-86; lectr. in field. Author: Growth and Finishing of Beef Cattle, A Class Handbook, 1982, La Charrette: Village Gateway to the American West, 2003; contbr. articles to profl. jours. Recipient Innovative Teaching award Tex. A&M U., 1978. Mem. Am. Soc. Animal Sci., Plains Nutrition Coun. (adv. bd. 1967-80, sec.-treas. 1994-95, founder), Nat. Assn. Colls. and Tchrs. Agr., Am. Registry Profl. Animal Scientists (dir. for Northeast 1987-89), Coun. for Agr. Sci. and Tech. World Conf. on Animal Prodn., Am. Soc. Dairy Sci., Gamma Sigma Delta. Clubs: Tiger (College Station) (pres.). Republican. Avocations: genealogy, fishing, gardening. Home: 13542 Carlos Fifth Ct Corpus Christi TX 78418-6913 E-mail: lschake@aol.com.

SCHALLENKAMP, KAY, academic administrator; b. Salem, S.D., Dec. 9, 1949; d. Arnold B. and Jennie M. (Koch) Krier; m. Ken Schallenkamp, Sept. 7, 1970; children: Heather, Jenni. BS, No. State Coll., 1972; MA, U. S.D., 1973; PhD, U. Colo., 1982. Prof. No. State Coll., Aberdeen, S.D., 1973-88, dept. chair, 1982-84, dean, 1984-88; provost Chadron (Nebr.) State Coll., 1988-92, U. Wis., Whitewater, 1992-97; pres. Emporia (Kans.) State U., 1997—. Cons. North Ctrl. Assn., nursing homes, hosps. and ednl. instns. Contbr. articles to profl. jours. Commr. North Ctrl. Assn., 1995-99. Bush fellow, 1980; named Outstanding Young Career Woman, Bus. and Profl. Women's Club, 1976. Mem. NCAA (pres.'s coun. 2000—), Kans. C. of C. (bd. dirs. 2000—), Am. Speech and Hearing Assn. (cert.), Rotary. Avocation: martial arts. Office: Emporia State U 1200 Commercial St Emporia KS 66801-5087 E-mail: schallka@emporia.edu.

SCHANFIELD, MOSES SAMUEL, geneticist, educator; b. Mpls., Sept. 7, 1944; s. Abraham and Fanny (Schwartz) Schanfield; m. Patricia A. McCarthy. BA in Anthropology, U. Minn., 1966; AM in Anthropology, Harvard U., 1969; PhD in Human Genetics, U. Mich., 1971. Postdoctoral fellow in immunology U. Calif. Med. Ctr., San Francisco, 1971-74, rsch. geneticist, 1974-75; head of blood bank Milw. Blood Ctr., 1975-78; asst. dir. ARC, Washington, 1978-83; exec. dir. Genetic Testing Inst., Atlanta, 1983-85; lab. dir. Analytical Genetic Testing Ctr., Atlanta and Denver, 1985-2000; adminstr. Monroe County Pub. Safety Lab., Rochester, NY, 2000—02; prof., chair dept. forensic sci. George Washington U., 2002—. Adj. asst. prof. Med. Coll. Wis., Milw., 1976—78; adj. assoc. prof. George Washington U., Washington, 1979—83, Emory U., Atlanta, 1984—89, U. Kans., 1992—; affiliated faculty Colo. State U. Ft. Collins, 1992—2000; mem. Nat. Forensic DNA Rev. Panel, Nat. Inst. of Justice, 1996—2000; pres. 1st European-Am. Intensive Course in PCR, Split, Croatia, 1997; co-organizer 2d European-Am. Intensive Course in PCR, Dubrovnik, Croatia. Author, editor: book Immunobiology of the Erythrocyte, 1980, International Methods of Forensic DNA Analysis, 1996, contg. author: book Immunogenetic Factors and Thalassaemia of Hepatitis, 1975; contbr. articles to profl. publs. Recipient Gold medal, Latin Am. Congress Hemotherapy and Immunohematology, 1979, R&D 100 award, 1993. Fellow: Am. Acad. Forensic Sci.; mem.: Human Biology Coun., Am. Soc. Human Genetics, Am. Soc. Crime Lab. Dirs., Phi Kappa Phi. Achievements include discovery of of the biological function of GC protein as vitamin D transport protein; of 2 sources of errors in DNA sizings; detection of the presence of HIV in Africa in the 1950's. Office: Monroe County Pub Safety Labtr Pub Safety Bldg Rm 524 150 Plymouth Ave S Rochester NY 14614-2277 E-mail: mschanfield@netscape.net.

SCHANTZ, ALLEN RAY, retired school administrator; b. East Greenville, Pa., Sept. 24, 1937; s. Clifford Charles and Laura (Kasperowicz) S.; m. Christine Fern Schantz, Aug. 3, 1959 (div. 1982); children: Allen Ray, Christopher Lyon, Lorie Ann Schantz Bounds; m. Linda Frances Bythrow, Aug. 21, 1993. BS in Edn. Math. & Geography, Millersville State Coll., 1959; MS in Edn., Westchester State Coll., 1971; MS in Math. Edn., Pa. State U., 1975; MS in Adminstrn., U. Pa., 1980. Cert. math. secondary prin., elem. prin., supr., supt. Tchr. math. Columbia (Pa.) Borough Schs., 1959; asst. instr. Kent (Ohio) State U., 1959-60; tchr. math. Millersville (Pa.) Borough Schs., 1960-61; systems computer program GE, Phila., 1961-64; systems analyst, programmer Honeywell, Inc., Bala Cynwyd, Pa., 1964-66; data processing mgr. Inter County Hospitilization, Glenside, Pa., 1966-67; tchr. math., computer cons. Rose Tree Media (Pa.) Schs., 1967-72, supr. K-12 math., 1972-98; ret. Adj. prof. Pa. State U., King of Prussia and Harrisburg, 1973-84, Widener U., Chester, Pa., 1981—; computer programming tchr. Assn. of 74, Valley Forge, Pa. Editor: Sophisticated Ciphers, 1978. Mem. Nat. Assn. Secondary Sch. Prins., Nat. Coun. Tchrs. of Math., Pa. Coun. Tchrs. of Math., Math. Assn. of Phila. and Vicinity, Phi Delta Kappa. Avocations: golf, skiing, gardening, photography, carpentry and cabinet making. Home: 1211 Anna Rd West Chester PA 19380-4079

SCHAPIRO, MORTON OWEN, university administrator; BA in economics, Hofstra U., 1975; PhD, U. Pa., 1979. Prof. econs. Williams Coll., pres., 2000—; head dept. econs. U. So. Calif., dean. Commentator Pub. Radio Internat; expert witness on econ. issues in higher edn. U.S. Congress. Author: The Student Aid Game; contbr. articles to profl. jours. Office: Office of the President Williams Coll PO Box 687 Williamstown MA 01267

SCHAPPELL, LOLA IRENE HILL, school system administrator; b. Rochester, N.Y., Feb. 17, 1940; d. Harrison Albert and Bertha May (McIntyle) Hill; m. Kerry W. Washburn, June 11, 1960 (div. Oct. 1968); children: Yvonne Marie Washburn White, Valerie Lee Washburn Anderson; m. Robert Nathaniel Schappell, Dec. 18, 1976. BS in Elem. Edn., SUNY, Brockport, 1962; MS in Edn., Purdue U., 1969; EdD, U. Mass., 1972. Cert. tchr., N.Y., N.C., curriculum specialist, adminstr., N.C. Ednl. psychologist Belchertown (Mass.) Sch. for Mentally Retarded, 1970-71; dir. reading Albion (N.Y.) Cen. Schs., 1972-73, Mexico (N.Y.) Cen. Schs., 1973-75; asst. prof. Fed. City Coll., Washington, 1975-76; curriculum specialist/reading Charlotte (N.C.)-Mecklenburg Schs., 1976-78, program specialist, 1978-81, asst. prin., 1981-84, elem. prin., 1984-88, Greensboro (N.C.) Pub. Schs., 1988-91, coord. spl. projects and grants, 1991-93; fgn. tchr. Guangzhou (China) Sr. Fin. Coll., 1995-96. Mem. adv. bd. Gethsemane Enrichment Ctr., Charlotte, 1984-88; bd. dirs. Am. Field Svc., Attica, N.Y., 1964-67, N.Y. Baha'i Dist. Teaching Com., Mexico, 1973-75; exec. dir. GPS Excellence Fund, Greensboro, 1991-93; mem. Nat. Baha'i Edn. Task Force, 1995—; speaker in field. Prin. creator acceleration/enrichment program. Participant Guildord Women for Race Rels., Greensboro, 1991-92, Race Rels. Forum, Greensboro, 1992; resource developer Black Child Devel., Greensboro, 1992. Mem. AAUW, ASCD, Phi Delta Kappa. Mem. Baha'i Faith. Avocations: water skiing, swimming, walking, gardening, reading. Home: 401 Chancery Park Ct Kernersville NC 27284-8338 Office: Guilford Co Pub Schs 701 N Eugene St Greensboro NC 27401-1621

SCHARFENBERG, MARGARET ELLAN, retired elementary school educator; b. Lansing, Mich., Mar. 22, 1924; d. John Milton and Florence Lucille (Craig) Amiss; m. Howard Edward Scharfenberg, June 29, 1946; children: Ann Derr Scharfenberg White, Joan Carol Scharfenberg Anderson, John Howard Scharfenberg. Student, Oberlin Coll., 1942-44; BA, Mich. State U., 1946; MA in Teaching, Rollins Coll., 1966. Cert. tchr., elem. supr., Fla. Tchr. Hill Elem. Sch., Maitland, Fla., 1964-65, Cheney Elem. Sch., Orlando, Fla., 1965-66; reading lab. tchr. Richmond Heights Elem. Sch., Orlando, 1966-68; supr. perceptual planning, oral clinician Orange County Schs., Orlando, 1968-69; reading lab. tchr. Winter Park (Fla.) H.S., 1969-72; from perceptual trainer to exptl. reading lab. tchr. Gateway Sch., Orlando, 1972-74; tchr. of migrant children Zellwood (Fla.) Elem. Sch., 1974-93; ret., 1993. Pioneer white/black sch. staffing Richmond Heights Elem. Sch., 1966-68; dir. Learning Skills Profl. Ctr., Orlando, 1971-74; speaker numerous symposia and convs. in field, 1968—; cons. in field. Author, editor (newsletter) Paper Meeting, 1968-69, (perception package) Patterns for a Purpose, 1968-69; producer films on perceptual tng., 1968-69. Chaplain, Oleander Garden Cir.; chaplain, past sec., Lakes and Hills Garden Club; sec. Tangerine Garden Club; chaplain, historian, past v.p. and pres. Women's Soc., Tangerine Cmty. Ch.; vol. Women of Hospice, Hospice Hope Chest; mem. Humane Soc. U.S.A. Named Tchr. of Yr., Zellwood Elem. Sch., 1993. Mem.: NEA, AAUW, Internat. Reading Assn. (sec. Orange County coun. 1965, pres. 1969), Rosicrucian Order (A.M.O.R.C.), Lions (staff mem. seminars on perception, recipient various certs. and plaques), Gamma Phi Beta (past pres. alumna group). Republican. Presbyterian. Avocations: reading, boating, gardening, animal study. Home: 6492 Dora Dr Mount Dora FL 32757-7064

SCHARFFE, WILLIAM GRANVILLE, academic administrator, educator; b. Saginaw, Mich., Mar. 12, 1942; s. William Edward and Marion Kittie (Granville) S.; m. Mary Jo Whitfield, Sept. 4, 1965; children: Sue L., William W. BA, Mich. State U., 1965, MA, 1969, PhD, 1977. Tchr. English Webber Jr. High Sch., Saginaw, 1965-66; tchr. speech Arthur Hill High Sch., Saginaw, 1966-68; staff asst. for pers. Saginaw City Schs., 1968-73, dir. pers., 1977-94, dir. employee devel. and media ops., 1994-99; prin. Zilwaukee Jr. High Sch., Saginaw, 1973-74; asst. prin. North Intermediate Sch., Saginaw, 1974-75, 1975-77; dir. policy svcs. Mich. Assn. Sch. Bds., Lansing, 1999—. Adj. asst. prof. Mich. State U., East Lansing, 1977; pvt. practice pers. cons., Saginaw, 1978—; adj. lectr. Ctrl. Mich. U., Mt. Pleasant, 1987, Mich. State U., 1977, Saginaw Valley State U., 1991. Author: (children's book) Elfred Alanzo & Santa's Surprise, 1987. Bd. dirs. Japanese Cultural Ctr. and Tea House, Saginaw, 1986-97, pres., 1993-95. Recipient Key Man award United Way Saginaw County, 1978, Outstanding Svc. award, 1978. Mem. Mich. Assn. Sch. Pers. Assn. (sec., bd. dirs. 1988-90, pres., bd. dirs. 1992-93), Mich. Mid. Cities Pers. and Labor Rels. Task Force (pres. 1980-82), Soc. For Human Resource Mgmt., Exch. Club (Saginaw chpt. pres. 1981), Saginaw Club (pres. 1996-97), Phi Delta Kappa. Republican. Episcopalian. Avocations: writing, golf, photography, public speaking. Home: 2812 Adams Blvd Saginaw MI 48602-3103

SCHATTSCHNEIDER, DORIS JEAN, mathematics educator; b. N.Y.C., Oct. 19, 1939; d. Robert W. Jr. and Charlotte Lucile (Ingalls) Wood; m. David A. Schattschneider, June 2, 1962; 1 child, Laura E. AB, U. Rochester, 1961; MA, Yale U., 1963, PhD, 1966. Instr. in math. Northwestern U., Evanston, Ill., 1964—65; asst. prof. U. Ill., Chgo., 1965—68; prof. Moravian Coll., Bethlehem, Pa., 1968—2002, prof. emerita, 2003—. Project dir. Fund for the Improvement of Post-Secondary Edn. U.S. Dept. Edn., 1991—93, 1995—97. Author (with W. Walker): (books and models) M.C. Escher Kaleidocycles, 1977, 1987; co-author: (videos and activities) Visual Geometry Project, 1986—91; author: Visions of Symmetry, 1990—2004; co-author: (videos and activities) A Companion to Calculus, 1995; editor: Geometry Turned On, 1997, M.C. Escher's Legacy, 2003. Exhbn. curator Allentown Art Mus., 1979, Payne Gallery, 1987. Grantee NEH rsch. grantee, 1988—90. Mem.: Assn. for Women in Math., Am. Math. Soc., Math. Assn. Am. (editor 1980—85, gov. 1980—89, 1st v.p. 1994—96, Allendoerfer award 1979, Meritorious Svc. award 1991, Dist. Math. Tchg. award 1993), Pi Mu Epsilon (councillor 1990—96). Mem. Moravian Ch. Office: Moravian Coll Math Dept 1200 Main St Bethlehem PA 18018-6650 E-mail: schattdo@moravian.edu.

SCHATZ, LILLIAN LEE, playwright, molecular biologist, educator; d. Joseph Louis and Rose S. BA in Biology, SUNY, Buffalo, 1965, MA in Biology, 1970. Cert. h.s. tchr. biology, chemistry, gen. sci., N.Y., 1968. Rsch. asst. dept. biology SUNY, Buffalo, 1965-68, rsch. asst. dept. pharmacology sch. medicine, 1969, rsch. assoc. dept. biology, 1971-74; cancer rsch. scientist dept. viral oncology Roswell Park Meml. Inst., Buffalo, 1969-70; tchr. biology Kenmore East Sr. H.S., Buffalo, 1970-71; playwright, 1976—. Presenter workshop Rosa Coplon Jewish Home and Infirmary, Buffalo, N.Y., 1982, N.Y. State Community Theater Assn., 1982. Author: (plays) Solomon's Court, 1979, Neshomah, 1983, Bernie, 1985, The Jonah Men, 1991, For the Love of Jake, 2001; contbr. rsch. articles to sci. jours. Charter mem. B'not Israel Group, Hadassah, life mem. Recipient N.Y. State Regents Coll. Scholarship, 1961-65; semi-finalist Sergel Drama prize Ct. Theatre, U. Chgo., 1985, Nat. Play Award Competition Nat. Repertory Theatre Found., 1981; Playwriting fellow, N.Y. State Creative Artists Pub. Svc. fellow, 1980-81, Roswell Park Meml. Inst. fellow, 1962, Summer Sci. fellow. Avocations: art, genealogy.

SCHATZ, MONA CLAIRE STRUHSAKER, social worker, educator, consultant, researcher; b. Phila., Jan. 4, 1950; d. Milton and Josephine (Kivo) S.; m. James Fredrick Struhsaker, Dec. 31, 1979 (div.); 1 child, Thain Mackenzie. BA, Metro State Coll., 1976; postgrad., U. Minn., 1976; MSW, U. Denver, 1979; D in Social Work/Social Welfare, U. Pa., 1986. Teaching fellow U. Pa., Phila., 1981-82; asst. prof. S.W. Mo. State U., Springfield, 1982-85; prof. Colo. State U., Ft. Collins, 1985—, field coord., 1986-88, dir. non-profit agy. adminstrn. program, 1995-97, project dir. Edn. and Rsch. Inst. for Fostering Families, 1987—, dir. youth agy. adminstrn. program Am. Humanics, 1988-90; mem. coun. foster care cert. program Western Gov.'s U., 1998—. Cons. Mgmt. and Behavioral Sci. Ctr., The Wharton Sch. U. Pa., 1981-82; resource specialist So. N.J. Health Sys. Agy., 1982; adj. faculty mem. U. Mo., Springfield, 1994; med. social worker Rehab. and Vis. Nurse Assn., 1985-90; mem. Colo. Child Welfare Adv. Com., Family Conservation Initiative; internat. cons. and trainer Inst. for Internat. Connections, Azerbaijan, Russia, Latvia, Albania, U.S., Hungary, Ukraine, Romania, 1992—. Contbr. articles to profl. jours. including Jour. Social Work Edn., New Social Worker, Chosen Child: Internat. Adoption Mag., others. Cons., field rep. Big Bros./Big Sisters of Am., Phila., 1979-83; acting dir., asst. dir. Big Sisters of Colo., 1971-78; owner Polit. Cons. in Colo., Denver, 1978-79; active Food Co-op, Ft. Collins, Foster Parent, Denver, Capital Hill United Neighbors, Adams County (Denver) Social Planning Coun., Co., Colo. Justice Coun., Denver, Regional Girls Shelter, Springfield; bd. dirs. Crisis Helpline and Info. Svc. Scholar Lilly Endowment, Inc., 1976, Piton Found., 1978; recipient Spl. Recognition award Big Bros./Big Sisters of Am., 1983, Recognition award Am. Humanics Mgmt. Inst., 1990, Innovative Tchg. award, Ctr. for Tchg. and Learning/Colo. State U. Mem. Inst. Internat. Connections (bd. dirs., mem. adv. bd.), Coun. Social Work Edn., Group for Study of Generalist Social Work, Social Welfare History Group, Nat. Assn. Social Workers (nominating com. Springfield chpt., state bd. dirs., No. Colo. rep.), Student Social Work Assn. Colo. State U. (adv. 1986-89), Permanency Planning Coun. for Children and Youth, NOW (treas. Springfield chpt. 1984-85), Student Nuclear Awareness Group (advisor), Student Social Work Assn. (advisor), Har Shalom (tchg. in youth edn. program), Alpha Delta Mu. Democrat. Avocations: cooking, travel, reading, biking, sewing. Office: Colo State U Social Work Dept Fort Collins CO 80523-0001 E-mail: schatz@cahs.colostate.edu.

SCHATZ, PAUL FREDERICK, laboratory director; b. Cin., Aug. 24, 1944; s. Frederick Vincent and Nell (Sarles) S.; m. Eleanor Mae Smith, Aug. 19, 1967; children: Alexander, Christopher. BA, Colgate U., 1966; PhD in Chemistry, U. Wis., 1971. Lab. dir. U. Wis., Madison, 1971—. Author various computer programs. Mem. Am. Chem. Soc. Office: Univ Wis Dept Chemistry 1101 University Ave Madison WI 53706-1322

SCHATZ, PAULINE, dietitian; b. Sioux City, Iowa, Sept. 25, 1923; d. Isaac and Haya (Kaplan) Epstein; m. Hyman Schatz, Sept. 2, 1951; children: Barbara, Larry. BS, UCLA, 1945, MS, 1950, MS in Pub. Health, 1963; EdD, U. So. Calif., 1984. Head dietitian VA, 1946-54; assoc. prof. L.A. City Coll., 1958-56; prof. home econs. Calif. State U., L.A., 1968-83, prof. emeritus, 1983—, dir. ctr. dietetic edn., 1979—, Northridge, 1988-90. Adv. Mid-Career Mentoring Proj., Calif. Dietetic Assn., 1999-00. Author: Manual for Clinical Dietetics, 1978, 3d edit., 1983, Developing a Dietetics Education Program, 1994; co-author: Mentoring, The Human Touch, 1994; contbr. articles to profl. jours. Grantee VA, Kellogg Found. Mem. Am. Dietetic Assn. (disting. Svc. award 1986), Calif. Dietetic Assn. (advisor mid-career mentoring project 1999-2000, Zellmer grantee 1966-69, Disting. Svc. award 1986, Excellence in Edn. 1993, Dolores Nyhus Meml. award 1997), L.A. Dietetic Assn., Kappa Omicron Nu. E-mail: paulineschatz@netscape.net.

SCHATZ, WAYNE ARDALE, district technology coordinator, computer educator; b. Cody, Wyo., July 27, 1947; s. Albert R. and Leona Mildred (Johnston) S.; m. Roanne Longwith, Dec. 16, 1966; children: Heidi Edith, Robert, Leon, Dale, Anne. BS, Ea. Mont. Coll., 1969; MEd, Lesley Coll., 1987. Cert. Elem. tchr., Wyo. Tchr. Coffeen Elem. Sch., Sheridan, Wyo., 1969-78, Woodland Park Elem., Sheridan, 1978-87; computer tchr. Cen. Mid. Sch., Sheridan, 1987-94; in-svc. instr. Sch. Dist. #2, Sheridan, 1987—, dist. tech. coord., 1994-97; computer tchr. Sheridan Jr. H.S., Sheridan, 1997—. Extension instr. U. Wyo., Laramie, 1989—. Bd. dirs. Bighorn Audobon Soc., Sheridan, 1966-77, pres., 1977-80; active Sheridan County Red Cross, Sheridan. Mem. Sheridan Cen. Edn. Assn. (pres. 1979-80, Tchr. of the Month 1988, 92, Tchr. of Yr. 1992), Wyo. Edn. Assn. (bd. dirs. 1980-82, treas. 1982-84), Wyo. Ednl. Computing Coun. (pres. 1989-92), Wyo. Bus. Edn. Assn. (pres. 2002-03), Wyo. Assn. Career & Tech. Edn. (bd. dirs. 2001-03). Republican. Mem. Lds Ch. Home: 955 Lewis St Sheridan WY 82801-3423

SCHAUB, THERESA MARIE, early childhood educator; b. Milw, Oct. 12, 1951; d. Joseph and Mary (Huberty) S. BS in Early Childhood, U. Wis., 1975. Cert. exceptional-edn.-early childhood, Wis. Kindergarten tchr. Sacred Heart, Milw., 1981-82, Ebenezer Child Care, Milw., 1982-83; presch.-head tchr. Ragamuffin Child Care, Milw., 1984-85, 86-87; asst. dir., head tchr. Country Kare, Albuquerque, 1985-86; kindergarten tchr. Holy Angels Sch., Milw., 1987-90, St. Rose Sch., Milw., 1990-94; head start tchr. Children's Outing Assn., Milw., 1994-96, Parkman Sch., Milw., 1996, Andrew S. Douglas Sch., Milw., 1996-97; kindergarten tchr. Sage program Maple Tree Sch., 1997—2000, Burbank Sch., 2000—. Supportive cons. St. Rose Sch., Milw., 1990-94, peer mediation supr., 1991-94, AV coord., 1990-94; parent vol. com. Children's Outing Assn., 1995-96 Author: ABC's of Peace, 1990. Pres. Young Dems.; vol. Homeless Shelter Casa Maria Hospitality, Milw., 1975-80; vol. tchr. Peacemakers Camp, Milw., 1992; bd. dirs. Clear Horizons Food Coop., Milw., 1978. Mem. Milw. Peace Ctr., NAEYC, Sierra Club, NOW, Nat. Audubon Soc., Wis. Edn. for Social Responsibility, Habitat for Humanity. Avocations: hiking, snowshoeing, traveling, listening to music, aerobics. Office: Burbank Sch 6035 W Adler Milwaukee WI

SCHAUBERT, DANIEL HAROLD, electrical engineering educator; b. Galesburg, Ill., Feb. 15, 1947; s. Robert Harold and Carolyn Virginia (Dunkle) S.; m. Joyce Marie Conard, June 15, 1968; 1 child, Karen Louise. BSEE, U. Ill., 1969, MS, 1970, PhD, 1974. Rsch. engr. U.S. Army Harry Diamond Labs., Adelphi, Md., 1977-80; rsch. engr., program mgr. U.S. Bur. Radiol. Health, Rockville, Md., 1980-82; prof. elec. engring. U. Mass., Amherst, 1982—, dept. head elec. and computer engring., 1994-98. Patentee in field. 1st lt. U.S. Army, 1974-77. Fellow IEEE (Third Millennium medal), IEEE Antennas and Propagation Soc. (membership chair 1980-82, editor newsletter 1982-84, sec.-treas. 1984-88, v.p. 1998, pres. 1999). Office: U Mass Elec and Computer Engring Amherst MA 01003

SCHAUBLE, JOHN EUGENE, physical education educator; b. Paterson, N.J., Aug. 14, 1949; s. Charles Eugene and Rosemary (White) S.; children: Sarah, Angela. BA, Bemidji State U., 1973, BS, 1974; MA, U. Ala., 1984. Cert. tchr. health, phys. edn., K-12; cert. swimming coach/level 4; cert. aquatic mgr.; cert. pool operator, ARC water safety instr., lifeguard instr., waterfront lifeguard instr., lifeguard mgmt. instr., first aid instr., CPR instr., water safety instr. trainer, AED essentials instr., disease prevention instr., oxygen adminstrn. instr., safety tng. for swim coaches instr.; cert. U.S.A. Track & Field level II. Northeast area dir. Phys. Fitness Inst. of Am., Albany, N.Y., 1974-75; head swim coach Lake Forest (Ill.) Swim Club, 1975-78; asst. swim coach/grad. asst. U. Ala., Tuscaloosa, 1978-79; head swim coach Palm Springs (Calif.) Swim Team, 1979-80; asst. swim coach Ft. Lauderdale (Fla.) Swim Team, 1980-82; aquatic dir., head swim coach Briarwood of Richmond Aquatic Club, Richmond, Va., 1982-83; head swimming coach, intramural coord. William Rainey Harper Coll., Palatine, Ill., 1983-85; boys/girls asst. swim coach Sch. Dist. 211, Palatine, 1985-90; nat. coach Palatine Swim Team, 1983-92; head boys and girls swim coach Adlai E. Stevenson High Sch., Lincolnshire, Ill., 1990-96, aquatic coord., 1990—, asst. girls track and field coach, 1992-99, varsity cross-country coach, 1999—, boys distance track and field coach, 1999—. Head coach Patriot Aquatic Club, 1992-94, head coach sr. team, 1994-99; fund raising com. U.S. Swimming, Inc., Colorado Springs, Colo., 1990-94; coaches rep. Ill. Swimming, Inc., Aurora, 1990-94, bd. dirs., tech. planning com., others. Nominated Coach of Yr., Nat. Jr. Coll. Athletic Assn., Ft. Pierce, Fla., 1984; named Boys Sectional Coach of Yr., Ill. High Sch. Assn., 1992. Mem. Ill. Swimming Assn. (nominated Coach of Yr. coll. divsn. boys 1984), Nat. Interscholastic Swimming Coaches Assn., Am. Swimming Coaches Assn., Am. Coll. Sports Medicine, Nat. Strength and Conditioning Assn., Ill. Track and Cross Country Coaches Assn., AAPHERD, NEA. Republican. Roman Catholic. Avocations: computer, running, swimming, tennis, weight tng. Home: 608 Applegate Ln Lake Zurich IL 60047-2363 Office: 1 Stevenson Dr Lincolnshire IL 60069-2824

SCHAUENBERG, SUSAN KAY, retired counseling administrator; b. Taylor Ridge, Ill., Oct. 23, 1945; d. Albert George and Elizabeth (Stedman) Grill; m. Robert Dale Schauenberg Jr.; 1 child, Trevor Alan. BA, Marycrest Coll., 1967; MA, U. Iowa, 1968. Prof. Black Hawk Coll., Moline, Ill., 1971—, prof. emerita, 2001—. Bus. cons., Taylor Ridge, 1984—; v.p. faculty senate Black Hawk Coll., 1980-82. Author: Career Bingo, 1999. Planning com. United Way Orgn., Quad-Cities, Ill., 1981-84, agy. rels. com., 1981-82, allocations com., 1980-82; den mother Rock Island chpt. Boy Scouts Am., 1978-79; sponsor Christmas fundraiser for 100 children, yearly. Named one of Most Admired Women of the Quad-Cities, 1975; won L.I.V.E. Volunteerism honor for peer counselor-aide program, 1991. Mem. Am. Fedn. Tchrs., Ill. Guidance and Personnel Assn. (Black Hawk chpt.), U. Iowa Alumni Assn., Phi Gamma Delta (mem. Parents Assn.). Avocations: stained glass window designer, travel. Home: 8428 104th Ave W Taylor Ridge IL 61284-9210 Office: Black Hawk Coll 6600 34th Ave Moline IL 61265-5870

SCHAUER, FREDERICK FRANKLIN, law educator; b. Newark, Jan. 15, 1946; s. John Adolph and Clara (Balayti) S.; m. Margery Clare Stone, Aug. 25, 1968 (div. June, 1982); m. Virginia Jo Wise, May 25, 1985. AB, Dartmouth Coll., 1967, MBA, 1968; JD, Harvard U., 1972. Bar: Mass. 1972, U.S. Supreme Ct. 1976. Assoc. Fine & Ambrogne, Boston, 1972-74; asst. prof. law W.Va. U., Morgantown, 1974-76, assoc. prof., 1976-78, Coll. William and Mary, Williamsburg, Va., 1978-80, Cutler prof., 1980-83; prof. of law U. Mich., Ann Arbor, 1983-90; Frank Stanton prof. of 1st Amendment Kennedy Sch. of Govt., Harvard U., Cambridge, Mass., 1990—, acad. dean, 1997—2002, acting dean, 2001. Vis. scholar, mem. faculty law Wolfson Coll. Cambridge (Eng.) U., 1977-78; vis. prof. Law Sch., U. Chgo., 1990; vis. fellow Australian Nat. U., 1993, 98; William Morton Disting. Sr. fellow in humanities Dartmouth Coll., 1991; vis. prof. law Harvard Law Sch., 1996, 97, 2000; Ewald Disting. vis. prof. law U. Va., 1996, vis. prof. govt. Dartmouth Coll., 1997; disting. vis. prof. law U. Toronto, 2000. Author: The Law of Obscenity, 1976, Free Speech: A Philosophical Enquiry, 1982 (ABA cert. merit 1983), Supplements to Gunther Constitutional Law, 1983-96, Playing by the Rules: A Philosophical Examination of Rule Based Decision-Making in Law and Life, 1991, The First Amendment: A Reader, 1992, 2d edit., 1995, The Philosophy of Law, 1995, Profiles, Probabilities and Sterotypes, 2003; editor: Legal Theory, 1995-2000; contbr. articles to profl. jours. Mem. Atty. Gen.'s Commn. on Pornography, 1985-86. Served with Mass. Army N.G., 1970-71. NEH fellow, summer 1980, Guggenheim fellow, 2001-02. Fellow Am. Acad. Arts and Scis., Radcliffe Inst. for Adv. Studies; mem. Am. Philos. Assn., Am. Soc. for Polit. and Legal Philosophy (v.p. 1996-99), Assn. Am. Law Schs. (chmn. sect. constl. law 1984-86). Office: Kennedy Sch of Govt Harvard U Cambridge MA 02138 E-mail: fred_schauer@harvard.edu

SCHAUMANN, CAROLINE, language educator; b. Berlin, Sept. 7, 1969; arrived in U.S., 1991; d. Frank and Cora-Beate S.; m. Jeffrey Thomas Ransdell, June 30, 1997 (div. Aug. 1999). BA, Free U., Berlin, 1992; MA, U. Calif., Davis, 1994, PhD, 1999. Asst. prof. Middlebury (Vt.) Coll., 1999—2002, Emory U., Atlanta, 2002—. Author: Our Own Private Ezahlraum, 2001. Summer Seminar grant Ctr. for Advanced Holocaust Studies, 2000; Quadrille Ball scholar Office Internat. Edn., 1999. Mem. MLA, German Studies Assn., Am. Assn. Tchrs. German, Women in German, Computer Assisted Lang. Instrn. Consortium. Avocations: rock climbing, mountaineering, running. Office: Emory U Dept German Studies 637 Ashbury Cir Trimble Hall Atlanta GA 30322 E-mail: cschaum@emory.edu.

SCHECHTER, JOEL, magazine editor, writer, educator; b. Washington, June 21, 1947; s. Henry Bear and Ruth (Lindauer) S. BA, Antioch Coll., 1969; DFA, Yale U., 1973. Lit. advisor Am. Place Theater, N.Y.C., 1973-77; asst. prof. SUNY, Stony Brook, 1974-77; prof. Sch. Drama Yale U., New Haven, 1977—92; editor Theater Mag., New Haven, 1977—92; prof. theatre arts San Francisco State U., 1992—. Polit. satire columnist New Haven Independent, 1988-90. Author: Durov's Pig, 1985, Satiric Impersonations, 1994, The Congress of Clowns, 1998, The Pickle Clowns, 2001, Popular Theatre: A Sourcebook, 2003; (play) The Complete Aristophanes, 1988. State senate candidate New Haven Green Party, 1988, 90. Fox fellow Yale U., Moscow, 1991. Mem. Lit. Mgrs. & Dramaturgs Am. (v.p. 1989—), Am. Soc. Theatre Rsch. Office: San Francisco State U Dept Theatre Arts 1600 Holloway Ave Dept Theatre San Francisco CA 94132-1722

SCHECHTER, MARTIN, mathematician, educator; b. Phila., Mar. 10, 1930; s. Joshua and Rose (Shames) S.; m. Naomi Deborah Kirzner, Dec. 23, 1957; children: Sharon Libby, Arthur Irving, Isaac David, Raphael Morris. BS, CCNY, 1953; MS, NYU, 1955, PhD, 1957. Instr. NYU, N.Y.C., 1957-59, from asst. prof. to assoc. prof., 1959-65, prof., 1965-66, Yeshiva U., N.Y.C., 1966-83, U. Calif., Irvine, 1983—. Vis. assoc. prof. U. Chgo., 1961; vis. prof. Hebrew U., Jerusalem, 1973, Autonomous U., Mexico City, 1979. Author: Principles of Functional Analysis, 1971, 2d edit., 2002, Spectra of Partial Differential Operators, 1971, 2d edit., 1986, Modern Methods in Partial Differential Equations, 1977, Operator Methods in Quantum Mechanics, 1981, Linking Methods in Critical Point Theory, 1999; contbr. more than 180 articles to profl. jours. Achievements include new results and theorems concerning boundary value problems for partial differential equations; operators on Banach and Hilbert spaces; spectral theory of partial differential operators; nonlinear functional analysis, critical point theory. Office: U Calif Math Dept Irvine CA 92697-0001

SCHEER, JANET KATHY, mathematics educator; b. Bklyn., Apr. 22, 1947; d. Seymour and Hilda (Shoer) S. BA, Bklyn. Coll., 1968; MS, Syracuse (N.Y.) U., 1969; PhD, Ariz. State U., 1977. Cert. tchr., N.Y., Ariz.; cert. prin., Ariz. Math. tchr. Jamesville (N.Y.) DeWitt Middle Sch., 1969-72; math. tchr., middle sch. coordinator Am. Internat. Sch., Kfar Shmaryahu, Israel, 1972-74; from asst. prof. to assoc. prof. So. Ill. U., Carbondale, 1977—86; sr. nat. math. cons. Holt, Rinehart & Winston, 1986—89; nat. product devel. specialist Scott, Foresman and Co., Glenview, Ill., 1989-90, dir. field svcs. for math., 1991—; exec. dir. Create A Vision, Foster City, Calif. Sr. nat. math. cons. Holt, Rinehart & Winston, N.Y.C., 1986-89, Harcourt Brace-Jovanovich/Holt, 1989. Editor Ill. Math. Tchr. jour., 1980-83; author: Manipulatives in Mathematics Unlimited, 1987, Harcourt Math, 2002, 04, Holt Middle School Math, 2004; columnist Learning Mag., 1996-97; contbr. to textbooks and profl. jours. Named one of Outstanding Young Women Am., 1978, 81-85, Outstanding Tchr. Yr. So. Ill. U., 1978-79; recipient numerous grants. Mem. Nat. Council Tchrs. Math., Research Council for Diagnostic and Prescriptive Math. (charter mem., v.p. 1984-86), Ill. Council Tchrs. Math. (various offices), Phi Delta Kappa, Kappa Delta Pi. Avocations: swimming, golf, tennis. Office: Create A Vision 1175 Chess Dr Ste 206 Foster City CA 94404-1108

SCHEER, TERRI LYNN, special education educator; b. St. Charles, Mo., Oct. 1, 1961; d. Michael Vincent Sr. and Christine May (Stepp) Brush. Student, U. Mo., 1984. Mental retardation profl. Community Living for Handicap, St. Charles, 1984-85; tchr. adult spl. edn. St. Louis Assn. for Retarded Citizens, 1985-86; tchr. spl. edn. Fransic Howell Sch. Dist., St. Charles, 1986-89; tchr. vocat. spl. edn. Spl. Sch. Dist., St. Louis, 1989-96; spl. edn. dept. chairperson, tchr. Ft. Zumwalt Sch. Dist., 1996—; instr. Lindenwood Coll., 1998—. Mem. adv. bd. Lewis and Clark Tech. Sch., St. Charles, 1987-88; student coun. advisor West County Tech. Sch., St. Louis, 1989—, sr. class advisor, 1991—, mem. adv. bd. Vocat. Indsl. Clubs Am., 1991—. Explorer leader Boy Scouts Am., St. Louis, 1991-91. Mem. Mo. Vocat. Assn., Nat. Assn. Vocat. Edn. Spl. Needs Personnel.

SCHEFFEL, DONNA JEAN, elementary school educator; b. Balt., Sept. 20, 1953; d. G. Donald Scheffel and Mary LaVerne (Perry) Jones; 1 child, Amanda Lynne. BS, Salisbury (Md.) State Coll.; Cert., Baldwin-Wallace Coll., Berea, Ohio, 1983. Tchr. Wadsworth (Ohio) city schs., 1984-85, Parma (Ohio) city schs., 1984-85; elem. tchr. St. Leo the Great Sch., Cleve., 1985-91. Mem. team Early Prevention Sch. Failure; faculty rep. bd. dirs. Parent Tchr. Unit. Parma city schs., 1997—; 1st aux. svcs. computer sci. tchr. Bethel Christian Acad., Parma. Named one of Outstanding Young Women of Am., 1986. Mem.: ASCD, PEA, NEA, NAFE, Ohio Edn. Assn., N.E. Ohio Edn. Assn. Office: Bethel Christian Acad 12901 W Pleasant Valley Rd Parma OH 44130-5702

SCHEFFER, LUDO CAREL PETER, educational researcher, consultant; b. Bussum, The Netherlands, Sept. 3, 1960; s. Lukas Albert and Alida Johanna Theodora (Kassenaar) S.; m. Gwynne Rochelle Smith, oct. 1, 1994; 1 child, William Alexander. PhD, Free U., Amsterdam, The Netherlands, 1987, U. Pa., 1995. Cons., trainer Shell Netherlands, Rotterdam, 1987-88; cons. trainer Hollandse Beton Groep, The Hague, The Netherlands, 1988; rsch. asst. lit. rsch. ctr. U. Pa., Phila., 1988-90; rsch. asst. Nat. Ctr. on Adult Lit., Phila., 1990-91, lit. fellow, 1991-93, project dir., 1993—; owner S2 Dynamics. Vis. asst. prof. psychology Drexel U., Phila. Co-author: Students At Risk: Pitfalls and Promising Plans, 1993; (newsletter) NCAL Connections, 1994. Bd. dirs. CHAMP, Phila., 1991. Recipient Cmty. Leadership award Internat. Ho. of Phila., 1991; named Phi Beta Delta scholar, 1992. Mem. APA (assoc.), Am. Ednl. Rsch. Assn., Jean Piaget Soc., Amnesty Internat., Habitat for Humanity, So. Poverty Law Ctr., Phila. Concerned About Housing. Avocations: reading, arts, sports. Home: 507 S 45th St Philadelphia PA 19104-3913

SCHEFFING, DIANNE ELIZABETH, special education educator; b. St. Louis, Mar. 17, 1963; d. Eugene Shibley Scheffing Jr. and Sarah Ann (Lukens) Scheffing. BS, Mo. Bapt. Univ., 1988; MA, Fontbonne Univ., St. Louis, 1999; postgrad., Webster U., St. Louis, 2002. Cert. elem. edn. grades 1-8 Mo., mild/moderate cross-category grades K-12 Mo., severely developmentally delayed 2002. Kindergarden tchr. asst. Andrews Acad., St. Louis, 1989—91; sci. tchr. edn. dept. St. Louis Sci. Ctr., 1994—96; tchr. asst. multi-handicapped Kehrs Mill Elem./Rockwood Sch. Dist., St. Louis, 1996—2000; tchr. spl. edn. Gateway/Hubert Wheeler State Sch. for Severely Handicapped, St. Louis, 2000—. Mem., sec. St. Louis Young Reps. Club, 1988—94; majority mem. Bethel #44 Internat. Order of Job's Daughters, Ballwin, 1978—84. Named Woman of Yr., St. Louis Young Reps. Club, 1992, 1994. Mem.: Am. Cancer Soc. Methodist. Avocations: Olympic supporter, bowling, traveling. Office: Gateway/Hubert Wheeler State Sch 100 S Garrison Saint Louis MO 63103

SCHEFFLER, ISRAEL, philosopher, educator; b. N.Y.C., Nov. 25, 1923; s. Leon and Ethel (Grünberg) S.; m. Rosalind Zuckerbrod, June 26, 1949; children: Samuel, Laurie. BA, Bklyn. Coll., 1945, MA, 1948; M.H.L., Jewish Theol. Sem., 1949; PhD (Ford fellow 1951), U. Pa., 1952; A.M. (hon.), Harvard U., 1959; D.H.L. (hon.), Jewish Theol. Sem., 1993. Mem. faculty Harvard U., 1952-92, prof. edn., 1961-62, prof. edn. and philosophy, 1962-64, Victor S. Thomas prof. edn. and philosophy, 1964-92, professor emeritus, 1992—, hon. research fellow in cognitive studies, 1965-66, co-dir. Research Ctr. for Philosophy of Edn., 1983-98, dir. Rsch. Ctr. Philosophy of Edn., 1998—2003; scholar-in-residence The Mandel Ctr., Brandeis U., 2003—. Fellow Center for Advanced Study in Behavioral Scis., 1972-73 Author: The Language of Education, 1960, The Anatomy of Inquiry, 1963, Conditions of Knowledge, 1965, Science and Subjectivity, 1967, Reason and Teaching, 1973, Four Pragmatists, 1974, Beyond the Letter, 1979, Of Human Potential, 1985, Inquiries, 1986, In Praise of the Cognitive Emotions, 1991, Teachers of My Youth, 1995, Symbolic Worlds, 1997; co-author: Work, Education and Leadership, 1995; editor: Philosophy and Education, 1958, 66; co-editor: Logic and Art, 1972, Visions of Jewish Education, 2003; contbr. articles to profl. jours. Recipient Alumni award of merit Bklyn. Coll., 1967, Disting. Svc. medal Tchrs. Coll., Columbia, 1980, Benjamin Shevach award Boston Hebrew Coll., 1995; Guggenheim fellow, 1958-59, 72-73; NSF grantee, 1962, 65. Mem. Am. Acad. Arts and Scis., Am. Philos. Assn., Philosophy Edn. Soc., Nat. Acad. Edn. (charter), Philosophy of Sci. Assn. (prs. 1973-75), Charles S. Peirce Soc. (pres. 1998). Address: 3 Woodside Rd Newton MA 02460

SCHEFFLER, LEWIS FRANCIS, pastor, educator, research scientist; b. Springfield, Ohio, Oct. 13, 1928; s. Lewis Francis and Emily Louise (Kloker) S.; m. Willa Pauline Cole, Aug. 9, 1949 (div. 1978); children: Lewis F. Fischer, Richard Thomas, Gary Arlen, Tonni Kay; m. Mary Lee Smith, Apr. 18, 1978; stepchildren: Kimberly McCollum, Jeffrey McIlroy, Kerry Buell. BA in Liberal Arts, Cin. Bible Seminary, 1950; AA in Bus., Jefferson Coll., 1989; MAT, Webster U., 1989. Quality assurance Tectum Corp., Newark, 1954-57; rsch. group leader Owens-Corning Fiberglas, Granville, Ohio, 1957-64; tech. asst. to v.p. R&D and Engring., 1960-63; pres. Ohio Glass Fibers Cons., 1962-68; rsch. adminstr. Modiglas Fibers Corp., Bremen, Ohio, 1965-68; dir. R & D Flex-O-Lite Corp., St. Louis, 1968-71; pastor Christian Ch., St. Louis, 1972-75; police commns. Brentwood (Mo.) Police Dept., 1975-87; pastor Christian Ch., Potosi, Mo., 1988-89, Slater (Mo.) Christian Ch., 1989-93, Clark (Mo.) Christian Ch., 1996-99; asst. prof. English lang. and lit. Mo. Valley Coll., Marshall, 1989-94; adj. prof. theology Mo. Sch. Religion, 1993-97; adj. prof. English Moberly Area C.C., 1996-98; min. Ctrl. Union Cmty. Ch., Vaudalia, Mo., 1998—. Organizing co-chmn. aerospace composite materials com. ASTM, 1961; mem. exec. bd. Northwest Area Christian Ch., 1989-93; mem. Coun. of Areas of Mid-Am. Region Christian Ch., 1990-93; cons. and lectr. in field. Contbr. articles to profl. jours. Patentee in field. Money raiser United Appeal, chaplaincy Blessing Hosp., Quincy, Ill., 1974; vol. Ill. Divsn. Children and Family Svcs., 1972-75; sec. exec. com. N.W. Area Christian Ch. (Disciples of Christ), 1992-94. Mem. Medieval Acad. Am., Mo. Philol. Assn. Avocation: philosophy and pomology. Home: 701 Walnut St Ladonia MO 63352-1137

SCHEIB, GERALD PAUL, fine art educator, jeweler, metalsmith; b. L.A., Dec. 26, 1937; s. Harry William and Olive Bauer (Cartwright) S.; m. Elizabeth Ann Galligan, Dec. 27, 1965 (div. 1978); children: Gregory Paul, Geoffrey Paul; m. Dedra Lynn True, Oct. 1, 1983; 1 child, Adam True. AA, East L.A. Jr. Coll., 1959; BA, Calif. State U., L.A., 1962, MFA, 1968. Cert. life teaching credential in fine arts, secondary and coll. tchr., Calif. Secondary tchr. art L.A. Unified Sch. Dist., 1963-77; prof. fine art L.A. Community Coll. Dist., 1977-2001; ret., 2001; pres. faculty senate L.A. Mission Coll., San Fernando, Calif., 1983-84. Bargaining unit rep., AFT Coll. Guild Local 1521; elected Arts and Letters chair L.A. Mission Coll., 1993; owner, mgr. Artificers Bench, Sylmar, Calif., 1976—; cons. to Edward H. Bohlin Co. Custom Silver Works, 1998. Mem. policy bd. The Calif. Arts Project, 1995-97; chair L.A. County Art Edn. Coun., 1997-98; plank owner U.S. Naval Meml., Washington; trustee L.A. Artcore, 2001. With USNR, 1955-97, ret. Recipient of tribute City of L.A., 1983, Citizen of Month award, Los Angeles County, 1983, Cold War Cert. of Recognition,

Sec. of Def., 2000. Mem. Calif. Art Edn. Assn. (membership chmn. 1985-87, pres.-elect 1989-91, pres. 1991-93, Calif.'s Outstanding Art Educator in Higher Edn. 1994-95), San Fernando Active 20-30 Club (pres. 1981-82), Nat. Assn. Scholars, Sons of Union Vets of Civil War, U.S. Naval Cryptologic Vets. Assn., L.A. Artcore (bd. dirs. 2001--). Republican. Avocations: collecting antiques, Civil War reenacting, creating custom jewelry. Office: 13356 Eldridge Ave Sylmar CA 91342-3200

SCHEIBEL, ARNOLD BERNARD, psychiatrist, educator, research director; b. N.Y.C., Jan. 18, 1923; s. William and Ethel (Greenberg) S.; m. Madge Mila Ragland, Mar. 3, 1950 (dec. Jan. 1977); m. Marian Diamond, Sept. 1982. BA, Columbia U., 1944, MD, 1946; MS, U. Ill., 1952. Intern Mt. Sinai Hosp., N.Y.C., 1946-47; resident in psychiatry Barnes and McMillan Hosp., St. Louis, 1947-48, Ill. Neuropsychiat. Inst., Chgo., 1950-52; asst. prof. psychiatry and anatomy U. Tenn. Med. Sch., 1952-53, assoc. prof., 1953-55, UCLA Med. Ctr., 1955-67, prof., 1967—, mem. Brain Rsch. Inst., 1960—, acting dir. Brain Rsch. Inst., 1987-90, dir., 1990-95. Cons. in field. Contbr. numerous articles to tech. jours, chpts. to books.; mem. editl. bd. Brain Rsch., 1967-77, Developmental Psychobiology, 1968—, Internat. Jour. Neurosci., 1969—, Jour. Biol. Psychiatry, 1968—, Jour. Theoretical Biology, 1980—; assoc. editor News Report, 1989—. Mem. Pres.'s Commn. on Aging, Nat. Inst. Aging, 1980—. Served with AUS, 1943-46; from lt. to capt. M.C. AUS, 1948-50. Guggenheim fellow (with wife), 1953-54, 59; recipient Disting. Svc. award Calif. Soc. Biomed. Rsch., 1998. Fellow Am. Acad. Arts and Scis., Norwegian Acad. Scis., Am. Psychiat. Assn. (life, Harriet and Charles Luckman Disting. Tchg. award 1997) AAAS; mem. Am. Neurol. Assn., Soc. Neurosci., Pyschiat. Rsch. Assn., Soc. Biol. Psychiatry, So. Calif. Psychiat. Assn. Home: 16231 Morrison St Encino CA 91436-1331 Office: UCLA Dept Neurobiology Los Angeles CA 90024 E-mail: scheibel@ucla.edu.

SCHEIBER, HARRY N. law educator; b. 1935; BA, Columbia U., 1955; MA, Cornell U., 1957, PhD, 1961; MA (hon.), Dartmouth Coll., 1965; D.Jur.Hon., Uppsala U., Sweden, 1998. Instr. to assoc. prof. history Dartmouth Coll., 1960-68, prof., 1968-71; prof. Am. history U. Calif., San Diego, 1971-80; prof. law Boalt Hall, U. Calif., Berkeley, 1980—. Chmn. jurisprudence and social policy program, 1982-84, 90-93, assoc. dean, 1990-93, 96-99; The Stefan Riesenfeld prof., 1991—; vice chair Univ. Academic Senate, 1993-94, chair 1994-95; dir. Earl Warren Legal Inst., 2002-; Fulbright disting. sr. lectr., Australia, 1983, marine affairs coord. Calif. Sea Grant Coll. Program, 1989-2000; vis. rsch. prof. Law Inst. U. Uppsala, Sweden, 1995, hon. prof. DiTella U., Buenos Aires, 1999; cons. Calif. Jud. Coun., 1992-93; acting dir. Ctr. for Study of Law and Soc., 1999-2001; co-dir. Law of the Sea Inst., 2002—; Cassel lectr., Stockholm U., 2003—. Author: The Wilson Administration and Civil Liberties, 1960, Ohio Canal Era, 1970; co-author: American Law and the Constitutional Order, 1988, The State and Freedom of Contract, 1998; author: Inter-Allied Conflicts and Ocean Law (1945-1953), 2001; co-author: American Law and the Constitutional Order, 1978, Law of the Sea: The Common Heritage and Emerging Challenges, 2000, numerous others; editor: Yearbook of the California Supreme Court Historical Society, 1994—; contbr. articles to law revs. and social sci. jours., 1994. Chmn. Littleton Griswold Prize Legal History, 1985-88; pres. N.H. Civil Liberties Union, 1969-70; chmn. Project '87 Task Force on Pub. Programs, Washington, 1982-85; dir. Berkeley Seminar on Federalism, 1986-95; cons. judiciary study U.S. Adv. Commn. Intergovernmental Rels., 1985-88; dir. NEH Inst. on Constitutionalism, U. Calif., Berkeley, 1986-87, 88-91. Recipient Sea Grant Colls. award, 1981-83, 84-85, 86-2002; fellow Ctr. Advanced Study in Behavioral Scis., Stanford Calif., 1967, 71; Guggenheim fellow, 1971, 88; Rockefeller Found. humanities fellow, 1979, NEH fellow, 1985-86; NSF grantee 1979, 80, 88-89. Fellow AAAS, Am. Acad. Arts and Scis., U. Calif. Humanities Rsch. Inst., Am. Soc. for Legal History (hon., pres. 2003—), Japan Soc. for Promotion of Sci. (invitational fellow); mem. Am. Hist. Assn., Orgn. Am. Historians, Agrl. History Soc. (pres. 1978), Econ. History Assn. (trustee 1978-80), Law and Soc. Assn. (trustee 1979-81, 96-99), Nat. Assessment History and Citizenship Edn. (chmn. nat. acad. bd. 1986-87), Marine Affairs and Policy Assn. (bd. dirs. 1991-96), Ocean Governance Study Group (steering com. 1991—), Internat. Coun. Environ. Law, Calif. Supreme Ct. Hist. Soc. (bd. dirs. 1993—, v.p. 1997-98). Office: U Calif Berkeley Law Sch Boalt Hall Berkeley CA 94720-2150 E-mail: scheiber@law.berkeley.edu.

SCHEIE, PAUL OLAF, physics educator; b. Marietta, Minn., June 24, 1933; s. Olaf Johan and Selma Pricilla (Varhus) S.; m. Mary Anna Harrison, may 18, 1963; children: Eric, Maren. BA, St. Olaf Coll., Northfield, Minn., 1955; MS, U. N.Mex., 1957; PhD, Pa. State U., 1965. Asst. prof. physics Oklahoma City U., 1958-63; asst. prof. biophysics Pa. State U., State Coll., 1965-73; prof. physics Tex. Luth Univ., Seguin, 1973-2001, prof. emeritus, 2001—. Interim acad. dean, 1976. Contbr.a rticles to profl. publs. Recipient Faculty Alumni award, Tex. Luth., Coll., 1965. Mem. Biophys. Soc., AAAS, Am. Assn. Physics Tchrs., Am. Phys. Soc., Royal Micros. Soc., Sigma Xi. Lutheran. Lodge: Lions. Home: 207 Leonard Seguin TX 78155 Office: Tex Luth Univ Dept Physics 1000 W Court St Seguin TX 78155-5978 E-mail: pscheie@tlu.edu.

SCHEITHE, JEANNE MARIE, language educator; b. Waterburg, Conn., Apr. 9, 1952; d. Robert Ernest and Jane (Smith) Crosby; m. Frederick Raymond Scheithe, Oct. 7, 1983. BS in elem. edn. cum laude, Southern Conn. State Coll., 1974, MS in reading cum laude, 1981. Sub. tchr. Naugatuck (Conn.) Bd. Edn., 1976-77, tchr., 1977-79, mid. sch. tchr., 1979—2003, Hup Brook Intermediate Sch., 2003—. Advisor, chaperone, acad., cultural and social activities Hillside Mid. Sch., 1977-2003, Conn. Thinking Cap Quiz Bowl advisor, 1995-2001, vol. tutor to athletes in need, 1985-2003, organizer student fair, 1990-95, report card revision com., 1988-89, 94-95; creator math. remediation program, 1987-94. Contbg. writer Math. Curriculum, 1986-87. Treas., bldg. rep. Naugatuck Tchrs. League, 1981-84; treas. CARE, 1988, 89. Mem. Conn. Edn. Assn., NEA, Nat. Honor Soc. Avocations: aerobics, swimming, attending student events, golf. Home: 243 Millville Ave Naugatuck CT 06770-3848 Office: Hup Brook Intermediate School 75 Crown St Naugatuck CT 06770-4018

SCHELL, JACQUELYN ANN, speech pathology/audiology services professional; b. Binghamton, N.Y., Apr. 15, 1947; d. Robert Emory and Eleanor Bernadine (Shea) Finch; m. Michael William Schell, Aug. 30, 1969; children: Amy, Julie, Amanda, Carey, Kate. BS, Ithaca (N.Y.) Coll., 1969; MS magna cum laude, SUNY, Potsdam, 1983. Speech therapist pub. schs., NY, 1969—, Sci-Tech Ctr. of No. N.Y., Watertown, 1989—99. Mem. sch. bd. Watertown City Sch. Dist., 1983-98; mem. coll. coun. Oswego (N.Y.) Coll., 1990-99; trustee Herrings Coll., Watertown, 1993—, WPBS, 2002, Lyme Cmty. Found., 2002; pres. bd. North County Children's Clinic, 1999; mem. Dem. Rural Conf., 2000—, Dem. State Com., 2000—. Democrat. Roman Catholic. Home: PO Box 184 Chaumont NY 13622

SCHELL, MARY ELIZABETH, secondary education educator; b. Ft. Worth, Tex., May 13, 1922; d. Walter John and Marie Magdalene (Connelly) Nobles; m. James Hays Schell, Sept. 8, 1943; children: James Schell Jr., Elizabeth Jean. BS, North Tex. State U., 1941, MS, 1943. Cert. counselor coord., dir., Tex.; cert. tchr., Tex., Fla., Okla. Tchr. h.s., Peaster, Tex., 1941-42, Andrews, Tex., 1942-43, Lawton, Okla., 1943-44; supr. North Tex. State U., Denton, 1945-47; tchr., writer, coord., dir. Houston Ind. Sch. Dist., 1960-86; owner Schell Puppet Prodns., Houston, 1986—. Writer U.S. Army, Ft. Monmouth, N.J., 1945-46. Author: (radio programs) Texas School of the Air, 1946, (book series) The Adventures of Mrs. Sea Shell. Vol. leader Cub Scouts, Houston, 1955-57, Brownies, Houston, 1958-59; vol. ch. tchr., Houston, 1970-73; dir. Citizens Patrol, Houston, 1988-94; vol. dir. summer workshops, Houston, 1994-95. Nominee Nat. Contest for Outstanding Tchr., 1947; named Area II Outstanding Tchr., Iota Lambda Sigma, 1979-80. Mem. Delta Kappa Gamma (v.p. 1973—). Avocations: writing, directing plays, music. Home and Office: Schell Puppet Prodns 4402 Lorinda Dr Houston TX 77018-1113

SCHELLIN, PATRICIA MARIE BIDDLE, secondary school educator; b. Columbus, Wis., Apr. 1, 1955; d. Charles Westly Sr. and Dorothy (Madigan) Biddle; m. Edwin O. Schellin, June 21, 1980; children: Jennifer, Jeremy, Jonathan. BS, U. Wis., LaCrosse, 1978. Cert. tchr., Wis. Tchr., coach Freedom (Wis.) Schs., 1978-80, Fall River (Wis.) Schs., 1983-84; tchr. St. Jerome's Sch., Columbus, 1984-86, 90—, Dickason Mid. Sch., Columbus, 1987; substitute tchr. Columbus Schs., 1980—. Swimming instr. Columbus Recreation Dept., 1979—; coach girls basketball, Columbus High Sch., 1983—, varsity girls soccer, 1993—; instr. CPR ARC, Columbus, 1986—, water safety chair, 1984—. Coach soccer, baseball Columbus Recreation Dept., 1988—; recreation dir. City of Columbus, 1993—. Mem. AAHPERD. Lutheran. Avocations: travel, sports, family. Home: 549 Hibbard St Columbus WI 53925-1241 Office: Saint Jeromes Sch 156 W James St Columbus WI 53925-1569

SCHEMAN, BLANCHE, reading specialist; b. N.Y.C., Oct. 17, 1917; d. Adolf and Rose (Bistrong) Kirsch; m. Paul Scheman, June 29, 1941 (dec. Dec. 1987); children: Naomi, Carol, Judith. BA, Bklyn. Coll., 1939; MA, Columbia U., 1941. Guidance counselor U.S. Employment Svc., N.Y.C., 1942-46; reading therapist Reading and Learning Clinic Reading and Learning Ctr. Adelphi U., Garden City, N.Y., 1957-66; reading specialist Cold Spring Harbor (N.Y.) Sch. Dist., 1958-85; vol. reading specialist English as Second Lang. and Lit. Vol., Huntington, N.Y., 1988-92. Lectr. in field. Vol. Huntington Cinema Arts Ctr. Named Woman of Yr. Anti-Defamation League, B'nai B'rith, Freeport, L.I., N.Y., 1953. Mem. AAUW (edn. chair, exec. com. 1988-91), Cold Spring Harbor Tchr. Assn. (chair retiree chpt. exec. com. 1987—). Democrat. Jewish. Avocations: reading, theatre, concerts, knitting, needlepoint, travel. Home: Waterside Retirement Estates 4540 Bee Ridge Rd Apt 229 Sarasota FL 34233-2552

SCHEMMEL, RACHEL ANNE, food science and human nutrition educator, researcher; b. Farley, Iowa, Nov. 23, 1929; d. Frederic August and Emma Margaret (Melchert) Schemmel. BA, Clarke Coll., 1951; MS, U. Iowa, 1952; PhD, Mich. State U., 1967. Dietitian Children's Hosp. Soc., L.A., 1952-54; instr. Mich. State U., East Lansing, 1955-63, from asst. prof. to prof. food sci., human nutrition, 1967—. Author: Nutrition Physiology and Obesity, 1980; contbr. articles to profl. jours. Recipient Disting. Alumni award Mt. Mercy Coll., 1971, Borden award, 1986, Outstanding Alumni award U. Iowa, 1996, Mich. State U., 2002, Outstanding Achievement award Clarke Coll., 1997. Fellow: Am. Soc. Nutrition Scis.; mem.: Soc. for Nutrition Edn., Brit. Nutrition Soc., Am. Diet Assn. (pres. Mich. 1976—77, pres. Lansing 1960, Outstanding Dietetic Educator award 1988), Inst. Food Technologists, Am. Assn. Family and Consumer Scis. (chair nutrition health and food mgmt. divsn. 1995—97, Outstanding Leader award 1998), Phi Kappa Phi (pres. 1994—95), Sigma Xi (pres. Mich. State U. chpt. 1983—84, Sr. Rsch award 1986). Roman Catholic. Home: 1341 Red Leaf Ln East Lansing MI 48823-1339 Office: Mich State U Dept Food Sci Nutrit East Lansing MI 48824 E-mail: schemmel@msu.edu.

SCHENK, SUSAN KIRKPATRICK, nurse educator, consultant, business owner; b. New Richmond, Ind., Nov. 29, 1938; d. William Marcius and Frances (Kirkpatrick) Gaither; m. Richard Dee Brown, Aug. 13, 1960 (div. Feb. 1972); children: Christopher Lee, David Michael, Lisa Catherine; m. John Francis Schenk, July 24, 1975 (widowed Apr. 1995). BSN, Ind. U., 1962; postgrad., U. Del., 1973-75. RN, PHN, BCLS; cert. community coll. tchr., Calif.; cert. vocat. edn. tchr., Calif. Staff nurse, then asst. dir. nursing Bloomington (Ind.) Hosp., 1962-66; charge nurse Newark (Del.) Manor, 1967-69; charge nurse GU Union Hosp., Terre Haute, Ind., 1971-72; clin. instr. nursing Ind. State U., Terre Haute, 1972-73; clin. instr. psychiatric nursing U. Del., Newark, 1974-75; psychiatric nursing care coord. VA Med. Ctr., Perry Point, Md., 1975-78; from nurse educator to cmty. rels. coord. Grossmont Hosp., La Mesa, Calif., 1978—91; dir. psychiat. svcs. Scripps Hosp. East County, El Cajon, Calif., 1991-97; nursing instr., adult edn. Grossmont Union H.S. Dist., La Mesa, 1996—. Tech. advisor San Diego County Bd. Supervisors, 1987; tech. cons. Remedy Home and Health Care, San Diego, 1988; expert panelist Srs. Speak Out, KPBS-TV, San Diego, 1988; guest lectr. San Diego State U., 1987. Editor: Teaching Basic Caregiver Skills, 1988; author, performer tng. videotape Basic Caregiver Skills, 1988. Mem. patient svcs. com. Nat. Multiple Sclerosis Soc., San Diego, 1986-89; bd. dirs. Assn. for Quality and Participation, 1989. Adminstrn. on Aging/DHHS grantee, 1988. Mem. Ind. U. Alumni Assn. (life), Calif. Coun. Adult Edn., Mensa, Sigma Theta Tau. Avocations: piano, gardening, reading. Home and Office: 9435D Carlton Oaks Dr Santee CA 92071-2582 E-mail: susansks@aol.com.

SCHENKEL, SUSAN, psychologist, educator, author; came to U.S., 1949; BA, U. Wis., 1967; MA in Clin. Psychology, SUNY, Buffalo, 1970, PhD in Clin. Psychology, 1973. Lic. psychologist, Mass. Psychologist Fitchburg (Mass.) State Coll., 1972-75, instr. in psychology, 1973-74; staff psychologist div. of alcoholism Boston City Hosp., 1975-76; chief psychologist Cambridge (Mass.) Ct. Clinic, 1976-80; instr. in psychology dept. psychiatry Med. Sch. Harvard U., 1976-80; pvt. practice psychology Cambridge, 1976—; instr. in psychology U. Mass., Boston, 1978. Speaker in field. Author: Giving Away Success, 1984, German edit., 1986, Brazilian edit., 1988, rev. edit. 1991, Chinese edit., 1991; contbr. articles to profl. jours. USPHS fellow, 1967-70; N.Y. State Regents scholar, 1968-70; SUNY Rsch. Found. grantee, 1971-72. Mem. Am. Psychol. Assn., Mass. Psychol. Assn., Am. Soc. Tng. and Devel., Assn. for Advancement of Behavior Therapy.

SCHENKER, ALEXANDER MARIAN, Slavic linguistics educator; b. Cracow, Poland, Dec. 20, 1924; came to U.S., 1946, naturalized, 1952; s. Oskar and Gizela (Szaminski) S.; m. Krystyna Czajka, Oct. 15, 1970; children: Alfred R., Michael J., Catherine I. Student, Stalinabad Pedagogical Inst., 1943-46, U. Paris, 1947-48; MA, Yale U., 1950, PhD, 1953. Asst. in instrn. Yale U., New Haven, 1950-52, instr., 1952-56, asst. prof., 1956-63, asso. prof., 1963-67, prof. Slavic linguistics, 1967—. Vis. prof. Slavic linguistics U. Calif., Berkeley, 1969-70 Author: Polish Declension, 1964, Beginning Polish, 2 vols., rev. edit., 1973, The Dawn of Slavic: Introduction to Slavic Philology, 1996; editor: Fifteen Modern Polish Short Stories, 1970, American Contributions to the 10th Internat., Congress of Slavists Linguistics, 1988; co-editor: For Wiktor Weintraub, 1975, The Slavic Literary Languages, 1980, Studies in Slavic Linguistics and Poetics, 1982. Recipient Scaglione prize for Slavic Studies, MLA. Mem. Conn. Acad. Arts and Scis., Polish Inst. Arts/Scis., Am. Assn. Tchrs. Slavic and Eastern European Langs., Am. Assn. Advancement Slavic Studies, Polish Acad. Arts and Scis. Home: 145 Deepwood Dr Hamden CT 06517-3451 Office: Yale U Dept Slavic Langs and Lits PO Box 208236 New Haven CT 06520-8236 E-mail: alexander.schenker@yale.edu.

SCHENKER, MARC BENET, preventive medicine educator; b. L.A., Aug. 25, 1947; s. Steve and Dosella Schenker; m. Heath Massey; children: Yael, Phoebe, Hilary. BA, U. Calif., Berkeley, 1969; MD, U. Calif., San Francisco, 1973; MPH, Harvard U., Boston, 1980. Instr. medicine Harvard U., Boston, 1980-82; asst. prof. medicine U. Calif., Davis, 1982-86, assoc. prof., 1986-92, prof., 1992—, chmn. dept. epidemiology and preventive medicine, 1995—. Fellow ACP; mem. Am. Thoracic Soc., Am. Pub. Health Assn., Soc. Epidemiologic Rsch., Am. Coll. Epidemiology, Soc. Occupl. Environ. Health, Internat. Commn. Occupl. Health, Assn. Tchrs. Preventive Medicine, Phi Beta Kappa, Alpha Omega Alpha. Office: Dept Epidemiology and Preventive Medicine TB 168 One Shields Ave Davis CA 95616-8638

SCHENTAG, JEROME JOHN, pharmacy educator; b. St. Clair, Mich., Jan. 25, 1950; s. John and Rose Schentag; m. Rita R. Sloan, June 26, 1976; 1 child, Annie. BS in Pharmacy, U. Nebr., 1973; D. Pharmacy, Phila. Coll. Pharmacy, 1975. Postdoctoral fellow SUNY, Buffalo, 1975-76, asst. prof. of pharmacy, 1976-81, assoc. prof., 1981-86, prof., 1986-2000; CEO CPL assoc., LLC, 2001—. Dir. Clin. Pharmacokinetics Lab., Millard Fillmore Hosp., Buffalo. Editor: Applied Pharmacokinetics, 1981, 4th edit. edit., 2000; contbr. articles to profl. jours. Am. Coll. Clin. Pharmacy fellow, 1985; recipient Disting. Young Alumni award Phila. Coll. of Pharmacy, 1989. Fellow Am. Assn. Pharm. Scientists; mem. Am. Soc. Microbiology. Office: U Buffalo Sch Pharms 543 Hochstetter Hall Buffalo NY 14260 E-mail: Schentag@Buffalo.edu.

SCHEPPERLEY, KAREN L. special education educator; b. Royal Oak, Mich., June 11, 1961; d. James L. Moore and Audrey M. Cairns; children: Jenna L. Staten, Jason A. Staten; m. William E. Schepperley, Aug. 17, 1996. A in Elem. Edn., Mid MIch. C.C., 1991; BS in Spl. Edn., Ctrl. Mich. U., 1994, MA in Spl. Edn., 2002. Cert. elem., emotionally impaired, learning disabled tchr. Mich. Receptionist Renosol Corp., Farwell, Mich., 1986—88; student asst. Mid-Mich. C.C., Harrison, 1989—91; spl. edn. tchr. Chippewa Hills Pub. Sch., Weidman and Barryton, Mich., 1995—96, Farwell (Mich.) Area Schs., 1996—. Counselor Albright UMC, Reed City, Mich.; Headstart dir. Ctr. Mich. CAA, Evart. Sunday sch. tchr., Vacation Bible Sch. tchr., Clare, Mich. Mem.: Coun. for Exceptional Children, Beta Sigma Phi. Methodist. Avocations: golf, skiing, walking, cooking, reading. Office: Farwell Mid Sch 470 Ohio St Farwell MI 48622

SCHER, STEVEN PAUL, literature educator, educator; b. Budapest, Hungary, Mar. 2, 1936; came to U.S., 1957, naturalized, 1963; Diploma in piano, Bela Bartok Conservatory of Music, Budapest, 1955; BA cum laude, Yale U., 1960, MA, 1963, PhD, 1966. Instr. German, Columbia U., N.Y.C., 1965-67; asst. prof. German, Yale U., New Haven, 1967-70, assoc. prof., 1970-74; prof. German and comparative lit. Dartmouth Coll., Hanover, N.H., 1974—, chmn. dept., 1974-80, 93-96, acting chmn. dept., 1982-83, Ted and Helen Geisel 3d Century prof. humanities, 1984-89, Daniel Webster prof. German and comparative lit., 2000—. Vis. prof. U. Paderborn, Fed. Republic Germany, summer 1980, Karl-Franzens-U. Graz, Austria, summer 1984; grant reviewer Guggenheim Found., NEH, Am. Council Learned Socs., others; cons. univ. presses and scholarly jours.; lectr. throughout world Author: Verbal Music in German Literature, 1968; editor: (with Charles McClelland) Postwar German Culture: An Anthology, 1974, 2d edit., 1980, Interpretationen: Zu E.T.A. Hoffmann, 1981, (with Ulrich Weisstein) Literature and the Other Arts. Proc. of IXth Congress of Internat. Comparative Lit. Assn., Innsbruck, vol. 3, 1981, Literatur und Musik. Ein Handbuch zur Theorie und Praxis eines komparatistischen Grenzgebietes, 1984, Music and Text: Critical Inquiries, 1992 (with Walter Bernhart and Werner Wolf) Word and Music Studies: Defining the Field, 1999; contbr. articles and essays to scholarly jours. Morse fellow, 1969-70; Humboldt fellow, 1972-73; Yale Coll. scholar, 1957-60, grad. fellow, 1960-62; DAAD grantee U. Munich, 1964-65 Mem. MLA (chmn. bibliography com. of div. lit. 1972-86), Am. Comparative Lit. Assn., Internat. Comparative Lit. Assn., Internat. P.E.N. Club Home: 6084 Dartmouth Hall Hanover NH 03755-3511 Office: Dartmouth College Dept German Studies 6084 Dartmouth Hall Hanover NH 03755-3511 E-mail: steven.p.scher@dartmouth.edu.

SCHERER, RONALD CALLAWAY, voice scientist, educator; b. Akron, Ohio, Sept. 11, 1945; s. Belden Davis and Lois Ramona (Callaway) S.; children: Christopher, Maria. BS, Kent State U., 1968; MA, Ind. U., 1972; PhD, U. Iowa, 1981. Research asst. U. Iowa, Iowa City, 1979-81, asst. research scientist, 1981-83, adj. asst. prof., 1983-88, adj. assoc. prof., 1988—; adj. asst. prof. U. Denver, 1984-86; asst. adj. prof. U. Colo., Boulder, 1984-93, adj. assoc. prof., 1993-96; research scientist The Denver Ctr. for the Performing Arts, 1983-88, sr. scientist, 1988-96; lectr. voice and speech sci. Nat. Theatre Conservatory, Denver, 1990-94; asst. clin. prof. Sch. Medicine U. Colo., Denver, 1988-96; assoc. prof. Bowling Green State U., Ohio, 1996—2001, prof., 2001—. Adj. assoc. prof. U. Okla., 1992-96; affiliate clin. prof. U. No. Colo., 1993-96; Oberlin Coll. affiliate scholar, 1996—; mem. exec. and legis. bd. Nat. Ctr. for Voice and Speech, 1990-96; G. Paul Moore lectr., The Voice Found., 2002. Author: (with Dr. I. Titze) Vocal Fold Physiology: Biomechanics, Acoustics and Phonatory Control, 1983; contbr. articles to profl. jours. Nat. Inst. Dental Research fellow, 1972-76. Fellow: Internat. Soc. Phonetic Scis. (auditor 1988—91); mem.: Am. Assn. Phonetic Scis. (nominating com. 1985—87, counselor 2000—03, councelor 2000—03), Internat. Assn. Logopedics and Phoniatrics, Acoustical Soc. Am., Am. Speech-Lang.-Hearing Assn., Internat. Arts Medicine Assn., Collegium Medicorum Theatri, Sigma Xi, Pi Mu Epsilon (G. Paul Moore lectr.). Office: Bowling Green State U Dept Comm Disorders Bowling Green OH 43403-0001

SCHERER, SUZANNE MARIE, artist, educator; b. Buffalo, Sept. 12, 1964; d. Robert Henry Scherer and Judith Louise Le Bar; m. Pavel Victorovich Ouporov, Oct. 25, 1991. AA, Broward C.C., 1984; BFA magna cum laude, Fla. State U., 1986; MFA summa cum laude, Bklyn. Coll., 1989; postgrad., Surikov State Art Acad., Moscow, 1989-91. Educator Bklyn. Mus., 1987-89, Newark Mus., 2000-01; profl. artist N.Y.C., 1989—. Guest lectr. Bklyn. Coll., 1992, Pa. Sch. Art and Design, Lancaster, 1996; artist-in-residence Lancaster Mus. and Pa. Sch. Art and Design, 1996; lectr. Lancaster Mus. Artist: The Trouble with Testosterone and Other Essays on the Biology of the Human Predicament, by Robert M. Sapolsky, 1997, Bataille's Eye, 1997, The Basics of Buying Art, 1996, Monumental Propaganda, 1994, Genesis: A Living Conversation, 1996; artist (jour.) The Scis. 1995-97, (TV) Genesis: A Living Conversation, 1996, (radio) Radio Free Europe: Interview with Raya Vail, 1995, WBAI-FM: Interview with Charles Finch, 1994; solo exhbns. include Lancaster (Pa.) Mus. Art, 1996, H. Ferzt Gallery, N.Y.C., 1994, Ctrl. House of Artist-New Tretyakov Gallery, Moscow, 1991, Spaso House Gallery, Residence of Am. Amb., Moscow, 1991; group exhbns. include Bass Mus. Art, Miami Beach, Fla., 1996, Schmidt Bingham Gallery, N.Y.C., 1996, Kemper Mus. Contemporary Art, Kansas City, Mo., 1995, Smithsonian Instn., 1995, Dalaenas Mus., Fawn, Sweden, 1995, Brit. Consulate, 1995, DeSaisset Mus., Santa Clara, Calif., 1994, N.Y. Acad. Scis., N.Y.C., 1996; pub. collections include N.Y. Pub. Libr., N.Y.C., Met. Mus. Art, N.Y.C., Harvard U. Fogg Art Mus., State Russian Mus., St. Petersburg, Binghamton (N.Y.) Art Mus., Ekaterinburg (Russia) Mus. Fine Art, Bob Blackburn's Printmaking Workshop Collection, N.Y.C., Lancaster Mus. Art, Min. Culture, Moscow, Russian Acad. Art, Moscow. Mem. Internat. Women's Orgn., Moscow, 1989-91. Grantee Internat. Rsch. and Exchs. Bd., 1989; Visual Arts Residency grantee Mid-Atlantic Arts Found., 1996. Democrat. Avocations: reading, visiting museums, collecting art and artifacts, photography. Home and Office: Scherer and Ouporov 594 16th St Brooklyn NY 11218-1201

SCHERGER, JOSEPH EDWARD, family physician, educator; b. Delphos, Ohio, Aug. 29, 1950; m. Carol M. Wintermute, Aug. 7, 1973; children: Adrian, Gabriel. BS summa cum laude, U. Dayton, 1971; MD, UCLA, 1975. Family practice residency U. Wash., Seattle, 1975-78; clin. instr. U. Calif. Sch. Medicine, Davis, 1978-80, asst. clin. prof., 1980-84, assoc. clin. prof., 1984-90, clin. prof., 1990—, dir. predoctoral program, 1991-92; med. dir. family practice and community medicine Sharp Healthcare, San Diego, 1992-96; assoc. dean primary care, chair dept. family medicine U. Calif., Irvine, 1996—2001, prof. dept. family medicine, 1996—2001; dean Fla. State U., Coll. Medicine, Tallahassee, 2001—03; clin. prof. family and preventive medicine U. Calif., San Diego, 2003—. Recipeient Hippocratic Oath award UCLA, Calif. Physician of Yr. award

Am. Acad. Family Physicians. Mem. NAS (mem. Inst. Medicine), Am. Acad. Family Physicians, Soc. Tchrs. Family Medicine. Home: 13188 Windbreak Rd San Diego CA 92130 Office Fax: 858-755-6537. E-mail: jscherger@aol.com.

SCHERR, BARRY PAUL, foreign language educator; b. Hartford, Conn., May 20, 1945; s. Joseph and Helen Lillian (Shapiro) S.; m. Sylvia Egelman, Sept. 8, 1974; children: Sonia, David. AB magna cum laude, Harvard U., 1966; AM, U. Chgo., 1967, PhD, 1973. From acting asst. prof. to asst. prof. U. Washington, Seattle, 1970-74; from asst. prof. to prof. Russian, Dartmouth Coll., Hanover, NH, 1974—, chmn. dept. Russian, 1981-90, 96-97, chmn. program linguistics and cognitive sci., 1989-96, assoc. dean for humanities, 1997—2001, assoc. provost, 2001, provost, 2001—. Co-organizer Internat. Conf. Russian Verse Theory, 1987, Internat. Conf. Anna Akhmatova and the Poets of Tsarskoe Selo, 1989, Internat. Conf. Eisenstein at 100: A Reconsideration, 1998. Author: Russian Poetry: Meter, Rhythm and Rhyme, 1986, Maxim Gorky, 1988; co-trans. The Seeker of Adventure, Alexander Grin, 1989; mem. editorial bd. Slavic and East European Jour., 1978-88; co-editor: Russian Verse Theory: Procs. of the 1987 Conference at UCLA, 1987, O RUS! Studia litteraria Slavica in honorem Hugh McLean, 1995, A Sense of Place: Tsarskoe Selo and Its Poets, 1993, Twentieth-Century Russian Literature, 2000, Eisenstein at 100: A Reconsideration, 2001; co-translator, co-editor Maksim Gorky: Selected Letters, 1997; contbr. articles to profl. jours. Scholar Harvard Coll., 1963-66; fellow NDEA, 1966-69; grantee Internat. Rsch. and Exchange Bd., 1969-70, NEH, 1987, 89, U.S. Dept. Edn., 1987-89, Dartmouth Coll. Sr. Faculty, 1988; summer rsch. grantee Grad. Sch., Inst. Comparative and Fgn. Area Studies U. Wash., 1973. Mem. MLA (mem. exec. com. assoc. dept. fgn. langs. 1983-85, del. assembly 1986-88), Am. Assn. Advancement Slavic Studies, Am. Assn. Tchrs. Slavic and East European Langs. (pres. 1987-88, founder, past pres. No. New England chpt., numerous coms.). Office: Dartmouth Coll Russian Dept Reed Hall Hanover NH 03755-3506 E-mail: Barry.scherr@Dartmouth.edu.

SCHERR, STEPHEN A. educational association administrator; b. Omaha, Dec. 5, 1938; m. Janice Akins, Aug. 16, 1968; children: Joseph M., Anna K. Nubel, Michael A., Peter T. BA, St. Louis U., 1963, MA in History, 1968; JD, George Washington U., 1971. Staff atty., law clk. U.S. Gen. Acctg. Office, 1970—72; dep. Adams County atty., 1972—74; Adams County pub. defender, 1974—81; mem. Hastings Bd. Edn., 1983—87; Adams County atty., 1990—95; atty. Whelan & Scherr; pres. Nebr. State Bd. Edn., Hastings, 2001—. Youth athletic coach, Hastings, 1973—93; 3rd dist. chmn. Dem. Party, 1973—74, Adams County chmn., 1976—78, state platform chmn., 1982, 1996; mem. South Ctrl. Cmty. Mental Health Bd., 1974—78, pres., 1975—78; bd. mem. Western Nebr. Legal Svcs., 1983—94, Hastings Libr. Found., 1985—89, Hastings Area Coun. on Alcoholism, 1990—98, Crossroads Ctr., 1995—97. Office: Dist 5 PO Box 2004 Hastings NE 68902*

SCHETLIN, ELEANOR M. retired university official; b. NYC, July 15, 1920; d. Henry Frank and Elsie (Chew) Schetlin. BA, Hunter Coll., 1940; MA, Tchrs. Coll., Columbia U., 1942, EdD, 1967. Playground dir. Dept. Parks, N.Y.C., 1940-42; libr. Met. Hosp. Sch. Nursing, N.Y.C., 1943-44, dir. recreation and guidance, 1945-58, historian Alumnae Assn., 2000—03; coord. student activities SUNY, Plattsburgh, 1959-63, asst. dean students, 1963-64; asst. prof., coord. student personnel svcs. CUNY, Hunter Coll., 1967-68; asst. dir. student personnel Columbia U., Coll. Pharm. Scis., N.Y.C., 1968-69, dir. student personnel, 1969-71; assoc. dean students Health Scis. Ctr. SUNY, Stony Brook, 1971-73, asst. v.p. student svcs., 1973-74, assoc. dean students, dir. student svcs., 1974-85. Founding mem. Sea Cliff unit 300 Nassau County Aux. Police; founding mem. Nassau NOW Women of Color Task Force. Contbr. articles to profl. jours. Recipient NOW Alliance PAC award, 1991, 1999, Lifetime Achievement award, Nassau NOW, 1992, Task Force Women of Color award, NOW, 1994. Mem.: So. Poverty Law Ctr., Wellesley Ctrs. Rsch. Women, Nat. Women's History Project, Women's Environment and Devel. Orgn., Nat. Women's Studies Assn., Nat. Assn. Women Edn., Nat. Mus. Women in the Arts. Home: 60 Hildreth Pl East Hampton NY 11937

SCHETTINO, MARIA CARMEN, preschool educator; b. N.Y.C., Mar. 12, 1949; d. Aniello and Mary Louise (Bove') S.; m. Albert Zezulinski (div. Apr. 1986); 1 child, Kerri; m. Michael J. Pulitano, June 24, 1989. A in Early Edn., SUNY, Farmingdale, 1969. Interviewer N.Y. State Planning Commn., Farmingdale, N.Y., 1969-70; Albany, 1970; asst. tchr. Alphabet Pre-Sch., 1971-72; tchr. art Montessori Sch., St. Thomas, V.I., 1975; substitute tchr. Miss Sue's Nursery Sch. and Kindergarten, Plainview, N.Y., 1975-80; asst. tchr. Bethpage (N.Y.) Nursery Sch., 1979-85, tchr., 1985-89, Kiddie Junction Pre-Sch. and Camp, Levittown, NY, 2000—. Coach Mid Island Gymnastics Sch., Hicksville, N.Y., 1986—, dir. presch. program, 1992-95; dir. M.A.T.S.S. Kids Gym, Syosset, N.Y., 1995-2000; gymnastics specialist 1st Class Child Care, Uniondale, N.Y., 1990. Fin. sec. Lantern Road Civic Assn., Hicksville, 1976. Mem. Early Childhood Ednl. Counsel. Democrat. Avocation: phys. fitness. Home: 90 Lantern Rd Hicksville NY 11801-6210 Office: Kiddie Junction Pre-Sch and Camp 3 N Village Green Levittown NY 11756

SCHEUSNER, DALE LEE, microbiologist, educator; b. Watertown, S.D., Feb. 10, 1944; s. E. Leonard and Amy B. (Buchholz) S.; m. Theresa A. Mahder, July 10, 1971; children: John, David. BS, S.D. State U., 1966; MS, N.C. State U., 1968; PhD, Mich. State U., 1972. Rsch. microbiologist S.C. Johnson & Son, Inc., Racine, Wis., 1971-82; tchr., adminstr. Living World, Racine, Wis., 1982-86; dept. head, tchr. Christian Life Sch., Kenosha, Wis., 1986-95; assoc. prof. Evangel U., Springfield, Mo., 1995—. Contbr. articles to profl. jours. Recipient Sci. World Award Wis. Dept. Edn., 1990. Mem. Am. Soc. Microbiology, Inst. Food Technologists. Avocations: gardening, photography. Home: 2506 S Blackman Rd Springfield MO 65809-3406 Office: Evangel U 1111 N Glenstone Ave Springfield MO 65802-2125

SCHEVING, LAWRENCE EINAR, anatomy educator, scientist; b. Hensel, N.D., Oct. 20, 1920; s. Einar L. and Mary (Brown) S.; m. Virginia M. Krumdick, Aug. 6, 1949; children: Lawrence, Mary, John, Jennifer, Patricia (dec.). BS in Biology, DePaul U., 1949, MS in Zoology, 1950; PhD, Loyola U., Chgo., 1957. Mem. faculty Lewis Univ., Lockport, Ill., successively instr., asst. prof., assoc. prof., prof. and head dept. biol. sci., 1950-57; prof. anatomy Chgo. Med. Sch., 1957-67, La. State U. Med. Sch., New Orleans, 1967-70, U. Ark. Coll. Med., Little Rock, 1970-74, Rebsamen prof. anat. sci., 1974-91, Rebsamen prof. emeritus, from 1991. Vis. prof. U. Bergen, Norway, 1952, The Med. Sch. Hannover, Fed. Republic Germany, 1973; dir. chronobiology course Chautauqua series NSF, 1979; dir. NATO Advanced Study Insts., 1979, Workshop on chronobiotech. and chronobiol. engring., 1985; dir. Fedn. Am. Socs. Exptl. Biology summer research conf., Copper Mountain, Colo., 1988; mem. breast cancer task force Nat. Cancer Inst.; mem. U.S. Army med. research and devel. adv. com., 1982—; cons. to VA. Author: Biological Rhythms in Structure and Function, 1981; editor: Chronobiology, 1974, Chronobiotech. and Chronobiol. Engring. 1986, Research Advance in Chronobiology, 1987; numerous chpts. to books, over 200 articles in field of chronobiology and other biol. areas to profl. jours.; mem. editorial bd.: Chronobiologia, Chronobiology Internat., Am. Jour. Anatomy. Served to capt. AUS, 1940-45; col. Res. Decorated Bronze Star, Disting. Svc. medal, others; recipient Research award Chgo. Med. Sch. Bd. Dirs., 1962, Most Helpful Prof. award La. State U., 1968, award for Excellence in Nat. Leadership and Lifes Work, Gov. N.D., 1992; named Prof. Year Student Council Chgo. Med. Sch., 1964; recipient Golden Apple award student body U. Ark. Med. Sch., 1972; Alexander von Humboldt Sr. Scientist prize German govt., 1973, Highest Faculty award U. Ark. Med. Soc., 1987, others; spl. lecture and symposium dedicated in his honor Am. Assn. Med. and Chronotherapeutics, 1999. Mem. AAAS, Am. Soc. Anatomists, Am. Assn. Cancer Research, Am. Soc. Zoologists, Am. Soc. Photobiology, Internat. Soc. Chronobiology (hon., sec.-treas. 1971-83, pres.-elect 1983-85, pres. 1985-89, symposium dedicated in his honor 1993), So. Assn. Anatomists (past councillor), Am. Indsl. Hygiene Assn. (traditional workshifts com. 1983-89), Sigma Xi (chpt. pres. 1964-65) Roman Catholic. Home: Brookfield, Wis. Died Apr. 14, 2000.

SCHEWEL, ROSEL HOFFBERGER, education educator; b. Mar. 1, 1928; d. Samuel Herman and Gertrude (Miller) Hoffberger; m. Elliot Sidney Schewel, June 12, 1949; children: Stephen, Michael, Susan. AB, Hood Coll., 1949; MEd, Lynchburg Coll., 1974, EdS, 1982, EdD (hon.), 2000. Reading resource tchr. Lynchburg Pub. Schs., Va., 1967-75; adj. prof. edn. Lynchburg Coll., 1973-79, assoc. prof. edn., 1980-92. Cons., seminar leader Woman's Resource Ctr., Lynchburg, 1980-92. Trustee, chair bd. trustees Lynchburg Coll., Va., 1992-98, 99—; bd. dirs. Va. Found. for Humanities and Pub. Policy, 1985-90, New Vistas Sch., Lynchburg Human Rights Commn., 1992-2000, Lynchburg Youth Svcs., 1993-97; bd. dirs. Venture Enterprising Women, Planned Parenthood of the Blue Ridge; trustee Va. Mus. of Fine Arts, 1985-90; apptd. Commn. on Edn. for All Virginians, 1990; bd. dirs. Action Alliance for Virginia's Children and Youth, 1995-2002; trustee Amazement Sq. Children's Mus., 1996—; vol. Ct. Apptd. Spl. Advocate, Riverviews Art Space Bd., 2002—. Recipient Disting. Svc. award NCCJ, 1973, Outstanding Woman in Edn. award YWCA, 1988, Disting. Alumni award Lynchburg Coll., 1993. Mem. Phi Kappa Phi. Democrat. Jewish. Address: 4316 Gorman Dr Lynchburg VA 24503-1948

SCHGIER, LINDA PRIEST, musician, educator; b. Cullman, Ala., Nov. 16, 1942; d. Isaac Columbus and Frances Elene (Woodall) Priest; m. William Meyer Schgier, July 12, 1969. AA, Sacred Heart Coll., 1962; BS, U. N. Ala., 1965; postgrad., U. Ala., 1967-68. Tchr. Annapolis (Md.) Jr. H.S., 1965-66, Whitesburg Elem., Huntsville, Ala., 1966-69, West Elem. Sch., Cullman, 1970-83; music assoc., pianist 1st Bapt. Ch., Cullman, 1970—2000; music asst., pianist, dir. children's choir, dir. youth and children's handbells St. John's Evang. Protestant Ch., 2001—. Tchr. music summer camps, Older Children's Music Week Shocco Springs Bapt. Assembly, Talladega, Ala.,. 1982—; pvt. piano and organ tchr. Mem. Am. Music Tchrs. Assn., Cmty. Concerts Assn. (bd. dirs. 1972—), Coterie (historian 1997-98), Symphony Club (pres. 1996-97), DAR. Avocations: reading, music, travel, puzzles, model trains. Home: 166 County Road 1473 Cullman AL 35058-0792

SCHIAVELLI, MELVYN DAVID, academic administrator, science educator, researcher; b. Chgo., Aug. 8, 1942; s. Gene James and Frances Elizabeth (Giacomo) S.; m. Virginia Farrell, Sept. 10, 1966; children—Timothy, Karen BS in Chemistry, DePaul U., 1964; PhD in Chemistry, U. Calif., Berkeley, 1967. Rsch. assoc. Mich. State U., East Lansing, 1967-68; from asst. prof. to assoc. prof. chemistry Coll. William and Mary, Williamsburg, Va., 1968-80, prof. chemistry, 1980-94, chmn. dept. chemistry, 1978-84, dean Faculty Arts and Scis., 1984-86, provost, 1986-93, acting pres., 1992; prof. chem. and biochem., provost U. Del., Newark, 1994—. Contbr. articles to profl. jours., 1969— Grantee NSF Petroleum Rsch. Fund, 1969-90. Mem. Am. Chem. Soc., Royal Inst. Chemists, Sigma Xi. Roman Catholic. Office: U Del Office Provost 129 Hullihen Hall Newark DE 19716

SCHIAVONI, THOMAS JOHN, social studies educator; b. Sag Harbor, N.Y. s. Francis G. and Ann M. (O'Rourke) S. BA, SUNY, Cortland, 1986; MA in Liberal Arts, SUNY, Stony Brook, 1993. Social studies tchr. The Desisto Sch., Stockbridge, Mass., 1986-87, Bd. Coop. Ednl. Svcs. 1, Southampton, N.Y., 1987-90, Center Moriches (N.Y.) Union Free Sch. Dist., 1988—. Adj. instr. sociology Syracuse U.; com. mem. The Social Studies K-12 Curriculum com., Center Moriches UFSD, 1991, com. chmn. com. on middle sch. reform. Office: Center Moriches UFSD 311 Frowein Rd Center Moriches NY 11934-2217

SCHIAZZA, GUIDO DOMENIC (GUY SCHIAZZA), educational association administrator; b. Phila., May 17, 1930; s. Guido and Claudina (DiPrinzio) S.; m. Irmgard Heidi Reissmueller, May 15, 1954. BA, Pa. State U., 1952; postgrad., St. Joseph's U., 1954-55, Villanova U., 1954-55, Temple U., 1955-58. Cert. tchr., Pa.; cert. clinician, ednl. specialist, instructional specialist, sch. psychologist, guidance counselor, reading specialist. Speech therapist, lang. arts instr. Commonwealth of Pa., Dept. Edn., 1956-59; founder, clinician, instr., dir., bd. pres. Communicative Arts Ctr., Inc., Drexel Hill, Pa., 1958, Comm. Skills, Cmty. Resources Ctr., Inc., Drexel Hill, Pa., 1958, 1964—; charter mem. exec. bd., bd. pres. United Pvt. Acad. Schs., Assn. of Pa., Drexel Hill, 1966—; exec. bd. govs., bd. chmn. The Accrediting Commn., Drexel Hill, 1971—. Charter mem. Pa. State Univ. Radio and TV Guild, University Park, Pa., 1951—; mem. legis. action com., Pa. State U., Univ. Park, 1988—; cons. communications skills, The Accrediting Commn., 1971—, United Pvt. Acad. Schs. Assn., Pa., 1966—. Founder, chmn., CEO Am. Ednl. Group, 1991—; chmn. CEO Internat. Ednl. Group, 1991—; CEO Cmty. Resources Ctr., Drexel Hill, 1991—, project coord. Energy Quest, 1992—; active Nat. Com. to Preserve Social Security and Medicare, Washington, 1986—, Am. Immigration Control Found., Monterey, Va., 1987—, English First, Springfield, Va., 1988—; mem. pres.'s coun. Rep. Nat. Com., 1989—, Nat. Rep. Senatorial Com., 1989—, Rep. Presdl. Task Force, 1989—; mem. Congrl. Legis. Agenda steering com. Empower Am., 1999. 1st Lt. Signal Corps, U.S. Army, 1952-54. Recipient Svc. award United Pvt. Acad. Sch. Assn. Pa., Monroeville, Pa., 1978, Disting. Achievement and Svc. award Bd. Govs. of the Accrediting Commn., Downington, Pa., 1980, Dr. Charles Boehm Edn. of Yr. award University Park, Pa., 1990, Loyal and Dedicated Svc. award The Accrediting Commn., 1974. Mem. NEA, Libr. Congress (chartered), Internat. Platform Assn., Pa. Edn. Assn., Jefferson Ednl. Found., World Affairs Coun. Phila., Heritage Found., Nat. Trust for Hist. Preservation, Nat. Congl. Club, Pa. State U. Nittany Lions Club, Pa. State U. Alumni Assn., Pa. State U. Football Lettermen's Club, Pa. State U. Varsity "S" Club. Republican. Roman Catholic. Avocations: music, home and garden design, automotive design, reading, golf. Office: The Accrediting Commn 436 Burmont Rd Drexel Hill PA 19026-3630

SCHICHLER, ROBERT LAWRENCE, English language educator; b. Rochester, N.Y., May 16, 1951; s. Alfred James and Elizabeth Johanna (Flugel) S. BA in English, SUNY, Geneseo, 1974, MA in English, 1978; PhD of English, Binghamton U., 1987. Writer, asst. administr. Artists-in-Residence Program, Rochester, N.Y., 1978-79; substitute tchr. City Sch. Dist., Rochester, 1980-82; instr. English Talmudical Inst. Upstate N.Y., Rochester, 1981-82, Binghamton (N.Y.) U., 1983-84; rsch. asst. Medieval and Renaissance Texts and Studies, Binghamton, 1985-86; adj. asst. prof. Rochester Inst. Tech., 1987-89; asst. prof. English Ark. State U., State University, 1989-94, assoc. prof., 1994-99, prof., 1999—. Adj. asst. prof. Monroe C.C., Rochester, 1987-89. Author: King of the Once Wild Frontier: Reflections of a Canal Walker, 1993; editor: Lady in Waiting: Poems in English and Spanish, 1994, Abstracts of Papers in Anglo-Saxon Studies, 1988-2003, Ctr. for Medieval and Early Renaissance Studies, Binghamton, 1986-94, Spillway Publs., Rochester, 1992—; asst. editor: Old English Newsletter, 1986-87, Mediaevalia, Binghamton, 1988-89; contbr. articles to profl. jours. Mem. Internat. Soc. Anglo-Saxonists, Medieval Acad. Am., Am. Numismatic Assn. Home: Apt M1 726 Southwest Dr Jonesboro AR 72401-7045 Office: Ark State U Dept English and Philosophy State University AR 72467-1890 E-mail: rschich@mail.astate.edu., boonzither@hotmail.com.

SCHICK, BRIAN KEITH, middle school educator; b. St. Louis, Aug. 21, 1968; s. Dennis Alexander and Joan Frances (Jedlink) S.; m. Patricia Ann McNutt, Aug. 16, 1991. BS in Edn., U. Mo., 1989; MA in Teaching, Webster U., 1991. Lang. arts/social studies tchr. Mehlville Sch. Dist., St. Louis, 1989-94; reading tchr. Rockwood Sch. Dist., Eureka, Mo., 1994—. Presenter workshop Critical Thinking-Mehlville Staff Devel., 1991; com. mem. Mehlville Strategic Planning Facilities Com., St. Louis, 1991-94; ex-officio exec. mem. Mehlville-Oakville Sch. Dist. Found., St. Louis, 1993-94; com. mem. Mehlville Strategic Planning Mid. Sch. Com., St. Louis, 1993-94; core team leader Oakville Jr. Sch. Improvement Leadership Team, St. Louis, 1993-94. Author: (song lyrics) Constitution Rap, 1990. Com. mem., advisor March of Dimes-Walk Am., St. Louis, 1994. Grantee Mehlville-Oakville Found., 1994; Personal Responsibility Edn. Program grantee, 1995; Rockwood Profl. Devel. grantee, 1995. Mem. ASCD, NEA, Nat. Coun. Social Studies, Mehlville Community Tchrs. Assn. (bldg rep. 1989-94). Roman Catholic. Avocations: music, pets, reading, hallmark ornament collecting, travel. Office: LaSalle Springs Mid Sch 3300 Highway 109 Glencoe MO 63038-2201

SCHICK, IRVIN HENRY, academic administrator, educator; b. Wilkes-Barre, Pa., Aug. 10, 1924; s. Irvin and Elizabeth (Valentine) S.; m. Marilyn Freeman, July 17, 1954 (dec. Aug. 1961); m. Marjorie Bletch Beach, Dec. 23, 1967; 1 child, Carolyn Patricia. Diploma, Bliss Elec. Sch., 1947; BEE with distinction, George Washington U., 1958; MSEE (NSF fellow), U. Md., 1961. Engring. asst. Jeddo-Highland Coal Co., Pa., 1942-43; instr. Bliss Elec. Sch., Washington, 1947-50; prof. math. and elec. engring., dept. head Montgomery Coll., Rockville, Md., 1950-65, dir. ext., 1965-67, dean adminstrn., 1967-75, adminstrv. v.p., 1975-78, prof. emeritus, adminstrv. v.p. emeritus, 1978—. Tchr., tutor, cons. indsl. cos., 1949—. Served with USAAF, 1943-46. Mem. AAUP, IEEE, Am. assn. Sch. Adminstrs., Internat. Platform Assn., Md. State Tchrs. Assn., Montgomery County Edn. Assn., Bliss Elec. Soc. (bd. govs., past pres.), Tent Troupe Theatrical Orgn. (bd. govs.), Theta Tau, Sigma Tau (past pres.), Sigma Pi Sigma, Tau Beta Pi. Home: 105 Fleetwood Ter Silver Spring MD 20910-5512

SCHIEBER, CHRISTIANA ELIZABETH, secondary education educator; b. Blacksburg, Va., Feb. 11, 1949; d. Dorothy (Carrick) Turner; m. Dennis Lee Schieber, Oct. 18, 1973; children: Brian Dennis Schieber, John Michael Schieber. EdB in Elem. Edn., U. Ctrl. Okla., 1976, MS summa cum laude, 1978. Tchr. Star Spencer High Sch., Oklahoma City, 1976-79, Darlington Sch., El Reno, Okla., 1982-88, Kingfisher (Okla.) High Sch., 1988—, Redlands Jr. Coll., El Reno, Okla., 1986—. Trainer and advisor Star Spencer Reading Across the Curriculum; entry yr. tchr. supr., staff devel. com. and chmn., pub. rels. person, gifted tchr. vol., cheerleader sponsor, hon. soc. sponsor, acad. team coach, cheerleader sponsor/coach, yearbook sponsor, Darlington Sch.; student coun. sponcer, Kingfisher High Sch., 1989—, chair staff devel., 1993—; reading setting panel, nat. review com. Nat. Assessment Edn. Progress Level, 1993. Named Kingfisher Tchr. of Yr., 1990, Zone Five Tchr. of Yr., 1986, Darlington Tchr. of Yr., 1986, 88; grantee Okla. Humanities Found. Mem. AAUW (exec. com. bylaws), Internat. Reading Assn. (grantee, team leader southwest region Young Adult Choices 1994-96), Okla. Edn. Assn., Okla. Reading Assn. (regional dir. 1991-94, sec. 1994-95), Okla. Dept. Edn., (Priority Academic Student Skills com. guide, Reading com. for h.s.), Delta Kappa Gamma (state v.p., internat. commn. com.). Democrat. Lutheran. Avocations: reading, crafts, gardening. Home: RR 4 Box 93 Okarche OK 73762-9384 Office: Kingfisher High School 9th and Toronto Kingfisher OK 73750

SCHIEBER, PHYLLIS, writer, learning disabilities specialist; b. NYC, Feb. 18, 1953; d. Kurt and Henia Schieber. BA, Herbert H. Lehman Coll., 1973; MA in English Lit., NYU, 1974; MS, Devel. Specialist, Yeshiva U., 1977. Cert. tchr. English and spl. classes of handicapped, N.Y. English tchr. Norwalk (Conn.) H.S., 1976-84; learning disabilities specialist Iona Coll., New Rochelle, N.Y., 1989-95, Mercy Coll., Dobbs Ferry, NY, 1991—2003. Freelance writer and editor. Author: (novels) Strictly Personal, 1986, Willing Spirits, 1998. Home: 48 Lefurgy Ave Hastings On Hudson NY 10706-2504 E-mail: phylsheba@aol.com.

SCHIEBLER, GEROLD LUDWIG, pediatrician, educator; b. Hamburg, Pa., June 20, 1928; s. Alwin Robert and Charlotte Elizabeth (Schmoele) Schiebler; m. Audrey Jean Lincourt, Jan. 8, 1954; children: Mark, Marcella, Kristen, Bettina, Wanda, Michele. BS, Franklin and Marshall Coll., 1950; MD, Harvard U., 1954. Intern pediat. and internal medicine Mass. Gen. Hosp., Boston, 1954—55, resident, 1955—56; resident pediat. U. Minn. Hosp., Mpls., 1956—57, fellow pediatric cardiology, 1957—58, rsch. fellow, 1958—59; rsch. fellow sect. physiology Mayo Clinic and Mayo Found., 1959—60; asst. prof. pediatric cardiology U. Fla., 1960—63, assoc. prof., 1963—66, prof., 1966—92, Disting. Svc. prof., 1992—2000, adj. Disting. Svcs. prof., 2001—, chmn. dept. pediat., 1968—85, assoc. v.p. for health affairs for external rels., 1985—2000. Dir. divsn. Children's Med. Svcs. State of Fla., 1973—74. Author (with L.P. Elliott): The X-ray Diagnosis of Congenital Cardiac Disease in Infants, Children and Adults, 1968, 1979; author: (with L.J. Krovetz and I.H. Gessner) Pediatric Cardiology, 1979. Named Children's Med. Svcs. Pediatrician of Decade, Gov. Jeb Bush, 1999. Mem.: AMA (Benjamin Rush award 1993), AAAS, Fla. Med. Assn. (past v.p., bd. govs., pres. 1991—92), Fla. Heart Assn. (past pres.), Fla. Pediat. Soc. (exec. com.), Soc. Pediatric Rsch. (emeritus), Am. Coll. Cardiology, Am. Acad. Pediat. (Abraham Jacobi award 1993), Inst. Medicine NAS, Alpha Omega Alpha, Phi Beta Kappa. Home: 408 Beachside Villas Amelia Island Plantation Amelia Island FL 32034-6551

SCHIEFFELIN, GEORGE RICHARD, educational consultant; b. N.Y.C., July 3, 1930; s. George McKay and Louise (Winterbotham) S. BA, Hobart Coll., 1953. Ednl. cons., Denver, 1956-62, New Haven, 1962-89, Tampa, Fla., 1989—. Dir. Charles Scribner's Sons, N.Y.C., Scribner Book Stores, N.Y.C., Pubs. Realty Co., N.Y.C., 1962-83, Macro Communications, N.Y.C., 1975-83; asst. to lt. gov. of Colo., 1958-59. Trustee Hobart and William Smith Colls., 1969-78, Rocky Mountain Coll., 1989-93, adv. com. Rocky Mountain Coll., 1993—. With AUS, 1953-55. Mem. Morristown Field Club, Univ. Club (Denver), Princeton Club (N.Y.C.), Williams Club.

SCHIELDS, VICKIE MARIE, elementary educator; b. Hazen, N.D., July 9, 1957; d. Richard Carl and Leona Irene (Wetzel) S. BS in Elem. Edn. cum laude, Dickinson State U., 1979. Cert. tchr., Mont. Tchr. elem. sch. Lambert (Mont.) Pub. Schs., 1979—. Negotiator Lambert Edn. Assn., 1984-85; judge Richland County Spelling Bee, Sidney, Mont, 1979—; chmn. I Love to Read program, Lambert, 1980-82, Grandparents Day program, 1987; coord. Book It program, 1988—; rep. OBE Conv., Rochester, Minn., 1992, Gifted & Talented Conf., Mpls., 1993; coord. travel group Nat. Finals Rodeo, 1990. Game chmn. Farmers Union, Golden Valley, N.D., 1978—; Bible sch. tchr. St. Paul's Luth. Ch., Dodge, N.D., 1978-83, organist, 1978—, ch. janitor, 1978—; judge Dunn County 4-H, Killdeer, N.D., 1979-85; crusader Am. Cancer Soc., 1980—; cook Lion's Den Teen Ctr., Lambert, 1991—. Named one of Outstanding Young Women of Am., 1987; recipient Outcome Based Edn. award, Lambert Pub. Sch. Mem. Mont. Edn. Assn., Lambert Edn. Assn., PTA, Lambert Domestic Club (sec. 1990—), Women of Moose, Guys and Gals Square Dance Club, Richey Rodeo Club. Lutheran. Avocations: travel, reading, piano, gardening, baking bread. Home: PO Box 126 Lambert MT 59243-0126 Office: Lambert Pub Sch PO Box 236 Lambert MT 59243-0236

SCHIELE, PAUL ELLSWORTH, JR., education business owner, writer; b. Phila., Nov. 20, 1924; s. Paul Ellsworth Sr. and Maud (Barclay) S.; m. Sarah Irene Knauss, Aug. 20, 1946; children: Patricia Schiele Sommers, Sandra Schiele Kicklighter, Deborah Schiele Hartigan. AT, Temple U., 1949; BA, LaVerne U., 1955; MA, Claremont Grad. U., 1961; PhD, U.S. Internat. U., San Diego, 1970. Cert. sec. tchr., Calif. 1961. Tchr. sci. and math. Lincoln High Sch., Phila., 1956-57, Ontario (Calif.) Sch. Dist., 1957-65; math. and sci. cons. Hacienda La Puente U. Sch. Dist., Calif., 1965-75; asst. prof. Calif. State U., Fullerton, 1975-83; pres., owner

Creative Learning Environments and Resources, Glendora, Calif., 1983—, cons. sci. curriculum, 1985—. Dir. title III project ESEA, 1974-75, cons. for project, 1975-77; cons. in field. Author: (student workbook) Beyond the Earth, 1969, Primary Science, 1972, 2d edit., 1976, (novel) Under Cover of Night, 1995, Chasing the Wild Geese, 1996, Deceptive Appearances, 1997; editor: A Living World, 1974, 2d edit., 1986; writer 9 sound filmstrips, model units for sci. and math. activity books, 10 sci. activities for L.A. Outdoor Edn. Program, 1980; editor 21 sci. and math. activity books, 1975-76; writer, co-dir. (TV) Marine Biology Series, 1970-71; contbr. munerous articles to profl. mags., 1960-85; writer and designer of 2 sci. ednl. games; designer in field. Apptd. adv. com. Sci. and Humanities Symposium Calif. Mus. Sci. and Industry, 1974; mem. State Sci. Permit Com., Tide Pools of Calif. Coast, 1974-75; mem. Friends of Libr., Friends Libr. Found. Mem. Internat. Platform Assn., Internat. Soc. Photographers, Glendora Hist. Soc., ABI Rsch. Assn. (bd. govs.), Calif. Elem. Edn. Assn. (hon.), Nat. PTA (hon.), Calif. Inter-Sci. Coun. (pres., chmn. 1971, 72), Elem Sch. Scis. Assn. (past pres., bd. dirs.), Paddlewheel Steamboating Soc. of Am., Phi Delta Kappa (chartered). Republican. Lutheran. Avocations: travel, etchings, art collecting, fencing. Home: 231 Catherine Park Dr Glendora CA 91741-3018

SCHIERINGA, PAUL KENNETH, special education educator, entertainer; b. Holland, Mich., Mar. 28, 1934; s. Peter and Mary (Van Kampen) Schieringa; m. Patti Ann Poling, Dec. 27, 1987. BA in Bus. Adminstrn., Hope Coll., 1957; MDiv, Founding Ch., Washington, 1963. Cert. nursing home adminstr., Ill. Quality control officer U.S. R.R. Retirement Bd., Chgo., 1957—61; entertainer, 1961—; med. mgr. hosps., nursing homes, mental health agencies, Chgo. and Ionia, Mich., 1971—87; theater adminstr. Croswell Opera House, Adrian, Mich., 1987—88; tchr. music/spl. edn./career edn. Guam Dept. Edn., Hagatna, 1991—2001. Cons. various nursing homes, Chgo., 1977—83, Betty's Learning Ctr., Upper Tumon, Guam, 1997—2001; mem. diabetes policy adv. bd. Mich. Dept. Pub. Health, Lansing, 1983—88; chairperson Citizens' Adv. Coun. for Southgate (Mich.) Mental Health Ctr., 1984—88. Composer: (songs) Free As A Gull, 1964, 23rd Psalm, 1972, He Cared So Much For Me, 1991, Lo, He Comes, 1992, It Still Took Calvary, 1997, (Chaplains Verse for Navy Hymn) Eternal Father Strong to Save, 1992. Co-chair restoration adv. bd. Naval Air Sta., Hagatna, 1993—2001; bd. dirs. Friends of Guam Pub. Libr., Hagatna, 1996—2001. Named to Ancient Order of the Chamorri, Gov. of Guam, 2001. Avocations: writing childrens' books, World War II historian, organ, fishing. Home: 879 W 32d St Holland MI 49423

SCHIFF, ERIC ALLAN, physics educator; b. LA, Aug. 29, 1950; s. Gunther Hans and Katharine Shepherd (MacMillan) S.; m. Nancy Ruth Mudrick, Aug. 12, 1973; children: Nathan, Evan. BS, Calif. Inst. Tech., 1971; PhD, Cornell U., 1979. Rsch. assoc. U. Chgo., 1978-81; asst. prof. Syracuse (N.Y.) U., 1981-87, assoc. prof., 1987-95, prof., 1995—, dept. chair, 1997—2003, assoc. dean sci. and math., 2003—. Vis. Brown U., Providence, R.I., 1988-90, Xerox Palo Alto Rsch. Ctr., 1995. Contbr. articles to profl. jours. Rsch. grant NSF, 1983-86. Mem. Am. Phys. Soc. (exec. com. NY state chpt. 1991-94), Materials Rsch. Soc. (symposium organizing com. 1992-97, 2003—), Internat. Conf. Amorphous and Microcrystlaline Semiconductors (organizing com. 1999). Office: Syracuse U Dept Physics Syracuse NY 13244-0001

SCHIFF, GARY STUART, academic administrator, educator, consultant; b. Bklyn., Mar. 27, 1947; s. Jacob and Lillian (Grumet) S.; children: Jeremy Jay, Rina Joy. BA, Bin Hebrew Lit., Yeshiva U., 1968; MA, Columbia U., 1970, Cert. in Middle East Studies, PhD, Columbia U., 1973; DHL (hon.), Gratz Coll., 1997. Asst. prof. Jewish studies and polit. sci. CUNY, 1973-76; dir. Mid. East affairs Nat. Jewish Cmty. Rels. Coun., N.Y.C., 1976-78; exec. asst. to pres. Acad. for Ednl. Devel., N.Y.C., 1978-83; pres., prof. Middle East studies Gratz Coll., Melrose Park, Pa., 1983-97. Vis. prof. Balt. Hebrew U., 1997, Washington Coll., Md., 1999-2000, 2000-2001; vis. asst. prof. polit. sci. Yeshiva U., 1973-77. Author: Tradition and Politics: The Religious Parties of Israel, 1977, The Energy Education Catalog, 1981; contbr. articles to profl. jours. Grantee NEH, Ford Found., Danforth Found., Woodrow Wilson Found., William Penn Found., Pew Charitable Trusts. Mem. Assn. of Colls. of Jewish Studies (bd. dirs.), Assn. for Israel Studies (v.p.), Coun. for Jewish Edn. (bd. dirs.), Assn. for Jewish Studies, World Jewish Congress (governing bd.), Am. Jewish Com. (N.Y. chpt. bd. dirs., Phila. chpt. communal affairs commn.). Avocations: cantorial music, boating, cats. Home: 29182 Ricks Landing Rd Kennedyville MD 21645-3306 E-mail: garygrant@aol.com.

SCHIFLETT, PEGGY L. KUCERA, secondary school educator, consultant; b. Dallas, June 27, 1953; d. John Henry Kucera, Jr. and Mary Frieda Evelyn (Fischer) Kucera; m. Joseph Raymond Schiflett III, Aug. 6, 1977; children: Shayna Louise, Joseph Raymond IV. BA in English and History maxima cum laude, St. Edward's U., 1975; postgrad., S.W. Tex. State U. at U. Kent, 1995. Cert. education St. Michael Sch./ Houston, Tex., 1975. Sci. and reading tchr. St. Michael Sch., Houston, 1975-81; English tchr. Oak Ridge Jr. and Sr. HS, Conroe, Tex., 1981-83; English tchr., co-chmn. San Marcos HS, San Marcos, Tex., 1986—. Advanced Placement cons., presenter for English lit. Coll. Bd., Austin, 1996—; mem. vertical team English San Marcos Consol. Ind. Sch. Dist., 1996—; weather watcher Sta. KVUE, Channel 24 TV, Nat. Weather Svc. Vol. dispatcher North Hays County and Wimberley Emergency Med. Svc.; ambulance medic, driver Wimberley Emergency Med. Svc., 1987-93; coach Girls HS Fastpitch Softball, 1990-94, Sr. Little League Fastpitch Softball coach, Wimberley, 1995. Grantee Mellon Found., 1994, San Marcos Ind. Sch. Dist. Edn. Found., 1995; named Ctrl. Tex. Softball Coach of Yr. Austin Am. Statesman, 1993. Mem. Nat. Coun. Tchr. English, Tex. Coun. of Tchr. of English, Assn. of Tex. Profl. Educators, Tex. Assn. for Gifted and Talented. Episcopalian. Avocations: baseball, camping, reading, travel. Home: 447Hill Country Trl Wimberley TX 78676 Office: San Marcos HS 1301 Highway 123 San Marcos TX 78666-7843

SCHILD, RUDOLPH ERNST, astronomer, educator; b. Chgo., Jan. 10, 1940; s. Kasimir A. and Anneliese (Schuricht) S.; m. Jane H. Struss, July 28, 1982. BS, U. Chgo., 1962, MS, 1963, PhD, 1966. Rsch. fellow Calif. Inst. Tech., Pasadena, 1966-69; scientific dir., 1.5m Telescope Program Smithsonian Astrophysical Obs., Amado, Ariz., 1969-74; astronomer Harvard-Smithsonian Ctr. for Astrophysics, Cambridge, Mass., 1974--. Lectr. Harvard U., 1975-83. Author: (slide set) The Electronic Sky: Digital Images of the Cosmos, 1985, (CD-ROM) Voyage to the Stars: The Rudy Schild Collection; contbr. over 100 articles to scholarly and profl. jours. Mem. Am. Astronomical Soc., Internat. Astronomical Union. Achievements include 2 patents; discovery of gravitational microlensing. Office: Ctr for Astrophysics 60 Garden St Cambridge MA 02138-1516 E-mail: rschild@cfa.harvard.edu.

SCHILDKRAUT, JOSEPH JACOB, psychiatrist, educator; b. Bklyn., Jan. 21, 1934; s. Simon and Shirley (Schwartz) S.; m. Elizabeth Rose Beilenson, May 22, 1966; children: Peter Jeremy, Michael John. AB summa cum laude, Harvard U., 1955; MD cum laude, Harvard Med. Sch., 1959. Intern medicine U. Calif. Hosp., San Francisco, 1959-60; resident in psychiatry Mass. Mental Health Center, Boston, 1960-63; dir. neuropsychopharmacology lab., 1967—98; founding dir., 1998—; sr. psychiatrist, 1967—; research psychiatrist NIMH, Bethesda, Md., 1963-67, cons., 1967-68; asst. prof. psychiatry Harvard Med. Sch., Boston, 1967-70, assoc. prof., 1970-74, prof., 1974—. Dir. psychiat. chemistry lab. Mass. Mental Health Ctr., 1977-98, founding dir., 1998-. Author: over 200 publ. including, Neuorpsychopharmacology and the Affective Disorders, 1970; editor: Depression and the Spiritual in Modern Art: Homage to Miró, 1996, U.S. patent, 2002; editor-in-chief Jour. Psychiat. Rsch., 1982-92; mem. editorial bd. Psychophysiology, 1968-74, Jour. Psychiat. Rsch., 1968-82, Psychopharmacology, 1970-84, Sleep Revs., 1972-79, Communications in Psychopharmacology, 1974-81, Psychotherapy and Psychosomatics, 1974-91, Rsch. Communications in Psychology, Psychiatry and Behavior, 1976—, Jour. Clin. Psychopharmacology, 1980—, Integrative Psychiatry, 1982-89, 91—, others. Bd. dirs. Med. Found., Boston, 1991-97 chair clin. rsch. com., 1994-96; trustee Mind/Body Med. Inst. Deaconess Hosp., Harvard Med. Sch., Boston, 1988-2002, chair sci. adv. bd., 1988-95. Served as surgeon USPHS, 1963-65. Recipient Anna-Monika Found. prize, 1967, Hofheimer award Am. Psychiat. Assn., 1971, hon. mention award, 1968; McCurdy-Rinkel prize No. New Eng. Dist. br. Am. Psychiat. Assn., 1969; William C. Menninger award ACP, 1978; Neuropsychiatry Classics, 1995; Lifetime Achievement award Soc. of Biological Psychiatry, 1996; Award for Rsch. in Mood Disorders The Am. Coll. of Psychiatrists, 1999. Fellow: Am. Psychiat. Assn. (disting. life); mem.: AAAS, Soc. Neurosci., Collegium Internat. Neuropsychopharmacologicum, Assn. Rsch. in Nervous and Mental Disease, Group Without a Name, Am. Soc. Neurochemistry, Am. Soc. Pharmacology and Exptl. Therapeutics, Am. Coll. Psychiatrists, Am. Psychopath. Assn., N.Y. Acad. Scis., Soc. Biol. Psychiatry, Am. Psychosomatic Soc., Am. Coll. Neuropsychopharmacology, Psychiat. Rsch. Soc., World Psychiat Assn. (sec. sect. biol. psychiatry 1972—77), Phi Beta Kappa. Achievements include patents in field. Home: 35 Jefferson Rd Chestnut Hill MA 02467-2341 Office: Mass Mental Health Ctr 74 Fenwood Rd Boston MA 02115-6113

SCHILLACI, PATRICIA ANN, secondary school educator; b. Pittston, Pa., June 8, 1954; d. Marino Frank and Eleanor (Pepe) S. BA, Wilkes Coll., Wilkes-Barre, Pa., 1976; MS, U. Scranton, 1979. Cert. math. supr., 1993, secondary prin., 1994. Permanent substitute Wyoming Area High Sch., Exeter, Pa., 1976-79; secondary math./Spanish tchr. Pittston Area Jr. High Sch., 1979-84; tchr. secondary math. and Spanish Pittston Area High Sch., Yatesville, Pa., 1984—, chair dept. math., 1999—. Recipient Gerard M. Musto Honor Soc. award, 1990. Mem. ASCD, Nat. Assn. Student Activity Advs., Nat. Coun. Tchrs. Math. (mid. states evaluator 1988-93), Pa. Coun. Tchrs. Math. (advisor Key Club, advisor sr. class), Luzerne County Coun. Tchrs. Math., Northeastern Pa. Coun. Tchrs. Math. Office: Pittston Area Sr High Sch 5 Stout St Pittston PA 18640-3391

SCHILLING, EYDIE ANNE, science educator, consultant; b. Columbus, Ohio, June 17, 1965; d. Phyllis Anne (Helsel) Radugge. BS in Bilog. Scis., Ohio State U., 1989, MA in Sci. Edn., 1994. Cert. tchr., Ohio; comprehensive sci., biology sci. gen. sci. Tchr. integrated 7th and 8th grade sci. Wynford Middle Sch., Bucyrus, Ohio, 1989-93; tchr. tech. biology and integrated 8th grade sci. Ridgedale Jr./Sr. H.S., Marion, Oho, 1993-94, tech. chemistry and integrated 8th grade sci., 1994-95; tchr. biology, chemistry, tech. biology Teays Valley H.S., Asheville, Ohio, 1995-96. Cons. Tech.-Prep. Consortium, Marion, 1993-95, Marion County Schs., 1993-95, Buckeye Assessment Teams in Sci., Columbus, 1995—; mem. math-sci. adv. subcom. Ctrl. Ohio Regional Profl. Devel. Ctr., Columbus, 1995—; instr. Project Discovery, Columbus, 1995—; tchr. biology, chemistry Tech. Prep II Teays Valley H.S., Ashville, Ohio, 1995—; coach high sch. girls track, high sch. cross country Teays Valley Schs., Ashville, 1995—. Grantee Project Discovery, Columbus, 1991; intern Young Exptl. Scientist C.O.S.I., Columbus, 1991, 92. Mem. Nat. Sci. Tchrs. Assn., Sci. Elem. Coun. Ohio (presenter conf. 1995-96), Ohio State Univ. Alumni, Phi Delta Kappa. Republican. Lutheran. Home: 1039 Vernon Rd Bexley OH 43209-2467 Office: Teays Valley Schs SR 752 Ashville OH 43103

SCHILLING, KATHERINE LEE TRACY, retired principal; b. Mitchell, S.D., May 31, 1925; d. Ernest Benjamin and Mary Alice (Courier) Tracy; BA, Dakota Wesleyan U., 1947; MA, U. S.D., 1957; postgrad. U. Wyo., U. Nebr., Kearney State Coll.; m. Clarence R. Schilling, Oct. 14, 1951; 1 child, Keigh Leigh. Tchr. elem. and secondary schs., also colls., S.D. and Nebr. Mem. staff S.D. Girls' State, 1950-51; mem. S.D. Gov.'s Com. on Library, Nebr. Gov.'s Com. on Right to Read; prin. Mitchell (S.D.) Christian Sch., 1987-94; ret., 1994. Recipient Outstanding Tchr. award S.D. High Sch. Speech Tchrs., 1966. Mem. NEA, Nebr., Thurston County (pres.) edn. assns., Winnebago Tchrs. Assn., Delta Kappa Gamma. Clubs: Internat. Toastmistress (internat. dir. 1963-65, Mitchell Toastmistress of Year 1959), Order Eastern Star. Contbr. articles to profl. jours., also poetry. Home: 39 S Harmon Dr PO Box 578 Mitchell SD 57301-0578

SCHILLING, RHONDA CHRISTINE, music educator; b. Ithaca, N.Y., Nov. 8, 1968; d. Frederick Erle Chalone and Joy Frances (Lanphear) Toscano. MusB, U. Ill., 1990, MusM, 1991. Grad. tchg. asst. U. Ill., Champaign, 1990-91; gen. music tchr., choir dir. St. Matthew's Sch., Champaign, 1991-92; keyboard instr., music history and midi tech. Wayland Acad., Beaver Dam, Wis., 1992-95; program assoc. Wis. Sch. Music Assn., 1995; K-5 music tchr. Madison (Wis.) Sch. Dist., 1999—. Pvt. piano tchr., Madison; freelance arranger Hal Leonard Corp., Milw., 1995; dir. music Immaculate Heart of Mary Ch., Monona, Wis., 1997. Recorded Within the Garden compact disc, 1997. Pianist St. James Luth. Ch., Verona, Wis., 1998— Mem. NAFE, Music Educators Nat. Conf., Music Theory Midwest, Phi Kappa Phi, Pi Kappa Lambda, Golden Key. Avocations: reading, walking, computer technology, Tae Kwon Do. Home: 210 S Shuman St Verona WI 53593-1345 Office: Thoreau Elem Sch 3870 Nakoma Rd Madison WI 53711

SCHILLING, WARNER ROLLER, political scientist, educator; b. Glendale, Calif., May 23, 1925; s. Jule Frederick and Pauline Frances de Berri (Warner) S.; m. Jane Pierce Metzger, Jan. 27, 1951 (dec. Nov. 1983); children: Jonathan, Frederick. AB, Yale U., 1949, MA, 1951, PhD, 1954. Research fellow Center Internat. Studies, Princeton U., 1953-54; asst. prof. internat. relations Mass. Inst. Tech., 1957-58; mem. faculty Columbia, 1954—, prof. govt., 1967-73, James T. Shotwell prof. internat. relations, 1973—; dir. Inst. War and Peace Studies, 1976-86. Cons., occasional lectr. in field. Co-author: Strategy, Politics and Defense Budgets, 1962, European Security and the Atlantic System, 1973, American Arms and a Changing Europe, 1973; Contbr. numerous articles to jours. Served with USAAF, 1944-46. Guggenheim fellow, 1964-65; resident fellow Bellagio Study and Conf. Center, 1975 Mem. Internat. Inst. Strategic Studies, Council Fgn. Relations. Clubs: Leonia Democratic. Home: 496 Park Ave Leonia NJ 07605-1243 Office: 420 W 118th St New York NY 10027-7213

SCHILLING-NORDAL, GERALDINE ANN, retired secondary school educator; b. Springfield, Mass., Feb. 4, 1935; d. Robert Milton and Helen Veronica (Ewald) Schilling; m. Reidar Johannes Nordal. BS, Boston U., 1956, MEd, 1957; postgrad., Springfield Coll., Anna Maria Coll. Tchr. art Agawam (Mass.) Jr. H.S., 1957-58, Agawam H.S., 1958—2003, K-12 art acad. coord., 1995-96, head art dept., 1970-95. Instr. oil painting univ. ext. course Agawam Night Sch., 1957-58; instr. creative arts Agawam Evening Sch., 1973-80. Active Agawam Town Report Com., 1967-77, Agawam Hist. Commn., 1979-87, Agawam Arts and Humanities Com., 1979-85, Agawam Minerva Davis Libr. Study Com., 1987-88, Agawam Cultural Coun., 1994-97; sec. Agawam Town Beautification Com., 1974-87; mem. town tchrs. rep. Agawam Bicentennial Com., 1975-77; chmn. 40th anniversary St. John the Evangelist Ch., Agawam, 1986, co-chmn. 50th anniversary com., 1996, mem. renovation com., 1983; decoration chmn. town-wide Halloween parties, Agawam, 1971-93; recruiter Miss Agawam Pageant; appeal vol. Cath. Charity, 1995-2002; mem. Agawam Cath. Womens Club, 1995—, banquet com., 1997, 99, co-chmn., 2003-04. Mem. NEA, Agawam Edn. Assn. (sec. 1970-74, 76-77, h.s. addition dedication com. 1998-99, scholarship com., 1997, Agawam Tchrs. Wall of Fame for 45 Yrs. Svc. 2002), Hampden County Tchrs. Assn., Mass. Tchrs. Assn., Mass. Art Edn. Assn., Nat. Art Edn. Assn., New Eng. Art Edn. Assn., Am. Assn. Ret. Persons, Mass. Cath. Order Foresters, West Springfield Neighborhood House Alumni Assn. (pres. 1966, advisor 1968), West Springfield H.S. Alumni Assn. (3d v.p. 1968-70, 1st v.p. 1970-71, pres. 1972-74), Boston U. Alumni Club Springfield Area (organizer area giving campaigns 1957-62, class agt. 1985—, mem. area scholarship com. 1995—), Retired Educators Assn. of Mass., Hampden W. Chap., Am. Legion (life), Zeta Chi Delta (pres. 1955-56), Delta Kappa Gamma (Alpha chpt., art chairperson, reservation chmn. art work and hist. archives, hospitality 50th and 60th ann. com.). Office: PO Box 291 Agawam MA 01001

SCHILLINGS, DENNY LYNN, retired history educator, educational and grants consultant; b. Mt. Carmel, Ill., June 28, 1947; s. Grady Lynn and Mary Lucille (Walters) S.; m. Karen Krek; children: Denise, Corinne. AA, Wabash Valley Coll., 1967; BEd, Ea. Ill. U., 1969, MA in History, 1972; MA in Adminstrn., Govs. State U., 1996; postgrad., Ill. State U., No. Ill. U. Grad. asst. dept. history Ea. Ill. U., Charleston, 1969; tchr. Edwards County High Sch., Albion, Ill., 1969-70, Sheldon (Ill.) High Sch., 1971-73, Homewood-Flossmoor (Ill.) High Sch., 1973—2003, grants and devel. mgr., 1994—2003; supr. History dept. Coll. Liberal Arts and Scis, No. Ill. U., Dekalb; ret., 2003. Participant, con. Atlantic Coun. U.S. and NATO, Washington, 1986, Internat. Soviet-U.S. Textbook Project Conf., Racine, Wis., 1987; moderator Soviet-U.S. Textbook Study: Final Report, Dallas, 1987; chair history content adv. com. Ill. Tchr. Certification Requirements Com. 1986; mem. Ill. State Bd. Edn., Com. to Establish Learner Outcomes, 1984, Joint Task Force on Admission Requirements Ill. State Bd. on Higher Edn., 1986—; mem. adv. com. for Jefferson Found. Sch. Programs, 1987-90, Ill. State Bd. Edn.'s Goals Assessment Adv. Com., 1987-90; chair Ill. Learning Standards Project, 1996-97. Author: (with others) Economics, 1986, The Examination in Social Studies, 1989, Links Across Time and Place: A World History, 1990, Illinois Government Text, 1990, 99, 2003, Challenge of Freedom, 1990; author: The Living Constitution, 1991, 3d edit., 2002; co-editor: Teaching the Constition, 1987; reviewer, cons. for ednl. instns. and organizations; chair editorial bd. Social Edn., 1983; contbg. editor Social Studies Tchr., 1987-88. Mem. steering com. Homewood-Flossmoor High Sch. Found., 1983-84; elected bd. edn. Homewood Elem. Dist. 153, 1999—. Mem. NEA, Am. Hist. Assn. (James Harvey Robinson prize com. 1990-91), Ill. Coun. Social Studies (v.p. 1981, editor newsletter 1979-84, pres. 1983), Ill. Edn. Assn. (Gt. Lakes coord. com. 1982-83), Nat. Coun. Social Studies (publs. bd. 1983-86, bd. dirs. 1987-90, 94-96, exec. com. 1989-90, chair conf. com. 1989-90, pres. 1993-94, program planning com. 1989, 91), Phi Alpha Theta. Avocations: computers, reading. Home and Office: 18447 Aberdeen St Homewood IL 60430-3525 E-mail: dschillingsl@comcast.net.

SCHILPLIN, YVONNE WINTER, educational administrator; b. Mahnomen, Minn., May 26, 1946; d. Milo Joseph and Lucille Margaret (Schoenborn) Winter; m. Frederick Colegrove Schilplin III, Dec. 30, 1975; children: Frederick IV, Chad. Student, St. Cloud State U., 1964. Retail fashion buyer Fandel's Dept. Store, St. Cloud, Minn., 1968-75; mem. graduation standards exec. com. Minn. Dept. Edn., Mpls., 1988—; mem. Annandale (Minn.) Sch. Bd. Dist. 876, 1988-94, chmn., 1991-94; co-owner, cons. Am. Rsch. Grant Writing & Tng., Inc., 1993—. Edn. chmn. Minn. PTA, Mpls., 1989-91; mem. legis. com. St. Cloud Reading Rm., 1991-92, v.p., 1996—; liaison for sch. bd. Annandale PTA, 1989-94; co-chmn. Living Wax Mus., Minn. Pioneer Park, 1991-92; mem. facilities planning com. Sch. Dist. 876, mid. sch. steering com. Recipient Minn. Sch. Bd. Mem. of Yr., 1994. Mem. Stearns County Hist. Soc., Minn. Sci. Mus., St. Cloud Country Club. Avocations: reading, tennis, herb and flower garden, fishing, fashion modeling. Home: RR 3 Annandale MN 55302-9803

SCHILSKY, RICHARD LEWIS, oncologist, researcher; b. N.Y.C., June 6, 1950; s. Murray and Shirley (Cohen) S.; m. Cynthia Schum, Sept. 24, 1977; children: Allison, Meredith. BA cum laude, U. Pa., Phila., 1971; MD with honors, U. Chgo., 1975. Diplomate Nat. Bd. Med. Examiners, Am. Bd. Internal Medicine (subspecialty med. oncology); lic. physician, Mo., Ill. Intern, resident medicine Parkland Meml. Hosp., Southwestern Med. Sch., Dallas, 1975-77; clin. assoc. medicine br. and clin. pharmacology br. Divsn. Cancer Treatment, Nat. Cancer Inst., Bethesda, Md., 1977-80, cancer expert clin. pharmacology br., 1980-81; asst. prof. dept. internal medicine U. Mo. Sch. Medicine, Columbia, 1981-84; asst. prof. dept. medicine U. Chgo. Pritzker Sch. Medicine and Michael Reese Med. Ctrs., 1984-86, assoc. prof. dept. medicine, 1986-89; assoc. dir. joint sect. hematology and med. oncology U. Chgo. and Michael Reese Med. Ctrs., 1986-89; assoc. prof. dept. medicine, assoc. dir. sect. U. Chgo. Pritzker Sch. Medicine, 1989-91, prof. dept. medicine sect. hematology-oncology, 1991—; dir. U. Chgo. Cancer Rsch. Ctr., 1991-99; chmn. Cancer and Leukemia Group B, Chgo., 1995—; assoc. dean clin. rsch. biol. scis. divsn. U. Chgo., 1999—. Vivian Saykaly vis. prof. oncology McGill U., 1992; sci. com. Internat. Congress on Anti-Cancer Chemotherapy, 2002; adv. panel on hematologic and neoplastic disease U.S. Pharmacopeial Conv., 1991-95; bd. dirs. Assn. Am. Cancer Insts., 1995-99; cancer ctr. support grant rev. com. Nat. Cancer Inst., NIH, 1992-95; expert panel on advances in cancer treatment, 1992-93; mem. Cancer Ctrs. Working Group, 1996-97; oncologic drugs adv. com. FDA, 1996-2000, chmn., 1999-2000; mem. NCI Clin. Trials Implementation com., 1997-98; bd. scientific advisors Nat. Cancer Inst., 1999—. Mem. editl. bd. Investigational New Drugs, 1988-95, Jour. Clin. Oncology, 1990-93, Contemporary Oncology, 1991-95, Jour. Cancer Rsch. and Clin. Oncology, 1991—, Seminars in Oncology, 1997—; assoc. editor Clin. Cancer Rsch., 1994—, Cancer Therapeutics, 1997-99, Cancer, 2000—; contbr. articles to profl. jours., chpts. to books. With USPHS, 1977-80. Recipient Spl. Advancement for Performance award VA, 1983, Fletcher Scholar award Cancer Rsch. Found., 1989; grantee VA, 1981-87, Am. Cancer Soc., 1983-86, 92-95, Ill. Cancer Coun., 1985-86, Michael Reese Inst. Coun., 1985-86, Nat. Cancer Inst., 1987, 88-90, Burroughs-Wellcome Co., 1987-88, NIH/Nat. Cancer Inst., 1988— Fellow ACP; mem. AAAS, Am. Soc. Clin. Oncology (chmn. pub. rels. com. 1994-96, bd. dirs. 2002-), Am. Assn. Cancer Rsch. (chmn. Ill. state legis. com. 1992—), Am. Fedn. Clin. Rsch. (senator Midwest sect. 1983-84, councilor 1983-86, chmn.-elect 1987-88, chmn. 1988-89), Am. Cancer Soc. (bd. dirs. Ill. divsn. 1997—), Am. Assn. Cancer Edn., Am. Soc. Clin. Pharmacology and Therapeutics, Ctrl. Soc. Clin. Rsch., N.Y. Acad. Scis., Assn. Am. Cancer Insts. (bd. dirs. 1995-99), Chgo. Soc. Internal Medicine, Sigma Xi, Alpha Epsilon Delta, Alpha Omega Alpha. Office: U Chgo Biol Scis Divsn 5841 S Maryland Ave Chicago IL 60637-1463 E-mail: rs27@uchicago.edu.

SCHIMMEL, PAUL REINHARD, biochemist, biophysicist, educator; b. Hartford, Conn., Aug. 4, 1940; s. Alfred E. and Doris (Hudson) S.; m. Judith F. Ritz, Dec. 30, 1961; children: Kirsten, Katherine. AB, Ohio Wesleyan U., 1962; postgrad., Tufts U. Sch. Medicine, 1962-63, Mass. Inst. Tech., 1963-65, Cornell U., 1965-66, Stanford U., 1966-67, U. Calif., Santa Barbara, 1975-76; PhD, Mass. Inst. Tech., 1966; DSc (hon.), Ohio Wesleyan U., 1996. Asst. prof. biology and chemistry MIT, 1967-71, assoc. prof., 1971-76, prof. biochemistry and biophysics, 1976-92, John D. and Catherine T. MacArthur prof. biochemistry and biophysics, 1992-97; prof. Scripps Rsch. Inst. and The Skaggs Inst. for Chem. Biology, 1997-2001, Ernest and Jean Hahn prof. molecular biology and chemistry, 2001—. Mem. study sect. on physiol. chemistry NIH, 1975-79; indsl. cons. on enzymes and recombinant DNA; bd. dirs. Cubist Pharms., 1993-2002, Repligen Corp., Alkermes, Inc. Author: (with C. Cantor) Biophysical Chemistry, 3 vols., 1980; mem. editl. bd. Archives Biochemistry, Biophysics, 1976-80, Nucleic Acids Rsch., 1976-80, Jour. Biol. Chemistry, 1977-82, Biopolymers, 1979-88, Internat. Jour. Biol. Macromolecules, 1983-89, Trends in Biochem. Scis., 1984—, Biochemistry, 1989—, Accounts of Chem. Rsch., 1989-94, European Jour. Biochemistry, 1991-96, Protein Sci., 1991-94, Proc. Nat. Acad. Scis., 1993-99. Alfred P. Sloan fellow, 1970-72; recipient Emily M. Gray award Biophys. Soc., 2000. Fellow AAAS, Am. Acad. Arts and Scis. (chmn. Amory prize com. 1995-96); mem. NAS (class II biochemistry sect. rep. 1995-96), Am. Philos. Soc., Am. Chem. Soc. (Pfizer award 1978, chmn. divsn. biol. chemistry 1984-85) Am. Soc. for

Biochemistry and Molecular Biology (chmn. nominating com. 1990, awards com. 1995-97), Ribonucleic Acid Soc. Office: The Scripps Rsch Inst 10550 N Torrey Pines Rd La Jolla CA 92037-1000

SCHIMMELFENNIG, LADONA BETH, special education educator, management analysis and compliance specialist; b. Tulsa, Apr. 29, 1948; d. James Wyatt and Ladona Babe (Robertson) Holder; m. Bryan Anapuni Schimmelfennig, July 4, 1988; 1 child, Malia M. BS in Spl. Edn., U. Tulsa, 1969; MA in Edn., Pepperdine U., Malibu, Calif., 1976. Tchr. asst. Sarasota (Fla.) Head Start, 1968; spl. edn. tchr. S.E.C.O., Honolulu, 1969-70, Monroe Jr. High Sch., Tulsa, 1970-73, Honolulu Community Action prog., Project Head Start, 1973-76; spl. edn. coord. Oahu Head Start, Honolulu, 1976-77; dir. spl. edn. Govt. of Am. Samoa, Pago Pago, 1977-79; ednl. specialist II for emotionally handicapped Dept. Edn., Oahu, Hawaii, 1984; dist. edn. specialist II for spl. edn. Windward Oahu Dept. Edn., Hawaii, 1979—2002; mgmt. analysis and civil rights compliance specialist Hawaii Dept. Edn., Honolulu, 2002—. Dir. 1st Am. Samoa Spl. Olympics, 1978, 79. Contbr. articles to profl. jours. Bd. dirs., pub. rels. chmn. Hawaii Spl. Olympics, 1980-84; bd. dirs. Spl. Parent Info. Network, Wai Nani Way Hoeke; sec.-treas. Pacific Basin Consortium, 1977-79; adv. panel on edn. handicapped children Southwestern Reg. Deaf-Blind Ctr., 1977-79, others in past. Mem. Coun. for Exceptional Children (chpt. pres. 1969), Nat. Assn. State Dirs. Spl. Edn., Nat. Info. for Spl. Edn. Mgmt., S.W. Deaf/Blind Assn. Avocations: aerobics, jogging, scuba diving, shopping. Home: 739 W Hind Dr Honolulu HI 96821-1805 Office: Hawaii Dept Edn Queen Liliuokalani Bldg 1390 Miller St Honolulu HI 96813

SCHINDLER, BARBARA FRANCOIS, education educator; b. Chgo., Oct. 28, 1935; d. Harry and Nellie Irene (Lewis) Francois; m. Charles A. Schindler, Jan. 29, 1955; children: Marian, Susan, Neal. BA, U. Tex., 1960; MA, U. Okla., 1975, PhD, 1984. Cert. tchr., Okla. Tchr. Norman (Okla.) Pub. Schs., 1972-86; exec. dir. Dem. Party Okla., Oklahoma City, 1986-87; tchr. Moore (Okla.) Pub. Schs., 1987-88; curriculum supr. Oklahoma City Pub. Schs., 1988-96; adj. prof. U. Okla., 1996—. Mem. sch. bd. Moore-Norman Vocat.-Tech. Sch., Norman, 1979-83; bd. dirs. Law-Related Edn., Oklahoma City; chair Okla. Close-Up, Oklahoma City, 1990-92; community planner U.S.-Japan Ednl. Initiative, 1993. Contbr. chpt. to book For the Man, the Myth and the Era, 1987; author: (supplementary materials) The Oklahoma Story, 1980. Nat. Del. Dem. Party Conv., N.Y.C., 1980, Atlanta, 1988; county party chair Dem. Party, Cleveland County, 1985-87. Recipient Excellence in Teaching award Profl. Educators, 1975; Fulbright fellow, 1992, 97, NEH fellow, 1988, 96; grantee Japan Study Tour Found., 1990. Mem. ASCD, Nat. Coun. for Social Studies (com. mem. 1988—, pres. 1999), Nat. Coun. for Econ. Edn. (bd. dirs. 1990—), Okla. Edn. Assn. (bd. dirs. 1978-85), Phi Delta Kappa. Avocations: bridge, hiking. Home: 2000 Morgan Dr Norman OK 73069-6525

SCHINDLER, LAURA ANN, piano teacher, accompanist; b. St. Louis, Aug. 17, 1943; d. Francis Joseph and Alice Binkley (Hurtgen) Schindler; m. John Charles Noto, Dec. 27, 1986. BM cum laude, Fontbonne Coll., St. Louis, 1970; MAT, Washington U., St. Louis, 1972; student, Ecole Normale de Musique, Paris, 1973-74. Nat. cert. tchr. of music; cert. Orff Schulwerk, Mozarteum Acad., Salzburg, Austria. Organist, choir dir. St. John's Basilica, St. Louis, 1971-73; piano tchr. Cmty. Music Sch., St. Louis, 1971-73, St. Louis Inst. Music, 1972-73; accompanist Robert McFerrin, Sr., N.Y.C., Chgo.,Springfield, St. Louis, 1974-77; piano tchr., Orff instr. St. Louis Conservatory, 1974-82; pvt. piano tchr. and accompanist St. Louis, 1982—. Vocal accompanist Affiliate Artist Program, St. Louis, 1977; accompanist MTNA West. Ctr. Divsn. Auditions, St. Louis, 1979, Forest Park C.C. Chorus, 1980-82, Ethical Soc. Chorus, 1980-83, Washington U. Music Sch., 1970-72; adjudicator piano competitions, Mo. and Ill., 1978—; clinician Piano Tchr. Workshops, Mo./Ill., 1979—. Contbr. articles to profl. jours.; performer Today Show, NBC, 1976, Capella Soloists Sunset concerts, 1976, Bicentennial Horizons of Am. Music, 1976, Rubinstein Music Club Meetings, 1997—, Benefit for Mo. Com. for Firearms Safety, 1982; performer, composer Am. Composers Concert, 1976. Recipient Mid-Am. Disting. Ind. Piano Tchr. award N.W., 1997, Disting. Piano Tchr. award Cedarhurst Chamber Music and Beethoven Soc., 1992; Acad. fellow Washington U., 1970-72. Mem.: Piano Tchrs. Round Table (pres. 1999—2001, exec. bd. mem. 2003—), Musical Diversions Soc. (bd. dirs. 1995—), St. Louis Area Music Tchrs. Assn. (v.p. for programs 1986—88, pres. 1988—92, chair nominating com. 1996—2000), Rubinstein Music Club. Democrat. Mem. Ethical Soc. Avocations: travel, walking, reading, eastern european folk dancing, ballroom dancing. Home: 7567 Lindbergh Dr Saint Louis MO 63117-2173

SCHIPANI, SISTER KATHLEEN MONICA, special education educator; b. Phila., Apr. 21, 1955; d. Louis and Patricia Ann (Murdock) S. BA in Theology and English, Immaculata (Pa.) Coll., 1980; MA in Edn., Trenton (N.J.) State U., 1989; postgrad., Gallaudet U., Washington, 1990. Joined Immaculate Heart of Mary Sisters, Roman Cath. Ch., 1973; cert. tchr., spl. edn. tchr., Pa. Elem. tchr., dir. religious spl. edn. St. Thomas More Sch., Arlington, Va., 1976-79; jr. high sch. tchr., dir. religious spl. edn. St. Martin of Tours, Phila., 1980-85; jr. high sch. tchr. Cathedral Sch., Raleigh, N.C., 1985-87; tchr. spl. edn. St. William Sch., Phila., 1987-95; dir. religious edn. for deaf Archdiocese of Phila., 1995—2001, adminstr. dept. disabilities and deaf ministry, 2001—. Recipient Most Disting. Cath. Educator, Archdiocese of Phila., 1991; UNICO grantee, 1988. Mem. Coun. Exceptional Children, N.E. Phila. Learning Disabilities Assn. (founding, profl. advisor 1989—), Kappa Delta Pi (alumni chpt.). Avocations: art work, tennis, jogging. Office: 222 N 17th St Philadelphia PA 19103

SCHIPPA, JOSEPH THOMAS, JR., psychologist, educational consultant, hypnotherapist; b. North Tarrytown, N.Y., Mar. 29, 1957; s. Joseph Thomas Sr. and Viola Elizabeth (De Marco) S. MusB, Manhattanville Coll., 1978, MA in Teaching, 1981; PD, Fordham U., 1989, MSEd, 1995, PhD, 1971; Dr of Clin. Hypnotherapy, Am. Inst. Hypnotherapy, 1991. Lic. psychologist; cert. sch. psychologist, clin. mental health counselor, addictions counselor, hypnotherapist, Nat. Cert. Counselor. Tchr. Sch. of St. Gregory the Gt., Harrison, N.Y., 1978-81; learning specialist Blind Brook High Sch., Rye Brook, N.Y., 1981-83; tchr. spl. edn. Ossining (N.Y.) High Sch., 1983-88; clin. intern in psychology Westchester County Med. Ctr. Psychiat. Inst., Valhalla, N.Y., 1988-89; sch. psychologist Putnam Valley (N.Y.) Elem. Sch., 1989—; pres. Learning Alternatives, Sleepy Hollow, N.Y.; psychologist Hudson Behavioral Health, Sleepy Hollow, 1995—. Theodore Presser Found. scholar, 1976, 77, 78. Mem. APA, Am. Bd. Hypnotherapy, Nat. Assn. Sch. Psychologists, Orton Dyslexia Soc., Assn. for Transpersonal Psychology, Nat. Assn. Alcohol and Drug Addiction Counselors, Am. Mental Health Counselors Assn. Avocation: music. Office: Learning Alternatives 239 N Broadway Ste 6 Sleepy Hollow NY 10591-2654

SCHIRBER, ANNAMARIE RIDDERING, speech and language pathologist, educator; b. Somerset County, N.J., Dec. 18, 1941; d. Pieter C. and Marie Louise (Kerk) Riddering; m. Eric R. Schirber, Aug. 25, 1960; children: Stefan Rene, Ashley Brooke. BA in Speech and Hearing Therapy, Rutgers U., 1964; MA in Edn. of Deaf and Hard of Hearing, Smith Coll., 1968; postgrad., Rutgers U., 1987-93. Cert. tchr. of deaf, hard of hearing, spl. edn., speech correctionist, speech-lang pathologist, N.J. Speech therapist Manatee County Bd. Edn., Bradenton, Fla., 1968-69; speech-lang. specialist Lawrence Twp. Pub. Schs., Lawrenceville, NJ, 1969—2002, Montgomery Twp. Bd. Edn., Skillman, NJ, 2003—, Rock Brook Sch., Skillman, 2003—. Adj. instr. comm. dept. Trenton (N.J.) State Coll., 1983-87; vis. lectr. Rutgers U., New Brunswick, 1993. Author: Teaching Auditory Processing Skills to Children, 1994; co-author: (with Erica Winebrenner) Speech Activities for Children, 1994, Language Activities to Teach Children at Home, 1994. Mem. exec. com. Women's Coll. Symposium, Princeton, N.J., 1982-84; mem. nat. alumnae admissions com. Smith Coll., Northampton, Mass., 1984-86. Grantee Lawrence Twp. Bd. Edn., 1973, 89, 90, Lawrence Twp. Edn. Found., 1999, 2001. Mem. N.J. Speech-Lang. and Hearing Assn. (legis. com. 1996), Ctrl. Jersey Speech-Lang. and Hearing Assn. (exec. com. 1996—, v.p. 1985, pres. 1986-87), Princeton Area Smith Coll. Club (exec. com. 1996—, pres. 1998-2000). Home: 10 Sycamore Ln Skillman NJ 08558-2013

SCHIRMER, BARBARA ROSE, special education educator; b. N.Y.C., Dec. 23, 1948; d. Jack and Bella (Schiller) Edberg; m. John M. Schirmer, Aug. 22, 1971; children: Alison, Todd. BS, U. Buffalo, 1970; MEd, U. Pitts., 1971; EdD, U. Buffalo, 1983. Cert. spl. edn. tchr., N.Y. Tchr. W.Va. Sch. for the Deaf, Romney, 1971-72; tchr. Boston Sch. for the Deaf, Mass., 1972-74; asst. prof. Univ. Wis., Milw., 1982-83; assoc. prof. Lewis and Clark Coll., Portland, Oreg., 1985—97, assoc. dean, 1993—97; chair and prof. Kent State U., 1997—2001; dean, prof. Miami U., Oxford, Ohio, 2001—. Author: Language and Literary Development in Children Who Are Deaf, 2000, Psychological, Social and Educational Dimensions of Deafness, 2001; mem. editl. adv. bd. Jour. Deaf Studies and Deaf Edn., Jour. Literacy Rsch., Tchg. Exceptional Children; contbr. articles. Mem.: Internat. Reading Assn., Am. Ednl. Rsch. Assn., Coun. Exceptional Children, Con. Am. Instn. Deaf. Home: PO Box 623 Oxford OH 45056-0623 Office: Miami U McGuffey Hall Oxford OH 45056

SCHIRMER, DAVID WAYNE, coach; b. Sharon, Pa., Jan. 3, 1956; s. David Clemens and Carol Joy (Sager) S.; m. Linda Jo Gulnac, June 21, 1986; children: Cameron, Lynda, Grant. BS in Agr. Edn., Pa. State U., 1978. Svc. technician Sears Roebuck, Sharon, 1974-79, Sperry Rand, Greenvale, Pa., 1973; lab technician Pa. State U., Sharon, 1974-78; tchr. Clarion-Limestone High Sch., Strattanville, Pa., 1978—. Computer cons. Schirmer Computer Svc., Summerville, Pa., 1986—; athletic dir. Clarion-Limestone, Strattanville, 1987-96; asst. coach track and field Clarion U., 1996-1999, gold coach, 1999-2001, football coach, 2002—. Contbr. articles to profl. jours. Mem. com. Young Democrats, Mercer County, Pa., 1978. Named Tchr. in Space NASA, 1985, Young Tchr. of Yr, Clarion Rotary, 1981. Mem. Pa. State Edn. Assn., Pa. State Athletic Dirs. Assn., Alpha Tau Alpha, Gamma Sigma Delta. Lutheran. Avocations: hunting, fishing, music, electronics, sports. Home: 1018 Aaron Rd Summerville PA 15864-3606 Office: Clarion Limestone Schs PO Box 285 Strattanville PA 16258-0285

SCHKADE, ANTHONY ROLAND, academic administrator; b. Shackelford County, Tex., Aug. 10, 1941; s. August Paul Schkade and Margaret Lenore Mickan; m. Mary Luella Hett, July 29, 1972; children: Lisa Susan, Todd Ryan. Diploma, Concordia Luth. Coll., Austin, Tex., 1961; BSE, Concordia U., Seward, Neb., 1963; MEd, Concordia U., 1972; PhD, U. Nebr., 1989. Tchr. elem. sch., youth dir. St. Paul Luth. Sch., San Antonio, 1963-67; asst. registrar Concordia Tchrs. Coll., Seward, Nebr., 1968-72; registrar Barat Coll., Lake Forest, Ill., 1972-76; asst. dir. registration and records U. Nebr., Lincoln, 1976—. Mem. Bethesda Luth. Home for the Retarded Assn., Wis., 1976—; mem. bd. elders Christ Luth. Ch., 1979-90; mem. Good Shepherd Luth. Ch., 1999—. Mem. Am. Assn. Collegiate Registrars and Admissions Officers (placement com., past pres. Nebr. chpt.), U. Assn. for Adminstrv. Devel. Democrat. Avocations: home repairs, wood working, socializing, U. Nebr. football fan. Home: 6531 Tanglewood Ln Lincoln NE 68516-2357 Office: U Nebr 109 Adminstrn Bldg 17th and R St Lincoln NE 68588-0416 E-mail: aschkade@unl.edu., schkade@navix.net.

SCHLACHTER, DEBORAH BRISTOW, special education educator, consultant; b. Ajo, Ariz., Dec. 21, 1957; d. John Edward Jr. and Anne Elizabeth (Butler) Bristow; m. James Martin Schlachter Jr., July 25, 1981; children: James Martin, Katie Elizabeth, Joshua Timothy, Jacob Leslie, Jean Nicole. BE, Stephen F. Austin, 1981; MEd, U. N. Tex., 1991. Cert. tchr., Tex. Pvt. practice spl. needs tutor, Dallas/Ft. Worth, 1981-91; pvt. practice family in home child care Lancaster, Tex., 1982-89; instr., coord. Cedar Valley Coll., Lancaster, 1989—; tchr. DeSoto (Tex.) Ind. Sch. Dist., 1990-91; kindergarten tchr. Dallas Ind. Sch. Dist., 1991-92, ESL tchr. 1st grade, 1992-93; 4-6th grade Montessori tchr. Dallas Pub. Sch., 1993-95. Co-leader strategic planning Lancaster Ind. Sch. Dist., 1992-93. Co-editor: Resource Handbook for Educators on American Indians, 1993-94. Vol. tutor Women's Halfway House, Nacogdoches, Tex., 1980-81; trainer in spl. needs children PTA, Dallas-Ft. Worth, 1990—, active Dallas-Lancaster, 1984—; voting mem. Dallas Native Am. Parent Adv. Com., 1992-94; vol. Harry Stone Montessori Acad. PTA, v.p., 1995-96, 96-97, legis. chmn., 1997-98, mem. sch. ctr. edn. team; leader Harry Stone Montessori Ptnrs. in Edn.; leadership trainer Tex. PTA, 1996—; mem. mem. to mem. network Nat. PTA, 1997—. Mem. ASCD, AAUW, Nat. Assn. Edn. Young Children, Nat. Indian Edn. Assn., Nat. Mus. Am. Indian, Am. Montessori Soc., So. Assn. Children Under Six, Dallas Assn. Edn. Young Children, Native Am. Rights Funds, Am. Indian Resource and Edn. Coalition. Episcopalian. Avocations: reading, horseback riding, swimming, cooking, travel. Home: 532 Laurel St Lancaster TX 75134-3220

SCHLAGETTER, JEANNE LOUISE, elementary education educator; b. Piqua, Ohio, Nov. 15, 1947; d. Paul Edwin and Bernadette (Hoying) Gaier; m. Mark Thomas Schlagetter, Dec. 13, 1969; children: Monica, Kari, Travis, Blaine, Lindsay. BS in Edn., Bowling Green State U., 1970; MS in Edn., U. Dayton, 1992. Cert. elem. tchr., Ohio. Sub. tchr. Sidney (Ohio) City Schs., 1970; elem. tchr. Piqua City Schs., 1970-71; 7th-8th grade social studies tchr. Holy Angels Sch., Sidney, 1971-74; 3d grade tchr., 1974-75; 5th grade lang. arts tchr., 1977-98; 6th grade tchr., 1998—. Mem. adv. bd. Holy Angels Youth Group, Sidney, 1990-2000. Asst. coach, worker Shelby County Youth Soccer, Sidney, 1990-2002; com. chairperson, worker Sidney HS Soccer Boosters, 1990-93, 98-2002. Frank J. Gleason Ednl. Enrichment Program grantee Copeland Corp., 1989, Copeland Edn. grantee, 1993, 95, 2003; recipient Outstanding Cath. Educator award, Miami Valley Cath. Edn. Coun., 1990. Mem. Nat. Cath. Edn. Assn., Internat. Reading Assn., Ohio Cath. Edn. Assn. (program presenter 1988), Ohio Coun. Internat. Reading Assn. (Dr. Lois B. Bing Honor grant 1991), Shelby County Internat. Reading Assn. (sec. 1988-90, historian 1993-95), Newman Club (pres. 1993-94, sec. 1995-96, v.p. 2000-01), Delta Kappa Gamma (sec. 1994-96, Annie Webb Blanton scholarship 1991). Roman Cath. Avocations: reading, gardening, listening to music, family activities. Office: Holy Angels Sch 120 E Water St Sidney OH 45365-3199 E-mail: mschlagetter@woh.rr.com.

SCHLAX, SHARON LYNN NEWELL, physical education educator; b. Oxnard, Calif., Feb. 14, 1950; d. Ruth Nana (Pool) Horton; 1 child, Amber Lynn Gould. BA, Calif. Bapt. Coll., Riverside, 1971; MS, Azusa Pacific U., 1985. Cert. tchr., Calif. Tchr. phys. edn. Mission Mid. Sch., Riverside, 1971—, dept. head, 1987-95, Mira Loma Mid. Sch., Riverside, 1995—. Tchr. spl. edn. Summer Sch., Riverside County Schs., 1981—; tchr. Teens Learn Choices Mission Mid. Sch., 1986—; tennis coach; softball, track and intramural sports coach. Mem. Calif. League of Mid. Schs. Democrat. Avocations: skiing, bowling, tennis, other sports, dancing. Home: 21409 Webster Ave Perris CA 92570-7669 Office: Mira Loma Mid Sch 5051 Steve St Riverside CA 92509-3548

SCHLEEDE, LORI GERAINE, primary education educator; b. East Patchogue, N.Y., Mar. 20, 1964; d. Robert Hupfer and Sandra Jean Geraine; m. John F. Schleede, June 25, 1989. BS in Edn., Seton Hall U., 1986; MS in Edn., L.I. U., 1990. Notary public. Kindergarten tchr. So. County Sch. Dist., East Patchogue, 1988-93; pres. Cedar Key Seafood Distbrs., Inc., 1997—. Sch. rep. union-ednl. problems com. So. Country Sch. Dist., East Patchogue, mem. bldg. planning team, mem. assessment com., trainer perceptual screening; adminstr. for Head Start, Brevard County, Fla., 1994-97. Dir. programs Space Coast Early Intervention Ctr., 1997—. EDm. Internat. Reading Assn., Nat. Assn. for Edn. Young Children, Assn. for Edn. Young Children Internat., North Shore Reading Coun. (treas. 1992-93). Avocations: gardening, boating, biking, reading, photography.

SCHLEGEL, JOHN P. academic administrator; b. Dubuque, Iowa, July 31, 1943; s. Aaron Joseph and Irma Joan (Hingtgen) S. BA, St. Louis U., 1969, MA, 1970; BDiv, U. London, 1973; DPhil, Oxford U., 1977. Joined Soc. of Jesus, 1963, ordained priest Roman Cath. Ch., 1973. From asst. prof. to assoc. prof. Creighton U., Omaha, 1976-79, asst. acad. v.p., 1978-82; dean Coll. Arts and Scis. Rockhurst Coll., Kansas City, Mo., 1982-84, Marquette U., Milw., 1984-88; exec. and acad. v.p. John Carroll U., Cleve., 1988-91; pres. U. San Francisco, 1991-2000, Creighton U., Omaha, 2000—. Cons. Orgn. for Econ. Devel. and Cooperation, Paris, 1975-76. Author: Bilingualism and Canadian Policy in Africa, 1979; editor: Towards a Redefinition of Development, 1976; contbr. articles to profl. jours. Mem. Milwaukee County Arts Coun., 1986—88, Mo. Coun. on Humanities, Kansas City, 1984; trustee St. Louis U., 1985—91, Loyola U., Chgo., 1988—95, Loyola U. New Orleans, 1995—98, St. Ignatius H.S., Cleve., 1990—91, Loyola Coll. in Md., 1992—98, Xavier U., 1998—. Oxford U. grantee, 1974-76; Govt. of Can. grantee, 1977-78. Mem.: Am. Coun. Edn., Bohemian Club. Avocations: racquet sports, classical music, cooking, hiking. Office: Creighton U Office Pres 2500 Calif Plz Omaha NE 68178 E-mail: jpschlegel@creighton.edu.

SCHLEI, ROBIN, gifted and talented education coordinator; d. Sam and Dorothy (Baer) Mesirow; m. Howard Schlei; children: Stephen, Kevin. BA, Cornell U., 1970; MS, U. Wis., Milw., 1986. Cert. elem., secondary tchr., Wis. Spanish tchr., dept. chairperson Sussex-Hamilton High Sch., Sussex, Wis., 1970-74; bilingual elem. tchr. Milw. Pub. Schs., 1975-87; instr. Cardinal Stritch Coll., Milw., 1987—; K-12 gifted/talented coord. Mequon-Thiensville Sch. Dist., Mequon, Wis., 1987—. Rsch. on The Effects of First Language Syntax When Learning a Second Language. Named Mequon-Thiensville Tchr. of the Yr., 1989; recipient PLT Lura B. Carruthers scholarship. Mem. ASCD, NEA, Wis. Assn. Talented and Gifted (pres.; sec. 1993), Wis. Assn. of Educators of the Gifted/Talented (treas. 1989-92), Wis. Assn. Supervision and Curriculum Devel., Phi Beta Kappa, Pi Lambda Theta, Phi Delta Kappa. Home: 1935 W River Bend Ct Thiensville WI 53092-2925

SCHLENKER, SHIRLEY MAY, secondary education educator; b. McLaughlin, S.D., Aug. 22, 1949; d. Reuben and Ruth Ida (Hinez) S. BS in Edn., Black HIlls State U., 1972. Cert. tchr. Nebr. Phys. edn. tchr. Alliance (Nebr.) Mid. Sch., 1972—. Title IX advisor Alliance Sch. Dist., 1988-92; Sch. Cmty. Intervention Program team leader Alliance Middle Sch., 1989-94, coach basketball, volleyball, 1972-94; coach girls' tennis Alliance High Sch., 1990-2003, head softball coach, 1999-2000, asst. softball coach, 2001-02. Coord. Am. Heart Assn. Jump-a-thon, Alliance, 1979-94; officer, mem. Alliance Bus. and Profl. Women Assn., 1979-89; vol. Spl. Olympics YMCA, Alliance, 1980-90; usher First Presbyn. Ch., Alliance, 1982-92, ordained elder, 1994—. Named Outstanding Young Educator Jaycees, 1979, Young Career Woman Bus. and Profl. Women, Alliance, 1979, Outstanding Young Women Am., 1979, 80, 84. Mem. AAHPERD, Nebr. Coaches Assn., Nebr. Edn. Assn., Alpha DElta Kappa (historian, recording sec., sargent at arms). Democrat. Presbyterian. Avocations: softaball, tennis, fishing, walking, jigsaw puzzles. Home: 120 W 25th St Apt 310 Alliance NE 69301-2124

SCHLENNER, DIANE MARIE, elementary school educator; b. Phila., Aug. 31, 1971; d. Robert Joseph and Donna Catherine (Janthor) S. BEd, Bloomsburg U., 1993. Sales clk. Party Parrot, Chester, N.J., 1987-88; dietary aide Heath Village Retirement Home, Hackettstown, N.J., 1988-89; aide Campus Child Ctr., Bloomsburg, Pa., 1990; sec. First Gen. Svcs., Flanders, N.J., 1990; clk. typist Picatinny Arsenal, Rockaway, N.J., 1990-91; clk. typist, sec. sociology dept. Bloomsburg (Pa.) U., 1992. Mem. Assn. Childhood Edn. Iternat., Pa. State Edn. Assn., Psychology Assn., Kappa Delta Pi, Phi Iota Chi. Roman Catholic. Home: 21 Nestlingwood Dr Long Valley NJ 07853-3526

SCHLESINGER, CAROLE LYNN, elementary education educator; b. Detroit, May 13, 1961; d. Robert Schlesinger and Regenia Compere. Student, Kalamazoo Coll., 1981-84; BA, U. Mich., 1986; teaching cert., Eastern Mich. U., 1992. Cert. elem. tchr., Mich. Bank teller U. Mich. Credit Union, Ann Arbor, 1987; rsch. asst. dept. postgrad. medicine U. Mich., Ann Arbor, 1987; fin. planner IDS Fin. Svcs., Ann Arbor, 1988-89; telemarketer U. Mich. Telefund, Ann Arbor, 1989-90; enumerator U.S. Bur. Census, Ann Arbor, 1990; reading and math. tutor Reading and Learning Skills Ctr., Ann Arbor, 1991-92; interpreter Living Sci. Found., Wixom, Mich., 1992-94. Intern planning and mgmt. info. div. Peace Corps., Washington, 1985; intern Com. for Econ. Devel., Washington, 1985. Elder 1st Presbyn. Ch., Ann Arbor, 1992-94; canvasser, vol. Pub. Interest Rsch. group in Mich., Ann Arbor, 1986-87; trainee Groundwater Edn., Eastern Mich. U., Ypsilanti, 1991, mem. dean's adv. com., 1992; mem., group leader Ann Arbor Dems., 1984-87. Mem. ASCD, Mich. Reading Assn., Washtenaw Reading Coun., Mich. Coun. Tchrs. Math., Nat. Coun. Tchrs. Math., Mich. Sci. Tchrs. Assn., Kappa Delta Pi.

SCHLESINGER, LEONARD ARTHUR, retail executive; b. N.Y.C., July 31, 1952; s. Joe and Edith (Smukler) S.; m. Phyllis Barbara Fineman, Dec. 23, 1972; children: Rebecca, Emily, Katharine. BA, Brown U., 1972; MBA, Columbia U., 1973; DBA, Harvard U., 1979. Mgr. Procter & Gamble, Green Bay, Wis., 1973-75; asst. prof., assoc. prof. bus. sch. Harvard U., Boston, 1978-85, prof. bus. adminstrn., 1988-98; exec. v.p., COO Au Bon Pain, Inc., Boston, 1985-88; sr. v.p. Brown U., 1998-99; exec. v.p., COO Limited Brands, 1999—2003, vice chmn., 2003—. Bd. dirs. GC Companies, Chestnut Hill, Mass., 1997-2000, Borders Group, Inc., Ann Arbor, Mich., 1995-00, Limited Brands, Columbus, Ohio, 1996—, Pegasystems, Inc., Cambridge, Mass., 1996-00. Editor: Human Resources Mgmt. Jour., Jour. Mgmt. Inquiry; contbr. 40 articles to profl. jours. Jewish. Avocations: travel, music, bicycling. Home: 12 Edge of Woods New Albany OH 43054 Office: Limited Brands 3 Limited Pkwy Columbus OH 43230-1467 E-mail: lschlesinger@limitedbrands.com.

SCHLESINGER, MICHAEL EARL, atmospheric sciences educator; b. L.A., Feb. 23, 1943; s. Samuel and Berle D. (Robinson) S.; m. Barbara Joyce Brownstein, Apr. 13, 1969; children: Mylynda Beryl, Michelle Louran; m. Natalie Gennadievna Andronova, Sept. 17, 1991; 1 child, Samuel Michael. BSE, U. Calif., L.A., 1965, MSE, 1970, PhD, 1976. Engr. Ralph M. Parsons Co., L.A., 1965, 65-66, N.V. Philips, Eindhoven, The Netherlands, 1965; rsch. asst. U. Calif., L.A., 1966-69, 71-74, cons., 1971, 77; resident cons. Rand Corp., Santa Monica, Calif., 1973-76; asst. prof. atmospheric scis. Oreg. State U., Corvallis, 1976-82, assoc. prof. atmospheric scis., 1982-89; prof. atmospheric scis. U. Ill., Urbana-Champaign, 1989—. Editor: Physically-Base Modelling and Simulation of Climate and Climate Change, Parts 1 and 2, 1988, Climate-Ocean Interaction, 1990, Greenhouse-Gas-Induced Climatic Change: A Critical Appraisal of Simulations and Observations, 1991; contbr. articles to Jour. Atmospheric Sci., Nat. Geol. Rsch. and Exploration, Chemosphers, Jour. Geophys. Rsch., Nature, Eos Trans., Jour. Climate, Acta Meteorologica Sinica, Climatic Change, Climate Dynamics, Sci., Revs. Geophysics, also others. Grantee NSF, U.S. Dept. Energy; recipient Spl. Creativity award NSF, 1993, 98. Mem.: Academia Europaea (fgn. mem.). Achievements include discovery of a 65-70 year oscillation in the instrumental record of global average surface temperature. Home: 3 Holmes Ct Champaign IL 61821-6503 Office: U Ill Dept Atmospheric Scis 105S Gregory Ave Urbana IL 61801

SCHLESSINGER, ARTHUR JOSEPH, physical education educator; b. Mineola, N.Y., June 9, 1945; s. Albert J. and Gladys (Russell) S.; m. Frances D. Schulman, July 23, 1967; children: James R., Caren R. BS in Edn.,

SUNY, Cortland, 1967; MS in Health Edn., Adelphi U., 1975. Cert. phys. edn. tchr., N.Y. Tchr. phys. edn. Monroe (N.Y.) Woodbury Sch. Dist., 1967-68, Harborfields Sch. Dist., Greenlawn, N.Y., 1968-70, Comsewogue Sch. Dist., Port Jefferson Station, N.Y., 1970—, track coach, 1972—, soccer coach, 1984-95. Recipient Jack Ault Meml. award N.Y. State Sportswriters and Coaches Orgn. for Girls Sports, 1991; named Man of Yr., Port Jefferson, 1991, Section XI Track Coach of Yr., 1987, 89, 90, Section XI Soccer Coach of Yr., 1984, 86, 87, 91. Mem. AAHPED, N.Y. Assn. for Health, Phys. Edn. and Dance, N.Y. United Tchrs., Nat. Soccer Coaches Assn. Am., Port Jefferson Station Tchrs. Assn. (sr. bldg. rep. 1975-85, v.p. 1985-91), Suffolk County Track Coaches Assn. (league chair 1990—), Suffolk County Girls Soccer Coaches Assn. (pres. 1990-95). Home: 7 Cottonwood Ave Port Jefferson Station NY 11776-3110

SCHLICHTING, CATHERINE FLETCHER NICHOLSON, librarian, educator; b. Huntsville, Ala., Nov. 18, 1923; d. William Parsons and Ethel Loise (Breitling) Nicholson; m. Harry Fredrick Schlichting, July 1, 1950 (dec. Aug. 1964); children: James Dean, Richard Dale, Barbara Lynn. BS, U. Ala., 1944; MLS, U. Chgo., 1950. Asst. libr. U. Ala. Edn. Libr., Tuscaloosa, summers 1944-45; libr. Sylacauga (Ala.) H.S., 1944-45, Hinsdale (Ill.) H.S., 1945-49; asst. libr. Centre for Children's Books, U. Chgo., 1950-52; instr. reference dept. libr. Ohio Wesleyan U., Delaware, 1965-69, asst. prof., 1969-79, assoc. prof., 1979-85, prof., 1985—, curator Ohio Wesleyan Hist. Collection, 1986—, student pers. libr., 1966-72. Author: Introduction to Bibliographic Research: Basic Sources, 4th edit., 1983, Checklist of Biographical Reference Sources, 1977, Audio-Visual Aids in Bibliographic Instruction, 1976, Introduction to Bibliographic Research: Slide Catalog and Script, 1980; info. cons. (documentary) Noble Achievements: The History of Ohio Wesleyan 1942-1992, 1992, 150 Years of Excellence: A Pictorial View of Ohio Wesleyan University, 1992. Mem. adminstrv. bd. Meth. Ch., 1973-81, chmn. adminstrv. bd., 1985—, mem. coun. on ministries, 1975-81, chmn., 1975-77, trustee, 1999—2003. Recipient Algernon Sidney Sullivan award U. Ala., 1944, Hon. Alumna award Ohio Wesleyan U., 1997; Ohio Wesleyan U.-Mellon Found. grantee, 1972-73, 84-85; GLCA Tchg. fellow, 1976-77. Mem. ALA, Ohio Libr. Assn., Midwest Acad. Libr. Conf., Acad. Librs. Assn. Ohio (dir. 1984-86), AAUP (chpt. sec. 1967-68), United Meth. Women (pres. Mt. Vernon dist. 1994-97, newsletter editor 1998—), Ohio Wesleyan Woman's Club (exec. bd. 1969-72, 77-79, 81-84, pres. 1969-70, sec. 1977-78), History Club (pres. 1971-72, v.p. 1978-79) Fortnightly Club (pres. 1975-76, 87-88), Am. Field Svc. (pres. Delaware chpt. 1975-76), Kappa Delta Pi, Alpha Lambda Delta. Democrat. Home: 57 Willow Brook Way S Delaware OH 43015 Office: Ohio Wesleyan U La Beeghly Library Delaware OH 43015

SCHLITT, JEAN WANAMAKER, secondary school educator; b. Gary, Ind., July 27, 1944; d. John Edward and Louise Margarette (Bach) Wanamaker; m. Raymond John Schlitt, June 29, 1968; children: Theresa M., Carol A., Rachel L. Student, Eckerd Coll., 1962-64; BA, U. Fla., 1966, MEd, 1967. Cert. tchr., Fla. Tchr. St. John's Sch. Bd., St. Augustine, Fla., 1967-68, Alachua Sch. Bd., Gainesville, Fla., 1968-69, Okaloosa Sch. Bd., Niceville, Fla., 1985—. Councilwoman Town of Mary Esther, 1982-86. Mem. APA, Nat. Coun. Tchrs. Social Studies, Okaloosa County Edn. Assn., Delta Kappa Gamma. Home: 38 Magnolia Ave Shalimar FL 32579-1110 Office: Niceville HS 800 John Sims Pky E Niceville FL 32578-1210

SCHLOSS, MARTIN, educational administrator; b. Bklyn., May 18, 1947; s. Albert and Marian Lois (Finkelstein) S.; m. Caroline B. Adler, Mar. 8, 1970; children: Zev, Shani, Naomi. BA in Sociology, Yeshiva U., 1969, ABD in Adminstrn. and Supervision, 1990; MS in Spl. Edn., Bklyn. Coll., 1975. Ordained rabbi, Yeshiva Chaim Avraham, 1971; cert. tchr., N.Y. Coord. religious edn. Maimonides Inst., Queens, N.Y., 1969-77, coord. religious activities, 1975-77, tchr. spl. edn., 1977-78, P.S. 205 M., Bklyn., 1978-79; instr. Stern Coll., Yeshiva U., N.Y.C., 1980; dir. spl. edn. ctr. Bd. Jewish Edn., N.Y.C., 1980—, dir. divsn. sch. svcs., 1992—. Adj. undergrad. instr. Coll. of S.I., N.Y.C., 1982, grad. instr., 1992; co-founder Consortium of Spl. Edn., N.Y.C. and Washington, 1986—; co-chair Task Force on Spl. Edn., N.Y.; chair subcom. Task Force-Handicapped, N.Y.; supr. Vols. in Spl. Edn., 1989—; supr. BJE/Scheuer Family Found. Resource Rm. Program, 1987—, Three R's Program, 1981—, Vocat. Prep. Program, 1983—, Jewish Heritage Program, 1980—, Substance Abuse Prevention Program, 1985—; numerous presentations in field. Exec. editor jour. The Jewish Special Educator, 1992; contbr. articles to profl. publs.; author curriculum in field; co-editor Learning Disabilities - A Handbook for Jewish Educators, 1985, Resource Room Programming - A Handbook for Educators in Jewish Schools, 1988; contbr. articles to profl. publs.; editor Purim Kit. Mem. adv. com. N.Y. State Edn. Dept., Albany, 1988, mem. nonpub. sch. office, 1986; mem. nat. leadership commn. U.S. Dept. Edn., Washington, 1988. Recipient award of distinction Worcester (Mass.) Jewish Cmty., 1973, Ednl. Leadership award OTSAR, 1982, Sam and Rose Hurrowitz award Fedn. of Jewish Philanthropies, 1983. Mem. Coun. for Exceptional Children, Inst. for Spl. Edn. Enrichment (founder, coord. 1989—), Assn. Jewish Spl. Educators (founder, mem. editl. bd. spl. edit. 1988-92), Am. Assn. for Mentally Retarded. Democrat. Avocations: sports, computers. Home: 1831 53rd St Brooklyn NY 11204-1526 Office: Bd Jewish Edn 426 W 58th St New York NY 10019-1190

SCHLOSSBERG, FRED PAUL, elementary education educator; b. N.Y.C., May 30, 1944; s. Alexander and Mae S.; divorced; 1 child, Elan. BSBA, Boston U., 1966; M of Phys. Edn., NYU, 1983. Tchr. elem. sch. N.Y.C. Bd. Edn., 1966—. Coach local basketball team, North Bellmore, N.Y., 1988—, local baseball team, North Bellmore, 1988-92. Vol. Alcoholics Anonymous, West Hempstead, N.Y., 1987-93; tutor Literacy Vols. Am. Democrat. Avocations: physical fitness, dealer of sports and non-sports cards, comic books and memorabilia, music, travel. Home: 3678 Ocean Ave Seaford NY 11783-3432

SCHLUETER, DAVID ARNOLD, law educator; b. Sioux City, Iowa, Apr. 29, 1946; s. Arnold E. and Helen A. (Dettmann) S.; m. Linda L. Boston, Apr. 22, 1972; children: Jennifer, Jonathan. BA, Tex. A&M U., 1969; JD, Baylor U., 1971; LLM, U. Va., 1981. Bar: Tex. 1971, D.C. 1973, U.S. Ct. Mil. Appeals 1972, U.S. Supreme Ct. 1976. Legal counsel U.S. Supreme Ct., Washington, 1981—83; assoc. dean St. Mary's U., San Antonio, 1984—89, prof. law, 1986—, Hardy prof. trial advocacy, dir. advocacy programs, 2000—; reporter Fed. Adv. Com. on Criminal Rules, 1988—. Chmn. JAG adv. coun., 1974-75. Author: Military Criminal Justice: Practice and Procedure, 1982, 5th edit., 1999; (with others) Military Rules of Evidence Manual, 1981, 4th edit., 1997, Texas Rules of Evidence Manual, 1983, 6th edit., 2002, Texas Evidentiary Foundations, 1992, 2d edit., 1998, Military Evidentiary Foundations, 1994, 2d edit., 2000, Military Criminal Procedure Forms, 1997, Federal Evidence Tactics, 1997, Texas Rules of Evidence Trial Book, 2000; editor-in-chief: Emerging Problems Under the Federal Rules of Evidence, 3d edit., 1998; contbr. articles to legal publs. Maj. JAGC, U.S. Army, 1972-81. Fellow Am. Law Inst., Tex. Bar Found. (life), Am. Bar Found. (life); mem. ABA (vice-chmn. criminal justice sect. coun. 1991-94, vice-chmn. com. on criminal justice and mil. 1983-84, chmn. standing com. on mil. law 1991-92, mem. standing com. on armed forces law, chmn. editl. adv. bd., Criminal Justice Mag., 1989-91, 2000-), Tex. Bar Assn. Republican. Lutheran. Office: St Marys U Sch Law 1 Camino Santa Maria St San Antonio TX 78228-8603

SCHLUETER, LINDA LEE, law educator; b. L.A., May 12, 1947; d. Dick G. Dulgarian and Lucille J. Boston; m. David A. Schlueter, Apr. 22, 1972; children: Jennifer, Jonathan. BA, U. So. Calif., 1969; JD, Baylor U., 1971. Bar: D.C. 1973, U.S. Supreme Ct. 1976, Ct. Mil. Appeals, 1990, Tex. 1997. Govt. rels. specialist hdqrs. U.S. Postal Svc., Washington, 1973-75; staff atty. Rsch. Group, Inc., Charlottesville, Va., 1979-81; pvt. practice Washington, 1981-83; asst. prof. law Sch. Law St. Mary's U., San Antonio, 1983-87, assoc. prof., 1987-90, prof., 1990-94. Presenter law Tex. Women Scholars Program, Austin, 1986, 87; bd. dirs Inst. for Comparative and Internat. Legal Rsch. Author: Punitive Damages, 1981-89, 4th edit., 2000, ann. suppls., Legal Research Guide: Patterns and Practice, 1986, 4th edit., 2000; editor Cmty. Property Jour., 1986-88, Cmty. Property Alert, 1989-90; editor Modern Legal Sys. Cyclopedia, 20 vols., 1990, ann. suppls. Mem. ABA, Bexar County Women's Bar Assn., San Antonio Conservation Soc., Order of Barristers, Phi Alpha Delta. Republican. Lutheran.

SCHLUTER, DOLPH A. biologist, educator; b. Montreal, Que., Can., May 22, 1955; s. Antoine Leon and Leny (Neiman) S. BS, U. Guelph, Ont., Can., 1977; PhD, U. Mich., 1983. Postdoctoral fellow U. Calif., Davis, 1983-84, U. B.C., Vancouver, Can., 1984-85, rsch. fellow, 1985—, asst. prof. biology, 1989-91, assoc. prof., 1991—. Contbr. articles to profl. publs. Recipient Young Investigators prize Am. Soc. Naturalists, 1984; rsch. grantee Natural Sci. and Engring. Rsch. Coun., U. B.C., 1985-90; rsch. fellow Natural Sci. and Engring. Rsch. Coun., 1983, 85. Achievements include research on natural selection, co-evolution of competing species. Office: U BC Dept Zoology 6270 University Blvd Vancouver BC V6T 1Z4 Canada

SCHMALBECK, RICHARD LOUIS, university dean, lawyer; b. Chgo., Dec. 31, 1947; s. George Louis and Betty Jeanne Schmalbeck; m. Linda Michaels; children: Suzanne, Sabine. AB in Econs. with honors, U. Chgo., 1970, JD, 1975. Bar: Ohio 1975, D.C. 1977. Asst. to dir. and economist Ill. Housing Devel. Authority, Chgo., 1971-73; assoc. Vorys, Sater, Seymour & Pease, Columbus, Ohio, 1975-76; spl. asst. to assoc. dir. for econs. and govt. Office of Mgmt. and Budget, Washington, 1976-77; assoc. Caplin & Drysdale, Washington, 1977-80; assoc. prof. law Duke U., Durham, N.C., 1980-84, prof. law, 1984-90, 93—, vice chmn. acad. coun., 1984—85, 2001—02; dean U. Ill. Coll. Law, Champaign, 1990-93. Assoc. editor U. Chgo. Law Rev., 1974-75; contbr. articles to profl. jours. Mem. ABA (articles editor jour. 1977-80), Am. Law Inst., Phi Beta Kappa. Office: Duke University Sch of Law PO Box 90360 Durham NC 27708-0360

SCHMALENSEE, RICHARD LEE, dean, economist, former government official, educator; b. Belleville, Ill., Feb. 16, 1944; s. Fred and Marjorie June (Veigel) S.; m. Edeth Diane Hawk, Aug. 19, 1967; children: Alexander Clayton, Nicholas Hawk. SB, MIT, 1965, PhD, 1970. From asst. prof. to assoc. prof. econs. U. Calif., San Diego, 1970-77; assoc. prof. applied econs. Sloan Sch. Mgmt. MIT, Cambridge, Mass., 1977-79, prof., 1979-86, prof. econs. and mgmt., 1986—, Gordon Y Billard prof., 1988-99; dir. MIT Ctr. for Energy and Environ. Policy Rsch., Cambridge, Mass., 1991-99; dep. dean Sloan Sch., Cambridge, Mass., 1996—98, John C Head III dean, 1998—. Bd. dirs. Internat. Securities Exch., MFS Investment Mgmt.; mem. Pres.'s Coun. Econ. Advisers, 1989—91. Author: The Economics of Advertising, 1972, The Control of Natural Monopoly, 1979; co-author: Markets for Power, 1983, Economics, 1988, Paying with Plastic, 1999, Markets for Clean Air, 2000; co-editor: Handbook of Industrial Organization, 1989; mem. editl. bd. Jour. Indsl. Econs., 1981-89, Am. Econ. Rev., 1982-86, Internat. Jour. Indsl. Orgns., 1982-89, Jour. Econs. & Mgmt. Strategy, 1993-98, Jour. Econ. Perspectives, 1993-98. NSF grant, 1975-77, 81-83; Rsch. fellow U. Louvain, Belgium, 1973-74, 85. Fellow: AAAS, Econometric Soc.; mem.: Am. Econ. Assn. (nominating com. 1987, exec. com. 1993—95). Home: 20 Malia Ter Chestnut Hill MA 02467-1326 Office: MIT Sloan Sch Mgmt 50 Memorial Dr Rm E52-473 Cambridge MA 02142-1347

SCHMALSTIEG, WILLIAM RIEGEL, retired Slavic languages educator; b. Sayre, Pa., Oct. 3, 1929; s. John William and Dorothy Augusta (Riegel) S.; m. Emily Lou Botdorf, Mar. 28, 1952; children: Linda, Roxanne. BA, U. Minn., 1950; postgrad., Columbia U., 1952; MA, U. Pa., 1951, PhD, 1956; PhD (hon.), Vilnius U., 1994. Instr. U. Ky., Lexington, 1956-59; asst. prof. Lafayette Coll., Easton, Pa., 1959-63; assoc. prof. U. Minn., Mpls., 1963-64; prof. Pa. State U., University Park, 1964—2002, head dept. Slavic langs., 1969-91. Mem. Internat. Commn. Balto-Slavic Linguistics, 1973—; appointed Edwin Erle Sparks prof. Slavic Lang., 1990. Author: (with L. Dambriunas and A. Klimas) An Introduction to Modern Lithuanian, 1966, 4th edit., 1990, 5th edit., 1993, reprinted as Beginner's Lithuanian, 1999, An Old Prussian Grammar, 1974, Studies in Old Prussian, 1976, Indo-European Linguistics, 1980, An Introduction to Old Church Slavic, 1976, 2d edit., 1983, A Lithuanian Historical Syntax, 1988; (with Warren Held and Janet Gertz) Beginning Hittite, 1988, A Student Guide to the Genitive of Agent in the Indo-European Languages, 1995, An Introduction to Old Russian, 1995, The Historical Morphology of the Baltic Verb, 2000; editor Gen. Linguistics, 1971-82; mem. editl. adv. bd. Jour. Indo-European Studies, Baltistica, Linguistica Baltica, Acta Linguistica Lithuanica, Archivum Lithuanicum, Lietuviu Kalbotyros Klausimai, Baltu Filologija. Served to 1st lt. U.S. Army, 1952-54. NEH grantee, 1978-79, Fulbright grantee and exch. scholar Acad. Scis., Vilnius, USSR, 1986; recipient Humanities medal Pa. State U., 1983, Friend of Lithuania award Knights of Lithuania, 1990, Lithuanian Govt. Mazvydas medal, 1997; named Disting. Alumnus Breck Sch., 1990. Mem.: Assn. Advancement Baltic Studies (pres. 1982—84). Episcopalian. Home: 814 Cornwall Rd State College PA 16803-1430 E-mail: wxsl@psu.edu.

SCHMEHL MORLEY, SUSAN LINDA, fine arts educator, artist; b. Aug. 29, 1949; BFA, U. Mass., Amherst, 1971; postgrad., Studio Art Ctr. Internat., Florence, Italy; MFA in Painting, Md. Inst. Coll. Art, 2003. With Peace Corps, 1973-76; studio arts, Spanish tchr., 1976-97; chair of fine and performing arts Berkshire Sch., Sheffield, Mass., 1997-2000. Fellow Skidmore Coll., 1994. Recipient Scholastic Art and Writing award, 1998, Outstanding H.S. Tchr. award, U. Chgo., 1999, Scholastic Art and Writing award, 2000, Outstanding Nat. Sculpture Tchr. award, Internat. Sculpture Ctr., 2001, Outstanding H.S. Tchr. award, Internat. Artist Residency, Jingdezhen Sanbao Ceramic Art Inst., China, 2002; Fulbright Meml. Fund scholar, Japan, 2002. Mem.: Nat. Assn. Art Educators, Ind. Sch. Art Instrs. Assn. Home: 245 N Undermountain Rd Sheffield MA 01257 E-mail: slsmorley@yahoo.com.

SCHMERTMANN, JOHN HENRY, civil engineer, educator, consultant; b. N.Y.C., Dec. 2, 1928; s. Johannes Conrad Schmertmann and Margaret Anna-Marie (Carstens) Schmertmann Ottesen; m. Pauline Anne Grange, Aug. 11, 1956; children: Carl, Gary, Neil, Joy. BSC.E., MIT, 1950; MSC.E., Northwestern U., 1954, PhD in Civil Engring., 1962. Registered profl. engr., Fla. Soils engr. Mueser Rutledge Cons. Engrs., N.Y.C., 1951-54; soils engr. C.E., U.S. Army, Wilmette, Ill., 1954-56; asst. prof. civil engring. U. Fla., Gainesville, 1956-62, assoc. prof., 1962-65, prof., 1965-79, adj. prof., prof. emeritus; prin. Schmertmann & Crapps, Inc., Gainesville, 1979-97, LoadTest Inc., Gainesville, 1991—, Office John H. Schmertmann Inc., Gainesville, 1997—. Postdoctoral fellow Norwegian Geotech. Inst., Oslo, 1962-63; vis. scientist div. bldg. research NRC Can., Ottawa Ont., 1971-72 Author numerous profl. papers Fellow ASCE (br. pres. 1972, Collingwood prize 1956, Norman medal 1971, State of the Art award 1977, Middlebrooks award 1981, Terzaghi lectr. 1989), Fla. Engring. Soc.; mem. Nat. Acad. Engring. Lutheran. Avocation: sport fishing. Office: Office John H Schmertmann Inc 4509 NW 23rd Ave Ste 19 Gainesville FL 32606-6570

SCHMERTZ, ERIC JOSEPH, lawyer, educator; b. N.Y.C., Dec. 24, 1925; married; 4 children. AB, Union Coll., 1948, LL.D. (hon.), 1978; cert., Alliance Francaise, Paris, 1948; JD, NYU, 1954. Bar: N.Y. 1955. Internat. rep. Am. Fedn. State, County and Mcpl. Employees, AFL-CIO, N.Y.C., 1950-52; asst. v.p., dir. labor tribunals Am. Arbitration Assn., N.Y.C., 1952-57, 59-60; indsl. relations dir. Metal Textile Corp. subs. Gen. Cable Corp., Roselle, N.J., 1957-59; exec. dir. N.Y. State Bd. Mediation, 1960-62, corp. dir., 1962-68; labor-mgmt. arbitrator, N.Y.C., 1962—; mem. faculty Hofstra U. Sch. Bus., 1962-70; prof. Hofstra U. Sch. Law, 1970—, Edward F. Carlough disting. prof. labor law, 1981-98, dean Sch. Law, 1982-89, disting. prof. emeritus of law, 1998—; of counsel The Dweck Law Firm, N.Y.C., 1999—; commr. labor rels. City of N.Y., 1990-91. Scholar-in-residence Pace U. Sch. Law, 1998—; 1st Beckley lectr. in bus. U. Vt., 1981; bd. dirs. Wilshire Oil Co.; mem. N.Y. State Pub. Employment Rels. Bd., 1991-97; cons. and lectr. in field. Co-author: (with R.L. Greenman) Personnel Administration and the Law, 1978; contbr. chpts. to books, articles to profl. jours., to profl. law confs., seminars and workshops. Mem. numerous civic orgns. Served to lt. USN, 1943-46. Recipient Testimonial award Southeast Republican Club, 1969; Alexander Hamilton award Rep. Law Students Assn.; Eric J. Schmertz Disting. Professorship Pub. Law and Pub. Svc. established Hofstra Law Sch., 1993. Mem. Nat. Acad. Arbitrators, Am. Arbitration Assn. (law com., Whitney North Seymour Sr. medal 1984), Fed. Mediation and Conciliation Svc., N.Y. Mediation Bd., N.J. Mediation Bd., N.J. Pub. Employment Rels. Bd., Hofstra U. Club, Princeton Club. Office: The Dweck Law Firm 230 Park Ave Rm 416 New York NY 10169-0422 E-mail: schmertz@dwecklaw.com.

SCHMID, HARALD HEINRICH OTTO, biochemistry educator, academic director; b. Graz, Styria, Austria, Dec. 10, 1935; Came to U.S., 1962; s. Engelbert and Annemarie (Kletetschka) S.; m. Patricia Caroline Igou, May 21, 1977. MS, U. Graz, 1957, LLD, 1962, PhD, 1964. Rsch. fellow Hormel inst. U. Minn., Austin, 1962-65, rsch. assoc., 1965-66, asst. prof., 1966-70, assoc. prof., 1970-74, prof., 1974—. Cons. NIH, Bethesda, Md., 1977—; acting dir. Hormel inst. U. Minn., 1985-87, exec. dir., 1987-01; faculty mem. Mayo Med. Sch., Rochester, Minn., 1990—. Mng. editor Chemistry and Physics of Lipids, Elsevier Sci. Publs., Amsterdam, The Netherlands, 1984-01; contbr. numerous articles to profl. jours. Rsch. grantee NIH, 1967—. Mem. AAAS, Am. Soc. Biochemistry and Molecular Biology, Am. Chem. Soc., The Oxygen Soc. Avocations: yacht racing, downhill skiing, classical music. Home: 2701 2nd Ave NW Austin MN 55912-1195 Office: U Minn Hormel Inst 801 16th Ave NE Austin MN 55912-3679

SCHMID, RUDI (RUDOLF SCHMID), internist, educator, academic administrator; b. Switzerland, May 2, 1922; arrived in U.S., 1948, naturalized, 1954; s. Rudolf and Bertha (Schiesser); m. Sonja D. Wild, Sept. 17, 1949. BS, Gymnasium Zurich, 1941; MD, U. Zurich, 1947; PhD, U. Minn., 1954. Intern U. Calif. Med. Ctr., San Francisco, 1948—49; resident medicine U. Minn., 1949—52, instr., 1952—54; rsch. fellow biochemistry Columbia U., 1954—55; investigator NIH, Bethesda, Md., 1955—57; assoc. medicine Harvard Med. Sch., 1957—59; asst. prof. Harvard U., 1959—62; prof. medicine U. Chgo., 1962—66, U. Calif., San Francisco, 1966—91, dean Sch. Medicine, 1983—89, assoc. dean internat. rels., 1989—95. Cons. to U.S. Army surgeon gen. NIH; hon. prof. Peking Union Med. Coll., Shanghai Second Med. U., Xian U. of Med. Sci., Jillin U. Medicine. Mem. editl. bd.: Blood, 1962—75, Jour. Clin. Investigation, 1965—70, Jour. Gastroenterology, 1965—70, Jour. Investigative Dermatology, 1968—72, Annals Internal Medicine, 1975—79, Procs. Soc. Exptl. Biology and Medicine, 1974—84, Chinese Jour. Clin. Scis., Jour. Lab. Clin. Medicine, 1991—, Hepatology Rsch., 1993—, World Jour. Gastroenterology, 2002, cons. editor: Gastroenterology, 1981—86. Mem. Swiss Nat. Ski Team, 1941—44. With Swiss Army, 1943—48. Master: ACP; fellow: Royal Coll. Physicians, N.Y. Acad. Scis., Am. Acad. Arts and Scis.; mem.: NAS, German-Am. Acad. Coun. (exec. com. 1992—99), Leopoldina, Swiss Acad. Med. Scis., Am. Assn. Study Liver Disease (pres. 1965), Am. Gastroenterol. Assn., Am. Soc. Hematology, Am. Soc. Biol. Chemistry and Molecular Biology, Am. Soc. Clin. Investigation, Assn. Am. Physicians (pres. 1986), Internat. Assn. Study Liver (pres. 1980—82), IOM (sr.). Achievements include research in biochemistry, metabolism of hemoglobin, heme, prophyrins, bile pigments, liver and muscle. Home: 211 Woodland Rd Kentfield CA 94904-2631 Office: U Calif Med Sch Office Dean PO Box 0410 San Francisco CA 94143-0410 Personal E-mail: s.d.schmid@worldnet.att.net. Business E-Mail: schmidr@medsch.ucsf.edu.

SCHMID, WILFRIED, mathematician, educator; b. Hamburg, Germany, May 28, 1943; came to U.S., 1960; s. Wolfgang and Kathe (Erfling) S. BA, Princeton U., 1964; MA, U. Calif., Berkeley, 1966, PhD, 1967. Asst. prof. math. U. Calif., Berkeley, 1967-70; prof. math. Columbia U., 1970-78, Harvard U., 1978—. Vis. mem. Inst. for Advanced Study, Princeton, 1969-70, 75-76; vis. prof. U. Bonn, 1973-74; hon. prof. U. Cordoba, Argentina, 1989; math. advisor Mass. Dept. Edn., 2000-02. Editor: Letters in Mathematical Physics, Jour. Algebraic Geometry; contbr. articles to profl. jours. Recipient Prix Scientifique de l'UAP, 1986; Sloan fellow, 1968-70, Guggenheim fellow, 1975-76, 88-89. Mem.: Am. Acad. Arts and Scis. Home: Silver Hill Rd Lincoln MA 01773 Office: Harvard U Dept Mathematics Cambridge MA 02138

SCHMIDER, MARY ELLEN HEIAN, American studies educator, academic administrator; b. Chippewa Falls, Wis., Apr. 17, 1938; d. A. Bernard and Ellen Dagmar (Gunderson) Heian; m. Michael Heaton Leonard, June 16, 1962 (div. Oct. 1969); 1 child, William Gunerius Leonard; m. Carl Ludwig Schmider, June 17, 1970; 1 child, Dagmar Heian (née Schmider) Meinders. BA in English Lit. magna cum laude, St. Olaf Coll., Northfield, Minn., 1960; MA in English Lit., U. So. Calif., 1962; PhD in Am. Studies, U. Minn., 1983. Mem. founding faculty in English, Calif. Luth. Coll., Thousand Oaks, Calif., 1961-64; instr. dept. English U. Vt., Burlington, Vt., 1964-70; instr. Univ. writing program U. RI, South Kingston, RI, 1973-77; grad. asst. dept. rhetoric U. Minn., Mpls., 1975-76; dir. continuing edn./cmty. svc. Moorhead State U., Minn., 1977-86, dean grad. studies and grad. faculty, 1983-95; US Fulbright lectr. Lanzhou U., China, 1997. Mem. bd. pensions Luth. Ch. in Am., Mpls., 1982—87; mem. bd. higher edn. and schs. Evang. Luth. Ch. in Am., Chgo., 1987—95; cert. coll. mgmt. Carnegie Mellon U., 1987; lectr. USIA in Austria, Italy, Japan, Iceland; bd. dirs. Luth. Brotherhood, Mpls., 1988—2001; collegiate full prof. U. Md., U. Coll., Europe, Heidelberg, Germany, 2000—. Author: (biog. sketches) Biog. Dictionary of Social Welfare, esp. Jane Addams. Mem. exec. comm. Minn. Humanities Commn., St. Paul, 1983-89, chair, 1987-88. Bush Leadership fellow, 1987. Mem. US Fulbright Assn., Am. Studies Assn., Phi Beta Kappa, Phi Kappa Phi. Lutheran. Avocation: swimming, design, music, internat. travel, family activities.. Home: 7701 180th St Chippewa Falls WI 54729-6440 E-mail: mehsels@yahoo.com.

SCHMIDGALL, RAYMOND STANLEY, accounting and finance educator; b. Bloomington, Ill., Nov. 12, 1945; s. Raymond Klein and Myrtle Louise (Sosamon) S.; m. Barbara Marie Roehl, Mar. 16, 1968; children: Erica Leigh, Monica Rae, Kristina Marie, Joanna Lynn. BBA, Evangel Coll., 1967; MBA, Mich. State U., 1969, PhD, 1980. CPA, Mich. Auditor Ernst & Ernst, Lansing, Mich., 1971-73; contr. AH&MA Ednl. Inst., East Lansing, Mich., 1973-75; lectr. Mich. State U., East Lansing, 1975-76, instr., 1976-80, asst. prof., 1980-84, assoc. prof., 1984-89, Hilton Hotels prof. of hospitality fin. mgmt., 1989—. V.p. Hospitality Fin. Cons., Inc., Okemos, Mich., 1982—; pres. Hospitality Publs., Inc., Okemos, 1982—; adv. bd. mem. Chi Alpha, East Lansing, 1993—. Author: Managerial Accounting for Hospitality Industry, 5th edit., 2002; co-author: Basic Financial Accounting for Hospitality Industry, 1982, Financial Management for the Hospitality Industry, 1993, Financial Accounting for Hospitality Industry, 2d edit., 2000; contbr. more than 170 articles to profl. jours. With U.S. Army, 1969-70, Vietnam. Mem. Coun. Hotel, Restaurant and Inst. Educators (treas. 1993-97), Assn. Hospitality Fin. Mgmt. Educators (sec. 1985—), Hospitality Fin. and Tech. Profls., Am. Hotel and Motel Assn. Mem. Assembly of God Church. Avocation: jogging. Office: Mich State Univ 240 Eppley Ctr East Lansing MI 48824-1121 E-mail: schmidga@msu.edu.

SCHMIDLY, DAVID J. university president, biology educator; b. Levelland, Tex., Dec. 20, 1943; m. Janet Elaine Knox, June 2, 1966; children: Katherine Elaine, Brian James. BS in Biology, Tex. Tech U., 1966, MS in Zoology, 1968; PhD in Zoology, U. Ill., 1971. From asst. prof. to prof. dept. wildlife fisheries scis. Tex. A&M U., College Station, 1971-82, prof., 1982-96, head dept. wildlife, 1986-92, CEO, campus dean Galveston, 1992-96; chief curator Tex. Coop. Wildlife Coll., College Station, 1983-86; v.p. Tex. Inst. Oceanography, 1992-96; v.p. rsch. and grad studies, dean grad. sch., tech. transfer Tex. Tech U., Lubbock, 1996—, prof. biol. scis., 1996—, pres., 2000—. Cons. Nat. Park Svc., Wildlife Assocs., Walton and Assocs., Continental Shelf Assn., LGL; lectr. in field; press adv. com. Tex. A&M U., 1983-96; charter mem. Tex. A&M U. Faculty Senate, 1983-85, chmn. Scholarship Com., 1978-82. Author: The Mammals of Trans-Pecos Texas including Big Bend National Park and Guadalupe Mountains National Park, 1977, Texas Mammals East of the Balcones Fault Zone, 1983, The Bats of Texas, 1991, The Mammals of Texas, 1994, Texas Natural History: A Century of Change, 2002; contbr. articles to profl. jours. Trustee Tex. Nature Conservancy, 1991—; mem. adv. bd. Ft. Worth Zoo, 2000. Recipient Dist. Prof. award Assn. Grad. Wildlife and Fisheries Scis., 1985, Donald W. Tinkle Rsch. Excellence award Southwestern Assn. Naturalists, 1988, Diploma Recognition La Universidad Autonoma de Guadalajara, 1989, La Universidad Autonoma de Tamaulipas, 1990. Fellow Tex. Soc. Sci. (bd. dirs. 1979-81); mem. AAAS, Am. Soc. Mammalogists (life, editor Jour. Mammalogy 1975-78), Am. Inst. Biol. Scis. (bd. dirs. 1993—, coun. affiliate socs. 1989—), Am. Naturalist, Soc. Marine Mammalogy (charter mem.), Soc. Systematic Zoology, The Wildlife Soc. Soc. Conservation Biology, Nat. Geog. Sci. Soc., S.W. Assn. Naturalists (life mem., bd. govs. 1980-86, 91—, pres. 1981, trustee 1986—), Tex. Mammal Soc. (pres. 1985-86), Assn. Systematic Collections (bd. dirs.), Chihuahuan Desert Rsch. Inst. (v.p. bd. scientists 1982—, bd. dirs. 1991), Mexican Soc. Mammalogists, Sigma Xi (v.p. 1986-87, pres. 1987-88), Disting. Scientist award 1991), Coun. Pub. Univ. Pres. and Chancellors (exec. com. 2000), Golden Key, Beta Beta Beta, Phi Sigma, Phi Kappa Phi. Home: 4607 9th St Lubbock TX 79416 Office: Tex Tech U PO Box 42005 Lubbock TX 79409-2005 E-mail: david.schmidly@ttu.edu.

SCHMIDT, CAROLYN LEA, elementary school educator; b. Waterloo, Iowa, Apr. 5, 1949; d. Carl George and Leola Marie (Flater) S. Student, Wartburg Coll., 1967-69; BS, Iowa State U., 1971; MA, U. Iowa, 1980. Cert. elem., learning disabilities, chpt. I reading tchr., Iowa. 5th grade tchr. Midland Cmty. Schs., Wyoming, Iowa, 1971-78; 4th grade tchr. Walnut Ridge Acad., Waterloo, Iowa, 1978-79; learning disabilities tchr. Ft. Dodge (Iowa) Cmty. Schs., 1980-82, chpt. I reading tchr., 1982—. Active dist. in-svcs. and confs. in field. Active First Evang. Free Ch., Ft. Dodge, 1980-89. Mem. Internat. Reading Assn. Avocations: macintosh computers, classical guitars, reading, sports.

SCHMIDT, JANIS ILENE, elementary education educator; b. Wyandot County, Ohio., Feb. 4, 1930; d. Floyd Dale and Edith June (Clark) Herbert; m. William Frederick Schmidt, Aug. 27, 1950; children: Lon William, Randy Floyd. BS, Findlay Coll., 1968; MEd, Ashland Coll., 1986. Cert. elem. tchr., Ohio. Elem. tchr. Wharton (Ohio) Elem., 1950-52, Upper Sandusky (Ohio) Schs., 1967—. Author: Improvement of Retention, 1986. Officer Beta Usando Literary Club, Upper Sandusky, 1993; mem. Wyandot Meml. Hosp. Guild, 1980-95, North Salem Luth. Ch. Tchr., officer, 1950—, Tri-G Mothers League, 1953-80. Jennings scholar The Martha Holden Jennings Found., Ohio, 1969-73. Mem. Internat. Reading Assn. (com. chmn. 1990). Republican. Lutheran. Avocations: golf, boating, bicycling, gardening, sewing. Home: 569 N Warpole St Upper Sandusky OH 43351-9332 Office: East Sch 401 3rd St Upper Sandusky OH 43351-1105

SCHMIDT, JOHN GERHARD, neurologist, educator, researcher; b. Rock Springs, Wyo., Oct. 17, 1956; s. Gerhard Daniel and Phillys Elaine (Score) S.; m. Lenore Ann Ilg, May 2, 1987; children: Kirstin, Joseph, Rebecca. BS in Phys. Scis., Colo. State U., 1980; MD, U. Minn., 1985. Diplomate Am. Bd. Psychiatry and Neurology, Nat. Bd. Med. Examiners. Intern in internal medicine Med. Coll. Wis. Affiliated Hosps., Milw., 1985-86, resident in neurology, 1986-88, chief resident, 1988-89; fellow in neurorehab. Burke Rehab. Ctr., Cornell U. Med. Coll., White Plains, N.Y., 1989-90; med. dir. PremierCare Neurorehab. Ctr., St. Louis, 1990-93; instr., dir. divsn. neurologic rehab. dept. neurology St. Louis U., 1990-93; dir. stroke rehab. Souers Stroke Inst., St. Louis, 1991-93; sr. instr. dept. neurology U. Rochester (N.Y.) Sch. Medicine and Dentistry, 1993-95, asst. prof. neurology, 1995—2001; asst. prof. rehab. U. Rochester (N.Y.) Sch. Medicine, 1997—2001, assoc. prof. neurology and rehab., 2001—; assoc. attending neurologist Strong Hosp. U. Rochester, 1998—; attending neurologist dept. phys. medicine and rehab. St. Mary's Hosp., Rochester, 1993—2002; attending neurologist Rochester Gen. Hosp., 2002—; med. dir. St. Mary's Hosp., Rochester, 1993-96, secondary appointment, asst. prof. of rehab., 1997—2001. Mem. cardiovascular health care team Preferred Care, 1999—; mem. ethics com. Unity Health Systems, 1996-99; presenter in field. Contbg. author: Comprehensive Neurologic Rehabilitation, Vol. 5: Orthotics in Neurologic Rehabilitation, 1992, Neurotrauma, 1996; contbr. articles and abstracts to med. jours. Bd. dirs. Rochester Rehab., 2003—, med. dir. PRALID (People Rebldg. and Living in Dignity), Rochester, 1994-2000, treas., 1998-2000; mem. stroke edn. com. Am. Heart Assn., St. Louis, 1991-93; mem. Operation Stroke; mem. Am. Stroke Assn., 2000—, chair subcom. rehab. and recovery Genesee Valley chpt., nat.lobbyist, 2002—; mem. stroke coun. Am. Heart Assn., 2002—. Recipient Burke award Winifred Masterson Burke Found., 1990, lifetime achievement award N.Y. Easter Seals Soc., 1994, Outstanding Vol. award Am. Heart Assn., 2002; Army and Navy ROTC scholar, 1975-79; NSF fellow Colo. Sch. Mines, 1974 Fellow Am. Heart Assn.; mem. Am. Acad. Neurology, Am. Soc. Neurorehab. (cert.), Phi Kappa Phi. Lutheran. Avocations: fishing, skiing, mountain climbing, photography. Office: Rochester Gen Hosp Dept Neurology 1425 Portland Ave Rochester NY 14621 E-mail: schmidtjohng@netscape.net.

SCHMIDT, JOHN RICHARD, agricultural economics educator; b. Madison, Wis., July 3, 1929; s. Oscar John and Alma Theodora (Ula) S.; m. Rosemary Pigorsch, Oct. 7, 1951; children: Janet, Deborah, Allen. BS, U. Wis., 1951, MS, 1953; PhD, U. Minn., 1960. Asst. prof. agr. econs. U. Wis., Madison, 1956-61, assoc. prof., 1961-65, prof., 1965-95, prof. emeritus, 1995—, chmn. dept., 1966-70; owner, mgr. JRS Computing Svcs., Madison, 1995—. Farm mgmt. cons. Am. Farm Bur. Fedn., Chgo., 1962; cons. Banco de Mexico, 1972-84, IBRD (World Bank), 1973-94, Agrl. Devel. Bank Iran, 1974-76; adv. bd. Internat. Devel. Inst., 1983; faculty Salzburg Seminar, 1983, 85. Contbr. articles to tech. jours., also monographs, bulls. Bd. dirs. U. Wis. Credit Union, 1968-77, pres., 1969-75; mem. com. Wis.-Upper Mich. Synod Sem., 1972-75, ch. coun. 1967-69, 72-75, pres. 1974-75. Mem. Rotary (pres. Madison West 1994-95), Delta Theta Sigma (nat. sec. 1962-64), Gamma Sigma Delta (pres. Wis. chpt. 1975). Lutheran. Home: 106 Frigate Dr Madison WI 53705-4426 Office: JRS Computing Svcs 6601 Grand Teton Plz Ste 4 Madison WI 53719-1049 E-mail: jrschmi1@facstaff.wisc.edu.

SCHMIDT, KATHLEEN MARIE, lawyer; b. Des Moines, June 17, 1953; d. Raymond Driscoll and Hazel Isabelle (Rogers) Poage; m. Dean Everett Johnson, Dec. 21, 1974 (div. Nov. 1983); children: Aaron Dean, Gina Marie; m. Ronald Robert Schmidt, Feb. 7, 1987. BS in Home Econs., U. Nebr., 1974; JD, Creighton U., 1987. Bar: Nebr. 1987, U.S. Dist. Ct. Nebr. 1987, U.S. Ct. Appeals (8th cir.) 1989, U.S. Supreme Ct. 1991. Apprentice printer, journeyman Rochester (Minn.) Post Bull., 1978-82; dir. customer info. Cornhusker Pub. Power Dist., Columbus, Nebr., 1982-83; artist Pamida, Omaha, 1983; offset artist Cornhusker Motor Club, Omaha, 1983-84; assoc. Lindahl O. Johnson Law Office, Omaha, 1987-88; pvt. practice Omaha, 1988-90; ptnr. Emery, Penke, Blazek & Schmidt, Omaha, 1990-91; pvt. practice, Omaha, 1992—. Atty. in condemnation procs. Douglas County Bd. Appraisers, Omaha, 1988-99, Sarpy County Bd. Appraisers, Omaha, 1999—; presenter Nebr. Sch. Bd. Assn., 1991, 92. Mem. Millard Sch. Bd., Omaha, 1989-96, treas. 1991, 92; mem. strategic planning com. Millard Sch. Dist., 1990; mem. Omaha Mayor's Master Plan Com., 1991-94. Named hon. mem. Anderson Mid. Sch., Omaha, 1991; recipient Award of Achievement, Nebr. Sch. Bd. Assn., 1991, 94. Mem. Nebr. Bar Assn., Omaha Bar Assn. (spkrs. bur. 1992—), Nat. Sch. Bd. Assn. (del. federal rels. network 1991-96, cert. recognition 1991). Republican. Lutheran.

SCHMIDT, LAURA LEE, elementary and middle school gifted and talented educator, special education educator; b. South Bend, Ind., Sept. 6, 1960; d. Max A. and Sandra Lee (Engmark) Tudor; m. William Michael Schmidt, Aug. 7, 1982; children: Sandra Lorena, Charlotte Lee. BA, U. Ky., 1982; postgrad., Augustana Coll., Sioux Falls, S.D., U. S.D.; MEd, S.D. State U., 1991. Cert. elem. K-8, spl. edn. K-12, mid./jr. h.s., gifted edn. K-12, S.D. Spl. edn. tchr. Owen County Sch. Dist., Owenton, Ky.; elem. sch. tchr. White River (S.D.) Sch. Dist.; elem. and music tchr. St. Liborius Sch., Orient, S.D.; spl. edn. and chpt. I tchr. Cresbard (S.D.) Sch.; gifted edn. tchr., spl. edn. tchr. Douglas Mid. Sch., Douglas Sch. Dist., Box Elder, S.D. Easter seals camp counselor; vol. Spl. Olympics; accompianist high sch. choir. Mem. Dir. Spl. Edn., Mortar Board, Lambda Sigma. Home: 614 Bluebird Dr Box Elder SD 57719-9509

SCHMIDT, LAWRENCE KENNEDY, philosophy educator; b. Rochester, N.Y., Oct. 2, 1949; s. Paul Frederick Schmidt and Rebecca Jane Gilford; m. Monika Reuss, Sept. 2, 1984; 1 child, Kassandra Gaya Reuss-Schmidt. BA, Reed Coll., 1972; MA, U. N.Mex., 1978; PhD, U. Duisburg (Germany), 1983. Instr. philosophy U. Duisburg, 1979-83, U. N.Mex., Albuquerque, 1984; asst. prof. philosophy Hendrix Coll., Conway, Ark., 1984-89, chair dept. philosophy, 1987-92, 96-98, 2000—, assoc. prof. philosophy, 1989-99, prof. philosophy, 1999—. Bd. dirs. Marshall T. Steel Ctr. for the Study of Religion and Philosophy. Author: The Epistemology of H-G Gadamer, 1985, 2d edit., 1987; editor: The Specter of Relativism, 1995, Language and Linquisticality in Gadamer's Hermeneutics, 2000; translator: Hans-Georg Gadamer on Education, Poetry, and History, 1992; contbr. articles to profl. jours. Fulbright scholar, Duisburg, 1977-79, Fulbright sr. scholar Heidelberg, 1999; faculty rsch. grantee Hendrix Coll., 1985, 88, 91, 93, 96, 99. Mem.: Soc. for Phenomenology and Existential Philos., Am. Philos. Assn., Ark. Philos. Assn., AAUP (pres. Hendrix chpt. 1987—91, 1995—97, 1999—2001), Phi Beta Kappa. Avocations: travel, skiing, hiking. E-mail: schmidt@Hendrix.edu.

SCHMIDT, MARY BERRY, educational administrator; b. Roswell, N.Mex., Feb. 9, 1956; d. Philip Leslie and Carmen Estella (Colon) Berry; 1 child, Jennifer Marie Schmidt. BS, U. Tex. at El Paso, 1983; MEd, 1985. Cert. mid-mgmt., provisional generic spl. edn., provisional early childhood edn. handicapped child, provisional elem., profl. reading specialist, provisional kindergarten, computer literacy. Tchr. 3rd grade El Paso ISD Burnet Elem., 1983-85, tchr. 1st grade, 1985-87; gifted and talented tchr. 6th grade El Paso ISD Edgar Park Elem., 1987-88; gifted and talented tchr. 5th grade El Paso ISD Omar Bradley Elem., 1988-89; gifted and talented, computer lit. tchr. 5th grade El Paso Coldwell Elem. Intermediate, 1989-92; asst. prin. El Paso ISD Mesita Elem., 1992—. Bd. mem. Nat. Cmty. for Prevention of Child Abuse, 1985-91, Our Lady of Assumption Sch. Bd., 1986-90, El Paso; fashion show coord. Loretto Acad., El Paso, 1993-94; presenter in field. Sec. Monterey Park Assn., El Paso, 1986-90; leader Girl Scouts Am., El Paso, 1987-90, Leadership El Paso, 1993-94. Named Top 10 Tchrs. El Paso ISD, 1988. Mem. PTA, Tex. Elem. Prin. Assn., Paso del Norte Assn. Supervision and Curriculum, Tex. Assn. Gifted and Talented, Internat. Reading Assn., Assn. Childhood Edn., El Paso Techs. Assn., Delta Kappa Gamma. Roman Catholic. Avocations: snowmobiling, reading, crafts, shopping. Home: 3432 Clearview Ln El Paso TX 79904-4528

SCHMIDT, NANCY CHARLENE LINDER, English and journalism educator; b. Canton, Ohio, May 10, 1940; d. Charles William Masters and Mona Louise (Branch) Masters Swindell; m. Walter C. Linder, Sept. 6, 1958 (div. 1974); children: Karen Linder Heard, Cynthia Linder Webb, Walter Charles Jr.; m. Charles Mathew Schmidt, Aug. 19, 1978; children: John, Michael, Greta Schmidt Wacker. BS in Edn., Kent State U., 1974, BS in English, 1979, BS in Journalism, 1985. Cert. elem. tchr., English tchr., journalism tchr. Jr. high sch. reading tchr. New Philadelphia (Ohio) City Schs., 1974-77; jr. high sch. tchr. Plain Local Schs., Canton, 1977-78; high sch. tchr., advisor yearbook, newspaper Nordonia Hills City Schs., Macedonia, Ohio, 1979—. Coun. pres. Village of Boston Heights, Ohio, 1983-86; leader Girl Scouts USA, 1965-73; children's choir dir. Broadway United Meth. Ch., 1965-74, Sun. sch. supt., 1965-73; pres. New Phila. Welcome Wagon Club, 1964-66. Mem. ASCD, Nat. Coun. English Tchrs., Nordonia Hills Educators Assn. (pres. 1989-91, v.p. 1991-93, bd. dir. 1993—). Republican. Avocations: boating, fishing, ceramics, reading. Home: 630 Fairfield Ln Aurora OH 44202-7836 Office: Nordonia High Sch 8006 S Bedford Rd Macedonia OH 44056-2025

SCHMIDT, PATRICIA RUGGIANO, education educator; b. Ft. Bragg, N.C., Jan. 13, 1944; d. Samuel and Elva (Beckmann) Ruggiano; m. Thomas Jay Schmidt, Nov. 11, 1967; children: Thomas Jay Jr., Anthony Charles. BA cum laude, Potsdam (N.Y.) Coll., 1965; MEd, U. Mass., 1966; EdD, Syracuse U., 1993. Cert. elem. tchr., N.Y., K-12 reading tchr., N.Y. Elem. tchr. Liverpool (N.Y.) Pub. Schs., 1966-68; reading specialist Fayetteville-Manlius (N.Y.) Schs., 1973-91; grad. asst. Syracuse U., 1991-92, adj. instr., 1992-93, Oswego (N.Y.) Coll., 1992-93, Le Moyne Coll., Syracuse, 1992-93; asst. prof. edn. LeMoyne Coll., Syracuse, 1993—. Treas., negotiator for N.Y. State United Tchrs., Fayetteville-Manlius Tchrs. Assn., 1984-91; N.Am. del. to Eastern Europe for rsch. exchange and study People to People, Budapest, St. Petersburg, Moscow, 1993; presenter in field. Author: One Teacher's Reflections: Implementing Multicultural Literacy Learning, 1996, Cultural Conflict and Struggle: Literacy Learning in a Kindergarten Program, 1998; co-editor: (with P. Mosenthal) Reconceptualizing Literacy in the New Age of Multiculturalism & Pluralism; contbr. articles to profl. jours. William Sheldon fellow, 1992-93. Mem. Internat. Reading Assn., Am. Ednl. Rsch. Assn., Nat. Reading Conf., N.Y. State Reading Assn., Kappa Delta Pi, Phi Delta Kappa. Avocations: skiing, golf, gardening, hiking, travel. Home: RR 3 Canastota NY 13032-9803 Office: Le Moyne Coll 101 Reilly Hall Syracuse NY 13214

SCHMIDT, PHILIP S. mechanical engineering educator; Prof. dept. mech. engring. U. Tex., Austin, Douglass prof. Recipient Ralph Coats Roe award ASEE, 1992; named Carnegie Found./Case Tex. Prof. of Yr., 1994. Office: Univ Tex Dept Mech Engring Austin TX 78712 E-mail: pschmidt@mail.utexas.edu.

SCHMIDT, ROBERT, retired mechanics and civil engineering educator; b. Reshetylivka, Ukraine, May 18, 1927; came to U.S., 1949, naturalized, 1956; s. Alfred and Aquilina (Konotop) S.; m. Irene Hubertine Bongartz, June 10, 1978; children: Ingbert Robert. Student, UNRRA-Univ., Munich, 1946-47, Technische Hochschule Karlsruhe, Germany, 1947-49, Vorpruefung; BS, U. Colo., 1951, MS, 1953; PhD, U. Ill., 1956. Tech. draftsman, Kalisch, Poland, 1943-45; rsch. asst. U. Ill., 1953-56, asst. prof. mechanics, 1956-59; assoc. prof. U. Ariz., Tucson, 1959-63; prof. mechanics and civil engring. U. Detroit, 1963-99, chmn. civil engring. dept., 1978-80; ret., 1999. Lectr. Oakland U., 1997-98; rschr. in linear and nonlinear theory of elasticity, theories of arches, plates, and shells, and approximate methods of analysis. Editor: Indsl. Math., 1969—; book reviewer Applied Mechanics Rev., Indsl. Math. Jour.; contbr. numerous articles to profl. jours. With C.E., U.S. Army, 1951-52. Grantee NSF 1960-78. Mem. AAUP, ASCE, ASME (cert. recognition 1972), Am. Acad. Mechanics (a founder), Indsl. Math. Soc. (pres. 1966-67, 81-84, 1st Gold award 1986), Sigma Xi. Avocations: biosophy, walking, bicycling, swimming.

SCHMIDT, ROBERT MILTON, physician, scientist, educator, administrator; b. Milw., May 7, 1944; s. Milton W. and Edith J. (Martinek) S.; children Eric Whitney, Edward Huntington. AB, Northwestern U., 1966; MD, Columbia U., 1970; MPH, Harvard U., 1975; PhD in Law, Medicine and Pub. Policy, Emory U., 1982; MA, San Francisco State U., 1999. Diplomate Am. Bd. Preventive Medicine. Resident in internal medicine Univ. Hosp. U. Calif.-San Diego, 1970-71; resident in preventive medicine Ctr. Disease Control, Atlanta, 1971-74; commd. med. officer USPHS, 1971; advanced through grades to comdr., 1973; dir. hematology div. Nat. Ctr. for Disease Control, Atlanta, 1971-78, spl. asst. to dir., 1978-79, inactive res., 1979—; clin. asst. prof. pediatrics Tufts U. Med. Sch., 1974-86; clin. asst. prof. medicine Emory U. Med. Sch., 1971-81, clin. assoc. prof. community health, 1976-86; clin. assoc. prof. humanities in medicine Morehouse Med. Sch., 1977-79; attending physician dept. medicine Wilcox Meml. Hosp., Lihue, Hawaii, 1979-82, Calif. Pacific Med. Ctr., San Francisco, 1983—; dir. Ctr. Preventive Medicine and Health Rsch., 1983—, dir. Health Watch, 1983—; sr. scientist Inst. Epidemiol. and Behavioral Medicine, Inst. Cancer Rsch., Calif. Pacific Med. Ctr., San Francisco, 1983-88; prof. hematology and gerontology, dir. Ctr. Preventive Medicine and Health Rsch., chair health professions program San Francisco State U., 1983-99, prof. medicine, 1983—, prof. emeritus, Calif. State U. Sys., 1999—; founding dir. Health Watch Internat., 1994—, CEO, pres. Cons. WHO, FDA, Washington, NIH, Bethesda, Md., Govt. of China, Mayo Clinic, Rochester, Minn., Northwestern U., Evanston, Ill., Chgo., U. R.I., Kingston, Pan Am. Health Orgn., Inst. Pub. Health, Italy, Nat. Inst. Aging Rsch. Ctr., Balt., U. Calif., San Diego, U. Ill., Chgo., Columbia U., NYC, Harvard U., Johns Hopkins U., U. Chgo., UCLA, U. Calif. Berkeley, Brown U., Providence, U. Calif., San Francisco, Stanford U., Boston, Emory U., Atlanta, Duke U., NC, U. Tex., Houston, Ariz. State U., U. Hawaii, Honolulu, U. Paris, U. Geneva, U. Munich, Heidelberg U., U. Frankfurt, U. Berlin, Cambridge U., England, U. Singapore, others; vis. rsch. prof. gerontology Ariz. State U., 1989—90; mem. numerous sci. and profl. adv. bd., panels, com. Mem. editorial bd. Am. Jour. Clin. Pathology, 1976-82, The Advisor, 1988—, Generations, 1989—, Contemporary Gerontology, 1994—, Alternative Therapies in Health and Medicine, 1995—, Aging Today, 1997—; book and film reviewer Sci. Books and Films, 1988—, many other jours.; author: 17 books and manuals including Hematology Laboratory Series, 4 vols., 1979-86, CRC Handbook Series in Clinical Laboratory Science, 1976—; assoc. editor: Contemporary Gerontology, 1993—; contbr. more than 300 articles to sci. jours. Alumni regent Columbia U. Coll. Physicians and Surgeons, 1980—. Northwestern U. scholar, 1964-66; NSF fellow, 1964-66; Health Professions scholar, 1966-70; USPHS fellow, 1967-70; Microbiology, Urology, Upjohn Achievement, Borden Rsch. and Virginia Kneeland Frantz scholar awards Columbia U., 1970; recipient Am. Soc. Pharmacol. and Exptl. Therapy award in pharmacology, 1970, Commendation medal USPHS, 1973, Meritorious Performance and Profl. Promise award, 1989, Student Disting. Teaching and Svc. award Pre-Health Professions Student Alliance, 1992, Leadership Recognition awards San Francisco State U., 1984-89, 91-96, Meritorious Svc. award, 1992. Fellow: ACPM, AAAS (med. scis. sect.), ACP (commentator ACP Jour. Club/Annals of Internal Medicine 1993—), Internat. Soc. Hematology, Am. Soc. Clin. Pathology, Am. Coll. Preventive Medicine (sci. com.), Am. Geriat. Soc., Royal Soc. Medicine (London), Gerontol. Soc. Am.; mem.: APHA, AMA, Calif. Coun. Gerontology and Geriat., Nat. Assoc. Adv. for Health Professions, Internat. Health Eval. Assn. (v.p. for Ams. 1992—94, bd. dirs. 1992—, pres. 1994—96), Calif. Med. Assn., San Francisco Med. Soc., NY Acad. Sci., Am. Soc. Aging (editl. bd. 1990—, Dychtwald Pub. Speaking award 1991), Am. Soc. Microbiology, Assn. Tchr. Preventive Medicine (edn. com., rsch. com.), Am. Coll. Occupl. and Environ. Medicine, Calif. Coun. Gerontology and Geriat., Am. Assn. Med. Info., Nat. Assn. Advisors for Health Professions (bd. dirs.), Am. Assoc. Blood Banks, Acad. Clin. Lab. Physicians and Scientists, Internat. Soc. Thrombosis and Hemostasis, Internat. Commn. Standardization in Hematology, Am. Soc. Hematology (hon.; emeritus), Am. Assn. Med. Info. (chair prevention and health evaln. informatics WG), Nat. Gallery of Art (Washington), Columbia U. Club No. Calif., Northwestern U. Club. No. Calif., Harvard Club (NY and San Francisco), Golden Key (hon. faculty mem.), Army and Navy Club, Cir. Club, Cosmos Club (mem. art com. 1997—), Knights of Malta, Sigma XI, Phi Beta Kappa. Home: Whaleship Plaza 25 Hinckley Walk San Francisco CA 94111-2303 Office: Health Watch Med Ctr PO Box 7999 San Francisco CA 94120-7999 Fax: 415-956-8950. E-mail: rmschmidtmd@aol.com.

SCHMIDT, SANDRA JEAN, secondary school educator; b. Limestone, Maine, Mar. 21, 1955; d. Dale Laban and Marie Audrey (Bailey) Winters; m. Lee Lloyd Schmidt, Oct. 20, 1973; children: Colby Lee, Katrina Leesa. AA summa cum laude, Anne Arundel Community Coll., 1987; BS summa cum laude, U. Balt., 1990; MAT, Johns Hopkins U., 2003. CPA, Md. Enlisted U.S. Army, 1973, traffic analyst, 1973-85, resigned, 1985; auditor Md. State Office of Legislative Audits, Balt., 1990-93; fin. analyst Md. Ins. Adminstrn., Balt., 1993-2000; tchr. math. Baltimore City Pub. Schs., 2000—. Tutor Anne Arundel County Literacy Coun., Pasadena, Md., 1990-97; mentor U. Balt., 1991; host family Am. Intercultural Student Exchange, 1992-98. Named Tchr. of Yr., Balt. City Coun. of PTAs, 2001. Mem.: Md. Coun. Tchrs. Math., Nat. Coun. Tchrs. Math., U. Balt. Alumni Assn., Phi Theta Kappa, Beta Gamma Sigma, Alpha Chi. Republican. Baptist. Home: 7716 Pinyon Rd Hanover MD 21076-1585 E-mail: beadmaniac@hotmail.com.

SCHMIDT, STANLEY EUGENE, retired speech educator; b. Harrington, Wash., Dec. 14, 1927; s. Otto Jacob and Ella Genevieve (Wilson) S.; m. Jayne Brown; children: Randall Lee, Stephen Douglas. BS in Edn., U. Idaho, 1956; MEd in Adminstrn., U. Oreg., 1958; MA in Speech, Wash. State U., 1975. Supt., tchr., coach Rose Lake (Idaho) Sch. Dist. #35, 1949-55; forensics coach, speech tchr., dir. forensics Jefferson H.S., Portland, Oreg., 1955-65; dir. forensics Portland C.C., 1965-93, lead speech instr., 1979-82, subject area chmn., 1986-90; adj. prof. speech U. Portland, 1987-93; ret., 1993. Parliamentarian faculty senate, 1975-80. Co-author anthology: The Literature of the Oral Tradition, 1963. Chmn., precinct committeeman Rep. Party, Kootenai County, Idaho, 1951-53; mem. Easter Seal Soc.; pres. Kootenai County Tchrs. Assn., 1953-54, North Idaho Edn. Assn., 1954-55, Oreg. Speech Assn., 1960-61, Oreg. C.C. Speech Assn., 1971-72. Recipient Excellence award U.S. Bank, Portland, 1993, Merit award N.W. Forensic Assn., 1992, Faculty Merit award Portland C.C., 1984. Mem.: Oreg. Speech Assn. (pres.), Speech Comm. Assn., Western Speech Comm. Assn., Oreg. Ret. Tchrs. Assn, Am. Rose Soc., Portland Rose Soc., Tualatin Valley Shrine Club (pres. 1994), Benevolent and Protective Order of the Elks, Royal Ark Mariners, York Rite Sovereign Coll., Order of Ea. Star (Worthy Patron 1970, 1953), Royal Rosarian, Masons (worshipful master 1984—85, dist. dep. 1986—90, jr. grand deacon 1990—91, jr. grand steward 1991—92, grand orator 1992—93), Cryptic Masons of Oreg. (grand orator 1994—95, illustrious master 1997), Knights Templar (knight comdr. of temple of grand encampment), Red Cross of Constantine (dir. of the work 1989—2001, recorder 1993—97, sovereign 2000—01, St. Laurence Conclave), Royal Order Scotland, Scottish Rite Found. (comdr. multnomah coun. kadosh 1990—91, pres. 2002—), Elks, Royal Arch Masons, Shriners, Beta Theta Pi. Baptist. Avocations: rose gardening, stamps, coins, fishing, sports. Home: 5460 SW Palatine St Portland OR 97219-7259

SCHMIDT-BOVA, CAROLYN MARIE, career and technical school administrator; b. Jacksonville, Fla., Sept. 1, 1948; d. Leonard Stephen and Marianne Vesta (Ruscher) S.; m. Edward W. Bova. EdB, SUNY, Buffalo, 1980, MEd, 1981; cert. advanced study, SUNY, Brockport, 1988. Cert. tchr., N.Y., SDA Work Study Coord. Instr. Erie Bd. Coop. Edn. Svcs., Lancaster,

N.Y., 1977-82, Orleans-Niagara Bd. Coop. Ednl. Svcs., Medina, N.Y., 1982-88. Adj. instr. SUNY, Buffalo, 1988—2002, student adv.; cons. N.Y. Dept. Edn., Albany, 1982—92, facilitator, 1982—85, regional resource person, 1985—91; bd. dirs. Inst. for Curriculum Advancement; mem. adv. com. Sch. Dist. Reorganization Ctrl. Western Regional Study; regional rep. N.Y. State Alternative Sch. Educators Adminstrn. Leader Girl Scouts U.S.A., Buffalo; vol. Skills-USA, NY. Tchr. Intern award Tchrs. Ctr., Lockport, N.Y., 1989, Disting. Occupational edn. award N.Y., 1991, Lifetime Achievement award Buffalo (N.Y.) State Coll. Career and Tech. Edn., 2003. Mem.: ASCD, United Univ. Profls., Sch. Adminstrs. Assn. N.Y. State, N.Y. State Tchr. Educators, N.Y. State Tchrs. Vocat. Assn., Career and Tech. Clubs Am. (advisor, Advisor of Yr. N.Y. State 1994—95, Buffalo State Coll. Career Tech. Edn. Excellence award 1995—96), Am. Career and Tech. Assn., Am. Career and Tech. Skills Edn. Adminstrs., So. Poverty Law Ctr., Buffalo State Coll. Alumni, Western N.Y. Women in Adminstrn., Nefane Hist. Soc., Iota Lambda Sigma, Epsilon Pi Tau, Phi Delta Kappa. Home: 5894 Fisk Rd Lockport NY 14094-9224 Office: Orleans-Niagara Bd Ednl Svc 3181 Saunders Settlement Rd Sanborn NY 14132-9487

SCHMIEDEKAMP, ANN MARIE BOUDREAUX, physicist, educator; b. Houston, Sept. 11, 1948; d. Philip Henry and Leah Marie Boudreaux; m. Carl W. Schmiedekamp; children: Lumelle, Mendel, Brendan, Briana. BS, U. Tex., 1970, PhD, 1976. Vis. scientist Inst. of Physics, Budapest, Hungary, 1974; asst. prof. Pa. State U., Abington, 1978-84, assoc. prof., 1984—; a. Vis. scientist Princeton (NJ) U., 1985—86, Nat. Cancer Inst., Frederick, Md., 1992—93; cons. Smithkline Beecham Pharm., 1999—2000. Office: Pa State U Abington 1600 Woodland Rd Abington PA 19001-3918

SCHMIEL, DAVID GERHARD, clergyman, religious education administrator; b. Cedarburg, Wis., Dec. 10, 1931; s. Gerhard August and Frieda Helena (Labrenz) S.; m. Shirley Ann Friede, July 6, 1957; children: Mark, Peter, Steven, Daniel, Julia. BA, Northwestern Coll., 1953; ThD, Concordia Sem., 1967. Pastor St. Paul's Luth. Ch., Gresham, Nebr., 1958-60, Onalaska, Wis., 1960-62; prof. St. Paul's Coll., Concordia, Mo., 1962-70; prof., dean Concordia Coll., St. Paul, 1970-81; dir. instrn. Concordia Sem., St. Louis, 1981-82; pres. Concordia Coll., Ann Arbor, Mich., 1983-91; dir. theol. edn. svc. Luth. Ch.-Mo. Synod, St. Louis, 1991-93; pres. Concordia Theol. Sem., Ft. Wayne, Ind., 1993-95, ret., 1995. Author: Via Propria and Via Mystica...Gerson, 1969. Found. for Reformation Rsch. Jr. fellow, Southeastern Inst. for Medieval and Renaissance Studies, Jr. fellow, 1965, 66, 68.

SCHMIT, SHARYN KEARNEY, secondary school educator; b. New Orleans, Sept. 10, 1945; d. William Frank and Mercedese Marie (Marks) Kearney; m. Kenneth Arthur Schmit, Dec. 29, 1973; children: Kenneth Kearney, Allison Katherine. BS, Southeastern La. U., 1967; MA, Ga. State U., 1971, Southeastern La. U., 1974. Tchr. Andrew Jackson High Sch., Chalmette, La., 1967-68, Floyd Jr. High Sch., Mableton, Ga., 1968-71, Lockett Elem. Sch., New Orleans, 1972-75, Jos. S. Clark Sr. High Sch., New Orleans, 1975-80; curriculum area specialist New Orleans Pub. Schs., 1980; tchr. Livingston Mid. Sch., New Orleans, 1980-81, Sixth Ward Jr. High Sch., Pearl River, La., 1981-82; tchr., dept. chair Northshore High Sch., Slidell, La., 1982-97, asst. prin., 1997—. Cognitive coach tng. St. Tammany Parish, Covington, La., 1991—, prospective adminstr., math. articulation com. mem., 1992—; model career options La. State Dept. Edn., Baton Rouge, 1991-93; master tchr. assessor for intern tchrs., 1994—. Tchr. Sunday sch. 1st United Meth. Ch., Slidell, La., ch. edn. com. Mem. Nat. Coun. Tchrs. Math., St. Tammany Fedn. Tchrs., La. Assn. Sch. Adminstrs. Home: 97 Live Oak Dr Slidell LA 70461-1305 Office: Northshore High Sch 100 Panther Dr Slidell LA 70461-9103 E-mail: skschmit@bellsouth.net., sks@stpsb.k12.la.us.

SCHMITT, DIANA MAE, elementary education educator; b. Dubuque, Iowa, Jan. 19, 1950; d. Raymond J. and Marie Arlen Schmitt. BA, U. Iowa, 1972; MA, Clarke Coll., Dubuque, 1981; postgrad., U. Wyo. 6th grade tchr. Shelby County Sch. Dist., Shelby, Iowa, 1972-73; 4th and 5th grade tchr. Dist. 200, Woodstock, Ill., 1973-76; rural sch. tchr. Albany County Sch. Dist., Laramie, Wyo., 1976-83, 1st, 3d, 5th and 6th grade tchr., 1983-98; chmn. outdoor classrm. devel. Indian Paintbrush Elem., 1992—. Mem. rev. com. for excellence in sci. edn., adv. com. Western Edn. Adv. Com. for Wyo., 1989; tchr. sci. methods for elem. sch. U. Wyo., 1990-91; mem. Higher Edn. Grant Reading State Com., 1994; participant Sci. Grasp, 1990, Inst. Chemical Edn. Fundamental, 1992; presenter 1st Soviet-Am. Sci. Conv., Moscow, 1991; mem. workshop on water, Nat. Geog. Soc., 1993; presenter NSTA nat. and regional convs., state Wyo. Interdisciplinary Conf. convs., No. Iowa Beginning Reading conf. Recipient Delta award, 1993; named Dist. Exemplary Sci. Tchr., 1986-87; Wyo. Game and Fish grantee, 1993-95, Nat. Geog. Soc. grantee, 1997. Mem. NEA, Internat. Reading Assn., Nat. Sci. Tchrs. Assn., Wyo. Sci. Tchrs. Assn. (sec.), Alpha Delta Kappa (pres.). Home: 5737 Southview Rd Laramie WY 82070-6801 Office: Indian Paintbrush 1653 N 28th St Laramie WY 82072-9200 E-mail: msdmschmitt@yahoo.com.

SCHMITT, JOHANNA MARIE, plant population biologist, educator; b. Phila., Mar. 12, 1953; d. William Francis and Laura Belle (Wear) S.; m. Darrell Marion West, Aug. 6, 1983. BA, Swarthmore (Pa.) Coll., 1974; PhD, Stanford U., 1981. Postdoctoral rsch. assoc. Duke U., Durham, N.C., 1981-82; asst. prof. Brown U., Providence, 1982-87, assoc. prof. biology, 1987-94, prof., 1994—. Mem. R.I. Task Force, New Eng. Plant Conservation program, 1991—; mem. regional advisory com. New Eng. Plant Conservation program, 2000-. Assoc. editor Evolution, 1990-92, Am. Naturalist, 2000-2001; contbr. articles to profl. jours. including Evolution, Ecology, Am. Naturalist, Genetics, Nature. Bd. dirs. Sojourner House, Providence, 1989-92. NSF grad. fellow, 1974, mid. career fellow, 1992-93; rsch. grantee, 1984—; recipient faculty award for women, 1991—. Mem. Soc. for Study of Evolution (coun. mem. 1990-92, exec. v.p. 1994-95, v.p. 1999), Bot. Soc. Am., Ecol. Soc. Am., Am. Soc. Naturalists (v.p. 1997, pres. 2002). Achievements include research on ecological genetics and genomics of natural plant populations: density-dependent phenomena, gene flow and population structure, inbreeding depression, the evolution of sex, maternal effects, seed ecology, natural selection, evolution of plasticity, adaptive significance of phytochrome, ecological risks of transgenic plants. Office: Brown Univ Dept Ecology & Evolution Providence RI 02912-0001

SCHMITT, PAUL JOHN, history and geography educator; b. Pitts., Jan. 25, 1951; s. Phillip John and Adeline Marie (Barnhart) S.; m. Ruth Margaret Glass, June 20, 1987. BS, Ariz. State U., 1976, BA in Edn., 1978; MA, U. Nev., Las Vegas, 1994. Registration clk. Hermosa Inn Resort, Scottsdale, Ariz., 1978-79, asst. mgr., 1979-82; convention svc. mgr. Carefree (Ariz.) Inn Resort, 1982-84; tchr. Tonopah (Nev.) High Sch., 1984-85; reservation clk. Desert Inn Country Club and Spa, Las Vegas, Nev., 1985-92; prof. history C.C. of So. Nev., Las Vegas, 1992—. Mem. Assn. Am. Geographers, Orgn. Am. Historians, Am. Western History Assn., Orgn. Am. Historians, Phi Alpha Theta, Gamma Theta Upsilon. Avocations: reading, photography, horseback riding. Office: CC So Nev Cheyenne Campus Dept Regional Studies 3200 E Cheyenne Ave # C North Las Vegas NV 89030-4228

SCHMITT, PHYLLIS MARY, elementary education educator; b. Muenster, Tex., Jan. 20, 1940; d. Edward Martin and Margaret Mary (Hess) S. BS, U. Tex., 1970. Permanent elem. teaching credential, Tex.; life multi-subject teaching credential, Calif. Elem. tchr. Holy Souls Sch., Little Rock, 1957-61, tchr. 7, 8, 1965-68; tchr. St. Joseph Sch., Rhineland, Tex., 1961-65; tchr. adult basic edn. Austin (Tex.) State Hosp., 1969-70; tchr. Resurrection Sch., Sunnyvale, Calif., 1970-72; tchr. mid. sch. Harmony Sch., Occidental, Calif., 1972-73, elem. tchr., 1973—2002; ret., 2002. Tchr. rep. Harmony Ark Com., Harmony Union Sch. Dist.; marine sci. mentor tchr. Harmony Union Sch., 1985-86. Co-author, editor: For Sea Book 1-2, 1988, For Sea 3 Estuaries, 1993. Ag lit. edn. com. Farm Bur. Sonoma County, Santa Rosa, 1992-98. Grantee Marine Sci. Inst. NSF, Santa Cruz, Calif., 1985, Univ. Rsch. Expeditions, Mendocino, Calif., 1989, Inst. Chemistry Edn., Greeley, Colo., 1988, Sea Edn., Woods Hole, Mass., 1994. Mem. Nat. Marine Edn. Assn., Southwestern Marine Educators, Calif. Ret. Tchrs. Assn., Calif. Tchrs. Assn. (local treas. 1972-76), Calif. Native Plant Soc., Audubon Soc. (edn. com. Madrone chpt. 1994—, rec. sec. 2000-01), Sonoma County Hist. Soc. (bd. dirs. 1996—, pres. 1999-2003, Nat. History Week Edn. award 1989), Sonoma County Mus. Soc., Calif. Acad. Scis. (edn. mem.), San Francisco Fine Arts Mus., Sierra Club. Democrat. Roman Catholic. Avocations: birding, hiking, photography, reading, travel.

SCHMITT, RICHARD, philosopher, educator; b. Frankfurt/Main, Ger., May 5, 1927; came to U.S., 1946, naturalized, 1952; s. Julius and Elisabeth Dorothea S. BA, U. Chgo., 1949, MA, 1952; PhD, Yale U., 1956. Instr. philosophy Yale U., 1956-58; mem. faculty Brown U., 1958—, prof. philosophy, 1968—2001, emeritus prof. philosophy, 2001—. Vis. prof. Stanford U., 1966-67, U. Calif., Santa Barbara, 1971-72, Miles Coll., summer 1964, U. Mass., Boston, 1974 Author: Martin Heidegger on Begin Human, 1967, Alienation and Class, 1983, Introduction to Marx and Engels: A Critical Reconstruction, 1987, Beyond Separateness: The Relatioinal Nature of Human Beings, Their Autonomy, Knowledge, and Power, 1995, Alienation adn Freedom, 2002, also articles on phenomenology and existentialism Marxist theory. Alfred Hodder fellow, 1963-64; Guggenheim fellow, 1965-66 Mem. Am. Philos. Assn. Office: Brown U Dept Philosophy 79 Waterman St Providence RI 02912-9079

SCHMITT, ROLAND WALTER, retired academic administrator; b. Seguin, Tex., July 24, 1923; s. Walter L. and Myrtle F. (Caldwell) S.; m. Claire Freeman Kunz, Sept. 19, 1957; children: Lorenz Allen, Brian Walter, Alice Elizabeth, Henry Caldwell. BA in Math, BS in Physics, U. Tex., 1947, MA in Physics, 1948; PhD, Rice U., 1951; DSc (hon.), Worcester Poly. Inst., 1985, U. Pa., 1985; DCL (hon.), Union Coll., 1985; DL (hon.), Lehigh U., 1986; DSc (hon.), U. S.C., 1988, U. Tech. De Compeigne, 1991; DL (hon.), Coll. St. Rose, 1992, Russell Sage, 1993, Hartford Grad. Ctr., 1995, Ill. Inst. Tech., 1996, Rensselaer Polytechnic Inst., 1997. With GE, 1951-88, R & D mgr. phys. sci. and engring., 1967-74, mgr. energy sci. and engring. R & D, 1974-78, v.p. corp. R & D, 1978-82, sr. v.p. corp. R & D, 1982-86, sr. v.p. sci. and tech., 1986-88, ret., 1988; pres. Rensselaer Poly. Inst., Troy, N.Y., 1988-93; ret., 1993. Bd. dirs. Blasch Precision Ceramics, GlobalSpec-.com, Logical Net, Value Innovations; chair adv. bd. NYSTAR; bd. advisors LearnLinc, 1996-2000; tech. adv. bd. Chrysler Corp., 1990-93; tech. adv. coun. Mobil Corp., 1997-99; mem., past pres. Indsl. Rsch. Inst., 1978-88; energy rsch. adv. bd. U.S. Dept. Energy, 1977-83; mem. Nat. Sci. Bd., 1982-94, chmn., 1984-88; chmn. CORETECH, 1988-93; mem. Com. on Japan, NRC, 1988-90, Comml. Devel. Ind. Adv. Group, NASA, 1988-90; exec. com. Coun. on Competitiveness, 1988-93; chmn. NRC Panel on Export Controls, 1989-91; mem. Dept. Commerce Adv. Commn. on Patent Law Reform, 1990-92; adv. bd. Oak Ridge Nat. Lab., 1993-98; chair Rev. NATO Sci. program, 1998; mem. NRC panel rev. state dept. use sci. tech. and health, 1999—; chmn. Motorola's Sci. Adv. Bd., 1995-99; chmn. rsch. priority panel for NRC Future of Space Sci., 1994-95. Trustee N.E. Savs. Bank, 1978-84; bd. advisors Union Coll., Schenectady, 1981-84, Argonne Univs. Assn., 1979-82, RPI, 1982-88; bd. govs. Albany Med. Ctr. Hosp., 1979-82, 88-90; bd. dirs. Sunnyview Hosp. and Rehab. Ctr., 1978-86, Coun. on Superconductivity for Am. Competitiveness, 1987-89; mem. exec. com. N.Y. State Ctr. for Hazardous Waste Mgmt., 1988-89; chmn. Office of Tech. Assessment adv. panel on industry and environment; mem. Nat. Commn. Ill. Inst. Tech., 1993-94; chair NSF Acad. Rsch. Fleet Rev., 1998-99. With USAAF, 1943-46. Recipient RPI Community Svc. award, 1982, award for disting. contbns. Stony Brook Found., 1985, Rice U. Disting. Alumni award, 1985, IRI Medalist award, 1989, Royal Swedish Acad. of Engring. Sci., 1990, Arthur M. Bueche award Nat. Acad. of Engring., 1995, N.Y. State Bus. Coun.'s Corning award, 2001; named Fgn. Assn. of Engring. Acad. of Japan, U. Albany Found. Acad. Laureate, 1997; named to Jr. Achievement Capital Region Bus. Hall of Fame, 1996; inducted RPI Hall of Fame, 1999. Fellow AAAS, IEEE (Centennial medal 1984, Engring. Leadership award 1989, Founders medal 1992, Hoover medal 1993), Am. Phys. Soc. (Pake award 1993), Am. Acad. Arts and Scis.; mem. NAE (coun.), Am. Inst. Physics (chmn. 1993-98), Coun. Sci. Soc. Pres. (chair 1993-97), N.Y. Acad. Scis. (pres. coun. 1993—), Dirs. Indsl. Rsch., Rensselaer Alumni Assn. (Disting. alumni award 1993), Eta Kappa Nu (eminent mem.) Office: PO Box 240 Rexford NY 12148-0240

SCHMITZ, ALICE J. secondary education educator; b. Milw., Sept. 27, 1951; d. Roy Frederick and Loraine Anna (Schmidt) Schoeni; m. Gerald Wayne Schmitz, June 30, 1984; 1 child, Tyler Gerald. BS, U. Wis., Whitewater, 1973, MS, 1983; cert. in sch. adminstrn., Northern Ill. U., 1989. Secondary sch. tchr., dept. chmn. Richland Ctr. (Wis.) H.S., 1973—80, Nicolet H.S., Glendale, Wis., 1980—84; secondary sch. tchr. Township H.S., Palatine, Ill., 1984—2001; tech. coord. Township H.S. Dist. 211, Palatine, Ill., 2001—. Mem. awards com. and staff devel. com. Hoffman Estates (Ill.) H.S., 1995-2003, lead tchr. Project Link for at-risk students, 1993-99. Webmaster Lake Zurich Cougars Travel Baseball. Named Tchr. of Month, Coca Cola N.W. Suburban Ill., 1997; recipient Those Who Excel award, Ill. State Bd. Edn., 1998, Prin.'s award of excellence, 1996, Prin.'s award in celebration of learning, 2003. Mem. Nat. Bus. Edn. Assn., Ill. Bus. Edn. Assn., Ill. Computer Educators, Parent Tchr. Orgn. (sec. 1999-2002, editor newsletter 2002—), Delta Pi Epsilon (pres. 1983-85). Avocations: reading, son's sporting events, computers. Office: Hoffman Estates HS 1100 W Higgins Rd Hoffman Estates IL 60195-3050

SCHMITZ, DENNIS MATHEW, English language educator; b. Dubuque, Iowa, Aug. 11, 1937; s. Anthony Peter and Roselyn S.; m. Loretta D'Agostino, Aug. 20, 1960; children— Anne, Sara, Martha, Paul, Matthew. BA, Loras Coll., 1959; MA, U. Chgo., 1961. Instr. English Ill. Inst. Tech., Chgo., 1961-62, U. Wis., Milw., 1962-66; asst. prof. Calif. State U., Sacramento, 1966-69, assoc. prof., 1969-74, prof., 1974-99; ret., 1999. Poet-in-residence, 1966-99. Author: We Weep for Our Strangeness, 1969, Double Exposures, 1971, Goodwill, Inc., 1976, String, 1980, Singing, 1985, Eden, 1989, About Night: Selected and New Poems, 1993, The Truth Squad, 2002. Recipient Discovery award Poetry Center, N.Y.C., 1968; winner First Book Competition Follett Pub. Co., 1969; di Castagnola award Poetry Soc. Am., 1986; Shelley Meml. award Poetry Soc. Am., 1987; NEA fellow, 1976-77, 85-86, 92-93, Guggenheim fellow, 1978-79. Mem. PEN, Assoc. Writing Programs. Roman Catholic.

SCHMITZ, DOLORES JEAN, primary education educator; b. River Falls, Wis., Dec. 27, 1931; d. Otto and Helen Olive (Webster) Kreuziger; m. Karl Matthias Schmitz Jr., Aug. 18, 1956; children: Victoria Jane, Karl III. BS, U. Wis., River Falls, 1953; MS, Nat. Coll. Edn., 1982; postgrad., U. Minn., Mankato, 1969, U. Melbourne, Australia, 1989, U. Wis., Milw., 1989, Carroll Coll., 1990, Cardinal Stritch Coll., 1990. Cert. tchr., Wis. Tchr. Manitowoc (Wis.) Pub. Schs., 1953-56, West Allis (Wis.) Pub. Schs., 1956-59, Lowell Sch., Milw., 1960-63, Victory Sch., Milw., 1964, Palmer Sch., Milw., 1966-84, 86-94, unit leader, 1984-86; ret., 1994. Co-organizer Headstart Tchg. Staff Assn., Milw., 1968; insvc. organizer Headstart and Early Childhood, Milw., 1969-92; pilot tchr. for Whole Lang., Hi-Scope and Math. Their Way, 1988-93; bd. dirs. Curriculum Devel. Ctr. of Milw. Edn. Ctr., 1993-94. Author: (curriculum) Writing to Read, 1987, Cooperation and Young Children (ERIC award 1982), Kindergarten Curriculum, 1953. Former supporter Milw. Art Mus., Milw. Pub. Mus., Milw. County Zoo, Whitefish Bay Pub. Libr., Riveredge Nature Ctr.; vol. fgn. visitor program Milw. Internat. Inst., 1966-94, holiday folk fair, 1976-94, Earthwatch, 1989; lobbyist Milw. Pub. Sch. Bd. and State of Wis., 1986-93; coord. comty. vols., 1990-94. Grantee Greater Milw. Ednl. Trust, 1989. Mem. NEA (life), ASCD, Milw. Kindergarten Assn. (rec. sec. 1986-93), Nat. Assn. for Edn. of Young Children, Tchrs. Applying Whole Lang., Wis. Early Childhood Assn., Milw. Tchrs. Ednl. Assn. (co-chmn. com. early childhood 1984-86), Assn. for Childhood Edn. Internat. (charter pres. Manitowoc chpt. 1955-56), Milw. Educating Computer Assn., Alpha Psi Omega. Roman Catholic. Avocations: bicycling, nature, world travel. Home: 1355 Pinellas Bayway S Apt 22 Tierra Verde FL 33715-2140 E-mail: dolintv@aol.com.

SCHMITZ, ROGER ANTHONY, chemical engineer, educator, academic administrator; b. Carlyle, Ill., Oct. 22, 1934; s. Alfred Bernard and Wilma Afra (Aarns) Schmitz; m. Ruth Mary Kuhl, Aug. 31, 1957; children: Jan, Joy, Joni. BSChemE, U. Ill., 1959; PhD in Chem. Engring., U. Minn., 1962. Prof. chem. engring. U. Ill., Urbana, 1962-79; Keating-Crawford prof. chem. engring. U. Notre Dame, Ind., 1979—, chmn. dept. chem. engring., 1979-81, dean engring., 1981-87, v.p., assoc. provost, 1987-95. Cons. Amoco Chems., Naperville, Ill., 1966—77; vis. prof. Calif. Inst. Tech., L.A., 1968—69. Contbr. articles to profl. jours. With U.S. Army, 1953—55. Fellow, Guggenheim Found., 1968. Mem.: AIChE (A.P. Colburn award 1970, R.H. Wilhelm award 1981), Am. Soc. Engring. Edn. (George Westinghouse award 1977), Nat. Acad. Engring. Roman Catholic. Home: 16865 Londonberry Ln South Bend IN 46635-1444 Office: U Notre Dame 301 Cushing Hall Notre Dame IN 46556 E-mail: schmitz.1@nd.edu.

SCHMOEKER, PETER FRANK, secondary school educator; b. St. Louis, Oct. 1, 1957; s. Ernst Alfred and Annemarie Dora (Kawohl) S.; m. Maggy Noelle Taunay, Sept. 29, 1979; children: Adrienne Nepenthe, Camille Aureli, Genevieve Helena. BA in Biology and German, Washington U., St. Louis, 1980; MEd, U. Mo., St. Louis, 1990. Cert. tchr. German, biology, gen. sci., Mo. Med. rsch. tech. II Washington U., 1979-85; sci. and German tchr. Pattonville Sch. Dist., St. Louis, 1985—. Math. and sci. tutor Loretto Learning Ctr., Webster Groves, Mo., 1986—. Leader Boy Scouts Am., 1990—; del. leader People to People Amb. Program, 1994. Mem. NEA, PTA, Eagle Scout Assn., CIM Floaters (pres. 1990—), Goethe Inst. Lutheran. Avocations: sailing, climbing, hiking, caving, camping. Home: 6907 Mitchell Ave Saint Louis MO 63139-3650 Office: Pattonville Heights Mid Sch 195 Fee Rd Maryland Heights MO 63043-2709

SCHMOLDT, PEGGY SUE, cosmetology educator; b. International Falls, Minn., Apr. 11, 1959; d. John Herbert and Elizabeth Ann (Powers) Hauptli; m. Stephen Michael Schmoldt, Jan. 5, 1980 (div. Feb. 1996); children: Jillian Marie, Megan Elizabeth. Student, U. Iowa, 1977-78; diploma, Capri Cosmetology Coll., 1979; student, Regis U., 1993—. Lic. cosmetologist, Colo., Fla.; cert. pvt. cosmetology tchr., vo-tech. tchr., Colo. Hair designer Fashion Ave., Dubuque, Iowa, 1979-81, LaVonne's, Denver, 1981-83, A Unique Boutique, Destrehan, La., 1984-85, V.I.P. Salon, Boca Raton, Fla., 1987-89; sch. mgr., instr. LaVonne's Acad. of Beauty, Denver, 1981-83; nat. platform educator Anion Labs., Inc., Harvey, La., 1984-85; salon mgr., designer, publ. rels. specialist, educator Lord & Taylor Salons, Boynton Beach/Boca Raton, Fla., 1985-87; dir. edn. Cantwell/Creative Sch. Beauty, Pompano Beach, Fla., 1988-91; dir. cosmetology edn. Boca Raton Inst., 1991-92; freelance cosmetologist, educator Profl. Salon Svcs., Westminster, Colo., 1993—. Mem., educator La. Hair Fashion Com., New Orleans, 1985; tchr. Le Team Styles Group, Ft. Lauderdale, Fla., 1986-87; mem. Colo. Edn. Com., Denver, 1993; educator Inter Mountain Beauty Supply, Denver, 1995; cosmetology educator Inst. Hair Design, Arvada, Colo., 1996-97; mem. Nexxus Design Team, 1994, Nat. Hair Am., 1994; framesi technician, educator Bottenfield's/Freeman Beauty Supply, Denver, 1997-99; hair designer, chemical specialist Red Frog Salon, Golden, Colo., 1998—. Pres. New Orleans Cosmetology Assn., 1984; treas., membership chair Palm Beach Cosmetology Assn., 1986-88; vol. Look Good-Feel Better program Am. Cancer Soc., Palm Beach/Broward County, Fla., 1989, Denver, 1993; mem. nat. planning com. trainer's panel LGFB, 1995; sec., mem. legislation/edn. com. Broward County Cosmetology Assn., 1990-92; mem. spkrs. bur. Planned Parenthood of Rocky Mountains, Denver, 1993. Mem. Denver Cosmetology Assn. (pres. 1993, 94), Colo. Cosmetology Assn. (3d v.p. 1993, 1st v.p. 1994, mem. legislation/by-laws com., pres. 1995-96), Colo. Edn. Commn. (co-chmn. 1997-98, 99, Denver affiliate pres., 1998-99.). Roman Catholic. Avocations: swimming, ballet, skiing, hiking, biking.

SCHMOLL, HARRY F., JR., lawyer, educator; b. Somers Point, N.J., Jan. 20, 1939; s. Harry F. Sr. and Margaret E. S.; m. Rita L. Miescier, Aug. 29, 1977. BS, Rider Coll., 1960; JD, Temple U., 1967. Bar: Pa., D.C. 1969, N.J. 1975. With claims dept. Social Security Adminstrn., Phila., 1960-67; staff atty. Pa. State U., State College, 1968-69, instr. criminal justice University Park, 1969-74; regional dir. Pa. Crime Commn., State College, 1969-70; campaign aide U.S. Senator Hugh Scott, Harrisburg, Pa., 1970; pvt. practice law State College, 1970-74, Manahawkin, NJ, 1975-96; prof. criminal justice, prof. emeritus bus. law Burlington County Coll., Pemberton, NJ, 1974—2002; assoc. Mattleman, Weinroth & Miller, P.C., Cherry Hill, NJ, 2003—. Judge mcpl. ct., Stafford Twp., 1982-85. Author: New Jersey Criminal Law Workbook, 1976, 2nd edit., 1979, Absecon Diary of Margie Roth, 1933-37, 2000. Former gen. counsel German Heritage Coun. N.J., Inc.; mem. Barnegat Twp. Rent Control Bd., 1991, Barnegat Twp. Zoning Bd., 1994; mem. fund distbn. com. United Way of Burlington County, N.J., 1987—; trustee H.B. Smith Indsl. Village Conservancy, 1988—; bd. trustees Holiday Village East Cmty. Svcs. Assn., 2003—; mem. Stafford Twp. Com., 1979-81; dep. mayor, 1979. Mem. Pa. Bar assn., N.J. Bar Assn., German-Am. Club So. Ocean County (past pres.), Tri-State Jazz Soc. (bd. dirs.). E-mail: HarrySchmoll2@comcast.net.

SCHNABEL, DIANE SUSAN, speech pathologist, educator; b. Logansport, Ind., Nov. 5, 1945; d. Estal Thomas and Mabel Ethelyn (Benner) Mullin; m. Mark Schnabel, Dec. 18, 1982. BS, Purdue U., 1968; MA, Ball State U., 1977. Cert. tchr., spl. edn. tchr., Ind.; cert. speech pathologist, Ind. Speech therapist Taylor Community Schs., Center, Ind., 1968-72, Woodlawn Ctr., Logansport, 1972-75, dir. children's svcs., 1975-80, program dir., 1980-82; speech therapist Porter County Assn. Retarded Citizens, Valparaiso, Ind., 1984-85, programs and svcs. cons., 1985-86; speech pathologist Four Rivers Rehab. Svcs., Linton, Ind., 1986—. Adviser in health careers Logansport Community Schs., 1975—. Mem. Coun. Exceptional Children, Ind. Speech-Lang.-Hearing Assn. (honors com. 1989-92), Purdue Alumni Assn., Ind. Assn. Rehab. Svcs., Kappa Kappa Kappa. Lutheran. Avocations: travel, reading, cross-stitch, music. Office: Four Rivers Rehab Svcs PO Box 249 Linton IN 47441-0249

SCHNAPP, DIANA CORLEY, speech communication educator; b. Russellville, Ark., Dec. 4, 1946; d. Robert Eston and Claudie (Cates) C. BS, Ill. State U., Normal, 1968, MS, 1970; PhD., U. Md., 1986. Tchr. Davenport (Iowa) Schs., 1968-69; prof. speech communication Black Hawk Coll., Moline, Ill., 1970-92; prof. speech comm. Johnson County C.C., Overland Park, Kans., 1993—97; adj. prof. McHenry Coll., Kans. City, Mo., 1992—93. Cons. U.S. Army Corps Engrs., Hosp. Groups, Cooperative Extension Service, Moline, Rock Island, East Moline, 1973—;adj. prof. Coll. of DuPage, 1993, Rockhurst U., 2000-03 Contbr. articles to profl. jours. and mags. Vol. Sta. WQPT-TV, Luth. Hosp., Moline, 1983-85; tchr., coord. Overland Pk. Ch. of Christ, Women's Ministry Dir., 1999-02; bd. dirs. Towncrest Homeowners Assn., Moline, 1983-86, Coop. Extension Found., Women's Ministry Leader Ch. of Christ, 1993, Children's Family Svcs., Kans. City Health Ministry; Assoc. docent John Wornall House Mus.. Mem. Nat. Communication Assn., Internat. Listening Assn. Democrat. Avocations: reading, collecting art objects, walking, theatre, writing. Home: 9107 W 132nd St Overland Park KS 66213-4321 E-mail: dschnapp@kc.rr.com.

SCHNEIDER, ADELE GOLDBERG, librarian, educator; b. N.Y.C., May 13, 1924; d. Abraham and Anna (Levy) Goldberg; m. Noel Schneider, Jan. 1, 1950; children: Adam Matthew, Tracy Lynn. BA, Bklyn. Coll., 1945;

MLS, Pratt Inst., 1965; MA, L.I. Univ., 1971. Field interview Gallup Poll, N.Y.C., 1941-48; social worker N.Y.C. Dept. Social Svcs., 1949-52; editor Bklyn. Coll. Alumni Quar., 1961-65; instr. Kingsborough C.C./CUNY, 1965-70, asst. prof. dept. libr., 1970-72, assoc. prof., 1972-88, prof., 1988-92, prof. emeritus, 1992—. Contbr. articles to profl. jours. Recipient lifetime achievement award Bklyn. Coll., 2000. Mem. ALA, Libr. Assn. CUNY, N.Y. Tech. Svcs. Librs., Beta Phi Mu. Home: 124 Oxford St Brooklyn NY 11235-2311 Office: 2001 Oriental Blvd Brooklyn NY 11235-2333 E-mail: lordduffy@msn.com.

SCHNEIDER, CARL EDWARD, law educator; b. Exeter, N.H., Feb. 23, 1948; s. Carl Jacob and Dorothy (Jones) S.; m. Joan L. Wagner, Jan. 6, 1976. BA, Harvard Coll., 1972; JD, U. Mich., 1979. Curriculum specialist Mass. Tchrs. Assn., Boston, 1972-75; law clk. to judge U.S. Ct. Appeals (D.C. cir.), Washington, 1979-80; law clk. Potter Stewart U.S. Supreme Ct., Washington, 1980-81; asst. prof. law U. Mich., Ann Arbor, 1981-84, assoc. prof. law, 1984-86, prof. law, 1986—, prof. internal medicine, 1998—, Chauncey Stillman prof. ethics, morality and practice of law; vis. prof. U. Tokyo, 1998. Author: The Practice of Autonomy: Patients, Doctors and Medical Decisions, 1998, (with Margaret F. Brinig) An Invitation to Family Law, 1996, (with Marsha Garrison) The Law of Bioethics, 2003; editor: (book) The Law and Politics of Abortion, 1980, Family Law in Action: A Reader, 1999 (with Margaret F. Brinig and Lee E. Teitelbaum), Law at the End of Life: The Supreme Court and Assisted Suicide, 2000; contbr. articles to profl. jours. Fellow Am. Council of Learned Socs., Ford Found., 1985, Hastings Ctr.; life fellow Clare Coll., Cambridge. Mem. Order of Coif. Office: U Mich Law Sch 801 Monroe St Ann Arbor MI 48109-1210

SCHNEIDER, CAROL GEARY, educational association administrator; B in History magna cum laude, Mount Holyoke Coll.; postgrad., U. London; PhD in History, Harvard U. Instr. U. Chgo., DePaul U., Chgo. State U., Boston U.; exec. v.p. Assn. Am. Colls. and Univs., Washington, 1988—98, pres., 1998—. Contbr. articles to profl. jours. Woodrow Wilson fellow, Harvard U., Kent fellow, Harvard Prize fellow, Mina Shaughnessy fellow, U.S. Dept. Edn., 1982. Mem.: Phi Beta Kappa. Office: Am Assn Colls and Univs 1818 R St NW Washington DC 20009*

SCHNEIDER, CAROLYN ALICE BRAUCH, elementary education educator; b. N.Y.C., Dec. 15, 1946; d. Elliott David and Marie Alice (Giroux) B.; m. Thom J. Schneider, Aug. 3, 1978; children: Logan, Whitney, Brock. BS, U. Bridgeport, 1968. Tchr. phys. edn. Westview (Colo.) Elem. Sch., 1968-72, McElwain (Colo.) Elem. Sch., 1972-75; tchr. phys. edn., health Northglenn (Colo.) Mid. Sch., 1975—, coach gymnastics, 1975-84, coach track, volleyball, 1975—, coach softball, 1998—. Coach North Area Soccer Assn., Thornton, Colo., 1995-96, 96-97 Rec. (competitive), 97— U-11B/Explosion White coach traveling competitive team, U-12B/Colo. XTreme competitive soccer team; instr., bldg. supr. Northglenn Recreation Dept., 1969-84, mem. sch. improvement team, rep. Dist. Sch. Improvement Team. Mem. NEA, AAHPERD, Colo. Edn. Assn., Am. Health Assn. Roman Catholic. Avocations: sports, reading, travel.

SCHNEIDER, ELAINE FOGEL, special education educator, consultant; b. Bklyn., Mar. 6, 1947; d. Maurice Seymour and Lillian (Marowitz) F.; m. Jack Schneider, June 12, 1977; 1 child, Karli. BA, Hunter Coll., 1967; MA, Queens Coll., 1969, NYU, 1977; PhD, Calif. Coast U., 1985. Cert. tchr.; registered dance/movement therapist; infant massage instr. Speech-lang. pathologist N.Y. Dept. Edn., 1969-72; dir. Dance Theatre, Coconut Grove, Fla., 1972-75; chmn. dept. lang.and speech Lancaster (Calif.) Sch. Dist., 1978-81; exec. dir. Antelope Valley Lang. Movement Therapy, Lancaster, 1981—, Babu Steps, Lancaster, 1983—; exec. dir. First Touch Antelope Valley Infant Devel., Lancaster, 1995—, exec. dir. Santa Clarita Baby Steps, SCV therapies, 1996—. Author: Pictures Please! Adult Language Supplement, 1990, The Power of Touch: Infant Massage, 1995, In Infants and Young Children, 1996; contbr. articles to profl. jours.. Bd. dirs. Families for Families Resource Ctr., Lancaster, 1993—, United Way, Lancaster, 1988-96; mem. adv. bd. L.A. County Child Care, 1991—; mem. L.A. County teen pregnancy program State of Calif. Interagy. Coord. Coun., 1988—, state coun. appointee, 1988—; mem. Assistance League of Antelope Valley, 1992-94. Recipient L.A. County award Bd. Suprs., 1993, 1994, People Who Make a Difference award Antelope Valley Press, 1994; grantee March of Dimes, 1993. Mem. Am. Speech-Lang.-Hearing Assn. (dir.-elect dist. 7), Am. Dancer Therapy Assn., Am. Speech-Lang. Pathologists in Pvt. Practice, Infant Devel. Assn., Internat. Assocs. Infant Message, Nat. Assn. for Edn. Young Children, So. Calif. Assn. Edn. of Young Children, Calif. Speech Lang. Assn. Avocations: yoga, skiing, dancing. Office: Antelope Valley Therapies Inc First Touch 540 W Lancaster Blvd Ste 106 Lancaster CA 93534-2534 also: 27616 Newhall Ranch Rd Santa Clarita CA 91355-4015

SCHNEIDER, FRANK DAVID, family physician; b. Brookline, Mass., Aug. 12, 1961; s. Morris I. and Shirley R. (Freedman) S.; m. Peggy S. Lorton, Aug. 14, 1993; children: Michael, Brian, Daniel, Allison. BA, Boston U., 1983, MD, 1987; MS in Pub. Health, U. Mo., 1992. Diplomate Am. Bd. Family Practice; lic. physician N.C., Tex. Intern Duke U., Fayetteville, NC, 1987—88, resident in family practice, 1988—90; acad. fellow, clin. instr. dept. family and cmty. medicine U. Mo., Columbia, 1990—92; asst. prof. U. Tex. Health Sci. Ctr., San Antonio, 1992—98, dir. med. student edn. dept. family practice, 1993—99, assoc. prof., 1999—, residency dir., 1999—2002. Mem. staff Univ. Hosp., San Antonio, 1992, U. Mo. Hosp. and Clinics, Columbia, 1990, Santa Rosa Hosp., 1997; lectr. in field. Contbr. articles on family violence and med. edn. to profl. jours. Am. Acad. Family Physicians Found. grantee, 1994, HHS grantee, 1995, 98, 2000; recipient Tex. Acad. Family Physicians Rsch. award, 1996. Mem.: AMA (nat. adv. coun. violence and abuse 2001—, chair edn. com.), Tex. Med. Assn., Bexar County Med. Soc., Tex. Acad. Family Physicians (pres. 2003—), Soc. Tchrs. Family Medicine (chmn. group on fellowship tng. 1991—93, chmn. group on violence edn. 1996—2000, edn. com. 1997—2001, family medicine curriculum project adv. com. 2001—), Am. Acad. Family Physicians (commn. on pub. health 2001—), Assn. Am. Med. Colls. (group on ednl. affairs 1998—). Office: U Tex Health Sci Ctr Dept Family Practice 7703 Floyd Curl MSC 7794 San Antonio TX 78229-3900 E-mail: fschneider@uthscsa.edu.

SCHNEIDER, GRETA, economist, speaker, author, security consultant; b. Bklyn. Student, Bklyn. Conservatory of Music, 1961—66; BA, MA, CUNY, 1975, MA, 1976. Writer, cons., Pitts., 1972-73; cons. Flushing, N.Y., 1973-85; sr. writer, cons. Buck Cons. Inc., N.Y.C., 1985-86; chmn., CEO Schneider Cons. Inc., N.Y.C., 1986-90; pvt. cons. Greta Schneider Cons., N.Y.C., 1991—; prin. Schneider Consulting Group, 1996—. Lectr. The Learning Annex, 1995-96, 2002, Seminar Ctr., N.Y.C., 1998-, others; advisor Am. Women's Econ. Devel. Corp., 1988—; adv. bd. Women's Profl. Coun., 1998; guest mem. discussion Reuters Bus. Report, 1998; mem. Women's Econ. Round Table, 1998; mem. Profl. Women's Adv. Bd., 1998; spkr. in field. Author: Exploding the Bankruptcy Mystique, 1993, Holistic Bankruptcy, 1998, 2002. Mem. Little Theatre Group, Marathon Cmty. Ctr., Little Neck, N.Y., 1980-83; founder, pres. Bankruptcy Anonymous, 1996; mem. Bklyn. Conservatory of Music, 1961-66. Cambridge Biographical Inst. fellow, 1993. Mem. AFTRA, Nat. Assn. Women Bus. Owners, Nat. Assn. Bus. Communicators, Internat. Platform Assn. (spkr. 2001), Employee Assistance Profls. Assn., Soc. Human Resource Mgmt., U.S. C. of C., Writers Guild Am., Rotary. Avocations: chef, pilot, tennis, chess, speech coach. Office: 130 W 30th St New York NY 10001-4004

SCHNEIDER, JAMES JOSEPH, military theory educator, consultant; b. Oshkosh, Wis., June 18, 1947; s. Joseph Edward and Virginia Gertrude Schneider; m. Peggy L. Spees, July 28, 1973 (dec. May 1976); m. Claretta Virginia Burton, Nov. 11, 1984; children: Kevin, Jason, Jenifer, Julie. BA, U. Wis., Oshkosh, 1973, MA, 1974; PhD, U. Kans., 1992. Planning evaluator Winnegago County, Oshkosh, 1978-80; ops. rsch. analyst Tng. and Doctrine Command Analysis Ctr., Ft. Leavenworth, Kans., 1980-84; prof. mil. theory Sch. Advanced Mil. Studies U.S. Army Command and Gen. Staff Coll., Ft. Leavenworth, 1984—. Adj. assoc. prof. history Russian and East European Studies Ctr., U. Kans., 1994—; vis. assoc. prof. philosophy St. Mary Coll., Leavenworth, Kans., 2000. Author: (monograph) Exponential Decay of Armies in Battle, 1985, The Structure of Strategic Revolution, 1994; also numerous articles. With U.S. Army, 1965-68, Vietnam. Recipient medal for civilian achievement Dept. Army, 1989, superior civilian svc. award, 2001, Bronze Order of St. George, U.S. Cav. Assn., 1990 Mem. Am. Hist. Assn., Mil. Ops. Rsch. Soc., Soc. Mil. History, Phi Beta Delta. Office: U S Army Command/Gen Staff Coll Sch Advanced Mil Studies Fort Leavenworth KS 66027

SCHNEIDER, JANICE KAY, secondary education educator; b. Pana, Ill., Feb. 7, 1951; d. Raymond Chris and Beulah A. (Hill) Brinkman; m. Charles L. Schneider, Apr. 27, 1974; children: Bryce (dec.), Alayna, Alyssa, Charles L. IV. BS in Edn., Ea. Ill. U., 1972; MA in Lit., Sangamon State U., Springfield, Ill., 1978. Cert. tchr., Ill. Tchr. Waverly (Ill.) High Sch., 1972-73; tchr. Spanish and English Nokomis (Ill.) High Sch., 1973—. Avocations: paso fino horses, gardening, antiques. Office: Nokomis High Sch 511 Oberle St Nokomis IL 62075-1015

SCHNEIDER, JAYNE BANGS, school librarian; b. Cin., Nov. 9, 1950; d. Neil Kendrick and Edith (Dilworth) Bangs; m. James R. Bronn, June 9, 1973 (div. 1979); m. Arthur Schneider, July 11, 1986; 1 stepdaughter, Heather. BS in Elem. Edn., Ea. Ky. U., 1973; MA in Libr. Sci., Spaulding U., 1978. Tchr., 1st & 2d grades Fort Thomas (Ky.) Pub. Schs./Ruth Moyer Elem., 1973; libr. Lassiter Middle Sch., Ky., 1973-2000; part-time libr. Jefferson County Pub. Schs. Profl. Libr.; part-time libr., Jefferson County Pub. Schs. Profl. Libr. Gheens Acad. Presenter Nat. Mid. Sch. Assn., St. Louis, 1988, Denver, 89, Assn. Ind. Media Educators, 1992; part-time libr. Jefferson County Pub. Schs., Profl. Libr., Gheens Acad. Co-capt. Block Watch; tree bd. mem. City of Kingsley; mem. Ky. Hist. Soc., Friends of the Libr. Recipient Outstanding Media Librarian award Jefferson County, 1998; named Superstar Ky. Ednl. TV; Owen Badgett grantee Louisville Community Grant, 1988. Mem. NEA, ALA, AASL, PTSA (life), Nat. Mid. Sch. Assn., Jefferson County Sch. Media Assn. (treas. 1982-83, sec. 1991-92, newsletter editor 1992-93, pres.-elect 1993-94, pres. 1994-95, nomination chairperson 1996-97, bd. dirs. 1997-2000, named Jefferson County's Outstanding Sch. Media Librarian 1998), Ky. Sch. Media Assn. (bd. dirs. 1994-95, 97-98). Presbyterian. Avocations: genealogy, collecting antique glass, knitting. Home: 2553 Kings Hwy Louisville KY 40205-2646 E-mail: jaynesch@aol.com.

SCHNEIDER, KATHLEEN ANN, secondary school educator; b. Wisconsin Rapids, Wis., Jan. 5, 1949; d. Walter Edward and Darlene Emma (Schwoch) Reynolds; m. Gregory Russell Schneider, June 17, 1972; children: Gregory John. BA, Luther Coll., 1971; MED, Nat. Louis U., 1988. Cert. speech educator. Tchr. Sts. Mary and Joseph, Fond du Lac, Wis., 1973-75, St. Mary Sch., Pewaukee, Wis., 1975-78, Sch. Dist. Kettle Moraine, Wales, Wis., 1979—, writing coord., 1988-93. Mem. WCTE, Nat. Coun. Tchrs. English (newsletter editor 1981, dir. 1994-2003), Wis. Edn. Assn. Coun., Phi Delta Kappa. Roman Catholic. Home: 183 Willow Dr Hartland WI 53029-1313 Office: Kettle Moraine High Sch PO Box 902 Wales WI 53183-0902 E-mail: schneidk@kmsd.edu.

SCHNEIDER, LOIS ALENE, elementary education educator; b. Baxter Springs, Kans., Aug. 17, 1937; d. Wayman Oscar Fain and Laura Marie (Matthews) Fain-Stephens; m. Donald L. Schneider, Mar. 7, 1959; children: Timothy Mark, James Royce. BS in Edn., S.E. Mo. U., 1959, MEd, 1967. Tchr. Cape Girardeau (Mo.) Pub. Schs., 1960-62, Dexter (Mo.) Pub. Schs., 1962-67, Shawnee Mission Sch. Dist., Prairie Village, Kans., 1967-71, Parkway Sch. Dist., Chesterfield, Mo., 1971—99. Treas. Boy Scouts, Florissant, 1973-82. Mem. ASCD, Mo. State Tchrs. Assn., Internat. Reading Assn., Parkway Ind. Community Tchrs. Assn. (treas. 1976-86), Nat. Coun. for Social Studies. Home: 11807 Spruce Orchard Dr Saint Louis MO 63146-4823

SCHNEIDER, MARY LOUISE, retired elementary education educator; b. Waterville, Wash., Oct. 17, 1918; d. John Steve and Alice Ray (Jones) S. BA in Edn., Holy Names Coll., 1940. Cert. elem. tchr. Wash., 1940. Tchr. Mud Springs/Douglas County, Mansfield, Wash., 1941-42; elem. tchr. Mansfield Sch. dist., Douglas County, Wash., 1942-43, Waterville (Wash.) Sch. Dist., Douglas County, Wash., 1943-49, Lewis and Clark Elem. Sch., Wenatchee, Wash., 1949-60; spl. reading tchr. H.B. Ellison Jr. High, Wenatchee, 1960-62, Orchard Jr. High, Wenatchee, 1962-67; lang. arts tchr. Pioneer Jr. High, Wenatchee, 1967-77; retired, 1977. Author lang. arts learning packages for students, 1967; co-author: Name on the Schoolhouse, 1989. Vol. Am. Heart Assn., Wenatchee, 1975-90, Am. Cancer Soc., Wenatchee, 1975-88. Recipient Cert. of Recognition, Wash. State Ct. Cath. Daus. of the Ams., 1970, 72, 74. Mem.: AAUW (treas. 1973—75), PEO (pres. 1980—82, 1988—90), Chelan-Douglas County Sch. Retirees Assn. (com. chmn. 1989—90), Cath. Daus. of the Ams. (state pres. 1984—86, nat. evangelization chmn. 1986—88, local ct. pres. 1958—60, 1999—2001, author Wash. State Ct. of Cath. Daus. 1988). Avocation: sewing.

SCHNEIDER, MAX ALEXANDER, physician, educator; b. Buffalo, N.Y., June 29, 1922; s. Henry Nathanial and Ruth Irene (Alexander) S.; life ptnr. Ronald F. Smelt. MD, SUNY Buffalo, 1949. Cert. Am. Soc. Addiction Medicine; diplomate Am. Bd. Med. Examiners. Residency internal medicine Buffalo Gen. Hosp., 1950-52, internship, 1949-50; instr. in medicine SUNY, Buffalo, 1953-64; fellow Harvard Med. Sch., Boston, 1952-53; clinical assoc. prof. Univ. Calif., Irvine, 1989-96; medical dir. Beverly Manor/Care Hosp., Orange, Calif., 1969-76; clinical prof. U. Calif., Irvine, 1996—; edn. dir. chem. dependency recovery svcs. St. Joseph Hosp., Orange, Calif., 1976-88, medical dir., 1988-97; dir. of edn. Positive Action Ctr. Chapman Med. Ctr., Orange, 1997—. Cons. N.Am. Rockwell, 1970—80; mem. sci. adv. bd. Am. Coun. Drug Addiction, 1993—99; mem. drug abuse adv. com. FDA, 1993—96, chair, 1996—97, cons., 1997—2001; chair Ruth Fox Meml. Endowment Fund Am. Soc. Addiction Medicine, 1995—; bd. chair Nat. Coun. Alcoholism and Drug Dependency, 1999—2000; pres. Med. Edn. and Rsch. Found., 1981—2002, bd. dirs.; established tng. of addiction medicine U. Calif., Irvine, 1972—; lectr. on addiction medicine. Contbr. numerous articles to profl. jours.; lectr. in field. Recipient Disting. Svc. award Jr.C of C., Buffalo, 1956, Citation for Civic Svc., City Anaheim, 1981, Disting. Svc. award Nat. Assn. State Alcohol & Drug Abuse., 1985, Disting. Cmty. Svc. award Elections Com. Orange County, 1986, Man of Yr. award Orange County Cultural Pride, 1992, Disting. Svc. award Am. Soc. Addiction Medicine, 1993, Silver Key award Nat. Coun. Alcoholism & Drug Dependence, 1993, Physician of Yr. award Orange County Medical Assn., 1995, Disting. Svc. award Pasadena Coun. Alcoholism & Drug Dependence, 1996, John Wallace Life-Time Achievement award Merrill Scott Symposium on Alcoholism, 1997, and numerous others. Fellow Am. Coll. Addiction Treatment Adminstrs., Am. Soc. Addiction Medicine (pres. 1985-87), Calif. Soc. Addiction Medicine (pres. 1983-85); mem. AMA, ACP, Am. Soc. Internal Medicine, Calif. Medical Assn., Orange County Calif. Jewish. Avocations: travelling, organizing trips to foreign countries, classical music, opera. Office: Max A Schneider MD Inc 3311 E Kirkwood Ave Orange CA 92869-5211 Fax: (714) 639-0987. E-mail: masmdinc@aol.com.

SCHNEIDER, THOMAS AQUINAS, surgeon, educator, retired surgeon; b. St. Charles, Mo., Dec. 22, 1934; s. Vincent Augustine and Anna Maria (Marheineke) Schneider; m. Joyce Elaine Diehr, June 7, 1958; children: Lisa, Thomas, Dawn, Tracy. BS, Loras Coll., 1954; MD, St. Louis U., 1958. Diplomate Am. Bd. Surgery. Resident surgery St. Louis City Hosp., 1958—63; pvt. practice St. Charles, 1963—2001; ret., 2001. Clin. instr. St. Louis U., 1966—91, asst. clin. prof., 1991—; med. dir. vascular lab. St. Joseph Health Ct., St. Charles, 1991—, dir. trauma svc., 1981—91. Fellow: ACS; mem.: St. Louis Vascular Soc. (pres. 1993—95), St. Louis Surg. Soc. (councilor 1988—91, v.p. 1996—97), Mo. Com. on Trauma, Hodgen Club (pres. 1988), Alpha Omega Alpha. Roman Catholic. Avocations: golf, music, history.

SCHNITZLER, BEVERLY JEANNE, designer, art educator, writer; b. Berkeley, Calif. children: Erich Gregory. BS, Ariz. State U., 1954; MA, Calif. State U., L.A., 1959; postgrad., Claremont Grad. Sch., 1956-59, Chouinard Art Inst., L.A., 1960-63. Spl. art tchr. and cons. Alhambra (Calif.) City Sch. Dist., 1958—60; prof. art Calif. State U., L.A., 1960—2002, prof. emeritus, 1998—. Cons. in art and creative fabric art Calif. State U., L.A., 1960—; lectr. in field; Calif. State U. del. for internat. acad. exch. guidelines to Yunnan Art Inst., Kunming, China, 1993. Author: New Dimensions in Needlework, 1978; project dir. and head designer heraldic banners Calif. State U., L.A., 1986-87; exhibiting artist in fiber art; exhibited at Regional Golden Thimble Exhbn., 1990 Participant student/prof. exch. program Kunming, 1993; lifetime sponsor Pasadena Fine Arts Club, sponsor student scholarship com., 1996-98, historian, 2003—. Calif. State U. L.A. instl. grantee, 1978, 79; AAUW Found. grantee, 1988; recipient Award for Outstanding Artistic Merit, Calif. State U. L.A. Assoc. Students, 1987; scholar conf. Spain and Portugal of the Navagators: The Age of Discovery to the Enlightenment, Georgetown U., 1990, scholar conf. participant Portugal and Spain of the Navigators: The Age of Exploration, George Washington U., 1992; recipient Emily Gates Nat. Alumna Achievement award Sigma Sigma Sigma, 1995. Mem. Nat. Surface Design Assn., Costume and Textile Coun. of L.A. County Mus., Internat. Designers Assn., Internat. World Conf. of Educators, AAUW, Costume Soc. Am., Fine Art Club of Pasadena. Office: Calif State U Art Dept 5151 State University Dr Los Angeles CA 90032-4226

SCHNOSE, LINDA MAE, special education educator; b. Herington, Kans., May 13, 1952; d. Ralph William and Agnes Mae (Sander) Schrant; m. Gregory Dean Schnose, June 5, 1976; children: Christina, Elise. BA in Human Devel. and Family Life, U. Kans., 1974; BA in Edn., Wichita (Kans.) State U., 1978, MEd, 1979. Secondary tchr. learning disabled Unified Sch. Dist. 497, Lawrence, Kans., 1980—. Staff develop. bldg. rep., 1993—99, inclusion com. chmn. 1994-95, collaborative tchr. in math. West Jr. H.S., 1996—. Tchr. Corpus Christi Ch., Lawrence, 1988—98, mem. jr. high activities com., 1994-95; sec. Lawrence Aquahawks Swim Club, 1994-95, pres., 1995-96, treas., 1996—98; co-chmn. reading task force, 2001—, mem. continuous improvement team, 2001—, prin. selection com., 2003 Grantee, NEH, 1998—2003. Mem. Coun. for Exceptional Children (chair membership com. 1989-91), Coun. for Learning Disabilities, NEA, Kans. Med. Aux., Nat. Med. Aux., Kans. Edn. Assn., Lawrence Edn. Assn. (bldg. rep. 1987-91), Douglas County Med. Aux., Nat. Staff Devel. Coun., Phi Delta Kappa. Roman Catholic. Avocations: reading, sailboarding, sewing, biking, travel. Home: 1708 Lake Alvamar Dr Lawrence KS 66047-9303 Office: West Jr High Sch 2700 Harvard Rd Lawrence KS 66049-2629

SCHNUCKER, ROBERT VICTOR, history and religion educator; b. Waterloo, Iowa, Sept. 30, 1932; s. Felix Victor and Josephine (Maasdam) S.; m. Anna Mae Engelkes, Sept. 18, 1955; children: Sarai Ann, Sar Victor, Christjahn Dietrich. AB, NE Mo. State U., 1953; BD, U. Dubuque, 1956; MA, U. Iowa, 1960, PhD, 1969. Ordained to ministry Presbyn. Ch., 1956/. Pastor United Presbyn. Ch. USA, Springville, Iowa, 1956-63, Meth.-Presbyn. Ch., Labelle, Mo., 1976-97; asst. prof. N.E. Mo. State U., Kirksville, 1963-65, assoc. prof., 1963-65, prof., 1969—99; interim pastor Bethel Presbyn. Ch., Grundy Center, Iowa, 1999—2001, First Presbyn. Ch., Aplington, 2002—. Dir. Thomas Jefferson U. Press; supr. Bible exam. Presbyn. Ch. USA, Louisville, 1977-89; bd. dirs. Ctr. for Reformation Rsch., St. Louis, 1984-99; pres. Conf. of Hist. Jours., 1993; adj. prof. religion U. No. Iowa, 1999-2001, vis. prof. religion and humanities, 2001-2002, adj. prof. humanities, 2003—. Author: A Glossary of Terms for Western Civilization, 1975, Helping Humanities Journal Survive, 1985, History Assessment Test, 1990; editor: Calviniana, 1989, Historians of Early Modern Europe, 1976-93, 97, Network News Exch.., 1978-88; pres. 1st and 2d Editing History, Conf. for Hist. Jour., 1985-97; book rev. editor, mng. editor 16th Century Jour., 1972-97; pub. 16th Century Essays and Studies, 1980-97; contbr. articles to profl. jours. Recipient 16th Studies Conf. medal for Significant Achievement in Early Modern Studies, 1997, Presdl. Citation for Contbns. to the Univ., Truman State U., 1997; fellow Soc. Sci. Study of Religion, 1988, Sixteenth Century Studies conf., 1998; NEH grantee for jour. pubs., 1980. Mem. AAUP, Am. Acad. Religion, Renaissance Soc. Am., Am. History Assn. (chmn. Robinson prize com. 1987), Am. Soc. Ch. History, Soc. History of Edn., Soc. Bibl. Lit., Soc. for Reformation Rsch., Soc. Scholarly Pubs., Soc. for Values in Higher Edn., Conf. for Hist. Jour., Am. Coun. Learned Soc. (exec. bd. conf. adminstr. officers 1993-96, sec. 1994, chmn. 1995-96), Conf. Faith and History, 16th Century Studies Cons. (exec. sec. 1972-97). Office: U No Iowa Dept Philosophy & Religion Baker Hall 148 Cedar Falls IA

SCHOBERT, MELODY A. counseling educator; b. Creston, Iowa, May 8, 1953; d. Joseph C. and Donna J. Schobert; children: Arlen D. Chase, Benjamin M. MusB, Iowa State U., 1976, M in Counselor Edn., 1987; PhD in Counselor Edn., U. Iowa, 2000. Lic. counselor 7-12, tchr. K-12 music, 7-12 secondary tchr., postsecondary counselor, postsecondary psychology tchr., Iowa. Student devel. specialist William Penn Coll., Oskaloosa, Iowa, 1987-90; acad. advisor III Iowa State U., Ames, 1990-2000; asst. prof. U. Memphis, 2000—03; clin. instr. counseling, sch. and ednl. psychology SUNY, Buffalo, 2003—. Presenter in field. Performer River City Concert Band; bd. mem. Tenn. Initiative for Gifted Edn. Reform (TIGER), 2003. Mem.: ACA, Am. Sch. Counseling Assn., Am. Assn. for Counselor Edn. and Supervision. Avocations: musical groups, counted cross-stitch. Office: SUNY Buffalo 407 Baldy Hall Buffalo NY 14260-1000 E-mail: ms246@buffalo.edu.

SCHOCH, JACQUELINE LOUISE, retired academic administrator; b. DuBois, Pa., July 17, 1929; d. Horace Gordon and Cora (Wineberg) S.; B.Sc. in Health and Phys. Edn., Pa. State U., 1951, M.Ed. in Counseling and Psychology, 1960, D.Ed. in Counseling and Psychology, 1965; cert. Inst. Ednl. Mgmt., Harvard U., 1979. Tchr. girls' phys. edn. Jr.-Sr. High Sch., Ford City, Pa., 1951-52; tchr. girl's phys. edn., acad. U.S. history DuBois Area Sr. High Sch., 1952-56, girls' guidance counselor, 1956-65; dir. guidance DuBois Area Sch. Dist., 1965-67, dir. instrn., 1967-70; asst. dir. for resident instrn. DuBois campus Pa. State U., 1970-76, assoc. dir. acad. affairs, 1976-78, dir. DuBois campus, 1978-90, campus exec. officer, also mem., chmn. univ. coms., faculty senate, ret., 1990. Instr. polit. action courses local C. of C., 1963; instr. adult swimming classes local YMCA, 1953-55; instr. continuing edn. program Pa. State U., 1967-70, also asst. prof. edn., 1970—. Cons. Appalachia project, W.Va., 1967-68; mem. evaluating teams for evaluating secondary schs. Middle States Evaluation Com., 1960-62; chair Penelec Consumer Adv. Com.; mem. Penelec Ednl. Com.; mem. commn. for women Pa. State U.; mem. adv. com. Pa. State U. Alumni Assn. Bd. dirs. DuBois area United Fund, co-chmn. fund raising campaign, 1967-68, 2d v.p., 1970— ; bd. dirs. DuBois council Girl Scouts, 1954-56, Family Life Center-Luth. Services, 1972-76; treas. DuBois Ednl. Found., 1981—; bd. dirs. DuBois Area YMCA; v.p. bd. dirs. Clearfield County Area Agy. on Aging; elder St. Peters United Ch. of Christ. Named Boss of Yr., Internat. Secs. Assn., 1977; recipient Disting. Citizens award

Jaycees, 1990. Mem. Delta Mu Sigma, Delta Psi Omega, Iota Alpha Delta, Delta Kappa Gamma, Pi Lambda Theta, Phi Delta Kappa. Lodge: Rotary (Paul Harris fellow 1989). Office: DuBois Campus Pa State U Du Bois PA 15801

SCHOCHOR, JONATHAN, lawyer, educator; b. Suffern, N.Y., Sept. 9, 1946; s. Abraham and Betty (Hechtor) S.; m. Joan Elaine Brown, May 31, 1970; children: Lauren Aimee, Daniel Ross. BA, Pa. State U., 1968; JD, Am. U., 1971. Bar: D.C. 1971, U.S. Dist. Ct. D.C. 1971, U.S. Ct. Appeals (D.C. cir.) 1971, Md. 1974, U.S. Dist. Ct. Md. 1974, U.S. Supreme Ct. 1986. Assoc. McKenna, Wilkinson & Kittner, Washington, 1970-74, Ellin & Baker, Balt., 1974-84; ptnr. Schochor, Federico & Staton, Balt., 1984—. Lectr. in law; expert witness to state legis. Editor-in-chief: Am. U. Law Rev., 1970—71. Mem. ABA, ATLA (state del. 1991, state gov. 1992-95), Am. Bd. Trial Advs. (membership com. 1994—), Am. Bd. Trial Advs., Am. Judicature Soc., Md. State Bar Assn. (spl. com. on health claims arbitration 1983), Md. Trial Lawyers Assn. (bd. govs. 1986-87, mem. legis. com. 1985-88, chmn. legis. com. 1986-87, sec. 1987-88, exec. com. 1987-92, v.p. 1987-88, pres.-elect 1989, pres. 1990-91), Balt. City Bar Assn. (legis com. 1986-87, spl. com. on tort reform 1986, medicolegal com. 1989-90, cir. ct. for Balt. City task force-civil document mgmt. sys. 1994-95), Bar Assn. D.C., Internat. Platform Assn., Phi Alpha Delta. Office: Schochor Federico & Staton PA 1211 Saint Paul St Baltimore MD 21202-2783

SCHOEN, RICHARD MELVIN, mathematics educator, researcher; b. Celina, Ohio, Oct. 23, 1950; s. Arnold Peter and Rosemary (Heitkamp) S.; m. Doris Helga Fischer-Colbrie, Oct. 29, 1983; children: Alan, Lucy. BS, U. Dayton, 1972; PhD, Stanford U., 1976. Lectr. U. Calif.-Berkeley, 1976-78, prof. math., 1980-85; asst. prof. Courant Inst. NYU, 1978-80; prof. math. U. Calif.-La Jolla, 1985-87, Stanford U., 1987—. Contbr. articles to profl. jours. Fellow NSF, 1972, Alfred P. Sloan Found., 1979, MacArthur Found. prize, 1983, Bôcher prize, 1989. Mem. Am. Acad. Arts and Scis., Am. Math. Soc., Nat. Acad. Sci. Democrat. Office: Stanford U Mathematics Dept Stanford CA 94305

SCHOENBECK, AUDREY KAY, parochial school educator; b. Geneva, Nebr., Oct. 23, 1949; d. Arthur and Martha Lois (Bartels) S. BSEd, Concordia Tchrs. Coll., Seward, Nebr., 1972; MA in Edn., Concordia Tchrs. Coll., 1982. Tchr. Dist. 55, Burwell, Nebr.; English tchr. Aoyama Gakuin Jr. Coll., Tokyo; tchr. Faith Luth. Sch., Ft. Lauderdale, Fla. Mem. Assn. for Supervision and Curriculum Devel. Home: RR 1 Box 58 Daykin NE 68338-9801

SCHOENBERG, MARGARET MAIN, former English language educator; b. Winnipeg, Manitoba, Can., Apr. 2, 1923; came to U.S., 1948; d. George Knowles and Catherine Bruce (Oswald) Main; m. Emanuel Schoenberg, Oct. 23, 1953 (dec. Aug. 1977); children: Paul, Roberta S. Johnson. BA in English, U. Manitoba, 1946; MA, Radcliffe Coll., 1950; PhD, Harvard U., 1958; AASc, RN, Adirondack C.C., 1987; BA in Music, SUNY, Potsdam, 1992. Licentiate Royal Schs. Music, London. Lectr. English U. Manitoba, Winnipeg, 1946-48; instr. English U. Akron, Ohio, 1956-60; assoc. prof. English Kent (Ohio) State U., 1964-82, prof. emeritus, 1982—. Performer concert piano, 1965-87, dramatic reader, writer, 1994. Departmental scholar Crane Sch. Music SUNY, 1993. Mem. Pi Kappa Lambda. Home: Rte 28 Box 372 Indian Lake NY 12842 E-mail: manx@capital.net., margaretschoenberg@hotmail.com.

SCHOENEBERG, JOYCE EILEEN, secondary school biology educator; b. St. Louis, Jan. 13, 1944; d. John F. and Sophie A. (Nachowiak) Zielinski; m. Carl M. Schoeneberg, Dec. 18, 1971; children: C. Jason, Jennifer. BA in Zoology, Washington U., St. Louis, 1965; MEd in Biology, So. Ill. U., 1972. Cert. secondary biology tchr., Mo. Life sci. tchr. Normandy (Mo.) Sch. Dist., 1965-69; biology tchr. Hazelwood (Mo.) Sch. Dist., 1969-73, Parkway Sch. Dist., St. Louis County, Mo., 1983—. Sci. chair Parkway Sch. Dist., St. Louis County, Mo., 1992—. Mem. Sci. Tchrs. Mo., Nat. Assn. Biology Tchrs., Phi Mu (pres. 1964-65). Methodist. Avocations: travel, gardening, tennis, photography. Office: Parkway N High Sch 12860 Fee Fee Rd Saint Louis MO 63146-4498

SCHOENFELD, ALAN HENRY, mathematics and education educator; b. N.Y.C., July 9, 1947; s. Neil Howard and Natalie (Weinberg) S.; m. Jean Snitzer, June 14, 1970. BS in Math., Queens Coll., 1968; MS in Math., Stanford U., 1969, PhD in Math., 1973. Lectr. U. Calif., Davis, 1973-75; from asst. prof. to assoc. prof. Hamilton Coll., Clinton, N.Y., 1978-81, U. Rochester, N.Y., 1981-84; lectr. U. Calif., Berkeley, 1975-78, assoc. prof. edn., math., 1985-86, prof., 1986—, chmn. div. edn. in math., sci. and tech., 1987—98, chmn. Sch. Edn., 1994—98. Chmn. Grad. Group in Sci. and Math. Edn., U. Calif., Berkeley, 1985-87; chief organizer IV Internat. Conf. Math. Edn., 1984. Author: Mathematical Problem Solving, 1985, Mathematical Association of AmericaNotes # 1, Problem Solving, 1983; editor: Cognitive Science and Mathematics Education, 1987, A Source Book for College Mathematics Teaching, 1990, Mathematical Thinking and Problem Solving, 1994, Research in Collegiate Mathematics Education, vol. 1, 1994, vol. 2, 1996, vol. 3, 1998, vol. 4, 2000. Mem. State Calif. Math. Framework Com., 1988-90; mem. adv. panel Calif. Assessment Program, 1988—; mem. Supt.'s Math. Task Force, 1995. Grantee NSF, 1979, 85, 87, 90-92, 96-97, 2001, Sloan Found., 1984, 87, Spencer Found., 1983, 93. Mem. Nat. Acad. Edn. (exec. bd. 1995—, v.p. 2001—), Math. Assn. Am. (chmn. teaching undergrad. math. com. 1982-89, mem. editorial bd. Jour. Rsch. Math. Edn. 1982-85, chmn. 1984-85), Am. Ednl. Rsch. Assn. (exec. com. Spec. Int. Group Math. Edn. 1984-86, chair pubs. com. 1994—, pres. 1998-2000), Am. Math. Soc. (com. on edn. 1992-97), Cognitive Sci. Soc., Nat. Coun. Tchrs. Math. (mem. rsch. adv. com. 1990-93, chair 1992-93, leader prins. and stds. 1997-2000), Nat. Bd. for Profl. Teaching Standards (mem. math. panel 1990—), Nat. Rsch. Coun. (math. sci. edn. bd. task force on K-12 1986-88, bd. testing/assessment 1993-98). Avocations: food, wine. Home: 830 Colusa Ave Berkeley CA 94707-1839 Office: U Calif Dept Edn Berkeley CA 94720-0001

SCHOENFELD, DIANA LINDSAY, photographer, educator; b. Knoxville, Tenn., Sept. 3, 1949; d. David Lindsay and Martha Jane (Zigler) S. Student, Fla. Presbyn. Coll., 1967-69, U. Neuchâtel, Switzerland, 1969-70; B in Visual Arts in Art and Art History, Ga. State U., 1972; MA in Studio Art, U. N.Mex., 1974, MFA in History, Practice of Photography, 1984. Instr. Rio Hondo Coll., Whittier, Calif., 1975-76, Coll. of Redwoods, Eureka, Calif., 1976-85; vis. asst. prof. U. Nebr., Lincoln, 1985, U. Mich., Ann Arbor, 1986-87; vis. asst. prof., guest curator U. Hawaii at Manoa, Honolulu, 1987, 88-89; vis. asst. prof. U. Oreg., Eugene, 1994; vis. lectr., artist in residence Ohio State U., Columbus, 1996-97; instr. art studies in Am. West Ohio Wesleyan U., Mont. State U., Bozeman, 1999; instr. mus. and gallery Humboldt State U., 2003, instr. mus. and gallery practices, 1999—. Diversity cons. Calif. Arts Project, 1995-96, instr./participant summer insts. and visual arts wokshops, 1994—; rep. Calif. Arts Project Leadership Acad., 2002; exhbn. curator and co-curator Rio Hondo Coll., Clarke Mus., Coll. Redwoods, Ohio State U., U. Hawaii, Maine Photog. Workshops, Rockport, others, 1975—; exhbn. dir., juror Coll. of Redwoods with Eureka C. of C., 1983; presenter on art and rehab., instns. including U.S. HHS, Soc. for Photog. Edn., U. Mich., Nat./Internat. Head Injury Conf., Family Survival Project San Francisco, Sta. KOLN-TV, Lincoln, 1983, others; lectr. U. Hawaii, Claremont Coll., Pomona, Calif., nat. conf. Soc. for Photog. Edn., New Orleans, 1990, Humboldt State U., Arcata, Calif., 1999-2000, 02; juror Humboldt Cultural Ctr., Eureka, Calif., 1999, Humboldt County Fair, Ferndale, Calif., 2002; instr., 2000; cons. Redwood Arts Project, Klamath-Trinity Schs., Calif., 2001-02; actor, Castle Rock Prodns., 2001; photographer Ferndale Repertory Theater, Calif., 2002; lectr., spkr., presenter in field. Author, curator exhbn. and illus. catalog with essay Symbol and Surrogate: The Picture Within, 1989-90; artist, author, Fractures and Severances: Patient as Artist, 1982-84, 84—; artist: Illusory Arrangements, 1978; exhibited photog. Albuquerque Mus. Art., Vietnam Vets' State Memls. West of Miss.; illustrated brochure Diana Schoenfeld: Landscape and Memory sponsored by Humboldt State U. and First St. Gallery, 1999; interviewed by KHSU radio, Arcata, Calif., 2000-01; exhibited in group shows at San Francisco Mus. Modern Art, 1980 (Print awards 1978, 79), 1st St. Gallery, Eureka, 1999, Alinder Gallery, Gualala, Calif., 1992-93, 95, Art Ctr., Eureka, 1992, Ink People Gallery, Eureka, 1992, Solomon-Dubnick Gallery, Sacramento, 1994, Tokyo Inst. Polytechnics, 1995, Ohio State U., 1996, B.C. Space, Laguna Beach, Calif., 1997, Internat. Ctr. Photography, N.Y.C., 1997, Humboldt State U., Arcata, Internat. Photography Hall of Fame and Mus. Okla. City, 1999-2000, Morris Graves Mus. Art, Eureka, 2000; one-woman shows include Humboldt Bay Nat. Wildlife Refuge Welcome Ctr., Loleta, Calif., 2001-02, Travel Advantage, Eureka, 1999, Art Ctr., 1991, Orange Coast Coll., Costa Mesa, Calif., 1991, A.G. Edwards, Eureka, 1992, Ambiance, Eureka, 1993, Iris Inn, Eureka, 1994, Redwood Arts Project, Arcata, 1996, Humboldt State U., 1997-99, Players' Theatre, Ukiah, Calif., 1997, 1st St. Gallery, Eureka, 1999, Morris Graves Mus. Art, 2002, Humboldt Sr. Resource Ctr., Eureka, 2002, others; represented in permanent collections including Houston Mus. Art, Ctr. Creative Photography, Tucson, Ariz., Graham Nash Collection, Barrow Neurol. Inst., Phoenix, Avon Collection, Mus. Contemporary Photography, Chgo., L.A. Ctr. for Photog. Studies, Nat. Mus. Women in Art, Washington, San Francisco Mus. Modern Art, Princeton U., Laguna Beach Mus. Art, Ohio Wesleyan U., Women Photographers Internat. Archive, Yale U., pvt. collections, others; creator CD-ROM multimedia presentation Schoolhouse Odyssey. Exploring Remote, Rural and Ghost Schools-A Photographer's Notes, 1998. Ctr. for Internat. Media Rsch., Internat. Conf. Visual Sociology, Bielfield, and others. Vol. Women's Resource Ctr., Eureka, 1996, Lewis Rathburn Wellness Ctr., Asheville, N.C., 1997. Selected for Gov. of Ga. Honors Program in Art, Wesleyan Coll., summer 1966; Marion Crowe scholar Atlanta Press Photographers Assn., 1971; Nat. Endowment for Arts Emerging Artist fellow/grantee, 1980; recipient Reva and David Logan award for New Writing in Photography, Boston U., 1985, Discovery award Art of Calif. jour., 1992. Mem. Soc. for Photog. Edn., Friends of Photography (presenter). Avocations: carpentry and construction, camping, hiking, writing, gardening. Home and Office: PO Box 596 Wildbird Ln Loleta CA 95551-0560

SCHOENGOOD, JO-ANN, physical education and health educator; b. N.Y.C., Jan. 24, 1952; d. Arthur Edward and Elaine Frances (Levy) S. BS, Russell Sage Coll., 1974; MEd with honors, William Paterson Coll., 1991. Cert. health, phys. edn. tchr., supr., N.J. Water safety instr. Passaic County Tech. and Vocat. High Sch., Wayne, N.J., 1972—, mem. faculty, 1974—. Asst. to dir. on phys. edn., project adventure coord. Passaic County Tech. and Vocat. Edn. Assn.; coach field hockey, swimming/diving, volleyball, and waterfront dir. in field; mem. faculty Erase, rep. coun.; Principal's liason com., Conflict Mgmt. Trainers; participant Ctr. Grad. Studies and Profl. Edn. Active Nat. Mus. Women in Arts. Recipient Sage Circle award for Leadership, 1974. Mem. NEA, ASCD, ARC (Essex/Passaic chpt. 1972—), N.J. Edn. Assn., Am. Assn. Univ. Women, Acad. Advancement Tchg. and Mgmt., Russell Sage Coll. Alumni Assn., William Patterson Coll. Alumni Assn., N.J. Phys. Edn., Health, Recreation, Dance, U.S. Golf Assn affiliate. Democrat. Jewish. Avocations: theatre, clarinet, golf, tennis, travel. Home: 43 Hinchman Ave Apt 2A Wayne NJ 07470-8030

SCHOENING, RUTH IRENE, retired music educator, musician; b. Moline, Ill., Mar. 23, 1922; d. Karl John and Cora Irene (Reynolds) Wilhelmsen; m. Raymond Edward Schoening, Apr. 28, 1945; children: Stephen Ray, Carol Irene Haertel, John Edward. MusB Edn., U. Wis., 1945, MusM, 1979. Cert. music tchr. Pvt. piano instr., Racine, Wis., 1945—; music instr. Racine Christian Sch., 1960-75; workshop presenter Music Educators Nat. Confs., 1975-82; instr. music U. Wis.-Parkside, Racine, 1985-90, 95, 98. Author, editor: From Sound to Symbol, 1969, Can You Do This?, 1984, Shortcuts for the Older Beginner, 1987. Organist Luth. Ch. Resurrection, Racine, 1960—; accompanist Racine Symphonic Chorus, 1987-98; vol. accompanist Racine Pub. Schs., 1983-93, Park High Sch. Concert Choir, 1998—; active vol. Christian Coalition, Chesapeake, Va., 1990—, nat. and state Rep. coms., 1993—. Mem. Am. Guild Organists, Music Tchrs. Nat. Assn. Avocations: reading, walking, computers, entertaining. Home: 923 Illinois St Racine WI 53405-2223 E-mail: ruth_schoening22@juno.com.

SCHOENROCK, CHERI MICHELLE, principal; b. Renton, Wash., Mar. 10, 1961; d. Bruce A.E. and Roberta M. Schoenrock. AA, Bellevue (Wash.) C.C., 1981; BA, N.W. Coll., 1985; MEd, Seattle Pacific U., 1989, prin.'s credentials, 1998. Lic. tchr. Wash.; lic. prin., Wash. Tchr. Spanaway Christian Sch., Tacoma, 1985-92, Neighborhood Christian Sch., Bellevue, 1992-94, Renton Christian Sch., Wash., 1994—2003, prin., 2003—. Author: (bible curriculum) Assn. Christian Schs. Internat., 1993-94. Rep. precinct com. officer, Issaquah, Wash., 1991-93. Mem. Delta Epsilon Chi. Mem. Assembly of God Church. Avocations: softball, hiking, biking, traveling, skiing. Home: 8230 Renton Issaquah Rd SE Issaquah WA 98027-5428 Office: Renton Christian Sch 15717 152nd Ave SE Renton WA 98058-6330

SCHOEPPNER-GRUNDER, MARY CATHERINE, mathematics educator; b. Canton, Ohio, Mar. 3, 1967; d. Thomas William Sr. and Catherine Irene (Von Almen) S. BS, Mt. Union Coll., 1989; MA, Kent State U., 1998. Tchr. math. St. Thomas Aquinas High Sch., Louisville, Ohio, 1989—2001, Minerva (Ohio) Local Schs., 2001—. Mem. Nat. Coun. Tchrs. Math., Greater Canton Coun. Tchrs. Math. Roman Catholic. Avocations: gardening, music, sports. Home: 2270 Rummell Ave NE Paris OH 44669-9758 Office: Minerva HS 501 Almeda Ave Minerva OH 44657 E-mail: mcg1@minerva.stark.k12.oh.us.

SCHOFF, PAMELA ANN, elementary school educator; b. Pontiac, Mich., Mar. 30, 1949; d. Marce Thomas and Peggy Joyce (Coleman) S. BA in Social Studies, William Tyndale Coll., Farmington Hills, Mich., 1971; cert., U. Mich., Dearborn, 1983. Cert. tchr., Mich. Substitute tchr. Waterford (Mich.) Sch. Dist., 1984-87; 4th and 5th grade tchr. Highland (Mich.) Hills Christian Sch., 1987-91, Oakland Intermediate Sch. Dist., Pontiac, 1991—; subs. tchr. Waterford Sch. Dist., 1991—, Clarkston Sch. Dist., 1991—, Rochester Sch. Dist., NY, 1991—. Chief coord. Pioneer Girls Waterford Community Ch., 1989—. Avocations: baseball, basketball, volleyball, ventriloquism, painting. Home: 2500 Mann Rd Lot 322 Clarkston MI 48346-4226 Office: Oakland Intermediate Dist 2100 Pontiac Rd Auburn Hills MI 48326-2455

SCHOLER, MARGARET D. adult education educator; b. La Habra, Calif., June 14, 1920; d. James Robards Darling and Ula McWhorter; m. Emerson C. Scholar, 1964 (dec.); m. Philip Lynden Evans, 1941 (div. 1960); children: Lynden Anthony Evans, Conrad St. George Evans, Madelon Blythe Evans Mitchell. AB, U. Calif., Berkeley, 1942. Rsch. crew U. Calif., Berkeley, 1942—43; asst. Robert Johnson, Interiors, Oakland, Calif., 1948; libr. asst. Oakland Pub. Libr., 1960—62; asst. mgr. Fairyland Dutchess Caterers, Oakland, 1962—63; mgr. art gallery Bret Harte Board Walk, Oakland, 1962—63; lectr. Am. Antiques Normandale Coll., Mpls., 1969—90, Ohio State U. Continuing Edn., Columbus, 1990—97, Cuesta Coll. Continuing Edn., San Luis Obispo, Calif., 1998—99, Elderhostel, Calif. Poly. U., Cambria Pines, 2000—01. Acquisitions co-chair Godfrey Ho. Mus., Mpls., 1978—90; bd. dirs. decorative arts coun. Mpls. Inst. Arts, 1980—90; lectr., Mpls. and St. Paul, 1970—90. Mem.: AAUW (co-chair programs Morro Bay chpt. 2000—02, garden tour chair 2003). Democrat. Episcopalian. Home: 2751 Ironwood Ave Morro Bay CA 93442

SCHOLL, ALLAN HENRY, retired school system administrator, educational consultant; b. Bklyn., May 6, 1935; s. Joseph Arnold and Edith (Epstein) S.; m. Marina Alexandra Mihailovich, July 3, 1960. BA, UCLA, 1957; MA, U. So. Calif., 1959, PhD in History, 1973. Lic. gen. secondary tchr. (life), administrv. svcs. (life), jr. coll. tchr. (life) Calif. Tchr. social studies L.A. Unified Sch. Dist., 1960-82, adviser social studies sr. high schs. div., 1982-84, dir. secondary history, social scis. Office Instrn., 1984-91; instr. history L.A. City Coll., 1966-69, U. So. Calif., L.A., 1968-69, Community Coll., Rio Hondo, Calif., 1972-74, Cerritos (Calif.) Coll., 1973-74; dir. ALMAR Ednl. Cons., Pasadena, Calif., 1991—. Curriculum developer, writer history tchg. and resource guides; cons. Pasadena Unified Sch. Dist., 1987-88, Coll. Bd., 1980-88, Autry Mus. Western Heritage, 1992—, L.A. Unified Sch. Dist. Office Gifted Programs, 1995—; sch. edn. field supr. Secondary History-Social Scis., Calif. State U., Dominquez Hills, 1997—; edn. cons. Am. Odyssey, 1991; cons. H.S. govt. and U.S. history textbooks, 1987; lectr. in history and art history, developer and writer, Interdisciplinary Teaching Guide to the Roots of Photography: The Monterey Legacy (Monterey Art Mus. and UC Santa Cruz),2001 Author: United States History and Art, 1992; co-author: History of the World: The Modern Era, 1994, History of the World, 1995; co-developer, contbr.: The Treatment of People of African Descent in Nazi Occupied Europe, 1995, The Holocaust Timeline, 1995, Those Who Dared: Rescuers and Rescued, 1995; cons. Anne Frank in Historical Perspective, 1995; contbr. articles to profl. jours. Bd. dirs. Pasadena Chamber Orch., 1977-78, Pasadena Symphony Orch., 1984-85, Pasadena Centennial Com., 1985; mem. exec. bd., chmn. edn. com. Martyrs Meml. and Mus. of Holocaust of L.A., 1992—; mem. Ednl. adv. bd. Autry Mus. of Western Heritage, 1992—. With U.S. Army, 1958-59. NDEA fellow Russian lang. studies, San Francisco State U., 1962; Chouinard Art Inst. scholar, 1952. Mem. Am. Hist. Assn., Nat. Coun. Social Studies, Calif. Coun. Social Studies, Soc. Calif. Social Studies Assn. (bd. dirs. 1982-84), Assoc. Adminstrs. L.A. (legis. coun. 1983-85), Crohn's and Colitis Found. Am., Phi Alpha Theta. Avocations: reading, hiking, travel, art history, opera.

SCHOLL, GLEN, principal; b. Newhall, Calif., Nov. 5, 1946; s. Thomas and Charlotte Avis (Levey) S.; m. Judith Anne Jones, Sept. 10, 1965; children: Marilee, Glena, Douglas, Arlen, Wesley, Laura, Keith. BS, U. Utah, 1969; MA in Edn., No. Ariz. U., 1972. specialist in ednl. adminstrn. Tchr. Fredonia (Ariz.) Pub. Schs., 1969-72; acting prin. Bullhead City (Ariz.) Sch. #15, 1974-75; prin. Bullhead Primary Sch., 1975-78, Bullhead City Intermediate Sch., 1978-89, Copper Rim Elem. Sch., Globe, Ariz., 1989—. Pres., v.p. Bullhead City PTA, 1975-76; pres. Bullhead City Roadrunner Bobbysox, 1976-77, Mohave County Sch. Adminstrn., Kingman, Ariz., 1979-80. Dist. commr. Gila Dist. Boy Scouts Am., Globe, 1994 (Silver Beaver award 1987), dist. River Valley Dist., Bullhead City, 1979 (Dist. award Merit 1980). Mem. Nat. Assn. Elem. Sch. Prins., Ariz. Sch. Adminstrs. Assn., Rotary (pres. 1994). Republican. Mem. Lds Ch. Avocations: family history research, woodworking, camping. Office: Copper Rim Elem Sch 501 E Ash St Globe AZ 85501-2206 Home: 162 W 100 S Ivins UT 84738-6213

SCHOMMER, TRUDY MARIE, pastoral minister, religion education; b. Wayzata, Minn., May 18, 1937; d. Edward and Gertrude (Mergen) S. BA, Coll. St. Catherine, St. Paul, 1966; MA, Manhattanville Coll., 1971, Pacifica Grad. Inst., 1996. Joined Order of Franciscan Sisters of Little Falls, Minn., 1955. Dir. religious edn. St. Pius X, White Bear Lake, Minn., 1971-77; campus min., theology tchr. St. Cloud (Minn.) State Univ., 1977-81; pastoral min. St. Galls, St. Elizabeth, Milw., 1981-85; dir. religious edn. St. Alexander's, Morrisonville, N.Y., 1985-90; pastoral min. of religious edn. St. Mary's, Bryantown, Md., 1990-91; diocesan dir. religious edn. Diocese of New Ulm, Minn., 1991—. Exec. bd. mem. Nat. Assembly Religious Women, Chgo., 1974-78. Author: Easiest Gospel Stories Ever, 1993; book reviewer Sister's Today, 1988-91. Mem. Network, Washington, 1978—. Mem. Nat. Cath. Edn. Assn., Nat. Parish Coords. and Dirs. Democrat. Roman Catholic. Home and Office: 113 Saint Paul St NW Apt 13 Preston MN 55965-8906

SCHONAUER, ANNE MILLER, music educator; b. Houston, July 29, 1965; d. George Louquet and Marilyn Ann (Rhoades) Miller; m. Paul Richard Schonauer, July 2, 1988 (div. June 2001); children: Paul David, Joanna Louquet. BA in Music, BMusEd, Southwestern Okla. State U., 1987; MA, 1991; PhD in Music Edn., U. Okla., 2002. Cert. music tchr., Okla., Tex., Ala., Ga. Tchr. band 5-6 Dallas Ind. Schs., 1988-89; tchr. gen. music, K-5 Norman (Okla.) Pub. Schs., 1991—96; vis. instr. U. Okla., 1997—99; tchr. gen. music K-6 Moore Pub. Schs., Okla., 1999—. Mem. NEA, Orgn. of Am. Kodaly Educators, Music Edn. Nat. Conf. Office: Plaza Towers Elem 852 SW 11th St Moore OK 73160

SCHONFELD, RUDOLF LEOPOLD, secondary school educator; b. La Paz, Bolivia, Feb. 2, 1942; came to U.S. 1958; s. Walter and Eva (Fuchs) S.; m. Sonia Nussbaum, July 7, 1963; children: Walter, Miriam Schonfeld Giotta. BA, Wilkes Coll., 1963; MA, Seton Hall U., 1972; PhD, Ludwig Maximillian U., Heidelberg, Ger., 1974. Tchr. Parsippany (N.J.) High Sch., 1963-69, tchr. Spanish and German, 1969-82; supr. world langs. Parsippany-Troy Hills Sch. Dist., 1982—; vice-prin. Brooklawn Mid. Sch., Parsippany, N.J. Author: Voces y Vistas, 1989, Pasos y Puentes, 1989, Arcos y Alamedas, 1989. Mem. Masons (master 1990). Avocations: soccer, reading, counseling, values clarification. Office: Parsippany-Troy Hills 5 Lincoln Ave Lake Hiawatha NJ 07034-2409

SCHOOLAR, JOSEPH CLAYTON, psychiatrist, pharmacologist, educator; b. Marks, Miss., Feb. 28, 1928; s. Adrian Taylor and Leah (Covington) S.; m. Betty Jane Peck, Nov. 2, 1960; children— Jonathan Covington, Cynthia Jane, Geoffrey Michael, Catherine Elizabeth, Adrian Carson AB, U. Tenn., Knoxville, 1950, MS, 1952; PhD, U. Chgo., 1957, MD, 1960. Diplomate Am. Bd. Psychiatry and Neurology. Chief drug abuse research TRIMS, Houston, 1966-72; assoc. prof. U. Tex. Grad. Sch. Biomed. Scis., Houston, 1968—; prof. psychiatry Baylor Coll. Medicine, Houston, 1975—, prof. pharmacology, 1974—2002, prof. emeritus pharmacology and psychiatry, 2003—, chief div. psychopharmacology, 1973-82; dir. Tex. Research Inst. Mental Scis., Houston, 1972-85. Mem. Nat. Bd. Med. Examiners' Task Force on Drug Abuse and Alcoholism, 1982— ; mem. Drug Abuse Adv. Com., FDA, Washington, 1983-85, chmn., 1984; chmn. profl. needs planning task force Nat. Inst. Drug Abuse, Washington, 1977— Editor: Current Issues in Adolescent Psychiatry, 1973, Research and the Psychiatric Patient, 1975, The Kinetics of Psychiatric Drugs, 1979, Serotonin in Biological Psychiatry - Advances in Biochemical Psychopharmacology, 1982. Cons. Parents' League Houston, 1972-74; mem. coordinating com. Citizens Mental Health Service, Houston, 1976; mem. acad. com. for study of violence Houston Police Dept., 1979; bd. dirs. Can-Do-It, Houston, 1982— . Served with U.S. Army, 1945-47, to 1st lt. USAR, 1950-62. Recipient Eugen Kahn award Baylor Coll. Medicine, Houston, 1964, Alumni award for Disting. Svc., U. Chgo., 1995, Psychiat. Excellence award Tex. Soc. Psychiat. Physicians, 1995. Fellow Am. Psychiat. Assn., Am. Coll. Psychiatrists, Am. Coll. Neuropsychopharmacology, Collegium Internationale NeuroPsychopharmacologicum, Am. Soc. Pharmacology and Exptl. Therapeutics. Episcopalian. Home: 1111 Hermann Dr Unit 17E Houston TX 77004-6930 Office: Baylor Coll Medicine One Baylor Pla PO Box 66575 Houston TX 77265-6575

SCHOOLEY, ROBERT T. medical educator; b. Denver, Nov. 10, 1949; s. Robert Enoch and Lelia Francis (Barnhill) S.; m. Constance Benson; children: Kimberly Dana, Elizabeth Kendall. BS, Washington and Lee U., 1970; MD, Johns Hopkins U., 1974. Diplomate Am. Bd. Internal Medicine. Intern Johns Hopkins Hosp., Balt., 1974-75, resident, 1975-76; clin. assoc. lab. clin. investigation Nat. Inst. Allergy & Infectious Disease, NIH, Bethesda, Md., 1976-77, chief clin. assoc. lab. clin. investigation, 1977-78, med. officer lab. clin. investigation, 1978-79; from instr. to assoc. prof. medicine Harvard Med. Sch., Boston, 1979-90; prof. medicine U. Colo.,

Denver, 1990—. Dir. Colo. Ctr. for AIDS Rsch., 2003—. Mem. editl. bd.: Antimicrobial Agts. and Chemotherapy, 1987—2000, Biotherapy, 1987—95, Jour. Acquired Immune Deficiency Syndromes, 1988—, Clin. and Diagnostic Lab. Immunology, 1992, assoc. editor: Clin. Infectious Diseases, 2002—; contbr. articles to profl. jours. Clin. and rsch. fellow Infectious Disease Unit, Mass. Gen. Hosp., Boston, 1979-81; rsch. fellow Medicine Harvard Med. Sch., 1979-81; recipient Bonfils-Stanton award for sci. and medicine. Fellow Infectious Disease Soc. Am.; mem. AAAS, Am. Assn. Immunologists, Am. Soc. Clin. Investigation, Assn. Am. Physicians, Omicron Delta Kappa. E-mail: robert.schooley@uchsc.edu.

SCHOPP, JAMES A. secondary education educator; B of Music Edn., Ill. Wesleyan U., 1975; M of Ednl. Adminstrn., Northeastern Ill. U., 1992; postgrad., Ill. State U., U. Tulsa, No. Ill. U. Cert. tchr. elem. edn., music specialist, adminstr. Tchr. music appreciation and reading, choir dir. Northlawn Sch., Streator, Ill., 1975-85; tchr. 2d grade Pritchett Elem. Sch., 1985—; dir. choral activities and mus. Aptakisic Jr. High Sch., Buffalo Grove, Ill., 1985—. Mem. math. com., ednl. devel. com., reading com., social studies com., Pritchett Elem. Sch., 1985—; mem. grad. com. Aptakisic Jr. High Sch., Buffalo Grove, 1985—; dir. dist. # 102 Summer Sch., 1990, 91, 92. Guest voice recitalist North Ctrl. Coll., 1991; soloist Chgo. Symphony, St. Louis Symphony, Tulsa Symphony, Boston Symphony, Aurora Festival Chorus, Naperville Community Chorus; performer leading opera roles with Santa Fe Opera, Tulsa Opera, San Francisco Opera, Ravinia Summer Festival. Dir. Chancel Choir Aldersgate Meth. Ch., Wheaton, Ill. Mem. ASCD, Music Educators Nat. Conf., Phi Delta Kappa.

SCHOPPMEYER, MARTIN WILLIAM, education educator; b. Weehawken, N.J., Sept. 15, 1929; s. William G. and Madeleine M. (Haas) S.; m. Marilyn M. Myers, Aug. 9, 1958; children: Susan Ann, Martin William. BS, Fordham U., 1950; EdM, U. Fla., 1955, EdD, 1962. Tchr. Fla. pub. sch., 1955-59; instr., then asst. prof. U. Fla., 1960-63; assoc. prof., then prof. edn. Fla. Atlantic U., Boca Raton, Fla., 1963-68, dir. continuing edn., 1965-67; mem. faculty U. Ark., Fayetteville, Ark., 1968—, prof. edn., 1971-93, Univ. prof., 1993—99, Univ. prof. emeritus, 1999—, program coord. for ednl. adminstrn., 1983-90. Mem. Nat. Adv. Coun. Edn. Professions Devel., 1973-76; exec. sec. Ark. Sch. Study Coun., 1976—; evaluator instructional tng. program Nat. Tng. Fund, 1978; bd. dirs. Women's Ednl. and Devel. Inst., 1977-80, Nat. Sch. Devel. Coun., sec., 1989-90, v.p. 1990, pres., 1990-92; mem. oversight com. South Conway (Ark.) County Sch. Dist.; mem. state commn. to study effect of Amendment 59 to Ark. Constn.; cons. Lake View V. Huckabee, 1994-2002. Author books, monographs, articles in field. Mem. president's coun. Subiaco Acad., 1984-90; chmn. Subiaco Sch. Bd., 1990-93, mem., 1993-97. With U.S. Army, 1951-53, Korea. Recipient numerous fed. grants. Mem. V.F.W., Ark. Edn. Assn. (past chpt. pres.), Ark. Assn. Ednl. Adminstrs., KC, Rotary, Kappa Delta Pi, Phi Delta Kappa, Delta Tau Kappa. Roman Catholic. Home: 2950 Sheryl Ave Fayetteville AR 72703-3542 E-mail: MSCHOPPMEYER@cox.com.

SCHORSCH, ISMAR, clergyman, Jewish history educator; b. Hannover, Germany, Nov. 3, 1935; m. Sally Korn; children: Jonathan, Rebecca, Naomi. BA, Ursinus Coll., 1957; MA, Columbia U., 1961, PhD, 1969; MHL, Jewish Theol. Sem. Am., 1962; LittD (hon.), Wittenberg U., 1989, Ursinus Coll., 1990, Gratz Coll., 1995, Russian State U., 1996, Tufts U., 2000. Ordained rabbi, 1962. Instr. Jewish Theol. Sem., N.Y.C., 1964-68; asst. prof. Jewish Theol. Sem. Am., N.Y.C., 1970-72, assoc. prof., 1972-76, prof., 1976—, dean Grad. Sch., 1975-79, provost, 1980-84; chancellor, 1986—; asst. prof. Jewish history Columbia U., N.Y.C., 1968-70. Bd. dirs. Leo Baeck Inst., 1976, mem. exec. com., 1980, pres., 1985-86, 90—, mem. editorial bd. of yearbook, 1987; participant symposium Spirit and Nature: Religion, Ethics and Environ. Crisis, Middlebury Coll.; organizer Nat. Religious Partnership for the Environment. Author: From Text to Context: The Turn to History in Modern Judaism, 1994, (monograph) Sacred Cluster: The Core Values of Conservative Judaism, 1995; contbr. articles to profl. publs. Chaplain U.S. Army, 1962—64. Recipient Clark F. Ansley award Columbia U. Press, 1969; NEH fellow, 1979-80 Fellow Am. Acad. Jewish Rsch. Jewish. Office: Jewish Theol Sem 3080 Broadway New York NY 10027-4650

SCHOU, GAYLE EVELYN, academic administrator; b. Morrison, Ill., Oct. 6, 1941; d. Francis Kneale and Dorothy Pearl (Hockman) Nelson; m. Thomas Gordon Mode, Oct. 5, 1961 (dec. Oct. 1972); 1 child, Laurel Mode; m. Wayne Albert Schou, May 29, 1976. BS, No. Ill. U., 1970, MS, 1977, EdD, 1980. Tchr. Thomson (Ill.) Pub. Schs., 1963-76; dir. spl. programs St. Mary's U., San Antonio, 1980-82; asst. prof. S.W. Tex. State U., San Marcos, 1982, U. Tex., San Antonio, 1983; assoc. dean Coll. St. Mary, Omaha, 1983-86; assoc. dean continuing edn. George Washington U., Washington, 1986-89; assoc. dean Rio North Rio Salado CC, Phoenix, 1989-92; dean gen. edn. and spl. programs Clarkson Coll., Omaha, 1992-94; exec. dir. St. Louis Ctr. Nat. Louis U., 1994-95; exec. dir., v.p. corp. ednl. svcs. Clarke Coll., 1995-99; prof. Grand Canyon U., Phoenix, 1999—2002; dept. head edn. programs Argosy U., Phoenix, 2002—. Democrat. Avocations: music, travel. Office: 2301 W Dunlop Ave Phoenix AZ 85021 Personal E-mail: gschou@msn.com. Business E-Mail: gschou@argosyu.edu.

SCHOWE, SHERAL LEE SPEAKS, special education educator; b. San Francisco, June 14, 1953; d. Veral John and Myrtle Lee (Hunter) Speaks; m. Derryll Boyd Schowe, Aug. 7, 1982; 1 child, Devin. B degree, Brigham Young U., 1977, M degree, 1979; AA, Ricks Coll., Rexburg, Idaho, 1974; fellow, Gallaudet Coll., 1978. Lic. therapeutic recreation specialist; cert. spl. edn. instr.; cert. edn. adminstrn. Asst. Calif. Jud. Edn. and Rsch., Berkeley; coord. Cottonwood Elem. Community Sch., Holladay, Utah; founder, coord. handicap svcs. Granite Dist. Community Edn., Salt Lake City; founder, coord. ind. living skills program Hartvigsen Community Sch., Salt Lake City; area dir., exec. dir. Utah Spl. Olympics, Sandy, Utah. Fund raising cons. non-profit orgns.; spl. edn. instr. Granite Sch. Dist, Salt Lake City; developer, instr. Transition Intervention program for Behaviorally Disordered Elem. Students, 1994—; owner, dir. Wasatch Acad. Wine. Contbr. numerous articles to profl. jours. Mem. archtl. barriers com. Salt Lake 504 Coun., 1978-80; mem. Salt Lake County Cmty. Devel. Citizens Adv. Coun., 1981, vice chair, 1982, chair, 1983; mem. panel Salt Lake County Title XX Adv. Coun., 1984-87; pres., moderator Presbyn. Women United Cottonwood Presbyn. Ch., 1992, 93, deacon, 1992, 93, 94; v.p. PTA Truman Elem. Sch., 1991, 92, 93, PTA rep. 1992, 93, tchr. v.p., mem. Granite Dist. Coun.; rep. Granite Edn. Assn., 1992, 93. Named Edn. of Handicapped of Yr. Mental Retardation Assn., 1982, Woman of Yr. Salt Lake City JayCees, 1982; recipient Outstanding Contribution to Fitness award Utah Gov's. Coun. on Health & Physical Fitness, 1990. Mem. Utah Community Edn. Assn. (Profl. Community Educator of Yr. 1987), Nat. Assn. Spl. Olympics Profls. (bd. dirs. 1990), Coun. Exceptional Children, Zonta (svc. com. chair 1987, bd. dirs. 1988, pub. rels. chair 1990, '91, Soviet Art Exch.chair 1991, '92, '93), Exec. Women's Svc. Orgn., Russian Cultural Exch. Program (chair 1992, 93), Presbyn. Women's Assn. Democrat. Presbyterian. Home: 11454 High Mountain Dr Sandy UT 84092-5661 Office: Granite Sch Dist Dept Spl Edn 340 E 3545 S Salt Lake City UT 84115-4697

SCHRAD, ROGER WILLIAM, elementary physical education educator, coach; b. Carroll, Iowa; BS in Phys. Edn., U. S.D., 1980; MA in Edn. Adminstrn., San Diego State U., 1983. Tchr. phys. edn. K-5 Clark Elem, East Elem, Brown Elem., Evanston, Wyo., 1980-82, Uinta Meadows Elem. Sch., Evanston, 1982—; coach varsity football Evanston High Sch., 1980—, coach varsity wrestling, 1980-85, coach freshman basketball, 1989, 91, 92, coach varsity track, 1991—. Superivsing tchr. student-tchrs. U. Wyo., Evanston, 1989. Cons. Evanston Recreation Dept., 1980; coord. Jump for Heart, Am. Heart Assn., Evanston, 1984-87, 1991—; donor 4000 trees to elem. students to plant on Arbor Day, 1986—, Evanston; neighborhood vol. Am. Diabetes Assn. Recipient Merit award U.S. Dept. Edn., 1988. Mem. NEA, AAHPERD, Wyo. Alliance Health, Phys. Edn. Recreation and Dance, Wyoming Edn. Assn., Evanston Edn. Assn., Evanston Coaches Assn. (pres. 1990-91), Wyo. Coaches Assn., Nat. Coaches Assn., Nat. Assn. Sports and Phys. Edn. (Inspiration award 1993). Office: Uinta County Sch Dist # 1 931 Summit St Evanston WY 82930-3450

SCHRADE, ROLANDE MAXWELL YOUNG, composer, pianist, educator; b. Washington, Sept. 13; d. Harry Robert and Isabelle Martha (Maxwell) Young; m. Robert Warren Schrade, Dec. 21, 1949; children: Robelyn, Rhonda Lee, Rolisa, Randolph, Rorianne. Pupil, Harold Bauer, N.Y.C., Vittorio Giannini; student, Manhatten Sch. Music, Juilliard Sch. Music. Debut as concert pianist Town Hall, N.Y.C., 1953, Nat. Gallery, Washington, 1954; concert pianist Constitution Hall, Washington, 1972; founder, dir. ann. performances Sevenars Concerts, Inc., Worthington, Mass., 1968—, music dir., 1975—, also broadcasts, 1984, 85; recitalist Radio Sta. WGMS-FM, Washington; mem. music faculty Allen-Stevenson Sch., N.Y.C., 1968-89; co-founder, v.p., treas. Sevenars Music House, Inc., N.Y.C., 1968—. Concerts include Lincoln Ctr., Alice Tully Hall, 1980, 93, Sevenars Concerts, Inc., 1968—, Lincoln Ctr., 2000; Lifetime T.V. film Tour, N.Z., 1982-84; featured NBC Today Show with Schrade family pianists, 1993; named to Steinway Piano Co. Global Artist List; appearances PM Mag., TV film, 1980-81; composer, pub., recs. of more than 100 songs; albums include America 76, Original and Traditional Songs for Special Days, 1988; editor: songs of Carrie Jacobs Bond, Boston Music Co.; TV feature film with Schrade Family Pianists, 1997; performed in Schrade-James Family Concert Lincoln Ctr., N.Y.C., 2000, Lifetime TV showing. Mem. ASCAP, DAR (Bicentennial award 1972), Mut. Artists Mgmt. Alliance (founder, bd. dirs.). Episcopalian. Home and Office: 30 East End Ave Ste 3A New York NY 10028-7053 Office: Sevenars Concerts Ireland St S at Rte 112 Worthington MA 01098

SCHRADER, DIANA LEE, secondary education educator; b. N.Y.C., Oct. 9, 1946; d. Edward Schrader and Virginia (Felleman) Buck. Assocs. degree, Concordia Coll., 1966, BA, 1968. Cert. tchr., N.Y. Tchr. grade 1 Emanuel Luth., Patchogue, N.Y., 1968-70; tchr. grades 3-4, 1-2 Grace Luth., Bronx, N.Y., 1970-74; tchr. grades 3-4, 5 Queens Sch., Kew Gardens, N.Y., 1974-77; writer, home tutor N.Y.C., 1977-79; tchr. grade 8 St. Matthew Luth. Sch., N.Y.C., 1979—90; co-dir. upper sch. program grades 5-8, 1991—2000; tchr. grades 5 and 6 Manhattan Christian Acad., N.Y.C., 2000—02; founder learing resources nonprofit orgn. F.L.O.C.K., 2002. Author: Television in Classroom, 1978, Take My Hands, 1980; contbr. articles to ednl. jours. and mags. Pres. congregation St. Matthew Ch., N.Y.C., 1991-96, choir dir., 1990-2000. Mem. ASCD, Luth. Schs. Assn. (Tchr. of Yr. 1990). Lutheran. Avocations: reading, piano, crafts, travel. Office: Apt 4F 678 Warburton Ave Yonkers NY 10701-1618

SCHRADER, LAWRENCE EDWIN, plant physiologist, educator; b. Atchison, Kans., Oct. 22, 1941; s. Edwin Carl and Jenna Kathryn (Tobiason) S.; m. Elfriede J. Massier, Mar. 14, 1981 BS, Kans. State U., 1963; PhD, U. Ill., 1967; grad., Inst. Ednl. Mgmt., Harvard U., 1991. Asst. prof. dept. agronomy U. Wis., Madison, 1969-72, assoc. prof., 1972-76, prof., 1976-84; prof., head dept. agronomy U. Ill., Urbana, 1985-89; dean Coll. Agr. and Home Econs. Wash. State U., Pullman, 1989-94, prof. dept. horticulture, 1994—. Chief competitive rsch. grants office Dept. Agr., Washington, 1980-81; trustee, treas. Agrl. Satellite Corp., 1991-94. Contbr. chpts. to books, articles to profl. jours. Active Consortium for Internat. Devel., 1989-94, chair fin. com., vice chair exec. com., 1990-92, trustee 1989-94; mem. exec. com. Coun. Agrl. Heads of Agr., 1992-94. Capt. U.S. Army, 1967-69. Recipient Soybean Researchers Recognition award 1983, Disting. Service award in Agriculture Kansas State U., 1987; Romnes Faculty fellow U. Wis., 1979 Fellow AAAS (steering group sect. agr. 1991-95, chair-elect sect. on agr., food and renewable resources 1995-96, chmn. 1996-97, past chmn. 1997-98, coun. mem. 1997-98), Am. Soc. Agronomy, Crop Sci. Soc. Am.; mem. Internat. Soc. for Hort. Sci., Am. Soc. for Hort. Sci., Am. Soc. Plant Biologists (sec. 1983-85, pres.-elect 1986, pres. 1987), Am. Chem. Soc., Coun. for Agrl. Sci. and Tech., Blue Key, Sigma Xi, Gamma Sigma Delta (Outstanding Alumnus award, 2003), Phi Kappa Phi, Phi Eta Sigma, Alpha Zeta (named to Centennial Honor Roll 1997). Methodist. Home: 3504 Crestview Rd Wenatchee WA 98801-9668 Office: Wash State U Tree Fruit Rsch & Extension Ctr 1100 N Western Ave Wenatchee WA 98801-1230 E-mail: schrader@wsu.edu.

SCHRAGE, CHRISTINE ROSETTA, swine production executive, educator; b. Burlington, Iowa, June 10, 1953; d. Roland Lee and Janet Elaine (Kapotas) Wiemann; m. Neal Schrage, Nov. 22, 1994; 1 child, Nolan Robert. Assoc. of Animal Sci., Hawkeye Inst. Tech., 1977; Degree in Mktg. and Internat. Bus., U. No. Iowa, 1996, MBA, 1997. Draftsman Confinement Specialists, Mediapolis, Iowa, 1973-75; herdsman X-L Pork, Cedar Falls, Iowa, 1976-77; livestock specialist Tasco, Inc., Shell Rock, Iowa, 1977-81; problem accounts specialist I.F.G. Leasing, Parkersburg, Iowa, 1981-86; pres. Pork Purveyors, Ltd., Parkersburg, 1986-88, 89-95; gen. mgr. div. Pork Purveyors Doane Farm Mgmt. Co., Parkersburg, 1988-89; founder div. Pork Purveyors, Ltd. Craft Store, Parkersburg, 1990-92; adj. instr. U. No. Iowa, Cedar Falls, 1997—, Wartburg Coll., Waverly, Iowa, 1999—. Mem. adv. com. animal sci. dept. Hawkeye Inst. Tech., Waterloo, Iowa, 1988-94; coord. Parkersburg Econ. Devel., 1990-92; mem. Iowa Small Bus. Adv. Bd., 1992-96; mng. dir. Surg. Device Internat., Inc., 1992-96. Producer children's album with 5 original songs, 1989; contbr. articles to profl. jours. Mem. jud. nominating commn. Iowa Dist. Two-A, 1992—98; Mediator Iowa Farmer/Creditor Mediation Svc., 1987—98; dir. choir Calvary Bapt. Ch., 1991—92; mem. small bus. adv. coun. IDED, 1992—95; mem. Parkersburg Depot Park Bd., 1991—; Act-UNI adviser Internat. Club Bus. Students; membership sec. Missions NOW team leader Parkersburg United Meth. Named Outstanding Alumni All Agrl. Club, Hawkeye Inst. Tech., 1979, Citizen of Yr., Parkersburg, Iowa, 1991; recipient Iowa Community Betterment Leadership award, 1991, Gov.'s Volunteerism award, 1992, Iowa Cmty. Betterment 1st pl. award, 1999—2000. Mem.: Am. Legion (life), Dobro Slava, Mu Kappa Tau, Omicron Delta Kappa, Beta Gamma Sigma. Avocations: cross-stitching, volleyball, singing. Home: PO Box 596 Parkersburg IA 50665-0596 Office: U No Iowa CBB 357 Cedar Falls IA 50614-0001

SCHRAGE, ROSE, educational administrator; b. Montelimar, France, Apr. 15, 1942; came to U.S., 1947; d. Abraham and Celia (Silbiger) Levine; m. Samuel Schrage, Dec. 12, 1935 (dec. 1976); children: Abraham, Leon. BRE, Beth Rivkah Tchrs. Sem., Bklyn., 1968; Paralegal, Manpower Career Devel. Agy., Bklyn., 1973; MS, L.I. U., 1975; Advanced Cert. Ednl. Adminstrn., Bklyn. Coll., 1983. Cert. sch. dist. adminstr., guidance counselor, tchr., asst. prin. Sec., N.Y.C., 1964-68; police adminstrv. aide N.Y.C. Police Dept., 1974-75; coord. state reading aid program Sch. Dist. 14, Bklyn., 1977-78, project dir. Title VII, 1978-81, asst. dir. reimbursable fed. and state programs, 1981-85, dist. bus. mgr., 1985-94, asst. prin., 1994—99, spl. edn. instrn. specialist, adminstr., 1999—; ednl. adminstr. Ctrl. Liaison Office for Impartial Hearings, divsn. student support svcs. Dept. Edn., N.Y.C., 2001—. Chmn. N.Y.C. Bd. Edn. IMPACT Com., Bklyn., 1986—. Author (poem): Never Again, 1983; contbg. editor Chai Today; contbr. articles on current affairs and concerns to profl. jours. Del. Republican. Jud. Conf., 1968; founder, pres Concerned Parents, Bklyn., 1977; radio co-host Israeli War Heroes Fund-Radiothon, Bklyn.; family counselor local social agys., Bklyn.; co-founder cmty. vol. ambulance Hatzalah, 1977. Recipient Cert. of Appreciation as vol. regional coord. N.Y. State Mentoring Program N.Y. Gov. Cuomo, 1991, Proclamation, N.Y. City Coun., 2003. Mem. Am. Assn. Sch. Adminstrs., Assn. Orthodox Jewish Tchrs. (v.p. exec. bd., Orgn. award 2003), N.Y. State Assn. Sch. Bus. Ofcls., N.Y.C. Assn. Sch. Bus. Ofcls., Coun. Suprs. and Adminstrs. Avocations: tennis, needlepoint, piano, reading, communal activities.

SCHRAMM, BEATRICE GRIFFIN, retired teacher; b. Clinton, Ill., June 6, 1914; d. Tully and Mary Griffin; m. Marvin C. Schramm, Sept. 13, 1939 (dec. Oct. 1963); children: Ellen McGlothin, Roselyn Drew, Janice Hultman. BE, Ill. State U., Normal, 1933; MS, Purdue U., Lafayette, 1968; postgrad, Ball State U., Muncie, 1966. Cert. tchr., Ill., Ind. Tchr. Clinton, Attica (Ind.) and Lafayette (Ind.) pub. schs., 1934-76. Author: Sounds and Symbols in American English, 1994. Home: 1705 S 12th St Lafayette IN 47905-2108

SCHRECKENBERGER, PAUL CHARLES, clinical microbiologist, educator; b. Buffalo, N.Y., Oct. 4, 1947; s. Charles Louis and Dorothy Magdalen (Roll) S.; m. Ann Louise Dye; Aug 1, 1970; children: Scott, Laura, Adam. AAS, Erie Community Coll., Williamsville, N.Y., 1968; BS, SUNY, Buffalo, 1970; MS, U. Minn., 1974; PhD, U. Ill., Chgo., 1989. Instr. Erie Community Coll., Williamsville, N.Y., 1970-72; med. technologist U. Minn. Hosp., Mpls., 1973-74; asst. prof. med. lab. scis. U. Ill. at Chgo., 1974-77; supr. microlab. U. Ill. Hosp., Chgo., 1977-85, sect. head bacteriology, 1985-89; asst. prof. of pathology U. Ill. Coll. Medicine, Chgo., 1989—; dir. clin. microbiology lab. U. Ill. Hosp., Chgo., 1989—. Cons. Clin. Microbiology Lab., Elmhurst Hosp., Ill, 1995-, Clin. Microbiology Lab., Edward Hosp., Naperville, Ill, 2001-, Clin. Microbiology, Sherman Hosp., Elgin, Ill, 2001-. Co-author: Bacterial Vaginosis, 1984, 1991 Yearbook of Clinical Microbiology, 1991, Color Atlas and Textbook of Diagnostic Microbiology, 4th edit., 1992, 5th edit., 1997; author: (self study courses) Enterobacteriacae, 1989, Nonfermenters, 1990; contbr. articles, abstracts and revs. to profl. jours. Named Outstanding Alumnus Dept. Med. Technology, SUNY, Buffalo, 1976; recipient Sch. of Assoc. Med. Scis. grant, U. Ill. at Chgo., 1976-77, Campus Rsch. Bd. grant, 1983 (co-investigator). Mem. Am. Soc. for Med. Tech. (vice chmn. microbiology sci. assembly 1975-77, Profl. Achievement award in microbiology 1982, Difco scholar in microbiology 1985), Am. Soc. for Microbiology (editorial bd. jour. clin. microbiology 1990—), Chgo. Med. Mycol. Soc., Chgo. Soc. for Med. Tech. (pres. 1982-83, Mem. of Yr. 1984), Ill. Med. Tech. Assn., South Ctrl. Assn. for Clin. Microbiology (pres. 1990, Outstanding Contbr. 1988), Ill. Soc. Microbiology (pres. 1991, Tanner Shaughnessy Merit award 1992). Avocations: playing guitar, racketball. Home: 914 Clinton Pl River Forest IL 60305-1504 Office: U Ill at Chgo 840 S Wood St Rm 750 Chicago IL 60612-7317

SCHREIBER, EVERETT CHARLES, JR., chemist, educator; b. Amityville, N.Y., Nov. 13, 1953; s. Everett Charles Sr. and Mary S.; m. Jane Karen Sklenar, July 19, 1980. BS, Pace U., 1975; PhD, U. Nebr., 1980. Rsch. assoc. SUNY, Stony Brook, 1980-82; asst. dir. rsch. Muscular Dystrophy Assn., N.Y.C., 1983-84; rsch. assoc. SUNY, 1984-86; spectroscopist G.E. NMR Instruments, Fremont, Calif., 1986-87; quality assurance engr. Varian NKMR Instruments, 1987—89; tech. tng. specialist Varian NMR Instruments, Palo Alto, Calif., 1989-95, sr. tech. support chemist, 1995-96, sr. chemist, 1996-2000, sr. tech. writer, 2000—. Author of tng. texts in engring. and computers; editor Megabytes. V.p. Old Bailey Pl. Home Owners Assn., Fremont, 1989, 95-97, pres., 1990-93, bd. mem., 1994-95, v.p., 1995-96, pres., 1996-97; treas. Young Life, Mission Valley, Fremont, 1993-96, young life com., 1998-2000; mem. money mgmt. com. Centerville Presbyn. Ch., Fremont, Calif., 1997—. Mem. Am. Chem. Soc., N.Y. Acad. Scis. Republican. Roman Catholic. Avocations: photography, computers, model trains, music. Office: Varian NMR Systems 3120 Hansen Way Palo Alto CA 94304-1030

SCHREINER, HELEN ANN, special education educator; b. Lancaster, Pa., Oct. 1, 1949; AA, York Coll. of Pa., 1969; B of Edn., Millersville U., 1971, MEd, 1979. Cert., spl. edn. tchr., supr., Pa. Tchr. Solanco Sch. Dist., Quarryville, Pa., 1971—. Adult edn. tchr./GED, Intermediate Unit 13, Lancaster, Pa., 1974-78. Recipient mini-computer grant, Intermediate Unit 13, 1983. Mem. Coun. for Exceptional Children, Assn. for Retarded Citizens, Learning Disabilities Assn., United Comml. Travelers, Phi Delta Kappa, Pi Lambda Theta, Fraternal Order of Police. Democrat. Roman Catholic. Avocations: travel, collecting menus from restaurants. Home: 5 Bentley Ln Lancaster PA 17603-6203 Office: Solanco Sch Dist 585 Solanco Rd Quarryville PA 17566-9615

SCHRENKER, VIRGINIA MCCRARY, math and Latin educator; b. Nashville, Jan. 20, 1949; d. James Watts and Georgia Ruth (Kesterson) McC.; m. Carl James Schrenker, Jr., Aug. 17, 1974; children: Michael James, David Alexander. BA, Memphis State U., 1970; MA, Fla. State U., 1973. Cert. tchr., Fla. Tchr. Dade County Pub. Schs., Coral Gables, Fla., 1973—2003. Advanced placement faculty cons. Coll. Entrance Examination Bd., Princeton, N.J., 1993-98; adv. com. for Nat. Latin Exam. Am. Classical League, Oxford, Ohio, 1990-93; ednl. cons. Fla. Dept. Edn., Tallahassee, 1987-88; textbook evaluation com. for fgn. langs. Dade County Pub. Schs., Miami, 1983. Asst. editor Archaeological News, 1971-73; editor (newsletter) Bromeliadvisory, 1988-94. Finalist Dade County Math. Tchr. of Yr., 2000, Fla. Latin Tchr. of Yr., 2001; named to Fla. Fgn. Lang. Assn. Hall of Fame, 2002. Mem. Classical Assn. Fla. (exec. sec. 1986-93), Am. Classical League, Classical Assn. Midwest and South, Cryptanthus Soc. (pres. 1996-2000), Bromeliad Soc. Internat. (internationally accredited judge), Am. Orchid. Soc., Eta Sigma Phi, Pi Mu Epsilon. Avocations: growing bromeliads and orchids, sewing, quilting, collecting antiques.

SCHRIER, ARNOLD, historian, educator; b. N.Y.C., May 30, 1925; s. Samuel and Yetta (Levine) S.; m. Sondra Weinshelbaum, June 12, 1949; children— Susan Lynn, Jay Alan, Linda Lee, Paula Kay. Student, Bethany Coll., W.Va., 1943-44, Ohio Wesleyan U., 1944-45; BS, Northwestern U., 1949, MA, 1950, PhD (Social Sci. Research Council fellow, Univ. fellow), 1956. Asst. prof. history U. Cin., 1956-61, assoc. prof., 1961-66, prof., 1966-95, dir. grad. studies history, 1969-78, Walter C. Langsam prof. modern European history, 1972-95; Walter C. Langsam prof. history emeritus, 1995—. Vis. asst. prof. history Northwestern U., Evanston, Ill., 1960; vis. assoc. prof. history Ind. U., Bloomington, 1965-66; vis. lectr. Russian history Duke U., 1966; disting. vis. prof. U.S. Air Force Acad., 1983-84; dir. NDEA Inst. World History for Secondary Sch. Tchrs., U. Cin., 1965; Am. del. Joint U.S.-USSR Textbook Study Commn., 1989. Author: Ireland and the American Emigration, 1958, reissued, 1970, paperback edit., 1997, The Development of Civilization, 1961-62, Modern European Civilization, 1963, Living World History, 1964, rev., 1993, Twentieth Century World, 1974, History and Life: the World and Its People, 1977, rev., 1993, A Russian Looks at America, 1979, Irish Immigrants in the Land of Canaan, 2003. Pres. Ohio Acad. History, 1973-74, Midwest Slavic Conf., 1980. Served with USNR, 1943-46, 52-54. Recipient Disting. Svc. award Ohio Acad. History, 1992; Am. Council Learned Socs. fgn. area fellow, 1963-64 Mem. World History Assn. (v.p. 1986-88, pres. 1988-90). Home: 10 Diplomat Dr Cincinnati OH 45215-2073 E-mail: arnsond@aol.com.

SCHRIESHEIM, ALAN, research administrator; b. N.Y.C., Mar. 8, 1930; s. Morton and Frances (Greenberg) Schriesheim; m. Beatrice D. Brand, June 28, 1953; children: Laura Lynn, Robert Alan. BS in Chemistry, Poly. Inst. Bklyn., 1951; PhD in Phys. Organic Chemistry, Pa. State U., 1954; DSc (hon.), No. Ill. U., 1991; Laureate, Lincoln Acad., 1996; PhD (hon.), Ill. Inst. Tech., Chgo., 1992, Pa. State U., 2001. Chemist Nat. Bur. Standards, 1954—56; with Exxon Rsch. & Engring. Co., 1956—83, dir. corp. rsch., 1975—79; gen. mgr. Exxon Engring., 1979—83; sr. dep. lab. dir., COO Argonne Nat. Lab., 1983—84, lab. dir., CEO, 1984—96, dir. emeritus, 1996—; prof. chemistry dept. U. Chgo., 1984—96, lectr. Bus. Sch., 1996—99; prin. Washington Adv. Group, 1996—. Karcher lectr. U.

Okla., 1977; Hurd lectr. Northwestern U., 1980; Rosensteil lectr. Brandeis U., 1982; Welsh Found. lectr., 87; com. svc. NRC, 1980—; vis. com. chemistry dept. MIT, 1977—82; mem. vis. com. mech. engring. and aerospace dept. Princeton (N.J.) U., 1983—87, mem. vis. com. chemistry dept., 1983—87; mem. Pure and Applied Chemistry Com.; del. to People's Republic of China, 1978; mem. Presdl. Nat. Commn. on Superconductivity, 1989—91, U.S.-USSR Joint Commn. on Basic Sci. Rsch., 1990—93; mem. U.S. nat. com. Internat. Union Pure and Applied Chemistry, 1982—85; mem. magnetic fusion adv. com. Divsn. Phys. Scis. U. Chgo. Magnetic Fusion adv. com. to U.S. DOE, 1983—86; mem. Dept. Energy Rsch. Adv. Bd., 1983—85, Congl. Adv. Com. on Sci. and Tech., 1985—96; mem. vis. com. Stanford (Calif.) U., U. Utah, Tex. A&M U., Lehigh U.; bd. govs. Argonne Nat. Lab., 1984—96; mem. adv. com. on space sys. and tech. NASA, 1987—93; mem. nuc. engring. and engring. physics vis. com. U. Wis., Madison; mem. Coun. Gt. Lakes Govs. Regional Econ. Devel. Commn., 1987—, rev. bd. Compact Ignition Tomamak Princeton U., 1988—91; advisor Sears Investment Mgmt. Co., 1988—89; bd. dirs. HEICO, Smart Signal Corp.; adv. bd. Batterson Venture Ptnrs., Influx, UHV Aluminum, Valley Indsl. Assn., Coun. on Superconductivity for Am. Competitiveness; mem. State of Ill. Commn. on the Future of Pub. Svc., 1990—92; co-chair Indsl. Rsch. Inst. Nat. Labs./Industry Panel, 1984—87; mem. Nat. Acad. Engring. Adv. Commn. on Tech. and Soc., 1991—92, Sun Electric Corp. Bd., 1991—92, U.S. House of Reps. subcom. on Sci.-Adv. Group on Renewing U.S. Sci. Policy, 1992—96, Chgo. Acad. Scis. acad. coun., 1994—; mem. adv. bd. Chemtech; mem. sr. action group on R&D investment strategies Ctr. for strategic and Internat. Studies, 1995; bd. vis. Astronomy and Astrophysics Pa. State U., 1995—; bd. overseers Fermi Nat. Lab., 2003—. Adv. bd.: Chemtech, 1970—85, editl. bd.: Rsch. & Devel., 1988—92, Superconductor Industry, 1988—95; patentee in field. Mem. spl. vis. com. Field Mus. of Natural History, Chgo., 1987—88; trustee The Latin Sch. of Chgo., 1990—92; adv. bd. WBEZ Chicagoland Pub. Radio Cmty., 1990—96; mem. Conservation Found. DuPage County, 1983—96, Econ. Devel. Adv. Commn. of DuPage County, 1984—88, Ill. Gov.'s Commn. on Sci. and Tech., 1986—90, Inst. for Ill. Coun. Advisors, 1988—, Ill. Coalition Bd. Dirs., 1989—, Inst. for Ill. Adv. Rev. Panel, 1986—88, NASA Sci. Tech. Adv. Com. Manpower Requirements Ad Hoc Rev. Team, 1988—91, Ill. Sci. and Tech. Adv. Com., 1989—, chmn., 1997; mem. U. Ill. Engring. Vis. com., Urbana-Champaign, 1986—95; trustee Tchrs. Acad. for Math. and Sci. Tchrs. in Chgo., 1990—96; bd. visitors astronomy and astrophysics Pa. State U., 1995—; bd. dirs. LaRabida Children's Hosp. and Rsch. Ctr., 1987—95, Children's Meml. Hosp., Children's Meml. Inst. for Edn. and Rsch. Recipient Outstanding Alumni Fellow award, Pa. State U., 1985, laureate, Lincoln Acad. Ill., 1996, Disting. fellow, Poly. U., 1989. Fellow: AAAS (coun. del. chem. sect. 1986—92, sci. engring. and pub. policy com. 1992, standing com. audit 1992, bd. dirs. 1992—96, selection com. to bring FSU scientists to ann. mtg. 1995—), N.Y. Acad. Scis.; mem.: AIChE (award com. 1992—), NAE (adv. com. tech. and soc. 1991—92, mem. program adv. com. 1992—94, chair study fgn. participation in U.S. R&D 1993—96, NRC com. on dual use tech. 1996—97, com. to assess policies and practices of Dept. of Energy to design, ma 1998—99), Ctr. Strategic and Internat. Studies (sr. action group 1995—96), Indsl. Rsch. Inst. (fed. adv. com. to Fed. Sci. and Tech. Com. 1992—96, co-chmn. Nat. Labs. Indsl. Panel 1984—87, sr. action group on R&D Investment Strategies), Am. Nuc. Soc., Am. Petroleum Inst. (rsch. coord. coun.), Nat. Conf. Advancement Rsch. (conf. com. 1985—, site selection com. 1994, conf. com. 50th ann. 1996), Am. Mgmt. Assn. (R&D coun. 1988—), Am. Chem. Soc. (joint bd. coun. on sci. 1983—87, chmn. petroleum divsn. 1983—91, councilor, com. on chemistry and pub. affairs 1983—91, petroleum chemistry award 1969, 1995—96), Econ. Club, Comml. Club, Cosmos Club, Carleton Club (bd. govs. 1992—), Phi Lambda Upsilon, Sigma Xi. Home: 1440 N Lake Shore Dr Apt 31ac Chicago IL 60610-5927 Office: Argonne Nat Lab 9700 S Cass Ave Argonne IL 60439-4803

SCHRIMSHER, JOANNE JOHNSON, professional counselor; b. Miami, May 23, 1944; d. Alfred Peter and Patricia (Pearson) Johnson; m. Geoffrey Schrimsher, Dec. 21, 1964; children: John Alfred, Jana. BS in Home Econs., Tex. A&I U., 1964; MS in Counseling and Human Devel., Troy State U., 1979, EdS in Sch. Counseling, 1980. Lic. profl. spl. edn. counselor, profl. edn. diagnostician; registered play therapist-supr. Home econs. tchr. William Adams H.S., Alice, Tex., 1964-66, Sharyland (Tex.) H.S., 1967-68; home econs. and substitute tchr. Panama Canal Co., 1974-77; psychometrist, counselor Wiregrass MHMR and Family Life Ctrl., Dothan and Ft. Rucker, Ala., 1979; cons. Region III Edn. Svc. Ctr., Victoria, Tex., 1980-82; ednl. diagnostician Region III ESC, Victoria, Tex., 1982-86, ednl. diagnositician, LPC, 1988—97; ednl. diagnostician, spl. edn. counselor Jackson County Spl. Svcs. Coop., Edna, Tex., 1997—. Mem. Tex. Counseling Assn., Tex. Ednl. Diagnosticians Assn., Tex. Assn. for Play Therapy, Victoria African Violet Soc. (pres.), Assn. for Play Therapy. Office: Jackson County Spl Svcs Coop Box 919 Edna TX 77957

SCHRIVER, MARTHA LOUISE, middle school educator; b. Martinsburg, W. Va., Aug. 2, 1947; d. George Henry and Christine Louise S. BS in Edn., Bowling Green State U., 1970; MEd, U. Toledo, 1988, PhD in Edn., 1992. Cert. tchr., Ohio, permanent. Tchr. 7th and 8th grades Clyde (Ohio) Jr. High Sch., 1970-89; grad. teaching asst. U. Toledo, 1989-91; asst. prof. Ga. So. U., Statesboro, Ga., 1991—. Evaluation com. mem. Forensic Med. Sci. Day Conf., NW Ohio, 1989; mem. programs planning and evaluation com. N.W. Ohio Jr. Sci. and Humanities Symposium, 1990-91, N.W. Ohio Sci. Day Com., 1991-92, steering com. Science Math. Tech. Edn. Ctr., Univ. Toledo, 1991-92. Mem. AAUW, ASCD, Nat. Assn. for Rsch. and Sci. Teaching, Nat. Sci. Tchrs. Assn., Nat. Middle Level Sci. Tchrs. Assn., Sci. Educators Coun. Ohio, Phi Kappa Phi. Office: Ga So U Middle Grade & Secondary Ed Landrum 8134 Statesboro GA 30460-8134

SCHRÖDER, DIETER KARL, electrical engineering educator; b. Lübeck, Germany, June 18, 1935; arrived in U.S., 1964; s. Wilhelm and Martha (Werner) S.; m. Beverley Claire (Parchment), Aug. 4, 1961; children: Mark, Derek. BS, McGill U., Montreal, Que., Can., 1962, MS, 1964; PhD, U. Ill., 1968. Sr. engr. rsch. and devel. sect. Westinghouse Electric Corp., Pitts., 1968-73; fellow engr. rsch. and devel. sect. Westinghouse Electric Corp., Pitts., 1973-77, adv. engr., 1977-79, mgr., 1979-81; prof. elec. engring. Ariz. State U., 1981—. Rsch. Inst. Solid State Physics, Freiburg, Fed. Republic Germany, 1978-79. Author: Advanced MOS Devices, 1987, Semiconductor Material and Device Characterization, 1998; patentee in electrical field; contbr. articles to profl. jour. Life Fellow IEEE (life, disting. nat. lectr. 1993-2003); mem. Electrochem. Soc., Sigma Xi, Eta Kappa Nu. Mem. Baha'i Faith. Home: 10572 E Firewheel Dr Scottsdale AZ 85255-1911 Office: Ariz State U Dept Elec Engring Tempe AZ 85287-5706

SCHRODI, TOM, instructional services director; b. Belleville, Ill., Sept. 24, 1942; s. Walter Joseph and Emma Elizabeth (Bleiker) S.; m. Elizabeth Agnes Clark Schrodi, Aug. 19, 1967; children: Lisa, Tammy, Dawn. BS, Ea. Mich. U., Ypsilanti, 1964; MS, Ea. Mich. U., 1965. Calif. Adminstrv. Credential K-12 and Adult, Calif. Standard Svcs. Credential, Supr. 7-12, Calif. C.C. Credential in History, Calif. Standard Teaching Credential in History. Federal and state project writer Orange Unified Sch. Dist., 1975-80, coord. spl. programs, 1976-79, adminstrv. asst. spl. programs, 1979-80, adminstr. of curriculum, 1980-85, dir. instrnl. svcs., 1985—. Coord. career edn. Orange County Consortium K-14, 1972-75; instr. Ctrl. County Regional Occupation Program, 1973-75, Whittier Coll., 1974-82; guest lectr. Calif. State U., Long Beach, 1972-80; cons. Calif. State Dept. Edn., Imperial County Dept. Edn. Author: Visual Communications Cluster Curriculum Guide, 1977, Social Studies Review, 1974, Le Mot Educational Services, 1972; co-author: California's Career Education State Plan, 1978, Comprehensive Career Education System, 1977, Monograph, 1973, Needs Assessment, 1972. Named ASCA Adminstr. of Yr. Curriculum and Instrn., 1993. Mem. Business Industry Coun., Orange Unified Curruculum Coun., Articulation Coun., Partnership Network, Dist. Negotiation Team, ASCD, Calif. Indsl. Edn. Assn., Intercultural Edn. Commn., Orange Suburbia Kiwanis Club, Orange High Sch. Faculty Club, Profl. Assn. Orange Educators. Office: Orange Unified Sch Dist 370 N Glassell St Orange CA 92866-1032

SCHROEDER, EDWIN MAHER, law educator; b. New Orleans, June 25, 1937; s. Edwin Charles and Lucille Mary (Maher) S.; m. Marietta Louise DeFazio, Aug. 1, 1936; children: Edwin Charles II, Jonathan David, Margaret Louise. AA, St. Joseph Sem., St. Benedict, La., 1957; PhB, Gregorian U., Rome, 1959; JD, Tulane U., 1964; MS, Fla. State U., 1970. Bar: Mass. 1964. Asst. prof. law U. Conn., 1965-68; asst. prof., asst. law libr. U. Tex., 1968-69; asst. prof. Fla. State U., 1969-71, assoc. prof., 1971-75, prof., 1975—, dir. Law Libr., 1969—, asst. dean Coll. Law, 1979-83, assoc. dean Coll. Law, 1983-93. Mem. ABA, Am. Assn. Law Librs. (v.p. Southwestern chpt. 1983-84, pres. 1984-85), Order of Coif, Beta Phi Mu. Roman Catholic. Home: 806 Middlebrooks Cir Tallahassee FL 32312-2439 Office: Fla State U Coll Law Law Libr Tallahassee FL 32306-1600 E-mail: eschroed@law.fsu.edu.

SCHROEDER, HENRY NICK, secondary education educator; b. Dickinson, N.D., Oct. 13, 1950; s. Henry C. and Susan K. (Krebs) S.; m. Cindy K. Jost, June 2, 1973; children: Chris, Mandy, Brett. BS in Secondary Math and Phys. Edn., Dickinson State Coll., 1972; M Math., Minot State U., 1996. Tchr., coach Halliday (N.D.) Pub. Sch., 1972-74, Mandan (N.D.) Pub. Schs., 1974—. Ind. crop adjustor, 1976—. Western Math. scholars appointee edn. grantee, 1991, 92. Mem. NEA, N.D. Edn. Assn., Nat. Coun. Tchrs. Math., Nat. Coaches Assn., N.D. Coaches Assn., Nat. Ofcls. Assn., N.D. Ofcls. Assn., Elks, K.C. Avocations: sports, camping, sightseeing. Office: Mandan High Sch 905 8th Ave NW Mandan ND 58554-2400 E-mail: Henry.Schroeder@sendit.nedak.edu.

SCHROEDER, LEILA OBIER, retired law educator; b. Plaquemine, La., July 11, 1925; d. William Prentiss and Daisy Lavinia (Mays) Obier; divorced; 1 child, James Michael Cutshaw; m. Martin Charles Schroeder Jr., Sept. 19, 1969. BA, Newcomb Coll., 1946; MSW, La. State U., 1953, JD, 1965. Bar: La. 1965. Exec. dir. Evangeline Area Guidance Ctr. La. Dept. Hosps., Lafayette, 1955-57, dir. social services dept. East La. State Hosp. Jackson, 1957-60, cons. psychiat. social work Baton Rouge, 1960-61; research assoc. La. State U., Baton Rouge, 1965-68, asst. prof., 1968-73, assoc. prof., 1973-80, prof., 1980-96; ret., 1996. Author: The Legal Environment of Social Work, 1982, The Legal Environment of Social Work, 1995; contbr. articles to profl. jours. Fellow Am. Orthopsychiat. Assn.; mem. ABA, Nat. Assn. Social Workers, Acad. Cert. Social Workers, La. State Bar Assn., Baton Rouge Bar Assn. Home: 4336 Oxford Ave Baton Rouge LA 70808-4651

SCHROEDER, THOMAS LEONARD, mathematics educator; b. Akron, June 26, 1947; s. Charles H. Schroeder and Marion B. (Buzenberg) Schroeder Hirtreiter; m. Susan Guthiel, May 30, 1976; children: Peter H., David N. AB in Math., Princeton U., 1969; PhD in Math. Edn., Ind. U., 1983. Vol. Peace Corps, Eastern Caribbean, 1969-74; from asst. to assoc. prof. U. Calgary, Alta., Canada, 1980-88; assoc. prof. edn. U. B.C., 1988-93; assoc. prof. Grad. Sch. Edn. SUNY, Buffalo, 1993—, faculty senator, 1994-96, chair dept. Learning and Instrn., 2000—03. Vis. assoc. prof. Simon Fraser U., Vancouver, 1987; dir. U. Credit Union, 1995-. Author: (with others) Professional Standards for Teaching Mathematics, 1991; contbr. articles to profl. jours. Bd. dirs., pres. U. Calgary Credit Union, 1981-86, pres., 1982-85. Recipient Outstanding Profl. Achievement award Can. Assn. for Studies in Ednl. Adminstrn., 1986. Mem. Am. Ednl. Rsch. Assn., Internat. Group for the Psychology of Math. Edn., Nat. Coun. Tchrs. Math. (com. chair 1989-90, tchg. stds. commn. 1989-91). Democrat. Episcopalian. Office: SUNY Learning and Instrn Dept 505 Baldy Hall Buffalo NY 14260-1000 E-mail: tls7@buffalo.edu.

SCHROEDER, W(ILLIAM) WIDICK, religion educator; b. Newton, Kans., Nov. 12, 1928; s. William Fredric and Irene (Widick) S.; m. Gayle Eadie, Sept. 1, 1956; children: Scott David, Carla Gayle. BA, Bethel Coll., 1949; MA, Mich. State U., East Lansing, 1952; BDiv, Chgo. Theol. Sem., 1955; PhD, U. Chgo., 1960; DD (hon.), Chgo. Theol. Seminary, 1995. Ordained to ministry Congl. Christian Ch., 1955. Instr. Mich. State U., East Lansing, 1953-54, U. Chgo., 1958-60; from asst. prof. to prof. religion and society Chgo. Theol. Sem., 1960-94, prof. emeritus, 1994—. Vis. fellow Mansfield Coll., Oxford, Eng., 1966; vis. lectr. Yale U., 1970; vis. scholar Ctr. for Process Studies, Claremont, Calif., 1976; vis. lectr. in ethics and soc. Divinity Sch. U. Chgo., 1967-71, 76; editor Rev. of Religious Rsch., 1964-69. Author: (with Victor Obenhaus) Religion in American Culture: Unity and Diversity in a Midwestern County, 1964; Cognitive Structures and Religious Research, 1970; (with Victor Obenhaus, Larry A. Jones and Thomas P. Sweetser) Suburban Religion: Churches and Synagogues in the American Experience, 1974; (with Keith A. Davis) Where Do I Stand? Living Theological Options for Contemporary Christians, 1973, rev. edit., 1975, 3d edit., 1978; Flawed Process and Sectarian Substance: Analytic and Critical Perspectives on the United Church of Christ General Synod Pronouncement, Christian Faith: Economic Life and Justice, 1990; Toward Belief: Essays in the Human Sciences, Social Ethics, and Philosophical Theology, 1996; co-editor: (with Philip Hefner) Belonging and Alienation: Religious Foundations for the Human Future, 1976; (with Gibson Winter) Belief and Ethics: Essays in Ethics, the Human Sciences and Ministry in Honor of W. Alvin Pitcher, 1978; (with John B. Cobb, Jr.) Process Philosophy and Social Thought, 1981; (with Perry LeFevre) Spiritual Nurture and Congregational Development, 1984, Pastoral Care and Liberation Praxis: Essays in Personal and Social Transformation, 1986, Creative Ministries in Contemporary Christianity, 1991; (with Franklin I. Gamwell) Economic Life: Process Interpretations and Critical Responses, 1988; co-editor Studies in Religion, Society and Personality, Center for the Scientific Study of Religion, 1972-2001. Mem. Religious Rsch. Assn., Soc. Christian Ethics. Home: 6315 Longwood Rd Libertyville IL 60048-9447

SCHROLL, EDWIN JOHN, retired secondary educator, stage director; b. Watertown, NY, Feb. 14, 1941; s. Clarence Edwin and Frances Lucille (Snyder) S. BS, Lyndon State Coll., 1966; MS, Oswego State U., 1971. Cert. tchr. N.Y. English tchr. jr. h.s. Watertown (N.Y.) Sch. System, 1966-67; English tchr. h.s. Belleville (N.Y.) Cen. Sch., 1967-71, Massena (N.Y.) Cen. Sch., 1971-96, drama and speech tchr., 1988-96, drama coach, 1975-96, forensics coach; ret., 1996. Engr., announcer, programmer Pathways to Peace program Sta. WNCQ, Watertown, 1967-92; dir. Family History Ctr., Watertown, N.Y. Cinematographer, writer, narrator, prodr. (documentaries) The United States: A Bicentennial Tour, 1976, Europe on $100 a Day, 1986; cinematographer: (TV) Wish You Were Here in Cape Vincent, 2000, Partying, 1989; co-author: Standard Operations Procedures and Duties of a Desk Clerk, 1963, Wish You Were Here in Cape Vincent, 2000; prodn. supr. (hist. pageant) 1,000 Seasons, 2001; dir. various high sch. prodns.; actor various community prodns. Bd. dirs. Youth in Action, 1993-94; active Nat. Family Opinion, 1991—; state advocate Ednl. Theatre Assn., 1996; del. Citizens Ambassador Program of People to People Internat. Theatre Edn. Delegation to China, 1996; active Cape Vincent Arts Coun., 1997—, Gravelly Point Players, 1997—, Breakwater Art Gallery, 1997—. Mem. Nat. Geog. Soc., Ednl. Theatre Assn., Archaeology Inst. Am., Am. Film Inst., Nat. Trust Hist. Preservation, Cinerama Preservation Soc. Republican. Mem. Lds Ch. Avocations: stamp and coin collecting, gardening, historical research, genealogy, travel. Home: PO Box 216 143 S Murray St Cape Vincent NY 13618 Office: Massena Sch System Nightengale Ave Massena NY 13662-1901 E-mail: edschroll@tds.net.

SCHROLL, MARK, research and development electronics educator; b. Denver, May 2, 1964; s. Evelyn Mary Przybilla; m. LuAnn Cecilia Schaefer, July 23, 1994; children: Katelyn Ann, Jennifer Marie. BS in Indsl. Tech. Edn., St. Cloud State U., 1988; MS in Edn. in Ednl. Tech. Leadership, George Washington U., 1998. R&D, electronics educator Sci. Acad. South Tex., Mercedes, 1989—. Presenter Tex. Edn. Adminstrn., Austin, 1993-96, 99, High Schs. That Work, So. Region, Louisville, Ky., 1996, Assn. Tex. Tech. Educators, Austin, 1993, 95, Miss. Valley Tech. Tchr. Edn. 89th conf., 2002; summer tchr. trainer Project Lead the Way Found., Rochester (N.Y.) Inst. Tech., 1999-. Author: Technology Systems Laboratory Activity Guide, 1992, Communication Systems Curriculum Guide, 1992, Energy Systems Curriculum Guide, 1992, Technology Systems Curriculum Guide, 1991; co-author sr. level course Project Lead the Way. Mem. Internat. Tech. Edn. Assn. (presenter conf. 1998), Aircraft Owners and Pilots Assn. Avocations: sailing, flying, scuba diving. Home: 2618 Lou Ann Ln Harlingen TX 78550-3349 Office: Science Academy of S TX Tech Dept 100 Med High Dr Mercedes TX 78570-9702

SCHROM, ELIZABETH ANN, writer, educator; b. Princeton, Minn, June 7, 1941; d. Raymond Alois and Grace Eleanor (Hayes) S. Student, U. Minn., 1960; BA, St. Scholastica Coll., Duluth, Minn., 1963; postgrad., Princeton U., 1965; MEd, Temple U., 1972; MLS, Drexel U., 1974; postgrad., NYU, 1981, Russian Temple U., 1983. Tchr. Strandquist HS, Minn., 1963-64, Hutchinson HS, Minn., 1964-65, Peace Corps, Ankara, Turkey, 1965-67, Phila. Sch. Dist., 1968-80; children's libr. Laurel Pub. Libr., Del., 1983; writer Ortonville (Minn.) Ind. Sch. Dist., 1983—. Mem. Jewish Com. on Middle East, Washington, 1988-90, 93, Nat. Coun. Returned Peace Corps. Vol., Washington, 1989-99, Nat. Taxpayers Union, Washington, 1988-92; mem. bd. policy Liberty Lobby, Washington, 1989-2000; mem. Arkadashlar, 2003. Populist. Roman Catholic. Avocations: writing, cooking, history, travel, sewing. Home: 1141 US Hwy 12 Lot 8 Ortonville MN 56278

SCHROTH, PETER W(ILLIAM), lawyer, management and law educator; b. Camden, N.J., July 24, 1946; s. Walter and Patricia Anne (Page) S.; children: Laura Salome Erickson-Schroth, Julia James. AB, Shimer Coll., 1966; JD, U. Chgo., 1969; M in Comparative Law, U.Chgo., 1971; SJD, U. Mich., 1979; postgrad., U. Freiburg, Fed. Republic Germany, Faculté Internationale pour l'Enseignement de Droit Comparé; MBA, Rensselaer Poly. Inst., 1988; DHL, Shimer Coll., 2000; MSc, Sch. Oriental and African Studies, 2000. Bar: Ill. 1969, N.Y. 1979, Conn. 1985, Mass. 1990; solicitor Supreme Ct. England and Wales 1995. Asst. prof. So. Meth. U., 1973-77; fellow in law and humanities Harvard U., 1976-77, vis. scholar, 1980-81; assoc. prof. N.Y. Law Sch., 1977-81; prof. law Hamline U., St. Paul, 1981-83; dep. gen. counsel Equator Bank Ltd., 1984-87; v.p., dep. gen. counsel Equator Holdings Ltd., 1987-94, v.p., gen. counsel, 1994-2000. Adj. prof. law U. Conn., 1985-86, Western New Eng. Coll., 1988—, adj. prof. of mgmt. Rensselaer Poly. Inst., 1988-98, prof., 1999—, dir. Ctr. for Global Bus. Studies, 2000—. Author: Foreign Investment in the United States, 2nd edit., 1977; author: (with Stiefel) Products Liability: European Proposals and American Experience, 1981; author: Doing Business in Sub-Saharan Africa, 1991; bd. editors Am. Jour. Comparative Law, 1981—84, 1991—, mem. editl. bd. Conn. Bar Jour., 1988—, sr. editor, 1993—2000, editor-in-chief, 2000—, recent decisions editor N.Y. Internat. Law Rev., —, mem. editl. rev. bd. Jour. Bus. in Developing Nations, 1996—2000, editor-in-chief, 2000—, co-editor-in-chief Jour. Legal Studies in Bus. Treas., mem. bd. trustees Shimer Coll. Mem. ABA (editor in chief ABA Environ. Law Symposium 1980-82), Am. Soc. Comparative Law (bd. dirs. 1978-84, 91—), Am. Fgn. Law Assn., Internat. Bar Assn., Internat. Law Assn. (com. multinat. banking), Acad. Internat. Bus., Conn. Civil Liberties Union (bd. dirs. 1985-92), Environ. Law Inst. (assoc.), Columbia U. Peace Seminar (assoc.), Hartford Club (bd. govs. 1995-98), Am. Corp. Counsel Assn. (pres. Conn. chpt.1997-2000), Conn. Bar Assn. (chair sect. of internat. law 1997-2000). Office: Rensselaer Poly Inst Lally Sch Mgmt and Tech 275 Windsor St Hartford CT 06120-2910

SCHUBERT, E. FRED, electrical engineer, educator; b. Stuttgart, Germany, Feb. 8, 1956; came to U.S., 1985; s. Konrad and Martha Ruth (Reichert) S.; m. Jutta Maria Lukai, Feb. 22, 1980; children: Anne F., Martin F., Ursula V. Diploma in Engring. with honors, U. Stuttgart, 1981, D in Engring. with honors, 1986. Rsch. assoc. Max Planck Inst., Stuttgart, 1981-85; tech. staff, prin. investigator AT&T Bell Labs., Murray Hill, N.J., 1985-95; prof. dept. elec. and computer engring. Ctr. for Photonics Rsch., Boston U., 1995—2002; constellation chmn., prof. Rensselaer Poly. Inst., Troy, 2002—. Author: Doping in III-V Semiconductors, 1993; editor: Delta Doping of Semiconductors, 1996; patentee in field. Postdoctoral fellow AT&T, 1985-87; recipient Alexander von Humboldt Rsch. prize, 2000, Discover Mag. award, 2000. Fellow IEEE, Internat. Soc. Optical Engring., Am. Phys. Soc., Optical Soc. Am.; mem. Verein Deutscher Elektrotechniker (lit. prize 1994), Material Rsch. Soc. Roman Catholic. Achievements include several patents involving doping of III-V semiconductors and several patents on high efficiency light emitting diodes. Home: 49 Angela St Canton MA 02021-2251 Office: Rensselaer Poly Inst Dept Elec Computer and Sys Engring 110 8th St Boston MA 12180

SCHUBERT, JANET LEE, middle school educator; b. Cleve., Apr. 22, 1952; d. Melvin Gene and Lillian Ester (Adams) Jewett; m. Terry Lee Schubert, June 14, 1980; children: Jill Marie Schubert Clark, Lisa Ann. BA, Miami U., Oxford, Ohio, 1974; MA, Kent State U., 1977. Learning disabled/behaviorally disordered tchr. Berea (Ohio) City Schs., 1974-83, health specialist, 1983-90, classroom of the future tchr., 1990-93; ednl. cons. Jostens Learning, 1993-94; 6th grade team educator Ford Mid. Sch., Brook Park, Ohio, 1994—. Summer sch. prin., cons. Cuyahoga County Spl. Edn., Brook Park, Ohio, 1974-79; in-svc. workshop leader. Vol. S.W. Gen. Hosp., Middleburg Heights, Ohio, 1984-89, jr. bd., 1985-87. Martha Holden Jennings Found. scholar, 1981-82, master tchr., 1982. Mem. Berea Fedn. Tchrs. (rep. 1985-91, mem. negotiating com. 1991-92), Cuyahoga County Agrl. Soc. (bd. dirs. 1985-95). Avocations: traveling, snow skiing, flying, reading, challenging projects. Office: Ford Mid Sch 17001 Holland Rd Cleveland OH 44142-3523

SCHUBERT, RUTH CAROL HICKOK, artist, educator; b. Janesville, Wis., Jan. 24, 1927; d. Fay Andrew and Mildred Wilamette (Street) Hickok; m. Robert Francis Schubert, Oct. 20, 1946; children: Stephen Robert, Michelle Carol. Student, DeAnza Coll., 1972—73; AA Scholarship, Monterey Peninsula Coll., 1974; BA with honors, Calif. State U., San Jose, 1979. Owner, mgr. Casa De Artes Gallery, Monterey, Calif., 1977—86; dir. Monterey Peninsula Mus. Art Coun., 1975—76; quick-draw artist So. Oreg. Pub. TV, KSYS; leader painting workshops; demonstrator, lectr., judge in U.S., B.C. Can., New Zealand and Loreto, Baja, Mexico. One-woman shows include Aarhof Gallery, Aarau, Switzerland, 1977, Degli Agostiniani Recolletti, Rome, 1977, Wells Fargo Bank, Monterey, 1975, 1978, 1979, Seaside (Calif.) City Hall Gallery, 1979, 1989, Village Gallery, Lahaina, Hawaii, 1983, 1986, 1989, 1984, Portola Valley Gallery, 1984, 1985, Rose Rock Gallery, Carmel, 1984—86, Taupo (N.Z.) Arts Soc., 1988, Geyserland Art Mus., Rotorua, N.Z., 1988, Wanganui (N.Z.) Art Soc., 1988, Hallei Brown Ford Gallery, Roseburg, Oreg., 1991, 1995, Collection of Ann Cunningham, Carmel, 1993—95, catalog nat. group juried shows include, Sierra Nev. Mus. Art, Reno, 1980, Bard Hall Gallery, San Diego, 1980, San Diego Nat. Watercolor Show, Mid-West Nat. Watercolor Show, Rahr-West Mus., Manitowoc, Wis., 1980, Rosicrucian Mus., San Jose, 1981, 1984, Calif. State Agri-Images, Sacramento, 1984, XVII Watercolor West, Brea Civic Cultural Ctr., 1985, Watercolor West XXIII, Grand Art Galleries, Glendale, Calif., 1991, Watercolor West XXV, Riverside (Calif.) Art Mus., 1993, Nat. Pen Women at Marjorie Evans Gallery, Carmel, 1986, Monterey County Juried Expo, Monterey Peninsula Mus. Art, 1986, 1987, Am. Artists Group Exhbn., 1993, 1994, 1995, Gallery Hirose, Tsukuba, Ibaragi, Japan, Internat. Art Show for End of World Hunger, Ashland, Oreg., 1990, biann. art exhbn. Sumner Mus., Washington, D.C., 1992, State of the Art, New

Eng. Fine Arts, Boston, 1993, N.W. Wildlife, Nightingale Gallery, Ea. Oreg. Coll., La Grande, 1993, N.W. Visual Arts Ctr. 19th Ann., Panama City, Fla., 1993, NWWS Waterworks N.W. Julie Tolles Gallery, Mercer Island, Wash., 1994, Represented in permanent collections Rogue Valley Manor Spl. Svcs., Medford, Oreg., Monterey Calif. Peninsula Mus. Art, Nat. Biscuit Co. subs. RJR Nabisco, San Jose, Waikato Mus. Art, Hamilton, N.Z., Muscular Dystrophy Assn., San Francisco, Old Sch. Hous Mus., Qualicum Bay, Vancouver Island, B.C., USS George Washington Aircraft Carrier, Adm. Robert Sprigg, Pres. Bill Clinton, Barbara Bush, George Montgomery, Marilyn Horne, Alison Krauss, also numerous pvt. collections. Recipient 1st prize, Monterey County Fair, 1979, Jade Fon Watercolor award, Hall of Flowers, San Francisco, 1980, 1st Nat. Art Show, NY Am. Artist mag., 1980, Nat. Art Appreciation award, 1984, award, Norcal State Art Fair, 1985, Watercolor award, 25 Ann. Aqueous Media Show, Salem, Oreg., 1990, Watercolor Transparent award, NWWS, Mercer Island, 1994, NWWS Signature Artist Waterworks, Seattle, 1999, award, Calif. Watercolor Soc., 2001, numerous other awards for watercolor paintings. Mem.: Watercolor West (signature), Women Artists Registry N.Am., Nat. Mus. Women in Arts, Art Alumni San Jose State U., Nat. League Am. Pen Women (pres. 1983—84, 1986—87), Cen. Coast Art Assn. (pres. 1982—85), Mid-West Watercolor Soc., Arts Coun. So. Oreg. (Silver award 2000), Watercolor Soc., Monterey Peninsula Watercolor Soc., Rogue Valley Art Gallery (bd. officer), LaHaina Arts Soc., Watercolor Soc. Oreg., Artists Equity Assn., Nat. Watercolor Soc. (assoc.), Am. Watercolor Soc. (assoc.). Achievements include Artwork selected for inclusion in profl. pubs. including "Best of Watercolor" in Rockport Publr. and "The California Art Preview" in Les Krantz. Home: 3533 Southvillage Dr Medford OR 97504-9283

SCHUBERT, WILLIAM HENRY, curriculum studies educator; b. Garrett, Ind., July 6, 1944; s. Walter William and Mary Madeline (Grube) S.; children by previous marriage: Ellen Elaine, Karen Margaret; m. Ann Lynn Lopez, Dec. 3, 1977; children: Heidi Ann, Henry William. BS, Manchester Coll., 1966; MS, Ind. U., 1967; PhD, U. Ill., 1975. Tchr. Fairmount, El Sierra and Herrick Schs., Downers Grove, Ill., 1967-75; clin. instr. U. Wis., Madison, 1969-73; tchg. asst., univ. fellow U. Ill., Urbana, 1973-75, asst. prof. Chgo., 1975-80, assoc. prof., 1981-85, prof., 1985—, coord. secondary edn., 1979-82, coord. instrnl. leadership, 1979-85, dir. grad. studies Coll. Edn., 1983-85, coord. grad. curriculum studies, 1985—, coord. edn. studies, 1990-94, 96—, chair area curriculum and instrn., 1990-94. Vis. assoc. prof. U. Victoria (B.C., Can.), 1981; disting. vis. prof. U. S.C., 1986; presenter in field. Author (with Ann Lopez Schubert): Curriculum Books: The First Eighty Years, 1980; author: Curriculum: Perspective, Paradigm and Possibility, 1986, with Edmund C. Short and George Willis, 1985; author: (with J. Dan Marshall and James T. Sears) Turning Points in Curriculum: A Contemporary American Memoir, 2000; author: (with Ann Lopez Schubert, Thomas P. Thomas, Wayne M. Carroll) Curriculum Books: The First Hundred Years, 2002; editor (with Ann Lopez): Conceptions of Curriculum Knowledge: Focus on Students and Teachers, 1982; editor: (with George Willis) Reflections from the Heart of Educational Iquiry: Understanding Curriculum Teaching Through the Arts, 1991; editor: (with William Ayers) Teacher Lore: Learning From Our Own Experience, 1992, re-pub., 2001; editor: (with George Willis, R. Bullugh, C. Kridel, J. Holton) The American Curiculum: A Documentary History, 1993; assoc. editor, mem. editl. bd. Ednl. Theory, mem. editl. bd. Catalyst: Voices of Chicago School Reform, Taboo: The Jour. of Culture and Edn., former mem. editl. bd. Ednl. Studies, former cons. editor Phenomenology and Pedagogy, adv. bd. Tchg. Edn., Pi Lamda Pubs., 1995—, Jour. Curriculum and Supervision, —, mem. editl. bd. Curriculum and Teaching, —, emeritus editl. bd. Jour. Curriculum Theorizing, 1999—; editor: (book series) Student Lore, 1990—; cons. editor Jour. Curriculum Discourse and Dialogue, —, mem. adv. bd. Jour. Critical Issues in Curriculum and Instrn., 2000—, contbr. over 200 articles to profl. jours., —, chpt. to books., —. Mem.: ASCD (steering com. curriculum com. 1980—83, publs. com. 1987—90, internat. polling panel 1990—), Soc. Profs. of Edn. (exec. bd. 1988—97, pres.-elect 2000—01, pres. 2001—02), John Dewey Soc. (bd. dirs. 1986—95, chair awards com. 1988—90, co-chair lectures commn. 1989—91, 1989—91, pres.-elect 1990—91, pres. 1992—93), Inst. Dem. in Edn., Nat. Soc. Study Edn., World Coun. Curriculum and Instr., Am. Ednl. Studies Assn., Am. Ednl. Rsch. Assn. (chmn. creation and utilization of curriculum knowledge 1980—82, program chmn. curriculum studies divsn. 1982—83, sec. dvisn. B 1989—91, v.p. 2000—01), Am. Assn. Colls. Tchr. Edn., Soc. Study Curriculum History (sec.-treas. 1981—82, pres. 1982—83, founding mem.), Profs. of Curriculum (factotum 1984—85), Internat. Acad. Edn., Scottish Rite, Masons, Phi Kappa Phi (pres. U. Ill. Chog. chpt. 1981—82), Phi Delta Kappa. Office: U Ill Coll Edn M/C 147 1040 W Harrison St Chicago IL 60607-7129 E-mail: schubert@uic.edu.

SCHUCK, PETER HORNER, lawyer, educator; b. N.Y.C., Apr. 26, 1940; s. Samuel H. and Lucille (Horner) S.; m. Marcy Cantor, June 26, 1966; children: Christopher, Julie. BA with honors, Cornell U., 1962; JD cum laude, Harvard U., 1965, MA, 1969; LLM, NYU, 1966; MA (hon.), Yale U., 1982. Bar: N.Y. State 1966, D.C. 1972. Practiced law, N.Y.C., 1965-68; teaching fellow in govt. Harvard U., 1969-71; cons. (Center for Study of Responsive Law), Washington, 1971-72; dir. Washington office Consumers Union, 1972-77; dep. asst. sec. for planning and evaluation HEW, Washington, 1977-79; vis. scholar Am. Enterprise Inst. for Public Policy Research, Washington, 1979; assoc. prof. law Yale U., 1979-81, prof., 1981-86, Simeon E. Baldwin prof. law, 1986—, dep. dean, 1993-94. Vis. prof. Georgetown U. Law Ctr., 1986-87, NYU Law Sch., fall 1994, N.Y. Law Sch., spring 1997, 98, 99 Author: The Judiciary Committees, 1975, Suing Government, 1983, Citizenship Without Consent, 1985; co-author: Agent Orange on Trial, 1986, enlarged edit., 1987, Citizens, Strangers and In-Betweens: Essays on Immigration and Citizenship, 1998, The Limits of Law: Essays on Democratic Governance, 2000, Diversity in America: Keeping Government at a Safe Distance, 2003; editor: Tort Law and the Public Interest, 1991, Foundations of Administrative Law, 1994, 2d edit., 2003; co-editor: Paths to Inclusion, 1998, Immigration Stories, 2004; contbr. articles and revs. to profl. and popular publs. Recipient Silver Gavel award ABA, 1987; Guggenheim fellow, 1984-85; Fulbright scholar, 2004. Jewish. E-mail: peter.schuck@yale.edu.

SCHUELE, DONALD EDWARD, physics educator; b. Cleve., June 16, 1934; s. Edward and Mildred (Matousek) S.; m. Clare Ann Kirchner, Sept. 5, 1956; children: Donna, Karen, Melanie, Judy, Rachel, Ruth. BS, John Carroll U., Cleve., 1956, MS, 1957; PhD, Case Inst. Tech., 1962. Instr. physics and math. John Carroll U., 1956-59; part-time instr. physics Case Inst. Tech., 1959-62, instr., asst. prof., assoc. prof., 1962-70; mem. tech. staff Bell Telephone Labs., 1970-72; assoc. prof. physics Case Western Res. U., 1972-74, prof., 1974—, dean undergrad. coll., 1973-76, chmn. dept. physics, 1976-78; vice dean Case Inst. Tech., 1978-83, v.p. for undergrad. and grad. studies, 1983-84, dean, 1984-86, prof. physics, 1986-88, dean math. and natural sci., 1988-89, Albert A. Michaelson prof. physics, 1989—, acting chmn. elec. engring. and applied physics, 1992-93. Cons. in field. Co-editor: Critical Revs. in Solid State Scis, 1969-84; contbr. articles to profl. jours.; patentee in field. Mem. adv. bd. St. Charles Borromeo Sch., 1970-72; pres. Seed Found., 1986-89; trustee St. Mary's Sem., 1980-93; mem. Olympic Sports Equipment and Tech. Com., 1982-93; trustee Newman Found., 1983—, Northeastern Ohio Sci. Fair, 1983—; mem. Diocesan Pastoral Coun., 1992-94; active Rep. Presdl. task force. Recipient Disting. Physics Alumnus award John Carroll U., 1983; NSF Faculty fellow, 1961-63; Sam Givelber fellow Case Alumni Assn., 2001. Mem.: North Coast Thermal Analysis Soc., Am. Assn. Physics Tchrs., Am. Phys. Soc. (vice chair Ohio sect. 1995—96, chair 1996—97), Newman Apostolate, Case Alumni Coun. (life; 3d v.p. 2001—02, 1st v.p. 2002—03, treas. 1992, pres. 2003—), Tau Beta Pi, Sigma Xi, Alpha Sigma Nu. Republican. Roman Catholic. Achievements include patents fluid pressure device, impact wrench torque calibrator, detection of wear particles and other impurities in industrial fluids, electrical oil analysis instrument. Home: 4892 Countryside Rd Cleveland OH 44124-2513 Office: Case Western Res U 10900 Euclid Ave Cleveland OH 44106-1712 E-mail: des3@po.cwru.edu.

SCHUELEIN, MARIANNE IDA, neurologist, educator; b. Stuttgart, Germany, Apr. 16, 1934; d. Curt Charles and Gertrude (Weil) S.; m. Ralph Mack Krause, June 26, 1960; children: Peter C., Steven C. AB, Wellesley Coll., 1955; MD, NYU, 1959. Diplomate Am. Bd. Pediatrics; diplomate in neurology and child neurology Am. Bd. Psychiatry and Neurology. Intern in pediatrics Yale U., New Haven, 1959-60; resident in pediatrics Michael Reese Hosp., Chgo., 1960-62; fellow in neurology Children's Hosp., Washington, 1962-63; resident in neurology Georgetown U., Washington, 1964-67, asst. prof. neurology and pediatrics, 1967—; chair divsn. neurology Sibley Meml. Hosp., Washington, 2001—02. Mem. Bd. Medicine, Washington, 1988—2001, acting chair, 2001; lectr. Georgetown U.. Law Sch., 1992; mem. staff Georgetown U. Hosp., Children's Hosp. D.C., Fairfax Hosp., Prince George's Hosp. Ctr., Washington, Sibley Meml. Hosp., Va. Hosp. Ctr.; bd. dirs. St. John's Devel. Svcs.; mem. Folger Poetry Bd.; examiner Am. Bd. Psychiatry and Neurology, 1980—2000; cons. USLME. Contbr. articles to profl. publs. Recipient Cert. of Recognition, MD Assn., 1978, Disting. Svc. award Epilepsy Fedn., 1981, Newmyer award Sidwell Friends, 1985, Vicennial medal Georgetown U. Med. Ctr., 1987, presdl. cert. of Appreciation Med. Soc. of the D.C., 1995. Fellow: Am. Acad. Pediatrics, Am. Acad. Neurology; mem.: Nat. Tuberous Sclerosis Assn. (bd. dirs. 1986—), Med. Soc. D.C. (chmn. neurology sect. 1992—93), Child Neurology Soc., Am. Acad. Devel. Medicine, NYU Med. Sch. Alumni Assn. D.C. (pres. 1993), Cosmos Club (bd. mgmt. 1994—2003, sec. 1998—2000, v.p. 2000—01, pres. 2001—02). Office: Georgetown U Sch Medicine Kober-Cogan #307 3800 Reservoir Rd NW Washington DC 20057

SCHUELER, JAN FRANCES MENIER, early childhood special education administrator; b. Port Clinton, Ohio, July 3, 1955; d. Vito Joseph and Isabelle Mae (Robron) Menier; m. Jerold Douglas Schueler, Mar. 18, 1977; children: Ryan, Blair, Chase. BEd in Spl. Edn., Bowling Green State U., 1977; MEd in Early Childhood, U. Toledo, Ohio, 1991. Cert. spl. edn. tchr., elem. prin., supr., pre-sch. and K-8 tchr., Ohio. Kindergarten tchr. Sandusky County (Ohio) Ednl. Svc. Ctr., 1977-80, Huron (Ohio) City Schs., 1986-89, pre-sch. tchr., 1989-90, pre-sch. spl. edn. tchr., 1989-90; early childhood svcs. coord. No. Ohio Spl. Edn. Regional Resource Ctr., Oberlin, Ohio, 1991-94; early childhood spl. edn. dir. Sandusky County Office of Ednl. Svcs., Fremont, Ohio, 1994—. Developer Huron City Schs. Pre-sch. Program, 1989-91; cons. No. Ohio SERRC, Oberlin, 1991-94, Early Childhood divsn. Ohio Dept. Edn., Columbus, 1991-94; mem. adv. bd. Berlin-Milan (Ohio) Schs. Pre-sch., 1992-94, Lorain County Office of Edn. Pre-schs., Elyria, Ohio, 1992-94. Supr. Middleground Family Reunification Program, Norwalk, Ohio, 1993-95; mem. com. Huron Athletic Boosters, Inc., 1992—, sec. 1995—; concession co-chair Huron Baseball Program, Inc., 1993-95. Mem. ASCD, Nat. Assn. for Edn. of Young Children, Coun. for Exceptional Children, Assn. for Early Childhood Edn. Internat., Children and Adults with Attention Deficit Disorder (chpt. coord. 1993-95), Phi Delta Kappa (v.p. membership Firelands chpt. 1996—), Pi Lambda Theta. Home: 307 Wexford Dr Huron OH 44839-1459 Office: Sandusky County Ednl Svc Ctr 602 W State St Fremont OH 43420-2534

SCHUELLER, WOLFGANG AUGUSTUS, architectural educator, writer; b. Aachen, Germany, Sept. 10, 1934; came to U.S., 1964; s. Sepp and Mathilde (Kalff) S.; m. Ria Herpers, Apr. 22, 1960; 1 child, Uschi. Diploma in Engring. in Civil Engring., FH Aachen, Germany, 1960; BS in Archtl. Engring. with honors, N.D. State U., 1966; MSCE in Structural Engring., Lehigh U., 1968; BArch, Syracuse U., 1971. Registered profl. engr., N.Y., Pa. Supr. constrn., structural engr. Hochtief A.G., Munich and Essen, Fed. Republic of Germany, 1960-63; structural designer Green Blanksteen Russel Assocs., Winnipeg, Man., Can., 1963-64; structural engr. Pioneer Svc. and Engring. Co., Chgo., 1966-67, Richardson, Gordon Assocs., Pitts., 1968-69; prof. architecture Syracuse U (N.Y.), 1971-82, Va. Poly. Inst., Blacksburg, 1982-94, U. Fla., Gainesville, 1994—. Vis. prof. Ministry Univ. Affairs Thailand, 1996, Suzhou (China) U., 1999, 2001, Manipal (India) Inst. Tech., 2001, China U. Mining Tech., Xuxhou, China, 2002, Xuxhou, 03, LiaoNing Tech. U., Fuxin, China, 2002, Chongqing (China) U., 2003, Hebei U. Tech., Tianjin, China, 2003. Author: Highrise Building Structures, 1977, Horizontal-Span Building Structures, 1983, The Vertical Building Structure, 1990, The Design of Building Structures, 1996. Mem. ASCE, Nat. Soc. Archtl.Engrs., Soc. for History of Tech., Coun. on Tall Bldgs. and Urban Habitat, Sigma Xi, Phi Kappa Phi, Tau Beta Pi. Achievements include rsch., presentation of papers, workshops, book critiques, seminars, and pub. lects. on relationship between bldg. sci., structures in particular, and architecture in the U.S., Japan, India, Singapore, Cambodia, Indonesia, China, Guatemala and Thailand. Office: U Fla Coll Arch Gainesville FL 32611-5702

SCHUESSLER, ISABELLE SWEENY, school administrator; b. Washington, May 12, 1934; d. Charles Amos and Barbara (Crosser) Sweeny; m. Donald Charles Schuessler, Aug. 8, 1953; children: Donald C. Jr., Janet L., Douglas P., David J. AA, AB, George Washington U., 1962. Dir. St. Patrick's Episcopal Day Sch., Washington, 1962-86; founding head Washington Episcopal Sch., Bethesda, Md., 1986—2001. Cons. St. Andrew's Episcopal Sch., Bethesda, 1976-79, St. James' Children's Ctr., Potomac, 1991-1996, Cadence Episcopal Sch., Washington, 1992-1995; v.p. Nat. Assn. Episcopal Schs., N.Y.C., 1981-84, pres., 1984-86; evaluator Middle States Assn. Colls. and Schs.; cons. to schs. and sch. founding groups, churches for fundraising. Democrat. Episcopal. Avocations: volunteering, crafts. Home and Office: 9 Orchard Way South Potomac MD 20854

SCHUH, G(EORGE) EDWARD, university dean, agricultural economist; b. Indpls., Sept. 13, 1930; s. George Edward and Viola (Lentz) S.; m. Maria Ignez, May 23, 1965; children: Audrey, Susan, Tanya. BS in Agrl. Edn, Purdue U., 1952, DAgr (hon.), 1992; MS in Agrl. Econs., Mich. State U., 1954; MA in Econs, U. Chgo., 1958, PhD, 1961; prof. (hon.), Fed. U. Vicosa, Brazil, 1965; hon. doctorate, Purdue U., 1992. From instr. to prof. agrl. econs. Purdue U., 1959-79; dir. Center for Public Policy and Public Affairs, 1977-78; dep. undersec. for internat. affairs and commodity programs Dept. Agr., Washington, 1978-79, chair bd. for internat. food and agrl. devel., 1995—2002; prof. agrl. and applied econs., head dept. U. Minn., Mpls., 1979-84; dir. agr. and rural devel. World Bank, Washington, 1984-87; dean Humphrey Inst. for Pub. Affairs U. Minn., 1987—96; Orville and Jane Freeman Endowed chair Humphrey Inst. for Pub. Affairs, U. Minn., 1996—; regents prof. U. Minn., 1998—. Program advisor Ford Found., 1966-72; sr. staff economist Pres.'s Coun. Econ. Advisors, 1974-75; bd. on agr. NRC, 1998—; trustee Internat. Food Policy Rsch. Inst., 1997-2003, Internat. Potato Ctr., 2003—. Author, editor profl. books; contbr. numerous articles to profl. publs. Trustee Sasakawa Africa Assn., 1998—. Served with U.S. Army, 1954-56. Recipient 60 at 60 award, Internat. Insts. for Cooperation in Agr. Fellow: AAAS, Am. Agrl. Econs. Assn. (bd. dirs. 1977—80, pres.-elect 1980—81, pres. 1981—82, Thesis award 1962, Pub. Rsch. award 1971, Article award 1975, Policy award 1979, Publ. of Lasting Value award 1988), Am. Acad. Arts and Scis.; mem.: Brazilian Soc. Agrl. Economists, Am. Econ. Assn., Internat. Assn. Agrl. Econs. Office: Humphrey Ctr U Minn 301 19th Ave S Minneapolis MN 55455-0429 E-mail: geschuh@hhh.umn.edu.

SCHUH, MARTHA SCHUHMANN, mathematics educator; b. Boston, Oct. 12, 1941; d. Reinhardt and Betsy (Hancock) Schuhmann; 1 child, Erika. BA in Math., Oberlin Coll., 1962; MA in Math., U. Ill., 1963. Tchr. math. Sandburg HS, Orland Park, Ill., 1964-66, Centennial HS, Champaign, 1966-71; lectr. in math. U. Wis., Stevens Point, 1971-75; tchr., math. dept. chair Baraboo Jr. HS, 1976-82; prof. math. U. Wis., Manitowoc, 1982—. Mem. Math. Assn. Am., Am. Math. Assn. Two-Yr. Colls., Nat. Coun. Tchrs. Math., Wis. Math. Coun. Home: 1118 Fairmont Ln Manitowoc WI 54220-2712 Office: U Wis Viebahn St Manitowoc WI 54220 E-mail: mschuh@uwc.edu.

SCHUKER, STEPHEN ALAN, historian, educator; b. N.Y.C., Feb. 16, 1939; s. Louis A. and Millicent (Milchman) S.; m. Elisabeth Glaser, 1998. AB summa cum laude, Cornell U., 1959; AM, Harvard U., 1962, PhD, 1969; children: Lauren, Daniel. Asst. head hist. rsch. naval history div. Office Chief Naval Ops., 1959-61; instr. history Harvard U., Cambridge, Mass., 1968-69, asst. prof., 1969-74, lectr., 1974-75; vis. assoc. prof. European studies Sch. Advanced Internat. Studies, Johns Hopkins U., Washington, 1977, adj. prof., 1978-83; assoc. prof. history Brandeis U., Waltham, Mass., 1977-82, prof., 1982-91; Commonwealth prof. history U. Va., Charlottesville, 1991-92, William W. Corcoran prof., 1992—; syndic U. Press New Eng., 1979-81; cons. Nat. Commn. Documents and Records Federal Ofcls., 1976, Rockefeller Found., 1981. Lt. USNR, 1959-61. Nat. Endowment Humanities fellow, 1972-73; Am. Council Learned Socs. fellow, 1976-77, 85; sr. fellow USIA-Fulbright Commn., 1984, fellow internat. security John D. and Catherine T. MacArthur Found., 1987-89, fellow Historisches Kolleg, Bayerische Akademie der Wissenschaften, 1996—, fellow German Marshall Fund, 1998-99. Mem. Am. Hist. Assn., Soc. Historians Am. Fgn. Relations. Author: The End of French Predominance in Europe (George Louis Beer prize, Gilbert Chinard prize), 1976, American "Reparations" to Germany, 1919-1933: Implications for the Third World Debt Crisis, 1988; editor: Deutschland und Frankreich vom Konflikt zur Aussöhnung, 2000; contbr. articles to profl. jours. Office: U Va Corcoran Dept History University Station Charlottesville VA 22904 E-mail: sas4u@virginia.edu.

SCHULER, ROBERT HUGO, chemist, educator; b. Buffalo, Jan. 4, 1926; s. Robert H. and Mary J. (Mayer) S.; m. Florence J. Forrest, June 18, 1952; children: Mary A., Margaret A., Carol A., Robert E., Thomas C. BS, Canisius Coll., Buffalo, 1946; PhD, U. Notre Dame, 1949. Asst. prof. chemistry Canisius Coll., 1949-53; asso. chemist, then chemist Brookhaven Nat. Lab., 1953-56; staff fellow, dir. radiation research lab. Mellon Inst., 1956-76, mem. adv. bd., 1962-76; prof. chemistry, dir. radiation research lab. Carnegie-Mellon U., 1967-76; prof. chemistry U. Notre Dame, Ind., 1976—, dir. radiation lab., 1976-95, dir. emeritus, 1995—, John A. Zahm prof. radiation chemistry, 1986—; Raman prof. U. Madras, India, 1985-86. Vis. prof. Hebrew U., Israel, 1980. Author articles in field. Recipient Curie medal Poland, 1992. Fellow AAAS; mem. Am. Chem. Soc., Am. Phys. Soc., Chem. Soc., Radiation Research Soc. (pres. 1975-76), Sigma Xi. Clubs: Cosmos. Office: U Notre Dame Radiation Lab Notre Dame IN 46556 E-mail: schuler.1@nd.edu.

SCHULL, MYRA EDNA, librarian; b. Vienna, May 3, 1951; came to U.S., 1952; d. Verlin Watson and Wiltraud Ingeborg (Oftner) Miller; m. Terence William Schull, May 26, 1972; 1 child, Michael William. AB, Ball State U., 1973, MA, 1977; MLS, Ind. U., 1992. Tchr. English, German Shenandoah Sch. Corp., Middletown, Ind., 1973-84; head audio visual Muncie (Ind.) Pub. Libr., 1985-86; media specialist Delaware Cmty. Sch. Corp., Muncie, 1988—. Mem. libr. adv. bd. High St. Meth. Ch., Muncie, 1991—. Tchr. Creativity grantee Lilly Endowment Inc., Indpls., 1993. Mem. Assn. Ind. Media Educators, Job's Daus. (life, honored queen), Internat. Assn. Sch. Librs., Internat. Reading Assn., Coun. for Basic Edn. Avocations: travel, reading, dog obedience training. Home: 218 N Riley Rd Muncie IN 47304-3946 Office: Delaware Cmty Sch Corp 7821 N State Road 3 Muncie IN 47303-9401

SCHULMAN, LEE S. educational association administrator; Mem. faculty Mich. State U., Lansing, 1963—82; 1st Charles E. Ducommun prof. of edn. and (by courtesy) prof. of psychology Stanford U., Stanford, Calif., 1982—97; pres. Carnegie Found For Advancement of Teaching, Menlo Park, Calif., 1997—. Contbr. articles to profl. jours. and other publs. Recipient E.L. Thorndike award, Am. Psychol. Assn. Divsn. of Ednl. Pschology, 1995. Fellow: Am. Acad. Arts and Scis.; mem.: Nat. Acad. Edn., Am. Ednl. Rsch. Assn. Achievements include development of (with others) studies that supported the creation of Nat. Bd. for Profl. Teaching Standards. Office: Carnegie Found Advancement Tchg 555 Middlefield Rd Menlo Park CA 94025 Office Fax: 650-326-0270.

SCHULTE, MATTHEW LEE, secondary school educator; b. Belmond, Iowa, June 19, 1964; s. Eldon Lee and Mary Ann (De Master) S.; m. Carol Lynn Van Norden, July 23, 1988; children: Heidi Lynn, Erica Leigh, Austin Matthew, Jenna Carolyn. BA in Math. and Computer Sci., Ctrl. Coll., Pella, Iowa, 1986; MSM, Iowa State U., 1996. Cert. secondary tchr., coach., Iowa; nat. bd. cert. in AYA math., 2000. Tchr./coach Belmond Cmty. Schs., 1986-93, Pella Cmty. Schs., 1993—. Mem. Nat. Coun. Tchrs. Math., Profl. Educators of Iowa. Republican. Ref. Ch. in Am. Avocations: woodworking, landscaping. Office: Pella High School 212 E University St Pella IA 50219-1970

SCHULTHEIS, EDWIN MILFORD, dean, business educator; b. N.Y.C., Apr. 15, 1928; s. Milford Theodore and Lillian May (Hill) S.; m. Joan Edna Bruckner, June 23, 1956. BS, Hofstra Coll., 1950; MBA, NYU, 1958, EdD, 1972. Officer mgr., sales rep. Topton Rug Mfg. Co., N.Y.C., 1950-54; area mgr., trainer Mobil Oil Co., N.Y.C., 1954-62; coord. distributive edn. North Babylon (N.Y.) Pub. Schs., 1962-88, chmn. bus. mktg. and indsl. edn. depts., 1988-91; prof. bus. adminstrn. SUNY, Farmingdale, 1970-91; asst. prof. edn. NYU, 1973—; dir. edn. Syracuse (N.Y.) U., 1973-78; chmn. dept. bus. adminstrn. Five Towns Coll., Seaford, N.Y., 1991-92, divsn. chmn. bus. and tech. Dix Hills, N.Y., 1992-98, dean instrn., 1993-98, dep. dean of faculty, 1993-98, assoc. dean, 1996-97, prof. emeritus, 1998—. Test writer, cons. N.Y. State Dept. Edn., Albany, 1965—; textbook reviewer McGraw-Hill Book Co., N.Y.C., 1967-69; cons. Cornell U., 1975; dist. adviser Distributive Edn. Clubs N.Y., 1970, bd. govs., trustee, 1975-78; mem. curriculum adv. coun. Suffolk County (N.Y.) Distributive Edn. Assn., 1967—. Author: Modern Petroleum Marketing, 1971, Content and Structure of Belief-Disbelief Systems, 1972. Elder Presbyn. Ch., U.S.A. Named N.Y. State Tchr. of Yr., 1976, Outstanding Tchr. in N.Y. State, 1978; recipient Outstanding Svc. award Distributive Edn. Clubs N.Y., Suffolk County Distributive Edn. Assn., Tchr. Excellence award N.Y. State, 1980, Citation for Excellence in Edn. Gov. Mario Cuomo N.Y., 1991, Citation Excellence in Teaching Babylon Twp., 1991. Mem. Acad. Mgmt., Am. Petroleum Inst., Am. Security Coun., Suffolk County Assn. Distributive Edn. Tchrs. (mem. exec. bd. 1962-74), N.Y. State (pres. 1975-78), L.I. Distributive Edn. Assns. (hon. life, exec. bd. 1972-75), N.Y. State Occupl. Edn. Assn. (v.p. 1975-78), L.I. Bus. Edn. Chmns. Assn. (hon. life, exec. bd. 1972-75), N.Y. State Occupl. Edn. Assn. (v.p. 1975-78), L.I. Bus. Edn. Chmns. Assn. (hon. life), Distributive Edn. Clubs Am. (regional leader 1972-75, hon. life 1991), Bellport (N.Y.) Golf Club, Phi Delta Kappa, Kappa Delta Pi, Sigma Alpha Lambda, Phi Sigma Etz. Presbyterian (ordained ruling elder). Home: 14 Thorn Hedge Rd Bellport NY 11713-2616

SCHULTZ, ALBERT BARRY, engineering educator; b. Phila., Oct. 10, 1933; s. George D. and Belle (Seidman) S.; m. Susan Resnikov, Aug. 25, 1955; children: Carl, Adam, Robin BS, U. Rochester, 1955; MEngring., Yale U., 1959, PhD, 1962. Asst. prof. U. Del., Newark, 1962-65; asst. prof. U. Ill., Chgo., 1965-66, assoc. prof., 1966-71, prof., 1971-83; Vennema prof. U. Mich., Ann Arbor, 1983-99. Contbr. numerous articles to profl. jours. Served to lt. USN, 1955-58 Rsch. Career award NIH, 1975-80; Javits Neurosci. Investigator award NIH, 1985-92 Mem. NAE, Internat. Soc. for

Study Lumbar Spine (pres. 1981-82), ASME (chmn. bioengring. div. 1981-82, H.R. Lissner award 1990), Am. Soc. Biomechanics (pres. 1982-83, Borelli award 1996), U.S. Nat. Com. on Biomechanics (chmn. 1982-85), Phi Beta Kappa

SCHULTZ, ALVIN LEROY, retired internist, endocrinologist, retired university health science facility administrator; b. Mpls., July 27, 1921; s. Maurice Arthur and Elizabeth Leah (Gershin) S.; m. Martha Jean Graham, Aug. 14, 1947; children: Susan Kristine, David Matthew, Peter Jonathan, Michael Graham. BA, U. Minn., 1943; MD, 1947. Diplomate Am. Bd. Internal Medicine. Intern Ohio State U., Columbus, 1946-47; resident in internal medicine U. Minn. Hosps., Mpls., 1949-52, instr. medicine, 1952-54; asst. prof., 1954-59; assoc. prof., 1959-65; prof., 1965-88; prof. emeritus, from 1988; asst. chief medicine Mpls. VA Hosp., 1952-54; dir. endocrine clinic U. Minn., 1954-59; dir. medicine and rsch. Mt. Sinai Hosp., Mpls., 1959-65; chief of medicine Hennepin County Med. Ctr., Mpls., 1965-88; chmn. bd. acad. practice plan Hennepin Faculty Assocs., 1983-87; sr. v.p. med. affairs HealthOne Corp., 1988-92; med. affairs officer Health-Span, 1993-94; dir. strategic planning, chmn. med. adv. coun. Phoenix Alliance, Inc., St. Paul. Assoc. editor: Jour. Lab. and Clin. Medicine, 1966-69, Modern Medicine, 1960—; editl. bd. Minn. Medicine, 1965-94, Data Centrum, 1984-87; contbr. articles to profl. jours. Bd. dirs. Planned Parenthood of Minn., 1970-75, Hennepin County Med. Philanthropic Found., 1976-86. Capt. U.S. Army, 1947-49. Fellow ACP (Minn. gov. 1983-86, chmn. bd. govs. 1987-88, regent 1988-94); mem. Ctrl. Soc. Clin. Rsch., Am. Fedn. Clin. Rsch., Endocrine Soc., Am. Thyroid Assn., Minn. Med. Assn. (ho. of dels. 1980-85), Coun. of Med. Splty. Socs. (bd. dirs. 1987-92, v.p. 1988-89, pres. 1990-91), Minn. Assn. Pub. Tchg. Hosps. (pres. 1983-84), Hennepin County Med. Soc. (dir. 1977-81, pres. 1988-89, chmn. bd. dirs. 1989-90), Golden Valley Country (Mpls.), N.W. Racquet (Mpls.). Jewish. Avocations: golf, photography, music, reading, computer science. Home: Minneapolis, Minn. Died Jan. 19, 2001.

SCHULTZ, CAROLYN JOYCE, nursing educator; b. Johnstown, Pa., Aug. 26, 1949; d. Robert Charles and Marion Elizabeth (Beatty) Miller; children: Melissa Lynn, Allison Marie. ADN, Mt. Aloysius Coll., 1972; BSN, Indiana U. Pa., 1979; MSN, W.Va. U., 1984, postgrad., 1997—. RN, Pa. Staff nurse Conemaugh Valley Meml. Hosp., Johnstown, 1975-94, faculty Sch. of Nursing, 1984-92; clin. rsch. nurse Laurel Highlands Cancer Program, Johnstown, 1992-94; with Pa. State Nursing Faculty, 1998, Mt. Aloysius Coll. Nursing Faculty, 1998-00; staff nurse UPMC Lee Regional, 2000—. Mem. faculty St. Francis Coll., Loretta, Pa., 1983-84; chair svc. and rehab. com., bd. dirs. Johnstown unit Am. Cancer Soc., 1985-94, Cambria dist. dir., Johnstown, 1992-94. Recipient Vol. of Yr. award Am. Cancer Soc., 1990. Home: 330 Phillips St Johnstown PA 15904-1226 E-mail: coco120208@aol.com.

SCHULTZ, DARRELL LEE, art educator; b. Hettinger, N.D., Apr. 14, 1959; s. Glenn Arthur and Katie Gisela (Schwantje) S.; m. Tricia May (Perry) Langner, Aug. 7, 1981 (div. Jan. 1989); 1 child, Christopher Ryan Schultz; m. Rhonda Reana Myers, June 23, 1989 (div. Jan. 1997); 1 child, Stephanie Kate Schultz; m. Teresa J. Calcote Bowles, July 7, 2000. AA, Southeastern C.C., West Burlington, Iowa, 1979; BA, Southwestern Okla. State U., 1981; MEd, Southwestern Okla. U., 1991. Art tchr. grades 7-12 Cache (Okla.) Pub. Schs., 1981-99; assoc. prof. Lake City (Fla.) C.C., 1999; classroom and internet adj. Lake City C.C., Austin C.C. and Tarrant County Coll., Tex., 2000—. Named one of Outstanding Young Men of Am., 1988. Mem. Alpha Phi Sigma (Iota chpt.), Kappa Delta Pi, Phi Alpha Theta. Avocations: photography, watercolor painting, airbrush painting. Home: 7324 Old Mill Run St Fort Worth TX 76133-7025 E-mail: artdoc7@charter.net.

SCHULTZ, JOHN EDWARD, principal; b. Milw., Aug. 28, 1954; s. Edward Arthur and Marion Imogene (Nee McCool) S.; m. Ruth Ellen Burger. BA, Concordia Coll., 1977; M in Edn., Profl. Devel., U. Wis., Whitewater, 1980. Tchr., vice-prin. St. Paul's Luth., Janesville, Wis., 1977-94; tchr., prin. St. John's Luth., Adrian, Mich., 1994-97; prin. Evansville (Ind.) Luth., 1997—. Sec. Luth. Ch. Missouri Synod-Mich. dist. Mich. Luth. Prins., Ann Arbor, 1996-97; presenter in field; spkr. in field. Official In H.S. Athletic Assn., Evansville, 1997—; sec. bd. dirs. S. Wis. Dist. Conv., Milw., 1994; chmn South West Ind. Adminstr.; pres. Ctrl. H.S. Volleyball Boosters. Mem. ASCD, Internat. Reading Assn., Nat. Assn. Student Activity Advisors, Nat. Assn. Secondary Sch. Prins. (nominated Prin. of Yr. MetLife 1997), Am. Alliance Health, Ind. Dist. Prins. Luth. Schs. 21st Century, Luth. Edn. Assn. Lutheran. Home: 740 Lancaster Ct Evansville IN 47711-7210 Office: Evansville Luth Sch 120 E Michigan St Evansville IN 47711 E-mail: jeschult@evansville.net.

SCHULTZ, JUDITH, educational administrator, consultant; b. Boston, Oct. 2, 1960; d. William Leonard and Jeanne Anne (Parker) Schultz; m. Mark Devon Betourne. BA in Psychology, Plymouth (N.H.) State Coll., 1982; MA in Counseling Psychology, Antioch New Eng. Grad. Sch., Keene, N.H., 1989. Recreation therapist Laconia (N.H.) Devel. Svcs., 1982-85, program dir. recreation dept., 1985-86, behavior specialist vocat. svcs., 1986-87, tng. and devel. therapist, psychology dept., 1987-89, psychologist for the state, 1989-90; program supr. Spaulding Youth Ctr., Tilton, N.H., 1990-92, program dir., 1992—. Adv. bd. N.H. Vocat. Tech. Inst., Laconia, 1993—, assoc. prof., 1991; cons. in field. Song writer, profl. musician, 1977—. A founder youth sailing program Winnipesaukee Sailing Assn., Gilford, N.H., 1988. Mem. Winnipesaukee Yacht Club. Avocations: yacht racing, skiing, hiking, travel. Home: PO Box 7171 Gilford NH 03247-7171 Office: Spaulding Youth Ctr PO Box 189 Tilton NH 03276-0189

SCHULTZ, KAREN ROSE, clinical social worker, author, publisher, speaker; b. Huntington, N.Y., June 16, 1958; d. Eugene Alfred and Laura Rose (Palazzolo) Squeri; m. Richard S. Schultz, Apr. 8, 1989; children: Carlos, Sarah Rose. BA with honors, SUNY, Binghamton, 1980; MA, U. Chgo., 1982. Lic. clin. social worker, Ill. Unit dir., adminstr. Camp Algonquin, Ill., 1981; clin. social worker United Charities Chgo., 1982-86; social worker Hartgrove Hosp., Chgo., 1986-87; pvt. practice, Oak Brook, Ill., 1987—. Owner, founder Inner Space pub. Co., 1993; trainer, speaker various groups, schs. and orgns., 1988-89; group leader Optifast Program, Oak Park and Aurora, Ill., 1989-90; instr. social work Moraine Valley C.C., Palos Hills, Ill., 1989-90; instr. eating disorders Coll. of Dupage, Glen Ellyn, Ill., 1990-92, tchr. intuition and counseling, 1995—; spkr. in field. Author: The River Within, 1993, Shelter in the Forest, 1998, Flashes of Brilliance, 2002; editor, contbg. author: The River Within newsletter, 1989—2000. Mem. NASW (registered, diplomate), Acad. Cert. Social Workers. Avocations: creative writing, aerobics, yoga, personal growth. Office: 900 Jorie Blvd Ste 234 Oak Brook IL 60523-3841

SCHULTZ, SAMUEL JACOB, clergyman, educator; b. Mountain Lake, Minn., June 9, 1914; s. David D. and Anna (Eitzen) S.; m. Eyla June Tolliver, June 17, 1943; children: Linda Sue, David Carl. Grad., St. Paul Bible Inst., 1936; AA, Bethel Coll., 1938; BA, John Fletcher Coll., 1940; BD, Faith Theol. Sem., 1944; MST, Harvard U., 1945, ThD, 1949. Ordained to ministry Christian and Missionary Alliance Ch., 1944; pastor First Meth. Ch., Pine River, Minn., 1940-41, Waldo Congl. Ch., Brockton, Mass., 1944-45, Evang. Bapt. Ch., Belmont, Mass., 1945-47; prof. Gordon Coll., Boston, 1946-47, Bethel Coll. and Sem., St. Paul, 1947-49, St. Paul Bible Inst., 1948-49, Wheaton (Ill.) Coll., 1949-80, prof. emeritus, 1980—, Samuel Robinson prof. Bible and theology, 1955-80, chmn. Bible and philosophy dept., 1957-63, chmn. div. Bibl. edn. and philosophy, 1963-67, chmn. div. Bibl. studies, 1972-79; prof. Old Testament and Bible Exposition Trinity Coll. Grad. Sch. (name now Tampa Bay Theol. Sem.), Dunedin (now Holiday), Fla., 1987-93. Prof. Old Testament St. Petersburg (Fla.) Theol. Sem., adj. prof. St. Petersburg Jr. Coll., 1995-98; interim supply pastor Bible Ch. Winnetka, Ill., 1951, 60; resident supply pastor South Shore Bapt. Ch., Hingham, Mass., 1958-59. Author: The Old Testament Speaks, 1960, 5th edit., 2000, Law and History, 1964, The Prophets Speak, 1968, Deuteronomy-Gospel of Love, 1971, The Gospel of Moses, 1974, 79, Interpreting the Word of God, 1976, Leviticus-God Dwelling Among His People, 1983, The Message of the Old Testament, 1986; contbr. Deuteronomy commentary to The Complete Biblical Libr., 1996, First Samuel commentary, 1998, Minor Prophets commentary, 1999. Mem. bd. edn. Bethel Coll. and Sem., 1960-65; historian Conservative Congregation Christian Conf., 1980-86; bd. dirs. Inst. in Basic Youth Conflicts, 1965-80, Congl. Christian Hist. Soc., 1984-96, Brookwoods Christian Camps and Confs., Inc., Alton, N.H., 1978—; trustee Gordon-Conwell Sem., South Hamilton, Mass., 1980—, Lexington (Mass.) Christian Acad., 1987-98. NYU study grantee Israel, 1966, Wheaton Coll. Alumni research grantee, 1958; recipient Alumnus of the Yr. award Crown Coll., 1996. Mem. Soc. Bibl. Lit., Evang. Theol. Soc. (editor Jour. 1962-75), Near East Archaeol. Soc. (sec., bd. dir.), Wheaton Coll. Scholastic Honors Soc., Phi Sigma Tau. Book the Living and Active Word of God dedicated in his honor, 1983. Home: 11403 Oakmont Ct Fort Myers FL 33908-2822

SCHULTZ, STANLEY GEORGE, physiologist, educator; b. Bayonne, N.J., Oct. 26, 1931; s. Aaron and Sylvia (Kaplan) S.; m. Harriet Taran, Dec. 25, 1960; children: Jeffrey, Kenneth. AB summa cum laude, Columbia U., 1952; MD, N.Y. U., 1956. Intern Bellevue Hosp., N.Y.C., 1956-57, resident, 1957-59; research assoc. in biophysics Harvard U., 1959-62, instr. biophysics, 1964-67; assoc. prof. physiology U. Pitts., 1967-70, prof. physiology, 1970-79; prof., chmn. dept. physiology U. Tex. Med. Sch., Houston, 1979-96, prof. dept. internal medicine, 1979—, prof. dept. integrative biol. pharm. physiology, 1997—, vice chmn., 1999—, interim dean Sch. Medicine, 2003—, Fondren chair in cell signalling, 1999—. Cons. USPHS, NIH, 1970—; mem. physiology test com. Nat. Bd. Med. Examiners, 1974-79, chmn., 1976-79 Editor Am. Jour. Physiology, Jour. Applied Physiology, 1971-75, Physiol. Revs., 1979-85, Handbook of Physiology: The Gastrointestinal Tract, 1989-91—; mem. editl. bd. Jour. Gen. Physiology, 1969-88, Ann. Revs. Physiology, 1974-81, Current Topics in Membranes and Transport, 1975-81, Jour. Membrane Biology, 1977—, Biochim. Biophys. Acta, 1987-89; assoc. editor Ann. Revs. Physiology, 1977-81; assoc. editor News in Physiol. Scis., 1989-94, editor, 1994-2003; contbr. articles to profl. jours. Served to capt. M.C. USAF, 1962-64. Recipient Rsch. Career award NIH, 1969-74, Solomon Berson award NYU, 2003; overseas fellow Churchill Coll., Cambridge U., 1975-76 Mem. AAAS, Am. Heart Assn. (estab. investigator 1964-68), Am. Physiol. Soc. (councillor 1989-91, pres.-elect 1991-92, pres. 1992-93, past pres. 1993-94, Guyton award 1997, Orr Reynolds award 1999, Daggs award 2003), Fed. Am. Soc. Exptl. Biology (exec. bd. 1992-95), Biophys. Soc., Soc. Gen. Physiologists, Internat. Cell Rsch. Orgn., Internat. Union Physiol. Scis. (chmn. internat. com. gastrointestinal physiology 1977-80, chmn. U.S. nat. com. 1992-98), Assn. Am. Physicians, Am. Assn. Ob-Gyn. (hon. fellow), Assn. Chmn. Depts. Physiology (pres. 1985-86), Houston Philos. Soc., Sigma Xi, Phi Beta Kappa. Home: 4955 Heatherglen Dr Houston TX 77096-4213

SCHULTZ, T. PAUL, economics educator; b. Ames, Iowa, May 24, 1940; s. Theodore W. and Esther (Werth) S.; m. Judith Hoenack, Sept. 16, 1967; children: Lara, Joel, Rebecca. BA, Swarthmore Coll., 1961; PhD, MIT, 1966; MA (hon.), Yale U., 1974. Cons. Joint Econ. Com., Washington, 1964; rschr. econ. dept. Rand Corp., Santa Monica, Calif., 1965-72, dir. population rsch., 1968-72; prof. econ. U. Minn., Mpls., 1972-75, Yale U., New Haven, 1974—, dir. Econ. Growth Ctr., 1983-96; prof. econ. Malcolm K. Brachman, 1977. Cons. World Bank, Rockefeller Found., InterAm. Devel. Bank; mem. com. on population NAS, Washington, 1987-89, 90-93. Author: Structural Change in a Developing Country, 1971, Economics of Population, 1981; editor: (books) The State of Development Economics, 1988, Investment In Women's Human Capital, 1995, (periodical) Research in Population Economics, 1985, 88, 91, 96; assoc. editor Jour. Population Econs., 1991—. Econ. of Edn. Rev., 1993—, China Econ. Rev., 1994—. Mem. commn. on behavioral sci. and edn. Nat. Rsch. Coun., 1997-2002. Fellow: AAAS (population resources environ. com. 1985—89, nomination com. 1987—90); mem.: Econ. Rsch. Forum for Arab Countries (trustee 1993—2001), European Soc. for Population Econs. (bd. dirs., pres. 1997), Soc. for Study Social Biology (bd. dirs. 1986—89), Internat. Union for Sci. Study Population, Population Assn. Am. (bd. dirs. 1979—81), Econometrics Soc., Am. Econ. Assn. Office: Yale U Econ Growth Ctr PO Box 208269 27 Hillhouse Ave New Haven CT 06520-8269 E-mail: paul.schultz@yale.edu.

SCHULTZE, SYDNEY PATTERSON, language educator; b. Louisville, Jan. 20, 1943; d. Jack Howard and Marion Loel (Patterson) S.; m. Thomas Anthony Buser, May 11, 1974; children: Jack Schultze Buser, Adrian Schultze Buser. BA, U. Louisville, 1965; MA, Ind. U., 1968, PhD, 1974; postgrad., Oxford U., England, 1965-66. Vis. asst. prof. Ind. U., Bloomington, 1974-75; prof. U. Louisville, 1970—. Author: Structure of Anna Karenina, 1982, Culture and Customs of Russia, 2000; editor: Meyerhold the Director, 1982. Mem. Am. Assn. Advancement Slavic Studies, Am. Assn. Teachers Slavic and East European Langs., Am. Coun. Teaching Russian, Assn. Women in Slavic Studies. Democrat. Avocations: painting, reading, cooking. Home: 3601 Sudbury Ln Louisville KY 40220-2737 Office: Univ Louisville Louisville KY 40292-0001 E-mail: sydney.schultze@louisville.edu.

SCHULZ, RENATE ADELE, German studies and second language acquisition educator; b. Lohr am Main, Germany, Feb. 24, 1940; came to U.S., 1958; 1 child, Sigrid Diane. BS, Mankato State Coll., 1962; MA, U. Colo., 1967; PhD, Ohio State U., 1974. Edn. officer U.S. Peace Corps, Ife Ezinihitte, Nigeria, 1963-65; asst. prof. Otterbein Coll., Westerville, Ohio, 1974-76, State U. Coll. N.Y., Buffalo, 1976-77; from asst. to assoc. prof. U. Ark., Fayetteville, 1977-81; from assoc. to prof. U. Ariz., Tucson, 1981—, chair dept. German, 1984-90, chair PhD program in second lang. acquisition and teaching, 1994-97. Disting. vis. prof. USAF Acad., Colorado Springs, Colo., 1990-91. Recipient Creative Tchg. award, U. Ariz. Found., Tucson, 1984, Stephen A. Freeman award, N.W. Conf. Tchg. Fgn. Langs., 1984, Bundesverdienstkreuz, Fed. Govt. Germany, 1990, Anthony Papalia award for excellence in tchr. edn., Am. Coun. Tchrs. Fgn. Langs./N.Y. State Assn. Fgn. Lang. Tchrs., 2002. Mem.: MLA (del. 1989—91), Am. Assn. Applied Linguistics, Tchrs. of ESL, Am. Assn. Tchrs. German (v.p. 1988—90, pres. 1990—91), Am. Coun. Tchrs. Fgn. Langs. (exec. coun. 1979—81, Florence Steiner award 1993). Office: U Ariz Dept German Studies Tucson AZ 85721-0105 E-mail: schulzr@u.arizona.edu.

SCHULZ, ROBERT ADOLPH, management educator, management consultant; b. Long Branch, N.J., Aug. 20, 1943; s. Robert Adolph and Anna Elizabeth (Fuga) S. BA in Math., St. Vincent Coll., Latrobe, Pa., 1965; BS in Mech. Engring., U. Notre Dame, 1966; MBA, U. Pitts., 1967; PhD in Bus. Adminstrn., Ohio State U., 1971. Rsch. asst. Tech. and Bus. Svcs., Ohio State U., Columbus, 1967-68; teaching asst. dept. mktg. Ohio State U., 1968-70; sr. assoc. Mgmt. Horizons, Inc., Columbus, 1970-71; dir. tech. edn. Mgmt. Horizons Data Systems, Columbus, 1971-72, dir. edn., 1972-73; assoc. prof., Faculty of Mgmt. U. Calgary, Alta., Can., 1973-88, acad. dir. petroleum land mgmt., 1983—, prof. mgmt., 1988—. Coord. tchg. devel. office U. Calgary, Alta., 1991-98; pres. Scenario Mgmt. Cons. Ltd., Calgary, 1987—; bd. dirs. Wi-Lan, Inc. Chmn. align to 21st century task force Calgary Econ. Devel. Authority, 1989-92, bd. govs., 1994-96; chmn. coord. com. Calgary Cath. Diocese Synod, 1990-94, co-chmn. Synod implementation com., 1994-2001; bd. dirs. Calgary Sponsor and Refugee Soc., 1981-83. 3M Tchg. fellow, 1987; recipient awards for teaching and coaching acad. teams, Hon. Life Mem. award U. Calgary Students' Union, 1991, City of Calgary award for edn., 1995. Mem. Soc. for Teaching and Learning in Higher Edn., Can. Assn. Petroleum Landmen (hon.), Order of the U. Calgary, Beta Gamma Sigma. Roman Catholic. Avocations: golf, basketball, jogging. Home: 24-1815 Varsity Estates Dr NW Calgary AB Canada T3B 3Y7 Office: U Calgary Faculty of Mgmt Calgary AB Canada T2N 1N4

SCHULZ, SANDRA E. art educator; b. Dallas, July 2, 1963; d. Lionel Leigh and Ida Maria Johanna Schulz. BS in Art Edn., Tex. Woman's U., 1985, MFA in Sculpture, 1990. Cert. tchr. art all levels, Tex. Clk. and advt. Bartos Inc., Dallas, 1982—90; art tchr. 7th and 8th grades Harry Stone Mid. Sch., Dallas, 1990—91; art tchr. 9-12th grades Thomas Jefferson H.S., Dallas, 1992—. Art club sponsor, robotics team sponsor Thomas Jefferson H.S., Dallas. Chair publicity and decoration Tex. Cultural Partnership, Dallas, 1994-2001; publicity chair Am. Czech Culture Soc., Dallas, 1992-2001. Named Citizen of the Week, KRLD Radio Sta., 2002; recipient Brookhaven Coll. Pyramid award for tchg., 2001, Tex. Senate Excellence award for outstanding tchrs., Outstanding H.S. Tchr. award, Dallas Rotary Club, 2001—02. Mem. Nat. Art Educators Assn., Tex. Art Educators Assn., Dallas Art Educators Assn. (publicity chair 1996-98), Sculpture Assn. (sec. 1993-95). Lutheran. Avocations: camping, fishing, gardening, music, electric trains. Home: 9218 Clear Dr Sanger TX 76266 Office: Thomas Jefferson HS 4001 Walnut Hill Ln Dallas TX 75229-6239

SCHUMACHER, CYNTHIA JO, retired elementary and secondary education educator; b. Sebring, Fla., Sept. 24, 1928; d. Floyd and Espage S. BA, Fla. State U., 1950, MA, 1951; MS, Nova U., 1978; postgrad., Fla. State U., 1968-69. English tchr. Grady County Sch. System, Cairo, Ga., 1951-53; elem. tchr. Brevard County Sch. System, Melbourne, Fla., 1953-55; elem. tchr., curriculum generalist, secondary tchr. Lake County Schs., Tavares, Fla. area, 1955-85; retired, 1985. Mem. Edn. Standards Commn., Fla., 1980-85, Quality Instrn. Incentives Coun., Fla., 1983-84. Author: (poetry) Seeds from Wild Grasses, 1988, Creekstone Crossings, 1993, Soul Candles, 1998, Wellspring Legacies, 2000; (poetry and stories) Butterfly Excursions, 1996; (children's books) Colorful Character, 1998, Searching for S, 1998. Pres. League of Women Voters of Lake County, 1989-91; mem. Lake Conservation Coun., The Nature Conservancy, Habitat for Humanity of Lake County. Named Fla. Tchr. of Yr., Fla. Fedn. Women's Clubs, 1966, Lake County Tchr. of Yr., Lake County Sch. Sys., 1985, East Cen. Fla. Tchr. of Yr. finalist, State of Fla., 1986; recipient Good Egg award, Leesburg Area C. of C., 1991, Lifetime Achievement award, Fla. Edn. Assn. United, 2000. Mem. Lake County Edn. Assn. (pres. 1971-72, cons. 1985—). Democrat. Roman Catholic. Avocations: environ. support activities, gardening, creative writing, macrobiotic cooking,.

SCHUMACHER, GEBHARD FRIEDERICH BERNHARD, obstetrician-gynecologist; b. Osnabrueck, Fed. Republic Germany, June 13, 1924; came to U.S., 1962; s. Kaspar and Magarete (Pommer) S.; m. Anne Rose Zanker, Oct. 24, 1958; children: Michael A., Marc M. MD, U. Goettingen and Tuebingen, 1951; Sc.D. equivalent in obstetrics and gynecology, U. Tuebingen, 1962. Intern U. Tuebingen Med. Sch., 1951-52; tng. biochemistry Max Planck Inst. Biochemistry, Tuebingen, 1952-53; tng. biochemistry and immunology Max Planck Inst. Virus Research, 1953-54; resident in ob-gyn U. Tuebingen, 1954-59, tng. internal medicine, 1959, asst. scientist in ob-gyn and biochem. research, 1959-62, dozent in ob-gyn, 1964-65; Research assoc. in immunology Inst. Tb Research, U. Ill. Coll. Medicine, 1962-63; research assoc., asst. prof. ob-gyn U. Chgo., 1963-64; assoc. prof. ob-gyn asst. prof. biochemistry Albany Med. Coll. of Union U., 1965-67; research physician, div. labs. and research N.Y. State Dept. Health, Albany, 1965-67; assoc. prof. ob-gyn U. Chgo.-Chgo. Lying-In Hosp., 1967-73, prof. Immunology, 1974-91; chief sect. reproductive biology U. Chgo., 1971-91, prof. ob-gyn., 1973—91; prof. Biol. Sci. Collegiate Divsn. U. Chgo., 1982-96; prof. emeritus U. Chgo., 1996—. Cons. WHO, NIH, other nat. and internat. orgns.; mem. tech. and sci. adv. bds. Family Health Internat., Cistron Tech. Inc. Author: (with Beller) The Biology of the Fluids of the Female Genital Tract, 1979; (with Dhindsa) Immunological Aspects of Infertility and Fertility Regulation, 1980; (with Kaiser) Human Reproduction, Fertility, Sterility, Contraception, German edit., 1981, Spanish edit., 1986; contbr. articles to profl. jours. Fellow Am. Coll. Obstetricians and Gynecologists; mem. Soc. Gynecologic Investigation, Am. Soc. Reproductive Medicine, Soc. Study of Reprodn., Am. Soc. Cytology, Am. Soc. Investigative Pathology, Am. Soc. Andrology, Chgo. Assn. Reproductive Endocrinologists (pres. 1985-86), N.Y. Acad. Scis., Deutsche Gesellschaft für Gynakologie und Geburtshilfe, Gesellschaft für Biologische Chemie, Deutsche Gesellschaft für Immunologie, Gesellschaft Deutscher Naturforscher und Aerzte. Home and Office: 557 Hamilton Wood Homewood IL 60430-4403

SCHUMACHER, JEFFREY DAVID, principal; b. Peoria, Ill., Oct. 29, 1962; s. Harold and Verlene (Baute) S.; m. Carla Jane Sturdevant, Oct. 10, 1989. BS in Elem. Edn. and Spl. Edn., Drake U., Des Moines, 1985; MS in Elem. and Secondary Adminstrn., U. Iowa, 1991. Cert. tchr. K-9, spl. edn. tchr. K-9, adminstr. pre K-12. Spl. edn. tchr. grades 6-8 Des Moines Pub. Schs., 1985-86; spl. edn. sci. tchr. grades 5-9 Orchard Place Campus Sch., Des Moines, 1986-89; tchr. sci. Vinton Shellsburg (Iowa) Sch. Dist., 1989-91; system-wide prin. Nishna Valley Cmty. Schs., Hastings, Iowa, 1991—. Founding mem. Nishna Valley Am. Field Svc., Hastings, 1992; bd. dirs. S.W. Iowa Prins. Acad., Council Bluffs, 1993—; advisor spl. edn. Area Edn. Agy., Council Bluffs, 1992—; pres. Corner Conf. Prins., 1993-94. Des Moines Ind. Schs. grantee, 1988-89. Mem. Nat. Assn. Sch. Prins., Am. Assn. Sch. Prins., Nat. Middle Sch. Assn., Sch. Adminstrs. of Iowa, Nat. Assn. Elem. Sch. Prins., Phi Delta Kappa. Avocations: reading, outdoor activities, travel. Home: 909 NE 15th St Ankeny IA 50021-4566 Office: Nishna Valley Cmty Sch Dist RR 1 Box 80B Hastings IA 51540-9763

SCHUMACHER, MARY LOU, secondary education educator; b. Cando, N.D., Mar. 1, 1946; d. Harold J. and Ella (Baerwald) Campbell; m. Herbert Don Schumacher, Apr. 3, 1969; 1 child, Marissa Dawn. BS, Mayville State U., 1967; MS, U. Ariz., 1974. Tchr. San Manuel (Ariz.) High Sch., 1967-69, Flowing Wells High Sch., Tucson, 1969—2000, chmn. math. dept., 1988—2000, tchr., 2000—. Supr. U. Ariz., 2000—. Mem. NEA, Ariz. Tchr. Math., Nat. Coun. Tchrs. Math., Con Sortium for Math. Home: 6338 N Carapan Pl Tucson AZ 85741-3401 E-mail: schuma3@comcast.net.

SCHUMACHER, SUZANNE LYNNE, artist, art educator; b. San Francisco, Apr. 20, 1951; d. Martin John and Evelyn Lucinda (Andrews) S.; m. Timothy Van Ert, June 24, 1983 (div. Aug. 1988). BA, St. Marys Coll., 1972; MFA, San Francisco Art Inst., 1983. Instr. art Coll. Marin (Calif.), 1984-90; tchr. Montera Jr. High Sch., Oakland, Calif., 1989-92; prof. art St. Marys Coll., Moraga, Calif., 1990—. Developer, dir. Myrtle Street Art Studios, Oakland, 1978—. Avocations: ballet, tennis, languages. Home: 3037 Myrtle St Oakland CA 94608-4526 Office: St Mary's Coll Dept Art St Mary's Rd Moraga CA 94575

SCHUMACKER, RANDALL, educational psychologist; b. Oakes, N.D., May 26, 1951; s. Ernest and Helen S.; m. Joanne Cummins, July 24, 1952; children: Rachel Ann, Jamie Maureen. AA, William Rainey Harper Jr. Coll, Palatine, Ill., 1970; BS, Western Ill. U., 1972; MS, So. Ill. U., 1978, PhD, 1984. Rsch. asst. So. Ill. U., Carbondale, 1980-84, assoc. dir. computing, 1984-87; asst. prof. U. North Tex., Denton, 1988-90, assoc. prof., 1991-97, prof. ednl. tech. and rsch., 1998—, prof. biostat.; clin. prof. psychiatry U. Tex. Southwestern Med. Ctr., 2002—. Adj. prof. med. edn. U. North Tex. Health Scis. Ctr., 1996—; vis. prof. So. Ill. U., 1980-84; vis. scholar U. Chgo., 1996; cons. Tex. Acad. Math. & Sci., Denton, 1993, Carrollton-Farmers Br., Tex., 1991-94, Profl. Devel., 1989-92; pres. Southwest Ednl. Rsch. Assn., 2002-03; presenter in field. Author: Beginners Guide to Structural Equation Modeling, 1996, Advanced Structural Equation Modeling: Issues and Techniques, 1996, Interaction and Non-Linear Effects in Structural Equation Modeling, 1998, Understanding Statistical Concepts

Using S-Plus, 2001, New Development and Technologies in Structural Equation Modeling, 2001; editor Structural Equation Modeling: A Multidisciplinary Jour., 1994-98; editor Multiple Linear Regression Viewpoints, 1998—; editor emeritus Structural Equation Modeling, 1999—, Beginner's Guide to Structural Equation Modeling, 2nd edit., Basic Concepts, Principles, and Practice, 2004.; contbr. articles to profl. jours. Mem. APA, Am. Ednl. Rsch. Assn., S.W. Ednl. Rsch. Assn. (pres. 2002-03), Am. Statis. Assn., Nat. Coun. Measurement Edn. Republican. Lutheran. Avocations: sailing, golf. Office: U North Tex Coll Edn PO Box 311335 Denton TX 76203-1335 E-mail: rschumacker@unt.edu.

SCHUMAN, ELLIOTT PAUL, psychoanalyst, mediator, arbitrator, facilitator; BS, U.S. Naval Acad., 1949; MA, Columbia U., 1955, PhD, profl. diploma in counseling psychology, Columbia U., 1958. Diplomate Am. Bd. Psychotherapy, Am. Bd. Profl. Psychology, Am. Acad. Pain Mgmt., Am. Bd. Med. Psychotherapists; lic. psychologist, N.Y., N.J. From lectr. to asst. to Dean and counselor, Columbia Coll. Columbia U., N.Y.C., 1955-58; lectr., counselor Bklyn. Coll., 1958-60; adj. asst. prof., dir. testing and counseling L.I. U., 1960-62, asst. prof. to prof. psychology, 1962—; coord. grad. programs in psychology Long Island U., N.Y.C., 1984—; faculty Mid-Manhattan Inst. Modern Psychoanalysis, N.Y.C., 1992—. Psychologist Morningside Mental Hygiene Clinic, 1960-66; psychotherapist Community Guidance Svc., N.Y.C., 1962-69, supr., 1969-87; psychoanalyst Theodore Reik Consultation Ctr., 1966-69, tng. analyst, 1969—; mem. faculty Am. Inst. for Psychotherapy and Psychoanalysis, 1972-73, Ctr. for Modern Psychoanalytic Studies, 1973—, Nat. Psychol. Assn. for Psychoanalysis, 1974, Inst. for Expressive Analysis, 1980-81, Inst. for Modern Psychoanalysis, 1981-86; supervisor dept. psychiatry Mt. Sinai Hosp., 1979—. Author: Guide for Evaluation of Instruction, Navy Dept., 1958; contbr. numerous articles to profl. jours. Recipient fellowship Found. for Econ. Edn. Mem. AAAS, APA, AAUP, N.Y. State Psychol. Assn., N.Y. Acad. Scis., N.Y. Soc. Clin. Psychologists, Ea. Psychol. Assn., Soc. Projective Techniques, Nat. Assn. for Advancement Psychoanalysis, Coun. for Nat. Register Health Svc. Providers in Psychology, Am. Group Psychotherapy Assn., Am. Acad. Psychotherapists, N.Y. Soc. for Ericksonian Psychotherapy and Hypnosis, Assn. Family and Conciliation Cts., Sigma Xi, Phi Delta Kappa, Kappa Delta Pi. Home and Office: 116 Prospect Park W Brooklyn NY 11215-3710

SCHUMANN, ALICE MELCHER, medical technologist, educator, sheep farmer; b. Cleve., Sept. 1, 1931; d. John Henry and Marian Louise (Clark) M.; m. Stuart McKee Struever, Aug. 21, 1956 (div. June 1983); children: Nathan Chester, Hanna Russell; m. John Otto Schumann, July 3, 1985. BS, Colby Coll., New London, N.H., 1953. Cert. tchr.; cert. med. technologist. Rschr. Lakeside Hosp., Cleve., 1953-54, Bambridge (Ohio) Schs., 1954-55, Shalersville (Ohio) Schs., 1955-56, Richtnior Sch., Overland, Mo., 1956-57; tchr. sci. Tonica (Ill.) H.S., 1956-58, Morton Grove (Ill.) H.S., 1958—60, U. Chgo. Lab Sch., 1960-65; co-founder Ctr. for Am. Archeology, dir. flotation rsch. U. Chgo. Campus, Kampsville, Ill., 1957-71, head supplies distbn., dir. food svcs. dept.; head mailing dept. Found. for Ill. Archeology, Evanston and Kampsville, Ill., 1971-83; sheep farmer, wool processor Gravel Hill Farm, Kampsville, 1983—. Vol. Mt. Sinai Hosp., Cleve., 1948-49; tchr. Title I Dist. 40, Kampsville, 1970-71. Recipient Beverly Booth award Colby Coll., 1953, 1st prize for hand spun yarn DeKalb County Fair, Sandwich, Ill., 1987, 88. Mem. Precious Fibers Found., Natural Colored Wool Growers Assn., Farm Bur. of Calhoun County. Avocations: wool growing, custom wash and spinning wool and cotton, knitting, raising great pyrenees guard dogs for sheep, gardening. Home and Office: Gravel Hill Farm RR 1 Box 121A Kampsville IL 62053-9720

SCHUMANN, GAIL L. plant pathologist, educator; BS in Botany, U. Mich., 1972; MS in Plant Pathology, Cornell U., 1976, PhD in Plant Pathology, 1978. From vis. lectr. to assoc. prof. U. Mass., Amherst, Mass., 1984—94, assoc. prof., 1994—. Sr. editor APS Press, 1992; chair APS Press Illustrations of Plant Pathogens and Disease Com.; mem. editl. adv. bd. Plant Disease; mem. editl. bd. Phytopathology News; sec.-treas. N.E. divsn. APS, 1992-95, pres.-elect 1995. Author: Plant Diseases: Their Biology and Social Impact, 1991; co-author: IPM Handbook for Golf Courses, 1998. Recipient Genesis Tchg. award APS Found., 1988, Excellence in Tchg. award, 1993. Office: Univ Mass Amherst Fernald Hall Rm 209E 270 Stockbridge Rd Amherst MA 01003-9320*

SCHUPPERT, ROGER ALLEN, retired university official; b. Milw., Feb. 14, 1947; s. Arnold William and Harriet Mary (Hayward) S. BA in English, Ga. State U., 1972, MEd in Secondary Edn., 1977, M Comm. in Print Journalism, 1990. Clk. III, Ga. State U., Atlanta, 1973-85, records coord. I, 1985—2001, customer svc. specialist II, 2000—, ret. Chmn. policies and procedures com., staff adv. coun. Ga. State U., 1995-98 Mem. Dem. Nat. Com., Washington, 1988—. With USAF, 1965-68, Vietnam. Recipient Tech. Theatre award Ga. State U. Players, 1980, 90, 91. Avocations: reading, volleyball, theater. Home: PO Box 403 Atlanta GA 30301-0403

SCHURE, ALEXANDER, university chancellor; b. Can., Aug. 4, 1920; s. Harry Joshua and Bessie (Ginsberg) S.; m. Dorothy Rubin, Dec. 8, 1943 (dec. June 1981); children: Barbara, Matthew, Louis, Jonathan; m. Gail Doris Strollo, Sept. 12, 1984. AST in Elec. Engring, Pratt Inst., 1943; BS, CCNY, 1947; MA, NYU, 1948, PhD, 1950, EdD, 1953; D in Engring. Sci. honoris causa, Nova U., 1975; DSc, N.Y. Inst. Tech., 1976; LLD, Boca Raton Coll., 1976, LI U., 1983; LHD, Columbia Coll., Calif., 1983; D of Pedagogy, N.Y. Chiropractic Coll., 1985. Asst. dir. Melville Radio Insts., N.Y.C., 1945-48; pres. Crescent Sch. Radio and TV, Bklyn., 1948-51, Crescent Electronics Corp., N.Y.C., 1951-55; founder, pres., CEO N.Y. Inst. Tech., Bklyn., 1955—82, chancellor, CEO, 1982-91, chancellor emeritus, 1991—, founder computer graphics lab., 1970-91; pres., CEO, chancellor The Univ. Fedn., Inc., 1995—; chancellor, CEO Nova U. (now NSY), 1970-86; mem. Fla. State Bd. Ind. Colls. and Univs., 1991—; pres. Vidbits, Inc., 1992, N.Y. Coll. for Wholistic Health Edn. and Rsch., Syosset, L.I., NY, 2000—. Cons. N.Y. State Dept. Edn., U.S. Office Edn., UNESCO, tech. educator sent to Venezuela to study needs, UNESCO, 1960; mem. Regents Regional Coordinating Council for Post-Secondary Edn. in N.Y.C., 1973—; mem., 1st inductee Nassau County Consortia on Higher Edn., L.I., 1971—, Alfred P. Sloan Found. adv. com. for expanding minority opportunities in engring., 1974; rep. to Nat. Assn. State Adv. Council, 1975—; chmn. N.Y. Title IV Adv. Council, 1975-77; mem. steering com. L.I. Regional Adv. Council, 1974—; chair Regents Adv. Council on Learning Techs., 1986-88; mem., trustee exec. com. Commn. Ind. Colls. and Univs.; mem. adv. council learning technologies N.Y. State Dept. Edn., 1982—; mem. Accreditation Task Force for Council on Postsecondary Accreditation/SHEEBO Project on Assessing Long Distance Learning Via Telecommunications (Project ALLTEL), 1982—; mem. N.Y. State Motion Picture and TV adv. bd., chairperson tech. com.; dir. numerous research projects; expert witness Ho. Reps. com. of Commn. on Sci. and Astronautics; mem. adv. coun. Fla. State Bd. Ind. Colls. and Univs.; vis. tech. exec. Hofstra U., L.I., N.Y., 1998, 99. Author and-or editor textbooks, film producer; designer automatic teaching machine; built one of first computer-controlled anthropomorphic speech devices, 1959; contbr. articles to tech. publs.; patentee in field. Pres. bd. dirs., trustee L.I. Ednl. TV Coun., Garden City; bd. dirs. Coun. Higher Ednl. Instns., N.Y.C., 1973-83; pres. The Univ. Fedns., Fla., 1995--. Served with Signal Corps AUS, 1942-45. Recipient (2) Clio awards; 1st inductee Fine Arts Mus. of Long Island's Computer Hall of Fame, 1986. Mem. IEEE (L.I. sect. Gruenwald award 1988), N.Y. Acad. Sci., Am. Inst. Engring. Edn., N.E.A., Electronic Industries Assn. (chmn. task force curriculum devel.), Phi Delta Kappa, Delta Mu Delta, Eta Kappa Nu. E-mail: schure1ufi@aol.com.

SCHURIG ROLLINS, SANDRA L. academic administrator; b. Phila., May 16, 1952; d. Joseph and Leola Schuriq; divorced; 1 child, Gregory Clay Rollins. BA in Edn., LaSalle U., 1975; MA in Ednl. Adminstrn., Rider U., 1998. Counselor fin. aid Jefferson Med. Coll., Thomas Jefferson U., Phila., 1975-77, asst. to dean of admissions, 1977-81; coord. admissions and fin. aid Coll. Grad. Studies, Thomas Jefferson U., 1984-90; asoc. dir. fin. aid U. Medicine and Dentistry N.J., Stratford, 1990—. Chair Am. Assn. Colls. Osteo. Medicine Coun. Fin. Aid Officers, 1999. Mem. AAUW, N.J. Assn. Student Fin. Aid Adiminstrs. (tng. chair 1992-94, grad. and prof. concerns com. 1994-95), Nat. Assn. Student Fin. Aid Adminstrs., Middestates Assn. Coll. Registrars and Officers of Admission, com. chair conf. 1987-90). Home: 2 Cobblestone Ln Shamong NJ 08088-8404 Office: U Medicine & Dentistry NJ 40 Laurel Rd E Stratford NJ 08084-1350

SCHUSSLER, THEODORE, lawyer, physician, educator, consultant; b. July 27, 1934; s. Jack and Fannie (Blank) Schussler; m. Barbara Ann Gordon, June 18, 1961; children: Deborah, Jonathan, Rebecca. BA in Polit. Sci., Bklyn. Coll., 1955; LLB, Bklyn. Law Sch., 1958, JD, 1967; MD, U. Lausanne, Switzerland, 1974. Bar: N.Y. 1959, U.S. Dist. Ct. (so. and ea. dists.) N.Y. 1975, U.S. Tax Ct. 1961, U.S. Ct. Appeals (2nd cir.) 1962, U.S. Supreme Ct. 1975. Clerkship and practice, N.Y.C., 1956, 1958—59; legal editor tax divsn. Prentice-Hall, Inc., Englewood Cliffs, NJ, 1956; vol. criminal law divsn. Legal Aid Soc., N.Y.C., 1959; atty. legal dept. N.Y.C. Dept. Welfare, 1959—60; sole practice N.Y.C., 1960—. Sr. staff asst. IBM-Indsl. Medicine Program, 1969—70, 1974—76; intern in medicine St. Vincent's Med. Ctr. of Richmond, S.I., NY, 1976—77, resident emergency medicine, 1977—79; resident in gerontology, chief house physician Carmel Richmond Nursing Home, S.I., 1978—80; surg. rotation emergency dept. Met. Hosp. Ctr., 1979; house physician dept. medicine Richmond Meml. Hosp. and Health Ctr., 1979—80; gen. practice medicine, 1980—; attending physician, former chief dept. family practice, former chmn. med. care evaluation, med. records and by-laws coms., former physician Cmty. Hosp. Bklyn., 1980—94, advisor emergency dept., former mem. blood transfusion, credential's, emergency dept. coms., 1980—94, mem. med. staff, 1980—94; attending physician Meth. Hosp., Bklyn., 1984—92, supervising emergency dept. physician, dept. ambulatory care, 1980—83; attending physician Kings Hwy. Hosp., 1981—88, coord. emergency dept., 1981; clin. instr. dept. preventive medicine and cmty. health Downstate Med. Ctr. SUNY, Bklyn., 1981—88, clin. asst. prof., 1988—95, SUNY Health Sci. Ctr.; med. dir. divsn. devel. disabilities Mishkon-Jewish Bd. Family & Children's Svc., Bklyn., 1982—2000; primary care physician Jewish Home and Hosp. for Aged, N.Y.C., 1993—94; cons. in gerontology Palm Beach Home for Adults, Bklyn., 1980—92; cons. indsl. medicine IBM, 1990—92; tchr., instr., lectr., prof., 1954—95; med.-legal cons. to professions of medicine and law. Author: Torts, 1961, 1965, 1974, Jurisdiction and Practice in Federal Courts, 1967, Constitutional Law, 1973; contbr. articles to profl. jours. Recipient Pub. and Cmty. Svc. award, United Ind. Dems. 44th Assembly Dist., Bklyn. Fellow: Am. Coll. Legal Medicine; mem.: United Univ. Professions, Assn. Arbitrators of Civil Ct. of N.Y. (small claims divsn., arbitrator), Bklyn. Law Sch. Alumni Assn. (past bd. dirs.), Delta Sigma Rho. Home and Office: 760 E 10th St Apt 6H Brooklyn NY 11230-2352

SCHUSTER, PHILIP FREDERICK, II, lawyer, writer, law educator; b. Denver, Aug. 26, 1945; s. Philip Frederick and Ruth Elizabeth (Robar) S.; m. Barbara Lynn Nordquist, June 7, 1975; children: Philip Christian, Matthew Dale. BA, U. Wash., 1967; JD, Willamette U., 1972. Bar: Oreg. 1972, Wash. 2002, U.S. Dist. Ct. Oreg. 1974, U.S. Ct. Appeals (9th cir.) 1986, U.S. Ct. Appeals (D.C. cir.) 2001, U.S. Supreme Ct. 1986. Dep. dist. atty. Multnomah County, Portland, Oreg., 1972; title examiner Pioneer Nat. Title Co., Portland, 1973-74; assoc. Buss, Leichner et al, Portland, 1975-76; from assoc. to ptnr. Kitson & Bond, Portland, 1976-77; pvt. practice Portland, 1977-95; ptnr. Dierking and Schuster, Portland, 1996—; adj. prof. law Lewis & Clark Coll., 2002. Arbitrator Multnomah County Arbitration Program, 1985—; student mentor Portland Pub. Schs., 1988—. Author: The Indian Water Slide, 1999; contbg. author OSB CLE Publ., Family Law; contbr. articles to profl. jours. Organizer Legal Aid Svcs. for Community Clinics, Salem, Oreg. and Seattle, 1969-73; Dem. committeeman, Seattle, 1965-70; judge Oreg. State Bar and Classroom Law Project, H.S. Mock Trial Competition, 1988—. Mem. ABA, ATLA, NAACP (exec. bd. Portland, Oreg. chpt. 1979-98), ACLU, Multnomah Bar Assn. (Vol. Lawyers Project), Internat. Platform Assn., Alpha Phi Alpha. Avocations: river drifting, camping, swimming, walking, writing. Office: 3565 NE Broadway St Portland OR 97232-1820 E-mail: schuster@pcez.com.

SCHUSTER, SANDRA JEAN, women's basketball coach, educator; b. Anna, Ill., Dec. 18, 1956; d. Myron F. and Imogene Schuster. Assoc., Shawnee C.C., Ullin, Ill., 1976; B, Murray (Ky.) State U., 1979; M, No. Ill. U., DeKalb, 1991. Tchr., H.S. head coach Cobden (Ill.) Unit Sch., 1979-89; grad. asst. coach No. Ill. U., DeKalb, 1989-91; assoc. prof., head women's basketball coach Eureka (Ill.) Coll., 1991—. Named Coach of Yr., Ill. Basketball Coaches Assn., 1986-87, 91-92, NAIA Dist. 20, 1991-92, Chicagoland Collegiate Athletic Conf., 1993-94. Mem. Women's Basketball Coaches Assn. Home: 394 Circle Shore Dr Washington IL 61571-9565 Office: Eureka Coll 300 E College Ave Eureka IL 61530-1562 E-mail: sschuster@eureka.edu.

SCHUSTER, SEYMOUR, mathematician, educator; b. Bronx, N.Y., July 31, 1926; s. Oscar and Goldie (Smilowitz) S.; m. Marilyn Weinberg, May 2, 1954; children: Paul Samuel, Eve Elizabeth. BA, Pa. State U., 1947; A.M., Columbia U., 1948; PhD, Pa. State U., 1953; postgrad. (fellow), U. Toronto, 1952-53. Instr. Pa. State U., 1950-52, Poly. Inst. N.Y., 1953-54, asst. prof., 1954-56, assoc. prof., 1956-58; vis. assoc. prof. Carleton Coll., Northfield, Minn., 1958-59, assoc. prof., 1959-63, prof. math., 1968—, chmn. dept., 1973-76, William H. Laird prof. math. and liberal arts, 1992-94, William H. Laird prof. emeritus, 1994—. Vis. assoc. prof. U. N.C., Chapel Hill, 1961; research assoc. math. dept. U. Minn., Mpls., 1962-63, assoc. prof., 1963-65; assoc. prof. Minn. Math Center, 1965-68, dir. coll. geometry project, 1964-74; dir. Acad. Year Inst. for Coll. Tchrs., 1966-67, NSF Faculty fellow, 1970-71; vis. scholar U. Calif., Santa Barbara, 1970-71, U. Ariz., 1990; guest scholar Western Mich. U., 1976, 81; vis. prof. Western Wash. U., 1983, U. Oreg., 1986. Author: (with K. O. May) Undergraduate Research in Mathematics, 1961, Elementary Vector Geometry, 1962, (with P.C. Rosenbloom) Prelude to Analysis, 1966; also research articles on geometry, graph theory, and analysis.; cons. editor Xerox Pub. Co., 1962-71; assoc. editor, editorial bd. Am. Math. Monthly, 1969-86; assoc. editor: Indian Jour. Math. Edn, 1976-86; co-producer 12 films on geometry. With USNR, 1944—46. Recipient Honor award Am. Film Festival, 1967, Golden Eagle award Cine Film Festival, 1967, 68; named found. fellow Inst. for Combinatorics and Applications. Mem. Math. Assn. Am., Am. Math. Soc., Sigma Xi, Pi Mu Epsilon. Home: 316 Sumner St E Northfield MN 55057-2843

SCHUSTER, SYLVIA M. education educator; b. Germany, July 16, 1949; d. Morris N. and Gena Bergstein; 1 child, Maggie Noah. BA in English Lit., CUNY, 1972, MA in English Lit. and Creative Writing, 1976. Cert. English tchr. NY. Tchr. Brandeis H.S., N.Y.C., 1978—80; homebound English tutor Plainview (NY) H.S., 1984—; asst. dir. RISE program L.I. U., C.W. Post Campus, Brookville, NY, 1992—96, dir. RISE program, 1996—2000; lectr. in English BOCES Cultural Arts Ctr., Syosset, NY, 1999—. Adj. prof. english L.I. U., 1986—, Nassau (NY) C.C., 1994—, SUNY, Farmingdale, 2001—; owner pvt. tutoring bus., L.I., NY, 1984—. Contbr. poetry to anthologies, photographs to mags. Mem. com. L.I. Jr. Soccer League, 1992—; vol. Am. Cancer Assn., 1997, Am. Diabetes Found., 1999. Recipient Pres.' award, Iliad Press, 1996. Mem.: Am. Acad. Poets, Nat. Author's Registry, Nat. Coun. Tchrs. English, Nat. Soc. Poets, Internat. Soc. Poets (Outstanding Achievement award 1997—2002), Nat. Writers Club. Avocations: writing, photography, music, theater, art.

SCHUT, DONNA SUE, elementary education educator; b. Sioux Center, Iowa, Mar. 23, 1961; d. James Martin and Gertrude (Buyert) Intveld; m. Eric Peter Schut, July 21, 1958; 1 child, Alyssa Nichole. BA, Northwestern Coll., Orange City, Iowa, 1983, MA, 1990. Lic. tchr., Iowa. Tchr. Sioux Center Community Schs., 1983—, dept. head social studies dept., 1989-91, 4th grade team leader, 1994-96. Supr. student tchrs. Northwestern Coll., Orange City, 1986-87, 88-89, 90-91, 92-93, 94-95, 96-97. Mem. N.W. Iowa Reading Assn. (bldg. rep. 1983—), Sioux Center Edn. Assn., Nat. Coun. for Tchrs. Math., Iowa Coun. for Social Studies, Geographic Alliance Iowa, Assn. Supervision and Curriculum Devel., Internat. Reading Assn. Avocations: reading, baking, collecting cats, spending time with family. Office: Kinsey Elem Sioux Center Community Schs 397 10th St SE Sioux Center IA 51250

SCHUTH, MARY MCDOUGLE, interior designer, educator; b. Kansas City, Mo., Jan. 19, 1942; d. William Darnall and Marie DeArmond (Meiser) McDougle; m. Howard Wayne Schuth, Sept. 4, 1965; 1 child, Andrew Wayne. BS in Interior Design, Comm., Northwestern U., 1964; cert. basic mgmt., U. Mo., 1966. Registered interior designer La. Interior designer Cottington's Interiors, Glen Ellyn, Ill., 1964-65, Robnett-Putman Interiors, Columbia, Mo., 1966-67, Nu-Idea Furniture Co., New Orleans, 1973, Maison Blanche, New Orleans, 1974-75, Mary M. Schuth Interior Design, Metairie, La., 1977—; instr. interior design divsn. continuing edn. U. New Orleans, 1973-97; instr. interior design non credit program Tulane U., 1998. Judge model homes U.S. Homes, Mandeville, La., 1978, Mandeville, 80; bd. dirs. Interior Design Adv. Com., Delgado Coll., New Orleans, 1981—2000; mem. Alpha Chi Omega Frat. housing rev. com., 1991—96; guest lectr. Delta Queen Steamboat Co., 1995—2001; lectr. ASID Super Campus for Longue Vue Home and Garden Tour, New Orleans, 2002. Co-author: cookbook From the Privateers' Galley, 1980; design work featured in profl. jours.; contbr. to Metairie Mag., 1993-94. Recipient 3rd place Batik Design Juried Art Show Columbia (Mo.) Art League, 1969. Mem. AIA (profl. affiliate), Am. Soc. Interior Designers (profl.), New Orleans Old Garden Rose Soc., Alpha Chi Omega Alumnae Club (New Orleans).

SCHUTTE, ANNE JACOBSON, historian, educator; b. Palo Alto, Calif., Apr. 24, 1940; d. David Samuel and Mildred Rose (Ashworth) J.; m. William Metcalf Schutte, Dec. 21, 1967 (div. Jan. 1990). BA in History magna cum laude, Brown U., 1962; AM in History, Stanford U., 1963, PhD in History and Humanities, 1969. Instr. Lawrence U., 1966-69, asst. prof., 1971-77, assoc. prof., 1977-85, prof., 1985-91, U. Va., Charlottesville, 1992—. Bd. dirs. Ctr. for Reformation Rsch., 1980-83; mem. exec. com. Newberry Libr. program Assoc. Colls. Midwest, 1981-83, 86-88, 90-91; mem. steering com. Com. Women's Concerns, 1984-85. Author: Pier Paolo Vergerio: The Making of an Italian Reformer, 1977, Printed Italian Vernacular Religious Books, 1465-1550: A Finding List, 1983, Pier Paolo Vergerio e la Riforma a Venezia, 1489-1549, 1988 (trans. Virginia Cappelletti, Anna Maria Fabbrini), Aspiring Saints: Pretense of Holiness, Inquisition and Gender in the Republic of Venice, 1618-1750, 2001; editor: Cecilia Ferrazzi, Autobiografia di una santa mancata, 1990, English edit., 1996; translator: Heavenly Supper: The Story of Maria Janis (Fulvio Tomizza), 1991, also articles and numerous revs. We. Regional Alumnae scholar Brown U., 1957-59, 60-62, Stanford U., 1963-65, Stanford U./Italian Govt., 1965-66, Newberry Libr., 1978, S.E. Inst. Medieval and Renaissance Studies, 1979, NEH, 1979-80, 88-89, Gladys Krieble Delmas, 1985, 96; scholar Inst. Reformation Rsch., 1965; Grantee Fulbright Found., 1965-66, Pro Helvetia Found., 1966, Am. Philos. Soc., 1971, NEH 1979-80, 88-89, 95. Mem. Am. Hist. Soc., Am. Soc. Ch. History (coun.), Coordinating Com. for Women in History, Renaissance Soc. Am., 16th Century Studies Conf. (editorial bd. jour. 1972—, v.p. 1973-74, 79-80, pres. 1980-81), Soc. Italian Hist. Socs., Soc. Reformation Rsch. (nominating com. 1981-83, exec. coun. 1987-90, program sec. 1992-95, editor your. 1998—). Office: U Va Dept History Charlottesville VA 22903

SCHUTTE, PAMELA KAY, elementary school educator; b. Enid, Okla., June 6, 1952; d. Lawrence George Elbert and Naomi Jean (Hudson) Keener; m. David James Schutte, May 28, 1978; children: Dawn Renee, Caroleah Lynn. B in Elem. Edn., U. No. Colo., Greeley, 1977. Cert. elem. tchr., Ariz. Paraprofl. Fairmont Elem. Sch., Denver, 1974-75; instructional aide Jackson Elem. Sch., Greeley, Colo., 1975-77; 3d grade classroom tchr. Big Springs (Nebr.) Elem. Sch., 1977-79; homebound tutor, substitute Riverdale Elem. Sch., Port Byron, Ill., 1979-82; spl. edn. aide, substitute Ruth Fisher Elem. Sch., Tonopah, Ariz., 1986-87; 4th grade classroom tchr. Scott L. Libby Elem. Sch., Litchfield Park, Ariz., 1987-90, Longview (Wash.) Christian Sch. Tchr. rep. gifted task force Litchfield Park Elem. Sch. Dist., 1988-91. Vice-pres. Riverdale Elem. Sch. PTA, Port Byran, Ill., 1980, Scott Libby Elem. Sch. PTA, Litchfield Park, 1988. Mem. NEA, ASCD, Ariz. Educators Assn., Litchfield Park Sch. Dist. Educators Assn. (sec. 1989). Baptist. Home: 10719 Gill Rd Reedsville WI 54230-8912

SCHUYLER, JANE, fine arts educator; b. Flushing, N.Y., Nov. 2, 1943; d. Frank James and Helen (Oberhofer) S. BA, Queens Coll., 1965; MA, Hunter Coll., 1967; PhD, Columbia U., 1972. Asst. prof. art history Montclair State Coll., Upper Montclair, N.J., 1970; assoc. prof. C.W. Post Coll., L.I. Univ., Greenvale, N.Y., 1971-73, adj. assoc. prof, 1977-78; coord. fine arts, asst. prof. York Coll., CUNY, Jamaica, 1973-77, 78-87, assoc. prof., 1988-92, prof. 1993-96, prof. emerita 1996—. Author: Florentine Busts: Sculpted Portraiture in the Fifteenth Century, 1976; contbr. articles to profl. jours. Mem. fine arts com. Internat. Women's Arts Festival, 1974-76; pres. United Cmty. Dems. of Jackson Heights, 1987-89. N.Y. Columbia U. summer travel and rsch. grantee, 1969; recipient PSC-CUNY Rsch. award, 1990-91. Mem. Coll. Art Assn., Nat. Trust for Hist. Preservation, Renaissance Soc. Am. Roman Catholic. Home: 35-37 78th St Jackson Heights NY 11372

SCHWAB, GEORGE DAVID, social science educator, author; b. Nov. 25, 1931; s. Arkady and Klara (Jacobson) S.; m. Eleonora Storch, Feb. 27, 1965; children: Clarence Boris, Claude Arkady, Solan Bernhard. BA, City Coll. N.Y., 1954; MA, Columbia U., 1955, PhD, 1968. Lectr. Columbia Coll., N.Y.C., 1959, CUNY, 1960-68; asst. prof. history, 1968-72; assoc. prof. history, 1973-79; prof., 1980—2000; prof. emeritus, 2001—. Mem. Columbia U. Seminar on Law and Polit. Thought and Institutions; dir. Conf. History and Politics CUNY; with Nat. Com. Am. Fgn. Policy. Author: Dayez: Beyond Abstract Art, 1967, Enemy oder Foe, 1968, Switzerland's Tactical Nuc. Weapons Policy, 1969, The Challenge of the Exception: An Introduction to the Polit. Ideas of Carl Schmitt, 1970, 2nd edit., 1989, Appeasement and Detente, 1975, 81, Carl Schmitt: Polit. Opportunist?, 1975; translator: The Concept of the Polit. with Comments by Leo Strauss (Carl Schmitt), 1976, 96, Legality and Illegality as Instruments of Revolutionaries in Their Quest for Power, Remarks Occasioned by the Outlook of Herbert Marcuse, 1978, The German State in Hist. Perspective, 1978, Ideology: Reality or Rhetoric, 1978, Ideology and Fgn. Policy, 1978, 81, The Decision: Is the Am. Sovereign at Bay?, 1978, State and Nation: Toward a Further Clarification, 1980, Am. Fgn. Politics at the Crossroads, 1980, Carl Schmitt: Through a Glass Darkly, 1980, From Quantity and Heterogeneity to Quality and Homogeneity: Toward a New Foreign Policy, 1980, Toward an Open-Society Bloc, 1980, Eurocommunism: The Ideological and Political Theoretical Foundations, 1981, Am. Fgn. Policy at the Crossroads, 1982, A Decade of the Nat. Com. on Am. Fgn. Policy, 1984, (trans.) Polit. Theology: Four Chapters on the Concept of Sovereignty (Carl Schmitt), 1985, 88, The Destruction of a Family, 1987, Elie Wiesel: Between Jerusalem and New York, 1990, The Broken Vow, The Good

Obtained, 1991, Thoughts of a Collector, 1991, Carl Schmitt Hysteria in the US, 1992, Contextualizing Carl Schmitt's Concept of Grossraum, 1994; (translator) The Leviathan in the State Theory of Thomas Hobbes (Carl Schmitt), 1996, Carl Schmitt, A Note on a Qualitative Authoritarian Bourgeois Liberal, 2000, The Nat. Com. on Am. Fgn. Policy's Focus on Russia, 2000, U.S. National Security Interests Today, 2003; editor Am. Fgn. Policy Interests; series Global Perspectives in History and Politics. Trustee, pres. mem. exec. com. Nat. Com. Am. Fgn. Policy; mem. Coun. on Fgn. Rels. Decorated Order of the Three Stars (Latvia); recipient Ellis Island medal of honor. Office: Nat Com Am Fgn Policy 320 Park Ave New York NY 10022-6815 E-mail: ncafp@aol.com.

SCHWAB, PAUL JOSIAH, psychiatrist, educator; b. Waxahachie, Tex., Jan. 14, 1932; s. Paul Josiah and Anna Marie (Baeuerle) S.; m. Martha Anne Beed, June 8, 1953; children: Paul Josiah III, John Conrad, Mark Whitney. BA, North Ctrl. Coll., 1953; MD, Baylor U., 1957. Diplomate Am. Bd. Psychiatry and Neurology. Intern Phila. Gen. Hosp., 1957-58; clin. assoc. Nat. Cancer Inst., Bethesda, Md., 1958-60; resident in internal medicine U. Chgo., 1960-62, resident psychiatry, 1962-65, chief resident, instr. psychiatry, 1965, clin. instr. psychiatry, lectr. psychiatry, 1968-74, assoc. prof., 1974-79; clin. assoc., 1979-86; clin. assoc. prof., 1986—; dir. residency tng. U. Chgo., 1976-79, dir. in-patient unit and day treatment program, 1975-79; pvt. practice Naperville, Ill., 1965—; cand. Chgo. Psychoanalytic Inst., 1970-72. Clin. instr. dept. psychiatry U. Ill., Chgo., 1965—66; vis. lectr. in psychology North Ctrl. Coll., 2002—03. Contbr. articles to profl. jours. Bd. trustees North Ctrl. Coll., chair liaison com., 1983—, vice-chmn. acad. and student affairs com., 1983-92, vice chair admissions, fin. aid and student devel., 1992-95; pres. North Ctrl. Coll. Alumni Assn., 1979-80. Recipient Outstanding Alumnus, North Ctrl. Coll., 1983, Gael D. Swing award, 2001. Mem.: Am. Soc. Clin. Psychopharmacology, Am. Psychiat. Assn. (disting. life fellow, Nancy C.A. Roeske award 1991), Alpha Omega Alpha. Republican. Methodist. Home and Office: 1200 Tall Oaks Ct Naperville IL 60540-9494 E-mail: pauljschwab@earthlink.net.

SCHWABE, CALVIN WALTER, veterinarian, medical historian, medical educator; b. Newark, Mar. 15, 1927; s. Calvin Walter and Marie Catherine (Hassfeld) S.; m. Gwendolyn Joyce Thompson, June 7, 1951; children: Catherine Marie, Christopher Lawrence. BS, Va. Poly. Inst., 1948; MS, U. Hawaii, 1950; DVM, Auburn U., 1954; MPH, Harvard U., 1955, ScD, 1956. Diplomate Am. Coll. Vet. Preventive Medicine (disting.). From assoc. prof. to prof. parasitology and epidemiology, chmn. dept. tropical health, and asst. dir. Sch. Pub. Health, Am. U. Beirut, 1956-66; mem. Secretariat of WHO, Geneva, 1964-66; prof. epidemiology Sch. Vet. Medicine, also Sch. Medicine, U. Calif., Davis, 1966-91, chmn. dept. epidemiology and preventive medicine, 1966-70; assoc. dean Sch. Vet. Medicine, U. Calif., Davis, 1970-71, adj. prof. Agrl. History Ctr., 1984-91, prof. emeritus, 1991—. Cons. WHO, UN Environ. Program, FAO, NIH, Pan Am. Health Orgn., UNICEF, Nat. Rsch. Coun.; univ. lectr. U. Sask.; Fulbright vis. prof. Univ. Coll. East Africa, Cambridge (Eng.) U., U. Khartoum; Srinivasan Meml. lectr. U. Madras; Spink lectr. comparative medicine U. Minn.; Franklin lectr. scis. and humanities Auburn U.; Entwhistle lectr. Cambridge U.; Schofield lectr. U. Guelph; mem. Am. Rsch. Ctr. Egypt. Author: Veterinary Medicine and Human Health, 1969, 84, What Should a Veterinarian Do?, 1972, Epidemiology in Veterinary Practice, 1977, Cattle, Priests and Progress in Medicine, 1978, Unmentionable Cuisine, 1980, Development Among Africa's Migratory Pastoralists, 1996; also articles. Recipient Karl F. Meyer Gold Headed Cane award Am. Vet. Epidemiology Assn., 1985, Disting. Alumnus award Auburn U., 1992, Calvin Schwabe Career Achievement award Assn. Vet. Epidemiology and Preventive Medicine, 2002. Fellow Am. Pub. Health Assn. (governing coun. 1974-76); mem. AVMA, Am. Soc. Tropical Medicine and Hygiene, History of Sci. Soc. Democrat. Mem. Soc. Of Friends. Avocations: collecting musical instruments, cooking, raising bamboos. Home: 3300 Darby Rd Apt C801 Haverford PA 19041-1065 also: Apartado 90 Pedreguer Alicante 03750 Spain

SCHWABE, MARCUS CHRISTOPHER, medical foundation executive; b. Winnipeg, Man., Can., Dec. 20, 1960; s. Lothar and Hanna (Ludwinski) S.; m. Lorie Ann Bustard, Aug. 16, 1986; children: Adam, Noah, Kayleigh. BS, U. Alta., 1982, BEd, 1984. High sch. tchr. Strathcona County, Sherwood Park, Alta., Can., 1985-87; real estate sales Re/Max Real Estate, Edmonton, Alta., Can., 1987-88; dir. alumni and ch. rels. Augusta Univ. Coll. (formerly Camrose Luth. U. Coll.), Camrose, Alta., 1988-92, dir. alumni, 1992-95; sr. devel. officer U. Alta., Edmonton, 1995-98; owner Lifecare, 1985-96; exec. dir. Caritas Hosp. Found., Edmonton, Alta., Can., 1998—. Cons., presenter Lifecare, 1985—; owner Kidz-Own, 1993-96. Editor Kaluko mag., 1988-90, 94-95. Mem. coms. Evang. Luth. Ch. Can., chairperson synod youth com., 1982-88, mem. Alta. and the Ters. synod stewardship com., chairperson Office for Resource Devel., mgr. convs., coach slow pitch baseball team. Mem. Nat. Soc. Fundraising Execs., Assn. Univs. and Colls. Can., Assn. Can. Alumni Adminstrn., Can. Coun. for Advancement of Edn., Coun. for Advancement and Support of Edn., Nat. Soc. Fund Raising Execs. (treas. 1996—), Assn. Alta. Fund-Raising Execs. (program chair), Augustana U. Coll. Alumni Assn. (exec. dir., bd. dirs. 1995). Avocations: golf, squash, racquetball, baseball. Home: 7 Courtenay Bay Sherwood Park AB Canada T8A 5S2 Office: Caritas Hosp Found #3660 11111 Jasper Ave Edmonton AB Canada T5K OL4 E-mail: mschwabe@caritas.ab.ca.

SCHWAN, LEROY BERNARD, artist, retired art educator; b. Dec. 8, 1932; s. Joseph L. and Dorothy (Papenfuss) S.; children from previous marriage: David A., Mark J., William R., Catherine L., Maria E. Student, Wis. State U., River Falls, 1951-53, Southeastern Signal Sch., Ga., 1954; BS, U. Minn., 1958, MEd, 1960, postgrad., 1961-64, No. Mich. U., 1965, Tex. Tech. U., 1970, So. Ill. U., 1978, U. Iowa, 1980, EdD (hon.), 1988. Head art dept. Unity Pub. Schs., Milltown, Wis., 1958-61; instr. art Fridley Pub. Schs., Mpls., 1961-64; asst. prof. art No. Mich. U., Marquette, 1964-66, Mankato (Minn.) State Coll., 1966-71, assoc. prof., 1971-74; tchr. off-campus grad. classes Northeast Mo. State U., John Wood Cmty. Coll.; dir. Art Workshop Educultural Ctr., 1968; dir. art edn. Quincy (Ill.) Pub. Schs., 1974-78, art tchr., 1978-88, ret., 1988. Tchr. art to mentally retarded children, Faribault, Minn., Owatonna, Minn., Mankato, Lake Owasso Children's Home, St. Paul; dir. art workshops, Mankato, 1970, St. Paul, 1972, 73, 74, 75; dir. workshops tchrs. mentally retarded Mankato, 1971, Faribault, 1972, Omaha, 1972-73, Quincy, 1974, 79, 82, 84-86, asst. adj. Ill. VA Home, 1980—. Author: Art Curriculum Guide Unity Public Schs., 1961, Portrait of Jean, 1974, Schwan's Art Activities, 1984, Poems of Life, 1995, LeRoy Remembers, 2003; co-author: Bryant-Schwan Design Test, 1971, Bryant-Schwan Art Guide, 1973; contbr. articles to profl. jours., author numerous poems; one-man shows: Estherville Jr. Coll., 1968, Mankato State Coll., 1968, 71, 73, 75, 97, Farmington, Wis., 1970-71, 91, Good Thunder, Minn., 1972, Quincy, 1975, 77, 84, Western Ill. U., 1979, St. Croix River Valley Arts Coun. Gallery, Osceola, Wis., 1993-96, The Northern Ctr. for the Arts, Amery, Wis., 1994, 2001, Borders Books Gallery, Woodbury, Wells Fargo Gallery, Woodbury, Health Ptnrs. Gallery, Woodbury, 2000, Gallery at Fortes Ins., Woodbury, 2001; exhibited in group shows at Pentagon, Washington, 1955, U. Minn., 1958, No. Mich. U., 1965, St. Cloud State Coll., 1967, Moorhead State Coll., 1967, Bemidji (Minn.) State Coll., 1967, MacNider Mus., Mason City, Iowa, 1969, 72-74, Gallery 500, Mankato, Minn., 1970, Rochester, Minn., 1972, Minn. Mus., St. Paul, 1973, Hannibal, Mo., 1976, 77-78, Quincy, Ill., 1976-77, 85, Ill. Art Educators Show, 1984-85, Tchrs. Retirement Art Show, Springfield, Ill., 1987, Phipps Ctr. Arts, Hudson, Wis., 1997-99, 2000-01, 03; prodr. ednl. TV series, 1964-65, also 2 shows Kids Komments, Sta. WGEM, Quincy; mural commd. Gem City Coll., 1977. Webelos leader Twin Valley coun. Boy Scouts Am., 1968-69; bd. dirs. Quincy Soc. Fine Arts, 1975-85, Polk County Hist. Soc., 1993—. With Signal Corps., AUS, 1954-56. Recipient cert. of accomplishment Sec. Army, 1955, Golden Poet award, 1985, 86, 88, 90, 91, Silver Poet award 1989. Mem. Nat. Art Edn. Assn., Ill. Art Edn. Assn., Cath. Order Foresters, Am. Legion, Phi Delta Kappa. Home: 849 County Road H New Richmond WI 54017-6209

SCHWANK, JOHANNES WALTER, chemical engineering educator; b. Zams, Tyrol, Austria, July 6, 1950; came to U.S., 1978; s. Friedrich Karl and Johanna (Ruepp) S.; m. Lynne Violet Duguay; children: Alexander Johann, Leonard Friedrich, Hanna Violet, Rosa Joy. Diploma in chemistry, U. Innsbruck, Austria, 1975, PhD, 1978. Mem. faculty U. Mich., Ann Arbor, 1978—, assoc. prof. chem. engring., 1984-90, acting dir. Ctr. for Catalysis and Surface Sci., 1985-90, prof., interim chmn. dept. chem. engring., 1990-91, assoc. dir. Electron Microbeam Analysis Lab., 1990—2000; chmn. dept. chem. engring., 1991-95; prof. chem. engring. U. Mich., Ann Arbor, 1995—. Vis. prof. U. Innsbruck, 1987-88, Tech. U. Vienna, 1988; cons. in field. Contbr. over 125 articles to profl. jours. Fulbright-Hays scholar, 1978. Mem. Am. Chem. Soc., Am. Inst. Chem. Engrs., Mich. Catalysis Soc. (sec.-treas. 1982-83, v.p. 1983-84, pres. 1984-85). Achievements include patents for bimetallic cluster catalysts, hydrodesulfurization catalysts and microelectronic gas sensors. Home: 5633 Meadow Dr Ann Arbor MI 48105-9368 Office: U Mich Dept Chem Engring 2300 Hayward St Ann Arbor MI 48109-2136 E-mail: schwank@umich.edu.

SCHWARCZ, VERA, history educator, poet; d. Elmer and Katherine Savin; m. Jason Wolfe, July 31, 1983; children: Elie, Esther. BA in French Lit. and Oriental Religions, Vassar Coll., 1969; MA in East Asian Studies, Yale U., 1971; PhD in Chinese History, Stanford U., 1977. Instr. Stanford (Calif.) U., 1973; lectr. Chinese history Wesleyan U., Middletown, Conn., 1975-77, asst. prof. Chinese history, 1975-83, assoc. prof. history, 1983-87, prof. history, 1987—, chair East Asian studies, 1985-88, 94-96, Mansfield Freeman prof. East Asian Studies, 1987—; dir. Ctr. East Asian Studies, 1998—99. Dir. Mansfield Freeman for East Asian Studies, 1987-88, 94-96; exch. scholar Beijing U., 1979-80, vis. scholar, 1983, 86, 89; vis. scholar Ctr. de Documentation sur la Chine Contemporaine, Paris, 1985, DAO Assn., Cluj, Romania, 1993, Miskenot Sha'ananim, Jerusalem, 1991; vis. prof. East Asian studies Hebrew U., Jerusalem, 1996-97; mem. editl. bd. History and Theory, 1981-84, 96-99, China Rev. Internat., 1994—; bd. dirs. Sino-Judaic Inst., 1993-96; presenter, referee for various jours. in field. Author: Long Road Home: A China Journal, 1984, Chinese Enlightenment: Intellectuals, and the Legacy of the May Fourth Movement in Modern China, 1986, Zhongguo de qimeng yundong, 1989, Time for Telling Truth is Running Out: Conversations with Zhang Shenfu, 1992, Bridge Across Broken Time: Chinese and Jewish Cultural Memory, 1998, (poem) A Scoop of Light, 2000, Zhang Shenfu Fang Tan Lu, 2001 co-editor: China: Inside the People's Republic, 1972; contbr. articles, revs., poetry and fiction to profl. publs. Fellow Danforth Found., 1971-73, NDFL, 1973-74, NAS, 1979-80, Guggenheim Found. fellow, 1989-90, Great River Arts Inst. poetry fellow, 2000, founders fellow AAUW, 1988-89, faculty fellow Ctr. for Humanities Wesleyan U., 1988; grantee AAUW, 1974-75, Am. Philos. Soc., 1985, Am. Coun. Learned Socs., 1978, 96; finalist Nat. Jewish Book award in History, 1999; recipient Wesleyan Writers Conf. Poetry scholarship, 1999; poetry fellow Great River Arts Inst., Mex., 2000; recipient Poetry prize Taproot Lit. Rev., 2002-03. Mem. Assn. for Asian Studies (coun. on confs. 1989—, mem. Levenson prize com. 1991-92, chair 1992-93), New Eng. Assn. for Asian Studies (pres. 1988-89). Home: 42 Seneca Rd West Hartford CT 06117-2245 Office: Wesleyan U History Dept Middletown CT 06459-0001 Fax: 860-685-2781.

SCHWARTZ, ARLENE HARRIET, secondary school educator; b. Passaic, N.J., Feb. 28, 1944; d. Sol and Jeanette (Brody) Eigen; m. Peter Edward Schwartz, Aug. 13, 1966; children: Bruce, Andrew, Kenneth. BS, Boston U., 1965; MA, NYU, 1967; postgrad., So. Conn. State U., 1992. Cert. Spanish, French, Latin and social studies tchr., Conn. Instr. Spanish U. Ky., Lexington, 1966-67, Amity Regional Jr. High Sch., Orange, Conn., 1967-70; tchr. English as second lang. Jewish Community Ctr., Houston, 1973-74; part-time tchr. Spanish Adult Edn. Amity Regional Schs., Orange, 1979-83; part-time tchr. Spanish, French, Latin Amity Regional Jr. High Sch., 1983-84; lectr. English secondary schs., People's Rep. China, summer 1987, 1987, Novi Sad, Yugoslavia, 1988; lectr. English secondary schs. Seoul, Korea, 1993; fgn. lang. and social studies tchr. Branford (Conn.) High Sch., 1984—. Author: Student Life Book for Branford High School, 1992. Mem. Orange Transp. Com., 1979; mem. adv. bd. to study mass transit Dept. Transp., Orange, 1979; pres. Parents Music Group, Woodbridge, Conn., 1989-91. Mem. ASCD, NEA, Assn. Tchrs. of Spanish and Portuguese, Conn. Orgn. Lang. Tchrs., Phi Delta Kappa. Avocations: travel, exercise, skiing. Home: 1001 Pleasant Hill Rd Orange CT 06477-1115

SCHWARTZ, DANIEL JOEL, education administrator; b. Buffalo, Apr. 23, 1957; s. Tobias Louis and Helen Wilma (Silverstein) S.; m. Charla Beth Reinganum, June 7, 1987; children: Rachel Mara, Ilyana Rose. BA, U. Conn., 1980; MEd, Lesley Coll., 1994; postgrad., Nat. Louis U. Cert. secondary history tchr., Mass. Exhibit producer Conn. Humanities Coun., Hartford, 1979-81; vocat. instr. Gen. Dynamics Shipyard, Quincy, Mass., 1981-85; history tchr. Brookline (Mass.) H.S., 1987-89, New Perspectives Sch., Brookline, 1987-88, Boston Pub. Schs., 1988-90; dir. edn. USS Constitution Mus., Boston, 1990-93; asst. prin. Peabody Sch., Cambridge, Mass., 1993-94, Carleton W. Washburne Sch., Winnetka, Ill., 1994-98, prin., 1998—. Mem. educators bd. People and Places Program, Boston, 1990-94; adj. faculty Nat. Louis U., 1998-2001; mem. bd. internat. network of prins. ctrs. Harvard U. Photographer: Guide to Quincy Market, 1980; author curriculum, monograph in field. Grantee Conn. Humanities Coun., 1979, Mass. Culutral Coun., 1991, 92, Mass. Charitable Mechanics Assn., 1991, 92, Lowell Inst., 1990, 91, 92, Jeremiah E. Burke High Sch., 1989. Avocations: woodworking, photography. Home: 530 Audubon Pl Highland Park IL 60035-1204 Office: Carleton W Washburne Sch 515 Hibbard Rd Winnetka IL 60093-1600 E-mail: schwartd@nttc.org.

SCHWARTZ, DAVID ALAN, infectious diseases and placental and obstetrical pathologist, educator, epidemiologist; b. Phila., May 20, 1953; s. Harold Martin and Thelma (Bell) S; m. Stephanie Baker, May 16, 1993; 1 child, Jessica Lynn. BA, U. Pitts., 1974, MS in Hygiene, 1977; D in Medicine, Far Eastern U., Manila, The Philippines, 1984. Intern, resident in anatomic pathology sch. medicine Hahnemann U., Phila., 1984-87, chief resident sch. medicine, 1987-88; instr. Harvard U. Sch. Medicine, Boston, 1988-89; asst. prof. pathology Emory U. Sch. Medicine, Atlanta, 1989-94, assoc. prof., 1994—99; guest scientist Ctrs. for Disease Control, Atlanta, 1992—; assoc. prof. medicine (infectious disease) Emory U. Sch. Medicine, Atlanta, 1995—99. Vis. prof. U. Mayor San Simon, Bolivia, 1993—, Vanderbilt U. Med. Sch., 2001—; cons. in AIDS, CDC, Atlanta, 1992—; cons. in Chagas' disease U.S. AID, Washington, Bolivian Min. Health, La Paz, 1992—; chmn. pathology subcom. Women and Infants Transmission study NIH; pathology cons. Bangkok-CDC HIV Study, 1993—. Co-editor: Pathology of Infectious Diseases; mem. editl. bd. Ann. clin. Lab. Sci., Arch. Pathol. Lab. Medicine; mem. editl. rev. com. Human Pathology; contbr. numerous articles to profl. jours. and chpts. to texts. Recipient Pathology Resident Rsch. award Am. Soc. Clin. Pathologists, 1985; Pediat. AIDS Found. scholar, 1993—; Syphilis Rsch. grantee Ctrs. for Disease Control, 1991, Placental Infections Rsch. grantee Emory Med. Care Found., 1991—, Placental HIV Rsch. grantee NIH, 1991—. Fellow Coll. Am. Pathologists, Coll. Physicians Phila., Assn. Clin. Scientist. Jewish. Achievements include characterization of pathologic features of emerging infections; development of new diagnostic methods for pathologic identification of infectious agents; diagnosis of placental, perinatal and obstetrical diseases; research in obstetric, placental and maternal pathology.

SCHWARTZ, DAVID TAYLOR, urologist, educator; b. Cleve., May 7, 1937; s. Gilbert A. Schwartz and Rose Taylor; m. Claudette Fortier, Mar. 9, 1974; 1 child, Candice Webster. AB, Harvard U., 1959; MD, Columbia U., 1963. Diplomate Am. Bd. Urology. Intern St. Luke's Hosp., N.Y.C., 1963-64, asst. resident in surgery, 1964-65; resident in urology Presbyn. Hosp., N.Y.C., 1965-69; practice medicine specializing in urology Washington, 1971—94; asst. clin. prof. urology George Washington U., Washington, 1982—. Pres. Met. Med. Care, Inc., Washington, 1978—. Served to maj. USAF, 1969-71, Vietnam. NIH grantee. Fellow ACS; mem. Am. Urol. Assn., D.C. Med. Soc. Home: 11437 Hollow Timber Ct Reston VA 20194-1980

SCHWARTZ, ELEANOR BRANTLEY, academic administrator; b. Kite, Ga., Jan. 1, 1937; d. Jesse Melvin and Hazel (Hill) Brantley; children: John, Cynthia. Student, U. Va., 1955, Ga. Southern Coll., 1956-57; BBA, Ga. State U., 1962, MBA, 11963, DBA, 1969. Adminstrv. asst. Fin. Agy., 1954, Fed. Govt., Va., Pa., Ga., 1956-59; asst. dean admissions Ga. State U., Atlanta, 1961-66, asst. prof., 1966-70; assoc. prof. Cleve. State U., 1970-75, prof. and assoc. dean, 1975-80; dean, Harzfeld prof. U. Mo., Kansas City, 1980-87, vice chancellor acad. affairs, 1987-91, interim chancellor, 1991-92, chancellor, 1992-99; prof. mgmt. U. Mo. Block Sch., Kansas City, 1999—2003, prof. emeritus, 2003—. Disting. vis. prof. Berry Coll., Rome, N.Y. State U. Coll., Fredonia, Mons U., Belgium; cons. pvt. industry U.S., Europe, Can.; bd. dirs. Rsch. Med. Ctr., Waddell & Reed Funds, Inc., Toy and Miniature Mus., Menorah Med. Ctr. Found., NCAA, NCCJ, Econ. Devel. Corp. of Kansas City, Silicon Prairie Tech. Assn. Author: Sex Barriers in Business, 1971, Contemporary Readings in Marketing, 1974; (with Muczyk and Smith) Principles of Supervision, 1984. Chmn., Mayor's Task Force in Govt. Efficiency, Kansas City, Mo., 1984; mem. comm. unity planning and rsch. coun. United Way Kansas City, 1983-85; bd. dirs. Jr. Achievement, 1982-86. Named Career Woman of Yr., Kansas City, Mo., 1989; named one of 60 Women of Achievement, Girl Scouts Coun. Mid Continent, 1983; recipient Disting. Faculty award, Cleve. State U., 1974, Disting. Svc. award, Kans. State U., 1992, YWCA Hearts of Gold award, 2002. Mem.: Alpha Iota Delta, Golden Key, Phi Kappa Phi.

SCHWARTZ, ELIEZER LAZAR, psychologist, educator; b. Arad, Romania, Dec. 14, 1947; came to U.S., 1974; s. George and Elka (Rothschild) S.; m. Susan Ellen Lorge; children: Dafna, Michal, Amitai. BA in Psychology, Hebrew U., Jerusalem, Israel, 1973; MS in Psychology, Ill. Inst. Tech., 1975, PhD in Psychology, 1977. Cert. clin. psychologist, Ill. Psychologist, chief svc. Chgo.-Read Mental Health Ctr., 1979-80; prof. Ill. Sch. Profl. Psychology, Chgo., 1981—. Clin. psychologist Ray Graham Assn. for Handicapped, Elmhurst, Ill., 1981-89; dir. clin. svcs. Michael Solomon Psychology Ctr., Chgo., 1989-91; instr. Northwestern U., Evanston, Ill., summers 1988—99; dir. neuropsychology Brownstone Ctr., Chgo., 1991-92; cons. Jewish Vocat. Svcs., Chgo., 1983-84, 91-92, North Suburban Spl. Edn. Orgn., Arlington Heights, Ill., 1985-91, Grant Hosp., Chgo., 1991-95; dir. clin. tng. Ill. Sch. Profl. Psychology, 1996-97, dean, prof., 1997—2000. Author: (with others) Severe Developmental Disabilities, 1987, The Mental Status Exam, 1989; contbr. articles to profl. jours. Mem. APA, ASCD, Ill. Psych. Assn., Coun. for Exceptional Children. Jewish. Avocations: reading, listening to classical music. Office: 20 S Clark St Chicago IL 60603

SCHWARTZ, GORDON FRANCIS, surgeon, educator; b. Plainfield, NJ, Apr. 29, 1937; s. Samuel H. and Mary (Adelman) S.; m. Rochelle DeG. Krantz, Sept. 5, 1959; children— Amory Blair, Susan Leslie AB, Princeton U., 1956; MD, Harvard U., 1960; MBA, U. Pa., 1990. Intern N.Y. Hosp.-Cornell Med. Ctr., N.Y.C., 1960-61; resident in surgery Columbia-Presbyterian Med. Ctr., N.Y.C., 1963-68; instr. surgery Columbia U., N.Y.C., 1966-68; assoc. in surgery U. Pa., Phila., 1968-70; dir. clin. services Breast Diagnostic Ctr., Jefferson Med. Coll., Phila., 1973-78, asst. prof. surgery, 1970-71, assoc. prof., 1971-78, prof., 1978—. Practice medicine specializing in surgery and diseases of breast, Phila., 1968—; founder, chmn. acad. com, sec. of Med. bd. Breast Health Inst., 1990—; edtl. bd. The Breast Jour., 1994—. Author: (with R.H. Guthrie, Jr.) Reconstructive and Aesthetic Mammoplasty, 1989, (with Douglas Marchant) Breast Disease: Diagnosis and Treatment, 1981; mem. editl. bd. The Breast-Ofcl. Jour. of the European Soc. of Mastology, 1996—, Cancer, 1997—; co-editor Seminars Breast Disease, 1997; mem. editl. bd. ONE, Oncology Econs., 1999—; contbr. some 200 articles to profl. jours. Mem. Pa. Gov.'s Task Force on Cancer, 1976-82; mem. breast cancer task force Phila. chpt. Am. Cancer Soc.; mem. clin. investigation rev. com. Nat. Cancer Inst., 1992-95. Served to capt. AUS, 1961-63. NIH Cancer Control fellow, 1968-69 Mem. ACS, AMA, AAUP, Assn. for Acad. Surgery, Allen O. Whipple Surg. Assn., Soc. Surg. Oncology, Internat. Cardiovasc. Soc., Soc. for Surgery Alimentary Tract, John Jones Surg. Soc., Am. Soc. Clin. Oncology, Soc. for Study Breast Diseases (pres. 1981-83), Soc. Internat. Senologie (treas. 1982-90, v.p. 1990-92, sci. com. 1992—), Am. Soc. Breast Surgeons, N.Y. Acad. Scis., Am. Soc. Artificial Internal Organs, Am. Radium Soc., Philadelphia County Med. Soc. (chmn. com. on econs. 1999-2000, bd. dirs. 1999-2000), Internat. Sentinel Node Soc. (founding mem. 2003), Italian Soc. Senology (hon.), Greek Surg. Soc. (hon.), The Phila. Club, Union League, Princeton Club Phila. (pres. 1989-91), Princeton Club (N.Y.C.), Princeton Terrace Club, Nassau Club, Phi Beta Kappa, Sigma Xi, Alpha Omega Alpha, Nu Sigma Nu. Republican. Jewish. Office: 1015 Chestnut St Ste 510 Philadelphia PA 19107-4305 E-mail: gordonschwartz@yahoo.com.

SCHWARTZ, HOWARD WYN, business/marketing educator, consultant; b. Mpls., June 12, 1951; s. Jerry Schwartz and Geraldine (Berg) Brooks; m. Jeannie Marie Holtzmann, Aug. 2, 1975; children: Abigail Jorene, Rachel Elizabeth. BA cum laude, U. Minn., 1973, MBA, 1982, MEd, 1999. Acct. Med. Sch., U. Minn., 1973-77, bus. mgr. dept. neurology, 1977-79, adminstr. found. edn. dept., 1979-82, assoc. to chmn. dept. radiology, 1982-99; chmn. bus./mktg. edn. dept. Robbindale-Cooper H.S., New Hope, Minn., 1999—. Adj. instr. dept. radiology U. Minn., 1982—; pres. Bus. Mgmt. Svcs., Golden Valley, Minn., 1979—; lectr., author topics in bus./mktg. edn., 2000—. Editor-in-chief: RADWORKS Workload Measurement Manual, 1985-87; editor: Radiology Management, 1985-87, Purchasing the Radiology Information System, 1991, Current Concepts in Radiology Management, 1991; contbr. articles to profl. jours. Mem. Cystic Fibrosis Found., Minn., 1980—; chmn. Human Rights Commn., Robbinsdale, 1982-84; sec. Coord. Coun. Minority Concerns, 1984-85; chmn. imaging tech. adv. com. Univ. Hosp. Consortium, 1989-92; dir. Univ. Hosp. Consortium Svcs. Corp., 1990-92, Nat. Summit on Manpower, 1989-92; treas. Tech. Learning Campus Site Coun., Dist. 281, 1990-91, chmn. Bond Referendum campaign, 1995; pres. Armstrong H.S. Parent Assn., Dist. 281, 1991-92. Fellow Am. Healthcare Radiology Adminstrn. (regional pres. 1986-87, nat. pres. 1988-89, sec. edn. found. 1990-91, bd. dirs. edn. found. 1993-95, 97-98, Outstanding Author award 1990, 93, 96, Midwest Region Disting. Mem. award 1991, Gold award 1991); mem. Radiologists Bus. Mgrs. Assn., Delta Kappa Epsilon. Home: 7400 Winnetka Heights Dr Golden Valley MN 55427-3549 Office: PO Box 27405 Minneapolis MN 55427-0405 E-mail: Schwa006@ix.netcom.com., howard_schwartz@rdale.k12.mn.us.

SCHWARTZ, JANET SINGER, secondary school educator; b. Hartford, Conn., Aug. 13, 1951; d. Frederick Arthur and Elizabeth (Rothauser) Singer; m. Jonathan Robert Schwartz, Jan. 1, 1983; children: Rebecca Rose, Andrew David. BS in English, Cen. Conn. State U., 1973, MS in English, 1977. Cert. tchr., Conn. Tchr. English Avon (Conn.) Bd. Edn., 1973—. Tour guide Nook Farm, Hartford, Conn., 1969-73, Antiquarian and Landmarks Assn., Hartford, 1973-83; tchr. ESL, Northwestern Conn. Community Coll., Winsted, 1979; cons. Mark Twain-Harriet Beecher Stowe Inst. Learning, Hartford, 1988-89; sec. Conn. Consortium Law-Related Edn., Hartford, 1982-85; mem. exec. bd. Mark Twain Meml. Network, 1988-91; participant in assessment devel. Lab. of the Nat. Bd. for Profl. Teaching Standards, 1990-92. 4d. dirs. Burlington (Conn.) Hist. Soc., 1983-88; sec. Schwarzmann Mill Com., Burlington, 1988—. Recipient Celebration of Excellence award State of Conn., 1989, John F. Kennedy Libr. award, 1990; named Avon Tchr. of the Yr., 1995, Outstanding Tchr. of the Yr. Cen. Conn. State U. Alumni Assn., 1995. Mem. Nat. Coun. Tchrs. English, New Eng. Tchrs. English, Conn. Coun. Tchrs., Delta Kappa Gamma (sec. 2003-). Home: 39 Village Ln Burlington CT 06013-1403 Office: Avon Mid Sch 375 W Avon Rd Avon CT 06001-2208

SCHWARTZ, JERROLD BENNETT, school system administrator; b. Pitts., Jan. 19, 1942; s. Norman D. and Selma (Bass) S.; m. Nancy Feldman, Dec. 29, 1963; children: Mindy Cohen, Cathy Backal, Michael. EdB, U. Miami, 1963; MEd, U. Ga., 1969, specialist in adminstrn. and supervision, 1974; PhD, Ga. State U., 1983. Tchr. Dade County Sch. System, Miami, Fla., 1963-64, DeKalb County Sch. System, Decatur, Ga., 1966-70, prin., 1970-84, instructional coord., 1984-85, coord. staff devel., 1985-86, asst. dir. staff devel., 1986-94, dir. staff devel., 1994—. Adj. asst. prof. Ga. State U., Atlanta, 1986—. 1st Lt. U.S. Army, 1964-66. Named Outstanding Young Educator, DeKalb County Jaycees, Decatur, 1970, Hon. Llife Mem., Ga. PTA, 1976; recipient Cert. Appreciation, Alliance for Arts Edn., Washington, 1980, Assn. Children With Learning Disabilities, Decatur, 1982. Mem. ASCD. Nat. Staff Devel. Coun., Ga. Staff. Devel. Coun. (Disting. Staff Developer award 1995), DeKalb Assn. Educators (newsletter editor, 25 Yr. Svc. award 1991), Met. Atlanta Tchrs. Edn. Group (pres. 1994). Jewish. Avocations: basketball, aerobics, collecting inspirationals, poetry. Office: DeKalb County Sch System 3770 N Decatur Rd Decatur GA 30032-1005

SCHWARTZ, MIRIAM CATHERINE, biology educator; b. Tarlac, Luzon, Philippines, Mar. 9, 1964; came to U.S., 1980; d. Conrado Palarca and Elena Obcena (Domingo) Estanislao; m. Jason Jay Schwartz, July 20, 1987. BS in Biology, Calif. State U., L.A., 1985; PhD, Purdue U., 1992. Rsch. asst., rsch. assoc. dept. biol. sci. Purdue U., West Lafayette, Ind., 1988-93, teaching asst., instr., 1988-93; postdoctoral fellow sch. med. Emory U., Atlanta, 1993-94; biology lectr. Spelman Coll., Atlanta, 1994-95. Contbr. articles to profl. jours. Aux. vol. Emory Univ. Hosp., Atlanta, 1993-95. Mem. Phi Kappa Phi, Golden Key Nat. Honor Soc. Avocations: playing piano, reading business history and political science, hiking, cooking. Office: Spelman Coll Atlanta GA 30314

SCHWARTZ, MISCHA, electrical engineering educator; b. N.Y.C., Sept. 21, 1926; s. Isaiah and Bessie (Weinstein) S.; m. Lillian Mitchnick, June 23, 1957 (div.); 1 son, David; m. Charlotte F. Berney, July 12, 1970. B.E.E., Cooper Union, 1947; M.E.E., Poly. Inst. Bklyn., 1949; PhD in Applied Physics (Sperry Gyroscope grad. scholar), Harvard U., 1951. Project engr. Sperry Gyroscope Co., 1947-52; mem. faculty Poly. Inst. Bklyn., 1952-74, prof. elec. engring., 1959-74, head dept., 1961-65; prof. elec. engring. and computer sci. Columbia U., N.Y.C., 1974-88, Charles Batchelor prof. elec. engring., 1988-96, Charles Batchelor prof. emeritus, 1996—, dir. Ctr. for Telecommunications Research, 1985-88. Part-time tchr. Adelphi Coll., 1951-52, CCNY, 1952; cons. radiation physicist Montefiore Hosp., N.Y.C., 1954-56; vis. prof. sys. sci. dept. UCLA, 1964; vis. prof. dept. elec. engring. and computer sci. Columbia U., 1973-74; vis. prof. dept. electronic and elec. engring. U. Coll., London, 1995; vis. prof. dept. elec. and computer engring. U. Calif., San Diego, 1997; chmn. Commn. C, U.S. Nat. Com. Internat. Union Radio Sci., 1977-80; vis. scientist IBM Rsch., 1980, 94, NYNEX Sci. and Tech., 1986; vis. mem. tech. staff AT&T Bell Labs., 1995; cons. in field. Author: Information Transmission, Modulation and Noise, 4th edit., 1990, (with L. Shaw) Signal Processing, 1975, Computer Communication Network Design and Analysis, 1977, Telecommunications Networks, 1987, Broadband Integrated Networks, 1996; editor, contbr.: Communication Systems and Techniques, 1966, reissued, 1995. Trustee Gt. Neck Libr., 1997-2001, pres., 1998, 99. Served with AUS, 1944-46. NSF sci. faculty fellow, 1965-66; recipient Disting. Vis. award Australian-Am. Ednl. Found., 1975, Vis. Scientist award Nippon Tel. & Tel., 1981, Tchg. award Columbia U., 1984, Gano Dunn award Cooper Union, 1986, Mayor's award for excellence in tech., City of N.Y., 1995; finalist Mayor's Awards for Excellence in Sci. & Tech., City of N.Y., 1992, recipient Okawa award for contbns. comm., computer networks, engring. edn., 2003. Fellow AAAS, IEEE (chmn. adminstrv. com. profl. group info. theory 1964-65, bd. dirs. 1978-79, bd. govs. Comm. Soc. 1973-79, v.p. 1982-83, pres. 1984-85, Edn. medal 1983, IEEE Centennial Hall of Fame 1984, Region 1 award for leadership in mgmt. Ctr. for Telecom. Rsch. 1990, Edwin Armstrong award for contbns. to telecomm. 1994, Millennium medal 2000); mem. NAE, AAUP (chpt. pres. 1970-72), Assn. for Computing Machinery, Sigma Xi, Tau Beta Pi, Eta Kappa Nu (eminent mem. 1999). Home: 66 Maple Dr Great Neck NY 11021-1928 Office: Columbia U Schapiro CEPSR Rm 806 New York NY 10027 E-mail: schwartz@ctr.columbia.edu., mcschw66@aol.com.

SCHWARTZ, RICHARD BRENTON, English language educator, dean, writer; b. Cin., Oct. 5, 1941; s. Jack Jay and Marie Mildred (Schnelle) S.; m. Judith Mary Alexis Lang, Sept. 7, 1963; 1 son, Jonathan Francis. AB cum laude, U. Notre Dame, 1963; AM, U. Ill., 1964, PhD, 1967. Instr. English U.S. Mil. Acad., 1967-69; asst. prof. U. Wis.-Madison, 1969-72, assoc. prof., 1972-78, prof., 1978-81; assoc. dean U. Wis.-Madison (Grad. Sch.), 1977, 79-81; prof. English, dean Grad. Sch., Georgetown U., Washington, 1981-98, interim exec. v.p. for main campus academic affairs, 1991-92; interim exec. v.p. for the main campus Georgetown U., Washington, 1995-96; prof. English, dean Coll. Arts and Sci. U. Mo., Columbia, 1998—. Mem. exec. bd. Ctr. Strategic and Internat. Studies, 1981-87. Author: Samuel Johnson and the New Science, 1971 (runner-up Gustave O. Arlt prize), Samuel Johnson and the Problem of Evil, 1975, Boswell's Johnson: A Preface to the Life, 1978, Daily Life in Johnson's London, 1983, Japanese edit., 1990, After the Death of Literature, 1997, Nice and Noir: Contemporary American Crime Fiction, 2002, (novels) Frozen Stare, 1989, The Last Voice You Hear, 2001, After the Fall, 2002, Into the Dark, 2002, (short stories) The Biggest City In America, 1999 (Choice Mag. citation); editor: The Plays of Arthur Murphy, 4 vols., 1979, Theory and Tradition in Eighteenth-Century Studies, 1990; contbr. articles to profl. jours. Served to capt. U.S. Army, 1967-69. Decorated Army Commendation medal; recipient Presdl. medal Georgetown U., 1998; Nat. Endowment Humanities grantee, 1970, 87; Inst. for Research in Humanities fellow, 1976; Am. Council Learned Socs. fellow, 1978-79; H.I. Romnes fellow, 1978-81. Mem. Mystery Writers Am., Johnson Soc. So. Calif., Johnson Soc. of London, Am. Soc. Eighteenth-Century Studies, Coun. Grad. Schs., N.E. Assn. Grad. Schs. (exec. com. 1986-88), Assn. Grad. Schs. in Cath. Univs. (exec. com. 1984-87), Assn. Literary Scholars and Critics, Nat. Assn. Scholars, N.Am. Conf. Brit. Studies, Jefferson Club, Mosaic Soc., Alpha Sigma Nu, Alpha Sigma Lambda. Roman Catholic. Home: 5800 Highlands Pkwy Columbia MO 65203-5125 Office: U Mo Coll of Arts and Sci 317 Lowry Hall Columbia MO 65211-6080 E-mail: SchwartzRB@missouri.edu.

SCHWARTZ, RICHARD EVAN, mathematician, educator; BS in Math., UCLA, 1987; PhD in Math., Princeton U., 1991. Postdoctoral staff CUNY, IHES, MSRI, 1992—93; asst. prof. U. Chgo., 1996; assoc. prof. U. Md., 1997—2001, prof., 2001—. Contbr. articles to profl. jours. Fellow, John Simon Guggenheim Meml. Found., 2003; grantee, NSF, 1998—; grad. fellow, 1988—90, postdoctoral fellow, 1993—95, Sloan Dissertation fellow, 1990—91, Sloan Rsch. fellow, 1996—99. Office: Dept Math Univ Md College Park MD 21044*

SCHWARTZ, RICHARD FREDERICK, electrical engineering educator; b. Albany, NY, May 31, 1922; s. Frederick William and Mary Hoyle (Holland) S.; m. Ruth Louise Feldman, Oct. 25, 1945 (div. Oct. 1977); children: Kathryn Gail, Frederick Earl, Karl Edward, Eric Christian, Frieda Diane; m. Margaret Camp Boes, May 29, 1982. BEE, Rensselaer Poly. Inst., Troy, N.Y., 1943, MEE, 1948; PhD, U. Pa., 1959. Registered profl. engr., Pa., Mich. Instr. Rensselaer Poly. Inst., Troy, 1946-48; engr. Radio Corp. Am., Camden, N.J., 1948-51; instr. U. Pa., Phila., 1951-53, rsch. assoc., 1953-59, asst. prof. electrical engring., 1959-62, assoc. prof. electrical engring., 1962-73; prof. elec. engring. Mich. Tech. U., Houghton, 1973-85, dept. head, 1973-79; prof. elec. engring. SUNY, Binghamton, 1985-95, prof. emeritus, 1995—; pvt. practice Endicott, N.Y., 1999—. Vis. asst. prof. U. Mich., Ann Arbor, 1960; cons. Pa. Bar Assn. Endowment, Armstrong Cork Co., Am. Electronics Labs., Inc., IBM, RCA, City of Phila., GE. Co-author: The Eavesdroppers, 1959; contbr. articles to profl. jours. Active Delaware County Symphony, Pa., 1967-72, Keeweenaw Symphony Orch., Houghton, 1973-85, Vestal Cmty. Band, 1993—; mem. exec. bd. Broome County Peace Action, 1995—, sec. bd., 1998-2001; active Broome County Interfaith Caregivers, 1997—; mentor Schs. to Careers Partnership. 1995—. With U.S. Army, 1942-46. Fellow Acoustical Soc. Am.; mem. IEEE (sr., life, vice chmn. Binghamton sect. 2000—), AAAS (life), NSPE (life), Am. Soc. Engring. Edn. (life), N.Y. Soc. Profl. Engrs. (life, Broome chpt., bd. dir. 2000—, treas. 2001—, Engr. of Yr. 1995, Contbns. to Edn. award 1996), Audio Engring. Soc. (life), Found. for Engring. Edn. Inc.(bd. dirs. 2000—. sec. 2001-03), Order of the Engr., Sigma Xi, Eta Kappa Nu, Tau Beta Pi. Democrat. Unitarian Universalist. Patentee tuning sys., oscillator frequency control, transistor amplifier with high undistorted output. Home and Office: 2624 Bornt Hill Rd Endicott NY 13760-8231

SCHWARTZ, SUSAN LYNN HILL, principal; b. Portland, Ind., Aug. 15, 1951; d. Leland Alfred and Marjorie (Halberstadt) Hill; m. William Samuel Schwartz, July 6, 1974; children: Angelica Martinique, Allysia Dominica. BA, DePauw U., 1973; MA, Ball State U., 1976; postgrad., Tri-Coll. U., Fargo, N.D., 1986, Ind. U., 1993—. Cert. tchr. and aminstr., Ind., N.D. 2d and 3d grade tchr. Jay Sch. Corp., Portland, 1973-76; 1st to 3d grade tchr. Minot (N.D.) Pub. Schs., 1976-80; prin. elem. sch. Ward County Schs., Minot, 1980-82, LaPorte (Ind.) Schs., 1988-96; prin. kindergarten to 5th grade Western Wayne Schs., Cambridge City, Ind., 1996-97; prin. pre-K through 6th Cloverdale (Ind.) Elem. Sch., 1997—. Mem. State Sch. Evaluation Team, Bismarck, N.D., 1980-81. Bd. dirs. Am. Cancer Soc., Muncie, Ind., 1985-88, Richmond, Ind., 1992—, Suzuki Music Assn., Muncie, 1986-87; mem./leader Work Area on Edn.-Meth., Muncie, 1985-87; philanthropic chair Delaware County Welcome Wagon, Muncie, 1982-88; treas./fin. sec. Christian Women's Club, Muncie, 1983-86; pres. N.D. State U. Sch. Adminstrs. Assn., Fargo, 1980-81; mem. Wayne County Step Ahead Edn. Com., 1991—; bd. mem. United Way; Putnam County, safe sch. summit rep., 1997—. Named Outstanding Young Educator, Jaycees, 1980, Outstanding Young Career Woman, Bus. and Profl. Women, 1981. Mem. Phi Delta Kappa, Pi Lambda Theta, Delta Kappa Gamma, Psi Iota Xi. Methodist. Avocations: golf, racquetball, bridge. Office: Cloverdale Elem 311 E Logan St Cloverdale IN 46120-8707

SCHWARTZ, WILLIAM, lawyer, educator; b. Providence, May 6, 1933; s. Morris Victor and Martha (Glassman) S.; m. Bernice Konigsberg, Jan. 13, 1957; children: Alan Gershon, Robin Libby. AA, Boston U., 1952, JD magna cum laude, 1955, MA, 1960; postgrad., Harvard Law Sch., 1955-56; LHD (hon.), Hebrew Coll., 1996, Yeshiva U., 1998. Bar: D.C. 1956, Mass. 1962, N.Y. 1989. Prof. law Boston U., 1955-91, Fletcher prof. law, 1968-70, Roscoe Pound prof. law, 1970-73, dean Sch. of Law, 1980-88, dir. Ctr. for Estate Planning, 1988-91; univ. prof. Yeshiva U., N.Y.C., 1991—; of counsel Swartz & Swartz, 1973-80; v.p. for acad. affairs, chief acad. officer Yeshiva U., N.Y.C., 1993-98; counsel Cadwalader, Wickersham and Taft, N.Y.C., Washington, Charlotte, London, 1988—; mem. faculty Frances Glessner Lee Inst., Harvard Med. Sch., Nat. Coll. Probate Judges, 1970, 77, 78, 79, 88; gen. dir. Assn. Trial Lawyers Am., 1968-73; reporter New Eng. Trial Judges Conf., 1965-67; participant Nat. Met. Cts. Conf., 1968; dir. Mass. Probate Study, 1976—; chmn. spl. com. on police procedures City of Boston, 1989, 91. Bd. dirs., chmn. UST Corp., 1993—94, chmn. bd. dirs., 1996—2000; bd. dirs. Viacom Inc., Viacom Internat., Inc., chmn., nominating mem. governance com.; mem. adv. com. WCI Street, Inc.; mem. legal adv. bd. N.Y. Stock Exch. Author: Future Interests and Estate Planning, 1965, 77, 81, 86, Comparative Negligence, 1970, A Products Liability Primer, 1970, Civil Trial Practice Manual, 1972, New Vistas in Litigation, 1973, Massachusetts Pleading and Practice, 7 vols., 1974-80, Estate Planning and Living Trusts, 1990, The Convention Method: The Unused Amending Superhighway, 1995, Jewish Law and Contemporary Dilemmas and Problems, 1997, Does Time Heal All Wrongs?, 1999, Amending Irrevocable Trusts, 2003, others; note editor: Boston U. Law Rev., 1954-55; property editor: Annual Survey of Mass. Law, 1960—; contbr. articles to legal jours. Rep. Office of Pub. Info., UN, 1968—73; chmn. legal adv. panel Nat. Commn. Med. Practice, 1972—73; examiner of titles Commonwealth of Mass., 1964—; spl. counsel Mass. Bay Transp. Authority, 1979; pres. Fifth Ave. Synagogue, N.Y.C., 1997—2001, hon. pres., 2001—; trustee Hebrew Coll., 1975—, Salve Regina U., Yeshiva U. Recipient Homer Albers award Boston U., 1955, John Ordronaux prize, 1955; Disting. Service award Religious Zionists Am., 1977; William W. Treat award; William O. Douglas award. Fellow Am. Coll. Probate Counsel; mem. ABA, Am. Law Inst., Mass. Bar Assn. (chmn. task force tort liability), N.Y. State Bar Assn., Assn. Bar City N.Y., Nat. Coll. Probate Judges (hon. mem.), Phi Beta Kappa. Office: 100 Maiden Ln New York NY 10038-4818

SCHWARTZBECK, PATRICIA ANN, retired elementary school educator; b. Saratoga Springs, N.Y., Aug. 20, 1948; d. Andrew Arthur and Ellen (Norman) Mousin; m. Richard Alan Schwartzbeck, July 1, 1972; children: Russell, Patricia L., Cathlene. BS, SUNY, Plattsburgh, 1970. Cert. math. tchr. N-9, N.Y. 1st grade tchr. Schuylerville (N.Y.) Ctrl. Sch., 1970-79, 3d grade tchr., 1980—2002. Mem. Effective Schs. Bldg. Team, Schuylerville, 1991—92, 1993, 1995—; owner Mom & Pop's Country Store, Porter Corners, 1976—. Leader 4-H Club, Porter Corners, N.Y., 1982-91; tchr. religious edn. St. Joseph's Ch., Greenfield Center, N.Y., 1990-98. Roman Catholic. Home: 236 Plank Rd Porter Corners NY 12859-1915

SCHWARZ, BARBARA RUTH BALLOU, elementary school educator; b. East Orange, N.J., Aug. 8, 1930; d. Robert Ingram Ballou and Ruth Edna Sweeney; m. Eugene A. Schwarz, Jr., Dec. 24, 1954 (div. 1977); children: Ruth Ellen, Eugene A. III. BS, Trenton State Coll., 1952. Tchr. West Orange N.J. Schs., 1952-54, Franklin Sch., Ft. Wayne, Ind., 1955-56, Parliament Place Sch., North Babylon, N.Y., 1965-91. Trustee welfare trust fund North Babylon Tchrs. Orgn., N.Y., 1988-91. Vol. Safe Home, Suffolk County Coalition Against Domestic Violence, Bayshore, N.Y., 1979-90; sec. Victims Info. Bur., Suffolk, 1987-88, v.p., 1989-90, pres. bd. dirs., 1990-94, regional bd. dirs., 2002—, rep. to Women's Equal Rights Coalition, Suffolk County Human Rights Commn., 1989-94; mem. adv. bd. Suffolk County Women's Svcs., 1990-96, vice-chair, 1991-93; rep. LD 14 Suffolk County Women's Adv. Commn., 2001—; bd. dirs. Suffolk Abortion Rights Coun., 1992-96; mem. Suffolk-Nassau Abortion Def., 1991-94; pub. affairs com. Planned Parenthood Suffolk County, 1990-92; mem. Long Islanders for Fairness and Equality 1994-97; mem. subcom. Islip Presbyn. Ch. on Legis. Com. of N.Y. State Coalition Against Domestic Violence, 1999—; steering com. Save Our Svcs., Long Island, 1998—; mem. coun. on women, L.I. Presbytery, 2002—. Women's History Month Community Svc. honoree Town of Babylon, 1997. Mem. AAUW (mem. v.p. Islip area br. 1982-84, pres. 1984-88, legis. chair 1988-93, mem. com. promoting individual liberties Nassau-Suffolk dist. VI 1989-91, pro-choice coord. N.Y. state 1990-92, rep. to women on job task force 1986-98, chair dist. VI inter-br. 1991-92, chair N.Y. state pub. policy 1992-96, rep. on L.I. and N.Y. State Pro-Choice Coalitions, chair N.Y. state voter edn. campaign, 1995-98, assoc. pub. policy com. 1996-98, L.I. Achievement award 1996), N.Y. State Ret. Tchrs. Assn., Western Suffolk Ret. Tchrs. Assn., Coalition Ret. Tchrs. L.I., North Babylon Tchrs. Orgn. (retirees chpt.). Republican. Avocations: lobbying, reading, handcrafts, gourmet cooking, volunteer activities. Home: 23 Wyandanch Ave Babylon NY 11702-1920 E-mail: bbschwarz@webtv.net.

SCHWARZ, CHERYL MARITA, special education educator; b. Waukegan, Ill., Aug. 25, 1956; d. Walter George and Catherine Mary Nieds; children: Lindsay, Sarah. BS in Spl. Edn., Western Ill. U., 1978; MA in Learning Disabilities, Northeastern Ill. U., 1992; postgrad. in Ednl. Adminstrn., No. Ill. U., 2002—. Learning disabilities tchr. Golf Jr. HS, Morton Grove, Ill., 1978—81; learning disabilities tchr., coord. Dept. Spl. Edn. Wauconda (Ill.) HS, 1986—. Recipient Citizenship Edn. award, Dept. Ill. VFW, 1999—2000. Avocations: tennis, golf, reading, yoga, walking, running. Home: 1189 Hunters Ln Lake Zurich IL 60047-2249

SCHWARZ, LOUISE A. band director; H.s. band dir. Bethlehem Ctrl. H.S., Delmar, N.Y. Recipient Castleman award for excellence in chamber mus. teaching, 1993. Office: Bethlehem Ctrl High Sch 700 Delaware Ave Delmar NY 12054-2436

SCHWARZ, RALPH JACQUES, retired engineering educator; b. Hamburg, Germany, June 13, 1922; naturalized, 1944; s. Simon J. and Anna (Schoendorff) S.; m. Irene Lassally, Sept. 9, 1951; children: Ronald Paul, Sylvia Anne. BS, Columbia U., 1943, MS, 1944, PhD, 1949; postgrad., Poly. Inst. Bklyn., 1944-45, N.Y. U., 1946-47. Registered profl. engr., N.Y. Mem. faculty Columbia U., 1943-92, prof. elec. engring., 1958-92, chmn. dept., 1958-65, 71-72, assoc. dean acad. affairs Faculty Engring. and Applied Sci., 1972-75, acting dean, 1975-76, 80-81, vice dean, Thayer Lindsley prof., 1976-92, Thayer Lindsley prof. emeritus, 1992—; cons. systems analysis, communications and noise theory, 1945—. Vis. assoc. prof. UCLA, 1956; adviser Inst. Internat. Edn., 1952-65; vis. scientist IBM Research Center, 1969-70 Author: (with M.G. Salvadori) Differential Equations in Engineering Problems, 1954, (with B. Friedland) Linear Systems, 1965. Bd. dirs. Armstrong Meml. Research Found.; trustee Associated Univs., Inc., 1980-92. Fellow: IEEE (chmn. circuit theory group 1963—65, Centennial medal 1984). Home: 1270 North Ave # 5G New Rochelle NY 10804-2601 E-mail: rjs613@aol.com.

SCHWARZKOPF, GLORIA A. education educator, psychotherapist; b. Chgo., Apr. 20, 1926; m. Alfred E. Grossenbacher. BE, Chgo. State U., 1949, ME in Libr. Sci., 1956. Cert. nat. recovery specialist, reality therapist; libr. sci. endorsement; cert. hypnotherapist; cert. nat. forensic counselor; nat. cert. domestic violence counselor. Tchr. Chgo. Bd. Edn., 1949-91, inservice trainer in substance abuse, 1990—91; co-therapist ATC outpatient unit Ingalls Meml. Hosp., Chgo., 1981-86; recovery specialist Interaction Inst., Evergreen Park, Ill., 1993-95; ct. watcher Cook County, Chgo., 1994—2003; quality assurance evaluation Ill. State Bd. Edn., 1997-2000; libr. aide Chgo. Bd. Edn., 2001—03. Instr. Govs. State U., University Park, Ill., 1987, University Park, 91, South Suburban Coll., South Holland, Ill., 1991, Prairie State Coll., Chicago Heights, Ill., 1993, Chicago Heights, 96; with CP5 Project Assist Program, 2000—03; presenter in field; co-facilitator CPS Summer Sci. Camp Intervention project, 2000, 03. Columnist Peoples Choice Weekly, 1991-93. Del. to Russia and Czechoslovakia, Citizens Amb. Program. Recipient Sci. Tchr. of Yr. award, 1976, Svc. Recognition award, 1985, IMSA Recognition award. 1988; grantee Chgo. Pub. Sch., 1981. Mem. NEA, Nat. Assn. Forensic Counselors, Sci. Tchrs. Assn., Ill. Alcoholism Counselors Alliance, Nat. Alcoholism Coun., Am. Assn. Hypnotherapists, Am. Assn. Behavioral Therapists, Soc. of Am. for Recovery (nat. cert. recovery specialist), South Suburban Coun. on Alcoholism, Ill. Alcoholism and Other Drug Abuse Profl. Cert. Assn. Home: 2216 W 91st St Chicago IL 60620-6238

SCHWEDLER, JILLIAN MARIE, political science educator; b. Warren, Mich., Feb. 9, 1966; d. Marvin Charles and V. Diana (Keller) S.; m. Joel Allan Sherman, Nov. 14, 1992. BA, NYU, 1988, MA, 1992, PhD, 2000. Program officer Civil Soc. Project, N.Y.C., 1992-95; asst. prof. dept. govt. and politics U. Md., College Park, 2000—. Chair bd. dirs. MERIP/Mid. East Report, Washington. Author: Toward Civil Society in the Middle East, 1995, Islamist Movements in Jordan, 1997; mem. editl. bd. New Eng. Jour. Polit. Sci. Internat. rsch. fellow Social Sci. Rsch. Coun., Jordan & Yemen, 1995, Fulbright fellow, 1996-97, Am. Inst. Yemeni Studies fellow, 1997, Fulbright New Century scholar, 2003. Mem. Am. Polit. Sci. Assn., Mid. East Studies Assn., Law and Soc. Assn., Internat. Studies Assn. Avocations: scuba diving, dance, travel. Home: 131 Sprague Rd Scarsdale NY 10583-6347 Office: U Md Dept Govt and Politics 3140 Tydings Hall College Park MD 20742-7215 Fax: 301-314-9690. E-mail: jschwedler@gvpt.umd.edu.

SCHWEICHLER, MARY ELLEN, childhood education educator, consultant; b. Buffalo, N.Y., Oct. 19, 1931; d. Joseph John and Teresa Mary (McVey) Carter; divorced; children: Michele, Richard, Maria Regina, Beth, David. Cert. Indsl. and Labor Rels., Cornell U., 1983; BS magna cum laude, SUNY, Buffalo, 1986, postgrad., 1986—. Cert. early childhood edn. Postulant and tchr. Missionary Servants Blessed Trinity Pre-Sch., Phila., 1950-51; tchr., adminstr., founder Southtowns Pre-Sch. Devel., Blasdell, N.Y., 1975-82; asst. doord. dept. surgery 3d yr. student program SUNY, Buffalo, 1982-84, asst. to chair Health and Behavioral Scis., 1984-88. Lectr. early childhood edn. Orchard Pk. (N.Y.) Sch. Dist., 1975-82, SUNY Buffalo, 1975-82; cons. early childhood edn. Day Care Assn. Resource Ctr., Buffalo, 1987—. Contbr. articles profl. publs.; author numerous poems. Vol. Head Start, Lackawanna, N.Y., 1970-75, P.R. Teen Ctr., Lackawanna, 1970-72; mem. Orchard Pk. Enrollment and Bldg. Utilization Com., 1982, Orchard Pk. Edn. Adv. Bd., 1988, Nat. Multiple Sclerosis Soc., 1990—, Found. for Internat. Cooperation, 1965-69, Christian Family Movement, 1962-70, U-U Task Force on Domestic Violence, 1993—; founding mem. West N.Y. chpt. Reyes Syndrome Found., 1979-83; ombudsman ARC, Buffalo, 1989—; workshop leader Career Devel. Ctr. for Women in Govt., Albany, N.Y., 1982-84; trainer Smoking Cessation Am. Lung Assn., Buffalo, 1984-86; mem. elderly and disabled adv. coun. Jefferson County, 2003; vol., Ky. Assn. Sr. Svcs. Corps Program, Srs. Saving Medicare. Recipient Appreciation award, Orchard Park Sch. Bd., 1988. Mem. AAUW, Women's Aux. Am. Phys. Therapy Assn. (founder, pres. 1965-72), Nardin Acad. Alumni (bd. dirs. 1965-70), Alpha Sigma Lambda (sec. 1987—). Unitarian Universalist. Avocation: reading. Home: Masonic Home Village 200 Masonic Home Dr Apt 105 Masonic Home KY 40041-9011

SCHWEICKERT, RICHARD JUSTUS, psychologist, educator; b. Madison, Wis., July 19, 1946; s. Carl E. and Marie E. (Dilzer) S.; m. Carolyn M. Jagacinski, Dec. 27, 1980; children: Patrick, Kenneth. BS in Math., U. Santa Clara, 1968; MA in Math., Ind. U., 1972; PhD in Psychology, U. Mich., 1979. Statistician Bellevue Psychiatric Hosp., N.Y.C., 1969-71; asst. prof. Purdue U., West Lafayette, Ind., 1978-83, assoc. prof., 1984-91, prof., 1992—. Adv. panel on human cognition & perception NSF, 1993-96. Author: (with others) Handbook of Human Factors, 1987; editor Jour. Math. Psychology; assoc. editor Psychol. Bull. and Rev., 1993-98; mem. editl. bd. Jour. Exptl. Psychology; Learning, Memory and Cognition, 1985-89, 91-94, Jour. Math. Psychology, 1986-94; contbr. articles to profl. jours. Grantee NSF, 1981-84, 92-2000, NIMH, 1983-89. Fellow AAAS, Am. Psychol. Soc.; mem. Soc. for Math. Psychology (pres. 1990-91, bd. dirs.), Psychonomic Soc., Informs. Office: Purdue U Dept Psychol Scis Lafayette IN 47907

SCHWEIZER, KARL WOLFGANG, historian, educator, author; b. Mannheim, Fed. Republic Germany, June 30, 1946; came to U.S., 1988; m. Elizabeth Wild, 1969; 1 child, Paul. BA in History, Wilfrid Laurier U., Can., 1969; MA, U. Waterloo, Can., 1970; MA, PhD, Cambridge U., 1976. Prof. history Bishop's U., Lenoxville, Que., Can., 1976-88, chmn. dept., 1978-79,

82-84, 86; prof., chmn. humanities dept. N.J. Inst. Tech., Newark, 1988-93, prof. dept. social sci. and policy studies, 1993—, chmn. dept. humanities and social scis., 2000—03, prof. dept. humanities, 2003—; assoc. Ctr. for Study of Global Change Rutgers U., 1995—. Grad. faculty Rutgers U., 1993—; vis. lectr. U. Guelph, Can., 1978-80; rsch. assoc. Russian Rsch. Ctr., Ill., 1979-80, 99; acad. visitor London Sch. Econs., 1986, 94, vis. scholar, 1986-87, Queens U., Ont., Can., 1986-87; vis. fellow Darwin Coll., Cambridge, 1987, 94, 2003, Princeton U., 1994, Yale U., 1994; vis. prof. dept. polit. sci. Rutgers U., 1997—; sr. rsch. assoc. Peterhouse Coll., Cambridge, 2003. Author: The Art of Diplomacy, 1983, Lord Bute: Essays in Reinterpretation, 1988, England, Prussia and the Seven Years War, 1989, Frederick the Great, William Pitt and Lord Bute, 1991, Lord Chatham, 1993, François de Callières: Diplomat and Man of Letters, 1995, War, Politics and Diplomacy: The Anglo Prussian Alliance, 1756-1763, 2001, Seeds of Evil: The Gray/Snyder Murder Case, 2001, Statesmen, Diplomats and the Press, 2002; co-author: The Origins of War in Early Modern Europe, 1987, The War of the Spanish Succession, 1994, British Prime Ministers, 1997, Hanoverian Britain and Empire, 1998, Oxford Dictionary of the Enlightenment, 2003, Scribners Dictionary of Modern European History, 2003; co-author: (with J. Osborne) Cobbett in His Times, 1990; editor: The Devonshire Political Diary, 1757-1762, 1982, Diplomatic Thought 1648-1815, 1982, Warfare and Tactics in the 18th Century, 1984, Herbert Butterfield: Essays on the History of Science, 1998; co-editor: Essays in European History 1648-1815 in Honour of Ragnhild Hatton, 1985, Politics and the Press in Hanoverian Britain, 1989; contbr. articles to profl. jours.; gen. editor: Studies in History and Politics, 1980—91, editl. cons.: Scribner's Dictionary of Modern European History, Oxford Dictionary of National Biography. Mem. NJ Gov.'s Adv. Panel on Higher Edn. Restructuring, 1994; trustee NJ Literary Hall of Fame, 1988—92. Recipient thesis defence award Can. Coun., 1976, travel awards Peterhouse Coll., 1971-73, Adelle Mellen prize for outstanding contbn. to scholarship Edwin Mellen Press, 1989, Author's award N.J. Writer's Conf., 1993, Tchg. award N.J. Inst. Tech., 2000; fellow U. Waterloo, 1969-70, Province of Ont., 1969-70, Can. Coun., 1970-75; named Wilfred Laurier Proficiency scholar, 1966-69; rsch. grantee Bishop's U., 1977, 78, 80, 82, 83, postdoctoral rsch. grantee Can. Coun., 1977-78, 82-83, grantee Inter-Univ. Ctr. for European Studies, 1978, 81, conf. grantee S.S.H.R.C., 1985; travel grantee NEH, 1991, N.J. Com. for Humanities, 1988-1992; Mellon fellow Harvard U., 1978. Fellow Royal Hist. Soc.; mem. Internat. Commn. on History of Internat. Rels., Hist. Soc., Cambridge Hist. Soc., North American Conf. on Brit. Studies, Can. Assn. Scottish Studies, Can. Assn. 18th Century Studies. Avocations: music, writing, reading. Home: 49 South Passaic Ave Apt 24 Chatham NJ 07928 Office: NJ Inst Tech Dept Social Sci and Policy Newark NJ 07102

SCHWENNESEN, CAROL ANN, artist, educator; b. Orange, Calif., Aug. 28, 1945; d. Jarvis Larson and Marie Theresa (Riedel) S.; children: Aaron, Molly, Leslie. BA in Art History magna cum laude, BFA, Western Wash. U., Bellingham, 1984; MFA, Claremont (Calif.) Grad. U., 1987. Cert. tchr., Calif. Lectr. art Cypress (Calif.) Coll., 1987, Mt. San Antonio Coll., Walnut, Calif., 1987-89, Chaffey Coll., Alta Loma, Calif., 1988-90; asst. prof. Scripps Coll., Claremont, Calif., 1988-90; instr. Blue Heron Art Ctr., Vashon Island, Wash., 1990-96; adj. faculty Crafton Hills Coll., Yucaipa, Calif., 1997—2001. Cons. ABC-TV, N.Y., Calif., 1990, Fortune 500, Washington, 1996; juror Art in Pub. Places, King County/Metro Seattle, 1993, King County Work-Study Acad. Tng. Program, Vashon H.S., Seattle, Tacoma, Vashon Island, Wash., 1994-97. Artist paintings, drawings in Beetlejuice, 1988; group shows include Silverwood Gallery, Vashon Island, Wash., Art Works Gallery, Riverside, Calif, Gallery Oresti Marchesi, Copparo, Italy. Recipient merit scholarship Swedish Club L.A., 1985, travel grant Coll. Art Assn., N.Y., 1994. Mem. Coll. Art Assn. Avocations: physics, psychoneuroimmunology, systems of teaching/learning. Home and Office: PO Box 2282 Vashon WA 98070-2282

SCHWEPKER, CHARLES HENRY, JR., marketing educator; b. St. Charles, Mo., Jan. 21, 1963; s. Charles Henry Sr. and Mary Regina (Halter) S.; m. Laura Ann Pirrone, Dec. 1992; children: Charles Henry III, Anthony Peter, Lauren Nicole. BSBA, S.E. Mo. State U., 1984, MBA, 1988; PhD, U. Memphis, 1992. Asst. mgr. WalMart, Lubbock, Tex., 1985; prof. mktg. Cen. Mo. State U., Warrensburg, 1992—. Mktg. cons. Mem. editl. rev. bd. Jour. Personal Selling and Sales Mgmt., 1993—, Jour. Mktg. Theory & Practice, 1993—, Jour. Bus. and Indsl. Mktg., So. Bus. Rev., Jour. Relationship Mktg.; contbr. articles to profl. jours. and books; co-author: Sales Management: Analysis and Decision Making, Professional Selling: A Trust Based Approach. Chpt. advisor for Student Am. Mktg. Assn. at Ctrl. Mo. State U., 1992—, internat. study tour coord. Recipient Excellence in Reviewing award, Jour. Mktg. theory and Practice, 1996, Award for Jour. Personal Selling and Sales Mgmt., 1996. Mem. Am. Mktg. Assn., Acad. Mktg. Sci., Mktg. Mgmt. Assn. (nat. conf., Outstanding Paper award 2003). Roman Catholic. Avocations: golf, basketball, camping, fishing. Office: Ctrl Mo State U Coll Bus & Econs Dept Mktg and Legal Studies Warrensburg MO 64093

SCHWERDT, LISA MARY, English language educator; b. Coral Gables, Fla., Feb. 7, 1953; d. Henry G. and Dilys Doris (Bandurske) S. BS, Fla. Internat. U., 1973, BA, 1977; MA, Purdue U., 1979, PhD, 1984. Cert. secondary educator English, spl. edn., Fla. Tchr. English, Green Sch. English, Tokyo, 1973-75; tchr. spl. edn. Carol City (Fla.) Elem. Sch., 1975-77; grad. instr. Purdue U., West Lafayette, Ind., 1977-85; asst. prof. U. North Ala., Florence, 1985-89; adj. lectr. U. Ctrl. Fla., Orlando, 1989-90, Rollins Coll., Winter Park, Fla., 1989-90; prof. English, California U. Pa., 1990—, interim assoc. dean, 1995-98. Author: Isherwood's Fiction, 1989; contbr. articles and book revs. to profl. jours. Grantee Purdue Found., 1982; recipient Excellence in Teaching award Purdue U., 1979, 81. Mem. MLA, Coll. English Assn., Nat. Assn. Scholars, Nat. Coun. Tchrs. English, N.E. MLA, Pa. Coll. English Assn., Soc. for the Study of Narrative Lit., Soc. for Health and Human Values. Unitarian Universalist. Home: 5337 California Ave Bethel Park PA 15102-3821 Office: California U of Pa Dept English California PA 15419 E-mail: schwerdt@cup.edu.

SCHWERIN, ALAN KENNETH, philosophy educator; b. Johannesburg, Mar. 16, 1953; came to U.S., 1985; s. Kenneth Charles and Loretta May (Colyn) S.; m. Helen Griffiths, Jan. 29, 1977; children: Brett, Mia. BComm, U. Witwatersrand, Johannesburg, 1974; BA with honors, Rhodes U., Grahamstown, South Africa, 1977, MA, 1979; PhD, Rice U., 1988. Sr. lectr., philosophy dept. head U. Transkei, South Africa, 1980-85; asst. prof. philosophy McNeese State U., La., 1988-95, Monmouth U., Long Branch, N.J., 1996—. Author: The reluctant Revolutionary, 1989; editor: The Expanding Universe, 1993, Apartheid's Landscape and Ideas: A Scorched Soul, 2001, Bertrand Russell on Nuclear War, Peace and Language, 2002, Reason and Belief, 2002; contbr. articles to profl. jours. Recipient South Africa Nat. Photographic prizes, 1979; Rice U. fellow, 1986-88; Shearman Rsch. grantee; Human Scis. Rsch. Coun. scholar, 1977, 78. Mem. Am. Philos. Assn., Leibniz Soc., Hume Soc., Acad. Model Aeronautics, So. Soc. for Philosophers and Psychologists, Bertrand Russell Soc. (pres. 1999—). Avocations: photography, model sailplane design and construction. Home: 1 Cutter Dr Asbury Park NJ 07712-3225

SCHWERT, GEORGE WILLIAM, JR., biochemist, educator; b. Denver, Jan. 27, 1919; s. George William and Agnes (Buhler) S.; m. Margaret Houlton, June 23, 1943 (dec. Sept. 1975); children: George, Janet; m. Jean Stubbs Coplin, Nov. 20, 1979. BA, Carleton Coll., 1940; PhD, U. Minn., 1943. Rsch. biochemist Sharp and Dohme, Inc., Glenolden, Pa., 1943-44; asst. prof. biochemistry Duke U. Sch. Medicine, Durham, N.C., 1946-52, assoc. prof. biochemistry, 1952-57, prof. biochemistry, 1957-59; prof. U. Ky., Lexington, 1959-85, prof. emeritus, 1985—, chmn. dept. biochemistry, 1959-74. Mem. physiol. chemistry study sect. NIH, Bethesda, Md., 1959-64; mem. biochem. panel wooldridge com. Office Sci. Tech., Washington, 1964. Mem. editl. bd. Jour. Biol. Chemistry, 1965-69, 72-77; contbr. articles to profl. jours. Lt. (j.g.) USNR, 1944-46, PTO. Markle scholar in med. sci. John and Mary Markle Found., 1949-54. Mem. Am. Soc. for Biochemistry and Molecular Biology (emeritus), Am. Chem. Soc. (emeritus), Biochem. Soc. Great Britain (emeritus). Avocation: model railroads. Home: 3316 Braemar Dr Lexington KY 40502-3376

SCHWIND, MICHAEL ANGELO, law educator; b. Vienna, July 2, 1924; came to U.S., 1951; s. Siegfried and Sali (Salner) S. JD, U. Central, Ecuador, 1949; LL.M. in Internat. Law, NYU, 1953, LL.B., 1957. Bar: Ecuador 1949, N.Y. 1957, U.S. Supreme Ct. 1967. Pvt. practice, N.Y.C., 1957-69; Lectr. law NYU Sch. Law, 1959-63, adj. asst. prof., 1963-64, assoc. prof., 1964-67, prof., 1967-94, prof. emeritus, 1994—. Dir. Inter-Am. Law Inst., Inst. Comparative Law, NYU Sch. Law, 1967-71. Contbr. International Encyclopedia of Comparative Law, vol. 5; Bd. editors Am. Jour. Comparative Law, 1971-97. Mem.: Am. Fgn. Law Assn. (bd. dirs. 1980—83, 1984—87, 1988—91, 1993—96, 1997—2000, v.p. 1983—84, 1991—93, 1996—97, 2000—), Am. Assn. Comparative Study Law (NYU rep. on bd. dirs. 1971—2000). Office: NYU Sch Law 40 Washington Sq S Rm 321 New York NY 10012-1005 E-mail: schwindm@juris.law.nyu.edu.

SCIALDO, MARY ANN, music educator, musician; b. Westchester, NY, Sept. 21, 1942; d. Camille George Scialdo. MusB, Seton Hill Coll., 1963; MusM, Pius XII Inst. Fine Arts, Florence, Italy, 1964; profl. diploma, Manhattan Sch. Music, 1978; postgrad., Peabody Cons. Cert. tchr. NY, Fla. Supr. music Great Barrington (Mass.) Sch. Sys., 1967—68; music, theater prof. Simons Rock Coll., Great Barrington, 1968—70, Cath. U. PR, Ponce, 1971; performing arts instr. Briarcliff Sch. Dist., 1981, Ossining (NY) Sch. Dist., 1982, Albert Leonard Jr. H.S., 1983, Pleasantville (NY) Sch. Dist., 1984; theater and music tchr. Briarcliff Manor Schs., 1984—98; music tchr. Hillsborough County Schs., Tampa, Fla., 1999—. Dir., prodr., mus. and vocal dir., set and costume numerous student prodns. Debut concert: Merkin Hall, N.Y.C., internat. debut concert: Glinka Mus.; performer: (fund raising concert) Chopin Found. NY, (Giannini retrospective) WQXR, WNCN, (CD) Scriabin 24 Preludes, Opus 11, 1998—99. Recipient Outstanding Drama Tchr. award, Emerson Coll., 1st place award, Young Artist Nat. Competition, Nat. Fedn. Music Clubs competition, Disting. Alumna Leadership award, Seton Hill U. Mem.: Sigma Alpha Iota (life). Democrat. Roman Catholic. Office: Webb Middle Sch 6035 Hanley Rd Tampa FL 33634-4913

SCIBELLI, ANDREW M. academic administrator; BA, St. Anselm Coll.; MEd, Boston State Coll.; EdD, U. Mass. Tchr. Springfield (Mass.) Pub. Schs., 1965-69; prof. biology Springfield Tech. Community Coll., 1969-70, 78-83, registrar, 1970-73, asst. to pres., 1974-78, dir. community rels., 1981-83, pres., 1983—. Bd. dirs. Mfg. Partnership of Western Mass., Springfield Ctrl.; trustee Pioneer Valley Planning Commn.; mem. chancellor's coun. U. Mass.; chmn. New Eng. Tech. Edn. Project New Eng. Bd. Higher Edn., Statewide Collective Bargaining Negotiating Team for Mass. C.Cs.; presenter nat. convs. Alliance for C.C. Innovation, 1991, 94, 95; active Toronto Trade Mission, 1992, Hartford Trade Mission, 1992; corporator Chicopee Savs. Bank. Apptd. commr. MASSJOBS West Commn., mem. Massjobs Coun.; chmn., co-host United Cerebral Palsy Telethon, 1981—, past. pres. bd. dirs. western Mass. chpt.; mem. exec. com., bd. dirs. Pvt. Industry Coun. and Regional Employment Bd.; dir. Italian Cultural Ctr.; pres. Make-A-Wish Found. Western Mass.; chmn. maj. firms unit United Way, 1989; bd. dirs. Springfield Edn. Ptnrship, Corp. Pub. Mgmt.; numerous other civic roles and activities. Mem. Am. Assn. Community and Jr. Colls. (presenter nat. conv.), Nat. Coun. Resource Devel., Nat. Inst. Staff and Organizational Devel. (Outstanding Chief Exec. Officer Mass. 1987), Nat. Coun. Community Svcs. and Continuing Edn. (Regional Person of the Yr. awd, 1993), Am. Assn. Higher Edn., Nat. Coun. Occupational Edn. (rep. New Eng.), Nat. Coalition Advanced Tech. Ctrs., Nat. Coun. Pres., Coop. Colls. Greater Springfield (chmn. 1987-88). Avocations: golf, sailing, bicycling, skiing. Office: Springfield Tech C C Office Pres Armory Sq Springfield MA 01105

SCILEPPI, JOHN A. psychologist, educator; b. Bklyn., Aug. 30, 1946; s. Aldoph G. and Marie Theresa (Saccaro) S.; m. Lynn A. Ruggiero, Nov. 27, 1982; 1 child, Luke M.R. BA magna cum laude in Psychology, Marist Coll., Poughkeepsie, 1967; MA, Loyola U., Chgo., 1969, PhD in Social Psychology, 1973. Lic. psychologist, N.Y. NDEA rsch. and tchg. fellow Loyola U., Chgo., 1969-71, lectr., 1971-73; v.p. acad. affairs Oglala Sioux C.C., Pine Ridge, S.D., 1975-76; assoc. prof. psychology Marist Coll., Poughkeepsie, NY, 1973-75, 76-88, prof., 1988—. Dir. MA Psychology program, 1990-2002; psychol. cons. for program evaluation, survey research and interpersonal communication. Abstrator: Psychological Abstracts, 1977-81; author: A Systems View of Education: A Model of Change, 1984, rev. edit., 1988, Community Psychology: A Common Sense Approach to Mental Health, 2000. Chmn. bd. Sch. of the New Cmty. of Chgo., 1970-72; bd. dirs. Rehab. Programs Inc., Poughkeepsie, 1981-94, Hyde Park Free Libr., 1996-2002, pres. 2001-02; mem. planning com. United Way of Dutchess County (N.Y.), 1979-80. Mem. Am. Psychol. Assn., Soc. for Psychol. Study of Social Issues, Eastern Psychol. Assn., Psi Chi, Alpha Sigma Nu. Democrat. Roman Catholic. Home: 1 River Rd Hyde Park NY 12538-1323 Office: Marist Coll Psychology Dept Poughkeepsie NY 12601

SCLAFANI, SUSAN K. federal official; b. Albany, NY, Sept. 22, 1944; AB in German and Math. cum laude, Vassar Coll., 1996; MA in German Lang. and Lit., U. Chgo., 1967; ME in Ednl. Adminstrn., U. Tex., Austin, 1985, PhD, 1987. Cert. Tchr.Math. Ill., N.Y., Lifetime Tchr. Math. and German 6-12 Tex., Adminstr., Supt., Supr., Midmgr. Tex. Tchr. Ctrl. YMCA H.S., Chgo., 1971—72, Woodson Jr. H.S. Houston Ind. Sch. Dist., Tex., 1972—74, H.S. for Engring. Professions, Houston Ind. Sch. Dist., Tex., 1975—78; coord. magnet sch. Washington H.S. Houston Ind. Sch. Dist., 1978—83; ctrl. office coord. instrnl. tech. Houston Ind. Sch. Dist., Tex., 1983—84, exec. dir. curriculum devel., 1987—89, asst. supt. constrn. mgmt. and program planning, 1989—92, assoc. supt. dist. adminstrn., 1992—94, chief of staff, 1994—96, chief of staff ednl. svcs., 1996—2001; counselor to Sec. of Edn. U.S. Dept. Edn., Washington. V.p. and gen. mgr. Quantum Access, Inc., 1986—87; adj. prof. dept. curriculum and instrn. U. Houston, Tex., 1988—94, adj prof. dept. ednl. leadership, 1999—2001; presenter to numerous ednl. groups. Co-author (with R. Paige): (Book) Strategies for Reforming Houston's Schools; School Choice or Best Systems, What Improves Education, 2001; contbr. articles to profl. jours. Vol. Star of Hope Women and Family Shelter, Houston, 1988—90; mem. com. Tex. Alliance for Minorities in Engring., Houston, 1975—85; activity vol., conf. spkr. Coun. for Exceptional Children, Houston, 1989—91; com. mem. Tex. Task Force for the Homeless, 1990—92; mem. Hispanic Youth Leadership Forum Steering Com., Houston, 1990—, Pub. Policy, Comty. and Agy. Support, Success by Six Coms., United Way, Houston, 1987—2001; chair Children's Policy Com. United Way, Houston, 1987—2001. Office: US Dept Edn 400 Maryland Ave SW Washington DC 20202 E-mail: susan.sclafani@ed.gov.

SCODEL, RUTH, humanities educator; b. Columbus, Ohio, Feb. 29, 1952; d. Alvin and Barbara (Keith) S.; 1 child, Anna Gabrielle. AB, U. Calif., Berkeley, 1973; PhD, Harvard U., 1978. Asst. prof. Harvard Coll., Cambridge, Mass., 1978-83; assoc. prof. classics of Greek and Latin U. Mich., Ann Arbor, 1983-87, prof., 1987—, dir. LSA Honors program, 1991—97. Author: Trojan Trilogy of Euripides, 1980, Sophocles, 1984, Credible Impossibilities, 1999, Listening to Homer, 2002; editor Transactions of Am. Philol. Assn., 1986-91. Office: Univ Mich Dept Classical Studies Ann Arbor MI 48109

SCOGIN, MARTHA ADUDDELL, public information officer; b. Brice, Tex., Jan. 16, 1933; d. Jeff and Elizabeth Dale Aduddell; m. Andrew J. Scogin Jr., May 3, 1977; childern: Jerry Don Taylor, Sherri Carol Drobil, Charlotte Jean Taylor, Sherry Denise Stewart. BA, Tarleton State U.; MA, PhD, Tex. Women's U., 1986. Lic. profl. counselor, marriage & family therapist, chem. dependency specialist. Pvt. practice, Granburg, Tex.; affiliate Psychiat. Inst.; advt. and pub. rels. cons., instr. in psychology Hill Jr. Coll.; cons. Johnson County Ctrs.; pub. info. coord. City of Dallas. Speaker in field; creator (workshops) on motivational topics. Named Profl. Woman of Yr., Bus. & Profl. Women, Granbury, 1992. Mem. Am. Assn. Counseling Devel., Nat. Coun. Family Rels., Tex. Coun. Family Rels., Tex. Assn. Family Rels., Tex. Mental Health Assn. Home: 9617 Divot Dr Granbury TX 76049-4466

SCORDIAS, MARGARET ANN, education educator; b. St. Louis, July 17, 1955; d. Robert Lennolan and Helen Margaret (Brannon) Lovan; m. George Joseph Scordias, Jan. 11, 1975; children: Stephen Michael, Anthony James. BA, Washington U., St. Louis, 1977; MEd, U. Mo., St. Louis, 1985. Cert. elem., learning disabilities, remedial reading tchr. Mo., libr. media specialist. Curriculum/ instrnl. specialist Maplewood-Richmond Heights Sch. Dist., Mo. Project dir. U. Mo., St. Louis, 2003—. Mem.: ASCD, NEA, Tchr.'s Acad. Internat. Reading Assn., Phi Delta Kappa.

SCOTCHMER, SUZANNE ANDERSEN, economics educator; b. Seattle, Jan. 23, 1950; d. Toivo Matthias and Margaret (Sangder) Andersen. BA in Econ., U. Wash., 1970; MA in Stats., U. Calif., Berkeley, 1979, PhD in Econ., 1980. From asst. to assoc. prof. econ. Harvard U., Cambridge, Mass., 1981-86; prof. econ. and pub. policy U. Calif., Berkeley, 1986—. Vis. prof. Toronto Sch. Law, 1993, Tel Aviv U., 1994, U. Paris, Sonbonne, 1992, New Sch. of Econ., Moscow, 1993, U. Aukland, 2002; prin. investigator NSF, 1986-2002; lectr. in law. Mem. editl. bd. Am. Econ. Rev., 1991-95, Jour. Pub. Econ., 1986-2001, Jour. Econ. Perspectives, 1994-97, Regional Sci. and Urban Econ., 1991—, Jour. Econ. Lit., 1998—; contbr. articles to profl. jours. Hoover Nat. fellow Stanford U., 1989, Olin fellow Yale Sch. Law, 1991, Sloan fellow, 1979, Phi Beta Kappa fellow, 1978; France/Berkeley Fund grantee, 1994-95. Office: Univ Calif 2607 Hearst Ave Berkeley CA 94720-7320

SCOTT, AMY ANNETTE HOLLOWAY, nursing educator; b. St. Albans, W.Va., Apr. 10, 1916; d. Oliver and Mary (Lee) Holloway; m. William M. Jefferson, June 22, 1932, (div. Oct. 1933); 1 child, William M. Jefferson, m. Vann Hyland Scott, Mar. 15, 1952, (dec. Dec. 1972). BS in Nursing Edn., Cath. U., Washington, 1948; cert. in psychiat. nursing, U. Paris, 1959. Indsl. nurse Curtiss Wright Air Plane Co., Lambert Field, St. Louis, 1941-44; faculty St. Thomas U., Manila, The Philippines, 1948-50; pub. health nurse St. Louis Health Dept., 1951-56; mem. faculty St. Louis State Hosp., 1960-67; dept. head St. Vincents Hosp., St. Louis, 1967-68; faculty RN, creator psychiat. program Sch. of Nursing Jewish Hosp., 1968-72; adminstrv. nurse St. Louis State Hosp., 1972-84. Initiated first psychiat. program sch. nursing, Jewish Hosp. Author: (short story) Two Letters, 1962, (novel) Storms, 1987, Life's Journey, 1993. Past bd. dirs. county bd. Mo. U., 1984-88; hon. citizen Colonial Williamsburg, Va.; mem. Rep. Presdl. Task Force; mem. Women in the Arts '94. Maj. nursing corps, USAF, 1956-60. Recipient Key to Colonial Williamsburg, Va., Medal of Merit, Rep. Presdl. Task Force, 1992; named to Rep. Presdl. Task Force Honor Roll, 1993, Nat. Women's Hall of Fame, 1995, Women's Hall of Fame, 1996. Mem. AAUW, NAFE, N.Y. Acad. Scis., Internat. Fedn. Univ. Women, Internat. Soc. Quality Assurance in Health Care, N.Y. Acad. Scis., Am. Biog. Inst. (life, mem. governing bd.), Women in the Arts, Cambridge Ctr. Engring., Internat. Platform Assn. Roman Catholic. Avocations: music, boating, horseback riding, dog sled riding, travel. Home: Washington, DC. Died Jan. 31, 2002.

SCOTT, ANNA MARIE PORTER WALL, sociology educator; b. South Fulton, Tenn. d. Thomas Madison and Jevvie Roggie (Porter) P.; m. John T. Scott Sr. (dec.); 1 child, Harvey G. BA, MEd, MSW, U. Ill. Cert. tchr. and social worker, Ill. Caseworker Dept. Pub. Aid, Champaign, Ill.; psychiat. social worker Vets. Hosp., Danville, Ill.; prof. sociology Parkland Coll., Champaign, Ill. Head Dem. 21st Congl. Dist., 1974-78; del. Nominating Conv./Mini Conv., 1975, 76; commr. Ill. Banking Bd.; mem. AME Ch., Hadassah; mem. Vet. of Armed Svcs. Named Outstanding Black Alumni, U. Ill., Urbana. Mem. LWV, NAACP, Nat. Coun. Negro Women (past pres.), Am. Legion (comdr. post 559), AMVETS, Champaign-Urbana Symphony Guild, Order Ea. Star (grand organist Eureka Grand chpt.). Avocations: pub. speaking, piano, baking, gardening, politics. Home: 309 W Michigan Ave Urbana IL 61801-4945 Office: Parkland Coll 2400 W Bradley Ave Champaign IL 61821-1806

SCOTT, BARBARA ANN, sociology educator, feminist, peace activist; b. NYC, Jan. 3, 1937; d. Richard W. and Lia (Varell) Scott; m. Josiah Bartlett Page, June 8, 1958 (div. 1975); children: Evan Bartlett, Eric Scott. BA magna cum laude, Pembroke Coll., Brown U., 1958; MA in Sociology Grad. Faculty, New Sch. for Social Rsch., 1972, PhD in Sociology, 1979. Elem tchr. The Harley Sch., Rochester, NY, 1958-61, Poughkeepsie Day Sch., NY, 1968; instr. sociology SUNY, New Paltz, 1973-79, asst. prof., 1979-84, assoc. prof., 1984—2002, prof. emeritus, 2002—. Co-organizer, co-chmn. intercollegiate conf. Liberal Arts in a Time of Crisis, 1981; vis. scholar Ctr. Def. Info., Washington, 1986-87, mem. adv. bd., cons.; mem. bd. adv. editors Sociol. Inquiry, 1990—; spkr. FLACSO U. Havana, Cuba, 1993, Camaguey, Holguin, Cuba, 1994. Author: Crisis Management in American Higher Edn., 1983 (Albert Salomon Meml. award 1980); editor: The Liberal Arts in a Time of Crisis, 1991; contbr. articles to profl. jours. Founder, coord. Mid-Hudson chpt. Educators for Social Responsibility, 1983-87; trustee Shoreline Found. for Folk Lit. and Art, Branford, Conn., 1983—; alumni spkr. Grad. Faculty New Sch. for Social Rsch., 1977; del. Salvador/U.S. women-to-women dialogue sponsored by Found. for Compasionate Soc., Cuernevaca, Mex. 1989, del. conf. on Media in a Time of Crisis, Sweden, 1989, delegate conferences on Women and Peace in Crete, Greece (1992) on women Refugees in a Time of War (Athens, Greece, 1994) and on Media in Wartime (Athens, Greece, 1997), expert group of U.N. Divsn. of Advancement of Women, meeting on women in pub. life, Vienna, 1991; spkr. various symposia. Recipient 2nd prize Quest for Peace Essay contest, Citizen Edn. for Peace Project, 1988; grantee rsch. grantee, Am. Coun. Learned Socs., 1990, SUNY Rsch. Found., 1984, 1986, 1987, 1989, 1990, 1991, 1996, 2000. Mem.: NOW, AAUW (Issue Focus grant 1988—89), International Advisory bd of Radio for Peace Internat., Internat. Action Ctr., Women's Internat. League for Peace and Freedom, NY State Sociol. Assn. (bd. dirs. 1974—75), Assn. for Humanist Sociology (spkr. annual meeting 2001), Am. Sociol. Assn., Soc. Study Social Problems, World Federalist Assn., War Resisters League, Internat. Peace Rsch. Assn. (del. to 25th Ann. Conf. Netherlands 1990, chair N.Am. sect., women and peace commn. 1990—91, Malta 1994), Phi Beta Kappa. Home: 160 Hurley Rd Salt Point NY 12578-3140 Office: SUNY Sociology Dept New Paltz NY 12561

SCOTT, BRADWELL DAVIDSON, educational administrator, writer, consultant; b. L.A., Sept. 12, 1949; s. Clifford Norton and Florence Marguerite (Jafraty) S.; m. Darian Jeanne Garritson, June 30, 1974; children: Nathan Hunter, Jamieson Fair. BFA, Calif. Inst. Arts, 1971; MA, Pacific Sch. Religion, 1978. Dir. Sherwood Oaks H.S., Van Nuys, Calif., 1971-73; sr. editl. assoc. U. and Coll. Orgn. Activities, Boston, 1979-89; headmaster Chgo. Jr. Sch., Elgin, Ill., 1989-92; ednl. affairs dir. Kumon Ednl. Inst., Boston, from 1992. Adv. grad. study Grad. Theol. Union/U. Calif., Berkeley, 1978-84; introducer, accreditation evaluator Ind. Schs. Assn. of the Ctrl. States, 1990; co-founder, publicist Fox Valley Ill. Phi Delta Kappa Ednl. Fraternity, Elgin, 1990-92; prin.'s mentor Raymond (Wash.) Pub. Schs. Dist., 1992-94; ednl. writer cons., sr. assoc. Diversified

Creative Svcs., Boston, 1992—. Editor, author (ednl. newsletter) Approaching Thunder: Developments on the American Educational Horizon, 1993—; author Regional Lab., Edn. Devel. Ctr., and Inst. for Responsive Edn. Mem. ASCD, Ednl. Press Assn. Avocations: video prodn., writing poetry. Home: Hampstead, NH. Died Jan. 25, 2002.

SCOTT, C. PAUL, psychiatrist, educator; b. Pitts., June 2, 1943; m. Nancy Ipp, Aug. 17, 1969; children: Rebecca, John. AB, U. Pa., 1964; MD, Case Western Res. U., 1968; postgrad., Pitts. Psychoanalytic Inst., 1984. Diplomate Am. Bd. Psychiatry and Neurology. Intern Mt. Sinai Hosp., Cleve., 1968-69; resident in gen. medicine Univ. Hosp., Cleve., 1969-70; resident in psychiatry Western Psychiat. Inst., Pitts., 1972-75, pres. med. staff, 1985-87; v.p. med. staff U. Pitts. Med. Ctr., 1995-97, clin. prof. Sch. Medicine; clin. assoc. prof. psychiatry M.C.P. Hahnemann U. With USPHS, 1970-72. Fellow Am. Psychiat. Assn. (Falk fellow 1972-75, disting.); mem. Pa. Psychiat. Assn., Pitts. Psychiat. Assn., Pitts. Psychoanalytic Assn. Avocation: golf. Office: 401 Shady Ave Apt C202 Pittsburgh PA 15206-4800

SCOTT, CAROL LEE, child care educator; b. Monte Vista, Colo., Jan. 10, 1944; d. Robert A. and Thelma G. (Allen) Jay; m. Bates E. Shaw, June 4, 1966 (dec. Feb. 1976); children: Crystal A., Sharon L.; m. James W. Scott, July 23, 1977. BA in Home Econs., Friends U., 1965; MS, Okla. State U., 1973. Cert. in family and consumer scis., child and parenting specialist; lic. profl. counselor. Receptionist Cen. Assembly of God Ch., Wichita, Kans., summer 1965; office worker Henry's Inc., Wichita, 1965-66; tchr. home econs. Wichita High Sch. South, 1966, Cir. High Sch., Towanda, Kans., 1966-68, Fairfax (Okla.) High Sch., 1968-74; tchr. vocat. home econs. Derby (Kans.) High Sch., 1974-75; child devel. specialist Bi-State Mental Health Found., Ponca City, Okla., 1975-87; instr. child care Pioneer Tech. Ctr., Ponca City, 1987-98, dir., 1987-89, 93-98; training, curriculum splist. Tinker AFB, Ponca City, Okla., 1998—2001; dir. CDC East Tinker AFB, Okla., 2001—. Cons. Phil Fitzgerald Assocs. Archs., Ponca City, 1980, Head Start Okla., 1981-86; trainer, paraprofl. Child Care Careers, 1980—; validator Early Childhood programs, Nat. Assn. Edn. Young Children 1992—; adj. faculty Rose State Coll., Midwest City, Okla., 2002-. Contbg. author Child Abuse Prevention Mini Curriculum. Mem. sch. bd. Ponca City Schs., 1982-85, title IV-A parent com., 1985-89; area chmn. Heart Fund, 1985; chmn. edn. com. Dist. XVII Child Abuse Prevention Task Force, Okla., 1985-98, treas., 1989-98; mem. cultural affairs com. Ponca City Adv. Bd., 1986-89; co-chair Week of the Young Child Com. for Kay County, 1991-98; mem. curriculum adv. com. Ctr. Early Childhood Profl. Devel., Univ. Okla., 1998-. Mem. Am. Assn. Family and Consumer Scis., Okla. Assn. Family and Consumer Scis., Early Childhood Assn. Okla., (sec. 1999, 2000), So. Early Childhood Assn., No. Okla. Early Childhood Assn. (chmn. 1992-93, 93-94, exec. com. at-large 1994-98), Mid Del. Early Childhood Assn. (pres. 2002—), Nat. Assn. for Edn. Young Children. Republican. Methodist. Home: 205 Wimbledon Rd Midwest City OK 73130-4917 Office: 72SPTG/SVYE 6120 Arnold St Tinker AFB OK 73145-8106

SCOTT, CHARLOTTE H. business educator; b. Yonkers, NY, Mar. 18, 1925; d. Edgar B. and Charlotte Agnes (Palmer) Hanley; m. Nathan Alexander Scott, Jr., Dec. 21, 1946; children: Nathan Alexander Scott, Leslie Kristin Scott Ashamu. AB, Barnard Coll., 1947; postgrad., Am. U., 1949-53; MBA, U. Chgo., 1964; LL.D., Allegheny Coll., 1981. Research asso. Nat. Bur. Econ. Research, N.Y.C., 1947-48; economist R.W. Goldsmith Assos., Washington, 1948-55, U. Chgo., 1955-56, Fed. Res. Bank, Chgo., 1956-71, asst. v.p., 1971-76; prof. bus. adminstrn. and commerce, sr. fellow Tayloe Murphy Inst., U. Va., Charlottesville, 1976-86; prof. commerce and edn. U. Va., Charlottesville, 1986-98, prof. emeritus, 1998—. Bd. dirs. Atlantic Rural Expn., Inc.; mem. adv. bd. NationsBank Charlottesville, 1991-93; mem. nat. adv. bd. coun. SBA, 1979-82; mem. consumer adv. coun. bd. govs. FRS, 1979-82, vice chmn., 1980-81, chmn., 1981-82. Mem. editorial bd. Jour. Retail Banking, 1978-85, Jour. Internat. Assn. Personnel Women, 1981-85; contbr. articles to profl. jours. Pres. women's bd. Chgo. Urban League, 1967-69; mem. Va. Commn. on Status of Women, 1982-85, Gov.'s Commn. on Va.'s Future, 1982-85, Gov.'s Commn. on Efficiency in Govt., 1985-87; treas. Va. Women's Cultural History Project, 1982-85; bd. dirs. Boys and Girls Club of Charlottesville/Albemarle; governing bd. Charlottesville/Albemarle Found., 1993—; mem. adv. bd. Ash Lawn-Highland Mus.; treas. Episcopal Diocese, Coun. Region XV, 1999—. Mem. Internat. Assn. Personnel Women (v.p. mems.-at-large 1980-82), Assn. Study of Higher Edn., Va. Assn. Econs., Acad. Mgmt., Barnard Coll./Columbia U. Alumnae Assn. (bd. dirs. 1977-81, trustee 1977-81). Episcopalian. Office: U Va McIntire Sch Commerce Monroe Hall Charlottesville VA 22903 Home: 250 Pantops Mountain Rd Charlottesville VA 22911

SCOTT, DAVID MICHAEL, pharmacy educator; b. St. Paul, July 5, 1949; s. David Marvin and Cecelia (Ventura) S.; m. Patti L. Anderson, May 1, 1976; children: Michael, Justin, Nathan. BS, U. Minn., 1972, MPH, 1982, PhD, 1987. Lic. pharmacist, Minn. Pharmacy intern United Hosps., St. Paul, 1972-73, staff pharmacist, 1973-75; pharmacy dir. Cmty.-Univ. Health Care Ctr., Mpls., 1975-84; clin. instr. pharmacy U. Minn., Mpls., 1975-86; assoc. dir. orthop. rsch. St. Paul Ramsey Med. Ctr., 1984-86; asst. prof. U. Nebr. Med. Ctr., Omaha, 1986-95, assoc. prof., 1996—2003, N.D. State U., Fargo, 2003—. Project epidemiologist Toward a Drug-Free Nebr., Nebr. Dept. Edn., Lincoln, 1989-94; mem. Springville Elem. Sch. Drug Abuse, Omaha, 1988-97; faculty advisor Acad. Student Pharmacists, APHA, Omaha, 1994-2003. Contbr. articles to sci. jours. Coach Keystone Little League, Omaha, 1991-94; bd. dirs. Butler-Gast YMCA, Omaha, 1992-96; vice chmn. bd. dirs., 1994-95; chmn. Nebr. PACT (Pulling Am. Cmtys. Together) Sch. Truancy Task Force, Lincoln, 1994-97. Grantee, Am. Assn. Colls. Pharmacy, Alexandria, Va., 1995—97, U.S. Dept. Edn., Washington, 1996—97, U.S. Dept. Health and Human Svcs. Health Resources and Svcs. Adminstrn., 2000—03. Avocations: jogging, softball, golf, reading, basketball. Office: ND State Univ Coll of Pharmcy 123 Sudro Hall Fargo ND 58105

SCOTT, DAVID ROBIN, electrical engineering educator; b. Duluth, Minn., June 2, 1950; s. Howard McKenzie and Doris Christine (Anderson) S.; m. Jane Carol Robertstad, Dec. 27, 1973; children: Eric Daniel, Nathan Wesley. BS in Elec. Engring., S.D. State U., 1972, MS in Elec. Engring., 1974; PhD in Elec. Engring., N.Mex. State U., 1990. Electronics engr. USAF, Ft. Worth, 1974, Anaheim, Calif., 1974-77; gen. engr. Def. Contract Adminstrn. Svc., Mpls., 1977-81; lectr. U. Tex., El Paso, 1981-83; instr. N.Mex. State U., Las Cruces, 1983-90; asst. prof. No. Ariz. U., Flagstaff, 1990-97, assoc. prof., 1997—, asst. chmn., 1998—2000, interim. chmn., 2000—02. Named Civil Servant of Yr. U.S. Govt., Mpls., 1981; Wakonse fellow No. Ariz. U., Flagstaff, 1994. Mem. IEEE (outstanding student 1972), Resna, Phi Kappa Phi, Eta Kappa Nu, Tau Beta Pi. Republican. Avocations: bicycling, woodworking. Home: 3920 E Kokopelli Ln Flagstaff AZ 86004-7873 Office: No Ariz U PO Box 15600 Flagstaff AZ 86011-0001

SCOTT, DAVID WARREN, statistics educator; b. Oak Park, Ill., July 16, 1950; s. John V. and Nancy (Mellers) S.; m. Jean Charlotte Madera, June 15, 1974; children: Hilary Kathryn, Elizabeth Alison, Warren Robert. BA, Rice U., 1972, MA, PhD, Rice U., 1976. Asst. prof. Baylor Coll. Medicine, Houston, 1976-79, Rice U., Houston, 1979-80, assoc. prof., 1980-85, chmn. stats. dept., 1990-93, Noah Harding prof. stats.; vis. prof. Stanford U., Palo Alto, Calif., 1985-86. Vis. prof. Dept. Def., Ft. Meade, Md., 1993-94, 99-2000. Author: Multivariate Density Estimation, 1992; mem. editl. bd. John Wiley & Sons Probability and Stats. Series, 1994—; past editor jour. Computational Stats. and Jour. Statis. Scis.; editor Jour. Computational and Graphical Stats., 2000—03; contbr. articles to profl. publs. Mem. applied and Theoretical stats. com. Nat. Rsch. Coun., 2001-03. Grantee NASA, 1982-84, Office Naval Rsch., 1985-93, NSF, 1993—. Fellow Internat. Stats. Inst., Inst. Math. Stats., Am. Statis. Assn. (assoc. editor jour. 1983-94); mem. Inst. Math. Statis. (cons.). Avocations: woodworking, hiking, family. Home: 4143 Marlowe St Houston TX 77005-1953 Office: Rice U Dept Stats 6100 Main St # Ms-138 Houston TX 77005-1827 E-mail: scottdw@rice.edu.

SCOTT, DONALD MICHAEL, writer, educator; b. L.A., Sept. 26, 1943; s. Bernard Hendry and Marguerita (Baroni) Scott, Barbara (Lannin) Scott (Stepmother); m. Patricia Ilene Pancaost, Oct. 24, 1964 (div. June 1971); children: William Bernard, Kenneth George. BA, San Francisco State U., 1965, MA, 1986. Cert. tchr. Calif. Tchr. Mercy HS, San Francisco, 1968-71; pk. ranger Calif. State Pk. Sys., Half Moon Bay, 1968-77; tchr. adult divsn. Jefferson Union HS Dist., Daly City, Calif., 1973-87; dir. NASA-NPS Project Wider Focus, Daly City, 1983-90, also bd. dirs., dir. Geo. Sci. Spl. Projects San Francisco, 1990—; nat. pk. ranger, naturalist Grant-Kohrs Ranch Nat. Hist. Site, Deer Lodge, Mont., 1987-88; nat. pk. ranger pub. affairs fire team Yellowstone Nat. Pk., 1988. Rsch. subject NASA, Mountain View, Calif., 1986—90; guest artist Yosemite (Calif.) Nat. Pk., 1986; nat. pk. ranger Golden Gate Nat. Recreation Area Nat. Pk. Svc., San Francisco, 1986, nat. pk. svc. history cons. to Bay Dist., 1988—94; adj. asst. prof. Skyline Coll., 1989—94, Coll. San Mateo, 1992—94; aerospace edn. specialist NASA/OSU/AESP, 1994—; state rep. Mont. and Nev. AESP, 1999—2003; cons. Friends Eastern State Penitentiary Project, Phila., 1993. Co-author: (book) From Montana to Mars, 2003; contbr. articles and photographs to profl. jours., mags., chapters to books. Panelist Cmty. Bds. San Francisco, 1978—87; active CONTACT Orgn., 1991—, bd. dirs., 1995—; mem. edn. working group Case for Mars VI, Boulder, 1996; pres. Youth for Kennedy, Lafayette, Calif., 1960; city chair Yes on A Com., So. San Francisco, San Mateo County, Calif., 1986. Mem.: Orange County Space Soc., Mars Soc. (founding mem., mem. ednl. task force), Planetary Soc. (charter mem.), Internat. Tech. Edn. Assn., Nat. Coun. Tchrs. Math., Nat. Sci. Tchrs. Assn., Nat. Assn. Interpretation (founding mem.), Friends George R. Stewart, Wider Focus, Yosemite Assn. (life). Avocations: photography, hiking, camping, travel. Home and Office: PO Box 978 Oceano CA 93445

SCOTT, DOROTHY ELAINE, elementary education educator; b. Gideon, Mo., Apr. 22, 1939; d. Harold Augustus and Louise Leone (Nickens) Jones; married, June 6, 1959; children: Robin Jennifer, Scott. BS in Edn., Tex. Christian U., 1980, MEd, 1985. Cert. elem. tchr., elem. art tchr., Tex. Sec. acctg. West Coast Airlines, Seattle, 1959-61; exec. sec. Geophys. Svcs., Inc., Dallas, 1961-68, Gifford-Hill, Inc., Dallas, 1969; tchr. Arlington (Tex.) Ind. Sch. Dist., 1980-90; coord. gifted edn. Grand Prairie (Tex.) Ind. Sch. Dist., 1990-92; tchr. Hurst-Euless-Bedford Ind. Sch. Dist., Bedford, Tex., 1992—. Cons. Tex. Christian U., Ft. Worth, 1986, 89; active staff devel. various Tex. sch. dists., 1985—; citizen Amb. Reading Delegation to Russia, 1995; Literacy '96 Delegation to the Republic of So. Africa, 1996; Mission in Understanding to the Three Gorges of the Yangtze River, Beijing, and Shanghai People's Republic of China, 1998. Troop leader Girl Scouts U.S., Dallas, 1976-80; pres. local PTA, Grand Prairie; active Girls Club Am., Arlington, 1980—. Recipient A.W.A.R.E. Found. award, Arlington, 1990, Thanks to Tchrs. award Apple Computer Co., Dallas, 1990. Mem. Nat. Assn. Gifted Children, Nat. Art Edn. Assn. (presenter), Am. Craft Coun., Tex. Reading Assn., Nat. Coun. Tchrs. of English, Nat. PTA (life), Tex. Coun. Tchrs. of Math., Tex. Assn. Supervision and Curriculum Devel., Nat./State Leadership Tng. Inst. on Gifted and Talented, Metroplex Assn. Tchrs. of Elem. Sci., Tex. Art Edn. Assn. (presenter), Internat. Reading Assn. (chairperson S.W. conv. 1990), Tex. Alliance for Arts (founding), Gifted Student Inst., Tex. Assn. Gifted/Talented, Arlington Reading Assn., Kappa Delta Pi. Avocations: art appreciation, travel, readinig, sports, music. Home: 1909 Rock Creek Dr Grand Prairie TX 75050-2235

SCOTT, JACQUELINE DELMAR PARKER, educational association administrator, business administrator, consultant, fundraiser, educator; b. L.A., May 18, 1947; d. Thomas Aubrey and Daisy Beatrice (Singleton) Parker (div.); children: Tres Mali, Olympia Ranee, Stephen Thomas. AA in Theatre Arts, L.A. City Coll., 1970; BA in Econs., Calif. State U., Dominguez Hills, Carson, 1973; MBA, Golden Gate U., 1979; EdD, Pepperdine U., 1999. Cert. parenting instr., 2000; holder various Microsoft certs. Sales clk. Newberry's Dept. Store, L.A., 1963-65; long distance operator Pacific Telephone Co., L.A., 1965-66; PBX operator Sears, Roebuck & Co., L.A., 1966-68; retail clk. Otey's Grocery Store, Nashville, 1968-69; collector N.Am. Credit, L.A., 1970-71; office mgr. Dr. S. Edward Tucker, L.A., 1972-74; staff coord. sch. edn. dept. Calif. State U., 1973-74; from bank auditor to corp. loan asst. Security Pacific Bank, L.A., 1974-77; from dist. credit analyst to asst. v.p. Crocker Nat. Bank, L.A., 1977-80; from capital planning adminstr. to project bus. mgr. TRW, Inc., Redondo Beach, Calif., 1980-87, lab. sr. bus. adminstr., 1984-86, project bus. mgr., 1986-87, div. sr. bus. adminstr., 1987-92; ptnr., co-author, co-facilitator, cons. Diversified Event Planners, Inc., L.A., 1990-93; asst. area devel. dir. United Negro Coll. Fund, L.A., 1993-96; cons. parenting edn., 1994—. Cmty. coll. instr.; cons. in field. Co-founder career growth awareness com. TRW Employees Bootstrap, Redondo Beach, Calif., 1980, pres., 1983-84; role model Inglewood High Sch., TRW Youth Motivation Task Force, Redondo Beach, 1981-83, Crozier Jr. High Sch., 1981-83, Monroe Jr. High Sch., Redondo Beach, 1981-83, Frank D. Parent Career Day, TRW Affirmative Action Com., Redondo Beach, 1987, St. Bernard's Career Day, 1991; chairperson community involvement com., 1981, chairperson disaster com., 1989-90; chairperson gen. and local welfare com. TRW Employees Charitable Orgn., 1989-90, disaster com. chair, 1988-89, bd. dirs. 1987-89; pres. Mgmt. Effectiveness Program Alumnae, L.A., 1982-83, TRW Employees Bootstrap Program Alumnae, 1983-84; group leader Jack & Jill of Am., Inc., South L.A., 1980-81, parliamentarian, 1986-87, v.p., 1981-82, chpt. pres., 1984-86, regional dir., 1987-89, nat. program dir., 1992-96, liaison to Young Black Scholars Program, 1986—; bd. dirs. Adolescent Pregnancy Child Watch, 1993—; nat. program dir., bd. dirs. Jack & Jill Am. Found., 1992-96; L.A. mem. Nat. Black Child Devel. Inst., 1994—; vol. ARC, 1994; parenting instr. Am. Red Cross, 1994-96; founder Jack & Jill of Am. Leadership Devel. Program, 1993. Recipient commendation NAACP, 1985, United Negro Coll. Fund, 1986, United Way, 1988, Austistic Children's Telephon, 1980, Inglewood Sch. Dist., 1981, Pres. award Harbor Area Chpt. Links, Inc., 1985, Women of Achievement award City of L.A., Black Pers. Assn., 1994. Mem. Black Women's Forum (sponsor), Phi Delta Kappa, Delta Sigma Theta. Avocations: reading, dancing. E-mail: jscott4@earthlink.net.

SCOTT, JOHN ROLAND, business law educator; b. Wichita Falls, Tex, May 13, 1937; s. John and Margaret S.; m. Joan Carol Redding, Sept. 5, 1959; 1 child, John Howard. LLB, Baylor Sch. Law, Waco, Tex., 1962. Bar: Tex. 1962, Alaska 1970, Tex., 1965, U.S. Dist. Ct. (we. dist.), U.S. Dist. Ct. Alaska 1975. Assoc. litigation sect. Lynch & Chappell, Midland, Tex., 1962-65; regional atty. Atlantic Richfield Co., Midland, 1965-79; sr. atty. Anchorage, 1969-77, Dallas, 1977-80; v.p., assoc. gen. counsel Mitchell Energy & Devel. Corp., Houston, 1980-82; asst. gen. counsel Hunt Oil Co., Dallas, 1982-84, v.p., chief counsel, 1984-91, sr. v.p. gen. counsel, 1994-2001; adj. prof. bus. law Dallas Bapt. U., Dallas, 2001—. Bar examiner in Alaska, 1974-77 Mem. State Bar Tex. (lectr.), Dallas Bar Assn., ABA, Phi Alpha Delta. Republican. Office: 3801 Hanover Ave Dallas TX 75225-7117

SCOTT, JOHN PAUL, medical educator; b. Kamunting, Malaysia, June 26, 1956; came to U.S., 1991; s. Joseph and Agnes (Beldon) S.; m. Lesley Carol Poole, Dec. 5, 1981; children: Christopher Michael, Elizabeth Mary, David Matthew. MB ChB, Otago U., Dunedin, New Zealand, 1979, MD, 1990; MS, Cambridge U., England, 1992; MS in Econs., U. London, 1999; LLB (hon.), U. Wolverhampton, 2000; LLM, U. Glamorgan, 2003, U. Glasgow, 2002. Resident Otago U., Dunedin, New Zealand, 1979-83; assoc. prof. transplantation Mayo Clinic, Rochester, Minn., 1991-96, prof., 1996—. Internat. advisor, 2000—. Contbr. articles to profl. jours. Fellow dept. pulmonary medicine Otago U., 1984-85, Cambridge U., 1985-88, sr. fellow, 1988-91. Fellow Royal Coll. Physicians (internat. advisor 2000—), Royal Australian Coll. Physicians, Am. Coll. Physicians, Royal Statis. Soc.; mem. Am. Thoracic Soc. (Minn. rep. 1993-96), Royal Soc. New Zealand, Internat. Soc. Philosophical Enquiry, Mayo Thoracic Soc. (pres. 1996-99). Avocations: philosophy, economics, chess, climbing, travel. Office: Mayo Clinic 200 1st St SW Rochester MN 55905-0002

SCOTT, JUDITH MYERS, elementary education educator; b. Loredo, Mo., Dec. 29, 1940; d. Wilbur Charles and Dora Emma (Frazier) Myers; m. David Ronald Scott, Dec. 18, 1965; children: Russell Myers, Geoffrey Douglas. BA in Edn., Ariz. State U., 1962, MA in edn., 1970. Cert. tchr., Ariz. Tchr. 2d grade Scottsdale (Ariz.) Elem. Dist., 1962-64; tchr. 1st grade Cahuilla Sch., Palm Springs, Calif., 1965, Palm Crest Sch., La Canada, Calif., 1968-69; tchr. Ak Chin Community Sch., Maricopa, Ariz., 1969-70; grad. asst. Ariz. State U., Tempe, 1970-71; pvt. tutor Tempe, 1970-77; tchr. Dayspring Presch., Tempe, 1978-83; tchr. 3d grade Waggoner Elem. Sch., Kyrene, Ariz., 1984-86; reading specialsit Tempe Elem. Sch. Dist., 1986-90, tchr., trainer collaborative literacy intervention project, 1990—. Exec. dir. Beauty for All Seasons, Tempe, 1982-86; presenter in field. Coord. New Zealand Tchr. Exch., Tempe Sister Cities, 1992—. Mem. NEA, ASCD, IRA, ARA, Ariz. Sch. Adminstrs., Ariz. Edn. Assn. Methodist. Avocations: painting, reading, hiking. Home: 1940 E Calle De Caballos Tempe AZ 85284-2507 Office: Tempe Elem Sch Dist 3205 S Rural Rd Tempe AZ 85282-3853

SCOTT, KENNETH EUGENE, lawyer, educator; b. Western Springs, Ill., Nov. 21, 1928; s. Kenneth L. and Bernice (Albright) S.; m. Viviane H. May, Sept. 22, 1956 (dec. Feb. 1982); children: Clifton, Jeffrey, Linda; m. Priscilla Gay, July 30, 1989; children: Ashley (dec. Apr. 2002), Shaler. BA in Econs., Coll. William and Mary, 1949; MA in Polit. Sci., Princeton U., 1953; LLB, Stanford U., 1956. Bar: N.Y. 1957, Calif. 1957, D.C. 1967. Assoc. Sullivan & Cromwell, N.Y.C., 1956-59, Musick, Peeler & Garrett, L.A., 1959-61; chief dep. savs. and loan commr. State of Calif., L.A., 1961-63; gen. counsel Fed. Home Loan Bank Bd., Washington, 1963-67; Parsons prof. law and bus. Stanford (Calif.) Law Sch., 1968-95, emeritus, 1995—; sr. rsch. fellow Hoover Instn., 1978-95, emeritus, 1995—; fellow Am. Acad. Berlin, 2001. Mem. Shadow Fin. Regulatory Com., 1986—, Fin. Economists Roundtable, 1991—; bd. dirs. Am. Century Mut. Funds, Mountain View, Calif. Author: (with others) Retail Banking in the Electronic Age, 1977; co-editor: The Economics of Corporation Law and Securities Regulation, 1980. Mem. ABA, Calif. Bar Assn., Phi Beta Kappa, Order of Coif, Pi Kappa Alpha, Omicron Delta Kappa. Home: 610 Gerona Rd Stanford CA 94305-8453 Office: Stanford Law Sch Stanford CA 94305-8610 E-mail: kenscott@stanford.edu.

SCOTT, L. CAROL, educational consultant; b. L.A., Jan. 27, 1954; d. Robert Lincoln and Nancy Jane (Kastman) Scott; m. Lynn Richter Toburen, Apr. 18, 1976 (div. May 1979); m. Constance Fleming, Dec. 24, 1989. BA in Human Devel. and Family Life, U. Kans., 1975, MA in Early Childhood Edn., 1979, PhD in Devel. and Child Psychology, 1995. Supr., instr. Child Study Ctr., U. Maine, Orono, 1979-82; contracting cons. LC Assocs, Kansas City, 1985—; lab. supr. U. Kans., Overland Park, 1982-89; exec. dir. Child Care Assocs. Johnson County, Overland Park, 1989-91; project dir. TRANSITION Independence (Mo.) Pub. Schs., 1992-95; dir. Met. Coun. Child Care, Kansas City, 1995-99. Program rep. nat. transition rsch. adv. panel Civitan Internat. Rsch. Ctr., U. Ala., Birmingham, 1993—95; mem. facilitator, chair coms. Met. Coun. Child Care/Mid. Am. Regional Coun., Kansas City, 1989—95; co-chair adv. com. child care and devel. block grants Olathe Area Social and Rehab. Svcs., 1991; mem. Kans. State Child Care Adv. Com., Salina, 1989—91. Co-author: (instr.'s manual) Mainstreaming in Early Childhood Education, 1980; contbr. articles to profl. jours. Mem. dir. Kansas City Women's Chorus, 1985—93; mem. adv. com. corp. child care provider resource and referral network Heart Am. Family Svcs., Kansas City, 1986—87. Named Outstanding Vol. Svc., Coaliation Prevention Child Abuse-Johnson County, 1987. Mem.: Nat. Assn. Edn. Young Children (co-chair Week Young Child 1989—90, 2d v.p. 1988—91, pres. Mo. bd. dirs. 2002—, Outstanding Yearly Svc. award 1988, Outstanding Extended Svc. award 2000). Avocations: choral singing, guitar, needle and bead work, reading, creative writing. E-mail: lcassoc@starband.net.

SCOTT, LINDA ANN, principal, elementary education educator; b. St. Louis, Jan. 21, 1955; d. Jay R. and Bernadette (Hogan) S. BS, Youngstown State U., Ohio, 1979; MS, Gov.'s State U., Park Forest, Ill., 1991. Tchr. Bishop Blanchette, Joliet, Ill., 1981-85, St. Joseph's, Joliet, Ill., 1985-86, Hufford Jr. H.S., Joliet, Ill., 1986-92; asst. prin. Washington Jr. H.S., Joliet, 1992-99; prin. A.O. Marshall Sch., 1999—. Ednl. coord. Warren-Sharpe Community Ctr., Joliet, 1990-98. Mem. life PTA, 1990—. No. Ill. U. grantee, 1990, Argonne Nat. Lab. grantee, 1990, U. Ill. grantee, 1991. Mem. Ill. Coun. Tchrs. of Math. Home: 7324 Heritage Ct Frankfort IL 60423-9587 Office: AO Marshall Sch 319 Harwood St Joliet IL 60432-2797

SCOTT, MELLOUISE JACQUELINE, educational media specialist; b. Sanford, Fla., Mar. 1, 1943; d. Herbert and Mattye (Williams) Cherry; m. Robert Edward Scott, Jr., July 1, 1972; 1 child, Nolan Edward. BA, Talladega Coll., 1965; MLS, Rutgers U., 1974, EdM, 1976, EdS, 1982. Media specialist Seminole County Bd. Edn., Sanford, 1965-72, Edison (N.J.), 1972-98; ret. Edison (N.J.) Bd. Edn., 1999. Mem. ALA, N.J. Ret. Educators Assn., NEA. Baptist. Home: PO Box 1771 Sanford FL 32772-1771

SCOTT, MICHELLE WILLIAMS, elementary education educator; b. Daytona Beach, Fla., Nov. 19, 1956; d. Lee Arthur and Marian (Nattiel) Gibson; m. William Randolph Scott, Aug. 12, 1978; children: Maury Darnell, Natalya Chivon, Trenton Demonz. BS, Fla. Agrl. and Mech. U., 1978. Cert. early childhood, elem. educator, middle grade English, social studies educator, reading and ESOL. Tchr. Sebastian (Fla.) River Middle Jr. High Sch., 1989-91, Tchrs.-Parents Helping Their Child, Sebastian, 1989. Sixth grade dept. chair Sebastian River Middle Jr. High Sch., 1988-93, reading club sponsor, 1989-91, faculty coun., 1988-91, tchr. support team, 1988-92, sch. improvement team, 1992-93, blue ribbon task force, 1989-90. Mem. Progressive Civic League, Gifford, Fla., 1988—, Fla. Agrl. and Mech. U. Alumni, Vero Beach, Fla., 1978—, Fla. Edn. Assn., Indian River County, 1978—. Recipient Golden apple award Indian River County Sch. Bd., 1990, Tchr. of Yr., 1990, 91, Svc. award, 1990. Mem. Alpha Kappa Alpha Sorority. Democrat. Baptist. Avocations: reading, sewing, travel. Home: 4275 47th Pl Vero Beach FL 32967-1136 Office: Sebastian River Mid Sch 9400 State Road 512 Sebastian FL 32958-6402

SCOTT, PAULA LAGRUE, special education educator; b. New Orleans, Dec. 22, 1955; d. Irvin and Selena (Columbus) Lagrue; m. Joe Scott, Jr., June 9, 1979; 1 child, Elizabeth Denise. BA, Southeastern La. U., 1977; MA, So. U., Baton Rouge, 1986; postgrad., So. U., 1989, Southeastern La. U., 1989. Cert. parish or city sch. supr., dir. spl. edn., parish or city sch. supr. instrn., elem. tchr., mentally retarded, learning disabled, mild-moderate elem., supr. student tchrs., elem. sch. prin., La. Tchr. Tangipahoa Parish Sch. Bd., Amite, La., 1978; tchr. spl. edn. Livingston Parish Sch. Bd., Livingston, La., 1978—. Named Regional Spl. Edn. Tchr. of Yr., State Dept. Edn., 1993. Mem. Coun. for Exceptional Children, Am. Fedn. Tchrs., La. Fedn. Tchrs., Livingston Fedn. Tchrs. Sch. Employees. Democrat. Pentecostal. Avocations: sewing, crafts, singing, crossword puzzles. Home: PO Box 778 Albany LA 70711-0778 Office: Albany Lower Elem Sch PO Box 970 Albany LA 70711-0970

SCOTT, PHYLLIS WRIGHT, coach, music educator; b. Lancaster, Pa., Nov. 9, 1925; d. George Bronson and Edythe Heckroth Wright; m. Edgar Lee Arthur Mixon, Oct. 12, 1946 (div. Nov. 1954); children: Thomas Lee, Raymond Dean, Michael George; m. Gilbert Henry Scott, June 23, 1976 (dec. May 1995). Grad., H.S., 1963; studied music, studied skating. Skating tchr. Health Ctr., Norfolk, Va., 1947, Ringing Rocks Park, Pottstown, Pa., 1945, Gt. Leopard Roller Rink, Chester, Pa., 1946—47, Ringing Rocks Park Roller Rink, Lancaster, Pa., 1948—49, Playland Roller Rink, York, Pa., 1950—51, Skateland Roller Rink, Camden, NJ, 1952—55, Exton (Pa.) Roller Rink, 1956—57; music tchr. Holiday Music, Pennsauken, NJ, 1962—64; pvt. music tchr. Bellmawr, NJ, 1965—98, Keyboard Am., Lewes, Del., 1998—. Prodr.: (skating shows), 1944—62. Den mother Cub Scouts of Am., Bellmawr, NJ, 1950—54. Recipient Silver-Bronze Dance medal, Roller Skating Rinks Operator Assn., 1943, Bronze Figures award, 1944. Mem.: Order of Eastern Star. Republican. Baptist. Avocations: needlepoint, playing keyboard instruments. Home: 29261 White Pine Rd Milton DE 19968 E-mail: Pscott1152@aol.com.

SCOTT, RALPH C. physician, educator; b. Bethel, Ohio, June 7, 1921; s. John Carey and Leona (Laycock) S.; m. Rosemary Ann Schultz, June 26, 1945; children: Susan Ann, Barbara Lynne, Marianne Elizabeth. BS, U. Cin., 1943, MD, 1945. Diplomate: Am. Bd. Internal Medicine (subspecialty cardiovascular disease). InternUniv. Hosps. U. Iowa, 1945-46; resident, asst. dept. pathology Coll. Medicine U. Cin., 1948-49, fellow internal medicine Coll. Medicine, 1949-53, fellow cardiology Coll. Medicine, 1953-57, mem. faculty Coll. Medicine, from 1950, prof. medicine Coll. Medicine, from 1968; staff clinics Cin. Gen. Hosp., 1950-75, clinician in internal medicine, 1952-75, dir. cardiac clinics, 1965-75, attending physician med. service, from 1958. Staff VA Hosp., Cin. 1954-86, 1992—, cons., 1961-86, 92—; attending physician Med. Svc., Christian R. Holmes Hosp., Cin., 1957-86; attending staff USAF Hosp., Wright Patterson AFB, 1960—; staff Good Samaritan Hosp., Cin., 1961—, cons., 1967—; staff Jewish Hosp., Cin., 1957—, cons., 1968—; cons. Children's Hosp., Cin., 1968—; attending physician Providence Hosp., Cin., 1971—, dir. cardiology, 1971-94. Contbr. articles to med. jours.; editorial bd. Am. Heart Jour, 1967-79, Jour. Electrocardiology, 1967—; editor: Electro-Cardiographic-Pathologic Conf., Jour. Electrocardiology, 1967—, Clin. Cardiology and Diabetes, 5 vols, 1981. Capt. AUS, 1946-48. Nat. Heart Inst. grantee, 1964-68, 67-74, 76-82, 1985-90. Fellow ACP, Am. Coll. Cardiology, Am. Coll. Chest Physicians, Coun. Clin. Cardiology, Coun. Clin. Epidemiology and Prevention; mem. Ohio State Med. Assn., Cin. Acad. Medicine, Cen. Soc. Clin. Rsch., Am. Heart Assn., Cin. Soc. Internal Medicine, Heart Assn. Southwestern Ohio, Am. Fedn. for Clin. Rsch., Internat. Cardiovascular Soc., Am. Soc. Preventive Cardiology, Sigma Xi, Alpha Omega Alpha, Phi Eta Sigma, Phi Chi. Home: Cincinnati, Ohio. Died Aug. 9, 2002.

SCOTT, REBECCA ANDREWS, retired biology educator; b. Sunny Hill, La., June 4, 1939; d. Hayward and Dorothy (Nicholson) Andrews; m. Earl P. Scott, June 8, 1957; children: Stephanie Scott Dilworth, Cheryl L. BS, So. U., 1962; MS, Eastern Mich. U., 1969. Biology thr., Detroit, 1966-68; sci. tchr. Ann Arbor (Mich.) Pub. Schs., 1968-69; biology tchr. North H.S., Mpls., 1972-2001, coord. math., sci. tch. magnet, 1986-2001, advisor Jets Sci. Club, ret., 2001. Mem. AAUW, LVW (pres. 1981-83, 87-89, treas. 1989-94), NSTA, Minn. Sci. Tchrs. Assn., Minn. Acad. Sci., Nat. Assn. Biology Tchrs., U. Minn. Women's Club, Iota Phi Lambda (pres. 1995-99, fin. sec., 1999—). Democrat. Baptist. Home: 3112 Wendhurst Ave Minneapolis MN 55418-1726

SCOTT, ROBERT ALLYN, academic administrator; b. Englewood, N.J., Apr. 16, 1939; s. William D. and Ann. F. (Waterman) S.; children: Ryan Keith, Kira Elizabeth. BA, Bucknell U., 1961; PhD, Cornell U., 1975; LLD, Ramapo Coll., 2000. Mgmt. trainee Procter & Gamble Co., Phila., 1961-63; asst. dir. admissions Bucknell U., Lewisburg, Pa., 1965-67; asst. dean Coll. Arts and Scis. Cornell U., Ithaca, 1967-69, assoc. dean, 1969-79, anthropology faculty, 1978-79; dir. acad. affairs Ind. Commn. for Higher Edn., Indpls., 1979-84, asst. commr., 1984-85; pres. Ramapo (N.J.) Coll., 1985-2000, Adelphi U., 2000—. Cons. Sta. WSKG Pub. TV and Radio, 1977-79, also to various colls. and univs., pubs., 1966—; mem. curriculum adv. com. Ind. Bd. Edn., 1984-87, Lilly Endowment Think Tank, 1984-86; mem. nat. adv. panel Ind. 21st Century Schooling Project, 1990-92; U.S. rep. to creation of U. Mobility Asian-Pacific, 1993—; U.S. rep. to meetings of Coun. European Rectors, 1991—; sr. advisor to U.S. State Dept. on Higher Edn. in Unesco European Region, 1997—; U.S. del. to UNESCO N.Am. and World Confs. on Higher Edn., 1998; sr. cons., chair N.J. Higher Edn. Restructuring Team, 1994; bd. dirs. iRV. Author books and monographs; editl. bd. Cornell Rev., 1976-79; book rev. editor Coll. and Univ., 1974-78; cons. editor Change mag., 1979-95; cons. editor Jour. Higher Edn., 1985—; exec. editor Saturday Evening Post book div. Curtis Pub. Co., 1982-85; contbr. articles to sociols., ednl. and popular publs. Trustee Bucknell U., 1976-78, First Unitarian Ch., Ithaca, 1970-73, 78-79, chmn., 1971-73, Unitarian Universalist Ch. of Indpls., 1980-85. With USNR, 1963-65. Spencer Found. rsch. grantee, 1977; recipient Sagamore of the Wabash award, 1986, Prudential Found. Leader of Yr. award, 1987, Disting. Svc. award West Bergen Mental Health Ctr., 1991, NYU Presdl. medal, 1994, Sci. and Edn. award Boy Scouts Am., 1993, Raoul Wallenberg Humanitarian Leadership award, 2000. Fellow Am. Anthrop. Assn.; mem. Am. Sociol. Assn., Am. Assn. Higher Edn., Coun. on Liberal Arts and Scis. (chair 1990-93), Am. Coun. on Edn. Commn. On Internat. Edn. (chair 1991-93), L.I. Assn., Global Kids, Inc., Regional Plan Assn., Nat. Fgn. Lang. Ctr., Brookings Instn. Study Group, Higher Edn. Colloquium (chmn. 1982-84, 96-98), N.J. Assn. of Coll. and Univs. (chair 1991-92), Bucknell U. Alumni Assn. (bd. dirs. 1971-80, pres. 1976-78, Outstanding Achievement 1991), Indian Trail Club, Century Assn., Phi Kappa Psi, Phi Kappa Phi. Office: Adelphi U Garden City NY 11530

SCOTT, ROBERT EDWIN, dean, law educator; b. Nagpur, India, Feb. 25, 1944; came to U.S., 1955; s. Roland Waldeck and Carol (Culver) S.; m. Elizabeth (Loch) Shumaker, Aug. 14, 1965; children: Christina Elaine, Robert Adam. BA, Oberlin (Ohio) Coll., 1965; JD, Coll. of William and Mary, 1968; LLM, U. Mich., 1969, SJD, 1973. Bar: Va. 1968. From asst. to prof. Law Sch. Coll. of William and Mary, Williamsburg, Va., 1969-74; prof. law Sch. of Law U. Va., Charlottesville, 1974-82, Lewis F. Powell, Jr. prof. Sch. of Law, 1982—2003, dean and Arnold H. Leon prof., 1991—2001; Justin W. D'Atri Prof. Law, Bus. & Soc. Columbia Law Sch., 2001—02; David & Mary Harrison Dist. Prof. U. Va., Charlottesville, Va., 2003—. Author: Commercial Transactions, 1982, 91, Sales Law and the Contracting Process, 1982, 91, Contract Law and Theory, 1988, 93, Payment Systems and Credit Instruments, 1996. Fellow Am. Bar Found., Am. Acad. Arts and Scis.; mem. Va. Bar. Democrat. Methodist. Home: 1109 Hilltop Rd Charlottesville VA 22903-1220 Office: U Va Rm WB179e Sch of Law Charlottesville VA 22903 Personal E-mail: res8f@virginia.edu.*

SCOTT, RONALD WILLIAM, educator, physical therapist, lawyer, writer; b. Pitts., Dec. 19, 1951; s. Richard Jack and Leone Florence (Gore) S.; m. Maria Josefa Barba-Garces, Aug. 5, 1973; children: Ronald William Jr., Paul Steven. BS in Phys. Therapy summa cum laude, U. Pitts., 1977; JD magna cum laude, U. San Diego, 1983; MBA, Boston U., 1986; LLM, Judge Adv. Gen. Sch., Charlottesville, Va., 1988; postgrad., Samuel Merritt Coll., Oakland, Calif. Bar: Calif. 1983, Tex. 1994; cert. orthopaedic phys. therapist. Commd. 1st lt. U.S. Army, 1978, advanced through grades to maj., atty.-advisor, 1983-87, malpractice claims atty. Ft. Meade, Md., 1988-89, chief phys. therapist Ft. Polk, La., 1989-92; phys. therapist, clin. instr. Brooke Army Med. Ctr., San Antonio, 1992-94; assoc. prof. dept. phys. therapy Sch. of Allied Health Scis., U. Tex. Health Sci. Ctr., San Antonio, 1994-98; dir. phys. therapy program Lebanon Valley Coll., Annville, Pa., 1998—. Presenter numerous profl. seminars on health law, ethics, and quality and risk mgmt.; guest lectr. phys. therapy program Hahnemann U., Phila., 1991—, Samuel Merritt Coll., Oakland, Calif., 1997—. Author: Healthcare Malpractice, 2d edit., 1999, Legal Aspects of Documenting Patient Care, 1994, Promoting Legal Awareness, 1996, Professional Ethics: A Guide for Rehabilitation Professionals, 1998; editor: Law Rev., U. San Diego, 1982-83, Issues on Aging Jour., 1996—; also articles; mem. editl. adv. bd. PT: The Mag. of Phys. Therapy, 1991—. Merit badge counselor Boy Scouts Am. Mem. Am. Phys. Therapy Assn. (past chair ethics and jud. com., McMillan scholar 1976), Am. Health Lawyers Assn., Pa. Phys. Therapy Assn., Soc. for Human Resource Mgmt. (presenter Geriatric Rehab. Conf. Cambridge U. 1995, Trinity Coll., Dublin 1996). Democrat. Methodist. Avocations: guitar, collecting rare records and books, golf, skiing, hiking. Home: 24 Hickory St Palmyra PA 17078-2943 Office: Lebanon Valley Coll Dir's Office MPT Program 101 N College Ave Annville PA 17003-1404

SCOTT, ROSA MAE, artist, educator; b. East Hampton, N.Y., Apr. 12, 1937; d. James Alexander and Victoria (Square) Nicholson; m. Frank Albert Hanna, Apr. 1, 1957 (div. Mar. 1985); 1 child, Frank Albert Hanna III; m. Warner Bruce Scott, Aug. 3, 1985 (dec. Oct. 2002); children: Bernadine, John, Patricia, Charlene, Lawrence. AA, Dabney Lancaster, 1989; BA, Mary Baldwin, 1992. Cosmetologist Rosa's Beauty Shop, East Hampton, 1962-68; sec. Frank Hanna's Cleaning Co., East Hampton, 1962-77; cashier, clk. Brook's Pharmacy, East Hampton, 1992; lead tchr. East Hampton Day Care, 1992-94, 97-98; substitute tchr. Lexington (Va.) Schs., 1994—, East Hampton Sch. Sys., 1996-97; lead tchr. Suffolk C.C. Child Care Ctr., River Head, N.Y., 1999; substitute tchr. East Hampton Sch., 2000—03; lead tchr. after sch. program Springs Sch., 2000—02, substitute tchr., 2000—03; receptionist Montauk Artist Assn., 2003—. Receptionist, Montauk (N.Y.) Artist Assn., 2003; sec. Lylburn Downing Cmty. Ctr., Inc., Lexington, 1985-92; arts and crafts tutor, supr. East Hampton Town Youth After Sch. Program, 1996—. Acrylic painter. Pres. Rockbridge Garden Club, Lexington, 1996; co-organizer Va. Co-op. Ex. Garden Clubs, Lexington, 1995; bd. dirs. Rockbridge Area Pres. Homes, 1996, Fine Arts of Rockbridge, 1985-92, Friends of Lime Kiln, Lexington, 1985-92. Mem.: Guild Hall, East End Arts, Montauk Artists Assn. (receptionist 2003), Artist Alliance East Hampton, L.I. Black Artists (v.p. 2000—03), Rockbridge Arts Guild. Avocations: collecting emmett kelly clowns, art, reading, theater, tennis.

SCOTT, SAMUEL RUSSELL, internal medicine educator; b. Mt. Airy, N.C., Feb. 11, 1943; s. J.R. and Mattie (Cooke) S. BS, Guilford Coll., 1965; MD, Wake Forest U., 1969; MS in Adminstrv. Medicine, U. Wis., 1990. Diplomate Am. Bd. of Internal Medicine. Intern U. Ky., Lexington, 1969-70, resident, 1970-72, asst. prof. medicine, 1972-78, assoc. prof., 1978-84, prof., 1984—, asst. dean for continuing med. edn., 1989-95, med. dir. physician asst. program, 1980-97. Med. dir. U. Ky. Home Care, 1987-97. Chmn. formulary subcom. Ky. Dept. Human Resources, Frankfort, 1985-94. Fellow ACP; mem. Am. Geriatrics Soc., Am. Soc. Internal Medicine, Soc. Gen. Internal Medicine. Mem. Soc. Of Friends. Home: 132 S Ashland Ave Apt 4 Lexington KY 40502-1799 Office: Ky Clinic Dept Internal Medicine Lexington KY 40536-0001

SCOTT, STEPHEN CARLOS, academic administrator; b. Greenville, S.C., Sept. 20, 1949; s. Carlos O'Dell and Christina (Nikitas) S.; m. Patsy Jordan, Apr. 13, 1968; children: Stephanie Christina, Lance Stephen. BA, Clemson (S.C.) U., 1971, MEd, 1975, EdD, 1987. Owner, mgr. Scotty's Inc., restaurant, Clemson, 1967-71; tchr. math. Pickens (S.C.) Sr. High Sch., 1972-74; instr. bus. Tri-County Tech. Coll., Pendleton, S.C., 1974-76, head dept., 1976-78, dir. br. campus Easley, S.C., 1978-80; dean bus. Greenville Tech. Coll., 1980-85, assoc. v.p., 1985-88; pres. Southeastern C.C., Whiteville, N.C., 1988-99; exec. v.p. N.C. C.C. Sys., 1999—2002; pres. Lenoir C.C., Kinston, NC, 2002—. Cons. P.C.E. Fed. Credit Union, Liberty, S.C., 1975-88, Jacobs Mfg. Co., Clemson, 1979-80, Flat Rock Shelter Ctr., Easley, 1980-85; bd. mem. N.C. Rural Ctr. Contbr. articles to profl. jours. and mags. Pres. So. Shelter Ctr., Greenville, 1986—88, Good Shepherd Found., Whiteville, 1990—92; bd. dirs. Good Shepherd, 1988—91; chmn. Columbus County Sch. Bond. Dr., 1989, Am. Heart Fund Drive Columbus County, 1992; co-chmn. Columbus County Long Range Planning Com., 1989—91; vice chmn. Pvt. Industry Coun. Region O, 1992—99; funding dir. Habitat for Humanity Columbus County, 1992; pres. bd. dirs. Columbus County Rural Health Ctr., 1994; bd. dirs. N.C. Rural Ctr., 2000—02. Recipient award for patriotism U.S. Savs. Bonds Program, 1987. Mem. Am. Assn. Cmty. and Jrs. Colls. (Pres.'s Acad.), Greater Kinston C. of C. (exec. bd. 2003—), Rotary (bd. dirs. Whiteville 1990-92, pres. 1992-93). Presbyterian. Avocations: running, chess, numismatics, reading. Home: 1306 Par Dr Kinston NC 28504- E-mail: scs320@lenoircc.edu.

SCOTT, SUSAN CLARE, art history educator, editor; b. Drexel Hill, Pa., July 13, 1942; d. William Edwin and Clar-Monna (Darby) S. BS in Art Edn./English, Pa. State U., 1964, MA in Art History, 1978, PhD in Art History, 1995. Art/English tchr. Phoenixville (Pa.) Area H.S., 1964-65; art tchr. K-6 Newark (Del.) Spl. Sch. Dist., 1965-70; art/English 7-9 Emmaus (Pa.) Jr. H.S., 1970-71; instr. art history Pa. State U., University Park, 1980—95, editor, papers in art history, 1983—2001, asst. prof. art history, 1995—2001, McDaniel Coll, Westminster, Md., 2001—. Editor, author: Projects and Monuments..., 1984; editor: Light on the Eternal City, 1987, The Age of Rembrandt, 1988, Paris, Center of Artistic Enlight, 1988 and subsequent vols. in 1989-90, 92-93, 95-96, 97-98, 2001; contbg. author: (exhbn. catalogue): Triumph of the Baroque, 1999, Aequa Potestas, 2000; author articles. Mem. Internat. Soc. for Chinese Archtl. History Studies, Soc. Archtl. Historians, Brit. Soc. for Eighteenth-Century Studies, Internat. Fulbright Assn., Alpha Delta Kappa. Office: McDaniel Coll Dept Art and Art History 2 College Hill Westminster MD 21157 Home: 259 Race Horse Rd Hanover PA 17331-7808 E-mail: sscott@mcdaniel.edu.

SCOTT, SUSAN SHATTUCK, secondary education educator; b. Cambridge, Mass., Sept. 12, 1945; d. Kenneth Elton and Phyllis Shattuck; m. Robert Allen Scott, Dec. 27, 1968 (div. 1973); 1 child, Kenneth Charles. BS in Edn., Boston State Coll., 1967; M in Math., Worcester Poly. Inst., 1990. Cert. secondary math. tchr., Mass. Tchr. South Jr. H.S., Weymouth, Mass., 1967-73; editor Houghton-Mifflin Co., Boston, 1973-74; tchr. Ctrl. Jr. H.S., Weymouth, 1974-81, South H.S., Weymouth, 1981-90, Weymouth H.S./Vocat. Tech. H.S., 1990—2002; ret., 2002. Freelance editor Houghton Mifflin, Boston, 1974-75. Treas. Singles' Group, Duxbury Bapt. Ch., 1976-78, Stone Village Condo. Assn., Wareham, Mass., 1993-. Mem. Nat. Coun. Tchrs. Math. Avocations: walking, swimming, reading, gardening, cooking. Home: 234 Rand Hill Rd Alton Bay NH 03810

SCOTT, TERRY ALAN, science education educator; b. Cin., Sept. 17, 1963; s. Wilson Earl and Barbara Joy (Kincaid) S. BA in Elem. Edn., U. Cin., 1986; MEd in Curriculum and Instrn., Wright State U., 1989. Cert. tchr. Program dir. Wildwood Christian Edn. Ctr., Milford, Ohio, 1984-86; tchr. Milford (Ohio) Exempted Village Schs., 1986-89; sci. edn. instr., researcher Purdue U., West Lafayette, Ind., 1989—. Cons. Dayton (Ohio) Pub. Schs., 1989, Mariemont (Ohio) Schs., 1990; sr. staff resident Purdue Residence Halls, West Lafayette, 1991—. Mem. ASCD, Nat. Assn. Rsch. in Sci. Teaching, Nat. Sci. Tchrs. Assn., Am. Edn. Rsch. Assn., Internat. Reading Assn. Democrat. Presbyterian. Avocations: bird watching, gardening, hiking, cooking, reading. Office: Purdue U 410 Engring Adminstrn Buil West Lafayette IN 47906

SCOTT, VICKI SUE, school system administrator; b. Pine Bluff, Ark., Feb. 16, 1946; d. John Wesley and Ruby Gray (Whitehead) and Hannah (Lewis) S. BA, Hendrix Coll., 1968; MS in Edn., U. Cen. Ark., 1978, postgrad., 1979-84, U. Ark., 1983-85, Ark. State U., 1993-94. Cert. adminstrn., secondary sch. prin., middle sch., secondary health and phys. edn. Tchr., coach Brinkley (Ark.) Pub. Schs., 1968-76, Lonoke (Ark.) Jr. and Sr. High Schs., 1976-77, S.E. Jr. High Sch., Pine Bluff, 1978-92, asst. prin., 1992-2000, dir. summer sch., 1991, 92; prin. White Hall (Ark.) Jr. H.S., White Hall, Arkansas, 2000—. AIDS educator Arkansas River Edn. Svc. Coop., Pine Bluff, 1989-92. Active Leadership Pine Bluff, 1993-94. Scholar Assn. Women Ednl. Suprs., 1985; named Outstanding Young Women of Am., 1974, AAMLA Bd., 2002-, Ark. Leadership Acad. Mem.: DAR, ASCD, NMSA, AAMLA (bd. dirs. 2002—), Nat. Assn. Sch. Secondary Prins., Ark. Activities Assn., Ark. Assn. Ednl. Adminstrs., Order Ea. Star, Phi Delta Kappa, Delta Kappa Gamma (Epsilon chpt. pres., scholar 1994). Baptist. Avocations: tennis, reading, hiking, travel, golf. Home: 3215 S Cherry St Pine Bluff AR 71603-5983 Office: White Hall Jr HS 8106 Dollarway Rd White Hall AR 71602-6999 E-mail: scottv@whjr.arsc.k12.ar.us., vscott@seark.net.

SCOTT, WALTER NEIL, physiologist, educator; b. Evansville, Ind., Mar. 2, 1935; s. Paul Kruger and Pauline Virginia (Kimbley) S.; children: Walter David Kimbley, Benjamin Bray. BS, Western Ky. State Coll., 1956; MD, U. Louisville, 1960. Intern New Eng. Ctr. Hosp., Boston, 1960-61, resident, 1961-62; NIH fellow medicine Mass. Meml. Hosps., Boston, 1962-63; USPHS fellow biophys. lab. Harvard Med. Sch., Brookline, Mass., 1963-65; spl. NIH fellow biochemistry MIT, Cambridge, 1965-66; biochemist Sch. Aerospace Medicine, San Antonio, 1966-68, acting chief biochem. pharmacology div., 1967-68; asst. prof. Mt. Sinai Grad. Sch., N.Y.C., 1968-71; mem. grad. faculty CUNY, N.Y.C., 1968-82; asst. prof. ophthalmology Mt. Sinai Med. Sch., N.Y.C., 1971-74, assoc. prof. ophthalmology, 1974-79, research prof. ophthalmology, 1979-82, asst. dean research, 1976-81, assoc. dean, 1981-82; chmn. dept. biology NYU, N.Y.C., 1982-87, prof., 1982—. Lancaster vis. prof. Western Ky. U., 1980; mem. cornea task force Nat. Eye Inst., 1972, vision rsch. program com., 1975—79; cons. metabolic biology program NSF, 1976—91; cons. VA Hosp. Dept. Medicine, 1998—2000; attending physician divsn. endocrinology Beth Israel Med. Ctr., 2001—. Contbr. articles to sci. publs. Trustee Inst. Applied Biology, 1986—. Served to capt. USAF, 1966-68 Fellow N.Y. Acad. Scis. (gov. 1978-82, pres. 1983, chmn. conf. organizing com. 1980-81, 87-88); mem. Am. Physiol. Soc., Am. Soc. Biol. Chemists, Biophys. Soc., Soc. Exptl. Biology and Medicine (editorial bd. procs.), Am. Heart Assn., AAAS, Am. Chem. Soc., Am. Soc. Nephrology, N.Y. Acad. Medicine (com. pub. health 1986—), Endocrine Soc., Soc. Cell Biology, Sigma Xi, Alpha Omega Alpha. Office: NYU Dept Biology 1009 Main Bldg Washington Sq E New York NY 10003 E-mail: walter.scott@nyu.edu.

SCOTT, WILLIAM CORYELL, medical executive; b. Sterling, Colo., Nov. 22, 1920; s. James Franklin and Edna Ann (Schillig) S.; m. Jean Marie English, Dec. 23, 1944 (div. 1975); children: Kathryn, James, Margaret; m. Carolyn Florence Hill, June 21, 1975; children: Scott, Amy Jo, Robert. AB, Dartmouth Coll., 1942; MD, U. Colo., 1944, MS in OB/GYN, 1951. Cert. Am. Bd. Ob-Gyn., 1956, 79, Am. Bd. Med. Mgmt., 1991. Intern USN Hosp., Great Lakes, Ill., 1945-46, Denver Gen. Hosp., 1946-47; resident Ob-Gyn St. Joseph's Hosp., Colo. Gen. Hosp., Denver, 1946-51; practice medicine specializing in Ob-Gyn Tucson, 1951-71; assoc. prof. emeritus U. Ariz. Med. Sch., Tucson, 1971—; v.p. med. affairs U. Med. Ctr., Tucson, 1984-94. Contbr. articles to med. jours. and chpt. to book. Pres. United Way, Tucson, 1979-80, HSA of Southeastern Ariz., Tucson, 1985-87; chmn. Ariz. Health Facilities Authority, Phoenix, 1974-83. Served to capt. USNR, 1956-58. Named Man of Yr., Tucson, 1975. Fellow ACS, Am. Coll. Ob-Gyn, Pacific Coast Ob-Gyn Soc., Ctrl. Assn. of Ob-Gyn; mem. AMA (coun. on sci. affairs 1984-93, chmn. 1989-91), Am. Coll. Physician Execs., Ariz. Med. Assn. Republican. Roman Catholic. Avocations: golf, gardening, photography. Address: HC 1 Box 923 Sonoita AZ 85637-9705 E-mail: cbarc3@hotmail.com.

SCOTT, W(ILLIAM) RICHARD, sociology educator; b. Parsons, Kan., Dec. 18, 1932; s. Charles Hogue and Hildegarde (Hewit) S.; m. Joy Lee Whitney, Aug. 14, 1955; children: Jennifer Ann, Elliot Whitney, Sydney Brooke. AA, Parsons Jr. Coll., 1952; AB, U. Kans., 1954, MA, 1955; PhD, U. Chgo., 1961; PhD in Econs. (hon.), Copenhagen Sch. Bus., 2000, Helsinki Sch. Econs., 2001. From asst. prof. to assoc. prof. sociology Stanford (Calif.) U., 1960-69, prof., 1969-99, prof. emeritus, 1999—, chair dept. sociology, 1972-75; sr. scholar John Gardner Ctr./Stanford U., 2002—. Courtesy prof. Sch. Medicine, Stanford U., 1972—, Sch. Edn., Grad. Sch. Bus., 1977—; fellow Ctr. for Advanced Study in Behavioral Scis., 1989-90; resident fellow Bellagio Study and Conf. Ctr., 2002; dir. Orgns. Rsch. Tng. Program, Stanford U., 1972-89, Ctr. for Orgns. Rsch., 1988-96; mem. adv. panel Sociology Program NSF, Washington, 1982-84; mem. epidemiol. and svc. rsch. rev. panel NIMH, Washington, 1984-88; mem. Commn. on Behavioral and Social Scis. and Edn., NAS, 1990-96; vis. prof. Kellogg Grad. Sch. Mgmt., Northwestern U., winter 1997, Hong Kong U. Sci. and Tech., fall 2000. Author: (with O.D. Duncan et al) Metropolis and Region, 1960; (with P.M. Blau) Formal Organizations, 1962, Social Processes and Social Structures, 1970; (with S.M. Dornbusch) Evaluation and the Exercise of Authority, 1975, Organizations: Rational, Natural and Open Systems, 1981, rev. edit., 2003; (with J.W. Meyer) Organizational Environments: Ritual and Rationality, 1983, edit., 1992; (with A.B. Flood) Hospital Structure and Performance, 1987; (with J.W. Meyer), Institutional Environments and Organizations: Structural Complexity and Individualism, 1994, Institutions and Organizations, 1995, rev. edit., 2001; (with S. Christinsen) The Institutional Construction of Organization, 1995; (with M. Ruef et al) Institutional Change and Healthcare Organizations: From Professional Dominance to Managed Care, 2000; editor Ann. Rev. of Sociology, 1986-91; (with R. Cole) The Quality Movement and Organization Theory, 1999, (with J. Davis et al) Social Movements and Organization Theory, 2004. Fellow Woodrow Wilson, 1954-55; mem. Nat. Commn. Nursing, 1980-83; chair Consortium Orgns. Rsch. Ctrs., 1989-91; elder First Presby. Ch., Palo Alto, Calif., 1977-80, 83-86. Named Edmund P. Learned Disting. Prof., Sch. Bus. Adminstrn., U. Kans., 1970—71; recipient Cardinal Citation for Disting. Svc., Labette C.C., Parsons, 1981, Disting. Scholar award, Mgmt. and Orgn. Theory divsn. Acad. Mgmt., 1988, Richard D. Irwin award for scholarly contbns. to mgmt., Acad. Mgmt., 1996; Social Sci. Rsch. Coun. fellow, U. Chgo., 0959, resident fellow, Bellagio Conf. Ctr., 2002. Mem. Inst. Medicine, Am. Sociol. Assn. (chmn. sect. on orgns. 1970-71, mem. coun. 1989-92), Acad. Mgmt., Sociol. Rsch. Assn., Macro-Organizational Behavior Soc., Phi Beta Kappa. Democrat. Presbyterian. Home: 940 Lathrop Pl Stanford CA 94305-1060 Office: Stanford U Dept Sociology Bldg 120 Stanford CA 94305 E-mail: scottwr@stanford.edu.

SCOTTI, DENNIS JOSEPH, educator, researcher, consultant; b. N.Y.C., Apr. 20, 1952; s. Joseph Charles and Theresa (Giancola) S. BS, Stony Brook U., 1974; MBA, Adelphi U., 1977; MS, Temple U., 1980, PhD, 1982. Bd. cert. in healthcare mgmt.; cert. healthcare fin. profl., managed care profl.; diplomate Am. Coll. Healthcare Execs. Dep. chief adminstr. Dept. Mental Health Devel. Ctr., Suffolk, N.Y., 1975-77; asst. prof. Rutgers U., N.J., 1980-83; assoc. prof. Fairleigh Dickinson U., N.J., 1983-88, prof., 1989—. Exec. v.p. Presscott Assocs., Ltd., Avon, Conn., 1989—. Author: Strategic Management in the Health Care Sector, 1988; contbr. articles to profl. jours. Mem. Regents Adv. Coun. N.J. Recipient Tchg. Excellence award Exec. Master of Bus. Adminstrn., 1997, William G. Fulmer Bronze award for meritorious svc., 1997, Robert H. Reeves Silver award for meritorious svc., 2001; co-recipient Helen M. Yerger Spl. Recognition award, 2002. Fellow Healthcare Fin. Mgmt. Assn.; mem. Assn. for Health Svcs. Rsch., Med. Group Mgmt. Assn., Health Planning and Mktg. Soc., Acad. Mgmt., Peoples Med. Soc., Health Decisions Assembly, Phi Theta Kappa, Delta Mu Delta. Office: Fairleigh Dickinson U 1000 River Rd Teaneck NJ 07666-1996

SCOTT-WABBINGTON, VERA V. elementary school educator; b. Holland, Tex., Jan. 17, 1929; d. John Leslie Scott and Willie Mattie (Dickson) Stafford. BA, Huston-Tillotson Coll., 1950; MA, Roosevelt U., 1965. Cert. elem. tchr., Tex. Tchr. Ft. Hood/Killeen (Tex.) Ind. Sch. Dist., 1951-58, Gary (Ind.) Sch. Dist., 1958-83, Ft. Worth Pub. Schs., 1983—, key tchr. minority math. and sci. edn. coop., 1989-92. Mem. mentorship program Ft. Worth Ind. Sch. Dist.; mem. Nat. Rev. Panel to Review Nat. Coun. of Social Studies Curriculum Stds., 1993; adj. prof. Tex. Weslyan U., Ft. Worth. Active in several polit., civic and social orgns. Recipient Outstanding Achievement in Edn. award Baker Chapel African Meth. Episc. Ch., 1991, NAACP Edn. award, 1992. Mem. Nat. Alliance Black Sch. Educators (tchr. 1991, Mary McLeod Bethune award 1991), Am. Fedn. Tchrs., Tex. Fedn. Tchrs. Avocations: reading, live theater, museums, shopping. Home: 7212 Misty Meadow Dr S Fort Worth TX 76133-7117

SCOTT-WILSON, SUSAN RICE, vice principal; b. Brownsville, Tenn., Aug. 11, 1942; d. Moreau Estes and E. Estelle (Walker) Rice; m. Charles E. Scott, Feb. 28, 1969 (div. July 1985); children: Tamera W., David W.; m. Lloyd Curlin Wilson, Apr. 7, 1994. BS, U. Tenn., Martin, 1964; EdM, Memphis State U., 1979, EdD, 1989. Cert. master tchr., Tenn. Elem. tchr. Lauderdale County Bd. Edn., Ripley, Tenn., 1964-65; exchange tchr. USIA, Washington, Netherlands, 1986-87; chmn. English dept. Am. Sch. of The Hague, Netherlands, 1987-88; secondary tchr. Haywood County Bd. Edn., Brownsville, Tenn., 1974-86, tchr. vocat. English, 1989-90, dir. adult basic edn., 1990-95; vice prin. Haywood H.S., Brownsville, Tenn., 1995—. Mem. curriculum task force Tenn. Dept. Edn., Nashville, 1985-86, mem. collaborative task force, 1989-92; chair Tenn. Acad. Decathlon Bd., 1998—. Local elector Tenn. Pres.'s Trust, Knoxville, 1989—; mem. Sister Cities Commn., Brownsville, 1990; com. mem. Ptnrs. in Edn., Brownsville, 1992—93; mem. West Star Leadership, 1993, Tenn. Reorgnl. Improvement Mgmt. Sys., 1994—95; mem. steering com. Fayette County-Haywood County Cmty. Enterprise, Brownsville, 1994—2000; bd. dirs. YMCA, Brownsville, 1996—2001. Named Outstanding Tchr. by students U. Chgo., 1989. Mem. NEA, Nat. Coun. Tchrs. English (regional composition judge 1984-86), Tenn. Edn. Assn., Tenn. Tchrs. Study Coun. (state steering com. 1984-86), Tenn. Prins. Study Coun., Sigma Tau Delta, Phi Delta Kappa. Methodist. Avocations: reading, travel. Home: 321 N Washington St Brownsville TN 38012-2063 Office: Haywood HS 1175 E College St Brownsville TN 38012-2208

SCOVILLE, JAMES GRIFFIN, economics educator; b. Amarillo, Tex., Mar. 19, 1940; s. Orlin James and Carol Howe (Griffin) S.; m. Judith Ann Nelson, June 11, 1962; 1 child, Nathan James. BA, Oberlin Coll., 1961; MA, Harvard U., 1963, PhD, 1965. Economist ILO, Geneva, 1965-66; instr. econs. Harvard U., Cambridge, Mass., 1964-65, asst. prof., 1966-69; assoc. prof. econs. and labor and indsl. relations U. Ill.-Urbana, 1969-75, prof., 1975-80; prof. indsl. rels. Indsl. Rels. Ctr., U. Minn., Mpls., 1979—, dir., 1979-82, dir. grad. studies, 1990-97. Cons. ILO, World Bank, U.S. Dept. Labor, Orgn. for Econ. Cooperation and Devel., USAID; labor-mgmt. arbitrator. Author: The Job Content of the US Economy, 1940-70, 1969, Perspectives on Poverty and Income Distribution, 1971, Manpower and Occupational Analysis: Concepts and Measurements, 1972, (with A. Sturmthal) The International Labor Movement in Transition, 1973, Status Influences in 3rd World Labor Markets, 1991. Mem. Am. Econ. Assn., Indsl. Rels. Rsch. Assn. (v.p. internat. sect. 1998, pres. 1999), Internat. Indsl. Rels. Assn. Office: U Minn Ind Rels Ctr 3-289 CSOM Minneapolis MN 55455 E-mail: jscoville@csom.umn.edu.

SCOVILLE, LYNDA SUE, special education educator, writer; b. Pampa, Tex., Jan. 5, 1945; d. Kenneth E. and Opal Myrle (Turner) Scoville; m. Bruce C. Ward, Oct. 1, 1976 (div. Nov. 1997); children: J. Wade Bainum, Jennifer L. Manzoor. BS in Edn., Emporia (Kans.) State U., 1967; MS in Edn., U. Kans., 1973; AS, Wichita (Kans.) State U., 1997. Cert. learning disabled, educable mentally handicapped, psychology, composition and lit., Ariz., Calif., Kans., Tex. Tchr. educable mentally handicapped and learning disabled Shawnee Mission (Kans.) Pub. Schs., 1967-69; tchr. headstart program Hutchinson Pub. Schs., 1968; tchr. educable mentally handicapped Chanute High Sch., Iola, Kans., 1974-76; tchr. learning and behavior disabled Sedgwick County Area Spl. Edn. Svcs. Coop., Goddard, Kans., 1979-80; tchr. learning disabled Butler County Sch. Bd. Coun. Spl. Edn. Coop., El Dorado, Kans., 1986-87, tchr. educable mentally handicapped Augusta Mid. Sch., 1999-2000; tchr. learning disabled Wichita Pub. Schs., 1987-89; writer, rschr. Andover, Kans., 1989-91; legal adminstrv. asst., 1992-94; tchr. learning and behavior disabled So. Tex. Ind. Sch. Dist., Mercedes, 1995-96; paralegal Legal Temps, 1999-2000; tchr. resource specialist program Alvord Pub. Schs., Riverside, Calif., 2000—01; tchr. cross categorical bilingual Wakefield Mid. Sch., Tucson, 2002—, Tucson Unified Sch. Dist., Ariz., 2002—03. Author: A Scoville Branch in America: A Genealogy and Story (1660-1990). U. Kans. grant. Mem. AAUW, ASCD, NAFE, DAR (Eunice Sterling chpt. registrar), Nat. Fedn. Paralegal Assns., Coun. for Exceptional Children, Kans. Paralegal Assn., Psi Chi. Home: Apt 15203 10700 N La Reserve Drive Oro Valley AZ 85737-8776 E-mail: lynda7071@aol.com.

SCRANTON-KRAEMER, LYNDA KAY, secondary education educator; b. Quincy, Ill., Aug. 6, 1947; d. Charles Leslie and Dorothy Blanche (Schnellbecher) S. BS in Phys. Edn., U. Ill., 1970; MA in Guidance, Roosevelt U., 1981. Cert. tchr., Ill. Phys. edn. tchr., coach Barrington (Ill.) High Sch., 1970-94, guidance counselor, 1994—. Orchesis sponsor Barrington (Ill.) High Sch., 1971-78, girls tennis coach, 1973-88; mem. adv. bd. Ill. High Sch. Assn. Tennis, Bloomington. Mem. NEA, Ill. Edn. Assn., Am. Assn. Health, Phys. Edn., Recreation and Dance, Ill. Assn. Health, Phys. Edn., Recreation and Dance. Avocations: music performance, golf, dance, counseling, remodeling properties. Home: 335 Park Ln Lake Bluff IL 60044-2320 Office: Barrington High Sch 616 W Main St Barrington IL 60010-3099

SCRASE, DAVID ANTHONY, German language educator; b. Upton, Dorset, Eng., Nov. 27, 1939; came to U.S., 1969; s. Robert Stanley and Dorothy Adelaide (Ridgewell) S.; m. Mary Ellen Martin, May 5, 1973 (div. Apr. 1985); 1 child, Anna Rachel Martin-Scrase; m. Mary McNeil, July 15, 1995. (div. Feb., 1998). BA, Bristol U., 1962; PhD, Ind. U., 1972. Lectr. Zurich U., Switzerland, 1964-68; asst. prof. Oxford Poly., Eng., 1968-69; prof. U. Vt., Burlington, 1971—. Author: Wilhelm Lehmann, A Critical Biography, 1984, Understanding Johannes Bobrowski, 1995, Joseph Hahn: Holocaust Poems, 1998; author: (with W. Mieder) The Holocaust: Introductory Essays, 1996, The Holocaust: Personal Accounts, 2001, Reflections on the Holocaust, 2002; contbr. articles to profl. jours. Fellow Brit. Acad., London, 1973, Humboldt Found., Bonn, Germany, 1974, 79. Avocations: reading, music, woodwork, sport. Office: U Vt Dept German Waterman Bldg Burlington VT 05405-0001

SCRIBNER, MARGARET ELLEN, educational consultant, consultant; b. Pana, Ill., Oct. 20, 1948; d. William M. and Beatrice Faye (Springman) Scribner; m. John E. McNeal, Aug. 15, 1977 (div. Oct. 1981); m. Leonard P. Basak, Jr., Mar. 13, 1986; children: L. Phillip Basak III, Cassandra Basak. BS in Social Work, Spalding U., 1970. Coord. Gov.'s Inaugural Com., Springfield, Ill., 1972; sr. cons. Ill. State Bd. Edn., Chgo., 1970—, acting divsn. supr., 2001—. Bd. dirs., corp. sec. Ventura 21, Inc., Roselle, Ill., 1984—87; mem. Ill. Common Performance Mgmt. Project Team, 1996—2001. Mem. Uptown Cmty. Orgn., Chgo., 1978—80; charter mem., organizer Margate-Ainslie Block Club, Chgo., 1979—80. Mem.: Internat. Leadership Tng. Inst. (cert. 1974), Bus. and Profl. women Chgo. (historian 1978—79), Nat. Assn. State Adminstrs. and Suprs. Pvt. Schs. (sec. 1999—2002, pres.-elect 2002—04), Brookwood Country Club (Wood Dale, Ill.), Ill. Athletic Club (Chgo.). Republican. Roman Catholic. Avocations: golf, clarinet, water colors, writing. Office: Ill State Bd of Edn 100 W Randolph St Ste 14-300 Chicago IL 60601-3283

SCROGAN, LEN CRAIG, school district administrator; b. New Orleans, Nov. 20, 1952; m. Janis Sue Clutter, July 16, 1976; children: Kirstin, Michael, Steffan. BA with honors, U. Denver, 1974; MA with honors, U. No. Colo., 1981. Cert. adminstr., Colo., N.J., Oreg. Tchr. Jefferson County Schs., Arvada, Colo., 1974-81; asst. prin. Greeley (Colo.) Schs., 1981-86; coord. computer edn. Albuquerque Schs., 1986-88; dir. planning and tech. Princeton (N.J.) Schs., 1988-90; dir. tech. Beaverton (Oreg.) Sch. Dist., 1990-92, Boulder (Colo.) Schs., 1992—. Adj. faculty mem. Lesley Coll., Cambridge, Mass., 1982—; adj. researcher EISD, N.Y.C., 1992; cons. in field. Co-author text and workbook: Telecommunications: Concepts and Application, 1992; contbr. articles to profl. publs.; author ednl. software. Recipient Disting. Achievement award Ednl. Press Assn., 1988, 89. Mem. Internat. Soc. for Tech. in Edn., Confedn. of Oreg. Sch. Adminstrs., Phi Beta Kappa. Avocation: competitive volleyball. Home: 637 S Broadway St Ste B302 Boulder CO 80305-5961

SCRUGGS, BETTY JOYCE CLENNEY, public school administrator; b. Edison, Ga., Sept. 14, 1928; d. Robert Lee and Mollie (Henley) Clenney; m. Herbert Harry Scruggs, July 15, 1949 (dec. Sept. 1982); children: Nancy S. Pennington, Emily S. Morgan, Herbert Harry Jr. AA, Andrew Coll., Cuthbert, Ga., 1947; BS, Valdosta (Ga.) State Coll., 1966, MEd, 1971, EdS, 1986. Tchr. Lowndes County Bd. Edn., Valdosta, 1947-50, 66-73, sch. psychometrist, 1974-78, dir. spl. edn., 1978-81, dir. pupil personnel services, 1981-87, adminstrv. asst. for personnel, from 1987. Cons. Ga. Dept. Edn., Atlanta, 1971; instr. Valdosta State Coll., 1971-81. Councilwoman City of Hahira, Ga., 1985-86; mem. Lowndes County-South Ga. Regional Library Bd., Valdosta, 1975-82. Mem. NEA, Ga. Edn. Assn., Lowndes Edn. Assn., Ga. Council Adminstrs. Spl. Edn., Council for Exceptional Children (sec., membership chmn. 1976-80, Administrator of Yr. 1980), Phi Delta Kappa, Sigma Chi, Delta Kappa Gamma. Lodges: Elks. Democrat. Baptist. Avocations: cross-stitching, bridge, clogging. Home: Apopka, Fla. Died Apr. 15, 2000.

SCUDDER, SALLIE ELIZABETH, secondary education educator; b. Tampa, Fla., Apr. 12, 1968; d. Roderick Williams and Martha Thelma (Mills) S. BA in Math., U. Miami, 1989; MEd in math. Edn., U. Fla., 1990. Cert. math. tchr., Fla. Student trainee U.S. Geol. Survey-Water Resources Div., Tampa, 1986-89; grad. asst. U. Fla.-Coll. Edn., Gainesville, 1989-90; writer Scott, Foresman, Ill., 1990; tchr. math. B.T. Washington Jr. High Sch., Tampa, 1990-91, H.B. Plant High Sch., Tampa, 1991—. Presenter Hillsborough County Profl. Day, Tampa, 1992; tchr. key scholars program Nat. Merit Prep., Tampa, 1992. Author: (activity book) Graphing, Probability and Stats Workshop, 1990. Vol. tchr. Davis Islands Community Ch. Sunday Sch., Tampa, 1991—; vol. softball coach Bayshore Little League, Tampa, 1992—. Mem. Math. Assn. Am., Nat. Coun. Tchrs. Math., Fla. Coun. Tchrs. Math., Hillsborough County Tchrs. Secondary Math. Democrat. Avocations: volleyball, softball, tennis, classical music, broadway. Home: 4316 S Hale Ave Tampa FL 33611-1332 Office: H B Plant High Sch S Himes Ave Tampa FL 33629

SCUDDER, THAYER, anthropologist, educator; b. New Haven, Aug. 4, 1930; s. Townsend III and Virginia (Boody) S.; m. Mary Eliza Drinker, Aug. 26, 1950; children: Mary Eliza, Alice Thayer. Grad., Phillips Exeter Acad., 1948; AB, Harvard U., 1952, PhD, 1960; postgrad., Yale U., 1953-54, London Sch. Econs., 1960-61. Rsch. officer Rhodes-Livingstone Inst., No. Rhodesia, 1956-57, sr. rsch. officer, 1962-63; asst. prof. Am. U., Cairo, 1961-62; rsch. fellow Ctr. Middle East Studies, Harvard U., 1963-64; asst. prof. Calif. Inst. Tech., Pasadena, 1964-66, assoc. prof., 1966-69, prof. anthropology, 1969-2000, prof. emeritus, 2000—; dir. Inst. for Devel. Anthropology, Binghamton, NY, 1976—2002; commr. World Commn. on Dams, 1998-2000. Cons. UN Devel. Program, FAO, IBRD, WHO, Ford Found., Navajo Tribal Coun., AID, World Conservation Union, Lesotho Highlands Devel. Authority, South China Electric Power Joint Venture Corp., U.S. Nat. Rsch. Coun., Que.-Hydro, Environ. Def. Fund, Ministry of Industry and Handicrafts, Lao People's Dem. Republic. Author: The Ecology of the Gwembe Tonga, 1962; co-author: Long-Term Field Research in Social Anthropology, 1979, Secondary Education and the Formation of an Elite: The Impact of Education on Gwembe District, Zambia, 1980, No Place to Go: The Impacts of Forced Relocation on Navajos, 1982, For Prayer and Profit: The Ritual, Economic and Social Importance of Beer in Gwembe District, Zambia, 1950-1982, 1988, The IUCN Review of the So. Okavango Integrated Water Development Project, 1993. John Simon Guggenheim Meml. fellow, 1975; recipient (1st) Lucy Mair medal for applied anthropology Royal Anthropol. Inst., 1998. Mem. Am. Anthrop. Assn. (1st recipient Solon T. Kimball award for pub. and applied anthropology 1984, Edward J. Lehman award 1991), Soc. Applied Anthropology (Bronislaw Malinowski award 1999), Am. Alpine Club. Office: Calif Inst Tech # 228 77 Pasadena CA 91125-0001 E-mail: tzs@hss.caltech.edu.

SCULLEN, THOMAS G. superintendent; Supt. Indian Prairie Community Unit Sch. Dist. 204, Naperville, Ill. Recipient State Finalist for Nat. Supt. of Yr. award, 1993. Office: Indian Prairie CUSD204 PO Box 3990 Naperville IL 60567-3990

SCURLOCK, JUDY B. early childhood educator; b. Florence, S.C., May 19, 1950; d. Charles James Jr. and Catherine (Finklea) Brockington; m. Gregory Blair Scurlock, June 10, 1972; children: Blair, Brian. BA, Columbia Coll., 1972; MEd, U. S.C., 1989. Tchr. Aiken (S.C.) County Schs., 1972-74, Richland County Schs., Columbia, S.C., 1974-76, Episcopal. Day Sch., Augusta, Ga., 1978-89; instr., dept. chair Aiken Tech. Coll., 1989—. Mem. Visions for Youth, Aiken, 1992-94; validator early childhood programs Nat. Acad. Early Childhood Programs. Recipient Gov. Disting. Prof. award, 1994. Mem. S.C. Assn. Edn. Young Children (pres. 1994-95, pub. rels. chair 1990-93, conf. chair 1993, pub. policy/advocacy chair 1996), S.C. Early Childhood Assn., Nat. Coalition Campus Child Care (conf. com. 1993), Nat. Assn. Edn. Young Children (affiliate pres. 1994-95), Sandhills Assn. Edn. Young Children (pres. 1993-94), Phi Delta Kappa. Presbyterian. Avocations: child advocate, golf, walking, exercise. Home: 821 Heard Ave Augusta GA 30904-4205 Office: Aiken Tech Coll PO Box 696 Aiken SC 29802-0796

SCUTT, ED, English language educator; b. Poughkeepsie, N.Y., Sept. 5, 1943; s. Edward Alvin Scutt and Helen (Jones) Lutz; m. Barbara Scutt, Aug. 25, 1986 (div. June 1989). AA, Dutchess C.C., 1963; BA, Houghton Coll., 1965; MA, SUNY, Buffalo, 1972. Cert. tchr., N.Y. Tchr. LaSalle Sr. High Sch., Niagara Falls, N.Y., 1965-66, Royalton-Hartland Jr.-Sr. High Sch., Middleport, N.Y., 1966-71, Hilton (N.Y.) Ctrl. High Sch., 1972—. Summer theater dir. Buck's Rock Camp, New Millford, Conn., 1974-79; presenter, cons. various confs., Washington, Niagara Falls, 1989-92; mem. steering com. Genesse Valley Devel. Learning Group, Rochester, N.Y., 1991—, founding mem., sec. whole lang. support group, 1989—; exec. bd. dirs. Hilton Ctrl. Teaching Assn. Mem. Nat. Coun. Tchrs. English. Avocations: community theater, reading, writing. Home: 65B Hill Court Cir Rochester NY 14621-1149 Office: Hilton Ctrl High Sch 400 East Ave Hilton NY 14468-1254

SCUZZARELLA, CARLA ANN, dean; b. Winthrop, Mass., Aug. 7, 1958; d. Carl Forbes and Anna Maria (Digregorio) Saunders; m. Frank Joseph Scuzzarella, Jr., Apr. 30, 1983; children: Robert Joseph, Michael James. BA in History, Salem State Coll., 1980, MEd, 1988, MA in European History. cert. tchr. secondary sch., prin., Mass. Tchr., coach girls' gymnastics Saugus (Mass.) High Sch., 1980-81; tchr. Winchester (Mass.) High Sch., 1981-83, coach girls' gymnastics, 1981-84; tchr. Watertown (Mass.) High Sch., 1983-94; dean student affairs Westford (Mass.) Acad., 1994—. Coach Women's Gymnastics Salem (Mass.) State Coll., 1984-91; class 1994 advisor Watertown High Sch., 1991— Mem. sch. com. Town of Saugus, Mass., 1991—; clk. Saugus Bus. and Edn. Collaboration, 1991—. Recipient Kennedy Libr. Teaching award, Boston, 1991; fellow Mass. Acad. for Tchrs., Ctr. for Teaching and Learning, U. Mass., Boston, 1991; Horace Mann grantee State of Mass., 1990; James Madison Meml. fellow, 1993. Mem. ASCD, NEA, Mass. Tchrs. Assn., Mas. Sch. Bd. Assn., Nat. Coun. for Social Studies, Mass. Coun. for Social Studies. Office: Westford Acad 30 Patten Rd Westford MA 01886-2943

SEAB, CHARLES GREGORY, astrophysicist, educator; b. Ft. Benning, Ga., May 26, 1950; s. James A. and Ruby (Jones) S.; m. Peggy R. McConnell, May 9, 1979; 1 child, Jenna R. McConnell-Seab. BS in Physics, La. State U., 1971, MS in Physics, 1974; PhD in Astrophysics, U. Colo., 1982. Engring. analyst, programmer Mid. South Svcs., New Orleans, 1974—77; NRC rsch. assoc. NASA Ames Rsch. Ctr., Mountain View, Calif., 1983—85; rsch. scientist U. Calif., Berkeley, 1985, Va. Inst. Theoretical Astronomy, Charlottesville, 1985—87; vis. asst. prof. U. New Orleans, 1987—89, asst. prof., 1989—91, assoc. prof. astrophysics, 1991—96, prof., 1996—. Bd. dirs. Freeport McMoran Obs., New Orleans; univ. tchg. fellow, chmn. physics dept., 2002—. Author: Astronomy, 1994, Study Guide for Universe, 1997; contbr. articles to profl. jours., chpts. to books. Capt. USAR, 1971-80. Nat. Merit scholar, 1967-71. Mem. Am. Assn. Physics Tchrs., Am. Astron. Soc., Astron. Soc. Pacific, Pontchartrain Astronomy Soc., Planetary Soc., Phi Kappa Phi, Sigma Pi Sigma. Avocations: amateur astronomy, tennis. Office: U New Orleans Physics Dept Lakefront Frnt New Orleans LA 70148-0001

SEABURG, GLEN T. chemistry educator; BA in chemistry, UCLA, 1934, PhD in chemistry, 1937. Recipient Nobel Laurette award, 1951, George C. Pimentel award in Chemical Edn.,1994. Home: Lafayette, Calif. Deceased.

SEADLER, STEPHEN EDWARD, social scientist; s. Silas Frank and Doris Amy Seadler; children: Einar Austin, Anna Carin. AB in Physics, postgrad. in atomic and nuclear physics, Columbia U., 1947; postgrad. with George Gamow in relativity, cosmology, and quantum mechanics, George Washington U., 1948—50. Electronic engr. Cushing & Nevell, Warner Inc., N.Y.C., 1951—54; seminar leader, leader trainer world politics Am. Found. for Continuing Edn., N.Y.C., 1955—57; exec. dir. Medimetric Inst., 1957—59; mem. long range planning com., chmn. corporate forecasting com., mktg. rsch. dir. W.A. Sheaffer Pen Co., Ft. Madison, Iowa, 1959—65; founder Internat. Dynamics Corp., Ft. Madison and N.Y.C., 1965, pres., 1965—70; originator DELTA program for prevention and treatment of violence, 1970; founder, pres. ID Ctr., Ft. Madison, Dover, N.J., 1968—. Mgmt. cons. in human resources devel. and conflict reduction, N.Y.C., 1970-73; pres. UNICONSULT computer-based mgmt. and computer scis., N.Y.C., 1973-76; speaker on decision support systems, internat. affairs and ideological arms control; author/speaker (presentation) Holocaust, History and Arms Control; originator social sci. of ideologics and ideotopology; spl. works collection accessible via On-line Computer Lib. Ctr. Instr. polit. sci. Ia. State Penitentiary, 1959-62; guest speaker on radio and television. Author: Principia Ideologica: A Treatise on Combatting Human Malignance, 1999, Ending the Bronze Age, 2001, Terror War and Peace, 2003; contbr. ideologics and ideotopology sects. to Administrative Decision Making, 1978, Management Handbook for Public Administrators, 1978, statement on ideological arms control in Part 4 of Sen. Fgn. Rels. Com. hearing on Salt II Treaty, 1979, Ideologics Extended to treat ethnic, racial, religious conflict, 1992, with first call for Abrahamic Reformation, Morristown (N.J.) Unitarian Ch., 1993; contbr. articles to profl. jours. Served with AUS, 1944—46. Recipient 20th Century Achievement Award medal Internat. Biographical Ctr., U.K., 1995; named to The Wisdom Hall of Fame by The Wisdom Soc., 1997. Mem.: IEEE, UN Assn.-USA, Forum on Physics and Soc., Fgn. Policy Assn., Am. Mgmt. Assn. (lectr. 1963—68), Am. Sociol. Assn., N.Y. Acad. Scis., Acad. Polit. Sci., Am. Statis. Assn., Am. Phys. Soc., West Point Soc. NJ, Union of Concerned Scientists, Friends of West Point, Scottish Rite. Office: ID Ctr PO Box 824 Dover NJ 07802-0824 E-mail: ses146@columbia.edu.

SEAGER, DANIEL ALBERT, university librarian; b. Jacksonville, Fla., Jan. 1, 1920; s. Harry James and Albertina Adeline (Klarer) S.; m. Helen Ruthe Medearis, Mar. 6, 1943; children: Mary Adele, Susan Kathleen, Dana Ruthe. AA, St. John's Coll., Winfield, Kans., 1941; AB, Okla. Bapt. U., 1948; BA in L.S, U. Okla., 1950, MA, 1953; postgrad., Colo. State Coll. (now U. No. Colo.), 1956-59. Head librarian, prof. English Southwest Bapt. U., Bolivar, Mo., 1949-53; head librarian, asst. prof. library sci., chmn. dept. Ouachita U., Arkadelphia, Ark., 1953-56; head librarian, head library sci. edn., assoc. prof. library sci. U. No. Colo., Greeley, 1956-66, dir. library services, 1966-71, coordinator library research and devel., 1971—, prof. library sci., 1984—, chief bibliographer/editor library publns., cons., instr. ednl. media program, 1968-71. Libr. cons., 1968—; cons. Ency. Brit. ultramicrofiche project, 1967-69; lectr. in field. Contbr. articles to profl. jours. Mem. book adv. coun. Edn. for Freedom Found.; mem. Com. library standards Colo. pub. schs., 1960-62; mem. exec. bd. Rocky Mountain Bibliog. Ctr. Research, 1959-60, 65-74, sec., 1961-63; sec. Colo. Council Librarians State-Operated Instns., 1966, chmn., 1968-70; mem. exec. bd. Weld County Assn. Mental Health, 1966, mem. library com., 1969; mem. Colo. Civil Service Examining Bd., 1961—; mem. U. N.C. Friends Libr., 1984—; Rep. com. chmn., Weld County, 1985-86; deacon, elder Christian Ch.; mem. The Srs. Coalition, 1995—. With U.S. Army Signal Corps, WWII, 1942-44, ETO, 1944-45, USAR Corps, 1945-48. Recipient several citations of merit profl. orgns. Fellow Intercontinental Biog. Assn.; mem. NEA, AAUP, Am. Library Assn. (library recruitment com. 1957—), Nat., Colo. assns. higher edn., United Profs. for Acad. Order Nat. Hist. Soc., Colo. Assn. Sch. Librarians (cons.), Spl. Libraries Assn., ALA (region recruitment rep. 1958—), Utah Library Assn., Kans. Library Assn., Wyo. Library Assn., Nebr. Library Assn., N.D. Library Assn., S.D. Library Assn., Nev. Library Assn., Mountain Plains Library Assn. (treas. 1959-63, exec. sec. 1963-76, spl. hons. plaque 1968, archivist 1974-84, constitution com. 1979, 83, chmn. nominating com. 1980, awards com. 1984, by-laws and amendments coms. 89-91, Pres.'s and Assn.'s Spl. award 17 Years Service award, Spl. Presdl. award 1994), Colo. Library Assn. (auditor), Tex. Library Assn., Southwestern Library Assn., Ill. Library Assn., Calif. Library Assn., Cath. Library Assn., Mich. Library Assn., Ohio Library Assn., N.Y. Library Assn., Pa. Library Assn., Midcontinent Med. Library Assn., Library Automation Research and Cons. Assn., U N.C. Friends of the Libr., 1984, Intercollegiate Studies Inst., Am. Security Council, Alumni Assn. U. No. Colo., Black Silent Majority Com. (hon.), Colo. Council Higher Edn., Colo. Edn. Assn. (mem. coms., del. to convs.), U. No. Colo. Edn. Assn. (treas. 1980-84, sec.-treas. 1984-85), U. Colo. Safety Com., Assn. Coll. and Reference Libraries, Colo. Hist. Soc., Assn. Research Libraries, Colo. Audiovisual Assn., Air Force Assn., Internat. Platform Assn., Acad. Polit. Sci. Columbia, Nat. Geog. Soc., Weld County Assn. Mental Health (mem. bd., chmn. library com.), Am. Judicature Soc., Emeritus Faculty Assn. U. No. Colo., Am. Numis. Assn., Am. Sci. Affiliation, Council on Consumer Info., Smithsonian Assocs., Chem. Abstracts Service Panel, Colo. Gerontol. Soc., Western Gerontol. Soc., Am. Assn. Retired Persons (vote com.), Am. Legion, Audubon Nature Program, Forest History Soc., Journalism Edn. Assn., Greeley Numis. Club, Greeley C. of C., U. No. Colo. Emeritus Faculty Assn., Nat. Travel Club, Civitan (lt. gov. Mountain Plains dist. 1960-62), Knife and Fork Club, Rep. Club (Washington), Rep. Congl. Club (Washington), Eagles Club, Phi Delta Kappa. Mem. Reformed Christian Ch. Am. Home: 1230 24th Ave Greeley CO 80634-3516

SEALE, JAMES LAWRENCE, JR., agricultural economics educator, international trade researcher; b. Memphis, Mar. 12, 1949; s. James Lawrence and Mary Helen (Keefe) S.; divorced. BA, U. Miss., 1972; postgrad., U. Chgo., 1978-79; PhD, Mich. State U., 1985. Agrl. vol. Peace Corps, Tondo, Zaire, 1973-75; agrl. advisor Harvard Inst. for Internat. Devel., Abyei, Sudan, 1978; specialist Mich. State U., Fayoum, Arab Republic of Egypt, 1980-83; asst. prof. agrl. econs. U. Fla., Gainesville, 1985-90, assoc. prof. agrl. econs., 1990-95, prof. agrl. econs., 1995—. Vis. prof. U. Leicester (Eng.), 1992, 94, hon. vis. fellow, 1995. Author: (with H. Theil and C.F. Chung) International Evidence on Consumption Patterns, 1989; editor: Journal of Agricultural and Applied Economics, 1998-2001, spl. edit., 2002-03; contbr. articles to profl. jours. Vol. Farmer to Farmer, UOCA, Namibia, 1994, Farmer to Farmer, Wenrock Internat., 1994; vol. agrl. bus. svcs. Wenrock Internat., Far Eastern Russia, 1998. NIMH scholar U. Chgo., 1978-79; traveling scholar U. Mich., 1979; rsch. fellow Cairo U., 1980-83; McKethan-Matherly rsch. fellow, 1986-88, McKethan-Matherly sr. rsch. fellow, 1991-94. Mem. Am. Econs. Assn., Am. Agrl. Econs. Assn., Internat. Assn. Agrl. Economists, Econometrics Soc., Caribbean Agro-Econ. Soc., Internat. Agrl. Trade Rsch. Consortium, Gamma Sigma Delta. Episcopalian. Avocations: scuba diving, Karate. Home: 408 W University Ave 7D Gainesville FL 32601 Office: U Fla Dept Food and Resource 2111 McCarty PO Box 110240 Gainesville FL 32611-0240

SEAMAN, JEFFREY RICHARD, academic administrator; b. Roslyn, N.Y., Feb. 22, 1949; s. Richard MacAvoy and Jane Louise (Decker) S.; m. I. Elaine Allen, Jan. 21, 1978; children: Christopher, Julia. BS, Cornell U., 1971, MA, MS, 1977, PhD, 1984. Lectr. Cornell U., Ithaca, N.Y., 1976-77; rsch. assoc. U. Pa., Phila., 1978-86, lectr. stats., 1979-84, dir. rsch. project, 1982-84, dir. microcomputer svcs., 1984-85, dir. computing resource, 1985-92, assoc. vice provost, 1990-92; pres. Pond View Assocs., Dover, Mass., 1992—; exec. dir. tech. Lesley Coll., Cambridge, Mass., 1994-98, chief info. officer, 1998—. Cons. Schuykill Twp., Valley Forge, Pa., 1990-92; mem. adv. bd. Apple Computer, 1985-90, Word Perfect, Orem, Utah, 1989-91, IBM, 1984-86. Office: Lesley Coll 29 Everett St Cambridge MA 02138-2702

SEAMANS, PATRICK WILLIAM, international education consultant, architect; b. Munich, Feb. 9, 1952; s. William Alberto and Francine (Latapy) S. BA in Architecture, U. Calif., Berkeley, 1975, MArch, 1979; MS in Internat. Pub. Adminstrn., U. So. Calif., L.A., 1999, MS TESL, 1997, postgrad., 1999—. Registered architect, Calif. Founder, pres. Hearing Impaired Archtl. HIAN, L.A., 1986—89. Translator in French, L.A., 1983—; architect various firms, So. Calif. and London, 1976—; lectr. in field. Author: A Socio-Anthropological Perspective of American Deaf Education, 2001, Critical Thinking About ASL, 1998; translator: Biographical Note on the Abbé de l'Epée, 1997; contbr. articles to profl. jours. Cons. L.A. Cmty. on Disabilities, 1988. Recipient Outstanding Leadership award, Office of Internat. Svcs., U. So. Calif., L.A., 2000, Profl. of the Yr. award - Architect, Calif. Gov.'s Com. for the Employment of Persons with Disabilities, 1994, Award of Excellence in State Examination in Indsl. Drafting, Acad. d'Orléans, France, 1971, Editor's Choice award and pub. poet, Nat. Libr. of Poetry, 1993, numerous others; fellow Cal Grant Grad. fellow, State of Calif., 1994—98; scholar Stoops Phi Delta Kappa scholar, 2001, Rossier Sch. of Edn. scholar, 2001, Mary S. and Howard L. Reed Endowed scholar, 2001, Merit scholar, Sch. Pub. Adminstrn., U. So. Calif., L.A., 1995—96, Cal Disabled Alumni Merit scholar, U. Calif.-Berkeley, 1975. Mem.: AIA, L'Amicale des Anciens Elèves de l'Institution des Jeunes Sourds d'Orléans, Am. Assn. of People with Disabilities, World Recreation Assn. Deaf (acting sec. U.S. bd. dirs. 1989—92, sec. internat. bd. dirs. 1992—98, 1st v.p. internat. bd. dirs. 1998—, ofcl. French-English and English-French translator), TESOL, Am. Coun. on Tchg. Fgn. Langs., Am. Lit. Translators Assn., Semiotic Soc. Am., Linguistic Soc. Am., Am. Assn. for Applied Linguistics, Brit. Deaf History Soc., History of Edn. Soc., Soc. Archtl. Historians, Am. Hist. Assn., European Cmty. Studies Assn., Am. Polit. Sci. Assn., Am. Soc. for Pub. Adminstrn., Assn. of Internat. Educators, Comparative and Internat. Edn. Soc., Am. Ednl. Rsch. Assn., Assn. for Study of Modern and Contemporary France, U. So. Calif. Archtl. Guild, Union Internationale des Architects, Internat. Freelance Photographers Orgn. (life), French Alliance of L.A., Soc. for Calligraphy, Libr. of Congress Assocs., Nat. Parks and Conservation Assn., Nat. Trust for Hist. Preservation, Internat. Soc. Poets, L.A. Press Club, Mensa, Intertel, Pi Sigma Alpha, Pi Alpha Alpha, Phi Beta Delta, Phi Delta Kappa. Roman Catholic. Avocations: photography, philosophy, linguistics, art, history.

SEARCY, JANE BERRY, retired educational administrator, counselor; b. Birmingham, Ala., Dec. 21, 1951; d. Francis Clifford and Mary Jacqueline (Meeks) Berry; m. Joseph Alexander Searcy III, July 3, 1982; children: Margaret Alice, Joseph Alexander IV. BA in Elem. Edn., Birmingham So. Coll., 1973; MA in Spl. Edn., U. Ala., 1975, EdS in Spl. Edn., 1977, EdD in Spl. Edn., 1982. Cert. elem. and spl. edn. tchr., Ala. Tchr. spl. edn. Tuscaloosa (Ala.) County Schs., 1974-75, Montgomery (Ala.) County Schs., 1975-77, Tuscaloosa City Schs., 1977-79, curriculum assoc., 1979-86, dir. spl. edn., 1986-99; counselor K-12 Tuscaloosa Acad., 1999—. Instr. W. Ala. U. Coll. Edn., 1985-87, adj. prof., 1988—; cons. L.E.A.D. Acad., Montgomery, 1989-90; agy. rep. Child Protection Team, Tuscaloosa, 1986—, Tuscaloosa Autism Coun., 1988—; mem. Ala. Legis. Task Force, West Ala. Early Intervention Coun., Tuscaloosa, 1982—. Adv. bd. Rural Infant Stimulation Environment, U. Ala., Tuscaloosa, 1988—; bd. dirs. Tuscaloosa Assn. for Retarded Citizens, 1987-94, 2000—, Child Protection Team, 1982—, Miracle Riders of West Ala., 1994-2000, RISE program, U. Ala, 1980—, Sheriff's Kids Act Program, Children's Ctr. Tuscaloosa, 1998—, pres. 1998-2000; sec. bd. dirs. Ala. Choir Sch., 1996-99; bd. dirs. Tombigbee coun. Girl Scouts U.S., 1994-97, disabilities coord., fin. com., 1993—, coun. trainer, 1997—, tri-state chair tng. for trainers, 2001; assoc. chair, 1997-2001; active Women Committed to Excellence, 1998, Forerunners Edn. Com., 1996—. Recipient Profl. of the Yr. award Tuscaloosa Assn. for Retarded Citizens, 1994. Mem. ASCD, Coun. Exceptional Children, Ala. Coun. Exceptional Children (Outstanding SPE Coord. in Ala. 1995), Tuscaloosa Coun. Exceptional Children, Ala. Coun. Sch. Adminstrn. and Supervision (bd. dirs. 1994-97), Ala. ASCD, Nat. Coun. Adminstrs. in Spl. Edn. (nat. bd. dirs.), Ala. Counseling Assn., Ala. Coun. Adminstrs. in Spl. Edn. (state pres. 1992-94, CASE del. to Sino-Am. conf. on exceptionality, Beijing, China 1995, Southeastern area CASE conf. chair 1996), Leadership Tuscaloosa (bd. dirs. 1996—), Alpha Delta Kappa (v.p. Epsilon chpt. 1984-86, pres. 1986-88, State Leadership Appreciation award 1988), Phi Delta Kappa, Alpha Omicron Pi (chpt. rels. adv. 1983-85, 2000—), Kappa Delta Pi. Home: 505 Rice Valley Rd NE Tuscaloosa AL 35406-2704

SEARLES, ANNA MAE HOWARD, educator, civic worker; b. Osage Nation Indian Terr., Okla., Nov. 22, 1906; d. Frank David and Clara (Bowman) Howard; A.A., Odessa (Tex.) Coll., 1961; BA, U. Ark., 1964; M.Ed., 1970; postgrad. (Herman L. Donovan fellow), U. Ky., 1972—; m. Isaac Adams Searles, May 26, 1933; 1 dau., Mary Ann Rogers (Mrs. Herman Lloyd Hoppe). Compiler news, broadcaster sta. KJBC, 1950-60; corr. Tulsa Daily World, 1961-64; tchr. Rogers (Ark.) H.S., 1964-72; tchr. adult class rapid reading, 1965, 80; tchr. adult edn. Learning Center Benton County (Ark.), Bentonville, 1973-77, supr. adult edn., 1977-79; tchr. North Ark. C.C., Rogers, 1979-90, CETA, Bentonville, 1979-82; tchr. Joint Tng. Partnership Act, 1984-85; coordinator adult edn. Rogers C. of C. and Rogers Sch. System, 1984—. Sec. Tulsa Safety Council, 1935-37; leader, bd. dirs. Girl Scouts U.S.A., Kilgore, Tex., 1941-44, leader, Midland, Tex., 1944-52, counselor, 1950-61; exec. sec. Midland Community Chest, 1955-60; gray lady Midland A.R.C., 1958-59; organizer Midland YMCA, Salvation Army; dir. women's div. Savings Bond Program, Midland; mem. citizens com. Rogers Hough Meml. Library, women's aux. Rogers Meml. Hosp.; vol. tutor Laubach literacy orgn., 1973—; tutor Laubach Lit. Orgn., 1973-96; sec. Beaver Lake Literacy Council, Rogers, 1973-83, Little Flock Planning Commn., 1975-77, Benton County Hist. Soc., 1981—; pub. relations chmn. South Central region Nat. Affiliation for Literacy Advance, 1977-79; bd. dirs. Globe Theatre, Odessa, Tex., Midland Community Theatre, Tri-County Foster Home, Guadalupe, Midland youth centers, DeZavala Day Nursery, PTA, Adult Devel. Center, Rogers CETA, 1979-81; vol. recorder Ark. Hist. Preservation Program, 1984—; docent Rogers Hist. Mus., 1988—, vol. tutor; with Ptnrs. in Edn., 1995-96. Recipient 21 yr. pendant Benton Hist. Soc., Nice People award Rogers C. of C., 1987, Thanks badge Midland Girl Scout Assn., 1948, Appreciation Plaque award Ark. Natural Heritage Commn., 1988; Cert. of recognition, Rogers Pub. Schs., 1986, Cert. of Recognition, Beaver Lake Literacy Coun., 1993; Instr. of Yr. award North Ark. Community Coll. West Campus, Conservation award Woodmen of the World Life Ins. Soc., 1991, Vol. of Yr. award Rogers Hist. Mus., 1993, 95. Mem. NEA (del. conv. 1965), Ark. Assn. Public Continuing and Adult Edn. (pres. 1979-80), South Central Assn. for Lifelong Learning (sec. 1980-84), PTA (life), Future Homemakers Am. (life; sec. 1980—), Benton County Hist. Soc. (life, pub. rels. chmn. 1990-96, recording sec. 1990-96), Delta Kappa Gamma (Disting. Acheivement award Beta Pi chpt. 1992). Episcopalian. Clubs: Altrusa (pres. 1979—), Apple Spur Community (Rogers), Garden Club Rogers (publicity chmn. 1994-95, garden therapy 1994-96). Home: 2808 N Dixieland Rd Rogers AR 72756-2146

SEARLS, EILEEN HAUGHEY, retired lawyer, librarian, educator; b. Madison, Wis., Apr. 27, 1925; d. Edward M. and Anna Mary (Haughey) S. BA, U. Wis., 1948, JD, 1950, MS in LS, 1951. Bar: Wis. 1950. Cataloger Yale U., 1951-52; instr. law St. Louis U., 1952-53, asst. prof., 1953-56, assoc. prof., 1956-64, prof., 1964-2000, law libr., 1952-2000. Chmn. Coun. Law Libr. Consortia, 1984-90; sec. Bd. of Conciliaton and Arbitration, Archdiocese of St. Louis, 1986-98. Named Woman of Yr. Women's Commn., St. Louis U., 1986. Mem. ABA, ALA, Wis. Bar Assn., Bar Assn. Met. St. Louis, Am. Assn. Law Librs. (Marian Gould Gallagher Disting. Svc. award 1999), Mid Am. Assn. Law Librs. (pres. 1984-86), Mid Am. Law Sch. Libr. Consortium (chmn. 1980-84), Southwestern Assn. Law Librs., Altrusa Club. Office: 3700 Lindell Blvd Saint Louis MO 63108-3412

SEARS, DAVID O'KEEFE, psychology educator; b. Urbana, Ill., June 24, 1935; s. Robert R. and Pauline (Snedden) S.; divorced; children: Juliet, Olivia, Meredith. BA in History, Stanford U., 1957; PhD in Psychology, Yale U., 1962. Asst. prof. to prof. psychology and polit. sci. UCLA, 1961—, dean social scis., 1983-92. Dir. Inst. for Social Sci. Rsch., 1993—. Author: Public Opinion, 1964, Politics of Violence, 1973, Tax Revolt, 1985, Political Cognition, 1986, Social Psychology, 11th edit., 2003, Racialized Politics, 2000, Oxford Handbook of Political Psychology, 2003. Fellow Am. Acad. Arts and Scis.; mem. Soc. for Advancement Socio-Econs. (pres. 1991-92), Internat. Soc. Polit. Psychology (pres. 1994-95). Office: UCLA Psychology Dept Los Angeles CA 90095-0001 E-mail: sears@psych.ucla.edu.

SEARS, JAMES THOMAS, educator, researcher; b. Tipton, Ind., Aug. 12, 1951; s. Virgil M. and Kathy (Cooper) S. BS magna cum laude, So. Ill. U., 1974; MS, Ind. U., 1975, PhD, 1984; MA, U. Wis., 1976. Vis. instr. Trinity U., San Antonio, 1983-84; prof. U. S.C., Columbia, 1984—; sr. rsch. fellow S.C. Ednl. Policy Ctr., Columbia, 1989-92. USIA rschr., lectr., The Philippines, 1989, 91; cons. S.C. Dept. Edn., Columbia, 1984-85; rsch. assoc. Far West Lab., San Francisco, 1986, J. Paul Getty Ctr. for Edn. and Arts, 1991, Office Ednl. Rsch. and Improvement, 1991—; vis. scholar Ctr. for Feminist Rsch., U. So. Calif., 1993-94; rsch. fellow ONE Inst., 1997; vis. minority scholar U. Wis., Madison, 1998; vis. prof. Harvard U., 2001; disting. cons. prof. Coll. Charleston. Author: Teaching and Thinking about Curriculum, 1990, Growing Up Day in the South, 1991, Sexuality and Curriculum, 1992, When Best Doesn't Equal Good, 1994, Bound by Diversity, 1994, Overcoming Heterosexism and Homophobia, 1997, Lonely Hunters, 1997, Curriculum, Religion and Public Education, 1998, A Dangerous Knowing, 1999, Queering Elementary Education, 1999, Turning Points in Curriculum, 2000, Rebels, Rubyfruit and Rhinestones, 2001, Democratic Curriculum Theory and Practice, 2001, Curriculum Work as Public Moral Enterprise, 2003; editor Empathy Jour., 1988-94, Teaching Edn. Jour., 1989-98, Jour. Gay and Lesbian Issues in Education, 2002—; mem. editl. bd. Jour. Curriculum Theorizing, Jour. Homosexuality. Bd. dirs., founder Gay and Lesbian Adv. Rsch. Project, Inc., Columbia, 1986-97. Recipient First Amendment award ACLU, 1993, Lit. award Gay Lesbian Straight Educators Network, 1999, Choice Outstanding Acad. Book, 2002; Fulbright Rsch. scholar, 1994-95. Fellow Profs. of Curriculum, Internat. Acad. Sex Rsch.; mem. ASCD (nat. conf. planning com.), Curriculum Tchrs. Network (pres. 1987-88), Am. Ednl. Rsch. Assn. (lesbian and gay studies SIG, 1989—), Nat. Writers Union. Avocation: play writing. Office: U SC Carolina Plaza 908 Columbia SC 29208-0001

SEARS, JOANN MARIE, academic librarian; b. Lafayette, Ind., Aug. 3, 1974; d. Robert E. and Teresa A. Sears. BS, Purdue U., 1996; MLS, Ind. U., 1998. Sci. and tech. reference libr. Auburn U. Libr., Ala., 1998—2002; math. and physics libr. U. Mich., 2002—. Contbr. articles to profl. jours. Mem.: Spl. Libraries Assn., Phi Beta Kappa. Office: 3026-D Shapiro Libr 919 S University Ann Arbor MI 48109-1185 Business E-Mail: josears@umich.edu.

SEARS, RICHARD BRUCE, speech and language pathologist; b. London, Ont., Can., Mar. 20, 1950; came to U.S., 1953; s. Edward Mervin and Helen Barbara (MacNamara) S.; m. Mary Lynn Power, Jan. 21, 1972; children: Evan, Ethan, Erin. BS, Ea. Mich. U., 1978, MA, 1979. Clin. intern VA Med. Ctr., Allen Park, Mich., 1979; speech and lang. diagnostician Lake-McHenry Regional Program, Crystal Lake, Ill., 1980; tchr. speech and lang. impaired Dearborn (Mich.) Pub. Schs., 1980-83, 85—; speech and lang. pathologist St. Joseph's Hosp., Sarnia, Ont., Can., 1983-85, Sarnia Gen. Hosp., 1983-85; speech and lang. pathologist, cons. Sarnia-Lambton Home Care, 1983-85. Mem. adv. bd. Metrostaff home Care, Southfield, Mich., 1986-90; adj. instr. U. Mich., Dearborn, 1998—. Lyricist, songwriter various music, 1986—. Chmn. Local Spiritual Assembly, Bahá'í, Dearborn, 1991—. Mem. Am. Speech, Lang. and Hearing Assn. Baha'I. Avocations: songwriting, golf, skiing, bicycling, sailing. Office: Dearborn Pub Schs 18700 Audette St Dearborn MI 48124-4222

SEARS, ROBERT STEPHEN, finance educator, university dean; b. Odessa, Tex., May 27, 1950; s. William Bethel and Leola Vernon (Little) S.; Reva Dana Flournoy, Aug. 17, 1973; children: Matthew Stephen, Elizabeth Rea. AAS, Odessa Jr. Coll., 1970; BA summa cum laude, Tex. Tech. U., 1973, MS, 1976; PhD, U. N.C., 1980. Supr. Bethel Enterprises, Odessa, Tex., 1973-74; tchg. asst. Tex. Tech U., Lubbock, 1974-76, dir. Inst. Banking and Fin. Studies, 1988-98; tchg. asst. U. N.C., Chapel Hill, 1976-79; asst. prof. U. Ill., Champaign, 1979-85, assoc. prof., 1985-88; rsch. prof. Bur. Econ. and Bus., Champaign, 1984; tchg. asst. Lubbock Bankers Assn., 1990—; chmn. dept. fin. Tex. Tech U., 1997-2001, interim dean Coll. Bus., 2000, sr. exec. assoc. dean, Coll. Bus, 2001—. Cons. Cameron Brown Mortgage Co., Raleigh, N.C., 1978-80, Howard Savs. Bank, Livingston, N.J., 1980; asset mgr., trustee, pvt. investors, 1984—. Author: Investment Management, 1993, (chpt), Modern Real Estate, 1980, 84; assoc. editor Rev. of Bus. Studies, 1989-95, Jour. Fin. Rsch., 1990-96, Internat. Chmn. fin. com. Temple Bapt. Ch., Champaign, Ill., 1982, bd. deacons, 1982-88, chmn. deacons, lay leader, 1983; Sunday sch. tchr. Carrboro (N.C.) Bapt. Ch., 1977-79; bd. deacons Ind. Ave. Bapt. Ch., Lubbock, 1989-96, Sunday sch. tchr., 1991-92, master design com., 1993-96; trustee All Saints Episcopal Sch., 1995—, treas., 2000; bd. deacons Southcrest Bapt. Ch., Lubbock, 1998—. Rsch. grantee Cameron Brown Mortgage Co., Raleigh, N.C., 1978-80, U Ill, Champaign, 1980-84, 86-87, Investors in Bus. Edn., Champaign, 1980-81, 84; recipient Excellence in Undergrad. Tchg. award U. Ill. Champaign, 1984-85, Award for Outstanding Coll. Educator Champaign-Urbana, Ill. Jaycees, 1983-84, Coll. of Commerce Alumni Assn. Undergrad. Excellence in Tchg. award U. Ill., 1981-82; Mortar Bd., Omicron Delta Kappa Leadership scholarship and Svc. award Tex. Tech U., 1997-98, Pres.'s Excellence in Tchg. award Tex. Tech U., 1993-94, Acad. Achievement award Tex. Tech U., 1994-95. Mem. Am. Fin. Assn., Southwestern Fin. Assn. (pres. 1989-90, v.p., program chmn. 1988-89, sec., treas. 1986-88, bd. dirs. 1984-86, mem. program com. 1985-86, 89—), Fin. Mgmt. Assn. (mem. program com. 1986, 89-94, 97, 99-2001), So. Fin. Assn. (mem. program com. 1986), Western Fin. Assn. (mem. program com. 1986), Ea. Fin. Assn., Lake Ridge Country Club. Republican. Baptist. Avocations: golf, walking, participating in sports with my children. Office: Tex Tech U COBA Lubbock TX 79409-2101

SEATON, ALBERTA JONES, biologist, educator, consultant; b. Houston, Dec. 31, 1924; d. Charles Alexander and Elizabeth (Polk) Jones; m. Earle Edward Seaton, Dec. 24, 1947 (dec. Aug. 1992); children: Elizabeth Wamboi, Dudley Charles. BS in Zoology and Chemistry, Howard U., 1946, MS in Zoology, 1947; ScD in Zoology, U. Brussels, 1949. Asst. prof. Spelman Coll., Atlanta, 1953-54; assoc. prof. biology Tex. So. U., Houston, 1954-60, prof. biology, 1960-72, 91-95; adminstr. Ministry Edn., Bermuda, 1973-76; lectr. biology Bermuda Coll., Devonshire, 1976-78; prof. anatomy Sch. Allied Health U. Tex. Health Ctr., Houston, 1979-80; cons. sci. sect. Nat. Inst. Pedagogy Ministry of Edn., Victoria, Seychelles, 1980-89. Head dept. biology Wiley Coll., Marshall, Tex., 1950-51; dir. NSF Summer Sci. Inst. Tex. So. U., 1957-59, gen. studies program, 1970-72, undergrad. and grad. rsch. in biology, 1954-72; mem. Univ. Honors Program Com., Tex. So. U., 1960-70; chair self-study com., Tex. So. U., 1969-71, ednl. policies com., 1968-72; lectr. biology U. Md., USN Air Sta., Bermuda, 1972-78; supr. adminstrn. and budget Office of Ministry Edn., Bermuda, 1973-76; lectr. in field. Author, editor: Conserving the Environment, Part 1, 1984; editor: Reprints of Agrinews, 1982; co-author, co-editor: Conserving the Environment, Part 2, The Seychelles, 1986, Conserving the Environment, Part 3, Focus on Aldabra, 1991; contbr. articles to profl. jours. Evaluator grant proposals NSF, 1957-72; active regional meetings Com. on Undergrad. Edn. in Biol. Sci., 1967-72, AAC-AAUP confs. on curriculum improvement, 1970-72; chair nurses licensing bd., Hamilton, Bermuda, 1973-75; mem. Endangered Species Com., Hamilton, 1974-77. Postdoctoral fellow Calif. Inst. Tech., Pasadena, 1959-60, NSF postdoctoral fellow Roscoe B. Jackson Lab., Bar Harbor, Maine, 1959, U. Brussels, 1965-66. Mem. AAAS, AAUP (apptd. to ad hoc coms. 1968-71, sec.-treas. Tex. State Conf. 1968-70), AAUW, Am. Assn. Zoologists, Assn. des Anatomistes, Assn. Women in Sci., Tex. Acad. Sci., Beta Kappa Chi, Beta Beta Beta. Episcopalian. Home and Office: 3821 Gertin St Houston TX 77004-6503 E-mail: seatonstar@aol.com.

SEAVER, JAMES EVERETT, historian, educator; b. Los Angeles, Oct. 4, 1918; s. Everett Herbert and Gertrude Lillian (Sharp) S.; m. Virginia Stevens, Dec. 20, 1940; children— Richard Everett, William Merrill, Robert Edward. AB, Stanford U., 1940; PhD, Cornell U., 1946. Asst. instr. history Cornell U., 1940-42, 44-46; instr. Mich. State U., 1946-47; mem. faculty U. Kans., Lawrence, 1947—, prof. history, 1960—; prof. emeritus, 1989—; pres. faculty U. Kans., 1972-74, 82-83. Author: The Persecution of the Jews in the Roman Empire, 313-438 A.D, 1952, also articles. Fulbright-Hays grantee Italy, 1953-54; Fulbright-Hays grantee Israel, 1963-64; Carnegie grantee Costa Rica, 1966-67 Mem.AAUP, Am. Hist. Assn., Am. Philol. Assn., Am. Numismatic Soc., Am. Acad. Rome, U.S. Archives of Recorded Sound. Clubs. Democrat. Episcopalian. Home: 600 Louisiana St Lawrence KS 66044-2336 Office: U Kans Dept History Lawrence KS 66045-0001

SEAVER, ROBERT LESLIE, retired law educator; b. Brockton, Mass., June 13, 1937; s. Russell Bradford and Lois (Marchant) S.; m. Marjorie V. Rote, Aug. 21, 1960 (div. 1974); children: Kimberly, Eric, Kristen; m. Elizabeth A. Horwitz, May 22, 1984. AB cum laude, Tufts U., Medford, Mass., 1958; JD, U. Chgo., 1964. Bar: Ohio 1964, U.S. Ct. Appeals (6th cir.) 1964, U.S. Dist. Ct. (so. dist.) Ohio 1965. Assoc. Taft, Stettinius and Hollister, Cin., 1964-66; v.p., sec., gen. counsel IDI Mgmt. Inc., Cin., 1966-74; pvt. practice Cin., 1974-75; prof. law emeritus No. Ky. U. Salmon P. Chase Coll. Law, Highland Heights, 1975—; of counsel Cors & Bassett, Cin., 1993-99; ret., 1999. Cons. in field, 1975-00. Author/editor: Ohio Corporation Law, 1988; contbr. chpts. to books. Advisor subcom. on pvt. corps of Ky. Commn. on Constl. Rev., 1987. With USMC, 1958-61. Recipient Justice Robert O. Lukowsky award of Excellence Chase Law Sch. Student Bar Assn., 1986. Republican. Unitarian Universalist. Avocations: duplicate bridge (life master), history. E-mail: rseaver@cinci.rr.com.

SEAWRIGHT, GAYE LYNN, education consultant; b. San Angelo, Tex., Dec. 20, 1958; d. Denson Woodrow and Eddie Carolyn (Dusek) Henry; m. Jimmy Don Seawright, Aug. 17, 1980; children: John Weston, Emily Kaye. BS in Poultry Sci., Tex. A&M U., 1981; MEd in Edn. Adminstrn., East Tex. State U., 1995. Cert. tchr. secondary biology, English. With Security State Bank, Pecos, Tex., 1976-77; bookkeeper Lowake (Tex.) Gin, 1978; cashier, pharmacy asst. K-Mart, College Station, Tex., 1980-81; sec./land title rsch. asst. Bosque Title Co., Meridian, Tex., 1981-82; cake decorator/instr. Lagniappe Bakery, M.J. Designs, DeSoto, Duncanville, Tex., 1987-88; tchr. sci. Red Oak (Tex.) Ind. Sch. Dist., 1988-93; poultry sci. instr. Cedar Valley Coll., Lancaster, Tex., 1989; outside sci. cons. Region 10 Edn. Svc. Ctr., Richardson, Tex., 1990-93, edn. cons., 1993-96; cons. Greater Learning Svcs., Stephenville, 1996—. Cons. Tex. Learn and Serve Program Region 14 Edn. Svc. Ctr., 1996, state rep. for True Colors, Corona, Calif., 1996. Commr. Tex. Animal Health Commn., Austin, 1988-95; mem. Ellis County 4-H youth adv. bd. Ellis County Ext. Svc., Waxahachie, Tex., 1990-94; dir. youth poultry show Ctrl. Tex. Youth Fair, Clifton, 1981-83; adv. bd. Garland (Tex.) Ind. Sch. Dist. Single Parent Program, 1993-96; adv. bd., coord. 21st Century Work Study Program, Celina, Tex., 1993-96; Johnson County campaign chmn. Gov. Bill Clements Campaign, Cleburne, Tex., 1985-86; DeSoto campaign chmn. George Bush campaign, 1988; del. Rep. Senatorial Dist. Meeting, Duncanville, 1988; del., nominee for state officer Rep. State Conv., Houston, 1988. Recipient Cert. of Appreciation, Operation We Care, Mayor Bruce Todd, Austin, 1995, 96; Tex. Edn. Agy. grantee, 1994, 95. Mem. AAUW, ASCD, NAFE, Sigma Tau Delta. Republican. Presbyterian. Avocations: reading, cake decorating, wildlife rehabilitation, children's musical performance (piano, flute, clarinet), children's activities. Home: RR 1 Box Aa-161 Stephenville TX 76401-9771 Office: Region 10 Edn Svc Ctr 1913 Linda Dr Stephenville TX 76401-9409

SEAY, GREG WAYNE, principal; BS in Elem. and Early Childhood Edn., So. Nazarene U., 1982, MA in Elem. Edn., 1987; cert. elem. prin., Ctrl. State U., 1989; EdD in Ednl. Adminstrn., Okla. State U., 1992. Office mgr. State Farm Ins. Agy., Odessa, Tex., 1975-78; tchr. math. Western Heights Sch. Dist., Oklahoma City, 1982-88; elem. prin. Putnam City Sch. Dist., Oklahoma City, 1988—. Mem. pers. evaluation workshop State Dept. Edn., 1982; mem. Policy Com., 1983-84; student coun. advisor, 1985-90. Mem. Am. Heart Assn., 1989-90. Mem. ASCD, Nat./Okla. Assn. Elem. Sch. Prins., Okla. Sch. Adminstrs. (coop. coun.).

SEAY, SUZANNE, financial planner, educator; b. Tulsa, May 3, 1942; d. James Paul and Ann (Maxey) S. BS, Hardin-Simmons U., 1964; MA, Ariz. State U., 1966. Cert. fin. planner; registered investment advisor. Tchr. Baker (Oreg.) Pub. Schs., 1964-65, Govt. of Guam, Agana, 1966-68, Hollister, Calif., 1968-74, Tehran (Iran) Am. Sch., 1974-75, Am. Sch. Isfahan, Iran, 1975-78; internat. pubs. rep. World Editions, Hollister, 1978-87; fin. planner, investment adviser Clock Tower Fin. (name now Royal Alliance), Monterey, Calif., 1984—; tchr. fin. planning Gavilan Coll., Gilroy, Calif., 1988-95, Monterey Peninsula Coll., 1988-94, Hartnell Coll., Salinas, Calif., 1989-94. Spkr. in field. Fin. columnist RVing Women mag., 1995—; talk show host Fin. Planning for Peace of Mind, Phoenix, 2002. Mem. Am. Field

Svc., Hollister, 1987-96; treas. San Benito Hospice, Hollister, 1987-91; bd. trustees. St. Bonaventure Indian Mission and Sch., 2000-03. Mem.: Fin. Planning Assn., RVing Women (bd. dirs. 2000—02). Democrat. Avocations: motorhome, traveling, reading. Home and Office: 2571 N Avenida San Valle Tucson AZ 85715-3404 E-mail: suzyseay@aol.com., suzanne@suzanneseay.com.

SEBALD, JAMA LYNN, academic administrator; b. Dayton, Ohio, Jan. 16, 1949; d. James Arthur and Betty Jean Sebald. BA, Ohio U., 1971; MA, U. Northern Colo., 1973, ednl. specialist cert., 1975. Grad. asst., fin. aid counselor U. Northern Colo., Greeley, 1974—75; asst. dir. fin. aid Med. Coll. Ga., Augusta, 1975—76; student fin. aid advisor U. Idaho, Moscow, 1976—. Mem. affirmative action com. U. Idaho, Moscow, 1987—90, mem. student employee of yr. com., 1996—, mem. parking task force, 2001, mem. parking com., 2001—. Recipient Outstanding Young Woman of Am. award, 1978. Mem.: AAUW (Moscow br. topic chair 1977—79, Moscow br. chair sr. honor awards com. 1979—80, Moscow br. sr. honor awards com. 1979—81, Moscow br. bylaws officer 1980—81, Moscow br. hospitality chair 1981—82, Moscow br. nominations com. chair 1982, Moscow br. treas. 1982—84, Moscow br. corr. sec. 1984—86, Moscow br. pres. elect 1986—87, Moscow br. pres. 1987—88, Idaho divsn. bd. dirs. 1987—88, Moscow br. ednl. found. program officer 1988—89, Moscow br. pres. elect 1991—92, Idaho divsn. bd. dirs. 1992—93, Moscow br. pres. 1992—93, Moscow br. ednl. found. program officer 1993—94, Moscow br. program v.p. 1995—96, Moscow br. co-pres. 1998—99, Idaho Division Board of Directors 1998—99, Moscow br. pres. 1999—2000, Ednl. Found. Name Gift award 1991, 1995), U. Idaho Women's Caucus (chair 1978—80), Idaho Student Fin. Aid Adminstrs. (pres. 1989—90), Idaho Student Fin. Aid Adminstrs. (sec., treas. 1978—79), Western Assn. Student Fin. Aid Adminstrs. (mem. exec. coun. 1989—90), Nat. Assn. Student Fin. Aid Adminstrs., Moscow Pregnancy Counseling Svc. (bd. dirs. 1984—86), Athena. Home: 615 N Washington Moscow ID 83843-2626 Office: U Idaho Student Fin Aid Svcs Moscow ID 83844-4291 Office Fax: 208-885-5592. Business E-Mail: jama@uidaho.edu.

SEBASTIAN, JAMES ALBERT, obstetrician, gynecologist, educator; b. Milw., Feb. 20, 1945; s. Milton Arthur and Bernice Marian (Friske) S.; m. Jacqulin Victoria Johnson, June l4, l969; children: Mila, Joel, Jon, Marnie. BS, U. Wis., l966, MD, l969. Diplomate Am. Bd. Ob-Gyn. Commd. officer USN, l965, advanced through grades to lt. comdr., 1972; intern U.S. Naval Hosp., St. Albans, N.Y., l969-70; resident in ob-gyn. Naval Regional Med. Ctr., Portsmouth, Va., l970-72, mem. staff, l976-77, Naval Hosp., Taipei, Taiwan, l972-76; resigned, l977; pvt. practice, l977—. Clin. prof. ob-gyn U. Minn. Med. Sch., Duluth, 2003—, clin. prof., 2003—; pres. clin. faculty dept. ob-gyn. U. Minn., Mpls., 1999-02. Fellow Am. Coll. Ob-Gyn. (bd. dirs. Minn. sect. 1996-99, best rsch. paper award Armed Forces dist. 1976); mem. Am. Fertility Soc., Minn. Perinatal Assn. (bd. dirs. 1978-87, pres. 1985-86), Kiwanis (pres. 1989-90). Office: Northland Ob-Gyn Assocs 1000 E 1st St Ste 204 Duluth MN 55805-2297

SEBASTIAN, LUCIA VILLA, principal; b. Osaka, Japan, Sept. 27, 1951; d. Frank Benedict and Margaret (Jacob) Villa; m. Richard J. Sebastian; children: Matthew John, Shanna Maria. BS, East Carolina U., Greenville, N.C., 1973; MA Ed, Coll. William and Mary, Williamsburg, Va., 1986, EdS in Adminstrn., 1992, EdD candidate, 1995—. Cert. elem., mid., secondary prin., elem. supr., dir. instrn., gen. supr., asst. supt. instrn., tchr. K-7. Tchr. 1st grade Williamsburg-James City County Pub. Schs., 1973-74; kindergarten tchr. Walsingham Acad., 1974-75; tchr. 6th grade York County Pub. Schs., Yorktown, Va., 1982-88, instrnl. specialist, 1988-92, asst. prin. Bethel Manor Elem. and Dare Elem. Schs., 1992—, prin. elem. summer sch., 1992-95; prin. Clara Byrd Baker Elem., Williamsburg, Va., 1995—. Fellow Hampton Rds. Ctr. for Advancement of Teaching, Norfolk, Va., 1987—. Campaign chair United Way, York County, 1992; prenatal instr. March of Dimes; Lamaze instr. Health Dept.; singer St. Bede's Folk Group. Mem. NEA, ASCD, Va. Edn. Assn., York Edn. Assn., York Mgmt. Assn., Va. Assn. Supervision and Curriculum Devel. (conf. chair 1991-94, treas. 1992, pres. elect 1993, pres. 1994), Delta Kappa Gamma (sec. 1990, Emily Nelson scholarship 1994), Phi Kappa Phi, Kappa Delta Pi. Roman Catholic. Avocations: singing, soccer. Home: 105 Little John Rd Williamsburg VA 23185-4907 Office: Clara Byrd Baker Elem Sch 3131 Ironbound Rd Williamsburg VA 23185-2320

SEBO, STEPHEN ANDREW, electrical engineer, educator, researcher, consultant; b. Budapest, Hungary, June 10, 1934; s. Emery Sebo and Elizabeth Thieben; m. Eva Agnes Vambery, May 25, 1968. MSEE, Budapest Poly-tech. U., 1957; PhD, Hungarian Acad. Sci., 1966. Engr. Budapest Elec. Co., 1957-61; asst. prof. Budapest Poly. U., 1961-66, assoc. prof., 1966-68, Ohio State U., Columbus, 1968-74, prof., 1974—82, Am. Electric Power prof. in power sys. engring., 1982—95, Neal A. Smith prof., 1995—. Recipient Power Educator award Edison Elec. Inst., 1981, Tech. Person of Yr. award Columbus Tech. Coun., 1994. Fellow IEEE (Prize Paper award 1981). Office: Ohio State U Elec Engring 2015 Neil Ave Columbus OH 43210-1272

SEBREN, LUCILLE GRIGGS, retired private school educator; b. Chesterfield, S.C., May 21, 1922; d. Manley Oscar and Clara Blanche (Rivers) Griggs; m. Herbert Lee Sebren, Dec. 19, 1943; children: Herbert Lee Jr., George Hall, Samuel Robert Franklin. BA, Flora Macdonald Coll., Red Springs, N.C., 1942; MEd, Coll. of William and Mary, 1966. Cert. tchr., Va., N.C., S.C. Tchr. Cheraw (S.C.) Elem. Sch., 1942-44; tchr. kindergarten Larchmont Meth. Ch., Norfolk, Va., 1951-53; tchr. Norfolk Acad., 1953-89, supr., cons., adminstr. primary dept., 1970-89, master tchr., cons. elem. grades, 1970-89, asst. to dir. of admissions, 1987—. Contbr. articles to profl. jours. Mem. Va. Symphony and Symphony Aux., Norfolk, 1946—, Norfolk Soc. Arts, 1970—, Chrysler Mus., Norfolk, 1965—, Va. Opera Assn., Norfolk, 1974—, Norfolk Forum, 1980—, U.S. Capitol Hist. Assn., 1983—, ODU Roundtable, 1990-, Smithsonian Instn., Met. Opera Guild, Va. Hist. Assn., World Affairs Coun., 2001—, Heritage Found., Nat. Trust Historic Preservation, Hermitage Mus. Found. Aux.; pres. Philanthropic Ednl. Orgn., 1993-96, v.p., 2001—; bicentennial mem. Libr. Congress. Recipient Disting. Svc. award Norfolk Acad., 1991. Mem. AAUW (sec. exec. bd. 1974-76), Joie de Vivre (treas. 1994—), Old Dominion U. Faculty Wives Club (pres. 1958-60), Town-N-Gown (bd. dirs. 1992—, chaplain 1993-96, v.p. 1995-96, pres.-elect 1996-97, pres. 1997-98), Old Dominion U. Town-N-Gown (pres.-elect 1998-99, pres. 1999-2001), bd. dirs. Old Dominion U. Town-N-Gown, 1992—, parliamentarian, 2001-03, Nat. Cathedral Assn., Nat. Trust for Historic Preservation, Nat. M.I. Hummel Club, Hon. Order Ky. Cols., Internat. Assn. Torch Clubs, Inc., Alpha Delta Kappa Internat. (pres., past state, provincial, nat. pres. 1995—, pres. Va. 1978-80, S.E. region 1981-83, internat. grand chaplain 1983-85, internat. grand pres.-elect 1985-87, internat. grand pres. 1987-89, internat. exec. bd. 1985-91, pres.-elect internat. past state pres. 1993-95, pres. 1995—), Kappa Delta Pi. Republican. Baptist. Avocations: reading, travel, collecting antique glassware and hummels, music. Office: Norfolk Acad 1585 Wesleyan Dr Norfolk VA 23502-5591

SECCO, ANTHONY SILVIO, chemistry educator; BS, St. F.X. U., Antigonish, Nova Scotia, 1978; PhD, U. British Columbia, Vancouver, 1982. Postdoctoral fellow U. Pa., Phila., 1982-84; prof. U. Manitoba, Winnipeg, Canada, 1984—. Mem. AAAS, Can. Soc. Chemistry, Am. Crystallographic Assn., Chem. Inst. Can. Office: U Manitoba Dept Chemistry Winnipeg MB Canada R3T 2N2

SECHRIST, CHALMERS FRANKLIN, JR., electrical engineering educator; b. Glen Rock, Pa., Aug. 23, 1930; s. Chalmers F. and Lottie V. (Smith) S.; m. Lillian Beatrice Myers, June 29, 1957; children: Jonathan A., Jennifer N. BE in Elec. Engring., Johns Hopkins U., 1952; MS, Pa. State U., 1954, PhD in Elect. Engring., 1959. Sr. engr. Bendix Corp., summers 1952, 53, 54; instr. elec. engring. Pa. State U., 1954-55; staff engr. HRB-Singer, Inc., State College, Pa., 1959-65; from asst. prof. to prof. elec. engring. U. Ill., Urbana, 1965-96, assoc. head instructional programs dept. elec. and computer engring., 1984-86, asst. dean engring., 1986-96, prof. Emeritus, 1996—; program dir. divsn. undergrad. edn. NSF, Washington, 1992-96; adj. prof. engring. Fla. Gulf Coast U., 1998—. Acting sci. sec. Sci. Com. on Solar-Terrestrial Physics, 1981; chmn. publs. com. Middle Atmosphere Program, 1980-86, editor handbook, 1981-86; mem. adv. com. on tech. edn. Fla. Dept Edn., 2001-. Editor: Proc. Aeronomy Confs, 1965, 69, 72; contbr. articles to profl. jours. Grantee NSF. Fellow: IEEE (edn. activities bd. 1990, tech. activities bd. 1991—92, edn. activities bd. 1992—93, chmn. com. on pre-coll. edn. ednl. activities bd. 1997—99, edn. activities bd. 1997—99, awards and recognition com. edn. activities bd. 2000—01, oversight subcom. Virtual Mus. 2000—02, precoll. edn. coord. com. edn. activities bd. 2000—03, Millennium medal 2000); mem.: Internat. Tech. Edn. Assn., Am. Soc. Engring. Edn., Am. Meteorol. Soc., Am. Geophys. Union, Edn. Soc. of IEEE (v.p. 1989—90, pres. 1991—92, Achievement award 1993). Home: 14315-C Harbour Links Ct Fort Myers FL 33908-7952 Home Fax: 239-454-3383. E-mail: csechrist@comcast.net.

SEDACCA, ANGELO ANTHONY, protective services official, educator; b. Bronx, N.Y., Mar. 14, 1971; s. Joseph and Marie Ann (Rella) Sedacca; m. Diane Bockino (div.); children: Christopher Michael, Nicholas Anthony. BA in French Studies, BA in Italian Studies, Fordham U., 1993; MA in French Lang. and Civilization, NYU, 1995; MA in Religious Studies, St. Joseph's Sem., 2003. Notary pub. N.Y. Fin. officer premium financing A.I. Credit Corp., N.Y.C., 1996-97; bartender Pelham Country Club, New Rochelle, NY, 1997-98; police acad. NYPD, 1998—99, police officer 40th precinct, 1998—99. Adj. prof. French Fordham U., 2001—. Eucharistic min., lector Secular Franciscan Order, 1990—. Recipient Internat. Sash of Acedemia, Internat. Cultural Diploma of Honor, Man of the Yr. medals, 1998—99, Cavalier, World Order Sci., Edn. and Culture. Mem.: London Diplomatic Acad. (founder counsellor 2000), Internat. Police Assn., Fraternal Order Police, Nat. Notary Assn., Order Internat. Fellowship, Cath. League, Fordham Club, Amb. Grand Eminence, KC (4th degree), Noble Order Internat. Ambs., Order of Malta Aux., Gamma Kappa Alpha, Alpha Mu Gamma. Roman Catholic. Avocations: martial arts, philosophy, civil and canon law, country music, theater. Home: 2066 Yates Ave Bronx NY 10461-1709

SEDERHOLM, SARAH KATHLEEN (KATHY SEDERHOLM), primary education educator; b. Herrin, Ill., Apr. 17, 1945; d. Clifford Clark and Sarah Kathleen (Cockrum) Hatcher; m. Karl Alexander Sederholm, Aug. 12, 1966; 1 child, Scott Alexander. BS in Edn., No. Ariz. U., 1967; MEd, U. Ariz., 1972. Primary classroom tchr. Tucson Unified Sch. Dist., 1967-69, Marana (Ariz.) Unified Sch. Dist., 1978—. Mem. Ariz. Edn. Assn. (student rels. com. 1992-94), Marana Edn. Assn. (assn. rep. 1985-89, 91-93, treas. 1993-95), Delta Kappa Gamma (pres. chpt. 1992-94, treas. chpt. 1994—). Home: 4302 N Stanley Pl Tucson AZ 85705-1734 Office: Marana Unified Sch Dist 11279 W Grier Rd Marana AZ 85653-9609

SEDGWICK, THOMAS FARRINGTON, secondary school educator; b. Seattle, Apr. 10, 1940; s. Thomas D. and Suzanne Sedgwick; m. Georgia Ann Sedgwick, June 17, 1967; children: David, Peter. BA, Carleton Coll., Northfield, Minn., 1962; MS, U. Oreg., 1966. Tchr. math. Tacoma (Wash.) Pub. Schs., 1962-94, math. dept. chair, 1972-87, 91-94, program mgr., 1985-91; math. tchr., dept. chair Life Christian Acad., Tacoma, 1994—. Dir., founding dir. Nat. Bd. Profl. Teaching Standards, Detroit, 1986-95; adv. cons. Channel One-Whittle Communications, Knoxville, Tenn., 1989-91. Recipient Presdl. award for excellence in math. teaching NSF, Washington, 1983. Mem. ASCD, Math. Assn. Am., Nat. Coun. Tchrs. Math., Coun. Presdl. Awardees in Math., Wash. State Math. Coun. (treas. 1988-93), Puget Sound Coun. Tchrs. Math., Oreg. Coun. Tchrs. Math. Office: Life Christian Acad 1717 S Union Ave Tacoma WA 98405-1911

SEDLAK, JO ANN, special education educator; b. Kansas City, Mo., Sept. 29, 1945; d. Lawrence Elmer and Margaret Elizabeth (Nichols) Leimkuehler; m. Daniel J. Sedlak, July 7, 1974; children: Sarah Anna, Mark Timothy. BS in Edn., Mo. Valley Coll., 1968; MS in Edn., Cen. Mo. State U., 1973; MEd in Spl. Edn., Washburn U., 1993. Elem. tchr. Lee's Summit (Mo.) Sch Dist. 7, 1968-74; reading specialist Ft. Leavenworth (Kans.) Unified Sch. Dist. 207, 1974-78; tchr. learning disabled Leavenworth County Spl. Edn. Coop. Unified Sch. Dist. 453, 1990—; with Eisenhower Elem. Sch., Ft. Leavenworth, 1991—98; tchr. Howard Wilson Elem. Sch., Leavenworth, Kans., 1998—. Sabbath sch. tchr. Reformed Presbyn. Ch., Winchester, Kans., 1978—. Mem.: Leavenworth Edn. Assn., Kans. Learning Disabilities Assn., Nat. Learning Disabilities Assn. Republican. Avocations: sewing, crafts, reading, family activities. Home: PO Box 152 Winchester KS 66097-0152

SEDLAK, VALERIE FRANCES, retired English language educator, retired academic administrator; b. Balt., Mar. 11, 1934; d. Julian Joseph and Eleanor Eva (Pilot) Sedlak; 1 child, Barry. AB in English, Coll. Notre Dame of Md., 1955; MA, U. Hawaii, 1962; PhD, U. Pa., 1992. Grad. teaching fellow East-West Cultural Ctr. U. Hawaii, 1959-60; adminstrv. asst. Korean Consul Gen., 1959-60; tchr. Boyertown (Pa.) Sr. High Sch., 1961-63; asst. prof. English U. Balt., 1963-69; assoc. prof. Morgan State U., Balt., 1970-2000, assoc. prof. English emerita, 2001—, asst. dean Coll. Liberal Arts, 1995-2000, sec. to faculty, 1981-83, faculty rsch. scholar, 1982-83, 92-93, comm. officer, 1989-90, dir. writing for TV program, 1990-97; exec. dir. Renaissance Inst. Coll. of Notre Dame of Md., 2000—03, ret., 2003—. Cons. scholar Md. Humanities Coun., 1992—. Author numerous poems and lit. criticism; editor Liberal Arts Rev., 1996-2000; mem. editl. bd., assoc. editor Md. English Jour., 1994-2000, Morgan Jour. Undergrad. Rsch., 1995-2000, CEA MAGazine, 2002—; assoc. editor, CEA Critic, 2003—; contbr. articles to lit. jours. Coord. Young Reps., Berks County, Pa., 1962-63; chmn. Md. Young Reps., 1964; election judge Baltimore County, Md., 1964-66; regional capt. Am. Cancer Soc., 1978-79; mem. adv. bd. Md. Our Md. Anniversary, 1984, The Living Constitution: Bicentennial of the Fed. Constitution, 1987 Morgan-Penn Faculty fellow, 1977-79, Nat. Endowment Humanities, 1984; named Outstanding Teaching Prof., U. Balt. Coll. Liberal Arts, 1965, Outstanding Teaching Prof. English, Morgan State U., 1987. Mem. MLA, South Atlantic MLA, Coll. Lang. Assn., Coll. English Assn. (Mid-Atlantic Group v.p. 1987-90, pres. 1990-92, exec. bd. 1992—, nat. bd. dirs. 2001—, nat. liaison officer 1993—), Women's Caucus for Modern Langs., Md. Coun. Tchrs. English, Md. Poetry and Lit. Soc., Md. Assn. Depts. English (bd. dirs. 1992—), Mid. Atlantic Writers' Assn. (founding 1981, exec. assoc. editor Mid. Atlantic Writers' Assn. Rev. 1989-2000), Delta Epsilon Sigma (v.p. 1992-94, pres. 1994-96), Pi Kappa Delta. Roman Catholic. Home: 17049 Keeney Mill Rd New Freedom PA 17349 Personal E-mail: vfsedlak@aol.com.

SEED, ALLEN H. elementary and secondary education educator, science educator; b. Lakewood, Ohio, June 9, 1953; s. Hugh A. and Patricia (Peattie) S.; m. Laura Seed, Aug. 11, 1979; children: David, Vicki. BS, Miami U., Oxford, Ohio, 1975; MEd, Miami U., 1980, PhD, 1994. Tchr. Hamilton (Ohio) city schs., Summit County Day Sch., Cin.; sci. curriculum coord. Maderia City Schs., Cin., tchr.; asst. prof. curriculum devel. and rsch. U. Memphis, Tenn., 2002—. Mem. adj. faculty Bowling Green State U., Miami U. Recipient Gov.'s award for Sci., Ohio, 1987, 1988; grantee, Greater Cin. Found., Tchr. Quality grant. Mem. ASCD, Nat. Staff Devel. Coun., Nat. Sci. Tchrs. Assn., Staff Devel. Coun. Ohio, Nat. Mid. Sch. Assn., Phi Delta Kappa. Home: 696 Fort Sumpter CV Collierville TN 38017

SEEDS, JOHN WILLIAM, obstetrician-gynecologist, educator; b. Vancouver, Wash., July 7, 1946; MD, U. Va., 1972. Cert. in ob-gyn. Intern Naval Hosp., Bethesda, Md., 1972-73, resident, 1973-76; fellow U. N.C., Chapel Hill, 1980-82, mem. faculty, 1982—91; prof., dir. residency program U. Ariz., Tucson, 1991—94; prof. Med. Coll. Va., 1994—, prof., chair, 1997. Office: Med Coll Va Dept Ob-Gyn PO Box 980034 Richmond VA 23298-0034

SEEFER, CAROLYN MARIE, business educator, curriculum developer; b. Rochester, N.Y., Apr. 9, 1962; d. Francis Michael and Joan Louise (Haitz) Brault; m. Christopher Paul Seefer, July 4, 1991; 1 stepchild, Christopher Jacob. BBA in Indsl. Rels., U. Ga., 1984, Cert. in Bus. Edn., 1987; MBA in Fin. Mgmt., John F. Kennedy U., 1996. Cert. secondary edn. tchr., bus. edn. tchr., adult edn. tchr., online tchr. UCLA, tech. comm. U. Calif., Berkeley, 1999. Personnel adminstr. U. Ga., Athens, 1985-86; substitute tchr. Clarke County Sch. Dist., Athens, 1987-90; edn. dir. Interactive Learning Systems, Athens, 1987-90; corp. trainer Martinez (Calif.) Unified Sch. Dist., 1990-91; tchr. Ctr. for Employment Tng., San Francisco, 1991; tchr., curriculum developer Heald Bus. Coll., Concord, Calif., 1991-96; instr. Diablo Valley Coll., Pleasant Hill, Calif., 1996—. Cons. Holton & Assocs., Ltd., Walnut Creek, Calif., 1992-95, SRD Assocs., Walnut Creek, 1993-95, Fitzpatrick and Assocs., Walnut Creek, 1993-95; curriculum advisor Heald Bus. Coll., Concord, 1993-96. Vol. Ga. Spl. Olympics, Athens, 1987, Nat. Pk. Svc., Alcatraz Island, March of Dimes, No. Calif. Spl. Olympics. Mem.: NAFE, ASTD, NEA, ASCD, Fine Arts Mus. San Francisco, Internat. Assn. Bus. Communicators, Internat. Soc. Bus. Educators, Calif. Bus. Educators Assn., World Affairs Coun., Assn. Bus. Comm., Nat. Bus. Edn. Assn., Commonwealth Club Calif., Delta Pi Epsilon (sec. 1989—90), Kappa Delta Pi, Alpha Omicron Pi (historian 1980—84, pledge advisor 1984—85, fin. advisor 1985—87). Republican. Roman Catholic. Avocations: travel, photography, reading, music, hiking. Home: 574 Cesar Ct Walnut Creek CA 94598-2229 Office: Diablo Valley Coll Bus Divsn 321 Golf Club Rd Pleasant Hill CA 94523-1529 E-mail: cseefer@dvc.edu.

SEELIGSON, MOLLY FULTON, professional life coach, education consultant, academic administrator; b. Dallas, Sept. 4, 1942; d. Bernard L. and Helen (Smith) Fulton; m. John M. Seeligson, Nov. 26, 1965; 1 child, Michael Bernard. BS, So. Meth. U., 1964. Cert. tchr., Tex.; cert. Heart Math coach. Pvt. tutor, Dallas, 1957-71; co-founder, bd. dirs., adminstr. Clear Spring Sch., Eureka Springs, Ark., 1974-93, exec. dir., 1993-95; head of sch. Fulton Acad., Heath, Tex., 2002—. Bd. dirs. Eureka Springs Child Devel. Ctr., 1975-78, Legacy, Inc., Dallas, First Arvest Bank, 1994—, Fulton Acad., 1993-, Org. for Atma Vidya Ednl. Found.; founding bd. The Wellness Ctr., 1994; designer La Poynor Ednl. Project, La Rue, Tex.; life and bus. coach; cons. in field. Author, pub. Sidereal Almanac, 1987-98. V.p. Hist. Dist. Mchts. Assn., Eureka Springs, 1972-73. Avocations: calligraphy, indian culture, scrapbooking, jewelry making, gardening.

SEELMAN, JANNET GENEVIEVE, secondary school educator; b. Constableville, N.Y., Sept. 23, 1954; d. Carl Francis and Genevieve Eve (Jarecki) S. AA, Jefferson Community Coll., 1974; BA, SUNY, Potsdam, 1976, MS, 1979. Cert. elem. and secondary tchr., N.Y. Para-tchr. Potsdam Middle Sch., 1978-79; 7th-12th grade tchr. remedial reading, writing, math. Harrisville (N.Y.) Cen. Sch., 1979—. Tchr. computer word-processing PSEN students; tchr. alternative English, math. and social studies to learning disabled students. Troop leader Girl Scouts U.S., 1980-96, mem. secondary shared decision making com. Mem. ASCD, Internat. Reading Assn., Lewis County Opportunities, Inc. (bd. dirs., sec., 1987-91, 97-2001, 2003), Parent-Tchr. Orgn. (sec. 1997-2003). Home: 7373 State Rte 12 Lowville NY 13367-9701 Office: One Pirate Ln Harrisville NY 13648-0200

SEGAL, BERNARD LOUIS, physician, educator; b. Montreal, Quebec, Canada, Feb. 13, 1929; came to U.S., 1961, naturalized, 1966; s. Irving and Fay (Schecter) S.; m. Idajane Fischman, Feb. 17, 1963; 1 dau., Jody Segal Reinbold. BSc cum laude, McGill U., 1950, postgrad., 1950-51, MD, C.M. high standing, 1955. Diplomate Am. Bd. Internal Medicine. Intern Jewish Gen Hosp., Montreal, 1955-56; resident Balt. City Hosp., 1956-57, Beth Israel Hosp., Boston, 1957-58, Georgetown Med. Ctr., Washington, 1958-59, St. George's Hosp., London, 1959-61; pvt. practice internal medicine and cardiology Phila., 1961—; prof. medicine Med. Coll. Pa., Hahnemann U., 1996—; prof. medicine, sr. attending physician Jefferson Med. Coll./Thomas Jefferson U., 1998—. Dir. cardiology Thomas Jefferson U., 1998. Author: Auscultation of the Heart, 1965; Editor: Theory and Practice of Auscultation, 1964, Engineering in the Practice of Medicine, 1966, Your Heart, 1972, Arteriosclerosis and Coronary Heart Disease, 1972; mem. editl. bd. Am. Jour. Cardiology, 1970—, Clin. Echocardiography, 1978; contbr. articles to profl. jour. Fellow ACP, Am. Coll. Cardiology (chmn. scholar-trainee com., trustee 1969-71), Am. Coll. Chest Physicians; mem. NY Acad. Sci., Alpha Omega Alpha. Home: 1156 Red Rose Ln Villanova PA 19085-2121 Office: Jefferson Heart Inst 925 Chestnut St Mezzanine Philadelphia PA 19107-4824 also: 401 E City Line Ave Ste 525 Bala Cynwyd PA 19004-1125

SEGAL, JACK, mathematics educator; b. Phila., May 9, 1934; s. Morris and Rose (Novin) S.; m. Arlene Stern, Dec. 18, 1955; children: Gregory, Sharon. BS, U. Miami, 1955, MS, 1957; PhD, U. Ga., 1960. Instr. math. U. Wash., Seattle, 1960-61, asst. prof., 1961-65, assoc. prof., 1965-70, prof., 1970-1999, chmn. dept., 1975-78, prof. emeritus, 2000—. Author: Lecture Notes in Mathematics, 1978, Shape Theory, 1982. NSF postdoctoral fellow Inst. Advanced Study, Princeton, N.J., 1963-64; Fulbright fellow U. Zagreb, Croatia, 1969-70, U. Coll. London hon. rsch. fellow, 1988; Nat. Acad. Sci. exch. prof. U. Zagreb, Croatia, 1979-80. Mem. Am. Math. Soc. Home: 8711 25th Pl NE Seattle WA 98115-3416 Office: U Washington Dept Mathematics Seattle WA 98195-0001 E-mail: segal@math.washington.edu.

SEGALL, JOANN BUTTERS, retired school librarian; b. Des Moines, Aug. 26, 1924; d. S. Donald and Aileen Blose (Mutchlar) Butters; m. Edwin Esar Segall, July 17, 1923; children: Jeffrey, Lewis, Becky. MLS, Cath. U., 1983. Asst. children's libr. Des Moines Pub. Libr., 1948; sec., mail clk. Am. Legation, Bucharest, Romania, 1956; USAID libr. Am. Embassy, Bamako, 1977; upper sch. libr. Sidwell Friends Sch., Washington, 1978-85, head libr., 1985-97. Tchr. ESL Lang. Inst., Washington, 1972-74. Vol. libr. Janney Elem. Sch., Washington, 1966; sec. sch. bd. Internat. Sch., Belgrade, 1963-66, chair, sec., Djakarta, Indonesia, 1968-71, girl scout leader, 1967-71, Washington, 1971-75. Recipient Internat. prize Amateur 3-Gaited Horse Show, 1953. Mem. Am. Libr. Assn., Beta Phi Mu (Honor award 1983). Avocations: reading, golf, gardening, cooking, needlecraft. Home: 4333 46th St NW Washington DC 20016-2475

SEGARS, TRUDY W. mathematics educator; b. Baton Rouge, July 17, 1953; d. Augustus Ray and Ethel Mae (Smith) Williams; m. Leandrew Segars Jr., Dec. 18, 1976 (div. May 13, 1992); children: Tamara, Tara, Teresa. BS, Southern U., Baton Rouge, 1973; MA, Atlanta U., 1977. Math. tchr., sci. tchr. E. Baton Rouge Sch. Bd., 1974-78; LSM clk. U.S. Postal Svc., Baton Rouge, 1978-79; math. tchr. E. Baton Rouge Sch. Bd., 1979-93; site coord. Southern U., Baton Rouge, 1993—. Middle sch. math. task. force E. Baton Rouge Sch. Bd., 1984—; cons. D.C. Health Textbooks, Inc., Austin, 1990; La. Math. Assessment Panel, La. State Dept. Edn., Baton Rouge, 1993—. Co-author: E. Baton Rouge School Math Guide, 1987. Mem. Parkwood Terrace Improvement Assn. Baker, La., 1990—; sec. 1st PResbyn. Ch. Scotland, Baton Rouge, 1993—. Named Tchr. of Yr. Northwestern Middle Sch., Zachary, La., 1985-86, 90; Black Role Model of Baton Rouge, 1st Presbyn. Ch. Scotland, Baton Rouge, 1994. Mem. NEA, Nat. Coun. Tchr. Math., Baton Rouge Area Coun. Tchrs. Math., Math. for

Edn. Reform, La. Edn. Assn., La. Assn. Tchrs. Math. Presbyterian. Avocations: cross-stitch, reading, playing piano. Home: 13445 Ector Dr Baker LA 70714-4655 Office: Southern University PO Box 9759 Baton Rouge LA 70813-9759

SEGERSON, MICHAEL P(ETER), elementary school administrator; b. Newport, R.I., Sept. 7, 1947; s. Arthur J. and Rita M. (Kaczenski) S.; m. Kathleen M. Clemens, Feb. 17, 1973; 1 child, Sean. BS, R.I. Coll., 1969; MEd, Providence Coll., 1977. Cert. elem./mid. sch. prin., elem. tchr., R.I. Elem. tchr. Newport (R.I.) Sch. Dept., 1969-87, prin./tchr., 1978-80, prin., 1982—. Cons. R.I. Edn. Leadership Acad., Providence, 1988-90; project coor. Newport Sch. Dept. Gifted/Talented, 1980-82. External v.p. Newport County Jaycees, 1972; mem. steering com. Newport County YMCA, 1983-91; bd. dirs. Vols. in Newport Edn., 1989—; mem. governing bd. Sullivan Sch./Florence Gray Family Ctr., 1994—. Mem. Nat. Assn. Elem. Sch. Prins., ASCD, Nat. Sci. Tchr. Assn., Nat. Coun. Tchrs. of Math., Green Valley Golf Assn. Avocations: golf, folk and classical music, reading. Home: 168 Carriage Dr Portsmouth RI 02871-2228 Office: Michael Sullivan Sch Dexter St Newport RI 02840

SEGGEV, MEIR, radiologist, educator; b. Burgas, Bulgaria, Jan. 23, 1939; came to U.S., 1969, naturalized, 1976; s. Bouco and Helen (Bejerano) S.; m. Ruth Lerner, Dec. 30, 1964 (div. Apr. 1978); 1 child, Yael.; m. Sandra Lee Slarsky, Apr. 7, 1979. MD, Hebrew U. Hadassah, Jerusalem, 1969. Diplomate Am. Bd. Radiology. Resident in radiology Harvard Med. Sch., Beth Israel Hosp., Boston, 1970-73; radiologist Peter Bent Brigham Hosp., Boston, 1973-74, Hale Hosp., Haverhill, Mass., 1974—; assoc. radiologist Beth Israel Hosp., Boston, 1974—; clin. instr. radiology Harvard Med. Sch., Boston, 1973—. Mem. AMA, Am. Inst. Ultrasound in Medicine, Am. Roentgen Ray Soc., Radiol. Soc. N.Am., Am. Coll. Radiology, Mass. Med. Soc., Harvard Club. Home and Office: 236 Fairview Rd Palm Beach FL 33480-3320

SEGUIN, LILLIAN ANGELIN, secondary school educator, mathematics educator; b. Brownsville, Tex., May 28, 1954; d. Frank DeWaine and Victoria Angelin (Muschamp) Preston; m. James William Seguin, Dec. 18, 1988. BS in Math., Tex. A&M U., 1976, MS in Math., 1992. Cert. tchr., Tex., Tex. Supr. Cert. Math. tchr. Pace H.S., Brownsville, 1984-86; math. tchr., dept. chair Hanna H.S., Brownsville, 1986-92; math. specialist Brownsville Ind. Sch. Dist., 1992-94; math. tchr., dept. chair Porter H.S., Brownsville, 1994—. Adj. instr. U. Tex., Brownsville, 1987—; textbook reviewer Houghton Mifflin, 1992. Deaconess Seventh Day Adventist Ch., Brownsville, 1990, 91. Mem. ASCD, Nat. Coun. Tchrs. Math., Tex. Assn. Suprs. Math., Rio Grande Valley Coun. Tchrs. Math., Assn. Tex. Profl. Edn., Alpha Delta Kappa.

SEHR, SISTER CECILIA ANNE, chemistry and physics educator; b. Chgo., Sept. 29, 1942; d. William and Elsie E. Sehr. BA, Dominican U., 1965; MA in Teaching, Harvard U., 1966; MS, Rensselaer Poly. Inst., 1972; EdD, Tex. A&M U., Commerce, 1993. Tchg. cert., Tex., Wis., Minn. Tchr. Regina H.S., Mpls., 1966-72, Dominican H.S., Whitefish Bay, Wis., 1972-82, Bishop Lynch H.S., Dallas, 1982—. Author: Objectives of Secondary School Physics Teaching, 1993. Recipient Carolene Hengsden Tchr. Yr. award Diocese of Dallas, 1990, Presdl. award for excellence in sci. and math. tchg. finalist Tex. Edn. Agy., 1996; named Outstanding Sci. Fair Tchr., Dallas Morning News, 1993, 96, 98, 99, 2000, 01, 02, 03, Fine Arts Tchr. Yr., Tex. Assn. Private and Parochial Sch. 5A, 2002. Mem. NSTA, Am. Chem. Soc. (recipient Werner Schultz High Sch. Tchg. award, 2003), Am. Assn. Physics Tchrs.

SEHRING, HOPE HUTCHISON, library science educator; b. Akron, Ohio; d. Wesley Harold and Jane (Brown) H.; m. Frederick Albert Sehring, July 15, 1978. BS, Slippery Rock U., 1968; MEd, U. Pitts., 1973; MLS, Seton Hill U., 2002. Cert. instructional media specialist. Reference libr.-intern Carnegie Mellon U., Pitts., 1981; libr. media specialist Gateway Sch. Dist., Monroeville, Pa., 1968—. Contbr. articles to profl. jours. Active Pa. Citizens for Better Libraries, Friends of Monroeville Pub. Libr. Recipient Gift of Time Tribute Am. Family Inst., 1992, 96; Henry Clay Frick Found. U. of London scholar, 1969, 73. Mem. NEA, ALA, Pa. Sch. Librs. Assn. (treas. 1982-84), Pa. State Edn. Assn., Pa. Citizens for Better Librs., Gateway Edn. Assn., Alpha Xi Delta. Avocation: culinary arts. Home: RR 2 Box 467 New Alexandria PA 15670-9634 Office: Gateway Sch Dist 9000 Campus Blvd Monroeville PA 15146 E-mail: hsehring@gator.gasd.k12.pa.us.

SEIBERLING, DANIEL R. principal; b. Akron, Ohio, Aug. 22, 1946; s. Carol J. Flemm, June 28, 1969; children: Phillip, Kurt. BS in Edn., Wittenberg U., Springfield, Ohio, 1968; MEd, Kent (Ohio) State U., 1972, Edn. Specialist in Adminstrn., 1977. Tchr. Cuyahoga Falls (Ohio) City Schs., 1968-69, Hudson (Ohio) Local Schs., 1969-76, 80-88, tech. coord./math. cons., 1976-80, adminstrv. asst., tchr., 1988-91, asst. prin., 1991-92, prin., adminstrv. asst., 1992-94, prin., pupil svcs. adminstr., 1994—. Tchr., author, team mem. indsl arts activities integrated in curriculum Tech. for Children, 1970-73. Author, coord. study packets/primary aged gifted children Packets for Advancing Thinking Skills, 1982. Coach Stow (Ohio) Soccer Assn., 1985-94; com. chmn. troop 273 Boy Scouts Am., 1988—; dir. leader MOE dist. Day camp, Akron, Ohio, 1992, 93, 94. Jennings Found. scholar, Cleve., 1984-85. Mem. ASCD, Ohio Assn. Elem. Sch. Adminstrs., Phi Delta Kappa. Avocations: reading, camping, travel. Office: Hudson Local Schs 34 N Oviatt St Hudson OH 44236-3042

SEIBERT, BARBARA ANN WELCH, business educator; b. Hagerstown, Md., Mar. 31, 1949; d. William Ridings Welch and Betty Louise (Timmons) Welch Clipp; m. Paul Alan Seibert, Aug. 22, 1970; children: Paul Matthew, Gretchen Elizabeth. AA, Hagerstown Jr. Coll., 1969; BS, Shepherd Coll., Shepherdstown, W.Va., 1971; MEd, Tex. A&M U., 1972. Cert. preK-12 libr., 7-12 bus. edn. tchr., Va. Instr. Lynchburg (Va.) Coll., 1980-83, Ctrl. Va C.C., Lynchburg, 1983-85; libr. James River Day Sch., Lynchburg, 1985—99; prof. Hagerstown Bus. Coll., 1999—. Mem. Lynchburg Pub. Libr. Bd., 1989-92. Mem. ALA, Va. Libr. Assn., Piedmont Area Reading Coun., Va. Reading Assn. (Young Readers Com. 1993—). Avocations: reading, travel, bridge, crafts. Home: 7872 Golf Vista Dr Greencastle PA 17225-9247 Office: Hagerstown Bus Coll 18618 Crestwood Dr Hagerstown MD 21740

SEIDE, PAUL, civil engineering educator; b. N.Y.C., July 22, 1926; s. Julius David and Sylvia (Eiler) S.; m. Joan Cecilia Matalka, Jan. 7, 1951; children: Richard Laurence, Wendy Jane Seide Kielsmeier. B.C.E., CCNY, 1946; M. Aero. Engring, U. Va., 1952; PhD, Stanford U., 1954. Aero. research scientist Nat. Adv. Commn. for Aeros., Langley AFB, Va., 1946-52; research asst. Stanford Calif. U., 1952-53; research engr. Northrop Aircraft Co., Hawthorne, Calif., 1953-55; head methods and theory sect. TRW Inc., Los Angeles, 1955-60; head methods and research sect. Aerospace Corp., El Segundo, Calif., 1960-65; prof. civil engring. U. So. Calif., L.A., 1965-91, prof. emeritus, 1991—, assoc. chmn. dept. civil engring., 1971-73, 81-83; Albert Alberman vis. prof. Technion-Israel Inst. Tech., Haifa, 1975; vis. prof. U. Sydney, Australia, 1986, U. Canterbury, N.Z., 1986. Cons. Northrop Inc., 1972-77, Aerospace Corp., 1966-68, Rockwell Inc., El Segundo, 1982-85 Author: Small Elastic Deformations of Thin Shells, 1975; contbr. numerous articles to profl. jours. NSF fellow, 1964-65 Fellow (life) ASME, Am. Acad. Mechanics; mem. ASCE (life), Tau Beta Pi, Sigma Xi. Democrat. Jewish. Home: 300 Via Alcance Palos Verdes Peninsula CA 90274-1105

SEIDEL, SELVYN, lawyer, educator; b. Long Branch, N.J., Nov. 6, 1942; s. Abraham and Anita (Stoller) S.; m. Deborah Lew, June 21, 1970; 1 child, Emily. BA, U. Chgo., 1964; JD, U. Calif., Berkeley, 1967; diploma in law, Oxford U., 1968. Bar: N.Y. 1970, D.C. Ct. Appeals 1982. Ptnr. Latham & Watkins, N.Y.C., 1985—. Adj. prof. Sch. Law, NYU, 1974-84; instr. Practicing Law Inst., 1980-81, 84. Contbr. articles to profl. jours. Bd. dirs. Citizen Scholarship Fund Am., 1995-2000. Mem. ABA, N.Y. County Bar Assn., N.Y.C. Bar Assn. (mem. fed. cts. com. 1982-85, internat. law com. 1989-92, 95-96, art law com. 1997-2000), Boalt Hall Alumni Assn. (bd. dirs. 1980-82). Office: Latham & Watkins 885 3rd Ave New York NY 10022-4802 E-mail: selvyn.seidel@lw.com.

SEIDENBERG, RITA NAGLER, education educator; b. N.Y.C., Mar. 24, 1928; d. Jack and Anna (Weiss) Nagler; m. Irving Seidenberg, Apr. 10, 1949; children: Jack, Melissa Kolodkin. BA, Hunter Coll., 1948; MS, CCNY, 1968; PhD, Fordham U., 1985. Cert. reading tchr., specialist, N.Y. Reading tchr. East Ramapo (N.Y.) Sch. Dist., 1967-68, clinician reading ctr., 1968-83, reading diagnostician, 1983-85, student support specialist, 1985-94. Instr. N.Y. State Dept. Edn., 1978; presenter Northeastern Rsch. Assn., 1978, 85, N.Y. State Reading Assn., 1986-94, 96, 97, Parents and Reading: IRA, 2000; adj. asst. prof. Fordham U. Grad. Sch. Edn., 1986-89, adj. assoc. prof., 1989—. Mem. Internat. Reading Assn., N.Y. State Reading Assn. (presenter 1997, 2000), Phi Delta Kappa, Kappa Delta Pi. Avocations: reading, art mus., opera, travel. Office: Fordham U Grad Sch Edn 113 W 60th St New York NY 10023-7484

SEIDERMAN, ARTHUR STANLEY, optometrist, consultant, author; b. Phila., Nov. 28, 1936; s. Morris and Anne (Roseman) S.; children: David, Leeann, Scott. Student, U. Vienna (Austria) Med. Sch., 1965; OD, Pa. Coll. of Optometry, 1963; AB, W.Va. Wesleyan Coll., 1959; MA, Fairleigh Dickinson U., 1973. Pvt. practice, Elkins Park, Pa., 1971-94, Plymouth Meeting, Pa., 1994-99. Vision cons. U.S. Olympic Teams, Phila. Flyers Hockey Team. Co-author: The Athletic Eye, 1983, 20/20 Is Not Enough, 1990; mem. editoral adv. bd. Jour. of Learning Disabilities, 1979—. Vice pres. Jewish Nat. Fund, Phila., 1988—. Capt. U.S. Army, 1963-68. Fellow Am. Acad. Optometry, Coll. of Optometrists in Vision Devel.; mem. Multidisciplinary Acad. of Clin. Edn. (pres.), Internat. Reading Assn. (pres. disabled group 1987-89). Home: 427 Springview Ln Phoenixville PA 19460

SEIDMAN, MICHAEL DAVID, surgeon, educator; b. Detroit, Oct. 14, 1960; s. Melvin and Rita Seidman; m. Lynn Ann Gaberman; children: Jake, Marlee, Kevin. BS in Human Nutrition, U. Mich., 1981, MD, 1986. Resident in Otolaryngology, Head and Neck Surgery Henry Ford Hosp., Detroit, 1986-91, attending physician, surgeon, 1992—, regional coord. Oto-HNS West Bloomfield, Mich., 1996-00, dir. divsn. oto/neuroto, 2000—; fellow in Otology, Neurotology, Skull Base Surgery Ear Rsch. Found., Sarasota, Fla., 1991-92; staff physician Sarasota Mem. Hosp., 1991-92; assoc. staff physician Doctors Hosp., Sarasota, 1991-92; asst. clin. prof. Wayne State U., Detroit, 1993—. Med. advisor Self Help Hard of Hearing People Inc., Bethesda, 1988—, mem. healthcare com., 1990-93; bd. dirs. Ear Rsch. Found., 1992—. Contbr. chpts. to books including Common Problems of the Ear, 1996, others; contbr. articles to profl. jours.; mem. editl. bd. Oto-HNS Jour., Hearing Rsch. Recipient Clin. Investigator Devel. award NIH, 1994-99, Fowler award Best Scientific Thesis, 2000; nominated Ams. Best Doctors, 2002. Fellow ACS; mem. AAAS, Am. Neurotology Soc., Am. Tinnitus Assn., Assn. Rsch. Otolaryngology (edn. com. 1992—), Sir Charles Bell Soc., Am. Acad. Oto-HNS. Avocations: downhill and water skiing, tennis, exercising. Achievements include patents in therapeutic treatment for mitochondrial function, health scan-nutritional survey and in a supplement that improves age-related hearing loss. Office: Henry Ford Health Systems 6777 W Maple Rd West Bloomfield MI 48322-3013

SEIDNER, STANLEY S. academic administrator, educator; b. N.Y.C., June 26, 1945; m. Maria Medina Seidner, Feb. 24, 1980; children: Jacqueline Elinor, Ariel Joseph. BA, Bklyn. Coll., 1968; MA, St. John's U., 1970, PhD, 1975; 6th yr. degree, CUNY, Richmond, 1976; MEd, U. Ulster, No. Ireland, 1992. Adminstr. N.Y.C. schs., 1971-75; assoc. prof. Tchrs. Coll., Columbia U., N.Y.C., 1975-79; dir. bilingual tchr. tng. U. Miami, Fla., 1979-80; acad. dean Nat. Coll. Edn., Chgo., 1980-85; supt. Caribbean Schs., P.R., 1985-86; v.p. M.S. Assocs., Chgo., 1986-88; dean/dir. acad. rsch. and 2nd lang. programs DeVry Inst. Tech., Chgo., 1988-92; prof., univ. supr. S.W. Tex. State U., San Marcos, 1993—. Cons. IBM Corp., P.R., 1980-92, Ministry of Edn., Spain, 1989-91. Author: In the Wake of Conservative Reaction, 1982, Issues of Language Assessment, 3 vols., 1981-88; (with others) Teaching the Soviet Child, 1980, Handbook for Secondary Bilingual Education, 1981. Recipient award Polish Acad. Arts and Scis., 1978, Italian Acad. Arts and Scis., Rome, 1987; recipient Acad. Recognition award NEA, 1983, Outstanding Acad. Achievement award U.S. Sec. of Edn., Washington, 1986; named NAAS Educator of Yr., 1985. Avocations: judo (3rd degree black belt), jiu jitsiu (2nd degree black belt), classical piano.

SEIFER, MARC JEFFREY, psychology educator; b. Far Rockaway, N.Y., Feb. 17, 1948; s. Stanley Cyclone and Thelma (Imber) S. BA, U. R.I., 1970; postgrad., New Sch. for Social Rsch., 1970-72, Sch. Visual Arts, 1971; MA, U. Chgo., 1974; PhD, Saybrook Inst., 1986. Cert. handwriting expert. Investigator neurol. study hand writing of schizophrenics Billings Hosp., Chgo., 1972-73; coll. instr. Providence Coll. Sch. of Continuing Edn., 1975-90, U. R.I. Extension, Providence, 1975-80, Bristol C.C., Fall River, Mass., 1980—, C.C. of R.I., Warwick, 1988—; expert handwriting neurol. investigation epileptic split brain writers UCLA, 1986; handwriting expert U. R.I. Crime Lab, Kingston, 1974-75; assoc. editor Jour. of Occult Studies, Providence, 1977-79; editor MetaScience, Kingston, 1979—, Jour. Am. Soc. Profl. Graphologists, Bethesda, Md., 1989—; instr. Roger Williams U., Bristol, R.I., 2000—; investigator handwriting and MRI of MS patients R.I. Hosp., 2002. Dir. MetaSci. Found., Kingston, 1979—; handwriting expert Dept. Social Svcs. and R.I. Atty. Gen.'s Office, Providence, 1990—2001; lectr. in field; cons. The Am. Experience, 60 Mins. Author: Startez Encounter, 1988, The Man Who Harnessed Niagara Falls, 1991, Polish transl., 2001, Handwriting and Brainwriting, 1992, Hail to the Chief, 1991, Mr. Rhode Island: The Stephen Rosati Story, 1994, Wizard: The Life and Times of Nikola Tesla, 1996 (designated as a book of unusual interest and merit, Publishers Weekly, 1996, designated as serious piece of scholarship, Sci. Am., 1997, high recommendation AAAS, 1997), The Space/Time/Mind Continuum, 2003, The Big Frame: A True-Life Courtroom Thriller, 2003, Inward Journey: From Freud to Gurdjieff, 2003, (screenplay) Tesla: The Lost Wizard (performed at Producer's Club Theater, 1996, video docudrama 1997), 1992, video, 1984; contbr. chapters to books; contbg. editor: Extraordinary Science, 1996, 2000, The Tesla Journal, 1997, Wired, 1998, Civilization, 2001, Cerebrum, 2003, Jour. Conscientology, 1999; contbr. articles to profl. jours. and mags. Fellow Am. Coll. Forensic Examiners (bd. dirs. 1992-93); mem. APA, Am. Soc. Profl. Graphologists (bd. dirs. 1989—), Tesla Soc., Nat. Bur. Document Examiners, Nat. Soc. for Graphology. Avocations: snorkeling, bridge. Home: PO Box 32 Kingston RI 02881-0032 E-mail: mseifer@cox.net.

SEIFERT, AVI, aerodynamic engineering educator and researcher; b. Rechovot, Israel, Aug. 8, 1959; s. Yitshak and Betty Seifert; m. Tamy Serfaty, Sept. 4, 1983; children: Meirav, Adi, Eyal, Jhonathan, Amir. MSc in Engring., Tel-Aviv U., 1986, PhD in Engring., 1992. Lectr, rschr. dept. engring. fluid mechanics and heat transfer Tel-Aviv U., 1990-96; rsch. assoc. NRC NASA, Langley AFB, 1996-99; sr. lectr., dept. fluid mechanics and heat transfer Faculty of Engring., Tel-Aviv U., 1999—. Cons. engr. "Ramot" Tel-Aviv U. R&D, 1987-96, 1999—. Contbr. articles to Jour. Fluid Mechanics, Procs. of the RAS B.L. Stability Conf., AIAA Jour., Jour. Engring. Math., Atmos. Environ., Jour. Aircraft. Mem. AIAA (fluid dynamic tech. com.). Achievements include first to construct a fully automated wind tunnel boundary layer stability experiment; first demonstration of active flow control in flight Reynolds numbers, first demonstration of active control of shock-induced separation; co-inventor oscillatory suction for separation control; research in the insight to the prospects of point source disturbances non linear interaction and control in boundary layers, and proving the superior relative efficiency of boundary layer separation control by oscillatory blowing, on airfoils at low and high Reynolds numbers, also in compessible speeds, finite wing planform and swept wing; developed actuators for flow control; patents for Method and Apparatus for Controlling the Motion of a Solid Body or a Fluid Stream and active control of dynamic stall and enhanced effectiveness of periodic excitation due to the superposition of weak steady suction. Home: 7/6 Kashani St Tel Aviv 69499 Israel Office: Dept Fluid Mech Engring Tel-Aviv U Ramat-Aviv 69978 Israel also: ICASE Nasa Langley Ms 170 Hampton VA 23681-0001

SEIFERT, TERESA DISTEFANO, physical education educator; b. Alexandria, Va., Aug. 9, 1957; d. S. John and Evelyn M. (Bender) diS.; children: Steven Robert, Lisa Ann, Gina Marie. BS, U. Md., 1979; MEd, Bowie State U., 1983. Dept. chair Acad. of the Holy Name, Silver Spring, Md., 1981-83; grad. asst. U. Md., College Park, 1984-85; prof. Prince George's C.C., Largo, Md., 1983—; asst. women's basketball coach Prince Georges C.C., Largo, Md., 1985-88, head women's basketball coach, 1988-94, prof. Mem. 23d legis. dist. Prince George's Rep. Cen. Com., 1988-94, treas.; 1st vice chmn. 5th dist. Congl. Rep. Com., Md., 1992—; chmn. Md. Fedn. Young Reps., 1990-95; mem. Calvert County Rep. Ctrl. Com., 1994-2002. Named Young Rep. Woman of Yr., Young Rep. Nat. Fedn., 1993. Mem. AAHPERD, Nat. Jr. Coll. Athletic Assn. Basketball Coaches Assn., Nat. Assn. for Sport and Phys. Edn., Assn. for Rsch., Adminstrn., Profl. Couns. and Socs., Md. Assn. for Health, Phys. Edn., Recreation and Dance. Roman Catholic. Avocations: cross-stitching, gardening.

SEILER, CHARLOTTE WOODY, retired educator; b. Thorntown, Ind., Jan. 20, 1915; d. Clark and Lois Merle (Long) Woody; m. Wallace Urban Seiler, Oct. 10, 1942 (dec. Aug. 2002); children: Patricia Anne Seiler Bootzin, Janet Alice Seiler Sawyer. AA, Ind. State U., 1933; AB, U. Mich., 1941; MA, Ctrl. Mich. U., 1968. Tchr. elem. schs., Whitestown, Ind., 1933-34, Thorntown, 1934-37, Kokomo, Ind., 1937-40, Ann Arbor, Mich., 1941-44, Willow Run, Mich., 1944-46; instr. English divsn. Delta Coll., Univ. Ctr., Mich., 1964-69, asst. prof., 1969-77; ret., 1977. Organizer, dir. Delta Coll. Puppeteers, Midland, Mich., 1972—77. Mem. Friends of Grace A. Dow Meml. Libr., 1974—, treas., 1974-75, 77-79, corr. sec., 1975-77; mem. Midland Art Assn.; adv. bd. Salvation Army, 1980-91, sec., 1984-87; leader Sr. Ctr. Humanities program Midland Sr. Ctr., 1977—; vol. Quality Health Care, 2002—; bridge refresher Harbor Cove, 2002—. Mem. AAUW (fellow 1979), Mich. Libr. Assn., Midland Symphony League, Tuesday Rev. Club (pres. 1979-80), Seed and Sod Garden Club (v.p. 1986-87, pres. 1987-88), Harbor Cove Civic Assn. (vol. 2001—), Pi Lambda Theta, Chi Omega. Presbyterian. Home: 652 Blackburn Blvd North Port FL 34287

SEILER, JEROME SAUL, obstetrician, gynecologist, educator; b. Bklyn., Apr. 22, 1938; s. Max W. and Pauline (Feller) S.; m. Harriet Silverstein, June 15, 1958; children: Sharon Rachel, Cynthia Beth, Stephanie Hope. BA, U. Vt., 1959; MD, Chgo. Med. Sch., 1964. Diplomate Am. Bd. Ob-Gyn, Nat. Bd. Med. Examiners. Intern Mt. Sinai Hosp., Chgo., 1964-65; resident in ob-gyn. NYU-Bellevue Med. Ctr., N.Y.C., 1965-69; pvt. practice, Flushing, N.Y., 1971—. Assoc. chmn., dir. med. edn. dept. ob-gyn Booth Meml. Med. Ctr., Flushing, 1978-95; assoc. prof. clin. ob-gyn. NYU Sch. Medicine, N.Y.C., 1987-95, adj. assoc. prof. clin. ob-gyn., 1995—; clin. assoc. prof. Cornell U. Med. Coll., N.Y.C.; assoc. chmn., dir. med. edn. dept. ob-gyn. N.Y. Hosp. Med. Ctr. Queens, 1995-2001. Contbr. articles to Ob-Gyn., Extracta Gynaecologica, Rev. Ob.-Gyn. Survey, Internat. Jour. Fertility, Jour. Reproductive Medicine. Lt. comdr. USNR, 1969-71. Fellow ACOG, ACS. Jewish. Office: 800A Fifth Ave New York NY 10021

SEILER, MARK WILLIAM, technology education educator; b. Algona, Iowa, July 20, 1963; s. Michael William and Cheryl Louise (Houchins) S.; m. Kellie MaDonna Howard, Aug. 8, 1987. BS in Tech. Edn. magna cum laude, Mankato State U., 1987; diploma in occupational proficiency, Willmar Tech. Inst., 1983. Cert. tchr., Minn. Tech. edn. tchr. Mankato (Minn.) East High Sch., 1987—. Adj. faculty Mankato State U., 1992—; mem. adv. bd. Minn. State Dept. Edn., St. Pual, 1985-86, chair dept., 1993—; tech. edn. club advisor, supermileage team advisor, engring. team adv. curriculum writing teams Mankato East High Sch., 1988—; presenter in field. Contbr. articles to profl. jours. Morris J. Nelson scholar Mankato State U., 1986; named Disting. Alumnus Willmar Tech. Coll., 1991, World Champion Oddyssey the Mind, 1986. Mem. NEA, Internat. Tech. Edn. Assn., Minn. Tech. Edn. Assn. (membership dir. 1988-90, pub. rels. chmn. 199--92, Spl. Recognition award 1991), Minn. Edn. Assn., So. Minn. Tech. Edn. Assn. (pres. 1990-92, chmn. Spring Tech. Fair 1987, 88), Mankato Tchrs. Assn., Coun. on Tech. Tchr. Edn., Phi Kappa Phi. Roman Catholic. Avocations: computers, family, golf, construction, sports. Home: 354 Terrace Vw W Mankato MN 56001-8626 Office: Mankato East High School 2600 Hoffman Rd Mankato MN 56001-6830

SEILER, MICHAEL JOSEPH, finance educator, researcher; b. Hahn, Germany, Mar. 18, 1970; m. Vicky Seiler. DBA, Cleve. State U., 1997. Assoc. prof. of fin. Hawaii Pacific U., Honolulu, 1997—. Cons., Honolulu, 1998—. Author: Becoming Fiscally Fit: How To Control Your Financial Future, 2002, Performing Financial Studies: A Methodological Cookbook, 2003. Grantee multiple grants, various orgns., 1997—2002. Office: Hawaii Pacific U Ste 504 1132 Bishop St Honolulu HI 96813 Office Fax: 808-544-0835.

SEITZ, JAMES EUGENE, retired college president, freelance writer; b. Columbia, Pa., July 27, 1927; s. Joseph Stoner and Minnie (Frey) S.; m. Florence Arlene Dutcher, Apr. 6, 1950; children: Diane Louise, Ellen Kay, Linda Marie, Karl Steven. BS, Millersville State Coll., 1950; MEd, Pa. State U., 1952; PhD, So. Ill. U., 1971. Tchr. pub. schs., Pa., 1950-56; lectr. Temple U., Phila., 1956-62; asst. prof. engr. tech. Kans. State U., Pitts., 1962-65; dean Mineral Area Coll., Flat River, Mo., 1965-69, Coll. of Lake County, Gravslake, Ill., 1969-73; founding pres. Edison State Community Coll., Piqua, Ohio, 1973-85; freelance writer Sidney, Ohio, 1985—. Founding sec.-treas. Ohio Tech. and C.C. Assn., Columbus, 1976; speaker in field. Author: Woodcarving: A Designer's Notebook, 1989, Country Creations, 1991, Selling What You Make, 1992, Effective Board Participation, 1993, Substance for the Soul, 1999, Practical Woodcarving Design and Application, 2003; contbr. articles to profl. jours. Founding pres. Exch. Club Grayslake, 1970; pres. Epicurian Soc., Sidney, Ohio, 1978-79; mediator Mcpl. Ct., Sidney, 1992-2003; sr. citizens' steering com. Arbor Day Found.; founding pres. Sr. Ctr. of Sidney-Shelby Co., 1996—, choir, 2001—, named Outstanding Sr. Citizen, 2001. Recipient Leadership and Svc. award, Pa. State U. Alumni Soc., 1990. Mem. Am. Assn. Ret. Persons (founding chpt. pres. 1990-91), Assn. for Career & Tech. Edn., VFW (charter Post 8757), Am. Legion (scholarship com. and judge Post 217 1996-97, exec. com. 1997—, publicity dir. 1998-2000), Sidney Singing Soldiers, 1996— (pres., 1998), Shelby Woodcarvers Guild (founding pres. 1999), Iota Lambda Sigma. Avocations: woodworking, lecturing. Home: 55 Brown Rd Sidney OH 45365-8949 E-mail: jseitz@voyager.net.

SEITZ, MARY LEE, mathematics educator; BS in Edn. summa cum laude, SUNY, Buffalo, 1977, MS in Edn., 1982. Cert. secondary tchr., N.Y. Prof. math. Erie C.C.-City Campus, Buffalo, 1982—. Reviewer profl. jours. and coll. textbooks. Reviewer profl. jours. Mem. N.Y. Maths. Assn. Two Yr. Colls., Assn. Maths. Tchrs. N.Y., N.Y. Assn. Two Yr. Colls., Inc., Internat.

Platform Assn., Pi Mu Epsilon. Avocations: gardening, photography, bird watching. Office: Erie C C-City Campus 121 Ellicott St Buffalo NY 14203-2601 E-mail: seitzm@ecc.edu.

SEITZ, SHARON ELIZABETH, elementary school educator; b. Newton, N.C., Dec. 12, 1950; d. Glenn Lloyd and Lorene Elizabeth (Sigmon) S. BS magna cum laude, Appalachian State U., 1973, MA, 1974. Cert. tchr., N.C. Intern tchr. corps. project Mable Sch., Zionville, N.C., 1972-74; tchr. Asheboro (N.C.) City Schs., 1974—. Mem. Sch. Leadership Team, 1991-93; cons. Comm. Skills Com. New Curriculum, Asheboro, 1992-93; sch. rep. Supt.'s Adv. Coun., Asheboro, 1992-93. Vol. ARS, Asheboro, 1988-90; mem. Luth. Ch. coun., 1988-90, witness com. chairperson, 1994—. Mem. N.C. Assn. Educators (treas., chair com. 1983-84), N.C. Coun. Tchrs. Maths., N.C. Zool. Soc., Internat. Assn. Childhood Edn. (treas. 1985-86), Community Concert Assn., Randolph Arts Guild. Avocations: reading, traveling. Office: Donna Lee Loflin Sch 405 S Park St Asheboro NC 27203-5629

SEIVERS, LANA C. commissioner of education; b. Clinton, Tenn, 1951; BEd, Middle Tenn. State U.; MA in Ednl. Adminstrn., D in Ednl. Leadership, U. Tenn. Speech pathologist Spl Edn. Oak Ridge Sch. System, Tenn.; adminstr. early childhood and edn programs Oak Ridge Sch. System, prin. Linden Elem. Sch.; supt. Clinton City Schs., Tenn., 1989—2003; commr. Tenn. Dept. Edn., Nashville, 2003—. Design cons. Inst. Sch. Leaders; mem. adv. coun. Edn of Childen with Disabilities. Mem.: Assn. Ind. and Mcpl. Schs. (bd. dirs.), Tenn. Orgn. Sch. Supts. (treas.), E. Tenn. Supts. Stidy Coun. (chair), So. Assn. Colls. and Schs. (chair). Office: Tenn Dept Edn 6th Fl Andrew Johnson Twr 710 James Robertson Pkwy Nashville TN 37243

SEKERA, CYNTHIA DAWN, secondary education educator; b. Stockton, Calif., Mar. 23, 1959; d. Donald Dean and Frances Lee (Cox) Penner; m. Carl Joseph Sekera, June 21, 1981; children: Matthew Carl, Samantha Dawn. BA, Calif. State U., 1981, postgrad., 1983, MA in Edn., 1984, postgrad., 1991. Cert. tchr., Calif. Tchr. KinderCare Schs., Santa Ana, Calif., 1981-84, Long Beach (Calif.) Sch. Dist., 1984-87, Tracy (Calif.) Adult/Elem. Dist., 1987-95; tech. tchr. Tracy High Sch. Dist., 1995-96; math. tchr. San Ramon Valley Sch. Dist., 1996—, dept. chair, 1997—, SIP coord., 1999—. Mem. Tracy Dist. Tech. Steering Com., 1991-96; tech. mentor tchr. Tracy Elem. Dist., 1992-95; pub. C.U.E. (Computer Using Educators) Newsletter, 1994-95. Contbr. articles to profl. jours. Tchr. McHenry House for the Homeless, Tracy, 1990-93. Mem. AAUW (vol. coord. 1988-90, v.p. 1990-91). Avocations: computers, children, music, laughter. Office: San Ramon Valley High Sch 151 Love Ln Danville CA 94526-2432

SELAMET, AHMET, science educator; b. Istanbul, Turkey, July 20, 1957; s. Sabahattin and Nermin S.; m. Emel Evren, May 30, 1983; children: Mert Evren. BSME, Tech. U. Istanbul, 1980, MSME, 1982; MS in Aerospace Sci., U. Mich., 1987, PhD in Mech. Engr., 1989. Rsch. scientist U. Mich., Ann Arbor, 1989-95; asst. prof. mech. engring. Ohio State U., Columbus, 1996-98, assoc. prof. mech. engring., 1998-2001, prof. mech. engring., 2001—. Cons. U. Mich., Ann Arbor, 1989-95. Guest editor: Noise Control Engring. Jour. and Applied Accoustics, 1994; contbr. articles to profl. jours. Recipient NATO Scholarship for PhD, Scientific and Tech. Rsch. Coun., Turkey, 1982-85. Mem. ASME, Acoustical Soc. Am., Soc. Automotive Engrs., Inst. of Noise Control Engring. Office: The Ohio State Univ Dept Mech Engr 1085 Robinson Lab 206 W 18th Ave Columbus OH 43210-1189

SELBIN, JOEL, chemistry educator; b. Washington, Aug. 20, 1931; s. Abram Jacob and Rose (Aronson) S.; m. Marion F. Kilsheimer, Aug. 28, 1955; children: Eric Allyn, Jeffrey Lynn, Deborah Lyn, Jonathan David. BS, George Washington U., 1953; PhD, U. Ill., 1957. Asst. prof. chemistry La. State U., Baton Rouge, 1957-61, assoc. prof., 1961-67, prof., 1967-91, also dir. Summer Inst. for High Sch. Tchrs., 1984-87, prof. emeritus, 1991—; spl. vis. prof. U. Colo., Denver, 1991-98, prof. Boulder, 1999—2002. Spkr. Union of Concerned Scientists, 1980—. Author: Theoretical Inorganic Chemistry, 2d edit., 1969; patentee in field; contbr. articles to profl. jours. Grantee Am. Chem. Soc., NSF, Rsch. Corp. Fellow AAAS; mem. Am. Chem. Soc. (Charles E. Coates award 1973), Phi Beta Kappa, Sigma Xi.

SELBY, ROBERT IRWIN, architect, educator; b. Evanston, Ill., Jan. 26, 1943; s. William Martin and Alice (Irwin) S.; m. Barbara Jean Kenaga, June 19, 1965; 1 child, Michael Scott. BArch, U. Ill., 1967, MArch, 1985. Registered architect, Ill. V.p. The Hawkweed Group Ltd., Chgo., Soldiers Grove and Osseo, Wis., 1971-84; prin. Robert I. Selby, Architect, Champaign, Ill., 1984—; asst. prof. architecture U. Ill. Sch. Architecture, Champaign, 1984—88, assoc. prof., 1988—, chmn. design divsn., 1988—93, coord. China program, 1988—91, assoc. dir. grad. studies, 2002—. Cons. housing rsch. and devel. program U. Ill., Urbana, 1985—; bd. editors U. Ill. Sch. Architecture jour., 1986-89, 96-97; chair exec. com. East St. Louis action rsch. project, 1995-96, 99-2001, sec. 1997-98, treas. 1998-99, dir., 2001-2002; presenter papers at internat. confs. on rebuilding cities and creating affordable housing. Author: (with others) The Hawkweed Passive Solar House Book, 1980; editor: (monograph) Urban Synergy: Process, Projects and Projections, 1993; contbr. chpt. to book and articles to profl. jours.; exhbn. of work (with E.N. Bacon) New Visions for Phila., 1993; featured soloist on trumpet and flugelhorn Parkland Big Band, 1998—. Served with USAFR, 1966-72. Mem. AIA (sec. Champaign-Urbana sect. 1985, pres. 1987, v.p., pres.-elect Ctrl. Ill. chpt. 1989, pres. 1990, pres.-elect AIA of Ill. 2001, pres. 2002, nat. bd. dirs., dir. Ill. region 2003-2005), Environ. Design Rsch. Assn. (chmn. 21st ann. internat. conf., co-editor conf. procs. 1988-90), Gargoyle Honor Soc., Alpha Rho Chi, Delta Upsilon (bd. dirs. U. Ill. 1991). Avocations: music, photography. Home: 909 W Union St Champaign IL 61821-3323 Office: U Ill Sch of Architecture 611 Taft Dr Champaign IL 61820 E-mail: rselby@uiuc.edu.

SELCHERT, DIANNE KAY, elementary school educator; b. Mitchell, SD, Oct. 26, 1953; d. Pete and Margaret Elaine (Walker) Mulder; m. David Albert Selchert, July 25, 1973; children: Craig David, Michelle Kay. BS in Edn., Dakota State U., 1981; MEd in Adminstrn., U. Nebr., 2002. Cert. elem. tchr., S.D. 5th and 6th grade tchr., spl. edn. tutor Carthage (S.D.) Pub. Sch., 1981-83; chpt. I tchr. Artesian (S.D.) Pub. Sch., 1983-88, 5th and 6th grade tchr., 1988-91; tchr. 5th grade Artesian-Letcher (S.D.) Middle Sch., 1991—98; instr. tech. and tchg. and learning acads., 1998—99; instr. distance tchg. learning acads., 2001—. Co-owner, bookkeeper Dakota Uniforms, Letcher, 1980—. Bible sch. tchr. Christian Reformed Ch., Corsica, S.D., 1970-73, Carthage Luth. Ch., 1982-83; Sunday sch. tchr. St. John's Lutheran Ch., Dempster, S.D., 1979-80, United Ch. of Christ, Letcher, S.D., 1986-87; mem. PTA, Tchr. Assistance Team, presenter, Technology and Innovation in Edn. State Conf., 1995— . Mem. S.D. Edn. Assn. (sec.-treas. local chpt. 1991-93, chair tchrs. com. prin. selection 1993, chair 1993—). Avocations: golf, aerobics, movies, gardening. Home: Ponderosa Plz # 105 Letcher SD 57359 Office: Artesian/Letcher Mid Sch 100 Railway St Letcher SD 57359

SELDOMRIDGE, DEBORAH MCBEE, secondary education educator; Math. tchr. Keyser (W.Va.) High Sch. Named W.Va. State Math. Tchr. of Yr., 1993. Mem.: Potomac Valley Coun. Tchrs. Math.*

SELIG, MICHAEL EMIL, communications educator; b. Galveston, Tex., Nov. 5, 1954; s. Oury Levy and Miraim Claire (Pozmantier) S.; m. Michelle Graham, May 28, 1989. BS, U. Tex., 1977, MA, 1980; PhD, Northwestern U., 1983. Visiting asst. prof. U. Vt., Burlington, 1983-86; asst. prof. Emerson Coll., Boston, 1986-91, assoc. prof., 1991—; dir. film program, 1992-93, 94—. Editor (acad. jour.) Jour. Film and video, 1987-92, book rev. editor, 1992-94; assoc. editor Mass. Jour. Comms., 1992—; contbr. articles to comms. publs. Mem. Soc. for Cinema Studies, Univ. Film and Video Assn. (bd. dirs. 1987-92). Office: Emerson Coll 120 Boylston St Boston MA 02116-4624

SELIG, WILLIAM GEORGE, university official; b. Prince Rupert, B.C., Can., Sept. 25, 1938; s. George Oliver Selig and Minerva Junuetta (Brand) Goodale; m. Judith Margaret Sprague, June 20, 1964; children: Cheryl, Cynthia. BA, Cen. Washington State Coll., 1961, MA, 1968; CAGS, U. Mass., 1972, EdD, 1973. Tchr. Sharon (Mass.) High Sch., 1963-64, Hydaburg (Alaska) Grade Sch., 1964-65, W. Puyallup (Wash.) Jr. High Sch., 1966-69; dir. spl. edn. Northampton (Mass.) Schs., 1969-73, 1974-76; asst. prof. Westfield (Mass.) State Coll., 1973; dir. pupil svcs. Longmeadow (Mass.) Pub. Schs., 1976-80; prof. Regent U., Virginia Beach, Va., 1980-83, dean, prof., 1984-89, provost, 1989-2000; Disting. prof. ednl. leadership, 2000—. Bd. dirs. Set Net, Virginia Beach; pres. Motivational Teaching Systems, Inc.; spl. edn. adv. bd. dirs. Virginia Beach Pub. Schs.; bd. trustees Klingberg Family Ctrs., New Britain, Conn., 1991—2000. Author: Training for Triumph, 1984, Loving Our Differences, 1989, Handbook of Individualized Strategies for Classroom Discipline, 1995; editor Or Gavett Meanliffe, 2001; contbr. chpt. to book. Episcopalian. Avocations: skiing, tennis. Office: Regent University 1000 Regent University Dr Virginia Beach VA 23464-9800 E-mail: georsel@regent.edu.

SELIGMAN, JOEL, dean; b. N.Y.C., Jan. 11, 1950; s. Selig Jacob and Muriel (Bienstock) S.; m. Friederike Felber, July 30, 1981; children: Andrea, Peter. AB magna cum laude, UCLA, 1971; JD, Harvard U., 1974. Bar: Calif. 1975. Atty., writer Corp. Accountability Rsch. Group, Washington, 1974-77; prof. law Northeastern U. Law Sch., 1977-83, George Washington U., 1983-86, U. Mich., Ann Arbor, 1986-95; dean law U. Ariz., Tucson, 1995-99; dean sch. law Washington U., St. Louis, 1999—. Cons. Fed. Trade Commn., 1979-82, Dept. Transp., 1983, Office Tech. Assessment, 1988-89; chair adv. com. on mkt. info. SEC, 2000-2001; reporter Nat. Conf. of Commrs. on Uniform State Laws, Uniform Securities Act, 2002. Author (with others) Constitutionalizing the Corporation: The Case for the Federal Chartering of Giant Corporations, 1976, The High Citadel: The Influence of Harvard Law School, 1978, The Transformation of Wall Street: A History of the Securities and Exchange Commission and Modern Corporate Finance, 1982, 3d edit., 2003, The SEC and the Future of Finance, 1985, (multi-volume) Securities Regulation, The New Uniform Securites Act, 2003; contbr. articles to profl. jours. Mem. State Bar Calif., Am. Law Inst. (adv. com., advisor corp. governance project), AICPAs (profl. ethics exec. com. 2000-2002). Office: Wash U Sch Law CB 1120 1 Brookings Dr Saint Louis MO 63130-4862

SELIGMAN, MARTIN E.P. psychologist, educator; b. Albany, N.Y., Aug. 12, 1942; s. Adrian and Irene Seligman; m. Mandy M. Seligman; children: Amanda, David, Lara, Nicole, Darryl, Carly, Jenny. AB, Princeton U., 1964; PhD in Psychology, U. Pa., 1967; PhD (hon.), Uppsala (Sweden) U., 1989, Mass. Coll. Profl. Psychology, 1997. Cert. psychologist Pa. Asst. prof. Cornell U., 1967-70; assoc. prof. psychology U. Pa., 1972-76, prof., 1976—, Fox Leadership prof., 1999—, dir. clin. program, 1980-94. Vis. fellow Maudsley Hosp. Inst. Psychiatry, U. London, 1975; hon. prof. psychology U. Wales, Cardiff. Author: Helplessness, 1975, Learned Optimism, 1991, What You Can Change & What You Can't, 1993, The Optimistic Child, 1995, Authentic Happiness, 2002 (Best Psychology Book 2003); contbr. numerous articles to profl. jours. Recipient MERIT award, 1991, William James fellow award Am. Psychol. Soc., 1992, James McKeen Cattell Fellow award, 1995; NIMH grantee, 1969—; NSF fellow, 1963-64, Woodrow Wilson fellow, 1964-65, Guggenheim fellow, 1974-75, Ctr. Advanced Study in Behavioral Scis. fellow, 1978-79, Theodore Roosevele fellow, AAPSS. Fellow AAAS, APA (pres. divsn. clin. psychology 1993-95, pres. 1997-99); mem. Ea. Psychol. Assn. (bd. dirs.), Psychonomic Soc., Assn. Advancement Behavior Therapy, Am. Psychopathol. Assn., Am. Psychosomatic Soc., Phi Beta Kappa, Sigma Xi. Office: 3815 Walnut St Philadelphia PA 19104-6196

SELIGSON, MITCHELL A. Latin American studies educator; b. Hempstead, N.Y., Nov. 12, 1945; m. Susan Berk, June 18, 1967; 1 child, Amber Lara. BA cum laude, Bklyn. Coll., 1967; MA, U. Fla., 1968; PhD, U. Pitts., 1974. Vol. U.S. Peace Corps, Costa Rica, 1968-70; asst. prof./assoc. prof. U. Ariz., Tucson, 1974-85; prof. U. Pitts., 1986-93, Daniel H. Wallace prof. polit. sci., 1994—, dir. Latin Am. studies, 1986-92, rsch. prof., 1992—. Cons. to U.S. AID, Guatemala, Honduras, Nicaragua, Costa Rica, Ecuador, Jamaica, Panama, El Salvador, Peru, Bolivia, Paraguay, 1980—. Author, editor: Peasants of Costa Rica and the Development of Agrarian Capitalism, 1980, The Gap Between Rich and Poor, 1984, Authoritarians and Democrats, 1987, Elections and Democracy in Central America, 1989, rev. edit. 1995, Development and Underdevelopment, 1993, The Political Economy of Global Inequality, 2003. Fulbright fellow, Costa Rica, 1986, Rockefeller Found. fellow, 1985-86; grantee Social Sci. Rsch. Coun., Ford Found., NSF, Mellon Found., Heinz Endowment. Mem. Am. Polit. Sci. Assn., Latin Am. Studies Assn. (chmn. fin. com. 1991). Office: U Pitts Dept Polit Sci Pittsburgh PA 15260 E-mail: seligson@pitt.edu.

SELKE-KERN, BARBARA ELLEN, university official, writer; b. Houston, Dec. 14, 1950; d. Oscar Otto Jr. and Edith Hicks (Hardey) Selke; m. Homer Dale Kern, May 31, 1985. BS, U. Colo., 1973; MA, U. Tex., 1981, PhD, 1986. Cert. elem. and secondary tchr., Tex. Co-owner Colo. Sound, Denver, 1972-76; tchr. Jefferson County Schs., Lakewood, Colo., 1974-76; dir. Harvest Time Day Care Ctr., Austin, 1976-77; mgr. TourService, Inc., Austin, 1977-82; from curriculum specialist to ednl. resources coord. U. Tex., Austin, 1982-88, ednl. resources dir., 1988-92; coord. adult vocat. programs Austin (Tex.) C.C., 1992-95, exec. asst. to pres., 1995-97, dean bus. svcs. and continuing edn., 1997-98; dir. orgnl. advancement Tex. State Tech. Coll. Sys., 1998-99, vice chancellor, 1999—. Author: Retail Travel Marketing, 1983, Communication Skills, 1984, Orientation to Cosmetology Instructor Training, 1984, Resumes and Interviews, 1984, Competency in Teaching, 1985, Guidelines for the Texas Cosmetology Commission Instructor Licensing Examination, 1985, Effective Communication, 1986, Effective Teaching, 1986, Balancing the Curriculum for Marketing Education, 1987, Bulletin Board Designs for Marketing Education, 1987, Marketing Education I, 1988, Flashcards for Marketing Education, 1988, Glossary for Marketing Education, 1988, Validated Task Lists for Apparel And Accessories Marketing, 1991; co-author: Higher Level Thinking in Marketing Education, 1990; author (computer software): Emergency Aid, 1986, 2nd edit., 1989, Measuring Employee Productivity, 1986, Retail Pricing in Action, 1987, Marketing Fibers and Fabrics, 1989, Physical Distribution, 1991; editor: Training Plans for Marketing Education, 1987, Correspondence, 1988, Instructional Planning, 1988; contbr. articles to profl. jours. Am. Bus. Women's Assn. scholar, 1985. Mem. Phi Delta Kappa, Kappa Delta Phi, Phi Kappa Phi. Office: Tex State Tech Coll 3801 Campus Dr Waco TX 76705-1607

SELL, WILLIAM EDWARD, law educator; b. Hanover, Pa., Jan. 1, 1923; s. Henry A. and Blanche M. (Newman) S.; m. Cordelia I. Fulton, Aug. 20, 1949 (dec.); 1 son, Jeffrey Edward. AB, Washington and Jefferson Coll., 1944, LHD, 1973; JD, Yale U., 1947; LLD, Dickinson Sch. Law, 1968. Bar: D.C. 1951, Pa. 1952. Instr. law U. Pitts., 1947-49, asst. prof. law, 1949-51, assoc. prof. law, 1953-54, prof. law, 1954-77, assoc. dean, 1957-63, dean, 1966-77, disting. svc. prof. law, 1977-94; emeritus dean, emeritus disting. svc. prof. law, 1994—; sr. counsel firm Meyer, Unkovic & Scott, Pitts., 1977-94. Vis. prof. U. Mich. Law Sch., 1957; past pres. Pa. Bar Inst.; bd. dirs., past pres. St. Clair Health Corp.; bd. dirs. Little Lake Theatre; sec. Little Lake Manor Corp.; cons. jud. edn. Supreme Ct. Pa., 1998-2002. Author: Fundamentals of Accounting Lawyers, 1960, Pennsylvania Business Corporations, 3 vols., 1969, revised, 1991, Sell on Agency, 1975, also articles; editor: Pennsylvania Keystone Lawyers Desk Library. Past pres., bd. dirs. St. Clair Meml. Hosp., St. Clair Hosp. Found.; bd. dirs. Exec. Svc. Corps, 1997-2003. With USAAF, WWII. Fellow Am. Bar Found. (life), Pa. Bar Found. (life); mem. ABA, Pa. Bar Assn., Allegheny County Bar Assn., Assn. Am. Law Schs., Am. Law Inst. (life), Univ. Club, Phi Beta Kappa, Order of Coif, Pi Delta Epsilon, Phi Gamma Delta, Phi Delta Phi, Omicron Delta Kappa. Presbyterian (elder, deacon). Home: 106 Seneca Dr Pittsburgh PA 15228-1029 Office: U Pitts Sch Law 531 Law Bldg Pittsburgh PA 15260 Fax: (412) 531-9203. E-mail: sell@law.pitt.edu.

SELLE, ELEANOR BLAKE, secondary education educator; b. Frankfort, Ind., June 7, 1933; d. Shirley J. and Ruth E. (Waymire) Blake; m. James E. Selle, May 10, 1958; children: David, Marjorie. AA, Stephens Coll., 1953; AB, Ind. U., 1955; MA, U. Colo., 1986. Pvt. piano instr., Miamisburg, Ohio, 1959—74; histology technician for rsch. in cancer Oak Ridge Associated U., 1975-79; now tchr. Accelerated Schs., Denver. Instr. biology Front Range Community Coll., Westminster, Colo. Home: 4755 W 101st Pl Westminster CO 80031-2521

SELLECK, BRUCE W. geologist, educator; AB, Colgate U., 1971; PhD, U. Rochester. Harold Orville Whitnall prof. geology Colgate U., Hamilton, NY, 1974—, assoc. dean of faculty, 1988, dean of faculty and provost, 1990—94. Office: Dept Geology and Environ Studies 304 Lathrop Hall Colgate Univ Hamilton NY 13346*

SELLERS, ANNETTE CABANISS, secondary education educator; b. Tuscaloosa, Ala., Mar. 3, 1947; d. Jack A. and Ruth (Gilliland) Cabaniss; m. Ronald A. Sellers, Aug. 24, 1968; children; Melanie, Brian. BS in Maths., U. Ala., Tuscaloosa, 1968, MA in Secondary Edn., 1971. Cert. secondary tchr., Miss. Tchr. math. and English Gordo (Ala.) High Sch., 1968-69; tchr. maths. Killeen (Tex.) High Sch., 1971-72, Tuscaloosa Acad., 1973-74; tchr. chpt. I math. Guin (Ala.) Elem. Sch., 1974-75; tchr. maths. and English Hamilton (Ala.) High sch., 1975-81; tchr. maths. Winfield (Ala.) High Sch., 1981-87; tchr. aid Shrine Sch. for Exceptional Children, Jasper, Ala., 1987-89; tchr. maths. Caledonia (Miss.) High Sch., 1989—. Tchr. asst. math. camp Miss. State U., Starkville, 1993; presenter workshops and sessions. Mem. com. Troop 9 Boy Scouts Am., Caledonia, 1991-01; tchr. Sunday sch. 1st United Meth. Ch., Columbus, Miss., 1992—. Named Tchr. of Yr., Lowndes County Sch. Dist., 1992, Educator of Yr., Columbus-Lowndes C. of C., 1994, STAR Tchr. Miss. Econ. Coun., 1993, 98, 2003, Tchr. Talk mini-grant Miss. Dept. of Edn., 1997; D.D. Eisenhower grantee, 1991, 93. Mem. Nat. Coun. Tchr. Maths., Miss. Coun. Tchrs. Maths., Miss. Profl. Educators, Kappa Delta Pi.

SELLERS, SUSAN TAYLOR, principal; b. Melrose, Mass., Jan. 8, 1948; d. Walter Edmund and Lucille (Clark) Taylor; m. Burton Chance Sellers, Oct. 6, 1989; children: Heather, Heidi. BA in English, Syracuse U., 1970; MA in Ednl. Leadership, Immaculata (Pa.) Coll., 1993; ABD in Ednl. Leadership, Immaculata Coll., 1997. Cert. early childhood elem. tchr., elem. prin., Letter of Eligibility. Dir. Head Start The Neighborhood Ctr., Utica, N.Y., 1970; tchr. Mt. Markham Sch. Dist., Bridgewater, N.Y., 1970-72; dir. Little People Day Sch., Malvern, Pa., 1987-88; tchr. Friendship Elem. Sch., Coatesville, Pa., 1988-93; asst. prin. Rainbow Elem. Sch., Coatesville, 1993-97; prin. Carl Benner Elem. Sch., Coatesville, 1997-98, New Hope-Solebury (Pa.) Elem. Sch., 1999—. Grad. adv. bd. Immaculata Coll., 1993-97. Recipient Artist in Edn. award Pa. Coun. Arts, 1990, 91, 92, Presdl. award for excellence in elem. math. Pa. Dept. Edn., 1991. Mem. ASCD, Internat. Reading Assn., Nat. Assn. Edn. Young Children, Nat. Coun. Tchrs. Math., Pa. Coalition Arts in Edn., Pa. Lit. Coun., Local Children's Team. Avocations: classical music, opera, visiting museums, photography, football. Office: New Hope-Soleburg Elem Sch 3020 N Sugan Rd Solebury PA 18963 Home: 145 Mountain View Dr West Chester PA 19380-1480

SELLS, BRUCE HOWARD, biomedical sciences educator; b. Ottawa, Ont., Can., Aug. 15, 1930; s. Charles Henry and Nell (Worth) S.; m. Bernice May Romain, Sept. 19, 1953; children: Jennifer, Monica, David, Lisa. BS, Carleton U., 1952; MA, Queen's U., 1954; PhD, McGill U., 1957. Demonstrator McGill U., Montreal, Ont., Can., 1954-57; rsch. assoc. Columbia U., N.Y.C., 1961-62; asst. prof. St. Jude Children's Hosp.-U. Tenn., Memphis, 1962-68; assoc. prof. St. Jude Children's Hosp., Memphis, 1964-72, mem., 1968-72; prof., dir. molecular biology Meml. U. Nfld., St. John's, Can., 1972-83, assoc. dean, 1979-83; prof. molecular biology U. Guelph, Ont., Can., 1983-96, dean biol. sci., 1983-95, univ. prof. emeritus, 1997—; exec. dir. Can. Fed. Biol. Socs., 1999—; interim dir. Nat. Inst. Nutrition, 2003—. Adv. com. Ont. Health Rsch. Coun., 1992. Contbr. articles to profl. jours. Rsch. fellow Damon Runyon Meml. Fund, Brussels, 1957-59, Copenhagen, 1959-60; Killam Sr. Rsch. fellow U. Paris, 1978-79; grantee NIH, 1963-72, NSF, 1965-69, Med. Rsch. Coun. Can., 1972-93, Damon Runyon Meml. Fund for Cancer Rsch., 1962-76, Nat. Found.-March of Dimes, 1974-78, Muscular Dystrophy Assn. Can., 1974-78, Nat. Cancer Inst. Can., 1979-83, Nat. Scis. and Engring. Rsch. Coun., 1990-2001, Vis. Prof. award Institut Pasteur, Paris, 1989; Exch. fellow Natural Scis. and Engring. Rsch. Coun. of Can., 1994. Fellow Royal Soc. Can. (rapporteur microbiology and biochemistry divsn. 1985-87, convenor 1987-89); mem. Acad. Sci. of Royal Soc. Can. (life scis. divsn. fellowship rev. com. 1990-92), Am. Soc. Microbiologists, Am. Soc. Biol. Chemists, Am. Soc. Cell Biology, Can. Biochemistry Soc. (pres. 1981-82, Ayerst award selection com. 1990), Med. Rsch. Coun. (Centennial fellowships com., chmn. com. on biotech. devel. grants 1983-85, standing com. for Can. Genetic Disease Network 1991-92, chmn., 1992-97), Nat. Rsch. Coun. Can. (biol. phenomena subcom. 1983-86, chmn. steering group, sci. criteria for environ. quality com. 1986, E.W.R. Steacie Prize com. 1986-88), Assn. Can. Deans of Sci. (co-founder 1989). Home: 277 Coutts Bay Rd RR # 5 Perth ON Canada K7H 3C7 Office: Can Fedn Biol Socs 305-1750 Courtwood Crescent Ottawa ON Canada K2C 2B5 E-mail: bsells@CFBS.org., Bruce.Sells@sympatico.ca.

SELMAN, MINNIE CORENE PHELPS, elementary school educator; b. Freedom, Okla., Mar. 25, 1947; d. Maxwell Jack and Mary Elizabeth (Mountain) Phelps; m. Thomas O. Selman, Aug. 8, 1966; children: T. Justin, Jeffrey L. BS in Elem. Edn., Northwestern Okla. State U., 1969; diploma in aerospace sci. and tech. edn., Okla. City U./Internat. Space Academy, 1996. Cert. elem. tchr., early childhood edn. tchr., elem. sci. tchr., Okla.; cert. early experiences insci., Okla. Tchr. Woodward (Okla.) Pub. Sch., 1969-72; pre-sch. tchr. Free Spirit Pre-sch., Woodward, 1974-75; tchr. Montessori Discovery World Pre-sch., Woodward, 1975-78; tchr. kindergarten Woodward Pub. Sch., Woodward, 1978—. Host Leaderhip Okla. in the Classroom, 1991; tng. tchr. Okla. State U., Stillwater, 1987, 90. Benefit vol. Western Plains Shelter Orgn., Woodward, 1990, 91; life mem. Plains Indians and Pioneers Hist. Found., Woodward. Woodward Pub. Schs. Ednl. Found. grantee, 1990, 91, 92, 97, NASA/NSTA grantee, 1995. Mem. NEA, Okla. Edn. Assn., Woodward Edn. Assn. (pub. rels. com. 1990—, v.p. 1997—, mem. chair 1997-98, 98—, kindergarten grade level chairperson 1998-99, 99-2000), Nat. Sci. Tchr. Assn. (cert. in elem. sci., presenter convs.), Nat. Earth Sci. Tchrs. Assn., Okla. Sci. Tchrs. Assn. Democrat. Home: 318 Spruce Park Dr Woodward OK 73801-5945

SELTZER, VIVIAN CENTER, psychologist, educator; b. Mpls., May 27, 1931; d. Aaron M. and Hannah (Chazanow) Center; m. William Seltzer; children: Jonathan, Francesca S. Rothseid, Aeryn S. Fenton. BA summa cum laude, U. Minn., 1951; MSW, U. Pa., 1953; PhD, Bryn Mawr Coll., 1976. Lic. psychologist, cert. sch. psychologist, marriage and family therapist; lic. social worker Pa. Family counselor, Phila., Miami, Fla., 1953-60; pvt. practice Phila., 1965—; prof. human devel. and behavior U. Pa., Phila., 1976—. Exch. prof. U. Edinburgh, Scotland, 1979—80; vis. prof. Hebrew U., Jerusalem, 1984—85; chair internat. com. U. Pa., Phila., mem. various coms., chair faculty senate. Author: (book) Adolescent Social Development: Dynamic Functional Interaction, 1982, The Psychosocial Worlds of the Adolescent, 1989; contbr. articles to profl. jours. Mem. bd. regents Gratz Coll., Phila., 1965—, chair acad. affairs com., 1980—, v.p., 1989—97. Mem.: APA, Internat. Coun. Psychologists, Phila. Soc. Clin. Psychologists (bd. dirs. 1975—86, 1999—, program chair 1980—86, 2001—), Pa. Psychol. Assn., Phi Beta Kappa. Fax: 215-573-2099. E-mail: seltzer@ssw.upenn.edu.

SELVADURAI, ANTONY PATRICK SINNAPPA, civil engineering educator, applied mathematician, consultant; b. Matara, Sri-Lanka, Sept. 23, 1942; arrived in Can., 1975; s. Kanapathiyar Sinnappa and W. Mary Adeline (Fernando) S.; m. Sally Joyce; children: Emily, Paul, Mark, Elizabeth. Diploma in Engring., Brighton Poly., U.K., 1964; Diploma, Imperial Coll./London U., 1965; MS, Stanford U., 1967; PhD in Theoretical Mechanics, U. Nottingham, 1971; DSc, U. Nottingham, Eng., 1986. Registered profl. engr., Can.; chartered mathematician, UK. Staff rsch. engr. Woodward Clyde Assoc., Oakland, Calif., 1966-67; rsch. assoc. dept. theoretical mechanics U. Nottingham, 1969-70; lectr. dept. civil engring. U. Aston, Birmingham, England, 1971-75; asst. prof. civil engring. Carleton U., Ottawa, Canada, 1975-76, assoc. prof., 1976-81, prof., 1982-93, chmn. dept., 1982-90, Davidson Dunton Rsch. lectr., 1987; prof., chmn. dept. civil engring./applied mechanics McGill U., Montreal, Canada, 1993-96. Vis. rsch. sci. Bechtel Group, Inc., San Francisco, 1981-82; vis. prof. U. Nottingham, 1986, Inst. de Mécanique de Grenoble, France, 1990; cons. Atomic Energy of Can. Ltd., Pinawa, Man., 1983-96—, Ministry of Transp. Ont., Toronto, 1984-97, Fleet Tech., Ottawa, 1988—, Atomic Energy Control Bd., 1987—. Author: Elastic Analysis of Soil Foundation Interaction, 1979, (with R.O. Davis) Elasticity and Geomechanics, 1996, (with R.O. Davis) Plasticity and Geomechanics, 2002; editor: Mechanics of Structured Media, 1981, (with G.Z. Voyiadjis) Mechanics of Material Interfaces, 1986, Developments of Mechanics, 1987, (with M.M. Zaman and C.S. Desai) Recent Accomplishments and Future Trends in Geomechanics in the 21st Century, (with M.J. Boulon) Mechanics of Geomaterial Interfaces, 1995, Mechanics of Poroelastic Media, 1996, Partial Differential Equations in Mechanics, Vol. 1, Fundamentals, Laplace's Equation, Diffusion Equation, Wave Equation, 2000, Vol. 2, The Biharmonic Equation, Poisson's Equation, 2000. Recipient Rsch. award Alexander von Humboldt Found., 1997; King George VI Meml. fellow English Speaking Union of Commonwealth, 1965, rsch. fellow SRC, UK, 1969, Erskine fellow U. Canterbury, New Zealand, 1992, 98, Killam rsch. fellow Can. Coun. for Arts, 2000-02. Fellow Am. Acad. Mechanics, Can. Soc. Civil Engring. (Leipholz medal 1991), Assoc. Prof. Engrs. of Ont. (Engring. medal for rsch. 1993), Engring. Inst. Can., Inst. Math. and Its Applications; mem. Internat. Assn. for Computer Methods and Advances in Geomechanics (award for significant paper in the category theory computational analytical 1994, paper prize computational and analytical theory category 1997, John Booker medal 2001). Roman Catholic. Office: McGill U Dept Civil Engring Montreal QC QC Canada H3A 2K6 E-mail: patrick.selvadurai@mcgill.ca.

SEMANIK, ANTHONY JAMES, instructional technology supervisor; b. Cleve., Mar. 2, 1942; s. Anthony Joseph and Angela Theresa (Peters) S.; m. Elaine Maria Christian, Apr. 20, 1968. BS in Edn., Kent State U., 1965, MEd, 1969. TV coord. Kent (Ohio) State U., 1967-71; TV producer/dir. High/Scope Ednl. Rsch. Found., Ypsilanti, Mich., 1971-72; dir. learning resource ctr. Mercy Coll. of Detroit, 1972-78; ind. media designer/cons. Detroit, 1972—; pub. affairs specialist Detroit bn. recruiting command U.S. Army, 1980-84, pub. affairs specialist tank-automotive command, 1984-85; dir. learning resource ctr. U. Detroit Mercy, 1985-96; dir. media svcs. Wayne State U., 1996-97; supr. learning techs. Ctr. Advanced Tech., Focus: Hope, Detroit, 1997—. Chair Detroit Ednl. Cable Consortium, 1992-97; 1st v.p. Southeast Mich. TV Edn. Consortium, 1999-2000, pres., 2001—. Producer, designer, dir., editor instructional-educational multimedia and video programs-series for univ. and cable TV, 1985—; editor: (video programs) Elders in the New Japan, 1987, China and its Elders, 1989. Chmn. Detroit Ednl. Cable Consortium, 1992-97. With U.S. Army, 1965-67. Mem. Consortium of Coll. and Univ. Media Ctrs., Assn. for Ednl. Comms. and Tech., U.S. Distance Learning Assn., Mich. Assn. Media in Edn., Detroit Tech. Coalition (steering com.), Phi Delta Kappa. Avocations: photography, videography, music, reading, computers. Home: 7176 Green Farm Rd West Bloomfield MI 48322-2824 Office: Focus Hope Ctr Advanced Tech 1400 Oakman Blvd Detroit MI 48238-2848 E-mail: semanit@focushope.edu., semanika@sprynet.com.

SEMAS, PHILIP WAYNE, editor; b. Gilroy, Calif., Feb. 23, 1946; s. Louis Alexander and Marian (Crapper) S.; m. Robin Lucille Tuttle, Sept. 7, 1967; children: Katherine Lucille, Anna Marian, Ellis Jeremy. Student, U. Oreg., 1963-67. Editor Coll. Press Service, Washington, 1967-68; free-lance writer Berkeley, Calif., 1968-69; asst. editor Chronicle of Higher Edn., Balt. and Washington, 1969-76, sr. editor, 1976-78, mng. editor, 1978-88; editor Chronicle of Philanthropy, Washington, 1988—95; editor, news media Chronicle of Higher Edn. Inc., 1995—2002; editor in chief Chronicle of Higher Edn, Washington, 2002—. Recipient Higher Edn. Writers award, AAUP, 1974 Mem. Am. Soc. Mag. Editors Office: Chronicle of Higher Edn 1255 23rd St NW Ste 700 Washington DC 20037-1125*

SEMBER, JUNE ELIZABETH, retired elementary education educator; b. Apr. 3, 1932; d. Charles Benjamin and Cora Emma (Miller) Shoemaker; m. Eugene Sember, Oct. 18, 1975. BS with honors, Ea. Mennonite, 1957; postgrad., Columbia U., 1958, U. W.Va., 1960. Tchr. grades 1-6 Cross Roads Pvt. Sch., Salisbury, Pa., 1953-55; tchr. grade 5 Connellsville (Pa.) Area Schs., 1957-58, tchr. grade 2, 1958-66, tchr. grade 1, 1967-92, classroom vol., 1992—. Supervising tchr. California (Pa.) U., 1970-90. Mem. Delta Kappa Gamma (pres. 1978-80). Presbyterian. Avocations: writing, traveling, reading nonfiction. Home and Office: 1125 Pittsburgh St Scottdale PA 15683-1630

SEMMEL, JOAN, artist, educator; b. N.Y.C., Oct. 19, 1932; d. Lawrence and Sarah (Zucker) Alperstein; children; Patricia, Andrew. Diploma, Cooper Union Art Sch., N.Y.C., 1952; student, Art Students League, N.Y.C., 1958-59; BFA, Pratt Inst., 1963, MFA, 1972. Teaching positions Md. Inst. Art, Balt., 1973, Rutgers U., Livingston, N.J., 1974-75, Bklyn. Mus. Art Sch., 1976-78, Mason Gross Sch. Arts, Rutgers U., New Brunswick, N.J., 1978—. Mem. jury Nat. Endowment for Arts, Washington, 1983, N.J. State Coun. on the Arts, 1990, 93. One-woman shows include Ateneo de Madrid, 1966, Mus. Plastic Arts, Montevideo, Uruguay, 1968, Juana Mordo Gallery, Madrid, 1969, Pratt Inst., N.Y.C., 1972, Lerner-Heller Gallery, N.Y.C., 1975, 78, 79, 81, Manhattanville Coll., Purchase, N.Y., 1985, Benton Gallery, Southampton, N.Y., 1987, Skidmore Coll., Saratoga Springs, N.Y., 1992, SUNY, Albany, 1992, SUNY Oswego, 1992, Pratt Manhattan Ctr., N.Y.C., 1993, Brenda Taylor Gallery, N.Y.C., 1996, Guild Hall Mus., 1998, Mitchell Algys, N.Y.C., 1999, 2003, Jersey City Mus., N.J., 2000; exhibited in group shows at Mus. Modern Art, Barcelona, Salon Nacional, Madrid, Concurso Nacional, Madrid, Moravian Coll., Bethlehem, Pa., Bronx Mus., Whitney Mus., N.Y.C., Bklyn. Mus., Mus. of U. Tex., Chrysler Mus., Norfolk, Va., Henry St. Settlement, N.Y.C., Ball State U. Art Gallery, Ft. Wayne (Ind.) Art Mus., Indpls. Art League, Mint Mus., Charlotte, N.C., L.I. U., Brookville, N.Y., Tampa (Fla.) Mus. Art, Richard Anderson Gallery, N.Y.C., David Zwirner Gallery, N.Y.C., N.J. State Mus., Trenton, Mathew Marks Gallery, N.Y.C., 1999, Snag Harbor Cultural Ctr., .I., N.Y., 2000, numerous others; represented in collections at Mus. Fine Art, Houston, Tex., Mus. of Univ. Tex., Austin, Chrysler Mus., Norfolk, Va., N.J. State Mus. Art, Mus. of Women in the Arts, Washington, Greenville County Mus., Greenville, S.C., numerous others; numerous commns for portraits; subject of articles and book chpts. Grantee Nat. Endowment for the Arts, 1980, 85, Yaddo Colony, 1980, MacDowell Colony, 1977, others. Address: 109 Spring St New York NY 10012-5219

SEMMES, SALLY PETERSON, choreographer, educator, performer; b. Rockford, Ill., Nov. 17; d. Edwin Carl and Eva Victoria Peterson; m. David Hamilton Semmes, Jan. 8, 1955; children: Melissa Kay Semmes-Thorne, Laurie Ruth. BS in Edn., U. Wis., 1953, postgrad., 1957-58, 61-62, San Diego State U., London campus, 1976, Northwestern U., 1977. Cert. English, speech/theater tchr., Wis. Tchr. English and speech Oshkosh (Wis.) H.S., 1953-54, Madison (Wis.) East H.S., 1955; instr. Patricia Stevens Finishing Sch., 1956; pvt. tchr. dance Phillips, Wis., 1957-60; project asst. Wis. Idea Theatre U. Wis, Madison, 1963-66; test adminstr. Manitowoc (Wis.) Counseling Ctr., 1967; tchr. English and speech Valders (Wis.) H.S., 1978-81; pub. info. U. Wis., Manitowoc, 1970-72, instr. dance, 1972-78, instr. pub. speaking, 1983—, instr. remedial Coll. English, 1992, freelance instr. dance, 1982-95, tchr. Hatrack Kids classes reading motivation, 1982—; owner Sally Semmes Ednl. Workshops, 1983—; staff Next Act Theatre, 2000. Narrator Green Bay (Wis.) Symphony Childrens Concerts, 1977-81, Manitowoc Symphony Orch., 1992; founder, pres., treas. The Hatrack Storytellers, Inc., 1967—; mem. Readers Theatre Reading Incentive Program for Children, 1967—. Choreographer (musicals) Anything Goes, Mame, Guys and Dolls, The Fantasticks, Broadway Bound, Joseph and the Amazing Technicolor Dreamcoat, (mus. revues including) 7 Showtime Shows, Manitowoc; dir.: (plays) Anything Goes, The Male Animal, The Boor, The Ugly Duckling, Our Town, The Sandbox, The Staring Match, The Imaginary Invalid; performer: (numerous productions) Daytrips, Trip to Bountiful, Tuck Everlasting, Love Letters, Dancing at Lughnasa, Lovers, Rules of the Game, The Resounding Tinkle, Baby with the Bathwater, The Man Who Came to Dinner, Blithe Spirit, The Glass Managerie, The White House, The Royal Family, See How They Run, Talking With, Marvin's Room, Eleemosynary, (groups) Milw. Repertory Theater, First Stage Milw., Kohler Arts Ctr., Next Act Theatre, Renaissance Theatreworks. Pub. svc. videos City of West Allis, Am. Cancer Soc., assisted living, 1998; lay reader St. James Episcopal Ch., Manitowoc, 1984—97; dir. Miss Manitowoc pageant, 1972—75, Miss Calumet County pageant, New Holstein, Wis., 1974; guest artist Creative Arts Week Minn. Episcopal Cathedral, Mpls., 1997; editor's asst. Wis. Mag. of History of Wis. State Hist. Soc., 1958. Recipient Cultural Achievement award Manitowoc and Two Rivers C. of C., 1984, Cert. of Appreciation Manitowoc Pub. Libr., 1987; named Sec. of Yr. Manitowoc Manpower, 1983; elected to Natl. Museum of Women in the Arts, 2002. Mem.: AAUW, AARP, LWV, Nature Conservancy, Environ. Defense, Arthritis Found., Wis. Alumni Assn., World Wildlife Fedn., PEO Sisterhood, Sierra Club, Phi Beta. Avocations: baking, travel, reading, film. Home and Office: 8501 Old Sauk Rd 305 Middleton WI 53562

SEMOFF, DEIRDRE PAULA, special education administrator, academic director; b. Albuquerque, Oct. 5, 1944; d. Milton C. F. and Padrice (McLaughlin) S. BA in Psychology, San Diego State U., 1971, MA, 1982; doctoral student, Claremont Grad. Sch. Cert. tchr., Calif., learning handicapped tchr., Calif. Specialist San Diego City Schs., 1977-79; coord. for program for learning disabilities San Diego State U., 1980-89; cons., writer Emerson & Stern Software Co., San Diego, 1986-87; faculty spl. edn. San Diego State U., 1987-89; counselor, coord. U. Calif., Berkeley, 1989—. Staff advisor for learning disabled diversity in learning. Joint PhD program scholar San Diego State U., 1986, Mus. Dept. scholar U. Ariz., 1964. Mem. Assn. on Higher Edn. and Disability, Calif. Assn. Post-Secondary Educators of Disabled, Coun. for Exceptional Children, Assn. for Hearing Disabilities, Coun. for Learning Disabilities, Computer Using Educators, Pi Lambda Theta. Avocations: swimming, horseback riding, theater, poetry, animal and environmental issues. Office: U Calif Berkeley 230 Cesar Chavez Ctr Berkeley CA 94720-4250

SEMON, MARK DAVID, physicist, educator; b. Milw., Mar. 27, 1950; s. Milton K. and Joyce Gloria (Kupper) S. Student, Imperial Coll., London, 1973-74; AB magna cum laude, Colgate U., 1971; PhD, U. Colo., 1976. Rsch. asst. Kitt Peak Nat. Obs., Tucson, Ariz., 1970, Los Alamos (N.Mex.) Sci. Lab., 1974; asst. prof. physics Bates Coll., Lewiston, Maine, 1976-83, assoc. prof., 1983-88, prof. physics, 1990—. Vis. prof. physics Amherst (Mass.) Coll., 1988-90; accident reconstructionist Med. and Tech. Cons., Portland, Maine, 1986—; referee Am. Jour. Physics, 1988—, Founds. of Physics, 1989—. Asst. editor Am. Jour. Physics, 1988-90; contbr. articles to Phys. Rev., Il Nuovo Cimento, other profl. jours. Woodrow Wilson fellow, 1971; grantee NSF, 1980, Nat. Rsch. Corp., 1978. Mem. Am. Phys. Soc., Am. Acad. Forensic Scientists, Am. Assn. Physics Tchrs., Am. Coll. Forensic Examiners, Coun. Undergrad. Rsch., Soc. Woodrow Wilson Fellows. Achievements include evaluation of expectation values in Aharonov-Bohm Effect; co-authoring new equation of state for liquid/gas systems near critical point, alternative formulation of quantum electrodynamics; new interpretation of the electromagnetic vector potential, new geometric model of velocity addition in special relativity. Office: Bates Coll Dept Physics 44 Campus Ave Lewiston ME 04240-6018 E-mail: msemon@bates.edu.

SEMONCHE, JOHN ERWIN, history educator, lawyer, consultant; b. Alpha, N.J., Feb. 9, 1933; s. John and Anna (Lukachek) S.; m. Barbara Lou Potts, June 16, 1962; 1 child, Laura Semonche Jones. BA, Brown U., 1954; MA, Northwestern U., 1955, PhD, 1962; JD, Duke U., 1967. Instr. U. Conn., Storrs, 1960-61; prof. history U. N.C., Chapel Hill, 1961—. Bd. editors History Microcomputer Review, Pittsburg, Kans., 1992-2003. Author: Ray Stannard Baker: A Quest for Democracy in Modern America, 1870-1918, 1969, Charting the Future: The Supreme Court Responds to a Changing Society 1890-1920, 1978, Religion and Constitutional Government in the United States, 1985, Keeping the Faith: A Cultural History of the U.S. Supreme Court, 1998; author (software) Computer Simulations in U.S. History, 1988. Served to lt. (j.g.) USN, 1955-58. Recipient Higher Edn. Software award EDUCOM/Nat. Ctr. Rsch. to Improve Postsecondary Tchg. and Learning, 1988; inclusion in 101 Success Stories of Information Technology in Higher Edn., Joe Wyatt Challenge Com., 1993. Office: Univ NC Dept History CB 3195 Hamilton Hl Chapel Hill NC 27599-3195

SEMONIN, RICHARD GERARD, retired state official; b. Akron, Ohio, June 25, 1930; s. Charles Julius and Catherine Cecelia (Schooley) S.; m. Lennie Stuker, Feb. 3, 1951; children: Cecelia C., Richard G. Jr. (dec.), James R., Patricia R. BS, U. Wash., 1955. With Ill. State Water Survey, Champaign, 1955-91, chief, 1986-91, chief emeritus, 1991—; co-chmn. Ill. Water Rsch. & Land Use Planning Task Force, 1992-94. Adj. prof. U. Ill., 1975-91; chmn. Ill. Low-Level Radioactive Waste Task Group, 1994-96. Contbr. chpts. to books and articles to profl. jours.; co-editor: Atmospheric Deposition, 1983. Staff sgt. USAF, 1948-52. Grantee NSF, 1957-76, U.S. Dept. Energy, 1965-90. Fellow AAAS, Am. Meteorol. Soc. (councilor 1983-86); mem. Nat. Weather Assn. (councilor 1978-81), Weather Modification Assn., Ill. Acad. Scis., Sigma Xi. Roman Catholic. Avocations: civil war, golf, fishing, geneology. Home: 1002 Devonshire Dr Champaign IL 61821-6620 Office: Ill State Water Survey 2204 Griffith Dr Champaign IL 61820-7495 E-mail: semonin@uiuc.edu.

SENDER, MARYANN, director; b. Fairview, Ohio, Aug. 6, 1956; d. Edward John and Annamay Knecht; m. Emil Robert Syarto, Sept. 9, 1978 (div. Nov. 1991); 1 child, Shannon Syarto; m. John Peter Sender, July 20, 2001. B in Edn./Therapy, Ohio State U., 1978; M in Counseling/Art Psychology, Ursuline Coll., 1989. Cert. rehab. counselor. HPER and program dir. Lakewood (Ohio) YWCA, 1978—80; activity therapy dir. Northside Hosp., Youngstown, Ohio, 1980—87; instr. art therapy Cleve. State U., 1989—93; acad. counselor Cuyahoga C.C., Cleve., 1989—91, ACCESS dir., 1991—. NOCSD chair No. Ohio Consortium, 1993—; spkr. in field. Chair Nat. Disability Awareness Day, Cleve., 1990—; com. mem., BAC/Global Issues, Cleve. and Atlanta, 1998, 1999, 2001; creator Ed Sparre Scholarship Cuyahoga C.C., 1999—; hon. mem. adv. bd. Cleve. Rapid Transit Authority, 1995—98. Mem.: Advocates for Disabled Ohioans, Assn. for Learning Disabilities, Assn. for Higher Edn., Transition and Comm. Consortium on Learning Disabilities, Dir. of Activities Assn., Profl. Activities Therapy Assn., Assn. Higher Edn. and Disability, Mental Health Assn., Am. Heart Assn., Ams. with Disability Act (coll. chairperson 1991—), Dance Exercise Assn., Am. Dance Assn. Avocations: swimming, dancing, art, reading, hiking. Home: 5874 Hickory Trl North Ridgeville OH 44039 Office: Cuyahoga C C 4250 Richmond Rd Highland Hills OH 44122 Fax: 440-327-5957. E-mail: maryann.sender@tri-c.cc.edu.

SENDLENSKI, LINDA STACHECKI, secondary education educator; b. Southampton, N.Y., May 4, 1946; d. Floryan C. and Irene L. (Maks) Stachecki; m. Robert Francis Sendlenski, Jan. 27, 1968; children: Robert P., Michael P., Thomas P., Kevin P. BS, St. Lawrence U., 1968; MS in Edn., L.I. U., 1990. Math tchr. Westhampton Beach (N.Y.) H.S., 1968-70, title I reading tchr., 1994-95; math tchr. Pierson H.S., Sag Harbor, N.Y., 1995—; pvt. tutor, 1970—. Tutor coord. L.I. U., Southampton, N.Y., 1990-94, adj. instr. math. and edn., 1991-96, literacy corps dir., 1993-94, reading specialist Ctr. for Acad. Achievement, 1990-92; Bd. Coop. Ednl. Svcs. cons. tchg. calculus II and complex variables Suffolk Bd. Coop. Edn., Westhampton Beach, 1994-95. Editor, pub. Southampton Sch. Dist. Newsletter, 1983-86. Trustee Southampton (N.Y.) Village Bd., 1986-88. Mem. Suffolk County Math. Assn., Phi Beta Kappa. Roman Catholic. Avocations: cooking, sports, reading. Home: 29 Wooley St Southampton NY 11968-3434 Office: Pierson HS 200 Jermain Ave Sag Harbor NY 11963-3549 E-mail: shsendl@sagharbor.k12.ny.us.

SENECAL, CONNIE MONTOYA, special education educator; b. Iloilo, Panay, Philippines, Oct. 23, 1945; came to U.S., 1968; d. Pedro Altaya Montoya and Esperanza Canoy Tupino; m. William S. Goodyear Jr., Oct. 26, 1968 (div. Nov. 1981); children: Stacy, Katie; m. John Joseph Senecal, Dec. 31, 1982; 1 child, Amy (died 3/29/98). BA, U. Guam, Agana, 1967; MA, U. No. Colo., 1970. Cert. tchr., Colo., Tex. Med. social worker Dept. Pub. Health and Welfare, Agana, 1967-68; tchr. emotionally disturbed-behavior disordered students Boulder (Colo.) Valley Pub. Schs., 1970-83, Dept. of Def. Dependents Schs., Mannheim, Germany, 1989, cons., behavior mgmt. specialist Heidelberg, Germany, 1986-89; resource tchr. Ft. Campbell (Ky.) Schs., 1983-86; tchr. Northside Ind. Schs., San Antonio, 1990-95, N.E. Ind. Sch., San Antonio, 1995—. Presenter workshops. Recording sec. Panay/Negros Filipino Assn., Agana, 1967; sec. AAUW, Agana, 1968. Tchr. of Year, Stahl Elem., NEISD, 1997-98. Mem. NEA, Coun. Exceptional Children. Democrat. Roman Catholic. Avocations: collecting russian lacquer boxes, fairy tale plates, german tins. Office: Stahl Elem Sch 5222 Stahl Rd San Antonio TX 78247-1798

SENECAL, KRISTIN SCHWARTZ, librarian; b. Mpls., Mar. 15, 1955; d. John Bernard and Avonne Gold Schwartz; m. Keith Evan Senecal; 1 child, Kathryn Eileen. BA, U. Del., 1976; MS in Libr. Sci., U. N.C., 1977; MA, Shippensburg U., 1990. Asst. libr. Med. Coll. Pa., Phila., 1977—79; circulation mgr. Linfield Coll. Libr., McMinnville, Oreg., 1979—80; reference libr. Wilson Coll., Chambersburg, Pa., 1985—88; libr. Dickinson Coll., Carlisle, Pa., 1988—2003, PALINET, Carlisle, 2003—. V.p. OCLC Mems. Coun., Dublin, 2001—02, pres., 2002—. Contbr. articles to profl. jours., chapters to books. Docent Cumberland County Hist. Soc., Carlisle, 2000—; vol. Domestic Violence Svcs. Cumberland & Perry Counties, Carlisle, 1990—. Grantee, Coun. Libr. Resources, 1994—97. Mem.: ALA, Assn. Coll. Librs. Ctrl. Pa. (chair user svcs. com. 1996—99, del.-at-large, exec. com. 2000—01), Assn. Coll. and Rsch. Librs. (treas. DV chpt. 1994—96). Avocations: travel, gardening. Office: PALINET 3000 Market St Philadelphia PA 19104-2801 Office Fax: 717-245-1439. Business E-mail: senecal@dickinson.edu.

SENELICK, LAURENCE PHILIP, theatre educator, director, writer; b. Chgo., Oct. 12, 1942; s. Theodore Senelick and Evelyn Marder. BA, Northwestern U., Evanston, Ill., 1964; AM, Harvard U., 1965, PhD, 1972. Asst. prof. English Emerson Coll., Boston, 1968-72; from asst. to prof. drama, Fletcher prof. drama and oratory Tufts U., Medford, Mass., 1972—, Disting. prof., 2002. Hon. curator Russian drama & theatre Harvard Theatre Collection, Cambridge, Mass., 1991—. Author: A Cavalcade of Clowns, 1978, Tchaikovsky's Sleeping Beauty, 1978, Gordon Craig's Moscow Hamlet: A Reconstruction, 1982, Serf Actor: The Life and Art of Mikhail Shchepkin, 1984, Anton Chekhov, 1985, The Prestige of Evil: The Murderer as Romantic Hero, 1987, (with P. Haskell) The Cheese Book, 1985, The Chekhov Theatre, 1996, The Changing Room: Sex, Drag and Theatre, 2000; editor: National Theatre in Northern and Eastern Europe 1743-1900, Cabaret Performance: Europe 1890-1940, 2 vols., Gender in Performance, Wandering Stars, The Chekhov Theatre, Russian Comedy of the Nikolaian Era, Tavern-Singing in Early Victorian London, Lovesick: Modernist Plays of Same-sex Love 1895-1925, 1999; dir.: (plays) The Merchant of Venice, Dead Souls, You Never Can Tell, Tartuff, The Magic Flute, Le Nozze de Figaro, Il Barbiere di Siviglia, numerous others; contbr. articles to profl. jours. Recipient rsch. award NEH, 1994-96, George Freedley award Theatre Libr. Assn., 1988, George Jean Nathan prize, 2001; fellow Guggenheim Found., 1979-80, 87-88, Wissenschaftskolleg zu Berlin, 1984-85. Mem. Am. Soc. Theatre Rsch. (exec. bd. dirs. 1992—, Disting. Scholar 2002), Internat. Fedn. Theatre Rsch. (univ. commn. 1992—). Avocations: collecting theatricalia, cooking. Office: Tufts U Dept of Drama Leir Hall Medford MA 02155

SENGUPTA, MRITUNJOY, mining engineer, educator; b. Cuttack, Orissa, India, Oct. 24, 1941; came to U.S., 1968; s. Chandi P. and Bani S.; m. Nupur Bagchi, Jan. 15, 1981; children: Shyam S. ME, Columbia U., 1971, MS, 1972; PhD, Colo. Sch. of Mines, 1983. Mining engr. Continental Oil Co., Denver, 1977-78, United Nuclear Corp., Albuquerque, 1978-80, Morrison-Knudson Co., Boise, Idaho, 1975-77, 80-82; assoc. prof. U. Alaska, Fairbanks, 1983-88, prof., 1989-95. Cons. UN Devel. Program, 1987. Author: Mine Environmental Engineering, vols. I and II, 1989, Environmental Impacts of Mining, 1992, Bioremediation Engineering for Mining and Mineral Processing Wastes, 1997, Mineral Industry of India: Planning, Development and Foreign Investment Opportunities, 2001; contbr. articles to profl. publs. Recipient Gold medal Mining Metall. Inst. of India, 1976, Nat. Merit scholarship Govt. of India, 1959-63. Mem. NSPE, AAAS, So. Mining Engrs. Achievements include development of new concepts for mine design in oilshale in Colo. Home: PO Box 13713 Mill Creek WA 98082-1713 E-mail: msengupta@msn.com.

SENHAUSER, DONALD A(LBERT), pathologist, educator; b. Dover, Ohio, Jan. 30, 1927; s. Albert Carl and Maude Anne (Snyder) S.; m. Helen Brown, July 22, 1961; children: William, Norman. Student, U. Chgo., 1944-45; BS, Columbia U., 1948, MD, 1951; grad. with honors, U.S. Naval Sch. Aviation Medicine, 1953. Diplomate Am. Bd. Pathology. Intern Roosevelt Hosp., N.Y.C., 1951-52; resident Columbia-Presbyn. Hosp., N.Y.C., 1955-56, Cleve. Clinic, 1956-60; instr. in pathology Columbia U., 1955-56; fellow in immuno-pathology Middlesex Hosp. Med. Sch., London, 1960-61; mem. dept. pathology Cleve. Clinic Found., 1961-63; assoc. prof. pathology U. Mo., 1963-65; prof., asst. dean Sch. Medicine U. Mo., 1969-70, dir. teaching labs., 1968-70, prof., vice-chmn. dept. pathology, 1965-75; prof., chmn. dept. pathology Coll. Medicine Ohio State U., 1975-92, chair emeritus, 1992, prof. Sch. Allied Med. Professions, 1975-95, prof. emeritus, 1995—, named prof., 2003. Dir. labs. Ohio State U. Hosps., 1975-92; pres. Univ. Reference Lab., Inc., 1984-86, CEO, 1986-92; bd. dirs. Columbus area chpt. ARC, 1978-82; cons. in field; WHO-AMA Vietnam med. edn. project mem. U. Saigon Med. Sch., 1967-72; vis. scientist HEW, 1972-73; acting dir. Ctrl. Ohio Regional Blood Ctr., 1976-79. Mem. editorial bd. Am. Jour. Clin. Pathology, 1965-76. With USN, 1945-46; lt. M.C. USNR, Korea, China; now capt. USNR ret. Served with USN, 1945-46; served as lt. M.C. USNR, Korea, China; now capt. USNR, Ret. Recipient Lower award, Bunts Ednl. Found., 1960—61; professorship endowed in his name, Ohio State U. Med. Sch., 2003. Mem. AAAS, Coll. Am. Pathologists (bd. govs. 1980-86, v.p. 1989-90, pres.-elect 1990-91, pres. 1991-93, immediate past pres. 1993—, Pathologist of Yr. 1994, Hartman award 1998), Am. Soc. Clin. Pathologists, Assn. Pathology Chmn., Am. Assn. Pathology, Internat. Acad. Pathology, Assn. Am. Med. Colls., Am. Assn. Blood Banks, Ohio Soc. Pathologists (gov. 1979, pres. 1987-89), Ohio Hist. Soc., Masons, Sigma Xi. Lutheran. Home: 1256 Clubview Blvd N Columbus OH 43235-1226 E-mail: donaldsenhauser@cs.com.

SENHOLZI, GREGORY BRUCE, secondary school educator; b. Amityville, N.Y., Apr. 16, 1952; s. Joseph Bruce and Beverly Ann (Sullivan) S.; m. Rochelle Ann Birnbaum, Nov. 20, 1976; children: David, Vicki. BA, Iona Coll., 1974; MLS, SUNY, Stony Brook, 1976. Salesman, printer R.H. Macy's, Huntington, N.Y., 1967-74; math. and computer tchr. Sachem Sch. Dist., Lake Ronkonkoma, N.Y., 1974—; math. chair Seneca Jr. H.S., Lake Ronkonkoma, NY, 2001—. Computer specialist Tex. Instruments, N.Y., 1982-84; audio video specialist Dart Audio Video, Centereach, N.Y., 1984-88; consulate, curriculum specialist Sachem Sch. Dist., 1978-2001. Deacon local Roman Cath. ch., Wading River, N.Y., 1989—, spiritual dir. 2001—. Mem. Adoptive Parents Com. (bd. dirs., workshop leader 1984—), K.C. (treas. 1988—). Avocations: swimming, acting, skiing, singing, travel. Home: 129 Gregory Way Calverton NY 11933-1138 Office: Sachem Sch Dist Main St Holbrook NY 11742 E-mail: gsenholz@optonline.net.

SENNETT, HENRY HERBERT, JR., theatre arts educator and consultant; b. Atlanta, Feb. 28, 1945; s. Henry Herbert and Betty Ruth (Wilson) S.; m. Beverly Ann Rodgers, Dec. 9, 1967; children: Cristie Aline, Herbert Alan. BS in Edn., Ark. State U., Jonesboro, 1968; MA, Memphis State U., 1971; MDiv, So. Bapt. Sem., Louisville, 1978; DMin, Midwestern Bapt. Sem., Kansas City, Mo., 1988; MFA, Fla. Atlantic U., 1989; PhD, La. State U., 2002. Endorsed Military Chaplain So. Baptist Conv.; cert. tchr. Tchr. speech and English Covington (Tenn.) High Sch., 1971-72; freelance designer Lighting by Herb, Memphis, 1972-73; tchr. speech and English Augusta (Ark.) High Sch., 1973-76; instr. drama Jefferson Community Coll., Louisville, 1977-78; pastor Dublin (Ohio) Bapt. Ch., 1979-83, Trinity Bapt. Ch., Searcy, Ark., 1983-85; asst. prof. theatre arts, dept. chair Palm Beach Atlantic Coll., West Palm Beach, Fla., 1985-96. Stress mgmt. cons. Palm Beach County Bd. Edn., West Palm Beach, 1988-94; freelance cons. theatrical lighting and design, West Palm Beach, 1986—; cons. drama edn. Fla. Dept. Edn., 1991-94; vis. prof. Midwestern Bapt. Sem., Kansas City, Mo., 1988; dept. coord., assoc. prof. Commn. Arts, La. Coll., 1996-2001; assoc. prof. theatre Southeastern Coll., Lakeland, Fla., 2001-2003 Author: Religion and Dramatics: Essays on the Relationship Between Christianity and Theatrical Arts, 1994, (plays) Stars, 1989, the Antigone Act, 1999, The Viewing, 2002, (play collection) Unexpected Encounters with Eternity, 1998. 1st lt. U.S. Army, 1968-70, Vietnam; lt. col. (chaplain) USAR, 1983—. Mem. Nat. Assn. Schs. Theatre, Southeastern Theatre Conf., Assn. Theatre in Higher Edn., Christians in Theatre Arts, Blue Key, Pi Kappa Phi (chpt. pres. 1965-66). Republican. Baptist. Avocations: pastor, author. E-mail: hsennettjr@cs.com.

SENTMAN, LEE H. aerospace engineer, educator; b. Chgo., Jan. 27, 1937; s. Lee H. Jr. and Esther (Dore) S.; m. Janice Gillespie; children: Jeanne, Charles, Christopher, Jessica. BS, U. Ill., 1958; PhD, Stanford U., 1965. Sr. dynamics engr. Lockheed Missiles and Space Co., Sunnyvale, Calif., 1959-65; prof. aero and astro engring. U. Ill., Urbana, 1965—2002, prof. emeritus, 2002—. Cons. to various aerospace cos. Contbr. articles to profl. jours. Fellow: AIAA (Plasmadynamics and Lasers award 1999, Sustained Svc. award 2002); mem.: Optical Soc. Am. Achievements include research in fundamental and overtone HF chemical lasers. Office: U Ill Dept Aero Engring 306 Talbot Lab Urbana IL 61801

SEPTER, ELIZABETH BYRNSIDE, secondary education educator; b. Harrodsburg, Ky., May 29, 1939; d. Minor Colonel and Esther Katherine (Christman) Byrnside; divorced; children: Gregory, Michael. Student, Ea. Ky. U., 1957-60; BS, Austin Peay U., 1962; social studies cert., Holy Family Coll., Phila., 1966; MEd, spl. edn. cert., Antioch Coll., Phila., 1989. Tchr. English Lumpkin County Schs., Dahlonega, Ga., 1963-65, 68-89, Washington County Schs., Springfield, Ky., 1967-68, Pennsbury Schs., Fairless Hills, Pa., 1970-80, Hightstown (N.J.) H.S., East Windsor Schs., 1980—. Mem. Delta Kappa Gamma. Home: 17 New School Ln Levittown PA 19054-3405 Office: Hightstown H S 25 Leshin Ln Hightstown NJ 08520-4001 E-mail: bsepter@aol.com.

SÉQUIN, CARLO H. computer science educator; b. Winterthur, Switzerland, Oct. 30, 1941; came to U.S., 1970; s. Carl R. and Margrit (Schaeppi) S.; m. Margareta Frey, Oct. 5, 1968; children: Eveline, Andre. BS, U. Basel, Switzerland, 1965, PhD, 1969. Mem. tech. staff Bell Labs., Murray Hill, N.J., 1970-76; vis. Mackay lectr. U. Calif.-Berkeley, 1976-77, prof. elec. engring. computer scis., 1977—, assoc. chmn. computer sci., 1980-83, assoc. dean capital projects, 2001—. Contbr. over 230 articles to profl. jours.; author first book on charge-coupled devices; patentee integrated circuits. Fellow IEEE, Assn. Computing Machinery, Swiss Acad. Engring. Scis. Office: U Calif Dept EECS Computer Scis Divsn Soda Hall Berkeley CA 94720-1776

SERAFIN, JOHN ALFRED, art educator; b. Washington, Nov. 3, 1942; s. John Bernard and Elizabeth (Pichette) S.; m. Josephine Azzarello, Apr. 12, 1969 (div. 1990); children: John Calvin, Michael Joseph, Mary Elizabeth. Student, Syracuse U., 1967-69, MS, 1974; BFA, U. Utah, 1971. Cert. tchr., N.Y. Graphic artist Sears, Roebuck and Co., Syracuse, 1967-68; dir. advt. Around the Town mag., Syracuse, 1969; tchr. art Blodgett Jr. High Sch., Syracuse, 1971-76, Roberts Elem. Sch., Syracuse, 1986-87, Fowler High Sch., Syracuse, 1976—. Yearbook adviser Blodgett Jr. High Sch., 1971-75, coach track, 1971-74, coach cross-country, 1972-74; jr. class adviser Fowler High Sch., 1977-78. Artist mag. cover design U. Utah Pharmacy Mag., 1970, Fine Art Index Internat., 1995 edit., Chgo.; group exhbns. include Syracuse Stage, 1989-92, N.Y. State Fair, 1977, 89, 90, Everson Mus., Syracuse, 1985, Cooperstown (N.Y.) Nat. Show, 1991, Westmoreland Nat. Art Show, Latrobe, Pa., 1995, Nat. Design Congress of Art & Design Exhbn. Art Reach '95, Salt Lake City, Tex. Nat. Show, Stephen Austin State U., 1996, Stad Diksmuide World Show, Brussels, 1996; represented by Montserrat Art Gallery, N.Y.C., Limner Gallery, N.Y.C., Agora Gallery, N.Y.C.; painting included in Mut. of N.Y. M.O.N.Y. Art Collection, N.Y.C. Recipient award of Excellence, Manhattan Arts Mag., N.Y.C. Mem. N.Y. State United Tchrs., Syracuse Tchrs. Assn. (rep. 1972-75), Associated Artists Galleries, Allied Artists of N.Y., Nat. Art Educators Assn., Syracuse U. Orange Pack and Alumni Assn., Crimson Club U. Utah Alumni Assn., N.Y. State Art Tchrs. Assn., Cooperstown Art Assn., Elks, Moose. Democrat. Avocations: syracuse university sports, brewing, blues music, working out, travel. Office: Fowler H S 227 Magnolia St Syracuse NY 13204-2796 Home: 113 Euclid Dr Fayetteville NY 13066-1919

SERAFINE, MARY LOUISE, psychologist, educator, lawyer; b. Rochester, N.Y., July 2, 1948; BA in Music with honors, Rutgers U., 1970; PhD, U. Fla., 1975; JD, Yale U., 1991. Bar: Calif. 1992, D.C. 1993, N.Y. 1999, U.S. Tax Ct. 1995. Tchg. and rsch. fellow U. Fla., Gainesville, 1970-76; vis. asst. prof. U. Tex., San Antonio, 1976-77, asst. prof. Austin, 1977-79; postdoctoral fellow dept. psychology Yale U., New Haven, 1979-83, lectr., 1981-83; asst. prof. dept. psychology Vassar Coll., Poughkeepsie, N.Y., 1983-88; with O'Melveny & Myers, L.A., 1991-96, Chadbourne & Parke, L.A., 1996-97, Fried, Frank, Harris, Shriver & Jacobson, L.A., 1997-99; pvt. practice, 1999—. Author: Music as Cognition: The Development of Thought in Sound, 1988; editl. reviewer Child Devel., Devel. Psychology, Am. Scientist, Jour. Exptl. Child Psychology, Jour. Applied Developmental Psychology, Yale Law Jour.; contbr. articles to profl. jours. Grantee State of Fla., 1974-75, U. Tex.-Austin, 1977, Spencer Found., 1979-85. Office: c/o Law Offices Thomas A Earls 102 B Fountainbrook Cir Cary NC 27511 Home: 311 W Whitaker Hill Raleigh NC 27608

SERFAS, RICHARD THOMAS, architecture educator, urban planner, county official; b. Reading, Pa., Nov. 24, 1952; s. Clifford Donald and Helen Catherine (McGovern) S. Student, Jacksonville U., 1970-72; BA, Colo. State U., 1974; MPA, Pa. State U., 1977; MS in Real Estate Devel., Columbia U., 1995. Project coord. ACTION Peace Corps, VISTA, Gary, Ind., 1974-75; city adminstr. City of Beverly Hills, Mo., 1975; grad. rsch. asst. dept. pub. adminstrn. Pa. State U., Middletown, 1976-77; community planner St. Louis County Dept. Planning, 1977-78; mgmt. analyst Clark County Sanitation Dist., Las Vegas, Nev., 1978-79; environ. planner Clark County Dept. Comprehensive Planning, Las Vegas, 1979-80, prin. planner, 1980-84, asst. coord. planning, 1984-85, coord. advance planning, 1985-89, asst. dir., 1989-94; project mgr. Focus 2000, Las Vegas, 1996-99; v.p. comml. planning and design Am. Nev. Corp., Henderson, Nev., 2000—. Instr. U. Nev. Sch. Architecture, Las Vegas, 1989-94; student advisor Las Vegas chpt. AIA, 1989-94. Staff advisor Clark County Comprehensive Plan Steering Com., 1980-94, Environ. Task Force, Las Vegas, 1984-94, Archtl. Design Task Force, Las Vegas, 1984-94, Devel. Sector Task Force, Las Vegas, 1984-94; mem. Transit Tech. Com., Las Vegas, 1989-94. Recipient achievement award Nat. Assn. Counties, 1983-90. Mem. Am. Inst. Cert. Planners, Urban Land Inst., Comml. Retail Coun., Nat. Assn. Corp. Real Estate Execs., Nat. Coun. for Urban Econ. Devel., Am. Planning Assn. (treas. Nev. chpt. 1979-91, pres. 1992-96, Appreciation award 1981, 83, 85, 87, 89, 91, Outstanding Pub. Sector Planning Accomplishment award 1987, 88, 90, 91), Cmty. Assns. Inst. So. Nev. (bd. dirs. 1990-92, sec. 1993-95). Democrat. Roman Catholic. Avocations: tennis, skiing, hiking, photography. Home: 2129 Stone Croft St Las Vegas NV 89134-2543 E-mail: rserfas@aol.com.

SEROW, WILLIAM JOHN, economics educator; b. N.Y.C., Apr. 8, 1946; s. William John and Dorothea (Goyette) S.; m. Elizabeth Goetz, Aug. 24, 1968; 1 child, Erika. BA, Boston Coll., 1967; MA, Duke U., 1970, PhD, 1972. Rsch. dir. Univ. Va., Charlottesville, 1970-81; prof., dir. Fla. State U., Tallahassee, 1981—. Editor: Handbook of International Migration, 1990; author: Population Aging in the United States, 1990. Capt. U.S. Army, 1967-73. Grantee Fla. Health Care Cost Containment Bd., 1988-90, Nat. Instn. Aging, 1983-89, NIMH, 1984-86, Govt. of Indonesia, 1992-98, TVA, 1997-98, 99-00, Fla. Dept. Environ. Protection, 2002-03. Mem. Internat. Union for Scientific Study of Population, Population Assn. Am., Am. and Western Econ. Assns., So. Demographic Assn. (pres. 1986-87), So. Regional Sci. Assn. (pres. 1982-83), Gerontol. Soc. Am. Avocations: railroads, sherlock holmes, baseball rsch. Office: Fla State U Ctr Demography and Population Health Tallahassee FL 32306-2240

SERPE-SCHROEDER, PATRICIA L. elementary education educator; b. La Porte, Ind., Feb. 1, 1949; d. Fred J. and Priscilla (Nowak) Serpe; children: Matthew Aaron, Scott Allan. BA, Purdue U., 1971, MS in Edn., 1976, PhD in Ednl. Aminstrn., 1999. Cert. tchr., administr., Ind. Tchr., grades 1-2 Westville (Ind.) Sch.; tchr., grade 2 Lincoln Sch., Highland, Ind.; tchr. grades 1, 2, 4 Iddings Sch., Merrillville, Ind., 1985-92; prin. Hudson Lake Elem. Sch., New Carlisle, Ind., 1992-94; title I coord. New Prairie Sch. Corp., New Carlisle, 1994-98; prin. Morgan Twp. Elem. Sch., Valparaiso, Ind., 1998—2001; dir. day svc. program Dungarvin Ind. Inc., LaPorte, Ind., 2002; dir. edn. Midwest Ctr. for Youth and Families, Kouts, Ind., 2002—03; prin. St. Joseph Cath. Sch., LaPorte, Ind., 2003—. Mem. drug-free, sci. textbook, elem. computer coms. New Prairie United Sch. Corp.; presenter in field; com. of practitioners for title I Ind. State Dept. of Edn. Recipient Ind. State grant. Mem. NEA, ASCD, Ind. Tchrs. Assn., Merrillville Tchrs. Assn. (sec., membership chmn., mem. computer and tech. coms. for sch. corp., bldg. adv. com.), Nat. Assn. Sch. Prins., Ind. Assn. Sch. Prins., Ind. Prins. Leadership Acad., New Prarie Classroom Tchrs. Assn. (sec.), Kappa Delta Pi, Delta Kappa Gamma, Pi Delta Phi, Phi Kappa Phi. Home: 804 Pennsylvania Ave La Porte IN 46350-2957

SERRIE, HENDRICK, retired anthropology and international business educator; b. Jersey City, July 2, 1937; s. Hendrick and Elois (Edge) S.; m. Gretchen Tipler Ihde, Sept. 3, 1959; children: Karim Jonathan, Keir Ethan. BA with honors, U. Wis., 1960; MA, Cornell U., 1964; PhD with distinction, Northwestern U., 1976. Dir. Solar Energy Field Project, Oaxaca, Mex., 1961-62; instr. U. Aleppo, Syria, 1963-64; asst. prof. Beloit (Wis.) Coll., 1964-69, Calif. State U., Northridge, 1969-70, Purdue U., West Lafayette, Ind., 1970-72, New Coll./U. South Fla., Sarasota, 1972-77; tchr. Pine View Sch., Sarasota, 1978; prof. anthropology, internat. bus. Eckerd Coll., St. Petersburg, Fla., 1978—2002, dir. internat. bus. overseas programs, 1981—2002; ret., 2002. Sr. rsch. assoc., Human Resources Inst., St. Petersburg, 1988—. Author, editor: Family, Kinship, and Ethnic Identity Among the Overseas Chinese, 1985, Anthropology and International Business, 1986, What Can Multinationals Do for Peasants, 1994, The Overseas Chinese: Ethnicity in National Context, 1998; writer, dir. films: Technological Innovation, 1962, Something New Under the Sun, 1963; contbr. articles to Wall Street Jour. and Wall Street Jour. Europe. Tchr. Sunday sch., North United Methodist Ch., Sarasota, 1977—. Exxon scholar, So. Ctr. for Internat. Issues, Atlanta, 1980-81; Presdl. fellow Am. Grad. Sch. Internat. Mgmt., 1991; recipient Leavy award, Freedoms Found., Valley Forge, Pa., 1989. Fellow Am. Anthropol. Assn., Soc. Applied Anthropology; mem. So. Ctr. Internat. Issues, Acad. Internat. Bus., Tampa Bay Internat. Trade Coun., Internat. Soc. Intercultural Edn., Tng. and Rsch. Republican. Avocations: singing, drawing, beach walking, cycling, sailing. Home: 636 Mecca Dr Sarasota FL 34234-2713 E-mail: serrieh@eckerd.edu.

SERRIN, JAMES BURTON, mathematics educator; b. Chgo., Nov. 1, 1926; s. James B. and Helen Elizabeth (Wingate) S.; m. Barbara West, Sept. 6, 1952; children: Martha Helen Stack, Elizabeth Ruth, Janet Louise Sucha. Student, Northwestern U., 1944-46; BA, Western Mich. U., 1947; MA, Ind. U., PhD, 1951; DSc, U. Sussex, 1972; DSc in Engring., U. Ferrara, Italy, 1992; DSc in Math., U. Padova, Italy, 1992. With MIT, Cambridge, 1952-54; mem. faculty U. Minn., Mpls., 1955—, prof. math., 1959-95, Regents prof., 1968—, head Sch. Math., 1964-65; emeritus, 1995. Vis. prof. U. Chgo., 1964, 75, Johns Hopkins U., 1966, U. Sussex, 1967-68, 72, 76, U. Naples, 1979, U. Modena, 1988, Ga. Inst. Tech., 1990. Author: Mathematical Principles of Classical Fluid Mechanics, 1957. Mem. Met. Airport Sound Abatement Council, Mpls., 1969— . Recipient Disting. Alumni award Ind. U., 1979 Fellow AAAS; mem. NAS, Am. Math. Soc. (G.D. Birkhoff prize 1973), Math. Assn. Am., Soc. for Natural Philosophy (pres. 1969-70), Finnish Acad. Sci. and Letters. Home: 4422 Dupont Ave S Minneapolis MN 55409-1739

SERVAGE, BONNIE LEE, nursing educator, administrator; BSN, Niagara U., 1981; MS in Health Edn., SUNY, Cortland, 1986; MSN, SUNY, Utica, 2001. cert. nurse adminstr. ANA; cert. trauma nurse core course provider, instr.; cert. emergency nurse; cert. adult nurse practitioner. Staff nurse ICU St. Luke's Meml. Hosp., Utica, N.Y., 1981-84, staff nurse emergency dept., 1984-86, charge nurse emergency dept., 1986-87, nursing supr., 1987-88, asst. dir. nursing, 1988-89, dir. nursing edn., asst. dir. nursing, 1989-90; dir. nursing Mohawk Valley Hosp., Ilion, N.Y., 1990-91; dir. staff devel. Mercy Ctr. for Health Svc., Watertown, N.Y., 1991-95; DON Genesis Healthcare N.Y., 1995-97; health occupations coord. Madison-Oneida BOCES, Verona, N.Y., 1997-98; asst. prof. nursing Jefferson C.C., Watertown, NY, 1998—2003; adult nurse practitioner Watertown Internists, 2003—. Mem. planning bd. Sackets Harbor (N.Y.) Village, 1994-98; sec. Mohawk Valley Chpt. Ins. Edn., Utica, 1992-94. Mem. nursing adv. com. Mohawk Valley Coll., Utica, 1989-90, 97-98. Mem. Nat. League Nursing, Am. Coll. Nurse Practitioners, Am. Acad. Nurse Practitioners, Am. Heart Assn. (profl. educators com., emergency cardiac care com. 1991-94), N.Y. State Nurse Practitioners, Sigma Theta Tau.

SESSIONS, BETTYE JEAN, humanities educator; b. Jacksonville, FL, Jan. 29, 1934; d. John Henry and Willene Porter Hayes; m. Malcolm G.A. Sessions, July 7, 1956; children: Sabrina F., Malcolm G.A. II, Byron Craig. BA, Fla. A&M U., 1956; MAT, Jacksonville U., 1967. Tchr. English, humanities Duval County Pub. Schs., Jacksonville, Fla., 1957—72; prof. humanities Fla. C.C., Jacksonville, Fla., 1972—90; news corr. Fla. Times - Jacksonville Jour., 1981—86; profl. writer, author and poet Jean-Aubrey Ideas, Inc., Jacksonville, 1985—2001.

SESSIONS, WILLIAM LAD, philosophy educator, administrator; b. Somerville, N.J., Dec. 3, 1943; s. William George and Alice Edna (Billhardt) Sessions; m. Vicki Darlene Thompson, Aug. 28, 1965; children: Allistair Lee, Laura Anne. BA magna cum laude, U. Colo., 1965; MA in Comparative Study of Religion, Union Theol. Sem., N.Y.C., 1967; postgrad., Oxford (Eng.) U., 1967-68; PhD, Yale U., 1971; postdoctoral studies, Stanford U., 1976, Harvard U., 1977-78. Tchg. fellow Yale U., 1969; instr. U. Conn., Waterbury, 1970-71; asst. prof. philosophy Washington and Lee U., 1971-77, assoc. prof., 1977-83, prof., 1983—, Ballengee 250th Anniversary prof., 1999—. Instr. So. Sem., 1972; vis. prof. St. Olaf Coll., 1985—86; assoc. dean Coll. Washington and Lee U., 1992—95, acting dean, 1995—96, 2001—02, head philosophy dept., 1996—. Author: The Concept of Faith, 1984, Reading Hume's Dialogues, 2002; contbr. Ruling elder Lexington (Va.) Presbyn. Ch., 1983—89, tchr. Sunday sch., 1984—, ruling elder, 2002—. Grantee Glenn grantee, Washington and Lee U., 1975—, Babcock Found., 1976, NEH, 1977, 1983, 1986, Mellon Found., 1978—79, Mellon East Asian Studies, 1990. Mem.: Soc. Christian Philosophers (steering com. ea. region 1986—90, 1992—95, 1997—98, exec. com. 1987—90), Soc. for Philosophy of Religion (exec. coun. 1988—94, v.p. 1991, pres. 1992), Va. Philos. Assn., Am. Philos. Assn., Phi Beta Kappa (exec. com. W&L chpt. 1986—95, 1998—2000, v.p. 1989—91, pres. 1991—93). Office: Washington & Lee U Dept of Philosophy Lexington VA 24450 E-mail: sessionsl@wlu.edu.

SESSLER, JANE VIRGINIA, retired secondary school educator; b. Mineola, N.Y., June 10, 1940; d. Howard George and Virginia Tuthill (Craft) S. BA, Cornell U., 1961; MS, U. Bridgeport, 1964; MA, Ohio State U., 1966; profl. diploma, L.I. U., 1984. Cert. tchr., guidance counselor, adminstr., N.Y. Tchr. math. Fairfield (Conn.) Pub. Schs., 1961-65, Manhasset (N.Y.) Pub. Schs., 1966—2000, chair math. dept., 1978-92, dist. math. coord., 1992—2000. Test item writer ACT, Iowa City, Iowa, 1989-90; adv. bd. Merrill Pub. Co., Columbus, Ohio, 1989-90; spkr. at profl. confs.; tchr. liaison Sch.-Cmty. Assn., Manhasset, 1985-92; mem. Citizen's Adv. Com. on Finance, 1992—; math. cons. Nassau BOCES, 2002-03. Trustee Goudreau Mus. Math. Mem. Assn. Math. Tchrs. N.Y. State, Nassau County Assn. Math. Suprs. (exec. bd. 1995—), Nat. Coun. Tchrs. Math., Coun. Adminstrs. and Suprs., Manhasset Adminstrs. and Suprs. Assn. (pres. 1997-99).

SESSOMS, ALLEN LEE, academic administrator, former diplomat, physicist; b. NYC, Nov. 17, 1946; s. Albert Earl and Lottie Beatrice (Leff) Sessoms; children from previous marriage: Manon Elizabeth, Stephanie Csilla. BS, Union Coll., Schenectady, N.Y., 1968; PhD, Yale U., 1972; DSc (hon.), Union Coll., 1998; PhD (hon.), Soka U., Japan, 2000. Sci. assoc. CERN, Geneva, 1973-78; asst. prof. physics Harvard U., Cambridge, Mass., 1974-81; sr. tech. advisor OES, State Dept., Washington, 1980-82; dir. Office Nuclear Tech. & Safeguards, State Dept., Washington, 1982-87; counselor for sci. and tech. U.S. Embassy, Paris, 1987-89, polit. minister, counselor Mexico City, 1989-91, dep. chief of mission, 1991-93; exec. v.p., v.p. for acad. affairs U. Mass. Sys., Boston, 1993-95; pres. CUNY Queens Coll., Flushing, N.Y., 1995-2000; lectr., fellow Belfer Ctr. for Sci. and Internat. Affairs, JFK Sch. Govt., Harvard U., Cambridge, Mass., 2000—03; pres. Del. State U., 2003—. Mem. adv. com. U.S. Sec. Energy, 1995-2002; mem. NCAA Pres. Coun., 1996-2000; mem. nuc. energy rsch. adv. com. U.S. Dept. Energy.. Contbr. articles to profl. jours. Bd. dirs. Milestone Fund, Drawing Ctr., Big Apple Circus; mem. adv. coun. Toda Internat. Ford Found. travel/study grantee, 1973-74; Alfred P. Sloan Found. fellow, 1977-81; recipient Wilbur Cross medal Yale Grad. Sch. Alumni, 1999, Medal of Highest Honor, Soka U., 1999; officer dans l'Order des Palmes Académiques, 1999. Mem. AAAS, Am. Phys. Soc., N.Y. Acad. Sci., Cosmos Club. Office: Office of the Pres Del Staet U 1200 N Dupont Hwy Dover DE 19901 Personal E-mail: vonsessoms@aol.com. Business E-Mail: asessoms@desu.edu.

SESTINI, VIRGIL ANDREW, retired biology educator; b. Las Vegas, Nov. 24, 1936; s. Santi and Merceda Francesca (Borla) S. BS in Edn., U. Nev., 1959; postgrad., Oreg. State U., 1963-64; MNS, U. Idaho, 1995; postgrad., Ariz. State U., 1967, No. Ariz. U., 1969. Cert. tchr., Nev. Tchr. biology Rancho H.S., 1960-76; sci. chmn., tchr. biology Bonanza H.S., Las Vegas, 1976-90, ret., 1990. Co-founder, curator exhibits Meadows Mus. Nat. History, 1993-94; part-time tchr., sci. chmn. Meadows Sch., 1987-94; ret., 1994; edn. specialist, cell biologist SAGE Rsch., Las Vegas, 1993, ret., 1998; founder Da Vinci Enterprises, Las Vegas, 1995. Author: Lab Investigations for High School Honors Biology, 1992, Laboratory Investigations in Microbiology, 1992, Genetics Problems for High School Biology, 1995, Science Laboratory Report Data Book, 1995, Field and Museum Techniques for the Classroom Teacher, 1995, Selected Lab Investigations and Projects for Honors and AP Biology, Vol. I Microbiology, 1995, Telecommunications: A Simulation for Biology Using the Internet, 1995; co-author: A Biology Lab Manual for Cooperative Learning, 1989, Metrics and Science Methods: A Manual of Lab Experiments for Home Schoolers, 1990, Experimental Designs in Biology I: Botany and Zoology, 1993, Designs in Biology: A Lab Manual, 1993, Integrated Science Lab Manual, 1994, Supplemental Experiments and Field Studies for AP Biology, 1998; contbr. articles to profl. jours. including The Sci. Tchr., Am. Biology Tchr., Fine Scale Models, Ships in Scale, IPMS Jour. With USAR, 1959-65. Reciepient Rotary Internat. Honor Tchr. award, 1965, Region VIII Outstanding Biology Tchr. award, 1970, Nev. Outstanding Biology Tchr. award Nat. Assn. Biology Tchrs., 1970, Nat. Assn. Sci. Tchrs., Am. Gas Assn. Sci. Tchg. Achievement Recognition award, 1976, 80, Gustov Ohaus award, 1980, Presdl. Honor Sci. Tchr. award, 1983; Presdl. award excellence in math. and sci. tchg., 1984, Celebration of Excellence award Nev. Com. on Excellence in Edn., 1986, Hall of Fame award Clark County Sch. Dist., 1988, Excellence in Edn. award, 1987, 88, Spl. Edn. award 1988, NSEA Mini-grants, 1988, 89, 92, World Decoration of Excellence medallion World Inst. Achievement, 1989, Cert. Spl. Congrl. Recognition, 1989, Senatorial Recognition, 1989, mini-grant Jr. League Las Vegas, 1989, Excellence in Edn. award Clark Country Sch. Dist., 1989; named Nev. Educator of Yr., Milken Family Found./Nev. State Dept. Edn., 1989; grantee Nev. State Bd. Edn., 1988, 89, Nev. State Edn. Assn., 1988-89. Mem. AAAS, NEA, Nat. Assn. Taxidermists, Nat. Sci. Tchrs. Assn. (life, Nev. state membership chmn. 1968-70), Nat. Assn. Biology Tchrs. (life, OBTA dir. Nev. state 1991-93), Am. Soc. Microbiology, Coun. for Exceptional Children, Am. Biographic Inst. (rsch. bd. advisors 1988), Nat. Audubon Assn., Nat. Sci. Suprs. Assn., Am. Inst. Biol. Scis., Nautical Rsch. Guild, Internat. Plastic Modelers Soc., So. Nev. Scale Modelers (Las Vegas coord., Modeloberfest, 1995), Silver State Scale Modelers Guild. Avocations: scale models, military figures, scale models circus, photography. E-mail: v.sestini@lvcm.com.

SETO, THEODORE PAUL, lawyer, educator; b. Kermanshah, Iran, Feb. 18, 1951; came to U.S., 1951; s. Paul Susumu and Genevieve (Reynolds) S.; m. Lenore T. Rothman, Aug. 2, 1980 (div. 1999); 1 child, Kira Rothman Seto; m. Sande Lynn Buhai, July 8, 2000; children: Samantha Elizabeth,

Genevieve Danielle. BA, Harvard U., 1973, JD, 1976. Bar: Mass. 1977, U.S. Dist. Ct. Mass. 1978, U.S. Dist. Ct. (ea. dist.) Pa. 1983, U.S. Tax Ct. 1985, U.S. Ct. Appeals (1st cir.) 1983, U.S. Ct. Appeals (3d cir.) 1990, U.S. Supreme Ct. 1983, U.S. Claims Ct. 1990. Law clk. to Hon. Judge Mansfield U.S. Ct. Appeals (2nd cir.), N.Y.C., 1976-77; assoc. Foley, Hoag & Eliot, Boston, 1977-83, Drinker Biddle & Reath, Phila., 1983-86, ptnr., 1986-91; assoc. prof. Loyola Law Sch., L.A., 1991-97, prof., 1997—. Author: A Uniform System of Citation, 12th edit. 1976; contbr. articles to profl. jours. Mem. ABA. Democrat. Office: Loyola Law Sch 919 Albany St Los Angeles CA 90015-1211

SETTEDUCATI, ANTHONY DAVID, secondary/elementary educator, English; b. N.Y.C., Oct. 4, 1947; s. Anthony Joseph and Julia Ann (Rushinski) Sette; m. Paula Marguerite Cali, July 29, 1972; children: Matthew David, Christopher Anthony. BA, SUNY, Stony Brook, 1969, MA in Liberal Studies, 1973; cert. sch. adminstr. and supr., cert. sch. dist. adminstr., Coll. New Rochelle, 1992. Cert. staff developer, N.Y. Tchr. English Farmingdale (N.Y.) Sr. High Sch., 1969-96, asst. prin., 1996-97, Saltzman East Meml. Elem. Sch., 1998—. Mentor N.Y. State Mentor Intern Program, Farmingdale, 1989-94; peer coaching coord. Farmingdale Sr. High Sch., 1990—; policy bd. mem. for staff devel. ctr. Farmingdale Sch., 1994. Author: Portfolio Self-Assessment For Teachers: A Reflection on the Farmingdale Model; guitarist (CDs): Acoustic Summer, My Guitar, Solitare for Guitar. Recipient N.Y. State Educator of Excellence, N.Y. State English Coun., 1994. Mem. ASCD, Nat. Coun. Tchrs. English, L.I. Lang. Arts Coun. Democrat. Roman Catholic. Avocations: musician, guitarist and bandleader. Office: Saltzman East Memorial Elem Sch 25 Mill Lane Farmingdale NY 11735 E-mail: dsette@optonline.net.

SETTERS, PAULA LOUISE HENDERSON, physics educator; b. Kay Jay, Ky., July 18, 1949; d. Louis and Lora (Bruce) H.; m. Charles Mullikin Setters; children: Philip Bennett, Lora Elizabeth. BS in Physics, Western Ky. U., 1970, postgrad., 1992; MA in Sci. Edn., U. Ala., 1974. Cert. tchr. Ky., 1970. Tchr. Warren Ctrl. H.S., Bowling Green, Ky., 1970-71, Homewood (Ala.) H.S., 1971-75, LaRue County H.S., Hodgenville, Ky., 1976-99, ret., 1999; adj. inst. Campbellsville U., 1998—2002, physics instr., 2002—03, adj. inst., 2003—. Profl. devel. presenter AEL, Charleston, W.Va., 1995-98, Ky. Instrnl. Tech. Leaders, Frankfort, Ky., 1994-98; rsch. asst. Dept. of Energy TRAC at Los Alamos (N.Mex.) Nat. Lab., 1991; strategic planning com. LaRue County Bd. Edn., 1992-99; site-based coun. LaRue County H.S., 1996-99. Chair spl. programs United Meth. Women, Hodgenville, 1990; pres. Hodgenville Elem. PTO, 1980-81; chair LaRue County Relay for Life, 2000-01. Mem.: Elizabethtown Hardin LaRue Ret. Tchrs. Assn., Ky. Assn. Physics Tchrs., Ky. Sci. Tchrs. Assn., Am. Assn. Physics Tchrs., Nat. Sci. Tchrs. Assn. Republican. Methodist.

SETTLES, WILLIAM FREDERICK, secondary and university educator, administrator; b. Aurora, Ill., Sept. 24, 1937; s. Arnold Joseph and Cleo Dorothy (Frazier) S.; m. June Ardith Cooper, Dec. 22, 1967; children: Sandi, Jim, Amanda, Caryn. BS, No. Ill. U., 1959, MS, 1961. Educator Aurora East Schs., 1959-62, Anaheim (Calif.) Union H.S. Dist., 1962-63, Joliet (Ill.) H.S. Dist., 1963-67; dean Sandburg H.S., Orland Park, Ill., 1967-68; asst. prin. St. Charles (Ill.) Pub. H.S., 1968-70; asst. prof. Western Ill. U., Macomb, 1970-72; educator social scis. Glenbard H.S. Dist., Glen Ellyn, Ill., 1972-96. Author: Life Under Communism, 1982; weekly newspaper columnist Ill. Copley Newspapers, Aurora, 1965-67; contbr. articles to profl. jours. Avocations: world travel, writing, photography. Home: PO Box 1121 Aurora IL 60507-1121

SETZER, KATHLEEN RUSSELL, special education educator; b. Long Beach, Calif., July 14, 1949; d. Robert Donald and Alice Nadine (Linton) Russell; m. Byron Douglas Cantrell, July 11, 1970 (div. Dec. 1986); children: Kristine, Julie, David; m. Paul Merritt Setzer, July 2, 1988; children: Lisl, Eric. BS in Bus. Adminstrn., Gallaudet U., 1971; MEd, Ga. State U., 1973. Cert. tchr. hearing impaired, Calif. Tchr. Ga. Sch. for the Deaf, Cave Spring, Ga., 1971-78, Calif. Sch. for the Deaf, Berkeley-Fremont, Calif., 1978-87; instr. Gallaudet U., Washington, 1987—95, Md. Sch. for the Deaf, 1995—. Recipient Tchr. of Yr. award Ga. Sch. for Deaf, 1974. Republican. Avocations: nature work, cooking, camping, canoeing. Home: 16 Young Branch Dr Middletown MD 21769-8137 E-mail: rgrib@stc.net.

SEVALSTAD, SUZANNE ADA, accounting educator; b. Butte, Mont., Mar. 26, 1948; d. John Cornelius and Ivy Jeanette (Cloke) Pilling; m. Nels Sevalstad, Jr., Mar. 11, 1975. BS in Bus. with high distinction, Mont. State U., 1970, MS in Bus., 1972. CPA, Mont. Internal auditor Anaconda Co., Butte, 1970-71; mgr. Wise River (Mont.) Club, 1976-79; instr. acctg. Bozeman (Mont.) Vocat./Tech. Ctr., 1970-72, Ea. Mont. Coll., Billings, 1972-73, Mont. State U., Bozeman, 1973-76, U. Nev., Las Vegas, 1979—. Recipient Women of Month award Freshman Class Women, 1976, Disting. Tchr. Coll. Bus. U. Nev., 1983, 86, 89, 93, Prof. of Yr. award Student Acctg. Assn. U. Nev., 1984, 87, 88, 90, 91, Outstanding Acctg. Prof. award Acctg. Students of U. Nev., 1987, 88, 89, Spanos Disting. Teaching award, 1989, 94, U. Nev. Disting. Tchg. award, 1998. Mem. AICPA, Am. Acctg. Assn., Nat. Inst. Mgmt. Acctg. (campus coord. 1988—), Inst. Mgmt. Accts., Assn. for Female Execs., Golden Key Soc. (hon.). Avocations: horseback riding, hiking, tennis, golf. Office: U Nev Dept Acctg 4505 S Maryland Pky Las Vegas NV 89154-9900

SEVCENKO, IHOR, history and literature educator; b. Radosc, Poland, Feb. 10, 1922; came to U.S., 1949, naturalized, 1957; s. Ivan and Maria (Cherniatynska) S.; m. Oksana Draj-Xmara, Apr., 1945 (div. 1953); m. Margaret M. Bentley, July 16, 1953 (div. 1966); m. Nancy Patterson, June 18, 1966 (div. 1995); children: Catherine, Elisabeth. Dr.Phil., Charles U., Prague, Czechoslovakia, 1945; Doct. en Phil. et Lettres, U. Louvain, Belgium, 1949; PhD (hon.), U. Cologne, Germany, 1994; D in Hist. Scis. (hon.), U. Warsaw, Poland, 2001. Fellow in Byzantinology Dumbarton Oaks, 1949-50, dir. studies, 1966, prof. Byzantine history and lit., 1965-75, sr. research assoc., 1975—; lectr. Byzantine and ancient history U. Calif., Berkeley, 1950-51; fellow Byzantinology and Slavic lit., research program USSR, 1951-52; instr., then asst. prof. Slavic langs. and lit. U. Mich., 1953-57; mem. faculty Columbia U., 1957-72, prof., 1962-65, adj. prof., 1965-72; vis. prof. Harvard U., 1973-74, prof., 1974-92, emeritus, 1992. Vis. fellow All Souls Coll., Oxford U., 1979—80, Wolfson Coll., Oxford U., 1987, 93, Onasis Found., Athens, 2002; vis. mem. Princeton Inst. for Advanced Study, 1956; vis. prof. Munich U., 1969, Coll. de France, 1985, Cologne U., 1992, 96, Ctrl. European U., Budapest, 1995, Budapest, 97; treas., acting treas., bd. dirs. Am. Rsch. Inst. in Turkey, 1964—66, 1967, 1975—; assoc. dir. Harvard Ukrainian Rsch. Inst., 1973—89, acting dir., 1977, 1985—86; chmn. Nat. Com. Byzantine Studies, 1966—77; mem. Internat. Com. for Greek Paleography, 1983—; guest of the rector Collegium Budapest, 1998. Author: Etudes sur la polémique entre Théodore Métochite et Nicéphore Choumnos, 1962, Society and Intellectual Life in Late Byzantium, 1981, Ideology, Letters and Culture in the Byzantine World, 1982, Byzantium and the Slavs in Letters and Culture, 1991, Ukraine Between East and West, 1996; co-author: Der Serbische Psalter, 1978, Life of St. Nicholas of Sion, 1984; contbr. articles to profl. jours. Recipient Hrusevs'kyj medal, Sci. Ševcenko Soc., 1996, Antonovych Lit. prize, Kiev, 2000; Guggenheim fellow, 1963, Humboldt-Forschungspreistraeger, 1985. Fellow Mediaeval Acad. Am., Brit. Acad. (corr.); mem. Am. Philos. Soc., Am. Acad. Arts and Scis., Ukrainian Acad. Arts and Scis. (hon. pres. 2003-), Sci. Sevcenko Soc., Société des Bollandistes Belgium (adj.), Accademia di Palermo (fgn.), Internat. Assn. Byzantine Studies (v.p. 1976-86, pres. 1986-96, hon. pres. 1996—), Christian Archeological Soc. of Athens (hon.), Austrian Acad. Sci. (corr.), Accademia Pontaniana of Naples (fgn.), Nat. Acad. of Sci. Ukraine (fgn.), Acad. Humanities Rsch. (Moscow), Cosmos Club (Washington), Harvard Club (N.Y.C.), Phi Beta Kappa (hon.). Office: Harvard Univ 204 Boylston Hall Cambridge MA 02138

SEVERANCE, JERI-LYNNE WHITE, elementary school educator; b. El Paso, Tex., Nov. 30, 1965; d. James Claude and Carol Ann (Magee) White; m. Scot Clark Severance, Dec. 30, 1989; children: Jacie, Jared. BA in Music Edn., Eckerd Coll., 1987; M in Music Edn., U. Tex., Austin, 1989. Cert. music K-12 Fla., English spkrs. of other langs.(ESOL) K-12, exceptional student edn. (ESE) K-12. Music tchr. Dunnellon (Fla.) H.S., 1989—90, Gateway H.S., Kissimmee, Fla., 1990—91, Grover C. Fields Middle Sch., New Bern, NC, 1991—92; pres-sch. tchr. 1st Alliance Ch., Orlando, Fla., 1992—93; fine arts tchr. Vanguard Sch., Lake Wales, Fla., 1993—94; music tchr. Midway Elem., Sanford, Fla., 1994—95; instr. Barry U., Orlando, Fla., 1995—97; music tchr. Pleasant Hill Elem., Kissimmee, 1995—98, tchr. exceptional student edn.., 1998—. Co-founder, co-chair Pleasant Hills Elem. Festival of Arts, Kissimmee; sch. rep. Osceola County Edn. in Park, Kissimmee; exceptional student edn. rep. child study com., Kissimmee. Pre-K choir dir. First United Meth. Ch., Kissimmee. Mem.: AAUW (sec., com. chair 1995—2001), Coun. for Exceptional Children (com. chair 2000—02), Phi Delta Kappa (mem. exec. bd. 2003—, com. chair 2003—04), Alpha Delta Kappa (chaplain, pres.-elect 1996—2002, pres. 2003—). Democrat. Methodist. Avocations: reading, sewing, dancing. Office: Pleasant Hill Elem Sch 1253 Pleasant Hill Rd Kissimmee FL 34741

SEVERINO, ROBERTO, foreign language educator, academic administration executive; b. Catania, Italy, July 19, 1940; s. Giuseppe and Alba (Scroppo) S. Student, State U. Catania, Italy, 1960-62; BA, Columbia Union Coll., 1967; MA, U. Ill., 1969, PhD, 1973. Head acct., pers. dir. Industria Nazionale Apparecchiature Scientifiche, Milan, 1961-63; teaching asst., lang. lab. supv. Columbia Union Coll., Takoma Park, Md., 1965-67; grad. teaching asst. U. Ill., Urbana, 1967-70, coord. Corr. Sch., 1970-71; instr. dept. French and Italian U. Mass., Amherst, 1971-73; prof. dept. Italian Georgetown U., Washington, 1973—, acting chmn., 1987, chmn. dept., 1988—; pres., co-founder Nat. Inst. Contemporary Italian Studies, 1986—; co-founder Associazione Internazionale del Diritto e dell'Arte, 1994—; pres. emeritus Am. U. of Rome, 1990-93, chair. Lit. dir. Georgetown U. Elec. Text Repository, Italian Archive, 1988-91, Ultramarina, 1992-96; mem. adv. bd. Nat. Italian Am. Found. Nat. Christopher Columbus 1992 Celebration; mem. U.S. delegation to 1st Conf. on Italian lang. and culture in U.S., 1987; lectr., speaker in field; founder Georgetown Poetry Series; pres. Coun. Promotion of Italian Lang. in Am. Schs., 1999—; hon. pres. U.S. Assn. Internat. Antonietta Labisi, 2000—. Author: Le soluzioni immaginarie, 1985, The Signs and Sounds of Italian, 1985, A carte scoperte, 1990, Presente imperfetto ed altri tempi, 1992, The Battle for Humanism, 1994, A Dumas: Mariano Stabile Sindaco di Palermo, 1994; co-author: Periscopio, 1986, International Nuclear Agreements Multilingual Glossary, 1988, United Nations Organization Multilingual Glossary, 1988, Regularizing the Irregular Italian Verb, 1990, Preserving and Promoting Italian language and Culture in North America, 1997, Napoleon: One Image, Ten Mirrors, 2002; translator; The Next 6000 Days by Saverio Avveduto, 1987; editor: (serials) Segni, 1985-88, Hispano-Italic Studies, 1976, 79; mem. editorial bd. Educazione Comparata, 1993—; contbr. articles to profl. jours.; translator: Angelo Scandurra: The Hot-Tempered Musician and Other Poems, 1996, M. Rotelli's E. Sanguineti, If, For Me, You Write a Poem, 1999, Francesco Battiato: Amnesia of the Blue, 2000; editor: Giuseppe Severino: Ricordi di Castelnuovo primi '900. Scene di vita paesana, 1992; co-founder, U.S. editor: Colophon, An Internat. Jour. Arts and Letters, 1997—. Trustee Joel Nafuma Refugee Ctr., Rome, 1993—; chmn. Strega Lit. Prize, Washington D.C. Jury, 1997-2001; mem. jury Prima Parete in Concerto, Lion's Internat. Art Prize, Catania, 1998—, Spoleto Poetry Prize, 1999—. Rsch. grantee Interuniversity Ctr. European Studies, 1977; recipient Accademia Internazionale di Lettere, Scienze, Arti medal, 1983, Internat. Poetry prize, 1986, Gold Cross Cavaliere dell'Ordine al Merito della Repubblica Italiana, 1983, Gold medal Italian Ministries of Univs. and Sci. Rsch., 1988, Marranzano d'Argento prize, 1989, Gold Commander class Cross al Merito della Repubblica Italiana, 1990, Georgetown U. Vicennial Disting. Svc. medal, 1994, Telamone prize, 1995, Top Sprint: Siciliani nel Mondo award, 2000. Mem. MLA, So. Atlantic Modern Lang. Assn., Nat. Assn. Secondary Sch. Prins. (mem. sch. partnerships internat. Italian adv. coun. 1988—), Italian Am. Cultural Found., Italian Cultural Soc. (pres. 1979-81, 83-85, Outstanding Svc. award 1983, chmn. acad. policy com. 1981—), Assn. Internationale Critiques Literaires and Associazione Italiana Critici Letterari, Greater Washington Assn. Tchrs. Fgn. Langs. (mem. award selection com. 1983-85), Manuscript Soc., Renaissance Soc. Am., Circolo Culturale Italiano (hon.), Am. Club (Rome), Touring Club Italiano (hon.), Gamma Kappa Alpha (v.p. 1990—, sec.-treas. and chpt. advisor 1985-90), World Jurist Assn. Ctr. Assocs. (U.S. pres. 1993—, chmn. program devel. and fin. com. 2000—), Associazione Internazionale del Diritto e dell'Arte (v.p. 1994—), Nat. Italian Am. Found. Coun. of 1,000, Napoleonic Soc. Am., Soc. di Studi Valdesi, Istituto Internazionale di Epistemologia la Magna Grecia, Unione Nazionale per la lotta contro l'Analfabetismo, Sons of Italy. Home: 4949 Quebec St NW Washington DC 20016-3230 Office: Georgetown U Dept Italian 37th And O Sts NW ICC 307 Washington DC 20057-0001 E-mail: Severiro@gunet.georgetown.edu.

SEVERY, LAWRENCE JAMES, psychologist, educator; b. Detroit, Mar. 30, 1943; m. Linda Andrea Anstensen, Aug. 20, 1966; children: Beth Andrea, Lisa Ellen. BS in Psychology, Wayne State U., 1965; MA in Psychology, PhD in Psychology, U. Colo., 1970. Rsch. asst. Inst. Behavioral Sci., U. Colo., Denver, 1968-69; predoctoral trainee Inst. Genetics and Behavior for Psychologists, U. Colo., Denver, 1969; asst. prof. psychology, sr. rsch. scientist Ark. Rehab. Rsch. and Tng. Ctr., U. Ark., 1970-71; various positions to prof., dept. psychology U. Fla., Gainesville, 1971—, R. David Thomas Endowed Legis. prof. psychology, 1988—, assoc. dean for student affairs Coll. Liberal Arts and Scis., 1990-98. Rsch. fellow Inst. Population Studies, U. Exeter, Devon, Eng., 1982, sr. rsch. assoc. Behavioral Rsch. Inst., 1976-77, postdoctoral trainee, U. N.C. Population Ctr.'s summer inst., 1973 and others; scholar-in-residence Family Health Internat., Research Triangle Park, N.C., 1998-99, tech. advisor for behavioral rsch., 2000-02, dir. divsn. behavioral and social scis., 2002—; cons. in field. Author: A Contemporary Introduction to Social Psychology, 1976, Advances in Population: Psychosocial Perspectives, Vol. 1 1993, Vol. 2, 1994, Vol. 3, 1999; contbr. articles, book chpts. and monographs to profl. publs. Recipient numerous grants in population and health fields. Fellow APA (numerous coms. divsn. population and environ., pres. 2002-03); mem. APHA, Population Assn. Am. (psycho-social workshop program chmn. 1982, 92), Assn. Consumer Rsch., Internat. Assn. Applied Psychology. Home: 10127 SW 48th Pl Gainesville FL 32608-7174 Office: U Fla Coll Liberal Arts and Scis Dept Psychology PO Box 112250 Gainesville FL 32611-2250

SEVIGNY, MAURICE, dean; b. Amesbury, Mass., July 24, 1943; m. Shirley Randall; 1 child, Marc Kendall. Grad., Mass. Coll. Art, Ohio State U. Dean fine arts Coll. Fine Arts, Tucson, 1991—; tchr., adminstr. Western Ky. U., Bowling Green State U.; Marguerite Fairchild Endowed prof. art, dept. head U. Tex., Austin. Mem. nat. adv. bds. NAEA, NCAA, ICFAD. Mem.: Internat. Coun. Fine Arts Deans. Office: Coll Fine Arts Music Bldg Rm 111 PO Box 210004 Tucson AZ 85721-0004*

SEVILLA-GARDINIER, JOSEFINA ZIALCITA, biology educator, musician; b. Manila, June 19, 1931; came to U.S., 1959; d. Paulino J. and Caridad (Zialcita) Sevilla; m. David E. Gardinier, July 2, 1966; children: Kenneth, Annemarie, Lourdes Marie. BS in Edn., U. Santo Tomás, Manila, 1951, MusB, 1958; MS, U. Mich., 1961, PhD, 1966. Tchr. sci. U. Santo Tomás High Sch., Manila, 1951-59; asst. prof. biology Mt. Mary Coll., Milw., 1966-68, Marquette U., Milw., 1968-71; asst. prof. microbiology Med. Coll. Wis., Milw., 1971-73; tchr. biology Divine Savior High Sch., Milw., 1984-88; instr. biology Milw. Area Tech. Coll., 1988—. Contbr. articles to profl. jours. Officer, bd. dirs. Filipino-Am. Assn. Wis., Milw., 1966—; mem. U. Santo Tomas Alumni Assn. Wis., Milw., pres. 1987-89; sect. leader Bel Canto Chorus and Its Piccolo, 1967—; mem. Archdiocesan Sch. Bd., Milw., 1986-89, East Side Cath. Sch. Bd., 1994-98; founder, dir. Gesu Ch. Choir, Milw., 1967-80, Allegro Chorale Old St. Mary's Ch., Milw., 1980—, mem. parish coun.; founder, dir. Tinigbayan, 1994—; minister music St. Philip Neri Parish, Milw., 1984-91. Fulbright scholar, 1959-65; fellow NSF, 1964-65, Argonne Nat. Labs., 1967. Mem. AAUW, Wis. Music Tchrs. Assn., Nat. Assn. Pastoral Musicians, Nat. Guild Piano Tchrs. (cert., chmn. Milw. chpt. 1993—), Milw. Music Tchrs. Assn. Roman Catholic. Avocation: creative crafts. Home: 21845 Gareth Ln Brookfield WI 53045-3926

SEWITCH, DEBORAH E. health science association administrator, educator, sleep researcher; b. Perth Amboy, N.J., Nov. 21, 1954; d. Myron David and Barbara A. (Werner) S. BA, Duke U., 1976; MA, CCNY, 1980; MPhil and PhD in Psychology, CUNY, 1982. Diplomate Am. Bd. Sleep Medicine, Am. Bd. Forensic Examiners. Assoc. dir. Sleep Disorders Ctr. Columbia-Presbyn. Med. Ctr., N.Y.C., 1980-81; sr. clinician Sleep Evaluation Ctr. Western Psychiat. Inst. & Clinic, Pitts., 1982-84; assoc. dir. Sleep Evaluation Ctr. U. Pitts., 1985, instr. in psychiatry Sch. of Medicine, 1984-85; dir. Sleep Disorders Ctr. The Griffin Hosp., Derby, Conn., 1985-89; asst. clin. prof. psychiatry Sch. of Medicine Yale U., New Haven, 1987-89; rsch. dir. unit for exptl. thermoregulation Inst. of Pa. Hosp., Phila., 1989-91; clin. asst. prof. psychology U. Pa., Phila., 1990-91; dir. Sleep Disorders Ctr. Hampstead (N.H.) Hosp., 1991-98; dir. Prescription for Sleep, LLC, Exeter, N.H., 1998—. Chair PhD part II exam. subcom. for bd. certification in clin. sleep disorders Am. Bd. Sleep Medicine, Rochester, Minn., 1989-92; cons. reviewer Jour. Sleep, Jour. Psychophysiology, Jour. Biol. Psychiatry; cons. in clin. sleep disorders and rsch. dept. psychiatry U. Pa., 1990-91. Mem. APA, Am. Acad. Sleep Medicine, Am. Coll. Forensic Examiners, Internat. Brain Rsch. Orgn., Soc. for Neurosci., Sleep Rsch. Soc. Jewish. Avocations: singing, horseback riding, antique collector. Office: Prescription for Sleep LLC 474 N Lake Shore Dr Apt 2703 Chicago IL 60611-3441

SEXSON, STEPHEN BRUCE, education writer, educator; b. Silver City, N.Mex., May 29, 1948; s. Ralph Dale and Wanda Claudean (McMahan) S.; m. Barbara Jane Davis, May 24, 1968; children: David Paul, Linda Carol. BA in Rhetoric and Pub. Address, Pepperdine U., 1969, MA in Pub. Comm., 1975; PhD in Higher Edn., Okla. State U., 1990. Asst. to supt. Morongo Unified Sch. Dist., Twentynine Palms, Calif., 1973-77; corp. trainer Merrill Lynch Realty, Dallas, 1979-81; sch. psychologist Texhoma (Tex.) Sch. Dist., 1982-83; assoc. prof., dir. Christian Student Ctr. Okla. Panhandle State U., Goodwell, 1982-84; rsch. resident Okla. State U., Stillwater, 1984-87; spl. programs staff LA Unified Sch. Dist., 1987—93; dir. Edwest Edn. Rsch., Burbank, Calif., 1991—; prof. Copper Mountain Coll., 2003—. Lectr. Chapman U., 1998—, Verbal Comm. Inst., Palm Desert, Calif., 2001—; guest lectr. edn. Okla. State U., Stillwater, 1993-94, U. Tulsa, 1993-94; spkr. Merrill Lynch Realty-Relo, Atlanta, 1979; prof. Chapman U., 1998—. Author: The Magic Classroom, 1995, The Values Rich Teacher, 1996, Dad's Role in the New Age, 2003; contbr. articles to profl. jours. Mem. ASCD, Am. Assn. Sch. Adminstrs., Nat. Assn. of Sch. Psychologists, Lions Club, Phi Delta Kappa. Avocations: computing, travel, theatre. Home: PO Box 845 Twentynine Palms CA 92277-0845 Office: Chapman U Coachella Valley Campus 42-600 Cook St Ste 134 Palm Desert CA 92211 E-mail: SteveSexson@aol.com.

SEXTON, DONALD LEE, retired business administration educator; b. New Boston, Ohio, June 14, 1932; s. Benjamin Franklin and Virgie Marie (Jordan) S.; m. Levonne Bradley, June, 1954 (div. June 1964); 1 child, Rhonda Jane; m. Carol Ann Schwaller, Dec. 18, 1965; children: David Lee, Douglas Edward. BS in Math. and Physics, Wilmington Coll., 1959; MBA, Ohio State U., 1966, PhD in Mgmt., 1972. Indsl. engr. Detroit Steel Corp., Portsmouth, Ohio, 1959-61; sr. rsch. engr. Rockwell Internat., Columbus, Ohio, 1961-68; v.p. merchandising R.G. Barry Corp., Columbus, 1968-74; v.p., gen. mgr. Henri Fayette, Inc., Chgo., 1976; gen. mgr. M.H. Mfg. Co., Jackson, Miss., 1976-77; assoc. prof. Sangamon State U., Springfield, Ill., 1977-79; Caruth prof. entrepreneurship Baylor U., Waco, Tex., 1979-86; Davis prof. entrepreneurship Ohio State U., Columbus, 1986-94, prof. emeritus, 1994—; dir. Nat. Ctr. for Entrepreneurial Rsch. Kauffman Found., Kansas City, Mo., 1994-97, scholar-in-residence, 1997-2000. Adj. faculty Nova Southeastern U., Ft. Lauderdale, Fla., 1997-99; mem. adv. bd. SBA, Columbus, 1986-94; rsch. adv. bd. U. So. Calif., L.A., 1986-90. Co-author: Entrepreneurship Education, 1981, Experiences in Small Business, 1982, Starting A Business in Texas, 1983; co-editor: Encyclopedia of Entrepreneurship, 1981, Art and Science of Entrepreneurship, 1986, Women Owned Business, 1989, Entrepreneurship: Creativity and Growth, 1990, The State of the Art of Entrepreneurship, 1991, Leadership and Entrepreneurship, 1996, Entrepreneurship: 2000, 1996, The Handbook of Entrepreneurship, 1999, Strategic Entrepreneurship, 2002. Served to staff sgt. USAF, 1951-55. Recipient Leavy Free Enterprise award Freedoms Found. Valley Forge, 1985, Cert. Appreciation SBA, Washington, 1984, 85, Outstanding Contbn. to Entrepreneurship Edn. award Assn. Coll. Entrepreneurs, 1991, Disting. Alumni award Wilmington Coll., 1993, Entrepreneurship Adv. of the Yr., 1997; named Adv. of Yr.-Innovation SBA, Dallas, 1982, 83, 84. Mem. Internat. Coun. for Small Bus. (sr. v.p. 1986), U.S. Assn. for Small Bus. (v.p. pub. rels. 1987), Acad. Mgmt. (chmn. entrepreneurship com. 1981, mem. adv. bd. 1984-85), Masons, Shriners, Eagles, Am. Legion, Alpha Tau Omega. Republican. Baptist. Avocation: golf. Home: 196 Bellerive Ln Summerville SC 29483-5032 E-mail: dlsexton@aol.com.

SEXTON, JOHN EDWARD, academic administrator, law educator; b. Bklyn., Sept. 29, 1942; s. John Edward and Catherine (Humann) S.; m. Lisa Ellen Goldberg; children: Jed, Katherine. BA, Fordham U., 1963, PhD, 1978; JD, Harvard U., 1979. Bar: NY 1981, US Supreme Ct. 1984. Prof. religion St. Francis Coll., Bklyn., 1965-75; law clk. U.S. Ct. Appeals, Wash., 1979, 80, U.S. Supreme Ct., Wash., DC, 1980-81; prof. law NYU, NYC, 1981—, dean law sch., 1988—2002, pres., 2002—. Dir. Washington Sq. Legal Services, NYC, 1983-2002, Pub. Interest Law Found., N.Y.C., 1983-85. Author: A Managerial Model of the Supreme Court, 1985, Federal Jury Instructions-Civil, 1985, How Free Are We? A Study of the Constitution, 1985, Cases and Materials in Civil Procedure, 1988. Dir. Root-Tilden Scholarship Program, 1984-88. Mem. Assn. of Am. Law Schs. (pres. 1997-98). Home: 29 Washington Sq W New York NY 10011-9180 Office: NYU Sch Law 70 Wash Sq S Rm 1216 New York NY 10012-1385

SEXTON, JOHN JOSEPH, oral and maxillofacial surgeon, educator; b. Boston, Dec. 4, 1947; s. Bernard Thomas and Margaret Theresa (Carrigg) S.; m. Judith Whelden, Aug. 21, 1971; 1 child, Benjamin. BS, Boston Coll., 19770; DMD, Tufts U., 1975; MScD, Boston U., 1978, CAGS, 1979. Diplomate Am. Bd. Oral and Maxillofacial Surgery. Orthognathic fellow Boston U. Inst. for Correction of Facial Deformities, 1976-77; intern, jr. resident, chief resident Boston U./Tufts U., 1975-79; asst. prof. Goldman Sch. Dental Medicine, Boston U., 1979-81; chief oral and maxillofacial surgery Beth Israel Hosp., Boston, 1981—2001, dir. maxillofacial trauma svc., 1990—2001, dir. mucosal disorders unit, 1990—2001; chief oral and maxillofacial surgery Lahey Clinic Med. Ctr., Burlington, Mass., 2001—. Cons. dermatology Beth Israel Hosp.; asst. prof. oral and maxillofacial surgery Harvard Med. Sch., Boston. Contbr. numerous articles to profl. jours. Avocations: philosophy, physics, history, travel. Office: 372 Washington St Wellesley MA 02481 also: Beth Israel Deaconess and Oral Maxillofacial Surgery 372 Washington St Ste 2500 Wellesley MA 02481-6202

SEXTON, ROBERT FENIMORE, educational organization executive; b. Cin., Jan. 13, 1942; s. Claude Fenimore and Jane (Wisenall) S.; m. Pam Peyton Papka, Sept. 15, 1985; children: Rebecca, Robert B., Ouita Papka, Paige Papka, Perry Papka. BA, Yale U., 1964; MA in History, U. Wash., Seattle, 1968, PhD in History, 1970; DHL (hon.), Berea Coll., 1990, Georgetown Coll., Ky., 1993, Eastern Ky. U., 2000. Asst. prof. history Murray (Ky.) State U., 1968-70; dir. Office Acad. Programs, Commonwealth of Ky., Frankfort, 1970-73; assoc. dean, exec. dir. Office Exptl. Edn. U. Ky., Lexington, 1973-80; dep. exec. dir. Ky. Coun. Higher Edn., Frankfort, 1980-83; exec. dir. Prichard Com. for Acad. Excellence, Lexington, 1983—; founder, pres. Ky. Ctr. Pub. Issues, Lexington, 1988—. Vis. scholar Harvard U., Cambridge, Mass., 1992, 94; chair Nat. Ctr. for Internships, Washington, 1973-80, Coalition for Alternatives in Post-Secondary Edn., Washington, 1977-80; bd. dirs. Editl. Projects in Edn., Consortium Policy Rsch. in Edn., Ky. Long Term Policy Rsch. Ctr., Edn. Commn. of the States; adv. bd. Consortium for Prodn. in Schs., 1992-94. Pub. The Ky. Jour., 1988-2001; editor book series: Public Papers of Governors of Kentucky, 1973-86; contbr. articles to profl. jours. Co-chmn. Carnegie Ctr. for Literacy, Lexington, 1990-93; mem. Gov.'s Task Force on Health Care, Frankfort, 1992—; bd. dirs. Ky. Inst. Edn. Rsch. Fund for Improvement in Postsecondary Edn., 1993-2000; chair Bluegrass Edn. Work Coun., Lexington, 1978-80; founder, steering com. Gov.'s Scholars Program, Frankfort, 1983-85. Recipient Charles A. Dana award for pioneering achievement, 1994. Mem. Am. Assn. Higher Edn. (bd. dirs. 1979-83). Democrat. Avocations: fishing, travel. Office: Prichard Com Acad Excell 167 W Main St Ste 310 Lexington KY 40507-1702

SEYDOUX, GERALDINE, molecular biologist; BS, U. Maine, 1986; PhD in Molecular Genetics, Princeton U., 1991. Postdoctoral trainee Carnegie Instn. Washington, Balt., 1991—95; asst. prof. molecular biology and genetics Sch. Medicine Johns Hopkins U., Balt., 1995—. Recipient Jr. Faculty Rsch. award, Am. Cancer Soc., 1996, Searle Scholars award, 1997, Presdl. Early Career award for scientists and engrs., NIH, 1999; fellow, Packard Found., 1996, MacArthur Found., 2001; scholar Basil O'Connor Starter scholar, March of Dimes, 1996. Office: Johns Hopkins U Sch Medicine 725 N Wolfe St 1515 PCTB Baltimore MD 21205*

SEYFERT, WAYNE GEORGE, secondary education educator, anatomy educator; b. Roslyn Park, N.Y., Nov. 23, 1947; s. George William Seyfert and Helen Francis (Weiss) Marks; m. Kathleen A. Kearns, May 23, 1970 (div. 1980); children: Sean Francis, Kerry Noelle, Adam Wayne. BS in Biology, SUNY, Cortland, 1969; MS in Biology, L.I. U. at C.W. Post, 1973; profl. diploma in sch. adminstrn., CUNY at Queen's Coll., N.Y.C., 1988. Cert. biology and secondary sci. tchr., N.Y.; cert. sch. adminstr. and supr., N.Y.; cert. sch. dist. adminstr., N.Y. Jr. h.s. sci. tchr. Port Washington (N.Y.) Schs., 1969-70; sci. tchr. Lawrence (N.Y.) Pub. Schs., 1970—2003; instr. North Shore Sci. Mus., Plandome, NY, 1973—75; adj. prof. human anatomy and physiology Nassau C.C., Garden City, NY, 1975—, N.Y. Inst. Tech., 1994—. Summer program dir. Sci. Mus. L.I., Plandome, 1976-85; environ. cons. Town of Brookhaven, L.I., 1978-80. Contbr. articles to profl. publs. Membership chmn. Boy Scouts Am., Sunrise dist., N.Y., 1978-79; mem. conservation adv. coun. Town of Brookhaven, 1977-79; mem. L.I. Sci. Congress exec. bd., 1985-98. Recipient Ednl. Leadership award Lawrence Ednl. Found., 1998, named L.I. Educator of Month, Hofstra U./TV Channel 12, L.I., 1995, Person of the Yr., Nassau Herald, 1998, STANYS Nassau County H.S. Sci. Tchr. of Yr., 1998. Mem. AAAS, Am. Fedn. Tchrs., Adj. Faculty Assn., Nat. Sci. Tchrs. Assn., Nat. Biology Tchr. Assn., Am. Philatelic Soc., Am. 1st Day Cover Soc., Am. Revenue Assn., Am. Perfin Soc., Am. Precanceled Stamp Soc., United Postal Stationary Soc., Meter Stamp Soc., State Revenue Assn., Am. Airmail Soc., Aerogramme Soc., Christmas Seal and Charity Seal Soc., N.Y. Acad. Scis., N.Y. State United Tchrs., Sci. Tchrs. Assn. N.Y. State, Lawrence Tchrs. Assn. (1st v.p. 1984-2001), MACUB Soc. for Neutobiology. Achievements include writing first history of America's first prairie and performance of first environmental study to trace an area's environmental change since first European encroachment. Home: PO Box 116 Woodmere NY 11598-0116

SEYFERTH, DIETMAR, chemist, educator; b. Chemnitz, Germany, Jan. 11, 1929; arrived in U.S., 1933; s. Herbert C. and Elisabeth (Schuchardt) S.; m. Helena A. McCoy, Aug. 25, 1956; children— Eric Steven, Karl Dietmar, Elisabeth Mary. BA summa cum laude, U. Buffalo, 1951, MA, 1953; PhD, Harvard, 1955; Dr. honoris causa, U. Aix-Marseille, 1979, Paul Sabatier Univ., Toulouse, France, 1992. Fulbright scholar Tech. Hochschule, Munich, Germany, 1954-55; postdoctoral fellow Harvard U., 1956-57; faculty MIT, 1957—, prof. chemistry, 1965-2000, prof. emeritus, 2000—, Robert T. Haslam and Bradley Dewey prof., 1983-99. Cons. to industry, 1957—; prof. emeritus, 2000—. Author: Annual Surveys of Organometallic Chemistry, 3 vols, 1965, 66, 67; regional editor: Jour. Organometallic Chemistry, 1963-81; coordinating editor revs. and survey sects., 1964-81; editor: Organometallics, 1981— ; contbr. research papers to profl. lit. Recipient Disting. Alumnus award U. Buffalo, 1964, Alexander von Humboldt Found. sr. award, 1984, Clifford C. Furnas Meml. award SUNY-Buffalo, 1987; Guggenheim fellow, 1968. Fellow AAAS, Am. Inst. Chemists, Inst. Materials, Am. Acad. Arts and Scis.; mem. NAS, Am. Chem. Soc. (Frederic Stanley Kipping award in organosilicon chemistry 1972, disting. svc. award advancement inorganic chemistry 1981, award in organometallic chemistry, 1996, Arthur C. Cope Sr. Scholar award 2003), Materials Rsch. Soc., Am. Ceramic Soc., Royal Soc. Chemistry, Gesellschaft Deutscher Chemiker, German Acad. Scientists-Leopoldina, Phi Beta Kappa, Sigma Xi. Office: MIT 77 Massachusetts Ave Rm 4-382 Cambridge MA 02139-4307 E-mail: seyferth@mit.edu.

SEYHUN, HASAN NEJAT, finance educator, department chairman; b. Ankara, Turkey, May 19, 1954; came to U.S., 1972; s. Niyazi and Serife (Sayilgan) S.; m. Tamara Z. Cleland, Aug. 10, 1992; children: Kent E., Jon C. and Evan G. BEE, Northwestern U., 1976; MA in Econs., U. Rochester, 1981, PhD in Fin., 1984. Elec. engr. Sungurlar, Istanbul, 1976-77; asst. prof. fin. U. Mich., Ann Arbor, 1983-91, assoc. prof., 1991-93, prof., 1993—, Jerome B. and Eilene M. York prof. bus. adminstrn., 1998—, chmn. fin. dept., 1994-95, 97-00. Vis. prof. Koc U., Istanbul, 2000-01, vis. assoc. prof. U. Chgo., 1988-89, 92, Wissenschaftliche Hochschule für Unternehmens führung, Koblenz, Germany, 1994; co-dir. banking and fin. svcs. program, cons. Citibank, Zurich, Switzerland, 1991; cons. Tweedy Brown, N.Y.C., 1993—, Towneley Capital, N.Y.C., 1994—. Mem. Am. Fin. Assn., Western Fin. Assn., European Fin. Assn., Beta Gamma Sigma. Avocations: volleyball, running. Office: U Mich 701 Tappan Ave Ann Arbor MI 48109-1217 E-mail: nseyhun@umiu.edu.

SEYMOUR, JOYCE ANN, elementary school educator; b. Lafayette, Ind., Nov. 24, 1947; d. Richard Max and Helen Lois (North) Taylor; m. Timothy Joe Seymour, Dec. 27, 1969; children: Christy Nicole, Chad Richard. BS, Purdue U., 1970; MA, Wright State U., 1974. Cert. tchr. elem. edn.; cert. counselor. Tchr. grade 5 Fairborn (Ohio) City Schs., 1970-84, elem. guidance counselor, 1984-94, tchr. grade 6, 1994-95, elem. guidance counselor, 1995—. Adv. com. Sch. Counseling, Wright State U., Dayton, 1986-88. Contbr. poem to A Treasury of Famous Poems, 1997. Mem. NEA, Ohio Sch. Counselor Assn., Phi Delta Kappa. Lutheran. Avocations: flying (pvt. pilot), water skiing. Home: 1100 Medway Carlisle Rd Medway OH 45341-9745 Office: Palmer-South Elementary 1020 S Maple Fairborn OH 45324-3735

SEYMOUR, RICHARD BURT, health educator; b. San Francisco, Aug. 1, 1937; s. Arnold Burt-Oakley and Florence Marguerite (Burt) S.; m. Michelle Driscoll, Sept. 15, 1963 (div. 1972); children: Brian Geoffrey, Kyra Daleth; m. Sharon Harkless, Jan. 5, 1973. BA, Sonoma State U., 1969, MA, 1970. Freelance writer, Sausalito, Calif., 1960—; coord., adminstr. Coll. of Mendocino, Boonville, Calif., 1971-73; bus. mgr. Haight Ashbury Free Clinics, San Francisco, 1973-77; exec. adminstr., dir. tng. and edn. projects Height Ashbury Free Clinics, San Francisco, 1977-87; instr. John F. Kennedy U., Orinda, Calif., 1986—; asst. prof. Sonoma State U., Rohnert Park, Calif., 1985—; pres., chief exec. officer Westwind Assocs., Sausalito, Calif., 1988—. Cons. Haight Ashbury Free Clinics, San Francisco, 1987—, treas., bd. dirs.; chmn. World Drug Abuse Treatment Network, San Francisco, 1988—; coord. Calif. Collaborative Ctr. for Substance Abuse Policy Rsch., 1997—; bd. dirs. Slide Ranch. Author: Physician's Guide to Psychoactive Drugs, 1987, Drug Free, 1987, The New Drugs, 1989, The Psychedelic Resurgence, 1993, Compost College, 1997, Clinicians' Guide to Substance Abuse, 2001; editor-in-chief Internat. Addictions Infoline, 1995; editor-in-chief Jour. of Psychoactive Drugs, 1996; exec. editor: Alcohol MD.com, 1999—; contbr. articles to profl. jours. Mem. Calif. Health Profls. for New Health Policy, Washington, 1976-80; chmn. Marin Drug Abuse Adv. Bd., San Rafael, Calif., 1979-81, CalDrug Abuse Svcs. Assn., Sacramento, 1975-79; mem. Alcohol and Drug Counselors Edn. Project, 1985—, San Francisco Delinquency Prevention Commn., 1981—, Calif. Primary Prevention Network, 1980—. Grantee NIMH, 1974—, Nat. Inst. on Drug Abuse, 1974—. Mem. Internat. Platform Assn., Commonwealth Club of Calif., Internat. Soc. Addiction Jour. Editors (bd. dirs., treas. 2000—). Democrat. Episcopalian. Avocations: travel, writing, landscape painting, camping. Office: Westwind Assocs 90 Harrison Ave Apt C Sausalito CA 94965-2240 E-mail: journal@hafci.org.

SEYMOUR, RICHARD DEMING, technology educator; b. Shelby, Ohio, Oct. 3, 1955; s. G. Deming and Elizabeth (Peterson) S.; m. Vicki Stebleton; 1 child, Ryan. BS in Edn., Ohio State U., 1978; MA, Ball State U., 1982; EdD, W.Va. U., 1990. Tchr. Crestview Sr. High Sch., Ashland, Ohio, 1978-81; from instr. to assoc. prof. Ball State U., Muncie, Ind., 1982—. Vis. instr. W.Va. U., Morgantown, 1985, Oreg. State U., 1990-91. Co-author: Exploring Communications, 1987, rev. edit., 2000; co-editor: Manufacturing in Technology Education, 1993. Advisor 4-H Clubs, Richland County, Ohio, 1978-81; dir. tech. in-svc. workshops Ind. Dept. Edn., Indpls., 1988-2000. Named technology tchr. educator of yr. Coun. on Technology Tchr. Edn., 1998. Mem.: Tech. Edn. Collegiate Assn. (internat. advisor 1990—92, nat. contest coord. 1992—), Am. Soc. Engring. Edn., Tech. Educators Ind. (pres. 1995—96), Ind. Math., Sci., Tech. Alliance (bd. dirs. 1994—), Coun. on Tech. Tchr. Edn. (v.p. 2003—), Soc. Mfg. Engrs., Internat. Tech. Edn. Assn. (bd. dirs. 1992—94, chmn. internat. conf. 1999, award of distinction 1999), Phi Delta Kappa, Epsilon Pi Tau. Methodist. Avocations: model railroads, sports, travel. Office: Ball State U Dept Industry Tech Muncie IN 47306-0255 E-mail: rseymour@bsu.edu.

SGRO, BEVERLY HUSTON, day school administrator, educator, state official; b. Ft. Worth, Jan. 12, 1941; d. James Carl and Dorothy Louise (Foster) Huston; m. Joseph Anthony Sgro, Feb. 1, 1964; children: Anthony, Jennifer. BS, Tex. Woman's U., 1963; MS, Va. Poly. Inst. and State U., 1974, PhD, 1990. Cert. tennis teaching profl. Instr. of deaf Midland (Tex.) Ind. Sch. System, 1963-64; speech pathologist Arlington (Tex.) Pub. Sch. System, 1964; rsch. asst. Tex. Christian U., 1964-65; tennis profl. Blacksburg (Va.) Country Club, 1977-81; from coord. for greek affairs to exec. asst. to v.p. student affairs Va. Poly. Inst. and State U., Blacksburg, 1981-89, dean of students, 1989-93; sec. of edn. Commonwealth of Va., Richmond, 1994-98; interim head Collegiate Sch., Richmond, 1998-99; head Carolina Day Sch., Asheville, N.C., 1999—. Adj. faculty Coll. Edn., Va. Poly. Inst. and State U.; lectr., presented papers at numerous symposia and convs., 1983—. Trustee Foxcroft Sch., Middleburg, Va., 1989-98, pres. bd. trustees, 1993-96; bd. dirs. Habitat Humanity. Mem. AACD, Nat. Assn. Student Pers. Adminstrs., Am. Coll. Pers. Assn. (sec., com. mem. 1986-88), Omicron Delta Kappa, Phi Kappa Phi, Phi Upsilon Omicron, Pi Lambda Theta, Sigma Alpha Eta, Zeta Phi Eta. Avocations: reading, travel, theatre. Home: 22 Hilltop Rd Asheville NC 28803-3030 Office: Carolina Day Sch 1345 Hendersonville Rd Asheville NC 28803-1923

SHAAR, H. ERIK, academic administrator; V.p. acad. affairs Shippensburg U. of Pa., until 1986; pres. Lake Superior State U., Sault Sainte Marie, Mich., 1986-92, Minot (N.D.) State U., 1992—. Office: Minot State U Office of Pres 500 University Ave W Minot ND 58707-0002

SHABICA, CHARLES WRIGHT, geologist, earth science educator; b. Elizabeth, N.J., Jan. 2, 1943; s. Anthony Charles and Eleanor (Wright) S.; m. Susan Ewing, Dec. 30, 1967; children: Jonathan, Andrew, Dana. BA in Geology, Brown U., 1965; PhD, U. Chgo., 1971. Prof. earth sci. Northeastern Ill. U., Chgo., 1971—; disting. prof., 1991; pres. Shabica & Assocs. Coastal Cons., Inc., Northfield, Ill., 1985—. Chmn. bd. dirs. Aesti Corp., 1991-96; rsch. collaborator Nat. Park Svc., 1978-82, 89—; adj. prof. Coll. V.I., St. Thomas, 1980, adj. prof. environ. sci. Northwestern U., Evanston, 1999—; Kellogg fellow Northeastern Ill. U., 1979—; chmn. Task Force on Lake Michigan, Chgo., 1986-89; mem. Chgo. Shoreline Protection Commn., 1987-88; cons. Shedd Aquarium, Chgo., 1991; mem. Ft. Sheridan Commn., 1989-90; bd. dirs. Winnetka (Ill.) Hist. Soc. Editor: (with Andrew A. Hay) Richardson's Guide to the Fossil Fauna of Mazon Creek, 1997. Commr., packmaster Boy Scouts Am., Winnetka, Ill., 1984-88. Coop. Inst. for Limnology and Ecosystems Rsch. Lab. fellow. Mem. Internat. Assn. for Great Lakes Rsch., Am. Shore and Beach Preservation Assn. (bd. dirs., pres. Great Lakes chpt.), Sigma Xi. Home: 326 Ridge Ave Winnetka IL 60093-3842 Office: 550 W Frontage Rd Ste 3400 Northfield IL 60093-1246

SHADARAM, MEHDI, electrical engineering educator; b. Tehran, Iran, Apr. 19, 1954; came to U.S., 1976; s. Ali and Masoumeh (Bayram) S.; m. Luz Elena Inungaray, Mar. 24, 1990; 1 child, Jacob Benjamin. BSEE, U. Sci. and Tech., Tehran, 1976; MSEE, U. Okla., 1981, PhD, 1984. Registered profl. engr., Tex. Lab. asst. elec. engring. dept. U. Okla., Norman, 1979-81, lab. instr. elec. engring. dept., 1982-84; project engr. Ra Nav Lab., Oklahoma City, 1981-82; asst. prof. elec. engring. dept. U. Tex., El Paso, 1984-90, assoc. prof. elec. engring dept., 1990-97, prof. elec. engring dept., 1997—2003, Schellenger prof., chmn. elec. engring. dept., 1999—, Brisco disting. prof., chmn. elec. engring. San Antonio, 2003—. Chmn. elec. engring. dept. U. Tex., El Paso, 1999-2000. Contbr. articles to profl. jours. Recipient Faculty Fellowship award Assoc. Western U., 1990, 1991, Advising the Best Thesis award U. Tex. El Paso, 1990, ASEE Faculty fellow, 1995-96. Mem. IEEE (sr. mem., chmn. 1988-90, treas. 1987), Optical Soc. Am., Soc. Photo Optical and Instrumentation Engrs., Eta Kappa Nu. Home: 6518 Jim De Groat Dr El Paso TX 79912-7319 Office: U Tex at San Antonio Elec Engring Dept 6900 N Loop 1604 West San Antonio TX 78249 E-mail: shadaram@utep.edu.

SHADLE, DONNA A. FRANCIS, principal; b. Canton, Ohio, Oct. 29, 1944; d. Gerald W. and Virginia M. (Kerker) Francis; m. Joseph E. Shadle, Apr. 24, 1965; children: Joseph, Paul, Ann, Mary. Student, Walsh Coll., 1964; BS in Edn., Kent State U., 1980, MS in Edn., 1989. Cert. early childhood, kindergarten, elementary edn., Ohio. Tchr. grade 4 St. Joseph's Elem., Canton, Ohio, 1964-65; dir., adminstr. Community Pre-sch., Canton, 1969-79; substitute tchr., K-8 Diocese of Youngstown, Canton, 1965-80; tchr. kindergarten St. Paul's Elem., North Canton, Ohio, 1980-95; prin. Sacred Heart of Mary Elem. Sch., Harrisburg, Ohio, 1995—. Reading pubs. cons.; tchr. rep. Home & Sch. Assn., North Canton, 1985; tech. com., 1992—; dir. drama Ctrl. Cath. H.S., Canton, 1987—; workshop presenter various ednl. conventions, 1989—; adv. bd. ADD Partnership of Ohio, North Canton, 1992—; invited to participate in various dept. projects Ohio State Dept. Edn.; cons. Sadlier Pub. Editor, pub. (newsletter) KinderKindlings, 1989—, pub. cons., 1994. Troop Leader Girl Scouts Am., North Canton, 1977-93; dir. Mime Easter drama, North Canton, 1983-89; vol. United Way, March of Dimes, Heart Fund Canton, Canton, 1965—. Recipient spl. recognition award for Ohio Tchr. of Yr. Ashland Oil, 1989. Mem. ASCD, Assn. Childhood Edn. Internat., Nat. Assn. Edn. Young Children, Nat. Cath. Ednl. Assn. (regional rep. to exec. bd.), Nat. Assn. Elem. Sch. Prins., Ohio Assn. Edn. Young Children, Canton Area Assn. Edn. Young Children. Home: 5544 Frazer Ave NW North Canton OH 44720-4040 Office: Sacred Heart of Mary 8276 N Nickelplate St Louisville OH 44641-9543

SHADLER, BARBARA GORDON, reading specialist; b. Pitts., July 31, 1952; d. Charles D. and Philomena (Konieczny) Gordon; m. Donald L. Shadler, Jan. 5, 1980; 1 child, Drew G. BA in Elem. Edn., Morehead State U., 1973; Reading Specialist, Shippensburg U., 1979, M Equivalency, 1990. Reading specialist Antietam (Pa.) Jr. High Sch., 1977-83, tchr. reading, 1984; reading specialist Mowrey Elem. Sch., 1983-84; implementor Waynesboro Mid. Sch., 1986-89, reading specialist, 1989—, developmental reading tchr., 1992—, coord. student assistance program, 1992—. Mem. NEA, Pa. State Edn. Assn., Waynesboro Area Tchrs. Assn. Avocations: computers, volleyball, camping, travel. E-mail: bshadler@supernet.com.

SHAEFFER, THELMA JEAN, primary school educator; b. Ft. Collins, Colo., Feb. 1, 1949; d. Harold H. and Gladys June (Ruff) Pfeif; m. Charles F. Shaeffer, June 12, 1971; 1 child, Shannon Emily. BA, U. No. Colo., 1970, MA, 1972. Cert. profl. tchr., type B, Colo. Primary tchr. Adams County Dist 12 Five Star Schs., Northglenn, Colo., 1970-84, Title I lang. arts tchr., 1984—2003, Title I reading tchr., 1992—2001; tchr. McElwain Elem. Sch., Denver, 1999—2003, Title I resource coach for staff, 2003—. Mem. policy coun. Adams County Dist. # 12 Five Star Schs., Northglenn, 1975-79, dist. sch. improvement team, 1987-89; presenter Nat. Coun. Tchrs. of English, 1990; assessor Nat. Bd. Tchrs., 2000. Vol. 1992 election, Denver, alumni advisor for Career Connections U. No. Colo., 1993-97; mem. supervisory bd. Sch. Dist. 12 Credit Union. Mem. Colo. Tchrs. Assn. (del. 1992), Dist. Tchrs. Edn. Assn. (exec. bd. mem. 1991-93), Internat. Reading Assn. (pres. Colo. coun. 1988), Internat. Order of Job's Daus. (coun.), Order Ea. Star, Delta Omicron. Episcopalian. Home: 2575 Urban St Lakewood CO 80215 Office: McElwain Elem Sch 1020 Dawson Dr Denver CO 80229-4909

SHAFER, CHRISTINE MARY, elementary school educator; b. Lawrence, Mass., Aug. 16, 1948; d. Charles A. and Jessie T. (Nahill) Morris; m. Alan P. Shafer, Aug. 23, 1970; children: Todd Alan, Jodie Lynn. BS in Elem. Edn., U. Mass. at Lowell, 1970. 4th grade tchr. Fisk Sch., Salem, N.H., 1970, 71; 2d grade tchr. Barron Sch., Salem, 1984-85, 6th grade tchr., 1985-87, Haigh Sch., Salem, 1987-93, 4th grade tchr., 1993—. Mem. PTA, Salem N.H., Salem Boosters Club. Mem. Salem Edn. Assn. (treas. 1991-94, chmn. membership com. 1994-95), Wellness (sec. 1994-95), Alpha Delta Kappa (chmn. membership com. 1992-94, profl. devel. com. 1995—, sec 2000-02). Avocations: reading, writing, crafts, music. Home: 35 Joseph Rd Salem NH 03079-2021

SHAFER, SUSAN WRIGHT, retired elementary school educator; b. Ft. Wayne, Dec. 6, 1941; d. George Wesley and Bernece (Spray) Wright; 1 child, Michael R. BS, St. Francis Coll., Ft. Wayne, 1967, MS in Edn., 1969. Tchr. Ft. Wayne Community Schs., 1967-69, Amphitheatre Pub. Schs., Tucson, 1970-96; ret., 1996. Odyssey of the Mind coord. Prince Elem. Sch., Tucson, 1989-91, Future Problem Solving, 1991-95. Tchr. Green Valley (Ariz.) Cmty. Ch., Vacation Bible Sch., 1987-89, dir. vacation bible sch., 1989-93. Mem.: PEO (pres. chpt. 2001—02), AAUW, NEA (life), Phi Delta Kappa, Alpha Delta Kappa (historian Epsilon chpt. 1990—96, Fidelis chpt. 1996—), Delta Kappa Gamma (pres. Alpha Rho chpt.). Republican. Methodist. Avocations: reading, traveling, walking. Home: 603 W Placita Nueva Green Valley AZ 85614-2827

SHAFF, BEVERLY GERARD, education administrator; b. Oak Park, Ill., Aug. 16, 1925; d. Carl Tanner and Mary Frances (Gerard) Wilson; m. Maurice A. Shaff, Jr., Dec. 20, 1951 (dec. June 1967); children: Carol Maureen, David Gerrard, Mark Albert; m. Carol Bernick, 1992. MA, U. Ill., 1951; postgrad., Colo. Coll., 1966, 73, Lewis and Clark Coll., 1982, Portland State U., 1975-82. Tchr. Haley Sch., Berwyn, Ill., 1948-51; assoc. prof. English, Huntingdon Coll., Montgomery, Ala., 1961-62; tchr. English, William Palmer High Sch., Colorado Springs, Colo., 1964-67, 72-76, dir., 1967-72; tchr. English, Burns (Oreg.) High Sch., 1976-78; tchr. English as 2d lang. Multnomah County Ednl. Svc. Dist., Portland, Oreg., 1979-85; coord. gen. studies Portland Jewish Acad., 1984-90; with Indian Edn. Prog./Student Tng. Edn. Prog. (STEP) Portland Pub. Schs., 1990-92, 95—; tchr. St. Thomas More Sch., Portland, 1992-95; tchr. Indian Edn. Act Program Portland Pub. Schs., 1995—. Del. Colorado Springs Dem. Com., 1968, 72; active Rainbow Coalition, Portland; ct. apptd. spl. adv. CASA; mem. Lake Oswego Libr. Bd., Citizens Rev. Bd. Mem. Nat. Assn. Admnstrs., Nat. Assn. Schs. and Colls., Nat. Coun. Tchrs. Math., Nat. Coun. Tchrs. English. Home: 430 NE 16th Ave Apt 201 Portland OR 97232-2886

SHAFFER, BECKY MARIE, secondary mathematics educator; b. Cleve., June 14, 1969; d. Robert Earle and Bonnie Barbara (Hantl) S. BS in Edn. magna cum laude, Bob Jones U., 1991; MA in Math., Ohio State U., 1992. Substitute tchr., math. tutor Mentor (Ohio) Bd. Edn., 1992-94, tchr. math., 1994—. Asst. track coach Ridge Jr. H.S., Mentor, 1995—, cross country coach, 2003—; math club advisor, 2000-2002, yearbook advisor, 2001—. Mem. Nat. Coun. Tchrs. Math., Greater Cleve. Coun. Tchrs. Math., Ohio Coun. Tchrs. Math. Avocations: running, bicycling, friends and family, sports. Office: Ridge Jr HS 7860 Johnnycake Ridge Rd Mentor OH 44060-5530 E-mail: Shaffer@MentorSchools.org.

SHAFFER, GAIL DOROTHY, secondary education educator; b. Summit, N.J., May 7, 1936; d. Franklin Clifford Jr. and Mildred Edna (Burgmiller) S. AB, Hood Coll., 1958. Tchr. Sherman Sch., Cranford, N.J., 1959-60, Gov. Livingston High Sch., Berkeley Heights, N.J., 1960—. Vol. intake worker Covenant House, N.Y.C., 1982-92, spkrs. bur., 1986—, bd. dirs., Newark, 1993—; mem. juvenile conf. Family Ct. Union County, Elizabeth, N.J., 1968—; project dir. Berkeley Heights (N.J.) Alliance Against Drugs and Alcohol, 1990-95; active Berkeley Heights Youth Com., 1960-65. Named Berkeley Heights Citizen of Yr. by Jr. C. of C., Speaker of Yr. by Covenant House Corp., Vol. of Yr. by Covenent House, Union County Tchr. of Yr., 1992-93, N.J. State Tchr. of Yr., 1992-93. Mem. DAR (Beacon Fire chpt.), ASCID, NEA, N.J. Edn. Assn., N.J. State Tchrs. of the Yr. (pres.), Union County Edn. Assn. Republican. Methodist. Avocations: reading, travel, U.S. history, needlework, Victoriana. Home: 522 Plainfield Ave Berkeley Heights NJ 07922-1919 also: 7 Embury Ave Ocean Grove NJ 07756-1354 Office: Gov Livingston High Sch 175 Watchung Blvd Berkeley Heights NJ 07922-2799

SHAFFER, JOYE COY, reading specialist; b. Lorain, Ohio; d. Harold Russell and Rose Marie (Uhrig) Jenkins; m. Robert H. Shaffer; children: John Coy, William Coy, Connie Coy Weeks, Teri Coy McLean. BS in Edn. cum laude, Kent State U., 1966; MA in Edn. summa cum laude, Calif. State U., Long Beach, 1971; EdD in Edn., U. No. Colo., 1975; postgrad., Oxford U., summer 1987, 89. Evaluator Colo. Dept. Edn., 1978; dir. Summer Reading Clinic U. Sask., Saskatoon, 1974; dir. U.S. Office Edn. Right-to Read Project U. No. Colo., Greeley, 1975-78; external evaluator ERIC Clearinghouse on Reading and Comm. Ind. U., Bloomington, 1989; asst. to dean Fla. State U., Panama City, 1982-86, dir. info. svcs., 1987-89; reading resource specialist, tchr. Orange County Schs., Orlando, Fla., 1989-95. Vis. scholar Ind. U., Bloomington, 1988-89. Contbr. articles to profl. jours. Bd. mem. Women's Resource Ctr. Gulf Coast Community Hosp., 1986-89. Grantee Right-To-Read, 1975-78; recipient Cert. of Distinction Colo. Assn. Adult and Continuing Edn., 1978, Cert. of Appreciation City of Greeley Human Rels. Commn., 1979. Mem. LWV (program chairperson Bay County, Fla. 1987-89), Fla. Reading Assn. (v.p. 1990-91, pres. 1992-93), Internat. Reading Assn. (chairperson basic edn. and reading com. 1978-79, pres. Weld County coun. 1975-76), Fla. Literacy Coalition, AAUW Hist. Preservation Project. Avocations: art, golf, tennis, travel. Home: Seascape Towers # 426 5207 S Atlantic Ave New Smyrna Beach FL 32169

SHAFFER, MARY LOUISE, art educator; b. Blufton, Ind., Nov. 23, 1927; d. Gail H. and Mary J. (Graves) S. AB, Northwest Nazerene U., 1950; MA, Ball State U., 1955; EdD, MS, Ind. U., 1964. Art and music tchr. Kuna (Idaho) H.S., 1950-55; asst. prof. art Northwest Nazarene U., Nampa, Idaho, 1955-56, head art dept., 1971-98, dir. Friesen Art Galleries, 1997-2000, faculty emeritus, 1998; asst. prof. art Pasadena (Calif.) U., 1956-61; prof. art Olivet Nazarene U., Kankakee, Ill., 1964-71. Dir. music Kankakee Congl. Ch., 1964-71, Nampa Christian Ch., 1971-76, Nampa Meth. Ch., 1976-81; juror Nampa Art Guild Painting Show, 1994, 2003; head art policy coun. Northwest Nazarene U.; spkr. in field. One-woman show Friesen Art Galleries, 1999; participant European Images Art Show, 1989; cover artist Nazarene Internat. Mag., 1989; painting retrospective, 1999. Dir. music Van Nuys (Calif.) Nazarene Ch., 1957-60. E.I. Lilly grantee, 1961-62; women's singles tennis champion Kankakee, Ill., 1966, 67, 68, Boise (Idaho) Racquet and Swim Club, 1973, Idaho Sr. Tennis champion Sun Valley, 1984; watercolor Sun Valley Mountain selected to go to moon on Endeavour Space Shuttle, 1992. Mem. NAFE, Nat. Art Edn. Assn., Idaho Arts Edn. Assn., Nat. Assn. Univ. Women, Nat. Mus. Women in the Arts, Boise Racquet Swim Club, Boise Art Mus. Avocations: travel, music, renovating buildings, watercolor painting, tennis. Home: Shaffer Studios 4755 E Victory Rd Meridian ID 83642-7011

SHAFFER, SHEILA WEEKES, mathematics educator; b. Syracuse, N.Y., Oct. 20, 1957; d. Carroll Watson and Reina Lou (Yonker) Judd; m. Jason Craig Shaffer, June 4, 1983 (div. Sept. 1994). BA, SUNY, Albany, 1979, MS, 1982. Cert. tchr. English/Math., N.Y. English tchr. Cortland (N.Y.) HS, 1979-81, Prince George's County, Upper Marlboro, Md., 1984-86, math. tchr., 1986-87, math. tchr./coord., 1990-95, 96-99; math./English tchr. Camden HS, St. Mary's, Ga., 1988-90; math tchr. Frederick County, Va., 1995-96, Kingston City (N.Y.) Schs., 1999—. Mem. SAT com. The Coll. Bd., N.Y.C., 1993-96. Mem.: Nat. Coun. Tchrs. Math. Avocations: reading, hiking, gardening. Office: Kingston City Schools 61 Crown St Kingston NY 12401-3833

SHAGAM, MARVIN HÜCKEL-BERRI, private school educator; b. Monongalia, W.Va. s. Lewis and Clara (Shagam) S. AB magna cum laude, Washington and Jefferson Coll., 1947; postgrad., Harvard Law Sch., 1947-48, Oxford (Eng.) U., 1948-51. Tchr. Mount House Sch., Tavistock, Eng., 1951-53, Williston Jr. Sch., Easthampton, Mass., 1953-55, Westtown (Pa.) Sch., 1955-58, The Thacher Sch., Ojai, Calif., 1958—; English dept. head Kurasini Internat. Edn. Centre, Dar-es-Salaam, Tanzania, 1966-67; dept. head Nkumbi Internat. Coll., Kabwe, Zambia, 1967-68. Vol. visitor Prisons in Calif., 1980-95, Calif. Youth Authority, 1983-93; sr. youth crisis counsellor InterFace, 1984-94. With U.S. Army, 1942-46, 1st lt. M.I. res.,1946-57. Danforth Found. fellow, 1942; Coun. for the Humanities fellow, Tufts U., 1983. Mem. Western Assn. Schs. and Colls. (accreditation com.), Great Teaching (Cooke chair 1977—), Phi Beta Kappa, Delta Sigma Rho, Cum Laude Soc. Republican. Avocations: hiking, camping, travel. Home: 5025 Thacher Rd Ojai CA 93023-8304 Office: The Thacher Sch 5025 Thacher Rd Ojai CA 93023-9001 Fax: 808-646-9490. E-mail: mshagam@thacher.org.

SHAH, HARESH CHANDULAL, civil engineering educator; b. Godhra, Gujarat, India, Aug. 7, 1937; s. Chandulal M. and Rama Shah; m. Mary-Joan Dersjant, Dec. 27, 1965; children: Hemant, Mihir. BEngring., U. Poona, 1959; MSCE, Stanford U., 1960, PhD, 1963. From instr. to assoc. prof. U. Pa., Phila., 1962-68; assoc. prof. civil engring. Stanford (Calif.) U., 1968-73, prof., 1973—, chmn. dept. civil engring., 1985-94, John A. Blume prof. engring., 1988-91, Obayashi prof. engring., 1991-97, dir. Stanford Ctr. for Risk Analysis, 1987-94, Obayashi prof. engring. emeritus, 1998—. Trustee Geohazards Internat.; bd. dir. OYO-RMS, Inc., Japan, ERS, R.M. Software Ltd., India, Risk Mgmt. Solutions, Inc., World Seismic Safety Initiative, Buildfolio, Inc.; cons. in field; pres. World Seismic Safety Initiative, 1994—. Author 1 book; contbr. over 250 articles to profl. jours. Mem. ASCE, Am. Concrete Inst., Earthquake Engring. Rsch. Inst., Seismol. Soc. Am., Sigma Xi, Tau Beta Pi. Avocations: hiking, climbing, travel. Office: Risk Mgmt Solutions Inc 149 Commonwealth Dr Menlo Park CA 94025-1133 E-mail: shah@cive.stanford.edu., hareshs@riskinc.com.

SHAH, SHIRISH KALYANBHAI, computer science, chemistry and environmental science educator; b. Ahmedabad, India, May 24, 1942; came to U.S., 1962, naturalized, 1974; s. Kayyanbhai T. and Sushilaben K. S.; m. Kathleen Long, June 28, 1973; 1 son, Lawrence. BS in Chemistry and Physics, St. Xavier's Coll. Gujarat U., 1962; PhD in Phys. Chemistry, U. Del., 1968; cert. in bus. mgmt., U. Va., 1986; PhD in Cultural Edn. (hon.), World U. West, 1986. Asst. prof. Washington Coll., Chestertown, Md., 1967-68; dir. quality control Vita Foods, Chestertown, Md., 1968-72; asst. prof., assoc. prof. sci., adminstr. food, marine sci. and vocat. programs Chesapeake Coll., Wye Mills, Md., 1968-76; assoc. prof., prof. sci., chmn. dept. tech. studies C.C. of Balt., 1976-91; assoc. prof. chemistry Coll. Notre Dame of Md., 1991—2002. Chmn. computer sys. and engring. techs., 1982-89, project facilitator telecom. curriculum and lab., 1985-89, coord. tech. studies, 1989-91; adj. prof. Phys. Sci. Coppin State Coll., 1996-98; mem. Balt. City Adult Edn. Adv. Com., 1982-89, Distance Learning Task Force, 1996-97; chmn. Coll. wide computer user com., 1985-91; coun. mem. Faculty R&D, 1994-97; adj. prof. chemistry Townson U., 1998—, Morgan State U., 1999—; lectr./prof. chemistry Villa Julie Coll., 2002—; cons. joint apprentice com. Baltimore City Govt., 1980-91. Contbr. articles to profl. jours. Permanent mem. Rep. Senatorial Com.; charter mem. Rep. Presdl. Task Force; mem. Congl. Adv. Com., 1983—; adviser Young Reps., 1992-2002. Recipient Phoenix award Am. Chem. Soc., 1996, 97, Pub. Rels. award, 1996, Sci. Policy award, 2000. Fellow Am. Inst. Chemists (co-chair internat. com. 2002); mem. IEEE, APHA, NSTA, Am. Lung Assn. (chair environ. affairs com., 1976-80), Am. Lung Assn. Md. (bd. dirs. 1971-80), Am. Chem. Soc. (chmn.-elect Md. sect. 1995-96, chmn. 1996-98, chair kids and chemistry program of Md. sect. 1996-99, sec. Mid-Atlantic regional conf., 2002-, chmn. com. govt. rels. Md. sect. 1998—, chair pub. rels. com. 2000--, pres.-elect Chesapeake sect. 2002-2003), Data Processing Mgmt. Assn., Assn. Indsl. (pres. elect 2002-03, pres. 2003-04), Nat. Environ. Tng. Assn., Nat. Assn. Indsl. Tech. (dir. local region, bd. accreditors 1989-95), Am. Vocat. Assn., Am. Tech. Edn. Assn., Am. Fedn. Tchrs., Md. State Tchrs. Assn., Md. Assn. Cmty. and Jr. Colls. (v.p. 1977-78, pres. 1978-97), Sigma Xi, Epsilon Pi Tau, Iota Lambda Sigma Nu. Roman Catholic. Home: 5605 Purlington Way Baltimore MD 21212-2950 Office: Chemistry Dept Towson University Towson MD 21252- E-mail: sshah@towson.edu., dr.shah@juno.com.

SHAH, SUBHASH NANDLAL, petroleum engineering educator; b. Gujarat, India, Aug. 23, 1945; s. Nandlal and Tara Shah; m. Jaya Subhash; children: Nimesh S., Monil S. B Chem. Engring., M.S. U. Baroda, Gujarat, 1968; MSChemE, U. N.Mex., 1971, PhD in Chem. Engring., 1974. Registered profl. engr., Okla. Rsch. engr. Halliburton Energy Svcs., Duncan, Okla., 1976-80, 1982-84, 85-89, group supr., 1984-85, disting. staff mem., 1989-94; sr. rsch. engr., group leader Allied Corp., Solvay, N.Y., 1980-82; Stephenson chair, prof., dir. WCTC rsch. facility U. Okla., Norman, 1994—, interim dir. Melbourne Sch. Petroleum and Geol. Engring., 2000—02. Vis. prof. U. Okla., 1991, dir. Ctr. for Advanced Gas Tech., 1994—. Contbr. articles to profl. publs., chpts. to books. Troop treas. Boy Scouts Am., Duncan, 1985-93, den leader, 1986-87; chmn. Stephens County Sci. Fair, Duncan, 1977-78. Mem. AIChE, Soc. Rheology, Am. Chem. Soc., Soc. Petroleum Engrs. (editl. rev. bd. 1984—, dir. SPE chpt., chmn. membership, tech. editor, publicity and scholarship coms., Recruitment award 1990), Am. Petroleum Inst. (mem. tech. adv. com. GRI sponsored rsch. group 1984-90), Internat. Coiled Tubing Assn. (bd. dirs.), Sigma Xi. Achievements include contribution to advancement of technical knowledge in the areas of fluid rheology and fluid mechanics as applied to hydraulic fracturing/stimulation, drilling, and well completions in petroleum industry. Office: U Okla 100 Sarkeys Energy Ctr T301 Norman OK 73019-0001

SHAH, SYED-WAQAR, science educator; m. Ulfat Zahara Bukhari; children: Syed Hassan Waqar, Syed Ahsan Bilal, Syed Annis Waqar, Mansoora Marriam Bukhari, Shala Sharif Bukhari. Faculty of Sci., Govt. Coll., Lahore, Pakistan, 1970; BSc Biology, Govt. Saadiq Egerton Coll., Bahawalpur, Pakistan, 1973; B.Ed. in Sci. Edn., B. Zakariya U., Multan, Pakistan, 1977; M.Ed. in Secondary Edn., U. Punjab, Lahore, 1980; M.Ed. in Ednl. Leadership, Wayne State U., 1996. Tchr. sci., botany, zoology and gen. sci. Govt. H.S., M.Ghar, Pakistan, 1977-79; tchr. sci., math. and social studies U. Lab. Sch. IER, Lahore, Pakistan, 1980-83; assoc. prof. U. Punjab, Lahore, 1984-99; tchr. Wayne County RESA, Mich., 1990-91; substitute tchr. Dearborn and Hamtramck Pub. Schs., Mich., 1995-96; faculty. U. Punjab Inst. Edn. and Rsch., Lahore, 1999—. Chmn. acad. affairs com. U. Punjab, Lahore, 1997-99, mem. acad. staff assn., 1983-99, chmn. estate and maintenance com., 1993-94, mem. budget and purchase com., 1994-94. sec. student affairs com., 1986-88. Scholar Sch. Bd. Edn., Multan, Pakistan, 1965. Mem. Wayne State Alumni Assn. Home: PO Box 4244 Falls Church VA 22044 E-mail: waqara@yahoo.com.

SHAHANDEH, AROUSHA, secondary school educator; b. Tehran, Iran, 1971; arrived in U.S.A, 1981; d. Pasha Dean Shahandeh and Soudabeh Rahgerai. BSc, Fla. State U., 1994, MS in English Edn., 1996. Am. lit.& composition tchr. Stranahan H.S., Fort Lauderdale, Fla., 1997—. Master: Broward Tchrs. Union. Avocations: pottery, reading, gardening, restoring antique furniture, nature excursions.

SHAHIED, ISHAK I. science educator; BA, Eastern Nazarene Coll., 1959; MS, U. Tenn., 1964; PhD, Colo. State U., 1973. Sr. rsch. chemist Aerospace Med. Rsch. Lab. USAF, Dayton, 1973—74; prof., dept. chmn. St. George's Med. Coll., Grenada, 1977—86; prof. Cleveland Coll., Kansas City, Mo., 1986—89; prof., head biochemist Life U., Marietta, Ga., 1989—94; prof. St. Matthew's Med. Coll., Belize, 1997—98, Ctrl. Bapt. Coll., Conway, Ark., 2001—02; prof., exec. dean St. James Sch. Medicine, Bonaire, Netherlands Antilles, 2002—. Taught at Cleve. Chiropractic Coll., Kansas City, Mo., 1976-77, 86-89. Author: Biochemistry of Foods and the Biocatalysts, 1977, (textbook) Physiology, 1980. Named Hon. fellow Truman Libr. Inst.; recipient Best Instr. award, 1984. Mem. N.Y. Acad. Sci. Avocations: writing, swimming.

SHAKESPEARE, EDWARD ORAM, III, retired secondary school educator; b. Villanova, Pa., May 29, 1924; s. Edward Oram and Henrietta MacDonald (Wilson) S.; m. Sarah Harrison Lowry, June 12, 1947 (dec. Mar. 1983); children: Edward O. IV (dec.), John L., David D.; m. Shirley Winter Mason, Apr. 13, 1985. AB, Haverford Coll., 1949; MA, Cornell U., 1950. English and sci. tchr. Park Sch., Balt., 1950-52, Haverford (Pa.) Sch., 1952-56; copy editor W. B. Saunders Co., Phila., 1956-58; English tchr. William Penn Charter Sch., Phila., 1958—71, dir. dramatics, 1961—71, chmn. English dept., 1961—66, dir. curriculum, 1968-71; tchr. English and biology Friends' Ctrl. Sch., Overbrook, Pa., 1971-75, chmn. English dept., dir. dramatics, 1972—75; English tchr. Baldwin Sch., Bryn Mawr, Pa., 1975-81, Shipley Sch., Bryn Mawr, Pa., 1981-87; ret., 1987. Chmn. English com. Nat. Assn. Ind. Schs., Boston, 1969-76, Ind. Sch. Tchr. Assn. Greater Phila., 1969-71. Author: Drama: From Print to Performance, 1973; prin. editor: Understanding the Essay, 1966, 3d edit., 1991, A Teacher's Notebook: English, 5-9, Vol. I, 1975, Vol. II, 1977. Bd. mgrs. Haverford Coll., 1975-80, mem. corp., 1981—; bd. trustees Green Tree Sch., Phila., 1972-84, 85—; bd. dirs. Del. Valley Friends Sch., Paoli, 1990-99; chmn. bd. trustees First Unitarian Ch. Phila., 1971-72, trustees Alternative Sch. West, Lower Merion/Radnor, 1971-73; mem. Dem. Com. Radnor Township, Wayne, Pa., 1964-84, chmn. 1976-78; bd. dirs. Greater Phila. Coun. Tchrs. of Englishy, 1967-68; mem. Dem. Com. Lower Merion/Narberth, 1986-94. With U.S. Army, 1943-45, ETO. Braitmayer fellow, Nat. Assn. Ind. Schs., 1967. Mem. Franklin Inn Club. Democrat. Avocations: acting, writing, painting, poetry. Home: Cathedral Village 600 E Cathedral Rd K102 Philadelphia PA 19128-1933

SHAKOW, DAVID JOSEPH, lawyer, former educator; b. N.Y.C., May 26, 1945; s. Jacob and Rae (Levine) S.; m. Kineret Piltch, Aug. 3, 1980; children: Rachel Esther, Chava Leah, Yaakov, Tuvia Simcha, Rivka Sara, Chana Miriam. BA, Harvard U., 1967, JD, 1970; LLM, NYU, 1976. Bar: N.Y. 1971. Law clk. to Hon. William H. Hastie, Phila., 1970-71; assoc. Davis Polk & Wardwell, N.Y.C., 1971-77; atty., adviser Office Tax Legis. Counsel U.S. Treasury, D.C., 1977-79, assoc. tax legis counsel, 1979-80, dep. tax legis. counsel, 1980-81; assoc. prof. U. Pa., Phila., 1981-87, prof. law, 1987-2000, prof. law emeritus, 2000—; of counsel King & Spalding, Washington, 1998-99; dir. KPMG, Washington, 2000—. Author: The Taxation of Corporations, Partnerships, and Their Owners, 2d edit., 1997; co-reporter Taxation of Pass-through Entities, Am. Law Inst. Fed. Income Tax Project, 1994-99. Office: KPMG 2001 M St NW Washington DC 20036-3389 E-mail: dshakow@kpmg.com.

SHALALA, DONNA E. university administrator, former federal official, political scientist, educator; b. Cleve., Feb. 14, 1941; d. James Abraham and Edna (Smith) S. AB, Western Coll., 1962; MSSC, Syracuse U., 1968, PhD, 1970; 39 hon. degrees, 1981-91. Vol. Peace Corps, Iran, 1962-64; asst. prof. polit. sci. CUNY, 1970-72; assoc. prof. politics and edn. Tchrs. Coll. Columbia U., 1972-79; asst. sec. for policy devel. and research HUD, Washington, 1977-80; prof. polit. sci., pres. Hunter Coll., CUNY, 1980-87; prof. polit. sci., chancellor U. Wis., Madison, 1987-93; sec. Dept. HHS, Washington, 1993-2001; pres. U. Miami, 2001—. Dir., treas. Mcpl. Assistance Corp. for the City of N.Y., 1975—77. Author: Neighborhood Governance, 1971, The City and the Constitution, 1972, The Property Tax and the Voters, 1973, The Decentralization Approach, 1974. Mem. Trilateral Commn., 1988—92, Knight Commn. on Intercollegiate Sports, 1989—91; bd. govs. Am. Stock Exch., 1981—87; trustee TIAA, 1985—89, Com. Econ. Devel., 1982—92, Brookings Inst., 1989—92; bd. dirs. Children's Def. Fund, 1980—93, Am. Ditchley Found., 1981—93, Spencer Found., 1988—92, M&I Bank of Madison, 1991—92, NCAA Found., 1991, Inst. Internat. Econs., 1981—, Gannett Co., Inc., McLean, Va., United Health Group, Mpls., Lennar Corp., Miami; trustee emeritus Kennedy Ctr. Bd. of Trustees, Washington. Ohio Newspaper Women's scholar, 1958, Western Coll. Trustee scholar, 1958-62; Carnegie fellow, 1966-68; Guggenheim fellow, 1975-76; recipient Disting. Svc. medal Columbia U. Tchrs. Coll., 1989. Mem. ASPA, Am. Polit. Sci. Assn., Nat. Acad. Arts and Scis., Nat. Acad. Pub. Adminstrn., Coun. Fgn. Rels., Nat. Acad. Edn. (Spencer fellow 1972-73). Office: U Miami Office of Pres 230 Ashe Bldg Coral Gables FL 33146*

SHALLCROSS, DORIS JANE, creative behavioral educator; b. Cranford, N.J., Feb. 28, 1933; d. John William and Ethel Belle (Ruth) S. BA, Montclair State Coll., 1955; MA, Wesleyan U., Middletown, Conn., 1962; EdD, U. Mass., 1973. Tchr. Hunterdon Cen. High Sch., Flemington, N.J., 1955-61, Roosevelt Jr. High Sch., Cleveland Heights, Ohio, 1961-65, Cleveland Heights H.S., 1965-67; adminstr. Cleveland Heights Pub. Schs., 1967-69; dir. humanistic edn. Montague (Mass.) Pub. Schs., 1972-75; program devel. specialist Tchr. Corps., SUNY, Oneonta, N.Y., 1976-78; asst. prof. edn. divsn. home econs. U. Mass., Amherst, 1978-82, prof., dir. grad. studies in creativity, 1982-95; pres. Shallcross Creativity Inst., Haydenville, Mass., 1995—. Pres. bd. trustees Creative Edn. Found., Buffalo, 1989-94; co-dir. Global Odyssey, 1992—; bd. dirs. Ctr. for Critical and Creative Thinking, Hartford, Conn., 1989-92, 95—; prof. internat. grad. program in creativity U. Santiago, Santiage de Compostela, Spain, 1999. Author: Teaching Creative Behavior, 1981; co-author: The Growing Person, 1985, Leadership: Making Things Happen, 1987, Intuition: An Inner Way of Knowing, 1989; cons. editor Jour. Creative Behavior, 1967—; contbr. articles to profl. jours. Mem. Planning Bd., Town of Williamsburg, 1981-89; v.p. bd. dirs. Pioneer Valley Performing Arts H.S., 1995-98, pres., 1998—; chair edn. com. Arts in Edn. Ctr., 1997—, pres. 2002-; bd. dirs. Mass. Charter Schs. Assn., 2001—; mem. Creative Problem Solving Inst. Coun. Recipient Disting. Leader award, Creative Edn. Found., 1986; grantee, NSF, 1987-89, U. Mass., 1987-89. Mem. NEA, Mass. Soc. of Profs., Inst. for Noetic Scis., Am. Creativity Assn. (bd. dirs. 1990-93). Avocations: music, golf, reading, gardening. Home and Office: 26 S Main St Haydenville MA 01039-9735

SHAMBAUGH, CATHERINE ANNE, elementary education educator; b. Urbana, Ohio, Dec. 5, 1958; d. Richard Parke and Elizabeth Anne (Hubbard) S. BA, Wittenberg U., Springfield, Ohio, 1981; MEd, Kent State U., 1988. Cert. elem. tchr., math. clinician, Spanish 1-8, Ohio. Tchr. Strongsville (Ohio) City Schs., 1981—. Bd. dirs. Caesar's Forum Theatre Co., 1999—. Martha Holden Jennings Found. grantee, 1985, Strongsville Assn. for Gifted and Talented grantee, 1989. Mem. Nat. Coun. Tchrs. Math., Ohio Coun. Tchrs. Math. (v.p. elem. 1995-98, Outstanding Math. Classroom Tchr. award 1994), Greater Cleve. Tchrs. Math. (Outstanding Math. Classroom Tchr. award 1991), Strongsville Edn. Assn. (v.p. 1989-92, 2001—), Nat. Tchr. Tng. Inst. (master tchr.), Phi Delta Kappa, Delta Kappa Gamma (rec. sec. 2000-02). Episcopalian. Avocations: horseback riding, reading, crafts, bird watching. Home: 741 Walwick Ct Berea OH 44017-2760 Office: Edith Whitney Elem Sch 13548 Whitney Rd Strongsville OH 44136-1951

SHAMBAUGH, IRVIN CALVIN, JR., aptitude test firm executive; b. Harrisburg, Pa., June 7, 1943; s. Irvin Calvin and Viola Mary (Deibler) S.; m. Amy Willcox, Jan. 3, 1975. BS in Geol. Sci., Pa. State U., 1964; postgrad. MIT, 1964-65, Tex. Christian U., Ft. Worth, 1974-76, East. Tex. State U., 1976-77. Rsch. coord. Johnson O'Connor Rsch. Found., Ft. Worth, 1965-76; pres., chief scientist Aptitude Inventory Measurement Svc., Dallas, 1976—; centennial fellow Coll. Earth and Min. Scis. Penn. State U., 1996. Author: The Test-Taker's Guide to Career Literature, 1982, Test Manual for Selected AIMS Worksamples, 1986, Books About Careers, 1986, Career Facts: Where to Find Them and How to Use Them, 1992, The AIMS Guide to Career Facts, 1997; co-author: AIMS Information About Aptitudes, 1979, The Aptitude Handbook: A Guide to the AIMS Program, 1996, 2d edit., 1998; co-author, editor: You and Your Aptitudes, 1983; developer Activity Preference Questionnaire, 1994, psychometric instrument III Interest Inventory, 1996; contbr. numerous reports and rsch. bulls. to profl. publs.; developer AIMS test battery, 1976—. Served with USMC, 1966-68. Mem. ACA, APA, AAAS, Assn. Assessment in Counseling and Edn., Am. Psychol. Soc., Nat. Coun. Measurement in Edn., Am. Statis Assn., Nat. Assn. Coll. Admissions Counselors, Nat. Assn. Test Dirs. Home: 934 Westbrook Dr Garland TX 75043-5243 Office: Aptitude Inventory Measurement Svc 12160 Abrams Rd Ste 314 Dallas TX 75243-4525

SHAMMAS, NAZIH KHEIRALLAH, environmental engineering educator, consultant; b. Homs, Syria, Feb. 18, 1939; came to U.S., 1991; s. Kheirallah Hanna and Nazha Murad (Hamwi) S.; m. Norma Massouh, July 28, 1968; children: Sarmed Erick, Samer Sam. Engring. degree with distinction, Am. U., Beirut, Lebanon, 1962; MS in Sanitary Engring., U. N.C., 1965; PhD in Civil Engring., U. Mich., 1971. Instr. civil engring. Am. U., Beirut, Lebanon, 1965-68, asst. prof. civil engring., 1972-76; tchg. fellow U. Mich., Ann Arbor, 1968-71; asst. prof. civil engring. King Saud U., Riyadh, Saudi Arabia, 1976-78, assoc. prof., 1978-91; prof. environ. engring. Lenox (Mass.) Inst. Water Tech., 1991-2001, dean edn., 1992-93; sr. prof. Sr. U., 1994—. Adj. prof. environ. sci., Berkshire C.C., 1995—; cons., ptnr. Cons. and Rsch. Engrs., Beirut, 1973-76; advisor, cons. Riyadh Water and Sanitary Drainage Authority, 1979-83; Ar-Riyadh Devel. Authority, 1977-93, Assoc. Cons. Engring. Team, 1994-99; assoc. cons. Vakakis Internat., 1995—; planning assoc. Berkshire Regional Planning Commn., 1999—. Co-author: Environmental Sanitation, 1988, Wastewater Engineering, 1988; contbr. over 30 articles to profl. jours. and confs. Recipient block grant U. Mich., 1968-70, Excellence in Tchg. award King Saud U., 1981, 84. Mem. ASCE, Water Environ. Fedn., Am. Water Works Assn., New Eng. Water Environ. Assn., New Eng. Water Works Assn., Internat. Water Assn., Assn. Environ. Engring. and Sci. Profs. Achievements include research on biological and physicochemical remediation processes, math. modeling of nitrification process, water and wastewater mgmt. in developing countries, water conservation, wastewater treatment and reuse, appropriate tech. for developing countries, multidisciplinary studies in environmental management and planning. Home: 35 Flintstone Dr Pittsfield MA 01201 E-mail: nshammas@localnet.com.

SHANAHAN, EILEEN FRANCES, secondary education educator; b. Bethlehem, Pa., Sept. 10, 1949; d. Edward Vincent and Geraldine Mary (Gilligan) S. BA, Moravian Coll., 1971. Cert. secondary tchr. in Spanish, English, N.J. Tchr. Kingsway Regional High Sch. Dist., Swedesboro, N.J., 1971—. Mem. NEA, N.J. Edn. Assn., Gloucester County Edn. Assn., Fgn. Lang. Educators N.J., Kingsway Edn. Assn. (sec. membership), Archaeol. Soc. N.J., Hellertown Hist. Soc., Gloucester County Hist. Soc. Democrat. Roman Catholic. Avocations: archaeology, historical research, genealogy.

SHANAHAN, ELIZABETH ANNE, art educator; b. High Point, N.C., Apr. 5, 1950; d. Joe Thomas and Nancy Elizabeth (Moran) Gibson; m. Robert James Shanahan, Aug. 31, 1969 (div. Mar. 1987); children: Kimberly Marie Shanahan Conlon, Brigette Susanne Shanahan Foshee. Student, Forsyth Tech. Coll., 1974-83, Tri-County Tech. Coll., 1989, Inst. of Children's Lit., 1989. Owner cleaning bus., Winston-Salem, N.C., 1985-86, 87; instr. Anderson (S.C.) Arts Coun., 1987—, Tri-County Tech. Coll., Pendleton, S.C., 1987-98. Artist Wild Geese, 1985 (Best in Show). Active Libr. of Congress, 1994. Mem. Anderson Art Assn. (con. 1987—), Met. Arts Coun. (Upstate Visual Arts divsn.), Triad Art Assn. (pres. Kernersville, N.C. chpt. 1984-85), Nat. Mus. Women in Arts (charter), Libr. of Congress (charter). Avocations: writing, sewing, traveling, decorating. Home: 2519 Mountain View Church Rd King NC 27021-7645

SHANAHAN, TIMOTHY EDWARD, urban education educator, researcher; b. Detroit, Mich., Aug. 10, 1951; s. Ignatius and Irene Alida (Duncan) S.; children: Erin Rachael, Meagan Rebecca; m. Cynthia Tullis Hynd. BA, Oakland U., 1972, MA in Tchg. of Reading, 1974; PhD, U. Del., 1980. Prof. U. Ill., Chgo., 1980—. Dir. Project Flame, Chgo., 1988-2000, Ctr. for Literacy, U. Ill., Chgo., 1989—; mem. adv. panel Nat. Assessment of Ednl. Progress, Princeton, NJ, 1991—; bd. dirs. Ill. Literacy Resource Devel. Ctr., Urbana, 1992—, pres., 1999-2001; mem. Nat. Reading Panel, 1998-2000; chair Nat. Literacy Panel for Language Minority Youth, 2002-,chair, Nat. Early Literacy Panel, 2002-. Author: Understanding REading and Writing Research, 1984, Academic Research Libraries in the Teaching of English, 1993, (reading instrn. program) Treasury of Literature, 1995; editor: Reading and Writing Together, 1990, Multidisciplinary Perspectives on Literacy Research, 1992, Teachers Thinking, Teachers Knowing, 1994, Dir. of reading, Chgo. Pub. Sch, 2001-2002. Mem. dels. assembly Sch. Dist. 101, LaGrange, Ill., 1991-93 Recipient Outstanding Tchr. award Amoco Found., 1982, Presdl. Citation for outstanding achievement U. Del., 1994, Albert J. Harris award for outstanding rsch., 1997, Ill. Reading Coun. Reading Hall of Fame, 2002. Fellow Nat. Conf. Rsch. in English (dir. coop. rsch. 1988-91); mem. Am. Ednl. Rsch. Assn., Internat. Reading Assn. (bd. dirs. 1998-2001, nat. English lang. arts stds. com. 1994-95, Milton D. Jacobson award 1982), Phi Kappa Phi. Democrat. Jewish. Home: 208 W Washington St #711 Chicago IL 60606 Office: Univ Ill Ctr for Literacy M/C 147 1040 W Harrison St Chicago IL 60607-7129

SHAND, ROSA, English educator; b. Wilmington, NC, May 8, 1937; d. Gadsden Edwards and Mary Boykin (Heyward) Shand; m. Philip Williams Turner III, Sept. 13, 1958 (div. Apr. 1986); children: Philip Gadsden Turner, Mary Cantey Meigs, Kristin Shand Turner. BA in English and Art, Randolph-Macon Woman's Coll., Lynchburg, Va., 1959; MA, U. Tex., 1981, PhD, 1983. English tchr. Va. Pub. Schs., 1958-61, Bishop Tucker Coll., Mukono, Uganda, 1962-69, Episcopal Sem. S.W., Austin, Tex., 1974-77; writer for ednl. TV S.W. Ctr. for Ednl. TV, Austin, 1978-80; instr. English Iona Coll., New Rochelle, N.Y., 1982-83, U. Tex., Austin, 1984-85; Larrabee prof. English Converse Coll., Spartanburg, SC, 1985—2001; vis. writer Wofford Coll., Spartanburg, 2001—. Bd. govs. S.C. Acad. Authors, 1992-97; bd. dirs. Emrys Found., Greenville, S.C., 1994-96; vis. writer Wofford Coll., Spartanburg, 2001--. Author: The Gravity of Sunlight, 2000, (short stories) New Southern Harmonies, 1998; contbr. short stories to So. Rev., Va. Quarterly Rev., Shenandoah, Mass. Rev., Am. Ficton, Chelsea, others. Recipient Katherine Ann Porter fiction award, NIMROD-Coun. for Arts, 1991, Libr. of Congress Reading prize, PEN, 1993, Jesse Jones award for best fiction, Tex. Inst. Letters, 2001, Stephen Turner award for best 1st fiction, 2001; fellow, Va. Ctr. for the Creative Arts, 1992—2001, Yaddo Corp., 1993, Macdowell Colony, 1995, 2000, 2002, NEA fellow in fiction, 2000, Dakins fellow, Sewanee Writers Conf., 2000; Sr. fellow in fiction, S.C. Arts Commn., 1994—95. Mem. Tex. Inst. Letters, Assoc. Writers Programs. Hub City Writing Project, Amnesty Internat., Phi Beta Kappa. Democrat. Home: 189 Clifton Ave Spartanburg SC 29302-1435

SHANE, PAUL GAUGUIN, social worker, educator, sociologist; b. N.Y.C., NY, Apr. 29, 1935; s. Sinclair Lewis and Belle (Schwartz) Shane; m. Ana Marjanovic, Oct. 28, 1984; children: Giga M., Eliezer A. BA, Cornell U., 1956; MS in Social Work, Columbia U., 1959; MPH, Johns Hopkins U., 1970, DSc, 1974. Unit dir., program asst., counselor Wel-Met Camps, N.Y.C., 1957—59, 1970; social group worker Jewish Community Ctr., Albany, NY, 1959—61; asst. pers. psychologist U.S. Army Main Induction Ctr., Albany, NY, 1959—61; social group worker Jewish Community Ctrs. Chgo., 1961—62, Hull House Assn., Chgo., 1962-65; project dir. Chgo. Assn. Retarded Citizens, 1965—67; community orgn. rep. Pa. Dept. Pub. Welfare, Harrisburg, 1967—69; dir. planning, then dep. dir. Woodhaven Project for Retarded People, 1972—74; vis. asst. prof. Sch. Social Adminstrn., Temple U., Phila., 1972—74, vis. assoc. prof., 1974—75; assoc. prof. social welfare/social work dept. Rutgers U., Newark, 1975—, dir., 1975—83, chair, 1983—85. Adj. instr. Community Coll. Balt., 1970-72; dir. Social Welfare in Israel summer program, Hebrew U. Sch. Social Work, Jerusalem, 1980-89; part-time prof. U. Belgrade, Yugoslavia, 1989-91, U. Zagreb, Yugoslavia, 1989-91; cons. Nat. Network Runaway and Youth Svcs., 1985-89, Garden State Coalition Youth and Family Concerns, 1982-89, Serbian Inst. Social Policy, Belgrade, 1989-91. Author: Policemen, Society's Untrained Service Deliverers?, 1975, Adoptions: Needs, Rights and Conflicts, 1975, Police and People: A Comparison of Five Countries, 1980, What About America's Homeless Children: Hide and Seek, 1996; spl. issue editor: Jour. of Health & Social Policy, 1991; contbr. articles to profl. jours.; reviewer Jour. Social Svc. Rsch., 1984-2000, Readings: A Jour. of Revs. and Commentary in Mental Health, 1985-2001. Recipient Honorable Mention, NSF, 1971; Fulbright scholar U. Belgrade and Inst. of Social Policy, Yugoslavia, 1989-90; fellow U.S. Nat. Inst. Mental Health, 1969-74. Mem. Internat. Assn. Schs. Social Work, AAUP, NASW, Am. Orthopsychiatric Assn., Am. Pub. Health Assn., Am. Sociol. Assn., Soc. Advancement of Field Theory, Soc. Psychol. Study Social Issues, Soc. Social Study of Jewry. Democrat. Jewish. Office: Rutgers Univ Social Work Dept Newark NJ 07102-1801

SHANE, RITA, opera singer, educator; b. N.Y.C. d. Julius J. and Rebekah (Milner) S.; m. Daniel F. Tritter, June 22, 1958; 1 child, Michael Shane. BA, Barnard Coll., 1958; postgrad., Santa Fe Opera Apprentice Program, 1962-63, Hunter Opera Assn., 1962-64; pvt. study with, Beverly Peck Johnson, Elizabeth Schwartzkopf, Bliss Hebert. Adj. prof. voice Manhattan Sch. of Music, 1993-95. Prof. voice Eastman Sch. Music Rochester U., 1989—, Aspen Music Sch., 1999, Hamamatsu, Japan, 2000—02; pvt. tchr., N.Y.C., 1978—; judge Richard Tucker Music Found., Met. Opera Regional Auditions, Licia Albanese Puccini Found. Performer with numerous opera cos., including profl. debut, Chattanooga Opera, 1964, Met. Opera, San Francisco Opera, N.Y.C. Opera, Chgo. Lyric Opera, San Diego Opera, Santa Fe Opera, Teatro alla Scala, Milan, Italy, Bavarian State Opera, Netherlands Nat. Opera, Geneva Opera, Vienna State Opera, Phila., New Orleans, Balt. Opera, Opera du Rhin, Strasbourg, Scottish Opera, Teatro Reggio, Turin, Opera Metropolitana, Caracas, Portland Opera, Minn. Opera, also others; world premiere Miss Havisham's Fire, Argento; Am. premieres include Reimann-Lear, Schat-Houdini, Henze-Elegy for Young Lovers; participant festivals, including Mozart Festival, Lincoln Center, N.Y.C., Munich Festival, Aspen Festival, Handel Soc., Vienna Festival, Salzburg Festival, Munich Festival, Perugia Festival, Festival Canada, Glyndebourne Festival, performed with orchs. including Santa Cecilia, Rome, Austrian Radio, London Philharmn., Louisville, Cin., Cleve., Phila., RAI, Naples, Denver, Milw., Israel Philharm., rec. artist, RCA, Columbia, Louisville, Turnabout, Myto labels, also radio and TV. Recipient Martha Baird Rockefeller award, William Matheus Sullivan award. Mem. Am. Guild Mus. Artists, Screen Actors Guild, Nat. Assn. Tchrs. Singing. Office: care Daniel F Tritter 330 W 42nd St New York NY 10036-6902 E-mail: rtritter@earthlink.net.

SHANK, RUSSELL, librarian, educator; b. Spokane, Wash., Sept. 2, 1925; s. Harry and Sadie S.; m. Doris Louise Hempfer, Nov. 9, 1951 (div.); children: Susan Marie, Peter Michael, Judith Louise. BS, U. Wash., 1946, BA, 1949; MBA, U. Wis., 1952; DrLS, Columbia U., 1966. Reference libr. U. Wash., Seattle, 1949; asst. engring. libr. U. Wis.-Madison, 1949-52; chief pers. Milw. Pub. Libr., 1952; engring.-phys. scis. libr. Columbia U., N.Y.C., 1953-59, sr. lectr., 1964-66, assoc. prof., 1966-67; asst. univ. libr. U. Calif.-Berkeley, 1959-64; dir. sci. libr. N.Y. Met. Reference and Rsch., 1966-68; dir. librs. Smithsonian Instn., Washington, 1967-77; univ. libr. prof. UCLA, 1977-89, asst. vice chancellor for libr. and info. svcs. planning, 1989-91, univ. libr., prof. emeritus, 1991—. Cons. Indonesian Inst. Sci., 1970; bd. cons. Pahlavi Nat. Library, Iran, 1975-76; pres. U.S. Book Exchange, 1975; bd. trustees Freedom to Read Found., 1989—. Trustee OCLC, Inc., 1978-84, 87, chmn., 1984; mem. library del. People's Republic of China, 1979; bd. dirs. Am. Council on Edn., 1980-81. Served with USNR, 1943-46. Recipient Disting. Alumnus award U. Wash. Sch. Librarianship, 1968, Role of Honor award Freedom to Read Found., 1990, Disting. Alumnus award Columbia U. Sch. Libr. Sci., 1992; fellow Coun. on Libr. Resources, 1973-74. Fellow AAAS; mem. ALA (pres. 1978-79, coun. 1961-65, 74-82, exec. bd. 1975-80, chmn. internat. rels. com. 1980-83, pres. info. sci. and automation div. 1968-69), Assn. Coll. and Rsch. Librs. (pres. 1972-73, Hugh Atkinson award 1990), Assn. Rsch. Librs. (bd. dirs. 1974-77), Beta Phi Mu. Home: 12919 Montana Ave Apt 101 Los Angeles CA 90049-4843 E-mail: RShank@ucla.edu.

SHANKLIN, ANNIE THOMAS, retired education educator; b. Crosby, Tex., Oct. 20, 1930; d. James Alexander and M. Pauline (Drenon) Thomas; m. Austin Don Shanklin III, Feb. 11, 1956; children: Penelope Dawn, Wandalyn Ylonde, Miriam Daphne, Donna Lynn, Adrienne Dee, Mia Johnee. BA, Tex. So. U., 1953; MS, U. Houston, 1992. Cert. spl. edn. tchr., Tex. Tchr. Crosby Ind. Sch. Dist., 1954-58, Houston Ind. Sch. Dist., 1959-87; mgmt. positions, 1988-93; adj. prof. S.E. Coll., Houston, 1993-94; ret., 1994. Author: Precious Memories, 1997 (Plaque); participant film Fire Drill-The Life Saving Mission, 1985. Del. Dem. State Conv., San Antonio, 1973; organizer presentation of debutants FLC Pagteant-South Park Ch., 1985; block capt. Cloverland Civic Club, Houston, 1986; libr. South Park Bapt. Ch., 1974-82; del. Impact II Conv., Boston, 1987. Recipient Plaque, South Park Bapt. Ch., 1982, Regional Granny Smith award Kroger Stores, 1996; Impact II grantee, 1986. Mem. NAFE, Crosby C. of C., Elias Carson Civic Club (founder, pres. 1993-97), Phi Delta Kappa, Sigma Gamma Rho (chaplain). Avocations: crafts, reading, writing, computer games, walking. Home: 5826 Avenue C Crosby TX 77532-8705

SHANKMAN, GARY CHARLES, art educator; b. Washington, Sept. 30, 1950; s. Bernard and Barbara Emeline (Robertson) S. BFA, Boston U., 1972; MFA, Am. U., 1975; postgrad., Koninklijke Academie, Antwerp, 1975-76, Skowhegan Sch. Painting and Sculpture, Maine, 1978. Instr. No. Va. Community Coll., Woodbridge, Va., 1978-85; instr. continuing edn. dept. U. D.C., Washington, 1978-86, Md. Coll. Art and Design, Silver Spring, 1981-86, Smithsonian Instn., Washington, 1978—; prof. Sage Coll. of Albany, NY, 1986—. Judge Ea. N.Y. State regional scholastic art exhbn. N.Y. State Mus., Albany, 1987—, Marblehead (Mass.) Festival of Arts, 1997; artist-in-residence, City of Rockville, Md., 1977, State of Okla., 1980, Byrdcliffe Art Colony, 1997, Constance Saltonstall Found. for the Arts, 2001, I-Park Artists' Enclave, 2002. One-man shows include Seta House, Antwerp, Belgium, 1976, H.C. Dickens, London, 1982, Mickelson Gallery, Washington, 1981, 85, 88, 92, 96, Shelnutt Gallery, RPI, Troy, N.Y., 1989, Yates Gallery, Siena Coll., Loudonville, N.Y., 1999, Canterbury Gallery, Albany, N.Y., 1997, The Canajoharie (N.Y.) Libr. and Art Gallery, 2001; 2 person show at Oakroom Artists Gallery, Schenectady, N.Y., 2000, 2003; group exhbns. include Miller Gallery, Cin., 1992, The Nisk-Art Gallery, Niskayuna, N.Y., 1993, Rathbone Gallery, Sage Coll., Albany, N.Y., Dietel Gallery, Troy, 1993, Broadway Gallery, Albany, 1994, 95, Mickelson Gallery, 1978-99, Cert. Framing and Gallery, Loudonville, N.Y., 1995, The Artworks Gallery 21, Glens Falls, N.Y., 1995, Fulton St. Gallery, Troy, N.Y., 1997, Stage Gallery, Merrick, N.Y., 2000, 01, Colonial Nat. Morningside Gallery, Latham, N.Y., 1999, 2000, Carrie Haddad Gallery, Hudson, N.Y., 2000, Trudy Labelle Fine Art, Naples, Fla., 2001, Train Sta. Gallery, West Stockbridge, Mass., 2001, 2002, 2003, Parker Gallery, Washington, 2002, Fine Arts Bldg. Gallery, Chgo., 2002, State of the Art Gallery, Ithaca, N.Y., 2002, Schcnetady Mus, N.Y., 2003, Bennington (Vt.) Ctr. Arts, 2003, others; represented in permanent collections Mabee-Gerrer Mus. of Shawnee, Okla., Superior Ct. Art Trust, Washington. Internat. Telephone and Telegraph fellow to Belgium, 1975. Home: 86 Lawnridge Ave Albany NY 12208-3118 Office: Sage Coll 140 New Scotland Ave Albany NY 12208-3425 E-mail: shankg@sage.edu.

SHANMUGAM, KEELNATHAM T. microbiology educator; b. Keelnatham, India, Oct. 15, 1941; came to U.S., 1965; s. K. Theivasigamani and Mangayarkarasu (Sundharam) Thirunavukkarasu; m. Valli Narayanaswamy, Aug. 27, 1972; 1 child, Nataraj. BS, Annamalai U., Chidambaram, India, 1963; MS, Utter Pradesh Agr. U., Pant Nagar, India, 1965; PhD, U. Hawaii, 1969. Assoc. res. microbiologist U. Calif., Berkeley, 1969-71; asst. prof. Birla Inst. Tech., Pilani, India, 1971-72; asst. res. chemist U. Calif., San Diego, 1973-75, asst. rsch. agronomist Davis, 1975-80; asst. rsch. scientist U. Fla., Gainesville, 1980-81, assoc. prof. microbiology and cell sci., 1981-89, prof. microbiology and cell sci., 1989—. Co-patentee in field. Grantee NIH, NSF, Dept. Energy, 1980—, USDA, USAID. Mem. Am. Soc. Microbiology (Robert G. Eagon award for outstanding svc. and accomplishments in microbial physiology). Achievements include patent on ethanol producing genetically engineered organism. Office: Univ Fla Dept Microbiology and Cell Sci Museum Rd Gainesville FL 32611

SHANNON, CYNTHIA JEAN, biology educator; b. Phila., Feb. 19, 1961; d. Foster Lloyd and Nancy Ellen (Chapman) Shannon. AA, Fullerton (Calif.) Coll., 1981; BA in Psychology, Calif. State U., Fullerton, 1986; BS in Zoology, Calif. Poly. State U., 1985, MS in Biology, 1991; postgrad. in ecology and evolution, Riverside. Biology instr. Calif. State Poly. U., Pomona, Calif., 1986-91, Mt. San Antonio Coll., Walnut, Calif., 1986—, chair biology dept., 1996-97. Mem. AAAS, Ornithological Soc. N.Am., So. Assn. Naturalists, Golden Key, Phi Kappa Phi. Democrat. Avocations: bird watching, hiking, dogs, food and wine, reading. Office: Mt San Antonio Coll 1100 N Grand Ave Walnut CA 91789-1341 E-mail: cshannon@mtsac.edu.

SHANNON, DONALD SUTHERLIN, accounting educator; b. Tacoma Park, Md., Dec. 28, 1935; s. Raymond Corbett and Elnora Pettit (Sutherlin) S.; B.A., Duke, 1957; M.B.A., U. Chgo., 1964; Ph.D., U. N.C., 1972; children— Stacey Eileen, Gail Allison, Michael Corbett. Mem. auditing staff Price Waterhouse & Co., N.Y.C., 1957-61; sr. accountant Price Waterhouse, Chgo., 1964-65; instr. Duke U., Durham, N.C., 1964-69; asst. prof. fin. U. Ky., Lexington, 1969-76, assoc. prof., 1976-81; assoc. prof. acct. Depaul U., Chgo., Ill., 1981-87; prof. acctg., 1987—. Mem. Am. Inst. C.P.A.s, Bus. Valuation Assn. (pres. 1986-88), Am. Finance Assn., Beta Gamma Sigma. Office: DePaul U Acct Dept 1 E Jackson Blvd Chicago IL 60604-2287

SHANNON, LYLE WILLIAM, sociology educator; b. Storm Lake, Iowa, Sept. 19, 1920; s. Bert Book and Amy Irene (Sivits) S.; m. Magdaline W. Shannon, Feb. 27, 1943 (dec. Sept. 2001); children: Mary Shannon Will, Robert William, John Thomas, Susan Michelle. BA, Cornell Coll., Mount Vernon, Iowa, 1942; MA, U. Wash., 1947, PhD, 1951. Acting instr. U. Wash., 1950-52; mem. faculty dept. sociology U. Wis., Madison, 1952-62, assoc. prof., 1958-62; prof. sociology U. Iowa, Iowa City, 1962—, chmn. dept. sociology and anthropology, 1962-70, dir. Iowa Urban Community Research Ctr., 1970-91; dir. emeritus, 1991—; prof. emeritus U. Iowa, Iowa City, 1991—. Vis. prof. Portland State U., Wayne State U., U. Wyo., U. Colo. Author: Underdeveloped Areas, 1957, Minority Migrants in the Urban Community, 1973, Criminal Career Continuity: Its Social Context, 1988, Changing Patterns of Delinquency and Crime: A Longitudinal Study in Racine, 1991, Developing Areas, 1995, Socks and Cretin: Two Democats Helping Bill with the Presidency, 1995, Alcohol and Drugs, Delinquency and Crime, 1998; editor: Social Ecology of the Community series, 1974-76. With USNR, 1942-46. Mem. AAAS, Am. Sociol. Assn., Midwest Sociol. Soc., Population Assn. Am., Soc. Applied Anthropology, Am. Soc. Criminology, Kiwanis, Phi Beta Kappa. Democrat. Home: River Heights Iowa City IA 52240-9147 Office: Univ Iowa W140 Seashore Hall Iowa City IA 52242-1407

SHANNON, MARCIA RUCKER, mental health nurse, educator; b. LaPorte, Ind., July 3, 1951; d. Glen Howard and Jacqueline B. (Severs) Rucker; m. David Michael Shannon, May 26, 1973; children: Ryan Patrick, Erin Kathleen. BSN, Valparaiso U., 1973; MSN, Wayne State U., 1979. RN, clin. specialist, Mich. Head nurse Midland (Mich.) Hosp., 1974-78; instr. Saginaw Valley State U., University Center, Mich., 1979-83; owner cons. firm Impact, Midland, Mich., 1983—2000; clin. nurse specialist VA Med. Ctr., Saginaw, Mich., 1984-91; dir. St. Luke's Health Ctr., Saginaw, 1990-91; ass. prof. Saginaw Valley State U., University Center, 1993—. Mem. adv. com. RN program Saginaw Valley State U., University Center, 1986; cons. Ctrl. Mich. Cmty. Hosp., Mt. Pleasant, 1992-94, Health Source Saginaw, Saginaw, 1993-2001, Tri-City Mental Health Mgrs., Saginaw, 1994-1999. Vol. park project Fun Zone, Midland, Mich., 1994; vol. coord. Tall in the Saddle, Midland, 1995; disaster mental health cons. to Midland-Glawwin chpt. ARC, disaster svcs. vol., 1997—. Mem. Midland Dist. Nurses' Assn. (pres. 1982-85), Sigma Theta Tau (pres.-elect 1988-92, 98-02, Nurse of Yr. award 1988). Avocations: backpacking, hiking, travel. Home: 3203 Whitewood Dr Midland MI 48642-6682 Office: Saginaw Valley State U 7400 Bay Rd University Center MI 48710-0001

SHANNON, THOMAS ALFRED, retired educational association administrator emeritus; b. Milw., Jan. 2, 1932; s. John Elwood and Eleanor Ann (Mitchell) S.; m. Barbara Ann Weidner, June 26, 1954; children: Thomas Alfred, Paul J., Suzanne L., Terrence D. BS, U. Wis, 1954; JD, U. Minn., 1961. Bar: Minn. 1961, Calif. 1963, U.S. Supreme Ct. 1965, D.C. 1977, Va. 1984; Life cert. as sch. adminstr., Calif.; cert. assoc. exec. Am. Soc. Assn. Execs. Pvt. practice law, Mpls., 1961-62; schs. atty. San Diego City Schs., 1962-73; dept. supt., gen. counsel, 1973-77; exec. dir. Nat. Sch. Bds. Assn., Washington, 1977-97, ret., 1997. Adj. prof. law and edn. U. San Diego; vis. prof. edn. U. Va.; adv. mem. Edn. Commn. of States; prof. Nat. Acad. Sch. Execs., 1971-77; legal counsel Am. Assn. Sch. Adminstrs., 1973-77; adj. prof. ednl. adminstrn. George Washington U., 1996-97. Exec. pub. The Am. Sch. Bd. Jour., 1977-96, Exec. Educator, 1978-96, Sch. Bd. News, 1981-96. Chmn. San Diego County Juvenile Justice Commn., 1973-74; mem. nat. coun. Boy Scouts Am., 1979-97; bd. dirs. Found. for Teaching Econ., San Francisco, 1993-2003. With USN, 1954-59. Mem. VFW (life), Am. Bar Assn. (chmn. com. public edn. 1978-82), Nat. Orgn. on Legal Problems of Edn. (pres. 1973), Nat. Sch. Bds. Assn. (chmn. council sch. attys. 1967-69) Home: 3811 26th St N Arlington VA 22207-5241 E-mail: tombar2@juno.com.

SHANNON, WILLA L. community college instructor, data analyst; b. Bellingham, Wash., Sept. 2, 1945; d. Harold Milton and Katherine Elizabeth Amundson; m. Robert A. Jamieson, July 4, 1970 (div. 1981); children: Aaron, Neal, Kyle; m. Paul Dennis Shannon, Dec. 29, 1984; 1 child Edward. BA, Whitman Coll., 1967; MS, U. So. Calif., 1995. Tchr. Muroc Unified Sch. Dist., Edwards, Calif., 1967-73, Ingram Nursery Sch., North Andover, Mass., 1973-74; library clerk Coast Cmty. Coll., Costa Mesa, Calif., 1979-80; systems engineer Rockwell Internat., Seal Beach, Calif., 1980-95; project mgr. Boeing Space Systems, Seal Beach, 1995-97; cmty. liaison Lower Umpqua Vicitms' Svcs., Reedsport, Oreg., 1998—2000; data analyst Reedsport Sch. Dist., 2000—. Instr. S.W. Oreg. C.C., 2000—. Mem. Troop Com. Boy Scouts Troop 761. Recipient certificate of Appreciation Naval Rsch. Lab. Code 7600, Wash., D.C., 1997. Mem.: Kiwanis. Avocations: music, quilting. Home: 2795 Ridgeway Dr Reedsport OR 97467-1881 Office: Southwestern Oreg CC 1988 Newmark Ave Coos Bay OR E-mail: bshannon@socc.edu.

SHANNON, WILLIAM NORMAN, III, marketing and international business educator, food service executive; b. Chgo., Nov. 20, 1937; s. William Norman Jr. and Lee (Lewis) S.; m. Bernice Urbanowicz, July 14, 1962; children: Kathleen Kelly, Colleen Patricia, Kerrie Ann. BS in Indsl. Mgmt., Carnegie Inst. Tech., 1959; MBA in Mktg. Mgmt., U. Toledo, 1963. Sales engr. Westinghouse Electric Co., Detroit, 1959-64; regional mgr. Toledo Scale, Chgo., 1964-70; v.p. J. Lloyd Johnson Assoc., Northbrook, Ill., 1970-72; mgr. spl. projects Hobart Mfg., Troy, Ohio, 1972-74; corp. v.p. mktg. Berkel, Inc., La Porte, Ind., 1974-79; gen. mgr. Berkel Products, Ltd., Toronto, Can., 1975-78; chmn. Avant Industries, Inc., Wheeling, Ill., 1979-81; chmn., pres. Hacienda Mexican Restaurants, South Bend, Ind., 1978—; chmn. Ziker Shannon Corp., South Bend, 1982-88, Hacienda Franchising Group, Inc., South Bend, Ind., 1987—. Assoc. prof. mktg. and internat. bus. St. Mary's Coll., Notre Dame, Ind., 1982—; chmn. Hacienda Franchise Group, Inc., 1987-96, Hacienda Mex. Restaurants Mgmt., Inc., 1994-96; sr. chmn. Hacienda Mex. Restaurants, 1996—; mem. London program faculty, 1986, 89, 92, 94, coord. internat. bus. curriculum, 1989—, mktg. curriculum, 1983, 88, 95—; advisor Coun. Internat. Bus. Devel., Notre Dame, 1991—; mng. dir. Alden & Torch Lake Railway, 1995—. Co-author: Laboratory Computers, 1971; columnist Bus. Digest mag., 1988—; mem. editl. bd. Jour. Bus. and Indsl. Mktg., 1986—, South Bend Tribune Business Weekly, 1990—; contbr. articles to profl. jours. V.p. mktg. Jr. Achievement, South Bend, Ind., 1987-90; pres. Small Bus. Devel. Coun., South Bend., 1987-90; bd. dirs. Ind. Small Bus. Coun., Indpls., 1986—, Mental Health Assn., South Bend, 1987-90, Michiana World Trade Orgn., Internat. Bus. Edn., 1989-91; Entrepreneurs Alliance Ind., 1988-92, Nat. Small Bus. United, Washington, 1989-92, Women's Bus. Initiative, 1986-90, dir. ednl. confs., 1986-90; chmn. bd. trustees, Holy Cross Coll., Notre Dame, Ind., 1987—, chmn. edn. com., 1993—; chmn. St. Joseph County Higher Edn. Coun., 1988-91, Nat. Coun. Small Bus., Washington, 1988—; Midwest region adv. coun. U.S. SBA, 1988-91; at-large mem. U.S. Govt. Adv. Coun. on Small Bus., Washington, 1988-90, 1994—, chmn. Bus. and Econ. Devel. Com., 1988-90, 1994—; vice chmn. Internat. Trade Com., 1994—; nat. adv. coun. Women's Network for Entrepreneur Tng., 1991—; vice chmn. State of Ind. Enterprise Zone Bd., 1991—; elected del. White House Conf. Small Bus., Washington, 1986; bd. dirs. Ind. Small Bus. Devel. Ctrs. Adv. Bd.; co-pres. Helena Twp. Downtown Devel. Authority, 2002—. Named Small Bus. Person of the Yr., City of South Bend, 1987, Small Bus. Advocate of the Yr., State of Ind., 1987, Ind. Entrepreneur Advocate of the Yr., 1988. Mem. Am. Mktg. Assn. (chmn. Mich./Ind. chpt., pres. 1985-86), U.S. Assn. Small Bus. and Entrepreneurship (nat. v.p. for entrepreneurship edn. 1991-92, nat. v.p. entrepreneurship devel. 1992—), Ind. Inst. New Bus. Ventures (mktg. faculty 1987-91), Michiana Investment Network (vice chmn. 1988-91), SBA (adminstrn. adv. coun. 1988—, contbg. editor Our Town Michiana mag. 1988-91), U.S. C. of C., Nat. Coun. Small Bus. (Washington), South Bend C. of C. (bd. dirs. 1987—, vice chmn. membership 1993—), Assn. for Bus. Communications (co-chmn. Internat. Conf. 1986), Univ. Club Notre Dame (vice chmn.), Shamrock Club Notre Dame (exec. dir., trustee 1993—), Rotary. Roman Catholic. Home: 2920 S Twyckenham Dr South Bend IN 46614-2116 Office: Saint Mary's Coll Dept Bus Adminstrn Eco Notre Dame IN 46556

SHANNON-HALLAM, ISABELLE LOUISE, education director; b. Newton, Mass., Sept. 5, 1934; d. Clarence Edward and Evelyn Florence (Peters) Overlock; m. Albert M. Shannon, Dec. 20, 1970 (div. 1982); children: Clare Louise Lord, William Christopher Lord; m. O. Keith Hallam, July 18, 1998. BA in French, Wheaton (Ill.) Coll., 1956; MA in French Lit., Boston U., 1970; PhD in Comparative and Internat. Edn., Mich. State U., East Lansing, 1977. Cert. French tchr., instrnl. supr., Va., French tchr., Mass. Tchr. French Belmont (Mass.) High Sch., 1966-70, East Lansing Pub. Schs., 1973-77; outreach dir. Can. Studies Ctr. Duke U., Durham, N.C., 1977-79; prof., dir. secondary edn. Va. Wesleyan Coll., Norfolk, 1979-98, coord. edn. dept., 1997-98, prof. emeritus, 1998—. Presenter in field; reviewer Longman Pubs., N.Y.C., 1987-98; evaluator, tchr. edn. programs Va. Dept. Edn., 1985-87. Host, program cons. Options in Edn., WHRV-FM, Norfolk, 1991-95; contbr. articles to profl. jours. Mem. adminstrv. bd. Cmty. United Meth. Ch., Virginia Beach, Va., 1985-92, chair, 1988, chair staff parish com., 1995-97, mem. bldg. com., 1999-2003; mem. Va. Symphony League, Norfolk, 1986-89; bd. dirs. Norfolk Sister Cities, 1987-92. Mem. ASCD, Assn. Tchr. Educators, Va. Assn. Colls. Tchr. Edn. (exec. bd. 1985-86, 90-94, pres.-elect 1992-94), Am. Assn. Coll. Tchr. Edn. (chief instl. rep. 1992-98), Assn. Ind. Liberal Arts Colls. Tchr. Edn. Avocations: reading, genealogy, bridge, art, travel. E-mail: ihallam@cox.net.

SHANTZ, CAROLYN UHLINGER, psychology educator; b. Kalamazoo, Mich., May 19, 1935; d. James Roland and Gladys Irene (Jerrett) Uhlinger; m. David Ward Shantz, Aug. 17, 1963; children: Catherine Ann, Cynthia Anne. BA, DePauw U., 1957; MA, Purdue U., 1959, PhD, 1966. Rsch. assoc. Merrill-Palmer Inst., Detroit, 1965-71; prof. Wayne State U., Detroit, 1971—. Com. mem. grant rev. panel NIMH, NIH, Washington, 1979-81, 84-86; reviewer grant proposals NSF, Washington, 1978—; cons. Random House, Knopf, Guilford, others. Editor Merrill-Palmer Quar., 1981—; contbr. articles to profl. jours. Rsch. grantee NSF, NICHHD, OEO, Edn., Spencer Found., 1966-89. Fellow Am. Psychol. Assn. (pres. div. on devel. psychology 1983-84), Am. Psychol. Soc.; mem. Soc. for Rsch. in Child Devel., Sigma Xi, Phi Beta Kappa. Office: Wayne State U Dept Psychology Detroit MI 48202 E-mail: cshantz@sun.science.wayne.edu.

SHAO, JOHN JIANPING, educator; b. Xinyu, China, Apr. 26, 1963; came to U.S., 1985; s. Zhikui and Juying (Li) S.; m. Diana Wang, Mar. 10, 1990; children: Matthew Stephen, Sarah Gladys. MA in Internat. Bus., U Tex., 1987; MS in Statistics, Va. Tech. Inst., 1990, PhD in Fin., 1991. CFA. Prof. fin. Oklahoma City U., 1991—; pres. Pinnacle Fin. Mgmt., Oklahoma

City, 1991—. Mem. Assn. Investment Mgmt. & Rsch. Office: Oklahoma City U 2501 N Blackwelder Ave Oklahoma City OK 73106-1493 Home: 12716 Whitefield Cir Oklahoma City OK 73142-3129

SHAPIRO, CARL, economics educator and consultant; b. Austin, Tex., Mar. 20, 1955; s. Sherman and Ellen S.; m. Dawn Boyer, Apr. 16, 1978; children: Eva, Benjamin. BS, MIT, 1976, PhD, 1981; MA, U. Calif., 1977. Prof. econs. and pub. affairs Princeton (N.J.) U., 1981-90; prof. bus. and econs. Univ. Calif., Berkeley, 1990—. Sr. cons. Charles River Assocs., 1998—; dep. asst. atty. gen. U.S. Dept. Justice, 1995-96; founder The Tilden Group, 1996. Assoc. editor Rand Jour. Econs., 1984-85, Quar. Jour. Econs., 1984-87; co-editor Jour. Econ. Perspectives, 1986-93, editor, 1993-95. NSF grantee, 1982, 84, 86, 88, 91; Sloan Found. fellow, 1984. Mem. Am. Econ. Assn., Econometric Soc. Avocations: frisbee, camping, bicycling. Office: U Calif Haas Sch Bus Berkeley CA 94720-0001

SHAPIRO, DEE, artist, educator; b. Bklyn., Nov. 30, 1936; BA, Queens Coll., MS, 1960. Former instr. art Adelphi U., Garden City, N.Y.; tutor Empire State Coll., Westbury, N.Y., 1982—. Curator North Shore Cmty. Arts Ctr., Great Neck, N.Y., 1978-79. Selected mus. collections: Guggenheim, N.Y.C., Neuberger, Everson Albright-Knox; corp. and pvt. collections; contbr. articles to cultural publs., featured in radio broadcasts, TV programs and videotapes. Coord. Cen. Hall Gallery, Port Washington, N.Y., 1975-76; lectr., instr. Nassau County (N.Y.) Office Cultural Devel., 1975-79; condr. pvt. art workshops, 1982—. Finalist N.Y. State Coun. Arts, 1979-80, NEA, 1981. Mem. Coll. Arts Assn. Home: 28 Clover Dr Great Neck NY 11021-1819

SHAPIRO, HAROLD TAFLER, former academic administrator, economist; b. Montreal, Que., Can., June 8, 1935; s. Maxwell and Mary (Tafler) Shapiro; m. Vivian Bernice Rapoport, May 19, 1957; children: Anne, Marilyn, Janet, Karen. BComm, McGill U., Montreal, 1956; PhD in Econs. (Harold Helm fellow, Harold Dodds sr. fellow), Princeton U., 1964. From asst. prof. to assoc. prof. econs. U. Mich., 1964—70, prof., 1970-76, prof. econs. and pub. affairs, 1977, chmn. dept. econs., 1974-77, v.p. acad. affairs, 1977-79, pres., 1980-87; rsch. adv. Bank Can., 1965-72; pres. Princeton (N.J.) U., 1988-2001, pres. emeritus, prof. econ. and pub. affairs Woodrow Wilson Sch., 2001—. Trustee N.J. Commn. Sci. and Tech., 1988—91; mem. Pres.'s Coun. Advisors Sci. and Tech., 1990—92; chmn. com. employer-based health benefits Inst. Medicine, 1991; bd. overseers Robert Wood Johnson Med. Sch., 2000—; bd. dirs. Dow Chem., DeVry Inst., Hastings Ctr., HCA. Editor (with William G. Bowen): (book) Universities and Their Leadership, 1998. Chair Nat. Bioethics Adv. Commn., 1996—2001; trustee Alfred P. Sloan Found., 1980—, Interlochen Ctr. Arts, 1988—95, U. Pa. Med. Ctr.; chmn. spl. Presdl. com. Rsch. Librs. Group, 1980—91; mem. Gov.'s High Tech. Task Force, Mich., 1980—87, Gov.'s Commn. Jobs and Econ. Devel., Mich., 1983—87, Carnegie Commn. Coll. Retirement, 1984—86, Pres. Bush Coun. Advisors Sci. and Tech., 1990—92; dir. Am. Coun. Edn., 1989—92; trustee Univ. Corp. Advanced Internet Devel., 2000—, Ednl. Testing Svc., 1994—, mem., 1994—2000. Recipient Lt. Gov.'s medal in commerce, McGill U., 1956. Fellow: Am. Acad. Arts and Scis., Mich. Soc. Fellows (sr.); mem.: Am. Philos. Soc., Inst. Medicine of NAS, Univs. Rsch. Assn. (trustee 1988—). Office: Princeton U Woodrow Wilson School 355 Wallace Hall Princeton NJ 08544-1013

SHAPIRO, IRWIN IRA, physicist, educator; b. N.Y.C., N.Y., Oct. 10, 1929; s. Samuel and Esther (Feinberg) S.; m. Marian Helen Kaplun, Dec. 20, 1959; children: Steven, Nancy. AB, Cornell U., 1950; A.M., Harvard U., 1951, PhD, 1955. Mem. staff Lincoln Lab. MIT, Lexington, 1954-70; Sherman Fairchild Distinguished scholar Calif. Inst. Tech., 1974; Morris Loeb lectr. physics Harvard, 1975; prof. geophysics and physics MIT, 1967-80, Schlumberger prof., 1980-84; Paine prof. practical astronomy, prof. physics Harvard U., 1982-97; sr. scientist Smithsonian Astrophys. Obs., 1982—; dir. Harvard-Smithsonian Ctr. for Astrophysics, 1983—; prof. Harvard U./Timken, 1997—. Cons. NSF, NASA. Contbr. articles to profl. jours. Recipient Albert A. Michelson medal Franklin Inst., 1975, award in phys. and math. scis. N.Y. Acad. Scis., 1982, Einstein medal Einstein Soc. Bern, 1994; Guggenheim fellow, 1982. Fellow AAAS, Am. Geophys. Union (Charles A. Whitten medal 1991, William Bowie medal 1993), Am. Phys. Soc.; mem. AAAS, NAS (Benjamin Apthorp Gould prize 1979), Am. Astron. Soc. (Dannie Heineman award 1983, Dirk Brouwer award 1987, Gerard Kuiper award 1997), Am. Philos. Soc., Internat. Astron. Union, Phi Beta Kappa, Sigma Xi, Phi Kappa Phi. Home: 17 Lantern Ln Lexington MA 02421-6029 Office: Harvard-Smithsonian Ctr Astrophysics 60 Garden St Cambridge MA 02138-1516 E-mail: ishapiro@cfa.harvard.edu.

SHAPIRO, JUDITH R. academic administrator, anthropology educator; b. N.Y.C., Jan. 24, 1942; Student, Ecole des Haute Etudes Inst. d'Etudes Politiques, Paris, 1961—62; BA, Brandeis U., 1963; PhD, Columbia U., 1972. Asst. prof. U. Chgo., 1970—75; fellow U. Calif., Berkeley, 1974—75; Rosalyn R. Schwartz lectr., asst. prof. anthropology Bryn Mawr Coll., Pa., 1975—78, assoc. prof., 1978—85, prof., 1985—94; pres. Barnard Coll., 1994—. Chmn. dept. Bryn Mawr Coll., 1982—85, acting dean undergrad coll., 1985—86, provost, 1986—94. Contbr. articles to profl. jours. Nat. adv. com. Woodrow Wilson Nat. Fellowship Found.; chair bd. dirs. Consortium on Financing Higher Edn.; bd. dirs. Fund for the City of N.Y.; chair bd. dirs. Women's Coll. Coalition. Fellow, Woodrow Wilson Found., 1963—64, Columbia U., 1964—65, Younger Humanist fellow, NEH, 1974—75, Am. Coun. Learned Socs., 1981—82, Ctr. for Advanced Study in the Behavioral Scis., 1989; grantee Summer Field Tng. grant, NSF, 1965, Ford Found., 1966, NIMH, 1974—75, Social Sci. Rsch. Coun., 1974—75. Mem.: Social Sci. Rsch. Coun. (com. social sci personnel 1977—80), Am. Anthrop. Assn. (ethics com. 1976—79, bd. dirs. 1984—86, exec. com. 1985—86), Am. Ethnol. Soc. (nominations com. 1983—84, pres. elect 1984—85, pres. 1985—86), Phila. Anthrop. Soc. (pres. 1983), Women's Forum, Sigma Xi, Phi Beta Kappa. Office: Barnard Coll Office of the Pres 3009 Broadway New York NY 10027-6501*

SHAPIRO, LUCILLE, molecular biology educator; b. N.Y.C., July 16, 1940; d. Philip and Yetta (Stein) Cohen; m. Roy Shapiro, Jan. 23, 1960 (div. 1977); 1 child, Peter; m. Harley H. McAdams, July 28, 1978; stepchildren: Paul, Heather. BA, Bklyn. Coll., 1962; PhD, Albert Einstein Coll. Medicine, 1966. Asst. prof. Albert Einstein Coll. Medicine, N.Y.C., 1967-72, assoc. prof., 1972-77, Kramer prof., chmn. dept. molecular biology, 1977-86, dir. biol. scis. div., 1981-86; Eugene Higgins prof., chmn. dept. microbiology, Coll. Physicians and Surgeons Columbia U., N.Y.C., 1986-89; Joseph D. Grant prof. devel. biology Stanford U. Sch. Medicine, 1989-97, chmn. dept. devel. biology, 1989-97, Virginia and D.K. Ludwig prof. of cancer rsch. dept. devel. biology, 1998—; dir. Beckman Ctr. Molecular & Genetic Medicine Stanford U., 2001—. Mem. bd. sci. counselors NIH, Washington, 1980—84; mem. bd. sci. advisors G.D. Searle Co., Skokie, Ill., 1984—86; mem. sci. adv. bd. SmithKline Beecham, 1993—2000, GlaxoSmithKline, 2001—, bd. dirs., 2001—; mem. sci. adv. bd. PathoGenesis, 1995—2000, Ludwig Found., 2000—; trustee Scientists Inst. for Pub. Info., 1990—94; lectr. Harvey Soc., 1993; DeWitt Stetten disting. lectr., 89, 2002; John M. Lewis lectr. Rockefeller U., 1998; Marker lectr. Pa. State U., 1999; Lundberg lectr. Gothenburg U., Sweden, 1999; honors lectr. NYU, 1998; disting. scientist lectr. NAS, 1999; Crawford lectr. U. Iowa, 1999; Oshman lectr. Baylor U., 2000; Adam Neville lectr. U. Dundee, Scotland, 2001; Genome lectr. Harvard U., 2001; Jesup lectr. Columbia U., 2002; Hopwood lectr. John Ennes Inst., Norwich, England, 2003; mem. grants adv. coun. Bechman Found., 1999—; mem. sci. adv. bd. Anacor Pharms., Inc., 2002—, bd. dirs. Editor: Microbiol. Devel., 1984; mem. editorial bd. Jour. Bacteriology, 1978-86, Trends in Genetics, 1987—, Genes and Development, 1987-91, Cell Regulation, 1990-92, Molecular Biology of the Cell, 1992-98, Molecular Microbiology, 1991-96, Current Opinion on Genetics and Devel., 1991—; contbr. articles to profl. jours. Mem. sci. bd. Helen Hay Witney Found., N.Y.C., 1986-94, Biozentrum, Basel, 1999-2001, Hutchinson Cancer Ctr., Seattle, 1999; mem. grants adv. bd. Beckman Found., 1999—; co-chmn. adv. bd. NSF Biology Directorate, 1988-89; vis. com., bd. overseers Harvard U., Cambridge, Mass., 1987-90, 2003—; mem. sci. bd. Whitehead Inst., MIT, Boston, 1988-93; mem. sci. rev. bd. Howard Hughes Med. Inst., 1990-94, Cancer Ctr. of Mass. Gen. Hosp., Boston, 1994; mem. Presidio Coun. City of San Francisco, 1991-94; mem. pres. coun. U. Calif., 1991-97. Recipient Hirschl Career Scientist award, 1976, Spirit of Achievement award, 1978, Alumna award of honor Bklyn. Coll., 1983, Excellence in Sci. award Fedn. Am. Soc. Exptl. Biology, 1994; Jane Coffin Child fellow, 1966; resident scholar Rockefeller Found., Bellagio, Italy, 1996. Fellow AAAS, Am. Acad. Arts and Scis., Am. Acad. Microbiology, Calif. Coun. on Sci. and Tech.; mem. Nat. Acad. Sci., Inst. Medicine of Nat. Acad. Sci., Am. Philos. Soc., Am. Soc. Biochemistry and Molecular Biology (nominating com. 1982, 87, coun. 1990-93), Am. Heart Assn. (sci. adv. bd. 1984-87), Am. Philos. Soc. Avocation: watercolor painting. Office: Stanford U Sch Medicine Beckman Ctr Dept Devel Biology Stanford CA 94305

SHAPIRO, MARCIA HASKEL, speech and language pathologist; b. N.Y.C., Nov. 6, 1949; d. Ben and Edna Haskel; m. Louis Shapiro, Aug. 1, 1981. BA, Hunter Coll., 1982; MA, NYU, 1983; MA in Speech Pathology, U. Ctrl. Fla., 1991; PhD, Barrington U., 2001. Cert. deaf educator, Fla. Tchr. deaf Pub. Sch. 47, N.Y.C., 1983-84; speech pathologist St. Francis Sch. for the Deaf, Bklyn., 1984-86, Seminole County Schs., 1986-87, Lake County Schs., 1987-89, Orange County Schs., Orlando, Fla., 1989-91, West Volusia Meml. Hosp., Deland, Fla., 1991-93, Orlando Regional Med. Ctr., 1993, Sand Lake Hosp., 1993-98; staff head swallowing dept. Leesburg Regional Med. Ctr., 1994; dir. speech pathology Fla. Hosp., Waterman, 1995—, rsch. assoc. dysphasia study. Mem. adv. bd. Libr. Spl. Edn., 2002—. Mem. AFTRA, EQUITY, Am. Speech and Hearing Assn. (v.p. continuing edn. Fla. 2002—), Annals of Deaf, Coun. Am. Instrs. of the Deaf, Alexander Graham Bell Assn. for Deaf. E-mail: marcy6116@aol.com.

SHAPIRO, MARK HOWARD, physicist, educator, academic dean, consultant; b. Boston, Apr. 18, 1940; s. Louis and Sara Ann (Diamond) S.; m. Anita Rae Lavine, June 8, 1961; children: David Gregory, Diane Elaine, Lisa Michelle. AB with honors, U. Calif., Berkeley, 1962; MS (NSF coop. fellow), U. Pa., 1963, PhD, 1966. Research fellow Kellogg Radiation Lab., Calif. Inst. Tech., Pasadena, 1966-68; vis. assoc. divsn. math., physics and astronomy Calif. Inst. Tech., 1976—; research assoc. Nuclear Structure Research Lab. U. Rochester (N.Y.), 1968-70; mem. faculty Calif. State U., Fullerton, 1970—2002, prof. physics, 1978—2002, acting assoc. dean Sch. Math., Sci. and Engring., 1985-86, acting dir. Office Faculty Research and Devel., 1986-87, chmn. physics dept., 1989-96, 98-01, prof. physics emeritus, 2002—; dir. tchr. enhancement program NSF, Washington, 1987-88. Tour speaker Am. Chem. Soc., 1983-85 Editor, publisher: The Irascible Professor, 1999; contbr. over 125 articles to profl. jours. Pres. Pasadena Young Democrats, 1967-68; mem. pub. info. and edn. com. Calif. Task Force on Earthquake Preparedness, 1981-85; bd. dirs. Calif. State U. Fullerton Found., 1982-85. Grantee Research Corp., 1971-74, Calif. Inst. Tech., 1977-78, U.S. Geol. Survey, 1978-85, Digital Equipment Corp., 1982, NSF, 1985-87, 90—. Mem. AAAS, Am. Phys. Soc., Am. Assn. Physics Tchrs. (profl. concerns com. 1990-93, chmn. 1991-93), Am. Geophys. Union, N.Y. Acad. Scis., Materials Rsch. Soc., Coun. on Undergrad. Rsch. (physics/astronomy councillor 1993—). Achievements include research in experimental nuclear physics, experimental nuclear astrophysics, geophysics and atomic collisions in solids. Office: Calif State Univ Physics Dept Fullerton CA 92834-6866 E-mail: mshapiro@fullerton.edu.

SHAPIRO, MATTHEW DAVID, economist, educator; b. Mpls., Apr. 11, 1958; s. Irving and Janet (Reinstein) S.; m. Susan L. Garetz, Oct. 21, 1989; children: Benjamin Avigdor, Molly Kendall. BA summa cum laude, MA, Yale U., 1979; PhD, MIT, 1984. Jr. staff economist Coun. Econ. Advisers, Washington, 1979-80, sr. economist, 1993-94; asst. prof. Yale U., New Haven, 1984-89; assoc. prof. U. Mich., Ann Arbor, 1989-95, prof., 1995—, sr. rsch. scientist, 2000—. Rschr. Nat. Bur. Econ. Rsch., Cambridge, Mass., 1986—; mem. acad. adv. coun. Fed. Res. Bank Chgo., 1995-; mem. com. on nat. stats. NAS, 1999-2002; mem. Fed. Econ. Stats. Adv. Com., 2000-. Bd. editors Am. Econ. Rev., 1993-96, 00—, co-editor, 1997-00; contbr. articles to profl. jours. Recipient Paul A. Samuelson Cert. of Excellence, TIAA-CREF, 1997; Olin fellow Nat. Bur. Econ. Rsch., Cambridge, 1986-87, Alfred P. Sloan fellow Sloan Found., 1991-93. Mem. Am. Econ. Assn., Econometric Soc., Phi Beta Kappa. Office: U Mich Dept Econs 611 Tappan Ave Ann Arbor MI 48109-1220

SHAPIRO, MEL, playwright, director, drama educator; b. Bklyn., Dec. 16, 1935; s. Benjamin Shapiro and Lillian (Lazarus) Bestul; m. Jeanne Elizabeth Shapiro, Feb. 23, 1963; children: Joshua, Benjamin. BFA, MFA, Carnegie-Mellon U., 1961. Resident dir. Arena Stage, Washington, 1963-65; producing dir. Tyrone Guthrie Theater, Mpls., 1968-70; master tchr. drama NYU, N.Y.C., 1970-80; guest dir. Lincoln Ctr. Repertory, N.Y.C., 1970; dir. N.Y. Shakespeare Festival, N.Y.C., 1971-77; prof. Carnegie Mellon U., Pitts., 1980-90, head. dept., 1980-87. Head acting UCLA Sch. Theater, Film and TV, 1990—. Dir. N.Y.C. prodns. The House of Blue Leaves, 1970, Bosoms and Neglect, 1978, Marco Polo Sings a Solo, 1998, Taming of the Shrew, 1999, Big Love (L.A.), 2002; co-adaptor mus. Two Gentlemen of Verona, 1971 (Tony award); author: (plays) The Price of Admissions, 1984 (Drama-Logue mag. award), The Lay of the Land (Joseph Kesselring award 1990), A Life of Crime, 1993; (books) An Actor Performs, 1996, The Director's Companion, 1998. With U.S. Army, 1955-57. Recipient N.Y. Drama Critics award, 1971, 72, Obie award Village Voice, 1972, Drama Desk award, 1973, Drama-logue award, 1993. Mem. Soc. Stage Dirs. and Choreographers (founder, editor The Jour. 1978). Office: UCLA Sch Theatre Film & TV 405 Hilgard Ave Los Angeles CA 90095-9000 E-mail: mshapiro@ucla.edu.

SHAPO, MARSHALL SCHAMBELAN, lawyer, educator; b. Phila., Oct. 1, 1936; s. Mitchell and Norma (Schambelan) S.; m. Helene Shirley Seidner, June 21, 1959; children: Benjamin, Nathaniel. AB summa cum laude, U. Miami, 1958, JD magna cum laude, 1964; AM, Harvard U., 1961, SJD, 1974. Bar: Fla. 1964, Va. 1977, Ill. 1993. Copy editor, writer Miami (Fla.) News, 1958-59; instr. history U. Miami, 1960-61; asst. prof. law U. Tex., 1965-67, asso. prof., 1967-69, prof., 1969-70; prof. law U. Va., 1970-78, Joseph M. Hartfield prof., 1976-78; Frederic P. Vose prof. Northwestern U. Sch. Law, Chgo., 1978—; of counsel Sonnenschein, Nath & Rosenthal, Chgo., 1991-2001. Vis. prof. Juristisches Seminar U. Gottingen (Fed. Republic Germany), 1976; cons. on med. malpractice and tort law reform U.S. Dept. Justice, 1978-79; mem. panel on food safety Inst. Medicine, NAS, 1978-79; vis. fellow Centre for Socio-legal Studies, Wolfson Coll., Oxford, vis. fellow of Coll., 1975, Wolfson Coll., Cambridge, 1992, 2001; mem. Ctr. for Advanced Studies, U. Va., 1976-77; cons. Pres.'s Commn. for Study of Ethical Problems in Medicine and Biomed. and Behavioral Rsch., 1980-81; reporter Spl. Com. on Tort Liability System Am. Bar Assn., 1980-84; del. leader People to People Citizen Amb. program delegation to East Asia Tort and Ins. Law, 1986; lectr. appellate judges' seminars ABA, 1977, 83, 90; reporter symposium on legal and sci. perspectives on causation, 1990; advisor Restatement of the Law, Third, Torts: Products Liability, 1992-97. Author: Tort Law and Culture, 2003, Towards a Jurisprudence of Injury, 1984, Tort and Compensation Law, 1976, The Duty to Act: Tort Law, Power and Public Policy, 1978, A Nation of Guinea Pigs, 1979, Products Liability, 1980, Public Regulation of Dangerous Products, 1980, The Law of Products Liability, 1987, Tort and Injury Law, 1990, 2d edit., 2000, The Law of Products Liability, 2 vols., 2d edit., 1990, 4th edit., 2001, supplements, 1991, 92, 93, 95, 96, 97, 98, 99, 2002, 03, Products Liability and the Search for Justice, 1993, (with Helene Shapo) Law School Without Fear, 1996, 2d edit., 2002, Basic Principles of Tort Law, 1999, 2d edit., 2003; (with Page Keeton) Products and the Consumer: Deceptive Practices, 1972, Products and the Consumer: Defective and Dangerous Products, 1970, (with D. Jacobson & A.N. Weber) International e-Commerce: Business & Legal Issues, 2001, (with G. Hernandez & others) eBusiness & Insurance, 2001, Concise Hornbook on Tort Law, 2003; mem. editl. bd. Jour. Consumer Policy, 1980-88, Products Liability Law Jour.; author: A Representational Theory of Consumer Protection: Doctrine, Function and Legal Liability for Product Disappointment, 1975; mem. adv. bd. Loyola Consumer Law Reporter; contbr. articles to legal and med. jours. Recipient Andrew J. Hecker award Fedn. Ins. and Corp. Counsel, 2001; NEH sr. fellow, 1974-75 Mem. Am. Law Inst., Am. Assn. Law Schs. (chmn. torts compensation systems sect. 1983-84, torts round table coun. 1970). Home: 1910 Orrington Ave Evanston IL 60201-2910 Office: Northwestern U Sch Law 357 E Chicago Ave Chicago IL 60611-3059

SHAPPELL, VAUGHN SCOTT, education director, educator; b. Allentown, Pa., Feb. 18, 1953; s. Scott Henry and Elizabeth Susan (Gruver) S.; m. Janile Martinez, Aug. 27, 1983. BA, Susquehanna U., 1975; MEd, Lehigh U., 1977. Cert. spl. edn. tchr., supr. of spl. edn., elem. and secondary prin., Pa. Tchr. Carbon-Lehigh Intermediate Unit 21, Schnecksville, Pa., 1976-79, Wiley House, Bethlehem, Pa., 1979-83, supr. of edn., 1983-85, dir. edn., 1985—. Mem. Coun. for Exceptional Children (pres. 1981), Pa. Assn. Fed. Program Coords., Coun. Adminstrs. of Spl. Edn., Mid. States Assn. Colls. and Schs. (vis. team chairperson 1987-94). Avocations: running, cross country skiing, hiking, camping. Office: Kids Peace Nat Ctrs Kids in Crisis 5300 Kidspeace Dr Orefield PA 18069-2098

SHARBONEAU, LORNA ROSINA, artist, educator, author, poet, illustrator; b. Spokane, Wash., Apr. 5, 1935; d. Stephen Charles Martin and Midgie Montana (Hartzel) Barton; m. Thomas Edward Sharboneau, Jan. 22, 1970; children: Curtis, Carmen, Chet, Cra, Joseph. AA in Arts, Delta Coll., 1986; studies with Steve Lesnick, Las Vegas, Nev.; studies with Bette Myers/Zimmerman, Phoenix and Bonners Ferry, Idaho. Prin. Sharboneau's Art Gallery, Spokane, 1977-80; tchr. art Michell's Art Gallery, Spokane, 1978-79; art therapist Vellencino Sch. Dist., Calif., 1981-83; ind. artist Lind, Wash., 1948—. Dir., producer, stage designer Ch. of Jesus Christ of LDS, San Jose, Sonora, Modesto, Calif., 1978 (1st. place road show San Jose); dir. Sharboneau's Art Show, Spokane, 1979, Hands On-Yr. of the Child; platform spkr., poet, fundraiser, libr., 1984-87; asst., apprentice to Prof. Rowland Cheney, Delta Coll., Stockton, Calif., 1985, 86, 87; demonstrated drip oil technique, Bonners Ferry, Idaho, Spokane, Wash., Stockton, Calif., Delta Coll. Author, illustrator: Through the Eyes of the Turtle Tree, The One-Armed Christmas Tree, The Price of Freedom, 1994, William Will, Bill Can, Song of the Turtle Tree, Chet's Ottle-Bottle: The Unbreakable Bottle, One Drop of Water and a Grain of Sand, The Price of Freedom; poet; prolific artist completed over 4000 paintings and drawings, displayed works in galleries through western states; featured in Magnolia News, Seattle, Delta Coll. Impact, Stockton, Calif., Stockton Record, Union Democrat, Sonora, Calif., Lincoln Center Chronicle, Stockton, Calif., Spokesman Rev., Spokane, Wash., Modesto (Calif) Bee, Angels Camp, Calif., Union Democrat, Sonora, Calif., New-Letter, Ch. of Jesus Christ of L.D.S 1st ward, Sonora; artist mixed media, oil, drip oil works, sculptures, pastel, watercolor; illustrations pen and ink, acrylic; sculptor bronze, lost wax method, ceramic art, soap stone, egg-tempra, original techniques, collage, variation on a theme. Dir., programmer, fundraiser Shelter Their Sorrows, Sonora, Calif., 1989-92, vol. Cmty. Action Agy. and Homeless Shelter; fundraiser for Homeless Flood Victims of No. Calif., 1997. Recipient Golden Rule award J.C. penny, 1991, Recognition award Pres. George Bush, cert. Spl. Congl. Recognition Congressman Richard H. Lehman, 3rd Pl. Best Show East Valley ARtists/Pala Show, 1973, 74, 75, 3d Pl. Artist of Yr., 1974, Valley Fair, Santa Clara, Calif., 1974, 1st and 2d Pl. Spokane County Fair, 1978, 3 honorable mentions, 4 premiums, 1979, 3 1st Pl., 3 2d Pl., 2 3rd Pl., honorable mention Calaveras County Fair/Angels Camp, Calif., 1983, 1st and 3rd Pl. Unitarian Art Festival, Stockton, Calif., 1984, 2d Pl., 1985, 3d Pl., 1986, 1st Pl. Lodi Art Ann., 1985, 3rd Pl., 1986, 1st Pl. 1987, 1st Pl., 1988, honorable mental SJCAC Junque Art Show, Stockton, 1985, 1st Pl Ctrl. Calif. Art League, Modesto, 1986, 88, 2d Pl. 1995; 3d Pl. Camilla Art Show, San Jose, Calif., 1974, and numerous others; 1st, 2d, and 3d Pl., Spokane County Fair, 1978; 4 honorable mentions, Sonora, Calif., 1993, 2nd Pl. Ctrl. Calif. Art Show, 1996. Mem. Ctrl. Sierra Arts Coun., Mother Lode Artists Assn., Sacramento Fine Arts Ctr., Inc., Internat. Platform Assn. (Judges Choice conv. arts competition 1993), The Planetary Soc., The Nat. Mus. of Women of Arts. Mem. Ch. of Jesus Christ of LDS. Achievements include: homeless shelter kitchen named in her honor, Sonora. Office: PO Box 5015 Sonora CA 95370-2015

SHARETT, ALAN RICHARD, lawyer, environmental and disability litigator, mediator and arbitrator, law educator; b. Hammond, Ind., Apr. 15, 1943; children: Lauren Ruth, Charles Daniel; m. Cherie Ann Vick, Oct. 15, 1993. Student, Ind. U., 1962-65; JD, DePaul U., 1968; advanced postgrad. legal edn., U. Mich. and U. Chgo., 1970-71; postgrad. in human resource law, Fla. Internat. U., 1999-2000; cert. mediator, Am. Arbitration Assn., 1994; cert. tng. and human resource devel., Fla. Internat. U., 2000. Bar: Ind. 1969, N.Y. 1975, U. S. Ct. Appeals (2d cir.) 1975, U.S. Ct. Appeals (7th cir.) 1974, U.S. Supreme Ct. 1973. Assoc. World Peace Through Law Ctr., Washington, 1967-68, Call, Call, Borns and Theodoros, Gary, Ind., 1969-71; judge protem Gary City Ct., 1970-71; environ. dist. atty. 31st Jud. Cir., Lake County, Ind., 1971-75; counsel Dunes Nat. Lakeshore Group, Ind., 1971-75; mem. Cohan, Cohan and Smulevitz, 1971-75; town atty. Independence Hill, Ind., 1974-75; judge pro tem Superior Ct. (31st cir.), Lake County, Ind., 1971-75; pvt. practice Flushing, N.Y., 1980-82, Miami Beach, Fla., 1988—; lead trial counsel, chmn. lawyers panel No. Ind. ACLU, 1969-71; liaison trial counsel Lake County and Ind. State Health Depts., and Atty. Gen., 1971-75. Professorial dir. NYU Pub. Liability Inst., N.Y.C., 1975-76; adj. faculty prof. constl. law Union Inst., Miami, Cin., 1990-92; adj. prof. environ. litigation and alternative dispute resolution Ward Stone Coll., Miami, 1994; guest prof. internat. environ. law Dept. Internat. and Comparative Law, U. Miami, 1992—; mem. adv. panel internat. environ. law Hemispheric Interam. Dialogue on Water Mgmt.(U.N. Agenda 21), 1993; mem. Nat. Dist. Attys. Assn., 1972-75, mem. environ. protection com.; pres. ESI Group, Nat. Environ. Responsibility Cons. Inc.; spkr. in field. Editor-in-chief DePaul U. The Summons, 1967-68; mem. staff DePaul Law Rev., 1968; contbr. articles to profl. jours. Gen. counsel Marjory Stoneman Douglas Friends of Everglades, 1992-93; asst. atty. gen., chair fed. and constnl. practice litigation group N.Y. State, N.Y.C., 1976-78; mem. Coalition Fla. Save Our Everglades Program; diplomate, vice chancellor Law-Sci. Acad. Am., 1967. Recipient Honors award in forensic litigation Law-Sci. Acad. Am., 1967; Presidential Medal Coalition Recipient, Washington D.C., 1992-93; Internat. fellow, Eco-Ethics Internat. Union, 2003-. Mem. ABA (nat. article editor law student divsn. 1967-68, nat. com. environ. litigation, com. fed. procedures, com. toxic torts, hazardous substances and environ. law, com. energy resources law, com. internat. environ. law, com. internat. litigation, environ. interest group, sect. natural resources, energy and environ. law, judge negotiation competition championship round, law student divsn., midyr. meeting 1995, sect. sci. and tech., biotech. com., environ. law and pub. health com., standing com. sci. evidence, spl. com. legal edn., nat. toxic and hazardous substances and environ. law com., sect. tort and ins. practice, corp. gen. counsel com., non-profit orgns. com., media law and defamation torts com., tort and hazardous substances and environ. law com., govt. and pub. sector lawyers divsn.), Judicature Soc., Soc. Am. Arbitration Assn. (cert. program in mediation 1993), N.Y. County Lawyers Assn. (com. on fed. cts., environ. law, insurance and health law, arbitration and alternative dispute resolution, labor relations and employment law, tech. and automation), ATLA (nat.

coms. toxic, environ. and pharm. torts, environ. litigation), Ill. State Bar Assn. (staff editor 1967-68), N.Y. State Bar Assn. (environ. law sect., family law sect.), Ind. State Bar Assn. (environ. law sect., internat. law sect., trial practice sect.), Greater Miami C. of C. (trustee 1993-94, com. environ. awareness, environ. econs., biomed. exch., planning and growth mgmt., internat. econ. devel., bus. and industry econs. devel., govtl. affairs, ins., internat. banking, Europe/Pacific), The Planetary Soc. Office: ESI Grp Nat Environ Resp Cons 1625 Vega Ave Merritt Island FL 32953-3175

SHARIFY, NASSER, educator, author, librarian; b. Tehran, Iran, Sept. 23, 1925; came to U.S., 1953, naturalized, 1972; s. Ebrahim and Eshrat (Saghafy) S.; m. Homayoun Taslimy, June 14, 1950 (div. 1978); children: Sharareh, Shahab. Licencie es Lettres, U. Tehran, 1947; MS, Columbia U., 1954, Dr. L.S., 1958. Editorial staff Teheran jours. Rah-e Now, Jahan-e Now, Saba, Jonb va Jush, 1943-51; translator, announcer All India Radio, 1948-49; librarian, dep. dir. Library of Parliament Iran, Tehran, 1949-53; cataloger Library of Congress, 1954-55; program asst. libraries devel. sect. UNESCO, Paris, 1959-61; acting chief servicing sect. Dept. Edn., 1962-63; dir. gen. Ministry Edn., Tehran, 1961-62; asst. prof. library and info. scis. and internat. edn. U. Pitts., 1963-66; founder, dir. Internat. Library Info. Center, 1964-66; vis. lectr. SUNY Albany Sch. Library Sci., summer, 1966; dir. internat. librarianship and documentation, internat studies and world affairs SUNY, Oyster Bay, 1966-68; dean, prof. grad. sch. library and info sci. Pratt Inst., Bklyn., 1968-87, chmn. inst. research council, 1971-89, disting. prof., dean emeritus sch. computer, info. and library scis., 1987—; pres. B.E.L.T., Inc., internat. planning cons., 1981—. Dir. Grad. Library Tng. Program, UNESCO Mission, Nat. Tchrs. Coll., Tehran, 1960; Iran's Ofcl. del. to UNESCO Conf. Ednl. Pubs., Geneva, 1961, SE Asia Edn. Secs. Conf., Murree, Pakistan, 1961, Internation Conf., on Cataloging Prins., Paris, 1961, CENTO Libr. Devel. Conf., Ankara, Turkey, 1962; chmn. standing com. for preparation reading materials for new literates UNESCO, Tehran, 1961-62; mem. U.S. AID Mission, Turkey, Iran, Pakistan, 1966; dir. Conf. on Internat. Responsibility Coll. and Univ. Librarians, Oyster Bay, 1967; U.S. del. 33d Conf. and Internat. Congress on Documentation, Tokyo, 1967; ALA del. UN Conf. on Non-Govtl. Orgn., 1969; cons. U.S. AID, Conf. on Book Devel., 1967; mem. adv. bd. Ency. Libr. and Info. Scis., 1969—; chmn. Pre-Am. Library Assn. Conf. Inst. on Internat. Libr. Manpower, Edn. and Placement in N.Am., Detroit, 1970; mem. Am. del. Internat. Fedn. Libr. Assn. Conf., Liverpool, Eng., 1971, Budapest, 1972, Grenoble, France, 1973, Washington, 1974, Brussels, 1977, Montreal, 1982, Chgo., 1985, Barcelona, 1992; organzier USAID sponsored Global Info. Village Conf., Rabat, Morocco, Bklyn., N.Y., 1997, spkr., 1997; bldg. cons. Learning Resources Center, Nat. Tchrs. Coll., Iran, 1972-73, cons. campus planning, 1972-73; UNESCO cons. missions to plan and evaluate Nat. Sch. Info. Sci., Morocco, 1973-74, 79-81, 89; cons. U.S. Info. Agy., Morocco, 1991, 92, 95; chmn. Conf. on Orgn. and Control of Info for Islamic Research, 1982; chmn. bd. cons. to Nat. U. Iran, 1974-75, Pahlavi Nat. Library of Iran, 1975-77; speaker Symposium Internat. sur l' information Economique, Casablanca, Morocco, 1990; inaugural speaker Ctr. Documentation et D'Information Multimedia, Rabat, Morocco, 1995. Author: cataloging of Persian works Including Rules for Transliteration Entry and Description, 1959, Book Production, Importation and Distribution in Iran, Pakistan and Turkey, 1966; Beyond the National Frontiers: The International Dimension of Changing Library Education for a Changing World, 1973; The Pahlavi National Library of the Future, 17 vols., 1976, other books; contbr. to Ency. of Library and Info. Sci., 1969, ALA World Ency. Library and Info. Services, 1980, 86, library jours., 1973—, Bookmark, 1972, Library Education in the Middle East, 1991, Remembering Rangathan: A Sentimental Reflection, 1992; contbr. poetry to various jours. and anthologies, 1947-51, 67, 91-93 lyrics to Iranian motion pictures and recs., 1948-52; works on display at Archieves of Hoover Inst. on War Revolution and Peace, Stanford U.; Contbr. to: film script for motion picture Morad, 1951-52. Trustee Bklyn. Public Library, 1970-82; pres. Maurice F. Tauber Found., 1981— . Recipient Taj (crown) medal and citation for disting. svc. Mohammad Reza Shah Pahlavi, Shah of Iran, 1978, Kaula Gold medal and citation for disting. svc. to internat. librarianship, 1985; named for Annual Nasser Sharify Lecture Series, Sch. of Computer Info. and Libr. Scis., Pratt Inst., 1988—; writings by and about Nasser Sharify are preserved at Archives of Hoover Instn. on wars, revolutions and peace., Stanford U., Stanford, Calif. Mem. ALA (chmn. com. equivalencies and reciprocity 1966-71, mem. UNESCO panel, mem. nominating com. 1970-71, chmn. Pakistan, Iran, Turkey, Morocco, and Middle East Resource panels, internat. library edn. com. 1973—, mem. com. internat. library schs. div. library edn. 1968-72, coordinator country resources panels, internat. library edn. com. library edn. div. 1973-78), N.Y. Library Assn. (dir. library edn. sect. 1969-72), Pub. Library Assn. (task force on internat. relations 1981-86), Am. Assn. Library Schs. (chmn. govtl. relations com., 1984-88), Am. Soc. Info. for Sci., Spl. Librarian Assn., Internat. Fedn. Library Assns. (adv. group library edn. 1971-73, v.p. library schs. sect. 1973-77). Home: 252 Jericho Tpke Westbury NY 11590-1213 Office: Pratt Inst Sch Info and Libr Sci 200 Willoughby Ave # 4 Brooklyn NY 11205-3899 E-mail: nsharify@aol.com.

SHARMA, BRAHAMA D. chemistry educator; b. Sampla, Punjab, India, June 5, 1931; naturalized Am. citizen; s. Des Raj and Kesara Devi (Pathak) S.; m. Millicent M. Hewitt, Dec. 22, 1956 (div. 1996); children: Nalanda V. Sharma Bowman, Renuka D; m. Katharine A. McAfee, June 17, 2001. BS with honors, U. Delhi, India, 1949, MS, 1951; PhD, U. So. Calif., 1961. Chemist Govt. Opium Factory, Ghazipur, India, 1951-52; lab. assoc., sci. asst. Nat. Chem. Lab., Poona, India, 1952-55; lab. assoc. U. So. Calif., L.A., 1955-61; research fellow Calif. Inst. Tech., Pasadena, 1961-65; asst. prof. chemistry U. Nev., Reno, 1963-64, Oreg. State U., Corvallis, 1965-70, Calif. State U., Northridge, 1973-75, assoc. prof., 1975-76; prof. L.A. Pierce Coll., Woodland Hills, Calif., 1976-96. Part-time assoc. prof. chemistry Calif. State U., L.A., 1973-85, prof., 1985—; vis. assoc. Calif. Inst. Tech., 1979, 82; pres. L.A. Pierce Coll. Senate, 1981-82, chmn. profl. and acad. stds., 1989-92. Contbr. articles to profl. jours. Key leader sci. and tech. 4-H U. Calif., San Luis Obispo County. Grantee E.I. duPont de Nemours, L.A., 1961, NSF, 1967-69. Mem. Am. Chem. Soc. (chmn. edn. com. So. Calif. chpt. 1981-82, rsch. grantee 1965-69), Royal Soc. Chemistry (chartered chemist), Am. Inst. Parliamentarians (sec., adminstr., lt. gov. region VII, exec. lt. gov.), Nat. Assn. Parliamentarians (registered parliamentarian, life), Calif. Assn. Parliamentarians (pub. rels. chmn., statewide edn. chmn. So. area, pres. Calif. Sigma unit), San Luis Obispo Gem and Mineral Club Inc. (pres. 1998, sec. 1999, v.p. 2000). Avocations: playing bridge, reading, history, classical music, crystal models. Office: LA Pierce Coll Chem Dept Woodland Hills CA 91371-0001 E-mail: mercury610@aol.com.

SHARMAN, DIANE LEE, secondary school educator; b. Harvey, Ill., May 12, 1948; d. Eric Melvin and Josephine A. (Kut) Van Patten; m. Richard Lee Sharman, Nov. 3, 1973; children: Daria Lee, Deedra Lee. BS, Purdue U., 1970; MBA, U. Chgo., 1973. Cert. secondary sch. math. tchr., Tex. Computers sales rep. GE, Chgo., 1970-73; mgr. sold equipment Xerox Corp., Rochester, N.Y., 1973-81, mgr. fin. ops. analysis worldwide Stamford, N.Y., 1981-84; math. tchr. Conroe (Tex.) Ind. Sch. Dist., 1993—. Mem. DAR, Nat. Coun. Tchrs. of Math., Assn., Tex. Profl. Educators, Purdue Alumni Assn. (life), Nat. Charity League, U. Chgo. Alumni Assn., Chi Omega. Avocations: golf, horseback riding. Home: 26 Fernglen Dr The Woodlands TX 77380-3955 Office: Knox HS 12104 Sawmill Rd The Woodlands TX 77380-2133 E-mail: rshar45854@aol.com., dsharman@conroe.isd.tenet.edu.

SHARP, CHRISTINA KRIEGER, nursing educator, researcher; b. Fort Montgomery, NY, Aug. 4, 1928; d. Joseph Lewis and Mary Agnes Krieger; m. Andrew Asa Jr. Sharp, Feb. 3, 1957 (dec. Jan. 31, 1969); children: Shawn Patrick, Sharon Paula Zegers. RN, cadet nurse, St. Lukes Hosp., N.Y.C., 1948; BS, Coll. William and Mary, 1955; MA, NYU, 1974. RN NY. Staff nurse Vets. Hosp., Richmond, Va., 1948—53, Army Hosp., West Point, NY, 1954—56; instr. nursing Orange County C.C., Middletown, NY, 1956—57, Santa Rosa (Calif.) Jr. Coll., 1961—62; supr. nursing Vocat. Edn. and Extension Bd., New City, NY, 1957—60; coord. practical nursing program Newburgh (NY) Sch. Dist., 1963—83. Cons. NY State Edn. Dept. Nursing, Albany, 1983—84. Editor: (yearbooks) Fla. Soc. RN, Ret., Inc., 1997—. Mem.: AAUW (sec. 1999—2001), Fla. Soc. RNs Ret., Inc. (Orlando dist. pres. 1998—2002, Fla. state coun. 43 pres. 2001—), NY State United Tchrs. (pres. 1997—, Cmty. Svc. award 1998), Widow and Widowers Soc. Ctrl. Fla. (pres. 1999—2002). Avocations: travel, opera, ballet, Broadway shows, ice shows. Home: 2735 Mystic Cove Dr Orlando FL 32812-5344 E-mail: tisharp@aol.com.

SHARP, DOUGLAS ANDREW, secondary school educator, educator; b. Austin, Tex., July 19, 1945; s. Jack Weston and Jean Ernestine (Beeman) S.; m. Marylin Gene Martin, Jan. 20, 1977. BA in Math., Tex. A&M U., 1967, MS in Math., 1970, postgrad., 1969-71; EdD, La Salle U., Mandville, La., 1993. Teaching fellow dept. math. Tex. A&M U., College Station, 1967-71; chmn. math. dept., asst. coach/coach athletics dept. Southfield Sch., Shreveport, La., 1972-73; coach athletics dept. St. John's Sch., Houston, 1975, chmn. math. dept., 1981-93, master teaching chair math., 1987-89; disting. vis. lectr. U. Houston, 1989-90, adj. prof., 1990. Contbr. articles to profl. jours. Recipient Excellence in Teaching award Fin. Dept. U. Houston, 1993, Outstanding Tchr. award Tandy Technol. Scholars, 1993-94. Mem. Am. Math. Soc., Am. Soc. Composer, Authors and Pubs., Am. Statistical Assn., Math. Assn. Am. (Edyth May Stiffe award 1991, 97), Calculus and Elem. Analysis Tchrs. Houston, Nat. Coun. Tchrs. Math., Cum Laude Soc. Office: St John's Sch 2401 Claremont Ln Houston TX 77019-5897

SHARP, GLENN (SKIP SHARP), college administrator; b. Stroud, Okla., Nov. 19, 1938; s. Charles W. and Adeline M. Sharp; m. Sherry Caroline Waddle, Aug. 29, 1959; children: Stephanie, Patricia, Nancy, Christopher. BS, Emporia State U., 1960, MS, 1966. Bus. educator Windthorst High Sch., Spearville, Kans., 1960-64, Northwest Kans. Tech. Coll., Goodland, 1964-66, asst. dir., 1966—97; dean of students Colby (Kans.) C.C., 1997—. Commr. Goodland City Commn., 1986-87; mem. State Scholar Com., Topeka, 1984-85; county chmn. Am. Cancer Soc., Sherman County, Kans., 1981-82; bloodmobile chmn. ARC, Sherman County, 1978-80; cubmaster Boy Scouts Am., Goodland, 1976— (Silver Beaver award 1992, Award of Merit 1989, James E. West Fellowship 1995); bd. dirs. Goodland Regional Med. Ctr., 1993—. Recipient Outstanding Svc. award Kans. Jaycees, 1972, Silver Beaver award Boy Scouts Am., 1992, Award of Merit, 1989, named Eagle Scout, 1952, Employee of Yr. Goodland C. of C., 1988. Mem. Nat. Assn. Fin. Aid (bd. dirs. 1988-91), Am. Vocat. Assn. (life, Nat. Leadership award 1995), Rocky Mountain Assn. Fin. Aid (pres., bd. dirs. 1985-91, Disting. Svc. awards 1985, 87, Hall of Fame 1992), Kans. Vocat. Assn. (life), Kans. Assn. Fin. Adminstrs. (pres., bd. dirs. 1983-93, Outstanding Svc. award 1986, Hall of Fame 1996, Meritorious Achievement award 1995, 35 Yr. award 2003), Kiwanis (pres. 1968-69, 92-93, Outstanding Kiwanian 1968, 94, 95), Phi Delta Kappa (life, pres. 1983-84, Outstanding Educator 1985-86, Svc. Key 1991). Democrat. Christian. Avocations: camping, collecting, travel. Home: 1812 Harvey Ct Colby KS 67701-1518

SHARP, J(AMES) FRANKLIN, finance educator, portfolio manager; b. Johnson County, Ill., Sept. 29, 1938; s. James Albert and Edna Mae (Slack) S. BS in Indsl. Engring., U. Ill., 1960; MS, Purdue U., 1962, PhD, 1966, cert. mgmt. acctg., 1979. Chartered fin. analyst, 1980; cert. in fin. mgmt., 1997. Asst. prof. engring., econs. Rutgers U., New Brunswick, N.J., 1966-70; assoc. prof. NYU Grad. Sch. Bus., N.Y.C., 1970-74; supr. bus. research AT&T, N.Y.C., 1974-77, dist. mgr. corp. planning, 1977-81, dist. mgr. fin. mgmt. and planning, 1981-85; prof. fin. Grad. Sch. Bus. Pace U., N.Y.C., 1975-91; chmn. Sharp CFA Rev. & Inst. for Investment Edn., 1987-96, Sharp Seminars, 1996—. Speaker, moderator meetings, 1965—; cons. Sharp Investment Mgmt., 1967—. Contbr. numerous articles to profl. publs.; corr.: Interfaces, 1975-78; fin. editor: Planning Rev., 1975-78. Mem. N.Am. Soc. Corp. Planning (treas. 1976-77, bd. dirs. at large 1977-78), Inst. Mgmt. Sci. (chpt. v.p. acad. 1972-74, chpt. v.p. program 1974-75, chpt. v.p. membership 1975-76, chpt. pres. 1976-77), Internat. Affiliation Planning Socs. (coun. 1978-84), N.Y. Soc. Security Analysts (CFA Rev. 1985-87), Ops. Rsch. Soc. Am. (pres. corp. planning group 1976-82), AAUP (v.p. Pace U. chpt. 1988-90), Theta Xi. Republican. Office: 315 E 86th St Apt 7H New York NY 10028-4740

SHARP, JOLLY KAY, English language educator; b. Corbin, Ky., Dec. 22, 1954; d. Joshua Pleas and Emma Olive (Patrick) Sharp; children: Jessica Ruth, Joshua Paul. BA, Cumberland Coll., 1974; MA, Wright State U., 1988; post grad., Mid. Tenn. State Univ., 2003. English tchr. Cumberland (Ky.) H.S., 1982-83; English educator Cumberland Coll., Williamsburg, Ky., 1991—. Mem. Williamsburg PTA, 1991-2000, sec., 1993-94. Mem. MLA, South Atlantic MLA, Flannery O'Connor Soc., Jesse Stuart Found., Popular Culture Assn., Delta Kappa Gamma (Alpha Lambda chpt.). Republican. Baptist. Avocations: reading, counted cross-stitch. Office: Cumberland Coll English Dept 7828 College Station Dr Williamsburg KY 40769-1389

SHARP, KAREN DEAN, art educator; b. Farmerville, La., Mar. 7, 1960; d. Gladden Everette and Elva Gray (Nolan) Dean; m. Thomas Richard Sharp, Nov. 20, 1982; children: Sylver Gray, Hunter Roe. Ed., Comml. Coll., 1979; BFA, La. Tech. U., 1982; cert. in art edn., N.E. La. U., 1990. Cert. art educator. Graphic artist Ken Juneau, Alexandria, La., 1983-85; art dir. Sharp Graphics, Monroe, 1985-87, Ad Creations, Monroe, La., 1987-88; tchr. art Ouachita Christian Sch., Monroe, 1989—. Active Miss. Mus. Recipient Addy award Ctrl. Ad Group, Alexandria, La., 1985, 86, Judges award Monroe Ad Group, 1989, Art Educator of Yr. award La. Gov., 1996. Mem. Nat. Art Edn. Assn., Women in the Arts. Republican. Mem. Ch. of Christ. Avocations: drawing, painting. Home: 7811 Westlake Rd Sterlington LA 71280-3235 Office: Ouachita Christian Sch 7065 Highway 165 N Monroe LA 71203-9718

SHARP, PHILLIP ALLEN, biologist, educator; b. Ky., June 6, 1944; s. Joseph Walter and Katherin (Colvin) S.; m. Ann Christine Holcombe, Aug. 29, 1964; children: Christine Alynn, Sarah Katherin, Helena Holcombe. BA, Union Coll., Barbourville, Ky., 1966, LHD (hon.), 1991; PhD, U. Ill., 1969; DSc (hon.), U. Ky., 1994, Bowdoin Coll., 1995, U. Tel Aviv, Israel, 1996, Albright Coll., 1996; hon. degree (hon.), U. Glasgow, 1998, U. Uppsala, 1999, Thomas Moore Coll., 1999, U. Buenos Aires, 1999, No. Ky. U., 1999, PhD (hon.), 2001. NIH postdoctoral fellow Calif. Inst. Tech., 1969—71; sr. research investigator Cold Spring Harbor (N.Y.) Lab., 1972—74; assoc. prof. MIT, Cambridge, 1974—79, prof. biology, 1979—99, Inst. prof., 1999—, head dept. biology, 1991—99, dir. Ctr. Cancer Rsch., 1985—91. Dir. The McGovern Inst., 2000—; co-founder, mem. sci. bd., dir. BIOGEN, 1978—, chmn. sci. bd., 1987—2002; mem. Pres.'s Adv. Coun. on Sci. and Tech., 1991—97; mem. presdl. appt. Nat.Cancer Adv. Bd. NIH, 1996—2000; chmn. GM Cancer Rsch. Found. Awards Assembly, 1994—; mem. sci. bd. Ludwig Inst., 1998—; mem. bd. scientific govs. Scripps Rsch. Inst., 1999—; trustee Mass. Gen. Hosp., 2001—02; co-founder, chair of sci. bd. and mem. of bd. dirs. Alnylan Pharm. Inc., 2002—; bd. advisors Polaris Venture Ptnrs., 2002; co-founder, chmn. sci. bd., dir. Alnylam Pharm., 2002—; mem. Corp. Ptnrs. HealthCare Systems, Inc., 2003—. Mem. editl. bd.: Cell, 1974—95, Jour. Virology, 1974—86, Molecular and Cellular Biology, 1974—85, RNA, 1995—. Trustee Alfred P. Sloan Found., 1995—. Co-recipient Nobel Prize in Physiology of Medicine, 1993; named Class of '41 chair, 1986—87, John D. MacArthur chair, 1987—92, Salvador E. Luria chair, 1992—99; recipient awards, Am. Cancer Soc., 1974—79, Eli Lilly, 1980, Nat. Acad.Sci./U.S. Steel Found., 1980, Howard Ricketts award, U.Chgo., 1985, Alfred P. Sloan Jr. prize, Gen. Motors Rsch. Found., 1986, award, Gairdner Found. Internat., 1986, N.Y. Acad.Scis., 1986, Louisa Horwitz prize, 1988, Albert Lasker Basic Med. Rsch. award, 1988, Dickson prize, U. Pitts., 1990, Fourth Ann. Biotech. Heritage award, 2002, Alumni Achievement award, U. Ill., 2003. Fellow: AAAS, Royal Soc. Edinburgh (hon.); mem.: Corp. Ptnrs. HealthCare Systems, Inc. (elected mem.), Inst. of Medicine of NAS (elected mem.), Am. Philos. Soc. (elected mem.) (The Benjamin Franklin medal 1999), Am. Soc. Biochemistry and Molecular Biology (elected mem. coun.), European Molecular Biology Orgn. (assoc.), Am. Acad. Arts and Scis., Am. Soc. Microbiology, NAS (councilor 1986). Home: 36 Fairmont Ave Newton MA 02458-2506 Office: MIT Ctr for Cancer Rsch 40 Ames St Rm E17529B Cambridge MA 02139-4307 E-mail: sharppa@mit.edu.

SHARP, RONALD ALAN, English literature educator, dean, author; b. Cleve., Oct. 19, 1945; s. Jack Trier and Florence (Tenenbaum) S.; m. Inese Brutans, June 22, 1968; children: Andrew Janis, James Michael. BA, Kalamazoo Coll., 1967; MA, U. Mich., 1968; PhD, U. Va., 1974. Instr. in English Western Mich. U., Kalamazoo, 1968-70; from instr. to acting pres. Kenyon Coll., Gambier, Ohio, 1970—2002, acting pres., 2002—03; dean of the faculty Vassar Coll., Poughkeepsie, NY, 2003—. Dir. Keats Bicentennial Conf., Harvard U., 1995. Author: Keats, Skepticism and the Religion of Beauty, 1979, Friendship and Literature: Spirit and Form. 1986; translator: Teatro Breve (Garcia Lorca), 1979, editor (with Eudora Welty) The Norton Book of Friendship, 1991, (with Nathan Scott) Reading George Steiner, 1994, (with Robert Ryan) The Persistence of Poetry: Bicentennial Essays on John Keats, 1998, Selected Poems of Michael Harper, 2002; co-editor Kenyon Rev., 78-82; contbr. articles to profl. jours. Recipient award for editl. excellence Ohioana Assn., 1980; fellow Nat. Humanities Ctr., 1981, 86, NEH, 1981, 84-87, 93, 94, 96, 98, Ford Found., 1971, Mellon Found., 1980, Danforth Found., 1971, English Speaking Union, 1973, Am. Coun. Learned Socs., 1986. Mem. MLA, NEH (chmn's. adv. group humanities edn. 1987), Wordsworth-Coleridge Assn., Keats-Shelley Assn. Jewish. Office: Dean of Faculty Vassar Coll Box 4 Poughkeepsie NY 12604

SHARP, RONALD ARVELL, sociology educator; b. Vivian, La., Sept. 29, 1941; s. Walter Arvell and Virginia (Refield-King) S.; m. Imelda Idalia Pena, Sept. 16, 1967; children: Ronald Arvell II, Donald Allen. BS in Edn., Cameron U., 1976; BA in Sociology, SUNY, Albany, 1977; MEd in Counseling Psychology, U. Okla., 1978; PhD in Sociology, Clayton U., 1985. Ret. radiologic technologist and instr. U.S. Army, 1960-82; radiologic technologist VA Hosp., Temple, Tex., 1983-84; vets. counselor Vets. Outreach Program, San Antonio, 1982-83; dir. personnel & mktg. Heran Pharms., San Antonio, 1988-91; prof. sociology Ctrl. Tech. Coll., Killeen, 1991-95; instr. sociology Tex. State Tech. Coll., Waco, 1995-96, Academia Assocs., 1996—. Part-time instr. Ctrl. Tex. Coll., 1980-82, City Coll. Chgo., 1981, Big Bend C.C., Mannheim, Germany, 1981-82; instr. Acad. Health Scis., 1977-79. Contbr. articles to profl. jours. Coach Youth Soccer Orgns., San Antonio and Mannheim, 1976-82. Nat. Coll. Radiology Technologists fellow, 1968. Mem. AAUP, DAV (past comdr.), VFW (past comdr.), Uniformed Svcs. Disabled Retirees (nat. vice-commdr., treas.), Am. Sociol. Assn., Soc. Applied Sociology, Nat. Assn. Medics and Corpsmen (PNC), Am. Mil. Ret. Assn. (PNVP), Combat Medics Assn. (nat. dir.), La. Archeol. Soc., Choctaw Nation of Okla., Okla. Anthrop. Soc., La. Archeol. Conservancy, Caddoan Hist. Soc., Okla. Anthropol. Survey, Order of Alhambra, KC, Masons, Soc. for the Study of Social Problems, Four Winds Intertribal Soc., Hokshichankiya Soc., Psi Beta (chpt. sponsor), Alpha Kappa Delta, Psi Chi, Sigma Eta Sigma (nat. dir.). Roman Catholic. Avocations: soccer, golf, paleo-historic anthropology. Home: 9310 Oak Hills Dr Temple TX 76502-5272 Office: Academia Assocs Waco TX 76705 Office Fax: 254-870-3444.

SHARPE, AUBREY DEAN, college administrator; b. Miami, Fla., Oct. 4, 1944; s. William Gibson and Ila-Mae (Albritton) S.; m. Linda Lee Rush, Dec. 22, 1973. BA, E. Tex. Bapt. U., 1967; MDiv, Southwestern Bapt. Theol. Sem., Ft. Worth, 1970; MA, southwestern Bapt. Theol. Sem., Ft. Worth, 1972; EdD, U. No. Tex., 1993. Assoc. pastor edn. Trinity Bapt. Ch., Ft. Worth, Tex., 1970-72; minister edn. Polytechnic Bapt. Ch., Ft. Worth, Tex., 1972-73; dean community svcs. Tarrant County Jr. Coll., Ft. Worth, Tex., 1973-84, religion inst., 1976-78; nat. dir. tng. Presbyn. Ministers Fund, Phila., 1984-89; v.p. The Pat Petersen Collection, Ft. Worth, 1984-91; owner ADS Investments, Ft. Worth, 1984—; dean continuing studies, Regional Tng. and Devel. Complex Tyler (Tex.) Jr. Coll., 1989—. Bd. mgrs. Synergy Capital Mgmt., LLC, 1997-99; chmn. bd. dirs. Sentinel Holdings Ltd., 1999—. Pres. Ft. Worth Boys Club, 1979; allocations chmn. United Way Tarrant County, Ft. Worth, 1981-87, Sr. Citizens, Inc., Ft. Worth, 1985-86, Tyler Metro YMCA, 1992-93; bd. dirs. United Way Tyler and Smith County, 1991-98, v.p. allocations/funding, trainer for loaned exec. program, 1991-95, Pacesetter Campaign chair 1996, campaign chair, 1997, bd. chair, 1998, bd. chair 1998; adv. bd. North Tex. Small Bus. Devel. Ctr., 1995-96; commr. Civil Svc. Commn., City of Tyler, Tex., 1997—; coun. mem. Tyler Indsl. Devel. Coun., City of Tyler, 1997—; bd. dirs. United Ways Tex., 1999—, Heart of Tyler-Main Street, 2001—. Recipient Nat. Sales Achievement award Nat. Assn. Life Underwriters, 1987, Nat. Sales Leader award 1987; recipient Achievers award Presbyn. Ministers Fund, 1987, Vol. Svc. Award, United Way of Tarrant County, 1987. Mem. ASTD (pres.-elect 1991, pres. 1992-93), Tex. Assn. Community Svcs. and Continuing Edn., Tex. Jr. Coll. Tchrs. Assn., Nat. Coun. for Community Svcs./Continuing Edn., Nat. Coun. for Cont. Ednl. and Tng. (south ctrl. regional dir., bd. dirs. 1999—), Tex. Adminstrs. Continuing Edn., Tyler Area C. of C. (bd. dirs. 2000—), Phi Delta Kappa. Republican. Baptist. Avocations: reading, collecting old books, landscaping. Office: Tyler Jr Coll Regional Training Complex 1530 S Southwest Loop 323 Tyler TX 75701-2556 Home: 3306 Lakepine Cir Tyler TX 75707-1728 E-mail: asha@tjg.tyler.cc.tx.us., asharpe@cox-internet.com.

SHARPE, DOROTHY JONES, secondary education educator, researcher; b. Suffolk, Va., Feb. 22, 1928; d. James Winton and Helen Rebecca Jones; m. Joseph Lee Sharpe, June 27, 1954 (div. Aug. 1969); 1 child, Alexandra Camille. BS in English and History, Miner Tchrs. Coll., 1950; MA in Edn., The Am. U., 1953; postgrad., U. So. Calif., 1976-82. Tchr. English, dept. chair Randall Jr. H.S., Terrell Jr. H.S., Washington, 1950-66; tchr. trainer English and reading Trinity Coll., D.C. Pub. Schs., Washington, 1966-72; project dir. street acad. Nat. Inst. Edn. and Washington Urban League, Washington, 1972-76; v.p. programs Washington Urban League, 1976-81; proposal developer, writer Match Inst., Washington, 1981; rschr., planner, writer Sterling Tucker Assn., Washington, 1982-84; planning cons. Techworld Trade Assocs., Washington, 1986-88; rsch. analyst Youth Policy Inst., Washington, 1997—. Planning cons., spkr. Nat. 4-H Ctr., D.C. Pub. Schs. Youth Policy Inst., 1981—; conf. chair, planner, writer D.C. U., Mckendree UMC, Washington, 1989-91. Author: Lagnuage Arts and Reading, 1968-79; designer urban youth think tank Youth Futures Inst., 1997—. Com. mem. Dixon Commn. Mental Health Law Project, Washington, 1980—; sr. assoc., bd. dirs. Youth Policy Inst., Washington, 1992-96. Recipient San Juan Barnes award Sr. Neighbors and Companions, 1985, others. Avocations: reading, writing poetry, arbouretums, museums, visiting mountains and rivers. Home: 2706 Brentwood Rd NE Washington DC 20018-2608

SHARPE, WILLIAM FORSYTH, economics educator; b. Cambridge, Mass., June 16, 1934; s. Russell Thornley Sharpe and Evelyn Forsyth (Jillson) Maloy; m. Roberta Ruth Branton, July 2, 1954 (div. Feb. 1986); children: Deborah Ann, Jonathan Forsyth; m. Kathryn Dorothy Peck, Apr. 5, 1986. AB, UCLA, 1955, MA, 1956, PhD, 1961; DHL (hon.), DePaul U., 1997; D (hon.), U Alicante, Spain, 2003. Economist Rand Corp., 1957—61; asst. prof. econs. U. Wash., 1961—63, assoc. prof., 1963—67, prof., 1967—68, U. Calif., Irvine, 1968—70; Timken prof. fin. Stanford U., 1970—89, Timken prof. emeritus, 1989—92; prin. William F. Sharpe

Assocs., 1986—92; prof.fin. Stanford U., 1993—95, STANCO 25 prof. fin., 1995—99, emeritus, 1999—; chmn. Financial Engines, Inc., 1996—2003. Author: The Economics of Computers, 1969, Portfolio Theory and Capital Markets, 1970; co-author: Fundamentals of Investments, 1989, Fundamentals of Investments, 2d edit., 1993, Fundamentals of Investments, 3d edit., 2000, Investments, 6th edit., 1999. With U.S. Army, 1956—57. Recipient Graham and Dodd award, Fin. Analysts' Fedn., 1972, 1973, 1986—88, Nicholas Molodovsky award, 1989, Nobel prize in econ. scis., 1990, UCLA medal, 1998. Mem.: Am. Econ. Assn., Ea. Fin. Assn. (Disting. Scholar award 1991), Western Fin. Assn. (Enduring Contbn. award 1989), Am. Fin. Assn. (v.p. 1979, pres. 1980), Phi Beta Kappa.

SHARPE, WILLIAM NORMAN, JR., mechanical engineer, educator; b. Chatham County, N.C., Apr. 15, 1938; s. William Norman and Margaret Horne (Womble) S.; m. Margaret Ellen Strowd, Aug. 21, 1959; children: William N., J. Ashley. BS, N.C. State U., 1960, MS, 1961; PhD, Johns Hopkins U., 1966. Registered profl. engr., Mich., La., Md. Assoc. prof. Mich. State U., East Lansing, 1970-75, prof., 1975-78; prof., chmn. dept. mech. engring. La. State U., Baton Rouge, 1978-83; prof., dept. mech. engring. Johns Hopkins U., Balt., 1983—, Decker prof. mech. engring., 1985—. Recipient Alexander von Humboldt award, Fed. Republic Germany, 1989 Fellow ASME (Nadai award 1993), Soc. Exptl. Mechanics (Tatnall award, exec. bd. 1979-81, pres. 1984-85); mem. ASTM, Am. Soc. Engring. Edn. Home: 220 Ridgewood Rd Baltimore MD 21210-2539 Office: Johns Hopkins U Dept Mech Engring 200 Latrobe Hall Rm 122 Baltimore MD 21218

SHATKIN, AARON JEFFREY, biochemistry educator; b. Providence, July 18, 1934; s. Morris and Doris S.; m. Joan A. Lynch, Nov. 30, 1957; 1 son, Gregory Martin. AB, Bowdoin Coll., 1956, DSc (hon.), 1979; PhD, Rockefeller Inst., 1961. Sr. asst. scientist NIH, Bethesda, Md., 1961-63, rsch. chemist, 1963-68; vis. scientist Salk Inst., La Jolla, Calif., 1968-69; assoc. mem. dept. cell biology Roche Inst. Molecular Biology, Nutley, N.J., 1968-73, full mem., 1973-77, head molecular virology lab., 1977-86, head dept. cell biology, 1983-86; dir. N.J. Ctr. Advanced Biotech. Medicine, 1986—; prof. molecular genetics UMDNJ, 1986—; univ. prof. molecular biology Rutgers U., New Brunswick, N.J., 1986—. Adj. prof. cell biology Rockefeller U.; vis. prof. molecular biology Princeton U. Mem. editl. bd. Jour. Virology, 1969-82, Archives of Biochemistry and Biophysics, 1972-82, Virology, 1973-76, Comprehensive Virology, 1974-82, Jour. Biol. Chemistry, 1977-83, 94-99, RNA Jour., 1995-96, Procs. of NAS, 1997-2001; editor Advances in Virus Rsch., 1983—, Jour. Virology, 1973-77; editor-in-chief Molecular and Cellular Biology, 1980-90. Served with USPHS, 1961-63. Recipient U.S. Steel Found. prize in molecular biology, 1977, N.J. Sci. and Tech. Pride award, 1989, Thomas Edison Sci. award State of N.J., 1991; Rockefeller fellow, 1956-61 Fellow AAAS, Am. Acad. Arts and Scis., Am. Acad. Microbiology, N.Y. Acad. Scis.; mem. NAS, Am. Soc. Microbiology, Am. Soc. Biol. Chemists, Am. Soc. Virology, Am. Chem. Soc., Am. Soc. Cell Biology, Harvey Soc. Home: 1381 Rahway Rd Scotch Plains NJ 07076-3452 Office: Ctr Advanced Biotech and Medicine 679 Hoes Ln Piscataway NJ 08854-5627 E-mail: shatkin@cabm.rutgers.edu.

SHATTUCK, LAWRENCE WILLIAM, admissions director; b. Nashua, N.H., Aug. 24, 1951; s. Fred and Shirley (Lundeen) S. AS, Middlesex C.C., Mass., 1975; MEd, Cambridge (Mass.) Coll., 1990. Admissions officer Tufts U. Sch. Dental Medicine, Boston, 1976-90; dir. admissions New Eng. Coll. Optometry, Boston, 1990—. Mem. Nat. Assn. Grad. Admissions Profls. (mem. membership com.), Nat. Assn. Advisors for the Health Professions, N.E. Assn. Advisors to the Health Professions. Home: 50 Lakeshore Dr Marlborough MA 01752- Office: New Eng Coll Optometry 424 Beacon St Boston MA 02115-1129

SHATTUCK, ROGER WHITNEY, author, educator; b. N.Y.C., Aug. 20, 1923; s. Howard Francis and Elizabeth (Colt) S.; m. Nora Ewing White, Aug. 20, 1949; children— Tari Elizabeth, Marc Ewing, Patricia Colt, Eileen Shepard. Grad., St. Paul's Sch., Concord, N.H., 1941; BA, Yale U., 1947; DHC (hon.), U. Orléans, France, 1990, Univ. of the South (Sewanee), 2003, St. Michael's Coll., Burlington, Vt., 2003. Information officer UNESCO, Paris, France, 1947-48; asst. editor Harcourt, Brace & Co., 1949-50; mem. Soc. Fellows, Harvard, 1950-53, instr. French, 1953-56; faculty U. Tex., Austin, 1956-71, prof. English, French, 1968-71, chmn. dept. French and Italian, 1968-71; Commonwealth prof. French U. Va., Charlottesville, 1974-88; univ. prof., prof. modern fgn. langs. Boston U., 1988-97. Mem. adv. bd. Nat. Translation Center, 1964-69, chmn., 1966-69; proveditieur gen. Coll. de Pataphysique, Paris, 1961—; Fulbright prof. U. Dakar, Senegal, 1984-85, elected bd. mem. Mt. Abraham Union H.S., 2000—. Author: The Banquet Years, 1958; poems Half Tame, 1964, Proust's Binoculars, 1963, Marcel Proust, 1974 (Nat. Book award 1975), The Forbidden Experiment, 1980, The Innocent Eye, 1984, Forbidden Knowledge, 1996, Candor and Perversion, 1999, Proust's Way, 2000; editor or co-editor: Selected Writings of Guillaume Apollinaire, 1950, Mount Analogue, (René Daumal), 1959, The Craft and Context of Translation (with William Arrowsmith), 1961, Selected works of Alfred Jarry, 1965, Occasions by Paul Valèry, 1970, The Story of My Life (by Helen Keller), 2003; mem. editl. bd. PMLA, 1977-78. Capt. USAAF, 1942-45. Decorated Ordre Palmes Academiques (France).; Guggenheim fellow, 1958-59; Fulbright rsch. fellow, 1958-59; ACLS rsch. fellow, 1969-70. Fellow AAAS; mem. Assn. Literary Scholars and Critics (pres. 1995-96).

SHAUGHNESSY, MICHAEL FRANCIS, psychology educator; b. N.Y.C., May 1, 1951; s. Daniel and Agnes (Antol) S.; m. Virginia Anne Shaughnessy, July 3, 1984; children: Lauri, Kaaren, Kurt, Travis. BA, Mercy Coll., Dobbs Ferry, N.Y.C., 1973; MEd, PhD, Bank State Coll. Edn., 1976; MS, Coll. New Rochelle, 1981; DEd, U. Nebr., 1983. Cert. sch. psychologist. Counselor Children's Village, Dobbs Ferry, 1971-74; tchr. Sch. Sts. Peter and Paul, Bronx, N.Y., 1974-76; social worker Crystal Run Sch., Fallsburg, N.Y., 1976-80; instr. S.E. Community Coll., Lincoln, Nebr., 1980-83; prof. psychology Eastern N.Mex. U., Portales, 1983—. Past editor Creative Child and Adult Quar.; contbr. articles to profl. jours. Recipient Cooper Found. award Nebr. State Dept. Edn., 1982. Mem. Nat. Assn. Creative Children and Adults (pres. 1985-86), Rocky Mountain Psychol. Assn., Inst. Logotherapy. Lodges: Lions. Office: Ea NMex U Dept Edn Station 23 Portales NM 88130

SHAVELSON, RICHARD, education educator; BA in Psychology, U. Oreg., 1964; MA in Psychology, San Jose State Coll., 1967; PhD in Ednl. Psychology, Stanford U., 1971. Asst. prof. edn. UCLA, 1973—75, assoc. prof. edn., 1975—79; dean Grad. Sch. Edn. U. Calif., Santa Barbara, 1987—93, prof. edn., 1987—96, affiliated appointment in stats. and applied probability, 1993—96; prof. edn. Stanford (Calif.) U., 1995—. Mem.: Spencer Found. (bd. dirs.), Am. Ednl. Rsch. Assn. (bd. dirs. grants bd. com.), Yosemite Nat. Insts. (bd. dirs.). Office: Stanford U Sch Edn 485 Lasuen Mall Stanford CA 94305-3096*

SHAW, BONITA LYNN, school administrator; b. Eau Claire, Wis., Jan. 4, 1944; d. Orrin Emil and Jennie (Eide) Indrebo; m. Robert Terry Shaw, Oct. 4, 1962; children: Chad Robert, Brooke Erin. BS in Spl. Edn., U. Wis., Eau Claire, 1968, MS in Spl. Edn., 1973; edn. specialist, U. Wis., Superior, 1992. Cert. tchr., adminstr., Wis. Tchr. spl. edn. Bullock Creek Jr.-Sr. High Sch., Midland, Mich., 1968-69, Wausau (Wis.) Sch. Dist., 1970-71; tchr. Hayward (Wis.) Elem. Sch., 1969-70, Chippewa Falls (Wis.) Sch. Dist., 1971-89; asst. prin. South Mid. Sch., Eau Claire, 1989—. Tchr. summer sch. program, gifted and talented program, U. Wis., Eau Claire, 1975; presenter at profl. confs. Author handbook for student tchr. in spl. edn. Mem. ASCD, Wis. Assn. Mid. Level. Edn., Assn. Wis. Secondary Adminstrs., Nat. Assn. Secondary Sch. Adminstrs., Nat. Mid. Sch. Assn. Avocations: hunting, golf, refinishing antiques, reading. Office: South Mid Sch 2115 Mitscher Ave Eau Claire WI 54701-7723 Home: 2528 Gregerson Dr Eau Claire WI 54703-9680

SHAW, DANNY WAYNE, educational consultant, musician; b. Detroit, Jan. 18, 1947; s. George L. and Nina Margarete (Smith) Shaw; m. Nancy Rivard, Feb. 29, 1980; 1 child, Christina Marie. BS, Wayne State U., 1973, MusM, 1975, EdS, 1979, PhD, 1982. Tchr. Dearborn (Mich.) Pub. Schs., 1973-74, Lincoln Park (Mich.) Schs., 1974-98, Beaufort County (SC) Schs., 1998—. Rsch. asst. Wayne State U., 1980—81, adj. faculty, 1981—85; pres. Sys. Support Svcs., Lincoln Park, Trenton, Mich., 1982—98; adj. faculty Marygrove Coll., Detroit, 1984. Mem. music adv. panel Mich. Coun. Arts, 1976—84; mem. cultural commn. City of Trenton, 1997—98; mem. Leadership Beaufort (S.C.) Class 2000; pres. Beaufort Orch., 2001—02, bd. dirs. With USMC, 1965—68, Vietnam. Decorated Presdl. Unit citation, Campaign medal Republic of Vietnam; recipient cert. for outstanding acad. achievement, Mich. Ho. Reps., 1975. Mem.: VFW, Shriners, Masons, Phi Delta Kappa. Home: 22 Brisbane Dr Beaufort SC 29902-5296 E-mail: dshaw@islc.net.

SHAW, DAVID WILLIAM, engineering educator; b. Whittier, Calif., Jan. 10, 1961; s. William Franklin and Mary Lou (LeMahieu) S.; m. Valerie Anne Arnold, Aug. 24, 1985; children: Kirsten, Rebecca, Evan, Adam. BSME, Geneva Coll., Beaver Falls, Pa., 1983; MSME, Ohio State U., 1986, PhD in Mech. Engring., 1988. Registered profl. engr., Pa. Grad. rsch. assoc. combustion lab. dept. mech. engring. Ohio State U., Columbus, 1983—88; mech. engr. process and reactor engring. br. Morgantown Energy Tech. Ctr., U.S. Dept. Energy, 1988-90; assoc. prof. mech. engring. Geneva Coll., Beaver Falls, 1996—2001, prof. mech. engring., 2001—. Mech. engr. high temp. reacting flows group Nat. Bur. Stds., summers, 1984, 85; summer faculty rschr. Oak Ridge Assoc. Univs., Pitts. Energy Tech. Ctr., summer 1992-95, 96, 99, Nat. Energy Tech. Lab., Pitts., 2000-03. Contbr. articles to profl. jours. Dept. of Energy grad. trainee, 1985-86 Mem. ASME, Am. Soc. Engring. Edn. Republican. Presbyterian. Avocations: camping, music, canoeing, triathlon. Office: Geneva College Dept Engring 3200 College Ave Dept Engring Beaver Falls PA 15010-3599

SHAW, DENNIS LEE, academic administrator; b. Beloit, Wis., Sept. 16, 1955; s. Glen Wellington and Mary Irene (Collier) S.; m. Mary Ann Baker, June 5, 1983 (div. Mar. 1990); 1 child, Michael Wellington; m. Dawn Marie Heinle, Feb. 13, 1993 (div. Aug. 1995). AS, U. Wis. Ctr. System, Rock County Campus, 1983; BBA, U. Wis., Whitewater, 1986, MBA, 1992; cert., CACUBO Mgmt. Inst., 1995. Cert. Cacubo Mgmt. Inst. Security supr. Martin Security, Inc., Beloit, 1974—78; security opns. mgr. Beloit Coll., 1978—89, security dir., 1989—93; coll. instr. (part-time) Blackhawk Tech. Coll., Janesville, Wis., 1987—93; dir., sec. & police svcs. U. Wis.-Stout, Menomonie, 1993—99, asst. to asst. vice chancellor, 1999—; adv. Collegiate Mgmt. Inst., 2001—. Mgmt. cons. Peripheral Visions, Ltd., Janesville, 1989-92; computer cons. Carlson & Shaw Mktg. Assocs., Beloit, 1988-89; owner-ptnr. Computer Odyssey, Janesville, 1990-94. Author: (computer programs) Coresort, 1987, Key Sort I, 1985. Bd. dirs. The Bridge to Hope Domestic Abuse Program, Menomonie, 1997-, bd. dirs. Oaklawn Harmony Ctr., 1999-; chmn. Rep. Party of Dunn County, 1999-2001, chmn. 3d Congl. Dist. Rep. Party, 2001-. Mem. Am. Soc. Indsl. Security (bd. dirs. 1990-93, coord. No. Ill. chpt. Am. Soc. Indsl. Security Found., Rockford 1988-93), Assn. MBA Execs., Internat. Assn. Chiefs of Police, Internat. Assn. Campus Law Enforcement Adminstrs., Jaycees (pres. Menomonie area 1993-94), Rotary Club of Menomonie. Republican. Avocation: play by mail computer gaming. Home: 2820 Edgewood Dr Apt 1 Menomonie WI 54751-5719 Office: U Wis-Stout Rm 113 1110 Broadway Rm 170 Menomonie WI 54751-2473

SHAW, DONALD LESLIE, Spanish language educator; b. Feb. 11, 1930; s. Stephen Leslie and Lily (Hughes) S.; m. Maria Concetta Cristini, June 30, 1958; children: Andrew Leslie, Sylvia Maria Pierina. BA, U. Manchester, Eng., 1952, MA, 1953; PhD, U. Dublin, Ireland, 1960. Asst. lectr. U. Dublin, 1955-57, U. Glasgow, Scotland, 1957-64, U. Edinburgh, Scotland, 1964-69, sr. lectr., 1969-72, reader, prof. spanish, 1972-86; prof. spanish U. Va., Charlottesville, 1986—. Vis. prof. Brown U., Providence, 1967, U. Va., Charlottesville, 1983. Author: Historia de la Literatura Española, Siglo XIX, 1973, La Generación del 98, 1977, Nueva Narrativa Hispanoamericana, 1981, Alejo Carpentier, 1985, Borges' Narrative Strategies, 1992, Antonio Skármeta and the Post-Boom, 1994, The Post-Boom in Spanish American Fiction, 1998, A Companion to Spanish American Fiction, 2001. Served with RAF, 1953-55. Avocation: cycling. E-mail: dls6h@vriginia.edu. Home: 1800 Jefferson Park Ave Charlottesville VA 22903-3554 Office: U Va 115 Wilson Hall Charlottesville VA 22903-3238 Business E-Mail: dlsbh@virginia.edu.

SHAW, GLORIA DORIS, art educator; b. Huntington, W.Va., Nov. 10, 1928; d. Charles Bert and Theodosia Doris (Shimer) Haley; m. Arthur Shaw, July 13, 1954 (dec. Aug. 1985); children: Deirdra Elizabeth, Stewart N. Student, SUNY, 1969-70, Art Students League, N.Y.C., 1969-70, 74; BA, SUNY, N.Y.C., 1980; postgrad., U. Tenn., 1982, Nat Kaz, Pietrasanta, Italy, 1992. Sculptor replicator Am. Mus. Natural History, N.Y.C., 1976-77; adj. prof. sculpture Fla. Keys C.C., Key West, 1983—. Prof. TV art history Fla. Keys C.C., 1989—; host moderator Channel 5 TV, Fla. Keys, 1982—; presenter Humanities Studies and Art History Channel 19 TV, 1995—, TV Jour. Channel 16, 1997—. Sculptor (portrait) Jimmy Carter, Carter Meml. Libr., 1976, Tennessee Williams, Tennessee Williams Fine Arts Ctr., 1982, UNICEF, 1978-79, (series) Fla. Panther and Audubon Wall Relief, 1985, (bust) AIDS Meml., 1990; one woman shows include Bank Street Coll., 1979, Hollywood Mus. of Art, 1985, Islander Gallery, 1983, Martello Mus., 1984, Greenpeace, 1987, FKCC Gallery, 2003; exhibited in group shows at Montoya, West Palm Beach, Fla., 1989, N.Y.C. Bd. of Edn. Tour of Schs., 1979, Earthworks East, N.Y., 1987, Man and Sci., 1978, Cuban Club, Key West, Fla., 1991, Leda Bruce Gallery, Big Pine, 1992, Kaz, Pietrasanta, Italy, 1992, Fla. Keys C.C. Gallery, 1993, Tennessee Williams Fine Arts Ctr., Key West, 1993, Internat. Woman's Show, Fla. Keys, 1994, Joy Gallery, 1994, 95, 96, Baron Gallery, Girls of Mauritania to UNICEF, 1996; designer Windows at Greenpeace Bldg., Key West, 1985-88, Pieta at St. Paul's Key West, 1997, Ceramic bird murals, FKCC, 1997; curator Women's Art, Key West, 1999, murals, Tennessee Williams Fine Arts Ctr., 1999, relief nudes Fine Arts Bldg., 1999, St. Francis sculpture and seated figures Garden Club, 2001, FKCC Gallery, 2003; retrospective: Gallery Florida Keys, 2003. Recipient Children and Other Endangered Species award Thomas Cultural Ctr., 1980, Purchase award Cuban C. of C., 1982, Sierra Club, 1983, Blue Ribbon, Martello Towers Art and Hist. Soc., 1985, Red Ribbon, South Fla. Sculptors, 1986, Endangered Species award Greenpeace, 1986. Mem. Nat. Sculpture Soc. of N.Y.C., Internat. Sculpture Ctr., Art Students League of N.Y.C. (life), Art and Hist. Soc. Democrat. Avocation: naturalist.

SHAW, HELEN LESTER ANDERSON, retired dean, nutrition educator, researcher; b. Lexington, Ky., Oct. 18, 1936; d. Walter Southall and Elizabeth (Guyn) Anderson; m. Charles Van Shaw, Mar. 14, 1988. BS, U. Ky., 1958; MS, U. Wis., 1965, PhD, 1969. Registered dietitian. Dietitian Roanoke (Va.) Meml. Hosp., 1959-60, Santa Barbara (Calif.) Cottage Hosp., 1960-61; dietitian, unit mgr. U. Calif., Santa Barbara, 1961-63; rsch. asst., NIH fellow U. Wis., Madison, 1963-68; from asst. prof. to prof. U. Mo., Columbia, 1969-88, assoc. dean, prof., 1977-84; prof., chair dept. food and nutrition U. N.C., Greensboro, 1989-94, dean Sch. Human Environ. Scis., 1994-2000; ret., 2000. Cluster leader Food for 21st Century rsch. program U. Mo., 1985-88. Contbr. articles to rsch. publs. Elder 1st Presbyn. Ch., Columbia, 1974-89, Greensboro, 1992—. Recipient Teaching award Home Econ. Alumni Assn., 1981, Gamma Sigma Delta, 1984; rsch. grantee Nutrition Found., 1971-73, NIH, 1972-75, NSF, 1980-83. Mem. Am. Soc. for Nutrition Scis., Am. Bd. Nutrition, Am. Soc. for Clin. Nutrition, Am. Dietetic Assn., Am. Family and Consumer Sci. Assn., Sigma Xi, Phi Upsilon Omicron, Kappa Omicron Nu. Democrat. Avocations: tennis, choral singing, art, volunteering.

SHAW, JOSEPH THOMAS, Slavic languages educator; b. Ashland City, Tenn., May 13, 1919; s. George Washington and Ruby Mae (Pace) S.; m. Betty Lee Ray, Oct. 30, 1942 (dec. Sept. 2002); children: David Matthew, Joseph Thomas, James William (dec. Jan. 1999). AB, U. Tenn., 1940, AM, 1941, Harvard, 1947, PhD, 1950. Asst. prof. Slavic langs. Ind. U., 1949-55, assoc. prof., 1955-61; prof. Slavic langs. U. Wis., 1961-89, prof. emeritus, 1989—, chmn. dept. Slavic langs., 1962-68, 77-86, chmn. div. humanities, 1964-65, 72-73, assoc. dean Grad. Sch., 1965-68. Author: The Letters of Alexander Pushkin, 1963, Pushkin's Rhymes: A Dictionary, 1974, Baratynskii: A Dictionary of the Rhymes and a Concordance to the Poetry, 1975, Batiushkov: A Dictionary of the Rhymes and a Concordance to the Poetry, 1975, Pushkin: A Concordance to the Poetry, 1985, American Association Teachers Slavic and East European Languages: The First Fifty Years 1941-91, 1991, Pushkin's Poetry of the Unexpected: The Nonrhymed Lines in the Rhymed Poetry and the Rhymed Lines in the Nonrhymed Poetry, 1994, Pushkin, Poet and Man of Letters, and His Prose (collected works, vol. 1), 1995, Pushkin Poems and Other Studies (collected works vol. 2), 1996, The Letters of Alexander Pushkin (collected works vols. 3-5), 3d edit., 1997, Konkordans k stikham Pushkina, 2000, Pushkin's Rhymes: A Dictionary (collected works, vol. 6-7), 2d edit., 2001, Batiushkov: A Dictionary of the Rhymes & A Concordance to the Poetry (collected works, vol. 8), 2d edit., 2001, Baratynskii: A Dictionary of the Rhymes & A Concordance to the Poetry (collected works, vol. 9), 2d edit., 2001, Poeziia neozhidannogo u Pushkina, 2002, Studies in Pushkin's Rhyming: Theory from Practice (collected works, vol. 10), 2002; editor: The Slavic and East European Jour., 1957-70; contbr. articles to profl. jours. Served to capt. USNR, 1942-46, 51-53. Mem. Am. Assn. Tchrs. Slavic and East European Langs. (mem. exec. council 1953-70, 73-80, pres. 1973-74) Home: 4505 Mineral Point Rd Madison WI 53705-5071

SHAW, LAQUETTA AVEITTE, computer specialist; b. Dallas, June 20, 1964; d. Lawrence James and Lillian Marie (Jefferies) S. BBA, East Tex. State U., 1985, MEd, 1992. Cert. tchr., adminstr., Tex. With Dallas County, Dallas, 1986-87, City of Dallas, 1987-88; tchr. Allstate Bus. Coll., Dallas, 1988-90, Phillips Sch. Bus. and Tech., Dallas, 1990, Nat. Edn. Ctr., Dallas, 1991; tchr., computer specialist Dallas Ind. Sch. Dist., 1988—. Personal computer cons., Dallas, 1985—. Program cons., troop leader Tejas coun. Girl Scouts U.S.A., 1991—. Recipient Pub. Svc. award Tejas coun. Girl Scouts U.S.A., 1992, Outstanding Technologist award House of Reps., 1995. Mem. ASCD, Assn. for System Mgrs., Delta Sigma Theta (Pub. Svc. award 1990). Avocations: computers, reading, aerobics, public speaking. Office: Sequoyah Learning Ctr 3635 Greenleaf St Dallas TX 75212-1520

SHAW, LAURIE JO, counseling and assessment center administrator; b. Morris, Minn., Feb. 23, 1956; d. Edgar Allen and Dorothy Ruth (Harms) S.; m. Grant William Carlson, July 23, 1983 (div. Feb. 1986). Tchr. aide degree, Hutchinson Area Vocat. Tech., Minn., 1975; audio visual prodn., Hutchinson (Minn.) AVTI, 1976; BA in Psychology, S.W. State U., 1982; MA in Counseling, N.Mex. State U., 1987. Libr. tech. S.W. State U., Marshall, Minn., 1976-84; student svcs. coord. Mohave C.C., Bullhead City, Ariz., 1987-91; counselor, instr. Prestonsburg C.C., Pikeville, Ky., 1992-93; project dir. So. W.Va. C.C., Williamson, W.Va., 1993-99; counseling dir. U. Ark., Monticello, 1999—. Mem. AAUW (v.p. 1990-92, 97-99), Nat. Assn. Student Pers. Adminstrs., Nat. Assn. Colls. and Employers, Ark. Assn. Colls. and Employers, Ky. Assn. Student Fin. Aid Adminstrs., Bus. and Profl. Women (pres. 1990-91, Young Career Woman award 1989), W.Va. Assn. Edn. Opportunity Program Pers., Mid.-East Assn. Edn. Opportunity Program Pers. Democrat. Methodist. Avocations: cross country skiing, oriental cooking, collecting hummels. Office: Bradley Co Med Ctr 404 S Bradley Warren AR 71671

SHAW, LEONARD GLAZER, electrical engineering educator, consultant; b. Toledo, Aug. 15, 1934; s. A. Daniel and Mary (Glazer) S.; m. Susan Gail Weil, Dec. 24, 1961; children: Howard Benjamin, Mitchell Bruce, Jenny Louise. BSEE, U. Pa., 1956; MSEE, Stanford U., 1957, PhD, 1961. From asst. to assoc. prof. Polytech. U. N.Y., Bklyn., 1960-75, prof., 1975—98, prof. emeritus, 1998—, head dept. elec. engring. and computer sci., 1982-90, dean Sch. Elec. Engring. and Computer Sci., 1990-94, vice provost for undergrad. studies, 1995-96. Vis. prof. Tech. U., Eindhoven, Netherlands, 1970, Ecole Nationale Superieure de Mecanique, Nantes, France, 1977, U. Sussex, Brighton, Eng., 1998; cons. Sperry Systems Mgmt. Div., Great Neck, N.Y.; mem. grant rev. panels NSF, 1986-98. Co-author: Signal Processing, 1975; contbr. articles to profl. jours. Rsch. grantee NSF, 1973, 81. Fellow: IEEE (mem. pub. bd. 1961—92, mem. various coms., editor-in-chief IEEE Press 1988—91, gen. chmn. Conf. of Decision and Control 1989, chmn. Tech. Field Award Coun. 1995—97), Control Sys. Soc. of IEEE (fin. v.p. 1992—93, 2000, pres.-elect 2001, pres. 2002). Office: Polytech U 6 Metrotech Ctr Brooklyn NY 11201-3840 E-mail: lshaw@poly.edu.

SHAW, MARY M. computer science educator; b. Washington, Sept. 30, 1943; d. Eldon Earl and Mary Lewis (Holman) Shaw; m. Roy R. Weil, Feb. 15, 1973. BA cum laude, Rice U., 1965; PhD, Carnegie Mellon U., Pitts., 1972. Asst. prof. to prof. computer sci. Carnegie Mellon U., Pitts., 1972—, assoc. dean computer sci. for profl. programs, 1992-99, Alan J. Perlis chair computer sci.; co-dir. Sloan Software Industry Ctr., Pitts., 2001—. Chief scientist Software Engring. Inst., Carnegie Mellon U., Pitts., 1984-88; mem. Computer Sci. and Telecommunications Bd., NRC, Washington, 1986-93. Author: (with W. Wulf, P. Hilfinger, L. Flon) Fundamental Structures of Computer Science, 1981, The Carnegie Mellon Curriculum for Undergraduate Computer Science, 1985, (with David Garlan) Software Architecture: Perspectives on an Emerging Discipline, 1996, (with Roy Weil) Free Wheeling Easy in Western Pennsylvania, 1995, 1996, 1999; contbr. articles to profl. jours. Recipient Warnier prize, 1993, (with Roy Weil) Recreation and Outdoor Stewardship award, 2003; named Woman of Achievement, YWCA of Greater Pitts., 1973. Fellow AAAS, IEEE (disting. lectr.), Assn. for Computing Machinery (SIGPLAN exec. com. 1979-83, Recognition of Svc. award 1985, 90); mem. Sigma Xi. Office: Carnegie Mellon U Dept Computer Sci Pittsburgh PA 15213

SHAW, MICHAEL LEE, social studies educator; b. Joliet, Ill., July 27, 1954; s. Richard James and Geneva B. (Briggs) S. AAS, Joliet Jr. Coll., 1979; BS, Ea. Ill. U., 1982. Cert. tchr. K-9. Tchr. 6th grade social studies St. Clement, Chgo., 1982—. With U.S. Army, 1975-77. Recipient Heart of Sch. award Archdiocese of Chgo., 1989-90. Mem. Nat. Coun. for Social Studies. Office: St Clement Sch 2524 N Orchard St Chicago IL 60614-2536 Home: Apt 232 528 W Oakdale Ave Chicago IL 60657-5724

SHAW, NANCY RIVARD, museum curator, art historian, consultant; b. Saginaw, Mich. d. Joseph H. and Jean M. (O'Boyle) Marcotte; m. Danny W. Shaw, Feb. 29, 1980; 1 stepchild, Christina Marie. BA magna cum laude, Oakland U., 1969; MA, Wayne State U., 1973. Asst. curator Am. art Detroit Inst. Arts, 1972-75, curator, 1975-98, curator emeritus, 1998—. Adj. prof. art and art history Wayne State U., Detroit, 1991-98; lectr. in field.; organizer exhibns. Contbg. author: American Art in the Detroit Institute of Arts, 1991, Vol. I, 1991, Vol. II, 1997; contbr. articles to exhbn. catalogues and profl. jours. Mem. Wayne State U. Alumni Assn. Roman Catholic. Avocations: knitting, painting, golf. Address: 22 Brisbane Dr Beaufort SC 29902-5296 E-mail: dshaw@islc.net.

SHAW, RICHARD DAVID, marketing and management educator; b. Pitts., Kans., Aug. 25, 1938; s. Richard Malburn and Jessie Ruth (Murray) S.; m. Adolphine Catherine Brungardt, Aug. 21, 1965; children: Richard David Jr., John Michael, Shannon Kathleen. BSBA, Rockhurst Coll., 1960; MS in Commerce, St. Louis U., 1964. Claims adjuster Kemper Ins. Group, Kansas City, Mo., 1961; tchr. acctg. Corpus Christi High Sch., Jennings, Mo., 1961-63; assoc. prof. econs. Fontbonne Coll., St. Louis, 1963-70, chmn. social behavioral sci. dept., 1968-70; mem. faculty, chmn. bus. div. Longview Community Coll., Lee's Summit, Mo., 1970-81, coord. mktg., 1979-81; workshop leader Rockhurst U., Kansas City, 1975—, prof. mktg., 1981—, chmn. mgmt. and mktg., 1983-85, co-chair MBA program, 1996—, co-chair Sch. of Mgmt. Undergrad. Programs, 1998—. Faculty moderator Jr. Execs. Assn., The Rock yearbook, Rockhurst U. Reps., Rockettes, co-chair undergrad. Sch. of Mgmt. programs, 1998—; pvt. cons., 1981—, chmn. freshman seminar com., 1994; instr. principles of mktg. on The Learning Channel on Cable TV for the PACE Program, 1994; chmn. sch. mgmt. curriculum com., 1993—; co-chair Task Force on Diversity, 1997. Author: Personal Finance, 1983, Principles of Marketing Study Guide, 1993, Contemporary Marketing Study Guide, 1994, Consumer Behavior Study Guide, 1997, Instructor's Manual for Michael Solomon's Consumer Behavior; co-author: Instructor's Resource Manual and Video Guide for Philip Kotler's Marketing Management, 9th edit.; cooperating author: Philip Kotler's Marketing Management. Mem. alumni bd. assessment task force Rockhurst U., 1971-73, 78-80, chmn. 30 yr. reunion com., 1990, 35 yr. reunion com., 1995, chmn. curriculum com., curriculum task force; chmn. Eastwood Hills Coun., Kansas City, 1974-76, bd. dirs., 1988-91, co-chmn. of Solid Rocks Faculty-Staff Fund Raising Campaign, 1994; lead couple Marriage Preparation Classes, Kansas City St. Joseph Dioceses, 1983--; co-chmn. Kansas City Vols. Against Hunger, 1975-80; campaign mgr. Larry Ferns for City Coun., Kansas City, 1975; bd. govs. Citizens Assn., 1976—. With USAR, 1960-64. Recipient Gov.'s Excellence in Teaching award, Mo., 1993, Harry B. Kies award Rockhurst U.; Hallmark fellow Rockhurst U., 1981-86; faculty devel. grantee Sch. Mgmt., Rockhurst U., 1984, 93, 95, 99. Mem. Am. Mktg. Assn., Soc. for Advancement of Mgmt., Mid-Am. Mktg. Assn., Alpha Sigma Nu, Kappa Delta Pi. Roman Catholic. Avocations: gardening, genealogy, photography. Home: 11014 Washington St Kansas City MO 64114-5177 Office: Rockhurst U 1100 Rockhurst Rd Kansas City MO 64110-2508 E-mail: dickshaw@everestkc.net., shaw.manor@att.net.

SHAW, THERESA (TERRI) S. federal official; married; 2 children. BS, George Mason U., 1960; Grad. Exec. Devel. Program, George Washington U., 1991. From staff to sr. v.p. and chief info. officer SLM Corp., Reston, Va., 1988—99; exec. v.p., COO eNumerate Solutions, Inc, McLean, Va., 2000—02; COO Fed. Student Aid U. S. Dept. Edn., Washington, 2002—. Office: US Dept Edn 400 Maryland Ave SW Washington DC 20202 Office Fax: 202-377-3003.

SHAW, VALEEN JONES, special education educator, elementary school educator; b. Coalville, Utah, June 19, 1930; d. G. Allen and Mabel Leon (Clark) Jones; m. Melvin Francis Shaw, June 21, 1948; children: C. Allene Shaw Fuhriman, Denise Ellen Shaw Call, Sharon Marie Shaw Williams. BS, Weber State U., Ogden, Utah, 1966; postgrad., U. Utah, Utah State U., Brigham Young U. Cert. tchr. elem. edn., early childhood edn., spl. edn. Tchr. 3rd grade Morgan (Utah) Sch. Dist., 1965-66; tchr. 6th grades N. Summit Sch. Dist., Coalville, Utah, 1966-67, tchr. 2d grades, 1967-82, tchr. resource, spl. edn., 1982-92, teaching specialist elem. summer sch. prog., 1967-92; elementary resource and spl. edn. tchr. North Summit Sch. Dist., Coalville, 1982-92. Mentor N. Summit Elementary Sch., 1988-89. Tchr./trainer Coalville Ch. of Jesus Christ of Latter-day Saints. &D Mem. NEA, ASCD Inst., Utah Edn. Assn., Morgan Edn. Assn., North Summit Edn. Asssn, Utah Fedn. Coun. for Exceptional Children.

SHEA, PATRICK A. lawyer, educator; b. Salt Lake City, Feb. 28, 1948; s. Edward J. and Ramona (Kilpack) S.; m. Deborah Fae Kern, Sept. 1, 1980; children: Michael, Paul. BA, Stanford U., 1970; MA, Oxford U., Eng., 1972; JD, Harvard U., 1975. Bar: Utah 1976, D.C. 1979. Mem. profl. staff majority leader's office U.S. Senate, 1971, asst. staff dir. intelligence com., 1975—76; assoc. VanCott, Bagley, Salt Lake City, 1976—79, ptnr., 1980—85; counsel fgn. relations com. U.S. Senate, 1979—80; gen. counsel KUTV, Comm. Investment Corp., Std. Comm., 1985—91; dir. Bur. of Land Mgmt. Dept. of Interior, 1997-98; dep., asst. sec. interior Land & Minerals Mgmt., 1998-2000; of counsel Ballard, Spahr, Andrews & Ingersoll LLP, Salt Lake City, 2000—. Cons. judiciary com. U.S. Ho. of Reps., 1972-73; adj. prof. polit. sci. U. Utah, Salt Lake City, 1981-97, Kans. State U., 2002—. Chmn. Utah Democratic Party, Salt Lake City, 1983-85; v.p. Tomorrow-Today Found., Salt Lake City, 1982-84. Mem. Am. Rhodes Scholar Assn., Utah Bar Assn., D.C. Bar Assn., Stanford Alumni Assn. (pres.-elect 1983-84). Clubs: Alta. Roman Catholic. Office: Ballard Spahr Andrews & Ingersoll LLP One Utah Ctr Ste 600 201 S Main St Salt Lake City UT 84111-2221 Fax: 801-596-6802. E-mail: sheap@ballardspahr.com.

SHEA, ROBERT STANTON, retired academic administrator; b. Quincy, Mass., Oct. 15, 1928; s. Arthur Joseph and Isabella (Crowley) S.; m. Ruth Eva Summers, May 30, 1952; children: Robert S. Jr., Stephen D., Lisa A., Louise M., David R. BS in Math., Boston Coll., 1952; MBA, Calif. State U., Fullerton, 1969. CLU, Chartered Fin. Cons. Test equipment engr. Hughes Aircraft Co., El Segundo, Calif., 1952-56; rsch. engr., project engr. Rockwell Internat., Anaheim, Calif., 1956-70; acctg. systems analyst Safeguard Bus. Systems, Van Nuys, Calif., 1971-76; cons. Am. Grad. U., Covina, Calif., 1987-94; registered rep. Mut. of N.Y., Anaheim, Calif., 1987-94; fin. cons. Empcom Ins. Svcs., Inc., Long Beach, Calif., 1984-94, also bd. dirs.; dean Coll. of Bus. Adminstrn. Pacific States U., L.A., 1972-94; ret., 1994. Track and field official The Athletics Congress. L.A., 1958-88; mem. Anaheim East chpt. Rotary Internat., Anaheim, 1973-85, pres. 1980; patrol leader Boy Scouts Am., Anaheim, 1964-75. With USN, 1946-48. Recipient Merit award Rotary Internat., 1978, Award of Merit, The Athletics Congress, 1977. Mem. Beta Gamma Sigma. Republican. Roman Catholic. Avocations: bicycling, backpacking, fishing, electronics, amateur radio. Home: 43815 Pioneer Ave Hemet CA 92544-6662

SHEA, ROSANNE MARY, artist, art educator; b. Waterbury, Conn., Oct. 29, 1957; d. John Patrick and Helen Gertude (Goodridge) S.; children: Matthew Shea, Wyatt Shea-Levandoski. BFA, U. Conn., 1980; MFA, Vermont Coll., 1996. Freelance artist, Waterbury, Conn., 1980-90; art tchr. Creative Summer program Mead Sch., Greenwich, Conn., 1991, 92, 93, 94; art tchr. W. Conn. State U., Danbury, 1994, Sacred Heart/St. Peter's Sch., New Haven, Conn., 1995—, Holy Cross H.S., Waterbury, 1996—. Arts and crafts program dir. Futures Initiative Program, Bridgeport, Conn., 1989; adj. art tchr. Naugatuck Valley Coll., Waterbury, Conn., 1991—; v.p. Bank Street Artists, Waterbury, Conn., 1993-94. Appeared as lead character in play Tropical Blues, 1996; one-woman exhbns. include Mattatuck C.C., Waterbury, Conn., 1992, A Frame Come True Gallery, Torrington, Conn., 1992, Discovery Mus., 1999, Mattatuck Mus., 2000; group exhbns. include Waterbury Arts Resource Coun., 1992 (mem.), Bank St. Artists Gallery, Waterbury, 1994 (mem.), Northampton Coll., Bethlehem, Pa., 1995, Talk of the Town Coffee House, Torrington, 1996, Sacred Ground Coffee House, Watertown, Conn., 1996, Wood Gallery, Montpelier, Vt., 1996, Women Only, Waterbury, 1996. Leader Boy Scouts Am., Waterbury, Conn., 1990-94; state visitation mgr. Conn. chpt. Nat. Holiday Project, 1986-87; course vol., mem. bd. Bridgeport (Conn.) Youth at Risk, 1986-88, ropes course leader, vol. enrollment mgr., 1987-99. Scholar AAUW, 1993, Philanthropic Ednl. Orgn., 1993; Inner City Cultural Devel. Program grantee Conn. Commn. Arts, 1997-98. Avocations: scuba diving, rock climbin, philosophy, health, camping.

SHEA, THOMAS JOSEPH, educator; b. Owatonna, Minn., July 14, 1950; s. Joseph Richard and Doris Elizabeth (Johnson) S.; m. Stephanie Tisdale, July 20, 1979; children: Joseph Tisdale, Kerry Abigail, Maggie Margaret. Student, U. Minn., Mpls., 1969-73, Mankato (Minn.) State U., 1973-74. Mem. Minn. Ho. of Reps., St. Paul, 1981-84; gen. mgr. Shea Dist. Co. Inc., Owatonna, Minn., 1984-88; owner, pub. Owatonna Photo News, 1988-92; editor Photo News Owatonna Peoples Press, 1992-93; comml. lending mktg. mgr. Premier Bank, Owatonna, 1993-95; mem. Steele County Bd. Commrs., Owatonna, Minn., 1991—, chmn., 2000—; instr. small bus. mgmt. Riverland C.C., Austin, Minn., 1995—2000; voices program officer So. Minn. Initiative Fund., 2000—. Bd. mem. Owatonna City Charter commn., 1986-92. Named Outstanding Young Man, Owatonna Jaycees, 1985. Mem. Izaak Walton League, Steele County Hist. Soc., Eagles, K.C., Elks. Democrat. Roman Catholic. Avocations: family activities, golf. Office: PO Box 187 Owatonna MN 55060-0187 E-mail: sunshea@msn.com.

SHEAR, THEODORE LESLIE, JR., archaeologist, educator; b. Athens, Greece, May 1, 1938; s. Theodore Leslie and Josephine (Platner) S.; m. Ione Doris Mylonas, June 24, 1959; children: Julia Louise, Alexandra. AB summa cum laude, Princeton U., 1959, MA, 1963, PhD, 1966. Instr. Greek and Latin Bryn Mawr Coll., 1964-66, asst. prof., 1966-67; asst. prof. art and archaeology Princeton (N.J.) U., 1967-70, assoc. prof., 1970-79, chmn. program in classical archaeology, 1970-85, assoc. chmn. dept. art and archaeology, 1976-78, 82-83, prof. classical archaeology, 1979—; prof. archaeology Am. Sch. Classical Studies, Athens, 1988-94. Mem. mng. com. Am. Sch. Classical Studies, Athens, 1972—; mem. archaeol. expdns. to Greece and Italy, including Mycenae, 1953-54, 58, 62-63, 65-66, Eleusis, 1956, Perati, 1956, Corinth, 1960, Morgantina, Sicily, 1962; mem. Ancient Agora of Athens, 1955, 67, field dir., 1968-94; trustee William Alexander Procter Found., 1982-89, Princeton Jr. Sch., 1983—, pres., 1994—. Author: Kallias of Sphettos and the Revolt of Athens in 286 B.C., 1978; contbr. articles to profl. jours. White fellow Am. Sch. Classical Studies, 1959-60 Mem. Archaeol. Inst. Am., Am. Philol. Assn., Coll. Art Assn., Archaeol. Soc. Athens (hon.), Phi Beta Kappa. Clubs: Century Assn. (N.Y.C.); Nassau (Princeton); Princeton (N.Y.C.); Hellenic Yacht (Piraeus, Greece). Republican. Episcopalian. Home: 87 Library Pl Princeton NJ 08540-3015 also: 30 Deinokratous St Athens Greece

SHEARER, CAROLYN JUANITA, secondary school educator; b. Heber Springs, Ark., May 20, 1944; d. James A. and Juanita Ruth (Wallace) S. BS, U. Colo., Boulder, 1966, MA, 1972. Cert. tchr., Colo. Tchr. Aurora (Colo.) Pub. Schs., reading resource tchr. Presenter writing process workshops. Author curriculum materials. Mem. PTA. Mem. NEA, ASCD, Colo. Edn. Assn., Aurora Edn. Assn. (bd. dirs., bargaining support team), Internat. Reading Assn., Colo. Reading Assn., Aurora Reading Assn. Pi Lambda Theta (v.p. Denver Metro chpt.). Democrat. Methodist. Office: West Mid Sch 10100 E 13th Ave Aurora CO 80010-3302

SHEARER, CHARLES LIVINGSTON, academic administrator; b. Louisville, Ky., Nov. 23, 1942; s. Guy Cooper and Kathryn (Aufenkamp) S.; m. Susan Pulling Shearer, Nov. 30, 1968; children: Todd A., Mark G., Scott B. BS, U. Ky., 1964, MA, 1967, Mich. State U., 1973, PhD, 1981. Instr. Henderson (Ky.) Community Coll., 1967-69; asst. prof. Ferris State Coll., Big Rapids, Mich., 1969-71; grad. asst. Mich. State U., East Lansing, 1971-73; dir. mgmt. program Albion (Mich.) Coll., 1973-75, dir. ops., 1975-79; v.p. fin. Transylvania U., Lexington, Ky., 1979-83, pres., 1983—. Bd. dirs. Lexington Philharm. Soc., 1983-89; mem. adv. bd. Salvation Army, Lexington, 1983-87; mem. Henry Clay Meml. Found., Lexington, 1983-89. Capt. U.S. Army Nat. Guard, 1966-76. Named One of Outstanding Young Men in Am., 1978. Mem. Am. Econs. Assn., Lexington C. of C. (bd. dirs. 1985—), Rotary. Mem. Disciples Of Christ Ch.

SHEARER, RICHARD EUGENE, educational consultant; b. Connellsville, Pa., Dec. 30, 1919; s. H.D. and Florence (Prinkey) S.; m. Ruth Mansberger, June 16, 1944 (dec. Mar. 1993); children: Patricia (Mrs. Richard Wilson), Suzanne (Mrs. Terry Jones), Richard J.; m. Marilyn Likeness Erdman, May 7, 1994. AB, Eastern Bapt. Coll. and Sem., Phila., 1943, D.D., 1953; B.D., New Brunswick Theol. Sem., 1945; MA, Columbia, 1948, Ed.D., 1959; LL.D., Denison U., 1958; H.H.D., Bishop Coll., 1977. Ordained to ministry Bapt. Ch., 1943; minister Atlantic Highlands, N.J., 1943-45, New Brunswick, N.J., 1945-5O; pres. Alderson-Broaddus Coll., Philippi, W.Va., 1951-83; ind. cons., 1983—; cons., interim dir. W.Va. Found. Ind. Colls.; prin. resdl. devel. Bridgeport, W.Va., 1983—; v.p., exec. dir. United Health Found., Clarksburg, W.Va., 1987—; pres. R. Shearer & Assocs., Philippi, W.Va., 1984. Lectr. Mex. Pastor's Conf., summer 1955; past pres. W.Va. Found. Ind. Colls.; mem. Commn. on Instnl. Funding, Am. Bapt. Chs., U.S.A.; coordinator (Central Europe Coll. Program); pres. Am. Bapt. Assn. Sch. and Coll. Adminstrs., 1977; mem. W.Va. Ednl. Found., W.Va. State Scholarship Commn. Bd. regents W.Va. Assn. Pvt. Colls.; bd. dirs. W.Va. Found. Independent Colls.; sr. min. Bridgeport (W.Va.) Bapt. Ch., 1988-93; bd. dirs. Eastern Bapt. Theol. Sem., Phila. Named Phi Delta Kappa Profl. Educator of Year, 1964 Mem. Am. Assn. Sch. Adminstrs., W.Va. Assn. Coll. and Univ. Presidents (sec. mem. exec. com. 1963—), Assn. Am. Colls. (commn. coll. and soc.), Kiwanis. Office: 300 Shearerwood Dr Philippi WV 26416

SHEARER, RICK LELAND, university official; b. Wichita, Kans., Jan. 8, 1955; s. Jack Leland and Marjorie Louise (Pearson) S. BSc, U. Calgary, Alberta, Can., 1979; MBA in Fin., Nat. U., 1984; MA in Edn., San Diego State U., 1992. V.p., gen. mgr. Direction Holdings Ltd., Calgary, 1979-81; cons. Ethic Mgmt. Ltd., Calgary, 1981-82; from dir. computer based edn. to dir. rsch. and evaluation Nat. U., San Diego, 1985-92, dir. instl. rsch., founding assoc. distance edn. system, 1992-96, dir. rsch. and instrnl. systems, 1996-97; sr. instrnl. designer Pa. State U., University Park, 1997-99, asst. dir. Instrnl. Design and Devel., 2000—. Presenter conf. procs. Distance Teaching and Learning, 1993-94, 95-96, 96-97, 97-98, 98-99, 99-2000, Ed Media 93, 1993, Assn. Edn. Comm. and Tech., 1994, 95, 97, 98, 99, 1998, Asynchronous Learning Network Conf., 1998, 99, 2000. Author: Am. Jour. Distance Edn., 1994, 97. Mem. Assn. Edn. Comm. & Tech., Am. Coun. Distance Edn. Avocations: fitness, skiing, sailing, skating. Office: Pa State U 210 Rider II University Park PA 16801 E-mail: rx557@psu.edu.

SHEARER, VALLORY ANN, mathematics educator; b. Newark, Feb. 15, 1952; d. Andrew Charles Sr. and Carmela Lucia (Sarrecchia) Leone; m. Wilfred Charles Shearer Sr., July 31, 1976; children: Kere, Danielle, Willy. BS, Towson State U., 1974; MEd, Western Md. Coll., 1986. Cert. tchr., Md. Tchr. math. Baltimore County Bd. Edn., Towson, Md., 1974-81; instr. math. Villa Julie Coll., Stevenson, Md., 1982—; tchr. algebra Sacred Heart Sch., Glyndon, Md., 1988-89. Instr. religious edn. St. Bartholomew's Sch., Manchester, Md., 1989—. Treas. Hampstead Elem. Sch. PTA, 1991-93; team rep. North Carroll Mid. Sch., Manchester, Md., 1992. Mem. Lions (softball commr. Hampstead club 1992, softball mgr. 1989—), Phi Sigma Sigma (advisor 1992). Democrat. Roman Catholic. Avocations: reading, swimming, stitchery, softball. Home: 4497 Foxtail Rd Hampstead MD 21074-1433 Office: Villa Julie Coll Green Spring Valley Rd Stevenson MD 21153

SHEATH, ROBERT GORDON, botanist, educator; b. Toronto, Ont, Canada, Dec. 26, 1950; arrived in U.S., 1978; s. Harry Gordon and Shirley Irene (Rose) Sheath. BSc, U. Toronto, 1973, PhD, 1977. Nat. Rsch. Coun. Can. postdoctoral fellow U. B.C., 1977-78; asst. prof. aquatic biology U. RI, Kingston, 1978-82, assoc. prof., 1982-86, chmn. dept. botany, 1986-90, prof., 1987-91; head dept. biology Meml. U., St. Johns, Canada, 1991-95; dean coll. biol. sci. U. Guelph, Ont., 1995-2001; provost Calif. State U., San Marcos, 2001—. Mem. evolution and ecology grant selection com. NSERC, 1994—97, chair, 1996—97, selection com. life scis., 1996, chair maj. facilities access life scis. subcom., 2001; mem. Can. Rsch. Chairs Coll. of Reviewers, 2000—01. Editor (with M. M. Harlin): Freshwater and Marine Plants of RI, 1988; editor: (with K. M. Cole) Biology of the Red Algae, 1990; editor: (with J.D. Wehr) Classification and Ecology of Freshwater Algae of North America, 2003; contbr. over 120 articles to profl. jours. Recipient G. A. Cox Gold medal, U. Toronto, 1973, Darbaker prize, Bot. Soc. Am., 1997, T. Christensen prize panel, 2000; grantee, NSF, 1980—91, 2001—, NSERC, 1991—2002. Mem.: Japanese Phycological Soc. (editl. bd. 2000—02), Brit. Phycological Soc. (freshwater flora com. 1993—2002, overseas v.p. 1997—99, assoc. editor 1999—2001), Arctic Inst. N.Am., Am. Soc. Limnology and Oceanography, Phycological Soc. Am. (editl. bd. 1983—86, assoc. editor 1984—89, pres. 1991—92, editl. bd. 1996—2000, publs. com. chair 2001—, bd. trustees 2001—, Bold award 1976), Internat. Phycological Soc. (editl. bd. 1993—95, nominating com. 2000—01, T. Christensen prize panel 2000). Office: U Calif San Marcos Office of Provost San Marcos CA 92096-0001 E-mail: rsheath@csusm.edu.

SHEATS, RACHEL GAY, computer and reading educator, videographer; b. Cassville, Mo., Feb. 15, 1964; d. R.G. Edmondson and Mary Louise Shultz; m. Charles Drew Sheats, Apr. 6, 1990; children: Zachariah, Joshua. AA in Country Music, Rogers State Coll., 1986; BS in Edn., Mo. So. State Coll., 1989; MEd in Ednl. Tech., U. Ark., 1996. Cert. tchr. 1-9 gen. edn. and reading specialist, Mo. Substitute tchr. Cassville Schs., Exeter (Mo.) Schs., Purdy (Mo.) Schs., 1989-90; reading specialist Cassville R-IV Schs., 1990—, computer literacy educator, 1998—. Tchg. intern U. Ark., 1994-95; prodn. cons. Jones TV Network, Springdale, Ark., 1995-96; curriculum cons. KOZK-TV, Springfield, Mo., 1994-96; instr. Crowder Coll., 2002—. Author: (ednl. workshops) The News and You!, 1991, The Book Report Alternative, 1992, Reading Buddies: A Community Effort, 1993, Reading Across the Curriculum with Style!, 1994, Internet Uses in Today's Classrooms, 1995, Teachers and Paraprofessionals: Building a Winning Team!, 1999, (video curriculum) Let's Start Cooking, 1995. Vol. Family Life Ctr., Cassville, 2000—. Recipient outstanding ednl. achievements award U. Mo. Ext. Ctr., 1992-93. Mem. Mo. Mid. Sch. Assn. (S.W. regional rep. 1999-2001). Home: Rt 4 Box 4188 Cassville MO 65625 Office: Cassville Mid Sch 1501 Main St Cassville MO 65625 Fax: (417) 847-3156. E-mail: rsheats@mo-net.com., rsheat@cassville.k12.mo.us.

SHEDD, PETER JAY, law educator; b. Ponca City, Okla., Feb. 15, 1953; s. Charlie W. and Martha B. (Petersen) S.; m. Margaret A. Mayberry, Sept. 2, 1972; children: Jarrett P., Anna C., Sarah E. BBA, U. Ga., 1974, JD, 1977. Law clk. U.S. Dist. Judge, Augusta, Ga., 1977-78; asst. prof. law U. Ga., Athens, 1978-82, assoc. prof., 1982-88, assoc. dean Coll. Bus., 1985-86, exec. asst. to pres., 1986-88, prof. legal studies, 1988—, chair instructional adv. com., 1992-93, chair exec. com. univ. coun., 1989-90, assoc. v.p. for instrn., 1999—2001, interim v.p. for instrn., 2002, sr. assoc. v.p. for instrn., 2002—03. Exec. com. Acad. Legal Studies in Bus., Athens, 1994-2000, Consortium on Negotiation and Conflict Resolution, 1995—. Author: Legal and Regulatory Environment of Business, 12th edit., 2002, Business Law, 1993; contbg. editor: Prentice Hall's Legal Studies Business Law Series, 1993. Chair ch. coun. First United Meth. Ch., Athens, 1995-98; mem. Cmty. Oriented Policing Coun., Athens, 1993. Named Ga. Prof. of the Yr., Coun. for Advancement and Support of Edn., 1993, Faculty Award of Excellence, Am. Bus. Law Assn., 1980. Mem. Am. Arbitration Assn. (3d party neutral 1993—), State Bar of Ga., Acad. Legal Studies in Bus. Avocations: reading, jogging, yardwork. Office: Univ of Ga 212 Brooks Hall Athens GA 30602-6255 Business E-Mail: pshedd@uga.edu.

SHEEHAN, DENNIS MICHAEL, physical education educator; b. Kingston, N.Y., Mar. 16, 1952; s. Daniel R. and Marie (Ziffert) S.; m. Katherine N. Nocton, June 15, 1974; children: Joseph, Lizabeth. AS in Recreation Leadership, Ulster County C.C. Real estate sales assoc., Saugerties, N.Y.; tchr. phys. edn., coord. athletics St. Josephs Cath. Sch., 1985—, Kingston Cath. Sch.; head baseball coach Ulster County C.C., Stone Ridge, N.Y., 1988—, asst. athletic dir. Home: 194 Union St PO Box 584 Glasco NY 12432-0584

SHEEHAN, DONALD THOMAS, retired academic administrator; b. Winsted, Conn., Jan. 2, 1911; s. James J. and Louise (Coffey) S.; m. Betty Young, June 25, 1941; 1 son, Michael Terrence. Grad., Gilbert Sch., Winsted, 1931; BS in Edn, Syracuse U., 1935; student, Sch. Pub. Affairs, Am. U., 1936. Dir. health edn. D.C. Tb. Assn., 1937-39; dir. Washington office NCCJ, 1939-41; dir. Bur. Info. Nat. Cath. Welfare Conf., Washington, 194-42; spl. cons. to U.S. Commr. Edn., 1946; staff mem. John Price Jones Co., Inc. (pub. relations cons.), 1946-51; cons. civil def. edn. program, asst. adminstr. charge vol. manpower FCDA, 1951-54, cons. vol. manpower, 1954—; dir. pub. relations U. Pa., 1954-76, sec. corp., 1975-76, sec., v.p. emeritus, 1976—; spl. lectr. pub. relations Drexel U., 1957-72; cons. Nat. Bd. Med. Examiners, 1964—, Coll. Physicians Phila., 1973—, Citizens' Action Com. to Fight Inflation, 1974-75, Wistar Inst. Anatomy and Biology, 1979, Univ. Mus., U. Pa., 1982—, Inst. Environ. Medicine, 1983—. Mem. adv. com. Nat. Trust for Hist. Preservation; cons. Am. Philos. Soc., 1988—. Served from 1st lt. to lt. col. USAAF, 1942-46. Decorated Bronze Star medal. Fellow Coll. Physicians Phila. (hon. assoc.), ; mem. Public Relations Soc. Am., Pi Gamma Mu. Clubs: Nat. Press. Roman Catholic. Address: Cathedral Village A-410 600 E Cathedral Rd Philadelphia PA 19128

SHEEHY, JANICE ANN, education technology coordinator; b. Jersey City, Mar. 18, 1955; d. Thomas Patrick and Norma Grace (Hultman) Sheehy; m. L. Hillen, June 19, 1976 (div. 1982); 1 child, Adrienne Grace; m. I. Richard Feingold, May 17, 1987. BA, Jersey City State Coll., 1977; student, Fairleigh Dickinson U., 1978-80; EdM, Rutgers U., 1992; EdD, Nova Southeastern U., 1997. Cert. elem. tchr., supr. K-12, adminstr. K-12. Tchr. 2d grade Roosevelt Sch., Union City, N.J., 1977-88, tchr. math., 1988-98, chair sch. improvement team, 1994-98; tech. coord. Christopher Columbus Sch., Union City, N.J., 1999—. Mem. N.J. Math. Coalition, 1994—, N.J. Math. Curriculum Frameworks Dist. Leadership Team, Framework, 1994—. Com. woman Dem. Com., Hudson County, N.J., 1985-86. Mem. ASCD, AAUW, Nat. Coun. Tchrs. Math., Assn. Math. Tchrs. N.J., Kappa Delta Pi, Phi Delta Kappa. Avocations: travel, reading, computers. Home: 360 Roosevelt St Fairview NJ 07022-1716 Office: Christopher Columbus Mid Sch 1500 New York Ave Union City NJ 07087-4324

SHEELEY, SHARON KAY, elementary education educator; b. Kenton, Ohio, Dec. 5, 1947; d. Harry Robert and Ruth Iretta (Gardner) Grunden; m. Charles Earl Sheeley, Sept. 19, 1970. BS, Bowling Green State U., 1974; MEd, Wright State U., 1986. Cert. elementary tchr. 1st grade tchr. Huntsville (Ohio) Elem., Indian Lake Dist., 1970-71, 2d grade tchr., 1971-72, Belle Center (Ohio) Elem., Benjamin Logan Dist., 1976-93, 1993-95, Benjamin Logan Elem., Bellefontaine, 1995—. Cons. Logan County Reading Coun., Bellefontaine, Ohio, 1988-2000; adv. bd. dirs. Faculty Adminstrv. Coun., Benjamin Logan, 1986-94; coord. Right-to-Read, Belle Center, 1980-1995; coord, 1995—. Feature writer Belle Center News, 1990-94. Sec. King's Daus., Belle Center, Ohio; mem. com. Ch. of Christ, Belle Center; mem., voting del. Weekday Religious Edn., Logan County, Ohio. Recipient Tchr. Spotlight award for excellance in edn., 1985; named Edn. Amb., Edn. Ctr. Inc., 1993-94. Mem. NEA, Internat. Reading Assn., Ohio Reading Coun., Ohio Edn. Ass., Logan County Reading Coun. (sec. 1989-91, v.p. 1991-92, pres. 1992-93, participant Ohio Reads), Ben Logan Edn. Assn. (bldg. rep. 1984-87, 1995-2000, v.p. 1987-94, 1996-2002, 2003—). Avocations: reading, boating, collecting. Office: Ben Logan Schs 4560 County Rd 26 Bellefontaine OH 43311

SHEELY, CINDY JEAN, elementary education educator; b. Renton, Wash., July 21, 1956; d. Leonard Ivan and Adeline Elaine (Waddington) Backman; m. Kevin Dee Sheely, July 17, 1982. BA, Seattle Pacific U.,

1978. Cert. tchr. K-9, Wash. Tchr. second/third grade Rainier Valley Christian, Seattle, 1978-80; tchr. first/second grade Seattle Christian Sch., 1980—. Mem. Skyway Ch. of God. Avocations: crafts, drawing, music, drama, reading. Home: 12214 SE 179th Pl Renton WA 98058-6522 Office: 18301 Military Rd S Seatac WA 98188

SHEERIN, MARILYN RITA, elementary school educator; b. Long Island City, N.Y., Dec. 28, 1949; d. Clyde Ralph and Anne Rita (Manzelli) Pittelli; m. Edward F. Sheerin, May 1, 1971; children: Matthew, Janine, Suzanne, Kate. BS, St. John's U., 1970; MS, Queens Coll., 1973. Elem. sch. tchr. Pub. Sch. 31, N.Y.C. Pub. Schs., 1970-74; substitute tchr. Manhasset (N.Y.) Pub. Schs., 1989-92, North Shore Pub. Schs., N.Y., 1992—. Mid. Sch. Pres. Manhasset Sch. Community Assn., 1990-92.

SHEETS, DOROTHY JANE, retired school librarian and educator; b. Grant, Ala., Jan. 17, 1933; d. Walker Samuel and Floria Mae (Parks) Campbell; m. Paul Beauford Sheets, Jan. 1, 1958 (div. July 1972); children: Wanda Kay, Jeffrey Lee, Sue Ann Sheets Cagle. AS, Snead Jr. Coll., 1953; BS, U. Ala., Tuscaloosa, 1956; MEd, Auburn U., 1968; grad., Writer's Digest Sch., Cin., 1996, Inst. Children's Lit., 1992; student, Nat. Radio Inst., Washington, 1997. Cert. tchr. and sch. libr., Ala. Children's libr. Cleve. Pub. Libr., 1956-58; tchr. reading Marshall County Bd. Edn., Guntersville, Ala., 1962-76, elem. libr., 1976-91. Pvt. tutor, Albertville, Ala., 1968—. Vol. tax preparer RSVP, Guntersville, 1992—. DAR scholar, 1955. Mem. NEA (life), Ala. Edn. Assn., Ala. Ret. Tchrs. Assn., Marshall County Ret. Tchrs. Assn., Am. Assn. Ret. Persons. Avocations: reading, storytelling, volunteering, gardening. Home: 407 Pecan Ave Albertville AL 35950-2733 E-mail: djsheets3@juno.com.

SHEFFEY, RUTHE GARNET, English and humanities educator, speaker; m. Vernon R. Sheffey, Dec. 29, 1950; children: Illona Sheffey Rawlings, Renata Sheffey Strong. BA, Morgan State U., Balt., 1947; MA, Howard U., 1949; PhD, U. Pa., 1959. Prof. English Morgan State U., Balt., 1949—, chair dept. English, 1970-76. Author: Impressions in Asphalt, 1969, Trajectory (My Collected Essays), 1989; editor Zora Neale Hurston Forum, 1986—. Named Md. Outstanding Faculty Mem. of Yr., 1994, Disting. Scholar in African-Am. Studies for Yr., Towson State U., 2002, Sheroe as Honor, Women for Responsive Govt., Inc., 2003; named to Morgan State U. Hall of Fame, 2000. Mem. Nat. Coun. Tchrs. English (past mem. coll. bd.), Coll. English Assn. (past pres. Mid. Atlantic Group), Zora Neale Hurston Soc. (founder, 1984, pres.), Langston Hughes Soc. (past pres.), other lit. socs. Mem. United Ch. of Christ. Avocations: reading, theatre-going, dancing.

SHEFFIELD, ELIZABETH BAKER, special education educator, lecturer, consultant; b. Cin., Oct. 28, 1926; d. Charles Wentworth Jr. and Beatrice (Carmichael) B.; m. Samuel Sanford Jr., Dec. 27, 1949; children: Samuel III, Anne Vanoy, William C., Charles T. BA magna cum laude, Smith Coll., 1948; MA in Spl. Edn., U. Cinn., 1972. Cert. learning disabilities and behavioral disorders tchr., Ohio. Reading specialist Lotspeich Schs., Cin., 1968-72, head spl. reading dept., 1972-78; dir. summer reading program 7 Hills Schs., Cin., 1973-76; tchr. aux. svcs. Cin. Pub. Schs., 1974-75; coop. tchr. U. Cin., 1975-76; adj. instr. Spl. Edn. Regional Resource Ctr., Cin., 1977—; pvt. practice learning disabilities Cin., 1978—; master tchr. Butler U., 1987-88. Lectr. in learning disabilities, 1972—, tchr. grad. course, Miami U. Ohio, 1992—. Recipient Outstanding Svc. award Southwestern Ohio Speech, Lang. and Hearing Assn., 1992, Lifetime Achievement award, Internat. Dyslexia Assn., 2001. Mem. Orton Dyslexia Soc. (founder Ohio Valley br. 1979, nat. v.p. 1986-92), Greater Cin. Lit. Network (v.p.), Cin. Tennis Club, Jr. League, Phi Beta Kappa, Sigma Xi. Home: 3054 Griest Ave Cincinnati OH 45208-2430

SHEHEEN, FRED ROUKOS, education agency administrator; b. Camden, S.C., July 7, 1936; s. Austin M. and Lucile (Roukos) S.; m. Rose Maria Serio, Nov. 26, 1966; children: Maria, Vincent, Margaret Rose. AB Polit. Sci., Duke U., 1958; postgrad., Harvard U., 1990; LLD (hon.), Claflin Coll., 1990; HHD, Lander Coll., 1992; AA honoris causa, Tech. Coll. Lowcountry, Beaufort, S.C., 1992. Bureau chief Charlotte (N.C.) Observer, Rock Hill, Columbia, S.C., 1958-63; press sec. to Gov. Donald Russell, Columbia, 1963-65; exec. asst. to Sen. Donald Russell, Washington, 1965-66; asst. to dir. S.C. State Devel. Bd., Columbia, 1967-68; v.p. & sec., pres. & publisher Banner Publishers Inc., Chronicle Publishers Inc., N.C., S.C., 1968-76; founder, pres., prin. owner Camden (S.C.) Co., 1976-87; commr. of higher edn. S.C. Commn. on Higher Edn., Columbia, 1987—; interim dir. pub. affairs U. S.C. Bd. dirs. S.C. Rsch. Authority, Columbia, 1983-86; mem. S.C. Commn. Human Affairs, 1971-72, S.C. Commn. Higher Edn., 1971-75, 79-86, (chmn. 1983-86), Edn. Improvement Act Selection com., 1983-86, Commn. Future S.C., Columbia, 1987-89. Contbr. chpt. to book, article to profl. jour. Pres. Kershaw County Mental Health Assn., Camden, S.C., 1971, 76; mem. S.C. Tuition Grants Commn., 1988—, Nat. Edn. Goals Panel task force Collegiate Attainment and Assessment, 1988—, S.C. Edn. Goals Panel, 1992—, So. Regional Coun. Coll. Bd., 1993—; adv. bd. Master Pub. Adminstrn. program U. S.C. Coll. Charleston, 1992—; trustee Springdale Sch., Camden, 1976-84, Boyland-Haven-Mather Acad., Camden, 1976-83, S.C. Gov's. Sch. Sci. and Mathematics, 1987—; bd. dirs. Kershaw County Cancer Soc. Recipient Sertoma Svc. to Mankind award Sertoma club, 1973; named Educator of Yr. S.C. Tech. Edn. Assn., 1990. Mem. State Higher Edn. Exec. Officers (exec. com. 1990—, Nat. Ctr. Edn. Statistics Network adv. com. 1990—), S.C. Agy. Dir's. Orgn. (pres. 1992). Roman Catholic. Avocations: racquetball, water sports, reading. Home: 2107 Washington Ln Camden SC 29020-1723 Office: SC Commn Higher Edn 1333 Main St Ste 200 Columbia SC 29201-3245

SHELAN, DEBBIE LEVIN, travel agency administrator, school system administrator; b. Dallas, Sept. 27, 1951; d. Sol and Charlotte (Yonack) Levin; m. Evan B. Shelan, June 10, 1973; children: Erin N., Stephanie L. BS in Elem. Edn., U. Tex., 1973, MA in Early Childhood Edn., 1983. Tex. Teaching Cert. Kindergarten tchr. Dallas I.S.D., 1973-74; preschool tchr. Methods Inst., Sacramento, 1974-75, preschool dir., 1975; 2nd grade tchr. Gay Ave. Elem., Gladewater, Tex., 1976; kindergarten tchr. Longview (Tex.) I.S.D., 1976-80; v.p. Evan's World Travel, Inc., Longview, Tex., 1980—. Elected sch. trustee Pine Tree I.S.D., Longview, Tex., 1991-97; chmn. Pine Tree Z Club, Longview Zenta Club, 1992—. Bd. mem. Longview (Tex.) Commn. on Arts and Culture, 1985-91; placement adv. Jr. League of Longview (Tex.), 1988-89; chmn. Gregg Co. Early Childhood Devel. Ctr. Enrichment Program, Longview, Tex., 1992, Longview (Tex.) Preschool Lang. and Devel. Program, 1991, Longview (Tex.) Preshcool Devel. Parenting and Curriculum Libr., 1992, Pine Tree Odyssey, 1992-97; vol. Junior Achievement, 1991-95; advisor Temple Emanu-El Youth Group, 1994—, chmn. 1995—. Named Best Chmn. Jr. League of Longview, Tex., 1991. Mem. Tex. Assn. Sch. Bds. Avocations: travel, reading.

SHELANSKI, MICHAEL L. cell biologist, educator; b. Phila., Oct. 5, 1941; s. Herman Alder and Bessie B.; m. Vivien Brodkin, June 9, 1963; children: Howard, Samuel, Noah. Student, Oberlin Coll., 1959-61; MD (Life Ins. Med. Research Fund fellow), U. Chgo., 1966, PhD, 1967. Intern in pathology Albert Einstein Coll. Medicine, N.Y.C., 1967-68, fellow in neuropathology, 1968-70, asst. prof. pathology, 1969-74; staff scientist NIH, Bethesda, Md., 1971-73; vis. scientist Inst. Pasteur, Paris, 1973-74; assoc. prof. neuropathology Harvard U., Cambridge, Mass., 1974-78; sr. research assoc., asst. neuropathologist Children's Hosp. Med. Center, Boston, 1974-78; prof., chmn. dept. pharmacology N.Y. U. Med. Center, N.Y.C., 1978-86; Delafield Prof., chmn. dept. pathology Coll. Physicians and Surgeons, Columbia U., N.Y.C., 1987—; dir. pathology services Presbyn. Hosp., N.Y.C., 1987—; co-dir. Taub Inst. for Rsch. on Alzheimer's Disease and the Aging Brain, N.Y.C., 1998—. Mem. Neurology A study sect. NIH, 1974-78; Pharmacological Scis. study sect., 1986-90; mem. sci. and med. adv. bd. Alzheimer's Disease and Related Disorders Assn., 1985-92, sec., 1987-92, mem. Zenith award panel, 1993-95; chmn. overhead powerline adv. panel State of N.Y., 1981-87; dir. Alzheimer's disease rsch. ctr. Columbia U., 1989—; mem. Am. Cancer Soc. IRG Panel, 1989-93, sci. adv. bd. Dystonia Assn., Amyotrophic Lateral Sclerosis Assn; elected mem., Inst. of Medicine, 1999. Mem. editl. bd. Jour. Neurochemistry, 1982-90, Jour. Neuropathology and Exptl. Neurology, 1983-85, Neuroscis., 1985—, Neurobiology of Aging, 1988-95, Lab. Investigation, 1989—, Brain Pathology, 1990-93. Served as sr. asst. surgeon USPHS, 1971-73. Guggenheim fellow, 1973-74 Mem. Am. Soc. Cell Biology, Inst. Medicine NAS, Am. Assn. Neuropathologists, Assn. Med. Coll. Pharmacologists, Am. Soc. Neurochemistry, Am. Assn. Physicians. Achievements include research on fibrous proteins of brain, aging of human brain, devel. neurobiology. Office: Columbia U Coll Physicians and Surgeons Dept Pathology 630 W 168th St New York NY 10032-3702

SHELBURNE, MERRY CLARE, public information officer, educator; b. L.A., Oct. 29, 1945; d. John Bartholomew and Geneva (Hedges) Delbridge; m. David Michael Shelburne, July 20, 1968. BA, Calif. State U., L.A., 1968; MA, Calif. State U., Northridge, 1993. Editl. asst. pub. affairs Calif. State U., L.A., 1968-71; publs. supr. Papercraft Specialty Co., L.A., 1973-74; creative dir. Family Record Plan, L.A., 1975-76; pub. info. asst. Glendale (Calif.) C.C., 1977-81, pub. info. officer, asst. prof. mass. comms., 1981—. Journalism advisor CourseWise, Atomic Dog, Internet, 1997—. Author: Walking the HighWire: Effective Public Relations, 1998, Effective Public Relations: A Practical Approach, 2001; songwriter Slow Dancin', If It Feels Good, 1990. Publicist Tim Richards Found. Annual Fundraiser Cmty. Faire, La Crescenta, 1980s. Mem. Calif. C.C. Pub. Rels. Orgn. (Radio Advt. 1st pl. award, Sports Publs. 1st pl. award). Avocations: songwriting, gardening, golf, dried flower decorations, golden retrievers. Office: Glendale CC 1500 N Verdugo Rd Glendale CA 91208-2809 E-mail: mshelbur@glendale.cc.ca.us.

SHELBY, NINA CLAIRE, special education educator; b. Weatherford, Tex., Oct. 23, 1949; d. Bill Hudson and Roselle (Price) S.; m. Richard Dean Powell, May 29, 1971 (div. 1973); 1 child, Stoney Hudson. BA in English, Sul Ross State U., 1974, MEd, 1984; MA in English, U. Tex., 1995. Jr. high lang. arts educator Liberty Hill, Tex., 1974-75; H.S. resource educator Georgetown (Tex.) I. S. D., 1976-77; intermediate resource educator Raymondville (Tex.) I. S. D., 1977-81; educator of severe profound Napper Elem. Pharr (Tex.) San Juan Alamo Ind. Sch. Dist., 1981-90; H. S. life skills educator Pharr (Tex.) San Juan Alamo ISD North H.S., 1990-93; intermediate inclusion educator Carman Elem. Pharr (Tex.) San Juan Alamo Ind. Sch. Dist., 1993—2000, chair dept. spl. edn. Carman Elem., 1998—2000; primary resource/inclusion educator Elgin (Tex.) Primary Sch., 2000—, chair dept. spl. edn., 2002—. Coach asst. Tex. Spl. Olympics, Pharr, 1981—, sponsor vocat. adj. club, 1990-93, adaptive asst. device team, Edinburg, Tex., 1993-95; spl. edn. rep. to Elgin Primary Campus Performance Adv. Coun., 2000-. Asst. cub scout leader Boy Scouts Am., 1994-95, sec. parental com. bd. rev., 1997—; parent vol. boy's and girl's Club McAllen, 1992-96. Mem. DAR, Assn. of Tex. Profl. Educators, Alpha Delta Kappa. Democrat. Mem. Ch. Of Christ. Avocations: reading, horticulture, piano, opera. Home: PO Box 426 Elgin TX 78621-0426 Office: Elgin Primary Sch Elgin ISD 1001 W 2d St Elgin TX 78621

SHELBY, TIM OTTO, secondary education educator; b. Longview, Wash., Mar. 23, 1965; s. William Richard and Ruth (Masser) S. BA in Edn., Eastern Wash. U., 1989; MA in Counseling, U. LaVerne, 2003. Cert. grades 4-12 English tchr., Wash., Calif. English tchr., head basketball and football coach Kahlotus (Wash.) H.S., 1989-90; tchr. various dists., 1990-92; English tchr., asst. basketball coach Kalama (Wash.) H.S., 1992-95; tchr. English, head basketball coach Frazier Mountain H.S., Lebec, Calif., 1995-97; English tchr., asst. basketball coach Shafter (Calif.) H.S., 1997-98; English tchr., asst. basketball coach, English dept. chmn. Mojave (Calif.) H.S., 1998—. Mem. ASCD, Nat. Coun. Tchrs. Eng., Calif. Edn. Assn. Roman Catholic. Avocations: travel, reading, coaching sports, theatre, movies. Home: 21330 Santa Barbara Dr Tehachapi CA 93561-8715 Office: Mojave Unified Sch Dist Mojave CA 93501

SHELDON, J. MICHAEL, lawyer, educator; b. Mt. Carmel, Pa., Sept. 1, 1951; s. Lloyd Loomis and Helen Roberta (Sosnoski) S. AA, Harrisburg (Pa.) Community Coll., 1978; BS, Pa. State U., 1980; M in Journalism, Temple U., 1991; JD, Widener U. Sch. Law, 1996. News announcer Sta. WNUE-AM, Ft. Walton Beach, Fla., 1974-76, Sta. WFEC-AM, Harrisburg, 1977-78; announcer Sta. WCMB-AM, Wormleysburg, Pa., 1979-80; writer newspaper Pa. Beacon, Harrisburg, 1982-85; media specialist Commonwealth Media Svcs., Harrisburg, 1982-86; dir. communications Pa. Poultry Fedn., Harrisburg, 1986-89; news anchor Sta. WGAL-TV, Lancaster, Pa., 1989-90; dir. pub. rels. Profl. Ins. Agts. - Pa., Md., Del., Mechanicsburg, Pa., 1990-92; v.p. comm. and mktg. United Way of the Capital Region, Harrisburg, Pa., 1992-93, Widener U. Sch. of Law, 1994-96; pres. Open Mike Comm., Harrisburg, 1994—. Mem. adj. faculty dept. journalism Temple U., 1992; mem. faculty dept. humanities Pa. State U., 1995-97, 99—. Contbg. author: Pa. 12th Annual Civil Litigation Update, Spoliation of Evidence: Why You Can't Have Your Cake and Eat it Too, 1999; contbg. editor: A Practical Guidebook to Massachusetts Aviation Law, 1999; Contbr. articles to profl. jours. Pub. rels. advisor Cen. Pa. Leukemia Soc., Harrisburg, 1989-90; media advisor Polit. Campaign, Hershey, Pa., 1990. With USAF, 1969-73. Mem. U.S. Fed. Mid. Dist. Bar, Pa. Bar, Dauphin County Bar, VFW (life), Am. Legion, Knights of Columbus (4th degree Knight), Chi Gamma Iota, Delta Tau Kappa. Republican. Roman Catholic. Avocations: motorcycles, music, electronics, martial arts. Office: 6059 Allentown Blvd Harrisburg PA 17112-2672

SHELL, MARY BELINDA JOHNSON, elementary school educator; b. Milton, Fla., Aug. 1, 1957; d. Francis Leo and Norma Jean (Farrow) Johnson; m. Leroy Oliver Shell, Dec. 5, 1981; children: Lee Wesley, Ashlyn Elizabeth, Seth Johnson. AA, Pensacola Jr. Coll., Milton, Fla., 1976; BS, U. West Fla., 1978. Cert. tchr., Fla. Tchr. 2nd and 3rd grades Santa Rosa County Sch. Bd., Jay, Fla., 1978-79; tchr. 1st grade S.S. Dixon Elem. Sch., Pace, Fla., 1979-81; tchr. 3rd grade Berryhill Elem. Sch., Milton, Fla., 1988-89; pre-kindergarten tchr. Jay Elem. Sch., 1989—. Mem. Nat. Assn. for Edn. of Young Children, Santa Rosa Profl. Educators. Baptist.

SHELLMAN-LUCAS, ELIZABETH C. special education educator, researcher; b. Thomas County, Ga., Feb. 5, 1937; d. Herbert and Juanita (Coleman) Smith; m. John Lee Lucas, Jr. (div.); 1 child, Sandie Juanita Lucas Boyce; m. Eddie Joseph Shellman; 1 child, Eddie Joseph Shellman, Jr. MS in Edn., CUNY, 1990. Cert. tchr., N.Y. Pvt. practice cosmetologist, N.Y.C., 1959—; tchr. N.Y.C. Bd. of Edn. High Sch. Dist., 1984—. Vol. various community orgns.; citizen amb. del. People to People Internat., 1994. Mem. Coun. for Exceptional Children. Avocations: reading, music, dancing, jogging, languages.

SHELTON, BESSIE ELIZABETH, school system administrator; b. Lynchburg, Va. d. Robert and Bessie Ann (Plenty) Shelton. BA (scholar), W.Va. State Coll., 1958; student, Northwestern U., 1953-55, Ind. U., 1956; MS, SUNY, 1960; diploma, Profl. Career Devel. Inst., 1993. Young adult libr. Bklyn. Pub. Libr., 1960-62; asst. head cen. ref. divsn. Queens Borough Pub. Libr., jamaica, N.Y., 1962-65; instrnl. media specialist Lynchburg Bd. Edn., 1966-74, ednl. rsch. specialist, 1974-77; ednl. media assoc. Allegany County Bd. Edn., Cumberland, Md., 1977—. Guest singer Sta. WLVA, 1966—, WLVA-TV Christmas concerts, 1966—;cons. music and market rsch. Mem. YWCA, Lynchburg, 1966—, Fine Arts Ctr., Lynchburg, 1966—; ednl. adv. bd., nat. research bd. Am. Biog. Inst.; mem. U.S. Congl. Adv. Bd., USN Nat. Adv. Coun.; amb. goodwill Lynchburg, Va., 1986. Named to Nat. Women's Hall of Fame. Mem. AAUW, NEA, NAFE, Md. Tchrs. Assn., Allegany County Tchrs. Assn., Va. Edn. Assn., State Dept. Sch. Librs., Internat. Entertainers Guild, Music City Songwriters Assn., Vocal Artists Am., Internat. Clover Poetry Assn., Internat. Platform Assn., Nat. Assn. Women Deans, Adminstrs. and Counselors, Intercontinental Biog. Assn., World Mail Dealers Assn., N.Am. Mailers Exch., Am. Assn. Creative Artists, Am. Biog. Inst. Rsch. Assn., Tri-State Cmty. Concert Assn., Pi Delta Phi, sigma Delta Pi, Nat. Travel Club, Gulf Travel Club. Democrat. Baptist. Home: PO Box 187 Cumberland MD 21501-0187

SHELTON, DEBORAH KAY, elementary education educator; b. Lynchburg, Va., July 10, 1952; d. Edward O. and Gloria (Keesee) S. BS, Nova U., 1979, MS, 1983, EdD, 1995. Cert. elem. tchr., elem. prin., supr. Legal sec. Bunnell & Assocs., Ft. Lauderdale, Fla., 1978-79; tchr. Davie Elem. Sch., Ft. Lauderdale, 1979-87, Altavista (Va.) Elem. Sch., 1987—. Mem. Supt.'s Adv. Com., 1989—. Mem. ASCD, Am. Ednl. Rsch. Assn., Va. Edn. Assn. (state com., lobbyist), Campbell County Edn. Assn. (pres. 1988-91, faculty rep. 1992—), Va. State Reading Assn., Internat. Reading Assn., Delta Kappa Gamma, Phi Delta Kappa (v.p. membership). Avocation: aerobics. Home: 315 Kitty Hawk Sq Lynchburg VA 24502-3466 Office: Altavista Elem Sch School Rd Altavista VA 24517

SHELTON, ELIZABETH ANNE, elementary school educator; b. Carbondale, Ill., June 26, 1952; d. William E. and Helen Vivian (Roth) S. BS, So. Ill. U., 1970, MS, 1979. Cert. tchr., Ill., Colo., Wash. 1st grade tchr. Lakeland Sch., Carbondale, Ill., 1973-80, Winkler Sch., Carbondale, Ill., 1980-83; kindergarten lead tchr. Graland Country Day Sch., Denver, 1983-97, pre-sch. dir., 1990-97; ednl. resource specialist Naval Ave. Elem. Sch., Bremerton, Wash., 1997—. Mem. Nat. Assn. for Edn. Young Children, Assn. for Childhood Edn. Internat., Colo. Coun. Internat. Reading Assn. (presenter 1993—), Colo. Assn. Edn. Young Children. Avocations: snow skiing, scuba diving, hiking, traveling. Office: Naval Ave Elem Sch 900 Birch St Bremerton WA 98312

SHELTON, JAMES KEITH, journalism educator; b. Altus, Okla., Oct. 28, 1932; s. Willis Oscar and Theodosia Agnes (Rupert) S.; m. Deborah Kennedy Evans, Dec. 26, 1953; children: Leslie Lynn, Lawrence Evans. BA, Midwestern State U., 1954; MA, U. North Tex., 1972. Reporter Lawton (Okla.) Constn., 1954; wire editor Wichita Falls (Tex.) Record-News, 1956-59; city hall reporter, polit. writer Dallas Times Herald, 1959-65; mng. editor, exec. editor Denton (Tex.) Record-Chronicle, 1965-69, 79-88; faculty mem., dir. pub. info. U. North Tex., Denton, 1969-79, journalist-in-residence, 1988—2002; ret. Author: What Journalists Should Know About Business, 1993. Mem. Supreme Ct. Task Force on Jud. Ethics, Austin, 1992-94. with U.S. Army, 1954-56. Mem. Soc. Profl. Journalists, Freedom on Info. Found. of Tex., Inc. (sec., bd. dirs.). Democrat. Methodist. Home: 621 Grove St Denton TX 76209-7323 E-mail: shelton@unt.edu.

SHELTON, JODY, educational association administrator; b. Norton, Kans., Aug. 4, 1944; d. James Pratt and Rita Merle (Thompson) Shelton. BA, Ottawa U., 1967; MEd, Emporia State U., 1977; EdD, Kans. U., 1991. Tchr. Belvoir Elem. Sch., Topeka, 1967-68, Ctrl. Elem. Sch., Olathe, Kans., 1968-77; prin. Westview Elem. Sch., Olathe, Kans., 1977-80, Tomahawk Elem. Sch., Olathe, Kans., 1980-88; asst. supt. human resources Olathe Dist. Schs., 1988-97, asst. supt., 1997—2002; exec. dir. Am. Assn. Sch. Pers. Adminstrs., 2002—. Cons. Master Tchr., Manhattan, Kans., 1981-86; adj. prof. Emporia (Kans.) State U., 1990—; chair North Ctrl. Edn. Team, 1984; mem. adv. coun. Sch. Edn., Kans. U., Lawrence, 1992—; mem. com. Five Yr. Tech. Plan, Olathe, 1991—. Contbr. articles to profl. jours. Bd. dirs. Temporary Lodging for Children. Recipient Outstanding Jayne award Jaycees, 1972, Outstanding Young Woman Kans., 1980. Mem. NAESP (Nat. Disting. Prin. award 1987-88), AASPA (affiliate), Kans. Career Devel. and Placement Assn., Kans. Assn. Elem. Sch. Prins. (pres., Nat. Disting. Prin. award 1987-88, Olathe C. of C., United Sch. Adminstrs. (bd. dirs.), Optimist. Avocations: theatre, reading, aerobics, bridge, dancing, traveling. Home: 11546 S Brentwood Dr Olathe KS 66061-9388 Office: Exec Dir Am Assn Sch Pers Adminstrs 533 B North Mur-len Olathe KS 66062 E-mail: jodysks@comcast.net.

SHELTON, LESLIE HABECKER, adult literacy and learning specialist; b. Lancaster, Pa., Feb. 15, 1948; d. William Powell and Mary Louise (Habecker) S. BS in Health and Phys. Edn., West Chester U., 1970; MA in Student Pers. Work, U. Iowa, 1972; Cert. in Graphic Design, U. Calif., Santa Cruz, 1980; postgrad. in Transformative Learning, Union Inst., 1997—. Cert. cmty. coll. instr., Calif., tchr., counselor, Iowa, tchr., Pa. Student devel. specialist U. Maine, Farmington, 1972-74; rsch. asst. career counseling U. Colo., Boulder, 1974-75; coord. student activities Iowa Lakes C.C., Estherville, 1975-76, coord. counseling svcs., 1976-78; career counselor, apt. mgr. Loyola Marymount U., L.A., 1978-79; exec. dir. Am. Cancer Soc. Monterey, Calif., 1979-82; patient svcs. coord. Am. Cancer Soc. San Mateo County, Calif., 1982-85; dir. Project READ South San Francisco Pub. Libr., 1985-98. Author: Honoring Diversity: A Multidimensional Learning Model for Adults, 1991, The Dinner Buffet Approach to Learner Support, 1994; illustrator: The Tree Deva. Facilitator, moderator Nat. Issues Forums, South San Francisco, 1987-94; cons., co-creator Easy Reader Voter Guide New Reader Coun. San Francisco Bay Area, 1994; founding bd. dirs. Salinas Valley (Calif.) Hosp. Assn., 1979-81; c.c. rep. Iowa Alliance for Arts in Edn., 1977-78. Grant honoree AAUW, 1989; Literacy Leader fellow Nat. Inst. Literacy, 1995-96. Mem. Calif. Libr. Assn. (coun. rep. 1991-94, chair literacy chpt. 1988-92), Bay Area Libr. Literacy Programs (chair 1987, 88, 92), New Reader Coun. Bay Area (staff coord. 1989-95), AAUW (chair edn. San Bruno br. 1988), North County Literacy Coun. (chair 1986-94, coord. Calif. statewide adult learner conf. 1996). Avocations: painting, photography, skiing, creating multimedia productions, writing.

SHEMANSKY, CINDY ANN, nursing educator; b. Mt. Holly, N.J., Sept. 27, 1959; d. Richard and Joan Mary (Schiehle) Wright; m Paul Joseph Shemansky, Feb. 14, 1981; 1 child, Craig Richard. RN, Mercer Med. Ctr., 1980; BA in Edn., St. Joseph's Coll., Maine, 1993; MEd, City U., Washington, 1997. Cert. in gerontology; lic. nursing home adminstr., N.J. Preceptor, staff nurse med.-surg. area Mercer Med. Ctr., Trenton, N.J.; dir. edn. Masonic Home N.J., Burlington. Task force mem. N.J. Dept. of Health Nurse Aide Curriculum. Contbr. articles to profl. jours. Recipient Excellence in Nursing Practice cert. N.J. Dept. Health, 1991, N.J. Dirs. Nursing Excellence in LTC cert., 1992, RN Splty. award in edn. N.J. Dirs. Nursing Adminstrn., 1993, Nat. Recognition award Nat. Nursing Staff Devel. Orgn., 1994. Mem. ANA, Nat. Gerontol. Nurses Assn. (edn. com., N.E. regional chmn. 2000-01, Innovations in Practice award 1997), N.J. State Nurses Assn., Nat. Nursing Staff Devel. Orgn. (Promoting Excellence in the Climate for Edn. award 1994, Belinda E. Puetz award 1995), Trenton Regional Assn. Insvc. Nurses (past pres., v.p., sec.).

SHEN, JI YAO, mechanical engineering educator; b. Shanghai, June 17, 1944; came to U.S., 1985; s. Bao Rong and Rui Wen (Han) S.; m. Rui Xian; children: Su, Yun. BS, Northwestern Polytech U., Xian, China, 1966; MS, Nanjing Aero. U., Nanjing, China, 1981; PhD, Old Dominion U., 1991. Sr. engr., aircraft designer Aircraft Flight Rsch. and Test Ctr., Xian, China, 1966-78; assoc. prof. Aero. Inst. Tech., Xian, 1980-85; vis. scholar U. So. Calif.-Old Dominion U., Norfolk, Va., 1985-88; rsch. asst. Old Dominion U.-NASA Langley Rsch. Ctr., Hampton, Va., 1988-91; asst. prof. N.C. A&T State U., Greensboro, 1992-95, assoc. prof., 1995—. Contbr. over 76 articles to profl. jours., scientific papers. Mem. AIAA, ASCE (com. mem. 1991—, bd. editors 1993, 94). Office: NC A&T State U Dept Manufacturing Greensboro NC 27411-0001

SHENINGER, ARTHUR WAYNE, retired principal; b. Phillipsburg, N.J., June 28, 1947; s. William A. and Helen I. Sheninger; m. Jean A. Lewis, Dec. 20, 1969; children: Robert, Eric, James. BA, Moravian Coll., 1969; MA, Rider U., 1974. Cert. tchr.; cert. supr. and prin.; cert. sch. adminstr. Tchr. White Twp., Belvider, N.J., 1969-74; adminstrn. prin. Alpha, N.J., 1974-77; prin. Hatchery Hill, Hackettstown, NJ, 1977—2003, ret., 2003. Cons. Geraldine R. Dodge Found., Morristown, 1996—. Mem. bd. White Twp. Bd. Edn., Belvidere, 1986-90; pres. White Twp. Athletic Assn., Belvidere, 1987-92; v.p. Warren County Athletic Assn., Belvidere, 1992; pres. Belvidere H.S. All Sports Boosters, 1993. Mem. NAESP (mem. adv. childcare com. 1993—), Nat. Assn. Elem. Prin., N.J. Prins. and Suprs. (mem. exec. com. 1977), N.J. Coun. Edn., N.J. PTA (life), Warren County Elem. Prins. (pres. 1976-77), Warren Lodge. Methodist. Avocation: travel. Office: Hatchery Hill Sch 5th Ave Hackettstown NJ 07840

SHENKER, JOSEPH, academic administrator; b. N.Y.C., Oct. 7, 1939; s. George and Isabelle (Schwartz) S.; m. Adrienne Green (div. 1979); children: Deborah, Karen; m. Susan Armiger, Jan. 2, 1988; children: Sarah Gabrielle, Jordan. BA in Psychology, Hunter Coll., 1962, MA in Econ., 1963; EdD in High Edn., Tchrs. Coll., 1969. Dean, community coll. affairs CUNY, 1967-69; acting pres. Kingsborough Community Coll., N.Y.C., 1969-70; chief negotiator for mgmt. CUNY, 1977; acting pres. Hunter Coll., N.Y.C., 1979-80; founding pres. LaGuardia Community Coll., N.Y.C., 1970-88; pres. Bank St. Coll. Edn., N.Y.C., 1988-95; provost C.W. Post Campus, L.I. U., 1995—. Bd. dirs. Sch. & Bus. Alliance, N.Y.C.; ptnr. N.Y.C. Partnership, 1990—; advisor Consortium for Worker Edn., 2001--; bd. dirs. DeWitt Wallace Reader's Digest Fund, 2001--. Chmn. Liberty Scholarship Adv. Com., Albany, N.Y., 1989—; co-chmn. Task Force on Early Childhood Edn., N.Y.C., 1989—, Agenda for Children Tomorrow, 1989—; chmn. Chancellor's Com. on U./Sch. Collaboratives, N.Y.C., 1988. Recipient Distinguished Alumni award Tchrs. Coll. Columbia, N.Y.C., 1990. Office: C W Post Campus Long Island U 720 Northern Blvd Greenvale NY 11548-1319

SHEN-MILLER, JANE, research biologist; b. Shanghai; came to U.S., 1951; d. Yi and Inyeening Shen; m. J. William Schopf, Jan. 16, 1980. BS, Wash. State U., 1955; MS, Mich. State U., 1956, PhD, 1959; postgrad., Argonne Nat. Lab., 1959-62. Asst. botanist Argonne (Ill.) Nat. Lab., 1963-72, botanist, 1972-79; assoc. program dir. NSF, Washington, 1977-79; UCLA vis. rsch. scholar UCLA, 1979-83, rsch. chemist, 1983-85, asst. vice chancellor rsch., 1985-86, rsch. biologist, 1986—. Contbr. articles to profl. jours. NASA rsch. grantee, 1962-86, NSF travel grantee, 1964, various other travel grants, 1970-82. Mem. Soc. Gravitational and Space Biology, Am. Soc. Plant Physiology (editl. bd. 1972-77), Am. Inst. Biol. Scis. (governing bd. 1973-80), Internat. Soc. Plant Molecular Biology (germination world's oldest seed Sacred Lotus from China 1994, cultivation of offspring from hundreds of years-old lotus seeds). Avocations: architecture, painting, planting, tennis, skiing. Office: UCLA-Dept Organismic Biology Ecology Evolution 5687 Geology Bldg Hilgard Ave Los Angeles CA 90095-1567

SHEPARD, ANNA RICHARDSON, elementary educator, tutoring company executive; b. Portsmouth, Va., Dec. 1, 1947; d. Curtis Leo and Lois (Bailey) Richardson; m. Ronald Lee Shepard, Dec. 28, 1968 (div. 1985) m. Feb. 14, 1990; 1 child, Kelly Suzanne. BA in Elem. Edn., U. Ky., Lexington, 1969. Tchr. 4th grade Churchland Elem., Portsmouth, Va., 1969-70, tchr. 5th grade, 1970-72; substitute tchr. Monterey (Calif.) Unified Sch. Dist., 1972, Prince Georges County Pub. Schs., Laurel, Md., 1973-76; tchr. 2d grade Lakeview Elem., Portsmouth, Va., 1976-80; substitute tchr. Portsmouth Pub. Schs., 1980-83, Chesapeake (Va.) Pub. Schs., 1980-83; tchr. 6th grade Churchland Elem., Portsmouth, 1983-90; tchr. 7th grade math. Churchland Jr. High., Portsmouth, 1990—96; founder Shepard's Tutoring Svc., 1996—. Author: What Could Our Child Possibly Teach Us?, 2002. Sunday sch. tchr. Aldersgate United Meth. Ch., Chesapeake, 1990-91. Mem. Tidewater Coun. Tchrs. Math. (bd. mem. 1990-91), Delta Kappa Gamma (recording sec. 1986-88). Republican. Methodist. Avocations: being with friends, stitchery, reading, writing.

SHEPARD, JEANNIE, elementary school educator; b. Lee County, S.C., Mar. 24, 1950; d. Leroy and Helen (Myers) Butler; m. Sept. 27, 1980; 1 child, LaVaughn Emil Blanding. BA in Edn., St. Peter's Coll., 1979. Cert. elem. tchr., early childhood, English, home health care. Tchr. kindergarten, tchr. pre-kindergarten Sch. #5, Linden, N.J., 1979-81; tchr. basic skills Sch. #2, Linden, N.J., 1981-82; tchr. grade 4 Sch. #4 Annex, Linden, N.J., 1982-83; tchr. grade 4, grade 2 Public Sch. #8, Jersey City, 1983-84; tchr. pre-sch. JFK Day care Ctr. Rahway (N.J.) Community Action Orgn. Inc., 1986-87; tchr. grade 7 18th Ave. Sch., Newark, 1987-89; tchr. grade 5 South 17th St. Sch., Newark, 1989-90, tchr. grade 6, 1989—. Coord. JFK Day Care Ctr., Rahway, N.J., 1987—. Treas. PTA South 17th St. Sch., 1992—, ch. community rels. com. First Bapt. Ch. of Linden, 1992—. Mem. N.J. Edn. Assn., Newark Tchrs. Edn. Assn., Operation PUSH. Avocations: reading, dancing, traveling, floral arranging, singing. Home: 307 Carnegie St Linden NJ 07036-2213

SHEPARD, ROBERT CARLTON, English language educator; b. Akron, Ohio, Dec. 20, 1933; s. Robert and Mildred Lucille (Stewart) S.; m. Marjorie Alma Mackey, June 9, 1956; children: Robert Lincoln, Donald Ward. BA, U. Oreg., 1970, MA, 1971; postgrad., England, 1979, 1991. Prof. English Southwestern Oreg. C.C., Coos Bay, 1971-94, chair divsn. English, 1976-78, prof. emeritus, 1994—. Liaison Oreg. Com. for Humanities, 1985-86; judge statewide writing contests Nat. Coun. Tchrs. English, Urbana, Ill., 1987-88; founder Willamette Valley Vineyards, Turner, Oreg., 1991; co-founder Nor 'Wester Brewing Co., Portland, 1993, Breweries Across Am., Portland, 1994. Author, photographer, producer: (multi-image show) Christmas Fiestas of Oaxaca (Mexico), 1985; editl. cons., 1996—; developer ednl. software, 1993—. With USMCR, 1954-58. Grad. Teaching fellow U. Oreg., 1970-71. Democrat. Avocations: bicycling, photography, music appreciation, world travel. Home: 3280 Sheridan Ave North Bend OR 97459-3043

SHEPHARD, MARK SCOTT, civil and mechanical engineering educator; b. Buffalo, Oct. 27, 1951; s. William N. and Beatrice (Hass) S.; m. Sharon L. Nirschel, Nov. 25, 1972; children: Steven W., Kari L. BS, Clarkson U., 1974; PhD, Cornell U., 1979. Asst. prof. civil engring. and mech. engring. Rensselaer Poly. Inst., Troy, N.Y., 1979-84, assoc. prof., 1984-87, prof., 1988—, dir. Sci. Computation Rsch. Ctr., 1990—, Samuel A. and Elisabeth C. Johnson Jr. prof. engring., 1993—; assoc. dir. Rensselaer Design Rsch. Ctr., Troy, N.Y., 1980-90. Vis. rsch. fellow GE Corp., R & D Schenectady, 1985, cons., 1984-87; cons. GM Rsch. Lab., Detroit, 1980—, also other orgns.; mem. tech. adv. bd. Aries Tech., Lowell, Mass., 1987-89. Editor: Engring. with Computers; mem. editl. bd. Internat. Jour. Numerical Methods Engring., Computer Methods in Applied Mechanics and Engring., Engring. Applications of Artificial Intelligence, Internat. Jour. Engring. Analysis and Design, Computational Mechanics; contbr. articles to profl. jours., chpts. to books. Fellow ASME, AIAA (assoc.), U.S. Assn. for Computational Mechanics (past pres.), Internat. Assn. for Computational Mechanics (exec. bd.); mem. Am. Soc. Engring. Edn., Am. Acad. Mechanics, Sigma Xi, Tau Beta Pi, Phi Kappa Phi. Home: 305 Algonquin Beach Rd Averill Park NY 12018-6007 Office: Rensselaer Poly Inst 110 8th St Troy NY 12180-3522

SHEPHEARD, LINDA JUNE, elementary education educator; b. Granite City, Ill., Dec. 12, 1949; d. Bernard Thomas Brewer and Alda Berniece Greene Roady; m. Warren DeWayne Shepheard Jr., Jan. 29, 1971; 1 child, Erick Warren. Student, Ill. State U.; BS in Elem. Edn., So. Ill. U., 1977, MS in Elem. Edn., 1986, postgrad., 1992—. Cert. tchr., Ill. Kindergarten tchr. Belle Valley Sch., Belleville, Ill., 1976—, tchr. 3d grade, 1992; asst. prin. Mascoutah C.U.S.D., Belleville, 1993—. Computer instr. So. Ill. U., Edwardsville, 1984, 85. Recipient Golden Apple award St. Clair County, 1993. Mem. ASCD, Ednl. Adminstrn. Leadership Orgn. (sec.-treas. 1992-93), Belle Valley Edn. Assn. (sec., v.p., pres. 1976-92), Assn. for Edn. of Young Children (v.p. so. Ill.). Avocations: golfing, boating. Home: 1324 Salem Dr Belleville IL 62221-5730 Office: Belle Valley Sch 100 Andora Dr Belleville IL 62221-4399

SHEPHERD, DEBORAH GULICK, elementary education educator; b. Edenton, N.C., Oct. 21, 1953; d. Lyman Mark and Rena (Bakker) G.; m. R.W. Shepherd. AA, Centenary Coll., Hackettstown, N.J., 1974; BA, Oral Roberts U., 1976; MA, Fairleigh Dickinson U., 1981. Cert. elem. and mid. sch. tchr., K-12 supr., N.J. Tchr. Mt. Olive Twp. Bd. Edn., Budd Lake, N.J., 1976—. Editor (newsletter) Mountain View News, 1986-97, Light from the Steeple, 1998—. Mem. Chancel Choir, United Presbyn. Ch., Flanders, NJ, 1988—92; mem. sr. choir First Presbyn. Ch., Hackettstown, NJ, 1993—, Sunday sch. treas., 1996—2000; bd. dirs. Heaven Sent Nursery Sch., 1997—99. Recipient Gov.'s Tchr. Recognition award State of N.J., 1991. Mem. Edn. Assn. Mt. Olive (treas. 1986-88, 99-2003), Morris County Coun. Edn. Assn. (rep. 1987-93). Avocations: cross-stitching, sewing, knitting, reading, singing. Home: 663 Rockport Rd Hackettstown NJ 07840-5222 Office: CMS Elem Sch 99 Sunset Dr Budd Lake NJ 07828

SHEPHERD, ELIZABETH POOLE, health science facility administrator; b. Bulape, Kasai, Congo, Mar. 16, 1937; (parents Am. citizens); d. Mark Keller and Sara Amelia (Day) Poole; m. Donald Ray Shepherd, June 6, 1958; children: Lisa, Stephanie, Leslie, Don Poole. BA magna cum laude, Austin Coll., 1958. Cert. secondary and elem. tchr., Tex. Tchr. Thomas Jefferson High Sch., Dallas, 1958, Edward H. Cary Jr. High Sch., Dallas, 1959-60; bus. mgr. Donald R. Shepherd, M.D., P.A., Conroe, Tex., 1972-96; bus. mgr., co-owner Profl. Labs, Inc., Houston, 1975-82; bus. mgr. Profl. Pathology Labs., Ltd., Conroe, 1997-2000, ret., 2000. Brownie leader Girl Scouts Am., 1967-69; dist. chmn. San Jacinto council Boy Scouts Am., Conroe, 1977; pres. Women of Ch. First Presbyn. Ch., Conroe, 1973-74, Montgomery County Med. Soc. Aux., Conroe, 1974-75; bd. dirs. ARC, Conroe, 1970-80; bd. dirs., officer Med. Ctr. Hosp. Vols., Conroe, 1978-81. Mem.: AAUW, Llano Women's Culture Club (pres. 2003—04), Alpha Delta, Alpha Chi. Republican. Presbyterian. Avocations: gardening, reading. Home: PO Box 306 Tow TX 78672

SHEPHERD, MARY ANNE, elementary education educator; b. Washington, Jan. 26, 1950; d. Edwin Joseph and Louise Therese (McKay) Zabel; m. Robert A. Shepherd, June 25, 1988. BS, U. Md., 1972; MEd, George Mason U., 1976; postgrad., U. Akron, 1991-93. Cert. mid. childhood generalist tchr., nat. bd. cert. tchr. 2000. Tchr. elem. schs. Montgomery County Public Schs., Rockville, Md., 1972-74, Fauquier County Pub. Schs., Warrenton, Va., 1974-76, Wooster (Ohio) Pub. Schs., 1976—; mem. faculty East Region Ohio Sch. Net, 1996-98. Master tchr, 1998-99; vestrywoman St. Paul's Episcopal Ch., Akron, Ohio, Ohio, 1996-99, jr. warden, 1998-99 Mem. Wooster Edn. Assn. (treas. 1984-91). Republican. Avocations: needlecrafts, exercising, gardening. Home: 4872 Medina Rd Akron OH 44321-1122 Office: Wooster City Schs 144 N Market St Wooster OH 44691-4810

SHEPLER, JACK LEE, mathematics educator; b. Vandergrift, Pa., Apr. 4, 1938; s. Howard Moses and Doris Lee (Davis) S.; m. Gloria Ann Morith, Apr. 7, 1962; children: David, Betsy, Stephen, Kathryn. BA, Roberts Wesleyan Coll., 1960; MA, San Diego State U., 1964; PhD, U. Wis., 1969. Secondary math. tchr. Batavia (N.Y.) Sch. Dist., 1960-62, Wheatland-Chili Ctrl. Sch. Dist., Scottsville, N.Y., 1962-63; secondary math. tchr., dept. chair Port Washington Union Free Sch. Dist., 1964-66; U.S. Dept. Edn. rsch. fellow U. Wis., Madison, 1966-69; prof. math. Indiana U. Pa., 1969—2001, statis. cons. Grad. Sch., 1969-75, 87-89. Contbr. articles to profl. jours. Elder Graystone Presbyn. Ch., Indiana, 1970-2001. Grantee Eisenhower Higher Edn., 1992-2001. Mem. Assn. Pa. State Coll. U. Ret. Faculty, Pa. Coun. Tchrs. Math. Home: 174 Appledale Lane Indiana PA 15701-8814 E-mail: jshepler@yourinter.net.

SHEPP, JUDITH ROSSER, elementary education educator; b. Dayton, Ohio, Mar. 11, 1942; d. Rollin Labarr and Eloise (Comstock) Rosser; m. John W. Shepp, July 12, 1969; children: David, Edward, Cynthia. BS, Eastern Ky. U., Richmond, 1964. Tchr. 5th grade Audubon Elem. Sch., Merritt Island, Fla., 1964-65, Ocean Breeze Elem. Sch., Indian Harbor Beach, Fla., 1965-66; tchr. 4th, 5th grades Audubon Elem. Sch., Merritt Island, Fla., 1966-69; spl. edn. tchr. Eustis Mid. Sch., Fla., 1988-89; tchr. 2nd, 4th, 5th grades Orange County Pub. Sch., 1992—2001; 3rd and 5th grades Maxey Elem. Sch., Winter Garden, Fla., 1991—2000; spl. ed. tchr. Lovell Elem. Sch., 2001—. Faculty rep. Orange County Classroom Tchrs. Assn., Orlando, Fla., 1994-97, 2001-03; primary team leader Maxey Elem. Sch., Winter Garden, Fla., 1994-95, 97-98, mem. adv. coun., 1996-98. Pres. West Pasco Jr. Woman's Club, New Port Richey, Fla., 1973-75, Magnolia Garden Circle, Mount Dora, Fla., 1984-86, Woman's Commn. of Fine Arts, Mount Dora, Fla., 1986-90. Mem. NEA, Internat. Reading Assn., Fla. Reading Coun., Orange County Reading Coun., Orange County Classroom Tchrs. Assn., Gen. Fedn. of Women's Club Mount Dora (pres. 1990-92, newsletter editor 1996-2003, Clubwoman of Yr. 1992). Avocations: reading, golf. Home: 30627 S Round Lake Rd Mount Dora FL 32757-9211 Office: Lovell Elem Sch 815 Roger Williams Rd Apopka FL 32703 E-mail: booknose@LCIA.com., sheppj@ocps.k12.fl.us.

SHEPPARD, DEBORAH CODY, hearing handicapped educator, clinician; b. Atlanta, Aug. 4, 1959; d. Jack Benar and Wilma (Shoffner) Cody; m. Kenneth Louis Sheppard, Nov. 14, 1987. BA in Speech Correction, Columbia (S.C.) Coll., 1981; MS in Edn. of Hearing Handicapped, U. Tenn., 1983; EdS in Spl. Edn. and Early Childhood, U. S.C., 1991, postgrad., 1998—. Cert. speech pathologist, S.C., cert. early childhood edn. tchr., cert. in hearing handicapped, S.C., nat. cert. in exceptional needs. Speech/lang. clinician Dist. 60 of Abbeville, S.C., 1981-82, Dist. of Pickens (S.C.) County, 1984-85; tchr. hearing handicapped Dist. 50 of Greenwood, S.C., 1985-88; speech/lang. clinician Saluda (S.C.) Dist. 1, 1989-91; tchr. hearing impaired Millbrook Elem. Sch., Aiken, S.C., 1991—. Tchr. Am. sign lang. Saluda Dist. 1, 1989-91, 91—. Grantee, 1993-94, 94-95, 95-96, 96-97, 97-98. Mem.: Nat. Assn. of the Deaf. Baptist. Avocations: aerobics, gardening, travel. Home: 301 Chime Bell Church Rd Aiken SC 29803-9365 Office: Chukker Creek Elem Aiken SC 29803

SHEPPERD, SUSAN ABBOTT, special education educator; b. Pekin, Ill., May 12, 1942; d. Robert Fred and Martha Mae (Abbott) Belville; m. Thomas Eugene Shepperd, Oct. 7, 1960; children: Scott Thomas, Allison Marie Shepperd-Henry, Michele Lea. BA, Maryville Coll., 1990; MEd, U. Mo., 1994. Cert. elem. edn. tchr. grades 1-8, spl. reading tchr. grades K-12. Resource tchr. reading grades K-8 St. Joseph Sch., Ardiocese of St. Louis, Cottleville, Mo., 1990-98. Mem. Pi Lambda Theta (pres. 1992-94), Assn. in Edn. (Gamma Zeta chpt.), Phi Kappa Phi, Delta Epsilon Sigma. Episcopalian. Avocations: golfing, music, swimming. Home: 15977 Chamfers Farm Rd Chesterfield MO 63005-4717

SHER, PHYLLIS KAMMERMAN, pediatric neurology educator; b. N.Y.C., Aug. 13, 1944; d. Seymour K. and Shirley (Parmit) Kammerman; m. Kenneth Swaiman, Oct. 6, 1985. BA, Brandeis U., 1966; MD, U. Miami, 1970. Diplomate Am. Bd. Psychiatry and Neurology. Pediatric intern Montefiore Hosp., Bronx, N.Y., 1970-71; resident in neurology U. Miami (Fla.) Med. Sch., 1971-73, fellow in pediatric neurology, 1973-75, asst. prof. neurology, 1975-80; rsch. assoc. NIH, Bethesda, Md., 1980-83; asst. prof. neurology and pediatrics U. Minn. Med. Sch., Mpls., 1983-86, assoc. prof., 1986-96; mem. Hennepin Faculty Assocs., 1996-99. Dir. Ripple program United Cerebral Palsy Found., Miami, 1972-75; chmn. med. svcs. com. 5-yr. action plan State of Fla., 1975; cons. Minn. Epilepsy Program for Children, 1983-85; vis. prof. Japanese Soc. Child Neurology, 1985, Chinese Child Neurology Ctr., 1989, Hong Kong Soc. Child Neurology & Devel. Pediat., 1995. Mem. editl. bd. Pediatric Neurology, 1991—, Brain and Devel., 1994-99; contbr. articles and abstracts to med. jours., chpts. to books. Comdr. USPHS, 1980-83. Fellow United Cerebral Palsy Found., 1972-73; rsch. grantee Gillette Children's Hosp., U. Minn. Grad. Sch., Viking Children's Fund, Minn. Med. Found. Fellow Am. Neurol. Assn., Am. Acad. Neurology; mem. Child Neurology Soc. (exec. com., councillor 1993-95), Upper Midwest Child Neurology Soc., So. Clin. Neurology Soc. Office: Pediatric Neurology 1821 University Ave W Ste N188 Saint Paul MN 55104-2870

SHER, RICHARD B. historian, educator; b. Newark, Mar. 29, 1948; m. Doris S. Holstein, Jan. 4, 1977; 1 child, Jeremy. BA, George Washington U., 1970; MA, U. Chgo., 1971, PhD, 1979. Spl. lectr. N.J. Inst. Tech., Newark, 1979-85, asst. prof. history, 1985-86, assoc. prof. history, 1986-92, prof. history, 1992-2000, disting. prof. history, 2000—, assoc. dean coll. sci. and liberal arts, dir. honors program, 1985-91, chair dept. history, 1999—; mem. grad. faculty Rutgers U., Newark, 1991—. Vis. prof. N.Y.U., 1982; with grad. faculty Rutgers U., New Brunswick, N.J., 2000—. Author: Church and University in the Scottish Enlightenment, 1985; editor: Eighteenth-Century Scotland, 1987—, Scotland and America in the Age of the Enlightenment, 1990, Sociability and Society, 1991, The Glasgow Enlightenment, 1995, Works of William Robertson, 1997. Fellow Royal Hist.Soc.; mem. Eighteenth Century Scottish Studies Soc. (exec. sec. 1986—). Office: NJ Inst Tech Dept History University Heights Newark NJ 07102-1982 E-mail: sher@njit.edu.

SHERBINSKI, LINDA ANNE, nurse anesthetist, nursing educator; b. Rochester, N.Y., Jan. 17, 1956; d. Edward Marion and Helen Marie (Kindzera) S. Student, Genesee Hosp. Sch. Nursing, Rochester, N.Y., 1977; BSN, Alfred U., 1978; grad. in anesthesia, Univ. Health Ctr. Pitts., 1987; MSN, Duquesne U., 1991. RN, Pa. Leader day team CCU The Genesee Hosp., 1978-84, staff nurse operating rm., 1984-85; staff nurse ICU Forbes Met. Hosp., Pitts., 1985-87; staff anesthetist Presbyn. Univ. Hosp., Pitts., 1987-92, preceptor anesthetist, 1991-92; instr. Univ. Health Ctr. Pitts. Sch. Anesthesia, 1987-90, U. Pitts. Grad. Anesthesia Program, 1990-92; staff anesthetist Meml. Med. Ctr., Springfield, Ill., 1992-94; anesthetist Rochester (N.Y.) Gen. Hosp., Highland Hosp., Genesee Hosp., N.Y., 1994-98, Emory U. Hosp., Atlanta, 1998—. Item writer Acad. Item Writers AANA, Chgo., 1991—. Contbr. articles to profl. jours., chpt. to book. Med. vol. Pitts. Marathon, 1990, 91. Mem. Am. Assn. Nurse Anesthetists (cert. nurse anesthetist, program dir. internship grant 1990), Nat. League Nursing, Sigma Theta Tau (sec. Delta Sigma chpt. 1978-80, Rsch. scholar Epsilon Phi chpt. 1991). Roman Catholic. Home: 1404 Treelodge Pkwy Atlanta GA 30350-6013 Office: Emory U Hosp 1364 Clifton Rd NE Atlanta GA 30322-1061

SHERBURNE, DONALD WYNNE, philosopher, educator; b. Proctor, Vt., Apr. 21, 1929; s. Hermon Kirk and Alma May (Bixby) S.; m. Elizabeth Statesir Darling, July 30, 1955; children— Kevin Darling, Nancy Elizabeth, Lynne Darling. AB, Middlebury Coll., 1951; BA, Balliol Coll., Oxford U., 1953; MA, Yale U., 1958, PhD, 1960. Instr. philosophy Yale, 1959-60; asst. prof. Vanderbilt U., Nashville, 1960-64, asso. prof., 1964-68, prof. philosophy, 1968-95, chmn. dept., 1973-80, 90-94, prof. emeritus, 1995. Cowling vis. prof. philosophy Carleton Coll., 1990; chmn. editorial adv. com. Vanderbilt U. Press, 1991-95. Author: A Whiteheadian Aesthetic, 1961, A Key to Whitehead's Process and Reality, 1966; editor: Soundings— An Interdisciplinary Jour, 1980-85; co-editor: Corrected Edition of Whitehead's Process and Reality, 1978. Troop leader Cub Scouts, 1965-67. Served with U.S. Army, 1954-56. Recipient Jeffrey Nordhaus award for excellence in teaching, 1984; Dutton fellow Oxford U., 1951-53; sr. fellow NEH, 1977-78. Mem. AAUP (pres. Vanderbilt chpt. 1966-67), Metaphys. Soc. Am. (governing coun. 1969-73, 86-90, pres.-elect 1992-93, pres. 1993-94), So. Soc. Philosophy and Psychology (governing coun. 1971-74, treas. 1974-77, pres.-elect 1977, pres. 1978, Jr. award for Excellence 1961), Am. Philos. Assn. (program com. 1982, com. on status and future of profession 1989-92, nominating com. 1994-95), Am. Soc. Aesthetics, Acad. Sr. Profls. Eckerd Coll., Phi Beta Kappa (pres. Vanderbilt chpt. 1975-77). Home: 3 Jefferson Ct S Saint Petersburg FL 33711-5144

SHERIDAN, KATHARINE JANE, elementary school educator; b. Somers Point, N.J., Dec. 4, 1971; d. Mary Elizabeth (Mroz) Goodman. BA in Spl. Edn., William Paterson U., 1995; MA in tchg., Marygrove Coll., 2001. Cert. tchr. of handicapped, N.J., elem. educator. Tchr. asst. emotionally disturbed classroom Indian Hills H.S., Oakland, N.J., 1995-96; spl. edn. tchr. perceptionally impaired classroom Maywood (N.J.) Sch. Dist., 1996-97; spl. edn. tchr. perceptually impaired Egg Harbor Twp. (N.J.) Sch. Dist., 1997—, basic skills instr., 1998-99, tchr. 1st grade, 1999—. Vol. coach Somers Point (N.J.) Recreation, 1997. Mem. Coun. for Exceptional Children, N.J. Edn. Assn., Am. Aerobic Assn. Internat. (instr. 1992-95), Kappa Delta Pi. Avocations: reading, writing, travel. Office: Egg Harbor Twp Sch Dist Egg Harbor Township NJ 08215

SHERIDAN, THOMAS BROWN, mechanical engineering and applied psychology educator, researcher, consultant; b. Cin., Dec. 23, 1929; s. Mahlon Brinsley and Esther Anna (Brown) S.; m Rachel Briggs Rice, Aug. 1, 1953; children: Paul Rice, Richard Rice, David Rice, Margaret Lenore. BS, Purdue U., 1951; MS, UCLA, 1954; ScD, MIT, 1959; Dr. (hon.), Delft U. Tech., The Netherlands, 1991. Registered profl. engr., Mass. Asst. prof. mech. engring. MIT, Cambridge, 1959-65, assoc. prof., 1965-70, prof., 1970-78, prof. engring. and applied psychology, 1978-94, prof. aeronautics and astronautics, 1994—, Ford prof., 1995—. Lectr. U. Calif., Berkeley, Stanford U., 1968; vis. prof. U. Delft, The Netherlands, 1972, Stanford U., 1989, Ben Gurion U., Israel, 1995; chmn. com. human factors, mem. com. aircrew-vehicle interaction, com. on commercially developed space facility, com. on human factors in air traffic control, NRC, mem. com. on nat. automated hwy. sys., com. on setting and enforceing speed limits, com. on intelligent vehicle initiative; mem. adv. com. on applied phys., math. and biol. scis. NSF; mem. life scis. adv. com., study group on robotics, oversight com. flight telerobotic servicer NASA; mem. task force on appropriate tech. U.S. Congress Office Tech. Assessment; mem. study sect. accident prevention and injury control NIH; mem. Def. Sci. Bd. Task Force on Computers, Tng. and Gaming, Nuclear Regulatory Commn. on Nuclear Safety Rsch. Rev. Com. Author: Telerobotics, Automation and Human Supervisory Control, 1992, Humans and Automation; co-author: Man Machine Systems, 1974; editor: (with others) Monitoring Behavior and Supervisory Control, 1976, Perspectives on the Human Controller, 1997; assoc. editor Automatica, 1982-94; co-editor: Perspectives on the Human Controller, 1997; mem. edtl. adv bd. Tech. Forecasting and Social Change, Computer Aided Design, Advanced Robotics, Robotics and Computer Integrated Mfg.; sr. editor Presence: Telerobots and Virtual Environments, 1991—. Served to 1st lt. USAF, 1951-53. Recipient Nat. Engring. award Am. Assn. Engring. Socs., 1997, Rufus Oldenburger medal ASME, 1997. Fellow IEEE (pres. Systems, Man and Cybernetics Soc. 1974-76, Centennial medal 1984, Norbert Wiener award 1993, Joseph G. Wohl award 1995, Millenium medal 2000), Human Factors Soc. (Paul M. Fitts award 1977, Arnold Small award 2000, pres. 1990-91, Pres. Disting. Svc. award 2000), Nat. Acad. Engring. Democrat. Mem. United Ch. of Christ.

SHERIF, S. A. mechanical engineering educator; b. Alexandria, Egypt, June 25, 1952; came to U.S., 1978; s. Ahmed and Ietedal H. (Monib) S.; m. Azza A. Shamseldin, Feb. 6, 1977; children: Ahmed S., Mohammad S.; m. Vitrell Lynn McNair, May 30, 2003. BSME (hon.), Alexandria U., 1975, MSME, 1978; PhD in Mech. Engring., Iowa State U., 1985. Tchg. asst.

mech. engring. Alexandria U., 1975-78; tchg. assoc. mech. and environtl. engring. U. Calif., Santa Barbara, 1978-79; rsch. asst. mech. engring. Iowa State U., Ames, 1979-84; asst. prof. No. Ill. U., Dekalb, 1984-87, U. Miami, Coral Gables, Fla., 1987—91; assoc. prof. mech. engring. U. Fla., Gainesville, 1991-2001, prof. mech. engring., 2001—, mem. doctoral rsch. faculty, 1992—, founding dir. Wayne K. and Lyla L. Masur HVAC Lab., 1995—, asst. dir. Indsl. Assessment Ctr., 2001—. ABET coord. for mech. engring., 1997—; coord. for mech. engring. So. Assn. Colls. and Schs., 2001—; affiliate Inst. for Sci. and Health Policy U. Fla., 2001—; cons. Solar Reactor Techs., Inc., Miami, 1988-91, Dade Power Corp., Miami, 1988-91, Ind. Energy Sys., Miami, 1988-91, Carey Dwyer Eckhart Mason Spring & Beckham, P.A. Law Offices, Miami, 1988-89, Michael G. Widoff, P.A., Attys. at Law, Ft. Lauderdale, Fla., 1989-93, Law Offices Pomeroy and Betts, Ft. Lauderdale, 1991-92, Ctr. for Indoor Air Rsch., 1994-2000; cons. Fla. Power and Light Co., 1996-98; external examiner U. Roorkee, 1994-95, 98—, Indian Inst. Tech., Delhi, 2002-, Alexandria U., Egypt, 2000-; adj. faculty cons. Kennedy Western U., Thousand Oaks, Calif., 1994-97; resident assoc. Argonne (Ill.) Nat. Lab., Tech. Transfer Ctr., summer 1992; faculty fellow NASA Kennedy Space Ctr., Cape Canaveral, Fla., summer 1993; rsch. assoc. summer faculty rsch. program USAF Office Sci. Rsch., Arnold Engring. Devel. Ctr., Arnold AFB, Tenn., 1994; faculty fellow NASA Marshall Space Flight Ctr., Huntsville, Ala., 1996, 97; ABET coord. for aerospace engring., 2002-; coord. for aerospace engring., Southern Assn. Coll. and Sch., 2002-. Co-editor: Industrial and Agricultural Applications of Fluid Mechanics, 1989, The Heuristics of Thermal Anemometry, 1990, Heat and Mass Transfer in Frost and Ice, Packed Beds, and Environmental Discharges, 1990, Industrial Applications of Fluid Mechanics, 1990, rev. edit., 1991, Mixed Convection and Environmental Flows, 1990, Measurement and Modeling of Environmental Flows, 1992, Industrial and Environment Applications of Fluid Mechanics, 1992, rev. edit., 1998, Thermal Anemometry-1993, 1993, Developments in Electrorheological Flows and Measurement Uncertainty-1994, 1994, Heat, Mass and Momentum Transfer in Environmental Flows, 1995, Thermal Anemometry, 1996, Fluid Measurement Uncertainty Applications, 1996, Devices for Flow Measurement and Analysis, 1997, Heat and Mass Transfer in Environmental Flows, 1998, Industrial and Environmental Applications of Fluid Mechanics, 1999, rev. edit., 2001, Measurement and Modeling of Environmental Flows, 2002, Industrial and Environmental Applications of Fluid Mechanics, 2003, Fluid Measurement Uncertainty Applications, 2003; reviewer more than 35 internat. jours., more than 150 conf. procs.; mem. editl. com. SECTAM XXI, 2001-2002; book rev. editor ASME Applied Mech. Revs., 2001-; assoc. tech. editor Solar Energy jour., 2002—; guest editor: Solar Energy Journal (special issue on Hydrogen Production), 2003-; contbr. numerous articles to profl. jours. NASA ambassador, 1996-98, lab. host student sci. tng. program Ctr. for Precollegiate Edn. and Tng., 1997—; mem. environ. awareness adv. com., Dade County Pub. Schs., 1989-91, lab. dir. cmty. lab. rsch. program, 1989-91, also faculty liaison design svcs. dept.; active Com. for Nat. Inst. for Environ., 1992—; mem. senate U. Fla., 1994-95, mem. OUTREACH Spkrs. program, 1996-98. Recipient Kuwait prize for applied scis., 2002, cert. recognition for rsch. contributions, NASA, 1993, 1996, 1997. Fellow ASME (mem. energy resources bd. 2001-03, steering com. internat. energy conversion engring. conf., 2002-03, chmn. 2002-03, coord. group fluid measurements, fluids engring. divsn. 1987—, vice chmn. 1990-92, chmn. 1992-94, fluids engring. divsn. adv. bd. 1994—, fed. honors and awards com. 1995-2001, mem. fluid mechs. tech. com. 1990—, fluid mech. com. 1987-90, K-19 com. on environ. heat transfer 1987—, chmn. 2003—, mem. K-6 com. on heat transfer in energy systems, 2001—, mem. fluid applications and systems tech. com. 1990—, systems analysis tech. com. advanced energy sys. divsn. 1989—, newsletter editor advanced energy sys. divsn. 1995-98, exec. com., 1999—, mem.-at-large honors awards 1999-2000, sec., treas. 2000-2001, vice chmn., 2001-02, chmn., 2002-03, sr. mem. and past chmn., 2003-04, fundamentals and theory tech. com. solar energy divsn. 1990-97, chmn. CGFM nominating com. 1992-94, mem. 1994-98, chmn. profl. devel. com. Rock River Valley sect. 1987, tech. activities operating com. Gator sect. 1994-96, MFFCC subcom. 1 on uncertainties in flow measurements 1995-2000), ASHRAE (mem. heat transfer fluid flow com. 1988-92, 93-97, corr. mem. 1992-93, 97—, mem. thermodynamics and psychrometrics com. 1988-92, 96-2002, corr. mem. 1992-96, vice chmn. 1990-92, mem. liquid to refrigerant heat exchs. com. 1989-93, 96-97, sec. 1990-92, corr. mem. 1993-96, 97-2001, corr. mem. air-to-refrigerant heat transfer com., 2000—, chmn. stds. project com. on measurement of moist air properties 1989-95, corr. mem. refrigeration load calculations com., 1999—, E.K. Campbell award of merit 1997, recipient ASHRAE dist. svc. award, 2003), AIAA (assoc., mem. terrestrial energy systems tech. com. 2001—); mem. AIChE (sr.), Internat. Assn. Hydrogen Energy, Internat. Solar Energy Soc., Am. Soc. for Engring. Edn., Internat. Energy Soc. (mem. sci. coun.), European Assn. Laser Anemometry (ASME/FED rep., mem. steering com.), Internat. Inst. Refrigeration (U.S. nat. com.), ABI (hon. mem. rsch. bd. adv. 1994—), Sigma Xi. Moslem. Avocations: reading, soccer, basketball, history, astronomy. Office: U Fla Dept Mech and Aerospace Engring 228 MAE Bldg B PO Box 116300 Gainesville FL 32611-6300 Home: 3440 NE 41st Pl Ocala FL 34479 E-mail: sasherif@ufl.edu.

SHERIFF, JIMMY DON, accounting educator, academic dean, administrator; b. Greenville, S.C., Dec. 8, 1940; s. James Donald and Gladys Ellie (Chapman) S.; m. Gwen Anne Campbell, Aug. 31, 1969. BA, So. Wesleyan U., 1964; MBA, U. Ga., 1970, PhD, 1976. Acct. Maremont Corp., Greenville, 1965-68; instr. U. Ga., Athens, 1970-73; asst. prof. Presbyn. Coll., Clinton, S.C., 1973-74; prof. Clemson (S.C.) U., 1974-87, assoc. dean, dir. rsch., 1987-92, acting dean, 1992-93, sr. assoc. dean, 1993—, chmn. bus. sch. adv. bd., 1995-97, asst. v.p. for econ. devel., 1999—. U.S. rep. Network Internat. Bus. Schs. Chmn. Pickens County Aeros. Commn., 1980-91; founding pres. Pickens County Property Owners Assn.; chmn. S.C. N.G. Scholarship Found., 1990-2000, pres., 2000—. Brig. gen. Army N.G. Home: 988 Old Shirley Rd Central SC 29630-9337 Office: Clemson U Office of VP 130 Lehotsky Hl Clemson SC 29634-0101 E-mail: sheriff@clemson.edu.

SHERMAN, ALAN ROBERT, psychologist, educator; b. N.Y.C., Nov. 18, 1942; s. David R. and Goldie (Wax) S.; m. Llana Helene Tobias, Aug. 14, 1966 (div. 1989); children: Jonathan Colbert, Relissa Anne; m. Ann Marie Redington, Aug. 22, 2002. BA, Columbia U., 1964; MS, Yale U., 1966, PhD, 1969. Lic. psychologist, Calif. Faculty psychology U. Calif., Santa Barbara, 1969—; clin. psychologist in pvt. practice Santa Barbara, 1981—. Cons. in field. Author: Behavior Modification, 1973; contbr. articles to profl. jours. and chpts. in books. Pres. Santa Barbara Mental Health Assn., 1978, 84-85, 91, Mountain View Sch. Site Coun., Santa Barbara, 1978-84. Recipient Vol. of Yr. award Santa Barbara Mental Health Assn., 1979, Tchg. Excellence awards Delta Delta Delta, Alpha Chi Omega, Gamma Phi Beta, Santa Barbara; NIMH predoctoral rsch. fellow, 1964-69; grantee in field. Fellow Behavior Therapy and Rsch. Soc.; mem. APA, AAUP (chpt. pres. 1978-79), Calif. Psychol. Assn., Assn. for Advancement of Behavior Therapy, Santa Barbara County Psychol. Assn. (pres. 1985), Phi Beta Kappa (chpt. pres. 1977-78), Sigma Xi, Psi Chi (chpt. faculty advisor, 1979—). Office: Univ of Calif Dept Psychology Santa Barbara CA 93106-9660 E-mail: sherman@psych.ucsb.edu.

SHERMAN, ALAN THEODORE, computer science educator; b. Cambridge, Mass., Feb. 26, 1957; s. Richard Beatty and Hanni Fey Sherman; m. Tomoko Shimakawa, Aug. 2, 1986; m. Pamela C. Steele, Oct. 20, 2001. ScB in Math. magna cum laude, Brown U., 1978; SM in Elec. Engring and Computer Sci., MIT, 1981, PhD in Computer Sci., 1987. Instr. Tufts U., Medford, Mass., 1985-86, asst. prof., 1986-89, U. Md. Balt. County, Catonsville, 1989-95, assoc. prof., 1995—; mem. Inst. for Advanced Computer Studies U. Md., College Park, 1989-92, 95-98. Rsch. affiliate MIT Lab. for Computer Sci., Cambridge, 1985-88. Author: VLSI Placement and Routing: The PI Project, 1989; co-editor: Advances in Cryptology: Proceedings of Crypto 82, 1983; contbr. articles to profl. jours. Mem. Assn. for Computing Machinery, IEEE, Internat. Assn. for Cryptologic Rsch., AAUP, Soc. for Indsl. and Applied Maths., Phi Beta Kappa, Sigma Xi. Avocations: tennis, Aikido, piano, chess. Home: 3618 Ordway NW Washington DC 20016 Office: U Md Baltimore County Dept Comp Sci Elec Engring Baltimore MD 21250-0001 E-mail: sherman@umbc.edu.

SHERMAN, ARTHUR, theater educator, writer, actor, composer, sculptor; b. Dec. 5, 1920; s. Herman and Fay (Epstein) S.; m. Margery Frost Sherman, Apr. 15, 1974 (div. Sept. 1989); children: Claudia, Andrew Jay. MusB, Juilliard Sch. Music, 1955; M in Music Edn., Manhattan Sch. Music, 1957; Doctoral Equivalency, CUNY, 1969. Dir. performing arts N.Y.C. (N.Y.) Tech. Coll., 1964-72; prof. speech and theatre John Jay Coll., N.Y.C., 1990—, Borough Man C.C., N.Y.C., 1990—. Judge Film Award Com., Australia, 1972-89, Acad. Awards, 1990; cons. Min. for Edn., Tasmania, Australia, 1977; presenter in field. Author: (screenplays) Thistle and Thorn, 1982, Same Difference, 1983, (book and lyrics) Lenore and the Wonder House, 1964, Prisms in the Looking Glass, 1993, Once Upon a Crime, We the Common Earth; (children's novel) Paradise Lagoon, 1989, (book) Picture Book for Young Adults Paintings, Music and Lyrics, 1998, An Adventure in the New Mythology, 1999, Songwriting Is Easy and Fun, 1996, Red Herr, 2003; (comedy theater) But Its Not Chekhov, 1999; (comic screenplay) Weaning, 1999; (7-book novel) The Pleiades, Burning in Heaven, Freezing in Hell, Bloody Mooring, Scoring in Limbo, Chasing the Phoenix, The Pleiades and Beyond Adventure Etc., Betrayal of Self; (with Edward Mapp) The Road to Mainstream, 1999; (play) To Hell with Buffalo Wings-Anyone for Eagle Wings?, 1999, Warsaw Ghetto Uprising, 2001; actor, dir. films, TV, theater in U.S. and Australia; actor: (films) The Punisher, 1979, Death of a Soldier, 1985, Les Patterson Saves the World, 1988, The Last Bastion, 1987; sculptures displayed YWCA, Hamilton, Ont., Can., 1967, Lincoln Ctr., N.Y.C., 1969, State Bank, Sydney, Australia, 1974; bust of Louis Armstron Meml. Mus. and House, Dame Judith Anderson Australian Consulate N.Y. Pres. United Fedn. Coll. Tchrs., N.Y.C., 1971. With USN, 1943-46. Grantee Australian Film Commn., 1981. Mem. ASCAP, Australasian Performing Rights Assn., Actors' Equity U.S. and Australia. Home: 315 W 57th St New York NY 10019-3158 Office: John Jay Coll 58th St 10th Ave New York NY 10019 E-mail: asherman@jjaycuny.edu.

SHERMAN, EDWARD FRANCIS, dean, law educator; b. El Paso, Tex., July 5, 1937; s. Raphael Eugene and Mary (Stedmond) S.; m. Alice Theresa hammer, Feb. 23, 1963; children: Edward F. Jr., Paul. BA, Georgetown U., 1959; MA, U. Tex., El Paso, 1962, 67; LLB, Harvard U., 1962, SJD, 1981. Bar: Tex. 1962, Ind. 1976. Aide to gov. Nev., state govt. fellow, Carson City, 1962; law clk. judge U.S. Dist. Ct. (we. dist.), El Paso, Tex., 1963; ptnr. Mayfield, Broaddus & Perrenot, El Paso, 1963-65; tchg. fellow Law Sch. Harvard U., Cambridge, Mass., 1967-69; prof. Sch. Law Ind. U., Bloomington, 1969-77; Edward Clark Centennial prof. U. Tex., Austin, 1977-96; prof., dean Tulane U. Law Sch., 1996—. Fulbright prof. Trinity Coll., Dublin, 1973-74; vis. prof. Stanford Law Sch., 1977, U. London, 1989, Sch. Pub. Adminstrn., Warsaw, Poland, 1995, Chuo U., Tokyo, 1995, U. New South Wales, Australia, 2002; counsel Tex. County Jail Litigation, 1978-85; bd. dirs., officer Travis County Dispute Resolution, 1993—; mem. arbitrtor panel, course dir. Internat. Ctrs. Arbitration. Co-author: The Military in American Society, 1979, Complex Litigation, 1985, 3d edit., 1998, Processes of Dispute Resolution, 1989, 3d edit., 2002, Civil Procedure: A Modern Approach, 1989, 3d edit., 2000, Rau & Sherman & Shannon's Texas ADR and Arbitration Statutes, 1994, 3d edit., 1999. Capt. U.S. Army, 1965-67, lt. col. Res., 1970-90. Fellow Tex. Bar Found.; mem. ABA (reporter civil justice improvements project 1993, offer of judgement task force 1995, com. on pro bono and pub. svc. 1997—, chmn. task force class action legis. 2002-03), Am. Arbitration Assn. (arbitrator panel), AAUP (gen. counsel 1986-88), Am. Law Inst., Tex. State Bar Assn. (alternative dispute resolution com. 1985-96, chair pattern jury charge com. 1983-94, Evans award for excellence in dispute resolution 1998), Tex. Civil Liberties Union (gen. counsel 1985-91), La. Law Inst., La. State Bar (bd. govs. 1997-99, com. on codes of lawyer and jud. conduct 1999—, com. on multi-juris. practice 2000—); La. Bar Found. (jud. liason com. 1999—), Assn. Am. Law Schs. (chmn. Sect. Litigation 1999, chmn. Sect. ADR 1995, com. on clin. legal edn. 1999—. Office: Tulane Law Sch 6329 Freret St New Orleans LA 70118-6231 Home: 21 Newcomb Blvd New Orleans LA 70118

SHERMAN, GORDON RAE, computer science educator; b. Menomenee, Mich., Feb. 24, 1928; s. Gordon E. and Myrtle H. (Evenson) S.; m. Lois E. Miller, July 3, 1951; children: Karen Rae, Gordon Thorstein. BS, Iowa State U., 1953; MS, Stanford U., 1954; PhD, Purdue U., 1960. Instr. math., rsch. assoc. Statis. and Computational Lab., Purdue U., Lafayette, Ind., 1956-60; dir. Computing Ctr., U. Tenn., Knoxville, 1960—, prof. computer sci., 1960-93, prof. emeritus, 1993—. Program dir. techniques and systems Office of Computing Activities, NSF, 1971-72; chmn. membership com. EDUCOM Coun., 1983-85. Contbr. articles on computer sci. to profl. jours. Served with USAF, 1946-49, 50-51. Recipient Chancellor's citation U. Tenn., 1983; NSF grantee, 1974. Fellow Brit. Computer Soc.; mem. Am. Statis. Assn., Assn. for Computing Machinery, Data Processing Mgmt. Assn. (Internat. Computer Sci. Man of Yr. award S.E. REgion VIII 1973, Profl. of Yr. Region VIII 1979), Ops. Rsch. Soc. Am., Soc. for Indsl. and Applied Math., Sigma Xi, Phi Kappa Phi. Republican, Lutheran. Home: 301 Cheshire Dr Apt 105 Knoxville TN 37919-5849 Office: U Tenn De[001b]t Computer Sci 107 Ayres Hall Knoxville TN 37916

SHERMAN, KENNETH ELIOT, medicine educator, researcher; b. Long Branch, NJ, Dec. 21, 1955; s. Emanuel and Gertrude Sherman; m. Susan Nacht, Nov. 30, 1980; children: Marc, Amy. BS, Rutgers U., 1976, PhD, 1980; MD, George Washington U., 1985. Diplomate Am. Bd. Internal Medicine, Am. Bd. Gastroenterology. Commd. capt. U.S. Army, 1985, advanced through grades to lt. col., 1995; intern, then resident in medicine Tripler Army Med. Ctr., Honolulu, 1985-88; fellow in gastroentrology Fitzsimmons Army Med. Ctr., Aurora, Colo., 1989-91; gastroenterologist Fitzsimons Army Med. Ctr., Aurora, Colo., 1991-94, chief dept. clin. investigation, 1992-94; resigned, 1994; assoc. prof. medicine and pathology U. Cin. Med. Ctr., 1994—2002, dir. hepatology and liver transplant medicine, 1998—, Gould prof. medicine, 2002—. Adv. com. FDA, 2003—. Author, editor: Viral Insecticides for Biological Control, 1985; reviewer Hepatology, 1993—, Am. Jour. Gastroentrology, 1994—; mem. editorial bd. Am. Jour. Gastroenterology, 1998—; contbr. articles to med. jours., chpt. to book; inventor composition and method. Asst. cubmaster Boy Scouts Am., Aurora, 1993-94. Recipient heroism award Kiwanis, 1982, rsch. award William Beaumont Soc., 1991; Busch predoctoral fellow Waksman Inst. Microbiology, 1976. Fellow ACP, Am. Coll. Gastroent.; mem. Am. Assn. for Study Liver Disease, Am. Soc. for Microbiology, Am. Gastroent. Assn., Am. Fedn. of Med. Rsch., Am. Soc. for Gastrointestinal Endoscopy, Am. Assn. of Transplantation, European Assn. for Study of the Liver. Avocations: skiing, camping, fishing. Office: U Cin Med Ctr Liver Unit Divsn Digestive Diseases Cincinnati OH 45267-0595

SHERMAN, MARTIN, entomologist, educator; b. Newark, Nov. 21, 1920; s. Louis and Anna (Norkin) S.; m. Ruth Goldsmith, Sept. 25, 1943 (div. Nov. 1975); children: Laurel Deborah Sherman Englehart, Susan Leslie Sherman Kitakis. BS, Rutgers U., 1941, MS, 1943; PhD, Cornell U., 1948. Research fellow in entomology Rutgers U., 1941-43; research asst. Cornell U., 1945-48; entomologist Beech-Nut Packing Co., Rochester, N.Y., 1948-49; mem. faculty U. Hawaii, Honolulu, 1949—, prof. entomology, 1958-86, prof. emeritus entomology, 1986—. Fulbright scholar U. Tokyo, 1956-57, Royal Vet. and Agrl. Coll. of Denmark, 1966; vis. prof. Rutgers U., 1973 Editorial bd.: Pacific Sci, 1962-66, Jour. Med. Entomology, 1968-72. Served to 1st lt. USAAF, 1943-45. Fellow: Am. Inst. Chemists; mem.: Internat. Soc. for Study Xenobiotics, Hawaiian Entomology Soc. (pres. 1969—70), Japanese Soc. Applied Entomology and Zoology, Am. Registry Profl. Entomologists, Soc. Environ. Toxicology and Chemistry, Soc. Toxicology, Am. Chem. Soc., Entomol. Soc. Am. (gov. bd. 1974—77, pres. Pacific br. 1970), Torch Club, Jewish War Vets. U.S.A., Am. Legion, VFW, Sigma Xi, Gamma Sigma Delta, Phi Kappa Phi, Delta Phi Alpha. Address: 1121 Koloa St Honolulu HI 96816-5103

SHERMAN, MAX RAY, lawyer, academic executive, former state senator; b. Viola, Ark., Jan. 19, 1935; s. Ernest and Eva (Davenport) S.; m. Gene Alice Wienbroer, July 29, 1961; children: Lynn Ray, Holly Ruth. BA in History, Baylor U., 1957, LLD (hon.), 1978; JD with honors, U. Tex., 1960. Ptnr. Gibson, Ochsner and Adkins, Amarillo, Tex., 1960-77; Tex. State Senator, 1971-77; pres. West Tex. State U., Canyon, 1977-82; spl. counsel to Tex. gov. State of Tex., Austin, 1983; dean Lyndon B. Johnson Sch. Pub. Affairs, Austin, 1983—97. Mem. exec. com. So. Regional Edn. Bd., 1986-87; mem. rev. com. for Harry S Truman Scholarship Found.; mem. Nat. Commn. on Innovations in State and Local Govt., 1985-98. Contbr. articles to law revs. Served to capt. USAR, 1960-64. Recipient Austinite of Yr. award Greater Austin C. of C., 1997, Texan of Yr. award Tex. Legis. Conf., 1999; named One of Ten Best Legislators, Tex. Monthly, 1973, 75, 77. Mem. ABA, Tex. Bar Assn., Nat. Assn. Schs. of Pub. Affairs and Adminstrs. (exec. counc. 1983-87, 88—, pres., 1988-89), Nat. Acad. Pub. Adminstrn., Assn. for Pub. Policy Analysis and Mgmt. (exec. com. 1983-86). Democrat. Presbyterian. Avocations: racquetball, tennis. Office: Univ Tex LBJ Sch Pub Affairs Drawer Y Univ Sta Austin TX 78713-8925

SHERMAN, MONA DIANE, school system administrator; b. N.Y.C., Aug. 28, 1941; d. Hyman and Lillian (Baker) Ginsberg; m. Richard H. Sherman, May 9, 1964; children: Holly Baker, Andrew Hunter. BS, Hunter Coll., CUNY, 1962; MS, CUNY, 1965. Cert. elem. tchr., K-12 reading endorsement specialist, ESL tchr., elem. adminstrn. and supervision, instrnl. supervision, spl. edn. learning disabilities and neurologically impaired edn., Ind. Elem. tchr. N.Y.C. Pub. Schs., 1962-77; team leader Tchr. Corps Potsdam (N.Y.) State Coll., SUNY, 1977-79; dir. Tchr. Ctr., Sch. City of Hammond, Ind., 1979-87; lab. coord. PALS, Gary (Ind.) Sch. Corp., 1987-93, mentor, 1988—, facilitator of staff devel., 1993—. Instr. Tex. Instrument Computer Co., Lubbock, 1983-84, Performance Learning Sys., Emerson, N.J., 1984—; cons. in classroom discipline and computer instrn. Gary Staff Devel. Ctr., 1987—; mentor Urban Tchr. Edn. program Ind. U. N.W., Gary, 1991—; chair sch. improvement team, tchr. of yr. com., 1993-94; mem., grantswriter Gary Tech. Com., Gary Distance Learning Com. Mem. Lake Area United Way Lit. Coalition NW Ind., 1990, Gary Reading Textbook Adoption Com.; sec. Martin Luther King Jr. Acad. PTSA, mem. sch. improvement team. Recipient Recognition NW Ind. Forum, 1988, Tchr. of Yr. award Merrillville (Ind.) Lions Club, 1988, Outstanding Tchr. of Yr. award Inland Ryerson, East Chicago, Ind., 1989. Mem. Ind. Reading Assn., Gary Reading Assn., Phi Delta Kappa, Delta Kappa Gamma. Avocations: theatre, crafts, tennis. Home: 7576 Granville Dr Tamarac FL 33321-8740

SHERMAN, RICHARD ARTHUR, nephrologist, educator; b. N.Y.C., Jan. 3, 1950; s. Stanley L. and Gloria L. (Wisotsky) S.; m. Rosa Y. Rabbach, March 18, 2000; children: Eric, Gregory, Stefano. BS, CCNY, 1971; MD, Yeshiva U., 1975. Intern, then resident Met. Hosp. Ctr., 1975-77; fellow in nephrology Bronx Mcpl. Hosp. Ctr., 1977-79; asst. prof. medicine Robert Wood Johnson Med. Sch., New Bruswick, 1979-85, assoc. prof., 1985—93, prof., 1993—. Med. adv. bd. Kidney and Urology Found. Am., 2002—; creator, organizer confs. hemodialysis therapy, N.Y., San Diego, 1984, 85. Editor-in-chief jour. Seminars in Dialysis, 1987—. Mem. coun. on dialysis Nat. Kidney Found., 1996—. Mem. Internat. Soc. Nephrology, Am. Soc. Nephrology, Nephrology Soc. N.J. (pres. 1984-85). Office: Robert Wood Johnson Med Sch Dept Medicine POB 19 1 Robert Wood Johnson Pl New Brunswick NJ 08903-0019

SHERMAN, RICHARD BEATTY, history educator; b. Somerville, Mass., Nov. 16, 1929; s. James Beatty and Hilda Louise (Ford) S.; m. Hanni Fey, June 13, 1952; children: Linda Caroline, Alan Theodore. AB, Harvard U., 1951, PhD, 1959; MA, U. Pa., 1952. Instr. history Pa. State U., State College, 1957-60; asst. prof. Coll. of William and Mary, Williamsburg, Va., 1960-65, assoc. prof., 1965-70, prof., 1970-87, chancellor prof., 1987-92, Pullen prof., 1992-94, prof. emeritus, 1994—. Fulbright prof. Am. history U. Stockholm, 1966-67. Author: The Negro and the City, 1970, The Republican Party and Black America, 1973, The Case of Odell Waller, 1992; co-author: The College of William and Mary: A History, 1993; contbr. articles to profl. jours. Served with U.S. Army, 1952-54. Am. Philos. Soc. grantee, 1964, 66, faculty rsch. grantee Coll. William and Mary, 1962, 63, 65, 80, 87. Mem. ACLU, Phi Beta Kappa. Democrat. Home: 205 Matoaka Ct Williamsburg VA 23185-2810 Office: Coll William and Mary Dept History Williamsburg VA 23185

SHERMAN, RICHARD H. education educator; b. Yonkers, N.Y., Jan. 5, 1941; m. Mona D. Sherman, May 9, 1964; children: Holly Baker, Andrew Hunter BA, Hunter Coll., 1962; MA, Iowa U., 1965; MS, Queens Coll., 1970; EdD, Yeshiva U., 1977. Cert. tchr., Ind., Ill., N.Y. Asst. prof. edn. SUNY, Potsdam; instr. Herbert H. Lehman Coll., CUNY; asst. prof. edn. Purdue U., Hammond, Ind.; assoc. dean Ind. Vocat. Tech. Coll., Gary; chmn., assoc. prof. Calumet Coll. St. Joseph, Whiting, Ind. Edn. dir. Mus. Broadcast Comms., Chgo., founding prin. Coral Springs Jr./Sr.High Charter Sch., Online/Onground Facilitator, U. Phoenix Online and at Ft. Lauderdale; dir. Zarem/Golde ORT TECH Inst., Chgo.; workshop leader; presenter and spkr. in field; exec. dir. Allied Ednl. Svcs. Co-editor: The Middle River Review; author, playwright, poet, critic. Bd. dirs. Jewish Fedn. N.W. Ind.; chmn. events "Walk for Israel", Lake Area United Way, v.p. mobilization and resources devel, needs and assessment priorities com., chmn. section campaign; active Lake County chpt. ARC, N.W. Ind. Film Commn. Recipient N.W. Ind. Forum Svc. Recognition award, Jewish Fedn. N.W. Ind. Young Leadership award, Harlem Arts Svc. award. Mem. Internat. Reading Assn., Am. Assn. Theatre Critics, Dramatists Guild, Ind. Reading Coun., Ind. Reading Profs. (treas.), Hammond Reading Coun. (pres.), Ind. State Coun., N.W. Ind. Arts Assn. (subcom.), Soc. Children's Writers and Illustrators, Rotary Club, Fla. Playwright Workshop, Sigma Tau Delta, Phi Delta Kappa.

SHERMAN, RUTH TODD, government advisor, counselor, consultant; b. Memphis, July 3, 1924; d. Robbie M. and Lillie M. (Shreve) Todd. BS, Memphis State U., 1972, MEd, 1975; MA, Western Mich. U., 1986; PhD, Ohio State U., 2001. Cert. tchr., counselor. Youth leader Assembly of God Ch., Memphis, 1962-64, youth dir., 1964-66; counselor Teen Challenge, Memphis, 1973-74; marriage and family therapist Memphis, 1976-77; govt. tng. advisor Def. Logistics Agy., Battle Creek, Mich., 1982-87, advisor Alexandria, Va., 1987-94, ret., 1994; tchr. computer graphics Ohio State U., Columbus, 1998—. Agy. to Mil. Svc. cons. Def. Logistics Agy., Oklahoma City, 1990-94. Author: Federal Catalog Training Books/Videos, 1987 (Sustained Superior Performance award 1987). Mem. Internat. Assn. Marriage and Family Counselors, Nat. Employment Counseling Assn., Am. Mental Health Counseling Assn. Avocations: drawing, creating computer animations, photography. Home: 257 Vista Dr Gahanna OH 43230-2986

SHERMAN, SUSAN JEAN, writer, educator, editor; b. N.Y.C., Oct. 30, 1939; d. Monroe and Gertrude (Horn) S.. BA, Sarah Lawrence Coll., 1969, MA in Lit., 1971. Tchr. English Dwight-Englewood, 1970-72, Riverdale Country Sch., NY, 1972-97; writer Riverdale, NY, 1997—. Author: Give Me Myself, 1961, (rec.) Promises to Be Kept, 1962; editor: Forward Into the Past, 1992, May Sarton: Among the Usual Days, 1993, May Sarton: Selected Letters, 1916-1954, 1997, To Bid Us Still Rejoice, 1998, Dear Juliette: Letters of May Sarton to Juliette Huxley, 1999, May Sarton:

Selected Letters, 1955-1995, 2002, May Sarton: Catching Beauty, The Earliest Poems (1924-1929), 2002, May Sarton: At Fifteen: A Journal, 2002.

SHERMAN, THOMAS FAIRCHILD, biology educator; b. Ithaca, N.Y., May 25, 1934; s. James Morgan Sherman and Katherine (Keiper) Sherman Rogers; m. Diane Elizabeth Bell; children: Catherine Lee Sherman (dec.), Anita Sherman, Elizabeth Bell Sherman (dec.); m. Laurel Ann Galbraith; children: Caroline Reynolds Sherman, Claire Galbraith Sherman; m. Katia Brahemcha, July 18, 1991. BA, Oberlin Coll., 1956; DPhil, Oxford U., 1960. Vis. asst. prof. zoology Oberlin (Ohio) Coll., 1960-61, from asst. prof. to prof. biology, 1966-96, emeritus prof., 1996—; postdoctoral rsch. fellow Yale U., 1961-62; vis. asst. prof. zoology Pomona Coll., Claremont, Calif., 1962-65; postdoctoral rsch. fellow Harvard U., 1965-66. Author: A Place on the Glacial Till, 1996; co-author: Biology: The Integrity of Organisms, 1977. Rhodes scholar, 1956-58. Home: 34 Hemlock Rd Brunswick ME 04011-3416

SHERMAN, THOMAS FRANCIS, education educator; b. Salamanca, NY, Dec. 20, 1946; s. Harry and Ione (Schultz) S.; m. Janice Ann Wade, Aug. 17; children: Piper Lee, Wade Thomas. AA, Paul Smith's Coll., 1967; BA, SUNY, Buffalo, 1970; MEd, Colo. State U., 1975; EdD, U. Colo., 1980. Tchr. Buffalo Pub. Schs., 1970, Poudre R.I. Pub. Schs., Ft. Collins, Colo., 1971, tchr., reading specialist, 1973-80; sr. resident supr. Lookout Mountain Schs. for Boys, Golden, Colo., 1972; faculty, dir. reading ctr. Ea. N.Mex. U., Portales, 1981-84; faculty Bemidji (Minn.) State U., 1985-90, Winona State U., Rochester, Minn., 1990-92; interim asst. v.p. acad. affairs S.W. State U., Marshall, Minn., 1992-93; interim asst. vice chancellor acad. affairs Minn. State Univ. System, St. Paul, 1993; prof. Winona State U., Rochester, 1994-2000; disting. faculty fellow Sheldon Jackson Coll., Sitka, Alaska, 2001—. System quality facilitator team Minn. State U., 1990-93; chair Winona State Outcomes/Indicators, 1990-92; coord. WSU/Minn. High Success Consortium Grad. Program; chmn. Minn. State Colls. and Univs. Grad. Coun., 2003—. Contbr. articles on reading edn. to profl. jours. Bd. dirs. Dodge/Fillmore/Olmstead Counties Corrections Bd., 1990-93; elder Presbyn. Ch.; coun. chair Minn. State Coll. and Univs., 2003-04. Mem. Internat. Reading Assn. (pres. Minn. Coun., cert. of merit, sub chair evaluation team Nat. Coun. Accreditation Tchr. Edn., mem. nat. media award com.), Rochester Kiwanis (bd. dirs. 1992-95), Alpha Upsilon Alpha Internat. (chair steering com.1995-98). Democrat. Avocation: skiing. Home: 1735 Walden Ln SW Rochester MN 55902-0901 Office: Winona State U Highway 14 E Rochester MN 55904

SHERNOFF, ELISE RUBIN, special education educator; b. Savannah, Ga., Aug. 16, 1951; d. Irving and Madeline (Sadler) Rubin; m. Victor Harvey Shernoff, June 4, 1972; children: Jason Noah, Heather Toby. BA in History, Armstrong State Coll., 1973, MEd in Spl. Edn., 1977. Cert. spl. edn. tchr., Ga. Tchr. Myers Mid. Sch., Savannah, 1973, Bartlett Mid. Sch., Savannah, 1973-74, Jenkins High Sch., Savannah, 1976-81, Beach High Sch., Savannah, 1986—. Bd. dirs. Rambam Day Sch., Savannah; presenter CEC conf., Denver, 1994, Indpls., 1995, NEA so. regional conf., Biloxi, Miss., 1995. Mem. Coun. for Exceptional Children, Jewish Edn. Alliance (bd. dirs. 1992—), Agudath Achim Synagogue-Sisterhood (life), Hadassah (life), B'nai B'rith Women. Democrat. Jewish. Avocations: cooking, baking, fitness walking.

SHERR, RICHARD JONATHAN, educator; b. NYC, Mar. 25, 1947; s. Solomon and Claire S. BA, Columbia U., 1969; MFA, Princeton U., 1971, PhD, 1975. Lectr. UCLA, L.A., 1973-74; asst. prof. Smith Coll., Northampton, Mass., 1975-80, assoc. prof., 1980-86, prof., 1986—, Caroline L. Wall '27 prof., 2000—. Vis. lectr. U. Wis., Madison, 1974—75. Author: Papal Music Manuscripts in the Late Fifteenth and Early Sixteenth Centuries, 1996, Music and Musicians in the Renaissance Rome and Other Courts, 1999, (series) Sixteenth Century Motet, 1987-99; author, editor: Papal Music and Musicians in Late Medieval and Renaissance Rome, 1998, The Josquin Companion, 2000; contbr. articles to profl. jours. Recipient Lions Club Palestrina prize, Italy, 1992; fulbright grantee, 1972, Leopold Schepp Found. fellow, 1982, medal of the City of Tours, France,2003. Mem. Am. Musicological Soc. (editl. bd. 1990-92), Renaissance Soc. Am. (discipline rep. 1997-99), Internat. Musicological Soc. Office: Smith Coll Dept Music Northampton MA 01063-0001

SHERRATT, GERALD ROBERT, retired academic administrator; b. Los Angeles, Nov. 6, 1931; s. Lowell Heyborne and Elva Genevieve (Lamb) S. BS in Edn., Utah State U., 1953, MS in Edn. Adminstrn., 1954; PhD in Adminstrn. Higher Edn., Mich. State U., 1975. Staff assoc. U. Utah, Salt Lake City, 1961-62; dir. high sch. relations Utah State U., Logan, 1962-64, asst. to pres., 1964-77, v.p. for univ. relations, 1977-81; pres. So. Utah U., Cedar City, 1982-97; mayor Cedar City, UT, 2002—. Dir. Honeyville Grain Inc., Utah; mem. coun. pres. Utah Sys. Higher Edn., 1982-97; chmn. bd. Utah Summer Games, Cedar City, 1984-97; chmn. pres.'s coun. Rocky Mountain Athletic Conf., Denver, 1984-85 Author hist. pageant: The West: America's Odyssey, 1973 (George Washington Honor medal 1973); musical review: How the West Was Won, 1998. Chmn. Festival of Am. West, Logan, Utah, 1972-82; chmn. bd. Utah Shakespearean Festival, Cedar City, 1982-86; chmn. bd. dirs. Salt Lake City Br. of the Fed. Res. Bank of San Francisco, 1996-98; bd. trustees Salt Lake Organizing Com. Winter Olympics 2002. 1st lt. USAF, 1954-57. Recipient Editing award Indsl. Editors Assn., 1962, Robins award Utah State U., 1967, Disting. Alumnus award Utah State U., 1974, So. Utah U., 1991, Total Citizen award Cedar City C. of C., 1993, Minuteman award Utah Nat. Guard, 1997; named to Utah Tourism Hall of Fame, 1989; Centennial medal So. Utah U., 1997; Imperial Order Utah Shakespearean Festival, 1997; named to Hall of Honor Utah Summer Games, 1997, Utah Educators Hall of Fame, 1999. Mem. Am. Assn. State Colls. and Univs., Cache C. of C. (bd. dirs. 1980-82), Cedar City Civic Club (pres.), Phi Kappa Phi, Phi Delta Kappa, Sigma Nu (regent 1976-78) Mem. Lds Ch.

SHERREN, ANNE TERRY, chemistry educator; b. Atlanta, July 1, 1936; d. Edward Allison and Annie Ayres (Lewis) Terry; m. William Samuel Sherren, Aug. 13, 1966. BA, Agnes Scott Coll., 1957; PhD, U. Fla., Gainesville, 1961. Grad. tchg. asst. U. Fla., Gainesville, 1957-61; from instr. to asst. prof. Tex. Womans U., Denton, 1961-66; rsch. participant Argonne Nat. Lab., 1973-80, 93-94; assoc. prof. chemistry North Cen. Coll., Naperville, Ill., 1966-76, prof., 1976-2001, prof. emeritus, 2001—. Contbr. articles to profl. jours. Ruling elder Knox Presbyn. Ch., 1971—, clk. of session, 1976-94. Mem. Am. Chem. Soc., Am. Inst. Chemists, Sigma Xi, Delta Kappa Gamma (chpt. pres. 2002—), Iota Sigma Pi (nat. pres. 1978-81, nat. dir. 1972-78, nat. historian 1989—). Presbyterian. Office: North Ctrl Coll Dept Chemistry Naperville IL 60566 Office Fax: 630-637-5180. E-mail: ats@noctrl.edu.

SHERRILL, BARBARA ANN BUKER, elementary school educator; b. Hamilton, Mont., July 11, 1952; d. Emery Orville and Helen (Hackett) Buker; m. Mark Warren Sherrill, Oct. 7, 1978; children: Kristopher Kain, Ashley Ann. BS in Elem. Edn., Western Mont. Coll., 1973, postgrad., 1984; M. Human Svcs., U. Gt. Falls, 1991. Cert. tchr., Mont. Tchr. elem. grades Ramsay (Mont.) Sch., 1974-90; tchr. Sch. Dist. 1, Butte, Mont., 1990-2000; media coord. Creativity Factory Presch., Butte, 1974-87; ednl. coord. R.O.C.K.I.E.S. 20th Century Cmty. Learning Ctr. Grant for Sch. Dist. 1, 2000—. Sci. mentor West Elem. Sch., 1997-2000; facilitator labor history workshop Internat. Brotherhood Teamsters, U. Wis., 1987, U. Calif., Berkeley, 1988; writer, rschr., 1987-88; Mont. Keystone Project mentor, 1997—; mem. Exploratium Inst. for Inquiry, 1998; early career mentor, 1999—; adult edn. instr. Butte Sch. Dist., 2002—; cmty. outreach instr. U. Mont. Western, 2002—; mem. Mont. Out-of-Sch. Time task force, 2001—; grant reader Montano OPI, 2003. Co-author: Teaching Labor Studies in the Schools, vol. 1, 1988, Gezel Developmental Tester, 1991—. Parent vol. Silver Bow Amateur Wrestling Assn. Butte, pairings master. Mem. AAUW, Am. Fedn. Tchrs., Mont. Fedn. Tchrs., AFL-CIO, Ramsay Fedn. Tchrs. (pres. 1975-79), Butte Tchrs. Union, Mont. Energy Edn. Coun. (bd. dirs. 1991, v.p. 1995—, presenter workshop, negotiating com. 1999—), Alpha Delta Kappa (pres. Mu chpt. 1994-96, corr. sec. Mont. chpt. 1996-98, scholarship com. 1998-2000). Democrat. Avocations: reading, skiing, swimming, computers. Office: Curriculum Office 119 N Montana St Butte MT 59701-9219

SHERRILL, GLADYS MARIE, elementary education educator; b. Little Rock, Sept. 8, 1940; d. Henry and Elcano Sherrill. BS in Edn., Ctrl. State U., Wilberforce, Ohio, 1963; MA in Edn., St. John Coll., Cleve., 1975. Tchr. Cleve. City Schs., 1963-70, Detroit City Schs., 1970-71; edn. dir. Head Start, Cleve., 1972-73; elem. tchr. Cleve. City Schs., 1973—. Mem. NEA (Black caucus, peace and justice caucus, fine arts com.), Ohio Edn. Assn., Zeta Pi Beta, Phi Delta Kappa. Republican. Mem. Unity Ch. Home: 1701 E 12th St Cleveland OH 44114-3206

SHERVE-OSE, ANNE, music educator; b. Minot, N.D., Feb. 11, 1953; d. Albin Gustav and Alvhild Margaret (Slen) Sherve; m. Alan Kent Ose, Jan. 19, 1980; children: Samuel Sherve Ose, Rachel Sherve Ose. BA in Phys. Edn. and Health, St. Olaf Coll., 1975; MusB in Music Composition, Iowa State U., 1982; MA in Music Edn., U. St. Thomas, 1998. Cert. tchr., Iowa. Asst. instr. Minn. Outward Bound Sch., Ely, 1977; tchr. phys. edn. and music Am. Girls Sch., Izmir, Turkey, 1978—79; tchr. elem. music N.E. Hamilton Schs., Blairsburg, Iowa, 1985—88, St. Thomas Aquinas Sch., Webster City, Iowa, 1992—98; dir. music Ellsworth C.C., Iowa Falls, Iowa, 1998—, chmn. dept. humanities, 2002—. Tchr. Blairsburg Community Presch., 1982-85, Iowa. Church organist Blairsburg United Ch. of Christ, 1980—; cmty. chorus dir. Williams (Iowa) Cmty. Chorus, 1988—; bd. dirs. William Pub. Libr., 1990-98; asst. scout leader Girl Scout Troop 234, Webster City, 1992-97. Home: 2230 Wilson Ave Williams IA 50271-7571 Office: Ellsworth CC 1100 College Ave Iowa Falls IA 50126

SHERWIN, BYRON LEE, religion educator, college official; b. N.Y.C., Feb. 18, 1946; s. Sidney and Jean Sylvia (Rabinowitz) S.; m. Judith Rita Schwartz, Dec. 24, 1972; 1 child, Jason Samuel. BS, Columbia U., N.Y.C., 1966; B of Hebrew Lit., Jewish Theol. Sem. of Am., 1966, M of Hebrew Lit., 1968; MA, NYU, 1969; PhD, U. Chgo., 1978; DHL (hon.), Jewish Theol. Sem. Am., 1996. Ordained rabbi, 1970. Prof. Jewish philosophy and mysticism Spertus Coll. Judaica, Chgo., 1970—, v.p. acad. affairs, 1984-2001. Author: Judaism, 1978, Encountering the Holocaust, 1979, Abraham Joshua Heschel, 1979, Garden of the Generations, 1981, Jerzy Kosinski: Literary Alarm Clock, 1981, Mystical Theology and Social Dissent, 1982, The Golem Legend, 1985, Contents and Contexts, 1987, Thank God, 1989, In Partnership with God: Contemporary Jewish Law and Ethics, 1990, No Religion Is an Island, 1991, Toward a Jewish Theology, 1991, How To Be a Jew: Ethical Teachings of Judaism, 1992, The Theological Heritage of Polish Jews, 1995, Sparks Amongst the Ashes: The Spiritual Legacy of Polish Jewry, 1997, Crafting the Soul: Creating Your Life as a Work of Art, 1998, Why Be Good?, 1998, John Paul II and Interreligious Dialogue, 1999, Perché Essere Buonil?, 1999, Per Que Ser Bueno?, 1999, Jewish Ethics for the Twenty-First Century, 2000, Creating an Ethical Jewish Life, 2001; contbr. articles to profl. jours. Recipient Man of Reconciliation award Polish Coun. Christians and Jews, 1992, Presdl. medal, Officer of Order of Merit, Republic of Poland, 1995. Mem. Midwest Jewish Studies Assn. (founding pres.), Am. Philos. Assn., Assn. for Jewish Studies, Rabbinical Assembly, Am. Acad. Religion, The Authors Guild. Republican. Avocations: cooking, book collecting. Office: Spertus Coll Judaica 618 S Michigan Ave Chicago IL 60605-1901 E-mail: bsherwin@spertus.edu.

SHERWOOD, JAMES ALAN, physician, scientist, educator; b. Oneida County, N.Y., Jan. 4, 1953; s. Robert Merriam and Sally (Trevett-Edgett) S. AB, Hamilton Coll., 1974; MD, Columbia U., 1978. Diplomate Nat. Bd. Med. Examiners, Am. Bd. Internal Medicine. Intern Duke U. Med. Ctr., Durham, N.C., 1978-79; resident physician Strong Meml. Hosp., Rochester, N.Y., 1979-81; fellow U. Rochester Sch. Medicine and Dentistry, 1981-83, NIH, Bethesda, Md., 1983-86; rsch. investigator Walter Reed Army Inst. Rsch., Washington, 1986-92; vis. scientist Clin. Rsch. Ctr., Kenya Med. Rsch. Inst., Nairobi, 1987-92; physician Saradidi Rural Health Programme, Nyilima, Kenya, 1987-92; rsch. cons. Rockville, Md., 1992-93; physician St. Mary's Hosp., Waterbury, Conn., 1993—; clin. instr. Sch. Medicine, Yale U., 1993-98; pvt. practice Conn., 1998—. Founding donor Yale Univ.-Kazan State Med. U. Russian Fedn. fellow exch. program. Contbr. chpt. to book, articles to profl. jours. Cmty. svc. vol. The Door, N.Y.C., 1976-77; vol. physician Washington Free Clinic, 1985-87; charity Sisters of St. Joseph of Chambery, 1993-98, Mulago Hosp., Makerere U., Kampala, Uganda. Lt. col. M.C., USAR, 1986-92. Recipient Norton prize in chemistry, 1974, Underwood prize in chemistry, 1974. Fellow Am. Coll. Physicians; mem. Med. Soc. D.C., Am. Fedn. Clin. Rsch., Am. Soc. Tropical Medicine and Hygiene, Conn. State Med. Soc., New Haven County Med. Assn., Muthaiga Club, Phi Beta Kappa, Sigma Xi. Avocations: drawing, book collecting. Home and Office: PO Box 850 Watertown CT 06795-0850

SHERWOOD, JOAN KAROLYN SARGENT, retired career counselor; b. Wichita, Kans., July 11, 1934; d. James Wirth and Ann K. (Freeburg) Sargent; m. Howard Kenneth Sherwood, Jan. 26, 1956 (div. 1966); children: Diane Elizabeth, Karolyn Sherwood, David Matthew. BS, Kans. State U., 1956; MA, Wichita State U., 1964; PhD, U. Kans., 1978. Asst. dir. student fin. aid U. Kans., Lawrence, 1973-78, asst. vice chancellor/student affairs, 1978-81, U. Mo., Kansas City, 1981-84; v.p. student affairs Western Wash. U., Bellingham, 1984-87; pres./owner Corp. Tng. Assurance, Kansas City, 1987-95; career coord. Park Univ., Parkville, Mo., 1995-01; ret., 2001. Program chair Phi Delta Kappa, Lawrence, 1983-84; initiation chair Phi Kappa Phi, Kansas City, 1983-84; organizer Singles Connection, Kansas City, 1983-84; creator SummerStart, Bellingham, 1988-89. Contbr.: Theatre Companies of the World, 1986; female voice: (film) Junction City, 1973; editor Case Studies in the Governance of Higher Edn., 1982, Nat. Assn. of Student Personnel Adminstrs. Alcohol Policies and Practices Among Colls. and Univs., 1987. Long range planning coord. Ch. Redeemer, Kansas City, 1994; workshop facilitator South Side Jr. C. of C., Kansas City, 1991; presenter Centurians, Kansas City, 1982; spkr. Pi Lambda Theta, 1983; vol., resident mgr. Hillcrest Ministries, 1996-99. NDEA fellow, 1969. Mem. ASTD, Phi Kappa Phi. Democrat. Roman Catholic. Avocations: creative writing, reading, films. Home: Unit 2204 2421 Yellowstone Wichita KS 67215 Office: Vista Vols Cmtys in Schs Alcott Acad 3400 E Murdock Wichita KS 67208

SHERWOOD, PATRICIA WARING, artist, educator; b. Columbia, SC, Dec. 19, 1933; d. Clark du Val and Florence (Yarbrough) Waring; widowed; children: Cheryl Sherwood Kraft, Jana Sherwood Kern, Marikay Sherwood Taitt. BFA magna cum laude, Calif. State U., Hayward, 1970; MFA, Mills Coll., Oakland, Calif., 1974; postgrad., San Jose State U., 1980-86. Cert. tchr., Calif. Tchr. De Anza Jr. Coll., Cupertino, Calif., 1970-78, Foothill Jr. Coll., Los Altos, Calif., 1972-78, West Valley Jr. Coll., Saratoga, Calif., 1978—. Artist-in-residence Centrum Frans Masereel, Kasterlee, Belgium, 1989. One-woman shows include Triton Mus., Santa Clara, Calif., 1968, 2002, RayChem Corp., Sunnyvile, Calif., 1969, Palo Alto (Calif.) Cultural Ctr., 1977, Los Gatos (Calif.) Mus., 1992, Stanford U. faculty club, Palo Alto, 1993, d.p. Fong Gallery, San Jose, Calif., 1995, 97, Heritage Bank, San Jose, 1997, City Jr. Coll., d.p. Fong Gallery, San Jose, 1997, City Coll., San Jose, Calif., 1997, West Valley Coll., Saratoga, Calif., 1998, Mus. West, Palo Alto, 2000-2001, Triton Mus., Santa Clara, 2001; exhibited in group shows at Tressider Union Stanford U., 1969, Oakland (Calif.) Mus. Kaiser Ctr., 1969, Sonoma (Calif.) State Coll., 1969, Bank Am., San Francisco, 1969, Alrich Gallery, San Francisco, U. Calif. Santa Clara, 1967, Charles and Emma Frye Mus., Seattle, 1968, Eufrat Gallery DeAnza Coll., Cupertino, 1975, San Jose Mus. Art, 1976, Lytton Ctr., Palo Alto, 1968 (1st award), Zellerbach Ctr., San Francisco, 1970, Works Gallery, San Jose, 1994, Inst. Contemporary Art, San Jose, 1997, Triton Mus. Art, Santa Clara, Calif., 1997, 98, San Jose Inst. Contemporary Art, 1998, San Jose City Coll. Artists Forum, 1998, West Valley Jr. Coll., Saratoga, Calif., 1998, Calvin Charles Gallery, Scottsdale, Ariz.; represented in permanent collections Mills Coll., Bank Am., San Francisco, Heritage Bank, San Jose, Stanford U., Palo Alto, Calif., San Jose U., Smithsonian Inst. Nat. Mus. Am. Art, WAshington, 2002. Art judge student show Stanford U., Palo Alto, 1977; mem. d.p. Fong Gallery, San Jose, Calif., 1994, J.J. Brooking Gallery, San Francisco, Mus. West Gallery, Palo Alto, Calif., Gallery Ocean Avenue, Carmel, Calif., 2002, Bryant Street Gallery, Palo Alto, 2003, Calvin Charles Gallery, Scottsdale, Ariz. Nat. Endowment for Arts/We. States Art Fedn. fellow, 1994. Mem. NEA, Calif. Print Soc., Womens Caucus for Arts, Internat. Platform Assn., Smithsonian Instn., Nat. Mus. Am. Art. Home: 1500 Arriba Ct Los Altos CA 94024-5956

SHERWOOD, ROBERT PETERSEN, retired sociology educator; b. Black Diamond, Wash., May 17, 1932; s. James Brazier and Zina (Petersen) S.; m. Merlene Burningham, Nov. 21, 1951; children: Robert Lawrence, Richard William, Rolene, RaNae. BS, U. Utah, 1956, MS, 1957; EdD, U. Calif., Berkeley, 1965. Tchr. Arden-Carmichael Sch. Dist., Carmichael, Calif., 1957-59, vice prin. jr. high, 1960-61, prin. jr. high, 1962-65; v.p., prin. San Juan Unified Sch. Dist., Sacramento, 1966-70; assoc. prof. Calif. State U., Sacramento, 1966-71; dir. outreach progs. Am. River Coll., Sacramento, 1971-73, acting assoc. dean of instrn., 1973-74, prof. sociology, 1970-92, chmn. sociology/anthropology dept., 1980-86, retired, 1992. Pres. acad. senate Am. River Coll., 1990-91. With USN, 1953-55. Recipient Merit Recognition award, Boy Scouts Am., 1989. Mem. NEA, Calif. Tchrs. Assn., Faculty Assn. Calif. Community Colls., Western Assn. Schs. and Colls., Calif. Fedn. Coll. Profs., Phi Delta Kappa (life). Mem. Lds Ch. Avocations: reading, writing, woodworking, travel. Home: 4053 Esperanza Dr Sacramento CA 95864-3069

SHESKA, JEROME WALLACE, physical education educator; b. Allentown, Pa., July 27, 1946; s. Wallace and Mary (Thorrick) S.; m. Cynthia Ippolito, Nov. 21, 1976; children: Tara, Mark. BS, East Stroudsburg U., 1968, MEd, 1981. Tchr. So. Cayuga Cen. Sch., Poplar Ridge, N.Y., 1968-69, Morris Hills Regional Sch. Dist., Denville, N.J., 1969-87; asst. prof. East Stroudsburg (Pa.) U., 1987—. Bd. dirs. Polono Cup Soccer Camps, Inc., East Stroudsburg; "A" lic. coach U.S. Soccer Fedn., Colo., 1979—; presenter profl. confs.; guest panelist L.I. Soccer Conv., 1989; participant Nat. Divsn. II Soccer Ethics Com., 1989-92. With U.S. Army, 1969-71, Vietnam. Named Coach of Yr., Mid. Atlantic region Intercollegiate Soccer Assn. Am., 1985, 87, 89. Mem. AAHPERD, Pa. State Athletic Conf. (past pres., Coach of Yr. 1989), Nat. Soccer Coaches Assn., Kiwanis. Republican. Roman Catholic. Office: East Stroudsburg Univ Koehler Field House East Stroudsburg PA 18301

SHETH, JAGDISH NANCHAND, business administration educator; b. Rangoon, Burma, Sept. 3, 1938; came to U.S., 1961, naturalized, 1975. s. Nanchand Jivraj and Diwaliben Sheth; m. Madhuri Ratilal Shah, Dec. 22, 1962; children: Reshma J., Raju J. B.Com. with honors, U. Madras, 1960; MBA, U. Pitts., 1962; PhD, 1966. Research asso., asst. prof. Grad. Sch. Bus., Columbia U., 1963-65; asst. prof. M.I.T., 1965-66, Columbia U., 1966-69; asso. prof. bus. adminstrn. U. Ill., Urbana, 1969-71, acting head dept., 1970-72, prof. and research prof., 1971-73, I.B.A. Disting. prof. and research prof., 1973-79, Walter H. Stellner Disting. prof. and research prof., 1979-83; Robert E Brooker Disting. prof. mktg. and research U. So. Calif., Los Angeles, 1983-91; Charles H. Kellstadt prof. mktg. Emory U., Atlanta, 1991—. Founder, dir. Ctr. for Telecommunications Mgmt. U. So. Calif, 1985—, Ctr. Relationship Mktg. Emory U., 1992; vis. prof. Indian Inst. Mgmt., 1968; vis. lectr. Internat. Mktg. Inst., Harvard U., 1969; Albert Frey vis. prof. mktg. U. Pitts., 1974; condr. seminars for industry and govt.; cons. to industry. Author: (with John A. Howard) The Theory of Buyer Behavior, 1969, (with S.P. Sethi) Multinational Business Operations: Advanced Readings, 4 vols, 1973, (with A. Woodside and P. Bennett) Consumer and Industrial Buying Behavior, 1977; (with Bruce Newman): A Theory of Political Choice Behavior, 1986; (with Dennis Garrett) Marketing Theory, 1986; (with S. Ram) Bringing Innovation to Market; (with Gary Frazier) Theories of Marketing Practice; (with Milind Lele) The Customer is Key; editor: Models of Buyer Behavior, 1964, (with Peter L. Wright) Marketing Analysis for Societal Problems, 1974, Multivariable Methods for Market and Survey Research, 1977, Winning Back Your Market, 1984, (with David Gardener and Dennis Garrett) Marketing Theory: Evolution and Evaluation, 1988, also (with Abdol Reza and Goli Eslghi) 9 vols. on global bus., 1989-90, (with Bruce Newman and Barbara Gross) Consumption Values and Choice Behavior, 1990; (with Bruce Newman and B. Miltal) Customer Behavior: Consumer Behavior and Beyond, 1998; (with Banwari Mittal) Value Space, 2001; (with Rajendra Sisodia) The Rule of Three, 2002; series editor Research in Marketing, 1978—00, Research in Consumer Behavior, 1984—86, (with A. Sobel) Clients for Life, 2000, (with A. Parvatiyar) Handbook of Relationship Marketing, 2000, Internet Marketing, 2000; contbr. articles profl. jours. Recipient Viktor Mataja medal Austrian Rsch. Soc., 1976, Mktg. Educator award Sales and Mktg. Execs. Internat., 1991, 99; Mgmt. Program for Execs. fellow, S & H Green Stamps fellow, 1963-64, Disting. fellow Internat. Engring. Consortium, 1997. Fellow APA, Acad. Mktg. Sci. (Disting. fellow 1996, Mktg. Educator award 1989); mem. Am. Mktg. Assn. (P.D. Converse award 1992). Home: 1626 Mason Mill Rd NE Atlanta GA 30329-4133

SHETTY, TARANATH, neurologist, educator; b. Mangalore, India, Apr. 29, 1938; s. Shankar and Bhavani Shetty; m. Urmila Shetty, Dec. 1972; children: Neeta, Teena, Geema. MBBS, Madras U., 1962; MD, Lucknow U., 1965. Diplomate Am. Bd. Pediatrics; diplomate in neurology with spl. competence in child neurology Am. Bd. Psychiatry and Neurology; diplomate with added qualification in clin. neurophysiology Am. Bd. Electroencephalography. Resident in pediatrics Children's Hosp. Med. Ctr., Boston, 1967-68, fellow in neurology, 1968-69; rsch. fellow in neurology Harvard U., Boston, 1968-69, tchg. fellow, 1971-72; resident in neurology Boston City Hosp., 1969-72; instr. Brown U., Providence, 1973-74, asst. prof., 1974-79, clin. assoc. prof., 1979—; dir. pediatric neurology R.I. Hosp., Providence, 1976—. Fellow Am. Acad. Neurology, Royal Coll. Physicians Can., Univ. Cub (Providence). Hindu. Home: 80 Clarendon Ave Providence RI 02906-5826 Office: 120 Dudley St Providence RI 02905-2436 E-mail: tara_shetty@hotmail.com.

SHEVIN, DAVID A. English literature educator; b. June 1, 1951; MFA, Bowling Green State U., 1976; PhD, U. Cin., 1986. Assoc. prof. English Miami U., Oxford, Ohio, 1985-87; prof. English Tiffin (Ohio) U., 1987—2001; assoc. prof. English Central State U., Wilberforce, Ohio, 2001—. Address: Apt 6 1453 N Broad St Fairborn OH 45324-5576

SHEWMAKER, KENNETH EARL, history educator; b. L.A., June 26, 1936; s. James Virgil and Jeanette M. (Greenberg) S.; m. Elisabeth L. Spalteholz, June 12, 1960; children: Richard Glenn, Nancy Jeanette. BS, Concordia Tchrs. Coll., 1960; MA, U. Calif., Berkeley, 1961; PhD, Northwestern U., 1966. Instr. Northwestern U., Evanston, Ill., 1965-66; asst. prof. Coll. William and Mary, Williamsburg, Va., 1966-67; from asst. prof. to assoc. prof. Dartmouth Coll., Hanover, N.H., 1967-78, prof. history, 1978—, acting chair dept. history, 1985-86, chmn. dept. history, 1986-89. Author: Americans and Chinese Communists, 1927-45: A Persuading Encounter, 1971 (Stuart L. Bernath prize 1972); editor: Papers of Daniel Webster, Diplomatic Papers, Vol. 1, 1841-1843, 1983, Vol. 2, 1850-1852, 1987, Daniel Webster, The Completest Man, 1990; contbr. articles to profl.

jours. Recipient Disting. Tchg. awards Dartmouth Coll., 1986, 96. Mem. N.H. Hist. Soc., Orgn. Am. Historians, Soc. Historians Am. Fgn. Rels. Lutheran. Avocations: fly fishing, fly tying. Office: Dept History Dartmouth Coll Hanover NH 03755

SHIBLEY, RALPH EDWIN, JR., special education and career-technical education; b. Columbus, Ohio, Dec. 31, 1944; s. Ralph Edwin and Dorothy Ann (Evans) S.; m. P. Kathleen Phillips, July 23, 1966; children: Christine Marie, Margot Marie. BSc in Edn., Ohio State U., 1971, MA, 1981, PhD, 1984. Cert. spl. edn. supr., Ohio. Spl. edn. tchr. Columbus City Schs., 1974—80; dir. R & D Six Pence Sch., Columbus, 1980—81; grad. rsch. assoc. Ohio State U., Columbus, 1980—84, program dir. Nisonger Ctr., 1984—87; prof. edn. U. Rio Grande, Ohio, 1987—, dir. Career-Tech. Tchr. Edn. Program, 1998—. Adj. prof. Bowling Green State U., 1994—, Ohio Dominican Coll.; vis. prof. W.Va. U., 1997; cons. Gallipolis (Ohio) Devel. Ctr., 1989-90; project site coord. U. Cin., Gallipolis, 1990-91. Author articles and textbook revs. Apptd. State of Ohio Com. Practitioners for Career-Tech. and Adult Edn., 2000-2002; mem. 1st Class Nat. Leadership Inst. Career Tech. Edn. Named Tchr. of Yr. Cen. Ohio Soc. for Autistic Children, 1977; recipient cert. of appreciation Coalition of Handicapped Students, 1988; Ohio Career Tech. Leadership Inst. fellow, 1999. Mem. ASCD, Coun. for Exceptional Children (past pres., editor Ohio fedn. tchr. edn. divsn.), Ohio Fedn. Coun. for Exceptional Children (past pres.), Interuniv. Coun. for Tchr. Edn., Am. Career-Tech. Assn., Epsilon Pi Tau (Laureate citation), Phi Delta Kappa. Democrat. Roman Catholic. Avocations: photography, golf, fishing. Bus. Home: 3590 Milton Ave Columbus OH 43214-4045 Office: U Rio Grande Sch of Edn Rio Grande OH 45674 E-mail: rshibley@rio.edu., rshibley@columbus.rr.com.

SHICK, RICHARD ARLON, finance educator; b. DuBois, Pa., July 17, 1943; s. Arlon Elmer and Melva Elizabeth (Bartell) S.; m. Linda B. Shick; children: Richard Arlon, Charles, Elizabeth. BS, SUNY, Buffalo, 1966, MBA, 1968, PhD, 1972. Asst. prof. banking and fin. U. Ga., Athens, 1970-75; assoc. prof. fin. St. Bonaventure (N.Y.) U., 1975-78, chmn. fin. dept., 1975-78, acting chmn. mktg. dept., 1976-99; assoc. prof. fin. Canisius Coll., Buffalo, 1978-99, prof. fin., 1999—, dean Richard J. Wehle Sch. Bus., 1979—2002. Bd. dirs. Better Bus. Bur., 1990-95, Statler Culinary program Emerson H.S., buffalo, 1992-98; sec., treas., bd. dirs. Chautauqua Brick Co., 1995—. Mem. editl. bd. Jour. Bus. Rsch., 1973-76, Jour. Fin. Rsch., 1977-81, Jour. Econs. and Bus., 1984-88, Fin. Rev., 1976-87, editor, 1981-82; contbr. articles to profl. jours. Chmn. mayor's rev. com. Buffalo Bd. Edn.; bd. dirs. Buffalo Alliance Edn., Old Ft. Niagara; bd. dirs. Buffalo Philharm. Orch., 1995-97, treas., 1996-97, chmn. devel. com.; mem. N.Y. State Com. to Promote Pub. Trust and Confidence in the Legal System, 1999; bd. dirs. Studio Arena Theatre, 2001—, v.p. bd., pres.-elect. NDEA fellow, 1966-68; U.S. Savs. and Loan League grantee, 1974, St. Bonaventure U. grantee, 1976, U.s. Govt. Title III grantee, 1999. Mem. Am. Fin. Assn., Ea. Fin. Assn., Southwestern Fin. Assn., So. Fin. Assn., Western Fin. Assn., Am. Mgmt. Assn., Jesuit Colls. and Univs. Deans of Bus. Schs. (treas. 1983-84, v.p. 1985-89, pres. 1987-88), Middle Atlantic Assn. Colls. and Schs. Bus. Adminstrn. (v.p. 1985-86, pres. 1986-87), Country Club Buffalo, Automobile Club Western N.Y. (bd. dirs. 1995-99, exec. com. 1998-99, 2001), Beta Gamma Sigma, Alpha Kappa Psi, Di Gamma, Alpha Sigma Lambda, Alpha Signa Nu. Republican. Home: 157 Crestwood Ln Buffalo NY 14221-1508 Office: Canisius Coll 2001 Main St Buffalo NY 14208-1035 E-mail: shick@canisius.edu.

SHIDELER, ROSS PATRICK, foreign language and comparative literature educator, writer, translator, poet; b. Denver, Apr. 12, 1936; BA, San Francisco State U., 1958; MA, U. Stockholm, 1963; PhD, U. Calif., Berkeley, 1968. Instr. in comparative lit. U. Calif., Berkeley, 1967-68; asst. prof. English Hunter Coll., N.Y.C., 1968-69; asst. prof. Scandinavian lang. and comparative lit. UCLA, 1969-73, assoc. prof., 1973-79, prof., 1979—; chmn. program in comparative lit., 1979-86, 92-96. Author: (monograph) Voices Under the Ground: Themes and Images in the Poetry of Gunnar Ekelof, 1973, Per Olov Enquist-A Critical Study, 1984, Questioning the Father: From Darwin to Zola, Ibsen, Strindberg and Hardy, 1999; translator: (plays) The Night of the Tribades (Per Olov Enquist), 1977, The Hour of the Lynx (Per Olov Enquist), 1990; co-editor (with Kathleen L. Komar): Lyrical Symbols and Narrative Transformations, Essays in Honor of Ralph Freedman, 1998; U.S. assoc. editor Swedish Book Rev., 1984—. Fellow, NDFL, 1964, NDEA, 1965, Fulbright-Hays, 1966—67. Mem. MLA (exec. com. divsn. Scandinavian Langs. and Lits. 1993-97), Soc. Advancement Scandinavian Studies (exec. coun. 1985-89, v.p. 1997-99, pres. 1999-2001), Am. Comparative Lit. Assn., Assn. Depts. and Programs Comparative Lit. (exec. com. 1993-94, 94-98). Office: UCLA Dept Comparative Lit Los Angeles CA 90024

SHIELDS, ANDREA LYN, psychologist, educator; b. Montgomery, Ala., Aug. 19, 1947; d. Theodore and Alma Lea Shields. BA, U. Ariz., 1969; MA in Psychology, U. of the Pacific, 1971; PhD in Clin. Psychology, Fielding Inst., Santa Barbara, Calif., 1977. Trainer So. Ariz. Mental Health Ctr., Tucson, 1968-69; rsch. asst. Stockton (Calif.) State Hosp., 1970; instr. psychology Modesto (Calif.) Jr. Coll., 1970-71, San Bernardino (Calif.) Valley Coll., 1971-72; instr. for Army recruiters Columbia (Mo.) Coll., 1974; instr., head psychology dept. Crafton Hills Coll., Yucaipa, Calif., 1972-88; adminstrv. dir. U. San Francisco, 1980-82; pvt. practice, Rancho Cucamonga, Calif., 1981—; fellow Prescribing Psychologists Register, 1997—. Presenter in field. Pres. inland unit Am. Cancer Soc., 1993-96. Mem. Rotary (bd. dirs. 1993-96. 2002--). Avocations: herbs, hiking. Office: 9045 Haven Ave Ste 107 Rancho Cucamonga CA 91730-5427

SHIELDS, CARLA FAYE, elementary school educator; b. Steubenville, Ohio, Mar. 3, 1961; d. Charles Lowell and Alice Jean (Weals) S. BS in Elem. Edn., Malone Coll., 1983; MS in Elem. Edn., U. Dayton, 1988. Cert. tchr., Ohio; validation in early edn. of handicapped, permanent cert., 2002. Substitute tchr. Buckeye Local Schs., Rayland, Ohio, 1983-84; learning disabled program tutor Smithfield (Ohio) Elem. Sch., 1984-88; self contained tchr. 4th grade, sci. tchr. 2d grade St. Joseph the Worker Sch., Weirton, W.Va., 1988-90, tchr. kindergarten and 2nd, 3rd, 6th grade sci., 1990-91; tchr. presch. spl. needs John Gregg Elem., Bergholz, Ohio, 1991—97, Irondale (Ohio) Elem. Sch., 1992—; itinerant presch. spl. needs, 2000—. Dir. flag corps Buckeye North H.S., Brilliant, Ohio, 1987. Democrat. Methodist. Avocations: camping, crafts, quilting. Home: 128 Linmar Ave Wintersville OH 43953-4249

SHIELDS, CLEVELAND GEORGE, family therapist, researcher, educator; b. Eldred, Pa., Dec. 4, 1953; s. George Nelson and Geneva (Kelly) S.; m. Linda Kay Dolby, May 6, 1978; children: Emily, Elliot. BS, Pa. State U., 1976; MDiv, Wesley Theol. Sem., 1980; PhD, Purdue U., 1987. Ordained to ministry United Meth. Ch., 1981. Assoc. pastor St. Joseph United Meth. Ch., Ft. Wayne, Ind., 1980-83; instr. U. Rochester, N.Y., 1987-88, sr. instr., 1988-89, asst. prof. family medicine and psychiatry, 1989-94, assoc. prof. family medicine and psychiatry, 1995—. Contbr. articles to profl. publs. Bd. dirs. Respite Care, Inc., Rochester, 1989-94, Alzheimer Assn., Rochester, 1989-97. Mem. Am. Assn. Marriage and Family Therapy, Gildas' Club. Office: Dept Family Medicine U Rochester Highland Hosp 885 South Ave Rochester NY 14620-2318

SHIELDS, CYNTHIA ROSE, college administrator; b. Monterey, Calif., June 1, 1954; d. William Lawrence and Rose Virdell Jackson; m. Franklin Shields, Sept. 19, 1981; 1 child, Brett. AA, San Francisco City Coll., 1980; BS, U. San Francisco, 1986; MPA, Golden Gate U., 1988; MS, Nat. U., 1994; EdD in Ednl. Leadership, U. Calif., Davis, 1997. Cert. community coll. instr., supr., Calif. Acct. exec. KFSN-TV, Fresno, Calif., 1982-85; instr. Merced County (Calif.) Schs., 1985-89; gen. mgr., owner Ad Line Advt., Merced, 1986-96; instr. Merced Coll., 1989-90; youth outreach specialist, 1990-91; re-entry coord., 1991-98; ednl. cons., 1998—. Sr. assoc. Sch. Leadership Ctr., Calif. Sch. Leadership Acad., 1989-92. Author curriculum materials. Bd. dirs. Merced Cmty. Med. Ctr. Found., 1991, MUHSD Found., 1992-94; mem. citizens adv. bd. Merced City Sch. Dist., 1985-87; chmn. Merced Conv. and Vis. Bur., 1991; coord. Merced Cmty. Housing Resource Bd., 1988-90; mem. Leaders program Nat. Inst. for Leadership Devel., 1996. Mem. AAUW, Merced City C. of C. (bd. dirs. 1991-93, v.p. fin. and ops. 1993-94), Phi Delta Kappa. Democrat. Avocations: community volunteer, reading, golf, cycling.

SHIELDS, JAMES JOSEPH, education administrator, educator, author; b. Phila., Feb. 11, 1935; s. James Joseph and Lena Josephine (Dyer) S. (dec.). BS in Polit. Sci., Saint Joseph's U., 1956; EdM, Temple U., 1959; EdD, Columbia U., 1963. Asst. dir. internat. studies Tchrs. Coll., Columbia U., N.Y.C., 1961, field rschr., Tchrs. for East Africa Program N.Y.C. and Kampala, Uganda, 1961-62; asst. prof. history and philosophy of edn. SUNY, New Paltz, 1962-64; asst. prof. comparative and internat. edn. CUNY, N.Y.C., 1964-69, assoc. prof., 1969-75, prof., 1975-98, prof. emeritus, 1998, head, Sch. Adminstrn. Program, 1983-85, chair dept. social and psychol. founds., 1988-90; dir. Japan Initiative, 1986-98; projects dir. Ctr. for Edn. Outreach and Innovation Tchrs. Coll. Columbia U., N.Y.C., 1998—. Cons. Inst. for Ednl. Devel., N.Y.C., 1968-71, Equitable Life Ins. Co., N.Y.C., 1981, N.Y.C. Bd. Edn. Dist. 4, 1996-97, Time Mag., 1998, Inst. Internat. Edn., 1998-99; vis. rsch. prof. Tokyo Met. U., 1986-95; vis. prof. Tchrs. Coll., Columbia U., 1965-67, 93-95, 98, 2000—, Yale U., 1997; mem. evaluation bd. Nat. Coun. on Accreditation of Tchr. Edn., Washington, 1970-75; assoc. Columbia U., Univ. Seminar on Modern Japan, N.Y.C., 1987—, chair, 1990-91. Author: Education in Community Development: Its Function in Technical Assistance, 1967, Problems and Prospects in International Education, 1968, Foundations of Education: Dissenting Views, 1974, Japanese Schooling: Patterns of Socialization Equality and Political Control, 1989, rev. edit. 1993; author numerous book chpts., monographs and book reviews; contbr. numerous articles to profl. jours. Mem. Pub. Edn. Assn. Task Force on a Reconstructed Ednl. Sys., N.Y.C., 1977-78, Pub. Edn. Assn. Task Force on Tchr. Selection, N.Y.C., 1981; mem. N.Y. Urban Coalition, 1982-84, Alumni Coun., Tchrs. Coll. Columbia U., 1993-99, 2000—. With USAR, 1959-59. Grantee SUNY Rsch. Found., 1964, Fulbright Travel grantee, 1964, N.Y. State Edn. Dept., 1969-72, Rsch. Found. CUNY, 1980-81, Japan-U.S. Friendship Commn., 1986-89, CUNY, City Coll. Provost Fund, 1988-89, 89-90; Japan Found. Ctr. for Global Partnership, 1994, The U.S.-Japan Found., 1994-96, The Tokyo Found, 1998-2000; recipient Wyo. Gov.'s Youth Coun. award, 1974, Higher Edn. award Holy Family Coll., Phila., 1990, Ann. Gertrude Langsam Ednl. Reconstrn. award Adelphi U., 1992; postdoctoral fellow Yale U., New Haven, 1967-68. Hon. fellow Comparative and Internat. Edn. Soc. (N.E. region conf. coord. 1984, bd. dirs. 1992-95); mem. Am. Ednl. Studies Assn. (founder, pres. 1973-74, exec. coun. 1970-75), Carnegie Coun. on Ethics and Internat. Affairs (bd. trustees 1998—, vice chmn. 2001—), Japan Soc. of N.Y., Internat. House of Japan, Soc. for Ednl. Reconstrn. (exec. com. 1973—), N.Y. Athletic Club (N.Y.C.), Beaux Arts Alliance. Avocations: collecting long island painters (1850-1950), travel, gardening. Address: Trump Pl 200 Riverside Blvd Apt 11N New York NY 10069-0911 also: 42 Old Town Xing Southampton NY 11968-5015 E-mail: jshieldsII@juno.com.

SHIELDS, JOHN CHARLES, American studies and African American studies and literature educator; b. Phoenix, Oct. 29, 1944; s. Granville Blaine and Elizabeth Merle (Hartgraves) S. BA, U. Tenn., Knoxville, 1967, MA in Coll. Teaching, 1969, PhD, 1978; EdS, George Peabody Coll., 1975. Tchr. English Sevier County High Sch., Sevierville, Tenn., 1967-68; head dept. English Battle Ground Acad., Franklin, Tenn., 1969-71; dir. academics Brentwood Acad., Nashville, 1971-73, Columbia (Tenn.) Mil. Acad., 1973-74; instr. U. Tenn., Knoxville, 1978-79; asst. prof. Ill. State U., Normal, 1979-86, assoc. prof. English, 1986-93, prof. English, 1993—. Cons. Ency. Britannica, Oxford Companion to African Am. Lit., Norton Anthology African Am. Lit., others; project dir. conf. on Phillis Wheatley NEH, 1983-85; faculty advisor Native Am. Student Soc. Ill. State U., 1990; Coll. of Arts and Sci. Lectr., Ill. State U., 2003—; mem. doctoral dissertation com. Assoc. editor Style, DeKalb, Ill., 1988-90, guest editor, 1990—; editor: The Collected Works of Phillis Wheatley, 1988, paperback, 1989; selected to be a mem. of the Adv. Bd. of The Greenwood Ency. of Am. Poetry, (7 vol.) contbr., adv. editor, contbr. Oxford Companion to African Am. Lit., 1997—, Am. Nat. Biography, 24 vol., 1994—; contbr. New Dictionary of Nat. Biography, Great Britain, 1995—; author: The Am. Aeneas: Classical Origins of the American Self, Univ. of Tenn. Press, 2001 (nominated for Ralph Waldo Emerson prize, John Hope Franklin award, Susan M. Glasscoch Interdisciplinary Book prize and Lora Romero First Book prize); contbr. articles to lit. jour. and chpt. to books; manuscript reviewer various presses and jour. Spokesperson for Native Am. citizens, 1990—. Ford Found. fellow, 1968-69, Soc. for Humanities fellow Cornell U., 1984-85, NEH fellow, 1983, 84, 89, 93, John C. Hodges Teaching Excellence award, 1969. Mem. MLA, Soc. Early Americanists, Internat. Soc. for 18th-Century Studies, Am. Studies Assn., Melville Soc., Coll. Lang. Assn., Phi Mu Alpha Sinfonia, Alpha Phi Omega, Sigma Nu. Unitarian Universalist. Avocations: piano, singing, native american culture, archaeology, rare book collecting. Home: 1412 Donegal Dr Normal IL 61761-5416

SHIELDS, LAWRENCE THORNTON, orthopaedic surgeon, educator; b. Boston, Oct. 2, 1935; s. George Leo and Catherine Elizabeth (Thornton) S.; m. Karen S. Kraus, Sept. 21, 1968; children: Elizabeth Coulter, Laura Thornton, Sarah Daly, Michael Lawrence. AB, Harvard U., 1957; MD, Johns Hopkins U., 1961. Diplomate Am. Bd. Orthopaedic Surgery. Intern Barnes Hosp., Washington U., St. Louis, 1961—62, resident, 1962—63; resident orthop. surgeon Children's Hosp. Med. Ctr., Boston, 1966—67, Mass. Gen. Hosp., Boston, 1967—68, Peter Bent Brigham, Robert Breck Brigham Hosps., Boston, 1968—69, Harvard Med. Sch., Boston, 1965—69, instr., 1969—; orthop. surgeon Peter Bent Brigham & Women's Hosp., Children's hosps., 1969—, Waltham (Mass.)-Weston Hosp. and Med. Ctr., 1969—, also chief orthop. surgery, pres. med. staff. Mem. Waltham-Weston Orthop. Assocs.; proprietor Boston Athenaeum; mem. staff Hahnemann Hosp., Boston, Newton-Wellesley (Mass.) Hosp.; cons. orthop. surgeon VA Hosp., Boston; mem. faculty Harvard Med. Sch.; vis. scholar Trinity Hall Cambridge U., 1987; hon. prof. New Eng. Coll., Henniker, NH, Sussex, England, 1995; bd. dirs. Wal-West Health Sys., 1986—; pres. Mass. Bay Investment Trust; dir. Waltham Investment Group. Contbr. articles to med. jours. Bd. dirs. Mass. Acad. Emergency Med. Technicians, Waltham Boys' Club; bd. of overseers Boston Lyric Opera, 1993—; trustee, exec. com. Waltham-Weston Hosp. and Med. Ctr. Lt. M.C. USNR, 1963-65. Fellow: ACS, Mass. Hist. Soc. Libr., Am. Acad. Orthop. Surgeons, Mass. Hist. Soc.; mem.: Thomas B. Quigley Sports Medicine Soc. (v.p., pres. 2001—), R. Austen Freeman Soc. (v.p.), Mass. Med. Soc. (v.p. 1982—83, councillor), Mass. Orthop. Assn. (sec. 1986—, bd. dirs.), Royal Soc. Medicine, N.Y. Acad. Scis., Cox & Co., Boston Lyric Opera (bd. overseers 1993), English Speaking Union (bd. dirs.), Academie Brillat-Savarin, Confrerie de La Chaine des Rotisseurs (elected 1996), Waltham Hist. Soc., Trollope Soc. (founding mem., bd. dirs., London), Thoreau Soc., Internat. Consular Corps (hon.), Charles River Dist. (pres. 1982—83, treas., exec. com.), Titanic Hist. Soc., Boston Opera Assn. (bd. dirs.), Harvard Mus. Assn., Emerson Soc., Handel and Hayden Soc. (bd. overseers), Les Amis d'Escoffier Soc., L'Ordre Mondial (elected 1999), St. Crisplin's Soc. Boston (pres. 1991—, founding mem.), USS Wasp CV-19 Assn., Theodore Roosevelt Assn. New Eng. (founding), East India, Devonshire Sports and Pub. Schs. Club (London), New Eng. Orthop. Club, Boston Orthop. Club, St. Botolph Club (Boston), Bull Dog Terries, Clover Club Boston, Union Club Boston, Harvard Club, Algonquin Club Boston (pres. 1990—, bd. dirs.), Rotary, Pi Eta (Harvard). Home: 9 Beverly Rd Newton MA 02461-1112 Office: 721 Huntington Ave Boston MA 02115-6010 also: 20 Hope Ave Ste 314 Waltham MA 02453-2717 E-mail: ltshields@mcb.harvard.edu.

SHIELDS, MARLENE SUE, elementary school educator; b. Denver, Apr. 7, 1939; d. Morris and Rose (Sniderman) Goldberg; m. Charles H. Cohen, Dec. 22, 1957 (dec.); children: Lee, Richard, Monica; m. Harlan Shields. BA magna cum laude, Met. State Coll., 1980; MA, U. No. Colo., 1986. Preschool tchr. Temple Emanuel, Denver, 1970-75; tchr. Kindergarten Temple Sinai, Denver, 1975-80; tchr. pre-Kindergarten St. Mary's Acad., Englewood, Colo., 1980-83; tchr. Beach Court Elem., Denver, 1983-86, Valverde Sch., Denver, 1984-85; tchr. third grade Brown Elem., Denver, 1985-86; tchr. learning disabilities Cowell Elem. Sch., Denver, 1986-87, Sabin Elem. Sch., Denver, 1987-88; tchr. second grade Sabin Elem., Denver, 1988—. Mem. curriculum com. Denver Pub. Sch., 1989—, pers. subcom., 2000-02; citizen amb. Spain joint tchr. conf., 1995. Mem. personal subcom. Sabin Elementary Sch., 2000. Mem. Colo. Coun. Internat. Reading Assn., Nat. Assn. for Young Children, Nat. Tchrs. Colo. Math., Internat. Reading Assn., Carousel of Intervention, Delta Kappa Gamma (sec., v.p., grade level chair), PRIDE (lang. curriculum com., math. curriculum com., impact com., CDM rep. 1994-95), Delta Kappa Gamma (state 1st v.p.). Home: 5800 Big Canon Dr Englewood CO 80111-3516

SHIELDS, PATRICIA LYNN, educational broker, consultant; b. Bklyn. BS in Biology, Bucknell U., 1984; BA in Biology, Rutgers U., 2002; MAT in Biol. Scis., Fairleigh Dickinson U., 2002. Pres., CEO Buttercup's Internat., Inc., Middletown, N.J., 1988—. Office: Buttercup's Internat Inc PO Box 148 Middletown NJ 07748-0148

SHIELDS, RANA COLLEEN, special education educator; b. Midland, Tex., Oct. 2, 1951; d. Robert Campbell and Edith Sue (Alexander) S.; m. Micheal Leggett; children: Daniel Robert Tilly, Casey Michelle Leggett; 1 stepchild, Laurie Ayn Leggett. B of Journalism, U. Tex., 1974; JD magna cum laude, South Tex. U., 1984; MEd in Spl. Edn., S.W. Tex. State U., 1993. Bar: Tex., 1985; cert. generic spl. edn., reading, Tex. City editor Huntsville (Tex.) Item, 1976-78; asst. county atty. Travis County Atty.'s Office, Austin, Tex., 1986-87; tchr. spl. edn. Liberty Hill (Tex.) H.S., 1990-91, Tex. Sch. for the Blind, Austin, 1991-93; grad. rsch. asst. in spl. edn. U. Tex., Austin, spring 1994, tchg. asst. spl. edn., 1995-96; tchr. spl. edn. Liberty Hill Middle Sch., 1997-98; contract spl. edn. monitor Tex. Edn. Agy., 1998—. Asst. casenotes editor: South Tex. Law Jour., 1983. Recipient 1st Pl. Spot News Photography award AP Mng. Editors, 1978, Am. Jurisprudence awards, 1979, 82, 83; named Outstanding Sophomore Journalist, Women in Comm., 1971; Univ. fellow, 1996-97. Mem. Assn. Tex. Profl. Educators, Kappa Delta Pi, Phi Kappa Phi, Pi Lambda Theta.

SHIER, GLORIA BULAN, mathematics educator; b. The Philippines; came to U.S., 1966. d. Melecio Cauilan and Florentina (Cumagun) Bulan; m. Wayne Thomas Shier; children: John Thomas, Marie Teresita, Anna Christina. BS, U. Santo Tomas, Manila, Philippines; MA, U. Ill., 1968; PhD, U. Minn., 1986. Tchr. Cagayan (Philippines) Valley Coll., St. Paul Coll., Manila, Manila Div. City Schs.; asst. prof. U. of East, Manila; rsch. asst. U. Ill., Urbana, 1968-69; instr. Miramar Community Coll., San Diego, 1974-75, Mesa Community Coll., San Diego, 1975-80, Lakewood Community Coll., St. Paul, 1984, U. Minn., Mpls., 1986-87, North Hennepin Community Coll., Brooklyn Park, Minn., 1987—. Cons. PWS Kent Pub. Co., Boston, 1989—. Chairperson Filipino Am. Edn. Assn., San Diego, 1978-79. Fulbright scholar U.S. State Dept., U. Ill., 1966-70; fellow Nat. Sci. Found., Oberlin Coll., 1967; recipient Excellence in Teaching award UN Ednl. Scientific Cultural Organ., U. Philippines, Cert. Commendation award The Gov. of Minn., 1990, Outstanding Filipino in the Midwest Edn. Cat. award 1992, Cavite Assn., 1998, Gintong Pamana Found.; Outstanding Filipino-Am. in Edn. Mem.: Am. Statis. Assn., Minn. Math. Assn. of Two Yr. Colls., Minn. Coun. Tchrs. Math., Internat. Group for Psychology of Math. Edn., Am. Math. Assn. for Two Yr. Colls., Nat. Coun. Tchrs. Math., Philippine-Am. Acad. Sci. and Engring., Math. Assn. Am., Am. Math. Soc., Fil-Minnesotan Assn. (bd. dirs. 1991—), Cultural Soc. Filipino-Ams. (pres. 2001—), Sigma Xi, Phi Kappa Phi. Roman Catholic. Avocation: piano. E-mail: gloria.shier@nhcc.mnscu.edu.

SHIERSHKE, NANCY FAY, artist, educator, property manager; b. St. Helens, Oreg., May 10, 1935; d. David Cline and Matilda Ruth (Pearce) Morrison; m. H. McNeal Kavanagh, Sept. 4. 1955 (dec. Dec. 1978); children: Marjorie L. Wood, David M. Kavanagh, Katherine F. Fiske; m. Richard M. Shiershke, Nov. 29, 1980. AA, Pasadena (Calif.) City Coll., 1956; BA, UCLA, 1965. Substitute elem. sch. tchr., Buena Park, Calif., 1967-69; property mgr. Pky. Cts., Arcadia, Calif., 1977—; libr. Reading Rm., Arcadia, 1979-87; freelance artist Kavanagh-Shiershke Art St., Arcadia, Calif., 1985—; art gallery hostess Descanso Gardens, La Canada, Flintridge, Calif., 1990—; display and sales person Village Fine Arts Gallery, Arcadia, 1991-92; art instr. Tri Cmty. Adult Edn., Covina, Calif., 1994—, Claremont (Calif.) Art Edn., 1998—. Art instr. Claremont (Calif.) Adult Edn. Group shows include Pasadena Presbyn. Ch., 1985—, Hillcrest Ch., 1992—, Descanso Gardens, 1994—, San Gabriel Fine Arts, 1994—. Named Artist of the Yr. Mid Valley art League, 1990; Recipient Best of Show San Gabriel Fine Arts, 1991, Hulsebus award Pasadena Prebyn. Ch., 1996, Best of Show Eagle Rock Rennaissance Pleín Air, 2002. Mem. Nat. Watercolor Soc., San Gabriel Fine Arts, Mid Valley Arts League (Artist of Yr. 1998), East Valley Art Assn., Valley Watercolor Soc., Foothill Creative Arts Group, Water Color West, Calif. Art Club. Home: 505 Vaquero Rd Arcadia CA 91007-6045 Office: 614 E Vine Ave West Covina CA 91791

SHIGEMOTO, APRIL FUMIE, secondary school English language educator; b. Lihue, Hawaii, Apr. 22, 1948; d. Warren Itaru and Edith Yuriko (Yoshimura) Tanaka; m. Tom Hideo Shigemoto, July 21, 1973; children: Taylor, Tyron, Tryson, Thomas-Jay. BA in English, U. Hawaii Manoa, 1970, profl. diploma secondary, 1971. English tchr. Kapaa (Hawaii) H.S. and Intermediate Sch., 1971-81, Kauai H.S. and Intermediate Sch., Lihue, Hawaii, 1981-90, core curriculum coord., 1990—, comprehensive student support svc. dist. resource tchr., 2001, sch. assessment liaison dist. resource tchr., 2002—. Leader Boy Scouts of Am., Lihue, Hawaii, 1982—. Recipient one of seven Status of Women awards, Kauai, Lihue, Hawaii, 1988, Den Leader of the Yr. award Boy Scouts of Am., 1988, Milken Educator's award, Milken Found., L.A., 1992; named Outstanding Working Mother, Garden Island Newspaper, Lihue, Hawaii, 1989, Kauai Dist. Tchr. of Yr., State Dept. Edn., Hawaii, 1990, State Tchr. of Yr., Scottish Rite Order of Free Masons, Honolulu, 1991, one of Kauai's Outstanding Families, Garden Island Newspaper, Hawaii, 1992. Mem. Nat. Coun. Tchrs. of English, Assn. for Supervision and Curriculum Devel., Phi Delta Kappa, Delta Kappa Gamma. Democrat. Avocations: traveling, reading, golfing. Office: Kauai Dist Office 3060 Eiwa St Lihue HI 96766

SHIH, CHIAHO, biomedical researcher, educator; b. Tainan, Taiwan, Jan. 9, 1950; came to U.S., 1975; s. Hai-Tsan and King-Hwa Shih; m. Min-Hui Lin, June 17, 1982; children: Justin, Kelvin. BS, Nat. Taiwan U., Taipei, 1973; PhD, MIT, 1982. Fellow Mass. Gen. Hosp./Harvard Med. Sch., Boston, 1982-85; asst. prof. U. Pa., Phila., 1986-92; assoc. prof. U. Tex. Med. Br., Galveston, 1992—2000, prof., 2000—. Contbr. articles to profl. jours. Pres. Houston chpt. N.Am. Taiwanese Prof. Assn., 1994-95. Recipient W.W. Smith Charitable Trust award, 1986, Rsch. Career Devel. award Nat. Cancer Inst./NIH, 1992-97. Mem. Am. Soc. Virology, Am. Soc. Microbiology, Soc. Chinese Bio-scientists in Am. (pres. Houston chpt. 1996-97). Achievements include discovery and isolation of the first human cancer gene ras and discovery of cancer gene neu, first defective interfering-like virus in human natural infection.

SHIH-CARDUCCI, JOAN CHIA-MO, cooking educator, biochemist, medical technologist, author; b. Rukuan, Chunghua, Taiwan, Dec. 21, 1933; came to U.S., 1955; d. Luke Chiang-hsi and Lien-chin (Chang) Shih; m. Kenneth M. Carducci, Sept. 30, 1960 (dec. July 1988); children: Suzanne R., Elizabeth M. BS in Chemistry, St. Mary Coll., Xavier, Kans., 1959; intern in med. tech., St. Mary's Hosp., Rochester, N.Y., 1960. Med. rschr. Strong Meml. Hosp. U. Rochester, 1960-61; pharm. chemist quality control Strasenburgh Labs., Rochester, 1961-62; cooking tchr. adult edn. Montgomery County Pub. Schs., Rockville, Md., 1973-79; tchr. The Chinese Cookery Inc., Rockville, 1975-86, Silver Spring, Md., 1986—, pres., bd. dirs., 1975—; chemist NIH, Bethesda, 1987-2000; analytical chemist NIH/WRAIR, Rockville, Md., 1994-96. Author: The Chinese Cookery, 1981, Hunan Cuisine, 1984, Vegetarian Cuisine, 2000, The Art of The Chinese Cookery, 2001. Mem. Am. Chem. Soc., Internat. Assn. Cooking Profls. (Woman of Yr. 1994-2000). Republican. Roman Catholic. Avocations: piano, music, dance, flowers, vegetables. Home and Office: The Chinese Cookery Inc 14209 Sturtevant Rd Silver Spring MD 20905-4448

SHILLING, ROY BRYANT, JR., academic administrator; b. Enville, Okla., Apr. 7, 1931; s. Roy Bryant and Lila M. (Prestage) S.; m. Margaret Riddle, Oct. 16, 1952; children: Roy Bryant III, Nancy Gale. BA, McMurry U., 1951, HHD, 1982; BD, So. Meth. U., 1957; MS, Ind. U., 1966, PhD, 1967. Presdl. asst. McMurry U., Abilene, Tex., 1959-61; asst. to pres. Tenn. Wesleyan Coll., 1961-64; asst. in devel. Ball State U., 1964-65; rsch. assoc. Ind. U., 1965-67; dir. planning and rsch. Baldwin Wallace Coll., 1967-68; exec. v.p. Southwestern U., 1968-69, pres., 1981-2000, pres. emeritus, 2000—; pres. Hendrix Coll., 1969-81; interim pres. McMurry Univ., 2002. Mem. Nat. Commn. on United Meth. Higher Edn., 1975-77. Mem. Ark. Arts and Humanities Coun., 1970-76, chmn., 1974-75; bd. dirs. Ark. Children's Hosp., 1981; mem. bd. higher edn. and ministry United Meth. Ch., 1972-80, mem. univ. senate, 1980-88, v.p. 1983-84, pres., 1984-88; chmn. Gulf dist. Rhodes Scholarship Selection Com., 1992, Ark. chmn., 1973-74, Tex. chmn., 1985-91; mem. Young Pres. Orgn., 1975-81; mem. bd. visitors Air U., 1991-94. With U.S. Army, 1952-54. Recipient Disting. Alumnus award McMurry U., 1980, Perkins Disting. Alumnus award So. Meth. U., 1987, Owen B. Sherrill award for leadership in econ. devel. Georgetown, 1988; named one of Top 100 Most Effective Coll. Pres. in Nation, Bowling Green State U./Exxon Edn. Found., 1986. Mem. North Ctrl. Assn. Colls. and Schs. (vice chmn., chmn. elect 1980-81), Nat. Assn Schs. and Colls. of United Meth. Ch. (v.p. 1975-76, pres. 1976-77), Nat. Coun. Ind. Colls. and Univs. (bd. dirs. 1984-88), So. U. Conf. (exec. com. 1974-78), 79-86, sec.-treas. 1979-86, v.p. 1991-92, pres. 1992-93), Am. Coun. Edn. (bd. dirs. 1989-91; mem. commn. on govt. and pub. rels. 1999-2000, spl. counselor to the pres. 2000-01), Inst. for Humanities (bd. dirs. Salado, Tex. chpt. 1985-91, mem. internat. coun. advs. 1994), NCAA Divsn. III Pres.'s Coun., 1998-2000, Philos Soc. Tex., Rotary, Masons, Alpha Chi, Phi Delta Kappa. Office: 1405 Mesa Ridge Ln Austin TX 78735-1639 E-mail: shilling@southwestern.edu.

SHILLINGBURG, HERBERT THOMPSON, JR., dental educator; b. Mar. 21, 1938; s. Herbert Thompson and Stefi Marie (Schuster) Shillingburg; m. Constance Joanne Murphy, June 11, 1960; children: Lisa Grace, Leslie Susan, Lara Stephanie. Student, U. N.Mex., 1955-58, 65-66; DDS, U. So. Calif., 1962. Gen. practice dentistry, Albuquerque, 1964-67; asst. prof. fixed prosthodontics sect. UCLA Sch. Dentistry, 1967-70, chmn., 1970-72; chmn. dept. fixed prosthodontics U. Okla. Coll. Dentistry, Okla. City, 1972—2003, David Ross Boyd Disting. prof., 1983, prof. emeritus, 2003—. Cons. VA Hosp., Muskogee, Okla., 1975—84, Oklahoma City, 1977—93, U.S. Army Dental Activity, Ft. Knox, Ky., 1980—94. Author: (also in Japanese, German, Greek, Spanish, Italian, French, Portuguese, Polish, Korean, Chinese and Russian) Preparations for Cast Gold Restorations, 1974, Fundamentals of Fixed Prosthodontics, 1976, Fundamentals of Fixed Prosthodontics, 2d edit., 1981, Fundamentals of Fixed Prosthodontics, 3d edit., 1997, Guide to Occlusal Waxing, 1979, Guide to Occlusal Waxing, 2d edit., 1984, Guide to Occlusal Waxing, 3d edit., 2000, Restoration of the Endodontically Treated Tooth, 1984, Fundamentals of Tooth Preparations for Cast Metal and Porcelain Restorations, 1987; co-editor: Quintessence of Dental Technology, 1984—88. Capt. U.S. Army, 1962—64. Named Disting. Lectr., O U Assoc., 1989; recipient Award for tchg. excellence, UCLA Sch. Dentistry, 1969, 1972, 1973, Okla. Coll. Dentistry, 1976, 1978, 1982, 1987, 1993, 1994, 1st prize, Am. Med. Writers Assn., 1988, Award for tchg. excellence, Okla. Coll. Dentistry, 1997, La Mèdaille de la Ville de Paris (èchelon Argent), 1990, Outstanding Profl. Achievement award, O U Coll. Dentristy, 2003. Fellow: Am. Coll. Dentists; mem.: ADA, Okla. State Dental Assn., Internat. Assn. Dental Rsch., Am. Coll. Prosthodontists (hon.), Am. Acad. Restorative Dentistry, Am. Acad. Fixed Prosthodontics (George H. Moulton award 1998), Acad. Operative Dentistry, Phi Kappa Phi, Omicron Kappa Upsilon (Stephen H. Leeper award for tchg. excellence 2000). Independent. Episcopalian. Avocations: travel, photography. Home: 1312 Brixton Rd Edmond OK 73034-3314 Office: U Okla Coll Dentistry PO Box 26901 Oklahoma City OK 73190-0001

SHILLINGSBURG, MIRIAM JONES, English educator, academic administrator; b. Balt., Oct. 5, 1943; d. W. Elvin and Miriam R. Jones; m. Peter L. Shillingsburg, Nov. 21, 1967; children: Robert, George, John, Alice, Anne Carol. BA, Mars Hill Coll., 1964; MA, U. S.C., 1966, PhD, 1969; BGS, Miss. State U., 1994. Asst. prof. Limestone Coll., Gaffney, S.C., 1969, Miss. State U., 1970-75, assoc. prof., 1975-80, prof. English, 1980-96, assoc. v.p. for acad. affairs, 1988-96, dir. summer sch., 1990-96, dir. undergrad. studies, 1994-96; dean arts and scis. Lamar U., Tex., 1996-99; dean liberal arts and scis. Ind. U., South Bend, 2000—. Disting. acad. visitor Mark Twain Ctr., 1993, 2001; Simms rsch. prof. U. S.C., 1998; vis. fellow Australian Def. Force Acad., 1989; Fulbright lectr. U. New South Wales, Duntroon, Australia, 1984-85. NEH fellow in residence, Columbia U., 1976-77. Author: Mark Twain in Australasia, 1988; editor: Conquest of Granada, 1988, The Cub of the Panther, 1997; mem. editl. bd. Works of W.M. Thackeray, Miss. Quar., So. Quar.; contbr. articles to profl. jours. and mags. Mem. South Ctrl. 18th Century Soc., Am. Lit. Assn., Pop Culture Assn., Sigma Tau Delta, Phi Kappa Phi, Simms Soc. (pres. 1996-97). E-mail: mimishill@hotmail.com.

SHILS, EDWARD B. management educator, lawyer, arbitrator and mediator; b. Phila., May 29, 1915; s. Benjamin and Dinah (Berkowitz) S.; m. Shirley Seigle, July 31, 1942; children: Ronnie Lois, Nancy Ellen, Edward Barry. BS in Econs., U. Pa., 1936, MA in Polit. Sci., 1937, PhD, 1940, JD, 1998, LLM, 1990, SJD, 1997; LLD (hon.), Phila. U., 1975; PhD (hon.), Tel-Aviv U., Israel, 1990. Bar: Pa. 1988, U.S. Dist. Ct. (ea. dist.) Phila. 1988, Pa. Supreme Ct. Rsch. assoc. FELS Inst. of Local and State Govt., U. Pa., 1937—38, Pa. Economy League, 1938—42; cons. job classification and wage adminstrn. Phila. City Council, 1942—43; chief coordination and planning VA, Phila., 1947—48; cons. tchr. salary schedules Phila. Bd. Pub. Edn., 1948—50; dir. pub. edn. survey Greater Phila. Movement, 1950—51; sr. dept. head U.S. Wage Stabilization Bd., Phila., 1951; methods cons. Budget Office Gov. Pa., 1951—55; cons., dir. Dental Mfrs. of Am., Inc., 1952—; cons. Phila. County Med. Soc., 1955—56; chmn. social sci. dept. Community Coll., Temple U., Phila., grad. lectr. pub. adminstrn., 1948—56; mem. faculty Wharton Sch. U. Pa., Phila., 1956—, prof. mgmt., chmn. mgmt dept., 1968—76, George W. Taylor prof. emeritus entrepreneurial studies, 1979, prof. emeritus polit. sci., 1985—, dir. Wharton Entrepreneurial Ctr., 1973—86; judicial adminstr. U. Pa., 1986—90; pvt. practice law Phila., 1988—; of counsel Sarner and Assocs., Phila.; disting. prof. entrepreneurial studies Tel Aviv U., 1991—95; atty., cons. Office Phila. Dist. Atty., 2001—. Pers. cons. Phila. Bd. Pub. Edn., 1946-75; cons. Phila. Psychiat. Ctr., 1971-76, Am. Bd. Internal Medicine, 1973-77, Girard Coll., 1974, Royal Coll. Physicians and Surgeons Can., 1977-80; cons. labor rels. Phila. Pub. Sch. Dist., 1951-68; cons. econ. Phila. New Conv. Ctr., 1988-90; mgmt. advisor to Phila. Dist. Atty., 1992-93; trustee Dental Sch. U. Pa., 2002—; cons. dir. Knitted Outerwear Mfrs. Assn. Pa., 1952—, Fashion Apparel Mfrs. of Pa., 1952—; dir. study to create Phila. CC, 1956; dir. study to create St. Louis Mo. Jr. Coll. Sys., 1960; dir., chmn. audit com. Vishay Intertech., Inc., 1983—; cons. in econs. to Phila. Profl. Sports Consortium, 1983-89, maj. leagues baseball, football, hockey and basketball, Washington, 1986-87. Author: Finances and Financial Administration of Philadelphia's Public Schools 1923-1939, 1940, Automation and Industrial Relations, 1963, Teachers, Administrators and Collective Bargaining, 1968, Industrial Peacemaker: George W. Taylor's Contribution to Collective Bargaining, 1979; co-editor: Frontiers of Entrepreneurship Research, 1985, The Shils Report, Impact of Mega Retail Chains on Small Enterprise, 1997. V.p. Fedn. Jewish Agys. for Phila., 1976-84, Life Trust Fedn. Jewish Agys., 1990—; pres. Jewish Publs. Soc. Am., 1978-81, Hon. pres., 1982-; Life trustee, hon. chmn. trustee com. on edn. Phila. U.; chmn. bd., hon. pres. Pathway Sch., Jeffersonville, Pa., 1970-84; pres. Philadelphians for Good Govt., 1991-93, hon. pres., 1992-95. Served as officer Signal Corps U.S. Army, 1943-46. Honored with a chair in his name at U. Pa. Law Sch., Edward B. Shils Professorship in Arbitration and Alternative Dispute Resolution, 1991, Wharton Sch. U. Pa., Edward B. and Shirley R. Shils Term Professorship Entrepreneurial Mgmt., 2001; recipient Joseph P. Wharton award, 1997, Alumni award of Merit U. Pa., 2001. Mem. Union League Pa. (pres. Wishbone Club 2003), Faculty Club U. Pa. (pres. 1966-69, 87-92, bd. govs. 1993—), Green Valley Country Club (Plymouth, Pa.), Masons (32 degree), Shriners. Home: 335 S Woodbine Ave Narberth PA 19072-1525 Office: U Pa Wharton Sch Philadelphia PA 19104 Also: 123 S Broad St Philadelphia PA 19109-1029

SHIN, EDWARD SUNG-SHIK, bilingual education educator; b. Seoul, Aug. 26, 1960; Came to U.S., 1977; s. Hyun-Woo and Sai-Shin (Jahng) S.; m. Rachel Youn-Kyung, Apr. 11, 1992; children: Calvin Joon Ho, Sarah Yerin, Timothy Jaetto. BA, UCLA, L.A., 1986; MEd, Harvard U., 1990. Cert. tchr., adminstrv. svcs., bilingual instr., Calif. Site/program dir. YMCA, L.A., 1984-86; bilingual tchr. L.A. Unified Sch. Dist., 1986-98, dist. bilingual adv., 1998—. Chair faculty Overland Ave. Sch., L.A., 1991-92; tchr. Korean lang. L.A. Christian Reformed Ch., 1987-90. Singer Olympic Honor Choir, L.A., 1984; group leader, counselor UCLA, 1985; vol. Neuropsychiatric Inst. UCLA, 1986. Chancellor's scholar UCLA, 1980; grantee Harvard Grad. Sch. Edn., 1989-90. Mem. ASCD, Assn. Calif. Sch. Adminstrs., United Teachers of L.A. Korean Presbyterian. Avocations: reading, singing, playing tennis with my children, guitar playing.

SHINAGEL, MICHAEL, English literature educator; b. Vienna, Apr. 21, 1934; came to U.S., 1941; s. Emanuel and Lilly (Hillel) S.; m. Ann Birdsey Mitchell, Sept. 1, 1956 (div. 1970); children: Mark Mitchell, Victoria Stuart; m. Rosa Joanne Bonanno, Dec. 6, 1973 (div. 1993); m. Marjorie Lee North, May 26, 1995. AB, Oberlin Coll., 1957; A.M., Harvard U., 1959, PhD, 1964; Doctorate (hon.), Internat. U. Ecuador, 1997; Doctorate (hon.), U. Argentina Empresa, 2003. Teaching fellow Harvard U., Cambridge, Mass., 1958-59, tutor in English, 1962-64, assoc. dir. career office, 1959-64, dean continuing edn., 1975—, lectr. extension, 1976—, sr. lectr. English, 1983—, master Quincy House, 1986—2001; asst. prof. English, Cornell U., Ithaca, N.Y., 1964-67; prof., chmn. dept. English, Union Coll., Schenectady, N.Y., 1967-75. Bd. dirs. Harvard Coop. Soc., publ. Harvard Rev.; pres. bd. dirs. Ednl. Exch. Boston, 1982-87; editor Continuing Higher Edn. Rev., 1997—. Author: Defoe and Middle-Class Gentility, 1968; co-author: (handbook) Summer Institutes in English, 1965; editor: Concordance to Poems of Swift, 1972, Critical Edition of Robinson Crusoe, 1975 (revised 1993); co-editor: Harvard Scholars in English (1890-1990), 1991. With U.S. Army, 1952—54, Korea. Woodrow Wilson fellow, 1957; NEH grantee, 1965 Mem. Univ. Continuing Edn. Assn., Assn. Continuing Higher Edn., Mass. Hist. Soc., Old South Meeting House, The Johnsonians, The Saturday Club, Harvard Faculty Club (pres. 1985-87), Phi Beta Kappa. Avocations: reading, cooking, music, tennis. Home: 22 Grozier Rd Cambridge MA 02138 Office: Harvard U Divsn Continuing Edn 51 Brattle St Cambridge MA 02138-3701 E-mail: shinagel@hudce.harvard.edu.

SHINEFLUG, ELIZABETH (NANA), theater educator, artistic director; b. Chgo., Dec. 21, 1935; d. Otto Ernst and Angelina (Ryan) Strohmeier; m. W.H. Shineflug; children: Otto, Lisa Farrell. BA, Northwestern U., 1957; MA, Columbia Coll., Chgo., 1986; grad. cert. in Laban movement analysis, Columbia Coll., 2002. Artistic dir. Chgo. Moving Co., 1972—; faculty interdisciplinary arts and theater dept. Columbia Coll., Chgo., 1973—. Choreographer 72 dances professionally performed, 1969—; solo performance artist, 1983—. Recipient Ruth Page Lifetime Svcs. to Field award Chgo. Dance Coalition, 1991, Livetime Achievement award Columbia Coll., 1996, Choreographic award Berlin, 1991; Nat. Endowment for Arts choreographic fellow, 1975, 77, 85, 86. Home: 800 Elm St Glenview IL 60025-4240

SHINER, NIKKI RAE, elementary educator; b. East Tawas, Mich, Jan. 28, 1955; d. Donald Earl and Hazel Geneva (Gordon) Meske; m. Donald William Shiner, Oct. 5, 1974; children: Donald Michael, Joel Matthew. BS, Bloomsburg (Pa.) State Coll., 1976; MSEd, Bloomsburg U., 1988. Cert. tchr., Pa. Math tchr. 7th grade Bloomsburg Sch. Dist., 1976-77, 1st grade tchr., 1977-80; kindergarten tchr. Berwick Sch. Dist., Pa., 1989-90, elem. gifted tchr., 1990-91, kindergarten, elem. gifted tchr., 1991-92, second grade tchr., 1992-94; kindergarten tchr. Nescopeck Elem. Sch., Pa., 1994—. Bd. dir. Berwick YMCA, 1988-91; bd. trustees Bethany United Meth. Ch., Berwick, 1989-91, 97-2001. Republican. Methodist. Avocations: sewing, skiing, reading, walking. Office: Nescopeck Elem Sch Dewey St Nescopeck PA 18635

SHIPE, KELLY ANN, music educator, director, professional harpist; b. Knoxville, Tenn., Sept. 24, 1960; Choral dir. Jefferson County H.S., Dandridge, Tenn. Harpist: (Audio Tape) And I Love You So, 1987, Praise Him With Harp, 1997. Avocations: skiing, ice skating, aerobics, travel, music. Home: 1912 John Sevier Hwy Knoxville TN 37920 Office: Jefferson County High Sch 115 W Dumplin Valley Rd Dandridge TN 37725-4501

SHIPLEY, MARILYN ELIZABETH, school system administrator; b. Cleve., May 19, 1942; d. Melvin James and Ethel Maude (Paddon) Bramley; m. Charles Hudson Shipley, Oct. 1, 1977. BA in Elem. Edn., Ariz. State U., 1965, MA in Elem. Edn., 1970; MS in Sch. Adminstrn., Calif. State U., 1975; EdD in Ednl. Mgmt., U. LaVerne, 1992. Elem. tchr. Garden Grove (Calif.) Unified Sch. Dist., 1965-69; elem. substitute tchr. Scottsdale (Ariz.) Pub. Sch., 1969-70; program asst. ESEA Title III project prolexia Riverside (Calif.) County Office Edn., 1970-75, coord. curriculum and instrn., 1975-89, coord./prin. spl. edn., 1987-89, coord./prin. pregnant minor-sch. age parents, 1989-92, coord. curriculum and staff devel., 1992—. Cons. in field, 1973-89. Co-author: Lexilogs, Lexileits, 1974, also student study folders. Mem. Assn. Calif. Curriculum Developers, Assn. Calif. Sch. Adminstrs., Western Riverside County Assn. Sch. Mgrs. (bd. reps. 1989-91, pres. 1992—), Calif. Alliance Concerned With Sch. Age Parents (sec. 1992, state bd. dirs.). Republican. Methodist. Avocations: quilting, swimming, writing. Home: 3702 Lomina Ave Long Beach CA 90808-2116

SHIPLEY, MELODY LEA, director, mathematician, educator; b. Endicott, NY, Apr. 21, 1961; d. Henry Lee Jackson and Leah Ann (Urick) Hart; m. Jerry Keith Shipley, Dec. 18, 1982; children: Savannah Lea, Jacob Aaron. BA in Athletic Tng., BA in Math. Edn., MidAm. Nazarene Univ., 1983, MEd, 1990. Cert. secondary math. tchr., Mo. 7-9th grade math. tchr. Gallatin (Mo.) Schs., 1983-84; 9-12th grade math. tchr. Copeland (Kans.) Schs., 1984-85; 8-12th grade math. tchr. Galt (Mo.) Schs., 1985—96; math prof., assoc. dean N. Ctrl. Mo. Coll., 1996—; dir. Academic Reinforcement Ctr., 2003—. Athletic trainer, Gallatin, 1983-84. Mem. Nat. Coun. Tchrs. of Math. Mem. Nazarene Ch. Avocations: drama, vocal music, reading, outdoor activities.

SHIPPEY, LYN, reading center director; b. Childress, Tex., Mar. 6, 1927; d. Robert Coke and Alta (Timmons) Elliott; m. James George Shippey, Mar. 29, 1947; children: James Robert, Deborah Shippey Meyer, Marilyn Shippey Buron. BS, U. Corpus Christi, 1963; MA in Edn., San Diego State U., 1977; EdD, U. San Diego, 1993. Cert. tchr., reading specialist, tchr. of learning handicapped, Calif. Substitute tchr. Dept. Edn., Guam, 1958-61; tchr. counselor, phys. edn. tchr. Robstown Ind. Sch. Dist., Tex., 1964-65; elem. tchr. Cupertino Union Sch. Dist., Calif., 1965-68, tchr., secondary, 1968-71; dir. PIRK Reading Center, Poway, Calif., 1973—. Cons., workshop presenter PIRK Reading Programs, Calif., Tex., 1974—; developer PIRK reading program Cupertino Union Sch. Dist., 1966-70. Author: Perceptual Integration Reading Kit, 1971, PIRK Reading Programs, 1977, rev. 1987. Mem. Alcala Soc. U. San Diego, Internat. Dyslexia Assn. (bd. dirs. San Diego br.), Learning Disabilities Assn. Avocations: research, writing. Office: PIRK Reading Center 16957 Cloudcroft Dr Poway CA 92064-1306

SHIREY, MARGARET (PEGGY SHIREY), elementary school educator; b. Sussex, N.J., Nov. 24, 1950; d. Steve and Grace (McGlew) Piniaha; children: Todd, Jessica. BS, Marymount Coll., Salina, Kans., 1972; M Elem. Edn., Ctrl. State U., 1985. Cert. elem. tchr., Okla. Tchr. Putnam City Sch. Dist., Oklahoma City, 1980—. Active Putnam City Reading Coun.; bargaining mem. Putnam City, 1993-95. Recipient Excellent Educator award; named One of Okla.'s Best Tchrs. Channel 5 Alive, Oklahoma City, 1991, Tchr. of the Yr. Harvest Hills Elem., 1998, 2002. Mem. NEA, ASCD, Okla. Edn. Assn., Putnam City Assn. Classroom Tchrs. (bldg. rep. 1983-86, legis. chairperson 1989-92). Democrat. Avocations: writing, reading, walking. Office: Putnam City Sch Dist 5401 NW 40th St Oklahoma City OK 73122-3302 Home: 5013 NW 26th St Oklahoma City OK 73127-1750

SHIRK, SHARON L. elementary education educator; b. Reading, Pa., Jan. 23, 1966; d. Kenneth M. and Donna L. (Henry) Mengel; m. Jeffrey L. Shirk, Sept. 19, 1987; children: Mitchell R., Hannah L. BS Edn., Kutztown U., 1987, M Reading, 1990. Cert. tchr. elem./spl. edn. visually impaired, reading, Pa. Tchr. third grade Wilson Sch. Dist., West Lawn, Pa., 1987—. Bible sch. tchr. Zion's United Ch. of Christ, Hamburg, Pa., 1980s-90s. Mem. Internat. Reading Assn., Kappa Delta Pi. Democrat. United Ch. of Christ. Avocations: reading, bowling, swimming. Home: 606 Hex Hwy Hamburg PA 19526-8900 Office: Wilson Sch Dist 2601 Grandview Blvd West Lawn PA 19609-1324

SHIRLEY, LAWRENCE HOYT, mathematician, educator; b. Flagstaff, Ariz., Nov. 13, 1947; s. Robert Albert and Shirley Amelia (Hoyt) S.; m. Alberta Ohenewah, Aug. 31, 1974; children: Jefferson, Emily. BS in Math., History, Calif. Tech., 1969; MEd in Comparative Edn., U. Ill., 1973; PhD in Math. Edn., Ahmadu Bello U., Zaria, Nigeria, 1984. Tchr. math. Bonthe (Sierra Leone) Secondary Sch./Peace Corps, 1969-71; advisor, peace corps math. Sierra Leone Ministry Edn., Bo, 1971-72; prof. math. edn. Ahmadu Bello U., 1974-88, dept. head., 1978-88; prof. math. edn. No. Ill. U., DeKalb, 1988-89, Towson U., Balt., 1989—, dept. vice chair, 1998-99,2000-01, acting dept. chair, 1999-2000, assoc. dean. grad. coll., 2001—. Cons., Nigeria Edn. Rsch. Coun., Lagos, 1978-88, Fed. U. Tech., Minna, Nigeria, 1986, Nat. Edn. Tech. Ctr., Kaduna, Nigeria, 1986-88, Peace Corps, 1995. Co-author, editor: Nigerian Primary Math, 1981; contbr. articles to profl. jours. Fellow Math. Assn. Nigeria; mem. Nat. Coun. Tchrs. Math., Md. Coun. Tchrs. Math., Internat. Study Group Ethnomath. (pres.), N.Am. Study Group History Pedagogy Math., Amnesty Internat., Planetary Soc. Democrat. Avocations: african affairs, history, astronomy. Home: 854 Bosley Ave Baltimore MD 21204-2610 Office: Towson U Dept Math Towson MD 21252-0001 E-mail: lshirley@towson.edu.

SHIRRELL, MARTHA HUGGINS, elementary school educator; b. Batesville, Ark., Nov. 13, 1937; d. Julius Edmond and Ida Pearl (James) Huggins; m. Jim G. Shirrell, Aug. 26, 1956; 1 child, James Franklin. BA, Ark. Coll., Batesville, 1959. Tchr. bus. Cord-Charlotte (Ark.) High Sch.; elem. tchr. Batesville (Ark.) Sch. Dist. 1, Little Rock Sch. Dist.; literacy specialist Ark. Dept. Edn., 1993—2000. Mem. Internat. Reading Assn., Nat. Coun. Tchrs. English, Assn. for Supervision and Curriculum Devel., AAUW (chpt. pres.), Ark. Reading Assn. (pres. 2000-2001). Home: 13 Cascades Dr Little Rock AR 72212-3315

SHIRVANI, HAMID, architect, educator, author, administrator, philosopher; b. Tehran, Iran, Oct. 20, 1950; came to US, 1974, naturalized, 1986; s. Majid and Taji (Granpisheh) Shirvani; m. Fatemeh Shokrollahi, Oct. 4, 2002. Diploma in architecture, Poly. of Cen. London, 1974; MArch, Pratt Inst., 1975; MS, Rensselaer Poly. Inst., 1977; MLA, Harvard U., 1978; MA, Princeton U., 1979, PhD, 1980; LHD (hon.), Soka U., Japan, 2003. Project designer London Borough of Barnet, 1973-74; asst. prof. architecture Pa. State U., 1979-82; prof., dir. grad. studies SUNY, Syracuse, 1982-85; prof., dir. Sch. Urban Planning and Devel., U. Louisville, 1985-86; prof. architecture and urban design U. Colo., Denver, 1986-92, dean Sch. of Architecture and Planning, 1986-91; prof. philosophy, dean Coll. Arts and Scis. U. Mass., Lowell, 1992-95; v.p. grad. studies and rsch., prof. urban studies CUNY Queens Coll., Flushing, 1995-2000; provost, exec. v.p., Martha Masters prof. art/architecture Chapman U., Orange, Calif., 2000—. Vis. faculty So. Calif. Inst. Architecutre, U. So. Calif.; lectr. in field, including U. Tex., San Antonio, Lehigh U., U. Waterloo (Can.), U. Sydney (Australia), Mo. State U., Columbia U., NYC, Amsterdam Acad. Art, U. Venice (Italy), Chinese U. Hong Kong, So. China Inst. U., U. Calif., Irvine, Villanova U., Rutgers U., Ariz. State U., Duke U., U. Pa., Yale U., U. Colo., U. NC Author: Urban Design: A Comprehensive Reference, 1981, Urban Design Review, 1981, Urban Design Process, 1985, Beyond Public Architecture, 1990; editor Urban Design Rev., 1982-85, Urban Design and Preservation Quar., 1985-88; mem. editorial bd. Jour. Archtl. Edn., 1988-94, Avant Garde, 1988-93, Jour. Planning Edn. and Rsch., 1987-93, Art and Architecture, 1974-78, Jour. Am. Planning Assn., 1982-88. Recipient Gold medal in Architecture and Urbanism, Faculty Honor award, Acad. Leadership award, Faculty Rsch. award, Commendation award AIA, 2003, Justice award SGI, 2003. Fellow Am. Soc. Landscape Archs. (recognition award), Royal Geog. Soc., Royal Soc. Arts; mem. Am. Inst. Cert. Planners, Am. Planning Assn. (chmn. urban design divsn. 1987-89, Disting. award 1984, Urban Design award 1985), Sigma Xi, Omicron Delta Epsilon, Tau Sigma Delta (Silver medal in archtl. edn. 1988), Tau Beta Pi, Sigma Lambda Alpha. Office: Chapman U Orange CA 92866-1099 Fax: 714-997-6801. E-mail: Ham@chapman.edu.

SHISHKOFF, MURIEL MENDELSOHN, education writer; b. Chgo., Mar. 5, 1917; d. Henry Robert and Anita (Arnow) Mendelsohn; m. Nicholas Shishkoff, Aug. 26, 1946; children: Andrew, Debra. BA, U. Chgo., 1936; MA, Northwestern U., 1940. Founding dir. Women's Opportunities Ctr., U. Ext., U. Calif., Irvine, 1970-72, asst. dir. Office Rels. with Schs. and Colls., 1974-82, cons. edn. improvement programs, 1993-95. UCI cons. to ASSIST, 1985-90; cons. Prins. Conf. for Acad. Excellence in Effective Schs., 1985-91, Jacob Javits Gifted and Talented Students Edn. program, Sherman Intertribal Acad., 1990-92, CAPP Scholars in Tng./Curriculum Devel., 1991-92, Native Am. Intertribal U., 1992-94; cons. CPEC-Eisenhower Math and Sci. Leadership Tng., 1993-96. Author: Transferring Made Easy, 1991, (with Kogee Thomas and Barbara Al-Bayati) Dream Catchers: A Transfer Guide for Native American College Students with Special Assistance for Those from Tribal Colleges, 2000. V.p. LWV, Palos Verdes Peninsula, CAlif., 1963. Lt. USNR (W-VS), 1942-45. Grantee Reachout, Dept. Mental Hygiene, Sacramento, 1972. Mem. Nat. Mus. Women in Arts (charter). Democrat. Home: 19542 Sandcastle Ln Huntington Beach CA 92648-3069 E-mail: mms9999@socal.rr.com.

SHIVAKUMAR, KUNIGAL NANJUNDAIAH, aerospace engineer, educator; b. Kunigal, Karnataka, India, Mar. 28, 1951; came to U.S., 1980; s. Kunigal H. Nanjundaiah; m. Netra D. Shivakumar, Nov. 1, 1984; children: Nishkala K., Nirmala K., Dhruva K. BE in Civil Engring., Bangalore (Karnataka) U., 1972; ME in Civil Engring., Indian Inst. Sci., Bangalore, 1974, PhD in Aeronautics, 1979. Rsch. assoc. Indian Inst. Sci., Bangalore, 1979, NRC, NASA Langley Rsch. Ctr., Washington, 1980-82; rsch. asst. prof. Old Dominion U., Norfolk, Va., 1982, rsch. assoc. prof., 1983-84; sr. scientist, group leader Analytical Svcs. & Materials, Hampton, Va., 1985-89, group leader, 1989-91; rsch. prof. N.C. Agrl. and Tech. State U., Greensboro, 1991—; dir. Ctr. Composite Materials Rsch., 1999—. Cons. Bharat Heavy Elecs., Hyderbad, 1979, Aerotech, Lockheed Corp., Hampton, 1990, AS&M, NASA Langley Rsch. Ctr., Hampton, 1991. Contbr. over 130 articles to profl. jours. Com. mem. Kannada Sanga, Bangalore, 1978; pres. India Assn. of Peninsula, Hampton, 1984. Recipient 9 Tech. awards NASA, I.I. Sc. Assoc. Fellow AIAA (assoc., sr., bd. dirs. 1991, gen. chair 37th SDM Conf., chair long-range planning com. 1996-97, chair materials TC, assoc. editor jour., awards); mem. ASTM, ASME, ASC. Hindu. Avocations: tennis, gardening. Home: 5124 Hedrick Dr Greensboro NC 27410-9320 Office: NC A&T State U Fort Irc Bldg Rm 205 Greensboro NC 27411-0001 E-mail: kunigal@ncat.edu.

SHOCKLEY, ALONZO HILTON, JR., school system administrator; b. Milford, Del., Sept. 30, 1920; s. Alonzo Hilton Sr. and Elizabeth (Hilton) S.; m. Kay Marilyn Falke, Aug. 13, 1979; children: Novella Lela Shockley Randolph, Cheryl Emmelyn Shockley Durant, Alonzo Hilton III. BS, Del. State Coll., 1943; MA, Mich. State U., 1947; cert., NYU, 1956, postgrad., 1980, Queens Coll., 1961-62, U. Maine, 1963. Cert. tchr., N.Y., Pa., Del. Tchr. sci. Brooks High Sch., Prince Frederick, Md., 1948; prin. elem., jr. high schs. dept. public instrn., Dover, Del., 1948-58; rsch. assoc. Del. State Coll., Dover, 1958-60; elem. sch. tchr. Cen. Sch. Dist. 4, Plainview, N.Y., 1960-62; asst. elem. prin. Union Free Sch. Dist., Wyandanch, N.Y., 1962-64; assoc. adminstrn. official N.Y. State Edn. Dept., Albany, 1964-65; edn. coord. Nassau County Commn. Econ. Opportunity, Garden City, L.I., 1965-66; dir. state and fed. programs Freeport (N.Y.) Pub. Schs., 1966-85; coord. state and fed. programs Amityville Pub. Schs., L.I., N.Y., 1985-91, ednl. cons., 1988—. V.p. Internat. Rotary, Ronkonkoma, N.Y., 1997; v.p. Phi Delta Kappa of L.I. #1020. Contbr. articles in field of ednl. adminstrn. to profl. jours. Pres. mid L.I. chpt. UN Assn. of U.S., bd. dir. so. N.Y. divsn., mem. coun. pres. steeringcom., pres. Suffolk County chpt., 1995—; organizer of 1997 Mcpl. Elections Bill contbg. to the implementation of the Dayton Peace Accord, 1987; 6 time supr. for Bosnia/Herzegovia elections. Served with U.S. Army, 1942-45, NATOUSA; mem. NYU Alumni Chorus, 1980—, Huntington Men's Chorus, L.I., 1985—. Recipient Cert. of Merit for supervising registration in Bosnia and Herzegovia, Ctrl. Bosnia Canton 6, 1997. Mem. Am. Assn. Sch. Adminstrs., NEA, N.Y. State Tchrs. Edn., Assn. Childhood Edn. Internat., Assn. Supervision and Curriculum Devel., Nat. Assn. Elem. Prins., Amityville Sch. Dist. Adminstrs., Am. Acad. Polit. and Social Sci., NYU Alumni Assn. (bd. dirs., v.p.), Sch. Health, Edn. and Nursing Arts Professionals (pres.), Rotary (pres. Ronkonkomas, L.I.), Phi Delta (v.p. Long Island N.Y. chpt. 1994—). Home: 49 Gaymore Rd Port Jefferson Station NY 11776-1354

SHOCKLEY, JAMES THOMAS, physics educator; b. Topaz, Mo., Sept. 16, 1925; s. William Ervin and Minnie Catherine (Turnbull) S.; m. Joan Elsie Griess, June 17, 1950 (div. Aug. 1968); 1 child, John William; m. Betty Jean Truitt, July 28, 1989. BA, Calif. State U., Fresno, 1951, MA, 1953; postgrad., Claremont Grad. Sch., 1955; PhD, U. So. Calif., 1961. Cert. secondary tchr., Calif.; cert. community coll. tchr., Calif. Aerodynamicist N.Am. Aviation, Los Angeles, 1953; instr. Calif. State U., Fresno, 1954-55, asst. prof. physics, 1956-63, instr. workshop in phys. sci. for elem. tchrs., 1961, credential advisor, supr. student teaching, 1956-86, assoc. prof., 1963-68, prof., 1968-90, prof. emeritus physics, 1990—. Cons. Fresno County Schs., 1971, USAF, Fresno, 1971, 72; validity cons. Commn. Tchr. Preparation and Licensing, San Francisco, 1977; instr. NSF Inst. for high sch. physics tchrs., 1962-63. Author: Physics and Astronomy for Liberal Arts Students, 1970; creator 7 Univ. Courses, 1958-85; textbook reviewer, 1965-77. Active mem. Civil Def., Fresno, 1952; mem. City-Univ. Edn. Liaison Com., Fresno, 1963-64; judge Bullard High Sch. Sci. Fair, Fresno, 1964-66; sponser Physics Club, Fresno, 1953-55. Recipient I Dare You award Danforth Found., Sanger, Calif., 1944, Tchr. grant Danforth Found., Fresno, 1958; Congress of Parents and Tchrs. scholar, San Diego, 1960. Mem. Am. Inst. Physics, Planetary Soc., Astron. Soc. Pacific, Aero Club, Phi Delta Kappa. Mem. Christian Ch. Avocations: flying, reading, photography, international travel, oil painting.

SHOEMAKER, CLARA BRINK, retired chemistry researcher; b. Rolde, Drenthe, The Netherlands, June 20, 1921; came to U.S., 1953; d. Hendrik Gerard and Hendrikje (Smilde) Brink; m. David Powell Shoemaker, Aug. 5. 1955; 1 child, Robert Brink. PhD, Leiden U., The Netherlands, 1950. Instr. in inorganic chemistry Leiden U., 1946-50, 51-53; postdoctoral fellow Oxford (Eng.) U., 1950-51; rsch. assoc. dept. chemistry MIT, Cambridge, 1953-55, 58-70; rsch. assoc. biochemistry Harvard Med. Sch., Boston, 1955-56; project supr. Boston U., 1963-64; rsch. assoc. dept. chemistry Oreg. State U, Corvallis, 1970-75, rsch. assoc. prof. dept. chemistry, 1975-82, sr. rsch. prof. dept. chemistry, 1982-84, prof. emerita, 1984—. Sect. editor: Structure Reports of International Union of Crystallography, 1967, 68, 69; co-author chpts. in books; author numerous sci. papers. Bd. dirs. LWV, Corvallis, 1980-82, bd. dirs., sec., Oreg., 1985-87. Fellow Internat. Fedn. Univ. Women, Oxford U., 1950-51. Mem. Metall. Soc. (com. on alloy phases 1969-79), Internat. Union of Crystallography (commn. on structure reports 1970-90), Am. Crystallographic Assn. (crystallographic data com. 1975-78, Fankuchen award com. 1976), Sigma Xi, Iota Sigma Pi (faculty adv. Oreg. State U. chpt. 1975-84), Phi Lambda Upsilon. Avocation: outdoor activities. Office: Dept Chemistry Oreg State U Corvallis OR 97331

SHOEMAKER, MELVIN HUGH, religious educator; b. Bryant, Ind., Feb. 11, 1940; s. H. Vaughn S. and Thelora Shoemaker (Avey) Mason; m. Glenna Joan Cockrell, Dec. 29, 1961; children: David Wesley, Diana Marie Thornton, Daniel Luther. BA, Ind. Wesleyan U., 1962; MDiv with honors, Asbury Theol. Sem., Wilmore, Ky., 1967; postgrad., U. Wis., 1966; MPhil, Drew U., 1988; D of Ministry, Fuller Theol. Sem., 1997. Ordained to ministry Wesleyan Ch. as elder, 1964. Instr. Ind. Wesleyan U., Marion, 1966-67; prof. Okla. Wesleyan Coll., 1979—84; prof. New Testament, dir. honors program and study abroad Azusa (Calif.) Pacific U., 1986—. Chmn. adv. coun. for Oxford (Eng.) U. honors semester Coun. for Christian Colls. & Univs.; sr. min. Hillside Wesleyan Ch., Marion, Ind., 1967-70, Houghton (N.Y.) Coll. Wesleyan Ch., 1970-73, Dearborn (Mich.) Free Meth. Ch., 1973-79, Sooner Park Wesleyan Ch., Bartlesville, Okla., 1980-82, 84-86; interim sr. min. Brethren in Christ Ch., Upland, Calif., 1989; asst. dist. supt. Tri-State Dist. Wesleyan Ch., Ark., Mo., Okla., 1985-86; N.T. adv. bd. Baker Book House, 1990-93; internat. edn. com. Nat. Collegiate Honor Coun., 1997—. Author: Eerdmans Bible Dictionary, 1987 (Gold medal 1988), Evangelical Dictionary of Biblical Theology, 1996. Youth affairs commr. City of Dearborn, 1976-78; pres. Dearborn Area Clergy, 1975-76; min.'s adv. coun. Youth for Christ of Greater Detroit, 1974-79. Mem.: Wesleyan Theol. Soc., Soc. Bibl. Lit., Theta Phi. Home: 208 Calle Concordia San Dimas CA 91773-3987 Office: Azusa Pacific U 901 E Alosta Ave Azusa CA 91702-2769

SHOEMAKER, PAMELA JEAN, educator; b. Chillicothe, Ohio, Oct. 25, 1950; d. Paul E. and Nettie K. (Steed) S.; m. F. Scott Sherman. BS in Journalism, MS in Comm., Ohio U., 1972; PhD in Mass Comm., U. Wis., 1982. Editl., advt. asst. Ohio Contractor Mag., Columbus, Ohio, 1972-74; advt. mgr. Uni-Tool Attachments, Inc., Columbus, 1974-76; mng. editor Ohio Dental Assn., Columbus, 1976-77; sec. to Council on Journalism ADA, 1977-79; lectr., teaching asst. dept. journalism and mass comm. U. Wis., Madison, 1980-82; asst. prof. journalism U. Tex., Austin, 1982-87, assoc. prof., 1987-91; dir. Ohio State U. Sch. Journalism, Columbus, 1991-94; John Ben Snow rsch. chair Syracuse (N.Y.) U., 1994—. Dir. Office of Survey Rsch., U. Tex., Coll. of Communication, 1986-89. Author: Gatekeeping, 1991 (vol. 3 of series) Communication Concepts, monograph Building a Theory of News Content, 1987; (with S.D. Reese) Mediating the Message: Theories of Influences on Mass Media Content, 1st edit., 1991, 2nd edit., 1996, How to Build Social Science Theories (with J. Tankard and D. Lasorsa); mem. editl. bd. Journalism Quar., 1984—, assoc. editor, 1990-92; editl. bd. Journalism Monographs, 1989-95, Jour. of Comm., 1991—, Mass Comm. Rev., 1990—, Polit. Comms., 1992-95; editor Comm. Campaigns on Drugs, Govt., Media, Pub., 1989; co-editor: Comm. Rsch., 1999—; contbr. articles to profl. jours, chpts. to books. Grantee AT&T Communications, 1984, Gannett Found., 1983, Am. Student Dental Assn., 1984; recipient research fellow Coll. of Communications U. Tex. at Austin, 1986-87. Mem. Assn. for Edn. in Journalism and Mass Communication (head, theory and methodology divsn. 1987-88, tchg. stds. com. 1987-93, chmn. 1988-89, Kreigenbaum Under-40 award 1990, pres.-elect 1994-95, pres. 1995-96, past pres. 1996-97), Internat. Comm. Assn. (chmn. membership com. 1985-86, sec. mass comm. divsn. 1987-89, vice chair 1991-93, chair 1993-95, chair nominating com. 1994-95), Coun. Comm. Assns. (chmn. bd. dirs. 1997), Am. Assn. Pub. Opinion Rsch., Nat. Comm. Assn. Democrat. Avocations: reading science fiction, needlework, music. Office: Syracuse U SI Newhouse Sch Pub Comm 215 University Pl Syracuse NY 13210-2816 E-mail: snowshoe@syr.edu.

SHOEMAKER, PATRICIA WASHABAUGH, reading specialist; b. Pitts., Nov. 1, 1952; d. Robert Widdup and Florence Mabel (Armstrong) Washabaugh; m. Richard Floyd Shoemaker; 1 child, Jillian Leigh. BEd, Shippensburg U., 1974; MEd in Reading, East Stroudsburg U., 1984. Cert. reading specialist Title I. Reading specialist Pocono Mountain Sch. Dist., Swiftwater, Pa., 1978-81, 85—. Mem. adv. bd. Pocono Mountain chpt. I Parent Adv. Coun., Swiftwater, 1986—. Children's ch. coord. East Stroudsburg (Pa.) United Meth. Ch., 1985-90, adminstrv. bd., 1993-96; asst. jr. high youth leader Meth. Youth Fellowship, East Stroudsburg, 1994-95; treas. East Stroudsburg Field Hockey Parents, 1997-2000. Mem. NEA, Internat. Reading Assn., Pocono Mountain Edn. Assn., Pa. State Edn. Assn., Keystone State Reading Assn. (program co-chair conf. 1993, presenter 1995, registration co-chair conf. 2001), Colonial Assn. Reading Educators (treas. 1992-95). Republican. Avocations: reading, travel. Home: RR 8 Box 8763 East Stroudsburg PA 18301-9652

SHOFFSTALL, SUSAN DIANE, secondary school educator; b. Metairie, La., Oct. 8, 1965; d. Robert James and Angela Ann Shoffstall. BS, U. North Tex., Denton, 1988, MEd, 2002. Cert. h.s.tchr. Tex. Tchr. 2d grade Mesquite (Tex.) Ind. Sch. Dist., 1989-95, Allen (Tex.) Ind. Sch. Dist., 1995—96; math. tchr. algebra and geometry Plano (Tex.) Ind. Sch. Dist., 1997—. Mem. Tex. Eagle Forum. Tex. Christian U. scholar, 1984-85. Mem.: ASCD, Assn. Tex. Profl. Educators, Mesquite Ednl. Assn., Nat. Coun. Tchrs. of Math., Tex. Fedn. of Tchrs., Golden Key. Republican. Baptist. Home: 430 Buckingham Rd Apt 925 Richardson TX 75081-5759

SHOGAN, MAUREEN GORDON, clinical nurse specialist, nursing consultant; b. Spokane, Wash., Mar. 4, 1950; d. Alvin E. and Marian K. (Wyatt) Gordon; m. Alexander Joseph Shogan, May 27, 1978. Diploma, Sacred Heart Sch. Nursing, 1971; BS in Nursing, Gonzaga U., 1985; MSN, Intercollegiate Ctr. Nursing, 1992. Cert. infant devel. instr. Staff nurse St. Joseph Hosp., Denver, 1971-75; neonatal transport nurse Deaconess Med. Ctr., Spokane, 1976-78, nurse mgr. neonatal ICU, 1977-78, clin. instr., 1978-94, coord. ednl. svcs., 1997-98. Motivational spkr.; cons. in field. Mem. editl. bd. Jour. Obstet., Gynecol. and Neonatal Nursing, 1997—. Named Student Nurse of Yr. Wash. State. Mem. AWHONN (cert.), Nat. Assn. Neonatal Nurses, Sigma Theta Tau. Avocations: research interests include prevalence of cocaine, marijuana and opiates on the meconium of infants born in spokane county, wash, effect of light on oxygen saturation of preterm infants. Home: 5726 N Sutherlin St Spokane WA 99205-7553 Office: Empire Health Svcs PO Box 248 Spokane WA 99210-0248

SHOHET, JUDA LEON, electrical and computer engineering educator, researcher, high technology company executive; b. Chgo., June 26, 1937; s. Allan Sollman and Frannye Ina (Turner) S.; m. Amy Lenore Scherz, Sept. 5, 1969; children: Aaron, Lena, William. BS, Purdue U., 1958; MS, Carnegie Mellon U., 1960; PhD, Carnegie-Mellon U., 1961. Registered profl. engr., Wis. Asst. prof. Johns Hopkins U., Balt., 1961-66; assoc. prof. U. Wis., Madison, 1966-71, prof., 1971—, chmn. dept. elec. and computer engring., 1986-90, dir. Torsatron/Stellarator Lab., 1974—99, dir. Engring. Rsch. Ctr. for Plasma-Aided Mfg., 1986—97. Pres. Omicron Tech., Inc., Madison, 1985—; cons. Hewlett-Packard Co., Abbott Labs, Trane Co., Oak Ridge Nat. Lab., McGraw-Edison Co., Princeton U., Los Alamos Sci. Lab., Nicolet Instruments, Lawrence Livermore Nat. Lab., Westinghouse Elec. Corp. Author: The Plasma State, 1979, Flux Coordinates and Magnetic Field Structure, 1991; contbr. over 140 articles to profl. jours.; author over 450 conf. papers; patentee in field. Recipient Frederick Emmons Terman award Am. Soc. for Engring. Edn., 1978, John Yarborough Meml. medal British Vacuum Coun., 1993. Fellow IEEE (Centennial medal 1984, Richard F. Shea Disting. Mem. award 1992), Am. Phys. Soc.; mem. IEEE Nuclear and Plasma Scis. Soc. (pres. 1980-82, Merit award 1978, Plasma Sci. and Applications prize 1990). Avocations: skiing, sailing, hiking. Home: 1937 Arlington Pl Madison WI 53726-4001 Office: U Wis Dept Elec & Computer Engring 1445 Engring Hall Madison WI 53706

SHOJI, HIROMU, orthopedic surgeon, educator; b. Chiba-Ken, Japan; Grad., Coll. Gen. Edn., 1959, U. Tokyo, Faculty Medicine, 1964. Diplomate Am. Bd. Orthopedic Surgery (examiner). Intern U. Tokyo Hosp., 1964-65, resident, 1965-67, Bklyn. Cumberland Med. Ctr., 1967-68, NYU Med. Ctr., 1968-69; Bone tumor clin. fellow Meml. Sloan-Kettering Med. Ctr., N.Y.C., 1969-70; orthopedic fellow Hosp. Spl. Surgery, N.Y.C., 1970-72; resident Bowman Gray Med. Sch., Winston-Salem, N.C., 1973-74; orthopedic surgeon pvt. practice, Sacramento, 1974-76, New Orleans, 1976-90, Riverside, Calif., 1990—. Mem. staff Parkview Hosp., Riverside Comty. Hosp., Corona Regional Hosp.; asst. prof. dept. orthopedic surgery U. Calif., Davis, 1974-76; assoc. prof. dept. orthopedic surgery La. State U. Med. Ctr., 1976-80, prof., 1980-90; clin. prof. Loma Linda U., 1990—. Contbr. numerous articles to profl. jours. Bone tumor clin. fellow Meml. Sloan-Kettering Med. Ctr., N.Y.C., 1966-70, orthopedic fellow Hosp. Spl. Surgery, N.Y.C., 1971-72. Mem. AMA, NAS, Am. Acad. Orthopaedic Surgeons, Am. Assn. Hip and Knee Surgeons, Japanese Orthopedic Assn., Orthopedic Rsch. Soc., Japanese Soc. Connective Tissue Rsch., Japanese Rehab. Assn., Am. Orthopedic Assn., So. Med. Assn., Am. Rheumatism Assn., Calif. Orthopedic Assn., Internat. Soc. Orthopedics and Traumatology, Knee Soc., Internat. Soc. Knee Surgery. Office: 3838 Sherman Dr Riverside CA 92503-4001 E-mail: hiros65@aol.com.

SHOLLENBERGER, SHARON ANN, secondary school educator; b. Pottstown, Pa., Sept. 13, 1947; d. John Clayton Sr. and Betty Jean (Sands) Lefever; m. Dennis Lee Shollenberger, May 3, 1980; 1 child, Jessica Lea. EdB, Indiana U. Pa., 1969. Cert. master's equivalency, Pa. Tchr. Downingtown (Pa.) Sch. Dist., 1969—. Advisor student coun., supr. store Lionville Mid. Sch. Recipient Gift of Time tribute Am. Family Inst., 1993. Mem. NEA, Pa. Edn. Assn., Nat. Bus. Edn. Assn. Democrat. Lutheran. Avocations: reading, embroidery, computers. Home: 415 Estate Rd Boyertown PA 19512-2223 Office: 550 W Uwchan Ave Exton PA 19341

SHONDELL, DONALD STUART, physical education educator; b. Fort Wayne, Ind., Jan. 1, 1929; s. Howard David and Elizabeth (Jones) S.; m. Betty Lou Hudson, Dec. 30, 1951; children: Steven, Kim, David, John. BS, Ball State U., 1952, MS, 1955; PED, Ind. U., 1970. Tchr. Brook (Ind.) High Sch., 1956-58; instr. Ball State U., Muncie, Ind., 1958--. Pres. U.S. Volleyball Assn., Colorado Springs, Colo., 1979-80, v.p. 1972-80; ch mn. NCAA Volleyball Com., Overland, Kans. Author: Volleyball, 1970. Recipient Leader in Volleyball award, 1971, William Morgan Pres.'s award U.S. Volleyball Assn., 1981, Tachikara 600 Victory Club award, 1989, H.T. Friermood award U.S. Volleyball Assn., Outstanding Faculty Tchr. award Ball State U, 1980, Dinsting. Alumni award Ball State U., 1984; named to Ball State Athletic Hall of Fame, 1984, Del. County Athletic Hall of Fame, 1987, Volleyball Hall of Fame, 1996; named outstanding alumnus Ball State Tchrs. Coll. Alumni Assn., 1980. Methodist. Avocations: racket sports, volleyball. Home: 1315 N Winthrop Rd Muncie IN 47304-2960 Office: Ball State U Muncie IN 47306-0001

SHONS, ALAN RANCE, plastic surgeon, surgical oncologist, educator; b. Freeport, Ill., Jan. 10, 1938; s. Ferral Caldwell and Margaret (Zimmerman) S.; children: Lesley, Susan. AB, Dartmouth Coll., 1960; MD, Case Western Res. U., 1965; PhD in Surgery, U. Minn., 1976. Diplomate Am. Bd. Surgery, Am. Bd. Plastic Surgery. Intern U. Hosp., Cleve., 1965-66, resident in surgery, 1966-67; rsch. fellow transplantation immunology U. Minn., 1969-72; resident surgery U. Minn. Hosp., 1972-74; resident plastic surgery NYU, 1974-76; asst. prof. plastic surgery U. Minn., Mpls., 1976-79, assoc. prof., 1979-84, prof., 1984; dir. divsn. plastic and reconstructive surgery U. Minn. Hosp., St. Paul Ramsey Hosp., Mpls. VA Hosp., 1976-84; cons. plastic surgery St. Louis Park Med. Ctr., 1980-84; prof. surgery Case Western Res. U., Cleve., 1984-93; dir. divsn. plastic and reconstructive surgery Case Western Reserve U., Cleve., 1984-92; prof. surgery, assoc. dir. comprehensive breast program, H. Lee Moffitt Cancer Ctr. and Rsch. Inst. U. South Fla., Tampa, 1992—. Examiner Am. Bd. Plastic Surgery, 1987-2000. Author: (with G.L. Adams and D. McQuarrie) Head and Neck Cancer, 1986; (with R. Jensen) Plastic Surgery Review, 1993. Capt. USAF, 1967-69. Fellow ACS (chmn. Minn. com. on trauma 1978-84); mem. AMA, Am. Soc. Plastic and Reconstructive Surgeons, Am. Assn. Plastic Surgeons, Minn. Acad. Plastic Surgeons (pres. 1981-82), Soc. Head and Neck Surgeons, Transplantation Soc., Plastic Surgery Rsch. Coun., Am. Soc. Aesthetic Plastic Surgery, Am. Soc. Maxillofacial Surgeons, Am. Assn. Immunologists, Soc. Exptl. Pathology, Am. Cleft Palate Assn., Am. Soc. Craniofacial Surg. Assn., Fla. Soc. Plastic and Reconstructive Surgeons, Sigma Xi. Office: 935 Northern Blvd Great Neck NY 11021

SHOOTER, ERIC MANVERS, neurobiology educator, consultant; b. Mansfield, Eng., Apr. 18, 1924; arrived in U.S., 1964; s. Fred and Pattie (Johnson) Shooter; m. Elaine Staley Arnold, May 28, 1949; 1 child, Annette Elizabeth. BA, Cambridge (Eng.) U., 1945, MA, 1949, PhD, 1950, ScD, 1986. DSc, U. London, 1964. Sr. scientist biochemistry Brewing Industry Rsch. Found., 1950—53; biochemistry lectr. Univ. Coll., London, 1953—63; assoc. prof. genetics Stanford U., 1963—68, prof. genetics and biochemistry, 1968—75, prof., chmn. neurobiology dept., 1975—87, prof. neurobiology, 1987—, chmn. Neurosci. PhD Program, 1972—82. Assoc. Neurosci. Rsch. Program, N.Y.C., 1979—89; mem. tchg. staff Internat. Sch. Neurosci., Praglia, Italy, 1987—93; sr. cons. Markey Charitable Trust, Miami, Fla., 1985—97; bd. dirs. Regeneron Pharm., Inc., Tarrytown, NY. Assoc. editor (book series) Ann. Rev. Neuroscis., 1984—2001; contbr. articles to profl. jours. Recipient Wakeman award, Duke U., 1988, Award for Disting. Achievement in Neurosci. Rsch., Bristol-Myers-Squibb, 1997; scholar, Josiah Macy Jr. Found., N.Y.C., 1974—75. Fellow: AAAS, Am. Acad. Arts and Scis., Royal Soc. (London); mem.: NAS, Am. Philos. Soc., Internat. Brain Rsch. Orgn., Internat. Soc. Neurochemistry, Am. Soc. Neurochemistry, Am. Assn. Biol. Chemists, Soc. for Neurosci. (Ralph W. Gerard prize 1995), Inst. Medicine of NAS, Alpha Omega Alpha (hon.). Avocation: travel. Home: 370 Golden Oak Dr Portola Valley CA 94028-7757 Office: Stanford U Sch Medicine Dept Neurobiology 299 Campus Dr Stanford CA 94305-5125

SHORE, HARVEY HARRIS, business educator; b. Cambridge, Mass., Apr. 14, 1940; s. Jacob and Freda Edna (Pearlman) S.; m. Roberta Ann Rogers, Jan. 29, 1967 (div. Oct. 1999); children: Nina Ellen, Elissa Amy. BA cum laude, Harvard U., 1961; MS, MIT, 1963; DBA, Harvard U., 1966. Asst. prof. indsl. adminstrn. U. Conn., Storrs, 1966-72, assoc. prof. indsl. adminstrn., 1972-77, dir. Hartford MBA prog., 1977-82, assoc. prof. mgmt. Storrs, 1982-95, assoc. prof. emeritus, 1995—. Contbr. articles to profl. jours.; editor Cubic Rev., 1975-78; author: Arts Administration and Management, 1987. Chmn. bus. adv. com. Tunxis Community Coll., Farmington, Conn., 1983-85; bd. dirs. Temple Beth Sholom, Manchester, Conn., 1987-90. Mem. Coll. and Univ. Bus. Instrs. Conn. (pres. 1975-76), Greater Nashua Human Resources Assn. (treas. 1997-98, pres. 1998-2000), Masons. Democrat. Jewish. Avocation: tennis.

SHORE, SHIRLEY WALTHER, retired secondary school educator; b. Wheeling, W.Va., 1931; d. George David and Elsie Walther; m. Curtis H. Shore, June 1, 1957; children: Laura Ann, Lisa Ann. BS in Edn., California U. of Pa., 1957. Lab technician West Penn Hosp., Pitts., 1952-54; tchr. English Monongahela (Pa.) Jr. High Sch., 1957-58; tchr. speech and drama Philipsburg-Osceola Sr. High Sch., Pa., 1958-63; instr. speech Pa. State U. Hosp., Philipsburg, 1967-72; tchr. English Philipsburg-Osceola Jr. High Sch., 1975-91, head English dept., 1987-91; tchr. English Philipsburg-Osceola Sr. High Sch., 1991—98, ret., 1998; instr. English C.C. Allegheny County, Pa., 2001—02. Tchr. speed reading Philipsburg-Osceola Sr. High Sch., 1957-72; columnist Centre Daily Times, State College, Pa., 1983-90. Chmn. Philipsburg Citizens Com. Against Pollution, 1970-72. Mem. DAR, Pa. Assn. Sch. Retirees, Daus. Am. Colonists, Colonial Dames 17th Century, Wetzel County Geneal. Soc. Democrat. Presbyterian. Avocations: genealogy, music, poetry, writing, theater. Home: 1104 Alton St Philipsburg PA 16866-2710

SHORT, BETSY ANN, elementary education educator; b. Macon, Ga., Mar. 18, 1958; d. Garland Brooks Jr. and Mary Eleanor (Jordan) Turner; m. Lynn Robin Short, July 21, 1984. BS in Early Childhood Edn., Ga. Coll., Milledgeville, 1981, M in Early Childhood Edn., 1993, EdS in Early Childhood Edn., 1995; EdS in reading, U. West Ga., 2001, cert. specialist in reading, 2001; intech cert., Macon State Coll., 2001; degree in Adminstrn. and Supervision, Ga. Coll. and State U., 2002. Cert. elem. tchr. and tchr. support specialist, Ga. Tchr. 3d grade Stockbridge (Ga.) Elem. Sch., 1983-84, tchr. kindergarten, 1984-93; tchr. augmented spl. instructional assistance Locust Grove (Ga.) Elem. Sch., 1993-97, kindergarten tchr., 1997-99, first grade tchr., 1999-2000, early intervention reading tchr., 2000—02, 2000—02; student support specialist Unity Grove Elem. and Ola Elem., 2002—03; asst. prin. Morgan County Primary Sch., Madison, Ga., 2003—; v.p. Henry Heritage Reading Coun., 1999—2000. Cons. Saxon Pub. Co.; v.p. Henry Heritage Reading Coun., 1999-2001; specialist in Reading, U. West Ga., Carrollton, 2001. Author: Spinning Yarns, 1995; mem. editl. adv. bd. Ga. Jour. Reading; contbr. articles to profl. jours.; artist oil painting/pen and ink drawing. V.p. Henry Heritage Reading Coun., 1999—2000. Mem. Profl. Assn. of Ga. Educators, Ga. Coun. Tchrs. Maths., Ga. Coun. Internat. Reading Assn., Ga. Coun. Social Studies, Ga. Sci. Tchrs. Assn., Henry Heritage Reading Coun. Baptist. Avocations: oil painting, cross-stiching, writing short stories, story telling. Office: Morgan County Primary Sch 993 East Ave Madison GA 30650 E-mail: bshort@morgan.k12.ga.us.

SHORT, ELIZABETH M. physician, educator, federal agency administrator; b. Boston, June 2, 1942; d. James Edward and Arlene Elizabeth (Mitchell) Meehan; m. Michael Allen Friedman, June 21, 1976; children: Lia Gabrielle, Hannah Ariel, Eleanor Elana. BA Philosophy magna cum laude, Mt. Holyoke Coll., 1963; MD cum laude, Yale U., 1968. Diplomate Am. Bd. Internal Medicine, Am. Bd. Med. Genetics. Resident internal medicine Yale New Haven Hosp., 1968-70; postdoctoral fellow in human genetics Yale Med. Sch., 1970-72; resident U. Calif., San Francisco, 1972-73; sr. chief resident Stanford (Calif.) Med. Sch., 1973-75; asst. prof. medicine Stanford Med. Sch., 1975-83, assoc. dean student affairs/med. edn., 1978-83; dep. dir. acad. affairs, dir. biomed. rsch. Assn. Am. Med. Colls., Washington, 1983-88; dep. assoc. chief med. dir. for acad. affairs VA, Washington, 1988-92, assoc. chief med. dir. for acad. affairs, 1992-96; health policy cons. HHS, 1996—2001; ret., 2001. Vis. prof. human biology Stanford U., 1983-86; mem. Accreditation Coun. Grad. Med. Edn., 1988-97; mem. White House Task Force on Health Care Reform, 1993. Assoc. editor Clin. Rsch. Jour., 1976-79, editor 1980-84; contbr. articles to profl. jours. Mem. Nat. Child Health Adv. Coun., NIH, 1991-97; mem. com. edn. and tng. Office Sci. and Tech. Policy, White House, Washington, 1991-96. Recipient Maclean Zoology award; Munger scholar, Markle scholar, Sara Williston scholar Mt. Holyoke Coll., 1959-63, Yale Men in Medicine scholar, 1964-68; Bardwell Meml. Med. fellow, 1963. Mem. AAAS, Am. Soc. Human Genetics (pub. policy com. 1984-95, chmn. 1986-94), Am. Fedn. Clin. Rsch. (bd. dirs. 1973-83, co-chmn. com. status women 1975-77, editor Clin. Rsch. Jour., 1978-83, nat. coun., exec. com., pub. policy com. 1977-87), Western Soc. Clin. Investigation, Calif. Acad. Medicine, Phi Beta Kappa, Alpha Omega Alpha. Home and Office: 3535 Ranch Top Rd Pasadena CA 91107 E-mail: elizshort@aol.com.

SHORT, JANET MARIE, principal; b. Boston, Sept. 18, 1939; d. Robert Emmett and Getta Agnes (Mills) Short. BS in Edn., Boston State Coll., 1962, MEd, 1967; LLD (hon.), Regis Coll., 1991; DPedagogy (hon.), Northeastern U., 2002. Tchr. Boston Pub. Schs., 1962-70, acting asst. dir. staff devel., 1970-71, tchr.-in-charge, 1971-75; prin. D.L. Barrett Sch., Boston, 1976-81; tchr. Boston Pub. Schs., 1981-82; prin. Maurice J. Tobin Sch., Boston, 1982—2001, lead cluster prin., 1995—2001; ret., 2001. Lectr. in field. Adv. bd. DiMaiti Stuart Found., Boston, 1990—97, Mission Hill and Camp Mission Possible, 1984—87; cmty. adv. bd. Harvard Sch. Pub. Health, Boston, 1990—; adv. bd. Boston Against Drugs, 1990—94. Recipient Women of Achievement award, Big Sister Assn. of Greater Boston, 1994, Thankful Recognition award, Channel 5 Boston, 1987, Recognition award, Boston Women's Mag., 1988, Pub. Svc. award, Henry L. Shattuck, Boston Mcpl. Bur. Rsch. award, 1988, Freedom's Found. Honor medal, 1990, Ann. Excellence in Edn. award, Alpha Gamma chpt. Pi Lambda Theta, 1993. Mem.: MESPA, ASCD, Boston Elem. Prins. Assn., Boston Mid. Sch. Assn., Boston Assn. Sch. Adminstrs. (exec. bd. 1984—93), Mass. Mid. Level Adminstrs. Assn., Delta Kappa Gamma (chpt. pres. 1978—80). Roman Catholic. Avocations: travel, bowling, reading, gardening. Home: 39 Ridgeway Dr Quincy MA 02169-2321

SHORT, LINDA MATTHEWS, retired elementary education educator; b. Winston-Salem, N.C., Mar. 25, 1949; d. Edwin Kohl and Nannie Mae (Bowen) Matthews; m. James Coy Short, June 18, 1972. BS, Appalachian State U., 1971, MA, 1981. Cert. elem. edn. tchr. Tchr. Mt. Airy (N.C.) City Schs., 1971-72, 88-01, Surry County Schs., Dobson, N.C., 1972-88. Mem. Mt. Airy City Schs. Adv. Bd., 1994-95. Pres.-elect Foothills Reading Coun., 1992-93; active Mt. Airy Women's Club, 1970s, Mt. Airy Jaycettes, 1970s; mem. adv. bd. State Employees Credit Union, 1998-2001. Mem. Foothills Reading Coun. (pres. 1993-96), N.C. Reading Assn. (area dir. 1995-96, com. chair 1996-97, conf. coord. 1998, sec. 1998-00, v.p. 2000-01, pres.-elect 2001-2002, pres. 2002-2003), N.C. Assn. Educators (dist. sec. 1996-97, 98), Internat. Reading Assn., Mt. Airy N.C. Assn. Educators (treas. 1992-94, v.p. 1996-97), Altrusa Club, Mayberry Reading Coun. (pres. 2000-01). Democrat. Avocations: music, painting, crafts, collecting dolls, ceramic cats. Home: 125 Brentwood Dr Mount Airy NC 27030-1860

SHORT, MARION PRISCILLA, neurogenetics educator; b. Milford, Del., June 12, 1951; d. Raymond Calistus and Barbara Anne (Ferguson) S.; m. Michael Peter Klein; 1 child, Asher Calistus Klein. BA, Bryn Mawr Coll., 1973; diploma, U. Edinburgh (Scotland), 1975; MD, Med. Coll. Pa., 1978. Diplomate Am. Bd. Psychiatry and Neurology, Am. Bd. Internal Medicine. Intern in internal medicine Hahnemann Med. Coll. Hosp., Phila., 1978-79; med. resident in internal medicine St. Lukes-Roosevelt Hosp., N.Y.C., 1979-81; neurology resident U. Pitts. Health Ctr., 1981-84; fellow in med. genetics Mt. Sinai Med. Ctr., N.Y.C., 1984-86; fellow in neurology Mass. Gen. Hosp., Boston, 1986-90, asst. neurologist, 1990-95; asst. prof. dept. neurology Harvard Med. Sch., Boston, 1990-95; assoc. prof. dept. neurology, pediat. and pathology U. Chgo., 1995—97; program dir. genetics, transplantation and clin. rsch. AMA, Chgo., 1997—2002; fellow McLean Ctr. for Clin. Med. Ethics U. Chgo., 2002—03, sr. fellow McLean Ctr. for Clin. Med. Ethics, 2003—. Recipient Clin. Investigator Devel. award, NIH, 1988—93; fellow, Inst. Medicine, Chgo., 1999, McLean Ctr. for Clin. Med. Ethics, U. Chgo., 2002—. Mem. AMA, Am. Acad. Neurology, Am. Soc. for Human Genetics, Am. Coll. Med. Genetics. Office: Pediat Neurosurgery U Chgo MC 4066 5481 S Maryland Ave Chicago IL 60637-4325 E-mail: priscilla_short@ama-assn.org., mpshort@surgery.bsd.uchicago.edu.

SHORTLIFFE, EDWARD HANCE, internist, medical educator, computer scientist; b. Edmonton, Alta., Can., Aug. 28, 1947; s. Ernest Carl and Elizabeth Joan Shortliffe. AB, Harvard U., 1970; PhD, Stanford U., 1975, MD, 1976. Diplomate Am. Bd. Internal Medicine. Trainee NIH, 1971—76; intern Mass. Gen. Hosp., Boston, 1976—77; resident Stanford Hosp., Palo Alto, Calif., 1977—79; asst. prof. medicine Stanford U. Sch. Medicine, Palo Alto, 1979—85, assoc. prof., 1985—90, chief divsn. gen. internal medicine, 1988—95, prof., 1990—2000; assoc. chair medicine Primary Care, 1993—95; assoc. dean info. resources and tech. Stanford U. Sch. Medicine, 1995—2000; prof., chair dept. biomed. informatics Columbia U. Coll. Physicians and Surgeons, N.Y.C., 2000—; deputy v.p. Information Technology, Health Sciences, Columbia U., N.Y.C., 2002—; bd. dirs. Medco Health Solutions, Inc., 2003—. Advisor Nat. Bd. Med. Examiners, Phila., 1987—93; pres. Symposium on Computer Applications in Med. Care, Washington, 1988—89; mem. Nat. Fed. Networking Adv. Coun., NSF, 1991—93; mem. computer sci. and telecomm. bd. NRC, 1991—96; bd. regents ACP-Am. Soc. Internal Medicine, 1996—2002; mem. President's Info. Tech. Adv. Com., 1997—2002; chmn. com. on healthcare and next generation internet NRC, 1998—2000; mem. Nat. Com. on Vital Health Stats., 2000—. Editor: Rule-Based Expert Systems, 1984, Readings in Medical Artificial Intelligence, 1984, Medical Informatics: Computer Applications in Health Care, 1990, Medical Informatics: Computer Applications in Health Care and Biomedicine, 2d edit., 2000. Mem. com. Sci. and Engring. Pub. Policy Nat. Acad. Sci., 2001—. Recipient Grace M. Hopper award, Assn. Computing Machinery, 1976, Young Investigator award, Western Soc. Clin. Investigation, 1987, Rsch. Career award, Nat. Libr. of Medicine, 1979—84; scholar, Kaiser Family Found., 1983—88. Fellow: Am. Coll. Med. Informatics (pres. 1992—94), Am. Assn. Artificial Intelligence; mem.: Am. Clin. and Climatol. Assn., Assn. Am. Physicians, Am. Med. Informatics Assn., Am. Soc. for Clin. Investigation, Inst. Medicine (mem. coun. 2000—), Soc. for Med. Decisionmaking (pres. 1989—90). Achievements include development of several medical computer programs including MYCIN. Avocations: skiing, jazz. Office: Columbia-Presbyn Med Ctr Vanderbilt Clinic Ste 550 622 W 168th St New York NY 10032-3720 E-mail: shortliffe@dbmi.columbia.edu.

SHOTTS, EMMETT BOOKER, JR., microbiology educator, researcher; b. Jasper, Ala., Sept. 23, 1931; s. Emmett Booker and Will Laceye (Brown) Shotts; m. Martha C. Monroe, Sept. 7, 1997; children: Elizabeth, Dan, Evelyn, Georgia Alice Maria. BS, U. Ala., 1952; MS, U. Ga., 1958, PhD, 1966. Epidemic intellegence svc. Ctr. for Disease Control, Atlanta, 1959-61; rsch. microbiologist Ctrs. for Disease Control, Atlanta, 1962-64; rsch. assoc. U. Ga., Athens, 1957-59, prof., 1966—97, prof. emeritus, 1997—; dir. Nat. Fish Health Rsch. Lab. US Dept. Interior, 1997—2001; cons., 2001—. Contbr. 35 chpts. to books, 175 abstracts and 242 articles to profl. jours. With U.S. Army, 1954-56. Recipient Rsch. award Beecham Pharm., 1986, 87, Edwards award Am. Soc. for Microbiology southeastern br., 1990, Feeley award, 1992, Disting. Svc. award Wildlife Disease Assn., 1992, Sneiszko award Fish Health Am. Fisheries Soc., 1995. Fellow Am. Acad. Microbiology (specialist med. microbiology); mem. Am. Soc. Clin. Pathology (med. technologist), Am. Coll. Vet. Microbiology (hon. diplomate), Am. Vet. Epidemiology Soc. (hon. diplomate). Office: Dept Med Microbiology U Ga Athens GA 30602 E-mail: emshotts@alltel.net.

SHOUB, EARLE PHELPS, engineer, industrial hygienist, educator; b. Washington, July 19, 1915; m. Elda Robinson; children: Casey Louis, Heather Margaret Shoub Dills. BS in Chemistry, Poly. U., 1938, postgrad., 1938-39. Registered profl. engr.; cert. safety profl. Chemist Hygrade Food Products Corp., N.Y.C., 1940-41, Nat. Bur. Stds., 1941-43; regional dir. U.S. Bur. Mines, 1943-62, chief div. accident prevention and health, 1962-70; dep. dir. Appalachian Lab. Occupl. Safety and Health, Nat. Inst. Occupl. Safety and Health, Morgantown, W.Va., 1970-77, dep. dir. divsn. safety rsch., 1977-79; mgr. occupl. safety, indsl. environ. cons. safety products Am. Optical Corp., Southbridge, Mass., 1979; cons., from 1979. Assoc. clin. prof. dept. anesthesiology W.Va. U. Med. Center, Morgantown, 1977-82, prof. Coll. Mineral and Energy Resources, 1970-79. Contbr. articles to profl. jours., chpts. to textbooks. Recipient Disting. Svc. award and gold medal Dept. Interior, 1959. Fellow Am. Inst. Chemists, Royal Soc. Medicine: mem. AIME, ASTM, NSPE, Am. Indsl. Hygiene Assn. (emeritus), Vets. of Safety, Am. Soc. Safety Engrs., Nat. Fire Protection Assn. (life), Am. Conf. Govtl. Indsl. Hygienists, Internat. Soc. Respiratory Protection (emeritus, past pres., William H. Revoir award 1993), Am. Nat. Stds. Inst., Soc. Mining Engrs., Sigma Xi. Methodist. Died Jan. 4, 2002.

SHOUN, ELLEN LLEWELLYN, retired secondary school educator; b. Germantown, Pa., Sept. 8, 1925; d. William Thomas and Ella (Hall) Llewellyn; m. Glenn Harte Shoun, June 25, 1949; children: Mary Deborah, Paul L., Eleanor C., Peter G., Elizabeth A. AB in Chemistry, Oberlin Coll., 1947; MA in Sci. Edn., Western Mich. U., 1972. Cert. libr. (ltd. profl.) Mich., secondary sch. tchr. Mich. Jr. chemist Am. Cyanamid, Stamford, Conn., 1947-49; Charles M. Hall Chem. instr. Oberlin (Ohio) Coll., 1949-51; br. libr. Bronson (Mich.) Pub. Libr., 1966-67; math. and sci. tchr. Bronson H.S., 1967-79; crew leader 1980 U.S. Census, Branch County, Mich., 1980; bus. mgr. Dr. C.F. Cole's Dental Office, Sturgis, Mich., 1982; reference aide Br. Dist. Libr., Coldwater, Mich., 1982-99; ret., 1999. Founder (with others) Bronson H.S. Cmty. Recycling Group, 1972—79. Trustee Bronson Pub. Libr., 1968—82, Housing Commn., 1975—; instr. CPR Cmty. health Ctr., Coldwater, Mich., 1978—80; cmty. chorus Cmty. Found., 1987—; chair refugee family com. Bronson United Meth. Ch., 1974—82, ch. choir, 1967—, sec. adminstrv. bd., 1987—, chair adminstrv. bd., 1984—86; bd. dirs., treas., mgr. Food Pantry, 5 Ch. Coop., Bronson, 1993—. Named Hon. Grand Marshal, Polish Festival Parade, Bronson, 2002; recipient Cmty. Vol. of Yr. award, Gleaner Life Ins. Soc., 2001. Mem.: Phi Beta Kappa. Democrat. Avocations: photography, knitting, Scrabble.

SHOVER, JOAN, retired secondary school educator; b. St. Joseph, Mo., Apr. 7, 1948; d. Jay S. and Clara Lillian (Burkett) Marquis; m. Rolland Craig Shover, May 31, 1975; children: Terra Jayne, Thomas Jay. BS in Edn., Ctrl. Mo. State U., 1971, MS in Edn., 1976, postgrad., 1989-96. Cert. tchr., edn. specialist, Mo. Phys. edn. tchr. Worth County H.S., Grant City, Mo., 1971-73, Blue Springs (Mo.) H.S., 1973—2003, ret., 2003. Rev. com. Mo. Dept. Elem. and Secondary Edn., Jefferson City, 1993—; mem. Mo. Quality Health/Phys. Edn. Cadre, 1998-2003. Mem. Mo. Gov.'s Council for Fitness and Health, 2002—. Named Educator of Yr., Am. Cancer Soc., 1989, Top 36 Am. Tchrs. award, Disney Corp., 1992, Mo. State Secondary Physical Educator of Yr., 1996. Mem. Am. Coun. on Exercise, Internat. Dance Exercise Assn., Mo. Assn. Phys. Edn., Health, Recreation and Dance (Kansas City rep. 1988—, pres. elect 1998-99, pres. 1998-99, past pres. 1999-2000, Kansas City Dist. Phys. Educator award 1989, Presdl. award 1988), Mo. State Tchrs. Assn., Delta Kappa Gamma. Avocations: reading, dancing, skiing, running. Home: 1418 NW A St Blue Springs MO 64015-3605 Office: 2000 Ashton Dr Blue Springs MO 64015 E-mail: jshover50@aol.com.

SHPIECE, MICHAEL RONALD, lawyer, educator; b. Detroit, Nov. 13, 1956; s. Harold Edwin and Rose Marie (Wheeler) S.; m. Tracy B. Schwartz; children: David E. Schwartz, Daniel E. Schwartz. PhB, Wayne State U., 1977; JD, U. Mich., 1984. Bar: Mich. 1985. Com. adminstr. Joint Legis. Com. on Aging, Lansing, Mich., 1979-81; policy analyst to commr. Mich. Ins. Bur., Lansing, 1981; legis. cons Cmty. Action Program Mich. UAW, Lansing, 1981-82; dep. dir. Mich. Dept. Licensing and Regulation, Lansing, 1983-85; assoc., ptnr. Honigman Miller Schwartz & Cohn, Detroit, 1985-93; adj. prof. law Wayne State U. Law Sch., Detroit, 1996—; of counsel Shapack, McCullough & Kanter, Bloomfield Hills, Mich., 1994-98; prin. Miller, Shpiece & Tischler, Southfield, Mich., 1998—. Pres. Friends of Child Abuse Prevention, Southfield, Mich., 1994—; bd. dirs. chmn. Mich. Freedom of Info. Com., Detroit, 1996-98. Contbr. articles to profl. jours. Pres. and trustee Farmington (Mich.) Bd. Edn., 1975-83; chairperson Farmington Hills Ad Hoc Com. on Ethics, 1990-96. Mem.: ABA (vice chair, chair-elect employee benefits com.), Oakland County Bar Assn., Am. Statis. Assn., Econ. Club Detroit. Democrat. Jewish. Home: 39372 Plumbrook Dr Farmington Hills MI 48331-2976 Office: Ste 200 26711 Northwestern Hwy Southfield MI 48034-2159 E-mail: mshpiece@msapc.net.

SHRACK, MARSHA CAROL, art educator, gallery director; b. El Dorado, Kans., June 14, 1952; d. Marvin Ray and Wanita June (Reynolds) Gates; m. Christopher George Shrack; children: Chelsea Christine, Emma Leigh, Gates Kipp. B Art Edn., Wichita (Kans.) State U., 1975, M Art Edn., 1978. Cert. art tchr., Kans. Grad. teaching asst. Wichita State U., 1975-76; secondary sch. art tchr. Unified Sch. Dist. 268, Cheney, Kans., 1976-77; K-12 art tchr. Bethel Life Sch., Wichita, 1979-81, Christian Ctr. Acad., Wichita, 1977-82; instr. art Pratt (Kans.) C.C., 1985—, art gallery dir., 1986-87, 93—. Graphic artist Peters and Assocs. Graphic Design, Wichita, 1982-84; freelance sign painter, Wichita, 1982-85; presenter in field; cons., art edn. advocate Haskins Elem. Sch., Pratt, 1992—. Exhibited in individual shows at Hutchinson (Kans.) Art Assn., 1991, Baker Arts Ctr., Liberal, Kans., 1992, Open Window Gallery, Pratt, Kans., 2001, Builders Block Gallery, Coffeeville, Kans., 2001, Mathews Gallery, Wichita, 2002, Stonehouse Gallery, Fredonia, Kans., 2003; exhibited in group shows at Lawrence (Kans.) Arts Ctr., 1993, Kans. Artist Craftsman, 1992-94, Faculty Art Exhibit Pratt C.C., 1986-2003, Baker Art Ctr., 1995. Art judge Hutchinson Art Assn. Art Fair, 1992, Acad. Olympics, Ctrl. Kans. H.S. Competition, 1985-2003, Nat. Fellowship Christian Schs., Waco, Tex., 1980. Mem. NEA, Nat. Art Edn. Assn., Kans. Art Edn. Assn., Pratt Higher Edn. Assn. (Tchr. of Yr. 1994), Kans. Artist Craftsman Assn. (bd. dirs., S.W. region rep.). Avocations: pottery, fibers and fabrics, gardening, church and family activities. Home: 226 NE 90th St Iuka KS 67066-9541 Office: Pratt Cmty Coll 348 NE State Road 61 Pratt KS 67124-8317 E-mail: marshas@prattcc.edu.

SHRADER, DOUGLAS WALL, JR., philosophy educator; b. Grundy, Va., May 22, 1953; s. Douglas Wall and Audrey Anne (Looney) S.; m. Barbara Frances Donahoe, June 15, 1975; children: Callie Hannah, Sterling Douglas. BA, Va. Polytech. Inst., 1974; MA, U. Ill., Chgo., 1975, PhD, 1979. Asst. to dean grad. studies U. Ill., Chgo., 1974-79; instr. philosophy U. Wis., Parkside, 1979; asst. prof. philosophy SUNY, Oneonta, 1979-85, assoc. prof. philosophy, 1985-92, prof. philosophy, 1992-99, chair dept. philosophy, 1988-91, 93—, dean humanities and fine arts, 1991-93, disting. teaching prof. philosophy, 1999—. Cons. Regents Coll., Albany, NY, 1994—, McGraw-Hill, N.Y., 1992—99, Prentice-Hall, NY, 1997, Jones and Bartlett, 1998, Oxford, 2001—02, SUNY Press, 2000—02, Wadsworth, 2003, Blackwell Publ., 2003. Author: Pathways to Philosophy, 1996; editor: Seeds of Wisdom, 1997, Language, Ethics and Ontology, 1998, The Fractal Self, 2000, Ethics, Theory and Practice, 1996, Children of Athena, 1999, Philosophy and the Public Realm, 2001, Thinking Outside the Box, 2002, Philosophical Dreams, 2003; mem. editl. bd., editor-in-chief Oneonta Philosophy Studies, 1991—, Ashgate World Philosophies Series, 1999—; mem. editl. bd. Ednl. Change, 1995—, Eidos: Studies in Ancient and Medieval Philosophy, 1991—, East-West Connections, 2000—. Bd. dirs. Catskill Area Hospice, Oneonta, 1985-88; troop treas. Boy Scouts Am., Oneonta, 1994-98, cubmaster, 1991-94; judge Odyssey of the Mind, Oneonta, 1994—. Rsch. grantee W.B. Ford Found., 1995, 98, 99, 2000, Henry Luce Found., 1999, 2002 Chinese Ministry of Edn., 2002; summer inst. fellow NEH, 1980, 85, 89, 95, 98; recipient Commendation for Acad. Excellence, SUNY-Oneonta Alumni Assn., 1995, Chancellor's award Excellence in Teaching, 1991 Mem. Soc. for Ancient Greek Philosophy, Soc. Comparative Study Civilizations, East-West Ctr. Assoc., N.Y. State Founds. Edn. Assn. Avocations: photography, music, construction, classic cars. Office: SUNY-Oneonta Ravine Pkwy Oneonta NY 13820-3414

SHRADER, LYNNE ANN, secondary school educator, coach; b. Concord, Mass., May 13, 1955; d. Arthur E. Jr. and Helen Louise (Eaton) Fay; m. John Neal Shrader, Nov. 11, 1978; children: Kristen Michelle, Michael Aaron. BS in Phys. Edn. and Health, Fla. So. Coll., 1978; postgrad., U. Tex., 1984; MEd in Ednl. Leadership, Augusta (Ga.) Coll., 2000; EdS in Ednl. Leadership, Ga. Coll. and State U., 2003. Cert. middle level sci., life phys. edn. and health tchr., Tex., health and phys. edn. tchr. (K-12), Ga. Tchr. sci. Copperas Cove (Tex.) Jr. High Sch., 1982-83; tchr., coach Manor Mid. Sch., Killeen, Tex., 1983-85; tchr. phys. edn. John Milledge Elem. Sch., Augusta, Ga., 1985-86, Blythe (Ga.) Elem. Sch., 1986-88, Terrace Manor Elem. Sch., 1988-90; tchr. phys. edn., health, coach, dept. chair Lakeside Mid. Sch., Evans, Ga., 1990—. Recreation specialist Frankfurt (Germany) Mil. Comty. Recreation Svcs., 1978-80, Richmond County Recreation and Parks Dept., Augusta, 1986-91; dir. Spl. Edn. Summer Camp Free-To-Be-Me, 1995; dir. transp. Summer Olympics, Atlanta, 1996. Mem. exec. com. Lakeside Mid. Sch. Booster Club, 1990-93; pres. Lakeside Mid. Sch. Parent-Tchr.-Student Orgn., 1992-93; mem. Ga. Leadership Resource Network. Recipient outstanding vol. award Hershey (Pa.) Track and Field Orgn., 1989, Tchr. of Month award Lakeside Mid. Sch., 1991. Mem. ASCD, AAHPERD, Profl. Assn. Ga. Educators (bldg. rep. 1991-). Republican. Congregationalist. Avocations: all sports, reading, sewing. E-mail: shraderjegte.net. Home: 716 Ashepoo Court Evans GA 30809 Office: Lakeside Mid Sch 527 Blue Ridge Dr Evans GA 30809-3605

SHRAGE, LAURETTE, special education educator; b. Montreal, Jan. 15, 1951; d. Ivan and Adela (Zupnik) Benda; m. William Lee Shrage, Oct. 30, 1977; children: Robert, Jaclyn. BS in Elem. Edn., Adelphi U., 1972; MS in Reading, Coll. New Rochelle, 1994. Cert. elem. edn., spl. edn., reading, bilingual edn., N.Y. Mgr. Century Operating Corp., N.Y.C., 1973-82; substitute tchr. New Rochelle (N.Y.) Sch. Dist., 1992-93, bilingual spl. edn. tchr., 1993—; substitute tchr. Keller Sch., Yonkers, N.Y., 1992-93; spl. edn. tchr., 1993—; co-owner Pet Store, 1998—. Parent rep. New Rochelle Com. Presch. Spl. Edn., 1990-91, New Rochelle Com. Spl. Edn., 1991-92; mem. adv. coun. Jefferson Sch., New Rochelle, 1993—, mem. Magnet Think Tank com., 1994—; mem. Ptnrs. in Policy Making N.Y. State, 1992; Instr. Family Sci. Workshop, 1996—; co-owner full svc. pet store. Pres. PTA Augustus St. Gardens Sch., N.Y.C., 1987-90; advt. mgr. Mitchell Lama Apt., N.Y.C., 1983-86; telethon vol. Channel 13, N.Y.C., 1977; sponsor Sagamore Children's Sch., Suffolk, N.Y., 1974. Recipient Parent Leadership award Coun. Suprs. and Adminstrs. City of N.Y., 1990. Avocations: spanish, french, tennis, piano, opera. Home: 110 Valley Forge Rd Weston CT 06883-1930 Office: Jefferson Sch 131 Weyman Ave New Rochelle NY 10805-1428

SHRAUNER, BARBARA WAYNE ABRAHAM, electrical engineer, educator; b. Morristown, N.J., June 21, 1934; d. Leonard Gladstone and Ruth Elizabeth (Thrasher) Abraham; m. James Ely Shrauner, 1965; children: Elizabeth Ann, Jay Arthur. BA cum laude, U. Colo., 1956; AM, Harvard U., 1957, PhD, 1962. Postdoctoral researcher U. Libre de Bruxelles, Brussels, 1962-64; postdoctoral researcher NASA-Ames Rsch. Ctr., Moffett Field, Calif., 1964-65; asst. prof. Washington U., St. Louis, 1966-69, assoc. prof., 1969-77, prof., 1977—. Sabbatical Los Alamos (N.Mex.) Sci. Lab., 1975-76, Lawrence Berkeley Lab., Berkeley, Calif., 1985-86; cons. Los Alamos Nat. Lab., 1979, 84, NASA, Washington, 1980, Naval Surface Weapons Lab., Silver Spring, Md., 1984. Contbr. articles on transport in semiconductors, hidden symmetries of differential equations, plasma physics to profl. jours. Fellow Am. Phys. Soc. (sr. divsn. plasma physics, exec. com. 1980-82, 96-98); mem. IEEE (sr.; sr. exec. com. of standing tech. com. on plasma sci. and applications 1996-98), AAUP (local sec.-treas. 1980-82), Am. Geophys. Union, Univ. Fusion Assn., Phi Beta Kappa, Sigma Xi, Eta Kappa Nu, Sigma Pi Sigma. Home: 7452 Stratford Ave Saint Louis MO 63130-4044 Office: Washington U 1 Brookings Dr Dept Elec Saint Louis MO 63130-4899 E-mail: bas@ee.wustl.edu.

SHREEVE, JEAN'NE MARIE, chemist, educator; b. Deer Lodge, Mont., July 2, 1933; d. Charles William and Maryfrances (Briggerman) Shreeve. BA in Chemistry, U. Mont., 1953, DSc (hon.), 1982; MS in Analytical Chemistry, U. Minn., 1956; PhD in Inorganic Chemistry, U. Wash., 1961. From asst. prof. to assoc. prof. chemistry U. Idaho, Moscow, 1961—67, prof., 1967-73, 2000—, acting chmn. dept. chemistry, 1969-70, 1973, head dept. and prof., 1973-87, v.p. rsch. and grad. studies, prof. chemistry, 1987-99. Mem. nat. com. Stds. Higher Edn., 1965—67, 1969—73; Lucy W. Pickett lectr. Mt. Holyoke Coll., 1976; George H. Cady lectr. U. Wash., 1993; chmn. Pres.'s Com. Medal Sci., 2003—. Mem. editl. bd. Jour. Fluorine Chemistry, 1970—, Jour. Heteroatom Chemistry, 1988—95, Accounts Chem. Rsch., 1973—75, Inorganic Synthesis, 1976—; contbr. articles to sci. jours. Mem. bd. govs. Argonne (Ill.) Nat. Lab., 1992—98. Named Hon. Alumnus, U. Idaho, 1972; named to Idaho Hall of Fame, 2001; recipient Disting. Alumni award, U. Mont., 1970, Outstanding Achievement award, U. Minn., 1975, Sr. U.S. Scientist award, Alexander Von Humboldt Found., 1978, Excellence in Tchg. award, Chem. Mfrs. Assn., 1980; NSF Postdoctoral fellow, U. Cambridge, Eng., 1967—68, U.S. Hon. Ramsay fellow, 1967—68, Alfred P. Sloan fellow, 1970—72. Mem.: AAUW (officer Moscow chpt. 1962—69), AAAS (bd. dirs. 1991—95), Idaho Acad. Sci. (Disting. Scientist 2001, Shirley B. Radding award Santa Clara Valley sect. 2003), Am. Chem. Soc. (bd. dirs. 1985—93, chmn. fluorine divsn. 1979—81, mem. adv. bd. Petroleum Rsch. Fund 1975—77, mem. women chemists com. 1972—77, Harry and Carol Mosher award Santa Clara Valley sect. 1992), Göttingen (Germany) Acad. Scis. (corr.), Phi Beta Kappa. Avocations: fishing, gardening. Office: U Idaho Dept Chemistry Moscow ID 83844-2343 Fax: 208-885-9146. E-mail: jshreeve@uidaho.edu.

SHREEVE, SUSANNA SEELYE, educational planning facilitator; BA in Dance, Arts and Humanities, Mills Coll.; MA in Confluent Edn., U. Calif., Santa Barbara, 1989; postgrad., U. Calif., 1990, San Diego State U., 1992. Cert. elem. tchr., C.C. adminstr., tchr., Calif. Comm. instr. Brooks Inst., 1982; initiator Santa Barbara County Arts and Aging Forum, 1982; co-planner PARTners "How Kids Learn" Conf., 1985; dir. Los Ninos Bilingual Head Start Program, 1986-87; writing counselor Am. and internat. students S.B. City Coll., 1988, U. Calif., Santa Barbara, 1989-90; writing counselor Upward Bound, 1989-90; edn. coord. Santa Barbara County Urban Indian Project, Santa Barbara, 1989-90; instr. Santa Barbara Youth Cultural Arts, 1993; planner/staff Tri-County Regional Team Youth Summit, 1993-94, staff/planner Discovering Individual Identity, 1993—; planner SIG confluent edn. AERA, 1994-98; DQ-U. math/sci. resources for tchrs. Indian Edn., 1992—; multi-cultural cmty. Regional Alliance Info. Network

Internet Youth Programs, Santa Barbara, 1991—. Pro-Youth Coalition planner City Santa Barbara, NetDay 1996—, Native Ams., 1996—; planner, adv., website liaison Nuc. Age Peace Found, World Indigenous Peoples Edn. Confs. Networker Native Am. Rights Fund, mem. youth commn.; mem. steering com. Santa Barbara Cmty. Currency; charter mem. Smithsonian Mus. Am. Indians (Friends of the Lakota); active Adopt a (Oglala) Grandparent, 1994—; founder, cons., facilitator, writer, spkr. William Samuel and Friends Native Am. Voices semi-ann. Cir. of Sharing; rep. Am. Religions Spl. Collection Archives U. Calif.-Santa Barbara. Mem. Cmty. Urban Agr., Intertribal Bison Coop., SB's Foothills Coalition, Sensory Awareness Found., Native Am.Writers Wordcraft Cir., Cmty. Youth Journalists, Nat. Congress Am. Indians (life), Kappa Delta Pi. Office: PO Box 3887 Santa Barbara CA 93130-3887 E-mail: susanna@glimpsesandglimmers.com., susanna@rain.org.

SHREINER, CURT, educational technologist, consultant; b. Ephrata, Pa., June 27, 1952; s. Paul H. and Grace B. BS in Edn., Millersville U., 1974; MS in Integrative Edn., Marywood Coll., 1977; MEd in Tech. and Media, Temple U., 1982; EdD in Tech. and Media, Columbia U., 1989. Tchr. Lebanon (Pa.) Sch. Dist., 1974-76; instr., researcher Millersville (Pa.) State U., 1976-77; writer, pub. Instrnl. Design Assocs., Lancaster, Pa., 1977-80; tchr. trainer Mainland (Pa.) Inst., 1980-81; videodisc designer WNET/THIRTEEN, Pub. TV, N.Y.C., 1981-82; computer software designer Academic Tech., Inc., Moorestown, N.J., 1982-86; audio scriptwriter Learn Inc., Mt. Laurel, N.J., 1986-87; CAI curriculum developer Constructive Alternatives, Inc., Phila., 1987-88; GUI designer Resolute, Ltd., Phila., 1988-91; multimedia designer Remtech Svcs. Inc., Newport News, Va., 1991-92; database design and info. mgmt. trainer The Work Group, Pennsauken, N.J., 1992; multimedia project dir. Vocat. Rsch. Inst., Phila., 1993-95; owner Curt Shreiner Prodns., 1995-96; multimedia designer Galaxy Scientific Corp., Warminster, Pa., 1996—. Computer cons. Phila. Mayor's Commn. on Literacy, 1987-91; learning cons. for Pub. Health Videos, Phila. Dept. Pub. Health, 1989-90. Co-author: Straight Talk Parenting Series, 1988, Teacher Revitalization, 1982, The Giggle Kids Present, 1978; designer: Ollie and Seymour, 1986 (Media and Materials Portfolio award); prodr., writer Maria's Story, 1995 (Telly award). Mem. Am. Soc. Tng. & Devel., Soc. for Applied Learning Tech., Internat. Soc. Performance Improvement. Avocations: fine art, photography, travel. E-mail: curt.shreiner@galaxyscientific.com.

SHRESTHA, BIJAYA, nuclear scientist, electrical engineering educator; b. Kathmandu, Nepal, July 8, 1955; came to U.S., 1985; s. Kalidas and Kamala M. (Joshi) S.; m. Puja, May 7, 1975; children: Anjana, Anjaya, Srijana, Samjhana. MS in Plasma Physics, Tribhuvan U., Kathmandu, Nepal, 1978; MS in Nuclear Physics, La. State U., 1988; PhD, U. Mo., Rolla, 1995. Asst. lectr. Tribhuvan U., Kathmandu, Nepal, 1979-82, lectr., 1982-85; teaching asst. La. State U., Baton Rouge, 1985-88; rsch. teaching asst. U. Mo., Rolla, 1988-95, postdoctoral fellow, 1995-96, adj. faculty dept. elec. engring., 1996—. Author: Campus Physics, 1982. Treas. Univ. Tchrs. Assn., Kathmandu, 1982. Recipient Fulbright scholarship, 1985. Mem. Am. Phys. Soc., Am. Nuclear Soc., Nepal Phys. Soc., Am. Math. Soc., Sigma Pi Sigma, Alpha Nu Sigma (pres. U. Mo. at Rolla chpt.), Tau Beta Pi. Home: 604 Fox Creek Rd Rolla MO 65401-3676 Office: U Missouri Dept Elec Computer Engring Rolla MO 65401

SHREVE, GENE RUSSELL, law educator; b. San Diego, Aug. 6, 1943; s. Ronald D. and Hazel (Shepherd) S.; m. Marguerite Russell, May 26, 1973. AB with honors, U. Okla., 1965; LLB, Harvard U., 1968, LLM, 1975. Bar: Mass. 1969, Vt. 1981. Appellate atty. and state extradition hearing examiner Office of Mass. Atty Gen., 1968-69; law clk. U.S. Dist. Ct., Dallas, 1969-70; staff and supervising atty. Boston Legal Assistance Project, 1970-73; assoc. prof. Vt. Law Sch., Royalton, 1975-81; vis. assoc. prof. George Washington U., Washington, 1981-83; assoc. prof. law N.Y. Law Sch., N.Y.C., 1983-84, prof., 1984-87; vis. prof. law Ind. U., Bloomington, 1986, prof., 1987-94, Richard S. Melvin Prof. Law, 1994—. Author: A Conflict of Laws Anthology, 1997; co-author: Understanding Civil Procedure, 2d edit., 1994; mem. editl. bd. Am. Jour. Comparative Law, 1994—, Jour. Legal Edn., 1998-2001; contbr. numerous articles to legal jours. Mem. Am. Law Inst., Am. Soc. for Pol. and Legal Phil., Assn. Am. Law Schs. (civil procedure sect. chair 1997, conflict of laws sect. chair 1998). Democrat. Episcopalian. Office: Ind U Sch Law Bloomington IN 47405

SHRINER, JOAN WARD, secondary school educator; b. Bemidji, Minn., Mar. 15, 1938; d. Robert Francis and Ruby Mae (Hagelberg) Ward; m. Larry J. Shriner; 1 child, Natasha. BS, Bemidji State U., 1960; MS, Nova U., 1987. Tchr. Franklin Jr. H.S., Brainerd, Minn., 1960-61, Evanston (Wyo.) H.S., 1963-65, Western H.S., Las Vegas, Nev., 1965-66, Rancho H.S., Las Vegas, 1966-91; chair English dept., 1980-91; tchr. Cheyenne H.S., Las Vegas, 1991—; chair English dept., 1991—. Table leader Proficiency Testing, Nev., 1986-2001, Analytical Trait Assessment, Nev., 1992-2001; head reader Nev. H.S. Proficience Exam, Nev. State Writing Proficiency, 1998—; mem. curriculum com. Clark County, 1980-2001, mem. adv. team N.E. Tchrs., 2001—, Clark County Dist. N.E. Area; mem. Nev. Curriculum Framework Com., 1995, state stds. com., 1999. Mem. NEA, ASCD, Nat. Coun. Tchrs. English, Nev. State Edn. Assn., Nev. English Lang. Arts Network, Clark County Edn. Assn., Clark County English/Lang. Arts Bd. Democrat. Avocations: reading, arts and crafts, aviculture, swimming. Home: 2825 Michael Way Las Vegas NV 89108-4171 E-mail: jmshriner@aol.com.

SHRIVER, DUWARD FELIX, chemistry educator, researcher, consultant; b. Glendale, Calif., Nov. 20, 1934; s. Duward Laurence and Josephine (Williamson) S.; m. Shirley Ann Clark; children: Justin Scott, Daniel Nathan. BS, U. Calif., Berkeley, 1958; PhD, U. Mich., 1961. From instr. to assoc. prof. chemistry Northwestern U., Evanston, Ill., 1961-70, prof., 1970-87, Morrison prof. of chemistry, 1987—, chmn. dept. chem., 1992-95; mem. Inorganic Syntheses Inc., 1974—, pres., 1982-85. Vis. staff mem. Los Alamos (N.Mex.) Nat. Lab., 1976-85, cons., 1985-92; vis. prof. U. Tokyo, 1977, U. Wyo., 1978, U. Western Ont., Can., 1979. Author: The Manipulation of Air-Sensitive Compounds, 1969, edit., 1987; co-author: Inorganic Chemistry, 1990, 2d edit., 1994, 3d edit., 1998; editor-in-chief Inorganic Syntheses, vol. 19, 1979; co-editor: The Chemistry of Metal Cluster Complexes, 1990; editl. bd. Inorganic Synthesis, 1979—, Advances in Inorganic Chemistry, 1986—, Jour. Coordination Chemistry, Inorganic Chimca Acta, 1988—, Chemistry of Materials, 1988-90, 92—, Jour. Cluster Sci., 1990-97, Organometallics, 1993-95; contbr. articles to profl. jours. Alfred P. Sloan fellow, 1967-69; Japan Soc. Promotion of Sci. fellow, 1977; Guggenheim Found. fellow, 1983-84. Fellow AAAS; mem. Am. Chem. Soc. (Disting. Svc. in Inorganic Chemistry award 1987), Royal Soc. Chemistry London (Ludwig Mond lectr. 1989), Electrochem. Soc., Materials Rsch. Soc. (medal 1990). Home: 1100 Colfax St Evanston IL 60201-2611 Office: Northwestern U Dept Chemistry Evanston IL 60208-0001 E-mail: shriver@chem.nwu.edu.

SHRIVER, PHILLIP RAYMOND, academic administrator; b. Cleve., Aug. 16, 1922; s. Raymond Scott and Corinna Ruth (Smith) S.; m. Martha Damaris Nye, Apr. 15, 1944; children: Carolyn (Mrs. William Shaul), Susan (Mrs. Lester LaVine), Melinda (Mrs. David Williams), Darcy, Raymond Scott II. BA, Yale U., 1943; MA, Harvard U., 1946; PhD, Columbia U., 1954; LittD, U. Cin., 1966; LLD, Heidelberg Coll., 1966, Eastern Mich., 1972, Ohio State U., 1973; DH, McKendree Coll., 1973; DPS, Albion Coll., 1974; LHD, Central State U., 1976, No. Ky. State U., 1980, Miami U., 1984, U. Akron, 1988. Mem. faculty Kent (Ohio) State U., 1947-65, prof. Am. history, 1960-65; dean Coll. Arts and Scis., 1963-65; pres. Miami U., Oxford, Ohio, 1965-81, pres. emeritus, prof. Am. history, 1981-99. Pres. Ohio Coll. Assn., 1974-75; chmn. coun. pres.'s Mid-Am. Conf., 1971-77; chmn. Ohio Bicentennial Commn. for NW Ordinance and U.S. Constn., 1985-89, Ohio Tuition Trust Authority, 1989-92; chmn. coun. pres.'s Nat. Assn. State Univs. and Land Grant Colls., 1975-76, mem. exec. coun., 1976-78. Author: The Years of Youth, 1960, George A. Bowman: The Biography of an Educator, 1963, (with D.J. Breen) Ohio's Military Prisons of the Civil War, 1964, A Tour to New Connecticut in 1811: The Narrative of Henry Leavitt Ellsworth, 1985, Miami University: A Personal History, 1998, (with C.E. Wunderlin Jr.) The Documentary Heritage of Ohio, 2000, (with E.F. Puff) The History of Presbyterianism in Oxford, Ohio, 2000. Bd. dirs. Cin. Ctr. Sci. and Industry, 1965-70; trustee Ohio Coll. Library Center, 1968-74; chmn. bd. Univ. Regional Broadcasting, 1975-76, 78-79. Served to lt. (j.g.) USNR, 1943-46, PTO. Decorated Order of Merit Grand Duchy of Luxembourg, 1976; recipient Disting. Acad. Svc. award AAUP, 1965, Gov.'s award 1969, A.K. Morris award, 1974, Ohioana Career medal, 1987, Converse award, 1990, Award of Merit, Am. Assn. for State and Local History, 1993, Bjornson award Ohio Humanities Coun., 2001. Mem. Orgn. Am. Historians, Ohio Acad. History (pres. 1983-84, Disting. Svc. award 1991), Archaeol. Inst. Am., Ohio Hist. Soc. (trustee 1982-91, v.p. 1983-84, pres. 1984-86), Ohio Humanities Council (Bjornson award 2001), Am. Studies Assn., Mortar Board, Phi Beta Kappa, Omicron Delta Kappa, Phi Alpha Theta, Alpha Kappa Psi, Kappa Delta Pi, Phi Eta Sigma, Phi Kappa Phi, Kappa Kappa Psi, Alpha Lambda Delta, Beta Gamma Sigma, Sigma Delta Pi, Alpha Phi Omega, Delta Upsilon (Disting. Alumni Achievement award 1985) Clubs: Rotary. Presbyterian. Home: 5115 Bonham Rd Oxford OH 45056-1428 Office: Miami U Oxford OH 45056 E-mail: shrivepr@muohio.edu.

SHRIVER, WILLIAM RUSSELL, secondary education educator; b. Garfield Heights, Ohio, Aug. 15, 1950; s. William Washington and Olive Elizabeth (Doutt) S.; m. Karen Ann Wolfe, June 20, 1987; children: Lauren, Matthew. BA, Coll. of Wooster, 1972; MA, U. Chgo., 1973; postgrad., Cleve. State U., 1973-74. Cert. tchr. Summer staff Philmont Scout Ranch, Cimarron, N.Mex., 1968-76; tchr. Mt. Vernon (Ohio) Sr. H.S., 1974—. Tchr. Kenyon Acad. Partnership Kenyon Coll./Mt. Vernon Sr. H.S., 1983—; vice chair state tchr. edn. cert. adv. commn. Ohio Bd. Edn., Columbus, 1991-99, state tchr. cert. standards revision com., 1992-95; mem. bd. examiners Nat. Coun. Accreditation of Tchr. Edn., Washington, 1993-02; mem. Ohio Gov.'s Commn. on Tchg. Success, 2001-03. Bd. of session First Presbyn. Ch., Mt. Vernon, 1980-87, 89-95, 2001—. Eagle Scout Boy Scouts Am., 1966. Mem. NEA (assembly del. 1983-99), Ohio Edn. Assn. (exec. com. 1987-93, 96-2002), North Ctrl. Ohio Edn. Assn. (pres. 1984-85, exec. sec. 1993—), Mt. Vernon Edn. Assn. (pres. 1976-78). Avocations: photography, geneology. Office: Mt Vernon HS 300 Martinsburg Rd Mount Vernon OH 43050-4246 E-mail: wshriver@mt-vernon.k12.oh.us.

SHRUM, ALICIA ANN, elementary school educator, librarian; b. Miami, Okla., Sept. 8, 1946; d. Harold Richard Moye and Novella (Fields) Steen; m. Jimmie Ray Shrum, May 15, 1971. BS in Elem. Edn., Northeastern State U., Tahlequah, Okla., 1969, MS in Elem. Edn., 1978; student pubs. course, Inst. Children's Lit., 1990-91. Cert. elem. tchr., libr. media specialist, Okla. Tchr. 1st grade Justus Sch., Claremore, Okla., 1969-74, tchr. 3rd grade, 1974-81, tchr. remedial math., libr., 1981-83, libr./enrichment educator, 1983—. Co-chair centennial com. Justis Sch., 1989; coach teams for 6th and 7th grades, 7th and 8th grades Acad. Bowl, 1993—. Justus Sch. rep. United Way, 1989-93. Mem. NEA, Okla. Edn. Assn. (grantee to establish new libr. 1984-87), Justus-Taiwah Edn. Assn. (sec./treas. 1988-90, pres. 1990-91, sec. 96-97). Democrat. Avocations: quilting, handicrafts, reading. Office: Justus Libr 3 Mile E Hwy # 20 Claremore OK 74018

SHTOHRYN, DMYTRO MICHAEL, librarian, educator; b. Zvyniach, Ukraine, Nov. 9, 1923; came to U.S., 1950; s. Mykhailo and Kateryna (Figol) S.; m. Eustachia Barwinska, Sept. 3, 1955; children: Bohdar O., Liudoslava V. Student, Ukrainian Free U., Munich, 1947-48, U. Minn., 1954; MA in Slavic Studies, U. Ottawa, Can., 1958, B.L.S., 1959, PhD in Slavic Studies, 1970. Slavic cataloger U. Ottawa, 1959; cataloger NRC Can., Ottawa, 1959-60; Slavic cataloger, instr. library adminstrn. U. Ill., Urbana, 1960-64, head Slavic cataloging, asst. prof. library adminstrn., 1964-68, head Slavic cataloging, assoc. prof., 1968-75, head Slavic cataloging, prof., 1975-85, lectr. Ukrainian lit., 1975-91, assoc. Slavic librarian, prof., 1985-95, prof. Ukrainian lit., 1991-95, prof. emeritus, 1995—. Vis. prof. Ukrainian lit. U. Ottawa, 1974; assoc. prof. Ukrainian lit. Ukrainian Cath. U., Rome, 1978— ; prof. Ukrainian lit. Ukrainian Free U., Munich, 1983—, Ukrainian lang. and lit., U. Ill., 1991-95, Ukrainian culture, 1996—; chmn. Ukrainian Research Program U. Ill., 1984—. Editor: Catalog of Publications of Ukrainian Academy of Sciences, 1966, Ukrainians in North America: A Bibliographical Directory, 1975; author: Ukrainian Literature in the U.S.A.: Trends, Influences, Achievements, 1975, The Rise and Fall of Book Studies in Ukraine, 1986, Oleh Kandyba-Olzhych: Bibliography, 1992; editor: Bull. Ukrainian Libr. Assn. Am., 1982-88; mem. editl. bd. Ukrainian Historian, 1985-98, Ethnic Forum, 1985-95, Crossroads, 1986-97, Ukrainian Quar., 1993—, Ukrainian Problems, 1997—, Ukrainian Rev., 1997-99. Counselor Boy Scouts Am., Champaign, Ill., 1967-85; bd. dirs. Ukrainian-Am. Found., Chgo., 1978-87. Recipient Grant Future Credit Union Toronto, 1956, Grant U. Ill., 1977, 1982, Silver medal, Parliament of Can. Librarian, Ottawa, 1959, award, Glorier Soc. Can., 1959, citation plaque, Ukrainian Congress Com. Am., Chgo., 2000, Medal, V. Stefanyk Subcarpathian State U., 2001. Fellow Shevchenko Sci. Soc. (exec. com., M. Hrushevsky medal 1998); mem. ALA (chmn. Slavic and East European sect. 1968-69), Ukrainian Libr. Assn. Am. (pres. 1970-74, 82-87), Ukrainian Acad. and Profl. Assn. (charter, sec. 1985-89, pres. 1989—), I. Franko Internat. Soc. (founding mem., pres. 1978-79, 81-82), Ukrainian-Am. Assn. Univ. Profs. (exec. com. 1981-96), Ukrainian Hist. Assn. (exec. com. 1983-97), Ukrainian Acad. Arts and Scis. in U.S. (exec. com. 1993-98), Ukrainian Congress Com. of Am. Scholarly Coun., Ukrainian Writers' Assn. Slovo, Libr. Congress Assocs. (charter mem.). Ukrainian Catholic. Home: 403 Park Lane Dr Champaign IL 61820-7729 Office: Dept Slavic Langs & Lits 3092 Fgn Langs Bldg 707 S Mathews Ave Urbana IL 61801-3625 E-mail: shtohryn@uiuc.edu.

SHU, CHI-WANG, mathematics educator, researcher; b. Beijing, People's Republic of China, Jan. 2, 1957; arrived in U.S., 1982, naturalized, 1993; s. Kuang-Yao and Ding-Zhen (Shi) Shu; m. Din-Sui Loh, May 1, 1984; 1 child, Hai-Shuo. BS, U. Sci. and Tech. of China, 1982; PhD, UCLA, 1986. Rsch. assoc. U. Minn., Mpls., 1986-87; asst. prof. applied math. Brown U., Providence, 1987-91, assoc. prof., 1992-96, prof., 1996—, chmn., 1999—. Mng. editor: Math. of Computation, 2002—, co-chief editor: Jour. Sci. Computing, 2000—; contbr. Recipient Pub. Svc. Group Achievement award for pioneer work in computational fluid dynamics, NASA, 1992, First Feng Kang prize of Sci. Computing, Chinese Acad. Sci., 1995; grantee, NSF, NASA, Army Rsch. Office. Mem.: Soc. for Indsl. and Applied Maths., Am. Math. Soc. Achievements include research in in numerical solutions for discontinuous problems. Home: 135 Woodbury St Providence RI 02906-3511 Office: Brown U Div Applied Maths 182 George St Providence RI 02912-9056

SHU, WENLONG, environmental engineer, educator; b. Shanghai, Nov. 28, 1932; s. Junde and Yuying (Wang) S.; m. Manqing Chen, Mar. 10, 1957; children: Minmin, Hongmin. B in Engring., Qing Hua U., Beijing, China, 1953; MS in Environ. Engring., U. N.C., 1982. Cert. sr. engr. in water and wastewater engring. Bur. Staffs of Sci. and Tech., State Coun. China. Asst. tchr. Harbin (China) U. Tech., 1953-56; engr. Rsch. Inst. Bldg. and Constrn., Beijing, 1956-80; vis. scholar U. N.C., Chapel Hill, 1980, rsch. assoc., 1981-82; sr. engr. and vice chief engr. Rsch. Inst. Environ. Protection, Beijing, 1982-90, rsch. prof., 1990—. Presenter in field; appraiser for proposals in environmental sciences of the Natl. Natural Science Found. of China, 1984—. Contbr. articles to profl. jours.; inventor in field. Recipient Lifelong Achievement award State Coun. China, Beijing, 1993—; Continuation Edn. grantee Ministry of Edn., Beijing, 1980-82; grantee UNEP Asia & Pacific Region Office, Bangkok, 1992. Mem. Am. Water Works Assn., Pacific Basin Consortium for Hazardous Waste Rsch., Chinese Soc. Water and Wastewater Engring. (com. 1985—), Rsch. Inst. Environ. Protection Metall. Industry (advisor to grads. 1984—). Avocations: travel, writing, handiwork. Home: 33 Xitucheng Rd Beijing 100088 China Office: Rsch Inst Environ Protect 33 Xitucheng Rd Beijing 100088 China E-mail: wenlong_shu@yahoo.com.

SHUART, JAMES MARTIN, retired academic administrator; b. College Point, N.Y., May 9, 1931; s. John and Barbara (Schmidt) S.; m. Marjorie Strunk, Apr. 5, 1953; children: James Raymond, William Arthur. BA, Hofstra U., 1953, MA, 1962; PhD, NYU, 1966; D (hon.), L.I. U., 2000. Group rep. Home Life Ins. Co., 1955-57, N.Y. Life Ins. Co., 1957-59; adminstr. Hofstra U., Hempstead, N.Y., 1959-70, asst. dir. admissions, asst. dean faculty, asst. pres., exec. dean student services, assoc. dean liberal arts scis., trustee, 1973-75, v.p. adminstrv. svcs., 1975-76, pres., 1976-2001, pres. emeritus, 2001—. Mem. higher edn. adv. com. N.Y. State Senate, 1979-95; trustee Commn. on Ind. Colls. and Univs., N.Y. State, 1982-89, 92-95, chmn., 1988-89; mem. Am. Coun. on Edn.'s Labor/Higher Edn. Coun., 1983-88, Am. Coun. on Edns. Commn. on Leadership Devel., 1987-89, Peat Marwick Higher Edn. Pres.'s Adv. Com., 1988-96; bd. dirs. European Am. Bank, 1990-2001, Travelers-Solomon, Smith Barney World Funds, 1995-2000; chair Nassau County Property Tax Relief Commn., 1990-92; co-chair N.Y. State Temporary Commn. for L.I. Tax Relief, 1990-93. Trustee Molloy Coll., 1973-77; mem. adv. bd. Adelphi U. Sch. Social Work, 1973-84; dep. county exec. Nassau County, 1973-75, commr. social svcs., 1971-73, commr. L.I. Reg. Planning Bd., 1978-83, chmn., 1981-83; bd. dirs L.I. Assn., 1986-90; trustee Uniondale (N.Y.) Pub. Libr., 1966-68, L.I. Hosp. Planning Coun., 1971-75; pres., bd. dirs. Health Welfare Coun. Nassau County, 1971-80; chmn. Nassau Bd. Social Svcs., 1971-73; bd. dirs. Winthrop U. Hosp., 1979-86; mem. Nassau County Charter Revision Commn., 1993-96. Decorated officer Order of Orange Nassau (The Netherlands); recipient Founders Day award NYU, 1967, Alumnus of Yr. award Hofstra U., 1973, George M. Estabrook Disting. svc. award Alumni Assn., 1974, Leadership in Govt. award C.W. Post coll., L.I. U., 1978, Man of Yr. award Hempstead C. of C., 1978, L.I. Pers. and Guidance Assn., award, 1977, Lincoln Day award Syosset-Woodbury Rep. Club, 1981, L.I. Bus. disting. Leadership award 1982, 96, Joseph Giacalone award 1986, Medal of Honor L.I. Assn., 1988, L.I. Achievement award Pub. Rels. Profls. of L.I., 1995, Award L.I. Bus. Devel. Coun., 1994, 98, WLIWCh21 Educator of the Yr. award, 1999, Lifetime Achievement award L.I. Assn., 2001, L.I. Software and Tech. Network award L.I. Software and Tech. Network, 2001; others; named to L.I. Hall of Fame, 1985, Lifetime Achievement award Met. Lacrosse Found., 2001. Home: 111 Cherry Valley Ave # M35 Garden City NY 11530-1570

SHUBART, DOROTHY LOUISE TEPFER, artist, educator; b. Ft. Collins, Colo, Mar. 1, 1923; d. Adam Christian and Rose Virginia (Ayers) Tepfer; m. Robert Franz Shubart, Apr. 22, 1950; children: Richard, Lorenne. AA, Colo. Women's Coll., 1944; grad., Cleve. Inst. Art, 1946; student, Western Res. U., 1947—48; BA, St. Thomas Aquinas Coll., 1974; MA, Coll. New Rochelle, 1978; student, Santa Fe C.C., 2001—03. Art tchr. Denver Mus., 1944—50; art tchr. adults and children Cleve. Recreation Dept., 1950—60; portrait painter, 1947—50; adult edn. art tchr. Nanuet Pub. Sch., 1950-65, Pearl River Adult Edn., 1960—75. Rec. sec. Van Houten Fields Assn., West Nyack, NY, 1964—66. Exhibited in group shows at Hopper House, Rockland Ctr Arts, CWC, Cleve. Inst. Arts, Coll. New Rochelle, Rockland County Ann. Art Fair, Gonzalez Sr. Ctr.; co-author, photographer: Windmills & Dreams, 1997; co-author: (book and brochure) Van Houten Fields 1937-87, 1987; group show, Watercolor show, Santa Fe Cmty. Coll., 2003, exhibited in group shows at Santa Fe C.C. Leader 4-H Club, Nanuet, 1960—80, Girl Scouts U.S., Nanuet, 1961—68; mem. scholarship com., gen. com. PTA, Nanuet, 1964—68; rec. sec. Van Houten Fields Assn., West Nyack, NY, 1960—74; com. mem. Eldorado Cmty. Improvement Assn.-Arterial Rd. Planning Com., Santa Fe, 1992—94, Environ. Def. Fund, Union Concerned Scientists, Nat. Com. to Preserve Social Security and Medicare; capt., organizer Neighborhood Watch; mem. Eldorado chpt. Security Com., Eldorado Conservation Greenbelt Com., 1996—97; campaign vol. Jim Baca for Gov., N.Mex., 1996, Tom Udall for Congress, 1999—, Gore for Pres., Santa Fe, 2000; mem. Eldorado Hist. Com., 1995—97, Shakespeare in Santa Fe Guild, 1998, Mil. Hist. Found., 2000—; vol. Santa Fe Libr., 1998—, Eldorado's Vista Grande Libr., 2001—03, Cerro Grande Food Bank, 1998—; bd. dirs. Friends of Santa Fe Libr., 2003—. Gund traveling scholar, Cleve. Inst. Arts, 1946. Mem.: NOW, AAUW, Audubon Soc., Action on Smoking and Health, Union Concerned Scientists, Am. Dem. Action, Environ. Def. Fund, Wilderness Club, Phi Delta Kappa, Delta Tau Kappa. Democrat. Avocations: books, gardening, photography, bicycling, writing. Home: 8 Hidalgo Ct Santa Fe NM 87508-8898

SHUCART, EVELYN ANN, artist, educator; b. Covington, Ky., May 29, 1942; d. Frederick Holroyd and Evelyn Ann (Thomson) Eastabrooks; m. Rexford Lee Hill III, Sept. 12, 1964 (div. 1983); children: Eric Douglas, Rexford Alan, Gerald Alexander, Andrew David; m. James Wood Shucart, Sept. 21, 1991. BS in Design, U. Cin., 1965. Freelance artist, St. Louis, 1960—; office mgr. United Ch. of Christ, St. Louis, 1983-84; program coord. Acme Premium Supply, St. Louis, 1984-86, mgr., 1986-93; v.p. I.B.A. Inc., St. Louis, 1993-97; tchr. fine arts Meramec C.C., St. Louis, 2000—. Illustrator: Life Through Time, 1975. Coord./advisor Guardian Angels N.Y., St. Louis, 1981-82; advisor Pres.'s Commn. on Continuing Edn., Eden Sem., St. Louis, 1982-83; advisor Ecumenical Task Force on Hunger, 1982; cons. Women's Task Force on Employment, 1975-76; cons. Nat. Bd. Homeland Ministries, United Ch. of Christ, 1982, mem. St. Louis Assn. United Ch. of Christ, pres., 1981-82; bd. dirs. Women's Caucus for Art, St. Louis, 2000—, pres. St. Louis chpt. 2003—; bd. dirs. art sect. St. Louis Artist's Guild, 2002. Recipient Best of Show award, Siegfried Reinhardt County Artists, 1976, J.McCall Meml. prize, 1997. Mem. LWV, Amnesty Internat., League Women Voters, Sierra Club. Avocations: gardening, golf, painting, reading, tai chi. Home and Office: 2039 Brookcreek Ln Saint Louis MO 63122-2254 E-mail: evieart@sbcglobal.net.

SHUCH, H. PAUL, radio astronomer; b. Chgo., May 23, 1946; s. Ben Aaron Wakes and Phyllis Anita (Greenwald) S.; m. M. Suk Chong, Mar. 24, 1969 (div. 1990); children: Erika Chong, Andrew Pace; m. Muriel Hykes, Dec. 30, 1996. AS, West Valley Coll., Saratoga, Calif., 1972; BS, San Jose State U., 1975, MA, 1986; PhD, U. Calif., Berkeley, 1990. Lic. FAA comml. pilot and instrument flt. instr. Engring. technician TransAction Systems, Inc., Palo Alto, Calif., 1969-71; rsch. and devel. engr. Applied Tech., Sunnyvale, Calif., 1972-75; electronics instr. West Valley Coll., Saratoga, Calif., 1973-77; sr. engring. instr. Lockheed Missiles and Space Co., Sunnyvale, 1975-77; avionics lectr. San Jose (Calif.) State U., 1984-87; head microwave instr. San Jose City Coll., 1977-90; prof. electronics Pa. Coll. Tech., Williamsport, 1990-97. Chief engr. Microcomm, San Jose, 1975-90; accident prevention counselor FAA, San Jose and Harrisburg, Pa., 1983—; exec. dir. SETI League, 1995—. Author: Conquering Communications, 1997, Tune in the Universe!, 2001; co-author: ARRL UHF/Microwave Experimenter's Manual, 1990; contbr. Radio Handbook, 1975; contbr. articles to profl. jours. Chmn. Santa Clara County Airport Commn., San Jose, 1983-87; faculty sen. San Jose City Coll., 1979-81; chmn. ARRL/CSVHFC Joint FCC Briefing Com., Washington, 1991-95; fellowship interviewer Fannie and John Hertz Found., 1992—; guest lectr. Air Safety Found., Frederick, Md., 1992. Sgt. USAF, 1965-69, SE Asia. Named Flt. Instr. of Yr., FAA, Harrisburg, 1992; recipient Doctoral Thesis prize Fannie & John Hertz Found., Livermore, Calif., 1990, Prof. Robert Horonjeff Meml. grant U. Calif. Berkeley Inst. Transp. Studies, 1990, Robert Goddard Meml. scholarship Nat. Space Club, Washington, 1988, fellowship in applied phys. sci. Fannie & John Hertz Found., Livermore,

Calif., 1989, Tech. Excellence award Dayton Hamvention, 2000. Fellow Brit. Interplanetary Soc., Radio Club Am.; mem. Am. Coun. Edn. (mil. program evaluator 1991—), Am. Radio Relay League (adv. com. chmn. 1983-87, Internat. Acad. Astronautics (corr. mem.), Tech. Achievement award 1999), WESCON (tech. session organizer 1979). Democrat. Jewish. Achievements include design and prodn. of world's first comml. home satellite TV receiver, 1978; patent for aircraft binaural doppler collision alert system, 1987, adaptive microwave antenna array; design and implementation of Project Argus all-sky SETI survey, 1996. Office: SETI League PO Box 555 Little Ferry NJ 07643-0555 E-mail: drseti@cal.berkeley.edu.

SHUCK, ANNETTE ULSH, education educator; b. Harrisburg, Pa., Apr. 4, 1946; d. David Addison and Florence (Scholl) Ulsh; children: Ryan David Summers, Kirsten Annette Shuck. BS, Bloomsburg U., 1967; MS, W.Va. U., 1968, EdD, 1976; cert., Albert Ellis Inst., 1993. Cert. elem., secondary, spl. edn. tchr., Pa., W.Va., sch. psychologist, W.Va. Elem. tchr. Pa. and W.Va. schs., 1968-70; instr. W.Va. U., Morgantown, 1972, grad. asst., 1972-75, instr. spl. edn. dept., 1976-77, asst. prof., 1977-83, assoc. prof., 1983-87; vis. assoc. prof. divsn. edn. U. V.I., Charlotte Amalie, St. Thomas, 1987-88, assoc. prof., 1988, prof. divsn. edn., 1989—. Instr. Lebanon Valley Coll. and Temple U., Harrisburg, Pa., 1970-72; cons. sch. psychology program Coll. Grad. Studies, Institute, W.Va., 1986; mem. Gov. of V.I. Spl. Edn. Task Force, 1988—. Author: International Family Interventionist Booklet, 1976, 1988, rev. edit., 1997; contbr. chpt. to book and articles to profl. jours. Active Environ. Awareness and Action Com., St. Thomas, 1991—; bd. dirs. V.I. Women's Bus. Ctr; hearing officer State Dept. Spl. Edn.; family edn. interventionist, 1979—. NDEA fellow, 1967-68. Mem. Coun. for Exceptional Children, Am. Assn. Coll. Tchr. Edn., Phi Delta Kappa (v.p. 1975-76, pres. 1976-77). Avocations: research, writing, snorkeling, sailing, architectural design. Office: U VI Tchr-Edn-209 St Thomas VI 00802

SHUGART, JILL, retired school system administrator, educational consultant; b. Dallas, July 15, 1940; d. Claude Ernest and Allie Merle (Hamilton) S. BA, Baylor U., 1962; MA, Tex. Woman's U., 1972, PhD, 1980. Middle sch. English tchr. Garland (Tex.) Ind. Sch. Dist., 1962-63, high sch. social studies tchr., 1963-76, high sch. asst. prin., 1976-79, dir. communications, 1979-82, asst. supt., 1982-85, supt., 1985—99, ret., 1999—. Mem. legis. coun. U. Interscholastic League, Tex., 1989-99; chmn. Dist. III music com., Tex., 1989-99; adj. prof. Tex. Women's U., Denton, 1983; chmn. Region X ESC Adv. Coun., rep. to commr.'s supt.'s com., 1993-95; cons. Richardson and Carrollton-Farmers Br. Sch. Dists., 2000-2002; coord. Region 10 ESC Supr.'s Acad., 2000-2002. Gen. chmn. Boy Scouts Am. Scouting Night, Dallas, 1988-89; chmn. City of Garland Comty. Action Com., 1995-99; sec. Tex. Sch. Alliance, 1995-96, chmn., 1998-99; life mem. Tex. and nat. PTA; pres. Garland br. Am. Heart Assn., 1990-91; co-chmn. sustaining dr. Garland YMCA, 1995-96; mem. Adv. Com. to Gov. and State Legisture, 1998; mem. steering com. Garland Econ. Devel. Partnership, 1994-99, Tex. Fast Growth Sch. Coalition; chair Tex. Sch. Alliance, 1998—. Recipient Lamar award for excellence Masons, Award of Distinction, Tex. Ret. Tchrs. Assn.; named Top 100 Educators to Watch, Executive Educator mag., 1985, Finalist as Outstanding Tex. Sch. Supt., 1990, Woman of Distinction, Soroptimist Club; Paul Harris fellow. Mem. Quality Tex. Bd. Examiners, Garland Edn. Found. (bd. dirs. 1999-2002), Baylor Med. Ctr. Garland (bd. dirs. 2001-2002). Republican. Baptist. Avocations: travel, lake activities.

SHULDES, L(ILLIAN) JUNE, elementary school educator; b. Chgo. d. Clarence Andrew Sr. and Lillian (Evans) Baldwin; m. Robert William Shuldes, June 19, 1954; children: Eugene Robert, Judith Yvonne Shuldes Turley. BS in Edn., Northwestern U., 1951, MA in Edn., 1956. Tchr. elem. sch. Chgo. Bd. Edn., 1951-87. Lectr. Chgo. Workshop, 1982; speaker in field. Vice chair 13th Congl. Dist. Rep. Women Orgn., Evanston, Ill., 1958-62; chmn. Am. history essay contest Signal Hill chpt. NSDAR, Barrington, Ill., 1988-92, chaplain, 1994-96; hon. condr. Elgin (Ill.) Symphony Orch., 1988. Recipient George Washington Honor medal Freedoms Foun., Valley Forge, Pa., 1971,72, Valley Forge Tchrs. medal, 1972, Pageant Honor cert., 1973. Mem.: AAUW, Concerned Women for Am., Barrington Hist. Soc., Chgo. Collie Club, Collie Club Am., Barrington Women's Club, South Barrington Garden Club, Christian Women's Club, Green Thumbs Garden Club, Barrington Lyric Opera, Delta Kappa Gamma. Baptist. Avocations: raising and showing collies, travel, gardening, early american forts. Home: 1 W Penny Rd Barrington IL 60010-9576

SHULER, SCOTT CORBIN, art education administrator; b. Detroit, Nov. 23, 1953; s. John Hays and Marilyn (Corbin) S.; m. Monica Ascui, Aug. 13, 1977; children: Stephanie Ascui, Nathan Corbin. BMus in Instrumental Music, U. Mich., 1975; MS in Edn., U. Ill., 1976; PhD in Music Edn., Eastman Sch. Music, 1987. Cert. music tchr. presch.-12. Music tchr. The Tatnall Sch., Wilmington, Del., 1976-78, Kohler (Wis.) Pub. Schs., 1978-83; vis. instr. Eastman Sch. Music, Rochester, N.Y., 1983-85; assoc. prof., music edn. coord. Calif. State U., Long Beach, 1985-88; arts cons. Conn. Dept. Edn., Hartford, 1988—; prof. music edn. New Eng. Conservatory, Boston, 1992-93. Adj. prof. U. Del., Newark, 1977-78, Hartt Sch. Music, West Hartford, Conn., 1990-97; vis. prof. Ctrl. Conn. State U., New Britain, 1989-90; co-chair Nat. Assessment Ednl. Progress Planning Com., Washington, 1993-96, State Collaborative on Assessment, Washington, 1993-98; mem. task force Nat. Stds. in the Arts, Washington, 1992-94. Author: (monograph) Music Educators Nat. Conf. Words of Note series, 1990; editor, author: (spl. focus issue) Music Educators Jour., 1992 (Edn. Press Assn. Am. award 1992); contbr. articles to profl. jours. V.p., pres. Edn. Adminstrs. Union, Hartford, 1989-94, 2002—; assoc. music dir. Comty. United Meth. Ch., Huntington Beach, Calif., 1985-88; dir. of music Grace United Ch. of Christ, Kohler, Wis., 1981-82; co-chair bd. trustees Congregational Ch. in South Glastonbury, Conn., 1996-97. Recipient Disting. Svc. award Conn. Art Edn. Assn., 1993, 2000, Young Writers award Design for Arts in Edn., 1988, Disting. Svc. award Conn. Drama Assn., 2001, Outstanding Music Educator award Nat. Fedn. Interscholastic Music Assn., 2001. Mem. ASCD, Nat. Art Edn. Assn., Conn. Music Educators Assn. (exec. bd. dirs. 1988—, Outstanding Adminstr. award 1992), Conn. State Employees Assn. (v.p., pres., Pres.'s award for commitment and svc. 1993), Nat. Coun. State Suprs. Music (pres.-elect 1996-98, pres. 1998-2000), Conn. Alliance for Arts Edn. (exec. bd. dirs. 1990—), Phi Delta Kappa. Office: Conn Dept Edn 165 Capitol Ave Rm 205 Hartford CT 06106-1659 E-mail: scott.shuler@po.state.ct.us.

SHULLICH, ROBERT HARLAN, systems analyst; b. Bklyn., Feb. 20, 1954; s. William and Vivian (Polowitz) Shullich; m. Phyllis Elaine Strickland, June 5, 1979 (dec. Oct. 1991). AS in Liberal Arts, Staten Island CC, 1976; BS in Computer Sci., Coll. S.I., 1985, MS in Computer Sci., 1988; MBA in Mgmt., Baruch Coll., 1993; MS in Telecom. Network, Polytech U., 1998. MCSE, Microsoft cert. database adminstr., Microsoft cert. sys. adminstr., cert. info. sys. security profl., computing profl., info. sys. auditor, Cisco cert. network assoc., sys. security cert. practitioner, cert. SSCP, CISSP, MCSA, MCDBA, TICSA, CCA, Master CIW Adminstr., Master CWP Adminstr., CCNA. Sr. sys. analyst ednl. adminstrv. sys. Coll. S.I., NY, 1981—. Mem.: IEEE, Nat. Sys. Programmer Assn., Data Processing Mgmt. Assn., Assn. Computing Machinery, Am. Mgmt. Assn., Math. Assn. Am., Alpha Iota Delta, Tau Alpha Pi. Roman Catholic. Avocations: bowling, concerts. Home: PO Box 026156 Brooklyn NY 11202-6156 Office: Coll SI 2800 Victory Blvd Staten Island NY 10314-6609 E-mail: rshullic@bigfoot.com.

SHULMAN, ABRAHAM, otolaryngology educator, hospital administrator; b. N.Y.C., Feb. 24, 1929; s. Ben and Libby (Sarnoff) S.; m. Arlene P., Sept. 8, 1957; children: Rachel, Melanie. BS, CCNY, 1950; MD, U. Berne, Switzerland, 1955. Diplomate Am. Bd. Otolaryngology. Rotating surg. intern Queens County Gen. Hosp., 1955-56; resident in otolaryngology Kings County Hosp., Bklyn., 1957-60; clin. instr. Downstate Med. Ctr., SUNY, 1962-64, assoc. prof., 1975-89; prof. clin. otolaryngology SUNY Health Sci. Ctr., Bklyn., 1989—92, prof. emeritus clin. otolaryngology, 1992—; clin. instr. Albert Einstein Coll. Medicine, 1966-68, asst. clin. prof. otolaryngological surgery, 1968-75. Asst. surgeon Bklyn. Eye & Ear Hosp., 1966-69; otology cons. College Point chief of otolaryngology Lincoln Hosp., 1967-70, Bklyn. VA Med. Ctr., 1977-85, chief otolaryngology, staff attending otolaryngologist, 1985—, acting chief of otolaryngology, 1990-91; lectr., asst. attending otolaryngologist Mt. Sinai Hosp., 1974; chief otolaryngology Lincoln Hosp., 1967-1970; asst. attending otolaryngology Bronx Mcpl. Hosp., 1967-75; chief Otolaryngologist, asst. attending otolaryngologist, Kings County Hosp., 1962-64, dir. otolaryngology, 1975-92, attending otolaryngologist, 1975—, Brookdale Med. Ctr., 1982-86; chief otolaryngology Cath. Med. Ctr., Bklyn. and Queens, 1969-94, attending otololaryngologist St. John's Queens Hosp., 1969-94; chmn. Internat. Tinnitus Forum, 1982—; Martha Entenmann Tinnitus Rsch. Ctr., Inc., dir. otology neurotology 1994—. Editor (co-chief): Internat. Tinnitus Jour., 1994—; editor: (text) Tinnitus Diagnosis and Treatment, 1991—. Cons. Children's Devel. Ctr., 1975; med. cons. Office Vocat. Rehab., 1974; dir. med. svc. Lexington Sch. of the Deaf, 1972-74. Lt. comdr. USNR, 1960-62. Recipient Cert. of Appreciation, Am. Speech and Hearing Assn., 1989—, Hocks award, Am. Tinnitus Assn., 1990, Honor award, Am. Acad. Otolaryngology, 1994, Myrtle Reed award, Hadassah Zionist Orgn. Am., honoree, Neuro Equilibrimetric Soc., 1998. Fellow ACS, AMA, Am. Acad. Ophthalmology and Otolaryngology, Am. Neurotology Soc., Am. Audiology Soc., Am. Soc. Ophthalmologic and Otolaryngology Allergy, Am. Soc. Facial Plastic Surgery, Internat. Coll. of Surgeons, Adam Politzer Soc.; mem. Am. Coun. Otolaryngology, Am. Soc. Contemporary Medicine and Surgery, Pan-Am. Assn. Otorrhinolaryngology and Bronchoesophagology, N.Y. Acad. Sci., Soc. for Cryosurgery, Queens County Med. Soc., Soc. Univ. Otolaryngologists, Bklyn. Oncology Soc., Assn. for Rsch. in Otolaryngology, Centurion Club, Sigma Xi. Office: SUNY Health Sci Ctr Bklyn Div Otolaryngology 450 Clarkson Ave Brooklyn NY 11203-2056

SHULMAN, GERALD I. physician, scientist, educator; b. Detroit, Feb. 8, 1953; BS with high honors and distinction, U. Mich., 1974; MD, PhD, Wayne State U., 1979; MA, privatim (hon.), Yale Univ., 1997. Intern Duke U., Durham, N.C., 1979-80, residency, 1980-81; fellowship in endocrinology and metabolism Mass. Gen. Hosp., Boston, 1981-84; asst. prof. medicine Harvard U., Boston, 1985-87; assoc. prof. Sch. Medicine Yale U., New Haven, 1989-96; assoc. dir. Yale MD-PhD Program Sch. Medicine Yale U., New Haven, 1993—, prof. medicine, cellular and molecular physiology, 1996—. Albert Weinstein vis. prof., Vanderbilt U., 1994, Harold Rifkin vis. prof., Albert Einstein Coll. Med., 1999, Sam Grant vis. prof., Washington U. Sch. Med., 2001, 1st Eli Lilly vis. prof., Cambridge U., 2002; assoc. dir. Yale Diabetes Endocrine Rsch. Ctr., 1996—; investigator Howard Hughes Med. Inst., 1997—; program dir. Yale/New Haven Hosp. Gen. Clin Rsch. Ctr.; Pfizer prof. U. Colo.; lectr. in field. Mem. editl. bd. Diabetes Jour. Am., Am. Jour. Physiology, Diabetic Medicine, Jour. Clin. Investigation, Am. Jour. Medicine, Diabetologia, Internat. Jour. Molecular Medicine, Am. Jour. Physiology, Jour. Biol. Chemistry; contbr. articles to profl. jours. Recipient of the Outstanding Investigator award for Clinical Rsch. 1994, Young Investigator award Am. Fed. for Med. Rsch., 1997, Boehriger Mannheim/ Juvenile Diabetes Found. Internat., Diabetes Care Rsch. award, 1997, Young Investigator award in diabetes Novartis, 1999, Mary June Kugel award, Juvenile Diabetes Rsch. Found. Internat. 1999, E.H. Ahrens Jr. award, Assoc. for Patient-Oriented Rsch., 2001, Josiah Brown award in Diabetes, UCLA, 2002. Fellow ACP, Internat. Soc. Magnetic Resonance in Medicine, 1998, Am. Soc. Clin. Investigation; mem. Am. Diabetes Assn. (clin. rsch. grantee 1996, Outstanding Sci. Achievement Lilly Lectr. award 1997, Mentor award 1997, 99); mem. Assn of Am. Physician, Endocrine Soc., Am. Physiol. Soc., European Assn. for Study of Diabetes, Interurban Clin. Club, NIH Metabolism Study Section 1992-1996 Office: Howard Hughes Med Inst Yale U Sch Medicine PO Box 9812 New Haven CT 06536-0812 Fax: 203-737-4059. E-mail: gerald.shulman@yale.edu.

SHULMAN, ROBERT GERSON, biophysics educator; b. N.Y.C., Mar. 3, 1924; s. Joshua S. and Freda (Lipshay) S.; m. Saralee Deutsch, Aug., 1952 (dec. Oct. 1983); children: Joel, Mark, James; m. Stephanie S. Spangler, May 11, 1986. AB, Columbia U., 1943, MA, 1947, PhD, 1949. Rsch. assoc. Columbia U. Radiation Lab., N.Y.C., 1949; AEC fellow in chemistry Calif. Inst. Tech., Pasadena, 1949-50; head semicondr. research sect. Hughes Aircraft Co., Culver City, Calif., 1950-53; mem. tech. staff Bell Labs., Murray Hill, N.J., 1953-66, head biophysics rsch. dept., 1966-79; prof. molecular biophysics and biochemistry Yale U., 1979-94, dir. divsn. biol. scis., 1981-87, Sterling prof. molecular biophysics and biochemistry, 1994—2002, Sterling prof. emeritus molecular biophysics 2nd biochemistry, 2002—, sr. rsch. scientist dept. diagnostic radiology, 2002—. Rask Oersted lectr. U. Copenhagen, 1959; vis. prof. Ecole Normale Superieur, Paris, 1962; Appleton lectr. Brown U., 1965; vis. prof. physics U. Tokyo, 1965; Reilly lectr. U. Notre Dame, Ind., 1969; vis. prof. biophysics Princeton U., 1971-72; Regents lectr. UCLA, 1978 Lt. (j.g.) USNR, 1944-46. Guggenheim fellow in lab. molecular biology MRC Cambridge (Eng.) U., 1961-62; recipient Havinga medal Leiden U., 1983, Gold medal Soc. Magnetic Resonance in Medicine, 1984, Mem. Nat. Acad. Scis., Inst. Medicine. Achievements include research in spectroscopic techniques applied to physics, chemistry and biology. Office: Dept Diagnostic Radiology MRRC Yale U PO Box New Haven CT 06520-8043 E-mail: Robert.Shulman@Yale.edu.

SHULMAN, YECHIEL, engineering educator; b. Tel Aviv, Jan. 28, 1930; came to the U.S., 1950; s. David and Rachel (Chonowski) S.; m. Ruth Danzig, June 29, 1950; children: Elinor D., Ron E., Orna L. BS in Aero. Engring., BS in Bus. and Engring. Adminstrn., MS in Aero. Engring., MIT, 1954, DSc Aero. and Astro., 1959; MBA, U. Chgo., 1973. Assoc. prof. mech. engring. Northwestern U., Evanston, Ill., 1959-67; v.p. adv. engring. Anocut, Inc., Elk Grove Vill., Ill., 1967-72; v.p. corp. devel. Alden Press, Elk Grove Vill., Ill., 1973-84; pres. MMT Environ., Inc., Shoreview, Minn., 1984-87; cons. Shulman Assocs., Mpls., 1987-89; prof. mech. engring. dept. U. Minn., Mpls., 1989-2000, H. W. Sweatt chair in technol. leadership and dir. ctr. for devel. technol. leadership, 1989-2000, dir. grad. studies mgmt. of tech. program, 1990-2000, prof. emeritus mech. engring. dept, 2000—. Mem. ASME, Internat. Assn. for Mgmt. of Tech. Office: U Minn 109 ME Bldg 111 Church St SE Minneapolis MN 55455-0150

SHULTIS, ROBERT LYNN, finance educator, cost systems consultant, retired professional association executive; b. Kingston, N.Y., June 30, 1924; s. Albert H. and Dorothy Elizabeth (Jenkins) S.; m. Bernice Elizabeth Johnson, Jan. 20, 1946; 1 son, Robert Lee. BS, Columbia Univ. Sch. Bus., 1949, postgrad., 1949-51. Staff acct. Price Waterhouse, N.Y.C., 1949-52; credit mgr., controller Organon, Inc., West Orange, N.J., 1952-68; v.p., treas., chief fin. officer Arwood Corp., Rockleigh, N.J., 1968-72; v.p., controller Technicon, Tarrytown, N.Y., 1972-80; exec. dir. Inst. of Mgmt. Accts., Montvale, N.J., 1980-86; faculty, exec. dir. Ctr. for Exec. Devel. Coll. William & Mary, Williamsburg, Va., 1987-91. Instr. Rutgers U., 1964-74, Fairleigh Dickinson U., 1967-68; mem. Fin. Acctg. Standards Adv. Coun., 1981-86; lectr., seminar leader, cons. on controllership, activity-based costing, cost mgmt., cost sys. design Boston U., U. Calif., Berkeley, U. Minn., Michigan State U., So. Meth. U., Baldwin Wallace Coll., George Mason U., James Madison U., U. N.C., Colo. State U., others, 1990—. Editor: Management Accountants' Handbook, and supplements, 1991-94; contbr. articles to profl. jours. Mem. bd. advs. U. Fla. Sch. Accountancy, James Madison U. Sch. Accountancy; mem. fin. and budget com. Kingsmill Cmty. Svcs. Assn.; interpreter Historic Jamestowne Island, 1997—. Served with USAF, 1943-45. Decorated Presdl. Unit Citation, ETO Ribbon, eight battle stars. Mem. AAUP, VFW, Am. Legion, Fin. Execs. Internat. (editl. adv. bd.), Inst. Mgmt. Accts., Am. Acctg. Assn., Assn. for Preservation of Va. Antiquities, Kingsmill Club, Beta Alpha Psi (adv. forum).

SHULTZ, GEORGE PRATT, former government executive, economics educator; b. N.Y.C., Dec. 13, 1920; s. Birl E. and Margaret Lennox (Pratt) S.; children: Margaret Ann Shultz Tilsworth, Kathleen Pratt Shultz Jorgensen, Peter Milton, Barbara Lennox Shultz White, Alexander George; m. Charlotte Mailliard, Aug. 15, 1997. BA in Econs., Princeton U., 1942; PhD in Indsl. Econs., MIT, 1949; Hon. degree, Yeshiva U., U. Tel Aviv, Technion-Israel Inst. Tech., Keio U., Tokyo, Brandeis U., U. Notre Dame, Princeton U., Loyola U., U. Pa., U. Rochester, Carnegie-Mellon U., Baruch Coll., Northwestern U., Tblisi State U., Columbia U. Mem. faculty M.I.T., 1949-57; assoc. prof. indsl. relations MIT, 1955-57; prof. indsl. relations Grad. Sch. Bus., U. Chgo., 1957-68; dean sch. Grad. Sch. Bus. U. Chgo., 1962-68, fellow Ctr. for Advanced Study in Behavioral Scis., 1968-69; U.S. sec. labor, 1969-70; dir. Office Mgmt. and Budget, 1970-72; U.S. sec. treasury, also asst. to Pres., 1972-74; chmn. Council on Econ. Policy, East-West Trade Policy com.; exec. v.p. Bechtel Corp., San Francisco, 1974-75, pres., 1975-81, vice chmn., 1977-81; also dir.; pres. Bechtel Group, Inc., 1981-82; prof. mgmt. and pub. policy Stanford U., 1974-82, prof. internat. econs., 1989-91, prof. emeritus, 1991—; chmn. Pres. Reagan's Econ. Policy Adv. Bd., 1981-82; U.S. sec. of state, 1982-89; Thomas W. and Susan B. Ford disting. fellow Hoover Instn., Stanford, 1989—. Bd. dirs. Charles Schwab & Co., Bechtel Group, Inc., Gilead Scis.; mem. adv. coun. Bechtel Inc.; chmn. J.P. Morgan Chase Internat. Coun.; chmn. Accenture Energy adv. bd.; chmn. adv. coun. Inst. Internat. Studies, 1990-98; mem. Calif. Gov.'s Econ. Policy Adv. Bd., 1995-98.. Author: Pressures on Wage Decisions, 1950, (with Charles A. Myers) The Dynamics of a Labor Market, 1951, (with John R. Coleman) Labor Problems: Cases and Readings, 1953, (with T.L. Whisler) Management Organization and the Computer, 1960, (with Arnold R. Weber) Strategies for the Displaced Worker, 1966, (with Robert Z. Aliber) Guidelines, Informal Controls and the Marketplace, 1966, (with Albert Rees) Workers and Wages in the Urban Labor Market, 1970, Leaders and Followers in an Age of Ambiguity, 1975, (with Kenneth W. Dam) Economic Policy Beyond the Headlines, 1977, 2d edition, 1998, Turmoil and Triumph: My Years as Secretary of State, 1993; also articles, chpts. in books, reports, and essays. Served to capt. USMCR, 1942-45. Recipient Medal of Freedom, 1989, Seoul Peace prize, 1992, Eisenhower medal for Leadership and Svc., 2001, Reagan Disting. Am. award, 2002, Ralph Bunche award for diplomatic excellence, 2002. Mem. Am. Econ. Assn., Indsl. Relations Research Assn. (pres. 1968), Nat. Acad. Arbitrators. Republican. Office: Stanford U Hoover Instn Stanford CA 94305-6010

SHULTZ, KENNETH LOWELL, athletic director; b. St. Louis, Aug. 15, 1948; s. Lowell Vern and Nellie Pauline (Rusk) S.; m. Kathleen Mary McElderry, Sept. 10, 1967; children: Amy Kathleen, Brandy Lynn, Michael Kenneth. BS with high honors, U. Ill., 1970, MS, 1971. Cert. tchr., adminstr., athletic adminstr., Ill. Instr. Western Ill. U., Macomb, 1972-73; tchr., coach Morris (Ill.) High Sch., 1973-79; assoc. athletic dir. Homewood-Flossmoor (Ill.) High Sch., 1979-81; athletic dir. North Olmsted (Ohio) City Schs., 1981-83, Homewood-Flossmoor (Ill.) High Sch., 1983—. Speaker 5 clinics athletic drug testing program Homewood-Flossmoor High Sch., 1990-91. Contbr. articles to athletic jours. Mem. AAHPERD, Nat. Strength and Conditioning Assn., Nat. Interscholastic Athletic Dirs. Assn. (bd. dirs. 2002—), Ill. Athletic Dirs. Assn. (pres. 2003-04, Athletic Dir. of Yr. 1992), Ill. Assn. Health, Phys. Edn., Recreation and Dance, Nat. Coun. Secondary Sch. Athletic Dirs. (named midwest regional athletic dir. of the year 1993), Nat. Interscholastic Athletic Adminstrn. Assn. (profl. devel. com. 1996—). Avocation: golf. Home: 9078 Charrington Dr Frankfort IL 60423-9449

SHUM, MARGARET, market economy educator; b. Downers Grove, Ill., June 11, 1973; d. Raymond Hing-Yan and Julia (Miao) S. BA, Northwestern U., 1995. Asst. project mgr. Planned Parenthood of Greater No. N.J., Morristown, 1995-97; lectr. in market economy and bus. english Dalian (China) U. Tech., 1997—. Mktg. cons. Williamson Techs. Inc., Livingston, N.J., 1991-92. Editor, author: Dr. Sun Yat-Sen and My Grandfather General Shum Hung-Ying, 1996. Art collection libr. Northwestern U., Evanston, Ill., 1994-95, rsch. asst. Chinese art, dept. art history, 1993-94. NSF fellow, 1992. Mem. Assn. Asian Studies, Chinese History Soc., Chinese Social Scientists in Am. Avocations: reading, jogging, bicycling, travel, photography. Home: 339 Walnut St Livingston NJ 07039-5011 Office: Dalian U Tech Guest-house Apt 310 Dalian China

SHUMARD, ELLEN BLAINE, school librarian, artist; b. Chgo., Ill., Oct. 12, 1925; d. Engval Siverin and Theresa Marie Stevenson; m. Harold D. Shumard, Apr. 10, 1953 (dec. Oct. 1957); children: Christopher, Theresa, Gerold, Richard, Charles. BA, Chgo. State U., Ill., 1971, MS in Libr. Sci., 1973. Lic. tchr. Ill., 1971. Artist Amer Sch., Chgo., 1948—55, Hiccoch Assn., Chgo., 1950; artist, draftsman designer W. Blancy & Assn., Chgo., 1950—52; libr. Glenwood Sch. for Boys, 1972—73, Kerly Dist. 140, Tinley Pk., Ill., 1973—74, Chgo. Pub. Sch., 1974—2000. 2d lt. USAF, 1952. Mem.: Ret. Officer Assn.(MOAA) (treas. 1955—58, v.p. 1955—58), AAUW. Republican. Lutheran. Avocations: needlepoint, painting, gardening. Home: 8101 W 129th St Palos Park IL 60464-2160

SHUMATE, GLORIA JONES, retired education administrator; b. Meridian, Miss., Jan. 8, 1927; d. Thomas Marvin and Flora E. (Suggs) Jones; m. Jack B. Shumate, Nov. 19, 1946; children: Jack B. Jr., Thomas Edward. BS, Miss. State U., 1960; MA, U. South Fla., 1969, postgrad. in vocat. edn., 1970-72. Cert. guidance counselor, psychology and social studies specialist, Fla. High sch. tchr. Lauderdale County Schs., Meridian, 1952-56; tchr. vocat. edn. Manpower Devel. and Tng., St. Petersburg, Fla., 1964-69; counselor City Ctr. for Learning St. Petersburg Vocat.-Tech. Inst., 1969-70, registrar, 1970-72, asst. dir., 1972-80, exec. dir., 1980-85; dir. vocat.-tech., adult edn. ops. Pinellas County Schs., Largo, Fla., 1985-89. Chmn. Fla. Equity Council, 1980-81; mem. Fla. Adv. Council on Vocat. Edn., 1980-85, Fla. Job Tng. Coordinating Council, 1983-84. Named Outstanding Educator Pinellas Suncoast C. of C., 1980. Mem. Nat. Council Local Adminstrs., Am. Vocat. Assn., Fla. Vocat. Assn., So. Assn. Colls. and Schs. (standards com. 1975-81), Phi Delta Kappa, Kappa Delta Pi. Democrat. Baptist. Avocations: crafts, reading, walking, genealogy, travel. Home: 2314 Foxworth Dr Panama City FL 32405-1938

SHUREN, JEFFREY ELIOT, behavioral neurologist, lawyer; b. Bklyn., June 19, 1963; m. Allison Weber, Aug. 31, 1991. BS, Northwestern U., Evanston, Ill., 1985; MD, Northwestern U., Chgo., 1987; JD, U. Mich., 1998. Diplomate Am. Bd. Psychiatry and Neurology. Asst. prof. dept. neurology U. Cin., Coll. Medicine; med. officer, Office Policy Food and Drug Adminstrn.; divsn. dir. coverage and analysis group Ctrs. Medicare and Med. Svcs. Asst. commr. policy Food and Drug Adminstrn. Mem. Am. Acad. Neurology, Internat. Neuropsychol. Soc., Alpha Omega Alpha. Office: 5600 Fishers Lane Rockville MD 20857

SHUTER, DAVID HENRY, foreign language educator; b. Portsmouth, Ohio, Apr. 26, 1961; s. Paul H and Mary E. (Carr) S. BS in Edn., Ohio State U., 1982; MEd, U. Dayton, 1990; postgrad., Ohio U., 1991—. Cert. tchr., Ohio. Tchr. Amanda (Ohio) Clearcreek Local Sch. Dist., 1982-85, Vinton County Consol. Sch. Dist., McArthur, Ohio, 1986-91, 93—; instr. Ohio U., Athens, 1991-93. Supr. Ohio U., Athens, 1992. Recipient Citizenship award, Lions Club, MInford, Ohio, 1979. Mem. ASCD, Inst. for Democracy in Edn., Ohio State U. Alumni Assn., Phi Delta Kappa. Avocations: farming, sports. Home: PO Box 116 Minford OH 45653-0116 Office: Vinton County High Sch 63910 Us Highway 50 Mc Arthur OH 45651-8400

SHUTT, FRANCES BARTON, special education educator; b. Pryor, Okla., Nov. 12, 1912; d. Edwin Harley and Bonnie (Heflin) Barton; m. John Paul Shutt, Dec. 24, 1932; children: Jon Edwin, Frances Paulette. BA, Northeastern Tchrs. U., 1941; MA, U. N.Mex., 1954, cert. in spl. edn., 1958. Classroom tchr., Pryor, Okla., 1932-40; classroom tchr. Albuquerque, 1941-55; homebound tchr. in spl. edn., 1955-72; substitute tchr. Las Cruces, N.Mex., 1973-75; ESL tchr., 1974-97; ret., 1997. Author: First Grade Guide, 1952. Mem. AAUW, 1962-68, Daus. of Nile, 1953; mission work in Japan, 1964, Samoa, 1972. Mem. N.Mex. Assn. Ednl. Retirees, Coun. for Exceptional Children (state pres. 1963-65), Ret. Tchrs. N.Mex. (sec. 1996), Las Cruces (N.Mex.) Ret. Tchrs. Assn. (sec. 1996-97, pres. 1998—), Order Eastern Star (worthy matron 1938), Pi Lambda Theta (pres. 1958-60), Alpha Delta Kappa (pres. 1968-70), Delta Kappa Gamma (pres. 1986-88), Kappa Kappa Iota (pres. 1990-93). Democrat. Baptist. Home: PO Box 697 Mesilla Park NM 88047-0697

SHYERS, LARRY EDWARD, mental health counselor, educator; b. Middletown, Ohio, Aug. 16, 1948; s. Edward and Ruth Evelyn (Davis) S.; m. Linda Faye Shearon, July 31, 1970; children: Jami Lynn, Karen Lindsey. BA, David Lipscomb Coll., Nashville, 1970; MA, Stetson U., Deland, Fla., 1973; MEd, U. Ctrl. Fla., 1981; PhD, U. Fla., 1992. Lic. mental health counselor, Fla.; nat. cert. counselor, psychologist, approved clin. supr.; diplomate Nat. Registry Neurofeedback Providers; ordained to ministry non-denominational Ch. of Christ, 1969. Minister Ch. of Christ, Ocala, Fla., 1970-75, Mt. Dora, Fla., 1975-80; tchr. Christian Home and Bible Sch., Mt. Dora, Fla., 1970-77, dir. guidance, 1977-86; pvt. practice individual and family counseling Mt. Dora, Fla., 1980—. Apptd. to state regulatory bd. for clin. social work, marriage, family therapy, mental heatlh counseling, 1987-95, vice-chmn., 1987-88, chmn., 1989-95, legis. liaison, 1988-95, probable cause panel, 1996—; adj. prof. Nova. U., 1986—, U. Ctrl. Fla., 1988—, psychology St. Leo Coll., 1985—, Rollins Coll., 1991—, Reformed Theol. Sem., 1995—; adj. instr. Lake Sumter C.C., 1989—, Stetson U., 1990—, Rollins Coll., 1991—; mem. individual manpower tng. sys. bd. Vocat.-Tech. Sch., Eustis, 1984-87; mem. adv. bd. U.S. Achievement Bd., 1983—; cons. in field. Dir. edn. Mt. Dora Ch. of Christ, 1983-86; mem. Leadership Lake County Class of 1999. Mem. Fla. Mental Health Counselors Assn. (chmn. award and profl. devel. coms. 1985, chmn. govt. rels. com., pres. 1986-87), ACA (govt. rels. com. 1990-95, publs. rev. com. 1991—), Am. Mental Health Counselors Assn. (govt. rels. com. 1987-90, chmn. 1988-90, publs. coun. 1991—, PP&I com. 1992-95), Am. Orthopsychiat. Assn., Am. Assn. Christian Counselors, Internat. Assn. Marriage adn Family Counselors, Assn. of Assessment in Counseling, Am. Assn. Profl. Hypnotherapists, Lake Sumter Assn. for Counseling and Devel. (pres. 1987-88), Assn. for Applied Psychophysiology and Biofeedback, Mount Dora C. of C. (mem. youth com. 1984), Leadership Lake County Class of 1999, Kiwanis, Kappa Delta Pi, Pi Lambda Theta, Chi Sigma Iota. Republican. Avocations: amateur radio, target shooting. Office: 3750 Lake Center Loop Mount Dora FL 32757-2211

SHYMANSKI, CATHERINE MARY, health facility administrator; b. Omaha, Jan. 23, 1954; d. Leo Michael and Mildred Mary (Swank) Shymanski. AAS in Nursing, Iowa Western C.C., 1977; BSN, Pacific Western U., 1982; BFA, Drake U., 1980; MSN, Pacific Western U., 1992. Charge nurse Nebr. Psychiat. Inst., Omaha, 1977-78; staff nurse Menninger Found., Topeka, 1978-79; staff devel. instr., clin. coord. Stormont Vail Regional Med. Ctr., Topeka, 1979-80; charge nurse Allen County Hosp., Iola, Kans., 1980-81; asst. dir. nursing Arkhaven at Erie, Kans., 1980; dir. shift ops. Truman Med. Ctr., Kansas City, Mo., 1983; nursing supr. Osawatomie (Kans.) State Hosp., 1981-91; nursing orientation and insvc. coord. Topeka State Hosp., 1991-94, dir. nursing edn., 1993-94; coord. health occupation Kaw Area Tech. Sch., Topeka, Kans., 1994-95; supr. outpatient and partial hospitalization svcs. St. Catherine Hosp., Garden City, Kans., 1995; DON, Garden Valley Retirement Village, Garden City, Kans., 1995-96; coord. quality assurance and edn. Beautiful Savior Home and Manor, Belton, Mo., 1996-97, Pk. Pl. Care Ctr., Raytown, Mo., 1997—. Mem. River City Players, Osawatomie, 1984-88. Mem. Bus. and Profl. Women (pres. Osawatomie chpt. 1985-86, 88-89, dist. dir. 1987-88, Young Career Woman award 1982, 84, Woman of Yr., 1982-83), Am. Psychiat. Nurses Assn., Kans. Nursing Assn. (pres. dist. 1985-86), Am. Cat Fanciers Assn., Topeka Cat Fanciers. Avocations: raise and show cats, gardening, reading. Office: Pk Pl Care Ctr 11901 Jessica Ln Raytown MO 64138-2639

SHYY, WEI, aerospace and mechanical engineering researcher, educator; b. Tainan, Taiwan, China, July 19, 1955; arrived in U.S., 1979; s. Chiang-Chen and June-Hua (Chao) S.; m. Yuchen Shih; children: Albert, Alice, Andrew Chang, Kevin Chang. BS, Tsin-Hua U., Taiwan, 1977; MSE, U. Mich., 1981, PhD, 1982. Postdoctoral rsch. scholar U. Mich., Ann Arbor, 1982-83; rsch. scientist GE Corp. Rsch. and Devel. Ctr., Schenectady, NY, 1983-88; faculty mem. of aeronautics and astronautics Nat. Cheng-Kung U., Taiwan, 1987; assoc. prof. aerospace engring., mechanics and engring. sci. U. Fla., Gainesville, 1988-92, prof. aerospace engring., mechanics and engring. sci., 1992—, chmn. dept. aerospace engring, mechs. and engring. sci., 1996—2002, chmn. dept. mech. and aerospace engring., 2002—; dir. NASA URETI: Inst. for Future Space Flight, Gainesville, 2002—. Dir. Space Grant Consortium NASA, Fla., 1998—2000, dir. Univ. Rsch., Engring. and Tech. Inst. on 3rd Generation Reusable Launch Vehicle; cons. in field; lectr. in field. Editor: Recent Advances in Computational Fluid Dynamics, 1989; author: Computational Modeling for Fluid Flow and Interfacial Transport, 1994; co-author: Computational Fluid Dynamics with Moving Boundaries, 1996, Computational Techniques for Complex Transport Phenomena, 1997; editor: Fluid Dynamics at Interface, 1999; assoc. editor Jour. Applied Mechanis Rev., Computer Modeling in Engineering and Sciences, mng. editor Cambridge U. Press.: Aerospace Book Series, mem. editl. adv. bd. Numerical Heat Transfer Jour., Progress in Computational Fluid Dynamics, Internat. Jour. Numerical Methods for Heat and Fluid Flow; contbr. articles. Fellow AIAA (Pendray Aerospace Lit. award 2003), ASME; mem. Minerals, Metals and Materials Soc., Am. Phys. Soc., Combustion Inst. Office: U Fla Dept Aerospace Engring 231 Aero Bldg Gainesville FL 32611

SI, JENNIE, engineering educator; b. Changchun, Jilin, China, Mar. 16, 1963; d. Quanyou Si and Baolin Jiao; m. Jun Shen, July 27, 1988. BS, Tsinghua U., Beijing, 1985, MS, 1988; PhD, U. Notre Dame, 1992. Rsch. asst. U. Notre Dame, South Bend, Ind., 1988-91; asst. prof. Ariz. State U., Tempe, 1991-96, assoc. prof., 1996-2000, prof., 2000—. Cons. Intel Corp., Chandler, Ariz., 1996, Ariz. Pub. Svc., Palo Verde, 1997, Medtronic, Tempe, Ariz., 2002—; proposal panelist/reviewer NSF/NRC, Washington, 1995—; adviser Assn. Chinese Sci. Engr., Tempe, 1996-99, 2002—; adv. com. Social, Behavioral and Econs. Scis. divsn. NSF, 1998-99. Assoc. editor IEEE Transaction on Automatic Control, 1998, 99, IEEE Transaction on Semiconductor Mfg., 1998-2002, Neural Networks, 2001-. Presdl. Faculty fellow The White House/NSF, Washington, 1995-2000; recipient Rsch. Initiation award NSF, Washington, 1993-96, Motorola Excellence award Motorola, Semicon. Prod. Sector, Tempe, 1995. Mem. IEEE (voting mem. neural network coun. 1995—). Avocation: skiing. Office: Ariz State U Dept Elec Engring Tempe AZ 85287 E-mail: si@asu.edu.

SIATRA, ELENI, English educator; b. Kozani, Greece, Oct. 22, 1961; came to U.S., 1985; d. Athanasios and Alexandra (Lanaras) S.; m. Todd Alan Reda, May 30, 1991. B of English, Aristotle U., 1983; MLS, Kent State U., 1986; MA in English, Miami U., 1990, ABD in English, 1996. Tchr. English as a 2d lang. Fgn. Langs. Inst., Kozani, Greece, 1983-85; asst. to dir. of ethnic studies ctr. Kent (Ohio) State U., 1986, student reference asst., 1985-86, instr., libr. adminstr., 1987; libr. readers' svcs. Bloomsburg (Pa.) U., 1987-88; grad. rsch. asst. Miami U., Oxford, Ohio, 1988-90, King Libr., Miami U., Oxford, Ohio, 1990-91; coord., portfolio rater Miami U., Oxford, Ohio, 1994-97, teaching assoc., 1991-94; instr. English Ind. U. East, Richmond, 2003—. Vis. instr. Miami U., 1994-97, tchr. ESL, Synchronon, Kozani, Greece, 1999-2001; mem. coll. of Arts and Scis. Comparative Lit. Com., Miami U., 1995-96. Sinclair Meml. scholar, 1995-96. Fulbright scholar, 1985-86; recipient Gordon Wilson award, 1994. Fellow Phi Kappa Phi; mem. ALA, Am. Soc. 18th Century Studies, Nat. Coun. Tchrs. English, Modern Lang. Assn., Internat. Soc. Study of European Ideas (workshop chair, 1996. Greek Orthodox. Home: PO Box 416 West College Corner IN 47003-0416 Office: Ind U East 2325 Chester Blvd Richmond IN 47374

SIBITZ, MICHAEL WILLIAM, school system administrator; b. San Francisco, July 22, 1937; s. Michael Jacob and Erna Anna Elsa (Altendorf) S.; m. Marilyn Joyce Pricco, Nov. 19, 1966; children: Elizabeth, Ryan. BA, San Francisco State U., 1959, MA, 1964; EdD, U San Francisco, 1980; postgrad., Notre Dame Coll. of Calif., Stanford U. Tchr., Pacifica, Calif., 1959-64, Dept. Def., 1964-65, Belmont, Calif., 1965-70; specialist Los Alto, Calif., 1970-71; adminstr. Belmont, Calif., 1971-80; supr. instrn., prin. Los Altos, Calif., 1980-84; asst. supt. Sylvan Union Sch. Dist., Modesto, Calif., 1984-97; supr., interim program dir. St. Mary's Coll., Moraga, Calif., 1998—99. mem. adj. faculty St. Mary's Coll., 1989—. Contbr. articles to profl. jours. Bd. dirs. Modesto Symphony, 1993-2002; mem. Stanislaus Arts Commn.; past pres. United Way Stanislaus County, Stanislaus County Industry Edn. Coun. Served with U.S. Army, 1960-66. Mem. NEA (life), ASCD, Assn. Calif. Sch. Adminstrs. (charter-life), Calif. Assn. Supervision and Curriculum Devel. (bd. dirs. 1997, treas. 1999-2001), Phi Delta Kappa. Roman Catholic. Home: 1400 Brickyard View Point Richmond CA 95801 Office: St Mary's Coll PO Box 4350 Moraga CA 94575-4350 E-mail: m2sibitz@aol.com.

SIBLEY, WILLIAM ARTHUR, academic administrator, physics educator, consultant; b. Ft. Worth, Nov. 22, 1932; s. William Franklin and Sada (Rasor) S.; m. Joyce Elaine Gregory, Dec. 21, 1957; children: William Timothy, Lauren Shawn, Stephen Marshall. BS, U. Okla., 1956, MS, 1958, PhD, 1960. Tchg., rsch. asst. U. Okla., 1956-60; postdoctoral rsch. in defect solid state Kernforschungsanlage Julich and Tech. U. Aachen, Germany, 1960-61; rsch. solid state divsn. Oak Ridge Nat. Lab., 1961-70; prof., head physics Okla. State U., Stillwater, 1970-76, dir. Sch. Phys. and Earth Scis., 1976-78, asst. v.p. rsch., 1978-88; v.p. acad. affairs U. Ala., Birmingham, 1990-96; program dir. NSF, Washington, 1988-89, acting dir. divsn. materials rsch., 1990, program dir., 1996-99, acting divsn. dir. rsch., evaluation and comm. divsn., 1998-99; pres. Okla. Ctr. for Advancement of Sci. and Tech., 2000—02; CEO, dir. Okla. Sci. and Tech. R & D, 2002—. Mem. solid state sci. com. NAS, 1977-83; bd. dirs. Oak Ridge Assoc. Univs., 1982-88, Coun. on Govt. Rels., 1987-93, Okla. Ctr. for Advancement Sci. and Tech., 1987-88; trustee, chmn. materials rsch. counsel Southeastern Univ. Rsch. Assn., 1992-95; cons. univ. edn. and rsch. Author: University Management 2010, 1998; contbr. articles to profl. jours. Pres. Stillwater Indsl. Found., 1985-86. Served to lt. AUS, 1951-53. Maj. USAR, 1953-60, Korea. Fellow Am. Phys. Soc.; mem. Omicron Delta Kappa, Sigma Xi, Sigma Pi Sigma, Pi Mu Epsilon. Baptist. Home: 2517 Thunderwind Cir Edmond OK 73034-6880 Office: OCAST 4545 Lincoln Blvd Ste 116 Oklahoma City OK 73105 E-mail: bsibley@ocast.state.ok.us.

SIBOLSKI, ELIZABETH HAWLEY, higher education administrator; b. Gt. Barrington, Mass., Aug. 18, 1950; d. William Snyder and Frances Harrington (Smith) Gallup; m. John Alfred Sibolski Jr., Aug. 15, 1970. BA, The Am. U., 1973, MPA, 1975, PhD, 1984. Acting dir. acad. adminstrn. Am. U., Washington, 1974, planning analyst, 1974-79, asst. dir. budget and planning, 1980-83, dir. instl. rsch., 1984-85, exec. dir. univ. planning and rsch., 1985-2000; exec. assoc. dir. Middle States Commn. on Higher Edn., Phila., 2000—. Trustee Mortar Bd. Nat. Found., 1989-95. Recipient Comencement award Am. U. Women's Club, 1973. Mem. Soc. Coll. and Univ. Planning (bd. dirs. 1995-2000, pres. 1998-99), Mortar Bd. (sect. coord. 1975-82), Pi Alpha Alpha, Phi Kappa Phi (chpt. officer 1986-92), Pi Sigma Alpha, Omicron Delta Kappa. Avocations: breed, raise and show morgan horses. Home: 565 Wayward Dr Annapolis MD 21401-6747 Office: Middle States Commn on Higher Edn 3624 Market St Philadelphia PA 19104-2614 E-mail: esibolski@msache.org.

SICES, DAVID, language educator, translator; b. N.Y.C., June 10, 1933; s. Harry and Henrietta (Finger) S.; m. Joan Picker, May 25, 1956 (div. 1961); children: Andrew M., Anne; m. Jacqueline Boulon, July 25, 1963; children: Laura, Harry J. AB, Dartmouth Coll., 1954, MA (hon.), 1971; PhD, Yale U., 1962. Instr. Dartmouth Coll., Hanover, N.H., 1957-62, asst. prof., 1962-67, assoc. prof., 1967-71, prof. French and Italian, 1971-75; prof. emeritus, 1995—. Cons. NEH, Washington, 1986—, Can. Arts Council, Ottawa, 1979; mem. screening com. French Govt. Assistantships, N.Y.C., 1978-83. Author: Harmony of Contrasts, 1968, Theater of Solitude, 1974; co-author: French Idioms, 1996; co-author: 2001 French Idioms, 1996; translator: Comedies and Proverbs of Musset, 1994, Michel Zink, Historical Dramas of Musset, 1997, The Invention of Literary Subjectivity, 1998; co-translator: Machiavelli's Discourses, 2002; co-editor, translator: Comedies of Machiavelli, 1985, Machiavelli and His Friends, 1996, The Sweetness of Power, 2002. Fulbright-Hays fellow, Paris, 1956-57, Fulbright-Hays summer seminar, Rome, 1966; fellow Am. Council Learned Socs., 1969-70; humanities devel. grant Dartmouth Coll., Hanover, 1976. Mem. AAUP, Am. Assn. Tchrs. French, Am. Assn. Tchrs. Italian, Dante Soc. Am. Avocations: music, travel, photography. E-mail: david.sices@dartmouth.edu.

SICHEL, WERNER, economics educator; b. Munich, Sept. 23, 1934; came to U.S., 1940; s. Joseph and Lilly (Greenwood) S.; m. Beatrice Bonne, Feb. 22, 1959; children: Larry, Linda. BS, NYU, N.Y.C., 1956; MA, Northwestern U., Evanston, Ill., 1960, PhD, 1964. Instr. Lake Forest (Ill.) Coll., 1959-62; asst. prof. Roosevelt U., Chgo., 1959-60; instr. Western Mich. U., Kalamazoo, 1960-64, asst. prof., 1964-67, assoc. prof., 1967-72, prof., 1972—, prof., chair dept. econs., 1985—2001. Fulbright sr. lectr. U. Belgrade (Yugoslavia), 1968-69; vis. scholar Hoover Instn., Stanford, Calif., 1984-85; coord. Mich. Pub. Utility Confs., Ann Arbor, 1974-93; cons. Squire, Sanders and Dempsey, Cleve., 1980-90. Author: Basic Economic Concepts, 1974, 1977, Economics, 1984, 1987, 1990, Economic Journals, 1986 (Choice award, 1987); editor: 12 books and numerous jours., 1975—. Pres. Kalamazoo Jewish Fedn., 1989-93. Grantee NSF, 1966, Sperry & Hutchinson, 1963, Fulbright, 1968, W.E. Upjohn Inst., 1988. Mem. Am. Econ. Assn., Indsl. Orgn. Soc., Econs. Soc. Mich. (pres. 1975-76), Internat. J.A. Schumpeter Soc., Midwest Bus. Econ. Assn. (pres. 1989-90), Midwest Econ. Assn. (pres. 1995-96). Jewish. Home: 123 Merriweather Ln Kalamazoo MI 49006-4105

SICHERMAN, ROBBIN MERYL, library media specialist; b. N.Y.C., Sept. 13, 1949; d. Lester and Helen (Schnei) S. BA, Bklyn. Coll., 1970; MS in Libr. Sci., Palmer Sch. of Libr. & Info. Sci., 1972; MS in Reading, Adelphi U., 1981; MEd in Edn. Technology, Lesley U., 2001. Mem. asst. Queens (N.Y.) Borough Pub. Libr., 1972-73, asst. children's libr., 1973, children's libr., 1973-81, asst. br. mgr./children's libr., 1981-88; libr. media specialist # 4 Sch., Lawrence, N.Y., 1988—. Mem. Am. Libr. Assn., N.Y. Libr. Assn., Nat. Coun. Tchrs. of English, Internat. Reading Assn., Nat. Assn. for Edn. of Young Children, Internat. Soc. Tech. Edn. Avocations: computers, needlepoint, sewing, reading. Home: 2371 E 26th St Brooklyn NY 11229-4920

SICILIANO, ELIZABETH MARIE, secondary school educator; b. Mansfield, Ohio, Apr. 22, 1934; d. Samuel Sevario and Lucy (Sferro) S. BS in Edn., Ohio State U., 1957; MA in Edn., Ea. Mich. U., 1971; MFA, Bowling Green U., 1975. Cert. tchr., Mich. Instr. adult edn. The Toledo (Ohio) Mus. Art, 1972-81; tchr. art Monroe (Mich.) Pub. Schs., 1975-2001. Workshop facilitator; presenter in field; art tchr. computer graphics. Artist, working in oils, pastels and fabricating jewelry. Judge Monroe Bicentennial, Monroe Arts and Crafts League, other shows. Mem. NEA, Mich. Edn. Assn., Nat. Art Edn. Assn., Mich. Art Edn. Assn., Stratford Festival for the Arts, Toledo Craft Club, Toledo Fedn. Art Socs., Toledo Mus. Art. Avocations: swimming, skiing, classic cars, designing and creating jewelry, portraiture and landscape in oils. Home: 7179 Edinburgh Dr Lambertville MI 48144-9539 Office: Monroe High Sch 901 Herr Rd Monroe MI 48161-9744

SICURO, NATALE ANTHONY, academic and financial administrator, consultant; b. Warren, Ohio, July 19, 1934; s. Gaetano and Antonette (Montecalvo) S.; m. Linda Lou Rockman, Aug. 3, 1957; children: Michael, Christine, Paul. BS, Kent State U., 1957, PhD, 1964; MS in Pub. Health, U. N.C., Chapel Hill, 1958. Tchr., coach, recreation adminstr. schs. in, N.E. Ohio, 1958-62; instr., grad. asst., teaching fellow Kent State U., 1962-64; asst. supt. Geauga (Ohio) County schs., 1964-65; dir. program planning, asst. dean regional campuses Kent State U., 1965-68, 70-72, dean continuing edn., assoc. provost med. affairs, 1972-78; sr. cons., mgr. Peat, Marwick, Mitchell, Washington and L.A., 1968-70; pres. So. Oreg. State Coll., Ashland, 1979-86, Portland State U., 1986-88, Roger Williams U., Bristol, R.I., 1989-93, Roger Williams U. Sch. Law, Bristol, 1992-93; Jones Disting. Univ. prof. Jones Inst. for Ednl. Excellence Tchrs. Coll., Emporia (Kans.) State U., 1993-94; pres. SICURO Ednl. Cons., 1994-96; investment mgmt. cons. Paine Webber Princeton Portfolio Mgmt. Group, Princeton, N.J., 1996-97; retired, 1997. Pres. Ohio Council Continuing Edn., 1975-76; bd. dirs. So. Oreg. Coll. Found., 1979-86; state rep., chmn. fed. relations com. Am. Assn. State Colls. and Univs., 1979-86, bd. dirs. 1987-88, chmn.-elect, 1988; chmn. Govtl. Relations Commn., Am. Council on Edn., 1983-86; mem. council of presidents Nat. Assn. Intercollegiate Athletics; chmn. council of presidents Evergreen Conf.; co-chmn. council of presidents Columbia Football League; dir. Rogue Valley Physicians Service. Pres. United Way of Jackson County, Oreg., 1982; bd. dirs. Ashland YMCA, 1980-81, Ashland Indsl. Devel. Corp., 1982-85; mem. Jackson County Econ. Devel. Com., 1981-86, Am. Council on Edn., 1986-87. Mem. Nat. Challenges Commn. Higher Edn., Ashland Rotary, Bristol Rotary, Phi Delta Kappa, Phi Kappa Phi. Roman Catholic.

SIDDALL, PATRICIA ANN, retired English language educator; b. North Adams, Mass., May 20, 1947; d. William W. and Shirley M. (Ogert) Hartman; 1 child, Michael William. BA in English, North Adams State Coll., 1969. Cert. secondary edn. tchr., English, Social Studies. English tchr. Bay Path Regional Vocat. Tech. High Sch., Charlton, Mass., 1977-98, humanities cluster chmn., 1987-91; ret., 1998. Del. Mass. Dem. State Conv., 1986, 87, 89, 90, 94. Mem. ASCD, NEA (bd. dirs. 1994-98), Am. Vocat. Assn., Nat. Coun. Tchrs. English, Mass. Vocat. Assn. (sec. Ctrl. chpt. 1982-85), Mass. Tchrs. Assn. (exec. com. 1988-94, bd. dirs. 1984-98). Roman Catholic. Avocations: photography, golf, environ. concerns, writing. Home: 124 Lake Point Ln Naples FL 34112-7043

SIDDAYAO, CORAZON MORALES, economist, educator, consultant; b. Manila, July 26, 1932; came to U.S., 1968; d. Crispulo S. and Catalina T. (Morales) S. Cert. in elem. teaching, Philippine Normal Coll., 1951; BBA, U. East, Manila, 1962; MA in Econs., George Washington U., 1971, MPhil, PhD, 1975. Cert. Inst. de Francais, France. Tchr. pub. schs., Manila, 1951-53; exec. asst. multinational oil corps., 1953-68; asst. pensions officer IMF, Washington, 1968-71; cons. economist Washington, 1971-75; rsch. assoc. Policy Studies in Sci. and Tech. George Washington U., Washington, 1971-72, teaching fellow dept. econs., 1972-75; natural gas specialist U.S. Fed. Energy Adminstrn., Washington, 1974-75; sr. rsch. economist, assoc. prof. Inst. S.E.A. Studies, Singapore, 1975-78; sr. rsch. fellow energy/economist East-West Ctr., 1978-81, project dir. energy and industrialization, 1981-86; vis. fellow London Sch. Econ., 1984-85; sr. energy economist in charge energy program Econ. Devel. Inst., World Bank, Washington, 1986-94, ret., 1994. Affiliate prof. econs. U. Hawaii, 1979—94; co-dir. UPecon Inst. Resource Studies, 1995—; vis. prof. econs. U. Montpellier, France, 1992, France, 1995—96, France, 1997—; vis. prof. pub. policy Duke U., 1997; lectr. pub. policy George Mason U., 2000; tchr. coord. English for Hispanic program Parish, 2002; cons., spkr. in field. Author or co-author: Increasing the Supply of Medical Personnel, 1973, The Offshore Petroleum Resources of Southeast Asia: Some Potential Conflicts and Related Economic Factors, 1978, Round Table Discussion on Asian and Multinational Corporations, 1978, The Supply of Petroleum Resources in Southeast Asia: Economic Implications of Evolving Property Rights Arrangements, 1980, Critical Energy Issues in Asia and the Pacific: The Next Twenty Years, 1982, Criteria for Energy Pricing Policy, 1985, Energy Demand and Economic Growth, 1986; editor, co-author: Energy Policy and Planning series, 1990-92, Energy Investments and the Environment, 1993; co-editor: Investissements Energetiques et Environnement, 1993; co-editor: (series) Energy Project Analysis for the CIS Countries (Russian), 1993, Politique d'Efficacité de l'Energie et Environnement, Expérience pratiques, 1994, Matérial Pedagogique sur la Politique d'Efficacité de l'Energie et Environnement, 1994; contbr. chpts. to books, articles to profl. jours. Grantee in field. Mem.: Alliance Francaise, Internat. Assn. Energy Economists (charter 1986—2003), Am. Econ. Assn., Perpetual Adoration Soc. of St. Agnes (Arlington), John Carroll Soc., World Bank 1818 Soc. (bd. dirs. 1999—2000), Eucharistic Frat. 3d Order of St. P.J. Eymard, Chorale de St. Louis de France, Omicron Delta Epsilon. Roman Catholic. Office: 1201 S Eads St Ste 1712 Arlington VA 22202-2845

SIDIE, STEVEN L. secondary school educator; b. Westby, Wis., Nov. 10, 1951. BS in Math., U. Wis., Whitewater, 1973; MA in Edn., Viterbo U., 1997. Tchr. Mukwonago (Wis.) Sr. H.S., 1975—. Mem.: Wis. Learning Found. (founder, treas. bd. govs. 1991), Wis. Edn. Assn. (sec.-treas. 1985—91), Nat. Bd. for Profl. Tchg. Stds. (bd. mem.). Office: Mukwonago Sr HS 605 W School Rd Mukwonago WI 53149*

SIDJANSKI, DUSAN, economist, educator; b. Belgrade, Yugoslavia, Oct. 23, 1926; arrived in Switzerland, 1943; s. Vlastimir and Mara (Yankovitch-Petrovich) Sidjanski; m. Monique Foex Petrovich, Sept. 2, 1963 (dec. 1984); 1 child, Sacha; life ptnr. Clarina Firmenich. D. in Polit. Sci., U. Lausanne, Switzerland, 1954. From collaborator to asst. prof. Ctrl. U. Venezuela, 1950-53; head rsch. Intergovernmental Com. European Migrations, Geneva, 1956—57; head rsch., dir. Denis de Rougemont European Centre Culture, 1957—80; pvt. tchr. U. Geneva, 1959, from lectr. to prof. polit. sci. Inst. European Studies, 1963—68, prof., 1968—98, emeritus prof., 1995—, past dir. dept. polit sci. faculty econ. and social scis., former vice-dean faculty social and econ. scis. Former hon. advisor permanent del. Venezuela, Geneva. Author: (book) Fédéralisme amphictyonique, 1956, Partis politiques face à l'intégration européenne, 1961, Dimensions européennes de la science politique, 1963, Federative Aspects of the European-Community in Studies, in Conjecture, 1965, Décisions closes et décisions ouvertes, 1965, Dimensiones institucionales de la integracion latinamericano, 1967, Verso l'Europa Unita Gruppi di Promozione, 1968, The Federal Future of Europe, 2000, The Federal Approach to the European Union, 2001, others; contbr. articles to profl. jours. Bd. dirs. Latsis Found., 2003—. Mem.: EUSA, ECPR, Assn. Inst. Europe (gen. sec.), Hellenic Inst. Internat. Law (collaborator-corr.), French and Swiss Assn. Polit. Sci. (former pres.), European Cultural Ctr. (pres. 2003—), Internat. Assn. Polit. Sci. Avocations: music, sports, skiing, tennis, swimming. Home: 16 chemin de La Rippaz 1223 Cologny-Geneva Switzerland Office: Latsis Foundation 33 ch de l'Avanchet 1216 Geneva Switzerland E-mail: dusan.sidjanski@politic.unige.ch.

SIDON, CLAUDIA MARIE, psychiatric and mental health nursing educator; b. Bellaire, Ohio, Feb. 6, 1946; d. Paul and Nell (Bernas) DePaulis; m. Michael Sidon; children: Michael II, Babe. Diploma, Wheeling (W.Va.) Hosp. Sch., 1966; BSN summa cum laude, Ohio U., 1979; MSN, W.Va. U., 1982. Lic. cert. social worker Bd. Social Worker

Examiners, W.Va.; RN, Ohio. Various staff positions Bellaire City Hosp., 1966-67, 72-77; adj. nursing faculty W.Va. No. C.C., Wheeling, 1977-82; nurse clinician, psychotherapist Valley Psychol. and Psychiat. Svcs., Moundsville, W.Va., 1984; psychotherapist, nurse clinician, case mgr. No. Panhandle Behavioral Health Ctr., Wheeling, 1984-88; assoc. prof. ADN program Belmont Tech. Coll., St. Clairsville, Ohio, 1988—; nurse neurosci. dept. Ohio State U., Columbus, 2002—. Presenter in field. Mem. Tri-State Psychiat. Nursing Assn. (past pres., v.p., program chmn.), Nat. League for Nursing (presenter), Phi Kappa Phi, Sigma Theta Tau. Home: 52295 Sidon Rd Dillonvale OH 43917-9538 Office: Belmont Tech Coll 120 Fox Shannon Pl Saint Clairsville OH 43950-9766

SIEBE, CAROL ANN, elementary school educator; b. Petaluma, California, Aug. 30, 1946; d. Ernest Henry and Minnie Corda; m. Norman Thomas, Mar. 21, 1970; children: David Henry,and Meredith Ann. BA, U. San Francisco, 1968; tchg. credential, Calif., 1970; MA edn. leadership, St. Mary's Coll., 1996. Elem. tchr. Two Rock Sch., Petaluma, Calif., 1970—72, supr. primary curriculum, 1986-92, lead tchr., 1996—, 1975—. Leader Wilson 4-H Club, Petaluma, 1981; softball coach Petaluma Girl's Softball Assn., 1984-85; active Children's Home Soc., Petaluma. Mem. ASCD, Gateway Reading Coun., Delta Kappa Gamma (2d v.p. Gamma Tau chpt. 1988—, pres. 1995-97). Republican. Roman Catholic. Avocations: reading, cooking, aerobic walking. Office: Two Rock Sch 5001 Spring Hill Rd Petaluma CA 94952-4634

SIEBERT, WILLIAM MCCONWAY, electrical engineering educator; b. Pitts., Nov. 19, 1925; s. Charles Theodore Jr. and Isabel (McConway) S.; m. Anne Decker, Sept. 10, 1949 (dec.); children: Charles R. (dec.), Thomas McC., Peter W., Terry A., Theodore D. SB, MIT, 1943, ScD, 1952. Jr. engr. Westinghouse Rsch. Labs., 1946-47; group leader Lincoln Lab. MIT, Cambridge, Mass., 1953-55, mem. faculty, 1952-95, prof. elec. engring., 1963-95, sr. lectr., 1995—. Cons. to govt. and industry, 1952—. With USNR, 1943-46. Fellow IEEE; mem. Acoustical Soc. Am., Sigma Xi, Tau Beta Pi, Eta Kappa Nu. Achievements include research in applications of communication theory to radar and biol. systems. Home: PO Box 505 17 Mountain View Rd Jackson NH 03846-0505 Office: MIT 77 Massachusetts Ave Cambridge MA 02139-4307

SIEDE, WOLFRAM, research scientist; b. Darmstadt, Germany, Sept. 10, 1958; s. Werner Heinrich and Ilse (Schütt) S. PhD, U. Frankfurt, Germany, 1986. Postdoctoral rsch. fellow Stanford (Calif.) U. Med. Ctr., 1986-90; instr. in pathology U. Tex. Southwestern Med. Ctr., Dallas, 1990-94, asst. prof. pathology, 1994-96; asst. prof. radiation oncology Emory U. Sch. Medicine, 1996—2002; assoc. prof. cell biology genetics U. No. Texas Health Sci. Ctr., Fort Worth, 2003—. Mem. editl. bd. Jour. Mutation Rsch. DNA Repair, 1994-2001; co-author: DNA Repair and Mutagenesis, 1995. Office: U No Texas Health Sci Ctr Dept Cell Biology & Genetics 3500 Camp Bowie Blvd Fort Worth TX 76107

SIEDLECKI, PETER ANTHONY, English language and literature educator; b. North Tonawanda, N.Y., May 19, 1938; s. Anthony Paul and Mary Barbara (Litwin) S.; m. Rose Mary Murphy, June 25, 1960 (div. 1978); children: Christopher, Gregory, Jeffrey, William; m. Lynnette Noreen Mende, Apr. 26, 1980; children: Peter Emmanuel Mende-Siedlecki. BA, Niagara U., 1960, MA, 1966; PhD, SUNY, Buffalo, 1982. Tchr. English Lewiston-Porter Sr. H.S., Youngstown, NY, 1960—64, Grand Island (N.Y.) Sr. H.S., 1964—65; prof. English Rosary Hill Coll., Amherst, NY, 1965—74, Daemen Coll., Amherst, NY, 1974—, dean, divsn. arts and scis., 2001—, chair divsn. humanities and social scis., 1998—2001; prof. Am. Lit. Jagiellonian U., Krakow, Poland, 1982-84, Friedrich-Schiller U., Jena, 1988-89. Commentator pub. radio, 1995—. Author (poetry) Voyeur; contbr. articles to profl. jours. Fulbright Sr. lectr., Council for Internat. Exchange of Scholars, 1982-84, 88-89. Mem. MLA, Fulbright Alumni Assn. Democrat. Home: 249 Winspear Ave Buffalo NY 14215-1035 Office: Daemen College 4380 Main St Buffalo NY 14226-3592 E-mail: psiedlec@daemen.edu.

SIEGAL, GENE PHILIP, pathology educator; b. Bronx, N.Y., Nov. 16, 1948; s. Murray H. and Evelyne (Philips) S.; m. Sandra Helene Meyerowitz, Aug. 3, 1972; children: Gail Deborah, Rebecca Stacey. BA, Adelphi U., Garden City, N.Y., 1970; MD, U. Louisville, 1974; PhD, U. Minn., 1979; cert. in hosp. mgmt., U. N.C., 1988. Diplomate Nat. Bd. Med. Examiners, Am. Bd. Pathology. Intern, resident, rsch. fellow Mayo Clinic Found., Rochester, Minn., 1974-79; rsch. assoc. Lab. Pathophysiology, Nat. Cancer Inst., NIH, Bethesda, Md., 1979-81; fellow surg. pathology U. Minn., Mpls., 1981-82; asst. prof. pathology U. N.C., Chapel Hill, 1982-88, assoc. prof. pathology, 1988-90; mem. Lineberger Comprehensive Cancer Ctr., Chapel Hill, 1983-90; prof. pathology U. Ala., Birmingham, 1990—, prof. cell biology, prof. surgery, 1991—, sr. scientist, group leader breast, ovary, prostate program, Comprehensive Cancer Ctr., 1993—99. Mem. Children's Cancer Study Group, 1987-90, Pediatric Oncology Group, 1990-2000, Children's Oncology Group, 2001—, mem. osteosarcoma pathology com.; sr. scientist Ctr. for Aging, Cell Adhesion and Matrix Rsch. Ctr., 1995—, Ctr. Metabolic Bone Disease, 1997—, Gene Therapy Ctr., 2000—. Co-editor: Molecular Antibodies in Diagnostic Immunohistochemistry, 1988; sr. assoc. editor Am. Jour. Pathology, 2003—; assoc. editor Archives of Pathology and Lab. Medicine, 1989-90; mem. editl. bd. Yearbook of Pathology, 1983-91, Archives of Pathology and Lab. Medicine, 1990-91, Am. Jour. Clin. Pathology, 1990—, Modern Pathology, 1996—, Advances in Anat. Pathology, 1999-, Am. Jour. Surg. Pathology, 2000-, Annals Diagnostic Pathology, 2003—. With USPHS, 1979-81. Clin. fellow Am. Cancer Soc., Chapel Hill, 1981-82, jr. faculty fellow, 1983-86, Jefferson-Pilot fellow in acad. medicine, U. N.C., Chapel Hill, 1985-86. Fellow Am. Soc. Clin. Pathologists (coun. on edn. and rsch.), Coll. Am. Pathologists (inspector 1990—), Royal Soc. Medicine (London); mem. AMA, AAAS, Internat. Skeletal Soc., AOA, Am. Soc. for Investigative Pathology (councilor 2002-), U.S. and Can. Acad. Pathology (abstract rev. bd. 1989-91, 99—), A.P. Stout Surg. Pathologists (pres.-elect exec. bd.), Metastasis Rsch. Soc., Am. Assn. Cancer Rsch., Assn. Dirs. Anatomic and Surg. Pathology (coun. 2000--), Sigma Xi (pres. U. N.C. chpt. 1989-90), Phi Beta Delta. Democrat. Jewish. Office: Univ Ala at Birmingham Dept Pathology 506 Kracke Birmingham AL 35233

SIEGAN, BERNARD HERBERT, lawyer, educator; b. Chgo., July 28, 1924; s. David and Jeannette S.; m. Sharon Goldberg, June 15, 1952 (dec. Feb. 1985); m. Shelley Zifferblatt, Nov. 19, 1995. AA, Herzl. Jr. Coll., Chgo., 1943, 46; Student, Roosevelt Coll., Chgo., 1946-47; JD, U. Chgo., 1949. Bar: Ill. 1950. Practiced in, Chgo.; partner firm Siegan & Karlin, 1952-73; pres., sec. various small corps. and gen. partner in partnerships engaged in real estate ownership and devel., 1955-70; weekly columnist Freedom newspaper chain, other papers, 1974-79. Cons. law and econs. program U. Chgo. Law Sch., 1970-73; adj. prof. law U. San Diego Law Sch., 1973-74, Disting. prof., 1975—; adj. scholar Cato Inst., Washington, 1991—, Heritage Found., 1992—; cons. windfalls and wipeouts project HUD, 1973-74; cons. FTC, 1985-86, U.S. Justice Dept., dir. constl. bibliog. project, 1986-88; keynote speaker 5th Internat. Conf. on Urbanism, Porto Alegre, Brazil, 1989; nominated by Pres. Reagan to U.S. Ct. Appeals (9th cir.) Feb. 2, 1987, confirmation denied July 14, 1988 by party line vote Senate Judiciary Com. Author: Land Use Without Zoning, 1972, Spanish edit., 1995, Other People's Property, 1976, Economic Liberties and the Constitution, 1980, The Supreme Court's Constitution: An Inquiry Into Judicial Review and Its Impact on Society, 1987, Drafting a Constitution for a Nation or Republic Emerging into Freedom, 1992, 2d edit., 1994, Portuguese, Ukrainian, Polish and Spanish edits., 1993, Property and Freedom: The Constitution, Supreme Court and Land Use Regulation, 1997, Adapting a Constitution to Protect Freedom and Provide Abundance (in Bulgarian), 1998, Property Rights: From Magna Carta to the Fourteenth Amendment, 2001; editor: Planning without Prices, 1977, The Interaction of Economics and the Law, 1977, Regulation, Economics and the Law, 1979, Government, Regulation and the Economy, 1980. Mem. pres.-elect's Task Force on Housing, 1980-81; mem. Pres.'s Commn. on Housing, 1981-82; mem. Nat. Commn. on bicentannial of U.S. Constn., 1985-91; chmn. adv. com. Affordable Housing Conf., San Diego, 1985, Rights of Regulated Conf., Coronado, Calif., 1976; chmn. Conf. on the Taking Issue, 1976; mem. Houston Regional Urban Design Team, Study of Houston, 1990; mem. U.S. team Bulgarian Econ. Growth and Transition Project, 1990; mem. devel. bd. Mingei Internat. Mus. World Folk Art, 1981-84. Served with AUS, 1943-46. Research fellow law and econs. U. Chgo. Law Sch., 1968-69; Urban Land Inst. research fellow, 1976-86; recipient Leander J. Monks Meml. Fund award Inst. Humane Studies, 1972, George Washington medal Freedom Founds. at Valley Forge, 1981, Spl. award Liberal Inst. of Rio Grande do Sul, Porto Alegre, Brazil, 1989, Thorsnes award for outstanding legal scholarship, 1998; named Univ. Prof., U. San Diego, 1997-98.

SIEGEL, ABRAHAM J. economics educator, academic administrator; b. N.Y.C., Nov. 6, 1922; s. Samuel J. and Dora (Drach) S.; m. Lillian Wakshull, Dec. 22, 1946; children: Emily Jean Siegel Stangle, Paul Howard, Barbara Ann Pugliese. BA summa cum laude, CCNY, 1943; MA, Columbia U., 1949; PhD, U. Calif., Berkeley, 1961. Instr. dept. econs. CCNY, 1947-49; research economist Inst. Indsl. Relations, U. Calif., Berkeley, 1952-54; instr. dept. econs. M.I.T., Cambridge, 1954-56, asst. prof., 1956-59, assoc. prof., 1959-64, prof. dept. econs. Sloan Sch. Mgmt., 1964-93, assoc. dean Sloan Sch. Mgmt., 1967-80, dean, 1980-87, prof. emeritus, sr. lectr., 1993—. Spl. lectr. Trade Union Program, Harvard U., 1961-64; vis. prof. Brandeis U., 1956-60; vis. prin. mem. div. Internat. Inst. Labour Studies, Internat. Labour Office, Geneva, 1964-65; asso. staff dir. Com. Econ. Devel., Study Group on Nat. Labor Policy, 1960-61; trustee, chmn. adminstrv. com. M.I.T. Retirement Plan for Staff Mems., 1970-91. Co-author: Industrial Relations in the Pacific Coast Longshore Industry, 1956, The Public Interest in National Labor Policy, 1961, The Impact of Computers on Collective Bargaining, 1969, Unfinished Business: An Agenda for Labor, Management and the Public, 1978. Bd. dirs. Whitehead Inst. Biomed. Rsch., Analysis Group, Inc., Internat. Data Group; mem. adv. group Internat. Inst. for Applied Systems Analysis, Laxenburg, Austria; mem. Framingham Sch. Com., South Middlesex Regional Dist. Vocat. Sch. Com., 1968-71. With USAF, 1943-46. Mem. Am. Econ. Assn., Indsl. Relations Research Assn., Nat. Acad. Arbitrators, Am. Arbitration Assn. (mem. various panels), Inst. Mgmt. Scis. Bus. Roundtable (exec. com.), Phi Beta Kappa. Clubs: Comml, St. Botolph's. Home: 112 Gardner Rd Brookline MA 02445-4537 Office: MIT Sloan Sch Mgmt 50 Memorial Dr Cambridge MA 02142-1347

SIEGEL, CAROL J. special education educator; b. Chgo., Sept. 6, 1966; d. Alan and Patricia Siegel. BA, Rosary Coll., 1988, MS, 1991. Asst. dir. Richter, Brown Jr. Citizens' Ctr., River Forest, Ill., 1988-91; tchr. kindergarten Lemont, Ill., 1993—96, Riverforest, Ill., 1996—99; tchr. early childhood spl. edn. East Sch., Franklin Park, Ill., 1999—.

SIEGEL, SHARON BARBARA, middle school educator; b. Bklyn., Nov. 18, 1942; d. Harold and Constance Ruth (Silberman) Dunayer; m. Murray Harvey Siegel, Aug. 9, 1964; children: Roy, Andrew. BS, SUNY, Cortland, 1964; MEd, Ga. State U., 1977. Cert. Tchr. Ariz., N.Y., Ga. 1st grade tchr. Turin Rd. Sch., Rome, N.Y., 1965-67; elem. sch. tchr. Fulton County Schs., Atlanta, 1975-90; 8th grad. math. tchr. Dodgen Mid. Sch., Marietta, Ga., 1990-92; 4th grade tchr., math. tchr. Four Peaks Elem. Sch., Fountain Hills, Ariz., 1992-94; 7th grade at-risk program tchr. Marietta Mid. Sch., 1994-95; 5th grade math. tchr. Dunleith Elem. Sch., Marietta, 1995—. Mem. NSTA, Nat. Coun. Tchrs. Math., Ga. Coun. Tchrs. Math., Ga. Sci. Tchrs. Assn. Avocation: racewalking. Office: Dunleith Elem Sch 120 Saine Dr SW Marietta GA 30008-3878 Address: 944 Elkins Lk Huntsville TX 77340-8808

SIEGEL, STANLEY, lawyer, educator; b. NYC, Mar. 2, 1941; s. David Aaron and Rose (Minsky) S. BS summa cum laude, NYU, 1960; JD magna cum laude, Harvard U., 1963. Bar: N.Y. 1963, D.C. 1964, Mich. 1970, Calif. 1976; CPA, Md. Atty. Office Sec. of Air Force, 1963-66; asst. prof. law U. Mich., Ann Arbor, 1966-69, assoc. prof., 1969-71, prof., 1971-74; ptnr. Honigman, Miller, Schwartz & Cohn, Detroit, 1974-76; prof. law UCLA, 1976-86, NYU, 1986—, assoc. dean, 1987-89. Vis. prof. Stanford Law Sch., 1973, Ctrl. European U., Budapest, 1993—2001, U. Konstanz, Germany, 1996, Tel Aviv U., 1998; fellow Max-Planck Inst., Hamburg, 1988; cons. reorgn. U.S. Postal Svc., 1969—71; exec. sec. Mich. Law Revision Commn., 1973; mem. bd. examiners AICPA, 1980—83. Author: (with Schulman and Moscow) Michigan Business Corporations, 1979, (with Conard and Knauss) Enterprise Organization, 4th edit., 1987, (with D. Siegel) Accounting and Financial Disclosure: A Guide to Basic Concepts, 1983, (with others) Swiss Company Law, 1996; mem. editl. bd. Lexis Electronic Author's Press, 1996-98. Served to capt. USAF, 1963-66. Mem. ABA, D.C. Bar Assn., Calif. Bar Assn., Assn. of Bar of City of N.Y., Am. Law Inst., AICPA. Office: NYU Law Sch 40 Washington Sq S New York NY 10012-1099

SIEGEL, STUART ELLIOTT, physician, pediatrics educator, cancer researcher; b. Plainfield, N.J., July 16, 1943; s. Hyman and Charlotte Pearl (Freinberg) S.; m. Linda Wertkin, Jan. 20, 1968; 1 child, Joshua. BA, MD, Boston U., 1967. Diplomate Am. Bd. Pediatrics, Am. Bd. Pediatric Oncology. Intern U. Minn. Hosp., Mpls., 1967-68, resident, 1968-69; clin. assoc. NIH, Bethesda, Md., 1969-72; asst. prof. pediatrics U. So. Calif. Sch. Medicine, L.A., 1972-76, assoc. prof., 1976-81, prof., 1981—, vice chmn. dept. pediat., 1994—; head div. hematology-oncology Childrens Hosp. L.A., 1976—, dep. physician-in-chief, 1987-90; dir. Childrens Ctr. for Cancer and Blood Diseases, L.A., 1996—. Mem. clin. cancer program project com. NIH, Nat. Cancer Inst., HEW, Bethesda, Md., 1978-82; pres. So. Calif. Children's Cancer Services, L.A., 1977-95. Bd. dirs. Nat. Leukemia Broadcast Coun., 1987—, Ronald McDonald Children's Charities, 1988-95, Make-A-Wish Found., 1987-95, Children's Hosp. L.A. Found., 1994-2000, Ronald McDonald House Charities, 1995—, L.A. Regional Coun. Am. Cancer Soc., 1996—, Nat. Childhood Cancer Found., 1995—; pres. Ronald McDonald House Charities So. Calif., 1996—; bd. trustees, Children's Hosp., L.A., 2000—; treas. Padres Contra El Cancer, 2003—. Surgeon USPHS, 1969-72. Fellow Am. Acad. Pediatrics. Office: Childrens Hosp LA Divsn Hematology Oncology MS#54 PO Box 54700 Los Angeles CA 90054-0700 E-mail: ssiegel@chla.usc.edu.

SIEGEL, WILMA BULKIN, oncologist, educator, artist; b. Phila., Dec. 2, 1936; d. Morris and Minnie (Staffin) Bulkin; m. Jesse Sanders Siegel, Nov. 11, 1976 (div. 1975); children: Hillary Siegel Levin, Nancy Siegel Jaffee. BA, U. Pa., 1958; MD, Women's Med. Coll. Pa., 1962; student, Nat. Acad. Design, N.Y., 1989-93, New Sch., 1974-84; studied with Rowena Smith, Ft. Lauderdale, 1991-94. Lic. physician, Pa., N.Y. Rotating intern Mt. Sinai Hosp., N.Y.C., 1963; resident in internal medicine Temple U. Hosp., 1964-65; fellow in hematology Mt. Sinai Hosp., N.Y.C., 1966; fellow in cancer chemotherapy Meml. Sloan Kettering Hosp., 1967; asst. attending physician divsn. neoplastic medicine Montefiore Med. Ctr., N.Y.C., 1967-74; clin. asst. physician Mt. Sinai Hosp., N.Y.C., 1974-75; pvt. practice Extra Greenspan, M.D. and Assocs., 1974-75; attending physician Trafalgar Hosp., N.Y.C., 1975; asst. attending physician Montefiore Med. Ctr., N.Y.C., 1976-81, attending physician, 1981—; med. dir. Beth Abraham Hosp., Ritter-Scheuer Hosp., N.Y.C., 1983-87; dir. hospice edn. and rsch. Beth Abraham Hosp., N.Y.C., 1988—. Asst. prof. medicine dept. oncology Albert Einstein Coll. of Medicine, Bronx, 1979-90, asst. prof. medicine dept. epidemiology and social medicine, 1988—, emeritus prof., 1990—; mem. cancer com. Montefiore Med. Ctr., mem. adv. com. home care dept.; mem. adv. com. Bronx Comty. Home Care, Hospice Visiting Nurse Svc. of the Bronx. One-person shows include AIDS Resource Ctr. of Wis., Hotel Pfister, Milw., 1997; exhibited in group shows Bailey Hall Exhibits, Ft. Lauderdale, 1992-97, Ft. Lauderdale City Hall, 1992, Lauderhill Libr., Ft. Lauderdale, 1993, LeGrange (Ga.) Mus., 1995, Marcella Geltman Gallery, No. N.J., 1995, Women for the Visual Arts, Boca Raton, Fla., 1995, Northwood U. Art Gallery, West Palm Beach, Fla., 1995-97, Gwinnett Fine Arts Ctr., Duluth, Ga., 1996, San Diego Watercolor Soc. Internat. Exhbn., 1996, North Valley Art League Nat. Show, Redding, Calif., 1997, San Bernardino (Calif.) Art Assn. Nat. Show, 1997, Hollywood (Fla.) Art and Culture Ctr., 1997, Ky. Watercolor Soc., Elizabethtown, 1997; represented in pvt. collections; contbr. articles to med. jours. Mem. AMA, Am. Soc. Clin. Oncology, Ea. Pain Assn., Acad. Hospice Physicians, Found. Thanatology, Found. for Rsch. on Sexually Transmitted Diseases, N.Y. Cancer Soc., N.Y. County Med. Soc., Ea. Clin. Oncology Group, Bronx PSRO, Nat. Assn. Women Artists Inc. (juried, 1st Place award 1999, Moore Greenblatt Meml. award 1995), 2+3 Artist Group Inc. (juried), Fla. Artist Group Inc. (juried), Gold Coast Watercolor Soc. (Dick Blick award 1994), Ga. Watercolor Soc., Fla. Watercolor Soc., Catherine Lorillard Wolfe Assn. (assoc.), Internat. Arts-Medicine Assn., Am. Physicians Art Assn. Home: 2504 Lajune Terr Fort Lauderdale FL 33316

SIEGFRIED, CHRISTINE LOUISE, principal; b. Center Valley, Pa., Jan. 16, 1968; d. Charles A. and Gloria A. (Slutter) Spohn; m. David P. Siegfried, June 26, 1993; children: Jacob, Kendra. BSBA, Bloomsburg U., 1989. Cert. bus. tchr. Bus. instr. Chubb Inst., Swarthmore, Pa., 1989-90; bus. edn. educator Easton H.S., 1990-95; asst. prin. Allen H.S., Allentown, Pa., 1995-98, So. Lehigh H.S., Center Valley, Pa., 1998—. Advisor Future Bus. Leaders of Am., Easton H.S., 1991-95; coach 7th and 8th grade field hockey, Easton, 1991-95; testing adminstr. ETS-SAT Program at Easton H.S., 1992-95. Mem. Nat. Bus. Edn. Assn. (Outstanding Bus. Edn. Student 1989), Pa. Bus. Edn. Assn. Avocations: crafts, biking, golfing. Home: 463 Kevin Dr Bethlehem PA 18017-2455 Office: So Lehigh HS 5800 Main St Center Valley PA 18034

SIEGLER, MARK, internist, educator; b. N.Y.C., June 20, 1941; s. Abraham J. and Florence (Sternlieb) S.; m. Anna Elizabeth Hollinger, June 4, 1967; children:Dillan, Alison, Richard, Jessica. AB with honors, Princeton U., 1963; MD, U. Chgo., 1967. Diplomate Am. Bd. Internal Medicine. Resident, chief resident internal medicine U. Chgo., 1967-71; hon. sr. registrar in medicine Royal Postgrad. Med. Sch., London, 1971-72; asst. prof. medicine U. Chgo., 1972-78, assoc. prof. medicine, 1979-85, acting dir. div. gen. internal medicine, 1983-85, dir. MacLean Ctr. Clin. Med. Ethics, 1984—, prof. medicine, 1985—, Lindy Bergman prof., 1997-2000, Lindy Bergman Disting. Svc. prof., 2000—, dir. fellowship tng. program in clin. med. ethics, 1986—. Vis. asst. prof. medicine U. Wis., Madison, 1977; vis. assoc. prof. medicine U. Va., Charlottesville, 1981-82. Co-author: Clinical Ethics, 1981, 2d edit., 1986, 3d edit., 1992, 4th edit., 1998, 5th edit., 2002, An Annotated Bibliography of Medical Ethics, 1988, Institutional Protocols for Decisions About Life-Sustaining Treatment, 1988; co-editor: Changing Values in Medicine, 1985, Medical Innovations and Bad Outcomes, 1987; editl. bd.: Am. Jour. Medicine, 1979—94, 1997—, Archives Internal Medicine, 1979—90, Bibliography of Bioethics, Jour. Med. Philosophy, 1978—89, Jour. Med. Philosophy, 1978—89, Jour. Clin. Ethics, 1989—, Jour. Med. Ethics (London), 2002—; contbr. articles to profl. jours. Mem. adv. bd. Bioethics Inst., Madrid, Notre Dame Ctr. for Ethics and Culture. Grantee Andrew W. Mellon Found., Henry J. Kaiser Family Found., Pew Charitable Trusts, Field Found. Ill., Ira De Camp Found., Gaylord & Dorothy Donnelley Found.; Phi Beta Kappa vis. scholar, 1991-92, Chirone prize Italian Nat. Acad. Medicine, 1996; mem. NAS Cloning Panel, 2001-02, others. Fellow ACP (human rights com., ethics com. 1985-90), Hastings Ctr.; mem. ACS (ethics com. 1992—), Assn. Am. Physicians, Chgo. Clin. Ethics Program (pres. 1989-90). Office: Univ Chgo MC 6098 MacLean Ctr Clin Med Ethics 5841 S Maryland Ave Chicago IL 60637-1463

SIELOFF, DEBRA ANN, educational administrator, consultant; b. Mt. Clemens, Mich. BA in Journalism, Oakland U., 1990; postgrad., U. Ariz. Instrnl. sys. designer Chrysler Corp., Detroit, 1978-80, Boeing Vertol, Phila., 1980-82; engring. stds. analyst E.I. DuPont Biomed. Engring. Divsn., Wilmington, Del., 1982-83; computer sys. job performance aid designer Dayco Corp. Internat., Ohio, 1983-84; mng. editor Arabians Mag., Mich., 1984-85; midsize market configuration mgr. GM, Mich., 1985-92; tech. awareness tng. mgr. Ford-UAW Nat. Tng. Ctr., Mich., 1992-93; edn. program mgr. Biosphere 2, Oracle, Ariz., 1993-96; ednl. devel. mgr. Harris Corp., Fla., 1996—. Mem. adv. bd. Tucson Resource Ctr. for Environ. Edn., Tucson Children's Mus., 1994, 95; mem. curriculum rev. com. Ariz. Riparian Coun., Phoenix, 1993; nat. edn. advisor Environ. Health Found., Ariz., 1994—. Recipient Wildlife Artist award Cranbrook Mus. of Natural History, 1975. Mem. NSTA, ASCD, Internat. Assn. Bus. Communicators (renaissance awards chairperson 1992-93), Sierra Club. Home: 2637 Aston Cir Melbourne FL 32940-7171

SIERLES, FREDERICK STEPHEN, psychiatrist, educator; b. Bklyn., Nov. 9, 1942; s. Samuel and Elizabeth (Meiselman) S.; m. Laurene Harriet Cohn, Oct. 25, 1970 (div. Aug. 1990); children: Hannah Beth Alterson, Joshua Caleb. AB, Columbia U., 1963; MD, Chgo. Med. Sch., 1967. Diplomate Am. Bd. Psychiatry and Neurology. Intern Cook County Hosp., Chgo., 1967-68; resident in psychiatry Mt. Sinai Hosp., N.Y.C., 1968-69, Chgo. Med. Sch., 1969-71, chief resident, 1970-71; staff psychiatrist U.S. Reynolds Army Hosp., Ft. Sill, Okla., 1971-73; assoc. attending psychiatrist Mt. Sinai Hosp., Chgo., 1973-74; instr. psychiatry Chgo. Med. Sch., North Chicago, 1973—, asst. prof., 1974-78, assoc. prof., 1978-88; prof. Finch U. Health Scis., Chgo. Med. Sch., North Chicago, 1988—, vice chmn., 1990-94, acting chmn., 1994-95, chmn., 1995—2002, chmn. ednl. affairs com., 1983-85, 86-01, residency dir., 1999-2001. Cons. psychiatry Cook County Hosp., 1974-79, St. Mary of Nazareth Hosp., 1979-84, Gt. Lakes Naval Hosp., 1987-90, Jackson Park Hosp., 1987-89, Mt. Sinai Hosp., 1988—, Elgin Mental Health Ctr., 1997—; chief mental health clinic, North Chicago VA Hosp., 1982-85, chief psychiatry svc., 1983-85. Author: (wth others) General Hospital Psychiatry, 1985, Behavioral Science for the Boreds, 1987, rev. 2d edit., 1989, rev. 3d edit., 1993, USMLE Behavioral Science Made Ridiculously Simple, 1998; editor: Clinical Behavioral Science, 1982, Behavioral Science for Medical Students, 1993; mem. editl. bd. Acad. Psychiatry, 2000—; contbr. articles to profl. jours. Coach Glenview (Ill.) Youth Baseball, 1987-89, mgr. 1990 (age 10-12 Glenview World Series winner 1990), Glenview Tennis Club, 1986-90 (3.5 Men's Doubles League winner 1989-90). Maj. M.C., U.S. Army, 1971-73. N.Y.State Regents scholar, 1959-63; NIMH grantee, 1974-83, Chgo. Med. Sch. grantee, 1974-83; recipient Seymour Vestermark award NIMH/Am. Psychiat. Assn., 2003. Fellow Am. Psychiat. Assn. (coun. edn. and career devel. 1993-95, Disting. Fellow, 2003—); mem. Am. Coll. Psychiatrists, Ill. Psychiat. Soc. (fellowship com. 1985-99), Columbia Coll. Alumni Secondary Schs. Com., Assn. Dirs. Med. Student Edn. in Psychiatry (exec. coun. 1985-99, chmn. program com. 1987-88, treas. 1989-91, pres-elect 1991-93, pres. 1993-95, immediate past pres. 1995-99), Alliance for Clin. Edn., Am. Assn. Chmn. Depts. Psychiatry, Chgo. Consortium for Psychiat. Rsch. (sec. 1996-97, treas. 1997-99), Am. Assn. Dirs. Psychiat. Residency Tng. (exec. coun. 2000-03, chair workforce coalition 2000-03), Sigma Xi, Alpha Omega Alpha, Phi Epsilon Pi. Office: Finch U Health Sci Chgo Med Sch 3333 Green Bay Rd North Chicago IL 60064-3037 E-mail: sierlesf@finchcms.edu.

SIERRA MILLAN, DANIEL, school administrator; b. San Juan, P.R., Apr. 3, 1965; s. Rubén and Carmen Gloria (Millán) Sierra. BA cum laude, U. P.R., 1987. Cert. music tchr., prin., P.R. Music tchr. Univ. Elem. Sch., Río Piedras, P.R., 1986; band conductor Congregación de Mita's Ch., Río Piedras, 1985-87; music tchr. Bayamón (P.R.) Mil. Acad., 1985-86; registrar

Bayámón (P.R.) Mil. Acad., 1986-88, vice prin., 1988-90, secondary sch. prin., 1990-94, registrar, 1994-95, 95-96, dir. admission and finance, 1996-97, exec. dir., 1997—. Mem. steering com. for MSACS accreditation Bayámón Mil. Acad., 1990-94; mem. PIENSE steering com. Coll. Bd., 1993-94; bd. dirs. Pvt. Edn. Assn. of P.R., 1997—. Mem. ASCD, Pvt. Edn. Assn. P.R. Avocations: music, baking, photography, travel. Home: PO Box 194826 San Juan PR 00919-4826 Office: Bayamón Mil Acad PO Box 172 Sabana Seca PR 00952-0172

SIESS, ALFRED ALBERT, JR., engineering executive, management consultant; b. Bklyn., Aug. 16, 1935; s. Alfred Albert and Matilda Helen (Suttmeier) S.; m. Gale Murray Scholes, Dec. 17, 1966; children: Matthew Alan, Daniel Adam. BCE, Ga. Inst. Tech., 1956; postgrad. in bus., Boston Coll., 1968; MBA, Lehigh U., 1972. With fabricated steel constrn. divsn. Bethlehem (Pa.) Steel Corp., 1958-76, project mgr., 1969-76, engr. projects and mining divsn., 1976-86; sr. cons. T.J. Trauner Assocs., Phila., 1986-87; assoc. S.T. Hudson Internat., Phila., 1987-90; dir. mktg. SWIN Resource Sys., Inc., Bloomsburg, Pa., 1989-90; mem. adj. faculty Drexel U., 1976-96. Weekly columnist Economic and Environmental Issues, East Pa. edit. The Free Press, 1981-86; co-patentee suspension bridge erection equipment. Founder S.A.V.E. Inc., Coopersburg, Pa., 1969, pres., 1970, 75, 81, bd. dirs. 1970—. Served with C.E., USN, 1956-58. Recipient Environ. Action award S.A.V.E., Inc., 1975. Mem. ASCE (chmn. environ. tech. com. Lehigh Valley sect. 1971-83, life), Lions, Chi Epsilon. Republican. Mem. United Church of Christ. Home: 6460 Blue Church Rd Coopersburg PA 18036-9371 Office: C E Resource Group PO Box 39 Coopersburg PA 18036-0039 E-mail: siess@quixnet.net.

SIEVEKE-PEARSON, STARLA JEAN, language educator; b. Deadwood, S.D., Nov. 10, 1963; d. Alfred Frank and Ivis Irene (Zirbel) S.; m. Darin L. Pearson, Feb. 14, 1988; children: Drew, Kaitlyn. BS, Black Hills State Univ., 1986; MA, Univ. No. Colo., 1994; postgrad., Univ. Colo., 1998—. Eng. tchr. White Pine H.S., Ely, Nev., 1987-90; secondary edn. faculty Metro State Coll., Denver, 1994—2001; eng., arts tchr. Flood Middle Sch., Englewood, Colo., 1990—99; tchr. mentor, staff developer Sierra Mid. Sch., Parker, Colo., 1999—. Pres. Nev. State Coun. Tchrs., 1988-90; exec. bd. Blue Spruce Awards Com., 1997-2000. Mem. Nat. Coun. Tchr. Eng., ASCD, Colo. Lang. Arts Soc. (exec. bd. 1997-2002), Colo. Lang. Arts Soc. (1st v.p. 2003). Lutheran. Avocations: reading, playing piano, interior decorating, traveling. Home: 448 Benton St Castle Rock CO 80104-8593 Office: Sierra Mid Sch 6651 Pine Lane Ave Parker CO 80138

SIEVERT, MARY ELIZABETH, small business owner, retired secondary school educator; b. Sioux City, Iowa, Sept. 28, 1939; d. Arthur Harry and Bertha Busboom Sievert. BS, Morningside Coll., 1960; MA, U. Nebr., 1962; postgrad., U. Iowa, Hope Coll., U. Calif., Irvine. Instr. chemistry lab. Morningside Coll., Sioux City, Iowa, 1959—60; tchr. chemistry Davenport Schs., Iowa, 1962—86, Blackhawk Coll., Moline, Ill.; admissions officer St. Luke's Hosp., Davenport; SSTP counselor U. Iowa, Iowa City; computer instr. Grinnell Coll., Iowa, 1983; P/K-12/A sci. coord. Davenport Schs., 1986—96, AGATE dept. chair, 1995—99; pres., CEO Memorabilia ExtraOrdinaire, Davenport, 1996—. Exchange tchr. Rowley Regis Coll., Birmingham, England, 1975; pres., CEO Quad Cities Sci. and Engring. Fair, Davenport, 1962—99; adv. evaluation coun. Antique Am., Davenport, 2000—01; antiques and collectibles lectr. Ea. Iowa C.C., Davenport, 2001—, Blackhawk Coll., Moline, Ill., 2002—. Contbr. articles to profl. jours. Fundraising v.p. Miss Iowa Bd., Davenport, 1999—2001; mem. plan and zone commn. City of Davenport, 1988—94; WelcomeAires mem. QC vol. bur. QC Internat. Airport, 2000—; charter mem. 1st in the Nation in Edn. Rschr. Found., 1986—97; 63 com. woman Scott County Rep. Party; handbell ringer, former dir. vacation Bible sch. Holy Cross Luth. Ch., Davenport; mem. bd. Christ Lutheran Ch., 2002—. Named Outstanding H.S. Chemistry Tchr. of Yr. in Iowa, Iowa Acad. Scis., 1969, Outstanding Young Educator, Davenport Jaycees, Centennial Tchr. of Yr. in Iowa, NIH, 1987; named to Iowa Sci. Tchrs. Hall of Fame, 2002; recipient Regional Catalyst award for outstanding chemistry tchr., Chem. Mfg. Assn., 1985, Golden Apple award for top educator, Scott County Edn. Orgn., 1998; fellow Woodrow Wilson fellow for outstanding H.S. chemistry tchrs., Princeton U., 1982; scholar NSF. Mem.: AAUW (past pres. local br. and Iowa State), NEA (life), U. Nebr. Alumni Assn. (life), Morningside Alumni Assn. (life), Delta Kappa Gamma (former local and state parliamentarian, mem. Hapke scholarship com.), Pi Lambda Theta (life; mem. charter alumni chpt.), Sigma Kappa (life). Avocations: bridge, gardening, travel, theater, symphony. Office: Memorabilia ExtraOrdinaire Inc 2707 East Hayes St Davenport IA 52803

SIEWERT, GREGG HUNTER, language professional educator; b. Parkston, SD, Oct. 18, 1952; s. Roy Clifford and Evelyn Louise (Freier) S.; m. Mary Elizabeth Sims, Dec. 20, 1973. BA, Doane Coll., 1974; MA, U. Iowa, 1977, PhD, 1991. Assoc. prof. French Truman State U., Kirksville, Mo., 1991—. Vis. instr. Grinnell (Iowa) Coll., 1986-89; adv. bd. fin. Ctrl. States Conf., 1994-99. NEH fellow, 1994, 98, CIBER fellow San Diego State U., Montpellier, France, 1995; French Govt. scholar French Cultural Svcs., Paris, 1997. Mem.: MLA, Fgn. Lang. Assn. Mo. (exec. bd. 1994—, pres. 2003—), Am. Assn. Tchrs. French, Pi Delta Phi, Phi Kappa Phi. Democrat. Avocations: sailing, gardening, birding, celtic music. Home: 22372 Nutmeg Tr Kirksville MO 63501-8506 Office: Truman State U MC 320 100 E Normal St Kirksville MO 63501-4221

SIGAFUS, EVELYN, secondary school educator; b. Phila., Apr. 1, 1945; d. Herman and Claire (Frank) Weiss; m. Martin Lewis Sigafus, Aug. 20, 1967; children: Michelle, Brent. BA in Edn., U. Ariz., 1967. Cert. tchr., Ariz. Math. tchr. Marana (Ariz.) H.S., 1967-70, Sabino H.S., Tucson, 1982, 84-91, Tucson H.S., 1983-84, Santa Rita H.S., 1991—. Mem. math. core curriculum com. Tucson Unified Sch. Dist., 1988-92, mem. math. assessment com., 1992-93, mem. computer lab. com., 1993-95, mem. textbook selection com., 1993-94. Mem. com. advancement chair, sec. Troop 739, Boy Scouts Am., Tucson, 1986-93; pres. Wrightstown Neighborhood Assn., Tucson, 1988—; pres. Sahuaro High Drama Parents, Tucson, 1991-93; mem. 5-yr. planning com. Cong. Anshei Israel, Tucson, 1994—; mem. bd. trustees Cong. Anshei Israel, 1996—. Grantee NSF, 1990. Mem. NEA, Ariz. Edn. Assn., Tucson Edn. Assn., Nat. Coun. Thcrs. MAth. Avocations: reading, sewing, cooking, target shooting. Home: 9424 E Calle Bolivar Tucson AZ 85715-5840 Office: Santa Rita HS 3951 S Pantano Rd Tucson AZ 85730-4014

SIGLER, LOIS OLIVER, retired secondary school educator; b. Piney Flats, Tenn., Sept. 8, 1923; d. Willie Campbell and Lillie (Brown) Oliver; m. William Virgil Sigler Jr., Aug. 25, 1962; 1 child, William Oliver. BS, East Tenn. State U., 1944; MS, U. Tenn., 1952; postgrad., Memphis State U., U. Tenn. Home econs. tchr. Buchanan (Va.) pub. schs., 1944-46; area supr. home econs. edn. and sch. lunch prog. State Dept. Edn., Commonwealth of Va., 1946-54; asst. nat. advisor Future Homemakers of Am./New Homemakers of Am., HEW, Washington, 1954-56, nat. advisor, 1956-63; family living coord. Ohio State Dept. and Columbus (Ohio) Pub. Schs., Columbus Met. Housing Authority, 1963; tchr. Millington (Tenn.) High Sch., 1966-92; ret., 1992. Mem. Pres. Kennedy's Food for Peace Coun., Pres. Eisenhower's Adv. Com. on Youth Fitness. Named Tenn. Home Econs. Tchr. of Yr., 1975, Woman of Yr., 1991, Twentieth Century award for achievement, 1991, One of Top 2000 Outstanding People of 20th Century, 1998. Mem. NEA, Am. Home Econs. Assn., Tenn. Home Econs. Assn., Am. Voc. Assn., Tenn. Voc. Assn., Nat. Voc. Home Econs. Tchrs. Assn., Tenn. Voc. Home Econs. Tchrs. Assn. (hon. 1992, past sec.-treas., Outstanding Svc. award 1986), W. Tenn. Home Econs. Edn. Assn. (past sec.), Tenn. Edn. Assn. (bd. dirs. 1977-80), W. Tenn. Edn. Assn., Shelby County Edn. Assn. (past sch. rep.), Future Homemakers Am. (nat. hon. 1956, state hon. 1991, master advisor award 1988, advisor mentor 1991), Omicron Nu, Pi Lambda Theta. Home: 4785 Rolling Meadows Dr Memphis TN 38128-4868

SIGMUND, PAUL EUGENE, political science educator; b. Phila., Jan. 14, 1929; s. Paul Eugene and Marie (Ramsey) S.; m. Barbara Rowena Boggs, Jan. 25, 1964 (dec. 1990); children— Paul Eugene, David, Stephen. AB, Georgetown U., 1950; AB Fulbright scholar, U. Durham, Eng., 1950-51; MA, Harvard, 1954, PhD, 1959; postgrad., U. Paris, France, U. Heidelberg, U. Cologne, Germany, 1955-56. Teaching fellow Harvard, 1953-55, 58-59, instr., 1959-63; assoc. prof. politics Princeton, 1963-70, prof. politics, 1970—. Author: (books) Nicholas of Cusa and Medieval Polit. Thought, 1963; author: (with Reinhold Niebuhr) The Dem. Experience, 1969; author: Natural Law in Polit. Thought, 1971, 1981, The Overthrow of Allende and the Politics of Chile, 1977, Multinationals in Latin Am.: The Politics of Nationalization, 1980, Liberation Theology at the Crossroads: Democracy or Revolution?, 1990, 1992, The U.S. and Democracy in Chile, 1993, The Ideologies of the Developing Nations, 1963; editor, 1967, 1972, Models of Polit. Change in Latin Am., 1970; co-editor (with Pedro Aspe): The Polit. Economy of Income Distbr. in Mex., 1983; editor: Poder, Sociedad y Estado en USA, 1985, Evangelization and Religious Freedom in Latin Am., 1999; assoc. editor: jour. World Politics; translator: (books) The Mil. and the State in Latin Am. (A. Roquié), 1987, St. Thomas Aquinas, On Politics and Ethics, 1988, Nicholas Cusa, The Cath. Concordance, 1991, 1995. Served to 1st lt. USAF, 1956-57. Mem. Am. Polit. Sci. Assn., Latin Am. Studies Assn., Phi Beta Kappa. Home: 8 Evelyn Pl Princeton NJ 08540-3818

SIKES, CONNIE SUE BOND, nursing educator; b. Sherman, Tex., Nov. 24, 1946; d. Robert Earl and Thelma (Bloxom) Bond; children: Andrew Carl Sikes, Morgan Blake Sikes. BS, Tex. Woman's U., Denton, 1965; MA, Tex. Woman's U., 1973. Staff nurse technician Parkland Meml. Hosp., Dallas, 1967-69; instr. nursing Grayson County Coll., Denison, Tex., 1969-81; charge nurse circulator/educator operating rm. Wilson N. Jones Meml. Hosp., Sherman, Tex., 1982-89, dir. nursing resource, 1989-97; performance improvement educator perioperative svcs. Wilson N. Jones Health Sys. Mem. Am. Assn. Operating Room Nurses (cert., pres. 1987-89), Tex. Nurses Assn., Tex. Soc. Health Care Educators, Am. Heart Assn. (bd. dirs.). Home: 2324 Diana Dr Sherman TX 75092-2936

SIKES, JUANITA LOU, art educator; b. Belen, N.Mex., Dec. 22, 1951; d. Melvin Vernette and Doris Marie (McArthur) Lovelady; m. James Carroll Fulcher, May 30, 1970 (div. Aug. 1988); children: Lee Collins Fulcher, Amy Laura Fulcher; m. Robert Harry Sikes, Dec. 26, 1990. BS in Edn., Ea. N.Mex. U., 1983. Cert. tchr., N.Mex. Bookkeeper J & L Auto Salvage, Socorro, N.Mex., 1970-72, Navajo Mobil, Truth or Consequences, N.Mex., 1972-75; subs. tchr. Portales (N.Mex.) Schs., 1977-78, art aide, 1988-91; tchr., aide spl. edn. Ft. Summer (N.Mex.) High Sch., 1978-83, tchr. spl. edn., 1983-86; tutor ESL and GED Ea. N.Mex. U. Clovis Campus, Ft. Summer, 1986-87; fashion illustrator Slyduds Clothing, Roswell and Ft. Summer, N.Mex., 1987-88; instr. drawing Ea. N.Mex. U., Portales, 1989-90; tchr. art Portales Jr. High Sch., 1991—. Supt. art dept. DeBaca County Fair Bd., Ft. Summer, 1979-87; advisor Portales Elem. Spl. Art Program, Portales, 1989-91; coord. Portales Jr. High Spl. Art Program, Portales, 1991—; judge arts and crafts dept. Roosevelt County Fair, Portales, 1992. Exhibited in group shows Crafter's Crossing Gallery, Ft. Worth, numerous art fairs. Vol. Sierra County Rescue Squad, Truth or Consequences, 1973-75, Mayors Christmas Tree, Portales, 1989-90; coord., 1991—. Recipient Outstanding Citizenship award Sierra County Rescue Squad, 1974, 75; named Artist of Month Ft. Sumner Pub. Libr., 1987. Mem. NEA (pres. local chpt. 1992—), Nat. Art Edn. Assn., Gamma Zeta (pres. Beta Sigma Phi chpt. 1984-88). Democrat. Mem. Ch. of Christ. Avocations: painting, sewing, bowling. Home: 2108 W Beech St Portales NM 88130-9303 Office: Portales Jr High Sch 300 E 5th St Portales NM 88130-6082

SIKORA, JAMES ROBERT, educational business consultant, financial analyst; b. Sacramento, July 8, 1945; s. George Robert and Marian Frances (Fears) S.; m. Marie Lynore Nyarady, June 22, 1968. BEE, U. Santa Clara, 1967; postgrad., U. Calif., Santa Cruz, 1979—98, personal fin. planning cert., 1998. Electronic engr. GTE-Sylvania, Santa Cruz, 1967-69, sys. analyst, 1969-71, sr. support analyst, 1971-73; coord. bus. sys. Santa Clara County Office Edn., San Jose, Calif., 1973-76, dir. dist. payroll, pers. svcs., 1976-85, dir. dist. bus. svcs., 1985-95; self-employed sch. bus. cons. Omniserve, Ben Lomond, Calif., 1995—; interim dir. fin. San Jose Unified Sch. Dist., 2001, spl. fiscal asst., 2001—02. Cons. Milpitas Unified Sch. Dist., 1995—97, San Jose Unified Sch. Dist., 1997, 2000, Santa Clara County Office of Edn., San Jose, 1997—2000, Los Altos Sch. Dist., 1998—99, Fairfield-Suison Unified Sch. Dist., Fairfield, 1999, Burlingamor Sch. Dist., 1999, San Lorenzo Valley Unified Sch. Dist., Felton, 2003; interim bus. mgr. Healdsburg Unified Sch. Dist., 1999—2000; interim dep. supt. adminstrv. svcs. Gilroy Unified Sch. Dist., 1999; interim bus. mgr. Moraga Sch. Dist., 1999; interim asst. supt. bus. svcs. Mountain-View/Los Altos Union H.S. Dist., Mountain View, 1997; interim asst. supt. fiscal svcs. Cupertino Union Sch. Dist., 1997—98; interim CFO Union Sch. Dist., San Jose, 1998; spl. asst. Milpitas Unified Sch. Dist., 1998—2000; interim bus. mgr. Los Gatos Sch. Dist., 1997; interim budget mgr. Saint Helena Unified Sch. Dist., 2000; interim AB1200 coord. Napa County Office Edn., 2000; vice-chmn. Edn. Mandated Cost Network Exec. Bd., 1991—95; mem. Schs. Fin. Svcs. subcom., 1987—94. Author, co-editor Howdy Rowdy Memorial, 1979. Affiliate Ballet San Jose/Silicon Valley, Calif.; packards cir. honor roll Monterey Bay Aquarium; angel, seat donor San Jose Repertory Theater; sustaining mem. Bay Shore Lyric Opera Co.; patron Second Harvest Food Bank; active Ctr. Photog. Arts; charter mem. Friends of Long Marine Lab. Dirs. Cir.; mem. Team Shakespeare, Shakespeare Santa Cruz; treas. Mountain Parks Found., 1997—99; chmn. Unemployment Ins. Tech. Subcom., 1988—90; bd. dirs. Mountain Parks Found., 1997—2000. Mem.: Montalvo Assn. (patron), Santa Cruz Mus. Art and History, Am. Assn. Ret. Persons, Friends of Santa Cruz Pub. Librs., ARC Cmty. Friend, Nature Conservancy, Felton Cmty. Hall (supporter), Planned Parenthood, Waddell Creek Assn. (sponsor), Point Lobos Natural History Assn., Calif. State Parks Found., Calif. Trout, Amnesty Internat., Wine Investigation for Novices and Oenephiles, Santa Cruz Fly Fisherman, Golden Gate Nat. Park Assn., Norwegian Elkhound Assn. (pres. 1977—79), Calif. Assn. Sch. Bus. Ofcls. (subsect. pres. 1984—85, risk mgmt. com. 1985—87, sect. bd. dirs. 1987—93, legis. com. 1989—2000, sect. pres. 1991—92, schs. employer adv. com. rep. 1991—, strategic planning com. 1994, risk mgmt. com. 1996—97, 1999—2002, purchasing com. 1999—2002, state strategic planning com. 2001, bd. dirs. 1991—92, 1999—2002), Am. Diabetes Assn., Napa Valley Wine Libr. Assn. (life), Am. Assn. Individual Investors (life), Trout Unltd. (life), Alaska Natural History Assn., Rotary Internat. (club svcs. dir. 2000—, San Lorenzo Valley chpt.), Am. Dog Owners Assn., Maui Arts and Cultural Ctr. Ohia Club, Quyana Club, Easter Seals Ctrl. Calif. Century Club, Cabrillo Music Festival New Century Club, Sierra Club (life). Libertarian. Roman Catholic. Avocations: photography, travel, oenophilia, fishing, snorkelling. Home and Office: 400 Coon Heights Rd Ben Lomond CA 95005-9711

SIKORA, ROSANNA DAWN, emergency physician, educator; b. Weirton, W.Va., Nov. 16, 1955; d. Edward and Dorothy Ann (Wade) S.; m. Odus E. Brown, Nov. 25, 1994; stepchildren: Aza, Katherine, Hannah. AB in Biology, W.Va. U., 1978, MD, 1982. Cert. in emergency medicine; cert. in pediats., specialty in pediat. emergency medicine; cert. in internal medicine. Resident in pediat. internal medicine W.Va. U. Hosps. Inc., Morgantown, 1982-86, with. Assoc. prof. emergency medicine, pediats., internal medicine W.Va. U. Sch. Medicine, 1996—; mem. pediat. advanced life support subcom. Am. Heart Assn., Charleston, 1987-97, mem. pediat. advanced life support affiliate faculty, 1987-97. Physician men's/women's varsity swim/diving team W.Va. U., Morgantown, 1994—. Fellow Am. Coll. Emergency Physicians (bd. dirs. 1990—, sec.-treas. 1995-96, v.p. 1996-97, pres.-elect 1997-98); mem. AMA, ACP, Am. Acad. Pediats., Alpha Omega Alpha. Democrat. Roman Catholic. Office: W Va U Dept Emergency Medicine PO Box 9149 Morgantown WV 26506-9149

SIKORSKI, LORENA L. school system administrator; b. Sarasota, Fla., Nov. 28, 1951; d.Raymond J. and M. Louise (Fatjo) S. BA, Calif. State U., Fullerton, 1973, MS, 1984. Cert. educator. Tchr. music and sci. pub. schs., Garden Grove, Calif., 1974—. Adminstr., dir. Gay and Lesbian Educators So. Calif., Inc., Orange County, 1985-87; prof. Sikorski Music Studio, Huntington Beach, Calif., 1974-90; chair electives dept. Jordan Intermediate Sch., 2001, chair sci. dept. Lake Intermediate Sch., 2003. Composer: Just to Know Him, 1975, Happiest Christmas Ever, 1975, Epopee--Love's Quiet Song, 1991; co-author: Invisible Minority, 1988. Asst. condr. Oriental Chamber Orch., Bellflower, Calif., 1988, Gt. Am. Yankee Freedom Band, 1989; artistic dir. Pacific Coast Freedom Band, Long Beach, Calif., 1990-92; bass trombonist Huntington Beach Community Concert Band, 1992-93. Recipient Cmty. Svc. award Sunnyside Sch., 1984, Recognition award Calif. Assembly, 1989, Cmty. award So. Calif. Women for Understanding, 1989, Musicianship award Gt. Am. Yankee Freedom Band, LA, 1986, Gold Starr award Gay, Lesbian and Straight Educators So. Calif., 1989; Conducting Honors Pacific Coast Freedom Band, 1991. Mem. NEA, Calif. Tchrs. Assn., Garden Grove Edn. Assn. (intermediate segment dir.). Democrat. Avocation: dog training.

SILBER, JOHN ROBERT, university chancellor, philosophy and law educator; b. San Antonio, Aug. 15, 1926; s. Paul G. and Jewell (Joslin) S.; m. Kathryn Underwood, July 12, 1947; children: David Joslin (dec.), Mary Rachel, Judith Karen, Kathryn Alexandra, Martha Claire, Laura Ruth, Caroline Jocasta. BA summa cum laude, Trinity U., 1947; postgrad., Northwestern U., summer 1944, Yale Div. Sch., 1947-48, U. Tex. Sch. Law, 1948-49; MA, Yale, 1952, PhD, 1956; L.H.D., Kalamazoo Coll., 1970; many others. Instr. dept. philosophy Yale U., 1952-55; asst. prof. U. Tex., Austin, Austin, 1955-59, asso. prof., 1959-62, prof. philosophy, 1962-70, chmn. dept. philosophy, 1962-67, Univ. prof. arts and letters, 1967-70, chmn. (Comparative Studies Program), 1967, dean (Coll. Arts and Scis.), 1967-70; Univ. prof., prof. philosophy and law Boston U., 1971—, pres., 1971-96, prof. internat. rels., 1996—, chancellor, 1996—. Vis. prof. Bonn U., 1960; fellow Kings Coll. U. London, 1963-64; bd. dirs. Mut. Am. Inst. Funds, Inc. Author: The Ethical Significance of Kant's Religion, 1960, Straight Shooting: What's Wrong With America and How to Fix It, 1989, Ist Amerika zu retten?, 1992; editor: Kant's Religion Within the Limits of Reason Alone, 1960, Works in Continental Philosophy, 1967— ; assoc. editor: Kant-Studien, 1968-87; contbr. to profl. jours. Chmn. Tex. Soc. to Abolish Capital Punishment, 1960-69; mem. Nat. Commn. United Meth. Higher Edn., 1974-77; exec. bd. Nat. Humanities Inst., 1975-78; trustee Coll. St. Scholastica, 1973-85, U. Denver, 1985-89, WGBH Ednl. Found., 1971-96, Adelphi U., 1989-97; bd. visitors Air U., 1974-80; bd. dirs. Greater Boston coun. Boy Scouts Am., 1981-93, v.p. fin., 1981-93, Silver Beaver award, 1989, Disting. Eagle, 1997; mem. Nat. Humanities Faculty, 1968-73, Nat. Captioning Inst., 1985-94; bd. advisors Matchette Found., 1969-70; mem. Nat. Bipartisan Commn. on Ctrl. Am., 1983-84, Presdl. Adv. Bd. Radio Broadcasting to Cuba, 1985-92; adv. bd. Schurman Libr. of Am. Hist., Ruprecht-Karl U., Heidelberg, 1986—, Jamestown Found., 1989—; mem. def. policy bd. U.S. Dept. Def., 1987-90; mem. internat. coun.advisors Inst. for Humanities at Salado, 1988—; bd. dirs. New Eng. Holocaust Meml. Com., 1989—, Brit. Inst. of U.S., 1989—, Bette Davis Found., 1997—, Boston Police Found., 1997—; Dem. gubernatorial candidate of Mass., 1990; vice chmn. U.S. Strategic Inst.; bd. dirs., vice chmn. Americans for Med. Progress, 1992—, chmn., 1994-95, mem. exec. com. 1995—; chmn. Mass. Bd. Edn., 1996-99; bd. advisors Nat. Assn. Scholars. Recipient E. Harris Harbison award for disting. tchg. Danforth Found., 1966, Wilbur Lucius Cross medal Yale Grad. Sch., 1971, Outstanding Civilian Svc. medal U.S. Army, 1985, Disting. Pub. Svc. award Anti-Defamation League of B'nai B'rith, 1989, Horatio Alger award, 1992, Am.-Swiss Friendship award, 1991, Israel Peace medal, 1985, Ehrenmedaille U. Heidelberg, 1986, White House Small Bus. award for entrepreneurial excellence, 1986, Cross of Paideia, Greek Orthodox Archdiocese of North and South Am., 1988, Pro Bene Meritis award U. Tex., Austin, 1997; Fulbright rsch. fellow Germany, 1959-60; Guggenheim fellow Eng., 1963-64; decorated with Knight Comdr.'s Cross with Star of Order of Merit Fed. Republic of Germany, 1983; commandeur Nat. Order of Arts and Letters (France), 1985. Fellow Royal Soc. Arts; mem. Am. Philos. Assn., Am. Soc. Polit. and Legal Philosophy, Royal Inst. Philosophy, Am. Assn. Higher Edn., Nat. Assn. Ind. Colls. and Univs. (dir. 1976-81), Phi Beta Kappa. Office: Boston U 1 Sherborn St Boston MA 02215-1708

SILBERT, LINDA BRESS, educational counselor, therapist; b. New Rochelle, N.Y., Sept. 14, 1944; d. Abram H. and Ann (Dreizen) Bress; m. Alvin Jay Silbert, Aug. 14, 1966; children: Brian R., Cheryl J. BS, SUNY, New Paltz, 1966; MS, We. Conn. State U., Danbury, 1989; PhD in Ednl. Adminstrn., Walden U., Mpls., 1993. Cert. in sch. counseling and elem. edn., N.Y. Children's writer Phone Programs, N.Y.C., 1984-86; owner, pub. Silbert & Bress, Inc., Mahopac, N.Y., 1976—, children's author, 1976—; owner, dir. Silbert Tutoring and Guidance Svc., Mahopac, 1968—. Parttime prin. Temple Beth Shalom Hebrew Sch., Mahopac, 1985—; leader parent workshops Silbert Tutoring and Guidance, 1985—, leader gifted program, 1989; cons. Mahopac Ctrl. Sch. Dist., 1983-84; cons., developer Author in Your Sch. program, 1983-87. Author: Creative Thinking Workbooks, 1976, Understanding People Storybooks, 1978 (lifeskills programs) Strong Kids Program, 1991, Stong Kids Early Childhood Programs, 1993, Passport to Emotionally and Socially Strong Kids, 1995, Teacher's Handbook Strong Study Skills Program, 1997. Membership chair Temple Beth Shalom, Mahopac, 1980-85. Recipient Gabriel Schonfeld award for educator excellence Bd. of Jewish Edn. of Greater N.Y., 1991. Mem. Am. Counseling Assn., Orton Dyslexia Soc., Am. Mental Health Counselors Assn., United Jewish Fedn. (award 1983). Avocations: dancing, painting. Office: Silbert & Bress Inc PO Box 68 Mahopac NY 10541-0068

SILER, SUSAN REEDER, communications educator; b. Knoxville, Tenn., May 31, 1940; d. Claude S. Jr. and Mary Frances (Cook) Reeder; m. Theodore Paul Siler Jr., Sept. 3, 1960; children: Mary Siler Walker, Theodore Paul III. BS in Communications and Journalism, U. Tenn., Knoxville, 1988, MS in Mass Comms., 1994, postgrad. 2d grade tchr. Lawton (Okla.) Pub. Schs., 1961-62, substitute tchr., 1963-64; with By Design, 1987-88; English tutor, 1991-95; adj. instr. comm. U. Tenn., 1994—, U. Tenn., Pellissippi State Tech. C.C., Knoxville, Tenn. Bd. dirs. Hlen Ross McNabb Mental Health Ctr., Knoxville. Tutor Episc. Ch. Ascension, Knoxville, 1990—; instr. United Meth. Ch., Knoxville, 1985-92; chmn. Dogwood Arts Festival, Knoxville, 1980-85; chmn. Bd. Govs . of East Tenn. Presentation Soc., 1988-96, Dogwood Trails; chmn., sec. bd. dirs. YWCA, Knoxville, 1982-88, editor newsletter, membership chmn., placement adv., sec.; Knoxville Jr. League, 1979-95; bd. dirs. Knoxville Women's Ctr., 1993-94; spl. events chmn. St. Mary's Med. Ctr. Found., 1986-89; Pres. Knoxville area Literacy Assn., 1989-92, tutor Episcopal Ch. Literacy program, Knoxville, 1990-95. Mem. Internat. Mass Comm. Assn., Soc. Profl. Journalists, Am. Journalism Historians Assn., Assn. for Edn. in Journalism and Mass Comms., Kappa Tau Alpha, Golden Key. Home: 717 Kenesaw Ave Knoxville TN 37919-6662

SILFEN, ROBERTA DAWN, wildlife hospital administrator; b. Bklyn. children: Frederick, Richard. BA, CUNY, 1953; MA, U. Hawaii, 1970; MS, Troy State U., Montgomery, Ala., 1971; MA, U. Tex., San Antonio, 1983; EdD, Tex. A&M U., 1991. Cert. mid.-mgmt., supt., Tex. Tchr. Pearl Harbor Kai Elem. Sch., Honolulu, 1968-71, Montgomery Pub. Schs., 1971-76, East Cen. Ind. Sch. Dist., San Antonio, 1976-78, adminstr., 1978-95; exec. dir.

Wildlife Care Ctr., Ft. Lauderdale, Fla., 1995—. Adj. prof. Nova Southeastern U., Ft. Lauderdale, Fla., 1992—; spkr. in field. Author: Practical Guide to Teaching Adult Learning, 5 Minute Classroom Manager: Behavior Management in a Nutshell; contbr. articles to profl. jours. Named Hon. 1st Lady, Gov. State of Ala.; Fulbright scholar; grantee U.S. Dept. Edn., 1979, 82, 89, 92-93. Mem. ASCD, Fulbright Alumni Assn., Phi Delta Kappa. Avocations: snow skiing, horseback riding, piano. Home: 3880 Queens Way Boca Raton FL 33434-3309 Office: 3200 SW 4th Ave Fort Lauderdale FL 33315-3019 E-mail: SILFENR@BELLSOUTH.NET.

SILUK, CAROL LINDA, elementary school educator; b. Mpls., June 30, 1946; d. Gerhard and Karolyn Ericka (Skalnik) Hanson; m. Oct. 18, 1975 (div. Aug. 1992); children: Melissa, Natalie; m. Dennis L. Siluk, Aug. 13, 1993 (div. Aug. 1997). BA, Luther Coll., 1968. Cert. elem. tchr. Elem. tchr. St. Paul Pub. Schs., 1968—2003. Bldg. steward St. Paul Fedn. Tchrs., 1979-2001, chair profl. policies com., 1991-2002, social com., 1990-2003, com. of nine, 1996-98; del. St. Paul Trades and Labor Assembly, 1996-99. Mem. Fedn. of Tchrs. (exec. bd. 1991-98, chair fin. com., mem. sch. site coun. 1999-2001, 2002-2003). Home: 6727 Gretchen Ct N Oakdale MN 55128-3132 E-mail: clindasiluk30@aol.com.

SILVA, JAMES ANTHONY, soil scientist, educator; b. Kilauea, Hawaii, Sept. 4, 1930; s. Anthony Clarence and Alice (Fernandez) S.; m. Lorraine Marie Zirger, July 8, 1967; children: Nancy Jean, Malia Alice. BS, U. Hawaii, 1951, MS, 1959; PhD, Iowa State U., 1964. Asst. agronomist experiment sta. Hawaiian Sugar Planters Assn., Honolulu, 1953-59; asst. soil biochemist dept. agronomy Iowa State U., Ames, 1959-64; asst. soil scientist dept. agronomy and soil sci. U. Hawaii, Honolulu, 1964-70, assoc. soil scientist dept. agronomy and soil sci., 1970-76, sta. statistician Coll. Tropical Agrl. and Human Resources, 1970-77, prin. investigator benchmark soils project, 1978-83, prof. soil sci. dept. agronomy and soil sci., 1976-98, prof. emeritus soil sci. dept. agronomy and soil sci., 1998—. Editor: Experimental Designs for Predicting Crop Productivity, 1981, Soil Based Agrotechnology Transfer, 1985, Plant Nutrient Management in Hawaii's Soils, 2000; contbr. chpt. to Detecting Mineral Nutrient Deficiencies in Tropical and Temperate Crops, 1989. Mem. Internat. Soc. Soil Sci., Soil Sci. Soc. Am., Agronomy Soc. Am., Gamma Sigma Delta. Office: U Hawaii Dept Tropical Plant and Soil Scis 3190 Maile Way Honolulu HI 96822-2319 Business E-Mail: jsilva@hawaii.edu.

SILVA, LAWRENCE KEHINDE, physical education educator; b. Lagos, Nigeria, June 27, 1948; s. Jacob Olawumi and Leah Adetunmibi Rotimi-Silva; m. Moji Silva, Mar. 8, 1980; children: James, Emmanuel, Daniel, Grace. BS, Benedict Coll., 1976; MAT, U. S.C., 1978; PhD, Ahmadu Bello U., Zaria, Nigeria, 1987. Asst. edn. officer Ministry of Edn., Govt. of Nigeria, Kaduna, 1971-78; lectr. Ahmadu Bello U., Zaria, 1979-90; assoc. prof. Bowie (Md.) State U., 1990—. Chmn. phys. edn. dept. Advanced Tchrs. Coll., Zaria, 1982-86; phys. edn. specialist Inst. of Edn., Zaria, 1986-90; faculty athletic rep. Bowie State U., 1997-98. Author: Community and Public Health, 1988; contbr. articles to sci. and profl. jours. Mem. AAUP, AAHPERD, Md. Assn. for Health, Phys. Edn., Recreation and Dance, Internat. Coun. for Health, Phys. Edn. (aging commn. 1992—). Democrat. So. Baptist. Avocations: music, athletics, christian activities. Home: 9104 6th St Lanham Seabrook MD 20706 Office: Bowie State U 14000 Jericho Park Rd Bowie MD 20715 E-mail: lsilva@bowiestate.edu.

SILVA, MONICA, gifted education educator; b. Miami, May 13, 1927; d. Arthur E. and Laura E. (Fernandez) S.; m. Alfred Bethel, Apr. 30, 1955 (annulled 1959); 1 child, Leonard James. BA in Edn., Fordham U., 1970, MS in Adminstrn. Supervision, 1976. Cert. tchr. elem. edn., N.Y.; cert. math. tchr. K-8, Va.; cert. social studies tchr. 7-12, N.Y.; cert. adminstr., N.Y. Tchr., adminstrv. asst. Intermediate Sch. 10 Bd. of Edn., N.Y.C., 1970-73, St. Peter's U.F.S.D., Peekskill, N.Y., 1973-76; assoc. dir. Harlem Hosp. Med. Ctr., N.Y.C., 1976-78; tchr. math., K-8 Bd. Edn., N.Y.C., 1980-83; tchr. math. Middle. Sch., Newport News, Va., 1983-86; tchr. talented and gifted Pub. Sch. 31 Bd. Edn., N.Y.C., 1986-91. Dir. summer ednl. program Episcopal Diocese, N.Y., 1970-89; dir. Arista Honor Soc., Intermediate Sch. 10, N.Y. Pub. Schs., 1971-73. Co-editor: (handbook) Frederick Douglass Teacher's Handbook, 1971. Counselor/tutor N.Y.C. Pub. Schs., 1970-73, mem. PTA, 1970-76, 80-83; mem. Cancer Support Group, Newport News, Va., 1994; vol. tchr. Queen Street Bapt. Ch., Hampton, Va., 1993-94. Grantee Chase Bank, N.Y.C., 1972. Mem. Libr. Congress, AAUW, Smithsonian Inst. Democrat. Episcopalian. Avocations: reading, playing piano, gardening, sewing and numismatics. Home: 3423 Shell Rd Hampton VA 23661-1441

SILVER, DONALD, surgeon, educator; b. N.Y.C., Oct. 19, 1929; s. Herman and Cecilia (Meyer) S.; m. Helen Elizabeth Harnden, Aug. 9, 1958; children: Elizabeth Tyler, Donald Meyer, Stephanie Davies, William Paige. AB, Duke U., 1950, BS in Medicine, MD, 1955. Diplomate Am. Bd. Surgery, Am. Bd. Gen. Vascular Surgery, Am. Bd. Thoracic Surgery. Intern Duke Med. Ctr., 1955-56, asst. resident, 1958-63, resident, 1963-64; mem. faculty Duke Med. Sch., 1964-75, prof. surgery, 1972-75; cons. Watts Hosp., Durham, 1965-75, VA Hosp., Durham, 1970-75, chief surgery, 1968-70; prof. surgery, chmn. dept. U. Mo. VA Med. Ctr., Columbia, 1975-98, chmn. univ. physicians, 2003—. Cons. Harry S. Truman Hosp., Columbia, 1975— ; mem. bd. sci. advisers Cancer Research Center, Columbia, 1975— ; mem. surg. study sect. A NIH; dir surg. svcs. U. Mo. Health System, 2001-2003. Contbr. articles to med. jours., chpts. to books; editorial bds.; Jour. Vascular Surgery, Postgrad. Gen. Surgery, Vascular Surgery. Served with USAF, 1956-58. James IV Surg. traveler, 1977 Fellow ACS (gov. 1995-99), Deryl Hart Soc.; mem. AMA, AAAS, Mo. Med. Assn., Boone County Med. Soc., Internat. Cardiovascular Soc., Soc. Univ. Surgeons, Am. Heart Assn. (Mo. affiliate rsch. com.), Soc. Surgery Alimenatry Tract, Assn. Acad. Surgery, So. Thoracic Surg. Assn., Internat. Soc. Surgery, Soc. Vascular Surgery, Am. Assn. Thoracic Surgery, Am. Surg. Assn., Ctrl. Surg. Assn. (pres.-elect 1990-91, pres. 1991-92), Western Surg. Assn., Midwestern Vascular Surg. Soc. (pres. 1984-85), Ctrl. Surg. Assn. Found. (treas. 1992-93, 2d v.p. 1993-94, 1st v.p. 1994-95, pres. 1995-96). Home: 1050 W Covered Bridge Rd Columbia MO 65203-9569 Office: U Mo Med Ctr Dept Surgery N514 Columbia MO 65212-0001 E-mail: Silverd@health.missour.edu.

SILVER, MICHAEL, school superintendent; b. Landsberg, Germany, Jan. 30, 1948; came to U.S., 1949; s. Norman and Esther Silver; m. Beverley Ann Moss, May 16, 1971; children: Sabina, Joseph. AB, Washington U., 1970, MEd, 1973, PhD, 1982. Cert. supt. Mo., Wash. Tchr. Normandy Sch. Dist., St. Louis, 1970-72, Parkway Sch. Dist., St. Louis, 1972-75, asst. prin., 1976-79, adminstrv. asst., 1979-83, asst. to supt., 1983-84, asst. supt., 1984-86; supt. Tukwila Sch. Dist., Seattle, 1986—. Bd. dirs. Cities in Schs., Seattle; mem. adv. bd. Sta. KCTS, Seattle, 1990—; vis. exec. Seattle U. Sch. Edn., 1995. Author: Values Education, 1976, Facing Issues of Life and Death, 1976. Pres. SeaTac Task Force, Seattle, 1989; bd. dirs. Anti-Defamation League, Seattle, 1987—; mem. City of Tukwila (Wash.) 2000 Com., 1988-90. Recipient A Plus award Wash. Coun. Econ. Edn., 1992, Excellence in Ednl. Leadership award Univ. Coun. for Ednl. Adminstrn., 1998, Art Tribute award, Wash. Art Edn. Assn., 2001; named Exec. Educator, 100 Exec. Educator Mag., 1985, 1996 Assoc. for Inst. for Ednl. Inquiry Leadership Program; named to Homework Ctrl.; 100 Most Influential People in U.S. Pub. Edn.; I/D/E/A fellow Charles F. Kettering Found., 1978, 88, Title VI fellow Washington U., 1971-73; named Supt. of Yr. Wash. Libr. Media Assn., 2000. Mem. ASCD, Am. Assn. Sch. Adminstrs., Wash. Assn. Sch. Adminstrs. (met. chpt., pres. 1989-90), King County Supts. (chmn. adv. com. 1989-90, 95-96), Southcenter Rotary Club (Paul Harris fellow 1994), Southwest King County C. of C., Phi Delta Kappa. Home: 14127 SE 50th St Bellevue WA 98006-3409 Office: Tukwila Sch Dist 4640 S 144th St Seattle WA 98168-4134 E-mail: silverm@tukwila.wednet.edu.

SILVERA, ISAAC FRANKLIN, physics educator; b. San Diego, Mar. 25, 1937; s. Albert and Victoria (Nahem) S.; m. Lili Jean Wong, June 3, 1961; children: Michelle, Janine, Cherie, Christopher. BA, U. Calif., Berkeley, 1959, PhD, 1965. Postdoctoral fellow Centre National de la Recherche Scientifique, Grenoble, France, 1965-66; tech. staff Rockwell Internat., Thousand Lakes, Calif., 1966-71; prof. physics U. Amsterdam, The Netherlands, 1971-82, Harvard U., Cambridge, Mass., 1982—. Contbr. over 200 articles to profl. jours. Recipient Hewlett Packard Europhysics award European Physical Soc., 1983. Fellow Am. Phys. Soc., AAAS. Office: Harvard Univ Dept Of Physics Cambridge MA 02138

SILVERMAN, CHARLOTTE, epidemiologist, educator; b. N.Y.C., May 21, 1913; d. Harry and Gussie (Goldman) S. BA, Bklyn. Coll., 1933; MD, Woman's Med. Coll. Pa., 1938; MPH, Johns Hopkins U., 1942, DrPH, 1948. Diplomate Am. Bd. Preventive Medicine. Intern Beekman Hosp., N.Y.C., 1939-40; resident Sea View Hosp., Staten Island, N.Y., 1940-41; asst. dir., dir. Bur. Tuberculosis Balt. City Health Dept., 1946-56; chief epidemiology, planning and rsch. Md. State Dept. Health, Balt., 1956-62; med. officer in various programs NIMH, Bethesda, Md., 1962-68; dep. dir. div. biol. effects and other positions Bur. Radiol. Health USPHS, Rockville, Md., 1968-83; assoc. dir. for human studies FDA, Rockville, 1983-92. Mem. faculty dept. epidemiology Johns Hopkins U. Sch. Hygiene and Pub. Health, Balt., 1950—. Author: Epidemiology of Depression, 1968; contbr. articles to profl. jours. Sr. Surg. USPHS, 1944-45. Recipient Mary Pemberton Nourse Meml. award AAUW, 1941-42, Merit award FDA, 1974, Alumni Life Achievement award Bklyn. Coll., 1994. Fellow APHA, Am. Coll. Preventive Medicine, Am. Orthopsychiat. Assn., Am. Coll. Epidemiology; mem. Delta Omega. Home: 4977 Battery Ln Apt 1001 Bethesda MD 20814-4927

SILVERMAN, JUDITH, human resource educational services director, author, consultant; b. Bklyn., Aug. 26, 1933; d. David and Shirley Beatrice (Maltz) Marks; m. Myron Bernard Silverman, July 3, 1955; 1 son, Brian Scott. B.A. cum laude, Bklyn. Coll., 1960; M.L.S., Pratt Inst., 1963; P.D., L.I.U. 1985. Sec. Fairchild Publs., N.Y.C., 1954-56; tchr., librarian N.Y.C. Bd. Edn., Bklyn., 1956-62; sr. librarian Bklyn. Pub. Library, 1964-68, Queens Borough Pub. Library, Queens, N.Y., 1973-76; asst. dir. personnel Baldwin (N.Y.) Pub. Library, 1976-80; dir. of personnel Bd. Cooperative Ednl. Services Nassau County, Westbury, N.Y., 1980—; cons. books R.R. Bowker Co., N.Y.C., 1971—. Author: Index to Collective Biographies for Young Readers, 1970, 3rd edit., 1979. Mem. N.Y. State/Sch. Personnel Adminstrs., L.I. Assn. Sch. Personnel Adminstrs., Nat. Assn. Ednl. Negotiators, N.Y. State Assn. Sch. Personnel Adminstrs. (Jay Greene award 1991), N.Y. State United Tchrs. (Friend of Edn. award 1993), N.Y. Library Assn. (mem. com.), Nassau County Library Assn., Beta Phi Mu. Office: Bd Coop Ednl Svcs Nassau County Valentines And The Pla Rd Westbury NY 11590

SILVERMAN, MARTIN MORRIS BERNARD, secondary education educator; b. Boston, May 27, 1936; s. Joseph Lazarus and Sonya Lillian (Feldman) S.; m. Joseph Harvey. BS in Chemistry, U. Mass., 1960, MEd, 1962; EdM, Columbia U., 1974, EdD, 1985. Math. and sci. tchr. Northampton (Mass.) Pub. Schs., 1960-62, U.S. Dept. of Def., Korea and Bermuda, 1963-66; tchr. math, sci. N.Y.C. Bd. Edn., 1966-91. Rsch. scholar biophysics NYU, 1986—; biochemistry rsch. asst. Harvard U. Med. Sch., Boston, 1960; supr., dir. sci. fairs and competitions; cons. in field. Writer, musician, composer and performer; photographer Explorers Jour., U. Mo. Archives collection, Jour. Violin Soc. Am. Curator musical instrument collection, instrument restorer Abrons Arts Ctr., Henry Street Settlement, 2000—03. Internat. Ctr. Photography scholar, N.Y.C., 1975. Mem. Violin Soc. Am., Jour. Violin Soc. Am., Nat. Assn. Watch Clock Collectors Assn., Musical Box Soc. Internat., Mensa, Explorers Club. Home: 25 Montgomery St New York NY 10002-6557

SILVERMAN, NORMAN HENRY, cardiologist, educator; b. Johannesburg, Sept. 29, 1942; came to U.S., 1972; s. Simon Cecil and Jean (Krawitz) S.; m. Heather Silverman. DSc in Medicine, U. Witwatersrand, Johannesburg, 1985, postgrad. Diplomate Am. Bd. Pediatrics. Asst. prof. pediatrics Stanford U., Palo Alto, Calif., 1974-75; asst. prof. pediatrics U. Calif., San Francisco, 1975, assoc. prof. radiology, 1979, prof., 1985—2002; prof. pediatrics Stanford U. Med. Ctr., 2002—. Co-author: Two Dimensional Echocardiography, 1982, Congenital Heart Disease, 1990; author: Pediatric Echocardiography, 1993; co-editor: Fetal Cardiology, 2003. Lt. South African Def. Force, 1968-69. Grantee March of Dimes, 1977-79, Am. Heart Assn., 1978-80, 90-92. Fellow Am. Coll. Cardiology, Coll. Physicians South Africa, Soc. Pediatric Rsch., Am. Pediatric Soc. Achievements include research in echocardiography of congenital heart disease in infants and chiildren; fetal echocardiography and treatment. Office: Stanford U Med Ctr 750 Welch Rd #305 Palo Alto CA 94304 E-mail: norm.silverman@stanford.edu.

SILVERMAN, PAUL HYMAN, science administrator, former university official; b. Mpls., Oct. 8, 1924; s. Adolph and Libbie (Idlekope) S.; m. Nancy Josephs, May 20, 1945; children: Daniel Joseph, Claire. Student, U. Minn., 1942-43, 46-47; BS, Roosevelt U., 1949; MS in Biology, Northwestern U., 1951; PhD in Parasitology, U. Liverpool, Eng., 1955, DSc, 1968. Rsch. fellow Malaria Rsch. Sta., Hebrew U., Israel, 1951-53; rsch. fellow dept. entomology and parasitology Sch. Tropical Medicine, U. Liverpool, 1953-56; sr. sci. officer dept. parasitology Moredun Inst., Edinburgh, Scotland, 1956-59; head dept. immunoparasitology Glaxo, Allen & Hanbury, Ltd., Ware, Eng., 1960-62; prof. zoology and vet. pathology and hygiene U. Ill., Urbana, 1963-72, chmn., head dept. zoology, 1963-68; prof., chmn. dept. biology, v.p. for rsch. U. N.Mex., 1972-77; provost, rsch. and grad. studies Ctrl. Adminstrn. SUNY, Albany, 1977-79, pres. Rsch. Found., 1979-80; pres. U. Maine, Orono, 1980-84; biol. divsn. Lawrence Berkeley Lab. U. Calif., Berkeley, 1984-86; head biomed. divsn. Lawrence Berkeley Lab., 1986-87; adj. prof. med. parasitology Sch. Pub. Health U. Calif., Berkeley, 1986, assoc. lab. dir. for life scis., dir Donner Lab., 1987-90, dir. systemwide biotech. rsch. and edn. program, 1989-90; dir. Beckman's Scientific Affairs, Fullerton, Calif., 1990-93; assoc. chancellor Ctr. for Health Scis., adj. prof. medicine U. Calif., Irvine, 1993-96. Dir. Western Ctr., Am. Acad. Arts and Scis., 1997—; cons., Commn. Colls. and Univs., North Central Assn. Colls. and Secondary Schs., 1964—; chmn. Commn. on Instns. Higher Edn., 1974-76; Fulbright prof. zoology Australian Nat. U., Canberra, 1969; adjoint prof. biology U. Colo., Boulder, 1970-72; mem. bd. Nat. Council on Postsecondary Accreditation, Washington, 1975-77; dir. research in malaria immunology and vaccination US AID, 1965-76; bd. dirs. Inhalation Toxicology Research Inst., Lovelace Biomed. and Environ. Research Inst., Albuquerque, 1977-84, Hastings Ctr.; mem. N.Y. State Gov.'s High Tech. Opportunities Task Force; chmn. research and rev. com. N.Y. State Sci. and Tech. Found.; mem. pres.'s council New Eng. Land Grant Univs.; bd. advs. Lovelace-Bataan Med. Center, Albuquerque, 1974-77; adv. com. U.S. Army Command and Gen. Staff Coll., Ft. Leavenworth, Kans., 1983-84. Mem. editl. bd. Jour. Anti-Aging Medicine, 1997—; contbr. articles to profl. jours. Chmn. rsch. rev. com. N.Y. State Sci. and Tech. Found.; bd. dirs. Hastings Ctr., 1997—. Fellow Meridian Internat. Inst., 1992; assoc. The Hastings Ctr., 1995—. Fellow Royal Soc. Tropical Medicine and Hygiene, N.Mex. Acad. Sci.; mem. Am. Soc. Parasitologists, Am. Soc. Tropical Medicine and Hygiene, Am. Soc. Immunologists, Brit. Soc. Parasitology (coun.), Brit. Soc. Immunologists, Soc. Gen. Microbiology, Soc. Protozoologists, Am. Soc. Zoologists, Human Genome Orgn., Am. Inst. Biol. Scis., N.Y. Acad. Scis., N.Y. Soc. Tropical Medicine, World Acad. Art and Sci., B'nai B'rith, Sigma Xi, Phi Kappa Phi. Office: Am Acad Arts & Scis 3000 Berkeley Pl Irvine CA 92697-7425

SILVERMAN, RICHARD BRUCE, chemist, biochemist, educator; b. Phila., May 12, 1946; s. Philip and S. Ruth (Simon) S.; . Barbara Jean Kesner, Jan. 9, 1983; children: Matthew, Margaret, Philip. BS, Pa. State U., 1968; MA, Harvard U., 1972, PhD, 1974. Asst. prof. Northwestern U., Evanston, Ill., 1976-82, assoc. prof., 1982-86, prof., 1986—, Arthur Andersen teaching & rsch. prof., 1996-98, mem. Inst. Neurosci., 1990—, Charles Deering McCormick prof., 2001—. Cons. Procter and Gamble Co., Cin., 1984, Abbott Labs, North Chicago, 1987, Searle R&D, St. Louis, 1988-90, DuPont, 1991, Dow, 1991, Leytig, Voit & Mayer law offices, 1992—, DowElanco, 1993-95, G.D. Searle, 1995, Affymax, 1995, Kinetik Pharms., 1999, Guilford Pharms., 2001, Activ X Bioscis., 2001, Cytoclonal Pharms., 2001; mem. adv. panel NIH, Bethesda, Md., 1981, 83, 85, 87-91, 2001; expert analyst CHEMTRACTS; scientific adv. bd. Influx, Inc., 1998—. NIGMS adv. coun., 2002. Mem. editl. bd.: Jour. Enzyme Inhibition, 1988—2002, Archives Biochem. & Biophys., 1993—, Jour. Medicinal Chemistry, 1995—2000, Enzyme Inhibition and Medicinal Chemistry, 2002—, Letters in Drug Design & Discovery, 2003—, Bioorganic & Medicinal Chemistry, 2003—, Bioorganic & Medicinal Chemistry Letters, 2003—. Mem. adv. bd. Ill. Math. & Scis. Acad., 1988. With U.S. Army, 1969-71. Recipient Career Devel. award USPHS, 1982-87, E. LeRoy Hall award for tchg. excellence, 1999, Northwestern Alumni Tchg. award, 2000; postdoctoral fellow Brandeis U., Waltham, Mass., 1974-76, DuPont Young Faculty fellow, 1976, Alfred P. Sloan Found. fellow, 1981-85; grantee various govt. and pvt. insts., 1976—. Arthur C. Cope. Sr. scholar ACS, 2003. Fellow: AAAS; mem.: Am. Chem. Soc. (nat. elected nominating com. divns. biol. chemistry 1993—96, long-range planning com. divsn. med. chem. 1999—2002), Am. Soc. Biochem. Molecular Biology, Am. Inst. Chemists. Avocations: tennis, family, golf. Office: Northwestern U Dept Chemistry 2145 Sheridan Rd Evanston IL 60208-3113

SILVERSTEIN, ARTHUR MATTHEW, ophthalmic immunologist, educator, historian; b. NYC, Aug. 6, 1928; s. Sol and Beatrice (Pearl) S.; m. Frances Swimmer, 1950; children— Alison, Mark, Judith AB, Ohio State U., 1948, M.Sc., 1951; PhD, Rensselaer Poly. Inst., 1954; D.Sc. (hon.), U. Granada, Spain, 1986. Research asst. Sloan Kettering Inst., N.Y.C., 1948-49; biochemist N.Y. Health Research Lab., N.Y.C., 1949-52, sr. biochemist Albany, 1952-54; chief immunobiology Armed Forces Inst. Pathology, Washington, 1956-64; assoc. prof. Johns Hopkins Sch. Medicine, Balt., 1964-67, prof., 1967-89, prof. emeritus, 1989—. Cons. NIH, 1963-77. Author: Pure Politics and Impure Science: The Swine Flu Affair, 1981, A History of Immunology, 1989, Paul Ehrlich's Receptor Immunology, 2002; mem. editl. bd. various sci. jours.; contbr. articles to profl. jours. Served to 1st lt. U.S. Army, 1954-56. Recipient Doyne Meml. medal Oxford Ophthal. Congress, Eng., 1974, Endowed Professorship Ind. Order Odd Fellows, 1964-89; Congl. Sci. fellow Fedn. Am. Socs. Exptl. Biology, 1975-76. Mem. AAAS, Am. Assn. Immunologists, Brit. Soc. Immunology, Assn. Research in Vision and Ophthalmology (trustee 1984-87, pres. 1988), Phi Beta Kappa, Sigma Xi. Home: 2011 Skyline Rd Baltimore MD 21204-6442 Office: Johns Hopkins Inst History Medicine 1900 E Monument St Baltimore MD 21205-2113 E-mail: arts@jhmi.edu.

SILVERSTEIN, LINDA LEE, secondary school educator; b. Riverside, Calif., July 1, 1953; d. John Conrad and Libbie Lola (Slovak) Woodard; m. Jerry Silverstein, Mar. 24, 1983. BS in Secondary Sci. Edn., BS in Zoology, Ohio State U., 1976, MA in Ednl. Adminstrn., 1992. Cert. tchr., Ohio; cert. prin., adminstr., Ohio. Tchr. Hilliard (Ohio) City Schs., 1978—. Lectr. Dimensions of Learning, Hilliard, 1993-95; edn. vol. Ohio Wildlife Ctr., Dublin, 1985—. Co-author: Human Growth: Guide to a Healthier Your, 1992. Grantee Ohio Dept. Edn., 1994-95; named Martha Holden Jennings scholar Ohio State U., 1983, Tchr. Leader Ctrl. Ohio Regional Profl. Devel. Ctr., 1992-93. Mem. ASCD, Nature Conservancy, Phi Delta Kappa. Republican. Presbyterian. Avocations: gardening, traveling, skiing, volunteering. Home: 93 Garden Rd Columbus OH 43214-2131

SILVERSTONE, HARRIS J. chemistry educator; b. N.Y.C., Sept. 18, 1939; s. Sidney M. and Estelle Silverstone; m. Ruth C. Federman, 1960; children: Robert, Aron, Nancy, Murray. AB, Harvard U., 1960; PhD, Calif. Inst. Tech., 1964. Asst. prof. Johns Hopkins U., Balt., 1965-68, assoc. prof., 1968-71, prof., 1971—. Contbr. articles to profl. jours. NSF Postdoctoral fellow Yale U., 1964. Mem. Am. Phys. Soc., Am. Chem. Soc., Internat. Soc. Theoretical Chem. Physics. Office: Johns Hopkins U 3400 N Charles St Baltimore MD 21218-2685

SILVIUS, DONALD JOE, educational consultant; b. Kingman, Kans., July 30, 1932; s. Henry Edgar and Gladys Mae (Beaty) S.; m. Jean Anne Able, Aug. 30, 1951; children: Laurie Dawn Silvius Gustin, Steven Craig, Jonathan Mark, Brian James. Student, So. Calif. Coll., 1949-52; AA, Bakersfield Coll., 1962; BA, Fresno State Coll., 1963, MA, 1968. Radio/TV announcer, musician, music arranger and copyist; life ins. underwriter, other positions, 1953-62; jr. high sch. English tchr., elem. and jr. high counselor; child welfare, attendance and guidance supr.; supr. pupil personnel svcs. Standard Sch. Dist., Oildale, Calif., 1963-92; ret., 1992. Tchr. counseling/guidance, adminstr. and spl. edn. various colls.; cons. in field. Bd. dir.s, pres. North of the River Sanitation Dist. Recipient Standard PTA-Hon. Svc. award, Bakersfield "Up With People" award Standard Sch. Dist. Tchrs. Assn., Innovations award Calif. Tchrs. Assn., Hon. Svc. award Kern chpt. Calif. Assn. Sch. Psychologists, Outstanding Ednl. Leader award West Kern chpt. Assn. Calif. Sch. Adminstrs., 1977-78, 7th Dist. PTA-Silver Svc. award, Continuing Svc. award Highland-Wingland PTA, Outstanding Cmty. Svc. for Developmentally Disalbed award. Mem. NEA, Calif. Tchrs. Assn., Oildale Lions Club, Phi Delta Kappa. Personal E-mail: j2498s@yahoo.com.

SIMA, ANDERS ADOLPH FREDRIK, neuropathologist, neurosciences researcher, educator; b. Jönköping, Sweden, Dec. 3, 1943; came to the U.S., 1990; s. Karl Jonas Simon and Svea Gunhild (Nilsson) S.; children: Patricia, Alexander, Vanessa. BS, U. Vienna, Austria, 1967; MD, U. Göteborg, Sweden, 1973, PhD, 1974. Asst. prof. pathology U. Goteborg, Sweden, 1973-83, U. Toronto, Ont., 1978-81, assoc. prof. pathology, 1981-82, U. Manitoba, Winnipeg, 1982-85, prof. pathology, 1985-90, dir. Diabetes Rsch. Ctr., 1988-90; prof. pathology U. Mich., Ann Arbor, 1990-96, prof. internal medicine, 1991-96; dir. neuropathology core MADRC Mich. Alzheimer Disease Rsch. Ctr., Ann Arbor, 1992—; prof. pathology and neurology Wayne State U., Detroit, 1996—, dir. Morris Hood Jr. Comprehensive Diabetes Ctr., 1998—. Hon. prof. neurosci. Med. Univ., Shanghai, China, 1988; cons. Pfizer, Inc., N.Y.C., 1987—, FDA, Washington, 1988—, Miles Pharm. Inc., West Haven, Conn. 1990—; mem. internat. adv. bd. Hoffman La Roche, Basel, Switzerland, 1992—. Assoc. editor: Jour. PNS, Internat. Jour. Diab.; editor-in-chief Frontiers in Animal Diabetes Research, Internat. Jour. Exptl. Diabetic Rsch., Internat. Jour. Diabetes Rsch.; assoc. editor Diabetes/Metabolism Rsch. and Revs.; mem. editl. bd. mem. for 8 nat. and internat. jours.; contbr. numerous articles to profl. jours. Recipient Chinese Acad.'s award for Sci. Achievement, 1981, Acad. Achievement award Toku Med. Soc., Sendai, Japan, 1985, Gold medal Consiglio Nat. delle Ricerche, Rome, 1987, Internat. Order of Merit, 1999, Order of Internat. Ambs., 1999; Diabetes Rsch. grantee NIH, Bethesda, Md., 1991, 92, Dementia Related grantee NIH, Bethesda, Md., 1994, Ednl. Tng. grantee Pfizer, Inc., N.Y.C., 1994. Fellow Royal Coll. Physicians and Surgeons Can., Internat. Study Group on Diabetes in Animals, Am. Assn. Pathologists, Juvenile Diabetes Found. (hon. chmn. 1984, Appreciation award 1984, Spl. Achievement award 1989, 97). Achievements include major contributions to the pathogenesis of diabetic neuropathy; description of genetically linked senile dementias. Office: Wayne State U Dept Pathology 540 E Canfield St Detroit MI 48201-1928 E-mail: asima@med.wayne.edu.

SIMHA, ROBERT, chemistry educator, researcher; b. Vienna, Aug. 4, 1912; arrived in U.S., 1938; s. Merkado and Mathilda Simha; m. Genevieve Martha Cowling, June 7, 1941. PhD, U. Vienna, 1935; D Natural Sci. (hon.), U. Tech., Dresden, Fed. Republic Germany, 1987. Rsch. assoc. U. Vienna, 1935-38, Columbia U., N.Y.C., 1939-41; instr. Poly. Inst. Bklyn., 1941-42; asst. prof. Howard U., Washington, 1942-45; coord., cons. Nat. Bur. Standards, Washington, 1945-51; prof. chem. engring. NYU, N.Y.C., 1951-58; prof. chemistry U. So. Calif., L.A., 1958-67; prof. macromolecular sci. Case Western Res. U., Cleve., 1967—83, prof. emeritus, 1983—. Vis. prof. U. Tech., Dresden, Germany, 1985, 89, 90, 91, U. Tech., Eindhoven, The Netherlands, 1989-91, Albert Ludwig U., Freiburg, Germany, 1991; chmn. 1st West Coast Gordon Conf., 1963; cons. in field; lectr. in field. Former mem. editorial bd. Jour. Colloid Sci., Macromolecules, Jour. Polymer Sci.; contbr. articles to profl. jours. and monographs. Recipient Meritorious Svcs. award, U.S. dept. Commerce, 1949, Superior Accomplishment award, Nat. Bur. Stds., 1949, Cert. of Recognition, NASA, 1988, 89; faculty fellow Columbia U., 1939, fellow Lalor Found., 1940, J.F. Kennedy Meml. Found. fellow Weizmann Inst., 1966, fellow Brit. Sci. Rsch. Coun., 1967, 87. Fellow AAAS, Am. Inst. Chemists, Am. Phys. Soc. (vice chmn. polymer physics div. 1956, Polymer Physics prize 1980), N.Y. Acad. Scis. (Morrison prize 1948), Washington Acad. Scis. (Disting. Svc. award 1946); mem. AAUP, Am. Chem. Soc. (chmn. polymer chemistry div. 1963), Soc. Rheology (Bingham medal 1973), Fedn. Am. scientists (chmn. Washington chpt. 1949), Sigma Xi. Achievements include research in hydrodynamics of polymer solutions and colloidal suspensions; in thermodynamics of polymers; in kinetics and statistics of macromolecular systems. Office: Case Western Res U Dept Macromolecular Sc Cleveland OH 44106-7202 E-mail: rxs10@po.cwru.edu.

SIMITSES, GEORGE JOHN, retired engineering educator, consultant; b. Athens, Greece, July 31, 1932; came to U.S., 1951, naturalized, 1963; s. John G. and Vasilike (Goutoufas) S.; m. Nena Athena Economy, Sept. 11, 1960; children: John G., William G., Alexandra G. BS in Aerospace Engring., Ga. Tech. Inst., 1955, MS in Aerospace Engring., 1956; PhD in Aeronautics and Astronautics, Stanford U., 1965. From instr. to prof. engring. Ga. Inst. Tech., Atlanta, 1956-89; prof., head dept. aerospace engring., interim dean engring. U. Cin., 1989-2000, retired, 2000. Cons. Lockheed-Georgia Co., Marietta, Ga., 1965-70, King & Gavaris Engrs., N.Y.C., 1977-79, Ga. Power Co., Atlanta, 1971-72. Author: Stability of Elastic Structures, 1976, Dynamic Stability of Suddenly Loaded Structures, 1989; contbr. chpts. to books, articles to profl. jours. Cmty. rep. Am. Hellenic Inst., Washington, 1976-91; del. Ga. State Dem. Conv., Macon, 1969. Fellow AIAA (various coms. 1974—), ASME (coms. 1976—), Am. Acad. Mechs.; corr. mem. Acad. Athens; mem. Hellenic Soc. Theoretical and Applied Mechs. (founding hon. mem.), AHEPA (v.p. chpt. 1978-79, coms. 1975-90), Sigma Xi (Sustained Rsch. award 1980, Best Paper award 1985). Office: Ga Inst Technology Aerospace Engring Atlanta GA 30332-0150 E-mail: george.simitses@aerospace.gatech.edu.

SIMKINS, GREGORY DALE, secondary education educator; b. Providence, Mar. 30, 1970; s. Dale Edward and Marie S. (Olivier) S.; m. Nicole Elizabeth Segal, June 11, 1994; 1 child, Alexander Dale. BS of Edn., Plymouth State U., 1996. Cert. tchr. K-8, N.H.; cert. tchr. K-6 with mid. sch., R.I. Tchr. elem. edn. Dept. of Edn., Concord, N.H., 1996-97; tech. cord. Rundlett Mid. Sch. Concord Schs., 1996-97, tchr. Rundlett Mid. Sch., 1996—2002; tchr. Stacy Mid. Sch., Milford, Mass., 2002—03, Barrington (R.I.) Mid. Sch., 2003—. Tech. advisor Assn. Non-Trad. Students, Concord, 1992-96; computer cluster coord. Plymouth State Coll., 1994-96, tech. and curriculum dir. Mindflight Ednl. Programs, 1995—. Author: (booklet) Accessing Computer Information, 1995, Navigating the Internet, 1997, Complete Guide to Role-Playing, 1998. With U.S. Army, 1988-92. All-Am. scholar USAA, 1994-95, 95-96. Mem. NEA. Avocations: writing, reading.

SIMKINS, SANDRA LEE, middle school educator; b. N.Y.C. d. Charles and Ray (Abramowitz) Fox; m. Alan Bruce Simkins, May 28, 1967; 1 child, Andrea. BA, Queens Coll., 1965; MA in Human Svcs., Wilmington Grad. Sch., 1987. Cert. elem. educator, middle sch. educator, Del. Elem. tchr. Valley Stream (N.Y.) Sch. Dist., 1965-66, Abington (Pa.) Sch. Dist., 1966-68; tchr. math. Mt. Pleasant Sch. Dist., Wilmington, Del., 1968-74; tchr. computers Brandywine Sch. Dist., Wilmington, Del., 1976-92; algebra tchr. Talley Mid. Sch., Wilmington, Del., 1992—. Treas. Assn. for Computers in Edn., Newark, Del., 1987-89; coach Del. Math. League, Dover, 1990-92; proctor, sponsor Del. Computer Faire, Dover, 1990-92; workshop leader Brandywine Tech. Seminar, Wilmington, 1993; internet homepage Webmaster Talley Mid. Sch.; coord. NetDay 96, Del. Pres. Greenview Civic Assn., Wilmington, 1980; v.p. Citizens Action Com., Wilmington, 1990-91, Booster Club, Wilmington, 1991-92; chair Concord Prom Com., Wilmington, 1992. Named Del. State Tchr. of Yr., Chpt. I Parents Com., 1988; nominee Presdl. award for Tchrs. of Math., Dept. Pub. Instrn., 1992. Mem. NEA, Del. Edn. Assn., Brandywine Edn. Assn., Brandywine Dist. Tech. Com. Avocation: computer consultant and workshop presenter. Home: 3316 Cross Country Dr Wilmington DE 19810-3311 Office: Talley Middle Sch 1110 Cypress Rd Wilmington DE 19810-1908

SIMKO, HELEN MARY, school library media specialist; b. Trenton, N.J., Feb. 25, 1950; d. Matthew John and Helen Catherine Harbach; m. Thomas F. Simko, Oct. 13, 1973; children: Jesse Matthew, Ian Christopher. BS in Home Econs. Edn., Immaculata Coll., 1972; postgrad. Home Econs. Design, Drexl U., 1972; MLS, So. Conn. State U., 1993, 6th Yr. Degree in Ednl. Founds., 1996. Cert. tchr. Conn. libr. media specialist (provl.) Conn. Substitute tchr. Pub. Schs. of Litchfield, Sch. Dist. #6, Litchfield, Conn., 1988-89; spl. edn. asst. Ctr. Elem. Sch., Litchfield, 1989-93, Litchfield Intermediate Sch., 1993; sch. libr. media specialist Burr Elem. Sch., Hartford, Conn., 1993-94, Swift Jr. H.S., Oakville, Conn., 1994—. Mem. student handbook revision com. Ctr. Sch., Litchfield, 1992-93, mission statement revision com., 1992-93, faculty adv. com., 1992-93; mem. Litchfield adv. com. on Quality Edn. and Diversity, 1994; mem. libr. media selection policy revision com. Watertown Bd. Edn., 1994; mem. tech. planning com. Watertown Pub. Schs., 1995—; mem. Swift Jr. H.S. Tech. Com., 1996. Active mem. Civic Family Svcs., Litchfield, 1983-89, LWV, Litchfield, 1986-89. Mem. ALA, ASCD, Conn. Edn. Media Assn. (bd. dirs., mem. co-chair), Am. Assn. Sch. Librs., Kappa Omicron Phi, Beta Phi Mu. Roman Catholic. Avocations: sewing, cooking, reading, skiing, tennis. Home: 45 Baldwin Hill Rd Litchfield CT 06759-3305

SIMKO, JAN, English, foreign language and literature educator; b. Zlaté Moravce, Slovakia, Oct. 30, 1920; came to U.S., 1967; s. Simon Simko and Terezia Simkova; m. Libusa Safarikova, Dec. 20, 1950 (div. 1970); children: Jan, Vladimir (dec.). Diploma in English, U. Bratislava, 1942, Diploma in German, 1943, PhD in English, 1944; MPhil in English, U. London, 1967. Tchr. English and German various bus. schs., 1942-45; asst. depts. English and German U. Bratislava, 1945-46; instr. English Econom U., 1946-47; faculty U. Bratislava, 1950-68, from asst. prof. to assoc. prof. English, 1957-68; prof. English Rio Grande Coll., Ohio, 1968-75. Instr. Shakespeare Georgetown U., 1982-84; vis. prof. English, scholar-in-residence W. Va. U., Parkersburg, 1989-90; instr. Slovak Fgn. Svc. Inst., Washington, 1974, 96, fed. govt., 1989, 91-93, IMF & World Bank, 1994-95; examiner critical langs. program Kent (Ohio) State U., 1974-91; feature writer Voice of Am., 1983-94; translator U.S. Dept. State, 1997—; bd. linguistics Slovak Acad. of Scis., 1957-67. Author: 3 English textbooks, 2 bilingual dictionaries, 1 linguistic monograph; editor: Lectures in the Circle of Modern Philology, 2 vols., 1965-66; chief consulting editor: textbooks of Slovak and Czech, 1993-96; contbg. writer: The Review, 1995-2002; Am./Can.-Slovak press; contbr. articles to profl. jours. With inf. Czecho-Slovak Army, 1946. Grantee Brit. Coun., 1947-49, Folger Shakespeare Libr./U.S. Dept. State, 1967-68; Internat. Rsch. and Exch. Bd., 1982, others; recipient awards W.Va. U., 1990, Bratislava U., 1995, medal Pres. of Slovakia, 2002. Mem. MLA (life), Slovak Studies Assn., Soc. for Scis. and Arts, Met. Opera Guild, Shakespeare Theater Guild, Nat. Symphony Orch. Assn., English-Speaking Union. Roman Catholic. Avocations: classical music, opera, theatre, fine arts, hiking, swimming. Home: Apt 511 725 24th St NW Washington DC 20037

SIMMONDS, JAMES GORDON, mathematician, educator; b. Washington, July 26, 1935; s. James H. and Elisabeth (Welch) S.; m. Monique van den Eynde; children: Robin, Katherine. S.B. in Aero. Engring, S.M., MIT, 1958, PhD in Math, 1965. Aerospace technologist NASA, Langley AFB, 1958; prof. applied math. U. Va., Charlottesville, 1966—98. Contbr. articles to sci. jours. Served with USAF, 1959-62. NATO fellow, 1972; NSF grantee, 1972— Mem. Math. Assn. Am., Am. Soc. Mechanics, ASME, Soc. for Natural Philosophy, Delta Psi. Home: 2116 Morris Rd Charlottesville VA 22903-1723

SIMMONDS, RAE NICHOLS, musician, composer, educator; b. Lynn, Mass., Feb. 25, 1919; d. Raymond Edward and Abbie Iola (Spinney) Nichols; m. Carter Fillebrown, Jr., June 27, 1941 (div. May 15, 1971); children: Douglas C. (dec.), Richard A., Mary L., Donald E.; m. Ronald John Simmonds, Oct. 9, 1971 (dec. Nov. 1995). AA, Westbrook Coll., Portland, Maine, 1981; B in Music Performance summa cum laude, U. Maine, 1984; MS in Edn., U. So. Maine, 1989; PhD, Walden U., 1994. Founder, dir. Studio of Music/Children's Studio of Drama, Portsmouth, N.H., 1964-71, Studio of Music, Bromley, Eng., 1971-73, Bromley Children's Theatre, 1971-73, Oughterard Children's Theatre, County Galway, Ireland, 1973-74, Studio of Music, Portland, Maine, 1977-96, West Baldwin, Maine, 1997—; resident playwright Children's Theatre of Maine, Portland, 1979-81; organist, choir dir. Stevens Ave. Congl. Ch., Portland, 1987-95; field faculty advisor Norwich U., Montpelier, Vt., 1995. Field advisor grad. program Vt. Coll., Norwich U., 1995; cons./educator mus. tng. for disabled vets. VA, Portsmouth, N.H., 1966-69; show pianist and organist, mainland U.S.A., 1939-59, Hawaii, 1959-62, Rae Nichols Trio, 1962—; mus. dir. Theatre By the Sea, Portsmouth, N.H., 1969-70. Author/composer children's musical: Shamrock Road, 1980 (Blue Stocking award 1980), Glooscap, 1980; author/composer original scripts and music: Cinderella, If I Were a Princess, Beauty and the Beast, Baba Yaga - A Russian Folk Tale, The Journey - Musical Bible Story, The Perfect Gift - A Christmas Legend; original stories set to music include: Heidi, A Little Princess, Tom Sawyer, Jungle Book, Treasure Island; compositions include: London Jazz Suite, Bitter Suite, Jazz Suite for Trio, Sea Dream, Easter (chorale), Rae Simmonds Jazz Trio Songbook Series, (CD) Fascinatin' Gershwin Rae Simmonds Jazz Trio, 2000; contbr. Maine Women Writers Collection. Recipient Am. Theatre Wing Svc. award, 1944, Pease AFB Svc. Club award, 1967, Bumpus award Westbrook Coll., 1980; Nat. Endowment for Arts grantee, 1969-70; Women's Lit. scholar, 1980, Westbrook scholar, 1980-81, Nason scholar, 1983; Kelaniya U. (Colombo, Sri Lanka) rsch. fellow, 1985-86. Mem. ASCAP, Internat. Soc. Poets, Internat. League Women Composers, Music Tchrs. of Maine, Am. Guild of Organists, Music Tchrs. Nat. Assn., Internat. Alliance for Women in Music, Doctorate Assn. N.Y. Educators, Inc., Delta Omicron, Phi Kappa Phi. Democrat. Episcopalian. Avocations: travel, philately. Home: 230 Douglas Hill Rd West Baldwin ME 04091-9715

SIMMONS, DEBORAH ANNE, environmental educator; b. Oroville, Calif., Oct. 9, 1950; d. Daniel Fredrick and Jeanne (Marlow) Simmons; m. Ronald Eugene Widmar, May 17, 1980. BA in Anthropology, U. Calif., Berkeley, 1972; MS, Humboldt State U., Arcata, Calif., 1977, PhD in Natural Resources, 1983. Cert. secondary tchr., Calif. TESOL instr. U.S. Peace Corps, South Korea, 1973-75; postdoctoral scholar U. Mich., Ann Arbor, 1983-84; asst. prof. Montclair State Coll., Upper Montclair, N.J., 1984-87; asst. prof. dept. tchr. edn. No. Ill. U., DeKalb, 1987-92, assoc. prof., 1992-98, prof., 1998—. Cons. Mendocino County Schs., Ukiah, Calif., 1977-78, Acad. for Ednl. Devel., Washington, 1994-95, Lincoln Park Zoo, Chgo., 1990-92, Chgo. Acad. Scis., 1992-97; dir. Nat. Project for Excellence in Environ. Edn., 1994—. Author monograph; contbr. numerous articles to Jour. Environ. Edn., Environment and Behavior, Children's Environments, Women in Natural Resources, others. Recipient Rsch. award Progressive Architecture, 1987, 88, Outstanding Rsch. award N.Am. Assn. for Environ. Edn., 1996; U.S. Forest Svc. grantee, 1991—; EETAP grantee, 1995—. Mem. N.Am. Assn. for Environ. Edn. (treas. 1991-95, pres. 1996). Avocation: backpacking. Office: No Ill U Dept Tchg Lng Dekalb IL 60115

SIMMONS, DIANA A. elementary education educator; b. San Diego, Dec. 26, 1936; m. Lewis A. Simmons, Sept. 2, 1957; children: Lisa Simmons Hansen, Marcia Simmons Westfall, Jeffrey. BA, W.Va. Wesleyan Coll., 1975, MAT, 1977. Classroom tchr. Main St. Sch., Buckhannon, W.Va., 1975-78, B-U Intermediate Sch., Buckhannon, 1978—. Mem. AAUW (v.p., pres. 1992-94), Delta Kappa Gamma. Home: 50 Boggess St Buckhannon WV 26201-2145

SIMMONS, DOLORES BROWN, finance officer, accountant; b. Alexandria, La., Mar. 23, 1937; d. Edward Eugene and Anita Marie (Chaudoir) Brown; m. Gordon E. Simmons, July 13, 1956 (dec. Apr. 1982); children: Gordon E. II, Steven E. Student, La. State U., 1954-55, 73-74, La. Coll., 1955-56. Acctg. clk. La. State U., Baton Rouge, 1956-58; real estate assoc. Realty Mart, Syron Real Estate, Baton Rouge, 1971-73; acct. Tchr.'s Retirement System of La., Baton Rouge, 1973-76, chief acct., 1976-87, fiscal officer, 1987—. Mem. adv. com. La. Pub. Employees Deferred Compensation Plan, Baton Rouge, 1985—; mem. acctg. adv. com. State Dept. of Civil Svc., Baton Rouge, 1987. Vol. Our Lady of Lake Hosp., Baton Rouge, 1980-81, Tax Preparation for Elderly, Baton Rouge, 1984-85. Named Hon. Citizen of New Orleans, 1977. Mem. Nat. Assn. Govtl. Accts., Govtl. Fin. Officers Assn. Am. (Excellence in Fin. Reporting award 1990-91), Govtl. Fin. Officers La., La. Sch. Bus. Officials, Am. Assn. Individual Investors (steering com. Baton Rouge chpt. 1987-91). Democrat. Roman Catholic. Avocation: bowling. Home: 10343 Ridgely Rd Baton Rouge LA 70809-3223 Office: Tchrs Retirement System La 8401 United Plaza Blvd Baton Rouge LA 70809-7017

SIMMONS, ENID BROWN, retired state agency administrator; b. Washington, June 6, 1947; d. Charles Mathews Brown and Susie (Nickens) Ludlow; m. Warren Simmons, Nov. 30, 1985; children: Stacey Arlene Herndon, Robert Eric Herndon, Nicholas Maxville Simmons. BA cum laude, Howard U., 1970, MA, 1973. With D.C. Pub. Schs., 1970-73; sr. evaluation cons. CTB/McGraw-Hill, Washington, 1973-79; sr. policy fellow Nat. Inst. Edn., Washington, 1979-80, sr. rsch. assoc.; rsch. area team leader Office Edn. Rsch. U.S. Dept. Edn., Washington, 1980-87; dep. assoc. dir. Office of Policy and Program Evaluation, Exec. Office Mayor, Washington, 1987-90; dir. office of policy and program evaluation Office of the Mayor, 1991—. Cons. Mid-Atlantic Equity Ctr., Am. U., Washington, 1988—. Author: Your Child and Testing, 1980, 89; exec. producer TV series Who's Keeping Score?, 1981. Bd. dirs. Lowell Sch., Community Prevention Partnership and Consortium and Univs. of Washington. Mem. Jack and Jill. Avocation: aerobics. Office: Govt of DC 441 4th St NW Washington DC 20001-2714*

SIMMONS, LORNA WOMACK, elementary school educator, educator; b. Enid, Okla., Dec. 25, 1954; d. Doyle Alex and Ruth Phyllis (Wiens) Nunneley; m. Daniel Bruce Womack, June 7, 1975 (widowed Jan. 1981); children: Zachary Womack, Travis Womack, Shawn Simmons, Shayla Simmons; m. H. Lynn Simmons, Feb. 14, 1982. BS cum laude, U. Tex., 1977. Spl. edn. tchr. Sand Springs (Okla.) I.S.D., 1977-78; pvt. therapist Alphabetic Phonics, Big Spring, Tex., 1981-87; dyslexia cons. Big Spring (Tex.) I.S.D., 1987-88; chpt. I tchr. Forsan I.S.D., Big Spring, Tex., 1988-91; cons. Classroom Phonics, Big Spring, Tex., 1991—. Author: Classroom Phonics, 1989, Classroom Phonics II, 1991, Classroom Phonics Spelling, 1991, Classroom Phonics Kid Cards, 1994, Classroom Phonics Comprehension Tests, 1994, Saxon Phonics K, 1996, Saxon Phonics 1, 1996, Saxon Phonics 2, 1996, Saxon Homestudy Phonics K, 1998, Saxon Homestudy Phonics 1, 1998, Saxon Homestudy Phonics 2, 1998, Saxon Phonics Intervention, 2000, Saxon Early Learning, 2003, Saxon Phonics and Spelling K, 2003, Saxon Phonics and Spelling 1, 2003, Saxon Phonics and Spelling 2, 2003, Saxon Phonics and Spelling 3, 2003. Mem. Internat. Reading Assn., Assn. Tex. Profl. Educators. Republican. Mem. Ch. of God. Home: 15650 CR BB Childress TX 79201

SIMMONS, LYNDA MERRILL MILLS, retired principal; b. Salt Lake City, Aug. 31, 1940; d. Alanson Soper and Madeline Helene (Merrill) Mills; m. Mark Carl Simmons, Nov. 17, 1962; children: Lisa Lynn Simmons Morley, William Mark, Jennifer Louise, Robert Thomas. BS, U. Utah, 1961, MS, 1983. Cert. sch. adminstr., Utah. Tchr. Wasatch Jr. H.S./Granite Dist., Salt Lake City, 1961-64, Altamont (Utah) H.S./Duchesne Dist., 1964-66; tchr. spl. edn. Park City (Utah) H.S., 1971-73; resource tchr. Eisenhower Jr. H.S., Salt Lake City, 1979-88; tchr. specialist Granite Sch. Dist., Salt Lake City, 1985-90; asst. prin. Bennion Jr. H.S., Salt Lake City, 1990-93; prin. Hartvigsen Sch., Salt Lake City, 1993—2002; ret., 2002. Adj. prof. spl. edn. U. Utah, Salt Lake City, 1987—, Utah Prin. Acad., 1994-95, co-chair Utah Spl. Educators for Computer Tech., Salt Lake City, 1988-90; adv. com. on handicapped Utah State Office Edn., 1990-93; presenter in field. Author: Setting Up Effective Secondary Resource Program, 1985; contbr. articles to profl. jours. Dist. chmn. Heart Fund, Cancer Dr., Summit Park, Utah, 1970-82; pack leader Park City area Boy Scouts Am., 1976-80; bd. dirs. Jr. League Salt Lake City, 1977-80, cmty. bd., 1997—; cookie chmn. Park City area Girl Scouts U.S., 1981; dist. chmn. March of Dimes, 1982—. Recipient Amb. award Salt Lake Conv. and Vis. Bur., 1993; named Bus. Woman of Yr., South Salt Lake C. of C., 2001. Mem. Nat. Assn. Secondary Sch. Prins., Park City Young Women's Mut. (pres. 1989-93, family history cons. 1995-95), Women's Athanaeum (v.p. 1990-93, pres. 1994-2001), Gen. Fedn. Women's Clubs (pres. Salt Lake dist. 1998-2002, cmty.-improvement chairperson Utah 1996-98, chairperson Woman of Yr., 1998—) Coun. for Exceptional Children (pres. Salt Lake chpt. 1989-90, pres. Utah Fedn. 1991-93, Spl. Educator of Yr. 1995), Granite Assn. Sch. Adminstrs. (sec.-treas. 1992-94). Mem. Lds Ch. Avocations: reading, cooking, writing, sports, handiwork.

SIMMONS, MARSHA THRIFT, science and reading educator, musician; b. Brunswick, Ga., Jan. 18, 1953; d. James Russell II and Ouida (Tyre) Thrift; m. Samuel Leland Simmons, Aug. 2, 1975; 1 child, Natalie Renee. BA, Agnes Scott Coll., 1975; MEd, Coll. of Charleston, 1980; MA, Regent U., 2001. Cert. tchr., Tenn., postgrad. profl. lic., Va. Organist Epworth United Meth. Ch., Atlanta, 1975-76; tchr. 3d grade Hanahan (S.C.) Acad.; 1976-77; grad. asst. Coll. of Charleston, S.C., 1977-78, sub. tchr. Early Childhood Devel. Ctr., 1978-79; owner, tchr. Marsha's Music (Studio and Store), S.C., Ga., Tex., Tenn., Va., 1979—; tchr. presch. Sykes Daycare, Lawrenceville, Ga., 1994; sub. tchr. Glynn County Schs., Brunswick, Ga., 1994; tchr. 6th grade sci. and reading Jackson (Tenn.)-Madison County Schs.. 1995-97; sub. tchr. Virginia Beach (Va.) City Pub. Schs., 1997—. Treas Kingwood (Tex.) Music Tchrs. Assn., 1985-87; mem. local sch. adv. com. Gwinnett County Bd. Edn., Lawrenceville, Ga., 1993-94; Odyssey of the Mind coord., coach N.E. Mid. Sch., Jackson, 1995-97; lead tchr. sci. stds. implementation Jackson-Madison County Schs., 1996-97; subst. tchr. Va. Beach City Schs., 1997-99; tchr. asst. Regent U., 2002-03; adminstrv. asst. U. Psychol. Svcs. Ctr., 2003—. Leader Girl Scouts Am., St. Simons Island, Ga., 1988-89; PTA v.p. and cultural arts chmn. Benefield Elem. Sch., Lawrenceville, 1991-93; chmn. cmty. outreach West Tenn. Music Tchr.'s Assn., Jackson, 1996-97. Recipient Spl. Svc. award Girl Scouts Am., 1989, Outstanding Woman in Bus. and Edn. award Parker Chapel Christian Meth. Episcopal Ch., Tenn., 1996, Lockheed Martin fellow Lockheed Martin Corp., 1997. Mem. ACA, Am. Guild Organists, Music Tchrs. Nat. Assn., Am. Assn. of Christian Counselors, Am. Psychol. Assn. Avocations: reading, cooking, sewing, crafts, drawing, painting. Home: 313 Chase Arbor Ct Virginia Beach VA 23462-7407

SIMMONS, REBECCA ANN, secondary education educator; b. Jonesboro, Ark., Nov. 22, 1951; d. Reuben Dale and Esther Faye (Casebier) Reaves; m. Ralph Edward Simmons, July 27, 1974 (dec.); children: Jody Lynn, John Reese, Cary Lee. BSE in English, Ark. State U., 1973; postgrad., Austin Coll., 1975; MSE, Ark. State U., 1999; postgrad., U. Ark., 1976, 96, U. Ark., Monticello, 1997. With dir.'s office Carl R. Reng Ctr. Ark. State U., State University, Ark., 1969—70; with pers. and credit depts. Sears, Jonesboro, 1970—73; tchr. English Harrisburg Mid. Sch., Harrisburg, 1974—75; tchr. English and German Rector H.S., 1975—80, tchr. English, history, German, 1986—. Judge Ark. Times Acad. All-Star Team, Little Rock, 1995; field tester Animal Tracks Environ. Program, Ark. State U., 1994, reading program N.E. Ark. Ednl. Coop., Hoxie, 1993; tchr. cons. Ark. Geographic Alliance, 1996-2003; mem. pers. policy com. Rector H.S., 2000-03; presenter workshops in field. Mem. pastor-parish rels. com. 1st United Meth. Ch., Rector, 1990-95, Sunday sch. tchr., trustee, Bible study facilitator; vol. Ark. Dem. Party, Rector Labor Day Picnic, 1975-2003; founder Soul Survivors, 2003; founding/charter mem., adv. com. Hope Cir., 2003; facilitator Bereavement Support Group, 2003. Named Global Classroom Tchr. EF Global, 1994; recipient Golden Ruler award Ptnrs.-in-Edn. and Sta. KAIT-TV, 1993. Mem. NEA, Ark. Edn. Assn. (pub. rels. com. 1974), Ark. Coun. Social Studies, Ark. Assn. Tchrs. of German, Clay County Cen. Edn. Assn., Clay County Cen. Grievance Com. Avocations: reading, needlework, gardening, home canning, writing. Home: 1174 Cr 522 Rector AR 72451-8035 Office: Rector H S 5th and Greenville Rector AR 72451 E-mail: rsimmons@rectorarkansas.com.

SIMMONS, ROBERT BURNS, history and political science educator; b. Gadsden, Ala., Dec. 27, 1937; s. Burns Hunter and Grace Barbara (Armstrong) S.; m. Eleanor Conner, Nov. 11, 1959 (dec.); children: Kathleen D., Mary Ellen. BS in Chemistry, U. Ala., 1961; BA in Biology and History, Athens State Coll., 1968, MA in Tchg., 1969; EdS (Coll. Scholar, PhD, George Peabody Coll., 1976; MAS, U. Ala., 1978. Quality control chem. lab. supr. Goodyear Tire & Rubber Co., Gadsen, 1961-65; sect. leader, R&D chem. labs. Thiokel Chem. Corp., Redstone Arsenal, Huntsville, Ala., 1966-69; prof. history, polit. sci. and mgmt. John C. Calhoun State C.C., Decatur, Ala., 1969—. Adj. prof. Athes (Ala.) State Coll., 1988—, asst. coord. instnl. devel. grant, 1983-84; asst. acad. dean Vol. State C.C., Gallatin, Tenn., 1974; cons. Ala. govs. office, 1987; attended Internat. Rels. Conf. U.S. State Dept., 1989; program presenter Conf. Tchg. Excellence, U. Tex., 1991, found. grant award; presenter Ala. Geog. Assn., 1998, 99; del. Ala. Edn. Assn. Post Secondary Com. Conf., 1990-98, Ala. Edn. Assn. Del. Assembly, 1997-98. Author: texts on world regional geography and on western civilization. Chmn. coms. Decatur Band Boosters; program com. coord. Congressman James Martin of Ala.; mem. acad. affairs com. Commn. on Instnl. Self Study, chmn. Instnl. Effectiveness, Exec. Com. on Articulation Post Secondary Insts. Ala., Calhoun's Instnl. Effectiveness Com., 1998-2000; chmn. Post Secondary Social Sci. Articulation Com., 1996-99, Faculty Senate, 1989-2000, chmn. faculty senate, 1999-2000. Woodrow Wilson fellow Athens State Coll., 1968; E. U.S. Office Edn. grantee, 1970-71, grantee, 1985—, Master Tchr. award NISOD U. Tex., 1990. Mem. Am. Hist. Assn., So. Hist. Assn., Ala. Hist. Assn. (mem. post secondary polit. action com. 1990—), Ala. Coll. Assn. (history chmn. 1990-93, coord. 1990-95, mem. curriculum com. 1993-95, instnl. effectiveness 1993-94, mem. Calhoun pres. cabinet 1994—), C.C. Humanity Assn., Am. Assn. Higher Edn., Am. Chem. Soc., Archaeol. Inst.

Am., Burningtree Country Club, Decatur C. of C., Beta Beta Beta, Phi Delta Kappa. Achievements include patent for missile propellants. Home: PO Box 2328 Decatur AL 35602-2328 Office: Calhoun C C PO Box 2216 Bldg Decatur AL 35609-2216

SIMMONS, ROBERT RANDOLPH, principal; b. Phila., Aug. 27, 1935; s. Aaron J. Simmons and Lou (Randolph) Higgs; m. Patricia Ann Grace, June 26, 1975; children: Darris, William, Cynthia L., Tricia M., Robby R. BA in History, Mich. State U., 1958; MA in Community Sch. Leadership, Ea. Mich. U., 1967, Specialist of Arts, 1976; EdD, U. Mich., 1978. Cert. tchr., elem. sch. adminstr., Mich.; cert. primary and elem. sch. tchr., N.Y. Tchr. Flint (Mich.) Community Schs., 1962-68, asst. prin., 1968-70, prin., 1970—, elem. liaison prin., 1992—. Adj. prof. edn. Ea. Mich. U., Ypsilanti, 1988—; NEA Mastery In Learning sch. renewal site-based cons., 1987—, cons. parent edn. Flint Community Schs., 1970—, cons. sch. improvement, Mich., 1989—; presenter Mich. Dept. Edn., MSU, 1987—; co-sponsor Mentor's for At-Risk Males Program, Stewart Sch., 1989—. Contbr. to book: Parents and Schools: From Visitors to Partners, 1993; contbr. articles to ednl. publs.; contbg. author in-dist. teaching materials Flint Community Schs. Mem. adv. bd. Community Alliance Resource Environment (CARE), Flint, 1989—; bd. dirs., co-sponsor Stewart/Brennan Youth Clubs, Inc., 1987—; active Coalition for Positive Youth Devel., 1990—, Urban League Flint; mem. Leonard Floyd scholarship com. New Jerusalem Full Gospel Bapt. Ch., pres. Inspirational Voice Choir, 1983-85, 90—; mem. Flint Jr. C. of C., 1968-70. Recipient Drum Maj. award Mayor Woodrow Stanley, City of Flint, 1992, Staff Devel. Policy Bd. award Mich. State Bd. Edn., 1987, Chpt. 1 Excellence in Edn. scholarship award, 1986, Flint Tchr.'s Golf Champaionship award, 1974, 78, 79, 81, 83, 84, Golf award Greater Flint Olympian-CANUSA Assn., 1981, 84, Outstanding Achievement in Edn. cert. Ctrl. Flint Optimist, 1993, Gov. and Mich. Community Svc. Commn. award, 1993. Mem. NAESP (Presenter award 1988), ASCD, NAACP, Nat. Community Edn. Assn. (Presenter award 1973), Mich. Elem. and Mid. Sch. Prin. Assn. (Presenter awards 1987-91), Flint Assn. Elem. Sch. Prins., Congress Flint Sch. Adminstrs. (pres. 1991—), Mich. Community Edn. Assn. (Presenter award 1973), Phi Delta Kappa (treas. Flint chpt. 1985-87, 25 Yr. Svc. award 1992), Alpha Phi Alpha. Democrat. Avocations: golf, collecting jazz recordings, reading. Home: PO Box 804 Flint MI 48501-0804 Office: 1950 Burr Blvd Flint MI 48503-4232

SIMMONS, RUTH DORIS, retired women's health nurse, educator; b. Bklyn., July 30, 1942; d. Stanley George and Doris Louise (Beckert) S. LPN, Glen Cove (N.Y.) Community, 1964; AD, SUNY, Farmingdale, 1976; BS in Profl. Arts in Edn., St. Joseph's Coll., 1994. Nurse labor/delivery unit Syosset (N.Y.) Hosp., 1964-66; staff nurse ob./gyn. and pediatrics unit Glen Cove Community Hosp., 1966-76; staff nurse labor, delivery, postpartum units Mercy Hosp., Scranton, Pa., 1976-99, ret., disabled, 1999. Asst. childbirth edn. classes Mercy Hosp., Scranton, 1976-99. Home: 2083 Hickory Ridge Rd Factoryville PA 18419-9658

SIMMONS, RUTH J. academic administrator; b. Grapeland, Tex., July 3, 1945; 2 children. Student, Universidad Internacional, Saltillo, Mex., 1965, Wellesley Coll., 1965—66; BA, Dillard U., 1967; postgrad., Universite de Lyon, 1967—68, George Washington U., 1968—69; AM, Harvard U., 1970, PhD in Romance Langs., 1973; LLD (hon.), Amherst Coll., 1995; LHD (hon.), Howard U., 1996, Dillard U., 1996; LLD (hon.), Princeton U., 1996, Lake Forest Coll., 1997; LHD (hon.), U. Mass., 1997; LLD (hon.), Dartmouth Coll., 1997. Interpreter lang. svcs. divsn. U.S. Dept. State, Washington, 1968—69; instr. French George Washington U., 1968—69; admissions officer Radcliffe Coll., 1970—72; asst. prof. French U. New Orleans, 1973—75, asst. dean coll. liberal arts, asst. prof. French, 1975—76; adminstrv. coord. NEH liberal studies project Calif. State U., Northridge, 1977—78, acting dir. internat. programs, vis. assoc. prof. Pan-African studies, 1978—79; asst. dean grad. sch. U. So. Calif., 1979—82, assoc. dean grad. sch., 1982—83; dir. studies Butler Coll. Princeton U., NJ, 1983—85, acting. dir. Afro-Am. studies, 1985—87, asst. dean faculty, 1986—87, assoc. dean faculty, 1986—90, vice provost, 1992—95; provost Spelman Coll., 1990—91; pres. Smith Coll., Northampton, Mass., 1995—2001; pres Brown Univ., Providence, 2001—. Peer reviewer higher edn. divsn. NEH, 1980—83, bd. cons., 1981; mem. grad. adv. bd. Calif. Student Aid Commn., 1981—83; chair com. to visit dept. African-Am. studies Harvard U., 1991—; mem. strategic planning task force N.J. Dept. Higher Edn., 1992—93; mem. nat. adv. commn. EQUITY 2000 Coll. Bd., 1992—95; mem. adv. bd. ctrl. N.J. NAACP Legal Def. Fund, 1992—95; mem. Mid. States Assn. Accreditation Team, Johns Hopkins U., 1993; chmn. accreditation team Bryn Mawr Coll., 1999; chair rev. panel for model instns. planning grants NSF, 1993; mem. Conf. Bd., 1995—; bd. dirs. MetLife, JSTOR, Pfizer Inc., COFHE, Com. Econ. Devel.; mem. adv. coun. dept. Romance Langs. and Lit. Princeton U., 1996—; presenter, spkr. and panelist in field. Mem. editl. bd.: World Edn. series Am. Assn. Collegiate Registrars and Admissions Officers, 1984—86; contbr. articles to profl. jours. Mem. adv. bd. N.J. Master Faculty Program Woodrow Wilson Nat. Fellowship Found., 1987—90, bd. trustees, 1991—96; trustee Inst. Advances Study, 1995—98, The Clarke Sch. for Deaf, 1995—; chmn. bd. trustees Acad. Music, 1995—98; mem. adv. com. Healthy Steps for Young Children Program, 1996—98; mem. bd. advisors 1st Internat. Conf. on AIDS, Ethiopia, 1998—. Named Women of Yr., CBS, 1996, Glamour Mag., 1996, Woman of World, NASA, 1998, Disting. Fulbright Alumna, Inst. Internat. Edn., 1997; recipient Disting. Svc. award, Assn. Black Princeton Alumni, 1989, Pres.'s Recognition award, Bloomfield Coll., 1993, TWIN award, Princeton Area YWCA, 1993, Women's orgn. Tribute award, Princeton U., 1994, Leadership award, Third World Ctr. Princeton U., 1995, Tex. Excellence award, Leap Program, 1995, Benjamin E. Mays award, A Better Chance, 1995, Achievement award, Nat. Urban League, 1998, Centennial medal, HArvard U. Grad. Sch. Arts & Scis., 1997; fellow, Danforth Found., 1967—73, Sr. Fulbright fellow, 1981; scholar, KYOK, 1963, Worthing Found., 1963—67, Fulbright scholar, U. de Lyon, 1967—68. Fellow: Am. Acad. Arts & Scis.; mem.: AAAS, Am. Philos. Soc. Office: Office of the President Brown University 1 Prospect Street, Campus Box 1860 Providence RI 02912 Mailing: Brown University President's Office Box 1860 Providence RI 02912-1860

SIMMONS, SHARON DIANNE, elementary education educator; b. Woodruff, S.C., Apr. 5, 1961; d. James Madison and Lucy Nell (Carlton) Crow; m. Wayne Roy Simmons, Mar. 29, 1986; children: Zachary, Luke. BA in Elem. Edn., U. S.C., 1983, M of Elem. Edn., 1987. Tchr. 3d grade M.S. Bailey Elem. Sch., Clinton, S.C., 1984-85, tchr. 4th grade, 1985-86; tchr. 5th grade Eastside Elem. Sch., Clinton, S.C., 1986-88, tchr. 4th & 5th grades, 1988-90, 91-92, tchr. 5th grade, 1990-91, tchr. 4th grade, 1993-95, tchr. 3rd grade, 1995-96; tchr. R.P. Dawkins Middle Sch., Moore, S.C., 1996—. Pilot tchr. authentic assessment Eastside Elem. Sch., 1992-93, mem. sch. libr. com., 1993—96 tchr. chair 4th grade, 1993-94, tchr. grad. course authentic assessment, 1996. Pres. libr. coun. Spartanburg-Woodruff (S.C.) Br. Libr., 1993-95, v.p., 1995—. Recipient Ambassador award The Edn. Ctr., 1993-94. Mem. S.C. Math. Tchrs. Assn., Sch. Improvement Coun., Spartanburg County Internat. Reading Assn. Baptist. Avocations: piano, cross stitch, travel, sports, reading. Home: 651 Parsons Rd Woodruff SC 29388-8700 Office: RP Dawkins Middle Sch 1300 E Blackstock Rd Moore SC 29369-9656

SIMMONS, VIRGINIA GILL, educational administrator; b. Gauley Bridge, W.Va., Feb. 14, 1942; d. David Herman and Margaret Josephine (Cameron) Gill; m. James Edward Simmons, Dec. 21, 1962; children: Melissa Marie, Cameron David. BS, W.Va. State Coll., 1964; MS, Marshall U., Huntington, W.Va., 1969; PhD, Kent (Ohio) State U., 1984; LLD (hon.), W.Va. State Coll., 1997. Elem. tchr. Kanawha and Pocahontas County Schs., 1964-67; tchr. mentally retarded Pocahontas County Schs., Marlinton, W.Va., 1967-69; tchr. gifted Kanawha County Schs., Charleston, W.Va., 1974-79, 81-84, cmty. edn. coord., 1986-88, spl. edn. specialist, 1984-86; teaching fellow Kent State U., 1979-81; dean evaluation and tng. Governor's Cabinet on Children and Families, Charleston, 1991-93; state coord. gifted W.Va. Dept. Edn., Charleston, 1988—, state coord. of gov.'s schs., 1993—. Adj. prof. Marshall U., Huntington, 1974-85, Kent State U., 1979-83, Coll. Grad. Studies Inst., W.Va., 1984—; cons. on gifted; bd. mem., reader Nat. Rsch. Ctr. on Gifted and Talented, 1991. Editor, writer: Inside, 1987 (Gov.'s award), Expanded Learning Opportunities, 1989-92; editor: Building Your Own Railroad Tracks, 1991. Cand., Dem. Party, Kanawha County, 1974; lobbyist Women's Orgn., W.Va. Legis., 1973-79; chairperson Gov.'s Hwy. Safety Leaders, 1985-91; dir., pres. Russia and W.Va.: A Partnership for Exch. Found., Inc., 1993—. Kent State U. Ednl. Rsch. fellow, 1982-83. Mem. ASCD, Nat. Assn. Gifted Children, W.Va. Assn. Gifted Talented (pres.), Nat. Conference Gov.'s Schs. (pres.), State Dirs. Gifted Talented, Coun. Exceptional Children, Internat. Assn. for Gifted, Fedn. Women's Clubs (pres., state officer), Phi Delta Kappa. Methodist. Office: West Virginia Dept Edn Bldg 6 Rm 362 Charleston WV 25305

SIMMONS SMITH, MONA JEAN (MONICA SIMMONS), special education educator, writer; b. Sharon, Pa., Sept. 23, 1952; d. James Pearman and Michaelina (Votino) Simmons; children: Manley Taylor Smith, Rachael Christina Smith. BS, Ga. Coll., 1973; MEd, U. Ga., 1975, postgrad. Cert. tchr. T-5 learning disorders, hosp.-homebound edn., T-5 multi-physically handicapped edn., T-5 leadership in edn., Ga. Tchr. Clayton County Bd. of Edn., Jonesboro, Ga., 1973-74; fellow, instr. U. Ga., Athens, 1974-75, instr., 1978-80; tchr. self-contained learning disabilities Cobb County Bd. of Edn., Marietta, Ga., 1976-78; ednl. coord. Physicians and Surgeons Hosp., Atlanta, 1981-83, Parkway Regional Hosp., Atlanta, 1984-89; hosp. homebound tchr. DeKalb County Bd. of Edn., Atlanta, 1980-86; mktg. mgr. Atlanta, 1987-88. Ednl. cons. 1977-80; mem. psycho ednl. testing Ednl. Evaluations, Atlanta, 1976-80; ednl. cons. Comprehensive Care Corp., Atlanta; field based rschr. Prep Sch., Hilton Head, S.C., 1993; lectr. in field. Author: (with Susan Brown) 50 Strategies for Positive Single Parenting, 1996, The Lowcountry Child, 1996, The Island Child, 1997, The Aster-Planet Chronicles 1-5, 1998, Vol. 1, Uniworld, Vol. II, Aster Jungle, 1998, Vol. III, Aster Desert, 1998, AsterJungle, 1998, Vol. 2, 1998, AsterOcean, 1998, Vol. 5, Aster City, 1998; co-author: 365 Positive Strategies for Single Parenting, 1998. Mem. Atlanta Ballet Guild (life), 1988—; vol. North Arts Ctr. Docent, 1989-91. U. Ga. teaching assistantship, 1976. Mem. Coun. for Exceptional Children (divsn. Children Learning Disabilities), Reynolds Plantation Club, Phi Delta Kappa. Avocations: snow skiing, fishing, travel, dancing, water skiing. Home: 4804 Calais Ct NE Marietta GA 30067-4078

SIMMS, AMY LANG, writer, educator; b. Bryn Mawr, Pa., Sept. 21, 1964; d. Eben Caldwell and Anna Mary L.; children: Harrison Lang, Maud Whittington. BA in French and Sociology, Bucknell U., 1986; postgrad., Sch. Mus. Fine Arts, 1988, Bryn Mawr Coll., 1988, Vassar Coll., 1993, U. Pa., 1995-97. Assoc. dir. pub. rels. Haverford (Pa.) Coll., 1995-96; copywriter, media and prodn. asst. DBM Assocs., Cambridge, Mass., 1986-88; tchg. asst. sociology dept. Bucknell U., Lewisburg, Pa., 1989; staff reporter Lewisburg Daily Jour., 1989-92, asst. editor, 1991, Milton (Pa.) Standard, 1991; tchr. Gt. Valley Sch. Dist., Malvern, Pa., 1997—. Co-founder, co-editor Lewisburg Holiday Herald, 1990; co-founder Environ. Advisor Newsletter, Lewisburg, 1990-91. Assoc. editor: Main Line Life, 1996-97. Media corr. Elem. Related Arts Com., Lewisburg, 1989; mem. adv. bd. Union County Children and Youth Svcs., Lewisburg, 1991-92; trustee Sarah Hull Hallock Meml. Libr., Milton, N.Y., 1993-95. Recipient Hon. Speakers award Lewisburg Lions Club, 1990. Mem. AAUW. Avocations: cats, books, food, travel, photography. Home: 8020 Saint Martins Ln Philadelphia PA 19118

SIMMS, FRANCES BELL, retired elementary education educator; b. Salisbury, N.C., July 29, 1936; d. William Taft and Anne Elmira (Sink) Bell; m. Howard Homer Simms, June 24, 1966 (dec. Oct. 1993); 1 child, Shannon Lara. AB in English, U. N.C., 1958; MEd, U. Fla., 1962; postgrad., Boston U., 1963—, U. Va., Queen's Coll., Cambridge, U.K. Playroom attendant dept. neurology Children's Hosp., Boston, 1958-60; reading clinician Mills Ctr., Inc., Ft. Lauderdale, Fla., 1960-61; reading/lang. arts tchr. Arlington (Va.) Pub. Schs., 1962-99. Cons. Arlington Pub. Schs. curriculum devel.; adv. bd. mem. ad hoc com. Edn. Tech., Arlington, 1965-67; reading instr. Va. Poly. Inst. and State U., Arlington, 1974; prodr., dir. Barcroft Newsbag-CATV, Arlington, 1982—; chair self-study Elem. Sch., Arlington, 1987, 93; adv. bd. Reading is Fundamental of No. Va., Arlington, 1988—; guest lectr. Marymount U., cons.; instr. Arlington (Va.) Adult Edn., 2000—; lectr., presenter in field; bd. dirs. Cen. European Leadership Inst., 2001. Exhibitions include Lee Heights Gallery. Laborer Christmas in April, Arlington, 1990—; tutor, vol. instr. Henderson Hall Marine Corps, Arlington, 1990—; organizer, instr. Better Beginnings, Arlington, 1994—, The Reading Connection, PR, 1994—; usher Kennedy Ctr., Washington; mem. Spkrs.' Bur. with Hospice; lay leader, choir mem. Cherrydale Meth. Ch., Arlington, 1976—. Recipient Literacy award, Margaret McNamara award Reading is Fundamental of No. Va., 1994-95. Mem. Va. State Reading Assn. (mem. conf. coms.), Arlington Edn. Assn. (contbg. editor newsletter 1967-69), Art League of Alexandria, Arlington Artist's Alliance, Greater Washington Reading Coun. (com. chairperson 1962—, Tchr. of Yr. 1995-96), Delta Kappa Gamma (Alpha Omicron former news writer, v.p., program chairperson, news editor). Avocations: water color, singing in choir, writing poetry, traveling, producing children's musicals. Home: 6110 23rd St N Arlington VA 22205-3414 E-mail: fsimms@starpower.net.

SIMMS, JACQUELINE KAMP, secondary education educator; Tchr. sci. Recipient Tandy Tech. Scholars prize Tandy Corp., 1994, Regional Catalyst award for Excellence in Chemistry Tchg. Chem. Mfrs. Assn., 1994, Presdl. award for Excellence in Sci. and Math. Tchg., 1994, Educator award Continental Cablevision, 1997. Office: Sandalwood High Sch 2750 John Prom Blvd Jacksonville FL 32246-3921

SIMMS, JOHN CARSON, logic, mathematics and computer science educator; b. Columbus, Ind., Oct. 24, 1952; s. Roberta Ann (Cooke) Burns; m. Florence Chizue Miyamoto, June 22, 1974; 1 child, Carson Chizumi. BA with highest distinction, Ind. U., 1972, MA, 1974; PhD, Rockefeller U., 1979. Assoc. instr. Ind. U., Bloomington, 1973-74; grad. fellow Rockefeller U., N.Y.C., 1974-78; vis. lectr. Tex. Tech U., Lubbock, 1978-80; v.p. Custom Computation, Inc., Lubbock, 1980-81; computer programmer and analyst Furr's Inc., Lubbock, 1981-82; contract computer programmer Lubbock, 1982-83; asst. prof. math. and computer sci. Marquette U., Milw., 1983-92, assoc. prof. math. and computer sci., 1992—. Assoc. editor Modern Logic, Modern Logic Books, 1990—; contbr. articles to profl. jours. Mem. AAAS, Assn. for Symbolic Logic, Kurt-Gödel-Gesellschaft (Collegium Logicum lectr. 1990), Am. Math. Soc., Interest Group in Pure and Applied Logic, Pi Mu Epsilon, Sigma Xi, Phi Beta Kappa. Achievements include research on new semantics for second-order logic, on a natural argument against the continuum hypothesis, on a natural argument against the axiom of choice, on applications of natural probabilistic notions to the foundations of mathematics. Home: 8969 N Pelham Pky Bayside WI 53217-1954 Office: Dept Math Stats Computer Sci Marquette Univ PO Box 1881 Milwaukee WI 53201-1881

SIMMS, LILLIAN MILLER, nursing educator; b. Detroit, Apr. 13, 1930; d. John Jacob and Mary Agnes (Knight) Miller; m. Richard James Simms, Feb. 2, 1952; children: Richard James Jr., Frederick William, Andrew Michael. BSN, U. Mich., 1952, MSN, 1966, PhD in Ednl. Gerontology, 1977. Program dir., assoc. prof. nursing health svcs. adminstrn. U. Mich., Ann Arbor, 1977-82, interim assoc. dir. nursing, asst. dean clin. affairs, 1981-82, assoc. prof. nursing adminstrn. and health gerontology, 1982-90, assoc. prof. nursing, 1990—; prof. emeritus, 1995. Spkr., presenter in field; mem. spl. study sect. NIH, 1986; mem. adv. com., panel of judges for inquiry and practice of nursing svc. adminstr. Intra and Interdisciplinary Invitational Conf., 1990; series editor Delmar Pubs., Inc., 1991-93; mem. med. delegation People to People Citizen Amb. Program, Australia and New Zealand, 1982, People's Republic of China, Hong Kong and Korea, 1989; dir. China project that developed acad. relationships with schs. of nursing in People's Republic of China, 1991-94. Developer concept of work excitement; co-author: Administracion de Servicios de Enfermeria, 1986, A Guide to Redesigning Nursing Practice Patterns, 1992, The Professional Practice of Nursing Administration, 2d edit., 1994; contbr. chpts. to books, numerous articles to profl. publs.; reviewer for various publs. in field. Bd. dirs. Domino House Sr. Ctr., Ann Arbor, 1990-95; mem. nursing dels. to China, People to People Internat., 1994, to Russia and Romania, 1996. Recipient Excellence in Nursing Edn. award Rho chpt. Sigma Theta Tau, 1995; grantee U. Mich., 1983-84, 84-87, 87-88, Presdl. Initiatives, 1990-92, W.K. Kellogg Found., 1991-93. Fellow Am. Acad. Nursing; mem. ANA, Am. Orgn. Nurse Execs., Midwest Nursing Rsch. Soc., Coun. on Grad. Edn. for Adminstrn. in Nursing (sec. 1986-88, chair publs. com. 1988-89), U. Mich. Nursing Alumni Assn., Sigma Theta Tau. Avocations: reading, gardening, international travel. Home: 1329 Wines Dr Ann Arbor MI 48103-2543 Office: U Mich Sch Nursing 400 N Ingalls St Rm 2174 Ann Arbor MI 48109-2003

SIMON, DOUG, government educational administrator; b. Tampa, Fla. BS in edn., U. South Fla. Spec. asst. US Dept. Edn., Off. Edn. Tech., Wash., DC, 2002—; vp Hockaday Donatelli, Alexandria, Va.; sales dir. eContributor.com; dir. polit. edn. dept. Rep. Nat. Com., 1998; staff, sec. of state chmn. J. Kenneth Blackwell US Census Monitoring Bd., Ohio. Office: US Dept Edn Off Edn Tech Rm FB6-7E229 400 Maryland Ave SW Washington DC 20202 E-mail: douglas.simon@ed.gov.*

SIMON, JANE, psychiatrist, educator; d. John L. and Ruth (Breidenbach) S.; m. 1967 (div. 1976); children: Claire Simon-Lanks, Belinda Elizabeth Simon-Lanks. Student, Columbia U., 1960-63, U. P.R., 1963-65; MD, Temple U., 1967; cert., Am. Inst. Psychoanalysis, 1982. Diplomate Am. Bd. Psychiatry and Neurology, Am. Bd. Forensic Pathology, Am. Bd. Anatomic Pathology. Inter, resident in pathology Columbia-Presbyn. Hosp., N.Y.C., 1967-71, fellow dept. pathology, 1971-73; resident in psychiatry Roosevelt Hosp., N.Y.C., 1973-75, fellow in child psychiatry, 1975-77; pvt. practice, N.Y.C., 1977—; med. dir. Blanton-Peale Counseling Ctr., Blanton-Peale Inst., N.Y.C., 1978—. Instr. dept. forensic medicine NYU Sch. Medicine, 1971-73; cons. Odyssey House, 1971-75; jr. med. examiner Office Chief Med. Examiner, City of N.Y., 1971-72, assoc. med. examiner, 1972-73; staff psychiatrist Jewish Meml. Hosp., 1977-78; assoc. attending dept. psychiatry and assoc. attending outpatient svc. child and adolescent divsn. St. Luke's-Roosevelt Med. Ctr., N.Y.C.; mem. Faculty Columbia U.; med. dir. Blanton-Peale Grad. Inst.; presenter in field. Author: (poetry) Incisions, 1989; mem. editl. bd. Am. Jour. Psychoanalysis, Jour. Am. Acad. Psychoanalysis, Jour. Religion and Health, 2002—; contbr. articles and revs. to med. jours., poems to poetry jours. Vol. psychiatrist Project for Psychiat. Outreach to Homeless, 1992-96. Fellow Am. Acad. Psychoanalysis (Editor Acad. Forum), 1995-2000; mem. Am. Psychiat. Assn., Internat. Karen Horney Soc., Poets and Writers, Poetry Soc. Am., Am. Physicians Poetry Assn., Acad. Am. Poets, Road Runners Assn. Avocations: piano, running. Office: 145 Central Park W Ste 1A New York NY 10023-2004 Fax: (212) 877-3566. E-mail: js145@msn.com.

SIMON, JOHN GERALD, law educator; b. N.Y.C., Sept. 19, 1928; s. Robert Alfred and Madeleine (Marshall) S.; m. Claire Aloise Bising, June 14, 1958; 1 son, John Kirby (dec.). Grad., Ethical Culture Schs., 1946; AB, Harvard U., 1950; LLB, Yale U., 1953; LLD (hon.), Ind. U., 1989. Bar: N.Y. 1953. Asst. to gen. counsel Office Sec. Army, 1956-58; with firm Paul, Weiss, Rifkind, Wharton & Garrison, N.Y.C., 1958-62; mem. faculty Yale Law Sch., 1962—, prof. law, 1967-76, Augustus Lines prof. law, 1976—2003, Augustus Lines prof. emeritus law, 2003—, dep. dean, 1985-90, acting dean, 1991; dir., co-chmn. program on non-profit orgns. Yale U., 1977-88. Author: (with Powers and Gunnemann) The Ethical Investor, 1972. Pres. Taconic Found., 1967—; trustee, sec. Potomac Inst., 1961-93; mem. grad. bd. Harvard Crimson, 1950—; chmn. bd. dirs. Coop. Assistance Fund, 1970-76, vice chmn., 1977—; mem. governing coun. Rockefeller Archives Ctr., 1982-86; trustee The Found. Ctr., 1983-92, Open Soc. Inst.-N.Y., 1996—. 1st lt. U.S. Army, 1953-5 6. Recipient Certificate of Achievement Dept. Army, 1956 Mem. Phi Beta Kappa. Office: Yale U Law Sch PO Box 208215 New Haven CT 06520-8215

SIMON, LINDA DAY, assistant principal; b. Cleve., July 27, 1957; d. Charles Walker and Frances (Manaia) Day; m. Michael Patrick Simon, June 23, 1979; children: Claire Marie, Thomas Michael. BS in Edn., Bowling Green State U., 1978; MA in Edn., Cleve. State U., 1982; postgrad., Baldwin-Wallace Coll., 1989, 90, Kent State U., 1991-92. Tchr., counselor Positive Edn. Program, Cuyahoga County Bd. Edn., Rocky River, Ohio, 1978-80; asst. prin. Parmadale-St. Anthony Home for Boys, Parma, Ohio, 1980-83; learning disabled tchr. Maple Heights (Ohio) Bd. Edn., 1983-85; Severe Behavior Handicap tchr. Parma (Ohio) City Schs., 1985-89, elem. counselor, 1989-91, asst. prin., 1991—. Team leader Dist. Strategic Planner, Parma, 1991—; adv. bd. At-Risk Student Program, Parma, 1992—. Parent sponsor Boy Scouts Am., Strongsville, Ohio, 1990—. Named Leading Leader, Active Parenting, Inc., Marietta, Ga., 1991. Mem. Ohio Assn. Secondary Sch. Adminstrn. Avocations: camping, bicycling, hiking, reading, needle work. Office: Albion Jr High Sch 11919 Webster Rd Strongsville OH 44136-3719

SIMON, MARILYN WEINTRAUB, art educator, sculptor; b. Chgo., Aug. 25, 1927; d. William and Caroline Mabel (Bergman) Weintraub; m. Walter E. Simon, Mar. 19, 1950 (div. Sept. 1990); children: Nina Fay Simon-Rosenthal, Jacob Aaron, Maurine Joy Simon Rubinstein, Linda Gay Simon Shapiro. PhB, U. Chgo., 1947; MEd, Temple U., 1969. Cert. tchr., Pa. Bd. sec. Delaware Valley Smelting Corp., Bristol, Pa., 1957-89; art tchr. Calumet Sch. Dist., Ill., 1951-53; art tchr., chmn. elem. art program Cheltenham (Pa.) Sch. Dist., 1969-95. Real estate agt., Tullytown, Pa.; speaker in field; devel. dir., exec. bd. Art Forms, Manayunk, Pa. One woman show Hahn Gallery, Phila., 1985; permanent exhibits Elkins Park (Pa.) Libr., Univ. Hosp., Cleve., (bronze bust of Yitzhak Rabin) Van Pelt-Dietrich Libr. Ctr. U. Pa., Phila., (bronze sculptor) Elizabeth and Joseph Schwartz Libr. at Beth Sholom, Elkins Park, Pa., Frank Lloyd Wright Beth Sholom Congregation; also represented in med. offices, private collections; author publs. on using art reproductions in edn. Chmn. Phila. chpt. U. Chgo. Alumni Fund Assn., 1978-84. Recipient numerous art awards including 1st prize Doylestown Art League, 1986-87, Best Sculpture award Mummers's Mus. Phila., 1987, Juror's award Cheltenham Art Ctr., 1987-88, 3d prize Abington Art Ctr., 1988, 1st prize for sculpture Art Assn. of Harrisburg, 1989, Best in Show, Artists Cultural Exchange, 1992, Clifford Owens Meml. award Artist Equity, 1995, Print award Cheltenham Art Ctr., 1995, 2 Honorable Mentions, Jane Law Gallery, Long Beach Island, N.J., 1995. Mem. Nat. Art Edn. Assn., Pa. Art Educators Assn. (regional rep. 1988-89, Outstanding Art Educator of Yr. award 1987), Oil Pastel Assn. N.Y.C. (invited mem.). Democrat. Jewish. Office: PO Box 29722 Elkins Park PA 19027-0922

SIMON, MELVIN I. molecular biologist, educator; b. N.Y.C., Feb. 8, 1937; s. Hyman and Sarah (Liebman) S.; m. Linda, Jan. 7, 1959; children—Joshua, David, Rachel BS, CCNY, 1959; PhD, Brandeis U., 1963. Postdoctoral fellow Princeton U., N.J., 1963-65; prof. biology U. Calif.-San Diego, La Jolla, 1965-82, Calif. Inst. Tech., Pasadena, 1982—, chmn., 1995-2000, prof., 2000—. Pres., dir. Agouron Inst., La Jolla, 1980— Contbr. articles to profl. jours. Mem. Nat. Acad. Scis. (Selman A. Waksman microbiology award 1991), Am. Soc. Microbiology

SIMON, RAYMOND JOSEPH, school system administrator; m. Phyllis Simon; 1 child, Sandy. Math tchr. North Little Rock H.S.; with sch. food svcs. and computer svcs.; asst. supt. for fin. Conway Pub. Schs.; dir. Ark. Dept. of Edn., Little Rock, 1997—. Adj. prof. U. Ctrl. Ark. Grad. Sch., U. Ark. Little Rock, Ark. State U., Beebe. Mem. Conway Planning Commn.; exec. bd. Quapaw Area Coun., Boy Scouts Am.; bd. dirs. Conway Civic Orch. Mem. Conway Area C. of C. Office: Ark Dept of Edn 4 Capitol Mall Rm 304A Little Rock AR 72201-1011*

SIMON, SHEILA SANDRA, special education educator, administrator; b. N.Y.C., July 24, 1940; d. Leo and Frances (Wexler) Brown; children: Steven Marc, Scott Irwin, Sean Eric, Rebecca Shane. BA in Psychology, Lehman Coll., Bronx, 1974; MS in Spl. Edn., Coll. New Rochelle, N.Y., 1978; MS in Counseling, Loyola Marymount Coll., L.A., 1992; postgrad., UCLA, 1993—. Elem. tchr. spl. edn. N.Y.C. Pub. Schs., Bronx, 1974-79; tchr. spl. edn. Lincoln Spl. Sch., Palm Desert, Calif., 1979-83; tchr., chair dept. spel. edn. Mt. Vernon Jr. H.S. L.A. Unified Sch. Dist., 1983-86, resource specialist Revere Jr. H.S., 1986-91, outreach cons. Manual Arts H.S., 1991-94; exec. dir. spl. edn. commn. L.A. Unified Schs., 1994—. Mem. Los Angeles County Multicultural Collaborative, 1994, Los Angeles County Hate Crime Network, L.A. Roundtable for Children. Recipient Outstanding Sch. Svc. award Revere PTA, L.A., 1988. Mem. Coun. for Exceptional Children, Calif. Assn. of Resource Specialists, Calif. Assn. Counseling and Devel., Calif. Sch. Counselors, Kappa Delta Pi, Delta Kappa Gamma. Avocations: camping, music, travel, painting in oil and watercolor. Office: LA Unified Sch Dist Spl Edn Commn 450 N Grand Ave # H256 Los Angeles CA 90012-2123

SIMON, THEODORE RONALD, physician, medical educator; b. Hartford, Conn., Feb. 2, 1949; s. Theologos Lingos and Lillian (Faix) S.; m. Marcia Anyzeski, Apr. 5, 1974; children: Jacob T., Theodore H., Mark G. BA cum laude, Trinity Coll., Hartford, 1970; MD, Yale U., 1975. Diplomate Am. Bd. Nuclear Medicine, Diplomate Nat. Bd. Med. Examiners; lic. Calif., Tex. Intern in surgery Strong Meml. Hosp., Rochester, N.Y., 1975-76; resident in diagnostic radiology U. Calif., San Francisco, 1976-78; resident in nuclear medicine Yale-New Haven Hosp., Conn., 1978-80, chief resident, 1979-80; asst. prof. nuclear medicine U. Tex. Southwestern Med. Ctr., Dallas, 1980-88, assoc. prof., 1990—. Cons. nuclear medicine St. Paul's Hosp., Dallas, 1981-88; cons. internal medicine Presbyn. Hosp., Dallas, 1981-88, 90, Med. City Hosp., Dallas, 1989—; cons. nuclear medicine VA Med. Ctr., Dallas, 1981-82, chief nuclear medicine svc., 1982-88; nat. dep. dir. nuclear medicine VA, 1985-88; dep. chief nuclear medicine NIH, Bethesda, Md., 1988-90; mem. del. Taiwan Atomic Energy, U.S. State Dept., 1990. Mem. editorial bd. Jour. History of Med. and Allied Scis., 1974-75; contbr. articles to Internat. Jour. Radiol. Applications, Jour. Nuclear Medicine, Am. Jour. Cardiology, Clin. Nuclear Medicine, Circulation, Yale Jour. Biol. Medicine, Radiology, Surg. Radiology, and others. Pres. Christ Lutheran Ch., University Park, Tex. Mem. Soc. Nuclear Medicine (treas. correlative imaging coun. 1988-90, mem. exec. com 1988—). Achievements include patent for Complex Motion Device to Enhance Single Photon Emission Computed Tomography Uniformity; research in single photon emission computed tomography as it related to substance abuse, schizophrenia, depression, neurotoxicity and chronic fatigue syndrome. Home and Office: 4429 Southern Ave Dallas TX 75205-2622

SIMONDS, VALERIE DEVERSE, prehospital educator; b. Greensburg, Pa., Jan. 23, 1943; d. John Young and Margaret (McCommons) Woods. Diploma in nursing, Shady Side Hosp., 1963; BS, Johns Hopkins U., 1976, MS with honors, 1979. RN, Md., Pa.; CEN NREMT-P. Health educator U. Md. Sch. of Pharmacy, Balt., 1979-80; EMT dept. chair Anne Arundel C.C., Arnold, Md., 1979-2000; health educator, cons. Johns Hopkins Inst. Policy Studies, Balt., 2000—03; health professions text editor/reviewer, 1990—. Developed and implemented 1st EMT-Paramedic program, Md.; mem. Md. Region III EMS adv. bd., Balt., 1986-98. Recipient Disting. Program award Md. State Dept. of Edn., 1986. Home: 285 Laguna Cir Severna Park MD 21146-1360

SIMONE, ANGELA PAOLINO, elementary education educator; b. New Haven, Jan. 27, 1953; d. John L. and Mary (Solli) Paolino; 1 child, Dennis. BS, So. Conn. U., 1974, MS in Reading, 1976; AS, S. Cen. Community Coll., New Haven, 1972. Substitute tchr. City of West Haven, Conn., 1976-77; elem. tchr. St. Brendén's Sch., New Haven, 1985, St. Lawrence Sch., West Haven, 1985-99, co-coord. Writing to Read Program, 1994-99, coord. social studies program, 1997-99, coord. math. program, 1998-99; coord. primary sci. program Rainbow Program for All God's Children, West Haven, 1987-97; elem. tchr., sch. improvement com. mem. Bridgeport (Conn.) Pub. Schs., 1999—. Mem. We Are the World Com. of West Haven Pub. Schs. Mem. AAUW, ASCD, NEA, Nat. Cath. Edn. Assn., Internat. Reading Assn., Conn. Edn. assn., Bridgeport Edn. Assn. Office: Dunbar Sch 445 Union Ave Bridgeport CT 06607-1823

SIMONE, BEVERLY SUE, academic administrator; b. Evansville, Ind., Aug. 11, 1946; d. Lloyd C. and Edna Margaret (Steckler) Miller; 1 child, Andrellia Christina Acheson-Rupert. BA in Speech and Theatre, Butler U., 1969; MS in Edn. and Communications, Ind. U., 1973, EdD in Adult Edn., 1986. Co-owner, mgr. Tres Bien Catering, Indpls., 1969-71; instr. communications Ind. Vocat. Tech. Coll., Indpls., 1970-72, dir. learning resources, 1972-75, chair div. gen. edn., 1975-79, dir. external svcs., 1979-80; v.p. community and govtl. rels. Milw. Area Tech. Coll., 1980-85, provost, 1985-87; pres. Western Wis. Tech. Coll., La Crosse, 1987-89; pres., chief exec. officer Madison Area Tech. Coll., 1989—. Nat. bd. dirs. Am. Family Ins. Mem. Milw. Jr. League, 1980-94, past v.p.; mem. Madison Jr. League, 1994—; bd. dirs. United Way Dane County, Madison, Wis., 1991-96, Am. Players Theatre, Madison Cmty. Found. Recipient Nat. Recognition award Am. Coun. Edn., 1981, 85, 86, Outstanding Alumnus award Ind. U. Sch. Edn., 1993; named Woman of Achievement La Crosse Regional Bus. Assn., 1988, Woman Who Makes a Difference, Internat. Women's Forum, 1994. Mem. Am. Assn. Community and Jr. Colls. (chair 1992-93, chair elect 1991-92, bd. dirs. 1989-94, Futures Commn.), Am. Assn. Women in Community and Jr. Colls. (pres. 1985-87), Am. Coun. on Edn. (bd. dirs. 1994-97), Assn. C.C. Trustees (adv. mem. 1985-87), Internat. Women's Forum, Greater Madison C. of C. (bd. dirs.), Tempo, Vantage Point, Rotary. Office: Madison Area Tech Coll 3550 Anderson St Madison WI 53704-2520

SIMONEAU, CYNTHIA LAMBERT, newspaper editor, journalism educator; b. Central Falls, R.I., May 18, 1958; d. Roland and L. Jean Simoneau; m. Paul E. Lambert, Oct. 24, 1981; children: Thomas S. Lambert, Marc S. Lambert. BA, U. R.I., 1980. Asst. news editor Newtown (Conn.) Bee, 1980-82; reporter Bridgeport (Conn.) Post & Telegram, 1982-83, bur. chief, 1983-91; editor Woman Wise Conn. Post, Bridgeport, 1991-97, asst. mng. editor, 1997—. Adj. prof. So. Conn. State U., New Haven, 1993—, Fairfield U., 2003—. Eucharistic min., mem. parish adv. coun., religious edn. tchr., St. Thomas Aquinas Ch., Fairfield, Conn. Mem. Soc. Profl. Journalists (bd. dirs. Conn. chpt. 1983-2003, treas. Conn. chpt. 1985-95, 2003—, pres. Conn. chpt. 1995-97, Journalism Excellence awards for news stories and columns, Pres.'s award Conn. chpt.). Avocation: reading. Office: Conn Post 410 State St Bridgeport CT 06604 E-mail: csimoneau@ctpost.com.

SIMONES, MARIE DOLOROSA, parochial school educator, nun; b. Dubuque, Iowa, Feb. 21, 1926; d. Joseph P. and Florence Julia (Hagge) S. AB, Loretto Heights Coll., 1948; MA, Notre Dame U., 1967. Joined Sisters of Loretto, Roman Cath. Ch., 1948. Tchr. St. Ann Sch., St. Louis, 1951-55, Arlington, Va., 1955-61, St. Augustine Sch., Lebanon, Ky., 1961-63, St. Paul the Apostle Sch., St. Louis, 1963-67, St. Vincent de Paul Sch., Denver, 1967—. Mem. Nat. Coun. Social Studies, Archaeological Inst. Avocations: travel, stamps, foreign dolls.

SIMONICH, SANDRA SUE, elementary education educator; b. Moline, Ill., Aug. 8, 1942; d. Kenneth Fred and Vurl Barbara (Nicely) Liedtke; children: Cassandra Ann Oliver Phillips; m. Joseph Donald Simonich, Mar. 11, 1983. BS, Augustana Coll., 1974; MS, Western Ill. U., 1984. With Bank of Silvis, Ill., 1960; with farm implement John Deere Harvester, East Moline; with parts depot John Deere, East Moline, 1960-68; tchr. Millikin Sch., Geneseo, Ill., 1974-76; elem. tchr. S.W. Sch., Geneseo, 1976—. Program initiator Raindows-Counseling for Children with a Loss of Some Kind, 1990, Family Math Program, 1994—; officer IMPACT, elem. coord., 1990—. Mem. Ill. Reading Coun., Rock Island, Ill., 1980—, Jr. Women's Club-Geneseo, 1988; pres. PTA, 1992-94, life mem. Avocations: aerobics, tennis, boating, skiing. Home: 203 Longview Dr Geneseo IL 61254-9113

SIMONS, HELEN, school psychologist, psychotherapist, educator; b. Chgo., Feb. 13, 1930; d. Leo and Sarah (Shrayer) Pomper; m. Broudy Simons, May 20, 1956 (div. May 1972); children: Larry, Sheri. BA in Biol., Lake Forest Coll., 1951; MA in Clin. Psychology, Roosevelt U., 1972; D of Psychology, Ill. Sch. Profl. Psychology, 1980. Intern Cook County Hosp., Chgo., 1979-80; pvt. practice psychotherapist Chgo., 1980—; sch. psychologist Chgo. Bd. Edn., 1974-79, 80—. Faculty Internat. Soc. for Prevention of Child Abuse and Neglect; lectr., presenter at workshops. Contbr. articles to profl. jours. Mem.: APA, Internat. Assn. Applied Psychology, Internat. Soc. for Prevention of Child Abuse and Neglect, Internat. Coun. Psychologists, Chgo. Sch. Psychol. Assn., Chgo. Psychol. Assn., Ill. Sch. Psychologists Assn., Nat. Sch. Psychologists Assn. Avocations: music, dancing, reading. Home: 6145 N Sheridan Rd Apt 29D Chicago IL 60660-6855 Office: Logandale Mid Sch 3212 W George St Chicago IL 60618- E-mail: hpompers@aol.com.

SIMONS, LYNN OSBORN, state agency administrator; b. Havre, Mont., June 1, 1934; d. Robert Blair and Dorothy (Briggs) Osborn; m. John Powell Simons, Jan. 19, 1957; children: Clayton Osborn, William Blair. Tchr. Midvale (Utah) Jr. H.S., 1956-57, Sweetwater county Sch. Dist. 1, Rock Springs, Wyo., 1957-58, U. Wyo., 1959-61, Natrona County Sch. Dist. 1, Casper, Wyo., 1963-64; credit mgr. Gallery 323, Casper, 1972-77; Wyo. state supt. pub. instrn. Cheyenne, 1979-91; sec.'s regional rep. region VIII U.S. Dept. Edn., Denver, 1993—2001; mem. Denver Fed. Exec. Bd., 1995-2001; mem. exec. bd. combined Fed. campaign, 1994—2001; ednl. cons., 2001—03; state planning coord. Capitol Bldg., Cheyenne, Wyo., 2003—. Mem. State Bds. Charities and Reform, Land Commrs., Farm Loan, 1979-91; mem. State Commns. Capitol Bldg., Liquor, 1979-91; Ex-officio mem. bd. trustees U. Wyo., 1979-91; ex-officio mem. Wyo. Community Coll. Commn., 1979-91; mem. steering com. Edn. Commn. of the States, 1988-90, 2003; mem. State Bd. Edn., 1971-77, chmn., 1976-77; advisor Nat. Trust for Hist. Preservation, 1980-86. Mem. LWV (pres. 1970-71). Democrat. Episcopalian. Office: Capitol Building Cheyenne WY 82003 E-mail: isimon@state.wy.us.

SIMPSON, BRADFORD VAN, education association executive; b. Greensboro, N.C., July 2, 1957; s. Charles Harrison and Virginia Lee (Moser) S.; m. JoAnne Wright, Nov. 18, 1978; children: Charles, Kimberly, Harrison. Grad. high sch., Greensboro. Dept. mgr. City of Greensboro, 1975-84; sales rep. Document Tech., Inc., Greensboro, 1984—; pres. Simpson Rsch. Inst., Greensboro, 1989—. Tchr., Guilford Tech. Coll., Greensboro, 1989, sales tng. seminars, 1993. Author: 365 Times to Love Your Wife, 1990; author motivational tape series; dir., producer (children's TV program) Butterscotch Critters, 1990; developed learning software for children, 1993; pub. newsletter Rebirth of America, The Next Generation, 1993. Mem. Assn. Info. and Image Mgmt. (pres. 1988-89), Data Processing Mgrs. Assn. Republican. Mem. United Ch. of Christ. Avocations: reading, camping, outdoor activities. Home: 1802 Bailiff St Greensboro NC 27403-3310 Office: Simpson Rsch Inst PO Box 1919 Greensboro NC 27402-1919

SIMPSON, DAVID WILLIAM, artist, educator; b. Pasadena, Calif., Jan. 20, 1928; s. Frederick and Mary Adeline (White) S.; m. Dolores D. Debus, July 30, 1954; 1 stepchild, Gregory C. Vose; 1 child, Lisa C. B.F.A., Calif. Sch. Fine Arts, 1956; MA, San Francisco State Coll., 1958. Instr. art Am. River Jr. Coll., Sacramento, 1958-60, Contra Costa Jr. Coll., San Pablo, Calif., 1960-65; prof. art U. Calif., Berkeley, 1967-91, prof. emeritus, 1991—. Exhibited in one-man shows including Robert Elkon Gallery, NYC, 1961, 63, 64, San Francisco Mus. Art, 1967, Henri Gallery, Washington, 1968, Oakland Mus., 1978, Modernism, San Francisco, 1980-81, 84, 86, 2001, Sheldon Meml. Art Gallery, Lincoln, Nebr., 1990, Mincher/Wilcox Gallery, San Francisco, 1991, 92, 93, Angles Gallery, Santa Monica, Calif., 1991-92, 94, 99, Bemis Found., Omaha, Nebr., 1991, Anthony Ralph Gallery, NYC, 1992, John Berggruen Gallery, San Francisco, 1994, Charlotte Jackson Fine Art, Santa Fe, 1995, Laguna Art Mus., Laguna Beach, Calif., 1995 Haines Gallery, San Francisco, 1997, 99, 2000, Studio La Citta, Verona, Italy, 1998, 2002, Renate Schröder Gallery, Cologne, Germany, 2000-02, Artothek, Cologne, 2002; group shows include Mus. Modern Art, NYC, 1963, Carnegie Internat., Pitts., 1961-62, 66-67, LA Mus. Art, 1964, U. Ill., 1969, Expo '70, Osaka, Japan, 1970, Josly Art Mus., Omaha, 1970, John Berggruen Gallery, San Francisco, 1979, Angles Gallery, Santa Monica, 1988, 90, John Good Gallery, NY, 1992, John Berggruen Gallery, San Francisco, 1993, Cheryl Haines Gallery, San Francisco, 1996, Museo di Arte Moderna e Contemporanea, Trento, Italy, 1996, Studio La Citta, Verona, Italy, 1996, Llonja, Palma De Majorca, Spain, 1997, Museo Cantonale d'Arte, Lugano, Switzerland, 1997, Studio La Citta, Verona, Italy, 1997, Haines Gallery, San Francisco, 1997, Palazzo Ducale, Gubbio, Italy, 1999, Palazzo Ducale, Sassuolo, Panza Collection, Italy, 2002, Panza Della Gran Guardia, Verona, 2002; represented in permanent collections including Phila. Mus. Art, Nat. Collection Fine Arts, Washington, Seattle Art Mus., La Jolla (Calif.) Mus. Art, Mus. Modern Art, NYC, San Francisco Mus. Art, Oakland (Calif.) Mus., Panza Collection, Italy, Laguna Art Mus., Laguna Beach, Calif., U. Art Mus., Berkeley, Calif., Museo Cantonale d'Arte Lugano, Switzerland, Museo Di Arte Moderna e Contemporanea Di Trento e Rouerato. Home: 565 Vistamont Ave Berkeley CA 94708-1244 Office: U Calif Dept Art Berkeley CA 94720

SIMPSON, DICK WELDON, political science educator; b. Houston, Nov. 8, 1940; s. Warren Weldon and Ola Ela (Felts) S.; m. Sarajane Avidon, Mar. 22, 1987; children: Kate Donley, August Donley. BA, U. Tex., 1963; MA, Ind. U., 1964, PhD, 1968; MDiv, McCormick Theol. Sem., 1984. Ordained to ministry United Ch. of Christ, 1985. Rsch. asst. Ind. U., Bloomington, 1965; fgn. area fellow Ford Found., Africa, 1966-67; instr. U. Ill., Chgo., 1967-68, asst. prof., 1968-71, assoc. prof. polit. sci., 1972-96, prof., 1996—. Exec. dir. Inst. on Ch., Chgo., 1984-86, Clergy and Laity Concerned, Chgo., 1987-89. Author: Winning Elections, 1972, 74, 81, 96, Strategies for Change, 1976, Politics of Compassion, 1989; editor: Chicago's Future, 1976, 80, 83, 88, 93, Rogues, Rebels, and Rubber Stamps, 2001, Inside Urban Politics, 2003. Alderman Chgo. City Coun., 1971-79; campaign mgr. McCarthy for Pres., Ill., 1967-68; transition team Mayors Washington and Byrne, 1979, 83, State's Atty. O'Malley and County Clk. Orr, 1990, 91, Ill. Atty. Gen. Lisa Madigan, 2003; congl. candidate, 1992, 94. Humanities Inst. fellow U. Ill., Chgo., 1985-86; rsch. grantee Joyce, Amoco, Woods, McArthur, Carnegie, Wieboldt Founds., 1972-2003; recipient award Clarence Darrow Cmty. Ctr., Clergy and Laity Concerned, IVI-IPO. Mem. Am. Polit. Sci. Assn. (Excellence in Tchg. award, 2002), Midwest Polit. Sci. Assn., Ill. Polit. Sci. Assn. (past pres.), City Club Chgo. (v.p., award). Office: Dept Polit Sci U Ill M/C 276 1007 W Harrison St Chicago IL 60607-7137 E-mail: simpson@uic.edu.

SIMPSON, DOROTHY AUDREY, retired speech educator; b. Las Vegas, N.Mex., Feb. 29, 1944; d. Clyde Joseph and Audrey Shirley (Clements) Simpson; m. Gary Alan Beimer, May 13, 1972 (div. Apr. 1986); children: Laura Lea Beimer Nelson, Rose Anne Colleen Beimer; m. Ian B. Croxton, Dec. 27, 1992 (div. Oct. 1993); m. Doyle W. Hauschulz, Feb. 23, 2001 (div. June 2003). BA, N.Mex. Highlands U., 1965; MS, U. Utah, 1968; EdD, U. N.Mex., 1989. Cert. secondary edn., N.Mex. Tchr. West Las Vegas (N.Mex.) H.S., 1966-67, Santa Rosa (N.Mex.) H.S., 1968-71, Questa (N.Mex.) Consol. Schs., 1972-73; prof. speech comm., assoc. dean coll. arts and scis. N.Mex. Highlands U., Las Vegas, 1975—2003, prof. emeritus, 2003—. Ednl. cons. Rancho Valmora, 2003—. Author: Hovels, Haciendas, and House Calls: The Life of Carl H. Gellenthien, M.D., 1986, Speaking for Life: A Speech Communication Guide for Adults, 1990, Wreck of the Destiny Train, 1993 Active Calvary Bapt. Ch., Las Vegas, 1959—. Recipient Educator of Yr. award Pub. Svc. Co. of N.Mex., Albuquerque, 1990. Mem. P.E.O. Republican. Avocation: writing. Home: PO Box 778 Las Vegas NM 87701-0778

SIMPSON, ELIZABETH ANN, reading and language arts educator; b. Collins, Miss., Oct. 20, 1940; d. Clyde C. and Edna L. (Lewis) McRaney; m. Arthur Thomas Simpson, Dec. 15, 1962; children: Lisa Bukovnik, Art, Cindy Simpson-Scharff, Sheri Lucas. BS, U. So. Miss., 1978, MEd, 1982. Tchr. Biloxi (Miss.) Pub. Schs., 1978—. Conv. presenter Miss. Coun. Tchrs. of English, Jackson, 1992. Leader Girl Scouts Am., San Antonio, 1970, Biloxi, 1975; Sunday sch. tchr. Episcopal Ch. of the Redeemer, Biloxi, 1978. Fellow South Miss. Writing Project, 1991, 92. Mem. Internat. Reading Assn., Nat. Coun. Tchrs. of English, Nat. Coun. Tchrs. of Math., Miss. Reading Assn. (sec. Gulf Coast chpt. 1986), Phi Delta Kappa, Phi Kappa Phi. Home: 347 Saint Mary Blvd Biloxi MS 39531-3419 Office: Beauvoir Elem Sch 2003 Lawrence St Biloxi MS 39531-5108

SIMPSON, JULIETTE RICH, elementary educator; b. Bainbridge, Ga., Jan. 9, 1944; d. Robert Lloyd Jr. and Juliette (Lane) Rich; m. Ralph Felward Simpson, Aug. 13, 1966; children: Juliette, Elena. AB in Elem. Edn., Wesleyan Coll., 1966. Elem. tchr. Bibb County Sch. Sys., Macon, Ga., 1966-69, Tift County Sch. Sys., Tifton, Ga., 1974-77, 1977—. Alt. del. Nat. Rep. Conv., Houston, 1992, San Diego, 1996; mem. State Rep. Com., 1994—; 8th dist. Phil Gramm leadership chmn.; chmn. Tift County Rep. Party, 1994-99; co-pres. Tifton Cir. Bar Assn., 1990-91; active Annie Belle Clark Sch. PTO; v.p. Tifton Choral Soc., 1994-98, vice-chmn., 1995-96. Mem. Profl. Assn. Ga. Educators, Internat. Reading Assn., Tift County Found. for Ednl. Excellence (Outstanding Tchr. award), Ga. Coun. for Social Scis., Dogwood Garden Club. Presbyterian. Home: 1020 N College Ave Tifton GA 31794-3942 Office: Annie Belle Clark Sch 506 12th St W Tifton GA 31794-3999

SIMPSON, LINDA SUE, elementary educator; b. Rogers, Ark., Oct. 13, 1947; d. Richard Eugene and Shirley Joan (Kilpatrick) S. BS in Edn., Ohio State U., 1969, postgrad., 1989-91; MA in Edn., Ea. Ky. U., 1978. Cert. elem. tchr. Tchr. Conrad Sch., Newark, Ohio, 1969-71; tchr. 1-6 North Elem. Sch., Newark, 1971-89; tchr. K-3 Cherry Valley Elem., Newark, 1989—; primary literacy coordinator Cherry Valley Sch., 1999—. Adv. bd. Ohio Coun. of Social Studies, Columbus, 1994—; planning team Ctrl. Ohio Regional Profl. Devel., Columbus, 1994-95. Elder 1st Presbyn. Ch., Newark, 1990-93; tutor Licking County Children's Home, Newark, 1969-73. Jenning scholar Martha H. Found., 1987; named Newark Tchr. of the Yr., 1981; recipient Ashland Oil Tchg. award Ashland Oil Co., 1995. Mem. DAR (history and scholarship chair 1982—), Delta Kappa Gamma. Presbyterian. Avocations: genealogy, golf, bowling. Home: 579 Manor Dr Newark OH 43055-2119 Office: Cherry Valley Sch 1040 W Main St Newark OH 43055-2556

SIMPSON, MICHAEL WAYNE, lawyer, educator; b. Oklahoma City, Mar. 9, 1959; s. Darrell Wayne and Mary Ellen (Cooley) S.; children: Jeremy, Charity. BA, U. Okla., 1982, postgrad., 1999—; JD, Oklahoma City U., 1985. Bar: Kans. 1986, Mo. 1987, Okla. 1993. Assoc. Ed Schneeberger Chartered, Leavenworth, Kans., 1986-88, O'Keefe and Knopp, Leawood, Kans., 1988, Norton, White and Norton, Leavenworth, Kans., 1988-89, Pistotnik Law Offices, Merriam, Kans., 1989-91; ptnr. Bangs, Hursh and Simpson, Overland Park, Kans., 1991-92; pvt. practice, Moore, Okla., 1993-99; tchr. Seeworth Acad., 2001-02; rsch. asst. U. Okla., 2003—. Mediator Moore, 1992—99; adj. instr. Okla. City CC, 1984, St. Mary's Coll., Leavenworth, Kans., 1989. Contbr. articles to profl. jours. Instr., Upward Bound, summers 2000, 01, 03. Mem. Kans. Bar Assn. (legis. com. 1987-93), Kans. Trial Lawyers Assn. (bd. govs. 1989-93, chmn. workers compensation legis. com. 1989-90, ann. conv. 1990—), Coun. on Law in Higher Edn., Kiwanis. Avocations: walking, investment education, softball, golf. Home and Office: 1317 N Lincoln Ave Oklahoma City OK 73160-6515

SIMPSON, PAMELA HEMENWAY, art historian, educator; b. Omaha, Sept. 8, 1946; d. Myrle E. and Leone K. (Cook) Hemenway; m. Henry H. Simpson III, Apr. 4, 1970; 1 child, Peter Stuart Hay. BA, Gettysburg Coll., 1968; MA, U. Mo., 1970; PhD, U. Del., 1974. Instr. art history Pa. State Extension Campus, Media, 1973, Washington and Lee U., Lexington, Va., 1973-74, asst. prof., 1974-79, assoc. prof., 1979-85, prof. art history, 1985—, Ernest Williams prof., 1993, chair art dept., 1987—, assoc. dean of coll., 1981-86. Chair co-edn. steering com. Washington and Lee Univ., Lexington, 1984-86; cons., head county survey Va. Hist. Landmarks Commn., Richmond, 1977-81. Author: Architecture of Historic Lexington, 1977 (Am. Assn. for State and Local History award 1977), The Sculptor's Clay: Charles Gafly, 1862-1929, 1996 (SECAC award), Cheap, Quick and Easy: Imitative Architectural Materials, 1870-1930, 1999; book reviewer Women's Art Jour., columnist, 1990—; contbr. articles to profl. jours. Officer Rockbridge Hist. Soc., Lexington, 1980—, Rockbridge Valley Nat. Orgn for Women, Rockbridge County, Va., 1984—, Historic Lexington (Va.) Found., 1987—; founder, officer Rockbridge Area Coalition Against Sexual Assault, Lexington, 1990—; bd. dirs. Project Horizon, domestic violence, sexual assault, 1998—. Recipient Outstanding Faculty award State Coun. of Higher Edn., State of Va., 1995; grantee Nat. Endowment for Arts, 1974, NEH, 1975, 77, Glenn, Washington and Lee U., 1980-81, 91; NEH Summer Inst. scholar, 1989; Hagley-Winterthur Mus. fellow, 1991, 96. Fellow Nat. Humanities Ctr.; mem. Southeastern Soc. Archtl. Historians (bd. dirs. 1990-94, v.p. 1993-94, pres. 1994-95, editor Arris 1998—), Soc. Archtl. Historians (book rev. editor Am. section Jour. 1999—), Coll. Art Assn., Vernacular Architecture Forum (bd. dirs. 1982-84, 2d v.p. 1988-91, pres. 1997-99), Southeastern Coll. Art Conf. (pres. 1986-90, 2d v.p. 1994—, editor rev. 1979-82). Democrat. Episcopalian. Avocations: painting, reading mysteries. Office: Washington and Lee U Dupont Hall Lexington VA 24450

SIMPSON, RITA ANN, early childhood educator; b. Florence, Ala., Aug. 16, 1953; d. Raymond Turner and Lula Mae (Doxie) S. BS cum. laude, Ala. State U., 1974; MA, U. N. Ala., 1979. Cert. tchr. Ala. Kindergarten tchr. Russellville (Ala.) City Schs., 1975, Community Kindergarten, Tuscumbia, Ala., 1976-77, Florence (Ala.) City Schs., 1977—. Mem. Colbert-Lauderdale Day Care Coun., The Shoals, Ala., 1989; family day care provider, 1985-90; mem. pers. com. Florence City Sch. Adv. Coun., 1990-91. Sec., tutor Outreach, Reentry Ministries, Florence, 1992—; mentor Boys and Girls Club, Florence, 1992—. Named to Outstanding Young Women in Am., 1983. Mem. NEA, Ala. Edn. Assn. (Emerging Leader 1988), Florence Edn. Assn., Nat. Assn. for Edn. of Young Children, Delta Sigma Theta (Acad. Excellence 1979). Democrat. Baptist. Avocations: reading, music, drawing, travel, working with youth. Office: Harlan Elem Sch 2233 Mcburney Dr Florence AL 35630-1251

SIMPSON, ROBERT URQUHART, medical educator, researcher; b. Long Beach, Calif., May 12, 1950; s. John Robert Simpson, Marjorie Ann

Simpson; m. Julie Ann Spiroff; children: Anna, Elizabeth. PhD, U. Wis., 1979. Postdoctoral fellow biochemistry U. Wis., Madison, 1979—83; asst. prof. pharmacology U. Mich., Ann Arbor, 1983—89, assoc. prof. pharmacology, 1990—98, prof., 1998—. Chair study sect. NIH, Bethesda, 1993—2000. Author: (book) Calcium Regulated Hormones and Cardiovascular Disease, 1995 (awards including Am. Hypertension Assn., 1995); contbr. articles to sci. publs. Recipient numerous, NIH, 1983—; grantee, Am. Heart Assn., 1989—92. Mem.: AAAS (Member 1978—2001), Am. Soc. Pharmacology and Expl. Therapeutics (Member 1988—2001), Am. Heart Assn. (Member 1990—2001), Sigma Xi (Member 1978—2001). Avocations: traveling, gardening, fishing. Office: Univ Mich Med Sch Pharmacology: 1301 MSRB III #0632 Ann Arbor MI 48109 Office Fax: 734-763-4450. Personal E-mail: robsim@umich.edu. Business E-Mail: robsim@umich.edu.

SIMPSON, ROGER LYNDON, aerospace and ocean engineering educator, researcher; b. Roanoke, Va., Oct. 25, 1942; s. Carlyle Rodgers and Leona Dorothy (Austin) S.; m. Darlene Annette Brown; children: Scott Carlyle Simpson, Sarah Catherine. B of Mech. Engring., U. Va., 1964; MSME, Stanford U., 1965, PhD, 1968. Registered profl. engr., Tex. Devel. engr. GE, San Jose, Calif., 1968; prof. So. Meth. U., Dallas, 1969-83; Jack E. Cowling prof. of aerospace and ocean engring. Va. Poly. Inst. and State U., Blacksburg, 1983—. Contbr. over 140 articles to profl. jours. Fellow AIAA (bd. dirs. 1992-95, v.p. edn. 1995-98, v.p. publs. 2000-03), ASME. Baptist. Avocations: hunting, hiking, geneology. Office: Va Poly Inst State Univ Aerospace and Ocean Engring Blacksburg VA 24061

SIMPSON-STEEBER, MARYBETH, elementary school educator; b. Bayonne, NJ, Mar. 17, 1966; d. David B. and Rosanne L. (Setaro) S. BA, Douglass Coll., 1987; MEd, Rutgers U., 1988. Cert. tchr. Coord., day camp, art tchr. Y.W.C.A., Bayonne, N.J., 1984-87, tchr., group, 1987-88; substitute tchr. Bayonne Bd. Edn., 1985-87; tchr. South Bound Brook (N.J.) Bd. Edn., 1988—. Mem. N.J. Edn. Assn., Phi Beta Kappa, Kappa Delta Pi. Office: South Bound Brook Bd Edn 1 Zimmerman Pl South Bound Brook NJ 08880-1209

SIMS, DAYLA DIANNE, elementary school principal; b. Glendale, Calif., Apr. 12, 1957; d. Preston Paul Buby and Evangeline Ruth (Sickler) B.; m. Laurence J. Mahrenholtz, Nov. 21, 1987 (div. Feb. 1993); m. David Wesley Sims, June 30, 1997. AA, El Camino Jr. Coll., Torrance, Calif., 1975-77; BA, Calif. State U., Carson, 1979; MA, Calif. State U., L.A., 1990; EdD, U. LaVerne, Calif., 1996. Cert. edn. adminstr., Calif. Teller Ban of Am., Lawndale, Calif., 1977-79; tchr. Whittier (Calif.) City Sch. Dist., 1980-88, tchr., mentor, 1988-92; prin. Los Nietos Sch. Dist., Whittier, Calif., 1992-98; prin Redondo Beach (Calif.) Unified Sch. Dist., 1998—. Mem. AAUW, Calif. Assn. Bilingual Edn., Assn. Calif. Adminstrs., Computer Users in Edn., Whittier Area Sch. Adminstrs. (program chair 1993—). Democrat. Avocations: bird watching, running, bicycling, body building, reading. Office: Berly Hts Elem Sch 920 Beryl St Redondo Beach CA 90277-2236 Home: Apt 512 531 Esplanade Redondo Beach CA 90277-4097

SIMS, JANETTE ELIZABETH LOWMAN, educational director; b. Lincolnton, N.C., July 21, 1934; d. Lee Hobson and Myrtle Elizabeth (Travis) Lowman; m. Mickey Ray Sims, Feb. 2, 1951; children: Carol Lee, Rickey Ray. BS, Lenoir-Rhyne Coll., 1968; MAT, U. N.C., 1973; EdD, U. N.C., Greensboro, 1989. N.C. "G" tchg. cert; cert. devel. edn. specialist. Quality control supr. Kiser Roth Hosiery, Inc., Maiden, N.C., 1959-63; 9th grade phys. sci. and math. tchr. Cherryville (N.C.) Jr. H.S., 1968; phys. sci., chemistry and astronomy tchr. Maiden (N.C.) H.S., 1968-75; dir. studies lab. coord. Catawba Valley C.C., Hickory, N.C., 1975-79, physics, chemistry, math. and computer sci. instr., 1979-90, dir. developmental studies and learning assistance ctr., 1990-2001; ret., 2001. Apprentice program instr. Meredith/Burda Corp., Newton, NC, 1979—88; part-time instr. math. and physics Catawba Valley C.C. Mem. Conover Planning Bd., 2001—; trustee Catawba County Assn. for Spl. Edn., Conover, 1978—79, Catawba Valley Found., Hickory, 1993—96, chair, 1996; tchr., mem. choir Faith Luth. Ch., Conover, 1980—, mem. ch. coun., 1995—97, pres. congregation and ch. coun., 1997—98, v.p. congregation and ch. coun., 2001—03. Mem. NEA, N.C. Assn. Educators (local unit pres.), Nat. Assn. Developmental Educators, N.C. Assn. Developmental Educators (regional chair 1990), Atlantic Assn. Physics Tchrs. (chair nominations com. 1992), N.C. Math. Assn. Two-Yr. Colls. (chairperson devel. math. com. 1991-93, sec. 1996-2000), Am. Legion Aux., Delta Kappa Gamma. Avocations: sewing, cooking. Home and Office: 300 Parlier Ave NE Conover NC 28613-9312 E-mail: jsims721@conninc.com.

SIMS, LARRY KYLE, secondary school educator; b. Ft. Worth, Dec. 28, 1944; s. Kyle G. and Gladys (Holloway) S.; m. Stephenie Chandler, Aug. 30, 1968; children: Alan Dean (dec.), Roy B. BBA, Howard Payne, Brownwood, Tex., 1969; MEd, Colo. State U., 1975. Cert. tchr., Tex., Wyo.; lic. real estate broker, Tex., Wyo. Coord. Breckenridge (Tex.) High Sch., 1970-74; multi-occupations coord. Lander (Wyo.) Valley High Sch., 1974-76; diversified occupations coord. Riverton (Wyo.) Career Ctr., 1977-79; mktg. edn. coord. Stephenville (Tex.) High Sch., 1986—, tech prep coord., 1994—. Author: Little Spotted Moo, 1991. Mem. Am. Vocat. Assn., Nat. Mktg. Educators, Tex. Vocat. Assn. Consortium, Mktg. Educators Tex. (state pres. 1989-90). Baptist. Avocations: snow skiing, gold hunting, photography. Home: HC 51 Box 317A Stephenville TX 76401-9711 Office: 2655 W Overhill Dr Stephenville TX 76401-1971

SIMS, MARCIE LYNNE, English language educator, writer; b. Monrovia, Calif., Feb. 22, 1963; d. Charles Eugene and Delores May (Wonert) S.; m. Douglas Todd Cole; children: Marcus Anthony Cole, Thomas Halvor Cole. BA in English, Calif. State Poly., 1986; MA in English, San Diego State U., 1990. Page U.S. Senate, Washington, 1979; instr. Calif. Conservation Corps, San Diego, 1990; instr. in English Shoreline C.C., Seattle, 1990-94, Seattle Ctrl. C.C., 1990-94, Green River C.C., Auburn, Wash., 1994—. Founder Wild Mind Women Writers Workshop, Seattle, 1992—. Author: Soul-Making: John Keats and the Stages of Death, 1990; contbg. author Moms on Line, 1996—; editor Espial Lit. jour. Vol. cons. Camp Fire, Wash., 1994-96. Mem. Am. Fedn. Tchrs., The Keats-Shelley Orgn., Wash. Fed. Tchrs. (exec. bd. mem. 1993-94), Phi Kappa Phi, Sigma Tau Delta. Democrat. Avocations: cooking, tennis. Office: Green River CC 12401 SE 320th St Auburn WA 98092-3622 E-mail: msims@grcc.ctc.edu.

SIMSON, GARY JOSEPH, law educator; b. Newark, Mar. 18, 1950; s. Marvin and Mildred (Silberg) S.; m. Rosalind Slivka, Aug. 15, 1971; children: Nathaniel, Jennie Anne. BA, Yale Coll., 1971; JD, Yale U., 1974. Bar: Conn. 1974, N.Y. 1980. Law clk. to judge U.S. Ct. Appeals 2d Cir., 1974-75; from asst. prof. law to prof. law U. Tex., 1975-80; prof. law Cornell U., Ithaca, N.Y., 1980-97, prof. law, assoc. dean, 1997—. Vis. prof. law Cornell U., Ithaca, 1979-80, U. Calif., Berkeley, 1986; chmn. adv. bd. law casebook series Carolina Acad. Press. Author: Issues and Perspectives in Conflict of Laws, 1985, 3d edit., 1997; contbr. articles to profl. jours. Mem. ABA, ACLU, Phi Beta Kappa. Office: Cornell U Law Sch Myron Taylor Hall Ithaca NY 14853 E-mail: simson@law.mail.cornell.edu.

SIMSON, JO ANNE, retired anatomy and cell biology educator, biologist, educator; b. Chgo., Nov. 19, 1936; d. Kenneth Brown and Helen Marjorie (Pascoe) Valentine; m. Arnold Simson, June 1961 (div.); 1 child, Maria; m. Michael Smith, Nov. 10, 1971 (div.); children: Elisabeth Smith, Briana Smith. BA, Kalamazoo Coll., 1959; MS, U. Mich., 1961; PhD, SUNY, Syracuse, 1969. Fellow Temple U. Health Sci. Ctr., Phila., 1968-70; asst. prof. Med. U. S.C., Charleston, 1970-76, assoc. prof., 1976-83, prof. anatomy and cell biology, 1983-96, prof. emerita, 1996—2001. With overseas program U. Md., 1999-2001; featured in Smithsonian exhibit, Sci. in Am. Life, 1994—. Contbr. articles to profl. jours.; author short stories and poems. Active adult edn. Unitarian Ch., Charleston, 1973-75, social action, 1990-92. Grantee NSF, 1959-60, NIH, 1966-67, 72-87, 91-95. Mem. Am. Assn. Anatomists, Am. Soc. Cell Biology, Histochem. Soc. (sec. 1979-82, exec. com. 1985-89), Fogarty Internat. Fellowship Bioctr. (Basel, Switzerland, 1987-88), Amnesty Internat. (newsletter editor Group 168 1982-86), Phi Beta Kappa. Home: 1760 Pittsford Cir Charleston SC 29412-4110

SIMUN, PATRICIA BATES, education educator, consultant; b. Pitts., Apr. 20, 1931; d. A.E. Griffith and Mary Effa (Casey) Bates; m. Richard Vincent Simun, Dec. 31, 1961; children: Mary Bates-Alt, Ann Eugenia Simun-Park. BS in Edn., W.Va. U., 1952; MA, U. Pitts., 1962, PhD, 1967. Cert. tchr., Calif., Pa., W.Va.; cert. counselor, Pa. Tchr. Avonworth Union Sch. Dist., Ben Avon, Pa., 1955-57; tchr. placement dir. Carnegie-Mellon U., 1957-61; rsch. asst. U. Pitts., 1961-62, rsch. assoc., 1962-63; chair ednl. founds. Calif. State U., L.A., 1983-84, assoc. chair adminstrn., counseling and founds. dept., 1985, prof. edn., 1967-91, dir. Costa Rica travel study, 1988-98, prof. emerita, 1991—. Vis. disting. prof. Universidad Autonoma, Guadalajara, Mex., summer 1975; cons., evaluation project support Calif. State U./L.A. Unified Sch. Dist., 1992-95; cons., evaluation integration L.A. Unified Sch.Dist., 1981-91; cons. ACLU, L.A., 1976-80; participant Alternative Edn. Exch., 1975, Internat. Options in Pub. Edn., Pasadena, Calif., 1975, others; discussion leader Am. Edn. Rsch. Assn. evaluation conf., San Francisco, 1977; speaker in field. Editor Excellence Through Equity, 1984-87; contbr. articles to profl. jours. Bd. dirs. Cmty. Child Care, Inc., L.A., 1985-88; mem. L.A. High Cmty. Adv. Voun., 1980-84; advisor Inst. Tchr. Leadership, L.A., 1978-80; mem. edn. com. Cmty. Rels. Conf. So. Calif., L.A., 1980-84; docent Page Mus. of La Brea Discoveries, 2001—. Recipient Cert. of Merit Human Rels. Commn., L.A., 1978, Cert. of Outstanding Svc. So. Poverty Law Ctr., 1984, Cert. of Appreciation L.A. Unified Sch. Dist., 1977, Outstanding Svc. award Mid-City Alternative Sch., 1982; Docent George C. Page Mus., 2001—. Mem. Am. Ednl. Rsch. Assn. (SIG com. chair 1983-84, sec. 1984-89), Calif. Edn. Rsch. Assn., Phi Lambda Theta, Kappa Delta Pi, Phi Beta Delta. Avocations: knitting, hiking, stamp collecting, reading. Home: 1019 S Longwood Ave Los Angeles CA 90019-1755 Office: Calif State U 5151 State University Dr Los Angeles CA 90032-4226 E-mail: psimun@pacbell.net.

SIMUNS, JUDITH MATA, elementary school vice-principal; b. Danao, Cebu, The Philippines, Dec. 23, 1946; came to U.S., 1976; d. Casiano and Rosalia (Batiquin) Mata; m. M. J. Simuns, Jan. 19, 1976. BS in Elem. Edn. magna cum laude, Cebu Normal Coll., Cebu City, The Philippines, 1967; MA in Spl. Edn. for Gifted, U. Philippines, Diliman, 1970; MA in Ednl. Adminstrn. with distinction, Calif. State U., Fresno, 1987. Preliminary adminstrv., life multiple subject teaching credentials, Calif.; cert. life lang. devel. specialist, Calif. Elem. tchr. Danao (The Philippines) City Pub. Schs., 1967-76; tutor Lane Elem. Sch., Fresno, 1979-80, elem. tchr., 1980-81, Calwa Elem. Sch., Fresno, 1981-87, tchr. on spl. assignment, 1987-89; guidance instrnl. specialist Norseman Elem. Sch., Fresno, 1989-92; vice-prin. Jefferson Elem. Sch., Fresno, 1992—. Grad. instr. Cebu Normal Coll. Grad. Sch., 1971-75; tchr. Fresno County Migrant Edn. Summer Program, 1978-89; leadership trainee Fresno Unified Sch. Dist., 1985-87. Master tchr. scholar Calif. State U., 1986-88. Mem. Orgn. Filipino-Am. Educators (pres. 1985-87, treas. 1990-92), Assn. Calif. Sch. Adminstrs. (sec. Fresno Unified Sch. Dist. 1993—), Phi Kappa Phi. Avocations: travel, photography, gardening. Home: 6026 N Winchester Ave Fresno CA 93704-1639

SINCERO, ARCADIO PACQUIAO, engineering educator; b. Antipolo, Tuburan, Cebu, The Philippines, Nov. 13, 1938; came to U.S., 1973; s. Santiago Encarguiz Sincero and Guadiosa Lipar Pacquiao; m. Gregoria Managase Alivio, Nov. 16, 1969; children: Roscoe, Arcadio Jr. BSChemE, Cebu Inst. Tech., 1965; ME, Asian Inst. Tech., Bangkok, 1968; DSc in Environ. Engring., George Washington U., 1987. Registered profl. engr., Md., Pa. Assoc. prof. civil and chem. engring. Cebu Inst. Tech., 1969-72; assoc. prof. Inst. Tech. Far Ea. U., the Philippines, 1972-73; planner critical path method Consolidated Engring. Co., Balt., 1973-74; pub. works engr. City of Balt., 1974-75; pub. health engr. State of Md., Balt., 1975-78, water resources engr., 1978-79, chief permits divsn., 1979-88; assoc. prof. civil engring. Morgan State U., Balt., 1988—. Author: (with G. A. Sincero) Environmental Engineering: A Design Approach, 1996, Physical-Chemical Treatment of Water and Wastewater; contbr. articles to profl. jours. Mem. ASCE, AIChE, AAUP, Am. Soc. Engring. Edn., Asian Soc. Environ. Protection, Water Environment Fedn. Achievements include research in environmental engineering, water quality, treatment of water by reverse osmosis for removal of organic chemicals, pollution engineering. Office: Morgan State U Dept Civil Engring Baltimore MD 21239

SINCLAIR, LINDA DRUMWRIGHT, educational consultant; b. Norfolk, Va., Aug. 4, 1942; d. Raymond Edward and Evelyn Elizabeth (Edwards) Drumwright; m. Charles Armstrong Sinclair, Oct. 5, 1962; children: William, Dianne, Sandy. BS, U. S.C., 1974, MA, 1976, postgrad. Cert. tchr. in biology, chemistry, physics. Sci. tchr. Keenan H.S., Columbia, S.C., 1976-77; chemistry/physics tchr. Lexington (S.C.) H.S., 1977-93; talented/gifted tchr. U. S.C., Columbia, 1988; tchr. rsch. program Oak Ridge (Tenn.) Nat. Lab., 1989; rschr. Savannah River Ecology Lab., Aiken, S.C., 1991-92; state sci. edn. cons. S.C. Dept. Edn., Columbia, 1993—. Cons. Prentice Hall Pub., Princeton, N.J., 1992-93. Author: Operation Radon, 1993. Adv. bd. S.C. Forestry Commn., Columbia, 1993—, S.C. Environ. Coalition, Columbia, 1993—, S.C. Sci. Coun., Columbia, 1989—; mem., com. chair Lexington Woman's Club, 1986—; v.p. Lexington Garden Club, 1983—. Named S.C. Sci. Tchr. of the Yr., S.C. Acad. Sci., 1986, Sigma Xi, 1986, S.C. Chemistry Tchr. of the Yr., S.C. Chem. Soc., 1992; recipient Presdl. Award for Excellence in Sci. Teaching, NSF, 1993. Mem. S.C. Sci. Coun. (v.p., pres.), S.C. Chemistry Tchrs. Assn. (bd. dirs. 1987—), S.C. Acad. Sci. (bd. dirs. 1982—), S.C. Jr. Acad. Sci. (bd. dirs. 1980—), S.C. Environ. Edn. Assn. (bd. dirs. 1990—), Midlands Sci. and Math. Hub (bd. dirs. 1993—). Republican. Lutheran. Avocatins: horseback riding, gardening, swimming, water sports. Home: 107 Hermitage Rd Lexington SC 29072-2221 Office: SC Dept Edn 801-H Rutledge Bldg 1429 Senate St Columbia SC 29201-3730

SINCLAIR, ROBERT EWALD, physician, educator; b. Columbus, Ohio, Jan. 19, 1924; s. George Albert and Bertha Florence (Ewald) S.; m. Mary Almira Underwood, Mar. 31, 1945; children: Marcia Ann, Bonnie Sue. BA, Ohio State U., 1948, MD, 1952. Lic. physician, Ohio, Colo., Ala., Kans. Intern Mt. Carmel Hosp., Columbus, 1952-53; resident in neurology and psychiatry Columbus State Hosp., 1964-66, chief psychiatric resident adolescent unit, 1965-66; pvt. practice medicine Columbus, 1953-57, Granville, Ohio, 1957-64; dir. student health svc., prof. health edn., team physician Denison U., 1957-64; dir. student health svc., team physician U. Cin., 1966-70; dir. Lafene Student Health Ctr. and U. Hosp.; team physician Kans. State U., Manhattan, 1970-80; dir. Russell Student Health Ctr. and Hosp.; prof. medicine U. Ala., University, 1980-92, ret. Physician Westinghouse Electric Corp., Columbus, 1953-57; asst. zone chief Civilian Def., Columbus, 1954-57; mem. Licking County Bd. Health, Ohio, 1958-59. Bd. dirs. social health com. Cin. and Hamilton County, Ohio, 1967-70, drug abuse and edn. com., 1968-70. With USNR, 1943-46. Mem. AMA, Ohio Med. Soc., Kans. Med. Soc., Ala. Med. Soc., Columbus Acad. Medicine, Licking County Med. Soc. (Ohio), Riley County Med. Soc. (Kans.), Tuscaloosa County Med. Soc., Nat. Athletic Trainers Assn., Ohio Coll. Health Assn. (editor Newsletter 1968-70, pres. 1970-71), Central Coll. Health Assn. (pres. 1972-73), So. Coll. Health Assn. (pres. 1986), St. Andrews Soc., Delta Tau Delta (faculty advisor), Nu Sigma Nu, Nu Sigma Nu Alumni Assn. (pres. 1953-54), Kiwanis, Rotary. Home: 1 Rollingwood Tuscaloosa AL 35406-2261

SINCOFF, STEVEN LAWRENCE, chemistry educator; b. N.Y.C., Apr. 17, 1948; s. Murray B. and Lillian (Goldberg) S.; m. Marcella Seay, June 12, 1993; children by previous marriage: Kristina Lynne, Carolyn Suzanne. BSChemE, N.J. Inst. Tech., 1969, MSChemE, 1972; PhD in Analytical Chemistry, Ohio State U., 1980. Commd. 2d lt. USAF, 1969, advanced through grades to lt. col., 1987, retired, 1991, fuels mgmt. officer, 1970-74; chem. engr. Aero. Systems Div., Wright-Patterson AFB, Ohio, 1974-77; assoc. prof. chemistry USAF Acad., Colorado Springs, Colo., 1980-84, dir. continuing edn. dept. chemistry, 1982-84; chief gas analysis lab. McClellan (AFB) Cen. Lab., Calif., 1984-88; exec. officer to comdr. Tech. Ops. Div. McClellan AFB, Calif., 1988-89, chief info. officer, 1989-91; gen. mgr. ChemWest Analytical Lab., Sacramento, 1991-92; dir. ops. Barringer Labs., Inc., Golden, Colo., 1992-94; instr. chemistry C.C. Aurora, Colo., 1995-98, Butte Coll., Oroville, Calif., 1998—, Met. State Coll. of Denver, 1995—98. Reviewer chemistry textbooks Saunders Pub., Phila., 1983-84. Mem. Am. Chem. Soc., Air Force Assn. Jewish. Avocations: microcomputers, hiking. Home and Office: 14574 Carnegie Rd Magalia CA 95954-9647 Office: Butte Coll Dept Chemistry Oroville CA 95965 E-mail: sincoffst@butte.edu.

SINEATH, TIMOTHY WAYNE, library educator, university dean; b. Jacksonville, Fla., May 21, 1940; s. Holcombe Asbury and Christine Marcel (Cook) S.; m. Patricia Ann Greenwood, June 8, 1962; children: Philip Greenwood, Paul Byron. BA, Fla. State U., 1962, MS, 1963; PhD (Higher Edn. Act fellow), U. Ill., 1970. Reference librarian U. Ga., 1963-64, catalog librarian, 1964-66; acad. coordinator continuing edn. in library sci. U. Ill., 1966-68; asst. prof. library sci. Simmons Coll., 1970-74, coordinator doctoral program, 1974-77; prof., dean Coll. Libr. Sci. and Info. Sci. U. Ky., Lexington, 1977-87, prof., 1987-97, dir. sch. Libr. and Info. Sci., 1997—. Cons. to libraries, schs., chs., industry; mem. Lexington (Ky.) Public Library Bd., 1978— Author profl. reports; contbr. articles on library and info. sci., gen. info. mgmt., organizational and small group behavior to profl. jours. Mem. ALA, Am. Soc. Info. Sci., Assn. for Libr. and Info. Sci. Edn. (pres. 1993). Episcopalian. Home: 3418 Bay Leaf Dr Lexington KY 40502-3804 Office: U Ky Mi King Bldg Lexington KY 40506-0039 E-mail: tsineath@uky.edu.

SING, DORIS ANNE, music educator; b. Houston, Oct. 1, 1947; d. Theron Ponton Sr. and Anna Agnes (Dethlefsen) Spradley; m. William B. Sing, Sept. 1, 1967; children: Erin Elaine, Emily Elizabeth. BS in Edn. cum laude, U. Houston, 1970, BMus cum laude, 1990, MMus in Music Lit., 2000. Cert. tchr. elem. and spl. edn., Tex. Dir. children's choir St. Andrew's Presbyn. Ch., Houston, 1984-90; tchr. music St. Andrew's Presbyn. Sch., Houston, 1991-93; founder, dir. Arts a la Carte, Houston, 1993—. Elder St. Andrew's Presbyn. Ch., 1992-94. Mem. Early Childhood Music and Movement Assn., KinderMusik Educators Assn. (cert. tchr.), ORFF-Schulwerk Assn., Phi Kappa Phi, Kappa Delta Pi. Avocations: singing, listening to classical music, opera. Office: Arts a la Carte 3637 W Alabama St Ste 490 Houston TX 77027-5907 E-mail: dsing@artsalacarte.com., dsing@houston.rr.com.

SINGER, ARMAND EDWARDS, foreign language educator; b. Detroit, Nov. 30, 1914; s. Elvin Satori Singer and Fredericka Elizabeth (Edwards) Singer Goetz; m. Mary Rebecca White, Aug. 8, 1940; 1 child, Fredericka Ann Hill. AB, Amherst Coll., 1935; MA, Duke U., 1939, PhD, 1944; diplôme, U. Paris, 1939; postgrad., Ind. U., summer 1964. Teaching fellow in sci. Amherst Coll., 1935-36; instr. French and Spanish, part-time Duke, 1938-40; teaching fellow Romance langs. W.Va. U., Morgantown, 1940-41, instr., 1941-47, asst. prof., 1947-55, assoc. prof., 1955-60, prof., 1960-80, prof. emeritus, 1980—, chmn. program for humanities, 1963-72, chmn. dept. integrated studies, 1963, acting chmn. dept. religion and program for humanities, 1973, dir. ann. colloquium on modern lit. and film, 1976—80, 1985—86, 1996—97, 1999—2001. Author: A Bibliography of the Don Juan Theme: Versions and Criticism, 1954, The Don Juan Theme, Versions and Criticism: An Annotated Bibliography, 1965, Paul Bourget, 1975, The Don Juan Theme: A Bibliography of Versions, Analogues, Uses, and Adaptations, 1993, supplement, 2003, The Armand E. Singer Tibet, 1809-1975, 1995, supplement, 1998, The Armand E. Singer Nepal, 1772-1961 and Beyond, 1997, The Officials of Tibet, 1999, The Chinese Presence in Tibet, 2002, (with J.F. Stasny) Anthology of Readings: Humanities I, 1966, Anthology of Readings: Humanities II, 1967, (with R.F. Gould) A Graded Catalog of Himalayan Mountaineering Correspondence, 2002; editor: West Virginia George Sand Conference Papers, 1981, (with Jürgen E. Schlunk) Martin Walser: International Perspectives, 1987, Doctor Faustus: Archetypal Subtext at the Millennium, 1999; editor W.Va. U. Philol. Papers, 1948-50, 53-55, editor-in-chief, 1951-52, 1955—; editor: 1001 Horny Limericks by Ward Marden, 1996; editor, contbr. Essays on the Literature of Mountaineering, 1982; bd. editors, The European Legacy, 2003—; contbr. numerous articles to profl. and philatelic jours. Bd. dirs. Cmty. Concert Assn., Morgantown, 1959-60, Humanities Found. W.Va., 1981-87. Recipient 4th Ann. Humanities award, W.Va. Humanities Coun., 1990, Armand E. and Mary W. Singer Professorship in Humanities named in honor of Armand Singer and wife Mary Singer, 1999. Mem. MLA (internat. bibliography com. 1956-59, nat. del. assembly 1975-78), So. Atlantic MLA (exec. com. 1971-74), Am. Assn. Tchrs. Spanish and Portuguese, Am. Philatelic Soc., Nepal and Tibet Philatelic Study Cir. (pres. 1999—), Nepal Philatelic Soc., Collectors Club of N.Y., Phi Beta Kappa. Republican. Home: 248 Grandview Ave Morgantown WV 26501-6925

SINGER, HOWARD JACK, biology educator; b. Newark, Sept. 4, 1940; s. Nat I. and Rose (Alboum) S.; m. Helena Liisa Niskanen, May 29, 1986; children: Jamie Alexander Niskanen-Singer. BA, Oberlin Coll., 1962; MS, U. Minn., 1966; PhD, Tufts U., 1970. Prof. biology N.J. City U. (formerly Jersey City State Coll.), Jersey City, 1970—. Cons. Proforma Base Corp., Jersey City, 1985-87, Instructivision, Inc., Livingston, N.J., 1988-89; researcher SUNY Downstate Med. Ctr., Bklyn., 1987-89. Contbr. articles to profl. jours. Pres. Van Vorst Pk. Assn., Jersey City, 1977-78; treas. Environ. Voters Alliance, N.J., 1984-90; dir. Hudson County (N.J.) Toxic Task Force, 1980-86; active Scientists Com. for Pub. Info., N.Y.C., 1976-80. Am. Chem. Soc. scholar, 1958-62; fellow NIH, 1966-70, NSF, 1961. Mem.: Am. Fedn. Tchrs. (membership chmn. 1989—), Theobald Smith Soc. (pres. 1996—97, alt. nat. councilor 1997—99, nat. councilor 2000—, alt. nat. councilor 2002—03, chmn. program com., nat. councilor 2003—), Am. Soc. for Microbiology. Avocations: skiing, art nouveau, scuba, tennis. Home: 297 York St Jersey City NJ 07302-4016 Office: NJ City U 2039 John F Kennedy Blvd Jersey City NJ 07305-1527 E-mail: hsinger@njcu.edu.

SINGER, IRVING, philosophy educator; b. N.Y.C., Dec. 24, 1925; s. Isidore and Nettie (Stromer) S.; m. Josephine Fisk, June 10, 1949; children— Anne, Margaret, Emily, Benjamin. AB summa cum laude, Harvard U., 1948, MA, 1949, PhD, 1952. Instr. philosophy Cornell U., 1953-56; asst. prof. U. Mich., 1956-59; vis. lectr. Johns Hopkins U., 1957-58; mem. faculty M.I.T., 1958—, prof. philosophy, 1969—. Author: Santayana's Aesthetics, 1957, The Nature of Love: Plato to Luther, 1966, rev. edit., 1984, The Goals of Human Sexuality, 1973, Mozart and Beethoven, 1977, The Nature of Love: Courtly and Romantic, 1984, The Nature of Love: The Modern World, 1987, Meaning in Life: The Creation of Value, 1992, The Pursuit of Love, 1994, The Creation of Value, 1996, The Harmony of Nature and Spirit, 1996, Reality Transformed: Film as Meaning and Technique, 1998, George Santayana: Literary Philosopher, 2000, Feeling and Imagination: The Vibrant Flux of our Existence, 2001, Sex: A Philosophical Primer, 2001, Explorations in Love and Sex, 2001, Three Philosophical Filmmakers: Hitchcock, Welles, Renoir, 2004. Served with AUS, 1944-46. Fellow Guggenheim Found., 1965, Rockefeller Found., 1970, Bollingen Found., 1966; grantee Am. Council Learned Socs., 1966; Fulbright fellow, 1955. Mem. Am. Philos. Assn. Office: MIT Rm E39-351 Cambridge MA 02139

SINGER, ISADORE MANUEL, mathematician, educator; b. Detroit, May 3, 1924; married; 5 children. BS, U. Mich., 1944; MS, U. Chgo., 1948, PhD in Math., 1950; ScD (hon.), Tulane U., 1981; LLD (hon.), U. Mich., 1989, U. Ill., Chgo. Moore instr. math. MIT, Cambridge, 1950—52, prof. math., 1956—70, Norbert Wiener prof., 1970—79, John D. MacArthur prof. math. (1st holder), 1983—, Inst. prof., 1987—; asst. prof. UCLA, 1952—54; vis. prof. math U. Calif., Berkeley, 1977—79, prof., 1979—83, Miller prof. math., 1982—83, prof. math., 1977—83. Vis. asst. prof. math. Columbia U., N.Y.C., 1954—55; mem. Inst. Advanced Study, 1955—56; past steering com. Ctr. for Non-Linear Scis., Los Alamos Nat. Labs.; adv. bd. Inst. Theoretical Physics, U. Calif., Santa Barbara; bd. dirs. Santa Fe Inst.; mem. various organizing coms. ; editor procs. for confs. in field. Former editor profl. jours. Recipient Nat. medal of Sci., 1983, Steele prize Lifetime Achievement, 2000; fellow Alfred P. Sloan, 1959—62, Guggenheim, 1968—69, 1975—76. Mem.: NAS (past councillor, former mem. com. math. and phys. scis., other coms.), Internat. Congress Mathematicians (program com.; 1986, Wigner prize 1989), Am. Phys. Soc., Am. Math. Soc. (v.p. 1970—72, past exec. com., Bocher Meml. prize 1969, Pub. Svc. award 1993), Am. Acad. Arts and Scis., Am. Philos. Soc. Office: MIT Dept of Math Bldg 2 Rm 387 77 Massachusetts Ave Cambridge MA 02139-4307

SINGER, J. DAVID, political science educator; b. Bklyn., Dec. 7, 1925; s. Morris L. and Anne (Newman) S.; m. C. Diane Macaulay, Apr., 1990; children: Kathryn Louise, Eleanor Anne. BA, Duke U., 1946; LLD (hon.), Northwestern U., 1983; PhD, NYU, 1956. Instr. NYU, 1954-55, Vassar Coll., 1955-57; vis. fellow social relations Harvard U., 1957-58; vis. asst. prof. U. Mich., Ann Arbor, 1958-60, sr. scientist Mental Health Research Inst., 1960-82, assoc. prof., 1964-65, prof. polit. sci., 1965—, coordinator World Politics Program, 1969-75, 81-90; vis. prof. U. Oslo and Inst. Social Research, 1963-64, 90, Carnegie Endowment Internat. Peace and Grd. Inst. Internat. Studies, Geneva, 1967-68, Zuma and U. Mannheim (W. Ger.), 1976, Grad. Inst. Internat. Studies, Geneva, 1983-84; U. Groningen, The Netherlands, 1991; Nat. Chengchi U., Taiwan, 1998. Author: Financing International Organization: The United Nations Budget Process, 1961, Deterrence, Arms Control and Disarmament: Toward a Synthesis in National Security Policy, 1962, rev. 1984, (with Melvin Small) The Wages of War, 1816-1965: A Statistical Handbook, 1972, (with Susan Jones) Beyond Conjecture in International Politics: Abstracts of Data Based Research, 1972, (with Dorothy La Barr) The Study of International Politics: A Guide to Sources for the Student, Teacher and Researcher, 1976, Correlates of War I and II, 1979, 80, (with Melvin Small) Resort to Arms: International and Civil War, 1816-1980, 1982, Models, Methods, and Progress: A Peace Research Odyssey, 1990, (with Paul Diehl) Measuring the Correlates of War, 1998, (with D. Geller) Nations at War, 1998; monographs; contbr. articles to profl. jours.; mem. editorial bd. ABC: Polit. Sci. and Govt., 1968-84, Polit. Sci. Reviewer, 1971—, Conflict Mgmt. and Peace Sci., 1978—, Etudes Polemologigues, 1978—, Internat. Studies Quar., 1989—, Jour. Conflict Resolution, 1989—, Internat. Interactions, 1989—. With USNR, 1943-66. Ford fellow, 1956; Ford grantee, 1957-58; Phoenix Meml. Fund grantee, 1959,, 1981-82; Fulbright scholar, 1963-64; Carnegie Corp. research grantee, 1963-67; NSF grantee, 1967-76, 1986-89, 1992-94; Guggenheim grantee, 1978-79 Mem. Am. Polit. Sci. Assn. (Helen Dwight Reid award com. 1967, 95, chmn. Woodrow Wilson award com., chmn. nominating com. 1970), Internat. Polit. Sci. Assn. (chmn. conflict and peace rsch. com. 1974—), World Assn. Internat. Rels., Internat. Soc. Polit. Psychology, Internat. Soc. Rsch. on Aggression, Social Sci. History Assn., Peace Sci. Soc., Internat. Peace Rsch. Assn. (pres. 1972-73), Consortium on Peace Rsch., Fedn. Am. Scientists (nat. coun. 1991-95), Union Concerned Scientists, Arms Control Assn., Internat. Studies Assn. (pres. 1985-86), Com. Nat. Security, Am. Com. on East-West Accord, World Federalist Assn. Office: U Mich Dept Polit Sci 505 S State St Ann Arbor MI 48109-1045

SINGER, ROBERT NORMAN, motor behavior educator; b. Bklyn., Sept. 27, 1936; s. Abraham and Ann (Norman) S.; m. Beverly; children: Richard, Bonni Jill. BS, Bklyn. Coll., 1961; MS, Pa. State U., 1962; PhD, Ohio State U., 1964. Instr. phys. edn. Ohio State U., Columbus, 1963-64, asst. prof., 1964-65, Ill. State U., Normal, 1965-67, dir. motor learning lab., 1965-69, assoc. prof., 1968-69, asst. dean Coll. Applied Sci. and Tech., 1967-69; asso. prof., dir. motor learning lab. Mich. State U., East Lansing, 1969-70; prof. Fla. State U., Tallahassee, 1970-87, dir. motor learning lab., 1970-72, dir. div. human performance, 1972-75, dir. Motor Behavior Ctr., 1975-87; chair dept. of exercise and sport scis. U. Fla., Gainesville, 1987—. Lectr. in N.Am., S.Am., Africa, Australia, Asia and Europe; cons. in field. Author: Motor Learning and Human Performance, 1968, rev. edit., 1975, 80, Coaching, Athletics and Psychology, 1972, Physical Education, 1972, Teaching Physical Education, 1974, rev. edit., 1980, Laboratory and Field Experiments in Motor Learning, 1975, Myths and Truths in Sports Psychology, 1975, The Learning of Motor Skills, 1982, Sustaining Motivation in Sport, 1984, Peak Performance, 1986; editor: Readings in Motor Learning, 1972, The Psychomotor Domain, 1972, Foundations of Physical Education, 1976, Completed Research in Health, Physical Education and Recreation, 1968-74, Handbook of Research on Sport Psychology, 1993, Handbook of Sport Psychology, 2001; mem. editl. bd. Rsch. Quar., 1968-81, Jour. Motor Behavior, 1968-81, Jour. Sport and Exercise Psychology, 1979-92, The Sport Psychologist, 1986-94, The Internat. Jour. Sport Psychology, 1977-88, Jour. Applied Sport Psychology, 1987-95; reviewer numerous jours.; contbr. articles to numerous anthologies and profl. jours. Served with U.S. Army, 1955-58. Recipient Disting. Alumnus award Bklyn. Coll., 1989. Mem. AAHPERD, APA (pres. divsn. of exercise and sport psychology 1995-97), Am. Acad. Kinesiology and Phys. Edn. (pres. 1995-96), Internat. Soc. Sport Psychology (prex. 1985-89, 90-93), Am. Ednl. Rsch. Assn., N.Am. Soc. Sport Psychology and Phys. Activity. Home: 6305 NW 56th Ln Gainesville FL 32653-3116 Office: U Fla 100 Florida Gym Gainesville FL 32653

SINGER-CHANG, GAIL LESLIE, social sciences educator, assistant dean for student affairs; d. Frank Max (Stepfather) and Rona Jane Singer; m. Anthony Chang. BA in Journalism, San Diego State U., 1988; MS in Counseling, Calif. State U., Fullerton, 1992; MA in Clin. Psychology, Calif. Sch. Profl. Psychology, 1994, D of Psychology in Clin. Psychology, 1996. Pupil pers. svcs. credential Calif. Asst. prof. family medicine, social and behavioral scis., asst. dean student affairs Western U. of Health Scis., Pomona, Calif., 1999—. Orgnl. cons., Irvine, Calif., 1998—99; program dir., doctor-patient communication program Western U. of Health Sciences, Pomona, Calif., 1999—; post-doctoral psychology intern El Toro Marine Base Family Services Ctr., El Toro, Calif., 1997—99; psychology intern Kaiser Permanente, Tustin, Calif., 1995—96, Orange Coast Coll. Student Health Ctr., Costa Mesa, Calif., 1994—95; counseling intern Teen-Age Pregnancy and Parenting Program, Fullerton, Calif., 1991—91; adj. prof. Concordia U., Irvine, Calif., 1998—99, Calif. State U., Fullerton, 1999; presenter in field. Presenter (profl. presentation) Enabling Disability Education: The Value of Using Disabled Persons as Standardized Patients, 10th Internat. Ottawa Conf. Med. Edn., 2002 (Greatest Profl. Promise, 1992), Creative Use of Assessment and Feedback: Increasing Deep Learning and Professionalism, Western Assn. Schs. and Colls., 2002, Psychosocial Aspects of the Physician-Patient Intervention, Soc. Psychol. Anthropology, 2003. Mem.: Assn. Profl. Cons., Am. Anthropol. Assn., Assn. for the Behavioral Scis. and Med. Edn., Soc. of Teachers of Family Medicine. Office: Western U Health Scis 309 East 2d St Pomona CA 91766 Office Fax: 909-469-5514. E-mail: gsingerchang@westernu.edu.

SINGERMAN, DONA FATIBENO, reading specialist; b. Cleve., July 6, 1939; d. Pasquale and Mary (Del Priore) Fatibeno; children: Camille Swartz, David E. BA, Lake Erie Coll., 1967; MEd, Cleve. State U., 1977; cert. in supervision, John Carroll U., 1985; student, Cambridge (Eng.) U., 1990-91. Cert. tchr. and supr., prin., Ohio. Tchr. Painesville-Mentor Schs., Ohio, Mentor (Ohio) Schs., tchr. chpt. I reading, 1985—2002, ESL tchr., 2001—02. Mem. Gephart Symposium, U. Colo., summer 1992; chmn. Internat. Literacy, OCIRA, 1995, membership chair Lake coun., 2001-02; tchr. home instrn. grades 2-11; tchr. ESL Reynolds and Brentmoor Sch. k-8; home tutor, 2000-01. Vol. Lake County Hist. Soc.; sec. Friends of Mentor Pub. Libr., 1990-91. Joseph Nemeth scholar (OCIRA), 1995. Mem. AAUW (legis. chair Mentor br. 1990-91, treas. 1991-93, chair Ednl. Founds. 2000—), Coun. Exceptional Children, Internat. Reading Assn. (v.p. Lake-Geauga unit 1990-91, 91-92, pres. 1992-93, 98-99, chair internat. lit. com. Ohio 1996-97), Phi Delta Kappa (program v.p. N.E. Ohio unit 1990-91, pres. 1991-92, Gerald Read Internat. scholar 1992)

SINGH, INDERJIT, nephrologist, internist, medical educator; b. Patiala, India, Oct. 17, 1962; arrived in U.S., 1987; s. Charanjit Singh and Pritinder Kaur; m. Toniya Cheema Singh, June 5, 1994; children: Kunaal Inder, Kabir Inder. MBBS, U. Delhi, 1986. Diplomate Am. Bd. Internal Medicine, Am. Bd. Nephrology. Cert. ACLS. Intern U. Delhi Affiliated Hosps., 1985-86, resident in internal medicine, 1986-87, Easton Hosp.-Hahnemann U. Hosp., 1990-92; rsch. assoc. in endocrinology U. Health Scis.-Chgo. Med. Sch., 1987-88; intern Nassau County Med. Ctr., N.Y., 1988-89; rsch. assoc. in med. transplantation Presbyn. Hosp.-U. Pitts., 1989-90; clin. fellow divsn. nephrology U. Mich., 1992-93, rsch. fellow, 1993-95; clin. asst. prof. internal medicine So. Ill. U. Sch. Medicine, Carbondale, 1995-97; clin. asst. prof. medicine St. Louis U. Sch. Medicine; with Metro Hypertension and Kidney Ctr.; staff nephrologist BMA Carbondale Dialysis Unit, 1995-97, Marion Nephroplex Dialysis Unit, 1996-97; assoc. med. dir. Jefferson County Dialysis, Festus, Mo., 1998—; med. dir. Washington County Dialysis, Potosi, Mo., 1999—. Med. dir. Arrowhead Point Med. Clinic, Harrisburg, Ill., 1995-97; staff nephrologist BMA Carbondale Dialysis Unit, 1995—, Marion (Ill.) Nephroplex Dialysis Unit, 1996—, Christian NE Hosp., St. Louis, DePaul Hosp., St. Louis, Jefferson Meml. Hosp., Crystal City, Mo., others; chmn. infection control com. Marion Meml. Hosp., 1995-97; instr. Washington U. Sch. Medicine. Contbr. articles to profl. jours., chpts. in books; presenter in field. Fellow ACP; mem. Am. Soc. Nephrology, Nat. Kidney Found., Am. Soc. Internal Medicine. Sikh. Avocations: travel, sports, tennis, opera, music, broadway. Home: 843 Courtwood Ln Ballwin MO 63011-5110 Office: Metro Hypertension and Kidney Ctr 11155 Dunn Rd Ste 315E Saint Louis MO 63136-6111 Fax: (314) 355-2669. E-mail: ising@worldnet.att.net., ijsinghmd@yahoo.com.

SINGH, MANMOHAN, orthopedic surgeon, educator; b. Patiala, Punjab, India, Oct. 5, 1940; came to U.S., 1969; s. Ajmer and Kartar (Kaur) S.; m. Manjit Anand, Jan. 1, 1974; children: Kirpal, Gurmeet. MB, BS, Govt. Med. Coll., Patiala, 1964; MSurgery, Panjab U., Chandigarh, India, 1968. Diplomate Am. Bd. Orthopaedic Surgery. Mem. vis. faculty Mayo Grad. Sch., Rochester, Minn., 1969; rsch. fellow Inst. Internat. Edn., Chgo., 1969-74; resident in orthopedic surgery Michael Reese Hosp. and Med. Ctr., Chgo., 1974-78; pvt. practice, Chgo., 1979—; mem. attending staff, dir. orthopedic rsch. Michael Reese Hosp. and Med. Ctr., Chgo., 1979-94; fellow in orthopedic oncology Mayo Clinic and Mayo Found., Rochester, 1979; assoc. prof. U. Ill., Chgo., 1996—. Founder Quantum Health Cir./Enterprises for Holistic Medicine. Developer x-ray method (Singh Index) and bone density method (Radius Index) for diagnosis of osteoporosis. Fulbright travel grantee, 1968. Fellow Am. Acad. Orthop. Surgeons, Am. Orthop. Foot and Ankle Soc.; mem. Orthop. Rsch. Soc., Am. Soc. for Bone and Mineral Rsch., Internat. Bone and Mineral Soc. Democrat. Sikh. Avocations: stamp collecting, photography, meditation. Office: 110 Ridge Rd Munster IN 46321

SINGH, RAJENDRA, mechanical engineering educator; b. Dhampur, India, Feb. 13, 1950; came to U.S., 1973; s. Raghubir and Ishwar (Kali) S.; m. Veena Ghungesh, June 24, 1979; children: Rohit, Arun. BS with honors, Birla Inst., 1971; MS, U. Roorkee, India, 1973; PhD, Purdue U., 1975. Grad. instr. Purdue U., West Layfayette, Ind., 1973-75; sr. engr. Carrier Corp., Syracuse, N.Y., 1975-79; asst. prof. Ohio State U., Columbus, 1979-83, assoc. prof., 1983-87, prof., 1987—, Donald D. Glower chair in engring., 2001—. Adj. lectr. Syracuse (N.Y.) U., 1977-79; bd. dirs. Inst. of Noise Control Engring., 1994-96, 99—, v.p. tech. activities, 2000-02, pres., 2003; gen. chmn. Nat. Noise Conf., Columbus, 1985; leader U.S. delegation to India-U.S.A. Symposium on Vibration and Noise Engring., 1996; vis. prof. U. Calif., Berkeley, 1987-88; pres. Inter-Noise 2002 Congress; chmn. India-USA Symposium on Vibration and Noise, 2001; cons., lectr. in field. Author: Emerging Trends in Vibration and Noise Engineering, 1996; contbr. over 285 articles to profl. jours.; guest editor jours. Recipient Gold medal U. Roorkee, 1973, R. H. Kohr Rsch. award Purdue U., 1975, Excellence in Tchg. award Inst. Noise Control Engring., 1989, Rsch. award Ohio State U., 1983, 87, 91, 96, 2001, Educator of Yr. award GM Tech. Edn. Program, 1998. Fellow ASME, Acoustical Soc. Am.; mem. Soc. Auto Engring., Inst. Noise Control Engring.(cert.), Am. Soc. Engring. Edn. (George Westinghouse award 1993). Achievements include patent for rolling door; development of new analytical and experimental techniques in machine dynamics, acoustics, vibration and fluid control. Home: 4772 Belfield Ct Dublin OH 43017-2592 Office: Ohio State U 206 W 18th Ave Columbus OH 43210-1189 E-mail: singh.3@osu.edu.

SINGH, YADHU NAND, pharmacology educator, researcher; b. Suva, Fiji, Aug. 4, 1944; came to U.S., 1988, naturalized, 1995; s. Shri Ram and Janki Kumari Singh; m. Kamal Kuar, Feb. 14, 1976; children: Yatesh Nand, Kashmir Kaur. BS, U. Otago, Dunedin, New Zealand, 1967; MS, U. Strathclyde, Glasgow, Scotland, 1974, PhD, 1979. H.s. tchr. Marist H.S., Suva, 1967-70; lectr. biol. chemistry U. South Pacific, Suva, 1970-80, sr. lectr. biology, 1980-86; asst. prof. pharmacology S.D. State U., Brookings, 1988-91, assoc. prof., 1991-97, prof., 1997—. Lectr. pharmacology U. Alberta, 1986-88; adj. lectr. Fiji Sch. Medicine, 1980-84; Fiji dir. Commonwealth med. plants project, 1981-84; cons. on kava. Author: Kava Bibliography; author 6 book chpts., more than 60 articles to profl. jours. Recipient McCarthy prize, 1974; MRC fellow U. Strathclyde, 1976-79; AHFMR fellow 1984-86; NIH grantee. Mem. Am. Assn. of Colls. of Pharmacy, Am. Soc. Pharmacology and Exptl. Therapeutics, Internat. Soc. Toxinology, Brit. Pharmacol. Soc., Sigma Xi, Rho Chi. Democrat. Hindu. Avocations: soccer, chess, gardening, reading. Office: SDSU Coll Pharmacy Administration Ln Brookings SD 57007-0001 E-mail: yadhu_singh@sdstate.edu.

SINGLETARY, JAMES, JR., school board administrator; b. Buffalo, Jan. 24, 1947; m. Carolyn Price, July 24, 1971; children: Arien, Craig, Brandon, Evan. Cert. sheet metal, Erie C.C., Buffalo, 1974; BS, SUNY, Buffalo, 1990; MS, Canisius Coll., 1993. Cert. tchr. permanent, 1988, sch. adminstr. and supr., 1993. Sheet metal worker Buffalo Sheets Metal, 1970-77; customer engr. IBM, Buffalo, 1977-83; sheet metal worker, drafting tchr. Buffalo Pub. Schs., 1983-93; asst. prin. Seneca Vocat. H.S., Buffalo, 1993-97; dir. Bur. Pers. Svcs., Buffalo Bd. Edn., N.Y.C., 1997—. 2d v.p. bd. dirs. Rev. Marvin W. Robinson Cmty. Ctr., Inc.; mem. Ctrl. Office Adminstrs. Adv. coun. mem. SUNY and Buffalo Vocat. Tech. Edn. Coun., 1988-91. With USN, 1964-70. Mem. Am. Edn. Rsch. Assn., Am. Fedn. Sch. Adminstrs., N.Y. State Fedn. Suprs. and Adminstrs., Vocat. Tech. Guild Buffalo, Buffalo Coun. Suprs. and Adminstrs. (mem. grievance com., v.p. exec. com. 1997—, mem. ctrl. office adminstrs.), Buffalo Secondary Asst. Prins. Assn. (v.p., pres. 1997—), Buffalo State Coll. Alumni Assn., Canisius Coll. Alumni Assn., Jack and Jill of Am., Inc., Phi Delta Kappa. Avocations: bowling, tennis, roller skating. Home: 273 Humboldt Pky Buffalo NY 14208-1044 Office: Buffalo Bd Edn Bur Pers City Hall Rm 719 Buffalo NY 14202-3331

SINGLETON, GREGORY RAY, dean; b. Lexington, Tenn., Sept. 25, 1961; s. Bobby Ray and Shirley Aileen (Flowers) S. AS, Jackson State C.C., 1979; BS, Memphis State U., 1985, MS, 1994. Cert. elem. edn., Tenn. Ednl. and leadership cons. Kappa Alpha, Lexington, Va., 1985-86; ednl. instr. Memphis City Schs., 1986-87; coord. fraternity/sorority affairs Memphis State U., 1987-94; asst. dean of students Purdue U., West Lafayette, Ind., 1994—. Vol. Crisis Ctr. Greater Lafayette, Ind., 1994; pres. young alumni coun. Memphis State U., 1992, v.p., 1991; chmn. speakers' bur. Memphis in May, 1992, 93; bd. dirs. United Cerebral Palsy Mid-South, Inc., Memphis, 1993-94; regional advisor BACCHUS and Gamma Peer Edn. Network, Denver, 1991—. Named one of Outstanding Young Men Am. U.S. Jaycees, 1984; recipient Outstanding Advisor award Southeastern Interfraternity Conf., 1992, Southeastern Panhellenic Conf., 1990. Mem. Assn. Fraternity Advisors (exec. v.p. 1994-95), Nat. Assn. Student Pers. Adminstrs., Nat. Assn. Campus Activities, Kappa Alpha, Omicron Delta Kappa (pres. Memphis alumni chpt. 1989). Democrat. Avocations: tennis, golf, community service. Office: Purdue U 1096 Schleman Hall Rm 250 West Lafayette IN 47907-1096 Home: Apt 502 910 West Ave Miami Beach FL 33139-5237

SINGLETON, ROBERT, secondary school educator; Chmn. theatre dept. H.S. for the Performing and Visual Arts, Houston. Named Tchr. of the Yr., Houston Ind. Sch. Dist., 1999—2000; recipient Founders award, Tex. Edn. Theatre Assn., 1999; fellow, The English Speaking Union, 2001. Mem.: Nat. Bd. for Profl. Tchg. Stds. (bd. mem.). Office: High Sch for the Performing and Visual Arts 4001 Sanford St Houston TX 77006*

SINGPURWALLA, NOZER DARABSHA, statistician, engineer, educator; b. Hubli, Mysore, India, Apr. 8, 1939; came to U.S., 1961; s. Darabsha Burjorji and Goolan Nusserwnaji (Engineer) S.; m. Norah Jackson, June 15, 1969; children: Rachel, Darius. DME, B.V. Bhoomraddi Coll., Hubli, 1959; MS, Rutgers U., 1964; PhD, NYU, 1968. Rsch. statistician Western Electric, Princeton, NJ, 1964—68; tech. staff Hughes Aircraft, Fullerton, Calif., 1968—2003; prof. ops. rsch. and stats., disting. rsch. prof. George Washington U., Washington, 1969—. Vis. prof. Stanford U., Palo Alto, Calif., 1978-79, Carnegie Mellon U., Pitts., 1989-90, Garvin Disting. prof. computer sci. and stats. Va. Poly. Inst. & State U., Blacksburg, VA., 1991, Santa Fe Inst.; cons. Assn. Am. Railroads, Washington, 1984—; vis. faculty guest Los Alamos Nat. Labs, 1998—; vis. prof. Santa Fe Inst., 2001; vis. fellow St. Hugh's Coll., Oxford, Eng., 2002. Author: Methods for Statistical Analysis of Reliability, 1974, Statistical Methods in Software Engineering, 1999; contbr. over 150 articles to profl. jours. Nat. Inst. of Sci. and Tech. fellow, 1993-94, Vis. fellow St. Hughe's Coll.; recipient Wilks award U.S. Army Rsch. Office; Rockafeller Found. scholar. Fellow AAAS, Am. Stat. Assn., Inst. Math. Stat.; mem. Internat. Stat. Inst. Zoroastrian. Home: 2306 N Stafford St Arlington VA 22207-3949 Office: George Washington U Dept of Statistics Washington DC 20037-2526

SINGSEN, ANTONE G., III, lawyer, educator; b. New Haven, Conn., Oct. 3, 1942; s. Antone G. and Mary Ellen (McKee) S.; m. Ann C. Lammers, June 12, 1965 (div. 1977); children: Hope, Molly; m. Jayne B. Tyrrell, June 23, 1985. BA, Brown U., 1964; LLB, Columbia U., 1967. Bar: N.Y. 1967, Mass. 1985. Law clk. to Hon. Wilfred Feinberg U.S. Ct. Appeals (2d cir.), N.Y.C., 1967-68; atty. Legal Aid Soc. of Westchester County, White Plains, N.Y., 1968-72; asst. gen. counsel Community Action for Legal Svcs., N.Y.C., 1972-78; v.p. Legal Svcs. Corp., Washington, 1979-82, program counsel, 1994-96; exec. dir. Legal Asst Corp. Ctrl. Mass., 1996-97; cons. atty. Natick, Mass., 1982-93, Watertown, Mass., 1997—. Coord., dir. Harvard Program on Legal Profession, Cambridge, Mass., 1987-94; lectr. Harvard Law Sch., 1984-93; coord. Interuniv. Consortium on Poverty Law, Cambridge, 1988-94. Author, editor (newsletter) Consorting, 1990-94; contbr. articles to profl. jours. Mem. probono legal svcs. com. Supreme Jud. Ct. Mass., 1997-98. Grantee Ford Found., 1988-94. Mem. ABA (commn. non-lawyer practice, 1992-95, delivery of legal svcs. com., 1988-92). Avocations: soccer, reading, cooking, crosswords. Office: 361 School St Watertown MA 02472-1413 E-mail: gerrysings@aol.com.

SINK, JOHN DAVIS, chemist, clergyperson; b. Homer City, Pa., Dec. 19, 1934; s. Aaron Tinsman and Louella Bell (Davis) S.; m. Nancy Lee Hile, Nov. 9, 1956 (dec. Aug. 1961); 1 child, Lou Ann (dec. Aug. 1961); m. Claire Kaye Huschka, June 13, 1964 (div. Feb. 1987); children: Kara Joan, Karl John; m. Sharon Ferrando Padden, July 15, 1989; 1 child, Lisa Michelle Padden. BS in Animal/Vet. Sci., Pa. State U., 1956, MS in Biophys./Animal Sci., 1960, PhD in Biochem./Animal Sci., 1962; EdD in Higher Edn., U. Pitts., 1986; MDiv, Emory U., 2001. Adminstrv. officer, exec. asst. to sec. agr. State of Pa., Harriwburg, 1962; prof., group leader dept. food, dairy and animal sci. Inst. Policy Rsch. and Evaluation, Pa. State U., University Park, 1962-79; pres. Collegian, Inc., 1971-72; joint planning & evaluation staff officer Sci. & Edn. Adminstrn., U.S. Dept. Agr., Washington, 1979-80; prof., comm. intercoll. program food sci. & nutrition U.W.Va., Morgantown, 1980-85; pres., CEO Pa. State U., Uniontown, 1985-92; pres. Sink, Padden & Assocs., Atlanta, 1992—; pastor Sardis United Meth. Ch., 1995—2003; prof. chemistry and biochemistry So. Polytech. State U., Marietta, Ga., 1997—. Dir. S.W. Inst. Uniontown, 1989-92; gen. mgr. Cavert Wire Co., Inc., Atlanta, 1993-97; exec. asst. naval rep. to gov. and adj. gen. State W.Va., Charleston, 1981-84; cons. Allied Mills Inc., Am. Air Lines, Am. Home Foods, Inc., Apollo Analytical Labgs., Armour Food Co., Atlas Chem. Industries, others. Author: The Control of Metabolism, 1974, Citizen Extraordinarire, 1993, On Atlanta's Holy Mountain, 2000; contbr. articles to profl. jours. Mem. nat. adv. bd. Am. Security Coun., 1981-91; mem. nat. adv. coun. Nat. Commn. Higher Edn. Issues, 1980-82; bd. dirs. W.Va. Cattleman's Assn., 1981-83, W.Va. Poultry Assn., 1980-83, Pembroke Welsh Corgi Club, 1969-71, Greater Uniontown Idnsl. Fund, 1986-91, Fayette County Econ. Devel. Coun., 1985-93, Westmoreland-Fayette coun. Boy Scouts Am., 1986-91, Westmoreland-Fayette hist. Soc., 1986-91, Fayette County Soil Conservation Dist., 1990-93, Pa. Youth Found., 1989-93, Fayette County Coop. Extension Bd., 1992-93, Pa. Masonic Found., 1993, Ga. Meth. Commn. on Higher Edn. and Campus Min., 2000—. Capt. USNR, 1985-86, ret. Decorated Army commendation medal; recipient Nat. Merit Trophy award nat. Block and Bridle Club, 1956, Darbarker prize Pa. Aca.d Sci., 1967, W.Va. Disting. Achievement medal, Disting. Leadership award Am. Security Coun. Found., 1983; Pa. Meat Packers Assn. scholar, 1958-62; hon. fellow in biochemistry U. Wis., 1965, NSF postdoctoral fellow, 1964-65; Sherman scholar, 1996-2001. Fellow AAAS, Am. Inst. Chemists, Inst. Food Technologists; mem. Am. Meat Sci. Assn. (pres. 1974-75), Pa. Air N.G. Armory (trustee 1968-80), Pa. Acad. Sci., U.S. Naval Inst., Res. Officers Assn., Armed Forces Comm. and Elecs. Assn., Acad. Polit. Sci. (world affairs coun. Pitts. chpt.), Am. Assn. higher Edn., Am. Assn. Univ. Adminstrs., Am. Chem. Soc., Am. Soc. for Biochemistry and Molecular Biology, Biophys. Soc., Am. Soc. Animal Sci., Inst. Food Technologists, Soc. Rsch. Adminstrs., Am. Cancer Soc. (bd. dirs. 1988-91), Greater Uniontown C. of C. (bd. dirs. 1989-93), Greater Connellsville C. of C. (pres., bd. dirs. 1989-91), North Fayette C. of C. (bd. dirs. 1986-89), Mon Valley Tri-State Network, Inc. (chmn. bd. dirs. 1989-92), Rotary (sec. State Coll. 1969-71, Paul Harris fellow 1991), Elks, Internat. Assn. Turtles, Consistory, Shriners, Masons, Alpha Zeta, Omicron Delta Kappa, Gamma Sigma Delta, Sigma Xi, Phi Lambda Upsilon, Gamma Alpha, Phi Tau Sigma, Phi Sigma, Phi Delta Kappa, Pi Sigma Phi. Republican. E-mail: jsink@spsu.edu.

SINKIS, DEBORAH MARY, principal; b. Worcester, Mass., May 13, 1949; d. Peter Paul and Joanne Mary (Dumphy) Shemeth; m. Ben J. Sinkis, June 8, 1969; 1 child, Russell John. BS in Elem. Edn., Worcester State Coll., 1970, MEd, 1977, cert. in curriculum, 1981; cert. in interactive tech., Harvard U., 1989; EdD in Ednl. Adminstrn., U. Mass., 1993. Tchr. Worcester Pub. Schs., 1971-83; computer assisted instr., 1983-86, tchr. trainer for computers, 1986, citywide computer coord., 1986-89; prin. Millbury St. Sch., Worcester, 1989-90, F.J. McGrath Sch., Worcester, 1990—. Adj. prof. edn. Worcester State Coll., 1996—; cons. computer edn. Author curriculum materials. Mem. computer coop. regional adv. coun. Mass. Commn. for Deaf and Hard of Hearing, 1989-90; bd. dirs. Montachusett coun. Girl Scouts U.S., 1996—. Named Woman of Distinction, Montachusett coun. Girl Scouts U.S., 1994; recipient Knollwood award Notre Dame Acad., 1997. Mem. ASCD, NEA, Nat. Assn. Elem. Sch. Prins., Mass. Elem. Sch. Prins. Assn., Mass. Tchrs. Assn., Internat. Soc. Tech. in Edn., Internat. Cath. Deaf Assn., Harvard/Radcliffe Club, Quota Internat. (pres.-elect Worcester chpt. 1995, pres. 1996-98, Deaf Woman of Yr. 1991), Phi Delta Kappa (Adminstr. of Yr. 1994). Office: Worcester Pub Schs 20 Irving St Worcester MA 01609-2432

SINNOTT, JOHN PATRICK, lawyer, educator; b. Bklyn., Aug. 17, 1931; s. John Patrick and Elizabeth Muriel (Zinkand) Sinnott; m. Rose Marie Yuppa, May 30, 1959; children: James Alexander, Jessica Michelle. BS, U.S. Naval Acad., 1953; MS, USAF Inst. Tech., 1956; JD, No. Ky. U., 1960. Bar: Ohio 1961, NY 1963, NJ 1970, Ga 2000, US Patent Office 1963, US Supreme Ct 1977. Assoc. Brumbaugh, Graves, Donohue & Raymond, N.Y.C., 1961-63; patent atty. Bell Tel. Labs., Murray Hill, N.J., 1963-64, Schlumberger Ltd., N.Y.C., 1964-71; asst. chief patent counsel Babcock & Wilcox, N.Y.C., 1971-79; chief patent and trademark counsel Am. Std. Inc., N.Y.C., 1979-92; of counsel Morgan & Finnegan, N.Y.C., 1992-99, Langdale & Vallotton, Valdosta, Ga., 2000—. Adj lectr NJ Inst Technology, Newark, 1974—89; adj prof Seton Hall Univ Sch Law, Newark, 1989—98. Author: (book) Counterfeit Goods Suppression, 1998, World Patent Law and Practice, Vols 2-2P, 1999, A Practical Guide to Document Authentication, 2003; contbr. articles to profl jours. Mem. local Selective Serv Bd., Plainfield, NJ, 1971; bd dirs New Providence Community Swimming Pool, NJ, 1970. Capt. USAF, 1953—61, col. AUS ret., 1977—91. Decorated Legion of Merit, others. Mem. N.Y. Intellectual Property Law Assn. (bd. dirs. 1974-76), Squadron A Assn., Cosmos Club, Valdosta Country Club. Republican. Roman Catholic. Home: 2517 Rolling Rd Valdosta GA 31602-1244 Office: Langdale & Vallotton 1007 N Patterson St PO Box 1547 Valdosta GA 31603 Fax: (229) 244-9646. E-mail: specan23@aol.com.

SINNOTT, WILLIAM MICHAEL, social studies educator; b. Jersey City, Mar. 6, 1948; s. Myles and Agnes Bridget (Ryan) S.; m. Louise Rosemary DeStefano, Dec. 27, 1969; children: Daria, Jessica, Carrie Ann. BA cum laude, Bloomfield Coll., 1970; MA, NYU, 1971; MAT, Fairleigh Dickinson U., 1974. Cert. tchr. social studies K-12, N.J. Permanent substitute tchr. Jersey City Bd. of Edn., 1971-73; tchr. mid. sch. social studies New Providence (N.J.) Bd. of Edn., 1973-89; tchr. U.S. history and anthropology New Providence H.S., 1989—. Asst. track coach New Providence H.S., 1976-82, head coach boys track, 1983—. Mem. 11th N.J. Vols., Warren County, 1994, Oxford (N.J.) Hist. Soc., 1994, Friends of Shippen Manor, Oxford, 1994. Recipient Scholar's Tchr. award Star-Ledger, 1994; named Boys Track Coach of Yr., Star-Ledger, 1994, The Courier-News, 1987, 94, Mountain Valley Conf. Track Coaches Assn., 1992, 93, 94, N.J. Track mag., 1994. Mem. NEA, Nat. Coun. for Social Studies, Nat. Fedn. Interscholastic Coaches, N.J. State Coaches Assn. Roman Catholic. Avocations: civil war re-enactment, travel, track. Home: 15 Lincoln Ave Oxford NJ 07863-3056 Office: New Providence HS 35 Pioneer Dr New Providence NJ 07974-1515

SINTON, CHRISTOPHER MICHAEL, neurophysiologist, educator; b. Beckenham, Kent, Eng., Sept. 10, 1946; came to U.S., 1983; s. Leslie George and Evelyn Mabel (Burn) S. BA, Cambridge U., Eng., 1968, MA, 1977; BSc, London U., 1978; PhD, U. Lyon, France, 1981. Rsch. fellow U. Lyon, 1980-83; rsch. assoc. Princeton (N.J.) U., 1983-84; sr. scientist Ciba-Geigy Corp., Summit, N.J., 1984-88; dir. electrophysiology Neurogen Corp., Branford, Conn., 1988-94; asst. prof. U. Tex. Southwestern Med. Ctr., Dallas, 1994—. Rsch. asst. prof. medicine NYU, N.Y.C., 1986-94; vis. asst. prof. Harvard U. Med. Sch., Boston, 1999—. Contbr. Scholar Med. Rsch. Coun. France vis. scholar, Princeton U., 1983. Mem. N.Y. Acad. Scis., Soc. Neurosci., European Sleep Rsch. Soc., Sleep Rsch. Soc. Achievements include research on genetic basis of narcolepsy, fetal effects of in-utero caffeine exposure, possible functional role of REM sleep and neuropeptide modulation of synaptic input. Office: U Tex SW Med Ctr Dept Internal Medicine 5323 Harry Hines Blvd Dallas TX 75390-8874 E-mail: sinton@utsw.swmed.edu.

SIPER, CYNTHIA DAWN, special education educator; b. Bklyn., Apr. 16, 1965; d. Joel S. and Diana M. (Kessler) Rosenblatt; m. Alan Siper, Apr. 9, 1989; children: Rebecca Ruth, Daniel Louis. BS in Edn., SUNY, Plattsburgh, 1988; MEd, SUNY, New Paltz, 1992. Cert. K-12 spl. edn. tchr., N-6 elem. edn. tchr., N.Y. Tchr. spl. edn. Valley Cen. Sch. Dist., Montgomery, N.Y., 1988-90, Middletown (N.Y.) Enlarged City Sch. Dist., 1990—. Spl. edn. tchr. rep. Coun. on Spl. Edn., Middletown, 1990—. Mem. Coun. for Exceptional Children, Middletown Tchrs. Assn., Kappa Delta Pi. Avocation: collecting disneyana.

SIPES, JAMES LAMOYNE, landscape architect, educator; b. Elizabethtown, Ky., Jan. 28, 1957; s. William L. and Betty Jean (Miller) S.; m. Kimberly A. Blevins, Feb. 5, 1983; children: Matthew, Sara, Ally. BS in Landscape Architecture, U. Ky., 1982; M in Landscape Architecture, Iowa State U., 1984. Registered landscape architect, Tex. Teaching asst. U. Ky., Lexington, 1981-82; planning intern Lexington-Fayette Govt., 1982-83; teaching asst. Iowa State U., Ames, 1983-84; landscape architect Nat. Park Svc., Gunnison, Colo., 1984-85, Schrickel, Rollins Assocs., Arlington, Tex., 1985-88, U.S. Forest Svc., Dillon, Mont., 1989; computer graphic cons. Video Perspectives, Inc., Louisville, 1990; lectr. U. Idaho, Moscow, 1989-93; assoc. prof. landscape architecture Wash. State U., Pullman, 1988-94; dir. U. Okla., Norman, 1995—. Cons. Computer Graphics and Simulations, Salt Lake City, 1993-94; mem. adv. bd. Cmty. Childcare Ctr., Pullman, 1992—. Computer editor Landscape Architecture Mag., Washington, 1994—; producer Animated World, PBS, 1994—; contbr. articles to profl. jours. Mem. Pullman Civic Trust, 1993-94. Recipient Cert. of Appreciation, Soil Conservation Svc., 1992, Cert. of Appreciation, U.S. Forest Svc., 1990. Mem. Am. Soc. Landscape Architects (Honor award 1984, 94, Tex. Design award 1992), Coun. Educators in Landscape Architecture, Nat. Computer Graphics Assn., Pacific N.W. Recreation Consortium, Gamma Sigma Delta, Phi Kappa Phi. Avocations: sports, art, reading, technology. Office: U Okla Landscape Architecture Dept Landscape Architecture Norman OK 73019-0001

SIPFLE, DAVID ARTHUR, retired philosophy educator; b. Pekin, Ill., Aug. 29, 1932; s. Karl Edward and Louis Adele (Hinners) S.; m. Mary-Alice Slauson, Sept. 4, 1954; children: Ann Littlefield (dec.), Gail Elizabeth. BA in Math., Philosophy magna cum laude, Carleton Coll., 1953; MA, Yale U., 1955, PhD, 1958. Instr. philosophy Robert Coll., Istanbul, Turkey, 1957-58, Am. Coll. for Girls, Istanbul, 1957-60; asst. prof. Carleton Coll., Northfield, Minn., 1960-67, assoc. prof., 1967-70, chmn. dept., 1968-71, 89-92, prof., 1970-92, William H. Laird prof. philosophy and liberal arts, 1992-98, cross country ski coach, 1979—84. Vis. fellow Wolfson Coll., Cambridge U., 1975-76. Translator: (with Mary-Alice Sipfle) Emile Meyerson, The Relativistic Deduction: Epistemological Implications of the Theory of Relativity, 1985, Explanation in the Sciences, 1991; contbr. articles to profl. jours. NEH Younger Humanist fellow, Nice, France, 1971-72, NSF Sci. Faculty fellow, Cambridge, Eng., 1975-76; Carleton Coll. Faculty Devel. grantee, 1981-83, 86-87. Mem. Am. Philos. Assn., Metaphysical Soc. Am., Philosophy of Sci. Assn. Avocation: cross country skiing. Office: Carleton Coll 1 N College St Northfield MN 55057-4001 E-mail: dsipfle@carleton.edu.

SIPPLE, WILLIAM STANTON, ecologist, educator; b. Camden, N.J., Nov. 16, 1939; s. Gordon R. and Beulah K. (Stetser) S.; m. Geraldine Ann Ruggiano, Apr. 25, 1942; children: Michael W., Michele L., Sean D. BA in Biology, Glassboro State U., 1969; MS in Regional Planning, U. Pa., 1971; postgrad., U. Md., 1974-78. Natural resources planner Md. Dept. Natural Resources, Annapolis, 1971-79; ecologist U.S. EPA, Washington, 1979—2003; pres. W.S. Sipple Wetland & Environ. Tng. Cons., 2003—. Instr. grad. sch. USDA, Washington, 1972-90, No. Va. C.C., Woodbridge, 1993-97, Inst. for Wetland and Environ. Edn. and Rsch., Sherborn, Mass., 1993—, Johns Hopkins U., Balt., 1995—, Humboldt Field Rsch. Inst., Steuben, Maine, 1999—, Towson U., Md., 2003—; mem. scientific adv. bd. Jug Bay Wetlands Sanctuary, Lothian, Md., 1988—; mem. Nat. Tech. Com. for Hydric Soils, Washington, 1986—; mem. sci. adv. com. County of Anne Arundel, Annapolis, 1973-76. Author: Through the Eyes of a Young Naturalist, 1991, Days Afield: Exploring Wetlands in the Chesapeake Bay Region; contbr. articles to profl. jours. Mem. Ecol. Soc. Am., Soc. Wetland Scientists, So. Appalachian Botan. Club, Sigma Xi. Democrat. Avocations: natural history, bottle collecting, postcard collecting, book collecting. Home and Office: 512 Red Bluff Ct Millersville MD 21108-1478

SIQUELAND, EINAR, psychology educator; b. Glasgow, Mont., Nov. 15, 1932; s. Harald and Anna Lydia (Kristensen) S.; m. Marian McGrail, Dec. 1960 (div. May 1970); children: Lynne Ruth, Beth Ann; m. Jillian E.A. Godfree, June 29, 1973. BA, Pacific Luth. U., 1954; MS, U. Wash., 1962, PhD, 1963. Rsch. assoc. pharmacology U. Wash., Seattle, 1958-59; clin. intern psychology VA Mental Hygiene Clinic, Seattle, 1960-61; asst. prof. dept. psychology Brown U., Providence, 1965-69, assoc. prof., 1969-88, prof., 1988-99; rsch. scientist dept. Pediatrics Women's and Infants' Hosp., Providence, 1975-93; prof. emeritus Brown U., 1999—. Contbr. articles to profl. jours., chpts. to books. With U.S. Army, 1956-58, Korea. Predoctoral fellow USPHS, 1961-63, postdoctoral fellow, 1963-65. Fellow Am. Psychol. Soc.; mem. AAUP, APA, Soc. Rsch. in Child Devel., Sigma Xi. Office: Brown U Dept Psychology PO Box 1853 Providence RI 02912-1853 E-mail: sequel-e@cox.net.

SIRI, WALTER ALAN, retired science educator; b. Carlstadt, N.J., June 4, 1936; s. Henry Eugene and Mary (Walter) S.; m. Joyce Elenore Meyers, Dec. 20, 1960; children: Walter Alan Jr., John. BA in Sci., Montclair State Coll., Upper Montclair, N.J., 1963, MA in Sci., 1968. Cert. secondary tchr. sci., N.J.; cert. supr., prin., N.J. Tchr. East Rutherford (N.J.) H.S., 1963-71, dept. chmn., 1966-71; tchr., dept. chair Henry P. Becton Regional H.S., East Rutherford, 1971-2000, ret., 2000. Right to Know coord., 1988-89; adj. prof. Fairleigh Dickinson U., 1988-96; advisor Key Club, 1963-2000, N.J. Sci. League, 1976-2000; asst. coach boys basketball, head coach swimming, boys track, girls track, cross country; chmn. sci. com. Mid. Atlantic States Evaluating Com. Elder First Presbyn. Ch., Carlstadt, 1972—; mem. Carlstadt Bd. Edn., 1968-83, vol. umpire Carlstadt Little League, 1968-85; mem. Carlstadt Planning Bd., 2002—. With USAF, 1954-58, Res., 1958-62. Recipient Certificates of recognition Sigma Xi, 1958, Fairleigh Dickinson U., Am. Chem. Soc., Citation Edison Sci. and Youth Day, 1976, Cert. N.J. Sci. Tchrs. Assn. and N.J. Sci. Edn. Leadership Assn. (ACS tchr. affiliate). Mem. NEA (life, ret.), N.J. Ret. Edn. Assn., Bergen County Ret. Edn. Assn., Am. Assn. Retired Persons, Am. Legion (boys state chmn. 1985—, post adjutant 1995-97), Am. Legion Jersey Boys State Alumni Assn., Montclair State U. Alumni Assn., Masons (blood bank chairperson 1989—, sr. warden; trustee Eclipse Masonic Assn.), Carlstadt Sr. Friendship Club. Avocations: fishing, photography. Home: 433 Union St Carlstadt NJ 07072-1406 E-mail: jsws201@aol.com.

SIRICA, ALPHONSE EUGENE, pathology educator; b. Waterbury, Conn., Jan. 16, 1944; s. Alphonse Eugene and Elena Virginia (Mascolo) S.; m. Annette Marie Murray, June 9, 1984; children: Gabrielle Theresa, Nicholas Steven. MS, Fordham U., 1968; PhD in Biomed. Sci., U. Conn., 1977. Asst. prof. U. Wis., Madison, 1979-84; assoc. prof. Med. Coll. Va., Va. Commonwealth U., Richmond, 1984-90, prof. of pathology, 1990—, divsn. chair exptl. pathology, 1992-99, divsn. chair cellular and molecular pathogenesis, 1999—. Vis. prof., Pa. State U. Coll. Medicine, 2000, chmn. symposium on Pathobiology of Neoplasia, Am. Soc. Investigative Pathology, Richmond, Va., 1993; regular mem. sci. adv. com. on carcinogenesis and nutrition Am. Cancer Soc., Atlanta, 1989-92, metabolic pathology study sect., NIH, Bethesda, 1991-95, ad hoc mem. study sect., 1997, 98, 99, 2000, 02, 03; chmn. Fedn. Am. Socs. Expt. Biology Summer Rsch. Conf. on Growth Factor Receptor Tyrosine Kinases, Snowmass Village, Colo., 1999, 2001. Editor, author: The Pathobiology of Neoplasia, 1989, The Role of Cell Types in Hepatocarcinogenesis, 1992, Cellular and Molecular Pathogenesis, 1996; co-editor, author: Biliary and Pancreatic Ductal Epithelia: Pathobiology and Pathophysiology, 1997; mem. editl. bd. Pathobiology, 1990-99, Hepatology, 1991-94; rev. bd. In Vitro Cellular and Devel. Biology, 1987—, Exptl. and Molecular Pathology, 1999—; contbr. rsch. papers to Am. Jour. Pathology, Cancer Rsch., Hepatology, others. Mem.: AAAS, Internat. Soc. for Study of Comparative Oncology, Soc. Toxicology, Hans. Popper Hepatopathology Soc., Soc. Exptl. Biology and Medicine, NY Acad. Scis., Am. Gastroenterological Assn., Am. Assn. Study Liver Diseases, Am. Soc. Investigative Pathology (chair program com. 1994—96), Assn. Clin. Scientists, Soc. for In Vitro Biology, Am. Assn. Cancer Rsch. (chmn. Va. state legis. com. 1992—95), Am. Soc. Cell Biology. Achievements include development of collagen gel-nylon mesh system for culturing hepatocytes; first establishment and characterization of hyperplastic bile ductular epithelial cells in culture; research in hepato and biliary carcinogenesis, pathobiology of hepatocyte and biliary epithelial cells and molecular pathogenesis and experimental therapeutics of biliary cancer. Office: Med Coll Va Va Commonwealth U PO Box 980297 Richmond VA 23298-0297 E-mail: asirica@hsc.vcu.edu.

SIRONEN, LYNN JANE, secondary school educator; b. London, Dec. 15, 1951; came to U.S., 1953; d. Harold Walter and Jane Adele Markham; m. Jan Steven Sironen, June 5, 1971; children: Karen, Christina, Steven. BA in Elem. Edn., U. R.I., 1973, MA in Sci. Edn., 1986. Elem. tchr. North Kingstown (R.I.) Schs., 1973, 75, substitute tchr., 1974, 80, computer tchr., 1985-86, tchr. sci., 1986—, Westerly (R.I.) Schs., 1981, The Wheeler Sch., Providence, 1981-82; grad. asst. U. R.I., Kingston, 1982-84, part-time instr., 1987. Mem., vice comdr., exec. bd. North Kingstown Ambulance Corps, 1975-87; pres. North Kingstown Band Parents, 1992-94. Mem. Nat. Sci. Tchrs. Assn., NEA of North Kingstown (sec. 1994-96), North Kingstown Bus. and Profl. Women's Club (treas. 1993-94) Rotary (Tchr. of Month 1993). Episcopalian. Home: PO Box 152 North Kingstown RI 02852-0152 Office: North Kingstown High School 150 Fairway Dr North Kingstown RI 02852-6207

SIROTKIN, PHILLIP LEONARD, education administrator; b. Moline, Ill., Aug. 2, 1923; s. Alexander and Molly (Berghaus) S.; m. Cecille Sylvia Gussack, May 1, 1945; children— Steven Marc, Laurie Anne. BA (McGregor Found. scholar), Wayne State U., 1945; MA, U. Chgo., 1947, PhD (Walgreen Found. scholar, Carnegie fellow), 1951. Lectr. U. Chgo., 1949-50; instr. Wellesley Coll., 1950-52, asst. prof. polit. sci., 1953-57; asso. dir. Western Interstate Commn. Higher Edn., Boulder, Colo., 1957-60; exec. asst. to dir. Calif. Dept. Mental Hygiene, Sacramento, 1960-63; asst. dir. NIMH, 1964-66, asso. dir., 1967-71, cons., 1971-73; exec. v.p., acad. v.p. State U. N.Y. at Albany, 1971-76; exec. dir. Western Interstate Commn. Higher Edn., Boulder, Colo., 1976-90, sr. adviser, 1990—. Midwestern Legis. Higher Edn. Steering Com., Boulder, Colo., 1990-91; sr. cons. Midwestern Higher Edn. Commn., 1991—; mem. oversight com. Hispanic Agenda, Larasa, 1992-98. Cons. Nebr. Post-Secondary Edn. Commn., 1994; nat. adv. com. Soc. Coll. and Univ. Planning, 1976, adv. panel, rev. state system higher edn. in N.D., 1986, gov.'s com. on bi-state med. edn. plan for N.D. and S.D., 1988-90, Edn. Commn. States' Nat. Task Force for Minority Achievement in Higher Edn., 1989-91; cons. Bur. Health Manpower Edn., NIH, 1972-74, Nat. Ctr. Health Svcs. Rsch., 1975-85; spl. cons. AID, 1963-64; case writer Resources for the Future, 1954-55; mem. 1st U.S. Mission on Mental Health to USSR, 1967. Author: The Echo Park Dam Controversy and Upper Colorado River Development, 1959. Bd. dirs. Council Social Work Edn., 1959-60. 1st lt. AUS, 1943-46. Recipient Superior Svc. award HEW, 1967; Faculty Rsch. award Wellesley Coll., 1956 Home: 299 Green Rock Dr Boulder CO 80302-4745

SISKAR, JOHN FREDERICK, art educator; b. Kenmore, N.Y., May 27, 1957; s. Robert Michael and Marion Rose (Stuff) S.; m. Susan Schuessler, June 25, 1982; children: John William, Benjamin Mark. BS in art edn. cum laude, Buffalo State Coll., 1982; EdM, U. Buffalo, 1988, postgrad., 1991—. Curriculum cons. Arts Coun. Chautauqua County, Jamestown, N.Y., 1987; cons., writer N.Y. State Edn. Dept., Albany, 1987, trainer, 1987-90; instr. State U., Fredonia, N.Y., 1993; art educator Fredonia H.S., 1983-93, dir. art, 1988-93; curriculum cons. Burchfield-Penney Arts Cen., Buffalo, N.Y., 1994—; instr. art edn. dept. Buffalo State Coll., 1993—. Art educator Chautauqua County Sch. Bd. Assoc., Fredonia, 1986—; portfolio adj. N.Y. State Summer Sch. for Arts, Albany, 1993—. Editor, cons. curriculum guide Western N.Y. Arch. & Design, 1994—; coord. Billboard Design, 1987-88. Coord. of division Northern Chautouqua Soccer Assn., Dunkirk, N.Y., 1993; team coach, 1989-93, team coach Dunkirk Fredonia Soccer League, Fredonia, 1992; vol. Fredonia Preservation Soc., 1989-92. Recipient summer profl. grant Fredonia Cen. Schs., 1992, curriculum devel. grant, 1984, 86, 87, 88, 90, 92. Mem. Assn. Supervision and Curriculum Devel., N.Y. State Art Tchrs. Assn. (chair of mgmt. plan, coord. of student exhibits 1982—), N.Y. State Art Tchrs. Assn. One Western (v.p., pres.-elect, pres. 1983—, editorial adv. bd. mem. 1987-90), Nat. Art Edn. Assn., Fredonia Tchrs. Assn. (newsletter graphics editor 1983-93). Office: Buffalo State Coll Art Edn Dept 1300 Elmwood Ave Buffalo NY 14222-1004

SISSOM, LEIGHTON ESTEN, engineering educator, dean, consultant; b. Manchester, Tenn., Aug. 26, 1934; s. Willie Esten and Bertha Sarah (Davis) S.; m. Evelyn Janelle Lee, June 13, 1953; children: Terry Lee, Denny Leighton. BS, Middle Tenn. State Coll., 1956; BS in Mech. Engring., Tenn. Technol. U., 1962; MS in Mech. Engring., Ga. Inst. Tech., 1964, PhD, 1965. Diplomate Nat. Acad. Forensic Engrs.; registered profl. engr., Tenn. Draftsman Westinghouse Electric Corp., Tullahoma, 1953-57; mech. designer ARO, Inc., Tullahoma, 1957-58; instr. mech. engring. Tenn. Technol. U., Cookeville, 1958-62, chmn. dept. mech. engring., 1965-79, dean engring., 1979-88, dean of engring. emeritus, 1988—; prin. cons. Sissom & Assocs., Cookeville, Tenn., 1962—. Bd. dirs. Accreditation Bd. Engring. and Tech., N.Y.C., 1978-86, treas., 1982-86. Author: (with Donald R. Pitts) Elements of Transport Phenomena, 1972, Heat Transfer, 1977, 1,000 Solved Problems in Heat Transfer, 1991; contbr. An Attorney's Guide to Engineering, 1986; contbr. articles to various publs. Fellow ASME (sr. v.p. 1982-86, gov. 1986-88, Golden medallion), Am. Soc. Engring. Edn. (bd. dirs. 1984-87, pres. 1991-92), Accreditation Bd. Engring. and Tech.; mem. NSPE, Soc. Automotive Engrs., Nat. Engring. Deans Coun. (chmn. 1984-87), Order of the Engr. (chmn. bd. govs. 1994-96), Tau Beta Pi (v.p. 1986-89, councillor 1986-89). Home and Office: 1151 Shipley Church Rd Cookeville TN 38501-7730

SISSON, JEAN CRALLE, retired middle school educator; b. Village, Va., Nov. 16, 1941; d. Willard Andrew and Carolyn (Headley) Cralle; m. James B. Sisson, June 20, 1964 (div. Oct. 1994); 1 child, Kimberly Carol; m. donald Wimer (div. 1998). BS in Elem. Edn., Longwood Coll., 1964; MA in Adminstrn. and Supervision, Va. Commonwealth U., 1979. Tchr. 2nd grade Tappahannock (Va.) Elem. Sch., 1964-67; tchr. 2nd and 4th grades Farnham (Va.) Elem. Sch., 1967-71; tchr. 6th grade Callao (Va.) Elem. Sch., 1971-81; tchr. 6th and 7th grades Northumberland Mid. Sch., Heathsville, Va., 1981—2003; ret., 2003. Sr. mem. Supt. Adv. Com., Heathsville, 1986-93. Author: My Survival, 1994; author of children's books, short stories and poetry. Lifetime mem. Gibeon Bapt. Ch., Village, Va., 1942—. Mem.: IDEA, ASCD, NEA, Nat. Wildlife Fedn., Nat. Coun. English Tchrs., Exercise Safety Assn., Va. Mid. Sch. Assn., Aerobics and Fitness Assn., PETA, Alpha Delta Kappa. Republican. Avocations: aerobics, dance, music, art, travel. Home: 1068 Lodge Rd Callao VA 22435-2105 Office: Northumberland Mid Sch PO Box 100 Heathsville VA 22473-0100 E-mail: jsisson@nucps.com.

SISSON, VIRGINIA BAKER, geology educator; b. Boston, Apr. 8, 1957; d. Thomas Kingsford and Edith Virginia (Arnold) S.; m. William Bronson Maze, Oct. 14, 1989. AB, Bryn Mawr Coll., 1979; MA, Princeton U., 1981, PhD, 1985. Rsch. assoc. Princeton (N.J.) U., 1985-86, Rice U., Houston, 1986-87, lectr., 1987-92, asst. prof. geology, 1992-99, clin. prof., 1999-2001, rsch. scientist, 2001—. Cons. U.S. Geol. Survey, Anchorage, 1984-95; rsch. assoc. Am. Mus. Natural History, 2001—; rsch. assoc. prof. U. Utah, 2001—. Contbr. over 40 articles to profl. jours. Trustee Geol. Soc. Am. Found. Rsch. grantee, NSF, Houston and Calif., 1988, Houston and Scotland, 1990, Alaska, 1990, Venezuela, 1996, Alaska, 1998, Nat. Geographic, 1998. Fellow Geol. Soc. Am.; mem. Assn. Women Geoscientists, Am. Women in Sci., Am. Geophys. Union, Mineral Soc. of Am., Mineral Assn. Can. Avocations: pilot, cross-country skiing, recorder playing, warbirds. Home: 4118 Lanark Ln Houston TX 77025-1115 Office: Rice U Dept Earth Sci MS-126 6100 Main St Houston TX 77005-1892 E-mail: jinnys@rice.edu.

SISSONS, JOHN ROGER, educational administrator; b. Monroe, Wis., Aug. 10, 1938; s. John F. and Pearl J. (Eichstadt) S.; m. Patricia M. Wiese, May 21, 1960; children: John A., Theresa M. Sissons, Kirstein. BA, U. Wis., Whitewater, 1971, MA, 1980. Cert. elem. tchr., Wis. Tchr. Postville Sch., Blanchardville, Wis., 1959-62; jr. high sch. tchr. Hollandale (Wis.) Sch., 1962-64; jr. high tchr., prin. DeSoto (Wis.) Sch. Dist., 1964-65; jr. high math. and sci. tchr. Walworth (Wis.) Grade Sch., 1965-68; math. sci. tchr. Reek Elem. Sch., Lake Geneva, Wis., 1968-81; dist. mgr. World Book, Inc., Chgo., 1981-92; goal tchr. Black Hawk Tech. Coll., Janesville, Wis., 1990-92; CEO, adminstr. Kid's Sta., Inc., Walworth, 1990—. Computer cons. So. Lakes United Educators, Burlington, Wis., 1983-86. Mem. Am. Legion, K.C. Democrat. Roman Catholic. Avocations: rv camping, nature walks, classic cars. Office: Kid's Sta Inc PO Box 323 507 N Main St Walworth WI 53184-9787

SITARZ, PAULA GAJ, writer; b. New Bedford, Mass., May 25, 1955; d. Stanley Mitchell and Pauline (Rocha) Gaj; m. Michael James Sitarz, Aug. 26, 1978; children: Andrew Michael, Kate Elizabeth. BA, Smith Coll., 1977; MLS, Simmons Coll., 1978. Children's libr. Thomas Crane Pub. Libr., Quincy, Mass., 1978-84. Dir. Reader's Theatre Workshop Thomas Crane Pub. Library, Quincy Mass., 1985. Author: (book) Picture Book Story Hours: From Birthdays to Bears, 1986, More Picture Book Story Hours, 1989, The Curtain Rises: A History of Theater From Its Origins in Greece and Rome Through the English Restoration, 1991, The Curtain Rises Volume II: A History of European Theater from the Eighteenth Century to the Present, 1993, Story Time Sampler: Read Alouds, Book Talks, and Activities for Children, 1997; contbr. monthly column Bristol County Baby Jour., 1992-98, South Shore Baby Jour., 1992-98, First Tchr., 1992-98. Mem. New Eng. Libr. Assn., Libr. Sci. Honor Soc., Smith Club of Southeastern Mass. (v.p. 1987-89, pres. 1989-91), Dartmouth (Mass.) Arts Coun., Beta Phi Mu. Roman Catholic. Avocation: singer. Home and Office: 25 Stratford Dr North Dartmouth MA 02747-3843

SITES, JOHN MILTON, mathematics educator, computer consultant; b. Balt., June 28, 1966; s. John Edward and Nancy Christine (Kamynskie) S. BS in Math. cum laude, Allentown Coll., Center Valley, Pa., 1992, postgrad., 1995—. With Harmes & Assocs., Balt., 1983, 84; internat. arrival bag handler State Aviation Bd., Balt., 1984-86; customer svc. agt. United Airlines, Allentown, 1986-87, Henson Airlines, various locations, 1987-88; tutor Northampton C.C., Bethlehem, Pa., 1988-89, Allentown Coll., Center Valley, 1990-91; supr. ground svcs. Continental Express Airlines, Allentown, 1988-90; sr. chief operator Allentown Coll. Acad. Computing Ctr., Center Valley, 1990-92; computer sci. coord. Sacred Heart Sch., Bethlehem,

1992—; paraprofl. for disadvantaged, at-risk & handicapped students Career Inst. Tech., Easton, Pa., 1992—. Computer cons. and planner Bangor (Pa.) Area Sr. H.S., 1992—, Wilson H.S., Easton, 1992—, Easton H.S., 1992—; group supr. Pvt. Industry Coun. Career Awareness Program, 1993-94; adj. math. faculty mem. Northampton C.C., Bethlehem, Pa., 1993-94. Contbr. articles to profl. jours. Activity aide United Cerebral Palsy, Bethlehem, 1987-88. Mem. Math. Assn. Am. (v.p. 1991), Pa. Coun. Tchrs. Math. Christian Ch. Avocations: model railroading, photography, antiques, computer hardware and software evaluation. Home: 3843 Suncrest Ln Bethlehem PA 18020-3485 Office: Career Inst of Tech 5335 Kesslersville Rd Easton PA 18040-6720

SIVASUBRAMANIAN, KOLINJAVADI NAGARAJAN, neonatologist, educator; b. Coimbatore, Madras, India, May 9, 1945; came to U.S., 1971; s. Kolinjavadi Ramaswamy and Sukanthi (Subramanian) Nagarajan; m. Kalyani Hariharier, Feb. 5, 1975; children: Ramya, Rajeev, Ranjan. BSc, Madras U., 1964, MD, 1969. Diplomate Am. Bd. Pediatrics and Neonatal-Perinatal Medicine. Intern in pediat. Jewish Hosp. and Med. Ctr., Bklyn., 1971-72; resident in pediat. U. Md. Hosp., Balt., 1972-74; fellow in neonatology Georgetown U. Hosp., Washington, 1974-76, attending neonatologist, 1976—, dir. nurseries, chief neonatology, 1981—, vice chair pediat., 1988-98, prof. pediat. and ob-gyn. Editor: Trace Elements/Mineral Metablolism During Development, 1993; editor pub. SIDS Series, 1985; editor jour. Current Concepts in Neonatology, India, 1990—; internat. editor Indian Jour. Pediat., India, 1988—. Chmn. Siva Vishnu Temple, Lanham, Md., 1981-91; mem. Fetus and New Born Com., Washington, 1988; founder, bd. dirs. Coun. of Hindu Temples U.S.A.; founder, coord. United Hindu Temples of Met. Washington; 1st v.p. Interfaith Conf., Washington; mem. D.C. bd. dirs. Nat. Youth Leadership Forum. Recipient "Preemies" cover article Newsweek, 1988; featured in "Washingtonian" jour., 1996. Fellow Am. Coll. Nutrition, Am. Acad. Pediat.; mem. AAAS, N.Y. Acad. Scis., Internat. Soc. for Trace Element Rsch. in Humans, Soc. for Bioethics Consultation, Am. Soc. Law, Medicine and Ethics. Hindu. Achievements include research in neonatology, trace elements kinetics, reduction in infant mortality, neonatal immunology, and bioethics. Office: Georgetown U Hosp 3 South Hospital 3800 Reservoir Rd NW Washington DC 20007-2113

SIZEMORE, BARBARA ANN, Black studies educator; b. Chgo., Dec. 17, 1927; d. Sylvester Walter Laffoon and Delila Mae (Alexander) Stewart; m. Furman E. Sizemore, June 28, 1947 (div. Oct. 1964); children: Kymara, Furman G.; m. Jake Milliones, Sept. 29, 1979 (div. Feb. 1992). BA, Northwestern U., 1947, MA, 1954; PhD, U. Chgo., 1979; LLD (hon.), Del. State Coll., 1974; LittD (hon.), Cen. State U., 1974; DHL (hon.), Bal. Coll. of Bible, 1975; D of Pedagogy (hon.), Niagara U., 1994. Tchr., prin., dir. Chgo. Pub. Schs., 1947-72; assoc. sec. Am. Assn. Sch. Adminstrs., Arlington, Va., 1972-73; supt. schs. D.C. Pub. Schs., Washington, 1973-75; ednl. cons. Washington and Pitts., 1975—; prof. Black studies U. Pitts., 1977-92; dean Sch. of Edn. DePaul U., Chgo., 1992-98, prof. emeritus Sch. Edn., 1998—. Author: The Ruptured Diamond, 1981; bd. mem. Jour. Negro Edn., 1974-83, Rev. Edn., 1977-85. Candidate city coun. Washington, 1977; mem. NAACP. Recipient Merit award Northwestern U. Alumni Assn., 1974, Excellence award Nat. Alliance Black Sch. Educators, 1984, Human Rights award UN Assn., 1985, Racial Justice award YMCA, 1995, Harold Delaney Ednl. award, Am. Assn. for Higher Edn. Black Caucas, 1999, Disting. Scholarship award Am. Ednl. Rsch. Assn., 2001, Pres. award Nat. Alliance of Black Sch. Educators, 2002; named to U.S. Nat. Com., UNESCO, 1974-77. Mem. Nat. Coun. for Black Studies, African Heritage Studies Assn. (bd. mem. 1972—), Nat. Alliance Black Sch. Educators, Delta Sigma Theta. Democrat. Baptist. Avocations: reading, writing. Fax: 773-528-4485. E-mail: bsizemor@depaul.edu.

SIZEMORE, ROBERT DENNIS, school counselor, educational administrator; b. Indpls., July 30, 1943; s. George R. and Thelma L. (Lagle) S.; m. Leslie Ann, June 14, 1969; children: Christopher J., Kelly Ann. BS in Edn., Ind. U., 1967; MS in Secondary Edn., U. Bridgeport, 1972; cert., Portland State U., 1987. Cert. secondary tchr. and counselor, Oreg. Tchr. Marseilles (Ill.) Jr. High, 1967-69, Greenwich (Conn.) High Sch., 1969-76, Oregon City (Oreg.) High Sch., 1976-77; tchr., counselor, adminstr., asst. prin. curriculum Reynolds High Sch., Portland, Oreg., 1977-97; prin. Fairview (Oreg.) Elem. Sch., 1997—. Presenter Nat. Coun. Social Studies Conventions; mem. high sch. reform network N.W. Regional Ednl. Lab.; officer Congress of Oreg. Sch. Adminstrs.-Oreg. Assn. Secondary Sch. Adminstrs., 1995-97; cons. in field; adj. staff Lewis and Clark Coll. Mem. ASCD, NEA, AACD, Nat. Assn. Secondary Sch. Prins., Congress Oreg. Sch. Adminstrs. (conv. presenter). Office: 225 Main St Fairview OR 97024-3704

SIZEMORE, WILLIAM CHRISTIAN, retired academic administrator, county official; b. South Boston, Va., June 19, 1938; s. Herman Mason and Hazel (Johnson) S.; m. Anne Catherine Mills, June 24, 1961; children: Robert C., Richard M., Edward S. BA, U. Richmond, 1960; BD, Southeastern Bapt. Theol. Sem., Wake Forest, N.C., 1963; MLS, U. N.C., 1964; MLS (advanced), Fla. State U., 1971, PhD, 1973; postgrad., Harvard U., 1989. Library asst. U. N.C., Chapel Hill, 1963-64; assoc. librarian, instr. grad. research Southeastern Bapt. Theol. Sem., 1964-66; librarian, assoc. prof. South Ga. Coll., Douglas, 1966-71, acad. dean, prof., 1971-80, dean coll., prof., 1980-83, acting pres., 1982-83; pres. Alderson-Broaddus Coll., Philippi, W.Va., 1983-94, William Jewell Coll., Liberty, Mo., 1994-2000, chancellor, 2000—02; dir. bus. expansion Clay County Econ. Devel. Coun., Kansas City, Mo., 2003—. Cons. Continental R&D, Shawnee Mission, Kans., 1987-92, So. Assn. Colls. and Schs., Atlanta, 1977, S.C. Commn. on Higher Edn., Columbia, 1975-76, State Coun. Higher Edn. for Va., Richmond, 1969-70, Software Valley Corp., 1989-94; adv. bd. Software Valley Found., 1991-94. Contbr. articles to profl. jours. Active Barbour County Devel. Authority, Philippi, 1984-94, Barbour County Emergency Food and Shelter Bd., 1985-94, Barbour County Extension Com., 1990-94; mem. exec. coun. Yellow Pine area Boy Scouts Am., Valdosta, 1974-76; pres. Satilla Librarians Ednl. Coun., Douglas, 1969-71; lectr., workshop leader on Bible studies various orgns., 1966—; bd. advisors Swatow Kakwang Profl. Acad., Peoples Republic China; pres. bd. dirs. W.Va. Intercollegiate Athletic Conf., 1985-86, coun. of pres. Nat. Assn. Intercollegiate Athletics; bd. dirs., mem. exec. com. Broaddus Hosp., Philippi, 1983-94; chmn. W.Va. Productive Industry Efforts Found., 1989-92; mktg. com. W.Va. Life Scis. Park Found., 1989-94, Gov.'s Partnership for Progress, 1989-94; mem. adv. panel W.Va. Rural Health Initiative, 1991-94; gov. bd., bd. dirs. W.Va. Alliance of Hosps., 1991-94; bd. dirs. Clay-Platte Econ. Devel. Coun., 1996—; bd. dirs. ARC, Kansas City, 1996-2002, exec.com. 2000-02; adv. com. Mo. Conservation Heritage Found. Discovery Ctr. Campaign, 1998-2002; mem. Clay County Millennium Hist. Bd., 2002—; mem. Liberty HIstory Book Steering Com., 2001—. Joseph Ruzicka scholar N.C. Library Assn., 1963; recipient Douglas Pilot Club Edn. award, 1981, Good Citizenship medal Nat. Soc. Sons of Am. Revolution, 1999. Mem. ALA, Am. Assn. for Higher Edn., Am. Assn. Univ. Adminstrs., Nat. Coun. Instrnl. Adminstrs., W.Va. Assn. Coll. and Univ. Pres. (exec. com., v.p., pres. 1992), Mountain State Assn. Colls., W.Va. Found. for Ind. Colls. (dir. 1983-84, v.p. 1988-92), Mo. Colls. Fund (exec. com. 1997-98), Barbour County C. of C. (bd. dirs. 1988-94, v.p. 1988-90, pres. 1990-92, chmn. bd. 1992-94), Liberty Area C. of C. (bd. dirs. 1995-97), Kansas City Club. Democrat. Baptist. Avocations: woodworking, gardening. Home: 1417 Woodbury Dr Liberty MO 64068-1266 Office: Clay County Econ Devel Coun Office 110 NW Barry Rd Kansas City MO 64155

SIZER, REBECCA RUDD, performing arts educator, arts coordinator; b. Melrose, Mass., July 28, 1958; d. David William and Harriet Fay (Sart) Rudd; m. Theodore Sizer II, June 21, 1980; children: Caroline Foster, Lydia Catherine Rachel, Theodore Rudd. AB, Mount Holyoke Coll., 1980; MFA, Rochester Inst. Tech., 1983; postgrad., Eastman and Westminster Choir Coll. Cert. tchr. music and art K-12, N.J. Dir. music Christian Bros. Acad., Lincroft, N.J., 1991-93, Peddie Sch., Hightstown, N.J., 1993-94; chair dept. fine and performing arts, arts curriculum coord. Ranney Sch., Tinton Falls, N.J., 1994-97; tchr. music N.J. Ctr. for Performing Arts, 1997; tchr. music elem. schs. Lakewood Sch. Dist., N.J., 1997—; dir. music Christ Ch. United Meth., 1997—. Dir. after sch. art program Upstairs Youth Agy., Rochester, N.Y., 1984-85; music dir. Peninsula Opera Rep. Co., Rumson, N.J., 1986-88, local music. theatre, Red Bank, N.J., 1986—; freelance artist, musician. Illustrator: (books) China: A Brief History, 1981, Making Decisions, 1983. Joseph A. Skinner fellow Mt. Holyoke Coll., 1981, Dodge fellow Geraldine R. Dodge Found., 1993. Mem. Music Educators Nat. Conf., Local 399 Musicians Union. Avocation: tennis. Home: 385 Branch Ave Little Silver NJ 07739-1102

SIZER, THEODORE R. education educator; b. New Haven, Conn., June 23, 1932; m. Nancy Faust; 4 children. BA in English Lit., Yale U., 1953; MAT in Social Studies, Harvard U., 1957, Phd in Edn. and Am. History, 1961; PedD (hon.), Lawrence U., 1969; LittD (hon.), Union Coll., 1972; LLD (hon.), Conn. Coll., 1984; LHD (hon.), Williams Coll., 1984; MA ad eundem, Brown U., 1985; LHD (hon.), U Mass., Lowell, 1985, Dartmouth Coll., 1985, Lafayette Coll., 1991, Webster U., 1992, Ind. U., 1993, Mt. Holyoke Coll., 1993, U. Maine, 1993, Iona Coll., 1995, L.I. U., 1996, Bridgewater State Coll., 1996. English and math. tchr. Roxbury Latin Sch., Boston, 1955-56; history and geography tchr. Melbourne (Australia) Grammar Sch., 1958; asst. prof. edn., dir. MA in tchrs. program Harvard U., Cambridge, Mass., 1961-64, dean grad. sch. edn., 1964-72; headmaster, instr. in history Phillips Acad., Andover, Mass., 1972-81; chmn. A Study of High Schs., 1981-84; prof. edn. Brown U., Providence, 1984-96, chmn. edn. dept., 1984-89, Walter H. Annenberg prof. edn., 1993-94, dir. Annenberg Inst. Sch. Reform, 1994-96, univ. prof. emeritus, 1997—. Chmn. Coalition of Essential Schs., 1984—97, chmn. emeritus, 1997—; vis. prof. U. Bristol, England, 1971, Brown U., Providence, 1983. Author: Secondary Schools at the Turn of the Century, 1964, The Age of the Academies, 1964, Religion and Public Education, 1967; author: (with Nancy F. Sizer) Moral Education: Five Lectures, 1970; author: Places for Learning, Placeses for Joy: Speculations on American School Reform, 1972, Horace's Compromise: The Dilemma of the American High School, 1984, rev. edit., 1985, Horace's School: Redesigning the American High School, 1992, Horace's Hope: What Works for the American High School, 1996; author: (with Nancy Faust Sizer) The Students Are Watching: Schools and the Moral Contract, 1999. Active Nat. Adv. Coun., Scholastic, Inc., 1996. Capt. U.S. Army, 1953-55. Named Guggenheim fellow, 1971; recipient citations Am. Fedn. Tchrs., Nat. Assn. Secondary Sch. Prins., Phillips Exeter Acad., Boston C. of C., Andover C. of C., Lehigh U. Edn. Alumni, 1991, Nat. Assn. Coll. Admissions Counsellors, 1991, Anthony Wayne award Wayne State U., 1981, Gold medal for excellence in undergrad. teaching CASE, 1988, Tchrs. Coll. medal Tchrs. Coll., Columbia U., 1991, Harold W. McGraw prize in edn., 1991, James Bryant Conant award Edn. Commn. States, 1992, Disting. Svc. award Coun. Chief State Sch. Officers, 1992, Coun. Am. Private Edn., 1993, Nat. award of Distinction U. Pa., 1993, Alumni award Harvard Grad. Sch. Edn., 1994. Fellow Am. Acad. Arts and Scis., Am. Philos. Soc.; mem. Nat. Acad. Edn. Office: FW Parker Charter Essential Sch Tchrs Ctr Ayer MA 01432

SKAAR, SARAH HENSON, editor, educator; b. Bryan, Tex., June 19, 1958; d. James Bond Henson and Evie Leone (Callihan) Miller; m. Kent Skaar, Apr. 7, 1990. BS, Wash. State U., 1983, M in Adult and Continuing Edn., 1986. Asst. prof. U. Idaho Coop. Extension System, 1984-91; editor Horse Country, Idaho Falls, 1994—. Author: Risk Management: Strategies for Managing Volunteer Programs, 1988. Recipient Pub. Info. award Nat. Assn. County Agrl. Agts., 1989. Avocation: american quarter horses. Address: 2795A S 900 E Hagerman ID 83332-5617

SKABARDONIS, ALEXANDER, civil engineering educator; b. Athens, Greece, Mar. 19, 1954; came to U.S., 1982; s. Spyros and Maria (Tsaroucha) S.; m. Panorea Karageorgou, June 18, 1978; children: Maria, Alexander. Diploma in civil engring., Nat. Tech. U., Athens, 1977; MS, U. Southampton, Eng., 1979, PhD, 1982. Cert. civil engring. transp. Sr. civil engr. Pechlivanions CO, Athens, 1977-78; rsch. fellow U. Southhampton, Eng., 1981-82; adj. prof., rsch. engr. Civil Engring. Inst. Transp. Studies U. Calif., Berkeley, 1983—. V.p. DHS Inc., Berkeley, 1986—. Contbr. more than 50 articles, 100 reports to profl. jours. Graduate Studies scholar Greek Scholarship Found., Athens, 1972; rsch. fellow Sci./Engring. Rsch. Coun., London, 1990. Mem. Tech. Chamber Greece, Hellenic Inst. Transp. Engrs., Inst. Transp. Engrs., Transp. Rsch. Bd. Avocations: photography, sports. Office: ITS-UCB 109 Mclaughlin Hall Berkeley CA 94720-1720

SKALE, LINDA DIANNE, retired elementary education educator; b. Lansing, Mich., May 24, 1947; d. Louis and Dolores Louise (Clum) Pascotto; m. Arthur Skale, Sept. 9, 1967; children: Michelle, John, David, Jennifer. BA, Mich. State U., 1969, MA, 1971. Tchr. 3rd grade Ionia (Mich.) pub. schs., 1971—; reading cons. Benton Harbor (Mich.) schs.; elem. tchr. 3rd-5th grades, curriculum chair lang. arts portfolio assessment Berrien Springs (Mich.) Sch., reading tchr., coord.; interim prin. Sylvester Elem. Sch., 1994-95; ret., 2001. Named 1989 Outstanding Employee of the Yr., Berrien Springs Schs., 1988. Mem. ASCD, Internat. Reading Assn., Mich. Reading Assn. (lectr.), Tri County Reading Assn., Mich. Elem. and Mid. Sch. Prins. Assn. Home: 14188 Avery Pt Granger IN 46530

SKARR, MICHAEL W. state agency administrator; B in Mech. Engring., Marquette U.; MBA, Lewis U.; cert. in mgmt. arts, Aurora U. Mem. Ill. State Bd. Edn., Springfield, 1991-93, chairperson, 1993—96; pres. and CEO Naperville C. of C., Ill., 1996—. Mem. Joint Edn. Com., Ill.; past mem. Naperville Dist. 203 Bd. Edn., chmn. regulatory process com. Past chmn. Will County United Way Campaign; past pres., mem. exec. bd. Rainbow Coun. Boy Scouts Am.; past bd. dirs. Rialto Square Theatre Corp.*

SKEEN, DAVID RAY, systems engineer, consultant, engineering executive, educator; b. Bucklin, Kans., July 12, 1942; s. Claude E. and Velma A. (Birney) S.; m. Carol J. Stimpert, Aug. 23, 1964; children: Jeffrey Kent, Timothy Sean, Kimberly Dawn. BA in Math., Emporia State U., 1964; MS, Am. U., 1972; grad., Fed. Exec. Inst., 1983, Naval War Coll., 1984; DSc in Engring. Mgmt., George Washington U., 1998. Cert. office automation profl. Computer sys. analyst to comdr.-in-chief U.S. Naval Forces-Europe, London, 1967-70; computer sys. analyst Naval Command Sys. Support Activity, Washington, 1970-73; dir. data processing Office Naval Rsch., U.S. Navy Dept., Arlington, Va., 1973-78; dir. mgmt. info. sys. Naval Civilian Pers. Command, Washington, 1978-80; dep. dir. manpower, pers. tng. automated sys. Dept. Naval Mil. Pers. Command, Washington, 1980-85; dir. manpower, pers. tng. info. resource mgmt. Chief Naval Ops., Washington, 1985-91; assoc. dir. Office of IRM, USDA, Washington, 1992-96; dir. modernization of adminstrn. processes program, 1996-98; dep. dir. office of ops. USDA, Washington, 1998; sr. engring. manager, cons. Lockheed Martin, Washington, 1998—. Lectr. Inst. Sci. and Pub. Affairs, 1973-76; cons. Electronic Data Processing Career Devel. Programs, 1975—; detailed to Pres.'s Reorgn. Project for Automated Data Processing, 1978, spl. Navy IRM studies, SECNAV, 1991, USDA/Office of Mgmt. and Budget IRM, 1993, spl. USDA Field Structure Studies, 1997; adj. prof. Sch. Engring. and Applied Sci., George Washington U., 1985—; with Pres.'s Fed. Automated Data Processing Users Group, Washington, 1978-80. Contbr. articles to profl. jours. Capt. USNR, 1960-91. Recipient Outstanding Performance award Interagy. Com. Data Processing, 1976, Adminstrv. Staff Performance award, 1998, Sec.'s cert. Appreciation, 1998. Mem. IEEE, Internat. Coun. on Sys. Engring., Sr. Exec. Assn., Assn. Fed. IRM, Naval Res. Assn., Pres. Fed. Automated Data Processing Users Group. Home: 707 Forest Park Rd Great Falls VA 22066-2908 E-mail: david.r.skeen@lmco.com.

SKELLAND, ANTHONY HAROLD PETER, chemical engineering educator; b. Birmingham, Eng., Feb. 21, 1928; came to U.S., 1959; s. Harold and Hilda Skelland. BSChemE, U. Birmingham, 1948, PhD in Chem. Engring., 1952. Mgr. Procter and Gamble, Eng., 1954-56, R&D engr., 1956-59; asst. prof. Ill. Inst. Tech., Chgo., 1959-62; assoc. prof. U. Notre Dame, South Bend, Ind., 1962-66, prof., 1966-69; Ashland prof. U. Ky., Lexington, 1969-79; prof. Ga. Inst. Tech., Atlanta, 1979—. Cons. Monsanto, Babcock and Wilcox, Union Carbide, E.I. duPont de Nemours, FMC Corp., Westinghouse and others. Author: Non-Newtonian Flow and Heat Transfer, 1967, Diffusional Mass Transfer, 1974; contbr. over 80 articles to profl. jours. Fellow AIChE, Inst. Petroleum; mem. Royal Soc. Chemistry (Eng.), Inst. Chem. Engrs. (Eng.). Avocations: tennis, theatre, dining out.

SKELLY, DAVID K, education educator; A.B. in biology, Middlebury Coll., 1983—87; PhD, U. Mich., 1987—92. Tchg. asst. Dept. Biology, Middlebury Coll., 1986—87, Dept. Biology, U. Mich., 1987—91; postdoctoral rsch. fellow U. of Wollongong, New South Wales, Australia, 1992—93; NSF postdoctoral fellow U. Wash., Seattle, 1993—95; asst. prof. Sch. of Forestry and Environ. Studies, Yale U., New Haven, 1996—2000; adj. appt. Dept. of Ecology and Evolutionary Biology, Yale U., 1996—; assoc. prof. of ecology Sch. of Forestry and Environ. Studies, Yale U., 2000—; asst. prof. ecology Yale U., 2000—; vis. assoc. prof. Dept. Biology, Penn. State U., 2001. Assoc. curator Divsn. Vertebrate Zoology, Peabody Mus. of Nat. History, Yale U., 2000—; mem., endangered species adv. com. Dept. Environ. Protection, State of Conn., 2002; peer rev. site vis. U.S. Environ. Protection Agency, 2002; mem., sci. adv. bd. Bonefish & Tarpon Unlimited, 2002—; dir. of postdoctoral studies Sch. of Forestry and Environ. Studies, Yale U., 2002—. Fellowship, John Simon Guggenheim Meml. Found., 2003, Australian Flora and Fauna Rsch. Program grant, U. of Wollongong, 1992—93, NSF postdoctoral fellowship, 1993—95, NSF/EPA grant, 1997—2000, NSF grant, 1997—2003, NIH/NSF grant, 2000—. Office: Sch of Forestry and Environmental Studies Yale U 370 Prospect St New Haven CT 06511

SKELTON, DIANN CLEVENGER, elementary education educator; b. Kennett, Mo., Nov. 26, 1956; d. Opie O'Neal and D. Charlenene (Duke) C. BSEd in Early Childhood Edn., Ark. State U., 1978, MSEd in Spl. Edn., 1979, MSEd in Early Childhood Edn., 1989; EdS in Edn. Adminstrn., S.E. Mo. State U. Spl. edn. tchr. Blytheville (Ark.) Pub. Sch., 1978-82; tchr. early childhood edn. Hayti (Mo.) Pub. Schs., 1982-86, tchr. kindergarten, 1986-91, tchr. 2d grade, 1991-97, remedial reading tchr., 1998—; tchr. early childhood edn. Hayti (Mo) Pub. Sch., 2002—03. Adj. instr. Three Rivers Cmty. Coll., 2002—. Mem. NEA, NAEYC, Assn. Supervision and Curriculum Devel., Beta Sigma Phi, Kappa Delta Pi, Delta Kappa Gamma. Republican. Baptist. Avocations: cross stitch, sporting events, Am. Kennel Club registered Dobermans. Office: Hayti Pub Schs 500 N 4th St Hayti MO 63851-1116

SKELTON, GORDON WILLIAM, data processing executive, educator; b. Vicksburg, Miss., Oct. 31, 1949; s. Alan Gordon and Martha Hope (Butcher) S.; m. Sandra Lea Champion, May 1974 (div. 1981); m. Janet Elaine Johnson, Feb. 14, 1986; 1 stepchild, Brian Quarles. BA, McMurry Coll., 1974; MA, U. So. Miss., 1975, postgrad., 1975-77, MS, 1987; PhD, U. South Africa, 2001. Cert. in data processing. Systems analyst Criminal Justice Planning Commn., Jackson, Miss., 1978-80; cord. Miss. Statis. Analysis Ctr., Jackson, 1980-83; data processing mgr. Dept. Adminstrn. Fed.-State Programs, Jackson, 1983-84; mgr. pub. tech. So. Ctr. Rsch. and Innovation, Hattiesburg, Miss., 1985-87; internal cons. Sec. of State, State of Miss., Jackson, 1987; system support mgr. CENTEC, Jackson, 1987-88; instr. dept. computer sci. Belhaven Coll., Jackson, 1988—; v.p. info. svcs. Miss. Valley Title Ins. Co., Jackson, 1988—. Adj. instr. engring. grad. program telecom. U. Miss., 1997—. Author: (with others) Trends in Ergonomics/Human Factors, 1986; contbr. articles to profl. jours. With U.S. Army, 1970-73, Vietnam. Recipient Cert. of Appreciation, U.S. Dept. Justice/Bur. Justice Stats., 1982. Mem. IEEE Computer Soc., Assn. Info. Tech. Profls. (chpt. pres. 1991, 92, program chair 1990), Assn. Computing Machinery, Am. Soc. Quality (cert. software quality engr.). Presbyterian. Avocations: gardening, collecting civil war relics. Office: Miss Valley Title Ins Co 315 Tombigbee St Jackson MS 39201-4600

SKERKER, ARTHUR J. secondary education educator; Sci. tchr. Hartford (Conn.) Pub. H.S., 1995, computer resource tchr., 1995—. Named State Tchr. of Yr., Sci., Conn., 1993. Office: Hartford Public High Sch 55 Forest St Hartford CT 06105-3243

SKIERKOWSKI, SISTER TERESA MARIE, educational administrator; b. Balt., Mar. 31, 1951; d. John George and Freda Lucy (Oleski) S. AA, Assumption Coll., Mendham, N.J., 1971; BA, Felician Coll., Lodi, N.J., 1976; MA, St. Charles Coll., Phila., 1992. Cert. tchr., N.J.; joined Sisters of Christian Charity, Roman Catholic Ch., 1969. Tchr. St. Nicholas Sch., Jersey City, 1973-75, Immaculate Conception Sch., Bronx, N.Y., 1977-80, Kingston (N.Y.) Cath. Sch., 1980-81, 86-88, St. Gabriel's Sch., Greenville, N.C., 1981-82, St. Jude's Sch., Mountain Top, Pa., 1985-86; tchr., dir. religious edn. St. Mary's Sch., Wharton, N.J., 1982-85; prin. Sacred Heart Sch., Luzerne, Pa., 1988—. Coord. region 6, Diocese of Scranton, Pa., 1989—. Mem. ASCD, Nat. Cath. Edn. Assn., Mid. States Assn. Elem. Schs., Nat. Assn. Elem. Sch. Prins. Avocations: biking, roller skating, bowling, reading, swimming. Office: Sacred Heart Sch PO Box 125 Luzerne PA 18709-0125

SKILBECK, CAROL LYNN MARIE, elementary educator and small business owner; b. Seymour, Ind., May 1, 1953; d. Harry Charles and Barbara Josephine (Knue) S.; div.; 1 child, Michael Charles. Student, U. Cin., 1977, Wright State U., 1985-86, No. Ky. U., 1995—. Cert. tchr., Ohio. Sec. Procter & Gamble, Cin., 1971-76; classified typist The Cin. Enquirer, Cin., 1976; tchr. St. Aloysius Sch., Cin., 1977-79, St. William Sch., Cin., 1979-82; legal sec. County Dept. Human Svcs., Cin., 1982-86; tchr. St. Jude Sch., Cin., 1986-91; educator, owner CLS Tutoring Svcs., Cin., 1991—; comm. edn. tchr. No. Ky. U., 1996; photographer Interstate Studio and Am. Sch. Pictures, 1994—; sales rep. Am. Sch. Pictures, 1997-98; tchr. Blessed Sacrament Sch., Ft. Mitchell, Ky., 1998—, asst. libr., 2001—. Tchr. St. Martin Gifted Program, Cin., 1992-93, Oak Hills Schs. Cmty. Edn., Cin., 1990—. Super Saturday Gifted Program, Cin., 1990—; adult leader antidrug program Just Say No, Cin., 1989-92; photographer, sales rep. Am. Sch. Pictures; children's dance instr., 2000—. Author: Study Skills Workshop, 1993; writer, dir. Christmas play, 1993; contbr. poetry to lit. publs. Vol. interior designer for homeless shelter St. Joseph's Carpenter Shop, Cin., 1990; vol. Habitat for Humanity. Mem. Nat. Tchrs. Assn. Democrat. Roman Catholic. Avocations: writing, jazz/tap dance, community theatre, interior decorating, aerobics instructor. Address: 6840 Skies Edge Ct Apt 25 Cincinnati OH 45247-3249

SKILES, JAMES JEAN, electrical and computer engineering educator; b. St Louis, Oct. 16, 1928; s. Coy Emerson and Vernetta Beatrice (Maples) S.; m. Deloris Audrey McKenney, Sept. 4, 1948; children: Steven, Randall, Jeffrey. BSEE, Washington U., St. Louis, 1948; MS, U. Mo.-Rolla, 1951; PhD, U. Wis., 1954. Engr. Union Electric Co., St. Louis, 1948-49; instr. U. Mo.-Rolla, 1949-51; prof. elec. engring. U. Wis., Madison, 1954-89, prof. emeritus, 1989—, chmn. Dept. Elec. Engring., 1967-72, dir. Univ. Industry Rsch. program, 1972-75, dir. Energy Rsch. Ctr., 1975-95. Cons. in field Contbr. articles to profl. jours. Mem. Monona Grove Dist. Schs. Bd., Wis., 1961-69; mem. adv. com. Wis. Energy Office, Madison, 1979-80, Wis. Pub. Service Commn., 1980-81. Recipient Wis. Electric Utilities Professorship in Energy Engring. U. Wis., 1975-89; recipient Benjamin Smith Reynolds Teaching award, 1980, Kiekhofer Teaching award, 1955, Acad of Elec. Engring. award U. Mo.-Rolla, 1982 Mem. IEEE (sr.), Am. Soc. Engring.

Edn. Home: 8099 Coray Ln Verona WI 53593-9073 Office: Univ of Wisconsin Dept Elec & Computer Engring 1415 Engineering Dr Madison WI 53706-1607 E-mail: skiles@engr.wisc.edu.

SKILLERN, FRANK FLETCHER, law educator; b. Sept. 26, 1942; s. Will T. and Vera Catherine (Ryberg) S.; m. Susan Schlaefer, Sept. 3, 1966; children: Nathan Edward, Leah Catherine. AB, U. Chgo., 1964; JD, U. Denver, 1966; LLM, U. Mich., 1969. Bar: Colo. 1967, Tex. 1978. Pvt. practice law, Denver, 1967; gen. atty. Maritime Adminstrn., Washington, 1967-68; asst. prof. law Ohio No. U., 1969-71, Tex. Tech U., Lubbock, 1971-73, assoc. prof. law, 1973-75, prof. law, 1975—, George W. McCleskey prof. water law, 1998—. Vis. prof. U. Tex. Law Sch., summer 1979, U. Ark. Law Sch., 1979-80, U. Tulsa Coll. Law, 1981-82; cons. and speaker in field. Author: Environmental Protection: The Legal Framework, 1981, 2d edit. published as Environmental Protection Deskbook, 1995, Regulation of Water and Sewer Utilities, 1989, Texas Water Law, Vol. I, 1988, rev. edit., 1992, Vol. II, 1991; contbr. chpts. to Powell on Real Property, Zoning and Land Use Controls, others; author cong. procs. and numerous articles. Mem. ABA (mem. publs. com. Sect. Natural Resources Law 1984—, vice chair internat. environ. law com. Sect. Natural Resources Law 1987). Office: Tex Tech U Sch Law PO Box 40004 Lubbock TX 79409-0004

SKILLICORN, JUDY PETTIBONE, gifted and talented education coordinator; b. Cleve., June 16, 1943; d. C. Arthur and Dorothy Laura Pettibone; m. Robert Charles Skillicorn, Aug. 21, 1965; children: Jodie Lynn, Brian Jeffrey, Jennifer Laura. BS in Edn., Ohio State U., 1965; MEd, Cleve. State U., 1988. 6th grade tchr. Windermer Sch., Upper Arlington, Ohio, 1965-68; pvt. tutor, 1968-71; adminstr. Westshore Montessori Sch., Elyria, Lorain & Amherst, Ohio, 1981; ch. educator First Congl. Ch., Elyria, 1982-84, St. Peters United Ch. of Christ, Amherst, Ohio, 1984; tchr. gifted Clearview Local Schs., Lorain, 1985-90; coord. gifted Ednl. Svc. Ctr. Lorain County, Elyria, 1990—2003; implementation dir. county-wide sch. for integrated arts Lorain County Ednl. Svc. Ctr., Elyria. Founder Arts Advocacy of Lorain County, 1994, pres. 1996; founder Arts Connected Tchg. pilot program in 4 sch. dists., 1995-96; mem. planning com. and curriculum com. Lorain County Alternative Sch.; mem. plannng com. Vision 2000, Lorain County C.C., 1997; initiator collaboration of Oberlin Coll. students tchg. arts integration in classrooms with tchrs., 1997. Author: Young Authors Handbook, 1991-2003; co-chair Page to Stage integrated arts program with Chronicle-Telegram, 1997. Bd. dirs. Lorain County Health Dept., 1999-2002, v.p., 2002-03, pres., 2003—; pageant dir. Ch. Medieval Feast, Elyria, 1988-91; chmn. diaconate First Congl. Ch., Elyria, 1990-93, 99; mem. com. Lorain County Beautiful, Seventh Generation, 1995-97. Recipient Partnership in Edn. for Young Authors Program grades K-6 Nat. Assn. Coll. Stores, Oberlin, 1993-2003, for Writers conf. Program grades 7-9, 1993-97; Jennings scholar tchr. Martha Holden Jennings Found., 1990-91. Mem. Writing Tchrs. Network (publ. com. 1991-93), North Ctrl. Consortium for Gifted (treas., v.p. 1991-93), Lorain County Elem. Sch. Adminstrs. (sec.-treas. 1993, v.p. 1993-94, pres. 1994-95, nominating com. 1997), Consortium Ohio Coords. for Gifted, Ohio Assn. Gifted Children, Chautauqua Lit. Soc., Greater Cleve. Coords. Consortium. Avocations: reading including children's literature, travel, attending plays, arts actvities and concerts, gardening. Office: Ednl Svc Ctr Lorain County 1885 Lake Ave Elyria OH 44035-2551

SKILLINGSTAD, CONSTANCE YVONNE, social services administrator, educator; b. Portland, Oreg, Nov. 18, 1944; d. Irving Elmer and Beulah Ruby (Aleckson) Erickson; M. David W. Skillingstad, Jan. 12, 1968 (div. Mar. 1981); children: Michael, Brian. BA in Sociology, U. Minn., 1966; MBA, U. St. Thomas, St. Paul, 1982. Cert. vol. adminstr.; lic. social worker; lic. real estate agt. Social worker Rock County Welfare Dept., Luverne, Minn., 1966-68, Hennepin County Social Svc., Mpls., 1968-70, vol. coord., 1970-78, St. Joseph's Home for Children, Mpls., 1978-89, mgr. cmty. resources, 1989-94; exec. dir. Mpls. Crisis Nursery, 1994-97; mem. cmty. faculty Met. State U., St. Paul and Mpls., 1980-97; faculty U. St. Thomas Ctr. for Non Profit Mgmt., 1990—2001; asst. adminstr. St. Joseph's Home Children, Mpls., 1997-98; asst. dir. Cath. Charities of Archdiocese of St. Paul and Mpls., 1998-2000; dir. mem. svc. Minn. Coun. Founds., 2001—02; exec. dir. Prevent Child Abuse Minn., St. Paul, 2002—; pres. Golden Girl Homes, Inc., 2001—. Trainer, mem. adv. commn. Mpls. Vol. Ctr., 1978-90, cons., 1980—, chmn. Contbr. articles to Jour. Vol. Adminitrn. Mem. adv. bd. Mothers Against Drunk Driving, Minn., 1986-88, Stop It Now! Minn., 2003, Congregations Concerned for Children, 2002—; vice chmn., chmn. adminstrv. coun., lay leader Hobart United Meth. Ch.; lay rep. to Minn. Ann. Conf. of Meth. Chs., 1989-92; chmn. social concerns. commn. Pk. Ave United Meth. Ch., 1992—; bd. dir. Ctr. for Grief, Loss and Transition; mem. Initiative for Violence Free Families, 1998—. Named one of Oustanding Young Women Am., 1974, Woman of Distinction Mpls. St. Paul Mag./KARE-TV, 1995. Mem. Minn. Assn. Vol. Dir. (pres. 1975, sec., ethics chmn. 1987—), Assn. for Vol. Adminstrn. (v.p. regional affairs 1985-87, mem. assessment panel 1986-94, coord. nat. tng. team, cert. process for vol. adminstr. 1988-92, profl. devel. chair 1990-92), Minn. Social Svc. Assn. (pres. 1981, 98-99, bd. dir. 1996-2001, Disting. Svc. award 1987); Legis. Com. Mem. Dem.-Farmer-Labor Party. Methodist. Avocations: bridge, volleyball, accordion, travel, reading. Office: Prevent Child Abuse Minn Ste 202-S 1821 University Ave Saint Paul MN 55104 E-mail: cskillingstad@msn.com.

SKINNER, ANDREW CHARLES, history educator, religious writer; b. Durango, Colo., Apr. 25, 1951; s. Charles La Verne and Julia Magdalena (Schunk) S.; m. Janet Corbridge, Mar. 22, 1974; children: Cheryl Lyn, Charles Lon, Kelli Ann, Mark Andrew, Holly, Suzanne. BA with distinction, U. Colo., 1975; MA with distinction, Iliff Sch. Theology, Denver, 1978; ThM, Harvard U., 1980; PhD, U. Denver, 1986. Group mgr. May Co. Dept. Store, Denver, 1980-83; assoc. studio dir. Talking Books Pub. Co., Denver, 1984-88; instr. history Metro. State Coll., Denver, 1984-88; prof. history Ricks Coll., Rexburg, Utah, 1988-92; prof. ancient scripture Brigham Young U., Provo, Utah, 1992—, chmn. ancient scripture, 1997—, dean Coll. of Religious Edn., 2000—, dir. Religious Studies Ctr., 2000—. Vis. instr. ancient scripture Brigham Young U., 1987; vis. prof. Jerusalem Ctr. for Nr. Eastern Studies, Israel; cons. Univ. Without Walls, Loretto Heights Coll., Denver, 1985-88; mem. editl. staff Dead Sea Scrolls, publ. bd. Israel Antiquities Authority; gen. editor New Testament Commentary, Brigham Young U. Author chpts. numerous books including Gethsemane, 2002, Parables of the Latter Days; co-author: Jerusalem-The Eternal City, 1996, New Testament Apostles Testify of Christ, 1998, C.S. Lewis: The Man and His Message, 1999, Parables of the Latter Days, 2001, Discoveries in the Judaean Desert XXXIII-Qumran Cave 4; contbr. articles to profl. jours. Bishop Mormon Ch., Denver, 1986-88, Utah. 1996—; varsity scout leader Teton Parks coun. Boy Scouts Am., Rexburg, 1988-89; host Internat. Scholars Conf. on Holocaust and the Chs., 1995; bd. dirs. Children of Israel Found., 2001—, Inst. for Study and Preservation of Ancient Religious Texts, 2001—. Mil. history fellow U.S. Mil. Acad., 1989. Mem. Am. Hist. Assn., Soc. Bibl. Lit., Mormon History Assn., Phi Theta Kappa, Phi Alpha Theta. Mem. Lds Ch. Office: Brigham Young U Coll Religious Edn JSB 375-A Provo UT 84602

SKINNER, BRIAN JOHN, geologist, educator; b. Wallaroo, South Australia, Dec. 15, 1928; came to U.S., 1958, naturalized, 1963; s. Joshua Henry and Joyce Barbara Lloyd (Prince) S.; m. Helen Catherine Wild, Oct. 9, 1954; children: Adrienne Wild, Stephanie Wild, Thalassa Wild. B.Sc., U. Adelaide, Australia, 1950; A.M., Harvard U., 1952, PhD, 1955; D Engring. (hon.), Colo. Sch. Mines, 1998; DSc (hon.), U. Toronto, 1998. Lectr. U. Adelaide, 1955-58; research geologist U.S. Geol. Survey, 1958-62, chief br. exptl. geochemistry and mineralogy, 1962-66; prof. geology and geophysics, chmn. dept. Yale U., New Haven, 1966-73, Eugene Higgins prof., 1972—. Hugh Exton McKinstry Meml. lectr. Harvard U., 1978; Alex L. du Toit lectr. Combined Socs. South Africa, 1979; Cecil H. and Ida Green lectr. U. B.C., 1983; Thayer Lindsley Meml. lectr. Soc. Econ. Geologists, 1983; Soc. Econ. Geologists Overseas lectr., 1985; Hoffman lectr. Harvard U., 1986, Joubin-James lectr. U. Toronto, 1987; mem. exec. com. divsn. earth scis. NRC, 1966-69; chmn. com. mineral resources and the environment. Nat. Acad. Scis.-NRC, 1973-75; mem. Lunar Sample Analysis Planning Team, 1968-70, Lunar Sci. Rev. Bd., 1971-72, U.S. Nat. Com. for Geochemistry, 1966-67, U.S. Nat. Com. for Geology, 1973-77, 85-93, chmn., 1987-93, chmn. bd. earth scis. NRC, 1987-88, earth scis. and resources, 1989-90; mem. bd. Internat. Geol. Correlation Program, UNESCO-IUGS, 1985-89, 90-96, chmn., 1986-89; cons. Office Sci. and Tech. Policy, 1977-80, NSF, 1977-82; dir. Econ. Geology Pub. Co.; chmn. governing bd. Am. Jour. Sci., 1972—; pres. Econ. Geology Pub. Co., 1996-2000. Author: Earth Resources, 1969, 77, 86, Man and the Ocean, 1973, Physical Geology, 1974, 77, 87, Rocks and Rock Minerals, 1979, The New Iron Age Ahead, 1987, Resources and World Development, 1987, The Dynamic Earth, 1989, 92, 95, 2000, 03, The Blue Planet, 1995, 99, 2000, Environmental Geology, 1996, Geology Today, 1999, Oxford Companion to the Earth, 2000; editor: Econ. Geology, 1969-96, Oxford Univ. Press Monographs in Geological Sciences, 1979—, Internat. Geology Rev., 1995—; editl. bd. Am. Scientist, 1974-90, chmn., 1987-90. Trustee Hopkins Grammar Sch., 1978-83. Recipient Disting. Contbns. award, Assn. Earth Sci. Editors, 1979, medal, Geol. Assn. Can., 1998, Futer's medal, Inst. of Mining and Metallurgy, London, 2002; fellow, Guggenheim fellow, 1970. Fellow Geol. Soc. Am. (councillor 1976-78, chmn. spl. publs. com. 1980-81, chmn. com. on coms. 1983, pres. 1985); mem. Geochem. Soc. (pres. 1972-73), Conn. Acad. Sci. and Engring. (div. chmn. 1978-80, coun. 1982-87), Soc. Econ. Geologists (pres. 1995, Silver medal 1981, Marsden medal 2003). Home: PO Box 894 Woodbury CT 06798-0894

SKINNER, DANIEL THOMAS, language educator; b. Boston, May 1, 1916; s. Thomas Henson and Esther Hannetta (Jennings) Skinner; m. Vyna May Wingood, Oct. 15, 1944 (dec. Jan. 1995); children: David Edward, John Arnold. AB magna cum laude, Harvard U., 1938, PhD in Romance Lang., 1953; MA in Romance Lang., Boston Coll., 1939. Substitute instr. in French Va. State Coll., Ettrick, 1939—40; instr. in French and Spanish Dillard U., New Orleans, 1940—42; from asst. prof. to prof. French and Latin Morgan State Coll., Balt., 1946—81. Vis. prof. Tex. So. U., Houston, 1953—54, Houston, 1956, Towson State Coll., Balt., 1964; part-time prof. Sojourner-Douglass Coll., Balt., 1981—85, Coppin State Coll., Balt., 1985—90; mem. adv. bd. Directory of Am. Scholars, N.Y.C., 1970—80. Author: U.S. Teacher-Training Program: for France, 1959, Victor Hugo and L. Frechette, 1972, Ustaz Aswad (Black Professor), 1996. Pres. PTA, Balt., 1957. Named Rosenwald fellow, Rosenwald Found., Chgo., 1947—48, Fulbright prof. in France, Fulbright Found., Washington, 1956—57; recipient Nat. award, Urban League, Boston, 1949. Mem.: Frisby Hist. Soc. (fin. sec. 2001—02), Henson Family Soc., Phi Beta Kappa. Democrat. Roman Catholic. Avocations: movies, pinochle, sports, foreign travel. Home: 2033 Wheeler Ave Baltimore MD 21216-3225

SKINNER, G(EORGE) WILLIAM, anthropologist, educator; b. Oakland, Calif., Feb. 14, 1925; s. John James and Eunice (Engle) S.; m. Carol Bagger, Mar. 25, 1951 (div. Jan. 1970); children: Geoffrey Crane, James Lauriston, Mark Williamson, Jeremy Burr; m. Susan Mann, Apr. 26, 1980; 1 dau., Alison Jane. Student, Deep Springs (Calif.) Coll., 1942-43; BA with distinction in Far Eastern Studies, Cornell U., Ithaca, N.Y., 1947, PhD in Cultural Anthropology, 1954; LLD (hon.), U. Hong Kong, 2001. Field dir. Cornell U. S.E. Asia program, also Cornell Research Center, Bangkok, Thailand, 1951-55; rsch. assoc. in Indonesia, 1956-58; asso. prof., then prof. anthropology Cornell U., Ithaca, N.Y., 1960-65; asst. prof. sociology Columbia, 1958-60; sr. specialist in residence East-West Ctr. Honolulu, 1965-66; prof. anthropology Stanford, 1966-89; Barbara Kimball Browning prof. humanities and scis., 1987-89; prof. anthropology U. Calif., Davis, 1990—. Vis. prof. U. Pa., 1977, Duke U., 1978, Keio U., Tokyo, 1985, 1988, U. Calif., San Diego, 1986, Hong Kong U., 2002; field rsch. China, 1949-50, 77, S.E. Asia, 1950-51, Thailand, 1951-53, 54-55, Java and Borneo, 1956-58, Japan, 1985, 88, 95; joint com. on contemporary China Social Sci. Research Coun.-Am. Acad. Learned Socs., 1961-65, 80-81, internat. com. on Chinese studies, 1963-64, mem. joint com. on Chinese studies, 1981-83; mem. subcom. rsch. Chinese Soc. Social Sci. Rsch. Coun., 1961-70, chmn., 1963-70; dir. program on East Asian Local Systems, 1969-71; dir. Chinese Soc. Bibliography Project, 1964-73; assoc. dir. Cornell China Program, 1961-63; dir. London-Cornell Project Social Rsch., 1962-65; mem. com. on scholarly communication with People's Republic of China, Nat. Acad. Scis., 1966-70, social scis. and humanities panel, 1982-83; adv. com. Ctr. for Chinese Rsch. Materials, Assn. Rsch. Libraries, 1967-70; policy and planning com. China in Time and Space, 1993-96. Author: Chinese Society in Thailand, 1957, Leadership and Power in the Chinese Community of Thailand, 1958; also articles; Editor: The Social Sciences and Thailand, 1956, Local, Ethnic and National Loyalties in Village Indonesia, 1959, Modern Chinese Society: An Analytical Bibliography, 3 vols, 1973, (with Mark Elvin) The Chinese City Between Two Worlds, 1974, (with A. Thomas Kirsch) Change and Persistence in Thai Society, 1975, The City in Late Imperial China, 1977, The Study of Chinese Society, 1979. Served to ensign USNR, 1943-46. Fellow Center for Advanced Study in Behavioral Scis., 1969-70, Guggenheim fellow, 1969, NIMH spl. fellow, 1970 Mem. NAS, AAAS, Am. Anthrop. Assn., Am. Sociol. Assn., Assn. Asian Studies (bd. dirs. 1962-65, chmn. nominating com. 1967-68, pres. 1983-84), Soc. for Cultural Anthropology, Internat. Union for Sci. Study of Population, Social Sci. History Assn., Am. Ethnol. Soc., Population Assn. Am., Siam Soc., Soc. Qing Studies, Soc. Econ. Anthropology, Phi Beta Kappa, Sigma Xi. Office: U Calif Dept Anthropology 1 Shields Ave Davis CA 95616-5270

SKINNER, JAMES LAURISTON, chemist, educator; b. Ithaca, N.Y., Aug. 17, 1953; s. G. William and Carol (Bagger) S.; m. Wendy Moore, May 31, 1986; children: Colin Andrew, Duncan Geoffrey. AB, U. Calif., Santa Cruz, 1975; PhD, Harvard U., 1979. Rsch. assoc. Stanford (Calif.) U., 1980-81; from asst. prof. to prof. chemistry Columbia U., N.Y.C., 1981-90; Hirschfelder prof. chemistry, dir. Theol. Chemistry Inst. U. Wis., Madison, 1990—. Vis. scientist Inst. Theol. Physics U. Calif., Santa Barbara, 1987; vis. prof. physics U. Jos. Fourier, Grenoble, France, 1987, U. Bordeaux (France), 1995. Contbr. articles to profl. jours. Recipient Fresenius award Phi Lambda Upsilon, 1989, Camille and Henry Dreyfus Tchr.-Scholar award, 1984, NSF Presdl. Young Investigator award, 1984, Humboldt Sr. Scientist award, 1993; NSF grad fellow, 1975, NSF postdoctoral fellow, 1980, Alfred P. Sloan Found. fellow, 1984, Guggenheim fellow, 1993. Mem. AAAS, Am. Chem. Soc., Am. Phys. Soc. Achievements include fundamental research in condensed phase theoretical chemistry. Office: U Wis Dept Chemistry Theoretical Chem Inst 1101 University Ave Madison WI 53706-1322

SKINNER, LYNN STRICKLAND, secondary school mathematics educator; b. Newnan, Ga., July 30, 1959; d. Elonza Floyd and Irene (Smith) S.; m. Walter Winston Skinner, Jr., Sept. 8, 1979; children: Sara Irene (Sallie), Jane Golden. Student, Clayton State Coll., 1977-78, Ga. Southwestern Coll., 1981; BBA, U. Ga., 1981; MEd, West Ga. Coll., 1990; EdS, State U. West Ga., 1998. Bus. mgr. Lee County Ledger, Leesburg, Ga., 1980-82; ins. rep. West Ga. Med. Ctr., La Grange, Ga., 1982-83; advt. rep. Newnan Times-Herald, 1983-85; chmn. dept. math. Greenville (Ga.) H.S., 1985-92; project success math. tchr. E. Coweta H.S., Sharpsburg, Ga., 1992—. Greenville H.S. STAR tchr., 1988-89. Founding mem. Lee County Women's Club, Leesburg, 1982; local fund drive chmn. Nat. Kidney Found., Luthersville, Ga., 1985, Am. Heart Assn., Luthersville, 1992; Sunday sch. tchr., program chmn. Women's Missionary Union, Mt. Zion Bapt. Ch., Alvaton, Ga., 1986—; neighborhood chmn. March of Dimes, 1998. Mem. Nat. Coun. Tchrs. Math., Ga. Coun. Tchrs. Math. (life), Ga. Assn. Educators, Coweta Assn. Educators (publicity chmn.), Delta Kappa Gamma (treas. 1990—). Democrat. Baptist. Avocations: oil painting, gardening, reading. Home: 60 Temple Ave Newnan GA 30263-2023 Office: East Coweta HS 400 Sharpsburg Mccollum Rd Sharpsburg GA 30277-2317

SKINNER, MARY JANE PICKENS, secondary education educator; b. Tuscaloosa, Ala., Oct. 29, 1938; d. William Edward and Dovie Martin (Bridges) Pickens; m. Donald Glenn Skinner, Nov. 28, 1964; children: Mary Kathleen, Glenda Dilburn. BA, Agnes Scott Coll., 1960; MA, U. Ala., 1963. Tchr. Byers and Lake Jr. High Schs., Denver, 1962-64; tchr. and yearbook sponsor Choctaw County High Sch., Butler, Ala., 1964-68, 73-81; tchr., student coun. sponsor Demopolis (Ala.) High Sch., 1983-98, ret., 1998. Bd. dirs., pres. Marengo County Hist. Soc., Demopolis, Demopolis Pub. Libr.; bd. dirs. Ala. Hist. Assn.; pres. Music Study Club, Demopolis, Study Club, Demopolis, Demopolis Arts Com., Welcome Newcomers of the Ea. Shore, Presbyn. Women, Spanish Ft. Presbyn. Ch. Mem. Pi Beta Phi. Home: 688 Deer Ave Daphne AL 36526-4000 E-mail: donsk479@aol.com.

SKLADAL, ELIZABETH LEE, retired elementary school educator; b. NYC, May 23, 1937; d. Angier Joseph and Julia May (Roberts) Gallo; m. George Wayne Skladal, Dec. 26, 1956; children: George Wayne Jr., Joseph Lee. BA, Sweet Briar Coll., 1958; postgrad., U. Kans., 1966-67; EdM, U. Alaska, 1976. Choir dir. Main Chapel, Camp Zama, Japan, 1958-59, Ft. Lee, Va., 1963-65, Main Chapel and Snowhawk, Ft. Richardson, Alaska, 1968-70; tchr. Anchorage (Alaska) Sch. Dist., 1970-98; ret. Active Citizen's Adv. Com. for Gifted and Talented, Anchorage, 1981-83; mem. music com. Anchorage Sch. Dist., 1983-86; soloist Anchorage Opera Chorus, 1969-80, Cmty. Chorus, Anchorage, 1968-80; mem. choir First Presbyn. Ch., Anchorage, 1971—, deacon, 1988—, elder, 1996—, mission com. chair, 1996-99, mem. pastoral nominating com., 2001-03; participant 1st cultural exch. from Anchorage to Magadan, Russia with Alaska Chamber Singers, 1992; participant mission trip to Swaziland, Africa with First Presbyn. Ch., Anchorage, summer 1995. Named Am. Coll. Theater Festival winner Amoco Oil Co., 1974; recipient Cmty. Svc. award Anchorage U. Alaska Alumni Assn., 1994-95. Mem. AAUW, Anchorage Concert Assn. Patron Soc. (assocs. coun. of dirs.), Alaska Chamber Singers, Am. Guild Organists (former dean, former treas., mem.-at-large), Local Delta Kappa Gamma (1st v.p.). Republican. Presbyterian. Avocations: camping, travel, cycling, fishing, cross-country skiing, gardening. Home: 1841 S Salem Dr Anchorage AK 99508-5156

SKLOVSKY, ROBERT JOEL, naturopathic physician, pharmacist, educator; b. N.Y. BS, Bklyn. Coll., 1975; MA in Sci. Edn., Columbia U., 1976; PharmD, U. of Pacific, 1977; D in Naturopathic Medicine, Nat. Coll. Naturopathic Medicine, 1983. Intern Tripler Army Med. Ctr., Honolulu, 1977; pvt. practice Milwaukie, Oreg., 1983—. Recipient Bristol Labs. award, 1983. Mem.: N.Y. Acad. Sci. Avocations: classical and jazz music, tap dance, art, botany, acting. Office: 6910 SE Lake Rd Milwaukie OR 97267-2101

SKOLL, PEARL A. retired mathematics and special education educator; b. N.Y.C., Apr. 15, 1927; d. Samuel and Lillian Ruth Adler; m. Ralph Lewis Skoll (dec. 1959); children: Jeffrey A., Steve, Lyle. BA, Hunter Coll., 1950; MA in Adminstrn./Supervision, Calif. State U., Northridge, 1974. Math. tchr. various schs., L.A. and N.Y.C., 1954-71; program coord. The Mobilecomputer Math Lab L.A. Unified Sch. Dist., L.A., 1971-77, leader tchr. tng., 1967-83, mainstream tchr., 1977-83, spl. edn. vocat. assessment counselor, 1983-86; retired, 1986. Mem. task force State Dept. of Edn., Sacramento, Calif., 1976; instr. Calif. State U., Northridge, 1975-76, Pepperdine U., Malibu, Calif., 1975-76. Author (book) Coping with the Calculator, 1975; editor (book) The Calculator Book, 1975; contbr. articles to profl. jours. Reader tapes for literacy program U. Nev., Las Vegas, 1986-87; hon. mem. adv. coun. IBC, Cambridge, Eng. 3d Internat. Congress of Math. Edn. grantee U.S. Office of Edn., 1976, Internat. Biog. Ctr. (Cambridge, Eng.) 20th Century award for Meritorious Achievement, 1994, IB Citation of Meritorious Achievement in Math. Svcs., various miscellaneous honors from IBC, 1995; named Woman of Yr., Am. Biog. Inst., 1994. Mem. Calif. Math. Coun., Nat. Coun. of Tchrs. of Math., Calif. State U. Alumni Assn. Democrat. Jewish. Avocations: volunteer work, cooking, baking, jigsaw & crossword puzzles, gardening. Home: 7684 Keating Cir Las Vegas NV 89147-4908 E-mail: angel415@prodigy.net.

SKOLNICK ROTHENBERG, BARBARA, elementary education educator; b. Greenfield, Mass., Nov. 8, 1952; d. Simon and Lililan (Margolskee) Skolnick; m. David Rothenberg, Dec. 23, 1978; children: Jeffrey, Sarah. BA in Elem. Edn., Fairleigh Dickinson U., 1974; MEd in Reading, U. Mass., 1980, CAGS in Edn., 1985. Cert. in elem. edn., spl. needs, prin., reading, supervision, Mass. Tchr. Amherst (Mass.) Pub. Schs., 1975—. Presenter in field. Author, compiler: Songs We Sing, 1991. Choral dir. for children's choir Internat. Sunday, Amherst, 1991—; founder Amherst Cmty. theatre, 1993; founder children's choir Voices That Care, Amherst, 1989—. Recipient honorable mention UN World Children's Day Found., 1992; named World of Difference Tchr., Anti Defamation League, Boston, 1993, Walt Disney Am. Tchr., Walt Disney Co., 1994. Mem. NEA, Nat. Coun. for Social Studies (Tchr. of Yr. 1993), Mass. Tchrs. Assn. Avocations: community theatre, choral singing. Home: 84 Grantwood Dr Amherst MA 01002-1536 Office: Wildwood Elem Sch Strong St Amherst MA 01002

SKONEY, SOPHIE ESSA, educational administrator; b. Detroit, Jan. 29, 1929; d. George Essa and Helena (Dihmes) Cokalay; m. Daniel J. Skoney, Dec. 28, 1957; children: Joseph Anthony, James Francis, Carol Anne. PhB, U. Detroit, 1951; MEd, Wayne State U., 1960, EdD, 1975; postgrad., Ednl. Inst. Harvard Grad. Sch., 1986—. Tchr. elem. sch. Detroit Bd. Edn., 1952-69, remedial reading specialist, 1969-70, curriculum coord., 1970-71, region 6 article 3 title I coord., 1971-83, area achievement specialist, 1984-88; adminstrv. asst. Office Grant Procurement and Compliance, 1988-2000. Mem. dean's adv. coun. Coll. Edn. Wayne State U., 1995—; cons. in field. Editor newsletter Alliance to the Mich. Dental Assn., 1993-2000. Recipient Disting. Alumni award Wayne State U., 1993. Mem. ASCD, Wayne State U. Edn. Alumni Assn. (pres. bd. govs. 1979-80, newsletter editor 1975-77, 80—), Macomb Dental Aux. (pres. 1969-70), Mich. Dental Aux. (pres. 1980-81), Alliance Mich. Dental Assn. (pres. 1998-2000), Am. Assn. Sch. Adminstrs., Wayne State U. Alumni Assn. (dir., v.p. 1985-86), Internat. Reading Assn., Mich. Reading Assn., Mich. Assn. State and Fed. Program Specialists, Profl. Women's Network (newsletter editor 1981-83, pres. 1985-87, Anthony Wayne award for leadership 1981), Anthony Wayne Soc., Delta Kappa Gamma, Beta Sigma Phi, Phi Delta Kappa (v.p. 1988-90, pres. 1990-91, Educator of Yr. 1985, 91, 96, 2000). Roman Catholic. Home: 20813 Lakeland St Saint Clair Shores MI 48081-2104 E-mail: skoneys@aol.com.

SKORUPSKI, DIANE CHRISTINE, school library media specialist; b. Southbridge, Mass., Mar. 24, 1948; d. Axel Hector and Naomia Maxine (Willis) Johnson; m. Alfred Robert Skorupski, Oct. 9, 1971; children: Kurt (dec.), Gregory R., Kayle J. BS in Edn., North Adams State Coll., 1970; MLS, U. Ariz., 1988. Cert. tchr., Ariz. Tchr. Town of Dudley, Mass., 1970-71, Sowest Supervisory Sch. Union, Bennington, Vt., 1971-73; sch. libr. media specialist Sunnyside Sch. Dist. # 12, Tucson, 1987—99, tchr.-libr., 1999—; dist. coord. Reading is Fundamental Tucson Unified Sch. Dist., 2002—. Bd. mem. Sch. Libr. Media Divsn., 1988-91, pres.-elect, 1992-93, pres. 1993-94. Contbr.: Information Literacy: Educating Children for the 21st Century, 1994. Named Libr. of Yr., Ariz. Tech. in Edn. Alliance, 2003; grantee Tech. for Tchg. US West, Am. Assn. Sch. Adminstrs., Autodesk, AT&T, 1991-93, Turtle Island Project Nat. Indian Youth Leadership Project grantee, 1996-97, Ednl. Enrichment Found. grantee, 2002.

Mem. ALA, NEA, Am. Assn. Sch. Librs., Ariz. Libr. Assn., Ariz. Reading Assn., Tucson Area Reading Coun. (bd. dirs., v.p.-elect 1995-96). Avocations: reading, travel, camping, sewing, crafts. Home: 7810 N Rasmussen Ave Tucson AZ 85741-1448

SKOVIRA, ROBERT JOSEPH, information scientist, educator; b. Mt. Pleasant, Pa., May 4, 1943; s. Robert Joseph and Genevieve (Budney) S.; m. Mary Elizabeth Machuga, Aug. 21, 1971; 1 child, Suzanne Marie. BA, St. Vincent Coll., 1966; MA, U. Pitts., 1972, MS in Info. Scis., 1986, PhD, 1977. Cert. tchr., Pa.; cert. in computer programming and ops. Tchr. Greensburg Ctrl. Cath. HS, Pa., 1967-75; asst. visiting prof. U. Va., Va., 1977-78; archives fieldworker U. Pitts., Pa., 1979; asst. vis. prof. U. Houston, Victoria, Tex., 1980-81; instr. St. Vincent Coll., Latrobe, Pa., 1982-84; prof. Robert Morris Univ., Coraopolis, Pa., 1983—; vis. prof. Libr. and Info. Sci. Dept., Comenius Univ., Bratislava, Slovakia, 1997. Web designer IMAGINING Info. Mem. Am. Soc. for Info. Sci. and Tech. (chmn. spl. interest group FIS 1989-90, mem. spl. interest group cabinet steering com. 1989-92, chmn. Pitts. chpt. 1991), Internat. Assn. for Computer Info. Sys., Assn. for Computing Machinery, Assn. for Info. Sys., Information Resources Mgmt. Assocs., Slovak Studies Assn. Democrat. Byzantine Catholic. Avocations: fishing, hiking, reading, gardening and growing bonsai, history of Slovakia. Office: Robert Morris U University Blvd Coraopolis PA 15108-1189

SKUBBY, CHRISTOPHER DANIEL, political science educator, social sciences educator, department chairman; b. Cleve., Apr. 28, 1959; s. Daniel David and Mary Jane Skubby; m. Phyllis Ann Wargo, Aug. 17, 1959. BA magna cum laude, Cleve. State U., 1981; MA, Johns Hopkins U., 1984, PhD, 1995. Sr. lectr. Towson (Md.) State U., 1985-93; prof. Lakeland C.C., Kirtland, Ohio, 1993—. Instr. Cuyahoga C.C., Highland Hills, Ohio, 1996. Intern Coast Alliance, Washington, 1980; spkr. Lakeland Spkrs. Bur., Kirtland, Ohio, 1996—2001; v.p. Extended Housing, Inc., Painesville, Ohio, 1999—; advisor Model UN Program; vol. Kennedy for Pres., Cleve., 1980. Hart fellow Johns Hopkins U., 1985-86. Mem. NEA, ACLU, Am. Polit. Sci. Assn., Acad. Polit. Sci., Am. Polit. Items Collectors, Amnesty Internat. Avocations: golf, collecting political memorabilia, travel, reading. Home: 91 Tuckmere Dr Painesville OH 44077 Office: Social Sci Divsn Lakeland CC Kirtland OH 44094

SKUJA, ANDRIS, physics educator; b. Riga, Latvia, Mar. 1, 1943; came to U.S., 1976; s. Edvins Martins and Rita (Ozolnieks) S. BSc, U. Toronto, Can., 1966; PhD, U. Calif., Berkeley, 1972. Rsch. officer U. Oxford, Eng., 1972-76; asst. prof. U. Md., College Park, 1976-81, assoc. prof., 1981-89, prof., 1989—; vis. prof. McGill U., Montreal, Que., Can., 1981; vis. scientist DESY, Hamburg, Fed. Republic Germany, 1983. Mem. instn. bd. CMS experiment Large Hadron Collider, CERN, 1994—. Contbr. articles to profl. jours. Fellow Am. Phys. Soc. Achievements include rsch. on the study of structure of nuclei by deep inelastic lepton scattering, study of the decay of the Zo; pioneer of the first electronic measurement of neutrino-electron scattering; study of gamma gamma interactions; lead scientist constrn. of forward muon sys. for solenoidal detector collaboration experiment at superconducting super collider; chair instn. bd. Hadron Calorimeter Subsy. for compact muon solenoid experiment at large Hadron collider, European Lab. for Particle Physics (CERN); pioneer construction of the forward sys. for the solenoidal detector collaboration experiment of the superconducting super collider. Home: PO Box 702 7711 Lake Glen Dr Glenn Dale MD 20769-2028 Office: U Md Dept Physics College Park MD 20742-0001

SKUMMER, MARY ANNE, hearing impaired educator, coordinator; b. Chgo., Jan. 11, 1951; d. Joseph Frank and Marie Jane (Babiarz) S. BS in Biology, Loyola U., 1973, EdD Curriculum and Instruction, 1990; MA Edn. of Hearing Impaired, Northwestern U., 1975; MA EMH, Roosvelt U., 1982. Cert. tchr. deaf and hard of hearing, Ill., educable mentally handicapped, Ill., gen. supervisory, Ill. Cons. for hearing impaired State of N.D., Bismarck, 1975-76; educator Dept. Mental Health and Devel. Disabilities, Park Forest, Ill., 1976-92; spl. needs coord. State of Ill. DMHDD, Park Forest, 1992—. Adj. faculty mem. Prairie State Coll., Chgo. Heights, Ill., 1984—; expert witness Deaf and Hard of Hearing, Robert W. Karr & Assocs., Chgo., 1992-93. Extraordinary minister, mem. parish coun. St. Mary's Ch., Park Forest, Ill. Fellow Am. Biographical Inst., 1995. Democrat. Roman Catholic. Avocations: gardening, stamp collecting. Home: 3612 213th St Matteson IL 60443-2511 Office: State of Ill DMHDD 114 N Orchard Dr Park Forest IL 60466-1200

SKURDENIS, JULIANN VERONICA, librarian, educator, writer, editor; b. July 13, 1942; d. Julius J. and Anna M. (Zilys) S.; m. Lawrence J. Smircich, Aug. 21, 1965 (div. July 1978); m. Paul J. Lalli, Oct. 1, 1978; 1 adopted child, Kathryn Leila Skurdenis-Lalli. AB with honors, Coll. New Rochelle, 1964; MS, Columbia U., 1966; MA, Hunter Coll., 1974. Young adult libr. Bklyn. Pub. Libr., 1964-66; periodicals libr., instr. Kingsborough C.C., Bklyn., 1966-67; acquisitions libr. Pratt Inst., Bklyn., 1967-68; acquisitions libr., asst. prof. Bronx (N.Y.) C.C., 1968-75, head tech. svcs., assoc. prof., 1975-97, prof., 1998—. Acting dir. Libr. Resource Learning Ctr., 1994-97. Author: Walk Straight Through the Square, 1976, More Walk Straight Through the Square, 1977; contbg. editor Internat. Travel News, 1989—, Travel Your Way/N.Y. Times, 1996-98; travel editor Archaeology mag., 1986-89; contbr. over 400 travel, hist., and archaeol. pieces. N.Y. State fellow, 1960-66, Columbia U. fellow, 1964-66, Pratt Inst. fellow, 1965. Mem. AAUP, Libr. Assn. CUNY (chairwoman numerous coms.), Archaeol. Inst. Am. Avocations: archaeology, travel, travel writing. Office: CUNY Bronx CC University Ave Bronx NY 10453-6994 E-mail: julie13@optonline.net.

SKVARLA, LUCYANN M. college official; b. Kingston, Pa., Jan. 15, 1959; d. John T. and Sophie H. (Turel) S. AS, Lackawanna Jr. Coll., Wilkes-Barre, Pa., 1978; BS, King's Coll., Wilkes-Barre, 1992. Cert. profl. sec. Sec. King's Coll., Wilkes-Barre, 1978, sec./adminstrv. asst., 1978-87, asst. for instnl. rsch., 1987—. Part-time instr. non-credit workshops King's Coll., 1994—; part-time instr. McCann Sch. Bus., Wyoming, Pa., 1989-91. Lector St. Hedwig's Ch., Kingston, Pa., 1983-92. Mem. Assn. for Instnl. Rsch. (participant in inst. at No. Ky. U. 1993), N.E. Assn. for Instnl. Rsch., Delta Mu Delta, Delta Epsilon Sigma, Alpha Sigma Lambda. Avocations: country line dancing, bowling, plastic canvas needlepoint, crocheting. Office: Kings Coll 133 N River St Wilkes Barre PA 18711-0851

SLAATTÈ, HOWARD ALEXANDER, minister, philosophy educator; b. Evanston, Ill., Oct. 18, 1919; s. Iver T. and Esther (Larsen) S.; m. Mildred Gegenheimer, June 20, 1951; children: Elaine Slaatte Quaddur, Mark, Paul. AA, Kendall Coll., 1940; BA cum laude, U. N.D., 1942; B.D. cum laude, Drew U., 1945, PhD, 1956; Drew fellow, Mansfield Coll., Oxford (Eng.) U., 1949-50. Ordained to ministry Meth. Ch. as elder, 1943. Pastor Detroit Conf. United Meth. Ch., 1950-65; assoc. prof. systematic theology Temple U., 1956-60; vis. prof., prof. philosophy and religion McMurry Coll. (now named McMurry U.), 1960-65; prof. dept. philosophy Marshall U., Huntington, W.Va., 1965-89, prof. emeritus, 1989—, chmn. dept., 1966-81, mem. grad. council, 1970-73, mem. research bd., 1974-76, mem. acad. standards and policy com., 1975-77, research grantee, 1976, 77; mem. bd. Campus Christian Center, 1973-75; prof. ethics St. Leo (Fla.) Coll., 1993. Lectr. Traverse City (Mich.) State Hosp., 1966-71, Am. Ontoanalytical Assn. internat. conf., Acapulco, Mex., 1970, World Congress Logotherapy, San Diego, 1980, other orgns. Author: Time and Its End, 1962, Fire in the Brand, 1963, The Pertinence of the Paradox, 1968, The Paradox of Existentialist Theology, 1971, Modern Science and the Human Condition, 1974, The Arminian Arm of Theology, 1977, The Dogma of Immaculate Perception, 1979, Discovering Your Real Self, 1980, The Seven Ecumenical Councils, 1980, The Creativity of Consciousness, 1983, Contemporary Philosophies of Religion, 1986, Time, Existence and Destiny, 1988, Critical Survey of Ethics, 1988; co-author: The Philosophy of Martin Heidegger, 1983, Religious Issues in Contemporary Philosophy, 1988, Our Cultural Cancer and Its Cure, 1995, A Re-Appraisal of Kierkegaard, 1995, Plato's Dialogues and Ethics, 1999, A Purview of Wesley's Theology, 2000; contbr. Analecta Frankliana, 1981; gen. editor: (series) Contemporary Existentialism; contbr. to theol. and philos. jours. Mem. W.Va. Conf. United Meth. Ch., 1966-87, ret., 1987; bd. dirs. Inst. for Advanced Philos. Research, 1979-90; chmn. bd. dirs. Salvation Army of Huntington, W. Va.; courtesy prof. U. South Fla., 1993-99. Recipient Outstanding Educators of Am. award, 1975, Profl. Excellence award Faculty Merit Found., State of W.Va., 1986, U. N.D. Found. award, 2000; named to Honorable Order of Ky. Colonels, W.Va. Ambassador of Good Will; named Internat. Man of Yr., 1993; NSF fellow, 1965, Benedum Found. rsch. grantee, 1970, NSF rsch.-grantee, 1965, 71. Mem. W.Va. Philos. Assn. (pres., 1966-67, 83-84), Am. Philos. Assn., AAUP, Am. Acad. Religion. Home: 203N Foliage Cir Cary NC 27511

SLACK, DONALD CARL, agricultural engineer, educator; b. Cody, Wyo., June 25, 1942; s. Clarence Ralbon and Clara May (Beightol) S.; m. Marion Arline Kimball, Dec. 19, 1964; children: Jonel Marie, Jennifer Michelle. BS in Agrl. Engring., U. Wyo., 1965; MS in Agrl. Engring., U. Ky., 1968, PhD in Agrl. Engring., 1975. Registered profl. engr., Ky., Ariz. Asst. civil engr. City of Los Angeles, 1965; research specialist U. Ky., Lexington, 1966—70, agrl. engring. advisor Tha Phra, Thailand, 1970—73, rsch. asst. Lexington, 1973—75; from asst. prof. to assoc. prof. agrl. engring. U. Minn., St. Paul, 1975—84; prof. U. Ariz., Tucson, 1984—, head dept. agrl. and biosystems engring., 1991—. Mem. Mid. East and Mediterranean Desert Devel. Program, 1997—; vis. prof. dept. atmospheric sci. Fed. U. Paraiba, Campina Grande, Brazil, 1997; vis. prof. dept. irrigation Chapingo Autonomous U., Mexico, 2000; tech. adv. Ariz. Dept. Water Resources, Phoenix, 1985—, Tucson active mgmt. area, 1996—; cons. Winrock Internat., Morrilton, Ark., 1984, Water Mgmt. Synthesis II, Logan, Utah, 1985, Desert Agrl. Tech. Sys., Tucson, 1985—, Portek Hermosillo, Mexico, 1989—, World Bank, Washington, 1992—, Malawi Environ. Monitoring Project, 1996, Mex. Inst. for Water Tech., 1997, Nat. Agrl. Rsch. Inst., La Serema, Chile, 1997; dep. program support mgr. Rsch. Irrigation Support Project for Asia and the Near East, Arlington, Va., 1987—94; mem. adv. team Cearan Found. for Meteorology and Hydrology, Fortaleza, Brazil, 1995—; mem. internat. adv. panel Matrou Resources Mgmt. Project, World Bank, Egypt, 1996—2000; bd. dirs. Sonoita Vineyards, Ltd., Watershed Mgmt. Group, Inc. Contbr. articles to profl. jours. Fellow ASCE (Outstanding Jour. Paper award 1988), Am. Soc. Agrl. Engrs. (Ariz. sect. Engr. of Yr. 1993); mem. Am. Geophys. Union, Am. Soc. Agronomy, Soil Sci. Soc. Am., U.S. Com. on Irrigation and Drainage (life), Am. Soc. Engring. Edn. (program evaluator accreditation bd. for enring. and tech., 2001—), SAR, Brotherhood of Knights of the Vine (master knight), Rocky Mountain Elk Found. (life), Sigma Xi, Tau Beta Pi, Alpha Epsilon, Gamma Sigma Delta. Democrat. Lutheran. Achievements include 3 patents pending; developer of infrared based irrigation scheduling device. Home: 9230 E Visco Pl Tucson AZ 85710-3167 Office: U Ariz Agrl Biosystems Engring Tucson AZ 85721-0001 E-mail: slackd@u.arizona.edu.

SLADE, BARBARA ANN, art educator; b. Bklyn., N.Y., May 15, 1941; d. Steve Licata, Margie Licata; m. George Drakos, Sept. 16, 1961 (div.); 1 child, Matthew Drakos; m. Fred Slade, Aug. 18, 1996. Student, Sch. Art and Design, N.Y., 1955—59; AAS, Fash Inst. Tech., N.Y., 1961; student, Art Student League, N.Y., 1975—83. Instr. art U. Nev., Las Vegas, 1992—93, Las Vegas Art Mus., Las Vegas, 1993—97, Sun City Summelin Art Club, Las Vegas, 1995—. Lectr., demo in pastel Sun City DelWeb Art Club, 2001. Mem.: Nev. Pastel Soc. (pres., co-founder 1998—2001). Avocation: birdwatching. Home: 1775 Montessouri St Las Vegas NV 89117-1623

SLADE, BARBIE EVETTE DELK, special education educator; b. Orlando, Fla., Sept. 5, 1961; d. Jack Everett and Barbara Nell (Corley) Delk; m. Mark Anthony Slade, Sept. 22, 1984; children: Nicholas Mark, Wesley Evan. BS with honors, U. So. Miss., 1992, MS, 2000, postgrad. in spl. edn., 2001—. Specific learning disability (SLD) tchr. K-12 North Forrest H.S., Hattiesburg, Miss., 1992—. Mem. various coms. and couns. North Forrest H.S., 1996—. Vol. Spl. Olympics, cmty. elderly. Mem.: Am. Fedn. Tchrs., Coun. Exceptional Children. Baptist. Avocation: reading. Home: 72 Clinton Rd Moselle MS 39459 Office: North Forrest High Sch 693 Eatonville Rd Hattiesburg MS 39401 E-mail: BabsSlade@hotmail.com.

SLAGLE, ROBERT LEE, II, elementary and secondary education educator; b. Carlisle, Pa., Oct. 16, 1962; s. Robert Lee and Hilda Carolyn (Jones) S.; m. Cynthia Jean Phifer, Feb. 8, 1992; children: Robert Lee III, Theodore Calvin George. BA in Bus. and Acctg., Gettysburg Coll., 1984; MA in Adminstrn., George Washington U., 1988; MA in Edn., Beaver Coll., 1994. Cert. tchr. elem. and secondary social studies, Pa. Engr. officer U.S. Army, Ft. Belvoir, Eustis, Va., 1984-88; ptnr., constrn. mgr. Triple S Quality Builders, Mechanicsburg, Pa., 1988-90; constrn. dir. Rite Aid Corp., Harrisburg, Pa., 1989-92; tchr. history, econ., govt. Colonial Sch. Dist., Plymouth Meeting, Pa., 1992—. Graduation project dir. Plymouth Whitemarsh H.S., 1998—, student coun. sponsor, 1994—; coach Plymouth Whitemarsh H.S. Football, 1991—, weightlifting, 1991—, baseball, 1995—; coach Whitemarsh (Pa.) Twp. Big League Baseball, 1992-97, Plymouth Whitemarsh H.S. Baseball, 1993—. Lay reader St. Mary's Episcopal Ch., Andorra-Phila., Pa., 1992—. Capt. U.S. Army Corps of Engrs., 1984-88. Decorated Army Commendation medal U.S. Army Dept. Def., 1985, Meritorious Svc. medal U.S. Army Dept. Def., 1988. Mem. ASCD, Colonial Edn. Assn. Republican. Avocations: carpentry, weight training and conditioning, hunting, outdoor recreation, american history and politics. Home: 4033 Center Ave Lafayette Hill PA 19444-1425

SLAKEY, STEPHEN LOUIS, secondary school educator; b. Oakland, Calif., Feb. 7, 1946; s. Louis T. and Vivian (Torrey) S.; m. Sylvia Amanda Loud S., Feb. 5, 1971; children: Stephen Andrew, Stephanie Amanda. BA, Calif. State U., Hayward, 1969; MA, Calif. State U., Fullerton, 1974. Cert. K-12 sch. adminstrn., 7-12 social sci. tchr., Calif. Tchr. geography La Puente HS, Calif., 1969—, chmn. dept. geography, 1973-80, 2002—, dir. staff devel., 1985—, mentor tchr., 1984—88, tchr. on spl. assignment, 2002—; coord. Secondary Sch. partnership student exchanges, La Puente HS- Ternivska bymnasia, Kyruyi, Ukraine, 2000—03. Di. Summer Geography Inst., Calif. State Polu. U., Pomona, 1990; instr. geography Mt. San Antonio Coll., 1990-91, U. La Verne, 1992—; co-dir. Geographic Inst., UCLA, 1985; prin. instr. Nat. Geographic Soc. Inst., Washington, 1986-87; founder, prin. Geo-Ed Assoc. Edn. Cons. Svc.; cons. bilingual edn. Calif State Poly U., 1972; curriculum cons. Hacienda-La Puente Unified Sch. Dist., 1972-74. Editor Project Food, Land and People, 1989-1996. Pres. Glendora Beautiful, 1983-84; rschr. Glendora Hist. Resources Survey, 1983; Exchange tchr. to Ukraine, 1999. Named Good Neighbor Tchr., State Farm, 1998; recipient Tchr. of Excellence award, Am. Coun. Tchr. Russian, 1999. Mem. Nat. Geog. Soc., Calif. Geog. Soc. (bd. dir. 1977-78, 91—, v.p. 1994, pres. 1995-97, Disting. Tchg. award 1975, 79, Disting. Svc. award 1999), Calif. Geog. Alliance (founder), Calif. Tchr. Assn. (chmn. grievance com. 1981-82), Glendora Pride II (pres. 1999—). Avocations: tennis, volleyball, sailing, travel, photography. Home: 1149 Steffen St Glendora CA 91741-3736 Office: Hacienda-La Puente Unified Sch Dist 15615 Nelson Ave La Puente CA 91744-3910

SLATER, C. STEWART, chemical engineering educator; b. Feb. 24, 1957; s. Clarence S. and Elizabeth Slater. BS, Rutgers U., Piscataway, N.J., 1979, MS, 1981, MPh, 1982, PhD, 1983. Process devel. engr. Procter & Gamble Co., Cin., 1979-81; teaching asst., project mgr. Rutgers U., 1981-83; prof. chem. engring. Manhattan Coll., Riverdale, N.Y., 1983-95; prof. and chair chem. engring. dept. Rowan U., Glassboro, N.J., 1995—. Cons. to major U.S. corps. Contbr. over 100 articles to profl. publs., several chpts. to books. Recipient Ralph R. Teetor award Soc. Automotive Engrs., 1986. Fellow Am. Soc. for Engring. Edn. (divsn. chmn. 2003, program chmn. 1990, New Engring. Educator Excellence award 1987, Dow Outstanding Faculty award 1989, John Fluke award 1992, George Westinghouse award 1996, Chester Carlson award 1999, Joseph J. Martin award 1998, 99), Mem. am. Chem. Soc., Am. Inst. Chem. Engrs., N. Am. membrance Soc., Sigma Xi, Tau Beta Pi, Omega Chi Epsilon. Achievements include research in membrane technology. Office: Rowan Univ Dept Chem Engring 201 Mullica Hill Rd Glassboro NJ 08028-1702 E-mail: slater@rowan.edu.

SLATER, CONSTANCE, special education educator; b. Plymouth, Mass., Sept. 13, 1931; d. George Lewiston and Dorothy Mae (Darby) Finch; student Broward Community Coll., 1968-73; B.A., Shaw U., 1975; postgrad. Fla. Atlantic U., 1975-77; m. Fred Carl Slater, Nov. 22, 1952; children— Steven, Scott, Stacey Slater Owens, Sherrill Slater McCarthy. Office mgr. Comml. Union Assurance Co., Indpls., 1950, Family and Child Service Agy., San Bernardino, Calif., 1951, Gate City Sash and Door Co., Fort Lauderdale, Fla., 1952-54; tchr. aide Sundial Sch. for Retarded, Ft. Lauderdale, 1963-68; tchr. asst. Broward County Schs., Ft. Lauderdale, 1968-77, tchr. Wingate Oaks Center for Retarded, Ft. Lauderdale, 1977— ; owner-dir. Tall Pine Camp for Exceptional Citizens, Coker Creek, Tenn., 1971— . Sec., Parents and Friends of Sunland Tng. Center, 1961-68; vice-chmn. Dist. 10, Fla. Human Rights Advocacy Com. on Mental Retardation, 1978— ; tchr. rep. to N. Central Adv. Com., 1978-79, Supt. Schs. Dist. Adv. Com., 1979; bd. dirs. Broward County Assn. for Retarded Citizens. Vocat. Edn. for Handicapped fellow Fla. Internat. U., 1979-80. Mem. Council for Exceptional Citizens, Nat. Assn. for Retarded Citizens, Am. Assn. on Mental Deficiency. Democrat. Home: 3010 NE 16th Ave Apt 701 Oakland Park FL 33334-5249

SLATER, JOAN ELIZABETH, secondary education educator; b. Paterson, N.J., Aug. 27, 1947; d. Anthony Joseph and Emma (Liguori) Nicola; m. Francis Graham Slater, Nov. 16, 1974; children: David, Kristin, Kylie. BA in English, Montclair State Coll., 1968, MA in English, 1971. Cert. English, speech and theater arts tchr., N.J., Tex. Tchr. Anthony Wayne Jr. High Sch., Wayne, N.J., 1968-70, Wayne Valley High Sch., Wayne, N.J., 1970-74, Strack Intermediate Sch., Klein, Tex., 1987—. Cons. Tex. Assessment Acad. Skills, Houston Post Newspaper, 1994—; mem. adv. bd. Tex. Edn. Assn., winter 1993; sch. dist. rep. So. Assn. Colls. and Schs., 1993-98; editor, advisor Pawprints Lit. Mag., 1989—. Co-author: Klein Curriculum for the Gifted and Talented, 1992-93. Com. chairperson Klein After-Prom Extravaganza, 1994-98; parent supporter Challenge Soccer Club, Klein, 1993—; mem. Klein H.S. Girls Soccer Team Bd., 1995-96. Mem. North Harris County Coun. Tchrs. English (sec. 1992-95), Klein Edn. Assn., Nat. Coun. Tchrs. English, Tex. Mid. Sch. Assn., Internat. Reading Assn., Greater Houston Area Reading Coun., Nat. Charity League. Avocations: aerobics, interior decorating, reading. Office: Strack Intermediate Sch 18027 Kuykendahl Rd Ste S Klein TX 77379-8197

SLATER, REBECCA ANN, elementary educator; b. Endicott, N.Y., Feb. 13, 1957; d. Philip Carl and Marian Louise (Zorn) Nickels; m. James Arthur Slater, July 19, 1975; children: Jaime Ann, Joseph Abraham. AAS in Liberal Arts and Mental Health, Broome C.C., Binghamton, N.Y., 1986; BS in Edn. and Psychology magna cum laude, Elmira Coll., 1988; MEd in Reading Edn. magna cum laude, SUNY, Binghamton, 1992. Vietnamese refugee lang. tutor Owego (N.Y.) Apalachin Sch. Dist., 1976; spl. edn. teaching asst. Broome-Tioga Bd. Coop. Ednl. Svcs., Binghamton, 1982-84; elem. tchr. Candor (N.Y.) Cen. Sch. Dist., 1988-92. Ednl. cons. Zaner Bloser Ed. Pub., various sch. dist. and ednl. orgns.; freelance ednl. writer. Honors scholar Elmira Coll., 1987-88. Mem. N.Y. State assn. Compensatory Tchrs. (speaker, presenter 1991, 92), N.Y. State reading Assn. (speaker, presenter 1992, 93), Internat. Reading Assn., Phi Delta Kappa, Kappa Delta Pi, Psi Chi. Home and Office: 517 Vanhook Rd Owego NY 13827-6537

SLATTA, RICHARD WAYNE, historian, educator, writer; b. Powers Lake, N.D., Oct. 22, 1947; s. Jerome Elmer and Amy Irene (Solberg) S.; m. Zoya Maxine Atkinson, June 25, 1982; 1 child, Jerome David. BA in History, Pacific Luth. U., 1965-69; MA in History, Portland (Oreg.) State U., 1973-74; PhD in History, U. Tex., 1974-80. Vis. instr. U. Colo., Boulder, 1979-80; prof. history N.C. State U., Raleigh, 1980—. Author: Gauchos and the Vanishing Frontier, 1983, Cowboys of the Americas, 1990, The Cowboy Encyclopedia, 1994, Comparing Cowboys and Frontiers, 1997, The Mythical West, 2001, Simón Bolivar's Quest for Glory, 2003; editor: Bandidos, 1987; mem. editl. bd. History Microcomputer Rev., 1986—2003, Jour. of Third World Studies, 1986—91; mem. adv. bd.: Internat. Jour. Social Edn., 1986—92. With U.S. Army, 1971-73. Recipient H. Herring Book prize Pacific Coast Coun. on Latin Am. Studies, 1984, Grand prize Computer Learning Month, 1988, Western Heritage Book award Nat. Cowboy Hall of Fame, Oklahoma City, 1991. Mem. Am. Hist. Assn., Western Hist. Assn., Sigma Delta Pi, Phi Alpha Theta. Democrat. Avocations: photography, snorkling, travel, computers. Office: History Dept Box 8108 NC State U Raleigh NC 27695 E-mail: slatta@ncsu.edu.

SLATTERY, CHARLES WILBUR, biochemistry educator; b. La Junta, Colo., Nov. 18, 1937; s. Robert Ernest Slattery and Virgie Belle (Chamberlain) Tobin; m. Arline Sylvia Reile, June 15, 1958; children: Scott Charles, Coleen Kay. BA, Union Coll., 1959; MS, U. Nebr., 1961; PhD, 1965. Instr. chemistry Union Coll., Lincoln, Nebr., 1961-63; asst. prof., assoc. prof. chemistry Atlantic Union Coll., South Lancaster, Mass., 1963-68; rsch. assoc. biophysics MIT, Cambridge, Mass., 1967-70; asst. prof., then prof. biochemistry Loma Linda U., Calif., 1970-80; prof. biochemistry-pediatrics, 1980—; chmn. dept., 1983-99. Vis. prof. U. So. Calif., L.A., 1978-79. Contbr. articles to profl. jours. NIH grantee, 1979-82, 86-89, AHA (Calif.), 1981-83, 83-84. Mem. AAAS, Am. Chem. Soc. (biochemistry divsn.), Am. Dairy Sci. Assn., N.Y. Acad. Scis., The Protein Soc., Am. Soc. Biochemistry and Molecular Biology, Sigma Xi. Office: Loma Linda U Sch Medicine Dept Biochemistry Loma Linda CA 92350-0001

SLATTERY, WILLIAM JOSEPH, school psychologist; b. N.Y.C., May 11, 1955; s. William Joseph and Theresa Mary (Cummings) S. BA, Manhattan Coll., 1977; MS in Edn. with honors, Pace U., 1979; postgrad., U. Fla., 1988—. Cert. sch. psychologist, N.Y., Fla.; nat. cert. sch. psychologist. Team leader, therapy aide Bronx (N.Y.) Psychiat. Ctr., 1978-79; sch. psychologist Middletown (N.Y.) Pub. Schs., 1979-84, N.Y. State Div. for Youth, Middletown, 1983, Bd. Coop. Ednl. Svcs. Orange County, Goshen, N.Y., 1985-86; sch. psychologist, cons. group home div. Piux XII Youth and Family Svcs., Middletown, 1980-85, adminstrv. aide, psychologist foster care div., 1984-85; therapist IV, Univ. Hosp. Jacksonville, Fla., 1986-88; coord. dist. crisis team Duval County Pub. Schs., Jacksonville, 1988-90; sch. psychologist Sch. Bd. Alachua County, Gainesville, Fla., 1990-94; sch. psychologist, program mgr. multidisciplinary diagnostic and tng. program U. Fla., 1994—. Recipient Merit Edn. award Univ. Hosp. Jacksonville, 1988, Outstanding Svc. award Duval County Pub. Schs., 1990. Mem. NASP, Fla. Assn. Sch. Psychologists (rsch. com. 1990-92), Am. Assn. Suicidology, Sertoma (chater Gainesville chpt.), Phi Delta Kappa. Avocations: swimming, scuba diving. Office: U Fla Multidiscplinary Diagnostic & Tng Prog 1341 Norman Hall Gainesville FL 32611 Home: PO Box 12424 Gainesville FL 32604-0424

SLAUGHTER, JOHN BROOKS, professional society administrator; b. Topeka, Mar. 16, 1934; s. Reuben Brooks and Dora (Reeves) S.; m. Ida Bernice Johnson, Aug. 31, 1956; children: John Brooks, Jacqueline Michelle. Student, Washburn U., 1951-53; BSEE, Kans. State U., 1956, DSc (hon.), 1988; MS in Engring., UCLA, 1961; PhD in Engring. Scis, U.

Calif., San Diego, 1971; D Engring. (hon.), Rensselaer Poly. Inst., 1981; DSc (hon.), U. So. Calif., 1981, Tuskegee Inst., 1981, U. Md., 1982, U. Notre Dame, 1982, U. Miami, 1983, U. Mass., 1983, Tex. So. U., 1984, U. Toledo, 1985, U. Ill., 1986, SUNY, 1986; LHD (hon.), Bowie State Coll., 1987; DSc (hon.), Morehouse Coll., 1988, Kans. State U., 1988; LLD (hon.), U. Pacific, 1989; DSc (hon.), Pomona Coll., 1989; LHD (hon.), Alfred U., 1991, Calif. Luth. U., 1991, Washburn U., 1992. Registered profl. engr., Wash. Electronics engr. Gen. Dynamics Convair, San Diego, 1956-60; with Naval Electronics Lab. Center, San Diego, 1960-75, div. head, 1965-71, dept. head, 1971-75; dir. applied physics lab. U. Wash., 1975-77; asst. dir. NSF, Washington, 1977-79, dir., 1980-82; acad. v.p., provost Wash. State U., 1979-80; chancellor U. Md., College Park, 1982-88; pres. Occidental Coll., Los Angeles, 1988-99; co-chair Calif. Citizens Commn. on Higher Edn., 1996-99; ret., 1999. Res., pres, CEO NACME, Inc., N.Y.C.; bd. dirs., vice chmn. San Diego Transit Corp., 1968-75; mem. com. on minorities in engring. Nat. Rsch. Coun., 1976-79; mem. Commn. on Pre-Coll. Edn. in Math., Sci. and Tech. Nat. Sci. Bd., 1982-83; bd. dirs. Solutia, Inc., ARCO, Avery Dennison Corp., IBM, Northrop Grumman Corp.; chmn. advancement com. Music Ctr. of L.A. County, 1989-93. Editor: Jour. Computers and Elec. Engring., 1972—. Bd. dirs. San Diego Urban League, 1962-66, pres., 1964-66; mem. Pres.'s Com. on Nat. Medal Sci., 1979-80; trustee Rensselaer Poly. Inst., 1982; chmn. Pres.'s Com. Nat. Collegiate Athletic Assn., 1986-88; bd. govs. Town Hall of Calif., 1990; bd. dirs. L.A. World Affairs Coun., 1990. Recipient Engring. Disting. Alumnus of Yr. award UCLA, 1978, UCLA medal, 1989, Roger Revelle award U. Calif.-San Diego, 1991, Disting. Svc. award NSF, 1979, Svc. in Engring. award Kans. State U., 1981, Disting. Alumnus of Yr. award U. Calif.-San Diego, 1982, Martin Luther King Jr. Nat. award, 1997; Naval Electronics Lab. Ctr. fellow, 1969-70; elected to Topeka High Sch. Hall of Fame, 1983, Hall of Fame of Am. Soc. Engring. Edn., 1993; named Kansan of Yr. by Kans. Native Sons and Daus., 1994. Fellow IEEE (chmn. com. on minority affairs 1976-80), Am. Acad. Arts and Scis.; mem. NAE, Nat. Collegiate Athletic Assn. (chmn. pres. commn.), Am. Soc. for Engring. Edn. (inducted into Hall of Fame 1993), Phi Beta Kappa (hon.), Tau Beta Pi, Eta Kappa Nu. Office: NACME Inc Empire State Bldg 350 Fifth Ave Ste 2212 New York NY 10118-2299

SLAUGHTER, ROCHELLE DENISE, elementary school educator; b. Kansas City, Kans., Jan. 3, 1956; d. Theodore and Barbara Jean (Williams) Hall; m. Eddie Slaughter, Nov. 1, 1997. AA, Penn Valley C.C., Kansas City, Mo., 1976; BA, U. Mo., Kansas City, 1978, MA, 1985; Edn. Specialist Degree, U. Mo., 1992. Cert. specialist in reading, Mo. Tchr. Kansas City Sch. Dist., 1979-85, reading resource tchr., 1985-95, tchr. 1st grade, 1995—2000, tchr. 3d grade, 2000—; S.T.A.R.R. tchr., 2002. Del. Literacy and Lang. Arts Instrn. Delegation to Peoples Republic of China, 1995. Supt. Sunday sch. Emmanuel Bapt. Ch., 1992—; del. lang. arts & literacy delegation People to People Citizen Amb. Progra, China, 1995; vol. for adult basic edn. program; tutor Laubach Literacy Coun. Kansas City, 1996-97. Recipient IMPACT Reading award Kansas City Reading dept., 1990. Mem. ASCD, NAACP, Internat. Reading Assn. (chpt. v.p. 1994-95, pres.-elect 1995-97, pres. 1997-99), Phi Delta Kappa (youth advisor 1993-99). Democrat. Baptist. Avocations: reading, computer work, sewing. Office: E F Swinney Applied Skills 1106 W 47th St Kansas City MO 64112-1215

SLAUGHTER-DEFOE, DIANA TRESA, education educator; b. Chgo., Oct. 28, 1941; d. John Ison and Gwendolyn Malva (Armstead) S.; m. Michael Defoe (div.). BA, U. Chgo., 1962, MA, 1964, PhD, 1968. Instr. dept. psychiatry Howard U., Washington, 1967-68; rsch. assoc., asst. prof. Yale U. Child Study Ctr., New Haven, 1968-70; asst. prof. dept. behavioral scis. and edn. U. Chgo., 1970-77; asst. to assoc. prof. edn. and African Am. studies and Ctr. for Urban Affairs and Policy Rsch. (now Inst. for Policy Rsch.) Northwestern U., Evanston, Ill., 1977-90, prof., 1990-97; Constance E. Clayton prof. urban edn. Grad. Sch. Edn. U. Pa., 1998—. Mem. nat. adv. bd. Fed. Ctr. for Child Abuse & Neglect, 1979-82, coord. Human Devel. and Social Policy Program, 1994-97; mem. nat. adv. bd. Learning Rsch. and Devel. Ctr. U. Pitts., Ednl. Rsch. & Devel. Ctr., U. Tex., Austin; formerly chmn., dir. public policy program com. Chgo. Black Child Devel. Inst., 1982-84; dir. Ill. Infant Mental Health Com., 1982-83; mem. res. adv. bd. Chgo. Urban League, 1986-97. Contbr. articles to profl. jours. Fellow APA (mem. divsn. ethnic and minority affairs, com. on children, youth and families, devel. psychology, sch. psychology, bd. sci. affairs 1995-97, bd. advancement psychology pub. interest 2003-, assoc. editor, mem. editl. bd. Child Devel. 1995-98, Disting. Contbn. to Rsch. in Pub. Policy award 1993, mem. bd. for advancement of psychol. in the pub. intrest 2003—); mem. Soc. for Rsch. in Child Devel. (governing coun. 1981-87), Am. Ednl. Rsch. Assn. (editl. bd. Rev. Ednl. Rsch.), Nat. Assn. Edn. Young Children, Assn. Study African Ams. and History, Nat. Head Start (past mem. R & E adv. bd.), Nat. Acad. Scis. (com. on child devel. and publ. policy 1987-93), Delta Sigma Theta. Office: U Pa Grad Sch Edn 3700 Walnut St Philadelphia PA 19104-6216 Business E-Mail: dianasd@gse.upenn.edu.

SLAVENS, THOMAS PAUL, library science educator; b. Cincinnati, Iowa, Nov. 12, 1928; s. William Blaine and Rhoda (Bowen) S.; m. Cora Hart, July 9, 1950; 1 son, Mark Thomas. BA, Phillips U., 1951; MDiv, Union Theol. Sem., 1954; MA, U. Minn., 1962; PhD, U. Mich., 1965. Ordained to ministry Christian Ch., 1953. Pastor First Christian Ch., Sac City, Iowa, 1953-56, Sioux Falls, S.D., 1956-60; librarian Divinity Sch., Drake U., Des Moines, 1960-64; teaching fellow Sch. Info., U. Mich., Ann Arbor, 1964-65; instr. U. Mich., Ann Arbor, 1965-66, asst. prof., 1966-69, assoc. prof., 1969-77, prof., 1977—. Vis. prof. U. Minn., 1967, U. Coll. of Wales, 1978, 80, 93; vis. scholar U. Oxford, Eng., 1980; adv. bd. Marcel Dekker Inc., N.Y.C., 1982—; cons. Nutrition Planning Abstracts-UN, N.Y.C., 1977-79. Author-editor: Library Problems in the Humanities, 1981, (with John F. Wilson) Research Guide to Religious Studies, 1982, (with W. Eugene Kleinbaur) Research Guide to History of Western Art, 1982, (with Terrence Tice) Research Guide to Philosophy, 1983, Theological Libraries at Oxford, 1984, (with James Pruett) Research Guide to Musicology, 1985, The Literary Adviser, 1985, A Great Library through Gifts, 1986, The Retrieval of Information, 1989, Number One in the U.S.A.: Records and Wins in Sports, Entertainment, Business, and Science, 1988, 2d edit., 1990, Doors to God, 1990, Sources of Information for Historical Research, 1994, Introduction to Systematic Theology, 1992, Reference Interviews Questions and Materials, 3d edit., 1994. Served with U.S. Army, 1946-48. Recipient Warner Rice Faculty award U. Mich., 1975; H.W. Wilson fellow, 1960; Lilly Endowment fellow Am. Theol. Library Assn., 1963. Mem. Assn. Libr. and Info. Sci. Edn. (pres. 1972), Beta Phi Mu.

SLAVICK, ANN LILLIAN, retired art educator; b. Chgo., Sept. 29, 1933; d. Irving and Goldie (Bernstein) Friedman; m. Lester Irwin Slavick, Nov. 21, 1954 (div. Mar. 1987); children: Jack, Rachel. BFA, Sch. of Art Inst. of Chgo., 1973, MA in Art History, Theory, Criticism, 1991. Dir. art gallery South Shore Commn., Chgo., 1963-67; tchr. painting, drawing, crafts Halfway House, Chgo., 1972-73; tchr. studio art Conant H.S., Hoffman Estates, Ill., 1973-74; tchr. art history and studio arts New Trier H.S., Winnetka and Northfield, Ill., 1974-80; tchr. 20th century art history New Trier Adult Edn. Program, Winnetka, 1980-81; tchr. art adult edn. program H.S. Dist. 113, Highland Park, Ill., 1980-81; rschr., writer Art History Notes McDougall-Littel Pub., Evanston, Ill., 1984-85; tchr. art and art history Highland Park and Deerfield (Ill.) H.S., 1980-2000; tchr. art history Coll. of Lake County, Grayslake, Ill., 1986-88; ret., 2000. Faculty chair for visual arts Focus on the Arts, Highland Park H.S., 1981-85, faculty coord. Focus on the Arts, 1987—; panelist Ill. Arts Coun. Arts Tour, 1999, Evanston Arts Coun., 2000-02, Ill. Arts Coun. Multidisciplinary Grant Awards, 2001-03; reader advanced placement art history exams, 2003. One woman show Bernal Gallery, 1979, U. Ill., Chgo., 1983, Ann Brierly Gallery, Winnetka, 1984; exhibited paintings, drawings, prints and constrns. throughout Chgo. area; work represented by Art Rental and Sales Gallery, Art Inst. Chgo., 1960-87, Bernal Gallery, 1978-82; group shows at Bernal Gallery; work in pvt. collections in Ill., N.Y., Calif., Ariz., Ohio. Recipient Outstanding Svc. in Art Edn. award Ea. Ill. U., 1992, Mayors award for contbn. to the arts, Highland Park, 1995. Mem.: Ill. Art Edn. Assn., Nat. Art Edn. Assn. Avocations: cooking, reading, theatre. Home: 5057 N Sheridan Rd Chicago IL 60640-3127 Office: Highland Park High Sch 433 Vine Ave Highland Park IL 60035-2099

SLAVIN, SUSAN ANN, secondary educator; b. Green Bay, Wis., Oct. 9, 1942; d. John James and Mary Jane (Christophersen) Wheeler; m. Laurence E. Slavin, Dec. 8, 1962; children: Susan, Karen, Mary, Laurence Jr., Fred Obley, Marc, Edward, Scott. BA in English, Ariz. State U., 1968, MA in Polit. Sci./Govt. Cert. prin., ESL tchr. Acting asst. prin. Alhambra High Sch., Phoenix, tchr. computer assisted English composition. Course developer computer assisted English and govt. Rio Salado Jr. Coll. Remedial English; grant writer. Co-author ESL Curriculum Guides; contbr. articles to profl. jours. Recipient 1st place, Nat. Paper Microcomputer Conf. in Edn., 1989. Mem. ASCD, TESOL, English Speakers Other Langs., Nat. Assn. Secondary Sch. Prins., Ariz. Coaches Assn. (high sch. and coll. track and field ofcl.).

SLAVOFF, HARRIET EMONDS, learning disabilities teacher, consultant; b. Elmer, N.J., Mar. 18, 1931; d. Lewis Arthur and Margaret (Miles) Emonds; m. Eugene Victor Slavoff, Feb. 3, 1951; children: Stephen, Stephanie Slavoff Perry, Eugene Jr. BA, Glassboro Coll., 1969, MA, 1976. Cert. tchr., N.J. Tchr. kindergarten Olivet Sch., Pittsgrove Twp., N.J., 1953; remedial tchr. Upper Pittsgrove Sch., 1964-74; learning disabilities tchr. cons. Salem County Schs., Woodstown, N.J., 1976, Pittsgrove Twp. Sch., 1977-78, Oldmans Twp. Sch., Pedricktown, N.J., 1979-83, Logan Sch., Bridgeport, N.J., 1985; child study team coord. East Greenwich Schs., Mickleton, N.J., 1987-93; supr. student tchrs. Rowan Coll., 1992-94. Learning disabilties cons.; ct. clk., Elmer, N.J., 1976, chair Juvenile Conf. Com., 1976-82; adj. prof. Rowan Coll., 1993-96. Pub. History of Elmer, 1893-1993, 1993. Mem. election bd. Dem. com., Elmer; mem. ch. choir; pres. Elmer PTA. Mem.: DAR, Country Garden Club (pres. 2002—03). Avocations: library work, flowers, crafts, reading. Home: 111 Front St Elmer NJ 08318-2138

SLAY-BARBER, DORIS A. educational administrator; b. San Antonio, Sept. 22, 1952; d. Harold and Lottie (Pieniazek) Brietzke; m. H. Gene Barber, June 26, 1987; children: G. L. Slay, Gary, Mike. BA, St. Mary's U., 1974; MEd, Trinity U., 1983. Cert. elem. tchr., Tex. Cons. computer software Edn. Svc. Ctr.; tchr., coord. gifted/talented program East Central Ind. Sch. Dist., San Antonio; coord. grade reporting and scheduling Northside Ind. Sch. Dist., San Antonio. Mem. ASCD, Bus. and Profl. Womens Club Inc. of San Antonio, Phi Delta Kappa. Office: 5900 Evers San Antonio TX 78238 E-mail: slaybarb22@hotmail.com.

SLEBODNIK, TRESSA ANN, retired elementary education educator; b. Belle Vernon, Pa., Nov. 11, 1931; d. Michael Ferdinand and Elizabeth (Skruber) Nusser; m. Thomas Patrick Slebodnik, June 6, 1953; children: Thomas, Anita, Eleanor, Edward, Charles, Kathleen, Linda. BS, California (Pa.) State Tchrs. Coll., 1953. Cert. tchr., Pa. Tchr. kindergarten Yough Sch. Dist., West Newton, Pa., 1969-76, tchr. first grade Sutersville, Pa., 1976-80, Smithton, Pa., 1980-81, tchr. kindergarten Smithton and Ruffsdale, Pa., 1981-82, Ruffsdale, 1982-96; ret., 1996. Devel. Approach to Sci. and Health, Ruffsdale, 1990-96; grade level coord., mentor tchr. and curriculum coun. Past pres. St. Edward Bowling League, Herminie, mem. curriculum coun.; active Altar-Rosary Soc., Herminie. Mem. NEA, Pa. State Edn. Assn., Keyston State Reading Assn., Youth Edn. Assn. (bldg. rep.), Westmoreland County Reading Coun., St. Edward Sunshine Club. Republican. Roman Catholic. Avocations: bowling, cards, reading, Bingo, gardening. Home: RR 1 Box 200 Irwin PA 15642-9617

SLEDD, WILLIAM TAZWELL, mathematics educator; b. Murray, Ky., Aug. 25, 1935; s. William Tazwell Jr. and Faye (Wall) S.; m. Aug. 9, 1958 (div. 1987); children: Luanne, Jane. BA, Murray State U., 1956; MA, U. Ky., 1959, PhD, 1961. Asst. prof. math. Mich. State U., East Lansing, 1961-65, assoc. prof., 1965-69, prof., 1969—2003; retired, 2003. Office: Mich State U Math Dept East Lansing MI 48824

SLEEMAN, MARY (MRS. JOHN PAUL SLEEMAN), retired librarian; b. Cleve., June 28, 1928; d. John and Mary Lillian (Jakub) Gerba; m. John Paul Sleeman, Apr. 27, 1946; children: Sandra (Sleeman) Swyrydenko, Robert, Gary, Linda. BS, Kent State U., 1965, MLS. Children's libr. Twinsburg Pub. Libr., Twinsburg, Ohio, 1965—66; supr. libr. mid. sch. Nordonia Hills Bd. Edn., Northfield, Ohio, 1965—93, ret., 1993. Mem.: No. Eastern Ohio Tchr. Assn., Storytellers Assn., Summit County Librarians Assn., ALA. Meth. Home: 18171 Logan Dr Cleveland OH 44146-5236 Office: 72 Leonard Ave Northfield OH 44067-1945

SLEETH, JOAN MARIE, elementary school educator; b. Miles City, Mont., Apr. 14, 1960; d. Vincent Joseph and Sylvia (Taylor) Hafla; m. Timothy Everett Sleeth, Oct. 14, 1978; 1 child, Nathaniel. AA, Miles C.C., 1984; BS in Elem. Edn., Ea. Mont. Coll., 1986, MS in Spl. Edn., 1993. Cert. class 2 tchr., level 1 elem., reading K-12, spl. edn. K-12, class 1 tchr., level 1 elem. K-8, Mont. Tchr. Discovery Daycare and Presch., Billings, Mont., 1986-87; spl. edn. aide Lockwood Intermediate, Billings, Mont., 1987-89; spl. edn. tchr. Billings Pub. Schs., 1989—99, elem. sch. tchr., 1999—. Reading math. tutor Lockwood Cmty. Edn., Billings, 1990; storyteller Youth Author's Day Tumblewood Reading Coun., Miles City, 1994; cert. trainer David Mandt and Assocs., Billings, 1994-98; active parenting facilitator Sch. Dist. 2, Billings, 1994—, AWANA leader, 1997—, AWANA SPARKS leader, 1998—. Author: Easy and Inexpensive Christmas Ornaments, 1994. Cub scout leader Pack 93 Lockwood coun. Boy Scouts Am., Billings, 1986-88; reader Midland Empire Reading Coun., Billings, 1994, sch. rep., 1990-95; mem. Burlington PTA, 1990-95, mem. care team, 1993-95. Recipient Golden Promise award Sta. KTVQ-2 News, 1992. Mem. NEA, Mont. Edn. Assn., Billings, Edn. Assn. (bldg. rep. 1994-99, sec. 2000—, Tchr. of Yr. 1999). Baptist. Avocations: sewing, making Christmas ornaments, snowmobiling, walking, cake decorating. Home: 3437 Becraft Ln Billings MT 59101-7027

SLEITH, BARBARA ANN BALKO, special education educator; b. Elizabeth Twp., Pa., Jan. 29, 1946; d. Andrew and Elizabeth (Kurutz) Balko; m. Melvin R. Sleith, Dec. 18, 1971; 1 child, Melynda Sue. AA, Robert Morris Jr. Coll., 1966; BS, California U. (Pa.), 1968, MEd, 1970; postgrad., U. Pitts., 1976, U. Indiana (Pa.). Tchr. Elizabeth (Pa.) Forward Sch. Dist., 1968-70; learning disabilities tchr. Allegheny Intermediate Unit 3, 1970-77, I.E.P. specialist, 1977-80, tchr. socially, emotionally maladjusted students, 1980-97, learning support tchr., 1997—2001, 7th grade math tchr., 2001—. Distbr. Royal Am. Foods; cons. in field. Developer Math Pass game. Neighborhood chmn. Girl Scouts U.S.A., 1978-80, asst. leader, 1986, day camp dir., coach cadette/sr. leaders; adult cons. ch. youth group, 1975-78, craft persoon vacation bible sch.; program rep., mem. liaison bd. Allegheny Intermediate Unit Edn. Assn., 1970-74; active PTA, Jr. Olympic Archery Develop. coach; various lay positions Holy Family Ch. Mem. Assn. Children with Learning Disabilities, Three Rivers Reading Council, Phi Delta Gamma (chpt. exec. officer). Clubs: Confraternity of Christian Mothers (various offices). Democrat. Roman Catholic. Address: Sportman Rd West Newton PA 15089

SLEJKO, LINDA MARIE, principal; b. Rockwall, Tex., Feb. 20, 1961; d. Thomas Richard and Vera Eugene (Peace) Lofland; m. Stephen Robert Slejko, Oct. 27. 1989. AD, Kilgore Jr. Coll., 1981; BS in Elem. Edn., U. North Tex., 1983, MA in Mid. Mgmt., 1986; EdD, Nova Southeastern Univ. Coord. individual program planning Denton State Sch., Tex., 1983-84; tchr. Mesquite Ind. Sch. Dist., Tex., 1984-85, instr., art specialist, 1985-93, asst. prin., 1993-97, prin., 1997—. Chair SBDM Price Elem., Mesquite, 1992-93; sec. PTA, Mesquite, 1994-95; staff devel. chair Floyd Elem., Mesquite, 1993-2003. Rep. Mesquite, 1994-95; mem. Eastridge Park Christian Ch. Mem. ASCD, TEPSA, Delta Kappa Gamma, 1st v.p. Home: 1248 Wildflower Ln Mesquite TX 75149-2632 Office: Bonnie Gentry Elem Sch 1901 Twin Oaks Dr Mesquite TX 75181

SLIDER, MARGARET ELIZABETH, elementary education educator; b. Spanish Fork, Utah, Nov. 27, 1945; d. Ira Elmo and Aurelia May (Peterson) Johnson; m. Richard Keith Slider, Oct. 25, 1968; children: Thomas Richard, Christopher Alan. AA, Chaffey Coll., 1966; BA, Calif. State U., San Bernardino, 1968, MEd in English as Second Lang., 1993. Cert. elem. tchr., Calif. Tchr. Colton (Calif.) Unified Sch. Dist., 1968—; lead sci. tchr. McKinley Sch., 1994-96; mem. sci. steering com. Colton Joint Unified Sch. Dist., 1996—. Mem. kindergarten assessment com. Colton Joint Unified Sch. Dist., Colton, 1988-90, dist. math. curriculum com., 1992-94; trainer Calif. State Dept. Edn. Early Intervention for Sch. Success, 1993—, demonstrator on-site classroom, 1994. Treas. McKinley Sch. PTA, Colton, 1989-91. Mem. NEA, ASCD, AAUW, Calif. Tchrs. Assn., Calif. Elem. Edn. Assn., Calif. Assn. of Tchrs. of English to Students of Other Langs., Calif. Mathematics Coun., Assn. Colton Educators, Pi Lambda Theta. Avocations: needlework, reading, bicycling. Home: 1628 Waterford Ave Redlands CA 92374-3967 Office: Colton Unified Sch Dist 1212 Valencia Dr Colton CA 92324-1731

SLIGER, BERNARD FRANCIS, academic administrator, economist, educator; b. Chassell, Mich., Sept. 30, 1924; s. Paul and Hazel (MacLauchlin) S.; m. Greta Taube, Sept. 1, 1945; children: Nan, Paul, Greta Lee, Sten. BA in Econs. with high hons., Mich. State U., 1949, MA, 1950, PhD, 1955; postgrad., U. Minn., 1961-62. Mem. faculty La. State U., 1953-61, prof. econs., 1961, head dept., 1961-65, vice chancellor, dean academic affairs, 1965-68; sec. adminstrn. State of La., 1968—69; sec.-treas. La. Office Bldg. Corp., 1969-72; organizer, exec. dir. La. Coordinating Council Higher Edn., 1969-72; prof. econs. Fla. State U., Tallahassee, 1973—2003, prof. econ. emeritus, 2003—, exec. v.p., 1972-76, chief acad. officer, 1973-76, pres., 1977-91, interim pres., 1993, dir. univ.'s London Study Ctr., 1975, pres. emeritus, 1992—2003; ret., 2003. Mem. staff sci. and tech. com. Fla. Ho. of Reps., 1979; mem. V.P. Mondale's Select Com. on Sci. and Tech., 1980; mem. bd. dirs. Fed. Res Bank of Atlanta, 1983-88; cons. econ. theory and pub. fin. to pvt. and pub. commns., orgns.; mem., chief cons. Gov. La.'s tax study com., 1968; formerly La. commr. adminstrn. and chief budget officer; mem. NCAA pres.'s commn., 1987-91. Author: (text) Public Finance, 1964, rev. edit., 1970, (with others) Municipal Finance Administration, 1976, rev.; contbr. to profl. publs. Vol. economist Tallahassee C. of C., 1977, Fla. C. of C., 1978; mem. Acad. Task Force for Review of the Ins. and Tort Systems, 1986-88; trustee The Nature Conservancy, 1986—; trustee Am. Coll. Testing Corp., 1981-87, chmn. 1985-87; ex-officio mem. Fla. Coun. 100. With C.E., U.S. Army, 1943-46. Named Dir. Practical Politics La. Ho. of Reps., 1969; Bernard F. Sliger Eminent scholar Chair in Econ. Edn. created in his name by Fla. State U., 1987, Bernard F. Sliger Bldg. dedicated at univ.-related rsch. park, Bernard F. Sliger Tower in Univ. Ctr. Bldg. dedicated, 1999. Mem. Kiwanis, Phi Beta Kappa, Omicron Delta Kappa, Phi Kappa Phi, Omicron Delta Epsilon, Alpha Kappa Psi, Beta Gamma Sigma, Phi Eta Sigma. Presbyterian. Home: 3341 E Lakeshore Dr Tallahassee FL 32312-1440 Office: Gus A Stavros Ctr Adv Free Enterprise & Economic Edu 250 S Woodward Ave Tallahassee FL 32306-4220 Office Fax: 850-644-9866. E-mail: sliger@mailer.fsu.edu; sliger@garnet.acns.fsu.edu.

SLINKER, JOHN MICHAEL, academic director; b. Lafayette, Ind., Jan. 8, 1952; s. William Guy Mahan and Betty Lucille (Utterback) and Richard Earl Slinker; m. Pamela Jo Pickering, Mar. 15, 1975; children: Jacob, Daniel. BS, Ea. N.Mex. U., 1974, MA, 1979; EdD, No. Ariz. U., 1988. Cert. specialist in planned giving; cert. fund-raising exec. Asst. sports infor. dir., news writer Ea. N.Mex. U., Portales, 1970-74, news svc. dir., sports info. dir., 1974-82; dir. univ. news and publ. No. Ariz. U., Flagstaff, 1982-86; dir. pub. affairs Humboldt State U., Arcata, Calif., 1988-92, dir. univ. rels., 1992—2003, sr. comms. and mktg. officer, 1992—2003, sr. assoc. Office of the Pres., 2003—. Cons. Calif. Dept. Parks and Recreation, Sacramento, 1989-90. Vol. Boy Scouts Am., Eureka, Calif., 1991-93, dist. commr., 1991-92. Mem. Coun. for Advancement and Support of Edn. (Bronze medal), Sigma Nu (div. comdr. 1976-81, chpt. advisor, Outstanding Alumnus 1976, 79, 81, 82). Republican. Methodist. Avocations: sports, travel, woodworking, stained glass, genealogy. Home: 1971 Gwin Rd Mckinleyville CA 95519-3961 Office: Humboldt State U Office of the Pres Arcata CA 95521

SLOAN, DAVID JAMES, sonographer; b. Camden, N.J., Apr. 27, 1955; s. James Eugene and Donna Sloan; m. Marcia Ann Sloan, Dec. 2, 1978; children: Christopher, Brian. BA in Psychology, Framingham State Coll., 1979; AS in Diagnostic Med. Sonography, Middlesex C.C., Bedford, Mass., 1980. Cert. Am. Registry of Diagnostic Med. Sonographers; registered vascular technologist. Dept. head ultrasound Ludlow Hosp., Mass., 1980—81; ultrasound supr. Providence Hosp., Holyoke, Mass., 1981—83, 1988—89, mgr. diagnostic imaging, 1989—95; dept. head project hancock Maine Coast Meml. Hosp., Ellsworth, Mass., 1983—88; ultrasound supr. Mercy Med. Ctr., Springfield, Mass., 1996—98; dept. chair med. imaging, program dir. DMS degree program, assoc. prof. ultrasound Springfield Tech. C.C., 1998—2002. Ind. computer cons., 1996—. Author: (software) In-house fetal dating program, 1998. Mem.: Soc. Diagnostic Med. Sonographers. Office: Springfield Tech CC 1 Armory Sq Springfield MA 01105

SLOAN, F(RANK) BLAINE, law educator; b. Geneva, Nebr., Jan. 3, 1920; s. Charles Porter and Lillian Josephine (Stiefer) S.; m. Patricia Sand, Sept. 2, 1944; children: DeAnne Sloan Riddle, Michael Blaine, Charles Porter. AB with high distinction, U. Nebr., 1942, LLB cum laude, 1946; LLM in Internat. Law, Columbia U., 1947. Bar: Nebr. 1946, N.Y. 1947. Asst. to spl. counsel Intergovtl. Com. for Refugees, 1947; mem. Office Legal Affairs UN Secretariat, N.Y.C., 1948-78; gen. counsel Relief and Works Agy. Palestine Refugees, Beirut, 1958-60; dir. gen. legal divsn., dep. to the legal counsel UN Legal Office, N.Y.C., 1966-78, rep. of Sec. Gen. to UN Commn. Internat. Trade Law, 1969-78, rep. to Legal Sub-com. on Outer Space, 1966-78; rep. UN Del. Vietnam Conf., Paris, 1973; rep. UN Conf. on Carriage of Goods by Sea Hamburg, 1978; prof. internat. law orgn. and water law Pace U., 1978-87, prof. emeritus, 1987—. Law lectr. Blaine Sloan Internat., 1988—. Author: United Nations General Assembly Resolutions in Our Changing World, 1991; contbr. articles to legal jours. Cons. UN Office of Legal Affairs, 1983-84, UN Water Resources Br., 1983; supervisory com., Pace Peace Ctr.; legal advisor Korean Missions, 1951, 53, UNTSO, Jerusalem, 1952, UNEF I, Gaza, 1957-58; prin. sec.UN Commn. to investigate Sec.-Gen. Hammarskjold's crash, 1961-62. Navigator AC, U.S. Army, 1943-46 Decorated Air medal. Mem. Am. Soc. Internat. Law, Am. Acad. Polit. and Social Sci., Am. Arbitration Assn., Order of Coif, Phi Beta Kappa, Phi Alpha Delta (hon.). Republican. Roman Catholic. Home: HCR-68 Box 72 Foxwind-Forbes Park Fort Garland CO 81133 Office: 78 N Broadway White Plains NY 10603-3710 also: 375 Soubry Pl Forbes Park Fort Garland CO 81133

SLOAN, JUDI C. former physical education educator; b. Kansas City, Mo., July 17, 1944; d. Oscar H. Wilde and Florance (Janes) Wilde Graupner; m. Richard J. Sloan; children: Blake, Tracy. BS in Phys. Edn., No. Ill. U., 1966, postgrad.; MS in Phys. Edn., Ind. U., 1970; postgrad., U. Ill., DePaul U., Loyola U., Nat. Louis U. Tchr. phys. edn., coach Niles West High Sch., Skokie, Ill., 1966-99. Former coach gymnastics, tennis; coach cross-country; coop. tchr.; creator, dir. Galibo Gymnastics Show, 1968-75; founder, co-chair staff wellness com., Niles Township Sch. Dist., 1988—, curriculum coun., 1988-91; creator phys. mgmt. course, sophomore health and fitness program, evening children's, summer girls' gymnastics programs; co-dir. Indian Cross Country Invitational, Niles West Gymnastics Invitational; adv. com. cross country Ill. High Sch. Assn. Recipient All-Am. High Sch. Gymnastics Coach award U.S. Gymnastics Fedn., 1981, award of Honor Nat. Sch. Pub. Rels. Assn., 1990, Ill. Disting. Educator award, 1992; Named Ill. Tchr. Yr., 1992-93. Mem. AAHPERD, Am. Fedn. Tchrs., Nat. Assn. Secondary Physical Edn., Nat. Coaches Fedn., Ill. Fedn. Tchrs., Ill. Assn. Heatlh, Phys. Edn., Recreation, Dance (Outstanding Phys. Edn. award 1986), Nat. Assn. Girls' and Women's Sports, Ill. Track and Cross Country Coaches Assn., Ill. Girls' Coaches Assn. Office: Niles West High Sch 5701 Oakton St Skokie IL 60077-2681

SLOAN, MARJORIE HAWKINS, science educator, retired advertising executive; b. Kansas City, Kans., Oct. 22, 1923; d. Ernest Henry Hawkins and Louisa Eola Fouché; m. Raymond Charles Sloan, July 21, 1949 (dec. Mar. 1994); children: Roger Charles, Jeffrey Craig. BS, Kans. State U., 1945; MS, Iowa State U., 1948. Cert. life tchg. license Kans., Calif. Tchr. Fredonia (Kans.) H.S., 1945—47; blend chemist Phillips Petroleum Co., Kansas City, Kans., 1947; asst. prof. Whittier (Calif.) Coll., 1948—50, Sacramento State U., 1950—51; tchr. L.A. Unified Sch. Dist., 1951—52, Torrance (Calif.) Unified Sch. Dist., 1957—60, L.A. Unified Sch. Dist., 1962—81; advt. account exec. Sloan, Sloan & Charles, Reseda, Canoga Park, Eureka, Calif., 1981—93; ret., 1993. Pinochle facilitator Prescott Adult Ctr., Prescott, Ariz., 2000—; staff Prescott Sr. Olympic Games, 2002, 2003. Mem.: LWV, AAUW (bd. dirs. 1996—97, Eleanor Roosevelt award 2000), Iota Sigma Pi, Omicron Nu, Phi Kappa Phi. Avocations: book clubs, wine tasting, foreign and domestic travel. Home: 3070 Indian Meadow Dr Prescott AZ 86301

SLOAN, MICHAEL LEE, secondary education educator; b. Chgo., Jan. 24, 1944; s. Robert Earl Sloan and Cyril (Lewis) Glass; m. Claudia Ann Schultz, Sept. 27, 1969. BS in Physics, Roosevelt U., 1966, MS, 1971. Tchr. physics Glenbard West H.S., Glen Ellyn, Ill., 1966-79; computer cons. Midwest Visual, Chgo., 1979-82; sr. engr. Apple Computer, Rolling Meadows, Ill., 1982-85; tchr. math. and physics Ill. Math. and Sci. Acad., Aurora, Ill., 1987—. Asst. prof. Roosevelt U., 1971-73; instr. Harper Coll., Palatine, Ill., 1984. Author: AppleWorks: The Program for the Rest of Us, 1985, 2d edit., 1988, Working with Works, 1987, Word Power, 1989, Working with PC Works, 1989, Working with Works 2.0, 1990. Bd. dirs. Youth Symphony Orch., Chgo., 1977-78, Friends of Fermilab, Batavia, Ill., 1998—; trustee Body Politic Theatre, Chgo., 1981-82. Home: ON008 Evans Ave Wheaton IL 60187 Office: Ill Math and Sci Acad 1500 Sullivan Rd Aurora IL 60506-1000 E-mail: msloan@imsa.edu.

SLOAN, ROBERT HAL, computer science educator; b. Buffalo, Apr. 1, 1961; s. George and Helen (Cohen) S.; m. Maurine Jo Neiberg, June 27, 1993; children: Rose, Emma. BS, Yale U., 1983; MS, MIT, 1986, PhD, 1989. Postdoctoral fellow Harvard U., Cambridge, Mass., 1989-90; asst. prof. U. Ill., Chgo., 1990-96, assoc. prof., 1996—; prog. dir. Nat. Sci. Found., 2001—02. Contbr. articles to profl. publs. Recipient Rsch. Initiation award NSF, 1990; NSF grantee, 1994, 98, 2001. Mem.: IEEE Computer Soc., Assn. for Computing Machinery. Democrat. Avocations: tournament bridge, cooking, running. Office: U Ill Chgo EECS Dept M/C 154 851 S Morgan St Rm 1120 Chicago IL 60607-7042

SLOANE, BEVERLY LEBOV, writer, consultant; b. N.Y.C., May 26, 1936; d. Benjamin S. and Anne (Weinberg) LeBov; m. Robert Malcolm Sloane, Sept. 27, 1959 (dec. May 16, 2002); 1 child, Alison Lori Sloane Gaylin. AB, Vassar Coll., 1958; MA, Claremont Grad. U., 1975, postgrad., 1975-76; cert. in exec. mgmt., grad. exec. mgmt. program, UCLA Grad. Sch. Mgmt., 1982; grad. intensive bioethics course Kennedy Inst. Ethics, Georgetown U., 1987, advanced bioethics course, 1988; grad. sem. in Health Care Ethics, U. Wash. Sch. Medicine, Seattle, summer 1988-90, 94; grad. Summer Bioethics Inst., Loyola Marymount U., summer 1990; grad. Annual Summer Inst. on Teaching of Writing, Columbia U. Tchrs. Coll., summer 1990; grad. Annual Summer Inst. on Advanced Teaching of Writing, Columbia Tchrs. Coll., summer 1993; grad. Annual Inst. Pub. Health and Human Rights, Harvard U. Sch. Pub. Health, 1994; grad. pub. course profl. pub., Stanford U., 1982; cert. clin. intensive biomedical ethics, Ethics Fellow, cert. clin. intensive biomedical ethics, Loma Linda U. Med. Ctr., 1989; grad. exec. refresher course profl. pub., Stanford U., 1994; cert Exec. Mgmt. Inst. in Health Care, U. So. Calif., 1995; cert. in ethics corps tng. program, Josephson Inst. of Ethics, 1991; cert. advanced exec. program Grad. Sch. Mgmt., UCLA, 1995; grad. Women's Campaign Sch., Yale U., 1998. Circulation libr. Harvard Med. Libr., Boston, 1958-59; social worker Conn. State Welfare, New Haven, 1960-61; tchr. English Hebrew Day Sch., New Haven, 1961-64; instr. creative writing and English lit. Monmouth Coll., West Long Branch, NJ, 1967-69; writer, cons., 1970—. V.p. council grad. students, Claremont Grad. U., 1971-72, adj. dir. Writing Ctr. Speaker Series, 1993-2000, spkr., 1996-98; bd. visitors Claremont Grad. U. Ctrs. for Arts and Humanities, 2001—; adv. coun. tech. and profl. writing Dept. English, Calif. State U., Long Beach, 1980-82; adv. bd. Calif. Health Rev., 1982-83; mem. Foothill Health Dist. Adv. Coun. L.A. County Dept. Health Svcs., 1987-93, pres., 1989-91; vis. scholar Hastings Ctr., 1996; spkr. N.Y. State Task Force on Life and the Law, 1996; panel spkr. Annual Conf. Am. Assn. Suicidology, 1998. Author: From Vassar to Kitchen, 1967, A Guide to Health Facilities: Personnel and Management, 1971, 2nd edit., 1977, 3d edit., 1992, Introduction to Healthcare Delivery Organization: Functions and Management, 4th edit., 1999. Pub. rels. bd. Monmouth County Mental Health Assn., 1968—69; chmn. creative writing group Calif. Inst. Tech. Woman's Club, 1975—79; mem. task force edn. and cultural activities City of Duarte, 1987—88; chmn. creative writing group Yale U. Newcomers, 1965—66; dir. creative writing group Yale U. Women's Orgn., 1966—67; mem. Exec. Program Network UCLA Grad. Sch. Mgmt., 1987—2000; trustee Ctr. Improvement Child Caring, 1981—83; mem. League Crippled Children, 1982—, treas. for gen. meetings, 1990—91, chmn. hostesses com., 1988—89, pub. rels. com., 1990—91; del. Task Force on Minorities in Newspaper Bus., 1987—89; rep. cmty. County Health Network Tobacco Control Program, 1991; mentor NY Citizens Com. Health Care Decisions; chmn. 1st ann. Rabbi Camillus Angel Interfaith Svc. Temple Beth David, 1978, v.p., 1983—86; cmty. rels. com. Jewish Fedn. Coun. Greater L.A., 1985—87; bd. dirs. League Crippled Children, 1988—91; ethics com., human subjects protection com. Jewish Home for Aging, Reseda, Calif., 1994—97; various positions and coms. Claremont Grad. U., 1986—; bd. visitors Claremont Grad. U. Ctr. Arts and Humanities, 2001—; bd. dirs. L.A. Commn. Assaults Against Women, 1983—84; class corr. Vassar Coll. Quar. Alumnae Mag., 1993—98; class of 1958 coms. Vassar Coll., class v.p., 1998—2000, class co-pres., 2000—01, class pres., 2001—, program chmn. 40th reunion, 1998. Recipient cert. of appreciation City of Duarte, 1988, County of L.A., 1988, Ann. Key Mem. award L.A. Dept. Health Svcs., 1990, cert. of appreciation Alumni Coun. Claremont Grad Sch., 1996; Coro Found. fellow, 1979, Ethics fellow Loma Linda U. Med. Ctr., 1989; named Calif. Communicator of Achievement, Woman of Yr. Calif. Press Women, 1992. Fellow: Am. Med. Writers Asn. (Pacific S.W. del. to nat. bd. 1980—87, dir. 1980—93, chmn. nat. book awards trade category 1982—83, chmn. Nat. Networking Luncheon 1983—84, nat. chmn. freelance sect. 1984—85, workshop leader, Nat. Ann. Conf. 1984—89, gen. chmn. Asilomar Western Regional Conf. 1985, workshop leader, Asilomar Western Regional Conf. 1985, nat. exec. bd. dirs. 1985—86, nat. adminr. sects. 1985—86, pres.-elect Pacific Southwest chpt. 1985—87, chmn. gen. session nat. conf. 1986—87, chmn. Walter C. Alvarez Mem. Found award 1986—87, program co-chmn. 1987, program chmn. nat. conf. 1987, moderator gen. session. nat. conf. 1987, pres. Pacific S.W. chap. 1987—89, workshop leader, Asilomar Western Nat. Conf. 1988, spkr. Pacific S.W. chpt. 1988—89, program co-chmn. 1989, workshop leader, Asilomar Western Nat. Conf. 1989, Pacific Southwest deleg. to nat. bd. 1989—91, immediate past pres. 1989—91, workshop leader, Nat. Ann. Conf. 1990—92, bd. dirs. 1991—93, workshop leader, Nat. Ann. Conf. 1995, chmn. conv. coms., Appreciation award for outstandin leadership 1989, named to Workshop Leaders Honor Roll 1991); mem.: AAUP, APHA, AAUW (creative writing chmn. 1969—70, books and plays chmn. Arcadia Br. 1973—74, 1st v.p. program dir. 1975—76, legis. chmn. Arcadia Br. 1976—77, networking chmn. 1981—82, spkr. 1987, chmn. task force promoting individual liberties 1987—88, pres.-elect 1998—99, educ. equity chmn. 1998—99, chmn. deleg. to national conv. 1999, chmn. Technical Trek Sci. Camp Scholarship for Girls 1999, Career Day 1999, pres. Arcadia br. 1999—2000, writer in res Calif. State Comm. Com. 1999—2000, diversity chmn. Arcadia br. 2000—01, Interbr. Coun. Arcadia br. repr. 2000—02, Calif. State diversity com. 2000—02, program vice-chmn. LA County Interbr. Coun. 2000—02, Woman of Achievement Arcadia br. 1986, cert. of appreciation 1987), AAUW Calif. State Diversity Comt. (program co-v.p. 2002), Town Hall Calif. (vice chmn. cmty. affairs sect. 1982—87, faculty-instr. Exec. Breakfast Inst. 1985—86, Exec. Breakfast Inst. spkr. 1986), Pasadena Athletic, Claremont Cols. Faculty House, Women's City (Pasadena), Nat. Writer's Union, Authors Guild, Assn. Writing Programs, NY Acad. Medicine (met. NY Ethics Network), Soc. Health and Human Values, Kennedy Inst. Ethics, Soc. Technical Comt., Nat. Fedn. Press Women (chmn. state women of achievement comt. 1986—87, nat. co-chmn. task force recruitment minorities 1987—89, del. 1987—89, bd. dirs. 1987—93, nat. dir. spkrs. bur. 1989—93, Plenary past pres. state 1989—, editor spkrs. bur. directory 1991—92, editor spkrs. bur. addendum dir. 1992, workshop leader, spkr. annual nat. conf. 1990, cert. of appreciation 1991, 1st runner up, Nat. Communicator of Achievement 1992, cert. of appreciation 1993), Hastings Cent. (vis. scholar 1996), Ind. Writers So. Calif. (bd. dirs. corp. 1988—89, bd. dirs. 1989—90, dir. specialized groups 1989—90, dir. at large 1989—90, dir. speech writing group 1991—92), NY Acad. Scis., Calif. Press Women (v.p. programs L.A. chpt. 1982—85, pres. 1985—87, state pres. 1987—89, immediate past state pres. 1989—91, chmn. state speakers bur. 1989—95, deleg. nat. bd. 1989—95, dir. family literacy day Calif. 1990, moderator, ann. spring conv. 1990, chmn. nominating comt. 1990—91, Calif. literacy dir. 1990—92, dir. state literacy com. 1990—92, moderator, ann. spring conv. 1992, Cert. of Appreciation 1991, Calif. Communicator of Achievement 1992), Am. Soc. Law, Medicine, Ethics, AAUW Calif. State Comns. Comt. (writer in residence 1999—2000), Coro Nat. Alumni Assn. (bd. dirs. 1999—), Am. Assn. Higher Edn., Women in Comm. Inc. (N.E. area rep. 1980—81, bd. dirs. 1980—82, v.p. cmty. affairs 1981—82, chmn. awards banquet 1982, chmn. LA chpt. Agnes Underwood Freedom Info. Awards banquet 1982, nominating com. 1982—83, seminar leader, spkr., ann. nat. profl. conf. 1985, program adv. com. L.A. chpt. 1987, com. Women of the Press awards luncheon 1988, bd. dirs. 1989—90, v.p. activities 1989—90, Recognition award 1983), Duarte Rotary Club. Home and Office: 1301 N Santa Anita Ave Arcadia CA 91006-2419

SLOANE, CARL STUART, educator and management consultant; b. N.Y.C., Feb. 9, 1937; s. George and Dorothy (Cohen) S.; m. Toby Tattlebaum, Dec. 27, 1958; children: Lisa Beth, Amy Rachel, Todd Cowan. BA, Harvard U., 1958, MBA, 1960. Asst. to pres. Revlon, Inc., N.Y.C., 1960-62; mgmt. cons. Harbridge House, Inc., Boston, 1962-69; pres., CEO, chmn. Temple, Barker & Sloane, Inc., Lexington, Mass., 1970—91; prof. bus. adminstrn. Harvard Grad. Sch. Bus. Adminstrn., Lexington, 1991—2001. Policyholders' examining com. N.W. Mut. Life Ins. Co.; bus. adv. com. Transp. Ctr., Northwestern U., 1984-91; adv. com. Ctr. for Sci. and Internat. Affairs, Kennedy Sch. Govt., Harvard U., 1984-94; bd. dirs. Rayonier, Inc., Brinks Co., MedSource Techs. Bd. dirs. Harvard-Radcliffe Hillel, Cambridge, Mass., 1987-98, chmn., 1994-98; bd. dirs., trustee Beth Israel Deaconess Med. Ctr., Boston, 1993—, vice-chmn., 1996-2002, chmn. 2002—; nat. fund chmn. Harvard . Bus. Sch., 1987-89, vis. com. Mem. Assn. Mgmt. Cons. Firms (chmn. 1984-86), Harvard U. Bus. Sch. Alumni Assn. (v.p. 1989, pres. 1989-91), Boston Yacht Club (Marblehead), Kernwood County Club (Salem), Harvard Club N.Y.C. Home: 9 Sargent Rd Marblehead MA 01945-3744 Office: Harvard Bus Sch Soldiers Fld Boston MA 02163-1317

SLOAT, BARBARA FURIN, cell biologist, educator; b. Youngstown, Ohio, Jan. 20, 1942; d. Walter and Mary Helen (Maceyko) Furin; m. John Barry Sloat, Nov. 2, 1968; children: John Andrew, Eric Furin. BS, Denison U., 1963; MS, U. Mich., 1966, PhD, 1968. Lic. and cert. emergency med. technician, paramedic. Lab. asst. U. Ghent, Belgium, 1964; teaching fellow, lectr. U. Mich., Ann Arbor, 1964-66, 68-70, asst. rsch. biologist Mental Health Rsch. Inst., 1972-74, vis. asst. prof., lectr. Ann Arbor and Dearborn, 1974-76, dir. women in sci. Ann Arbor, 1980-84, assoc. dir. honors, 1986-87, rsch. scientist, 1976—, lectr. Residential Coll., 1984—; assoc. Inst. Humanities U. Mich., Ann Arbor, 1991—. Author: Laboratory Guide for Zoology, 1979, Summer Internships in the Sciences for High School Women (CASE Silver medal, 1985, Excellence in Edn. award, U. Mich., 1993). Recipient Acad. Women's Caucus award, U. Mich., 1984, Grace Lyon Alumnae Award, Denison U., 1988; grantee NSF, U.S. Dept. Edcn., Warner Lambert Found., others. Mem. AAAS, Am. Soc. Cell Biology, N.Y. Acad. Scis., Nat. Assn. Women Deans, Adminstrs. and Counselors, Assn. for Women in Sci. (councilor 1988-90, pres. elect 1990, mentor of yr. award Detroit area chpt. 1994), Phi Beta Kappa, Sigma Xi. Avocations: hiking, yoga, tibetology, Tibetan medicine. Home: 240 Indian River Pl Ann Arbor MI 48104-1825 Office: U Mich Residential Coll 216 Tyler East Quad Ann Arbor MI 48109-1245 E-mail: bsloat@umich.edu.

SLOMANSON, WILLIAM REED, law educator, legal writer; b. Johnstown, Pa., May 1, 1945; s. Aaron Jacob and Mary Jane (Reed) S.; m. Anna Maria Valladolid, June 24, 1972; children: Lorena, Michael, Paul, Christina. BA, U. Pitts., 1967; JD, Calif. Western U., 1974; LLM, Columbia U., N.Y.C., 1975. Bar: Calif. 1975. Assoc. Booth, Mitchel, Strange & Smith, L.A., 1975—77; prof. law Western State U., San Diego and Fullerton, Calif., 1977-95; prof. Thomas Jefferson Sch. of Law, 1996—. Judge Provisional Dist. World Ct., L.A., 1990-93. Author: (reference book) International Business Bibliography, 1989, (textbooks) Fundamental Perspectives on International Law, 1990, 2nd edit., 1995, 4th edit., 2002, California Civil Procedure, 1991, California Civil Procedure in a Nutshell, 1992, (practitioner's treatise) The Choice Between State and Federal Courts in California, 1994, supplement, 1996. Lt. USN, 1967-71, Vietnam. Mem. Am. Soc. Internat. Law (chair, editor newsletter on UN decade of internat. law), San Diego County Bar Assn. (co-chair internat. law sect. 1988-92). Office: Thomas Jefferson Sch Law 2121 San Diego Ave San Diego CA 92110-2986 E-mail: bills@tjsl.edu.

SLONAKER, CELESTER LEE, principal; b. Richmond, Va., Sept. 13, 1943; s. Troy Kent and Betty Lee (Ferguson) S.; m. Carol Preston Laws, Aug. 1, 1970; children: Allen Terrell, Sarah Lindsey. B Music Edn., Va. Commonwealth U., Richmond, 1965, MA, 1972. Music tchr. Chesterfield County (Va.)-Elem. and High Sch., 1965-71; asst. prin. Chesterfield County-Crestwood, 1971-75, prin., 1975-81, Chesterfield County-Greenfield, 1981-90, Chesterfield County-Woolridge, 1990-92; dir. elem. edn. Instrn. Div. Ctr., Richmond, 1992—. Organist/choirmaster Meth. Ch., Richmond, 1962-69, St. Andrew's Episcopal Ch., Richmond, 1969—; cellist Richmond Community Orch., 1955-73. Group leader Community Orgns., Richmond, 1970-85; chmn. sch. bd. Episcopal Parochial Sch., Richmond, 1975-85; bd. mem. Richmond Ballet, 1983-89. Recipient Sch. Community award County Coun. PTA, Chesterfield County, 1983. Mem. ASCD, Nat. Assn. Elem. Prins., Va. Assn. Elem. Prins., Chesterfield Assn. Elem. Prins. (pres. 1985). Avocations: antiques, gardening, music. Office: Instrn Div Ctr 2318 Mcrae Rd Richmond VA 23235-3028

SLONIM, CHARLES BARD, ophthalmic plastic surgeon, educator; b. July 25, 1952; BA, Johns Hopkins U., 1974; MD, N.Y. Med. Coll., 1978. Diplomate Am. Bd. Ophthalmology. Intern. flexible med., surg. Mt. Sinai Med. Ctr., Cleve., 1978-79, resident ophthalmology, 1979-81, chief resident ophthalmology, 1981-82; affiliate prof. ophthalmology U. South Fla. Coll. Medicine, Tampa, 1982—. Fellow ACS, Am. Acad. Ophthalmology (mem. numerous coms. 1987—, Honor award 1993); mem. AMA, Contact Lens Assn. of Ophthalmologists (bd. dirs. 1992-94, 98-99, Honor award 1998), Fla. Soc. Ophthalmology (1st v.p. 1992-93, treas. 1993-94), Fla. Med. Assn., Internat. Assn. Contact Lens Educators. Office: Ste D 4444 E Fletcher Ave Tampa FL 33613-4937 Fax: 813-977-2611.

SLORP, JOHN S. retired academic administrator; b. Hartford, Conn., Dec. 5, 1936; Student, Ocean Coll., Calif., 1956, Taft Coll., 1961; BFA Painting, Calif. Coll. Arts and Crafts, 1963, MFA Painting, 1965. Grad. tchr. U. N.D., Grand Forks, 1964; in house designer Nat. Canner's Assn., Berkeley, Calif., 1965; faculty Md. Inst. Coll. Art, Balt., 1965-82, chmn. Found. Studies, 1972-78; faculty Emma Lake program U. Sask., Can., 1967-68, 70; selection, planning group for Polish Posters Smithsonian Instn., Md. Inst. Coll. Art, Warsaw, 1977; planner, initiator visual arts facility, curriculum Balt. High Sch. Arts, 1979-81; adjudicator Arts Recognition and Talent Search, Princeton, N.J., 1980-82; mem. Commn. Accredation Nat. Assn. Schs. Art and Design, 1985-88; pres. Memphis Coll. Art, 1982-90, Mpls. Coll Art and Design, 1990—2002, prof. emeritus, 2002—. Com. Advanced Placement Studio Art Ednl. Testing Svc., Princeton, N.J., 1975-82; chair Assn. Memphis Area Colls. and Univs., 1986-88. Prodr. film A Romance of Calligraphy; calligrapher various brochures, manuscripts, album covers, children's books. Mem. Hotel adv. com. City of Memphis and Shelby County Convention Hotel, 1982; adv. bd. Memphis Design Ctr.; bd. trustees Opera Memphis, 1985—, ART Today Memphis Brooks Mus., 1988—. Avocations: painting, calligraphy, computer graphics.*

SLOTKIN, RICHARD SIDNEY, American studies educator, writer; b. Bklyn., Nov. 8, 1942; s. Herman and Roselyn B. (Seplowitz) S.; m. Iris F. Shupack, June 23, 1963; 1 child, Joel Elliot. BA, Bklyn. Coll., 1963; PhD, Brown U., 1967; MA (hon.), Wesleyan U., Middletown, Conn., 1976. Mem. faculty Wesleyan U., 1966—, prof. English, 1976—, Olin prof., 1982—, chmn. dept. Am. studies, 1976—. Author: Regeneration Through Violence: The Mythology of the American Frontier, 1600-1860, 1973 (Albert Beveridge award Am. Hist. Assn.), (with J.K. Folsom) So Dreadfull a Judgement: Puritan Responses to King Philip's War, 1675-1677, 1978, The Crater: A Novel of the Civil War, 1980, The Fatal Environment: The Myth of the Frontier in the Age of Industrialization, 1800-1890, The Return of Henry Starr, 1988, Gunfighter Nation: The Myth of the Frontier in Twentieth Century America, 1992 (National Book award nominee, 1993), Abe: A Novel of the Young Lincoln, 2000 (MIchael Shaara Civil War Fiction award, 2000); and articles. Fellow Center Humanities; fellow Wesleyan U., 1969-70, 74-75, 80— ; fellow NEH, 1973-74, Rockefeller Found., 1976-77; recipient Don D. Walker prize AQ; lit. award Little Big Horn Assocs., 1986 Fellow Soc. Am. Historians; mem. AAUP, PEN, Am. Film Inst., Am. Studies Assn. (Mary Turpie prize for tchg. and program-bldg. 1995), Am. Hist. Assn., Orgn. Am. Historians, Authors Guild. Jewish. Office: Wesleyan U Ctr For The Americas Middletown CT 06459-0001

SLOVIK, SANDRA LEE, retired art educator; b. Elizabeth, N.J., Mar. 22, 1943; d. Edward Stanley and Frances (Garbus) S. BA, Newark State Coll., 1965, MA, 1970. Cert. art tchr. Art tchr. Holmdel (N.J.) Twp. Bd. Edn., 1965-99, ret., 1999. Computer art in-sv. tng. Holmdel Bd. Edn., 1990; computer art workshop Madison (N.J.) Bd. Edn., 1991; presenter Nat. Edn. Computer Conv., 1999. Charter supporter, mem. Statue of Liberty/Ellis Island Found., 1976—; charter supporter Sheriffs' Assn. N.J., 1993—; mem. PTA, Holmdel, 1965—. Recipient Curriculum award N.J. ASCD, 1992; grantee Holmdel Bd. Edn., 1989, 90, N.J. Bus., Industry, Sci., Edn. Consortium, 1990. Mem. NEA, Nat. Art Edn., Assn., N.J. Art Educators Assn., N.J. Edn. Assn., Monmouth County Edn. Assn., Holmdel Twp. Edn. Assn. (sr. bldg. rep. 1977-79). Avocations: travel, sports. Office: Village Sch 67 Mccampbell Rd Holmdel NJ 07733-2299 E-mail: sslovik@hotmail.com.

SLUSSER, BRETT WILLIAM, vocational education educator; b. Topeka, Kans., Jan. 19, 1952; s. Robert Dean and Velda Marie (Beedy) S.; m. Dianah Sue Raliff, Oct. 21, 1972; children: Tonya Marie, Antia Louise. Grad. high sch., Nixa, Mo., 1970. Cert. vocat. tchr., Okla. Mech. maintenance Langston (Okla.) U., 1979-81; dir. transp. Rekkins-Tryon Sch., Perkins, Okla., 1981-85; technician Bridwell Equipment Co., Stillwater, Okla., 1985; repairman Okla. State U., Stillwater, 1985; installer Cimarron Glass Co., Cushing, Okla., 1985-86; svc. clk. tech. Dennis Equipment Co., Pawnee, Okla., 1986; technican Janzen Motor Co., Stillwater, Okla., 1986-91; instr. Kiamichi ARea Vo-Tech. Sch., Stigler, Okla., 1991—. Fire fighter County Fire Dept., Stigler, 1991, rescue dept., 1991, civil def. dept., 1991. With USCG, 1971. Mem. NRA, Am. Vocat. Assn., Okla. Vocat. Assn., Green Coutnry Pullers Assn., Nat. Vocat. Indsl. Clubs Am., Masons. Democrat. Baptist. Avocations: tractor pulling, fishing, boating, camping, horse riding. Home: 1012 S Jefferson St Stillwater OK 74074-5449 Office: Kiamich Area Vocat Tech Sch RR 2 Box 1005 Stigler OK 74462-9802

SLY, MARILYNN JANE, elementary education educator; b. Des Moines, Aug. 16, 1963; d. Loren Eugene and Barbara Jean (Grob) Meggison; stepchildren: Julie Michelle, Nicholas Burton; m. Gary Lee Sly, July 26, 1986; 1 child, Shelby Barbara. BS, Iowa State U., 1985; MEd, U. Nev., 1991. Dist. mgr. Westmark Property Mgmt., Des Moines, 1985-86; substitute tchr. Des Moines Pub. Schs., 1986-87, elem. tchr., 1991—; policy change clk. Am. Mutual Life, Des Moines, 1987-88; chpt. 1 tchr. Clark County Schs., Las Vegas, 1988-91. Dir., sec., treas. Sunbelt Investments, Ltd., West Des Moines, 1991—, Meggison Real Estate, Inc., West Des Moines, 1991—, Meggison Devl., Inc., West Des Moines, 1991—. Contbr. articles to profl. jours. Recipient Communicator award Miss Iowa USA, 1985. Mem. NEA, Iowa State Edn. Assn., Des Moines Edn. Assn., Internat. Reading Assn., Ctrl. Iowa Reading Coun., Alpha Omicron Pi. Episcopalian. Avocations: children's literature, needlework, reading, travel, investments. Home: 2336 Heatherwood Dr West Des Moines IA 50265-5738 Office: Des Moines Pub Schs 710 College Ave Des Moines IA 50314-2844

SMAGORINSKY, PETER, education educator; b. Princeton, N.J., Oct. 24, 1952; s. Joseph and Margaret (Knoepfel) S.; m. Anne O'Gorman, July 10, 1982 (dec. Aug. 1982); m. Jane E. Farrell, Oct. 12, 1985; children: Alysha, David. BA, Kenyon Coll., 1974; MA in Tchg., U. Chgo., 1977, PhD, 1989. English tchr. Westmont (Ill.) H.S., 1977-78, Barrington (Ill.) H.S., 1978-85, Oak Park (Ill.) and River Forest H.S., 1985-90; asst. prof. U. Okla., Norman, 1990-95, assoc. prof., 1995-98, U. Ga., Athens, 1998-2001, prof., 2001—. Author: Standards in Practice, 1996; co-author: How English Teachers Get Taught, 1995, The Language of Interpretation, 1995; co-editor Rsch. in the Tchg. of English, 1996-2003; mem. editl. bd. Rev. Ednl. Rsch., Am. Jour. Edn., Written Comm., Reading and Writing Quarterly. Recipient Steve Cahir award for rsch. in writing Am. Ednl. Rsch. Assn., 1991, Raymond B. Cattell award for disting. programmatic rsch. Am. Ednl. Rsch. Assn., 1999. Mem. Nat. Coun. Tchrs. English (chair standing com. on rsch. 1995-96, co-chair assembly for rsch. 1996, trustee rsch. found. 1997-2003, chair 2000-2003, pres. nat. conf. rsch. in lang. and literacy, 2001, English Jour. Writing award 1989, Edwin M. Hopkins award 2000, Janet Emig award 2003). Home: 175 Emerald Dr Athens GA 30605-4106 Office: U Ga 125 Aderhold Hall Athens GA 30602 E-mail: smago@coe.uga.edu.

SMAIL, LESLIE ANNE, librarian; b. Pitts., July 25, 1958; d. Laurence Mitchell and Nancy (Fried) S.; m. Eric D. Hunley, July 10, 1998. BA, Christopher Newport Coll., 1980; MSLS, Cath. U., 1982. Libr. intern Tng. and Doctrine Command, Ft. Monroe, Va., 1982-84; libr. Ft. Story (Va.) Libr., 1985-2000; libr. dir. Bryant & Stratton Coll. Libr., Virginia Beach,

Va., 2000; libr. Gwinnett County Pub. Libr., Lawrenceville, Ga., 2000—01; contractor retrospective conversion project Tortolita Vet. Svcs., PC, Tucson, 2002—03; reference libr. Davis-Monthan AFB Libr., 2003—. Recipient Exceptional Performance award U.S. Army, Ft. Eustis, Va., 1985-99, Comdr.'s award for civilian svc., 1995, 2000; Outstanding Program Mgr. TRADOC, Ft. Monroe, 1988-89. Mem.: Sigma Tau Delta. Avocations: arts and crafts, antiques, gardening, genealogy. Office: DM Base Libr 5427 E Madera St Davis Monthan Afb AZ 85707 E-mail: leslie.smail@flash.net.

SMAILI, AHMAD, mechanical engineering educator; b. Gaza, Lebanon, Nov. 4, 1955; came to U.S., 1976; s. Abdulkarim and Fatme (Mourad) S.; m. Maha Hazime, Aug. 10, 1989; children: Layla, Ali. BS, Tenn. Technol. U., 1979, MS, 1981, PhD, 1986. Asst. prof. Miss. State U., Starkville, 1987-91, Tenn. Technol. U., Cookeville, 1991-95, assoc. prof., 1995—99, prof., 2000—. Cons. Waste Policy Inst., Washington, 1992, U. Tenn. Space Inst., Tullahoma, 1993—94, Marine Gears, Greenville, Miss., 1990—91, Geka Thermal Sys., Atlanta, 1994—; assoc. prof. Am. Univ. Beirut, 1999—. Contbr. articles to profl. jours. Co-chmn. Cookeville Refugee Support Com., 1993—. Named Outstanding Faculty Mem., Student Assn. Miss. State U., 1989; recipient Kinslow Rsch. award Tenn. Technol. U., 1996, 99, Howard Watrous award 5th Applied Mechanisms and Robotics Conf., 1997. Mem. ASME (faculty advisor), Am. Soc. Engring. Edn., Pi Tau Sigma (Purple Shaft Trophy 1989, 90), Tau Beta Pi. Moslem. Achievements include introduction for the first time the concept of "Robomechs" parallel-drive linkage arms for multi-function task applications; establishment of a mechatronics laboratory at Tennessee Technological University. Home: 850 3rd Ave Fl 18 New York NY 10022-6222 E-mail: asmaili@aub.edu.lb.

SMALBACH, BARBARA SCHILLER, foreign language educator; b. N.Y.C., Feb. 18, 1942; d. Sylvan Bertram and Frances (Siegel) Schiller; m. Mervyn Stockman, Nov. 21, 1962 (div. Jan. 1965); m. David H. Smalbach, Aug. 29, 1969. BA Adelphi U., 1963, MA 1968. Tchr. fgn. langs. Long Beach Pub. Sch. System, N.Y., 1963-64; teaching fellow dept. fgn. langs. Queens Coll., Flushing, N.Y., 1964-65; tchr. fgn. langs. Farmingdale Pub. Sch. System, N.Y., 1966—. Mem. Rockville Centre BiCentennial Festival Com., 1975-76; founder, pres. Friends of Rockville Centre Pub. Library, 1980-82; founder, co-chmn. Hist. Homes Tour, 1980-84; co-chmn. Rockville Centre Anniversary Celebration, 1983; pres. Mus. of The Village of Rockville Centre, 1985-87, Rockville Centre Village historian, 1986—; treas. Assn. of Nassau County Hist. Orgns., 1984—. Mem. NE Conf. on Teaching Fgn. Langs., AAUW (N.Y. state div. br. council rep. 1987, Div. Com. on Pub. Support for Pub. Ed., Dist. VI, 1984-87; Div. Com. Br. Council, Dist. VI, 1982-84; Nassau County Br. Pres., 1980-82; L.I. Women of Achievement award 1980, co-founder and co-chair excellence & equality for women & girls conf. 1989-94, edn. area rep. 1987-89, 91-92, state nominations com. 1986-87, state membership v.p. 1989-91, assoc. com. (LAF) 1990-91, co-founder and chair L.I. AAUW Day, 1983-86, Area Coordinator Project WIPE, 1984-88, co-creator and co-developer of anti-censorship workshops); Delta Kappa Gamma, Sigma Delta Pi. Republican. Jewish. Club: Tam O'Shanter (Brookville, N.Y.); Gleneagles (Delray Beach, Fla.). Avocations: travel, golf, reading. Home: 10 Allen Rd Rockville Centre NY 11570-1201

SMALL, GLORIA JEAN, retired elementary school educator; b. Libertyville, Ill., Feb. 6, 1946; m. Lou G. Small, Jr., June 13, 1971; children: James, David, Andrea. BA, Carroll Coll., 1968; MA, Roosevelt U., Chgo., 1971. Elem. tchr. Libertyville Pub. Schs., Ill., 1967-76; tchr. Barne Hage Preschool, Washington Is., Wis., 1981-83; elem. tchr. Washington Is. Sch., 1983—2003, ret., 2003. Contbr. newspaper Observer. Mem.: Washington Island Women's Club (pres. 2002—03). Luth. Avocations: writing, reading, collecting old toys. Home: RR 1 Box 141 Washington Island WI 54246-9744

SMALL, HELEN AGNES, reading education specialist; b. Brunswick, Maine, Aug. 12, 1941; d. Arthur Adams and Alice Margaret (Crimmins) S. BEd, St. Joseph's Coll., North Windham, Maine, 1963; MEd, U. Maine, 1968; student, U. So. Maine, 1968—. Cert. tchr. reading, Maine. Tchr. Brunswick Sch. Dept., 1963-74, reading specialist, 1974—; tchr., reading specialist, 1994—2001; ret., 2001. Organist St. Charles Ch., Brunswick, 1963-89, dir. children's choir, 1973-78; mem. steering com. for formation of Big Bros. and Big Sisters, Brunswick, 1978-79; bd. dirs. Big Bros./Big Sisters So. Maine, Inc., 1984-86, mem. steering com. Bath-Brunswick Council for Portland Chpt. Big Bros. and Big Sisters of Am., 1979-84; chairperson Brunswick Adv. Council of Big Bros. and Big Sisters of So. Maine, Inc., 1984-86; dir. music St. Ambrose Ch., Richmond, Maine, 1989-03. Mem. NEA, Internat. Reading Assn., Maine Tchrs. Assn., Maine Reading Assn., Reading Support Group, Am. Guild Organists. Democrat. Roman Catholic. Avocations: playing and listening to music, aqua exercises, walking, correspondence. Home: 103 Union St Brunswick ME 04011-2425

SMALL, LESLIE JANE, special education administrator; b. Palo Alto, Calif., Nov. 9, 1948; d. John A. and Virginia M. (Canterbury) Monken; m. George N. Small, May 25, 1974; children: Jacob Emory, Amanda Catherine. BS, U. Ill., 1971; MS, U. N.C., 1971; MA, No. Ariz. U., 1974. Spl. edn. tchr. Mesa (Ariz.) Pub. Schs., 1975-78, program specialist, learning disabilities, 1978-81; program coord. Project Enrich, Mesa, 1981-84; edn. specialist child inpatient unit N.C. Meml. Hosp., Chapel Hill, 1985; edn. supr. U. N.C. Neuropsychiat. Hosp., Chapel Hill, 1985-91; assoc. dir. Carolina Community Re-entry Prog. for Adults w/Head Injury, Durham, N.C., 1991-94; program dir. Learning Svcs. South Ctrl. regional campus, 1994—97; v.p. neurorehab. divsn. Learning Svcs. Corp., 1997—98; dir. clin. scs. Paradigm Health Corp., Concord, Calif., 1998—. Edn. cons. Developmental Neuropsychiatry Clinic, Chapel Hill, 1987-89, Pediatric Neuropharmacology Clinic, Chapel Hill, 1987-89. Author book chpt., ednl. materials in field. Coun. rep. Chapel Hill-Carrboro PTA, 1989—; pres. Dancemakers Parent Orgn., Chapel Hill, 1990—; den mother Boy Scouts Am., Chapel Hill, 1984-85; Brownie leader Girl Scouts U.S.A., Chapel Hill, 1986-87. Named Educator of Yr., Assn. for Retarded Citizens, 1984. Mem. Coun. for Exceptional Childrenn (chmn. membership div. for learning disabilities 1982-83, pres. div. for early childhood 1983-84), N.C. Hosp. Tchrs. Assn. (chmn. govtl. rels. 1989-90), Phi Delta Kappa. Methodist. Avocations: reading, gardening, white water river rafting. Home: 403 Wesley Dr Chapel Hill NC 27516-1521 Office: Paradigm Health Corp 1001 Galaxy Way Ste 300 Concord CA 94520

SMALL, RALPH EDWARD, pharmacy educator, consultant; b. Welland, Ont., Can., Apr. 30, 1950; s. George Edward and Margaret Emma Verna (Young) S.; m. Sharon McRae Stevens, Sept. 21, 1985. BS in Pharmacy, U. Toronto, Ont., Can., 1973; PharmD, Duquesne U., 1975. Prof. pharmacy and medicine Med. Coll. of Va. Va. Commonwealth U., Richmond, 1975—. Chmn. med. adv. bd. Cen. Va. chpt. Lupus Found., Richmond, 1983—; pharmacy capt. United Way Greater Richmond, l988; pres. West End Manor Civic Assn., Richmond, l984, J.R. Tucker High Sch. Community Coun., Richmond, l986; bd. dirs. Va. chpt. Arthritis Found., Richmond, 1986. Recipient Pub. Svc. award Arthritis Found., 1986, Lifetime Achievement award Arthritis Found., 1986, Pub. award Arthritis Found., 1986, Dist. Vol. of Yr., 1992, Excellence award United Way, 1988, NARD Leadership award, 1990, Va. Commonwealth Univ. Disting. Svc. award, 1994. Fellow Am. Coll. Clin. Pharmacy, Am. Soc. Health System Pharmacists, Am. Pharm. Assn. (trustee 1996); mem. Am. Assn. Colls. Pharmacy, Am. Soc. Health System Pharmacists, Va. Pharm. Assn. (pres. 1990-91, Bowl of Hygeia 1988, Svc. award 1994, Outstanding Pharmacist award 2000), Richmond Pharm. Assn. (pres. 1986, Dist. Pres. award 1987). Avocations: sports, golf, tennis, traveling. Home: 1800 Locust Hill Rd Richmond VA 23233-4148 Office: Va Commonwealth U Med Coll Va PO Box 980533 Richmond VA 23298-0533

SMALLS, PEGGY ANN, educational consultant, retired elementary educator; b. Atlanta, Feb. 25, 1943; d. Calton D. and Alberta (Wardlaw) Lamar. BA, Clark Coll. (Clark Atlanta Univ.), 1965; MEd, U. Ga., 1975; EDS, Brenau U., 1995. Cert. elem. grades, 7-12 social studies, middle grades, gifted and instructional supervision. Tchr. Atlanta Pub. Schs.; self employed ednl. cons. Founder River Run Civic Assn., Dekalb County, Ga.; campaign worker AFL-CIO/AFT, Atlanta; mem. Greenforest Community. Baptist Ch. Reading grantee Apple Corps; named Technology Tchr. of Yr. IBM. Mem. AFT (zone coord., editor, 2d v.p., work shop presenter, editor, writer newsletter, service award Local 1564, 1991), ASCD, Internat. Reading Assn., Alpha Kappa Alpha (philactor, sec., v.p., pres.), Phi Delta Kappa, Alpha Kappa Alpha (Lambda Epsilon Omega chpt. officer of the year, soror of yr.), . Avocations: writing, mentoring high school students.

SMALLWOOD, ROBERT ALBIAN, JR., secondary education educator; b. Phila., Oct. 3, 1946; s. Robert Albian and Mildred May (Miller) S.; m. Geraldine Ann Boozan, May 27, 1972; children: Amy Lynn, Daniel James. BSC, Rider Coll., 1969, MA, 1976; EdS, Rutgers U., 1986. Cert. social studies tchr., secondary sch. prin., supr. curriculum and instrn., Pa.; cert. social studies and gen. bus. tchr., prin., supr., sch. bus. adminstr., asst. supt. bus., sch. adminstr. (supt.) N.J. Tchr. social studies Trenton Bd. Edn., 1973-76, tchr. bus. edn., 1975-76, sch. disciplinaerian, 1976-84, 94-97; acting asst. prin. Jr. High Sch. 2, 1980-83, tchr. U.S. history, 1983-87, chmn. social studies dept., 1984-85; acting asst. prin. Carroll Robbins Elem. Sch., Jr. High Schs. #1 and #5, 1987-88; tchr. gifted and talented social studies Dunn Jr. High Sch., 1989-93, social studies tchr., 1997-99, whole sch. reform site facilitator, 1999—. Mem. Dist.'s Affirmative Action Adv. Council; mem. Nat. Tchr. Corps Project, Trenton Area; fin. advisor M.S. Prin., 1998—. Asst. ops. officer Trenton CD Unit, 1974-76, asst. disaster analysis officer, 1976, disaster analysis officer, 1976-79; trustee N.J. Coun. for Alcohol/Drug Edn., 1983-99, mem. exec. com., 1985-95, 96-99, chmn. nominating com., 1985, 86, treas., 1987-95, acting exec. dir., 1994-95, v.p., 1996-98, pres. 1998-99. With U.S. Army, 1969-72. Decorated Bronze Star, Army Commendation medal with oak leaf cluster, Joint Svc. Commendation medal. Mem. NEA, Vietnam Vets. Am., Va. Geneal. Soc., Md. Geneal. Soc., Md. Hist. Soc., Geneal. Soc. Pa., Nat. Geneal. Soc., Assn. Profl. Genealogists, Phi Delta Kappa. Home: 2 Leese Ave Trenton NJ 08609-1828

SMARDON, RICHARD CLAY, landscape architecture and environmental studies educator; b. Burlington, Vt., May 13, 1948; s. Philip Albert and Louise Gertrude (Peters) S.; m. Anne Marie Graveline, Aug. l9, 1973; children: Regina Elizabeth, Andrea May. BS cum laude, U. Mass., 1970, MLA, l973; PhD in Environ. Planning, U. Calif., Berkeley, l982. Environ. planner, landscape architect Wallace, Floyd, Ellenzweig, Inc., Cambridge, Mass., l972-73; assoc. planner Exec. Office Environ. Affairs, State of Mass., Boston, 1973-75; environ. impact assessment specialist USDA extension svc. Oreg. State U., Corvallis, 1975-76; landscape architect USDA Pacific S.W. Forest and Range Expt. Sta., Berkeley, l977; rsch. landscape architect U. Calif., Berkeley, l977-79; prof. landscape architecture, sr. rsch. assoc. SUNY Coll. Environ. Sci. and Forestry, Syracuse, 1979-86, prof. environ. studies, 1987—, dir. Inst. for Environ. Policy and Planning, 1987-95, chair faculty of environ. studies, 1996—. Co-dir. Gt. Lakes Rsch. Consortium, Syracuse, 1986—; guest lectr. numerous univs.; adj. asst. prof. U. Mass., Amherst, 1974-75, dir. R.G. Pack Environment Inst., 1996—; Sea Grant trainee Inst. for Urban and Regional Devel., Berkeley, 1976; condr., presenter numerous seminars and workshops; cons. to numerous orgns.; mem. com. on environ. design and landscape Transp. Rsch. Bd.-NAS, 1985-95; mem. tech. adv. bd. Wetlands Rsch., Inc., Chgo., 1985; mem. adv. bd. Wetlands Fund, N.Y., 1985; v.p. Integrated Site, Syracuse, 1990-2002. Co-editor: Our National Landscape, 1979, spl. issue Coastal Zone Mgmt. Jour., 1982, The Future of Wetlands, 1983, Foundations for Visual Project Analysis, 1986, The Legal Landscape, 1993, Protecting Floodplain Resources, 1995, Adirondacks and Beyond, 1998, Environmental Knowledge, 2001; mem. editl. bd. Northeastern Environ. Sci. Jour., 1981-85, Landscape and Urban Planning, 1991—, Environ. Sci. and Policy, 1999—, The Sci. World, 2001—; contbr. over 100 articles to profl. jours. Bd. dirs. Sackets Harbor Area Hist. Preservation Found., Watertown, N.Y., 1984-90; pres. Save the County, Inc., Fayetteville, N.Y., 1986-88, 2002—; apptd. to Great Lakes (N.Y.) Adv. Commn., chmn., 1993-98, Great Lakes Legal Found., 1999, NY State Wetlands Forum Bd., 2000. Recipient Beatrice Farrand award U. Calif., 1979, Am. Soc. Landscape Architects award, 1972, Pub. Svc. award in edn., 1990, Progressive Architecture mag. award 1992, Pres.'s Pub. Svc. award 1994. Mem. AAAS, NAEP, N.Y. Acad. of Sci., Am. Land Resource Assn. (charter), Internat. Assn. for Impact Assessment, Coastal Soc., Alpha Zeta (life), Sigma Lambda Alpha. Avocations: folk guitar, hiking, skiing, travel. Office: SUNY Faculty Environ Studies Syracuse NY 13210

SMART, ANN CATHERINE, dean; b. Anderson, Ind., Nov. 27, 1946; d. Edward Vernon and Virginia Ruth (Hersberger) Dillie; m. Houston Wynnlee Crisp, Aug. 17, 1968 (div. 1980); m. William H. Smart, Aug. 16, 1987. BS in Edn., Ball State U., 1969; postgrad., U. Alaska, 1971—73; M in Home Econs., Oreg. State U., 1975, PhD, 1991. Youth nutrition specialist U. Alaska, Fairbanks, 1970—73, extension mgmt. info. coord., 1972—73; specialist nutrition edn. Oreg. State U., Corvallis, Oreg., 1975; parent edn. and home econs. coord. Linn-Benton C.C., Albany, NY, 1975—77, Albany (N.Y.) Ctr. dir., 1977—79, Benton Ctr. dir., 1979—85, cmty. edn. divsn. dir., 1985—89, spl. asst. to v.p. bus. affairs, 1987, interim v.p. instrn., 1989—90, dean student svcs. and extended learning, 1991—94, dean extended learning and info. svcs., 1994—; ret. Rsch. assoc. Western Oreg. State Coll., Monmouth, Oreg., 1983; chmn. task force Cmty. Edn. Dirs., Oreg., 1983. Author: Anotated Bibliography Nutrition Education Resources, 1975, Program Planning Activities Nutrition for Elderly, 1975; co-prodr.: (films) Alaskan Food Choices, 1973; contbr. articles to bulls. Founding pres. Oreg. Coast C.C. Svc. Dist., Newport, Oreg., 1987—88; chmn. task force Charting the Future of Corvallis, 1988—89; mem. UN Forum 85, Nairobi, Kenya, 1985; sec. Benton County United Way, 1984—87, pres., 1991—92, Zonta Svc. Found. Corvallis, 1991—92, treas., 1994—. Named Leader of the 80s, League Innovation in Cmty. Colls., 1982. Mem.: LWV, Oreg. Cmty. Edn., Am. Assn. Women in C.C., Oreg. C.C. Assn., Nat. Coun. Cmty. Svcs. and Continuing Edn. (Oreg. rep. 1994—, Regional Person of Yr. award 1993), Am. Assn. Adult and Continuing Edn. (v.p. region VIII 1987—89), Oreg. Home Econs. Assn. (sec. 1979—81, mem. joint bds. articulation commn. 1992—95, named Disting. Leader 1984), N.W. Adult Edn. Assn. (pres. 1984—85, named Adult Educator of Yr. 1987), Corvallis C. of C. (bd. dirs.), Rotary, Albany (N.Y.) Club, Zonta Club (pres. Corvallis club 1982—83, internat. del. 1982, alt. 1984, African study tour 1985, named Zontian of Yr. 1994), Phi Kappa Phi, Phi Theta Kappa, Sigma Zeta. Democrat. Office: Linn-Benton Community Coll 6500 Pacific Blvd SW Albany OR 97321-3755

SMARTSCHAN, GLENN FRED, school system administrator; b. Allentown, Pa., Dec. 11, 1946; s. Fred Gotfred and Joyce Isabel (Hensinger) S.; m. Linda Susan Bastinelli, Mar. 18, 1972; children: Erin Joy, Lauren Nicole. BS in Edn., Kutztown State Coll., 1968; MS in Edn., Temple U., 1972; EdD in Ednl. Adminstrn., Lehigh U., 1979. Cert. tchr. history and comprehensive social studies, secondary prin., supt., Pa. Tchr. 8th grade social studies South Mountain Jr. H.S., 1968-76; adminstrv. asst. to prin. to prin. Raub Jr. H.S., 1976-80, dist. dir. curriculum, 1980-84, asst. to supt. for curriculum and cmty. svcs., 1984-86; supt. schs. Brandywine Hts. Area Sch. Dist., Topton, Pa., 1986-90, Mt. Lebanon Sch. Dist., Pitts., 1990—2003. Adj. prof. Cedar Crest Coll., 1986-88, Duquesne U., 1997, U. Pitts., 2001; CEO Ednl. Dynamics Cons.; assoc. Transformation Sys., 2002—; spkr. and cons. Multiple Client Feedback (MCF). Pay for Performance Plans, match of written, taught and tested curriculum, criterion referenced testing, strategic planning; rsch. assoc. U. Pitts; ednl. planner Burt Hill Kosar and Rittlman, 2003—; cons. tri-state area study coun. Univ. Pitts for planning and accountability, 2003—. Bd. dirs. Alternative House, Inc., Bethlehem, Pa., 1976-81, chmn. program com., 1977-78, v.p., 1979, pres., 1980; adv. com. Lehigh County (Pa.) Hist. Mus., 1980-86; bd. dirs. Girls Club Allentown, 1983-86, v.p., 1985. Mem. ASCD, Pa. Assn. Supervision and Curriculum Devel. (exec. com., registrar ea. regional meeting, v.p. Ea. region, pres. 1988), Am. Assn. Sch. Adminstrs. (Pa. State Supt. of Yr. 1999), Pa. Assn. Sch. Adminstrs. (pres. 1996), Pa. Sch. Bds. Assn., Juvenile Diabetes Assn. (bd. dirs.), Alumni Coun. Lehigh U. (pres. 1986), Phi Delta Kappa, Fleetwood Club, Rotary (charter mem. Allentown club, exec. com. 1985). Roman Catholic. Home: One Spalding Cir Pittsburgh PA 15228 Office: Mt Lebanon Sch Dist 7 Horsman Dr Pittsburgh PA 15228-1107

SMAY, CONNIE R. educational media specialist, educator; b. Benton Harbor, Mich., May 27, 1953; d. Victor Wier and Lois Reynolds; m. James Robert Smay, Aug. 11, 1979; children: Robert James, Thomas Victor, Rebekah Josephine. Student, Western Mich. U., Kalamazoo, 1975, 76; BS in Edn., Ctrl. Mich. U., Mt. Pleasant, 1975; MS in Edn. with honors, No. Ill. U., DeKalb, 1979. Tchr.'s aide Coloma (Mich.) Migrant Program, 1971, 73-76, tchr., 1977; factory prodn. line worker Voice of Music, Benton Harbor, 1972; student tchr. Wyoming (Mich.) Sch. Dist., 1975; libr., media specialist Cmty. Sch. Dist. 300, Dundee, Ill., 1975-79, Cmty. Sch. Dist. 115, Oquawka, Ill., 1980; children's libr. Warren County Pub. Libr., Monmouth, Ill., 1980-81; ednl. media specialist Parsippany Troy Hills (N.J.) Bd. Edn., 1990—. Computer liaison Parsippany Troy Hills Bd. Edn., 1993-98, insvc. trainer for dist., 1995—, integrator of technology and N.J. Core Content Stds. into content curriculum areas, 1990—; Internet trainer, 1997—, coord. NetDay, 1997-98. Grantee EBSCO Pub., Ipswich, Mass., 1996-97; recipient dist. mini-grant Sci. Is for Everyone, 1996, Hit the Nail on the Head, 1997, Integrating Core Curriculum Stds. in Sci. and Math. Mem. DAR, ALA, N.J. Reading Assn., N.J. Statewide Systemic Initiative, N.J. Edn. Assn., Parsippany Tech. Com., Ednl. Media Specialists Assn., Disting. Flying Cross Soc. (assoc.). Methodist. Home: 152 Orben Dr Landing NJ 07850-1828 Office: Parsippany Troy Hills Sch Dist care Ctrl Mid Sch Parsippany NJ 07054 also: Brooklawn Mid Sch Parsippany NJ 07054

SMELLEY, JOYCE MARIE, special education supervisor; b. New Iberia, La., Oct. 17, 1937; d. Monroe Carroll and Ethel Marie (Williams) Simpson; m. John T. Williamson, Feb. 1967 (div. 1972); 1 child, Tamara Marie; m. Roy David Smelley Sr., Sept. 25, 1990; children: Rebecca Marie, Roy David Jr. BS, East Tex. Bapt. Coll., 1960; cert. in spl. edn., U. Denver, 1969; MEd, La. State U., Shreveport, 1981; cert., Northwestern Coll., Natchitoches, La., 1982. Cert. tchr., La., Tex., Colo. Elem. tchr. Pine Tree Ind. Sch. Dist., Longview, Tex., 1960-67, Paris Elem. Sch., Aurora, Colo., 1967-69, Mound Elem. Sch., Burleson, Tex., 1972-73; tchr. Stanley (La.) High Sch., 1973-75, tchr. spl. edn., 1978-79; tchr. Town and Country Sch., Mansfield, La., 1975-78; tchr. spl. edn. Second Ward Sch., Gloster, La., 1979-80; assessment tchr. DeSoto Parish Evaluation Team, Mansfield, La., 1980-87, coord. pupil appraisal, 1987-88; supr. spl. edn. DeSoto Parish Sch. System, Mansfield, 1988—. Mem. Coun. Exceptional Children, La. Edn. Assn., La. Assn. Sch. Execs., La. Assn. Spl. Edn. Adminstrs., Pilots Club (pres. Mansfield 1992—), Order Ea. Star (organist 1992, worthy matron 1995). Baptist. Home: 134 Hope St Mansfield LA 71052-2906 Office: DeSoto Parish Schs PO Box 975 Mansfield LA 71052-0975

SMETHURST, JACQUELINE, educational consultant; b. Buckinghamshire, England, July 18, 1942; came to U.S., 1967; d. Jack and Pattie (Pilgrim) S.; m. James Patrick Leheny, Apr. 12, 1966 (div. Jan. 1984); children: Emma, Claire; m. David Drinkwater, July 1, 1995. BA, Oxford U., 1963, MA, 1967; MEd, U. Mass., 1972, EdD, 1984. Tchr. English Slough High Sch. for Girls, England, 1965-67; adminstr., tchr. U. Mass., Amherst, 1967-82; dean residential life Northfield (Mass.) Mt. Hermon Sch., 1982-86, acad. dean, 1986-88, head, 1988-98; planning cons. to edn. Jacqueline Smethurst Assocs., 2003—. Bd. dirs. Saltwater Inst., 1988—, Am. Friends St. Hilda's Coll., Oxford, England, 1995—, Nat. Assn. Ind. Schs., 1997, Concord Acad., Mass., 1998—, Ursuline Acad., New Orleans, 2003—. Fulbright scholar, 1963, English-Speaking Union scholar, 1963-65. Mem. Nat. Assn. Prins. of Schs. for Girls, Headmistresses Assn. of East, Headmasters Assn.. Episcopalian. Avocations: literature, women's issues, leadership, organizational change. Office: Jacqueline Smethurst Assocs 370 Park Rd Metairie LA 70005

SMIACH, DEBORAH, accountant, educator, consultant; b. Johnstown, Pa., Mar. 10, 1960; d. Frank Raymond and Pearl Lillian (Rudeck) S. BA in Acctg., U. Pitts., Johnstown, 1982; MBA, Katz Grad. Sch. Bus., Pitts., 1989, M of Info. Systems, 1991. CPA Pa., CGFM Va. Staff acct. C.E. Wessel & Co., Johnstown, Pa., 1982-84; sr. acct. Sickler, Reilly & Co., Altoona, Pa., 1984-86; assoc. prof. acctg. U. Pitts., Johnstown, 1986—, chmn. dept. bus., 1995—. Cons. Cambria-Somerset Coun. for Health Profls., Johnstown, 1986—; internal inspector Walter Hopkins & Co., Clearfield, Pa., 1995, Wessel & Co., Johnstown, 1992—. Mem. bd. dirs. Bottleworks Ethnic Arts Ctr., Johnstown, Pa., 1993—, Am. Red Cross-Keystone chpt., 1995—; coun. mem. Our Lady of Mount Carmel, South Fork, Pa., 1993-95. Mem. AICPA, Pa. Inst. Cert. Pub. Accts., Pa. Bus. and Profl. Women (dist. 5 chair public relations com. 1993-95, chair woman of the yr. com. 1995-96, chair issues mgmt. 1996-97), Johnstown Bus. and Profl. Women (pres., pres-elect, v.p., treas.) Democrat. Roman Catholic. Avocations: exercising, baking, reading, crafts. Office: U Pitts Johnstown 104 Krebs Hall Johnstown PA 15904

SMILES, RONALD, management educator; b. Sunderland, Eng., June 15, 1933; s. Andrew and Margaret (Turns) S.; m. Evelyn Lorraine Webster, Apr. 12, 1959 (div. Jan. 1981); children: Tracy Lynn, Scott Webster, Wendy Louise; m. Linda Janet Miller, June 23, 1990. Assoc. in Bus. Adminstrn., U. Pa., 1968; BSBA, Phila. Coll. Textiles & Sci., 1969; PhD, Calif. Western U., 1977; MA, U. Tex., Arlington, 1985, PhD, 1987. V.p. Liquid Dynamics Corp., Southampton, Pa., 1968-71; pres., gen. mgr. Internat. Election Systems Corp., Burlington, N.J., 1971-76; plant mgr. Rack Engring. Co., Connellsville, Pa., 1977-80; v.p. Ft. Worth (Tex.) Houdaille, 1980-85; chmn. grad. sch. bus. Dallas Bapt. U., 1987-92, prof., 1987—, assoc. dean Coll. Bus., 1996-97. Author: Impact on Legislation of Competition in the Voting Machine Industry, 1978, A Study of Japanese Targeting Practices and U.S. Machine Tool Industry Responses, 1985, Occupational Accident Statistics: An Evaluation of Injury and Illness Incidence Rates, 1987. Mem. Burlington County (N.J.) Selective Svc. Bd., 1974-76. Served with Royal Arty., 1951-53. Mem. Greater Connellsville C. of C. (v.p. 1979-80), Night Watch Honor Soc., Sigma Kappa Phi, Alpha Delta Epsilon (award 1968). Office: Dallas Bapt Univ Dallas TX 75211

SMILEY, FREDERICK MELVIN, education educator, consultant; b. Yuba City, Calif., Apr. 13, 1943; s. Lester Boomer and Claire Leone (DeChesne) S. AA, Yuba Coll., 1963; BA, Chico State U., 1966; MA in Edn., Chapman Coll., 1973, MA in English, 1978, MA in Spl. Edn., 1982; PhD, U. Santa Barbara, 1982; EdD, Okla. State U., 1992. Tchr., coach, v.p. McDermitt (Nev.) High Sch., 1978-80; resource specialist Eagle Mt. (Calif.) High Sch., 1980-81; instr. spl. edn. Mary Stone Sch., San Mateo, Calif., 1981-86; dept. leader Quaczar Corp., Bridgeport, Conn., 1986-87; cons., researcher Multi-functional Resource Ctr., Stillwater and Norman, Okla., 1988-91; prof. edn. Cameron U., Lawton, Okla., 1991—. Contbr. articles to profl. jours.; contbg. editor Think!, The Writing Teacher, Okla. Assn. Tchr. Eductors Jour., ATE Jour. Mem. AAUP, Am. Assn. for Teaching and Curriculum, Am. Soc. Curriculum Devel., Am. Coun. Rural Spl. Edn., Am. Assn. Colls. for Tchr. Edn., Coun. for Exceptional Children, Okla. Assn. Tchr. Educators (pres. 2001—), Soc. Educators and Scholars, Kappa Delta Pi, Phi Delta Kappa, Phi Kappa Phi. Democrat. Lutheran. Avocations: reading, writing, racing, tennis, golf. Office: Cameron U 2800 W Gore Blvd Lawton OK 73505-6377 E-mail: freds@cameron.edu.

SMINK, MARY JANE, graphic communications technology educator; b. Charlotte, N.C., Feb. 19, 1939; d. Arthur Elmore and Louise (Belue) Moore; m. George Thomas Smink Jr.; children: George Thomas III, Karl Frederich. BS, Winthrop Coll., 1959; MA in Indsl. Arts, Appalachian State U., 1970; EdD in Indsl. Arts, N.C. State U., 1983. Cert. technology edn., N.C. Tchr. Columbia (S.C.) City Schs., 1959-61, Mars City/Adams Twp. Schs., Mars, Pa., 1962-63, Cleveland County Schs., Shelby, N.C., 1964-65, dir. audio visual, 1966-67; coord. adult edn. Wilkes C.C., Wilkesboro, N.C., 1967-70; dir. career exploration Wilkes County Schs., Wilkesboro, N.C., 1970-71; tchr. Wake County Schs., Raleigh, N.C., 1971-79; cons. N.C. Dept. Pub. Instrn., Raleigh, N.C., 1980-90; asst. prof. N.C. A&T State U., Greensboro, 1990—. Articulation adv. com. Guilford Tech. C.C., Greensboro, 1990—. Contbr. articles to profl. jours. Organist Milner Meml. Presbyn. Ch., Raleigh, 1971—; leader Boy Scouts Am., Raleigh, 1973-78. Edn. Profl. Devel. Act fellow, 1980; recipient William Warner Rsch. award Epsilon Pi Tau, 1983, Epsilon Pi Tau Laureate citation N.C. State U., 1987, Award of Distinction, Tech. Student Assn., Inc., 1988, Hall of Fame citation Ednl. Exhibitors Assn. and SHIP, 1995; named State Supr. of Yr., Internat. Tech. Edn. Assn. Coun. of Suprs., 1986. Mem. S.E. Tech. Edn. Assn., N.C. Tech. Edn. Assn. (pres.-elect 1994-95), Internat. Tech. Edn Assn. (Disting. Tech. Educator award 1991, Meritorious Svc. award 1992, pres. bd. 1988), Tech. Student Assn., Inc (bd. dirs., pres. bd. 1986-87), Nat. Assn. Indsl. Tech. (jour. rev. bd. 1993—), Phi Delta Kappa (capital area chpt.), Phi Kappa Phi. Avocation: model railroading. Home: 5907 S Sharon Dr Raleigh NC 27603-4665 Office: NC A&T State Univ Sch Of Technology Greensboro NC 27411-0001

SMIT, HANS, law educator, academic administrator, lawyer; b. Amsterdam, Netherlands, Aug. 13, 1927; came to U.S. 1952; s. Eylard Albertus and Trijntje (de Jong) S.; m. Beverly M. Gershgol, Aug. 1, 1954; children: Robert Hugh, Marion Tina. LLB with highest honors, U. Amsterdam, 1946, JD with highest honors, 1949; AM, Columbia U., 1953, LLB with highest honors, 1958; D. (hon.), U. Paris I, 1991. Bar: Supreme Ct. Netherlands 1946, N.Y. 1974. Ptnr. Bodenhausen, Blackstone, Rueb, Bloemsma & Smit, The Hague, 1952-58; assoc. Sullivan & Cromwell, N.Y.C., 1958-60; mem. faculty law Columbia U., N.Y.C., 1960—, assoc. prof., 1960-62, prof., 1962—, Stanley H. Fuld prof. law, 1978—. Dir. Parker Sch. Fgn. and Comparative Law; vis. prof. U. Paris, Sorbonne-Pantheon, 1975-76, 89-90, 92-94; dir. Project on Internat. Proc., Columbia U.; reporter U.S. Com. on Internat. Rules Jud. Procedure, 1960-67; bd. dirs. Project on European Legal Inst., 1968, Leyden-Amsterdam-Columbia Summer Program in Am. Law; cons. internat. comml. transactions, internat. litig.; arbitrator ICC and AAA. Author: International Co-operation in Litigation, 1963, (with others) Elements of Civil Procedure, 5th edit., 1985, International Law, 3d edit., 1993, (with Pechota) World Arbitration Reporter, 1986, (with Herzog) The Law of the European Economic Community, 1978; editor-in-chief Am. Rev. of Internat. Arbitration. Mem. All-Dutch Waterpolo team 1946-48, All-Am. Waterpolo team, AAU, 1954. Knight Order of Netherlands Lion, 1987. Mem. ABA, Internat. Bar Assn., Am. Fgn. Law Assn., Assn. of Bar of City of N.Y., Am. Soc. Internat. Law, German-Am. Lawyers' Assn., Internat. Assn. Jurists of U.S.A.-Italy, Internat. Acad. Comparative Law, Royal Dutch Soc. Arts and Scis. (assoc.), Am. Arbitration Assn., Internat. C. of C. Home: 351 Riverside Dr New York NY 10025-2739 Office: Columbia U Sch Law 435 W 116th St New York NY 10027-7297

SMITH, AGNES MONROE, history educator; b. Hiram, Ohio, Aug. 8, 1920; d. Bernie Alfred and Joyce (Messenger) Monroe; m. Stanley Blair Smith; children: David, Doris, Darl, Diane. BA, Hiram Coll., 1940; MA, W.Va. U., 1945; PhD, Western Res. U., 1966. Social sci. tchr. Freedom (Ohio) High Sch., 1940-44; instr. of history W.Va. U., Morgantown, 1945; instr. of social sci. Hiram Coll., 1946; inst. history and social sci. Youngstown (Ohio) State U., 1964-66, asst. prof. to prof. of history, 1966-84, prof. history emeritus, 1984—; vis. prof. history Hiram Coll., 1988-90. Co-editor: Bourgeois, Sans Culottes and other Frenchmen, 1981; contbr. articles to profl. jours. Mem. Ohio Acad. History, Delta Kappa Gamma, Phi Alpha Theta, Pi Gamma Mu. Mem. Christian Ch. (Disciples Of Christ). Home: 16759 Main Market Rd West Farmington OH 44491-9608

SMITH, ALAN JAY, computer science educator, consultant; b. N.Y.C., Apr. 10, 1949; s. Harry and Elsie Smith. SB, MIT, 1971; MS, Stanford (Calif.) U., 1973, PhD in Computer Sci., 1974. From asst. prof. to full prof. U. Calif., Berkeley, 1974—; assoc. editor ACM Trans. on Computers Systems, 1982-93. Vice-chmn. elec. engring. & computer sci. dept. U. Calif., Berkeley, 1982-84; nat. lectr. ACM, 1985-86; mem. editorial bd. Jour. Microprocessors and Microsystems, 1988—; subject area editor Jour. Parallel and Distbn. Computing, 1989—; mem. IFIP working group 7.3.; program chmn. Sigmetrics 89, Performance 1989, Hot Chips Symposium, 1990, 94, 97. Fellow: AAAS, IEEE (disting. visitor 1986—87), Assn. for Computing Machinery (chmn. spl. interest group on ops. sys. 1983—87, nat. lectr. 1985—86, bd. dirs. spl. interest group on performance evaluation 1989—89, chmn. spl. interest group on computer architecture 1991—93, bd. dirs. spl. interest group on computer architecture 1993—2003); mem.: Computer Measurement Group. Office: U Calif Dept Computer Sci Berkeley CA 94720-1776

SMITH, ALLISON LONDON, English language educator, real estate developer; b. Kansas City, Mo., Dec. 1, 1942; d. William Jay Sr. and Emily Ann (Allison) L.; m. Bruce Mitchell Smith, June 5, 1965; children: Travis Mitchell, Chase London. BS, U. Mo., 1964, postgrad., 1992-93, S.W. Mo. State U., 1966-68. Educator Overland Park Sch. System, Shawnee Mission, Kans., 1964-66, West Plains Sch. System, West Plains, Mo., 1967-72; legal aid R. Jack Garrett, Atty. at Law, West Plains, Mo., 1972-74; province collegiate dir. Gamma Phi Beta, Mo./Kans., 1974-77; legal aid Howell County Prosecuting Atty., West Plains, Mo., 1978-80; educator Southwest Mo. State Univ., West Plains, Mo., 1981--. V.p. Southern Hills Ctr., Ltd., West Plains, 1979--; sec. treas, K & S Devel., Ltd., Harrison, Ark., 1982--. Pres. Ozark Med. Ctr. Aux., 1971; sec., treas. Country Club Bd. Dirs., 1975; choreographer People's Park Players and H.S. Prodns., 1975—; bd. govs. S.W. Mo. State U., 1995—. Named Outstanding Young Women Am., 1970; recipient svc. award Gamma Phi Beta, Denver, 1982; Fanfare for Fifty Theta Kappa Phi, Columbia, Mo., 1980. Mem. Nat. Assn. Tchrs. Coll. English, Nat. Soc. Legal Secs., DAR, PEO Sisterhood, Jefferson Club U. Mo., Gamma Phi Beta, Phi Delta Theta Mothers Club. Republican. Episcopalian. Home: 4720 County Road 7000 West Plains MO 65775-7640 Office: SW Mo State U Central Hall 128 Garfield Ave West Plains MO 65775-2715

SMITH, ALMA DAVIS, elementary education educator; b. Washington, June 27, 1951; d. Wyatt Deeble and Martha Elizabeth (Lingenfelter) Davis; m. Perry James Smith, Jan. 1, 1979; children: Lauren, Hunter. BS, James Madison U., 1973; MEd, U. Va., 1978. Cert. elem. tchr. and prin., Va. Tchr. Robert E. Lee Elem. Sch., Spotsylvania, Va., 1973-79, Conehurst Elem. Sch., Salem, Va., 1979, Hopkins Rd. Elem. Sch., Richmond, Va., 1980-87, Reams Rd. Elem. Sch., Richmond, Va., 1987-95, asst. prin. summer sch., 1990; tchr. Crestwood Elem. Sch., Richmond, Va., 1995—. Bd. mem. PTA, 1994-95, life mem., 1995; ambassador Chesterfield County Pub. Schs. Chesterfield Co. ambassador, 1998-2000. Mem. NEA, Spotsylvania Edn. Assn. (numerous chair positions), Chesterfield Edn. Assn. Home: 2811 Ellesmere Dr Midlothian VA 23113-3800

SMITH, ANDREW MACLELLAN, business administration educator; b. Livonia, Mich., Aug. 18, 1960; BS, Purdue U., 1983; MBA, Butler U., 1989. Grad. teaching asst. Butler U., Indpls., 1986-89; asst. prof. bus. adminstrn. Marian Coll., Indpls., 1989—. Cons. to small bus., Indpls., 1988—. Author: An Introduction to DOS, 1992. Founding sponsor Challenger Ctr., Alexandria, Va., 1988. Mem. Assn. Computing Machinery, Soc. Advancement of Mgmt. Avocations: music, golf. Office: Marian Coll 3200 Cold Spring Rd Indianapolis IN 46222-1960

SMITH, ANN ELIZABETH, elementary school educator; b. Laurens, S.C., Jan. 19, 1950; d. John Richard and Melda Beatrice (Duvall) S. BA, Berry Coll., Mt. Berry, 1972; MEd, U. S.C., Columbia, 1975, EdD, 1981. Tchr. Whitten Ctr., Clinton, S.C., 1972-75, Greenwood. Dist. #50, Greenwood, S.C., 1975-90, Greenwood Dist. #52, Greenwood, S.C., 1990—; psychologist, instr. Piedmont Tech. Coll., Greenwood, S.C.; tchr., adult edn. Laurens Dist. #56, Clinton, S.C., 1974-75; pvt. practice Greenwood, 1985—. Sec. GCARC, Greenwood, 1985-86, area coord. S.C. Spl. Olympics, 1985-86; corrs. sec. GCEA, Greenwood, 1987-88. Author: Curriculum for Profound and Severe, A Measure of the Efficacy of Mainstreaming, Modifying a Language Program, The Struggle, Counseling Materials for the Developmentally Disabled. Presenter S.C. Council for Exceptional Children, Charleston, 1989. Mem. NEA, SCEA, GCEA, Internat. Reading Coun., GCARC, New Age Study Group, Writer's Guild, S.C. Soc. for Artistic Children, Soc. for Autistic Children, Piedmont Reading Coun. Avocations: painting, music.

SMITH, ANNIE LEE NORTHERN, school system administrator; b. Houston, Dec. 27, 1932; d. Lee Fletcher and Christine (Johnson) Williams; stepfather Leamer Williams; m. Louis Northern, Dec. 23, 1956 (dec. 1965); 1 son, Eric V.; m. 2d Jules Smith, Jan 28, 1967. B.S., Tex. So. U., 1954, M.Ed., 1959, postgrad., 1978, Tex. A & M U., 1988; CSD (hon.) Guadalupe Coll., San Antonio, 1988; cert. mid-mgmt., 1959. Tchr. Stone Crest Nursery Sch., Houston, 1954-57, Cypress Fairbanks Ind. Sch. Dist. (Tex.), 1957-59, Houston Ind. Sch. Dist., 1959-75; instructional coordinator, 1975-77, prin., 1977—; staff dir., Houston Ind. Sch. Dist., 1990-94; ret. 1994. instr. Nat. Bapt. Pub. Bd., Nashville; speaker in field. Active Houston YWCA; reporter, announcer, youth coord., pulpit com., St. John Bapt. Ch., 1977—. Recipient Outstanding Performance award Houston Ind. Sch. Dist., 1974, Merit award, 1978, Cert. Appreciation City of Houston, 1986, State of Tex., 1986, Achievement award Spinal Health Edn., Outstanding Leadership award Lovett Sch., Svc. award H.A.S.A., 1994, Elrod Sch. Houston Ind. Sch. Dist., 1994, Johnson Washington Family, 1994, Leadership award St. John Bapt. Ch. Youth Dept., Houston, 1994, Women of Distinction award Houston Women's Dist. Task Force, 1994,a Key to City award, City of Miami, Fla., 1995, Tchr. Retirement Svc. award H.H.C.R.T.A., 1996, others. Mem. NEA, NAACP, HAABSE, Nat. Coun. Negro Women, Nat. Coun. Black Educators, Assault on Illiteracy Process (Black Togetherness award 1995, nat. co-chair War Chest 1991-95, nat. bd. dirs. 1995—), Parent Tchrs. Orgn., Houston Tchrs. Assn., Houston Prins. Assn., Tex. State Tchrs. Assn., Tex. Elem. Sch. Tchrs. Assn., Nat. Women of Achievement (pres. 1961—, reg. dir. 1991—, nat. pres. 1991-95, service award so. ctrl. region 1993, bd. dirs. 1995—), Am. Legion Aux., Mamie Charity Club (youth sponsor, reporter, sec., Outstanding Leadership award 1976), Sigma Gamma Rho (service award 1976-80, Outstanding Educator award 1980, appreciation award 1994, spl. recognition cert. 1995), Eta Phi Beta (achievement award 1993). Address: 2922 S Peach Hollow Cir Pearland TX 77584-2032 also: St James Episcopal Sch 3129 Southmore Blvd Houston TX 77004-6214

SMITH, ARTHUR E. counseling educator, vocational psychologist; b. St. Louis, Feb. 28, 1926; s. Lee L. and Dorothea M. (Debrecht) S.; m. Jane C. Dooley; children: Greg, Laura, Terry, Chris. BS, St. Louis U., 1949, MEd, 1951, PhD, 1962. Diplomate Am. Bd. Vocational Experts; lic. psychologist. Tchr., counselor St. Louis Pub. Schs., 1949-60; Evening Coll. dir. and assoc. prof., St. Louis U., 1960-66; grad. dean St. Mary's Coll., Notre Dame, Ind., 1966-68; chmn. behavioral studies U. Mo., St. Louis, 1968—; pres. Clayton Bus. Sch., St. Louis, 1983—; dir. Affiliates in Psychology and Counseling, St. Louis, 1970-78. Contbr. articles to profl. jours. Served with USNR, 1944-46, PTO. Recipient Recognition award Am. Soc. Tng. Dirs. and Am. Pers. and Guidance Assn. Mem. AACD (pres. St. Louis 1965), Nat. Vocat. Guidance Assn., Assn. Counselor Educators and Supvs., Am. Coll. Vocat. Experts, Nat. Rehab. Assn. (pres. St. Louis 1979-80, Recognition award 1980). Office: U Mo 8001 Natural Bridge Rd Saint Louis MO 63121-4401

SMITH, ARTHUR JOHN STEWART, physicist, educator; b. Victoria, B.C., Can., June 28, 1938; s. James Stewart and Lillian May (Geernaert) S.; m. Norma Ruth Askeland, May 20, 1966; children: Peter James, Ian Alexander. BA, U. B.C., 1959, M.Sc., 1961; PhD, Princeton U., 1966. Postdoctoral fellow Deutsches Electronen-Synchrotron, Hamburg, W. Germany, 1966-67; mem. faculty dept. physics Princeton U., 1967—, prof., 1978—, Class of 1909 prof., 1992—, assoc. chmn. dept., 1979-83, chmn. dept. physics, 1990—. Vis. scientist Brookhaven Nat. Lab., 1967—, chair sci. and tech. steering com. Brookhaven Sci. Assocs.; vis. scientist Fermilab, 1974—, Stanford Linear Accelerator Ctr., 1996—, vis. prof., 2000—, spokesperson BaBar experiment, 2000—. Assoc. editor Phys. Rev. Letters, 1986-89; contbr. articles to profl. jours. Fellow Am. Phys. Soc. (chmn. divsn. of particles and fields 1991). Achievements include research on experimental high-energy particle physics; kaon decays, physics of the B particles and quark structure of hadrons. Home: 4 Ober Rd Princeton NJ 08540-4918 Office: PO Box 708 Princeton NJ 08544-0001

SMITH, ARTHUR KITTREDGE, JR., academic administrator, political science educator; b. Derry, N.H., Aug. 15, 1937; s. Arthur Kittredge and Rena Belle (Roberts) S.; m. June Mary Dahar, Nov. 28, 1959; children: Arthur, Valerie, Meredith. BS, U.S. Naval Acad., 1959; MA, U. N.H., 1966; PhD, Cornell U., 1970. Vis. prof. El Colegio de Mexico, Mexico City, 1968-69; asst. prof. polit. sci. SUNY-Binghamton, 1970-74, assoc. prof., 1974-84, prof., 1984-88, provost for grad. studies and research, 1976-83, v.p. for adminstrn., 1982-88; prof. govt. and internat. studies U. S.C., Columbia, 1988-91, exec. v.p. for acad. affairs, provost, 1988-90, 91, interim pres., 1990-91; pres., prof. polit. sci. U. Utah, Salt Lake City, 1991-97; chancellor U. Houston Sys., 1997—; pres., prof. polit. sci. U. Houston Main Campus, 1997—. Author: (with Claude E. Welch, Jr.) Military Role and Rule: Perspectives on Civil-Military Relations, 1975; contbr. articles to profl. jours. With USN, 1959-65. Lehman fellow, 1966-69, NDEA fellow, 1969-70 Mem. Am. Polit. Sci. Assn., L.Am. Studies Assn., Inter-Univ. Sem. on Armed Forces and Soc., Am. Coun. on Edn., World Affairs Coun. (pres. Binghamton chpt. 1976-76), Bus.-Higher Edn. Forum, Phi Beta Kappa, Pi Sigma Alpha, Omicron Delta Kappa, Phi Delta Kappa, Beta Gamma Sigma, Phi Kappa Phi. Home: 1505 South Blvd Houston TX 77006-6335 Office: U Houston Sys Office Of The Chancellor Houston TX 77204-0001 E-mail: aksmith@uh.edu.

SMITH, BARBARA ANN, gifted education coordinator; b. Oak Park, Ill., Mar. 20, 1950; d. William J. and Mary T. (Barlow) S. BS in Edn., No. Ill. U., 1971, MS in Edn., 1974, cert. advanced study in edn., 1977, EdS in Edn., 1988, EdD, 1994. Nat. bd. cert. tchr., 2001; adminstr. gifted edn., verification, Ill.; lic. counselor, Ill. Coord. gifted edn. Dist. 45 Elem. Schs., Villa Park, Ill., 1986—, counselor to group on leadership devel., tchr. Contbr. articles to profl. jours. Mem. AACD, ASCD, NEA (chpt. sec., treas.), ACA, Ill. West Suburban Reading Coun., AAUW (coord. families facing change group), Delta Kappa Gamma (chpt. pres.), Phi Delta Kappa. Office: Sch Dist 45 255 W Vermont St Villa Park IL 60181-1943

SMITH, BARBARA ANN, elementary education educator; b. Peoria, Ill., Dec. 21, 1933; d. Gerald Clyde and Kathryn Jane Smith. BS, Taylor U., Ft. Wayne, Ind., 1959; MS, St. Francis Coll., Ft. Wayne, 1967. Tchr. freshman phys. edn. Taylor U., 1957-58; tchr. James H. Smart Sch., Ft. Wayne, 1959-67, Southwick Elem. Sch., Ft. Wayne, 1967-95, Meadowbrook Elem., 1995—. Chair Young Authors, Ft. Wayne, 1990-92; chair Coalition of Essential Schs., Ft. Wayne, 1992-94; mem. coun. Region 8 Dept. Edn., Ind., 1992-94; chairperson Performance Based Assessment Climate Com., 1992-94; facilitator Ind. 2000, 1993-95; chair Parent/Staff Adv. Coun., Ft. Wayne, 1994-95; title I Home/Sch. Coord., 1995. Campaign worker Rick Hawks for Congress, Ft. Wayne, 1990. Recipient various teaching awards. Mem. NEA, Ind. Profls., Internat. Reading Assn. (sec. 1993-94, Fort Wayne chpt. Elem. Tchr. of Yr. 1993), East Allen Tchrs., Ind. State Tchrs. Assn. Republican. Avocations: reading, travel, western line dancing, aerobics, biking. Home: 2803 Cherokee Run New Haven IN 46774-2917

SMITH, BARBARA MARTIN, art educator, artist; b. St. Louis, Feb. 3, 1945; d. Charles Landon and Mary Louise (Nolker) Martin; m. Timothy Van Gorder Smith, Nov. 27, 1976; children: Brian Eliot, Marjorie Van Gorder. BA, Lawrence U., 1967; MFA, So. Ill. U., 1975; MA, Washington U., St. Louis, 2002. Cert. tchr., Mo. Art instr. Horton Watkins High Sch., Ladue, Mo., 1968-76; leader Experiment in Internat. Living, Brattleboro, Vt., 1974; art tchr. Michigan City (Ind.) Ctr. for the Arts, 1979-80, Cleve. Mus. of Art, 1981-83; art instr. Villa Duchesne, St. Louis, 1986—. Edn. dir. Dunes Art Found., Michigan City, 1979; co-chmn. Internat. Wives Group, Cleve. Coun. on World Affairs, 1982-84; bd. dirs. Webster Groves (Mo.) Sch. Found., 1992. Exhibited in shows at Art Inst. of Chgo., 1979, So. Ill. U. Alumnae Exhibit, 1982, Focus Fiber, Cleve. Mus. of Art, 1982, Nova, Wearable Art, Kuban Gallery, Cleve., 1983, Drawings & Prints, St. Louis Artist's Guild, 1986. Mem. vestry Ch. St. Michael and St. George, 2003—; bd. dirs. Lawrence U., Appleton, Wis., 2001—, Webster Hist. Soc., 2003—. Recipient Grad. Fellowship Ann. Grad. award So. Ill. U., 1975; named Artist in Residence/ Artist in Schs. Ind. Arts Commn./NEA, 1978-79; named to Honors Seminar for Advancement of Art Edn., R.I. Sch. of Design, 1988, Mem. Art Edn. Delegation to Japan, 1992. Mem. Nat. Art Edn. Assn., Internat. Soc. for Edn. through Art, St. Louis Art Mus., St. Louis Artist Guild, St. Louis Watercolor Soc. (co-chair exhbns.). Home: 135 Jefferson Rd Webster Groves MO 63119-2934

SMITH, BENJAMIN ALEXANDER, II, education educator, geography educator; b. Lakeland, Fla. s. Benjamin Alexander and Lily Faye (Cowden) S.; m. Sylvia Louise Sizemore, July 31, 1957; children: Jullia, Benjamin A. III, Daniel Belton. BS, East Tenn. State U., 1962; MEd, U. Ga., 1976, EdD, 1986. Tchr. Atlanta Pub. Schs., 1962-63, Pinellas County Schs., Clearwater, Fla., 1963-65; press rels. Sears Roebuck & Co., Atlanta, 1965-71; merchandise mgr. Oxford Industries, Toccoa, Ga., 1971-74; tchr. Habersham County Schs., Clarkesville, Ga., 1974-86; asst. prof. U. So. Miss., Hattiesburg, 1986-88; assoc. prof. edn. and geography Kans. State U., Manhattan, 1998-2001, prof. edn. and geog., 2001—02, prof. emeritus, 2002—. Editor Jour. Social Studies Rsch., 1993-98, Geographic Insights, 1989-2001; editor: Geography Lessons, 1993; author: American Geographers 1784-1812: A Bio-Bibliographic Guide to the First Generations. With U.S. Army, 1954-56. Mem. Kans. Geog. Alliance (pubs. editor 1989-2001, coord. 1999-2001), Kans. Coun. for Social Studies pres. 1994-95), Nat. Coun. for Geog. Edn. (Dissertation awards, Geog. Excellence in Media/Geog. Rsch., Disting. Geog. Tchg. Coll. and Univ. award, Disting. Mentor award), Nat. Coun. for the Social Studies (chair archives 1992-94), Manhattan (Kans.) Men's Garden Club (pres. 1992-93). Presbyterian. Avocations: geography textbook collecting, history of geography. Home: 118 Morningside Dr Sylvania GA 30467-8515 E-mail: geogben@hotmail.com.

SMITH, BETTY ELAINE, geography educator; b. Paterson, N.J., Oct. 28, 1949; d. Robert Francis and Elaine Gertrude Clough; m. Harrison John Smith, Sept. 6, 1975. BA in Geography, U. Calif., Davis, 1971; MA in Geography, Calif. State U., Chico, 1987; PhD in Geography, SUNY, Buffalo, 1994. Asst. planner City of Sacramento, Calif., 1973-75; real estate broker Sun Realty, Redding, Calif., 1976-88, Medley Realty, Redding, 1976-88; rsch./tchg. asst. SUNY, Buffalo, 1991-94, instr., 1993-94; lectr. U. Wis., Oshkosh, 1994-95; asst. prof. Ea. Ill. U., Charleston, 1995—. Contbr. articles to profl. jours. Mem. Assn. Am. Geographers, Conf. Latinamericanist Geographers, Regional Sci. Assn. Internat., Sigma Xi (assoc.). Office: Ea Ill U Dept Geology and Geography Charleston IL 61920

SMITH, BETTY ROBINSON, elementary education educator; b. Athens, Ga., Jan. 31, 1941; d. Willie Martin and Leila Mary Robinson; m. Freddie Smith; children: Natalie Yvonne, Rewa Patrice. BSEd, Tuskegee (Ala.) Inst., 1964; MS, Nova U., Ft. Lauderdale, Fla., 1979; cert. early childhood, U. S. Fla. Head tchr. in headstart program Perkins Elem. Sch., St. Petersburg, Fla., 1965; tchr. Orange Grove Elem. Sch., Tampa, Fla., 1967-68, Largo (Fla.) Ctrl. Elem. Sch., 1970-71, North Shore Elem. Sch., St. Petersburg, Fla., 1971-99, Gulfport Elem. Montessori Acad., 2000—; resource cons. Mt. Zion Christain Acad., 1999—; also bd. dirs. Head tchr. Early Success Program; active Appreciate Cultures Program for sch. improvement plan Pinellas County; chair Multicultural Club; organizer ann. Elem. workshop; network trainer, Gulfport Elem., 2000—. Dir. youth choir, active community and religious roles; mem. mass choir Mt. Zion Progressive Baptist Ch.; organizer 55+ Club; head multicultural com. North Shore Elem. Sch. Mem. PCTA, Zeta Gamma Zta, PREP (rep. for Pinellas County, Fla.). Home: 4301 Cortez Way S Saint Petersburg FL 33712-4024

SMITH, BEVERLY HARRIETT, elementary school educator; b. Cleve. d. William Nathaniel and Tommie Lee (Hooks) Stovall; m. Levi Smith, July 3, 1970; children: Kimberly Varese, Tommy Levi. BA in Edn., Ky. State U., 1970; MA in Curriculum and Instrn., Cleve. State U., 1975. Guidance liaison Almira Elem. Sch., Cleve., 1986—2002, drug liaison, 1988—2002, sci. lead tchr., 1993—2002; bldg. chairperson Cleve. Tchr. Union, 1990—2002, exec. bd. dirs., 1996—2002, chair salary and benefits, 1996—2002. Supt. tchr. for practicum tchrs., 1989-2000, supt tchr. for student tchrs., 1990-2001. Fin. sec. Shiloh Bapt. Ch. Ednl. Bd., Cleve., 1984-86. Recipient career edn. grant, 1989-90, Sunshine Energy award East Ohio Gas Co., 1984-85, 1988-89; named Educator of Yr., 1995; Martha Holden Jennings scholar, 1997. Mem. ASCD. Avocations: reading, arts and crafts, travel. Office: Almira Elem Sch 3380 W 98th St Cleveland OH 44102-4639

SMITH, BRENDA JOYCE, author, editor, social studies educator; b. Washington, Jan. 2, 1946; d. William Eugene and Marjorie (Williams) Young; m. Duane Milton Smith, Aug. 4, 1978. BA in History and Govt. cum laude, Ohio U., 1968, postgrad. in Am. and European History, 1972. Tchr. Jr. High Sch., Lancaster, Ohio, 1968-69, Reynoldsburg (Ohio) Mid. Sch. and High Sch., 1970-71; grad. teaching asst. Ohio U., Athens, 1969-70, 71-72; polit. speech writer Legis. Reference Bur., Columbus, Ohio, 1972-74; pub. rels. writer Josephinum Coll., Columbus, 1976-78; social studies editor Merrill Pub. Co., Columbus, 1979-91; freelance author/editor social studies Columbus, 1991—. Project editor: Human Heritage: A World History, 1985, 89, World History: The Human Experience, 1992; author: The Collapse of the Soviet Union, 1994, Egypt of the Pharaohs, 1995; writer-editor on African Am. history series, 5th grade; writer of 3 Am. history books; writer on state histories of N.Y. and Ind. Del. 1st U.S.-Russia Joint Conf. on Edn., 1994. Mem. Nat. Coun. Social Studies, Ohio Coun. Social Studies, Freelance Editl. Assn.

SMITH, BRENDA MARIE, vocational home economics educator; b. Winchester, Tenn., May 28, 1957; d. William Ralph and Mary Elizabeth (Wynne) Hall; m. Kevin Wayne Smith, Mar. 30, 1980; children: Jessica, Andrea. BS in Edn., S.W. Mo. State U., 1979, MS in Edn., 1989. Cert. tchr., home economist, Mo. Tchr. vocat. home econs., advisor Koshkonong (Mo.) Schs., 1979-80, Ava (Mo.) R-1 Sch. Dist., 1980-83, West Plains (Mo.) R-7 Schs., 1983—; advisor Future Homemakers Am., 1979—. Adj. faculty S.W. Bapt. U., Mountain View (Mo.) Ctr., 1992-93; mem. WPHS Better Edn. Techniques Team, West Plains, 1987—; mem. adv. bd. Step One Teen Parenting Program, West Plains, 1992—; mem. adv. bd. home econs. dept. S.W. Mo. State U., Springfield, 1983—. Sec., bd. dirs. Friendship Circle Pre-sch., West Plains, 1989-91, chair bd. dirs., 1991-92. Mem. Future Homemakers Am. Alumni Assn., Mo. Home Econs. Tchrs. Assn. (bd. dirs.

1987—, treas. 1989-93, pres.-elect 1993-94, pres. 1994-95), Am. Vocat. Assn., Mo. Vocat. Assn., Am. Home Econs. Assn. (sec. dist. E 1982-83, cert. home economist), Mo. Home Econs. Assn., Mo. State Tchrs. Assn., Cmty. Tchrs. Assn. (pres. 1989-90, 92-93), Bus. and Profl. Women. Methodist. Avocations: collecting antiques, sewing, camping, tennis, golf. Home: 702 Shuttee St West Plains MO 65775-2916 Office: West Plains Sr High 602 E Olden St West Plains MO 65775-3334

SMITH, BRUCE R. English language educator; b. Jackson, Miss., Mar. 21, 1946; Student, U. Birmingham, England, 1966-67; BA magna cum laude in English with honors, Tulane U., 1968; MA, U. Rochester, 1971, PhD with distinction, 1973. From asst. prof. to assoc. prof. English Georgetown U., Washington, 1972-87, prof. English, 1987—2003, U. So. Calif., 2003—; faculty Bread Loaf Sch. English, Middlebury Coll., 1994—. Seminar dir. Folger Inst., 1994, 98-99. Author: Ancient Scripts and Modern Experience on the English Stage 1500-1700, 1988, Homosexual Desire in Shakespeare's England: A Cultural Poetics, 1991, Roasting the Swan of Avon: Shakespeare's Redoubtable Enemies and Dubious Friends, 1994, The Acoustic World of Early Modern England, 1999, Shakespeare and Masculinity, 2000; editor: Shakespeare, Twelfth Night: Text and Contexts, 2001; editl. bd. Shakespeare Quar., 1995—, PMLA, 2000-02, Studies in English Lit., 2003—; contbr. chpts. to books, articles to profl. jours. Summer grantee Georgetown U. Acad. Rsch., 1976, 84, 87, 89, 91, 92, 99; grantee Intercultural Curriculum Devel., 1982, Agecroft Assn., 1991; Mellon fellow Huntington Libr., 1996, jr. fellow Folger Inst., 1979, 85, fellow, 1990, 96, ACLS fellow, 1979-80, NEH fellow, 1987-88, 99, Va. Found. Humanites fellow, 1989, Internat. Globe fellow Shakespeare's Globe, London, 1997, Guggenheim fellow, 2001-02; recipient Roland Bainton pize for lit. 16th Century Studies Assn., 2000, Disting. Scholar award U. Rochester, 2002. Mem. MLA, Soc. Study Early Modern Women, Renaissance Soc. Am., Shakespeare Assn. Am. (pres. 1994-95), Com. for Lesbian and Gay History. Office: U So Calif Dept English Taper Hall 420 Los Angeles CA 90089-0354

SMITH, CANDA BANKS, educational consultant; b. Suffolk, Va., Oct. 17, 1929; d. John Thomas Banks and Edla Ruth Eure; m. Robert Luther Smith, Aug. 18, 1951; children: Kimberley Smith Kidd, Valerie Smith Eudy, Alexandra Eure. AA, Anderson (S.C.) Coll., 1946; BA, Coll. Notre Dame, Balt., 1991, MA, 1995. Tchr. presch., 1980-95; treas. Interface Resources, Ltd., Alexandria, Va., 1985—. Ednl. cons., 1995—. Active vol. profl. and community orgns; mem. exec. bd. dirs. Alxeandria Early Childhood Commn., 1996-2000; pub. chmn. Inova Alexandria Hosp. Aux., 1997, 98, pres., 1998, 99, mem. Inova Alexandria Found. bd. trustees, 1999-, sect., 2002, bd. lady mgrs., 2001-, recording sect. 2002-, 1872 hosp. bd.; area chmn. Am. Heart Assn., 1975-2000; vol. Ptnrs. in Edn., 1998-2002. Mem. DAR (state judge essay contest 1997-2002), Alexandria Kiwanianne Club (v.p. 1998). Home: 1102 Bayliss Dr Alexandria VA 22302-3506

SMITH, CARL BERNARD, education educator; b. Feb. 29, 1932; s. Carl R. and Elizabeth Ann (Lefeld) S.; m. Virginia Lee Cope, Aug. 30, 1958; children: Madonna, Anthony, Regina, Marla. BA, U. Dayton, 1954; MA, Miami U., Oxford, Ohio, 1961; PhD, Case Western Res. U., 1967. Tchr. Cathedral Latin H.S., Cleve., 1954-57; customer corr. E.F. MacDonald Co., Dayton, 1958-59; tchr. Kettering (Ohio) H.S., 1959-61; editor Reardon Baer Pub. Co., Cleve., 1961-62; tchr., rschr. Case Western Res. U., Cleve., 1962-65, Cleve. Pub. Schs., 1966-67; asst. prof. edn. Ind. U., Bloomington, 1967-69, assoc. prof., 1970-72, prof., 1973—99, prof. emeritus, 1999—. Dir. ERIC Ctr., 1988—, Family Literacy Ctr., 1990—; pres. Grayson Bernard Pub. Co., 1988—, Am. Family Learning Corp., 1996—. Author: Reading Instruction through Diagnostic Teaching (Pi Lambda Theta Best Book in Edn. award 1972), Getting People to Read, 1978; sr. author: Series r, 1983, New View, 1993, Teaching Reading and Writing Together, 1984, Connect! Getting Your Kids to Talk to You, 1994, Word History A Resource Book, 1995, Self-Directed Learner Curriculum, 1998, (videotape) Make a Difference, 1996, Improving Your Child's Writing Skills, 1999, Gotcha Grandpa, 2000, Talk to Your Children About Books, 2001, Teaching Children to Learn, 2002, Reading to Learn, 2003., Parents Guide to Character Devel., 2003. Pres. Bd. Edn., St. Charles Sch., Bloomington, 1976-80. Recipient Sch. Bell award NEA, 1967, Literacy award Ind. State Reading Assn., 1997. Mem. ASCD, Internat. Reading Assn., Nat. Coun. Tchrs. of English, Am. Ednl. Rsch. Assn., Phi Delta Kappa. Republican. Roman Catholic. Home: 401 Serena Ln Bloomington IN 47401-9226 Office: ERIC Clearinghouse Smith Rsch Ctr Bloomington IN 47405 E-mail: smith2@indiana.edu.

SMITH, CATHY, academic administrator; b. Richlands, Va., May 18, 1954; d. James Alvin and Doris Janet (Wilson) Smith; 1 child, Erin Amanda; m. John G. Cox. AS, S.W. Va. Community Coll., 1974; BS, Clinch Valley Coll., 1978; MS, Radford U., 1983. Cert. elem. grades 4-7, reading specialist grades K-12, devel. edn. specialist. Chpt. I reading tchr. Russell County Schs., Lebanon, Va., 1978-90; adj. faculty, reading S.W. Va. C.C., Richlands, 1983-87; elem. tchr. Russell County Schs., Lebanon; instr. devel. and basic reading and study skills NE State Tech. C.C., Blountville, Tenn., 1990-93; reading faculty Heartland C.C., Bloomington, Ill., 1993-96, open learning coord., 1996—. Dir. transitional studies, title III coord. Lake Mich. Coll., 1999-2000. Mem. Nat. Assn. Devel. Edn., Nat. Assn. Devel. Educators, Kellogg Inst., Coll. Reading and Learning Assn. (mem. Mich. devel. edn. consortium). Office: 2755 E Napier Ave Benton Harbor MI 49022-1881 Address: 7622 Red Arrow Hwy Stevensville MI 49127-9250 E-mail: smithk@lmc.cc.mi.us.

SMITH, CHARLES EDWARD, electrical engineering educator; b. June 8, 1934; s. Roy L. and Emma E. (Boyd) S.; m. Evelyn Juanita Blow, July 1, 1960; children: Charles E. Jr., Steven A., Gary L. BEE with honors, Auburn U., 1959, MS, 1963, PhD, 1968. Rsch. engr. Auburn U., Ala., 1959—68; from asst. prof. dept. elec. engring. to assoc. prof. U. Miss., University, 1968—76, chmn. dept. elec. engring., 1975—2002, prof., 1977—2002, prof. emeritus, 2002—. Contbr. articles to profl. jours. With USAR, 1953-65. Named Outstanding Engring. Tchr., U. Miss. Alumni Engring., 1970-71, Outstanding Faculty Mem., 1980-81, 87-88, 93-94, 99-2000, Burlington No. Faculty Achievement award outstanding tchg. and scholarship, 1993. Mem. IEEE (sr., life), Am. Soc. Engring. Edn., Kiwanis (v.p., pres. 1975-77), Sigma Xi (pres. U. Miss. chpt. 1976-77), Tau Beta Pi, Eta Kappa Nu, Phi Kappa Phi (exec. com. U. Miss. chpt. 1985). Baptist. Office: U Miss Dept Elec Engring University MS 38677-1848 E-mail: cesee@olemiss.edu.

SMITH, CHARLES EDWARD, education consultant; b. White County, Tenn., May 19, 1939; s. Cecil Edward and Christine (Newsome) S.; m. Shawna Lea Hickerson, Dec. 15, 1962; children: Chip, Tandy. BS in Journalism, U. Tenn., 1961; MA in English, George Peabody Coll., Nashville, 1966, PhD in Higher Edn., 1976. Editor Sparta Expositor, Tenn., 1961-63; mng. editor Putnam County Herald-Cookeville Citizen, Cookeville, Tenn., 1963-64; asst. news editor Nashville Tennessean, 1964-67; news bur. dir. U. Tenn., Knoxville, 1967-68, pub. relations dir., 1968-70, exec. asst. to chancellor, 1971-73; exec. asst. to pres. U. Tenn. System, Knoxville, 1973-75; chancellor U. Tenn., Nashville, 1975-79; v.p. pub. service U. Tenn. System; editor Nashville Banner, 1979-80; chancellor U.Tenn.-Martin, 1980-85; v.p. adminstrn. state-wide system U. Tenn.-Knoxville, 1985-87; commr. edn. State of Tenn., Nashville, 1987-93; chancellor Tenn. Bd. Regents, Nashville, 1994-2000. Trustee Am. Coll. Testing Bd., Iowa City, 1987-93; mem. So. Regional Edn. Bd., 1989-95, exec. com., 1991-95, vice chmn., 1994-95. Contbr. articles to profl. jours. Mem. Peabody Coll. Alumni Bd., 1994-99, pres., 1998-99. Recipient Single Best Editorial award Tenn. Press Assn., 1962, Peabody Coll. Disting. Alumnus award, 1993; named Fulbright fellow, 1980, One of Nation's Top 100 Coll. Educators, Bowling Green State U., 1986. Mem. Phi Kappa Phi. Democrat. Mem. Ch. of Christ. Home: 6340 Chickering Cir Nashville TN 37215-5301 Office: # 100 5300 Virginia Way Brentwood TN 37027-7529

SMITH, CHARLES EDWIN, computer science educator; b. Columbia, Mo., Apr. 15, 1950; s. William Walter and Nelletha Pearl (Lavendar) S.; m. Mary L. Davis, July 27, 1991. AA, Edison C.C., Ft. Myers, Fla., 1971; BS, Troy State U., 1979; MA, Webster U., St. Louis, 1989. Adj. instr. Manatee C.C., Venice, Fla., 1989-90, Edison C.C., Punta Gorda, Fla., 1989-92, prof. computer sci., 1992—, Charles O'Neill endowed chair astronomy, 1997-2001. Cons. Charles E. Smith Consulting, North Port, Fla., 1989-91; owner SmithTech Dental Handpiece Repair. Served to maj. USAF, 1975-79, USAFR, 1979-96. Mem. Air Force Assn. Mem. Fla. Assn. C.C.s, Mil. Officers Assn. Am., Am. Legion. Avocations: reading, fishing, boating, astronomy, woodworking. Office: Edison C C 26300 Airport Rd Punta Gorda FL 33950-5748

SMITH, CHARLES H. education educator; b. Charleston, W.Va., Oct. 2, 1947; s. Jesse R. and Freda Ruth (Cobb) S. BS, Alderson-Broaddus Coll., 1969; AM, U. Mich., 1971; PhD, U. Md., 1975; MBA, Coll. William and Mary, 1981. Mathematician Navl Rsch. Lab., Washington, 1972-75; ops. rsch. analyst U.S. Army Tng. Support Ctr., Fort Eustis, Va., 1975-78, Army Procurement Rsch. Office, Fort Lee, Va., 1978-82; asst. prof. Va. Commonwealth U., Richmond, 1982-87, assoc. prof., 1987—. Mem. Inst. for Ops. Rsch. and the Mgmt. Scis. Office: Va Commonwealth U Sch of Bus PO Box 844000 Richmond VA 23284-4000

SMITH, CHERYL DIANE, music educator; b. Princeton, Ind., Jan. 17, 1952; d. Ralph Eugene and Beulah J. Smith. BA, Oakland City U., 1974; MS, Ind. State U., 1980. Substitute tchr. North Gibson Sch. Corp., Princeton, Ind., 1974—77, South Gibson Sch. Corp., Ft. Branch, 1974—77; tchr. choral, gen. music South Knox Sch. Corp., Vincennes, 1977, North Knox Sch. Corp., Birknell, 1977—. Co-author: Introduction to Theater, 1999. Mem. exec. com. North Knox Social Mins., 1997—. Mem.: Choral Dirs. Nat. Assn., Nat. Music Educators Assn. Avocations: cross stitch, piano, reading.

SMITH, CHERYLYNNE DIANE, middle school principal; b. Phila., Nov. 9, 1947; d. Stanley Leonard and Margaret Frances (Coston) Woods; m. Everett Newton Smith, Oct. 4, 1969; 1 child, Royce Wood-son. BA in Spanish, Bennett Coll., Greensboro, N.C., 1969; MA in Bilingual-Bicultural Studies, LaSalle U., Phila., 1984. Cert. tchr., Pa., N.J. Bilingual-ESL tchr. Centennial Sch. Dist., Warminster, Pa., 1972-76; coord. bilingual-GED program Berean Inst., Phila., 1976-80; adminstr. computerized learning ctr. Control Data Corp., Phila., 1980-81; tchr. ESL Camden (N.J.) Bd. Edn., 1982-88, adminstr. mid. sch., 1988-93, adminstr. summer sch., 1991-93; prin. Broadway Elem. Sch., Camden, 1993-94, Morgan Village Sch., Camden, 1994—. Mem. ASCD, Nat. Assn. Mid. Sch. Adminstrs., Nat. Assn. Secondary Prins. Office: Morgan Village Sch 10th & Morgan Blvd Camden NJ 08104

SMITH, CHRISTINE JEAN, secondary school educator; b. Manchester, N.H., June 11, 1960; d. Frederick C. and Evelyn F. (Hofer) Caton; m. Leonard A. Smith, July 29, 1990. BA in French, St. Anselm Coll., 1982; MA in English, Rivier Coll., 1991, postgrad. Cert. English and French tchr., N.H. English tchr. Pelham (N.H.) H.S., 1984-2000, Rivier Coll., Nashua, N.H., 1992, Trinity H.S., Manchester, NH, 2000—01, Timberlane Regional H.S., Plaistow, NH, 2001—. Summer sch. English tchr. Haverhill (Mass.) H.S., 1987-92. Mem. Nat. Coun. Tchrs. English, New Eng. Assn. Tchrs. English, N.H. Assn. Tchrs. English, New Eng. Assn. Tchrs. Fgn. Langs., Assn. Tchrs. World Langs., Phi Delta Kappa. Republican. Roman Catholic. Avocations: reading, skiing, golf, swimming, counted cross-stitch. E-mail: csmith@timberlanehs.com.

SMITH, CINDY THOMPSON, special education educator; b. Raleigh, N.C., Nov. 6, 1957; d. Donald Wayne and Alice (Dupree) T.; m. Paul Neil Smith, Jan. 2, 1982; 1 child, Paul Cody Ryan. BS, Appalachian State U., Boone, N.C., 1980, MA, 1981. Ednl. specialist Western Carolina Ctr., Morganton, N.C., 1981; day camp dir. Ft. Sill (Okla.) Moral Support Div., 1982; spl. edn. tchr. Carroll High/East Gate Middle Sch., Ozark, Ala., 1982-83; resource specialist Del Rey Woods/Foothill Elem. Sch., Monterey, Calif., 1983-84; spl. day class tchr. Del Rey Woods Elem. Summer Sch., Monterey, 1984; resource specialist Del Rey Woods/Stilwell Elem. Sch., Monterey, 1984-85, 85-86; resource spl. day class tchr. Highland Elem. Summer Sch., Monterey, 1985; spl. edn. resource tchr. East Gate Middle Sch., Ozark, Ala., 1986-89; spl. edn. tchr. Harding Middle Sch., Cedar Rapids, Iowa, 1989—. Named Tchr. of Yr., Ozark City Schs., 1988. Avocations: volleyball, tennis, softball, aerobics. Home: 4501 Pineview Dr NE Cedar Rapids IA 52402-1715 Office: Harding Mid Sch 4801 Golf St NE Cedar Rapids IA 52402-5799

SMITH, CLAIRE LAREMONT, language educator; b. Panama City, Panama, Dec. 30, 1939; came to U.S., 1965; d. Sebastian Hamlet and Ambrozine Beatriz (Simon) Laremont; m. Stephen E. Greaves, Nov. 29, 1961 (div. 1968); children: Liza N. Greaves Smith, Katia T. Laremont Smith; m. James Elliott Smith, Dec. 20, 1969; 1 child, Raquel J. Student, U. Panama, Panama City, 1959-62; BA, SUNY, Fredonia, 1968, MS, 1970; postgrad., SUNY, Buffalo, 1983-93. Cert. tchr. secondary social studies, elem. bilingual edn., secondary Spanish and ESL, N.Y. Bilingual stenographer, bookkeeper, cashier Foto Internat., Panama City, 1960-65; tchr. secondary social studies and Spanish Forestville (N.Y.) Cen. Schs., 1968-69; grad. asst. dept. history SUNY, Fredonia, 1969-70; substitute tchr. Am. Overseas Schs. of Army Dependents, Camp Livorno, Italy, 1983-95; tchr. early childhood bilingual Dunkirk (N.Y.) Migrant Daycare Ctr., 1972-73; tchr., home instr. Head Start program Durkirk Schs., 1973-74; tchr. adult basic edn. N.Y. State Migrant Workers Opportunities, Dunkirk, 1977-80; tchr. social studies, bilingual, Spanish and ESL Dunkirk Mid. Sch., 1973-98; adj. instr. ESL SUNY, Fredonia, 1992, 93. Mem. affirmative action com. on cultural ethnic rels. SUNY, Fredonia, 1989-98; mem. com. on discipline Dunkirk Sch. Dist., 1991-98, compact learning com., 1993-98, Youth Empowerment System, wellness com.; mem. sch. improvement team Dunkirk Med. Sch., 1991-92; presenter profl. confs., U.S., Mex.; guest speaker Hispanic Heritage Week Celebration, N.Y. State Migrant Daycare, Fredonia, 1991. Bd. dirs. North County Counseling Svc., Dunkirk, 1992-96, People's Action Coaliton, Dunkirk, 1992-95, v.p., 1993-94, 95—; chairperson cultural awareness task force Dunkirk Cmty. Challenge, 1993-95; bd. dirs. Chautauqua County Connections, 1993-96, First Night Internat. Alliance, Boston, 1994-99; chair First Night Dunkirk, 1994-96, exec. dir., 1996-97; harborfest com. City of Dunkirk, 1992-96; vol. ARC fundraiser, 1995; founder, advisor Dunkirk H.S. ASPIRA Leadership Club, 1994-98, Dunkirk Schs. Step and Drill Team, 1994-97; N.Y. State advisor, trainer Hispanic Youth Leadership Inst. Conf., Albany, 1994-98. Named Person of Yr., Dunkirk Kiwanis, 1995; recipient Cmty. Svc. award N.Y. State Senator Jess Present, 1997. Mem. AAUW, NAAPC (edn. com. 1976), N.Y. State Assn. Bilingual Educators, Tchrs. of English to Speakers of Other Langs., Nat. Assn. Bilingual Edn., Dunkirk Tchrs. Assn. (bilingual scholarship fund, annual dinner awards program, 1979-92, active voter registration drive 1992), N.Y. State United Tchrs., SUNY Buffalo Grad. Student Assn. (senator 1990-92, co-pres. dept. learning and instrn. 1991-92), Phi Delta Kappa (SUNY Buffalo chpt.). Democrat. Roman Catholic. Avocations: jogging, reading, travel. Home: 2138 King Rd Forestville NY 14062-9707 Office: SUNY Coll Fredonia Dept Edn Fredonia NY 14048-1328

SMITH, CLODUS RAY, retired academic administrator; b. Blanchard, Okla., May 15, 1928; s. William Thomas and Rachel (Hale) S.; m. Pauline R. Chaat; children: Martha Lynn, William Paul, Paula Diane. Assoc. degree, Cameron State Coll., 1948; BS in Agrl. Edn., Okla. A & M Coll., 1950; MS in Vocat. Edn., Okla. State U., 1955; EdD in Vocat. Edn., Cornell U., 1960. Grad. asst. Cornell U., 1957-59; asst. prof. U. Md., 1959-62, assoc. prof., 1962-63, dir. Summer Sch., 1963-72, adminstrv. dean, 1972-73; spl. asst. to pres. Cleve. State U., 1973-74, v.p. for univ. rels., 1974-83; pres. Rio Grande Coll. and Rio Grande Community Coll., Ohio, 1983-86, Lake Erie Coll., Painesville, Ohio, 1986-92, Okla. Ind. Coll. Found., Oklahoma City, 1993-96, Okla. Assn. Ind. Colls. and Univs., 1993-96. Cons. NEA, Naval Weapons Lab., Dehlgren, Va.; researcher Personal and Profl. Satisfactions; contract investigator Nat. Endowment for Humanities; dir. Human Resources and Community Devel., Prince George's County, Md. Author: Planning and Paying for College, 1958, Rural Recreation for Profit, 1971, A Strategy for University Relations, 1975, State Relations for the 1980 Decade, 1982. Amb. Natural Resources, Ohio, 1984, chmn. dept.; founder N.Am. Assn. of Summer Schs., 1979. Recipient Rsch. award Nat. Project in Agrl. Communications, 1959, Edn. award Prince George's C. of C., 1971, Disting. Alumni award Cameron U. Mem. Am. Assn. U. Adminstrs., Am. Assn. for Higher Edn., Nat. Soc. for Study Edn., Coun. for Support and Advancement Edn., Am. Alumni Coun., Al Koran Hunter's Club, Shriners. Methodist. Avocations: volunteering on international religious missions, hunting, fishing, volunteering. E-mail: clodus@theshop.net.

SMITH, CONSTANCE LEWIS, secondary school educator; b. Macon, Ga., May 29, 1936; d. Isiah and Anna (Duncan) Lewis; m. Willie S. Smith, Dec. 2, 1956; children: Glenda Smith Hubbard, Kristen Y. MA, Ft. Valley (Ga.) State Coll., l98l. Cert. early childhood edn. tchr., Ga. Tchr. pub. schs., Macon, 197l—. Mem. NEA, Ga. Assn. Educators, Bibb County Assn. Educators, Delta Sigma Theta. Roman Catholic. Avocations: reading, travel, music, ceramics, interior decorating. Home: 3703 Greenbriar Rd Macon GA 31204-4255

SMITH, CURTIS ALFONSO, JR., university administrator; b. Hot Springs, Ark., Jan. 28, 1934; s. Curtis Alfonso and Claudine (Collins) S.; m. Willa Mae Steger, May 16, 1956 (div. Sept. 1962); 1 child, Pamela Yvette; m. Barbara Joan Brunious, Dec. 20, 1962 (dec. Oct. 2001); children: Curtis Alfonso, Tasya Ayesha; m. Dolores Leon, Jan. 29, 2002. AA, Kans. Tech., Topeka, 1955; BE, Chgo. Tchr. Coll., 1963; MA, Roosevelt U., Chgo., 1968; EdD, Nova U., Ft. Lauderdale, 1985. comml. rated pilot. Water safety instr. ARC, Chgo., 1951-67; tchr. Chgo. Pub. Schs., Chgo., 1964-70, staff/asst., 1970-74, dir. govt. fund, 1974-76, adminstr., 1976-81, asst. to deputy, 1981-85, adminstr., 1985-91; instr. Roosevelt U., Chgo., 1977-92; assoc. dean grad. studies Concordia U., River Forest, Ill., 1990—92; site adminstr. Nova U., Ft. Lauderdale, Fla., 1990—. Author: Slang Soul & Soup, 1968, Help for the Bereaved, 1973, Loved Ones Remembered, 1987. Treas. Evang. Child & Family Agy., Chgo., 1977-82. Named Outstanding Tchr. Chgo City Bank & Trust, 1967. Mem. NAACP, Aircraft Owners and Pilots Assn., The Rosicrucian Order, Urban League, Am. Assn. Sch. Educators, Ednl. Devel. Assn. (pres. 1982-94), Phi Delta Kappa (v.p. NIU chpt., Svc. award 1986, Outstanding Educator 1988). Democrat. Avocation: flying aircraft. Home: 16645 Paxton Ave South Holland IL 60473-2634 Office: Concordia U 7400 Augusta St River Forest IL 60305-1402

SMITH, CYNTHIA MARIE, mathematics educator; b. Titusville, Fla., Mar. 3, 1965; d. Earl Edson and Diana Lynn (Smith) Smith; m. Bret Michael Sewell, May 16, 1987 (div. Dec. 1990); m. Vincent Anthony Miller, Dec. 18, 1993. BS in Math., Howard Payne U., Brownwood, Tex., 1987; MA in Math., U. North Tex., 1992. Part-time instr. U. North Tex., Denton, 1990-92; tchr. math. Edinburg (Tex.) H.S., 1992; part-time instr. U. Tex.-Pan Am., Edinburg, 1992, instr. math., 1992—. Part-time instr. South Tex. C.C., McAllen, 1994, curriculum cons., 1994—; math. cons. St. Joseph Cath. Sch., Edinburg, 1994—; Tex. pre-engring. program instr., Edinburg, 1994; tchr. trainer Pittman Elem. Sch., Raymondville, Tex., 1994, Elsa (Tex.) Mid. Sch., 1994, Chapa Primary Sch., LaJoya, Tex., 1994. Author: The Eulerian Functions of Cyclic Groups, Dihedral Groups and P-groups, 1992. Mem. Nat. Coun. Tchrs. Math., Rio Grande Valley Coun. Tchrs. Math. Republican. Roman Catholic. Avocations: skiing, hiking, painting. Office: Univ of Texas-Pan American Math/Computer Sci Dept Edinburg TX 78539

SMITH, DANI ALLRED, sociologist, educator; b. Natchez, Miss., Dec. 12, 1955; d. Paul Hollis and Mary Frances Allred; m. Ronald Bassel Smith, Aug. 9, 1980. BS in Social Sci., Lee Coll., 1977; MA in Sociology, U. Miss., 1980; PhD in Sociology, U. Tenn., 2001. Staff writer Natchez Dem., 1977; secondary tchr. Natchez Pub. Schs., 1977-78; instr. sociology U. Miss., 1980-81, 82, rsch. assoc., instr. mgmt. info. systems, 1982-87; secondary tchr. Coffeeville (Miss.) Schs., 1981-82; asst. prof. sociology Lee Coll., Cleveland, Tenn., 1988-96, Fisk U., Nashville, 1996—. Advisor sociology club Lee Coll., 2002—; advisor Lee Collegian (campus newspaper), 1988—93, Epsilon Lambda Phi, 1992—96, Alpha Kappa Delta, 1992—96; advisor sr. class Fisk U., Nashville, 1997—98, 2001—02. Contbr. articles to profl. jours. and newspapers. Mellon Appalachian fellow, 1993-94; named one of Outstanding Young Women Am., 1981. Mem. Am. Sociol. Soc., So. Sociol. Assn., Christian Sociol. Soc., Gt. Smoky Mountains Assn., Am. Hiking Soc., Habitat for Humanity Pres.' Cir., Phi Kappa Phi, Alpha Chi, Alpha Kappa Delta. Avocations: reading, hiking, camping, plate collecting, cross-stitching. Home: 430 20th St NE Cleveland TN 37311-3949 Office: Fisk U Dept Sociology 1000 17th Ave N Nashville TN 37208-3045 E-mail: dasmith@fisk.edu.

SMITH, DAVID EUGENE, business administration educator; b. Boise, Idaho, Dec. 14, 1941; s. Roy Arthur and Anna Margaret (Fries) S.; m. Patricia Stroy, Aug. 4, 1973; 1 child, Zachary Adam. BS in Applied Stats., San Francisco State Coll., 1964, MS in Mgmt. Sci., 1966; MBA, PhD in Bus. Adminstrn., U. Santa Clara, 1969. Asst. to dir. mgmt ctr. Grad. Sch. Bus., U. Santa Clara, Calif., 1966-69, lectr. mktg., 1968; asst. prof. bus. adminstrn. dept. mktg./decision Scis. San Jose State U., Calif., 1969—71, assoc. prof. bus. adminstrn. dept. mktg./decision Scis., 1971—76, prof. bus. adminstrn. dept. mktg./decision Scis., 1976—, chmn. dept. mktg./decision Scis., 1986—89. Author: Quantitative Business Analysis, 1977, Internat. Edit., 1979, 1982; contbr. articles to profl. jours. Mem.: DSI, INFORMS, Beta Gamma Sigma, Phi Kappa Phi. Republican. Avocations: tennis, fishing, skiing. Home: 22448 Tim Tam Ct Los Gatos CA 95033-8521 Office: San Jose State U Mktg/Decision Scis One Washington Sq San Jose CA 95192

SMITH, DAVID JULIAN, educational consultant; b. Boston, Apr. 24, 1944; s. Julian John and Anita Regina (Goldman) S.; m. Suzanne Marilla Shaw, June 18, 1966. AB, Harvard U., 1966; MAT, Reed Coll., 1967. Cert. elem. tchr., Mass., Hawaii, Oreg. 10th grade tchr. Punahou Sch., Honolulu, 1967-69; 7th, 9th grades tchr. U. Hawaii Lab. Sch., Honolulu, 1969-70; 7th grade head tchr. Shady Hill Sch., Cambridge, Mass., 1970-92; pvt. practice ednl. cons. Cambridge, Mass., 1992—. Author: Mapping the World By Heart, 1992, CEESA Web-Site Manual, 1998, If the World Were a Village, 1999; contbr. articles to profl. jours. Bd. dirs. Cambridge Mental Health Assn., 1991-96, Cambridge Ctr. for Adult Edn., 1988-98; active Cambridge Civic Assn. Recipient Breaking the Mold award US Dept. Edn., 1992. Mem. Nat. Coun. for Social Studies, Nat. Coun. for Geog. Edn., Assn. Am. Geographers (chair cartographic splty. group 1997—). Office: Mapping the World by Heart 4 Blanchard Rd Cambridge MA 02138-1009

SMITH, DAVID LYLE, art educator, artist; b. Harpersfield, N.Y., June 6, 1926; s. Thomas Howard and Grace Louisa Smith; m. Alyce Louise Oosterhouse, June 6, 1952; children: C Matthew, Markalan, Elizabeth, Leigh, Stuart. BD in Design, U. Mich., 1951, MA in Edn., 1953; DPhil, Mich. State U., 1966. Graphic artist Ednl. TV Program U. Mich., Ann Arbor, 1952-53; tchr. art C.W. Otto Jr. H.S., Lansing, Mich., 1955-63; tchr. elem. art. Lansing Pub. Schs., 1963-67; assoc. prof. Dept. Art and Design

U. Wis., Stevens Point, 1967-96, assoc. prof. emeritus, 1996—; CEO Scarabocchio Art, Stevens Point; founder, mem. Scarabocchio Art Found., Stevens Point. Dir. Stevens Point Program, 1975-86; site adminstr., semester abroad tchr., Poland, 1978, 83; chmn. State Art Edn. Cert. Stds., 1981-83. Exhbns. include U. Wis. Stevens Point Faculty Show, 1974-76, 87, 90-93, 95, 97, Packages-Carlsten Art Gallery, 1978, 79, New Visions Gallery, Marshfield, Wis., 1989, 92, 95, Milw. Art Mus., 1992, U. Colo. Mountainside Art Guild & Fiske Planetarium, 1992-96, N.Mex., Art League, 1993, 94, 96, Alexander House, Port Edwards, Wis., 1993, 95, Sacramento FAC, 1993, 94, 97, 98, Laredo Art League, Tex., 1994, 95, 96, L.I. Arts Coun., Freeport, N.Y., 1994, Green Bay Neville Pub. Mus., 1995, 96, 97, 98, An Art Pl., Chgo., 1995, 97, Akron Soc. Artists, 1994, 96, 98, Mable (Ga.) Cultural Ctr., 1994, 95, 96, 98, Wis. Painters-Sculptors, 1996, 97, 98, 99, Mac Rostie Art Ctr., 1996, 97, 98, Coastal Ctr. Arts, Ga., 1996, 97, 98, Ridgewood Art Inst., N.J., 1997, 98, 99, Salmagundi Club, 1999, Period Gallery, 1998, 99, Glen Eure's Ghost Fleet Gallery, 1998, 99, Eleven East Ashland, 1997, 98, Wis. Edn. Assn. Art Showcase, 1996, 98, Internat. Registry of Artists and Art calendar, 1998, Studio 107, Ridge Art Assn., 1998, 99, others; accepted in nat. juried art competitions, 15 in 1993, 49 in 1994, 22 in 1995, 26 in 1996, 21 in 1997, 20 in 1998, 25 in 1999; one-man shows include Lincoln Ctr., Stevens Point, Wis., 1989, 93, 95, Charles M. White Libr., Stevens Point, Northeast C.C., Whiteville, N.C., 1998, others.; two-man shows (with Richard Schneider) Alexander House 1993; also Ctr. for Visual Arts 1996, Wausau, Wis.; three person show Brown County Libr., Green Bay, Wis., 1996. Style judge State Odyssey of the Mind, 1990-99; dist. dir. ctrl. divsn. Very Spl. Arts Wis., 1985-88. Mem. Nat. Art Edn. Assn., Wis. Art Edn. Assn. (bd. dirs., higher edn. rep. 1978-82), NEA (life), Wis. Edn. Assn. Coun., Assn. U. Wis. Profls. (sec. 1993-96), Wis. Alliance for Arts Edn., Res. Officers Assn. U.S., Ret. Officers, Nat. Assn. Uniformed Svcs., Air Force Assn., Consumers Union. Republican. Presbyterian. Avocations: sketching, gardening, travel. Home: 4242 Janick Cir N Stevens Point WI 54481-2511 Fax: (715) 342-5688. E-mail: d3smith@uswp.edu.

SMITH, DAVID STUART, anesthesiology educator, physician; b. Detroit, May 29, 1946; s. Philip and Eleanor (Bishop) S.; m. Suzanne Wanda Zeleznik, Aug. 17, 1969; children: Katherine Michele, Lisa Anne. BA, Oakland U.; MD, PhD, Med. Coll. Wis., 1975. Intern dept. medicine Med. Coll. Wis., Milw., 1975-76; resident dept. anesthesia U. Pa., Phila., 1976-78, fellow dept. anesthesia, 1978-80; dir. divsn. neuroanesthesia Hosp. U. Pa., Phila., 1982-2001, attending anesthesiologist, 1980—; asst. prof. U. Pa., Phila., 1980-89, assoc. prof., 1989—. Co-editor: Anesthesia and Neurosurgery, 3d edit., 1994, 4th edit., 2001; mem. editl. bd. Jour. Neurosurg. Anesthesia, N.Y.C., 1987-97; author and co-author of numerous sci. papers, revs., and book chpts. Sr. fellow, Nat. Rsch. Svc. award, Phila., 1985-87. Fellow Coll. Physicians Phila.; mem. Am. Soc. Anesthesiologists, Soc. Neurosurg. Anesthesia and Critical Care (sec., treas. 1987-89, v.p. 1989-90, pres. elect 1990-91, pres. 1991-92), Assn. U. Anesthesiologists, Internat. Soc. Cerebral Blood Flow and Metabolism. Jewish. Office: Hosp U Pa Dept Anesthesia 3400 Spruce St Philadelphia PA 19104-4206

SMITH, DEAN GORDON, economist, educator; b. Flint, Mich., Feb. 23, 1959; s. David Wade and Janet Pearl (Hendrickson) S. AB, U. Mich., 1981; PhD, Tex. A&M U., 1985. Economist RRC, Inc., Bryan, Tex., 1984-85, Parke-Davis, Ann Arbor, 1995-96; prof. U. Mich., Ann Arbor, 1985—, dept. chair, 2003—. Faculty fellow Lincoln Nat. Life Ins. Co., Ft. Wayne, Ind., 1990; CEO Good Health Mich., 1997-99; bd. dirs. Molina Healthcare Mich. Contbr. articles to profl. jours. Economist, Mich. Med. Liability Rsch. Program, Lansing, 1990, Gov.'s Healthcare Cost Mgmt. Team, Lansing, 1989. Grantee Mercy Consortium for Rsch., 1990, Robert Wood Johnson Found., 1992-95. Mem. APHA, Am. Coll. Healthcare Execs., Am. Econ. Assn., Am. Fin. Assn., Assn. Univ. Programs in Health Adminstrn. (chair fin. faculty com. 1992-93, bd. dirs.), Care Am. Mich. (bd. dirs. 1996-98). Avocations: bicycling, tennis. Office: U Mich Dept HMP 109 Observatory St Ann Arbor MI 48109-2029

SMITH, DEAN ORREN, physiology educator; b. Colorado Springs, Colo., May 28, 1944; s. Everett Ellsworth and Margaret Elizabeth Smith; m. Julie L. Rosenheimer, Dec. 30, 1985; children: Curtis Dean, Corey Bryant. BA, Harvard U., 1967; PhD, Stanford U., 1971. Prof. of physiology U. Wis., Madison, 1976-95, assoc. dean grad. sch., 1984-91; sr. v.p., exec. vice chancellor U. Hawaii, Honolulu, 1995—2001, prof., 2001—. Office: U Hawaii 1960 East-West Rd Honolulu HI 96822

SMITH, DEBBIE ILEE RANDALL, elementary school educator; b. Pampa, Tex., Oct. 8, 1955; d. Lester R. and Launa I. (Elmner) Randall; m. Jimmie E. Smith, July 20, 1974; children: Christi I., James R., Stacy L. AA, Seward County Community Coll., Liberal, Kans.; student, Panhandle State U., Goodwell, Okla. Paraprofl. High Plains Edn. Coop., Garden City, Kans.; tchr. USD 480, Liberal; TESOL DISD, Dumas, Tex. Mem. Phi Theta Kappa.

SMITH, DENIS JOSEPH, mathematics educator; b. Boston, Mar. 19, 1949; s. Joseph P. and Margaret L. (Stapleton) S.; m. Mary P. MacDougall, Aug. 26, 1972; children: Brandon Edward, Shane F. AB in math. edn., Boston Coll., 1971; MEd, Cambridge Coll., 1990. Tchr. Xaverian Bros. High Sch., Westwood, Mass., 1971—; math. instr. Dean Coll., Franklin, Mass., 2000—. Advisor Xaverian Math. Team/New Eng. Math. League, Westwood, Mass.1980—, chmn. Math. Dept. Xaverian Bros High Sch., Westwood, 1982-84, 86-88, 95—; math instr. Dean Coll., 2000—; bd. dirs. Greater Boston Math. League, Canton, Mass., 1989—, advisor, 1980—; ednl. cons. St. Catherine of Sienna, Norwood, Mass., 1990-92; in house coord. Nat. High Sch. Math. Exam., 1980—, supr. Math Olympiad Level I Exam. Eucharistic min. St. Mary's Ch., 1984—; coach Dedham Youth Soccer, 1985-92; pres. St. Catherine's Homes and Sch. Assn., 1989-91; vice chmn. Cardinal Parish Planning Coun., 1990—2002. Grantee NSF, 1993. Mem. Nat. Coun. Tchrs., Nat. Cath. Ednl. Assn. Democrat. Roman Catholic. Home: 23 Charles St Dedham MA 02026-3049 Office: Xaverian Bros High Sch 800 Clapboardtree St Westwood MA 02090-1718 E-mail: dsmith@xbhs.com.

SMITH, DENTYE M. library media specialist; b. Atlanta, July 21, 1936; d. William Harry and Gladys Magdalene (Bruce) S. AB, Spelman Coll., 1958; MLM, Ga. State U., 1975. Cert. Libr., media specialist. Tchr. English Atlanta Pub. Schs., 1961-82, supr. tchr., 1968-69, tchr. journalism, 1975-80, libr. media specialist, 1982-94; media specialist West Fulton High Sch., 1982-92, West Fulton Mid. Sch., 1992, Booker T. Washington Comprehensive High Sch., Atlanta, 1992-94. Leader jur. gt. books Archer and West Fulton high schs.; coord. Atlanta Pub. Schs. reading cert., program West Fulton H.S.; vol. liaison Atlanta-Fulton Pub. Libr., 1987-94, local arrangements com. Atlanta Libr. Assn., 1990-91; seminar presenter in field; coord. study skills seminars Morris Brown Coll.'s Summer Upward Bound Program, 1993, 94, 95; mem. High Mus. of Art, Atlanta, Atlanta Hist. Soc., Ga. Pub. TV. Contbr. articles to profl. jours. Named to Acad. Hall of Fame, Atlanta Pub. Schs., 1990; recipient Tchr. of Yr. award West Fulton H.S., Atlanta, 1974, acad. achievement incentive program award in media APS, 1990. Mem. NEA, Nat. Ret. Tchrs. Assn., Soc. Sch. Librs. Internat., Ga. Assn. Educators, Atlanta Assn. Educators, Nat. Alumnae Assn. Spelman Coll., Ga. State U. Alumni Assn., Nat. Trust Hist. Preservation, Ga. Trust Hist. Preservation, Atlanta Ret. Tchrs. Assn., Atlanta Hist. Assn., Ga. Ret. Tchrs. Assn., the Smithsonian Assocs., Libr. of Congress Assocs.

SMITH, DIANA MARIE, business educator; b. Des Moines, Oct. 25, 1940; d. Nathan Henry and Helen (Hall) Kitchen; m. Robert Nelson Smith, Jan. 26, 1971; 1 child, Stephen. BA, Drake U., 1968, MA, 1971. Cert. tchr., Iowa. Stenographer Polk County Welfare Dept., Des Moines, 1960-67; typist Polk County Auditor, Des Moines, 1968, Cen. Life Assurance Co., Des Moines, 1976-79; computer oper. IRS, Des Moines, 1988; lead specialist II Norwest Bank, Des Moines, 1978—2002; sec. Shive-Hattery Engrs., Des Moines, 1976-90; adult edn. instr. Des Moines Ind. Dist., 1969—2001; tchr. bus., computers Des Moines Pub. Schs., 1968—2000; instr. computers St. Paul Ch. and Saks Inc., Des Moines, 2000—. Ind. computer cons.; instr.-authorized tng. assoc. program for Word Perfect, 1994; Mary Kay beauty cons., 1993—. Chair meml. com. Burns United Meth. Ch., Des Moines, 1988—, Sunday sch. tchr., 1961-83, 92-98, sec. adminstrv. bd. Democrat. Avocations: reading, computers. Office: Saks Inc 701 Walnut Des Moines IA 50309

SMITH, DON EDWARD, school system administrator; b. Kansas City, Mo., Feb. 4, 1950; s. Herbert Thurman and Ella Marie (Meador) S.; m. Alberta Allred, Dec. 26, 1978; children: Don E. Jr., Heather JoDon. BA, Ark. State U., Jonesboro, 1974, BS Edn., 1980, MS Edn., 1986. Cert. sch. administr. Tchr. Marked Tree (Ark.) Sch. Dist., 1980-81; tchr./coach Trumann (Ark.) Sch. Dist., 1981-90; supt. Stanford Sch. Dist., Paragould, Ark., 1990-94, Wonderview Sch. Dist., Hattieville, Ark., 1994—. Mem. Regional Leaders, Paragould, 1992—. With USN, 1974-77. Recipient Acad. and Music scholarship, Ark. State U., 1968, 69. Mem. Am. Assn. Sch. Adminstrs., Ark. Assn. Edn. Adminstrs., Ark. Assn. Secondary Adminstrs., Ark. Assn. Sch. Bus. Ofcls., Ark. Rural Edn. Assn., Greene County C. of C. (chmn.-elect edn. com. 1990-94), Masons, Phi Beta Kappa, Kappa Delta Pi. Avocations: fishing, racing cars. Home and Office: Wonderview Sch Dist 2560 Highway 42 Cherry Valley AR 72324-8799

SMITH, DONALD CAMERON, physician, educator; b. Peterborough, Ont., Can., Feb. 2, 1922; came to U.S., 1952, naturalized, 1960; m. Jean Morningstar, Sept. 11, 1946. MD, Queen's U., 1945; MSc in Medicine, U. Toronto, Ont., 1948, DPH, 1949. Diplomate Am. Bd. Preventive Medicine, Am. Bd. Pediat. Intern Victoria Hosp., London, Ont., 1945-46; fellow in physiology U. Toronto, 1947—49; med. officer health Kent County (Ont.) Health Unit, 1950—52; Commonwealth Fund fellow in pediat. U. Mich. Hosp., 1952-55; prof. maternal and child health U. Mich. (Sch. Pub. Health); prof. pediat. U. Mich. (Med. Sch.), 1961-79, chmn. dept. health and human devel., 1961-79; prof. psychiatry and behavioral scis. Northwestern U. Med. Sch., Chgo., 1979-85. Chmn. Medicaid Adv. Coun., 1969-72; prin. advisor on health and med. affairs to gov. Mich., 1972-78; dir. Mich. Dept. Mental Health, 1974-78; chmn. health care policy bd. Mich. Dept. Corrections, 1986-91; chmn. State Pub. Health Adv. Coun., 1982-90; med. dir. Sisters of Mercy Health Corp., 1981-91; pres. Mental Health Assn. Mich., 1992-94; vis. prof. maternal and child health Harvard U., 1969-72. Surgeon lt. Royal Canadian Navy, 1946-47. Address: # 408 807 Asa Gray Dr Ann Arbor MI 48105 E-mail: leelo@umich.edu

SMITH, DONALD L. social sciences educator; b. Richland, Wash., Feb. 1, 1949; s. Marcelle H. and Nettie B. (Lacher) S.; m. Sally Jane Carr, Aug. 15, 1971; children: Shannon, Stephanie. AA, Mesa Coll., 1969; BS in Edn., Southwest Mo. State U., 1971, MS in Edn., 1976. Cert. tchr., Mo. Tchr., chair dept. social scis. Ozark (Mo.) H. S., 1971-96, retired, 1996; supr. clinical field experiences Southwest Mo. State U., Springfield, Mo., 2000—. Rsch. technician Ctr. Archaeol. Rsch., S.W. Mo. State U., Springfield, 1978, rsch. assoc., 1979; adj. prof. Drury Univ., Springfield, 1983—; cons. mandatory statewide competency testing in social studies Mo. Dept. Elem. and Secondary Edn., Columbia, 1986. Special corr. Springfield Newspapers, Inc., 1996-97. V.p. Frisco Railroad Mus., Springfield, Mo., 1996-97. Nat. Endowment for Humanities scholar, 1985, Fulbright scholar U.S. Dept. Edn., Zimbabwe, Botswana, Malawi, 1991. Mem. Nat. Coun. Social Studies, Greater Ozarks Coun. Social Studies, Mo. State Tchrs. Assn. (pres. dept. social studies 1982-83, newsletter editor 1983-88), Archaeol. Inst. Am., Bibl. Archaeol. Soc. Avocations: travel, military history, aviation, computers, model railroading. Home: 1801 W Cherokee St Springfield MO 65807-2205

SMITH, DONALD RAYMOND, librarian; b. Highland, Ill., Sept. 25, 1946; s. Raymond Stanley and Gladys Loraine (Martin) S.; m. Elaine Marie Neudecker, Apr. 12, 1969; 1 child, Benjamin Christopher. BA, So. Ill. U., 1968, MA, 1972, MS, 1978; MLS, U. Mo., 1976. Acad. adv. So. Ill. U., Edwardsville, 1970-73, libr. instr., 1973-78, edn. libr., 1978-82; assoc. dir. pub. svc. and collection devel. U. Tulsa, 1982-88, assoc. dir. gen. svcs., 1988-93; dir. libr. N.E. La. U., Monroe, La., 1993-96; dean info. svcs. U. La., Monroe, 1996—2003, dean libr., 2003—. Cons. Hayner Pub. Libr., Alton, Ill., 1977-82, Tulsa City County Libr., 1984; cons. facilitator Tulsa Area Libr. Coop., 1987-88, 90; collection evaulator Okla. Jr. Coll., Tulsa, 1984. Author: Newspaper Indexing Handbook, 1981; editor and compiler newspaper index, 1976-77. Cataloger Our Lady Queen of Peace Sch., Belleville, Ill., 1979-82; campaign worker Dem. Party, Belleville, 1972; chair bd. dirs. Tulsa Area Libr. Coop., 1991-93. With U.S. Army, 1969-70. Recipient Millicent C. Palmer award Friends of Lovejoy Library, So. Ill. U., 1974, H.W. Wilson scholar, 1974, Higher Edn. Coordinating Act grantee Ill. State Library, 1980-81, Workshop award U. Okla. Sch. Library Sci., 1984. Mem.: ALA, La. Libr. Network Commn., Tech. Consortium Tchr. Edn., Trailblazer Libr. Dirs. Bd. and Commn., La. Acad. Libr. Info. Network Consortium (at-large exec. bd. dirs. 1994—96, chmn. rsch. and devel. com. 2001—03), La. Assn. Coll. and Rsch. Librs. (automation and tech. com. 2000—, v.p., pres.-elect 2003—), La. Libr. Assn. (sec. scholarship trust 1994—), Okla. Libr. Assn. (chmn. contg. edn. com. 1985—86, chmn. adminstrn. roundtable 1989—90, chair automation roundtable 1991—92), Assn. Coll. and Rsch. Librs., NOTIS Users Group, Phi Delta Kappa, Phi Kappa Phi. Roman Catholic. Avocations: travel, history, reading. Office: U La Univ Libr 700 University Ave Monroe LA 71209-0720

SMITH, DORIS VICTORIA, educational agency administrator; b. N.Y.C., July 5, 1937; d. Albin and Victoria (Anderson) Olson; m. Howard R. Smith, Aug. 21, 1960; children: Kurt, Steven, Andrea. BS in Edn., Wagner Coll., 1959; MA in Edn., Kean Coll., 1963, cert., 1980; EdD, Nova Southeastern U., 1995. Cert. adminstr., tchr. elem. edn., N.J. Thorough and efficient coord. East Hanover (N.J.) Twp. Sch. Dist., 1977-79; ednl. specialist N.J. State Dept. Edn., Morristown, 1979—, ednl. planner, 1982-87, ednl. mgr., 1987—. Pres. N.E. Coalition Ednl. Leaders, Inc.; founding mem. Morris County Curriculum Network. Author: Affirmative Action—Rules and Regulations, 1982, Supervising Early Childhood Programs, 1984. Past pres. bd. trustees Florham Park Libr.; founding mem. Morris Area Tech. Alliance; founding mem., pres. Calvary Nursery Sch.; bd. of trust office N.J. Coun. Edn.; pres. bd. trustees Madison/Chatham Adult Sch.; trustee Morris County Children's Svcs.; pres. Morris Sch. Dist. Cmty. Sch. Bd. Advisors. Tchr. insvc. grantee; recipient Disting. Svc. award N.E. Coalition Ednl. Leaders, 1991, Disting. Svc. award Morris County Prins. and Suprs. Assn., Outstanding Educator award N.J. ASCD, 1995, Morris County Freeholders Resolution in recognition of svc. to county. Mem. N.J. Coun. Edn., N.J. Schoolmasters Assn., Phi Delta Kappa.

SMITH, DORIS WILMA DUNN, retired mathematics and science educator, writer, poet, speaker; b. Greensboro, N.C., Aug. 21, 1933; d. David Harry and Wilma Gertrude (Kerns) Dunn; m. Ralpha Ray Smith, June 1, 1957; children: Glenn, Harriet, Marcus. BS in Biology, Flora Macdonald Coll., 1955; MA in Biology Sci. and Math., U. Calif., Irvine, 1973; PhD in Edn., U. Beverly Hills, 1980. Tchr. sci. St. Pauls (N.C.) City Schs., 1955-57; tchr. math. Belmont (N.C.) City Schs., 1962-64, Charlotte-Mecklenburg City Schs., Charlotte, N.C., 1964-65, Newport Mesa Unified Schs., Newport Beach, Calif., 1965-67; tchr. math. sci. Anaheim (Calif.) Union High Sch., 1967-81, Fontana (Calif.) Unified Sch., 1982-84, Long Beach Unified Schs., 1984-95; ret., 1995. Freelance writer, poet, 1978— ; speaker various religious and civic orgns., 1979—. Author: A Limb of Your Tree, 1981, A Daughter's Return to her Roots, 1998. Mgr. Far West Anaheim Bobby Sox Softball, 1969-71, all-star mgr., 1970, all-star coach, 1969-71; leader Girl Scouts Am., 1970. E.I. du Pont de Nemours fellow, 1956. Mem. NEA, Calif. Tchrs. Assn., Anaheim Secondary Tchrs. Assn., Tchrs. Assn. Long Beach, Nat. Council Tchrs. Math., Nat. Assn. Female Execs., AAUW, Internat. Women's Writers Guild, Woman's World Internat. Clubs: Toastmasters. Republican. Presbyterian. Home and Office: 1422 Belaire Dr Mc Kinney TX 75069-7914 E-mail: docdds1@home.com.

SMITH, DOROTHY BRAND, retired librarian; b. Beaumont, Tex., Oct. 4, 1922; d. Robert and Lula (Jones) Brand; m. William E. Smith, June 15, 1941; children: Wilson B., Lurinda. BS in Social Sci., Lamar U., 1954; MLS, U. Tex., 1971. Tchr. Beaumont Ind. Sch. Dist., 1954-62, Austin (Tex.) Ind. Sch. Dist., 1962-66; libr. Galindo Elem. Sch., Austin, 1966-94; ret., 1994. Cons. Edn. Svc. Ctr., Austin, 1974, 83; workshop leader Austin Ind. Schs., 1980; China del. Citizen Amb. Program People Internat., 1993. Author: Texas in Children's Books, a Bibliography, 1974. Recipient Siddie Joe Johnson award, Children's Roundtable of Tex. Libr. Assn., 1984. Mem. ALA, AAUW, Tex. Libr. Assn. (life), Tex. State Tchrs. Assn. (life), Delta Kappa Gamma, Phi Delta Kappa. Presbyterian. Home: 6108 Mountainclimb Dr Austin TX 78731-3824 E-mail: dorries@aol.com.

SMITH, DUANE ALLAN, history educator, researcher; b. San Diego, Apr. 20, 1937; s. Stanley W. and Ila B. (Bark) S.; m. Gay Woodruff, Aug. 20, 1960; 1 child, Laralee Ellen. BA, U. Colo., 1959, MA, 1961, PhD, 1964. Prof. history Ft. Lewis Coll., Durango, Colo., 1964—. Author: Horace Tabor, 1973 (Cert. of Commendation 1974), Mining America, 1987, Mesa Verde National Park, 1988, The Birth of Colorado, 1989, Rocky Mountain West, 1992, They Came to Play, 1997, A Tale of Two Towns, 1997, Colorado: Our Colorful State, 1999, No One Ailing Except a Physician, 2001, The Ballad of Baby Doe, 2002, Henry Teller, 2003, A Visit With The Tomboy Bride, 2003. Chmn. La Plata County Dem. Com., Durango, 1984-85; mem. Colo. Centennial Commn., 1974-76, Durango Hist. Preservation Commn., 1989-91, Durango Hist. Preservation Bd., 1991—, Gary Hart Campaign La Plata County, 1974, 80, 84. Huntington (Calif.) Libr. fellow, 1968, 73, 78; recipient Fred H. Rosenstock award Denver Westerners, 1987; named Colo. Humanist of the Yr., Colo. Endowment for the Humanities, 1989, Colo. Prof. of the Yr. 1990, Rodman Paul award, 1992. Mem. Soc. for Am. Baseball Rsch., Mining History Assn. (presiding chmn. 1989-90, pres. 1994-95), Western History Assn. (coun. 1985-88), Colo. Hist. Soc. Methodist. Avocations: writing, jogging, gardening, jeeps. Home: 2911 Cedar Ave Durango CO 81301-4481 E-mail: smith_d@fortlewis.edu.

SMITH, DWIGHT MORRELL, chemistry educator; b. Hudson, N.Y., Oct. 10, 1931; s. Elliott Monroe and Edith Helen (Hall) S.; m. Alice Beverly Bond, Aug. 27, 1955 (dec. 1990); children— Karen Elizabeth, Susan Allison, Jonathan Aaron; m. Elfi Nelson, Dec. 28, 1991. BA, Ctrl. Coll., Pella, Iowa, 1953; PhD, Pa. State U., 1957; ScD (hon.), Cen. Coll., 1986; LittD (hon.), U. Denver, 1990. Postdoctoral fellow, instr. Calif. Inst. Tech., 1957-59; sr. chemist Texaco Rsch. Ctr., Beacon, N.Y., 1959-61; asst. prof. chemistry Wesleyan U., Middletown, Conn., 1961-66; assoc. prof. Hope Coll., Holland, Mich., 1966-69, prof., 1969-72; prof. chemistry U. Denver, 1972—, chmn. dept., 1972-83, 99-01, vice chancellor for acad. affairs, 1983-84, chancellor, 1984-89; pres., bd. trustees Hawaii Loa Coll., Kaneohe, 1990-92. Mem. Registry for Interim Coll. and Univ. Pres.; mem. adv. bd. Solar Energy Rsch. Inst., 1989—91; mem. vis. com. Zettlemoyer Ctr. for Surface Studies Lehigh U., 1990—96; dept. chemistry and geochemistry Colo. Sch. Mines; mem. sci. adv. bd. Denver Rsch. Inst.; sr. advisor Rocky Mountain Ctr. Homeland Def. Editor Revs. on Petroleum Chemistry, 1975-78; editl. adv. bd. Recent Rsch. Devels. in Applied Spectroscopy, 1998—; contbr. articles to profl. jours.; patentee selective hydrogenation. Chmn. Chs. United for Social Action, Holland, 1968-69; mem. adv. com. Holland Sch. Bd., 1969-70; bd. commrs. Colo. Adv. Tech. Inst., 1984-88, Univ. Senate, United Meth. Ch., Nashville, 1987-88, 91-93; mem. adv. bd. United Way, Inst. Internat. Edn., Japan Am. Soc. Colo., Denver Winter Games Olympics Com.; mem. ch. bds. or consistories Ref. Ch. Am., N.Y., Conn., Mich., United Meth. Ch., Colo. DuPont fellow, 1956-57, NSF fellow Scripps Inst., 1971-72; recipient grants Research Corp., Petroleum Research Fund, NSF, Solar Energy Research Inst. Mem. AAAS, Am. Assn. Aerosol Rsch., Am. Chem. Soc. (chmn. Colo. 1976, sec. western Mich. 1970-71, joint coun. and bd. com. on sci. 1997-98, award Colo. sect. 1986), Soc. Applied Spectroscopy, Mile High Club, Sigma Xi. Home: 1931 W Sanibel Ct Littleton CO 80120-8133 Office: U Denver Dept Chem & Biochem Denver CO 80208-0001

SMITH, DWYANE, university administrator; b. St. Louis, Feb. 16, 1961; s. Magnolia Smith. BS in Psychology, N.E. Mo. State U., 1983, MA in Edn. Adminstrn., 1991; postgrad., Harvard U., 1995; PhD, U. Mo., Columbia, 2000; postgrad., Harvard U., 1995. Intern IRS, St. Louis, 1983; minority counselor N.E. Mo. State U., Kirksville, 1983-88, dir. minority svcs., 1988-91, asst. dir. admissions, asst. dean multicultural affairs, 1991—, assoc. dean multicultural affairs; clin. assoc. U. Mo., Columbia; assoc. v.p. for enrollment mgmt. Park U., Parkville, Mo., 2002—; ednl. cons. Mem. Alpha Phi Alpha (chair statewide conv. 1990, Mo. Man of Yr. 1985), Alpha Phi Omega, Phi Kappa Phi, Habitat for Humanity. Avocations: reading, writing. Home: 837 SE 11th Ter Lees Summit MO 64081-2153 E-mail: dsmith@mail.park.edu.

SMITH, EARL CHARLES, nephrologist, educator; b. Pitts., Mar. 1, 1936; s. Mose and Irene (Surloff) S. BS, Tufts U., 1957; MD, U. Pitts., 1961. Diplomate in internal medicine and nephrology Am. Bd. Internal Medicine. Intern Montefiore Hosp., Pitts., 1961-62; resident, fellow Cleve. Clinic, 1964-68; physician Cook County Hosp., Chgo., 1968-71; chief nephrology divsn. Mt. Sinai Hosp., Chgo., 1971—, pres. med. staff, 1985-87, vice chair medicine, 1987—; chief nephrology divsn. Chgo. Med. Sch., 1994—, prof. medicine, 1995—. Cons. Internat. Jour. Artificial Organs, Milan, 1996—; med. adv. bd. Kidney Found. Ill., Chgo., 1980—. Co-author: Medical Exam Book-Nephrology, 1976, Self Assessment in Internal Medicine, 1980; assoc. editor Kidney jour., 1991—; contbr. articles to profl. jours. Chair hypertension com. Chgo. Heart Assn., 1973-75. Capt. USAF, 1962-64. Recipient Meritorious Svc. award Chgo. Heart Assn., 1975. Fellow Am. Coll. Physicians; mem. Am. Soc. Artificial Internal Organs, Am. Soc. Nephrology, Am. Soc. Hypertension Specialist in Clin. Hypertension, Internat. Soc. Nephrology, Phi Beta Kappa, Alpha Omega Alpha, Sigma Xi. Office: Mount Sinai Hosp 15th and California Ave Chicago IL 60608

SMITH, EDWARD HERBERT, radiologist, educator; b. N.Y.C., Feb. 18, 1936; s. Nathan Leon and Rebecca Ada (Brodsky) S.; m. Anne Chantler Oliphant, June 27, 1971; children: Peter Chantler, Jeffrey Martin. AB, Columbia Coll., 1956; MD, SUNY, 1960. Intern U. Calif. Hosp., San Francisco, 1960-61; resident in internal medicine Montefiore Hosp., N.Y.C., 1961-62; resident in radiology Kings County Hosp. Ctr., Bklyn., 1964-67, radiologist, 1967-69; instr. SUNY-Bklyn., 1967-69; radiologist Children's Hosp. Med. Ctr., Boston, 1969-70, Peter Bent Brigham Hosp., Boston, 1969-80; dir. div. radiology Charles A. Dana Cancer Research Ctr., Boston, 1974-80; instr. Harvard Med. Sch., Boston, 1969-70, asst. prof., 1970-75, assoc. prof., 1975-80, lectr. radiology, 1980—; radiologist U. Mass. Med. Ctr., Worcester, 1980—2001, prof., chmmn. dept. radiology, 1980—2001; prof. U. Mass. Med. Sch., Worcester, 1980—2001, prof. dept. surgery in urology, 1983—2001. Vis. radiologist Rambam Govt. Hosp., Haifa, Israel, 1972; vis. prof. dept. ultrasound U. Copenhagen, Herlev, Denmark, 1977-78, Shanghai Med. Ctr., Peoples Republic China, 1987; cons. Tng. Program in Diagnostic Ultrasound for Physicians and Technologists, Va., 1974-75; reviewer profl. jours. Author: (with others) Abdominal Ultrasound: Static and Dynamic Scanning, 1980; contbr. articles to profl. jours. Fogarty sr. internat. fellow John E. Fogarty Internat. Ctr. for Advanced Study in Health Scis., NIH, Copenhagen, 1977-78 Fellow Am. Coll. Radiology, Soc. Radiologists in Ultrasound (charter, emeritis); mem. Radiol. Soc. N.Am., New Eng. Soc. Ultrasound in Medicine (charter, pres. 1978-79), New Eng. Roentgen Ray Soc. (pres. 1989-90), Mass. Radiologic Soc. (exec. coun. 1991-97). Office: St Elizabeth Hosp Brighton MA 01655

SMITH, ELDRED REID, library educator; b. Payette, Idaho, June 30, 1931; s. Lawrence E. and Jennie (Reid) S.; m. Judith Ausubel, June 25, 1953; children: Steven, Janet. BA, U. Calif.-Berkeley, 1956, MA, 1962; M.L.S., U. So. Calif., 1957. Aquisition reference librarian Long Beach State Coll. Library, 1957-59; reference librarian San Francisco State Coll. Library, 1959-60; bibliographer U. Calif.-Berkeley Library, 1960-65, head search div. acquisition dept., 1966-69, head loan dept., 1969-70, asso. univ. librarian, 1970-72, acting univ. librarian, 1971-72; dir. libraries, also prof. SUNY, Buffalo, 1973-76; univ. librarian U. Minn., 1976-87, prof., 1976-96. Lectr. Sch. Library Sci., U. Wash., 1972; bd. dirs. Center for Research Libraries, 1975-77 Author: The Librarian, The Scholar, and the Future of the Research Library, 1990; contbr. articles to libr. jours. Council on Library Resources fellow, 1970 Mem. ALA, Assn. Research Libraries (dir. 1979-85, pres. 1983-84), Assn. Coll. and Research Libraries (pres. 1977-78, dir. 1976-79, com. on academic status 1969-74, chmn. univ. libraries sect. 1974-75) Home: 847 Gelston Pl El Cerrito CA 94530-3046

SMITH, ELEANOR JANE, university chancellor, retired, consultant; b. Circleville, Ohio, Jan. 10, 1933; d. John Allen and Eleanor Jane (Dade) Lewis; m. James L. Banner, Aug. 10, 1957 (div. 1972); 1 child, Teresa M. Banner Watters; m. Paul M. Smith Jr. BS, Capital U., 1955; PhD, The Union Inst., Cin., 1972. Tchr. Columbus (Ohio) Pub. Schs., 1956-64, Worthington (Ohio) Pub. Schs., 1964-72; from faculty to administrator U. Cin., 1972-88; dean Smith Coll., Northampton, Mass., 1988-90; v.p. acad. affairs, provost William Paterson Coll., Wayne, N.J., 1990-94; chancellor U. Wis.-Parkside, Kenosha, 1994-97, ret., 1997; ind. cons. in higher edn. Dir. Afrikan Am. Inst., Cin., 1977-84; adv. bd. Edwina Bookwalter Gantz Undergrad. Studies Ctr., Cin.; mem. Gov.'s Tobacco Tax adv. coun. Performances include (concert) Black Heritage: History, Music and Dance, 1972—. Spl. Arts Night Com., Northampton, 1988-89; bd. dirs. Planned Parenthood No. and Ctrl. Ariz., Am. Lung Assn. Ariz./N.Mex. Named career woman of achievement YWCA, Cin., 1983. Mem. AAUW, Nat. Assn. Women in Higher Edn., Am. Assn. for Higher Edn., Leadership Am. (bd. dirs., treas. 1993-95), Nat. Assn. Black Women Historians (co-founder, co-dir. 1979-82), Am. Coun. on Edn. (mem. com. on internat. edn. 1994-97, bd. dirs. 1995-97), Am. Assn. State Colls. and Univs. (mem. com. on policies and purposes 1994-97). Avocations: music, pen and ink drawing, travel, reading. Home: 24823 S Lakestar Dr Sun Lakes AZ 85248-7465

SMITH, ERIC J. school system administrator; b. Ga., 1956; Supt. Anne Arundel County Pub. Sch. Sys., Annapolis, Md., 2002—, NC Sch. Sys., NC, 1995—2002, Charlotte-Mecklenberg Sch. Sys., 1996—2001, Newport News Pub. Sch., 1992, Danville Pub. Sch. Sys. Named Urban Educator of Yr., Coun. of Great City Sch., 2000; recipient McGraw prize in Edn., 2002. Office: Anne Arundel County Pub Schs c/o Pub Info Off 2644 Riva Rd Annapolis MD 21401

SMITH, ERIC MORGAN, virology educator; b. Lafayette, Ind., Feb. 13, 1953; s. James E. and Betty Carolyn (Hanlin) S.; m. Janice Marie Kelly, May 26, 1979; children: David Kendall, Ben Pham. BS cum laude, Syracuse U., 1975; PhD, Baylor Coll. of Medicine, 1980. Postdoctoral fellow dept. microbiology U. Tex. Med. Br., Galveston, 1979-81, asst. prof. dept. microbiology, 1982-85, assoc. prof. dept. microbiology, 1985-90, prof. dept. microbiology, 1990—, prof. dept. psychiatry and behavioral scis., 1990—. Editl. bd. Progress in Neuro-Endocrin Immunology, Washington, 1988-92, Behavior and Immunity, 1993—, Cellular and Molecular Neurobiology, 1994—; mem. mental health AIDS and immunity rev. com. NIMH, 1992-96. Founding co-editor Advances in Neuroimmunology, 1991; contbr. over 140 articles to profl. jours. Mem. Galveston Hist. Found., 1980—. Mem. AAAS, Am. Soc. for Microbiology, Am. Assn. Immunologists, Internat. Soc. Immunopharmacology, Internat. Working Group on Neuroimmunomodulation, Assn. Immuno-Neurobiologists (co-founding pres.), Galveston Yacht Club, Syracuse Scuba Soc. (v.p. 1975). Avocations: sailing, photography, scuba diving. Office: U Tex Med Br Dept Psychiatry Galveston TX 77555-0001 E-mail: esmith@utmb.edu.

SMITH, EVELYN ELAINE, language educator; b. Waco, Tex., July 25, 1952; d. Walstein Bennett and Evelyn Dougherty (Box) S. BA, Baylor U., 1974, MA, 1979; PhD, Tex. Christian U., 1995. Cert. secondary tchr., Tex. Grad. asst. Baylor U., Waco, Tex., 1975, proofreader, 1980, rsch. assoc., 1981-86; reporter Killeen (Tex.) Daily Herald, 1981; writing tchr. Waco (Tex.) Ind. Sch. Dist., 1989-90; grad. asst. Tex. Christian U., Ft. Worth, 1992-93; adj. prof. English McLennan C.C., Waco, Tex., 1993-94; adj. instr. English Tex. State Tech. Coll., Waco, 1993-94, 97; instr. English Hill Coll., Hillsboro, Tex., 1997, Ctrl. Tex. Coll., Killeen, 1997, So. Meth. U., Dallas, 1997, El Centro Coll., Dallas, 1998, North Ctrl. Tex. Coll., Lewisville, 1998. Adj. lectr. Ctrl. Tex. Coll., Killeen, 1997, So. Meth. U., Dallas, 1997; adj. instr. El Centro Coll., Dallas, 1998, North Ctrl. Tex. Coll., Lewisville, 1998; vis. asst. prof. Idaho State U., Pocatello, 1998—. Contbr. articles to profl. jours. Bd. dirs., newsletter editor Historic Waco Found., 1981-85, sec., exec., mem. nominating coms., 1994-96. Mem. MLA, South Ctrl. MLA, S.W./Tex. PGA/ACA, Nat. Conf. Tchrs. English, Conf. Coll. Composition and Comm. Democrat. Mem. So. Bapt. Ch. Avocation: historical preservation. Office: Idaho State U Dept English & Philosophy PO Box 8056 Pocatello ID 83209-0001

SMITH, F. LOUISE, elementary school educator; b. Balt., Nov. 4, 1946; d. Joseph L. and Catherine L. Lilley; m. Wayne F. Smith, Aug. 7, 1976; 1 child, Ryan. BA, Mt. St. Agnes Coll., 1968; MEd, Loyola Coll. Elem. tchr. St. Clement Sch. Diocese Balt., 1966—68, elem. tchr. St. Mark Sch., 1968—71; elem. tchr. Longfellow Elem. Howard County, Columbia, Md., 1971—72, elem. tchr. Hammond Elem. Laurel, Md., 1972—2002. Tutor, Catonsville, Md. Named Tchr. of Yr., Am. Legion, 1997, Sunpapers All-Star Reading Tchr., Balt. Sun, 2001. Mem.: State Md. Reading Assn., Md. Congress Parents and Tchrs. (life), State Md. Internat. Reading Coun. Home and Office: 312 Locust Dr Catonsville MD 21228

SMITH, GAIL MARIE, special education educator, educational consultant; b. Buffalo, June 7, 1947; d. Daniel James and Geraldine Francis (Whalen) Healy; children: Christopher Alan Southworth, Jennifer Morgan Elizabeth. Student, Trinity Coll., Dublin, Ireland, 1968; BA in English and Edn. with hons., St. John's U., N.Y., 1969; postgrad., U. Md., Okinawa, Japan, 1970; MS in Spl. Edn. with honors, So. Conn. State U., 1982; postgrad., Wesleyan U., 1985, Mattatuck C.C., 1989, Conn. Adult Devel. Program, 1993. Cert. ESL, Conn., comprehensive spl. edn., Conn., nursery, kindergarten, grades 1-8, Conn., English grades 7-12, Conn., h.s. credit diploma program, Conn., external diploma program/non-credit mandated programs, Conn., CAPP facilitator, Conn., program leader WERACE, psychol. mgmt. tng., crisis mgmt. tng., CPR, 1st aid, respite, CTH, Conn.; pub. svc. lic. Tchr. Machinato Elem. Sch. Dept. of Def. Overseas Dependent Schs., Okinawa, 1969-70, tchr., chair dept. English Port Wheel Nine Sch., 1970-71; tchr. grades 5 and 6 regular and spl. edn. Woodbridge (Conn.) Pub. Schs., 1971-81, tchr. spl. edn., 1981-82; tchr. adjusted curriculum program Trumbull (Conn.) H.S., 1982-83, tchr. elem. self-contained resource room programs, cons., 1983-88, tchr. spl. edn., 1994; tchr. spl. edn. and regular edn. grades 9-12 Trumbull Alt. Sch., 1988-94; tchr. spl. edn., vocat. liaison Trumbull Pub. Schs., 1994; tchr. grades 9-12 at-risk adolescents (regular/spl. edn.) Regional Alt. Sch., Trumbull, 1995—. Ednl., behavioral cons.; active Conn. Ind. Living Adult Residential Program, 1988-89, medically fragile program Trumbull Pub. Schs., 1989, Datahr Rehab. Inst., Conn., 1994-96, Western Regional Adult Continuing Edn. Program, 1989-96; enl. specialist State of Conn. Dept. Edn., summers 1987, 88, 90; mgr. semi-supervised apt. program, 1989-93. Advocate Lyme disease, 1991—, spl. edn., 1989—; mem. edn. com. Fed. Correctional Instn., Danbury, Conn., 1994; alt. schs. rep. Trumbull Ednl. Assn., 1989-99, mem. exec. bd., 1986-94, rep. coun., 1985; mem. coun. Fairfield County, State of Conn. Edn. Assn. Fairfield County, 1988-89; mem. adv. bd., 1988-89; Trumbull Edn. Assn. rep. supt.'s adv. com. Trumbull Pub. Schs., 1988-89, spl. edn. rep. tchr. evaluation com., 1988—, Middlebrook Elem. Sch. rep. tchr. evaluation com., 1986-88, mem. lang. arts com., 1984-85, Middlebrook Elem. Sch. PTA liaison, 1983-84, v.p. Trumbull H.S. PTSA Coun. and Exec. Bd., 1982-83; mem. bd. mgrs. State of Conn. PTA, 1983-86, advisor Key Club, 1982-83; mem. coun. Newtown (Conn.) PTA, 1984-85, v.p., legis. rep., bd. edn. liaison, 1982-86; co-sponsor spl. edn. svc. club Nonnewaug H.S., Woodbury, Conn., 1976-80; bd. dirs. Children's Adventure Ctr., Inc., Newtown, Conn., 1982-89; evaluator State of Conn. Spl. Edn. Network for Software, 1985-95; co-chairperson child abuse com. St. of Ct., 1984-85, Bd. of mgrs. PTA, 1984-86. Mem. AAUW, NEA, Conn. Edn. Assn., Conn. Assn. Learning Disabilities, Trumbull Edn. Assn. (v.p. 1988-89, alt. sch. rep. 1985—), Conn. Adult Profl. Program (cert.), Western Edn. Regional Acad. and Adult Continuing Edn., Cmty. Tng. Home (lic.). Avocations: skiing, swimming, hiking, antiques, camping. Office: Trumbull Alternate Sch Madison Mid Sch Madison Ave Trumbull CT 06611 Home: 419 Danswoth Rd Youngstown NY 14174-1318

SMITH, GERARD VINTON, chemistry educator; b. Delano, Calif., Oct. 14, 1931; s. Marion Lew and Marjorie Elsie (Ryland) S.; m. Jolynn Clayton Fenn, June 22, 1956; children: Kenneth Paul, Craig Stephen, Elise Patricia. BA in Chemistry, Coll. of Pacific, 1953, MS in Chemistry, 1956; PhD in Chemistry, U. Ark., 1959; D honoris causa, József Attila U., Szeged, Hungary, 1996. Rsch. assoc. Northwestern U., Evanston, Ill., 1959-60, instr. chemistry, 1960-61; asst. prof. chemistry Ill. Inst. Tech., Chgo., 1961-66; assoc. prof. chemistry So. Ill. U., Carbondale, 1966-73, prof. chemistry, 1973—, dir. molecular sci. program, 1978-96. Tech. cons. to ins. adjusters and attys. and industry in So. Ill.; chemistry tutor local high sch.; rsch. collaborator József Attila U., Szeged, Hungary, 1980—; lectr. organic catalysis Pohang (Korea) U. Sci. and Tech., 1994, vis. prof., 1996, chair of Chemistry, 2000—. Author: Catalysis in Organic Syntheses, 1977; co-author: Heterogeneous Catalysis in Organic Chemistry, 1999; contbr. over 120 articles and book revs. to sci. jours. Elder Ch. of Christ. Recipient Outstanding Rschr. award So. Ill. U. Coll. Sci., 1990, Kaplan rsch. award Sigma Xi, 1992, Paul N. Rylander award Organic Reactions Catalysis Soc. div. N.Am. Catalysis Soc., 1995, Henry J. Albert award Internat. Precious Metals Inst., 1998; grantee Free U. Iran, 1978-81, Monsanto Co., 1962-63, ACS-PRF, 1963-66, USPHS-NIH, 1963-66, 69-72, W.R. Grace Co., 1966-72, Ill. State Geol. Survey, 1977, 78, Dept. Energy, 1981-96, NSF, 1984-87, Ill. Coal Rsch. Bd., 1982-96, Office of Water Resources Rsch., 1967-69, Materials Tech. Ctr., So. Ill. U., 1983-96, Uniroyal Chem. Co., 1989-92, Ctr. for Rsch. on Sulfur in Coal, 1987-96, numerous others. Avocations: science fiction, fantasy. Home: 106 N Lark Ln Carbondale IL 62901-2017 Office: So Ill U Dept Chemistry Mailcode 4409 Carbondale IL 62901-4409 E-mail: gvs@chem.siu.edu.

SMITH, GLENDA IRENE, elementary school educator; b. St. Paul, May 4, 1940; d. Otis Alvin and Bella Gladys (Elven) Anderson; m. Herbert Smith, Dec. 22, 1962; 1 child, Melanie Marjorie. BA, N.W. Nazarene Coll., 1962. Cert. elem. tchr., Calif. Tchr. Spring Lake Park Dist. Schs., Mpls., 1962-63, 64-65, Parma (Idaho) Sch. Dist., 1965-66, Nampa (Idaho) City Schs., 1966-69, Modesto (Calif.) City Schs., 1969-70, 71-78, tchr., mentor, 1985—; tchr., vice prin. Turlock (Calif.) Christian Schs., 1978-82. Author: Stories, Songs, Puppets, 1972. Mem. Nat. Tchr. Assn., Calif. Tchr. Assn., Modesto Tchr. Assn. Democrat. Episcopalian. Avocations: catering, reading, music, travel. Home: 2749 La Palma Dr Modesto CA 95354-3228 Office: Robertson Rd Sch 1821 Robertson Rd Modesto CA 95351-3499

SMITH, GRANT WARREN, II, university administrator, physical sciences educator; b. Kansas City, Mo., Jan. 21, 1941; m. Constance M. Krambeer, 1962; 1 child, Grant Warren III. BA, Grinnell Coll., 1962; PhD, Cornell U., 1966, postgrad., 1967. Asst. prof. chemistry Cornell U., Ithaca, N.Y., 1966-68, vis. prof. Am. Coun. on Edn. fellow, 1973-74; assoc. prof. U. Alaska, Fairbanks, 1968-77, prof., 1977-78, head dept. chemistry and chem. engring., 1968-73, acting head dept. gen. sci., 1972-73; pres. univ. assembly U. Alaska Sys., 1976-77; prof. phys. scis., dean Sch. Scis. and Tech., U. Houston, Clear Lake, 1979-84; prof. chemistry Southeastern La. U., Hammond, 1984-95, honors prof. arts and scis., 1995-97, v.p. acad. affairs, 1984-86, pres., 1986-95, Slippery Rock U., 1997—. Bd. dirs. Houston Area Rsch. Ctr., 1982-83, Penn-Northwest Devel. Corp., 1998—, Cmty. Devel. Corp. Butler County, 1998—, 3 Rivers Connect, 2000—; violinist, pres. exec. bd. Clear Lake Symphony, 1980-84. NIH fellow, 1963-66, DuPont fellow, 1967. Fellow Royal Soc. Chemistry (London, chartered chemist), Explorers Club; mem. Am. Assn. Higher Edn., Am. Assn. Univ. Adminstrs. (bd. dirs. 1982-88, 99—, v.p. 1988-90), AAAS, The Coll. Bd., Am. Chem. Soc., Internat. Assn. Univ. Pres., Internat. Soc. Ethnopharmacology, Am. Soc. Pharmacognosy, Internat. Soc. of Ethnobiology, Nat. Speleological Soc., Am. Spelean History Assn., Am. Bot. Coun., Arctic Inst. N.Am., Soc. for the History of Discoveries, Leadership Pitts. XV, Hammond C. of C. (bd. dirs. 1988-90), World Future Soc., Rotary, Sigma Xi, Phi Kappa Phi, Beta Gamma Sigma, Phi Eta Sigma. Office: Slippery Rock U Office of Pres Old Main Slippery Rock PA 16057-1326 E-mail: gwsmith@sru.edu.

SMITH, GREGORY ALLGIRE, college administrator; b. Washington, Mar. 31, 1951; s. Donald Eugene and Mary Elizabeth (Reichert) Smith; m. Susan Elizabeth Watts, Oct. 31, 1980; 1 child, David Joseph Smith-Watts. BA, The Johns Hopkins U., 1972; MA, Williams Coll., Williamstown, Mass., 1974. Adminstrv. asst. Washington Project for the Arts, 1975; intern Walker Art Ctr., Mpls., 1975—76; asst. devel. officer The Sci. Mus. of Minn., St. Paul, 1977; asst. dir. Akron (Ohio) Art Inst., 1977—80; asst. to dir. Toledo Mus. Art, 1980—82, asst. dir. adminstrn., 1982—86; exec. v.p. Internat. Exhbns. Found., Washington, 1986—87; dir. The Telfair Mus. Art, Savannah, Ga., 1987—94, Art Acad. of Cin., 1994—98, pres., 1998—. Trustee Greater Cin. Consortium of Colls. and Univs., vice chmn., 2001—; trustee Assn. Ind. Colls. of Art and Design. Mem.: Coll. Art Assn., Ohio Found. on the Arts (v.p. 1981—83, trustee 1981—84), Assn. Art Mus. Adminstrs. (founder 1984—85), Am. Assn. Mus. (surveyor mus. assessment program 1988—), Rotary (dir. Cin. club 2000—01, sec.-treas. 2001—02, pres. 2002—03), Univ. Club. Avocation: collecting arts and crafts movement objects, landscape design, gardening.. Home: 8380 Springvalley Dr Cincinnati OH 45236-1356 Office: Art Acad of Cin 1125 Saint Gregory St Cincinnati OH 45202-1799 E-mail: gasmith@artacademy.edu.

SMITH, HAROLD ALLEN, education administrator, researcher, educator; b. Franklin, La., Nov. 28, 1944; s. Bernie Lloyd and Lily Madge (Thompson) S.; m. Pheny Shang Fen Zhou, May 27, 1985. MusB in Edn., Delta State U., 1966; MDiv, New Orleans Bapt. Theol. Sem., 1977; MEd, Ariz. State U., 1984; EdD, Miss. State U., 1989. Educator Matthews/Doniphan (Mo.) Schs., 1966-70, Phoenix Pub. Schs., 1970-71; pvt. sch. educator John Curtis Schs., New Orleans, 1974-77; founder, dir. Chattanooga Assn. for Resettlement, 1977-83; adult educator Phoenix Union High Sch. Dist., 1983-84; vis. prof. Cen. Fgn. Expert Bur., Beijing, People's Republic of China, 1984-86; dir. China study program Miss. State U., 1986-90, editor Internat. Newsletter, 1987-89, program coord. Asian Studies Ctr., 1990-92; editor Miss. Meets Asia, 1990-92; program coord. ESL Ctr., 1991-92; prof., divsn. chair Shenandoah U., 1993-2000; pres. Shenandoah Enterprises Editing, Writing & Pub. Svcs., Alexandria, Va., 2000—. Cons. AMG Internat., Chattanooga, 1977-79, Chattanooga Area Literacy Movement, 1979-83; vis. prof. Georgetown U., 1992—, Notre Dame Seishin Coll. (Japan), 1993. Author: Education and Culture in China, 1988, Mississippi Agriculture and World Hunger, 1988; editor: International Experience and Relationships, 1988, International Student Handbook, 1991, AMTESOL Newsletter, 1991-92, AMTESOL Jour., 1991-92, WATESOL News, 1997—, TESLEJ, 1999—, BRIEFME, 1999—, TESOL Matters, 1998-99; contbr. numerous articles to profl. jours. Bd. dirs. Chattanooga Area Literacy Movement, 1979-83, Maricopa Refugee Com., Phoenix, 1983-84. With U.S. Army, 1971-74. Mem. NAFSA: Assn. Internat. Educators, Tchrs. of English to Speakers of Other Langs., Japan Assn. Of Lang. Tchrs., Washington Area Tchrs. of English to Speakers of Other Langs., Ala.-Miss. Tchrs. of English to Speakers of Other Langs., Assn. Tchr. Educators, Mid-South Edn. Rsch. Assn., Assn. Multicultural Counseling and Devel., Assn. Comparative and Internat. Edn. (also So. and Western orgns.), Ea. Ednl. Rsch. Assn., Kiwanis (bd. dirs. breakfast club Starkville, Miss. chpt. 1988-89), Phi Delta Kappa. Republican. Baptist. Avocations: travel, tennis, running, reading. Office: Shenandoah Enterprises Box U501 8 S Van Dorn St Dr Alexandria VA 22304-4228 E-mail: hsmith_44@onebox.com.

SMITH, HAROLD CHARLES, biochemistry educator, academic administrator; b. Münich, Germany, Feb. 5, 1954; came to U.S., 1966; s. Harold Charles Sr. and Gisela (Pointer) S.; m. Jenny Marie Lyverse, Aug. 21, 1976; children: Charles, Owen, Hanna Marie, Sammy Jay. BS, Purdue U., 1975, MS, 1978; MA, SUNY, Buffalo, 1980, PhD, 1982. Postdoctoral assoc. dept. biochemistry SUNY, Buffalo, 1982-83; postdoctoral assoc. dept. pharmacology Baylor Coll. Medicine, Houston, 1983-85, postdoctoral fellow dept. genetics, 1983-85, rsch. assoc. dept. biochemistry, 1985-86; prof. dept. biochemistry and biophysics U. Rochester, N.Y., 1986—. Dir. grad. studies dept. pathology U. Rochester, 1993-97, dir. med. sch. biochemistry, 1997-2001, organizer 1st internat. meeting RNA editing, Albany, N.Y., 1994; first chair First Gordon Rsch. Conf. on RNA Editing. Contbr. articles to profl. jours.; mem. editl. bd. Molecular and Cellular Biochemistry. Rsch. grantee Office of Naval Res., 1989-92, NIH, 1992--, Coun. for Tobacco Rsch., 1993-2000, Alcoholic Beverage Med. Rsch. Found., 1998-2001, USAF, 2001--; George W. Merck dean's acad. scholar; recipient Jr. Faculty Mentor award Women in Sci., Dentistry and Medicine. Mem. AAAS, ASBMB, Am. Heart Assn., N.Y. Acad. Sci., RNA Soc., Sigma Xi (Rsch. award 1981). Lutheran. Achievements include first proposed hypothesis for apoB mRNA editing mechanism (The Mooring Sequence Hypothesis) and demonstrated the tripartite cis-acting elements for editing site recognition and the role of multiple proteins, as an editosome, in the editing activity; proposed the "Gating" hypothesis for the regulation of nuclear editing activity; identified and was first to characterize the RNA-binding proteins involved in apoB mRNA editing; discovered yeast mRNA C to U editing; first to demonstrate in vitro DNA replication in nuclear matrix presentations. Home: 1056 Farnsworth Rd S Rochester NY 14623-5447 Office: Univ Rochester Dept Pathology 601 Elmwood Ave Rochester NY 14642-0001

SMITH, HARRIET GWENDOLYN GURLEY, secondary school educator, writer; b. Goldsboro, N.C., Nov. 14, 1927; d. Charles Harvey and Sadye Reid (Morris) Gurley; m. Albert Goodin Smith, Aug. 29, 1953; children: Susan Reid Smith Erba, Alan English Smith. Grad., St. Mary's Coll., Raleigh, N.C., 1946; BA, U. N.C., 1948; MEd, La. State U., Shreveport, 1982. Cert. tchr., N.C., La. Tchr. English, Journalism, Social Studies Goldsboro City Schs., 1948-49, Rocky Mount (N.C.) City Schs., 1949-51, Durham (N.C.) City Schs., 1951-53, Durham County Schs., 1954-56; realtor assoc. Sam Fullilore and Assocs., Shreveport, 1984-87; contbg. editor, columnist The New Front Gallery Mag., Shreveport, 1988. Bridge tchr. Caddo Magnet High Sch., La. State U., Woman's Dept. Club, pvt. groups, 1978—. Pres. Shreveport Med. Soc. Aux., 1985-86, chmn. various coms., 1970—; pres. Faculty Women's Club La. State U. Med. Ctr., 1990; mem. women's bd. dirs. Centenary Coll.; active United Meth. Women, Symphony Guild, Opera Guild, Rep. Women. Mem. Am. Contract Bridge League (life master, cert. tchr.), Am. Bridge Tchrs. Assn. (master tchr., tchg. del. to Russia 1994), La. Real Estate Commn., Bull and Bear Stock Club (sec. 1973-74, pres. 1975-76), Kappa Delta Pi. Avocations: travel, cultural activities, tennis, health and fitness, volunteer work. Home: 8502 Rampart Pl Shreveport LA 71106-6226 E-mail: hsmith39@msn.com.

SMITH, HOKE LAFOLLETTE, university president; b. Galesburg, Ill., May 7, 1931; s. Clude Hoke and Bernice (LaFollette) Smith; m. Barbara E. Walvoord, June 30, 1979 (div. 2001); children from previous marriage: Kevin, Kerry, Amy, Glen. BA (Harold fellow), Knox Coll., 1953; MA, U. Va., 1954; PhD (fellow 1958), Emory U., 1958; hon. degree, Sung Kyun Kwan U., Korea, 1993, Knox Coll., 1995; prof. (hon.), St. Petersburg Electrotech. U., 2001. Asst. prof. polit. sci. Hiram Coll., Ohio, 1958-64, assoc. prof. polit. sci., 1964-67; asst. to pres., prof. polit. sci. Drake U., Des Moines, 1967-70, chmn. interim governing com., 1971-72, v.p. acad. adminstrn., 1970-79; pres. Towson (Md.) U., 1979—2001, pres. emeritus, 2001—. Vis. prof. U. Md., College Park, 2001—03; mem. univ. adv. coun. Life Ins. Coun. Am., 1969—71; mem. task force to study the governance, structure and funding U. Sys. Md., 1998—99. Chmn. exec. com. Coun. Econ. Edn., Towson, Md., 1979—; bd. dirs. Balt. Coun. on Fgn. Rels.; chmn. Very Spl. Arts of Md.; bd. dirs. Greater Homewood Cmty. Corp.; commr. Md. Higher Edn. Commn., 2003—. With U.S. Army, 1954—56. Recipient Eileen Tosney award, Am. Assn. Univ. Administrs., 1991; Congl. fellow, Am. Polit. Sci. Assn., 1964—65. Mem.: St. Petersburg Intenat. Consortium of Colls. and Univs. (co-chair 1997), Met. and Urban Colls. and Univs. (co-chair 1996—), Soc. for Coll. and Univ. Planning (bd. dirs. 1986—88), Am. Assn. Higher Edn., Am. Coun. Edn. (bd. dirs., exec. com. 1988—94, chmn. elect 1991—92, chmn. 1992—93, past chmn. 1993—94), Am. Assn. State Colls. and Univs. (bd. dirs. 1984—88, Found. bd. dirs. 1985—87, chmn. elect 1985—86, chmn. 1986—87), Renaissance Group (exec. com.), Balt. C. of C. (adv. coun.), Pi Sigma Alpha, Gamma Gamma, Delta Sigma Tho, Omicron Delta Kappa, Phi Kappa Phi, Phi Beta Kappa. E-mail: hsmith@towson.edu.

SMITH, HOWARD RAY, school system administrator; b. Carthage, Mo., Apr. 5, 1948; s. Francis Lee and Eva Bell (Baker) S.; m. Coleen B. Stanley, June 5, 1976; children: Scott Allen, Alicia C. BS in Elem. Edn., Mo. So. State Coll., 1970; MS in Adminstrn., Drury, 1975; EdS, Pitts. State U., 1982; EdD, U. Ark., 1989. Cert. elem. educator, adminstr. Elem. tchr. Carthage (Mo.) R-9 Dist., 1970-75; elem. prin. St. Elizabeth (Mo.) Pub. Schs., 1975-77, Carthage (Mo.) R-9 Dist., 1977-88, asst. supt. of schs., 1988-94; supt. schs. St. Elizabeth (Mo.) Pub. Schs., 1994-96; assoc. prof. Kans. Dept. Curriculum and Instrn. Pittsburg State U., 1996—. Exec. bd. Boy Scouts of Am., Joplin, Mo., 1989—. Recipient Outstanding Young Educator award Carthage Jaycees, 1974, A. Sterl Artley Reading award Jasper County Internat. Reading Assn., 1982, Point of Excellence award Rho Sigma Chpt., 1992. Mem. ASCD, Mo. Assn. Elem. Sch. Prins., Am. Assn. Sch. Adminstrs., Mo. State Tchrs. Assn., Kappa Delta Pi, Joplin Chpt. Phi Delta Kappa. Avocations: woodworking, fishing, golf.

SMITH, J. ROY, education educator; b. Washington, Ga., Sept. 13, 1936; s. James Roy and Nellie Irene (Mansfield) S. BA, Mercer U., 1956; postgrad., Brown U., 1957; cert., Oxford U., Eng., 1963. Tchr. City of Cranston, R.I., 1957-59; with Charleston County, Charleston, S.C., 1962-64, 76-79; tchr. Fulton County, Fairburn, Ga., 1965-76, Berkeley County, Moncks Corner, S.C., 1979-94. Lt. (j.g.) USN, 1959-62. Charleston Area Writing Project fellow; recipient English Speaking Union scholarship Oxford U., 1963; Newspaper Fund of the Wall Street Jour. fellow. Mem. SAR (sec./treas. S.C. Soc. 1977-78), Soc. Second War with Great Britain, Sons and Daus. of Pilgrims (gov. Ga. br. 1976, hon. gov. 1976—), S.C. Hist. Soc., Ga. Hist. Soc., Kappa Phi Kappa (registered tour guide, lectr.). Home and Office: 110 Coming St Charleston SC 29403-6103

SMITH, JAMES BROWN, JR., secondary school educator; b. Greenville, N.C., Apr. 6, 1943; s. James Brown Sr. and Clara Lucille (Avery) S.; m. Donna Drake, Aug. 12, 1967; children: Caryn Frances, James Brown III, Sarah Elizabeth. BS, East Carolina U., 1966; MEd, Va. State U., 1976. Cert. tchr., postgrad. prof., Va. Tchr. Great Bridge Jr. High Sch., Chesapeake, Va., 1966-68, Queen's Lake Sch., York County, Va., 1968-76; tchr., chmn. career tech. edn. dept. Bruton High Sch., York County, 1976—. Cons. Acad. Tech, Hampton, Va., 1992-93; tchr. intern Va. Peninsula C. of C., Hampton, 1992. Mem. York County Edn. Assn., Va. Edn. Assn., NEA, Va. Vocat. Assn., Va. Tech. Edn. Assn., Assn. Career and Tech. Edn., Kiwanis (bd. dirs. 1984-92). Methodist. Avocations: photography, gardening, auto repair, fishing. Home: 135 John Pott Dr Williamsburg VA 23188-6328 Office: Bruton High Sch 185 E Rochambeau Dr Williamsburg VA 23188-2121 E-mail: jbsmithjr@hotmail.com.

SMITH, JAMES FINLEY, economist, educator; b. Dallas, Nov. 4, 1938; s. Emerson Russell and Achsah Elizabeth (Foster) S.; children: Carter Emerson, Jamie, Curtis Noel, Marshall Edward; m. Linda M. Topp, Aug. 5, 2001. BA, So. Meth. U., 1961, MA, 1964, PhD, 1971. Math. analyst Sears, Roebuck & Co., Oak Brook, Ill., 1965-68, adminstrv. asst. to v.p. and treas. Chgo., 1968-69, dir. econometric rsch., 1969-75; sr. economist Bd. Govs. FRS, Washington, 1975-77; dir. credit rsch. Sears, Roebuck & Co., Chgo., 1977-80; chief economist Union Carbide Corp., Danbury, Conn., 1980-85; dir. regional svcs. and U.S. cons. Wharton Econometric Forecasting Assocs., Phila., 1986; dir., chief economist Bur. Bus. Rsch. U. Tex., Austin, 1987-88; prof. fin. U. NC, Chapel Hill, 1988—, sr. fellow Kenan Inst. Pvt. Enterprise, 2002—; chief economist Nat. Assn. Realtors, Washington, 1999—2000; sr. fellow, Ctr. for Bus. Forecasting; chief economist Soc. Indsl. and Office Realtors, Washington, 2002—. Econ. adv. bd. U.S. Dept. Commerce, 1977-80, 83-93; cons. Pres.'s Coun. of Econ. Advisers, Washington, 1978-83; pres. Nat. Bus. Econ. Issues Coun., N.Y.C., 1981-83; dir. Nat. Bur. Econ. Rsch., Cambridge, Mass., 1992-95; bd. advisors Thurston Arthritis Rsch. Ctr., Chapel Hill, N.C., 1994-99. Author: (quarterly) UNC Business Forecast, 1988—, (with others) Economic Growth and Investment in Higher Education, 1987, The New Texas Economy, 1988, (with Elsie Echeverri-Carroll) The Economic Impact of Travel on Texas Counties: 1986, 1988; contbr. articles to profl. jours. Served to lt. U.S. Army, 1961-62. Fellow NDEA, 1962—65. Fellow Nat. Assn. Bus. Econ. (v.p. 1988-89, pres. 1989-90, dir. 1980-92); Nat. Economists Club (bd. govs. 1984-87), Am. Econ. Assn., Economists Group Switzerland, Fin. Mgmt. Assn., Bus. Economists U.K. Methodist. Home: 201 Bolinwood Dr Chapel Hill NC 27514 Office: U NC Kenan Flagler Bus Sch Dept Fin McColl Bldg Campus Box 3490 Chapel Hill NC 27599-3490 E-mail: j_smith@unc.edu.

SMITH, J(AMES) SCOTT, elementary education educator; b. Pittsfield, Ill., Oct. 8, 1951; s. James H. and Joan (Johnson) S.; 1 child, Sydney Jacquelyn. BA in Sociology, Elem. Edn., Sangamon State U., 1973, MA in Ednl. Adminstrn., 1976; PhD in Edn. Studies, U. Utah, 2000. Tchr. grades 3-6 Pleasant Hill (Ill.) Community Sch. Dist., 1973-79; tchr. grade 5 Colegio Internacional de Carabobo, Valencia, Venezuela, 1979-80; tchr. grades 3-7 Pleasant Hill Community Sch. Dist., 1980-88; tchr. grades 5, 6 Salt Lake City Sch. Dist., 1988—. Adj. prof. U. Utah, Salt Lake City, 1989—. Mem. Nat. Edn. Asns., Utah Coun. for Self-Esteem, Salt Lake Tchrs. Assn. (associational rep. 1989-92). Republican. Baptist. Avocations: renovational carpentry, gardening. Office: Washington Sch 420 N 200 W Salt Lake City UT 84103-1207 Home: 1718 Oak Spring Drive Salt Lake City UT 84108

SMITH, JANET FAYE, special education educator; b. Rockford, Ill., June 26, 1936; d. Homer Fred and Edna Bernice (Betz) Green; m. Douglas Duane Smith, Aug. 19, 1961; children: Glen, Alice Stuhlmacher, Linda J. Bell. BS, U. Wis., Platteville, 1961; MS, No. Ill. U., 1977. Cert. elem. tchr., spl. edn. tchr., Ill. Tchr. Rockford (Ill.) Pub. Schs., 1960-62; spl. edn. tutor Hilliard (Ohio) Pub. Schs., 1969-72; learning disabilities resource tchr. Pecatonica (Ill.) Unified Sch. Dist. #321, 1977—. Co-author: Ideas From Everywhere, 1991. Mem. NEA, Ill. Edn. Assn., PEO, Coun. Exceptional Children, Ill. Assn. Agrl. Fairs, Kishwaukee Genealogists, Winn-Boone Geneal. Assn. (co-chair early pioneer project 1991—), Mingling Clowns (corr. sec. 1979-88), Cousin Otto's Clown Alley (clown ambassador 1985). Avocations: gardening, balloon sculpting, cooking, reading, writing. Home: PO Box 206 Rockton IL 61072-0206 Office: Pecatonica Unified Sch Dist PO Box 419 Pecatonica IL 61063-0419

SMITH, JANICE ALFREDA, secondary school educator; b. San Pedro, Calif., Jan. 4, 1938; d. Willis Alfred and Elsie Ann (Moser) S. AA, Compton (Calif) Jr. Coll., 1957; BA, Calif. State U., Long Beach, 1960. Tchr. Mayfair H.S., Lakewood, Calif., 1960-85, Redmond (Oreg.) H.S., Sch. Dist. 2J, 1985-98, O'Callaghan Middle Sch., Las Vegas, 2000—03. Drill team instr. Mayfair H.S. Athletic Dept., Lakewood, Calif., 1962-71, coach volleyball, basketball, softball, 1974-85. Coach 10 league championship teams, Mayfair H.S., Lakewood, Calif., 1974-82, 1 Calif. Interscholastic Fedn. So. Divsn. League Champion, 1979; recipient Youth Sports award Lakewood (Calif.) Youth Hall of Fame, 1983; named Tchr. of Yr., Wal-Mart Found., 1999. Mem. NEA, Redmond Edn. Assn. (bargaining chmn. 1996-97, co-pres. 1997-98). Avocations: travel, devel. lang. arts curricula, golf, dogs. Home: 5848 Sassa St Las Vegas NV 89130-7235

SMITH, JEAN BENZING, retired elementary and middle school educator; b. Washington, Oct. 12, 1942; d. Norman L. and Josephine (Rankin) Benzing; m. Alvan C. Smith, Mar. 27, 1965; children: Ashley, Allen. BBS, Fla. State U., 1963; postgrad., West Ga. Coll., Carrollton, 1987, U. Ga., Athens, 1988. Tchr. Rabun County Bd. Edn., Clayton, Ga., 1966-67, DeKalb County Bd. Edn., Decatur, Ga., 1963-66; tchr. math. and social sci. Clayton County Bd. Edn., Jonesboro, Ga., 1987—, Pointe South Middle Sch., Jonesboro, 1990—2001, Mundy's Mill Middle Sch., Jonesboro, 2001—02, ret., 2002. 20th Anniversary amb. Mailbox Mag. Taft scholar, 1989. Mem. NEA, CCEA, Nat. Coun. Tchrs. Math., Ga. Ednl. Assn., Am. Math. Assn., Ga. Math. Assn., Ga. Assn. Educators (del. fall and spring assemblys 1990), Clayton County Ednl. Assn. Home: 230 Dix Leeon Dr Fairburn GA 30213-3608

SMITH, JERILYNN SUZANNE, educational coordinator; b. Loma Linda, Calif., Aug. 15, 1944; d. Gerald A. and Maxine (McGowan) Smith; m. J. Michael McGinn, July 22, 1966; m. Lynn A. Choate, May 8, 1971; 1 dau., Catherine Anne; m. C. Alen Ritchie Feb. 17, 1981. BA, U. Redlands, Calif., 1966; MA in Tchg., U. Redlands, 1968; MA in Edn., Calif. State U., San Bernardino, 1980; EdD in Inernat. Multicultural Edn., U. San Francisco, 1993. Tchr. elem. sch. Redlands Unified Sch. Dist., 1966-69, tchr. educationally handicapped, 1969-71, tchr. intermediate grades, 1971-74, tchr. bilingual edn., 1975-79, resource specialist, 1979-84, categorical projects resource tchr., 1984-87, dist. tchr. coord. Bilingual/Gate Programs, 1987-89; coord. bi-lingual, ESL programs Fontana Sch. Dist., 1989-96, coord. instrnl. support, 1996-97; coord. child devel. programs Salinas City Elem. Sch. Dist., 1997—. Supr. student tchrs. Calif. State Coll., 1975; lectr. Nat. U., 1995, Chapman U., 1996, U. Redlands, 1997. Bd. dirs. San Bernardino County Mus. Assn., 1983-89. Recipient Hon. Svc. award Lugonia PTA, 1982, Tchrs. Hall of Fame award, 1982, Fontana Hispanic C. of C. award, 1992, Latina Women in Edn. award MANA de Salinas, 1998. Mem. Calif. Assn. Bilingual Edn. (mem. state exec. bd. 1985-92), Nat. Assn. Bilingual Edn. (nat. bd. dirs. 1990-92, Pres.'s award 1996), U. San Francisco Assn. Doctoral Fellowship Recipients and Colleagues (pres. 1994-95), Phi Delta Kappa, Pi Lambda Theta. Democrat. Office: Fontana Unified Sch Dist 431 W Alisal St Salinas CA 93901-1624

SMITH, JOAN COLVIN, elementary education educator, principal; b. Dubach, La., Sept. 4, 1948; BA, N.E. La. U., 1971; MEd, Stephen F. Austin, 1976, MEd, 1991. Cert. tchr., La., Tex.; cert. middle mgmt., Tex. Tchr. Iberia Parish Schs., New Iberia, La., 1971-74, Hudson Ind. Sch. Dist., Lufkin, Tex., 1976-82, Huntington (Tex.) Ind. Sch. Dist., 1982—; prin. Huntington Elem. Sch., 1993—. Mem. Supt.'s Adv. Coun., Huntington, 1989-90, Dist. Ednl. Improvement Com., 1990-92; prin.'s adv. coun. Huntington Ind. Sch. Dist., 1991-92. Sec. PTA, Huntington, 1992-93; mem. Ladies Aux. to VFW, Clute, Tex., 1989-93. Named Tchr. of Yr.-Huntington Elem. Sch., Angelina County C. of C., 1989-90. Mem. NAESP, ASCD, Tex. Classroom Tchrs., Assn. Tex. Profl. Educators. Republican. Baptist. Avocations: photography, travel, crafting, collecting old sch. memorabilia. Office: Huntington Ind Schs 408 Linn St Huntington TX 75949

SMITH, JOAN H. retired women's health nurse, educator; b. Akron, Ohio; d. Joseph A. and Troynette M. (Lower) McDonald; m. William G. Smith; children: Sue Ann, Priscilla, Timothy. Diploma, Akron City Hosp., 1948; BSN in Edn., U. Akron, 1972, MA in Family Devel., 1980. Cert. in inpatient obstetric nursing. Mem. faculty Akron Gen. Med. Ctr. Sch. Nursing, 1964; former dir. obstet. spl. procedures Speakers Bur., Women's Health Ctrs. Akron Gen. Med. Ctr., 1988; ret., 1990. Cons., speaker women's health care. Mem. Assn. Women's Health, Obstet. and Neonatal Nursing (charter, past sec.-treas., past vice chmn. Ohio sect., chmn. program various confs.). Home: 873 Kirkwall Dr Copley OH 44321-1751

SMITH, JOHN WEBSTER, retired energy industry executive, consultant; b. Atlanta, Del., May 3, 1921; s. Frank Louis and Dorothy (Andrew) S.; m. Patricia Catherine Metzner, Jan. 9, 1943 (div. 1958); 1 child, Edward Marc; m. Beverly Brabner, Aug. 21, 1958 (div. July 1983); 1 child, David Andrew; m. Sandra Seefeld, Jan. 6, 1985. BA, Washington Coll., Chestertown, Md., 1942; MS, George Washington U., 1973. Served to rear admiral USN, 1942-73, served in ETO, Korea, Vietnam, Pacific, other locations, 1942-73, ret., 1973; supt., prof. Tex. Maritime Coll.-Tex. A&M U., Galveston, 1973-78; v.p. Sealcraft Ops., Inc., Galveston, 1978-83; dir. tng. Tidewater Marine Svcs. Assn., New Orleans, 1983-84; pres. various cos. Houston, 1984-86; mng. dir. Grand Hotel, Houston, 1986-87; exec. asst. to CEO Taylor Energy Co., New Orleans, 1988-97; exec. dir. Patrick F. Taylor Found, New Orleans, 1988-97, sr. cons., from 1997. Cons. Soc. Marine Cons., New Orleans, 1986-88; chmn. Galveston County Pvt. Industry Coun., 1980-82; chmn. bd. dirs. Gulf Coast Coun. Fgn. Affairs, Galveston, 1979-82; asst. in devel. of world's 1st nuclear radiation course after Bikini Atom Bomb test at Navy Dept.; trustee Patrick F. Taylor Found., 1997—. Contbr. articles, papers to profl. publs. Decorated 2 Legion of Merit medals, Bronze Star medal, Combat V medal. Mem. Navy League of U.S. (bd. dirs. New Orleans coun.), Coun. Am. Master Mariners, La. Sheriffs Assn., Ret. Officers Assn., Pelican Club Galveston, Rotary (pres. Galveston chpt. 1983), Lions Internat., Am. Legion, Lambda Chi Alpha (Hall of Fame 1995). Republican. Methodist. Avocations: reading, maps and charts, travel. Home: Slidell, La. Died Feb. 26, 2002.

SMITH, JOYCE CAMILLE, elementary education educator; b. Houston, Nov. 28, 1940; d. Jack William and Aline Doris (Hays) Langerhans; m. Harold Wayne Smith, Dec. 30, 1961; children: Kenneth, DeWayne. BFA, U. Tex., 1962; MEd, Xavier U., 1977. Cert. secondary educator, elem. educator, adminstr. Elem. educator Houston Ind. Schs., 1965-67; tchr. 5th grade N.W. Local Schs., Cin., 1967-89, tchr. 6th grade, 1989—. Drama dir. N.W. Local Schs., Cin., 1980-82, Winton Woods City Schs., Cin., 1982-83, sch. bd. adv. coun., 1977-79; entrepreneur Weddings Unlimited, Inc. Author: (with others) Zoo Educational Curriculum. Charter pres. Ohio Jaycee Women, 1970s, nat. v.p., 1973-74. Recipient Golden Apple Achiever award, 1993; named one of Outstanding Young Women of Am., 1970s. Mem. NEA (congrl. contact team, 1990—), ASCD, N.W. Assn. Educators (v.p., pres. 1988-90), Ohio Edn. Assn., Phi Delta Kappa. Methodist. Avocations: photography, gardening, theatre. Home: 11355 Kenshire Dr Cincinnati OH 45240-2351 Office: Northwest Local Schools 3240 Banning Rd Cincinnati OH 45239-5207

SMITH, JUDITH ANN, academic administrator; b. Springfield, Mo., Jan. 1, 1950; d. Harley Jr. and Barbara Jean (Anderson) Cozad; m. Robert Eugene Smith, July 11, 1969. BS in Edn., S.W. Mo. State U., 1973, MA in English, 1976. Cert. tchr. (life), Mo. Tchr. R-12 Schs., Springfield, 1973-83; program/communications mgr. Performing Arts Ctr. Trust, Tulsa, 1983-84; gen. mgr. Springfield Symphony Assn., 1984-86; assoc. dir. devel., dir. planning giving S.W. Mo. State U., 1986-89, dir. devel. alumni rels., 1989—. Dir. Summerscape (gifted program), Springfield, 1980-82; mem. NCAA fiscal integrity com. S.W. Mo. State U., 1994-96. Vol. Springfield Symphony Guild, 1986—88; vol. fundraising advisor First Night, Springfield, 1993—99; appointee Greene County Hist. Sites Bd., 1994—, chair, 1995—96; mem. cmty. task force Arts and Heritage Collaborative, 1997—98; bd. dirs. Springfield Area Arts Coun., 1995—2001, pres., 2000—01; bd. dirs. Discovery Ctr. of Springfield, 1994—99; mem. Cmty. Cultural Plan, 1995—96; co-founder Assn. Vogue Picture Record Collectors, 1998. Named Outstanding Young Educator Springfield Jaycees, 1976, Mo. Jaycees, 1977. Mem. Coun. for Advancement and Support of Edn. (com. on women and minorities 1988-90, Merit and Excellence awards 1988, 89, 90), Leadership Springfield Alumni Assn., PEO, Rotary, Delta Kappa Gamma (past chpt. officer). Office: SW Mo State U 901 S National Ave Springfield MO 65804-0088 Personal E-mail: voguejudi@mchsi.net. Business E-Mail: jas234T@smsu.edu.

SMITH, JUDITH DAY, early childhood educator; b. Birmingham, Ala., Feb. 7, 1949; d. Robert Henry and Margaret Ann (Moulton) Day; m. Richard Monroe Smith, Aug. 22, 1970; 1 child, Wendy Elaine. BA in English, Jacksonville State U., 1971, MS in Edn., 1978. Cert. early childhood edn., elem. edn., lay speaker United Meth. Ch. Kindergarten tchr., dir. St. Mark United Meth. Ch., Anniston, Ala., 1973—78; kindergarten tchr. The Donoho Sch., Anniston, 1978—79, 1st grade tchr., 1979—80, tchr. 2nd grade, 1980—2001, lower sch. ann. advisor, 1987—94, primary dept. head, 1993—2003, lower sch. art and music tchr., 2001—03, tchr. 2d grade, 2003—. Adj. faculty Child Devl., Ayers State Tech. Coll., 2001-02, tchr. 2d grade, 2003-; Wee Deliver post office advisor, 1994-98; applicant Tchr.-in-Space NASA, Washington, 1984-85; conducted primary tchrs.' seminar, Kenya, 1996; participant field test CERES Astronomy Edn., 1998-99. Mem. Anniston Mus. Nat. History, Mus. League; vol. Boy Scouts Am. Recipient Golden Apple award Ala. Power and WJSU-TV, 1994; nominee Outstanding Educator for 1996, Women Committed to Excellence, sponsored by Cottaquilla Coun. of Girl Scouts. Mem. Alpha Delta Kappa (Lambda chpt. pres. 1998-2000). Republican. Methodist. Avocations: sewing, writing, drawing, computer programming, reading. Home: 3905 Cloverdale Rd Anniston AL 36207-7014 Office: The Donoho Sch 2501 Henry Rd Anniston AL 36207-6399

SMITH, JUNE BURLINGAME, English educator; b. Barrington, NJ, June 1, 1935; d. Leslie Grant and Esther (Bellini) Burlingame; m. Gregory Lloyd Smith, July 6, 1963; children: Gilia Cobb Burlingame Smith, Cyrus Comstock. BA, Reed Coll., 1956; MS, Ind. U., 1959; MA, Calif. State U., Dominquez Hills, 1986. Sec. to dean Reed Coll., 1956-57; residence hall supr. Ind. U., 1957-59; buyer Macy's Calif., 1959-63; residence hall supr. U. Wash., 1963, interviewer Tchr. Placement Bur., 1964; music tchr. Chinook Jr. High Sch., Bellevue, Wash., 1964-68; pvt. practice music tchr., 1971-83; gifted grant coord. South Shores/CSUDH Magnet Sch., 1981; tchr. cons. L.A. Unified Sch. Dist., 1981-82; prof. English LA CC, Harbor Coll., Wilmington, Calif., 1989—; sexual harrasment officer Harbor Coll., Wilmington, Calif., 1991-92, pres. acad. senate, 1997—2002, staff devel. coord., 2001—02. Chair Sex Equity Commn., L.A. Unified Sch. Dist., 1988-91; bd. dirs. Harbor Inter Faith Shelter, 1994—; chair San Pedro Coordinated Plan Com. for the Port of L.A.; mem., parliamentarian Coastal San Pedro Neighborhood Coun. Mem. AAUW (pres. San Pedro, Calif. br. 1989-90, mem. task force Initiative for Equity in Edn. 1991-95), Am. Acad. Poets, Phi Kappa Phi,. Democrat. Home: 3915 S Carolina St San Pedro CA 90731-7115 Office: LA Community Coll Harbor 1111 Figueroa Pl Wilmington CA 90744-2311

SMITH, JUNE ELLEN, secondary and special education educator; b. Wilmington, Del., Aug. 20, 1942; d. Samuel Medford and Audrey Iona (Yunt) S. AA, Wesley Coll., 1962; BS, Del. State Coll., 1973, MEd, 1988. Cert. spl. edn., phys. edn., health edn., drivers edn. tchr., Del. Child care counselor State of Del., Wilmington, 1970-73; phys. edn. tchr. Cath. Diocese, Elkton, Md., 1973-75, Wilmington, Del., 1973-75; occupational/recreational therapist St. Francis Hosp., Wilmington, Del., 1975-78; spl. edn. tchr. Christina Sch. Dist., Newark, Del., 1978—. Head coach Girls H.S. Athletics, Newark, Del., 1980-91; tutor Learning Ctr., Newark, 1991; presenter in field. Coord. Cmty. Watch-Collins Park, New Castle, Del., 1977, 78; bd. dirs. Girls Little League Softball, New Castle, 1972-81; mem. McDonald's LPGA Championship; mem. vol. corps Tournament Sponsors Assn. Vol. Network Internat. Mem. NEA, Del. Edn. Assn., Coun. for Exceptional Children (presenter state conf. 1990), Learning Disabilities Assn. Am. (presenter internat. conf. 1990), Dupont Country Club, Lions (treas. Capital Trail club 1990-94, pres. 1995—), McDonalds LPGA Championship, Tournament Sponsors Assn. Vol. Network Internat., LPGA Tournament Sponsors Assn. (vol. corps). Methodist. Avocations: boating, fishing, camping, tennis, golf. Home: 1127 Elderon Dr Wilmington DE 19808-1922

SMITH, JUNE SYLVIA KOLBE, artist, educator; b. Chgo., June 8, 1926; d. Clarence William and Marie Wilma Colby; m. Harold Eugene Reed, Sept. 23, 1947 (div. June 1948); m. Joseph Patric Smith, June 7, 1951; children: Donna Kaye, Craig Douglas. AA, UCLA, 1948; student, Occidental Coll., 1961, Am. Inst. Fine Arts, 1962. Artist Biltmore Hotel, L.A., 1966-78; docent, instr. pub. rels. San Gabriel (Calif.) Fine Arts Assn., 1997—; instr. Michael's Arts & Crafts, Pasadena, Glendale, Monrovia, Calif., 1998—99, 2001—02. Represented in permanent collections Millard Sheets Gallery, one-woman shows include San Gabriel Fine Arts, 1991; contbr. New Voices in American Poetry, 1979. Public rels. St. James Ch., S. Pasadena, 1991-99. Recipient 2d pl. Santa Paula Art C.C., 1963, 2d pl. Highland Park Art Assn., 1968. Mem. Calif. Art Club. Democrat. Episcopalian. Avocations: rollerskating, gardening. Home: 3129 Chadwick Dr Los Angeles CA 90032 Office: San Gabriel Fine Arts Assn Mission and Santa Anita San Gabriel CA 90032

SMITH, KAREN MARIE, middle school educator; b. Jersey City, Sept. 23, 1950; d. George A. and Marie M. (Sahr) Wolfstirn; m. Donald W. Smith, Jan. 8, 1972; children: Susan Marie, Sean Michael. BA, William Paterson. 2nd & 3rd grade tchr. Our Lady Queen of Peace, Maywood, N.J., 1972-77; 6th, 7th, 8th grade tchr. St. Peter's Acad., River Edge, N.J., 1985-94; 6th grade tchr. South Orange (N.J.) Middle Sch., 1994—. Girl scout leader Bergen County, N.J., 1983-94 (named Outstanding leader 1990, Honor pin, 1993). Mem. NEA, N.J. Edn. Assn., Nat. Coun. Tchrs. English, Nat. Coun. Tchrs. Math., South Orange/Maplewood Edn. Assn., Irish Dance Tchrs. N.Am. (reg. dir.). Roman Catholic. Avocations: computers, crafts, reading, camping, hiking. Home: 206 Rod Cir Middletown MD 21769-7826

SMITH, KATHERYN JEANETTE, music educator; b. Siloam Springs, Ark., July 6, 1944; d. Charlie H. and Victoria Virginia (Jameson) Porter; m. Curtis Barth Smith, Jan. 10, 1975; 1 child, Melody Jeanette. B in Music Edn., So. Nazarene U., 1966; M in Music Edn., Kent (Ohio) State U., 1970. Gen. music tchr. Duncan (Okla.) Jr. H.S., 1966-68; elem. music tchr. Akron (Ohio) Pub. Schs., 1971-72; music prof. MidAm. Nazarene U., Olathe, Kans., 1972—. Clinician Lillenas Music Confs., Olathe, Kans., 1994, 96, 97. Keyboard accompanist Coll. Ch. of the Nazarene, 1973—. Mem. Music Educators Nat. Conf., Music Tchrs. Nat. Assn., MidAm. Nazarene Univ. Women's Aux. (chairperson 1973-74, 94-98). Avocation: whale collection. Office: MidAm Nazarene Univ 2030 E College Way Olathe KS 66062-1831 E-mail: ksmith@mnu.edu.

SMITH, KATHLEEN ANN, mathematics educator; BA in Math., U. Dallas, 1970; MS in Math., U. Ctrl. Ark., 1975. Cert. secondary prin., elem. prin. and tchr., secondary math., phys. sci. tchr., Ark. Tchr. math. and sci. Sacred Heart H.S., Morrilton, Ark., 1970-73, West Jr. H.S., West Memphis, Ark., 1973, Mt. St. Mary Acad., Little Rock, 1974, 75-76, St. Joseph Sch., Conway, Ark., 1976-90, asst. prin., 1981-84, prin., 1986-90; instr. math. U. Ctrl. Ark., Conway, 1990-2000; tchr. math. Sacred Heart Cath. Sch., Morrilton, 2000—. Adj. prof. math. Hendrix Coll., Conway, 1990-93. Named Tchr. of Yr., St. Joseph Sch., 1979. Mem. Nat. Coun. Tchrs. Math., Ark. Coun. Tchrs. Math. Roman Catholic. Avocations: needlework, camping.

SMITH, KATHLEEN DANA, principal, consultant; b. Fargo, N.D., June 24, 1947; d. Dana Eugene and Georgia Caroline (Cook) S.; m. Thomas Donald Gash, June 7, 1980; children: Caroline, Kathryn. BA in Polit. Sci. and History, U. Denver, 1969, MA in Counseling and Guidance, 1970; EdD in Leadership and Mgmt., U. No. Colo., 1985. Cert. tchr., Colo.; lic. counselor, Colo. Tchr., counselor Denver Pub. Schs.-East H.S., 1969-71; counselor, tchr. Cherry Creek Schs.-Cherry Creek H.S., Englewood, Colo., 1971-77, chair counseling dept., 1977-80, asst. to prin., 1980-81, adminstrv. asst. to dep. supt., 1982-83, dir. of pupil svcs., 1983-88; asst. prin. Cherry Creek Schs./Horizon Mid. Sch., Aurora, Colo., 1988-89, prin., 1989-93, Cherry Creek H.S., Englewood, Colo., 1993—. Presenter in field; cons. in field; mem. faculty U. Phoenix, Denver, 1988-94. Mem. Gov.'s Task Force for Better Air, Denver, 1984-86; mem., various chairs Jr. League Denver, 1983—; bd. dirs. Cerebral Palsy Ctr., Denver, 1991-93; mem. adv. com. Colo. Bd. Land Commrs., 1992-94. Harvard U. fellow, 1989; Colo. Dept. of Edn. grantee, 1987. Fellow Inst. for Devel. Ednl. Activities; mem. ASCD, Nat. Assn. Secondary Sch. Prins., Am. Assn. Sch. Adminstrs., Phi Delta Kappa. Roman Catholic. Avocations: reading, gardening, skiing, family, volunteer activities. Office: Cherry Creek High Sch 9300 E Union Ave Englewood CO 80111-1395

SMITH, KATHY ANN, music educator; b. Syracuse, N.Y., July 2, 1953; d. Clifford Wayne Hirsh and Helen Erdine (Schlie) Warner; m. Kevin Joseph Smith, July 31, 1993. MusB magna cum laude, Crane Sch. of Music, Potsdam, N.Y., 1975; MS in Edn., Elmira Coll., 1980; Cert. of Advanced Study, SUNY-Cortland, 1993. Cert. music educator, sch. dist. adminstr., NY. Music tchr. Vernon Verona (N.Y.) Sherrill Ctrl. Sch., 1975—, music dept. chairperson, 1986-98. Pvt. instr. studio lessons, Oneida, N.Y., 1975—, jazzband dir., 2000—; facilitator for music boosters club and middle sch. panel tchrs. orgn., Vernon, 1991—; mem. Colgate Symphony Orch., 1992; chairperson Sch. Improvement Project, Verona, 1992-94. Recipient Profl. Recognition award Vernon Verona Sherrill Ctrl. Schs., 1990, 92. Mem. ASCD, N.Y. State Sch. of Music Assn., N.Y. State Coun. Adminstrs. in Music Edn., Music Educators Nat. Conf., N.Y. State Band Dirs. Assn., Madison County Music Educators Assn. (v.p., pres. 1998—). Democrat. Roman Catholic. Avocations: reading, art, music, camping, baseball. Office: Vernon Verona Sherril Ctrl Schs Rte 31 Verona NY 13478 E-mail: katsmith@america.net., ksmith@vvs-csd-high.moric.org.

SMITH, KENNETH ALAN, chemical engineer, educator; b. Winthrop, Mass., Nov. 28, 1936; s. James Edward and Alice Gertrude (Walters) S.; m. Ambia Marie Olsson, Oct. 14, 1961; children: Kirsten Heather, Edward Eric, Andrew Ian Beaumont, Thurston Garrett. S.B., MIT, 1958, S.M., 1959, Sc.D., 1962; postgrad., Cambridge (Eng.) U., 1964-65. Asst. prof. chem. engring. MIT, 1961-67, assoc. prof., 1967-71, prof., 1971—, Edwin R. Gilliland prof. chem. engring., 1989—, acting head dept., 1976-77, assoc. provost, 1980-81, assoc. provost, v.p. rsch., 1981-91, dir. Whitaker Coll. Health Sci. and Tech., 1989-91. Cons. chem. and oil cos. NSF fellow, 1964-65, Overseas fellow, Churchill Coll., (Eng.), 1993, 01. Mem. Am. Inst. Chem. Engrs., Nat. Acad. Engring., Am. Chem. Soc., AAAS, Sigma Xi, Phi Lambda Upsilon, Tau Beta Pi. Episcopalian. Home: 32 School St Manchester MA 01944-1336 Office: MIT Bldg 66-540 Cambridge MA 02139

SMITH, LAVERNE BYRD, educational association administrator; b. Richmond, Va., Dec. 14, 1927; d. Charles Edward and Lena (Dickens) Byrd; m. Lewis Jr. Smith, Nov. 25, 1948. BA, Va. Union U., 1948; MS, Va. State U., 1964; PhD, U. Md., 1985. Cert. elem. and secondary tchr., Va. Tchr. Richmond (Va.) Pub. Schs., 1948-64; asst. prof. Va. State Coll., Ettrick, Va., 1964-67; asst. prof. edn., dir. Reading Ctr. Va. Union U., Richmond, 1967-74; state supr. reading and lang. devel. Va. Dept. Edn., Richmond, 1974-90, ret., 1990; acad. skills coord. Va. Union U., Richmond, 1991-93; free lance writer, 1994—. Bd. dirs. J. Sgt. Reynolds C.C. Author; The Blessed Gentle Beast, 1997; compiling author: First Baptist Church South Richmond: A Historical Chronology 1821-1992, 1992, Traveling On...First Baptist, South Richmond Today and The First Fifty Years 1821-1871, vol. I, 1994, reprinted 1996, Traveling On...First Baptist, South Richmond: The 133 Year Journey After the Civil War 1865-1998, vol. II, 1999; contbr. articles, poems, stories. to profl. jours. Historian First Bapt. Ch., So. Richmond, 1991—. Recipient Gov. award for 42 years of Svc. to Public Edn. in Va., 1990, Outstanding Educators of Am., 1974, Outstanding Woman in Comm. Richmond, Va. 1995. Mem. ASCD, NAACP, Am. Ednl. Rsch. Assn., Richmond Area Reading Assn. (past pres.), Va. Reading Assn. (past pres.-elect, Literacy award), Internat. Reading Assn., Nat. Polit. Caucus of Black Women, Bapt. Hist. Soc., Continental Soc., Inc., Alpha Kappa Alpha, Phi Delta Kappa (past chpt. pres.).

SMITH, LEWIS, academic administrator, educator; b. Muncie, Ind., Jan. 18, 1938; s. Thurman Lewis and Dorothy Ann (Dennis) S.; m. Suzanne F. Metcalfe; children: Lauren Kay, Raymond Bradley. AB, Ind. U., 1959, PhD, 1964. Asst. embryologist Argonne (Ill.) Nat. Lab., 1964-67, assoc. biologist, 1967-69; assoc. prof. Purdue U., West Lafayette, Ind., 1969-73, prof. biology, 1973-87, assoc. head dept. biol. scis., 1979-80, head dept., 1980-87; prof. dept. devel. and cell. U. Calif., Irvine, 1987-94, dean Sch. Biol. Scis., 1987-90, exec. vice chancellor, 1990-94; pres. U. of Nebr., 1994—. Instr. embryology Woods Hole (Mass.) Marine Biology Lab., 1972-74, mem. Space Sci. Bd., Washington, 1984-91; chmn. Space Biology and Medicine, space sci. bd., 1986-91; cell biology study sect. NIH, Bethesda, Md., 1971-75; chmn., 1977-79, bd. sci. counselors Nat. Inst. Child Health and Human Devel., 1990-95, chmn. 1992-95; space biology peer rev. bd. AIBS, 1980-85. Active Bus. Higher Edn. Forum, 2001; bd. dirs. Nebr. Arts Coun., Nebr., Nebr. Indsl. Competitiveness Alliance. Fellow Guggenheim, 1987; Sci. Freedom and Responsibility award, AAAS, 2002. Mem. AAAS (Sci. Freedom and Responsibility award 2002), Am. Soc. Biochemistry and Molecular Biology, Internat. Soc. for Devel. Biology, Soc. for Devel. Biology, Am. Soc. Cell Biology, Am. Soc. for Microbiology. Home: 2524 Wilderness Ridge Cir Lincoln NE 68512 Office: 3835 Holdrege St Lincoln NE 68583-0745

SMITH, LINDA, middle school educator; b. Barnesville, Ga., July 15, 1949; d. Marion (Walton) S. BS, Morris Brown Coll., 1970; Ms, Fort Valley State Coll., 1976. Cert. middle sch., instr. supr., Ga. Instrnl. lead tchr. Lamar County Sch. System, Barnesville, Ga., 1970—. Mem. Staff Devel. Coun. and Tchr. Instructional Support, Barnesville. V.p. Vogue, Lamar County. Named Tchr. of Yr. Lamar County Sch. System, 1986-87, Career Woman of Yr., 1993. Mem. NEA, Ga. Assn. Educators, Ga. Coun. Tchrs. of English, Ga. Sci. Tchrs. Assn., Lamar County Assn. Educators, Phi Delta Kappa. Democrat. Baptist. Avocations: reading, crossword puzzles, gardening. Home: 172 Walton Rd Barnesville GA 30204-4206 Office: Lamar County Middle Sch 3 Trojan Way Barnesville GA 30204-1544

SMITH, LINDA S. music educator, musician; b. Topeka, Kans., Oct. 8, 1955; d. Wilbur Porter and Esther Nadine (Faith) Smith. MusB, Oklahoma City U., 1977; MusM, Eastman Sch. Music, 1979; postgrad., EAstman Sch. Music, 1979—81; degree preparatoire superieur, Conservatoire Nat. de Region, Paris, 1982. Organist Calvary Bapt. Ch., Topeka, 1965—73, Ctrl. Presbyn. Ch., Oklahoma City, 1973—77, 1st Reformed Ch., Rochester, NY, 1977—81, St. Michael's Ch., Paris, 1981—83, West Side Christian Ch., Topeka, 1983—; dir. music Accent Acad., Topeka, 1997—99. CEO, pres., founder Genesis Music Found., Inc., 1999—. Editor: Kids Music Jour., 1999—, composer more than 400 songs. Piano tchr. Salvation Army, Topeka, 1999. Mem.: Music Tchrs. Nat. Assn., N.E. Kans. Music Tchrs. Assn., Topeka Music Tchrs. Assn. (v.p. 2000—, publicist 1998—99, sec. 1999—2000, pres. 2001—). Home: 2416 SE Monroe Topeka KS 66605 E-mail: Smithlinmu@aol.com.

SMITH, LOIS COLSTON, secondary school educator, educator; b. Edgewater, Ala., Aug. 3, 1919; d. Roy Minnie and Rebecca (Hayes) Colston; children: Linnie Ree Colston Carter, Lois Louise Colston Smith, Jessie Mae Colston Smith, Johnniza Colston Purifoy, Johnny Colston, Dorothy Dean Colston Cottingham, Lillian Dolly B. Colston Tarver. BS, A&M U., 1939; MA, N.Y.U., 1957. Vocat. Home Econ. Edn. 3rd and 4th grade tchr., Sulligent, Ala., 1957-61; elem. prin. Millport, Ala., 1962-67; 11th grade sci. and social studies tchr. Vernon, Ala., 1967-70; 7th-9th grade gen. vocat. home econ. tchr. Tuscaloosa, Ala., 1970-80; 7th grade gen. and voca. home econ. tchr., 1980-92; ret., 1995. Chmn. Voters registration, Tuscaloosa, Ala., 1980; troop leader Girl Scouts Am., Tuscaloosa, Ala., 1967-92; mem. bd. dirs. Shelter State Community Coll. Wellness Coun., 1993. Recipient Tombigbee Girl Scout 15 yr. svc. pin, Cert. Appreciation, Valuable Svc. award, Girl Scouts; named Zeta of Yr., Beta Eta Zeta chpt., Stillman Coll., 1983, Golden Cert. of Appreciation and Admiration Ala. A&M U., Huntsville, 1993. Mem. Ala. Edn. Assn., NEA, Order of Eastern Star, Ala. Vocat. Assn., AAUW, Beta Eta Zeta. Democrat. Baptist. Avocations: sewing, cooking, crocheting, fishing, gardening, ceramics, singing. Home: 3238 18th Pl Tuscaloosa AL 35401-4102

SMITH, LORAN BRADFORD, education educator; b. Medford, Mass., July 23, 1946; s. Gordon T. and Edith A. S. BA, Salem State Coll., 1968; MA, Okla. State U., 1971; PhD, U. Nebr., 1980. Instr. Black Hills State Coll., Spearfish, S.D., 1971-74, Augustana Coll., Sioux Falls, S.D., 1974-77; asst. prof. Mo. So. State Coll., Joplin, 1980-82, Washburn U., Topeka, Kans., 1982-86, assoc. prof., 1988-92; grad. faculty U. Kans., Lawrence, 1988-89; prof. Washburn U., 1992—. Election analyst KSNT-TV, Topeka, 1984-92. Contbr. articles to profl. jours. Chair pilot task force City of Topeka, 1983-84, mem. charter rev. com., 1999; chair Univ. Coun.; mem. coll. faculty coun., chair CAC curriculum com., social sci. divsn. Mem. Am. Polit. Sci. Assn., Am. Soc. Pub. Adminstrs. (Kans. chpt. v.p. 1985-87, pres. 1987-88), Urban Affairs Assn., Kansas Delta Alumni Corp., Sigma Phi Epsilon (Disting. Alumnus award 1997). Home: 4301 SW 15th St Apt 309 Topeka KS 66604-4311 Office: Washburn U 1700 SW College Ave Topeka KS 66621-0001

SMITH, MARCIA JEANNE, secondary school educator; b. Carthage, N.Y., Apr. 27, 1935; d. Herman Leon and Vera Magdelena (Weir) Zahn; div.; 1 child, Patrick Brian. BA, Syracuse U., 1958; MA, Middlebury Coll., 1962. Cert. in secondary edn./English. Tchr. English, South Jefferson Ctrl. H.S., Adams, N.Y., 1958-98; asst. prof. extension and evening div. Jefferson C.C., Watertown, N.Y., 1967-69; ret., 1998. Adj. instr. project advance Syracuse U., 1984-91, mem. cabinet, 1989-91. Vol. Samaritan Med. Ctr., Watertown, NY. Mem. N.Y. State English Council (named High Sch. Tchr. of Excellence 1989), Nat. Council Tchrs. English, AAUW, Coll. Women's Club of Jefferson County (corr. sec. 1989-90), Jefferson County Hist. Soc., Pi Lambda Theta, Alpha Delta Kappa. Avocations: gardening (flowers), ceramics, travel, reading. Home: 26836 Ridge Rd Watertown NY 13601-5401

SMITH, MARILYN NOELTNER, retired science educator; b. LA, Feb. 14, 1933; d. Clarence Frederick and Gertrude Bertha (Smith) Noeltner; m. Edward Christopher Smith, Sept. 11, 1971 (dec. Oct. 1999). BA, Marymount Coll., 1957; MA, U. Notre Dame, 1966; MS, Boston Coll., 1969. Cert. tchr.; cert. community coll. tchr., Calif.; cert. adminstr., Calif. Tchr., chmn. sci. dept. Marymount High Sch., Santa Barbara, Calif., 1954-57, LA, 1957-58, 69-79, tchr., chmn. sci. and math. depts. Palos Verdes, Calif., 1959-69; tchr., chmn. math. dept. Corvallis High Sch., Studio City, Calif., 1958-59; instr. tchr. tng. Marymount-Loyola U., LA, 1965-71, instr. freshman interdisciplinary program, 1970-71; tchr. math. Santa Monica (Calif.) HS, 1971-72; instr. math., chemistry, physics Santa Monica Coll., 1971—79; tchr. sci. Beverly Vista Sch., Beverly Hills, Calif., 1972—2002; ret., 2002. Cons. Calif. State Sci. Framework Revision Com., LA, 1975; chmn. NASA Youth Sci. Congress, Pasadena, Calif., 1968-69, Hawaii, 1969-70; participant NASA Educators Conf. Jupiter Mission, Ames Research, San Francisco, 1973, NASA Educators Conf. Viking-Mars Ames Project, San Francisco, 1976-77, NASA Landsat Conf., Edward's AFB, Calif., 1978, NASA Uranus Mission, Pasadena, Calif., 1986, NASA Uranus-Voyager Mission, Pasadena, 1989, NASA Neptune-Voyager Mission, Pasadena, 1989; test scoring com. Calif. Learning Assessment System, U. Santa Barbara, 1993, writing com. Trainers Manual, 1993. Author books and computer progs. including NASA Voyager-Uranus Sci. Symposium for Educators, 1989, NASA Voyager 2 Neptune Encounter Conf., 1989, others; contbr. articles to profl. jours. Sponsor Social Svc. Club, Palos Verdes, 1959-69, moderator, sponsor ARC Youth Svc. Chmn., Beverly Hills, 1974-77, judge L.A. County Sci. Fair, 1969—, blue ribbon com. NATAS, 1971—; bd. dirs. Children First, Beverly Hills, 1990-91; vol. sch. initiative, Beverly Hills, 1989-90; steering com. on tech. Beverly Vista Sch., 1994-95; del. Congress of Am. Women Scientists to Cuba, People to People Amb. Program, 2001; active U. Notre Dame Badin Guild, 1989—. Recipient Commendation in Teaching cert. Am. Soc. Microbiology, 1962, Salute to Edn. award So. Calif. Industry Edn. Council, 1962, Outstanding Teaching citation Cons. Engrs. Assn. Calif., 1967, Cert. Honor, Silver Plaque Westinghouse Sci. Talent Search, 1963-68, Tchr. award Ford-Future Scientists of Am., 1968, Biomed. award Com. Advance Sci. Tng., 1971, Outstanding Tchr. award LA County Sci. Fair Com., 1975-76, Contbns. to Youth Service citation ARC, 1976-77, Outstanding Tchr. award Kiwanis, Beverly Hills, 1987, NAST Pres'. award, 1990, Woman of Yr. award, 1990, cert. appreciation Profl. Leadership and Support for Advancing Sci. Edn. Calif. Dept. Edn., 1992-93, Outstanding Tchr. Gifted Students award Johns Hopkins U., 1999-2000. Mem. We. Assn. Schs. and Colls. (vis. com. 1968, writing com. 1969—), Assn. Advancement Biomed. Edn. (pres. 1970-71), 1st Internat. Sci. Tchrs. Conf. (presider, evaluator 1977), Nat. Sci. Tchrs. Assn. (presider, evaluator 1976, chmn. contributed papers com. 1977-78, presenter 1990), Beverly Hills Edn. Assn.(pres. faculty coun. 1980-81, 85-86, sch. rep. 1990—, Ann. WHO award 1995, 96), Chemist's Club, Calif. Statewide Math. Adv. Com., So. Calif. Industry Edn. Council, Calif. Assn. Chemistry Tchrs. (program chmn. 1960), Calif. Sci. Tchrs. Assn., Am. Chem. Soc., AAAS, South Bay Math. League (sec. 1967-68, pres. 1968-69, 72, 1969-70), Calif. Math. Council, Nat. Assn. Biology Tchrs., U. Notre Dame Sorin Soc. Republican. Roman Catholic. Avocations: stone age architecture, Gaelic, Irish fisheries population samplings and contributions to data bank. Home: 3934 Sapphire Dr Encino CA 91436-3635 Office: Beverly Vista Sch 200 S Elm Dr Beverly Hills CA 90212-4011

SMITH, MARK ANTHONY, biochemist, educator; b. Leicester, Eng., Aug. 15, 1965; came to U.S., 1992; s. John and Rita Joyce (Haywood) S. BSc with honors, Durham (U.K.) U., 1986; PhD, Nottingham (U.K.) U., 1990. Postdoctoral biochemist Sandoz Forschungsinstitut, Vienna, 1990-91, Karl Landsteiner rsch. fellow, 1991-92; rsch. assoc. Case Western Res. U., Cleve., 1992-94, instr. in biochemistry, 1994-95, asst. prof., 1995—99, assoc. prof., 1999—2002, prof., 2002—. Cons. StressGen Biotechs. Corp., Victoria, B.C., 1999, Panacea Pharms., Potomac, 2000—, Prion Devel. Labs., Vernon Hills, 2001—, Voyager Pharmacies, Raleigh, NC, 2001—; chief exec. cons. World Events Forum, Chgo., 2001—. Editor Biomed. Jour., 1994-95; guest editor Molecular Chemistry Neuropathology; mem. editl. bd. Internat. Jour. Exptl. Pathology; contbr. articles to profl. jours.; rsch. findings presented on WQHS-TV 61 sta. Dalland fellow Am. Philos. Soc., 1995; recipient Ruth Salta Investigator award, 1995, Young Scientist Lectr. award Internat. Soc. Neurochem., Nathan Shock New Investigator award Gerontol. Soc. Am. Mem. AAAS, Am. Assn. Neuropathology, Microscopic Soc. Northeast Ohio (pres. elect 1997—), N.Y. Acad. Scis., Internat. Soc. Neurochemistry. Avocations: golf, soccer, music, current affairs. Home: 2084 W 26th St Cleveland OH 44113-4053 Office: Case Western Res U Inst Pathology 2085 Adelbert Rd Cleveland OH 44106-2622

SMITH, MARSHALL SAVIDGE, foundation executive; b. East Orange, NJ, Sept. 16, 1937; s. Marshall Parsons and Ann Eileen (Zulauf) S.; m. Carol Goodspeed, June 25, 1960 (div. Aug. 1962); m. Louise Nixon Claiborn, Aug. 1964; children: Adam, Jennifer, Matthew, Megan. AB, Harvard U., 1960, EdM, 1963, EdD, 1970. Systems analyst and computer programmer Raytheon Corp., Andover, Mass., 1959-62; instr., assoc. prof. Harvard U., Cambridge, Mass., 1966-76; asst., assoc. dir. Nat. Inst. Edn., Washington, 1973-76; asst. commr. edn. HEW, Washington, 1976-79, chief of staff to U.S. Dept. Edn. sec., 1980; prof. U. Wis., Madison, 1980-86, Stanford (Calif.) U., 1986—2003, dean Sch. Edn., 1986-94; under-sec. edn. U.S. Dept. Edn., 1993-2000, acting dep. sec. edn., 1996-2000; program dir. Hewlett Found., 2001—. Task force, chmn. Clinton Presdl. Transition Team, 1992-93; chmn. PEW Forum on Ednl. Reform; chmn. bd. internat. com. studies in edn. NAS, 1992-93. Author: The General Inquirer, 1967, Inequality, 1972; contbr. several articles to profl. jours, chpts. to books. Pres. Madison West Hockey Assn., 1982-84. Mem. Am. Ednl. Rsch. Assn. (chmn. orgn. instl. affiliates 1985-86), Nat. Acad. Edn. Democrat. Avocations: environmental issues, philanthropy. Home: 1256 Forest Ave Palo Alto CA 94301 Office: Wm & Flora Hewlett Found Menlo Park CA

SMITH, MARTHA VIRGINIA BARNES, retired elementary school educator; b. Camden, Ark., Oct. 12, 1940; d. William Victor and Lillian Louise (Givens) Barnes; m. Basil Loren Smith, Oct. 11, 1975; children: Jennifer Frost, Sean Barnes. BS in Edn., Ouachita Bapt. U., 1963; postgrad., Auburn U., 1974, Henderson State U., 1975. Cert. tchr., Mo. 2d and 1st grade tchr. Brevard County Schs., Titusville and Cocoa, Fla., 1963-65, 69-70; 1st grade tchr. Lakeside Sch. Dist., Hot Springs, Ark., 1965-66, Harmony Grove Sch., Camden, 1972-76; 1st and 5th grade tchr. Cumberland County Schs., Fayetteville, N.C., 1966-69; kindergarten tchr. Pulaski County Schs., Ft. Leonard Wood, Mo., 1970-72; 3d grade tchr. Mountain Grove (Mo.) Schs., 1976-99; ret., 1999. Chmn. career ladder com. Mountain Grove Dist., 1991-99. Children's pastor 1st Bapt. Ch., Vanzant, Mo., 1984-88. Mem. NEA (pres.-elect Mountain Grove chpt. 1995-97, pres. Mountain Grove chpt. 1997-99), Kappa Kappa Iota. Avocation: antique and classic cars.

SMITH, MARY BETH, radiographic technology educator, musician; b. Newark, N.Y., Mar. 31, 1942; d. Francis and Ann Elizabeth (Kelly) S. BS, SUNY, Rochester, 1982; MS in Edn., U. Rochester, 1985. Cert. radiographic technician, Am. Registry of Radiographic Technicians. Radiographic tech. tchr. Clifton Springs (N.Y.) Hosp./Clinic, 1973-79; string instrument instr. various pvt. instns., Newark and Rochester, 1982—; profl. musician, 1982—. Sec./treas. Upstate String Band, Rochester, 1983-90; mem. music liturgy adv. bd. St. Michaels Ch., Newark, 1987—. Author: String Things for Little Fingers, 1994; composer/arranger (musical works) solo and orch. pieces for banjo, violin, and strings; musician (albums) A Banjo Yuletide & More Banjo Yuletide; contbr. articles to jours. and mags. Vol. ARC, Newark, 1980-90, Rochester Philharmonic Orch., 1994-95. Recipient Best Lady-Banjo champion U.S. Open Banjo Championships, 1988—. Mem. Fretted Instrument Guild Am., Am. Banjo Fraternity (exec. sec. 1991—), Suzuki Assn. Am., Wayne/Ontario County Arts Couns. (cons.), Sodus Bay and Arcadia Hist. Soc. (bd. dirs., music coord. 1992—), Finger Lakes Symphony Orch. (corr. sec. 1990—, pres. 2000, grant facilitator 1990—). Roman Catholic. Avocations: antiques, sailing, painting. Home and Office: 636 Pelis Rd Newark NY 14513-9014

SMITH, MARY FRANCES, school administrator; b. Ashland, Ky., Oct. 22, 1950; d. Charles Raymond and Lillian Avoline (Brown) Clinger; m. Robert David Smith, Dec. 29, 1969; children: Stephanie Allison, Christopher David. BA, U. Cen. Fla., 1972; MA, Nova U., 1982. Tchr. Ormond Beach (Fla.) Elem. Sch., 1973-84, tchr., administrv. asst., 1979-84; asst. prin. Spruce Creek Elem. Sch., Port Orange, Fla., 1984-89, Silver Sands Mid. Sch., Port Orange, 1989-91; prin. W.F. Burns Elem Sch., Oak Hill, Fla., 1991—. Adjudicator Fla. Bandmasters Assn., 1980—, Music USA, Fla.,1 989—. Sponsor, tchr. Seabreeze High Sch. Aux., Daytona Beach, Fla., 1970-91; sponsor Oak Hill area Girl Scouts U.S., 1991—; charter ptnr. Oak Hill area Boy Scouts Am., 1991—. Mary Smith Day proclaimed by City of Oak Hill, Fla., May 20, 1993. Mem. Nat. Assn. Elem. Sch. Prins., Fla. Assn. Sch. Adminstrs., Volusia Assn. Sch. Adminstrs., Fla. Bandmasters Assn., Port Orange/South Daytona C. of C. (chair edn. com. 1990-91), Phi Delta Kappa. Methodist. Avocations: dance, baton twirling, boating, reading. Home: 92 S Saint Andrews St Ormond Beach FL 32174 Office: WF Burns Elem Sch 160 Ridge Rd Oak Hill FL 32759-9423

SMITH, MARY LEX, victim's advocate; b. Helena, Mont., Dec. 12, 1942; d. Ralph Irvin and Alexandria Mary (Blain) S. BA, St. Mary Coll., Leavenworth, Kans., 1971; MPS, Loyola U., Chgo., 1981; MS in Adult Edn., Kans. State U., 1989. Joined Sisters of Charity of Leavenworth, 1960. Tchr. Cath. Elem. Schs., 1963-72; tchr. sci. Bishop Ward H.S., Kansas City, 1972-74; advisor, registrar St. Mary Coll., Leavenworth, Kans., 1974-76; admitting registrar St. Francis Hosp., Topeka, 1977-79; pastoral assoc. Holy Trinity Ch., Lenexa, Kans., 1980-86; cons. Diocesan Office Christian Formation, Kansas City, 1986-87; dir. catechumenate Inter Parish Catechumenate, Kansas City, 1987-89; pastoral assoc. Ch. of Holy Cross, Overland Park, Kans., 1989-95; advocate at ct. for domestic violence SAFE HOME Inc., Overland Park, 1995-99; coord. victim assistance program Wyandotte County Dist. Atty.'s Office, Kansas City, 1999—. Planning com. mem. Heartland Conf. Steering Com., Kansas City, 1990-95, Leadership Conf. Women Religious Workshops, Kansas City, 1984, 94. Presenter Liturgy Workshops, Archdiocese of Kansas City, 1980-95; contbr. articles to profl. jours. Mem. Kans. Orgn. for Victim Assistance, Domestic Violence Network, Archdiocesan Dirs. RCIA (chair 1981-86), Archdiocesan Liturgical Commn. (sec. 1980-87), Pax Christi USA, Kans. Victim Assistance Assn., Phi Kappa Phi. Avocations: reading, sewing, handcrafts. E-mail: msmith@wycokck.org., mlsmith62@hotmail.com.

SMITH, MARY SCOTT, elementary school educator, education educator; b. Fordyce, Ark., Sept. 16, 1926; d. Arthur and Jo Anna Scott; m. Joe Cephas Smith, Apr. 13, 1952; children: Marylyn Joe Anna Washington, Reginald Joseá. BS, Ark. Bapt. Coll., Little Rock, 1949; MA, U. Wis., Madison, 1952; postgrad., U. Ark., Fayetteville, 1966—70. Tchr. Childs' Sch. Dist., Banks, Ark., 1944—48; registrar Ark. Bapt. Coll., 1950—52, bus. mgr., 1952—54; tchr. Dallas County Tng. Sch., Fordyce, Ark., 1954—66, Little Rock Sch. Dist., 1966—86; asst. prof. edn. Ark. Bapt. Coll., 1986—93. Bd. dirs. Ark Tchrs. Credit Union, Little Rock, 1985—90. Mem.: Ark. Edn. Assn., Nat. Edn. Assn., Classroom Tchrs. Assn. (bldg. rep. 1974—80), Am. Retired Educator Assn. (chairperson 1997—), AAUW, Order of Eastern Star (state treas. 1979—, worthy matron), Fed. Womans' Club (pres. 1995—), Pi Lambda Theta, Zeta Phi Beta (Ouststanding Educator 1996). Democrat. Baptist. Avocations: reading, traveling, singing, crossword puzzles. Home: 2400 Howard St Little Rock AR 72206

SMITH, MELANIE MAXTED, secondary education educator; b. Galveston, Tex., Nov. 9, 1940; d. Aubrey Clement and Mary Lanier (Munds) Maxted; m. Jesse Daley Smith, Feb. 27, 1960; children: Stephanie (dec.), Laura, Ron. BA, Rice U., 1962; MA, Howard Payne U., 1969; postgrad., U. Tex., 1979. Tchr., chair English dept. Richland Springs (Tex.) Ind. Sch. Dist., 1964-95; now ret. Cons. Region XV Svc. Ctr., Tex., 1980—, Tex. Coun. of Tchrs. of English, 1993—. Contbr. articles to profl. publs. Bd. dirs. cmty./sch. theater, Richland Springs. Mem. Nat. Coun. Tchrs. English, Tex. Coun. Tchrs. English (cons.), Tex. Ednl. Theatre Assn. (sec. K-12, cons. creative drama 1985—, Secondary Sch. Theatre Tchr. of Yr. 1990). Episcopalian. Avocations: reading, grandchildren, sewing, fishing, travel.

SMITH, MERELYN ELIZABETH, elementary and middle school educator; b. Providence, June 30, 1957; d. Arnold Hobson and Frances Louise (Carpenter) S. BS, Gordon Coll., 1979; postgrad., U. N.H., 1990-93. Cert. elem., mid., and secondary tchr., Mass. 5th and 6th grade tchr. Glen Urquhart Sch., Beverly Farms, Mass., 1979-80, 4th and 5th grade tchr., 1980-81, 5th grade tchr., 1981-87, 6th to 9th grade math. and computer tchr., 1987—96, math. specialist and tchr., 1996—. Diagnostician, ednl. therapist Inst. for Learning and Devel., 1996; adj. prof. Gordon Coll., Mass., 1996—, U. N.H., Durham, 1996; presenter workshops in field. Leader Beverly (Mass.) Group Home Fellowship, 1982-2000; vacation Bible sch. tchr. North Shore Community Bapt. Ch., Beverly Farms, 1982-85. Recipient Vol. Svc. award Assn. Retarded Citizens, 1987, 95. Mem. Nat. Coun. Tchrs. Math., Assn. Tchrs. Math. in Mass., Assn. Tchrs. Math. in New Eng. Avocations: piano, hiking, cross country skiing, reading, sports. Office: Glen Urquhart Sch 74 Hart St Beverly MA 01915-2195

SMITH, MERILYN ROBERTA, art educator; b. Tolley, N.D., July 24, 1933; d. Robert Coleman and Mathilda Marie (Staael) S. BA, Concordia Coll., Minn., 1953; MA, State U. of Iowa, Iowa City, 1956, MFA, 1966. Tchr. Badger (Minn.) High Sch., 1954; instr. in art Valley City (N.D.) State Tchrs. Coll., 1957, 58, U. Wis., Oshkosh, 1967, asst. prof. art, 1969, assoc. prof., 1977-91, prof., 1991-93, prof. emeritus, 1993—; represented by Miriam Perlman Gallery, Chgo. Counselor Luth. Student Ctr., U. Iowa, 1959-65, rsch. asst. in printmaking, 1960-65; owner, dir. James House Gallery, Oshkosh, 1972-77; dir. Allen Priebe Gallery, U. Wis., Oshkosh, 1975. Exhibited in group shows at N.W. Printmakers Internat., Seattle and Portland, Oreg., 1964, Ultimate Concerns 6th Nat. Exhbn., Athens, Ohio, 1965, 55th Nat. Exhbn., Springfield, Mass., 1974, 11th An. So. Tier Arts and Crafts, Corning, N.Y., 1974, Soc. of the Four Arts, Palm Beach, Fla., 1974, Appalachian Nat. Drawing Competition, Boone, N.C., 1975, Rutgers Nat. Drawing Exhbn., Camden, N.J., 1975, 8th and 9th Biennial Nat. Art Exhibit, Valley City, N.D., 1973, 75, Clary-Miner Gallery, Buffalo, 1988, Nat. Art Show, Redding, Calif., 1989, Internat. Printmaker, Buffalo, 1990, Westmoreland Nat. Juried Competition, Youngwood, Pa., 1990, Ariel Gallery, Soho, N.Y., 1990, Grand Prix de Paris Internat., Chapelle De La Sorbonne, Paris, 1990, Nat. Juried Exhbn., Rockford, Ill., 1991, Nat. Invitational Exhbn., Buffalo, 1991, East Coast Artists Nat. Invitational Art Exhbn., Havre de Grace, Md., 1991, Ariel Gallery, Soho, N.Y., 1991, N.Y. Art Expo, 1991, Milw. Art for AIDS Auction, 1991, 92, 94. Mem. Winnebago Hist. Soc., Oshkosh, 1987—. Lutheran. Avocation: gardening. Home: 226 High Ave Oshkosh WI 54901-4734

SMITH, MICHAEL, college president; b. St. Joseph, Mo., Jan. 30, 1941; s. Walton Joseph and Margaret Dorothy (Chubb) S.; m. Connie Stanton, Oct. 27, 1965; children: Jeffrey, Timothy. AD, Mo. Western Community Coll., 1960; BS, N.E. Mo. State U., 1967; PhD, U. Nebr., 1975. Ins. investigator Retail Credit Co., St. Joseph, Mo., 1963-65; instr. Havana (Ill.) High Sch., 1967-68, West Bend (Iowa) High Sch., 1968-70, U. Nebr., 1972-75; asst. prof. English Albany (Ga.) Jr. Coll., 1975-78; chmn. arts and scis., dir. internat. programs U. Minn., Crookston, 1978-80; chief exec. officer, coll. dean N.D. State U., Bottineau, 1980-87; provost, dean of faculty Richard Bland Coll., Coll. William and Mary, 1987-89; chancellor La. State U., Eunice, 1989-95; pres. Our Lady of the Lake Coll., Baton Rouge. Commr. North Cen. Assn. Colls. and Schs., 1984-, accreditation cons./evaluator, 1982-87, vis. prof. English, U. New Orleans, 1995-98. With U.S. Army, 1960-63. Office: Our Lady of the Lake Coll 7434 Perkins Rd Baton Rouge LA 70808-4374 E-mail: msmith@ololcollege.edu.

SMITH, MIRIAM A. broadcast and communications educator; b. Price, Utah; d. John W. Smith. AS with high honors, Coll. Ea. Utah, 1978; BA in European Studies summa cum laude, Brigham Young U., 1980, JD, 1985; MA in Comms. Mgmt., U. So. Calif., L.A., 1991. Bar: Utah 1985, Calif. 1990. Pub. opinion pollster Bardsley and Haslacher, Portland, Oreg., 1976-81; intern Nat. Assn. Counties, Washington, summer 1981; law clk. U.S. Army Judge Advocate Gen. Corps, Ft. Leonard Wood, Mo., summer 1984; law clk. to Hon. George E. Ballif 4th Jud. Dist. Ct. Utah, Provo, 1985-87; estate adminstr. U.S. Bankruptcy Ct., Salt Lake City, 1988; bus. affairs intern Warner Bros. TV, Burbank, Calif., summer 1989; grad. tchg. asst. Annenberg Sch. for Comm. U. So. Calif., L.A., 1990-91; of counsel DaCorsi & Cort, Woodland Hills, Calif., 1991-98; asst. prof. broadcast and electronic comm. arts dept. San Francisco State U., 1998—. Acctg. clk. H&J Supply, Price, summer 1979; asst. regional corr. The Deseret News, Salt Lake City, summer, 1980; spl. feature writer The Sun Advocate, Price, summer 1981; bus. affairs and contracts extern ABC Entertainment, L.A., 1992 Contbr. articles to profl. publs. and newspapers. Electronic media specialist Bay Area Multi-Stake Pub. Affairs Coun. of Jesus Christ of Latter-day Saints, 1999—; vol. instr. culture program Brigham Young U.-Missionary Tng. Ctr., Provo, 1985-88. Winner Mock Trial Competition, ATLA, 1985; Honors at Entrance scholar Coll. Ea. Utah, 1976, Presdl. scholar Brigham Young U., 1978-80, Merit scholar Brigham Young U., 1980-81, 83-85, scholar Annenberg Sch. for Comms., U. So. Calif., 1989; grad. fellow U. So. Calif., 1990. Mem. Broadcast Edn. Assn., J. Reuben Clark Law Soc. (pub. affairs chair on bd. govs. L.A. chpt. 1993-96, chair San Francisco chpt. 2003—), Phi Kappa Phi. Office: San Francisco State U 1600 Holloway Ave San Francisco CA 94132-1722 E-mail: miriam@sfsu.edu.

SMITH, NOEL WILSON, psychology educator; b. Marion, Ind., Nov. 2, 1933; s. Anthony and Mary Louise (Wilson) S.; m. Marilyn C. Coleman, June 17, 1954; children: Thor and Lance (twins). AB, Ind. U., 1955, PhD, 1962; MA, U. Colo., 1958. Asst. prof. psychology Wis. State U., Platteville, 1962-63, SUNY, Plattsburgh, 1963-66, assoc. prof., 1966-71, prof., 1971-95, prof. emeritus, 1995—; courtesy prof. U. Fla., 1997—. Author: Greek and Interbehavioral Psychology, 1990, rev. edit., 1993, An Analysis of Ice Age Art: Its Psychology and Belief, 1992, Current Systems in Psychology: History, Theory, Research, and Application, 2001; co-author: The Science of Psychology: Interbehavioral Survey, 1975; sr. editor: Reassessment in Psychology, 1983; editor: Interbehavioral Psychology newsletter, 1970-77; contbr. articles to profl. jours. Fellow APA; mem. AAUP (pres. SUNY coun. 1980-82), Am. Psychol. Soc., Cheiron Internat. Soc. History of Behavior Sci., Sigma Xi. Home: 3027 Willow Green Sarasota FL 34235 Office: SUNY Dept Psychology Beaumont Hall Plattsburgh NY 12901

SMITH, NONA COATES, academic administrator; b. West Grove, Pa., Apr. 1, 1942; d. John Truman and Elizabeth Zane (Trumbo) Coates; m. David Smith, Oct. 12, 1968 (div. May 1986); children: Kirth Ayrl, Del Kerry, Michael Sargent, Sherri Lee. BA, West Chester (Pa.) U., 1988; PhD, Temple U., 1998. Legal sec. Gawthrop & Greenwood, West Chester, 1968-73, MacElree, Gallagher, O'Donnell, West Chester, 1981-84; social sec. Mrs. John B. Hannum, Unionville, Pa., 1975-81; rsch. asst. West Chester U., 1984-88, cons., 1988; dir. sponsored rsch. Bryn Mawr (Pa.) Coll., 1989—, chair rsch./tchg. evaluation, 1993-95. Treas. Kennett Vol. Fire Co., Kennett Square, Pa., 1984-86; founding mem. Colls. of Liberal Arts-Sponsored Programs. Recipient Scholastic All-Am. award U.S. Achievement Acad., 1988, Rsch. award Truman Libr., 1992, Goldsmith Rsch. award Harvard U., 1993; fellow Truman Dissertation, 1997—. Fellow Phi Alpha Theta; mem. AAUW, Am. Hist. Assn., Soc. Historians of Am. Fgn. Rels., Nat. Coun. Univ. Rsch. Adminstrs. (mem. nat. conf. com. 1995-96). Republican. Presbyterian. Avocations: reading, gardening, travel, cultural events. Home: PO Box 239 Unionville PA 19375-0239 Office: Bryn Mawr Coll 101 N Merion Ave Bryn Mawr PA 19010-2859

SMITH, NORMAN DWIGHT, geological sciences educator; b. Natural Bridge, N.Y., Jan. 26, 1941; s. Charles C. and Doris Eileen (White) S.; m. Judith Ann Milone, June 3, 1967; children: Laurence Charles, Daniel Graeme. BS, St. Lawrence U., 1962; MS, Brown U., 1964, PhD, 1967. Asst. prof. U. Ill., Chgo., 1967-72, assoc. prof., 1972-78, prof., 1978-98, head dept. geol. scis., 1988-92; prof., chair U. Nebr., Lincoln, 1998—. Fellow Found. Rsch. Devel., South Africa, 1989, 95. Author, co-author book chpts.; contbr. articles to profl. jours. Recipient 22 rsch. grants NSF, U.S. Army, BP Exploration, Exxon Prodn. Rsch., Anglo-Am. Corp., 1972—; Fulbright scholar, India, 1982. Fellow Geol. Soc. Am. (chair sedimentary geology div. 1993-94); mem. Soc. for Sedimentary Geology (pres. Great Lakes sect. 1977-78, editor Jour. Sedimentary Petrology 1983-88, Dedicated Svc. award 1988). Home: 8101 W Denton Rd Denton NE 68339-3090 Office: U Nebr Dept Geoscis Lincoln NE 68588

SMITH, PAMELA JEAN, elementary education educator; b. Indpls., Oct. 1, 1954; d. Edwin William and JoAnn Lorraine (Blomgren) S. BA, Adams State Coll., 1976; M in Social Sci., U. Miss., 1977; postgrad., U. South Fla., 1978-91. Classroom aide Englewood (Fla.) Elem., 1978-79; kindergarten tchr. Nokomis (Fla.) Elem., 1979-92, tchr. 1st grade, 1992—. Mem. Sch. Adv. Coun. Blueprint 2000. Mem. Univ. Fla. Gator Boosters. Mem. Nat. Wildlife Fedn., Nat. Sci. Tchr. Assn., Fla. Coun. for Social Studies, Fla. Reading Coun., Fla. Assn. Children Under Six, Fla. Aerospace Edn. Assn., Sarasota Reading Coun., Tchrs. Applying Whole Lang., Assn. for Childhood Edn. Internat., Ellis Island Found., Ctr. for Marine Conservation, Cousteau Soc., Am. Legion Aux., Delta Kappa Gamma (treas. 1992—). Democrat. Lutheran. Avocations: scuba diving, snow skiing. Office: Nokomis Elem 1900 Laurel Rd E Nokomis FL 34275-3242

SMITH, PAMELA RODGERS, elementary education educator; b. Hartselle, Ala., Feb. 21, 1961; d. Jesse Gene and Zella Lurline (Brown) Rodgers; m. Jeffrey Neal Smith, July 21, 1990. Student, Calhoun C.C., Decatur, Ala., 1979-82; BS in Early Childhood and Elem. Edn., Athens (Ala.) State Coll., 1984; M in Early Childhood Edn., U. Ala., Birmingham, 1990, AA cert. early childhood specialist, 1992. Day care tchr. Little Red Schoolhouse, Hartselle, 1977-84; tchr. kindergarten Neel (Ala.) Elem. Sch., 1985-86, Crestline Elem. Sch., Hartselle, 1987-95, Barkley Bridge Elem. Sch., Hartselle, 1995—. Cons. whole lang. workshop No. Ala. Tchr. Exch., 1991—. Mem. NEA, Ala. Edn. Assn., Hartselle Edn. Assn., Internat. Reading Assn., Ala. Reading Assn., Tenn. Valley Reading Assn. (v.p. 1998-99), Constructivist Math. Network, Whole Lang. Network, Kappa Kappa Iota (pres. 1998-99, 99-00). Democrat. Baptist. Home: 210 Wayward Ave NW Hartselle AL 35640-7794 E-mail: pamesmit@hcs.k12.al.us.

SMITH, PATRICIA ANN, middle school educator; b. N.Y.C., Apr. 21, 1947; d. James and Ursula (Wedhorn) Mentesane; m. Ted Holton Smith, June 28, 1968; children: Monica Marie, Elizabeth Christine, Stephanie Nicole. BA, U. South Fla., 1968; MA in Tchg., Oklahoma City U., 1973. Cert. elem. K-8, reading specialist, jr. h.s. math, sci., social studies tchr., Okla., elem. and secondary adminstrn. Tchr. Oklahoma City Schs., 1970-74, Putnam City Schs., Oklahoma City, 1975-76, Hennessey (Okla.) Pub. Schs., 1976-88, Norman (Okla.) Pub. Schs., 1988—; asst. prin. Whittier Mid. Sch., Norman, 1999. Field experiences supr. U. Okla., 1991-95. Vol. Norman Regional Hosp., 1994—, Habitat for Humanity, Norman, 1995, St. Joseph's Cath. Ch., Norman. 1st lt. U.S. Army, 1968-70. Mem.: Nat. Coun. Tchrs. Math., Kappa Alpha Theta. Republican. Roman Catholic. Avocations: gardening, reading, skiing. Home: 613 Riverwalk Ct Norman OK 73072-4844 Office: Norman Pub Schs 2000 W Brooks St Norman OK 73069-4204

SMITH, PATRICIA ANN HOEHN, elementary school educator, music educator; b. Williston, N.Dak., June 21, 1948; d. Harold H. and Mildred Thyra (Siemon) Hoehn; m. Harry Richard Smith, Nov. 29, 1986; m. Ruben Carroll (Doc) Gaulke, June 21, 1975 (div. Mar. 1987). BS in Edn., U. N.Dak., 1970; student, UCLA, 1987; MEd, U. N.Dak., 1972; student, Mesa State Coll., 1998, student, 2003. Cert. Tchr. ND, 1970, Colo., 1977. Tchr. Lakota Pub. Sch., Lakota, ND, 1970—71, Balta Pub. Sch., Balta, ND, 1972—75, Montrose Sch. Dist., Montrose, Colo., 1977—; pvt. piano tchr. Montrose, 1977—. Pvt. piano tchr., Montrose, Colo.; rep. conf. on children The White House, Washington, 1970. Mem.: Colo. Music Tchrs. Assn., Nat. Music Tchrs. Assn., Phi Delta Kappa. Republican. Methodist. Avocations: camping, skiing, gardening, reading, music.

SMITH, PATRICIA ANNE, special education educator; b. West Chester, Pa., Aug. 19, 1967; d. William Richard and Carol Anne (Benn) S. BS in Spl. Edn. cum laude, West Chester U., 1989; postgrad., Immaculata Coll., 1993-98. Cert. mentally and physically handicapped tchr., Pa. Learning support tchr. Chester County Intermediate Unit, Downingtown, Pa., 1989-90, early intervention tchr., 1990-92; autistic support tchr. Coatesville (Pa.) Area Sch. Dist., 1992—, event coord. WOYC workshops, 1993-2000, event coord. WOYC ext. workshops, 1999-2000, event coord. WOYC childrens workshops, 1999-2000. Presenter ann. conf. Pa. Assn. of Resources for People with Mental Retardation, Hershey, 1994; co-presenter ARC, 1996, Paoli Meml. Hosp., 1997; presenter info. sessions ann. conf. Del. Valley Assn. for Edn. of Young Children, Phila., 1994, Lions, Downingtown, Pa., 1992, early childhood conf. Capital Area Assn. for Edn. of Young Children, Harrisburg, Pa., 1995, vols. Caln Athletic Assn. Challenger League, 1995-96, Chester County MH/MR Consultation and Edn. Adv. Bd. Com., 1997-2000; mentor West Chester U., 1995-98. Mem. recreation adv. bd. dirs. Assn. for Retarded Citizens, Exton, Pa., 1993-98, Daisy Girl Scout Leader, 1995-96; vol. tutor Chester County Libr. Adult Literacy Program, 1995-98, vol. monitor, Residential Living Options Home, 2001— . Recipient Outstanding Svc. award Coatesville Area Parent Coun., 1994, 96, Vol. award Friendship PTA, 1993, 96, 99, Pa. Early Childhood Edn. Assn. Workshop presenter award, 1993; grantee Pa.Dept. Edn., 1993, Coatesville Area Sch. Dist., 1990, Pa. Bur. Spl. Edn., 2001, 02. Mem.: ASCD, Coun. for Exceptional Children, Autism Soc. Am., Nat. Assn. for Edn. of Young Children, Kappa Delta Pi. Republican. Roman Catholic. Home: 501 Clover Mill Rd Exton PA 19341-2505 Office: Friendship Elem Sch 296 Reeceville Rd Coatesville PA 19320-1520

SMITH, PATRICIA JEAN, gifted and talented education educator; b. Dallas, Apr. 23, 1951; d. James M. and Billie Jean (Wyrick) S. BA, U. Tex., Arlington, 1973; MLA, So. Meth. U., 1978. Tchr. social studies Lancaster (Tex.) Mid. Sch., 1973-75; tchr. English and French, Lancaster High Sch., 1975-79; asst. continuing legal edn. dept. So. Meth. U. Sch. Law, Dallas, 1984-86; tchr. English and French, Mabank (Tex.) High Sch., 1980-84, tchr. English, French and Latin, coord. gifted-talented edn., 1986—, coord. advanced placement program, 1994—. Mem. accreditation team So. Assn., Austin, 1976-78; sponsor student trips to Europe. Dist. rep. Tex. Gov.'s Inauguration, Austin, 1990; tchr., mem. youth com., musician Clear Creek Bapt. Ch., 1991—. Recipient Outstanding High Sch. Tchr. award Mabank C. of C., 1992, Tex. Excellence award for outstanding high sch. tchr. U. Tex., Austin, 1992. Mem. Tex. Assn. for Gifted and Talented (presenter state conf. 1994-96), Mabank Fedn. Tchrs. (pres. 1988—). Democrat. Avocations: art, piano, needlework. Office: Mabank High Sch 124 E Market St Mabank TX 75147-2307 Address: 1204 S Bettie St Mabank TX 75147-3708

SMITH, PEGGY O'DONIEL, physicist, educator; b. Lakeland, Fla., Nov. 27, 1920; d. John Arthur and Carrie Mattie (Jackson) O'Doniel; m. Fenton Frederick Smith, Oct. 11, 1943; children: James Scott, Stephen Arthur, Melody Ann, Candy Lou. Aviation Pilot Lic., Stetson U., Deland, Fla., 1941; BS in Sci. and Math., Fla. So. Coll., 1942; MA in Edn., U.S. Internat. U., San Diego, 1968. Physicist degausser U.S. Navy, Key West, Fla., 1942, physicist compass compensator Charleston, S.C., 1943, physicist magnetic signature analyst Washington, 1944; tchr. Chula Vista (Calif.) Sch. Dist., 1963-73, math specialist, 1974-77; owner Mineral Store, Chula Vista, 1977-82; ret. Leader math. workshops for girls, 1992-96. Author: Laz Goes to New Zealand; contbr. articles to profl. jours. Del. White House Conf. on Edn., 1956; sec. Chula Vista Rep. Women, 1995-97; chmn. Orphans of Italy, 1957-58. Recipient Kazanjian award, Joint Coun. Econ. Edn., Chula Vista, 1972, Fla. So. Coll. Alumni Achievement citation, 1999; Chula Vista Sch. Dist. math grantee, 1975. Mem. AAUW (v.p. 1989, 2001-03), Inner Circle, Calif. Ret. Tchrs. Assn. (v.p. 1998-2000), San Diego Gem and Mineral Soc. Avocations: golf, mineral collecting, coin collecting, bridge, travel. Home: 87 K St Chula Vista CA 91911-1409

SMITH, PENNY, middle school educator; b. Dayton, Ohio, Sept. 28, 1940; d. Sidney North and Helen (Elliott) Correll; m. Mark Richard Smith, June 21, 1980 (dec. Nov. 1994); children: Adam Mark, Erica North. BS in Edn., Taylor U., 1963; MEd, Bowling Green State U., 1966. Cert. tchr., N.C., Fla., Hawaii, Ind. 3d grade tchr. East Auburn (Ind.) Elem. Sch., 1963-66, Skycrest Elem. Sch., Clearwater, Fla., 1972-73; 1st grade tchr. John Wilson Elem. Sch., Honolulu, 1966-67; 4th grade tchr. Harrison-McKinney Elem. Sch., Auburn, Ind., 1967-71; 4th-6th grade tchr. Prospect Elem. Sch., Monroe, N.C., 1973-75; 6th grade tchr. Parkwood Mid. Sch., Monroe, 1975-96, advisor yearbook, cheerleaders, outward bound. Internat. studies Soviet Union, 1988. Speaker Am. Cancer Soc., Charlotte, N.C.; actor Calvary Ch., Charlotte; singer/dancer Sweet Adelines, Charlotte. Recipient award Terry Sanford Orgn., 1980, Outstanding Young Educator award Auburn Jaycees, 1964; named Union County Tchr. of Yr., 1976, Parkwood Middle Sch. Tchr. of Yr., 1992; Fulbright scholar, India, 1992. Mem. NEA, N.C. Coun. Social Studies, Assn. English Tchrs., Assn. Classroom Tchrs., Assn. N.C. Educators. Republican. Avocations: photography, travel, reading, snorkeling. Address: 6181 S Zunis Ave Tulsa OK 74136-1014

SMITH, PETER HOPKINSON, political scientist, consultant, writer; b. Bklyn., Jan. 17, 1940; s. Joseph Hopkinson and Mary Edna (Sullivan) S.; children: Jonathan Yeardley, Peter Hopkinson Jr, Joanna Alexandra. BA, Harvard U., 1961; MA, PhD, Columbia U., 1966. Asst. prof. Dartmouth Coll., Hanover, N.H., 1966-68; from asst. prof. to prof. U. Wis., Madison, 1968-80; prof. MIT, Cambridge, 1980-86; Simón Bolívar prof. L.Am. studies U. Calif., San Diego, 1987—, dir. Ctr. for Iberian and L.Am. studies, 1989—. Cons. Ford Found., N.Y.C., 1984—; vis. mem. Inst. for Advanced Study, Princeton, N.J., 1972-73. Author: Politics and Beef in Argentina: Patterns of Conflict and Change, 1969, Argentina and the Failure of Democracy: Conflict among Political Elites, 1904-55, 1974, Labyrinths of Power: Political Recruitment in Twentieth-Century Mexico, 1979, Mexico: The Quest for a U.S. Policy, 1980, Mexico: Neighbor in Transition, 1984; co-author: Modern Latin America, 1984, 89, 92, editor: Statistics, Epistemology, and History, 1984, Drug Policy in the Americas, 1992, The Challenge of Integration: Europe and the Americas, 1993, Talons of the Eagle, 1995; co-editor: New Approaches to Latin Am. History, 1974, The Family in Latin America, 1978; series editor: Latin America in Global Perspective, 1995—; contbr. articles to profl. jours. Guggenheim fellow, 1975-76; disting. Fulbright lectr. Mexico, 1984. Mem. Latin Am. Studies Assn. (pres. 1981), Am. Polit. Sci. Assn., Am. Hist. Assn., Coun. for Internat. Exch. Scholars, Coun. on Fgn. Rels. Office: U Calif Ctr Iberian & LAm Studies 9500 Gilman Dr La Jolla CA 92093-0528

SMITH, PHILIP JOHN, industrial and systems engineering educator; b. Bradenton, Fla., July 11, 1953; s. John Fredrick and Valerie Eline (Polk) S. BA in Psychology, U. Mich., 1975, MS in Indsl. and Ops. Engring., 1976, PhD in Psychology and Indsl. Engring., 1979. Lectr. dept. indsl. engring. U. Mich., Ann Arbor, 1979-80, rsch. scientist Ctr. for Ergonomics, 1979-80; asst. prof. dept. indsl. engring. Ohio State U., Columbus, 1980-86, assoc. prof., 1986-92, prof. indsl. and sys. engring., 1992—, dir. Inst. for Ergonomics, 1998—. Cons. Ford, Dearborn, Mich., 1986—, Metron, Washington, 1998—, PPG, Columbus, Ohio, 1999-2000, Booz Allen Hamilton, 2001-02. Co-editor: Challenges in Indexing Electronic Text and Images, 1994; contbr. articles, paper to profl. publs. Mem. IEEE Sys., Man and Cybernetics, Am. Soc. for Info. Sci., Assn. Computing Machinery (spl. interest group for info. retrieval 1992-93), Human Factors Soc. Avocation: dressage. Home: 7197 Calhoun Rd Ostrander OH 43061-9335 Office: Ohio State U Engring Dept 1971 Neil Ave Columbus OH 43210-1210 Business E-Mail: Smith.131@osu.edu.

SMITH, RAYMOND KERMIT, former educational administrator; b. Hahnville, La., July 6, 1915; married, 2 children. B.A., Xavier U., 1946, M.A. in Adminstrn. and Supervision, 1951; postgrad. in reading No. Mich. U., 1962, La. State U., 1965-66, Loyola U., New Orleans, 1966-68, Internat. Grade Sch., New Orleans, 1973. Tchr.-prin. St. Charles Parish Schs., Luling, La., 1937-42, supr. instrn., 1942-79, asst. supt. instrn., 1979-81; ret., 1981; evening, weekend instr. reading Loyola U., New Orleans, 1968-75. Contbr. articles to profl. jours. Pres., United Givers Fund St. Charles Parish, 1971-72; v.p. Bayou-River Health Planning Council, 1974-77, pres., 1977— ; pres. New Orleans/Bayou River Health Systems Agy., 1978, St. Charles Parish Cancer Soc., 1987—; v.p. St. Charles Toy and Gift Fund, 1988-89; bd. dirs. United Way of St. Charles Parish, ARC, St. Charles Parish, v.p., 1992—; mem. adv. bd. St. Charles Parish Emergency Planning Com.; mem. econ. devel. sect. St. Charles Parish; mem. St. Charles chpt. La. Coun. on Child Abuse; chmn. bd. commrs. St. Charles Hosp., Luling; mem. St. Charles Community Adv. Panel; lector, commentator, eucharistic minister Holy Rosary Ch., Hahnville. Recipient citation for directing 10 years of Head Start, Sec. HEW, Outstanding Svc. award United Way St. Charles parish, 1993. Mem. NEA. Clubs: Famous G Social of New Orleans (v.p.); K.C., West St. Charles Rotary (pres. 1987-88). Home: PO Box 70 346 Gum St Hahnville LA 70057-2230

SMITH, RICHARD ALTON, mechanical contracting company executive; b. Florence, S.C., Nov. 12, 1955; s. Lemuel Alton and Mary (Ham) S.; m. Sandra Adell Bruorton, Feb. 26, 1977; children: Amy Colleen Smith, Ernest Alton Smith. AA in Bus., Trident Tech. Coll., Charleston, S.C., 1982; BS in Trades and Indsl. Edn., U. Ga., 1992. Cert. assoc. welding insp. Welding foreman General Dynamics, Goose Creek, S.C., 1975-78; maint. mechanic Exxon Co. USA, Charleston, S.C., 1978-80, Alumax of S.C., Mt. Holly, 1980-83; mech. trainer Kendall Co., Bethune, S.C., 1983-86; maint. supr. Hercules Inc., Covington, Ga., 1986-88; v.p. Indsl. Mech. Inc., Watkinsville, Ga., 1988—; tng. cons. pvt. practice, Conyers, Ga., 1988—; v.p. Reinicke Corp., Athens, Ga., 1992—. Tng. cons. Lanier Tech. Inst., Gainesville, Ga., 1992—, Athens (Ga.) Tech., 1984—. Served with U.S. Army N.G., Operation Desert Storm, 1991. Decorated Army Commendation medal. Mem. Am. Welding Soc., Fluid Power Soc. Am., Am. Vocat. Assn., Ga. Vocat. Assn., Nat. Guard Assn. Am., Nat. Guard Assn. Ga., Ga. Military Inst. Avocations: camping, boating. Home: 102 Wappoo Creek Dr Ste 8C Charleston SC 29412-2144 Office: Reinicke Corp 180 Hanover Pl Athens GA 30606-7114

SMITH, RICHARD JACKSON, elementary education educator; b. Mt. Airy, N.C., Feb. 17, 1947; s. Robert Wayne and Ruth (Jackson) S.; m. Sue Monday, Sept. 10, 1971 (dec. Nov. 21, 1981); 1 child, Richard Jackson Jr. BA, U. N.C., 1972; MA, Appalachian State U., 1975; EdD, U. N.C., 1994. Elem. tchr. Surry County Schs., Dobson, NC, 1967-96, Title I parent coord., 1992-96, K-5 instnl. specialist, 1996—2003; project coord. Reading Is Fundamental, 1996-2000. Part-time instr. grad. equivalency diploma/adult basic edn. and effective tchr. tng. classes Surry C.C., Dobson, 1988-92, tchr. literacy class, 1999-2000; adj. faculty Lees-McRae Coll., 2003—; cons. Eckerd Family Youth Alternatives, Inc., 1994-96. Local and dist. chmn., state treas. N.C. Polit. Action Com. for Edn., Raleigh, 1976-81; state exec. com. N.C. Dem. Party, Raleigh, 1981-83; trustee, deacon First Bapt. Ch. of Pilot Mountain, 1988—, Sunday sch. dir. 1991—, mem. nominating com., 1991—, sec. bd. deacons 1990-91, vice chmn. 1996-97, chmn. 1997-99; trustee Charles M. Stone Meml. Libr., 1997-2000, vice chmn., 1998-99, chmn., 1999-2000; chaplain Pilot Mountain Camp, 2000—; bd. dirs. Surry County chpt. ARC, chair nominating com., 2000—, vcie chair, 2003—. Mem. ASCD, NEA (congressional lobbying 1976-80), Internat. Reading Assn. (local unit chair 1986-90), N.C. Assn. Educators (local, dist. pres. 1979-81, local, dist., state chmn. legis. commn. 1980-81), Gideon Internat., Pilot Mountain Jaycees (life, charter, pres. 1979-80, Officer of Yr. 1978, 79), Geneal. Soc. Rockingham & Stokes Counties, Stokes County Hist. Soc., SCV (Stokes County camp 1994—), Masons (32 degree, Scottish Rite, amb. 1990—, lodge master 1990, edn. chmn. 1986—, scholarship chmn. 1986—, Cert. of Meritorious Svc. 1988, adv. bd. Masonic Home for Children at Oxford 2001—, dist. dep. grand master Grand Lodge of N.C. 2001—). Home: PO Box 127 517 E Main St Pilot Mountain NC 27041-8519 Office: Surry County Schs PO Box 364 Dobson NC 27017-0364 E-mail: drrichardsmith@yahoo.com., SmithR@SurryCountyk12.nc.us.

SMITH, RICHARD JOSEPH, history educator; b. Sacramento, Oct. 30, 1944; s. Joseph Benjamin and Margaret Elaine (Stoddard) S.; m. Alice Ellen Weisenberger, July 1, 1967; 1 child, Tyler Stoddard. BA, U. Calif., Davis, 1966, MA, 1968, PhD, 1972. Lectr. Chinese U. Hong Kong, 1972-73, U. Calif., 1972-73; asst. prof. history Rice U., Houston, 1973-78, assoc. prof., 1978-83, prof., 1983—, Minnie Stevens Piper prof., 1987, Sarofim Disting. Teaching prof., 1993-95, George and Nancy Rupp prof. humanities, 1999—. Adj. prof. U. Tex., Austin, 1983—; cons. FBI, CIA, Washington, 1985—, NEH, Washington, 1983—, various mus., Houston, Boston, N.Y.C., 1987—. Author: Mercenaries and Mandarins, 1978, Traditional Chinese Culture, 1978, China's Cultural Heritage, 1983, 2d edit., 1994, Entering China's Service, 1986, Fortune-Tellers and Philosophers, 1991, Robert Hart and China's Early Modernization, 1991, Chinese Almanacs, 1993, Cosmology, Ontology and Human Efficacy, 1993, H.B. Morse: Customs Commissioner and Historian of China, 1995, Chinese Maps, 1996. Adj. mem. Houston Mus. Fine Arts, 1986—; guest curator Children's Mus., Houston, 1987-89, 91—; pres. Tex. Found. for China Studies, Houston, 1988-93. Named Tex. Prof. Yr., Carnegie Found. for the Advancement Tchg., 1998. Mem. Assn. for Asian Studies (pres. S.W. conf. 1990-91), Asia Soc. (bd. dirs. Houston Ctr. 1976—), Houston-Taipei Soc. (bd. dirs. 1990—), Nat. Com. on U.S.-China Rels., Nat. Coun. on Asia in Schs., Phi Kappa Phi. Democrat. Avocations: sports, travel, music. Home: 2403 Goldsmith St Houston TX 77030-1813 Office: Rice U Dept History MS-42 6100 Main St Houston TX 77005-1892 E-mail: smithrj@rice.edu.

SMITH, ROBERT CARLISLE, department administrator, welding educator; b. St. Albans, W.Va., Sept. 2, 1939; s. Clarence Mack (stepfather) and Artimitia (Blake) Smith Fowler; m. Janet Lee Koehn, Dec. 28, 1958; children: Teresa Lynn, Stephen Carlisle. BA, Glenville State U., 1984; MSc, Marshall U., 1994. Cert. welding inspector, non-destructive tester. Br. mgr. Va. Welding, Charleston, W.Va., 1963-76; prin. Weld Inspection and Cons., St. Albans, W.Va., 1976-94; quality assurance mgr. Kanawha Mfg., Charleston, 1988—2003; dept. head, welding instr. W.Va. U., Parkersburg, 1981—2003. Contbr. articles. Lt. ROTC 1957-71; committeeman Rep. Party, Kanawha County, 1968-69; former Sun. sch. tchr. Highlawn Baptist Ch.; presenter Nat. Educators Workshop NASA, Langley Space Flight Ctr., 1993. Recipient Disting. West Virginian award Gov. W.Va., 1968. Mem. Am. Welding Soc. (chmn. 1971-72, program chairperson 1989-90, educator of yr. 1990, 92), Am. Soc. Non-Destructive Testing (membership recruiter 1988), W.Va. Edn. Assn., W.Va. C.C. Assn. Protestant. Avocations: autos, trucks, writing, fishing, banjo. Home: 2302 S Walnut Dr Saint Albans WV 25177-3947

SMITH, ROBERT LUTHER, management educator; b. Kutztown, Pa., Feb. 18, 1927; s. Paul Luther and Esther Florence (Schwoyer) S.; m. Canda Eure Banks, Aug. 18, 1951; children: Kimberley Smith Kidd, Valerie Smith Eudy, Alexandra. BS, U.S. Naval Acad., 1949; MSA, George Washington U., 1975, DBA, 1984. Commd. USN, 1949-72, advanced through grades to comdr.; commanding officer USS Grouper, 1962-65; engr. and repair officer U.S. Submarine Base, Groton, Conn., 1965-67; supt. of test Portsmouth Naval Shipyard, Portsmouth, N.H., 1967-70; asst. project mgr. Naval Systems Submarine Acquisition, Washington, 1970-72; project mgr. EG&G, Washington Analytical, Rockville, Md., 1972-80; pres. Interface Resources Ltd., Alexandria, Va., 1980—; lectr. George Mason U., Fairfax, Va., 1981-84; prof. Coll. of Notre Dame of Md., Balt., 1984-98. Faculty Dealer Mgmt. Inst., Columbus, Ohio, 1981—83; cons. in field of orgn. performance. Sr. warden St. Paul's Episcopal Ch., Alexandria, 1980-81; mem. Alexandria Health Svcs., 1983—. Mem.: Am. Soc. for Quality, Kena Shrine, Scottish Rite, Kiwanis Alexandria (pres. 1985—86, del. to internat. 1985), Masons, Beta Gamma Sigma. Republican. Home: 1102 Bayliss Dr Alexandria VA 22302-3506 E-mail: doc4orgztn@aol.com.

SMITH, ROBERT MASON, academic administrator; b. Sill, Okla., May 8, 1945; s. Arnold Mason and Lillyan (Scott) Smith; m. Ramona Lynn Stukey, June 15, 1968; children: David, Angela. BA, Wichita State U., 1967; MA, Ohio U., 1968; PhD, Temple U., 1976. Debate coach Princeton (N.J.) U., 1971-73; debate coach Wichita (Kans.) State U., 1973-87; assoc. dean Coll. Liberal Arts and Scis., 1977-87; dean coll. arts and scis. U. Tenn., Martin, 1987-99; provost and vice pres. for academic affairs Slippery Rock Univ., 1999—2002, interim pres., 2002—. Dir. Govt. Sch. for Humanities, 1996—99; spl. asst. U.S. Dept. Human Svcs., Washington, 1980—81. Mem. State Behavioral Sci. Regulatory Bd., Topeka, 1984—87; trustee Leadership Kans., Topeka, 1986—87; founder, bd. dirs. WestStar Regional Tenn. Leadership Program, 1989—99. Recipient Excellence in Tchg. award, Coun. for Advancement and Support of Edn., 1994, Crystal Apple award for Outstanding Tchg., 1995, Award for Disting. Leadership, Nat. Assn. Cmty. Leadership, 1995, Gov.'s Award for Outstanding Achievement, 1999, Preceptor award, 1999; fellow, Health Human Svc. Mem.: Tenn. Speech Comm. Assn., Tenn. Coun. Colls. Arts and Scis. (pres. 1993—94), Assn. for Comm. Adminstrn. (pres. 1988), Kans. Speech Comm. Assn. (pres. 1977, Outstanding Coll. Speech Tchr. award 1977), Rotary Club, Phi Theta Kappa, Beta Theta Pi, Phi Eta Sigma, Phi Kappa Phi. Baptist. Home: 106 Ojibwa Dr Butler PA 16001-0528 Office: Slippery Rock Univ Pres 300 Old Main Slippery Rock PA 16057

SMITH, ROGER LEWIS, mathematics educator secondary school; b. Palo Alto, Calif., Apr. 5, 1945; s. Arthur McEwen and Dorothy Irene (Rogers) S.; m. Patricia A. Maisch; stepchildren: Filix, Francisco. BA, Humboldt State U., 1978. Sch. bus driver No. Humboldt H.S., Arcata, Calif., 1968-72; rsch. asst. U. Calif. Davis, NSF, Nat. Geographic, Puno, Peru, 1972-73; truck driver La. Pacific Corp., Big Lagoon, Calif., 1973-76; driver moving truck Humboldt Moving and Storage, Eureka, Calif., 1978-81; farm hand Hartmann Bulb Farms, Dows Prarie, Calif., 1984-86; tchr. 8th grade Eureka City Schs., 1986-90; math. tchr. advanced placement calculus Eureka H.S., 1990—. Photographer (news mag.) Peruvian Times, 1972. With U.S. Coast Guard, 1964-68. Mem. Calif. Coun. Tchrs. of Math. (v.p. far N. br. 1990-91, pres. elect 1991-92, pres 1992-93), Phi Delta Kappa. Democrat. Avocation: farming. Home: 3040 Central Ave Mckinleyville CA 95519-9401 Office: Eureka HS 1915 J St Eureka CA 95501-3052 E-mail: smithroger@eurekacityschools.org.

SMITH, ROGER PERRY, obstetrics and gynecology educator; b. Tucson, Jan. 31, 1949; m. Barbara Ann Nason, May 25, 1974; children: Scott Andrew, Jeffrey Todd. BS, Purdue U., 1969; BSM, Northwestern U., 1969, MD, 1972. Intern Chgo. Wesley Meml. Hosp., 1972—73; resident in ob-gyn. Northwestern Meml. Hosp.-McGaw Med. Ctr., 1973—76, Prentice Women's Hosp. and Maternity Ctr., Chgo., 1973—76; clin. asst. prof. sch. clin. medicine U. Ill., Champaign-Urbana, 1979—85; ob-gyn. Med. Coll. Ga., Augusta, 1985—99, Talmadge Meml. Hosp., Augusta, 1985—92; prof. Ob-Gyn Med. Coll., Ga., 1992—99; prof., vice chair, program dir. U. Mo., Kansas City, 1999—. Attending staff Carle Found. Hosp., Urbana, 1976—85; mem. courtesy staff Burnham City Hosp., Mercy Hosp., McKinley Hosp.; attending staff Med. Coll. Ga. Hosp. and Clinic, 1985—99, Truman Med. Ctr., Kansas City, 1999—, St. Luke's Health System, Kansas City, 1999—. Contbr. articles to profl. jours. Fellow: ACOG (sec.-treas. 2002—, Purdue Frederick award 1987); mem.: AMA, Assn. Profs. Ob-Gyn., Ga. Med. Assn., Chgo. Med. Soc., Mo. State Med. Assn., Obstet. and Gynecol. Soc. (asst. sec. 1976—79, sec. 1979—85), Am. Inst. Ultrasound in Medicine, Assn. Advancement Med. Inst., Ctrl. Assn. Ob-Gyn. (Cmty. Hosp. award 1979, 1983), Alpha Epsilon Delta, Phi Eta Sigma. Office: UMKC Truman Med Ctr 2301 Holmes St Kansas City MO 64108

SMITH, ROGERS MOOD, political scientist, educator; b. Sept. 20, 1953; s. Henry Dale and Betty (Mood) Smith. BA in Polit. Sci., Mich. State U., 1974; MA, Harvard U., 1978, PhD, 1980. Asst. prof. Polit. Sci. Yale U., New Haven, 1980—85, assoc. prof., 1985—89, Alfred Cowles prof. Govt, 1989—2001; Browne Disting. prof. Polit. Sci. U. Pa., Phila., 2001—. Author: Liberalism and American Constitutional Law, 1985, Citizenship Without Consent, 1985, Stories of Peoplehood, 2003, The Unsteady March, 1999, Civic Ideals, 1997; contbr. articles to profl. jours. Mem.: New Eng. Polit. Sci. Assn. (Pres.'s award 1982), Social Sci. History Assn. (Sharlin award), Orgn. Am. Historians (Curie prize), Am. Polit. Sci. Assn. (Greenstone prize, Bunche prize, Easton prize). Avocation: baseball. Office: Univ Pa Dept Political Science 208 S 37th St Philadelphia PA 19104-6215

SMITH, RONALD AUBREY, theology educator; b. Pecos, Tex., Jan. 9, 1937; s. Aubrey William and Godie Jane (Richie) S.; m. Patricia Ann Hetzel, Sept. 14, 1958; children: Wayne Edward, Brian Lee, Linda Gay Flinsbaugh, Craig Fredrick. BA in Sociology, U. Calif., Berkeley, 1959; BD in Theology, Golden Gate Bapt. Theol. Sem., Mill Valley, Calif., 1962; PhD in Religion, Baylor U., 1972. Ordained to ministry Bapt. Ch., 1962. Pastor First Bapt. Ch., Newman, Calif., 1962-64, Pittsburg (Calif.) Bapt. Ch., 1964-66; instr. Bible and sociology McLennan C.C., Waco, Tex., 1966-68, instr. religion, chair humanities, 1968-72, instr. religion, dir. divsn. humanities, fine arts and comm., 1972-73, dean of instrn., 1973-79; v.p. for acad. affairs, prof. theology Hardin-Simmons U., Abilene, Tex., 1979-87, exec. v.p., provost, prof. theology, 1987-92, dir. instnl. rsch., 1992-95, prof., 1992-99, sr. prof., 1999—. Mem., sometime chmn. adminstrv. coun. Abilene Intercollegiate Sch. Nursing, 1980-92; trustee Abilene Libr. Consortium, 1990-92; cons. Higher Edn. Task Force, Abilene, 1990; testified before Congl.Reauthorization hearing NEH, Dallas, 1989. Chmn. Abilene Com. for the Humanities, Abilene, 1987-88; bd. dirs. Abilene Edn. coun./Abilene C. of C., 1991-92; steering com. working group on character ethics and bibl. interpretation Soc. Bibl. Lit.; mem. bioethics com. Hendrick Med. Ctr. Mem. Am. Acad. Religion, Nat. Assn. Bapt. Profs. of Religion (past pres. southwest region), Deans Conf. Assn. So. Baptist Colls. of Schs. (past pres.), Conf. Acad. Deans of So. States (past pres.), Tex. Assn. Acad. Deans and V.Ps. (past pres.). Office: Hardin-Simmons U Box 16235 2200 Hickory St Abilene TX 79698-6235 E-mail: rsmith@hsutx.edu.

SMITH, RONALD EHLBERT, lawyer, educator, pastor, public speaker, writer, motivator, real estate developer; b. Atlanta, Apr. 30, 1947; s. Frank Marion and Frances Jane (Canida) S.; m. Annemarie Krumholz, Dec. 26, 1969; children: Michele, Erika, Damian. BME, Stetson U., 1970; postgrad., Hochschule Fuer Musik, Frankfurt, Fed. Republic Germany, 1971-74; Masters in German Lit., Germany & Middlebury Coll., 1975; JD, Nova U., 1981; postgrad., Gammon Sem. Sch., 2000—. Bar: Fla. 1982, U.S. Dist. Ct. (mid. dist.) Fla. 1983, U.S. Ct. Appeals (11th cir.) 1990, Ga. 1994, U.S. Dist. Ct. (no. dist.) Ga. 1994; cert. ednl. leader, Ga. Asst. state atty. 10th Jud. Cir. Ct., Bartow, Fla., 1982-85; pvt. practice Lakeland, Fla., 1985-94, Atlanta, 1994—; of counsel Mark Boychuk & Assocs., 1998—. Asst. 10th Jud. Cir. Ct., Bartow, 1981-82; instr. Broward County C.C., Ft. Lauderdale, Fla., 1976-79, 91-94, pub. and pvt. schs., Broward County, Atlanta Schs., 1998-2002, Offenbach, Germany, 1971-78; instr. Polk C.C. and Police Acad., Winter Haven, Fla., 1981-94; adj. prof. English, Ga. State U., 1996—; adj. prof. law DeKalb Coll., 1997-2002; part-time police instr. Police Acad., Forsyth, Ga., 1996—; music instr. Atlanta Pub. Schs., 1999-2002. Tchr., drama dir. Disciples I and II, United Meth. Ch., Lakeland, 1980-94, Glenn Meml. United Meth. Ch., Atlanta, 1994—, cand. to ministry, 2000—; Billy Graham counseling supr., 1994—; promoter Promise Keepers, 1995—; spkr., promoter ProNet, 1996—; min. music Scott Blvd. Bapt. Ch., Decatur, Ga., 1998, Gideon Internat., 1999-2002; cert. candidate Ordained Ministry United Meth. Ch. Freedom Bridge fellow German Acad. Exch. Svc., Mainz, 1974-75. Mem. ABA, Christian Legal Soc., Lakeland Bar Assn., Am. Immigration Lawyers Assn., Phi Delta Kappa. E-mail: smith321@bellsouth.net.

SMITH, RUBY LUCILLE, retired librarian; b. Nobob, Ky., Sept. 19, 1917; d. James Ira and Myrtie Olive (Crabtree) Jones; m. Kenneth Cornelius Smith, Dec. 25, 1946; children: Kenneth Cornelius, Corma Ann. AB, Western Ky. State Tchrs. Coll., 1943, MA, 1966. Tchr. rural schs., Barren County, Ky., 1941-42; tchr. secondary sch. English, libr. Temple Hill Consol. Sch., Glasgow, Ky., 1943-47, 49-51, 53-56, sch. libr., 1956-83. Sec. Barren County Cancer Soc., 1968—70, Barren County Fair Bd., 1969—70; leader 4-H Club, 1957—72; coord. tax-aide program AARP, 1985—88, dist. dir., 1988—2000, local chpt. v.p., 1996—98, pres., 1999—2000, instr. 55 Alive Mature Driving, 1993—; sec. Oak Grove Bapt. Ch., 1979—; coun. mem. Barren County; bd. dirs. Barren County Hist. Found., Inc., 1997—; trustee Mary Wood Weldon Meml. Libr., 1964—, Barren County Pub. Libr. Bd., 1969—2001; sec. Barren County Pub. Libr., 1969—2001; trustee Barren County Hist. Found., 1996—. Mem. NEA (life), Ky. Edn. Assn., Ky. Sch. Media Assn. (sec. 1970-71), 3d Dist. Libr. Assn. (pres. 1944, 66), Barren County Edn. Assn. (pres. 1960-62, treas. 1979-80), 3d Dist. Ret. Tchrs. Assn. (pres. 1991-92), Ky. Ret. Tchrs. Assn. (v.p. 1992-93, pres.-elect 1993-94, pres. 1994-95), Glasgow-Barren County Ret. Tchrs. Assn. (pres. 1984-86, 96-98, sec. 1989, treas. 1990), Ky. Libr. Trustee Assn. (bd. dirs. 1985-98, pres. 1986-88, 93-95, dir. Barren River region 1985-97), Barren County Rep. Women's Club, Monroe Assn. Woman's Missionary Union (dir. 1968-72, 79-83, sec. 1985-98), Monroe Assn. Bapts. (libr. dir. 1972-88), Ky. Libr. Assn., South Ctrl. Hist. Soc. (v.p. 1997-98, pres. 1998-2000), DAR (chaplain Edmund Rogers chpt. 1998—), Delta Kappa Gamma (pres. Delta chpt. 1996-98). Home: 54 E Nobob Rd Summer Shade KY 42166-8405

SMITH, SAMUEL HOWARD, academic administrator, plant pathologist; b. Salinas, Calif., Feb. 4, 1940; s. Adrian Reed and Elsa (Jacop) Smith; m. Patricia Ann Walter, July 8, 1960; children: Samuel, Linda Kjelgaard. BS in Plant Pathology, U. Calif., Berkeley, 1961, PhD in Plant Pathology, 1964; D (hon.), Nihon U., Tokyo, 1989, Far Eastern State U., Vladivostok, Russia, 1997. NATO fellow Glasshouse Crops Research Inst., Sussex, England, 1964-65; asst. prof. plant pathology U. Calif., Berkeley, 1965-69; assoc. prof. Pa. State U., University Park, 1969—74, prof., 1974—85, head dept. plant pathology, 1976—81, dean Coll. Agr., dir. Pa. Agrl. Expt. Sta. and Coop. Extension Service, 1981—85; pres. Wash. State U., Pullman, 1985—2000, pres. emeritus, 2000—. Bd. dirs. Blethen Corp., 1994—, Met. Mortgage & Securities, 2000—, Nat. Assn. State Univs. & Land-Grant Colls., 1994—, chair, bd. dirs., 1999—2000, exec. dir., W.K. Kellogg Found., Food & Soc. Project, 2000—, mem. Audit & Fin. Com., 1999—2000, chair, Coun. Pres.', 1998—99, exec. dir., Com. Food & Soc., 2000—, mem. Ad-Hoc Com. Fed. Support Agrl. Sci., Ext., & Edn., 1998—2000, mem. Commn. Info. Tech., 1994—2000, chair, Commn. Info. Tech., 1994—96, mem. Pres.' Policy Bd. Info. Tech., 1997—2000, mem. Kellogg Commn. Twenty-First Century State & Land-Grant Univs., 1995—2000; chair, exec. com. NCAA, 1997—99, Div. I bd. dirs., 1997—99, mem. Pres.' Commn., 1994—97, chair, Pres.' Commn., 1996—97, div. I chair, Pres.' Commn., 1995; bd. dirs. The Tech. Alliance, 1996—2000, Assn. Western Univs., 1993—2000; mem. adv. com. Wash. Sch. Employees Credit Union, 1993—95, Battelle Pacific N.W. Lab., 1993—2000; mem. Wash. Coun. Internat. Trade; chair of pres.' and chancellors Pacific-10 Conf. CEOs, 1993—94; bd. dirs. Norman Borlaug U., 2000—02, Seattle Times, 1998—; pres., bd. dirs. Talaris Rsch. Inst., 2000—; bd. trustees Western Gov.'s U., 1997—, spl. adv. to pres., 2000—, chair, pres. adv. coun., 1996—, exec. com., 1997—, chair, acad. policy com., 1997—, mem., nominating com., 1997—. Bd. trustees Pilchuck Glass Sch., 2001—, Wash. State Hist. Soc., 2000—. Mem.: Am. Phytopath Soc., Pi Kappa Alpha (hon.).

SMITH, SANDRA JEAN, special education educator; b. Muncie, Ind., May 20, 1944; d. Joseph Eugene and Judith Rose (Atkinson) S. BA, Ind. U., 1966; MA, Ball State U., 1968; MBA, Keller Grad. Sch. Mgmt., 1980. Cert. elem. and secondary tchr., Ill., Ind. Tchr. New Castle (Ind.) Jr. High Sch., 1966-70, Proviso West High Sch., Hillside, Ill., 1971-73, Ridgewood High Sch., Norridge, Ill., 1981-84; clin. educator Riveredge Sch., Forest Park, Ill., 1984-93, Maywood (Ill.) Schs., 1993-94; tchr. spl. edn. for emotionally disturbed children Valley View Schs., Romeoville, Ill., 1994—. Contbr. articles to profl. jours. Commr. Westmont (Ill.) Park Dist., 1981—. Mem. Nat. Coun. for Social Studies, Ill. Coun. for Social Studies, Nat. Parks and Recreation Assn., U.S. Volleyball Assn. (nat. scorekeeper 1977-92), Ill. H.S. Assn. (volleyball referee 1984-94). Avocation: volleyball. Home: 441 S Park St Westmont IL 60559-2228 Office: Irene King Sch 301 Eaton Ave Romeoville IL 60446-1799

SMITH, SARAH STERDIVANT, educational administrator, educational consultant; b. Meridian, Miss., June 4, 1952; d. Clenton and Doris Katherine (Mitchell) Sterdivant; m. Melvin M. Smith, Dec. 18, 1977; children: Jamall, Cedric, Anthony. BS, Miss. State U., 1973, MEd, 1974, EdS, 1978. Cert. tchr., counselor, ednl. adminstr., vocat. tchr., Miss. Counselor Miss. State U., Starkville, 1974-77, Columbus (Ga.) Coll., 1977; dir. counseling Mary Holmes Coll., West Point, Miss., 1978-80; counselor Itawamba C.C., Tupelo, Miss., 1980-87, dir. program svcs., 1987-90; exec. intern Bur. Sch. Improvements, Jackson, Miss., 1990-91; asst. dir. Tupelo-Lee County Vocat.-Tech. Ctr., 1991—. Mem. vocat. evaluation team Miss. Dept. Edn., Jackson, 1989; mem. policy bd. Head Start, Tupelo, 1990-92; mem. Leadership Inst. for Women, Miss. Dept. Edn., 1987 Author: Career Education, 1979, Community Networking Manual, 1988. Mem. Miss. Econ. Coun., 1984-87; mentor Miss. Equity Program, Tupelo, 1991-92; St. Jude ptnr. St. Jude Hosp., Memphis, 1989-92; mem. community resource com. Child Care Task Force, Tupelo, 1987-90; mem. Lee County Vocat. Adv. Com., Tupelo, 1986-90; mem. parents as tchrs. bd. Lift, Inc., Tupelo, 1992—; mem. community adv. bd. Create, Inc., Tupelo, 1992—. Recipient Partnership in Excellence award Itawamba C.C., 1990, Woman of Distinction award Tupelo Bus. and Profl. Women's Club, 1992; grantee Miss. Dept. Edn., 1990-91. Mem. NEA, Am. Vocat. Assn., Miss. Assn. Vocat. Educators, Miss. Secondary Vocat. Dirs., NAFE, Christian Meth. Episcopal Women's Missionary Assn., Miss. Assn. Women in Ednl. Leadership (exec. bd. 1988—). Democrat. Methodist. Avocations: volunteering, painting and drawing, interior decorating, fashion designing. Home: 102 Clairemont Dr Ridgeland MS 39157-9708 Office: Tupelo Pub Schs 201 S Green PO Box 557 Tupelo MS 38802-0557

SMITH, SAREBA G. special education educator; b. High Point, N.C., Nov. 28, 1930; d. Shannon and Mahaley (Blackwell) Gripper; m. Harold F. Smith, June 21, 1958; children: Sabrina Denise, Etta Marie, Sheri Ann, Harold F. Jr. BA, Clark Coll., Atlanta, 1954; MEd, Boston U., 1973; postgrad., R.I. Coll., 1986, U. R.I., Kingston, 1987. Tchr., dir. music Thomaston (Ga.) Sch., So. Pines (N.C.) Schs.; supr. edn., tchr. Hayden Sch. for Boys, Boston; spl. edn. tchr. S. Kingstown Pub. Schs., Wakefield, R.I. Mem. Human Svc. Adv. Bd. Recipient Cert. of Merit in recognition and appreciation of active interest and concern in the ednl. community, Citation for dedicated svc. to youth of Mass., others. Mem. Nat. Tchrs. Assn., Coun. for Exceptional Children. Home: PO Box 198 Kingston RI 02881-0198

SMITH, SHELAGH ALISON, public health educator; b. Oak Ridge, Tenn., June 3, 1949; d. Nicholas Monroe and Elizabeth (Kimbrough) Smith; m. Milton John Axley, 1991; 1 child, Elizabeth Claire Axley. BS in Edn., U. Tenn., 1971, AS in Dental Hygiene, 1974; MPH in Health Svcs. Adminstrn., Johns Hopkins, 1979. Lic. cert. health edn. specialist 1989. Social sci. rsch. analyst Dept. Health and Human Svcs., Health Care Fin. Adminstrn., Balt., 1980-85; pub. health educator, evaluator Nat. Cancer Inst.-NIH, Bethesda, Md., 1985-90; sr. policy analyst NIMH, Rockville, Md., 1990-92; pub. health advisor Ctr. Mental Health Svcs., Rockville, Md., 1992-96, sr. pub. health advisor orgn. and financing, 1997—. Mem. profl. devel. bd. Nat. Commn. for Health Edn. Credentialing, Inc., 2003—. Nominee C. Shepard for Outstanding Contbn. to Pub. Health, CDC, 2003; recipient Adminstr.'s Citation, Health Care Fin. Adminstrn., 1981, Dir.'s award, Nat. Cancer Inst., 1989, Spl. Act Svc. award, 1997, 1999, 2000, 2001, 2002, 2003, Quality Step Increase, 2001. Mem.: APHA (chmn. fin. and reimbursement for prevention svcs. com. 1987—89, 1996, governing coun. 1996—98, resolutions chair 1999, del. coalition nat. health edn. orgn. 1999—, advocacy chair 2001, pub. health edn. sect.), Washington Ethical Soc., Soc. Pub. Health Edn. (legis. co-chmn. 1990—91, governing bd. and ho. of dels. 1993—95, profl. devel. chair 1996, chpt. pres. 1997, treas. 1998—2000, nat. capital area exec. bd., Honor award 1999), Phi Kappa Phi. Democrat. Avocations: swimming, cooking, animal activism, sailing. Home: 14106 Heathfield Ct Rockville MD 20853-2760 Office: SAMHSA Ctr Mental Health Svc Office of Orgn and Financing 5600 Fishers Ln Rockville MD 20857-0001 E-mail: ssmith@samhsa.gov.

SMITH, SHERRI LONG, journalist, secondary education educator; b. Lancaster, Ky., Nov. 21, 1963; d. William Gordon and Hazel Marie (Howard) L.; m. Benjamin Conway Smith, Aug. 3, 1991; 2 children: Malory Scott, Sara Peyton. BA, Ea. Ky. U., 1985, MA, 1993. Tchr. Garrard County Schs., Lancaster, 1985-87, Franklin County H.S., Frankfort, 1987—, coord. dept., 1994—; writing cluster leader, 1997—. Ofcl. nominator Nat. Youth Leadership Forum. Recipient Golden Apple Achiever award Ashland Oil, Inc., 1996. Mem. NEA, Ky. Edn. Assn., Nat. Coun. Tchrs. English. Democrat. Baptist. Avocations: reading, horseback riding, traveling, writing. Home: 353 Harrodswood Rd Frankfort KY 40601-3947 Office: Franklin County High 1100 E Main St Frankfort KY 40601-2551

SMITH, SHERYL VELTING, organization administrator; b. Grand Rapids, Mich., Apr. 5, 1946; d. Louis and Martha (Kamminga) Velting; children: Laura, Paul. BA in Elem. Edn., Western Mich. U., Kalamazoo, 1968; MA in Adminstrn. and Supr./Edn., Akron U., 1980. Cert. edn. adminstr. and supr. Elem. tchr. Northview Pub. Schs., Grand Rapids, Mich., 1968-69, Ft. Knox (Ky.) Dependent Schs., 1969-70, Dept. of Def., Okinawa, 1970-71, Jefferson County Schs., Louisville, 1971-76, Hudson (Ohio) Local Schs., 1976-80; dir., presch. tchr. The Treehouse Presch., 1981-83; exec. dir. High Meadows Sch., Roswell, Ga., 1993-96; exec. v.p. Rivers of World, Inc., Alpharetta, Ga., 1997-99; dir. ind. programs Eaton Acad., Inc., Roswell, Ga., 1997—2003; pres. S.S. Internat. Cons., Alpharetta, Ga., 2001—, Ind. Study Acad., 2003—. Mem. regional conf. bd. Assn. Gifted Children, Akron, Ohio, 1979; chmn. bd. dirs. Friends of High Meadows, Roswell, 1990-94;; mem. adv. bd. Mt. Pisgah Christian Sch., Alpharetta, 1991-92, mem. headmaster search com., 1998—; bd. dirs. North Fulton Cmty. Found., 1996—, Howling Wolf Ranch Found., Whitefish, Mont.; mem. adv. bd. Peer Learning. Avocations: sports, gardening, travel, reading.

SMITH, SHIRLEY ANN NABORS, retired secondary school educator; b. Lake Creek, Tex., Dec. 9, 1938; d. Herbert Lee and Golden Ann (George) Nabors; m. Don G. Smith, Mar. 31, 1962. BS, East Tex. State U., 1960, MEd, 1962. Jr. HS English tchr. Mesquite Ind. Sch. Dist., Tex., 1960-61, 65-66; tchr. English, drama Chisum HS, Paris, Tex., 1966—2003. Bd. mem. Delta County pub. Libr.; chmn. Delta County Hist. Commn., Delta County Mus. Bd. Mem. DAR, Tex. State Tchrs. Assn., Nat. Coun. Tchrs. English, Delta Kappa Gamma. Democrat. Methodist. Avocation: genealogy. Home: 9687FR895 Lake Creek TX 75450-3422

SMITH, STEPHEN AUSTIN, communications educator; b. Fayetteville, Ark., May 15, 1949; s. Austin Clell and Margaret (King) S.; m. Lindsley Farrar Armstrong, Aug. 6, 1994; children: Caleb Jefferson, Margaret Cecilia. BA in Comm., U. Ark., 1972, MA in Comm., 1974; PhD in Comm. Studies, Northwestern U., 1983. Chief staff Atty. Gen. Ark., Little Rock, 1977-78; exec. asst. Gov. Ark., Little Rock, 1979-80; prof. comm. U. Ark., Fayetteville, 1982—. Author: Myth, Media and the Southern Mind, 1985; author, editor: Clinton on Stump, State, and Stage, 1994. State legislator Ark. Ho. of Reps., Little Rock, 1971-75; v.p. Ark. Constl. Conv., Little Rock, 1979-80. Recipient Madison prize So. States Comm. Assn., 1991. Fellow Am. Comms. Assn.; mem. Speech Comm. Assn. (chair, vice-chair Commn. on Freedom of Expression 1987—, Golden Anniversary Monograph award 1992, Haiman award 1989, Wichelns award 1978). Democrat. Unitarian Universalist. Office: U Ark Dept Comm 417 Kimpel Hall Fayetteville AR 72701 E-mail: Libertas@uark.edu.

SMITH, STEPHEN MARK, special education educator, music educator; b. Columbia, Mo., Feb. 23, 1954; s. Elmer Lee and Josephine Ann Smith; m. Pamela Layne Snella, July 30, 1978; 1 child, Christopher Stephen. A of Music, Morton Coll., 1974; BS in Music Edn., U. Ill., 1977; M of Spl. Edn., U. North Fla., 1995, postgrad., 2001—02. Cert. tchr. Fla. Dept. Edn., 1988. Commd. ensign USN, 1978, advanced through grades to lt., ret., 1988; tchr. spl. edn. music resource Dist. Operated Programs Duval County Sch. Dist., Jacksonville, Fla., 1988—. Presenter in field. Cubmaster Boy Scouts of Am., Jacksonville, 1988—90, scoutmaster, 1992—93, merit badge counselor, 1994—2002. Decorated Sea Svc. Ribbon, Sea Svc. Ribbon First Star, Navy Expeditionary Medal, Pistol Marksman Ribbon, Rifle Marksman Ribbon, Navy Achievement Medal; named Arts Educator of Yr., Cultural Coun., Jacksonville, 1997, Feature Article Educator Teaches in the Key of Success, The Times Union Newspaper, Jacksonville, 1998; recipient cert. of Appreciation, Future Educators Am., 1998; grantee, U.S. Dept. Edn., 1995, 1996, Duval Pub. Edn. Found., Jacksonville, 1996, 1996, Duval Pub. Edn. Found., 1996, U.S. Dept. Edn., 1997, The Cultural Coun. Greater Jacksonville, 1997, U.S. Dept. Edn., 1998, Duval County Pub. Found., 1998, U.S. Dept. Edn., 1999, Duval Pub. Edn. Found., 1999, The Cultural Coun. of Greater Jacksonville, 1999, Jacksonville Elec. Authority and The Alliance for World Class Edn., 2000, The Alliance for World Class Edn., 2000. Mem.: Fla. Elem. Music Educators Assn. (state dist. rep. 1990—91), Fla. Music Educators Assn., The Am. Legion, Pi Lambda Theta, Delta Sigma Pi. Democrat-Npl. Roman Catholic. Avocations: guitar, sailing, camping, computer gaming, flying. Office: District Operated Programs TEAMS Ctr 4037 Blvd Ctr Dr Jacksonville FL 32207

SMITH, SUE PARKER, media administrator; b. Pendleton, N.C., June 19, 1946; d. Edward Eldridge and Mildred (Conner) Parker; m. Jay Wilson Smith Jr., Nov. 24, 1967; 1 child, Susan Leigh. BEd, East Carolina U., Greenville, N.C., 1967, MEd in LS, 1983. Cert. tchr., media coord., N.C. Librarian Fike High Sch., Wilson (N.C.) City Schs., 1968-72; media coord. Nash-Rocky Mount Sch. System, Elm City, N.C., 1978—. Contbr. articles to profl. jours. Deacon, Nashville (N.C.) Bapt. Ch., 1989—. Mem. N.C. Assn. Educators, N.C. Assn. Sch. Librarians, Order Ea. Star (worthy matron 1989-90). Democrat. Avocations: reading, gardening, walking. Home: PO Box 505 112 E Lucille St Nashville NC 27856-1340 Office: Coopers Elem Sch 6833 S NC58 Elm City NC 27822-9433

SMITH, SUSAN ELIZABETH, guidance director; b. Phila., Mar. 24, 1950; d. E. Burke Hogue and Janet Coffin Hogue Ebert; m. J. Russell Smith, June 17, 1972 (div. June 1989); 1 child, Drew Russell. BS in Elem. Edn., E. Stroudsburg Coll., 1972; MEd in Counseling, U. Okla., 1974, postgrad., 1976-77, Trenton State Coll., 1989-90; EdM in Devel. Disabilities, Rutgers

U., 1992, postgrad., 1994—. Cert. elem. tchr., N.C.; cert. elem. tchr., early childhood edn. tchr., guidance and counseling, Okla.; cert. elem. tchr., guidance and counseling, tchr. of handicapped, psychology tchr., supr. instrn., dir. student pers. svcs., N.J. Elem. tchr. Morton Elem. Sch. Onslow County Schs., Jacksonville, N.C., 1971-72; instr. U. Isfahan, Iran, 1974-76; guidance counselor Moore (Okla.) Pub. Schs., 1976-77; counselor Johnstone Tng. Ctr. N.J. Divsn. Devel. Disabilities, Bordentown, 1988-90; spl. edn. tchr. Willingboro (N.J.) Schs., 1990-91; guidance counselor Haledon (N.J.) Pub. Schs., 1991-92; spl. edn. adj. tchr. Gateway Sch., Carteret, N.J., 1991-93; guidance counselor Bloomfield (N.J.) Pub. Schs., 1992-94; dir. guidance Somerville (N.J.) Pub. Schs., 1994-95. Adj. prof. in spl. edn. Essex County (N.J.) Coll., 1994; guidance Ft. Lee (N.J.) Schs., 1995-2001; guidance dir. Bogota Schs., N.J., 2001-02, Closter Schs., Closter, N.J., 2002—; cons., seminar and workshop presenter on behavior mgmt., parenting skills, and behavior modification techniques; cons. N.J. Fragile X Assn. Author: Motivational Awards for ESL Students, 1993, Parent Contracts to Improve School Behaviors, 1996; contbr. articles to profl. jours. Leader Boy Scouts Am., Oklahoma City, 1983-87, com. chmn., Redmond, Wash., 1987-88. Recipient Rsch. award ERIC/CAPS, 1992, Svc. award N.J. Fragile X Assn., 1993. Mem. ACA, Am. Sch. Counselor Assn. (grantee 1992), N.J. Counseling Assn., N.J. Sch. Counseling Assn., Assn. for Multicultural Counseling and Devel., AAUW, Assn. for Counselor Edn. and Supervision, N.J. Assn. for Counselor Edn. and Supervision, N.J. Prins. and Suprs. Assn., Nat. Assn. Coll. Admissions Counselors (grantee 1995), Alpha Omicron Pi. Episcopalian. Home: 916 Lincoln Pl Teaneck NJ 07666-2572

SMITH, SUSAN K. elementary education educator; b. St. Louis, Aug. 28, 1946; d. Gilbert D. and Elizabeth L. (Doak) McGough; m. Ronald James Smith, June 15, 1968; children: Joshua, Sarah. BS in Elem. Edn., So. Ill. U., 1968. Tchr. River Forest (Ill.) Pub. Schs., 1968-72, Dept. of Def. Sch., Gaeta, Italy, 1980-81, Gloucester (Va.) County Pub. Schs., 1982—, Jacob's Ladder, Christchurch, Va., summer 1992-94. Mem. Five Rivers Woman's Club, Gloucester, 1992-94; pres. Gloucester High Sch. Athletic Boosters, 1990-91. Mem. NEA, Va. Edn. Assn., Gloucester Edn. Assn. (v.p. 1982—), Delta Kappa Gamma (pres. Gamma Nu chpt. 1994—). Home: PO Box 112 Gloucester Point VA 23062-0112 Office: TC Walker Elem Sch 6099 TC Walker Rd Gloucester VA 23061 E-mail: susans@gc.k12.va.us.

SMITH, THOMAS HUNTER, ophthalmologist, ophthalmic plastic and orbital surgeon; b. Silver Creek, Miss., Aug. 10, 1939; s. Hunter and Wincil (Barr) S.; m. Michele Ann Campbell, Feb. 27, 1982; 1 child, Thomas Hunter IV. BA, U. So. Miss., 1961; MD, Tulane U., 1967; BA in Latin Am. Studies, Tex. Christian U., 1987, MA in History, 1995, PhD in L.Am. History, 1999. Diplomate Am. Bd. Ophthalmology (bd. examiners 1983-90). Intern Charity Hosp., New Orleans, 1967-68; resident in ophthalmology Tulane U., New Orleans, 1968-71; dir., sec. bd. dirs. Ophthalmology Assocs., Ft. Worth, 1971-99; adj. prof. history of medicine and L.Am. history Tex. Christian U., Ft. Worth, 2000—01; adj. instr. history of medicine and pub. health, L.Am. history Tulane U., 2001—03. Clin. prof. Tex. Tech U. Med. Sch., Lubbock, 1979-99; guest lectr., invited speaker numerous schs., confs., symposia throughout N.Am., Ctrl. Am., South Am., Europe and India; hon. mem. ophthalmology dept. Santa Casa de São Paulo Med. Sch. Contbr. articles to profl. jours. Cons. ophthalmologist Helen Keller Internat.; deacon South Hills Christian Ch.; mem. Rocky Mountain Coun. Latin Am. Studies. Recipient Tex. Chpt. award Am. Assn. Workers for the Blind, 1978, Recognition award Lions Club Sight & Tissue Found., Cen. Am., 1977-79; named to Alumni Hall of Fame U. So. Miss., 1989. Fellow ACS, Am. Acad. Ophthalmology (bd. counsellors 1995-98), Am. Acad. Facial Plastic and Reconstructive Surgery; mem. Tex. Med. Assn. (com. socio-econs.), Pan-Am. Assn. Ophthalmology (adminstr. 1988-93, bd. dirs. 1993-99), Internat. Cos. Cryosurgery, Royal Soc. Medicine (affiliate), Tex. Soc. Ophthalmology and Otolaryngology, Peruvian Ophthalmol. Soc. (hon.), Santa Casa De São Paulo (hon. assoc.), Tex. Ophthalmol. Assn. (past mem. exec. coun., treas.), Tex. Med. Assn., Tarrant County Med. Soc., Byron Smith Ex Fellows Assn., Tarrant County Multiple Sclerosis Soc. (past pres.), Tarrant County Assn. for Blind, Tulane Med. Alumni Assn. (bd. dirs.), S.Am. Explorers Club, Colonial Country Club, Petroleum Club Ft. Worth, Sigma Xi, Omicron Delta Kappa. Mem. Christian Ch. (Disciples Of Christ). Avocations: hunting, fishing, flying, world travel.

SMITH, VALERIE GAY, school counselor; b. Austin, Tex., Oct. 31, 1947; d. James Griffin and Ida Mae (Routon) Black; m. James David Smith, July 20, 1993. BA in English, McMurry Coll., 1969; MEd in Counseling, U. North Tex., 1974. Lic. profl. counselor, Tex.; cert. sch. counselor, Tex. Tchr. Nimitz H.S., Irving, Tex., 1969-71, MacArthur H.S., Irving, Tex., 1971-74, counselor, 1974-89, Ditto Elem. Sch., Arlington, Tex., 1989-94, Withers Elem. Sch., Dallas, 1994—. Mem. ACA, Am. Sch. Counselor Assn., Tex. Sch. Counselor Assn. (elem. v.p. 1990-92, senator 1988-90, sec. 1986-88, Rhosine Fleming Outstanding Counselor award 1987, pres.-elect 1992-93, pres. 1993-94), Tex. PTA (life), Tex. Counseling Assn. (region 4 dir. 1990-93, pres.-elect 1995-96, pres. 1996-97, past pres. 1997-98), Phi Delta Kappa. Home: 2120 Nob Hl Carrollton TX 75006-2817 Office: Withers Elem Sch 3959 Northaven Rd Dallas TX 75229-2758

SMITH, VERNA MAE EDOM (VME EDOM SMITH), sociology educator, freelance writer, photographer; b. Marshfield, Wis., June 19, 1929; d. Clifton Cedric and Vilia Clarissa (Patefield) Edom; children: Teri Smith Freas, Anthony Thomas. AB in Sociology, U. Mo., 1951; MA in Sociology, George Washington, 1965; PhD in Human Devel., U. Md., 1981. Tchr. Alcohol Safety Action Program Fairfax County, Va., 1973-75; instr. sociology No. Va. C.C., Manassas, 1975-77, asst. prof., 1977-81, assoc. prof., 1981-84, prof., 1984-94, prof. emerita, 1995, coord. coop. edn., 1983-89, Chancellor's Commonwealth prof., 1991-93; adj. faculty Tidewater C.C., 1996—; freelance writer, editor and photographer, 1965—; dir. Clifton C. Edom Truth With a Camera (photography workshops), 1994—. Asst. prodr. history of photography program Sta. WETA-TV, Washington, 1965; rsch. and prodn. asst., photographer, publs. editor No. Va. Ednl. TV, Sta. WNVT, 1970—71; cons. migrant divsn. Md. Dept. Edn., Balt., 1977; rschr. photographer Roundabout presch. high sch. series Am. Values Sta. WNVT, 1970—71; documentary photographer Portsmouth (Va.) Redevel. and Housing Authority, 1998—2000. Author, photographer: Middleburg and Nearby, 1986; co-author: Small Town America, 1993; contbr. photography to various works including Visual Impact in Print (Hurley and McDougall), 1971, Looking Forward to a Career in Education (Moses), 1976, Child Growth and Development (Terry, Sorrentino and Flatter), 1979, Photojournalism (Edom), 1976, 80, Migrant Child Welfare, 1977, (Cavenaugh), Caring for Children, 1973 (5 publs. by L.B. Murphy), Dept. Health, Edn. and Welfare, Nat. Geog., 1961, Head Start Newsletter, 1973-74, Women in Photojournalism, Nat. Press Photographers Assn., Nat. Fedn. Press Women, Photographic Soc. Am., Va. Found. for Humanities and Pub. Policy exhibits. Mem. ednl. adv. com. Head Start, Warrenton, Va. Recipient Emmy, Ohio State Children's Programming award; Fulbright-Hays rsch. grantee, 1993, Va. Found. for Humanities and Pub. Policy grantee, 1997-99. Mem. Va. Assn. Coop. Edn. (com. mem.). Democrat. E-mail: vme@macs.net.

SMITH, WILDA MAXINE, history educator; b. Gove, Kans., May 17, 1924; d. Corwin Leroy and Mabel Luzelle (Roberts) S. A.B. in History, Fort Hays State Coll., 1953, M.S., 1957; Ph.D., U. Ill., 1960. Elem. sch. tchr. schs. in Gove County, Kans., 1943-49; tchr. history Hays High Sch., Kans., 1953-57; asst. prof. history Fort Hays State Coll., Kans., 1960-63, assoc. prof., 1963-66, prof. history, 1966-77; prof. history Fort Hays State U., 1977-86, chmn. dept., 1981-86, prof. emeritus, 1987—. Author: (with Eleanor A. Bogart) The Wars of Peggy Hull: The Life and Times of a War Correspondent; contbr. articles and book revs. to profl. jours. Mem. Kans. Com. for Humanities, Topeka, 1982-85; bd. dirs. Kans. State Hist. Soc., Topeka, 1982-94, Kans. State Hist. Records Adv. Bd., 1992-94. Univ. fellow U. Ill., Urbana-Champaign, 1958-60; recipient W.C. Wood award Fort Hays State U., 1975, Pilot award for Outstanding Faculty Woman, Srs. and Alumni Assn. Bd. Fort Hays State U., 1984. Mem. Nat. Women's Studies Assn. (nat. coordinating council 1977-80), Kans. History Tchrs. Assn. (exec. bd. 1973), NOW, Delta Kappa Gamma (pres. 1974-76), Phi Delta Kappa (Cunningham Outstanding Educator award Fort Hays State chpt. 1986), Phi Kappa Phi. Avocations: fishing, travel, research, writing. Home: 2924 Walnut St Hays KS 67601-1721

SMITH-ANSOTEGUI, SUSAN COONLEY, elementary school educator; b. Tokyo, Aug. 14, 1951; d. Franklin Leonard and Hanako (Kondo) Coonley; m. R. Michael Ansotegui, June 28, 1993; children: Johana, Ashley. BS in Elem. Edn., U. Nev., Reno, 1973; MEd in Curriculum and Instrn., Lesley U., 1996; MEd in Adminstrn. and Supervision, U. Phoenix, 2001. Home sch. tchr. Calvert Sch., Kauai, Hawaii, 1977-80; tchr. 1st grade Northside Elem. Sch., Fallon, Nev., 1973-77, 80-81; tchr. reading and history Minnie P. Blair Mid. Sch., Fallon, 1981-88; tchr. 6th grade E.C. Best Elem. Sch., Fallon, 1988-96, Numa Elem. Sch., Fallon, 1996—. Tchr. trainer in math. Nev. Dept. Edn., Carson City, 1990—; component mgr. elem. and middle sch. sci. Rural Alliance, Carson City, Nev., 1997-98; math. workshop coord. Churchill County Sch. Dist., 1997—. Recipient State and Nat. Presdl. award for excellence in math. and sci. tchg., 1997; named County Tchr. of the Yr., Churchill County, 1994. Mem. Nat. Coun. Tchrs. Math., Churchill County Edn. Assn. (sec. 1986—, disting. svc. award 1996), Nev. Math. Coun. (sec. 1995-97, 99—, pres. 1997-99). Home: 2677 Rice Rd Fallon NV 89406-7445 Office: Churchill County Sch Dist 545 E Richards St Fallon NV 89406-3498 E-mail: smith-ansoteguis@churchill.k12.nv.us., ansoteg@cccomm.net.

SMITH-COX, ELIZABETH SHELTON, art educator; b. Washington, Feb. 12, 1924; d. Benjamin Warren and Sarah Priscilla (Harrell) Shelton; m. John Edwin Smith, Aug. 16, 1947 (dec. July 1992); children: Shelley Hobson, Dale Henslee, John Edwin Jr.; m. Headley Morris Cox Jr., Dec. 30, 1994. BA in Art, Meredith Coll., 1946; MEd in Supervision and Adminstrn., Clemson U., 1974. Youth dir. St. John's Bapt. Ch., Charlotte, N.C., 1946-47; art tchr. Raleigh (N.C.) Pub. Schs., 1947-49, East Mecklenberg H.S., Charlotte, 1968-69, D. W. Daniel H.S., Central, S.C., 1970-86; art instr. U. S.C., Columbia, 1966-68; adj. prof. Clemson (S.C.) U., 1991-93; artist-in-residence edn. program S.C. Arts Commn., Columbia, 1991-2001. Exhibited in numerous one and two person shows and in group exhibits; solo show at Meredith Coll. Rotunda Gallery, Raleigh, 2002; invitational alumnae exhibit Meredith Coll., 2000; exhibited in 2-person show Pickens County (S.C.) Mus., 2000; featured artist F. Hanson Discovery Ctr., Clemson, 2003. Vol. worker, editor newsletter Pickens County Habitat for Humanity, Clemson, 1981—; vol. art tchr. St. Andrew's Elem. Sch., Columbia, 1962-68; vol. Habitat for Humanity Mission to Honduras, summers 1996—. Recipient Svc. to Mankind award Clemson Sertoma Club, 1997, Disting. Alumni award Meredith Coll., 1996; named S.C. Tchr. of Yr., S.C. Dept. Edn. and Ency. Britannica, 1976, Citizen of Yr., Clemson Rotary Club, 1979. Mem. S.C. Art Edn. Assn. (pres. 1978, Lifetime Svc. award 1990, Lifetime Achievement in Art Edn. award 1995), Nat. Art Edn. Assn. (ret. art educator affiliate, pres. 1994-97, Disting. Svc. award 1995, Electronic Gallery 1999, 2000, 01, 02, 03, Ret. Art Educator of Yr. award 2000, Elizabeth's O'Neil Verner S.C. Gov.'s award for individual in Arts Edn. 2003), Nat. Art Edn. Found. (trustee 1996-2002, S.C. Watercolor Soc. (Mem. with Excellence 1993), Upstate Visual Artists (Best in Show award). Baptist. Avocations: travel, reading, writing, music. Home: 1604 Six Mile Hwy Central SC 29630-9483 E-mail: lizhmcox@innova.net.

SMITH-FARNSWORTH, SHARON ANNE, elementary education educator; b. San Francisco, Aug. 6, 1945; d. Donald Franklin and Maxine Anna (Alterman) Steiner; m. Edward Earl Smith III, Nov. 7, 1968 (div. Dec. 1987); 1 child, Edward Earl IV; m. Matthew Lee Farnsworth, Jan. 15, 1988. BA in History, U. Calif., Berkeley, 1967; cert. in gifted and talented in edn., U. Calif., Riverside, 1986. Cert. elem. tchr., Calif. Tchr. Manhattan Beach (Calif.) City Sch., 1968-78, Moreno Valley (Calif.) Unified Sch. Dist., 1984—. Mem. ASCD, NEA, NAACP, Calif. Leadership Acad., Calif. Tchrs. Assn., Moreno Valley Educators Assn. (rep. 1984-91, v.p. 1991-94), Smithsonian Inst., Phi Sigma Sigma. Republican. Avocations: reading, writing poetry, traveling. Home: 10689 Willow Creek Rd Moreno Valley CA 92557-2953 Office: Badger Springs Mid Sch 24750 Delphinium Ave Moreno Valley CA 92553-5812

SMITH-GOMES, KATHLEEN MARIE, special education educator; b. Mineola, N.Y., June 27, 1963; d. Warren Henry and Mary Cecilia (O'Reilly) Smith; m. Rui Cameira Gomes, July 12, 1986; 1 child, Kayla Elizabeth. BS in Spl. Edn. and Elem. Edn., SUNY, Buffalo, 1985; MS in Spl. Edn. summa cum laude, SUNY, Albany, 1986; cert. in supervision, Kean Coll., 1993, MS in Administrn., 1995. Cert. tchr., N.Y., N.J. Spl. edn. intern Niskayuna H.S., Schenectady, N.Y., 1985, SUNY, Albany, 1986; elem. tchr. St. Hedwig Sch., Elizabeth, N.J., 1986-87; resource/inclusion tchr. Colts Neck (N.J.) Pub. Sch., 1987-88; spl. edn. tchr. Matawan (N.J.) Regional H.S., 1988-89; resource/inclusion tchr. Roselle (N.J.) Pub. Schs., 1989—, acting spl. edn. dept. chair, 1995—, spl. edn. dept. chair, 1995—, mem. curriculum revision team, 1993-94, inclusion pilot program trainer, 1993—, mem. drug and alcohol core team Abraham Clark H.S., 1991—. Adminstrv. intern spl. edn. Kean Coll., 1994; advisor AIDS presentation, 1993; presenter Inclusion Workshop CEC Annual Conf., 1995. Advisor Quilts for Kids, Roselle, 1989-90; mem. Fairway Civic Assn., Union Twp., N.J., 1995—. Recipient Vol. award Pres. Bush, 1990; grantee SUNY, 1985-86. Mem. ASCD, N.J. Edn. Assn., Coun. for Exceptional Children, Roselle Edn. Assn. (bldg. rep. 1989—), Phi Delta Kappa (pub. rels. com. 1992—). Republican. Roman Catholic. Avocations: aviculture, sewing, water skiing, boating, gardening. Home: 91 Tuthill Rd Queensbury NY 12804-8457 Office: Abraham Clark HS 122 E 6th Ave Roselle NJ 07203-2081

SMITH-JONES, MARY EMILY, elementary school physical education educator; b. Ducktown, Tenn., Jan. 9, 1949; d. Oscar Clinton and Mary Myrtice (Hayes) S. Student, Kennesaw (Ga.) Jr. Coll., 1967-69; BS in Edn., Ga. So. Coll., 1971; MEd, Delta State U., 1974; EdS, West Ga. Coll., 1991. Cert. tchr., Ga. Tchr. phys. edn. East Hall High Sch., Gainesville, Ga., 1971-73, Morrow (Ga.) Elem. Sch., 1974—. Mem. com. to write phys. edn. curriculum for grades kindergarten through 4 State of Ga.; mem. com. to write elem. phys. edn. curriculum Clayton County, Ga. Mem. AAHPERD (mem. conv. hospitality com. 1991), Ga. Assn. Health, Phys. Edn., Recreation and Dance (exhibits chairperson 1992, 93). Home: 180 Falling Waters Dr Jonesboro GA 30236-5485 Office: Morrow Elem Sch 6115 Reynolds Rd Morrow GA 30260-1151

SMITH-LEINS, TERRI L. mathematics educator; b. Salina, Kans., Sept. 19, 1950; d. John W. and Myldred M. (Hays) Smith; m. Larry L. Leins, May 26, 1984. BS, Ft. Hays (Kans.) U., 1973, MS, 1976; AA, Stephen Coll., Columbia, Mo., 1970. Math tchr. Scott City (Kans.) Jr. H.S., Howard (Kans.) Schs.; instr. math. U. Ark., Ft. Smith. Contbr. articles to profl. jours., chpts. to books. Mem. AADE, ASCD, Nat. Assn. Devel. Edn. (state sec. 1986-88, computer access com. 1980-85), Phi Delta Kappa (Kappan of Yr. 1985), Delta Kappa Gamma (state chairperson women in art 1993-95, area one leader 1999-2001, Kappa state corr. sec., 2003—). Home: PO Box 3446 Fort Smith AR 72913-3446 E-mail: tleins@uafortsmith.edu.

SMITH TARCHALSKI, HELEN MARIE, piano educator; b. Washington, Dec. 24, 1957; d. Albert John and Marie Ethel (Wellens) Smith; m. Stanislaw Edward Tarchalski, Sept. 26, 1981. MusB in Applied Piano, Peabody Conservatory Md., 1979. Master cert. music tchr. Ind. piano instr., accompanist, various cities, 1978—; edn. rep., clinician Baldwin Piano and Organ Co., various cities, 1982-94. Clinician various univs., 1984—; com. mem., seminar leader Nat. Conf. on Piano Pedagogy, Chgo., 1990-94; mem. adv. bd. Pacific Music Alliance, Pasadena, Calif., 1994-97; mem. organizing com. World Piano Pedagogy Conf., 1996—. Editor (periodical) Soundboard, 1989-94, (textbook) Teaching Toward Tomorrow, 1994; contbg. author Encyclopedia of Keyboard Instruments, 1994, various jours.; author (computer software) Symbol Simon, 1995. Mem. Am. Liszt Soc. (bd. dirs. 1996—), Music Tchrs. Nat. Assn., Md. State Music Tchrs. Assn. (tech. chair 1996—), Montgomery County Music Tchrs. Assn. (pres. 1999—), Anapolis Sch. Music, 1998—. Avocations: scuba diving, water skiing, sailing, biking, rollerblading. Home: 1802 River Watch Ln Annapolis MD 21401-2009

SMITH-THOMPSON, PATRICIA ANN, public relations consultant, educator; b. Chgo., June 7, 1933; d. Clarence Richard and Ruth Margaret (Jacobson) Nowack; m. Tyler Thompson, Aug. 2, 1992; children from previous marriage: Deborah, Kurt, Nancy, Janna, Gail, Lori. Student, Cornell U., 1951—52; BA, Centenary Coll., Hackettstown, N.J., 1983. Prodn. asst. Your Hit Parade Batten, Barton, Durstine & Osborne, 1953-54; pvt. practice polit. cons., 1954-66; legal sec., asst. Atty. John C. Cushman, 1966-68; field dep. L.A. County Assessor Office, 1968-69; pub. info. officer L.A. County Probation Dept., 1969-73; dir. consumer rels. Fireman's Fund, San Francisco, 1973-76; spl. projects officer L.A. County Transp. Commn., 1977-78; tchr. Calif. State U., Dominguez Hills, 1979-86. Editor, writer Jet Propulsion Lab., 1979—80; pub. info. dir. L.A. Bd. Pub. Works, 1980—82; pub. info. cons. City of Pasadena, Calif., 1982—84, pub. rels. cons., 1983—90; cmty. affairs cons. Worldport L.A., 1990—92; tchr. Kern County Schs., 2002—. Contbr. articles to profl. jours. Active First United Meth. Ch. Commn. Missions and Social Concerns, 1983—89; bd. dirs. Depot, 1983—87; mem. devel. com. Pasadena Guidance Clinics, 1984—85; pres. Cultural Arts Assn., Bear Valley Springs, 1999—2000, Calif. Press Women, Bay Area, 1975. Recipient Pro award, L.A. Publicity Club, 1978, Outstanding Achievement award, Soc. Consumer Affairs Profls. Bus., 1976, Disting. Alumni award, Centenary Coll., 1992. Mem.: Nat. Assn. Mental Health Info. Officers (3 regional awards 1986), Calif. Press Women (pres. Bay area 1975—76, award 1974, 1978, 1983, 1984, 1985, Cmty. Rels. 1st pl. winner 1986, 1987, 1988, 1989), Nat. Press Women (Calif. chpt. pres. 1975—76, Pub. Rels. award 1986), Pub. Rels. Soc. Am. (accredited mem., consumer program award 1977, 2 awards 1984, Joseph Roos Cmty. Svc. award 1985). Republican. Home and Office: 24145 Jacaranda Dr Tehachapi CA 93561-8309

SMITH-WILLOUGHBY, DOLORES ANNE, educator, computer consultant; b. Chickasha, Okla., Jan. 6, 1938; d. Loranzie Dawl and Anna Mae (Montgomery) Wilkes; m. Don Jeral Willoughby, Apr. 8, 1956 (dec. Apr. 1975); m. Clarence (John) Smith, Aug. 1, 1999; children: Danny Michael, Melissa Dawn Willoughby Onesalt. BS, U. Sci. and Arts Okla., 1969; MEd, Southwestern Okla. State U., 1976; postgrad. Okla. State U., 1985-90, Ctrl. State U., Edmond., 1975; postgrad., U. Okla., 1985-89, 92. Cert. K-8 sci., math., reading, and social studies tchr., Okla. Teller Okla. Nat. Bank, Chickasha, 1957-66; tchr. Verden (Okla.) Pub. Schs., 1969-82, Amber-Pocasset (Okla.) Schs., 1982-89; tchr. sci., computer coord. Chickasha Intermediate Sch., 1989-92; elem. tchr. Grand Avenue Sch., Chickasha, 1992—2001; sci. tchr. Chickasha Intermediate Sch., 2001—02. Mem. evaluation com. North Ctrl. Accreditation, Oklahoma City, 1993; mem. sci. curriculum alignment com. Chickasha Schs., 1992-93, site chmn. for sci. and computer programs, 1993-94; reviewer CHIME newsletter, 1986. Contbr. articles to profl. jours. Mem. adv. bd. Chickasha Pub. Libr., 1993—. Recipient Okla. medal of Excellence for Elem. Teaching Okla. Found. for Excellence, 1995, Okla. Elem. Sci. Tchr. of Yr. award Okla. Sci. Tchrs. Assn., 1995, Grady County Ret. Tchr. award, 2003. Mem. NSTA (space adv. bd. 1990-94, gen. rev. panel 1994-96, NASA Educators' Workshop Math and Sci. Tchrs. award 1990). Democrat. Baptist. Avocations: bobbin lace-making, travel, reading, telecommunication. Home: 116 S 13th St Chickasha OK 73018-3107

SMITS, RONALD FRANCIS, English educator, poet; b. Bayonne, N.J., Dec. 22, 1943; s. Edwin Joseph and Florence Ann Smits; m. Bonnie Lee Brown, June 10, 1970 (div. Mar. 1976); 1 child, Ronald Thomas. AB, Rutgers U., 1966; MS, Ind. State U., 1969; PhD, Ball State U., 1978. Instr. English, Kaskaskia Coll., Centralia, Ill., 1969-74; instr. Ball State U., Muncie, Ind., 1976-78; asst. prof. English, Indiana U. Pa., 1979-92, assoc. prof., 1992-96, prof., 1996—. Dir. faculty forum br. campus Indiana U. Pa., Kittanning, 1998—. Contbr. poems to jours. 1st lt. U.S. Army, 1966-68, Vietnam. Doctoral fellow Ball State U., 1974-78; Disting. Faculty Award, Creativ Arts, Indiana U. Pa, 1993; recipient Outstanding Faculty award English Assn. of Pa. State U., 2002. Avocations: walking, nature hikes, walks through city neighborhoods, nature study, reading. Home: PO Box 466 Ford City PA 16226-0466 Office: Ind U of Pa Armstrong County Campus Kittanning PA 16201

SMOKVINA, GLORIA JACQUELINE, nursing educator; b. East Chicago, Ind., July 29, 1937; Diploma in nursing, St. Margaret Hosp. Sch. Nursing, 1959; BSN, DePaul U., 1964; MSN, Ind. U., 1966; PhD in Nursing, Wayne State U., 1977. RN, Ind. Staff and charge nurse surgical units St. Catherine Hosp., East Chgo., Ind., 1959-61, charge nurse surgical units, 1962-64; asst. head nurse ICU El Camino Hosp., Mountain View, Calif., 1961-62; instr. nursing South Chgo. Community Hosp., Chgo., 1964-65; asst. prof. med.-surgical nursing U. Evansville, Ind., 1966-70; assoc. prof. nursing Purdue U. Calumet, Hammond, Ind., 1970-80, prof. nursing, 1980—, acting head dept. nursing, 1986-87, head dept. nursing, 1987—, head sch. nursing, 1996—, dean schs. of profl. programs, 1996—2002, dean Sch. of Nursing, 2002—. Bd. dir. Health East Chgo. Cmty. Bd., St. Catherine Hosp.; cons. ICU St. Catherine Hosp., 1971, 74, 77, 79, 81, staff nurse, 71, 74, 77, 79, 81; cons. Vis. Nurses Assn., 1979, 80, Klapper, Issac & Parish Law Firm, Indpls., 1995; mem. adv. com. Vis. Nurse Assn. of NW Ind., 1977—; mem. Statewide Task Force on Nursing in Ind., 1987—; mem. Health E. Chgo. Task Force, 1996—; peer reviewer Coll. Nursing Valparaiso U., Ind., 1989; mem. gov. bd. St. Margaret Mercy Healthcare Ctrs. Inc., 1992—, chair quality svcs. com., 1992—, v.p., 1998—2001; mem. gov. bd. Sisters of St. Francis Regional Bd.; expert witness in several cases. Contbr. chpt. to Normal Aging: Dimensions of Wellness, 1986, Medical-Surgical Nursing, 1981; contbr. articles to profl. jours.; numerous rsch. projects. Mem. planning com. Lake County Health Fair, 1975, 77, nursing chair, 1978-80; chmn. nominations com. Ind. League for Nursing, 1995—; mem. adv. bd. Horizon Career Coll., Merriville, Ind., 1994—; mem. adv. com. Community Ctr. Devel. Corp., Hammond, 1993—, Three City Empowerment Zone E. Chgo., Gary and Hammond, 1994-95, grad. edn. Ind. U. Purdue U., 1981-85, Westhaysen Med. Edn. Trust Com. Calumet Nat. Bank, Hammond, 1987—; mem. panel Healthy E. Chgo., 1994-96; mem. Community Health Assn., 1979-84; v.p. Am. Heart Assn. N.W. Ind. affiliate, 1984-87, mem. edn. com. 1982-87, bd. dirs. Our Lady of Mercy Hosp., Dyer, Ind., 1989-92, Health Adv., 1979-82; bd. dirs. Am. Heart Assn. Ind. affiliate, 1981-87, chair community programs, 1982-87; bd. dirs. Lakeshore Health Care System, 1988-89, quality assurance com. Grantee HHS, 1983-85, 84, 85-88, 90—, Helene Fuld Health Trust, 1989, 92, 93-94, Pub. Health Svc., 1989-90, 1990-91, Meth. Hosp., 1993-98; recipient Meritorious Svc. award Am. Cancer Soc. of N.W. Ind., 1979, Lake Area United Way, 1979, Cert. of Recognition Am. Heart Assn., 1983-84, Med. and Sci. Disting. Program award, 1985, Franciscan Award, Svc. Recogn. St. Margaret Mercy Healthcare Ctr., 2002. Mem. AACN, N.W. Ind. Orgn. Nurse Execs., Nurse Exec. Resource Group (U. Chgo.), Nat. League for Nursing, Ind. Deans and Dirs. of AD, BS and Higher Degree Programs, Nurse Exec. Forum, Wayne State Alumni Assn., St. Margaret Alumni Assn. (v.p. program com., chmn. scholarship com.), Ind. U. Alumni Assn., Mu Omega (chpt. commitment award 1994, chair fin. com. 1991—), Sigma Theta Tau (hon.). Office: Purdue U Calumet 2200 169th St Hammond IN 46323-2068 E-mail: smokvina@calumet.purdue.edu.

SMOLEN, CHERYL HOSAKA, special education educator; b. Fairview, Ohio, Dec. 17, 1959; d. James Yukio and Midori (Osaki) Hosaka; m. Alan Smolen; children: Tyler, Dylan. BA, Ohio U., 1983; M in Curriculum and Instrn., Cleve. State U., 1992. Tchr. devel. handicapped Scioto Valley Sch. Dist., Piketon, Ohio, 1983-85; tchr. learning disabled Darlington County Sch. Dist., Darlington, S.C., 1985-88; small group instrn. tchr. Upper Arlington (Ohio) Sch. Dist., 1988-89; tchr. handicapped presch. Euclid (Ohio) Sch. Dist., 1989-91, Cuyahoga County Bd. Edn., North Olmsted, Ohio, 1991—; tutor learning disabled Avon Lake City Schs., Ohio, 1991-92; presch. spl. needs tchr. Spl. Horizon, North Olmsted, Ohio, 2000—02, Lakewood (Ohio) Sch. Dist., 2002—03, primary tchr. autistic unit, 2003—. Coord. Spl. Olympics, Darlington County, 1987-88; counselor Snoopy Camp, Hartsville, S.C., 1987; tutor Project LEARN, Cleve., 1990-92; tchr. Spl. Horizon, North Olmsted, Ohio, summer, 1992; mem. spl. edn. curriculum devel. com., handicapped presch. curriculum devel. com., coord. spl. edn. newsletter; ESL tutor, 1992—; mem. adv. bd. Spl. Horizon. Asst. Cub Scout leader, 2000—01; mem. Hayes Elem. PTA, Avon Heritage Booster Club. Mem. NEA, Ohio Edn. Assn., Coun. for Exceptional Children. Avocations: aerobics, playing flute, cross-stitching, spectator sports, jogging. Home: 4298 S Fall Lake Dr Avon OH 44011

SMOLLER, IRENE MILDRED, artist, educator; b. Chgo., July 28, 1919; d. Frank and Martha (Rothwell) Volkert; m. Louis Ben Smoller (dec.); 1 child, William. Student, N.Y. Acad., 1937-40, Art Inst. Chgo., 1950-51. One-man shows include Chgo. Pub. Libr., Merchants and Mfrs. Club, Chgo., Bernheim and Jeune Galerie, Paris, O'Hanna Gallery, London, Broadway Galleries, Ltd., Milw., LeBow Gallery, Evanston, Ill., Thor Gallery, Louisville, Palm Beach (Fla.) Gallery, Price Gallery, Chgo.; exhibited in groups shows including St. Paul Gallery and Sch. Arts, Russell Gallery, Bloomington, Ill., Adele Rosenberg Gallery, Chgo., Harper Gallery, Chgo., Butler Inst., Youngstown, Ohio, N.Y. Acad., Evanston (Ill.) Art Ctr., Denver Mus., Art Inst. Chgo., Krannert Mus., Springfield, Ill., McKerrie Galleries, Pitts., Biennale Internationale France, Paris, Rual Askew Gallery, Dallas, Ft. Wayne (Ind.) Mus., Societe des Artistes Independants Annuelle, Paris, Berheim-Jeune Gallery, Paris, Memmel Gallery, Milw., Downtown Gallery, New Orleans, Thor Gallery, Louisville, Internat. Exhbn., Lucca, Italy, Palm Beach (Fla.) Gallery, others; represented in permanent collections Galerie Bernheim and Jeune, Paris, Vincent Price collection, Cedar Rapids (Mich.) Mus. Art; pvt. instr., Chgo., 1960—. Midwest regional dir. Nat. Arts Coun. Recipient Maxwell Pearl purchase award, London, 1960, 2d prize Solomon Art purchase award, Phila., 1960, 2d prize Lincolnwood (Ill.) Art Festival, 1967, 1st prize Suburban Art Ctr. Ann., Highland Park, Ill., 1965, 1st prize Midwest Regional Representational, Chgo., 1964, Silver medal Internat. Italian Exbn., Rome; diplome d'honneur Laureate la France, 1964. Mem. Artist Equity Am., Renaissance Soc. U. Chgo., Royal Acad. (London). Home: 5555 N Sheridan Rd Chicago IL 60640-1601

SMOOT, JOSEPH GRADY, university administrator; b. Winter Haven, Fla., May 7, 1932; s. Robert Malcolm and Vera (Eaton) S.; m. Florence Rozell, May 30, 1955 (dec.); m. Irma Jean Kopitzke, June 4, 1959; 1 child, Andrew Christopher. BA, So. Coll., 1955; MA, U. Ky., 1958, PhD, 1964. Tchr., Ky. Secondary Schs., 1955-57; from instr. to assoc. prof. history Columbia Union Coll., Takoma Park, Md., 1960-68, acad. dean, 1965-68; prof. history Andrews U., Berrien Springs, Mich., 1968-84, dean Sch. Grad. Studies, 1968-69, v.p. acad. adminstrn., 1969-76, pres., 1976-84; v.p. for devel. Pittsburg State U., Kans., 1984—; exec. dir. Pitts. State U. Found., 1985—; bd. dirs. 1st State Bank and Trust Co., Pitts., 1994—; founder Pitts. State U. Radio Sta.-KRPS-FM, 1988; commr. North Cen. Assn., 1987-91, cons., evaluator, 1978—; cons. internat. edn; trustee Loma Linda U., 1976-84, U. Ea. Africa, Baraton, Kenya, 1979-84, Hindsdale Hosp., Ill., 1973-84; chmn., bd. trustees Andrews Broadcasting Corp., 1976-84; bd. dirs. Internat. U. Thailand Found., 1987-95, trustee, 1994-95. Contbr. articles to profl. jours; editor: Spottiswoode Soc. Record, 1990—. Active Pitts. Area Festival Assn., 1984-86, bd. dirs. Pitts. United Way, 1987-92, Pitts. C. of C. Found., 1990-93; bd. advisors Pitts. Salvation Army, 1987-92, vice-chmn., 1990-91, chmn., 1991-92; bd. trustees Mt. Carmel Med. Ctr. Found., 1991-95; bd. dirs. S.E. Kans. Symphony Orch., 1995—. Recipient Disting. Pres. award Mich. Coll. Found., 1984. Mem. Inst. Early Am. History and Culture (assoc.), Am. Hist. Assn., So. Hist. Assn., Orgn. Am. Historians, Soc. for Historians of Early Am. Rep., Soc. History of Authorship, Reading & Pub., Phi Alpha Theta. Club: Crestwood Country. Lodge: Rotary (dist. chmn. scholarship com. 1986-88, Paul Harris Fellow) Home: 1805 Heritage Rd Pittsburg KS 66762-3556 Office: Office of V P for Development Pittsburg State U Pittsburg KS 66762

SMOOTS, RENE WAGNER, secondary school educator; b. Akron, Ohio, Oct. 5, 1959; d. Robert Henry and Evelyn Viqi (Verlaney) Wagner; m. John P. Smoots III, June 20, 1987; children: Matthew, Jessica. BA in Edn., Va. Tech. U., 1981. Cert. math., gen. math. tchr., 4-7 elem. tchr., NK-4 tchr., Va. Tchr. math. Roanoke (Va.) County Pub. Schs., 1982-87, Goochland (Va.) H.S., 1987-88, Midlothian (Va.) H.S., 1988-94, James River H.S., Midlothian, 1994-95, Midlothian H.S., 1996—. Office: 401 Charter Colony Pkwy Midlothian VA 23114-4366

SMOTHERMON, PEGGI STERLING, middle school educator; b. Dallas, Nov. 11, 1948; d. Kiel Sterling and Ann C. (Wolfe) Sterling; m. William C. Smothermon Jr., June 20, 1981; children: Kirsten, Melinda, William III. BA, So. Meth. U., Dallas, 1973; MLA, So. Meth. U., 1978. Tchr. Richardson (Tex.) Ind. Sch. Dist., 1973-90, Coppell (Tex.) Ind. Sch. Dist., 1990-96, 2002—. J.J. Pearce scholar. Mem. Nat. Coun. Tchrs. Math., NSTA, NEA (faculty rep., membership chmn., sec.), Tex. Tchrs. Assn., Assn. Coppell Educators, Tex. Computer Edn. Assn., Tex. Coun. Tchrs. Math., Kappa Delta Pi. Home: 408 Greenridge Dr Coppell TX 75019-5714

SMOTHERMON, REBA MAXINE, elementary education educator; b. Liberal, Kans., July 8, 1933; d. Albert Isaac and Georga Maxine (Long) Shank; m. Wendell Scott Smothermon, Sept. 6, 1953; children: Jennifer Lynn Smothermon Kirby, Wendell Brent Smothermon. BA in Edn., Wichita State U., 1955; MA in Ednl. Psychology and Guidance, U. No. Colo., 1959. Cert. tchr. Kans., Calif., Colo. Tchr. second grade Unified Sch. Dist. 480/Washington Sch., Liberal, Kans., 1955-57, Adams County Dist. Skyline Vista Sch., Westminster, Colo., 1957-61; elem. tchr. Ventura Unified Santa Ana Sch., Ojai, Calif., 1964-80, Unified Sch. Dist. #480, Southlawn McKinley Schs., Liberal, 1980-95; ret., 1995. Literary coun. mem. Southwest Reading Coun., Liberal, 1985-95. Participant devel. sch. curriculum, 1977-79. Sec. to pres. Evergreen Garden Club, Liberal, 1980—; youth sponsor, pres. women's group 1st United Meth. Ch., Liberal, 1945—; mem. Liberal Panhellenic, 1980-96; bd. dirs., pres. Community Concerts of Liberal, 1987-91; pres. Liberal Woman's Club, 1995—; mem. Kans. Coun. on Travel and Tourism, 2002—. Mem. AAUW (pres. local chpt. 1980—, Woman of Yr. 1985, state chmn. internat. rels. com. 1985-90), PEO (various to pres. 1985—), DAR, Ladies' Oriental Shrine N.Am., White Shrine, Delta Kappa Gamma (various to pres. 1981—). Republican. Avocations: music, reading. Home: 830 S Clay F3 PO Box 470 Liberal KS 67905-0470

SMUTNY, JOAN FRANKLIN, academic director, educator; b. Chgo. d. Eugene and Mabel (Lind) Franklin; m. Herbert Paul Smutny; 1 child, Cheryl Anne. BS, MA, Northwestern U. Tchr. New Trier H.S., Winnetka, Ill.; mem. faculty, founder, dir. Nat. H.S. Inst. Northwestern U. Sch. Edn., Chgo.; faculty, founder, dir. h.s. workshop critical thinking/edn. Nat. Coll. Edn., Evanston, Ill., exec. dir. h.s. workshops, 1970-75; founder, dir. Woman Power Through Edn. Seminar, 1969-74; dir. Right to Read Seminar in critical reading, 1973-74; dir. seminar gifted h.s. students, 1973; dir. gifted programs for 6th, 7th, 8th graders Evanston pub. schs., 1978-79; dir. gifted programs 1st-8th grade Glenview (Ill.) pub. schs., 1979—. Dir. gifted programs Nat.-Louis U., Evanston, 1980-82, dir. Ctr. for Gifted, 1982—; dir. Bright and Talented Project, 1986—, North Shore Country Day Sch., Winnetka, 1982—; dir. Job Creation Project, 1980-82; dir. New Dimensions for Women, 1973; dir. Thinking for Action in Career Edn. Program 1976-79; dir. TACE, dir. Humanities Program for Verbally Precocious Youth, 1978-79; co-dir., instr. seminars in critical thinking Ill. Family Svc., 1972-75; writer ednl. filmstrips in lang. arts and lit. Soc. Visual Edn., 1970-74; spkrs. bur. Coun. Fgn. Rels., 1968-69; adv. com. edn. professions devel. act U.S. Office Edn., 1969—; state team for gifted, Ill. Office Edn., Office of Gifted, Springfield, Ill., 1977; writer, cons. Radiant Ednl. Corp., 1969-71; cons. ALA, 1969-71, workshop leader and spkr. gifted edn., 1971—; coord. career edn. Nat. Coll.Edn., 1976-78, dir. Project 1987—, dir. Summer Wonders, 1986—, Creative Children's Acad., bd. dirs., Worlds of Wisdom and Wonder, 1978—; dir. Future Tchrs. Am. Seminar in Coll. and Career, 1970-72; cons. rsch. & devel. Ill. Dept. Vocat. Edn., 1973—; evaluation cons. DAVTE, IOE, Springfield, Ill., 1977, mem. Leadership Tng. Inst. Gifted, U.S. Office Edn., 1973-74; dir. workshops for h.s. students; cons., spkr. in field; dir. Gifted Young Writers and Young Writers confs., 1978, 79; dir. Project '92 The White House Conf. on Children and Youth; mem. adv. bd. Educating Able Learners, 1991—; chmn. bd. dirs. Barbereux Sch., Evanston, 1992—; asst. editor, editl. bd. Understanding our Gifted, 1994—. Author: (with others) Job Creation: Creative Materials, Activities and Strategies for the Classroom, 1982, A Thoughful Overview of Gifted Education, 1990, Your Gifted Child—How to Recognize and Develop the Special Talents in Your Child from Birth to Age Seven, 1987, paperback, 1991, Education of the Gifted: Programs and Perspectives, 1990, The Young Gifted Child: Potential and Promise: An Anthology, 1998, The Gifted Young Child in the Regular Classroom, 1997, Gifted Girls, 1998, Perspectives in Gifted Education: Young Gifted Children, 1999, Stand Up For Your Gifted Child, 2001, Understand Gifted Population, 2002; contbg. editor Roper Rev., 1994—; asst. editor Understanding Our Gifted, 1995—; editor, contbr. Maturity in Teching; writer ednl. filmstrips The Brothers Grimm, How the West Was Won, Mutiny on the Bounty, Dr. Zhivago, Space Odyssey 2001, Christmas Around the World; editor IAGC Jour. for Gifted, 1994—; adv. bd. Gifted Edn. Press Quar., 1995—; contbr. editor numerous books in field; contbr. articles to profl. jours. including Chgo. Parent Mag.; reviewer programs for Gifted and Talented, U.S. Office Edn., 1976-78; editor Creativity Series Ablex, 1998—. Mem. AAUP, Nat. Assn. Gifted Child (nat. membership chmn. 1991—, co-chmn. schs. and programs, co-editor newsletter early childhood divsn.), Nat. Soc. Arts & Letters (nat. bd., 1st and 3d v.p. Evanston chpt. 1990-92), Mortar Bd., Outstanding Educators of Am. 1974, Pi Lambda Theta, Phi Delta Kappa (v.p. Evanston chpt. rsch. chmn. 1990-92). Home: 633 Forest Ave Wilmette IL 60091-1713

SMYER, MICHAEL ANTHONY, dean, educator, gerontologist; b. New Orleans, Oct. 21, 1950; s. Anthony and Alyce Mary (McGraw) S.; m. Patricia Ellen Piper, May 24, 1975; children: Brendan Piper-Smyer, Kyle Piper-Smyer. BA in Psychology, Yale U., 1972; PhD in Psychology, Duke U., 1977. Lic. psychologist, Pa. Asst. to pres. S.I. Community Coll., CUNY, 1970-71, Duke U., Durham, N.C., 1976-77; asst. prof. human devel. Pa. State U., University Park, 1977-82, assoc. prof., 1982-87, prof., 1987-95, assoc. dean rsch. and grad. studies, 1988-92; dean grad. sch. arts and scis., assoc. v.p. rsch. Boston Coll., Chestnut Hill, Mass., 1994—. Assoc. chmn. gerontology ctr., Pa. State U., 1979-86, prof.-in-charge individual and family studies, 1982-87, grad. prof.-in-charge individual and family studies, 1983-85; peer rev. com. mem. NIMH, 1991-95. Co-author: Mental Health and Aging, 1983, rev. 2d edit. 1994, Mental Health Consultation in Nursing Homes, 1988, The ABCs of Behavior Change, 1994, Older Adults' Decision Making and the Law, 1996, Aging and Mental Health, 1999; mem. editl. bd. Psychology and Aging, 1985-88, 92-94, Internat. Jour. Geriat. Psychiatry, 1992—, Jour. Gerontology, 1981-83, 95-98, 2000-03, Generations, 1994-2000, Jour. Mental Health and Aging, 1996-99; editor John Wiley series in Adult Devel. and Aging; contbr. over 100 articles to profl. jours. Adv. com. Centre Region Sr. Citizens, State College, 1983-86; bd. dirs. The Meadows Clinic, State College, 1983-85, Foxdale Village Continuing Care Retirement Cmty., State College, 1986-91; elected mem. Town Meeting, Wellesley, Mass., 2000—. Am. Coun. on Edn. fellow, 1985-86, W.K. Kellogg Found. fellow, 1982-85. Fulbright fellow, Japan, 2000; rsch. grantee NIMH, Nat. Inst. Aging, Adminstrn. on Aging, Health Care Financing Adminstrn. Fellow APA (pres. div. 20 1992-93), Gerontol. Soc. Am., Sigma Xi; mem. AAAS, APHA. Mem. Soc. Of Friends. Avocations: tennis, golf, skiing, hiking, swimming. Home: 32 Dover Rd Wellesley MA 02482-7321 Office: Boston Coll McGuinn 221 Chestnut Hill MA 02467

SMYER, MYRNA RUTH, drama educator; b. Albuquerque, June 10, 1946; d. Paul Anthony and Ruth Kelly (Klein) S.; m. Carlton Weaver Canaday, July 5, 1980. BFA, U. N.Mex., 1969; MA, Northwestern U., 1971. Pvt. practice drama instr., Albuquerque, 1974-78; dir. drama Sandia Preparatory Sch., Albuquerque, 1977-98, chmn. dept. fine arts, 1980-98; exec./artistic dir. touring theater co. Once Upon A Theatre, 1998—. Dialect coach, dir. Chgo. Acting Ensemble, 1969-71; lectr., workshop instr., performer Albuquerque Pub. Schs. and various civic orgns., Albuquerque, 1974—; writer, dir., performer Arts in the Pks., Albuquerque, 1977-80; performer, crew various indsl. videos, 1981-86; instr. workshops and continuing edn. U. N.Mex. 1977-80. Writer, dir., designer children's plays including May The Best Mammal (Or Whatever) Win, 1977, A Holiday Celebration, 1977, Puppets on Parade, 1978, A Witch's Historical Switches, 1979, A Governess Wronged, Or He Betrayed Her Trust, 2001, The Magic of Shakespeare, 2002, Dirty Work at Clean Water Creek, 2003, Once Upon a Rhyme Series, 1987—, Little Red Riding Hood, 1987, 2001, Goldilocks and The Three Bears, 1988, 2000, Cinderella, 1989, Hansel and Gretel, 1990, 2003, Rumpelstiltskin, 1991, 2002, The Dancing Princesses, 1992, The Three Pigs, 1994, Sleeping Beauty, 1996; dir. numerous other children and adult plays. Instr., writer, dir. various cmty. theatres including Albuquerque Little Theatre, Corrales Adobe Theatre, Kimo Theatre, Albuquerque Civic Light Opera, Now We Are Theatre, South Broadway Cultural Ctr.; N.Mex. arts commr., 1999—2002; mem. task force City of Albuquerque Cultural Plan, 2001; mem. City of Albuquerque Cultural Plan Adv. Com., 2002—, Albuquerque Arts in Edn. Task Force, 2000—. Recipient Helen and Doug Bridges award for Outstanding Instr., 1990, 1st Place award for Quality in Edn. N.Mex. Rsch. and Study Coun. and U. N.Mex., 1990, Albuquerque Acad. grant (children theatre), 1993, 95, 97, Neighborhood Appreciation award Four Hills, 1993, Albuquerque Arts Alliance Bravo award for Outstanding Contribution to Arts in Edn., 1995, Zia award, U. N.Mex. Disting. Alumni, 1999. Mem.: Albuquerque Performing Arts Mgrs., Albuquerque Arts Alliance. Avocations: reading, hiking, dancing. Office: Once Upon a Theatre 13170B Central Ave SE # 130 Albuquerque NM 87123-3032

SMYTH, ANNE, elementary school educator; b. Oceanside, N.Y., Sept. 28, 1943; d. David Anthony and Filomena Mary (Pascale) Caruso; m. Denis Charles Smyth, apr. 6, 1968; children: Michael David, Carolyn Anne. BS in Edn. and Social Studies, Cabrini Coll., 1965; MS in Spl. Edn., Adelphi U., 1980. Cert. tchr., (life), N.Y. Tchr. Belmnot Elem. Sch., North Babylon, N.Y., 1965-68, Forrest Sherman Elem. Sch., Naples, Italy, 1968-71, Centre Ave. Elem. Sch., E. Rockaway, N.Y., 1971—. Supr. Great Books Club, E. Rockaway, 1988—; mem. Ctr. Ave Teacher Adv. Com., E. Rockaway, 1988—. Pub. rels. agt. (vol.) Boy Scouts Am., Troop 163, Rockville Ctr., N.Y., 1988—. Mem. Am. Fedn. Tchrs. Roman Catholic. Avocations: reading, skiing, aerobic dancing, hiking, family activities. Home: 92 Muirfield Rd Rockville Centre NY 11570-2701

SMYTH, CRAIG HUGH, fine arts educator; b. N.Y.C., July 28, 1915; s. George Hugh and Lucy Salome (Humeston) S.; m. Barbara Linforth, June 24, 1941; children: Alexandra, Edward Linforth (Ned). BA, Princeton U., 1938, MFA, 1941, PhD, 1956; MA (hon.), Harvard U., 1975. Sr. mus. aid, rsch. asst. Nat. Gallery Art, Washington, 1941-42; officer-in-charge, dir. Cen. Art Collecting Point, Munich, 1945-46; lectr. Frick Collection, N.Y.C., 1946-50; asst. prof. Inst. Fine Arts NYU, 1950-53, assoc. prof. Inst. Fine Arts, 1953-57, prof. Inst. Fine Arts, 1957-73, acting dir. Inst. Fine Arts, acting head dept. fine arts Grad. Sch. Arts and Scis., 1951-53, dir. inst., head dept. fine arts Grad. Sch., 1953-73; prof. fine arts Harvard U., 1973-85, prof. emeritus, 1985—; Samuel Kress prof. Ctr. for Advanced Study in Visual Arts Nat. Gallery Art, Washington, 1987-88; dir. Villa I Tatti Harvard U. Ctr. Italian Renaissance Studies, Florence, 1973-85. Art historian in residence Am. Acad. in Rome, 1959-60; mem. U.S. Nat. Com. History Art, 1955-85; alt. U.S. mem. Comité Internat. d'Histoire de l'Art, 1970-83, U.S. mem., 1983-85; chmn. adv. com. J. Paul Getty Rsch. Inst. History of Art and Humanities, 1982-99; mem. architect selection com. J. Paul Getty Trust, 1983-84; mem. organizing com., keynote speaker 400th Anniversary of Uffizi Gallery, 1981-82; vis. scholar Inst. Advanced Study, Princeton, N.J., 1971, mem., 1978, visitor, 1983, 85-86; vis. scholar Bibliotheca Hertziana, Max Planck Soc., Rome, 1972, 73; mem. vis. com. dept. art and archaeology Princeton U., 1956-73, 85-89; mem. adv. com. Villa I Tatti, 1985-92; trustee Hyde Collection, Glens Falls, N.Y., 1985-87, The Burlington mag., 1987—; mem. commn. Ednl. & Cultural Exch. between Italy and U.S., 1979-83. Author: Mannerism and Maniera, 1963, rev. edit. with introduction by E. Cropper, 1992, Bronzino as Draughtsman, 1971, Michelangelo Architetto (with H.M. Millon), 1988, English edit., 1988, Repatriation of Art from the Collecting Point in Munich After World War II, 1988; editor: Michelangelo Drawings (Nat. Gallery of Art), 1992; editor (with Peter M. Lukehart), contbr.: The Early Years of Art History in the United States, 1993; founding chmn. (periodical) I Tatti Studies: Essays in the Renaissance, 1984-85; contbr. to profl. jours. Hon. trustee Met. Mus. Art, N.Y.C., 1968— ; trustee Inst. Fine Arts, NYU, 1973—; mem. mayor's com. Piazza Della Signoria, Florence, 1975-78. Lt. USNR, 1942-46. Decorated Chevalier Legion of Honor France, U.S. Army Commendation medal, Netherlands Medal for Svc. to the State; sr. Fulbright Rsch. fellow, 1949-50, honored by establishment of CHS professorship, Inst. of Fine Arts NYU, 1999. Mem. Am. Acad. Arts and Scis., Am. Philos. Soc., Coll. Art Assn. Am. (bd. dirs. 1953-57, sec. 1956), Accademia Fiorentina delle Arti del Disegno (academician, assoc.), Accademia di San Luca (hon. 1995), Harvard Club (N.Y.C.), Century Assn. (N.Y.C.), Phi Beta Kappa. Address: PO Box 539 Cresskill NJ 07626-0039

SNAPP, ELIZABETH, librarian, educator; b. Lubbock, Tex., Mar. 31, 1937; d. William James and Louise (Lanham) Mitchell; m. Henry Franklin Snapp, June 1, 1956 (div. Dec. 2001). BA magna cum laude, North Tex. State U., Denton, 1968, MLS, 1969, MA, 1977. Asst. to archivist Archive of New Orleans Jazz Tulane U., 1960-63; catalog libr. Tex. Woman's U., Denton, 1969-71, head acquisitions dept., 1971-74, coord. readers svcs., 1974-77, asst. to dean Grad. Sch., 1977-79, instr. libr. sci., 1977-88, acting Univ. libr., 1979-82, dir. librs., 1982—2002, dir. librs. emeritus, 2002—, univ. historian, 1995—2002; adj. prof. dept. history and govt. Tex. Woman's U., Denton, 2002—; rsch. assoc. Tex. Woman's U. Libr., Denton, 2002—. Chair-elect Tex. Coun. State U. Librs., 1988—90, chmn., 1990—92; adv. com. on libr. forumla Coord. Bd. Tex. Coll. and Univ. Sys., 1981—92; Libr. Sys. Act adv. bd. Tex. State Libr. and Archives Commn., 1999—2002; del. OCLC Nat. Users Coun., 1985—87, by-laws com., 1985—86, com. on less-than-full-svcs. networks, 1986—87; trustee AMIGOS Libr. Svcs., 1994—2000, sec. bd. trustees, 1996—97, vice-chmn. bd. trustees, 1997—99, chair bd. trustees, 1999—2000; project dir. NEH consultancy grant on devel. core curriculum for women's studies, 1981—82; chmn. Blue Ribbon com. 1986 Gov.'s Commn. for Women to select 150 outstanding women in Tex. History; project dir. math./sci. anthology project Tex. Found. Women's Resources; co-sponsor Irish Lecture Series, Denton, 1968, 70, 73, 78. Co-editor: Read All About Her! Texas Women's History: A Working Bibliography, 1995; contbr. articles to profl. jours. Bd. trustees, treas. Adult Day Care of North Tex., 2002—; sec. Denton County Dem. Caucus, 1970. Recipient Ann. Pioneer award, Tex. Woman's U., 1986, Women's Studies Vision award, 1998. Mem.: AAUW (legis. br. chmn. 1973—74, br. v.p. 1975—76, br. pres. 1979—80, state historian 1986—88, treas. 1998—99), ALA (stds. com. 1983—85), AAUP, Tex. Assn. Coll. Tchrs. (pres. Tex. Woman's U. chpt. 1976—77), So. Conf. Brit. Studies, Women's Collecting Group (chmn. ad hoc com. 1984—86), Tex. Hist. Commn. (judge for Farenbach History prize 1990—93), Tex. Libr. Assn. (program com. 1978, Dist. VII chmn. 1985—86, archives and oral history com. 1990—92, co-chair conf. program com. 1994, Tall Texan selection com. 1995—96, treas. exec. bd. 1996—99, Centennial com. 2000—02), AAUW Ednl. Found. (rsch. and awards panel 1990—94), Alliance Higher Edn. (chair acad. libr. dirs. 1993—95), Rotary Internat. (sec. local chpt. 1999—2002), Soroptimist Internat. (pres. Denton chpt. 1986—88), Women's Shakespeare Club (pres. 1967—69), Pi Delta Phi, Alpha Lambda Sigma (pres. 1970—71), Alpha Chi, Beta Phi Mu (pres. chpt. 1976 1978, sec. nat. adv. assembly 1978—79, pres. 1979—80, nat. dir. 1981—83). Methodist. Home: 2513 Coffey Dr Denton TX 76207-0002 Office: TWU Sta PO Box 424093 Denton TX 76204-4093 E-mail: esnapp@twu.edu.

SNARE, LEROY EARL, physicist, physics educator; b. Garden City, Mo., Nov. 6, 1931; s. Joseph Claude and Mildred Ella (Harvey) S.; m. Mary Lou Seabright, Feb. 6, 1960; children: Jonathan Lee, Sarah Elizabeth, Judith Irene. BA in Physics and Maths., U. Mo., 1953, MS in Physics, 1959; MS in Aeronautics and Astronautics, MIT, 1962. Cert. sec. sch. tchr., Mo. Head dynamic analysis and simulation br. Naval Avionics Ctr., Indpls., 1963-72, applied rsch. sr. staff, 1972-76, dir. syss. analysis divsn., 1976-80, dep. dir. applied rsch., 1980-84, dep. dir. engring., 1984-86, rsch. and tech. coord., 1986-91; asst. prof. phys. sci. Ivy Tech. State Coll., Indpls., 1991—2000. Mem. nat. bd. advs. Rose-Hulman Inst. Tech., Terre Haute, Ind., 1984-91. Author: Ivy Tech. State Coll. Ctrl. Campus Physic, Physical Sci. Lanoratory Manuals.; contbr. Mem. Ind. state plan comm. Ind. State Corp. Sci. and Tech., Indpls., 1985-88. Scholar Donnelly Garment Co., Kansas City, 1949-53. Mem. IEEE (sr.), Am. Assn. Physics Tchrs., Masons (Scottish rite), Sigma Xi. Presbyterian. Achievements include definition (with others) of equipment and procedures to initialize all navy aircraft inertial guidance systems; upgraded curriculum, added labs. to Ivy Tech. State Coll. Physics Courses which enabled credit transfers to four year colls. Home: 6626 N Olney St Indianapolis IN 46220-3757 Office: 1 W 26th St Indianapolis IN 46208-4777

SNEAD, ELEANOR LEROY MARKS, secondary school educator; b. Florence, S.C., Oct. 21, 1943; d. Franklin Leroy and Hazel Eleanor (Wallace) Marks; m. Samuel Everette Snead, Aug. 14, 1965; children: Robin Lynne, Ashley Eleanor. BA, Meredith Coll., 1965; MA, U. N.C., Greensboro, 1985. Cert. secondary bus. and marketing tchr., N.C. Tchr. Selma (N.C.) H.S., 1965, Laurinburg (N.C.) H.S. (now Scotland H.S.), 1965—76, 1984—2002, Hoke County H.S., Raeford, N.C., 1980—84; ret., 1984; mktg. edn. cons. NC Dept. Pub. Instrn., 2002—. Pvt. cons., Snead Consulting, Inc., Laurinburg, 2002—; curriculum writer N.C. Dept. Pub. Instrn., Raleigh, 1985, 90; presenter workshops Mktg. Edn. divsn. Vocat. Edn., N.C. Dept. Pub. Instrn. Recipient N.C. DECA Profl. Divsn. award, 1997; named Scotland County Outstanding Young Educator. Mem. NEA, N.C. Assn. Educators, Mktg. Educator's Assn., N.C. Mktg. Educator's Assn. (treas. 1988-2000, Solid Gold Tchr. 1989, Gold Link Tchr. 1990, Outstanding Mem. of N.C. 1994, Mktg. Educator of Yr., 1999, 2001, Lifetime Achievement in Mktg. Edn. award 2000), Am. Vocat. Assn., N.C. Vocat. Assn., Scotland County Area C. of C., Delta Kappa Gamma (treas. Delta Omicron chpt.), Delta Pi Epsilon, Beta Gamma Sigma. Methodist. Avocations: flower and shrub gardening, needlework, sewing. Office: Snead Consulting Inc 17701 Aberdeen Rd Laurinburg NC 28352

SNEED, ALBERTA NEAL, retired elementary education educator; b. Tipton County, Tenn., Jan. 13, 1926; d. Robert and Mary Lou (Wilks) Neal; m. Sollie Jr. Sneed, Jan. 26, 1968; 1 child, Hortense Yolanda Johnson Jeans. BS, Lane Coll., 1949; MEd, Memphis State U., 1975, postgrad., 1982. Cert.

elem. and secondary tchr., Tenn., supr. and adminstr. Tchr. Ouachita Parish Sch. Bd., Monroe, La., Covington (Tenn.) City Bd. Edn., 1978-; cons. Tipton County Bd. Edn., Covington. Mem. ASCD, NEA, Tenn. Assn. Supervision and Curriculum Devel., Tenn. Edn. Assn, TCEA, WTEA, Delta Sigma Theta.

SNEED, BARBARA LYNN FOLLINS, retired secondary school educator, counselor; b. New Orleans, July 14, 1942; m. Felton Sneed; 1 child. BS, So. U., 1965; MEd, U. New Orleans, 1977; postgrad., Loyola U. New Orleans, 1982. Tchr. Orleans Parish Schs., New Orleans, 1965-99; counselor Upward Bound Program U. New Orleans. Mem. Am. Assn. Tchrs. French, 100 Black Women, Alpha Kappa Alpha (treas. 1995), Phi Delta Kappa (pres.). Avocations: cooking, reading, gardening, music. Home: PO Box 870701 New Orleans LA 70187-0701

SNEED, JOANNE LAWSON, elementary school educator, author; b. Barren County, Ky., Ky., Aug. 16, 1940; d. Bobby Lee and Mary Clorine (Jones) Lawson; m. Thomas Nelson Sneed, June 9, 1965 (dec. May, 1986); 1 child, Thomas Nelson II. AA, Freed Hardeman U., 1960; BS, Western Ky. U., 1962, MA, 1967. Cert. elem. tchr., Ky. Sec. to dean Freed-Hardeman U., Henderson, Tenn., 1960-61; tchr. Nebo (Ky.) Jr. High Sch., 1962-64, Waddill Elem. Sch., Madisonville, Ky., 1964-68, Hall St. Elem. Sch., Madisonville, 1968-74, Pride Elem. Sch., Madisonville, 1978—. Author: Buford The Big-Eared Mouse, 1978, Buford Tales, 1986, Buford and the New Car, 1987, Buford Listens, 1992. Outreach trainer Widowed Perons Svc., Madisonville, 1988-90. Named Outstanding Young Educator, Madisonville Jaycees, 1969. Mem. NEA, Ky. Edn. Assn., Hopkins County Edn. Assn. Democrat. Mem. Ch. of Christ. Avocations: sewing, painting, travel, writing, walking. Home: 107 Ayer Pky Madisonville KY 42431-9124 Office: Pride Elem Sch 861 Pride Ave Madisonville KY 42431-1275

SNEED, RONALD ERNEST, engineering educator emeritus; b. Oxford, N.C., Nov. 23, 1936; s. Henry Ernest and Jewel Leigh (Hughes) S.; m. Shelba Jean Walters, June 8, 1958; children: Kathy Geneva Grosvenor, Jennie Leigh Berrier. BS in Agrl. Engring., N.C. State U., 1959, PhD in Biol. and Agrl. Engring., 1971. Registered profl. engr., N.C.; cert. irrigation designer, contractor, landscape irrigation auditor, and irrigation specialist. Sales trainee John Deere Co., 1959-60; ext. specialist N.C. State U., 1960-62, ext. instr., 1962-69, 70, ext. asst. prof., 1971-75, ext. assoc. prof., 1971-80, prof., 1980-92, prof. emeritus, 1993—; project engr. Agri-Waste Tech., Inc., 1993-2000, Irrigation Consulting, Inc., 1995—; project engr. Divsn. Soil and Water N.C. Dept. Environ. and Nat. Resources, 1997-99. Cons. Lexington (N.C.) Swine Breeders, 1973, 1st Colony Farms, Creswell, N.C., 1977-78, Greek Tobacco Co. Uruguay, 1973-84, Internat. Potato Ctr., Lima, Peru, 1981-85, Philip Morris Tobacco Co., Richmond, Va., 1992-94, Stowe's Nursery, Inc., Belmont, N.C., 1993-94, Floyd Harrell Farms, Inc., Conetoe, N.C., 1994, Gilliam & Mason, Inc., Harrellsville, N.C., 1994, Craven County Com. of 100, Ltd., 1995, Murphy Family Farms, 1997-2000, Larry Eason Farms, 1998, Panoramic Farm, Inc., 1997-99, Latham's Nursery, Inc., 1998— and numerous others. Maj. gen. U.S. Army, 1960-95, ret. Recipient Outstanding Paper award So. region Am. Soc. Hort. Sci., 1986, 91; Ronald E. Sneed Irrigation Soc., Inc. scholarship established in his honor, 1991. Fellow Am. Soc. Agrl. Engrs. (ednl. aids competition Blue Ribbon 1963-64, 68, 78-79, 85, 89, 91-92, Gunlogson Countryside Engring. award 1992, Outstanding Paper award 1984), The Irrigation Assn. (life tech. mem., Man of Yr. 1981), N.C. Irrigation Soc., Inc. (Oustanding Contbn. to Irrigation award 1973, former tech. advisor), Soil and Water Conservation Soc., N.C. Land Improvement Contractors Assn. (former tech. advisor), Carolinas Irrigation Assn. (hon.), Res. Officers Assn. (life), Civitan (Civitan of Yr. 1998). Democrat. Baptist. Office: 3405 Malibu Dr Raleigh NC 27607-6505 E-mail: rsneed@intrex.net.

SNEIDERMAN, MARILYN SINGER, secondary and elementary school educator; b. Erie, Pa., Jan. 13, 1943; d. Albert E. and Nettie (Levick) Singer; m. Donald G. Sneiderman, Aug. 15, 1965; children: Steven, Russell. BA in Edn., Mercyhurst Coll., 1965. Cert. tchr., Ohio. Substitute tchr. Beachwood (Ohio) Sch. System, 1980-87; tutor Hilltop Sch., Beachwood, 1987-91, ESL tchr., instnl. tutor, 1991—. Mem. ASCD, Greater Cleve. Coun. Tchrs. Math., Phi Delta Kappa. Home: 26200 Fairmount Blvd Beachwood OH 44122-2220

SNELBECKER, GLENN EUGENE, psychologist, educator; b. Dover, Pa., Sept. 24, 1931; s. William S. and Anna M. Snelbecker; m. Janice C. Fixler, Sept. 23, 1962; children: David M., Karen A., Laura B. BS, Elizabethtown (Pa.) Coll., 1957; MS, Bucknell U., Lewisburg, Pa., 1958; PhD, Cornell U., 1961. Lic. psychologist, Pa. Clin. psychology postdoctoral intern Brockton (Mass.) VA Hosp. and Boston U., 1961—62; clin. psychologist U.S. VA Hosp., Brockton, 1961—67; prof. Temple U., Phila., 1967—. Cons., author in pvt. practice Mgmt. Assocs. for Tech., Comms. and Health, 1963—; investigator NSF computer project Retraining H.S. Tchrs. and Elem. Sch. Tchrs. Temple U., Phila., 1985-92; prin. investigator/dir. instructional tech. projects. Author: Learning Theory, Instructional Theory, 1985; co-author: The ASTD Instructional Technology Handbook, 1993, The Tools and Techniques of Financial Planning, 4th edit., 1993, Instructional Design Theories and Models: An Overview of Their Current Status, Vol. 2, 1999, Instructional Design Theories and Models: An Overview of Their Current Status, Vol. 2, 1999; contbr. articles and chpts. to profl. jours. and books. Sgt. U.S. Army, 1952—55. Fellow APA, Phila. Soc. Clin. Psychologists; mem. Am. Ednl. Rsch. Assn. Avocations: travel, family. Office: Temple U TU-004-00 1301 Cecil Moore Ave Philadelphia PA 19122-6091 E-mail: glenn.snelbecker@temple.edu.

SNELL, MICHELLE LOUISE, underwriter; b. Mascoutah, Ill., Feb. 25, 1970; d. Charles Edward Snell and Karen Louise (Squier) Benson. BA, Simpson Coll., 1992. Substitute tchr. grades K-6 Murray (Iowa) Cmty. Schs., 1992-96, Clarke Cmty. Schs., Osceola, Iowa, 1992-96, East Union Schs., Afton, Iowa, 1993-96; ins. underwriter Allied Group Ins., Des Moines, 1997—. Democrat. Home: Unit 407 7425 Wistful Vista Dr Des Moines IA 50266

SNIDER, CLIFTON MARK, English educator, writer, poet; b. Duluth, Minnesota, Mar. 3, 1947; s. Allan George and Rhoda Marion (Tout) S. BA, Calif. State U., Long Beach, 1969, MA, 1971; PhD, U. N.Mex., 1974. Lectr. English Calif. State U., 1974—; instr. English Long Beach City Coll., 1975—2002. Author: (poetry) Jesse Comes Back, 1976; Bad Smoke Good Body, 1980; Jesse and His Son, 1982; Edwin: A Character in Poems, 1984; The Stuff That Dreams Are Made On: A Jungian Interpretation of Literature, 1991; (poetry) Blood & Bones, 1988; Impervious to Piranhas, 1989; The Age of the Mother, 1992; The Alchemy of Opposites, 2000; (novels) Loud Whisper, 2000; Bare Roots, 2001; Wrestling with Angels: A Tale of Two Brothers, 2001. Former officer steering com. Long Beach Lambda Dem. Club. Resident Fellow Yaddo, Saratoga Springs, N.Y., 1978, 82; Helene Wurlitzer Found. N.M., Taos, 1984, 90, 98; Karolyi Found., Vence, France, 1986, 87. Home: 2719 Eucalyptus Ave Long Beach CA 90806-2515 Office: Calif State U 1250 Bellflower Blvd Long Beach CA 90840-0001 E-mail: csnider@csulb.edu.

SNIDER, GORDON B. retired medical educator; b. Columbus, Ohio, Dec. 19, 1928; s. James M. and Rose G. (Joyce) S.; m. Mary Louise Graham, July 19, 1952; children: Mary Katherine, Cynthia L., John M., James G., Martha R. BA in Bacteriology, Ohio State U., 1950, MD, 1954. Diplomate Am. Bd. Internal Medicine. Intern Mt. Carmel Hosp., Columbus, 1954-55, resident, 1955-57; Henry Ford Hosp., Detroit, 1957-58; pvt. practice Lancaster, Ohio, 1960-94; dir. med. edn. Fairfield Med. Ctr., Lancaster, 1994-97. Clin. assoc. prof. medicine Ohio State U. Coll. Med., Columbus, 1981—; bd. dirs. Fairfield Med. Ctr., Lancaster, 1990-96. Founder, dir. paramedic program Lancaster fire Dept., 1985. Capt., M.C., U.S. Army, 1958-60. Fellow ACP, Lancaster Rotary (past pres.); mem. Fairfield Med. Soc. (past pres.), Ohio State Med. Assn., Ohio Soc. Internal Medicine (past pres.). Roman Catholic. Avocation: golf. Office: Fairfield Med Ctr 401 N Ewing St Lancaster OH 43130-3372 E-mail: gbs@greenapple.com.

SNIDER, JANE ANN, elementary school educator; b. Inglewood, Calif., Nov. 18, 1939; d. Percy E. and Mamie D. (Gorman) S. MusB, U. So. Calif., 1962; MS, Azusa Pacific U., 1987. Cert. gen. elem. and spl. secondary music tchr. Tchr. 6th grade Centralia Sch. Dist., Buena Park, Calif., 1963—, mentor, tchr. computer tech., 1983-97. Home: 1433 Royer Ave Fullerton CA 92833-4719 E-mail: jsnider7@earthlink.net.

SNIDER, PATRICIA FAYE, retired theater educator, small business owner; b. Shawnee, Okla., Aug. 26, 1931; d. d. George Bernard and Cora Fay (Jones) Wilson; m. George Dale Snider, Aug. 5, 1955; children: Brad Lee, Sidney Wayne, Pamela Sinder. BS in Speech, Okla. Bapt. U., 1954; MFA in Theater, U. Okla., 1958. Tchr. theater Shawnee High Sch.; prof. theater St. Gregory's U., Shawnee, 1964-65, 79-98; ret. Founder, active Shawnee Little Theater, 1967—; dir. Miss Shawnee Pageant, 1960-85, Miss Wood Pageant, Shawnee; constrn. com. Sarkey's Performing Art Ctr.; Okla. state chair Kennedy Ctr. Am. Coll. Theatre Festival; judge community and high sch. play competitions. Actress summer stock plays, Pioneer Playhouse, Shawnee Little Theater, others; performer numerous roles at Shawnee Little Theater; performer voice-overs for polit. commls., local radio commls. Tchr. class Ch. Sch., 1964—. Recipient Aringlion award for Outstanding Coll. Theatre Tchr., 1992, Kenny Center medal Am. Coll. Theatre Festivals, 1998. Mem. Am. Speech Assn., Am. Theater Higher Edn., Shawnee Fine Arts Club. Democrat. Methodist. Avocations: writing, painting.

SNINCHAK, FAYE RITA, humanities educator; b. Ilion, N.Y., Aug. 18, 1947; d. John Michael and Rita Anna (Bass) S. BA in Classics, Coll. of St. Rose, Albany, N.Y., 1969; postgrad. in English, Russell Sage Coll., 1970-74. Cert. permanent Latin and English tchr., N.Y. Tchr. English, Chatham (N.Y.) Cen. High Sch., 1969—, also coord. dept. English item writer N.Y. State Edn. Dept., Albany, 1985—; mem. policy bd. greater Capital Region Tchr. Ctr., Schodack, N.Y., 1986—; coord. English Regents Rerating Com. N.Y. State Edn. Dept., Albany, 1992—; mem. nat. faculty for assessment Four Seasons Project Coalition of Essential Schs., Brown U., 1993. Chmn. Village of Nassau (N.Y.) Planning Bd., 1979-85. N.Y. State Regents scholar, 1965; Activities Devel. Fund grantee, 1988-89. Mem. ASCD, NEA (del. region 10 1987—), Nat. Coun. Tchrs. English, Chatham Cen. Sch. Tchrs. Assn. (pres. 1981-87, chief negotiator 1987-91). Republican. Office: Chatham Cen High Sch 50 Woodbridge Ave Chatham NY 12037-1317

SNODDY, CHRIS RAYMOND, athletic trainer; b. Nashville, Nov. 19, 1959; s. Raymond Thomas and Farris (Duke) S. BS, David Lipscomb Coll., 1981; MA, Appalachian State U., 1987. Lic. athletic trainer. Real estate salesperson McKinney & Co., Nashville, 1980-89; head athletic trainer David Lipscomb U., Nashville, 1981-91; sr. athletic trainer Ctr. Sports Medicine, Bapt. Hosp., Nashville, 1993—; coord. sports medicine Bapt. Hosp., Nashville, 1997—99, mgr., 1999—2001, dir., 2001—03; head athletic trainer Skyline Med. Ctr., 2003—. Dir. sports medicine Pinnacle Rehab., Nashville, 1991-92; cons. sports medicine David Lipscomb H.S., Nashville, 1982-91; adj. faculty Free Will Bapt. Bible Coll., Nashville; cons. Lipscomb U. Sports Medicine. Editor: Where to Go Camping Guide, 1980; contbr. articles to Flying Eagle mag. Recipient Mayor's medallion City of Nashville, 1986, Silver Beaver award Boy Scouts Am., 1995, named Eagle Scout, 1976, Clin. Athletic Trainer of Yr., 1992, 2003. Mem. Nat. Athletic Trainers Assn., Tenn. Athletic Trainers Soc. Mem. Ch. of Christ. Lodges: Civitan (bd. dirs. Nashville 1986-87, pres. 1990), Wa-Hi-Nasa (lodge advisor 1995—), Order of Arrow (assoc. advisor Tenn. and Ky. chpts. 1984-87, Founder's award 1976). Avocation: skiing. Home: 315 Bowwood Dr Nashville TN 37217-2301

SNODGRASS, TRACI MORTON, elementary education educator; b. Duncan, Okla., Jan. 2, 1966; d. Robert Oliver and Freda Ann (Curry) Morton; m. Richard Norman Snodgrass, Dec. 28, 1986; children: Richard Christopher, Lauren Hall, Emily Renea. Student, Mercer U., 1984-86; BS in Edn., Valdosta State Coll., 1989. Tchr. kindergarten St. Paul's Sch., Daytona Beach, Fla., 1989—93; tchr. Volusia County Schs., Port Orange, Fla. Home: 1212 Waverly Dr Daytona Beach FL 32118-3623 Office: Sugar Mill Elem Sch 1101 Charles St Port Orange FL 32129

SNOKE, ARTHUR WILMOT, geology educator, researcher; b. Balt., Oct. 5, 1945; s. Wilmot Arthur and Mildred (Sprecher) S.; m. Judith Gill, June 5, 1966; children: Cynthia Lynn, Alison Christine. AB, Franklin and Marshall Coll., 1967; PhD, Stanford U., 1972. Rsch. assoc. U.S. Geol. Survey, Menlo Park, Calif., 1971-73; lectr. Humboldt State U., Arcata, Calif., 1974; asst. prof. U. S.C., Columbia, 1974-78, assoc. prof. geology, 1978-84; prof. U. Wyo., Laramie, 1984—. Co-editor: Geology of Wyoming, 1993, Fault-related Rocks: A Photographic Atlas, 1998, Rocky Mountain Geology; contbr. articles to profl. jours. Recipient Pres.'s award U. Wyo., 1997. Fellow Geol. Soc. Am.; mem. Am. Geophys. Union, Rocky Mountain Assn. Geologists. Office: U Wyo Dept Geology and Geophysics Laramie WY 82071-3006

SNOOK, BEVERLY JEAN, elementary school educator; b. Fort Dodge, Iowa, Feb. 7, 1947; d. Francis B. Collins and Juanita Faye Bowers; m. Francis K. Snook, Aug. 9, 1969; children: Katherine, Jennifer, Megan, Ashley. AA, Centerville Community Coll., Iowa, 1967; BA, U. No. Iowa, 1969; MA, Marycrest Coll., Davenport, Iowa, 1990. Tchr. Wayne Community Sch., Corydon, Iowa, 1969-70; spl. edn. instr. Chariton (Iowa) Community Sch., 1972-75, Wayne County Schs., Corydon, Iowa, 1977—. Rsch. in field. Mem. PTA, Rural Schs. Network Project NCREL. Mem. NEA, Iowa Edn. Assn., Iowa Reading Assn., Wayne Cmty. Edn. Assn. Home: 1403 90th St Corydon IA 50060-8863 Office: Elementary Bldg Wayne Cmty Sch Corydon IA 50060

SNOUFFER, NANCY KENDALL, English and reading educator; b. Long Branch, N.J., Aug. 22, 1941; d. Percival Wallace and Ruby Mae (Braswell) Kendall; m. Eugene Joseph Snouffer, Aug. 27, 1966; 1 child, Kendall Ann. BA in English, Gettysburg (Pa.) Coll., 1962; MA in English and Journalism, U. N.C., 1964; MS in Edn. and Reading, Western Ill. U., 1974; postgrad., U. Mo., 1976-78. Instr. English U. N.C., Wilmington, 1963-65, Shaw U., Raleigh, N.C., 1965-66; from instr. to asst. prof. English Wright Coll. and Chgo. City Colls., 1967-74; from instr. to asst. prof. reading Western Ill. U., Macomb, 1974-81; prof. comm., lang. and reading Del Mar Coll., Corpus Christi, Tex., 1982—, reading coord., 2001—. Mem. adv. bd. Tex. A&M U., Corpus Chrisit, 1993—; cons. in field. Author: College Reading Power, 5th edit., 1976-82; assoc. editor jour. Epistle, 1980-83, mem. editorial bd., 1983-85; contbr. articles to profl. jours. Master Tchr. Del Mar, 1986. Grantee Western Ill. U., 1974-81, Del Mar Coll., 1982—, NISSOD Teaching Excellence award, 1993, coll. academic support program Tex. State level Lifetime Achievement award. Mem. Tex. Assn. Developmental Educators, Tex. Coll. Reading Learning Assn. (chair So. membership 1994—, state sec. 1995-97, pres.-elect 1997-98, pres. 1998-99, past pres. 1999-2000, Lifetime Achievement award 2002), Nat. Assn. Developmental Educators (co-chair nat. com., profl. liaison), Internat. Reading Assn., Corpus Christi Literacy Coun. (bd. dirs. 1986—, sec. 1988-93, vice-chair 1991-92, v.p.-elect 2000-01, chair 2001—), Harbor Playhouse (bd. dirs. 1988, 91-93, chair 2001-03), Alliance Francaise. Republican. Episcopalian. Avocations: tennis, travel, reading. Home: 4206 Acushnet Dr Corpus Christi TX 78413-2004 Office: Del Mar Coll 101 Baldwin Blvd Corpus Christi TX 78404-3805

SNOW, JAMES HARRY, metallurgist, educator, aircraft planning executive; b. Inglewood, Calif., Jan. 7, 1949; s. Jack Norman and Georgiann H. S.; m. Darlene Angeline Pollo, Aug. 27, 1976 (div. June 1979); m. Wilma Susan Lewis, Aug. 17, 1986; children: Megan, Jaclyn, Brendan. AA, Orange Coast Coll., Costa Mesa, Calif., 1981; BA, Calif. State U., Long Beach, 1990, MA with honors, 1993; EdD, U. Calif., LA, Calif. Cert. tchr., Calif. Metall. tech. ARCO Metals, Paramount, Calif., 1973-81; sr. quality control supr. Phelps Dodge Brass Co., City of Commerce, Calif., 1981-84; sr. prodn. controller Cerro Metals Co., Paramount, 1985-86; prin. specialist, group leader McDonnel Douglas Aircraft, Long Beach, 1986-94; adj. prof. Calif. State Univ., Long Beach, 1994—; rschr. Ctr. for Collaborative Rsch. in Edn. U. Calif., Irvine, 1998—. Tchr. Lakewood (Calif.) H.S., 1994—. Author: The Design and Construction of a Solar Powered Refrigeration System, 1993, American Kaizen, 1997. With USN, 1969-71, Vietnam. Mem. Am. Solar Energy Soc., Internat. Tech. Edn. Assn., Internat. Solar Energy Soc., Am. Philatelic Soc., Epsilon Pi Tau (pres. Alpha Phi 1994-95), Phi Kappa Phi (bd. dirs. 1994—), Phi Delta Gamma (bd.d irs. 1994—). Avocations: fishing, reading, philately. Home: 20951 Glencairn Ln Huntington Beach CA 92646-6409 Office: Applied Tech Magnet Sch Dept Chair 4400 Briercrest Ave Lakewood CA 92646

SNOW, MARLON O. trucking executive, state agency administrator; m. Ann; children. Gen. mgr. spl. commadities Milne Truck Lines, Phoenix, L.A., 1970-81; gen. mgr. spl. commodities, sales Motor Cargo, Salt Lake City, Utah, 1981-82; owner MST Trucking, Inc., Salt Lake City, Utah, 1982—. V.p. Utah Motor Carriers for State of Utah, 1997-98; bd. dirs. Zions Bank. Mem. State Bd. Edn., 1994-97, chair, 1995-97; trustee Utah Valley State Coll., 1998; mem. Ho. of Reps., Utah, 1999-2001; bd. regents Bd. Higher Edn. State of Utah, 2001—; bd. dirs. Children's Justice Ctr., State of Utah, 2002--. Mem. Utah Valley State Coll. Found. (bd. dirs. 1991—), Alpine Sch. Dist. Found. (bd. dirs. 1990-94). Office: 1247 E 430 N Orem UT 84097-5400

SNOW, SUE, principal; Math. tchr. Carrollton (Ga.) Jr. High Sch.; curriculum dir. Rockdale County Pub. Schs., Conyers, Ga.; prin. Conyers Mid. Sch. Named Ga. State Math. Tchr. of Yr., 1992.*

SNOW, VELMA JEAN, secondary education educator; b. Hardaway, Ala., Oct. 29, 1952; d. Oliver and Lucy Ann (Carter) Harris; m. Joe Lee Snow Jr., July 8, 1979; children: Joe Lee, Jeffrey Oliver. BS in Biology, Ala. State U., 1974, MS, 1976. Cert. secondary tchr., Mich. Tchr. Perry County Schs., Marion, Ala., 1974-76, Montgomery (Ala.) Pub. Schs., 1976-78, Detroit Pub. Schs., 1979—. Vol. NAACP, Southfield, Mich., 1993. Recipient educators Achievement award Booker T. Washington Bus. Assn., 1988; NIH fellow, 1992, Am. Physiol. Soc. fellow, 1994. Mem. Mich. Sci. Tchrs. Assn., Detroit Sci. Tchrs. Assn., Young Astronauts Pilots (chpt. leader, coord. 1990-94, cert. 1993). Democrat. Baptist. Avocations: reading, golfing, singing, computer graphics. Home: 20477 Willowick Dr Southfield MI 48076-1765 Office: Detroit Pub Schs 2200 W Grand Blvd Detroit MI 48208-1178

SNOWBERGER, JANE ARDETH, geriatrics nurse, educator, consultant; b. Coffeeville, Kans., Nov. 4, 1945; d. Carl Fredrick and Mary Jane Emaline (Wood) Sonenberg; m. David E. Snowberger, Apr. 13, 1973; children: Tammy, Deena, John. Cert., N.Mex. State U., Las Cruces, 1980; AA, N.Mex. State U., 1983, ADN, 1990; BA, Graceland Coll., 1995, BS, 1997; MS, Clayton Coll., 1998, postgrad., PhD, 2002. Med.-surg. nurse Gerald Champion Hosp., Alamogordo, N.Mex., 1980-82, ob-gyn staff nurse, 1990-91; office nurse Dr. A. Austin, M.D., Alamogordo, 1982-83; supr. charge nurse Betsy Ross ICF Facility, Rome, N.Y., 1984-86; med. records clk. Rome murphy Hosp., 1987-88; supr. charge nurse Planned Parenthood, Alamogordo, 1988-89; coord. NA program N.Mex. U., Alamogordo, 1991—; nurse educator N.Mex. State U., 1991-96; dir. nursing Betty Dare Facility, 1997-98; pvt. practice nurse cons. N.Mex., 1999—. Sewing instr. Sr. Citizens, Alamogordo, 1989—. Mem. Nat. League for Nursing. Republican. Baptist. Avocations: sewing, serging, reading, dancing, hand crafts. Home and Office: PO Box 1075 1306 Greenwood Ln Alamogordo NM 88310-5742

SNOWDEN, RUTH, artist, educator, legal secretary; b. Quincy, Ill., Apr. 29, 1939; d. Emil G. and Edith M. Pfaffe; m. Howard L. Snowden; children: Jim, David, Sam, Amy. BS, Quincy U., 1964, BFA, 1989; MFA, U. So. Ill., 1991. Math. tchr. Notre Dame H.S., Quincy, 1964-67; math. lectr. Quincy U., 1974-83; legal sec. Snowden & Snowden Attys., Quincy, 1983—. Curator Significant Arch. in Quincy, Bell Tel., Chgo., 1986; mem. multi-arts panel Ill. Arts Coun., Chgo., 1986-89; art lectr. Quincy U., 1994—. Artist, editor: Visualizing Revelation, 1993; artist: Artists of Illinois, 1995, Quincy Women, 1838-1996, 1996; exhbns. include Biblical Arts Ctr., Dallas, The Michael Stone Collection Gallery, Washington, Art and The Law at Kennedy Galleries, N.Y.C., Loyola Law Sch., L.A., Minn. Mus. Am. Art, St. Paul, State of Ill. Ctr., Chgo., Oak Knoll, St. Louis, Overland Park, Kans. Bd. dirs. YMCA and YWCA, Quincy, 1978-96, Quincy Mus., 1984; Adams County campaign coord. U.S. Senator Dick Durbin, Quincy, 1980. Mem. Quincy Art Ctr. (pres. 1984-86, chair exhbn. com. 1995-96, adv. bd.). Democrat. Lutheran. Avocations: international travel, bible study.

SNOW-SMITH, JOANNE INLOES, art history educator; b. Balt. d. Henry Williams and Elsie Orrick (Bagley) Snow; m. Robert Porter Smith (dec.); children: Joanne Tyndale Darby, Henry Webster Smith, III (dec.), Constance Elizabeth Bagley, Cynthia Porter Bloom, Robert Porter Smith, Jr.; m. Robert Edward Willstadter. BA, Goucher Coll.; MA, U. Ariz., 1968; PhD, UCLA, 1976. Prof. Italian Renaissance art history U. Wash., Seattle, 1981—. Program dir. of art history U. Wash. Rome Ctr. in Palazzo Pio, Rome, 1998, 2000, 2002. Author: (book) The Salvator Mundi of Leonardo da Vinci, 1982 (Internat. award 1983), The Primavera of Sandro Botticelli: A Neoplatonic Interpretaion, 1993; contbr. numerous articles to profl. jours. Recipient Rsch. Professorship to study in Oxford and London, U. Wash. Grad. Sch., 1986. Mem. Nat. Soc. Colonial Dames of Am., Renaissance Soc. of Am., Leonardo Soc./U. London, Coll. Art Assn., Seattle Art Mus., Met. Mus. Art, Ashmolean Mus. (Oxford, Eng.). Home: 1414 Shenandoah Dr E Seattle WA 98112-3730 Office: Univ Wash PO Box 353440 Seattle WA 98195-3440 E-mail: jsnowsmi@u.washington.edu.

SNYDER, ALLEGRA FULLER, dance educator; b. Chgo., Aug. 28, 1927; d. R. Buckminster and Anne (Hewlett) Fuller; m. Robert Snyder, June 30, 1951 (div. Apr. 1975, remarried Sept. 1980); children: Alexandra, Jaime. BA in Dance, Bennington Coll., 1951; MA in Dance, UCLA, 1967. Asst. to curator, dance archives Mus. Modern Art, N.Y.C., 1945-47; dancer Ballet Soc. of N.Y.C. Ballet Co., 1945-47; mem. office and prodn. staff Internat. Film Found., N.Y.C., 1950-52; editor, dance films Film News mag., N.Y.C., 1966-72; lectr. dance and film adv., dept. dance UCLA, 1967-73, chmn. dept. dance, 1974-80, 90-91, acting chair, spring 1985, chair of faculty Sch. of the Arts, 1989-91, prof. dance and dance ethnology, 1973-91, prof. emeritus, 1991—; pres. Buckminster Fuller Inst., Santa Barbara, Calif., chairwoman bd. dirs., 1984—. Vis. lectr. Calif. Inst. Arts, Valencia, 1972; co-dir. dance and TV workshop Am. Dance Festival, Conn. Coll., New London, 1973; dir. NEH summer seminar for coll. tchrs. Asian Performing Arts, 1978, 81; coord. Ethnic Arts Intercoll. Interdisciplinary Program, 1974-73, acting chmn., 1986; vis. prof. performance studies NYU, 1982-83; hon. vis. prof. U. Surrey, Guildford, Eng., 1983-84; cons. Thyodia Found., Salt Lake City, 1973-74; mem. dance adv. panel Nat. Endowment Arts, 1968-72, Calif. Arts Commn., 1974-91; mem. adv. screening com. Coun. Internat. Exch. of Scholars, 1979-82; mem. various panels NEH, 1979-85; core cons. for Dancing, Sta. WNET-TV, 1988—. Dir. film Baroque Dance 1625-1725, in 1977; co-dir. film Gods of Bali, 1952; dir. and wrote film Bayanihan, 1962 (named Best Folkloric Documentary at Bilboa Film Festival, winner Golden Eagle award); asst. dir. and asst. editor film The

Bennington Story, 1952; created films Gestures of Sand, 1968, Reflections on Choreography, 1973, When the Fire Dances Between Two Poles, 1982; created film, video loop and text Celebration: A World of Art and Ritual, 1982-83; supr. post-prodn. film Erick Hawkins, 1964, in 1973. Also contbr. articles to profl. jours. and mags. Adv. com. Pacific Asia Mus., 1980-84, Festival of the Mask, Craft and Folk Art Mus., 1979-84; adv. panel Los Angeles Dance Currents II, Mus. Ctr. Dance Assn., 1974-75; bd. dirs. Council Grove Sch. III, Compton, Calif., 1976-81; apptd. mem. Adv. Dance Com., Pasadena (Calif.) Art Mus., 1970-71, Los Angeles Festival of Performing Arts com., Studio Watts, 1970; mem. Technology and Cultural Transformation com., UNESCO, 1977. Fulbright research fellow, 1983-84; grantee Nat. Endowment Arts, 1981, Nat. Endowment Humanities, 1977, 79, 81, UCLA, 1968, 77, 80, 82, 85; recipient Amer. Dance Guild Award for Outstanding Achievement in Dance, 1992. Mem. Am. Dance Therapy Assn., Congress on Rsch. in Dance (bd. dirs. 1970-76, chmn. 1975-77, nat. conf. chmn. 1972), Coun. Dance Adminstrs., Am. Dance Guild (chmn. com. awards 1972), Soc. for Ethnomusicology, Am. Anthrop. Assn., Am. Folklore Soc., Soc. Anthropology of Visual Comm., Soc. Humanistic Anthropology, Calif. Dance Educators Assn. (conf. chmn. 1972), L.A. Area Dance Alliance (adv. bd. 1978-84, selection com. Dance Kaleidoscope project 1979-81), Fulbright Alumni Assn. Home: 15313 Whitfield Ave Pacific Palisades CA 90272-2548 Office: Buckminster Fuller Inst 111 N Main St Sebastopol CA 95472-3448

SNYDER, CAROLYN ANN, education educator, librarian; b. Elgin, Nebr., Nov. 5, 1942; d. Ralph and Florence Wagner. Student, Nebr. Wesleyan U., 1960-61; BS cum laude, Kearney State Coll., 1964; MS in Librarianship, U. Denver, 1965. Asst. libr. sci. and tech. U. Nebr., Lincoln, 1965-67, asst. pub. svc. libr., 1967-68, 70-73; pers. libr. Ind. U. Librs., Bloomington, 1973-76, acting dean of univ. librs., 1980, 88-89, assoc. dean for pub. svcs., 1977-88, 89-91, interim devel. officer, 1989-91; adminstrv. army libr. Spl. Svcs. Agy., Europe, 1968-70; dean libr. affairs So. Ill. U., Carbondale, 1991-2000, prof., dir. found. rels., 2000—. Team leader Midwest Univs. Consortium for Internat. Activities-World Bank IX project to develop libr. system and implement automation U. Indonesia, Jakarta, 1984-86; libr. devel. cons. Inst. Tech. MARA/Midwest Univs. Consortium for Internat. Activities Program in Malaysia, 1985; ofcl. rep. EDUCAUSE, 1996-2000; mem. working group on scholarly comm. Nat. Commn. on Librs. and Info. Sci., 1998-2000. Editor Library and Other Academic Support Services for Distance Learning, 1997; contbr. chpt. to book and articles to profl. jours. Active Humane Assn. Jackson County, 1991—, Carbondale Pub. Libr. Friends, 1991—, Morris Libr. Friends, 1991—. Cooperative Rsch. grant Coun. on Libr. Resources, Washington, 1984. Mem. ALA (councilor 1985-89, Bogle Internat. Travel award 1988, H.W. Wilson Libr. Staff devel. grant 1981), Libr. Adminstrn./Mgmt. Assn. (pres. 1981-82), Com. on Instnl. Coop./Resource Sharing (chair 1987-91), Coalition for Networked Info. (So. Ill. U. at Carbondale rep. 1991-2000), Coun. Dirs. State Univ. Librs. in Ill. (chair 1992-93, 99-2000), Coun. on Libr. and Info. Resources Digital Leadership Inst. Steering Com. (Assn. Rsch. Librs. rep. 1998-2000), Ill. Assn. Coll. and Rsch. Librs. (chair Ill. Bd. Higher Edn. liaison com. 1993-94), Ill. Network (bd. dirs.), Ind. Libr. Assn. (chair coll./univ. divsn. 1982-83), U.S. Grant Assn. (bd. dirs. 1992—), Ill. Libr. Computer Sys. Orgn. (policy coun. 1992-95, 96-2000), Nat. Assn. State Univs. and Land-Grant Colls. (commn. on info. tech. and its distance learning and libr. bds. 1994-96), NetIllinois (bd. dirs. 1994-96), OCLC Users Coun. (elected rep. 1995-98), Big 12 Plus Libr. Consortium (chair 1997-98), Nat. Commn. on Librs. and Info. Sci. Working Group on Scholarly Comms., Assn. Rsch. Libr. (vis. program officer 2000—01). Avocations: antiques, theater, movies, reading. Office: So Ill U Ctrl Devel Carbondale IL 62901-6632

SNYDER, DEBORAH JEAN, special education educator; b. N.Y.C., Nov. 8, 1953; d. James Fleming and Marguerite (Parker) S. BS, Keene State Coll., 1975; MA, Siena Heights U., 1979. Tchr. Manchester (N.H.) Pub. Schs., 1978, Monadnock Regional High Sch., Swanzey, N.H., 1980—. Actor: Old Homestead Players, 1985—. Bd. dirs. Childrens Performing Arts Ctr., 1989-92, AIDS Svcs. for the Monadnock Region, 2001-. Mem. Swanzey Lions Club. Avocations: gardening, crafts, travel, photography. Office: Monadnock Regional High Sch 580 Old Homestead Hwy Swanzey NH 03446-2301

SNYDER, DONALD CARL, JR., secondary education educator; b. Phila., Aug. 24, 1954; s. Donald Carl and Gloria (Nicklous) S. BS, Temple U., 1976, MS, 1980. Cert. tchr., Pa. Gen. sci. tchr. James Russell Lowell Sch., Phila., 1977-89; physics tchr. South Phila. High Sch., 1989—, biol. tchr., 1990-92. Rep. Phila Sci. Tchrs. Assn., Nat. Assn. Biol. Tchrs., 1992; mem. project 2061 Sch. Dist. Phila., 1992-93. Author: Science Assessment in the Service of Reform, 1991. Active U.S. Olympic Soc., 1980—. Mem. AAAS, Pa. Acad. Sci., Nat. Sci. Tchrs. Assn., Nat. Sci. Suprs. Assn., Nat. Assn. Biology Tchrs. (state rep. 1992—), ASCD, Fulbright Alumni Assn. (no. Ireland 1983-84), Phi Delta Kappa. Democrat. Lutheran. Avocations: traveling, reading, photography, theater. Home: 5210 Westford Rd Fl 1 Philadelphia PA 19120-3619 Office: South Phila High Sch Broad And Snyder Ave Philadelphia PA 19148

SNYDER, HENRY ALLEN, elementary education educator; b. Bloomsburg, Pa., Nov. 2, 1948; s. Clair Leroy and Ellen Alda (Willow) Snyder; m. Margo Ann Fetterolf, June 21, 1969; children: Cherie Lin, Trevor Allen. BA in Econs., Bloomsburg U., 1970; MS in Edn., SUNY, Cortland, 1976. Cert. tchr., N.Y. High sch. math. tchr., jr. varsity basketball coach Hancock (N.Y.) Cen. Sch., 1970-71; 5th grade tchr Windsor (N.Y.) Cen. Sch., 1971—, varsity softball coach, 1975, 76. Social studies curriculum writer BOCES of Broome and Tioga Counties, Binghamton, N.Y., 1988; mem. competency based edn. com. N.Y. State Edn. Dept., Albany, 1975, appt. mem. score certification, 1993—. Elder First Presbyn. Ch., Deposit, N.Y., 1979-86, chmn. pastor nominating com., 1990-91. Mem. Windsor Tchrs. Assn. (chief bldg. rep. 1972-74, 92), Lions (pres. Deposit club 1985, treas. 1989-91, past sec., zone chmn. south cen. dist.). Republican. Avocations: card and map collecting, softball, walking, travel. Home: 82 Pine St Deposit NY 13754-1125 Office: Windsor Cen Sch 213 Main St Windsor NY 13865-4134

SNYDER, JOHN HENRY, computer science educator, consultant; b. Wichita, Kans., Mar. 16, 1947; s. Melvin Henry and Cathleen Ann (Collins) S.; m. Patricia Reilly, Mar. 11, 1984; children: Matthew Melvin George, Mark John Joseph. BA, U. Kans., 1970; MS, Nova U., Ft. Lauderdale, Fla., 1984. Cert. tchr. Nev., N.D. Computer sci. tchr. Hyde Park Jr. High Sch., Las Vegas, Nev., 1981-86, Chapparal High sch., Las Vegas, 1986-91, Cimarron Meml. High Sch., Las Vegas, 1991-94; chair dept. sci. & tech. Advanced Tech. Acad., Las Vegas, 1994—. Copywriter pub. info. office CCSD, Las Vegas, 1982—84; chmn. gifted children spl. interest group Am. Mensa, 1984; mem. tech. com. Nev. State Network Internet Com., 1994—95; vice chair NW Accreditation Team, 2002—04; cons. Office Supt. Clark County Sch. dist., Las Vegas, 1984, Las Vegas, 85, IBM Corp., Atlanta, 1991—96; systems analyst Homes & Narver (summer), 1988; adminstrv. aide EG&G Energy Measurements, Las Vegas, 1989; adj. instr. computer sci. Nova U., 1984—93, U. Nev., Las Vegas, 1990—, The Meadows Sch., 1991—96; nat. coord. Milken Educator States Network, 2000—, Milken Educator Listserve, 2001—; chmn. Nev. State Tchrs. of the Yr., 2000—, 2d v.p., 2001—02, nat. conv. chmn., 2002. Newsletter editor Nat. State Tchrs. of Yr., 1991-93, nat. newsletter editor, webmaster, 1998—, 1999—; contbr. articles to profl. jours. Co-chmn. Ednl. Exposition, Las Vegas, 1984; tech. cons. Harry Reid for U.S. Senate, 1986, 92; mem. Nevada 2000 Tech. Subcom., 1993, Nev. State Network Internet Com., 1993—. Named Tchr. of Yr., State of Nev., 1989-90, Burger King, 1989-90, U. Nev., Las Vegas, Southland Tchr. of Yr., 1990, Tandy Tech. Scholar, 1991, Nev. Educator of Yr., Milliken Family Found., 1992, Nev. Tchr. of the Yr. Microsoft Corp./Technology & Learning Mag., 1995; recipient Innovative Teaching award Bus. Week Mag., 1990, McAuliffe fellowship, 1994, 97, Impact Innovator grantee, 1996. Mem. KC (sec., v.p., pres., past pres., local lodge newsletter editor), Am. Legion, Phi Delta Kappa (newsletter editor Overall Excellence award 1990). Democrat. Roman Catholic. Avocations: programming, didjeridu, classical music, website construction, virtual reality. Office: Advanced Tech Acad 2501 Vegas Dr Las Vegas NV 89106-1643 E-mail: jsnyder@atech.org.

SNYDER, LYNN NELSON, special education educator; b. L.A., Sept. 30, 1951; s. Donald Vernon and Marceline Opal (Nelson) S.; m. Arlene Frances Moon, Oct. 6, 1972; 1 child, Valerie Ann. BS, Christian Heritage Coll., 1980; MA, St. Mary's Coll. Calif., 1992. Cert. tchr., cert. adminstr., Assn. Christian Schs. Internat. Tchr. Tabernacle Bapt. Sch., Concord, Calif., 1981-87; vice prin. King's Valley Christian Sch., Concord, 1987-91; dir. learning ctr. Berean Christian High Sch., Walnut Creek, Calif., 1991-92; adminstr. New Vistas Christian Sch., Pleasant Hill, Calif., 1992-94, Kings Valley Christian Sch., Concord, Calif., 1994—. Mem. ASCD. Avocations: cattle ranching, horses. Office: Kings Valley Christian Sch 4255 Clayton Rd Concord CA 94521-2761

SNYDER, MARTHA JANE, elementary school educator, consultant; b. Brookline, Mass., Apr. 2, 1953; d. James Caldwell and Helen Rebecca (Magowan) Thompson; m. William I. Snyder, Dec. 28, 1983; 1 child, Rebecca Jane-Lee. BA, Maryville Coll., 1975; MEd, Boston State Coll., 1981; postgrad. Orton-Gillingham Tng. Program, Mass. Gen. Hosp., 1980. Cert. elem. tchr., reading specialist, Mass., N.H. Reading tutor Carroll Hall Sch. at Lesley Coll., Cambridge, Mass., 1979-80; reading tchr. Esma Lewis Elem. Sch., Rifle, Colo., 1980-85, 87-88; reading tutor Hopkinton (N.H.) Ind. Sch., 1988-89; pvt. practice Concord, N.H., 1989-92; tchr. Computer tots of N.H., Epsom, 1993-95. With Mass. Migrant Edn. Saturday Morning Program, Boston Indian Ctr., 1979-80. Mem. Internat. Dyslexia Assn., Mass. Gen. Alumni Assn., Phi Delta Kappa.

SNYDER, NANCY SUSAN, reading specialist; b. East Stroudsburg, Pa., Sept. 15, 1950; d. Robert Milton and Elinor Ackerly (Smith) Richards; m. William Robert Snyder, July 2, 1973. BSEdn., East Stroudsburg U., 1973, MEd, 1979, Reading Specialist, 1983. Cert. tchr. elem. edn., reading specialist. Office worker, supr. Burnley Workshop of Poconos, East Stroudsburg, 1969-73; remedial tchr. Colonial Northampton Intermediate Unit #20, Easton, Pa., 1973—. Mem. Act 178 Professional Devel. Com., Easton, 1985—. Mem. Nat. Coun. Tchrs. Math., Internat. Reading Assn., Colonial Intermediate Unit #20 Edn. Assn. 9sec. 1973—), Keystone Reading Assn. Republican. Avocations: piano and organ music performance, reading. Home: RR 2 Box 2030A Stroudsburg PA 18360-9802 Office: Colonial Northampton Int 20 6 Danforth Rd Easton PA 18045-7820

SNYDER, RICHARD GERALD, research scientist, administrator, educator, consultant; b. Northampton, Mass., Feb. 14, 1928; s. Grant B. and Ruth (Putnam) S.; m. Phoebe Jones, March 2, 1949; children: Dorinda, Sherrill, Paul, Jeff, Jon, David. Student, Amherst Coll., 1946-48; BA, U. Ariz., 1956, MA, 1957, PhD, 1959. Diplomate Am. Bd. Forensic Anthropology. Tchg. asst. dept. anthropology U. Ariz., Tucson, 1957-58, assoc. rsch. engr. Applied Rsch. Lab., Coll. Engring., 1958-60, mem. staff Ariz. Transp. and Traffic Inst., 1959-60, assoc. prof. sys. engring., 1960; chief phys. anthropology Civil Aeromed. Rsch. Inst. FAA, Oklahoma City, 1960-66, rsch. pilot, 1962-66, acting chief Protection and Survival Labs., 1963-66; mgr. biomechanics dept. Office Automotive Safety Rsch. Ford Motor Co., Dearborn, Mich., 1966-68, prin. rsch. scientist, 1968; assoc. prof. anthropology U. Mich., Ann Arbor, 1968-73, prof., 1973-85; rsch. scientist Hwy. Safety Rsch. Inst. U. Mich. Trans. Rsch. Inst., Ann Arbor, 1968—85; head biomed. dept. U. Mich., Ann Arbor, 1969-84, dir. NASA Ctr. of Excellence in Man-Vehicle Syss., 1984-85, prof. emeritus, 1985—, rsch. scientist emeritus, 1989—; pres. Biodynamics Internat., Tucson, 1986—. Pres., bd. dirs. George Snively Rsch. Found., 1992-98; assoc. prof. sys. engring. U. Ariz., 1950; adj. assoc. prof. U. Okla., 1963; rsch. assoc. Zoller Lab., U. Chgo., 1964-65, rsch. assoc. dept. anthropology, 1965-67; assoc. prof. Mich. State U., East Lansing, 1967-68; cons. USAF Aerospace Med. Rsch. Labs., Nat. Acad. Scis., U.S. Dept. Transp., adv. com. Office Naval Rsch. Dept. Navy, numerous others. Assoc. editor Jour. of Comm., 1961-63; cons. editor Jour. Biomechanics, 1967-81;mem. editl. bd. Product Safety News, 1973—; adv. bd. Aviation Space and Environ. Medicine, 1980-91, 94—; mem. editl. rev. bd. Stapp Car Crash Jour., 2001-03; contbr. chpts. to books and numerous articles to profl. jours. Judge Internat. Sci. Fair, Detroit, 1968; mem. coun. Explorer Scouts, Ann Arbor, 1968-70; dir. Am. Bd. Forensic Anthropology, 1978-84, 85-91; dir. Snell Meml. Found., 1990—; bd. dirs. N.Mex. Rsch. Inst., 1996-2000. 1st lt. USAF, 1949-54, Korea. Decorated Disting. Flying Cross, 3 Air medals; recipient Met. Life award Nat. Safety Coun., 1970, Admiral Luis de Flores Flight Safety award Flight Safety Found., 1981; named to Safety and Health Hall of Fame Internat., 1993, Ariz. Aviation Hall of Fame, 1998. Fellow AAAS, Aerospace Med. Assn. (Harry G. Moseley award 1975, Profl. Excellence award 1978, John Paul Stapp award in aerospace biomechanics 1994), Royal Anthrop. Inst., Am. Anthrop. Assn., Am. Acad. Forensic Scis. (T. Dale Stewart award 1992), Soc. Automotive Engrs. (Arch T. Colwell Merit award 1973, Aerospace Congress award 1982, Tech. Contbns. to Air Transport Safety), Explorers Club; mem. AIAA (assoc. fellow), Am. Assn. Phys. Anthropologists, Ariz.-Nev. Acad. Sci., Internat. Soc. Aircraft Safety Investigators, Aerospace Physiologists Soc., Sigma Xi, Beta Beta Beta. Republican. Congregationalist. Avocations: aviation, aerospace medicine, forensic anthropology. Home: 3720 N Silver Dr Tucson AZ 85749-9709 Office: Biodynamics Internat Tucson AZ 85749

SNYDER, SUSAN BROOKE, retired English literature educator; b. Yonkers, N.Y., July 12, 1934; d. John Warren and Virginia Grace (Hartung) S. BA, Hunter Coll., CUNY, 1955; MA, Columbia U., 1958, PhD, 1963. Lectr. Queens Coll., CUNY, N.Y.C., 1961-63; instr. Swarthmore Coll., Pa., 1963-66, asst. prof. English lit., 1966-70, assoc. prof., 1970-75, prof., 1975-93, Eugene M. Lang research prof., 1982-86, Gil and Frank Mustin prof., 1990-93; ret.; prof. emeritus Swarthmore Coll., from 1993. Scholar-in-residence Folger Shakespeare Libr., 1997—. Author: The Comic Matrix of Shakespeare's Tragedies, 1979, Pastoral Process, 1998; editor: Divine Weeks and Works of Guillaume de Saluste, Sieur du Bartas, 1979, Othello: Critical Essays, 1988, All's Well that Ends Well, 1993; mem. editl. bd. Shakespeare Quar., 1972—. Folger Library sr. fellow, 1972-73; Nat. Endowment for Humanities fellow, 1967-68; Guggenheim Found. fellow, 1980-81; Huntington Library summer grantee, 1966, 71; Folger Library grantee, 1969; Nat. Endowment for Humanities grantee, 1970; Nat. Endowment for Humanities summer grantee, 1976 Mem. Renaissance Soc. Am. (coun. 1979-81), Shakespeare Assn. Am. (trustee 1980-83). Home: Bethesda, Md. Died Sept. 14, 2001.

SNYDER, SUSAN LEACH, science educator, writer; b. Columbus, Ohio, Nov. 25, 1946; d. Russell and Helen Marie (Sharpe) Leach; m. James Floyd Snyder, June 18, 1988. BS in comprehensive sci. edn., Miami U., 1968; MS in entomology, U. Hawaii, 1970. Gen. and health sci. tchr. Columbus Pub. Schs., 1971-73; life, earth & physical sci. tchr. Upper Arlington (Ohio) Schs., 1975—2000. Author: The Ocean Environment, 1992, 96; co-author: Focus on Earth Science, 1987, 89, Merrill Earth Science, 1993, 95. Glencoe Earth Science, 1997, 99, 2002, The Air Around Us, 2002, The Changing Surface of Earth, 2002, The Water Planet, 2002; mem. author team: Science Interactions, 1993, 95, 98, Science Voyages, 2000, 2001, Glencoe Science, 2002, 2003, Integrated Science, 2003; contbr. articles to profl. jours. Trustee N.Am. Astrophys. Obs., Delaware, Ohio, 1983-97; pres. Consortium of Aquatic and Marine Educators Ohio, 1983-84; sec. Ohio chpt. Nat. Tchrs. of Yr., 1993-95; docent, vol. Conservancy of S.W. Fla. Mus. Natural History, 2000—. Named Outstanding Earth Sci. Tchr. of State of Ohio and East Cen Sect. Nat. Assn. Geology Tchrs., 1983, Ohio Tchr. of Yr. Ohio State Dept. Edn., 1987, Finalist Nat. Tchr. of Yr. Coun. of Chief State Sch. Officers, 1987; Pres. award for Excellence in Sci. and Math Teaching Nat. Sci. Tchrs. Assn., 1992, Outstanding Tchr. award Geological Soc. Am., 1992. Mem. Nat. Sci. Tchrs. Assn. (Exemplary Earth Sci. Teaching Team 1983, 84, 85, conf. workshop presenter 1985), Nat. Marine Educators Assn. (Nat. Outstanding Marine Sci. Tchr. 1984, bd. mem. 1984, 2000-03, conf. workshop presenter 1983, 84, 86, 92), Great Lakes Educators of Aquatic and Marine Scis. Avocation: photography. Home: 1361 Marlyn Dr Columbus OH 43220-3973

SOBOL, BRUCE J. internist, educator, researcher; b. N.Y.C., June 10, 1923; s. Ira J. and Ida S. S.; B.A., Swarthmore Coll., 1947; M.D., N.Y.U., 1950; m. Barbara Sue Gordon, Apr. 30, 1951; children: Peter Gordon, Scott David. Intern, Bellevue Hosp., N.Y.C., 1950-51, resident, 1951-52, N.Y. Heart Assn. fellow, 1953-55; resident VA Hosp., Boston, 1952-53; practice medicine specializing in internal medicine, White Plains, N.Y., 1955-59; dir. cardio-pulmonary lab. Westchester County (N.Y.) Med. Ctr., Valhalla, 1959-78; rsch. prof. medicine N.Y. Med. Coll., 1970-78; dir. med. rsch. Boehringer Ingelheim, Ltd., Ridgefield, Conn., 1978-83. Bd. dirs. Westchester Community Svcs. Coun., 1977-79; pres. Westchester Heart Assn., 1976-79. Served with inf. AUS, World War II; ETO. Diplomate Am. Bd. Internal Medicine. Fellow ACP, Am. Coll. Allergy, Am. Coll. Chest Physicians, N.Y. Acad. Scis.; mem. Am. Physiol. Soc., Am. Heart Assn., N.Y. Trudea Soc., Am. Thoracic Soc., Am. Fedn. Clin. Rsch. Contbr. numerous articles to profl. publs.

SOBOL, ELISE SCHWARCZ, music educator; b. Chgo., June 12, 1951; d. Morton and Harriet Jacobsohn Schwarcz; m. Lawrence Paul Sobol, Aug. 21, 1977 (div. Sept. 1989); children: Marlon I., Aaron L. AA, Simon's Rock of Bard Coll., 1971; student, Mannes Coll. Music, 1971—73, Juillard Sch. Music, 1973—74; BA, New Sch. for Social Rsch., 1985; MA, Columbia U., 1987. Staff auditorium events, concerts, lectures Met. Mus. Art, 1972-73; sec. to pres. Harry Beall Mgmt. Inc., N.Y.C., 1973-76; sales rep. M.L. Falcone Pub. Rels., N.Y.C., 1976-77; asst. to pres. Jacques Leiser Artist Mgmt., N.Y.C., 1977-78; artist rep. Elise Sobol Mgmt. Inc., South Huntington, N.Y., 1978-82; tchr. music Nassau Boces Elem., 1988—; dir. L.I. Music Workshop, 1992—. Adj. prof. NYU Steinhardt Sch. Edn., 2000—; advisor arts and humanities Internat. Biog. Ctr., Cambridge, England; guest lectr. NYU, 1999, Hofstra, 2000; adj. faculty C.W. Post Coll. L.I. U., 2000; instr. SUNY, Farmingdale, 1993—98; music tchr. The Roslyn Middle Sch., 1987—88; dir. Early Musical Devel. Program for Children at Calling All Kids, South Huntington, 1981—86; tchr. young and adult piano students, 1968; piano adj. educator N.Y. State, 1993—. Musician: (piano concerts) Chamber Music series at U.S. Mil. Acad., N.J. met. area, Disting. Artists series, 2002—03, Met. Area Concerts, 2003, Am. Assn. Univ. Women Commentary and Concerts, 2003; author: An Attitude and Approach for Teaching Music to Special Learners, 2001; musician: (commentary and concert) A Gentlewoman's Pursuit, AAUW, 2003. Active Nassau Boces Elem. Program PTA, cultural arts coord., 1988—. Recipient Award of Honor, L.I. Very Spl. Arts Festival, 1993, Spl. Citation N.Y. State Assembly Ames Elem. Program, 1998, Spl. Recognition Nassau Music Educators Assn., 1999, 1st prize Dr. Martin Luther King Jr. Performing Arts Competition for Exceptional Students Nassau County, 1999, 2000, 01, Internat. Peace Prize, United Cultural Convention, May 2002, Town of Oyster Bay citation, 2002. Mem. NAFE, ASCD, AAUW, N.Y. State Sch. Music Assn. (chair music for spl. learners 1993—), Amnesty Internat., Music Educators Nat. Conf., Music Tchrs. Nat. Assn., Nassau Music Educators Assn., Nat. Mus. for Women, Met. Mus. of Art. Home: 21 Saxon St Melville NY 11747

SOBOL, THOMAS, education educator; b. Jan. 11, 1932; m. Harriet Sobol; three children. BA in English, Harvard U., 1953, grad., 1954; PhD, Columbia U., 1969. Head dept. English pub. sch. system, Bedford, N.Y., 1961-65; dir. instrn., 1965-69; asst. supt. instrn. pub. sch. system, 1969-71; supt. sch. systems Scarsdale, N.Y., 1971-87; commr. N.Y. State edn. Albany, 1987-95; Christian A. Johnson Prof. Columbia Univ. Teacher's College, N.Y.C., 1995—, dir. ednl. adminstrs. Office: Columbia Univ Teachers College 525 W 120th St New York NY 10027-6625*

SOBOLEWSKI, JANE ANN, business educator; b. Ironwood, Mich., May 24, 1958; d. Edward A. and Betty A. (Olson) Blomquist; m. Robert Sobolewski; children: Jared, Ryan. AA, Gogebic Community Coll., 1978; BS, Ferris State Coll., 1980; MA, Northern Mich. U., 1987. Instr., bus. Ironwood (Mich.) High Sch., 1980-84, Gogebic Community Coll., Ironwood, 1983—. Sec. Mich. Assn. Higher Edn., Ironwood, 1985-93. Tchr., Sunday Sch., Salem Luth. Ch., Ironwood, 1990-91. Mem. Nat. Bus. Educators Assn., Mich. Bus. Educators Assn. (regional fall conf. co-chmn. 1989-90), Delta Pi Epsilon. Avocations: swimming, reading, travel, walking. Home: 203 W Michigan Ave Ironwood MI 49938-1127 Office: Gogebic Community Coll E4946 Jackson Rd Ironwood MI 49938-1365

SOCHACKI, TINA MARIE, secondary education educator; b. Evergreen Park, Ill., July 10, 1967; d. Alex Wayne and Judith Anne (Zicha) Spirakes; m. Matthew Zygmunt Sochacki, June 18, 1993. BA in French and Spanish Edn., U. Ill., 1989; postgrad., Gov.'s State U., University Park, Ill., 1994-96. Cert. 6-12 tchr., Ill.; Ill. type 75 cert. Tchr. fgn. lang. Bremen H.S., Midlothian, Ill., 1989-90, Acad. of Our Lady H.S., Chgo., 1990-91, Evergreen Park H.S., 1991—. Mem. ASCD, Am. Assn. Tchrs. French, Ill. Coun. on Tchg. Fgn. Langs., U. Ill. Alumni Assn., Golden Key. Avocations: billiards, reading, spending time with family and pet pug. Office: Evergreen Park HS 9901 S Kedzie Ave Evergreen Park IL 60805-3416

SOCKEY, FELICIA WILLENE, elementary school educator; b. Stigler, Okla., Sept. 17, 1957; d. Jessie Fredrick abd Genevieve Madeline (Garland) Venable; m. Leland L. Sockey. BS, Northeastern State U., Tahlequah, Okla., 1979; AS, Ea. State Coll., Wilburton, Okla., 1977. Cert. tchr., Okla. Elem. tchr. Pocola (Okla.) Pub. Schs.; elem. English tchr. Quinton (Okla.) Pub. Schs., 2001—. Mem. NEA, Okla. Edn. Assn., Internat. Soc. Poets.

SOCOL, SHELDON ELEAZER, university official; b. N.Y.C., July 10, 1936; s. Irving and Helen (Tuchman) S.; m. Genia Ruth Prager, Dec. 26, 1959; children: Jeffrey, Steven, Sharon, Robyn, Leslie, Steven Warren. BA, Yeshiva U., 1958; JD, NYU, 1963. From asst. bursar to dir. student fins. Yeshiva U., N.Y.C., 1958-70, sec., 1970—, chief fiscal officer, 1971-72, v.p. bus. affairs, 1972—. Mem. N.Y. State Adv. Coun. on Fin. Assistance to Coll. Students, 1969-76; asst. dir. Tng. Inst. for Fin. Aid Officers, Hunter, Coll., CUNY, 1970-71; mem. presdl. adv. com. Temple U., 1986; mem. regents adv. task force N.Y.C. Regional Plan for Higher Edn., 1971-73; bd. dirs. N.Y. Structural Biology Ctr., 2000; spkr. in field. Pres. Minyon Park Estates, Inc. Mem. NEA, Nat. Assn. Coll. and Univ. Attys., Met. N.Y.C. Fin. Aid Adminstrs. Assn., Ea. Assn. Student Fin. Aid Officers, Am. Mgmt. Assn., Am. Assn. for Higher Edn., Nat. Assn. Coll. and Univ. Bus. Officers, Soc. Coll. and Univ. Planning, Mid. States Assn. Colls. (evaluation team Commn. on Higher Edn., U. Medicine and Dentistry N.J., 1985, Upstate Health Sci. Ctr. 1986, Carnegie-Mellon U. 1988, Albany Med. Ctr. 1989). Office: Yeshiva U 500 W 185th St New York NY 10033-3299 E-mail: dses@ymail.yu.edu.

SOCZKIEWICZ, EUGENIUSZ STANISŁAW, physicist, educator; b. Inowrocław, Poland, Oct. 26, 1934; s. Stefan and Anna (Miętkiewicz) S. MS, U. Toruń, Poland, 1956; D in Tech. Scis., Polish Acad. Scis., Warsaw, Poland, 1973; DSc in Physics, U. Poznań, Poland, 1984. Lectr. physics Secondary Sch., Tuchola, Bydgoszcz, Poland, 1956-64, High Pedagogical Sch., Katowice, Poland, 1964-67, Silesian Tech. U., Gliwice/Katowice, 1967-86, asst. prof., 1986-93, assoc. prof., 1993—. Contbr. articles to profl. jours. Mem. IEEE, Polish Phys. Soc., Polish Acoustical Soc., European

Phys. Soc., European Acoustics Assn. Roman Catholic. Achievements include propagation of ultrasonic waves in liquids and randomly inhomogeneous media. Home: Derkacza 6/25 44-100 Gliwice Katowice Poland Office: Silesian Tech U Inst Physic Krzywoustego 2 44-100 Gliwice Katowice Poland Fax: 48 32 2372216. E-mail: soczkiewicz@gnom.matfiz.polsl.gliwice.pl.

SODEN, RUTH M. geriatrics nurse, educator; b. Tipton, Iowa, Nov. 29, 1940; d. Tony and Clarissa Arlene (Beall) Koreman; m. James D. Soden; children: Shannon, Scott, Suzan, Staci. AA, Highline Community Coll., Midway, Wash. Cert. in intravenous therapy. Charge nurse Wildwood Health Care Ctr., Puyallup, Wash.; admissions coord. Forestglen Nursing Ctr., Seattle, staff devel. dir.; charge nurse Green River Terrace Nursing Ctr., Auburn, Wash., Discovery Care Ctr., Hamilton, Mont.; nurse mgr. Tacoma Luth. Home; charge nurse and minimum data set coord. Discovery Care Ctr., Hamilton. Mem. Clover Park Tech. Coll., Tacoma. Mem. Nat. Gerontol. Nursing Assn. (practical nurse program adv. com.), Wash. State Nurses Assn., Assn. for Practitioners in Infection Control, Nat. Coun. on Family Rels., Phi Theta Kappa. Home: 157 West Hills Way Hamilton MT 59840-9316

SODER-ALDERFER, KAY CHRISTIE, counseling administrator; b. Evanston, Ill., Oct. 25, 1949; d. Earl Eugene and Alice Kathryn (Lien) Soder; m. David Luther Alderfer, May 15, 1976. BSE, No. Ill. U., 1972; postgrad., Luth. Sch. Theology, Phila., 1973; MA, Gov.'s State U., University Park, Ill., 1978; PhD, Walden U., 1985. Consecrated deaconess Luth. Ch., 1974. News reporter Suburban Life Newspaper, La Grange Park, Ill., 1972; counselor various orgns. Ill. & Pa., 1973—; parish worker Luth. Ch., De Kalb, Ill., 1973-74; counseling supr. Gov. State Cmty. Counseling Svc., 1977—78; pub. rels. asst. Luth. Ch. Women, Phila., 1974-76; editor Luth. Ch., Chgo., 1979—; spiritual dir. Gentle Pathways, Downers Grove, Ill., 1988—, psychotherapist, 1990—, also bd. dirs. Founder Wordsmith Wizards, 2002; cons. Evang. Luth. Ch. in Am., Chgo., 1988—, Lehigh Valley Hosp. Assn., Allentown, Pa., 1986, Luth. Social Ministry Orgns. of Pa. and N.J., 1997; cons. multinat. corps., 2001—. Author: Gentle Journeys, 1993, With Those Who Grieve, 1995, Help! There's a Monster in My Head, 2000; editor Entree, 1988-93, Multicultural Jour., 1992-99, project mgr., 1996-98; graphic designs exhbn. Franklin Mus., Phila., 1981; photography published in 4 books. Spokeswoman Progressive Epilepsy Network, Phila., 1980-85; chair spiritual life com. Luth. Deaconess Cmty., Gladwyne, Pa., 1990-92; founder Teens with Epilepsy and Motivation, 1995; vol. March of Dimes, Ill., 1991-93, Am. Cancer Soc., 2000—; amb. of goodwill Good Bears of the World, 1993-94; spiritual dir. Evang. Luth. Ch. in Am. Recipient Silver award Delaware Valley Neographics Soc., 1981; 50th anniversary scholar Luth. Deaconess Community, 1983. Mem. APA, AHF, Webmasters of the World. Avocations: painting, mixed media, story telling, traveling, native american studies. Office: Gentle Pathways 1207 55th St Downers Grove IL 60515-4810

SOEHREN, SHARON KAYE, school district administrator; b. Reeder, N.D., Jan. 28, 1943; d. Orville W. and Marian (Rose) Honeyman; m. Marvin D. Soehren, Aug. 11, 1964; children: Shannon, Shawn. BA, Dickinson State U., 1963; BS Elem. Edn., U. Mary, 1982. Tchr. Bowman (N.D.) Sch., 1963-65, Reeder (N.D.) Sch., 1966—2000; CEO Bison (S.D.) Sch. Dist. #52-1, 2000—. Prin. Reeder Sch., 1987—, dist. adminstr., 1993—; mem. State Health Curriculum, Bismarck, N.D., 1993—; tchr., trainer HIV/AIDS Dept. Pub. Instrn., Bismarck, 1992—. Eucharistic minister Sacred Heart Ch., Reeder, 1994. Named tchr. of yr. Farm Bur., Hettinger, N.D., 1993. Mem. NEA, N.D. Edn. Assn., Nat. Elem. Sch. Prins., N.D. Elem. Sch. Prins., S.D. Elem. Prin. Assn., S.D. Sch. Adminstrs. Avocations: reading, walking, singing, camping, fishing. Home: 201 E Carr St Bison SD 57620 Office: Bison Pub Sch #52-1 Bison SD 57620

SOFFER, REBA N. history educator; b. Nashville, Dec. 22, 1934; d. Phillip and Ida (Finesilver) Nusbaum; m. Bernard Harold Soffer, Jan. 28, 1956; 1 child, Roger Phillip. BA magna cum laude, Bklyn. Coll., 1955; MA in History with honors, Wellesley (Mass.) Coll., 1957; PhD, Harvard U., 1962. Asst. prof. history Calif. State U., Northridge, 1962-67, assoc. prof. history, 1967-71, prof. history, 1971—. Vis. prof. history UCLA, 1980; Christiansen vis. fellow St. Catherine's Coll., Oxford (Eng.) U., 1987; sr. panelist NEH; chmn. adv. screening com. in history Council for Internat. Exchange Scholars, 1980-83. Author: Ethics and Society in England, 1978, Discipline and Power, 1995; contbr. articles to profl. jours. Bd. dirs. environmentalist group Pacific Palisades (Calif.) Resident's Assn., 1977—, Los Angeles Theater Works, Los Angeles, 1984—. NEH fellow, 1981-82, 88; recipient Outstanding Prof. award for 19 campuses of the Calif. State System, 1985. Mem. Royal Hist. Soc.; mem. Am. Hist. Assn., Pacific Coast Conf. in Brit. Studies (pres. 1976-78), N.Am. Conf. in Brit. Studies (assoc. exec. sec. 1978-83, nominating com. 1989—, endowment com. 1987—, exec. sec. 1990—), Pacific Coast Am. Hist. Assn. (coun. 1980-83, 89, chair program com. 1988-89), Calif. Women in Higher Edn. (pres. Northridge chpt. 1986-88). Home: 665 Bienveneda Ave Pacific Palisades CA 90272-3339 Office: Calif State U Dept Of History Northridge CA 91330-0001

SOFFER, ROSEMARY S. community health nurse, consultant, educator; b. N.Y.C., June 29, 1953; d. E.F. Harvey and Paula L. Show. Diploma, Hosp. U. Pa. Sch. Nursing, 1975; BSN, Neumann Coll., 1980; postgrad., Temple U., 1983—; MSN, Neumann Coll., 1998. RN, Pa., Del.; cert. CPR instr. Educator nursing sch., consulting nurse practitioner, educator Ambilikkai Village Health Clinic, India; program devel., nurse cons. Anglican Ch. India, 1995; charge nurse Hosp. of U. Pa., Phila., audit ventricular tachycardia, 1980; community nurse Community Nursing Svc., Chester, Pa.; program devel. nurse cons. Anglican Ch. India, Phila./Delaware County, Pa., 1995; ind. nurse contractor, 1994, 95. Spkr. in field at Neumann Coll., chs. and orgns.; presenter numerous seminars on internat. nursing issues; exec. dir. Christian Ministry Internat. Author: The Real Rambo, 1989, Coping Mechanism of the Chronically Ill During Separation, 1983, Opened Eyes, 1990. Exec. com. Rambo Co., Inc. Sight for Curable Blind; bd. dirs. Ecumenical Caring Coalition-Chester Food Cupboard; elder Yeadon Presbyn. Ch., 1990-93; pres., dir. Ministry Internat., 1995—. Named one of Outstanding Young Women of Am., nominated by Dept. Atty. Gen. Harrisburg, 1991-92, Professionalism award Yeadon H.S., 1971. Mem. Internat. Nursing Soc., Pa. Med. Missionary Soc. (bd. dirs. 1990-95), Sigma Theta Tau.

SOHAILI, MONIRA, special education educator, writer; b. Pune, India, Nov. 4, 1933; d. Ispandiar and Keshvar Yaganegi; m. Shahpur Sohaili, Oct. 15, 1953 (dec. Dec. 2000). BA in Edn., Northeastern Ill. U., 1981, MA, 1982. Cert. behavioral therapy Behavioral Therapy Tng. Ctr., L.A., 1996. Tchr. Parramalta Marist H.S., Australia, 1970—71; guide Bahai House of Worship, Chgo., 1973—83; ESL instr. Cuban/Hatian Refugee Program, Chgo., 1983—84, Chgo. Bd. Edn., 1984—87; ESL and Eng. instr. Santa Monica (Calif.) City Coll., 1987—89; ESL, Eng. and reading tchr. Le Conte Mid. Sch., L.A., 1989—96; head dept. Ctr. Mid. Sch., 1994—96, spl. edn. tchr., 1996—, dept. head, 1996—2000; tchr. spl. edn. J. Burroughs Mid. Sch., L.A., 2000—. Storyteller in field, 2002—. Author: (children's book) Monira's Fables, 2000, From Earth and Beyond, 2003. Coord. childproof medicine vials donation, Papua New Guinea, 1995—97. Recipient Cert. of Achievement, L.A. USD Lang. Acquisition, 1993, I Made a Difference award, L.A. Dept. Edn., 1995. Mem.: NEA (reading and writing program 1990—), Calif. Tchrs. Assn. (assisted in program 1990—). Avocations: reading, writing, traveling, swimming. Office: John Burroughs HS 600 McCadden Pl Los Angeles CA 90005 Address: PO Box 95 Santa Monica CA 90406-0095

SOHN, CHANG WOOK, energy systems researcher, educator; b. Seoul, Jan. 10, 1947; parents Kye Taek and Young Bo (Koh) S.; m. Chung Hae Han Sohn, Aug. 24, 1974; children: Douglas Jemin, Sammy Sungmin. BS in Engring., Seoul Nat. U., 1969; MS in Mech. Engring., Tex. Tech. U., 1975; PhD in Mech. Engring., U. Ill., Urbana, 1980. Registered profl. engr., Ill. 1st lt. Korean Army, 1969-71; tchr. KyungGi H.S., Seoul, 1971-72; rsch. asst. Tex. Tech. U., Lubbock, 1973-74, U. Ill., Urbana, 1974-79, rsch. assoc., 1979-80; rsch. engr. U.S. Army Engring. R&D Ctr., Champaign, Ill., 1980-84, acting. team leader, 1992, prin. investigator, 1984—, project leader, 1995—2000. Adj. assoc. prof. U. Ill., Urbana, 1992-97; vis. rsch. fellow Korea Inst. Energy Rsch., 1995-96. Contbr. articles on fluid mechanics, heat transfer to profl. jours, ASHRAE transactions. Recipient Tech. Transfer award U.S. Army Corps of Engrs., Washington, 1991, Spl. Act award U.S. Army Yuma (Ariz.) Proving Ground, 1988; Korea Inst. Energy Rsch. fellow, 1995-96. Mem. ASME (K-19 com. 1993—2000), ASHRAE (com. chair Cool Storage Design Guide 1992, air conditioning rsch. ctr. industry adv. bd. mem. 1991-96). Home: 2910 Robeson Park Dr Champaign IL 61822-7609 Office: US Army ERDC-CERL PO Box 9005 Champaign IL 61826-9005 E-mail: c-sohn@cecer.army.mil.

SOHN, HONG YONG, chemical engineer, educator, metallurgical engineer, educator; b. Kaesung, Kyunggi-Do, Republic of Korea, Aug. 21, 1941; arrived in U.S., 1966; s. Chong Ku and Soon Deuk (Woo) Sohn; m. Victoria Bee Tuan Ngo, Jan. 8, 1971; children: Berkeley Jihoon, Edward Jihyun. BSChemE, Seoul (Republic of Korea) Nat. U., 1962; MSChemE, U. N.B., Can., 1966; PhD in Chem. Engring., U. Calif., Berkeley, 1970. Engr. Cheil Sugar Co., Busan, Republic of Korea, 1962-64; rsch. assoc. SUNY, Buffalo, 1971-73; rsch. engr. DuPont Co., Wilmington, Del., 1973-74; prof. metall. engring., adj. prof. chem. engring. U. Utah, Salt Lake City, 1974—. Cons. Lawrence Livermore Nat. Lab., 1976—, Cabot Corp., 1984—, DuPont Co., 1987—, Utah Power and Light Co., 1987—, H. C. Starck, 1997—. Co-author: (book) Gas-Solid Reactions, 1976; co-editor: Rate Processes of Extractive Metallurgy, 1979, Extractive Metallurgy of Refractory Metals, 1980, Advances in Sulfide Smelting, 2 vols., 1983, Recycle and Secondary Recovery of Metals, 1985, Gas-Solid Reactions in Pyrometallurgy, 1986, Flash Reaction Processes, 1988, Metallurgical Processes for the Year 2000 and Beyond, 1988, Metallurgical Processes for the Early Twenty-First Century, 2 vols., 1994, Proceeding of the Julian Szekely Memorial Symposium on Materials Processing, 1997, Value-Addition Metallurgy, 1998, Sulfide Smelting, 2002, Metallurgical and Materials Processing: Principles and Technologies, 3 vols., 2003; contbr. articles to profl. jours. Recipient Fulbright Disting. lectr., 1983; Camille and Henry Dreyfus Found. Tchr. scholar, 1977, Japan Soc. Promotion Sci. fellow, 1990. Mem.: AIChE, AIME (James Douglas Gold medal 2001), Korean Inst. Chem. Engrs. (Fellow award 1998), Korean Acad. Sci. and Tech., Minerals, Metals and Materials Soc. (past dir., Extractive Metallurgy Lectr. award 1990, champion H. Mathewson Gold medal award 1993, Extraction and Processing Sci. award 1990, 1994, 1999). Achievements include patents for process for treating sulfide-bearing ores, continuous solvent extraction with bottom gas injection. Office: U Utah 135 S 1460 E Rm 412 Salt Lake City UT 84112-0114 E-mail: hysohn@mines.utah.edu.

SOIFER, ALEXANDER, mathematics educator; b. Moscow, Aug. 14, 1948; came to U.S., 1978; s. Yuri and Rebbeca (Gofman) S.; m. Terza L. Zane, Mar. 7, 1980 (div. Dec. 1985); children: Mark, Julia; m. Maya Kikoin, Aug. 31, 1990; children: Isabelle, Leon. MA in Math. and Computer Sci., Moscow State Pedagogical Inst., 1971; PhD in Math., Moscow State Pedagogical Univ., 1973. Assoc. math. Karelsky (USSR) Pedagogical Inst., 1973-74; jr. rsch. staff mem. Inst. Machine Theory, Moscow, 1974-75, Inst. Info. Sys., Moscow, 1975-76; lectr. U. Mass., Boston, 1979; prof. math., film studies, art history U. Colo., Colorado Springs, 1979—. Pub. Ctr. for Excellence in Math. Edn., Colorado Springs, 1986—; mem. adv. bd. Quantum; vis. rschr. DIMACS, Rutgers U., 2003—; vis. fellow, mathematician Princeton U., 2003—. Author: Mathematics as Problem Solving, 1987, How Does One Cut a Triangle?, 1990, (with V. Boltyanski) Geometric Etudes in Combinatorial Mathematics, 1991, Colorado Mathematical Olympiad: The First Ten Years and Further Explorations, 1994; mng. editor, pub.: Geombinatorics, 1991—. Mem. Human Rels. Comm. of Colorado Springs, 1993-95; chair, founder Colo. Math. Olympiad, 1984—; mem. USA Math. Olympiad subcom., 1996—; sec. World Fedn. Math. Competitions, 1996—. Democrat. Jewish. Avocations: fine art, african/fang culture art, film history. Home: 885 Red Mesa Dr Colorado Springs CO 80906-4525 Office: U Colo 1420 Austin Bluffs Pkwy Colorado Springs CO 80918-3733 E-mail: asoifer@math.uccs.edu.

SOINSKI OPASKAR, GAIL V. secondary school administrator; b. Cleve., May 13, 1948; d. Victor R. and Angela (Penkal) Soinski; m. Frank A. Opaskar, Apr. 13, 1985; 1 child, Amanda. BS, U. Cin., 1971; MS, Cleve. State U., 1977. Tchr. phys. edn. Bolton Elem. Sch., Cleve. Bd. Edn., 1971-72; thcr. phys. edn. and health Jane Addams High Sch., Cleve. Bd. Edn., 1972-89, athletic dir., 1980-89, head coach, volleyball, 1972-87, head track coach, 1972-85; asst. prin. Patrick Henry Intermediate Sch., Cleve., 1989-91, Max Hayes Vocat. High Sch., Cleve., 1991-92, Lincoln West High Sch., Cleve., 1992—. Mem. ASCD, Cleve. Coun. of Adminstrs. and Suprs.

SOJKA, GARY ALLAN, biologist, educator, university official; b. Cedar Rapids, Iowa, July 15, 1940; s. Marvin F. and Ruth Ann (Waddington) Sojka Green; m. Sandra Kay Smith, Aug 5, 1962; children: Lisa Kay, Dirk Allan. BS, Coe Coll., 1962; MS, Purdue U., 1965, PhD, 1967, DSc (hon.), 2002; DL (hon.), Lycoming Coll., 1995. Rsch. assoc. Ind. U., Bloomington, 1967-69, asst. prof., 1969-73, assoc. prof., 1973-79, prof., 1979-84, assoc. chmn. biology, 1977-79, chmn. biology, 1979-81, dean arts and scis., 1981-84; pres. Bucknell U., Lewisburg, Pa., 1984-95, prof. biology, 1984—. Mem. higher edn. commn. Mid. States Assn. Colls. and Schs., 1992-96, chmn. task force on instnl. effectiveness, 1999-2000; chmn. tax policy subcom. Nat. Assn. Ind. Colls. and Univs., 1991-93; mem. study group on internat. edn. Am. Coun. Edn., 1992-94. Mem. So. Ind. Health Sys. Agy., Bedford; chmn. bd. dirs. Stone Belt Coun. Ret. Citizens, Bloomington, 1977—78; mem. nominating com. Ind. Assn. Ret. Citizens, Indpls., 1979; bd. dirs. Geisinger Med. Found., Danville, Pa., 1985—97, 2003—, mem. regional bd., 1997—2003; chmn. Pa. Assn. Ind. Colls. and Univs., 1989—90; mem. pres.'s commn. NCAA, 1993—95; mem. planning adv. com. Snyder County, Pa., 1996—98, mem. planning commn., 2001—; bd. dirs. Bethesda Found., Lewisburg, 1996—98; trustee, bd. dirs. Am. Livestock Conservancy, 2001—; gov. Inst. European Studies, 0989—1994, Citizen for the Future of Pa., 1999—. Recipient Ind. U. Sr. Class Tchg. award, 1975, Frederick B. Lieber award, 1977, Coe Coll. Alumni award of merit, 1982, Gary A. Sojka award Bucknell U., 1992, Cmty. Leadership award Susquahanna Valley Boy Scouts, 1994, Sheepskin award for Disting. Svc. to Higher Edn. Pa. Assn. Colls. and Univs., 2000, ECAC Officiation award, Bucknell U., 2003; named to Coe Coll. Athletic Hall of Fame, 1988; Gary A. Sojka Pavillion named in his honor, 2003. Mem.: AAAS, Pa. Assn. Coll. and Univs. (interim pres. 1997—98, exec. com., Sheepskin award 1999, Sheepskin award 2000), Phila. Soc. Promotion of Agriculture, Am. Coun. Edn. (study group on internat. edn. 1992—94), Nat. Assn. Independent Colls. and Univs. (subcom. chmn. 1991—93), Am. Soc. Biol. Chemists, Am. Acad. Microbiology, Am. Soc. Microbiology, Omicron Delta Kappa, Sigma Nu, Sigma Xi. Baptist. Office: Bucknell U Dept Biology Lewisburg PA 17837

SOKOL, LARRY NIDES, lawyer, educator; b. Dayton, Ohio, Sept. 28, 1946; s. Boris Franklin and Kathryn (Konowitch) S.; m. Beverly Butler, Aug. 3, 1975; children: Addie Teller, Maxwell Philip. BA, U. Pa., 1968; JD, Case Western Res. U., 1971. Bar: Oreg. 1972, U.S. Dist Ct. Oreg. 1972, U.S. Ct. Appeals (9th cir.) 1973, U.S. Supreme Ct. 1980. Law clk. chief judge Oreg. Ct. Appeals, Salem, 1971-72; pvt. practice Portland, Oreg., 1972—; prof. law Lewis and Clark Law Sch., Portland. Adj. prof. law sch. environ. litigation Lewis & Clark U., 1984— Commr. planning City of Lake Oswego, Oreg., 1981-84. Sgt. USAR, 1968-74. Mem. Oreg. State Bar Assn. (chmn. litigation sect. 1983, disciplinary rev. bd. 1982-85), Oreg. Trial Lawyers Assn. Democrat. Jewish. Avocations: running, swimming, squash, model trains, scuba diving. Office: 735 SW 1st Ave Portland OR 97204-3326

SOKOL, ROBERT JAMES, obstetrician, gynecologist, educator; b. Rochester, N.Y., Nov. 18, 1941; s. Eli and Mildred (Levine) S.; m. Roberta Sue Kahn, July 26, 1964; children: Melissa Anne, Eric Russell, Andrew Ian. BA with highest distinction in Philosophy, U. Rochester, 1963, MD with honors, 1966. Diplomate Am. Bd. Ob-Gyn (assoc. examiner 1984-86), Sub-Bd. Maternal-Fetal Medicine. Intern Barnes Hosp., Washington U., St. Louis, 1966-67, resident in ob-gyn., 1967-70, asst. in ob-gyn., 1966-70, rsch. asst., 1967-68, instr. clin. ob-gyn., 1970; Buswell fellow in maternal fetal medicine Strong Meml. Hosp.-U. Rochester, 1972-73; fellow in maternal-fetal medicine Cleve. Met. Gen. Hosp.-Case Western Res. U., Cleve., 1974-75, assoc. obstetrician and gynecologist, 1973-83, asst. prof. ob-gyn., 1973-77; asst. program dir. Perinatal Clin. Rsch. Ctr., 1973-78, co-program dir., 1978-82, program dir., 1982-83, acting dir. obstetrics, 1974-75, co-dir., 1977-83, assoc. prof., 1977-81, prof., 1981-83, assoc. dir. dept. ob-gyn., 1981-83; prof. ob-gyn. Wayne State U., Detroit, 1983-2000, 2000—, chmn. dept. ob-gyn., 1983-89, mem. grad. faculty dept. physiology, 1984—, interim dean Med. Sch., 1988-89, dean, 1989-99, pres. Fund for Med. Rsch. and Edn., 1988—99; chief ob-gyn. Hutzel Hosp. Detroit, 1983-89; interim chmn. med. bd. Detroit Med. Ctr., 1988-89, chmn. med. bd., 1989-99, sr. v.p. med. affairs, 1992-99, trustee, 1990-99; past pres. med. staff Cuyahoga County Hosps.; mem. profl. adv. bd. Educated Childbirth Inc., 1976-80; dir. C.S. Mott Ctr. for Human Growth and Devel., 1983-89, 99—. Sr. Ob cons. Symposia Medicus; cons. Grant Planning Task Force Robert Wood Johnson Found., Nat. Inst. Child Health and Human Devel., Nat. Inst. Alcohol Abuse and Alcoholism, Ctr. for Disease Control, NIH, Health Resources and Services Adminstrn., Nat. Clearinghouse for Alcohol Info., Am. Psychol. Assn.; mem. alcohol psychosocial research rev. com. Nat. Inst. Alcohol Abuse and Alcoholism, 1982-86; mem. ob/gyn adv. panel U.S. Pharmacopeial Conv., 1985-90, adv. com. on policy Am. Jour. Ob-Gyn., 1999-, internat. adv. bd. Karmanos Cancer Inst., Detroit, Mich., 2002-; mem. clin. rsch. task force Assn. Am. Med. Colls., 1998-2000. Mem. internat. editorial bd. Israel Jour. Obstetrics and Gynecology; reviewer med. jours.; mem. editorial bd. Jour. Perinatal Medicine; editor-in-chief Interactions: Programs in Clinical Decision-Making, 1987-90; researcher computer applications in perinatal medicine, alcohol-related birth defects, perinatal risk and neurobehavioral devel.; contbr. articles to profl. jours. Mem.Pres.'s leadership coun. U. Rochester, 1976—80; mem. exec. com. bd. trustees Oakland Health Edn. Program (OHEP), 1987—2000, permanent trustee, 2000—, U. Rochester, 1986—. Maj. M.C. USAF, 1970—72. Mem.: APHA, ACOG (chmn. steering com. drug and alcohol abuse contract 1986—87, rep. ctr. for disease control & prevention task force 2000—, editor-in-chief ACOG Update 2001—), NAS (Inst. of Medicine, com. to study fetal alcohol syndrome 1994—96), AMA, Wayne State U. Devel. Coun., Wayne State U. Acad. Scholars, Soc. Physicians Reproductive Choice and Health, World Assn. Perinatal Medicine, Internat. Soc. Computers in Obstetrics, Neonatology, Gynecology (v.p. 1987—89, pres. 1989—92), Soc. for Neuroscis. (Mich. chpt.), Am. Med. Soc. on Alcoholism and Other Drug Dependencies, Am. Gynecol. and Obstet. Soc., Neurobehavioral Teratology Soc., Soc. Perinatal Obstetricians (pres.-elect 1987—88, pres. 1988—89, v.p., achievement award 1995), Rsch. Soc. Alcoholism, Cen. Assn. Obstetricians-Gynecologists (pres.-elect 1997—99, pres. 1999—2000), Detroit Acad. Medicine (pres.-elect 1999—2001, pres. 2001—02), Wayne County Med. Soc., Mich. Med. Soc., Royal Soc. Medicine, Assn. Profs. Gyn.-Ob, Perinatal Rsch. Soc., Soc. Gynecologic Investigation, Am. Med. Informatics Assn., Chgo. Gyn. Soc. (hon.), Detroit Physiol. Soc. (hon.), Wayne State U. Acad. Scholars (faculty devel. coun. 2003—), Alpha Omega Alpha, Sigma Xi, Phi Beta Kappa. Republican. Jewish. Home: 7921 Danbury Dr West Bloomfield MI 48322-3581 Office: Wayne State U CS Mott Ctr for Human Growth and Devel Detroit MI 48201 E-mail: rsokol@moose.med.wayne.edu.

SOKOLOWSKI, DENISE GEORGIA, librarian, university administrator, educator; b. Oceanside, NY, Nov. 2, 1951; d. Charles John and Georgia Denis (Papadam) Sokolowski; m. Robert Harald Munoz, May 21, 1983. A.A., Modesto Jr. Coll., 1971; B.A., Calif. State Coll., Stanislaus, 1974; M.L.I.S., U. Calif., Berkeley, 1982. Sec. to support svcs. officer Stanislaus State Coll., Turlock, Calif., 1973—75; vet. asst. U. Md. European Div., Heidelberg, Germany, 1976—77, publs. asst., 1983—85, libr., 1985—. Tour guide, escort Great Pacific Tour Co., San Francisco, 1978—81; word processor Telegraph Ave. Geotechn. Assocs., Berkeley, 1982—83. Mem.: ALA, Assn. Coll. Rsch. Librs., Calif. Library Assn., Beta Phi Mu. Democrat. Office: U Md Unit 29216 Apo AE 09102 E-mail: dsoko@ed.umuc.edu.

SOLA, JANET ELAINE, secondary school educator; b. New Britain, Conn., Oct. 23, 1935; d. Walter Andrew and Helen (Mandl) Sinkiewicz; m. Raymond Albert Sola BS, Ctrl. Conn. State U., 1957; MS, So. Conn. State U., 1962; postgrad., U. Conn, 1969. Tchr. bus. Amity Regional High Sch., Woodbridge, Conn., 1957-60; bus. instr. Stone Coll., New Haven, 1962; instr. Manpower Devel. and Tng. Act, New Britain, 1970-74, So. Ctrl. C.C., New Haven, 1977, lectr., 1987; mgmt. lectr. II, Quinnipiac Coll., Hamden, Conn., 1981-87; mayor's aide Town of Hamden, 1987-89, recycling coord., 1989-92; tchr. bus. edn. Hamden High Sch., 1992—, coord. coop. work experience and diversified occupations, 1992—. Assessor credit for life Quinn Coll., Hamden, 1986-89; advisor Hamden Hub Student Interns, 2000. Author: (poetry) Flights of Fancy, 1991, Recycled Thoughts, 1992; contbr. poetry to Contemporary, The Hamden Chronicle, Treasured Poems of Am., Nat. Arts Soc. Campaigner Sola for Town Clk. Com., Hamden, 1981; community liaison Carusone for Mayor Com., Hamden, 1981-87; v.p., Am. Legion Aux. Unit 88, Hamden, 1985-95; treas. Green Dragon Enterprises, Inc., 2002—; chmn. unit 88 Laurel Girl States. Named Tchr. of Yr., Hamden H.S., 2000—01; recipient Laurel, Am. Legion Aux. Girl's State, 2002. Mem.: AAUW, NAFE, ASCD, Nat. Bus. Educators, Internat. Platform Assn., Nat. Assn. Italian Women, Internat. Soc. Poetry (disting. mem.), Lions Internat. Hamden chpt., Ctrl. Conn. U. State Alumni Assn. (bd. dirs., Disting. Alumni Svc. award, Disting. Alumni award 2003). Avocations: bowling, swimming. Home: 50 Vernon St Hamden CT 06518-2825 Office: Hamden HS 2040 Dixwell Ave Hamden CT 06514-2404 E-mail: jsola@hamdenschools.org.

SOLBERG, MYRON, food scientist, educator; b. Boston, June 11, 1931; s. Alexander and Ruth (Graff) S.; m. Rona Mae Bernstein, Aug. 26, 1956; children: Sara Lynn, Julie Sue, Laurence Michael. BS in Food Tech, U. Mass., 1952; PhD, MIT, 1960. Commd. 2d lt. USAF, 1952, advanced through grades to lt. col., 1973, ret., 1991; cons. to food industry, 1956-60 and from 64; mem. rsch. staff food tech. MIT, 1954-60; quality control mgr. Colonial Provision Co., Inc., Boston, 1960-64; sci. editor Meat Processing mag., Chgo., 1968-69; mem. faculty Rutgers U., 1964-2000, prof. food sci., 1970-2000, dir. Ctr. for Advanced Food Tech., 1984-2000, prof. emeritus, from 2000. Bd. dirs. NuVim Inc.; UN expert on food product quality control, 1973-74; vis. prof. Technion, Israel Inst. Tech., Haifa, 1973-74. Co-editor Jour. Food Safety, 1977-88; contbr. articles to profl. jours. Pres. Highland Park (N.J.) Bd. Health, 1971-72. Recipient numerous research grants, Sec.'s Honor award U.S. Dept. of Agrl., Lifetime Recognition for Disting. Leadership award Cook Coll./N.J. Agrl. Experiment Sta., Rutgers U. medal. Fellow AAAS, Am. Chem. Soc., Inst. Food Technologists (pres. N.Y. sect. 1971-72, Food Scientist of Yr. N.Y. sect. award 1981, Nicholas Appert award 1990, Carl R. Fellers award 2001); mem. Am. Soc. Microbiology, Am. Soc. Quality Control, Am. Meat Sci. Assn., N.Y. Acad. Scis., N.J. Acad. Sci. Home: Highland Park, NJ. Died July 28, 2001.

SOLBERG, RONALD LOUIS, investment adviser; b. Madison, Wis., May 15, 1953; s. Carl Louis and Gladys Irene Evelyn (Oen) S.; m. Anna Maria Teresa Gorgol, May 16, 1983 (div. Aug. 1992); m. Elizabeth Catherine Gillett, Dec. 24, 1996 (div. Oct. 2001). BA in Econs. with honors, U. Wis., 1975; MA, U. Calif., Berkeley, 1977, PhD, 1984. Country risk analyst Wells Fargo Bank, San Francisco, 1978-79; asst. v.p., economist Wells Fargo Ltd., London, 1979-81; cons. RAND Corp., Santa Monica, Calif., 1982-84; acting instr. econs. U. Calif., Berkeley, 1983; 1st v.p., portfolio risk policy mgr. Security Pacific Corp., L.A., 1984-92; internat. fin. cons., 1992-94; v.p., fixed-income credit rschr. Pacific Investment Mgmt. Co., 1994-95; mng. dir. head Asian econ. rsch. Chase Manhattan Bank, Hong Kong, 1995-98; acting head of emerging markets securities Asia, Chase Manhattan Asia Ltd., 1996-98; mng. dir., head mkt. and credit rsch. group Tokyo-Mitsubishi Internat. plc, London, 1998—2000; prin. Viking Asset Mgmt., Laguna Beach, Calif., 2001—. Adj. asst. prof. U. So. Calif., L.A., 1985-92. Author: (monograph with G. Grossman) The Soviet Union's Hard-Currency Balance of Payments and Creditworthiness in 1985, 1983; (book) Sovereign Rescheduling: Risk and Portfolio Management, 1988, Country Risk Analysis, 1992; contbr. articles to profl. jours. Research fellow Inst. Internat. Studies, Berkeley, 1982-84. Mem. Am. Econ. Assn., Asia Soc., Nat. Assn. for Bus. Economists, Soc. for Internat. Devel. Avocations: fly fishing, cross-country skiing, squash, billiards.

SOLBRIG, INGEBORG HILDEGARD, German literature educator, writer; b. Weissenfels, Germany, July 31, 1923; arrived in U.S., 1961, naturalized, 1966; d. Reinhold J. and Hildegard M.A. (Ferchland) S. Grad. in chemistry, U. Halle, Germany, 1948; BA summa cum laude, San Francisco State U., 1964; postgrad., U. Calif., Berkeley, 1964-65; MA, Stanford U., 1966, PhD in Humanities and German, 1969. Asst. prof. U. R.I., 1969-70, U. Tenn., Chattanooga, 1970-72, U. Ky., Lexington, 1972-75; assoc. prof. German U. Iowa, 1975-81, prof., 1981-93, prof. emerita, 1993—. Domestic and abroad lectr.; lectr. Conv. on Culture, Al-Sharja, United Arab Emirates, 2003. Author: Hammer-Purgstall und Goethe, 1973, Modulationen von Gold und Licht in Goethes Kunstmärchen, 1997, Momentaufnahmem, 2000, J.G. Herder: Echo of the Cultural Philospher's Ideas in Early African-American Intellectual Writing, 2000, Maria Sibylla Merian..., 2001; main editor: Rilke Heute, Beziehungen und Wirkungen, 1975; editor (and translator): Reinhard Goering: Seeschlacht/Seabattle, 1977; editor: Orient-Rezeption, 1996, Orient-Rezeption, Fischer Lexikon Literatur, 1996; mem. editl. bd.: Kairoer Germanistische Studien, vol. 9 & 10, 1998; contbr. articles to profl. jours., chpts. to books; editor: Orient-Rezeption, Fischer Lexikon Literatur, 2000. Mem. Iowa Gov.'s Com. on 300th Anniversary German-Am. Rels. 1683-1983, 1983. Recipient Hammer-Purgstall Gold medal Austria, 1974; named Ky. col., 1975; fellow Austrian Ministry Edn., 1968-69, Stanford U., 1965-66, 68-69; Old Gold fellow Iowa, 1977; Am. Coun. Learned Socs. grantee; German Acad. Exch. Svc. grantee, 1980; sr. faculty rsch. fellow in the humanities, 1983; NEH grantee, 1985; May Brodbeck fellow in the humanities, 1989; numerous summer faculty rsch. grants. Mem.: MLA (life), Soc. for the History of Alchemy and Chemistry, Internat. Herder Soc. (founding mem.), Goethe Soc. N.Am., Inc., Can. Soc. for 18th Century Studies, Am. Soc. for 18th Century Studies, Deutsche Schiller Gesellschaft, Goethe Gesellschaft, Internat. Vereinigung fur Germanische Sprach und Lit. Wiss., Egyptian Soc. Lit. Criticism (hon.). Achievements include research in transcultural, interdisciplinary studies. Avocations: horseback riding, photography, writing, travel. Home: 1126 Pine St Iowa City IA 52240-5711 E-mail: isolbrig@blue.weeg.uiowa.edu.

SOLIDAY, MICHAEL DAVID, secondary school and special educator; b. Durant, Okla., Feb. 25, 1955; s. David Norman and Patsy Marceille (Mansfield) S.; 7 foster children. BS in Edn., Utah State U., 1979; MEd in Deaf Edn., Western Md. Coll., Westminster, 1982; postgrad., Drake U., Des Moines, 1986. Itinerant tchr. for hearing impaired Heartland, AEA II, Des Moines, 1979-80, tchr. for hearing impaired, 1983-85, 86-87; tchr. Fla. Sch. for the Deaf, St. Augustine, 1982-83; liaison State of Iowa/Deaf Svcs., Des Moines, 1985-86; tchr. resource and 4th grade White Pine County Sch. Dist., Ely, Nev., 1987-94; tchr. h.s. deaf Brevard County Sch. Bd., Titusville, Fla., 1994—; resource tchr. White Pine County Sch. Dist., 1995—. Chairperson sch. improvement Nev. Dept. Edn., Ely, 1990-91. Soccer commr. Steptoe Valley Soccer Club, Ely, 1989-94, 95-96; foster parent Children's Svcs., State of Nev., 1989-93; bd. dirs. White Pine County Family Recreation Ctr., 1996—. Named Nev. Tchr. of the Yr., Dept. of Edn., Nev., 1993; recipient Supt.'s award White Pine County Sch. Dist., 1992, 93. Avocations: backpacking, bicycling, canoeing, fishing, dogs.*

SOLIMANDO, DOMINIC ANTHONY, JR., writer, consultant, pharmacist, educator; b. Bklyn., Apr. 4, 1950; s. Dominic Anthony and Grace Evelyn (Phillips) S. BS, Phila. Coll. Parm. and Sci., 1976; MA, Cen. Mich. U., 1980; postgrad., Purdue U., 1986-89. Bd. cert. oncology pharmacist. Pharmacist Walter Reed Army Med. Ctr. Pharmacy Svc., Washington, 1977; chief pharmacy svc. Andrew Rader USA Health Clinic, Ft. Myer, Va., 1977-79; oncology pharmacist Walter Reed Med. Ctr., Washington, 1979-82; clin. preceptor Sch. Pharmacy, Med. Coll. Va., Va., 1980; chief hem./oncology pharmacy Tripler Army Med. Ctr., Honolulu, 1983-86, Letterman Army Med. Ctr., San Francisco, 1989-90, 91-92; chief pharmacy svc. 28th Combat Support Hosp., Operation Desert Shield/Desert Storm, Saudi Arabia, 1990-91; chief hematology/oncology pharmacy sect. Walter Reed Army Med. Ctr., Washington, 1992-96, dir. hematology-oncology pharmacy residency program, 1992-96; oncology pharmacist Thomas Jefferson U. Hosp., Phila., 1996-98; oncology pharmacy mgr. Lombardi Cancer Ctr./Georgetown U. Med. Ctr., Washington, Pa., 1998-99; dir. oncology drug info. CancerEducation.com, 1999-2000; oncology cons., med. writer, 2000—; pres. Oncology Pharmacy Svc., Inc., 2000—. Adj. prof. Coll. Pharmacy, U. Pacific, Stockton, Calif., 1983-86, 89-91; mem. editorial panel Drug Intelligence and Clin. Pharmacy, Cin., 1984-88; clin. asst. prof. Coll. Pharmacy, U. Md., 1992-96, Coll. Pharmacy, U. Ark., 1995; clin. preceptor Coll. Pharmacy, Howard U., 1992-96, 2001—, clin. asst. prof., 2003—; clin. faculty Phila. Coll. Pharmacy and Sci., 1996-98, clin. assoc. prof., 1998—; clin. faculty Temple U. Coll. Pharmacy, 1998; adj. asst. prof. Coll. Pharmacy and Health Sci., Butler U., 2001-02; clin. assoc. prof. Bernard J. Dunn Sch. Pharmacy, Shenandoah U., 2001—. Ret. lt. col. U.S. Army, 1996. Recipient Upjohn rsch. grant Am. Coll. Clin. Pharmacy, 1988, Bristol award Phila. Coll. Pharmacy and Sci., 1976, WMSHP-Bayer Recognition award Washington Met. Area Soc. Health Sys. Pharmacists, 2000. Fellow: Am. Soc. Hosp. Pharmacists, Am. Pharm. Assn. (various coms.); mem.: Am. Med. Writers Assn., Fedn. Internat. de Pharm. (hosp.), Va. Pharmacists Assn. (various coms.), Washington Metro.Area Soc. Health-Sys. Pharmacists, Am. Inst. Hist. Pharmacy, Acad. Pharmacy Practice and Mgmt. (mem.-at-large 1989—90, chair clin./pharm. therapeutic practice sect. 1991—92, chair hosp. and instnl. practice sect. 1998—99, chair-elect adminstrv. practice sect. 2002—03, chmn. 2003—, Disting. Achievement award in Hosp. & Instnl. Practice 2001), Am. Coll. Clin. Pharmacy (various coms.), Internat. Soc. Oncology Pharmacy Practioners, Assn. US Army, Kappa Psi, Rho Chi. Avocations: bicycling, chess, history, cooking, travel. Home: 5204 22d St N Arlington VA 22205-3137 Office: # 110-545 4201 Wilson Blvd Arlington VA 22203 E-mail: OncRxSvc@aol.com.

SOLIS, LORI, special education educator; b. Ysleta, Tex., Dec. 9, 1948; d. Pablo and Pilar (Navarette) Rodriguez; m. Benito Granada Solis; 1 child, Joe Paul. BA, Sul Ross State U., 1970; MA, U. Tex., 1986. Cert. elem. tchr., high sch. speech, drama, spl. edn., bilingual, diagnostician, master tchr., Tex. Bilingual tchr. 1st grade Weslaco (Tex.) Ind. Sch. Dist., 1971-73; spl. edn. tchr. 1st grade Donna (Tex.) Ind. Sch. Dist., 1973-74; spl edn. tchr. k-6 Menard Spl. Edn. Coop., Sonora, Tex., 1974-82, ednl. diagnostician Rock Springs, Eldorado, Tex., 1986-88; tchr. 2nd grade Sonora Ind. Sch. Dist., 1982-84, bilingual tchr. ESL grades 2-5, 1990-92, spl. programs coord., 1992—; bilingual tchr. 2nd grade Austin (Tex.) Ind. Sch. Dist., 1985-86; spl. edn. coord. Menard Ind. Sch. Dist., Rock Springs, Eldorado, 1988-90. Participant bilingual spl. edn. grad. student rsch. project U. Tex., Austin, 1984-85. Tchr. St. Ann Cath. Ch., Sonora, 1981-82; mem. Vocat. Homemaking Adv. Com., Sonora Ind. Sch. Dist, 1989-91, Sutton County Welfare Bd., Sonora, 1990-92. Mem. ASCD, ATPE, Tex. Assn. Bilingual Edn., Tex. Ednl. Diagnosticians Assn. Democrat. Avocations: reading, fishing, camping. Office: Sonora Ind Sch Dist 807 S Concho Ave Sonora TX 76950-7002

SOLLORS, WERNER, English language, literature and American studies educator; PhD, Freie U., Berlin, 1975. Wissenschaftlicher asst., asst. prof. John F. Kennedy Inst. Freie U., Berlin; from asst. to assoc. prof. English and Comparative Lit. Columbia U.; Henry B. and Anne M. Cabot Prof. English Lit., prof. Afro-Am. studies Harvard U., Cambridge, Mass. Author: Amiri Baraka/LeRoi Joines: The Quest for a Populist Modernism, 1978, Beyond Ethnicity: Consent and Descent in American Culture, Neither Black Nor White Yet Both: Thematic Explorations of Interracial Literature, 1997; contbr. chapters to books Das amerikanische Drama der Gegenwart, 1976, The Harvard Encyclopedia of American Ethnic Groups, 1980, Reconstructing American Literary History, 1986, 1986, Columbia Literary History of the United States, 1988, 1988, Critical Terms for Literary Study, 1990, 1990, Looking Inward, Looking Outward: From the 1920s through the 1940s, 1990, 1990, Nationale und kulturelle Identitat: Studien zur Entwicklung des kollektiven Bewusstseins in der Neuzeit, 1991, Immigrants in Two Democracies: French and American Experience, 1992, Intersecting Boundaries: The Theatre of Adrienne Kennedy, 1992, Il razzismo e le sue storie, 1992, Swedes in America: Intercultural and Interethnic Perspectives on Contemporary Research, 1993, Multiculturalism and the Canon of American Culture, 1993, Configurations de l'ethnicite aux Etats-Unis, 1993, History & Memory in African-American Culture, 1994, Thematics: New Approaches, 1995, Thematics Reconsidered: Essays in Honor of Horst Jr. Daemmrich, 1995, Performances in American Literature and Culture, 1995, New Essays on Henry Roth's Call It Sleep, 1996, Families, 1996, Cultural Difference and the Literary Text, 1996, Beyond Pluralism, 1998, The Sally Hemings-Thomas Jefferson Relationship, 1999, Columbia Companion to 20th Century American Short Fiction, 2001, Dream-Fluted Cane: Essays on Jean Toomes and the Harlem Renaissance, 2001, Not English Only: Redefining "American" in American Studies, 2001, American Studies and Peace, 2001, Mixed-Race Literature, 2001; editor: A Bibliographic Guide to Afro-American Studies, 1972, A Bibliographic Guide to Afro-American Studies Supplement I, 1974; co-editor: Bibliographie amerikanistischer Veröffentlichungen in der DDR bis, 1968, 1976, Varieties of Black Experience at Harvard, 1986, The Invention of Ethnicity, 1989, The Life Stories of Undistinguished Americans as Told by Themselves, 1990, 1999, The Return of Thematic Criticism, 1993, Cane, 1993, Blacks at Harvard: A Documentary History of African-American Experience at Harvard and Radcliffe, 1993, The Black Columbiad: Defining Moments in African-American Literature and Culture, 1994, Theories of Ethnicity: A Classical Reader, 1996, The Promised Land, 1997, Multilingual America: Transnationalism, Ethnicity and the Languages of American Literature, 1998, The Multilingual Anthology of American Literature, 2000, The Norton Critical Edition of Olaudah Equiano, 2000, Interracialism: Black-White Intermarriage in American History, Literature and Law, 2000, The Adrienne Kennedy Reader, 2001, German? American? Literature?: New Directions in German-American Studies, 2002, Interracial Literature: An Anthology of Black-White Contacts in the Old World and the New, 2003; contbr. articles to profl. jours. Recipient Constance Rourke prize Am. Studies Assn., 1990; John Simon Guggenheim Meml. fellow, Andrew W. Mellon faculty fellow Harvard U., Walter Channing Cabot fellow Harvard U., 1997-98; NEH fellow, 1999-00. Fellow: Am. Acad. of Arts and Scis. Office: Harvard U Barker Center 12 Quincy St Cambridge MA 02138-3804

SOLLOWAY, MARY ELISE, elementary educator; b. Dallas, Nov. 25, 1956; d. Ray Oland and Wanda Lou (Wooldridge) Blakley; m. Robert Steven Solloway, May 28, 1977; 1 child, Jonathan Bartholomew. BS in Elem. Edn., U.Okla., 1979, M in Liberal Studies, 1992. Cert. tchr., Okla. Tchr. English Little Axe Pub. Schs., Norman, Okla., 1980; tchr. kindergarten Plaza Towers Elem. Sch., Moore, Okla., 1980-81; owner, dir., tchr. Sunburst Pre-Sch. and Day Care, Norman, 1982-85; tchr. transitional 1st grade McKinley Elem. Sch., Norman, 1985—. Rep. Profl. Educators of Norman, 1986-87, At-Risk task force com. Norman Pub. Schs., 1989-92; chmn. lang. arts site plan com. McKinley Elem. Sch., Norman, 1991—; workshop presenter Okla. Writing Project., 1993—. Recipient scholarship Okla. Summer Writing Inst., U. Okla., 1993. Mem. Coun. Exceptional Children, Nat. Ctr. Learning Disabilities, Learning Disabilities Assn. Norman (pres. 1990-91, sec. 1991-92, v.p. 1992—). Democrat. Presbyterian. Avocations: guitar, church choir, reading, hiking, needlecrafts.

SOLMSSEN, PETER, retired academic administrator; b. Berlin, Nov. 1, 1931; AB, Harvard U., 1952; JD, U. Pa., 1959. Atty. Ballard, Spahr, Andrews & Ingersoll, Phila., 1959-60; with U.S. Fgn. Service, 1961; vice consul Singapore, 1962-63; asst. to under sec. of state, 1963-65; 2d sec., 1965-67; Cultural attache U.S. Dept. State, Sao Paulo, Brazil, 1967-70; adviser on arts Washington, 1974-80; dep. ambassador at large for cultural affairs, 1981-83; pres. Phila. Coll. Art, 1983-87, U. of the Arts, Phila., 1987-2000. One-man photography exhbns. include: Mus. Art, Sao Paulo. Author and illustrator. Mem.: Philadelphia; Century Assn.*

SOLOMON, CHARLES FRANCIS, electronics educator; b. Newark, Feb. 1, 1932; s. Milton Casper and Anne Marie (Casgrove) S.; m. Alice Margret Morris, Feb. 5, 1955; children: Charles Michael, Theresa Marie, Elizabeth Ann, Thomas Francis. BS, Okla. State U., 1966; MEd, Tex. A&M U., 1971, PhD, 1984. Aircraft mech. electronics Spartan Sch. Aero., Tulsa, Okla., 1956-62; bldg. maintenance engr. student union Okla. State U., Stillwater, 1962-64, rsch. technician, 1964-66; assoc. prof. Tex. State Tech. Coll., Waco, 1966-69; program chair Tex. State Tech. Inst., Waco, 1969-83, master instr. electronics, 1983-90, program chmn., 1990-93, master instr. electronics tech. and elec. electronics core, 1993-99; ret., 1999—. Cons. in field. Author: Audio Circuit Analysis, 1976, (manual) Audio Circuits, 1976; contbr. articles to profl. jours.; reviewer book Introduction Electronic Devices and Circuits, 1989. Music dir. St. Joseph Catholic Ch., Bellmead, Tex., 1966-90. Airman 1st class USAF, 1951-55. Mem. Tex. Tech. Soc., Tex. Jr. Coll. Tchrs. Assn., Campus Colleague Computer Assn. (com. 1985-96, chmn. instnl. effectiveness com. 1992-94), Waco Civic Chorus, KC (trustee 1958-90). Avocations: music, hunting, fishing, camping, hiking, round dancing. Home: 399 Beaver Ln Waco TX 76705-4956 E-mail: charles.solomon@worldnet.att.net.

SOLOMON, EDWARD IRA, chemistry educator, researcher; b. N.Y.C., Oct. 20, 1946; s. Mordecai L. and Sally S. Solomon; m. Darlene Joy Spira, Sept. 15, 1984; children: Mitchell Landau, Paige Elana. BS, Rensselaer Poly. Inst., 1968; PhD, Princeton U., 1972. Rsch. assoc. Princeton (N.J.) U., 1972-73; postdoctoral fellow H.C. Ørsted Inst., Copenhagen, 1973-74, Calif. Inst. Tech., Pasadena, 1974-75; asst. prof. MIT, Cambridge, Mass., 1975-79, assoc. prof., 1979-81, prof., 1981-82, Stanford (Calif.) U., 1982-91, Monroe E. Spaght prof. humanities and sci., 1991—. Cons. prof., World Bank lectr. Xiamen U., People's Republic of China, 1984: O.K. Rice lectr. U. N.C., 1984, Reilly lectr. U. Notre Dame, 1985; invited prof. U. Paris, 1987; 1st Glen Seaborg lectr. U. Calif., 1990; Frontiers in Chem. Rsch. lectr. Tex. A&M U., 1990; ACS lectr., Argentina, 1992; invited prof. Tokyo Inst. Tech., 1992; Xerox lectr. U. Alta., 1993; lectr. NSC Republic of China, 1993; Leermakers lectr. Wesleyan U., 1994; Amoco lectr. Ind. U., 1995; Kahn lectr. U. N.Mex., 1996, Golden Jubilee invited prof. Tata Inst., India, 1996; Karcher lectr. U. Okla., 1997; Colloquium 3eme Cycle, Switzerland, 1998; FMC lectr. Princeton U., 1998; A.D. Little lectr. MIT, 1998, Nobel Found. lectr. Stockholm U., 2000; invited prof. Tata Inst. Bombay, India, 2000; numerous lectureships. Assoc. editor Inorganic Chemistry, 1985—; mem. editl. adv. bd. Chem. Revs., 1990—, Jour. Inorganic Biochemistry, Chemtracts, Chemistry and Biology, Jour. Biol. Inorganic Chemistry, Coord. Chem. Revs.; contbr. 350 articles to profl. publs., including Jour. Am. Chem. Soc., Inorganic Chemistry, Procs. of NAS, Phys. Rev. Sci. Mem. panels NIH, NSF, Washington; mem. vis. coms. Exxon, U. Calif., Santa Cruz. Recipient Ramsen award Md. ACS and Johns Hopkins U., 1994, NIH Merit award, 1995, Dean award for disting. tchg., 1990, G.W. Wheland medal, U. Chgo., 2001, ACS award Inorganic Chem., 2001, Frontiers Biol. Chem. award, Max Planck Inst., NIH Merit award, 2002, Centenary medal and lectureship Royal Soc. U.K., 2003; Sloan fellow. Fellow AAAS, Japan Soc. for Promotion of Sci., Am. Acad. Arts and Scis.; mem. Am. Chem. Soc. (chmn. bioinorganic divsn.), Am. Phys. Soc., Internat. EPR Soc., Soc. Biol. Inorganic Chenistry, Sigma Xi. Achievements include research in structure/function correlations in copper cluster proteins, in electronic structure of the blue copper active site, in spectroscopic definition of the active site in the Cu/ZnO methanol synthesis catalyst, in new spectroscopic probes of non-heme iron enzymes, in excited state potential energy surfaces of inorganic complexes and their contribution to reactivity, on new methods of inorganic spectroscopy; covalency in transition metal complexes. Office: Stanford U Dept Chemistry Roth Way Stanford CA 94305 E-mail: edward.solomon@stanford.edu.

SOLOMON, ELDRA PEARL BROD, psychologist, educator, biologist, writer; b. Phila., Apr. 9, 1940; d. Theodore and Freda Miriam (Warhaftig) Brod; m. Edwin Marshall Solomon, June 28, 1959 (div. Jan. 1985); children: Mical Kenneth, Amy Lynn, Belicia Efros. BS, U. Tampa, 1961; MS, U. Fla., 1963; MA, U. South Fla., 1987, PhD, 1989. Lic. clin. psychologist; cert. diplomate in clin. hypnotherapy Nat. Bd. Cert. Clin. Hypnotherapy. Adj. biology prof. Hillsborough C.C., Tampa, Fla., 1968-86; biopsychologist Ctr. for Rsch. in Behavioral Medicine, U. South Fla., Tampa, 1985-89; dir. rsch. Advanced Devel. Sys., Tampa, 1989-92; pvt. practice Tampa, 1990—; clin. dir. Ctr. for Mental Health Edn., Assessment and Therapy, Tampa, Fla., 1992—. Adj. prof., mem. grad. faculty U. South Fla., 1992—; expert witness, psychol. expert county and cir. cts., 1989—; health edn. cons. Advanced Devel. Sys., Tampa, 1985-92. Author: Human Anatomy and Physiology, 1990, The World of Biology, 5th edit., 1995, Introduction to Human Anatomy and Physiology, 2003; author: (book chpt.) Health Psychology: Individual Differences and Stress, 1988, Young Killers: The Challenge of Juvenile Homicide, 1999; sr. author: Biology, 6th edit., 2002; contbr. chpts. to books. Mem. APA, Am. Soc. Criminology, Fla. Psychol. Assn., Internat. Soc. for the Study of Dissociation (chair Tampa chpt., 1994-95, bd. dirs. 1993-99), Tampa Bay Assn. Women Psychotherapists (pres. 1998-99, bd. dirs. 1996-2002). Democrat. Jewish. Avocations: boating, swimming, reading. E-mail: epbsolomon@aol.com.

SOLOMON, ELINOR HARRIS, economics educator; b. Boston, Feb. 26, 1923; d. Ralph and Linna Harris; m. Richard A. Solomon, Mar. 30, 1957; children: Joan S. Griffin, Robert H., Thomas H. AB, Mt. Holyoke Coll., 1944; MA, Radcliffe U., 1945; PhD, Harvard U., 1948. Jr. economist Fed. Res. Bank Boston, 1945-48; economist Fed. Res. Bd. Govs., Washington, 1949-56; internat. economist U.S. State Dept., Washington, 1957-58; professorial lectr. Am. U., Washington, 1964-66; sr. economist antitrust div. U.S. Dept. Justice, Washington, 1966-82; prof. econs. George Washington U., Washington, 1982—. Econ. cons., Washington, 1982—; expert witness antitrust, fin. networks, electronic funds transfer cases, Washington, 1988—. Author: Virtual Money, 1997; author, editor: Electronic Funds Transfers and Payments, 1987, Electronic Money Flows, 1991; contbr. articles on econs., banking and law to profl. jours. Mem. Am. Econs. Assn., Nat. Economists Club (bd. govs. 1997-2000), The Cosmos Club (chair Digital Age series 1999-2001, chair Frontiers of Sci. 2001-2003). Home: 6805 Delaware St Chevy Chase MD 20815-4164 Office: George Washington U Dept Econs Washington DC 20052-0001

SOLOMON, JAMES EMORY, music educator; b. Jacksonville, Fla., Sept. 16, 1946; s. Crawford and Nancy (Adamson) S.; 1 child, James Tyler. BA in History, Stanford (Calif.) U., 1970; MAT in Music, Jacksonville U., 1980; master level Orff cert., Memphis State U., 1981. Cert. elem. and pre-sch. tchr., music tchr., Calif., Fla.; nat. bd. cert. tchr. Tchr. Stonewall Jackson Elem. Sch., Jacksonville, 1977-78; tchr. music St. Paul's By-The-Sea Elem. Sch., Jacksonville Beach, Fla., 1978-80; musician Defrates trio, Jacksonville Beach, 1981; tchr. music Evelyn Hamblen Elem. Sch., St. Augustine, Fla., 1981-91, Osceola Elem. Sch., St. Augustine, 1991-2000, R.B. Hunt Elem. Sch., St. Augustine, 2000—. Adj. prof. music Jacksonville U., 1980-92; instr. Orff tchr. Fla. Atlantic U., Boca Raton, Fla., 1984-85, 87-89, Jacksonville U., 1990-96, Eastman Sch. Music, Rochester, N.Y., 1992—; instr. Fla. Music Demonstration Sch., 1993-96. Author: (book) Monkey Business-Progress Lessons, 1987, Village Day, 1989, The Body Rondo Book, 1990, Conga Town, Percussion Ensembles, 1995, D.R.U.M., 1998; co-author: The Tropical Recorder, 1997; prodr.: (video) Congas, Bongos & Other Percussion--A Guide to Technique, 1988. Named Outstanding Fla. Educator, Fla. Dept. Edn., 1991-92, St. Johns County Tchr. of Yr., St. Augustine, 1991. Mem. Am. Orff-Schulwerk Assn. (presenter at nat. confs., regional rep. nat. bd., 1990-94), Music Educators Nat. Conf. (cert. music educator). Avocations: learning new percussion instruments, following sports, reading. Home: 838 Shoreline Cir Ponte Vedra Beach FL 32082-2740 Office: 125 Magnolia Dr Saint Augustine FL 32080-4684

SOLOMON, MARILYN KAY, educator, consultant; b. Marshall, Mo., Oct. 16, 1947; d. John W. and Della M. (Dille) S. BS, Ctrl. Mo. State U., 1969; MS, Ind. U., 1974. Cert. in early childhood and nursery sch. edn., Mo., Ind. Tchr. Indpls. Pub. Schs., 1969-74; dir. Singer Learning Ctrs., Indpls., 1974-78; v.p. ECLC Learning Ctrs., Inc., Indpls., 1978-95; pres., CEO, owner Early Learning Ctrs., Inc., Indpls., 1995—; owner, pres., CEO, Solomon Antique Restoration, Inc., Indpls., 1996—, The Shoppes at Guilford Junction, 2002—; pres., CEO, The Woodford Group, 1995—. Mem. OJT tng. task force Dept. Labor, Washington; mem. nat. task force for parenting edn. HEW, Washington; cons. to numerous corps. on corp. child care; built 29 child care ctrs. for corps., hosps. and govt. Co-author curricula. Founding bd. dirs. Mid City Pioneer, Indpls., 1977; mem. adv. bd. Enterprise Zone Small Bus. Incubator, Indpls., 1995-2002; founding bd. dirs. Family Support Ctr., Indpls., 1983, pres. bd. dirs., 1985-87; founding mem., co-chair Voices for Children, 1996—; mem. White Rivers Gardens State Park, Indpls. Mus. Art, 500 FEstival Assn. Recipient Outstanding Leadership award Ind. Conf. on Social Concerns, 1975, 76, 77, Children's Mus. Edn. award, 1974; named to Outstanding Young Women of Am., 1984. Mem. Indpls. Mus. Art, Ind. Lic. Child Care Assn. (v.p. 1992, pres. 1974, 75), State of Ind. Quality and Tng. Coun. (chair 1992), Step Ahead-Marion County (rep. for child care 1992—, co-chair educare com. 1999—), Ind. Alliance for Better Child Care (bd. dirs. 1992, adv. bd. 1990-95), Pub. Broadcasting (tng. com. 1992-99, child devel. tng. com. 1996-99), Order Ea. Star, Indpls. Zool. Soc. (charter). Office: Early Learning Ctrs Inc 1315 S Sherman Dr Indianapolis IN 46203-2210 E-mail: earlylearn@iquest.net.

SOLOMON, MARK RAYMOND, lawyer, educator; b. Pitts., Aug. 23, 1945; s. Louis Isadore and Fern Rhea (Josselson) S. BA, Ohio State U., 1967; MEd, Cleve. State U., 1971; JD with hons., George Washington U., 1973; LLM in Taxation, Georgetown U., 1976. Bar: Ohio, Mich., U.S. Dist. Ct. (ea. dist.) Mich., U.S. Ct. Appeals (6th cir.), U.S. Tax Ct., U.S. Ct. Fed. Claims. Tax law specialist corp. tax br. Nat. Office of IRS, 1973—75; assoc. Butzel, Long, Gust Klein & Van Zile, Detroit, 1976—78; dir., v.p. Shatzman & Solomon, P.C., Southfield, Mich., 1978—81; prof., chmn. tax/bus. law dept., dir. MS in Taxation Program Walsh Coll., Troy, Mich., 1981—; of counsel Meyer, Kirk, Snyder & Lynch, PLLC, Bloomfield Hills, Mich., 1981—. Adj. prof. law U. Detroit, 1977-81. Editor: Cases and Materials on Consolidated Tax Returns, 1978, Cases and Materials on the Application of Legal Principles and Authorities to Federal Tax Law, 1990. Mem. Mich. Bar

Assn., Phi Eta Sigma. Avocation: bridge (life master). Home: 2109 Golfview Dr Apt 102 Troy MI 48084-3926 Office: Meyer Kirk Snyder & Lynch PLLC 100 W Long Lake Rd Ste 100 Bloomfield Hills MI 48304-2773 also: Walsh Coll 3838 Livernois Rd Troy MI 48083-5066 E-mail: msolomon@walshcol.edu.

SOLOMON, MILDRED ZELDES, educational psychologist, health services researcher, medical ethics educator; b. Chgo., Apr. 7, 1949; BA in English, Smith Coll., 1971; MA, U. Newcastle-upon-Tyne, Eng., 1978; EdD, Harvard U., 1991. Lang. arts tchr. Gateway Regional Sch. Dist., Huntington, Mass., 1971-73; tchr. educator U.S. and U.K., 1974-76; tchr. trainer, 1975-76; dir. curriculum devel., tchr. preparation Edn. Devel. Ctr., Inc., Newton, Mass., 1976-82, project dir., 1982-86, sr. assoc. for devel., 1984-86, sr. scientist, 1987—2000, v.p., 2001—. Assoc. clin. prof. Social Medicine and Anaesthesia Harvard Med. Sch., Harvard U., 1988—; project dir. Teenage Health Tchg. Modules, 1982; prin. investigator Sexually Transmitted Disease Project, 1983-86, Decisions Near the End of Life, 1987—; dir. Ctr. for Applied Ethics and Profl. Practice, 1996—; chmn. Nat. Task Force on End-of-Life Care in Managed Care; presenter, lectr. in field. Author: The Diagnostic Teacher: Constructing New Approaches to Professional Development, 1999, Meeting the Challenge: Twelve Recommendations for Improving End-of-Life Care in Managed Care, 1999, Innovations in End-of-Life Care: Promising Practices and International Perspectives, Vol. 1, 2000, Vol. 2, 2001, Vol. 3, 2002; author curriculum materials in field; author audiovisual prodns. A Question of Burning, 1977, Regardless of Sex, 1979, It Just Happens Sometimes, 1984, So They Gave Me These Pills, 1986, Let's Do Something Different, 1986; editor-in-chief: Innovations in End-of-Life Care (a web-based jour.); contbr. articles to profl. publs., newspapers, mags., chpts. in books. Recipient Silver award Houston Internat. Film Festival, 1986, Finalist award Info. Film Prodrs. Am., 1979, Cindy award Audio-Visual Communicators Am., 1986, John R. Hogness award Lectureship, Assn. Acad. Health Ctrs., 1994; grantee Ctrs. for Disease Control, 1983, 84, 85, 86, W.K. Kellogg Found., 1987-94, Robert Wood Johnson Found., 1996-98, 98—, Open Soc. Inst., 1995-97, 2001, Mayday Fund, 1995-99, Nat. Cancer Inst., 1996-00, Agy. for Health Care Rsch. and Quality, 1996-00, Nathan Cummings Found., 1998—, Health Resources and Svcs. Adminstrn., 1999-2003, The Kohlberg Found., 2001. Mem. APHA, Am. Soc. Law, Medicine and Ethics, Am. Soc. Bioethics and Humanities. Office: Edn Devel Ctr 55 Chapel St Newton MA 02458-1060

SOLOMON, PAUL ROBERT, neuropsychologist, educator; b. Bklyn., Aug. 27, 1948; s. Maynard and Norma Harris (Roben) S.; m. Suellen Zablow, Aug. 16, 1970; children: Todd, Jessica. BA in Psychology, SUNY, New Paltz, 1970, MA in Psychology, 1972; PhD in Psychology, U. Mass., 1972. Diplomate Am. Coll. Forensic Examiners; lic. psychologist, Mass. Prof. psychology and neurosci. Williams Coll, Williamstown, Mass., 1976—, neurosci. program chmn., 1990-95; dir. memory disorders clinic S.W. Vt. Med. Ctr., Bennington, 1990—; pres. Clin. Neurosci. Rsch. Assocs., 1997—. Bd. dirs. No. Berkshire Mental Health Assn., North Adams, Mass. Author: Scientific Writings, 1985, Memory, 1989, Psychology 4th edit., 1993; contbr. articles to profl. jours. Bd. dirs. W. Mass. Alzheimers Assn., 1992—. Recipient Distinguished Teaching award U. Mass., Amherst, 1975; Rsch. grantee EPA, NIH, NSF, 1978—; Rsch. fellowships NIH, 1979, NSF, 1980. Fellow APA, AAAS, Am. Psychol. Soc.; mem. Soc. for Neuroscience. Home: 130 Forest Rd Williamstown MA 01267-2029 Office: Williams Coll Dept Psychology Williamstown MA 01262

SOLOMON, PHYLLIS LINDA, social work educator, researcher; b. Hartford, Conn., Dec. 6, 1945; d. Louis Calvin and Annabell Lee (Nitzberg) S. BA in Sociology, Russell Sage Coll., 1968; MA in Sociology, Case Western Res. U., 1970, PhD in Social Welfare, 1978. Lic. social worker, Pa. Rsch. assoc. Inst. Urban Studies Cleve. State U., 1970-71; program evaluator Cleve. State Hosp., 1971-74; project dir. Ohio Mental Health and Mental Retardation Rsch. Ctr., Cleve., 1974-75; rsch. assoc. Psychiat. Rsch. Found. of Cleve., 1975; project dir. Ohio Mental Health and Mental Retardation Rsch. Ctr., 1977-78; rsch. assoc. dirs. rsch. and mental health planning Fedn. for Community Planning, 1978-88; prof. dept. mental health scis., dir. sect. mental health svcs. and systems research Hahnemann U., Phila., 1988-94; prof. Sch. Social Work U. Pa., Phila., 1994—. Secondary appointment Prof. Social Work in Psychiatry U. Pa. Sch. Medicine, 1994—; adj. prof. dept. psychiatry Allegheny U., 1994-97. Author: (with others) Community Services to Discharged Psychiatric Patients, 1984; co-editor: New Developments in Psychiatric Rehabilitation, 1990, Psychiatric Rehabilitation in Practice, 1993; editl. adv. bd. Community Mental Health Jour., 1988—; editl. bd. Jour. Rsch. in Social Work, 1997-2000, Social Work Forum, 1997—, Health and Social Work, 1998-2000, Psychiat. Rehab. Jour., 1999—, Mental Health Svcs. Rsch. Jour., 2001—, Brief Treatment and Crisis Intervention, 2001—, Social Work, 2003—; contbr. articles to profl. jours. Trustee Cleve. Rape Crisis Ctr., 1981-84, CIT Mental Health Svcs., Cleve., 1985-88; mem. citizen's adv. bd. Sagamore Hills (Ohio) Children's Psychiat. Hosp., 1984-88. Named Evaluator of the Yr., Ohio Program Evaluators Group, 1987; recipient Ann. award Cuyahoga County Cmty. Mental Health Bd., 1988, Armin Loeb award Internat. Assn. Psychosocial Rehab. Svcs., 1999, Outstanding Non-Psychiatrist award Am. Assn. Cmty. Psychiatrists, 2002. Mem. NASW, Internat. Assn. Psychosocial Rehab. Svcs., Soc. for Social Work and Rsch. (1st place award for pub. article 1997). Jewish. Home: 104 Woodside Rd Apt A108 Haverford PA 19041-1831 Office: U Pa Sch Social Work 3701 Locust Walk Philadelphia PA 19104-6214

SOLOMON, ROBERT DOUGLAS, pathology educator; b. Delavan, Wis., Aug. 28, 1917; s. Lewis Jacob and Sara (Ludgin) S.; m. Helen Fisher, Apr. 4, 1943; children: Susan, Wendy, James, William. Student, MIT, 1934-36; BS in Biochemistry, U. Chgo., 1938; MD, Johns Hopkins U., 1942. Intern John's Hopkins Hosp., 1942-43; resident in pathology Michael Reese Hosp., 1947-49; lectr. U. Ill., Chgo., 1947-50, fellow NIH pathology, 1949-50; asst. prof. U. Md., Balt., 1955-60; assoc. prof. U. So. Calif., L.A., 1960-70; chief of staff City of Hope Nat. Med. Ctr., 1966-67; prof. U. Mo., Kansas City, 1977-78, SUNY, Syracuse, 1968-78; chief of staff The Hosp., Sidney, N.Y., 1985-86; adj. prof. biology U. N.C., Wilmington, 1989—. Cons. VA Hosp., Balt., 1955-60, Med. Svc. Lab., Wilmington, 1989-93; active in field of bariatrics, 1997—. Co-author: Progress in Gerontological Research, 1967; contbr. papers and profl. jours. and rsch. in biochemistry, revascular of heart, carcinogenesis, cancer chemotherapy, atherogenesis, discovery of reversibility of atherosclerosis, chemistry of urochrome pigments. V.p. Rotary, Duarte, Calif., 1967; v.p. and pres. Force for an Informed Electorate. Capt. Med. Corps, AUS, 1943-46, PTO. Grantee NIH, Fleischmann Found., Am. Heart Assn., Nat. Cancer Inst., 1958-70. Fellow ACP (pres. Md. chpt.), Western Geriatrics Soc. (founding); mem. Coll. Am. Pathologists (past pres. Md. chpt.), Am. Soc. Clin. Pathologists, Assn. Clin. Scientists, Am. Chem. Soc., Royal Soc. Medicine (London), Phi Beta Kappa, Sigma Xi. Achievements include development of fiber-optic arterial catheter for visualization and making movies of aortic endothelium in vivo. Home: 113 S Belvedere Dr Hampstead NC 28443-2504 E-mail: Rdsolomon@aol.com.

SOLOWAY, ROSE ANN GOULD, clinical toxicologist; b. Plainfield, N.J., Apr. 19, 1949; d. George Spencer Jr. and Rose Emma (Frank) Gould; m. Irving H. Soloway, Dec. 13, 1979. BSN, Villanova U., 1971; MS in Edn., U. Pa., 1976. Diplomate Am. Bd. Applied Toxicology. Staff nurse Hosp. of U. Pa., Phila., 1971-73; asst. clin. instr. Hosp. of U. Pa. Sch. Nursing, Phila., 1973-77; staff devel. instr. Hosp. of Med. Coll. Pa., Phila., 1977-78; dir. emergency nurse tng. program Ctr. for Study of Emergency Health Svcs., U. Pa., Phila., 1979-80; edn./comms. coord. Nat. Capital Poison Ctr. Georgetown U. Hosp., Washington, 1980-94; clin. toxicologist Nat. Capital Poison Ctr. George Washington U. Med. Ctr., Washington, 1994—; adminstr. Am. Assn. Poison Control Ctrs., Washington, 1994-99, assoc. dir., 1999—. Mem. clin. toxicology and substance abuse adv. panel U.S. Pharmacopeial Conv., Inc., Washington, 1990—2000, mem. expert panel clin. toxicology and substance abuse, 2000—. Contbr. articles to profl. jours. Mem.: APHA, Poison Prevention Week Coun. (vice-chair 1988—91, 2001—03, chair 1991—93, 2003—), Am. Acad. Clin. Toxicology (edn. com. 2000—), Am. Assn. Poison Control Ctrs. (co-chmn. pub. edn. com. 1985—90). Avocations: reading, cooking, knitting, jewelry making. Office: Am Assn Poison Control Ctrs Ste 330 3201 New Mexico Ave NW Washington DC 20016-2756

SOLPER, SHERRIE ANN, learning disabilities educator; b. Bottineau, North Dakota, May 13, 1955; m. David E. Solper, June 21, 1975; children: Trisha, Brandy, Jacob. BS in speech, lang., pathology and elem. edn., Minot State U., N.D., 1977, MS in learning disabilities, 1990. Cert. in teaching, N.D. Elem. tchr. Berthold Pub. Sch., ND, 1977-82; tchr. learning disabilities Minot Pub. Sch., ND, 1990—. Recipient: Citation for Excellence, Minot State U., N.D., 1990.

SOLTERO, MARY ANN, elementary education educator; b. Bellingham, Wash., Feb. 25, 1949; d. Thomas Redmond and Berniece Olive (Walker) Maloney; children: Ann Marie, Elizabeth Elaine. BS, Eastern Mont. Coll., 1971, MS, 1979. Third grade tchr. Cody (Wyo.) Pub. Schs., 1971-72; second grade tchr. Sunset Elem. Sch., Cody, Wyo., 1972-81, remedial reading tchr., 1981-89, third grade tchr., 1989—; ret. Writer lang. art curriculum com., Cody Pub. Schs., 1992-94. Recipient grant State of Wyo., 1994. Mem. NEA, Wyo. Edn. Assn., Cody Edn. Assn. (treas. 1987-88), Internat. Reading Assn., Nat. Coun. Tchrs. Eng., Delta Kappa Gamma (1st v.p. 1994). Democrat. Roman Catholic. Avocations: quilting, counted cross stitch, sewing. Home: 13210 SE 7th St #51 Vancouver WA 98683

SOLTES, JOANN MARGARET, retired music educator, realtor; b. Sewickley, Pa., Nov. 11, 1942; d. Mary Ann Soltes. BS in Music Edn., Duquesne U., 1964; MA, Mich. State U., 1977; student, Goethe Institut, Germany, 1992, Big Bend Coll., 1992. Music tchr. grades K-12 Ctr. Twp. Schs., Monaca, Pa., 1964—69; facilitator of masters program Nat.-Louis U., Heidelberg, Germany, 1995—99; music tchr., classroom tchr. Dept. Def. Dependent Schools Overseas, Okinawa, Turkey, Germany, Japan, 1969—99; realtor Coldwell Banker, Monaca, Pa., 1999—; substitute tchr. Facilitator The Study of Teaching Study Groups, Schweinufirt, Germany, 1992—95; presenter in field, Germany and Japan, 1992, Germany and Japan, 85. Mem. sch. advisory coun. Schweinfurt Am. Sch., Germany, 1995—96, mem. fine arts com., 1987—, chair grade level com., 1990—91, mem. sch. improvement com., 1989—90; vol. Adult Literacy Action, Beaver, Pa., 1999—2002; Ch. organist. Mem.: AAUW, Assn. for Supervision and Curriculum Devel., Beaver Falls Bus. and Career Women's Club (program chmn.), Beaver County Assn. Realtors, Nat. Assn. Realtors, Pa. Assn. Realtors, Community Concert Patron Board, Outlook Club, Phi Delta Kappa. Roman Catholic. Avocations: reading, cooking, bridge, singing, theatrical performance, church organist. Office: Coldwell Banker 3468 Brodhead Rd Monaca PA 15061

SOLYMOSY, HATTIE MAY, writer, publisher, storyteller, educator; b. Kew Gardens, N.Y., Apr. 1, 1945; d. Julius and Sylvia Becky (Glantz) Fuld (dec.); m. Abraham Edward Solymosy, Apr. 21, 1974 (div., Sept. 2000). BA, Queens Coll., 1966, MS in Edn., 1973. Cert. tchr., N.Y.C. and N.Y. Actress, model, 1950-60; elem. tchr. N.Y.C. Bd. of Edn., 1966—; owner Ultimate Jewelry, N.Y.C., 1976-80; tutor N.Y.C., 1983-91; children's writer, 1991—; romance writer, 1993—; owner Hatties' Tales, Cedarhurst, N.Y., 1993—, Cigar Box Factory, Cedarhurst, N.Y., 1993—. Bd. dirs. Hamajama Gifts; co-owner Cigar Box Factory, 1996—, Spouse-For-Hire, 1999—, Pen Pal psychic advisor, 1999, Psychic Line, 1999—, ATM Mktg., 1999—, Credit Card Machines, 2000—, Ads-in Motion, Hot Nuts, Teaching Kids to Cook!, 2003, Ally-for-Hire, 2003, Cool Kids Cook!, 2003. Author: (sound recs.) Delancy Dolphin, 1993, Thaddius Thoroughbred, 1993, Willie's War, 1993, Noodles-An Autobiography, 1993, (with Jared Marc Milk) Trapped With The Past, 1993, Thick Slick Tangled Webs, 1993, Cinderella Cockroach, 1993, A Christmas Tale, 1993, Chanukah Tale, 1993, Doc Simon, 1995, Mr. Music, 1996, Women on Film, 1996, Buying a Dream, 1996, Rock and Roll, 1996, The Psycho Line, 1999, Legally Raped, 1999; author: Myster of the Old Fishing Shack, 1999, Hot Nuts, 2000, Cool Kids Cook!, 2003. Social sec., fundraiser Children's Med. Ctr., N.Y.C., 1969-79; aux. mem. St. John's Hosp., N.Y., 1987—; storyteller children's stories Oklahoma City Fed. Bldg. bombing victims, Mo. flood victims, children's hosps.; assoc. mem. Mus. Natural History; fundraiser Lung Assn., 1997—, Am. Heart Assn., 1998—. Mem. Romance Writers of Am., Soc. of Children's Writers and Illustrators, Simon Wiesenthal Ctr., World Jewish Congress, del. People to People Internat. Missions in Understanding. Democrat. Jewish. Avocations: music, tennis, movies, gardening, dance. Home: Chatham Sq 326 A Peninsula Blvd Cedarhurst NY 11516 Office: Hatties Tales Cigar Box Factory and Spouse-for-Hire Psychic Line Pen Pal Psych PO Box 24 Cedarhurst NY 11516-0024

SOMASUNDARAN, PONISSERIL, surface and colloid engineer, applied science educator; b. Pazhookara, Kerala, India, June 28, 1939; came to U.S., 1961; s. Kumara Moolayil and Lakshmikutty (Amma) Pillai; m. Usha N., May 25, 1966; 1 child, Tamara. BS, Kerala U., Trivandrum, India, 1958; BE, Indian Inst. Sci., Bangalore, 1961; MS, U. Calif., Berkeley, 1962, PhD, 1964. Rsch. engr. U. Calif., 1964, Internat. Minerals & Chem. Corp., Skokie, Ill., 1965-67; rsch. chemist R.J. Reynolds Industries, Inc., Winston-Salem, N.C., 1967-70; assoc. prof. Columbia U., N.Y.C., 1970-78, prof. mineral engring., 1978-83, La Von Duddleson Krumb prof., 1983-97; dir. NSF Industry U. Coop. Rsch. Ctr. in Novel Surfactants, 1998—; hon. prof. Wuhan Inst. Chem. Tech., 2001—. Chmn. Henry Krumb Sch. Chem. Engring., Materials Sci. and Mining Engring., Columbia U., 1988—97; dir. Langmuir Ctr. for Colloids and Interfaces Columbia U., 1987—; cons. numerous agys., cos., including NIH, B.F. Goodrich, NSF, 1974, Alcan, 1981, UNESCO, 1982, Sohio, 1984—85, IBM, 1984, Am. Cyanamid, Duracell, 1988—89, DuPont, 1989, Canmet, 1990—93, Unilever, 1991—, Engelhard, 1991—94, UOP, Alcoa, 1991—92, Allied Signal, GAF, 1999—2000, INCO, Arch.Chem.; mem. panel NRC; chmn. numerous ianternat. symposia and NSF workshops; mem. adv. panel Bur. Mines Generic Ctr., 1983—91; keynote and plenary lectr. internat. meetings; hon. prof. Ctrl. South U. Tech., China; Brahm Prakash prof. metallurgy and material sci. Indian Inst. Sci., Bangalore, 1990; hon. rsch. advisor Beijing Gen. Rsch. Inst., 1991—; Henry Krumb lectr. AIME, 1988. Editor: (books) Fine Particles Processing, 1980; hon. editor-in-chief Colloids and Surfaces, 1980—, Ency. of Colloids and Interfaces, —; contbr. articles to profl. jours.; editor-in-chief: Encyclopedia of Colloid and Surface Chemistry. Pres. Keralasamajam of Greater N.Y., N.Y.C., 1974-75; bd. dirs. Fedn. Indian Assocs., N.Y.C., 1974-95, Vols. in Svc. to Edn. in India, Hartford, Conn., 1974—; mem. planning bd. Village of Piermont, N.Y., 1995-2000, mem. zoning bd. appeals, 2000—, mem. citizens adv. com., 2000—. Recipient Disting. Achievement in Engring. award, AINA, 1980, Antoine M. Gaudin award Soc. Mining Engrs.-AIME, 1983, Achievements in Applied Sci. award 2d World Malayalam Conf., 1985, Robert H. Richards award, AIME, 1986, Arthur F. Taggart award Soc. Mining Engrs.-AIME, 1987, honor award Assn. Indian in Am., 1988, VHP award of Excellence, Ellis Island medal of Honor, 1990, Commendations citation State of N.J. Senate, 1991; named Mill Man of Distinction, Soc. Mining Engrs.-AIME, 1983, Disting. Alumnus award Indian Inst. Sci., Bangalore, 1989, Outstanding Contbns. and Achievement award Cultural Festival India, 1991, Recognition award SIAA, 1992, Asian-Am. Heritage award Asian Am. Higher Edn. Coun., 1994. Fellow Russian Acad. Nat. Scis. (fgn.), Chinese Acad. Engring. (fgn.) Indian Nat. Acad. Engring., Instn. Mining and Metallurgy (U.K.); mem. AICE, NAE, Soc. Mining Engrs. (bd. dirs. 1982-85, Disting. mem. award, also others), Engring. Found. (chmn. bd. 1993-95, chmn. conf. com. 1985-88, bd. exec. com. 1985-88, bd. dirs. 1991—, Frank Aplan award 1992), Am. Chem. Soc., N.Y. Acad. Scis., Russian Acad. Natural Scis. (fgn.), Internat. Assn. Colloid and Surface Scientists (councillor 1989-92), Indian Material Rsch. Soc. (hon.), Chinese Acad. Engring., Sigma Xi. Achievements include patents for in field.

SOMBERG, JOHN CHARIN, medicine and pharmacology educator; b. N.Y.C., Oct. 8, 1948; AB, NYU, 1970; MD, N.Y. Med. Coll., 1974. Diplomate Nat. Bd. Med. Examiners. Intern Met. Hosp. Ctr., N.Y.C., 1974-75, med. jr. resident, 1975-76; chief med. resident N.Y. Med. Coll., 1976-77; fellow cardiovascular medicine Peter Bent Brigham Hosp., Harvard Med. Sch., Boston, 1977-79, instr. medicine, 1979-80; asst. prof. medicine and pharmacology Albert Einstein Coll. Medicine, Bronx, N.Y., 1985-88; chief cardiology sect. VA Med. Ctr., North Chicago, Ill., 1988-89; assoc. prof., chief divsn. clin. pharmacology Chgo. Med. Sch., North Chgo., 1988-89, prof. medicine and pharmacology, chief divsns. cardiology and clin. pharmacology, 1989—98; prof. medicine and pharmacology, chief divsn. clin. pharmacology, dir. Rush Analytical Laboratories Rush U., Chicago, Ill., 1998—. Founder and pres. Academic Pharmaceuticals, Lake Bluff, Ill. Editor Jour. Clin. Pharmacology, 1985-1994; editor-in-cheif Am. Jour. Therapeutics, 1994—; mem. editorial bd. Am. Jour. Cardiology; contbr. articles, revs., abstracts to profl. publs., chpts. to books. Fellow Am. Coll. Clin. Pharmacology (reagent 1986-1994); mem. Am. Heart Assn. (mem. bd. govs. Chgo. chpt.), Am. Fedn. Clin. Rsch., Fedn. for Advancement of Sci. and Exptl. Biology. Home: PO Box 869 Lake Forest IL 60045-0869

SOMERS, SARAH PRUYN, retired elementary school educator; b. Albany, N.Y., Oct. 15, 1936; d. Howard Sewall and Carolyn (Decker) Pruyn; m. Richard Moss Somers Jr., Aug. 15, 1959 (dec. Jan. 1986); children: Sewall Wendy Somers Hautzinger, Sarah Louise. BS in Edn., Wheelock Coll., 1958. Cert. elem. tchr., Mass., N.J. Elem. tchr. Madison (N.J.) Pub. Schs., 1960-63, 76-99; ret., 1999—. Group chmn., student tchr. sponsor Madison Pub. Schs., 1980-99, rep. roundtable, 1988-99; reading vol. Cold Spring Elem. Sch., Doylestown, 2000—. Vol. libr. Torey J. Sabatini Sch., Madison, 1970-76, room mother, 1970-81; room mother Kings Rd. Sch., 1976-77, Madison High Sch., 1976-81, The Gill/St. Bernards Sch., Bernardsville, N.J., 1977-82, The Morristown Beard Sch., 1982-86; vol. Cold Spring Elem. Sch. Doylestown, Pa., 2000—; chaperone, coach YMCA Nat. Swim Meet, 1979-81; mem. aquatic com. YMCA, Madison, 1973-80; mem. Jr. League Boston, Morristown; mem. Madison Hist. Soc., 1988-99; chaperone Madison Teen Ctr., 1991-99. Recipient Govs. Tchr. Recognition award, 1988. Fellow NEA (ret.); mem. N.J. Edn. Assn. (ret.), Morris County Edn. Assn. (ret.), Madison Edn. Assn. (rep. coun. 1992—), Bucks County Hist. Soc. Republican. Episcopalian. Avocations: reading, active sports, tennis, walking, tv. Home: 5126 Barness Ct Doylestown PA 18901-6240

SOMERSTEIN-CAMPBELL, JASMINE AURORA ABRERA, preschool administrator, educator; b. Manila, Feb. 17, 1943; d. Bernardo Paez and Rosalia (Sityar) Abrera; m. Jules Leon Somerstein, Dec. 10, 1967 (div. July 1995); children: Joseph, Sandra, Marc (dec. Mar. 2001); m. James Walter Campbell, Jan. 13, 2001. BA in English, U. Philippines, Manila, 1964; MA in English Edn., NYU, 1978, MA in Elem. Edn., 1987; postgrad., U. Pitts., Oxford (Eng.) U., 1964-66, 86. Cert. tchr., N.Y. Instr. U. Pitts., 1965-66, U. of the East, Manila, 1968-69; tchr. Am. Internat. Sch., Manila, 1966, Domenec High Sch., Pitts., 1967-68; substitute tchr. Lakeland and Peekskill Sch. Dist., NY, 1975-77; exec. dir. Internat. Pre-Sch. Ctr., Inc., NY, 1977—; instr. Bd. Coop. Ednl. Svcs., N.Y.C., 1989-97; exec. dir. Horas Alegres Bilingual Presch., Dallas, 1997—2003; early childhood coord. Good Shepherd Cath. Ch., Colleyville, 2000—; dir. Good Shepherd Little Lambs Program, 2002—; exec. dir. Internat. Tots, Inc., 2003—. Exec. sec. Ctr. Ednl. TV, Manila, 1964; sec. NYU, 1973—74, UN, N.Y.C., 1975; prodr., interviewer Continental Cablevision, N.Y.C., 1984—97; child devel. advisor Westchester County, N.Y.C., 1989—; cons. Hudson Valley Export-Import, Inc., N.Y.C., 1988—92; adj. instr. Tarrant County Coll., Hurst, 2001—. Vol. Philippine Band of Mercy, Manila, 1963-93. Mem. Nat. Child Care Assn., Nat. Assn. Edn. Young Children, Nat. Coun. Tchrs. English, N.Y. Child Care Assn., Assn. Childhood Edn. Internat., Child Care Coun. Westchester, Manitoga, Peekskill/Cortlandt C. of C. (bd. dirs. 1989-92), Greater Dallas Hispanic C. of C., Hispanic Bus. Alliance. Democrat. Avocations: reading, photography, music, travel, piano. Office: PO Box 93056 Southlake TX 76092-1056 E-mail: Jasminvale@aol.com.

SOMERVILLE, CAROLYN JOHNSON, educational administrator; b. Parkersburg, W.Va., Mar. 11, 1942; d. George Hughes and Nellie Maude (Cather) Johnson; m. Ron D. Somerville, Aug. 22, 1965 (div. 1981); children: Jennifer Nicole Somerville Moon, Ron Dean. BS, Asbury Coll., 1963; MEd, Ohio U., 1966. Cert. elem. prin., Okla. Tchr. jr. high Prince George County Schs., Md., 1963-64; grad. asst. Ohio U., Athens, 1964-65; social worker W.Va. Dept. of Welfare, Huntington, 1965-67; counselor jr. high Wood County Schs., Parkersburg, W.Va., 1972-78, tchr. jr. high, 1979-81; substitute tchr. Yukon (Okla.) Schs., 1982-83; asst. prin. elem. Western Heights Schs., Oklahoma City, 1983-85; asst. prin. Skyview Elem. Sch., Yukon, 1985-96, Lakeview Middle Sch., Yukon, 1995—, Independence Middle Sch., Yukon, 1995—. Presenter workshops; cons. in field; corr. editor Okla. Middle Level Edn. Assn. Mem. adv. bd. Planned Parenthood, Parkersburg, W.Va., 1974-77; counselor, speaker Gov. Com. on Crime and Delinquency, Parkersburg, 1974-77; tchr. Sunday sch. Trinity Bapt. Ch., Yukon, 1982-83; sponsor Alateen, 1988-93. Named Adminstr. of Yr. Dist. 11A, 1995. Fellow Nat. Prins. Assn., State of Okla. Prins. Assn.; mem. ASCD, Okla. Assn. Elem. Sch. Prins. (com.), Coop. Coun. Okla. Sch. Adminstrn., Yukon Curriculum Coun. Avocations: reading, writing, sewing, boating. Home: 113 W Vail Dr Yukon OK 73099-5829 Office: Lakeview Middle Sch 2700 N Mustang Rd Yukon OK 73099-3300 also: Independence Middle Sch 500 E Vandament Ave Yukon OK 73099-4803

SOMERVILLE, DAPHINE HOLMES, retired elementary education educator; b. Clinton, N.C., Jan. 19, 1940; d. George Henry and Mamie Estelle (Streeter) Holmes; m. Kalford Burton Somerville, Dec. 26, 1970 (div. Sept. 1992); 1 child, Daria Lynn. AA, Blackburn Coll., 1959, BA, 1961; MS in Edn., Hofstra U., 1967; postgrad., Columbia U., 1971, SUNY, Farmingdale, 1999-2000. Permanent teaching cert. common br. subjects grades 1-8. Tchr. East Islip (N.Y.) Sch. Dist., 1961-99, ret., 1999; tchr. computer/writing Opportunities Industrialization Ctr., 1998—, cert. webmaster, 2000—. Mem., instr. Outcome Based/Mastery Learning/Excellence in Learning Com., East Islip, 1984—89; mentor East Islip Sch. Dist., 1987—88, mem. sch. improvement team, 1989—91, staff devel. com., 1992—96; chair Ptnrs. in Edn., 1991—2001; instr. AARP's Driver Safety, 2001—; election inspector, 2001—02. Author: Beaman Family Reunion Journal, 2001, Baptist Training Union Study Guide; founder, co-author: tutoring program Adopt-A-School Child/Family, 1990. Mem. Bay Shore (N.Y.) Civic Assn. and Bay Shore Pub. Schs. Task Force for the Advancement of Equality of Ednl. Opportunity, 1967—69; sec. Islip Town NAACP, Bay Shore, 1965—90; dir. Bapt. Tng. Union, 1974—81; trustee First Bapt. Ch., Bay Shore, 1979—90. Recipient Cmty. Svc. award Town Bd.-Town of Islip, Suffolk County, 1982, Br. Recognition award Islip Town NAACP, 1987, Disting. Svc. award L.I. Region NAACP, 1993, Dedicated Svc. award Ptnrs. in Edn. First Bapt. Ch. of Bayshore, 1995, 98, Proclamation for genuine concern edn. residents Suffolk County Exec. Robert Gaffney, 1997, Cert. Spl. Congl. Recognition, Congressman Rick Lazio, 1997, African-Am. Educators award Martin L. King Commn. of Suffolk County, 1997, Editors Choice award The Nat. Libr. of Poetry, 1999, Citation, Town of Islip, 1999; L.I. Sch. to Career Partnership for Proposed Sch./Bus. Govt. Project grantee, 1998. Mem. Nat. Coun. Negro Women (life, ednl. involvement award 1993), East Islip Tchrs. Assn. (past bldg. rep.), N.Y. State

United Tchrs., Huntington Christian Women's Club (fin. coord.) 2003. Democrat. Avocations: theater, writing, tennis, reading, working with children, travel. Home: 130 Carman Rd Dix Hills NY 11746-5648

SOMERVILLE, RICHARD CHAPIN JAMES, atmospheric scientist, educator; b. Washington, May 30, 1941; s. James William and Mollie (Dorf) S.; m. Sylvia Francisca Bal, Sept. 17, 1965; children: Anatol Leon, Alexander Chapin. BS in Meteorology, Pa. State U., 1961; PhD in Meteorology, NYU, 1966. Postdoctoral fellow Nat. Ctr. Atmospheric Rsch., Boulder, Colo., 1966-67; rsch. assoc. geophysical fluid dynamics lab. NOAA, Princeton, N.J., 1967-69; rsch. scientist Courant Inst. Math. Scis., N.Y.C., 1969-71; meteorologist Goddard inst. space studies NASA, N.Y.C., 1971-74; adj. prof. Columbia U., NYU, 1971-74; head numerical weather prediction sect. Nat. Ctr. Atmospheric Rsch., Boulder, 1974-79; prof. meteorology Scripps Inst. Oceanography, U. Calif.-San Diego, La Jolla, 1979—. Author: The Forgiving Air: Understanding Environmental Change, 1996. Fellow: AAAS, Am. Meteorol. Soc.; mem.: Am. Geophys. Union. Office: U Calif San Diego Scripps Inst Oceanography 9500 Gilman Dr Dept 0224 La Jolla CA 92093-0224

SOMMA, BEVERLY KATHLEEN, medical and marriage educator; b. Bayonne, N.J., June 13, 1938; d. Leroy and Isabelle (Lysaght) Latourette; m. Louis Anthony Somma, Nov. 24, 1973; children: Francis, Keith. AS, Ocean County Coll., 1973; BA, Georgian Ct., 1977; MAT, Monmouth Coll., 1978; postgrad., U. Pa., 1980-85, 88-89. Nurse's aide Community Meml. Hosp., Toms River, N.J., 1971-72; with marriage coun. dept. psychiatry U. Pa. Sch. Medicine, Phila., 1993—; with Helene Fuld Med. Ctr. Edn., 1993—. Ednl. cons. Ctr. for Cognitive Edn., Yardley, Pa., 1990—, tng. program Archdiocese Phila., Penn Found., Inc., 1993; lectr. Marriage Coun. of Phila. dept. psychiatry, sch. medicine U. Pa., 1993—; with Helene Fuld Med. Ctr. Edn., 1993—. Voter svc. chmn. LWV, Toms River, N.J., 1971-72; contact rep. Pro Life Coalition, Phila.; vol. nursing tutor Ocean County Coll., Toms River, 1972; vol. tchr.'s aide St. Michael the Archangel, Levittown, Pa., 1987-88; vol. VITA; counselor Bucks County Coun. Alcoholism and Drug Dependence, Inc., 1984-93; active World Affairs Coun. Phila. All Am. scholar; recipient U.S. Achievement Acad. Nat. award. Mem. Nat. Soc. for Fund Raising Execs., Alumni Assn. Georgian Ct. Coll., Ocean County Coll., Bucks County C.C., Sigma Tau Delta. Republican. Methodist. Avocations: cooking, tennis, golf, jogging, ice-skating. Home: 1506 Kathy Dr Yardley PA 19067-1717

SOMMER, BARBARA, school administrator; b. N.Y.C. d. David and Rose (Weingarten) Melnick; m. Robert I. Sommer, Aug. 29, 1971; children: Mara, Adam. BA, Queens Coll., 1972, MS in Spl. Edn., 1975; MS in Edn. Adminstrn., Pace U., 1993. Cert. tchr. N.Y., sch. dist. adminstr. N.Y. Sub. tchr. Pub. Sch. # 20, Pub. Sch. # 21, N.Y.C., 1972; tchr. Creative Nursery Sch., N.Y.C., 1972, PS 20, N.Y.C., 1972-75; sub. tchr. PS 79, N.Y.C., 1973; tchr. PS 162, N.Y.C., 1975-78; tchr., curriculum developer Child Study Ctr. Pace U., N.Y., 1987-93, intern adminstrn. Child Study Ctr., 1991-92; dir. Westport (Conn.)-Weston Coop. Nursery Sch., 1993-95; edn. coord. White Plains (N.Y.) Child Day Care Assn., Inc., 1995—. Tchr. New Castle Recreation Dept., N.Y., 1985-86; supr. Saturday Recreation Program, New Castle, N.Y., 1985; tchr. North Westchester YM-YWHA, N.Y., 1974. Chair craft fair Grafflin Sch./Chappaqua PTA, 1985-86. Recipient Cert. Recognition Day Care In-Service Tng. Project, Family Support Early Intervention, N.Y. Med. Coll., MRI/Inst. for Human Devel., 1992, Cert. for Svc. Coord., Westchester Med. Ctr., 1993. Mem. NOW, AAUW, ASCD, Nat. Assn. for Edn. Young Children, Nat. Head Start Assn., Assn. for Childhood Edn. Internat., Westchester Assn. for Edn. Young Children, Westchester Edn. Coalition, Tau Delta Kappa, Phi Delta Kappa, Kappa Delta Pi.

SOMMERS, ALEXIS NIGEL, university administrator, engineering educator, manufacturer; b. London, Oct. 9, 1941. B. Mech. Engring., Cornell U., 1964; M.S., Rutgers U., 1966; Ph.D., Purdue U., 1968; s. Alexis and Joan (Lanchester) S.; children: Robin Alexis, Guinevere Rose; m. Pamela Coffey, Oct. 17, 1990. Chief project engr. El-Tronics, Inc., Warren, Pa., 1963-64; exptl. mathematician Allison div. Gen. Motors, Indpls., 1966-68; transp. systems analyst Vitro Labs., Silver Spring, Md., 1968-70; assoc. dean grad. sch. U. New Haven, 1970-74, provost, 1974-91, prof. indsl. engring., 1991—; interim pres. Newton-New Haven Co., Inc., North Haven, Conn., 1995-96. Contbr. articles to profl. jours. Chmn. South Cen. Conn. chpt. ARC, 1986-88; sec. Bethany Conservation Trust (Conn.), 1980-86; chmn. Bethany Conservation Commn., 1982-88; apptd. bd. zoning appeals Town of Guilford, Conn., 1991—. Recipient Sterling award ARC, 1988. Mem. Inst. Indsl. Engrs. (sr.), Ops. Research Soc. Am., Soc. Logistics Engrs. (Adm. Eccles medal 1994), Conn. Assn. Purchasing Mgrs. (pres. 2003—). Democrat. Congregationalist. Home: 71 Broad St Guilford CT 06437-2636 Office: U New Haven E244 Buckman Hall 300 Orange Ave North Haven CT 06516*

SOMMERS, BARBARA JEAN, secondary educator; b. Chgo., Mar. 22, 1962; d. Robert Casler and Karen Marina (Meister) E. BA in Spanish and Sociology, Gettysburg Coll., 1984; MA in Spanish Lang. and Lit., Middlebury Coll., 1994. Cert. Spanish tchr., Pa. GED instr. Ctr. for Human Svcs., Gettysburg, Pa., 1984-86; Spanish tchr. Hempfield High Sch., Landisville, Pa., 1986-87, Gettysburg Area Sch. Dist., 1987—2002; Spanish instr. Gettysburg Coll., Gettysburg, 2002—, Harrisburg (Pa.) Area C.C., 2003—. Recipient Patriotism award VFW, 1980. Mem. Am. Tchrs. Spanish and Portuguese, Phi Sigma Iota. Republican. Avocations: hiking, bicycling, skiing, reading. Office: Gettysburg Coll McKnight Hall Gettysburg PA 17325 E-mail: ganchogan@yahoo.com.

SOMMESE, ANDREW JOHN, mathematics educator; b. N.Y.C., May 3, 1948; s. Joseph Anthony and Frances (Lia) S.; m. Rebecca Rooze DeBoer, June 7, 1971; children: Rachel, Ruth. BA in Math., Fordham U., 1969; PhD in Math., Princeton U., 1973. Gibbs instr. Yale U., New Haven, 1973-75; asst. prof. Cornell U., Ithaca, N.Y., 1975-79; assoc. prof. U. Notre Dame, Ind., 1979-83, prof. of math., 1983—, chair dept. math., 1988-92, Vincent J. Duncan and Annamarie Micus Duncan chair math., 1994—. Mem. Inst. for Advanced Study, Princeton, N.J., 1975-76; guest prof. U. Bonn, Germany, 1978-79; guest rschr. Max Planck Inst. for Math., Bonn, 1992-93; cons. GM Rsch., Warren, Mich., 1986-97. Editor: Manuscripta Mathematica jour., 1986-93, Advances in Geometry, 2000;mem. editl. bd. Milan Jour. Math., 2002; contbr. articles to profl. publs. Recipient Rsch. award for Sr. U.S. Scientists Alexander Von Humboldt found., 1993; A.P. Sloan Found. rsch. fellow, 1979. Mem. Am. Math. Soc., Soc. for Indsl. and Applied Math., Phi Beta Kappa. Office: U Notre Dame Dept Math Notre Dame IN 46556 E-mail: sommese@nd.edu.

SOMORJAI, GABOR ARPAD, chemist, educator; b. Budapest, Hungary, May 4, 1935; came to U.S., 1957, naturalized, 1962; s. Charles and Livia (Ormos) S.; m. Judith Kaldor, Sept. 2, 1957; children: Nicole, John. BS, U. Tech. Scis., Budapest, 1956; PhD, U. Calif., Berkeley, 1960; Dr. Honoris Causa (hon.), Tech. U., Budapest, 1989, U. Pierre et Marie Curie, Paris, 1990, U. Libre Brussels, 1992, U. degli de Ferrara, Italy, 1998, Jozsef Attila U., Szeged, Hungary, 1999, Royal Inst. Tech., Stockholm, 2000; D (hon.), U. Manchester, Eng., 2001. Mem. research staff IBM, Yorktown Heights, N.Y., 1960-64; dir. Surface Sci. and Catalysis Program Lawrence Berkeley Lab., Calif., 1964—; mem. faculty dept. chemistry U. Calif.-Berkeley, 1964—, assoc. prof., 1967-72, prof., 1972—, Miller prof., 1978, univ. prof., 2002. Unilever prof. dept. chemistry U. Bristol, Eng., 1972; vis. fellow Emmanuel Coll., Cambridge, Eng., 1989; Baker lectr. Cornell U., Ithaca, N.Y., 1977; mem. editorial bds. Progress in Solid State Chemistry, 1973—, Jour. Solid State Chemistry, 1976-92, Nouveau Jour. de Chemie, 1977—, Colloid and Interface Sci., 1979—, Catalysis Revs., 1981, Jour. Phys. Chemistry, 1981-91, Langmuir, 1985—, Jour. Applied Catalysis, Molecular Physics, 1992—. Author: Principles of Surface Chemistry, 1972, Chemistry in Two Dimensions, 1981, Introduction to Surface Chemistry and Catalysis, 1994; editor-in-chief Catalysis Letters, 1988—; contbr. articles to profl. jours. Recipient Emmett award Am. Catalysis Soc., 1977, Kokes award Johns Hopkins U., 1976, Albert award Precious Metal Inst., 1986, Sr. Disting. Scientist award Alexander von Humboldt Found., 1989, E.W. Mueller award U. Wis., Chemical Pioneer award Am. Inst. of Chemists, 1995, Von Hippel award Materials Rsch. Soc., 1997; Guggenheim fellow, 1969, Wolf prize in chemistry, 1998. Fellow: AAAS, Am. Phys. Soc.; mem.: NAS, Catalysis Soc. N.Am., Am. Chem. Soc. (chmn. colloid and surface chemistry 1981, Surface and Colloid Chemistry award 1981, Peter Debye award 1989, Arthur W. Adamson award 1994, Award for creative rsch. in homogeneous and heterogeneous catalysis 2000, Cotton medal 2002), Hungarian Acad. Scis. (hon. Pauling medal 2000, Nat. Medal of Sci. 2001), Am. Acad. Arts and Scis. Home: 665 San Luis Rd Berkeley CA 94707-1725 Office: U Calif Dept Chemistry D 58 Hildebrand Hl Berkeley CA 94720-0001 E-mail: somorjai@socrates.berkeley.edu.

SOMVILLE, MARILYN F. retired dean; Dean Mason Gross Sch. Arts, New Brunswick, NJ; ret., 2000. Bd. dirs. Opus 118 Harlem Ctr. Strings. Office: Opus 118 Harlem Ctr for Strings PO Box 986 New York NY 10029*

SON, MUN SHIG, education educator; b. Hwanggan, South Korea, Feb. 5, 1950; came to the U.S., 1978; s. Young Hee and Jeong Poon (Park) S.; m. Ock Jhee Kim, June 7, 1978; children: Jennifer, John. BA in Statistics, Sung Kyun Kwan U., Seoul, 1975; MS in Statistics, Okla. State U., 1982, MS in Econs., PhD in Statistics, Okla. State U., 1984. Rsch. asst. Cen. Bank Korea, Seoul, 1975-78; lectr. Okla. State U., Stillwater, 1983-84; vis. asst. prof. U. Vt., Burlington, 1984-86, asst. prof., 1986-91, assoc. prof., 1991—. Cons. Green Mountain Power, Burlington, 1987, Sugarbush Ski Planning Com., Waitsfield, Vt., 1987—. With Korean Army, 1976-77. NSF grantee, 1986-91, Pak-Doo Rsch. Found. grantee, 1989—. Mem. Inst. Math. Statistics, Am. Statis. Assn., Korean Scientists and Engrs. Assn. Am., Korean Am. Univ. Profs. Assn. Home: 156 Old Stage Rd Essex Junction VT 05452-2513 Office: U Vt 16 Colchester Ave Burlington VT 05401-1455

SONBUCHNER, GAIL MURPHY, secondary special education educator; b. St. Paul, Aug. 26, 1942; d. Harold Alvin and Marian Rose (Erickson) Anderson; (div.); children: Marla Estelle, Sean Steven, Jason James Francis; m. Hugo Frank Sonbuchner, July 18, 1983; children: Gregory, Jon, Viktoria. BS in Elem. Edn., U. Minn., 1964; MS in Elem. Edn., Bemidji State U., 1980. Cert. elem. edn., elem. remedial reading, secondary remedial reading, secondary developmental reading, learning disabilities. Elem. classroom tchr. S.W. Elem. Sch., Grand Rapids, Minn., 1964-67; middle/H.S. spl. edn. tchr. Deer River (Minn.) H.S., 1979-80; spl. edn. tchr. Monticello (Minn.) H.S., 1980—. Spkr. Laubach Literacy Conv., Raleigh, N.C., 1992; mem. adv. bd. Hamline U. Collaborating for Learning and Studying Strategies, St. Paul, 1995, State Minn. Spl. Edn. Licensure Stds. Team, Bd. Tchg., 1996. Author: Help Yourself: How to Take Advantage of Your Learning Styles, 1991. Mem. Minn. Fedn. Tchrs. Roman Catholic. Avocations: quilting, writing. Home: 1504 W River St Monticello MN 55362-8957 Office: Monticello HS PO Box 897 Monticello MN 55362-0897

SONG, CHUNSHAN, chemist, chemical engineer, educator; b. Shijiazhuang, Hebei, China, Feb. 11, 1961; came to U.S., 1989; s. Jingsheng Song and Fengxian He; m. Lu Sun, Jan. 10, 1985; children: Lucy J., James J. BS in Chem. Engring., Dalian (China) U. Tech., 1982; diploma in Japanese, N.E. Shifan U., Changchun, China, 1983; MS in Applied Chemistry, Osaka (Japan) U., 1986, PhD in Applied Chemistry, 1989. Postdoc. rsch. assoc. Osaka Gas Co., 1989; rsch. assoc. Pa. State U., University Park, 1989-94, asst. prof. fuel sci., 1994-97, assoc. prof., 1997—2003, assoc. dir. lab. hydrocarbon process chemistry, 1995-98, dir. applied catalysis in energy lab., 1998—2003, prof., 2003—, dir. clean fuels and catalysis program, 2003—. Editor: Catalytic Conversion of Polycyclic Aromatic Hydrocarbons, 1996, Advances in Catalysis and Processes for Heavy Oil Conversion, 1998, Shape-Selective Catalysis, 1999, Catalysis in Fuel Processing and Environmental Protection, 1999, Chemistry of Diesel Fuels, 2000, CO2 Conversion and Utilization, 2002, Environmental Challenges and Greenhouse Gas Control for Fossil Fuel Utilization in the 21st Century, 2002, Fuel Processing for Fuel Cells, 2002; contbr. articles to Catalysis Today, Energy Fuels, Catalysis Letters, Fuel, Fuel Processing Tech., Ind. Engring. Chem. Rsch., Applied Catalysis, Studies in Surface Sci. and Catalysis, Chemtech. Agy. Recipient Outstanding Svc. award, Internat. Pitts. Coal Conf., 2001; fellow Agy. Ind. Sci. Tech. fellow, Japan, 1995, NEDO, Japan, 1998. Mem.: Am. Chem. Soc. (co-chair several symposia 1995—, program com. petroleum chemistry divsn. 1996—, exec. com. 1997—, chmn. website com. 1997—2000, chmn. program for fuel chem. divsn., exec. com. of fuel chem. divsn. 2000—, chair-elect 2003), AIChE, AAAS. Achievements include development of concept for designing sulfur-resistant noble-metal catalysts, tri-reforming process concept for production of synthesis gas using waste flue gas; discovery of new method for preparing highly active molybdenum sulfide catalysts by using water and Mo precursor; established several new shape-selective catalytic reactions of polycyclic hydrocarons, including ring-shift isomerization, conformational isomerization, shape-selective alkylation, and shape-selective hydrogenation; established the features and reaction pathways of thermal degradation and stabilization of coal-derived and petroleum-derived aviation jet fuels in pyrolytic regime; established a new desulfurization process concept of selective adsorption for removing sulfur (SARS). Office: Pa State U Energy and Geo-Environ Engring Dept Fuel Sci Program 206 Hosler Bldg University Park PA 16802-5001 E-mail: csong@psu.edu.

SONIN, AIN A. mechanical engineering educator, consultant; b. Tallinn, Estonia, Dec. 24, 1937; came to U.S., 1965; m. Epp Jurima, July 24, 1971; children: Juhan, Aldo. BA Sc., U. Toronto, Ont., Can., 1960, MA Sc., 1961, PhD, 1965. Rsch. fellow, teaching asst. U. Toronto, 1960-65; asst. prof. MIT, Cambridge, 1965-68, assoc. prof., 1968-74, prof. mech. engring., 1974—. Sr. scientist Thermo Electron Corp., Waltham, Mass., 1981-82; cons. in field. Contbr. over 70 articles to profl. jours. in fluid and thermal sciences. Mem. ASME, AAAS, Am. Phys. Soc. Achievements include 4 patents in field. Office: MIT Rm 3-256 Cambridge MA 02139

SONLEITNER, FRANK JOSEPH, zoology educator; b. Chgo., Jan. 23, 1932; s. Frank Joseph Sr. and Lucille (Hamilton) S.; m. Nancy Kate Pierce, Sept. 13, 1974 (div. Feb. 1987); children: Bonnie, Catherine, Carol. AB, U. Chgo., 1951, BS, 1956, PhD, 1959. Postdoctoral fellow NSF, Sydney, Australia, 1959-61; lectr. in zoology U. Calif., Berkeley, 1961-62; asst. prof. entomology U. Kans., Lawrence, 1962-65; asst. prof. zoology U. Okla., Norman, 1965-69, assoc. prof. zoology, 1969—2002; prof.zoology emeritus, 2002. Bd. dirs. Nat. Ctr. for Sci. Edn. With U.S. Army, 1954-55. Office of Surgeon Gen. U.S. Army rsch. grantee, 1963-65. Mem. AAAS, Am. Inst. Biol. Scis., Ecol. Soc. Am., Entomol. Soc. Am., Okla. Acad. Sci., Nat. Ctr. for Sci. Edn., Phi Beta Kappa. Office: U Okla Dept Zoology Norman OK 73019-0001

SONNENSCHEIN, HUGO FREUND, academic administrator, economics educator; b. N.Y.C., Nov. 14, 1940; s. Leo William and Lillian Silver Sonnenschein; m. Elizabeth Gunn, Aug. 26, 1962; children: Leah, Amy, Rachel. AB, U. Rochester, 1961; MS, Purdue U., 1963, PhD, 1964, PhD (hon.), 1996; PhD (hon.), Tel Aviv U., 1993; D (hon.), U. Autonoma Barcelona, Spain, 1994; PhD (hon.), Lake Forest Coll., 1995, North Ctrl. Coll., 2001, U. Chgo., 2002. Faculty dept. econs. U. Minn., 1964—70, prof., 1968—70; prof. econs. U. Mass., Amherst, 1970—73, Northwestern U., 1973—76, Princeton (N.J.) U., 1976—87, Class of 1926 prof., 1987—88, provost, 1991—93; dean, Thomas S. Gates prof. U. Pa. Sch. Arts & Scis., Phila., 1988—91; pres. U. Chgo., 1993—2000, Hutchinson disting. prof., pres. emeritus, 2000—. Vis. prof. U. Andes, Columbia, 1965, Tel Aviv U., 1972, Hebrew U., 1973, U. Paris, 1978, U. Aix-en-Provence, France, 1978, Stanford U., 1984—85; bd. dirs. Van Kampen Mutual Funds. Editor: Econometrica, 1977—84; mem. editl. bd.: Jour. Econ. Theory, 1972—75, Jour. Math. Econs., 1974—, SIAM Jour., 1976—80; contbr. articles to profl. jours. Trustee U. Rochester, 1992—, U. Chgo., 1993—. Fellow, Social Sci. Rsch. Coun., 1967—68, NSF, 1970—, Ford Found., 1970—71, Guggenheim Found., 1976—77. Fellow: Econometric Soc. (pres. 1988—89), Am. Acad. Arts and Scis.; mem.: NAS, Am. Philos. Soc.*

SONS, LINDA RUTH, mathematician, educator; b. Chicago Heights, Ill., Oct. 31, 1939; d. Robert and Ruth (Diekelman) Sons. AB in Math., Ind. U., 1961; MS in Math., Cornell U., 1963, PhD in Math., 1966. Tchg. asst. Cornell U., Ithaca, NY, 1961-63, instr. math., summer 1963, rsch. asst., 1963-65; from asst. prof. to assoc. prof. math. No. Ill. U., De Kalb, 1965—78, prof., 1978—, presdl. tchg. prof., 1994-98, disting. tchg. prof., 1998—, dir. undergrad. studies math. dept., 1971—77, exec. sec. univ. coun., 1978—79, chair faculty fund, 1982—. Author (with others): A Study Guide for Introduction to Mathematics, 1976, Mathematical Thinking in a Quantitative World, 1990, 2003; contbr. articles to profl. jours. Bd. dirs., treas. DeKalb County Migrant Ministry, 1967—78; pres. Luth. Women's Missionary League, 1974—87; mem. campus ministry com. No. Ill. Dist. Luth. Ch./Mo. Synod, Hillside, 1977—2001; mem. ch. coun. Immanuel Luth. Ch., DeKalb, 1978—85, 1987—89. Recipient Excellence in Coll. Tchg. award, Ill. Coun. Tchrs. Math., 1991; NSF Rsch. grantee, 1970—72, 1974—75. Mem.: London Math. Soc., Ill. Sect. Math. Assn. Am. (v.p. sect., pres.-elect, pres., past pres. 1982—87, bd. dirs. 1989—92, Disting. Svc. award 1988), Math. Assn. Am. (mem. nat. bd. govs. 1989—92, mem. com. undergrad. program math. 1990—96, chmn. coun. awards 1997—2003, Disting. Coll. or Univ. Tchg. Math. Sect. award 1995, Cert. Meritorious Svc. Nat. award 1998), Assn. Women in Math., Am. Math. Soc., Sigma Xi (past chpt. pres.), Phi Beta Kappa (pres. No. Ill. assn. 1981—85). Achievements include research in classical complex analysis, especially value distribution for meromorphic functions with unbounded characteristics in the unit disc. Office: No Ill U Dept Math Scis Dekalb IL 60115

SONTAG, FREDERICK EARL, philosophy educator; b. Long Beach, Calif., Oct. 2, 1924; s. M. Burnett and Cornelia (Nicholson) S.; m. Carol Furth, June 10, 1950; children: Grant Furth, Anne Burnett Karch. BA with great distinction, Stanford U., 1949; MA, Yale U., 1951, PhD, 1952; LLD (hon.), Coll. Idaho, 1971. Instr. Yale U., 1951-52; asst. prof. philosophy Pomona Coll., Claremont, Calif., 1952-55, assoc. prof., 1955-60, prof., 1970—, Robert C. Denison prof. philosophy, 1972—, chmn. dept. philosophy, 1960-67, 76-77, 1980-84; chmn. coord. com. in philosophy Clarement Grad. Sch. and Univ. Ctr., 1962-65. Vis. prof. Union theol. Sem., N.Y.C., 1959-60, Collegio de Sant' Anselmo, Rome, 1966-67, U. Copenhagen, fall 1972; theologian-in-residence Am. Ch. in Paris, fall 1973; fulbright regional vis. prof., India, East Asia, Pacific areas, 1977-78; mem. nat. adv. coun. Kent Fellowship Program of Danforth Found., 1963-66. Author numerous books, the most recent being; Love Beyond Pain: Mysticism Within christianity, 1977, Sun Myung Moon and the Unification Church, 1977, also German, Japanese and Korean transl.; (with John K. Roth) God and America's Future, 1977, What Can God Do?, 1979, A Kierkegaard Handbook, 1979, The Elements of Philosophy, 1984, (with John K. Roth) The Questions of Philosophy, 1988, Emotion, 1989, The Return of the Gods, 1989, Willgenstein and the Mystical, 1995, Uncertain Truth, 1995, The Descent of Women, 1997, The Acts of the Trinity, 1997, Truth and Imagination, 1998, 2001: A Spiritual Odyssey, 2001, The Mysterious Presence, 2002. Pres. bd. dirs. Claremont Family Svc., 1960-64; trustee The Coro Found., L.A. and San Francisco, 1967-71; bd. dirs., chmn. ways and means com. Pilgrim Place, Claremont, 1970-77. With AUS, 1943-46. Vis. scholar Ctr. for Study Japanese Religions, Kyoto, Japan, spring 1974; vis. fellow East-West Ctr., Honolulu, summer 1974; Wig Disting. prof. award, 1970, 76. Mem. Am. Philos. Assn., Metaphys. Soc. Am. Soc. on Religion in Higher Edn. (Kent fellow 1950-52), Am. Acad. Religion, Phi Beta Kappa. Congregationalist. Office: Pomona Coll 551 N College Ave Claremont CA 91711-4410

SOPER, JOHN TUNNICLIFF, obstetrician-gynecologist, educator; b. Iowa City, Mar. 15, 1952; MD, U. Iowa, 1978. Cert. in ob-gyn. Intern U. Utah Med. Ctr., Salt Lake City, 1978-82, resident in ob-gyn., 1978-82; fellow in gynecol. oncology Duke U., Durham, 1982-85; attending physician Duke U. Med. Ctr., Durham, 1982—, Rex Hosp., Raleigh, N.C., 1995—, Womens Hosp., Greensboro, N.C., 1995—, Wesley Long Hosp., Greensboro, 1995—; asst. prof. Duke U., 1982-83, 83-89, assoc. prof., 1989-95, prof., 1995—. Mem. ACOG, Am. Soc. Clin. Oncology, Soc. Gynecol. Oncologists, Mid-Atlantic Gynecologic Oncology Soc. Office: Duke U Med Ctr PO Box 3079 Durham NC 27715-3079

SORENSEN, HENRIK VITTRUP, electrical engineering educator; b. Skanderborg, Denmark, Jan. 17, 1959; came to U.S. 1983; s. Evan Anton and Anna Marie (Vittrup) S.; m. Karen Ann Taylor, Mar. 5, 1988; children: Amanda Elisabeth, Christian Henrik, Alexander Evan. MS, Aalborg U. Ctr., 1983; PhD, Rice U., 1988. Asst. prof. Dept. Electrical Engring. U. Pa., Phila., 1988-95; v.p. Ariel Corp., Cranbury, N.J., 1995-97, Lucent Techs., 1997—. Cons. AT&T Bell Labs., Murray Hill, N.J., 1990-95. Author: Handbook for Digital Signal Processing, 1992, The FFT Bibliography, 1995, A Digital Signal Processing Laboratory, 1997; contbr. articles to profl. jours. Fellow Rotary; mem. IEEE (editor 1990-94, vice chmn. Phila. sect. 1991-94), Sigma Xi, Eta Kappa Nu. Lutheran. Achievements include development of fast algorithms for the split radix fast Fourier transform and for the fast Hartley transform. Home: 75 Franklin Dr Plainsboro NJ 08536-2310

SORENSON, LIANE BETH MCDOWELL, women's affairs director, state legislator; b. Chgo., Aug. 13, 1947; d. Harold Davidson McDowell and Frances Elanor (Williams) Daisey Van Kleeck; m. Boyd Wayne Sorenson, June 30, 1973; children: Nathan, Matthew, Dana. BS in Edn., U. Del., 1969, M in Counseling with honors, 1986. Tchr. Avon Grove Sch. Dist., West Grove, Pa., 1969-70, Alexis I. duPont Sch. Dist., Wilmington, Del., 1970-73, Barrington (Ill.) Sch. Dist., 1973-75; counseling intern Medill Intensive Learning Ctr.-Christina Sch. Dist., Newark, Del., 1985; counselor Family Violence Shelter CHILD, Inc., Wilmington, 1985, 86-87, dir. parent edn. programs, 1987-88; dir. Office Women's Affairs, exec. dir. Commn. on Status of Women U. Del., Newark, 1988—; mem. Dist. 6 Del. Senate, Dover, 1992—, minority whip. Chair Del. Ho. Edn. Com., 1992—, Adv. Bd. Del. Breast Cancer Coalition, 1998—; commr. Edn. Commn. State Del.; mem. tng. com. Nat. Conf. State Legislatures; mem. Bd. Women's Network Nat. Conf. State Legislatures; mem. joint sunset com. Del. Legislature, Del. House of Reps., 1992-94, Del. Senate, 1994—, Del. Legis. Joint Fin. Com. Del. Legis., 1994—, Coun. State Govts. Toll Fellowship. Presenter papers various meetings & confs. Pres. bd. dirs. Nursing Mothers, Inc., 1980-81; trustee Hockessin Montessori Sch., 1982-84, enrollment chair, 1982-83; trustee Hockessin Pub. Libr., 1982-84, pres. bd., 1982-84; bd. dirs. Del. Coalition for Children, 1986-88; bd. dirs. Children's Bur. Del., 1984-87, sec., 1985-87; pres. Jr. League Wilmington, 1986-87, rsch. coun. v.p., 1985-86; bd. dirs. YWCA New Castle County, 1989-91; pres. Del. Women's Agenda, 1986-88; vice-chair Women's Leadership Ctr., 1992—; mem. Del. Work Family Coalition; bd. dirs. Del. divsn. Am. Cancer Soc., 1993—. Grantee Del. Dept. Svcs. to Children, Youth and Their Families, 1987-88, 1988, State of Del. Gen. Assembly, 1992; recipient Disting. Legis. Svc. award Del. State Bar Assn., 1997, Del Tufo award Delaware Humanities Forum, 1999. Mem.: Hockessin Hist. Soc. (bd. mem. 2000—), Del. Family Law Commn., Del. Alliance for Arts in Edn., Del. Greenway and Trails Coun., Am. Assn. for Higher Edn. (chair women's caucus 1991—92, program chair women's caucus 1990—91, pre-conf. workshop coord. women's caucus 1990 Ann. Conf.), Rotary (charter mem. Hackessin Pike Creek club 1994—). Republican. Methodist. Avocations: camping, hiking. Office: State of Delaware Legislative Hall Rm 210 PO Box 1401 Dover DE 19903-1401

SORENSON, SHARON ORILLA, language arts author and consultant; b. Evansville, Ind., Aug. 15, 1943; d. Orville C. and Viola C. (Savage) Blaser; m. Charles E. Sorenson, July 26, 1938. BA, U. Evansville, 1964, MA, 1968; postgrad., Ind. U., 1983. Tchr. English dept. Ctrl. H.S., Evansville, 1964-86, chairperson English dept., 1974-84; dir. writing lab. Evansville (Ind.)-Vanderburgh Schs., 1980-86; freelance lang. arts writer, 1986—; nat. lang. arts cons. Prentice hall Sch. Divsn., Upper Saddle River, N.J., 1990-2000. Asst. instr. U. Evansville, Ind., 1968-74; key note spkr. numerous profl. meetings, workshops and seminars, 1980—. Author: A Student's Guide to Writing Better Compositions, 1989, English Grammar and Usage Simplified and Self-Taught, 1989, Using Computers in the Language Arts Classroom, Grades K-12, 1990, Working With Special Students in English/Language Arts, Grades K-12, 1991, Easy Reference Grammar Guide Minilessons, 1991, Writing Skills Workbook for the GED, 1992, Webster's New World Student Writing Handbook, 1992, 4th edit., 2000, Composing: Prewriting, Response, Revision, 1993, The Research Paper: A Contemporary Approach, 1993, 2d edit., 1999, How to Write Short Stories, 1994, 2d edit., 1998, Introduction to Research, 1996, Writing: An Art- and Literature-based Approach, 1999, The Research Paper: A Quick Reference, 1999, The Complete Idiot's Guide to Living with Breast Cancer, 2000, Grammar: A Quick Reference, 2001; contbr. articles to profl. jours. Mem., vol. Nature Conservancy, 1985—, Wesselman Park Nature Ctr., Evansville, 1990—. Title IV C grantee Fed. Govt., 1979-82; named Boss of Yr., Bus. Women's Assn., Evansville, 1982; Hilda Maehling fellow NEA, 1985. Mem. Nat. Coun. Tchrs. English (co-chair coms. 1975-94, 86-90), Ind. Coun. Tchrs. English, Nat. Audubon Soc. Home and Office: 10776 Wolfe Ln Mount Vernon IN 47620-9630 E-mail: ssoren@sigecom.net.

SORESE, DENISE POWERS, reading and language arts consultant, educator; b. N.Y.C., Sept. 11, 1945; d. Daniel Dennis and Frances Louise (Kruft) Powers; m. Vincent James Sorese, Aug. 12, 1967; children: Jaclyn, Lauren. BS in Edn., SUNY, Cortland, 1967; M of Reading, U. Bridgeport, 1970; cert. advanced study in adminstrn., Fairfield U., 1993. Tchr. early childhood N.Y.C. Bd. Edn., 1965-67; tchr. elem. sch. Greenwich (Conn.) Bd. Edn., 1967-72, reading/language arts specialist, 1972-77, 91—, learning facilitator, 1995—, mainstreaming assoc., 1986-91, adminstr. summer sch., 1993—2000; dir., program coord. summer acad. Convent of Sacred Heart Sch., 1994—. Aftersch. adminstr. Hamilton Ave. Sch., Greenwich, 1993-96; state assessor Conn. State Dept. Edn., Hartford, 1993—, tech. advisor, 1993-97; presenter and author in field. Mem. project Charlie, chmn. Jr. League Greenwich, 1989-92; bd. dirs. St. Pauls Day Sch., Riverside, Conn., 1981-92, PTA, Greenwich, 1984-93, St. Catherines Players, Riverside, 1993-94; literacy amb. People to People Internat., 2000. Reading grantee State of Conn., 1973, 74. Mem. NEA, ASCD, Conn. Edn. Assn., Conn. Reading Assn. (bd. dirs., exemplary reading award, chairperson 1994-96), Conn. Coun. Tchrs. English, Internat. Reading Assn. (Exemplary Reading award for Conn. 2002), Delta Kappa Gamma (pres. chpt. 2002—03), Phi Delta Kappa. Roman Catholic. Avocations: tennis, reading, theatre. Office: Cos Cob Sch 300 E Putnam Ave Cos Cob CT 06807-2545 E-mail: de_sorese@greenwich.k12.ct.us.

SORGEN, ELIZABETH ANN, retired educator; b. Ft. Wayne, Ind., Aug. 21, 1931; d. Lee E. and Miriam N. (Bixler) Waller; m. Don DuWayne Sorgen, Mar. 8, 1952; children: Kevin D., Karen Lee Sorgen Hoeppner, Keith Alan. BS in Edn., Ind. U., 1953; MS in Edn., St. Francis Coll., Ft. Wayne, 1967. Tchr., bldg. rep. and math. book adoption rep. East Allen County Schs., Monroeville, Ind., 1953-94, ret., 1994. Founder nursery sch., choir mem. St. Marks Luth. Ch., Monroeville, 1960—; active Allen County Local Edn. Fund; vol. Sci. Ctrl.; pres. Heritage Homemakers, 1990-2000; substitute tchr. Recipient Golden Apple award East Allen County Schs., 1976, Monroeville Tchr. of Yr. award, 1993. Mem.: AAUW, Ft. Wayne Ret. Tchrs. Assn. Avocations: square and line dancing, camping, gardening. Home: 25214 Lincoln Hwy E Monroeville IN 46773-9710

SORGI, DEBORAH B(ERNADETTE), educational software company executive; b. NYC, May 2, 1955; d. Waldo L. and Maria N. (Santo) Sorgi. BA in Elem. Edn., St. Francis Coll., 1976; MS in Reading, St. John's U., 1979. Cert. tchr., NY. Adminstrv. asst. Will Darrah and Assoc., N.Y.C., 1976-77; classroom tchr. St. Rita Sch., Bklyn., 1977-80; ednl. cons. Jostens Learning Corp. (formerly, Prescription Learning Corp.), Phoenix, 1980-82, regional dir., 1982-86, regional mktg. mgr., 1986-90, sr. mktg. mgr., 1990-91, area sales mgr., 1991-92; v.p. Simon & Schuster Tech. Group/CCC, Sunnyvale, Calif., 1992; pres. EduStar Am., Inc., Orlando, Fla., 1992-93; gen. mgr. edn. Wang Labs., Inc., Billerica, Mass., 1994-95, bus. devel. mgr. pub. sector, 1995-96; regional v.p. Jostens Learning Corp., San Diego, 1996-98; v.p. sales Am. Cybercasting Corp., Solon, Ohio, 1998-99; v.p. sales and mktg. Computer Adaptive Techs., Evanston, Ill., 1999-2000; sr. v.p. Classwell Learning Group Houghton Mifflin, Boston, 2000—02. Republican. Roman Catholic. Avocations: piano, golf, reading, opera and classical music, tennis.

SORKIN, ROBERT DANIEL, psychologist, educator; b. N.Y.C., May 24, 1937; s. Harry and Cynthia (Erdreich) S.; m. Nancy Jayne Sloan, July 3, 1960; children: David, Susan. BEE, Carnegie Inst. Tech., 1958; PhD, U. Mich., 1965. Assoc. rsch. engr. Cooley Labs. U. Mich., Ann Arbor, 1960-65; asst. prof. psychology Purdue U., West Lafayette, Ind., 1965-68, assoc. prof., 1968-73, prof. dept. psychol. scis., 1973-88; prof., chair dept. psychology U. Fla., Gainesville, 1988-95, prof. dept. psychology, 1995—. Asst. dean sch. humanities, social scis. and edn. Purdue U., 1973-75; dir. psychobiology program NSF, Washington, 1975-76; chair Coun. Grad. Depts. Psychology, Blacksburg, Va., 1994-95; mem. com. on hearing and bioacoustics NRC, Washington, 1987-90. Co-author: Human Factors: Understanding People-System Relationships, 1983; contbr. articles to Jour. Acoustical Soc. Am., Perception and Psychophysics, Jour. Exptl. Psychology, Human Factors, Psychol. Rev., Psych. Sci. With U.S. Army, 1960. Fellow Acoustical Soc. Am., Am. Psychol. Assn., Am. Psychol. Soc.; mem. Human Factors Soc.

SORRELL, ANN JEAN, secondary education educator; b. Burlington, Vt., Sept. 18, 1949; d. George Robert and Jeannette Sylvia (Gaboriault) Nattress; children: Justin Owen, Sabreena Ann. BS, U. Vt., 1971; MA, Middlebury Coll., 1976; CAS in Supervision and Adminstrn., Trinity Coll., 1994. Tchr., computer tech. coord. South Burlington (Vt.) High Sch., 1971—. Adj. prof. U. Vt., Burlington, 1991—; translator and interpreter, Vt., 1971—; computer tech. cons., Vt., 1990—. Author: Oral Communication Testing, 1977, Oral Proficiency Manual Level 1, 1992, Oral Proficiency Manual Level II, 1993, Le Francais Vivant 3, 1991; contbr. articles to profl. jours. Treas. Bartlett's Bay Assn., South Burlington, 1979-86; team mem., leader New Am. Schs., 1993—; mem. com. Vt. State Cert. Appeals, Montpelier, 1980-83, Vt. State Commn. on Assessment, Montpelier, 1991; bd. dirs. Vt. State Tech. Coun., 1992. French Govt. scholar, 1983, Minitel scholar, 1991; Christa McAuliffe fellow, 1991. Mem. ASCD, Am. Coun. on Teaching Fgn. Lang. (tester), Am. Assn. Tchrs. French, Vt. Fgn. Lang. Assn. (bd. dirs., sec.), Vt. State Telecom. Consortium (bd. dirs.), Internat. Assn. Learning Labs., Northeast Coalition Ednl. Leaders, Delta Kappa Gamma. Avocations: hypercard development, reading, swimming, t'ai chi, multimedia production and implementation. Home: 9 Adams Ct South Burlington VT 05403-8708 Office: South Burlington High Sch 550 Dorset St South Burlington VT 05403-6233

SORRELL, REBECCA SUE, special education educator; b. Columbus, Ohio, Mar. 11, 1960; d. Richard Allen and Nancy Louise (Castor) R.; m. James Edward Sorrell Jr., June 28, 1980; children: James Richard, Nichola Alexander, Sarah Elizabeth. BA in Edn., U. Ky., 1985. Cert. tchr., Ohio, Va. Tchr. learning and behavior disorders program Saffell St. Elem. Sch., Lawrenceburg, Ky., 1985-89; tchr. learning disabilities program Benjamin Franklin Mid. Sch., Rocky Mount, Va., 1991—. Mem. Coun. Exceptional Children, Coun. Learning Disabilities, Roanoke Adult Flute Choir. Presbyterian. Avocations: flute, rug latching. Address: 113 Northwest Dr Gretna VA 24557

SORSTOKKE, ELLEN KATHLEEN, marketing executive, educator; b. Seattle, Mar. 31, 1954; d. Harold William and Carrol Jean (Russ) Sorstokke. MusB with distinction, U. Ariz., 1976; postgrad., UCLA Extension, 1979-83, L.A. Valley Coll., 1984-85, Juilliard Extension, fall 1987, U. Calif. Berkeley Extension, 1992-93. Pvt. practice music tchr., Tucson, 1975—77, Whiteriver, Ariz., 1977—78, L.A., 1980—85, S.I., N.Y.C., 1986—89; music tchr. Eloy (Ariz.) Elem. Schs., 1976-77, Whiteriver (Ariz.) Pub. Schs., 1977-78; svc. writer, asst. svc. mgr. Alfa of Santa Monica, Calif., 1978-79; purchasing agt. Advance Machine Corp., L.A., 1979-80; asst. mgr. Atlantic Nuclear Svcs., Gardena, Calif., 1980-81; mgr. Blue Lady's World Music Ctr., L.A., 1981-83; instrument specialist Baxter-Northup Music Co., Sherman Oaks, Calif., 1983-85; dir. mktg. Mandolin Bros., Ltd., S.I., N.Y., 1985-89; product mgr. Gibson Guitar Corp., Nashville, 1989; sales mgr. Saga Musical Instruments, South San Francisco, Calif., 1990-91, mktg. dir., 1991-95, mktg. analyst, 2002—. Freelance mktg. cons., S.I., Foster City, Atlanta, 1986—; freelance cons. www.fussycats.com, 2002; music cons. 20th Century Fox, L.A., 1984; freelance music copyist and orchestrator, Tucson, L.A., N.Y.C., 1972-89; freelance graphic designer and advt., N.Y.C., S.I., Foster City, Atlanta, 1986—. Contbr. articles to profl. jours. Campaign worker Richard Jones for Supr., Tucson, 1972; mem., program book designer Marina Del Rey-Westchester Symphony Orch., L.A., 1981-83. Scholar U. Ariz., 1973-76, ASCAP scholar UCLA, 1980-81. Mem. Tucson Flute Club (publicity chmn. 1974-75, v.p. 1975-76). Republican.

SORTER, BRUCE WILBUR, federal program administrator, educator, consultant; b. Willoughby, Ohio, Sept. 1, 1931; s. Wilbur David and Margaret Louise (Palmer) S.; m. Martha Ann Weirich, Sept. 2,1960 (div. 1967); 1 child, David Robert. BA, U. Md., 1967; MCP, Howard U., 1969; PhD, U. Md., 1972. Cert. community developer. Commd. USAFR, 1967, advanced through grades to lt. col., 1964; sr. planner, cons. Md. Nat. Capital Park and Planning Com., 1968-71; instr. psychology, sociology Howard and P.G. C.C., Columbia and Largo, Md., 1971-72; cmty. resource devel. dept. Md. Coop. Extension Svc., U. Md., College Park, Md., 1972-92; coord. rural info. ctr. Md. Coop. Ext. Svc., U. Md., College Park, 1989-92; affiliate prof. U. Md., 1985-92, ret., 1996. Ext. advisor USDA Internat. Programs, Washington, 1991-96; co-author, co-dir. Dept. Edn. Coun. Effectiveness Tng. Program, 1979-81; author First County Energy Conservation Plan, Prince George's County, 1978-85. Author, co-author 12 books; contbr. articles to profl. publs., chpts. to books. Developer, dir. teamwork tng. programs U.S. Dept. Edn., U.S. Dept. Agriculture, Brazil, Poland, Nat. Grange, 1972-92; cons. Fed. Power Commn. U.S., 1973-75, State Dept. Natural Resources, Md., 1978-79, Dept. Edn., Brazil, 1981-82, Nat. Grange, 1987, Edn. Ext. Svcs., Poland, 1991-92. Urban Planning fellow Howard U., 1968, Human Devel. fellow U. Md., 1970; recipient Meritorious Svc. award Dept. Def., 1983, Disting. Community Svc. award Md. Community Resource Devel. Assn., 1983, Citation for Outstanding Svc., Ptnrs. of Am., 1983, Excellence in Ednl. Programs award Am. Express, 1984, Project of Yr. award Am. Psychol. Assn., 1976, Award of Yr. Am. Vol. Assn., 1976, Achievement award Nat. Assn. of Counties, 1980. Mem. Internat. Cmty. Devel. Soc. (bd. dirs., Achievement award for outstanding contbn. to cmty. devel. 1985, Disting. Svc. award 1990), Md. Cmty. Resource Devel. Assn. (sec.-treas. 1979, pres. 1980, 88-89). Republican. Methodist. Avocations: volunteer work, tennis, sailing, skiing.

SORTLAND, TRUDITH ANN, speech and language therapist, educator; b. Butte, Mont., Dec. 3, 1940; d. Kenneth Hjalmer Sortland and Sigrid V. (Kotka) Strand. BS, Minot (N.D.) State U., 1965. Tchr. Westby (Mont.) Sch., 1960-61, Glasgow (Mont.) Southside Sch., 1962-65, Glasgow AFB, Mont., 1965-80; tchr., speech and lang. pathologist Mineral County Sch. Dist., Hawthorne, Nev., 1965-68, 78—, kindergarten tchr. Mina, Nev., 1968-72, elem. tchr., 1978-80, speech, language pathologist, 1980—; tchr. Dept. Def., Pusan, Republic of Kores, 1972-73, Illesheim, Fed. Republic Germany, 1973-78, Mohall (N.D.) Pub. Sch., 1964-65. Cons. Mary Kay Cosmetics, tchr. Glasgow AFB, 1965-68. Supt. Sunday sch. Bethany Luth. Ch., Hawthorne, 1987—, sec. Ladies Aid, 1987—. Mem. NEA, Nev. Edn. Assn., AAUW (past sec., pres.), Pair O Dice Square Dance Club (sec. 1989—), Delta Kappa Gamma. Avocations: square and round dancing, photography. Office: Mineral County Sch Dist A St Hawthorne NV 89415 Home: 332 Benson Circle Dr Pittsburgh PA 15227-1500

SOSA, ERNEST, philosopher, educator; b. Cardenas, Cuba, June 17, 1940; s. Ernesto and Maria (Garriga) S.; m. Sara Mercedes, Dec. 21, 1961; children: E. David, Adrian J. BA, U. Miami, 1961; MA, U. Pitts., 1962, PhD, 1964. Instr. U. Western Ontario, London, Ontario, Can., 1963-64, U. Pitts., 1964; postdoctoral fellow Brown U., Providence, 1964-66; asst. prof. U. Western Ontario, London, Ontario, 1966-67; asst. prof. to full prof. Brown U., Providence, 1967-74, chmn. of philosophy, 1970-76, full prof., 1974—, Romeo Elton prof., 1981—. Vis. prof. U. Miami, 1970, Nat. U. Mexico, 1979, 80, 81, Harvard U., Cambridge, Mass., 1982, U. Salamanca, 1995, 98, Oxford U., 1997; disting. vis. prof. Rutgers U., 1998—; co-chair program com. 20th World Congress of Philosophy, 1998. Author: Knowledge in Perspective, 1991; gen. editor book series, Cambridge Univ. Press, 1990—, Blackwell Publishers, 1991—; editor Philosophy and Phenomenol. Rsch.; co-editor: Nous; contbr. numerous articles to profl. jours. Grantee NSF, 1970-72, Exxon Ednl. Found., 1980-82; recipient Sr. fellowship NEH, 1988-89. Mem. Am. Acad. Arts and Scis., Am. Philos. Assn. (sec.-treas. 1974-82, chair internat. coop. com. 1984-89, ea. divsn. rep. 1995—, pres. ea. divsn. 2003-, v.p. ea. divsn. 2003-2004), Am. Coun. Learned Socs./Soviet Acad. Commn., Internat. Fedn. Philos. Soc. (steering com. 1988-98, v.p. 1988-93), Institut Internat. de Philosophie (exec. com. 1993-96). Avocations: running, travel. Office: Brown U Dept Philosophy Providence RI 02912-0001

SOSLOWSKY, LOUIS JEFFREY, bioengineering educator, researcher; b. Bklyn., Apr. 4, 1964; s. Martin and Phyllis (Popowitz) S. BS, Columbia U., 1986, MS, 1987, PhD, 1991. Rsch. asst. Bioengring. Inst., Columbia U., N.Y.C., 1983-86, rsch. fellow, 1986-91; asst. prof. bioengring., mech. engring., orthopedic surgery U. Mich., Ann Arbor, 1991-97; assoc. prof. orthopedic surgery and bioengring. U. Pa., Phila., 1997—, dir. orthopedic rsch., 1997—. Reviewer Jours. Biomech. Engring., Biomechanics, Orthopaedic Rsch., Surg. Rsch., 1991—; panelist Shoulder Workshop, Am. Acad. Orthopaedic Surgeons-ASES, NIH, Vail, Colo., 1992. Assoc. editor Jour. Biomech. Engring., Jour. Shoulder and Elbow Surgery; contbr. numerous articles to Biorheology Jour., Biomechanics Jour. Orthopaedic Rsch., Clinics in Sports Medicine, numerous chpts. in Biomechanics of Diarthrodial Joints, Basic Orthopedic Biomechanics, also others. Grantee Orthopaedic Rsch. and Edn. Found., 1991—, NSF, 1992—, Whitaker Found., 1992—, NIH, 1994—. Mem. ASME, AAUP, Orthopaedic Rsch. Soc., Am. Soc. Biomechanics, Sigma Xi, Tau Beta Pi, Chi Epsilon. Office: U Pa 424 Stemmler Hall Philadelphia PA 19104-6081

SOTO, PATRICIA MCFARLANE, elementary school educator; b. Oak Park, Ill., Aug. 21, 1948; m. Alex Soto. BA, Fla. State U., 1970; MSc in Edn., Fla. Internat. U., 1991. Nat. bd. cert. tchr. 1996. Tchr., sci. dept. chair George Washington Carver Middle Sch., Coconut Grove, Fla., 1984—. Named Outstanding Health Educator, Ednl. Devel. Corp. Mem.: Nat. Sci. Tchrs. Assn. (Optical Data Corps. Videodisc Tech. award 1992), Nat. Bd. for Profl. Tchg. Stds. (bd. mem.). Office: Carver Middle Sch 4901 Lincoln Dr Coconut Grove FL 33133-5699*

SOTOMORA-VON AHN, RICARDO FEDERICO, pediatrician, educator; b. Guatemala City, Guatemala, Oct. 22, 1947; s. Ricardo and Evelyn (von Ahn) S.; m. Eileen Marie Holcomb, May 9, 1990; m. Victoria Monzon, Nov. 26, 1971; children: Marisol, Clarisa, Ricardo III, Charlotte Marie. MD, San Carlos U., 1972; MS in Physiology, U. Minn., 1978. Diplomate Am. Bd. Pediats., Am. Bd. Pediat. Cardiology, Am. Bd. Neonatology-Perinatal Medicine. Rotating intern Gen. Hosp., Guatemala, 1971-72; pediat. intern U. Ark., 1972-73, resident, 1973-75; fellow in pediat. cardiology U. Minn., 1975-78; rsch. assoc. in cardiovasc. pathology United Hosps., St. Paul, 1976; fellow in neonatal-perinatal medicine St. Paul's Children's Hosp., 1977-78, U. Ark., 1981-82; instr. pediats. U. Minn., 1978-79; pediat. cardiologist, unit cardiovasc. surg. Roosevelt Hosp., Guatemala City, 1979-81; asst. prof. pediats. cardiology and neonatology U. Ark., Little Rock, 1981-83; pvt. practice Little Rock, 1983—. Fellow Am. Acad. Pediats., Am. Coll. Cardiology, Am. Coll. Chest Physicians, Am. Coll. Angiology; mem. ABA, AAAS, Ark. Med. Soc., N.Y. Acad. Scis., Am. Heart Assn., Soc. Pediat. Echocardiology, Guatemala Coll. Physicians and Surgeons, Ctrl. Ark. Pediat. Soc., So. Soc. Pediat. Rsch., Soc. Critical Care Medicine, Guatemala Acad. Genealogy, Heraldry and Hist. Studies (corr.), Soc. Genealogists London, Pleasant Valley Country Club (Little Rock), The Little Rock Club. Home: 25 River Ridge Cir Little Rock AR 72227-1523 Office: Ste 820 Medical Towers II Little Rock AR 72205 E-mail: rfsotomora@aol.com.

SOUCY, ROBERT JOSEPH, history educator; b. Topeka, June 25, 1933; s. William Joseph and Bernice Winefred (Riley) S.; m. Barbara Stone, May 10, 1960 (div. 1979); children: Anne Marie, Alissa Bernice; m. Sharon Fairchild, Jan. 2, 1986. AB, Washburn U., 1955; MA, Kans U., 1956; student, U. Dijon, France, 1956-57; PhD, U. Wis., 1963. Instr. Harvard U., Cambridge, Mass., 1963-64; asst. prof. Kent (Ohio) State U., 1964-66; assoc. prof. Oberlin (Ohio) Coll., 1966-69, prof., 1969—2003; ret., 2003. Author: Fascism in France, 1972, Fascist Intellectual, 1979, French Fascism, 1924-33, 1986, French Fascism, 1933-39, 1995; mem. editl. bd. French Hist. Studies, 1986-88. 1st lt. USAF, 1957-60. Fullbright scholar, 1956-57; grantee NEH, 1969, 88, ACLS, 1969, 89, Am. Philos. Soc., 1969, 73. Mem. Am. Hist. Soc., French Hist. Soc. (mem. editorial bd. 1986-88). Avocations: tennis, squash. Home: 143 E College St Oberlin OH 44074-1774

SOUKUP, DEBORAH CRAIG, elementary school educator; b. Columbus, Ga., Sept. 2, 1954; d. Douglas Broward and Peggie-Louise (Lee) C. BA, Wittenberg U., 1976; MEd, Lesley Coll., 1981. Tchr. Associacao Escola Graduada de Sao Paulo, Brazil, 1977-79, Hillsboro (N.H.)-Deering Schs., 1981—2000, Simi Valley Unified Sch. Dist., 2001—; cons. JPL-NASA, 2002—. Recipient N.H. Elem. Tchr. Sci. award, 1990, 91. Mem. Nat. Sci. Tchrs. Assn. Home: 187 Brooks Ct Simi Valley CA 93065-8230

SOUKUP, RODNEY JOSEPH, electrical engineer, educator; b. Faribault, Minn., Mar. 9, 1939; s. Joseph Edward and Lillian Margurite (Fierst) S.; m. Therese Marie Rockers, Dec. 18, 1965; children: Richard Joseph, Michael Harold, Stephen Rodney. BS, U. Minn., 1961, MSEE, 1964, PhD, 1969. Prin. devel. engr. Univac, St. Paul, 1969-71; instr. U. Minn., Mpls., 1972; asst. prof. U. Iowa, Iowa City, 1972-76; assoc. prof. U. Nebr., Lincoln, 1976-80, chmn., 1978-80, prof., chmn., 1980-2000, Henson coll. prof., chmn., 1998-2000, Henson coll. prof., 2000—. Contbr. articles to profl. jour. and conf. Coach men's softball, Mpls., 1963-71, Lincoln, 1984-90; coach Lincoln pk. and recreation grade sch. basketball, 1976-82, Little Chief's baseball, Lincoln, 1977-78. Fellow IEEE (def. R&D com. 1988, edn. soc. EAB 1991, Ad. Com 1991-94, treas. 1998—); mem. Am. Vacuum Soc., Nat. Elec. Engring. Dept. Heads Assn. (Chgo. chmn. steering com. 1992-94, v.p. 1989-90, pres. 1990-91, bd. dirs. 1988-94, 97-99, Outstanding Leadership and Svc. award 1998), KC, Tau Beta Pi, Eta Kappa Nu. Republican. Roman Catholic. Avocations: high fidelity, golf. E-mail: rsoukup@unl.edu., rsoukup@neb.rr.com.

SOULE, GEORGE ALAN, literature educator, writer; b. Fargo, ND, Mar. 3, 1930; s. George Alan and Ruth Georgia (Knudsen) S.; m. Carolyn Richards, Nov. 24, 1961; 1 child, Katherine. BA, Carleton Coll., 1947; postgrad., Corpus Christi Coll., Cambridge (Eng.) U., 1952-53; MA, Yale U., 1956, PhD, 1960. Instr. English lit. Oberlin (Ohio) Coll., 1958-60; asst. prof. U. Wis., Madison, 1960-62; from asst. prof. to prof. Carleton Coll., Northfield, Minn., 1962-95, prof. emeritus, 1995—, chair English dept., 1980—83; tchr. Cannon Valley Elder Collegium, 1998—2002, vice chair, 2003—, also bd. dirs. Cons. Ednl. Testing Svc., Princeton, NJ, 1967-84, 94-97; lectr. Wordsworth Winter Sch., Grasmere, UK, 2003. Author: Four British Women Novelists: An Annotated and Critical Secondary Bibliography, 1998; editor: Theatre of the Mind, 1974; contbr. articles to profl. jours. Mem. libr. bd. City of Northfield, 1997-2000; bd. dirs. Northfield Area Found., 2001-02. With U.S. Army, 1954-55. Internat. fellow Rotary, 1952-53, Sterling pre-doctoral fellow Yale U., 1957-58. Mem.: Anthony Powell Soc., The Iris Murdoch Soc., Friends of Dove Cottge, Boswell Soc. of Auchinleck, Johnson Soc. of Lichfield, Mayflower Soc., Oxford and Cambridge Club, Rotary, Phi Beta Kappa. Episcopalian. Avocations: cooking, travel, Jeopardy (Champion Sr. Tournament 1990). Home: 313 Nevada St Northfield MN 55057-2346 Office: Carleton Coll 1 N College St Northfield MN 55057-4001 Fax: 507-645-5099. E-mail: gsoule@charter.net.

SOULE, LUCILE SNYDER, pianist, music educator; b. Fargo, N.D., Sept. 21, 1922; d. Roy Henry and Gene (McGhee) Snyder; m. Leon Cyprian Soule Jr., Sept. 1, 1954 (dec. Dec. 1994); children: Robert Leon, Anne Lucile. MusB, MusB in Edn., MacPhail Coll. Music, 1943; MA, Smith Coll., Northampton, Mass., 1945; postgrad. diploma, Juilliard Sch. Music, 1948. Organist various chs., Mont., La., and Ohio, 1935-68; instr. Smith Coll., Northampton, 1945-46; freelance pianist, accompanist Juilliard Sch. Music, also pvt. groups and individuals, N.Y.C., 1946-49; from instr. to assoc. prof. Newcomb Coll., Tulane U., New Orleans, 1949-61; staff pianist, soloist New Orleans Symphony, 1954-61; guest artist Contemporary Music Festival La. State U., Baton Rouge, 1953-61; lectr. Lakewood br. Ohio State U., 1964-66; music tchr. East Cleveland (Ohio) Pub. Schs., 1969-85; music dir. East Cleveland Theater, 1985—2001; cons. and mgr. of spl. programs East Cleve. (Ohio) Theater, 2001—03; pianist Zhao Rong Chun, Cleve., 1995—; pianist for William Dempsey, Cleve., 1997—. Pres. New Orleans Music Tchrs. Assn., 1958-59; publicity chair Rocky River (Ohio) Chamber Music Soc., 1963-67; v.p. Cleve. chpt. Am. Orff Schluwerk Assn., 1974-75, presenter in field; mem. The Trio, 1998—. Pianist (compact disc with Zhao) Master of the Erhu, 1996; debut recital with Zhao at Weill Recital Hall, Carnegie Hall, 1999; composer Serenity Prayer, 1998, The Crown of Life, 1999. Mem. Citizens Adv. Group, East Cleveland, 1967-69; vocal coach, 1946—. Woolley Found. fellow, 1950-51, Tchg. fellow Case Western Res. U., 1967-68, Smith Coll., 1943-45; Juilliard Sch. Music scholar, 1946-48. Mem. Darius Milhaud Soc. (bd. dirs. 1984—), Fortnightly Mus. Club (corr. sec. 1996-2000), Lecture Recital Club (bd. dirs. 1993-95), Mu Phi Epsilon. Democrat. Christian Scientist. Avocations: church work, gourmet cooking, travel, art. Home and Office: 15617 Hazel Rd East Cleveland OH 44112-2904

SOULE, ROBERT D. safety and health educator, administrator; b. DeTour Village, Mich., July 8, 1941; s. Harold M. and Mildred M. (Abear) S.; m. Mary Ann Kretzschmar, June 13, 1964; children: Dawn Marie, Robert John, Rebecca Ann. BS, Mich. State U., 1963; MS in Chem. Engring., Purdue U., 1965; EdD in Higher Edn. Adminstrn., U. Pitts., 1993. Cert. safety profl.

cert in indsl. hygiene; registered profl. engr., Mich., Ind., Tex. Calif. Environ. health engr. Dow Chem. Co., Midland, Mich., 1965-69, sr. indsl. hygienist Freeport, Tex., 1969-70; v.p. Clayton Environ. Cons., Southfield, Mich., 1970-77; prof. safety and health Indiana U. of Pa., 1977—, assoc. dean health & human svcs., 1999-2000. Cons. in pvt. practice, Indiana, Pa., 1977—. Contbr. chpts. to books; mem. editorial bd. Am. Indsl. Hygiene Assn. Jour., 1979-85, Occupational Hazards, 1992-98, Professional Safety, 1998—. Fellow Am. Indsl. Hygiene Assn.; mem. Am. Conf. Govtl. Indsl. Hygienists, Am. Soc. Safety Engrs. (profl.), Am. Acad. Indsl. Hygiene (sec.-treas.). Office: Indiana U Pa Safety Scis Dept 123 Johnson Indiana PA 15705-1087 E-mail: bobsoule@iup.edu.

SOUSA, JOSEPH PHILIP, secondary education educator; b. Azores, Portugal, May 26, 1943; s. Agostinho and Emilia Augusta (Freitas) S.; m. Filomena Alice Castro, Apr. 1, 1967 (div. Aug. 1983); children: Yvette Marie, John Philip. BA in Math., San Jose State U., 1981. Cert. tchr., Calif., Ga.; ordained priest Cath. and Apostolic Ch. of Antioch, 1989, bishop, 1991. Tchr. math. Milpitas (Calif.) Unified Sch. Dist., 1981-93, mentor tchr., 1989-91; tchr. Cobb County Sch. Dist., 1993, South San Francisco Unified Sch. Dist., 1994—. Advisor math. engring. and sci. achievement San Jose (Calif.) State U., 1982—; cons. math. Coll. Bd., 1986-88. With USAR, 1965-83. Mem. NEA, Nat. Coun. Tchrs. Math., Calif. Tchrs. Assn., Calif. Union Portuguese (pres. 1984), Irmandade Divino Espirito Santo (sec. 1982-85). Avocations: collecting stamps, soccer, meditation, tai-chi, regenesis. Home: 4349 La Cosa Ave Fremont CA 94536-4721 E-mail: jps526@telis.net.

SOUSA, RONALD WAYNE, foreign language educator; b. Santa Cruz, Calif., Aug. 14, 1943; s. Daniel and Ulala Kathryn (Snyder) S.; m. Joyce Ann Burton, Mar. 16, 1968; children: Jonathan David, Benjamin Joseph. BA, U. Calif., Berkeley, 1966, MA, 1968, PhD, 1973. Asst. prof. Portuguese and Latin Am. studies U. Tex., Austin, 1971—74; asst. prof. Spanish and Portuguese U. Minn., Mpls., 1974—76, assoc. prof. Spanish and Portuguese, 1976—82, prof. Spanish, Portugese and comparative lit., 1982-93; prof. Portuguese, Spanish and comparative lit. U. Ill., Urbana, 1994—. Vis. prof. of Portuguese U. Calif., Berkeley, 1977; program chmn. dept. comparative lit. U. Minn., 1983-87, 90-92, chmn. dept. cultural studies and comparative lit., 1992-93; head dept. Spanish, Italian and Portuguese, U. Ill., 1994-2000. Author: The Rediscoverers, 1981; co-author: Reading the Harper, 1996, The Humanities in Dispute, 1998; editor-translator: Control of the Imaginary, 1988, Yes, Comrade, 1993; translator: The Passion According to G.H., 1988; translator: Yes Comrade, 1993, This Litle Lusitanian House, 2003; Memoirs of a Militia Sergeant, 1999; co-translator, The Murmuring Coast, 1995; contbr. articles to navies publs. and mags. Office: U Ill Spanish Italian Portuguese 4080 FLB/707 S Matthews Urbana IL 61801

SOUTH, STEPHEN A. academic administrator; Pres. South Coll., Knoxville, Tenn., 1989—. Office: South Coll Office of the President 720 N 5th Ave Knoxville TN 37917-6721

SOUTHERLIN, KENNETH GOWAN, principal; b. Greenville, S.C., May 29, 1950; s. William Bates and Nancy Ellen (Hightower) S.; m. Donna Elizabeth Sloan, Aug. 8, 1971; children: Kenneth Gowan Jr., Krystal Danielle. AA, North Greenville Coll., 1969; BS, Clemson U., 1971, MA, 1973. Tchr. James F. Byrnes H.S., Duncan, S.C., 1971-72, Blue Ridge H.S., Greer, S.C., 1972-74, asst. prin., 1974-77, prin., 1977—. Budget com. The Sch. of Greenville, 1993, sch. to work com., 1994. Mem. Tigerville Vol. Fire Dept., 1978-79, commr., 1979-84; mem. Blue Ridge Ruritan, Greer, 1974—; mem. Locust Hill. Bapt. Ch., 1985—; chmn. Locust Hill Bapt. Ch., 1994, deacons, 1994, fin. com., 1994. Named Outstanding Educator First Union Corp., 1994. Mem. ASCD, Assn. of Secondary Prins., Phi Delta Kappa. Home: 441 N Southerlin Rd Taylors SC 29687-7036 Office: Blue Ridge HS 2151 Fews Chapel Rd Greer SC 29651-4946

SOUTHERN, ANN GAYLE, nurse, educator; b. Radford, Va., Oct. 1, 1950; d. William Gale and Harless (Rogers) Farmer. Degree in nursing cum laude, Wytheville (Va.) C.C., 1985; BS, Radford (Va.) U., 1988, MS, 1995. RN. Nurse Pulaski (Va.) Cmty. Hosp., 1985-88, St. Alban's Psychiat. Hosp., Radford, 1988-98; clin. instr. Wytheville RN Program, 1996-98; nurse Sunbridge of New River Valley, Dublin, 1999—2003, Columbia Pulaski Cmty. Hosp., Pulaski, Va., 1999—2003. Counselor AIDS/hepatitis disease process cmty. support groups, Radford, 1992-2003; lectr. breast cancer and self-exam., Radford, 1995. Mem. ANA, Sigma Theta Tau. Methodist. Avocations: old movies, gardening. Home: 6746 Dudley Ferry Rd Radford VA 24141-8876

SOUTHERN, PAUL MORRIS, JR., internist, educator, microbiologist; b. Ft. Worth, June 26, 1932; s. Paul Morris and Margaret M. (Moore) S.; children: Sheryl Ann, Mark Lee. BS, Abilene Christian Coll., 1953; MD, U. Tex., 1959; DTM&H, London Sch. Hygiene/Trop. Med., 1993. Diplomate in internal medicine and infectious diseases Am. Bd. Internal Medicine; diplomate Am. Bd. Pathology. Intern Parkland Meml. Hosp., Dallas, 1959-60, resident, 1960-62; rsch. fellow in infectious diseases U. Tex. Southwestern Med. Sch., Dallas, 1962-63, 66-68; practice medicine, specializing in internal medicine Irving, Tex., 1963-66; asst. prof. internal medicine U. Tex. Southwestern Med. Sch., 1968-71, assoc. prof. pathology and internal medicine, 1973-81, prof., 1981—; assoc. prof. lab medicine Washington U. Sch. Medicine, St. Louis, 1971-73; dir. clin. microbiology Parkland Meml. Hosp., Dallas, 1973—. Vis. prof. dept. microbiology St. Thomas's Hosp. Med. Sch., London, 1980-81, Kuwait U. Faculty Medicine, 1981, 82. Contbr. articles to profl. jours. Fellow ACP; mem. Tex. Soc. Clin. Microbiology (pres. 1974-76), Acad. Clin. Lab. Physicians and Scientists, Am. Soc. Microbiology, Infectious Diseases Soc. Am., Tex. Infectious Diseases Soc. (pres. 1983-84), Am. Soc. Clin. Pathologists, So. Soc. Clin. Investigation, Southwestern Assn. Clin. Microbiology (pres. 1994-95), Royal Soc. Tropical Medicine and Hygiene, Am. Fedn. Clin. Rsch., Am. Soc. Tropical Medicine and Hygiene, Alpha Omega Alpha. Home: 2625 Thomas Ave Dallas TX 75204-2638 Office: U Tex Southwestern Med Ctr 5323 Harry Hines Blvd Dallas TX 75390-7208

SOUTHGATE, PAUL GREGORY, information administrator; b. Itasuke AFB, Japan, May 27, 1957; s. Herbert Fletcher and Joyce Elaine (Munford) S.; m. Denese White, Dec. 13, 1980; children: Karen Marie, Kelly Beth. Student, U. Ky., 1975-78; BBA, Ea. Ky. U., 1980. Cert. computer profl. Dir. computer systems Asbury Theol. Seminary, Wilmore, Ky., 1981-95; chief info. officer Asbury Coll., Wilmore, 1995-2000, Christian Appalachian Project, Lancaster, Ky., 2000—01, Ky. Assoc. for Comm. Action, Frankfort, Ky., 2002—03, St. Joseph Hosp., Lexington, Ky., 2003. Pres. bd. Wilmore Day Care Ctr., Inc., 1987-92. Pres. bd. T.R.U.C.K. Ministry, Inc., Frankfort, Ky., 1991—; stewardship chmn. Wilmore United Meth. Ch., 1988-90; city councilman City of Wilmore, 1994-2001. Sgt. USMC, 1977-81. Republican. United Methodist. Avocations: model trains, pool, volunteer work. Office: St Joseph Hosp One St Joseph Dr Lexington KY 40504 Home: 392 Dove Creek Rd Frankfort KY 40601 E-mail: pdkksouth@yahoo.com.

SOUTHWORTH, HORTON COE, educational educator, education scholar; b. Monroe, Mich., Apr. 2, 1926; s. Frederick Osgood and Bertha Southworth; m. Jannene MacIntyre, Apr. 1971; children: Sueann, Nancy, Jim, Janet, Jaye, Bradford, Alexandra. BS, Mich. State U., East Lansing, 1950, MA, 1953, EdD, 1962. Cert. K-8 tchr., elem. prin., Mich. Mid. sch. tchr. Bellevue (Mich.) Pub. Schs., 1950-51, elem. prin., 1951-53, supervising prin., 1953-55; elem. prin. Pontiac (Mich.) Pub. Schs., 1955-59; coord. Macomb Tchr. Ctr. Mich. State U., Warren, 1959-67, asst. prof., 1962-64, assoc. prof., 1964-67; prof. edn., chmn. elem. edn. dept. U. Pitts., 1967-91; scholar-in-residence Duquesne U., Pitts., 1990—, cons., 1991-92. Cons. Pa. Dept. Edn., Harrisburg, 1968-91; treas. Learning Tree Assocs. Pitts., 1974—. Chmn. Three Rivers dist. Boy Scouts Am., Pitts., 1980-90; pres. Univ. Childrens Sch., California, Pa., 1988—, mem. adv. com. grad. program in Pa., Nova Southeastern U., Harrisburg, 1989—; invited participant Leadership Conf., Oxford U., 1995, 97. With USNR, 1944-46, PTO. Recipient Chancellor's Disting. Tchr. award U. Pitts., 1988, Prof. Emeritus award, 1991, Presdl. citation Merit, 1997. Mem. Assn. Tchr. Educators (33 Yr. Mem. award 1991, 45 yr.award 2003), Pa. Assn. Colls. and Tchr. Educators (exec. bd. 1985-91), Masons (life), Kappa Delta Pi (5 Yr. Chpt. Counselor award 1989), Phi Delta Kappa (43 Yr. Mem. award 2003), Theta Chi. Democrat. Presbyterian. Avocations: skiing, reading, gardening. Home: 927 Lincoln Highlands Dr Coraopolis PA 15108-7736

SOUTHWORTH, JAMIE MACINTYRE, retired education educator; b. Ironton, Ohio, Oct. 16, 1931; d. Gaylord and Lydia Marcum (Adkins) MacIntyre; m. Horton C. Southworth; children: Jaye, Brad, Alexandra, Sueann, Janet, Jim. BS, Ball State U., 1952, MA, 1961; EdD, U. Pitts., 1981; attended, Oxford (Eng.) U., 1997. Cert. adminstr. and tchr., reading specialist, Pa. Instr. Mich. State U., East Lansing, 1964-67; instr., coord. U. Minn., Mpls., 1967-71; rsch. assoc. Pitts. Pub. Schs., 1971-80; assoc. prof. California U., Pitts., 1988, prof. edn., 1993—, state grants educator, 1990-95, dir. leadership tng. proposal, 1996-00; ret., 2000. Chancellor state adv. com., California U. rep., 1994—, faculty profl. devel. com. state rep., 1991-99; invited participant Oxford (Eng.) U. Leadership Studies, 1995, 97; cons. TITL project Duquesne U.; CEO Learning Tree Corp., 1975-2000; presenter, rsch. conf. 2000, Waikato U., New Zealand, rsch. young childrens conf. 2000-02, San Diego; chair-IRA, internat. conf. nat. Fulbright scholars, San Francisco, 2002. Contbr. articles to profl. jours. Recipient Seal of St. Peter's Coll., Oxford, 1997; U.S. Office of Edn. title III & IVC grantee; grantee Pa. Vocat. Tech. State, 1990-91, 93, Bibliotherapy Project California Univ. Pa., 1992, Pa. State, 1993, Pa. Campus Compac, 1993. Mem. Am. Assn. Colls. Tchr. Edn., NEA Young Children, Kappa Delta Pi (counselor), Phi Delta Kappa.

SOUTHWORTH, LINDA JEAN, artist, critic, educator, poet; b. Milw., May 11, 1951; d. William Dixon and Violet Elsie (Kuehn) S.; m. David Joseph Roger, Nov. 16, 1985 (div. July 1989). BFA, St. John's U., Queens, N.Y., 1974; MFA, Pratt Inst., Bklyn., 1978. Pvt. practice self-employed, N.Y.C., 1974—; art critic Resident Publs., N.Y.C., 1993-95. Adj. prof. art history St. Francis Coll., Bklyn., 1985-94; artist-in-residence Our Saviour's Atonement Luth. Ch., N.Y.C., 1993-95. One-woman shows include Galimaufry, Croton-on-Hudson, N.Y., 1977, Kristen Richard Gallery, N.Y.C., 1982, Gallery 84, 1990, The Bernhardt Collection, Washington, 1991, Netherland Club, N.Y.C., 1992, Chuck Levitan Gallery, Soho, 1996, Seventh and Second Photo Gallery, 1998, Pen & Brush Solo Award Show, 2001, N.Y.C. Pub. Libr., 2002, exhibited in group shows at Union St. Graphics, San Francisco, 1974, Nuance Gallery, Tampa, 1987, 1988, Illustrators Ann. Drawing Show, N.Y.C., 1989—90, Salmagundi Club, 1991, 1992, Henry Howells Gallery, 1992—93, Mus. Gallery, 1994, Cavalier Gallery, Greenwich, Conn., 1995, CaribGallery, N.Y.C., 1996, N.Y. State Mus., 1997, Knickerbocker Gallery, 1999, Maison Royale, New Orleans, La., 2002, Christmas Card/UNICEF, 1992, Represented in permanent collections Peltz,Walker & Dubinsky, Valois of Am., one-woman shows include New York City Pub. Libr., 2002. Recipient first prize award annual watercolor exhibit, Pen and Brush, 2000. Mem. Pen and Brush, Poetry Soc. Am. Mem. Collegiate Ch. Avocations: ballroom dancing, old inns and architecture. Home: 106 Cabrini Blvd Apt 5D New York NY 10033-3422 E-mail: linda@lindasouthworth.com.

SOUTO BACHILLER, FERNANDO ALBERTO, chemistry educator; b. Andújar, Jaen, Spain, Mar. 27, 1951; s. Manuel and Maria Encarnación (Bachiller Mora) Souto García; m. Josefina Melgar Gómez, July 20, 1974; children: Antonio Alberto, Fernando Jose, Natacha. Licenciate of Sci., U. Granada, Spain, 1973; PhD, U. Alta., Can., 1978; ScD, Ministerio de Educación, Madrid, 1988. Asst. prof. chemistry U. P.R., Mayagüez, 1979-82, assoc. prof., 1983-88, prof. Mayaguez, 1988—, dir. CRIL, 1986—. Vis. prof. U. Granada, 1988, EPFL, Lausanne, Switzerland, 1989, U. Málaga, Spain, 1990. Contbr. articles to profl. jours. Queen Elizabeth scholar, 1975; Fundación Juan March rsch. fellow, 1979. Fellow Royal Soc. Chemistry (London), Am. Inst. Chemists; mem. Am. Chem. Soc. (councilor 1989-91, chmn. 1987), Sigma Xi. Roman Catholic. Achievements include development of two interrelated areas of research in organic molecular photophysics and photochemistry of aromatic natural products and production of natural products by in vitro biosynthesis, rotating optical disk ring electrode; elucidation of geometry and spin multiplicity of cyclobutadiene C_4H_4 and C_4D_4. Home: H21 Calle Almirante Alturas de Mayaguez Mayaguez PR 00682-6239 Office: U of PR Chemistry Dept Mayaguez PR 00681

SOUZA, BLASE CAMACHO, librarian, educator; b. Kohala, Hawaii, Feb. 3, 1918; d. Lawrence Lorenzo Ramos and Mary Maria (Caravalho) Camacho; m. Alfred Patrick Souza, Nov. 26, 1949; children: Michelle Louise, Patricia Ann. EdB, U. Hawaii, Honolulu, 1939; PD, U. Hawaii, 1940; MLS with honors, Pratt Inst., 1947. Cert. tchr., Hawaii. Tchr. Honolulu Dept. Pub. Instruction, 1940-42, Lahaina (Maui, Hawaii) Dept. Pub. Instruction, 1941-42, Waialua (Oahu, Hawaii) Dept. Pub. Instruction, 1943-46, libr., 1947-66; rsch. libr. dept. of edn. U. Hawaii, Honolulu, 1967-68, adminstr., rsch. libr. dept. of edn., 1968-70; edn. officer, program specialist media svcs. Hawaii Dept. of Edn., Honolulu, 1970-75; local historian P.R. Heritage Soc. of Hawaii, Honolulu, 1976—. Cons. Hawaii Multi-Cultural Ctr., Honolulu, 1976-80, Hawaii Heritage Ctr., Honolulu, 1981—; lectr., cons. P.R. Heritage Soc. of Hawaii, Honolulu, 1984—. Author: Boricua Hawaiiana: Puerto Ricans of Hawaii, Reflections of the Past and Mirror of the Future, 1983, De Borinquen a Hawaii, 1985, A Puerto Rican Poet On The Sugar Plantations of Hawaii, 2000; co-author: Legacy of Diversity, 1975, MONTAGE-An Ethnic History of Women in Hawaii, 1977, A Puerto Rican Poet on the Super Plantations of Hawaii, 2000; contbr. articles to profl. jours. Bd. dirs. Friends of Waipahu Cultural Garden Park, 1983-92; active Hist. Hawaii Found., Honolulu, 1984, Bishop Mus., Honolulu, 1985—. Hawaii Com. for the Humanities grantee, 1980, 91. Mem. Hawaii Assn. Sch. Librs. (pres. 1965), Hawaii Libr. Assn. (pres. 1975), Hawaii Mus. Assn., P.R. Heritage Soc. Hawaii (founder, pres. 1980-84, 93-99), AAUW. Roman Catholic. Avocations: collect sculpture, music, reading. Office: 4220 Lafayette Pl Culver City CA 90232-2820

SOVERN, MICHAEL IRA, law educator; b. N.Y.C., Dec. 1, 1931; s. Julius and Lillian (Arnstein) S.; m. Lenore Goodman, Feb. 21, 1952 (div. Apr. 1963); children: Jeffrey Austin, Elizabeth Ann, Douglas Todd; m. Eleanor Leen, Aug. 25, 1963 (div. Feb. 1974); 1 child, Julie Danielle; m. Joan Wit, Mar. 9, 1974 (dec. Sept. 1993); m. Patricia Walsh, Nov. 12, 1995. AB summa cum laude, Columbia U., 1953, LLB (James Ordronaux prize), 1955, LLD (hon.), 1980; PhD (hon.), Tel Aviv U., 1982; LLD (hon.), U. So. Calif., 1989. Bar: N.Y. 1956, U.S. Supreme Ct. 1976. Asst. prof., then assoc. prof. law U. Minn. Law Sch., 1955-58; mem. faculty Columbia Law Sch., 1957—, prof. law, 1960—, Chancellor Kent prof., 1977—, dean Law Sch., 1970-79; chmn. exec. com. faculty Columbia U., 1968-69, provost, exec. v.p., 1979-80, univ. pres., 1980-93, pres. emeritus, 1993. Rsch. dir. Legal Restraints on Racial Discrimination in Employment, Twentieth Century Fund, 1962-66; spl. counsel to gov. N.J., 1974-77; cons. Time Mag., 1965-80; mem. panel of arbitrators N.J. Bd. Mediation, Fed. Mediation and Conciliation Svc.; bd. dirs. Sequa, Asian Cultural Coun., Shubert Orgn., Comcast Corp., Sta. WNET-TV, NAACP Legal Def. Fund, 1976-97, Freedom Forum Newseum; chmn. N.Y.C. Charter Revision Commn., 1982-83; co-chmn. 2d Cir. Commn. on Reduction of Burdens and Costs in Civil Litigation, 1977-80; chmn. Commn. on Integrity in Govt., 1986; pres. Italian Acad. Advanced Studies in Am., 1991-93, Shubert Found., 1996—; chmn. Japan Soc., 1993—, Am. Acad. Rome, 1993—; chmn. nat. adv. coun. Freedom Forum Media Studies Ctr., 1993-2001; chmn. Sotheby's, 2000—. Author: Legal Restraints on Racial Discrimination in Employment, 1966, Law and Poverty, 1969, Of Boundless Domains, 1994; host Sta. WNET-TV series Leading Questions. Mem. Pulitzer Prize Bd., 1980-93, chmn. pro tem, 1986-87; trustee Kaiser Family Found., 1994-2002, Presdl. Legal Expense Trust, 1994-98; chmn. Sotheby's, 2000. Decorated commendatore Order of Merit (Italy); recipient Alexander Hamilton medal Columbia Coll., 1993, Citizens Union Civic Leadership award, 1993, Town Hall Friend of the Arts award, 2001. Fellow Am. Acad. Arts and Scis.; mem. ABA, Coun. Fgn. Rels., Assn. Bar City N.Y., Am. Philos. Soc., Am. Arbitration Assn. (panel arbitrators), Am. Law Inst., Econ. Club, Nat. Acad. Arbitrators. Office: Columbia U Sch Law 435 W 116th St New York NY 10027-7297

SOWA, FRANK XAVIER, entrepreneur, futurist, educator, speaker; b. Akron, Ohio, Aug. 9, 1957; s. William Walter and Olga Susan (DeMay) S. BA in English and Chemistry, Muskingum Coll., 1979. Reporter Dix Publs., Cambridge, Ohio, 1976-78; editor Messenger Newspapers, Akron, 1978-79; mgr. corp. communications Davy McKee Corp., Cleve., 1979-81; mgr. market communications Roadway Package System, Pitts., 1984-85; owner, chief exec. officer Xavier Communications, Pitts., 1982-87, The Xavier Group, Ltd., Pitts., 1986—89, CEO, pres., 1990—, Seed.Net Computer Online Incubator, Pitts., 1994—98. Cons. C.C. Allegeny County, Pitts., 1986-88, instr., 1987, LaRoche Coll., Pitts., 1982-83, U. Aron, 1982, U. Pitts. Gov.'s Internat. Studies, 1988-91; chmn. Pitts. Quality and Productivity Exposion, 1991, 7th Ann. Pitts. Quality Conf., 1991; chmn. econ. devel. com. SMC Bus. Couns., 1993-95; bd. dirs. OMEGA Fed. Credit Union, 1994-98; tech. solutions cons. Ednl. Tech. Assocs., N.Y.C., 1998-2000; bd. dirs. Three Rivers Ednl. Tech. Conf.; presenter in field. Author: Pittsburgh Reinvented, 1985, National Quality Standards (ISO 9000) for Training and Instruction, (software) Chronometics Modeller, 1987; editor Pitts. Trends Newsletter, 1984-89; columnist Boardwatch Mag., 1994-98; contbr. articles to profl. jours. Chmn. N.H. Civic-Cultural Ctr., Pitts., 1987-88; adv. coun. Smaller Mfrs. Coun., 1987-93; sec., bd. dirs. Imaginarium Children's Theatre, Pitts., 1985; active World Affairs Coun., 1987-92, UN's 21st Century Studies, 1986-89, Pa. High-Tech. Coun., Greater Pitts. Reg. Econ. Revitalization Initative, 1994-95; nat. transport policy adv. unit Dept. Transp.; campaign mem. Muskingum Leadership Coun., 1994. Recipient Brownfield Pub. Svc., Pa. Jaycees, 1987. Mem. NSPE, Am. Soc. Quality Control (bd. dirs. Pitts. sect. 1990-95), Def. Preparedness Assn. (bd. dirs. Pa. 1991-95), Pitts. Inst. for the Future (pres., chmn. 1988-90), Assn. Online Profls. (founding mem.), World Future Soc., Am. Entrepreneurs Soc., Congl. Inst. for Future, Western Pa. Conservancy, Gov.'s Scanning Bd., Soc. Internat. Bus. Economists, Inst. Internat. Mgmt. Cons., Econs. Club.

SOWER, VICTOR EDMUND, management educator; b. Roanoke, Va., Sept. 3, 1946; s. Hammond Edmundson and Daphne Muriel (Dymond) S.; m. Judith Lynn Carroll, June 17, 1967; children: Diane C. Sower Fuller, Christopher Hammond. BS in Chemistry, Va. Poly. Inst. and State U., 1968; MBA, Auburn U., 1980; PhD, U. North Tex., 1990. Process engr. Radford (Va.) Army Ammunition Plant, 1968-69; process devel. engring. mgr. Ampex Corp., Opelika, Ala., 1971-80; gen. mgr. Tandy Magnetics, Ft. Worth, 1980-87; mfg. cons. Tandy Corp., Ft. Worth, 1987-90; prof. dept. mgmt. and mktg. Sam Houston State U., Huntsville, Tex., 1990—. Steering com. Ctr. Bus. and Econ. Rsch., Huntsville, 1990—; cons. various mfg. and svc. orgns. Author: Classic Readings in Operations Management, 1995, An Introduction to Quality Management and Engineering, 1999; mem. editl. rev. bd. Jour. Bus. Strategies, Huntsville, 1990—, Jour. Ops. Mgmt., 1995—; contbr. articles to profl. jours. Dist. com. mem. Bedford (Tex.) area Boy Scouts Am., 1987-90, dist. advancement chmn., 1988-89. Lt. U.S. Army, 1969-71. Mem. AIChE, Inst. Supply Mgmt., Am. Chem. Soc., Am. Soc. Quality Control (sr. cert.), Am. Prodn. and Inventory Control Soc., Decision Scis. Inst., Acad. Mgmt. Roman Catholic. Office: Sam Houston State U Dept Mgmt and Mktg Huntsville TX 77341

SOWERS, MARGARET ANN, home economics, family and consumer science educator; b. Pitts., Apr. 4, 1946; d. Richard Conwell and Ruth Eleanor (Springer) Westermann; m. Christopher Herr Sowers, Sept. 20, 1969; children: Heather Ross. BS in home econs., Carnegie-Mellon U., 1968; MS in edn., Temple U., 1974, postgrad., 1994—, Pa. State U. cert. family life educator, 1994. Sub. tchr. Lebanon (Pa.) Sch. Dist., 1981-87, home economics tchr., 1970-74, 84-85; home economics cons. Lebanon County Penn State Coop. Extension, 1986—; home economics, family and consumer sci. educator, curriculum leader Cedar Crest H.S., Lebanon, 1993—. Acting extension home economist, 1988-89, Train the Trainer Pa. Dept. Edn., 1993—; cons. Hershey Foods Test Kitchens, 1995-98; adj. prof. early childhood edn., adviser, facilitator Harrisburg Area C.C., Lebanon, Pa., 1999—. Bd. dirs. Am. Heart Assn., 1988-94, chairperson of Heart-At-Work Task Force, 1987-91, vice chairperson ctrl. program com., 1988-91, chairperson, 1991-94, health and cmty. site com., 1997—; co-chmn. Centennial Anniversary Celebration of Zion United Meth. Ch., Bible sch. tchr., mem. ch. choir, mem. bell choir; vol. Dietitian for Boost II, Lebanon, 1976-78. Recipient Educator's award Dept. Edn. Pa., 1985, Stds. for Excellence Sr. H.S. Home Econs. Program, 1995; named Vol. of Yr. Am. Heart Assn., 1991. Mem. ASCD, Am. Assn. Family and Consumer Scis., Pa. Assn. Family and Consumer Scis., Lebanon County Home Econs. Assn. (pres., v.p., treas.), Pa. Nutrition Coun., Nat. Assn. for Edn. Young Children, Nat. Coun. Family Rels., Family and Consumer Scis. Edn. Assn., Lebanon Valley Assn. Edn. Young Children (treas.), Phi Delta Kappa, Kappa Omicron Nu. Avocations: needlework, recreational activities, food preparation, educational resources. Home: 1015 Franklin Ave Lebanon PA 17042-7112 Office: Cedar Crest H S Cornwall-Lebanon Sch Dist 115 E Evergreen Rd Lebanon PA 17042-7505 E-mail: msowers@mail.clsd.k-12.pa.us.

SOYFER, VALERY NIKOLAYEVICH, geneticist, biophysicist; b. Gorky, RSFSR, USSR, Oct. 16, 1936; came to U.S., 1988; s. Nikolay Ilya Soyfer and Anna A. Kuznetsova; m. Nina I. Yakovleva, Aug. 12, 1961; children: Marina, Vladimir. BS in Agronomy, Timiryazev Agrl. Acad., Moscow, 1957; MS in Biophysics, Lomonosov State U., Moscow, 1961; PhD in Molecular Genetics, Kurchatov Inst. Atomic Energy, Moscow, 1964; D Phys. and Math. Scis., Moscow, 1994. Head Group Inst. Gen. Genetics, Moscow, 1966-70; dir. Lab. Molecular Genetics, Moscow, 1970-79; sci. dir. USSR Inst. Applied Molecular Biology and Genetics, Moscow, 1974-76; pres. Moscow Ind. U., 1985-88; disting. prof. Ohio State U., Columbus, 1988-90; Robinson prof. George Mason U., Fairfax, Va., 1990-93, disting. prof. molecular genetics, 1993—. Sci. sec. Coun. on Molecular Biology and Genetics, Moscow, 1972-80; mem. USSR Govtl. Coun. on Molecular Biology and Molecular Genetics, 1974-80; invited lectr. Halle-Wittenburg U., German Democratic Republic, 1975; prin. investigator USSR State Com. on Sci., 1972, 74, 78, NIH, 1990, Dept. of Energy, 1992, Open Soc. Inst., 1995-98. Author: Molecular Mechanisms of Mutagenesis, 1969, History of Molecular Genetics, 1970, Molekulare Mechanismen der Mutagenese und Reparatur, 1976, Power and Science, History of the Crushing of Soviet Genetics, 1989, Lysenko and the Tragedy of Soviet Science, 1994, Triple Helical Nuclec Acids, 1995; contbr. more than 200 articles on molecular genetics, biophysics and history of sci. to Nature, Science Mutation Rsch., Nucleic Acids Rsch., others. Chmn. bd. Friends of St. Petersburg Ind. U., N.Y., 1990—; pres. USSR Amnesty Internat. Group, Moscow, 1983-88. Recipient Gregor Mendel gold medals of Czech Nat. Acad. Scis. and Czech Soc. History Scis., 1995, 96, N. Vavilov silver medal, Russian Acad. Natural Scis., 2002. Mem. USSR Soc. Geneticists and Breeders (founding), Gt. Britain Genetical Soc., USSR Biochem. and Microbiol. Soc., Internat. Soc. for History, Philosophy and Social Studies of Biology (charter), European Culture Club (charter), Internat. Sci. Fedn. (bd. dirs. 1992-95, chmn. bd. Internat. Soros Sci. Edn. program), Nat. Acad. Scis. Ukraine, Russian Acad. Natural Sci., Am. Soc.

of Biochemistry and Molecular Biology, others. Achievements include discovery of DNA Repair in higher plants; establishment of correlation between structural damages in DNA and mitagenesis rate in higher plants; co-development of the method of photofootprinting of DNA triplexes, the role of environmental contamination in mutagenesis of organisms. Office: George Mason U Ste 3024 D King Hall Fairfax VA 22030

SPADY, BENEDICT QUINTIN, secondary education educator; b. Norfolk, Va., Mar. 17, 1967; s. Bennie Jr. and Beatrice (Sanderlin) S.; children: Quintin Cornelius, Raphawn Malik; m. Michelle Allen. BS cum laude, Norfolk State U., 1992. Cert. tchr., Va. Tchr. tech. edn., asst. basketball coach Tallwood H.S., Virginia Beach, Va., 1992—; head girls varsity basketball coach Bayside H.S., Virginia Beach, 1996—. Coord. Technology Student Assn., Tallwood HIgh Sch. Advancement dir. Norfolk area Boy Scouts Am., 1991—; tutor Bowling Green Recreation Ctr., Norfolk, 1991-92. Mem. Tidewater Turners Va., Alpha Phi Alpha (Boy Scout dir. 1991). Home: 2129 Haverford Dr Chesapeake VA 23320-2521

SPAEPEN, FRANS AUGUST, applied physics researcher, educator; b. Mechelen, Belgium, Oct. 29, 1948; arrived in U.S., 1971; s. Jozef F. M. and Ursula (Roppe) Spaepen; m. Moniek Steemans, Aug. 21, 1973; children: Geertrul M., Elizabet U., Hendrik J. L. Burgerlijk Metaalkundig Ingenieur, U. Leuven, Belgium, 1971; PhD, Harvard U., 1975. IBM postdoctoral fellow Harvard U., Cambridge, Mass., 1975-77, asst. prof. applied physics, 1977-81, assoc. prof., 1981-83, Gordon McKay prof. applied physics, 1983—2002, Franklin prof. applied physics, 2002—, dir. Materials Rsch. Lab., 1990—98, dir. Rowland Inst., 2002—. Vis. prof. U. Leuven, 1984, Deutsches Zentrum für Luft-und Raumfahrt-Köln, 2000, Forschungszentrum Jülich, 2001; chmn. Gordon Conf. on Phys. Metallurgy, 1988; NRC com. on solid state scis., 1990—93; NRC com. on condensed matter and materials physics, 1996—98; Krengel lectr. Technion, Israel, 1994; mem. summer rsch. group Los Alamos Nat. Lab., 1986—99; mem. sci. and tech. steering com. Brookhaven Nat. Lab.; chmn. scientific adv. bd. Netherlands Inst. for Metals Rsch. Co-editor: (series) Solid State Physics; mem. editl. bd. Jour. Applied Physics, Applied Physics Letters, 1990—93, 1999—2001, Applied Physics Revs., 1991—97, Phys. Rev., 1994—99, Jour. Non-Crystalline Solids, 1990—94; editor (prin. editor): Jour. Materials Rsch., 2001—; contbr. articles to profl. jours., chpts. to books. Recipient Best Paper award, Acta Metallurgica, 1994, Humboldt award, 1999, R.F. Mehl award, TMS Inst. Metals, 2002. Fellow: AIME-The Metall. Soc., Am. Phys. Soc. (chmn. divsn. materials physics 1992); mem.: Vlaamse Academie voor Wetenschappen en Kunsten (fgn.), Orde van den Prince, Böhimische Physikalische Gesellschaft, Vlaamse Ingenieurs Vereniging, Materials Rsch. Soc. (councillor 1986—88, 1990—92, co-chmn. fall meeting Boston 1990, chmn. program com. 1993—2000, Woody award 1998), Am. Soc. Metals (lectr.). Office: Harvard U Div Engring and Applied Scis 29 Oxford St Cambridge MA 02138-2901 E-mail: spaepen@deas.harvard.edu.

SPAETH, C. EDMOND, library media specialist; b. Yonkers, N.Y., May 3, 1945; s. Camille and Ida Mae (Therrien) S.; m. Merrill Hunting, Sept., 1973; 1 child, Erin Elise. BA, Mich. State U., 1974; MS, L.I. U., 1981. Cert. sch. libr. specialist, N.Y. Libr. media specialist West Park (N.Y.) Union Free Sch., Valley Central Schs., Kingston (N.Y.) City Schs.; reference libr. Newburgh (N.Y.) Free Libr. Freelance storyteller. Reviewer ABC/CLIO Video Rating Guide for LibRs.; contbr. entries premier edit. Hudson River Almanac; contbr. articles to JeMe Souviens. Chairperson Town of Fishkill Parks Bd.; trustee Mt. Gulian Historic Site. With USN, 1967-71. Recipient Storybook Garden grant. Mem. SLMSSENY (pres., v.p., editor newsletter), Ulster County Sch. Libr. System Bd., Kingston City Schs. Libr. Bd., Beta Phi Mu.

SPAFFORD, MICHELLE, special education educator; b. New Kensington, Pa., June 7, 1964; d. Del John and Joan Elizabeth (Dunlap) S. BA in Therapeutic Recreation, Alderson-Broaddus Coll., Philippi, W.Va., 1986; M in Spl.Edn., Clarion (Pa.) U., 1991. Cert. tchr. mentally and physically handicapped, Pa., therapeutic recreation specialist. Resident care specialist Verland Found., Sewickley, Pa., 1986; child care specialist Luth. Youth and Family Svc., Pa., 1986-87; mental health therapist DuBois (Pa.) Regional Med. Ctr., 1987-90, recreational therapist, 1990-91; supr. Clearfield (Pa.) County Child & Youth Svcs., Clearfield, Pa., 1990-91; grad. asst. Clarion U., 1990-91; spl. edn. tchr. DuBois Area Sch. Dist., 1992—; recreational therapist The Golden Age, DuBois, 1994-95. Perkins participatory planning com. Jefferson Tech., DuBois, 1994—; mem. Sandy Twp. Recreation Bd., 1995—, chair. Tchr. pioneer club Christian Missionary Alliance, DuBois, 1993; tchr., coach Spl. Olympics, DuBois, 1991; advisor Environ. Club, DuBois Area H.S., 1994—; chair Sandy Twp. Park and Recreation Bd. Mem. Council for Exceptional Children, Pa. Therapeutic Recreation Assn., The Wilderness Soc. Republican. Baptist. Avocations: swimming, water skiing, volleyball, cooking. Home: 1229 Treasure Lk Du Bois PA 15801-9029 Office: Du Bois Area Sch Dist Liberty Blvd Du Bois PA 15801

SPAGNOLO, SAMUEL VINCENT, internist, pulmonary specialist, educator; b. Pitts., Sept. 3, 1939; s. Vincent Anthony and Mary Grace (Culotta) S.; children: Samuel, Brad, Gregg; m. Dorcas R. Hardy, Sept. 29, 1996. BA, Washington & Jefferson Coll., 1961; MD, Temple U., 1965. Diplomate Am. Bd. Internal Medicine, Bd. Pulmonary Disease, lic. physician Fla., Calif., Md., D.C., Va., Ariz., Pa., Mass. Sr. resident in medicine VA Med. Ctr., Boston, 1969-70, chief resident in medicine, 1970-71; Harvard Clin. and Rsch. fellow in pulmonary diseases Mass. Gen. Hosp., Boston, 1971-72; asst. chief med. svc. VA Med. Ctr., Washington, 1972-75, acting chief med. svc., 1975-76, chief pulmonary disease sect., 1976-94, chief of staff, 1998-99, dir. respiratory care & sr. attending in pulmonary diseases, 1999—; instr. in medicine Boston U. Sch. of Medicine, Tufts U. Sch. Medicine, Boston, 1970-71; clin. and rsch. fellow in pulmonary diseases Harvard U. Sch. of Medicine, Mass. Gen. Hosp., Boston, 1971-72; attending physician George Washington U. Med. Ctr., 1972—; clin. asst. prof. medicine Georgetown U., Washington, 1975-77; asst. prof. medicine George Washington U. Sch. of Medicine and Health Scis., Washington, 1972-75, assoc. prof., 1975-81, prof. medicine, 1981—, dir. divsn. pulmonary diseases and allergy, 1978-93; assoc. chmn. dept. medicine George Washington U. Med. Ctr., Washington, 1986-89. Cons. in pulmonary diseases The Washington Hosp. Ctr., Washington, D.C., 1977—, Will Rogers Inst., White Plains, N.Y., 1980—, U.S. Dept. Labor, Washington, 1980—, Walter Reed Army Med. Ctr., Washington, 1987; rep. Am. Coll. Chest Physicians to Am. Registry Pathology, Washington, 1981-92; numerous radio tv appearances on Health Oriented Programs; invited lectr. in U.S., Russia, Jordan; chmn., mem. many coms. George Washington U. Sch. of Medicine, George Washington Med. Ctr., VA Med. Ctr., Washington; med. chest cons. in attempted assasination of former Pres. Regan. Author: Clinical Assessment of Patients with Pulmonary Disease, 1986; co-author: (with A.E. Medinger) Handbook of Pulmonary Emergencies, 1986, Handbook of Pulmonary Drug Therapy, 1993, (with Witorsch, P.) Air Pollution and Lung Disease in Adults, 1994; mem. editl. bd. CHEST, 2002—; contbr. numerous articles to profl jours. including Med. Clin. N.Am., Chest, So. Med. Jour., Am. Jour. Cardiology, Jour. Am. Med. Assn., Clin. Rsch., Am. Rev. Respiratory Disease, Am. Lung Assn. Bull., Clin. Notes on Respiratory Diseases, Jour. Nuclear Medicine, Drug Therapy; presenter abstracts at profl. meetings. Pres., chmn. Found. Vets. Health Care, 1998—. Lt. cmmdr. U.S. Pub. Health Svc., 1966-68; founder, chmn. bd. Found. Vets. Health Care, 1998—. Decorated Cavaliere in Order of Merit, Republic of Italy, 1983; nominated for Golden Apple award by med. students Geo. Washington Sch. of Medicine, Phila., 1977; recipient cert. appreciation D.C. Lung Assn., 1983. Fellow ACP (coun. critical care 1983-85), Am. Coll. Chest Physicians (gov. D.C., coun. of govs. 1989-96); mem. Am. Thoracic Soc. (exec. com. D.C. chpt. 1978, 85, 89, mem. adv. com. Tb control, 1978-84, pres. D.C. chpt. 1981-83), Nat. Assn. VA Physicians (sec. 1987-89, v.p. 1989-91, pres. 1992-98), Internat. Lung Found. (pres. 1991—). Achievements include first major review of patient outcome during early history of intensive care units; an analysis of mechanisms of hypoxemia in patients with chronic liver disease; first report of Pneumocystis Carinii Pneumonitis in patients with lung cancer; first prospective evaluation of short course therapy reported in U.S. using Isoniazid and Rifampin; first American report using laser through fiberoptic bronchoscope to treat lung cancer; first report to evaluate continuous intravenous morphine to control pain in cancer patients; description of a simple technique to measure the total lung volume non-invasively using the routing chest x-ray. Office: Geo Washington U 5-403A 2150 Pennsylvania Ave NW Washington DC 20037-3201

SPALDING, HELEN H. library director; BA in English, U. Iowa, 1972, MA in Libr. Sci., 1974; MPA, U. Mo., Kansas City, 1985. Serials records libr. Iowa State U. Librs., Iowa, 1974—76, serials cataloger, 1976—79; head tech. svcs. U. Mo. Kansas City Librs., 1979—85; assoc. dir. librs. U. Mo., Kansas City, 1985—. Coun. Libr. Resources Acad. Libr. mgmt. intern Northwestern U., 1983—84; spkr. in field. Mem.: Assn. Coll. and Rsch. Librs. (pres. 2002—03). Office: Univ Mo Kansas City 5100 Rockhill Rd Kansas City MO 64110-2499

SPANDORFER, MERLE SUE, artist, educator, author; b. Balt., Sept. 4, 1934; d. Simon Louis and Bernice P. (Jacobson) S.; m. Lester M. Spandorfer, June 17, 1956; children: Cathy, John. Student, Syracuse U., 1952-54; BS, U. Md., 1956. Mem. faculty Cheltenham (Pa.) Sch. Fine Arts, 1969—; instr. printmaking Tyler Sch. Art Temple U., Phila., 1980-84; faculty Pratt Graphics Ctr., N.Y.C., 1985-86. One woman shows include Richard Feigen Gallery, N.Y.C., 1970, U. Pa., 1974, Phila. Coll. Textiles and Sci., 1977, Ericson Gallery, N.Y.C., 1978, 79, R.I. Sch. Design, 1980, Syracuse U., 1981, Marian Locks Gallery, Phila., 1973, 78, 82, Temple U., 1984, Tyler Sch. Art, 1985, University City Sci. Ctr., 1987, Gov.'s Residence, 1988, Wenninger Graphics Gallery, Provinceton, Mass., 1989, Widener U. Art Mus., 1995, Gloucester County Coll., 1996, Mangel Gallery, 1992, 97, 2000, 03, Cabrini Coll., 1999; group shows Bklyn. Mus. Art, 1973, San Francisco Mus. Art, 1973, Balt. Mus. Art, 1970, 71, 74, Phila. Mus. Art, 1972, 77, Fundacio Joan Miro. Barcelona, Spain, 1977, Del. Mus. Art, Wilmington, 1978, Carlsberg Glyptotek Mus., Copenhagen, 1980, Moore Coll. Art, Phila., 1982, Tyler Sch. Art, 1983, William Penn Meml. Mus., Harrisburg, Pa., 1984, Ariz. State U., 1985, Tiajin Fine Arts Coll., China, 1986, Beaver Coll., Phila., 1988, The Port of History Mus., Phils., 1987, Sichuan Fine Arts Inst., Chong Qing, China, 1988, Glynn Vivian Mus., Swansea, Wales, 1989, Phila. Mus. Art, 1990, Fgn. Mus., Riga, Latvia, 1995, Woodmere Art Mus., Phila., 1996, Am. Coll., 1997, Cheltenham Ctr. for the Arts, Phila., 1997, Rowan Coll., 1997, Villanova U., 1998, U. Pa., 1999, U. of the Arts, 2001, others; represented in permanent collections Met. Mus. Art, N.Y.C., Whitney Mus. Am. Art, N.Y.C., Mus. Modern Art, N.Y.C., The Israel Mus., Balt. Mus. (gov.'s prize and purchase award 1970), Phila. Mus. Art (purchase award 1977), Toyoh Bijutsu Gakko, Tokyo, Library of Congress, Temple U.; commd. works represented in U. Pa. Inst. Comtemporary Art, 1991; co-author: Making Art Safely, 1993. Recipient award Balt. Mus. Art/Md. Inst. Art, 1971, Govs. prize and Purchase award Balt. Mus. Art, 1970, Outstanding Art Educators award Pa. Art Edn. Assn., 1982, Purchase award Berman Mus., 1995, Artist Equity award, 1996; grantee Pa. Coun. Arts, 1989. Mem. Am. Color Print Soc., Pa. Art Edn. Assn. Jewish. Office: 307 E Gowen Ave Philadelphia PA 19119-1023 E-mail: lesspand@home.com.

SPANGENBERG, RUTH BEAHRS, psychologist, educator; b. Eufaula, Ala., Nov. 17, 1918; m. Karl R. Spangenberg, Mar. 21, 1943 (dec. Sept. 1964); children: Kristin, Eric Karl, Karen, Karla, Kathy, Rudy. BA, Pomona Coll., 1940; MA, Stanford U., 1965. Cert. marriage, family and child counselor Calif. Math. and history tchr. Chaffey HS, Ontario, Calif., 1941-43; psychology prof. San Mateo (Calif.) Coll., 1965-69; pscyhologist, counselor Canada Coll., Woodside, Calif., 1969-85; pvt. practice Palo Alto, Calif., 1965—. Regent John F. Kennedy U., Orinda, Calif., 1985—; founder, pres. bd. dirs. Samaritan Counseling Ctr., Palo Alto, 1989—97; adv. bd. Foothill Coll., Los Altos Hills, Calif., 1996—. Contbr. articles to profl. jours. Vol. DeBakey U.S. Brigade The Uniformed Svcs. U. of Health Sci., Bethesda, Md., 2001; mem. DeBakey Brigade, 2001—; dedicated David Packard Hall Uniformed Svcs. U. Health Scis., 1998; pres. bd. dirs., trustee Meth. Ch. Conf., Calif.-Nev., 1980—93; founding bd. dirs. Am. Musical, Bay Area, 1986—; founder Com. Green Foothills, Bay Area, San Mateo, 1964—; bd. dirs., capital fund chair YWCA Palo Alto, Stanford, 1962—68. Named Ruth Beahrs Spangenberg Plz. in Concord in her honor, JFK U.; recipient Samaritan award, Samaritan Counseling Ctr., 1996, Kennedy citation, JFK U., 1997, Jacqueline Kennedy award, 1999, Lifetime Achievement award, Sr. Coord. Ctr., 1997, WAVE award, GirlSource, 2003. Mem.: Am. Assn. Family Therapists. Republican. Methodist. Avocations: music, gardening, reading, travel, creative crafts. Home and Office: 2100 Old Page Mill Rd Palo Alto CA 94304-1326

SPANGLER, CLEMMIE DIXON, JR., construction company executive; b. Charlotte, N.C., Apr. 5, 1932; s. Clemmie Dixon and Veva C. (Yelton) S.; m. Meredith Jane Riggs, June 25, 1960; children: Anna Wildy, Abigail Riggs. BS, U. N.C., 1954; MBA, Harvard U., 1956; LHD (hon.), Queens Coll., 1985; LLD (hon.), Davidson Coll., 1986, Furman U., 1993; LLD U. N. Carolina (hon.), 2003. Pres. C.D. Spangler Constrn. Co., Charlotte, 1958-86, Golden Eagle Industries, Inc., 1968-86; chmn. bd. Bank of N.C., Raleigh, 1973-82; dir. NCNB Corp., 1983-86; chmn. N.C. Bd. Edn., 1982-86; pres. U. N.C., Chapel Hill, 1986-97; CEO, chmn. C.D. Spangler Constrn. Co., Charlotte, 1997—. Bd. dirs. BellSouth Corp., Atlanta; chmn. bd. dirs. Nat. Gypsum Co., Charlotte. Past deacon Myers Park Bapt. Ch., vice-chmn. Charlotte-Mecklenburg Bd. Edn., Charlotte, 1972-76; past trustee Charlotte Symphony Orch., Crozer Theol. Sem.; past chmn. Charlotte adv. bd. Salvation Army; past bd. dirs. YMCA, Equitable Life Assurance Soc., Jefferson-Pilot Corp.; pres. bd. trustees Mint Mus. Art; bd. dirs. Union Theol. Sem., 1985-90, Assocs. Harvard Bus. Sch.; pres. bd. overseers Harvard Coll., 2003. With U.S. Army, 1956-58. Recipient Liberty Bell award Mecklenburg County Bar Assn., 1985, Alumni Achievement award Harvard Bus. Sch., 1988. Mem. Assn. Am. Univs., Bus. Higher Edn. Forum, Harvard Club (N.Y.C.), Univ. Club (N.Y.C.), Quail Hollow Country Club (Charlotte). Office: CD Spangler Constrn Co Office of Chmn Box 36007 Charlotte NC 28236-6007

SPANIER, GRAHAM BASIL, university president; b. Capetown, South Africa, July 18, 1948; s. Fred and Rosadele (Lurie) Spanier; m. Sandra Kay Whipple, Sept. 11, 1971; children: Brian Lockwood, Hadley Alison. BS, Iowa State U., 1969, MS, 1971; PhD, Northwestern U., 1973. Assoc. dean, prof. in charge Pa. State U., University Park, 1973—82, pres., 1995—; vice-provost, prof. SUNY, Stony Brook, 1982—86; provost, v.p. for acad. affairs Oreg. State U., 1986—91; chancellor U. Nebr., Lincoln, 1991—95. Chmn. Presdl. Adv. Group on Info. Tech., 1997—99, Kellogg Commn. on Future of State and Land-Grant Univs., 1997—2000; bd. dirs. Univ. Corp. for Advanced Internet Devel., U.S. Dept. Edn. Commn. on Opportunity in Athletics, 2002—03; host TV and radio programs, 1973—2003; bd. dirs. Citizens Bank of Pa.; vice-chmn. Worldwide U. Network, 2003—. Founding editor: Jour. Family Issues. Del. White House Conf. on Families, Washington, 1980; Pres., chmn. bd. dirs. Christian Children's Fund, Richmond, Va., 1985—94; bd. dirs. Nat. 4H Coun., 1997—2000. Named Named Outstanding Young Alumnus, Iowa State U., 1982; Woodrow Wilson fellow, 1972. Mem.: Assn. Am. Univs. (com. intellectual property 1997—), Acad. Health Ctrs. (commn. on future of acad. health ctrs. 1996—98), Am. Assn. State Colls. and Univs. (joint commn. on accountability report 1993—95), Nat. Collegiate Athletic Assn. (pres. commn. 1995—97, bd. dirs., exec. com. 1997—2001, divsn. I bd. dirs., chmn. 1998—2001), Am. Coun. on Edn. (commn. on women 1992—95), Nat. Assn. State Univs. and Land Grant Colls. (exec. com. coun. on acad. affairs 1990—91, bd. pres. commn. on info. technologies 1993—99, chmn. 1996—99, bd. dirs. 1997—, chmn. coun. of pres. 1999—2000, bd. chair 2002), Am. Assn. Family and Consumer Scis. (Moran award 1972), Am. Sociol. Assn. (family sect. chmn. 1983—84), Population Assn. Am., Nat. Coun. Family Rels. (pres. 1987—88, Outstanding Grad. Student award 1972), Am. Assn. for Marriage and Family Therapy, Worldwide Univs. Network (vice chair 2003—). Democrat. Avocations: aviation, magic, athletics, public broadcasting. Office: Pa State Univ Office of Pres 201 Old Main University Park PA 16802-1503

SPANN, WILMA NADENE, retired principal; b. Austin, Tex., Apr. 24, 1938; d. Frank Jamison and Nadene (Burns) Jamison Plummer; m. James W. Spann II, Aug. 2, 1958 (dec.); children: James III, Timothy, Terrance, Kemberly, Kelby, Elverta, Peter, Margo. BA, Marquette U., 1974; MS, U. Wis., 1985. Sec. Spandagle Coop., Milw., 1969-89; tchr. adult basic edn. Milw. area Tech. Coll., Milw., 1975-80; tchr. Milw. Pub. Sch. System, 1975-90, adminstrv. intern, 1990-91; asst. prin. Clara Barton Elem. Sch., Milw., 1992-93; asst. prin. in charge Greenfield Montessori Sch., Milw., 1993-94, 1993-94, prin., 1993—2003; ret., 2003—. Del. Inter Group Coun.; instr. Nat. Baptist Congress Christian Edn., Milw. Area Tech. Coll. (MATC); lectr. German Baptist Congress, Wiesbaden, Germany, 2003—. Contbr. articles to profl. jours. Dir. Vacation Bible Sch., Tabernacle Cmty. Bapt. Ch., Milw., 1977-80, bd. dirs. Christian edn., 1981-90; v.p. women's aux. Wis. Gen. Bapt. State Conv., 1985-95, pres. women's aux., 1995—; instr. Wis. Congress Christian Edn., 1982—; asst. dean Wis. Gen. Bapt. State Congress Christian Edn., 1985; mem. sr. retreat com. Nat. Bapt. Youth Camp; fin. sec. Interdenominational Min.'s Wives Wis; CEO Rev. James W. Spann Found. Recipient cert. of Recognition, women's auxiliary Wis. Gen. Bapt. State Conv., 1986, Bd. Edn. Tabernacle Bapt. Ch., 1990, Leadership award, NAACP, 2003; named Educator Yr., Career Youth Develop. (CYD), 2003; named one of Milw. 28 Women of Hon., Calilee Baptist Ch., 2003. Mem. NAACP, Internat. Assn. Childhood Edn. (sec. 1990-92), Met. Milw. Alliance Black Sch. Educators, Nat. Bapt. Conv. (life, del. intergroup coun., Myra Taylor scholar com.), Marquette U. Alumni Assn., Interdenominational Alliance Minister's Wives & Widows of Wis. (fin. sec.), Assn. Women in Adminstrn., N.Am. Baptist Women's Union, Ch. Women United (life, del. to intergroup), Milw. Elem. Principal's Assn., Phi Delta Kappa, Eta Phi Beta. Democrat. Avocations: writing, public speaking, traveling, reading. Home: 1906 W Cherry St Milwaukee WI 53205-2046 Office: Greenfield Montessori Sch 3239 S Pennsylvania Ave Milwaukee WI 53207-3131

SPARKS, CHARLES EDWARD, pathologist, educator; b. Peoria, Ill., July 29, 1940; s. William Joseph and Meredith (Pleasants) S.; m. Janet Lindsay Dehoff, Aug. 18, 1977; children: William, Debra, Robert. BS in Biology, MIT, 1963; MD, Thomas Jefferson U., 1968. Diplomate Am. Bd. Pathology, Am. Bd. Clin. Chemistry. Rsch. asst. Mass. Gen. Hosp., Boston, 1963; intern N.Y. Hosp., Cornell Naval Hosp., St. Albans, 1968-69; resident in clin. pathology Hosp. of U. Pa., 1972-75; fellow in cardiopulmonary medicine U. Pa., Phila., 1975-76; fellow in biochemistry Med. Coll. Pa., Phila., 1976-77; asst. instr. U. Pa., Phila., 1972-75; instr. Med. Coll. Pa., Phila., 1976-77, asst. to assoc. prof. biochemistry and physiology, 1977-82; assoc. prof. pathology U. Rochester (N.Y.), 1982-88, prof. pathology, 1988—. Advisor med. scientist tng. program U. Rochester (N.Y.), 1984-92; attending pathologist, dir. clin. chemistry unit Strong Meml. Hosp., 1982—, chair rsc. adv. com., assoc. chair pathology, 1994—, dir. grad. studies in Integrative Biomed. Scis., 1998—. Contbr. articles to profl. jours.; patentee in field. Lt. comdr. USN, 1969-72. Postdoctoral fellow NIH, 1975-77. Mem. AAAS, Am. Diabetes Assn. (co-chmn. nat. symposium meeting 1988), The Acad. Clin. lab. Physicians and Scientists, Am. heart Assn. (fellow coun. on arteriosclerosis, mem. nominating com.). Office: Dept Pathology U Rochester 601 Elmwood Ave Rochester NY 14642-0001

SPARKS, LARRY EDWARD, elementary school educator; b. Berea, Ky., Feb. 23, 1954; s. Clifton Eugene and Delores Jean (Robinson) S. BA in Elem. Edn., Berea Coll., 1976; exch. student, Newberry Coll., 1976; MA in Ednl. Adminstrn., George Peabody Coll. Tchrs., 1979; Rank I Ednl. Adminstrn., Ea. Ky. U., 1988. Cert. tchr. elem. k-8, prin. k-8, supr. instrn. k-12, Ky. Tchr. Sand Gap (Ky.) Elem. Sch., Jackson County Bd. Edn., 1976-78; substitute tchr. Garrard and Madison Counties, Ky., 1979-80; adminstrv. dir. Ky. Jr. Coll. Bus., Richmond, Ky., 1980-84; tchr. math. and social scis. grades 5 and 6 Paint Lick (Ky.) Elem. Sch., Garrard County Bd. Edn., 1984—, prin., 2002—. Sch. dist. tech. grant writer, 1986-87, mem. dist. tech. com., 1987-88, coord. sch. computer lab., 1984-87, basketball coach, 1986-87, yearbook sponsor, 1986-89, newspaper sponsor, 1990-91, mem. sch. handbook com., 1988—, mem. sch. guidance com., 1990-92, mem. sch. dedication com., 1988, mem. sch. primary action plan com., 1992, mem. sch. tech. com., 1990-94; sponsor Nat. Jr. Beta Club, 1991—; coach Elem. Acad. Team, 1991-95; chmn. Elem. Social Studies, 1994—. V.p. PTO, Paint Lick, 1984-86; mem. Nat. Trust for Hist. Preservation, 1992—, Ky. Farm Bur., Lancaster, 1980—. Coach dist. champions Elem. Acad. Team, 1994, Quick Recall champions, 1994, 95, Future Problem Solving champions, 1995; grantee Garrard County Sch. Dist., 1986-87; reciepient MESA award Ky. Coun. Mathematics Tchr. Elem. Mem. ASCD, Nat. Coun. Tchrs. of Math., Ky. Edn. Assn. (state del. 1984-85), Future Tchrs. of Am., Future Farmers of Am., Berea C. of C., Kappa Delta Pi. Democrat. Avocation: antique collector and dealer. Home: 102 Hughes Ave Berea KY 40403-1072

SPATT, HARTLEY STEVEN, humanities educator, educator; b. Bklyn., Nov. 21, 1947; s. Milton E. and Blanche S. (Bakstansky) S.; m. Wendy Doroshkin, June 13, 1971; children: Martin, Samantha. BA summa cum laude, Colgate U., 1970; MA, NYU, 1971, Johns Hopkins U., 1973, PhD, 1975. Asst. prof. Towson State U., Balt., 1974-76, SUNY Maritime Coll., Bronx, 1976-81, assoc. prof., 1981-87, prof., 1987—, assoc. v.p. for acad. affairs, 1999—2002. Writer, editor A.L. Fierst, Greatneck, N.Y., 1977-80, Reference Works, 1993-2001; bus. mgr. Victorian Studies Bulletin, N.Y.C., 1983—; writer Chernow Edit. Services, N.Y.C., 1985-90. Contbr. articles to Victorian Poetry, Walt Whitman Rev., other profl. jours. NEH fellow, 1979, 82, 86. Mem. MLA, N.E. Victorian Studies Assn. (chair nominations 1985—), William Morris Soc. U.S. (sec.-treas. 1984—), Phi Beta Kappa. Republican. Jewish. Office: Maritime Coll Suny Bronx NY 10465 E-mail: spatt@sunymaritime.edu.

SPAULDING, MELINDA DUNCAN, special education educator; b. Dayton, Ohio, June 23, 1966; d. Thomas Edmond and Ruth Naomi (Benbow) Duncan; m. John Ray Spaulding, June 24, 1989; 1 child, Olivia Hope. BS, Ea. Ky. U., 1988; MA in Edn., Georgetown (Ky.) Coll., 1994. Kindergarten spl. edn. tchr. Fayette County Pub. Schs., Lexington, Ky., 1989-97, primary spl. edn. tchr., 1997—. Co-presenter Early Childhood Conf., Lexington, 1993. Active United Way of Bluegrass, Lexington, 1992-94. Coun. for Exceptional Children grantee, 1993; named Spl. Edn. Tchr. of Yr., Fayette Co., 1994. Mem. Coun. for Exceptional Children, Coun. for Children with Learning Disabilities. Republican. Christian Ch. Avocations: tennis, singing, fashion, football. Home: 203 Idle Hour Dr Lexington KY 40502-1103 Office: Squires Elem Sch Fayette County Pub Schs 3337 Squire Oak Dr Lexington KY 40515-1400 E-mail: mspaulding7@excite.com.

SPEAR, ROBERT CLINTON, environmental health educator, consultant; b. Los Banos, Calif., June 26, 1939; s. Clinton Wentworth Spear and Maytie Izetta (Patten) Gill; m. Patricia Warner, Dec. 15, 1962; children: Andrew Warner, Jennifer Ellen. BS, U. Calif., Berkeley, 1961, MS, 1962; PhD, Cambridge U., 1968. Registered profl. engr., Calif. Sys. engr. U.S. Naval Weapons Ctr., China Lake, Calif., 1962-65, 68-69; from asst. prof. to assoc. prof. environ. health U. Calif. Sch. Pub. Health, Berkeley, 1970-81, prof., 1981—, dir. No. Calif. Occupational Health Ctr., 1980-89, assoc. dean, 1988-91, dir. environ. engring. and health scis. lab., 1991-96; assoc. dean U.

Calif. Coll. Engring., Berkeley, 1994-96; dir. Ctr. for Occupl. and Environ. Health U. Calif., Berkeley, 1992-2000. Vice-chair Berkeley divsn. Acad. Senate, 1998-99, chair, 1999-2000; hon. prof. Sichuan Inst. Parasitic Disease. Contbr. articles on engring. aspects of environ. health to profl. jours. Mem. Nat. Adv. Com. on Occupational Safety and Health, U.S. Dept. Labor, 1986-88. NSF grad. fellow Cambridge U., 1965-68, sr. internat. fellow Fogarty Ctr., NIH, Australian Nat. U., 1977-78, research grantee Nat. Inst. Occupational Safety and Health NIH, State of Calif., 1971— . Mem. ASME, AAAS, Am. Indsl. Hygiene Assn., Nat. Inst. Occupl. Safety and Health (bd. scientific counselors), Assn. Univ. Programs in Occupational Health and Safety (pres. 1984-85) Democrat. Avocation: sailing. Home: 1963 Yosemite Rd Berkeley CA 94707-1631 Office: U Calif Sch Pub Health Berkeley CA 94720-0001 E-mail: spear@uclink4.berkeley.edu.

SPEAR, THOMAS TURNER, history educator; b. Coral Gables, Fla., Dec. 23, 1940; BA, Williams Coll., 1962; MA, U. Wis., 1970, PhD, 1974; postgrad., Sch. Oriental and African Studies, 1976-77. Sr. lectr. La Trobe U., Melbourne, Australia, 1973-80; Charles R. Keller prof. Williams Coll., Williamstown, Mass., 1981-92; prof. U. Wis., Madison, 1993—, dir. African studies program, 1995-98, chair dept. history, 2001—. Reviewer NEH, Social Sci. Rsch. Coun./Am. Coun. Learned Socs., Am. Philos. Soc. Author: The Kaya Complex: A History of the Mijikenda Peoples of the Kenya Coast to 1900, 1978, Kenya's Past: An Introduction to Historical Method in Africa, 1981, (with Derek Nurse) The Swahili: Reconstructing the History and Language of and African Soc., 800-1500, 1985, Mountain Farmers: Moral Economics of Land and Agricultural Development in Arusha and Meru, 1997; editor: (with Richard Waller) Being Maasai: Ethnicity and Identity in East Africa, 1993, (with Isaria N. Kimambo) East African Expressions of Christianity, 1999; editor Jour. of African History, 1997-2001; contbr. articles to profl. jours. Grantee Williams Coll., 1984, 87-89, 91-92, NEH, 1984, Am. Coun. Learned Socs., 1982, La Trobe U., 1976-77; recipient A.C. Jordan prize U. Wis., 1972, Fgn. Area fellowship Social Sci. Rsch. Coun./Am. Coun. Learned Socs., 1970-72, Coll. Tchrs. fellowship NEH, 1987-88, Guggenheim fellowship, 1995-96, U. Wis., 1995—. Mem. Am. Hist. Soc. (contbr. Guide to Hist. Lit.), African Studies Assn., African Studies Assn. Australia (founder, exec. sec. 1978-80), Internat. African Inst. Office: U Wis Dept History 3211 Humanities 455 N Park St Madison WI 53706-1405

SPEARING, ANTHONY COLIN, English literature educator; b. London, Jan. 31, 1936; came to U.S., 1987; s. Frederick and Gertrude (Calnin) S. MA, Cambridge U., Eng., 1960. W.M. Tapp rsch. fellow Gonville-Caius Coll. Cambridge U., 1959-60, asst. lectr. in English, 1960-64, official fellow Queens' Coll., 1960-87, life fellow, 1987—, dir. studies in English, 1967-85, lectr. in English, 1964-85, reader in medieval English lit., 1985-87; vis. prof. English U. Va., Charlottesville, 1979-80, 84, prof. English, 1987-89, Kenan prof. English, 1989—. William Matthews lectr. Birkbeck Coll., London, 1983—84; invited lectr. numerous colls. and univs. Eng., Europe, Can., U.S.; Landsdowne vis. fellow U. Victoria, 1993; Benjamin Meaker vis. prof. U. Bristol, 2003. Author: Criticism and Medieval Poetry, 1964, rev. edit., 1972; (with Maurice Hussey and James Winny) An Introduction to Chaucer, 1965; The Gawain-Poet: A Critical Study, 1970, Chaucer: Troilus and Criseyde, 1976, Medieval Dream-Poetry, 1976, Medieval to Renaissance in English Poetry, 1985, Readings in Medieval Poetry, 1987, The Medieval Poet as Voyeur, 1993; editor: The Pardoner's Prologue and Tale (Chaucer), 1965, rev. edit., 1994, The Knight's Tale (Chaucer), 1966, rev. edit., 1995, The Franklin's Prologue and Tale (Chaucer), 1966, rev. edit., 1994; co-editor: (with Elizabeth Spearing) Shakespeare: The Tempest, 1971, Poetry of the Age of Chaucer, 1974, The Reeve's Prologue and Tale (Chaucer), 1979, Julian of Norwich: Revelations of Divine Love, 1998; translator: The Cloud of Unknowing and Other Works, 2001; contbr. numerous articles to profl. jours. Mem. Medieval Acad. Am., Internat. Assn. U. Profs. English, New Chaucer Soc. (trustee 1986-90). Office: Univ Va Dept English 219 Bryan Hall PO Box 400121 Charlottesville VA 22904-4121 E-mail: acs4j@virginia.edu.

SPEARING, KAREN MARIE, physical education educator, coach; b. Chgo., Apr. 17, 1949; d. John Richard and Naomi (Allen) Miller; m. Edward B. Spearing III, Apr. 28, 1973. BS in Phys. Edn., U. Wis., Whitewater, 1972; MS in Outdoor Edn., No. Ill. U., 1978. Cert. phys. edn. tchr., Ill.; cert. CPR instr., master hunter safety instr., boating safety instr., master snowmobile instr., Ill. Tchr., coach Glenside Mid. Sch., Glendale Heights, Ill., 1973—, athletic dir., 1981—92, 1995—98, chair dept., 1992-93. Hunter safety instr. State of Ill., 1988—, water safety instr., 1989—, snowmobile instr., 1990-2000, master snowmobile instr., 1995, CPR instr., 1996—. Amb. People to People Citizen Amb. Program, Russia and Belarus, 1993; awards chairperson U.S. Power Squadron, Chgo., 1987—93; mem. exec. com. DuPage Power Squadron., 1993—96, comdr., 2000—01, edn. officer, 1996—98, Adminst. Officer, 1998; mem. com. Ill. Hunting and Fishing Days, Silver Springs State Pk., 1993; mem. Outdoor Wilderness Leadership Class, 1997; pres. Allied Ill. Markswomen, 2001—02. Mem. AAHPERD, Ill. Assn. Health, Phys. Edn., Recreation and Dance, Ill. H.S. Assn. (volleyball referee). Avocations: clock collecting, hunting, fishing, boating. Office: Glenside Mid Sch 1560 Bloomingdale Rd Glendale Heights IL 60139-2734

SPEARMAN, DAVID LEROY, elementary education educator, administrator; b. Chgo., June 4, 1959; s. Lee Roy and Florida Lee (Gordon) S.; m. Tina R. Smith, Aug. 20, 1994; children: David Gordon, Dana Naomi. Student, Loyola U., Chgo., 1977-78, Moody Bible Inst., 1978-81; BA in Comm., Columbia Coll., Chgo., 1986; postgrad., DePaul U., 1987-89, Chgo. City Wide Colls., 1988—, Chgo. State U., 1992-93; MA in Ednl. Adminstrn., Governor's State U., 1994. Cert 03 tchr., lang. arts endorsement K-8, adminstrv. 020 endorsement, speech endorsement, Ill. Prodr., announcer, talk show host Sta. WYCA, Hammond, Ind., 1983-88; music dir., announcer Sta. WCFJ, Chicago Heights, Ill., 1988-89; tchr. Evang. Christian Sch., Chgo., 1987-89; truant officer Chgo. Bd. of Edn., 1990-92; tchr. Truth Elem. Sch., Chgo., 1992-99; tchr. 7th grade Richard Byrd Acad., 1999—2002; video instr. dept. learning tech. Chgo. Pub. Schs., 1999—2001; tchr. 6th grade Richard Byrd Acad., 2002; broadcsting instr. Kennedy King City Coll., Chgo., 2002—; master tchr., 6th grade Nat. Tchr. Acad., 2002—03; instr. videography Malcolm X City Coll., Chgo., 2003—. 4th grade facilitator Truth Elem. Sch., Chgo., 1994-95, 3rd grade facilitator, 1995-97, chair dept. sci., 1993-96, chair social com., 1994-95, dir. summer sch., 1994, coord. social ctr., 1994; freelance camera operator Sta. WCFC-TV, Chgo., 1989-92, Ctrl. City Prodns., Chgo., 1992-93, Chgo. Cable Acess Prodns., 1992-93; chief videographer DANA Videofilms Prodn. Co., 1995—, www.danaVideofilms.com. Author: (booklet) Teacher's Opinions of the Security and Safety Climate in Chicago Public Schools at Cabrini Green, 1993; contbr. articles to profl. jours., mags. and newspapers; producer documentaries Spirit Night, The Last Lifeboat. Youth counselor Cook County Juvenile Detention Ctr., 1979-80; scout leader Boy Scouts Am., Chgo., 1992-94, asst. scoutmaster Chgo. Housing Authority scouting program, 1992-95; bd. dirs. ISO Aeronautics Chgo. Bd. Edn., 1994—. Recipient Tchr. Incentive award Oppenheimer Found., 1993-94, 95-96, Rochelle Lee Found. award, 1993-94, 96-97; named one of Outstanding Young Men of Am., 1989, 98; Chgo. Found. for Edn. grnatee, 1993-94, 94-95, 95-96, mini-grant libr. winner Chgo. Pub. Schs., 1998; tchr. honoree Chgo. State of City Address Dinner by Mayor Richard Daley, 1995; honored by visitation by U.S. Sec. of Edn. Richard Riley and Chgo. Pub. Schs. CEO Paul Vallas, 1995. Mem. Chgo. Tchrs. Union, Moody Bible Inst. Alumni, Columbia Coll. Alumni Govs. State U. Alumni, Internat. Platform Assn., United Negro Coll. Fund. Evangelical Pentecostal. Avocations: video editing and producing, freelance filmmaking. Office: Nat Tchrs Acad 55 W Cermak Chicago IL 60616 E-mail: davidLspearman@aol.com.

SPEARMAN, LEONARD H. O., SR., federal official; b. Tallahassee, July 8, 1929; married; 3 children. BS, Fla. A&M U., 1947; MA, U. Mich., 1950, PhD, 1960. Prof. psychology So. Univ. of Baton Rouge, 1960—70, dean lower divsn., 1960—70; dir. div. student spl. svcs. Office Edn. HEW, Washington, 1970—72, dir. div. student fin. assistance, 1972—75, assoc. commr. for student assistance, 1975—78, acting dep. commr. for higher and continuing edn., 1976—78, assoc. dep. commr. for higher and continuing edn., 1978—80, assoc. dep. asst. sec. for higher and continuing edn., 1980; pres. Tex. So. U., 1980—86, disting. prof. psychology, 1986—88; amb. to Rwanda Kigali, 1988—91; amb. to Lesotho Maseru, 1993; exec. dir. White House Initiative on Historically Black Colleges and Universities, 2001—. Mailing: Exec Dir, White House Init on HBCU US Dept of Education 400 Maryland Ave SW Washington DC 20202

SPEARS, DIANE SHIELDS, artist, retired art academy administrator; b. Seattle, May 21, 1942; d. Richard Keene McKinney and Dorothy Jean (Shields) Thacker; m. Howard Truman Spears, Sept. 3, 1977; 1 child, Truman Eugene. BA in Art, English, Edn., Trinity U., 1964; MA in Christian Counseling, San Antonio Theol. Sem., 1986, D of Christian Edn., 1988. Cert. tchr. secondary edn., elem. edn., ednl. supervision, Tex. Instr. ESL Dliel-Geb (Def. Lang. Inst.), San Antonio, 1973-74, Ceta/Ace Bexar County Sch. Bd., San Antonio, 1975-78; tchr. elem. edn., art, music New Covenant Faith Acad., San Antonio, 1983-89; instr. ESL Jewish Family Svc., San Antonio, 1991; tchr. elem. art Edgewood Ind. Sch. Dist., San Antonio, 1992-93, dist. art specialist, 1993-95, fine arts coord., 1995-98, dir. visual arts, 1998-99; tchr. 5-6th gr./art tchr. Pipe Creek Christian Sch., Tex. Owner, operator Art for Kings, San Antonio, 1985—. Illustrator teacher-created materials-lit. activities for young children, 1989-90; author: (art curriculum) Art for Kings, 1987; editor: (art curriculum) Edgewood Ind. Sch. Dist. Elem. Art Curriculum, 1993; exhibited in group shows at Charles and Emma Frye Mus., Seattle, 1966, 68, Centro Cultural Aztlan Galerie Expression, 1998 (Best of Show 1998). Dir. intercessory prayer New Covenant Fellowship, San Antonio, 1980-90. Recipient awards for painting and graphics, San Antonio, 1996-98. Mem.: San Antonio Art Edn. Assn. (1st pl. 1995), Tex. Art Edn. Assn. (1st pl. graphics divsn. 1995), Nat. Mus. for Women in Arts (charter). Republican. Avocations: water skiing, motorcycle riding, sewing, writing. Home: 264 Mountain Dr Lakehills TX 78063-6725 E-mail: dshieldsspears@earthlink.net.

SPEARS, LOUISE ELIZABETH, minister, secondary school educator; b. Liberty, Miss., Feb. 2, 1945; d. Willie and Alice Gray Spears; 1 child, Guy Alice. BSc, Alcorn State U., 1966; MSc, Ind. U., 1969; PhD, U. N. Colo., 1975; MDiv, Garrett-Evang. Theol. Sem., 1983. Cert. African Meth. Episcopal Ch., 90; Tchr. Ga. Tchr. Hazlehurst H.S., Hazlehurst, Miss., 1967—68; tchg. asst. Ind. U., Bloomington, Ind., 1968—70; tchr. Ala. State U., Montgomery, Ala., 1970—72, Ky. State U., Frankfort, Ky., 1972—73, Jackson State U., Jackson, Miss., 1975—81; pastor United Meth. Ch., Keosauqua, Iowa, 1983—85, Detroit, 1985—88; tchr. Clarke County Sch. Dist., Athens, Ga., 1998—; pastor African Meth. Episcopal Ch., various, Ga., 2000—. Realtor Ga. Real Estate, Atlanta, 1989—92; academic adminstr. Emmanuel Bible Coll., Macon, Ga., 1992—93; substitute tchr. Atlanta Pub. Sch., Atlanta, 1994—98; co-chmn. Augusta Ga. Conf., Augusta, Ga., 2001, mem. stewardship commn.; fin. coord. Reach Out and Touch Club, Inc., 2002—03; mem. Athens-Clarke County Commn. on Disability, 2003; mem. career and tech. edn. exec. adv. bd. Athens-Clarke County Commn. on Disability; mem. career and tech. edn. adv. bd. Tech. Prep Awareness, 2003, mem. sub-com., 03. Co-author: National Poetry Book, 1995; featured cover story: Zebra Mag., 2001. Bd. dir. Reach Out & Touch Club, Inc., Athens, 2001—. Recipient Cmty. Svc. award, Reach Out & Touch Club, Inc., 2000. Mem.: NEA, Nat. Assn. Social Studies, Reach Out and Touch Club (fin. coord.). Democrat. African Meth. Episcopal. Avocations: reading, travel, writing, listening, helping. Home: 200 Crane Drive 18 Bogart GA 30622 Office: Alternative Education Program 440 Dearing Extension Athens GA 30606

SPEARS, MELINDA KATHARYNE, mathematics educator; b. Texarkana, Ark., Nov. 21, 1942; d. Marschall Caven and Paula Katharyne (Fenton) Rivers; m. Kenneth Wayne Spears, June 19, 1959; children: Kenneth Wayne Jr., Paula Jane Spears Owens, Susan Lynn Spears Parsons. BS, E. Tex. State U., Texarkana, 1976; MS, 1985. Elem. tchr. Texarkana (Ark.) Pub. Schs., 1976-84, secondary math. tchr., 1984—; adjunct faculty E. Tex. State U., Texarkana, 1987-90, Texarkana (Tex.) C.C., 1994—. V.p. Ark. County Tchrs. Math., 1992-93; participant Presdl. Coun. Awardees Internet Pilot Project, 1995. Sec. Miller County Tchrs. Fed. Credit Union, Texarkana, Ark., 1990—. Recipient Presdl. Award of Excellence in Math. Teaching, Nat. Sci. Found., 1993,Alumni Achievement award E. Tex. State U., Texarkana, 1994. Nat. Coun. Tchrs. Math., Southwest Ark. Coun. Tchrs. Math., Red River Coun. Tchrs. Math., Delta Kappa Gamma. Baptist. Avocations: piano, quilting, gardening. Office: Texarkana Arkansas Sch Dist 3512 Grand Ave Texarkana AR 71854-2232 E-mail: melindas@darkstar.swsc.k12.ar.us.

SPEARS, ROBERT KEITH, principal; b. Paintsville, Ky., July 23, 1951; s. Russell and Ola Jean (Picklesimer) S.; m. Barbara Lyn Finney, Aug. 12, 1972; children: Robert Andrew, Erin Rhea. BA, Georgetown (Ky.) Coll., 1974; MEd, U. Louisville, 1995. Cert. secondary adminstr., Ky. Tchr. Bullitt County Pub. Schs., Shepherdsville, Ky., 1974-77, Oldham County Pub. Schs., LaGrange, Ky., 1977-89, Ten Broeck Hosp., Louisville, 1990-91; dir. edn. Brooklawn Youth Svcs., Louisville, 1991-92; prin., dir. Cropper Day Treatment Alternative/Shelby County Bd. Edn., Cropper, Ky., 1992—. Mem. Coun. on Exceptional Children, Ky. Assn. Tchrs. History, Shelby County Assn. Sch. Adminstrs. Democrat. Baptist. Office: Shelby County Bd Edn Cropper Day Treatment Alternative 8472 Cropper Rd Pleasureville KY 40057-7011

SPEARS, SUZANNA D. educational administrator; b. East Rockaway, N.Y., Jan. 10, 1944; d. Rowland Fredrick and Christine E. (Stefanovich) Schwenker; m. James Lowell Spears, Dec. 28, 1985. BA in Elem. Edn. and Econs., U. Denver, 1966; MEd in Elem. and Early Childhood Edn., U. No. Colo., 1977. Lic. adminstrv. dir. child care ctrs., Colo., human resource instruments and tng. adminstr., Colo. Tchr. elem. sch. Mapleton Sch. Dist., 1966-68; dir. day care ctr., 1968-69; owner small bus., 1969-74; with Arapahoe C.C., 1974-84; dean divsn. extended studies Pike's Peak C.C., Colorado Springs, 1984—. Mem. adv. coun. Project: Going the Distance, Pub. Broadcasting System; south ctrl. regional rep. Instrnl. Telecom. Consortium. Bd. dirs. Women's Resource Agy. Colorado Springs, 1989-92. Named Regional Person of Yr., Nat. Coun. Community Svcs. and Continuing Edn., 1991-92. Mem. Zonta Internat. (pres. local chpt. 1988-90, dir. So. Colo. area 1990-92, dist. treas. 1992—, named Outstanding Zontian of Yr. 1989-90). Home: 309 Howell Ave Brush CO 80723-1731 Office: Pikes Peak Community Coll 5675 S Academy Blvd Colorado Springs CO 80906-5498

SPECHT, ALICE WILSON, university libraries dean; b. Caracus, Venezuela, Apr. 3, 1948; (parents Am. citizens); d. Ned and Helen (Lockwood) Wilson; m. Joe W. Specht, Dec. 30, 1972; 1 child, Mary Helen. BA, U. Pacific, 1969; MLS, Emory U., 1970; MBA, Hardin-Simmons U., 1983. Libr. social scis. North Tex. State U., Denton, 1971-73; reference libr. Lubbock (Tex.) City and County Libr., 1974-75; system coord. Big Country Libr. System, Abilene, Tex., 1975-79; assoc. dir. Hardin-Simmons U., Abilene, 1981-88, dir. univ. librs., 1988—. Apptd. Mayor's Task Force Libr. Svcs., 1995-96. Author bibliog. instrn. aids, 1981-90; editor; The College Man, For Pilots Eyes Only. Mem. mayor's task force Abilene Pub. Libr., 1995—96; mem. Libr. Sci. Art. Bd. for Tx. Recipient Boss of Yr., Am. Bus. Women's Assn., 1994. Mem.: ALA, Abilene Libr. Consortium (chair adminstrv. coun. 1990, coord. nat. conf. 1991, chair adminstrv. coun. 1993, coord. nat. conf. 1993, chair adminstrv. coun. 1998, 2002, coord. nat. conf. 2002), Tex. Libr. Assn. (chair com. 1978—84, sec.-treas. coll. and univ. librs. divsn. 1993—94, legis. com. 1994—), Texshare Ednl. Working Group (chair 1999, 2002, libr. systems act adv. bd. mem. 2001—), Rotary (chair com. 1989—90). Home: 918 Grand Ave Abilene TX 79605-3233 Office: Hardin-Simmons U PO Box 16195 2200 Hickory St Abilene TX 79698-6195

SPECHT-JARVIS, ROLAND HUBERT, fine arts and humanities educator, dean; b. Dortmund, Germany, Oct. 31, 1954; came to U.S., 1982; s. Otto and Waltraud Specht; m. Shawn Cecilia Jarvis, June 15, 1982; children: Alex Jarvis, Elly Jarvis. staatsexamen in German and pedagogy, Staatsexamen in Law and German, Ruhr U. Bochum, Germany, 1982, PhD, 1988. Instr. German St. Cloud (Minn.) State U., 1982-87, asst. prof. German, 1987-89, assoc. prof. German, 1989-92, prof. German, 1992—, dir. Ingolstadt program dept. fgn. langs. and lit., 1984-97, chmn. and dir. dept. fgn. langs., 1988-94, dir. quality enhancement programs State Minn., 1994-97, dean Coll. Fine Arts & Humanities, 1997—. Author: (with H. Walbruck) Deutsch Gestern und Heute, 1986, tchrs. annotated edit., 1986, audio tape program and manual, 1987, workbook, 1987, test series, 1988, Deutsch Aktuell 3 tchrs. edit., 1993, 4th edit. workbook, 1999, Compendium College of Fine Arts and Humanities, 1998, 2000, student edit., 1993, workbook, 1993, tape program manual, 1993, Microsoft Word. Textverarbeitung mit dem Macintosh, 1990, Die Ausbildung des Literarischen Diskurses Friedrich Schlegels zur Zeit der Herausgabe des Athenaeums, 1994, (with Shawn C. Jarvis and Isolde Mueller) Deutsch Aktuell 3, 1998, 5th edit., 2003. V.p., founder Förderverein Ingolstadt-St. Cloud, 1985; bd. dirs. Alexandria-St. Cloud Performing Arts Found., 1997—, St. Cloud State U. Alumni Assn., 1995, Theatre L'Homme Dieu, 1997—, St. Cloud Symphony Orch., 1998-2002, Herberger Coll. Bus., 2000—; mem. coun. Coll. of Arts and Scis., 1995. Mem. St. Cloud Rotary (sec. 1998-99, v.p. 2001-02, pres. 2002-03), Amnesty Internat. Avocations: kids, outdoors, chess, racquetball, motorcycles. Home: 1922 9th Ave SE Saint Cloud MN 56304-2118 Office: St Cloud State Univ 720 4th Ave S Saint Cloud MN 56301-4498 E-mail: roland@stcloudstate.edu.

SPECTOR, DANIEL EARL, historian, educator; b. Pensacola, Fla., Dec. 19, 1942; s. Joseph and Dorothy Margaret (Givens) S.; m. Esta Gelda Rappaport, Aug. 9, 1964; children: Warren Leigh, Susan Artemis (dec.). BA, George Washington U., 1963; postgrad., U. Fla., 1963-64; MA, U. Tex., 1972, PhD, 1975. Adj. instr. Jacksonville (Ala.) State U., 1975-77; chief skill qualification test br. U.S. Army Mil. Police Sch., Ft. McClellan, Ala., 1975-80; supr. edn. specialist U.S. Army Chem. Sch., Ft. McClellan, 1980-82; chief U.S. Army Chem. Sch. Standardization & Analysis Div., Ft. McClellan, 1982-84; dep. dir. U.S. Army Chem. Sch. Directorate of Tng. & Doctrine, Ft. McClellan, 1984-88; adj. prof. U. Ala., Birmingham, 1986—2001; chem. corps historian U.S. Army Chem. Sch., Ft. McClellan, 1988-94; adj. prof. Troy State U., Ft. Benning, Ga., 2003—. Accreditation coord. U.S. Army Chem. Sch., Ft. McClellan, 1984-90; accreditation team chief So. Assn. Colls. and Schs., Atlanta, 1985-90; U.S. Army rep. EURO-NATO nuc., biol. and chem. workgroups, 1984-90. Author: Chemical School Annual Historical Reviews, 1988-90. Mem. Jacksonville Kiwanis, 1981-92. Alumni scholar George Washington U., 1959-63; NDEA fellow U. Fla., 1963-64, NDFL fellow U. Tex. 1972-73. Mem. Middle Eastern Studies Assn., Middle East Inst., Am. Hist. Assn., Soc. Mil. History, Ala. Assn. Historians, MENSA, Temple Beth-El, Scottish Rite, Hiram Lodge, Ala. Master Gardener, Legion of Honor, Chapel of Four Chaplains, Phi Alpha Theta. Democrat. Jewish. Avocations: gardening, fishing, pistol shooting. Home: 1317 7th Ave NE Jacksonville AL 36265-1174 E-mail: drspector@nti.net.

SPEELHOFFER, THOMAS JOHN MICHAEL, mathematics and German language educator; b. Norristown, Pa., July 11, 1946; s. Francis Harold and Carolyn Joan (McGrogan) S. BS in Edn., Villanova U., 1969; MS In Humanistic Edn., Marywood Coll., 1979; postgrad., Telekolleg II, Coblenz and Munich, 1988-90, Inst. Français, Munich, 1989-90, Temple U., Pa. State U., Kent State U., West Chester (Pa.) State Coll. Cert. secondary school tchr., Pa. Vol. VISTA HEW, Washington, 1969-70; tchr. math. Beeville (Tex.) Ind. Sch. Dist., 1970-71; tchr. math. and German Marple Newtown Sch. Dist., Newtown Square, Pa., 1971—; educator Radio Shack Computer Ctrs., Phila. and Bala Cynwyd, Pa., 1981-82, Tandy Computer Ctrs., Munich, 1982. Tchr. adult edn. State Correctional Instn. Graterford, Pa., 1974-76, alternative evening Marple Newtown High Sch. Translator: Die Spinne (screenplay, Robert Sigl), 1989; author: children's computer books; editorial assistance jours. Arithmetic Tchr., Math. Tchr. Mem. exec. com. PTO, Supt.'s Dist. Adv. Coun. Grantee Fulbright Tchr. Exchange, Remagen, Fed. Republic Germany, 1988-89, NSF, 1971, 72, 78. Mem. Fulbright Assn. (life, officer Phila./Del. Valley chpt. 1993-95, pres. 1995-96, 96-97), Nat. Coun. Tchrs. of Math. (life), NEA (del. nat. rep. assembly), Pa. State Edn. Assn. (del. state ho. dels., participant leadership tng. conf., rep. S.E. region mtgs.), Marple Newtown Edn. Assn. (pres. 1983-85, 79-81, chmn. various coms.). Home: 2801 Stanbridge St Apt A-115 Norristown PA 19401-1645 Office: Marple Newtown Schs 120 Media Line Rd Newtown Square PA 19073-4696

SPEER, GLENDA O'BRYANT, middle school educator; b. Uvalde, Tex., Mar. 30, 1956; d. Harvey Glen and Mary (Miller) O'Bryant; m. Weldon Michael Speer, July 12, 1975; children: Janena Lea, Jon Michael. BS, Sul Ross State U., Alpine, Tex., 1978; MA, U. Tex., San Antonio, 1984. Tchr. math. Jackson Middle Sch., San Antonio, 1978-82; tchr. math., computers Bradley Middle Sch., San Antonio, 1982-86, chmn. dept. math., 1986—. Computer edn. tchr. trainer N.E. Ind. Sch. Dist., San Antonio, 1984—; acad. pentathlon coach Bradley Middle Sch., 1988-92; software reviewer Nat. Coun. Tchrs. Math., Reston, Va., 1994. Editor Math Matters newsletter, 1989—; writer curriculum guide: Computer Literacy Guide for Teachers, 1992. Black belt Karate and self-defense instr. Tang So Do Karate Assn., San Antonio, 1994—. Recipient Supt.'s award N.E. Ind. Sch. Dist., 1990, 92, 93, Red Apple Tchrs. award St. Mary's U., San Antonio, 1992. Mem. Nat. Coun. Tchrs. Math., Tex. Coun. Tchrs. Math., Bradley Middle Sch. PTA. Avocations: genealogy, southwest history. Office: Bradley Middle Sch 14819 Heimer Rd San Antonio TX 78232-4500

SPEER, MARY BLAKELY, French language educator; b. Bennettsville, S.C., June 13, 1942; d. Ralph Erskine and Ollie Mae B.; m. Eugene R. Speer, May 22, 1970. BA, Duke U., 1964; MA, Princeton U., 1967, PhD, 1971. From instr. to asst. prof. Boston U., 1969-72; lectr. Princeton (N.J.) U., 1973-75; from lectr. to asst. prof. Rutgers U., New Brunswick, N.J., 1977-82, assoc. prof., 1982-88, prof. Co-author: On Editing Old French Texts, 1979; editor: Le Roman des Sept Sages, 1989; co-editor: Translatio Studii: Essays...In Honor of Karl D. Utti; contbr. articles and revs. to profl. jours. Fulbright fellow, 1964-65; NEH grantee, 1979-80, 88-89. Office: Rutgers U Dept French 103 Ruth Adams Bldg New Brunswick NJ 08901-1414

SPEER, MAX MICHAEL, special education educator; b. Granite City, Ill., Nov. 10, 1949; s. Max J. and Betty L. (Butler) S.; m. Anita Christine Patton, June 12, 1971; children: Michael, Max. BS in Edn., So. Ill. U., Edwardsville, 1973. Cert. tchr. elem. social and emotional disorders. cert. tchr. learning disabled and educable mentally handicapped, Ill. Tchr. middle sch. spl. edn. Granite City Sch. Dist., 1973—. With U.S. Army, 1969-70. Mem. Coun. for Exceptional Children. Episcopalian. Avocations: tennis, bridge.

SPEERING, ROBIN, educator, computer specialist; b. Athens, Ga., Apr. 23, 1937; s. Harry and Effie (Adams) S. BS, U. Ga., 1962, MEd, 1970, EdS, 1974; MRE, Southwestern Bapt. Sem., 1964. Cert. tchr., Ga. Ind. audio-visual equipment specialist, Athens, 1957-69; mgr. Speering Printing Co., Athens, 1965-67, asst. mgr., computer specialist, 1986—; tchr. Oconee County H.S., Watkinsville, Ga., 1968-69, Barrow County Schs., Winder,

Ga., 1970-73, Comer (Ga.) Elem. Sch., 1974-76, Tadmore Elem. Sch., Hall County, Ga., 1976-77, Richmond County Schs., Augusta, Ga., 1977-85, Truett-McConnell Coll., Watkinsville, Ga., 1995-96. Freelance writer, Athens, 1986—. Contbr. articles to newsletters, area newspapers. Tchr. Christian Fellowship Ch., Athens, 1990—. Mem. ASCD, NEA, Ga. Assn. Educators, Printing Industry Assn. Ga., Kappa Delta Pi. Avocations: music, photography, electronics. Home: PO Box 6943 Athens GA 30604-6943 Office: Speering Printing Co 278 Hodgson Dr Athens GA 30606-2962

SPEES, EMIL RAY, philosophy educator; b. Rosiclare, Ill., July 25, 1935; s. Ray Clifton and Mattie (Clemens) S.; m. Edith Calvert, May 15, 1968; children: Edith Elizabeth, Ray Calvert. BA, So. Ill. U., 1957, MS, 1959; PhD, Claremont (Calif.) Grad. Sch., 1969. Asst. to dean of students Claremont Men's Coll.; rehab. counselor Rancho Los Amigos Hosp., Downey, Calif.; dean of student life So. Ill. U., Carbondale, assoc. prof. philosophy, women's studies, ednl. adminstrn. Rschr. in field and in Buddhism. Author: The Academic Profession, 1982, Higher Education: An Arena of Conflicting Philosophies, 1989; contbr. articles to profl. jours. Mem. Am. Coll. Pers. Assn. (media chmn., chmn. internat. student devel. commn., coms.), Soc. for Intercultural Edn., Tng., and Rsch. Internat. Home: 3925 Chautauqua Rd Carbondale IL 62901-7314 Office: So Ill U Dept Ednl Admin & Higher Edn Carbondale IL 62901-4606

SPEIER, PETER MICHAEL, mathematics educator; b. Bklyn., Nov. 4, 1946; s. Fred A. and Herta (Katz) S.; m. Patricia Carol Johnson, Nov. 27, 1976. BS, SUNY, Cortland, 1968; MEd, U. Ga., 1971; MS, Adelphi U., 1975. Dept. chair J. L. Mann High Sch., Greenville, S.C., 1971-72; tchr. Long Beach (N.Y.) Jr. High Sch., 1972-75; tchr., coord. Largo High Sch., Upper Marlboro, Md., 1975-89; tchr. Oxon Hill (Md.) High Sch., 1989-93; prof. Prince George's C.C., 1993—. Tchr. Cmty. Based Classroom, Lanham, Md., 1990; adj. prof. Prince George's C.C., Largo, Md., 1976-93. With U.S. Army, 1968-70, Vietnam. N.Y. State Regents scholar SUNY, 1964-68. Mem. NEA, VFW, DAV, Nat. Coun. Tchrs. Math., Am. Math. Assn., Two Yr. Colls., Md. Tchrs. Assn., Md. Coun. Tchrs. Math. Avocation: travel. Home: 6613 Pine Grove Dr Suitland MD 20746-3527 E-mail: speierpm@pg.cc.md.us.

SPEILLER-MORRIS, JOYCE, English educator; b. Utica, N.Y., Nov. 11, 1945; d. Arnold Leonard Speiller and Sybil (Sall) McAdam; m. Joseph Raymond Morris, Mar. 17, 1984. BS, Syracuse U., 1968; MA, Columbia U., 1969. Cert. tchr., N.Y., Fla. Chmn. upper sch. social studies dept., tchr. grade 6 social studies and English Cathedral Heights Elem. Sch., N.Y.C., 1969-74; adj. prof. Broward Community Coll., Hollywood, Davie and Pompano, Fla., 1982-90, St. Thomas U., Miami, Fla., 1982-84, 90, 99, Miami-Dade Community Coll., 1983, Nova Southeastern U., Miami and Davie, 1983-84; semester lectr. U. Miami, Coral Gables, 1985-98, master tchr., 1990, 92, 94, faculty fellow, 1990-94, mem. curriculum devel., 1991-94. Contbr. presentation to Fla. Coll. English Assn., 1991-92, Wyo. Conf. English, 1991; guest spkr. in field of svc.-learning, 1992-94, 97; cons. svc.-learning curriculum design, 1994; acad. advisor U. Miami, 1994, 95, 96; U. Miami rep. to Ctrl. and South Fla. Higher Edn. Diversity Coalition, 1998; faculty acad. coach football, UCLA. Reviewer textbook McGraw Hill, 1993; contbr. instr.'s manual of textbook, 1994; contbr. poetry to revs., articles to profl. jours. Founder, dir. Meet the Author program, Coral Gables, 1989-98. Recipient V.P. award U. Miami, 1992, cert. recognition West Palm Beach, Fla., TV sta., 1992; grantee Fla. Office for Campus Vols., 1992, Dade Community Found., 1992. Mem. MLA, Nat. Soc. Experiential Edn., Fla. Coll. English Assn., Coll. English Assn., Nat. Coun. Tchrs. English, Fla. Chpt. of Tchrs. of English to Spkrs. of Other Langs. (spkr. conf. 1992), Conf. on Coll. Composition and Comm., Am. Correctional Assn., Phi Delta Kappa, Phi Lambda Theta. Avocations: reading, community svc. Home: PO Box 292104 Davie FL 33329-2104

SPELLMAN, MITCHELL WRIGHT, surgeon, academic administrator; b. Alexandria, La., Dec. 1, 1919; s. Frank Jackson and Altonette Beulah (Mitchell) S.; m. Billie Rita Rhodes, June 27, 1947 (dec.); children: Frank A., Michael A. (dec.), Mitchell A., Maria S. Weaver, Melva A., Mark A., Manly A. (dec.), Rita S. Parks; m. Adrienne Foster Williams, Feb. 14, 2001 (dec. Dec. 2001). AB magna cum laude, Dillard U., 1940, LL.D. (hon.), 1983; MD, Howard U., 1944; PhD in Surgery (Commonwealth Fund fellow), U. Minn., Mpls., 1955; D.Sc. (hon.), Georgetown U., 1974, U. Fla., 1977. Intern Cleve. Met. Gen. Hosp., 1944-45, asst. resident in surgery, 1945-46, Howard U. and Freedmen's Hosp., Washington, 1946-47, chief resident in thoracic surgery, 1947-48, teaching asst. in physiology, 1948-49, chief resident in surgery, 1949-50, teaching asst. in surgery, 1950-51; asst. prof. surgery Howard U., 1954-56, assoc. prof., 1956-60, prof., 1960-68; dir. Howard surgery service at D.C. Gen. Hosp., 1961-68; fellow in surgery U. Minn., 1951-54; sr. resident in surgery U. Minn. Med. Sch. and Hosp., 1951—54; dean Charles R. Drew Postgrad. Med. Sch., Los Angeles, 1969-77, prof. surgery, 1969-78; asst. dean, prof. surgery Sch. Medicine, U. Calif. at Los Angeles, 1969-78; clin. prof. surgery Sch. Med., U. So. Calif., 1969-78; dean for med. svcs., prof. surgery Harvard Med. Sch., Boston, 1978-90, dean emeritus for med. svcs., 1990—, dean emeritus for internat. projects, 1990—, prof. surgery emeritus, 1990—; dir. internat. exch. programs Harvard Med. Internat., 1995—; exec. v.p. Harvard Med. Ctr., 1978-90. Fellow Ctr. for Advanced Study in Behavioral Scis.; vis. prof. Stanford, 1975-76; bd. dirs. Kaiser Found. Hosps., Kaiser Found. Health Plan, 1971-89; mem. D.C. Bd. Examiners in Medicine and Osteopathy, 1955-68; mem. Nat. Rev. Com. for Regional Med. Programs, 1968-70; mem. spl. med. adv. group, nat. surg. cons. VA, 1969-73; mem. Commn. for Study Accreditation of Selected Health Ednl. Programs, 1970-72; chmn. adv. com. br. med. devices Nat. Heart and Lung Inst., 1972; Am. health del. to visit People's Republic of China, 1973; hon. dir. State Mut. Cos., 1990—; mem. com. mandatory retirement in higher edn. NAS/NRC, 1989-91; mem. panel on internat. programs Nat. Libr. Medcine, 1996, 97. Mem. editorial bd.: Jour. Medicine and Philosophy, 1977-90; Contbr. articles on cardiovascular physiology and surgery, measurement of blood volume, and radiation biology to profl. jours. Past bd. dirs. Sun Valley Forum on Nat. Health; mem. ethics adv. bd. HEW, 1977-81; bd. dirs. Harvard Comty. Health Plan, 1979-84; former trustee Occidental Coll.; former bd. overseers com. to visit univ. health svc. Harvard, bd. overseers Harvard Comty. Health Plan, 1984-95; former regent Georgetown U., bd. dirs., 1986-92; former vis. com. U. Mass. Med. Ctr.; mem. bd. visitors UCLA Sch. Medicine; mem. corp. MIT; adv. bd. PEW Scholars Program in Biomed. Scis., 1984-86; bd. dirs. Med. Edn. for South African Blacks, 1985—. Recipient Distinguished Alumnus award Dillard U., 1963, Distinguished Postgrad. Achievement award Howard U., 1974, Outstanding Achievement award U. Minn., 1979, Surg. Alumnus of Yr. award U. Minn., 1991, Disting. Support citation Charles R. Drew U. of Medicine, 2002; named U. Minn. Dept. Surgery Alumnus of Yr., 1991; Markle scholar in med. scis., 1954-59. Mem. AMA, AAAS, AAUP, ACS, Nat. Med. Assn. (William A. Sinkler Surgery award 1968), Soc. Univ. Surgeons, Am. Coll. Cardiology, Am. Surg. Assn., Inst. of Medicine of Nat. Acad. Scis. (chmn. program com. 1977-79, governing coun. 1978-80), Nat. Acad. Practice in Medicine, Am. Assn. Sovereign Mil. Order of Malta (Knights and Dames of Malta), Soc. Black Academic Surgeons, MIT Corp. (life mem. emeritus), Cosmos Club. Roman Catholic. Office: Harvard Medical Internat 1135 Tremont St Suite 900 Boston MA 02120

SPENCE, A(NDREW) MICHAEL, dean, finance educator; b. Montclair, N.J., 1943; BA in Philosophy summa cum laude, Princeton U., 1966; BA, MA in Maths., Oxford U., 1968; PhD in Econs. with honors, Harvard U., 1972. Asst. prof. polit. econ. Kennedy Sch. Govt. Harvard U., Cambridge, Mass., 1971-75, prof. econs., 1977-83, prof. bus. adminstrn., 1979-83, George Gund prof. econs. and bus. adminstrn., 1983-86, vis. prof. econs. dept., 1976-77, chmn. bus. econs. PhD program, 1981-83, chmn. econs. dept., 1983-84, dean Faculty Arts and Scis., 1984-90; assoc. prof. dept. econs. Stanford (Calif.) U., 1973-75, Philip H. Knight prof., dean Grad. Sch. Bus., 1990-99, Philip H. Knight prof., dean emeritus, prof. econs., 1999—. Bd. dirs. BankAm. Corp., Gen. Mills, Inc., Nike, Inc., Siebel Syss., Sun Microsyss., VeriFone, Inc.; chmn. Nat. Rsch. Coun. Bd. on Sci., Tech. and Econ. Policy. Author: 3 books; mem. editl. bd. Am. Econs. Rev., Bell. Jour. Econs., Jour. Econ. Theory and Pub. Policy; contbr. over 50 articles to profl. jours. Mem. econs. adv. panel NSF, 1977-79; mem. econs. adv. com. Sloan Found., 1979—. Recipient Danforth fellow, 1966, Rhodes scholar, 1966, J.K. Galbraith prize for excellence in tchg., 1978, Nobel prize in econ. scis., 2001. Fellow AAAS, Econometric Soc.; mem. Am. Econ. Assn. (John Bates Clark medal 1981). Office: Stanford U Grad Sch Bus Bldg 350 Memorial Way Stanford CA 94305-5015

SPENCE, DIANNA JEANNENE, software engineer, educator; b. Mountain View, Calif., June 5, 1964; d. Ronald Kenneth and Susan (Durham) S. BA, Coll. William and Mary, 1985; MS, Ga. State U., 1996. Tchr. math. and computers Woodward Acad., College Park, Ga., 1985-90; software engr. Computer Comm. Specialists, Inc., Norcross, Ga., 1990-98; ind. cons., 1998—2003; instr. math. and computer sci. Ga. Perimeter Coll., 1999, 2002—; software engr. Knowlagent, Inc., Alpharetta, Ga., 2003—. Tutor, 1994-2002. Mem. Pi Kappa Phi, Pi Mu Epsilon. Jewish. Avocations: travel, writing, music, theater.

SPENCE, MARY LEE, historian, educator; b. Kyle, Tex., Aug. 4, 1927; d. Jeremiah Milton and Mary Louise (Hutchison) Nance; m. Clark Christian Spence, Sept. 12, 1953; children: Thomas Christian, Ann Leslie. BA, U. Tex., 1947, MA, 1948; PhD, U. Minn., 1957. Instr., asst. prof. S.W. Tex. State U., San Marcos, 1948-53; lectr. Pa. State U., State College, 1955-58; mem. faculty U. Ill., Urbana-Champaign, 1973—, asst. prof., assoc. prof., 1973-81, 81-89, prof. history, 1989-90, prof. emerita, 1990—. Editor (with Donald Jackson) The Expeditions of John Charles Fremont, 3 vols., 1970-84, (with Clark Spence) Fanny Kelly's Narrative of Her Captivity Among the Sioux Indians, 1990, (with Pamela Herr) The Letters of Jessie Benton Fremont, 1993, The Arizona Diary of Lily Fremont, 1878-1881, 1997; contbr. articles to profl. jours. Mem. Children's Theater Bd., Urbana-Champaign, 1965-73. Grantee Nat. Hist. Pub. and Records Commn., Washington, 1977-78, 87-90, Huntington Libr., 1992; recipient Excellent Advisor award Liberal Arts and Sci. Coll./U. Ill., 1986. Mem. Western History Assn. (pres. 1981-82), Phi Beta Kappa (exec. sect. Gamma chpt. 1985-89, pres. 1991-92), Phi Alpha Theta. Episcopalian. Home: 1107 Foley Ave Champaign IL 61820-6326 Office: U Ill Dept History 810 S Wright St Urbana IL 61801-3644

SPENCER, ALBERT FRANKLIN, physical education and education educator; b. Pitts., Dec. 31, 1943; s. Albert Clair and Ann Mary (Kielbas) S. BS in Edn., Slippery Rock (Pa.) State, Coll., 1966; MS, Clarion (Pa.) State Coll., 1981; PhD in LS, Fla. State U., Tallahassee, 1985, PhD in Phys. Edn., 1992. Phys. edn. tchr., libr., coach St. John's Indian Sch., Komatke, Ariz., 1976-77, Duncan (Ariz.) H.S., 1977-79; tchr. math. and sci. Army and Navy Acad., Carlsbad, Calif., 1979-80; phys. edn. tchr., libr., coach Baboquivari H.S., Sells, Ariz., 1980-81; asst. men's intercoll. basketball coach Fla. State U., Tallahassee, 1981-83; asst. prof. phys. edn., dir. audiovisual svcs. St. Leo (Fla.) Coll., 1983-86; asst. prof. Atlanta U. and Emory U., Atlanta, 1986-87; assoc. prof. phys. edn./athletics, libr. dir., coach Ga. Mil. Coll., Milledgeville, 1987-90; asst. prof. edn. U. Nev., Las Vegas, 1991-94; asst. prof. phys. edn., dept. human performance/health scis. Rice U., Houston, 1994—. Cons. ednl. tech. Atlanta Pub. Schs., 1986-87; profl. basketball scout Bertka Agy. and L.A. Lakers, 1985-91; deptl. dir. KMart, New Kensington, Pa., 1972-74; dir. athletics YMCA, Kittanning, Pa., 1969. Contbg. author: Twentieth-Century Young Adult Writers, 1994; contbr. articles and revs. to profl. jours. Fundraiser KC, Las Vegas; vol. coach for youth league St. Anthony Elem. Sch., San Antonio, Fla.; scoutmaster Boy Scouss Am., New Kensington. Mem. AAHPERD, ALA, Am. Libr. and Info. Sci. Educators, Fla. Assn. for Health, Phys. Edn., Recreation and Dance, Tex. Assn. for Health, Phys. Edn., Recreation and Dance, U.S. Phys. Edn. Assn., Tex. Faculty Assn., Beta Phi Mu, Omicron Delta Kappa. Roman Catholic. Avocations: writing, golf, basketball, hiking. Office: Rice U Dept Human Perf/Hlth Svcs PO Box 1892 Houston TX 77251-1892

SPENCER, CAROL BROWN, association executive; b. Normal, Ill., Aug. 26, 1936; d. Fred William and Sorado (Gross) B.; m. James Calvin Spencer, Dec. 18, 1965 (div. July 1978); children: James Calvin Jr., Anne Elizabeth. BA in English, Calif. State U., Los Angeles, 1964, MA in Pub. Adminstrn., 1986. Cert. secondary edn. tchr., Calif. Tchr. English Seneca Vocat. High Sch., Buffalo, 1966-70; pub. info. officer City of Pasadena, Calif., 1979-90, City of Mountain View, Calif., 1990-93; exec. dir. Calif. Assn. for the Gifted, 1993-98. Owner PR to Go, 1994—. Sec., bd. dirs. Calif. Music Theatre, 1987-90; bd. dirs. Pasadena Beautiful Found., 1984-90, Pasadena Cultural Festival Found., 1983-86, Palo Alto-Stanford Heritage, 1990-93, Mountain View Libr. Found., 1997-98, Las Vegas Art Mus.; mayoral appointee Strategic Planning Adv. Com., Pasadena, 1985-86; active Mountain View Lib. Found., 1997-98; trainer Clark County Election Dept.; mem. Nev. Arts Advocates. Mem. NOW, Pub. Rels. Soc. Am., Calif. Assn. Pub. Info. Ofcls. (Paul Clark Achievment award 1986, award for mktg. 1990), City/County Comms. and Mktg. Assn. (bd. dirs. 1988-90, Savvy award for mktg. 1990), Las Vegas Art Mus., Las Vegas Opera Guild. Democrat. Episcopalian. Home: 7915 Laurena Ave Las Vegas NV 89147-5064

SPENCER, CONSTANCE JANE, reading educator, consultant; b. Norfolk, Va., May 23, 1917; d. Thomas Sidney and Constance Lydia (Gordon) Richter; m. Harlie S. Spencer, Jr., June 2, 1937; children— Constance Spencer Mathis, Arline Spencer Johnson, Harlie S. III, Thomas, Janice Spencer Baxter. B.S., D.C. Tchrs. Coll., 1956; M.A., NYU, 1969. Cert. tchr., Washington. Tchr. pub. schs., Washington, 1956—, tchr. trainer, 1969-75, asst. dir. reading, 1975-77, tchr., 1977-88 (ret.); cons. D.C. Heath Co., N.Y.C., 1974-75. Author: The History of Norfolk State University, 1935-38: The First Three Years with Director Samuel Fischer Scott, 1993; editor, contbr. Fundamental Reading Skills, 1970, Advanced Reading Skills, 1971, editor, writer curriculum guide, 1972. Mem. NEA, Research Club, Internat. Reading Assn., Coll. Reading Assn. Home: 4907 New Hampshire Ave NW Washington DC 20011-4113 Office: DC Pub Schs 415 12th St NW Washington DC 20004-1905

SPENCER, CONSTANCE MARILYN, secondary education educator; b. New York, Jan. 2, 1942; m. Robert William Spencer, Dec. 30, 1966; children: Keane Thomas, Keith Lyle. BA, U. Calif., Santa Barbara, 1964; MA in English, U. West Fla., 1974. Cert. lang. devel. specialist, preliminary adminstr. Credentialed tchr. Valley Stream (N.Y.) N. H.S.; tchr. Workman Jr. H.S., Pensacola, Fla., Imperial Beach (Calif.) Elem. Sch.; substitute tchr. South Bay Union Sch., Imperial Beach; mgr. Geni, Inc., Pasadena, Calif., Avon Products, Inc., Pasadena; tchr. Walnut (Calif.) H.S., 1985—; pres. Am. Computer Instrn. Inc., Upland, Calif. Grant writer Walnut Valley Unified Sch. Dist., 1986-99, mentor tchr., 1988-2000; accreditation co-chair Walnut H.S., 1993-94. Mem., sec. Toastmistress, Ontario, Calif., 1977-86. Grantee Calif. Dept. Edn., 1987, Walnut Valley Unified Sch. Dist., 1988, Diamond Bar (Calif.) Walnut Valley Found., Rotary, 1994-2000. Republican. Roman Catholic. Avocation: writing. Home: 2238 Coolcrest Way Upland CA 91784-1290 Office: Walnut HS 400 Pierre Rd Walnut CA 91789-2535

SPENCER, EDGAR WINSTON, geology educator; b. Monticello, Ark., May 27, 1931; s. Terrel Ford and Allie Belle (Shelton) S.; m. Elizabeth Penn Humphries, Nov. 26, 1958; children: Elizabeth Shawn, Kristen Shannon. Student, Vanderbilt U., 1949-50; BS, Washington and Lee U., 1953; PhD, Columbia U., 1957. Lectr. Hunter Coll., 1954-57; mem. faculty Washington and Lee U., 1957—, prof. geology, head dept., 1962-95, Ruth Parmly prof. Pres. Rockbridge Area Conservation Coun., 1978-79, 95-98; NSF sci. faculty fellow, New Zealand and Australia; dir. grant for humanities and pub. policy on land use planning Va. Found., 1975; dir. grant Petroleum Rsch. Fund, 1981-82; leader field trip Ctrl. Appalachian Mts. Internat. Geol. Congress, 1989. Author: Basic Concepts of Physical Geology, 1962, Basic Concepts of Historical Geology, 1962, Geology: A Survey of Earth Science, 1965, Introduction to the Structure of the Earth, 1969, 3d edit., 1988, The Dynamics of the Earth, 1972, Physical Geology, 1983, Geologic Maps, 1993, 2nd edit., 2000, Earth Science-Understanding Environmental Systems, 2003. Recipient Va. Outstanding Faculty award Va. Coun. of Higher Edn., 1990. Fellow Geol. Soc. Am., AAAS; mem. Am. Assn. Petroleum Geologists (dir. field seminar on fold and thrust belts 1987, 88-91), Am. Inst. Profl. Geologists, Am. Geophys. Union, Nat. Assn. Geology Tchrs., Yellowstone-Bighorn Rsch. Assn., Phi Beta Kappa (hon.), Omicron Delta Kappa (hon.), Sigma Xi. Home: PO Box 1055 Lexington VA 24450-1055

SPENCER, GAYLE, b. Charlotte, N.C., Aug. 14, 1947; BA in Health and Phys. Edn., U. S.C., 1969, MA in Health and Phys. Edn., 1973; postgrad., U. N.C., Charlotte, 1983, Coastal Carolina Coll. Tchr. Keenan Jr. High, Columbia, S.C., 1969, Saluda (S.C.) High, 1969-70, Hyatt Pk. Elem., Columbia, 1970-72; tchr. high sch. Providence Day Sch., Charlotte, 1973-84, tchr. elem. and mid. sch., 1975-84; tchr. Waccamaw Elem., Conway, S.C., 1984-85, Conway Elem., 1984-85, Homewood Elem., Conway, 1986-93, Horry Elem., Aynor, S.C., 1986-91, St. James Mid. Sch., Surfside, 1994—97, Socastee Elem./Carolina Forest Elem., 97-98. Instr. Francis Marion Coll., Florence, S.C., 1973-74, Coastal Carolina Coll., Conway, 1974-75; dir. Tchrs. Understand Fun and Fitness (TUFF); mem. S.C. Tchr. Forum Leadership Coun., 1992-95; mem. Horry County Tchr. of Yr. Selection Com., 1992, 93, Horry County Tchr. Forum Steering Com., 1994—; coach various jr. high, high sch. and coll. athletic teams; presenter in field; running club coach, staff wellness coord., Socastee Elem., 1997-. Contbr. articles to profl. publs. Mem. Horry County Target 2000 Com., 1990, S.C. Health Frameworks Com., 1992-93; vol. ARC, Am. Heart Assn., Conway C. of C. Named Tchr. of Yr., Homewood Elem. Sch., 1991, 92, Horry County, 1992; scholar Sun News, 1990-91. Mem. NEA, S.C. Edn. Assn. (mem. delegate assembly 1993—), Horry County Edn. Assn. (sec. 1992-94, v.p. 1994-95, pres. 1995—), S.C Assn. Health, Phys. Edn., Recreation and Dance. Home: 182 Watersedge Dr Unit D3 Pawleys Island SC 29585-6449 E-mail: ggator2@aol.com., gspence@ses.sccoast.com.

SPENCER, HAROLD EDWIN, retired art educator, art historian, painter; b. Corning, N.Y., Oct. 1, 1920; s. Clayton Judson and Hazel Leona (McCaslin) Spencer; m. Editha Mary Hayes, Sept. 13, 1947; children: David Hayes, Robert Alan, Eric James, Mark Edward. BA, U. Calif., Berkeley, l948, MA, l949; PhD, Harvard U., 1968. Teaching asst., vis. instr. U. Calif., Berkeley, 1949, 50; chmn. art dept. Blackburn Coll., Carlinville, Ill., 1949-62; assoc. prof. art dept. Occidental Coll., L.A., 1962-68, chmn. dept., 1963—68; assoc. prof. art U. Conn., Storrs, 1968-69, prof., 1969-88, adminstrv. assoc. to dept. head, 1972-73, assoc. dept. head, 1977-79, coord. art history, 1984-87, prof. emeritus, 1988—. Guest curator William Benton Mus. Art, Storrs, 1979—80; mem. planning com. Weir Farm Trust, Wilton, Conn., 1988—89, bd. overseers, 1989—93, 2002—, bd. trustee, v.p., 1995—2002; trustee Lyme Acad. Fine Arts, Old Lyme, Conn., 1993—98. Author: The Image Maker, 1975, Wilson Henry Irvine and the Poetry of Light, 1998; co-author: Connecticut and American Impressionism, 1980, Connecticut Masters, Connecticut Treasures, 1989, A Connecticut Place: Weir Farm, An American Painter's Rural Retreat, 2000; editor: Readings in Art History, 2 vols., 1969, Readings in Art History, 3d rev. edit., 1983, American Art: Readings from the Colonial Era to the Present, 1980; contbr. articles to profl. jours.; guest curator Florence Griswold Mus., Old Lyme, 1995—98, guest co-curator Weir Farm Nat. Hist. Site, 1997—2000; exhibitions include in regional and nat. juried and pvt. and pub. collections. With U.S. Mcht. Marine, 1942—46. Recipient various awards for art, 1941—; fellow Harvard U. Faculty Arts and Scis., 1960—61, Frank Knox Meml., 1964—65; grantee U. Conn. Rsch. Found., 1969, 1974—78; scholar U. Calif. James Phelan, 1948—49. Mem.: AAUP, Conn. Acad. Arts and Scis., Coll. Art Assn., Phi Kappa Phi. Democrat. Avocations: reading, travel, poetry. Home: 426 Peachtree Court Paso Robles CA 93446

SPENCER, HEATHER LEIGH, middle school language educator; b. Barberton, Ohio, Feb. 18, 1970; d. James Allen and Margaret Jane (Boski) Stamp; m. Larry Lee Spencer, June 20, 1993. Student, Un. de Alcalá de Henares, Madrid, 1990-91; BA with honors, Mount Union Coll., 1992; MA, Bowling Green State U., 2000. Cert. K-12 Spanish tchr., 6-12 English tchr., Ohio. Spanish/English tchr., head Spanish dept. Arcadia (Ohio) H.S., 1992-94, girls basketball coach, 1992-93; Spanish/lang. arts tchr. Revere (Ohio) Mid. Sch., 1994—, girls volleyball coach, 1995—. Pvt. instrnl. tutor, Findlay, Ohio, 1992-93, Revere, 2000—; ednl. tour guide, Spain, 1995—. Author, editor: Listen and Learn a Language, 1994, (Am. Bookseller award). Mem. Ohio Edn. Assn., Revere Edn. Assn., Am. Fedn. Tchrs., Nat. Coun. Tchrs. English, Profl. Fgn. Lang. Educators Assn., Sigma Tau Delta, Alpha Mu Gamma, Alpha Chi Omega (pres. Alpha Eta chpt. 1991-92). Avocations: sewing, writing poetry, exercise, hiking, travel. Home: 2052 19th St Cuyahoga Falls OH 44223-1948

SPENCER, JAMES CALVIN, SR., humanities educator; b. Detroit, Oct. 21, 1941; s. Donald and Beulah S.; m. Linda J. Voloshen, Nov. 21, 1987; children: James, Anne. BA, Calif. State U., 1966; MA, SUNY, 1970, PhD in Philosophy, 1973. NDEA fellow SUNY, Buffalo, 1968-70, SUNY fellow, 1970-71; instr. Cuyahoga C.C., Parma, Ohio, 1971-73, asst. prof., 1973-77, assoc. prof., 1977-81, prof. philosophy and art, from 1981. Cons. continuing edn. divsn. Kans. State U., 1986, Case Western U., Cleve., 1973, Ford Motor Co., Brookport, Ohio, 1990, Campus Planning Inst., Cleve., 1991-94, PBS Nat. Faculty Referral Network, 1996—; pres. Spencer Enterprises, Brecksville, Ohio, 1991—; reviewer manuscripts for Wadsworth Pub. and McGraw-Hill Pub. Author: The Nightmare Never Ends, 1992; co-author: Instructor's Manual for the Voyage of Discovery: A History of Western Philosophy, 1996; contbr. articles to profl. jours. Ward com. Democratic Party, Ashland, Brecksville, Ohio, Libertarian Party, Buffalo, N.Y.; vice chancelier Argentier, Bailli de la Chaine des Rotisseurs, Chevalier Ordre Mondial, 1996—. NSF grantee, 1979, 87, 97, 99. Mem. Soc. Wine Educators, Am. Wine Soc. Home: Brecksville, Ohio. Died June 15, 2000.

SPENCER, PRISCILLA JAMES, physical education educator; b. Boston, Aug. 21, 1960; d. Richard P. and Gwendolyn (Williams) S. BA in Psychology, Bates Coll., Lewiston, Maine, 1983; MS in Phys. Edn. Recreation, So. Conn. State U., 1990; PhD in Phys. Edn., Temple U., 1999. Cert. educator in phys. edn. and health, Conn. Counselor Youth and Family Svcs., Westfield, Mass., 1983-85; phys. edn. tchr. Pleasant Valley Elem. Sch., South Winds, Conn., 1989-93; instr. kinesiology Pa. State U., 1998—. Cons. Pub. Schs., Conn., 1991—. Co-author: Popcorn's Travels Across America, 1992; author: Gymnastics for All, 1994. Named Outstanding Elem. Phys. Edn. Program Conn. Assn. Health, Phys. Edn. and Recreation, 1991; recipient Celebration of Excellence award State Conn. Dept. Edn., 1992; Fels Found. grantee, 1995; Pa. State Dept. Health cmty. grantee, 1999. Mem. AAHPERD. Home: 18 Saddle Ridge Dr West Hartford CT 06117-2330

SPENCER, REX LEROY, retired secondary school educator; b. Kendallville, Ind., Jan. 29, 1944; s. Richard Donald and Mildred Francis (Fourman) Spencer; m. Diana Carole Land, Nov. 21, 1981; children: Katie Jo, Emily Paige. BS, Defiance Coll., 1966; MA, Ball State U., 1970. Cert. tchr. Ohio. Tchr. Ansonia (Ohio) HS, 1966-80, 1986—2003, Ansonia Mid. Sch., 1982-86; ret.; 2003. Instr. Edison CC, Piqua, Ohio, 1983—88, Defiance (Ohio) Coll., 1989—92. Named Outstanding Am. History Tchr., Darke County DAR, 1992. Mem.: NEA, Am. Registry Outstanding Professionals, Ohio Coun. Social Studies, Nat. Coun. Social Studies, Ansonia Edn. Assn. (pres. 1976—77, treas. 1991—98), Ohio Edn. Assn., Defiance Coll. Alumni Assn. (bd. dirs. 1976—79, v.p. 1979—80, pres. 1980—82). Methodist. Avocations: golf, bicycling, walking, antique collecting, singing with gospel quartet.

SPENCER, WINIFRED MAY, art educator; b. Tulsa, Oct. 7, 1938; d. Len and Madge (Scofield) S. BA in Comml. Art, U. Tulsa, 1961. Cert. comml. art, K-12 art, English/journalism tchr. Freelance comml. artist, Tulsa, 1962-63; art/sci. educator Pleasant Porter Elem., Tulsa, 1963-65; art educator, supervising tchr. Kendall Elem. Kendall Elem., Tulsa, 1965-70; art educator, team leader pilot program Bunche Elem., Tulsa, 1970-75; art educator Carnegie Elem., Tulsa, 1975-81; art educator, fine arts dept. chair Foster Jr. High, Tulsa, 1982-83, Foster Mid. Sch., 1983-97; freelance comml. artist, photographer Tulsa, 1997—2002. Judge Okla. Wildlife Arts Festival, Okla. Wildlife Assn., Tulsa, 1988; supervising tchr., tchr. tng. U. Tulsa, 1965-70, Northeastern State U., Tahlequah, Okla, 1965-70; pres. Tulsa Elem. Art Tchrs., Tulsa Pub. Schs., 1967-68, curriculum writing/curriculum cons., 1970-75, 91—; coord. summer arts/artists in the schs. program Tchr. Adv. Bd., Summer Arts Tulsa Arts and Humanities Coun., 1986-94. Exhibited in group shows at Tulsa City-County Ctrl. Libr., 1989, Philbrook Art Mus., 1993-94, Gillies Art Show, Gilcrease Mus., 1999. Mem. Rep. Nat. Com., 1994-96, 2000; art adv. PTA, Tulsa, 1970—; mem. Christian Sci. Ch., Tulsa, 1960-2002; mem. task force on cultural affairs Tulsa Goals for Tomorrow, 1995-98; del. Arts Edn. Summit Arts at the Core of Learning: Organizing for Action, Arts and Humanities Coun., Tulsa, 1998; mem. Gillies docent program Gilcrease Mus., Tulsa, 1999, 2000, 2001. Invited U.S.-China Joint Conf. on Edn., Citizen Amb. Program People to People Internat., 1992, U.S.-Spain Joint Conf. on Edn., 1995. Mem. AAUW, NEA, Okla. Edn. Assn., Okla. Mid. Level Edn. Assn. (del. 1994), Nat. Art Edn. Assn. (del. 1992, 94, 96), Okla. Art Edn. Assn., Internat. Platform Assn., Libr. of Congress Assn. Avocation: travel. Home and Office: 439 S Memorial Dr Tulsa OK 74112-2203

SPERBER, MARILYN JANICE, special education educator; b. N.Y.C., Feb. 24, 1947; d. Max Schuman and Doris (Behr) Schuman Friedman; m. Mark Victor Sperber, Mar. 24, 1968; children: Dustin Cory, Jonathan Kyle. BS in Edn., SUNY, New Paltz, 1968, MS in Spl. Edn., 1976; postgrad., Fordham U., 1989-90. Cert. elem. tchr., K-12 spl. edn. tchr., N.Y. Elem. tchr. Mamaroneck (N.Y.) Ctrl. Sch., 1968-69, N.Y.C. Pub. Schs., 1969-70; edn. therapist Astor Day Treatment Ctr., Poughkeepsie, N.Y., 1976-80; spl. educator The Children's Annex, Kingston, N.Y., 1980-84; instr. Jr. Coll. of Albany, N.Y., 1984-87; spl. educator R.C.G. BOCES, Castleton, N.Y., 1984-87; asst. prof. Sullivan County C.C., Loch Sheldrake, N.Y., 1987-95; spl. educator resource rm. Benjamin Cosor Elem. Sch., Fallsburg, N.Y., 1987—. Author: Why Am I Doing This?, 1998. Grantee Fallsburg Ctrl. Schs., 1991, Hudson Valley Portfolio Project, 1993-96. Mem. Fallsburg Tchrs. Assn. (asst. treas. 1990—), Sullivan Reading Coun., N.Y. State Reading Coun., Phi Delta Kappa. Avocations: bicycling, walking, aquasize, skiing. Home: 96 Edwards Rd Monticello NY 12701-3420 Office: Benjamin Cosor Elem Sch Brickman Rd Fallsburg NY 12733

SPERDUTO, LEONARD ANTHONY, mathematics educator; b. Philadelphia, Jan. 19, 1958; s. Anthony and Lena (Maio) S. AAS, Camden County Coll., Blackwood, N.J., 1982, 87; BA, Rutgers U., 1989. Cert. tchr. math., N.J. Math. tutor Rutgers U., Camden, N.J., 1987-89; substitute tchr. Maple Shade (N.J.) Bd. Edn., 1989-90; math. tutor Camden County Coll., Blackwood, 1992-94, adj. instr. basic skills math., 1992—. Mem. Nat. Coun. Tchrs. Math. Home: 6849 Clark Ave Camden NJ 08110-6101 Office: Camden County Coll PO Box 200 Blackwood NJ 08012-0200

SPERELAKIS, NICHOLAS, SR., physiology and biophysics educator, researcher; b. Joliet, Ill., Mar. 3, 1930; s. James and Aristea (Kayaidakis) S.; m. Dolores Martinis, Jan. 28, 1960; children: Nicholas Jr., Mark (dec.), Christine, Sophia, Thomas, Anthony. BS in Chemistry, U. Ill., 1951, MS in Physiology, 1955, PhD in Physiology, 1957. Teaching asst. U. Ill., Urbana, 1954-57; instr. Case Western Res. U., Cleve., 1957-59, asst. prof., 1959-66, assoc. prof., 1966; prof. U. Va., Charlottesville, 1966-83; Joseph Eichberg prof. physiology Coll. Medicine U. Cin., 1983-96, chmn. dept., 1983-93, Eichberg prof. emeritus, 1996—. Cons. NPS Pharm., Inc., Salt Lake City, 1988-95, Carter Wallace, Inc. Cranbury, N.J., 1988-91; vis. prof. U. St. Andrews, Scotland, 1972-73, U. San Luis Potosi, Mex., 1986, U. Athens, Greece, 1994; Rosenblueth prof. Centro de Investigacion y Avanzades, Mex., 1972; mem. sci. adv. com. several internat. meetings, editl. bds. numerous sci. jours. Co-editor: Handbook of Physiology: Heart, 1979; editor: Physiology and Pathophysiology of the Heart, 1984, 2d edit., 1988, 3rd edit., 1994, 4th edit., 2000, Calcium Antagonists: Mechanisms of Action on Cardiac Muscle and Vascular Smooth Muscle, 1984, Cell Interactions and Gap Junctions, vols. I and II, 1989, Frontiers in Smooth Muscle Research, 1990, Ion Channels in Vascular Smooth Muscle and Endothelial Cells, 1991, Essentials of Physiology, 1993, 2d edit., 1996, Cell Physiology Source Book, 1995 (Outstanding Acad. Book, Choice Am. Libr. Assn. 1996, 98), 3d edit., 2001, Electrogenesis of Biopotentials, 1995; assoc. editor Circulation Rsch., 1970-75, 75-80, Molecular Cellular Cardiology; regional editor Current Drug Targets, 2000-2002; contbr. articles to profl. jours. Lectr. Project Hope, Peru, 1962. Sgt. USMC, 1951-53, Res., 1953-59. Recipient Disting. Alumnus award Rockdale (Ill.) Pub. Schs., 1958, Rsch. Excellence award Am. Heart Assn. Ohio, 1995, Visionary award Am. Heart Assn., S.W. Ohio, 1995; U. Cin. Grad. fellow, 1989; NIH grantee, 1959-99. Mem. IEEE, Engring. in Medicine and Biology, Am. Physiol. Soc. (chair steering com. sect. 1981-82), Biophys. Soc. (coun. 1990-93), Am. Soc. Pharmacology and Exptl. Therapeutics, Internat. Soc. Heart Rsch. (coun. 1980-89, 92-98), Am. Hellenic Ednl. Progressive Assn. (pres. Charlottesville chpt. 1980-82), Ohio Physiol. Soc. (pres. 1990-91), Phi Kappa Phi. Independent. Greek Orthodox. Avocations: ancient coins, stamp collecting. Office: U Cin Coll Medicine 231 Bethesda Ave Cincinnati OH 45229-2827

SPERLING, GEORGE, cognitive scientist, educator; s. Otto and Melitta Sperling BS in Math., U. Mich., 1955; MA in Psychology, Columbia U., 1956; PhD in Psychology, Harvard U., 1959. Rsch. asst. in biophysics Brookhaven Nat. Labs., Upton, N.Y., summer 1955; rsch. asst. in psychology Harvard U., Cambridge, Mass., 1957-59; mem. tech. rsch. staff Acoustical and Behavioral Rsch. Ctr., AT&T Bell Labs., Murray Hill, N.J., 1958-86; prof. psychology and neural sci. NYU, N.Y.C., 1970-92; disting. prof. cognitive scis., neurobiology and behavior U. Calif., Irvine, 1992—. Instr. psychology Washington Sq. Coll., NYU, 1962-63; vis. assoc. prof. psychology Duke U., spring 1964; adj. assoc. prof. psychology Columbia U., 1964-65; acting assoc. prof. psychology UCLA, 1967-68; hon. rsch. assoc. Univ. Coll., U. London, 1969-70; vis. prof. psychology U. Western Australia, Perth, 1972, U. Wash., Seattle, 1977; vis. scholar Stanford (Calif.) U., 1984; mem. sci. adv. bd. USAF, 1988-92. Recipient Meritorious Civilian Svc. medal USAF, 1993; Gomberg scholar U. Mich., 1953-54; Guggenheim fellow, 1969-70, APS fellow. Fellow: APA (Disting. Sci. Contbn. award 1988), AAAS, Am. Psychol. Soc. (William James fellow), Optical Soc. Am. (Tillyer award 2002), Am. Acad. Arts and Sci.; mem.: NAS, Soc. Math. Psychology (chmn. 1983—84, exec. bd. 1979—85), Soc. Exptl. Psychologists (Warren medal 1996), Psychonomic Soc., Soc. Computers in Psychology (steering com. 1974—78), Eastern Psychol. Assn. (bd. dirs. 1982—85), Ann. Interdisciplinary Conf. (founder, organizer 1975—), Assn. Rsch. in Vision and Ophthalmology, Sigma Xi, Phi Beta Kappa. Office: U Calif SS Plz A Dept Cognitive Scis Irvine CA 92697-5100 E-mail: sperling@uci.edu.

SPERLING, MARYLIN KURLAN, early childhood education educator; b. Bklyn., Dec. 22, 1940; d. Harvey and Ann (Crane) Kurlan; m. Norman M. Sperling, May 28, 1966; children: Harvey Jonathan, Elissa Sperling Lazev. BA in Edn., CUNY, 1962, MS in Early Childhood Edn., 1965. Cert. nursery-grade 2 tchr., N.Y.; lic. early childhood tchr., N.Y.C. Tchr. kindergarten Pub. Sch. 38K, Bklyn., 1962-67, tchr. grade 1 and 2, 1978-80; tchr. kindergarten Pub. Sch. 82Q, Jamaica, N.Y., 1981-84, Pub. Sch. 30Q, Jamaica, 1984-87; tchr. pre-kindergarten Pub. Sch. 182, Jamaica, 1987—2001. Workshop leader Impact II, N.Y.C. Bd. Edn., 1987; AFT del. convs., Cin., 1996, Washington, 1997, New Orleans, 1998, Niagara Falls, N.Y., 1999, Phila., 2000, Washington, 2003; mem. Dist. 28 com. N.Y.C. Universal Pre-Kindergarten, 1998-99; del. NY State United Tchrs. Conv. 1996, 98, 2000, 02. Exhibited in group shows at Cork Gallery, N.Y.C. Art Tchr.'s Assn., 1983, Bronx (N.Y.) Mus., 1984; contbr. articles to profl. jours., mags. Grantee N.Y.C. Bd. Edn., 1987, 89, 91, 93, 95. Avocations: photography, painting, singing, guitar and keyboard. Home: 73-07 177th St Fresh Meadows NY 11366

SPERLING, MINDY TOBY, social sciences and bilingual education educator; b. N.Y.C., Dec. 21, 1954; d. Albert and Jeanette (Klein) Goldweit; m. Jonathan Sperling, June 15, 1980; children: Joshua, Elliot Asher. BS, Cornell U., 1976; MA, New Sch. Social Rsch., 1978; PhD, Yeshiva U., 1989. Rsch. asst. Cornell U., Ithaca, N.Y., 1975; nursery sch. tchr. Women's and Children's Ctr., Pearl River, N.Y., 1976-77; instr. Cen. Colombo-Americano, Medellin, Colombia, 1979; translator Escuela Nacional de Salud Publica, Medellin, 1979; trilingual exec. sec. Bank Leumi Trust Co. N.Y., 1979-82; intern psychol. rsch. pediatrics unit Columbia Presbyn. Hosp., N.Y.C., 1983-84; adj. prof. Internat. Overseas Program, Coll. Edn. U. Ala., Tuscaloosa, 1984-85; instr. Yeshiva U., N.Y.C., 1985-89; program evaluation cons. multicultural edn. Office of Rsch. Evaluation and Assessment, Bklyn., 1990-91, field cons. spl. rsch. div., study on ltd. English proficient students, 1990-91. Adj. prof. Multicultural Ctr. Jersey City State Coll., summer 1990, bilingual/ESL program dept. langs. and culture, William Paterson Coll., Wayne, N.J., 1990-91; part-time faculty dept. English/fgn. langs., Howard C.C., 1993-94; bilingual listed leader Columbia II La Leche League, 1992-97; founder La Leche League of Savage/No. Laurel, 1993-97; provider instrnl. svcs. to non-English speaking students Elkridge (Md.) Elem. Sch., 1992-93; rep. N.Am. Conf. Ethiopian Jewry, Beinei'nu (Between Us) Project, 1992-93; tchr. hands-on-sci. outreach program Bollman Bridge Elem. Sch., 1993; coord. Chaverim Bi'Golah Program Consolidated Religious Sch., Md., 1992-94; part-time faculty, lectr. dept. Spanish and Portuguese U. Md., 1994—; adj. prof. U. Md. Univ. Coll., 1994-95, 97—; tchr. rep. Summer Abroad program in Taxco, Mex., U. Md.; invited mem. serving on the fgn. lang./ESL adv. coms., Howard County Bd. Edn., 1995-96, Magic Cir. Pre-Kindergarten, Running Brook Elem. Sch., FACTS; translator for sch. and cmty. programs Running Brook Elem. Sch., 1995-96; ESL tchr., program cons., bilingual tchr. of ednl. devel. and tchr. kindergarten readiness Family and Cmty. Together with Schs., 1995-96; grant application reviewer, field reader, panel expert U.S. Dept. Edn., 1995; presenter in field; cons. in field. Translator Further Studies on Family Formation Patterns and Health, 1981; reviewer in field; contbr. articles to profl. jours., poetry to mags. Storyteller Queensboro Pub. Libr., 1987-88; bilingual leader La Leche League Ctrol. Queens, 1991; mem. N.Y.C. Storytelling Ctr., 1987-88; bilingual project coord./parent liaison Dual Lang. Enrichment Program, Brook Ave. Sch., Bay Shore, N.Y., 1990-91; bilingual storyteller Bollman Bridge Elem. Sch., 1991-94; instr. Spanish classes on maternal child health topics for expectant parents Howard County Health Dept., 1994-95; water safety/swim instr. Columbia Swim Ctr., ARC, 1994—; coord. Beth Shalom Youth Group grades 3-5 pre-Passover get-together, 1996; invited guest spkr. Bollman Bridge Elem. Sch. Swim Fitness and Safety at Waterfronts for Wellness Day, 1996; tchr. conversational Hebrew Level VIII, coord. Israeli pen pal project at the Howard County Jewish Cmty. Sch., 1995-96; swim instr. Beth Tifiloh Camps, Balt., summer, 1996, Columbia Swim Ctr., 1993—98; parent liaison middle sch. parent adv. coun. Patuxent Valley Middle Sch., 1997—. U.S. Dept. Edn. fellow Yeshiva U., 1982-85; recipient Outstanding Tchr. award, cert. U. Md. Panhellenic Assn., 1994, Balt. Jewish Coun. for Ednl. Svcs. grant to attend Coun. on Alternatives in Jewish Edn. Conf. in Jerusalem, Israel, 1996. Mem. APA, AAAS, MLA, Psychology Soc. (chair 1977-78), Soc. Rsch. Child Devel., N.Y. Acad. Scis., Internat. Platform Assn., Nat. Assn. Bilingual Edn., Am. Acad. Polit. and Social Sci., Rockland Coun. for Young Children. Home: 9537 Sea Shadow Columbia MD 21046-2060 Office: U Md Dept Spanish and Portugese 2215 Juan Ram 332N Jim 248nez College Park MD 20742-0001 also: University Blvd At Adelphi Rd College Park MD 20742-0001

SPERO, DIANE FRANCES, school director; b. Glen Ridge, N.J., Sept. 4, 1949; d. Gerard Anthony and Frances Dolores (Duffy) Racioppi; m. John David Spero, Feb. 21, 1971; children: John, Lisa. BA in Elem. Edn., Trenton (N.J.) State Coll., 1971; postgrad., Ariz. State U. Tchr. Mount Laurel (N.J.) Twp. Schs., 1971-75, Chandler (Ariz.) Unified Schs., 1975-77, Madison Sch. Dist., Phoenix, 1977-78; dir., tchr. Creative Art Sch. for Youth, Scottsdale, Ariz., 1985—. Choir dir., youth choir dir. St. Patricks Ch., Scottsdale, 1986-92; vol. Am. Diebetes Assn., 1990—, Am. Cancer Soc., 1990-93. Mem. ASCD, Nat. Assn. for the Edn. of Young Children, Ariz. assn. for the Edn. of Young Children, Assn. for Childhood Edn. Internat. Roman Catholic. Avocations: writing musical shows, reading. Office: CASY Country Day Sch 7214 E Jenan Dr Scottsdale AZ 85260-5416 Home: 10398 E Mark Ln Scottsdale AZ 85255-7308

SPERO, KEITH ERWIN, lawyer, educator; b. Cleve., Aug. 21, 1933; s. Milton D. and Yetta (Silverstein) S.; m. Carol Kohn, July 4, 1957 (div. 1974); children: Alana, Scott, Susan; m. Karen Weaver, Dec. 28, 1975. BA, Western Res. U., 1954, LLB, 1956. Bar: Ohio 1956. Assoc. Sindell, Sindell & Bourne, Cleve., 1956-57, Sindell, Sindell, Bourne, Markus, Cleve., 1960-64; ptnr. Sindell, Sindell, Bourne, Markus, Stern & Spero, Cleve., 1964-74, Spero & Rosenfield, Cleve., 1974-76, Spero, Rosenfeld & Bourne, LPA, Cleve., 1977-79, Spero & Rosenfield Co. LPA, 1979—. Tchr. bus. law U. Md. overseas div., Eng., 1958-59; lectr. Case-Western Res. U., 1965-69; instr.; nat. panel arbitrators Am. Arbitration Assn. Author: The Spero Divorce Folio, 1966, Hospital Libaiblity for Acts of Professional Negligence, 1979. Trustee Western Res. Hist. Soc., 1984—2000, exec. com., 1992—2000; v.p., chmn. libr. display and collections com. Western Res. Hist. Soc, 1992—95, chmn. history mus. com., 1995—99; commodore Dugway Creek Yacht Club, 1985—87; bd. dirs. Vail Valley Inst., 2000—. 1st lt. JAG USAF, 1957—60, capt. Res. USAF, 1960—70. Fellow Am. Acad. Matrimonial Lawyers; mem. ABA, Ohio Bar Assn., Cleve. Bar Assn., Cuyahoga County Bar Assn., Ohio Acad. Trial Lawyers (pres. 1970-71), Assn. Trial Lawyers Am. (state committeeman 1971-75, bd. govs. 1975-79, sec. family law litigation sect. 1975-76, vice-chmn. 1976-77, chmn. 1977-79), Am. Bd. Trial Advs., Order of Coif, Masons, Sonnenalp Golf Club (Edwards, Colo.), Phi Beta Kappa, Zeta Beta Tau, Tau Epsilon Rho. Jewish. (trustee, v.p. congregation 1972-78). Office: 440 Leader Bldg E 6th and Superior Cleveland OH 44114-1214 E-mail: keith@vail.net.

SPETH, GERALD LENNUS, education and business consultant; b. Logan, Utah, July 14, 1934; s. Fredrick William and Elizabeth LaVern (Nuttall) S.; m. Dora Goff, Aug. 11, 1955; children: Camille, Michael Gerald, Mark Alan, Janell, Doreen. BS, Utah State U., 1956; MBA, Ind. U., 1969; EdD, Ball State U., 1988. Auditor Ernst & Ernst, Salt Lake City, 1956, 58-59; officer 1st and 2d lt. U.S. Army, 1956-58, officer capt. to col., 1959-82; controller Columbia Club, Indpls., 1982-83; sr. v.p. Allied Fidelity Corp., Indpls., 1983-85; adj. faculty Ind. Cen. U., Indpls., 1982-85; prof., dir. grad. bus. progs. U. Indpls., 1985-2001. Cons. in field. Counselor in stake presidency, bishop, area welfare dir., mission pres., high councilor LDS Ch., 1965—. Decorated Legion of Merit, Bronze Star medal. Mem. Am. Soc. Mil. Comptrollers, U.S. Govt. Accts. Assn., Beta Gamma Sigma, Sigma Iota Epsilon, Alpha Kappa Psi, Kappa Delta Psi, Delta Mu Delta. Home: 8337 Goldfinch Cir Indianapolis IN 46256-1629 Office: U Indpls 1400 E Hanna Ave Indianapolis IN 46227-3630 E-mail: speth@uindy.edu.

SPEWOCK, THEODOSIA GEORGE, principal, reading specialist, educator; b. Canton, Ohio, Sept. 11, 1951; d. George Eleftherios and Despina George (Ilvanakis) Sideropoulos; m. Michael Andrew Spewock, Aug. 23, 1974. BS, Kent State U., 1974; MEd in Reading, Pa. State U., 1978; postgrad., Ind. U. of Pa., 1989, 94, Pa. State U. Cert in early childhood edn., cert. elem. prin., Pa. Tchr. Winnisquam Regional Sch. Dist., Tilton, N.H., 1974-77; reading specialist Tyrone (Pa.) Area Sch. Dist., 1978-80, home-sch. liaison, 1980-98, title 1 coord., 1994—, elem. sch. prin., 1998—. Chair adv. bd. Family Ctr., Tyrone, 1994; steering com. Altoona Reading Inst., Altoona, Pa., 1991—; chair state reading conf. Keystone Reading Assn., 1994-96. Creator and host (weekly radio story hour): Mrs. Spewock & Friends, 1990-99; author: Just for Five's, 1995, Just for Four's, 1995, Just for Three's, 1995, Just for Two's, 1995, Just for One's, 1995, Just for Babies, 1995, Getting Ready to Read, 1996; contbr. articles to profl. jours. Mem. adv. bd. strategic planning Tyrone Area Sch. Dist., 1994; rep. Pa. in Washington D.C., 1992. Recipient Dist. Svc. award Tyrone Area Cmty. Orgn., 1992, Outstanding Employee award, 1989. Mem. Keystone State Reading Assn. (pres. 1995), Internat. Reading Assn., Blair County Reading Coun. (pres. 1986-88), Nat. Assn. Supervision and Curriculum Devel., Nat. Assn. Edn. Young Children, Nat. Assn. Elem. Sch. Prins., Pa. Assn. Fed. Program Coords., Phi Delta Kappa. Avocations: piano, reading, folk dancing, cross-country skiing, walking for fitness. Office: Tyrone Area Sch Dist 801 Clay Ave Tyrone PA 16686-1806 E-mail: tgspewock@tyrone.k12.pa.us.

SPICER, BARBARA JEAN WENTZ, elementary school educator; b. Hanover, Pa., Mar. 27, 1951; d. Elwood Frederick and Viola Grace (Wantz) Wentz; m. Edwin Franklin Spicer, June 16, 2001. BS, Shippensburg U., 1972, MEd, 1976. Substitute tchr. various schs. South Western Sch. Dist., Hanover, Pa., 1973, Littlestown (Pa.) Sch. Dist., 1973, Title I reading instr., tutor, 1973-74; elem. supr., tchr. New Freedom (Pa.) Christian Schs., 1974—. Vol. Landis Valley Mus., Lancaster, Pa., 1994, 95. Avocations: writing and directing school plays, sightseeing, sewing, reading. Office: New Freedom Christian Schs 222 N Constitution Ave New Freedom PA 17349-9513

SPICER, MICHAEL WILLIAM, university educator; b. Uffculme, Devon, England, July 18, 1949; arrived in U.S., 1967; s. William John Arthur and Annie Doreen Taverner Spicer; m. Claudia Ann (Bevinger), June 10, 1972; 1 child, Jeffrey Arthur. BS in bus. adminstrn., Ohio State U., 1971, MA in pub. adminstrn., 1972, PhD in pub. adminstrn., 1974. Lectr. in economics U. Exeter, England, 1974—76; vis. asst. prof., pub. adminstrn. Ohio State U., Columbus, 1976—77; asst. prof. econ. and pub. adminstrn. U. Colo., Colo. Springs, Colo., 1977—81, assoc. prof. econ. and and pub. adminstrn., 1981—86, assoc. dean grad. sch. pub. affairs, 1983—86; assoc. dean, oll. urban affairs Cleve. State U., 1986—92, prof. urban affairs and pub. adminstrn., 1986—. Bd. editors Adminstrv. Theory and Praxis, Omaha, 2000—03. Author: (book) The Founders, the Constn. and Pub. Adminstrn., 1995, Pub. Adminstrn. and the State: A Postmodern Approach, 2001; contbr. articles to profl. jour. Mem.: ASPA, Pub. Adminstrn. Theory Network, Am. Econ. Assn. Home: 23711 Cliff Dr Bay Village OH 44140 Office: Cleve State Univ 1717 Euclid Ave Cleveland OH 44115 Office Fax: 216-687-9342. Business E-Mail: mike@wolf.csuohio.edu.

SPIEGEL, ALLEN D. medical educator, consultant; b. N.Y.C., June 11, 1927; s. Max and Betty (Silver) S.; m. Lila Spiegel, Apr. 16, 1958; children: Merrill S., Marc B., Andrea M. AB, Bklyn. Coll., 1947; MPH, Columbia U., 1954; PhD, Brandeis U., 1969. Chief radio & TV unit N.Y.C. Health Dept., 1951-61; health edn. assoc. The Med. Found., Inc., Boston, 1961-69; prof. SUNY Downstate Med. Ctr. at Bklyn., 1969—. Cons. in field. Author, editor of numerous books including Strategic Health Planning, 1991, Home Health Care, 2d rev. edit., 1987, Risk Management in Health Care Institutions: A Strategic Approach, 1997, 2d rev. edit., 2003, A. Lincoln, Esquire: A Shrewd Sophisticated Litigator, 2002; mem. editl. adv. bd. Nation's Health; contbr. articles to profl. jours. NEH fellow, 1979, WHO study/travel fellow, 1974, Nat. Ctr. for Health Svcs. Rsch. fellow, 1966-69; recipient of citations from govtl. and pub. agys; seminar leader Profl. Continuing Edn. Programs (overseas), 1988. Mem. Am. Pub. Health Assn. (com. chmn.), Internat. Union for Health Edn., Columbia U. Sch. of Pub. Health Alumni Assn., Community Agy. Pub. Rels. Assn., Coun. on Med. Television, Soc. of Pub. Health Educators, Health Edn. Media Assn., Consumer Commn. on the Accreditation of Health Svcs. Home: 47 Jensen Rd Sayreville NJ 08872-1969 Office: SUNY Downstate Medical Ctr 450 Clarkson Ave Box 43 Brooklyn NY 11203-2056

SPIEGEL, HERBERT, psychiatrist, educator; b. McKeesport, Pa., June 29, 1914; s. Samuel and Lena (Mendlowitz) S.; m. Natalie Shainess, Apr. 24, 1944 (div. Apr. 1965); children: David, Ann; m. Marcia Greenleaf, Jan. 29, 1989. BS, U. Md., 1936, MD, 1939. Diplomate: Am. Bd. Psychiatry. Intern St. Francis Hosp., Pitts., 1939-40; resident in psychiatry St. Elizabeth's Hosp., Washington, 1940-42; practice medicine specializing in psychiatry N.Y.C., 1946—; attending psychiatrist Columbia-Presbyn. Hosp., N.Y.C., 1960—; faculty psychiatry Columbia U. Coll. Physicians and Surgeons, 1960—. Adj. prof. psychology John Jay Coll. Criminal Justice, CUNY, 1983— ; mem. faculty Sch. Mil. Neuropsychiatry, Mason Gen. Hosp., Brentwood, N.Y., 1944-46 Author: (with A. Kardiner) War Stress and Neurotic Illness, 1947, (with D. Spiegel) Trance and Treatment: Clinical Uses of Hypnosis, 1978; subject of book: (by Donald S. Connery) The Inner Source: Exploring Hypnosis with Herbert Spiegel, M.D.; Mem. editorial bd.: Preventive Medicine, 1972; Contbr. articles to profl. jours. Mem. profl. advisory com. Am. Health Found.; mem. pub. edn. com., smoking and health com. N.Y.C. div. Am. Cancer Soc.; mem. adv. com. Nat. Aid to Visually Handicapped. Served with M.C. AUS, 1942-46. Decorated Purple Heart. Fellow Am. Psychiat. Assn., Am. Coll. Psychiatrists, Am. Soc. Clin. Hypnosis, Am. Acad. Psychoanalysis, Internat. Soc. Clin. and Exptl. Hypnosis, William A. White Psychoanalytic Soc., N.Y. Acad. Medicine, N.Y. Acad. Scis.; mem. Am. Orthopsychiat. Assn., Am. Psychosomatic Soc., AAAS, AMA, N.Y. County Med. Soc. Office: 19 E 88th St New York NY 10128-0557

SPIEGEL, SAMUEL ALBERT, program director; b. Phila., Feb. 7, 1963; m. Mary C. Stewart, Oct. 23, 1993. Student, Temple U., 1981-85, Met. State Coll., Denver, 1987; BA in Biol. Sci., Fla. Atlantic U., 1989; MS in Sci. Edn., Fla. State U., 1993, PhD. Cert. tchr. biology, Fla. Rsch. assoc., tchr. asst. Fla. Atlantic U., Boca Raton, 1987-89; tchr. Forest Hill H.S., West Palm Beach, Fla., 1990, Havana (Fla.) Mid. Sch., 1990-92; grad. asst., instr. Fla. State U., Tallahassee, 1992; cons. Hubbard Sci./Redo Sci., Boulder, Colo., 1992-93; program dir. Sci. FEAT Fla. State U., Tallahassee, 1992—95; dir. R&D i4Learning, Tallahassee, Fla., 1995—. Adv. com. Knowles Sci. Tchg. Found. Recipient Innovation in Tchg. Sci. Tchrs. award, Assn. Edn. Tchrs. of Sci., 1997. Office: i4Learning 416 E Georgia St Tallahassee FL 32301 Office Fax: 850-577-1877.*

SPIEGELBERG, EMMA JO, business education educator, academic administrator; b. Mt. View, Wyo., Nov. 22, 1936; d. Joseph Clyde and Dorcas (Reese) Hatch; m. James Walter Spiegelberg, June 22, 1957; children: William L., Emory Walter, Joseph John. BA with honors, U. Wyo., 1958, MEd, 1985; EdD, Boston U., 1990. Tchr. bus. edn. Laramie (Wyo.) H.S., 1960-61, 65-93, adminstr., 1993-97; prin. McCormick Jr. H.S., Cheyenne, Wyo., 1997—2002; exec. dir. Wyo. Assn. Secondary Sch. Prins., 2001—. Author: Branigan's Accounting Simulation, 1986, London & Co. II, 1993; co-author: Glencoe Computerized Accounting, 1993, 2d edit., 1995, Microcomputer Accounting: Daceasy, 1994, Microcomputer Accounting: Peachtree, 1994, 3d edit., 2000, Microcomputer Accounting: Accpac, 1994, Computerized Accounting with Peachtree, 1995, 2000, 02. Mem. United Ch. of Christ; bd. dirs. Cathedral Home for Children, Laramie, 1967-70, 72—, pres., 1985-88, Laramie Plains Mus., 1970-79.

Named Wyo. Bus. Tchr. of Yr., 1982, Wyo. Asst. Prin. of Yr., 1997. Mem.: NASSP, NEA, Wyo. Assn. Secondary Sch. Prins. (sec., treas. 1997—2001), Albany County Edn. Assn. (sec. 1970—71), Wyo. Edn. Assn., Wyo. Bus. Edn. Assn. (pres. 1979—80), Internat. Soc. Bus. Edn., Mt. Plains Bus. Edn. Assn. (Wyo. rep. to bd. dirs. 1982—85, pres. 1987—88, Sec. Tchr. of Yr. 1991, Leadership award 1992), Nat. Bus. Edn. Assn. (bd. dirs. 1987—88, 1991—96, Sec. Tchr. of Yr. 1991), Wyo. Vocat. Assn. (exec. bd. 1978—80, pres. 1981—82, exec. sec. 1986—89, Outstanding Contbns. to Vocat. Edn. award 1983, Tchr. of Yr. 1985), Am. Vocat. Assn. (policy com. region V 1984—87, region V Tchr. of Yr. 1986), U. Wyo. Alumni Assn. (bd. dirs. 1985—90, pres. 1988—89), Laramie C. of C. (bd. dirs. 1985—88), Zonta Internat. (Laramie) (v.p. 2002—03, pres. 2003—), Delta Pi Epsilon, Pi Lambda Theta, Chi Omega, Alpha Delta Kappa (state pres. 1978—82), Phi Delta Kappa, Kappa Delta Pi. Home: 3301 Grays Gable Rd Laramie WY 82072-5031

SPIELBERGER, CHARLES DONALD, psychology educator, behavioral medicine, clinical and health psychologist; b. Atlanta, Mar. 28, 1927; s. A.R. and Eleanor (Wachman) S.; m. Carol Lee, June 4, 1971. BS, Ga. Tech., 1949; BA, U. Iowa, 1951, MA, 1953, PhD, 1954. Asst. prof. med. psychology Duke U., Durham, N.C., 1955-58, from asst. prof. to assoc. prof. psychology, 1955-63; prof. psychology Vanderbilt U., Nashville, 1963-66; tng. specialist in psychology NIMH, Bethesda, Md., 1965-67; prof. psychology, dir. clin. training program Fla. State U., Tallahassee, 1967-72; prof. psychology U. South Fla., Tampa, 1972—85, dir. clin. tng., 1972—78, disting. univ. rsch. prof., 1985—. Fellow Netherlands Inst. for Advanced Study, Wassenaar, 1979-80, 85-86; cons. FAA, NIMH, VA, USAF, others. Author: Anxiety and Behavior, 1966, Understanding Stress and Anxiety, 1979, Anxiety in Sports, 1989, Test Anxiety: Theory, Assessment and Treatment, 1995; editor: Stress and Anxiety Series, 16 vols., 1975—; gen. editor: Centennial Psychology Series, 1979—. Named Disting. scholar U. South Fla., 1973, Disting. Sci. Contbr., Fla. Psychol. Assn., 1977, 88, Outstanding Faculty Rschr., U. South Fla., 1985. Fellow APA (pres. 1991-92, nat. treas. 1987-90, pres. divsn. clin. psychology 1989, pres. divsn. cmty. psychol. 1975-76, pres. divsn. internat. psychol., 2002, Disting. Sci. Contbr. to Cmty. Psychology 1982, Disting. Sci. and Prof. Contbr. Clin. Psychology 1989, Disting. Contbr. Edn. 1992, Disting. Contbr. Profl. Practice 1993, APA/APF Gold Medal Disting. Contbr., 2003); mem. Southeastern Psychol. Assn. (pres. 1975-76), Soc. for Personality Assessment (pres. 1986-89, Disting. Sci. Contbr. 1990), Nat. Coun. Sci. Soc. Presidents (chair 1996-2000), Internat. Stress Mgmt. Assn. (pres. 1992-2000), Internat. Coun. Psychologists (pres. 1986-87), Internat. Assn. Applied Psychology (pres. 1998-2002), Psi Chi (nat. pres. 1980-83). Home: 11313 Carrollwood Dr Tampa FL 33618-3703 Office: U South Fla Dept Psychology Tampa FL 33620

SPIELHAGEN, FRANCES ROSE, secondary school educator; b. NYC, Feb. 1, 1946; d. Louis and Mary (Muscarella) Calabretta; m. Gerard Fredric Spielhagen, June 9, 1968; children: Amy, Jeremy. BA summa cum laude, Fordham U., 1967, MA in Classics, 1969, PhD, 2002; postgrad., L.I. U., 1975—77, U. Conn., 1981—82, postgrad., 1990—96. Tchr. 3d grade St. Anthony Sch., Bronx, 1968-69; tchr. grades 6-8 Cathedral of St. John the Divine, N.Y.C., 1969-74; tchr. grades 9-10 Warwick (N.Y.) High Sch., 1974-76; tchr. grades 9-12 Vernon (N.J.) Twp. High Sch., 1978—2002; prof. Mt. St. Mary Coll., Newburgh, NY, 2002—. Eleanor Roosevelt fellow, 1991, postdoctoral fellow AERA, 2003—; recipient A+ for Kids award WOR-TV-Impact II, Newark, 1990, Target Tchr. award, 1999, Time for Kids award, 2001. Mem.: NAGC, ASCD, AERA, AAUW, NEA, Am. Classical League. Roman Catholic. Avocations: travel, educational writing/publishing, needle arts, sketching. Office: Mt StMary Coll 330 Powell Ave Newburgh NY 12550

SPIELMAN, JOHN PHILIP, JR., historian, educator; b. Anaconda, Mont., June 16, 1930; s. John Philip and Lewanna (Coleman) S.; m. Danila B. Cole, Sept. 14, 1955. BA, U. Mont., 1951; MA, U. Wis., 1953, PhD, 1957. Instr. U. Mich., Ann Arbor, 1957-59; asst. prof. history Haverford (Pa.) Coll., 1959-65, assoc. prof., 1965-70, prof., 1970-85, Audrey Dusseau meml. prof. humanities, 1985-97, dean, 1966-68. Author: Leopold I of Austria, 1977, The City and the Crown, 1993; co-author 2 textbooks; translator: Simplicissimus (Grimmelshausen), 1981. Served with U.S. Army, 1953-55. Mem. Am. Hist. Assn., Soc. French Hist. Studies, Soc. Austrian and Hapsburg Historians. Home: 749 Millbrook Ln Haverford PA 19041-1210

SPIELMANN, DIANE RUTH, research center public services director; b. N.Y.C., May 27, 1951; d. Elias and Walli (Mischkowski) S. BA magna cum laude, Queens Coll. CUNY, Flushing, 1973; MPhil, CUNY Grad. Sch., N.Y.C., 1979; PhD, CUNY, N.Y.C., 1987. Editl. asst. Harcourt, Brace, Jovanovich, N.Y.C., 1973-74; archivist Leo Baeck Inst., N.Y.C., 1976-92, pub. svcs. and devel. coord., 1992-2000. German instr., lectr. CUNY Grad. Sch., N.Y.C., 1976-78, Queens Coll. CUNY, Flushing, 1978-81; judge nation-wide jr. high sch. essay contest U.S. Holocaust Meml. Coun., Washington, 1991; guest lectr. on archives Assn. Jewish Librs. Conf., Livingston, N.J., 1987; adj. asst. prof. German-Jewish history and culture Queens Coll., CUNY, Flushing, 1998—. Author in field. Chair Holocaust meml. com. Hillcrest Jewish Ctr., Flushing, 1988-91, lectr. in Holocaust history, 1988; 1st v.p. PhD Alumni Assn. CUNY Grad. Sch., 1995—. Recipient prize for Excellence in Interpretation of German Lit., Lit. Soc. Found., 1973, Alumni Achievement award CUNY, 2002; Grad. U. fellow CUNY, 1975, 78-79. Mem. MLA, German Studies Assn., Leo Baeck Inst., Phi Beta Kappa, Delta Phi Alpha. Jewish. Avocations: painting and drawing, creative design, sewing, accordion, sports.

SPIESS, ELIOT BRUCE, biologist, educator; b. Boston, Oct. 13, 1921; s. George Nicholas and Rena (Bunce) S.; m. Luretta Davis; children: Arthur Eliot, Bruce Davis. AB cum laude, Harvard Coll., 1943; AM, Harvard U., 1947, PhD, 1949. Instr. biology Harvard U., Cambridge, Mass., 1949-52; asst. prof. U. Pitts., 1952-56, assoc. prof., 1956-65, prof., 1965-66, U. Ill., Chgo., 1966-89, prof. emeritus, 1989—. Editor: Papers on Animal Polulation Genetics, 1962; author: (book) Genes in Populations, 1977, 2d edit., 1989; contbr. articles to profl. jours. 1st lt. U.S. Army Air Force, 1943-45. Grantee NSF, 1972-83, U.S. Atomic Energy Commn., 1966-72. Fellow AAAS; mem. Soc. for the Study of Evolution (assoc. editor 1956-58, 67-69, editor of Evolution 1975-78), Am. Soc. Naturalists (pres. 1981). Avocations: piano, photography, writing, reading, birding, hiking.

SPIKER, GEORGE DAVID, principal; b. Canton, Ohio, Apr. 17, 1942; s. George Donald and Mary Elizabeth (Allenbaugh) S.; children: George Daniel, Elizabeth Kay. BS, Mount Union Coll., 1964; M of Combined Scis., U. Miss., 1969; EdD, U. Akron, 1995. Tchr. Sandy Valley Local Schs., Magnolia, Ohio, 1964-72; supr. Stark County Dept. Edn., Louisville, 1972-76; elem. prin. Sandy Valley Local Schs., Magnolia, 1976-93, Garfield Local Schs., Garrettsville, Ohio, 1993—. Sch. edn. com. chmn. Quest Recovery Svcs., Stark County, Ohio, 1980-93; zone chmn. Dist. 13-D Lions, Ohio, 1985-87, 96-98.mem Mem. Nat. Assn. Elem. Sch. Prins., Ohio Assn. Elem. Sch. Adminstrs. (com. mem.), Portage County Elem. Sch. Adminstrs., Garrettsville Lions Club, Phi Delta Kappa. Republican. Methodist. Avocations: reading, sports, music, writing, travel. Home: 3670 Mogadore Rd Mogadore OH 44260 Office: James A Garfield Local Schs 10207 State Route 88 Garrettsville OH 44231-9205 E-mail: dspiker@mail.garfield.sparcc.org.

SPILLANE, ROBERT RICHARD, school system administrator; b. Lowell, Mass., Oct. 29, 1934; s. John Joseph and Catherine (Barrett) S.; children: Patricia, Robert Jr., Kathleen, Maura. BS, Ea. Conn. State Coll., 1956; MA, U. Conn., 1959, PhD, 1967. Elem. and secondary tchr., Storrs, Conn., 1956-60, Chaplin, Conn., 1960-62; elem. prin. Trumbull, Conn., 1962-63; secondary prin., 1963-65; asst. supt. Glassboro (N.J.) Pub. Schs., 1966-68, Roosevelt (L.I., N.Y.) Schs., 1968-70, New Rochelle (N.Y.) Pub. Schs., 1970-78; dep. commr. N.Y. State Dept Edn., Albany, N.Y., 1978-81; supt. Boston Pub. Schs., 1981-85, Fairfax (Va.) County Pub. Schs., 1985—97; regional officer Office Overseas Schs. U.S. Dept. State, 1997—. Bd. dirs. Council Great City Schs.; mem. adv. bd. Met. Ctr. Ednl. Research, Devel. and Tng. NYU, Instr. Mag.; chmn. pres.' adv. bd. Tchrs. Coll. Columbia U.; co-chmn. adminstrs. com. study on edn. and edn. of tchrs. U.S. Office Edn., Washington; mem. N.Y. State Sch. Officers Resolutions Com. on Legislation, Westchester County Chief Sch. Officers Legis. Com.; bd. dirs. Curriculum Devel. Council So. N.J., Impact II, N.Y.C.; adj. prof. sch. edn. Fordham U., N.Y.C., Iona Coll., New Rochelle, Bank St. Coll. Edn., N.Y.C., Glassboro State Coll.; instr. NYU; vis. lectr. U. Bridgeport, Conn. Author: You and Smoking, 1970, Management by Objectives in the Schools, 1978; contbr. articles to profl. jours. Trustee Mus. Fine Arts, Boston; bd. dirs. Jr. Achievement Ea. Mass., Inc.; mem. adv. com. Boston Pub. Library, The Statue of Liberty-Ellis Island Found., Inc., commn. on Bicentennial U.S. Constitution. Recipient Disting. Alumni award Ea. Conn. State Coll., 1969, Disting. Alumni award U. Conn., 1986; named one of Outstanding Young Men of Am. Mem. Am. Assn. Sch. Adminstrs. (Nat. Supt. of the Year award 1995), Mass., Conn., N.J., N.Y. Assns. Sch. Adminstrs., Sch. Mgmt. Study Group (pres. 1971-73, Hall of Fame award 1974), Assn. Supervision and Curriculum Devel., Nat. Sch. Pub. Relations Assn., Phi Delta Kappa. Avocations: swimming, sailing, skiing, theater and the arts, entertaining. Office: Office Overseas Schs US Dept State Rm 245 SA 29 Washington DC 20522-2902*

SPILLERS, BETSY ROSE, history educator; b. Athens, Greece, Dec. 26, 1944; d. Frank and Panayiota Spyridakis; m. Roger E. Spillers, Aug. 6, 1966; children: Daphne Rose, Heather Frances, Francis Eugene. BA, U Zambia, 1979; MA in Edn., S.W. State U., 2000. Tchr. Worthington Sr. High Sch., 1982—93, Alternative High Sch, Worthington, 1990-91; ESL tchr. Dist. 518, Worthington, Minn., 1990-91; tchr. social studies Round Lake (Minn.) HS, 1993—. Instr. African history Worthington C.C., 1989-91. Mem. AAUW (chmn. scholarships 1985, fin. com. 1986-87, pres. 1987-89), Minn. Edn. Assn. Avocations: archaeology, classical civilization, travel, swimming. Home: 417 8th Ave Worthington MN 56187-1501 Office: Round Lake High School 445 Harrison St Round Lake MN 56167

SPILLERS, WILLIAM RUSSELL, civil engineering educator; b. Fresno, Calif., Aug. 4, 1934; s. William Horton and Marguerite Ester (Johnson) S.; m. Priscilla Watson, Sept. 10, 1960 (div. 1981); children: Sarah, William, Lars; m. Sandra Lynn Newsome, July 15, 1983 (div. 1995); m. Joy Bechard, Mar. 13, 2000. Student, Fresno State Coll., 1951-53; BS, U. Calif., Berkeley, 1955, MS, 1956; PhD, Columbia U., 1961. Registered profl. engr., N.Y., N.J. Structural engr. John Blume Assocs., San Francisco, 1956-57; teaching asst. Columbia U., N.Y.C., 1957-61, prof. civil engring. and engring. mechanics, 1961-76; prof. civil engring. Rensellaer Poly. Inst., Troy, N.Y., 1976-90; prof., chmn. civil and environ. engring. N.J. Inst. Tech., Newark, 1990—, disting. prof. civil and environ. engring., 1995—. Cons. Weidlinger Assoc., N.Y.C., 1957-76, Geiger Berger Assoc., N.Y.C., 1957-76, DeLeuw Oh Eocha, Manchester, Eng., 1974, Parsons Hawaii, L.A., 1983, Horst Berger Ptnrs., N.Y.C., 1980; organizer NSF workshop on design theory, Troy, N.Y., 1988. Author: Automated Structural Analysis, 1972, Iterative Structural Design, 1975, Intro Structures, 1985; (with R. Levy) Analysis of Geometrically Nonlinear Structures, 1995, Introduction to Structures, 2002; editor 4 books including Design Theory, 1988; contbr. over 140 articles to profl. jours. Named Educator of Yr. award, Cons. Engrs. Coun. N.J., 1998; NSF fellow, 1976, Guggenheim fellow, 1968. Mem. ASCE (numerous coms., chmn. exec. com. TCCP, 1987), Internat. Assn. Bridge & Structural Engrs. Democrat. Achievements include contribution to the development of fabric structures; initiated the science of design theory; participated in development of applications of digital computers to large structural systems. Home: 7 Oak Ave West Orange NJ 07052-2409 Office: NJ Inst Tech Dept Civil & Environ Engring Newark NJ 07102

SPINDEL, ROBERT CHARLES, electrical engineering educator; b. N.Y.C., Sept. 5, 1944; s. Morris Tayson and Isabel (Glazer) S.; m. Barbara June Sullivan, June 12, 1966; children: Jennifer Susan, Miranda Ellen BSEE, Cooper Union, 1965; MS, Yale U., 1966, MPhil, 1968, PhD, 1971. Postdoctoral fellow Woods Hole Oceanographic Instn., Mass., 1971-72, asst. scientist, 1972-76, assoc. scientist, 1976-82, sr. scientist, 1982-87, chmn. dept. ocean engring., 1982-87; dir. applied physics lab. U. Wash., Seattle, 1987—. Mem. naval studies bd. NRC, 1987-99; mem. Naval Rsch. Adv. Com., 1998—. Contbr. articles to profl. jours.; patentee on underwater nav. Recipient A.B. Wood medal Brit. Inst. Acoustics, 1981, Gano Dunn medal The Cooper Union, 1989, Ocean Engr. Soc. Tech. Achievement award, 1990. Fellow IEEE (assoc. editor jour. 1982—), Acoustical Soc. Am., Marine Tech. Soc. (pres. elect 1991-93, pres. 1993-95), Oceanography Soc. (Munk award 2001). Independent. Jewish. Avocations: automobile restoration, hiking. Home: 14859 SE 51st St Bellevue WA 98006-3515 Office: U Wash Applied Physics Lab 1013 NE 40th St Seattle WA 98105-6606 E-mail: spindel@APL.Washington.edu.

SPINDLER, JUDITH TARLETON, elementary school educator; b. Dayton, Tenn., Mar. 4, 1932; d. Frank Willson and Julia Elizabeth (Venable) S. BS in Edn., Longwood Coll., 1953; MA in Edn., Va. Commonwealth U., 1976. Tchr. Oceana, King's Grant Sch., Virginia Beach, Va., 1953-66, Ginter Park Elem. Sch., Richmond, Va., 1966-67, Bon Air Elem. Sch., Chesterfield County, Va., 1967-87; ret., 1987. Charter mem. Web of Hope sponsored by ARC (Humanitarian award). Recipient 86 ribbons for 1st, 2nd and 3rd pl. awards various knitting competitions, 5 Best in Show awards rosette competition, including blue ribbons State Fair Va., 1998, 6 ribbons Best in Show rosette Chesterfield County Fair, 1998, 2 Best in Show Chesterfield County Fair, 1 Best in Show State Fair of Va., 3 Blue Ribbons Chesterfield County Fair, 2000, 2 Red Ribbons, 1 White Ribbon Va. State Fair, 2000, 3 Blue Ribbons Chesterfield County Fair, 2 Red Ribbons, 1 White Ribbon 1 Blue, 5 in Va. State Fair, 2002. Mem. NEA, Va. Edn. Assn., Knitting Guild Am. (qualified tchr.), Knit Wit Guild (founding mem.). Avocation: knitting. Home: 4103 Hyde Park Dr Chester VA 23831-4826

SPINELLA, DENNIS MICHAEL, education educator; b. Mt. Pleasant, Pa., Feb. 21, 1945; s. Michael Louis and Veronica Joan Spinella; m. Bernadette Marie Beitle, July 17, 1976; children: Melissa, Jennifer, Lauren. BS in Elem. Edn., Calif. U. Pa., 1966; MEd in Elem. Edn., U. Pitts., 1967, PhD in Sch. Adminstrn., 1986. Tchr. Allegheny Valley Sch. Dist., Springdale, Pa., 1966-71; lectr. in edn. U. Pitts., Pitts., 1971-74; asst. elem. sch. prin. Keystone Oaks Sch. Dist., Pitts., 1974-76; prin. elem. sch. North Hills Sch. Dist., Pitts., 1976-88, dir. edn., 1988-92; lectr. in edn. Carlow Coll., Duquesne U., Pitts., 1992—, U. Pitts., Pitts., 1995—. Bd. govs. Pa. Congress of Sch. Adminstrn., Pa., 1978-82; v.p. dean's alumni coun. U. Pitts., 1986—; pres. U. Pitts. Alumni Assn., 1995. Vol. sch. bd. election, Penn Hills, Pa., 1988; v.p. Northaven Civic Assn., Glenshaw, Pa., 1990-91. PEELS leadership sci. scholar Clarion U. Pitts., 1985. Mem. ASCD, Pa. Staff Devel. Coun. (charter mem.), U. Pitts. Assn. Doctoral Educators (v.p. 1994-95), Phi Delta Kappa (pres. 1992-94, Western Pa. Consortium of Educators rep. 1990—, Leadership award), Pitts. Oldies Music Assn. Democrat. Avocations: professional radio disk jockey, professional research reading, travel, dancing. Home: 17012 Burchfield Rd Allison Park PA 15101-4065 Office: Carlow Coll DuQuesne U Pittsburgh PA 15116

SPINELLI, ANNE CATHERINE, elementary education educator; b. Chgo., Dec. 19, 1943; d. Stanley J. and Lucy A. (Schmidt) Malaski; m. Joseph P. Spinelli Jr., May 28, 1966. BS in Edn., Ohio U., 1965; postgrad., Ashland U., 1989—. Lic. tchr. kindergarten - 8th grade. Tchr. K-3 North Olmsted (Ohio) City Schs., 1965-70, master tchr., 1970-71, kindergarten tchr., 1971-74, Cloverleaf Schs., Lodi, Ohio, 1974—99; ret., 1999. Seminar presenter sci. dept. Ednl. Rsch. Coun. Am., Cleve., 1969-74, State of Ohio Supr. Assn., Columbus, 1986, Great Lakes Internat. Reading Assn., Chgo., 1993; panelist Ohio Coun. Elem. Sch. Sci. Conv., Akron, 1969; speaker Nat. Sci. Tchrs. Assn. Great Lakes Conf., Cleve., 1971, State of Ohio Proficiency Conf., Cleve., 1996, 97, 98, 2000. Co-author: North Olmsted Schools Motor Perception Book for Kindergarten, 1970, Kindergarten Home Activities Book, 1991—2002. Mem. Zoning Commn., Westfield Twp., Medina County, Ohio, 1978-90; area coord. Cancer Soc., Medina County, 1983, 85, 89, 98; mem. Zoning Bd. Appeals, Westfield Twp Medina County, Ohio, 1996-99. Jennings scholar Jennings Found., N.E. Ohio, 1987-88; named Outstanding Educator/Acad. Subjects Mid East Ohio/Spl. Edn. Regional Resouce Ctr., 1994, Medina County (Ohio) Tchr. of the Year, 1995; finalist Tchr. of Yr. for Ohio, 1996. Mem. ASCD, NEA, Ohio Edn. Assn., No. Ohio Edn. Assn., N.E. Ohio Edn. Assn., Cloverleaf Edn. Assn. (bldg. reps. 1985-99), Internat. Reading Assn., Lizotte Reading Coun., Elem., Kindergarten, Nursery Sch. Educators. Avocations: travel, gardening. Office: Westfield Elem Sch 9055 S LeRoy Rd Westfield Center OH 44251

SPINGOLA, JEANNIE SAUNDRA, college, special education and adult educator, counselor; b. San Francisco, June 17; d. Frank and Camella Regina (Mazzaferro) S.; m. Peter William Connolly. BA, San Francisco Coll. Women, 1970; MA, U. San Francisco, 1974; student, Dominican Coll., 1971. Counselor Dept. Store Local 1100, San Francisco; cons. ESL Am. Fgn. Studies, San Francisco; counselor, instr. San Francisco Coll. Dist. Cons. Fgn. Lang. Inst., San Francisco. Composer and vocal performer classical and musical comedy Macy's California. Mem. ASCD, ICF, MEA/OSIA, CABE, Am. Fedn. Tchrs., AMA, CAMP, Nat. Assn. Hist. Preservation, Am. CB Radio Assn., Calif. Psychol. Assn., Friends of J. Paul Libr.

SPIRES, DENISE TATE, secondary education educator; b. Oxford, Ala., Sept. 4, 1956; d. Robert Lanier and Mary Bernice (Ginn) Tate; m. Wesley Davis Spires, Mar. 3, 1984. BS in Secondary Math., Auburn (Ala.) U., 1979; MEd in Secondary Math., Ga. Southwestern State U., 1990; EdS in Secondary Math. Edn., Columbus Coll., 1995. Tchr. math. Crisp County H.S., Cordele, Ga., 1979—, chairperson dept., 1992—. Mem. steering com. 10 yr. study Crisp County H.S., Cordele, 1992, student coun. advisor, 1988-93, 1999-2003, chmn. Graduation, 1999—. Named STAR Tchr., Crisp County C. of C., 1985-86. Mem. Nat. Coun. Tchrs. Math., Page. Presbyterian. Avocations: craft, reading, sewing, horseback riding. Home: 1972 Royal Rd Cordele GA 31015-5148 Office: Crisp County HS 2012 Frontage Rd Cordele GA 31015

SPIRNAK, JOHN PATRICK, urologist, educator; b. Cleve., Mar. 17, 1951; s. John Joseph and Mary Barbara (Mancos) S.; m. Diane Lynne Miller, Sept. 15, 1979; children: Jennifer, Patrick, Christopher. BS in Zoology, Ohio U., 1973; MD, Emory U., 1977; degree in urology, Case Western Reserve U., 1983. Diplomate Am. Bd. Urology. Intern, gen. surg. resident U. Hosp., Cleve., 1977-79, resident in urology, 1980-83; nephrology rsch. resident Metro Health Med. Ctr., Cleve., 1979-80, dir. urology, 1987—; sr. instr. divns. urology Case Western Reserve U., Cleve., 1983-85, asst. prof. urology, 1985-91, assoc. prof. urology, 1991-2000, prof., 2000—. Adv. panel U.S. Pharmacopeia Urology, Washington, 1986—. Editor Urologic Decision Making, 1991, New Diagnostic Tests, 1996; manuscript reviewer Jour. Endourology, 1989—, Urology, 1993—, Jour. Urology, 1994—; contbr. articles to profl. jours. and chpts. to books. Named One of Top Doctors Cleve. Mag., 1996, 99. Fellow ACS; mem. AMA, Am. Assn. Surgery Trauma, Am. Urol. Assn., Cleve. Urol. Soc. (sec.-treas. 1986-88, pres. 1988-89). Avocations: sports, gardening. Home: 2178 Silveridge Trl Westlake OH 44145-1797 Office: Metro Health Med Ctr 2500 Metrohealth Dr Cleveland OH 44109-1900

SPIRO, HOWARD MARGET, physician, educator; b. Cambridge, Mass., Mar. 23, 1924; s. Thomas and Martha (Marget); m. Marian Freelove Wagner, Mar 11, 1951; children: Pamela Marget, Carolyn Standish, Philip Marget, Martha Standish. BA, Harvard, 1944, MD, 1947; MA, Yale, 1967. Intern Peter Bent Brigham Hosp., Boston, 1947-48, resident, 1948-51, Mass. Gen. Hosp., 1953-55; practice medicine, specializing in gastroenterology New Haven, 1955—. Chief gastrointestinal unit Yale Sch. Medicine, 1955-82, prof. medicine, 1967-99, dir. program for humanities in medicine, 1983-99; sr. lectr. in medicine Columbia U. Sch. Medicine, 2000—. Author: Clinical Gastroenterology, 1970, 4th edit., 1993, Doctors, Patients and Placebos, 1986, The Power of Hope-A Doctor's Perspective, 1998; editor Jour. Clin. Gastroenterology, 1979-98, (with others) When Doctors Get Sick, 1987, Empathy and the Practice of Medicine, 1993, Facing Death—Where Culture, Religion and Medicine Meet, 1996, Doctors Afield, 1998, Yale Guide to Careers in Medicine and Allied Professions, 2003. Served with USNR, 1943-45; Served with AUS, 1951-53. Mem. ACP (master) Clubs: Madison Beach. Home: 89 Middle Beach Rd Madison CT 06443-3006 Office: Conn Gastroenterology Cons 40 Temple St New Haven CT 06510-2715 E-mail: Howard.spiro@yale.edu.

SPIRO, THOMAS GEORGE, chemistry educator; b. Aruba, Netherlands Antilles, Nov. 7, 1935; s. Andor and Ilona S.; m. Helen Handin, Aug. 21, 1959; children: Peter, Michael. BS, UCLA, 1956; PhD, MIT, 1960. Fulbright rschr. U. Copenhagen, Denmark, 1960-61; NIH fellow Royal Inst. Tech., Stockholm, 1962-63; research chemist Calif. Research Corp., La-Habra, 1961-62; mem. faculty Princeton U., 1963—, prof. chemistry, 1974—, head dept., 1979-88, Eugene Higgins prof., 1981—. Author: (with William M. Stigliani) Environmental Issues in Chemical Perspective, 1980, Chemistry of the Environment, 1996, 2002; contbr. articles to profl. jours. Recipient Bomem-Michelson award Bomem Corp., 1986; NATO sr. fellow, 1972, Guggenheim fellow, 1990. Fellow AAAS; mem. Am. Chem. Soc., Phi Beta Kappa, Sigma Xi. Office: Princeton U Dept Chemistry Princeton NJ 08544-0001 E-mail: spiro@princeton.edu.

SPITZE, GLENYS SMITH, retired educator; b. Rozel, Kans., May 20, 1919; d. Harry H. and Mary Louisa (Mishler) Smith; m. LeRoy A. Spitze, Dec. 31, 1942 (dec. Nov. 1995); children: Randall LeRoy, Kevin Lance, Kimett Alvin, Terril Christian, Shawn Smith; 1 fosterchild, Theo Ritz-Spitze. Cert. tchg., U. Kans., 1939; AA, San Jose (Calif.) City Coll., 1963; BA in Psychology, San Jose State U., 1965, MA in Child Devel., 1968. Cert. tchr., counselor, Calif. Elem. sch. tchr. Topeka County Schs., Richland, Kans., 1939-40, Kinsley (Kans.) Pub. Schs., 1940-42; presch. substitute tchr. AAUW Kindergarten, Newark, Ohio, 1945—46; presch. tchr. Meth. Ch. Facility, Campbell, Calif., 1956-58; guest lectr. Govt. Sch. Social Work, Colombo, Sri Lanka, 1965-66; instr. man-woman relationship San Jose State Free U., 1966-67; child devel. lab. psychol. examiner Child Labs San Jose State U., 1967-68; pvt. informal practice tchr., counselor, cons. San Jose, Kailua, Hawaii. Vocal music dir. grades 1-3 Southside Sch., 1940-41; 6th dist. Calif. Congress Parent-Tchrs. Social Welfare dir., officer 6th dist. com. Calif. Coun. on Crime and Delinquency, San Jose, 1956-62; mem. kindergarten com. AAUW, Newark, Ohio, 1945-46; coord. Sangha Symposium, Asian Philosophy Club, San Jose State U., 1964-65; lectr. in field. Contbr. articles, poems to profl. pubs. Hon. del. Gov. Brown's Conf. on Prevention of Juvenile Delinquency, Sacramento, 1963; co-organizer Post Polio Support Group, Kailua-Kona, HI, 2000. Mem. Psi Chi. Avocations: writing, reading, swimming, snorkeling, anthropology and archeology travel. Home: 78-6800 Alii Dr KKSRC 5-103 Kailua Kona HI 96740-4421 Home (Summer): 311 E Bowman Woodland Park CO 80863 also: PO Gen Delivery Woodland Park CO 80863 E-mail: GMGlenys@webtv.net.

SPITZER, MATTHEW LAURENCE, law educator, dean; b. L.A., June 23, 1952; s. William George and Jeanette Dorothy S.; m. Jean Fuksman, July 8, 1973; 1 child, Amanda Elizabeth. BA in Math., UCLA, 1973; JD, U. So. Calif., 1977; PhD in Social Scis., Calif. Inst. Tech., 1979. Assoc. Nossaman, Guthner, Knox & Elliott, L.A., 1977—79; asst. prof. Northwestern U., Chgo., 1979—81; William T. Dalessi prof. law U. So. Calif., L.A., 1987—2000, assoc. prof., 1981—84, prof., 1984—, dir. law and rational choice programs, 1990—2000, dir. Comms. Law and Policy Ctr., 1998—2000, dean, Carl Mason Franklin prof. law, 2000—; prof. law and social scis. Calif. Inst. Tech., Pasadena, 1992—2000. Vis. prof. law U. Chgo., 1996, Stanford (Calif.) U., 1997; mem. organizing com. Telecoms. Policy Rsch. Conf., Washington, 1991-94. Author: Seven Dirty Words and Six Other Stories, 1986; co-author: (with T. Hazlett) Public Policy Toward Cable Television, 1997. Recipient (shared with Elizabeth Hoffman) Ronald H. Coase prize U. Chgo., 1986. Mem.: Am. Law and Econs. Assn. (bd. dirs. 1997—2000). Avocations: paperweight collecting, audiophile. Office: U So Calif Law Sch Los Angeles CA 90089-0071

SPIVACK, FRIEDA KUGLER, psychologist, administrator, educator, researcher; b. N.Y.C., Aug. 21, 1932; d. David and Anna (Steir) Kugler; married; children: Alizah Brozgold, Ely. MA with honors, Hunter Coll., 1963; PhD, NYU, 1971. Prof. Manhattan Coll., N.Y.C., 1971-74, Queens Coll., Flushing, N.Y., 1974-76, Lehman Coll., N.Y.C., 1976-92; exec. dir. Hosp. Clinics Home Ctr. Instructional Programs, 1980—; project dir. Bushwick Even Start Program, N.Y.C., 2001—. Bd. dirs., pres. HCHC, Inc., Bklyn.; keynote spkr. N.Y. State Edn. Conf., N.Y.C., 1996, N.Y. Divsn. of Early Childhood Conf., 1997; spkr. N.Y.C. Interagy. Early Childhood Programs, 1995-2003; developer universal pre-sch. classes for Dist. 32, N.Y.C. Contbr. articles to profl. jours., chpts. to textbooks; author family guidance program curriculum in field, infant abecedary program, children's devel. assessments; editor, author: Learning to Function in Life, 1996; author: Perspective of Conductive Education, Infants and Young Children, Young Children's Journal. Mem. exec. bd. N.Y. State Divsn. Early Childhood, 1981—; del. Coun. for Exceptional Children, 1981—88; chmn. Empire State Consortium of Early Childhood Grants, 1990—91; exec. dir. Hosp. Clinic Home Ctr. Instrnl. Corp., 1976—, 1990—91; cmty. orgn. liaison ACE Integration Head Start; project dir. Danforth Found. Grant Transitions and Tracking of Presch. Children in the Pub. Sch., N.Y.C. Reggio Emilia program Parent Svcs. Project, Parent and Children Play and Project Enrichment and Coordination programs; chairperson N. Bklyn. Child Care Network, N. Bklyn. Child Health Care Adv. Coun.; project dir., author Bushwick Even Start Program, 2001—; chairperson Bushwilk Child Care Network, 1998—, No. Bklyn. Child Care Health Coun., 1997—; bd. dirs., pres. Inter-Am. Conductive Edn. for Motor Disabled, Bklyn.; bd. dirs., exec. dir. ACE Integration Head Start, 1994—; bd. dirs. sponsoring bd. coun. N.Y.C. Head Start; bd. dirs. Parent and Child Diagnostic Ctr., 1998—; grant project dir. Parent Across Parents, 2003—, United Way, 2003—. Grantee Fed. Grants, 2000-02, United Way, 2003—. Mem.: AAUP, Nat. Even Start Assn., Internat. Coll. Pediatrics (mem. exec. bd. 1986—), Assn. Edn. Young Children, Am. Fedn. Tchrs.-Profl. Staff Congress, Coun. Exceptional Children (lectr., keynoter 1994—98), Internat. Coun. Psychologists, Nat. Assn. Sch. Psychologists. Avocations: sculpture, writing, travel. Office: ACE Integration Head Start 1419-1423 Broadway Brooklyn NY 11221-4202 Address: HCHC Inc at Kingsbrook Jewish Med Ctr DMRI Rm 219C Schenectady Ave Brooklyn NY 11203 also: ACE Preschool 139 Menahan St Brooklyn NY 11221-3907 E-mail: FSpivack997@earthlink.net.

SPIVAK, STEVEN MARK, textile and standards engineer, educator; b. NYC, Oct. 11, 1942; s. Irving Samuel and Mollie E. S. BS in Textile Engrng., Phila. Coll. Textiles, 1963; MS in Textiles, Ga. Inst. Tech., 1965; PhD in Fiber Sci., U. Manchester, United Kingdom, 1967. Asst. prof. Phila. U., 1968—70, U. Md., College Park, 1970—74, assoc. prof., 1974—83, prof., 1983—2001, prof. emeritus, 2001—. Sr. standards analyst Nat. Inst. Standards and Tech., Gaithersburg, Md., 1974-75, 86-87; expert U.S.-Saudi Arabian Joint Com. for Econ. Cooperation, Washington, 1985-91, U.S. FTC, Washington, 1985-91; chmn. ISO/COPOLCO consumer policy and internat. standards com., Geneva, 1991-95; spl. asst. U.S. Gen. Svcs. Adminstrn., 1991-92. Co-author: Standardization Essentials, 2001; co-editor: A Sourcebook on Standards Information, 1991; contbr. articles to profl. jours. including Textile Rsch. Jour., Textile Chemist and Colorist, ASTM Standardization News, Standards Engrng., Jour. Applied Fire Sci., ISO Bull. Fellow Textile Inst. (chartered textile tech. 1979), Standards Engrng. Soc. (chmn. Washington sect. 1985-87), Am. Nat. Standards Inst. (bd. dirs. 1983-91, 96-2001), Fiber Soc. (pres. 1984), Soc. Fire Protection Engrs. Achievements include research in fiber and textile flammability, performance, care, and maintenance of textile furnishings, standardization, international trade and government standards policy, indoor air quality and textiles, consumer product standards and fire safety. Home and Office: 6301 Beachway Dr Falls Church VA 22044-1510

SPIVEY, SARAH EAKINS, retired elementary school educator; b. Wilmington, N.C., Dec. 29, 1943; d. Leo E. and Kathleen (Johnson) Eakins; divorced; children: Coleman, Christopher, Jonathan. BS, Campbell U., 1965; MEd, U. N.C., 1975; prin. certification, N.C. Cen. U., 1976. Cert. elem. tchr., N.C. Tchr. Wake County Schs., Wake County, N.C., 1965-75, prin., 1975-78; dir. community schs. and pub. rels. Rocky Mt. (N.C.) City Schs., 1978-80; prin. Parkwood Elem. Sch. and Hillandale Elem., Durham, 1980—95. Neighborhood fund collector Diabetes Assn., Raleigh, NC, 1991; family suppott exec. com. mem. N.C. Air Nat. Guard, 2002—03; officer Moores Creek Battleground Assn., 1999—; mem. Red Hat Soc. Named Tchr. of Yr., State of N.C., 1973, Tarheel of Week, News and Observer Newspaper, Raleigh, 1973, Outstanding Alumni, Campbell U., 1974; named to Nat. Tchr. of Yr. Honor Roll, Ency. Britannica, 1973; recipient ARC Profl. of Yr. award, Durham County, 1993. Mem. NEA, Nat. State. Tchrs. of Yr., Nat. Fedn. Sch. Adminstrs., N.C. Assn. Educators, DAR. Avocations: reading, gardening, travel, ethnic cooking. Home: PO Box 41 Harrells NC 28444-0041

SPLITTSTOESSER, SHIRLEY O. elementary school educator; b. Rochester, Minn., June 21, 1937; d. Edward and Rose (Kruger) O'Connor; m. Walter Splittstoesser; children: Pamela, Sheryl, Riley. BS with honors, Mankato State U., 1960; MEd, Purdue U., 1962; postgrad., U. Calif., Berkeley, U. Ill. Tchr. Dist. 2148, Steele County, Minn., 1956-59, Chrysler Sch., Modesto, Calif., 1963-64, North Davis (Calif.) Pub. Schs., 1964-65, Delphi (Ind.) Pub. Schs., 1960-61, 62-63, Dist. 116-Yankee Ridge Sch., Urbana, Ill., 1965—89, Wiley Sch., 1989-94; dir. Howard Hughes Med. Inst. Sci., Urbana, 1994—2002. Rsch. in field; dir. sci. fairs, nature ctrs. Recipient Disting. Educator awrd Milken Family Found., 1990. Mem. Univ. Women's Club (chair 1996—, Delta Kappa Gamma (pres. 1998-2000). Home: 2006 Cureton Dr Urbana IL 61801-6226 Business E-Mail: splitts@life.uiuc.edu.

SPODEK, BERNARD, early childhood educator; b. Bklyn., Sept. 17, 1931; s. David and Esther (Lebenbaum) S.; m. Prudence Debb, June 21, 1957; children: Esther Yin-ling, Jonathan Chou. BA, Bklyn. Coll., 1952; MA, Columbia U., 1955, EdD, 1962. Cert. early childhood edn. tchr., N.Y. Tchr. Beth Hayeled Sch., N.Y.C., 1952-56, N.Y. City Pub. Schs., Bklyn., 1956-57, Early Childhood Ctr., Bklyn. Coll., 1957-60; asst. prof. elem. edn. U. Wis.-Milw., 1961-65; assoc. prof. early childhood edn. U. Ill., Champaign, 1965-68, prof. dept. curriculum and instrn., 1968-97, dir. dept. grad. programs, 1986-87, chair dept., 1987-89, dir. hons. program, Coll. Edn., 1984-86, mem. faculty Bur. Ednl. Rsch., 1981-85, prof. emeritus, 1997—; adv. prof. Hong Kong Inst. of Edn., 1999-2001. Dir. insts. Nat. Def. Edn. Act, 1965-67, dir. experienced tchr. fellowship program, 1967-69, co-dir. program for tchr. trainers in early childhood edn., 1969-74; vis. prof. Western Wash. State U., 1974, U. Wis., Madison, 1980; vis. scholar Sch. Early Childhood Studies, Brisbane (Australia) Coll. Advanced Edn., Delissa Inst. Early Childhood Studies, S. Australia Coll. Advanced Edn., 1985, Beijing Normal U., Nanjing Normal U., E. China Normal U., Shangai, People's Republic China, 1986; rsch. fellow Kobe U., Japan, 1996; adj. prof. Queensland (Australia) U. Tech., 2000. Author or co-author 35 books including: (with others) A Black Studies Curriculum for Early Childhood Edication, 1972, 2d edit., 1976, Teaching in the Early Years, 1972, 3d edit., 1985, Early Childhood Education, 1973, Studies in Open Education, 1975 (Japanese trans.), Early Childhood Education: Issues and Perspectives, 1977, (with Nir-Janiv and Steg) International Perspectives on Early Childhood Education, 1982 (Hebrew trans.), with Saracho and Lee (Mainstreaming Young Children, 1984, (with Saracho and Davis) Foundations of Early Childhood Education, 1987, 2d edit. (Japanese trans.), 1991, (with Saracho) Right from the Start, 1994 (Chinese and Korean translations), Dealing with Individual Differences in the Early Childhood Classroom, 1994; editor: Handbook of Research in Early Childhood Education, 1982, Today's Kindergarten, 1986, (with Saracho and Peters) Professionalism and the Early Childhood Practitioner, 1988, (with Saracho) Early Childhood Teacher Education, 1990, Issues in Early Childhood Curriculum, 1991, Educationally Appropriate Kindergarten Practices, 1991, Issues in Childcare, 1992, Handbook of Research on the Education of Young Children (Portuguese translation), 1993, (Portuguese tranls.) (with Saracho), Language and Literacy in Early Childhood Education, 1993; (with Safford and Saracho) Early Childhood Special Education, 1994; (with Garcia, McLaughlin & Saracho) Meeting the Challenge of Cultural and Linguistic Diversity, 1995, (with Saracho) Issues in Early Childhood Educational Evaluation and Assessment, 1996, (with Saracho) Multiple Perspectives on Play in Early Childhood Education, 1998, (With Saracho and Pellegrini) Issues in Early Childhood Educational Research, 1998, (with Saracho) Contemporary Perspectives in Early Childhood Curriculum, 2002, (with Saracho) Contemporary Perspectives in Early Childhood Education, 2002, (with Saracho) Contemporary Perspectives on Play in Early Childhood Education, 2003, (with Saracho) Studying Teachers in Early Childhood Settings, 2003; series editor Yearbook in Early Childhood Education, early childhood edn. publs., 1971-79; guest editor Studies in Ednl. Evaluation, 1982, Early Education and Child Development, 1995; also contbr. chpts to books, articles to profl. jours. Mem. Am. Ednl. Rsch. Assn. (chair early childhood and child devel. spl. interest group 1983-84, publs. com. 1984-86), Nat. Assn. Edn. Young Children (sec. 1965-68, bd. govs. 1968-72, pres. 1976-78, editorial adv. bd. 1972-76, book rev. editor, 1972-74, cons. editor, 1985-87 Young Children jour., mem. tchr. edn. commn. 1981-88, chair commn. on appropriate edn. 4-5 yr. old children, 1984-85, cons. editor Early Childhood Rsch. Quar. 1987-90), Nat. Soc. for Study of Edn. (1972 yearbook com.), Pacific Early Childhood Edn. Rsch. Assn. (pres. 2000—). Office: U Ill Dept Curriculum & Instrn 1310 S 6th St Champaign IL 61820-6925 E-mail: b-spodek@uiuc.edu.

SPOHN, JANICE, elementary education educator, consultant; b. Pitts., Jan. 12, 1952; d. James Arthur and Jean Edna (Smithyman) Rowan; m. Chester Michael Spohn II, Oct. 23, 1972; children: Chester M. III, Lisa Marie. BE, Clarion U., 1973; ME, Slippery Rock U., 1989; supervisory cert., Duquesne U., 1992. Cert. reading specialist, gifted edn., supervisor reading, Pa. Group supr. Butler County (Pa.) Children Ctr., 1974-87; temp. instr. Slippery Rock U., Slippery Rock, Pa., 1989; reading specialist North Allegheny Schs., Pitts., 1990—. Coord. Pa. Framework Network, North Allegheny Schs., 1991—; Pa. Framework steering com. Allegheny Intermediate Unit, 1993-2001. Co-author/editor: (book) Pennsylvania Framework-Portfolio Implementation Guide, 1993; author, instr. online course on Emergent and Early Reading. Mem. ASCD, Nat. Coun. Tchrs. of English, Internat. Reading Assn., Keystone State Reading Assn., Three Rivers Reading Coun., Butler County Reading Coun. Avocations: reading, crafts, camping. Home: 520 Herman Rd Butler PA 16002-9157 Office: Peebles Elem N Allegheny Schs 8625 Peebles Rd Pittsburgh PA 15237-5720 E-mail: cspohn@zoominternet.net., jspohn@northallegheny.org.

SPOOR, KATHRINE SUE, elementary education educator; b. Springfield, Mass., Apr. 10, 1964; d. Kenneth Martin and Sara Estelle (Farnum) S. BS, The King's Coll., 1986; diploma, Inst. of Children's Lit., 1989; MEd, Castleton (Vt.) State Coll., 1993. Cert. tchr. N-8, Vt. Chpt. I reading Weathersfield Pub. Schs., Perkinsville, Vt., 1986-87, tchr. grade 5 Ascutney, Vt., 1988, tchr. grade 2 Perkinsville, 1988-91; tchr. grades 1-6 Chester Pub. Schs., Balt., 1987; tchr. LA/reading grade 4 Mid-Vt. Christian Sch., Quechee, 1993-94, tchr. grade 4, 1994—99, 2002—, tchr. grade 6, 1999—2002, curriculum coord. K-6, dir. academics, 2002—. Tchr. asst. team Perkinsville Elem. Sch., 1986-87, 88-89, 90-91. Avocations: reading, travel, bicycling, swimming, music.

SPRAGENS, WILLIAM CLARK, public policy educator, consultant; b. Lebanon, Ky., Oct. 1, 1925; s. Thomas Eugene and Edna Grace (Clark) S.; m. Elaine Jean Dunham, June 14, 1964. AB in Journalism, U. Ky., 1947, MA, 1953; PhD, Mich. State U., 1966. Instr. U. Tenn., Knoxville, 1962-64; part-time instr. Mich. State U., East Lansing, 1964-65; asst. prof. Millikin U., Decatur, Ill., 1965-67, Wis. State U., Oshkosh, 1967-69; assoc. prof. Bowling Green (Ohio) State U., 1969-82, prof., 1982-86, prof. emeritus, 1986—; chmn. Spragens and Skinner Assocs., Reston, Va., 1996—. Author: Electronic Magazines, 1995; editor-in-chief: Popular Images of American Presidents, 1988. Del. candidate McGovern for pres. campaign, Bowling Green, 1972; co-dir. Nat. Convs. Program, 1972, 76, 80, 84. Lyndon Baines Johnson Found. grantee, 1977, 78. Mem. AAAS, World Affairs Coun. Washington, Am. Polit. Sci. Assn., Internat. Soc. for Polit. Psychology, Am. Soc. for Pub. Adminstrn. Democrat. Presbyterian. Avocations: collectibles, psychology. Home and Office: PO Box 410 Herndon VA 20172-0410 E-mail: sprag1999@aol.com.

SPRALEY, JUDITH ANN, nursing educator, administrator; b. Gross Point, Mich., Jan. 11, 1936; d. Leonard Joseph and Margaret (McCloskey) S. BSN, Mount St. Joseph Coll., 1958; MEd, U. Cin., 1986. RN Ohio. Dir. nursing svc. Otto C. Epp Meml. Hosp., Cin.; nursing instr. Deaconess Hosp. Sch. Nursing, Cin.; nursing adminstr. U. Hosp., Cin.; chair surg. tech. program Cin. State Tech. Coll. and C.C., 1979-97; ednl. cons., instr. Optima Health Svcs., Inc., Bradenton, Fla., 1999—; ednl. cons. Fla. Career Inst., Lakeland, Fla., 2001; RN Immunization Clinic, East Coast Med. Network, Inc., Orlando, Fla., 2003—. Author, instr. operating rm. courses for nurses and surg. technologists; acute and long term patient advocate; cons. curriculum devel. and instrn. SHINE vol. Fla. Dept. Elder Affairs. Mem.: The Red Hat Soc., Lakeland Woman's Club. Home and Office: 3332 Songbird Ln Lakeland FL 33811-3016 E-mail: jjjsmith@strato.net.

SPRAYBERRY, ROSLYN RAYE, retired secondary school educator; b. Newnan, Ga., June 29, 1942; d. Henry Ray and Grace (Bernhard) S. BA, Valdosta State Coll., 1964; MA in Teaching, Ga. State U., 1976, EdS in Spanish, 1988; EdD, Nova U., 1993. Cert. tchr., Ga. Tchr. history Griffin (Ga.) High Sch., 1964-65; tchr. 6th grade Beaverbrook Elem Sch., Griffin, 1965-66; tchr. Spanish, chair fgn. lang. dept. Forest Park (Ga.) High Sch., 1969-77, Riverdale (Ga.) High Sch., 1977-99; ret., 1999. Correlator Harcourt, Brace, Jovanovich, 1989; adv. bd. So. Conf. Lang. Teaching, 1992-99; lectr. and speaker in field. Contbr. articles to The Ednl. Resource Info. Ctr. Clearinghouse on Langs. and Linguistics, Ctr. for Applied Linguistics, Washington; designed courses for the Gifted, Ga. Dept. of Edn. Cnvener Acad. Alliances-Atlanta II, Clayton County, Ga., 1982-99; advisor, workshop leader Ga. Fgn. Lang. Camp, Atlanta, 1983; dir. Clayton County Fgn. Lang. Festival, 1990-91. Recipient STAR Tchr. award Ga. C. of C., 1982; Fulbright-Hays scholar, 1978; NEH grantee, 1977, 84. Mem. NEA, Am. Coun. Tchrs. Fgn. Langs., Am. Assn. Tchrs. Spanish and Portuguese, Ga. Assn. Educators, Fgn. Lang. Assn. Ga. (treas. 1977-85, assoc. editor jour. 1981-86, Tchr. of Yr. award 1976), Clayton County Edn. Assn., So. Conf. Lang. Teaching, KPS Leadership Specialists (co-founder 1993). Methodist. Avocations: guitar playing, traveling, reading, writing. Home: 104 Hickory Trail Stockbridge GA 30281-7361

SPRENKLE, CASE MIDDLETON, economist, educator; b. Cleve., Aug. 18, 1934; s. Raymond E. and Helen K. (Middleton) Sprenkle; m. Elaine Elizabeth Jensen, June 22, 1957; children: David, Peter, Amy. BS, U. Colo., 1956; MA, Yale U., 1957, PhD, 1960. Instr. econs. Yale U., New Haven, 1959-60; mem. faculty U. Ill., Urbana, 1960-97, prof., 1970-97, prof. emeritus, 1997—, chmn. dept. econs., 1976-80, acting head dept. econs., 1995-96, asst. dean Coll. Commerce, 1962-65; dir. U. Ill.-U. Warsaw MBA program, 1991—. Cons. Ill. Revenue Commn., 1962; faculty Econs. Inst., Boulder, Colo., 1965, Boulder, 72, Boulder, 81; vis. scholar London Sch. Econs., 1967, 74, 81, 88; vis. lectr. City of London U., 1981; bd. dirs. Aggregate Equipment Co. Contbr. articles to profl. jours. Bd. dirs. Champaign-Urbana Symphony, treas., 1972—74, pres., 1975—77; bd. dirs. Champaign County Arts and Humanities Coun., 1977—79, Champaign-Urbana Mass Transit Dist., 1983—96, vice chmn., 1985, 1993—94. Am. Bankers Assn. grantee, 1970—71. Mem.: Am. Fin. Assn., Am. Econs. Assn., Omicron Delta Epsilon. Presbyterian. Home: 3403 S Persimmon Cir Urbana IL 61802-7128 Office: U Ill Dept Econs 1201 S 6th St Champaign IL 61820 E-mail: csprenkl@uiuc.edu.

SPRESSER, DIANE MAR, mathematics educator; b. Welch, W.Va., Dec. 12, 1943; d. Paul Mack and Rachel Jean (DeMario) S. BS with honors, Radford U., 1965; MA, U. Tenn., 1967; postgrad., Ohio State U., summers 1970-72; PhD, U. Va., 1977. Math. instr. James Madison U., Harrisonburg, Va., 1967-68, asst. prof. math., 1968-77, assoc. prof. math., 1977-82, prof. math., 1982—98, acting head dept. math., 1978-79, head dept. math. and computer sci., 1979-92, head dept. math., 1992-94, prof. emerita math., 1998—; 19709476. Tchr. enhancement program dir. NSF, Arlington, Va., 1994-2002; dir. divsn. elem., secondary and informal edn., NSF, 2001-02, sr. prgm. coord. Math. and Sci. Partnership, 2002—; mem. nat. question writing com. MathCounts, 1993-96. Reviewer Computing Revs. of Assn. for Computing Machinery, 1990—; contbr. articles and book/software revs. to profl. jours. Organist Blessed Sacrament Ch., Harrisonburg, 1969-81. Mem. Am. Math. Soc., Math. Assn. Am., Assn. Women in Math., Nat. Coun. Tchrs. Math., Assn. for Computing Machinery, Va. Acad. Sci. (rsch. com. 1991-96, co-chair arrangement com.). Roman Catholic. Avocations: classical music, theatre, movies. Office: NSF 4201 Wilson Blvd Rm 875 Arlington VA 22230-0001

SPRINGER, MARLENE, university administrator, educator; b. Murfreesboro, Tenn., Nov. 16, 1937; d. Foster V. and Josephine Jones; children: Ann Springer, Rebecca Springer. BA in English and Bus. Adminstrn., Centre Coll., 1959; MA in Am. Lit., Ind. U., 1963, PhD in English Lit., 1969. Chair English dept. U. Mo., Kansas City, 1980-81, acting assoc. dean grad. sch., 1982; Am. Coun. of Edn. Adminstrn. fellow U. Kans., Lawrence, 1982-83; dean of grad. sch. U. Mo., Kansas City, 1983-84, assoc. vice chancellor for acad. affairs and grad. studies, 1985-89; vice chancellor for acad. affairs East Carolina U., Greenville, N.C., 1989-94; pres. CUNY Coll., Staten Island, 1994—. Author: Edith Wharton and Kate Chopin: A Reference Guide, 1976; What Manner of Woman: Essays, 1977, Thomas Hardy's Use of Allusion, 1983, Plains Woman: The Diary of Martha Farnsworth, 1986 (Choice award 1986), Ethan Frome: A Nightmare of Need, 1993. Huntington Libr. fellow, 1988. Mem.: Coun. Grad. Schs. (chair 1986—88), Assn. Tchr. Educators (chair 1992), Acad. Leadership Acad. (exec. com. 1992—94), Am. Assn. State Colls. and Univs., Am. Coun. on Edn. (profl. devel. com. 1991—, invited participant Nat. Forum 1984, bd. dirs. 2001—). Office: Coll Staten Island 2800 Victory Blvd Rm 1a-404 Staten Island NY 10314-6609

SPRINGER, WILMA MARIE, retired secondary school educator; b. Goshen, Ind., Jan. 13, 1933; d. Noah A. and Laura D. (Miller) Kaufman; m. Walter Frederick Springer, May 25, 1957; children: Anita Daniel, Timothy, Mark. BA, Goshen Coll., 1956; MS, Bradley U., 1960. Tchr. Topeka Elem. Sch., Ind., 1956—57, Metamora Grade Sch., Ill., 1957—59, Bellflower Unified Sch. Dist., Calif., 1960—61, 1968—2001, Lindstrom Elem. Sch., 1970—89, Jefferson Elem. Sch., Bellflower, 1989—92, Woodruff Elem., 1992—93, Williams Elem. Sch., Lakewood, Calif., 1993—96; ret., 2001. Chmn. gifted and talented edn. Lindstrom Elem. Sch., Lakewood, 1986—89, Jefferson Elem. Sch., Bellflower, 1989—91, Baxter Elem., 1996—2001; stage mgr. Hour of Power TV Crystal Cathedral, 1983—; mem. program quality rev. team State of Calif., 1989—91; mem. adv. bd. Weekly Reader, 1989—96. Contbr. articles in field. Active sch. bd. campaign, 1984, Bellflower City Coun., 1988, state senator and assemblyman campaigns, 1986-87; petition circulator various state initiatives, 1987-88; bd. dirs. Women's Ministries of Crystal Cathedral, Garden Grove, Calif., 1978-88; educator del. People to People Ambassadors Program, South Africa, 2003. Instructional Improvement Program grantee State of Calif., 1986-87; recipient Recognition award Regional Ednl. TV Adv. Coun., 1986, Cathedral Star award Women's Ministries of Crystal Cathedral, 1985. Mem.: AAUW, NEA (del. nat. conv. 1986, 1987, 1990, 1992, 1993, 1994, 1995), Calif. Tchrs. Assn. (del. 1986, 1994), Bellflower Edn. Assn. (elem. dir. 1986—88, treas. 1988—89, v.p. 1989—91, pres. 1991—95), Toastmasters (Founder's Dist. Gov. 2001—02, disting., Distinguished Toastmaster, achieved Distinguished Dist.), Delta Kappa Gamma. Republican. Mem. Reformed Churches of Am. Avocations: quilting, water color painting. Home: 3180 Marna Ave Long Beach CA 90808-3246

SPRINGSTON, JAMES RAYMOND, college administrator, educator; b. Detroit, June 16, 1947; s. George Hatzel and Elizabeth Jane (Phelps) S.; m. Carol Sue Rhinehart, June 27, 1974 (div. Feb. 1984). BA, Mich. State U., 1971; MEd, Wayne State U., 1981. Cert. tchr. Mich. High sch. tchr., debate coach Wateford Sch. Dist., Pontiac, Mich., 1972-81; dir. debate, asst. prof. Marist Coll., Poughkeepsie, N.Y., 1985-91, dir. forensics, 1991-92; instr. speech, dir. of debate U. R.I., Kingston, 1992—. Adj. prof. debate coach U. Mich., Flint, 1981-85; adj. faculty Wayne State U., Detroit, 1984-85, Henry Ford Community Coll., Dearborn, Mich., 1984-85; dir. Nat. Ceda Debate Inst., 1991—, Boces Jr. High Debate Program, Poughkeepsie, 1988-92. Author: (with others) Prima Facie, 1989, Championship Debates, 1991. Mem. comm. com. Am. Heart Assn., Poughkeepsie, 1987-92; vol. trainer United Way, Poughkeepsie, 1991-92. Mem. Cross Examination Debate Assn. (rep. to nat. coun. 1991-93), Speech Communication Assn., Phi Kappa Delta. Baha'I. Avocations: photography, canoeing. Office: U RI 309 Independence Hall Kingston RI 02881

SPRINKLE, JAMES THOMAS, paleontologist, educator; b. Arlington, Mass., Sept. 2, 1943; s. Rex Thomas and Rose (Weiss) S.; m. G.K. Klizicki, Sept. 1, 1968; children: David, Diana. SB, MIT, 1965; MA, Harvard U., 1966, PhD, 1971. Postdoctoral assoc. NRC-U.S. Geol. Survey at Paleontol. and Stratigraphiy Br., Denver, 1970-71; asst. prof. dept. geol. scis. U. Tex., Austin, 1971—77; assoc. prof. dept. geolog. scis. U. Tex., Austin, 1977—83, prof., 1983-86, 1st Mr. and Mrs. Charles E. Yager prof., 1986—. Mem. Treatise adv. bd. U. Kans. Paleontol. Inst., Lawrence, 1991—. Contbr. articles to sci. and profl. jours.; co-author monographs, lab. manual in paleobiology, textbook chpts. Grantee NSF, 1977, 89, 93. Fellow Geol. Soc. Am. (treatise commn. 1982-86); mem. Paleontol. Soc. (councilor 1981-83, Schuchert award 1982), Soc. for Sedimentary Geology, Soc. Systematic Biologists. Achievements include proposal of new classes of fossil echinoderms (Ctenocystoidea), 1969, (Coronoidea, 1983); new subphylum of fossil echinoderms (Blastozoa), 1973; co-author paper reporting discovery of fossilized eggs in late Paleozoic blastoid, 1976. Home: 2801 Winston Ct Austin TX 78731-5539 Office: U Tex Dept Geol Scis Austin TX 78712 E-mail: echino@mail.utexas.edu.

SPRINKLE, MARTHA CLARE, elementary school educator; b. Tehachapi, Calif., Oct. 17, 1944; d. William Foote and Mildred Sprinkle; BA, U. Calif., Santa Barbara, 1966; MA in Orgn. Mgmt., U. Phoenix, 2000. Cert. tchr. Calif., water aerobics instr. 1986. Tchr. Muroc Unified Sch. Dist., Edwards, Calif., 1966—71, Elk Hills Sch., Tipman, Calif., 1971—79,

Tehachopi Valley Recreation and Pks., 1979—, So. Kern Unified Sch., Rosamond, Calif., 1985—2003. Planning commr. City of Tehachapi, Calif., 1984—. Home: PO Box 852 Tehachapi CA 93581

SPROUL, JOAN HEENEY, elementary school educator; b. Johnstown, Pa., July 17, 1932; d. James L. and Grace M. (Dunn) Heeney; m. Robert Sproul, July 31, 1957 (dec.); 1 child, Mary Claire. BS, Clarion U., 1954; MA, George Wash. U., 1963; postgrad., U. Va., 1966-88. Cert. tchr., Va. Kindergarten tchr. Jefferson Sch., Warren, Pa., 1954-55; primary grades tchr. Alexandria (Va.) Pub. Schs., 1955-64; elem. tchr. Fairfax County Schs., Springfield, Va., 1965-97; math. lead tchr. West Springfield (Va.) Sch., 1987-97, ret., 1997. Contbr. (with others) Virginia History, 1988. Advisor Springfield Young Organists Assn., 1971-83; mem. Fairfax County Dem. Com., 1988-94, West Springfield Civic Assn., 1965—, Women's Aux. Fairfax Co. Salvation Army. Grantee Impact II, 1985-86. Mem. AAUW, NEA, Nat. Fedn. Bus. and Profl. Women (pres., dir., dist. VIII 1984—, Woman of Yr. 1985, 88), Delta Kappa Gamma (2d v.p. Va. chpt. 1963—), Phi Delta Kappa, Sigma Sigma Sigma. Episcopalian. Avocations: reading, music, gardening, fashion design. Home: 8005 Greeley Blvd West Springfield VA 22152-3036

SPROULE, DEBORAH W. art educator, artist; b. Inglewood, Calif., Sept. 1, 1957; d. Joseph Fredrick and Martha Ann (Gross) Wagner; m. Dale Fenton Sproule, May 1, 1955; 1 child, Andrew Martin. BS Fine Art, U. Oreg., 1982; BS Art Edn., U. Minn., 1985; MA, U. Wis., 2000, MFA, 2001. Cert. art tchr. Wis., 1986. One-woman shows include, Oreg., Minn., Wis., 1980—2003, exhibited in group shows, 2000—03, Represented in permanent collections Soloman Kamm, Chgo., Mesa Gallery, Ariz. Refugee vol. Calvary Episcopal Ch., Rochester, Minn., 1991—98, channel 1 food shelf vol., 1991—98, youth min. vol., 1991—98; vol. Cmty. Svc., Refugee Resettlement. Mem.: Coll. Arts Assn., Am. Crafts Coun., U. Wis. Alumni Assn. Avocation: cmty. advocacy visual art. Home: 1617 Tarragon Dr Madison WI 53716

SPROUSE, CHERYL LYNNE, principal; b. Lynchburg, Va., May 29, 1951; d. Elwood Gleason and Essie Ellen (Campbell) S. AS in pre-teaching, Ctrl. Va. C.C., 1971; BS, Radford Coll., 1973; MS, Radford U., 1978. Cert. tchr. Va. 5th and 7th grade tchr. Amherst (Va.) County Pub. Schs., 1973-78; asst. prin., 4th and 5th grade tchr. Amherst Elem. Sch., 1978-79, asst. prin., 1979-80, prin., 1989-93; asst. prin. Amelon Elem. Sch., Madison Heights, Va., 1979-80, Monelison Jr. High Sch., Madison Heights, 1980-89; prin. Amherst (Va.) Elem. Sch., 1989-93, Check (Va.) Elem. Sch., 1993-95; ops. mgr. Sam's Club, Charlottesville, Va., 1995-99; grad. coord. Liberty U., Lynchburg, Va., 1999—. Family life facilitator Amherst County Pub. Schs., 1985-87, family life curriculum Va. Dept. Edn., 1986-87, chpt. 1 adv. bd., 1989-91. Dir. Young Musicians Choir, Grades 1 to 6, Rivermont Ave. Bapt. Ch., Lynchburg, 1990—, pres. adult choir, 1991-93; mem. adult choir 1st Bapt. Ch., Roanoke, 1994—, dir. young musicians grade 4 choir. Mem. ASCD, Va. Assn. Elem. Sch. Prins., Piedmont Assn. Elem. Prins., Radford U. Alumni (pres. 1983-85), Order Eastern Star (electa 1994-95, soloist 1991-93, worthy matron 1998-99), Phi Delta Kappa Republican. Avocations: singing, swimming, tennis, reading, crafts. Office: Liberty U University Blvd Lynchburg VA 24502 Address: 208 Graves Dr # B Forest VA 24551-2620 E-mail: csprouse@liberty.edu.

SPROUSE, EARLENE PENTECOST, special education educator; b. Hopewell, Va., Apr. 23, 1939; d. Earl Paige and Sophia Marlene (Chairky) Pentecost; m. David Andrew Koren, July 3, 1957 (div. Jan. 1963); children: David Andrew Jr., Elysia Marlene, Merri Paige; m. Wayne Alexender Sprouse, Sept. 2, 1964; 1 child, Michael Wayne. AS, Paul D. Camp C.C., Franklin, Va., 1973; BS in Comm. Disorders, Old Dominion U., 1975, MEd in Spl. Edn., 1977. Tchg. cert. with endorsement in speech lang. pathology, learning disabilities and emotional disturbance, Va. Speech lang. pathologist Southampton County Schs., Va., 1975-76; learning disabled tchr. itinerant Franklin (Va.) City Pub. Schs., 1976-78, emotionally disturbed/learning disabled tchr., 1978-85, speech lang. pathologist, 1986-91, ednl. diagnostician, 1992—2003, lead tchr. spl. edn., 2000—03; resource specialist TideWater Acad., 1999—; speech lang. pathologist South Hampton Co. Pub. Sch., 2003—. Project leader curriculum guide Listening and Lang. Processing Skills, 1990-91; speech/lang. pathologist Southampton County, 2003—. Mem. Career Edn. Adv. Com., Va. Dept. Edn., 1995—; mem. field-based cons. network Old Dominion U., Coll. of William and Mary, 1997—. Recipient Excellence in Edn. award C. of C., Hampton Roads, Va., 1988-89; grantee Va. Edn. Assn., Richmond, 1994—, Project UNITE Dept. Edn., Richmond, 1994—, Project Payroll, 1999-2000, DOE/VBEP Project Second Chance, 2000-01. Mem. Franklin City Edn. Assn. (pres. 1980, 91), Internat. Dyslexia Assn., Coun. for Learning Disabilities. Methodist. Avocations: fishing, music. Home: 272 Colonia Dr Surry VA 23883 E-mail: esprouse39@hotmail.com.

SPRUIELL, VANN, psychoanalyst, educator, editor, researcher; b. Leeds, Ala., Oct. 16, 1926; s. Vann Lindley and Zada (Morton) S.; m. Iris Taylor, Sept. 20, 1951 (div. Oct. 1966); children: Graham, Fain, Garth; m. Joyce Ellis, Feb. 11, 1967; stepchildren: Sidney Reavey, Catherine Ellis, Matson Ellis. BS, U. Ala., Tuscaloosa, 1948; MD, Harvard U., 1952. Resident Bellevue Hosp., N.Y.C., 1952-53, N.Y. Hosp., N.Y.C., 1953-55; fellow Tulane Sch. Medicine, New Orleans, 1955-57; pvt. practice New Orleans, 1957—. Vis. rschr. Anna Freud Ctr., London, 1972-73; co-pub. JOURLIT and BOOKREV; pres. and founding mem. Psychoanalytic Archives CD-ROM Texts (PACT), New Orleans, 1993—; clin. prof. psychiatry La. State U. Sch. Medicine, Tulane U. Sch. Medicine; sec. Ctr. for Advanced Studies in Psychoanalysis, 1989—. Editl. bd. Psychoanalytic Quarterly, 1973—; N.Am. editor Internat. Jour. Psychoanalysis, London, 1988-93; editor Psychoanalysis South, 1996—; mem. various other editl. bds.; contbr. articles to profl. jours. and books. Sgt. U.S. Army, 1944-46. Mem. Am. Psychoanalytic Assn. (sec. bd. on profl. stds. 1979-92), Wyvern Club. Avocations: interdisciplinary studies, sailing. Home: 215 Iona St Metairie LA 70005-4137

SPRUILL, HOWARD VERNON, former academic administrator, minister; b. South Norfolk, Va., Dec. 27, 1919; s. Veron B. and Mabel E. (Kirby) S.; m. Daisy Lee Singleton, Dec. 11, 1943; 1 child, Ruth Elaine. BS, Valley Forge Christian Coll., 1977; MDiv, Luther Rice Sem., 1978, DMin, 1980. Ordained to ministry Assemblies of God, 1953. Auditor U.S. Navy, Little Creek, Va., 1945-50; pastor Elk Garden, W.Va., 1950-52, Emporia, Va., 1952-57, Manassas, Va., 1957-69; dist. sec., treas., 1968-74; pastor Silver Spring, Md., 1974-79; dist. supt. Potomac Dist. Coun., Assemblies of God Ch., 1979-91. Pres. Valley Forge Christian Coll., 1982; chmn. bd. regents, 1968-91; pres. Prince William County Ministerial Assn., 1966-68. Author: Deacon Servant to God and Man, 1980. Served with U.S. Army, 1937-45. Home: 122 Southern Oak Dr Hagerstown MD 21740

SPURGEON, NANNETTE SUANN (SUSIE SPURGEON), special education educator; b. Crawfordsville, Ind., Nov. 15, 1962; d. Dwight Cordell and Nancy Mae (Meagher) Spurgeon. BS, Stephen F. Austin State U., 1985; MS, Purdue U., 1990. Cert. elem. edn. tchr., deaf edn. tchr., learning disabilities educator. Tchr. 1st grade Aldine Ind. Sch. Dist., Houston, 1985-86; tchr. pre-Kindergarten Cypress-Fairbanks Ind. Sch. Dist., Houston, 1986-88, Disabilities Svcs., Inc., Crawfordsville, Ind., 1989; elem. hearing impaired tchr. Pleasant Hill Elem. Sch. North Montgomery Community Sch. Corp., Crawfordsville, Ind., 1990-91; tchr. learning disabilites, title 1, hearing impaired, reading recovery Hoover Elem. Sch. Crawfordsville Community Sch. Corp., Crawfordsville, 1991—. Tchr. aide Crawfordsville Community Sch. Dist., 1988-89; interpreter Christ the Good Shepard Cath. Ch., Houston, 1986-87; coach 7th grade volleyball Northridge Mid. Sch., 1990; volleyball coach Tuttle Mid. Sch., Crawfordsville, 1991—. Named to Alpha Chi, Kappa Delta Pi. Mem. Reading Recovery Coun. of N.Am., Coun. for Exceptional Children, Kappa Sigma Phi. Avocations: volleyball, softball, signed song interpretations. Home: 307 Jennison St Crawfordsville IN 47933-2748 E-mail: sspurgeon@hoover.cville.k12.in.us.

SQUARCIA, PAUL ANDREW, school superintendent; b. Yukon, Pa., Nov. 17, 1939; s. Paul and Lucy (Nardonne) S.; m. Gena Maria Porreca, Aug. 18, 1962; children: Paul, Stephanie, Suzanne. BS, Boston U., 1961, cert. advanced studies, 1974; EdD, Boston Coll., 1987; MEd, U. N.H., 1967. Sci. tchr. Berlin (N.H.) Sch. Dept., 1961-63, asst. prin., 1963-66; prin. Oxford Hills High Sch., South Paris, Maine, 1967-70, Silver Lake Regional Dist., Kingston, Mass., 1970-72, asst. supt. schs., 1972-78, supt. schs., 1978—. Adj. prof. Bridgewater (Mass.) State Coll., 1980—, Lesley Coll., Cambridge, Mass., 1980—. Recipient Nat. Superintendent of the Yr. awd., Massachusetts, Am. Assn. of School Administrators, 1993. Mem. ASCD, Am. Assn. Sch. Adminstrs., Mass. Assn. Sch. Supts. (pres. 1992-93). Roman Catholic. Avocations: reading, traveling, spectator sports. Home: 28 Holmes Ter Plymouth MA 02360-4013 Office: Silver Lake Regional Dist 250 Pembroke St Kingston MA 02364-1066

SQUIBB, SANDRA HILDYARD, special education educator; b. Kansas City, Mo., May 23, 1943; d. Victor Herbert and Vivian Aline (Henderson) Hildyard; children: Jason, Trevor. BA, So. Meth. U., 1966; MS, FHSU, 1984. Cert. early childhood, spl. edn. tchr., Kans., Tex., cert. bldg. adminstr. K-12. Speech pathologist Edinburg (Tex.) Consolidated Sch. Dist., 1971-74; owner, audiologist Northwest Kans. Hearing Svc., Colby, Kans., 1976—; supr. Northwest Kans. Ednl. Svc. Ctr., Colby, 1980-87, coord. Oakley, Kans., 1987-92. Treas. Kans. Div. of Early Childhood, 1987-89. Precinct chmn. Dem. Party, Thomas County, 1980—, party chmn., 1988-90; mem. Parent Adv. Coun., Colby, 1984-87; mem. bd. Alcohol and Drug Abuse Coun.; cmty. rep. Head Start Policy Coun., 1994—; mem. Thomas County Econ. Devel. Comty. Liaison Group, 1998—. Recipient grants in field. Mem. Coun. for Exceptional Children (award of excellence 1991). Roman Catholic. Avocations: skiing, golf. Home: 425 La Hacienda Dr Colby KS 67701-3914 Office: NW Kans Hearing Svcs 175 S Range Ave Colby KS 67701-2931

SQUIRE, JAMES ROBERT, retired publisher, consultant; b. Oakland, Calif., Oct. 14, 1922; s. Harry Edwin and Ruby (Fulton) S.; m. Barbara Lyman, Jan. 20, 1946; children: Kathryn Elizabeth, Kevin Richard, David Whitford. BA, Pomona Coll., 1947, DLitt, 1966; MA, U. Calif., Berkeley, 1949, PhD, 1956. Tchr. secondary sch., Oakland, Calif., 1949-54; supr., lectr. English edn. U. Calif. at Berkeley, 1951-59; prof. English U. Ill., Urbana, 1959-67; exec. sec. Nat. Council Tchrs. English, 1960-67; editor-in-chief, sr. v.p. Ginn & Co., Lexington, Mass., 1968-74, sr. v.p., pub., 1975-80, sr. v.p., dir. research and devel., 1980-82, sr. v.p., sr. cons., 1983-84; cons., 1984-94. Lectr. grad. sch. edn. Harvard U., 1990-99; sr. rsch. assoc. Boston U., 1996-97; pres. Nat. Conf. Rsch. in English, 1982-83; pres. Hall of Fame in Reading, 1995-96; sr. rsch. assoc. Boston U., 1996-97. Author: (with W. Loban, M. Ryan) Teaching Language and Literature, 1961, 69, (with R.K. Applebee) High School English Instruction Today, 1968, (with B.L. Squire) Greek Myths and Legends, 1967, Teaching English in the United Kingdom, 1969, A New Look at Progressive Education, 1972; editor: Teaching of English, 76th Yearbook Nat. Soc. Study Edn., 1977, Dynamics of Language Learning, 1987, Writing K-12 Exemplary Programs, 1987, (with R. Iadrisano) Perspectives on Writing: Theory, Research, Practice, 2000, (with J. Jensen, D. Lapp, J. Flood) Handbook of Research on Teaching the English Language Arts, 1991, 2d edit., 2001, (with E.J. Farrell) Transactions in Literature: A Fifty Year Perspective; section editor: Ency. of English Studies and Language Arts, 1994. Bd. dirs. Am. Edn. Publ. Inst., 1968-70. With AUS, 1943-45. Recipient Creative Scholarship award Coll. Lang. Assn., 1961, Lifetime Rsch. award Nat. Conf. Rsch. in English, 1992; named Ky. col., 1966; named to Hall of Fame in reading, 1987. Mem. MLA, Assn. Am. Pubs. (vice chmn. sch. divsn. 1971-73, chmn. 1974-76, 81-82, Mary McNulty award 1983), Nat. Coun. Tchrs. English (Exec. Com. award 1967,l Disting. Svc. award 1991), Internat. Reading Assn., Coll. Conf. on Composition and Communication, Phi Delta Kappa. Home: 2807 Kings Crossing Apt 115 Kingwood TX 77345

SQUIRES, CONNIE JO, special education educator; b. Omaha, Nebr., July 14, 1933; d. Paul Sydney Hilt, Lillian Elvera (Holstrom) Hilt; m. Daryl Jessup Squires, Sept. 2, 1955; children: Stephen, Chadwick, Scott. BEd, Whitworth Coll., 1955; MEd, Seattle Pacific U., 1978; postgrad., U. Wash., Ea. Wash. U. Cert. tchr. spl. edn. and reading Wash., sch. psychologist Wash., drug and alcohol counselor Wash. Tchr. elem. Mead Sch. Dist., Spokane, Wash., 1955—59; tchr. spl. edn. Cle Elum Sch. Dist., 1959—60; tchr. elem. Goleta Sch., Santa Barbara, Calif., 1960—62, Anacortes Sch. Dist., Anacorte, Wash., 1962—63, Bellevue Sch. Dist., Bellevue, Wash., 1963—77; sch. psychologist/ednl. specialist Spokane Sch. Dist., 1977—88; sch. psychologist West Valley Sch. Dist., Spokane, 1990—98; ret., 1998. Counselor drug and alcohol, cons. Assocs. in Counseling, Spokane, 1984—99. Bd. dirs. Friends of Little Spokane River Valley. Named Sch. Psychologist of Yr., Washington State, 1995. Mem.: Spokane Ret. Tchrs. (bd. dirs.), Nat. Assn. Sch. Psychologists, Whitworth Women's Aux. Republican. Presbyterian. Avocations: writing, gardening, computers.

SREENIVASAN, KATEPALLI RAJU, mechanical engineering educator; b. Kolar, India, Sept. 30, 1947; married 1980; 2 children. BE, Bangalore U., 1968; ME, Indian Inst. Sci., 1970, PhD in Aeronautical Engring., 1975. JRD Tata fellow Indian Inst. Sci., 1972-74, project asst., 1974-75; fellow U. Sydney, Australia, 1975, U. Newcastle, 1976-77; rsch. assoc. Johns Hopkins U., Balt., 1977-79; from asst. prof. to assoc. prof. Yale U., New Haven, 1982-85, prof. mech. engring., 1985—, Harold W. Cheel prof. mech. engring., 1988—, prof. physics, 1990—, prof. applied physics, 1993—. Vis. scientist Indian Inst. Sci., 1979, vis. prof., 1982, Calif. Inst. Tech., Pasadena, 1986, Rockefeller U., 1989, Jawaharlala Nehru Ctr. Advancement Sci. Studies, 1992, chmn. mech. engring. dept., 1987-92; vis. sci. DFVLR, Gottingen, Germany, 1983; mem. Inst. for Advanced Study, Princeton, N.J., 1995. Recipient Narayana Gold medal Indian Inst. Sci., 1975, Disting. Alumnus award, 1992; Humboldt Found. fellow, 1983, Guggenheim fellow, 1989. Fellow AAAS, ASME, Am. Phys. Soc. (Otto Laporte award 1995), AIAA (assoc.), Am. Acad. Arts and Sci., Third World Acad. of Scis., Conn. Acad. Arts and Scis.; mem. NAE, Am. Math. Soc., Conn. Acad. Sci. and Engring., Sigma Xi. Achievements include research in origin and dynamics of turbulence; control of turbulent flows; chaotic dynamics; fractals. E-mail: k.sreenivasan@yale.edu.

SRINIVASAN, VENKATARAMAN, marketing and management educator; b. Pudukkottai, Tamil Nadu, India, June 5, 1944; came to U.S., 1968; s. Annaswamy and Jambagalakshmi Venkataraman; m. Sitalakshmi Subrahmanyam, June 30, 1972; children: Ramesh, Mahesh. B Tech., Indian Inst. Tech., Madras, India, 1966; MS, Carnegie-Mellon U., 1970, PhD, 1971. Asst. engr. Larsen & Toubro, Bombay, 1966-68; asst. prof. mgmt. and mktg. U. Rochester, N.Y., 1971-73, assoc. prof., 1973-74, Stanford (Calif.) U., 1974-76, prof., 1976-82, dir. PhD program in bus., 1982-85, Ernest C. Arbuckle prof. mktg. and mgmt. sci., 1982—2003, Adams. disting. prof. mgmt., 2003—; mktg. area coord., 1976—78, 1988—93, 2000—03. Cons. in field. Mem. editorial bd. Jour. Mktg. Rsch., 1988—, Mktg. Sci., 1980—, Mgmt. Sci., 1974-91; contbr. articles to profl. jours. Mem. Am. Mktg. Assn., Inst. Ops. Rsch./Mgmt. Scis. Hindu. Avocation: classical music.

STABA, EMIL JOHN, pharmacognosy and medicinal chemistry educator; b. N.Y.C., May 16, 1928; s. Frank and Marianna T. (Mack) P.; m. Joyce Elizabeth Ellert, June 19, 1954; children— Marianna, Joanna, Sarah Jane, John, Mark. BS cum laude, St. John's U., 1952; MS, Duquesne U., 1954; PhD, U. Conn., 1957. Asst. prof. U. Nebr., 1957-60, prof., chmn. dept., 1968; prof. dept. pharmacognosy U. Minn., 1968—95; interim dir. R&D Tom's of Main, Kennebunk, 1996. Pres. Plants Personified, Inc., 1995—; cons. econs. plants and plant tissue culture U.S. Army Q.M.C.; cons. on drug plants and plant tissue culture NASA; cons. N.C.I. at NIH on anti-cancer natural product prodn., 1991-92; cons. Govt. of Korea, food and pharm. industry cons. NSF-Egyptian Acad. Sci. Rsch. Tech., 1984—; internat. vis. prof. Dalhousie U., 1983; cons. on Indonesia biotech. devel. World Bank-Midwestern Univs. Consortium for Internat. Activities, 1985-90, Thailand, 1989; mem. natural products revision com. U.S. Pharmacopeia, 1980—, chair subcom. natural products, 1995-2000; mem. adv. coun. on life scis. NASA, 1984-87. Mem. editorial bd.: Jour. Plant Cell, Tissue and Organ Culture, 1980-86, plant cellular and developmental biology sect. of In Vitro, 1988— Served with USNR, 1945-46, PTO. Sr. fgn. fellow NSF, Poland, 1969; Fulbright fellow, Germany, 1970; Coun. Sci. and Indsl. Rsch.-NSF fellow, India, 1973, Pakistani Coun. Sci. and Indsl. Rsch.-NSF fellow, Pakistan, 1978; fellow U.K. Sci. Engring. Rsch. Coun., 1989. Fellow AAAS; mem. Am. Soc. Pharmacognosy (pres. 1971-72), Am. Assn. Colls. Pharmacy (chmn. tchrs. sect. 1972-73, dir. 1976-77), Tissue Culture Assn. (pres. plant sect. 1972-74), Am. Pharm. Assn. and Acad. (chmn. pharmacognosy and nat. products 1977), Soc. Econ. Botany, Am. Soc. Pharmacognosy (hon.), Am. Soc. Pharmacognosy, Plants Personified, Inc. (pres. 1995—). Home: 2840 Stinson Blvd Minneapolis MN 55418-3127 E-mail: staba001@tc.umn.edu.

STABY, DOROTHY LOUISE, elementary school educator; b. Washington, July 26, 1932; d. Charles Pemberton and Eleanor (Thompson) Sheffield; m. Jack Bradford Staby, Oct. 27, 1956; children: John Bradford, Robert Stanford, Mary Katherine. BS in Edn. with honors, James Madison U., 1954; MA, State U. Iowa, 1955; postgrad., Columbia U., 1957, Bklyn. Coll., 1957, SUNY, New Paltz, 1962, SUNY, Binghamton, 1993. Cert. elem., health and phys. edn. tchr., N.Y. Tchr. phys. edn. Garden City (N.Y.) High Sch., 1955-58; substitute tchr.1st-12th grades Amityville Sch., Capaigue Sch., Massapeque Sch., L.I., N.Y., 1958-63; tchr. 1st and 2d grades St. Patricks Elem. Sch., Owego, N.Y., 1969-70; tchr. 5th grade Glenwood Elem. Sch., Vestal, N.Y., 1970-83; tchr. 2d grade Clayton Ave. Elem. Sch., Vestal, N.Y., 1983—. Head, counselor Coll. Settlement Farm Camp, Willow Grove, Pa., 1954-55; instr. Iowa City Recreation Dept., 1955; counselor Garden City Recreation Dept., 1956-57, Country Day Camp, Plainedge, N.Y., 1960-62; tchr. computer Vestal Schs., 1983-87, Vestal Recreation Dept., Vestal, 1989-90, health tchr. Vestal High Sch., 1988. State U. Iowa scholar, 1954-55. Mem. NEA, AAUW, AAHPERD, N.Y. Edn. Assn., Nat. Sci. Tchrs. Assn., Vestal Tchrs. Assn. Democrat. Methodist. Avocations: computers, reading, sports. Home: PO Box 475 Little Meadows PA 18830-0475 Office: Clayton Ave Elem Sch Clayton Ave Vestal NY 13850

STACEY, WESTON MONROE, JR., nuclear engineer, educator, physicist; b. Birmingham, Ala., July 23, 1937; s. Weston Monroe and Dorothy (Toole) S.; m. Penny Smith; children: Helen Lee, Weston Monroe III, Lucia Katherine. BS in Physics, Ga. Inst. Tech., 1959, MS in Nuclear Sci., 1963; PhD in Nuclear Engring., MIT, 1966. Nuclear engr. Knolls Atomic Power Lab., Schenectady, N.Y., 1962-64, 66-69; assoc. dir. applied physics divsn. and dir. fusion program Argonne Nat. Lab., Chgo., 1969-77; Callaway Regents prof. Ga. Inst. Tech., Atlanta, 1977—. Author: Modal Approximation in Reactor Physics, 1967, Space-Time Nuclear Reactor Kinetics, 1969, Variational Methods in Nuclear Reactor Physics, 1972, Fusion Plasma Analysis, 1981, Fusion, 1984, Nuclear Reactor Physics, 2001; contbr. over 230 articles to profl. jours. Recipient Cert. Appreciation Dept. Energy, 1981, 88, Disting. Assoc. award Dept. Energy, 1990, Rsch. award Sigma Xi, 1998, Ga. Tech., 2003. Fellow: Am. Nuclear Soc. (bd. dirs. 1974—77, Outstanding Achievement award 1981, 1996, Seaborg medal 2001, Wigner award 2003), Am. Phys. Soc.; mem.: AAAS, Am. Soc. Engring. Edn. Office: Ga Inst Tech Nuclear Engring Dept 0425 Atlanta GA 30332-0001 E-mail: weston.stacey@nre.gatech.edu.

STACKHOUSE, MAX LYNN, Christian ethics educator; b. Ft. Wayne, Ind., July 29, 1935; s. C. Dale and Naomi Elizabeth (Graham) S.; m. N. Jean Hostetler, Aug. 19, 1959; children: Dale Emil, David Graham, Sara Elizabeth. BA, De Pauw U., 1957, LHD (hon.), 1995; cert., Nijenrode U., Breukelen, The Netherlands, 1958; BD, MDiv, Harvard U., 1961, PhD, 1965. Ordained to ministry United Ch. of Christ, 1961. Lectr. Harvard Divinity Sch., Cambridge, Mass., 1964-66; asst. prof. Andover-Newton (Mass.) Theol. Sch., 1966-69, assoc. prof., 1969-73, prof., 1973-78, Herbert Gezork prof., 1978-93; Stephen Colwell prof. Princeton (N.J.) Theol. Sem., 1993—. Vis. prof. United Theol. Coll., Bangalore, India, 1973, 76, 82, 87, 2000, Pacific Theol. Coll., Suva, Fiji, 1982, Das Sprackenkonvikt, East Berlin, 1983; pres. joint doctoral program Boston Coll. and Andover Newton Theol. Sch., 1988-89, also chmn. Rels. and Soc. Dept., 1975-93; dir. Kuyper Ctr. for Pub. Theology, 1994—; pres. Berkshire Inst. Theology and Arts, 1991—. Author: Creeds Society of Human Rights, 1984, Public Theology and Political Economy, 1987, Apologia, 1988 (Best Booklist Internat. Bull. Missiology 1988), On Moral Business, 1994, Christian Ethics in a Global Era, 1996, Covenant and Commitments, 1998, God and Globalization, vol. 1, 2000, vol. 2, 2001, vol. 3, 2002; author, editor 11 books; mem. ediorial bd. Jour. Religious Ethics, Christian Century; contbr. articles to religious jours. Mem. investigation team Am. Com. for Human Rights, Philippines, 1984; pres. James Luther Adams Found., 1987-93; exec. sec. Am. Com. for Higher Edn. in India, 1986-91. Rsch. grantee Ctr. for Urban Studies, Harvard U., 1965-66, Assn. Theol. Schs., 1986-87, Lilly Endowment, Indpls., 1989, 91, Pew Charitable Trusts, 1993, 98; recipient Outstanding Alumnus award DePauw U., 1988. Fellow Soc. for Sci. Study of Religion (bd. dirs. 1980-84), Soc. for Values in Higher Edn.; mem. NAACP, Amnesty Internat., Am. Theol. Assn., Soc. Christian Ethics (past pres., past exec. sec.), Stockbridge Club. Democrat. Office: Princeton Theol Sem PO Box 821 Princeton NJ 08542-0803

STACKNOWITZ, JANET, reading specialist; b. Queens, N.Y., Jan. 19, 1942; d. Joseph John and Charlotte (Reichold) Weber; m. Robert Stacknowitz, July 25, 1959 (div. June 1980); children: Debra Anne Lorraine, Karen Lynn. AA, Suffolk C.C., 1975; BS in Edn., L.I. U., 1980; MS in Edn., CUNY, 1991. Tchr. Pumpkin Patch Day Nursery, Commack, N.Y., 1971-76; reading tchr. Mt. Sinai Jr. H.S., N.Y., 1979-80; dir. Floral Park (N.Y.) Play Sch., 1981-90; head tchr., edn. dir. A Learning Ctr., N.Y.C., 1996—, edn. dir., 1998—, universal Pre-K tchr., 1999—. Vol. instr. Pelham Fritz Recreation Ctr.; ast. to City Coun. Woman, Harlem, 1991. Mem. N.Y. Women Against Rape (cert. counselor). Democrat. Home and Office: 23 E 124th St Apt B New York NY 10035-2727

STACY, BILL WAYNE, academic administrator; b. Bristol, Va., July 26, 1938; s. Charles Frank and Louise Nelson (Altwater) S.; m. Sue Varnon; children: Mark, Sara, James. BSEd., S.E. Mo. State U., 1960; MS, So. Ill. U., 1965, PhD, 1968. Tchr. Malden High Sch., Mo., 1960-64; faculty Southeast Mo. State U., Cape Girardeau, 1967-89, dean Grad. Sch., 1976-79, interim pres., 1979, pres., 1980-89, Calif. State U., San Marcos, 1989-97; chancellor U. Tenn., Chattanooga, 1997—. Bd. dirs. River Valley Ptnrs. Bd. dirs. United Way; mem. Allied Arts Bd. Mem. Am. Assn. Higer Edn., Chattanooga C. of C. (bd. dirs.). Presbyterian. Office: U Tenn 615 Mccallie Ave Chattanooga TN 37403-2504

STAEHELIN, LUCAS ANDREW, cell biology educator; b. Sydney, Australia, Feb. 10, 1939; came to U.S., 1969; s. Lucas Eduard and Isobel (Malloch) S.; m. Margrit Weibel, Sept. 17, 1965; children: Daniel Thomas, Philip Roland, Marcel Felix. Dipl. Natw., Swiss Fed. Inst. Tech., Zurich, 1963, PhD in Biology, 1966. Research scientist N.Z. Dept. Sci. and Indsl. Research, 1966-69; research fellow in cell biology Harvard U., Cambridge, Mass., 1969-70; asst. prof. cell biology U. Colo., Boulder, 1970-73, assoc. prof., 1973-79, prof., 1979—. Vis. prof. U. Freiburg, 1978, Swiss Fed. Inst. Tech., 1984, 92, U. Melbourne, Australia, 1998; mem. cellular biology and physiology study sect. NIH, Bethesda, Md., 1980-84; mem. DOE panel on rsch. directions for the energy bioscis., 1988, 92; mem. NSF adv. panel for cellular orgn., 1994-96; mem. plant biology panel NASA. Editor Jour. Cell Biology, 1977-81, European Jour. Cell Biology, 1981-90, Plant Physiology, 1986-92, Plant Jour., 1991-97, Biology of the Cell, 1996-99, Planta, 2003—; editor: (with C.J. Antzen) Encyclopedia of Plant Physiology, Vol. 19, Photosynthesis III, 1986; contbr. numerous articles to sci. jours. Recipient Humboldt award Humboldt Found., 1978, Sci. Tchr. award U. Colo., 1984, Outstanding Faculty award U. Colo.-Boulder Parents Assn., 2001; grantee NIH, 1971—, USDA, 1994—, NASA, 1997—; hon. sr. fellow U. Melbourne, Australia, 1998. Mem. AAAS, Am. Soc. Cell Biology, Am. Soc. Plant Physiology, German Acad. Natural Scis. Leopoldina. Home: 2855 Dover Dr Boulder CO 80305-5305 Office: Dept Molecular Cell U Colo 347 UCB Boulder CO 80309-0347 E-mail: staeheli@spot.colorado.edu.

STAFF, MARY CLARE, special education educator; b. Scranton, Pa., May 18, 1939; d. Martin Francis and Mary Owens Carroll; m. Thomas Robert Staff, Apr. 4, 1964 (dec. Aug., 1992); children: Thomas, David. BA in Elem. Edn., Art, Marywood Coll., 1961; postgrad., U. Scranton, 1961-64, Marywood Coll., 1972-74. Cert. elem., spl. edn. tchr., Pa. Elem. tchr. Scranton (Pa.) Sch. Dist., 1961-67, learning disabilities tchr., 1970-72, diagnosticiian, 1972-77, learning support tchr., 1977—. Dir. Art Workshop for Tchrs. of Handicapped Children, 1984. Dir. Spl. Events for Children, St. Patrick's Ch., Scranton, 1988—, bd. dirs. Youth Ministry, 1989—, pres. Women's Soc., 1992—; bd. dirs. Mental Health Assn. Northeastern Pa., 1987—, Nat. Coun. Cath. Women; exec. bd. dirs. Diocesan Coun. Cath. Women, 1993; vol. Friendship Seven for Mentally Handicapped, Scranton, 1990—; active Parish Vocation Team. Grantee; Chpt. II ECIA, 1983, Pa. Dept. Edn. Bur. Spl. Edn., 1984 Mem. Marywood Coll. Alumnae Assn., Phi Delta Kappa Avocations: bowling, dancing, catechist, lector. Home: 1717 Luzerne St Scranton PA 18504-2345

STAFFORD, BETTY TRAMMELL, psychiatric nursing educator; b. Atlanta, May 26, 1931; d. George G. and Bertha (Knopf) Trammell; m. William M. Stafford, Aug. 22, 1970 (div. May 1990); children: Donna Stafford Cash, William M. Jr. Diploma, Crawford W. Long Sch., 1952; BSN, U. Miss., 1969; MS, U. So. Miss., 1979. Staff nurse VA, Gulfport, Miss., 1952-54, Meml. Hosp. Gulfport, 1954-55, 90-2000, pvt. physicians' offices, Gulfport, 1955-57, U. Ark. Med. Ctr., Little Rock, 1958-59, asst. head nurse, 1965-67; instr. Miss. Gulf Coast C.C., Gulfport, 1969-70, 73-2000, Fla. Keyes C.C., Key West, 1970-71; insvc. edn. coord. El Cajon (Calif.) Valley Hosp., 1972, Miss. Gulf Coast C.C., 1972—98, Meml. Hosp., Gulfport, 1990—99; ret. Presenter at workshops in field. Vol. blood drives ARC; vol. Am. Heart Assn.; mem. exec. bd. dirs. Mental Health Assn. Harrison County, Gulfport, 1991-2000. Mem. ANA, Miss. Nurses Assn. (dist. treas., chmn. scholarship com., Psychiat.-Mental Health Nurse of Yr. award 1983, 93), Orgn. for ADN (chmn. state membership com. 1990—), Coun. Psychiat. and Mental Health Nursing, Faculty Asn., Spl. Interest Group Psychiatric and Mental Health Nursing Educators, Sigma Theta Tau. Methodist. Avocations: horseback riding, dog training, swimming, fishing, ballroom dancing. Home: 21173 D'Herde Rd Gulfport MS 39503 E-mail: schiefsan@aol.com.

STAFFORD, WILLIAM BUTLER, retired psychology educator; b. Pitts., Feb. 6, 1931; s. Lee Elmer and Helen Huston (Butler) S.; m. Barbara Anne Svoboda, Aug. 11, 1956; children: Mark William, Debra Anne. Student, Adrian (Mich.) Coll., 1949-50; AB, Ohio U., 1954, MA, 1955; EdD, Ind. U., 1965. Cert. tchr., dir. guidance svcs., Ind., nat. bd. cert. counselor. Residence counselor Ohio U., 1954-55; counselor dean of students' staff DePauw U., Ind., 1955-57; instr. Ind. U., Bloomington, 1957-65, asst. prof. edn., 1965-67; counselor Univ. Sch., Bloomington, Ind., 1957-65, dir. pupil pers. svcs., 1965-67; asst. prof. edn. Lehigh U., Bethlehem, Pa., 1967-72, assoc. prof. counseling psychology, 1972-94, prof. emeritus, 1994—. Mem. clin. staff Impact Project, 1996-98; cons. North Ctrl. Assn. Secondary Schs. and Colls., Ind. Dept. Public Instrn., Pa. Dept. Edn. Patients rights and rev. com. Allentown State Hosp. Author: Schools Without Counselors: Guidance Practices for the Teacher in the Elementary School, 1975. Mem. adv. bd. Lehigh Valley Child Care, Inc. Jesse Smith Noyes fellow, 1980; award given in his honor, William B. Stafford Leadership award, 2003- Mem. ACA, APA (counseling psychology divsn.), Am. Sch. Counselor Assn., Assn. Counselor Educators and Suprs., Am. Ednl. Rsch. Assn., Pa. Counseling Assn., Pa. Sch. Counselors Assn. (Pa. Counselor Educator of Yr. 1994), Internat. Alliance Invitational Edn. (adv. coun., mem. editl. bd., editor Jour. Invitational Theory and Practice), Pa. Alliance Invitiational Edn. (editor newsletter), Chi Sigma Iota (chpt. advisor). Episcopalian. Home: 1586 Pinewind Dr Alburtis PA 18011-2704 E-mail: wbs0@lehigh.edu.

STAHL, CHARLYN BETH, medical educator; b. Runge, Tex., Sept. 30, 1940; d. Valentine Dedrick and Sophia Anna (Juenger) Goehring; m. Eugene Jacob Stahl, Sept. 4, 1982; 1 stepchild, Bobby Joe. BS, Tex. Woman's U., 1961; MS, U. Houston Clear Lake, 1994. Cert. blood bank specialist, med. technology. Asst. supr. St. Paul Hosp., Dallas, 1963—66; technologist J.L. Goforth Lab., Dallas, 1966—67; chief technologist E. Tex. Pathologists Lab., Longview, 1967—71; lab. mgr. Pathology Assn., Longview, 1971—79; technologist blood bank Meth. Hosp., Houston, 1980—82; chief technologist Park Plz. Hosp., Houston, 1982—83; supr. blood bank M.D. Anderson Hosp., Houston, 1983; supr. day shift Beltway Cmty. Hosp., Pasadena, Tex., 1983—84; dir. med. lab. technology program San Jacinto Coll., Pasadena, Tex., 1984—. Reading mentor Pasadena Ind. Schs., 1998—. Avocations: reading, quilting. Home: 5229 Sycamore Ave Pasadena TX 77503 Office: 8060 Spencer Hwy Pasadena TX 77505-5903

STAHL, DIANE IRENE, parochial school educator; b. Ridgewood, N.Y., May 2, 1952; d. Frederick Martin and Stanislava Mary (Halunka) S. BS in Edn., Wagner Coll., 1974. 6th grade tchr. St. Mark's Luth. Sch., Bklyn., 1975-79, 8th grade tchr., asst. prin., 1979-81, 8th grade tchr., acting prin., 1981-82, 8th grade tchr., asst. prin., 1982-84; 6th grade tchr. Redeemer Luth. Sch., Glendale, N.Y., 1984-87, 8th grade tchr., 1987—. Named Tchr. of Yr. Luth. Schs. Assn., 1985. Avocations: collecting horse statues, reading, crocheting. Home: 64-40 Catalpa Ave Ridgewood NY 11385 Office: Redeemer Luth Sch 69-26 Cooper Ave Glendale NY 11385

STAHL, WILLIAM MARTIN, professional training director; b. Danbury, Conn., Dec. 13, 1945; s. William M. and Mary Elizabeth (Barrett) S.; m. Elizabeth Larkin, 1968 (div. 1979); 1 child, Nathaniel Edward; m. Pamela Putnam, July 13, 1984; 1 child, Julia Barrett. BA, Bard Coll., 1968; MS, Bank Street Coll., 1975. Asst. tchr., tchr. Willowbrook State Sch., S.I., 1968-70; tchr., supr. Bronx (N.Y.) Children's Hosp., 1970-75; sch. cons. Washington County Mental Health, Inc., Montpelier, Vt., 1975-80; behavioral cons. Peabody (Mass.) Pub. Schs., 1980-86; founder, dir. profl. tng., treas. Ctr. for Applied Spl. Tech., Inc., Peabody, 1984—. Grad. faculty Goodard Coll., Plainfield, Vt., 1977-80; clinician, supr. North Shore Children's Hosp., Salem, Mass., 1981-86, asst. dir. Med. Ednl. Evaluation Ctr. Clinic, 1986-88; dir. New Tools Inst., Harvard U./Ctr. for Applied Spl. Tech.d, 1989—; presenter in field. Mem. Nat. Assn. Sch. Psychologists, Nat. Assn. MacIntosh Trainers. Office: CAST Inc 39 Cross St Peabody MA 01960-1628

STAHR, BETH A. academic librarian; b. Elmhurst, Ill, June 13, 1951; d. John H. Pohlmann and Mary Anne Price; m. Charles Ward Stahr, Aug. 25, 1973; children: Margaret L., Andrew J. BS Engring., Purdue U., 1973; MLS, Syracuse U., 1999. Environ. specialist Owens Corning Fiberglas, Toledo, 1973—78; genealogical rschr. pvt. practice, Wausau, Wis., 1988—98; libr. Southeastern La. U., Hammond, La., 1999—; asst. prof. Southeastern La. Univ., Hammond, La., 2000—. V.p., trustee Wis. Genealogical Coun., 1992—98; treas., trustee Assn. Profl. Genealogists, Washington, 1994—95, Bd. Cert. Genealogists, 1998—; v.p. Louisiana Genealogical and Hist. Soc., 2001—. Vol. Birch Trails coun. Girl Scouts Am., Tomahawk, Wis., 1980—91; v.p., trustee La. Genealogical and Hist. Soc., La., 2001—. Mem.: ALA, ACRL. Episcopalian. Home: 55 Dogwood Ln Covington LA 70435

STALBAUM, BERNARDINE ANN, English language educator; b. Passaic, N.J., May 14, 1942; d. Michael and Anna (Filakowski) Vasel AB, Montclair State U., 1964; MA, Montclair (N.J.) State U., 1969, post grad., 1981. Cert. secondary Eng. tchr. acctg. and gen. bus.; reading specialist, supr., prin. English tchr. Clifton (N.J.) Bd Edn., 1964-82, 90—, reading specialist, 1982-96, dept. resource person, 1982—; G.E.D. instr., student tchr. supr. Clifton (N.J.) Evening Sch. Div., 1984-98; computer instr. lang. arts mid. and H.S., Clifton Bd. Edn., 2000—. Coach acad. deathlon team Clifton Bd. Edn., 1990—; rschr. in field; mem. clin. faculty Montclair State U., 1998—. Mem. NEA, Parent Tchr. Student Assn., Nat. Coun. Tchrs. English, N.J. Edn. Assn., Passaic County Edn. Assn., Clifton Tchrs.' Assn. (sch. del. 1964-92), N.J. Coun. Tchrs. English, N.J. Network Ednl. Renewal, Clifton HS Faculty Orgn. (welfare chmn.), Montclair State U. Alumni Assn. (v.p. membership and programming 1984-95). Home: 279 Pershing Rd Clifton NJ 07013-3718 Office: Clifton High Sch 333 Colfax Ave Clifton NJ 07013-1701

STALDER, FLORENCE LUCILLE, secondary education educator; b. Fairmont, W.Va., Jan. 3, 1920; d. Brooks Fleming and Sally May (Odewalt) Clayton; m. Bernard Nicholas Stalder, Sept. 14, 1946; children: Kathryn Lynn Stalder Mirto, Susan May Stalder Woodard. BA in Edn. with honors, Fairmont State Coll., 1966; MA, W.Va. U., 1973; postgrad., Kent State U., 1973, U. Va., Charlottesville, 1981. Cert. elem. tchr., W.Va. Sec. to mgr. Hall Agy., Inc., Fairmont, W.Va., 1941-43; sec. to supt. Westinghouse Electric Corp., Fairmont, 1943-47; sec. to purchasing agt. Fairmont Supply Co., 1947-48; sec. to dist. mgtr. Ea. Gas & Fuel Assoc., Gen. Stores Div., Grant Town, W.Va., 1948-50; sec. to pres., v.p. Hutchinson Coal Co., Fairmont, 1950-52; sec. to personnel mgr. Consolidation Coal Co., Fairmont, 1957-61; sec. and asst. to adminstr. Fairmont Clinic (Monongahela Valley Assoc. Health Ctrs.), 1965-70; instr. Fairmont Jr. High, Miller Jr. High Schs., 1968-85. Instr., dir. W.Va. Univ. Younger Youth Sci. Camps, Fairmont, 1966-72; workshop instr. W.Va. State Bd. Edn. Energy Workshops, Fairmont, 1973-74; adult edn. instr., Fairmont, 1985—; sec., exec. bd. mem. Score. Pres. PTA, 1958-61; troop leader Girl Scouts USA, 1961-64; sec., mem. League of Women Voters, Fairmont, 1968-97; charter mem. Lifelong Learners Fairmont State Coll.; counselor, charter mem. Mil. Order Fgn. Wars U.S. Mem. AAUW (pres. 1972-74), NEA, DAR (1st v.p. regent 1986-92, regent 1992-95,Marion County Edn. Assn., W.Va. Edn. Assn., W.Va. Adult Edn. Assn., Daus. of Founders and Patriots of Am. (pres. 1979-85, nat. officers club 1985—), Daus. of Am. Colonists (vice regent 1988-91, regent 1991-94), Daus. Am. Pioneers, Alpha Delta Kappa (pres. 1979-81). Republican. Methodist. Avocations: ecology and conservation issues, humane education, food preservation, gardening. Home: 1208 Bell Run Rd Fairmont WV 26554-1400

STALEY, LYNN, English educator; b. Madisonville, Ky., Dec. 24, 1947; d. James Mulford and Florine (Hurt) Staley. AB, U. Ky., 1969; MA, PhD, Princeton U., 1973. Grad. asst. Princeton (N.J.) U., 1971-73; instr. English Colgate U., Hamilton, N.Y., 1974-75, from asst. to assoc. prof., 1975-86, prof., 1986—. Author: The Voice of the Gawain-Poet, 1984, The Shepheardes Calendar: An Introduction, 1990, Margery Kempe's Dissenting Fictions, 1994, (with David Aers) The Powers of the Holy: Religion, Politics and Gender in Late Medieval English Culture, 1996; editor: The Book of Margery Kempe, 1996; translator: The Book of Margery Kempe, 2001; contbr. articles to profl. jours. NEH fellow, 2003—04, Guggenheim fellow, 2003—04. Mem. MLA, Medieval Acad. Am., Renaissance Soc. Am., New Chaucer Soc., Spenser Soc. Office: Colgate U Dept English 13 Oak Dr Dept English Hamilton NY 13346-1383

STALEY, MARSHA LYNN, elementary school educator, principal; b. California, Mo., July 19, 1950; d. David D. and Jenny L. (Howard) Hutchison; children: Timothy Jay Turley, Damon Andrew Turley; m. Richard Lynn Staley, June 30, 1989. AA, State Fair C.C., Sedalia, Mo., 1982; BS in Edn., Drury Coll., 1984; MS in Elem. Adminstrn., S.W. Mo. State U., 1993; doctoral student, U. Mo., 1994—. Cert. tchr. grades 1-8, Mo. Tchr. grade 5 Newburg (Mo.) Elem. Sch., 1986-88; tchr. grades 1, 4, 5 and 6 Sherwood Elem. Sch., Springfield, Mo., 1988-93, Westport Elem. Sch., Springfield, 1993-94; regional facilitator U. Mo.; elem. prin. Maherly Pub. Schs., 1999—. Mem. Pi Delta Kappa, Pi Lambda Theta (pres. Alpha chpt. 1996-97). Avocations: reading, horseback riding, bicycling, hiking. Office: U Mo 103 London Hall Columbia MO 65211-2240

STALEY, THOMAS FABIAN, language professional, academic administrator; b. Pitts., Aug. 13, 1935; s. Fabian Richard and Mary (McNulty) S.; m. Carolyn O'Brien, Sept. 3, 1960; children: Thomas Fabian, Caroline Ann, Mary Elizabeth, Timothy X. AB, BS, Regis Coll., 1957; MA, U. Tulsa, 1958; PhD, U. Pitts., 1962; D.H.L., Regis Coll. Asst. prof. English Rollins Coll., 1961-62; mem. faculty U. Tulsa, 1962-88, prof. English, 1969-88, dean Grad. Sch., 1969, dean Coll. Arts and Scis., 1981-83, provost, v.p. acad. affairs, 1983-88, McFarlin prof. modern lit., 1988; prof. English, dir. Ransom Humanities Rsch. Ctr. U. Tex., Austin, 1988—, Chancellor's Centennial prof. of the Book, 1989—92, Harry Huntt Ransom chair liberal arts, 1992—. Fulbright prof., Italy, 1966-67; Fulbright lectr., 1971; Danforth assoc., 1962-67; chmn. Internat. James Joyce Symposium; dir. Grad. Inst. Modern Letters, 1970-81. Author: James Joyce Today, 1966, James Joyce's Portrait of the Artist, 1968, Italo Svevo: Essays on His Work, 1969, (with H.J. Mooney) The Shapeless God: Essays on the Modern Novel, 1968, (with B. Benstock) Approaches to Ulysses: Ten Essays, 1970, Approaches to Joyce's Portrait: Ten Essays, Jean Rhys: A Critical Study; editor: Il Punto Su Joyce, 1973, Dorothy Richardson, Ulysses: Fifty Years, 1974, Twentieth-Century Women Novelists, 1982, British Novelists, 1890-1929, Traditionalists, Dictionary of Lit. Biography, Vols. 34, 36, 70, 77, An Annotated Critical Bibliography of James Joyce, 1989, Joyce Studies: An Annual edit., 1990—, Studies in Modern Literature Series, 1990—, Reflections on James Joyce: Stuart Gilbert's Paris Journal, 1993, Writing the Lives of Writers, 1998, James Joyce Quar., 1963-89; adv. editor Twentieth-Century Lit., 1966—, Jean Rhys Rev., 1986—; bd. dirs. Eighteenth-Century Short Title Catalogue/North America, 1990; editl. bd. Tulsa Studies in Women's Literature, Jour. Modern Lit., 1989—; contbr. articles to profl. jours. Bd. dirs. Tulsa Arts Coun., 1969-76, NCCJ, 1979—; pres. James Joyce Found., 1968-72; chmn. bd. Undercroft Montessori Sch., 1968-70, Marquette Sch., 1969-70; bd. dirs. Cascia Hall Prep. Sch.; chmn. disting. authors com. Tulsa Libr. Trust, 1984; mem. bd. commrs. Tulsa City-County Libr., chmn., 1980-82; mem. adv. coun. Tex. Inst. for Humanities; trustee Regis U., 1992—; bd. dirs. Libr. of Am., 1994—, Harlick Trust, 1994—; mem. symposium com. Lyndon Baines Johnson Presdl. Libr., 1993—. Recipient Am. Council Learned Socs. award, 1969, 80 Mem. MLA, Internat. Assn. Univ. Profs. English, Anglo-Irish Studies Assn., Am. Com. for Irish Studies, Assn. Internat. de Bibliophilie, James Joyce Soc., Hopkins Soc., Tex. Philos. Soc. (bd. dirs. 1991—), Internat. James Joyce Found. (hon. trustee), U.S. Tennis Assn., Tulsa Tennis Club, Westwood Country Club, The Athenaeum Club (London), Grolier Club (N.Y.), Edgecomb Tennis Club (Kennebunk, Maine), Tarry House, Phi Beta Kappa. Home: 2528 Tanglewood Trl Austin TX 78703-1540 also: 4 Surf Ln Kennebunk ME 04043

STALKER, JACQUELINE D'AOUST, academic administrator, educator; b. Penetang, Ont., Can., Oct. 16, 1933; d. Phillip and Rose (Eaton) D'Aoust; m. Robert Stalker; children: Patricia, Lynn, Roberta. Teaching cert., U. Ottawa, 1952; tchr. music, Royal Toronto Conservatory Music, 1952; teaching cert., Lakeshore Tchrs. Coll., 1958; BEd with honors, U. Manitoba, 1977, MEd, 1979; EdD, Nova U., 1985. Cert. tchr. Ont., Man., Can. Adminstr., tchr., prin. various schs., Ont. and Que., 1952-65; area commr. Girl Guides of Can., throughout Europe, 1965-69; administr., tchr. Algonquin Community Coll., Ottawa, Ont., 1970-74; tchr., program devel. Frontenac County Bd. Edn., Kingston, Ont., 1974-75; lectr., faculty advisor dept. curriculum, edn. U. Man., Can., 1977-79; lectr. U. Winnipeg, Man., Can., 1977-79; cons. colls. div. Man. Dept. Edn., 1980-81, sr. cons. programming br., 1981-84, sr. cons. post secondary, adult and continuing edn. div., 1985-88, dir. post secondary career devel. br. and adult and continuing edn. br., 1989; asst. prof. higher edn., coord. grad. program in higher edn. U. Man., 1989-92, assoc. prof., coord. grad. program in higher edn., 1992-95. Cons. lectures, seminars, workshops throughout Can. Contbr. articles to profl. jours.; mng. editor Can. Jour. of Higher Edn., 1989-93. Mem. U. Man. Senate, 1976-81, 86-89, bd. govs., 1979-82; Can. rep. Internat. Youth Conf., Garmisch, Fed. Republic of Germany, 1968; vol. Can. Cancer Soc.; mem. Assn. RN Accreditation Coun., 1980-85; chair Child Care Accreditation Com., Man., 1983-90; chair Task Force Post-Secondary Accessibility, Man., 1983; vol. United Way Planning and Allocations; provincial dir., mem. nat. bd. Can. Congress for Learning Opportunities for Women. Recipient award for enhancing the Outreach activities of the univ. U. Man., 1994. Mem. Can. Soc. Study Higher Edn., Man. Tchrs. Soc., U. Man. Alumni Assn., Women's Legal Edn. and Action Fund. Home: 82 McNulty Crescent Winnipeg MB Canada R2M 5H4

STALLINGS, PHYLLIS ANN, music educator; b. Little Rock, Feb. 24, 1944; d. Roy Edwin and Helen Lavern (Waters) Moseley; m. Paul Harold Stallings, Jan. 22, 1966; children: Kevin Scott, Michael Shane, Natasha Lynette, Clayton Lane. B in Music Edn., Ouachita Bapt. U., 1966; M in Music Edn., Ark. State U., 1971. Cert. vocal and band music tchr., Ark., Mo. Tchr. vocal music Glenwood (Ark.) Pub. Sch., 1966-67; tchr. elem. music DeSoto (Mo.) Pub. Sch., 1967-69; tchr. secondary music Richland Pub. Sch., Essex, Mo., 1969-71; tchr. elem. music Augusta (Ark.) Pub. Sch., 1971-82; tchr. vocal music Independence (Mo.) Christian Sch., 1982-87; tchr. secondary music Doniphan (Mo.) Region I Pub. Sch., 1988-91; vocal and band dir. grades K-12 Delaplaine (Ark.) H.S., 1992, Stanford (Ark.) H.S., 1992-93; band and choir dir. grades K-12 Delaplaine Schs., 1993-94; dir. K-12 vocal and band Southland C-9 Schs., Cardwell, Mo., 1994—2001; organist 1st Bapt. Ch., Paragould, Ark., 1998—2002; sub tchr. six local sch., 2001—. Camp music dir. YWCA/Camp Burgess Glen, Cedar Mountain, N.C., summer 1964; interum minister of music First Bapt. Ch., Paragould, Ark., 1988-89; pvt. piano and voice tchr., 1967—. Active PTA. Am. Coll. Musicians scholar, 1962; acad. and music scholar. Mem. Music Educators Nat. Conf., Cen. Tchrs. Assn., Mo. Tchrs. Assn. Avocations: cooking, composing, church, reading, vocal solo singing. Home: Sunset Hills Subdivsn 1700 Hillcrest Dr Paragould AR 72450-4057

STALLINGS, VIOLA PATRICIA ELIZABETH, systems engineer, educational systems specialist, retired information technology manager; b. Norfolk, Va., Nov. 6, 1946; d. Harold Albert and Marie Blanche (Welch) S.; m. (div. Oct. 1984); 1 child, Patricia N.P. Stallings. BS in Psychology, Va. State U., 1968; MBA with distinction, U. Pa., 1975; postgrad., Temple U., 1972-74, Calif. State U., San Francisco, 1973; EdD with specialization in tech., Nova Southeastern U., Ft. Lauderdale, Fla., 1996. Cert. exec. project mgr., project mgmt. profl. Project Mgmt. Inst. Tchr., supr. Peace Corps, Liberia, West Africa, 1968-71; tchr. Day Care Ctr., disruptive h.s. students Tioga Comm. Youth Ctr., 1972-73; tchr. Phila. Sch. Dist., 1972-76; bus. cons. Phila., 1976; sr. sys. engr./sr. industry svcs. specialist, project mgr. IBM/K-12 Edn. and IBM Global Industry, Mt. Laurel, N.J.; retiring cert. exec. project mgr. IBM Global Svcs. Task force leader IBM Corp., 1990—91. Bd. dirs. Unity Ch. of Christ, 1993—95, 2000—02, sec., 2000—01. Recipient Outstanding Svc. award IBM Black Workers Alliance, Washington, 1984. Mem. AAUW, World Affairs Coun., Project Mgmt. Inst., St. Joseph's Carpenter Soc. (bd. dirs. 1999—), Women of Arts, Beta Gamma Sigma. Baptist. Avocations: reading, writing, drawing, gardening, cooking, dancing, sewing.

STALLWORTH-BARRON, DORIS A. CARTER, librarian, educator; b. Ala., June 12, 1931; d. Henry Lee Carter and Hattie Belle Stallworth; m. George Stallworth, 1950 (dec.); children: Annette LaVerne, Vanzette Yvonne; m. Walter L. Barron, 1989. BS, Ala. State U., 1955; MLS, CUNY, 1968; postgrad., Columbia U., St. John's U., NYU. Cert. supr. and tchr. sch. libr. media, N.Y. Libr. media specialist N.Y.C. Bd. Edn.; head libr. Calhoun County High Sch., Hobson City, Ala. Cons. Libr. Unit, N.Y.C. Bd. Edn.; cons. evaluator So. Assn. Secondary Schs., Ala.; supr., adminstr., liason rep. Community Sch. Dist. #24 N.Y.C. Sch. System; previewer libr. media Preview Mag., 1971-73; mem. ednl. svcs. adv. coun. Sta. WNET, 1987-89; mem. coun. N.Y.C. Schs. Libr. System, 1987-90, mem. N.Y.C. bd. examiners for tchr. librs., 1972-89; turn-key tchr. trainer N.Y. State Dept. Edn., 1988; spl. guest speaker and lectr. Queens Coll., City U., Community Sch. Dist. #24, PTA, N.Y. City Sch. System, Libr. unit, 1980-90; curriculum writer libr. unit N.Y.C. Bd. Edn., 1985-86. Contbr. articles to ednl. publs. Mem. State of Ala. Dem. Exec. Com., 1994—; active A+ for Kids. Mem. NAFE, ALA, Am. Assn. Sch. Librs. (spl. guest speaker and lectr. for conv. 1987), Am. Sch. Libr.'s Assn., Nat. Assn. Black Pub. Adminstrs., N.Y. State Libr. Assn., N.Y.C. Sch. Librs. Assn., Nat. Forum for Black Pub. Adminstrs., N.Y. Coalition 100 Black Women, Lambda Kappa Mu Sorority, Inc., Alpha Kappa Alpha Sorority Inc.

STAMBAUGH, JOHN EDGAR, oncologist, hematologist, pharmacologist, educator; b. Everett, Pa., Apr. 30, 1940; s. John Edgar and Rhoda Irene (Becker) S.; m. Shirley Louise Fultz, June 24, 1961; 4 children. BS in Chemistry cum laude, Dickinson Coll., 1962; MD, Jefferson Med. Coll., 1966, PhD, 1968. Intern Thomas Jefferson U. Hosp., Phila., 1968-69, resident, 1968-69; oncology fellow Jefferson Med. Coll., 1970-72, instr. pharmacology, 1969-70, asst. prof., 1970-74, assoc. prof., 1974-82, prof., 1982—. Pvt. practice med. oncology, hematology and cancer pain, Woodbury, N.J.; staff physician Cooper Med. Ctr., Camden, N.J., 1972—, Underwood Meml. Hosp., Woodbury, 1972—, West Jersey Hosp., 1973—, J.F. Kennedy Hosp., 1978—, Our Lady of Lourdes Hosp., 1990—. Contbr. articles to profl. jours. Fellow: Am. Soc. Pain Mgmt., Am. Acad. Pain Mgmt., Am. Coll. Clin. Pharmacology; mem.: Am. Assn. Clin. Rsch., Am. Pain Soc., Internat. Assn. for Study of Pain, Am. Assn. for Cancer Rsch., Am. Soc. Clin. Oncology, Am. Soc. for Pharmacology and Exptl. Therapeutics, Camden County Med. Soc., Gloucester County Med. Soc., N.J. Med. Soc. (del.), Am. Soc. Clin. Pharmacology, AMA, ABA, Sigma Xi. Office: 17 W Red Bank Ave Ste 101 Woodbury NJ 08096-1630 also: 100 Carnie Blvd Voorhees NJ 08043-4512

STAMPER, JAMES M. retired English language educator; b. Roxana, Ky., Sept. 26, 1917; s. Marion and Amanda (Combs) S.; m. Diane C. Mahoney, Aug. 12, 1967. BS in Edn., Union Coll., 1941; MA in English, U. Ky., 1946. Subs. tchr. Ermine Elem. Sch., Dry Fork Elem. Sch., 1936-37; elem. tchr. various schs., 1937-41; h.s. Eng. tchr. Whitesburg H.S., Ky., 1941-46; instr. English U. Ky., Lexington, 1946-49, U. Md., College Park, 1949-52; instr. bus. English DePaul U., Chgo., 1952-62; English tchr., cons. in high sch. English Bd. Edn., Chgo., 1962-72; ret. Chgo. Area Schs., 1972; subst. tchr. Chgo. Area schs., 1972-82. Vis. instr. in English Jacksonville (Fla.) U. Co-author: A Handbook on Oral Reading Diagnosis, Resource Materials for Essential English in the Secondary Schools, A Syllabus in Basic English; contbr. articles to profl. jours. Scholar Knights of Columbus, Union Coll., U. Ky. Mem. AARP. Home: 4501 Concord Ln Northbrook IL 60062-7163

STANBERRY, D(OSI) ELAINE, English literature educator, writer; b. Elk Park, N.C. m. Earl Stanberry; 1 child, Anita St. Lawrence. Student in Bus. Edn., Steed Coll. Tech., 1956; BS in Bus. and English, East Tenn. State

U., 1961, MA in Shakespearean Lit., 1962; PhD, Tex. A&M U., 1975; postgrad., North Tex. State U., U. South Fla., NYU, Duke U., U. N.C. Prof. Manatee Jr. Coll., Bradenton, Fla., 1964-67; Disting. prof. English Dickinson State U., N.D., 1967-81; retired, 1981. Author: Poetic Heartstrings, Mountain Echoes, Love's Perplexing Obsession Experienced by Heinrich Heine and Percy Bysshe Shelley, Poetry from the Ancients to Moderns: A Critical Anthology, Finley Forest, Chapel Hill's Tree-lined Tuck, (plays) The Big Toe, The Funeral Factory; contbr. articles, poetry to jours., mags. Recipient Editor's Choice award Nat. Libr. Poetry, 1988, 95, Distinguished Professor of English Award, Dickinson State U., 1981; included in Best Poems of 1995. Mem. Acad. Am. Poets, N.C. Writers Network, N.C. Poetry Soc. (Carl Sandburg Poetry award 1988), Poetic Page, Writers Jour., Poets and Writers, Friday-Noon Poets, Delta Kappa Gamma. Home: Finley Forest 193 Summerwalk Cir Chapel Hill NC 27517-8642

STANDBERRY, HERMAN LEE, school system administrator, educational consultant; b. Oran, Mo., Feb. 22, 1945; s. Willie Standberry and Bettie Mae (Thompson) Standberry-Taylor; m. Barbara Irene Palmer, July 1, 1942; children: Donna, Debra, Nina, Miriam, Miranda, Gretchen, Charles, Mary, Dwayne, Helena, Regina, Lakesha. BS, So. Ill. U., 1968; MA, Newport U., 1981, LHD (hon.), 1990; EdD, Walden U., 1992; D Ministry, Am. Christian Coll. and Sem., 1992; MEd, Ind. Wesleyan U., 1997. Cert. supt., gen. adminstr., curriculum, tchr., sch. counselor; approved profl. devel. provider Ill. State Bd. Edn. and Ill. State Tchr. Cert. Bd. Tchr. Community H.S. Dist. 428, Blue Island, Ill., 1968-70; exec. dir., dep. dir. program planner, HeadStart dir. Kane County Coun. for Econ. Opportunity, Batavia, Ill., 1970—75; case mgr., youth supr., educator State of Ill., Dept. Pub. Aid., Dept. Corrections, Chgo., Joliet and St. Charles, Ill., 1975—85; adminstrv. asst. to prin. Bloom High Sch. Dist. 206, Chicago Heights, Ill., 1992-93; asst. prin. Rogers High Sch., Michigan City, Ind., 1994-95; prin. Mich. City (Ind.) Area Alternative H.S., 1995—; chmn. bd./CEO Dr. Herman Standberry and Assocs., 2000—. Chmn. bd. dirs. Greater Chgo. Coun. of Religious Orgns., 1985-89; mem. George Bush's Rep. Presdl. Task Force, Washington, 1989; nominated mem. U.S. Rep. Senatorial Inner Cir., Washington, 1989; interim supt. LaPorte Cmty. Schs., 2001; supt., prin. United Ednl. Cultural Acad., 2000—. Author (curriculum) Business Law I & II, 1968, Career Counseling and Survival, 1978. Bd. dirs. YMCA, Elgin, Ill, 1972, City of Elgin-Fremont Youth Orgn., 1971-72; host agy. rep. Dept. Human Svcs., Chgo., 1985-90; sustaining mem. Ill. Rep. Party, Springfield, 1989; host agy. Percy Julian High Sch., Chgo., 1989-90, 2000—, Ill. Dept. Pub. Aid, Chgo., 1987. Recipient NBC 5/Chgo. and AT&T Jefferson award; grantee Ill. Dept. Pub. Aid, 1984-87, hon. award Christian World Affairs Conf., 1985-86. Mem. Internat. Assn. Police and Community Rel. Officers, United Evangelistic Consulting Assn. (chmn. bd. dirs., pres. 1985-93). Home: 803 E 193rd St Glenwood IL 60425-2011 Office: United Evangelistic Assn 1236 W 103rd St Chicago IL 60643-2361

STANDIFORD, SALLY NEWMAN, technology educator; b. Berkeley, Calif., Dec. 25, 1941; d. Richard Lancaster and Eleanor June (Wagstaff) Newman; m. Jay Cary Standiford, Nov. 21, 1964; children: Barbara, Susan. AB, Georgian Ct. Coll., Lakewood, N.J., 1963; MA in Teaching, The Citadel, 1972; PhD, U. Ill., 1980. Tchr. Goose Creek High Sch., Hanahan, S.C., 1969-73; rsch. and teaching asst. U. Ill., Urbana, 1974-78, rsch. asst. Inst. Aviation, 1979-80, vis. asst. prof., 1980-84; adminstr. City Colls. Chgo., 1978; mgr. Control Data Corp., Champaign, Ill., 1978-79, instrnl. design specialist Savoy, Ill., 1979-80; asst. prof. U. St. Thomas, St. Paul, 1984-88; assoc. prof. tech. U. Wis., River Falls, 1988-92, prof., 1992—. Dir. Ednl. Tech. U. Wis., 1988—; tech. coord. telecomms. curriculum project, U. Wis., 1993—; advisor N.W. Instrnl. Broadcast Svc., 1989—; evaluator Wis. Dept. Pub. Instrn., Madison, 1990—; rschr. Saturn Sch. Tomorrow, St. Paul, 1991—; cons. Met. State U., Mpls., 1992—, Hamline U., St. Paul, 1994—; mem. U. Wis. Sys. Distance Edn. Policy Task Force, 1993—. Author: Computers in English Classroom, 1983; contbg. author: Language Arts Methods, 1987; also numerous articles; designer instrnl. software. Del. Minn. Dem.-Farmer-Labor Conv., Rochester, 1988; computer cons. Women Against Mil. Madness, Mpls., 1988-91; marcher Honeywell Project, Mpls., 1988-91; pres. faculty senate U. Wis., 1992-94. Grantee NSF, 1970-71, fellow, 1973-74; ssummer faculty rsch. fellow USAF, 1987; U. Wis. Lighthouse Tech. Innovation, 1994—. Mem. Am. Assn. Colls. of Tchr. Edn. (co-chair spl. study group on tech. in edn.), Nat. Coun. Tchrs. English (instrnl. tech. com. 1983-88, commn. on media 1985-88, cons. 1992—), Assn. Women in Computing, Western Wis. Alliance in Tech. (advisor 1990—), Computer Profls. for Social Responsibility (charter). Office: U Wis A12 Ames River Falls WI 54022

STANDING, KIMBERLY ANNA, educational researcher; b. Hagerstown, Md., Mar. 24, 1965; d. Thomas Townsend and Ruth Annadeane (Powell) Stone; m. Christopher G. Standing, May 20, 1989; children: Iain Christopher, Leah Elizabeth. BA in Math., St. Mary's Coll., 1988; MA in Higher Edn. Adminstrn., George Washington U., 1996, postgrad. Sr. analyst Westat, Inc., Rockville, Md., 1988—. Mem. Am. Ednl. Rsch. Assn., Assn. Study Higher Edn. Home: 11545 Brundidge Ter Germantown MD 20876-5500 Office: Westat Inc RW2564 1650 Research Blvd Rockville MD 20850-3195 E-mail: KimStanding@westat.com.

STANDING BEAR, ZUGGUELGERES GALAFACH, criminologist, forensic scientist, educator; b. Boston, Jan. 10, 1941; m. Nancy Lee Karlovic, July 13, 1978 (div. Aug. 1985); m. Virginia Anne Red Hawk, Mar. 22, 1988. BS, U. Nebr., 1971; MS in Forensic Sci., George Washington U., 1974; postgrad. cert. in forensic medicine, Armed Forces Inst. Pathology, 1974; MSEd, U. So. Calif., 1976; MPA, Jacksonville State U., 1981; PhD in Criminology, Fla. State U., 1986. Diplomate Am. Bd. Forensic Examiners, Am. Bd. Forensic Medicine, chmn. 2002-03; cert. coroner, Ga., 1988-92; cert. criminal justice instr., Calif., Ga. Criminal investigator U.S. Army, 1965; dist. comdr. 7th region U.S. Army Criminal Investigation Command, Seoul, 1974-77; course mgr. U.S. Army Mil. Police Sch., Ft. McClellan, Ala., 1978-81; ret. U.S. Army, 1981; instr. Fla. State U., Tallahassee, 1981-85; asst. prof. No. Ariz. U., Flagstaff, 1985-86; program coord., prof. Valdosta (Ga.) State U., 1986-95; assoc. prof. Colo. State U., Ft. Collins, 1995—2001, U. Colo., 2001—; adminstr. The Flash and Thelma Meml. Hedgehog Rescue of N.Am., Inc., 1998—. V.p. Bearhawk Cons. Group, Ft. Collins, 1986—; chair Am. Bd. Forensic Examiners. Editor Jour. Contemporary Criminal Justice, 1992. Mem., task group coord. Com. for Sexual Assault Evidence Stds., ASTM, 1993— Com. Colo State U.; mem. leadership coun. Cmty. Policing Project, Valdosta, Ga., 1993-95; treas. and v.p. edn. and rsch. No. Colo. WOLF rescue, edn., and rsch. project, LaPorte, Colo., 1995—; mem. Nat. Am. lang. preservation com. Colo. State Univ. Decorated Bronze Star medal, Meritorious Svc. medal (with oak leaf cluster). Fellow Am. Acad. Forensic Scis. (gen. sec. 1987-88, gen. chmn. 1988-90, gen. program co-chair 1995-96, Gen. Sec. Meritorious Svc. award 1996), Am. Coll. Forensic Examiners, Internat. Assn. Forensic Nurses (disting. fellow, mem. exec. bd. dirs., cons. and permissions exec., chmn. ethics com.); mem. ASTM (co-coord. sexual assault evidence stds. task group), Am. Sociol. Assn., Acad. Polit. Sci., Am. Soc. Criminology, Acad. Criminal Justice Scis. (program com. 1996-97), So. Criminal Justice Assn., Am. Assn. of U. Profs., Harley Owners Group, Internat. Hedgehog Assn, (treas.). Haudenosaunee (Native Am.). Avocations: hedgehog and wolf behavior, traditional Native American religious counseling, motorcycling. Office: Forensic Health Sci Programs Beth-El Coll Nursing and Health Scis U Colo Colorado Springs CO 80918 Home: 514 Hopi Circle Divide CO 80814

STANDLEY, MARK, school program administrator, consultant; b. Waco, Tex., Feb. 12, 1954; s. Troy and Julia (Crockett) S.; m. Christine Selin Standley, Dec. 31, 1986; children: Aron, Robin Joanne. BA, S.W. Tex. State U., 1976; MS, U. Oreg., 1993. Cert. tchr., adminstr. Vol. U.S. Peace Corps, South Korea, 1976-79; tchr. Northway (Ala.) Sch., 1985-90; prin. Mentasta (Ala.) Lake Sch., 1990-92; program mgr. Ala. Gateway Sch. Dist., Tok, 1993-95; account exec. Apple Computer, TOK, Alaska, 1995—. Co-founder Nat. Acad. for Ednl. Tech., Eugene, Oreg., 1993; ednl. advisor Dynamix Software, Eugene, 1993—; team leader Tech. Leadership Retreats, Ala., 1992—. Co-author: Technology Advisory Councils, 1993, Teacher's Guide to the Incredible Machine, 1994. Bd. dirs. No. Ala. Environ. Ctr., Fairbanks, 1983-84; v.p. Upper Tanana Natural History Assn., Tok, 1988-89; mem. Tom Snyder Prodns. Presenters Club, 1994—. Recipient Tchr. Fellowship grant Am. Indian Soc. for Engring. and Sci., 1987, Tech. Incentive grant Apple Computer, Inc., 1989. Mem. ASCD, Internat. Soc. for Tech. in Edn., Ala. Soc. for Tech. in Edn. (bd. dirs. 1992—, pres.-elect 1994—, Pres.'s award 1994). Avocations: kayaking, snow shoe racing. Home: 19913 Kalka Cir Eagle River AK 99577-8711

STANFORD, AMELIA JEAN, elementary education educator; b. Eudora, Miss., Oct. 29, 1940; d. Charles Loyd and Thelma Adelaide (Shelton) Sexton; m. Carl Dennis Stanford, June 30, 1961; children: Carla, Lesa, Dennis. Student, N.W. Jr. Coll., 1960; BS, Memphis State U., 1967. Cert. elem. edn. educator 1-6, Miss. 5th-6th grade tchr. Miss Lee's Sch., Memphis, 1962-63; 6th grade tchr. St. Paul Sch., Memphis, 1965; 3d grade tchr. Southaven (Miss.) Sch., 1965-68; 2d grade tchr. Sacred Heart Sch., Walls, Miss., 1968—. Co-editor: (filmstrip) Helping Children with Homework, 1977. Active Coalition Christian Voters, DeSoto County, Miss., 1993—; Sunday sch. tchr. Glenn's Chapel, Lake Cormorant, Miss., 1963—, Bible sch. dir., 1963—, children's ch. dir., 1990—. Mem. Nat. Cath. Edn. Assn. Methodist. Avocations: reading, grandchildren, church work, bicycling. Home: 291 Highway 301 N Lake Cormorant MS 38641-9506 Office: Sacred Heart Sch PO Box 96 Walls MS 38680-0096

STANFORD, JANE HERRING, management consultant and educator, author; b. Lockhart, Tex., Dec. 17, 1939; d. John William and Frances Argyra (Cheatham) H. Jr.; m. Rube Valton Stanford, Sept. 17, 1966; children: (Steven) Scott, Lisa Ann. BS, Texas A&M U., Kingsville; MS in Counseling, Texas A&M U., Corpus Christi; MBA, Texas A&M U., Kingsville; PhD in Orgn. Theory and Strategic Mgmt., U. North Tex. Instr. cmty. coll., Corpus Christi, 1981—88; tchg. fellow U. North Tex., Denton, 1988-90; assoc. prof. bus. policy and internat. mgmt., pres. faculty senate Texas A&M U., Kingsville, 1990—99, full mem. grad. faculty, 1992-99, grad. rsch. advisor, MBA program, Coll. Bus., 1992-98, head, asst. v.p. acad. affairs, 1998-99, ret., 1999; mgmt. cons. Strategic Mgmt. Solutions, Inc., 1999—, pres., primary cons., 2000—; adj. prof., mgmt. Texas A&M U., 2002—; vis. assoc. prof. mgmt. Coll. of Bus., Texas A&M U., Chorpus Christi, Tex., 2003—. Chair univ. assessment, budgeting and planning com. Tex. A&M U., 1997—98; internat. lectr. strategic mgmt. within internat. context, Columbia, Argentina; workshop leader and participant in acad. issues; paper presenter internat. conf. Soc. for the Advancement Mgmt., 1998—2003; initiator corp. learning cons. Key to Success guidebooks and workshops; vis. assoc. prof. mgmt. Tex. A&M U., Corpus Christi, 2003—. Author: Building Competitiveness: U.S. Expatriate Management Strategies in Mexico, 1995; contbr. articles to profl. jours. and conf. procs. Apptd. to water resources adv. com. City of Corpus Christi, 2003—. Named Leadership Corpus Christi Class of XXX, 2001—02; fellow Sys. Chancellor's fellow in leadership in higher edn. program, Tex. A&M U., 1997. Mem.: Soc. ADvancement Mgmt., Acad. Mgmt., Inst. Mgmt. Cons., Strategic Mgmt. Soc., Delta Sigma Pi, Kappa Delta Pi (life). Presbyterian. Avocations: book collecting, photography, travel. Home: 13526 Carlos Fifth Ct Corpus Christi TX 78418-6913 Office: Strategic Mgmt Solutions Inc 13526 Carlos Fifth Ct Corpus Christi TX 78418-6913 E-mail: planyourbiz@aol.com.

STANFORD, JANINE LYNETTE, secondary school educator; b. Lamar, Colo. d. Roger Irvin Smith and Dorothy Fay McBride; m. William Stanford, July 4, 1984. AA, Mesa Jr. Coll. (now Mesa State Coll.), Colo., 1969; BA/teaching cert., Colo. State U., 1971; MA, Ariz. State U., 1978. Cert. tchr., Ariz. Tchr. and coord. internat. baccalaureate program Paradise Valley High Sch., Phoenix, 1973—. Coord. internat. baccalaureate program N. Canyon High Sch., Phoenix, 1990—97. Campaign asst. Paradise Valley Edn. Assn., Phoenix, 1976—2002; cert. tchr. law-related edn. ctr. Ariz. Bar Assn., Phoenix, 1992. Mem. NEA, DAR, Nat. Coun. Social Studies, Clan Donald USA, Ariz. Edn. Assn. (bd. dirs. 1996-2000), Ariz. Coun. Social Studies, Paradise Valley Edn. Assn. (sr. bldg. rep., bd. dirs., v.p. 1990-92), Phi Beta Kappa. Democrat. Avocations: travel, knitting, geneaology, quilting, photography. Office: Paradise Valley High School 3950 E Bell Rd Phoenix AZ 85032

STANFORD, JENNIFER LAURA, nurse educator; b. St. Catherine, Jamaica, West Indies; came to U.S., 1978; d. Armon F. and Doris M. Stanford. BSN, George Mason U., 1980; MS in Nursing Edn., U. Md., 1997. Staff nurse, technician Holy Cross Hosp., Silver Spring, Md., 1974-85; asst. head nurse King Faisal Specialist Hosp., Riyadh, Saudi Arabia, 1986-89; clin. coord. Montgomery Surgery Ctr., Rockville, Md., 1990-93; clin. resource nurse Montgomery Gen. Hosp., Olney, Md., 1993-96, liaison nurse, 1996—. Treas. United Meth. Women, Rockville, 1996—; chairperson singles ministry Jerusalem Mt. Pleasant United Meth. Ch., Rockville, 1994-96; mentor Beale Elem. Sch., Rockville, 1993—. Mem. Am. Soc. Post Anesthesia Care Nurses, Chesepeak Bay Post Anesthesia Nurses (treas. 1995-97). Avocations: needlepoint, reading, walking. Home: 9263 Chadburn Pl Gaithersburg MD 20886-4036

STANFORD, KATHLEEN THERESA, secondary school educator; b. Belize City, Belize, Sept. 28, 1933; d. Frederick Gill and Ila Mae (Cherrington) Hyde; m. Herman Emanuel Stanford., Oct. 3, 1970 (dec. Feb., 1989). Student (summer), S. We. La. U., Lafayette, 1958; BA, Seton Hill Coll., 1962; student (summer), Xavier U., New Orleans, 1956, 68; postgrad., Southern U. and A&M Coll., 1962, 67, Adelphi U., 1988, C.W. Post, N.Y., 1988. Cert. sci. tchr., La. (life). Tchr. Mem. Sisters of Holy Family Order, various cities, U.S. & Belize, 1953-69; sci. tchr., moderator Sisters of Holy Family, Grand Coteau, La., 1967-68, Lafayette, La., 1968-70; laicized, 1970; sci. tchr., sponsor of sci. fair N.Y.C. Bd. of Edn., Bklyn., 1981—. Sci. coord. La. Sci. Acad., Lafayette, 1968-70; mem. U.F.T. /IHS sci. com., N.Y.C., 1984-85. Contbr. poetry to Poetry Mags., 1974—. Hon. mem. Pres. Clinton's 2d Term Com., Washington, 1997; sci. sponsor Ford Future Scientists of Am., 1968, Dist. Sci. Fair, Bklyn., 1984; sec. Belize Parkfest of N.Y., Inc., 1990-92 Recipient Commendation for pupils 20th Internat. Sci. Fair, 1969, poetry awards Am. Poetry Assn., 1989, 90, cert. for leadership, Dem. Nat. Com., Washington, 1997. Mem. Belize Cosmopolitan Benevolent Assn. (v.p.). Democrat. Avocations: writing poetry, photography, bird watching, swimming, walking, singing.

STANGER, ROBERT HENRY, psychiatrist, educator; b. N.Y.C., N.Y., May 19, 1937; s. Sidney and Mary (Strassner) S.; m. Andrea Rogin, Aug. 28, 1960; children: Lee Ann, David Neal. AB, Guilford Coll., 1959; MD, Emory U., 1964. Intern in internal medicine Wake Forest U., 1964-65; resident in gen. psychiatry U. Pitts., Western Psychiat. Inst. and Clinic, 1967-70; pvt. practice gen. psychiatry Monroeville, Pa., 1970-2001; med. dir. Allegheny Valley Mental Health-Mental Retardation Ctr., New Kensington, Pa., 1970-76; dir. psychiat. svcs. Allegheny Valley Hosp., Natrona Heights, Pa., 1983-96, chmn. dept. psychiatry and behavioral medicine, 1983-96; pvt. practice Natrona Heights, 1984-97. Clin. instr. psychiatry U. Pitts. Sch. Medicine, 1970-79, clin. asst. prof., 1980-2002, asst. prof. emeritus, 2002—; cons. Westinghouse Elec. Corp., East Pitts., 1977-87; mem. ethics com. human rsch. Allegheny Valley Hosp., 1976-97; chmn. dept. psychiatry Citizens Gen. Hosp., 1978-88. Capt. M.C., U.S. Army, 1965-67, Vietnam. Mem. AMA, Am. Psychiat. Assn. (del. 1986-88), Pa. Psychiat. Soc. (councilor 1976-79, treas. 1979-80, sec. 1980-81, v.p. 1981-82, pres.-elect 1982-83, pres. 1983-84), Pitts. Psychiat. Soc. (councilor 1974-76, sec. 1977-78, pres.-elect 1978-79, pres. 1979-80), Allegheny County Med. Soc. Home and Office: 3910 Old William Penn Hwy Pittsburgh PA 15235-4837

STANISLAO, JOSEPH, consulting engineer, educator; b. Manchester, Conn., Nov. 21, 1928; s. Eduardo and Rose (Zaccaro) S.; m. Bettie Chloe Carter, Sept. 6, 1960. BS, Tex. Tech. U., 1957; MS, Pa. State U., 1959; Eng.ScD, Columbia U., 1970. Registered profl. engr., Mass., Mont. Asst. engr. Naval Ordnance Research, University Park, Pa., 1958-59; asst. prof. N.C. State U., Raleigh, 1959-61; dir. research Darlington Fabrics Corp., Pawtucket, R.I., 1961-62; from asst. prof. to prof. U. R.I., Kingston, 1962-71; prof., chmn. dept. Cleve. State U., 1971-75; prof., dean N.D. State U., Fargo, 1975-94, acting v.p. agrl. affairs, 1983-85, asst. to pres., 1983—, dir. Engring. Computer Ctr., 1984—, prof. emeritus indsl. engring. and mgmt., 1994—; pres. XOX Corp., 1984-90; chmn. bd., chief exec. officer ATSCO, 1989-94, chief engr., 1993—; prof. emeritus N.D. State U., 1994. Adj. prof. Mont. State U., 1994—, dir. indsl. and mgmt. engring. program, 1996—, mfg. rsch., sponsored by Nat. Sci. Found. 1997—; v.p., co-owner, bd. dirs. D.T.&J., Inc., Fargo, N.D., 1999—, London, Eng., 1999—; v.p. engring. Roll-A-Ramp, Rolla-A-Latter, and Rolla-A-conveyor, 2000—; cons. to healthcare sys., 1999—. Contbr. chpts. to books, articles to profl. jours.; patentee pump apparatus, pump fluid housing; patents pending roll-a-ramp and roll-a-latter. Served to sgt. USMC, 1948-51. Recipient Sigma Xi award, 1968; Order of the Iron Ring award N.D. State U., 1972, Econ. Devel. award, 1991; USAF recognition award, 1979, ROTC appreciation award, 1982 Mem. Am. Inst. Indsl. Engrs. (sr.; y.p. 1964-65), ASME, Am. Soc. Engring. Edn. (campus coord. 1979-81), Acad. Indsl. Engrs. Tex. Tech U., Lions, Elks, Am. Legion, Phi Kappa Phi, Tau Beta Pi (advisor 1978-79). Roman Catholic. Home: 8 Park Plaza Dr Bozeman MT 59715-9343

STANISZEWSKI, SUE ANN KOBER, special education administrator; b. Waukesha, Wis., Sept. 9, 1947; d. Laurel Robert and Besse Louise (Bixby) Kober; m. James Henry Staniszewski, Aug. 8, 1970; children: Leigh Ann, Kristine Elizabeth. BEd, U. Whitewater, 1969, MSEd in Spl. Edn., 1973. Cert. spl. edn. tchr. K-12, elem. sch. adminstr., Level B & A spl. edn., dir. pupil svcs./spl. edn., specialist in adminstrv. leadership, Wis. Primary TMR tchr. Manitowoc (Wis.) County Handicapped Children's Edn. Bd., 1969-72, early childhood edn., 1972-90, unit leader, 1969-88, program support K-6, 1978-90, program support K-9, 1987-90, program supr., 1990-92, asst. adminstr., 1992-93, adminstr., 1993—. Adj. prof. Silver Lake Coll., Manitowoc, 1992; presenter workshops in field; active numerous coms. Policy coun. mem. Header Start, Manitowoc County, 1990-92; mem. Silver Lake Coll. Ednl. Adv. bd., 1991-92; edn. chmn. Edn. for Employment, Manitowoc County, 1991—; mem. Youth Svcs. Coord. Coun., 1990-91. Named Tchr. of Yr. Wis. chpt. Early Childhood: Exceptional Ednl. Needs, 1978. Mem. ASCD, Wis. Assn. Sch. Bds., Wis. Assn. Sch. Dist. Adminstrs., Coun. Exceptional Children, Phi Delta Kappa, Delta Kappa Gamma (pres. 1984-86). Avocations: skiing, tennis, travel. Office: Manitowoc County Handicapped Children's Edn Bd 4400 Michigan Ave Manitowoc WI 54220-3067

STANKEWICZ, MARY CHRISTINE, middle school educator; b. Perth Amboy, N.J., Aug. 8, 1949; d. Stephen Charles and Mary (Pinelli) S. BA, Trenton State Coll., 1971. Cert. tchr., N.J. Tchr. social studies Avenel (N.J.) Jr. High Sch., 1971-81; tchr. geography Woodbridge (N.J.) Mid. Sch., 1981—, social studies staff leader, 1990—. Named Tchr. of Yr. Am. Legion Post 471, Iselin, N.J., 1988; recipient Gov.'s Tchr. Recognition award, State of N.J., 1988. Mem. NEA, Nat. Coun. Geographic Edn., N.J. Coun. Social Studies, N.J. Geographic Alliance, Alpha Delta Kappa (historian Alpha Epsilon chpt. 1984-86, corr. sec. 1986-88, pres. 1988-90, state by-laws chair 1990-94). Roman Catholic. Avocations: bowling, reading, birdwatching, travel, stamp collecting. Home: 103 Howard St Hopelawn NJ 08861-1525 Office: Woodbridge Mid Sch 525 Barron Ave Woodbridge NJ 07095-3003

STANKIEWICZ, ANDRZEJ JERZY, physician, biochemistry educator; b. Lidzbark, Poland, Sept. 28, 1948; came to U.S., 1981; s. Wincenty and Zofia (Plawgo) S. MD, Med. Sch., Gdansk, Poland, 1972, PhD, 1976. Asst. prof. Med. Sch., Gdansk, 1972-77, adj. prof., lectr., 1978-81; rsch. fellow Harvard U. Med. Sch., Boston, 1981-84; resident Brown U. Sch. Medicine, Providence, 1984-87, fellow in oncology, 1987-90; pvt. practice Providence, 1990—. Contbr. articles to profl. jours. Fellow Internat. Union Biochemistry; mem. ACP, Societas Scientiarum Gedanensis. Roman Catholic. Achievements include evolution of adenine metabolizing systems, rare abnomalities of blood coagulation interactions between hemostasis and complement system. Office: St Josephs Hosp 200 High Service Ave North Providence RI 02904-5113

STANKIEWICZ, ANGELA L. principal elementary school; b. Fall River, Mass., Apr. 28, 1953; d. Joseph J. and Ruth C. (Morro) S. BS in Elem. Edn., Bridgewater State U., 1975; MEd, Lesley Coll., 1990. Cert. elem. tchr., Mass. Tchr. 1st grade Sts. Peter & Paul Sch., Fall River, 1978-85, tchr. 4th grade, 1985-92; prin. St. Mary's Sch., New Bedford, Mass., 1992—. Mem. kindergarten curriculum com., Diocese of Fall River, 1981-82. Bd. dirs. Algonquin Camp Fire Coun., Fall River, 1982. Recipient Our Lady of Good Counsel award Diocese of Fall River Camp Fire Girls, 1984, 3rd prize Computer Learning Found., 1989. Mem. AAUW, ASCD, Nat. Cath. Edn. Assn. Roman Catholic. Home: 252 Blackstone St Fall River MA 02721-2748 Office: St Mary's Sch 115 Illinois St New Bedford MA 02745-2596

STANLEY, CAROL JONES, academic administrator, educator; b. Durham, N.C. m. Donald A. Stanley. BS, N.C. Ctrl. U., Durham, 1969; MS, N.C. Ctrl. U., 1975; spl. student, U. N.C., Greensboro, 1987-90. Master's G teaching cert. Instr. Fayetteville (N.C.) State U., 1975-76, adj. instr., 1986-89; instr. Durham Tech. C.C., 1977; adminstrv. sec., adj. instr., rsch. asst. N.C. Ctrl. U., Durham, 1989, asst. dir. recruitment, 1994—; admissions, discharge coord., emergency dept. adminstrn. Duke U. Med. Ctr., Durham, 1991—. Asst. dir. recruitment N.C. Ctrl. U. Sch. Law, 1993—. Mem. ASCD, Nat. Bus. Edn. Assn., Delta Sigma Theta (scholarship 1989). Home: 508 Snowcrest Trl Durham NC 27707

STANLEY, DENISE ROSE, secondary school educator; b. Norton, Va., June 15, 1970; d. Gary Duane and Tina Leigh (O'Dell) Rose; m. Kenneth Darrell Stanley Jr., May 31, 1991; children: Andrew Kenneth Lee, Dakota Rose. BA in English, U. Va. Coll. at Wise, 1992. Cert. tchr. English, secondary sch., Va., S.C. Instr. English J.J. Kelly H.S., Wise, Va., 1992-93; English, speech and drama instr. Ervinton H.S., Nora, Va., 1993-97; English tchr. Clintwood (Va.) H.S., 1997—2001, forensics coach, 1998—2001; tchr. English and advanced grammar and composition Myrtle Beach (S.C.) H.S., 2001—. Forensic and drama coach Ervinton H.S., Nora, 1993-97; co-chair media cluster writing com., tech. prep comm. arts S.W. Va. C.C. Consortium, Richlands, 1994-97; mem. tech. com. Dickenson County Sch. System, Clintwood, Va., 1994; facilitator for reading to learn in-svc. project Dickenson County Schs., 1995; mem. steering com. ACE Educators, Mountain Empire C.C., 1999—. Dir. Miss EHS Pageant, 1994, 95, 96; admissions/pub. rels. asst. SVCC, 1995. Mem.: NEA, S.C. Edn. Assn., Horry County Edn. Assn. Republican. Mem. Ch. Of God. Avocations: reading, creative writing, recreational sports, acting. Home: 6634 Cinnamon Fern Ln Myrtle Beach SC 29588-6456 Office: Myrtle Beach HS 3302 Robert M Grissom Pky Myrtle Beach SC 29577

STANLEY, EDWARD ALEXANDER, geologist, forensic scientist, technical and academic administrator; b. NYC, Apr. 7, 1929; s. Frank and Elizabeth (Wolf) S.; m. Elizabeth Ann Allison, June 7, 1958; children: Karen (dec.), Scott. BS, Rutgers U., 1954; MS, Pa. State U., 1956, PhD,

1960. Rsch. geologist Amoco Petroleum Co., Tulsa, Okla., 1960-62; prof. U. Del., 1962-64, U. Ga., 1964-77; assoc. dean rsch., chmn. geology dept. Indiana (Pa.) U., 1977-81; supr. Phillips Petroleum Co., Bartlesvill, Okla., 1981-86; dir., comdg. officer NYC Police Dept. Crime Lab., 1986—94; pvt. practice, 1994—97; assoc. Internat. Environ. Svcs., 1997—. Cons. in field. Contbr. articles to profl. jours. Served to sgt. USAF, 1947-50. Grantee NSF, 1965-68, 74, Rsch. grant Office Water Resources, 1965-68; NAS exch. prof. Soviet Union, 1968-69, 73; invited guest Moscow Police Dept. Forensic Labs., 1990; invited speaker FBI Internat. Symposium on Forensic Trace Evidence, 1991, 98; recipient Commemorative medal of the lab. Dept. Botany, Jozsef Attilla U., Szeged, Hungary, 2000, Millenium medal, 2000. Fellow AAAS, Geol. Soc. Am.; mem. Am. Assn. Petroleum Geologists, Am. Acad. Forensic Sci., Am. Soc. Crime Lab Dirs., Am. Assn. Stratigraphic Palyologists, Sigma Xi. Presbyterian. Avocations: photography, music, firearms. Home: 2004 Haverford Rd Ardmore PA 19003-3010 E-mail: eas.aquila@verizon.net.

STANLEY, GEORGE DABNEY, JR., paleontology educator; b. Chattanooga, Jan. 25, 1948; s. George Dabney and Lucille (Proctor) S. BA, U. Tenn., Chattanooga, 1970; PHD, U. Kans., 1977. Lectr. in geology U. Calif., Davis, 1977-78; geologist, rsch. assoc. Smithsonian Instn., Washington, 1978-81; assoc. prof. U. Mont., Missoula, 1982-90, prof., 1990—. Organizing com. Internat. Com. on Fossil Cnidaria and Porifera, v.p., 1999; U.S. group leader Internat. Geol. Correlation Projects 335, 359, 458; mem. Internat. Subcommn. Triassic Stratigraphy. Contbr. over 100 articles to profl. jours. Recipient Burlington No. Found. award, 1988, U. Kans. Haworth award, 1999, Dennison award U. Mont., 2001; Orgn. Tropical Studies fellow, Fulbright fellow, Germany, 1981-82; Exch. fellow Kumamoto (Japan) U., 1992-93; grantee NSF, Nat. Geographic Soc.; U. Mont. Disting. scholar, 1992. Mem. Soc. Sedimentary Geology, Geol. Soc. Am. (treatise com. 2002—), Paleontol. Soc. Washington (pres. 1980-81), Paleontol. Soc. (medal com. 1990-93, dist. lectr. 1993-94), Paleontol. Assn. Gr. Britain.

STANLEY, H(ARRY) EUGENE, physicist, educator; b. Norman, Okla, Mar. 28, 1941; s. Harry Eugene and Ruth S.; m. Idahlia Dessauer, June 2, 1967 (dec. Mar. 2003); children: Jannah, Michael, Rachel. BA in Physics (Nat. Merit scholar), Wesleyan U., 1962; postgrad. (Fulbright scholar), U. Cologne, W. Ger., 1962-63; PhD in Physics, Harvard U., 1967; PhD (hon.), Bar-Ilan U., Ramat-Gan, Israel, 1994, Roland Eötvös U., Budapest, Hungary, 1997, U. Liege, 2001, U. Dortmund, 2001. NSF predoctoral rsch. fellow Harvard U., 1963-67; mem. staff Lincoln Lab MIT, 1967-68, asst. prof. physics, 1969-71, assoc. prof., 1971-73; Miller rsch. fellow U. Calif., Berkeley, 1968-69; Hermann von Helmholtz assoc. prof. health scis. and tech. Harvard U.-MIT Program in Health Scis. and Tech., 1973-76; vis. prof. Osaka U., Japan, 1975; univ. prof., prof. physics, prof. physiology Sch. Medicine, dir. Ctr. Polymer Studies Boston U., 1976—. Joliot-Curie vis. prof. Ecole Superieure de Physique et Chimie, Paris, 1979; vis. prof. Peking U., 1981, Seoul Nat. U., 1982, 30th Ann. Saha Meml. Lecture, 1992; Sigma Xi nat. lectr., 2002-03; dir. NATO Advanced Study Inst., Cargese, Corisca, 1985, 88, 90, IUPAP Internat. Conf. on Thermodynamics and Statis. Mechanics, 1986, Enrico Fermi Sch., Varenna, Italy, 1996, 2003, Gordon Rsch. Conf. on Water and Aqueous Solutions, 1998, NATO advanced rsch. workshop, 1999, 2001; cons. Sandia Nat. Lab., 1983-94, Dowell Schlumberger Co., 1982-92, Elscint Co., 1983-85; nat. co-chmn. Com. of Concerned Scientists, 1974-76. Author: Introduction to Phase Transitions and Critical Phenomena, 1971, From Newton to Mandelbrot: A Primer in Theoretical Physics, 1990, Fractal Forms, 1991, Fractal Concepts in Surface Growth, 1995, Cours de physique, 1999, Introduction to Econophysics: Correlations & Complexity in Finance, 2000; editor: Biomedical Physics and Biomaterials Science, 1972, Cooperative Phenomena Near Phase Transitions, 1973, On Growth and Form: Fractal and Non-Fractal Patterns in Physics, 1985, Statis. Physics, 1986, Random Fluctuation and Pattern Growth, 1988, Correlations and Connectivity: Geometric Aspects of Physics, Chemistry and Biology, 1990, Fractals in Science, 1994, Disordered Materials and Interfaces, 1996, Physics of Complex Systems, 1997, Statis. Mechanics in the Physical Biological and Social Sciences, 1997, Application of Statis. Mechanics to Practical Problems, 1999, Structure and Function of Biological Systems under Extreme Conditions, 2002, Statis. Physics, 2000, Statis. Mechanics: From Rigorous Results to Applications, 2000, Scaling in Disordered Systems, 2002, New Kinds of Phase Transitions, 2002; editor Physica A., 1988—. Named John Simon Guggenheim Meml. fellow, 1979—80; recipient Choice award, Am. Assn. Book Pubs., 1972, Macdonald award, 1986, Venture Rsch. award, Brit. Petroleum, 1989, Mass. Prof. of Yr. award, Coun. Advancement and Support of Edn., 1992, Floyd K. Richtmyer prize, 1997, Turnbull prize, 1998, Memory Ride prize, 2001, NSF Disting. Tchr.-Scholar prize, 2001, Fgn. mem. Hazilian Acad. of Sci., 2003. Fellow AAAS, Am. Phys. Soc. (chmn. New Eng. sect. 1982-83; Centennial lectr. 1999); mem. Non-Linear Sci. Panel of Nat. Acad. Sci., Hungarian Phys. Soc. (hon.), Brazilian Acad. Scis. (hon.). Home: 50 Metacomet Rd Waban MA 02468-1465 Office: Boston U Ctr for Polymer Studies Boston MA 02215 E-mail: HES@bu.edu.

STANLEY, JANICE FAYE, special education educator; b. Montgomery, Ala., Nov. 21, 1953; d. Holley Moring and Miriam Elizabeth (Long) S. BS in Edn., Auburn U., 1977, EdS, 1992; M of Spl. Edn., Troy State U., 1982. Spl. edn. tchr. Fews Elem. Sch., Montgomery, 1977-79, Vaughn Rd. Elem. Sch., Montgomery, 1979-81, Dunbar Elem. Sch., Montgomery, 1981-91, Catoma Elem. Sch., Montgomery, 1991-95, Chisholm Elem. Sch., 1995—. Edn. mgr. Civitan Club, Montgomery, 1992-93, bd. dirs., 1992—, sec. edn. meeting, 1996—, Civitan of Yr., 1997. Mem. Kappa Delta Pi. Methodist. Avocations: reading, swimming, attending plays. Home: 8500 English Oak Loop Montgomery AL 36117-6822 Office: Chisholm Elem Sch 307 E Vandiver Blvd Montgomery AL 36110-1800

STANLEY, JULIAN CECIL, JR., psychology educator; b. Macon, Ga., July 9, 1918; s. Julian Cecil and Ethel (Cheney) S.; m. Rose Roberta Sanders, Aug. 18, 1946 (dec. Nov. 1978); 1 child, Susan Roberta Willhoft; m. Barbara Sprague Kerr, Jan. 1, 1980 (dec. May 2001), m. Dorothy Lee Fahey, Oct.9, 2002. BS, Ga. So. U., 1937; Ed.M., Harvard U., 1946, Ed.D., 1950; D of Ednl. Excellence (hon.), U. North Tex., 1990; LHD (hon.), State U. of West Ga., 1997. Tchr. Fulton and West Fulton high schs., Atlanta, 1937—42; instr. psychology Newton (Mass.) Jr. Coll., 1946—48; instr. edn. Harvard U., 1948—49; assoc. prof. ednl. psychology George Peabody Coll. Tchrs., 1949—53; assoc. prof. edn., 1953—57; prof. edn., 1957—62; prof. ednl. psychology, 1962—67; chmn. dept., 1962—63; dir. lab. exptl. design U. Wis., Madison, 1961—67; prof. edn. and psychology Johns Hopkins U., 1967—71, prof. psychology, 1971—99, dir. study mathematically precocious youth, 1971—, prof. emeritus, 1999. Mem. rsch. adv. coun. Coop. Rsch. Br., U.S. Office Edn., 1962—64; mem. com. examiners for aptitude tests Coll. Entrance Exam. Bd., 1961—65, chmn., 1965—68; mem. rsch. com. Ednl. Testing Svc., 1962—67; fellow Social Sci. Rsch. Coun. Inst. Math. for Social Scientists U. Mich., summer, 1955; postdoctoral fellow stats. U. Chgo., 1955—56; Fulbright rsch. scholar U. Louvain, Belgium, 1958—59; Fulbright lectr. New Zealand and Australia, 1974; cons. U. Western Australia, 1980; fellow Ctr. for Advanced Study in Behavioral Sci., 1965—67, vis. scholar, 1983; hon. prof. Shanghai (People's Republic of China) Tchrs. U.; disting. tchr. Commn. on Presdl. Scholars, 1987, 92; vis. prof. U. Ga., 1947, U. Hawaii, 1960, Harvard U., 1963, U. North Tex., 1990, U. NSW, 1992; mem. adv. bd. Tex. Acad. Math. and Sci., 1988—99; trustee Ctr. for Excellence in Edn., 1989—93, Advanced Acad. Ga., 1999—, Ga. Acad. Math., Engring. and Sci., 1996—2001; cons. Ctr. for Talented Youth, 1998—; lectr. Esther Katz Rosen, 2002. Author: Measurement in Today's Schools, 4th edit., 1964, (with D.T. Campbell) Experimental and Quasi-Experimental Designs for Research, 1963, 66, (with Gene V Glass) Statistical Methods in Education and Psychology, 1970, (with K.D. and B. Hopkins) Educational and Psychological Measurement and Evaluation, 3d edit., 1990, (with K.D. Hopkins, G.H. Bracht) Perspectives in Educational and Psychological Measurement, 1972; editor: Improving Experimental Design and Statistical Analysis, 1967, Preschool Programs for the Disadvantaged, 1972, Compensatory Education for Children, Ages 2-8, 1973, (with D.P. Keating, L.H. Fox) Mathematical Talent: Discovery, Description, and Development, 1974, (with W.C. George, C.H. Solano) The Gifted and the Creative: A Fifty-Year Perspective, 1977, Educational Programs and Intellectual Prodigies, 1978, (with W.C. George, S.J. Cohn) Educating the Gifted: Acceleration and Enrichment, 1979, (with C.P. Benbow) Academic Precocity: Aspects of Its Development, 1983; adv. editor jours. Served with USAAC, 1942-45. Julian C. Stanley chair in ednl. psychology created U. Wis., Madison, 1995; recipient awards Mensa Ednl. Rsch. Found., 1989, 97, four awards for excellence in rsch., Lifetime Achievement award, 2000. Fellow APA (pres. div. ednl. psychology 1965-66, div. evaluation and measurement 1972-73, Thorndike award for disting. psychol. contbns. to edn. 1978, divsn. evaluation and measurement Lifetime Contbn. award 1997, divsn. gen. psychology George Miller award 1999), AAAS, Am. Statis. Assn., Am. Psychol. Soc. (J. McKeen Cattell award 1994) Am. Psychological Found., 2002; mem. Nat. Council Measurement Edn. (pres. 1963-64), Am. Ednl. Research Assn. (pres. 1966-67, award for disting. contbns. to research in edn. 1980), Nat. Assn. for Gifted Children (2d v.p. 1977-79, Disting. Scholar award 1982), Psychometric Soc. (past dir.), AAUP (past chpt. pres.), Tenn. Psychol. Assn. (past pres.), Nat. Acad. Edn., Phi Beta Kappa (past chpt. pres.), Phi Beta Kappa Assocs., Sigma Xi, Phi Delta Kappa Office: CTY 2701 N Charles St Baltimore MD 21218-4351 Fax: 410-964-8439. E-mail: jstanley@jhu.edu.

STANLEY, MYRTLE BROOKS, minister, educational and religious consultant; b. Balt., May 13, 1929; d. Benjamin Franklin and Ora Estell (Robinson) Brooks; m. Theodore Freeland Stanley, June 4, 1949; children: Theodora Stanley Snyder, Benjamin Brooks, Jonathan Stephen. BS, Morgan State Coll., 1951, MS, 1972; MA in Theology, St. Mary Sem. and U., Balt., 1987; postgrad., Fordham U., 1989-91; PhD, Am. U., 2001. Tchr., curriculum coord. Balt. City Pub. Schs., 1958-83; dir. propagation of faith Archdiocese of Balt., Roman Cath. Ch., Balt., 1984-95; coord. rite of Christian initiation for adults St. Matthew Roman Cath. Ch., Balt., 1996—; instr. Ch. Leadership Inst., Archdiocese of Balt., 1999—. Author, prodr. play It's Your Own Funeral, 1980, Miracle on 22d Street, 1980. Bd. dirs. Balt. Clergy and Laity Concerned, 1984-94, Towson (Md.) Cath. H.S., 1993-95, Good Samaritan Hosp., Balt., 1994-96; coord. Internat. Sisters in Struggle, 1991—. Mem. AAUW, Religious Sisters of Mercy of the Ams. (assoc.), Phi Delta Kappa.

STANLEY, PETER WILLIAM, former academic administrator; b. Bronxville, N.Y., Feb. 17, 1940; s. Arnold and Mildred Jeanette (Pattison) Stanley; m. Mary-Jane Cullen Cosgrove, Sept. 2, 1978; 1 child, Laura. BA magna cum laude, Harvard U., 1962, MA, 1964, PhD, 1970; LHD (hon.), Occidental Coll., 1994, Rhodes Coll., 2001. Asst. prof. history U. Ill., Chgo., 1970—72, Harvard U., 1972—78, lectr. history, 1978—79; dean of coll. Carleton Coll., Northfield, Minn., 1979—84; program officer in charge edn. and culture program Ford Found., 1984—87, dir. edn. and culture program, 1987—91; pres. Pomona Coll., Claremont, Calif., 1991—2003, pres. emeritus, 2003—. Lectr. Fgn. Service Inst., Arlington, Va., 1977—89. Author: A Nation in the Making: The Philippines and the United States, 1974; co-author: Sentimental Imperialists: The American Experience in East Asia, 1981; editor: Reappraising an Empire: New Perspectives on Philippine-American History, 1984; contbr. articles to profl. jours. Trustee The Coll. Bd., 1991—99, vice-chmn., 1993—94, chmn., 1994—96, Barnard Coll., 2000—; humanities and scis. coun. Stanford U., 1986—2002; nat. adv. coun. Nat. Fgn. Lang. Ctr., 1991—2002; bd. dirs. The James Irvine Found., 1997—, chmn., 2003—; bd. dirs. The Pacific Basin Inst., 1998—, chmn., 1998—2003; bd. dirs. The Hitachi Found., 1993—2000, Assn. Am. Colls. and Univs., 1995—2001, vice-chmn., 1998—99, chmn., 1999—2000; bd. fellows Claremont Grad. U. and Claremont U. Consortium, 1991—2003; bd. overseers Nat. Bd. Ednl. Testing and Pub. Policy, 2000—. Fellow Frank Knox Meml. fellow, Harvard U., 1962—63, Charles Warren Ctr. for Studies in Am. History fellow, 1975—76. Mem.: Coun. on Fgn. Rels., Assn. Asian Studies, Am. Hist. Assn., Phi Beta Kappa. Home: 65 Knollwood Dr Old Saybrook CT 06475 Office: Pomona Coll Pres Office Claremont CA 91711-6301

STANLEY, ROBERT ANTHONY, artist, educator; b. Defuniac Springs, Fla., Mar. 10, 1942; m. Jane Tumosa, May 11, 1973; children: Daiva, Thomas, Daniel. BA cum laude, U. Dayton, 1964; MS, Pratt Inst., N.Y.C., 1969. Dir. art program Upward Bound project Earlham Coll., Richmond, Ind., 1967-68; lectr. art dept. U. Dayton, Ohio, 1967-68; asst. prof. art and humanities Harrisburg (Pa.) C.C., 1969-71; prof. art Oakton Coll., Des Plaines, Ill., 1971—2002, prof. emeritus, 2002—. Mem. com. League for Humanities Study Grant, Des Plaines, 1988-89; assoc. dir. Inst. for Environ. Response, N.Y.C., 1968-70; Bd. dirs. So. Shore Art Assn., 2003; presenter League for Innovation Conf., 1994, Mid-Am. Art Conf., 1997. Author: Exploring the Film, 1968 (Maxi award 1969), (interactive multimedia) VisLang, 1994; contbr. articles to profl. jours.; shows include William Penn Mus., Harrisburg, Pa., New Horizons in Art Chgo., 1974, Internat. All on Paper, Buffalo, 1979, Zaner Gallery, Rochester, N.Y., 1983, Joy Horwich Gallery, Chgo., 1988, 95, U. Oreg., Portland, 1991, Atrium Gallery, N.Y.C., 1991, Shelter Gallery, Chgo., 1992, Matrix Gallery, Chgo., Museé d'Art Contemporain, Chamalieres, France, 1994, 97, Blank Arts Ctr., Michigan City, Ind., 1997, No. Ind. Ctr. Visual and Performing Arts, Munster, Ind., 1998, Contemporary Art Ctr., Peoria, Ill., 1999, Gov.'s Mansion, Indpls., 1998, Vichy, FR, 2000, Blank Art Ctr., M.C., Ind., 2001, Koehnline Gallery, Des Plaines, 2002, 59th Salon NIAA, Munster, 2002, Exhbn. Am. Art, Chgo., 2003, Gallery Artists, Chgo., 2003, Gallery 415, Chgo., 2003, 18th Ann. Juries Exhibit, Lubeznik Ctr. Arts, M.C., 2003. Bd. dirs. Kloempken Prairie Restoration, Des Plaines, 1987-89, Brickton Art Ctr., 1998—. Grantee OCC Ednl. Found., 1989; recipient 2d Place Paragon award for video Nat. Coun. Cmty. Rels., 1985, 1st place Gold award for graphics Art Ctr. Show, Dayton Art Inst., 1969, award of merit Internat. Works on Paper, 1979, Prix de la Ville de Vichy Chamalieres Triennial, 1997, Merit award Chesteron Ind. Regl. 2000; named Top 100, World Digotal Art, 2001. E-mail: rastanley@comcast.net.

STANLEY, SHERYL LYNN, college administrator; b. Moberly, Mo., Oct. 21, 1952; d. James Melvin and Gloria May (Bagby) S. BS, Coll. of the S.W., Hobbs, N.Mex., 1974. Salesman KHOB Radio, Hobbs, 1973-74; adminstrv. asst. Coll. of the S.W., 1974-80, pub. info. officer, 1980-82, dir. pub. info., 1982-84, dir. pub. affairs, 1984, dir. coll. communications, 1988—; community rels. coord. Lea Regional Hosp., Hobbs, 1985-88. Author, editor, photographer numerous univ. publs. Campaign co-chair United Way of Lea County, Hobbs, 1988. Recipient Excellence in Community Svc. award Hosp. Corp. Am., 1986. Mem. N.Mex. Pres Women, Eastern N.Mex. Rose Soc. (treas. 1986-88, sec. 1988-91). Methodist. Avocations: photography, dog training. Office: Coll of the SW 6610 N Lovington Hwy Hobbs NM 88240-9120

STANLEY-CHAVIS, SANDRA ORNECIA, special education educator, consultant; b. July 6, 1950; d. McKinley and Thelma Louise Stanley. BA, Ottawa (Kans.) U., 1972; MS in Edn., U. Kans., 1975, PhD (fellow), 1980; postgrad., St. George's U. Sch. Medicine, Grenada, W.I. Dir., head tchr. Salem Bapt. Nursery Sch., Jersey City, 1972—73; spl. edn. instr. Joan Davis Sch. Spl. Edn., Kansas City, Mo., 1975—76; instnl. media/materials trainee, then rsch. asst. U. Kans. Med. Ctr., 1976—79; rsch. asst. U. Kans., Lawrence, 1979; dir., coord. tng. and observation Juniper Gardens Children's project Bur. Child Rsch., U. Kans., Kansas City, 1979—82, rsch. assoc., 1980; psychol. assoc., ednl. cons. family crisis unit Internat. Youth Orgn., 1988—93; ednl. cons. Renaissance Ctr., 1994; exec. dir. 2000 Friends, 1994; asst. prof., coord. spl. edn. Albany (Ga.) State U., 1995—2000; pres. Ednl. Expansion, Inc., 2000—. Lectr., spkr., cons. edn. and med. sci. Author: papers and manuals in field. Past mem. adv. bd. Rainbows for All God's Children; mem. adv. bd. Albany Advocacy Resource Ctr., God's House of Human Svcs., Inc.; chmn. edn./workforce devel. com. C. of C.; vice chmn. Albany Mid. Sch. Ga. Sch. Coun.; bd. dirs. Victory Tabernacle Missions. Recipient various awards, plaques, certs of recognition; grantee, Easter Seals, 1975; scholar, Coll. Women, Inc., 1977; Christian Cmty. Health fellow. Mem.: ASCD, Nat. Coun. for Learning Disability, Coun. of Exceptional Children, Christian Med. and Dental Soc. Home: 2301 Beattie Rd Albany GA 31721-2105 E-mail: educationalexpansion@yahoo.com.

STANNARD, DAPHNE EVON, nursing educator; b. New Haven, Oct. 12, 1963; d. Jerry Wilmert and Katherine Evon (Moore) S.; m. Bertram C.H. Simon, July 18, 1992. BSN, Vanderbilt U., 1986; MS in Critical Care Nursing, U. Calif., San Francisco, 1991; PhD in Nursing, U. Calif. San Francisco, San Francisco, 1997. CCRN, Calif.; cert. ACLS. Critical care nurse U. Mich. Med. Ctr., Ann Arbor, 1986-87; nurse recovery room UCLA Med. Ctr., 1987; pub. health nurse L.A., 1988; surg. ICU critical care nurse Cedars-Sinai Med. Ctr., L.A., 1988-89; critical care nurse med. surg. ICU U. Calif. Med. Ctr., San Francisco, 1989-91, critical care nurse, adult critical care float unit, 1992-95; recovery rm. nurse Mt. Zion Med. Ctr./U. Calif. at San Francisco Med. Ctr., San Francisco, 1992-96; asst. clin. prof., critical care nurse med.-surg. ICU U. Calif. Med. Ctr., San Francisco, 1999—. Contbr. articles to profl. jours. Mem. ANA, AACN, Soc. Critical Care Medicine (bd. dirs. Calif. chpt. 1995—), Nat. Coun. Family Rels., Sigma Theta Tau. Home: 1265 Washington St Apt 9 San Francisco CA 94108-1062 Office: San Francisco State U Sch Nursing 1600 Holloway Ave San Francisco CA 94132-1722

STANNARD, WILLIAM A. mathematics educator; b. Whitefish, Mont., Sept. 5, 1931; s. Delbert Stannard and Ethel M. (Kearns) Bays; m. Beverly C. Paisley, Mar. 16, 1951 (dec. May 1988); children: Susan, Jon, Mark, Gail; m. Donna M. Freer, June 29, 1989. Diploma, No. Mont. Coll., 1951; BA in Edn., U. Mont., 1953; MAT in Math., Stanford U., 1958; EdD in Math., Mont. State U., 1966. Math tchr. Arlee (Mont.) Pub. Schs., 1953-54, Shelby (Mont.) Pub. Schs., 1954-57, Helena (Mont.) Pub. Schs., 1958-60; instr. math. No. Mont. Coll., Havre, 1960-62, Mont. State U., Bozeman, 1962-66, prof. math. Billings, 1966-84, prof. emeritus of math., 1984—; prof. math. Calif. State U., Bakersfield, 1984-88, Fresno, 1988-89, Hayward, 1989-90; math tchr. Fremont (Calif.) Pub. Schs., 1994—. Project dir. Nat. Sci. Found. Projects, Billings, 1979-84. Pres. Mont. Coun. Tchrs. Math., 1970-72. Mem. Nat. Coun. Tchrs. Math. (bd. dirs. 1976-79), Calif. Tchr. Math. (ctrl. sect. pres. 1982-84). Avocation: skiing. Home: 40384 Imperio Pl Fremont CA 94539-3032

STANO, CARL RANDOLPH (RANDY STANO), newspaper editor, art director, educator; b. Russellville, Ark., Apr. 1, 1948; s. Carl J. Stano and Martha Lee (Linton) Partain. AA, San Jacinto Coll., 1968; BS in Edn., U. Tex., Austin, 1971; MA, Syracuse U., 1979. Cert. tchr., Tex. Dir. student publs., tchr. A.N. McCallum High Sch., Austin, Tex., 1971-78; grad. asst. S.I. Newhouse Sch. Pub. Communications Syracuse (N.Y.) U., 1978-79; asst. editor, art dir. Kansas City (Mo.) Star Times, 1980-81; dir. graphic arts Democrat and Chronicle, Rochester, N.Y., 1981-85; dir. editorial art and design The Miami (Fla.) Herald, 1985-95; Knight prof. commn. U. Miami, Coral Gables, Fla., 1995—, assoc. dir. for the Advance Media Ctr., 1996—. Bd. dirs. PBC Internat. Publ.; instr. summer workshops U. Tex., Austin, U. Iowa, Ball State U., Columbia U., Tex. Tech U., U. Okla., U. Houston, N.Mex. State U., Syracuse U., Kans. State U., Ctrl. Mich. State U., Ouachita State Bapt. U., 1970—; instr., lectr. Syracuse U., 1980, 1982-83, St. John Fisher Coll., Rochester, 1983-85, U. Miami, 1985-95; instr. profl. seminars Poynter Inst. for Media Studies, So. Newpapers Pubs. Assn.; chmn. SND Quick Course, 1996. Newspaper redesigns Democrat and Chronicle, 1982, Olympian, Olympia, Wash., 1985, Sentinel Newspapers, East Brunswick, N.J., 1986, Jacksonville, N.C. Daily News,1988, El Nuevo Herald, 1987, Miami Herald, 1991, Daily Record, Dunn, N.C., 1996. Recipient numerous Tex. State H.S. awards, 1971-78, Edith Fox King Tchg. award Tex. Interscholastic League Press Conf., Austin, 1972, Tex. H.S. Jour. Tchr. of Yr. award, 1974, Lifetime Achievement award Am. Student Press Assn., 1989, Nat. Jour. Tchr. of Yr. award Newspaper Fund and Wall St. Jour., Princeton, N.J., 1974, mem. Pub. Svc. award team Miami Herald, 1993; mem. Pulitzer Prize reporting team Kansas City Times/Star, 1981; named to Nat. Scholastic Journalism Hall of Fame U. Okla., 1987, Gallery of Profls. S.I. Newhouse Sch. Pub. Commns. Syracuse U., 1994. Mem. Soc. Newspaper Design (contest chmn. 6th edit. 1985e, southeast chmn. 1985-89, competition chmn. 1987-90, sec. 1989, exec. bd. dirs. 1989-93, 2d v.p. 1990, 1st v.p. 1991, pres. 1992, immediate past pres. 1993, excellence awards 3d-17th edits., bronze award 1991, 92, 93, silver award 1983, 85, 89-95, gold award 1986, 89, 92, Best of Show, 1992), Fla. Soc. News Editors (illustration graphic award 1987, 88, 90-96, page design award 1988, 90-96, print mag. award 1989-92), Columbia Scholastic Press Advisors Assn. (Gold Key award 1980, five Trendsetter awards 1975-77), Nat. Scholastic Press Assn. (3 five-star/Pacemaker awards). Home: 4718 SW 67th Ave Apt 8B Miami FL 33155-5876 Office: U Miami Sch Comm 121C Merrick Way Coral Gables FL 33134

STANSBERY, DAVID HONOR, ecologist, malacologist; b. Upper Sandusky, Ohio, May 5, 1926; s. Honor Gerald and Daisy Elizabeth (Kirby) S.; m. Mary Lois Pease, June 16, 1948; children: Michael David, Mark Andrew, Kathleen Mary, Linda Carol. BS, Ohio State U., 1950, MS, 1953, PhD, 1960. Instr. Ohio State U., Columbus, 1956-62, asst. prof., 1962-66, assoc. prof., 1966-71; state curator of natural history Ohio State Mus., Columbus, 1962-72; vis. scientist Smithsonian Instn., Washington, 1973-74; sr. rsch. assoc. The Ohio State Mus., Columbus, 1972—; dir. mus. of zoology Ohio State U., Columbus, 1970-92, prof. zoology, 1971-91, curator of mollusks Mus. of Biol. Diversity, 1962-2000, prof. emeritus, 1991—, curator emeritus, 2001—. Adv. bd. Ohio Biol. Survey, 1961-72; exec. com. Ohio Acad. of Sci., 1961-69; chair collection stds. Coun. of Systematic Malacologists, 1977-81; bd. govs. The Nature Conservancy, 1979-86; rsch. adv., guest lectr. Huazhong Agrl. U., Wuhan, Hubei, China, 1992; mem. faculty Upper Cumberland Biol. Sta. Tenn. Tech U., 1987-91; presenter in field. Assoc. editor: Ohio Jour. Sci., 1960-61, editor, 1961-64; contbr. articles to profl. jours. Bd. trustees Columbus Audubon Soc., 1969-73; bd. dirs. Am. Rivers Cons. Coun., 1973-88. Recipient Oak Leaf award Nature Conservancy, 1977, Ohio Conservation Achievement award Ohio Dept. Natural Resouces, 1974, Lifetime Achievement award Freshwater Mollusk Conservation Soc., 1999, Herbert Osborn award Ohio Biol. Survey, 1999; grantees U.S. Dept. Interior, U.S. Dept. Commerce, U.S. Army Corps of Engrs., Battelle, Am. Electric Power, and others. Fellow: AAAS, Acad. Zoology, Ohio Acad. Sci.; mem.: Am. Malacol. Union (pres. 1970—71), Sigma Xi (pres. 1974—75). Achievements include building the world's largest freshwater bivalve mollusk collection at the Ohio State University Museum of Biological Diversity. Avocations: geology, history of science, evolution of ethics, linguistics. Home: 32 Amazon Pl Columbus OH 43214-3502 Office: Mus of Biol Diversity Ohio State Univ 1315 Kinnear Rd Columbus OH 43212-1157 Fax: 614-292-7774. Personal E-mail: mlpdhs@aol.com. Business E-Mail: stansbery.1@osu.edu.

STANSELL, LELAND EDWIN, JR., lawyer, mediator, educator; b. Central, S.C., July 13, 1934; s. Leland Edwin and Hettie Katherine (Hollis) S.; children: James Leland, Susan. BS, Fla. So. Coll., 1957; LLB, U. Miami, Fla., 1961, JD, 1968. Bar: Fla. 1961; cert. civil mediator Fla. Supreme Ct., U.S. Dist. Ct. Fla. Assoc. Wicker & Smith, Miami, 1961-62, ptnr., 1962-75; pvt. practice, Miami, 1975-99, Leland E. Stansell, Jr., P.A., Miami, 1995—. Chmn. Appellate Jud. Nominating Com., Dade County (Fla.), 1983-87; mem. adv. com. Am. Arbitration Assn., 1975-90. Served with U.S. Army, 1957. Mem. ABA (ho. of dels. 1982-86), Fla. Bar (bd. govs. 1966-70,

70-80), Dade County Bar Assn. (dir. 1969-72, exec. com. 1974-75, pres. 1975-76), U. Miami Law Alumni Assn. (dir., officer, pres. 1968-69), Fla. Criminal Def. Attys. Assn. (treas. 1964-66), Am. Judicature Soc., Am. Bd. Trial Advs., Internat. Assn. Def. Counsel, Fla. Acad. Profl. Mediators, Fedn. Ins. Counsel, Miami Beach Rod and Reel Club (pres.), Coral Reef Yacht Club, Bankers Club, Ocean Reef Yacht Club, Delta Theta Phi (pres. Miami alumni chpt. 1966, regional dir. 1968. Office: 19 W Flagler St Miami FL 33130-4400

STANSKY, PETER DAVID LYMAN, historian; b. N.Y.C., Jan. 18, 1932; s. Lyman and Ruth (Macow) S. BA, Yale U., 1953, King's Coll., Cambridge (Eng.) U., 1955, MA, 1959; PhD, Harvard U., 1961; D.L. (hon.), Wittenburg U., 1984. Teaching fellow history and lit. Harvard U., 1957-61, instr., then asst. prof. history, 1961-68; assoc. prof. history Stanford U., 1968-73, prof., 1973-74, Frances and Charles Field prof., 1974—, chmn. dept. history, 1975-78, 79-82, 89-90, assoc. dean humanities and scis., 1985-88. Chmn. publs. com. Conf. Brit. Studies, 1970-78; pres. Pacific Coast Conf. Brit. Studies, 1974-76, N. Am. Conf. Brit. Studies, 1983-85; vis. fellow Wesleyan Center Humanities, Middletown, Conn., 1972, All Soul's Coll., Oxford (Eng.) U., 1979, St. Catherine's Coll., Oxford (Eng.) U., 1983 Author: Ambitions and Strategies, 1964, England Since 1867, 1973, Gladstone, 1979, William Morris, 1983, Redesigning the World, 1985, On or About December 1910, 1996, Another Book That Never Was, 1998, From William Morris to Sergeant Pepper, 1999, Sassoon: The Worlds of Philip and Sybil, 2003; co-author: Journey to the Frontier, 1966, The Unknown Orwell, 1972, Orwell: The Transformation, 1979, London's Burning, 1994. Guggenheim fellow, 1966-67, 73-74; Am. Council Learned Socs. fellow, 1978-79; NEH fellow, 1983, 98-99, Royal Hist. Soc. fellow Ctr. for Advanced Study Behavioral Scis., 1988-89 Fellow Am. Acad. Arts and Scis. (coun. 1994-98, 2002—); mem. Am. Hist. Assn. (pres. Pacific Coast br. 1988-89), Conf. on Brit. Studies, Victorian Soc., William Morris Soc., AAUP, Century Assn. Home: 375 Pinehill Rd Hillsborough CA 94010-6612 Office: Stanford U Dept History Stanford CA 94305-2024 E-mail: stansky@stanford.edu.

STANTON, DENNIS JOE, secondary school educator; b. Bad Axe, Mich., Aug. 5, 1952; s. Carl Jr. and Lillian Olive (Edwards) S.; m. Kyle Elise Gordon-Stanton, July 25, 1973; children: Amy, Amanda. BS, Ctrl. Mich. U., 1974; M in Math., Western Mich. U., 1978. Cert. tchr., Mich. Tchr. adult edn. Union City (Mich.) Cmty. Schs., 1974-80, tchr., 1974—. Chess coach Mid. Sch. Chess Team, Union City, 1974-78; cross country coach Varsity Cross Country, Union City, 1982-89. Leader 4-H Poultry Club of Calhoun County, 1993—, 4-H Horse Club, 2000—; pres. 4-H Horse Leaders, 2000—; trustee Athens (Mich.) Bd. Edn., 1993-94, treas., 1994-95, pres., 1995—. Mem. Nat. Coun. Tchrs. Math., Mich. Coun. Tchrs. Math., Mich. Coun. Tchrs. Arithmetic, Union City Edn. Assn. (treas., membership chairperson 1974—), United Fedn. Pigeon Racing (treas. 1990-92), MIHA District XV (chmn. 1997—), Mich. Interscholastic Horseman Assn. Avocations: woodworking, horses. Home: 2380 M Dr S Athens MI 49011-9740 Office: Union City Cmty Schs 435 Saint Joseph St Union City MI 49094-1242

STANTON, DONALD SHELDON, academic administrator; b. Balt., June 8, 1932; s. Kenneth Gladstone and Dorothy Erma (Hetrick) S.; m. Barbara Mae Hoot, June 25, 1955; children: Dale Richard, Debra Carol, Diane Karen. AB, Western Md. Coll., 1953; Litt.D., Oglethorpe U., 1999; LLD, Western Md. Coll., 1981; MDiv magna cum laude, Wesley Theol. Sem., 1956; MA, Am. U., 1960; Ed.D., U. Va., 1965; L.H.D., Columbia Coll., 1979; Litt.D., Albion Coll., 1983. Ordained to ministry United Methodist Ch., 1956; pastor Balt. and Va. confs. United Meth. Ch., 1953-59; dir. Richmond (Va.) Area Wesley Found., 1959-63; chaplain, dean of students Greensboro Coll., 1963-65; chaplain Wofford Coll., 1965-69; dir. office coll. services United Meth. Div. Higher Edn., Nashville, 1969-75; v.p. for devel. Wesleyan Coll., 1975-78; pres. Adrian Coll., 1978-88, Oglethorpe U., Atlanta, 1988-99, pres. emeritus, 1999—. Adminstr., prof. European internat. ednl. programs, summers 1960, 69-71, 73; chmn. pres.'s assn. Mich. Intercollegiate Athletic Assn., 1986-87. Contbr. articles, revs. to profl. publs. in U.S., Japan, Argentina, chpts. to books; editor: Faculty Forum, 1972-74; bass-baritone soloist. Bd. dirs. Toledo (Ohio) Symphony, 1980-83, Lewanee County Jr. Achievement, 1980-83, Found. Ind. Higher Edn., 1996-99, Nat. Conf. for Cmty. and Justice, Atlanta Region, Atlanta Area Coun. Boy Scouts Am.; chair bd. trustees U. Ctr. Ga., 1994-96; chair So. Collegiate Athletic Conf., 1994-95. Adminstrn. bldg. at Adrian Coll. named in honor of Stanton and his wife, 1988. Mem. Am. Assn. Univ. Adminstrs. (bd. dirs. 1990-93), Ga. Assn. Colls. (pres. 1992), Soc. Wesley (Disting. Alumni Recognition award 1988), Ga. Found. for Ind. Colls. (vice chair 1992), Nat. Assn. Ind. Colls. and Univs. (past mem. pub. rels. com.), Assn. Pvt. Colls. and Univs. Ga. (treas. 1996-97), Rotary, Omicron Delta Kappa, Order of Omega, Tau Kappa Epsilon, Psi Chi, Phi Eta Sigma. Home: 312 Tillman Rd Lake Junaluska NC 28745-9779 E-mail: stantons2@earthlink.net.

STANTON, LEA KAYE, elementary school educator, counselor; b. Denver, Nov. 13, 1930; d. Edgar Malcolm and Eunice Lois (Chamberlain) Wahlberg; m. Charles M. Stanton, June 15, 1952; children: Gary Charles, Thomas Edgar, Brian Paul, Craig John, William Mayne. BS, Ea. Mich. U., 1954, MA, 1977, EdS in Counseling, 1984. 1st grade tchr. Taylor (Mich.) Pub. Schs., 1952-53; 1st-8th grade tchr., 7th-9th grade counselor Dearborn (Mich.) Pub. Schs., 1972-95; substitute tchr. grade 1-8 Estes Park (Colo.) Pub. Schs., 1995-2000. Tutor YWCA, Dearborn and Inkster, Mich., 1956-59; mem. sch. adv. com. Salina Elem. Sch., Dearborn, 1972-80. V.p. Dearborn Ink Human Rels. Coun., 1960-75; bd. dirs. Dearborn Interfaith Action Coun., 1960-75; union rep. McDonald Pub. Sch., Dearborn, 1985-90; mem. Vanguard Voices Cmty. Chorale, Dearborn, 1993-94; den mother Boy Scouts Am., Dearborn. Mem. AAUW (new mem. chmn.), Women's Internat. League for Peace and Freedom, Mich. Group Psychotherapy Soc., Nat. Bd. Cert. Counselors. Avocations: hiking, reading, singing, writing. Home: 13146 Hidden Beach Way Clermont FL 34711-5915

STANTON, ROBERT JOHN, JR., English language educator; b. Manhattan, NY, July 7, 1942; s. Robert John Stanton and Mary McGinty; m. Felicia Lena Giancola, Nov. 15, 1959; children: Robert III, Sharon. BA, Hofstra U., 1970; MA, U. Mass., Amherst, 1972, postgrad., 1974-79. Instr. English Flagler Coll., St. Augustine, Fla., 1972-74; tchg. asst. U. Mass., Amherst, 1974-77, lectr. in Rhetoric, 1979-81; English tchr. Bishop Kenny H.S., Jacksonville, Fla., 1982-83, Duval County Pub. Schs., Jacksonville, 1984-87; asst. prof. English Jacksonville U., 1987-91, assoc. prof. English, 1992—, chmn. divsn. humanities, 1993-97. Author: Seventeen British Novelists, 1978, Gore Vidal, 1978, Truman Capote, 1980, Views From A Window: Conversations with Gore Vidal, 1980; (poems) Collected Word Paintings, 2000; co-author: Beneath Mad River Mansion, 1992, Noah's Orbella, 1994, The Devil's Rood, 1996, Dangerous Words, 2003. Mem. MLA, Nat. Assn. Tchrs. English, Fla. Assn. Depts. English (pres. 1996), Swift River Hist. Soc. Democrat. Avocations: astronomy, reading, writing, observing the universe. Home: 614 15th Ave S Jacksonville Beach FL 32250 Office: Jacksonville Univ Jacksonville FL 32211 E-mail: bstanto@ju.edu.

STANTON, VIVIAN BRENNAN (MRS. ERNEST STANTON), retired guidance counselor; b. Waterbury, Conn.; d. Francis P. and Josephine (Ryan) Brennan; B.A., Albertus Magnus Coll.; M.S., So. Conn. State Coll., 1962, 6th yr. degree, 1965; postgrad. Columbia U.; m. Ernest Stanton, May 31, 1947; children— Pamela L., Bonita F., Kim Ernest. Tchr. English, history, govt. Milford (Conn.) High Sch., 1940-48; tchr. English, history, fgn. Born Night Sch., New Haven, 1948-54, Simon Lake Sch., Milford, 1960-62; guidance counselor, psychol. examiner Jonathan Law High Sch., Milford, 1962-73, Nat. Honor Soc. adv., 1966-73, mem. Curriculum Councils, Graduation Requirement Council, Gifted Child Com., others, 1940-48, 60-73; guidance dir. Foran High Sch., Milford, 1973-79, career center coordinator, 1976-79, ret., 1979. Active various community drives; mem. exec. bd. Ridge Rd PTA, 1956-59; mem. Parent-Tchr. council Hopkins Grammer Sch., New Haven; mem. Human Relations Council, North Haven, 1967-69; vol., patient rep. surg. waiting rm. Fawcett Meml. Hosp., P.C., Sun City Ctr. Emergency Squad, Good Samaritans. Mem. Nat. Assn. Secondary Schs. and Colls. (evaluation com.; chmn. testing com.), AAUW, LWV, Conn. Personnel and Guidance Assn., Conn. Sch. Counselors Assn., Conn. Assn. Sch. Psychol. Personnel, Conn., Milford (pres. 1945-47) edn. assns. Clubs: Univ., Charlotte Harbor Yacht, Sun City Ctr. Golf and Racquet. Home: 237 Courtyard Blvd Apt 202 Sun City Center FL 33573-5779

STANTON, WILLIAM JOHN, JR., marketing educator, author; b. Chgo, Dec. 15, 1919; s. William John and Winifred (McGann) S.; m. Imma Mair, Sept. 14, 1978; children by previous marriage: Kathleen Louise, William John III. BS, Ill. Inst. Tech., 1940; MBA, Northwestern U., 1941, PhD, 1948; D (hon.), Cath. U. Santo Domingo, Dominican Republic, 2003. Mgmt. trainee Sears Roebuck & Co., 1940-41; instr. U. Ala., 1941-44; auditor Olan Mills Portrait Studios, Chattanooga, 1944-46; asst. prof., asso. prof. U. Wash., 1948-55; prof. U. Colo., Boulder, 1955-90; prof. emeritus, 1990—; head mktg. dept. U. Colo., 1955-71, acting dean, 1963-64; assoc. dean U. Colo. (Sch. Bus.), 1964-67. Author: Econ. Aspects of Recreation in AK, 1953; author: (with Rosann Spiro and G.A. Rich) (also Spanish and Portuguese transl.); author: (with others) Challenge of Bus., 1975; author: (with M. Etzel and B. Walker) (also Spanish, Chinese, Portuguese, Indonesian and Korean transl.); author: (with R. Varaldo) Italian edit., 2d edit., 1990; author: (with others) South African edit., 1992; contbr. articles to profl. jour.; author (with K. Miller and R. Layton): Australian edit., 4th edit., 2000; author: (with M. Etzel and B. Walker) Marketing, 13th edit., 2003; author: (with Rosann Spiro and G.A. Rich) Mgmt. of a Sales Force, 11th edit., 2003; author: (with M.S. Sommers and J.G. Barnes) Can. edit. Fundamentals of Mktg., 11th edit., 2003. Mem. Am. Mktg. Assn., Mktg. Educators Assn., Beta Gamma Sigma. Roman Catholic. Home: 1445 Sierra Dr Boulder CO 80302-7846

STAPLES, LYNNE LIVINGSTON MILLS, retired psychologist, educator, consultant; b. Detroit, Sept. 18, 1934; d. Robert Livingston Mills Staples and Lyda Charlotte (Diehr) Staples; m. Lee Edward Burmeister, July 16, 1955 (div. 1982); children: Benjamin Lee, Lynne Ann. BS, Ctrl. Mich. U., 1957; MA, U. Mich., 1965; student, Marygrove Coll., Cen. Mich. U., 1971-74. Ltd. lic. psychologist, sch. psychologist; cert. social worker, elem. permanent cons. and tchr. for mentally handicapped. First grade tchr. Shepherd (Mich) Schs., 1957-59; tchr. Kingston (Mich.) Schs., 1959-65; tchr. educationally handicapped Rialto (Calif.) Unified Sch. Dist., 1965-66; tchr., cons. Tuscola Int. Sch. Dist., Caro, Mich., 1966-71; sch. psychologist Huron Int. Sch. Dist., Bad Axe, Mich., 1971-74, Tuscola Int. Sch. Dist., Caro, 1974-89; instr. Delta Coll., University Center, Mich., 1976-88; tchr. spl. day classes Victorville (Calif.) High Sch., 1989; sch. psychologist Bedford (Ind.) Schs., 1990-91; clin. psychologist ACT team and outpatient therapy Sanilac County Mental Health Svcs., Sandusky, Mich., 1991-99; ret., 1999. Cons. sch. psychologist Marlette (Mich.) Schs., 1982-86, Bartholomew Pub. Schs., Columbus, Ind., 1989, Johnson County Schs., Franklin, Ind., 1990; clin. psychologist Thumb Family Counseling, Caro, 1985-88; personnel com. Team One Credit Union, 1993; instr. St. Clair C.C., 1993. Conf. presenter in field. Del. NEA-Mich. Edn. Assn. Rep. Assemblies, 1970—89; pres., auction chmn. Altruesa Club, Marlette, 1982—88; style show chmn. Marlette Band Boosters, 1983; mem. exec. bd Lawrence County Tchrs. Assn., Bedford, 1991; mem. Meth. Choir, 2000; mem. pit orch. prodn. Bye Bye Birdie, Sandusky, 2001; dist. dir. social action United Meth. Women, 2000—02; precinct del. Dem. Party, 2000—; v.p. Port Huron dist. United Meth. Women, 2002—03; mem. Marlette First United Meth. Praise Band, 1999—2003; bd. dirs. Team One Credit Union, 1994—, Vassar City Band, 1998—2003, Flint Concert Band, 2000—03, Bay City Concert Band, 2000—02, Unionville-Sebewaing Cmty. Band, 2001—02, Vassar Orch., 2001, Honsinger Wind Ensemble, 2001—03; mem. Sanilac Three-Minute Band, 2001—03, Sanilac Symphonic Band, 1993—2000. Fed. govt. grantee Wayne State U., 1968. Mem.: Ind. Assn. Sch. Psychologists (pub. rels. bd. 1990—91), Ind. State Tchrs. Assn. (rep. assembly del. 1991), Am. Federated State and Mcpl. Employees (chairperson #15 chpt. 1993—96), Mich. Edn. Assn-Ret. Thumb Area (sec. 1996—2002, exec. bd. 2002—03), Emmaus Reunion Group, Lions (bd. dirs. 1996—99, 2d v.p. 1999). Democrat. Avocations: antiques, swimming, gardening, pets, traveling. Home: 6726 Clothier Rd Clifford MI 48727-9501

STAPLETON, CLAUDIA ANN, school director; b. Memphis, July 14, 1947; m. Mark Phillip Stapleton, Sept. 18, 1985. AS, Amarillo Coll., 1995; BS, Wayland Bapt. U., 1997, postgrad., 1997-98. Sch. dir. Acad. Profl. Careers, Amarillo, Tex., 2002—. Republican. Methodist. Home: 3321 Lenwood Dr Amarillo TX 79109-3345 Office: Acad Profl Careers 2201 S Western Ste 102-3 Amarillo TX 79109 Fax: 806-353-7172.

STAPLETON, JEAN, journalism educator; b. Albuquerque, June 24, 1942; d. James L. and Mary (Behrman) S.; m. John Clegg, Apr. 15, 1965 (dec. Sept. 1972); m. Richard Bright, Jan. 13, 1973 (div. 1985); children: Lynn, Paul Bright; m. William Walter Farran, Nov. 9, 1996. BA, U. N.Mex., 1964; MS in Journalism, Northwestern U., 1968. Reporter Glenview (Ill.) Announcements, 1967-68, Angeles Mesa News Advertiser, L.A., 1968-69, City News Svc., Radio News West, L.A., 1969-71; press sec. polit. campaign, 1972; instr. journalism East L.A. Coll., 1973-75, prof., dept. chair, 1975—. Author: Equal Marriage, 1975, Equal Dating, 1979. Mem. NOW (pres. L.A. chpt. 1973-74), Assn. Women in Comm., Soc. Profl. Journalists, Ninety Nines, L.A. Poets Writers Collective. Democrat. Methodist. Home: 3232 Philo St Los Angeles CA 90064-4719 Office: East LA Coll 1301 Avenida Cesar Chavez Monterey Park CA 91754-6001

STARACE, ANTHONY FRANCIS, theoretical atomic physicist; b. N.Y.C., July 24, 1945; s. Louis J. and Ione A. (Liva) S.; m. Katherine Anne Fritz, June 25, 1968; children: Alexander Fritz, Anne Katherine. AB cum laude, Columbia Coll., 1966; MS, U. Chgo., 1967, PhD, 1971. Rsch. assoc. Imperial Coll., London, 1971-72; asst. prof. dept. physics and astronomy U. Nebr., Lincoln, 1973-75, assoc. prof., 1975-81, prof., 1981—, chmn., 1984-95, assoc. dean for sci. rsch., 2000—01, George Holmes Univ. prof., 2001—. Mem. adv. bd. Inst. Theoretical Atomic and Molecular Physics Harvard-Smithsonian Ctr. Astrophysics, 1993-96, chmn., 1994-95; vis. fellow Harvard-Smithsonian Inst. Theoretical Atomic and Molecular Physics, Cambridge, Mass., 1995-96. Author: Theory of Atomic Photoionization, 1982; assoc. editor Revs. of Modern Physics, 1996—; mem. editl. bd. Phys. Rev. A, 1993-98. Rsch. fellow Albert-Ludwigs U., Freiburg, Germany, 1979-80; fellow Alexander von Humboldt, 1979-80, Alfred P. Sloan Found., 1975-79; Joint Inst. for Lab. Astrophysics vis. fellow U. Colo., Boulder, 1992-93. Fellow Am. Phys. Soc. (chmn. div. atomic molecular and optical physics 1990-91). Achievements include research in theoretical atomic physics; few-body dyanamics, properties of atoms in strong external fields, coherent control of atomic processes, intense laser interactions with atoms and quantum information. Office: U Nebr Dept Physics and Astronomy 116 Brace Lab Lincoln NE 68588-0111 E-mail: astarace1@unl.edu.

STARCHER-DELL'AQUILA, JUDY LYNN, special education educator; b. Cuyahoga Falls, Ohio, Sept. 20, 1956; d. James Calvin and Jane Yvonne (Hart) Starcher; m. Richard Paul Dell'Aquila, July 16, 1983; 1 child, Jessica Lynn Dell'Aquila. BS in Hearing & Speech Scis., Ohio U., 1978; MEd in Deaf Edn., U. Cin., 1980; PhD in Spl. Edn., Kent State U., 1996. Cert. supr. and tchr., Ohio. Tchr. deaf Parma (Ohio) City Schs., 1978-79, Mayfield (Ohio) City Schs., 1980-81; tchr. deaf, low incidence work study coord. Trumbull County Ednl. Svc. Ctr., Warren, Ohio, 1981-84; work study coord. Cuyahoga Ednl. Svc. Ctr., Valley View, Ohio, 1984-88; instr., student tchg. supr. Kent (Ohio) State U., 1993-95; project dir. Children's Hosp. Med. Ctr./Family Child Learning Ctr., Tallmadge, Ohio, 1995-2000; coord. spl. edn. Cleveland Heights/University Heights (Ohio) City Sch. System, 2000—. Am. Sign Lang. instr. Cuyahoga C.C., Cleve., 1993-2000; dir. adv. bd. Hearing Impaired Toddler Infant & Families Program, Tallmadge, 1995-2000; mem. County Collaborative Group, Medina, Summit counties, Ohio, 1995-2000; state trainer SKI—HI, Logan, Utah, 1997—. Mem. Coun. Exceptional Children. Grantee Job Tng. & Partnership Act, Cleve., 1982, 86-88; Univ. fellow Kent State U., 1991. Democrat. Avocations: antique collector, exercise, reading. Home: 151 E Pleasant Valley Rd Seven Hills OH 44131-5601 Office: Cleveland Hgts/Univ Hgts Bd Edn 2155 Miramar Blvd University Heights OH 44118

STARCHMAN, DALE EDWARD, medical educator; b. Wallace, Idaho, Apr. 16, 1941; s. Hubert V. and Lottie M. (Alford) S.; m. Erlinda Socrates, Dec. 13, 1969; children: Ann, Cindy, Julie, Mark. Student, Rockhurst Coll., 1959—61; BS in Physics, Pitts. (Kans.) State U., 1963; MS in Radiation Biophysics, U. Kans., 1965, PhD in Radiation Biophysics, 1968. Cert. Radiol. Physicist, Health Physicist, Med. Physicist. Chief health physicist IIT Rsch. Inst., Chgo., 1968-71; radiol. physicist Mercy Hosp. Inst. of Radiation Therapy, Chgo., 1968-71; prof., head radiation biophysics Northeast Ohio U. Coll. of Medicine, Rootstown, Ohio, 1971—; pres. Med. Physics Svcs., Inc., Canton, Ohio, 1971—. Author: (with Wayne R. Hedrick and David L. Hykes) Ultrasound Physics and Instrumentation, 3rd edit., 1995; contbr. numerous articles in profl. jours., chpts. in books, monographs. Fellow Am. Coll. Radiology; mem. Am. Assn. Physicists in Medicine (bd. mem. at large 1984-86, pres. Penn-Ohio chpt. 1975-76, rec. sec. midwest chpt. 1970, mem. edn. coun. 1980-83, chmn. Am. assn. med. dosimetrists task group 1976-78, mem. physics curriculum diagnostic residents task group 2003—, mem. numerous other coms. 1975-83), Health Physics Soc. (chmn. summer sch. sub. com. 1977-78), Radiol. Soc. N.Am. (assoc. scis. com. 1976-86, task force chmn. 1983-86, mem. 1975-86), Sigma Xi, Kappa Mu Epsilon. Achievements include research areas including selection, quality assurance and acceptance testing of diagnostic x-ray units, design of radiology facilities; effects of tissue inhomogeneities on electron therapy, radiation atrophy in bone, large field therapy swing technique, polymer dosimetry, photon spectra through thick shields, fetal effects, ultrasound, mammography. Home and Office: 5942 Easy Pace Cir NW Canton OH 44718-2216

STARK, AGNES GORDON, artist, educator; b. Balt, June 7, 1938; d. Alexander Gordon and D'Arcy (Hilles) Young; m. James Edward Stark, May 8, 1965; children: Gordon Metcalf. BFA, Carnegie Mellon U., 1962; grad. studies, U. Mich., 1962—63. Prodn. asst. The Peterborough Players, NH, 1958-60; asst. to designer Westport County Playhouse, Conn., 1961; lighting designer North Shore Music Theatre, Beverly, Mass., 1962; asst. to designer John Drew Theatre, Hampton, NY, 1963, Arena Stage, Washington, 1963-64, Front St Theatre, Memphis, 1964-65; artist, potter Memphis, 1970—. Crafts adv. panelist Tenn. Arts Commn., Nashville, 1970; adv. Memphis Arts Coun., 1989, judge, 1990—. Exhbns. include Ark. Arts Ctr., Little Rock, 1968, 70, 73, 77, 84, La. Crafts Coun. Juried Show, 1970, Memphis Brooks Mus. Art, 1973-77, Theatre Memphis, 1975, 78-95, Old Tyme Commissary Gallery, Greenwood, Miss., 1976, Memphis Area C. of C., 1977, Nat. Bank of Commerce, Memphis, 1978, 80, 84, Memphis Botanic Garden, 1978, 79, A.C.C. (Am. Crafts Coun.) Dallas Market Show, 1981, A.C.C. Balt. Winter Market, 1982, Turner Clark Gallery, Memphis, 1982, Rhodes Coll., Memphis, 1985, Univ. of Memphis, 1985, Ferguson Gallery, Memphis, 1995, Best of Tenn. Craft Artist Show, 1998-2001, 2003. Bd. dir. Art Today-Memphis Brooks Mus., 1985-91. Mem. Am. Crafts Coun., Tenn. Assn. Craft Artists (v.p. 1986), Memphis Assn. Craft Artists (pres. 1972-76), Memphis Potters Guild (pres.). Republican. Episcopalian. Avocations: gardening, bird watching, hiking, swimming. Home: 3598 Cowden Ave Memphis TN 38111-6002

STARK, JANICE ANN, elementary education educator; b. Oelwein, Iowa, July 25, 1940; d. Wilbert George and Martha Isabelle (Bulgur) Brown; widowed; children: Stephanie, Brad. BA, U. No. Iowa, 1962; MA, St. Thomas U., 1991. Lic. tchr. Tchr. 5th grade Roseville (Minn.) Schs., 1962-63; tchr. 4th grade Iowa City Schs., 1963-64, Calumet City (Ill.) Schs., 1964-65; tchr. 3d grade, substitute tchf. 6th grade Robbinsdale (Minn.) Schs., 1965-69, 74-78; tutor, W.I.S.E. vol. Mpls. Pub. Schs., 1969-72, 79-86, tchr. grades 3-5 Putnam Elem., 1986-92, tchr. 4th grade Hamilton Elem., 1992-93; guest tchr. Koln (Germany) Holweide Sch., 1993-94; with Tchr. Inst. Minn. Humanities Commn., Mpls., 1995; tchr. Burroughs Cmty. Sch., Mpls., 1995—; internat. teaching exchange grades 5 and 6 Manorvale Primary Sch., Werribeo, Australia, 1997. Mem. City-Wide Tchr. Adv. Com., 1987-89; bldg. contact rep. Lang. Arts and Social Studies, 1986-89; mem. Site Coun. Leadership Team, 1989-92; N.E. Mplw. tchr. contact person Whole Lang., 1991-92; mem. Mpls. Pub. Schs. Profl. Devel. Com., 1992-93, Local 59 Leadership Consortium, 1992-93. Mem. AAUW, Pi Lambda Theta. Avocations: travel, reading. Home: 8317 34th Ave N Minneapolis MN 55427-1828

STARK, JOAN SCISM, education educator; b. Hudson, N.Y., Jan. 6, 1937; d. Ormonde F. and Myrtle Margaret (Kirkey) S.; m. William L. Stark, June 28, 1958 (dec.); children: Eugene William, Susan Elizabeth, Linda Anne, Ellen Scism; m. Malcolm A. Lowther, Jan. 31, 1981. BS, Syracuse U., 1957; MA (Hoadly fellow), Columbia U., 1960; Ed.D., SUNY, Albany, 1971. Tchr. Ossining (N.Y.) High Sch., 1957-59; free-lance editor Holt, Rinehart & Winston, Harcourt, Brace & World, 1960-70; lectr. Ulster County Community Coll., Stone Ridge, N.Y., 1968-70; asst. dean Goucher Coll., Balt., 1970-73, asso. dean, 1973-74; assoc. prof., chmn. dept. higher postsecondary edn. Syracuse (N.Y.) U., 1974-78; dean Sch. Edn. U. Mich., Ann Arbor, 1978-83, prof., 1983-2001, prof. and dean emeritus, 2001—; dir. Nat. Ctr. for Improving Postsecondary Teaching and Learning, 1986—91. Editor: Rev. of Higher Edn., 1991-96; contbr. articles to various publs. Leader Girl Scouts U.S.A., Cub Scouts Am.; coach girls Little League; dist. officer PTA, intermittently, 1968-80; mem. adv. com. Gerald R. Ford Library, U. Mich., 1980-83; trustee Kalamazoo Coll., 1979-85; mem. exec. com. Inst. Social Research, U. Mich., 1979-81; bd. dirs. Mich. Assn. Colls. Tchr. Edn., 1979-81. Mem. Am. Assn. for Higher Edn., Am. Ednl. Rsch. Assn. (Div. J. Rsch. award 1998), Assn. Study Higher Edn. (dir. 1977-79, v.p. 1983, pres. 1984, Rsch. Achievement award 1992, svc. award 1998, Disting. Career award 1999), Assn. Innovation Higher Edn. (nat. chmn. 1974-75), Assn. Instl. Rsch. (disting. mem., Sidney Suslow award 1999), Assn. Colls. and Schs. Edn. State Univs. and Land Grant Colls. (dir. 1981-83), Acctg. Edn. Change Commn., Phi Beta Kappa, Phi Kappa Phi, Sigma Pi Sigma, Eta Pi Upsilon, Lambda Sigma Sigma, Phi Delta Kappa, Pi Lambda Theta.

STARK, NORMAN, secondary school educator; b. Bronx, N.Y., Sept. 15, 1940; s. Martin and Margaret (Neuman) S.; m. Betty Joanne Kelton, Sept. 4, 1994 (dec. May 1998); 1 child, Michelle Allison; m. Lois Marie Ricketson, Dec. 25, 2001. Student, Newark State Coll., Union, 1963-69. Creative writing tchr., acting tchr., singles forum tchr., film tchr. Plantation (Fla.) High Sch., 1988; Hoover Mid. Sch. and Palm Bay H.S., Melbourne, Fla., 1995. Editor West Palm Beach News, 1979; screenplay writer, actor. With U.S. Army, 1963—69. Avocations: reading, puzzles, movies. Home: 2732 Locksley Rd Melbourne FL 32935-2433 E-mail: norman915@msn.com.

STARKEY, LUCILLE A. music educator; b. East Liverpool, Ohio; d. William Oscar and Goldie May (Cline) Mansfield; m. James Richard, Apr. 6, 1968; 1 child, Karen Michelle. BA, Northland Coll., 1966. Tchr. 1st grade

Monroe Local Sch., Graysville, Ohio, 1967-68; tchr. music Caldwell (Ohio) Ex Village, 1969-71, Switzerland of Ohio, Woodsfield, 1971-99. Vol. Missionary N.Am. Mission Bd. Avocation: archery - tournament and 3d. Home: 3171 Lodwick Dr Apt 3 Warren OH 44485

STARKS, CAROL ELIZABETH, retired principal; b. Elizabeth, NJ, Oct. 16, 1941; d. Arthur E. and Argetha P. (Henderson) Starks. AA, Graceland Coll., Lamoni, Iowa, 1961; BA in Elem. Edn., Mich. State U., 1963; MA in Elem. Adminstrn., San Jose State U., 1972. Cert. elem. sch. tchr. Calif., life diploma for elem. edn. Calif., specialist tchr. in reading Calif., std. svc. credential in supervision Calif., elem. sch. tchr. N.J. Tchr. grade 3 Hayes Sch., Monterey, Calif., 1963—65; tchr. grade 2 Woodruff Sch., Berkeley Heights, NJ, 1965—67; tchr. remedial reading and educationally handicapped Ord Terrace Sch., Monterey, 1967—68, asst. prin., 1975—77, prin., 1984—88; tchr. grade 3 Manzanita Sch., Monterey, 1968—73; asst. prin. La Mesa Sch., Monterey, 1973—74, tchr. grade 6, 1974—75; prin. Foothill Sch., Monterey, 1977—80, Olson Sch., Monterey, 1980—84, Highland Sch., Monterey, 1988—95, Bay View Sch., Monterey, 1995—99. Interviewed as representative of elementary principals Calif. Commn. on the Tchg. Profession, 1984—85. Treas. Kans. City Coun., 2002; mem. world ch. pubs. com. Remnant Ch. Jesus Christ of Latter Day Saints, 2001—, music dir. Blue Springs congregation, 2001—, mem. hymnbook com., 2003—, World Ch., 2003—. Recipient Calif. Disting. Sch. Prin.'s award, 1989, 1993, Proclamation for profl. accomplishments and 19 yrs. of svc., City of Seaside (Calif.), 1995. Mem.: scholarship com. Kans. City Coun. (pres. 2000—01), Monterey Bay Sch. Adminstr. Assn. (pres. 1997—98), Assn. Calif. Sch. Adminstr. (sec./treas. Monterey Peninsula charter 1977—78, v.p. 1978—79, pres. 1979—80, treas. region X 1979—81, pres. region X 1981—82, mem. elem. adminstrn. com. 1982—86, del. to Nat. Assn. Elem. Sch.Prins. Convention 1983—84, state facilitator Elem. Adminstrn. Acad. North 1984—85, state dir. Elem. Adminstrn. Acad. North 1985—86, invited writer for case studies for Calif. sch. leadership acad. 1985—86, state del. to rep. assembly 1986—91, Region X Blanche Montague award for Outstanding Sch. Adminstr. 1987), Who's Who of Am. Women, Delta Kappa Gamma (1st v.p. Delta Lambda chpt. Calif. 1986—88, 2nd v.p. Delta Lambda chpt.Calif. 1988—90, pres. Delta Lambda chpt.Calif. 1990—92, Calif.membership task force 1991—93, Calif.personal growth and svcs. com. 1993—95, dir. area V Calif. 1995—97, state chairperson comms. com. 1997—99, mem. scholarship com. Kansas City coun. 2000—01, pres. Phi chpt. Mo. 2000—02, sec. Kansas City coun. 2001—02, state comm. com. 2001—03, treas. Kansas City coun. 2002—, chair state comm. com. 2003—, chmn. state comm. com. 2003—). Republican. Remnant Ch. Of Jesus Christ Of Latter Day Saints. Avocations: travel, reading, music, computer. Home: 3341 S Cochise Ave Independence MO 64057

STARKS, ELIZABETH VIAL, gifted/talented education educator; b. Chgo., Feb. 2, 1943; d. George McNaughton and Mary Margaret (Beatty) Vial; m. Edward Arnold Kearns, June 6, 1964 (div. 1978); m. Kevin James Starks, Aug. 4, 1979; children: Lauren Elizabeth Kearns, Jason Edward Kearns. BA, U. Ariz., 1964; MA, Denver U., 1994. Tchr. grade 6 Tucson Pub. Schs., 1965-66; gifted/talented tchr. grades 4-6 Sch. Dist Re-3(J), Keenesburg, Colo., 1988—. Gifted/talented coord. RE-3(J) Sch. Dist., 1992—, social studies curriculum com., 1993—, technology com., 1993-94. Bd. dirs. A Woman's Place (safe house), Greeley, Colo., 1994—; chmn. adv. bd. South County A Woman's Place, Ft. Lupton, Colo., 1994—; bd. dirs. Weld Mental Health Ctr., Greeley, 1984-87; County Dem. chairperson, Greeley, 1976-79. Mem. ASCD, ACLU, Nat. Assn. Gifted and Talented, Colo. Assn. Gifted and Talented, Phi Delta Kappa, Kappa Kappa Gamma. Avocations: reading, golf, swimming, gourmet cooking, theatre. Office: Hudson Elem Sch PO Box 278 Hudson CO 80642-0278

STARKS, FLORENCE ELIZABETH, retired special education educator; b. Summit, N.J., Dec. 6, 1932; d. Edward and Winnie (Morris) S. BA, Morgan State U., 1956; MS in Edn., CUNY, 1962; postgrad., Fairleigh Dickinson U., 1962-63, Seton Hall U., 1963, Newark State Coll. Cert. blind and visually handicapped and social studies tchr., N.J. Tchr. adult edn. Newark Bd. of Edn.; ret., 1995; tchr. N.Y. Inst. for Edn. of the Blind. Developer first class for multiple handicapped blind children in pub. sch. system, Newark, 1960; ptnr. World Vision Internat. Mem. ASCD, AFL-CIO, AAUW, Coun. Exceptional Children, Am. Assn. U. Women, Nat. Assn. Negro Bus. and Profl. Women's Club Inc., N.J. Edn. Assn., Newark Tchrs. Assn., Newark Tchrs. Union-Am. Fedn. Tchrs., World Vision Internat. (ptnr.). Home: 4 Park Ave Summit NJ 07901-3942

STARKS, ROSALYN JUNE, physical education and health educator; b. Phoenix, June 17, 1952; d. Ross Owen and Maribel Louise (Barnes) S. BS in Edn., U. Ariz., 1974; MA in Edn., No. Ariz. U., 1991. Tchr. Phys. Edn. K-12, Ariz. Phys. edn. tchr. Santa Cruz Valley Union High Sch., Eloy, Ariz., 1975-84; phys. edn., health tchr. Phoenix Union High Sch. Dist., 1985—. Coach Santa Cruz Valley Union H.S. and So. Mountain H.S., Phoenix, 1975—, facilitator student assistance program, 1987—; Phoenix 5A Metro Region Rep. State Softball Adv. Bd., 1990-94; mem. HIV/AIDS articulation com. Phoenix Union H.S. Dist., 1994—; mem. crisis intervention team South Mountain H.S., 1995—, dir. studies com., 1993—, title I literacy strategies cadre, 1995—. Del. People to People Internat. Citizen Amb. Program, Berlin Reflections, 1994; del. Sports Devel. Delegation to South Africa, 1997. Named Softball Coach of Yr., A Ctrl. Divsn., 1980. Mem. AAHPERD, NEA, Ariz. Edn. Assn., Ariz. AHPERD, Phoenix Union H.S. Dist. Classroom Tchrs. Assn. Avocation: bowling. Home: 4406 N 111th Dr Phoenix AZ 85037-5333 Office: S Mountain High School 5401 S 7th St Phoenix AZ 85040-3104

STARKWEATHER, TERESA MADERY, artist, educator; b. L.A., June 12, 1950; d. Earl and Maureen Madery; m. Lee A. Starkweather, May 29, 1977; children: Ashley, Chelsea. Student, Art Ctr. Coll. Design, L.A., 1970-72; BFA, Atlanta Coll. Art, 1973; credential, Calif. State U., Northridge, 1994-96. artist Chaleur, Torrance, Calif., 1991, Prestige Graphics, L.A., 1993-95; artist, designer Zarah Co., Topanga, Calif., 1991-95. Artistic dir. Echoes Cards, Topanga, Calif., 1991-94. Contbg. artist Am. Artist Mag., spring 1991, The Best of Watercolor, 1995, Splash 4 The Splendor of Light, 1996, Splash 5, 1997, Painting the Many Moods of Light, 1999, Keys to Painting Textures and Surfaces, 2000, Keys to Painting Fruit and Flowers, 2000; exhibited Lankershim Arts Ctr., Calif., 1990, L.A. City Hall, 1990, Orlando Gallery, Sherman Oaks, Calif., 1991, Watercolor West Nat. Exhbn., Calif., 1991, 95, 97, Century Gallery, L.A., 1992, L.A. Mcpl. Art Gallery, 1993, Artspace Gallery, L.A., 1993, Springfield Art Mus., Mo., 1994, Foothills Art Ctr., Colo., 1994, Orlando Gallery, Sherman Oaks, 1996, Nan Miller Gallery, Rochester, N.Y., 1998. Recipient Bronze medal Art Calif. Mag. Discovery Awards, 1992, 93, 1st pl. award Valley Watercolor Assn., Artspace Gallery, L.A., 1993, 98, Patron Purchase award Watercolor U.S.A., Springfield, Mo., 1994, 2d pl. award Nat. Watercolor Soc. Show, 1997, Best of Show award Valley Watercolor Soc. Show, 1998; finalist The Artist's Mag. Awards, 1996, 97; named Signature Mem., Watercolor West, 1997. Avocations: horseback riding, tennis.

STARNES, SUSAN SMITH, elementary education educator; b. Grinnell, Iowa, Oct. 8, 1942; d. Edwin Fay Smith Jr. and Miriam Jane (Spaulding) Smith Simms; m. Wayman J. Starnes, Apr. 25, 1964; children: Michele Ann Starnes Hoffman, Mary Shannon Starnes Zornes. BS in Edn. summa cum laude, Mo. Bapt. U., 1991. Cert. early childhood tchr., elem. tchr. 1-8. Adminstr. Presbyn. Ch. in Am. Hist. Ctr., St. Louis, 1985-90; tchr. 3rd grade Ctrl. Christian Sch., St. Louis, 1991-98; subst. tchr. Ctrl. Christian Sch., Kirk Day Sch., Twin Oaks Christian Sch., St. Louis, 1998—. Mem. chapel com. Ctrl. Christian Sch., St. Louis, 1991-98. Children's dir. Canaan Bapt. Ch., St. Louis, 1991—96, Bible Study Fellowship children's leader, 1986—89, mission trip vol., 1992, 1993, 1999—2003; camp counselor Youth for Christ, Kansas City, 1992, 1993, Awana leader, 1996—; mem. Mo. Bapt. Conv. Disaster Relief Childcare Unit, 1997—. Mem. Kappa Delta Pi. Avocations: biking, swimming, hiking.

STARNES, WILLIAM HERBERT, JR., chemist, educator; b. Knoxville, Tenn., Dec. 2, 1934; s. William Herbert and Edna Margaret (Osborne) Starnes; m. Maria Sofia Molina, Mar. 4, 1986. BS with honors, Va. Poly. Inst., 1955; PhD, Ga. Inst. Tech., 1960. Rsch. chemist Esso Rsch. & Engring. Co., Baytown, Tex., 1960-62, sr. rsch. chemist, 1962-64, polymer additives sect. head, 1964-65, rsch. specialist, 1965-67, rsch. assoc., 1967-71; instr. and rsch. assoc. dept. chemistry U. Tex., Austin, 1971-73; mem. tech. staff AT&T Bell Labs., Murray Hill, NJ, 1973-85; prof. chemistry Poly. U., Bklyn., 1985-89, head dept. chemistry and life scis., 1985-88, assoc. dir. polymer durability ctr., 1987-89; Floyd Dewey Gottwald Sr. prof. chemistry Coll. William and Mary, Williamsburg, Va., 1989—, prof. applied sci., 1990—. Invited lectr. several fgn. countries and U.S.; ofcl. guest USSR Acad. Scis., 1990, Russian Acad. Scis., 1992; disting. vis. prof. Beijing Inst. Tech., 1996; vis. scientist Tex. Acad. Scis., 1964—67; mem. bd. doctoral thesis examiners Indian Inst. Tech., New Delhi, 1988, McGill U., Montreal, 1989, MacQuarie U., Sydney, Australia, 1991, McMaster U., Hamilton, Canada, 1994; panelist, reviewer NSF Acad. Rsch. Facilities Modernization Program, 1990; channel program mentor U. Cairo, 1994—95; mem. opinion leader panel Wall St. Jour., 1995—; charter mem. dept. chemistry adv. coun. Va. Poly. Inst. and State U., 1998—; sci. advisor European Multinational Environ. Rsch. Project on PVC in Soil and Landfills, 1995—99; cons. numerous indsl. cos., govtl. and pvt. agys.; course dir. continuing edn. Editor-in-chief: Jour. Vinyl and Additive Tech., 1998—, mem. adv. bd., bd. reviewers: Jour. Vinyl Tech., 1981—83, mem. editl. bd.: Jour. Chem. and Biochem. Kinetics, 1992—, Polymer Degradation and Stability, 1997—, Internat. Jour. Coatings Sci., 2001—; contbr. chapters to books, articles to profl. jours. Named honoree Plastics History and Artifacts Program, Plastics Pioneers Assn., 2001; recipient Profl. Progress award, Soc. Profl. Chemists and Engrs., 1968, Disting. Tech. Staff award, AT&T Bell Labs., 1982, Polymer Sci. Pioneer award, Polymer News, 1988, Honor Scroll award, N.J. Inst. Chemists, 1989; fellow NSF, 1958—60; grantee, NSF, 1989—, Nat. Bur. Stds. Ctr. Fire Rsch., Internat. Copper Rsch. Assn., Va. Ctr. Innovative Tech., GenCorp Found., several indsl. cos. Fellow: AAAS (Project 2061 1985—86, chmn. chemistry subpanel 1985—86, mem. panel on phys. scis. and engring. 1985—86), Soc. Plastics Engrs. (nat. publs. com. 1998—2001, thesis advisor nat. award Vinyl Plastics divsn. 1996, 1998), N.Y. Acad. Scis., Am. Inst. Chemists (life); mem.: Va. Acad. Sci., Soc. Plastics Engrs., Am. Chem. Soc. (bd. dirs. southeastern Tex. sect. 1970, spkrs. bur. divsn. polymer chemistry 1976—, mem.-at-large exec. com. Va. sect. 1995), Phi Lambda Upsilon (pres. Va. Poly. Inst. chpt. 1954—55), Sigma Xi (M. A. Ferst award Ga. Inst. Tech. chpt. 1960), Phi Kappa Phi (life). Achievements include patents in field; research in degradation, stabilization, flammability, microstructures and polymerization mechanisms of synthetic polymers, especially poly(vinyl chloride); free radical chemistry; carbon-13 nuclear magnetic resonance and organic synthesis; subspecialities include organic chemistry, polymer chemistry. Office: Coll William and Mary Dept Chemistry PO Box 8795 Williamsburg VA 23187-8795 E-mail: whstar@wm.edu.

STAROST, DIANE JOAN, music educator; b. Huntington, N.Y., June 27, 1963; d. Frank Basil and Therese Basile Castrogivanni; m. Alan Francis Starost, May 20, 1990; children: Nicholas Francis, Arianna Marie. MusB in Music Edn., SUNY, 1985; MusM in Music Performance, Manhattan Sch. Music, 1988. Cert. tchr. N.Y. Pvt. practice, Greenlawn, NY, 1980—; vocal music tchr. Manetuck & Oquenock Elem. Schs., West Islip, NY, 1985—92, Udall Mid. Sch., West Islip, NY, 1992—97; dir. youth music Old First Presbyn. Ch., Huntington, NY, 1997—. String tchr. Northport (N.Y.)-East Northport Schs., 1987—91, summer music coord., 1991; colorguard dir., choreographer West Islip (N.Y.) Schs., 1987—91, all dist. chorus dir., 1991—94; musical theater dir., adv. Udall Middle Sch., West Islip, 1992—97. Soloist Old First Ch., Huntington, NY, 1984—. Recipient Crane Performers cert., Crane Student Tchg. award; Crane Merit scholar, SUNY, 1985. Mem.: Music Educators Nat. Conf., N.Y. State Sch. Music Assn., Suffolk County Music Educators Assn. Roman Catholic. Avocations: music, art, cooking, gardening. Home: 16 Geneva Pl Greenlawn NY 11740 E-mail: dialstar@yahoo.com.

STARR, DARLENE R. special education educator, education educator; b. Bucyrus, Ohio, Aug. 25, 1943; d. Dale H. and Helen J. (Rettig) Laipply; m. Douglas K. Rudy, Sept. 12, 1987; children: Kris, Kim, Kirk, Shane, Aubry. BS in Elem. Edn., St. Cloud State U., 1976; reading specialist, Avila Coll., 1981; MS in Spl. Edn., Kans. U., 1987. Cert. grades K-9 elem. reading/learning disabilities. Tchr. Wright Devel. Ctr., Monticello, Minn., 1977-78; tchr., dir. chpt. 1 Maple Lake (Minn.) Dist. Schs., 1978-80; chpt. 1 tchr. Olate (Kans.) Dist. Schs., 1980-82; first grade tchr. Spring Hill (Kans.) Dist. Schs., 1982-85; kindergarten tchr. Marietta (Ga.) City Schs., 1985-86; learning disabilites tchr. Louisburg (Kans.) Dist. Schs., 1987-90, tchr. grade 2, 1990-91; learning disabilities tchr. Olathe (Kans.) Dist. Schs., 1991—. Adj. prof. Ottawa U., Overland Park, Kans., 1993—; learning disabilities cons., Olathe, 1992—. Mem. Nat. Coun. for Tchrs. Math., Coun. for Learning Disabilities, Internat. Reading Assn., Kans. Reading Assn. (chair parents and reading com.), Delta Kappa Gamma. Lutheran. Avocations: golf, tennis, antiquing, reading. Home: RR 1 Box 51A Pleasanton KS 66075-9793

STARR, ILA MAE, elementary school educator; b. La Grande, Oreg., Dec. 27, 1917; d. Samuel Fulmer Andrew and Ida Luella Perry; m. James Marion Starr, Mar. 2, 1940; children: Jacqueline Ann Starr Brandon, James Steven Starr. BA, U. Wash., 1939; BS, Eastern Oreg. Coll., LaGrande, Oreg., 1960, Tchr. Cert. Oreg., 1940. Cert. Wash. 1962, Calif. 1974. Mus. tchr. La Grande (Oreg.) Pub. Schs., 1939-40; girl scout exec. Girl Scouts of Am., Grand Coulee, Wash., 1940-41; Elem. Sch. Tchr. Centralia (Wash.) Pub. Schs., 1954; elem. sch. tchr. Wenatchee (Wash.) Pub. Schs., 1956-64, Lancaster (Calif.) Pub. Schs., 1964-68, Marysville (Calif.) Pub. Schs., 1968-79. Pvt. mus. tchr., Seattle, Grand Coulee and Wenatchee, Wash., 1940—. Bd. dirs. Community Concert Assn., Yuba City, Calif., 1986-88; inspiration chmn. Republican Women, Yuba City, 1986-88. Recipient Hon. Pub. Sch. Award, Masonic Lodge 437, Lancaster, 1966; Nominee for Tchr. of Yr., Marysville Pub. Schs., 1978. Mem. Am. Assn. U. Women (program v.p. 1976; Grant Honoree 1977), PTA (hon. life mem. 1965), The Seminar Club (program chmn.), Innerwheel Club (pres. 1985-86). Mem. Lds Ch. Avocations: mus. vocal soloist, choir dir.

STARR, ISIDORE, law educator; b. Bklyn., Nov. 24, 1911; BA, CCNY, 1932; LLB, St. John's U., Jamaica, N.Y., 1936; MA, Columbia U., 1939; JSD, Bklyn. Law Sch., 1942; PhD, New Sch. Social Rsch., 1957. Bar: N.Y. 1937. Tchr. various high schs., N.Y.C., 1934-61; from assoc. prof. to prof. edn. Queen's Coll., 1961-75, prof. emeritus, 1975—. Dir. Inst. on Law-Related Edn., Lincoln-Filene Ctr., Tufts U., 1963; dir. Law Studies Inst., N.Y.C., 1974; adv. on Our Living Bill of Rights Film Series (6 films) Ency. Brit. Ednl. Corp.; mem. Ariz. Ctr. for Law-Related Edn.; mem. coun. on pub. legal edn. State of Wash., 2001—; cons. in field. Author: The Lost Generation of Prince Edward COunty, 1968, The Gideon Case, 1968, The Feiner Case, 1968, The Mapp Case, 1968, The Supreme Court and Contemporary Issues, 1968, Human Rights in the United States, 1969, The American Judicial System, 1972, The Idea of Liberty, 1978, Justice: Due Process of Law, 1981; co-editor Living American Documents, 1971. Bd. dirs. Phi Alpha Delta Juvenile Justice Program, 1981—. 1st lt. U.S. Army, 1943-46. John Hay fellow, 1952-53; recipient Outstanding Citizen award Philip Morris Cos., 1992. Mem. ABA (hon. chair adv. commn. on Youth Edn. for Citizenship, Isidore Starr award for Spl. Achievment in Law Studies, Leon Jaworski award 1989), Am. Judicature Soc., Am. Soc. Legal History, Am. Legal Studies Assn., Nat. Coun. Social Studies (past pres.), Washington Coun. Pub. Legal Edn., Phi Beta Kappa, Phi Alpha Delta (cert. of appreciation 1981). Address: 12501 Greenwood Ave N Apt C110 Seattle WA 98133-8000

STARR, JOYCE IVES, special education educator; b. Guilford, N.Y., Jan. 25, 1932; d. Paris Otto and Alta Lena (Wade) Ives; m. Leonard E. Cornell, July 7, 1956 (dec. Mar. 1973); children: Stephen, Lorrinda, Teresa, David; m. Donald Fay Starr, May 8, 1976 (dec. Apr. 1982); stepchildren: Donald Fay II, Matthew, Mark, Thor (dec. May 1986). Student, Rochester (N.Y.) Inst. of Tech., 1949-51; BS. in Edn., SUNY, New Paltz, 1955; student, Syracuse U., summers 1967-68. Art tchr. Oxford (N.Y.) Acad. and Cen. Sch., 1954-57; spl. edn. tchr. junior high sch. Liberty (N.Y.) Cen. Sch., 1966-67, spl. edn. tchr. primary grades, 1967-71; spl. edn. tchr. Del. Acad. and Cen. Sch., Delhi, N.Y., 1971-87; resource rm. tchr. Sidney Ctrl. Sch., N.Y., 1993. Pres. Tchrs. Assn., Bd. Coop. Sch. Ednl. Services, Liberty, N.Y., 1970-71; organizing com. of N.Y. Heartland Bioregion, 1996—; mem. Made in Chenago Gallery, Inc., 1997-99. Vol., coach Spl. Olympics, Liberty, Delhi, N.Y., 1974-87; chairperson Chenango County Environ. Mgmt. Coun., 1991-93; mem. Upper Catskill Community Coun. Arts; deacon Guilford Ctr. Presbyn. Ch., 1991-93, treas. ladies aid, 1995-99, elder, 1999; mem. planning bd. Town of Guilford, 1999. Mem. N.Y. State Tchrs. of Handicapped, Assn. Children with Learning Disabilities, Del. Acad. Faculty Assn. (region polit. action com. 1982-83), Three Rivers Project, Chenango County Bird Club (sec. 1995-96, editor newsletter 1997—), Tri-Town Hikers, Delhi Art Group. Avocations: gardening, hiking, freelance art, nature study. E-mail: jivesstarr@mkl.com.

STARR, MARTIN KENNETH, management educator; b. N.Y.C., May 21, 1927; s. Harry and Melanie (Krauss) S.; m. Polly Exner, Apr. 3, 1955; children: Christopher Herschel, Loren Michael. BS, MIT, 1948; MS, Columbia U., 1951, PhD, 1953. Ptnr., dir. M.K. Starr Assocs., 1956-61; prof. mgmt. sci. Columbia U., N.Y.C., 1961-96, dir. Ctr. for the Study of Ops., 1980-95, dir. Ctr. for Enterprise Mgmt., 1995-96, vice dean Grad. Sch. Bus., 1974-75; Disting. prof. ops. mgmt. Crummer Grad. Sch. Bus. Rollins Coll., Winter Park, Fla., 1996—2003, prof. emeritus, 2003—, dir. Ctr. for Enterprise Mgmt., 1996—2001; prof. emeritus Columbia U., 1996—. Guest lectr. Am. U., Beirut, 1964, MIT, 1964-67, U. Cape Town, S. Africa, 1976, 80, 82, 84, 86, 88; cons. GE, E.I. duPont de Nemours & Co., Eastman Kodak Co., Lever Brothers, TRW, R.J. Reynolds, Young & Rubicam, IBM. Author: (with David W. Miller) The Structure of Human Decisions, 1967, Inventory Control-Theory and Practice, 1972, Product Design and Decision Theory, 1963, (with David W. Miller) Executive Decisions and Operations Research, 2d edit., 1969, Systems Management of Operations, 1971, Management: A Modern Approach, 1971, Production Management: Systems and Synthesis, 2d edit., 1972, (with Irving Stein) The Practice of Management Science, 1976, Operations Management, 1978, (with G. Dannebring) Management Science: An Introduction, 1981, (with Earl K. Bowen) Statistics for Business and Economics, 1982, (with Marion Sobol) Statistics for Business and Economics: An Action Learning Approach, 1983, Managing Production and Operations, 1989, Global Corporate Alliances and the Competitive Edge, 1991, (with Marion Sobol) Introduction to Statistics for Executives, 1993, Operations Management: A Systems Approach, 1996, ED-text rev., 2000, Production and Operations Management, 2004; editor: Executive Readings in Management Science, 1965, (with Milan Zeleny) Multiple Criteria Decision Making, 1977, Global Competitiveness: Getting the U.S. Back on Track, 1988; editor-in-chief Mgmt. Sci., 1967-82; mem. editl. bd. Behavioral Sci., 1970—; editl. adviser Operational Rsch. Quar., 1970-85; cons. editor: Columbia Jour. World Business: Focus: Decision Making, fall, 1977, Quantitative Methods in Mgmt., McGraw-Hill Book Co., N.Y.C.; contbr. articles to profl. jours. Fellow Inst. for Ops. Rsch. and the Mgmt. Scis.; mem. Inst. Mgmt. Scis. (pres. 1974-75), Prodn. and Ops. Mgmt. Soc. (pres.-elect 1994—, pres. 1995, past pres., bd. dirs. 1996—, chair Coun. of Pres. 1999—), Beta Gamma Sigma. Home: 100 S Interlachen Ave Apt 304 Winter Park FL 32789-4450 Office: Rollins Coll 120 Crummer Grad Sch Bus Winter Park FL 32789

STARR, STEPHEN FREDERICK, academic administrator, historian; b. N.Y.C., Mar. 24, 1940; s. Stephen Z. and Ivy (Edmondson) S.; children: Anna, Elizabeth. BA in Ancient History, Yale U., 1962; MA in Slavonic Langs. and Lit., King's Coll., Cambridge U., 1964; PhD in History, Princeton U., 1968. Assoc. prof. dept. history Princeton U., 1968-74; sec. Kennan Inst. for Advanced Russian Studies, Woodrow Wilson Internat. Center for Scholars, Washington, 1974-79; v.p. acad. affairs Tulane U., New Orleans, 1979-82, prof. history, adj. prof. architecture, 1979-83; scholar-in-residence Historic New Orleans Collection, 1982-84; pres. Oberlin (Ohio) Coll., 1983-94, The Aspen Inst., Washington, 1994—. Spl. cons. President's Commn. Fgn. Langs. and Internat. Studies, 1978-81; v.p. Nat. Council for Soviet and East European Rsch., 1978-80. Author: Decentralization and Self Government in Russia, 1830-1870, 1972, Konstant in Melnikov: Solo Architect in a Mass Society, 1978, 2nd edit., 1981, Il padiglione di Melnikov, 1979, Bamboula! The Life and Times of Louis Moreau Gottschalk, 1994, (with Hans von Herwarth) Against Two Evils, 1981, The Russian Avant-Garde, 1981, Red and Hot: The Fate of Jazz in the USSR, 1983, New Orleans Unmasqued, 1985, Southern Comfort, The Garden District of New Orleans, 1800-1900, 1990. Mem. Greater New Orleans Found., 1983-91, La. Repertory Jazz Ensemble, 1980—; bd. dirs. Rockefeller Bros. Fund, 1984-94; trustee Eurasia Found., 1997—. Mem. Am. Assn. Advancement Slavic Studies, Coun. Fgn. Rels., Internat. Rsch. and Exch. Bd. (trustee), Nat. Fgn. Lang. Ctr. (bd. advisers). Office: Chm Ctrl Asia Inst Nitze Sch Adv Intl Studies/Johns Hopkins Univ 1619 Massachusetts Ave NW Washington DC 20036-2213

STARRS, JAMES EDWARD, law and forensics educator, consultant; b. Bklyn., July 30, 1930; s. George Thomas and Mildred Agatha (Dobbins) S.; m. Barbara Alice Smyth, Sept. 6, 1954; children: Mary Alice, Monica, James, Charles, Liam, Barbara, Siobhan, Gregory. BA, LLB, St. John's U., Bklyn., 1958; LLM, NYU, 1959. Bar: N.Y. 1958, D.C. 1966, U.S. Ct. Mil. Appeals 1959, U.S. Dist. Ct. (so. and ea. dists.) N.Y. 1960. Assoc. Lawless & Lynch, N.Y.C., 1958; tchg. fellow Rutgers U., Newark, 1959-60; asst. prof. law DePaul U., Chgo., 1960-64; assoc. prof. law George Washington U., Washington, 1964-67, prof. law, 1967—, prof. forensic scis., 1975—. Cons. Nat. Commn. Reform Fed. Criminal Laws, Washington, 1968, Cellmark Diagnostics, Germantown, Md., 1987—, Time-Life Books, 1993; participant re-evaluation sci. evidence and trial of Bruno Richard Hauptmann for Lindbergh murder, 1983; participant reporting sci. re-analysis of firearms evidence in Sacco and Vanzetti trial, 1986; project dir. Alfred G. Packer Victims Exhumation Project, 1989, A Blaze of Bullets: A Sci. Investigation into the Deaths of Senator Huey Long and Dr. Carl Austin Weiss, 1991, Meriwether Lewis Exhumation Project, 1992—, Frank R. Olson Exhumation Project, 1994, Jesse W. James Exhumation Project, 1995, Samuel Washington-Harewood Excavations, 1999, The Boston Strangler Re-Investigation, 2000, The Exhumation of Carl E. Williams, Sr., 2001, The Exhumation of Samuel Swan, 2002, The Gettysburg Excavations, Pa., 2002—; Snider lectr. U. Toronto, 1999, Boston Strangler Re-Investigation, 2000, Mutter Lectr. Coll. of Physicians, Phila., 2003. Author: (with Moenssens and Inbau) Scientific Evidence in Criminal Cases, 1986; (with Moenssens, Inbau and Henderson) Scientific Evidence in Civil and Criminal Cases, 1995; editor: The Noiseless Tenor, 1982; co-editor: (review) Scientific Sleuthing, 1976—; mem. editl. bd. Jour. Forensic Sci., 1980-98, Encyclopedia of Forensic Sciences; contbr. articles to profl. jours. Sgt. U.S. Army, 1950-53, Korea. Recipient Vidocq Soc. award, 1993; Ford Found. fellow, 1963; vis. scholar in residence USMC, 1984. Fellow Am. Acad. Forensic Sci. (chmn. jurisprudence sect. 1984, 1994, 1995, bd. dirs. 1986-89, 98-2001, Jurisprudence Sect. award 1988, Disting. fellow 1996); mem. ABA, Mid-Atlantic Assn. Forensic Sci. (emeritus), Assn. Trial

Lawyers Am., Internat. Soc. Forensic Sci. (chmn. jurisprudence sect. 1988), Internat. Assn. for Identification, Geol. Soc. Am. Roman Catholic. Home: 8602 Clydesdale Rd Springfield VA 22151-1301 Office: George Washington U Nat Law Ctr 720 20th St NW Washington DC 20006-4306 E-mail: jstarrs@main.nlc.gwu.edu.

STARZINGER, VINCENT EVANS, political science educator; b. Des Moines, Jan. 12, 1929; s. Vincent and Genevieve (Evans) S.; m. Mildred Hippee Hill, June 16, 1953; children: Page Hill, Evans. AB summa cum laude, Harvard U., 1950, LLB, 1954, PhD, 1959; AM (hon.), Dartmouth Coll., 1968. Bar: Iowa 1954. Practice with firm Bannister, Carpenter, Ahlers & Cooney, Des Moines, 1954; teaching fellow, then instr. govt. Harvard, 1957-60; mem. faculty dept. govt. Dartmouth, 1960-94, chmn. dept. govt., 1972-77, 83-85, Joel Parker prof. law and polit. sci., 1976-94, prof. emeritus, 1994—. Author: Middlingness: Juste Milieu Political Theory in England and France, 1815-48, 1965, repub. as The Politics of the Center, 1991; also articles. Served with AUS, 1955-56. Sheldon traveling fellow, 1950-51; Social Sci. Research Council fellow, 1958-59; Dartmouth faculty fellow, 1963-64; Am. Philos. Soc. award and Earhart Found. fellow, 1970-71 Mem. ABA, Am. Polit. Sci. Assn., Iowa Bar Assn., Am. Alpine Club, Cambridge (Mass.) Boat Club, Phi Beta Kappa.. Home: Elm St Norwich VT 05055 Office: PO Box 981 Hanover NH 03755-0981

STARZYNSKI, CHRISTINE JOY, secondary educator; b. Chgo. d. Stanley J. and Lottie (Wnek) Dudek; children: Karolyn, Katherine, Jeanne. BA, Northeastern U.; MA in Teaching, Webster U. Tchr. Des Plaines (Ill.) Dist. 62 Schs.; tchr. Spanish, Dist. 211 Schs., Hoffman Estates, Ill., dept. chmn.; with Spanish program Schaumburg (Ill.) Schaumburg Pub. Libr., 1984-92. Bd. dirs. Kohl Internat. Teaching Awards, 1992-94. Recipient Kohl Exemplary Teaching award, 1986; inducted into Adminstr's. Acad.; named Vol. of Yr. Schaumburg Twp., 1996. Mem. Am. Assn. Tchrs. Spanish and Portuguese (conv. presenter), Am. Coun. Tchrs. Fgn. Langs., Ill. Coun. Tchrs. Fgn. Langs. Avocation: travel. Home: 319 Mendon Ln Schaumburg IL 60193-1037 Office: Hoffman Estates High Sch 1100 W Higgins Rd Hoffman Estates IL 60195-3050

STASTNEY, AGNES FLORENCE, principal; b. Halliday, N.D., Aug. 1, 1935; d. Carl J. and Christina (Hausauer) Entzel; m. Ronald Charles Stastney, Mar. 27, 1967; children: Shadron, Hoyt. BS, Dickinson State U., 1965; MS, U. Mary, 1988. Cert. elem. tchr. and adminstr., N.D. Tchr. Hope & Big Flat Dists., Halliday, N.D., 1953-58, Killdeer (N.D.) Sch. Dist., 1958-59, Halliday (N.D.) Sch. Dist., 1959-63, Bismark (N.D.) Pub. schs., 1963-90, asst. prin., 1987-90, prin., 1990—. Chairperson North Ctrl. Assn. Self-Study, Bismarck, 1991-92. Mem. PTO, N.D. Elem. Prins. Assn., N.D. Coun. Sch. Adminstrs., N.D. South Ctrl. Reading Assn., Zonta, Delta Kappa Gamma (v.p. 1964, chair rsch. 1988, sec. 1991). Lutheran. Avocations: reading, camping. Office: Pioneer Elem Sch 1400 Braman Ave Bismarck ND 58501-2746

STATEN, DONNA KAY, elementary school educator; b. Temple, Tex., Apr. 17, 1958; d. Paul James and Doris Mary (Kleypas) Hoelscher; 1 child, Ryan. BS in Edn., U. Mary Hardin-Baylor, Belton, Tex., 1980. Cert. tchr. in art, elem. edn., health, phys. edn., recreation, gifted and talented edn., Tex. Art tchr. Meridith Magnet Sch., Temple, 1980-84, 1991—2000; bank officer mktg. Tex. Am. Bank, Houston, 1985-88; pvt. practice art tchr., designer Houston, 1989; tchr. ESL Aldine Ind. Sch. Dist., Houston, 1990; art tchr. Kennedy-Powell Acad., Temple, 2000—. Exec. dir. Visual Arts Friends of the Cultural Activities Ctr., Temple, 1993-95, Temple Sister Cities Corp., Temple, 1994-97; chmn. fine arts team Meridith Campus, 1993-96; state rev. panelist Tex. Edn. Agy., 1997; curator Artsonia.com student art gallery, 2002–; dir. Binney & Smith Camp Crayola, 2003. Curator Internat. Children's Art Exhbn., 1996, 2003, 04, art exhibit From Russia with Love, 1992-95. Mem. Contemporaries, Temple, 1994—2001; treas. Oaks Homeowners Assn., Temple, 1994—95, sec. bd. dirs., 1997—99; mem. Temple Mayor's Panel; bd. sec. Keep Temple Beautiful, 1997—99; Tchr.'s Honor Scroll Internat. Project, 2001—02; pres. Assn. Tex. Profl. Educators; singer St. Luke's Ch. Choir, Temple, 1991—; mem. St. Luke's Women's Soc., 1993—. Recipient honorable mention in Christmas Decorating Contest Women's Day mag., 1989, cert. of recognition Crayola/Binney & Smith, 1993-94, 95-96, 97-2001, 03-04, Golden Apple Tchr. award Sta. KWTX-TV, 2002; Focus on Edn. grantee, Wal-Mart, 2001. Mem. ASCD, AAUW, Fine Arts Network, Internat. Soc. for Edn. Through Art, Nat. Art Edn. Assn., Tex. Classrm. Tchrs. Assn., Am. Craft Coun., Soc. Craft Designers, Tex. Computer Edn. Assn., Tex. Fine Arts Assn., Tex. Art Edn. Assn., Nat. Mus. of Women in the Arts, Cultural Activities Ctr., Temple Assn. for the Gifted, Electronic Media Interest Group, Tex. Alliance Edn. and the Arts., Friends of the Temple Libr., Tex. Assn. Gifted and Talented. Roman Catholic. Avocations: gardening, painting and drawing, singing. Office: Kennedy-Powell Acad 3707 W Nugent Ave Temple TX 76504 Address: 2420 Holly Ln Temple TX 76502-2669 E-mail: donna.staten@tisd.org.

STATMAN, JACKIE C. career consultant; b. Kingman, Kansas, June 15, 1936; d. Jack Carl and Dorothy E. (Kendall) Pulliam; children: David Alan, Susan Gail Piotrowski. BA, U. Kans., 1958. Reg. music therapist Topeka State Hosp., Kans., 1958-59; caseworker Child Welfare, Pensacola, Fla., 1960-61; devel. rsch. tester Children and Youth Project, Dallas, 1973-74; middle sch. counselor Hockaday Sch., Dallas, 1981-84; career cons. Career Design Assocs., Inc., Garland, Tex., 1984-86; owner Career Focus Assocs., Plano, Tex., 1987-98. Pres. Assn. Women Entrepreneurs of Dallas, Inc., 1991-93; mem. career edn. adv. com. Plano Ind. Sch. Dist., 1993-97. Author: (newspaper column) "Career Forum", 1991-92. Mem. Cmty. Svcs. Commn., City of Plano, 1993-97, chmn., 1997; mem. Leadership Plano Alumnae Assn., 1990—; bd. dirs. Mental Health Assn. in Tex., 1989-93; founding pres. Mental Health Assn. Collin County, 1988-90; bd. dirs. Dallas/Ft. Worth chpt. Nat. Assn. Women Bus. Owners 1992-93. Recipient Child Advocacy award Mental Health Assn. of Greater Dallas, 1985, Golden Rule award JC Penney Comp., Inc., 1986, Humanitarian Vo. of the Yr. award Vol. Ctr. Collin County, 1990. Avocation: community and civic volunteering.

STATON, SHELLEY VICTORIA, secondary education educator; b. Perth Amboy, N.J., Nov. 16, 1957; d. Henry Thomas and Elaine (Edwards) S. BA, Spelman Coll., 1979; MA, Calif. State U., Dominquez Hills, 1993. Tchr. Sylmar (Calif.) High Sch., 1986-87, Fremont Adult Sch., L.A., 1986-88, Peary Middle Sch., Gardena, Calif., 1988—. Coach Peary Middle Sch. Speech Team, Gardena, 1990—. Recipient Shiny Apple award L.A. Unified Sch. Dist., 1991. Mem. ASCD. Home: 5275 Fox Path Stone Mountain GA 30088 Office: Peary Magnet Sch 1415 W Gardena Blvd Gardena CA 90247-4712

STAUB, AUGUST WILLIAM, drama educator, theatrical producer, director; b. New Orleans, Oct. 9, 1931; s. August Harry and Laurel (Elfer) S.; m. Patricia Gebhardt, Nov. 22, 1952; 1 child, Laurel Melicent. BA, La. State U., 1952, MA, 1956, PhD, 1960. Instr., tech. dir. La. State U., 1955; instr. Ea. Mich. U., 1956-58; assoc. dir. Dunes Summer Theatre, Michigan City, Ind., summers 1957-60; asst. prof., assoc. dir. univ. theatre U. Fla., 1960-64; assoc. prof. U. New Orleans, 1964-66, prof., chmn. dept. drama and communications, 1966-76; prof., head drama dept. U. Ga., 1976-95, prof. emeritus, 1996—. Exec. producer Jekyll Island Mus. Comedy Festival, 1984-88, Highlands (N.C.) Playhouse, 1989-2000, Ga. Repertory Theatre, 1991-95; staff dir. Theatre in the Square, Marietta, Ga., 1996—; exec. sec. Theatres of La.; v.p. New Orleans Internat. Jazz Festival, 1967-69; pres. S.W. Theatre Conf., 1973-74. Author: Lysistrata, 1968, The Social Climber, 1969, A Small Bare Space, 1970, Introduction to Theatrical Arts, 1971, Creating Theatre, 1973, Varieties of Theatrical Arts, 1980, 83, 94; gen. editor: Artists and Ideas in the Theatre (Peter Lang), 1989—; assoc. editor Speech Tchr., 1966-68, So. Speech Comm. Jour., 1974-77, Quar. Jour. Speech, 1977-79. Bd. dirs. Friends Ga. Mus., Athens, Ga. Symphony, Coun. Arts for Children, New Orleans, New Orleans Ctr. Creative Arts, Athens Arts. Commn., Ga. Alliance Arts Edn. Lt. AUS, 1952-54. Recipient Creativity in Rsch. medallion U. Ga., 1987, Disting. Svc. award S.W. Theater Conf., 1985; La. State U. Found. Disting. Faculty fellow, 1970-71. Fellow Coll. of Fellows of Am. Theatre (bd. dirs. 1999-2001), Coll. of Fellows of the S.W. Theatre Assn.; mem. Am. Theatre Assn. (pres. 1985-86, bd. dirs.), Univ. and Coll. Theatre Assn. (pres. 1974-75), Nat. Assn. Schs. Theatre (pres. 1981-83), Univ. Resident Theatre Assn. (bd. dirs. 1976-79), Inst. European Theatre, Nat. Theatre Conf., Am. Soc. Theatre Rsch., Internat. Fedn. Theatre Rsch. Home: 190 Ravenwood Ct Athens GA 30605-3340 E-mail: gusstaub@earthlink.net.

STAUB, MARTHA LOU, retired elementary education educator; b. Cumberland, Md., May 29, 1939; d. Walter W. and Velma Grace (Darr) McCoy; m. Paul L. Staub, Apr. 11, 1964; children: Desiree, Paul, Sharon, Lucy, Charles. BS, Frostburg State U., 1961; postgrad., We. Md. State U., 1983; MS, Towson State Coll., 1983; student, Loyola Coll., 1988. Cert. tchr. 1st-mid. sch., Md. Elem. tchr. Cumberland Valley, Bedord, Pa., Garrett County, Oakland, Md., Carroll County, Westminster, Balt. County Bd. Edn., Towson, Md. With peer coaching, 1990-93, master learning, 1989-91. Recipient Excellence in Edn. award Baltimore County, 1990-91; honored by Randallstown Elem. PTA, 1989; donation made in her honor Christa McAuliffe scholarship fund, 1990. Mem. ASCD, NEA (Excellence in Teaching honor 1992), Md. State Tchrs. Assn., Tchr.'s Assn. of Balt. County Orgn., PTA, Md. Coun. Tchrs. Math., Women Educators of Balt. County Orgn., Delta Kappa Gamma. Home: 710 Melendez Way Lady Lake FL 32159-9265

STAUBER, DONNA BETH, education educator; b. Belton, Tex., Dec. 18, 1955; d. William R. and Pansy Joan (Bell) Parmer; 1 child, Chassati Thiele; m. George Russell Stauber, July 25, 1987; children: Blake, Michal. BS, Tex. A & M U., 1978; MS in Edn., Baylor U., 1983; PhD in Health Edn., Tex. Woman's U., 1993. Cert. health edn. specialist. Tchr., coach Sand Springs (Okla.) Ind. Sch. Dist., 1978-80, McGregor (Tex.) Ind. Sch. Dist., 1980-82, Leander (Tex.) Ind. Sch. Dist., 1983-87; grad. asst. Baylor U., Waco, Tex., 1982-83, lectr., 1987-94, 1994; product devel. coord. WRS Group, Inc., Waco. Lectr. at various confs. on self-esteem, body image, and emotional healing to educators. Vol. Multiple Sclerosis Soc. Mem. AAHPERD, Tex. Assn. Health, Phys. Edn., Recreation and Dance, Soc. Pub. Health Edn., Nat. Wellness Assn., Assn. for Worksite Health Promotion, Am. Coll. Health Assn., Internat. Coun. Health, Phys. Edn., Recreation, Sport and Dance (health edn. commn. 1995). Home: 9601 Bryce Dr Waco TX 76712-3218

STAUBER, KARL NEILL, foundation administrator; b. Statesville, N.C., Jan. 4, 1951; s. Van G. and Dorthea (Mills) S.; m. Hollis Scott, Aug. 14, 1971. BA, U. N.C., 1973; Program for Mgmt. Devel., Harvard U., 1983; PhD, Union Inst., Cin., 1993. Asst. dir. Reynolds Babcock Found., Winston-Salem, N.C., 1974-79; exec. dir. Needmor Found., Toledo, 1979-83; pres. Econ. Devel., Inc., Boulder, Colo., 1983-86; v.p. program N.W. Area Found., St. Paul, 1986-93; dep. under sec. rsch., edn., and econ. USDA, Washington, 1993-94, under sec. rsch., edn., and econ., 1994—; CEO and pres. N.W. Area Found., St. Paul, 1996—. Contbr. editorials to newspapers. Adv. bd. mem. Found. Mid South, Jackson, Miss., 1988-93, Mpls. Found., 1991-93. Avocations: furniture building, tractor restoration. Office: Northwest Area Found 60 Plato Blvd East Ste 400 Saint Paul MN 55107*

STAUBER, MARILYN JEAN, retired secondary and elementary school; b. Duluth, Minn., Feb. 5, 1938; d. Harold Milton and Dorothy Florence (Thompson) Froehlich; children: Kenneth D. and James H. Atkinson; m. Lawrence B. Stauber Sr., Jan. 11, 1991. BS in Edn., U. Minn., Duluth, 1969, MEd in Math., 1977. Cert. elem. and secondary reading tchr., remedial reading specialist, devel. reading tchr., reading cons. Sec. div. vocat. rehab. State Minn., Duluth, 1956-59; sec. Travelers Ins. Co., Duluth, 1962-66; lead tchr. Title 1 reading and math. Proctor, Minn., 1969-98; ret. Mem. choirs and Choral Soc. John Duss Music, chairperson Outreach, Forbes Meth. Ch., proctor. Mem. NEA, VFW, Internat. Reading Assn., Nat. Reading Assn., Minn. Arrowhead Reading Coun., Elem. Coun. (pres. 1983-84, 86-87), Proctor Fedn. Tchrs. (recert. com. 1980—, treas. 1981-86), Proctor Edn. Assn. (chairperson recert. com.), Am. Legion, Euclid Ea. Star, Phi Delta Kappa. Home: 6713 Grand Lake Rd Saginaw MN 55779-9782

STAUFF, JON WILLIAM, history educator; b. Toms River, N.J., Sept. 5, 1965; s. John Henry and Regina (Fox) S. AA, Ocean County Coll., 1984; AB, Coll. William and Mary, 1986; MA, SUNY, Buffalo, 1990, PhD, 1994. Grad. teaching asst. SUNY, Buffalo, 1986-89, 90, lectr. history Millard Fillmore Coll., 1991; rsch. asst. German Bundestag Christian Dem. Union, Bonn, Germany, 1991; instr. history Ocean C.C., Toms River, 1992-93; asst. prof. history St. Ambrose U., Davenport, Iowa, 1993-2000, dir. Cath. Studies, 1997—, assoc. prof. history, 2000—. Tchg., rsch. fellow SUNY, 1986-89, Milton Plesur Dissertation fellow SUNY, 1990-91; Dissertation grantee German Acad. Exch. Svc., 1989-90; participant Fulbright German Studies Summer Seminar, 1995. Mem. Am. Hist. Assn., German Studies Assn., Phi Beta Kappa, Phi Alpha Theta (Lynn Turner prize 1986). Avocations: sports, stamp collecting. Address: St Ambrose Univ History Dept 518 W Locust St Davenport IA 52803-2829

STAUFF, WILLIAM JAMES, college official; b. Providence, Mar. 2, 1949; s. William A. and Charlotte A. (Thorpe) S.; m. Bertha Nichols, Jan. 22, 1972; children: William J., Heidi A., Anneliese C. BSBA, Northea. U., Boston, 1977; MBA, Suffolk U., 1983; ABS, Moody Bible Inst. Chgo., 1992-97; ThD, Bethany Theol. Sem., Dothan, Ala., 1997. Process writer, indsl. engr. Rockwell Internat., Hopedale, Mass., 1972-77; bus. mgr., acct. Luth. Svc. Assn. New Eng., Framingham, Mass., 1977-80; mgr. acctg. and fin. Office Info. Tech. Harvard U., Cambridge, Mass., 1980-89; dir. bus. ops. facilities mgmt. U. Va., Charlottesville, Va., 1989-97; mgr. commitment sys. Billy Graham Evangelistic Assn., Mpls., 1997-2000; v.p. Erskine Coll., Due West, S.C., 2000—. Pub. acctg. auditor Charles Murphy/Paul Haggerty, CPAs, Framingham, 1977-80. Mem. Assn. Higher Edn. Facilities Officers. Avocations: gardening, music, teaching. E-mail: stauff@erskine.edu.

STAUFFER, ELIZABETH CLARE, elementary school educator, music choral director, consultant; b. Waterbury, Conn., May 15, 1948; d. Harold Henry and Minerva May (Mattoon) S. B.A., Fairleigh Dickinson U., 1970; M.S., So. Conn. State U., 1973, 6th year diploma, 1978; postgrad., Christ Ch. Coll., Oxford (Eng.) U., 1994, 95—. Cert. tchr. elem. edn., music edn., intermediate adminstrn. and supervision, Conn., Sexual Assault Crisis Counselor, Conn. Tchr. music pub. schs., Clyde, N.Y., 1970-71; tchr. Children's Corner, Inc., Stamford, Conn., 1973-79; tchr. pub. schs., Naugatuck Conn., 1972— ; cons., adviser Children's Corner, Inc., Stamford, 1979-84; dir. Sweet Adelines, Inc., Waterbury, 1981— . Contbr. articles to profl. jours.; arranger songs for barbershop harmony, 1983. Mem. Republican Town Com., Seneca Falls, N.Y., 1971; edn. chmn. Town Bicentennial Com., Naugatuck, 1975-76; v.p. PTO, Naugatuck 1975-77. Mem. Naugatuck Tchrs. League (bldg. rep. 1972, 75, 78, 85, 99-03), Negotiations Com., 1985,87, 90, 92, 95, 98, 2001, 02, Conn. Edn. Assn. (rep. assembly), NEA, Adminstrn. and Supervision Assn., AAUW. Republican. Episcopalian. Avocations: tennis; sailing. Home: 50 Hickory Ln Naugatuck CT 06770-1725 Office: Naugatuck Bd Edn Naugatuck CT 06770

STAUFFER, LOUISE LEE, retired secondary school educator; b. Altoona, Pa., Mar. 31, 1915; d. William Thomas and Mary Hall (Schroyer) Lee; m. John Nissley Stauffer, Aug. 20, 1938 (dec. Sept. 1983); children: Thomas Michael, Nancy Kay, John Lee, Donald David. BA, Juniata Coll., 1936; postgrad., Columbia U., U. Pa., Pa. State U. Tchr. Latin, Middletown (Pa.) High Sch., 1936-41; tchr. English and Latin, Roosevelt Jr. High Sch., Springfield, Ohio, 1949-57; tchr. French, North High Sch., Springfield, 1957-63; ret., 1963. Mem. Moorings Property Owners Assn., Naples, Fla., 1983—; Emmanuel Luth. Ch., Naples, 1980—; bd. dirs., editor newsletter, membership chmn., rec. sec., corr. sec., parliamentarian Naples Cmty. Hosp. Aux., 1985-92; chmn. Patient Mail, 1992—. Mem. AAUW, Am. Assn. Ret. Persons, Women's League (Juniata Coll.), Founders Club (Juniata Coll.), Moorings Country Club. Lutheran. Avocations: golf, singing, reading, walking, volunteering.

STAUFFER, THOMAS MICHAEL, former university president; b. Harrisburg, Pa., Dec. 5, 1941; s. John Nisley and Louise Lee Stauffer; m. Marion Walker, Aug. 26, 1966 (div. 1989); children: Amity Juliet, Courtney Amanda, Winston Thomas; m. Deborah Whisnand, May 16, 1993 (div. 2003); 1 stepchild, Elizabeth Stinson. Student, Juniata Coll., 1959-61; BA cum laude, Wittenberg U., Ohio, 1963; Cert. in E. European Politics, Freie U. Berlin, 1964; MA, PhD, U. Denver, 1973; Doctorate (hon.), Jackson State U., 2002. Asst. dean coll., assoc. prof. polit. sci. Keene State Coll., 1968-72; dir. fellows in acad. adminstrn., office leadership devel. Am. Coun. on Edn., 1972-78, v.p., divsn. external rels., 1978-82; pres., prof. pub. policy U. Houston, 1982—91; pres., prof. pub. policy and internat. rels. Golden Gate U., 1992—99; CEO Young Pres. Orgn. Internat., 1999—2001; exec. dir. Lincoln Ctr. for Ethics in Internat. Mgmt., prof. applied global bus. Thunderbird--The Am. Grad. Sch. of Internat. Mgmt., 2003—; CEO Upper Mgmt. Internat., 1985—, pres., 1985—. Exec. sec. Fedn. of Assn. of the Acad. Health Care Professions, 1975-80; chmn. task force on the future of Am. Coun. on Edn., 1978; exec. dir. Bus.-Higher Edn. Forum, 1978-81, Nat. Commn. on Higher Edn. Issues, 1980-81; spl. asst. to adminstr. NASA, 1991-92; cons. NSF, Dept. State, Coun. for Internat. Exch. Scholars, Japan External Trade Orgn.; mem. dels. on higher edn. and econ. devel. to People's Republic of China, S.E. Asia, Japan, Rwanda, Sri Lanka, United Arab Emirates and other nations, 1972—. Exec. editor Ednl. Record and Higher Edn. and Nat. Affairs, 1978-82; author books and monographs; contbr. articles to profl. jours. and newspapers. Chmn. com. advanced tech. Tex. Econ. Devel., 1984, Houston Com. on Econ. Diversification Planning, 1984, Houston World Trade Ctr. Task Force, 1985, East Tex. 2000 Com. on Econ. Devel., S.E. Tex. Higher Edn. Coun., 1989, Clear Lake Area Econ. Devel. Found.; v.p. Inter-Am., U. Coun. for Econ. and Social Devel., Houston World Trade Assn.; co-chair Tex. Sci. and Tech. Coun., 1986; pres. St. John Hosp.; chair nat. bd. Challenger Ctr. for Space Sci. Edn., 1987-89, Ctr. for Advanced Space Studies, 1990-94; bd. dirs. Houston Hosp. Coun. Found., Tex. Coun. on Econ. Edn., Tex. Senate Space Industry Tech. Commn., Tex. Innovation Info. Network Sys., San Francisco C. of C.; vice-chair San Francisco World Trade Assn.; chair San Francisco Consortium on Higher Edn.; mem. steering com. Houston Econ. Devel. Coun., blue ribbon com. City Coll., Bay Area Coun., Silicon Valley Mfrs. Group; chair San Francisco Mayor's Blue Ribbon Com. on Econ. Devel. Recipient Disting. Alumni award Grad. Sch. Internat. Studies U. Denver, 1989, Tex. Senate Resolution of Commendation, 1991, Challenger Ctr. Nat. award, 1990, ACE Fellow Anniversary award, 1990, Leadership H.S. Do the Right Thing award, 1998; Am. Coun. on Edn. fellow in acad. adminstrn., 1971, Ford Found. and Social Sci. Found. fellow, 1963-68, sr. fellow Am. Leadership Forum. Mem. AAAS, Internat. Studies Assn. (co-chmn. ann. meeting 1978), Policy Studies Orgn., Bay Area Internat. Forum, Internat. Assn. Univ. Pres., Phoenix Com. on Fgn. Rels., Commonwealth Club, San Francisco World Trade Club. Home: 1806 Green St San Francisco CA 94123-4922 Office: 15249 N 59th Ave Glendale AZ 85306

STAVANS, ILAN, Latin American studies educator, writer; b. Mexico City, Mex., Apr. 7, 1961; came to U.S., 1985; s. Abraham Stavchansky and Ofelia Slomianski; m. Alison Sparks, June 25, 1988; children: Joshua, Isaiah. BA, U. Autónoma Met., 1984; MA, Jewish Theol. Sem., 1987, Columbia U., 1988, Mphil, 1989, PhD, 1990. Lewis Sebring prof. Latin Am. and Latino culture Amherst (Mass.) Coll., 1993—. Rsch. scholar Inst. Latin Am. Studies, U. London, 1998-99. Author: The Hispanic Condition, 1995, The One-Handed Pianist and Other Stories, 1996, Art and Anger, 1996, The Riddle of Cantinflas, 1998, The Oxford Book of Jewish Stories, 1998, Mutual Impressions: Writers of the Americas Reading One Another, 1999, Latino U.S.A.: A Cartoon History, 2000, The Essential Ilan Stavans, 2000, On Borrowed Words: A Memoir of Language, 2002, The Poetry of Pablo Neruda, 2003, Spanglish: The Making of a New American Language, 2003, Moterial, 2003others; editor-in-chief Hopscotch: A Cultural Review; series editor Jewish-Latin America and Latino Voices. Recipient Latino Lit. prize, 1992, Bernard M. Baruch Excellence award, 1993; named to Quality Paperback Book Month, 1994, 99; Constantiner fellow 1984-86; Acad. fellow Jewish Theol. Sem., 1984-86; Transl. fellow N.Y. State Coun. Arts, 1989; Guggenheim fellow 1998; NEH fellow, 2003. Office: Amherst Coll Amherst MA 01002

STAVROPOULOS, YVETTE, editor, writer, educator; b. West Chester, Pa., June 17, 1964; d. Vasilios and Era (Havelos) S. BA, West Chester (Pa.) U., 1986, MA, 1991. Corr. The Mercury, Pottstown, Pa., 1986-87, staff reporter, 1987-88; lectr. in English Pa. State U., Media, 1992—; adj. instr. English Widener U., Chester, Pa., 1992—. Textbook editor, bus. writing tutor Ins. Inst. Am., Malvern, Pa., 1994—. Recipient Phila. Pres. Assn. award, 1989. Mem. Hellenic U. Club of Phila. Greek Orthodox.

STAY, BYRON LEE, rhetoric educator, college administrator; b. Tacoma, Nov. 20, 1947; s. Werner Frederick and Georgia Elvira (Linstrom) S.; m. Claire Marie Moblard, Jan. 1, 2000. BA, Seattle Pacific Coll., 1970; MA, U. Del., 1975, PhD, 1980. Nstr. U. Md., College Park, 1978-80; asst. prof. rhetoric Mount St. Mary's Coll., Emmitsburg, Md., 1980-85, assoc. prof. rhetoric, 1985-95, prof. rhetoric, 1996—, assoc. dean, 1995—2000. Author: A Guide to Argumentative Writing, 1995; editor: Writing Center Perspectives, 1995, Censorship, 1996, Mass Media, 1999, Writing Ctr. Rsch., 2002; mem. edit. bd. Jour. of Tchg. Writing, 1993—, Writing Ctr. Jour., 1993—. Dir. Mkt. St. Mile, Frederick (Md.) Steeplechaser, 1983-99. With U.S. Army, 1970-72, Ft. Sill, Okla. Mem. Nat. Writing Ctrs. ASsn. (pres. 1995, gen. editor NWCA Press 1995—, Outstanding Svc. award 1997). Avocations: running, trumpet playing, chess. Home: 6744 Woodridge Rd New Market MD 21774 Office: Mount St Mary's Coll Rhetoric Dept Emmitsburg MD 21727

STAYTON, WILLIAM RALPH, psychologist, educator; b. Kelso, Wash., Dec. 25, 1933; s. Ralph Willard and Marguerite (Hunter) S.; m. Kathleen Boucher, Sept. 4, 1954; children: Mark, John, Cheryl, Paul. BA, U. Redlands, 1956; MDiv, Andover Newton Theol. Sem., 1960; ThD, Boston U., 1967; PhD, Inst. Advanced Study of Human Sexuality, 2002. Ordained to ministry Am. Bapt. Ch., 1959. Assoc. min. 1st Bapt. Ch. in Newton, Mass., 1956-61; min. 1st Bapt. Ch., Gloucester, Mass., 1961-68; chaplain New Eng. Bapt. Hosp., Boston, 1968-71; asst. prof. Sch. Medicine U. Pa., Phila., 1971-78, adj. assoc. prof. Grad. Sch. Edn., lectr., mem. faculty Grad. Sch. Edn., 1982—90; asst. prof. Jefferson Med. Coll./Thomas Jefferson U., 1978-83; marriage and family therapist Wm R. Stayton & Assocs., Ltd., P.C., Phila., 1978—. Mem. faculty La Salle U., Phila., 1983-2002; prof. and coord., human sexuality program Widener U., Chester, Pa., 1999—. Editor spl. issue Topics in Clin. Nursing, 1980; contbr. articles to profl. jours., chpts. to books. Pres. Cmty. Svcs. for Human Growth, Paoli, Pa., 1989-91, bd. dirs., 1981-97. Named Man of Yr., B'nai B'rith, Gloucester, Mass., 1968; recipient Outstanding Svc. award Community Svcs. for Human Growth, 1990, Richard J. Cross award U. Medicine and Dentistry N.J., 1997, Dean's award Sch Human Svc. Professions Widener U., 2002. Mem. APA, Am. Assn. Marriage and Family Therapists, Am. Assn. Sex Educators, Counselors and Therapists (bd. dirs. 1982-86, 88-90, chmn. dist. VI 1982-86, pres. 1996-98, Outstanding Svc. award 1978-87, 87, Disting. Svc.

award 2000), Sex Info. and Edn. Coun. U.S. (pres. 1985-87, sec. 1990-92), Soc. for Sci. Study Sex (chmn. ann. meeting 1983), Pa. Assn. Marriage and Family Therapists (continuing edn. com. 1985-90), Planned Parenthood Southeastern Pa. (bd. dir. 1999-, first v.p. 2001-), Phi Kappa Phi. Democrat. Home: 81 Andover Ct Wayne PA 19087-5616 Office: 987 Old Eagle School Rd Ste 719 Wayne PA 19087-1708 E-mail: wmstayton@cs.com.

STEADMAN, LYDIA DUFF, symphony violinist, retired elementary school educator; b. Hollywood, Calif., Dec. 31, 1934; d. Lewis Marshall and Margaret Seville (Williams) Duff; m. John Gilford Steadman, Apr. 14, 1961 (dec.). Student, Pepperdine U., 1952-55; BA in Music Edn., U. So. Calif., 1957. Cert. spl. secondary music, edn. tchr., Calif. Instrumental music tchr. Lancaster (Calif.) Sch. Dist., 1957-62, Simi Sch. Dist., Simi Valley, Calif., 1962-70, elem. tchr., 1970—2001. Tchr. Polynesian culture, dances, games, 1970—; hist. play wright for elem. grades, organizer elem. sch. dance festivals; dir. All Dist. Orch., Lancaster, Simi Valley Schs., 1957-70; compile Japanese Culture Study Unit for elem. grades Ventura County. 1st violinist San Fernando Valley Symphony, Sherman Oaks, Calif., 1962-75, Valley Symphony, Van Nuys, 2001--, Simi Valley's Santa Susana Symphony, Conejo Valley Symphony, Thousand Oaks, 1975-81, tour concert mistress, 1980; 2d violinist Ventura County Symphony, Santa Susana Symphony, 1981-95, L.A. Drs. Symphony, 2001-; prin. 2d violinist Calif. Luth. U. Orch. Pres. San Fernando Cmty. Concerts, Van Nuys, Calif., 1982-94; free lancing with pit orch. Cabrillo Music Theatre, Conejo Players Theater, Moorpark Coll. Theatre, Newbury Park H.S. Theater Orch., 2001—; 2d violinist L.A. Doctors Symphony, 2001—, Young Artists Ensemble, Civic Arts Plaza, Camarillo H.S. Theatre Orch., 2003, Loyola Marymount Orch., 2003; organizer ann. sch. Jump Rope-a-Thon for Am. Heart Assn., Nat. Geog. Geography Bee; bd. dirs. East Ventura County Cmty. Concert Assn. Mem. AAUW, NAFE, L.A. World Affairs Coun., Bus. and Profl. Women of Conejo Valley (pres. Golden Triangle chpg. 1988-90, 95-96, issues and mgmt. chair 1990, ways and means chair Coast chpt. 1990, editor Golden Triangle newsletter 1988-90, treas. 1992-93, sec. 1993-94, v.p. 1994—), Pacific Asia Mus., Armand Hammer Mus., Sigma Xi. Republican. Lutheran. Avocations: hula dancing, walking, collecting world coins, world traveling, violin. Home: 32016 Allenby Ct Westlake Village CA 91361-4001

STEARNS, PETER NATHANIEL, history educator; b. London, Mar. 3, 1936; (parents Am. citizens); s. Raymond P. and Elizabeth (Scott) S.; m. Nancy Driessel (div. 1976); children: Duncan, Deborah; m. Carol Zisowitz, Mar. 26, 1978 (div. 1999); children: Clio Elizabeth, Cordelia Raymond; m. Margaret Brindle. AB, Harvard U., 1957, MA, 1959, PhD, 1963. From instr. to assoc. prof. U. Chgo., 1962-65; prof., chmn. history dept. Rutgers U., New Brunswick, N.J., 1965-74; Heinz prof. history Carnegie Mellon U., Pitts., 1974—. chmn. dept. history, 1986-92, dean Coll. Humanities and Social Scis., 1992-2000; provost George Mason U., 2000—. Co-dir. Pitts. Ctr. for Social History, 1986-92; chmn. acad. adv. coun. N.Y.C. Coll. Bd., 1982-85; chmn. Pacesetter World History commn., Coll. Bd., 1992-95, Coll. Bd. Advanced Placement World History, 1997—; mem. adv. bd. Liberal Education, 2001—. Author: The Working Classes and the Rise of Socialism, 1971, European Society in Upheaval: Social History since 1800, 1967; : European Society in Upheaval: Social History since 1800, 1975, (3d ed.), 1991, Priest and Revolutionary: Lamennais and the Dilemma of French Catholicism, 1967, (Polish tranl.), 1967, Modern Europe, 1789—1914, 1969, Revolutionary Syndicalism and French Labor: a cause without rebels, 1971, (with Harvey Mitchell) Workers and Protest: The European Labor Movement, The Working Classes and the Rise of Socialism, 1890—1914, The European Experience since 1815, 1972, 1848: The Revolutionary Tide in Europe, 1974, (publ. in England) The Revolutions of 1848, Lives of Labor: Work in Maturing Industrial Society, 1975, (German tranl.), 1975, Old Age in European Society, 1977, Face of Europe, 1977, Paths to Authority: Toward the Formation of Middle Class Consciousness, 1978, Be A Man! Males in Modern Society, 1979, (rev. ed.), 1990, (with Linda Rosenzweig) Themes in Modern Social History, 1985, (with Carol Stearns) Anger: The Struggle for Emotional Control in America's History, 1986, World History: Patterns of Change and Continuity, 1987, (rev.ed.), 1994, (3d ed.), 1998, (4th ed.), 2001, (with others) Makers of Modern Europe, 1987, (rev. ed.), 1994, (with others) Documents in World History, Vol.1: The Great Tradition and Vol. 2: The Modern Centuries, 1987, Life and Society in the West, The Modern Centuries, 1987, Expanding the Past: A Reader in Social History, 1988, Life and Society in the West, The Modern Centuries, 1988, (with C. Stearns) Emotion and Social Change, Toward a New Psychohistory, 1988, (with Andrew Barnes) Social History and Issues in Consciousness and Cognition, 1989, Jealousy: Evolution of an Emotion in American History, 1989, Interpreting the Industrial Revolution, 1991, (with Michael Adas and Stuart Schwartz) World Civilizations, 1991, (rev. ed.), 1995, 2003, Meaning Over Memory: Issues in Humanities Education, 1993, The Industrial Revolution in World History, 1993, (rev. ed.), 1998, (Swedish tranl.), American Cool: Developing a 20th Century Emotional Style, 1994, Turbulent Passage: A Global History of the 20th Century, 1994, rev. edit., 2003, (with Ron Harre) Discursive Psychology in Practice, 1995, Millenium III, Century XXI, 1996, (rev. ed.), 1998, (with Hinshaw) Encyclopedia of the Industrial Revolution, 1996, (rev. ed.), 1998, Fat History: Bodies and Beauty in the West, 1997, Fat History: Bodies and Beauty in the West, rev. edit., 2002, Schools and Students in Industrial Society: Japan and the West, 1997, History in Documents, 1998, (with Lewis) Emotional History of the U.S., 1998, World History in Documents: and Comparative Analysis in World History, 1998, Battleground of Desire: The Struggle for Self-Control in Modern America, 1999, Experiencing World History, 2000, Teaching, Learning and Knowing History, 2000, Gender in World History, 2000, Consumerism in World History, 2001, (with Brindle) Facing Up to Management Faddism, 2001, Cultures in Motion, 2001; editor: Century for Debate, 1969, The Impact of the Industrial Revolution, 1972, (with Walkowitz) Workers in the Industrial Revolution, 1974, The Other Side of Western Civilization, 1979, (rev. ed.), 1984, (4th ed.), 1991, The Rise of Modern Women, 1977, (with Michael Weber) The Spencers of Amberson Avenue: A Turn-of-the-Century Memoir, 1983, (with Van Tassel) Old Age in a Bureaucratic Society, 1986, Encyclopedia World History, 2000, Encyclopedia of European Social History, 1999; contbg. editor: History of Emotions series NYU Press; author: Anxious Parents: A History of Modern American Childrearing, 2003, Western Civilization in World History, 2003; contbr. over 150 articles to prof. and popular jours. Guggenheim Found. fellow, 1973-74; NEH grantee, 1981-84, 86, 90, Rockefeller Found. grantee, 1982-83. Fellow Internat. Soc. for Rsch. on Emotion; mem. Am. Hist. Soc., World History Assn., Am. Hist. Assn. (v.p., head teaching div. 1995-98), Nat. Bd. Profl. Tchg. Standards. Democrat. Avocations: racquet sports, travel. Home: 7750 Wyckland Ct Clifton VA 20124 Office: George Mason Univ Fairfax VA 22030

STEARNS, WANDA JUNE, state and federal programs supervisor; b. Clarksburg, W.Va., Mar. 14, 1948; d. Walter David and Mary Eleanor (Ashburn) Zeitler; m. Calvin Edward Stearns, July 27, 1973; 1 child, Steven Walter. BS, Eastern Nazarene Coll., Quincy, Mass., 1972; MS, LaVerne U., 1976. Cert. elem. tchr., supr., adminstr. Tchr. Mansfield (Ohio) City Schs., 1970-82; dir. of presch. Sunshine Presch. and Day Care, Mansfield, 1985—93; dir. curriculum and instrn. Whitehall (Ohio) City Schs., 1993—97; supr. state and fed. programs Columbus City Schs., Ohio, 1997—. Bd. dirs. Sister Cities, Mansfield, 1988-93. Mem. LWV, ASCD, Internat. Reading Assn., Nat. Coun. Tchrs. English, Phi Delta Kappa. Avocations: reading, cooking, travel. Home: 146 Macenroe Dr Blacklick OH 43004-9344 Office: Shepard Ctr 873 Walcutt Ave Columbus OH 43219

STEBBINS, VRINA GRIMES, retired elementary school educator, counselor; b. Columbus, Ohio, Aug. 24, 1939; d. Marion Edward and Vrina Elizabeth (Davis) Grimes; m. Gary Frank Stebbins, Dec. 23, 1959; 1 child, Gregory Gary. Student, Ohio U., 1957-59; BS in Edn., Miami U., Oxford, Ohio, 1965; MS in Edn., St. Francis Coll., 1971; Counseling Endorsement, Ind.-Purdue U., Ft. Wayne, 1988. Cert. elem. classroom educator K-6, sch. counselor, social worker, Ind. 1st grade tchr. Greenville (Ohio) Pub. Schs., 1963-68; elem. educator East Allen County Schs., New Haven, Ind., 1969-84, elem. sch. counselor, 1984-98; ret., 1998. Presenter at Ind. profl. orgns., 1985-92, 1st Presbyn. Ch., Ft. Wayne, 1984—, Project 2000, Ft. Wayne, 1992—; participant Bus.-Edn. Exchange, Ft. Wayne C. of C., 1993. Mem. ACA, Ind. Counseling Assn. (com. mem. 1992-93, Ind. Elem. Counselor of Yr. 1991), East Allen Educators' Assn. (chair com. 1989-98, East Allen County Schs. Elem. Educator of Yr. 1989, 95), Arts United, Phi Delta Kappa, Delta Kappa Gamma (1st v.p. Ind. state 1993-95, Ind. state pres. 1995-97). Democrat. Presbyterian. Avocations: travel, collecting antiques and angels. Home: 5712 Sandra Lee Ave Fort Wayne IN 46819-1118 E-mail: vstebbinsg@aol.com.

STECKEL, RICHARD J. radiologist, academic administrator; b. Scranton, Pa., Apr. 17, 1936; s. Morris Leo and Lucille (Yellin) Steckel; m. Julie Raskin, June 16, 1960; children: Jan Marie, David Matthew. BS magna cum laude, Harvard U., 1957, MD cum laude, 1961. Diplomate Am. Bd. Radiology. Intern UCLA Hosp., 1961-62; resident in radiology Mass. Gen. Hosp., Boston, 1962-65; clin./rsch. assoc. Nat. Cancer Inst., 1965-67; faculty UCLA Med. Sch., 1967—, prof. radiol. scis. and radiation oncology, 1974—2000; chmn. dept. radiol. scis. UCLA Med. Ctr., 1994-2000, prof. emeritus, 2000—; pres. Assn. Am. Cancer Insts., 1981. Dir. Jonsson Comprehensive Cancer Ctr., 1974—94; mem. staff UCLA Med. Ctr., Cottage Hosp., Santa Barbara, Calif. Contbr. Fellow: Am. Coll. Radiology; mem.: Assn. Univ. Radiologists, Am. Roentgen Ray Soc., Radiol. Soc. N.Am. Office: 1126 Bel Air Dr Santa Barbara CA 93105-

STEDINGER, JERY RUSSELL, civil and environmental engineer, researcher; b. Oakland, Calif., June 22, 1951; s. Russell Phillip and Vivian Lavina (Nelson) S.; m. Robin Lee Gray, June 30, 1973; children: Matthew, Carolyn. BA, U. Calif., Berkeley, 1972; AM, Harvard U., 1974, PhD, 1977. Math. programmer Lawrence Livermore Lab., Livermore, Calif., 1973; rsch. asst., teaching fellow Engr. and Applied Physics, Harvard U., Cambridge, Mass., 1974-77; asst. prof. Civil and Environ. Engr., Cornell U., Ithaca, N.Y, 1977-83; hydrologist U.S. Geol. Survey, Reston, Va., 1983-84; assoc. prof. Civil and Environ. Engr., Cornell U., Ithaca, N.Y., 1989-93, prof., 1989—. Cons. Pacific Electric and Gas Co., San Francisco, 1989-98, U.S. Army Corps Engrs., 1999. Author: Water Resources Systems Planning and Analysis, 1981; contbr. articles to profl. jours. Scoutmaster Troop 2, Boy Scouts Am., Ithaca, N.Y., 1988-2003. Recipient Editor's Citation for Excellence in Reviewing award Am. Geophys. Union, 1983, 90, 93; named Presdl. Young Investigator, NSF, 1984-90, CEE Prof. of Yr., Chi Epsilon, 1979-80, 99-2000. Fellow Internat. Water Acad., Am. Geophys. Union; mem. ASCE (Huber Civil Engring. Rsch. prize 1989, Julian Hinds award 1997), Soc. for Risk Analysis. Office: Cornell U Sch Civil Environ Engring 213 Hollister Hall Ithaca NY 14853-3501

STEEL, DUNCAN GREGORY, physics educator; b. Cleve., Jan. 11, 1951; s. Robert John and Mildred (Graham) S.; children: Adam, Benjamin. BA, U. N.C., 1972; MS, U. Mich., 1973, 75, PhD, 1976. Physicist Exxon Rsch. and Engring., Linden, N.J., 1977-78, Hughes Rsch. Labs., Malibu, Calif., 1975-85; prof. U. Mich., Ann Arbor, 1985—; sr. rsch. scientist Inst. Gerontology Sch. Medicine, U. Mich., Ann Arbor, 1986—, sr. rsch. scientist biophys. rsch. divsn., 1992—, Peter S. Fuss prof. engring., 1999—, area chair optical scis., dir. optical scis. lab., 1989—. Topical editor Jour. Optical Soc., Washington, 1986-92. Contbr. articles to profl. jours. Guggenheim fellow, 1999. Fellow IEEE, Optical Soc. Am., Am. Phys. Soc. Achievements include development of first phase conjugate laser; first high resolution nonlinear laser spectroscopy of semiconductor heterostructures; research in of collision induced resonances in atoms; low noise (below the standard quantum limit) room temperature semiconductor lasers; of first demonstration of coherence optical control and wave function engineering in quantum dots; of first demonstration of wave function engineering; first deimonstration quantum entanglement in a single quantum dot; demonstration of in vitro tryptophan phosphorescence for studies of protein structure in solution; discovery of of structural annealing in proteins during protein folding. Office: U Mich Physics Dept 500 E University Ave Ann Arbor MI 48109-1120

STEELE, ANTONIO L. retired principal, educator; b. Charlotte Amalie, St. Thomas, V.I., Oct. 4, 1947; s. Oliver O. and Viola A. (Smith) Steele; m. Floria R.; children: Monifa N., Renael E., Renan O., Rissah M. BA, Coll of V.I., 1970; MA, NYU, Washington Sq., 1977; postgrad., U. Ill., Taff Inst. Elem. tchr. George Washington Sch., St. Thomas, 1970; tchr. Eulalie Rivera Sch., St. Croix, V.I., 1971-73, Alfredo Andrews Sch., St. Croix, 1973, tchr. environ. edn., 1974, asst. prin., 1975-80, Juanita Gardina Elem. Sch., St. Croix, 1980, Evelyn M. Williams Elem. Sch., St. Croix, 1981, prin., 1982-97, Claude O. Markoe Elem. Sch., 1998—2000. Leader and presenter workshops, task force leader; mem. V.I. Commn. on Edn. Active ch. and cmty. roles. Mem. LEAD (adv. bd.), Am. Fedn. Sch. Adminstrs., St. Croix Edn. Adminstrn. Assn. (pres. 1987-2000, adminstr. adult basic edn. 1989—), C.L.C. of V.I. (treas. 1996).

STEELE, BEVERLY J. elementary school educator; b. Gary, Ind., June 16, 1948; d. Earl Robert S. and Mandy Pearl Hearon; stepfather: James T. Hearon. BS in Edn., Lincoln U., 1970; MEd, Ind. U., 1974. Cert. elem. sch. tchr. Tchr. grades 2, 4, 6 Norton Sch. Gary (Ind.) Cmty. Sch. Corp., 1970-72, tchr. grades 3-5 Vohr Sch., 1972-83; tchr. grade 1 Vohr Sch., 1983-95; tchr. grade 4, 1995—. Tchr. challenge gratn program Gary Cmty. Sch. Corp., 1997, 98. Asst. min. music United Male Chorus Gary-Calumet Region, Gary, 1989—; mem. The Sounds of Peace Singing Ensemble, Gary and Calumet, 1974—; tchr. Voices of Praise Children's Choir; min. music Carter Meml. Christian Meth. Episcopal Ch., 1997, past bd. dirs. Recipient numerous plaques Carter Meml. CME Ch., Gary, 1993, 99. Mem. Delta Sigma Theta, Phi Delta Kappa. Democrat. Avocations: computers, piano and organ, teaching. Office: Vohr Elem Sch 1900 W 7th Ave Gary IN 46404-1408 E-mail: bjsteele51@hotmail.com.

STEELE, DAVID H. state legislator; m. Sharon Nauta; 7 children. BS in Math., Utah State U., 1971, MEd, 1978, postgrad., 1986, Calif. Poly, 1984. Cert. tchr. and adminstr., Utah. Dir. instructional tech., dir. adult and continuing edn. Davis Sch. Dist.; mem. Utah Senate, Dist. 21, Salt Lake City, 1986—; mem. transp. and pub. safety com., mem. edn. com.; co-chair exec. and natural resources appropriations. Mem. steering com. Edn. Commn. of the states; chair Edn. and Job Tng. Com.; co-chair Info. Tech. Commn. Utah. Republican. Office: 320 S 500 E Kaysville UT 84037-3307

STEELE, DOROTHY PAULINE, retired elementary education educator; b. Buffalo, Kans., Jan. 30, 1920; d. Lloyd and Clara E. (Pickering) Easley; m. Roy M. Steele, June 4, 1944 (dec. Apr. 1961); 1 child, Roylee Joan Steele Turley. AB, U. Mo., Kansas City, 1957, MA, 1966. Elem. tchr. Rushton Sch. Dist. 110, Mission, Kans., 1956-66; reading specialist Shawnee Mission (Kans.) Pub. Schs., 1966-86; ret., 1986. Del. World Coun. Teaching Profession, Calgary, B.C., Can., 1983. Elder Countryside Christian Ch. (Disciples of Christ), Mission, Kans., 1983-89; mem. Theatre Assocs., Kansas City, 1989-90; sec. Shawnee Mission Indian Hist. Soc., 1987—. Named to Kans. Tchr. Hall of Fame, 1990. Mem. Johnson County Ret. Tchrs. Assn., La Sertoma (Jewel award 1989), Delta Kappa Gamma (fin. com. 1984-90). Avocations: reading, organ, piano, violin, travel. Home: 6511 Reeds Dr Shawnee Mission KS 66202-4225

STEELE, JAMES EUGENE, retired school system administrator; b. South Norfolk, Va. s. James Edward and Blanche Eugenia (Munden) S. BS in Music Edn., William & Mary Coll., 1961; MEd in Ednl. Adminstrn. and Supervision, Temple U., 1972; EdD in Ednl. Adminstrn., Nova U., 1976. Cert. tchr., Va. Piccoloist Va. Symphony Orch., 1951-73; dir. choral music Hampton (Va.) City Schs., 1960-65, supr. music, 1965—2003; ret., 2003. Guest flute soloist Music Tchrs. Assn., Great Britain, 1962. Dir. fine arts divsn. Hampton Assn. Arts Humanities, 1967—. Mem. NEA, Va. Edn. Assn., Hampton Edn. Assn., Va. Assn. Sch. Execs., Hampton Instrnl. Suprs. Assn., Tidewater Regional Suprs., Va. Assn. Sch. Curriculum Devel., Va. Music Suprs. Assn., Va. Music Educators Assn., Music Educators Nat. Conf., Va. Choral Dirs. Assn., Va. Band and Orch. Dirs. Assn., Va. String Tchrs. Assn. Home: 132 Fayton Ave Norfolk VA 23505-4428

STEELE, JULIUS RAYNARD, special education educator; b. Little Rock, Ark., Oct. 18, 1952; s. D. J. Steele and Juanita (Thomas) Gilbert; children: Misty N., Sara M. BS, Northwestern U., Natchitoches, La., 1974; MA, La. Tech. U., 1978; EdS, Point Loma Nazarene Coll., 1992; EdD in Ednl. Leadership, No. Ariz. U., 1995. Cert. tchr. handicapped, severely handicapped, counseling, physical edn., edn. adminstrn, Calif. Tchr. learning handicapped Caddo Parish Schs., Shreveport, La., 1974-81; tchr. severely handicapped Pulaski County Schs., Little Rock, 1988-89, San Diego City Schs., 1989-93; asst. prin. Oxnard Union High Sch. Dist., 1993—. Cons. Point Loma Nazarene Coll., San Diego, 1992-93. Mem. adv. bd. San Diego Parks & Recreation Disabled Svcs., 1992-93, adv. com. Lincoln Prep. High Sch., San Diego, 1992-93. Mem. Assn. Calif. Sch. Adminstrs., Omega Psi Phi (treas.). Democrat. Avocations: cycling, wood carving. Home: 8705 Brannock Ct Bakersfield CA 93313-4285

STEELE, NANCY EDEN ROGERS, nonprofit corporation executive, former educator; b. Elgin, Ill., Aug. 18, 1946; d. Vance Donald and Barbara Marie (Yarwood) Rogers; m. James Frederick Steele, Apr. 12, 1976; children: Justin Vance Jabari, Barbara Marie Noni. BS, Centenary Coll., 1968; MA, U. Nebr., 1971. Program asst. Head Start & Follow Through, Lincoln, Nebr., 1971-74; K-12 resource tchr. Nantucket (Mass.) Pub. Schs., 1975-77; kindergarten lead tchr. Parkville Sch., Guaynabo, P.R., 1977-79; instr. in gen. psychology L.A. C.C., Sebana Seca, P.R., 1978-79; lang. arts and parent edn. tchr. Sweetwater Union H.S. Dist., Chula Vista, Calif., 1980-86; upper grade team leader Park View Elem. Sch., Chula Vista, 1986-91; upper grade tchr. Clear View Elem. Sch., Chula Vista, 1991-94; mentor tchr. Chula Vista Elem. Sch. Dist., 1990-94; acad. dir. AmeriCorps Nat. Civilian Cmty. Corps, San Diego, 1994-96; asst. prin. Harborside Elem. Sch., Chula Vista, 1996-98; prin. Burton C. Tiffany Elem. Sch., Chula Vista, 1998-2000; exec. dir. Interactions for Peace, 2000—. Cons. in field. Author: Peace Patrol: A Guide for Creating a New Generation of Problem Solvers, 1994 (Golden Bell award 1993), Primary Peacemakers, 2001; co-author: Power Teaching for the 21st Century, 1991. Recipient Peacemaker of Yr. award San Diego Mediation Ctr., 1993, Champion for Children award Children's Hosp. and San Diego Office of Edn., 1994, Leadership award San Diego Channel 10, 1998. Mem. ASCD, AAUW, Nat. Coun. for Social Studies, Assn. Calif. Sch. Adminstrs., Chula Vista Aquatics Assn. (bd. dirs. 1986-96), Optimist Club. Home: 1551 Malibu Point Ct Chula Vista CA 91911-6116

STEELE, ROBERT B. director vocational education; b. Pineville, W.Va., May 11, 1948; s. Hatler B. Steele and Pauline (Syck) Price; m. Sarah Lindbeck, Dec. 25, 1994; children: Jennifer, John. Assoc. degree, Cuyahoga C.C., 1972; BA, Cleve. State U., 1989; MEd in Spl. Edn. & Rehab., Kent State U., 1990, postgrad., 1992—. Cert. rehab. counselor. Psychiat. asst. State Dept. of Mental Health, Broadview, Ohio, 1972-74; instr. tech. English U. East Cen., Santo Domingo, San Pedro, Dominican Republic, 1974-77; behavior trainer Cuyahoga County Bd. Mental Retardation/Devel. Disabilities, Parma, Ohio, 1977-79; vocat. coord. Parma Adult Tng. Ctr., 1979-80; mobility and orientation specialist Cuyahoga County Bd. MR/DD, Cleve., 1980-85, employment and tng. specialist, 1985-91; supported employment coord. Kent (Ohio) State U., 1991-92; lectr., project coord. dept. teaching specialties U. N.C., Charlotte, 1992-94; coord. vocat. opportunities Collaborative Stark County Cmty. Mental Health Bd., Canton, Ohio, 1994—. Exec. bd. dirs. Supported Employment Tng. Inc., Charlotte; outcome based curriculum devel. com. Charlotte Mecklenburg Schs., Charlotte, 1992-94; cons. vocat. programming Hattie Larlham Found., Ravenna, Ohio, 1990-93; mem. Ohio interagy. employment tng. task force Ohio Interagy. Tng. Network, Akron, 1990-91; mem. N.C. State Vocat. Alternatives Task Force, 1992-94, Charlotte Mecklenburg Supported Employment Steering Com., Charlotte, 1992-94; mem. dirs. adv. com. Ohio State Dept. Mental Retardation and Devel. Disabilities, 1991-92; mem. vocational rehab. com. Ohio Coun. Cmty. Mental Health & Recovery Orgns., 1994—. Co-author: (book chpt.) Psychiatric Rehabilitation in Practice, 1993; author, editor: Job Placement Procedure Manual, 1991; co-author, editor: Cuyahoga Job Readiness Curriculum, 1990. Mem. human rights com. VOCA Residential Corp., 1993-94. Western Region Transition Svcs. tng. grantee N.C. Dept. Pub. Info., 1992, Undergrad. Specialization in Supported Employment grantee, Rehab. Svcs. Adminstrn., 1993, 94; doctoral leader fellow Kent State U., 1990-92. Mem. ASCD, Assn. for Persons in Supported Employment, Nat. Rehab. Assn., Am. Assn. on Mental Retardation, Assn. for Persons with Severe Handicaps, Vocat. Evaluation and Work Adjustment Assn., Internat. Assn. Psychosocial Rehab. Avocations: music, songwriting, camping, hiking. Home: 6350 Lake O Springs Ave NW Canton OH 44718-1128 Office: Vocat Opportunities Collab 500 Cleveland Ave NW Canton OH 44702-1542

STEELE, SANDRA ELAINE NOEL, nursing educator; b. Warren, Pa., May 8, 1939; d. Cecil Harry Johnson and Romaine Mae (Goodwin) Hamblin; children: Lynne Cerise, William Leslie. Diploma in nursing, Allegheny Gen. Hosp., 1961; postgrad., City U., Bellevue, Wash., 1988-89, Bus. Computer Tng. Inst., 1994. RN, Wash.; CNOR. Staff nurse oper. rm. Allegheny Gen. Hosp., Pitts., 1961-62, Dr.'s Hosp., Seattle, 1962-66; staff nurse immunization clinic Snohomish County Health Dept., Everett, Wash., 1969-77; staff nurse oper. rm. Gen. Hosp. Med. Ctr., Everett, 1977-82, clin. educator surg. svcs., 1982-93; patient coord. Cascade Regional Eye Ctr., Marysville, 1993-94; nursing educator Cascade Valley Hosp., Arlington, Wash., 1994-96, dir. hosp. edn., 1996—. Cons. Reed, McClure, Moceri, Thonn and Moriarty Legal Firm, Seattle, 1989—. Pres. Tulalip Elem. Sch. PTSA, Marysville, Wash., 1974-76, pres. Marysville PTSA Coun., 1976-80; leader Campfire Girls, Marysville, 1972-76; bd. dirs. N.W. Laser Network, Seattle, 1988-90. Recipient Outstanding Svc. award Washington State PTSA, 1974, Goledn Acorn award Marysville PTSA Coun., 1979, People Taking Significant Action award Marysville PTSA, 1978. Mem. Assn. Oper. Rm. Nurses, Nat. Nursing Staff Devel. Lutheran. Avocations: computers, sewing, hiking, travel, polar bears. Home: 418 Priest Point Dr NW Marysville WA 98271-6823

STEELE, SARAH JANE, elementary school educator; b. Scottsbluff, Nebr., May 28, 1947; d. Earl Roe and Mary Eleanor (Blakey) Cherry; m. Gary Gene Steele, May 19, 1968; children: Jason Linn, Sally Suzanne. BS, Chadron State Coll., 1970, MS, 1994. Tchr. k., 1, 2 grades Chadron (Nebr.) Elem. Sch., 1970-71; tchr. 6th grade Morrill (Nebr.) Elem. Sch., 1971—. Mem. NEA, Nebr. State Edn. Assn., Morrill Edn. Assn. (pres. 1983-84), Alpha Delta Kappa (pres. 1994-96), Phi Delta Kappa. Republican Congregationalist. Avocations: reading, sporting events, crafts. Home: 100777 County Road D Morrill NE 69358-2105 Office: Morrill Pub Schs PO Box 486 Morrill NE 69358-0486

STEELE-HUNTER, TERESA ANN, elementary education educator; b. Newark, Aug. 5, 1959; d. Frederick Douglas and Blanche (Terry) S. BA in Sociology, Kean Coll. N.J., 1981, MA in Ednl. Adminstrn., 1985. Cert. tchr. elem. edn., N.J. Recreation counselor Irvington (N.J.) Recreation Dept., 1978, 90; subs. tchr. Irvington Bd. Edn., 1981-86, tchr. social studies, 1986—. Office mgr. Onyx Sales and Mktg., Inc., East Orange, N.J., 1990-91. Corr. sec. Mayor Michael G. Steele Civic Assn., Irvington,

1990—; mem. edn. and scholarship com. Solid Rock Bapt. Ch., 1992—. Recipient Excellence in Edn. award N.J. Alliance Black Sch. Educators, 1992; named one of Outstanding Women in Community, Irvington Town Coun., 1992. Mem. NEA, ASCD, Nat. Coun. for Social Studies, N.J. Edn. Assn., Irvington Edn. Assn. Democrat. Avocations: crocheting, reading, traveling, collecting postcards, african statues and dolls. Home: 1590 Pershing Pl South Plainfield NJ 07080-3037

STEELY, ALLEN MERLE, secondary school educator; b. Geneva, Ill., Apr. 5, 1952; s. Merle Ashel and Vera Mae S.; m. Marcia Anne Limkeman, May 30, 1981; children: Rachel Anne, Joshua Allen, Jonathan David, Kathryn Elizabeth. BA in Psychology, Wheaton (Ill.) Coll., 1974. Lic. stationary engr. City of Elgin, Ill. Psychology tchr. Igbaja (Nigeria) Theol. Sem., 1974; info. officer for famine relief program Soc. Internat. Ministries, Ethiopia, 1975; sci. tchr. Bingham Acad., Addis Ababa, Ethiopia, 1975-76; stationary engr. Indeck Power Equipment Co., Wheeling, Ill., 1976-77; sci. tchr. Rockford (Ill.) Christian Jr. H.S., 1977—, sci. dept. chmn., 1996—. Soccer coach Rockford (Ill.) Christian Schs., 1978—; sch. coord. Invent Am., Rockford, 1993-96. Author: A God-Centered View of Salvation: A Theocentric Perspective of the Gospel. Bd. dirs First Evangelical Free Ch., Rockford, 1986-90, Rockford Reachout Jail Ministry; chmn. First Free Ch. Social Concerns Com., Rockford, 1989. Recipient Excellence in Sci. Tchg. award Ill. Math. and Sci. Acad., Aurora, 1988; nominee for Presidential award sci. and math. tchg., Washington, 1991. Mem. Nat. Fedn. Interscholastic Ofcls. Assn. (cert. soccer referee), Nat. Sci. Tchrs. Assn. Republican. Mem. Evangelical Free Ch. Avocations: pairs dance skating, soccer, rock climbing. Home: 420 Laurel Dr Rockford IL 61107-4829 Office: Rockford Christian Schs 1401 N Bell School Rd Rockford IL 61107-2872

STEEN, LYNN ARTHUR, mathematician, educator; b. Chgo., Jan. 1, 1941; s. Sigvart J. and Margery (Mayer) S.; m. Mary Elizabeth Frost, July 7, 1940; children: Margaret, Catherine. BA, Luther Coll., 1961; PhD, MIT, 1965; DSc (hon.), Luther Coll., 1986, Wittenberg U., 1991, Concordia Coll., Minn., 1996. Prof. math. St. Olaf Coll., Northfield, Minn., 1965—. Vis. scholar Inst. Mittag-Leffler, Djursholm, Sweden, 1970-71; writing fellow Conf. Bd. Math. Sci., Washington, 1974-75; exec. dir. Math. Sci. Edn. Bd., Washington, 1992-95. Author: Counterexamples in Topology, 1970, Everybody Counts, 1989; editor: Mathematics Today, 1978, On the Shoulders of Giants, 1990, Math. Mag., 1976-80, Why Numbers Count, 1997, Mathematics and Democracy, 2001; contbg. editor: Sci. News, 1976-82. NSF Sci. faculty fellow, 1970-71, Danforth Found. grad. fellow, 1961-65. Fellow AAAS (sec. math. sect. 1982-88); mem. Am. Math. Soc., Math. Assn. Am. (pres. 1985-86, Disting. Svc. award 1992), Coun. Sci. Soc. Pres. (chmn. 1989), Sigma Xi (Bd. Dirs. Spl. award 1989). Home: 716 Saint Olaf Ave Northfield MN 55057-1523 Office: St Olaf Coll Dept of Math Northfield MN 55057 E-mail: steen@stolaf.edu.

STEENO, PAULA HERRICK, special education administrator; b. Sedalia, Mo., Mar. 30, 1954; d. Warren Bishop and Clara Marie (Fowler) Herrick; m. Paul Alvin Steeno, June 4, 1977; children: Sarah Lynn, Benjamin Bishop, Rachel Leigh. BS, U. Mo., Columbia, 1976; MS, U. Mo., St. Louis, 1979; EdD, U. Mo., 1994. Cert. tchr. learning disabilities, speech-lang., mentally handicapped, spl. reading, behavioral disorder, spl. edn. adminstrn., sch. psychol. examiner, elem. sch. prin. Tchr., remedial reading So. Boone County R-I Schs., Ashland, Mo., 1976—77; tchr., second grade Archdiocese of St. Louis, 1977—78; resource tchr. City of St. Charles (Mo.) Pub. Schs., 1978—80, Spl. Sch. Dist./St. Louis County, 1981-85, itinerant dist. programming cons., 1985—86, psychol./ednl. examiner, 1987; supr. student tchrs. in learning disabilities U. Mo., Columbia, 1987—88, supr. master level practicum students, 1988; sch. psychol. examiner Columbia (Mo.) Pub. Schs., 1988—; process coordinator Columbia Pub. Schs., 1999—. Adj. prof., Columbia Coll., 1999-; cons./tutor college level students with learning disabilities, 1989-90; adj. instr. U. Mo., Columbia, 1988; mem. Project Impact Team, City of St. Charles, 1981; reading specialist Adult Basic Edn., Columbia Pub. Sch., 1976-77; others. Active Parenting With Pride/Insvc. on Parenting Skills for Parents With Handicapped Children, 1990, Leadership Acad., 1989, others; hearing officer, State of Mo., 1988, 90-. Recipient Doctoral Teaching Assistantship, 1987-88. Mem. Coun. on Learning Disabilities, Assn. for Children and Youth with Learning Disabilities (exhibits coord. state conf. 1986), Coun. Exceptional Children (Joan Davis Spl. Merit award 2002). Home: 3708 Woodridge Ct Columbia MO 65201-6532

STEEVES, ERIC WILLIAM, school administrator; b. Millinocket, Maine, June 8, 1958; s. William John and Helen Rose (Vitchner) S. BA, U. South Fla., 1981; MS, Husson Coll., 1984; diploma, Maine State Prins.' Acad., 1992; MEd, U. Maine, 1995. Cert. social studies, bus. edn. tchr., guidance counselor, prin., Maine. Asst. mgr. hardware div. C.R. Steeves & Sons Plumbing & Hardware, Millinocket, Maine, 1981-86; social studies tchr. Penobscot Valley High Sch., Howland, Maine, 1986-88, Katahdin High Sch., Sherman Station, Maine, 1988-91; vice prin. Katahdin Jr./Sr. High Sch., Sherman Station, 1991-93; guidance counselor Millinocket (Maine) Elem. Sch., 1994—, Stearns H.S., 1995—. Mem. MSAD (peer support tng. instr. 1989—, chmn. computer curriculum com. 1991—), ACA, Aroostoock County Athletic Dirs. Assn. (chmn. 1991-92, chmn. budget com. 1992—), Nat. Assn. Secondary Sch. Prins., Maine State Prins.' Assn., Maine Sch. Counselor's Assn., Katahdin Area Crisis Intervention Team, Millinochet Alcohol and Drug Edn. and Info. Team. Republican. Avocations: softball, basketball, golf, fishing, hunting. Home: 17 Canyon Dr Millinocket ME 04462-2303 Office: Stearns H S Guidance Office Millinocket ME 04462

STEFANE, CLARA JOAN, business education secondary educator; b. Trenton, N.J., Apr. 08; d. Joseph and Rose M. (Bonfanti) Raymond; m. John E. Stefane, July 19, 1975. BS in Bus. Adminstrn., Georgian Ct. Coll., Lakewood, N.J., 1968. Cert. tchr. gen. bus. and secretarial studies, N.J. Tchr. bus. Camden Cath. High Sch., Cherry Hill, N.J., 1960-68, Cathedral High Sch., Trenton, 1970-72; tchr., bus., chair dept. McCorristin Cath. High Sch., Trenton, 1972-95—. Mem. Mercer County Task Force for Bus. Edn., Trenton, 1989-90. Sustaining mem. Rep. Nat. Com.; del. mem. 1992 Presdl. Trust; mem. Rosary Altar Soc., Incarnation Ch. Named Tchr. of Yr., The Cittone Inst., Princeton, N.J., 1991. Mem. ASCD, N.J. Bus. Edn. Assn., Nat. Cath. Edn. Assn., Sisters of Mercy of the Ams. (assoc.). Roman Catholic. Avocations: reading, creative writing, attending operas and yankee baseball games. Home: 278 Weber Ave Trenton NJ 08638-3638 Office: McCorristin Cath High Sch 175 Leonard Ave Trenton NJ 08610-4807

STEFANELLI, LISA EILEEN, elementary education educator; b. Mineola, N.Y., Feb. 22, 1965; d. Anthony Joseph and Myrna Joan (Graber) S. BS in Elem. Edn. (cum laude), SUNY, Oneonta, N.Y., 1987; MS in Reading (with distinction), Hofstra U., 1991. Cert. tchr., N.Y. Tchr. asst. East Meadow (N.Y.) Sch. Dist., 1987-88, tchr. elem., 1988—. Cons. Bd. of Coop. Ednl. Svcs., Westbury, N.Y., 1991—; dance club advisor East Meadow Sch. Dist., 1992—. Organizer Parent-Tchr. Workshops, 1992; grade chair, 1989-90, 92-93. Mem. ASCD, Nassau Reading Coun., Internat. Reading Assn., Parkway Tchr. Assn. (treas. 1991-93), Parkway PTA. Avocations: dancing, reading, theatre, tennis.

STEFANIK, JEAN MARIANNE, retired education educator, naturalist; b. Springfield, Mass., June 10, 1949; d. Edward Carl and Suzanne Florence (Chelkonas) S. BS in Elem. Edn.; MEd, Am. Internat. Coll.; postgrad., Norwich U., U. Vt., Merrimack Valley Coll., Franklin Pierce Coll., U. Mass., U. Hawaii. Reading specialist Easthampton (Mass.) Schs., 1973-74; dir. curriculum Barre Town (Vt.) Sch. Dist., 1974-80; dir. extended edn. program Amherst (N.H.) Sch. Dist., 1980—2003, ret., 2003—. Part-time educator Computer Ctr., Tandy Corp., Manchester, N.H., 1981-82; part-time instr. Notre Dame Coll., Manchester, 1981-83, Merrimack Valley Coll., 1981-86, U. N.H. Coll. for Lifelong Learning, 1982-87, 92-96, sabbitical including work for Smithsonian Inst. Marine Sys. Lab. and New England Aquarium's Right Whale Rsch. Team, 1987-88; mem. Alaska Oil Spill and Ecology Info. Ctr., Juneau, 1989; mem. Earthwatch/Rsch. Teams Giant Clams of Tonga, 1988, Fijian Coral Reefs, 1993, field svc. rep., 1993-95. Mem. ASCD (internat., bd. dirs. 1979-80, 82-2000, mem. elem. global edn. pilot project 1992-94, issues com. 1995-96, mem. conf. local arrangements com. 1991), Vt. ASCD (pres. 1970-80, treas. 1977-79), N.H. ASCD (pres. 1982-84, 86-87, bd. dirs. 1981—, exec. dir. 1999-2000), Internat. Reading Assn., New Eng. Aquarium Self-Contained Underwater Breathing Apparatus Club (pres. 1990-93), United Divers N.H. (pres. 1996-97), N.H. Orchid Soc. (trustee 1996-98), Edn. Conservation (dir. 2001-), Seamark (chmn. 1993), Nature Conservancy, New Eng. Wildflower, Mensa, Phi Delta Kappa, Alpha Chi. Home: 285 Beaver St Manchester NH 03104-5569 E-mail: extedsearch@aol.com.

STEFANO, GEORGE B. neurobiologist, researcher; b. N.Y.C., Sept. 11, 1945; s. George and Agnes (Hendrickson) S.; 1 child, Michelle Laura. PhD, Fordham U., 1973. Mem. faculty N.Y.C. C.C., 1972-79, Medgar Evers Coll. CUNY, 1979-82; prof. cell biology, chmn. dept. biol. sci. SUNY, Old Westbury, 1982-86, asst. v.p. rsch., 1985-89, dir. Old Westbury Neurosci. Inst. and Geronotology Ctr., 1986—. Pres., dir. East Coast Neurosci. Found., Dix Hills, N.Y., 1977-82; rsch. coord. dept. anesthesiology St. Joseph Hosp. and Med. Ctr., Paterson, N.J., 1979-82; disting. teaching prof. SUNY, 1991; adj. prof. surgery, dir. cardiac rsch. program, vice-chair bd. dirs. SUNY, Stony Brook, 1995-98; rsch. assoc. dept. psychiatry Harvard Med. Sch., 1995-97; dir. Basic Rsch. Mind/Body Med. Inst., Harvard Med. Sch., 1998—. cons. NIDA; adv. bd. Acta Pharmacol. Sinica; vice chmn., bd. dirs. Rsch. Found. SUNY. Co-founder, mem. editl. bd. Molecular Cellular Neurobiology Advances in Neuroimmunology, 1991—96, Animal Biology, assoc. editor Jour. Neuroimmunology, 1998—99, Current Opinion in European Medicine, Current Opinion Exptl. Rsch.; editor: Modern Aspect of Immunobiology; co-editor: Placebo; mem. editl. bd. Internat. Jour. Molecular Medicine; editor: Med. Sci. Monitor; contbr. over 300 papers to sci. jours.; author: 5 textbooks in field. Project dir. NIMH-COR, 1983-00; bd. dirs. Rsch. Found. SUNY. Named CASE Prof. N.Y., 1991; Nat. Acad. Scis. grantee, 1978, 80, NIMH grantee, 1979—, NSF grantee, 1989-92, Nat. Inst. Drug Abuse grantee, 1993—. Mem. AAAS, Soc. Neurosci. (pres. Old Westbury chpt.), Assn. Immuno-Neurobiologists (exec. pres. 1991-98).

STEFANSEN, PEGGY ANN, special education educator; b. Newton, Kans., Sept. 16, 1953; d. Manny E. and Marjorie M. (Covalt) Osburn; m. Todd Stefansen, June 9, 1976; 1 child, Tyler. BA, Oral Roberts U., 1975; MA, Tulsa U., 1981. Tchr. learning disabilities Prague (Okla.) Pub. Schs., Chandler (Okla.) Pub. Schs., Skiatook (Okla.) Pub. Schs.; tchr. Prague Pub. Schs. Mem.: NEA, Okla. Edn. Assn., Leanring Disabilities Assn. Home: Rte 1 Box 22A Paden OK 74860 Office: Prague Elementary NBU # 3504 Prague OK 74864-2031

STEFFEL, SUSAN ELIZABETH, English language and literature educator; b. Muskegon, Mich., Feb. 9, 1951; d. Sherman Burgess and Geraldine (Westerman) Bos; m. Andrew John Steffel, July 12, 1975. BA, Hope Coll., 1973; MA in English, Mich. State U., 1978, PhD in English, 1993. Tchr. secondary English Maple Valley Schs., Vermontville, Mich., 1973-91; prof. English Ctrl. Mich. U., Mt. Pleasant, 1991—, Towle prof., 1998—. Supr. secondary student tchrs. dept. English Ctrl. Mich. U., 1991—, vice-chair profl. educators, 1994—95, chair profl. educators coun., 1995—96, chair com. on coms., 1997—98, mem. acad. senate, 1999—. Co-author: High School English: A Process for Curriculum Development, 1985, 20th Century Children's Authors, 1994, Fantasy Literature for Children and Young Adults, 2003. Recipient Excellence in Edn. award Lansing Regional C. of C., 1985, 86, 88, 89, 90, Excellence in Teaching award Ctrl. Mich. U., 1996, outstanding tchr. award Sigma Delta Tau, 1997, outstanding educator award Kappa Delta Pi, 2000; named Towle Prof., 1998. Mem.: AAUW, ASCD, Conf. English Edn., Assembly Lit. for Adolescents, Mich. Coun. Tchrs. English (steering com. 1985—, asst. editor jour. 1993—98, editor jour. 1999—2003, v.p. 2001—02, pres.-elect 2002—03, pres. 2003—), Nat. Coun. Tchrs. English (guest reviewer 1993—), Am. Ednl. Rsch. Assn., Am. Assn. Colls. for Tchr. Edn., Golden Key Honor Soc., Phi Delta Kappa (sec. 1995—96), Phi Kappa Phi. Avocations: reading, gardening, pets, needlework. Office: Ctrl Mich U 204 Anspach Hl Mount Pleasant MI 48859-0001

STEFFEN, LLOYD HOWARD, minister, religion educator; b. Racine, Wis., Nov. 27, 1951; s. Howard C. and Ruth L. (Rode) S.; m. Emmajane S. Finney, Feb. 14, 1981; children: Nathan, Samuel, William. BA, New Coll., 1973; MA, Andover Newton Theol. Sch., 1978; MDiv, Yale U., 1978; PhD, Brown U., 1984. Ordained to ministry United Ch. of Christ, 1983. Chaplain Northland Coll., Ashland, Wis., 1983-90, assoc. prof., 1982-90, Lehigh U., Bethlehem, Pa., 1990-97, chaplain, 1990—, prof., 1997—, chair dept. religion studies, 2000—. Mem. theol. com. Wis. Conf. United Ch. of Christ, Madison, 1985—87; mem. div. ch. and ministry NW assn. Wis. Conf., Eau Claire, 1987—90; mem. ecumenical commn. Penn N.E. Conf., 1994—96; mem. Common Ground, Bethlehem, Pa., 1994—97, chair, 1995—97; mem. ch. & ministry com. Pa. Northeast Conf., 1997—2000; mem. ethics com. St. Luke's Hosp., Bethlehem, Pa., 1998—; mem., vice-chair, bd. dirs. Religious Coalition for Reproductive Choice; non-govtl. org. rep. UN; 10th Curtis Lectr. Sacred Heart Univ., 1999; Frederick C. Wood Lectr. Cornell U., 2002. Author: Self-Deception and the Common Life, 1986, Life/Choice: The Theory of Just Abortion, 1994, Abortion: A Reader, 1996, Executing Justice: The Moral Meaning of the Death Penalty, 1998, The Demonic Turn: The Power of Religion to Inspire or Restrain Violence, 2003; contbr. articles to profl. jours. Town supr. Town of La Pointe, Wis., 1984-87. Recipient 1st Pilgrim Press Church and Soc. Book award, NEH Inst. award, Harvard U., 1988, East-West Ctr., 1995; fellow, Brown U., 1982; faculty devel. grant, Northland Coll., 1986, faculty devel. grantee, 1990, Lehigh U., 1994, 1998, 2003. Mem. Soc. Christian Ethics, Am. Acad. Religion, Assocs. for Religion and Intellectual Life, Assn. for Coordination of Univ. Religious Affairs. Home: 1349 Woodland Cir Bethlehem PA 18017-1636 Office: Lehigh U Johnson Hall # 36 Bethlehem PA 18015 E-mail: lhs1@lehigh.edu.

STEFFEN, PAMELA BRAY, secondary school educator; b. Bessemer, Ala., Mar. 9, 1944; d. James Ernest and Margaret Virginia (Parsons) Bray; m. Ted N. Steffen, June 17, 1972; children: Elizabeth, Thor. BA, U. Louisville, 1966; MA, Spalding U., 1975. Cert. tchr., gifted tchr., Ky. Tchr. English and German Louisville (Ky.) Pub. Schs., 1967-73; tchr. English to fgn. students Internat. Ctr., U. Louisville, 1970-78; bookkeeper T.N. Steffen PSC, Louisville, 1978-85; tchr. of adults Jefferson County Pub. Schs., Louisville, 1985-87, tchr. English and German, 1987—. Network participant, bd. dirs. Foxfire, Louisville, 1990—; spokesperson Coalition Essential Schs., Prividence, 1990—, Ctr. for Leadership in Sch. Reform, Louisville, 1990—; group leader AAUW, Louisville, 1983-88; presenter seminars; 94 AATG summer Austrian Inst. Graz; participant Austrian Landeskunde Internat., 1994. Bd. dirs. Jefferson County Med. Soc. Aux., Louisville, 1984-88, Highland Cmty. Ministries, Louisville, 1980-87, Highland Ct. Apts. for Elderly, Louisville, 1984-87; nat. v.p. Deafness Rsch. Found. Aux., 1984-88; mem. vestry and rector search com. St. Andrew's Episcopal Ch., Louisville, 1985-88; active Louisville Fund for Arts campaign, 1980-93; Louisville Orch. Assn. fundraiser. Fullbright fellow Goethe Inst., Munich, 1969; grantee Ky. Arts Coun., 1991-92, artist-in-residence, 1992—; grantee Ky. Humanities Coun. CES, 1993, fall forum presenter; named to Ky.'s Commonwealth Inst. Tchrs. and Vis. Tchrs. Inst.; selected for Landeskunde in Österreich, 1994; summer study scholar Goethe Inst., Freiberg, Germany, 1996. Mem. ASCD, Nat. Coun. Tchrs. English, Coalition Essential Sch., Greater Louisville Coun. Tchrs. English, Am. Assn. Tchrs. German. Avocations: swimming, travel, beagling, writing, reading. Home: 2404 Barret Hill Rd Louisville KY 40205-1635 Office: Fairdale High Sch 1001 Fairdale Rd Fairdale KY 40118-9744

STEFFENS, ANNIE LAURIE, sign language educator, interpreter; b. N.Y.C. d. Robert William and Irene Marie (Hoecker) S. Cert., U. Ariz., Tucson, NYU, Gallaudet U., Washington D.C. Cert. sign lang. interpreter, sign lang. educator. Sign language interpreter high sch., Brattleboro, Vt., Longmeadow, Mass.; tchr. sign language pvt. sch., Putney, Vt., Main Street Arts, Saxtons River, Vt., Cmty. Coll., Greenfield, Mass., Cheshire Hosp., Keene, N.H., YMCA, Keene, Brattleboro Sr. Ctr., Brattleboro Recreation Ctr.; pvt. practice. Developer new program using Am. sign lang., 1995—; mem. sign lang. choir Gallaudet U., NYU; poetry educator Main Street Arts; mem. new Am. Sign Lang. program Grace Cottage Hosp., Townsend, Vt., 1996; developer, designer Am. Sign Lang. Mentorship, 1997—, Am. Sign Lang. Linguistics program, 1998—. Author: (poem) Down Peaceful Paths. Advocate Women's Shelter, Brattleboro; counselor Vt. respite care project Mental Health of Southeastern Vt., Brattleboro. Named Am. Sign Language Tchr. of Excellence, 1998; recipient Bronze medal for excellence in Am. sign lang., 1999, Angel award, 2000. Mem. Nat. Assn. Deaf, Sign Instrs. Guidance Network. Avocations: signing to music, dancing, singing, poetry, painting abstract designs. Home: 14 Spruce St Brattleboro VT 05301-2716

STEFFENS, DONNA IRENE, gifted and talented education coordinator; b. Akron, Ohio, July 23, 1945; d. Harry Lee and Hazel Irene (Jay) Dye; m. Donald William Steffens, Dec. 18, 1971; children: Buddy Burgy, Jyl, Scott. BS in Edn., U. Akron, 1968, MS in Ednl. Adminstrn., 1972, postgrad., 1974. Cert. tchr., prin., supr./coord./dir. instrn., Wis. Tchr. elem. Copley (Ohio) Pub. Schs., 1966-74; insvc. cons. Summit County Svcs., Akron, Ohio, 1973; tchr. Title 1 Cedarbur (Wis.) Pub. Schs., 1975, mid. sch. tchr., 1988-90, dist. coord. gifted programming, 1990—, dir. summer enrichment acad., 1996—; pvt. tutor Columbia, Md., 1978; day care operator Ellicott City, Md., 1978-79. Instr. Cardinal Stritch Coll. of Edn., 1995 (curriculum coun. for dist., 1993-95, staff devel. com., 1993-95, assessment com., 1993-95); Christian edn. coord. Alliance Bible Ch., Cedarburg; adv. coun. chair Gifted Program, Cedarburg, 1988-92; enrichment program adv. com. U. Washington County. Mem. Libr. Bd., 1991, Cedarburg Cmty. Scholarship Bd., 1991, Jaycettes, 1979-81; bd. dirs. Workforce 2010; pres. WATG; chair Parents Supporting Parents; mem. bldg. and scholarship coms. Alliance Bible Ch., chmn. Christian edn. com. Recipient Meritorious Svc. award Wis. Assn. Edn. Gifted and Talented, 1991, Jennings grant Copley Pub. Schs., Award of Recognition, Kohl Found. Fellowship, 1996-97. Mem. ASCD, Wis. Coun. Gifted and Talented, Wis. Assn. Edn. Gifted and Talented, Wis. Assn. for Talented and Gifted (pres. 1997-98). Avocations: singing, crafts, travel. Office: Cedarburg Sch Dist W68n611 Evergreen Blvd Cedarburg WI 53012-1847 Fax: 414-376-5300. E-mail: donacdrbrg@aol.com.

STEGALL, DIANE JOYCE, school system administrator; b. Kansas City, Mo., Oct. 12, 1956; d. Dean Edward and Delma June (Veach) Wintermute; m. Thomas Scott Stegall, Nov. 22, 1975; children: Shawn Scott, Shelly Diane, Shey Thomas. BS, East Tex. State U., 1978, MS, 1982. Cert. secondary English tchr., Tex. Tchr. Cooper (Tex.) High Sch., 1978-93; asst. supt. Chisum Ind. Sch. Dist., Paris, Tex., 1993—2003, supt., 2003—. Adminstr. First United Meth. Ch., Cooper, 1975-93. Mem.: ASCD, Tex. Computer Edn. Assn. (region 8 dir.), Vocat. Home Econs. Assn. Tex., Assn. Tchrs. and Profl. Educators, N.E. Tex. Assn. Supervision and Curriculum Devel. (pres.), Delta Kappa Gamma (corr. sec. 1992—94, v.p. 2000—02, pres. 2002—). Avocations: reading, travel, family activities. Home: 1320 SW 8th St Cooper TX 75432-3714 Office: Chisum Ind Sch Dist 3250 S Church St Paris TX 75462-8909

STEGENGA, PRESTON JAY, international education consultant; b. Grand Rapids, Mich., July 9, 1924; s. Miner and Dureth (Bouma) S.; m. Marcia Jean DeYoung, July 28, 1950; children: James Jay, Susan Jayne. BA, Hope Coll., 1947; MA, Columbia U., 1948; PhD, U. Mich., 1952; LHD (hon.), Northwestern Coll., Iowa, 1989. Instr. history, polit. sci. Berea Coll., Ky., 1948-50, asoc. prof., 1952-55; assistantship U. Mich., 1950-52; pres. Northwestern Coll., Orange City, Iowa, 1955-66; chief Cornell U. Project, U. Liberia-U.S. AID Program, Monrovia, W. Africa, 1966-68; coordinator internat. program Calif. State U., Sacramento, 1968-71; dir. Calif. State U. (Internat. Center), 1971-88; acting v.p. acad. affairs Calif. State U., 1974-75, spl. asst. to pres., 1988-92; mem. Calif. State Liaison Com. for Internat. Edn.; ednl. cons. to Pres., Republic of Liberia, 1973-74; cons. internat. programs Am. Assn. State Colls. and Univs., 1975-89; cons. UN Devel. Programme, 1975-88; internat. edn. cons., 1992—. V.p. Sacramento chpt. UN Assn., U.S.A., 1969-71, pres., 1971-73, bd. dirs.; mem. Calif. UN Univ. Adv. Coun., 1976-80, internat. trade com. C. of C., 1984—, chair coll.-U. com., 1995—, com. World Trade Ctr., 1996—; pres. Tri-State Coll. Conf., 1963-64; dir. Fulbright project for Chinese scholars, 1985; cons. internat. projects Calif. State Fair, 1990—, cons. Sacramento Diplomatic Consular Corps Project, 1987—, N.C. Advocates for Global Edn., 2001—. Author: Anchor of Hope, 1954; asst. to editor History of Edn. Jour.; contbr. articles to profl. jours. Trustee Western Sem., Mich., Northwestern Coll., Iowa, 1955-66, 91-96, New Brunswick Sem., N.J., 1955-66, Global Calif. Coun., 1991-93; campus rep. Fulbright and Rhodes Scholarships, 1970-88; trustee, v.p. World Affairs Coun., 1976-77, 85-90, pres., 1990-92, trustee, 1993-; mem. Task Force for Improving Am. Competence in World Affairs, 1980-89; mem. internat. bd. Los Rios Coll. Found., 1980-85; mem. Am. Coun. for UN U., 1979-85, Interfaith Svc. Bd., 1985-90; bd. dirs. New Zealand-Sacramento Sister City, 1989—. With AUS, 1942-45. Decorated Purple Heart; named hon. chief Kpelle Tribe, West Africa, 1973, hon. commodore Port of Sacramento, 1983, Multi-Cultural Educators Hall of Fame, 1996; recipient Disting. Svc. award UN Assn., 1971, Republic of Venezuela Edn. award, 1979, Outstanding Svc. award Fed. Republic of Germany, 1985, Disting. Svc. award Calif. State U. Chancellor, 1988, Citation of Achievement, Calif. Sec. of State, 1988, U.S. Congl. Register Recognition Citation, 1988, President's Award, World Affairs Coun., 1992, Gov.'s award Calif. State Fair, 1993, Internat. award Sacramento C. of C., 1993, Disting. Svc. award Assn. Citizens & Friends of Liberia, 1995; Ministry of Edn. scholar Republic of China, 1981; German Acad. Exch. Svc. fellow U. Bonn, 1981; Hon. Legis. Resolutions, Calif. State Senate and Assembly, 1988; Stegenga Hall named in honor of 11 years of service as pres. Northwestern Coll., 2003. Mem. Assn. Iowa Coll. and Univ. Pres. (v.p. 1965-66), NEA, Calif. State Univ. Student Pers. Assn., Coun. for Internat. Visitors, Am. Acad. Polit. and Social Sci., Assn. for Advancement of Dutch-Am. Studies, Phi Delta Kappa, Phi Kappa Phi, Phi Beta Delta. Mem. Reformed Ch. Am. Home: 545 Mills Rd Sacramento CA 95864-4911

STEHLE, EDWARD RAYMOND, secondary education educator, school system administrator; b. Pitts., May 30, 1942; s. Edward August and Mary Josephine (Veverka) S.; m. Alberta McConnell; 1 child, Christian Dollison (dec.). BA, U. Pitts., 1964; MA, Columbia U., 1966, doctoral student, 1966-68. Instr. European history C.W. Post Coll., Long Island U., Greenville, N.Y., 1967-68, Middlebury (Vt.) Coll., 1968-69; history master The Lawrenceville (N.J.) Sch., Lawrenceville, N.J., 1969—, dir. day students, 1978-83, asst. dir. coll. counseling, 1983-88, chmn. history dept., 1988-94; asst. dir. The N.J. Scholars Program, Lawrenceville, 1981, dir., 1982-91, chmn. bd., 1988-96, also bd. dirs. Cons. U. Del. Sea Grant Coll., Newark, 1981-82; cons. on history of migrations Statue of Liberty-Ellis Island Found., N.Y.C., 1985-88; mem. selection com. Morris County (N.J.) Summer Opportunities for Tchrs. Program, Morristown, 1985-86; trustee Craftsbury Chamber Players, Greensboro, Vt., 1985-89; N.E.H. Coun. for Basic Edn. fellowship ind. study in the humanities, 1997. Co-author: A Guide to Programming in Basic Plus, 1975; contbr. Harper's Encyclopedia of the Modern World, 1972. Vice pres. Assoc. Mems., Ch. of Christ, Greensboro, 1974-76, pres., 1976-78. Vis. scholar Cambridge (Eng.) U., 1996. Mem. Am. Hist. Assn., Nassau Club (Princeton, N.J.), Mountainview Country Club (Greensboro, Vt.), N. Am. Conf. British Studies. Democrat.

Episcopalian. Avocation: painting. Home: 2810 Main St Lawrenceville NJ 08648-1017 Office: The Lawrenceville Sch Main St Lawrenceville NJ 08620-2310 E-mail: estehle@lawrenceville.org.

STEICHEN, JAMES MATTHEW, agricultural engineer, educator; b. Stillwater, Okla., Nov. 14, 1947; s. John Henry and Ione Elizabeth (Schroeder) S.; m. Ethel Marie Honeyman, Aug. 17, 1968; children: Christine, Laurel, Bethany. BS, Okla. State U., 1970, PhD, 1974. Registered profl. engr. State extension specialist U. Mo., Columbia, 1974-78; asst. prof. Kans. State U., Manhattan, 1978-80, assoc. prof., 1980-88, prof., 1988—. Contbr. articles to profl. jours. Senator faculty Kans. State U., 1987-90; commr. Kans. State Conservation Commn., 1990-95. Grantee U.S. Geol. Survey, 1988-91, Dept. Def., 1995—. Mem. Am. Soc. Agrl. Engrs. (chmn. soil and water divsn. 1989-90, Paper Honor award 1989), Soil and Water Conservation Soc. Am. (pres. 1998-99), Sigma Xi. Democrat. Roman Catholic. Avocations: reading, travel. Home: 3007 Tomahawk Cir Manhattan KS 66502-1974 Office: Kans State U Seaton Hall Dept Biol and Agrl Engring Manhattan KS 66506 E-mail: steichen@ksu.edu.

STEIDEL, CHARLES C. astronomy educator; AB, Princeton U., 1984; Ph.D., Calif. Inst. Tech., 1990. Prof. MIT, 1994; prof. astronomy Calif. Inst. Tech., Pasadena, 1995—. Recipient NSF Young Investigator Award, 1994, Helen B. Warner Prize, 1997; fellow Sloane Found., 1994, Packard Found., 1997, MacArthur Found., 2002. Office: California Inst Tech Dep't Astronomy 1201 E California Blvd Dept Pasadena CA 91125-0001*

STEIN, BELLE WEISS, retired elementary education educator; b. N.Y.C., Aug. 30, 1923; d. Leonard Edwin and Ruth (Scheinzeit) Weiss; m. Henry J. Stein, July 26, 1945; children: Joanne Stein Haiby, Joel, Jacqueline Stein Przytula, Janet Stein, Joyce Stein Schachter. BA, CUNY, 1943; MS, SUNY, New Paltz, 1962. Route mgr. New Manhattan Cleaners, Bklyn., 1942-43; asst. editor Beverage Market Guide, N.Y.C., 1943-45; mil. pers. contact ARC, Bastrop, Tex., 1945; tchr. Unified Free Sch. Dist. 3, North Babylon, N.Y., 1960-86, chmn. reading and social studies, 1968-82; ret., 1986. Contbr. articles to ednl. jours. Sec. Westwood Civic Assn., Babylon, 1950-56, Temple Beth Sholom, Babylon, 1956-58; pres. Sinai Reform Temple, Bay Shore, N.Y., 1992—. Outdoor edn. scholar Cornell U., 1977. Mem. North Babylon Retirees Orgn. (pres. 1989—), North Babylon Tchrs. Orgn. (sec. 1978-86, negotiations team 1974-86), Am. Fedn. Tchrs. (del. 1980—), AAUW, LWV, Hadassah (life). Democrat. Avocations: reading, tennis, gardening, writing, travel. Home: 32 Darcy Cir Islip NY 11751-3704

STEIN, DALE FRANKLIN, retired university president; b. Kingston, Minn., Dec. 24, 1935; s. David Frank and Zelda Jane S.; m. Audrey Dean Bloemke, June 7, 1958; children— Pam, Derek. BS in Metallurgy, U. Minn., 1958; PhD, Rensselaer Poly. Inst., Troy, N.Y., 1963. Metallurgist rsch. lab. GE, Schnectady, N.Y., 1958-67; assoc. prof. U. Minn., 1967-71; prof. metall. engring., head dept. Mich. Technol. U., Houghton, 1971-77, head mining engring., 1974-77, v.p. acad. affairs, 1977-79, pres., 1979-91; pres. emeritus, 1991—. Cons. NSF, Dept. of Energy, 1972-90; trustee Rensselaer Poly. Inst., 1989-95; chmn. com. on decontamination and decommissioning uranium enrichment facilities NRC, 1993-96; active Nat. Materials Adv. Bd., 1987-93; chmn. adv. com. Ctr. for Nuclear Waste Regulatory Analyses. Contbr. articles to profl. jours. Paul Harris fellow. Fellow Metall. Soc. (pres. 1979, inst. Hardy Gold medal 1965), Am. Soc. Metals (Geisler award Eastern N.Y. chpt. 1967); mem. AIME, AAAS, NAE, Sigma Xi, Phi Kappa Phi, Tau Beta Pi, Alpha Sigma Nu.

STEIN, JEROME LEON, economist, educator; b. Bklyn., Nov. 14, 1928; s. Meyer and Ida (Shapiro) S.; m. Hadassah Levow, Aug. 27, 1950; children: Seth, Gil, Ilana. BA summa cum laude, Bklyn. Coll., 1949; MA, Yale U., 1950, PhD, 1955; Docteur honoris causa, U. de la Méditerranée, 1997. Instr. Brown U., Providence, 1953-56, asst. prof., 1956-60, assoc. prof., 1960-62, prof., 1962-70, Eastman prof. polit. economy, 1970-94, prof. emeritus, 1994—. Vis. prof. Hebrew U., Jerusalem, 1965-66, 72-73, 78; Ford Found. rsch. prof. econs. U. Calif., Berkeley, 1979-80, Sorbonne, U. Paris, 1982, Tohoku U., Sendai, Japan, 1983, Haute Etudes Comml., France, 1987, Monash U., Melbourne U., Australia, 1989, U. Aix-en-Provence, Marseille, France, 1992, 95, 96, 97, 98, U. Munich, 1994, La Sapienza, Rome, 1994; vis. prof. applied math. Brown U., 1996—. Author: Essays in International Finance, 1962, (with G.M. Borts) Economic Growth in a Free Market, 1964, Money and Capacity Growth, 1971, Monetarism, 1976, Monetarist, Keynesian and New Classical Economics, 1982, Economics of Futures Markets, 1986, International Finance Markets, 1991, Fundamental Determinants of Exchange Rates, 1995; bd. editors Am. Econ. Rev., 1974-80; assoc. editor Jour. Fin., 1964-70. Ford Found. faculty fellow, 1961-62; Social Sci. Research Council grantee, 1965-66; Guggenheim fellow, 1972-73 Mem. Am. Econ. Assn. Home: 77 Elton St Providence RI 02906-4505 Office: Brown U 182 George St Providence RI 02912-9056 Fax: 401-863-1355. E-mail: Jerome_Stein@BROWN.EDU.

STEIN, MICHAEL ALAN, cardiologist, medical educator; b. Chgo., May 31, 1958; s. Harold Marc and Carlyne Mae (Skirow) S.; m. Ann Palmer Coe, June 9, 1984; children: Sarah Elizabeth, David Benjamin, Kathryn Marie. BA magna cum laude, Lawrence U., 1980; MD, U. Ill., 1984. Diplomate in internal medicine, cardiovas. diseases and interventional cardiology Am. Bd. Internal Medicine. Intern, resident in medicine U. Ill., Chgo., 1984-87; fellow in cardiology, then interventional cardiology U. Iowa, Iowa City, 1987-91; asst. prof. Emory U., Atlanta, 1991-95; dir. cardiology dept. Lower Fla. Keys Health Sys., 1997-98; clin. asst. prof. U. Wis., Madison, 1998—2001. Med. dir. CCU Atlanta VA Med. Ctr., Decatur, Ga., Ga., 1991—95; med. dir. cardiac catheterization lab. Dunwoody Med. Ctr., Atlanta, 1994—95; staff cardiologist Cardiology Cons., Pensacola, Fla., 1995—96, So. Med. Group, Key West, Fla., 1996—98, U. Wis., 1998—2001; staff cardiologists St. Mary's Hosp., Madison, Wis., 2001—02; dean Med. Ctr., 2001—02; v.p. Fond du Lac (Wis.) City Coun., 2000—01. Mem. Fond du Lac City Coun., 2000—01, v.p., 2000—01. Recipient clin. investigator award NIH, 1990-95. Fellow Am. Coll. Cardiology, Am. Heart Assn. (coun. clin. cardiology, Clin. Scientist award 1990-95), Soc. for Cardiac Angiography & Interventions; mem. AAAS. Avocations: sailing, sailboat racing, hiking, scuba diving, fishing. Home: 7668 Leta Way Verona WI 53593 E-mail: mastein@chorus.net.

STEIN, PAULA NANCY, psychologist, educator; b. N.Y.C., Aug. 23, 1963; d. Michael and Evelyn (Graber) S.; m. Andreas Howard Smoller, Sept. 2, 1991; children: Rebecca Leigh Smoller, Rachel Jordan Smoller. BA, Skidmore Coll., 1985; MA with distinction, Hofstra U., 1986, PhD, 1989. Lic. clin. psychologist, N.Y.; cert. in sch. psychology, N.Y. Intern NYU Med. Ctr.-Rusk Inst., N.Y.C., 1988-89; instr. Mt. Sinai Med. Ctr., N.Y.C., 1989-93, asst. prof. rehab. medicine, 1993-95. Psychologist Fishkill (N.Y.) Consultation Group, 1991—. Contbr. chpt. to book, articles to profl. jours. Kraewic scholar Skidmore Coll., 1985. Mem. APA, Assn. for Advancement of Behavior Therapy, Phi Beta Kappa. Jewish. Avocations: skiing, swimming. Office: Fishkill Consultation Group 1092 Main St PO Box 446 Fishkill NY 12524-0446

STEIN, THOMAS HENRY, social science educator; b. Elmhurst, Ill., May 17, 1949; s. Peter Leonard and Marion Edith (Zirbel) S.; m. Alberta Piazza, July 10, 1971; 1 child, Heather. BA in Polit. Sci., Loyola U., Chgo., 1971; postgrad., Loyola U., 1972-76; MS in Edn., Pacific Western U., 1988, PhD in Edn., 1989. Cert. tchr., Ill. Budget analyst, dean global studies divsn. U.S. Dept. Def., Gt. Lakes Naval Sta., Ill., 1971—72; global studies dean, tchr. social sci., coach bowling, softball Mother Guerin High Sch., River Grove, Ill., 1972—; tchr. Highland Park (Ill.) High Sch., 1981-84. Instr. Franklin Park (Ill.) Park Dist., 1977—; tchr. Triton Coll., River Grove, 1990-91; evaluator Chgo. Met. History Fair, 1980-89; faculty adviser Scholastic, Inc., N.Y.C., 1990—; dir. Students Against Animal Cruelty, River Grove, 1991—; moderator Nat. Honor Soc., 1993—; adj. faculty St. Mary's U., 2003--. With Ill. N.G., 1971-77. Recipient Outstanding Achievement award Am. Express/Assn. Am. Geographers, 1989, Heart of the Sch. award for Peace and Justice. Fellow Acad. Polit. Sci.; mem. ASCD, Nat. Coun. Social Studies, Nat. Hist. Soc., Ctr. Study of the Presidency, Nat. Cath. Edn. Assn., Orgn. History Tchrs., Am. Polit. Sci. Assn. Democrat. Roman Catholic. Home: 3601 Emerson St Franklin Park IL 60131-1713 Office: Mother Guerin High Sch 8001 W Belmont Ave River Grove IL 60171-1096

STEINBACH, DONALD ERVIN, middle school educator; b. Pevely, Mo., Oct. 14, 1938; s. Ervin Daniel Julius and Leona Emma (During) S.; m. Agnes Ann Miller, July 15, 1962; children: Jeffery, James, Jonathan, Joel, Janice, Jennifer. BA in Edn., Concordia Coll., River Forest, Ill., 1961; MA in Geography, Valparaiso U., 1972. Cert. tchr., Md. Tchr. Zion Luth. Sch., Marengo, Ill., 1959-60, Trinity Luth. Sch., Centralia, Ill., 1961-64, Concordia Luth. Sch., Hyattsville, Md., 1964—. Adj. tchr. Bible study Redeemer Luth. Ch., Hyattsville, 1971—; chmn. Washington Area Tchrs. Conf., 1980-82; treas. Southeastern Dist. Tchrs. Conf., Washington, 1982-87. Mem. Kiwanis, Midland, Mich., 1971-81. Mem. NRA, Nat. Coun. Social Studies, Md. State Coun. Social Studies, Luth. Edn. Assn. Lutheran. Avocations: hunting, fishing. Home: 4114 33rd St Mount Rainier MD 20712-1946

STEINBERG, ARTHUR IRWIN, periodontist, educator; b. Pitts., Sept. 16, 1935; s. Ben and Sylvia (Jacobs) S.; m. Barbara Fay Ehrenkranz, May 23, 1959; chldren: Sharon Jill, Mindy Ruth, Michael Eli. BS in Microbiology, U. Pitts., 1957, DMD cum laude, 1963, postgrad. in radiobiology, 1957-59; diploma in periodontology-immunology, Harvard U., 1966. Asst. prof. periodontology SUNY, Buffalo, 1966-67; assoc. prof. periodontology Temple U., Phila., 1967-68, assoc. prof. grad. periodontology, 1968-70; attending periodontist Phoenixville (Pa.) Hosp., 1971—; clin. assoc. prof. U. Pa. Sch. Dental Medicine, 1981—2002, clin. prof. of gen. restorative dentistry, 2002—. Mem. infections control com., by-laws com., religious affairs com., 1977—, credentials com., 1982—; mem. staff Suburban Gen. Hosp. Norristown, Pa., 1971-80, Phoenixville Hosp., 1968-95; asst. prof. periodontics U. Pa., 1973-82, clin. assoc. prof., 1982-2002, clin. prof. of general restorative dentistry, 2000—, admissions interviewer Sch. Dental Medicine, 2002—; lectr. continuing edn., off-campus program U. Pitts., 1973-93; Fulbright-Hays lectr. Nat. U. Ireland, Cork, 1970-71; vis. prof. Cork Dental Sch. and Hosp., 1971—; lectr. Periodontology Soc. Madrid, 1980, 5th Region Soc. Periodontology Viña Del Mar, Chile, 1985; dentist in pediatrics Charlestown (Mass.) Boys Club, 1965-66; spkr. Periodontists Conv., Chgo., 1966, N.J. Coll. Medicine and Dentistry, Conn. Dental Assn., 1967, U. Ind. Schs. Dentistry and Medicine, Phila. Ann. Dental Sci. Session, 1969, N.J. Dental Assn., 1970, Wilmington chpt. Sigma Epsilon Delta, 1974, Lehigh Valley Dental Soc.m 1974, Inst. Medicine, Bucharest, Romania, 1976, Irish Dental Assn., 1992, other confs., and convs.; participant Project Head Start, Childrens Hosp., Boston, 1966; mem. fund-raising subcom. Harvard U. Sch. Dental Medicine, 1980—; mem. faculty U. Pitts., 1988-93; commencement spkr. U. Pa. Sch. Dental Medicine, 1988, Harcum Coll. Dental Hygiene Program, 1994-95, C.C. of Phila. Dental Hygiene Program, 2002; presenter Phila. County Dental Soc., Ann. Meeting Liberty Dental Conf., 1988, 90, Acad. Gen. Dentistry Ann. Meeting, 1988; judge divsn. medicine and healthcare Del. Valley Sci. Fair, 1997; clin. prof. gen. restorative dentistry U. Pa., 2002; admissions interviewer U. Pa. Sch. Dental Medicine, 2002—. Contbg. author: The Fulbright Experience, 1987, Dentistry and the Allergic Patient, 1973; contbr. numerous articles to profl. jours. Named to Phoenixville Hosp. Hall of Honor, 1996; USPHS fellow. Fellow Acad. Dentistry Internat., Internat. Acad. Dental Studies, Am. Coll. Dentists, Coll. Physicians Phila., Pierre Fouchard Acad.; mem. AMA, AAUP, Harvard Dental Alumni Assn., Harvard Odontological Soc., Fulbright Assn., Nat. Fulbright Alumni Assn. (a founder 1976, v.p.fin. affairs 1976-79), Am. Acad. Periodontology (ins. com. 1969, hosp. care com. 1973-74, continuing edn. spkr. 1976 conv., 1983 conv., nominating com. chmn. Pa. region to exec. coun. 1975, nat. clin. affairs com. 1984), Am. Coll. Clin. Pharmacology, Northea. Soc. Periodontists, Acad. Stomatology Phila., Phila. Acad. Scis., Sigma Xi, Omicron Kappa Upsilon, Psi Omega (dep. councillor Zeta chpt. 1977-79), Masons (32 degree Shriner), Legion Honor Chapel Four Chaplains, Rotary (dir. 1973-76, chmn. found. com., chmn. internat. svc. 1974-76), B'nai B'rith, Hadassah (assoc. mem.), Harvard of Phila., 25 Yr. Club U. Pa., Area Study (pres. 1976-77), Am. Soc. Ret. Dentists, Omicron Kappa Upsilon. Home and Office: 1681 Pheasant Ln Norristown PA 19403-3331 E-mail: arthurst@pobox.upenn.edu.

STEINBERG, DAVID ISAAC, social sciences educator, consultant; b. Cambridge, Mass., Nov. 26, 1928; s. Naaman and Miriam (Goldberg) S.; m. Isabel Maxwell, 1951 (div. 1962); 1 child, Christopher; m. Ann Myongsook Lee, May 15, 1964; children: Alexander L., Eric D. BA, Dartmouth Coll., 1950; MA, Harvard U., 1955; DLitt (hon.), Sungkunkwan U., Seoul, Republic of Korea. Analyst Nat. Security Coun., Washington, 1951-53; program officer Asia Found., N.Y.C., 1956-58, asst. rep., 1958-62, 1962-63, rep., 1963-68, 1968-69; cons., sr. fgn. svc. officer AID, Washington and Bangkok (Thailand), 1969-86; ret., 1986; pres. Mansfield Ctr. for Pacific Affairs, Helena, Mont., 1986-87, Sr. Resources Internat., 1989-94; disting. prof. Korea Studies Georgetown U., Washington, 1990-94; rep. The Asia Found., Seoul, Republic of Korea, 1994-97; dir. Asian studies Sch. Fgn. Svc. Georgetown U., Washington, 1997—, Disting. prof. and dir. Asian studies, 1997—. Pvt. cons., Washington, 1987—, World Bank, 1987—, Woodrow Wilson Ctr. for Scholars of the Smithsonian Instn., Dept. of State and the Agy. for Internat. Devel., the Can. Internat. Devel. Agy., Devel. Assocs., Inc., and others; founding mem. Burma Studies Found., De Kalb, Ill., 1987. Author: Burma's Road Toward Development, 1981, Burma, 1982, The Republic of Korea Economic Transformation and Social Change, 1988, The Future of Burma, 1990, Burma: The State of Myanmar, 2001, Stone Mirror: Reflections on Contemporary Korea, 2003; co-editor Georgetown Southeast Asia Survey 2002-03, 2003. 1st lt. U.S. Army, 1953-55. Fellow Lingnan U., Canton, China, 1948, Dartmouth Coll., 1950; named Disting. Prof. of Korea Studies, Georgetown U. Mem. Assn. Asian Studies, Oriental Ceramic Soc., Asia Devel. Roundtable (chmn. 1984-86, 87—), Siam Soc., Royal Asiatic Soc. (life Korea br.), Burma Rsch. Soc. (life), Asia Soc. (cons. 1988—), Cosmos Club, Royal Bangkok (Thailand) Sports Club. Home: 6207 Goodview St Bethesda MD 20817-6101 Office: Georgetown U Sch Fgn Svc Washington DC 20057 E-mail: DSteinb620@aol.com, stienbdi@georgetown.edu.

STEINBERG, DAVID JOEL, academic administrator, historian, educator; b. N.Y.C., Apr. 5, 1937; s. Milton and Edith (Alpert) S.; m. Sally Levitt (div. Dec., 1986); children: Noah, Jonah; m. Joan Diamond, Aug. 28, 1987. BA magna cum laude, Harvard U., 1959, MA, 1963, PhD, 1964; LittD, Kyung Hee U., Seoul, Korea, 1989; LLD (hon), Keimyung U., Daegu, Korea. Prof. history U. Mich., 1964-73; exec. asst. to pres. Brandeis U., Waltham, Mass., 1973-77, v.p., univ. sec., 1977-83; pres. L.I. U., Brookville, N.Y., 1985—. Testified before Com. on Fgn. Affairs, U.S. Ho. of Reps., Fgn. Affairs Com. of U.S. Senate; cons. The Ford Found., UN Fund for Population Activities. Author: Philippine Collaboration in World War II, 1967 (Univ. Press award, 1969), The Philippines: A Singular and a Plural Place, 1982, The Philippines: A Singular and a Plural Place, rev. edit., 1987, Asia in Western and World History: A Guide for Tchg., 1993; co-author: S.E. Asia Transformed: A Modern History, 2004. Chmn. Commn. Ind. Colls. and Univs.; past pres. Cambridge (Mass.) Ctr. for Adult Edn., chmn. L.I. Group. English Speaking Union Exch. scholar, Malvern Coll., NDEA scholar, Fulbright Found. exch. scholar. Mem. Coun. Fgn. Rels., Assn. Asian Studies (chmn. fin. com.), Harvard Club (N.Y.C.), Century Club (N.Y.C.). Democrat. Jewish. Office: LI Univ Off Pres 700 Northern Blvd Greenvale NY 11548-1320

STEINBERG, JANET DEBERRY, optometrist, educator, researcher; b. Phila., July 28, 1940; d. Bill and Florence (Kurtz) DeBerry; 1 child, J. Douglas Milner. Student, Rider Coll., 1975-77; BS, Pa. Coll. Optometry, 1978, OD, 1981. Dir. Hopewell (N.J.) Valley Eye Assocs., 1982-99; also clin. assoc. Scheie Eye Inst., U. Pa., Phila., 1985—; dir. Penn Ctr. for Low Vision Rehab. and Rsch. dept. ophthalmology U. Pa., Phila., 1984—; physician U. Pa. Health Sys., Phila., 2000—; pres. Allen Vision Sys., Phila., 1997—. Asst. adj. prof. Pa. Coll. Optometry, Phila., 1983—85; mem. N.J. Low Vision Panel, 1981—; cons. healthcare industry, 1985—. Fellow Am. Acad. Optometry; mem. Am. Optometric Assn. (Optometric Recognition award 1983-89), N.J. Optometric Assn. (sci. achievement award 1999), Assn. Rsch. in Vision and Ophthalmology, Union League Phila., Corinthian Yacht Club, Beta Beta Beta. Avocations: sailing, snorkeling, scuba, golf. Office: Ralston/Penn Ctr Rm 141 3615 Chestnut St Philadelphia PA 19104-2689

STEINBERG, JOAN EMILY, retired middle school educator; b. San Francisco, Dec. 9, 1932; d. John Emil and Kathleen Helen (Montgomery) S. BA, U. Calif., Berkeley, 1954; EdD, U. San Francisco, 1981. Tchr. Vallejo (Calif.) Unified Sch. Dist., 1959-61, San Francisco Unified Sch. Dist., 1961-93, elem. tchr., 1961-78, tchr. life and phys. sci. jr. high sch., 1978-85, 87-93, sci. cons., 1985-87; lectr. elem. edn. San Francisco State U., 1993-94. Ind. sci. edn. cons., 1993—. Contbr. articles to zool. and edn. books and profl. jours. Recipient Calif. Educator award, 1988, Outstanding Educator in Tchg. award U. San Francisco Alumni Soc., 1989; Fulbright scholar U. Sydney, Australia, 1955-56. Mem. San Francisco Zool. Soc., Exploratorium, Am. Fedn. Tchrs., Calif. Acad. Scis., Calif. Malacozool. Soc., Nat. Sci. Tchrs. Assn., Elem. Sch. Sci. Assn. (sec. 1984-85, pres. 1986-87, newsletter editor 1994-99), Sigma Xi. Democrat.

STEINBERG, LEO, art historian, educator; b. Moscow, July 9, 1920; arrived in U.S., 1945; s. Isaac N. and Anna (Esselson) S. PhD, NYU Inst Fine Arts, 1960; PhD (hon.), Phila. Coll. Art, 1981, Parsons Sch. Design, 1986, Mass. Coll. Art, 1987, Bowdoin Coll., 1995. Assoc. prof. art history Hunter Coll., CUNY, N.Y.C., 1961-66, prof., 1966-75; prof. Grad. Ctr. CUNY, 1969-75; Benjamin Franklin prof. art. history U. Pa., Phila., 1975-91, prof. emeritus, 1991—. Charles Eliot Norton lectr. Harvard U., 1995-96; Mellon lectr. Nat. Gallery Art, 1981-82. Author: Other Criteria, 1972, Michelangelo's Last Paintings, 1975, Borromini's San Carlo alle Quattro Fontane, 1977, The Sexuality of Christ in Renaissance Art and in Modern Oblivion, 1983, 2d enlarged edit., 1996, Encounters with Rauschenberg, 2000, Leonardo's Incessant Last Supper, 2001. Recipient award in lit. Am. Acad. and Inst. Arts and Letters, 1983; fellow Am. Acad. Arts and Scis., 1978, Univ. Coll., London U., 1979, MacArthur Found., 1986; recipent Frank Jewett Mather award, 1956, 84; Disting. scholar 2002. Mem. Coll. Art Assn. Am. (Disting. Scholar award 2002). Home: 165 W 66th St New York NY 10023-6508

STEINBERG, MALCOLM SAUL, biologist, educator; b. New Brunswick, N.J., June 1, 1930; s. Morris and Esther (Lerner) S.; children: Jeffery, Julie, Eleanor, Catherine; m. Marjorie Campbell, 1983. BA, Amherst Coll., 1952; MA, U. Minn., 1954, PhD, 1956. Postdoctoral fellow dept. embryology Carnegie Instn., Washington, 1956-58; asst. prof. Johns Hopkins, Balt., 1958-64, assoc. prof., 1964-66; prof. biology Princeton U., 1966-90, Henry Fairfield Osborn prof. biology, 1975—, prof. molecular biology, 1990—. Instr.-in-charge embryology course Marine Biol. Lab., 1967-71, trustee, 1969-77; chmn. Gordon Rsch. Conf. on Cell Contact and Adhesion, 1985; apptd. to NAS/NRC Bd. on Biology, 1986-92. Mem. editl. bd. Bioscience, 1976-82, Integrative Biology, 1997-99; contbr. articles to profl. jours. Fellow AAAS; mem. AAUP, Soc. Comparative Integrative Biology (program officer divsn. devel. biology 1966-69, chmn. elect, then chmn. 1982-85), Am. Soc. Cell Biology, Internat. Soc. Devel. Biologists, Internat. Soc. Differentiation (bd. dirs. 1995-2000), Soc. Devel. Biology (trustee, sec. 1970-73), Sigma Xi. Home: 86 Longview Dr Princeton NJ 08540-5642 E-mail: msteinberg@princeton.edu.

STEINBERG, MARK DAVID, history educator; b. San Francisco, June 8, 1953; s. Norman Emanuel and Dina (Gilbert) S.; m. Jane Taylor Hedges, Aug. 10, 1980; 1 child, Alexander. BA, U. Calif., Santa Cruz, 1978; MA, U. Calif., Berkeley, 1982, PhD, 1987. Instr. U. Oreg., Eugene, 1987; asst. prof. Harvard U., Cambridge, Mass., 1987-89, Yale U., New Haven, 1989-94, assoc. prof., 1994-96, dir. undergrad. studies Russian and Eastern European studies, 1990-96; asst. prof. U. Ill., Urbana-Champaign, 1996-98, assoc. prof., 1996—2003, prof., 2003—, dir. Russian and Ea. European Ctr., 1998—. Lectr. Yale Alumni Assn., 1990-96. Author: Moral Communities, 1992, The Fall of the Romanovs, 1995, Voices of Revolution, 1917, 2001, Proletarian Imagination, 2002; co-editor: Cultures in Flux, 1994; mem. editl. bd. Annals of Communism, 1992—, Kritika, 2000; contbr. articles to profl. jours. Fellow Social Sci. Rsch. Coun., 1990-92, rsch. fellow IREX, 1991-92, fellow NEH, 1995, Ill. Program for Rsch. in Humanities, 2000-2001; NEH summer stipend, 1998. Mem. Am. Assn. for Advancement of Slavic Studies, Am. Hist. Assn. Jewish. Avocations: hiking, music, travel. Home: 1502 S Orchard St Urbana IL 61801-4816 Office: U Ill Dept History 810 S Wright St Urbana IL 61801

STEINBERG, MICHAEL P, education educator; PhD, U. Chgo., 1985. Instr. Humanities Divsn., Columbia Coll., Chgo., 1981—82; lectr. Social Sciences Collegiate Divsn. and Dept. History, U. Chgo., 1983—85; William Rainey Harper instr. U. Chgo., 1985—86; asst. prof. history Colgate U., 1986—89, Cornell U., 1989—93, prof. modern European history, 1989—. Dir. European Cultural Studies work group, Princeton U., 1983—85; faculty mem. Salzburg Seminar, Salzburg, Austria, 1987; vis. asst. prof. of history Cornell U., 1988; assoc. prof. Ecole des Hautes Etudes en Sciences Sociales, Paris, 1991; faculty fellow for the Humanities Cornell U., 1994; vis. prof. Inst. of Lit., Nat. Tsignhua U., Taiwan, 1994; vis. assoc. prof. Divinity Sch., U. of Chgo., 1995. Author: The Meaning of Salzburg Festival: Austra as Theater and Ideology, 1890-1938, 1990; assoc. editor The Musical Quarterly. Fellowship, John Simon Guggenheim Meml. Found., 2003. Office: Dept of History Cornell U 450 McGraw Hill Ithaca NY 14853 Home: 512 Highland Rd Ithaca NY 14850

STEINBERG, RICHARD IRA, physics educator; b. Phila., Apr. 1, 1942; s. Harry and Sophie S.; m. Shari Levine, June 14, 1964; children: Daniel G., Beth H., Champagne C. BA, Swarthmore Coll., 1963; PhD, Yale U., 1969. Instr. Yale U., New Haven, Conn., 1969-71; rsch. assoc. U. Grenoble, France, 1971-74; asst. prof. U. Md., College Park, 1974-76; rsch. asst. prof. physics U. Pa., Phila., 1976-84; prof. physics Drexel U., Phila., 1984—. Cons. Particle Data Group, Berkeley, Calif., 1975-85, Du Pont Corp., Wilmington, Del., 1989; vis. staff mem. Los Alamos (N.Mex.) Nat. Lab., 1985, 87. Contbr. articles over 400 on nuc. and particle physics to profl. jours. Achievements include rsch. on proof of time reversal symmetry in beta decay, tests for charge conservation and proton stability, searches for neutrino oscillations and magnetic monopoles; development of kiloton range scintillation detectors. Office: Drexel U Physics Dept 32nd and Chestnut Sts Philadelphia PA 19104

STEINBERG, WARREN LINNINGTON, school principal; b. N.Y.C., Jan. 20, 1924; s. John M. and Gertrude (Vogel) S.; m. Beatrice Ruth Blass, June 29, 1947; children: Leigh William, James Robert, Donald Kenneth. Student, U. So. Calif., 1943-44; BA, UCLA, 1949, MEd, 1951, EdD, 1962. Tchr., counselor, coach Jordan H.S., Watts, L.A., 1951-57; tchr., athletic coord. Hamilton H.S., L.A., 1957-62; boys' vice prin. Univ. H.S., L.A., 1962-67, Crenshaw H.S., L.A., 1967-68; cons. Ctr. for Planned Change, L.A. City Sch., 1968-69; instr. edn. UCLA, 1965-71; boys' vice prin. LeConte Jr. J.S., L.A., 1969-71, sch. prin., 1971-77; adminstrv. cons. on integration L.A. Unified Sch. Dist., 1977-81, adminstr. student-to-student interaction program, 1981-82; cprin. Gage Jr. H.S., Huntington Park, Calif.,

1982-83; prin. Fairfax H.S., L.A., 1983-90. Pres. Athletic Coords. Assn., L.A. Unified Sch. Dist., 1959-60; v.p. P-3 Enterprises, Inc., Port Washington, N.Y., 1967-77, Century City (Calif.) Enterprises, 1966-88. Contbr. articles on race rels., youth behavior to profl. jours. and newspapers. V.p. B'nai B'rith Anti-Defamation League, 1968-70; mem. adv. com. L.A. City Commn. on Human Rels., 1966-71, 72-76, commr., 1976—, pres., 1978-87, also chmn. edn. com.; mem. human rels. commn. L.A. Unified Sch. Dist., 1999—, mem. citizens adv. com. for student integration, 1976-79; mem. del. assembly Cmty. Rels. Conf. So. Calif., 1975-91; chmn. So. Calif. Drug Abuse Edn. Month com., 1970; bd. dirs. DAWN, The Seedling, 1993-95, Project ECHO—Entrepreneurial Concepts, Hands-On, 1996—; mem., chmn. case conf. human rels. West L.A. Coordinating Coun. With USMCR, 1943-46. Recipient Beverly Hills B'nai B'rith Presdl. award, 1965, Pres.'s award Cmty. Rels. Conf. So. Calif., 1990, Lifetime Achievement award L.A. City Human Rels. Commn., 1996, award L.A. Unified Sch. Dist. Bd. Edn., 1997, commendation L.A. City Coun., 1968, 88. Mem. Beverly-Fairfax C. of C. (bd. dirs. 1986-88), Lions (bd. dirs. 1960-62), Kiwanis. Home: 2737 Dunleer Pl Los Angeles CA 90064-4303

STEINBUCHEL, CARLA FAYE, pediatrics nurse, nursing educator; b. Wichita, Kans., Aug. 6, 1949; d. Conrad Vernon Sr. and Dolores Mae (Jacobs) Jansson; children: Carla Lara, Cara Nicole, Haley Elisabeth. BS in Nursing, Wichita State U., 1978, M of Nursing, 1985; Pediatric Nurse Practitioner, U. Ala., Birmingham, 1997. Nurse supr. Osteopathic Hosp., Wichita, 1978-85; nurse Wesley Med. Ctr., Wichita, 1982-85, Huntsville (Ala.) Hosp., 1985-86; neonatal outreach coordinator North Ala. Perinatal Outreach Ctr., Huntsville, 1986-90; clin. instr.Coll. Nursing U. Ala., Huntsville, 1990-92; pediatric and neonatal clin. nurse specialist Med. Ctr. Hosp. Huntsville, Huntsville, 1991-95; pediatric clin. nurse specialist Huntsville Hosp. Sys., 1995-98, pediatric nurse mgr., 1997-98, clin. edn. specialist, 1998-2000; dir. organizational devel. and tng., 2000—01; dir. Corp .U., 2002—03; clin. nurse III ambulatory surgery unit Crestwood Med. Ctr., 2003—. Manuscript reviewer Neonatal Network, Petaluma, Calif., 1987-88. Mem. AACN (past sec. pres.), Nat. Assn. Pediatric Nurses and Practitioners. Democrat. Methodist. Avocations: travel, reading, writing. Home: PO Box 4755 Huntsville AL 35815-4755

STEINE, LYNETTE HAZEL ANNE, secondary school educator, educator; b. Oceanside, N.Y., Sept. 9, 1948; d. Lyon and Hazel (McGinnis) S. AA, Oxford Coll. of Emory U., 1966-68; BA, Emory U., 1968-70; MEd, Ga. State U., 1971-73, specialist in edn., 1979. Mktg. Edn. Social studies tchr. Dekalb County Schs., Decatur, Ga., 1970-81; mktg. tchr. Fulton County Schs. Chattahoochee High Sch., Atlanta, 1981—. Secondary dir. Ga. Mktg. Edn. Assn., 1985-86; bd. mem. Ga. DECA Adv. Bd., 1985-87, 1988-91; v.p. Ga. Mktg. Edn. Assn., 1986-88. Author: Internal Planning Consideration, 1987; co-author: Private Enterprise, 1990. Del. County Dist. State Rep. Conv., 1980-81; alt. del. Rep. Nat. Cons., Detroit, 1980; mem., contbr. Atlanta Humane Soc., various local and nat. animal protections orgns., including Nat. Humane Edn. Soc. Recipient Crestwood Apreciates Personnel award Crestwood High Sch. PTSA, 1991; recipient 3rd place Ga. Coun. on Vocat. Edn., 1987. Mem. Ga. Mktg. Edn. Assn., Nat. Mktg. Edn. Assn., Ga. Vocat. Assn., Am. Vocat. Assn. Avocations: walking, reading, cooking, photography, animal work. Home: 8515 Haven Wood Trl Roswell GA 30076-3654

STEINER, BARBARA ANNE, secondary school educator; b. Lebanon, Oreg., June 17, 1944; d. Balf Wellington and Doris Ardell (Philpott) Bond; m. Ernest David Steiner, June 29, 1971; children: Julie Lanee, Jaime Michele. BA, Columbia Union Coll., 1967; MA, Andrews U., 1975. Tchr. piano, organ Ga.-Cumberland Acad., Calhoun, 1968-71; tchr. music Battle Creek (Mich.) Acad., 1975-76; ind. tchr. music, 1965—; tchr. music Emerald Jr. Acad., Pleasant Hill, Oreg., 1990-92, Reno (Nev.) Jr. Acad., 1995-98. Pres. aux. group Battle Creek Sanatorium/Hosp., 1978-79; v.p. Mich. Assn. Hosp. Aux., Lansing, 1979-81. Mem. Nat. Music Tchr. Assn., Nat. Guild Organists. Republican. Seventh-Day Aventist. Avocations: music composition and arrangements, photography, yard work. Home: 13794 Palomino Creek Dr Corona CA 92883-8965

STEINER, HENRY JACOB, law and human rights educator; b. Mt. Vernon, N.Y., June 14, 1930; s. Meier and Bluma (Henigson) S.; m. Pamela Pomerance, Aug. 1, 1982; stepchildren: Duff, Jacoba. BA magna cum laude, Harvard U., 1951, MA, LLB magna cum laude, Harvard U., 1955. Bar: N.Y. 1956, Mass. 1963. Law clk. to Hon. John M. Harlan U.S. Supreme Ct., 1957-58; assoc. Sullivan and Cromwell, N.Y.C., 1958-62; asst. prof. sch. law Harvard U., Cambridge, Mass., 1962-65, prof., 1965—, Jeremiah Smith Jr. prof. law, 1986—. Founder, dir. Law Sch. Human Rights Program, 1984—; chair univ. com. on human rights studies Harvard U., 1994—2002; bd. dirs. U. Middle East project, 1996—99, chair bd. dirs., 2000—; vis. prof. Yale U., 1972—73, Stanford U., 1965; cons. AID, 1962—64, Ford Found., 1966—69. Co-author: (textbook) Transnational Legal Problems, 4th edit., 1994, Tort and Accident Law, 2d edit., 1989, International Human Rights in Context: Law, Politics, Morals, 2d edit., 2000; author: Moral Argument and Social Vision in the Courts, 1987, Diverse Partners: Non-Governmental Organizations in the Human Rights Movement, 1991; former devels. editor Harvard Law Rev.; contbr. articles to profl. jours. Office: Harvard U Law Sch Cambridge MA 02138 E-mail: hsteiner@law.harvard.edu.

STEINER, JANET, educational association administrator; Bachelors Degree, Blackburn Coll.; Masters Degree, D in Ednl. Leadership, So. Ill. U. Instr. Blackburn Coll.; ret.; mem. Ill. State Bd. Edn., 1999—, chairperson, 2003—. Office: Ill State Bd Edn 100 N 1st St Springfield IL 62777*

STEINER, ROGER JACOB, linguistics educator, writer, researcher; b. South Byron, Wis., Mar. 27, 1924; s. Jakob Robert and Alice Mildred (Cowles) S.; m. Ida Kathryn Posey, Aug. 7, 1954 (dec. May 1992); children: David Posey, Andrew Posey, Anthony Wright. BA cum laude, Franklin & Marshall Coll., 1945; MDiv, Union Theol. Sem., 1947; MA, U. Pa., 1958, PhD, 1963. Ordained to ministry, Meth. Ch., 1947. Clergyman United Meth. Ch., N.Y., Wis., Pa., 1945-61; lectr. U. Bordeaux, France, 1961-63; instr. dept. langs. & lit. U. Del., Newark, 1963-64, asst. prof., 1964-71, assoc. prof., 1971-80, prof., 1980-85, dept. linguistics U. Del., Newark, 1985-96, prof. emeritus, 1998—. Cons. Charles Scribner's Sons, N.Y.C., 1972-75, Larousse, N.Y.C., 1981-84, Houghton-Mifflin, Boston, 1981-84, Macmillan, 1994-99. Author: Two Centuries of Spanish and English Bilingual Lexicography (1590-1800), 1970, New College French and English Dictionary, 1972, 1988; editor: Simon & Schuster's International Spanish Dictionary, 2d edit., 1997, Cuyás Spanish and English Dictionary, 3d edit., 1999, New College Spanish and English Dictionary, 3d edit., 2004; contbr. articles to profl. jours., chpts. to books. Recipient fellowship Am. Philos. Soc., Phila., 1971, Lilly Found., Phila., 1979-81. Mem. MLA (founder lexicography group 1974-75, chmn. 1976, 77, 80, 85), Dictionary Soc. N.Am., Phi Beta Kappa (pres. chpt. 1975-76). Republican. Avocations: languages, photography. Office: U Del Dept Linguistics Newark DE 19716-2551 E-mail: rsteiner@udel.edu.

STEINER, STANLEY F. literature educator; b. Richardton, N.D., July 18, 1952; s. John F. and Anna Maria (Greff) Steiner; m. Katherine Radloff, July 20, 1973 (div. May 1978); 1 child, Benjamin Matthew; m. Joy Lynn Berryman, Mar. 31, 1983; children: Lea Christine, Avi John. AA, Bismarck State Coll., 1972; BA, U. Mary, Bismarck, 1974; MS, Northern State U., Aberdeen, S.D., 1976; PhD, U. Wyo., 1992. Tchr., asst. prin. Bismarck Pub. Schs., ND, 1974—78, Teton County Sch. Dist., Jackson Hole, Wyo., 1978—89; prof. Boise State U., 1992—. Author: Promoting A Global Community, Through Children's Literature, 2001; editor: Frierian Pedagogy: Praxis, and Possibilities, 2000; author: Building Bridges: Books Bring Us Together, 2002. Literacy area coord.; adv. bd. dirs. Idaho Human Rights Commn. Mem.: NCTE, Am. Libr. Assn., Internat. Reading Assn. (Notable Books for Global Soc. award 2002—). Avocations: childrens literature specialist, woodworker, hiking, cooking. Home: 1105 Pueblo St Boise ID 83702-4152 Office: Boise State U 1910 University Dr Boise ID 83725 Business E-Mail: ssteine@boisestate.edu.

STEINFORT, JAMES RICHARD, financial consultant; b. Grand Rapids, Mich., Oct. 1, 1941; s. Gerald Gene and Harriett Lois (Stauffer) S.; m. Elizabeth Ann O'Laughlin, Mar. 14, 1964; children Dawn, Robin, Susan, Troy, Ginger. AA in Computer Sci., San Jacinto Coll., Pasadena, Tex., 1973; BS in Tech. Mgmt. cum laude, Regis Coll., 1987. Chartered cons., Am. Cons. League. Customer engr. Control Data Corp., Mpls., 1964-65; computer engr. GE, Phoenix, 1965-69; tech. analyst Manned Spacecraft Ctr., Houston, 1969-73, systems analyst, 1973-75; tech. support mgr. Ohio Med. Products, Houston, 1975-79; prodn. regional mgr. Johnson & Johnson Co., Denver, 1979-83; prin., internat. cons. J.R. Steinfort & Assocs., Boise, Idaho, 1983-90; univ. program dir. TIES (Tech. and Indsl. Ext. Svc.) Boise State U., 1990-95; exec. dir. Idaho Mfg. Alliance, Boise, 1995-97, Assn. of Idaho Mfrs., 1997-98. Cons. The Timberline Group, Boise, 1996—; instr. computer classes Snake River Correctional Inst., 2000—. Author: (nonfiction) Conspiracy in Dallas, 1975, rev. edit., 1992, 96; (tech. manuals) Medical/EDP Design Applications, 1985, Factory Quality Audit, 1991; editor newsletter Industry TIES, 1992-94, ISO-9000 Guidelines & Checklist, 1994. Chmn. subcom. Gov.'s Prayer Breakfast Commn., Boise, 1988-92; v.p. Full Gospel Businessman's Internat., Boise, 1990. With USAF, 1960-64. Univ. Ctr. grantee Econ. Devel. Adminstrn., Boise, 1990-96. Mem. Am. Soc. for Quality Control (sr.), Nat. Assn. Mgmt. and Tech. Assistance Ctrs. (bd. dirs. 1990-96), Am. Mgmt. Assn., Am. Cons. League (chartered cons.), Idaho Total Quality Inst. (bd. dirs. 1991-96, trustee 1995-97, Idaho Quality award), Tech. Transfer Soc. Avocations: hiking, camping, photography, writing, hunting. Home: 11934 Ginger Creek Dr Boise ID 83713-3677 also: The Timberline Group 3355 N Five Mile Rd # 281 Boise ID 83713-3925 E-mail: jstein@micron.net.

STEINHAUSER, JANICE MAUREEN, arts administrator, educator, artist; b. Oklahoma City, Okla., Apr. 3, 1935; d. Max Charles and Charlotte (Gold) Glass; m. Stuart Z. Hirschman, Dec. 30, 1954 (div. 1965); children: Shayle, David, Susan; m. Sheldon Steinhauser, May 2, 1965; children: Karen, Lisa Steinhauser Hackel. BFA, U. Colo., Denver, 1972; student, U. Mich., 1953-55. Community affairs adminstr. United Bank Denver, 1973-76; dir. visual arts program Western States Arts Found., Denver, 1976-79; exec. dir. Artreach, Inc., Denver, 1980-82; v.p. mktg. Mammoth Gardens, Denver, 1982-83; dir. pub. rels. Denver Ctr. for Performing Arts, 1983-86; founder, pres. Resource Co., Denver, 1986-88; dir. liberal studies div. Univ. Coll. U. Denver, 1992-97; sculptor, 1997—. Bd. dirs. Met. Denver Arts Alliance, 1982-85, Denver Internat. Film Festival, 1983-86, Colo. Nat. Abortion Rights Action League, 1991-95, Mizel Mus. Judaica, 1995-2000; mem. Women's Forum of Colo., 1981-2002. Mem. Nat. Assn. Women Artists, Colo. New Music Assn. (bd. dirs. 1987-91), Asian Performing Arts Colo. (bd. dirs.), Phi Beta Kappa, Kappa Delta Phi. Democrat. Jewish. Avocations: travel, reading, films. E-mail: jansart3@aol.com.

STEINHAUSER, SHELDON ELI, sociology and gerontology educator, diversity and development consultant; b. N.Y.C., Aug. 11, 1930; s. Charles W. and Helen (Rosenstein) S.; m. Frances Goldfarb, June 28, 1953 (div. 1963); children: Karen, Lisa Steinhauser Hackel; m. Janice M. Glass, May 2, 1965; children: Shayle, David, Susan Hirschman. BS, L.I. U., 1963; DPS (hon.), Regis U., 1994. Community cons. Anti-Defamation League, Columbus, Ohio, 1951-57, regional dir. Denver, 1957-85, dir. nat. field svcs., 1977-85, dir. nat. community svcs. divsn., 1979-81, western area dir., 1975-85; exec. v.p. Allied Jewish Fedn. of Denver, 1985-91; pres. Sheldon Steinhauser & Assocs., Denver, 1991—; instr. sociology Met. State Coll., Denver, 1969-71, assoc. prof., 1994—; diversity cons., trainer BG Svc. Solutions, Denver Internat. Airport, 1994—. Maj. gifts devel. cons., 1992—, Shalom Park Capital, Jewish Family Svcs., 1997, CV Found., 2000—; pres. Anti-Defamation League Profl. Staff Assn., Agy. Execs. Orgn., Denver, 1963; cons. in field. Mem. editl. bd. Sustainable Cmtys. Rev. Missions to Egypt and Israel, 1982, 83; staff dir. Mission to Israel, 1986, 87, 90; former mem. Denver Anti-Crime Coun.; chmn. Mountain States Inst. of Judaism, Denver, 1958-59; past pres. Adult Edn. Coun. Met. Dever; past mem. cmty. adv. bd. Jr. League Denver; cons. U.S. Dept. Justice Cmty. Rels. Svc., 1994; past mem. Colo. Martin Luther King Holiday Planning Com., Latin Am. Rsch. and Svc. Agy., founding bd. mem.; mem. adv. com. Regis U. Inst. Common Good; Equal Opportunity Adv. Coun., Met State Coll., Denver; past mem. cmty. working group Nat. Civilian Cmty. Corps.; congl. del. White House Conf. on Aging, 1995. Recipient M.L. King Jr. Humanitarian award Colo. M.L. King Commn., Denver, 1986, 1st Ann. Human Rels. award Colo. Civil Rights Commn., Denver, 1965, Humanitarian award NAACP, Denver, 1980, ADL Civil Rights Achievement award, 1989; named to Gallery of Fame, Denver Post, 1979, 80. Mem. Diversity Assocs. Internat., Western Social Sci. Assn., Am. Sociol. Assn. (sect. on aging), Colo. Jewish Reconstructionist Fedn., Am. Soc. on Aging, Sociol. Practice Assn., Assn. for Gerontology in Higher Edn. (nat. pub. policy com.), Gerontol. Soc. Am., Colo. Gerontol. Soc., B'nai B'rith. Avocations: travel, photography, tennis, running, cantorial music. E-mail: sheldons3@aol.com.

STEINHORN, IRWIN HARRY, lawyer, educator, corporate executive; b. Dallas, Aug. 13, 1940; s. Raymond and Libby L. (Miller) Steinhorn; m. Deborah Kelley Steinhorn, Apr. 7, 2002; 1 child, Leslie Robin. BBA, U. Tex., 1961, LLB, 1964. Bar: Tex. 1964, U.S. Dist. Ct. (no. dist.) Tex. 1965, Okla. 1970, U.S. Dist. Ct. (we. dist.) Okla. 1972. Assoc. Oster & Kaufman, Dallas, 1964-67; ptnr. Parness, McQuire & Lewis, Dallas, 1967-70; sr. v.p., gen. counsel LSB Industries, Inc., Oklahoma City, 1970-87; v.p., gen. counsel USPCI, Inc., Oklahoma City, 1987-88; ptnr. Hastie & Steinhorn, Oklahoma City, 1988-95; mem., officer, dir. Conner & Winters, Oklahoma City, 1995—. Adj. prof. law Oklahoma City U. Sch. Law, 1979—; lectr. in field. Mem. adv. com. Okla. Securities Commn., 1986—; mem. exec. adv. bd. Oklahoma City U. Sch. Law, 2000—; bd. dirs. Okla. Venture Forum, 2000—. Served to capt. USAR, 1964-70. Mem. ABA, Tex. Bar Assn., Okla. Bar Assn. (bus. assn. sect., sec.ptreas. 1986-87, chmn. 1988-89), Com. to Revise Okla. Bus. Corp. Act, Rotary, Phi Alpha Delta. Republican. Jewish. Home: 224 NW 18th St Oklahoma City OK 73103 Office: Conner & Winters One Leadership Sq 211 N Robinson Ave Ste 1700 Oklahoma City OK 73102-7136 E-mail: isteinhorn@cwlaw.com.

STEINLICHT, STEVEN, astrologer, mystic, educator; b. Bloomington, Ill., Mar. 13, 1950; s. Henry Jr. and Mary Elizabeth (Ritter) S. Student, U. Ill., 1968; Dr. in Metaphysics, Universal Life Ch., 1975. Lic. psychol. counselor, Universal Life Ch. Minister Temple of Truth, Universal Life Ch., Bloomington, Ill., 1977; co-founder Ascension, Bloomington, 1979; stockroom supr. Murray's Shoes, Bloomington, Ill., 1981-86; psychic Rainbow Place, Albuquerque, 1988-90; software mgr., corp. astrologer Computer Bazaar, Albuquerque, 1991-96; pres., founder Albuquerque Metaphys. Inst., 1993—. Tchr., healer Gold Key Ctr., Albuquerque, 1987-88, pub. spkr. New Age Connection, Albuquerque, 1987-96, psychic Metaphysical Crystal Palace, Albuquerque, 1987; detective N.M. Bur. Investigations, 1988. Author: Astarunum, The Portable Oracle, 1993; columnist Rainbow Place, 1988-90, Up Front! Mag., 1996-97; inventor of Midpointer/Aspectarian, 1997; volunteer photographer and cartoonist at "the sims Resource" online forums, 2001-. Min. Universal Life Ch., 1972—. Mem. Mensa Internat., Soc. for Creative Anachronism, S.W. Psychic Forum; held office of Ed./Public Rels. for Mars Explorer Model at New Mexico Mus. of Natural Hist., 2003. Avocations: photography, hiking, role-playing games, magic tricks, calligraphy.

STEINMAN, JOAN ELLEN, law educator; b. Bklyn., June 19, 1947; d. Jack and Edith Ruth (Shapiro) S.; m. Douglass Watts Cassel, Jr., June 1, 1974 (div. July 1986); children: Jennifer Lynn, Amanda Hilary. Student, U. Birmingham, Eng., 1968; AB with high distinction, U. Rochester, 1969; JD cum laude, Harvard U., 1973. Bar: Ill. 1973, Ill. 1973. Assoc. Schiff, Hardin & Waite, Chgo., 1973-77; asst. prof. law Chgo.-Kent Coll. Law Ill. Inst. Tech., 1977-82, assoc. prof., 1982-86, prof., 1986-98, Disting. prof., 1998—, interim dean, 1990-91. Cons. in atty. promotions Met. Dist. Greater Chgo., 1981, 85, mem. adv. com. on 7th cir. rules. Author: Wright & Miller et al., Federal Practice and Procedure Treatise, vols. 14B, 14C; contbr. articles to law jours. Coop. atty. ACLU Ill., Chgo., 1974, Leadership Coun. for Met. Open Cmtys., Chgo., 1975, Better Bus. Bur. Met. Chgo., 1987; apptd. bd. arbitrators Nat. Assn. Security Dealers, 1989—2000; apptd. to Ill. Gov.'s Grievence Panel, 1987; bd. dirs. Pro Bono Advocates, 1995—99. Recipient Julia Beveridge award Ill. Inst. Tech., 1996, Ralph L. Brill award Chgo. Kent Coll. Law, 1997; Norman and Edna Freehling scholar Chgo.-Kent Coll. Law, 1989-93. Mem. ABA, Am. Law Inst. (advisor Fed. Jud. Code Revision project 1996-2001, cons. group complex litig. project 1990-93, restatement of the law, third, torts, products liability 1993, transnat. rules of civil procedure 2000-03), Am. Assn. Law Schs. (exec. com. civil procedure sect. 1998-99), Soc. Am. Law Tchrs., Chgo. Coun. Lawyers, AAUW (legal advocacy network 1987-2000), Chgo.-Lincoln Am. Inn. of Ct. (master 1991), Order of Coif, Phi Beta Kappa. Democrat. Jewish. Office: Chgo Kent Coll Law 565 W Adams St Chicago IL 60661-3613

STEINMAN, LISA MALINOWSKI, English literature educator, writer; b. Willimantic, Conn., Apr. 8, 1950; d. Zenon Stanislaus and Shirley Belle Malinowski; m. James A. Steinman, Apr. 1968 (div. 1980); m. James L. Shugrue, July 23, 1984. BA, Cornell U., 1971, MFA, 1973, PhD, 1976. Asst. prof. English Reed Coll., Portland, Oreg., 1976-82, assoc. prof., 1982-90, prof., 1990—, Kenan prof. English lit. and humanities, 1993—. Cons. NEH, Washington, 1984-85. Author: Lost Poems, 1976, Made in America, 1987, All That Comes to Light, 1989, A Book of Other Days, 1992, Ordinary Songs, 1996, Masters of Repetition, 1998, Carslaw's Sequences, 2003; editor: Hubbub Mag., 1983—; mem. editl. bd. Williams Rev., 1991—, Stevens Jour., 1994—; contbr. articles to profl. jours. Fellow Danforth Found., 1971-75, NEH, 1983, 96, Oreg. Arts Commn., 1983, Nat. Endowment for Arts, 1984; Rockefeller Found. scholar, 1987-88; recipient Pablo Neruda award, 1987, Oreg. Inst. Lit. Arts award, 1993. Mem. MLA, Poets and Writers, PEN (N.W. chpt., co-founder, officer 1989-93). Home: 5344 SE 38th Ave Portland OR 97202-4208 Office: Reed Coll Dept English 3203 SE Woodstock Blvd Portland OR 97202-8138 E-mail: lisa.steinman@reed.edu.

STELLA, JANET LOUISE, special education educator, researcher; b. Pitts., Oct. 11, 1961; d. Adam John and Patricia Jean (Mitchell) S. BS in Child Devel./Child Care magna cum laude, U. Pitts., 1983; MEd in Mentally and/or Physically Handicapped, California U. Pa., 1992. Cert. tchr. mentally and/or physically handicapped, Pa. Devel. care specialist Allegheny Valley Sch., Pitts., 1983; tchr. Parents Anonymous Pitts. Therapeutic Children's Ctr., 1983-84; substitute child devel. specialist Craig House Technoma, Pitts., 1984-85; resident advisor, asst. site supr., then site supr. Chartiers Mental Health-Mental Retardation Ctr., Pitts., 1985-88; case mgr. for mentally retarded adults Allegheny East Mental Health and Mental Retardation Ctr., Pitts., 1989-93; spl. edn. tchr. Allegheny Intermediate Unit, Pitts., 1993—. Cons. on family and child support svcs. subcom. Pa. Protection and Advocacy, Inc., Pitts., 1987-89. Vol. Children's Hosp. Pitts., 1980-81. Presdl. scholar California U. Pa., 1992. Mem. Coun. for Exceptional Children, South Park Runners Club, Sigma Pi Epsilon Delta. Roman Catholic. Home: 3145 Belleville St Pittsburgh PA 15234-2739 Office: Allegheny Intermediate Unit 4 Station Sq Fl 2 Pittsburgh PA 15219-1129

STELLA, VALENTINO JOHN, pharmaceutical chemistry educator; b. Melbourne, Victoria, Australia, Oct. 27, 1946; came to U.S., 1968; s. Giobatta and Mary Katherine (Sartori) S.; m. Mary Elizabeth Roeder, Aug. 16, 1969; children: Catherine Marie, Anne Elizabeth, Elise Valentina. B of Pharmacy, Victorian Coll. Pharmacy, Melbourne, 1967; PhD, U. Kans., 1971. Lic. pharmacist, Victoria. Pharmacist Bendigo (Victoria) Base Hosp., 1967-68; asst. prof. Coll. Pharmacy U. Ill., Chgo., 1971-73; from asst. prof. to assoc. prof. to prof. Sch. Pharmacy U. Kans., Lawrence, 1973-90, Univ. disting. prof., 1990—. Dir. Ctr. for Drug Delivery Rsch.; cons. to 15 pharm. cos., U.S., Japan, Europe. Co-author: Chemical Stability of Pharmaceuticals, 2d edit., 1986; co-editor: Prodrugs as Novel Drug Delivery Systems, 1976, Directed Drug Delivery, 1985, Lymphatic Transport of Drugs, 1992; author numerous papers, revs., abstracts. Fellow AAAS, Am. Assn. Pharm. Scientists, Am. Acad. Pharm. Scientists. Roman Catholic. Achievements include 16 U.S. patents; rsch. in application of phys./organic chemistry to the solution of pharm. problems. Office: U Kans West Campus Dept Pharm Chemistry 2095 Constant Ave Lawrence KS 66047-3729 Home: 1135 W Campus Rd Lawrence KS 66044-3115

STELLAR, ARTHUR WAYNE, educational administrator; b. Columbus, Ohio, Apr. 12, 1947; s. Fredrick and Bonnie Jean (Clark) S. BS, Ohio U., 1969, MA, 1970, PhD, 1973. Tchr. Athens (Ohio) City Schs., 1969-71; curriculum coord., tchr. Belpre (Ohio) City Schs., 1971-72; prin. elem. schs., head tchr. learning disabilities South-Western City Schs., Grove City, Ohio, 1972-76; dir. elem. edn. Beverly (Mass.) Pub. Schs., 1976-78; coord. spl. projects and systemwide planning Montgomery County Pub. Schs., Rockville, Md., 1978-80; asst. supt. Shaker Heights (Ohio), 1980-83; supt. schs. Mercer County Pub. Schs., Princeton, W.Va., 1983-85, Oklahoma City Pub. Schs., 1985-92, Cobb County, Ga., 1992-93; dep. supt. Boston Pub. Schs., 1993-95, acting supt., 1995-96; supt. Kingston (N.Y.) Sch. Dist., 1996—2001; pres., CEO High/Scope Ednl. Rsch. Found., Ypsilanti, Mich., 2001—. Adj. prof. Lesley Coll., Cambridge, Mass., 1976-78; adj. faculty Harvard U., 1992-93. Author: Educational Planning for Educational Success, Effective Schools Research: Practice and Promise; editor: Effective Instructional Management; cons. editor, book rev. editor Jour. Ednl. Pub. Rels.; mem. editl. bd. Jour. Curriculum & Supervision, Reading Today's Youth; contbr. articles to profl. jours. Bd. govs. Kirkpatrick Ctr.; mem. Oklahoma City Com. Econ. Devel.; founding bd. dirs. Okla. Alliance Against Drugs, Okla. Zool. Soc. Inc.; selected for Leadership Oklahoma City, 1986; bd. dirs. Leadership Oklahoma City, ARC, Okla. Centennial Sports Inc., Rip Van Winkle Coun. BSA; mem. Okla. Acad. for State Goals, State Supt.'s Adv. Coun.; mem. clin. experiences adv. com. U. Okla. Coll. Edn.; trustee Arts Coun. Oklahoma City, Omniplex Sci. and Arts Mus., Oklahoma City Area Vocat.-Tech. Dist. 22 Found.; mem. Urban Ctr. Ednl. Adv. Bd., U.S. Dept. Edn. Urban Supt. Network, Coun. Great City Schs. Bd., Urban Edn. Clearing House Adv. com., U. Okla. Adminstrn. cert. program com., Cmty. Literacy Coun. Bd.; cmty. bd. dirs. Langston U.; chair United Way Greater Okla., Sch. Mgmt. Study Group, Okla. Reading Coun. (Okla. literacy coun. reading award 1-89), Oklahoma City PTA; bd. dirs. Oklahoma County chpt. ARC, Jr. Achievement Greater Oklahoma City Bd., Okla. State Fair Bd., Horace Mann League, 1993-2000, v.p. 2000-01, pres.-elect, 2001-02, pres. 2002-03, past pres. 2003-04; v.p. Last Frontier Coun. Bd., v.p. N.Y. State PTA, 1996-2000, Kingston chpt. Rip Van Winkle Coun.; v.p. Boy Scouts Am., 1996-2001, membership chmn., 1996-97; mem. exec. bd. Nat. Dropout Prevention Ctr. Network, 1998—, chmn., 2003—; mem. curriculum com. N.Y. State Coun. Sch. Supts., 1996-2001; bd. dirs. Friends Historic Kingston, 1996-2001, Friends Senate House, Kingston, 1996-2001. Named to Linden McKinley H.S. Acad. Hall of Fame, 2003; recipient Silver Beaver award, Boy Scouts Am., 1990, Am. award, Horace Mann League, 1995—2003; fellow, Charles Kettering Found. IDEA, 1976, 1978, 1980, NEH, Danforth Found., 1987—88. Mem. ASCD (life, exec. coun., pres.-elect 1993-94, pres. 1994-95, rev. coun. 1997-2002), Mich. ASCD, Mass. ASCD, Ohio ASCD, Okla. ASCD (Publ. award 1989), N.Y. ASCD, Internat. Soc. Ednl. Planning, Internat. Reading Assn. (mem. govt. rels. com. 2003—), Nat. Soc. Study Edn., Nat. Planning

Assn., Nat. Assn. Gifted Children (life), Nat. Assn. Educators Young Children (Mich. chpt.), Am. Assn. Sch. Adminstrn. (Mich. chpt.), Nat. Coun. Tchrs. English (life), Music Educators Nat. Conf. (life), Nat. Orgn. Legal Problems Edn., Nat. Policy Bd. Ednl. Adminstrn., Am. Assn. Sch. Adminstrs. (life, Leadership for Learning award 1991), Coll. Bd. Advanced Placement Spl. Recognition award 1991, Nat. Assn. Elem. Sch. Prins. (life), Am. Edn. Fin. Assn., Nat. Assn. Edn. Young Children (life), Nat. Sch. Pub. Rels. Assn. (Honor award 1991), Am. Mus. Natural Hist. (assoc.), World Coun. Curriculum and Instrn. (life, bd. dirs. N.Am. chpt. 1996-2000, pres. 2000-02), Coun. Basic Edn., Ohio Assn. Elem. Sch. Adminstrs., Buckeye Assn. Sch. Adminstrs., Ohio U. Coll. Edn. (disting. alumnus award 1991), Okla. Assn. Sch. Adminstrs., Mass. Assn. Sch. Adminstrs., Okla. Coalition Pub. Edn., Okla. Commn. Ednl. Leadership, Urban Area Supts. (Okla. br.), Ohio U. Alumni Assn. (nat. dir. 1975-78, pres. Ctrl. Ohio chpt. 1975-76, pres. Mass. chpt. 1976-78, life mem. trustees acad.), World Future Soc. (life) Greater Oklahoma City C. of C. (bd. dirs.), Oklahoma Heritage Assn., Heritage Hills Assn. (bd. dirs.), Victorian Soc. (New England chpt.), Nat. Eagle Scout Assn. (life), Aerospace Found. (hon. bd. dirs.), PLATO, Learning, Inc. (bd. dirs.), Am. Bus. Card Club, Coca Cola Collectors Club, Internat. Club, Mgmt. Consortium (bd. advisors), Detroit Inst. Arts, Henry Ford Mus., Greenfield Village; Rotary (Boston), Fulbright Alumni Assn. (life), Tau Kappa Epsilon Alumni Assn. (regional officer Mass. 1976-78, named Alumni Nat. Hall of Fame 1986, Nat. Alumnus of Yr. 1993, Excellence in Edn. award 1993), Kappa Delta Pi (life, advisor Ctrl. Okla. chpt., nat. publs. com.), Phi Delta Kappa (life). Methodist.

STELMACK, GLORIA JOY, elementary education educator; b. Chgo., Oct. 1, 1933; d. Raymond Thomas and Bess (Henneberry) Ibison; m. Carl Francis McGarrity, Feb. 7, 1953; children: Maureen, Thomas, Stephen, John; m. Stephen Stanley Stelmack, Dec. 22, 1979. BA with honors, U. Ill., 1972; MA in Reading, Northeastern Ill. U., 1977. Cert. tchr., Ill. Tchr., reading specialist St. Pius Sch., Chgo., 1972-82, St. Jane de Chantal Sch., Chgo., 1982—. Adv. com. St. Jane de Chantal Sch., Chgo., 1986—; v.p. Nat. Coun. of Tchrs. of English, Chgo., 1980-81. Nominated for Golden Apple award, 1990. Avocations: travel, reading, flower arranging, golf. Office: Saint Jane de Chantal Sch 5201 S Mcvicker Ave Chicago IL 60638-1497

STEMPLESKI, SUSAN, English language professional, writer; d. John Adam Stempleski and Helen Marie (Fitzgerald) Sutter. BA in English Lit., Boston U., 1964; MA in Bilingual, Bicultural Studies, Boston State Coll., 1973; MEd, Columbia U. Tchr.'s Coll., 1989, postgrad. Tchr. French, math. Matignon High Sch., Cambridge, Mass., 1964-65; rsch. asst. Boston U., 1965-66; coord. ABE, ESL Boston Pub. Schs., 1966-72; coord. ESL program Harvard U., Cambridge, 1972-74, tng. rep., 1974-76; lectr. ESL Emerson Coll., Boston, 1976-77; coord. bilingual programs Newbury Jr. Coll., Boston, 1976-77; tchr. EFL, tchr. trainer The Cleve. Inst., Paris, 1977-80; mng. dir. Caf(é)-Th(é)atre de la Rosais, Jugon-les-Lacs, France, 1980-81; instr. ESL CUNY, 1981-89; lectr. in TESOL Columbia U. Tchr.'s Coll., N.Y.C., 1988—. Cons. EFL/ESL materials devel., program design tchr. tng. and devel.; Fulbright lectr., Chile, 1987; mem. adv. bd. BBC English by TV, Encyclopedia Britannica; cons. ESL English Advantage Video, 1990; dir. ESL Hello America, 1991; advisor Encounter English, 1990, Am. Lang. Hello, 1991. Author: Getting Together, 1986, Explorations, 1988, Video in Action, 1990, Focus on the Environment, 1992, Video in Second Language Teaching, 1992, Earth Watch, 1993, Cultural Awareness, 1993, That's English, 1994, American English OK!, 1998, English Today, 1998, Film, 2001; contbr. articles to profl. jours. Recipient Duke of Edinburgh commendation, 1990; grantee U.S. Info. Agy. Acad. Specialist, 1985, 87, 89, 91, 94, Disting. Am. Specialist award, 1994; Fulbright scholar Bolivia, 1987. Mem. TESOL (exec. bd. 1993-96, founding chair video interest sect. 1989-90, local com. conv. N.Y.C. 1985, dir. video theater ann. conv. San Antonio 1989, San Francisco 1990, pres. Mass. affiliate 1976-77, v.p. 1975-76, mem.-at-large exec. bd. 1973-75, chair ann. conf. 1975, 76, video liaison officer 1987—), Internat. Assn. Tchrs. English as Fgn. Lang. (video spl. interest group com. 1987—), Assn. Binational Ctrs. in L.Am. (proposal com. 1989), Kappa Delta Pi. Avocations: theater, film, opera. Home: 504 W 111th St Apt 54 New York NY 10025-1939 Office: Columbia U Tchrs Coll Box 66 TESOL Program 525 W 120th St New York NY 10027-6625

STENBERG, CARL W., III, public administration educator, dean; b. Pitts., July 8, 1943; s. Carl W. and Mildred (Baggs) S.; m. Kirstin D. Thompson; children: Erik Anders, Kerry Cathryn, Kaameran Baird. BA, Allegheny Coll., 1965; MPA, SUNY, Albany, 1966, PhD, 1970. Research asst. N.Y. State Div. Budget, Albany, 1967; analyst, then sr. analyst U.S. Adv. Commn. on Intergovtl. Relations, Washington, 1968-77, asst. dir. for policy implementation, 1977-83, acting exec. dir., 1982; exec. dir. Council of State Govts., Lexington, Ky., 1983-89; prof., dir. Weldon Cooper Ctr. for Pub. Svc. U. Va., Charlottesville, 1989-95, Disting. prof. pub. svc., 1991-95; prof., dean Yale Gordon Coll. Liberal Arts U. Balt., 1995—2003; prof. Sch. Govt. U. N.C., Chapel Hill, 2003—. Mem. Am. Part Program USIA, 1987; adj. prof. George Washington U., 1971, 81, Am. U., 1972-80, 82, U. Md., 1976, U. So. Calif., 1984-87; v.p. Bureaucrat Inc., Washington, 1973-77, mng. editor, 1973-77. Feature editor Pub. Mgmt. Forum Pub. Adminstrn. Rev., 1977-83, editor U. of Va. newsletter, 1994-95; co-editor-in-chief The Regionalist, 1997-2002. Pres. Reston Home Owners' Assn., Va., 1973-74; mem. U.S. del. Ad Hoc Group on Urban Problems, OECD, 1980-82. Vivien Stewart vis. fellow Cambridge U., Eng., 1980; recipient Disting. Alumni award Polit. Sci. Dept. Rockefeller Coll., 1985. Fellow: Nat. Acad. Pub. Adminstrn. (chair bd. dirs. 2002—); mem.: Va. Alliance for Pub. Svc. (pres. 1991—92), Am. Soc. Pub. Adminstrn. (pres. 1990—91, Marshall E. Dimock award, Louis Brownlow award, Donald Stone award). Home: 301 Madera Ln Chapel Hill NC 27514 Office: U NC Sch Govt CB # 3330 Knapp Bldg Chapel Hill NC 27599-3330 E-mail: stenberg@109mail.109.unc.edu.

STENCER, MARK JOSEPH, healthcare administrator, consultant; b. Pitts., Mar. 19, 1955; s. Frank C. and Ramona (Calabrese) S. BFA, Carnegie-Mellon U., 1976; BA in Liberal Arts, U. Mich., 1979; MA in Mgmt., NYU, 1982. Asst. dir. NYU Office Acad. Devel., N.Y.C., 1980-82; program dir. John B. Cummings Co., Inc., Fundraising and Pub. Rels. Cons., N.Y.C., 1982-84; assoc. dir. The Statue of Liberty, Ellis Island Found., N.Y.C., 1984-86; dir. devel. Fordham U., N.Y.C., 1986-91; exec. v.p. Cambridge U., England, 1991-94; exec. campaign dir. Cmty. Counselling Svc. Co., Inc., N.Y.C., N.J., 1995-2000; exec. sr. dir. U. Chgo., N.Y. Regional Divsn., 2000—02; chief devel. officer Sisters of Mercy Health Sys., 2002—. Named Outstanding Young Man Am., 1985, 86. Mem. Ass. Fundraising Profls., Assn. Healthcae Philanthropy, Coun. Advancement and Support of Edn., Assn. for Healthcare Philanthropy. Republican. Roman Catholic. Avocation: pianist. Home: 1735-H Boulder Springs Dr Saint Louis MO 63146

STENGEL, ROBERT FRANK, engineering and applied science educator; b. Orange, N.J., Sept. 1, 1938; s. Frank John and Ruth Emma (Geidel) S.; m. Margaret Robertson Ewing, Apr. 8, 1961; children: Brooke Alexandra, Christopher Ewing. SB, MIT, 1960; MS in Engring., Princeton U., 1965, MA, 1966, PhD, 1968. Aerospace technologist NASA, Wallops Island, Va., 1960-63; tech. staff group leader C.S. Draper Lab., Cambridge, Mass., 1968-73, Analytic Scis. Corp., Reading, Mass., 1973-77; assoc. prof. Princeton (N.J.) U., 1977-82, prof. engring. and applied sci., 1982—, assoc. dean engring., 1994-97. Cons. GM, Warren, Mich., 1985-94; mem. com. strategic tech. U.S. Army NRC, 1989-92; vice chmn. Congl. Aero. Adv. Com., Washington, 1986-89; mem. com. on trans-atmospheric vehicles USAF Sci. Adv. Bd., 1984-85; mem. com. on low altitude wind shear and its hazard to aviation Nat. Rsch. Coun., 1983, Navy Theater Missile Defense com. NRC, 2000-01. Author: Stochastic Optimal Control: Theory and Application, 1986, reprinted as Optimal Control and Estimation, 1994; N.Am. editor Cambridge Aerospace Series, Cambridge Univ. Press, 1993-98; contbr. over 200 tech. papers to profl. publs.; patentee wind probing device. Lt. USAF, 1960-63. Recipient Apollo Achievement award NASA, 1969, Cert. of Commendation, MIT, 1969, Excellence in Aviation award FAA, 1997, John R. Ragazzini Edn. award, AACC, 2002. Fellow IEEE, AIAA (Mechanics and Control of Flight award 2000). Avocations: photography, music, bicycling. Home: 329 Prospect Ave Princeton NJ 08540-5330 Office: Princeton U D202 Engineering Quadrangle Princeton NJ 08544-0001 Fax: (609) 258-6109. E-mail: stengel@princeton.edu.

STENGER, JUDITH ANTOINETTE, middle school educator; b. Camp Blanding, Fla., Dec. 20, 1942; d. Jack Joseph DiSalvo and Judith Lorraine (Donnelly) DiSalvo-Kohser; m. Harry Richard Stenger, Feb. 4, 1967; children: Scott Joseph, Christopher Richard. BS in Art Edn., Indiana U. Pa., 1965; postgrad., Trinity Coll., 1983-84, Western Md. Coll., 1983-84. Tchr. art elem. sch. Elizabethtown (Pa.) Schs., 1965, Freedom (Pa.) Area Schs., 1966; tchr. art elem. and mid. schs. Carroll County (Md.) Schs., 1967-69; spl. educator Montgomery County (Md.) Schs., 1980-92, tchr. art mid. sch., 1992—. Co-leader Md. Student Assistance Program (drug intervention), Rockville, 1995—, mem., 1993—. Represented in 17 group shows. Named Outstanding Tchr. Coun. Exceptional Children, 1986. Mem. NEA, Md. State Tchrs. Assn., Montgomery County Tchrs. Assn., Nat. Art Edn. Assn., Nat. Artists Equity, Md. Art Edn. Assn., Rockville Arts Place. Avocations: printmaking, sculpture, painting. Office: Montgomery County Pub Schs Parkland Mid Sch 4610 W Frankfort Dr Rockville MD 20853-2721

STENMARK, JEAN KERR, mathematics educator; b. Davis, Calif., Aug. 25, 1922; d. Norman and Rachel Kerr; m. Roy M., Aug. 24, 1952, (div. July 1975); children: Ruthann, John, Jane. BA, U. Calif., Berkeley, 1942; MS, Calif. State U., Hayward, 1978. Cert. elem. tchr., Calif. With civil svc. U.S. Navy-Aviation Supply, Oakland, Calif., 1942-45; acct. various acctg. firms, San Francisco, 1945-56; tchr. Oakland Unified Sch. Dist., 1969-80; maths. specialist EQUALS and Family Math. Programs U. Calif., Berkeley, 1980-95. Cons. Calif. Assessment Program, Sacramento, 1975-92, New Standards Assessment Project, Oakland, Calif., 1991—. Editor: 101 Short Problems, 1995, Mathematics Assessment: Myths, Models, Good Questions and Practical Suggestions, 1991; author: Assessment Alternatives in Mathematics, 1989; co-author: Family Math, 1986, Math for Girls and Other Problem Solvers, 1981, Family Math for Young Children: Comparing, 1997; co-editor: Mathematics Assessment: a practical handbook for grades 3-5, 2001; co-writer, core advisor: Mathematics Assessment: A Video Library, K-12 Guide, 1998. Mem. Calif. Math. Coun., PTA (hon. life). Democrat. Protestant. Avocations: walking, reading. Home and Office: 242 Ashbury Ave El Cerrito CA 94530-4104 E-mail: jkstenmark@aol.com.

STENSVAAG, JOHN-MARK, legal educator, lawyer; b. Mpls., July 1, 1947; s. John Monrad and Hannah (Mehus) S.; m. Nancy Kay Strommen, June 19, 1970; children: Eric Paul, Nellie Marlene, Rebecca Gayle, Kirsten Elizabeth, Jonathan Michael. BA, Augsburg Coll., Mpls., 1969; JD, Harvard U., 1974. Bar: Minn. 1974, U.S. Dist. Ct. Minn. 1977, U.S. Ct. Appeals (D.C. cir.) 1978. Law clk. U.S. Ct. Appeals (8th cir.), Duluth, Minn., 1974-75, U.S. Dist. Ct. Minn., Mpls., 1975-76; spl. asst. atty. gen. Minn. Pollution Control Agy., Roseville, 1976-79; asst. prof. law Vanderbilt U., Nashville, 1979-83, assoc. prof., 1983-87, prof., 1987-88. Vis. prof. law U. Iowa, Iowa City, 1987-88, prof., 1988-2003, Charlotte and Frederick Hubbell prof. environ. and natural resource law, 2003—. Author: Hazardous Waste Law and Practice, vol. 1, 1986, vol. 2, 1989, Clean Air Act: Law and Practice, vol. 1, 1991, vol. 2, 1993, Materials on Environmental Law, 1999; contbr. articles to legal pubs. Danforth Grad. fellow, 1969-73. Lutheran. Home: 4 Heather Dr Iowa City IA 52245-3227 Office: U Iowa Coll Law Iowa City IA 52242 E-mail: J-Stensvaag@uiowa.edu.

STEPETIC, MARY LORRAINE, elementary school educator; b. Santa Fe, Feb. 21, 1956; d. Robert Newton and Alice Lorraine (Gibbs) Thompson; m. Thomas James Stepetic, Aug. 6, 1982; children: Kelly Michelle, Jamie Alyse. BA, U. N.Mex., 1979, cert. teaching, 1983, MEd, 1985. Substitute tchr. Albuquerque Pub. Schs., 1984; grad. intern Los Padillas Elem. Sch., Albuquerque, 1984-85; tchr. Lavaland Elem. Sch., Albuquerque, 1985-88, Sandia Base Elem. Sch., Albuquerque, 1989—. Assoc. ctr. teaching excellence Ea. N.Mex. U., Portales, spring 1993. Mem., calendar co-chair Mary Ann Binford Found., Albuquerque. Mem. ASCD, NSTA, Nat. Coun. Tchrs. Math., Pi Beta Phi Alumnae Assn. (treas. 1990-93). Avocations: cross stitch, gardening, reading, quilting. Home: 4101 Dietz Ct NW Albuquerque NM 87107-3206 Office: Sandia Base Elem Sch Bldg 21000 KAFB East Albuquerque NM 87116

STEPHAN, ALEXANDER FRIEDRICH, German language and literature educator; b. Lüdenscheid, Fed. Republic Germany, Aug. 16, 1946; arrived in US, 1968; s. Eberhard and Ingeborg (Hörnig) S.; m. Halina Konopacka, Dec. 15, 1969; 1 child, Michael. MA, U. Mich., 1969; PhD, Princeton U., 1973. Instr. German Princeton U., N.J., 1972-73; from asst. prof. to prof. German UCLA, 1973-85; prof. German U. Fla., Gainesville, 1985-2000, chmn., 1985-93; prof. German, Ohio Eminent Scholar, fellow Mershon Ctr., Ohio State U., 2000—. Author: (literature edition) Christa Wolf, 1976, Die deutsche Exilliteratur, 1979, Christa Wolf (Forschungsbericht), 1981, Max Frisch, 1983, Anna Seghers im Exil, 1993, Im Visier des FBI, 1995, paperback edit. 1998, English transl. Communazis, 2000, Anna Seghers: Das siebte Kreuz. Welt und Wirkung eines Romans, 1997; editor: Peter Weiss: Die Ästhetik des Widerstands, 1983, 3d edit., 1990, Exil. Literatur und die Künste, 1990, Exil-Studien, 1993—, (literature edition) Christa Wolf: The Author's Dimension, 1993, 2d edit., 1995, Themes and Structures, 1997, Uwe Johnson: Speculations about Jakob and Other Writings, 2000, Early 20th Century German Fiction, 2003, Anna Seghers, Die Entscheidung, 2003; co-editor: Studies in GDR Culture and Society, 1981—90, Schreiben im Exil, 1985, The New Sufferings of Young Werther and Other Stories from the GDR, 1997, Rot=Brau? Brecht Dialog, 2000, Nationalsozialismus und Stalinismus bei Brecht und Zeitgenossen, 2000; co-prodr.: (TV documentaries) Im Visier des FBI, 1995, Das FBI und Marlene Dietrich, 2000, Das FBI und Brechts Telephon, 2002, Exilanten und das OSS, 2002, Thomas Mann und der CIA, 2002. Grantee, Humboldt Found., 1988, 1994, 1998—99, 2002—03, Guggenheim Found., 1989, Feuchtwanger Meml. Libr., 1998, German Acad. Exch. Svcs., 1993, 1997, NEH, 1974, 1984, 1997, Am. Coun. Learned Socs., 1976, 1977, 1984, Am. Philos. Soc., 1979, 1981, 1992, Weichmann Stiftung, 1998. Mem.: German PEN, German Assn. for Am. Studies, Internat. Brecht Soc. (pres.), German Studies Assn., Internat. Anna Seghers Soc., Soc. for Exile Studies. Office: Ohio State U Dept Germanic Lang/Lit 314 Dieter Cunz Hall Columbus OH 43210-1229

STEPHAN, DIETRICH A. pediatrician, educator, geneticist; b. Pitts., Aug. 25, 1969; s. Thorsten and Aziza Stephan. PhD, U. Pitts., 1996. Sr. fellow Nat. Human Genome Rsch. Inst., Bethesda, Md., 1996—99; prof. pediat. Children's Nat. Med. Ctr., Washington, 1999—. Co-dir. - Microarray Ctr. Rsch. Ctr. for Genetic Medicine, Washington, 2000—02; chief sci. officer OrthoGene, Inc., N.Y.C., 2001—; mem. internat. adv. bd. Found. for Genetic Medicine, Leesburg, 2002—; guest rschr. Nat. Human Genome Rsch. Inst./NIH, Bethesda, 1999—; adj. prof. Johns Hopkins U., Balt., 2000—; prof. biochemistry and molecular biology George Washington U. Sch. of Medicine, Washington, 2000—; prof. genetics George Washington U. Sch. of Arts and Sciences, Washington, 1999—. Author (inventor): A gene expression-based method for distinguishing metastatic from non-metastatic forms of tumor, and use in designing therapeutics, 2001, Germline mutations in the ribonuclease L gene in families showing linkage with HPC1, 2002; contbr. chpt. in book, 1997; author (rsch. grant): molecular basis of cardiomyopathy in Rippling muscle disease, 2000 ($260,000, 2000), Prodn.of "sensory" array for the human eye, 2000 ($200,000, 2000), Expression profiling of cardiopulmonary disease, 2000 ($14,000,000, 2000), Skeletal Genome Anatomy Project, 2001 ($1,200,000, 2001), Biological basis of neurodevelopmental deficits in neurofibromatosis, 2002 ($460,697, 2002), Microarray Center for research on the nervous system, 2002 ($3,610,015, 2002), Predicting relapse in acute lymphoblastic leukemia, 2002 ($2,150,351, 2002); contbr. numerous articles to profl. jours. Bd. dir. Nat. Human Genome Rsch. Inst. Seminar Series, Bethesda, 1998—99; mem. NIH Fellows Assn., Bethesda, 1998—99. Recipient Nat. Rsch. Award Finalist, Am. Soc. Human Genetics, 2001; grantee Rsch. Grant, Alexander von Humbolt Found., 1997. Mem.: Soc. Pediat. Rsch. Office: Genetic Medicine Rsch Ctr 111 Michigan Ave NW Washington DC 20010 Office Fax: 202-884-6014. Business E-Mail: dstephan@cnmcresearch.org.

STEPHEN-COSSIE, ELIZABETH ANN, retired special education educator; b. Kansas City, Kans., Nov. 27, 1934; d. William Donald and Maryana (Seifert) Stephen; m. Leroy Fitzgerald Cossie, Dec. 7, 1984. BA, Sterling (Kans.) Coll., 1956; postgrad. U. Iowa, U. Kans., 1959. Elem. tchr. Bd. Edn. Dist. 500, Kansas City, 1956—68; tchr. hearing impaired spl. edn. Wyandotte County Spl. Edn. Coop. Dist. 500, Kansas City, 1968—94; ret. Mem. Delta Kappa Gamma. Presbyterian. Avocations: gardening, needlepoint, piano.

STEPHENS, BESS, computer company executive; Grad., Tuskegee Inst. Govt. and pub. affairs mgr. Hewlett Packard Co., human resources mgr., v.p. and global dir. philanthropy and edn., 2002—. Pres., exec. dir. Hewlett Packard Co. Found. Trustee Western Govs. U., Salt Lake City, Bay Area Sch. Reform Collaborative; mem. bd. fellows Santa Clara U., 1991—. Mem.: Nat. Bd. for Profl. Tchg. Stds. (bd. mem.), Gifts in Kind Internat. (bd. dirs.). Office: Hewlett Packard Co MS 1029 3000 Hanover St Palo Alto CA 94304*

STEPHENS, BETSY BAIN, retired elementary school educator; b. Bessemer, Ala., Apr. 1, 1927; d. Herman Merritt and Lorene Burnice (Waldrop) Bain; m. Merton Von Stephens, June 23, 1947; children: Marc Von, Timothy Merton, Martha Katherine. Diploma, Wheeler Bus. Coll., Birmingham, Ala., 1945; B, U. Montevallo, 1949; MA, U. Ala., Birmingham, 1972. Tchr. Lee County Bd. Edn., Auburn, Ala., 1950-52, Jefferson County Bd. Edn., Birmingham, Ala., 1964-89. Mem. Nat. Coun. Tchrs. of English, Bessemer Music Club, Jefferson County Ret. Tchrs. Assn., Ala. Ret. Tchrs. Assn., Soc. of Ala. Retirees, Alpha Delta Kappa. Home: 7373 Warrior River Rd Bessemer AL 35023-7019

STEPHENS, CECILE HIGDON, artist, art educator; b. Linden, Ala., July 12, 1925; d. Cecil Rudolph and Mildred (Thomas) Hinson; m. William Travis Higdon, Jr., June 28, 1947 (div. Dec. 1971); children: William Travis III, Kent Thomas, Dean Gregory; m. John Pearson Stephens, June 29, 1973. BFA, Auburn U., 1968; MA, U. South Ala., 1971; 2d MA, U. Miss., 1976; postgrad., Nova U., 1973-80. Head art program, art instr. Miss. Gulf Coast C.C., Gautier, 1968-80; art instr. William Carey Coll., Gulfport, Miss., 1982-83. Art instr. U. So. Miss., Hattiesburg, 1968-73; juror and judge various art shows, 1975-85. Exhibited in solo shows at Birmingham So. U., 1960, Auburn U., 1968, La Font Gallery, Pascagoula, Miss., 1991, U. Miss., Oxford, 1994, Singing River Depot Gallery, Pascagoula, 1995, Eastern Shore Art Ctr., Fairhope Ala., 1995, Space 504 Gallery, N.Y.C., 1996, others; group shows include U. Ala., Tuscaloosa, Birmingham So. U., Biloxi (Miss.) Art Mus., Montgomery (Ala.) Mus. Art, Mobile (Ala.) Coll., Palais des Congres, Paris, Auburn U., U. So. Miss., Hattiesburg, James Russell Gallery, Gautier, Miss., Nat. Mus. of Women in the Arts, Washington. Mem. Rep. Women, Pascagoula, 1984-97; past state chmn., pres. gen.'s project DAR, Pascagoula, 1988-92, past regent, Pascagoula, 1988-92; v.p., bd. mem. cmty. concerts, Gautier, Pascagoua and Moss Point, Miss., 1986-90; ship christening com. mem. Ingalls Ship Bldg., Pascagoula, 1997; mem. adv. bd. Melange Dance Co., Pascagoula, 1995-97. Recipient Exemplary Achievement Alumna award Auburn U. Centennial of the Admission of Women, 1992, Unsung Hero's award Moss Point Miss. C. of C., 1996. Mem. Am. Soc. Portrait Painters, Washington Soc. Portrait Artists (charter), Nat. Mus. Women in the Arts (charter), Jackson County Arts Coun. (bd. mem.), Mobile Mus. Art, Ea. Shore Miss. Mus. Art, Walter Anderson Mus. Art (mem. adv. bd.). Episcopalian. Avocations: gardening, antique collecting, traveling. Home: 3855 River Rd Moss Point MS 39563-3711

STEPHENS, ELISA, college president; Pres. Acad. of Art Coll., San Francisco, 1992—. Office: 79 New Montgomery St 6th Fl San Francisco CA 94105-3410*

STEPHENS, GARY RALPH, American literature and journalism educator; b. Wichita, Kans., Mar. 4, 1943; s. Hubert Hal and Iris Lenore (Edgar) S.; m. Swati Niru Desai, May 13, 1978; children: Anaar, Joshua. AB, Wichita State U., 1965; MA, Brandeis U., 1969, PhD, 1972. Asst. prof. English, Queens Coll., CUNY, Flushing, 1971-75, N.Y. Inst. Tech., Old Westbury, 1976-81, assoc. prof., 1982-88, chmn. dept., 1979—93, prof. N.Y.C., 1989—; assoc. in journalism Grad. Sch. Journalism, Columbia U., N.Y.C., 1986-97; chmn. dept. N.Y. Inst. Tech., N.Y.C., 1999—. Cons. in field. Contbr. articles to profl. publs. J.W. Fulbright fellow India, 1993; fellow Woodrow Wilson Found., 1965, Rockefeller Found., 1966, NEH, 1981. Office: NY Inst Tech 1855 Broadway New York NY 10023-7692

STEPHENS, LOWNDES FREDERICK, journalism educator; b. Frankfort, Ky., Sept. 27, 1945; s. James Willis and Harriet Connally (Barton) S.; m. Sally Lanier Smith, June 15, 1968; children: Sally Randolph, John Brent. BA in Econs., U. Ky., 1967, MA in Comms., 1969; PhD, U. Wis., 1975. Publs. officer Ky. divsn. Devel. Info., Frankfort, 1968-69; rsch. economist Spindletop Rsch., Inc., Lexington, Ky., 1969-72; content rsch. writer Ky. Ednl. TV Found., Lexington, 1972; editor Lake Superior project Inst. Environ. Studies, U. Wis., Madison, 1972-74; dir. Comms. Rsch. Ctr.; asst. prof. U. N.D., 1974-76; assoc. prof., prof. Coll. Journalism U. S.C., Columbia, 1976—, J. Rion McKissick prof. journalism, 2000—. Dir. Ctr. for Mass Comms. Rsch., 1999—; assoc. dean grad. studies and rsch., 1992-95, prof., 1986—; cons. Inst. for Def. Analyses, Dept. Def., Am. Newspaper Pubs. Assn., U.S. Office Edn., CPC Internat., U.S. Info. Agy., Edelman Worldwide Pub. Rels.; faculty cons. Army Command and Gen. Staff Coll., 1979-93; mem. nat. adv. panel George Polk Awards. Editl. bd. World Press Ency., Jour. Pub. Rels. Rsch., Mass Comm. Rev., Newspaper Rsch. Jour.; contbr. articles to profl. jours. Nat. Adv. bd. Am. Vets. Com., 1979—. Lt. col. USAR, 1985—. Rockefeller Found. grantee U. Wis., 1972-74; recipient Tchg. Excellence award Mortar Bd., 1988-89, Christa's Tchr. award Christa Corrigan McAuliffe Ctr. Edn. Tchg. Excellence Framingham State Coll., 1996. Fellow Inter-U. Seminar Armed Forces and Soc., So. Assn. Pub. Opinion Rsch. (pres. 1989-91); mem. AAUP, Internat. Comm. Assn., Am. Econ. Assn., Assn. Edn. Journalism and Mass Comms. (chmn. internat. comm. divsn. 1978-79, head Mass Comm. and Soc. divsn. 1986-87, Mortar Bd. Tchg. award 1987-88), Sigma Delta Chi, Ommicron Delta Kappa (Outstanding faculty leader 1988), Omicron Delta Epsilon, Kappa Tau Alpha. Democrat. Methodist. Home: 443 Brookshire Dr Columbia SC 29210-4205 Office: U SC Coll Journalism Columbia SC 29208-0001 E-mail: lfstephens@prodigy.net., stephens.lowndes@sc.edu.

STEPHENS, MARTHA LOCKHART, writer, researcher; b. Corpus Christi, Tex., Jan. 3, 1940; d. Hugh Rairdon and Amelia Virginia (McRee) Lockhart; m. David George Hmiel, June 10, 1961 (div. Oct. 1969); m. William Melvin Stephens Jr., June 2, 1971. BA in English Lit., Colo. Coll., 1961; MA in English Lit., U. Ariz., 1967; BFA in Drawing, U. Tex., San Antonio, 1989. Cert. tchr., Tex. English tchr. Colo., Ala., N.Y., Va. and Calif. pub. schs., 1961-68, San Antonio Ind. Sch. Dist., 1968-73, North East

Ind. Sch. Dist., San Antonio, 1973-82, level chmn. English, 1974-82, chmn. English lit. selection com., 1977, art and creative writing tchr., 1981-85, art tchr., head dept., 1986-94. Presenter in field; cons., tour guide, presenter workshops San Antonio Mus. Art, 1983-86; cons., docent McNay Art Mus., San Antonio, 1987; mem. adv. bd. San Antonio Coun. Tchrs. English, 1980. One woman show Art Ctr. Gallery, 1988; two-person show Chapman Grad. Ctr., Trinity U., 1979; numerous group exhbns. including Tex. Soc. Sculptors, 1979, NOW Art Show, San Antonio, 1980, Alternate Space Gallery, San Antonio, 1983, United Bank of Austin, 1985, U. Tex., San Antonio, 1986, N.E. Ind. Sch. Dist., 1986, others; contbr. articles to profl. publs.; authorized biographer Dorothy Dehner. Sponsor/recipient Gold Crown award Columbia Sch. Press Assn., 1992, citation for excellence Scholastic Art and Writing Awards, 1992, State Champion award Tex. H.S. Press Assn., 1990, 91, 92. Mem. NEA, Tex. State Tchrs.' Assn. (pres. Tchrs. of English sect. region 10 1979), North East Tchrs.' Assn., Nat. Art Edn. Assn., Tex. Art Edn. Assn. (regional rep. 1989-93, Merit award 1986, rep. region V 1989-93, capt. region V 1991-93), San Antonio Art Edn. Assn. (pres. 1990-92, Svc. award 1993, adv. bd. 1988-93). Democrat. Episcopalian. Avocations: painting, writing, gardening, cooking, computers. Home: 10935 Whisper Valley St San Antonio TX 78230-3617

STEPHENS, RALPH RENNE, massage therapy educator; b. Vinton, Iowa, Apr. 19, 1948; s. E.O. and Carrie D. S.; m. Sara Ann Beckley. BS in Indsl. Edn., Iowa State U., 1971; Natural Therapeutics Splst., N.Mex. Sch. Natural Therapeutics, 1986. Lic. massage therapist Iowa, N.Mex., massage therapy instr. N.Mex., cert. therapeutic massage and bodywork Nat. Cert. Bd. Therapeutic Massage and Bodywork, St. John method neuromuscular therapy. Pvt. practice Helping Hands Body Therapy Ctr., Iowa City, 1986-92; staff instr. Carlson Coll. Massage Therapy, Cedar Rapids, Iowa, 1987-92; instr. St. John Neuromuscular Therapy Seminars, 1991-99; pvt. practice Ralph Stephens Seminars, Cedar Rapids, 1992—; mem. tchg. staff Himalayan Inst. Yoga Sci. and Philosophy of U.S.A., Honesdale, Pa., 2001—. Dir. sports massage Iowa City Annual Hospice Road Race Com., 1986-88; cons., sys. engr., equipment supplier to workshop and seminar presenters Helping Hands Audio/Video, 1989-94; chairperson Iowa Bd. Examiners Massage Therapy, Des Moines, 1995-2000; sec. Iowa Bd. Examiners Massage Therapy, Des Moines, 1992-95; presenter in field. Author: Massage Therapy Principles and Practice, 1999; contbr. articles to profl. jours.; prodr. videos Seated Therapeutic Massage, Vol. 1, Back and Neck, 1995, Vol. 2, Shoulder, 1996, Vol. 3, Forearm, Wrist and Hand, 1996, Feel Great Hands on Health Series (4 tapes) Feel Great Every Day, Posture Yourself and Move Right, Massage Made Easy, Stretching that Works, 1998, Event Sports Massage, 1998, Side-Lying Therapeutic Massage, 1999, Therapeutic Sports Massage for the Lower Extremity, 1999, Anatomy of the Lower Extreminty, 1999, Medical Massage for the Cervical Region, 2001, Medical Massage for the Lumbar Region, 2002, Golf-Flexology, 2003; monthly editl. columnist Massage Today, 2000—, quar. columnist Up Close and Personal Newsletter, 2002-. Trustee Am. Massage Therapy Assn. Found., 1990-93, 95-96; chairperson Walford (Iowa) Disaster Preparedness Com., 1999. Mem. Am. Massage Therapy Assn. (cert. sports massage therapist, registered massage therapist cert., organizer, chair Iowa sports massage team 1986-88, 1st v.p., convention coord. Iowa chpt. 1988-89, edn. chair Iowa chpt. 1988-89, pres. Iowa chpt. 1989, ctrl. dist. rep. nat. bd. dirs. 1990-93, media spokesperson nat. media rels. team 1991-96, nat. nominating com. 1994, mem.-at-large nat. bd. dirs. 1995-96, nat. nominating commn. 1998-99, Disting. Nat. Officer award 1993, 96, Meritorious award Iowa chpt. 1997, Nat. Meritorious award 1997), Himalayan Inst. Yoga Sci. and Philosophy, tchg. staff, 2000. Republican. Avocations: golf, yoga, meditation. Home: PO Box 8267 Cedar Rapids IA 52408-8267 Office: Ralph Stephens Seminars LLC PO Box 8267 Cedar Rapids IA 52408-8267 Business E-Mail: ralph@ralphstephens.com.

STEPHENS, SALLIE L. retired assistant principal, commissioner; b. Crawfordville, Ga., May 23, 1931; d. Columbus and Bertha (Swain) Stephens; 1 child, Marilyn E. BA in Elem. Edn., Clark Coll., 1954; MS, Nova Southeastern U., 1975, EdD, 1998. Tchr. elem. sch. Broward County Sch. Dist., Ft. Lauderdale, Fla., 1954—78, asst. prin., 1978—2001. City commr. City of Miramar, Fla., 1999—, vice mayor, 1999—; vol., mentor Broward County Sch. Dist., 2002—. Mem.: Miramar Pembroke C. of C. (bd. dirs. 1982—), Phi Delta Kappa (bd. dirs. 1995—). Democrat. Baptist. Avocations: golf, dancing. Home: 2740 Huron Way Miramar FL 33025 Office: City of Miramar 6700 Miramar Pkwy Miramar FL 33023

STEPHENS, SUNNY COURINGTON, special education educator; b. Abilene, Tex., Mar. 13, 1943; d. Samuel Delmar and Delta Ree (Kniffen) Courington; m. Kenneth Edward Stephens, Apr. 6, 1967; 1 child, Lane Bradley. BS, Abilene Christian U., 1965; postgrad., U. Tex., 1972; MEd, Our Lady of the Lake Coll., San Antonio, 1977; PhD, Tex. Woman's U., 1983. Cert. secondary tchr., spl. edn. tchr., supr., bilingual tchr., early childhood tchr. Tchr. Poteet (Tex.) Ind. Sch. Dist., 1965-71, San Antonio Ind. Sch. Dist., 1971-79, South San Antonio Ind. Sch. Dist., 1979-80, dir. spl. edn., 1991—. Prof. Incarnate Word Coll., San Antonio, 1978-93; cons. Advocacy, Inc., Austin, Tex., 1981—, Easter Seal Rehab., San Antonio, 1978—, Children's Hosp., San Antonio, 1978—, Sch. Dists., Tex., Ariz., Colo., Ill., La., 1978—. Author: ABC Cookery, 1980, Curriculum Guide Early Childhood, 1978, (multimedia program) Learning Thru Success, 1980; contbr. articles to profl. jours. Named Outstanding Profl. Nat. Spina Bifida Assn., 1986, Tex. Prof. of Yr. Coun. for Advancement and Support of Edn., 1987, Estee Lauder Knowing Woman, 1988. Mem. Tex. Coun. Exceptional Children (pres. 1980-81), Tex. Spina Bifida Assn. (bd. dirs. 1983-93). Avocations: quilting, barbershop quartet singing. Home: 635 Meadows Rd Poteet TX 78065-9742 Office: South San Antonio Sch Dist 2415 W Southcross Blvd San Antonio TX 78211-1868

STEPHENSON, DONALD GRIER, JR., government studies educator; b. DeKalb County, Ga., Jan. 12, 1942; s. Donald Grier and Katherine Mason (Williams) S.; m. Ellen Claire Walker, Aug. 15, 1967; children: Todd Grier, Claire Walker. AB, Davidson Coll., N.C., 1964; MA, Princeton U., 1966, PhD, 1967. Research assoc. Nat. War Coll., Washington, 1968-70; asst. prof. govt. Franklin and Marshall Coll., Lancaster, Pa., 1970-73, assoc. prof. govt., 1973-81, prof. govt., 1981—, Charles A. Dana prof., 1989—, dept. chair, 1976—79, 1999—2002. Mem. adv. coun. to dean of the chapel Princeton U., 1974-85; Commonwealth lectr. Pa. Humanities Coun., Phila., 1987-88, 90, 92-95, 98-99. Co-author: American Constitutional Development, 1977, American Government, 1992, 1994, American Constitutional Law, 2002; author: The Supreme Court and the American Republic, 1981, An Essential Safeguard, 1991, Campaigns and the Court, 1999; contbr. articles to profl. jours. Elder, mem. session First Presbyn. Ch., Lancaster, 1973-76, 96-99; judge Pa. constl. competition Dickinson Coll., 1988-94. Capt. U.S. Army, 1968-70. Woodrow Wilson fellow, 1964-65, 66-67; Nat. Endowment for Humanities grantee, 1972, 85-89. Mem. Am. Polit. Sci. Assn. (Corwin award com. 1978, nominating com. Law and Courts sect. 1995), Pa. Polit. Sci. Assn. (editl. bd. Polity 1972-78), Supreme Ct. Hist. Soc. (editl. award 1990, 2002). Presbyterian. Home: 62 Oak Ln Lancaster PA 17603-4762 Office: Franklin and Marshall Coll PO Box 3003 Lancaster PA 17604-3003 E-mail: grier.stephenson@fandm.edu.

STEPHENSON, JANE ELLEN, educational association administrator; b. Banner Elk, N.C., Apr. 2, 1938; d. Braxton Leo and Mary Helen (Barlow) Baucom; m. John Bell Stephenson (dec. 1994); children: Jennifer Stephenson McLamb, Rebecca, David. AA, Lees McRae Coll., 1957; BS in Secretarial Adminstrn./Edn., U. N.C., Greensboro, 1959; MA in Bus. Edn., Appalachian State U., 1962; MS in Higher Edn. Adminstrn., U. Ky., 1976; Doctorate (hon.), Berea Coll., 1995. Acad. intern continuing edn. U. Ky., Lexington, 1977, coord. student svcs., 1978-80, dir. acad. support svcs., 1980-83, dir. human rels. ctr., 1983-84; exec. dir. Berea (Ky.) C. of C., 1988-89; found., dir. New Opportunity Sch. for Women, Berea, 1987—. Asst. prof. bus. and econs. Berea Coll., fall 1987. Author: (book) Courageous Paths: Stories of Nine Appalachian Women, 1995. Bd. dirs. Berea Hosp., 1985—, Mountain Assn. for Comty. Econ. Devel., 1995-96, Ky. Nat. Identification Program for Advancement of Women in Higher Edn. Adminstrn., 1984-86; mem. adv. bd. Ency. of Appalachia, 1996—; vol. coord. Berea Forum, 1985-95; mem. adv. bd. Ea. Ky. Women's Leadership, 1996—; mem. Leadership Madison County, Richmond, Ky., 1988; mem., bd. dirs. Ky. Women's Leadership Network, Lexington, 1993; chairperson state adv. bd. Elderhostel, 1987-94; mem. Foster Care Rev. Bd., 1990-91; commr. Ky. Commn. on Women, 1993-97, Ky. Appalachian Commn., 1995—; Appalachian dir. Steele-Reese Found., 1997—. Recipient Woman Advocate for Women award Women Mean Bus. Conf., 1996, Anderson medal Commonwealth of Ky., 1991, Women of Achievement State and Local award Bus. and Profl. Women Ky., 1988; named Citizen of Yr., Berea Lions Club, 1989. Mem. AAUW (Women as Agts. of Change award 1990), LWV. Presbyterian. Avocations: reading, piano. Home: 3121 Grantham Way Lexington KY 40509-2373 Office: New Opportunity Sch for Women 204 Chestnut St Berea KY 40403-1538

STEPHENSON, JOSEPH ANDERSON, vocational school educator; b. Richmond, Va., Jan. 19, 1960; s. Joseph Anderson Sr. and Marie (Beverly) S.; m. Laura Flowers, Sept. 24, 1983; children: William Kieth, Andrea Marie. BS in Indsl. Arts Edn., Ea. Ky. U., 1982, MS in Indsl. Tech. Edn., 1989. Indsl. arts tchr. Monticello (Ky.) Ind. Bd. Edn., 1983-88; tech. edn. tchr. Clark County Bd. Edn., Winchester, Ky., 1988-99; ind. tech. tchr. Scott County H.S., Georgetown, Ky., 1999—. Bd. dirs. Wayne County Little Leauge, Monticello, 1986-87. Recipient Class Act award Sta. WTVQ, 1992, Golden Apple Achievement award Ashland Oil, 1993. Mem. NEA, Ky. Edn. Assn., Ky. Indsl. Edn. Assn. (Tchr. of Yr. 1991), Internat. Tech. Edn. Assn. (Tchr. Excellence award 1992), Lions (v.p. Monticello chpt. 1986-88, zone chmn. dist. 43-C 1988, pres. Winchester chpt. 1990-91), Epsilon Pi Tau. Democrat. Baptist. Avocation: baseball and softball umpire. Home: 14 Village Dr Winchester KY 40391-1729 Office: Scott County HS 1080 Long Lick Pike Georgetown KY 40324-9442

STEPHENSON, JUDYTH ANN, secondary school educator; b. Altus, Okla., Dec. 23, 1940; d. Roy L. and Goldie Louise (Smith) Williams; m. Stanley D. Stephenson, June 9, 1963; children: Julia A., Susan L. B Music Edn., U. Okla., 1963; MA, U. Hawaii, 1973. Pvt. voice and piano tchr., Altus, 1963-65, Stillwater, Okla., 1965-67; choral dir. Griffess AFB, Rome, N.Y., 1967-68, Protestant Chapel, USAF Academy, Colo., 1970-71; tchr. elem. music Northside Ind. Sch. Dist., San Antonio, 1975-76, choral dir. Coke Stevenson Middle Sch., 1976-83, choral dir. John Marshall High Sch., 1983—95; assoc. dir. choral affairs Southwest Tex. State U., 1995—99; tchr. voice and piano pvt. practice, Stillwater, Okla. Fin. advisor Gamma Phi Beta, Southwest Tex. State U., 1989-90. Mem. Am. Choral Dirs. Assn., Tex. Music Educator's Assn. (regional chairperson 1983-86, v.p. 1988—), Tex. Choral Dirs. Assn., Tex. Music Adjudicators Assn. Avocations: walking, quilting, travel, gemology. Home: 912 Mission Hills Dr New Braunfels TX 78130-6603 E-mail: jasret99@earthlink.net.

STEPHENSON, MARY U. principal, educational administrator; b. Rocky Mount, N.C., Apr. 11, 1949; d. Walter James and Elizabeth (Hargrove) Umstead; m. Ralph Bernard Stephenson, July 30, 1976. BA, St. Augustine's Coll., 1971; MS, NC A&T State U., 1977; EdS, East Carolina U., 1989; postgrad., Tenn. Sch. of Religion; Doctorate, Nova Southeastern U., 1999. Cert. English tchr.; cert. prin.; cert. mentor, supt., supr. Tchr. Bertie Sr. H.S., Windsor, 1971-80, Seaboard (N.C.) Coates Elem. Sch., 1980-84, Conway (N.C.) Middle Sch., 1984-87, asst. prin., 1987-89, prin., 1989-93, Squire Elem. Sch., Gaston, NC, 1993—99; dir. fed. programs Northampton County Shcs., Jackson, NC, 1999—2001; adj. faculty Elizabeth City (NC) State U., 2002—; part-time faculty Halifax C.C., Weldon, NC. Mem. Middle Sch. Adv. Bd., Raleigh, 1992-93; mentor tchr. Conway Middle Sch., 1984-87; mem. Supt. Adv. Coun., Jackson, n.C., 1982-87; English dept. chairperson Bertie Sr. H.S., Windsor, 1979-80. Mem. Northampton County Schoolmaster, Jackson, 1990—; treas. St. Augustine Alumni, Raleigh, 1985—; youth leader First Bapt. Ch., Rich Square, 1982-86; mem. Oak Grove Bapt. Ch., 1990-94, Oak Grove Unity Choir, 1990-94. Named Miss Joyful Sounds Joyful Sounds Gospel Chorus, 1989; recipient Profl. Achievement award St. Augustine's Coll. Alumni, 1990. Mem. NEA, ASCD, N.C. Assn. of Educators, Simga Gamma. Democrat. Baptist. Avocations: reading, travel, singing. Home: 162 Wood Glenn Rd Roanoke Rapids NC 27870-6286 Office: Halifax CC Weldon NC E-mail: stephensonm@halifaxcc.edu.

STEPHENSON, PATRICIA ANN, public health researcher, educator; b. Washington, July 21, 1954; arrived in Sweden, 1990; d. Stanley Edwin and Mary Virginia (Brenneman) S.; m. Marsden Grigg Wagner, Dec. 14, 1990. BS, Calif. State U., Hayward, 1979; ScD, Johns Hopkins U., 1986. RN. Asst. prof. Sch. Pub. Health U. Wash., Seattle, 1986-90, adj. asst. prof. Sch. Nursing, 1987-90; sr. rschr. Ctr. for Pub. Health Rsch., Karlstad, Sweden, 1990-94; cons. health policy analyst, ops. rschr. Copenhagen, 1990-97; sr. advisor maternal, child health and nutrition USAID, Washington, 1998—. Vis. assoc. prof. Sch. Pub. Health U. Mich., Ann Arbor, 1995-96; cons. WHO, 1989, UNICEF, 1990—, World Bank, 1995-96. Mng. editor, co-founder European Jour. Pub. Health, 1991-94; author, editor: Tough Choices - InVitro Fertilization and the New Reproductive Technologies, 1993; contbr. articles to profl. publs. Women's health policy fellow John D. and Catherine T. MacArthur Found., 1995; recipient Commendation for work in fertility U.K. Parliament/House of Commons, 1989. Mem. APHA, Global Health Council, Delta Omega. Avocations: equestrian sports, dressage, show jumping, ballet, opera. Home: 123 Sherman Ave Takoma Park MD 20912 E-mail: pstephenson@usaid.gov.

STEPNEY, JOYCE HARRIETT, special education educator; b. Columbia, Miss., July 3, 1940; d. George Frank and Catherine E. (Brown) S. BS, Jackson State U., 1962, MS, 1970, ednl. specialist cert., 1979; postgrad., U. So. Miss., 1972, 77. Cert. ednl. specialist, Miss. Tchr. Marion Ctrl. High Sch., Columbia, 1962-68, Jefferson Middle Sch., Columbia, 1968-72, Columbia (Miss.) Elem. Sch., 1972—; exec. dir. Miss. Rural Ctr., 1996-97. Panelist U. So. Miss., 1979; sec. Columbia-Marion County Tchrs. Ctr. Policy Bd., 1980-81; pres. Columbia Assn. Classroom Tchrs., 1980-81; instr. Columbia (Miss.)-Marion County Tchrs. Ctr., 1982; tutor Sunflower Outreach Program, Columbia, 1988—; mem. adv. com. Pearl River Valley Equal Opportunity Emergency Sch. Assistance; mem. supts. adv. com., ins. and policy coms., local survey, assessment team and screening team for exceptional children Columbia Sch. Dist.; many others. Lay speaker, mission interpreter United Meth. Ch., Miss. Conf.; youth coord. Miss. United Meth. Conf., 1973-76; pres. Marion County Civicette Federated Club, 1973-75, Sixth Dist. Federated Clubs, 1975-77; bd. dirs. Marion County Assn. for Retarded Persons, 1975-77; sec. Miss. Rural Ctr. Bd. Dirs., 1980-84; mem. bd. dirs. Seashore Meth. Assembly, 1980-88; chairperson Miss. Conf. Commn. on the Status and Role of Women, 1982-84; sec.-treas. Lloyd Johnson Campaign, 1987; mem. Miss. Conf. Equitable Compensation Com.; Brookhaven Dist. Children Coord.; exec. dir. Miss. Rural Ctr., and others. Recipient Jackson State U. Outstanding Achievement award in edn., 1983. Mem. NEA, Miss. Assn. Educators, Columbia Assn. Educators (sec. 1976-77), Coun. for Exceptional Children, Miss. Fedn.-Coun. for Exceptional Children, Jackson State U. Nat. Alumni Chpt., Alpha Kappa Alpha, Columbia Progressive Arts Federated Club, Marion County Dem. Women, Heroines of Jericho, Lampton Ct. Methodist. Avocations: reading, sewing, traveling. Home: 95 Rankin Rd Columbia MS 39429-9141

STEPNITZ, SUSAN STEPHANIE, special education educator; b. Detroit, Mar. 1, 1948; d. N. Thomas and Dorothy (Richardson) Wagner; m. Kenneth H. Stepnitz Jr., July 25, 1970; children: Joshua, Zachary. BA in Polit. Sci., Olivet Coll., 1970; MA in Spl. Edn., Wayne State U., 1972. Tchr. Traverse Bay Area Intermed. Sch. Dist., Traverse City, Mich., 1973—, negotiator, ednl. profl. and support staff Travere City, Mich., 1982—. Mem. spl. edn. adv. com. Mich. Bd. Edn., 1992-96; mem. spl. delivery sys. edn. task force Mich. Dept. Edn., 1993-94, mem. spl. edn./gen. edn. com. Office of Spl. Edn.; mem. Comprehensive Sys. Pers. Devel. Task Force, 1996—; spl. edn. tchr. mentor, 1997—. Dir. Handicapped Accessibility Awareness Special Kid's Day Nat. Cherry Festival, 1987-98, vol. mgmt. coord. Nat. Cherry Festival, 1998—; asst. dir. youth handbell choir 1st Congl. Ch., 1998—. Recipient Anne Sullivan award Mich. Edn. Assn., 1993, Friend of the Physically Impaired Assn. of Mich. award, 1994. Mem. AAUW (pres. Mich. chpt. 1987-89, Outstanding Person in Edn. award 1986, strategic planning com.), Mich. Edn. Assn. (spl. edn. tng. cadre 1990—). Home: PO Box 6763 Traverse City MI 49696-6763

STEPONAITIS, VINCAS PETRAS, archaeologist, anthropologist, educator; b. Boston, Aug. 10, 1953; s. Vincas and Elena (Povydis) S.; m. Laurie Cameron, Dec. 31, 1976; children: Elena Anne, Lillian Kazimiera. AB in Anthropology magna cum laude, Harvard U., 1974; MA in Anthropology, U. Mich., 1975, PhD in Anthropology, 1980. From lectr. to assoc. prof. dept. anthropology SUNY, Binghamton, 1979-87; assoc. prof. U. N.C., Chapel Hill, 1988-94, prof., 1995—, dir. Rsch. Labs. Archaeology, 1988—. Guest worker Nat. Bur. Standards, 1979; adj. lectr. dept. anthropology SUNY, Binghamton, 1979; lectr. and presenter in field. Author: Ceramics, Chronology, and Community Patterns, An Archaeological Study at Moundville, 1983, Archaeology of the Moundville Chiefdom, 1998, (CD-Rom) Excavating Occaneechi Town, 1998; editor Southeastern Archaeology, 1984-87; regional editor Investigations in Am. Archaeology, 1987-91; mem. editl. bd. Prehistory Press, 1990-97, Southern Cultures, 1992—, Am. Archaeology, 1996-2000; contbr. articles to profl. jours. Smithsonian Instn. fellow, 1978-79; grantee NSF, 1978-80, 83, 89-92, 94, 2000, Wenner-Gren Found., 1981, 86-88, Nat. Geographic Soc., 1987-88, Z. Smith Reynolds Found., 1992-94. Fellow Am. Anthrop. Assn.; mem. Soc. Am. Archaeology (Presdl. Recognition award 1993-94, exec. com. 1983-84, treas. 1992-94, pres. 1997-99), Archaeological Conservancy (bd. dirs. 2000—, chmn. 2003—), Ctr. for Maya Rsch. (bd. dirs. 2002-), Southeastern Archaeol. Conf. (editor 1984-87, pres. 1990-92), N.C. Archaeol. Soc. (exec. sec. 1988-91, sec. 1991-96), N.C. Archaeol. Coun. (exec. com. 1988-92), Archaeol. Soc. S.C., Ala. Archaeol. Soc., Miss. Archaeol. Soc., La. Archaeol. Soc., Tenn. Anthrop. Assn. Office: U NC Rsch Labs Archaeology Alumni Bldg Cb 3120 Chapel Hill NC 27599-3120

STERIS, CHERYL LYNN, elementary school educator, reading coordinator; b. Denver, Aug. 28, 1948; d. David Hayes Gillard and Vera Agness (Downer) Rubino; children: Kirsten Dianne, Christopher William. BA, Bowling Green State U., 1970; MEd, Ashland U., 1992. Cert. edni. supr., Ohio. Tchr. U.S. Dependent Schs., Weisbaden, Germany, 1971-73, Berlin-Milan Schs., Milan, Ohio, 1973—; primary reading coord. Milan Elem. Sch., 1979—. Cooperating tchr. Bowling Green State U., Milan, 1983—; mem. profl. devel. team N.W. Ohio Regional Profl. Devel. Ctr., 1994—. Martha Holden Jennings scholar, 1994-95. Mem. NEA, Nat. Coun. Tchrs. of English, Delta Kappa Gamma, Phi Delta Kappa. Avocations: reading, cooking, skiing, travel. Home: 4902 Hollyview Dr Vermilion OH 44089-1619 Office: Milan Elem Sch S Main St Milan OH 44846

STERLING, KEIR BROOKS, historian, educator; b. N.Y.C., Jan. 30, 1934; s. Henry Somers and Louise Noel (de Wetter) S.; m. Anne Cox Diller, Apr. 3, 1961; children: Duncan Diller, Warner Strong, Theodore Craig. BS, Columbia U., 1961, MA, 1963, profl. diploma, 1965, PhD, 1973. Asst. to dean Sch. Gen. Studies Columbia U., N.Y.C., 1959-65; rsch. grantee Eng., 1965-66; instr. history Pace U., N.Y.C. and Pleasantville, N.Y., 1966-71, from asst. prof. to assoc. prof., 1971-77, adj. prof., 1977-83; ordnance br. historian U.S. Army Ordnance Ctr. and Sch., Aberdeen Proving Ground, Md., 1983-94, Ft. Lee, Va., 1994-98; historian U.S. Army Combined Arms Support Command, Ft. Lee, 1998—. Lectr. gen. counseling Bklyn. Coll., CUNY, 1967-68; asst. acad. dean, adj. asst. prof. history, coord. Am. studies program, dir. summer session Marymount Coll., Tarrytown, N.Y., 1968-71; asst. dean Rockland C.C., SUNY, Suffern, 1971-73; vis. prof. Mercy Coll., Westchester C.C., King's Coll., Nyack Coll., U. Wis., 1971, 75, 78-80, 83, Harford (Md.) C.C., 1987-94; adj. instr. Army Logistics Mgmt. Coll., Ft. Lee, 1995—; co-project dir. Am. Ornithologists Union Centennial Hist. Project, 1976-89; cons. Arno Press, Inc., 1973-78, Coun. State Colls. of N.J., 1984-85, NSF, 1983—, Am. Trust for Brit. Libr., 1986-89; active Columbia U. Seminar on History and Philosophy of Sci., 1976-83; archivist, historian mem. steering com. sect. mammalogy Internat. Union Biol. Scis., 1985—. Author: Last of the Naturalists: The Career of C. Hart Merriam, 1974, 77; editor: Notes on the Animals of North America (B.S. Barton), 1974; assoc. editor: Am. Nat. Biog., 1989-98; editor, contbr.: Natural Sciences in America, 1974, 68 vols., 1974, Biologists and Their World, 1978, 77 vols.; gen. editor, contbr.: The International History of Mammalogy, 1987—; sr. editor, contbr. (with R. Harmond, G. Cevasco, and L. Hammond) Biographical Dictionary of American and Canadian Naturalists and Environmentalists, 1997; contbg. author: Ground Warfare: An International Encyclopedia, 2002, Dictionary of Am. History, 3d edit., 2003, Encyclopedia of World Environmental History, 2003; editor, contbr. to numerous works in history, Am. natural scis., and Am. mil. history. With U.S. Army, 1954—56. Grantee Theodore Roosevelt Meml. Fund, Am. Mus. Natural History, 1967, Nat. Geog. Soc., 1977, NSF/Am. Soc. Mammalogists, 1978, NSF, 1981-82, IREX, 1982. Mem.: History of Sci. Soc., Orgn. Am. Historianan, Am. Hist. Assn., Assn. Bibliography of History (mem. coun. 1994—), Am. Soc. Environ. History (sec., mem. governing bd., editor newsletter), Am. Ornithologists Union (co-chmn. centennial hist. com., mem. archives com., grantee 1976, 1977), Am. Soc. Mammalogists (mem. archives com., mem. 75th ann. com.), Phi Delta Kappa, Sigma Tau Delta, Phi Alpha Theta. Democrat. Episcopalian. Home: 7104 Wheeler Rd Richmond VA 23229-6939 Office: 3901 A Ave Ste 100 Fort Lee VA 23801-1807 E-mail: kbs1934@cs.com., sterlink@lee.army.mil.

STERLING, RAYMOND LESLIE, civil engineering educator, researcher, consultant; b. London, Apr. 19, 1949; came to U.S., 1966; s. Richard Howard and Joan Valeria (Skinner) S.; m. Linda Lee Lundquist, Aug. 8, 1970 (div. Sept. 1982); children: Paul, Juliet, Erika; m. Janet Marie Kjera, Aug. 20, 1983; 1 child, Zoey. B in Civil and Structural Engring. with 1st class honors, U. Sheffield, Eng., 1970; MS in Geol. Engring., U. Minn., 1975, PhDCE, 1977. Registered civil engr., Minn.; chartered structural engr., Eng. Engr. trainee Met. Water Bd., London, 1968; civil engr. Egil Wefald and Assocs., Cons. Engrs., Mpls., 1969-71; structural engr. Husband and Co., Cons. Engrs., Eng., 1971-73; rsch. asst. U. Minn., Mpls., 1973-77, dir. Underground Space Ctr., 1977-95, asst. prof. dept. civil and mineral engring., 1977-83, assoc. prof., 1983-95; project. coord., structural engr. Setter, Leach and Lindstrom, Inc., Mpls., 1976-77; prin. cons. Itasca Cons. Group, Inc., Mpls., 1981-94; prof. civil engring. La. Tech. U., Ruston, 1995—, dir. Trenchless Tech. Ctr., 1995—. Vice-chmn. U.S. Nat. com. on tunneling tech. NRC, NAS, 1990-91, chmn. 1992-94, com. on infrastructure, 1991-93, bd. infrastructure and the constructed environment, 1994-96; acting co-dir. Minn. Cold Climate Bldg. Rsch. Ctr. U. Minn., 1987-89, co-dir. Bldg. Energy Rsch. Ctr., 1986, speaker's bur., other u. coms.; energy adv. com. Legis. Com. on Minn. Resources, 1989-95; com. on moisture control in bldgs. U.S. Bldg. Thermal Envelope Coordinating Coun., 1985-86; program planning com. on bldg. founds. U.S. Dept. Energy, 1985-95; adv. bd. for energy efficient residence demonstration project Nat. Assn. Home Builders, 1980; mem. Gov's. Exxon Oil Overcharge Adv. Task Force, 1986, Mpls. Energy Future Com., 1980-81, Scientist's Inst. for Pub. Info., N.Y.; cons. U.S. Army Corps. Engrs., UN, N.Y., Opus Corp., Mpls., Dames & Moore Internat., London, City of Mpls., Larson Engring., White Bear, Minn., Pilsbury Co., Mpls., Colgate Divsn. Sch., Rochester, N.Y., others; adv. prof. Chongqing Jianzhu U., Sichuan, People's Republic China, 1985—; vis. rschr. Nat. Inst. Pollution and Resources MITI, Japan, 1991; vis. prof. U. Mo., Rolla, 1979; Shimizu prof. civil and mineral engring., U.

Minn., 1988-95; adv. prof. Tongji U., Shanghai, 1996—; mem. eminent speaker program Instn. Engrs., Australia, 1993; hon. prof. Changsha Rwy. U., China, 1998—, Xian U. Arch. and Tech., China, 1999; lectr., presenter in field. Author: Earth Sheltered Housing Design: Guidelines, Examples and References, 1978, transl. into Chinese, French, Spanish and Russian, 2d. edit., 1985, (with others) Earth Sheltered Community Design: The Design of Energy-Efficient Residential Communities, 1980 (award for Best Book in Architecture and Urban Planning Profl. and Scholarly div. Assn. Am. Pubs. 1981), transl. into Spanish, 1981, Underground Building Design, 1983, translated into Japanese and Russian, others, Building Foundation Handbook, 1988, Underground Space Design, 1993, others; editor: (with others) Key Questions in Rock Mechanics: Proc. 29th U.S. Symposium on Rock Mechanics, 1988; contbr. articles to profl. jours. including Jour. Agrl. Engring., Internat. Jour. Rock Mechanics and Mining Scis., Exptl. Mechanics, many others. Named Most Valuable Profl., Gulf Coast Trenchless Assn., 1999; recipient Young Engr. of Yr. award, Minn. Fedn. Engring. Soc., 1982, Applied Rsch. award in rock mechanics, NRC, 1993, elected fgn. mem., Acad. Engring. of Russian Fedn., 1993, Person of Yr. award, Trenchless Tech. mag., 2001; grantee Shimizu Constrn. Co., 1987—93, Nat. Assn. Homebuilders, 1989, U.S. Dept. Energy, 1989—90, NSF, 1991, Minn. Dept. Transp., 1991, ASHRAE, 1991—92, many others. Fellow: ASCE (bd. dirs. 1985—92, pres. Minn. sect. 1990—91, Young Civil Engr. of Yr. award 1982, Stephen D. Bechtel Pipeline Engring. award 2003), Royal Soc. Arts, Mfrs. & Commerce, Inst. Structural Engrs., Instn. Civil Engrs.; mem.: NSPE, Internat. Soc. Trenchless Tech. (vice chmn. 1999—2002, chmn. 2002—), N. Am. Soc. Trenchless Tech. (bd. dirs. 1996—, treas. 1997, internat. rep. 1998—, vice chmn. 1999, chmn. 2000), Internat. Tunneling Assn. (coordinating editor jour. 1986—95, co-sr. editor 1996—, animateur working group on direct/indirect advantages of underground structures 1997—2000), Am. Underground Constrn. Assn. (Award of Distinction 2000). Achievements include research in underground construction, underground space utilization, trenchless technology, rock mechanics, and energy use in buildings. Office: Trenchless Technology Ctr Louisiana Tech U PO Box 10348 Ruston LA 71272-0046

STERLING, RICHARD LEROY, English and foreign language educator; b. Atlantic City, Feb. 18, 1941; s. Richard Leroy and Anne (Bass) S. BA, Am. U., 1968; MA, Cath. U., 1971; PhD, Howard U., 1990. Head Start tchr. D.C. pub. schs., summer 1968; tchr. French and English, adult and continuing edn. D.C. Pub. Schs., Washington, 1969-71, 76-83; instr. French Howard U., Washington, 1973-76, grad. teaching asst., 1983-85, instr., lectr. in French, 1985-89; tchr. English Community-Based Orgns., D.C. Pub. Schs., Washington, 1989-91; asst. prof. French and English Bowie (Md.) State U., 1991-97, assoc. prof. French, 1997—. Tchr. summer enrichment program for gifted children Sch. Edn., Howard U., summers 1985, 86; tchr. ESL, D.C. Pub. Schs., summer, 1989, 94; asst. coord. Humanities Immersion Program, Project Access for H.S. Students, Bowie State U., summer 1997-98; vice-chmn. World Centennial Conf.; French, Am. and Planetary Dimensions of Saint-John Perse, U. D.C., 1987; mem. adv. coun. Northeast Conf. Teaching Fgn. Langs; NAACP-ACT-SO competition humanities judge 1997-2000; adj. assoc. prof. English, Southeastern U. Washington, summer 1998—; judge D.C. Pub. Schs. World Langs. Festival, 2001; presenter, book reviewer in field. Author: The Prose Works of Saint-John Perse: Towards an Understanding of His Poetry, 1994; contbg. editor MaComere Rev., 2003—; contbr. articles to profl. jours. Active Assn. Democratique des Francais a L.Etranger, 1988—, Senegal friendship com. Office Cmty. and Ethnic Affairs, Prince George's County Govt., Md., 1993-94, Inst. for Haitian Cultural and Sci. Affairs, 1992-94, local arrangements com. Conf. Coll. Composition and Communication, Washington, 1995, Friends of the Corcoran, 1999; membership com. and outreach com. St. John's Ch., Washington, 1993, ch. growth com., 1995. With U.S . Army, 1964-66. Mem. MLA, Coll. Lang. Assn., Middle Atlantic Writers Assn. (chmn. essay contest com. 1995-2000, bd. dirs. 2000—), Samuel Beckett Soc., Societe des Professeurs Francais et Francophones d'Amerique, Zora Neale Hurston Soc., Am. Assn. Tchrs. French (sec.-treas. Washington chpt. 1986-90), Nat. Cathedral Assn., Md. Fgn. Lang. Assn. (bd. dirs. 1997-2001), Coun. Internat. d'Etudes Francophones, Friends D.C. Superior Ct. (bd. dirs. 1996—), Univ. Club (Washington), Pi Delta Phi, Sigma Tau Delta. Democrat. Episcopalian. Avocations: classical music, history, travel. Office: Bowie State U Dept English & Modern Langs Bowie MD 20715 E-mail: rsterling@bowiestate.edu.

STERN, FRITZ RICHARD, historian, educator; b. Breslau, Germany, Feb. 2, 1926; came to U.S., 1938, naturalized, 1947; s. Rudolf A. and Catherine (Brieger) S.; m. Margaret J. Bassett, Oct. 11, 1947 (div. 1992); children: Frederick P., Katherine Stern Brennan; m. Elisabeth Niebuhr Sifton, Jan. 1, 1996. BA, Columbia U., 1946, MA, 1948, PhD, 1953; DLitt (hon.), Oxford U., 1985; LLD (hon.), New Sch. for Social Rsch., 1997, Columbia U., 1998; LLD (hon.), U. Wroclaw, 2002. Lectr., instr. Columbia U., 1946-51, faculty, 1953—, prof. history, 1963—, Seth Low prof. history, 1967-92, univ. prof., 1992-96, provost, 1980-83; acting asst. prof. Cornell U., 1951-53; univ. prof. emeritus Columbia U., 1997—; tchr. Free U. Berlin, 1954, Yale U., 1963; permanent vis. prof. U. Konstanz, West Germany, 1966—; sr. adviser U.S. Embassy, Bonn, 1993-94. Élie Halévy prof. U. Paris, spring 1979; Phi Beta Kappa vis. scholar, 1979-80; Tanner lectr. Yale, 1993. Author: The Politics of Cultural Despair, 1961, The Failure of Illiberalism-Essays in the Political Culture of Modern Germany, 1972, rev. edit., 1992, Gold and Iron: Bismarck, Bleichroeder and the Bldg. of the German Empire, 1977 (recipient Lionel Trilling award Columbia U.), Dreams and Delusions: The Drama of German History, 1987, rev. edit. 1999, Einstein's German World, 1999; editor: The Varieties of History, 1956, 71, (with L. Krieger) The Responsibility of Power, 1967; mem. editorial bd. Foreign Affairs, 1978-92; contbr. articles to profl. jours.; reviewer Fgn. Affairs, 1963-95. Trustee German Marshall Fund, 1981-99, Aspen Inst. of Berlin, 1983—; senator Deutsche Nationalstiftung, 1994—; mem. Trilateral Commn., 1983-90. Decorated Officer's Cross Order of Merit Fed. Republic of Germany; fellow Center Advanced Behavioral Scis., 1957-58; fellow Social Sci. Research Council, 1960-61; fellow Am. Council Learned Socs., 1966-67; fellow Netherlands Inst. Advanced Study, 1972-73; mem. Nuffield Coll., Oxford, 1966-67, Inst. Advanced Study Princeton, 1969-70; Guggenheim fellow, 1969-70; Ford Found. grantee, 1976-77; vis. scholar Russell Sage Found., 1989, spring 1993; recipient Leopold-Lucas-prize Evang. Faculty U. Tübingen, 1984, Peace prize German Book Trade Frankfurt Book Fair, 1999, Bruno Snell medal U. Hamburg, 2002. Mem. Am. Hist. Assn., AAAS, Am. Philos. Soc., Coun. Fgn. Rels., Deutsche Akademie für Sprache und Dichtung (corr.), Berlin Brandenburgische Akademie der Wissenschaften (corr.), Orden Pour le Mérite, Germany, Phi Beta Kappa (senator-at-large 1973-78). Clubs: Century (N.Y.C.). Home: 15 Claremont Ave New York NY 10027-6802 E-mail: fs20@columbia.edu.

STERN, HARRIAN MICHA BURTTSCHELL, educational diagnostician; b. Houston, June 30, 1951; d. Henry August and Barbara Ruth (Banks) Burttschell; m. Stephen Stern, May 28, 1972; children: Barrett Avonn, Ashley Beth. BS in Spl. Edn./Psychology, Tex. Woman's U., 1973, MEd in Spl. Edn./Ednl. Diagnostician, 1975, PhD in Child Devel./Spl. Edn. Diagnostic, 1989. Cert. tchr., adminstr. elem. mentally retarded, ednl. diagnostician lang./learning disabilitis, spl. edn. supr., mid-mgmt. adminstr., emotionally disturbed, Tex.; registered profl. ednl. diagnostician. From spl. edn. resource tchr. to coord. diagnosticians Dallas (Tex.) Ind. Sch. Dist., 1972—2003, coord. diagnosticians, 2003—; ednl. diagnostician Irving (Tex.) Ind. Sch. Dist., 1982—83; pvt. practice in testing, cons., speaking, tutoring Psychoednl. Diagnostic Svcs., Dallas, 1982—. Tchr. U. Tex., Dallas, 1982, Richland Jr. Coll., 1990. Pres. Starlight B'nai B'rith Women, 1982-83, pres. Dallas coun., 1990-91; pres. Shearith Israel Sisterhood, 1987-89; v.p. S.W. br. Women's League for Conservative Judaism, 1987-92, nat. bd. dirs., 1988—, pres. S.W. br., 1992-94, nat. trainer, 1994—, mem. editl. bd. Outlook mag., 1994-96, 98—, nat. v.p. 1998-2002, nat. cons., 1999—, Outlook features editor, 2002—. Mem. Tex. Ednl. Diagnosticians Assn. (state pres. 1984-85), Tex. Profl. Edn. Diagnosticians Bd. of Registry (bd. dirs. 1983-89, chmn. 1987-89), Assn. Children with Learning Disabilities, Orton Dyslexia Soc., Coun. Exceptional Children, Phi Delta Kappa, Pi Lambda Theta. Avocations: reading, travel, gourmet cooking. E-mail: hbsphd13@aol.com.

STERN, JEANNETTE ANNE, secondary school educator; b. Bklyn., June 13, 1948; d. Samuel and Rosalie (Presler) Beckerman; m. William D. Stern, Aug. 10, 1974; children: Susan Rachel, Diana Lynne. BA, SUNY, Albany, 1970; MA, Hofstra U., 1972; MEd, Tchrs. Coll., N.Y.C., 1993, EdD, 1994. Cert. tchr. social studies 7-12, Spanish 7-12, adminstrn. and supervision. Tchr. Spanish Wantagh (N.Y.) Pub. Schs., 1970-73, tchr. social studies, 1973-92, chmn. dept. social studies, 1992—. Regional dir. N.Y. State Middle Sch. Assn., 1990—; cons. in field. Contbr. articles to profl. jours. Chairperson sch. bd. Congregation B'nai Israel, Freeport, N.Y., 1989—. Recipient Faculty Svc. award Am. Legion, 1983, PTA Svc. award, Wantagh, 1988. Mem. Nat. Middle Sch. Assn., Wantagh United Tchrs., Am. Fedn. Tchrs., SUNY at Albany Alumni Assn. (bd. dirs. 1970-73), Holocaust Mus. (charter), Phi Delta Kappa. Avocations: knitting, crochet, travel. Home: 17 Florence Ave Freeport NY 11520-5823 Office: Wantagh Pub Schs 3301 Beltagh Ave Wantagh NY 11793-3362

STERN, MARGARET BASSETT, retired special education educator, author; b. Bklyn., June 6, 1920; d. Preston Rogers and Jeanne (Mordorf) Bassett; m. Fritz R. Stern Oct. 11, 1947 (div. Dec. 1992); children: Frederick Preston, Katherine Stern Brennan. BA, Wellesley Coll., 1942; MEd, Bank Street Coll. Edn., N.Y.C., 1943, 74. Propr. Castle Sch., N.Y.C., 1944-51; dir. Mothers' Coop. Nursery Sch., Ithaca, N.Y., 1952-54; tchr. sci. and math. The Brearley Sch., N.Y.C, 1956-57. Cons., lectr. Head Start, Tuskegee, Ala., 1964; cons. in math. The Gateway Sch., N.Y.C., 1967-90; spl. lectr. Columbia U. Tchrs. Coll., N.Y.C., 1990-94; condr. workshops in Eng., 1960-88. Author: (with Catherine Stern and Toni Gould) Structural Reading Program, Workbooks and Teachers Guides A through E, 1963, 3d edit., 1978, Structural Arithmetic Workbooks and Teachers Guides Grades 1-3, 1965, 2d edit., 1966, (with Stern) Children Discover Arithmetic, 1971, (with Gould) Spotlight on Phonics, Four Workbooks and Teachers Guides, 1980, Sound/Symbol Activities and Decoding Activities, 1980, 2d edit., 1994; Experimenting with Numbers, 1988, Structural Arithmetic, 1-3, 1992. Recipient award, Orton Dyslexia Soc. N.Y., 1989, Bank St. Coll. Edn., 1998. Mem.: Nat. Coun. Tchrs. Math., Internat. Dyslexia Assn. Home: 3204 River Crescent Dr Annapolis MD 21401

STERN, RAUL ARISTIDE, physics educator, researcher; b. Bucarest, Romania, Dec. 26, 1928; came to U.S., 1950; s. Henry Herman and Anna (Schonbaum) S.; m. Ruth Nathan, Feb. 3, 1953; children: Gabriella C. A., Susanna V. BS, U. Wis., 1952, MS, 1953; PhD, U. Calif., Berkeley, 1959. Mem. tech. staff Bell Telephone Labs., Murray Hill, N.J., 1960-81; prof. U. Colo., Boulder, 1978—2002, prof. emeritus, 2002—. Vis. prof. and cons. in field. Assoc. editor: The Physics of Fluids, 1984-87; contbr. and reviewer to articles in sci. jours. Evinrude Found. fellow U. Wis., 1953; Sherman Fairchild Found. Disting. scholar Calif. Inst. Tech., 1986. Fellow Am. Phys. Soc. Achievements include research in physics and gaseous electronics. Home: 3260 Lafayette Dr Boulder CO 80305-7115 Office: U Colo PO Box 391 Boulder CO 80309-0391

STERN, ROBERT C. physician, educator; b. N.Y.C., Dec. 13, 1938; s. Samuel and Lily S. BA, Drew U., 1959; MD, Albert Einstein Coll. Medicine, 1963. Diplomate Nat. Bd. Med. Examiners, Am. Bd. Pediat., Am. Bd. Pediatric Pulmonology. Intern pediat. U. Hosps. Cleve., Babies and Childrens Hosp. Divsn., 1963-64, jr. asst. resident pediat., 1964-65; sr. asst. resident pediat. Bronx Mcpl. Hosp. Ctr., N.Y.C., 1965-66; fellow cystic fibrosis/pediat. pulmonary diseases Case Western Res. U. Sch. Medicine, Cleve., 1968-70; sr. instr. pediat. Case Western Res. U., Cleve., 1970-71, asst. prof., 1971-77, assoc. prof., 1977-83, prof., 1983—. Cons. Cystic Fibrosis Founds. various countries, 1990—, various pharm. and med. tech. cos., 1990—. Author: Treatment of Hospitalized Cystic Fibrosis Patients, 1998, Treatment of Cystic Fibrosis, 2000; contbr. numerous chpts. to Nelson's Textbook of Pediatrics, 1979—, also over 100 articles to med. jours. Pres., CEO, Children's Lung Found., Cleve., 1983—. Capt. USAF, 1966-68. Recipient David Stuckert award Cystic Fibrosis Rsch. Inst., San Francisco, 1997. Mem. Am. Thoracic Soc., Soc. Pediat. Rsch. Achievements include introduction of heparin lock for intermittent administration of intravenous drugs; research in cystic fibrosis. Home: 2300 Overlook Rd Apt 406 Cleveland Heights OH 44106-2391 Office: Univ Hosp Cleve 11100 Euclid Ave Cleveland OH 44106-1736 E-mail: rcs1@prodigy.net.

STERNBERG, LEONEL DA SILVEIRA LOBO, education educator; BS in math., Calif. State U. at Hayward, 1972; MS in biology, U. of Calif. at Riverside, 1975, PhD in biology, 1978. Prof. biology U. Miami, 1985—. NSF postdoctoral fellow U. of Calif. at Los Angeles, 1980—85. Fellowship, John Simon Guggenheim Meml. Found., 2003. Office: Dept Biology U Miami Coral Gables FL 33124-0421

STERNBERG, ROBERT JEFFREY, psychology educator, researcher; b. Newark, Dec. 8, 1949; s. Joseph Sternberg and Lillian Myriam (Politzer) Weingast; m. Elena Grigorenko, 2003; children from previous marriage: Seth, Sara. BA summa cum laude, Yale U., 1972; PhD in Psychology, Stanford U., 1975; D honoris causa, Complutense U., Madrid, Spain, 1994, U. Cyprus, 2000, U. Paris, 2000, U. Leuven, Belgium, 2001. Mem. faculty dept. psychology Yale U., New Haven, 1975—, asst. prof., 1975—80, assoc. prof., 1980—83, prof. psychology, 1983-86, dir. grad. studies, 1983—88, IBM prof. psychology and edn., 1986—, acting chmn. dept. psychology, 1992, dir. Yale Ctr. Psychology of Abilities, Competencies and Expertise, 2000—. Editor-in-chief Ency. of Human Intelligence, Psychol. Bull., 1991-96, Contemporary Psychology, 1999-2004; cons. editor Learning and Individual Differences, 1992—, Intelligence, 1977—, Devel. Rev., 1987-91, Jour. Personality and Social Psychology, 1989-91, Psychol. Rev., 1989-91; author: Intelligence, Information Processing and Analogical Reasoning, 1977, Beyond IQ, 1985, The Triarchic Mind, 1988, Metaphors of Mind, 1990, In Search of the Human Mind, 1995, 98, (with T. Lubart) Defying the Crowd, 1995, Successful Intelligence, 1997, Pathways to Psychology, 1997, Thinking Styles, 1997, Intelligence, Heredity and Environment, 1997, Love is a Story, 1998, Cupid's Arrow, 1998. Recipient award for Excellence Mensa Edn. and Rsch. Found., 1989, Disting. Lifetime Contbn. to Psychology Conn. Psychology Assn., 1999, Disting. Scientist and Scholar award Positive Psychology Network, 2002 ; Guggenheim Found. fellow, 1985-86. Fellow AAAS, APA (pres. 2003, past pres. divsns. 1, 10, 15, 24, McCandless Young Scientist award divsn. devel. psychology 1982, Disting. Sci. award for early career contbn. 1981, pres. 2003, Farnsworth award, E.L. Thorndike award 2003), Am. Acad. Arts and Scis., Am. Psychol. Soc., Soc. Exptl. Psychologists; mem. Am. Ednl. Rsch. Assn. (Rsch. Rev. award 1986, Outstanding Book award 1987, Sylvia Scribner award 1996), Soc. Multivariate Exptl. Psychology (Cattell award 1982), Nat. Assn. Gifted Children (Disting. Scholar award 1985), Phi Beta Kappa. Achievements include theory of successful intelligence; balance theory of wisdom. Avocations: physical fitness, travel, reading, cello. Home: 105 Spruce Bank Rd Hamden CT 06518-2233 Office: Yale Univ PACE Ctr PO Box 208358 New Haven CT 06520 E-mail: robert.sternberg@yale.edu.

STERNBERG, STEPHEN STANLEY, pathologist, educator; b. N.Y.C., July 30, 1920; s. Morris and Clara (Nussberg) Sternberg; m. Norma Wollner; children: Alessandra, Susan. BA, Colby Coll., 1941; MD, NYU, 1944. Diplomate Am. Bd. Pathology and Anatomic Pathology. Intern Mt. Sinai Hosp., Cleve.; resident in pathology Charity Hosp., New Orleans, 1947-49; fellow Meml. Hosp., N.Y.C., 1949-50, attending pathologist, 1972—; prof. pathology Cornell U. Med. Ctr., N.Y.C., 1979—. Mem. Sloan-Kettering Inst. for Cancer Rsch., N.Y.C., 1984—; prof. pathology Cornell U. Med. ctr., N.Y.C., 1979—. Editor: Diagnostic Surg. Pathology, 1989; contbr. articles to profl. jours. Capt. flight surgeon USAF, 1945—47. Fellow: N.Y. Acad. Scis.; mem.: Am. Coun. on Sci. and Health (chmn. bd. dirs. 1986—89), Soc. for Toxicology, Am. Assn. for Cancer Rsch. Republican. Jewish. Office: Meml Hosp 1275 York Ave New York NY 10021-6094

STERNFELS, RONALD JULIAN, academic program administrator; m. Rhonda Pancirer; children: Howard, Bradley. BS, CCNY, 1968; MS, U. Rochester, 1971; PhD, NYU, 1976; Exec. MBA, U. New Haven, 1986. Cert. med. lab. tech. Lab. planning cons. Technicon Instruments Corp., Tarrytown, N.Y., 1976-82; sr. engr. Norden Sys., Norwalk, Conn., 1982-88; program dir. Oak Ridge (Tenn.) Assoc. U., 1988-94, process improvement cons., 1994—. Mem. adv. bd. Consortium for Nano-Structured Materials, Richmond, Va., 1992—; mem. steering com. U.S. Dept. Edn., Washington, 1990. Bd. dirs. Oak Ridge Cmty. Playhouse, 1990-92. With USNG, 1969-75. Petroleum Rsch. Found. rsch. fellow, 1975; NSF undergrad. rsch. program rsch. grantee, 1967. Mem. Am. Chem. Soc. Home: 154 Whippoorwill Ln Oak Ridge TN 37830-8645 Office: PO Box 5496 Oak Ridge TN 37831-5496

STERNITZKE-HOLUB, ANN, elementary school educator; b. Oklahoma City, Okla., May 5, 1952; d. James Francis and Doris Josephine (Lahr) Sternitzke; m. James Robert Holub, Apr. 4, 1987. AA, Golden West Coll., Huntington Beach, Calif., 1972; BS, Calif. State U., Fullerton, 1975, postgrad., 1976. Cert. secondary multiple subject, phys. edn. and English tchr. grades kindergarten-12, Calif.; life cert. educator Calif. Cmty. Colls. Phys. edn. and fencing instr. Fullerton Coll., 1976-82; fencing instr. Golden West Coll., Huntington Beach, 1977-83, Calif. State U., Fullerton, 1983-86; elem. phys. edn. specialist Placentia-Yorba Linda (Calif.) Unified Sch. Dist., 1989-93, elem. tchr. Bryant Ranch Sch., 1993—. Puppeteer Adventure City Amusement Park, Anaheim, Calif., E. Free Ch., Fullerton, Everlasting Arms, Fullerton. Mem. support staff 1984 Olympics, Long Beach, 1984; entertainer Stagelight Family Prodns., Brea, Calif., 1993—. Recipient Calif. Dept. Agr. award, 1999; grantee, Placentia-Yorba Linda Found., 1997—98, 2003, Disney Performing Arts, 1996—2001, Org. County Music/Arts Adminstrs., 2001, Yorba Linda Rotary Club, 2003, others. Mem. AAHPERD, U.S. Fencing Assn., U.S. Fencing Coaches Assn., Calif. State U. Alumni Assn., Vets. Fencing Assn. Republican. Avocations: dance, musical theatre, puppetry, fencing, costuming. Office: Bryant Ranch Sch 24695 Paseo De Toronto Yorba Linda CA 92887-5116 E-mail: annholub@yahoo.com.

STETINA, PAMELA ELEANOR, nursing educator; b. Cambridge, Mass., Nov. 11, 1964; d. Charles and Eleanor Mary (Jennison) Toth; m. Francis Lee Stetina Jr., Aug. 15, 1987. BSN, Salisbury (Md.) State U., 1987; cert. in gerontology, U. Denver, 1990; M in Nursing, U. Phoenix, Englewood, Colo., 1996. RN. Grad. nurse, RN Dorchester Gen. Hosp., Cambridge, Md., 1987-89; staff nurse Salisbury Med. Ctr., 1988-89; staff/charge nurse Porter Care Hosp., Denver, 1989-91; float nurse Summit Health Profls., Denver, 1991—96; clin. nurse NMC Home Care, Englewood, 1992-95; mem. faculty, asst. dir. nursing Concorde Career Inst., Denver, 1994-96; coord. nursing Pueblo C.C.-S.W., Durango, Colo., 1996-2000; asst. prof. Tex. A&M U., Corpus Christi, 2000—. Mem. curriculum com., faculty whole com., libr. com. Tex. A&M U., Corpus Christi, 2000—. Contbr. Jour. Nursing Jocularity. Instr. CPR Am. Heart Assn., Colo., 1994—. Named Educator of Yr., Colo. Pvt. Sch. Assn., Denver, 1995. Mem. Nat. League for Nursing, Oncology Nursing Soc., So. Nursing Rsch. Soc., Sigma Theta Tau. Avocations: reading, hiking. Office: Tex A&M U Sch Nursing 6300 Ocean Dr Corpus Christi TX 78412 E-mail: pstetina@juno.com.

STEVENS, ADELE AMY KUBOTA, physical education educator; b. Waimea, Kauai, Hawaii, Jan. 21, 1945; d. Shigeomi and Bernice Aiko (Hamamura) Kubota; m. Donald Lynn Stevens, July 5, 1975; children: Abbie-Aiko Ke'ala, Mayumi Maile. Student, U. Hawaii, 1965-66; BA in Edn., Pacific Luth. U., 1967; postgrad., U. Mass., 1967-68, U. Oslo, 1970. Cert. tchr., Hawaii. Grad. teaching asst. U. Mass., Amherst, 1967-68; tchr. health, phys. edn., guidance Kauai (Hawaii) and Intermediate Sch., 1968-70; exec. dir. Hawaii Motorcycle Safety Found., Honolulu, 1979-81; tchr. phys. edn. Waipahu (Hawaii) H.S., 1970-93, tchr. career guidance, 1993—; tchr. driver edn. area high schs., 1976—, coord. Project Renaissance, 1992. Cooperating tchr. U. Hawaii, Honolulu, 1971-77, Brigham Young U., Laie, Hawaii, 1987; chair Sch. Climate com., 1994—. Adv. bd. Moanalua Gardens Day Care Ctr., Honolulu, 1984-87; active The Ch. at Our House, Mililani, Hawaii,1 987—; team mom Mililani Bobby Sox Softball, 1988-90; coach, referee Mililani Am. Youth Soccer Orgn., 1988-92; participant Mililani Community Volleyball League, 1990—; asst. coach Mililani Basketball Assn., 1992. Mem. NEA, AAHPERD, ASCD, Hawaii State Tchrs. Assn. (assoc. policy com.), Hawaii Assn. Health, Phys. Edn., Recreation and Dance, Am. Driver and Traffic Safety Edn. Assn., Leeward Oahu Tchrs. Assn. (sch. rep. 1991-92). Avocations: reading, tennis, travel. Office: Waipahu HS 94-1211 Farrington Hwy Waipahu HI 96797-3205

STEVENS, ALICE MARIE, educational consultant; b. Colorado Springs, Colo., Jan. 18, 1954; d. Charles C. and Gladys Marie (Craft) S. BS, S.W. Bapt. U., 1976; MEd, U. Mo., 1983; PhD, Purdue U., 2001. Cert. tchr. reading, learning disabilities, Mo. Sci. tchr. Lincoln County R-IV Schs., Winfield, Mo., 1976-78; sci. instr. Ricks Inst., Monrovia, Liberia, West Africa, 1978-79; learning specialist Total Learning Clinic, Columbia, Mo., 1982-89; homebound instr. Rusk Rehab. Ctr., Columbia, Mo., 1988-91; instr. Columbia Coll., Columbia, Mo., 1989, 91; learning disabilities specialist Columbia (Mo.) Pub. Schs., 1989-91; tchr., rsch. asst. Purdue U., West Lafayette, Ind., 1991-98; ednl. cons. West Lafayette, Ind., 1991-97; asst. dir. Cerebral Palsy Assn. Greater Lafayette, 1993-94; instr. Frostburg (Md.) State U., 1998-2000; dir. prevention programs Brain Injury Assn., Alexandria, Va., 2000—. Asst. dir. Cerebral Palsy Assn. Greater Lafayette, 1993-94. Mem. ASCD, AAE, Nat. Sci. Tchrs. Assn. (conf. presenter 1993), Coun. for Exceptional Children (conf. presenter), Soc. for Prevention Rsch., Kappa Delta Pi, Phi Delta Kappa. Office: Brain Injury Assn 105 N Alfred Alexandria VA 22314 E-mail: amstevens@biausa.org.

STEVENS, BRENDA ANITA, psychologist, educator; b. N.Y.C., Oct. 23, 1949; d. Henry Stevens and Frances Marie (Russo) Incorvaia; m. Edwin Randall Trinkle, Feb. 21, 1976 (div. 1987); m. John Alexander Czaja, Sept. 10, 1994; 1 child, Peter A. BS, EdM, Boston U., 1971, CAGS, 1973; PhD in Edn., U. Tenn., 1991. Nat. cert. sch. psychologist. Sch. adjustment counselor Dedham (Mass.) Pub. Schs., 1972-73; testing specialist Children's Hosp. Med. Ctr., Boston, 1973-74; sch. psychologist North Middlesex Regional Schs., Townsend, Mass., 1974-78; grad. asst. U. Tenn., Knoxville, 1978-79, 89-90, program evaluator, 1983-84, clinic coord., 1989-90; psychology assoc. Cherokee Mental Health Ctr., Morristown, Tenn., 1985; asst. prof. U. Nebr., Kearney, 1990-93, Miami U., Oxford, Ohio, 1993-2000; sch. psychologist Indian Hill Sch., Cin., 2000—. Psychol. cons. Roane County Pub. Schs., Kingston, Tenn., 1978-89; cons., adminstrv. intern Knox County Pub. Schs., Knoxville, 1984-85; sch. psychologist Jefferson County Pub. Schs., Dandridge, Tenn., 1986-88, Oak Ridge (Tenn.) Pub. Schs., 1989; cons. Psychol. Corp., 1994-96. Commr.'s appointee Mass. State Coun. for Hearing Impaired, Boston, 1976-78; bd. dirs. Luth. Social Ministries Tenn., Knoxville, 1989; exec. bd. Luth. Community Svcs., Knoxville, 1987-89; cons. Mass. State Dept. Edn., Boston, 1974-78. Head Start grantee, 1991-94, Project One to One grantee Dawson County, 1991; Trustee scholar Boston U., 1968-71; recipient Women of Achievement award Commn. Women, 1983. Mem. Am. Psychol. Assn., Nat. Assn. Sch.

Psychologists, Phi Kappa Phi, Pi Lambda Theta, Ohio Sch. Psychologists Assn, Phi Delta Kappa. Avocations: sailing, cooking, gardening, needlepoint. Office: 6845 Drake Rd Cincinnati OH 45243

STEVENS, CHERITA WYMAN, writer, educator; b. Erick, Okla., Jan. 12, 1938; d. Forrest Clarence and Wilma Peter Wyman; m. Paul Donald Stevens, May 30, 1958 (div. Nov. 10, 1978); children: Paul McDonald, Mark Liu. BA in Social Sci., Phillips U., 1961; MA in Sch. Law and Fin., Calif. State U., LA, 1976; cert. in ESL, U. Calif., LA. Adminstrv. credential K-12 and adult; LA, Calif. Classroom tchr. grades 7-9 South Pasadena (Calif.) Unified, 1966—74; assoc. regional pastor Disciples of Christ, Pacific Southwest, 1976—82; computer store owner Claremont (Calif.) Computer, 1982—87; tchr., adminstr. Cabrillo Unified Sch. Dist., Half Moon Bay, Calif., 1987—97; ESL computer lab. media instr. Chapman Edn. Ctr., Garden Grove, Calif., 1997—2003. Legis. intern Calif. State Assembly, Sacramento, 1978—80; fin. analyst Primerica Life/Citigroup, Orange, Calif., 2000—02; grant reviewer U.S. Dept. Edn., Washington, 2002. Editor: Direction Newspaper, 1976—82; author: (software) Apartment Maintenance, 1988, Grants Tracking, 1989, Financial Management, 1991, (articles) to newspapers, mags., (book lab curriculum, 500 pages) Curriculum and Lesson Plans for the INdependent Learning Lab, 1995; designer: lesson plan OTAN Website, 2003. Mem. Ams. for Dem. Action, Pasadena, 1963—80; civil rights activist, 1960—69; organizer first Martin Luther King Jr. celebration in U.S., 1972; active First Christian Ch., Orange, 1963—2002, Pasadena, Calif. Grantee Consortium grant adult edn., Calif. Dept. Edn./Joint Partnership Training Act, Half Moon Bay, 1996. Mem.: Assn. Calif. Sch. Adminstrs. (site rep. 1993—97). Avocations: golf, photography, genealogy. Home: 401 W La Veta Ave #220 Orange CA 92866

STEVENS, DIANA LYNN, elementary education educator; b. Waterloo, Iowa, Dec. 12, 1950; d. Marcus Henry and Clarissa Ann (Funk) Carr; m. Paul John Stevens; 1 child, Drew Spencer. BS, Mid Am. Nazarene Coll., 1973; M in Liberal Arts, Baker U., 1989. Elem. tchr. Olathe (Kans.) Sch. Dist. #233, 1975—. Artwork appeared in traveling exhibit ARC/Nat. Art Edn. Assn., 1968, Delta Kappa Gamma Bull., 2001. Pres. Artists' League, Olathe, 1990—. Olathe Sch. Dist. Action grantee, 1996-97. Mem. NEA, Kans. Edn. Assn., Olathe Edn. Assn. (social com.), Nat. Art Edn. Assn., Delta Kappa Gamma (profl. affairs com. mem.), Coll. Ch. of the Nazarene. Avocations: portrait art, reading biographies, power walking, exhibiting artwork. Home: 217 S Montclaire Dr Olathe KS 66061-3828

STEVENS, GAIL LAVINE, community health nurse, educator; b. Glens Falls, NY, June 10, 1938; d. Paul E. and Doris E. (Shippey) Lavine; m. Gary R. Stevens, Apr. 1, 1961; children: Ginelle Tonia, Gavin Wesley, Gordon Rickard. BSN, Syracuse (N.Y.) U., 1961; MA, U. South Ala., 1975, MS in Nursing, 1989; EdD, U. So. Miss., 1979. Instr. nursing Providence Sch. Nursing, Mobile, Ala., 1961-63, Mobile Infirmary Sch. Nursing, 1963—78; asst. and assoc. prof. nursing Mobile Coll., 1978—88; prof. nursing U. Mobile, 1989—, chair Baccalaureate Dept. Nursing, 2002—. Contbr. articles to profl. jours. Mem. ANA, Syracuse U. Nurses Alumni Assn., Sigma Theta Tau Internat. Home: 2710 Palao Ct Mobile AL 36693-2722 E-mail: drgstevens@comcast.net.

STEVENS, GEORGE EDWARD, dean, academic administrator; b. Phila., Mar. 7, 1942; s. George Edward Stevens and Marstella (Smalls) Harvey; m. Pamela Ann Giffhorn; children: Kwanza Baraka, Charles Edward. BS, Del. State U., 1971; BA, Thomas E. Edison Coll., 1976; MBA, Wash. U., 1973; DBA, Kent State U., 1979. Asst. to dir. employee rels. Rohm & Haas, Inc., Phila., 1973-75; tchg. asst., instr. Kent (Ohio) State U., 1973-75; from asst. to assoc. prof. Ariz. State U., Tempe, 1979-83; from assoc. prof. to prof. U. Ctrl. Fla., Orlando, 1983-89, prof., interim dean, 1989-90; prof., dean Oakland U., Rochester, Mich., 1991-95, Kent (Ohio) State U., 1995—. Chmn. bd. Kent Regional Bus. Alliance, St. Louis, 1992—; cons.=evaluator, mem. accreditation rev. com. Higher Learning Commn. Author: Cases in Human Resources Management, 1983, 6th edit., 1996. Mem. exec. com Mid-Am. Conf., 2003—, infectious dis. com.; bd. dirs. Kent State U. Found. Mem. Acad. Mgmt., Soc. Advancement of Mgmt. (dir.), Decision Scis. Inst., Rotary Club of Kent, Beta Gamma Sigma (bd. govs.), Delta Mu Delta, Delta Sigma Pi. Avocations: basketball, jogging, spectator sports, volleyball, reading. Home: 4031 Queensbury Cir Stow OH 44224-5417 Office: Kent State Univ PO Box 5190 Kent OH 44242-0001

STEVENS, GERALD D. secondary education educator, consultant; b. Seattle, Apr. 9, 1941; s. James Edward and Olga Rubina (Olsen) S.; m. Michele Christine Hayek, June 16, 1973; children: Heather Corrine, Wendy Jeannette, Gerald Michael. Student, U. Wash., 1963-65; BA in Polit. Sci., Calif. State U., L.A., 1989; MA, U. So. Calif., 1995, postgrad., 1995—. Cert. tchr., Calif. Bank auditor Nat. Bank Commerce, Seattle, 1965-72; pvt. practice GEMIC L.A., 1972-86; tchr. L.A. Unified Sch. Dist., 1986-96. Cons. model schs. program Fgn. Policy Assn., Washington, 1990; presenter coalition essential schs. L.A. Unified Sch. Dist., 1990-91. Author: Redistributive Econ. Justice, 1993. Vol. C.L.A.R.E. Found., Santa Monica, 1989-91. With USMC, 1960-63, PTO. Mem. So. Calif. Social Sci. Assn. (bd. dirs. 1990-94, v.p.), United Tchrs. L.A., Sierra Club. Avocations: songwriting, ceramic art. Home: Unit 2 2101 Ocean Ave Apt 2 Santa Monica CA 90405-2229 Office: LA Unified Sch Dist 450 N Grand Ave Los Angeles CA 90012-2123

STEVENS, JOHN GALEN, mathematics educator, consultant; b. Kansas City, Mo., Aug. 7, 1943; s. Albert Owen and Mildred Lucille (Embree) S.; m. Mary Lou Beilstein, Dec. 27, 1966; children: Sarah, Rachel. BS in Chemistry, Ind. U., 1965; PhD., NYU, 1972. Asst. prof. Montclair State U., Upper Montclair, N.J., 1969-74, assoc. prof., 1974-79, prof. math., 1979—. Cons. Exxon Mobil Rsch. and Engring. Co., Inc., Annandale, N.J., 1975—. Contbr. articles to profl. jours.; patentee in field. NSF grantee. Mem. Soc. for Indsl. and Applied Math., Am. Math. Soc. Presbyterian. Achievements include research in mathematical modeling of physical systems, especially combustion and pollution control. Home: 130 Gallows Hill Rd Westfield NJ 07090-1107 Office: Montclair State U Dept Math Scis Montclair NJ 07043 E-mail: stevensj@mail.montclair.edu.

STEVENS, LEONARD BERRY, educational consultant; b. Fall River, Mass., Sept. 19, 1938; s. Henry Bennett and Manetta (Berry) S.; m. Elizabeth Holihen, Aug. 17, 1963; children: Lisa M., Christopher M., Andrew B., Rosa B. A. BS, Boston U., 1960; EdD, U. Mass., 1978. Cert. supt., Mass. Edn. writer Providence Jour.-Bull., 1963-67; sr. editor Cowles Comms., Inc., N.Y.C., 1967-68; exec. editor Change in Higher Edn. Mag., N.Y.C., 1968-70; spl. asst. to Chancellor N.Y.C. Bd. Edn., 1970-73; rsch. asst. U. Mass., Amherst, 1973-76; dir. Greater Cleve. Project, 1976-78; dir. Office Sch. Monitoring and Cmty. Rels. U.S. Dist. Ct. (no. dist.) Ohio, Cleve., 1978-88; dir. Compact for Ednl. Opportunity, Milw., 1988-90; race-related sch. planning cons. Sarasota, Fla., 1990—. Cons. as racial/cultural diversity and sch. desegregation planning expert and analyst to state edn. depts., pub. sch. dists., parties in litigation; expert witness in over 25 sch. desegregation cases; lectr. in field at univs. and seminars. Co-author: Make Your Schools Work, 1975; contbr. articles to profl. jours. and mass media publs. Trustee Inst. Child Advocacy, Cleve.; bd. dirs. Com. on Cath. Cmty. Action, Cleve., 1981-88. Lt. (j.g.) USN, 1960-63. Office: PO Box 2479 Sarasota FL 34230

STEVENS, LEOTA MAE, retired elementary education educator; b. Waverly, Kans., Mar. 27, 1921; d. Clinton Ralph and Velma Mae (Kukuk) Chapman; m. James Oliver Stevens, Nov. 7, 1944 (dec.); children: James Harold, Mary Ann Hooker Tibbits. BA, McPherson Coll., 1954; MS, Emporia U., 1964, postgrad., 1969-77, Wichita U., 1977. Educator Pleasant Mound Sch., Waverly, 1940-41; prin. educator Halls Summit Sch., Waverly, 1941-42; educator Waverly Grade Sch., 1942-43, Ellinwood (Kans.) Jr. H.S., 1943-45, Hutchinson (Kans.) Grade Sch., 1945-48, Lincoln Sch., Darlow, Kans., 1948-49; educator prin. Mitchell-Yaggy Consol. Sch., Hutchinson, 1949-57; educator elem. Hutchinson Sch. Dist. 308, 1957-85, ret., 1985. V.p. Reno County Tchrs. Assn. Hutchinson, 1956-57, pres. Assn. Childhood Edn. Internat., 1978-79. Author of numerous poems; compiler The Alexander-Kukuk Descendants: 1754 to 1998. Mem. Worker ARC Blood Mobile, 1986—2000, Hutchinson Cmty. Concerts, 1970—; historian Women's Civic Ctr., 1988—92, art com. chmn, 1992—96; den mother Cub Scouts, 1963—66; leader Girl Scouts Ellinwood, 1944—45; bell ringer ARC Blood Mobile, 1986—2000; ch. sch. tchr. Trinity United Meth. Ch., 1959—71, attendance chair, 1994. Mem. AAUW (news reporter 1984-87, legis. chmn. program com. 1991-94, 2d v.p., 1994-95), Ret. Nation State and Local Edn. Assn., Reno County Tchrs. Assn. (v.p. 1956-57), Assn. Childhood Edn. Internat. (pres. 1978-79), Reno County Extension Homemaker Coun. (rep. 1987—), Rainbow Extension Club (pres. 1986-92), Hutchinson Area Ret. Tchrs. Assn. (historian 1996-99), Am. Legion Aux., Friends of Preservation, Delta Kappa Gamma (sec., v.p. 1972-80, grant chmn. 1980-88, publicity com. 1990-93, legis. chmn. 1994-2000). Republican. Avocations: art, music, traveling, gardening, camping, genealogy. Home: 805 W 23rd Ave Hutchinson KS 67502-3765

STEVENS, LINDA TOLLESTRUP, academic director; b. Salt Lake City, Feb. 7, 1963; d. Garn Alvin and Mary Ann (Cannon) Tollestrup; 1 child, Marli Brynn. BS, U. Utah, 1984, MS, 1989. Cert. sch. counselor, Utah. Tchr. pre-sch. Adventurer's Pre-Sch., Salt Lake City, 1984; adminstr. headstart program Creative Devel. Ctr., Salt Lake City, 1984-85; vocat. evaluator Utah Divsn. Rehab. Svcs. Vocat. Evaluation, Salt Lake City, 1985-86; human resource counselor Davis Applied Tech. Ctr., Kaysville, Utah, 1986-95; advising programs coord. Pa. State U., Hazleton, 1995—. Trainee Phoenix Inst., Salt Lake City, 1986, U. No. Colo., Greeley, 1986; instr. Utah State Turning Point, Salt Lake City and Provo, 1992. Mem. Golden Spike Dog Obedience Club, Ogden, Utah, 1986-90, Humane Soc. Utah, 1986—. Mem. NEA, ACA, Nat. Acad. Advising Assn., Am. Vocat. Assn., Am. Bus. Women's Assn. (v.p. 1992), Utah Vocat. Assn. (bldg. fund coord. 1989-90), Utah Fedn. Bus. and Profl. Women (Woman of Achievement award 1991), Golden Key Honor Soc., Delta Soc., Phi Eta Sigma. Mem. Lds Ch. Avocations: dog training, tennis, violin, piano, reading. Office: Pa State Univ Highacres Hazleton PA 18201

STEVENS, MARY JO THOMAS, librarian; b. Louisville, Ky., Feb. 15, 1952; d. Manuel Edward and Josephine Marie (Smith) Stevens; 1 child, Sarah Elizabeth. BA, U. Louisville, 1983; MS, U. Ky., 1985. Govt. documents libr. Ohio State Supreme Ct. Libr., Columbus, 1986; libr. Mercer County Pub. Libr., Harrodsburg, 1987-88; asst. libr. Lindsey Wilson Coll., Columbia, Ky., 1988-92; coll. libr. U. Ark. C.C., Hope, Ark., 1992—99; libr. dir. MacMurray Coll., Jacksonville, Ill., 1999—. Contbr. articles to profl. jours. Mem. steering com. Digital Acad. Libr., 2002—; chmn. Librs. of Jacksonville in Coop. Consortium. Mem. Sangamon Valley Acad. Libr. Consortium (chmn. 2001-). Office: Henry Pfeiffer Libr 447 E College Ave Jacksonville IL 62650

STEVENS, PHYLISS ELIZABETH, fine art dealer, consultant, publisher, lecturer; b. Balt., Dec. 30, 1953; d. Lawrence and Frances Elizabeth Stevens. BS, Va. Commonwealth U., 1977. Gallery dir. KenWest Gallery, L.A., 1979-84; fine art cons. La Mirage Gallery, L.A., 1984-86; gallery dir. West 43rd St. Gallery, L.A., 1986-89; pres. Vibrant Fine Art, L.A., 1990—. Pres., founder, organizer Art in Pub. Places, L.A., 1984-86; creative dir. The Black Child/Art, L.A., 1986-88; art cons. NBC-TV Segment Series, Hill St. Blues, Hollywood, Calif., 1982. Editor Art Forum, 1984, American Black Artists Newsletter, 1988. Recipient Top Cons. Design Workshop award West Coast Art Stars, 1978, Community Involvement In the Arts award Founder's Women Club, 1980. Mem. NAFE, Am. Artist Club (pres. 1986-88). Democrat. Avocations: reading, creative writing, theatre, travel. Office: Vibrant Fine Art 3931 W Jefferson Blvd Los Angeles CA 90016-4211 E-mail: vibrant2@earthlink.net.

STEVENS, REBECCA SUE, retired religious education administrator; b. Winchester, Ind., May 25, 1940; d. Cleo Gordon and Florence Elizabeth (Bockhofer) Parrish; m. John Vincent Stevens, June 18, 1961; children: Brenda, Michael, Matthew, Bonnie, Jason. AB, Taylor U., 1962; cert., Evang. Tchr. Tng. Assn., 1962. Tchr. kindergarten Neighborhood House, Kokomo, Ind., 1962-63; weekday religious tchr. Howard County Coun. Chs., Kokomo, 1965-69; substitute tchr. Kokomo Ctr. Schs., 1984-88; dir. Christian edn. United Ch. of Christ, Kokomo, 1978-84, 1st Christian Ch., Kokomo, 1988-94; dir. Joy Day Pre-Sch., Kokomo, 1984-95, ret., 1995. Mem.: Women's Christian Temperance Union (edn. and pub. rels. dir. state and county levels 1972—). Avocations: sewing, rocks, shells, collecting refrigerator magnets. Home: 3500 Robin Dr Kokomo IN 46902-4430

STEVENS, RICHARD GORDON, political scientist, educator; b. Chgo., Dec. 29, 1925; s. Philip Jacob and Almyra (DeVillery) Solomon; m. Norma Jean Duncan, Oct. 14, 1949; children: Dennis Gordon, Laura Louise, Patricia Jean. AM in Polit. Sci., U. Chgo., 1956, PhD in Polit. Sci., 1963. Asst. prof. Coll. William and Mary, Williamsburg, Va., 1959-62; tutor honors divsn. U. Santa Clara, Calif., 1963-66; asst. prof. U. Wash., Seattle, 1966-69; assoc. prof. U. Waterloo, Ont., Can., 1969-73; prof., chmn. Rockford (Ill.) Coll., 1973-75; prof. Georgetown U., Washington, 1981-85; prof., assoc. dean Def. Intelligence Coll., Washington, 1984-92; prof. Nat. Def. U., Washington, 1992-94; lectr. Inst. World Politics, Washington, 1994-2000; adj. prof. Am. U., Washington, 1994—. Cons. Pub. Adminstrn. Svc., McLean, Va., 1975—, Office Sec. Def., Washington, 1977; Fulbright prof. law U. Hong Kong, 1986-87. Author: The American Constitution and Its Provenance, 1997, Frankfurter and Due Process, 1987, Sober as a Judge, 1999; co-author: American Political Thought, 1973, 83; contbr. articles to profl. jours. Comdr. USNR, 1943—85. Carnegie fellow in law and govt. Harvard Law Sch., Cambridge, Mass., 1962-63; Salvatori fellow Free Congress Found., Washington, 1994-95. Mem. Am. Polit. Sci. Assn., Nat. Assn. Scholars, Naval Res. Assn., Assn. Former Crewmembers USS Intrepid, Harvard Law Sch. Assn., Mil. Officer's Assn. of Am. Home: 8350 Greensboro Dr # 307 Mc Lean VA 22102 E-mail: stevensrg@aol.com.

STEVENS, SHEILA MAUREEN, teachers union administrator; b. Glendale, Calif., Nov. 1, 1942; d. Richard Chase and Sheila Mary (Beatty) Flynn; m. Jan Whitney Stevens, Sept. 12, 1964; children: Ian Whitney, Bevin Michelle. AA in Liberal Arts, Monterey Peninsula Coll., Calif., 1963; BA in Anthropology, Calif. State U., Long Beach, 1969; postgrad. studies in Edn., U. Guam, 1976-77. Tchr. U.S. Trust Territory of the Pacific, Koror, Palau Island, 1968-72, Kolonia, Ponape Island, 1972-76, Dept. Edn., Agana, Guam, 1976-79; newspaper editor Pacific Daily News (Gannett), Agana, 1979-83; comm. dir. Guam Fedn. of Tchrs., Agana, 1983-84, exec. dir., 1984-85, Alaska Fedn. Tchrs., Anchorage, 1985-87; labor rels. specialist N.Y. State United Tchrs., Watertown, 1987-93, regional staff dir. Potsdam, 1993—2003; ret., 2003. Mem. Gov.'s Blue Ribbon Panel on Edn., Agana, Guam, 1983-85; leadership devel. coord. Am. Fedn. Tchrs., Washington, 1983—; trainer positive negotiations program Situation Mgmt. Sys., Hanover, Mass., 1988—. Author, editor: Pacific Daily News, 1981-83 (Guam Press Club awards 1981, 82, 83); contbr. articles to mag. and jours. Mem. task force on labor policy, com. on self determination, Govt. of Guam, Agana, 1984-85, Adult Basic Edn. Planning Com., 1985; mem. labor studies adv. bd., Anchorage, Alaska, 1989, regional compact coalition N.Y. State Edn. Dept., Albany, 1994. Named Friend of Edn., Carthage (N.Y.) Tchrs. Assn., 1990. Mem. NOW, ACLU, ASCD, AAUW, Am. Fedn. Tchrs. Comm. Assn. (Best Editorial award 1984), Indsl. Rels. Rsch. Assn. Democrat. Methodist. Avocations: travel, reading, free-lance writing, cross-country skiing. Office: NY State United Tchrs 12 Elm St Potsdam NY 13676-1812

STEVENS, SUZANNE DUCKWORTH, artist, educator; b. Richmond, Ind., Feb. 1, 1946; d. Delbert Raymond and Virginia (Grosvenor) Duckworth; married, 1970 (divorced 1979); 1 child, Neil D. Stevens. BA in Painting and Drawing with honors, Fla. State U., 1968; MA in Painting and Drawing, Goddard Coll., Plainfield, Vt., 1978. Substitute counselor Crisis Intervention Home, Virginia Beach, Va., 1978-85; art instr. Contemporary Art Ctr. Va., 1979—; pvt. art instr. and artist Fine Art Studio, Virginia Beach, 1978—. Artist in residence Virginia Beach Sch. Sys., 1991, 93; curator student shows Contemporary Art Ctr. Va., 1990—; instr. Va. Marine Sci. Mus., Virginia Beach, 1993. One-woman shows include Decker Studios, Virginia Beach, 1986, Contemporary Art Ctr. Va., 1990—, Commons Gallery, Norfolk, Va., 1990, Waterworks Visual Arts Ctr., Salisbury, N.C., 1991, Artists at Work Gallery, Virginia Beach, 1992, Ramada Plaza Resort, 1992—2000, exhibited in group shows at Peninsula Fine Arts Ctr., Newport News, Va., 1982, 1983, 1984, Contemporary Art Ctr. Va., 1986, 1988, 1994, 1995, 1996, Maritime Mus., Virginia Beach, 1988, Seashore State Park, 1992, Represented in permanent collections Chrysler Mus., Norfolk, Visions Mag. for Arts, Virginia Beach, 1996, Exhibited in group shows at Va. Waterfront Internat. Arts Festival Poster. Recipient Outstanding Tchr. award, Gov.'s Sch. for Visual and Performing Arts, U. Richmond, Va., 1990, 1992, 1998, 1999. Mem. Women in the Arts Mus., Classics Plus Dance Orgn., Tadems Dance Orgn. Democrat. Avocations: dancing, piano, tennis, reading, gardening. Home: 1401 Rylands Rd Virginia Beach VA 23455-3929

STEVENSON, CAROL WELLS, secondary education educator; b. Richmond, Va., Feb. 14, 1942; d. Alfred Hatcher and Laura Dowdy (Hobson) Wells; m. James Pendleton Stevenson, June 23, 1962; children: James Brian Stevenson, Anne Pendleton Stevenson. BS in Home Econ. Edn., James Madison U., Harrisonburg, Va., 1962; MA in Adult Edn., Va. Commonwealth U., 1981. Cert. Home Econ., Collegiate Profl. Cert., Va. Home econ. tchr. Patrick Henry High Sch., Ashland, Va., 1962-66, Liberty Middle Sch., Ashland, Va., 1976—. Named Va. Home Econ. Tchr. of Yr., 1988, Tchr. of Yr., Liberty Mid. Sch., 1983-84, 84-85, 85-86, Most Outstanding Home Econs. Tchr. in U.S., Home Baking Assn., 1994; Check Excellence regional winner State Dept. Edn., 1990. Mem. Am. Home Econs. Assn., Va. Home Econ. Assn. (Va. Home Econs. Tchr. of Yr. award 1988), Va. Home Econ. Tchr. Assn., Am. Vocat. Assn., Va. Vocat. Assn., Nat. Assn. Vocat. Home Tchrs., Future Homemakers Am. Found. Episcopalian. Home: 202 Hanover Ave Ashland VA 23005-1815 Office: Liberty Mid Sch RR 3 Box 2500 Ashland VA 23005-9803

STEVENSON, CHARLES BEMAN, business educator; b. Columbus, Ohio, Oct. 30, 1922; s. Arthur Edwin and Mary Lucille (Beman) S.; BA, George Washington U., 1960, MA, 1962; diploma U.S. Army Command and Gen. Staff Coll., 1962; postgrad. U. Pitts., 1968-74, 80-81; m. Sara DeSalles Gilroy, June 12, 1948. Enlisted in U.S. Army, 1942, commd. 2d lt., 1943, advanced through grades to lt. col., 1963, ret., 1968; prof. mil. sci. Indiana U. Pa., 1965-68, asst. prof. bus. mgmt., 1968-71, assoc. prof., 1972-89, also dir. IUP Econ. Edn. Ctr., prof. emeritus, 1991—, sec., founder IUP Coll. Bus. Adv. Coun., 1978—; founder Coll. Bus. Fgn. Student Intern. Program; v.p. Mgmt. Scis. Resources, 1988-89; pres., mgmt. cons. CBS & Assocs, 1990—; pub. policy expert Heritage Found., 1986—; founder IUP Wash. D.C. Leadership Tgn. Trips, 1987-91; lectr. in field. Mem. edn. com. Pa. C. of C. 1976-83; chmn. Indiana County ARC, 1975-76; trustee Episcopal Diocese of Pitts., 1975-78, 79-80, mem. planning commn., 1975-82; mem. vestry, sr. warden St. Peter's Episc. Ch., 1983-85; mem. Episc. Diocesan Council, 1983-85. Decorated Legion of Merit; recipient Achievement awards, honor certs. Freedoms Found. at Valley Forge, 1986, Pub. Svc. award Dept. Army, 1986; others. Mem. NRA, VFW, Ind. Personnel Assn. (pres. 1981-83) Am. Mgmt. Assn., Ret. Officers Assn., Mil. Order World Wars (comdr., founder chpt. 200), Assn. Pa. U. Bus. and Econ. Faculty (pres. 1985-88). Republican. Club: Army and Navy (Washington). Home: 1398 School St Indiana PA 15701-2567 Office: Indiana U Pa Coll Bus Indiana PA 15705-0001

STEVENSON, DAVID JOHN, planetary scientist, educator; b. Wellington, New Zealand, Sept. 2, 1948; came to U.S., 1971; s. Ian McIvor and Gwenyth (Carroll) S. BSc, Victoria U., New Zealand, 1971; PhD, Cornell U., 1976. Rsch. fellow Australian Nat. U., Canberra, Australia, 1976-78; asst. prof. UCLA, L.A., 1978-80; assoc. prof. Calif. Inst. Tech., Pasadena, 1980-84, prof., 1984—, George van Osdol prof., 1995—. Chmn. divsn. geol. & planetary scis. Calif. Inst. Tech., 1989-94. Contbr. about 100 articles to profl. jours. Named Fulbright scholar, USA, 1971-76. Fellow Am. Geophysical Union (Harry H. Hess medal 1998), Royal Soc. London, 1993; mem. AAAS, Am. Astron. Soc. (Urey prize 1984). Office: Calif Inst Tech 1200 E California Blvd Pasadena CA 91125-0001 E-mail: djs@gps.caltech.edu.

STEVENSON, HAROLD WILLIAM, psychology educator; b. Dines, Wyo., Nov. 19, 1924; s. Merlin R. and Mildred M. (Stodick) S.; m. Nancy Guy, Aug. 23, 1950; children: Peggy, Janet, Andrew, Patricia. BA, U. Colo., 1947; MA, Stanford U., 1948, PhD, 1951; DS (hon.), U. Minn., 1996. Asst. prof. psychology Pomona Coll., 1950-53; asst. to asso. prof. psychology U. Tex., Austin, 1953-59; prof. child devel. and psychology, dir. Inst. Child Devel., U. Minn., Mpls., 1959-71; prof. psychology, fellow Center for Human Growth and Devel., U. Mich., Ann Arbor, 1971—; dir. program in child devel. and social policy U. Mich., 1978-93. Adj. prof. Tohoku Fukushi Coll., Japan, 1989—, Peking U., 1990—, Inst. Psychology Chinese Acad. Scis.; mem. tng. com. Nat. Inst. Child Health and Human Devel., 1964-67; mem. personality and cognition study sect. NIMH, 1975-79; chmn. adv. com. on child devel. Nat. Acad. Scis.-NRC, 1971-73; exec. com. div. behavioral scis. NRC, 1969-72; mem. del. early childhood People's Republic of China, 1973, mem. del. psychologists, 1980; mem. vis. com. Grad. Sch. Edn., Harvard U., 1979-86; fellow Center Advanced Studies in Behavioral Scis., 1967-68, 82-83, 89-90. Recipient J.M. Cattell Fellow award in applied psychology Am. Psychol. Soc., 1994, William James Fellow award, 1995, Quest award Am. Fedn. Tchrs., 1995. Fellow Am. Acad. Arts and Scis., Nat. Acad. Edn.; mem. APA (pres. divsn. devel. psychology 1964-65, G. Stanley Hall award 1988, Bronfenbrenner award 1997, Dist. Sci. award Applications of Psychology 1997), Soc. Rsch. Child Devel. (mem. governing coun. 1961-67, pres. 1969-71, chmn. long-range planning com. 1971-74, mem. social policy com. 1977-85, mem. internat. affairs com. 1991-94, Disting. Rsch. award 1993), Internat. Soc. Study Behavioral Devel. (mem. exec. com. 1972-77, pres. 1987-91), Phi Beta Kappa, Sigma Xi. Home: 4001 Glacier Hills Dr # 322 Ann Arbor MI 48105-2847 E-mail: hstevens@umich.edu.

STEVENSON, JAMES RICHARD, radiologist, lawyer; b. Ft. Dodge, Iowa, May 30, 1937; s. Lester Lawrence and Esther Irene (Johnson) S.; m. Sara Jean Hayman, Sept. 4, 1958; children: Bradford Allen, Tiffany Ann, Jill Renee, Trevor Ashley. BS, U. N.Mex., 1959, JD, 1987; MD, U. Colo., 1963. Diplomate Am. Bd. Radiology, Am. Bd. Nuc. Medicine, Am. Bd. Legal Medicine, 1989; Bar: N.Mex. 1987, U.S. Dist. Ct. N.Mex. 1988. Intern U.S. Gen. Hosp., Tripler, Honolulu, 1963-64, resident radiology Brook, San Antonio, 1964-67; radiologist, ptnr. Van Atta Labs., Albuquerque, 1970-88, Radiology Assocs. of Albuquerque, 1988—, pres., 1994-96. Radiologist, ptnr. Civerolo, Hansen & Wolf, Albuquerque, 1988-89; adj. asst. prof. radiology U. N.Mex., 1970-71; pres. med. staff AT & SF Meml. Hosp., 1979-80, chief of staff, 1980-81, trustee, 1981-83. Author: District Attorney manual, 1987. Participant breast screening Am. Cancer Soc., Albuquerque, 1987-88; dir. profl. divsn. United Way, Albuquerque, 1975. Maj. U.S. Army, 1963-70, Vietnam; col. M.C. USAR, 1988—. Decorated Bronze Star; Allergy fellow, 1960; Med.-Legal Tort scholar, 1987. Fellow Am. Coll. Radiology (councilor 1980-86, mem. med. legal com. 1990-96), Am. Coll. Legal Medicine, Am. Coll. Nuc. Medicine, Am. Coll. Nuc. Physicians, Radiology Assn. Albuquerque; mem. AMA (Physicians' Recognition award 1969—), Am. Soc. Law & Medicine, Am. Arbitration Assn., Albuquerque Bar Assn., Soc. Nuc. Medicine (v.p. Rocky Mountain chpt. 1975-76), Am. Inst. Ultrasound in Medicine, N.Am. Radiol. Soc. (chmn. med. legal com. 1992-95), N.Mex. Radiol. Soc. (pres. 1978-79), N.Mex. Med. Soc. (chmn. grievance com.), Albuquerque-Bernalillo County Med. Soc. (scholar 1959), Nat. Assn. Health Lawyers, ABA (antitrust sect. 1986—), N.Mex. State Bar, Albuquerque Bar Assn., Sigma Chi, Albuquerque Country Club, Elks, Masons, Shriners. Republican. Methodist. Home: 3333 Santa Clara Ave SE Albuquerque NM 87106-1530 Office: Medical Arts Imaging Ctr A6 Med Arts Sq 801 Encino Pl NE Albuquerque NM 87102-2612

STEVENSON, MAROLANE, counselor; b. Bottineau, N.D., Mar. 31, 1942; d. Joseph and Lillian (Paryzek) Yellen; m. June 12, 1964. BA, Coll. of Idaho, 1964; MS, U. Utah, 1969; EdD, U. Mont., 1990. cert. psychology, sociology and guidance and counseling tchr./supr., prin., supt. Counselor Missoula County High Schs., dir. career ctr.; title I, ESL, edn1. counselor dept. continuing edn. U. Utah, Salt Lake City. Author: An Epxerimental Analysis of the Performance of Undergraduate Students on Verbal Reasoning Problems When Tested in Solitude and In A Non-Interacting Group. Recipient Gov.'s Citation for Meritorious Svc., State of Mont., 1980, YWCA Excellence award for Pub. Svc., 1992. Mem. NEA, Am. Counseling Assn., Am. Career Guidance Assn., Am. Sch. Counselor Assn., Mont. Counseling Assn. (pres. 1973-74, v.p., editor newsletter), Mont. Edn. Assn., Mont. Sch. Counselor Assn. (legis. chair, sec. vice chair, pub. rels. chair), Mont. Adv. Coun. for Vocat. Edn. (v.p. 1980-81), Phi Delta Kappa, Delta Kappa Gamma Soc. Internat. (N.W. regional dir. 1990-92, N.W. coord. of U.S. Forum, 1988-90, state pres. 1985-87). Home: 3910 Belle Ln Missoula MT 59801-8913

STEVENSON, MARY EVA BLUE, retired elementary education educator; b. Dillon, S.C., Nov. 20, 1928; d. Alex Adolphus and Artie Mishael (Carmichael) Blue; m Damon Stevenson, Feb. 22, 1951 (dec. Sept. 1984); children: Gwendolyn, Jean Stevenson Arzani, Mary Stevenson Miller, Martha Stevenson Jones, Michele. BA, Allen U., Columbia, S.C., 1950; MA, U. West Fla., Pensacola, 1977. Tchr. 1st grade Worth County Schs., Sylvester, Ga., 1956-57; substitute tchr. Dept. Def. Schs., Tachikawa, Japan, 1966-68; tchr. 1st grade Roswell (N.Mex.) Cath. Sch., 1968-69, Okaloosa County Sch. System, Ft. Walton Beach, Fla., 1970-93; ret., 1993. Coord. Each One-Teach One Tutorial Program, Ft. Walton Beach, 1980—. Named Outstanding Model Mother, Progressive Comty. Orgn., Ft. Walton Beach, 1984, educator of Yr., Delta Sigma Theta, Okaloosa Alumni chpt., Ft. Walton Beach, 1987; recipient Willie Bankston award for comty. svcs. So. Christian Leadership Conf., 1996. Fellow Alpha Kappa Alpha (v.p., past parliamentarian, philackter Sigma Omicron Omega chpt.); mem. Fla. Ret. Educators Assn., Emerald Coast/NEA Retirement Program, Order Ea. Star (assoc. matron 1983-94, worthy matron 1994-97). Democrat. Mem. African Methodist Episcopal Ch. Home: 226 Watson Dr NW Fort Walton Beach FL 32548-4270

STEVENSON, NANCY ROBERTA, physiologist, educator; b. Vinton, Iowa, Feb. 14, 1938; d. James Francis and Roberta Nelson (Hart) S.; m. John Lenard, Oct. 5, 1973; children: Eric, Keith, Karen, Steven. BS, U. No. Iowa, Cedar Falls, 1960; MS, Rutgers U., 1963, PhD, 1969. Tchr. home econs. Ewing (N.J.) Jr. H.S., 1960-61; instr. U. Medicine and Dentistry N.J.-R.W. Johnson Med. Sch., Piscataway, 1971-72, asst. prof., 1972-78, assoc. prof. physiology, 1978—. Cons., Highland Park, N.J., 1985—; step 1 material devel. com. for physiology U.S. Med. Lic. Exam., 1998—; physiology test com. Nat. Bd. Med. Examiners, 1998-2000. Contbr. articles to profl. jours. Fundraiser Rutgers Prep. Sch., Somerset, N.J., 1994, mem. com., 1991; parent aide Highland Park Recreational Campus Sports Program, 1985-88; Cub Scout leader Boy Scouts Am., Highland Park, 1985-87; bd. dirs. U. No. Iowa. Recipient Gender Equity award Am. Med. Women's Assn., 1995, Master Educator award U. Medicine and Dentistry N.J., 2001, others; grantee U. Medicine and Dentistry N.J., 1996; NIGMS fellow, 1967-18, VIAMD fellow, 1969-71. Mem. AAUP (chpt. pres. 2002—, coun. v.p. 2002—), Am. Gastroenterol. Assn., Am. Physiol. Soc., Am. Dietetic Assn., Internat. Assn. Med. Sci. Educators, N.J. Acad. Sci. (pres. 1996-98, past pres. 1998—), Achievements include research into mechanisms of intestinal absorption of ascorbic acid, chronobiology of intestinal digestive/absorptive functions. Office: UMDNJ-RW Johnson Med Sch Dept Physiol and Biophysics 675 Hoes Ln Piscataway NJ 08854-5627

STEVENSON, PAUL MICHAEL, physics educator, researcher; b. Denham, Eng., Oct. 10, 1954; came to U.S., 1983; s. Jeremy and Jean Helen (Jennings) S. BA, Cambridge (Eng.) U., 1976; PhD, Imperial Coll., London, 1979. Rsch. assoc. U. Wis., Madison, 1979-81, 1983-84; fellow European Orgn. for Nuclear Rsch., Geneva, 1981-83; sr. rsch. assoc. Rice U., Houston, 1984-86, asst. prof. physics, 1986-89, assoc. prof., 1989-93; prof. physics, 1993—. Contbr. articles to profl. jours. Avocation: music. E-mail: stevenson@physics.rice.edu.

STEVENSON, THOMAS HERBERT, management consultant, writer, executive coach; b. Covington, Ohio, Oct. 16, 1951; s. Robert Louis and Dolly Eileen (Minnich) S.; m. Jackie Lowe, June 1, 1997. BA in Econs./Comm., Wright State U., 1977; MA in Psychology, Cleve. State U., 2001. Cert. regulatory compliance mgr. Am. Bankers Assn., 1990; cert. Gestalt Practitioner, Gestalt Inst. Cleve., 1999. Teaching asst., rsch. asst. Wright State U., Dayton, Ohio, 1975-77; teaching asst. Bowling Green (Ohio) State U., 1978; loan officer Western Ohio Nat. Bank & Trust Co., 1979-80, asst. v.p. adminstrs., 1981-82, v.p. mgmt. svcs. div., 1983-85; bank mgmt. cons. Young & Assocs., Inc., Kent, Ohio, 1985-86, exec. v.p., 1987-2000; mem. faculty Gestalt Inst. Cleve., 2001—, Cleve. State U., 2002—; pres., CEO, Cleve. Cons. Group, Inc., 2002—. Legis. impact analyst Community Bankers Ohio, 1985-94, Community Bankers Ga., 1988-94; mem. exec. com. Owl Electronic Banking Network 1981-85; mem. faculty Gestalt Inst. Cleve., 2001—. Author: Compliance for Community Banks, 1987, Compliance Deskbook, 1988, Internal Audit for Community Banks, 1989, Truth in Lending for the Community Bank, 1989, Bank Protection for the Community Bank, 1989, Community Reinvestment Act for the Community Bank, 1989, Executive Management Guide to an Effective Board of Directors, 1990, The Board of Directors, 1990, The Home Mortgage Disclosure Guide, 1990, A Guide to Flood Insurance, 1990, Insider Lending, 1990, A Guide to the Equal Credit Opportunity Act, 1990, Investment Management, 1990, Contingency Planning, 1990, Insider Conduct, 1990, Currency Transaction Reporting Deskbook, 1990, Property Appraisal Deskbook, 1991, Bank Protection Deskbook, 1991, Regulatory Management Deskbook, 1991, Record Retention Deskbook, 1991, Environmental Deskbook for Financial Institutions, 1992, Deposit Compliance Deskbook, 1992, Fair Housing Deskbook, 1992, Insider Lending Deskbook, 1992, CRA Deskbook, 1992, Investment Mgmt. Deskbook, 1992, Internal Audit Deskbook, 1993; contbr. articles to profl. jours. Mem. adv. bd. Upper Valley Joint Vocat. Sch. for Fin. Instns., 1981-85, Am. Indian Edn. Ctr., Cleve. Cpl. USMC, 1972-73. Recipient George Washington medal of Honor Freedom's Found., 1974. Mem. Nat. Mus. Am. Indian (charter), Am. Inst. Banking (adv. bd. 1982-85), Native Am. Heritage Assn., Inst. Noetic Scis., Eagles Club, Gestalt Inst. Cleve. Republican. Mem. Ch. of Brethren. Home and Office: 3750 Chagrin River Rd Chagrin Falls OH 44022-1130 E-mail: Therbstevenson@aol.com.

STEVOS, JOYCE LOUISE, education director; b. Providence, May 22, 1943; d. Josephus Caldwell and Patricia Anita (Strong) Caldwell Smith; m. Manuel Joseph Stevos, Oct. 22, 1966 (div. Jan. 1981); 1 child, Manuel Joaquim. BEd, R.I. Coll., 1965. Cert. tchr. and prin., R.I. Tchr. Providence Sch. Dept., 1975-76, social studies dept. head, 1971-76, supr. social studies, 1976-90, dir. program and staff devel., 1990-92, dir. strategic planning and profl. devel., 1992—. Cons. in field. Author: The Constitution, 1977, 87. Pres. Urban League R.I., Providence, 1983-87. Recipient Never Again award Jewish Fedn. R.I., 1983, Community Svc. award John Hope settlement House, 1987, Edn. award Providence NAACP, 1991, Nat. Educator award Milken Family Found., 1992. Mem. NCCJ (trustee, program com.), DAR, Nat. Coun. for Social Studies (membership com., sec. 1979-80, Carter G. Woodson Book Award com. 1994—), Social Studies Suprs. Assn. (sec. 1979-80), R.I. Black Heritage Soc. (pres. 1989-95), Delta Sigma Theta (treas. 1989-91, scholarship). Avocations: cooking, family history, reading. Home: 57 Althea St Providence RI 02907-2801 Office: Providence Sch Dept 797 Westminster St Providence RI 02903-4045

STEWARD, LESTER HOWARD, psychiatrist, academic administrator, educator; b. Burt, Iowa, Nov. 6, 1930; s. Walter and Helen Steward; m. Patricia Byrness Roach, June 17, 1953; children: Donald Howard, Thomas Eugene, Susan Elaine, Joan Marsha. BS, Ariz. State U., 1958, MA in Sci. Edn., 1969; postgrad., Escuela Nat. U., Mex., 1971-80; PhD in Psychology, Calif. Coast U., 1974; MD, Western U. Hahnemann Coll., 1980. Rschr. drug abuse and alcoholism Western Australia U., Perth, Australia, 1970-71; intern in psychiatry Helix Hosp., San Diego, Calif., 1971-72; rschr. drug addiction North Mountain Behavioral Inst., Phoenix, 1975-77; exec. v.p., CEO James Tyler Kent Coll., 1977-80; pres., CEO Western U. Sch. Medicine, 1980-86; instr. psychology USN Westpac, Subic Bay, Philippines, 1988-91. Pvt. practice preventive medicine Tecate, Baja California, Mexico, 1971-88; instr. Modern Hypnosis Instrn. Ctr., 1974—, Maricopa Tech. Community Coll., Phoenix, 1975-77; mem. Nt. Ctr. Homeopathy, Washington, Menninger Found., Wichita, Kans. Contbr. numerous papers to profl. confs. Leader Creighton Sch. dist. Boy Scouts Am., Phoenix, 1954-58. Fellow Am. Acad. Med. Adminstrs., Am. Assn. Clinic Physicians and Surgeons, Internat. Coll. Physicians and Surgeons, Am. Coll. Homeopathic Physicians, Am. Counc. Sex Therapy; mem. numerous orgns. including Nat. Psychol. Assn., Am. Psychotherapy Assn., Royal Soc. Physicians, World Med. Assn., Am. Acad. Preventive Medicine, Am. Bd. Examiners in Psychotherapy, Am. Bd. Examiners in Homeopathy, Western Homeopathic Med. Soc. (exec. dir.), Ariz. Profl. Soc. Hypnosis (founder 1974). Home: Phoenix, Ariz. Died Sept. 28, 2001.

STEWART, ALBERT CLIFTON, college dean, marketing educator; b. Detroit, Nov. 25, 1919; s. Albert Queely and Jeanne Belle (Kaiser) S.; m. Colleen Moore Hyland, June 25, 1949. BS, U. Chgo., 1942, MS, 1948; PhD, St. Louis U., 1951. Chemist Sherwin Williams Paint Co., Chgo.; rsch. asst. dept. chemistry U. Chgo., 1947-48; instr. chemistry St. Louis U., 1949-51; exec. Union Carbide Corp., Danbury, Conn., 1951-84; prof. mktg. Western Conn. State U., Danbury, 1984—99, dean Sch. of Bus., 1987—90, 1994—95, prof. emeritus, 1999—. Cons. Ford Found., 1963-69, Union Carbide Corp., 1984-94; bd. dirs. Exec. Register, Inc., Danbury, 1985-90; assoc. Execom, Darien, Conn., 1986-90. Patentee in field. Bd. dirs. Am. Mus. Natural History, N.Y.C., 1976-85, N.Y.C. Philharm., 1975-80; arbiter Am. Arbitration Assn., N.Y.C., Danbury; active town Coun., Oak Ridge, Tenn., 1953-57. Lt. (j.g.) USNR, World War II. Recipient Cert. of Merit Soc. Chem. Professions, Cleve., 1962. Mem. Am. Mktg. Assn., Sigma Xi. Clubs: Rotary (Cleve., N.Y.C.). Home: 28 Hearthstone Dr Brookfield CT 06804-3006 Office: Western Conn State U 181 White St Danbury CT 06810-6826

STEWART, BARBARA LYNNE, geriatrics nursing educator; b. Youngstown, Ohio, May 10, 1953; d. Carl Arvid and Margaret Swanson; m. James G. Stewart, Mar. 17, 1973; children: Trevor J., Troy C. AAS, Youngstown State U., 1973, BS, 1982. Cert. gerontol. nurse, ANCC. Supr., dir. nursing svcs. Peaceful Acres Nursing Home, North Lima, Ohio; nurse repondent Health Sci. Ctr. U. Colo., Denver; charge nurse Westwood Rehab. Med. Ctr., Inc., Boardman, Ohio, Park Vista Health Care Ctr., Youngstown, Ohio; dir. nursing Rolling Acres Care Ctr., North Lima, Ohio; primary instr. Alliance (Ohio) Tng. Ctr., Inc.; asst. supr. Akron (Ohio) Dist. Office Divsn. Quality Assurance Bur. Long Term Care Quality, 2003—; supr. div. of quality assurance, bur. of Long Term Care Quality Ohio Dept. of Health. Former instr. CPR, ARC; mem. Western Res. Join Fire Dept. Emergency Med. Svcs., 1st responder, Poland, Ohio. Mem. Tri County Dir. Nurses Assn., Nat. Gerontol. Nursing Assn. (nomination com.), Youngstown State U. Alumni Assn.

STEWART, DAVID, school system administrator; BA, Anderson U.; MA, DEd, West Va. U. From tchr. to prin. Schs. in West Va. and Del., 1972—87; asst. supt. County Sch. System, West Va., 1990—93, supt., 1993; asst. divsn. chief West Va. Dept. Edn., 1993—96, asst. supt. adminstrv. svcs., 1998—2000, supt. of schs., 2000—. Mem. Toyota Families and Schs. adv. panel for Nat. Ctr. for Family Literacy. With USAF. Mem.: Internat. Assn. Sch. Bus. Officials, Am. Assn. Sch. Adminstrs. Office: West Va Dept Edn 1900 Kanawha Blvd E Charleston WV 25305 E-mail: nchatfie@access.k12.wv.us.

STEWART, DAVID LESLIE, secondary education educator; b. Hayward, Calif., Mar. 6, 1951; s. Thomas I. and F. Janice (Hines) S.; m. Karen Lee Clark, June 19, 1976; children: Matthew, Andrew, Lucas, Timothy, Samuel, Nathanael. BS in Math., Bowling Green U., 1973; MS in Math., Wright State U., 1987. Cert. secondary tchr., Ohio; cert. Nat. Bd. for Profl. Tchg. Standards, 1998. 5th grade tchr. Twin Wells Indian Sch., Sun Valley, Ariz., 1975-77; math. instr. Weisenborn Jr. H.S., Huber Heights, Ohio, 1977-78; adj. instr. Miami U., Oxford, Ohio, 1986—; math. instr. Lebanon (Ohio) H.S., 1978—. Deacon Lebanon Cmty. Ch., 1994-96, elder, 1998—. Recipient Excellence in Teaching award Area Progress Coun. of Warren County, 1991. Avocation: family activities. E-mail: Stewart.David@Lebanon.k12.oh.us., stewcrew@characterlink.net.

STEWART, DAVID PENTLAND, lawyer, educator; b. Milw., Dec. 24, 1943; s. James Pentland and Frederica (Stockwell) S.; children from previous marriage: Jason, Jonathan; m. Jennifer Kilmer, June 21, 1986; children: Daniel, Mary Elizabeth. AB, Princeton U., 1966; JD, MA, Yale U., 1971; LLM, N.Y.U., 1975. Bar: N.Y. 1972, U.S. Dist. Ct. (ea. and so. dists.) N.Y. 1973, U.S. Ct. Appeals (2d cir.) 1973, D.C. 1976. Assoc. Donovan, Leisure, Newton & Irvine, N.Y.C., 1971-76; atty. adviser, office of legal adviser U.S. Dept. State, Washington, 1976-82, asst. legal adviser, 1982—. Adj. prof. law Georgetown U., Washington, 1984—, Am. U., Washington, 1985-86, Johns Hopkins U. Sch. Advanced Internat. Studies, 2000—; vis. lectr. Sch. Law U. Va., 1993-96, Nat. Law Ctr., George Washington U., 1993—. Contbr. articles to profl. jours.; also editorial adv. bds. Mem. dean's adv. coun. internat. law Am. U., 1984-88. Served to maj. USAR, 1970-87. Mem. ABA, Fed. Bar Assn., Am. Soc. Internat. Law., Internat. Law Assn. (adv. coun. procedural aspects internat. law inst.). Office: US Dept State Office Legal Adviser Washington DC 20520-6310 E-mail: stewartdp@state.gov.

STEWART, DAVID WAYNE, marketing educator, psychologist, consultant; b. Baton Rouge, Oct. 23, 1951; s. Wesley A. Stewart, Jr. and Edith L. (Richhart) Moore; m. Lenora Francois, June 6, 1975; children: Sarah Elizabeth, Rachel Dawn. BA, N.E. La. U., 1972; MA, Baylor U., 1973, PhD, 1974. Rsch. psychologist HHS, La., 1974-76; rsch. mgr. Needham, Harper & Steers Advt., Chgo., 1976-78; assoc. prof. Jacksonville (Ala.) State U., 1978-80, Vanderbilt U., Nashville, 1980-86, sr. assoc. dean, 1984-86; prof. U. So. Calif., L.A., 1986-90, Ernest W. Hahn prof. mktg., 1990-91, Robert Brooker rsch. prof. mktg., 1991—, chmn. dept. mktg., 1995-99, dep. dean faculty, 1999-2001, dep. dean, 2001—. Mgmt. cons., 1978—. Author, co-author: Secondary Research: Sources and Methods, Effective Television Advertising: A Study of 1000 Commericals, Consumer Behavior and the Practice of Marketing, Focus Group: Theory and Practice, Attention, Attitude, and Affect in Repsonse to Advertising, Nonverbal Communication and Advertising; editor: Jour. of Mktg., 1999-2002; contbr. articles to profl. jours.; editor: Jour. of Mktg., 1999-2002; mem. edtl. bd. Jour. Mktg. Rsch., Jour. Consumer Mktg., Jour. Pub. Policy & Mktg., Jour. Mktg., Jour. Advt., Jour. Promotion Mgmt., Current Issues and Rsch. in Advt., Jour. Internat. Consumer Mktg., Jour. Managerial Issues, Jour. Promotion Mgmt.; past pres. policy bd. Jour. Consumer Rsch., Acad. Mgmt. Fellow APA (coun. rep.), Am. Psychol. Soc. (charter); mem. Soc. for Consumer Psychology (past pres.), Inst. Mgmt. Scis., Decision Sci. Inst., Am. Mktg. Assn. (pres. acad. coun. 1997-98, v.p. fin. 1998-99), Assn. for Consumer Rsch., Am. Statis. Assn. (chair sect. on stats. in mktg. 1997), Acad. of Mgmt. Republican. Baptist. Office: U So Calif Marshal Sch Bus Office Dep Dean HOH 802C Los Angeles CA 90089-1428 E-mail: david.stewart@marshall.usc.edu.

STEWART, JEAN CATHERINE, critical care and neuroscience emergency trauma nurse, educator; b. Pitts., July 12, 1948; d. Frank E. and Bertha G. (Drawdy) Henry. BSN, Ariz. State U., 1971; MSN, U. Tex., Houston, 1988. Cert. neurosci. RN; cert. emergency nurse; cert. trauma nurse; cert. in clin. trials design and mgmt., San Diego; cert. clin. trials adminstr. Neurosurg. nursing cons. The Meth. Hosp., Houston, 1981-84; staff devel. instr. M.D. Anderson Hosp. and Tumor Inst., Houston, 1984-85; staff nurse Ben Taub Gen. Hosp. Emergency Ctr., Houston, 1985-87; continuing edn. instr. Emergency Ctr. Ben Taub Gen. Hosp., Houston, 1987-91; clin. nurse specialist neurosci./orthopedics/trauma div. U. Calif. Med. Ctr., San Diego, 1991-96; surg clin. nurse specialist Kaiser Permanente, 1998-99; critical care internship program coord. San Diego Am. Assn. Critical Care Nurses, 1998—2000; clin. nursing coord. U. Calif. San Diego Mitochondrial and Metabolic Disease Ctr., 1999—2002. Announcer Dial A Shuttle program, Nat. Space Insts.; adj. clin. instr. ADN program Southwestern C.C., 2000—; trustee Neuroscience Nursing Found., 2001—; presenter meetings and confs. various profl. orgns. Mem. manuscript rev. bd. Jour. Neuroscis. Nurses.; editorial rev. bd. Dimensions in Oncology Nursing. Recipient Millie Fields Rsch. Assistance award U. Tex., 1987. Mem. AACN (Rsch. award 1987, rsch. grantee Houston Gulf Coast chpt.), Emergency Nurses Assn., Am. Assn. Neurosci. Nurses (founding mem., past treas. S.C. chpt., pres. and program dir. Houston chpt., bd. dirs. div. nursing affairs 1991-93), Am. Assn. Neurol. Surgeons, Harvey Cushing Soc. (assoc.), World Fedn. Neurosci. Nurses, Soc. Trauma Nursing, Nat. Assn. Clin. Nurse Specialists, Sigma Theta Tau. Home and Office: 1640 10th Ave # 103 San Diego CA 92101-2873

STEWART, JOAN HINDE, academic administrator; b. N.Y.C., Aug. 11, 1944; d. Wade and Dorothy (Ronning) H.; m. Philip Robert Stewart, Jan. 31, 1970; children: Anna Faye, Justin. Student, Université Laval Summer Sch, Quebec, 1963, Middlebury Coll. Summer Sch., 1964-65; BA summa cum laude, St. Joseph's Coll., 1965; student, Salzburg Summer Sch., Austria, 1966; MPhil, Yale U., 1969, PhD, 1970. Teaching assoc. Yale U., New Haven, 1967-69, acting instr., 1969-70; instr. Wellesley (Mass.) Coll., 1970-71, asst. prof., 1971-72, N.C. State U., Raleigh, 1973-77, assoc. prof., 1977-81, asst. head dept. fgn. langs. and lits., 1978-82, prof., 1981—99; prof., dean liberal arts U. S.C., 1999—2003; pres., prof. Hamilton Coll., Clinton, NY, 2003—. Asst. dean rsch. and grad. programs N.C. State U., 1983-85, acting head dept. fgn. langs. and lits., 1984-85, head 1985-97. Author: The Novels of Mme Riccoboni, 1976, Collette, 1983, 1996, Gynographs: French Novels by Women of the Late Eighteenth Century, 1993; editor: Mme Riccoboni's Lettres de Mistriss Fanni Butlerd, 1979; co-editor: Isabelle de Charrière's Lettres de Mistriss Henley, 1993, Marie Riccoboni's Histoire d'Ernestine, 1998. Chmn. N.C. Humanities Coun., 1988-89. Fellow Camargo Found., Cassis, France, 1979, Nat. Humanities Ctr., 1982-83, (sr.) ctr. for humanities Wesleyan U., 1990; NEH fellow Princeton U., 1980; NEH fellow Coll. Tchrs. and Ind. Scholars, 1990-91; stipend younger humanists NEH, 1973; travel grantee ACLS, 1983; travel to collections grantee NEH, 1984. Mem. AAUP, MLA, Am. Assn. Tchrs. French.

STEWART, JOANNE, director; b. Vancouver, Wash., Mar. 10, 1944; d. Edward Charles and Claudine Marie Spencer; m. William Lemley Stewart, Sept. 2, 1966 (dec. June 1983); children: Amy Diane Stemple, Nicholas William. BS, Wash. State U., 1966, MA, 1973. Cert. tchr., Mont., Idaho, Wash., Calif. Tchr. foods Seaside High Sch., Monterey, Calif., 1966-67; tchr. home econs. Marysville (Wash.) High Sch., 1967-68, Palouse (Wash.) High Sch., 1968-73, Ennis (Mont.) High Sch., 1973-76, Genesee (Idaho) High Sch., 1976-77; instr. young family Missoula (Mont.) County High Sch., 1983-84; tchr. home econs. Woodman Sch., Lolo, Mont., 1985-86; travel cons. Travel Masters, Missoula, 1984-87; ticketing mgr. Blue Caboose Travel, Missoula, 1987-91; tchr. family and consumer scis. Victor (Mont.) High Sch., 1991-2001; dir. Victor 21st Century Learning Ctr., 2001—, After Sch. Learning Ctr. Project dir. sch.-to-work implementation Victor Sch. Reaching Out for Positive Ednl. Success (ROPES), 1996—2002, project dir. Op. Green Thumb, gender equity Carl Perkins grant, 1997—98. Co-pres. Lolo PTO, 1980-81; v.p. Lolo Community Ctr., 1981; sec. Lolo Mosquito Control Bd., 1988—; mem. telecommunications com. Conrad Burns & Gov. Racicot; sec. state supt. edn. task force on vocat. edn., 1995-96; coord. Health Rocks!, Nat. 4-H Program, 2000-01. Marysville Edn. Assn. scholar, 1962, Future Homemakers Am. scholar, 1962. Mem. AAUW (sec. 1986, program chmn. 1987), Forestry Triangle (pres. 1981, editor cookbook 1982), Washington State Future Homemakers Am. (hon. mem.), Am. Family and Consumer Scis. Assn., Mont. Family and Consumer Scis. Assn. (bylaws chair 1994, pres. elect 1995-96, pres. 1996-97, Profl. of Yr. 1997), Mont. Vocat. Tchrs. Assn. (returning Rookie of Yr. 1992, Am. Federated Tchrs., Mont. Vocat. Family and Consumer Scis. Tchrs. (v.p. 1993-94, pres. 1994-95, Tchr. of Yr. 1998). Republican. Methodist. Avocations: homemaking, swimming. Home: 1200 Lakeside Dr Lolo MT 59847-9705 Office: Victor High Sch ROPES 425 4th Ave Victor MT 59875-9468

STEWART, KENT KALLAM, analytical biochemistry educator; b. Omaha, Sept. 5, 1934; s. George Franklin and Grace S.; m. Margaret Reiber, June 10, 1956; children: Elizabeth, Cynthia, Richard, Robert. Student, U. Chgo., 1951-53; AB, U. Calif., Berkeley, 1956; PhD, Fla. State U., 1965. Guest investigator Rockefeller U., N.Y.C., 1965-67, research assoc., 1967-68, asst. prof., 1968-69; research chemist U.S. Dept. Agr., Beltsville, Md., 1970-75, lab. chief Nutrient Composition Lab., 1975-82; prof., head dept. food sci. and tech. Va. Poly. Inst. and State U., Blacksburg, 1982-85, prof. biochemistry, anaerobic microbiology, food sci./tech., 1985—96, prof. emeritus of biochemistry; adj. prof. dept. chemistry and biochemistry U. Tex., Austin, 1996—. Editor Jour. Food Composition and Analysis, 1987-97, also 3 books; contbr. articles to profl. jours., co-author book; patentee in field. Capt. USMCR, 1956-59. Fellow Inst. Food Technologist, AAAS; mem. Am. Chem. Soc. Home: 3900 Glengarry Dr Austin TX 78731-3812 Office: Dept Chemistry and Biochemistry Mail Code A5300 1 University Sta U Tex Austin TX 78712 E-mail: kkstewart@mail.utexas.edu.

STEWART, LUCILLE MARIE, retired special education coordinator; b. Pitts., Feb. 24; d. William H. and Edna (Hoffman) S. BEd, Duquesne U.; MEd, U. Pitts.; postgrad., Columbia U., U. Calif., Calif. State U. Cert. elem. and secondary tchr., spl. edn. tchr., supr., adminstr. Tchr., group leader mentally retarded Ednl. Alliance, N.Y.C., 1950—53; tchr. Lincoln (Ill.) State Sch., 1953; tchr., program leader, sec. Edn. Alliance, N.Y.C., 1954-58; tchr. mentally retarded Ramapo Ctrl. Sch. Dist., Spring Valley, N.Y., 1958-60, tchr. seriously emotionally disturbed, 1960-64, supr. presch. program for educationally disadvantaged, 1965-67; program dir. Pomona (N.Y.) Camp for Retarded, summers 1960-63; tchr. mentally retarded Stockton Sch., San Diego, 1964-65; tchr. mentally retarded sch. Cathedral City Sch., 1967-78; program specialist spl. edn. Palm Springs (Calif.) Unified Sch. Dist., 1978-95; prin. elem. summer schs. Palm Springs (Calif.) Unified Sch. Dist., 1971-72; tchr. elem. mentally retarded sch. Palm Springs (Calif.) Unified; prin.-tchr. Summer Extended Sch. for Spl. Students, summer 1979-99. Exec. com. U. Calif. Extension, area adv. com.; spl. edn.

surrogate parent Palm Springs Unified Sch. Dist. Mem. NEA, AAUW, ASCD, Calif. Adminstrs. Spl. Edn. (desert cmty. mental health childrens com.), Coun. Exceptional Children (adminstrn. divsn., early childhood-learning handicap divsns.), Am. Assn. Childhood Edn., Autism Soc., Coachella Valley, Learning Disabilities Assn., Creative Desert, Desert Theater League, Alpha Kappa Alpha, Phi Delta Kappa, Delta Kappa Gamma.

STEWART, MARILYN EPSTEIN, educational administrator, consultant; b. Balt., Jan. 27, 1950; d. Charles and Ruth (Saks) Epstein; m. Marc F. Stewart, Aug. 10, 1972; children: Benjamin, Jack. BA, U. Pitts., 1970; MEd, Goucher Coll., 1971. Cert. fund raising exec., 1983. Tchr. Calhoun Sch., N.Y.C., 1977-80, dir. mid. sch., 1980-86, dir. devel. and external affairs, 1986-93; pres. Stewart Group, N.Y.C., 1993—. Ptnr. Personal Fin. Control, Waterbury, Conn., 1994; spkr. in field. Vol. fund raising cons. Housatonic Valley Assn., Cornwall Bridge, Conn., 1991-93, Ballet Manhattan, N.Y.C., 1990-93. Mem. Nat. Soc. Fund Raising Execs., Nat. Assn. Ind. Schs., Assn. Supervision and Curriculum Devel., Coun. Advancement Secondary Edn. Democrat.

STEWART, NANCY SUE SPURLOCK, education educator; b. Phoenix, Dec. 31, 1933; d. Ernest Neal and Ethel Ora (Boothe) Spurlock; m. Biven Stewart, Dec. 31, 1953 (div. 1962); 1 child, Sally K. BA in Edn., Ariz. State U., 1961, MA in Edn., 1968, Reading Specialist Cert., 1970. Cert. tchr. 1-12, Ariz. Elem. tchr., reading specialist Chandler (Ariz.) Pub. Schs. Dist. 80, 1961-92; instr. Greater Phoenix Area Writing Project Ariz. State U. and Chandler Unified Sch. Dist. 80, 1983—. Mem. AAUW, NEA, Chandler Edn. Assn., Ariz. Edn. Assn., Delta Kappa Gamma Soc. Internat., Kappa Delta. Mem. Ch. of Christ. Avocations: crafts, reading. Home: 750 W Detroit St Chandler AZ 85225-4413

STEWART, RICHARD BURLESON, law educator; b. Cleve., Feb. 12, 1940; s. Richard Siegfreid and Ruth Dysert (Staten) Stewart; m. Alice Peck Fales, May 13, 1967 (div. June 1992); children: William, Paul, Elizabeth; m. Jane Laura Bloom, Sept. 20, 1992; children: Emily, Ian. AB, Yale U., 1961; MA (Rhodes scholar), Oxford (Eng.) U., 1963; LLB, Harvard U., 1966; D (hon.), Erasmus U., Rotterdam, 1993. Bar: DC 1968, U.S. Supreme Ct. 1971. Law clk. to Hon. Potter Stewart U.S. Supreme Ct., 1966-67; assoc. Covington & Burling, Washington, 1967-71; asst. prof. law Harvard U., 1971-75, prof., 1975-82, Byrne prof. adminstrv. law, 1982-89, assoc. dean, 1984-86; asst. atty. gen. environment and natural resources div. Dept. Justice, Washington, 1989-91; prof. law NYU Law Sch., N.Y.C., 1992-94, Emily Kempin prof. law, 1994—2002, John Edward Sexton prof. law, 2002—, univ. prof., 2002—; of counsel Sidley & Austin, 1992—. Spl. counsel U.S. Senate Watergate Com., 1974; vis. prof. U. Calif., Berkeley Law Sch., 1979—80, U. Chgo. Law Sch., 1986—87, Georgetown U., 1991—92, Europen U. Inst., 1995; dir. Ctr. Environ. and Land Use Law, Health Effects Inst.; mem. adv. bd. Environ. Def. Author: (book) The Reformation of American Administrative Law (in Chinese), 2002; author: (with P. Menell) Environmental Law and Policy, 1994; author: (with S. Breyer, C. Sunstein and M. Spitzer) Administrative Law and Regulation, 1979, Administrative Law and Regulation, 5th edit., 2002; author: (with E. Rehbinder) Integration Through Law: Environmental Protection Policy, 1985, Integration Through Law: Environmental Protection Policy, paper edit., 1987; author: (with R. Revesz) Markets v. Environment?, 1995; author: (with R. Revesz and P. Sands) Environment, the Economy, and Sustainable Development, 2001; author: (with J. Wiener) Reconstructing Climate Policy, 2003; editor (with R. Revesz): (book) Analyzing Superfund: Economics, Science, and Law, 1995. Fellow: Am. Acad. Arts and Scis.; mem.: ABA, Am. Law Inst. Office: NYU Law Sch 40 Washington Sq S New York NY 10012-1099 E-mail: stewartr@juris.law.nyu.edu.

STEWART, SARAH, elementary school educator; BS in Edn., Ohio State U., 1963; MS, U. N.C., 1978. Reading recovery/reading resource tchr. McDougle Elem. Sch., Chapel Hill, NC, 1998—. Recipient N.C. Gov.'s Long Leaf Pine award, 1992. Mem.: Am. Fedn. Tchrs. in N.C. (past pres.), Nat. Bd. for Profl. Tchg. Stds. (bd. mem.). Office: Chapel Hill-Carrboro City Schs-McDougle 900 Old Fayetteville Rd Chapel Hill NC 27516*

STEWART, STEVEN ELTON, state agency administrator; b. Oklahoma City, July 12, 1952; s. Elton Alexander and Bonnie Kate (Elms) S.; m. Jana Richardson, Aug. 6, 1974; children: Stacey Anne, Scott Elton. BA in Edn., East Cen. U., 1976, MEd, 1978; M Sch. Adminstrn., Okla. U., 1983. Title XIV field coord. Region XIV Regional Edn. Svc. Ctr./Okla. Dept. Edn., 1976-78, psychometrist, 1978-80, asst. dir., 1980-82, adminstr., 1982—. Mem. Spl. Svcs. cadre Okla. Dept. Edn., Oklahoma City, 1989-90; mem. State Regional Edn. Svc. Ctr. Leadership Team, 1991—; mem. Okla. Policies and Procedures Compliance Team, 1992—, RESC Eval. Team, 1995. Mem. Coun. Exceptional Children, Coun. Adminstrs. Spl. Edn., Learning Disabilities Assn., Okla. Coun. on Children and Youth. Democrat. Mem. Ch. of Christ. Avocations: music, all-terrain vehicles, computers. Office: Ada Regional Edn Svc Ctr 704 N Oak Ave Ada OK 74820-3267

STEWART, TERESA ELIZABETH, elementary school educator; b. Cheverly, Md., Nov. 26, 1966; d. Richard Lynn and Sandra Lois (O'Neill) S. BS in Elem. Edn. cum laude, Bowie State U., 1988, MEd in Elem. Edn., 1996. Cert. elem. tchr., Md. Asst. tchr. Tom Thumb Day Care, Bowie, Md., 1989; elem. tchr. Berwyn Bapt. Sch., College Park, Md., 1989-95, Berkshire Elem. Sch., Forestville, Md., 1995-98, Paint Branch Elem. Sch., College Park, Md., 1998-99, Berwyn Bapt. Sch., College Park, Md., 1999—. Dir. vacation Bible sch., youth group leader Bowie United Meth. Ch., 1988-98, sec. adminstrv. coun., 1993-97, chairperson staff parish rels. com., 1996—, sec. membership com., 1993—, choir mem., 1980—, choir dir., 2000—; tchr. children's Bible class University Park Ch. of Brethren, 1990-94, Sun. sch. tchr., 1997-2000; instr., judge Belle-Aires Twirling Corp., Bowie, 1986—; pres. Md. Baton Coun., 1998—. Koonz, McKinney & Johnson Law Firm scholar, 1986-88. Mem. Kappa Delta Pi. Democrat. Avocations: camping, collecting postcards and teddy bears, twirling, choral singing. Home: 13202 11th St Bowie MD 20715-3707 Office: Berwyn Bapt Sch 4720 Cherokee St College Park MD 20740-1839 E-mail: tstwirl@aol.com.

STEWART, VERLINDSEY LAQUETTA, accounting educator; b. Birmingham, Ala., Dec. 27, 1965; d. Nathan Jr. and Shirley Ruth Brown; m. Kelvin Lorenzo Stewart I, June 22, 1991 (div. Feb. 1999); 1 child, Kelvin Lorenzo II. BS in Acctg., Ala. A&M U., 1988, MS in Bus. Edn., 1995, AA Cert. in Bus. Edn., 1997. Cert. tchr. bus. grades 7-12, Ala. Jr. acct. Childress Acctg., Huntsville, Ala., 1990-93; acctg. clk. Appeal Beauty Salon, Huntsville, 1988-94; receptionist Coop. Ext., Normal, Ala., 1992-94; grad. asst. Ala. A&M U., Normal, 1995; student tchr. J.O. Johnson H.S., Huntsville, Ala., 1995; acctg. instr. J.F. Drake State Tech., Huntsville, 1996—. Cons. Jr. Achievement, Huntsville, 1995—96. Post-reviewer: (book) College Accounting 9th, 1999 (Honorarium 1999). Vol. Habitat for Humanity, Huntsville, 1995-97; vol. asst. leader Girl Scouts North Ala., Huntsville, 1995-96. Recipient Adminstrv. Acad. award Rust Coll., 1999, Emerging Leaders Sch. award Ala. Edn. Assn., 1994, Ala. Master Tchr. Seminar, 2001. Mem. Nat. Bus. Edn., Ea. Star Mitzpah Ctr., Phi Beta Lambda (adviser 1998—), Delta Sigma Theta. Democrat. Baptist. Avocations: aerobics, weights, reading, listening to jazz music. Office: JF Drake State Tech Coll 3421 Meridian St N Huntsville AL 35811-1544 E-mail: vbdst28@aol.com.

STEWART, VIRGINIA L. CAUDLE, retired cosmetology educator; b. Winston-Salem, N.C., Aug. 8, 1925; d. William Henry and Katie (Sullivan) C.; m. Troy Thomas Stewart, June 22, 1946 (dec. Sept. 1991). Diploma, La Mae Beauty Coll., 1945; student, Winston-Salem Tchrs. Coll., 1953-55; BA, Nat. Inst. Cosmetology, 1969, MA, 1973, assoc. doctorate, 1975. Cert. N.C. Dept. Pub. Instruction. Tchr. cosmetology Winston-Salem/Forsyth County Schs., 1976-90. Leader vocat. club Vocat. Indsl. Career Ctr., Winston-Salem, 1987-90. Field worker United Fund, Winston-Salem, 1962-70; bd. dirs. YMCA Glade St. Winston-Salem, 1960-68; leader troop 10 Dreamland Ch. Girl Scouts U.S., Winston-Salem, 1948-52; youth choir dir. Dreamland Bapt. Ch., Winston-Salem, 1946-52, Mars Hill Bapt. Ch., Winston-Salem, 1953-72; clk. Carver Sch. East Ward Precint, Winston-Salem, 1968-70; treas. Carver/Monticello Community Club 1966-68; treas. Mt. Zion Bapt. Handbell Choir, 1989-91; sec. Mt. Zion Bapt. Chancel Choir, 1988-91; trustee Mt. Zion Bapt. Ch., 1993. Recipient plaque Carver/Monticello Community Club, 1986, award Mt. Zion Bapt. Handbell Choir, 1991, Mt. Zion Bapt. Chancel Choir, 1991, Past Matron's lapel pin Sisters of Bivouac Chpt 530, 1949, 6-1st prize ribbons, 3-2d prize ribbons, 1-3d prize ribbon Dixie Classic Fair, 1991, 4-1st prize ribbons, 3-2d prize ribbons Dixie Classic Fair, 1992. Mem. Nat. Beauty Culturists' League (trustee 1960-66, plaque 1966), Winston-Salem Beauticians #2 (pres. 1965-70, Beautician of Yr. trophy 1967, plaque 1970), Best Yet Flower/Garden Club (pres. 1976-80, plaque 1980), Fedn. Garden Clubs N.C. (4th dist. directress 1993, chairperson 4th dist. flower show 1993). Democrat. Avocations: swimming, gardening, basketball, singing, piano. Home: 3620 Kinghill Dr Winston Salem NC 27105-4026

STEWART, ZELMA BROWN, elementary school educator; b. St. Louis, Sept. 19, 1930; d. Floyd and Mateva (Lindsey) Brown; m. James Stewart, Sept. 21, 1948; children: James Roland, Glynis Marie. BS in Edn., Cleve. State U., 1975. Cert. tchr. religion, libr. skills, children's lit. Libr. St. Aloysius Sch., Cleve., 1965-75, tchr. grade 4, 1975-82; tchr. grade 5 St. Agatha-St. Aloysius Sch., Cleve., 1982—. Co-author: Black Christian Saints, 1987. Named Tchr. of the Yr., Cath. Diocese of Cleve., 1989, Excellence award, 1989, Cmty. Bus. Svc. Cath. Sch. award Cleve.-St. Vincent DePaul, 1989; recipient The Crystal Apple award Cleve. Plain Dealer (newspaper), 1995; established Zelma Stewart scholarship for students of St. Agatha-St. Aloysius Sch. Mem. N.E. Cath. Edn. Assn., St. Agatha-St. Aloysius Parent Tchr. Union., Cleve. Art Mus. Democrat. Roman Catholic. Avocations: reading classics, writing short stories, classical and jazz music. Office: St Agatha-St Aloysius Sch 640 Lakeview Rd Cleveland OH 44108-2606

STIENMIER, SAUNDRA KAY YOUNG, aviation educator; b. Abilene, Kans., Apr. 27, 1938; d. Bruce Waring and Helen E. (Rutz) Young; m. Richard H. Stienmier, Dec. 20, 1958; children: Richard, Susan, Julia, Laura. AA, Colo. Women's Coll., 1957; postgrad., U. Colo., 1959, 69; BS, Temple Buell Coll., 1969; ed., Embre Riddle Aviation U., Ramstein, Germany. Cert. FAA pilot. Dir. Beaumont Gallery, El Paso, Tex., 1972-77; mem. grad. studies faculty Embre Riddle Aviation U., 1979-80; mgr. Ramstein Aero Club, USAF, 1977-80, Peterson Flight Tng. Ctr., Peterson AFB, Colo., 1980-97, Flight Tng. Ctr., Rocky Mtn. AFB, Colo., 1997—. Named Outstanding S.W. Artist. Mem.: AAUW, Assn. Profl. Flight Tng. Ctrs., Soc. Arts and Letters, Women in Aviation, Colo. Pilots Assn., Nat. Pilot Assn., Aircraft Owners and Pilots Assn., Nat. Air Transp. Assn. (flight tng. com.), Interant. Women Pilots Assn., Scots Heritage Soc., Scottish Soc. Pikes' Peak, 99's Club, Order Eastern Star, Delta Psi Omega, Beta Sigma Phi. Office: PO Box 14123 Colorado Springs CO 80914-0123 E-mail: saundra@viawest.net.

STIER, WILLIAM FREDERICK, JR., academic administrator, educator; b. Feb. 22, 1943; m. Veronica Ann Martin, 1965; children: Mark, Missy, Michael, Patrick, Willy III. BA, St. Ambrose Coll., 1965; MA, Temple U., 1966; EdD, U. S.D., 1972; postdoct., Marquette U., 1976-77, U. Wis., summer 1977. Grad. asst. Coll. Edn. Temple U., Phila., 1965-66; various faculty positions dept. health, phys. edn., recreation, 1968-74; pres., CEO Fla. Breeders, Inc., Largo and St. Petersburg, 1974-76; treas. Charolais of Fla., Inc., St. Petersburg and Ft. Myers, 1975-76; adminstrv. campus Cardinal Stritch Coll., Milw., 1976-80; chmn. dept. profl. health and phys. edn., athletic dir. Ohio No. U., Ada, 1980-83; chmn., prof. phys. edn. and sports dept. SUNY, Brockport, 1983-86, dir. intercollegiate athletics, 1983-90, grad. coord. sport mgmt., 1990—, pres. faculty senate, 1992-93, grad. coord., 1994—, Disting. Svc. prof. Pres., CEO Ednl. and Sport Mgmt. cons., N.Y. and Ohio, 1980—; chmn. bd. dirs. Kreative Kids Learning Ctrs., Inc., 1978—; bd. dirs. Cretive Children Child Care Ctrs.; cons. MacMIllan Pub. Co., Inc., 1981-83, Sport Fedn., Hong Kong, Singapore and Malaysia, 1987, 88, Nat. Coll. Sport Coaches, Mexico City, 1990; speaker numerous confs. and convs. Author of 17 books and contbr. to several compendiums in field; contbr. more than 274 articles to profl. jours.; mem. editl. bd. and reviewer profl. jours.; editor The Phys. Educator, 1998—, Internat. Jour. Sport Mgmt., 1999—. Active ARC, 1975-90, Boy Scouts Am., 1955-59; mem. greater Milw. REgional day Care adv. Com., 1979-81; adv. bd. Nat. Ctr. Exploration Human Petential, Del Mar, Calif., 1981-84; nat. basketball coach, St. Kitts-Nevis, 1984; cons. on basketball, Mex., 1982, 90. Brockport scholar, 1984-86, 92, 93, 94, 98, 99. Mem. AAHPERD (reviewer jour. 1984—), N.Y. Assn. Health, Phys. Edn., Recreation and Dance (higher edn. sect. 1983—, pres. 1985-86, 87-88), Nat. Assn. sport and Phys. Edn., Nat. Assn. Girls and Women's Sports, Nat. Assn. Phys. Edn. in Higher Edn., Nat. Assn. Phys. Edn. in Higher Edn., Nat. Assn. Athletic Mktg. and Devel. Dirs., Nat. Assn. Collegiate Dirs. Athletics, Internat. Soc. Comparative Phys. Edn. and Sports, N.Am. Sport Mgmt., Eta Sigma Gama, Phi Epsilon Kappa, Phi Kappa Phi, Phi Epsilon Omega. Office: SUNY-Brockport Dept Phys Edn and Sport Brockport NY 14420 E-mail: bstier@brockport.edu.

STIGLITZ, JOSEPH EUGENE, economist, educator; b. Gary, Ind., Feb. 9, 1943; s. Nathaniel David and Charlotte (Fishman) Stiglitz; children: Siobhan, Michael, Edward, Julia. BA, Amherst Coll., Mass, 1964; DHL, Amherst Coll., 1974; PhD in Econs., MIT, 1966; MA (hon.), Yale U., 1970; D in Econs. (hon.), U. Leuven, 1994. Asst. prof. econs. MIT, 1966—67; asst. prof. Cowles Found., Yale U., New Haven, 1967—68, assoc. prof., 1968—70, prof. econs., 1970—74; vis. fellow St. Catherine's Coll., Oxford, England, 1973—74; Joan Kenney professorship Stanford U., 1974—76, prof. of economics and senior fellow, Hoover Inst., 1988—2001; Oskar Morgenstern dist. fellow Inst. Advanced Studies Math., Princeton, NJ, 1978—79; Drummond prof. polit. economy Oxford U., England, 1976—79; prof. econs. Princeton U., 1979—88; sr. v.p., chief economist World Bank, Washington, 1995—2000; sr. fellow Brookings Inst., Washington, 2000; Stern visiting prof. Columbia U., 2000; prof. of economics and finance Columbia U. Grad. Sch. of Bus., Dept. of Econ. and Sch. of Internat. and Public Affairs, 2001—; prof. of exec. MBA programs Columbia U. Tapp rsch. fellow Gonville and Caius Coll., Cambridge, England, 1966—70; vis. prof. dept. econs. U. Canterbury, Christchurch, New Zealand, 1967; sr. rsch. fellow social sci. divsn. Inst. for Devel. Studies U. Coll. Nairobi, 1969—71; mem. Pres.'s Coun. Econ. Advisers, 1993—95, chmn. coun. econ. advisers, 1995—97, sr. v.p. devel. econs. and chief econs., exec. dir.; cons. World Bank, State of Alaska, Seneca Indian Nation, Bell Comm. Rsch. Editor: Jour. Econ. Perspectives, 1986—93; Am. editor: Rev. of Econ. Studies, 1968—76, assoc. editor: Am. Econ. Rev., 1968—76, Energy Econs., Managerial and Decision Econs., mem. editl. bd.: World Bank Econ. Rev.; author: Whither Socialism?, 1996, Frontiers of Development Economics: The Future in Perspective, 2000, New Ideas About Old Age Security: Toward Sustainable Pension Systems in the 21st Century, 2001; author: (with C.E. Walsh) Principles of Macroeconomics, 2002, Economics, 2002; author: (with R. K. Sah) Peasants Versus City-Dwellers: Taxation and the Burden of Economic Development, 2002; author: Globalization and Its Discontents, 2002, The Rebel Within: Joseph Stiglitz and the World Bank, 2002; author: (with B. Greenwald) Towards a New Paradigm in Monetary Economics, 2003; author: The Roaring Nineties, 2003. Recipient John Bates Clark award, Am. Econ. Assn., 1979, Internat. prize, Accademia Lincei, 1988, Union des Assurances de Paris prize, 1989, The Nobel Prize in Economic Sciences, 2001, Rechtenwald Prize, Germany, 1998; fellow, Guggenheim, 1969—70; scholar guest, The Brookings Inst., Washington. Fellow: Inst. for Policy Rsch. (sr. 1991—93), Brit. Acad. (corr.); mem.: NAS (fellow, 1988), Econometric Soc., Am. Acad. Arts and Scis.(fellow, 1983), Am. Econ. Assn. (exec. com. 1982—84, v.p. 1985). Office: Columbia U Uris Hall Rm 814 Broadway and 116th St New York NY 10027*

STILES, ANNE SCOTT, nursing educator; b. Columbus, Ohio, Aug. 15, 1949; d. Raymond and Elizabeth (Isaly) Latham; children: Heather, Jeremy. BSN, Ohio State U., 1971; MSN, Oral Roberts U., 1986; PhD, Tex. Woman's U., 1990; postgrad., U. Ariz., 1992-94. Assoc. prof., dir. nursing rsch. Ga. So. U., 1994-99; assoc. prof. nursing U. Ark. for Med. Scis. Coll. Nursing, 1999—2002; faculty Kaplan Ednl. Ctr., Ltd., 1995-96; perdiem staff nurse Bulloch Meml. Hosp., 1995-96; prof. nursing Tex. Woman's U., 2002—. Contbr. articles to profl. jours. and books. Postdoctoral fellow U. Ariz., 1992-94; grantee March of Dimes, 1996, 97, 98. Mem. ANA, Ga. Nurses Assn. (chair cabinet on rsch. 1996-99), So. Nursing Rsch. Soc., Tex. Nurse's Assn., Sigma Theta Tau.

STILES, GARY LESTER, cardiologist, molecular pharmacologist, educator; b. N.Y.C., May 22, 1949; s. Robert L. and Vivian M. (Cano) S.; m. Alexis H. Stiles; children: Heather B., Wendy A. BS in Chemistry, St. Lawrence U., 1971; MD, Vanderbilt U., 1975. Diplomate Am. Bd. Internal Medicine, sub.-bd. Cardiovascular Medicine. Resident in internal medicine Vanderbilt U., Nashville, 1975-78; fellow in cardiology Duke U., Durham, N.C., 1978-81, mem. faculty, 1981—, assoc. prof., 1986-89, chief div. cardiology, 1989-99, prof. medicine, 1990—, prof. pharmacology, 1990—, Ursula Gellar prof. cardiology, 1999—; CMO, v.p. Duke Health Sys., 1999—. Mem. sci. adv. coun. Alta. Heritage Found., Edmonton, Can., 1990—; mem. pharmacology study sect. NIH, Bethesda, Md., 1988-91. Mem. editl. bd. Jour. Biol. Chemistry, 1990-95, Molecular Pharmacology, 1991-99. Recipient Katz prize Am. Heart Assn., 1983, award Am. Fedn. Clin. Rsch., 1989; grantee Am. Heart Assn., 1987-90. Fellow Am. Coll. Cardiology (award 1993); mem. Internat. Churchill Soc., Assn. Am. Physicians, Am. Soc. Clin. Investigation. Republican. Achievements include patent in field. Office: Duke U Med Ctr PO Box 3681 Durham NC 27710-0001 E-mail: glsmd@duke.edu.

STILL, MARY JANE (M. J. STILL), mathematics educator; b. Kingsport, Tenn., Apr. 14, 1940; d. James Charles and Allie Fair (Williams) S.; m. Michael S. Golden, 1962 (div. 1971); m. Thos L. Scruggs, 1972 (div. 1975); children: Amanda Fair, Jacob Charles. AB in English, Math., Edn-Psychology, Trevecca Nazarene Coll., 1962; MEd in Math., Statistics, Auburn U., 1969. File clk. FBI, Washington, 1958; tchr. Stratford Jr.-Sr. High Sch., Nashville, 1962-63; statistician Pub. Welfare Dept. State of Tenn., Nashville, 1963-65; math. and English tchr. Smiths Sta. High Sch., Smiths, Ala., 1965-66; math., English, psychology tchr. West Point High Sch., West Point, Ga., 1966-67; math. tchr. La Grange High Sch., La Grange, Ga., 1967-68; math. and English tchr. Townsend High Sch., Townsend, Tenn., 1968-72; math., English, physical edn. tchr. Northshore High Sch., West Palm Beach, Fla., 1974-75; prof. math. Palm Beach Community Coll., Lake Worth, Fla., 1975-78, Palm Beach Community Coll.-North Campus, Palm Beach Gardens, Fla., 1978—. Cons. Fla. Power & Light Co., North Palm Beach, 1989; lectr. Palm Beach Community Coll. Speakers, Palm Beach Gardens, 1986-89. Editor, advisor: College Mathematics, 1989; textbook editor, advisor Dellen Pub., Scott Foresman Pub., 1988—, Little Brown, McGraw Hill, 1989—, Wadsworth & Prindle/Weber/Schmidt, 1992—; contbr. to textbooks and profl. jours. Scorekeeper, coach, mgr. baseball and softball leagues Palm Beach area, 1980-90; supporter Jackson polit. campaign, West Palm Beach, 1988, Children's Mus. and Turtle Soc., Juno Beach, Fla., 1986; coach, mgr., sponsor boys' baseball little league, girls' softball, ladies' softball, Lake Park, Palm Beach Gardens, Fla., 1980-92, active softball and basketball coll. and cmty. leagues. NSF math. summer fellow Northeastern U., Boston, 1988; NSF grad. scholar, Auburn, Ala., 1967-69; Shakespeare scholar Shakespearean Soc. Palm Beach, Stratford-on-Avon, Eng., 1975; NSF grantee U. Fla., 1996. Mem. NEA, Math. Assn. Am., Fla. Assn. Cmty. Colls., Am. Statis. Assn., Dreher Sci. Mus., Bus. Women North Palm Beach, Animal Rescue League (West Palm Beach, life), Audubon Soc., NOW, Hist. Soc., Rwy. Club, Consortium for Math. and its Applications. Nazarene. Avocations: artist, music, drama, sports, church work. Office: Palm Beach Community Coll N 3160 P G A Blvd West Palm Beach FL 33410-2802

STILLINGER, JACK CLIFFORD, English educator; b. Chgo., Feb. 16, 1931; s. Clifford Benjamin and Ruth Evangeline (Hertzler) S.; m. Shirley Louise Van Wormer, Aug. 30, 1952; children: Thomas Clifford, Robert William, Susan, Mary; m. Nina Zippin Baym, May 21, 1971. BA, U. Tex., 1953; MA (Nat. Woodrow Wilson fellow), Northwestern U., 1954; PhD, Harvard U., 1958. Teaching fellow in English Harvard U., 1955-58; asst. prof. U. Ill., Urbana, 1958-61, assoc. prof., 1961-64, prof. English, 1964—; permanent mem. Center for Advanced Study, 1970—. Author: The Early Draft of John Stuart Mill's Autobiography, 1961, Anthony Munday's Zelauto, 1963, Wordsworth: Selected Poems and Prefaces, 1965, The Letters of Charles Armitage Brown, 1966, Twentieth Century Interpretations of Keats's Odes, 1968, Mill: Autobiography and Other Writings, 1969, The Hoodwinking of Madeline and Other Essays on Keats's Poems, 1971, The Texts of Keats's Poems, 1974, The Poems of John Keats, 1978, Mill: Autobiography and Literary Essays, 1981, John Keats: Complete Poems, 1982, Norton Anthology of English Literature, 1986, 3rd edit., 2000, John Keats: Poetry Manuscripts at Harvard, 1990, Multiple Authorship and the Myth of Solitary Genius, 1991, Coleridge and Textual Instability, 1994, Reading The Eve of St. Agnes, 1999; editor Jour. English and Germanic Philology, 1961-72. Guggenheim fellow, 1964—65. Fellow AAAS; mem. MLA, Keats-Shelley Assn. Am. (bd. dirs., editorial bd. Jour., Disting. Scholar award 1986), Byron Soc., Phi Beta Kappa. Home: 806 W Indiana Ave Urbana IL 61801-4838

STILLMAN-MYERS, JOYCE L. artist, educator, writer, illustrator, consultant; b. N.Y.C., Jan. 19, 1943; d. Murray W. and Evelyn (Berger) Stillman. BA, NYU, 1964; student, Art Students League, 1965, Pratt Inst., 1972; MFA, L.I. U., 1975; postgrad., Calif. Inst. Integral Studies, 1994—. Tchr. N.Y.C. Pub. Schs., 1964-71; artist, 1974-76, Louis K. Meisel Gallery, N.Y.C., 1975-84, Tolarno Gallery, Melbourne, Australia, 1976—, Allan Stone Gallery, N.Y.C., 1990—; founder CoCreative Inst. Art, Fingerlakes Region, N.Y. Vis. assoc. prof. Towson State U., 1982; tchr. Tompkins Cortland C.C., 1988; lectr. Cornell U., 1990; founder Ithaca Women Artists Salon, Artistic Applications Decorative Arts Ctr. One-woman shows include Ctrl. Hall Gallery, Port Washington, 1975, Tolarno Gallery, Melbourne, 1976, Louis K. Meisel Gallery, N.Y.C., 1977, 1980—82, Heckscher Mus., Huntington, N.Y., 1980, Holtzman Gallery, Towson (Md.) State U., 1982, Roslyn Oxley Gallery, Sydney, 1976, 1982, Tomasulo Gallery, Union Coll., N.J., 1983, Stages Keuka Coll., Keuka Park, N.Y., 1985, New Visions, Ithaca, N.Y., 1989, Her-Chambliss, Hot Springs, Ark., 1990, Artist on the Lake, Hector, N.Y., 1992, Mus. Modern Art Christmas Card Collection, 1994, Arnot Mus., Elmira, N.Y., 2002, over 75 group shows, designer, Mus. Modern Art Christmas Card Collection, 1978—81, 1994, Time-Life Poster, 1978, Doing Dionysos, Arts of the So. Trees, 2000—02. Mem. Literacy Vols. Am. Recipient Flower Painting award, Artist's Mag., 1986, Distinctive Merit award, Art Dir.'s Club 58th Ann., 1979; grantee Pub. Svc., N.Y. State Creative Artist's, 1979. Mem.: AAUW, Nat. Assn. Women Artists. Home: 112 Brooklyn Ter Odessa NY 14869-9786

STILLWELL, VALORIE CELESTE, secondary school mathematics educator; b. Merced, Calif., Nov. 26, 1960; d. Wallace Dee and Frances Estelle (Cagle) Sinclair; m. William Edward Stillwell, May 27, 1990. BS in Math. with highest honors, BS in Human Devel. with highest honors, U. Calif., Davis, 1982, track coaching credential with honors, 1983; MA in Edn., U.S. Internat., 1990. Cert. gifted and talented edn. and spl. edn.

educator. Asst. track coach Woodland (Calif.) and Vacaville (Calif.) H.S., 1980-83; gifted and talented edn. math tchr., head track and field coach Irvington H.S., Fremont, Calif., 1983-87; gifted and talented edn. math tchr. Mission San Jose H.S., Fremont, 1987-90; math tchr., math dept. chairperson Edna Hill Mid. Sch., Brentwood, Calif., 1990-95, math mentor tchr., 1994-96; math. dept. chairperson Bristow Mid. Sch., Brentwood, 1995—. Mem. liaison com. Irvington H.S., Fremont, 1983-87; mem. safety and facilities com. Mission San Jose H.S., Fremont, 1987-90; sch. site coun. chairperson Edna Hill Mid. Sch., 1990-93, reading com. chairperson, mem. transition team, mem. dist. math. com., 1994—, salary com. co-chairperson, 1994-96. Ednl. Initiatives grantee, 1990. Mem. ASCD, Nat. Coun. Tchrs. of Math., Nat. Math. League, Calif. Math. Coun., Contra Costa County Math. (mem. adv. coun.), Diablo Math. Educators, Math Counts (peer tutor competition team). Avocations: reading, sports. Office: Bristow Sch 855 Minnesota Ave Brentwood CA 94513-1802

STILWELL, CHARLOTTE FINN, vocational counselor; b. San Francisco, Oct. 31, 1947; d. Frederick William and Helen Carolyn (Watson) Finn; Bobby Gene Stilwell, Dec. 17, 1937; children: Robert, Shelley, James, Joel. AA, St. Petersburg Jr. Coll., 1967; BS, Fla. State U., 1969; MA, U. South Fla., 1971; attended, U. S.C., 1972. Nat. cert. counselor; cert. sch. counselor. Dir. tutorial program Hillsborough County Schs., Tampa, Fla., 1971-72, tchr., counselor, 1972-73, h.s. counselor, 1973-77; vocat. counselor Pinellas County Schs., Clearwater, Fla., 1977—. Dist. coord. Counseling for High Skills Kans. State, 1992—. Vol. Suicide & Crisis Ctrs., Tampa, St. Vincent DePaul's Soup Kitchen, St. Petersburg, Fla., 1993, Toy Shop, 1994-95, Spl. Olympics, 1996. General Electric Found. fellow. Mem. Am. Counseling Assn., Am. Sch. Counselor Assn. (Am. Sch. Counselor of Yr. 1995), Fla. Counseling Assn., Fla. Sch. Counselor Assn. (v.p. post secondary 1993-95), Phi Delta Kappa (historian 1993—), Pinellas Sch. Counselor Assn. (pres. 1991-95). Republican. Avocations: oil painting, snow skiing, sports. Office: PTEC Clearwater 6100 154th Ave N Clearwater FL 33760-2140

STILWELL, CONNIE KAY, secondary school educator; b. Frontenac, Kans., Feb. 26, 1947; d. Jerry Albert and Ann (Zortz) Scavezze; m. Richard W. Stilwell, June 7, 1969; 1 child, John Thomas. BS in Edn., Pittsburg State U., 1970; MS in Curriculum/Guidance, U. Kans., 1975. Tchr. Shawnee Mission (Kans.) Pub. Schs., 1970-76, 77—, curriculum writer math., social studies, sci., lang. arts, 1977-93. Adminstrv. asst. Learning Exch., Kansas City, Mo., 1976-77; instr. Webster Coll., Kansas City, 1978, U. Mo., Kansas City, 1979, Kans. U.-N.E. Kans. Math. Dissemination Project, summer 1993, curriculum coun. in lang. arts, 1992, mem. supt. coun., 1993-94, mem. math. coun., 1993-95, mem. science curriculum coun., 1994—, mem. profl. devel. coun., 2001-03; mem. regional conf. U.S. Dept. Edn., 1995; program advisor math curriculum Kansas City Pub. TV, 1993-95; math. mentor, 1995—. Co-author: Language Arts, 1979, Science Curriculum, 1983, Curriculum-Math., 1977-87, Social Studies Curriculum, 1990, Power Pack-Math Enrichment Activities, 1990; presenter insvc. and workshops. Mem. steering com. Imagination Celebration, Kennedy Ctr., Kansas City, 1983-84, Earthworks Pilot Program, Shawnee Mission PTA, 1985-93; mem. Kans. QPA Site Coun., 1993, Westwood View Ednl. Enhancement Fund Coun., mem. bldg. team, 1994-95; mem. long range planning team PTA; Co-chmn. fundraising Folly Theatre, Kansas City, 1986. Recipient Presdl. award for Excellence in Sci. and Math. Tchg., Kans. State Level, 1990, Tchrs. Who Make a Difference award Kansas City Chiefs, 1992; named Shawnee Mission Tchr. of Yr., 2003; finalist for Tchr. of Yr., Kans. Region III. Mem. NEA, ASCD, Nat. Assn. Tchrs. Math., U. Kans. Alumni Assn., Pittsburg State Alumni Assn., Friends of Art-Nelson Art Gallery, sec., Sigma Chi Mother's Club, Delta Kappa Gamma, Alpha Gamma Delta Alumni. Republican. Avocations: walking, bicycling, reading, tennis. Home: 14202 Benson St Shawnee Mission KS 66221-2513

STILWELL, WILLIAM EARLE, III, psychology educator, retired military officer; b. Cin., Ohio, July 28, 1936; s. William Earle Jr. and Frances (Hunt) S.; m. Doris Ann Nowak; children: Jane Belen Stilwell Angel, William Earle IV. AB, Dartmouth Coll., 1958; MS, San Jose State U., 1966; PhD, Stanford U., 1969. Lic. counseling psychologist, Ky.; cert. profl. qualification in psychology Assn. State of Provincial Psychology Bds. Rsch. assoc. Am. Inst. Rsch., Palo Alto, Calif., 1967-69; prof. psychology U. Ky., Lexington, 1969—. V.p. Ednl. Skills Devel., Lexington, 1969-85. Author: Psychology for Teachers and Students, 1981; mem. editl. bd. Counsel Edn. and Supervision, 1980-87; contbr. numerous (25) articles to profl. jour., chpts. to books. Assigned to patron nine, USNR, 1960-63, active res. in Alameda, Calif., Washington area, 1965-83, exec. officer, 1979-82. Recipient Natl. Def. and Armed Forces Res. with cluster, Tchr. Who Make a Difference Awd., UK Coll. of Edn., 1998, 2002, Svc. award, Coun. Univ. Depts. Clin. Psychology, 1998, Study Web Academic Excellence Awd., 1999, 2000, Web Homework Spot award, 2000. Mem. APA (life), Coun. Counseling Psychology Tng. Programs (Svc. award 2001), Am. Ednl. Rsch. Assn. (v.p. 1980-82), Ky. Psychol. Assn., Ky. Sch. Counseling Assn. (v.p. 1979-80, 81-82), Ohio Soc. of the Colonial Wars, Hon. Order Ky. Cols., Res. Officers Assn. US (life), Stanford Alumni Assn. (life). Avocations: hypertext mark up language, fishing in ontario. Home: 1919 Williamsburg Rd Lexington KY 40504-3013 E-mail: westil3@uky.edu.

STILWILL, TED, school system administrator; Tchr., adminstr.; asst. dir. of curriculum and instrn. Coun. Bluffs Cmty. Schs., 1980—83; head dept. elem. and secondary edn. Iowa Dept. of Edn., acting dir., 1995—96, dir., 1995—. Bd. dirs. North Ctrl. Regional Ednl. Lab.; chair sch. budget com.; mem. several bds. and commns. Office: State of Iowa Dept Edn Grimes State Office Bldg Des Moines IA 50319-0001 Fax: 515-242-5988.*

STIMPSON, CATHARINE ROSLYN, English language educator, writer; b. Bellingham, Wash., June 4, 1936; d. Edward Keown and Catharine (Watts) Stimpson. AB, Bryn Mawr Coll., 1958; BA, MA, Cambridge U., Eng., 1960; PhD, Columbia U., 1967. Mem. faculty Barnard Coll., N.Y.C., 1963—80; prof. English, dean of grad. sch., vice provost grad. edn. Rutgers U., New Brunswick, NJ, 1980—92, univ. prof., 1991—; chmn. bd. scholars Ms. Mag., N.Y.C., 1981—92; dir. fellows program MacArthur Found., 1994—97; univ. prof., dean Grad. Sch. Arts and Sci. NYU, N.Y.C., 1998—. Author: Class Notes, 1979, Where the Meanings Are, 1988; editor: Signs: Jour. Women in Culture and Soc., 1974—81, Women in Culture and Society book series, 1981; contbr. Change Mag., 1992—93. Chmn. N.Y. Coun. Humanites, 1984—87, Nat. Coun. Rsch. on Women, 1984—89; trustee Bates Coll., 1990—; pres. Assn. Grad. Schs., 2000—01; bd. dir. Stephens Coll., Columbia, Mo., 1982—85, Legal Def. and Edn. Fund, 1991—96. Fellow, Woodrow Wilson Found., 1958, Fulbright fellow, 1958—60, Nat. Humanities Inst., 1975—76, Rockefeller Humanities fellow, 1983—84. Mem.: PBS (bd. dirs. 1994—2000), NOW, AAUP, PEN, MLA (exec. coun., chmn. acad. freedom com., 1st v.p., pres. 1990). Democrat. Home: 29 Washington Sq W Apt 15C New York NY 10011-9199 Office: NYU 6 Washington Sq N New York NY 10003-6668 E-mail: catharine.stimpson@nyu.edu.

STINE, GORDAN BERNARD, dentist, educator; b. Charleston, SC, Feb. 10, 1924; s. Abe Jack and Helen (Pinosky) S.; m. Barbara Berlinsky, Jan. 20, 1951; children: Steven Mark, Robert Jay. BS in Chemistry, Coll. of Charleston, 1944; DDS, Emory U., 1950; DHL (hon.), Coll. of Charleston, 1999. Lic. dentist, Ga., S.C. Pvt. practice gen. dentistry, Charleston, 1953-87; spl. asst. to pres. Med. U. S.C., Charleston, 1983-97, clin. assoc. prof. cmty. dentistry, 1983-97, dir. Dental Continuing Edn., 1984-97, dental cons., 1997—, bd. visitors, 1982, 83, chmn., 1982, chmn. Cultural Projects Coun., 1984-97, mem. continuing edn. adv. com., 1986-89; dental coord. Area Health Edn. Ctrs., 1987-97. Dental cons., 1997—. Trustee Coll. Charleston, 1988—, vice-chmn., 1992-98, emeritus trustee, 1999—; instr. Trident Tech. Coll., 1981; trustee State Coll., 1987-88; dental adv. com. Divsn. Dental Health SC State Bd. Health, 1967-68; regional adv. group S.C. Regional Med. Program, 1974-75; chmn. S.C. Dental Polit. Action Com., 1973-74, 76-84, bd. dirs., 1973-85, chmn., 1973-83; bd. dirs. Coastal Carolina Fair Assn., 1957-61, 63-65, pres., 1965-66; bd. dirs. Charleston Symphony Assn., 1963-68, pres., 1965, pres.'s coun., 1983-84; bd. dirs. Charleston Civic Ballet, 1968, S.C. Art Alliance, 1973-74, Charleston Concert Assn., 1967-73, Charleston R.R. Hist. Soc., 1967-68; bd. dirs. Coastal Carolina coun. Boy Scouts Am., 1972, 74-75, 82-84, v.p. for So. Regional Coun. Exec. Com. Programs, 1985-86, pres., 1990-91, adv. com., 1972, 74-75, 82-85, chmn. Kiawah Dist., 1982, Gordan B. Stine Health Ctr., 1995, Boys Coun., 2001-2003; chmn. Coll. Prep. Sch., 1963-67, vice chmn., 1964-66, regional bd., 1992—; mem. Task Force for Martin Luther King Jr. Legal Holiday, YMCA of Greater Charleston, 1974-75; founder Charleston Mini Parks, 1969, bd. dirs., 1969-71, chmn., 1969, 71; bd. dirs. Charleston Pride, 1986-2003, chmn., 1973-75, 83-85; chmn. dental divsn. Trident United Way, 1962, 69, bd. dirs., 1970-76, 78—, cmty. welfare planning coun., 1967-68, chmn. pub. svc. sect., 1993, pres., 1982, chmn. fund drive, 1977, exec. com., 1977-79, 81-84; chmn. fundraising dental divsn. Cancer Soc., 1956, 61, 66, 70-71; chmn. Charleston County Dems., 1968-72; Charleston County councilman, 1975-84, chmn., 1979-80; alderman Ward 13 City of Charleston, 1971-75; active pub. svc. coms. including S.C. Assembly on Growth, 1981, Trident Devel. Coun., 1972; legis. com. S.C. Assn. Counties, 1979, 81-82, Charleston Waterfront Park Adv. Com., 1982-83, Charleston Neighborhood Housing Svcs. Bd., 1984; state senatorial candidate, 1975; vice chmn. Berkeley-Charleston-Dorchester Coun. of Govts., 1983—, sec., 1985-90, chmn., 1991-95, chmn. exec. bd. dirs., 1995—, mem. & chmn. various coms.; exec. com. Charleston Mus., 1980, bd. dirs., 1977-78, steering com., 1978-80; chmn. Charleston Bicentennial Com., 1972-75; bd. dirs. Carolina Art Assn., 1978; fund drive chmn. Roper Hosp., 1973; bd. dirs. Coastal Fed. Credit Union, 1979-80, pres., 1979; exec. com. Greater Charleston Safety Coun., 1976-85, v.p., 1986-88, pres., 1989; bd. dirs. Trident Area Found., 1977-80, adv. bd., 1981-82, life mem. bd. dirs., 1995; steering com. Charleston campaign United Negro Coll. Fund, 1972-73; bd. dirs. Robert Shaw Boys Ctr., 1975-77, Mil. Svcs. Ctr., 1979-82, Trident 100, 1980-81; chmn. State Health Fair Adv. Bd. for Nat. Health Screening Coun., 1984-85; pres. adv. coun. Winthrop Coll., 1984-85; extension adv. bd. Clemson U., 1985-86, chmn., 1987-89, statewide cmty. devel. adv. com., 1985; bd. mem. Hebrew Benevolent Soc., 1968—, pres., 1970, 71; mem. Hebrew Orphan Soc., 1972—, v.p., 1988-89, pres., 1990-92; trustee Congregation Beth Elohim, 1959-64, pres., 1967-68, Brotherhood pres., 1960, chmn. 250th ann. yr. 2001; pres. Jewish Welfare Bd., 1970-71, com. mem. With USMC, 1942, with USN, 1945-46, 51-53, res., 1953-72, res. ret., 1971-84. Named Coll. of Charleston Alumnus of Yr., 1966, Cmty. Leader Am., 1968-71; recipient Hettie Rickett Cmty. Devel. award, 1979, award adv. dental bd. Carolina Continental Ins. Co., 1983-84, Gov.'s Order of Palmetto award, 1985, 94, 96, Joseph P. Riley Leadership award, 2002. Fellow ACD, Royal Soc. Health; mem. ADA, APHA, Coastal Dist. Dental Soc. (pres. 1954), Charleston Dental Soc. (pres. 1957-58, Dentist of Yr. 1992), S.C. Acad. General Dentistry (Dentist of Yr. 1998, newsletter editor 1995—), Nat. Assn. Regional Couns. (bd. dirs. 1991-95), Israel Dental Assn., Hebrew Orphan Soc. (pres. 1991, 92, 93), Pierre Fauchard Acad. (state chmn. 1991, 93, State Dentist of Yr. 1994, trustee S.E. region U.S. 1997—), S.C. Dental Assn. (pres. 1974-75, edn. com. 1985-90, Cmty. Svc. award 1995), S.C. Downtown Devel. Assn. (bd. dirs. 1983—, pres. 1992-93), Charleston Trident C. of C. (pres. 1972, bd. dirs. 1968-74, 80), S.C. Assn. Regional Couns. (pres. 1986-87), Exch. Club Charleston (pres. 1962), S.C. State Exch. Club (bd. dirs. 1965-68), Alpha Omega (pres. 1949-50, Disting. Svc. award 1976-77, pres. Southeastern group 1960-78, charter mem., emeritus mem. 1993), Tau Epsilon Phi (chpt. pres. 1943). Avocations: gardening, community service. Home: 27 Wraggborough Ln Charleston SC 29403-6362 Office: 171 Ashley Ave Charleston SC 29425-0001

STINER, FREDERIC MATTHEW, JR., accounting educator, consultant, writer; b. Balt., Apr. 4, 1946; s. Frederic Matthew and Bertha Moulton (Kidd) S.; m. Martha Susan Scharper, June 21, 1969 (div. Jan. 2000); children: Frederic Matthew, John Alexander, James M ichael, Katherine Elizabeth. MS, U. Del., 1969; MBA, Marshall U., 1972; PhD, U. Nebr., 1976. CPA, W.Va. Staff acct. Goodman & Co., CPAs, Norfolk, Va., 1973-74; sr. acct. Snyder, Grant, Muehling, CPAs, Lincoln, Nebr., 1977-78; asst. prof. Iowa State U., Ames, 1978-79, U. Md., College Park, 1979-82; assoc. prof. acctg. U. Del., Newark, 1982—2001; prof., chmn. dept. acctg., taxation and law Long Island U., Bklyn., 2002—. Contbr. articles to acad. and profl. jours. Mem. AICPA, W.Va. Soc. CPAs. Home: 109 Autumn Horseshoe Newark DE 19702-2354 Office: LI U Dept Acctg Taxation and Law Brooklyn NY 11201

STINSON, MARY FLORENCE, retired nursing educator; b. Wheeling, W.Va., Feb. 11, 1931; d. Rolland Francis and Mary Angela (Voellinger) Kellogg; m. Charles Walter Stinson, Feb. 12, 1955; children: Kenneth Charles, Karen Marie, Kathryn Anne. BSN, Coll. Mt. St. Joseph, 1953, postgrad., 1983; MEd, Xavier U., Cin., 1967; postgrad., U. Cin., 1981. Staff nurse contagious disease ward Cin. Gen. Hosp., 1953-54, asst. head nurse med. and polio wards, 1955, acting head nurse, clin. instr., 1955-56; instr. St. Francis Hosp. Sch. Practical Nursing, Cin., 1956-57, Good Samaritan Hosp. Sch. Nursing, Cin., 1957—66; instr. refresher courses for nurses Cin. Bd.. Edn. and Ohio State Nurses Assn. Dist. 8, 1967-70; coord. sch. health office Coll. Mt. St. Joseph, Ohio, 1969-72, instr. dept. nursing, 1974-79, asst. prof., 1979-89; RN assessor Passport program Coun. on Aging Southwestern Ohio, 1989-90, quality assurance coord. Passport program, 1990-93; quality assurance supr. Passport and Elderly Svcs. Program, 1993-94; quality assurance mgr. Coun. Aging Southwestern Ohio, 1995-2000; ret., 2000. Staff nurse St. Francis/St. George Hosp., Cin., 1988-89. Charter mem. Adoptive Parents Assn. St. Joseph Infant and Maternity Home; women's com. for performing arts series Coll. Mt. St. Joseph; chmn. by-law com. Mt. St. Joseph Nursing Honor Soc., 1996—98; active St. Antoninus Rosary Altar and Sch. Soc., St. Antoninus Athletic Club, com. chmn., 1969—70; bd. dirs. Coll. Mt. St. Joseph Alumni Assn., 1982—84, sec., 1968—69, v.p., 1969—70, pres., 1970—71, chmn. revision of constn., 1976—77; homecoming chmn. Coll. Mt. St. Joseph, 1970, co-chmn., 1977, co-chair com. to celebrate 75 years of nursing edn., 2001—02; mem. com. to plan 50th ann. of graduation Coll. Mt. St. Joseph Alumni Assn. Democrat. Roman Catholic. Mem. River Squares Club (v.p. 1967), Sigma Theta Tau (charter Omicron Omicron chpt. 1998—). Home: 5549 Cleander Dr Cincinnati OH 45238-4266 E-mail: cstinson@fuse.net.

STINSON, RICHARD FLOYD, retired horticulturist, educator; b. Cleve., Feb. 4, 1921; s. Floyd Earl and Helen M. (Schiemann) S.; m. Lois D. Stinson; children: Leigh, Laurie, Glenn, Paul, Cathy. BS, Ohio State U., 1943, MS, 1947, PhD, 1952. Instr. floriculture SUNY, Alfred, 1947-48; asst. prof. floriculture U. Conn., Storrs, 1948-55; asst. prof. horticulture Mich. State U., East Lansing, 1955-59, assoc. prof. horticulture, 1959-67; assoc. prof. agrl. edn. and horticulture Pa. State U., University Park, 1967-73, prof., 1973-89, sr. faculty mem., 1979-89, prof. emeritus, 1990—. Cons. in field. Contbr. articles to profl. jours. Lt. (j.g.) USNR, 1943-46. Mem. N.Am. Assn. Colls. and Tchrs. Agr. (E.B. Knight Jour. award 1992), Sigma Xi, Alpha Tau Alpha, Gamma Sigma Delta, Phi Delta Kappa. Office: Pa State U 323 Agrl Adminstrn Bldg University Park PA 16802-2601 E-mail: rfs5@psu.edu.

STIPE, ROBERT EDWIN, design educator; b. Easton, Pa., July 18, 1928; s. J. Norwood and Ethel M. Stipe; m. Josephine Davis Weedon, 1952; children: Daniel W. Stipe, Frederick Norwood Stipe. AB in Econ., Duke U., 1950, LLB, 1953; MRP, U. N.C., 1959. Urban planning cons. City and Town Planning Assocs., Chapel Hill, N.C., 1956-57; asst. dir., prof. pub. law and govt. U. N.C. Inst. Govt., Chapel Hill, N.C., 1957-74; sr. Fulbright rsch. fellow London U., 1968-69; dir. Divsn. Archives and History N.C. Dept. Cultural Resources, Raleigh, N.C., 1974-75; vis. prof. U. N.C., Chapel Hill, 1975-77; prof. design N.C. State U., Raleigh, 1976-89, emeritus prof. design, part time prof. design, 1989—2000. Lectr. Inst. Advanced Studies, Bratislava, Slovak Republic, 1992-96; bd. trustees U.S. com. Internat. Coun. on Monuments and Sites, Preservation Action, Nat. Coun. on Preservation Edn., Hist. Preservation Fund N.C., Alliance for Preservation Hist. Landscapes, Old Salem Inc., Stagville Ctr. for Preservation Tech.; emeritus trustee Nat. Trust for Hist. Preservation; mem. bd. adv. Nat. Alliance Preservation Commn. Author, editor more than 100 articles and publs. in fields of historic preservation, landscape conservation, design, urban planning and planning law. Mem. Chapel Hill Design Review Bd.; trustee Chapel Hill Preservation Soc.; founder, trustee Chapel Hill HIstorical Soc. Fellow U.S. Com. Internat. Coun. on Monuments and Sites, 1986; recipient Disting. Svc. award Ruth Coltrane Cannon award, N.C. Soc. for Preservation of Antiquities, 1973, Sec. of Interior's Disting. Conservation Svc. award, 1978, Spl. award outstanding contbns. to landscape architecture Am. Soc. Landscape Archiects, N.C. chpt., 1985, Louise DuPont Crowninshield award for Superlative Lifetime Achievement in Historic Preservation, Nat. Trust for Historic Preservation, 1988, Dist. Svc. and Profl. Leadership award Nat. Coun. for Preservation Edn., 1989, Charles S. Murphy award, Duke U. Law Sch. Alumni Assn., 2003. Mem. Cosmos Club (Washington), Sigma Pi Kappa (First Disting. mem. 1994), Sigma Lambda Alpha (disting. mem. 1996), Phi Delta Phi. Home: 100 Pine Ln Chapel Hill NC 27514-4331

STIPEK, DEBORAH, education educator, dean; BS in Psychology, U. Wash., 1972; PhD in Devel. Psychology, Yale U., 1977. Prof. Grad. Sch. Edn. UCLA, 1977—2000; co-dir. NIMH Tng. Program in Applied Human Devel.; dir. Corinne Seeds U. Elme. Sch., Urban Edn. Studies Ctr.; I. James Quillen dean, prof. edn. Stanford (Calif.) U., 2001—. Mem. bd. on children, youth and families NRC; dir. MacArthur Found. Network on Tchg. and Learning. Author: Motivation to Learn: From Theory to Practice, 2002; author: (with A. Bohart) Constructive and Destructive Behavior: Implications for Family, School, and Society, 2001; author: (with K. Seal) Motivated Minds: Raising Children to Love Learning, 2001. Congl. Sci. fellow, Soc. for Rsch. in Child Devel., Office Senator Bill Bradley, 1983—84. Office: Stanford Univ Sch Edn 485 Lasuen Mall Stanford CA 94305-3096*

STIRLER, KAREN SUE, special education educator, adult education educator; b. Waterloo, Iowa, June 25, 1951; d. Walter Henry and Nadine Augusta (Boege) S. BS in Vocat. Home Econs., U. No. Iowa, 1973, MA in Spl. Edn., 1982. Tchr. vocat. home econs. and sci. Randolph (Nebr.) Pub. Schs., 1976-77; tchr. spl. edn. Highland Community Sch., Riverside, Iowa, 1978-82, New Hampton (Iowa) Schs., 1982-86, Roosevelt Mid. Schs., Cedar Rapids, Iowa, 1986-92, Kennedy High Sch., Cedar Rapids, 1992—. Tchr. adult basic edn. Kirkwood C.C., Cedar Rapids, 1987-99. Bd. dirs. Arc East Ctrl. Iowa. Mem. NEA, Am. Home Econs. Assn., Coun. for Exceptional Children, Iowa Edn. Assn., Cedar Rapids Home Econs. Assn., Cedar Rapids Tchr. Edn. Assn., Thursday Evening Optimist. Lutheran. Avocations: sewing, crafts, antiques, sports. Office: Kennedy High Sch 4545 Wenig Rd NE Cedar Rapids IA 52402-2298

STITES, M(ARY) ELIZABETH, architecture educator; b. N.Y.C., July 28, 1915; d. Otto and Olivia (Stites) Gaertner; m. Raymond S. Stites, Jul. 29, 1938; 1 child: Mary Elizabeth. BArch, NYU, 1940; postgrad., U. Vienna, 1961. Instr. U. Md. Coll. Arts & Scis., College Park, 1949-67, adminstrv. asst., 1959-76, assoc. prof., 1967-76; cons. Md. Coll. Art and Design, Silver Spring, 1976-89; asst. organist St. Luke's Ch., Bethesda, Md., 1976—95. Lectr. religious architecture, history architecture, archtl. studies of Leonardo da Vinci. Contbr. articles to Book of Knowledge Grolier Soc., 1952, New Cath. Ency., 1965. Past mem. Yellow Springs Town Planning Commn.; mem. Montgomery County com. Md. Hist. Trust for Archtl. Preservation. Mem. Coll. Art Assn., Soc. Archtl. Historians, Archaeol. Inst. Am., AIA. Episcopalian. Home: PO Box 98 Garrett Park MD 20896-0098

STITH, CHERYL DIANE ADAMS, elementary school educator; b. Birmingham, Ala., Oct. 15, 1950; d. Mack Jones and Joan (Logan) Adams; m. Hugh P. Stith, III, Jan. 7, 1972; children: Jennifer Dawn, Kristy Michelle. BS cum laude, U. Ala., Birmingham, 1986, MA in Edn., 1992, EdS, 1994. Cert. ednl. specialist, Ala. Substitute tchr. Homewood City (Ala.) Schs., 1986-87; tchr. Robert C. Arthur Elem. Sch., Birmingham, 1987-95; instrnl. support specialist Edgewood Elem. Homewood City Schs., 1995—. Mem. summer enrichment program U. Ala.-Birmingham, 1993; mem. State of Ala. Textbook Com., Montgomery, 1995; lectr. in field. Vol. Birmingham Soup Kitchens, 1988—, Habitat for Humanity, Birmingham, 1992—; spkr. Ala. Kidney Found., Birmingham, 1992—; vol. U. Ala.-Birmingham's Young Author's Conf., 1986-92; mem. Robert C. Arthur Elem. Sch. PTO. Named Tchr. of the Yr., Birmingham Pub. Schs., 1993-94, Outstanding Tchr., 1994; Beeson fellow Samford U. Writing Project, 1990; Ala. Ret. Tchrs. Found. scholar, 1994. Mem. NEA, Ala. Edn. Assn., Birmingham Edn. Assn., Internat. Reading Assn. (S.E. regional conf. presider and vol.), Ala. Reading Assn., Birmingham Reading Coun., Birmingham Tchrs. Applying Whole Lang., Nat. Coun. Tchrs. English, Phi Kappa Phi, Kappa Delta Pi. Methodist. Avocations: reading, writing, gardening. Home: 1034 Greystone Crst Birmingham AL 35242-7012

STITH, JAMES HERMAN, physics educator; b. Alberta, Va., July 17, 1941; s. Pierpont and Ruth (Stith) Morgan; m. Alberta Juanita Hill, Oct. 2, 1965; children: Adrienne, Andrea, Alyssa. BS, Va. State U., 1963, MS, 1964; DEd, Pa. State U., 1972; LHD, Va. State U., 1992. Instr. Va. State U., Petersburg, 1964-65; assoc. engr. RCA, Lancaster, Pa., 1967-69; commd. 2d lt. U.S. Army, 1965, advanced through grades to col., 1991; ret., 1993; assoc. prof. of physics U.S. Mil. Acad., West Point, NY, 1976—90, prof., 1991-93; vis. scientist USAF Acad., Colorado Springs, Colo., 1976-77; prof. physics Ohio State U., Columbus, 1993-98; vis. scientist Lawrence Livermore (Calif.) Nat. Lab., 1986-87; v.p. physics resources ctr. Am. Inst. Physics, 1998—. Contbr. articles to jour. Chmn. West Point Sch. Bd., 1984-86. Recipient Archie L. Lacey award N.Y. Acad. Sci., 1994, Disting. Svc. citation Am. Assn. Physics Tchrs., 1995; NSF fellow, 1973; named to Hall of Fame at Va. State U. ROTC, 1994. Fellow AAAS, Am. Phys. Soc.; mem. Am. Assn. Physics Tchrs. (v.p. 1990, pres.-elect 1991, pres. 1992), Am. Inst. Physics (governing bd. 1991-93), Nat. Soc. Black Physicists (chartered fellow 1992, pres. 1998-99), Coun. Sci. Soc. Pres. (mem. exec. bd. 1992-96, treas. 1993-96), NAACP, Va. State U., ROTC Alumni Assn., Sigma Pi Sigma, Phi Kappa Phi, Alpha Phi Alpha (pres. 1980-82, Man of Yr. 1980, 83), Sigma Xi. Baptist. Home: 2013 Clearwood Dr Mitchellville MD 20721-2511 Office: Am Inst Physics One Physics Ellipse College Park MD 20740-3843 E-mail: jstith@aip.org.

STITH, LEAH DRAKE, legislative aide, school system administrator; b. Portsmouth, Va., Nov. 18, 1949; d. Freddie Lee Sr. and Rebecca (Greene) Drake; m. S. DeLacy Stith, Sr., Oct. 20 1979; children: Maisha Kito, S. DeLacy Jr. BS in Polit. Sci., Norfolk State U., 1985, postgrad., 1992—. Substitute tchr. Portsmouth Schs., 1985-90; asst. sr. residential counselor Pines Treatment Facility, Portsmouth, 1986-90; legis. asst. del. Gen. Assembly, Richmond, Va., 1986-90; spl. asst. to lt. gov. Va. State Govt., Richmond, 1990—. Mem. sch. bd. Portsmouth Schs., 1991—; mem. adv. bd. WHRO Pub. TV, Portsmouth, 1991—; guest lectr. spl. edn. conf. Norfolk State U., 1994. Sec. Wesley Ctr. Bd., Portsmouth, 1991-92, Portsmouth Dem. Com., 1991-92; coord. Don Beyer for Lt. Gov., Portsmouth, 1989, United Negro Coll. Fund, Portsmouth, 1986. Recipient Disting. Alumnus award Norfolk State U., 1991, Sojourner Truth award Nat. Assn. Black Bus. and Profl. Women, Norfolk, 1992, Woman of Yr. award Black Women's Health Network, 1993, others. Mem. Am. Assn. Sch.

Adminstrs., Va. Sch. Bd. Assn. (fin. com., Cert. of Achievement award 1991-92). Episcopalian. Avocation: politics. Home: 3604 Cedar Ln Portsmouth VA 23703-3502 Office: Office of Lt Gov 101 N 8th St Richmond VA 23219-2305

STIVER, PATRICIA ABARE, elementary education educator; b. Plattsburgh, N.Y., Nov. 17, 1941; d. Joseph LaBarge and Janet Marcella (Downs) Abare. BA, SUNY, Fredonia, 1964; MS, SUNY, Albany, 1988. Cert. elem. educator N.Y. Tchr. elem. Randolph (N.Y.) Ctrl. Sch., 1964-66, Schoharie (N.Y.) Ctrl. Schs., 1966-86, asst. elem. math. coord., 1986-96, remedial math. tchr., 1986—, coord. elem. computer assisted instrn., 1986-90, math. coordinating spls., 1996—, elem. math. coordinating specialist, 1996—. Mem. ASCD, Nat. Coun. Tchrs. Math., Assn. Math. Tchrs. of N.Y. State, N.Y. State United Tchrs. and Affiliates, N.Y. State Assn. Comprehensive Edn. (U.S., Europe). Democrat. Avocations: gardening, clarinet, alto and tenor saxophone playing in bands, singing in choirs, computers, spectator sports. Home: 107 Brookside Pl PO Box 121 Schoharie NY 12157-0121 Office: Schoharie Ctrl Sch Main St Schoharie NY 12157

STIX, THOMAS HOWARD, physicist, educator; b. St. Louis, July 12, 1924; s. Ernest William and Erma (Kingsbacher) S.; m. Hazel Rosa Sherwin, May 28, 1950; children: Susan Sherwin Fisher, Michael Sherwin. BS, Calif. Inst. Tech., 1948; PhD, Princeton U., 1953. Mem. staff Plasma Physics Lab. Princeton U., 1953—, co-head exptl. div., 1961-78, asst. dir. acad. affairs, 1978-80, assoc. dir. acad. affairs, 1980-93; prof. astrophys. sci., 1962-96; assoc. chmn. dept. astrophys. sci., 1981-91; acting dir. Ctr. for Jewish Life Princeton U., 1994-95. Author: The Theory of Plasma Waves, 1962, Waves in Plasmas, 1992; mem. adv. bd. McGraw-Hill Advanced Physics Monograph Series, 1963-70; bd. editors: Physics of Fluids, 1966-68, Internat. Jour. Engring. Sci, 1969-77, Nuclear Fusion, 1975-80; assoc. editor: Phys. Rev. Letters, 1974-77. Chmn. Princeton United Jewish Appeal, 1954-55, 63-64, Princeton Hillel Found., 1972-76, pres., 1994-96. Served with AUS, 1942-45. Recipient award for disting. teaching Princeton U., 1991, Disting. Career award Fusion Power Assn., 1999; NSF sr. postdoctoral fellow physics Weizmann Inst. Sci., Rehovot, Israel, 1960-61; Guggenheim Meml. Found. fellow, 1969-70 Fellow Am. Phys. Soc. (chmn. div. plasma physics 1962-63, com. internat. freedom of scientists 1983-87, chmn. 1985; James Clark Maxwell prize 1980); mem. AAUP, Sigma Xi, Tau Beta Pi. Home: Princeton, NJ. Died Apr. 16, 2002.

STOCK, JEFFREY ALLEN, urologist, educator; b. Bronx, N.Y., May 24, 1962; MD, Mt. Sinai Sch. Medicine, 1988. Diplomate Am. Bd. Urology. Intern, resident gen. surgery, urology U. Medicine-Dentistry N.J.-U. Hosp., Newark, 1988-93; fellow U. Calif. San Diego-Children's Hosp., 1993-94; urologist West Orange, N.J., 1994—. Urologist St. Barnabas Med. Ctr., 1994—, Hackensack (N.J.) Med. Ctr., 1995—, Children's Hosp., N.J., 1994—, Newark Beth Israel Med. Ctr., 1994—, Morristown Meml. Hosp.; clin. assoc. prof. U. Medicine-Dentistry N.J., 1995—. Fellow ACS, Am. Acad. Pediatrics, Soc. Pediatric Urology; mem. Am. Urol. Assn. Office: 101 Old Short Hills Rd Ste 203 West Orange NJ 07052-1023

STOCKARD, ROBERT THOMAS, secondary school administrator; b. Alton, Ill., Jan. 29, 1940; s. John Charles and Girtha Isabelle (Smith) S.; m. Christle S. Foster, Apr. 2, 1966; 1 child, Gina Foster BS, So. Ill. U., 1963, MS, 1967; postgrad., Butler U., 1972. Cert. indsl. arts educator, guidance counselor, secondary adminstr. Tchr. Indpls. Pub. Schs., 1963-69, dean of student, 1969-70, vice prin., 1970-80, vice prin., dir., 1980-93, dir. adult edn., 1993—; rsch. cons. Ill. Dept. Edn., Springfield, 1969. Cons. Ind. Classroom Tchrs. Assn., 1969-70, Warren Twp. Schs., Indpls., 1971-72; proposal writing Indpls. Pub. Schs., 1969—, recruiter, 1965-69; workshop conf. leader IPS, 1981—; developer partnership between Ind. Career Edn. Ctr. and Auto Zone Corp. Asst. youth dir. Fall Creek YMCA, Indpls., 1963-65; bd. dirs. Near Eastside Multi-Svc. Ctr., Indpls., 1980-82, mem. adv. coun., 1982-84; adv. coun. Boy Scouts Am.; active Indpls. Urban League, Ind. Black Expo. Recipient Bus. Partnership Disting. Svc. award Indpls. C. of C., 1981, 85, Ptnrs. in Edn. Leadership award, 1983, 84, 85, 86, Disting. Recommender award Ind. U., 1986, Cmty. Svc. award Positive Change Network, 1995; grantee State of Ind., 1991, Nat. Ctr. for Rsch. in Vocat. Edn., 1992. Mem. ASCD, NAACP, Kiwanis (youth com. bd. 1990—), Am. Vocat. Assn., Ind. Vocat. Assn., Ind. Coun. of Vocat. Adminstrs., Ind. Urban League, Ind. Black Expo., 100 Black Men of Indpls., North Ctrl. Assn. Sch. Dists. (program reviewer 1975-81, mem. several sch. evaluation teams), Kappa Alpha Psi (polemarch 1992-94, bd. dirs. Indpls. chpt. 1994—, Disting. Svc. 1986, 87, 90, 91, 94, found. guide right program grantee 1993), Phi Delta Kappa, Iota Lambda Sigma. Avocations: bowling, woodworking, home maintenance, spectator sports. Home: 6565 Sunset Ln Indianapolis IN 46260-4166 Office: Indpls Pub Schs 2405 Madison Ave Indianapolis IN 46225-2106

STOCKER, ARTHUR FREDERICK, classics educator; b. Bethlehem, Pa., Jan. 24, 1914; s. Harry Emilius and Alice (Stratton) S.; m. Marian West, July 16, 1968. AB summa cum laude, Williams Coll., 1934; A.M., Harvard U., 1935, PhD, 1939. Instr. Greek Bates Coll., 1941-42; asst. prof. classics U. Va., 1946-52, assoc. prof., 1952-60, prof., 1960-84, prof. emeritus, 1984—, chmn. dept., 1955-63, 68-78, assoc. dean Grad. Sch. Arts and Scis., 1962-66; vis. asst. prof. classics U. Chgo., summer 1951. Editor: (with others) Servianorum in Vergilii Carmina Commentariorum Editio Harvardiana, Vol. II, 1946, Vol. III, 1965; assoc. editor: Classical Outlook. Served with USAAF, 1942-46; col. (ret.). Sheldon traveling fellow from Harvard, 1940-41 Mem. Va. Classical Assn. (pres. 1949-52), Mid. West and South Classical Assn. (pres. So. sect. 1960-62, pres. 1970-71), Nat. Huguenot Soc. (pres. gen. 1989-91), Am. Philol. Assn., Mediaeval Acad. Am., Poetry Soc. Va. (pres. 1966-69), Soc. Colonial Wars in the State of Va., Sons of the Revolution, S.A.R. (chpt. pres. 1972, 91), Huguenot Soc. Va. (pres. 1981-83), Raven Soc. (Raven award 1977), Phi Beta Kappa, Omicron Delta Kappa. Republican. Presbyterian (elder). Clubs: Masons, Red-Land (Charlottesville, Va.), Colonnade (Charlottesville, Va.), Farmington Country (Charlottesville, Va.), Commonwealth (Richmond, Va.), Williams (N.Y.C.), Army and Navy (Washington). Home: 250 Pantops Mountain Rd Charlottesville VA 22911-8694

STOCKER, JOYCE ARLENE, retired secondary school educator; b. West Wyoming, Pa., May 13, 1931; d. Donald Arthur and Elizabeth Mae (Gardner) Saunders; m. Robert Earl Stocker, Nov. 26, 1953; children: Desiree Lee Stocker Stackhouse, Rebecca Lois Stocker Genelow, Joyce Elizabeth Stocker Scrobola. Grad. cum laude, Coll. Misericordia, Dallas, 1953; Master's equivalency diploma, Pa. Dept. Edn., 1991. Cert. tchr., Pa. Tchr. music and lang. arts West Pittston (Pa.) Sch. Dist., 1953-60; tchr. music and choral Wyoming Area Sch. Dist., Exeter, Pa., 1970-78, tchr. English composition, 1978-93, chmn. lang. arts dept., 1982-90, dir. nat. history day activities, 1982-93. State cons. Nat. History Day, 1996—. Organist, choir dir. United Meth. Ch., Wyo., 1958—; dir. W. Wyo. Centennial Choir, 1998; mem. adminstrv. bd. West Wyo., 2000—; mem. worship com. United Meth. Ch. and Interch. Coun., Wyo. and West Wyo. Recipient DAR Tchr. of Yr. award, 1992-93, Wilkes U., 1990; named Outstanding Educator, Times Leader, 1993; honoree Wyo. United Meth. Ch. Choir, 1999. Mem. NEA, Pa. Edn. Assn., Wyo. Edn. Assn., N.E. Pa. Writing Coun., Nat. Coun. Tchrs. English, Women Educators Internat., Orgn. Am. History, Pa. Music Educators Assn., Music Educators Nat. Coun., Nat. Coun. Social Studies, Pa. Assn. Sch. Retirees (Vol. of Yr. 1998), Pa. Sch. Employees Retirement Sys. (social svcs. com.), Pa. Retired Pub. Sch. Employees Assn. (Luzerne-Wyoming counties chpt.), Pa. Coun. Social Studies, Delta Kappa Gamma (recording sec. 1991—, accompanist Pa. state chorus, 1999—, 2000—), Phi Mu Gamma. Methodist. Avocations: reading, writing, sewing, hunting, fishing. Office: Wyoming Area Sch Dist 20 Memorial St Exeter PA 18643-2659

STOCKING, GEORGE WARD, JR., anthropology educator; b. Berlin, Dec. 8, 1928; came to U.S., 1929; s. George Ward and Dorothé Amelia (Reichhard) S.; m. Wilhelmina Davis, Aug. 19, 1949 (div. 1965); children: Susan Hallowell, Rebecca, Rachel Louise, Melissa, Thomas Shepard; m. Carol Ann Bowman, Sept. 29, 1968. BA, Harvard U., 1949; PhD, U. Pa., 1960. From instr. to assoc. prof. history U. Calif., Berkeley, 1960-68; assoc. prof. anthropology and history U. Chgo., 1968-74, prof. anthropology, 1974—2000, Stein-Freiler Disting. Svc. prof., 1990—, prof. emeritus, 2000—, dir. Fishbein Ctr. for History Sci. and Medicine, 1981-92. Vis. prof. U. Minn., Mpls., 1974, Harvard U., Cambridge, Mass., 1977, Stanford U., Palo Alto, Calif., 1983, U. Ill., Urbana, 1999. Author: Race, Culture and Evolution, 1968, Victorian Anthropology, 1987, The Ethnographer's Magic, 1992, After Tylor, 1995, Delimiting Anthropology, 2001; author, editor: The Shaping of American Anthropology, 1974; editor History of Anthropology, 1983-97. Active labor union and radical polit. activity, 1949-56. Fellow Ctr. for Advanced Study in Behavioral Scis., 1976-77, John Simon Guggenheim Meml. Found., 1984-85, Inst. for Advanced Study, 1992-93; Getty Ctr. for History of Art and Humanities scholar, 1988-89, Dibner Inst., MIT, 1998. Fellow Am. Anthropol. Assn. (Franz Boas award 1998), Am. Acad. Arts and Scis.; mem. Royal Anthropol. Inst. (Huxley medal 1993), History Sci. Soc. Avocation: needlepoint. Office: Univ Chicago Dept Anthropology 1126 E 59th St Chicago IL 60637-1580 E-mail: g-stocking@uchicago.edu.

STOCKMAN, ROBERT HAROLD, religious organization administrator, educator; b. Meriden, Conn., Oct. 6, 1953; s. Harold Herman and Margery (Fothergill) S.; m. Mana Derakhshani, 1992; 1 child, Lua Bahiyeh. BA in Geology and Archaeology, Wesleyan U., 1975; MSc in Geology, Brown U., 1977; MTS, Harvard U., 1984, ThD, 1990. Coord. Inst. for Bahai Studies, 1990—. Grad. rsch. asst. geology dept., Brown U., Providence, 1975-77; instr. geology and oceanography, Cmty. Coll. R.I., Lincoln, 1977-80; instr. geology, Boston State Coll., 1980-82, U. Lowell, Mass., 1983-84; instr. geology and astronomy and operator of Astronomy Observatory, Bentley Coll., Waltham, Mass., 1983-90; teaching asst. Harvard U., 1986-89; instr. religion DePaul U., Chgo., 1990-95, 95-2003, vis. asst. prof. religious studies, 1995-96; spkr. on Baha'i Faith in America. Author: The Baha'i Faith in America, Vol. 1, Origins, 1892-1900, 1985, The Baha'i Faith in America, Vol. 2 Early Expansion, 1900-1912, 1995, Thornton Chase: First American Baha'i, 2002; mem. editl. bd. World Order, 1990—; contbr. articles to profl. jours. Mem. Am. Acad. Religion (mem. Baha'i studies unit 1984—, chairperson 1985-86, 89-2003), Mid. East Studies Assn., Soc. Iranian Studies, Assn. Baha'i Studies (mem. Internat. Com. 1990-98, chair study of religions sect. 1989—). Home: 224 Swanson Cir South Bend IN 46615-2549 Office: Baha'i Nat Ctr Office Rsch Wilmette IL 60091 E-mail: rstockman@usbnc.org.

STOCKSTILL, JAMES WILLIAM, secondary school educator; b. Springfield, Mo., Aug. 28, 1945; s. Arley Ian and Elma Jean Stockstill(m1964) (div. 1964) 1 child, Jamie Stockstill ; m. Vicki Bell, Aug. 20, 1966 (div. 1970); 1 child, Michelle LaDawn; m. Meredith Jeanine Spencer, Dec. 26, 1974; 1 child, Danielle. BS in Edn., S.W. Mo. State U., 1969. Head football coach, phys. edn. tchr. Golden City (Mo.) High Sch., 1969-70; coach, tchr. Mountain View (Mo.) High Sch., 1970-71; journeyman bricklayer Fort Lauderdale (Fla.) BMPI Union, 1971-74; masonry contractor Waynesville, N.C., 1974-86; masonry contractor, master stone and brick masonry contractor Hillsborough, N.C., 1986—; masonry instr. Orange High Sch., Hillsborough, 1986—. Owner Athenian Lady Fitness Ctr., Waynesville, 1984-86; gymnastics instr. Canton (N.C.) YMCA, 1976-80; pres. Trade and Industry Adv. Coun., Hillsborough, 1988-90; rep. VICA Skill Contest Orange High Sch., 1986-88. Author: A Collection of Poems, 1992, 93. Mem. Com. to Increase and Diversify Tax Base, Hillsborough, 1992; rebuilt Hist. Monument for Town of Hillsborough, 1997. Mem. AFT. Avocation: powerlifting. Office: Orange High Sch 500 Orange High School Rd Roxboro NC 27278-8415 Home: PO Box 1113 Roxboro NC 27573-1113

STOCKWELL, VIVIAN ANN, nursing educator; b. Hardy, Ark., Apr. 26, 1943; d. Belvin L. and Armilda L. (Langston) Cooper; m. R.D. Sneed, Mar. 16, 1963 (div. Jan. 1981); m. Homer E. Stockwell, Jan. 6, 1990; 1 child, Sherilyn. Diploma, St. Luke's Sch. Nursing, Kansas City, Mo., 1964; BS in Nursing summa cum laude, Avila Coll., Kansas City, 1987. Staff nurse operating rm. North Kansas City (Mo.) Hosp., 1972-76; pvt. scrub nurse Van M. Robinson, MD, North Kansas City, 1976-81; instr. health occupations Independence (Mo.) Pub. Schs., 1981-85; instr. Park Coll., Parkville, Mo., 1987-89, asst. to dir. dept. nursing, 1989-90. Ch. sch. tchr. Independence Blvd. Christian Ch., 1976-87, deacon, 1979-88, elder, 1988—, chmn. official bd., 2000, 02, chmn. elders, 2003; pres. Christian Women's Fellowship, 1994-97; mem. adult adv. bd. NCK Assembly, Internat. Order of Rainbow for Girls, 1983-94. Mem. DAR (1st vice regent Alexander Doniphan chpt. 2002—), Order Eastern Star, Sigma Theta Tau, Kappa Gamma Pi, Delta Epsilon Sigma.

STODDARD, ROBERT H. geography educator; b. Auburn, Nebr., Aug. 29, 1928; s. Hugh P. and Nainie L. (Robertson) S.; m. Sally E. Salisbury, Dec. 10, 1955; children: Martha, Andrew R., Hugh A. BA, Nebr. Wesleyan, Lincoln, 1950; MA, U. Nebr., 1960; PhD, U. Iowa, 1966. Instr. Nebr. Wesleyan, 1961-63, asst. prof., 1963-67, U. Nebr., Lincoln, 1967-71, assoc. prof., 1971-81, prof., 1981—2001. Vis. prof. Tribhuvan U., Kathmandu, Nepal, 1975-76, U. Columbo, Sri Lanka, 1986; inst. instr. Okla. State U., Stillwater, 1966; TV instr. Nebr. Ednl. TV Higher Edn., Lincoln, 1969; instr. Career Opportunity Program, Lincoln, 1973; dir. Geog. Edn. of Nebr., Lincoln, 1989-95. Author: Field Techniques, 1982; contbg. author: Human Geography, 2d edit., 1989; editor: Sacred Places, 1997. Mem. subcom. Lincoln-Lancaster Planning Com., 1974-78. Mem. Assn. Am. Geographers, Nat. Coun. for Geog. Edn. (Disting. Tchg. Achievement award 1992). Democrat. Unitarian Universalist. Office: U Nebr Dept Geography Lincoln NE 68588-0368

STODGHILL, RONALD, school system administrator; b. White Plains, N.Y., Dec. 21, 1939; s. Joseph and Marian (Wynn) Stodghill; children: Kimberly, Denise, Ronald. BS, Ea. Mich. U., 1961; MS, We. Mich. U., 1967; EdD, Wayne State U., 1981. Dir. edn. New Detroit, Detroit; deputy supt. St. Louis Pub. Schs., Mo.; supt. Wellston Pub. Schs., Mo. Mem. ASCD (sec.), Am. Assn. Advancement of Sci., Nat. Assn. Bilingual Edn. Home: 6574 Saint Louis Ave Saint Louis MO 63121-5725

STOECKLIN, SISTER CAROL ANN, education educator; b. Detroit, July 20, 1953; d. Andrew Charles and Ernestine (Roselli) S. BA, Mercy Coll. of Detroit, 1974; M in theol. studies, St. John's Provincial Sem., 1986; MA, St. Louis U., 1991, PhD, 1993. Joined Religious Sisters of Mercy. Tchr. Bishop Borgess High Sch., Redford, Mich., spring 1976, St. Agatha High Sch., Detroit, 1976-79; adminstrv. asst., campus minister, religion dept. chair Muskegon (Mich.) Cath. Ctrl. High Sch., 1979-84; adminstrv. asst., dir. ministries Nouvel High Sch., Saginaw, Mich., 1984-85; acad. dean, counselor, tchr. St. Joseph's on the Rio Grande High Sch., Albuquerque, 1985-87; tchr. Holy Ghost Elem. Sch., Albuquerque, 1988-89; grad. asst. edn. dept. St. Louis (Mo.) U., 1991-93; from asst. to assoc. prof. edn. U. Detroit Mercy, 1993—; project adminstr. Our Lady of Guadalupe Mid. Sch., Detroit, 1997-99; dir. cert. and field experiences U. Detroit Mercy, 1999—. Mem. edn. com. Sisters of Mercy, Farmington Hills, Mich., 1990-93; CHRPN, 1993-96; literacy program evaluator Macomb County Headstart, Mt. Clemens, Mich., 1990; curriculum cons. St. Mary's H.S., St. Louis, 1991. Co-author: Valuing Our Differences, 9-12, 1992, K-8, 1993. Mem. ASCD, Assn. Univ. Women, Mercy Secondary Edn. Assn., Mercy Elem. Edn. Network, Phi Delta Kappa, Pi Lambda Theta. Roman Catholic. Avocations: writing poetry, photography, calligraphy. E-mail: stoeckca@udmercy.edu.

STOELTJE, BEVERLY JUNE, liberal studies educator; b. Rotan, Tex., Apr. 1, 1940; d. Roger Caswell and Laura Inez (Kennedy) Smith; children: Gretchen, Rachael; m. Richard Bauman, Nov. 26, 1977; children: Mark, Andrew. BA, U. Tex., 1961, MA, 1975, PhD, 1979. Asst. prof. English U. Tex., Austin, 1983-86; assoc. prof. anthropology, folklore/ethnomusicology Ind. U., Bloomington, 1986—, also mem. African studies faculty, Am. studiesEat. Cons. S.W. Ednl. Devel. Lab., Austin, 1976, Tex. Women's History Project, San Antonio, 1981; dir. Folk Arts Survey Tex., Austin, 1977, 78; dir. USIA linkage on performance Ind. U. and U. Ghana, 1989-93; assoc. dir. Ind. Ctr. on Global Change and World Peace, 1994-95. Author: Children's Handclaps, 1979; editor: (with C.B. Cohen and R. Wilk) Beauty Queens on the Global Stage, 1996; editor (essay collection) Feminist Revision in Folklore Studies, 1988, Women, Language, and Law in Africa, 2002; contbr. articles to profl. jours. and chpts. in books. Fulbright rsch. fellow Ghana, 1989-90; grantee Tex Commn. for Humanities, 1980; Weatherhead scholar Sch. Am. Rsch., 1997-98. Mem. African Studies Assn., Am. Folklore Soc. (exec. bd. 1981-84), Am. Anthropol. Assn., Law and Soc. Office: Dept Anthropology Student Bldg Ind U Bloomington IN 47405

STOFFREGEN, GERTRUDE BOETTCHER, retired gifted education educator; b. Altenburg, Mo., Feb. 25, 1929; d. Albert G.L. and Rose Maria (Schulz) Boettcher; m. H. Jack Stoffregen, Dec. 28, 1952 (dec. Apr. 1990); children: Jonathan, Nathan. BS, Concordia U., 1956, MA, 1963. Tchr. 1st St. Paul Luth. Ch., Jackson, Mo., Our Savior Luth. Ch., Chgo., Cmty. Consol. Sch. Dist. 59, Elk Grove Village, Ill., tchr. of gifted children, chair lang. arts, sec. Presenter in field. Author: History of Lutheran Church of the Holy Spirit. Pres. ForestView Homeowners Assn., Elk Grove Village, 1968-74; sec. Detroit Island Landowners Assn., Door County, Wis., 1971—; chairperson Luth. Ch. Bd. Edn., 1989-94; pres. Luth. Ch. Holy Spirit, 1989-94. Avocations: choral singing, handbell ringing, gardening, reading, travelling. Home: 314 Forest View Ave Elk Grove Village IL 60007-4325

STOKELY, JOAN BARBARA, retired elementary school educator; b. Cleve., May 6, 1945; d. Paul Warner and Florence Leona (Sorensen) S. BS, Lamar U., 1967, M Elem. Edn., 1970. Cert. tchr., adminstr., Tex. 4th grade tchr. Vidor (Tex.) Ind. Sch. Dist., 1967-74, 88-94, 5th grade tchr., 1974-77, 7th and 8th grade tchr., 1979-88; grad. equivalency diploma tchr. Beaumont Ind. Sch. Dist., Vidor, 1977-81, kindergarten to 4th grade Apple Lab Mastery tchr., 1994—2001, 2nd grade tchr., 2001—02, ret., 2002—; tchrs. aide mothers day out, 2002—. K-4th grade computer lab mastery tchr. of basic skills in math and reading. Pres. Vidor Tchrs. Fed. Credit Union, 1985—2000; mem. troop com. Boy Scouts Am., Vidor, 1972-83; tchr. Roman Cath. Chs., Beaumont, Tex., 1967-87; tchr's aide Mother's Day Out, 2003—. Mem. AAUW, DAR, Tex. State Tchrs. Assn. (pres. Vidor chpt. 1990-94, chmn. uniserve adv. coun. region 15 1991-92, sec. region 15 1993-96), Tex. Computer Edn. Assn., Colonial Dames (chpt. registrar 1997-99, treas. 1999—). Avocations: genealogy, handicrafts, writing, travel.

STOKER, HOWARD W. former education educator, educational administrator, consultant; b. Highland Park, Ill., July 20, 1925; s. Howard W. and Elsie S.; m. M. Annette Stoker, July 9, 1949; children: Joanne, Dianna, Patricia, Robert. EdB, Wis. State U., Whitewater, 1949; MA, State U. Iowa, 1950; PhD, Purdue U., 1957. H.S. tchr. Dixon (Ill.) Pub. Schs., 1950-55; prof. Fla. State U., Tallahassee, 1957-84; head instrnl. devel. and evaluation U. Tenn., Memphis, 1984-88, vis. prof. Knoxville, 1988-89, rsch. prof. Coll. Edn., 1989-92; ednl. cons. H.W. Stoker, Inc., Knoxville, 1992—. Sr. assoc. prof. Ednl. Testing Svc./So. Regional Office, Atlanta, 1979-80; test devel. cons. State of Tenn., 1989—; cons. in field. Editor Fla. Jour. Ednl. Rsch., 1974-83; contbr. chpts. to books and articles to profl. jours. With USN, 1944-46. Mem. Am. Edn. Rsch. Assn., Nat. Coun. on Measurement in Edn. (bd. mem.). Avocations: crafts, carving, swimming.

STOKES, ALLISON, pastor, researcher, religion educator; b. Bridgeport, Conn., Aug. 17, 1942; d. Hugh Vincent and Mildred Roberta (Livengood) Allison; m. Jerome Walter Stokes, June 1, 1964 (div. 1977); children: Jonathan Jerome, Anne Jennings. BA, U. N.C., 1964; MPhil, Yale U., 1976, PhD, MDiv, Yale U., 1981; ThM, Harvard U., 1997. Ordained to ministry United Ch. of Christ, 1981. Acting univ. min. Wesleyan U., Middletown, Conn., 1981; assoc. pastor Orange Congl. Ch., Conn., 1981-82; chaplain, asst. prof. religion Vassar Coll., Poughkeepsie, N.Y., 1982-85; assoc. univ. chaplain Yale U., New Haven, 1985-87; pastor Congl. Ch., West Stockbridge, Mass., 1987—; rsch. assoc. Hartford (Conn.) Sem., 1987-92; founding dir. Women's Interfaith Inst. in the Berkshires, 1992—. Bd. dirs. Dutchess Interfaith Coun., Poughkeepsie, 1984-85; bd. dirs. Gould Farm, Monterey, Mass., 1992—, pres. bd. dirs., 1997—. Author: Ministry after Freud, 1985, Finding Time, Finding Energy, 1996; co-author: Defecting in Place, 1994, Women Pastors, 1995; contbr. articles to profl. jours. Kanzer Fund Psychoanalysis and Humanities grantee, 1977; AAUW fellow, 1978, Merrill fellow Harvard Div. Sch., 1994. Mem. Am. Acad. Religion, Kiwanis. Home: PO Box 422 Housatonic MA 01236-0422 Office: Conregational Church 45 Main St West Stockbridge MA 01266-9707

STOKES, CATHERINE ANN, elementary education educator; b. N.Y.C., Jan. 26, 1951; d. Matthew John and Joanna Elizabeth (McEllen) Coffey; m. Edward Martin Stokes, Aug. 10, 1974; children: Matthew, Michael. AA, Suffolk Community Coll., 1970; BA, SUNY, Potsdam, 1972; MEd, SUNY, New Paltz, 1974; postgrad., L.I. U., 1988. Cert. elem. tchr., N.Y. 6th grade tchr. Rombout Sch., Beacon, N.Y., 1972-77; 5th grade tchr. S. Ave. Elem. Sch., Beacon, 1978-91, elem. sci. coord., 1989-91; tchr. Rombout Mid. Sch., Beacon, 1991—. Troop program coord. Boy Scouts Am., 2001—; coord. Beacon Young Playwrights Festival, 2002—03. Recipient award Nat. Energy Edn. Day Com., 1987, Outstanding Sci. Tchrs. award Sci. Tchrs. Assn. N.Y. State, 1987; NSF grantee, 1986-88. Mem. NEA, Nat. Sci. Tchrs. Assn. Avocations: science magic, reading, sports, crafts. Office: Rombout Mid Sch Mattewan Rd Beacon NY 12508

STOKES, MELISSA ANNE, special education educator; b. Washington, July 10, 1968; d. Ronald Blaine and Jane Ellen (Morrison) S. BA in Psychology magna cum laude, Coll. Notre Dame Md., Balt., 1991; MEd in Spl. Edn., Loyola Coll. Md., Balt., 1993. Cert. secondary spl. edn. tchr., Md. Tchr. St. Elizabeth Sch. and Habilitation Ctr., Balt., 1992-93; spl. educator Perryville (Md.) Elem. Sch., 1993-94, Perryville High Sch., 1994—, reading specialist, 1993—. Mem. Kappa Gamma Pi, Delta Epsilon Sigma, Psi Chi. Avocations: running, weight lifting, rock climbing, camping, walking. Office: Perryville High Sch 1696 Perryville Rd Perryville MD 21903-2541

STOKES, ROSA, educational administrator; 1 child from previous marriage, Kellé Marie; m. James Milton Stokes. BS in Sociology and Social Work, Morgan State U., Balt., 1971; MS in Spl. Edn., Coppin State U., Balt., 1983; postgrad., Johns Hopkins U., 1992—. Cert. in advanced studies, evaluation, group process and leadership advanced proficiency, Md. Med. social worker Balt. City Hosp., 1971-73; salesperson Equitable Life Assurance Soc., Balt., 1977-79; tchr. Balt. City Pub. Schs., 1985-92, asst. prin. J. Briscoe Sch., 1992—, coord. Project Respond, 1992-94, exec. dir. Project Respond, 1994—. Mem. adv. bd. Project Succeed, Balt., 1990-92, Project Raise, Morgan State U., 1991-92; cons. Family Preservation Initiative, Balt., 1994—. Coord. bicentennial N.W. Area Ctrl. Md., Girl Scouts U.S.A., Balt., 1976; sec. Jack and Jill, Balt., 1991-93; advisor Balt. State U.-Friends Sch., 1992-94. Mem. ASCD, NEA, Pub. Sch. Tchrs. Am., Balt. City Internat. Reading Assn., NAACP, Phi Delta Kappa.

STOLL, SARAH MAY REICHERT, elementary school educator; b. Torrington, Wyo., Nov. 8, 1967; d. Fred L. and Delores J. (See) Reichert. AA, Ea. Wyo. Coll., 1988; BA, U. Wyo., 1990. Tutor math. and English Ea. Wyo. Coll., Torrington, 1987-88; sec. range mgmt. dept. U. Wyo., Laramie, 1989-90; Tchr. 4th grade Fremont County Sch. Dist. #38, Arapahoe (Wyo.) Sch, 1991—. Mem. NEA, ASCD, Wyo. Edn. Assn., U. Wyo. Alumni Assn.

STOLLAR, VICTOR, microbiology educator; b. Saskatoon, Sask., Can., Dec. 6, 1933; s. Percy and Rose (Dirnfield) S.; children: Lisa, Miriam, Anna. MDCM, Queens U., 1956. Intern Montreal (Que.) Gen. Hosp., 1956-57; resident Boston City Hosp., 1957-58; research fellow biochemistry dept. Brandeis U., Waltham, Mass., 1958-60, 61-62; cardiology fellow Beth Israel Hosp., Boston, 1960-61; research fellow Weizmann Inst., Rehovot, Israel, 1962-65; asst. prof. microbiology Rutgers Med. Sch., Piscataway, N.J., 1965-70, assoc. prof., 1970-75; prof. microbiology Robert Wood Johnson Med. Sch., Piscataway, 1975—. Mem. study sect. virology NIH, Bethesda, Md., 1980-83. Assoc. editor Virology, 1975—; mem. editl. bd. Jour. Virology, 1997-2003; contbr. articles to profl. jours. Recipient Univ. Excellence award in biomed. rsch., U. Medicine and Dentistry of N.J., 1995. Democrat. Jewish. Office: Robert Wood Johnson Med Sch 675 Hoes Ln Piscataway NJ 08854-5627

STOLOFF, CAROLYN, artist, poet, educator; b. N.Y.C., Jan. 14, 1927; Student, U. Ill., 1944-46; pupil of, Zavier Gonzalez, Eric Isenburger, Hans Hofmann, Stanley Kunitz; BS in Painting, Columbia U., 1949. Tchr. painting and drawing Manhattanville Coll., Purchase, N.Y., 1957-74, chmn. art history and studio art, 1960-65, seminar in writing and poetry, 1969-74; tchr. English and creative writing Baird House, 1973; vis. writer Stephens Coll., 1975; instr. Hamilton Coll., 1985. Vis. writer summer writers' workshop U. Rochester, NY, 1985. One-woman shows include Dubin Gallery, Phila., Manhattanville Coll. Gallery, 1957, 67, Arts and Crafts Gallery, Wellfleet, Mass., Open Studio, 1984, 87, Atlantic Gallery, 1985, Donnell Libr., Fine Pub. Libr., N.J., 1989, Pine Pub. Libr., Fairlawn, N.J., 1989, Tom Kendall Gallery, N.Y.C., 1990, others; exhibited in group shows at Whitney Mus., 1951, ACA Gallery, Audubon Artists, Pa. Acad. Fine Arts, Silvermine Guild, Nat. Assn. Women Artists, Krasner Gallery, City Ctr. Gallery, Laurel Gallery, Knickerbocker Artists, L.I. League of Painters and Sculptors, N.J. Soc. Painters and Sculptors, Nat. Exhbn. Contemporary Art U.S. in Los Angeles, Oakland Art Mus., Arthur Brown Gallery, Nat. Assn. Women Artists, 1986, Graphics Jury Audubon Artists, 1987, others. Author: Stepping Out, 1971; Dying to Survive, 1973; In the Red Meadow, 1973; Lighter-than-Night Verse, 1977; Swiftly Now, 1982; A Spool of blue, New and Selected Poems, 1983, You Came to Meet Someone Else, 1993, (collection of poetry) Reaching for Honey, 2003; contbr. poems to mags., anthologies. Vol. tutor Poets in Pub. Svc., 1989—90, Pub. Schs., 1995—96. Grantee MacDowell Colony, 1961, 62, 70, 76, Helene Wurlitzer Found., 1972, 73, 74, Ossabaw Island Project, 1976, R.I. Creative Arts Ctr., 1981, Michael Karolyi Meml. Found., 1983, Va. Ctr. Creative Arts, 1985, 1988, Millay Colony for th eArts, 1987, UCROSS Found., 1992; recipient Theodore Roethke award Poetry Northwest, 1967, Silver Ann. medal Audubon Artists, 1967, Achievement award Nat. Council on Arts, 1968, 1st prize for poetry Miscellany, 1972, Michael M. Engel Sr. Meml. award Audubon Artists, 1982, 3d place Concrete Poetry Competition, Gamut, 1983, Robert Philipps Meml. award for painting, 1990, Daler-Rowney award for oil painting, 1994, Art Students League award for oil, 1995, Grumbacher Gold medal for oils, 1998, Vi Gale award for poetry, 1999, Emily Lowe award for oil painting, 2000. Home: 24 W 8th St New York NY 10011-9019 Office: 32 Union Sq E Rm 911 New York NY 10003-3209

STOLOFF, DAVID L. education educator, academic administrator, web site designer; b. Bronx, N.Y., June 17, 1952; s. Martin and Florence (Rosen) S.; m. Deborah Leah Narotsky, Nov. 10, 1985; children: Nathan Benjamin, Charles Abraham, Daniel Harry, Florence Rose. BS in Biology, SUNY, Brockport, 1973; MA in Ednl. Tech., Concordia U., Montreal, 1977; PhD in Comparative and Internat. Edn., UCLA, 1982. Cert. life scis. tchr. N.Y., Tex., Calif. Sci., TEFL tchr. Peace Corp., Kinshasa, Chibambo, Zaire, 1973-75; tchr. Mollie Goodman Acad. H.S., Ashkelon, Israel, 1975-76; ednl. rschr. Dallas Indep. Sch. Dist., 1977-78; tchr. Long Beach (Calif.) Poly. H.S., 1982-84; asst. prof. SUNY, Plattsburgh, N.Y., 1984-86; assoc. prof. Calif. State U., L.A., 1986-90; prof. Sonoma State U., Rohnert Park, Calif., 1990-95; prof. edn., chmn. dept. East Conn. State U., Willimantic, 1995-97, 98—, interim dean Sch. Edn. and Profl. Studies, 1997-98. Co-prodr.: (video) Mosaic City, 1977; web page developer. Bd. dirs. Temple B'nai Israel, Willimantic, 1997-2001, Windham Hosp., Willimantic. Calif. Acad. Partnership Program grant Calif. State U., 1987-90; grant Conn. State U., 1997; fellow Bush Program Child Devel. and Social Policy, 1980-82. Mem. Conn. Distance Learning Consortium, Assn. State Tech. Using Tchr. Educators (pres. 1993-95), Calif. Faculty Assn. (Sonoma State chpt., pres. 1993-95), Phi Delta Kappa. Avocations: travel, gardening, science fiction. Home: 86 Pigeon Rd Willimantic CT 06226-1321 Office: Eastern Conn State U 83 Windham St Willimantic CT 06226-2211

STOLOFF, NORMAN STANLEY, materials engineering educator, researcher; b. Bklyn., Oct. 16, 1934; s. William F. and Lila (Dickman) S.; m. Helen Teresa Arcuri, May 15, 1971; children: Michael E., Linda M., David M., Stephen L. BMetE, NYU, 1955; MS, Columbia U., 1956, PhD, 1961. Metall. engr. Pratt & Whitney Aircraft, East Hartford, Conn., 1956-58; prin. rsch. scientist Ford Sci. Lab., Dearborn, Mich., 1961-65; asst. prof. materials engring. Rensselaer Polytechnic Inst., Troy, N.Y., 1965-68, assoc. prof., 1968-71, prof., 1971-97, prof. emeritus, 1997—. Cons. Electric Boat div. Gen. Dynamics, New London, Conn., 1987-89, Martin Marietta Rsch. Labs., Balt., 1990, Rockwell Internat., Thousand Oaks, Calif., 1989, Cummins Engine Co., Columbus, Ind., 1991. Editor: (with others) High Temperature Ordered Intermetallic Alloys, 1985, Superalloys II, 1987, Physical Metallurgy and Processing of Intermetallic Compounds, 1996, others; contbr. articles to profl. jours. Recipient Fulbright Rsch. award U.S. State Dept., 1968-69, DOE Fellowship Assoc. Western U., 1995. Fellow Am. Soc. Materials Internat.; mem. The Minerals, Metals and Materials Soc., Materials Rsch. Soc. Avocations: hiking, fishing, reading. Office: Rensselaer Polytechnic Inst Dept Materials Sci Engring MRC Bldg Troy NY 12180-3590 E-mail: stolon@rpi.edu.

STOLPER, EDWARD MANIN, secondary education educator; b. Boston, Dec. 16, 1952; s. Saul James and Frances A. (Liberman) S.; m. Lauren Beth Adoff, June 3, 1973; children: Jennifer Ann, Daniel Aaron. AB, Harvard U., 1974; M Philosophy, U. Edinburgh, Scotland, 1976; PhD, Harvard U., 1979. Asst. prof. geology Calif. Inst. Tech., Pasadena, 1979-82, assoc. prof. geology, 1982-83, prof. geology, 1983-90, William E. Leonhard prof. geology, 1990—, chmn. divsn. geol. and planetary sci., 1994—. Marshall scholar Marshall Aid Commemoration Commn., 1974-76, recipient Newcomb Cleve. prize AAAS, 1984, F.W. Clarke medal Geochem. Soc., 1985, Arthur Holmes medal European Union Geosci., 1997; Geochemistry fellow The Geochem. Soc. and The European Assn. for Geochemistry, 1997. Fellow Meteoritical Soc. (Nininger Meteorite award 1976), Am. Geophys. Union (James B. Macelwane award 1986), Mineral Soc. Am., Am. Acad. Arts and Scis.; mem. NAS, Geol. Soc. Am., Sigma Xi. Office: Calif Inst Tech Div Geol Planetary Sci Pasadena CA 91125-0001

STOLWIJK, JAN ADRIANUS JOZEF, physiologist, biophysicist; b. Amsterdam, The Netherlands, Sept. 29, 1927; came to U.S., 1955, naturalized, 1962; s. Leonard and Cornelia Agnes (Van Der Bijl) S.; m. Deborah Rose, 1990. BS, Wageningen U., The Netherlands, 1948, MS, 1951, PhD, 1955. Biophysicist John B. Pierce Found., New Haven, 1957-61; assoc. fellow John B. Pierce Found. Lab., 1961-64, fellow, 1964, assoc. dir., 1974-89; instr. dept. physiology Yale U. Sch. Medicine, New Haven, 1962-63, asst. prof., 1964-68, asst. prof. epidemiology, 1968-69, assoc. prof., 1969-75, prof., 1975-99, dir. grad. studies, dept. epidemiology and public health, 1992-99, chmn. dept. epidemiology and pub. health, 1982-89; rsch. fellow Harvard U., 1955-56. Cons. divsn. disease prevention Conn. Health Dept., 1977-99; cons. vehicle inspection program Dept. Motor Vehicles, 1979-83; mem. sci. adv. bd. EPA, 1985-93; mem. tech. adv. bd. Dept. Commerce, 1972-77. Mem. Am. Physiol. Soc., Biophys. Soc., Aerospace Med. Soc., Am. Public Health Assn., AAAS, Internat. Biometeorol. Soc., Soc. Occupational and Environ. Health, Am. Conf. Govt. Indsl. Hygienists, ASHRAE, Conn. Acad. Sci. and Engring. Clubs: Cosmos. Home: 165 Dromara Rd Guilford CT 06437-2391 Office: PO Box 8034 60 College St New Haven CT 06510-3210 E-mail: stolwijk@prodigy.net.

STOLZENBERG, LISA ANN, education educator; b. Hollywood, Fla., July 15, 1963; d. Joel and Doris S.; m. Stewart John D'Alessio, July 19, 1999. PhD, Fla. State U., Tallahassee, 1993. Rsch. asst. Fla. State U., Tallahassee, 1985—86; rsch. analyst Fla. Dept. Corrections, Tallahassee, 1986—88; program evaluator Fla. Dept. Health and Rehab. Svcs., Tallahassee, 1988—90; social sci. analyst Westat Inc., Rockville, Md., 1990—91; rsch. assoc. Justice Rsch. and Statistics Assn., Washington, 1992—93; asst. prof. Fla. Internat. U., Miami, 1996—2002, assoc. prof., 2002—. Cons. Nat. Rsch. Coun. Washington, 1990, Westat, Inc., Rockville, Md., 1992-93, Ind. U.-Purdue U., Indpls., 1994-96. Author: Criminal Courts for the 21st Century, 1999, 2d edit., 2002; contbr. articles to profl. jours. Grantee Ind. U., 1994, Ind. U.-Purdue U. Indpls., 1994, Purdue U., 1996, Nat. Inst. Justice, 1996, 2003, Fla. Dept. Children and Families, 2000. Mem. Nat. Inst. Justice, Am. Soc. Criminology, Acad. Criminal Justice Scis., Am. Sociol. Assn., So. Sociol. Soc. Avocation: motorcycle riding. Office: Fla Internat U University Park PCA-260A Miami FL 33199 Fax: 305-348-5848. E-mail: stolzenb@fiu.edu.

STOMFAY-STITZ, ALINE MARIA, education educator; b. Newark, N.J. d. Adolph and Irene (Badowska) Wegrocki; m. Emery Stomfay-Stitz (dec.); children: Peter, John, Robert. BA, Barnard Coll.; MA, Case Western Reserve U.; EdD, No. Ill. U., 1984. Asst. prof. Coll. St Scholastica, Duluth, Minn., 1984-85, St. Leo (Fla.) Coll., 1985-87, Nicholls State U., Thibodaux, La., 1989-91; assoc. prof. edn. Christopher Newport U., Newport News, Va., 1991-96. Vis. prof., assoc. prof. edn. U. No. Fla., Jacksonville, 1996-2003; assoc. editor Joun. Early Childhood Tchr. Edn. Author: Peace Education in America 1828-1990, 1993; author (book chpt.): Toward Education That is Multicultural, 1992, Multicultural Education for the 21st Century, 1993; contbr. articles to profl. jours. Mem.: Internat. Peace Rsch. Assn., Nat. Assn. for Early Childhood Tchrs. Educators, Am. Ednl. Rsch. Assn. (SIG exec. com.). E-mail: stitzA@bellsouth.net.

STONE, ALAN JAY, retired college administrator; b. Ft. Dodge, Iowa, Oct. 15, 1942; s. Hubert H. and Bernice A. (Tilton) S.; m. Jonieta J. Smith; 1 child, Kirsten K. Stone Morlock. BA, Morningside Coll., 1964; MA, U. Iowa, 1966; MTh, U. Chgo., 1968, DMin, 1970; PhD (hon.), Kyonggi U., Korea, 1985; LLD, Stillman Coll., 1991, Sogong U., Korea, 1992, Alma Coll., 2001; HD, Morningside Coll., 2001. Admissions counselor Morningside Coll., Sioux City, Iowa, 1964-66; dir. admissions, asso. prof. history George Williams Coll., Downers Grove, Ill., 1969-73; v.p. coll. relations Hood Coll., Frederick, Md., 1973-75; v.p. devel. and fin. affairs W.Va. Wesleyan Coll., Buckhannon, 1975-77; dir. devel. U. Maine, 1977-78; pres. Aurora (Ill.) U., 1978-88, Alma (Mich.) Coll., 1988-2000; pres., CEO Alzheimer's Assn., Chgo., 2001—02; ret., 2002. Home: 28897 N 94th Pl Scottsdale AZ 85262 E-mail: stone5613@earthlink.net.

STONE, ALFRED WARD, educator; b. Meadville, Pa., Aug. 13, 1925; s. Clifford Alsworths and Freda (Bruehl) S.; m. Dolores Stone, Dec. 1, 1951 (div.); children: Clifford, John, Bonalyn, David; m. Mary L. Girardat, June 1, 1968; 1 child, 1 Scott. BA in Econs., Allegheny Coll., 1950, MEd, 1957; PhD in Psychology, U. Pitts., 1978; postgrad., U. So. Calif., L.A., 1979. Phys. boys sec. YMCA, Meadville, 1952-57, state sec. Harrisburg, Pa., 1957-62, acting exec. sec. Allentown, Pa., 1962-63; exec. dir. War on Poverty, C.A.P., Meadville, 1964-67; prof. emeritus psychology dept., co-dir. gerontology program Edinboro (Pa.) U., 1967—93. Host TV program Understanding People, 1970—; chmn. Regional Cmty. Svcs., Inc.; coord. gerontology programs Edinboro U. Bd. dirs. Westbury Meth. Cmty., West Pa. Health Smart; pres., mem. Profl. Assn. of Specialists of Aging, N.W. Pa., 1978-86; dir. programs for children Milkhaus Found. With U.S. Mcht. Marine, USCG, 1943-46, U.S. Army, 1950-52. Mem. APHA, APA, Gerontol. Soc. Am. Avocations: painting, reading, golfing. Home: 220 Meadville St Edinboro PA 16412-2558 Office: Edinboro U Intergenerational Ctr Edinboro PA 16444-0001

STONE, CYNTHIA MARIE BEAVERS, dancing and gymnastics educator; b. Roanoke, Va., Mar. 3, 1952; d. Thomas Lane and Nannie Ruth (Brown) Beavers. BA, Birmingham So. Coll., 1974. Dance dir. Cobb County Parks and Recreation, Marietta, Ga., 1974-77; program dir. Camp Chattoga, Tallulah Falls, Ga., 1974—; dir. Chattooga Sch. of Gymnastics and Dance, Marietta, 1976—. Coach Cobb County YMCA, Marietta, 1976; tchr. Peachtree Presbyn. Ch., Atlanta, 1980—; Chattooga dir. Friendship Ambs., Upper Montclair, N.J., 1983, 92. Choreographer opening ceremony Ga. State Games, 1991, 92; internat. choreographer compulsory routines Spl. Olympics, 1991; asst. choreographer closing ceremonies Skate Am., Atlanta, 1992. Dir. rhythmic gymnastics competition Ga. Spl. Olympics, 1992—; counselor Camp Sunshine, Atlanta, 1988—, sport chmn. Ga. State Games, Atlanta, 1990—. Mem. U.S. Gymnastics Fedn. (safety cert., level I coach cert., rhythmic state chmn. 1985-91, rhythmic regional chmn. region VIII 1991—), Ga. Gymnastic Coaches Assn. (pres. 1978-80), Ga. Presch. Assn., Mortar Bd., Phi Beta Kappa, Alpha Lambda Delta. Methodist. Avocations: horseback riding, ballet. Home: 500 Marsh Creek Ct NW Atlanta GA 30328-2111 Office: Chattooga 4005 Canton Rd Marietta GA 30066-2739

STONE, DEBRA LYNN (DEBBIE STONE), elementary education educator; b. Washington, Ind., Aug. 18, 1956; d. Gerald Leo and Agnes Ilene (Wade) Mangin; m. Richard Brice Stone, June 10, 1978; children: Jonathan, Christopher. AS in Elem. Edn., Vincennes U., 1976; BS, Ind. State U., 1978, MS, 1984. Cert. K-6 tchr., 7-8 tch., Ind. Sec. Ind. U., Bloomington, 1978-79; Chpt. I tchr. reading and math. Barr Reeve Intermediate Sch., Montgomery, Ind., 1979-80; 3d grade tchr. Edgewood Intermed Sch., Bloomington, 1980. Faculty chair Ellettsville Elem. Sch., 1990-94, 86-88, mem. tchr. assistance team, 1992—. Mem. bd. edn. St. John's Cath. Ch., Bloomington, 1988-89, eucharistic min., mass coord., 1995—; band parent Edgewood Jr. H.S., Ellettsville, 1993-95; treas. PTA Ellettsville Elem. Sch., 1994-95. Mem. Alpha Delta Kappa (pres. Beta Zeta chpt. 1994-96). Avocations: sons' sporting and show choir activities, family activities, reading, gardening. Home: 4103 Jay Stewart Ln Ellettsville IN 47429-9594 Office: Edgewood Intermed Sch 7600 W Reeves Rd Bloomington IN 47404

STONE, EDWARD C. physicist, educator; b. Knoxville, Iowa, Jan. 23, 1936; s. Edward Carroll and Ferne Elizabeth (Baber) Stone; m. Alice Trabue Wickliffe, Aug. 4, 1962; children: Susan, Janet. AA, Burlington Jr. Coll., 1956; MS, U. Chgo., 1959, PhD, 1964, DSc (hon.), 1992, Washington U., St. Louis, 1992, Harvard U., 1992; BA (hon.), U. So. Calif., 1998. From rsch. fellow in physics to prof. Calif. Inst. Tech., Pasadena, Calif., 1964—94, v.p., 1964—91, Voyager project scientist, 1972—, David Morrisioe prof. physics, fellow, 1994—, chmn. divsn. physics, math. and astron., 1983—88, v.p. jet propulsion lab., 1991—2001, Morrisroe prof. physics, 1994—; mem. of lab. Draper Lab., 2001. Cons. Office of Space Sci., NASA, 1969—85, adv. com. outer planets, 1972—73; high energy astrophysics mgmt. oper. working group NASA, 1976—84, cosmic ray program working group, 1980—82, outer plantets working group, 1981—82, solar sys. exploration com., 1981—83, U. rels. study group, 1983; exec. com. Com. on Space Rsch. Interdisciplinary Sci. Commn., 1982—86; com. on space astronomy and astrophysics Space Sci. Bd., 1979—82, steering group study on maj. directions for space sci., 1984—85; mem. Space Sci. Bd., NRC, 1982—85; commn. on phys. sci., math. and resources NRC, 1986—89; adv. com. vis. sr. scientist program NASA/Jet Propulsion Labs., 1986—90; com. on space policy NAS/NAE, 1988—89; chmn., chief sci. advisor The Astronomers, KCET, 1989—91; chmn. adv. panel NAS/WQED TV program "Sail on, Voyager!", 1989—90; Morrisive prof. physics Jet Propulsion Lab., 1994—; v.p., COSPAR Bur., 2001—. Mem. editl. bd. Space Sci. Instrumentation, 1975—81, Space Sci. Rev., 1982—85, Astrophysics and Space Sci., 1982—, Sci. mag. Bd. dir. W.M. Keck Found., 1994—. Named an asteroid Edward C. Stone in his honor, 1996; named to Hall of Fame, Aviation Week and Space Tech., 1997, Hall of Honor, Burlington Comm., 1999; recipient medal for exceptional sci. achievement, NASA, 1980, Am. Edn. award, 1981, Disting. Svc. medal, 1981, 1998, 2001, Dryden award, 1983, Disting. Pub. Svc. medal, 1985, Outstanding Leadership medal, 1986, 1995, Achievement award, Soc. for Tech. Comm., 1984, Space Achievement award, AIAA, 1986, Oppenheimer Mem. Lecture Aviation Week and Space Tech. Aerospace Laureate, 1989, Sci. Man of Yr. award, ARCS Found., 1991, Nat. Medal of Sci., 1991, Golden Plate award, Am. Acad. Achievement, 1992, COSPAR award, 1992, LeRoy Randle Grumman medal, 1992, Disting. Pub. Svc. award, Aviation/Space Writers Assn., 1993, Internat. von Karman Wings award, 1996, Space Flight Award, Am. Astron. Soc., 1997, Alumni award, S.E. C.C., Burlington, Iowa, 1997, CEO of Yr. award, ARC, 1998, Allan D. Emil Meml. award, Internat. Astronautical Fedn., 1999, Carl Sagan award, Am. Astronautical Soc. and Planetary Soc., 1999, Prof. Achievement award, Alumni, U. Chgo., 2002, Nat. Award for Op., Assn. for Unmanned Sys., Nat. Medal of Sci., Pres. Bush; fellow Sloan Found., 1971—73. Fellow: AAAS (award 1993), AIAA (assoc.; Calif. coun. sci. and tech. 1996—2001, Space Sci. award 1984, von Karman lectureshp in astronautics 1999), Internat. Aero. Union, Am. Geophys. Union, Am. Phys. Soc. (exec. com. 1974—76, chmn. cosmic physics divsn. 1979—80); mem.: NAS, Sci. Edit. Bd., Comm. of Phys. Sci., Math., and Applications, NRC, Am. Phil. Soc., Calif. Assn. Rsch. in Astronomy (vice-chmn. 1986—2003, chmn. bd. dirs. 1994—97, 2000—03, bd. dir., vice-chmn. 1986—88, 1991—94, 1997—2000), Astron. Soc. Pacific (hon.), Royal Aeronautical Soc., Nat. Space Club (bd. gov., Sci. award 1990), Am. Philos. Soc. (Magellanic award 1992), Am. Astron. Soc. (divsn. planetary sci. com. 1981—84, Space Flight award 1997), Internat. Acad. Astronautics (trustee 1989—2001, v.p. 2001—). Office: Calif Inst Tech Space Radiation Lab M/C 220-47 Pasadena CA 91125

STONE, ELIZABETH CECILIA, anthropology educator; b. Oxford, Eng., Feb. 4, 1949; d. Lawrence and Jeanne Cecilia (Fawtier) S.; m. Paul Edmund Zimansky, Nov. 5, 1976. BA, U. Pa., 1971; MA, Harvard U., 1973; PhD, U. Chgo., 1979. Lectr. anthropology SUNY, Stony Brook, 1977-78, asst. prof., 1978-85, assoc. prof., 1985-95, prof., 1995—2002. Participated archaeol. in Eng., Iran, Iraq, Afghanistan; dir. archaeol. projects Ain Dara, Syria,, Tell Abu Duwari, Iraq, Ayanis Survey, Turkey. Author: Nippur Neighborhoods, 1987; co-author: (monograph) Old Babylonian Contracts from Nippur 1, 1976, Adoption in Old Babylonian Nippur and the Archive of Mannum-meshu-lissur, 1991, The Iron Age Settlement at Ain Dara, Syria, 1999; co-editor: The Cradle of Civilization Recent Archaeology in Iraq-Biblical Archaeologist, 1992, Velles Paraules: Ancient Near Eastern Studies in Honor of Miguel Civil on the Occasion of His 65th Birthday, 1991; mem. editl. bd. Bull. Am. Schs. Oriental Rsch., 1993-95, 99—; contbr. articles to profl. jours. Assoc. trustee Am. Schs. of Oriental Rsch., 1983-90. Fulbright fellow, 1986-87; rsch. grantee Ford Found., 1974, Nat. Geog. Soc., 1983, 84, 88, 90, 97-99, 2002, 03, Am. Schs. of Oriental Rsch., 1987, 88, NSF, 1989-92, 2000-02, NEH, 1989-93. Office: SUNY Dept Anthropology Stony Brook NY 11794-0001 E-mail: estone@notes.cc.sunysb.edu.

STONE, ELIZABETH WALKER, English educator; b. Washington, Aug. 17, 1921; d. Micajah Theodore and Isabelle Morris (Grinnage) Walker; m. Frank Daniel Reeves (div.); children: Deborah E., Daniel R.; m. French Franklin Stone. BA in English, Howard U., 1940, MA in Am. Lit., 1942; MFA in Drama, Cath. U. Am., 1948; EdD in Speech and Drama, Columbia U., 1956. From instr. to asst. prof. liberal arts Howard U., Washington, 1944-55; supr. speech therapists D.C. Pub. Schs., Washington, 1955-58; assoc. prof. speech and drama D.C. Tchrs. Coll., Washington, 1958-62; edn. specialist ISIA, Washington, 1965-67; dep. dir. Internat. Agy. Com. on Mexican-Am. Affairs, Washington, 1967-69; dir. univs. and founds. divsn. U.S. Dept. of Commerce, Washington, 1969-71; dir. stds. for edn. instns. Social and Rehab./HEW, Washington, 1971-73, dir. tng., 1973-75; dir. comm. skills Howard U. Sch. Law, Washington, 1975-90; writer, 1990—. Editor: Higher Education Aid for Minority Business, 1970; author, dir. (TV documentary) High Expectations, 1988 (Gannett award 1989); contbr. articles to profl. jours. Writer seconding nomination speech J.F. Kennedy Campaign, L.A. Conv., 1960; spl. asst. White House Conf. on Civil Rights, Washington, 1966; writer, dir. TV campaign commls. Doug Wilder, State of Va., 1985; writer, cons. Project Vote, Washington, 1987; mem. bd. visitors Mount Vernon, Va., 1988-95. Recipient First Outstanding Alumna award Howard U. Sch. Comm., Washington. Mem. Federally Employed Women (adv. bd., bd. mem. 1978—), Black Women's Agenda (founding nat. pres., 1st pres. 1978—, Outstanding Svc. award 1990), Nat. Smart Set (nat. pres., Spl. Svc. award 1991), Nat. Gallery Art (vice chair widening horizons program), Woman's Nat. Dem. Club (co-chair art in overseas embassies). Episcopalian. Avocation: creative writing. Home: 2795 Windham Ct Delray Beach FL 33445-7110

STONE, GAIL ANN, elementary and secondary education educator; b. Chgo., Mar. 7, 1943; d. Leonard Oscar and Bernice L. (Grunwald) Johnson; m. Joe Thomas Stone, Dec. 28, 1963; children: Jason, Brandon. BS, U. Wash., 1968; MS, U. Rochester, 1988. Cert. math. educator K-12, spl. educator K-12. Math. paraprofessional, tchr. Pittsford (N.Y.) Schs., 1975-82; tchr. math. Norman Howard Schs., Rochester, N.Y., 1984—. Dir. coll. guidance Norman Howard Schs., 1985—; spkr. in field; core group tchr./writer NSF grant, 1992—. Dir. YWCA, Rochester, 1971-74; counselor CPT Housing, Rochester, 1969-75. Named Writer Computer Program NSF. Mem. Nat. Coun. Tchrs. Math., Assn. Math. Tchrs. N.Y. State, Coun. Exceptional Children. Avocations: gardening, hiking, cooking, swimming. Office: Norman Howard Sch 275 Pinnacle Rd Rochester NY 14623-4103 E-mail: gsswim@aol.com.

STONE, GEOFFREY RICHARD, law educator, lawyer; b. Nov. 20, 1946; s. Robert R. and Shirley (Weliky) S.; m. Nancy Spector, Oct. 8, 1977; children: Julie, Mollie. BS, U. Pa., 1968; JD, U. Chgo., 1971. Bar: N.Y. 1972. Law clk. to Hon. J.S. Kelly Wright U.S. Ct. Appeals (D.C. cir.), 1971-72; law clk. to Hon. William J. Brennan, Jr. U.S. Supreme Ct., 1972-73; asst. prof. U. Chgo., 1973-77, assoc. prof., 1977-79, prof., 1979-84, Harry Kalven Jr. disting. svc. prof., 1984—, dean Law Sch., 1987-93, provost, 1994—2002. Author: Constitutional Law, 1986, 4th edit., 2001, The Bill of Rights in the Modern State, 1992, The First Amendment, 1999, Eternally Vigilent: Free Speech in the Modern Era, 2001; editor The Supreme Ct. Rev., 1991—; contbr. articles to profl. jours. Bd. dirs. Ill. divsn. ACLU, 1978-84; bd. advisors Pub. Svc. Challenge, 1989; bd. govs. Argonne Nat. Lab., 1994—. Fellow AAAS; mem. Chgo. Coun. Lawyers (bd. govs. 1976-77), Am. Law Inst. Assn. Am. Law Schs. (exec. com. 1990-93), Legal Aid Soc. (bd. dirs. 1988), Order of Coif. Office: U Chgo 1111 E 60th St Chicago IL 60637-5418

STONE, HAZEL L. educator; b. Sept. 27, 1936; d. Rayford Howard and Hazel L. (Howell) Adams; m. Frank Alvin Stone, July 10, 1965; children: Jeffrey Lynn, Amy Luan. BS, Abilene Christian U., 1960; MA, U. Tex., Odessa, 1987. 3rd grade tchr. McCamey Ind. Sch. Dist., Tex., 1960—62;

6th grade tchr. Ross Elem., Ector County Ind. Sch. Dist., Odessa, 1962—92. Am. Heritage fellow. Mem. Tex. State Tchrs. Assn., Delta Kappa Gamma, Phi Theta Kappa, Kappa Delta Pi. Home: 1444 Pagewood Ave Odessa TX 79761-3452

STONE, MARILYN, foreign language educator, consultant; b. N.Y.C., Jan. 14, 1935; d. Paul Ference Moskowitz and Anna Schwartz; m. Joseph Stone, Aug. 30, 1959; children: Sara Jean, Edward, Hillary, Daniel. BA in Spanish/French, Queens Coll.; MA in Spanish Lit., Columbia U.; PhD in Spanish Lit., NYU. Cert. Spanish/English translator, medieval/modern paleography profl. Spanish/English interpreter Nassau County Ct., 1985-86; Spanish lang. cons. Fine Arts Mus. of L.I., Hempstead, N.Y., 1986-87; Spanish instr. Dominican Coll., Blauvelt, N.Y., 1987, Nassau C.C., Blauvelt, N.Y., 1987, 92; instr. in translation methods NYU, N.Y.C., 1990—; ind. lang. cons. Chase Manhattan Bank, Bergen Lang. Inst., Teaneck, N.J., 1991—; asst. prof. transl. NYU. Presenter papers in field; adj. asst. prof. Spanish, Kingsborough C.C., CUNY, 1987-90; lectr. in field. Author: A Handbook of Courtroom Terms in Spanish and English, 1981, Marriage and Friendship in Medieval Spain, 1990, Women at Work in Spain From the Middle Ages to Early Modern Times, 1998; contbr. articles to profl. jours.

STONE, MARVIN JULES, physician, educator; b. Columbus, Ohio, Aug. 3, 1937; s. Roy J. and Lillian (Bedwinek) S.; m. Jill Feinstein, June 29, 1958; children: Nancy Lillian, Robert Howard. Student, Ohio State U., 1955-58; SM in Pathology, U. Chgo., 1962, MD with honors, 1963. Diplomate Am. Bd. Internal Medicine, (Hematology, Med. Oncology). Intern ward med. svc. Barnes Hosp., St. Louis, 1963-64, asst. resident, 1964-65; clin. assoc. arthritis and rheumatism br. Nat. Inst. Arthritis and Metabolic Diseases, NIH, Bethesda, Md., 1965-68; resident in medicine, ACP scholar Parkland Meml. Hosp., Dallas, 1968-69; fellow in hematology-oncology, dept. internal medicine U. Tex. Southwestern Med. Sch., Dallas, 1969-70, instr. dept. internal medicine, 1970-71, asst. prof., 1971-73, assoc. prof., 1974-76, clin. prof., 1976—, chmn. bioethics com., 1979-81; mem. faculty and steering com. immunology grad. program, Grad. Sch. Biomed. Scis., U. Tex. Health Sci. Ctr., Dallas, 1975, adj. mem., 1976—. Dir. Charles A. Sammons Cancer Ctr., chief oncology, dir. immunology, co-dir. divsn. hematology-oncology, attending physician Baylor U. Med. Ctr., Dallas, 1976—; v.p. med. staff Parkland Meml. Hosp., Dallas, 1982. Contbr. chpts. to books, articles to profl. jours. Chmn. com. patient-aid Greater Dallas/Ft. Worth chpt. Leukemia Soc. Am., 1971-76, chmn. med. adv. com., 1978-80, bd. dirs., 1971-80; mem. v.p. Dallas unit Am. Cancer Soc., 1977-78, pres., 1978—; mem. adv. bd. Baylor U. Med. Ctr. Found. With USPHS, 1965-68. Recipient Wings of Eagles award, Baylor Health Care Sys., 2001, Disting. Svc. award, U. Chgo., 2002. Master ACP (gov. No. Tex. 1993-97, laureate Tex. chpt. 2000); fellow Royal Soc. Medicine (London); mem. AMA, Am. Assn. Immunologists, Am. Soc. Hematology, Internat. Soc. Hematology, Coun. Thrombosis, Am. Heart Assn. (established investigator 1970-75), Am. Soc. Clin. Oncology (edn. com. 2002—, career devel. com. 2002—), Am. Osler Soc. (bd. govs. 1997-2000, v.p. 2001-03, pres. 2003-04), Am. Assn. for Cancer Rsch., So. Soc. Clin. Investigation, Tex. Med. Assn., Dallas County Med. Soc., Clin. Immunology Soc., Phi Beta Kappa, Sigma Xi, Alpha Omega Alpha. Office: Baylor U Med Ctr Charles A Sammons Cancer Ctr 3500 Gaston Ave Dallas TX 75246-2096 E-mail: marvins@baylorhealth.edu.

STONE, PETER HUNTER, atmospheric scientist, educator; b. Bklyn., May 10, 1937; s. Lauson Harvey and Jane Hunter (Colwell) S.; m. Paola Diana Malanotte, Dec. 19, 1987. BS, Harvard U., 1959, PhD, 1964. From asst. prof. to assoc. prof. dynamical meteorology Harvard U., Cambridge, Mass., 1966-72; staff meteorologist NASA Goddard Inst. Space Studies, N.Y.C., 1972-74; dir. Ctr. Meteorology and Phys. Oceanography MIT, Cambridge, 1983-89, prof. meteorology, 1974-98, prof. climate dynamics, 1998—. Editor: Jour. of Climate, 1990-92, Dynamics of Atmospheres and Oceans, 1988-98. Recipient Group Achievement award Galileo Sci. Team/NASA, 1996, Pioneer Venus Orbiter Sci. Team/NASA, 1980; Alfred P. Sloan fellow Sloan Found., 1968-70. Fellow Am. Meteorol. Soc., Am. Assn. for the Advancement of Sci.; mem. Am. Geophys. Union. Office: MIT 77 Massachusetts Ave Rm 54-1718 Cambridge MA 02139-4307

STONE, ROBERT CHRISTOPHER, computer scientist, educator; b. Norman, Okla., Aug. 19, 1964; s. Robert Joseph and Billie Dee (Combs) S.; m. Yvette Marie Hewes, May 2, 1983; children: Katherine Angelica Stone, Nicholas Christopher Stone. BS in Psychology, Regents Coll., 1989; DO, U. North Tex. Health Sci. Ctr., Ft. Worth, 1995; cert. med. asst., Western Coll., San Leandro, Calif., 1987. Cert. med. asst., ACLS. Psychiat. counselor CareUnit, Ft. Worth, 1985-86; med. office nurse Bay Area Health, San Francisco, 1986-88; guest lectr. U. North Tex., Denton, 1989-92; rschr. U. North Tex. Health Sci. Ctr., 1989-97, instr., 1992—; CEO Edn. Rsch. Labs., Inc., Ft. Worth, 1993-95, also chmn. bd. dirs.; intern. Texas A&M Sch. Med. Scott & White Hosp. and Clinic, Temple, TX, 1997-98, resident Psychiatry, 1998-99; resident psychiatry U. Texas Southwestern Med. Ctr., Dallas, 1999-2000, resident psychiatry sr. rsch. track, 2000-2001, dir. mental health, assoc. med. dir., 2001—. V.p. Exec. Edn. Rsch., Inc., Ft. Worth, 1990-95; v.p. edn. CyberMed, Ft. Worth, 1994-95; edn. cons. Diocese of S.W., Dallas, 1993-94, instructor of psychiatry, U. Texas Southwestern Med. Ctr. Dept. Psychiatry, 2001—; presenter and investigator in field. Author: (electronic editions) DSM-IV, Diagnostic Criteria, Little Black Book of Primary Care Pearls and References, Current Clinical Strategies Series, Lexi-Comp Seris, 1995; contbr. articles to profl. jours. Pres. parish coun. St. Barbara's Orthodox Ch., Ft. Worth, 1994, choir dir., 1992-94. Recipient tchg. fellowship U. North Tex. Health Sci. Ctr., 1992-95; computer adaptive testing grantee Found. for the Improvement of Post Secondary Edn., Washington, 1993-95. Mem. AMA, Am. Osteo. Assn., Soc. for Acad. Emergency Medicine, Undergrad. Acad. Osteopathy, Emergency Medicine Club (v.p.). Republican. Russian Orthodox. Achievements include specializing in the assessment and treatment of victims of cviolencem including deomstiv violence victims and victims of internat. torture seeking political asylum in the US.

STONE, SUSAN RIDGAWAY, marketing educator; b. Coronado, Calif., Oct. 30, 1950; d. Lester Jay and Marguerite Ridgaway (King) Stone; m. Martin Zachary Sipkoff, Oct. 27, 1984; 1 child, Benjamin. AB, Wilson Coll., 1977; MBA, Shippensburg U., 1980; DBA, George Washington U., 1992. Assoc. prof. mgmt. and mktg. Shippensburg (Pa.) U., 1983—; dir. mktg. VSP Wastewater Tech., Gettysburg, Pa., 1982; pres. Ridgaway Rose Internat., Inc., 1999—. Mktg. cons. Svcs. Unltd., Gettysburg, 1975—; bd. dirs., chair pers. Survivors, Inc.; lectr. in field. Author: (with Stephen J. Holoviak) Managing Human Productivity: People are Your Best Investment, 1987, 2nd printing 1991; contbr. articles to profl. jours. Bd. dir. Survivors Inc., chmn. personnel com. Recipient Excellence in tchg. award, Corning Found., 1993, Outstanding Svc. award, 1994, 2002, Sprint Tchg. Excellence award, 1998, Orrston Bank Tchg. Excellence award, 2001, Panhellenic Coun. Tchg. award, 1999, Martin Babinee Outstanding Adv. award, 2003; fellow John L. Grove Rsch. fellow, 2002. Mem.: DAR, NOW, Southwest Acad. of Mgmt., S.E. Acad. Mgmt., Am. Mktg. Assn., Acad. Mktg. Sci., Survivors, Inc. (bd. dirs., chair pers. com.), Mensa, Adams County Literacy Coun., Nat. Hist. Trust, Kappa Kappa Gamma, Beta Gamma Sigma. Democrat. Episcopalian. Avocations: gardening, writing, sailing. Office: Shippensburg Univ 1871 Old Main Dr Shippensburg PA 17257-2299 E-mail: srston@ship.edu.

STONE, VICTOR J. law educator; b. Chgo., Mar. 11, 1921; s. Maurice Albert and Ida (Baskin) S.; m. Susan Abby Cane, July 14, 1951; children: Mary Jessica, Jennifer Abby, Andrew Hugh William. AB, Oberlin Coll., 1942; JD, Columbia U., 1948; LLD, Oberlin Coll., 1983. Bar: N.Y. 1949, Ill. 1950. Assoc. Columbia U., N.Y.C., 1948-49, Sonnenschein, Chgo., 1949-53; rsch. assoc. U. Chgo., 1953-55; asst. prof. law U. Ill., Champaign, 1955-57, assoc. prof. law, 1957-59, prof. law, 1959-91, prof. law emeritus, 1991—, assoc. v.p. acad. affairs, 1975-78. Mem. jud. adv. coun. State Ill., 1959-61; mem. com. jury instrns. Ill. Supreme Ct., 1963-79, reporter, 1973-79; mem. Ill. State Appellate Defender Commn., 1973-83, vice-chmn., 1973-77, 79-83; bd. dirs. Champaign County Ct.-Apptd. Spl. Advocate Program, 1995-99, pres., 1998-99. Co-editor: Ill. Pattern Jury Instructions, 1965, 71, 77; Civil Liberties and Civil Rights, 1977. Trustee Oberlin Coll., 1982-97, AAUP Found., 1983-90. Lt. USNR, 1942-46. Ford Found. fellow, 1962-63. Fellow Ill. Bar Found. (charter 1986—); mem. ABA, CASA (bd. dirs. 1994-98, pres. 1998-99), Ill. Bar Assn. (chmn. individual rights and responsibilities 1971-72, mem. coun. civil practice and procedure 1978-82, Elmer Gertz award in civil liberties and civil rights, 2003), Chgo. Bar Assn., AAUP (gen. counsel 1978-80, pres. 1982-84, pres. Ill. conf. 1968-70, pres. Ill. chpt. 1964-65, mem. coun. 1982-90), ACLU (bd. dirs. Ill. div. 1986-96, exec. com. 1991-96, Roger Baldwin award for lifetime achievement 2002), Am. Bar Found. (life 1986), State Univs. Annitants Assn. (pres. 1994-95, mem. state exec. com. 1995-97). Office: U Ill Coll Law 504 E Pennsylvania Ave Champaign IL 61820-6909 E-mail: v-stone@uiuc.edu.

STONE-MAGNER, ROSE MARIE, vocational educator; b. Emporia, Kans., Sept. 9, 1945; d. Sherman Albert and Martha Marie (Brough) Kellum; m. Walter Lee Stone, July 18, 1965; children: Leah Marie, Zenetta Ann; m. Edmund Magner, Mar. 29, 1998. Diploma in cosmetology, St. John's Sch., 1963, Capitol Beauty Sch., 1964; AAS, DelMar Coll., 1985; BA in Occupational Edn., Corpus Christi State U., 1989. Cert. cosmetology instr., tchr., Tex. Mgr. Rose Marie's Beauty Salon, Bellaire, Ohio, 1964-66; asst. mgr. Linden Lady Wigs, Columbus, Ohio, 1966-68; owner, mgr. Rose Marie's, Mt. Vernon, Ohio, 1969-76; hairstylist Clara's North Pole Beauty Salon, Corpus Christi, Tex., 1976-80; tchr. cosmetology Flour Bluff Ind. Sch. Dist., Corpus Christi, 1981-85, S.W. Ind. Sch. Dist., San Antonio, 1985-86, Carrollton (Tex.) Farmers Br. Ind. Sch. Dist., 1986-92; ednl. dir. Concept Chem., Houston, 1992; owner, ednl. dir. Rose Marie's Hair Salon, Corpus Christi, 1993—. Mem. legis. com. Tex. Hairdressers and Cosmetology Assn., Corpus Christi, 1985-86; editor Magner Pub., 1998—; owner Rose Marie Collectibles, Corpus Christi, 1999—. Mem. Nat. Cosmetology Assn., Cosmetology Instrs. in Pub. Schs. (chmn. 1987-88, chair workshop 1989), Romance Writers of Am., Tex. Hairdressers Assn., Tex. Indsl. Vocat. Assn., Vocat. Indsl. Clubs Am. (dist. adv. com. 1983-88, state adv. com. 1986-88, Texan award for Statesman 1990, State Leader 1985, Judging award 1985), Corpus Christi Execs. Assn. (bd. dirs. 1997—), Gulfway Mchts. Assn. (pres. 1998—), Christian Bus. and Profl. Women's Club Corpus Christi, Corpus Christi Bus. and Profl. Women's Club, Inc., Iota Lambda Sigma. Democrat. Mem. Ch. of Christ. Avocations: fishing, hunting. Office: Rose Marie's Hair Salon PO Box 2259 Rockport TX 78381-2259

STONER, CONNIE KAY, special education educator; b. Versailles, Mo., Apr. 18, 1949; d. Norman Francis and Helen Pauline (Kreissler) Schnirch; m. Gerald Alan Winter, Feb. 27, 1967 (div. 1971); children: Julie Marie Winter Stuart Brainard, Kimberly Lynn; m. Larry Dean Stoner, 1971; children: Grant, Colin. BS, Northeast Mo. State U., 1970, MA, 1971. Cert. speech pathology, audiology, Mo. Speech pathologist Cameron (Mo.) Pub. Schs., 1971-73, Independence (Mo.) Pub. Schs., 1973-78, self-contained lang. devel. tchr., 1978-96, speech pathologist, reading clinician, 1996—. Author: Language for Learners, 1981. Sec. Am. Field Svc.; v.p. Truman Music Boosters. Recipient Excellence in Teaching award, 1991; named Young Educator of Yr., Jaycees, 1986; HEW fellow, 1971. Mem. Mo. State Tchrs. Assn. (pres. 1997-99). Avocations: reading, aerobics, collecting music boxes. Office: Santa Fe Trail Elem 1301 Windsor St Independence MO 64055-1179

STONNINGTON, HENRY HERBERT, physician, medical executive, educator; b. Vienna, Feb. 12, 1927; arrived in U.S., 1969; m. Constance Mary Leigh Hamersley, Sept. 19, 1953. MB, BS, Melbourne U., Victoria, Australia, 1950; MS, U. Minn., 1972. Diplomate Am. Bd. Phys. Medicine and Rehab., 1973. Pvt. practice, Sydney, N.S.W., Australia, 1955-65; clin. tchr. U. N.S.W., Sydney, 1965-69; resident in Phys. Medicine and Rehab. Mayo Clinic, Rochester, Minn., 1969-72, mem. staff, 1972-83; assoc. prof. Mayo Med. Sch., Rochester, 1975-83; chmn. dept rehab. medicine Med. Coll. Va., Va. Commonwealth U., Richmond, 1983-88, prof. rehab. medicine, 1983-89, dir. rsch. tng. ctr., 1988-89; v.p. med. svcs. Sheltering Arms Hosp., Richmond, 1985-92; prof. and chmn. dept. phys. medicine and rehab. U. Mo., Columbia, 1992-94; med. dir. Meml. Rehab. Ctr., Savannah, Ga., 1994-97; clin. prof. rehab. medicine Emory U., Atlanta, 1997—2000; clin. prof. medicine sect. phys. medicine and rehab. La. State U., 2001—. Med. dir. rehab. svcs. Meml. Hosp., Gulfport, Miss., 1998—; clin. prof. phys. med. and rehab. La. State U. Med. Sch., 2001—. Editor: Brain Injury, 1987—2001, Pediatric Rehabilitation, 1997—2000; contbr. articles to profl. jours. Recipient award Rsch. Tng. Ctr. Model Sys., Nat. Inst. Disability and Rehab. Rsch., Washington, 1987, 88, Disting. Clinician award Am. Acad. Phys. Medicine and Rehab., 2002. Fellow Australian Coll. Rehab. Medicine, Australasian Faculty Rehab. Medicine, Royal Coll. Physicians Edinburgh (Scotland), Am. Acad. Phys. Medicine and Rehab. (named Disting. Physician 2002), Am. Coun. Rehab. Medicine, Am. Assn. Acad. Physiatrists; mem. Internat. Brain Injury Assn. (v.p. for sci. affairs 1998—, bd. govs.). E-mail: hencon2731@aol.com.

STOOKEY, GEORGE KENNETH, retired director, retired dental educator; b. Waterloo, Ind., Nov. 6, 1935; s. Emra Gladison and Mary Catherine (Anglin) Stookey; m. Nola Jean Meek, Jan. 15, 1955; children: Lynda, Lisa, Laura, Kenneth. AB in Chemistry, Ind. U., 1957, MSD, 1962, PhD in Preventive Dentistry, 1971. Asst. dir. Preventive Dentistry Rsch. Inst. Ind. U., Indpls., 1968-70, assoc. prof. preventive dentistry Sch. Dentistry, 1973-78, prof., 1978-98, disting. prof., 1998—, prof. emeritus, 2001, assoc. dir. Oral Health Rsch. Inst., 1974—81, 1999—2001, dir., 1981-99, assoc. dean rsch. Sch. Dentistry, 1987-97, 00-01, acting dean, 1996, assoc. dean acad. affairs, 1997-98, exec. assoc. dean, 1998-2000. Cons. USAF, San Antonio, 1973—, ADA, Chgo., 1972—, Nat. Inst. Dental Rsch., Bethesda, 1978—82, Bethesda, 1991—95. Author (with others): (book) Introduction to Oral Biology and Preventive Dentistry, 1971, Preventive Dentistry in Action, 1972 (Meritorious award, 1973), Preventive Dentistry for the Dental Assistant and Dental Hygienist, 1977; contbr. articles to profl. jours. Mem.: ADA, Am. Assn. Lab. Animal Sci., European Orgn. Caries Rsch., Internat. Assn. Dental Rsch. Republican. Office: Ind U Emerging Techs Ctr 351 W 10th St Ste 222 Indianapolis IN 46202-4119 E-mail: gstookey@iupui.edu.

STORCK, THOMAS CHARLES JOLIFFE, author, librarian; b. Bklyn., Jan. 25, 1951; s. John Norman and Elizabeth Marian (Gabbert) S.; m. Martha Goddard Furman, May 11, 1974 (dec. July 1987); children: Michael Hector, Mary Gwyn, Clare Marie, Gabriel Charles; m. Inez Marie Fitzgerald, Dec. 12, 1987. BA, Kenyon Coll., 1973; MLS, La. State U., 1978; MA, St. John's Coll., Santa Fe, 1980. Documents libr. Okla. State U., Stillwater, 1979-81; libr. Christendom Coll., Front Royal, Va., 1981-85; philosophy instr. Mt. Aloysius Coll., Cresson, Pa., 1986; libr. Mount de Sales Acad., Catonsville, Md., 1986-88; lectr. philosophy Catonsville C.C., 1988; law libr. U.S. Treasury Dept. Libr., Washington, 1989—. Author: The Catholic Milieu, 1987, Foundations of a Catholic Politicl Order, 1998, Christendom and the West, 2000; contbr. numerous articles to profl. jours. and mags. Mem. K. Roman Catholic. E-mail: tstorck@alumni.kenyon.edu.

STOREY, J. BENTON, horticulturalist, educator; BS in Horticulture, Tex. A&M U., 1949, MS, 1952; PhD in Botanical Sci. and Plant Physiology, U. Calif., LA, Calif., 1957. Prof. Tex. A & M Univ., College Station, 1950—. Editor: The Pecan Quar., 1967—81. Recipient Outstanding Grad. Educator award, 1992. Office: Texas A&M University Dept Horticultural Scis College Station TX 77843-0001*

STORM, SANDY LAMM, secondary education educator; b. Shelbyville, Ill., Aug. 6, 1949; d. Raymond Ralph and Hazel Clara (Sands) Lamm; m. David Michael Storm, Aug. 24, 1968; children: Michael Lee, Marc David, Michelle Kimberly. BS in Edn., Eastern Ill. U., 1967-70, MSEd, 1990-91. Cert. tchr. and sch. guidance, Ill. Substitute tchr. Shelby County, Shelbyville, Ill., 1989-90; family and consumer sci. tchr. Shelbyville Sch., Shelbyville, 1990—; counselor, sports cons. Human Excellence, Shelbyville, 1991—. Ill. ROE #11 SCAT Team mem. Mem. NEA. Democrat. Avocations: counted cross stitch, reading, cooking, travel. Home and Office: PO Box 506 Shelbyville IL 62565-0506 Fax: 217-774-5346.

STOUT, GLENN EMANUEL, retired science administrator; b. Fostoria, Ohio, Mar. 23, 1920; AB, Findlay U., 1942, DSc, 1973. Head atmosphere scis. sec. Ill. State Water Survey, 1952—71; sci. coord. NSF, 1969-71; asst. to chief Ill. State Water Survey, Champaign, 1971-74; prof. Inst. Environ. Studies, Urbana, Ill., 1973-94, dir. task force, 1975-79; dir. Water Resources Ctr. U. Ill., Urbana, 1973-94; rsch. coord. Ill.-Ind. Sea Grant Program, 1987-94; emeritus, 1994—. Mem. Ill. Gov.'s Task Force on State Water Plan, 1980-94; bd. dirs. Univ. Coun. Water Resources, 1983-86, chmn. internat. affairs, 1989-92; mem. nomination com. for Stockholm Water Prize, 1994-96. Contbr. articles to profl. jours. Bd. govs. World Water Coun., 1996-98. Mem. Am. Water Resources Assn., Internat. Water Resources Assn. (sec. gen. 1985-91, v.p. 1992-94, exec. dir. 1984-95, pres. 1995-97, hon.), Am. Meteorol. Soc., Am. Geophys. Union, N.Am. Lake Mgmt. Soc., Ill. Lake Mgmt. Assn. (bd. dirs. 1985-88), Am. Water Works Assn., Kiwanis (pres. local club 1979-80, lt. gov. 1982-83), Sigma Xi (pres. U. Ill. chpt. 1985-86). Achievements include on April 9, 1953 we recorded on film the first radar pattern of the hooked echo, depicting a major tornado. Home: 920 W John St Champaign IL 61821-3907 E-mail: g-stout@uiuc.edu.

STOUT, LINDA KAY, elementary education educator; b. Marshall, Mo., Sept. 6, 1944; d. David Fowler and May Marchess (Neff) S.. BS in Edn., Ohio State U., 1966; MEd, Bowling Green State U., 1977; postgrad., U. Toledo, 1995—. Tchr. 5th grade Battle Creek (Mich.) Pub. Schs., 1966-67; tchr. 4th grade Sylvania (Ohio) Schs., 1967-79, tchr. 5th grade, 1979—. Peer leader, instr. Summer Inst. Reading Intervention, Ohio, 2001—03; tchr. edn. adv. com. Bowling Green State U., Ohio, 1980—; presenter in field. Past advisor 4-H, Toledo; written composition coord. Sylvania Schs., 1997-98; regional problem capt. and trainer for spontaneous Odyessy of the Mind, 1995-98. Jennings scholar, 1988—89. Mem. IRA, Nat. Coun. Tchrs. English, Ohio Coun. Tchrs. English Lang. Arts, Ohio Coun. IRA (chmn. mid. sch. literacy com., conf. com. 2003); Toledo Coun. IRA (past treas., past pres.) Office: Highland Elem Sch 7720 Erie St Sylvania OH 43560-3729

STOUT, MARY WEBB, education program specialist; b. Richmond, Va., Dec. 24, 1947; d. Frank Edmond Webb and Edith Diuguid (Harris) Webb Steger; m. Teddy Alvin Stout, July 8, 1972. BA, Mary Washington Coll., 1970; MEd, U. Va., Charlottesville, 1972; Edn. Specialist, Coll. William and Mary, 1991, EdD, 1995; cert. in Multimedia Devel., George Mason U., 2003. Tchr. Harrisonburg City Sch., Va., 1970-71, Buckingham County Sch., Va., 1972-73; guidance counselor So. European Task Force US Army, Vicenza, Italy, 1973-78, edn. specialist Quartermaster Sch. Ft. Lee, Va., 1978-80, edn. specialist Tng. Support Ctr. Ft. Eustis, Va., 1980-82; edn. specialist Hdqs. Tng., Doctrine Command, Ft. Monroe, Va., 1982-83; edn. svc. specialist Combined Arms Ctr., Ft. Leavenworth, Kans., 1983-88; instrnl. systems specialist Hdqs. TRADOC, Ft. Monroe, 1988-98; supervisory edn. svc. specialist Hdqs. US Army Pers. Command, Alexandria, Va., 1998-2000; edn. program specialist OSD Office of Chancellor Edn. and Profl. Devel., Arlington, Va., 2000—; online faculty U. Phoenix, 2002—. Mem. devel. bd. Sch. Edn. Coll. William and Mary, 2002—. Legis. affairs rep. Running Man Homeowners Assn., Yorktown, Va., 1996—98; treas. Massanetta Springs Alumni Assn., Harrisonburg, Va., 1988—2000, membership chmn., 1998—2002. Recipient Alumni award Massanetta Springs Alumni Assn., 1996. Mem.: Assn. for Instnl. Rsch., Am. Assn. for Adult and Continuing Edn., Mary Washington Coll. Alumni Assn., U. Va. Alumni Assn., Coll. William and Mary Alumni Assn., Assn. Advancement of Computing in Edn., Assn. Ednl. Comm. and Tech., Am. Assn. Higher Edn., Assn. Study Higher Edn., Kappa Delta Pi. Presbyterian. Avocations: running, red cross water safety instructor. Home: 6006 River Dr Mason Neck VA 22079-4127 Office: Dept Def Chancellor Edn and Profl Devel Civilian Pers Mgmt Svcs 1400 Key Blvd Ste B-200 Arlington VA 22209 E-mail: MSTOUT8895@aol.com., mary.stout@cpms.osd.mil.

STOVALL, RICHARD L. retired academic administrator; b. Springfield, Mo., Mar. 28, 1944; s. Wilbern Lee and Ernestine Patricia (Putman) S.; m. Susannah K. Young; children: Richard Christopher, Stacy Suzanne. BA, SW Mo. State U., 1966; MA, C.W. Post Coll. L.I. U., 1969; PhD, Ohio State U., 1975. Instr. SW Mo. State U., Springfield, 1969-72; asst. prof. U. S.C., Columbia, S.C., 1975-77; prof., asst. dept. head SW Mo. State U., Springfield, 1977—2003, ret., 2003. Cons. Cedar Hills High Sch., Dallas, 1986, Andrews Ins. Agy., 1984, Mo. Cosmetology Assn., 1983-84, Springfield Pers. Assn., 1982, Syntex Corp. 1981-82; pub. rels. Halcyon of Dallas, 1988-96, Hawthorne Group of Washington, 1995-96, The Harrell Group, Dallas, 1999. Contbr. articles to profl. jours. Tabulation room coord. for MSHSAA Dist. Speech Festival; lectr. Springfield Pub. Schs., City Utilities Citizens Adv. Bd.; pres. Boy Scouts Am. With ES USNR-TAR, 1962-69. Mem. Pub. Rels. Soc. Am., Am. Forensics Assn., Speech Communication Assn. Am., So. Speech Communication Assn., Pub. Rels. of the Ozarks, Pub. Rels. Soc. Mid-Mo., Cen. States Speech Assn., Speech and Theatre Assn. Mo., Cherokee Homeowners Assn. (past pres.). Episcopal. Home and Office: 3 Whiterock Ln Kimberling City MO 65686 E-mail: richardstovall@msn.c.

STOVER, CAROLYN NADINE, middle school educator; b. Martinsburg, W.Va., May 30, 1950; d. Norman Robert and Garnet Agnes (Zombro) Whetzel; m. James Stenner Stover Sr., Nov. 20, 1971; children: Heather N., James S. Jr. BA in Home Econs., Shepherd Coll., 1972; cert. in advanced studies, W.Va. U., 1978; cert. in tchg. methods, Marshall U., 1973; cert. in spl. edn., Shippensburg Coll., 1972. Cert. tchr., W.Va., N.Mex.; reg. EMT. Substitute tchr. Berkeley County Schs., Martinsburg, W.Va., 1972, adult edn. instr., 1972-77, home econs. instr., 1973-83; substitute tchr. Ruidoso (N.Mex.) Mcpl. Schs., 1984-90, child find coord. Region 9 edn. coop., 1990, life skills and at-risk educator, 1991—, coord. coun., 1991-93, mem. budget com., 1993. Elder First Presbyn. Ch., Ruidoso, 1984-90, 94-96, 2002--; sponsor Acad. Booster Club, Ruidoso, 1993—; instr. CPR, 1980. Named Outstanding Young Women of Am., 1981. Mem. NEA, Nat. Middle Sch. Assn., Ruidoso Edn. Assn. (reporter, membership chair), Ruidoso Bowling Assn. (sec. 1999-2001), Rotary (youth leadership councilor 1991—). Democrat. Avocations: cross-stitching, needlework, family, sports, youth. Home: Box 7837 PO Box 7837 Ruidoso NM 88355-7837 Office: Ruidoso Mid Sch 100 Reese Dr Ruidoso NM 88345-6016

STOVER, CURTIS SYLVESTER, retired vocational school educator; b. Glenmore, Ohio, Dec. 18, 1933; s. Paul R. and Sarah J. (Jones) Stover; m. Betty J. Christian, Oct. 3, 1953; children: Anita, Brenda, Linda, Curtis, Brian, Russell. BS, So. Ill. U., 1976; MS, Ctrl. State U., Edmond, Okla., 1989. Cert. secondary and vocat. tchr. Ill. Vocat. Ctr. Indsl. maintenance instr. Belleville Area Coll., Granite City, Ill., 1976-83; elec., mechanical, automated indsl. systems instr. Moore-Norman Area Votech Sch., Norman, Okla., 1983—. Tng. cons. Nat. Steel Co., Granite City Steel Co., 1976—83. Author: (book) Life & Other Illusions, 1995, Blind Justice, 2003; co-author: The Yankee Dollar Conspiracy, 2000. Mem.: Vocat. Indsl. Clubs Am. (advisor, mem. tech. com. robotics workcell 1989—90), Okla. Trade and Indsl. Assn. (chmn. indsl. maintenance tech. trade group), Fluid Power Soc. Internat. (cert. fluid power mechanic instr., cert. hydraulic technician instr., cert. pneumatic technician instr.), Nat. Assn. Trade and Indsl. Instrs. (sec.-treas. 1989—92), Okla. Vocat. Assn., Am. Vocat. Assn., Aniad Shrine, Masons, Iota Lambda Sigma. Home: 808 N Stout Cir Moore OK 73170-1118 Office: Moore-Norman Votech Sch 4701 12th Ave NW Norman OK 73069-8399 E-mail: smokey@itlnet.net.

STOVER, GARY LEE, special education educator; b. Springfield, Ill., May 23, 1960; s. Robert T. and Mary Jane (Woods) S.; m. Laurie Lynn Redick, June 23, 1984; children: Gary Lee Jr., Sarah Lynn. AA, Lincoln Land C.C., 1981; BS, Ill. State U., 1983. Phys. edn. tchr. Springfield Devel. Ctr., 1984-85; adapted phys. edn. tchr. Hope Sch., Springfield, 1986-94; spl. edn. tchr.-BD Lanphier H.S., 1994—, head wrestling coach, 1994—. Mem. AAHPERD, Ill. Coaches Assn. Home: RR 3 Box 22 Sherman IL 62684-9803 Office: Lanphier HS 1300 N 11th St Springfield IL 62702-4099

STOWE, CHARLES ROBINSON BEECHER, management consultant, educator, lawyer; b. Seattle, July 18, 1949; s. David and Edith (Andrade) Beecher S.; m. Laura (Everett), Mar. 9, 1985. BA, Vanderbilt U., 1971; MBA, U. Tex., Dallas, 1975; JD, U. Houston, 1982; PhD, U. Warsaw, Poland, 1998. Bar: Tex., 1982; US Dist. Ct. (so. dist.) Tex. 1984; US Tax Ct. 1984. Acct. exec. Engleman Co., Dallas, 1974-75; dir. Productive Capital Assoc., Tex., 1975-81; instr. Richland Coll., Dallas, 1976; acct. Arthur Andersen and Co., 1976-78; pres. Stowe and Co., 1978—; asst. prof. dept. gen. bus., fin. Coll. Bus. Adminstrn., Sam Houston State U., 1982—, dir. office internat. programs, 1997-2001; part-time pub. rels. cons. Bd. dir. Office Internat. programs; adminstrv. intern asst. to pres., 1985. Author: Bankruptcy I Micro-Mash Inc., 1989, rev. edit., 1995; The Implications of Foreign Financial Institutions on Poland's Emerging Entrepreneurial Economy, 1999; co-author: CPA rev.; co-editor: Knowledge Cafe for Intellect Product and Intellectual Entrepreneurship, 2001; editor, ACET Journal of Computor Education and Research, 2002-, Houston Jour. Internat. Law, 1981-82; contbg. articles to profl. jour. Trustee Stowe-Day Found., 1979-80; mem. nat. adv. bd. Young Am. Found., 1979—; vol. faculty State Bar Tex. Profl. Devel. Program, 1988—; vol., mediator Dispute Resolution Ctr. Montgomery County; mediator so. dist. US Dist. Ct. Tex. 1993; team chief US Mil. liaison Rep. Poland, 1994; pub. affairs officer George C. Marshall European Ctr. Security Studies, 1997. Capt. Res. USNR, 1971—74. Navy Achievement Medal, Gold Star; Legion of Merit; Def. Meritorious Svc. Medal(oak leaf cluster), Navy Meritorious Svc. Award; Summer Fellow Tex. Coordinating Bd., 1988; Prince-Babson Fellow Entrepreneurship Symposium, 1991; recipient Freedoms Found. Award. Mem. ABA; Am. Arbitration Assn., State Bar Tex. (vol. faculty profl. devel. program 1988-90; vice-chmn. profl. efficiency and econ. rsch. com. 1993; chmn. law office mgmt. com. 1993-94, (bd. dirs., 2002—, Walker County Bar Assn. (pres. 1987-88); Tex. State Bar Coll. (bd. dirs. 2001—), Assn. for Computer Educators Tex. (bd. dirs. 2001-03); Pub. Rels. Soc. Am.; Tex. Assn. Realtors; US Navy League; Naval Res. Assn.; Res. Officers Assn.; Dallas Vanderbilt Club (pres. 1977-78); bd. dir. Assoc. Computer Educators Texas, 2000-, State Bar Coll. Tex., 2002-. Office: PO Box 2144 Huntsville TX 77341-2144

STOWE, WILLIAM WHITFIELD, English language educator; b. New Haven, Dec. 7, 1946; s. Arthur Clifford Jr. and Barbara (Borst) S.; m. Karin Ann Trainer, May 8, 1976. BA magna cum laude, Princeton U., 1968; MPhil, Yale U., 1977, PhD, 1978; MA ad eundem gradum, Wesleyan U., 1992. Tchr. Coleytown Jr. High Sch., Westport, Conn., 1968-73; lectr. Princeton (N.J.) U., 1976, 77; instr. Rutgers U., New Brunswick, N.J., 1977; asst. prof. Wesleyan U., Middletown, Conn., 1979-84, assoc. prof., 1984-90, prof., 1990—, chair English dept., 1992-95, Benjamin Waite prof. of English lang., 1998—. Vis. lectr. Yale U., New Haven, 1978; vis. asst. prof. Wesleyan U., 1978-79; vis. prof. Princeton (NJ) U., 2003. Author: Balzac, James and the Realistic Novel, 1983, Going Abroad: European Travel in Nineteenth-Century American Culture, 1994; editor: The Poetics of Murder, 1983 (Edgar Allen Poe award nominee 1983); contbr. articles to profl. jours. Yale U. fellow, 1973-77. Home: PO Box 217 Middlefield CT 06455-0217 Office: Wesleyan U Dept English Middletown CT 06459-0001

STOWELL, EWELL ADDISON, botany educator, forestry consultant; b. Ashland, Ill., Sept. 2, 1922; s. Leslie Rockwell and Margaret Virginia (Flatt) S.; m. Barbara Joanne Edwards, June 21, 1953. BEd, Ill. State Normal U., Normal, 1943; MS in Botany, U. Wis., 1947, PhD, 1955. Instr. botany U. Wis., Milw., 1947-49, teaching asst. Madison, 1949-53; from instr. to assoc. prof. biology Albion (Mich.) Coll., 1953-65, prof., 1965-88, prof. emeritus, 1988—, chmn. dept., 1972-76. Vis. lectr. U. Wis., Madison, 1963; vis. prof. U. Mich., Ann Arbor, 1964. Co-author lab. manuals; contbr. articles to profl. jours. Cpl. U.S. Army, 1943-46, ETO. Stowell Arboretum at Albion Coll. named in his honor, 1988, Stowell Endowed Scholarship established 1996. Mem. Albion Acad. Advanced Learning, Am. Inst. Biol. Sci., Mich. Acad. Sci., Arts and Letters (chmn. botany sect. 1970-71, 89-90), Mich. Bot. Club (v.p. 1981-85), Mycological Soc. Am., Nat. Audubon Soc., Albion Acad. for Lifelong Learning, Sigma Xi (local pres. 1961, 73). Methodist. Avocations: birding, botanizing, gardening. Home: 1541 E Michigan Ave Albion MI 49224-9200 Office: Albion Coll 611 E Porter St Albion MI 49224-1831

STRAATSMA, BRADLEY RALPH, ophthalmologist, educator; b. Grand Rapids, Mich., Dec. 29, 1927; s. Clarence Ralph and Lucretia Marie (Nicholson) S.; m. Ruth Campbell, June 16, 1951; children: Cary Ewing, Derek, Greer. Student, U. Mich., 1947; MD cum laude, Yale U., 1951; DSc (hon.), Columbia U., 1984; JD cum laude, U. West LA, 2002. Diplomate Am. Bd. Ophthalmology (vice chmn. 1979, chmn. 1980). Intern New Haven Hosp., Yale U., 1951-52; resident in ophthalmology Columbia U., N.Y.C., 1955-58; spl. clin. trainee Nat. Inst. Neurol. Diseases and Blindness, Bethesda, Md., 1958-59; assoc. prof. surgery/ophthalmology UCLA Sch. Medicine, 1959-63, chief div. ophthalmology, dept. surgery, 1959-68, prof. surgery/ophthalmology, 1963-68, prof. ophthalmology, 1968—2001, dir. Jules Stein Eye Inst., 1964-94, chmn. dept. ophthalmology, 1968-94, prof. emeritus, 2001—; ophthalmologist-in-chief UCLA Med. Ctr., 1968-94. Lectr. numerous univs. and profl. socs. 1971—; cons. to surgeon gen. USPHS, mem. Vision Research Tng. Com., Nat. Inst. Neurol. Diseases and Blindness, NIH, 1959-63, mem. neurol. and sensory disease program project com., 1964-68; chmn. Vision Research Program Planning Com., Nat. Adv. Eye Council, Nat. Eye Inst., NIH, 1973-75, 75-77, 85-89; mem. med. adv. bd. Internat. Eye Found., 1970-79; mem. adv. com. on basic clin. research Nat. Soc. to Prevent Blindness, 1971-87; mem. med. adv. com. Fight for Sight, 1960-83; bd. dirs. So. Calif. Soc. to Prevent Blindness, 1967-77, Ophthalmic Pub. Co., 1975-93, v.p. 1990-93, Pan-Am. Ophthalmol. Found., 1985-95; chmn. sci. adv. bd. Ctr. for Partially Sighted, 1984-87; mem. nat. adv. panel Found. for Eye Research, Inc., 1984-94; mem. cons. com. Palestra Oftalmologica Panamericana, 1976-81; coord. com. Nat. Eye Health Edn. Program, 1989; mem. sci. adv. bd. Rsch. to Prevent Blindness, Inc., 1993—. Editor-in-chief Am. Jour. Ophthalmology, 1993-2002; mem. editorial bd. UCLA Forum in Med. Scis., 1974-82, Am. Jour. Ophthalmology, 1974-91, Am. Intra-Ocular Implant Soc. Jour., 1978-79, EYE-SAT Satellite-Relayed Profl. Edn. in Ophthalmology, 1982-86; mng. editor von Graefe's Archive for Clin. and Exptl. Ophthalmology, 1976-88; contbr. over 500 articles to med. jours. Trustee John Thomas Dye Sch., Los Angeles, 1967-72. Lt. USNR, 1952-54. Recipient William Warren Hoppin award N.Y. Acad. Medicine, 1956, Univ. Service award UCLA Alumni Assn., 1982, Miguel Aleman Found. medal, 1992, Benjamin Boyd Humanitarian award Pan Am. Assn. Ophthalmology, 1991, Lucian Howe medal, Am. Ophthalmological Soc., 1992, Internat. Gold Medal award 3rd Singapore Nat. Eye Ctr. Internat. Meeting and 11th Internat. Meeting on Cataract, Implant, Microsurgery and Refractive Keratoplasty, 1998, award of merit in retinal rsch. Retina Rsch. Found., 2002. Fellow Royal Australian Coll. Ophthalmologists (hon.); mem. Academia Ophthalmologica Internationales (pres. 1998-2002), Am. Acad. Ophthalmology (bd. councillors 1981, Life Achievement award 1999), Found. of Am. Acad. Ophthalmology (trustee 1989, chmn. bd. trustees 1989-92), Am. Acad. Ophthalmology and Otolaryngology (pres. 1977), Am. Soc. Cataract and Refractive Surgery, AMA (asst. sec. ophthalmology sect. 1962-63, sec. 1963-66, chmn. 1966-67, coun. 1970-74), Am. Ophthalmol. Soc. (coun. 1985-90, v.p. 1992, pres. 1993), Assn. Rsch. in Vision and Ophthalmology (Mildred Weisenfeld award 1991), Assn. U. Profs. of Ophthalmology (trustee 1969-75, pres.-elect 1973-74, pres. 1974-75), Assn. VA Ophthalmologists, Calif. Med. Assn. (mem. ophthalmology adv. panel 1972-94, chmn. 1974-79, sci. bd. 1973-79, ho. of dels. 1974, 77, 79), Chilean Soc. Ophthalmology (hon.), Columbian Soc. Ophthalmology (hon.), Glaucoma Soc. Internat. Congress of Ophthalmology (hon.), Heed Ophthalmic Found. (chmn., bd. dirs. 1990-98), Hellenic Ophthalmol. Soc. (hon.), Internat. Coun. Ophthalmology (bd. dirs. 1993), Internat. Coun. Ophthalmology Found. (pres. 2002—), LA County Med. Assn., LA Soc. Ophthalmology, Pan-Am. Assn. Ophthalmology (coun. 1972—, pres. elect 1985-87, pres. 1987-89), Peruvian Soc. Ophthalmology (hon.), Retina Soc., Barraquer Inst. Ophthalmology (pres. 1996—), Academia Ophthalmol. Internat. (pres. 1998-2002), Internat. Coun. Ophthalmology (pres. Found. 2002—, Jules Francois medal 2002), The Jules Gonin Club. Republican. Presbyterian. Avocations: music, scuba diving. Home: 3031 Elvido Dr Los Angeles CA 90049-1107 Office: UCLA 100 Stein Plz Los Angeles CA 90095-7065

STRAAYER, CAROLE KATHLEEN, retired elementary education educator; b. Jackson, Mich., Jan. 4, 1934; d. Joseph and Maude Vivian (Whitney) Kerr; m. Richard Lee Straayer, Feb. 1, 1958; children: Steven Jay, Susan Kay Straayer Maxson. A, Jackson Community Coll., Mich., 1953; BS, Ea. Mich. u., 1957, MA, 1961. Cert. elem. tchr., Mich. Tchr. Napoleon (Mich.) Sch. Dist., 1954-56, Waterford (Mich.) Twp. Sch. Dist., 1957, Jackson (Mich.) Pub. Schs., 1957-98. Mem. choir 1st Presbyn. Ch., Jackson, 1983—; mem. Jackson Recycling Task Force, 2002—. Jackson Citizen Patriot scholar, 1971. Mem. NEA, AAUW (group leader 1989-92, chmn. edn. com. 1998-2000, program v.p. 1999-2001, pres. 2002-2004), Mich. ASCD (region 3 rep. 1989-90), Mich. Edn. Assn. (ret.), Jackson Edn. Assn. (bldg. rep., chmn. tenure com. 1974-80, mem. negotiating team 1995, bd. dirs. 1996), Jackson/Hillsdale Profl. Devel. (rep. 1988-90), Delta Kappa Gamma (pres. Beta Beta chpt. 1986-88, 98—, mem. state nominating com. 2001—03, state chmn. profl. affairs 2001-03, state chmn. personal growth and svcs. 2003-2005). Avocations: playing bridge, giving parties, tutoring at school and home. Home: 2220 Pioneer Dr Jackson MI 49201-8900

STRACK, SHARON ANN, educator, musician; b. Perth Amboy, N.J., May 29, 1954; d. Peter Paul and Lucille Catherine (Anderson) McCann. BA, Jersey City State Coll., 1976; MEd, Trenton State Coll., 1980. Music specialist Woodbridge (N.J.) Twp. Bd. Edn., 1976—2002; prin. Ross St. Sch., Woodbridge, NJ, 2002—. Music coord. Our Lady of Fatima Ch., Piscataway, N.J., 1987-2002. Columnist, Tempo mag. Facilitator, coord. Metuchen Diocese Family Life, N.J., 1985-2002. Recipient Govs. Tchr. Recognition award, 1995, Govs. award for disting. leadership in music edn., 1998, Excellence in Edn. award Woodbridge Twp. Edn. Found., 1999; named Tchr. of Yr., Woodbridge Twp., 1999. Mem. N.J. Music Educators Assn. (bd. dirs. 1984-2001, exec. com. 1989-91, membership chairperson 1991-93, pres.-elect 1993-95, pres. 1995-97), Cen. Jersey Music Educators Assn. (bd. dirs. 1982-2000, sec. 1983-87, pres. 1989-91), Alliances for Arts Edn./N.J., Alpha Delta Kappa. Roman Catholic. Avocations: fishing, gardening, flower arranging, calligraphy, cooking. Home: 106 Anita Dr Piscataway NJ 08854-2463 Office: Ross St Sch #11 110 Ross St Woodbridge NJ 07095

STRADA, CHRISTINA BRYSON, retired humanities educator, librarian; b. Dunoon, Argyll, Scotland; d. Alexander Paul and Margaret (Spencer) Bryson; m. Joseph Anthony Strada (dec.); children: Michael, David, Elaine, Mary Margaret. AB, SUNY, Fredonia, 1968, MS, 1970; MLS, U. Buffalo, 1973. Library media specialist. Tchr. English Dunkirk (N.Y.) H.S., 1969-70, Cardinal Mindzenty H.S., Dunkirk, 1970-71, Lake Shore Cen. H.S., Angola, N.Y., 1971-72, libr., tchr., 1973-77; libr. dir. Darwin R. Barker Libr. and Mus., Fredonia, 1977-86; tchr., libr. Cassadaga (NY) Valley Sch. Dist., Fredonia, 1990—95; ret., 1995; instr. and librarian Fredonia (N.Y.) HS and BOCES Ednl. Ctr., Fredonia, 1995—2001. Instr. English composition, English lit., libr. rsch. Empire State Coll. N.Y., State Univ. Coll., Fredonia; cons. Friends of Barker Libr. and Mus., 1986—. Author short stories. Rschr. Fredonia Hist. Preservation Soc., 1986—; v.p. Friends of Barker Libr., 2001—; active Patterson Libr. Lit. Discussion Group; sec. NY State Victorian Soc., 2001—02; bd. dirs. Chautauqua County br. Lit. Vols. of Am., Dunkirk, NY, 1998—2001; bd. dirs., v.p. D.R. Barber Friends' Libr., 1997—2003. Mem. AAUW (chmn. telephone and reservations com. 1969—), NY State Libr. Assn., N.Y. State Tchr. Assn., LWV, Fredonia Shakespeare Club (v.p. 1988-89, pres. 1997-98, treas. 2002-03). Republican. Roman Catholic. Avocations: writing, reading, gardening, walking. Home: 15 Carol Ave Fredonia NY 14063-1207

STRAHILEVITZ, MEIR, inventor, researcher, psychiatry educator; b. Beirut, July 13, 1935; s. Jacob and Chana Strahilevitz; m. Aharona Nattiv, 1958; children: Michal, Lior. MD, Hadassah Hebrew U. Med. Sch., 1963. Diplomate Am. Bd. Psychiatry and Neurology, Royal Coll. Physicians and Surgeons Can. Asst. prof. Washington U. Med. Sch., St. Louis, 1971-74; assoc. prof. So. Ill. U., Springfield, 1974-77, U. Chgo., 1977, U. Tex. Med. Br., Galveston, 1978-81; chmn. dept. psychiatry Kaplan Hosp., Rehovot, Israel, 1987-88; clin. assoc. prof. U. Wash., Seattle, 1981-88; prof. U. Tex. Med. Sch., Houston, 1988-92. Contbr. articles to profl. jours. Fellow Am. Psychiat. Assn., Royal Coll. Physicians and Surgeons Can. Achievements include patents for immunological and affinity adsorption methods and devices for removing species from the blood circulatory system; specific adsorption devices with automatic regeneration of adsorben -t utilized in automated fluid purification and analytical and preparatory applications; for treatment methods for psychoactive drug dependence; for immunological methods for treating psychoactive drug intoxication; methods of improved targeting of drugs and visualization ligands, particularly in the treatment and diagnosis of cancer; invention of use of antibodies to receptors and their fragments as drugs, of immunoadsorption treatment of hyperlipidemia, cancer, autoimmune disease, atherosclerosis and coronary artery disease; immunoassay methods for psychoactive drugs; discovery of the protective effects of Nitric Oxide (NO) on psychiatric patients. Office: PO Box 25008 Seattle WA 98125-1908

STRAIN, LINDA ROGERS, elementary art educator; b. Greensburg, Ind., Sept. 10, 1943; d. Horace Sterling Rogers and Marguerite Coombs Caldwell; m. Harold Trenton Strain, Feb. 13, 1976; 1 child, Roger Lee. AA, Hinds Jr. Coll., Raymond, Miss., 1963; BA, Miss. Coll., Clinton, 1965. Art resource tchr. Jacksonville (Fla.) Pub. Schs., 1966-67; art tchr. Hapeville H.S., Atlanta, 1967-68, Nortan Elem. Sch., Louisville, 1968-71; elem. tchr. Gardendale Elem. Sch., Merritt Island, Fla., 1971-73; Congl. appointee Washington, 1973-75; art tchr. Clinton Jr. H.S., 1975-79, Pillow Acad., Greenwood, Miss., 1981-85, Warren (Ark.) H.S., 1985-86, Brown Elem. Sch., Star City, Ark., 1986—. Tchr. liaison At The Arts and Sci. Ctr., Pine Bluff, Ark., 1992—; mem. Ark. Arts Coun., Little Rock, 1994—; reader Winthrop Rockefeller Found., Little Rock, 1993—. Author: Jefferson County Art Curriculum Guide, 1970. Recipient award for patriotic svc. U.S. Savs. Bonds, 1994; Rockefeller grantee, 1992. Mem. DAR, Ark. Art Educators (newsletter editor 1991—, named Elem. Art Educator for Ark. 1992, Ark. Art Educator 1996), Ark. Edn. Assn. Democrat. Baptist. Avocations: reading, travel. Home: 303 Marie Dr Warren AR 71671-3435 Office: Brown Elem Sch 201 Ashley Star City AR 71667

STRAITON, T(HOMAS) HARMON, JR., librarian; b. Selma, Ala., June 28, 1941; s. Thomas Harmon and Marie (Khoeler) S. BS in Ornamental Horticulture, Auburn U., 1963; MLS, U. Ala., Tuscaloosa, 1979. Math. tchr. Tallassee (Ala.) City Schs., 1965-66, math., sci. tchr., 1966-68, head math. and sci. depts., 1968-78; head microforms and documents dept. Auburn (Ala.) U. Librs., 1980—, asst. dean info. svcs., 1998—2002, assoc. dean, 2002—. Adj. faculty Grad. Sch. Libr. Svc., U. Ala., 1988, 90, 95, 96—; chmn. Govt. Documents Roundtable, Southeastern Libr. Assn., 1986-88; condr. numerous workshops, seminars, presentations include 1992-93, 96 Notis Users Group meetings, Ala. Virtual Libr., 1997—; cons. Southeastern Libr. Network, 1997—. Contbr. numerous articles on microforms to fed. publs. and profl. jours. including The Ala. Librarian, Microform Rev.; pub.: Major Microform Sets Held by Alabama Libraries, 1988, Alabama's Major Microform Collections: The Enlarged and Revised Edition, 1991, Alabama's Major Microform Collections: The Electronic Edition, 1996. Group cond. United Way, 1981-83. Recipient Award of Excellence, Univ. Microfilm Internat., 1994, Eminent Librn. Ala. Lib. Assn., 1998. Mem. ALA (chmn. bylaws com. 1988-89, Govt. Documents Roundtable 1986-88, v.p. 1985-86, exec. coun. 1985-86, Eminent Libr. award 1998), Ala. Libr. Assn. (numerous editl. and ednl. coms., rep. 1991—, chmn. handbook com. 1986-90, chmn. awards com. 1995-03, bibliographic com. 1993—), Southeastern Libr. Assn. (Ala. rep., exec. bd. dirs., handbook com. 1995—, nominations com. 1995—), Alpha Zeta, Beta Phi Mu (Ala. chpt. Libr. of Yr. 1992), Gamma Sigma Delta, Pi Alpha Sigma. Democrat. Baptist. Avocations: gardening, reading. Home: PO Box 132 Auburn AL 36831-0132 Office: Assoc Dean Auburn U Librs Auburn AL 36849-5606 E-mail: strait@auburn.edu.

STRAKA, ROBERT JOHN, JR., music educator, band director; b. Pitts., Oct. 1, 1959; s. Robert John and Elaine Barbara S. MusB, West Va. U., 1981; MusM, Yale U., 1983. Cert. music tchr. Conn. Band dir. Betsy Ross Arts Magnet Sch., New Haven, Conn., 1983-89, Regional Sch. Dist. #16, Prospect, Beacon Falls, Conn., 1989—. Music specialist project Talent of Conn., New Haven, 1983-84; clarinet instr. Neighborhood Music Sch., 1988—; mem. steering com. Waterbury (Conn.) Regional Arts Project, 1989-92; co-presenter Conn. Inst. for Teaching and Learning, Hartford, 1991. Co-author: More Ideas for Kids: Classroom Principles and Activities in the Creative Arts for Use with Handicapped Students, 1984. Mem. Hamden (Conn.) Arts Commn., 1992 Named Tchr. of Yr. Regional Sch. Dist. # 16 Bd. Edn., Prospect, Conn., 1992-93. Mem. NEA, Conn. Edn. Assn., ASCD, Music Educators Nat. Conf., Conn. Music Educators Assn. (festival chmn. 1992, 93, so. regional dir. 1993-95), Conn. Alliance for Arts Edn. Democrat. Roman Catholic. Avocations: cooking, visual arts, travel, reading. Office: Regional Sch Dist # 16 30 Coer Rd Prospect CT 06712-1614

STRAND, MELVIN LEROY, English educator; b. Waseca, Minn., Mar. 15, 1936; s. Carl Morris and Dorothy Mae Robran S. BS, Minn. State U., Mankato, 1961, MS in Edn., 1968; MS, Bemidji (Minn.) State U., 1972; EdD, U. S.D., 1976. Tchr. English Rockford (Ill.) Secondary Schs., 1960-61, Rochester (Minn.) Secondary Schs., 1961-63, Richfield (Minn.) Secondary Schs., 1963-82; asst. prof. English King Saud U., Abha, Saudi Arabia, 1982-92; prof. English Saudi Arabian Am. Oil Co., Dhahran, Saudi Arabia, 1994, Royal Saudi Navy, Dhahran, 1995-96, Ctrl. Tex. Coll., Killeene, 1996—. Author: The Basic Sentence, 1989, Sentence to Paragraph, 1990; subject of nat. Saudi Arabian telecast Guest of Kingdom, 1991; contbr. articles to jours. in field. Vol., instr. AARP 55-Alive; active Minnesotans for Responsible Recreation, Nat. Arbor Day Found., Internat. Rescue Com.; com. mem. Dem. Congrl. Campaign; active Grace Luth. Ch. With USAF, 1955—59. Recipient, USAF Missile Badge, 1958. Mem. NEA, AARP, Minn. Edn. Assn., Nat. Coun. Tchrs. of English, Edn. Minn., Am. Fedn. of Tchrs., Ret. Educators Assn. Minn., Edn. Minn., Sierra Club, World Wildlife Fund, Nature Conservancy, Nat. Parks Conservation Assn., Childreach Plan Internat., Pi Delta Epsilon. Democrat. Lutheran. Avocations: world travel, reading, writing, environmental concerns. Home: 13342 382nd Ave Waseca MN 56093

STRANG, WILLIAM GILBERT, mathematician, educator; b. Chgo., Nov. 27, 1934; s. William Dollin and Mary Catherine (Finlay) S.; m. Jillian Mary Shannon, July 26, 1958; children— David, John, Robert. SB, MIT, 1955; BA (Rhodes scholar), Oxford (Eng.) U., 1957; PhD (NSF fellow), UCLA, 1959. Asst. prof. mathematics MIT, 1959-63, assoc. prof., 1963-66, prof., 1966—. Pres. Wellesley-Cambridge Press; hon. prof. Xian Jiaotong U., People's Republic of China, 1980. Author: An Analysis of the Finite Element Method, 1973, Linear Algebra and Its Applications, 1976, Introduction to Applied Mathematics, 1986, Calculus, 1990, Introduction to Linear Algebra, 1993, Wavelets and Filter Banks, 1996, Linear Algebra, Geodesy, and GPS, 1997. Recipient Chauvenet prize Math. Assn. Am., 1977; Sloan fellow, 1966-67, Hon. fellow Balliol Coll., Oxford, 1999; Fairchild scholar, 1981. Mem. Soc. Indsl. and Applied Math. (pres. 1999-2000). Home: 7 Southgate Rd Wellesley MA 02482-6606 Office: MIT Math Dept Rm 2-240 Cambridge MA 02139 E-mail: gs@math.mit.edu.

STRANGE, FRANCES RATHBUN, financial aid administrator, therapist; b. Wichita Falls, Tex., Aug. 14, 1949; d. Willie and Viola Gertrude (Loesby/Jarrell) Rathbun; m. Douglas William Strange, 1967 (div. Apr. 1992); children: Chad Douglas, Cameron Todd, Cooper Lane, Chance (dec.). B of Behavioral Sci., Hardin-Simmons U., 1988, MEd, 1992; M of Human Rels., U. Okla., 1990. Lic. profl. counselor. Bus. officer Hardin-Simmons U., Abilene, Tex., 1983-85; admissions office Hardin Simmons U., Abilene, Tex., 1986-88, asst. fin. aid dir., 1989-93, dir. fin. aid, 1993-96; grant coord. fin. aid Baylor U., Waco, Tex., 1985-86; social worker Dept. Human Svcs., Duncan, Okla., 1988-89; dir. fin. aid U. Sci. and Arts of Okla., Chickasha, 1996-99, Oklahoma City Meth. U., 1999—. Contract counselor Harmony Family Svcs., Abilene, 1992-96. Mem. APA, ACA, Nat. Assn. Student Fin. Aid Adminstrs., Okla. Assn. Student Fin. Aid Adminstrs., S.W. Assn. Student Fin. Aid Adminstrs., Alpha Chi. Baptist. Avocations: camping, traveling, fishing. Home: PO Box 66 Union City OK 73090

STRANGES, ANTHONY NICHOLAS, science history educator; b. Niagara Falls, NY, Sept. 28, 1936; s. Victor Anthony and Maria Theresa (Serianni) S.; m. Sonya Michelene Rudy, Aug. 24, 1963; children: Krista, Kara. BS in Chemistry, Niagara U., 1958, MS in Chemistry, 1964; PhD in History of Sci., U. Wis., 1977. Secondary tchr. Notre Dame Coll. Sch., Welland, Ont., Can., 1959-63, Lewiston-Porter H.S., Youngstown, N.Y., 1963-69; prof. Tex. A&M U., College Station, 1977—. Author: Electrons and Valence, 1982; contbr. articles to profl. jours. Recipient Faculty Disting. award for Tchg. Assn. of Former Students, Tex. A&M U., 1987. Mem. Am. Hist. Assn., Can. Sci. and Tech. History Assn., Soc. for the History of Tech., Hist. of Sci. Soc. Democrat. Roman Catholic. Avocations: music, collecting stamps. Home: 1205 Barak Ln Bryan TX 77802-3202 Office: Tex A&M U Dept History College Station TX 77843-0001 Business E-Mail: a-stranges@tamu.edu.

STRASBURG, LINDA ANN, corporate radio trainer, talk show host speaker; b. Price, Utah, Dec. 1, 1948; d. William Henry and Lillyan (O'Berto) Loomis; m. Jerry R. Bell, Sept. 11, 2002; children: Sundee A., Sean T. Cert. in Design, Utah Tech. Coll., 1970, BS in Human Resource Mgmt. cum laude, 1987; M in Profl. Commn. Writing. Cert. clin. hypnotherapist, leadership trainer, Jump Start Entrepreneur Program. Telephone operator Mountain Bell Telephone Co., Salt Lake City, 1969-71; owner, operator Strasburg machine, West Jordan, Utah, 1976-90; v.p. publs. Utah

Tech. Coll., Salt Lake City, 1984—; sr. cust. svc. agent Delta Air Lines, Salt Lake City, 1988—; owner Brauns & Co., Lights On-Network, 1993—; talk show host trainer, 1992—. Arbitrator Better Bus. Bureau.; talk show host KTALK Radio. Group shows include West Jordan Women's Art Show, Granite Art Show, Utah Tch. Coll. Comml. Art Show. Pres. West Jordan Cmty. Crime Watch, 1976-79; pub. spkr. West Jordan Crime Prevention, Utah, 1976-78; commr. Utah Crime Prevention Assn., Salt Lake City, 1978; mem. masterplan com. West Jordan City, 1979, mem. assessment panel, 1980; mem. instl. coun. Salt Lake C.C., 1986—, alumni coun., 1986-88; pres. Westland PTA, West Jordan, 1980-82, West Jordan Elem. PTA, 1982-83. Mem. Nat. Spkrs. Assn., Am. Soc. Tng. Devel., Utah Women's Bus. Coun., Toastmasters. Home: 2303 Straw Cir West Jordan UT 84084-2106

STRASSER, GERHARD FRIEDRICH, German language and comparative literature educator; b. Landshut, Germany, Sept. 13, 1940; came to the U.S., 1967; s. Friedrich Ludwig and Josephine (Buchner) S. MA, Bavarian Ministry Edn., Munich, 1965, MAT, 1967; PhD in Comparative Lit., Brown U., 1974. Studienreferendar Goethe-Gymnasium, Regensburg, Germany, 1965-66; asst. tchr. secondary sch. Gymnasium Cham, Germany, 1966-67; instr. German Trinity Coll., Hartford, Conn., 1967-68, instr. French, 1968-69; libr. reference asst. Brown U., Providence, 1972-73; asst. prof. German and comparative lit. Northwestern U., Evanston, Ill., 1973-79, Pa. State U., University Park, 1979-86, assoc. prof., 1986-96, prof., 1996—, head dept. Germanic and Slavic langs. and lits., 1997-2000. Author: Lingua Universalis, 1988, Mnemonik und Emblematik der Fruehen Neuzeit, 2000; co-author: Assoziationen, 1991, Alles Gute!, 4th edit., 1994; co-editor Comparative Literature Studies, 1988-2001, assoc. editor, 2001-; Johann Joachim Becher 1635-1682, 1993; editl. cons. McGraw-Hill, Inc., N.Y.C., 1984-97, Klett Verlag, Stuttgart, Germany, 1988-97; contbr. articles to profl. jours. Recipient Pa. State U. Class of 1933 award, 1989; grantee Am. Coun. Learned Socs., 1978, Am. Philos. Soc., 1985, 92, German Acad. Exch. Svc., 1987, Thyssen Found., 1988; Volkswagen Found. fellow, 1977, 78, 81-82; Fulbright Found. lectr., 1967-68, scholar, 1960-61; named to faculty honor roll Northwestern U., 1976-77. Mem. MLA, German Soc. for History Sci., Am. Comparative Lit. Assn., Am. Assn. Tchrs. German, Thomas-Mann-Gesellschaft. Avocations: classical music, travel, cross-country skiing. Home: 3702 Plaza Dr State College PA 16801-4668 E-mail: gfs1@psu.edu.

STRATING, SHARON L. elementary school educator, college instructor; b. Jamestown, ND, Jan. 20, 1949; d. Walter and Evelyn Darlene (Lang) Remmick; m. Rick Donald Strating, Dec. 24, 1978 (presently divorced); children: Heather Dawn, Amber Nicole, Ashley Renee. BS in Secondary Edn., So. Mo. State U., 1971; MEd in Sci. Edn., N.W. Mo. State U., 1992. Cert. elem. tchr., Mo. Tchr. Cassville R-III Sch., 1971-76, Savannah R-III Sch. Sys., Mo., 1976-91; instr. 4th grade Horace Mann Lab. Sch., Maryville, Mo., 1991—. Facilitator for Environ. Edn. Pilot Project Kans. U., Lawrence; co-chair EPA Pollution Prevention Adv. Task Force; mem. biol. sci. curriculum study Elem. Tchr. Module Project, 1993; instr. for coll. practicum students; Map 2000 Sr. Leader for performance-based assessment sys., Mo., 1994—. Author: Living the Constitution Through the Eyes of the Newspaper, 1987, Tabloid Teaching Tool, 6 edits., 1986-91; tchr. guides in lit. revised editions for Sadako and the Thousand Paper Cranes, The Kid in the Red Jacket, Missing Gator of Gumbo Limbo, Owls in the Family, Where the Waves Break: Life at the Edge of the Sea, 2000-2001; author: Open the Eyes of Children to the World of Literacy Through Copmprehensive Literacy, Prof. Develop. Program, 2002. Chairperson March of Dimes, 1972-76, Cystic Fibrosis, 1972-78; scout leader Brownies, 1976-77; exec. bd. dirs. PTA, 1976-82, fund raising chairperson, 1976-83; program chairperson presch. PTA, 1976-80;chairperson community environ. activities, 1976—, Adopt a Hwy. Program, 1976-91; mem. Mo. Stream Team Effort, 1976—. Recipient Nat. Pres. Environ. Youth award, 1988, 89, Presdl. award State of Mo., 1992, 93, Nat. Presdl. award, 1992-93; named Mo. State Tchr. of Yr., 1990-91, Disney Salutes the Am. Tchr. award, 1995. Mem. Nat. Hist. Soc., Internat. Reading Assn., Nat. Bd. for Profl. Tching. Standards and Mid.-Age Child in Sci., Nat. Sci. Tchrs. Assn., Nat. Assn. Lab. Schs. (sec. 1994-95), Sci. Tchrs. Mo. Lutheran. Avocations: travel, ecology, creative writing, motivational speaking, arts and crafts. Office: Northwest Mo State U Horace Mann Lab Sch Brown Hall Rm 108 Maryville MO 64468 Home: 3A Faustiana Pl Maryville MO 64468

STRATIS, GEORGE, finance educator; b. N.Y.C., Oct. 10, 1947; s. James and Mary (Manias) S.; m. Tina Candiloros, June 21, 1970; children: Justin, Diana Christine. BSEE, Poly. Inst. Bklyn., 1969; MSEE, NYU, 1972, MBA, 1975; DBA, Nova Southeastern U., 1997. Devel. engr. def. activities div. Western Electric, Whippany, N.J., 1969-72, planning engr. engring. div. N.Y.C., 1972-75; dir. svc. costs AT&T, Basking Ridge, N.J., 1975-81, product mgr., 1981-84; dir. licensing Bellcore, Livingston, N.J., 1984-88, dir. market planning and analysis, 1988-90, dir. total quality mgmt. team bus. planning and benchmarking, 1990—94, dir. strategic market planning, 1994—97, dir. global alliance devel., 1997—99; prof. bus. and fin. Nyack (NY) Coll., 1999—. Comptroller Millington (N.J.) Bapt. Ch., 1983-84; ranger Boys Brigade Chatham, N.J., 1987—; facilities mgr. Long Hill Chapel Chatham, N.J., 1991-92, Sunday Sch. supt., 1992-94, ch. treas., 1994-97; mem. Cornerstone Bible Ch. Mem. Planning Forum (treas.). Avocations: golf, tennis, swimming. Office: Nyack Coll 1 South Blvd Nyack NY 10960

STRATMAN, DEBORAH, filmmaker, film and video educator; BFA, Sch. of the Art Inst. of Chgo., 1990; MFA, Calif. Inst. of the Arts, 1995. Adj. asst. prof. Film, Video and New Media, 1998; filmmaker and adj. asst., prof. film and video Sch. of Art Inst. of Chgo., 1998—. John Simon Guggenheim Meml. Found., 2003. Office: 37 South Wabash Chicago IL 60603-3103

STRATT, RICHARD MARK, chemistry researcher, educator; b. Phila., Feb. 21, 1954; s. Stanford Lloyd and Florence Clair (Sussman) S. SB in Chemistry, MIT, 1975; PhD, U. Calif., Berkeley, 1979. Postdoctoral rsch. assoc. U. Ill., Champaign, 1979-80; NSF postdoctoral rsch. assoc., 1980; asst. prof. chemistry Brown U., Providence, 1981-85, assoc. prof., 1986-88, prof., 1988—, dept. chair, 1996—99, Harrison S. Kravis prof., 1999—2000. Mem. editl. bd. Jour. Chem. Physics, 2002—; mem. adv. bd. Jour. Phys. Chemistry, 1999—; contbr. articles to profl. jours. Alfred P. Sloan fellow, 1985-89; Fulbright scholar Oxford U., 1981-82. Fellow Am. Phys. Soc.; mem. Am. Chem. Soc. (chmn.-elect theoretical chem. subdivsn. 1997-98, chair 1998-99, program chair phys. chem. divsn. 2000-01, chair 2001-02), Sigma Xi, Phi Lambda Upsilon. Office: Brown U Dept Chemistry Providence RI 02912-0001 Business E-Mail: Richard_Stratt@brown.edu.

STRATTA, TERESE MARIE, physical education educator; b. Chgo., Mar. 4, 1959; d. Peter Joseph and Lillian Mae (Peretto) S. BS magna cum laude, East Stroudsburg State Coll., 1982; MS, East Stroudsburg U., 1984; PhD, So. Ill. U., Carbondale, 1994: Cert. phys. edn./health instr. grades K-12, Pa. Elem. phys. edn. tchr., coach Mountain View Sch. Dist., Kingsley, Pa., 1982-83; grad. coaching asst. East Stroudsburg (Pa.) U., 1983-84; cardiac rehab. coord. Highland Physicians, Ltd., Honesdale, Pa., 1984-85; adminstr., instr., coach The Pa. State U., Worthington-Scranton Campus, Dunmore, 1985-87; corp. fitness dir. Owens-Ill., TV Products Div., Pittston, Pa., 1987-88; grad. teaching and rsch. asst. So. Ill. U., Carbondale, 1988-92; asst. prof. Anderson Coll. Contbr. chpts. to books. Recipient Athletic Volleyball scholarships So. Ill. U., 1977-79, Ill. State U., Normal, 1979-80. Mem. Internat. Assn. Phys. Edn. and Sport for Girls and Women, N.Am. Soc. for Sports Mgmt., N.Am. Soc. for Sociology of Sport, Nat. Assn. Collegiate Women Athletic Adminstrs., Nat. Assn. Girls' and Women's Sport (rsch. network mem. 1990—, minority rep. divsn. 1992—), AAHPERD, Am. Coll. Sports Medicine (cert. exercise specialist), AAUW. Avocations: jogging, hiking. Home: 20433 Ithaca Rd Olympia Fields IL 60461-1341

STRATTON, CHARLOTTE ETHEL, retifed secondary education educator; b. Kearney, N.J., June 4, 1932; d. Philip Sr. and Ethel (Irwin) Coombe; m. Vernon E. Stratton, June 5, 1954; children: Lynn Stratton McDonald, Vernon Jr., Elaine C. Stratton Iatauro, Laurie. BS, Beaver Coll., 1954. Mem. supts. cabinet TriValley Ctrl., Grahamsville, N.Y., 1989-90; team leader grade 8 Tri-Valley Ctrl. Sch., Grahamsville, N.Y., 1991-93; mem. bldg. leadership team Tri-Valley, Grahamsville, N.Y., 1991-98. Recipient Tchr. of Yr. award Tri-Valley Tchrs. Assn., 1990, nominated for Sullivan County Tchr. of Yr., 1993. Avocations: stenciling, gardening, knitting. Home: 697 S Hill Rd Grahamsville NY 12740-5108

STRAUB, SUSAN MONICA, special education educator; b. Tampa, Fla., Jan. 31, 1954; d. Paul Ferdinand and Betty Hew (Wellacott) S. AA, Hillsborough Community Coll., 1975; BA, U. S. Fla., 1978. Lifeguard, swimming instr. Tampa Recreation Dept., 1970-74 summers, pool mgr., 1975-76 summers, office asst. sec., 1977-78 summers; tchr. Hillsborough Assn. Retarded Citizens, Tampa, 1978-79, Hillsborough County Sch. Bd., Tampa, 1979—, Sch. of Hope, 1979-81, Mango Elem. Sch., 1981-85, Lopez Elem Sch., Seffner, Fla., 1985-93, Wilson Elem. Sch., Plant City, Fla., 1993-98, Mann Mid. Sch., Brandon, Fla., 1998-2000, Armwood H.S., Seffner, Fla., 2000—. Coach Spl. Olympics, Tampa, 1980, 2000—, games ofcl., 1982, steering com., Hillsborough County, 1984-92. Sec., treas. Superstar Bowling League for Handicapped, Tampa, 1988-89, 1st v.p., 1989-91. Recipient Spl. Olympics award Hillsborough County, State of Fla., 1980; named Vol. of Yr. Mass. Mutual, 1982, Coach of Yr. Hillsborough County Spl. Olympics, 1982, Tchr. of Yr. U. So. Fla. Alumni Assn., 1990. Mem. Coun. Exceptional Children (hospitality chair, Dept. Exceptional Student Edn. Person of Yr. 1987-88, Chpt. Tchr. of Yr. 1990), Soroptimist Internat. (1st v.p., 2d v.p. 1990-91, Team Leader 1985-91, 92-93). Democrat. Roman Catholic. Avocations: soccer, swimming. Home: 517 Somerstone Dr Valrico FL 33594- Office: Armwood H S 12000 Hwy 92 Seffner FL 33584-3418

STRAUGHAN, WILLIAM THOMAS, engineering educator; b. Shreveport, La., Aug. 2, 1936; s. William Eugene and Sara Chloetilde (Harrell) S.; m. Rubie Ann Barnes, Aug. 20, 1957; children: Donna Ann, Sara Arlene, Eugene Thomas. BS, MIT, 1959; MS, U. Tex., 1986; PhD, Tex. Tech. U., 1990. Registered profl. engr., Fla., Ill., Iowa., La., Tex., Wash. Project engr. Gen. Dynamics Corp., Chgo., 1959-60; chief project, design engr. Gen. Foods Corp., Kankakee, Ill., 1960-64; mgr. plant engring. Standard Brands Inc., Clinton, Iowa, 1964-66; regional mgr. Air Products & Chems., Inc., Creighton, Pa., 1966-68; gen. mgr. Skyline Corp., Harrisburg, N.C., 1968-70; cons. Charlotte, N.C., 1970-72; dir. engring. and Fla. ops. Zimmer Homes Corp., Pompano Beach, 1972-73; v.p. engring. and mfg. Nobility Homes, Inc., Ocala, Fla., 1973-78, Moduline Internat., Inc., Lacey, Wash., 1978-85; rsch. engr. U. Tex., Austin, 1985-86; lectr., rschr. Tex. Tech. U., Lubbock, 1987-90; assoc. prof. U. New Orleans, 1990-92; asst. prof. dept. civil engring. La. Tech. U., Ruston, 1992-98. Tchr. 26 different courses, 1987—; adj. prof. Coll. Engring., La. Tech. U., 2001--; cons. in field, Dubach, La., 1992—; condr. workshops in field; apptd. spokesman Mfrd. Housing Industry before U.S. Congress. Contbr. articles to profl. jours. Vol. engring. svcs. Lubbock Fire Safety House, 1990; judge sci. fair Ben Franklin H.S., New Orleans, 1990. Recipient T.L. James Svc. award La. Tech. U., 1994; grantee Urban Waste Mgmt. and Rsch. Ctr., New Orleans, 1991, Shell Devel. Co., 1993, La. Edn. Quality Support Fund, Insituform Techs., Inc., Trenchless Tech. Ctr., PABCO, Inc., InLiner USA, Inc., 1995, others; numerous grants in field. Mem. ASME (life), ASCE (Student chpt. Tchr. of Yr. award 1995, 98), Phi Kappa Phi, Sigma Xi, Chi Epsilon. Achievements include design, construction and management of first plant for the production of intermediate moisture pet food (Gainesburgers) in the world; organization and direction of all activities to allow Clinton, Iowa plant with a 1 mile shoreline to continue operations during the greatest flood of the upper Mississippi River in 1965. Avocations: flying, skiing, backpacking, golf, photography. Home: 199 Sellers Rd Dubach LA 71235-3218 E-mail: drtomstraughan@msn.com.

STRAUGHN, LAURA HAMILTON, special education educator; b. LaGrange, Ky., Nov. 11, 1961; d. Bruce Ross and Hilda Ann (King) Hamilton; m. Leonard Ray Straughn, Dec. 27, 1986. Student, Eastern Ky. U., 1979-81; BA, U. Ky., Lexington, 1983; Masters, U. Louisville, 1990. Cert. spl. edn. tchr., Ind., Ky. Tchr. spl. edn. Oldham County Schs., 1984-89; edn. specialist Jefferson (Ind.) Hosp., 1989-93; state cons. Ky. Dept. of Edn., Frankfort, 1993; cons. Floyd County Schs., New Albany, Ind., 1993-94, spl. edn. tchr., 1994—. Presenter Floyd County Schs. and Jefferson Hosp., 1990—, Ky. Dept. Edn., Frankfort, 1993—; mem. task force on emotional behavioral disability Ky. Dept. Edn., Frankfort, 1993. Presenter Floyd County Schs. and Jefferson Hosp., 1990—, Ky. Dept. Edn., Frankfort, 1993—; mem. tasl force on emotional behavioral disability Kt. Dept. Edn., Frankfort, 1993; adj. instr. Ind. U., 1996. Mem. ASCD, Coun. for Exceptional Children, Coun. for Children with Behavior Disorders (v.p. 1994). Avocations: antiques, horse-back riding. Home: 7425 W Highway 524 Westport KY 40077-9705 Office: New Albany HS 1020 Vincennes St New Albany IN 47150-3148

STRAUS, KATHLEEN NAGLER, education administrator, consultant; b. N.Y.C., Dec. 3, 1923; d. Maurice and Mildred (Kohn) Nagler; m. Everet M. Straus, May 29, 1948 (dec. Nov. 1967); children: Peter R., Barbara L. BA in Econs., Hunter Coll., 1944; postgrad., Columbia U., 1944-45, Am. U., 1946-47, Wayne State U., 1976-78. Various positions, 1944-50, 66; dep. dir. Model Neighborhood Agy., City of Detroit, 1968-70; dir. social svcs. Southeastern Mich. Coun. Govts., Detroit, 1970-74; staff coord. Edn. Task Force, Detroit, 1974-75; exec. dir. People and Responsible Orgns. for Detroit, 1975-76; staff dir. edn. com. Mich. Senate, Lansing, 1976-79; assoc. exec. dir. Mich. Assn. Sch. Bds., Lansing, 1979-86; dir. community rels. and devel. Ctr. for Creative Studies, Detroit, 1986-87, pres., 1987-91; mem. Mich. Bd. Edn., 1992—, pres., 2003. Mem. Mich. Bd. for Pub. Jr. and C.C.s, Lansing, 1980-92, v.p., 1989, pres., 1991; cons. Met. Columbus (Ohio) Schs. Com., 1975-76; mem.. steering com. Mich. Edn. Seminars, 1979-86; mem. Adv. Com. on Higher Edn. Needs in S.W. Mich., 1971-72, Ad Hoc Com. on Equal Access to Higher Edn., 1970-71, Citizens Action Com. on Sch. Fin. Contbr. articles to profl. jours. Active numerous civic orgns.; vice chmn. downtown br. Met. Detroit YWCA, 1970-74; bd. dirs. Citizens for Better Care, Inc., 1973-78; mem. edn. com. New Detroit, Inc., 1972—; trustee Detroit Sci. Ctr., Inc., 1975—; founder, pres. Mich. Tax Info. Coun., 1982—; v.p. bd. dirs. Univ. Cultural Ctr. Assn., 1986-91; trustee Comprehensive Health Planning Coun. Southeastern Mich., 1977-78; mem. Wayne County Art and History Commn., 1988; co-chmn. Nat. Arts Program, 1987-88. Recipient Amity citation Congress, Detroit, 1966, Disting. Community Svc. award Am. Jewish Com., 1988, Disting. Community Svc. award Common Coun., Detroit, 1976, resolution Mich. Ho. of Reps., 1986, Mich. Senate, 1988, Educator of Yr. Wayne State U., 1999, Disting. Warrior award Detroit Urban League, 2000; named to Mich. Edn. Hall of Fame, 1997; inducted into Mich. Women's Hall of Fame, 2000. Mem. LWV (pres. Detroit 1961-63), Alpha Chi Alpha.. Democrat. Avocations: travel, theater, concerts. Home: 8801 Kingswood St Detroit MI 48221-1569 Office: State Bd Edn PO Box 30008 Lansing MI 48909-7508

STRAUS, LORNA PUTTKAMMER, biology educator; b. Chgo., Feb. 15, 1933; d. Ernst Wilfred and Helen Louise (Monroe) Puttkammer; m. Francis Howe Straus II, June 11, 1955; children: Francis, Helen, Christopher, Michael. BA magna cum laude, Radcliffe Coll., 1955; MS, U. Chgo., 1960, PhD, 1962. Rsch. assoc. dept. anatomy U. Chgo., 1962-64, instr., 1964-67, asst. prof., 1967-73, assoc. prof., 1973-87, prof., 1987—, asst. dean, then dean students Coll., 1967-82, dean admissions Coll., 1975-80, univ. marshal, 1999—. Trustee Radcliffe Coll., Cambridge, Mass., 1973-83; chmn. Cmty. Found., Mackinac Island, Mich., 1994—. Recipient silver medal Coun. for Advancement and Support Edn., 1987. Mem.: North Ctrl. Assn. (commr. 1998—, pres.-elect 2001—02, pres. 2002—), Harvard U. Alumni Assn. (bd. dirs. 1980—83), Phi Beta Kappa. Avocations: travel, gardening. Home: 5642 S Kimbark Ave Chicago IL 60637-1606 Office: U Chgo 5845 S Ellis Ave Chicago IL 60637-1476 E-mail: l-straus@uchicago.edu.

STRAUSER, BEVERLY ANN, education educator; b. Dunkirk, N.Y., July 19, 1956; d. Henry Frank and Agnes Frances (Bielat) Rutkowski; m. Edward Britton Strauser, Oct. 9, 1982; children: Nicholas, Douglas, Thomas. BS, Regents Coll., Albany, N.Y., 1985; MS, SUNY, Fredonia, 1990; postgrad., U. Sarasota, 1998—. Cert. tchr. early childhood, bus. adminstrn., N.Y. Tchr. gifted edn. and computer literacy North Collins (N.Y.) Ctrl. Sch., 1986-87; tchr. pre-sch. St. Anthony's Sch., Fredonia, 1988-91; asst. prof. edn., tchr. edn. portfolio coord. Armstrong Atlantic State U., Savannah, Ga., 1992—2000; supr. student tchrs. Ga. So. U., Statesboro, 2000—. Cons. Jamestown (N.Y.) Cmty. Schs., 1989-91, Jewish Ednl. Allance, Savannah, 1991-92, Meth. Daysch. of Richmond Hill, Ga., 1992-93, Cath. Diocese Savannah, 1998-99; presenter in field. Recipient Key award Jamestown Cmty. Schs., 1990. Mem. Nat. Assn. for the Edn. of Young Children, Ga. Assn. on Young Children (bd. dirs., sr. dist. rep. 1992-94), Internat. Reading Assn., Assn. Childhood Edn. Internat. Avocations: travel, reading. Home: 264 Boyd Dr Richmond Hill GA 31324-4155 Office: Ga So Univ Statesboro GA

STRAUSER, EDWARD B. psychologist, educator; b. Dunkirk, N.Y., June 6, 1953; s. Fredrick Edward and Lucille Ruth (Mayott) S.; m. Beverly Ann Rutkoswki; children: Nicholas, Douglas, Thomas. BS, SUNY, Fredonia, 1975; MS, Canisius Coll., 1980; EdD, SUNY, Buffalo, 1986. Tchr. Pioneer Mid. Sch., Yorkshire, N.Y., 1977-82; sch. psychologist BOCES, Orchard Park, N.Y., 1982-91; asst. prof. Pembroke (N.C.) State U., 1987-88; from asst. prof. to prof. ednl. psychology Armstrong State Coll., Savannah, Ga., 1991—2001; coord. profl. devel. Wurzburg (Germany) H.S., 2001—. Cons. ACT/PEP Test Svc., Albany, NY, 1988, SUNY, Fredonia, 1988—89, Cleve. City Schs., 1992; vis. prof. Andhra U., Visakapatnam, India, 1998; coord. profl. devel. Wurzburg (Germany) H.S., 2001—. Contbr. chpts. to books and articles to profl. jours. Mem. exec. bd. Erie County Spl. Olympics, Orchard Park, 1983-84; bd. dirs. N.Y. Assn. Sch. Psychologists, 1990. Recipient Citation for Contribution to field of electrothermal biofeedback research, 1986, Citation of Appreciation for Profl. Contbn., Nat. Mid. Sch. Assn., 1988, Outstanding Svc. Awd. Project Safe Place, 1995. Mem. AAUP, Am. Assn. Tchg. and Curriculum, Nat. Assn. Sch. Psychologists, N.Y. State Tchrs. of Handicapped, Ga. Mid. Level Educators, Phi Delta Kappa. Avocation: travel. Home: 264 Boyd Dr Richmond Hill GA 31324-4155 Office: Armstrong State Coll 11935 Abercorn St Savannah GA 31419-1909

STRAUSER, SIMEON JOHN, academic administrator; b. Coatesville, Pa., July 21, 1958; s. Charles Elwood and AnnaMae (Garrahan) S.; divorced; 1 child, Nathan Charles. Grad. Theology, Full Gospel Bible Inst., 1981; ThM (hon.), Evang. Theol. Sem., 1986. Stewardship dir. mission outreach Full Gospel Missions, Coatesville, Pa., 1983—; also exec. bd. mem.; v.p. student affairs Full Gospel Bible Inst., Coatesville, 1989—; also exec. bd. mem. Adv. bd. mem. Full Gospel Assemblies Internat., 1986—, conf. lectr., 1983—; adminstrv. counsel Philippine Benguet Bible Inst., 1983-84; classroom asst., tutor Rainbow Elem. Sch. Coatesville Area Sch. Dist., 1987-90. Editor news report/quarterly Full Gospel Ministries Mission Outreach Report, 1990-92; exec. prodr. edn. video, 1992. Mem. Full Gospel Bible Inst. Alumni Assn., Full Gospel Assembly of Parkesburg, Pa. Avocations: travel, hiking, biking, 18th century real estate restorations. Office: Full Gospel Missions PO Box 1230 Coatesville PA 19320-0157

STRAUSS, ALBRECHT BENNO, English educator, editor; b. Berlin, May 17, 1921; came to U.S., 1940; s. Bruno and Bertha (Badt) S.; m. Nancy Grace Barron, July 30, 1978; 1 child, Rebecca Ilse; stepchildren: Carolyn, Kathryn BA, Oberlin Coll., 1942; MA, Tulane U., 1948; PhD, Harvard U., 1956. Instr. English Brandeis U., 1951-52; teaching fellow gen. edn. Harvard U., 1952-55; instr. English Yale U., 1955-59; asst. prof. English U. Okla., Norman, 1959-60, U. N.C., Chapel Hill, 1960-64, assoc. prof., 1964-70, prof., 1970-91, prof. emeritus, 1991—; lectr. Duke Inst. for Learning in Retirement, 1993—. Editor Studies in Philology, 1974-80; sec. editorial com. Yale Edit. of Works of Samuel Johnson, 1975— ; mem. editorial com. Ga. edit. works of Tobias Smollett, 1973—; contbr. articles to lit. publs. Served with U.S. Army, 1942-46 Recipient Tanner Teaching award U. N.C., 1966; Fulbright fellow, Germany, 1983-84 Mem. MLA, South Atlantic MLA, Am. Soc. Eighteenth-Century Studies (pres. Southeastern group 1980-81), Johnsonians Republican. Jewish. Home: 396 Lakeshore Ln Chapel Hill NC 27514-1728

STRAUSS, DIANE JAYNE, elementary school educator, small business owner; b. Crawfordsville, Ind., July 6, 1940; d. Harold and Madge Virginia Wright. BS, Purdue U., 1964; MS, Butler U., 1971, postgrad., 1974—, Ind. Vocat. Tech. Coll., 1983—, Ind.-Purdue U., 1980—. With Am. United Life Ins. Co., Indpls., 1959-64; tchr. St. Matthews Elem. Sch., Indpls., 1962-63, Decatur Twp. Sch. System, Indpls., 1964-71; reading coord. Benton County Sch. System, Fowler, Ind., 1971-73; tchr. Ctr. Grove High Sch., Greenwood, Ind., 1978-79; coord. title 1 dept. corrections curriculum projects Ind. U.-Purdue U., Indpls., 1980-82; tchr. Indpls. Pub. Schs., 1986—2002, instrl. coach, 2002—. Owner, co-dir. Bus. Personal Devel. Ctr., Indpls., 1971-86, Strauss Learning Ctr., Indpls., 1971-90, Strauss Enterprises, 1991—. Pres. Decatur Twp. Tchrs. Assn., Indpls., 1970, ednl. lobbist, 1964-97. Mem.: Mem. ASCD, NEA, Indt. State Tchrs. Assn., Indpls. Edn. Assn. (life), Phi Delta Phi. Home and Office: 7370 Lions Head Dr A Indianapolis IN 46260-3460

STRAUSS, HERBERT LEOPOLD, chemistry educator; b. Aachen, Germany, Mar. 26, 1936; came to U.S., 1940, naturalized, 1946; s. Charles and Joan (Goldschmidt) S.; m. Carolyn North Cooper, Apr. 24, 1960; children: Michael Abram, Rebecca Anne, Ethan Edward. AB, Columbia U., 1957, MA, 1958, PhD, 1960; postgrad, Oxford U., 1960-61. Mem. faculty U. Calif., Berkeley, 1961—, prof. chemistry, 1973—, vice chmn. dept. chemistry, 1975-81, 92-95, asst. dean. Coll. Chemistry, 1986-92, assoc. dean, 1995—. Vis. prof. Indian Inst. Tech., Kanpur, 1968-69, Fudan U., Shanghai, 1982, U. Tokyo, 1982, U. Paris du Nord, 1987; mem. IUPAC Commn. I.1, 1994—. Author: Quantum Mechanics, 1968; assoc. editor Ann. Rev. Phys. Chemistry, 1976-85, editor, 1985-2000. Recipient Bomen-Michaelson award Coblentz Soc., 1994, Ellis Lippincott award Optical Soc. Am., 1994, The Berkeley citation, 2003; Alfred P. Sloan fellow, 1966-70. Fellow Am. Phys. Soc., AAAS; mem. Am. Chem. Soc., Sigma Xi, Phi Beta Kappa, Phi Lambda Upsilon. Achievements include research in elucidation of vibrational spectra associated with large amplitude molecular motion in gases, liquids and solids. Home: 2447 Prince St Berkeley CA 94705-2021 Office: U Calif Dept Chemistry Berkeley CA 94720-1420 E-mail: hls@cchem.berkeley.edu.

STRAUSS, JEROME FRANK, III, physician, educator; b. Chgo., May 2, 1947; s. Jerome Frank (Jr.) and Josephine (Newberger) Strauss; m. Catherine Blumlein, June 20, 1970; children: Jordan L., Elizabeth J. BA, Brown U., 1969; MD, U. Pa., 1974, PhD, 1975. Asst. prof. Sch. of Medicine U. Pa., Phila., 1976—83, assoc. prof. Sch. of Medicine, 1983—85, prof. Sch. of Medicine, 1985—, assoc. chair Sch. of Medicine, 1987—, assoc. dean Sch. of Medicine, 1990—; Luigi Mastroianni jr. prof. and founding dir. Ctr. Rsch. on Women's Health and Reproduction, Phila., 1990—94; prof. Inst. of Medicine NAS, 1994—. Biochem. endocrinology study sect. NIH, 1983—87, Nat. Adv. Child Health and Human Devel. Coun., 2002—; chmn. population rsch. com. Nat. Inst. Child Health and Human Devel., 1989—92; chair Reproductive Scientist of the Ams. Network, 1995—; dir. Ctr. Excellence in Women's Health, 1996—2002; co-chair Indo-U.S. Joint Workers Group on Reproductive Sci. and Contraceptive Tech., 1999—; bd.

dirs. Burroughs Wellcome Fund, 2003—. Editor: Lipoprotein and Cholesterol Metabolism in Sterodogenic Tissues, 1985, Current Topics in Membrane Research, 1987, Uterine and Embryonic Factors in Early Pregnancy, 1991, New Achievements in Research of Ovarian Function, 1995, Cell Death in Reproductive Physiology, 1997, Molecular Biology in Reproductive Medicine, 1999, Ovarian Function Research: Present and Future, 1999, Reproductive Medicine Molecular, Cellular and Genetic Fundamentals, 2002, Steroids jour., 1993—; assoc. editor Ency. of Reproduction, 1998—, assoc. editor, mem. editl. bd. Jour. Lipid Rsch., 1982—90, corr. editor Jour. Steroid Biochem. and Molecular Biology, 1990—99, mem. editl. bd. Endocrinology, 1986—90, 1997—2000, Biology of Reprodn., 1986—90, 1999—, Jour. of Women's Health, 1991—, Jour. Soc. Gynecologic Investigation, 1993—, Placenta, 1995—98, Trends in Endocrinology and Metabolism, 1999, Reference en Gynecologie Obstetrique, 1999—, Seminars in Reproductive Endocrinology, 2000—, Jour. Endocrinology, 2000—, Human Reproduction Update, 2001—. Recipient Transatlantic medal, Brit. Endocrine Soc., 1998. Fellow: Internat. Acad. Human Reproduction; mem.: Perinatal Rsch. Soc., Am. Soc. for Reproductive Medicine, Soc. for Study of Reprodn. (bd. dirs. 1989—91, Rsch. award 1992), Endocrine Soc., Soc. Gynecologic Investigation (pres. 2003, Pres.'s Achievement award 1990), Am. Physiol. Soc., Am. Assn. Pathologists. Office: U Pa Dept Ob/Gyn 421 Curie Blvd Philadelphia PA 19104-4218 E-mail: jfs3@mail.med.upenn.edu.

STRAUSS, JON CALVERT, academic administrator; b. Chgo., Jan. 17, 1940; s. Charles E. and Alice C. (Woods) S.; m. Joan Helen Bailey, Sept. 19, 1959 (div. 1985); children: Susan, Stephanie; m. Jean Anne Sacconaghi, June 14, 1985; children: Kristoffer, Jonathon. BSEE, U. Wis., 1959; MS in Physics, U. Pitts., 1962; PhD in E.E., Carnegie Inst. Tech., 1965; LLD (hon.), U. Mass., 1996. Assoc. prof. computer sci., elec. engring. Carnegie Mellon U., Pitts., 1966-70; dir. computer ctr., prof. computer sci. Tech. U. Norway, Trondheim, Norway, 1970; vis. assoc. prof. elec. engring. U. Mich., Ann Arbor, 1971; assoc. prof. computer sci. Washington U., St. Louis, Mo., 1971-74, dir. computing facilities, 1971-73; dir. computing activities U. Pa., Phila., 1974-76, faculty master Stouffer Coll. House, 1978-80, prof. computer, info. scis., prof. decision sci. Wharton Sch., 1974-81, exec. dir. Univ. Budget, 1975-78, v.p. for budget, fin., 1978-81; prof. elec. engring. U. So. Calif., Los Angeles, 1981-85, sr. v.p. adminstrn., 1981-85; pres. Worcester Poly. Inst., Mass., 1985-94; v.p., chief fin. officer Howard Hughes Med. Inst., Chevy Chase, Md., 1994-97; pres. Harvey Mudd Coll., Claremont, Calif., 1997—. Cons. Electronics Assocs., Inc., 1965, IBM Corp., 1960-64, Westinghouse Elec. Corp., 1959-60; bd. dirs. Transamerica Income Fund, Variable Ins. Fund, United Educators Ins. Contbr. articles on computer systems and university mgmt. to profl. jours.; co-holder patent. Bd. dirs. Presbyn.-U. Pa. Med. Ctr., Phila., 1980-81, U. So. Calif. Kenneth Norris Jr. Cancer Hosp., L.A., 1981-85, Med. Ctr. of Ctrl. Mass., 1986-94, Worcester Acad., 1986-91, Mass. Biotech. Rsch. Inst., 1985-94. Mem. New. Eng. Assn. Schs. and Colls., Inc., Commn. on Instns. of Higher Edn., Nat. Collegiate Athletic Assn. (pres.'s commn. 1990-94). Avocations: rowing, running, sailing, swimming. Office: Harvey Mudd Coll 301 E 12th St Claremont CA 91711-5901

STRAUSS, PETER L(ESTER), law educator; b. N.Y.C., Feb. 26, 1940; s. Simon D. and Elaine Ruth (Mandle) S.; m. Joanna Burnstine, Oct. 1, 1964; children: Benjamin, Bethany. AB magna cum laude, Harvard U., 1961; LLB magna cum laude, Yale U., 1964. Bar: D.C. 1965, U.S. Supreme Ct. 1968. Law clk. U.S. Ct. Appeals D.C. Cir., 1964-65, U.S. Supreme Ct., 1965-66; lectr. Halle Selassie U. Sch. Law, Addis Ababa, Ethiopia, 1966-68; asst. to solicitor gen. Dept. Justice, Washington, 1968-71; assoc. prof. law Columbia U., 1971-74, prof., 1974—, Betts prof., 1985—, vice-dean, 1996, 2001—02. Gen. counsel NRC, 1975-77, Adminstrv. Conf. U.S., 1984-95; Byrne vis. prof. Sch. Law Harvard U., Cambridge, Mass., 1994; bd. dirs. Ctr. for Computer Assisted Legal Instrn., 2002—. Mem. adv. bd. Lexis Electronic Author's Press, 1995-99; editor: SSRN Administrative Law Abstracts, 1997—; author: (with Abba Paulos translator) Fetha Negast: The Law of the Kings, 1968; (with others) Administrative Law Cases and Comments, 2003, Administrative Justice in the United States, 2002; contbr. articles to profl. jours. Recipient John Marshall prize Dept. Justice, 1970, Disting. Svc. award NRC, 1977. Mem. ABA (chair sect. administrv. law and regulatory practice 1992-93, Disting. Scholarship award 1988), Am. Law Inst. Office: Columbia U Law Sch 435 W 116th St New York NY 10027-7201

STRAVINSKA, SARAH, dance educator; b. Pitts., Nov. 12, 1940; d. Robert Edwin Williams and Alice Elizabeth Markey Hildeboldt; m. George Lawrence Denton, May 10, 1959 (div. 1973); children: Kathryn, Michael, Laura, David. BFA in Dance, Fla. State U., 1977, MFA in Dance, 1979; Cert. in Ballet, Vaganova Inst., Leningrad, Russia, 1990; Cert., Raoul Gelabert Kinesiology Ins, N.Y.C., 1980. Dancer Ballet Russe, N.Y.C., 1957-58; dance choreographer Dutchess County Ballet, Beacon, N.Y., 1960-65; instr. Brevard C.C., Cocoa, Fla., 1969-73; chair dept. dance Randolph/Macon Woman's Coll., Lynchburg, Va., 1979-84; asst. prof. dance U. So. Miss., Hattiesburg, 1984-86; prof. and coord. dance U. La., Lafayette, 1986—. Dir. State of La. Danse Project, Lafayette, 1991-94. Choreographer original dance works: Mama! Stop the Bombs, 1989, The Yellow Wallpaper, 1990, Spring Night, 1998, Serrano!, 2002; reconstructor of classical ballets: Les Sylphides, 1991, Giselle, 1992, Swan Lake, 1993, Raymonda, Pas de Quatre, 1994. Dir. concerns for children La Danse with Acadiana Arts Coun., Lafayette, 1987-93; mem. Arts in Edn. Program, Lafayette, 1987—. Grantee Mellon Found., 1982. Mem. Am. Coll. Dance Festival Assn. (bd. dirs., festival coord. 1989-91), Dance History Scholars, CORPS de Ballet Internat. (founding mem.), Phi Kappa Phi. Episcopalian. Avocations: writing, music, reading, biking. Office: Univ of La PO Box 43690 Lafayette LA 70504-3690

STRAZZELLA, JAMES ANTHONY, law educator, lawyer; b. Hanover, Pa., May 18, 1939; s. Anthony F. and Teresa Ann Strazzella; m. Judith A. Coppola, Oct. 9, 1965; children: Jill M., Steven A., Tracy Ann, Michael P. AB, Villanova U., 1961; JD, U. Pa., 1964. Bar: Pa. 1964, D.C., 1965, U.S. Dist. Ct. (ea. and mid. dist.) Pa. 1969, U.S. Ct. Appeals (3rd cir.) 1964, U.S. Ct. Appeals (D.C. cir.) 1965, U.S. Ct. Appeals (4th cir.) 1983, U.S. Supreme Ct. 1969. Law clk. to Hon. Samuel Roberts Pa. Supreme Ct., 1964-65; asst. U.S. atty. D.C., 1965-69; vice dean, asst. prof. law U. Pa., Phila., 1969-73; faculty Temple U., Phila., 1973—; James G. Schmidt chair in law, 1989—; acting dean, 1987-89. Chief counsel Kent State investigation Pres.'s Commn. Campus Unrest, 1970; chmn. Atty. Gen.'s Task Force on Family Violence, Pa., 1985-89; mem., chmn. justice ops. Mayor's Criminal Justice Coordinating Commn., Phila., 1983-85; Pa. Joint Coun. Criminal Justice, 1979-82; mem. Com. to Study Pa.'s Unified Jud. Sys., 1980-82; Jud. Coun. Pa., 1972-82; chmn. criminal procedural rules com. Pa. Supreme Ct., 1972-85; mem. task force on prison overcrowding, 1983-85, rsch. adv. com., 1988, Pa. Commn. on Crime and Delinquency; chmn. U.S. Magistrate Judge Merit Selection Com., 1991, mem., 1989, 90, 91; co-chair Mayor's Transition Task Force on Pub. Safety, Phila., 1992; designate D.C. Com. on Adminstrn. of Justice Under Emergency Conditions, 1968; del. D.C. Jud. Conf., 1985, 95. Contbr. articles to profl. jours. and books. Mem. adv. bd. dirs., past pres. A Better Chance in Lower Merion; dir. Hist. Fire Mus., Phila., 1978—, 1st v.p., 2002—; bd. dirs. Lower Merion Hist. Soc., 1998—2000, Neighborhood Civic Assn., Bala-Cynwyd, Pa., 1984—87, Smith Meml. Playground in Fairmount Pk., 1997—, Coun. Legal Edn. Opportunity Bd., 1997—; bd. trustees Bala Cynwyd Pub. Libr., 1999—. Recipient award for disting. tchg. Linback Found., 1983, Advancement of Justice award Pa. Atty. Gen., 1989, Disting. Pub. Svc. award Assn. State and County Detectives, 1989, Spl. Merit award Pa. Assn. Police Chiefs, 1989, significant contbn. to legal scholarship and edn. Beccaria award Phila. Bar Assn. and Nat. IAB Assn., 1995. Fellow: Am. Bar Found.; mem.: St. Thomas More Soc. (pres. 1985—86, past dir. Phila. area, St. Thomas More award 1996), Phila. Bar Assn. (criminal justice sect., appellate cts. com.), Pa. Bar Assn. (commn. profl. stds. 1981—84, chmn. criminal law sect. 1986—88, Merit award 1987), FBA (Phila. crim. law com. adv. bd. 1988—93, chmn. nat. criminal law com. 1991—92), Am. Law Inst., ABA (faculty appellate judges seminars 1975—, various coms., acad. advisor appellate judges edn. com. 1993—, reporter task force on federalization criminal law 1998—99), Order of the Coif (exec. bd. U. Pa.). Roman Catholic. Home and Office: 100 Maple Ave Bala Cynwyd PA 19004-3017 Office: Temple U Law Sch 1719 N Broad St Philadelphia PA 19122-6002

STREET, CECILIA REGINA, elementary school educator, administrator; b. Mobile, Ala., June 18, 1935; d. Joseph Monroe and Regina (Cain) S. BA in Elem. Edn., Mt. St. Agnes Coll., 1958; MRE, Cath. U. Am., 1968; M in Elem. Adminstrn., U. South Ala., 1977, M in Counseling, 1991. Tchr. 1st grade St. Mary Sch., Rockville, Md., 1958-59, St. Joseph Sch., Macon, Ga., 1959-62; tchr. 1st and 2d grades St. Mary Sch., Mobile, 1962-65; adminstr. St. Joseph Sch., Mobile, 1965-67, St. Mary Sch., Huntsville, Ala., 1967-69, St. Aloysius Sch., Bessemer, Ala., 1969-71, Corpus Christi Sch., Mobile, 1971-90; tchr. Meadowlake Sch., Mobile, 1990-91; adminstr. Palmer Pillans Mid. Sch., Mobile, 1991-92. Founder, dir. Parish Day Care Ctr., Mobile, 1983-87, Corpus Christi Day Ctr., Mobile, 1983-87; adminstr. Meadowlake Elem. Sch., Mobile, 1992-95. Dir. parish religious edn. Corpus Christi Ch., 1971-82. Named Career Woman of the Yr. Gayfer Career Club, Mobile, 1993; recipient Blue Ribbon plaque Nat. Fedn. Elem. Sch. Prins., Mobile, 1990. Roman Catholic. Home: 1151 Cody Rd S Lot 19 Mobile AL 36695-4464

STREET, LELA KATHRYN, retired secondary education educator; b. Sullivan, Ind., May 2, 1942; d. Harold Seward and Kathryn Nell (Leach) Gambill; m. Robert Wayne Street, Aug. 18, 1963; children: Erin Wynne, Heather Leigh. BS, Ind. State U., 1964, MS, 1971. Tchr. Northeast Sch. Corp., Farmersburg, Ind., 1965-66, Southwest Sch. Corp., Sullivan, Ind., 1966-99; ret., 1999. Sponsor Young Astronaut-NASA, Sullivan, 1986-94, Sci. Club, 1994-99; dir. Jr. High-Elem. Sci. Fair, 1967-99; coach Sci. Olympics, Sullivan, 1990-99, Thinking Cap Quiz Bowl, Sullivan, 1992-99, Odyssey of Mind, Sullivan, 1989-90, Sullivan High and Jr. H.S. Track, 1975-96. Named Educator of Yr. Sullivan Jaycees, 1972; nominee Golden Apple award WTHI TV, Terre Haute, Ind., 1991, 92. Mem. NEA, Nat. Mid. Sch. Sci. Tchrs. Assn., Ind. State Tchrs. Assn., S.W. Sullivan Edn. Assn. (treas., com. mem. 1966-99), Hoosier Assn. Sci. Tchrs., Delta Kappa Gamma (past rec. sec., sec., com.), Phi Delta Kappa. Baptist. Avocations: travel, music, antiques, reading, walking.

STREET, PATRICIA LYNN, secondary education educator; b. Lillington, N.C., May 3, 1940; d. William Banks and Vandalia (McLean) S.; m. Col. Robert Gest, June 2, 1962 (div. 1985); children: Robert, Roblyn Renee. BS, Livingstone Coll., 1962; MEd, Salisbury State U., 1974; postgrad., various, 1968—. Tchr. Govt. of Guam Marianas Island, Agana, Guam, 1962-64; sec., typist USAF, Glasgow AFB, Mont., 1964-65, Syracuse (N.Y.) U. AeroSpace Engring., 1966-67; tchr. Syracuse (N.Y.) City Sch. System, 1967-69; lectr. U. of Md., Eastern Shore, Princess Anne, Md., 1970-72; tchr. Prince George's County Pub. Schs., Upper Marlboro, Md., 1973—. Instr. U. Guam, Anderson AFB, 1963, U.S. Armed Forces Inst., Anderson AFB, 1963, Yorktowne Bus. Inst., Landover, Md., 1987-90, Cheseapeake Bus. Inst., Clinton, Md., 1983-89; asst. advisor student tchrs. U. Md. Ea. Shore, Princess Anne, 1972; adj. instr. Bowie State U., 1990—; conv. speaker. Mem. AAUW, NEA, ASCD, Am. Vocat. Assn., Md. Bus. Edn. Assn. (pres.-elect 1987-88, pres. 1988-89, Educator of Yr. 1989), Md. Vocat. Assn. (regional rep. 1986-89, audit chmn. 1987-89, Vocat.-Tech. Educator of Yr. 1989), Ea. Bus. Edn. Assn. (co-editor newsletter 1990-91, secondary exec. dir. 1991-94, pres.-elect 1997-98, pres. 1998-99), Md. State Tchrs. Assn., D.C. Bus. Edn. Assn., Nat. Bus. Edn. Assn., Nat. Bus. Edn. Assn. (exec. bd. dirs. 1998-99), Internat. Soc. for Bus. Edn., Md. Bus. Edn. Com., Prince George's County Edn. Assn., Delta Pi Epsilon. Democrat. Baptist. Avocations: sewing, singing, modern creative dancing. Home: 10107 Welshire Dr Upper Marlboro MD 20772-6204 Office: Prince George's Pub Sch Upper Marlboro MD 20772

STREET, TERRI EVANS, counselor, consultant; b. Marion, Va., Dec. 9, 1950; d. Edward Henry and Elizabeth (Burris) Evans; 1 child, Edward Brian Evans. BA in English and Edn., Emory and Henry Coll., 1972; MS in Edn. and Psychology, Radford Coll., 1977; MS in Counseling and Human Svcs., Radford U., 1992; cert. advanced grad. studies, Va. Poly. Inst. and State U., 1995, PhD in Counselor Edn., 1996. Nat. cert. counselor; cert. in secondary guidancce, speech, pub. speaking, English, grades 4-7, tchr. effectiveness and student achievement, Va. Tchr. social studies Austinville (Va.) Elem. Sch.cc, 1974-80; tchr. lang. arts Scott Meml. Elem. Sch., Wytheville, Va., 1980-85; tchr. English, speech and drama George Wythe H.S., Wytheville, 1985-91, counselor, 1991-94; grad. asst. Va. Poly. Inst. and State U. Coll. Edn., Blacksburg, 1995-96; counseling coord. Roanoke Valley Gov.'s Sch. for Sci. and Tech., Roanoke, Va., 1996—. Evening adminstr. Wytheville C.C., 1993; presenter in field, 1995—; mem. Wythe County Child Study Team, 1992-94; mem. steering com. Crossroads Tech. Prep. Consortium, 1991-94. Recipient presdl. citation U. Richmond Gov.'s Sch. for Visual and Performing Arts, 1990, 92. Mem. ACA, NEA, Nat. Assn. for Coll. Admission Counseling, Nat. Career Devel. Assn., Va. Edn. Assn. (resolutions com. 1983-85), Va. Career Devel. Assn., Va. Counselors Assn., Roanoke Edn. Assn., Roanoke Valley Counselors Assn., Wythe County Edn. Assn. (reporter 1976-77, 79-80, v.p. 1981-82, 92-93, treas. 1985-86), Chi Sigma Iota. Avocations: reading, spending time outdoors, theatre, dance. Home: 655 E Pine St Wytheville VA 24382-2019 Office: Roanoke Valley Gov's Sch for Sci and Tech 2104 Grandin Rd SW Roanoke VA 24015-3528

STREETEN, BARBARA WIARD, ophthalmologist, medical educator; b. Candia, N.H., Mar. 3, 1925; d. Robert Campbell Wiard and Gertrude Sarah Matheson; m. David Henry Palmer Streeten, Aug. 2, 1952; children: Robert Duncan, Elizabeth Anne, John Palmer. AB magna cum laude, Tufts U., 1945, MD cum laude, 1950. Diplomate Am. Bd. Ophthalmology. Jr. resident in gen. pathology Mallory Inst., Boston City Hosp., 1951-52; fellow in ophthalmic pathology Mass. Eye and Ear Infirmary, Boston, 1952-53; resident in ophthalmology Wayne County Gen. Hosp., Eloise, Mich., 1953-56; from jr. to sr. clin. instr. ophthalmology U. Mich. Med. Sch., Ann Arbor, 1956-60; from asst. prof. to prof. ophthalmology SUNY Health Sci. Ctr. (now called SUNY Upstate Med. U.), Syracuse, 1964—, dir. eye pathology lab., 1966—; from asst. prof. to prof. pathology SUNY Health Sci. Ctr., Syracuse, 1968—. Contbr. articles Contbr. over 114 articles to profl. jours., chpts. to textbooks. Mem. vision study sect. Nat. Eye Inst., NIH, Bethesda, Md., 1977-80, mem. bd. sci. counselors, 1982-86; mem. editl. bd., mem. editl. adv. com. Ophthalmology jour., 1982-94; gen. editor Investigative Ophthalmology and Visual Sci., 1979-82, mem. editl. bd., 1987-92. Grantee Nat. Eye Inst., NIH, 1975—2002. Mem. Am. Assn. Ophthalmic Pathologists (charter, past pres., bd. dirs., Zimmerman medal 1997), Am. Acad. Ophthalmology (honor award 1990), Verhoeff Ophthalmic Pathology Soc. (past pres.), Assn. for Rsch. in Vision and Ophthalmology (past sect. chmn.), Internat. Soc. Ophthalmic Pathology (co-v.p. N.Am. 1990-92), Phi Beta Kappa, Alpha Omega Alpha. Episcopalian. Achievements include establishment of elastic system nature of the suspensory ligament of the ocular lens; ultrastructural and immunopathologic contributions to diseases of the ocular connective tissue matrix, particularly those related to cataract and glaucoma. Home: 334 Berkeley Dr Syracuse NY 13210-3000 Office: SUNY Upstate Med Univ WH Rm 2107 766 Irving Ave Syracuse NY 13210-1602 E-mail: streeteb@upstate.edu.

STREETER, PATRICIA ELLEN, elementary school educator; d. Edward William and Helen Katherine; m. Earl Louis Streeter, June 20, 1958 (dec. 1995); 1 child, Michelle Lynn. BA, Whittier Coll., 1958; MEd, UCLA, 1963; EdD, Brigham Young U., 1976. Cert. elem. tchr., K-8, adminstrv. credential, life adult edn. credential, lang. devel. specialist credential. Tchr. Guam Pub. Schs., Agana, 1959-60, LA Unified Schs., 1961—98, bi-lingual coord., 1979-80, reading specialist, 1980-82; learning lab specialist, adult divsn. LA Unified Sch. Dist., 1977—98, bilingual tchr., 1982—98, ESL instr., 1983-89, educator, 1989—. Career day chmn., Montague Street Sch., Pacoima, Calif., 1986—; bd. dirs. Kollege Bound Kids, Montague, Pacoima, Young Astronauts, Pacoima; grant writer Montague Charter Acad., 1998-2000, tchr., 1999—. Contbr. articles to profl. jours. Program chmn. UCLA Bd. dirs. Grad Sch. Edn., 1988-2003; patron McGowan Theater Arts, UCLA, 1966-89; bd. dirs. Whittier Coll. West Alumni Club, 1987-89. Recipient scholarship UCLA, Thomas Lang. Sch., 1981; grantee LA Edn. Partnership, 1987-89, Montague St. Sch., Pacoima, Calif., 1989, Senate of Calif., 1992, State of Calif., 1993, Assn. Calif. Sch. Adminstrs., Calif. Ednl. Initiatives Fund (author SB 1274 restructuring grant and title VII transitional bilingual edn., authored $2 million and won grants); gained $2 million in Grants for Montague Charter Academy. Mem. Tarzana Taxpayers Assn., Pi Lambda Theta (pres. Santa Monica chpt. 1987-89, v.p. region IV 1986-88, v.p. so. chpts. 1986-88, pres. 1992-93), Alpha Delta (pres. UCLA chpt. 1989—), UCLA grad. sch. edn. alumni assn. (pres. 1992-94). Republican. Congregationalist. Avocations: piano, writing, reading, genealogy, aerospace. Home: 18331 Tarzana Dr Tarzana CA 91356-4215

STREETMAN, BEN GARLAND, electrical engineering educator; b. Cooper, Tex., June 24, 1939; s. Richard E. and Bennie (Morrow) S.; m. Lenora Ann Music, Sept. 9, 1961; children: Paul, Scott. BS, U. Tex., 1961, MS, 1963, PhD, 1966. Fellow Oak Ridge Nat. Lab., 1964-66; asst. prof. elec. engring. U. Ill., 1966-70, assoc. prof., 1970-74, prof., 1974-82; rsch. prof. Coordinated Sci. Lab., 1970-82; prof. elec. engring. U. Tex., Austin, 1982—, dir. Microelectronics Rsch. Ctr., 1984—, Dula D. Cockrell Centennial chair engring., 1989-96, dean Coll. Engring., 1997—. Bd. dirs. Nat. Instruments, Zix Corp. Author: Solid State Electronic Devices, 5th edit., 2000. Recipient Frederick Emmons Terman award Am. Soc. Engring. Edn., 1981, AT&T Found. award, 1987; named Disting. Alumnus, U. Tex. at Austin, 1998. Fellow IEEE (Edn. medal 1989), Electrochem. Soc.; mem. NAE, Am. Acad. Arts and Scis., Tau Beta Pi, Eta Kappa Nu, Sigma Xi. Office: U Tex at Austin Dean of Engring 1 University Sta C2100 Austin TX 78712-0284

STREIB, VICTOR LEE, dean; b. Marion, Ind., Oct. 8, 1941; s. Albert Wolfe and Melba Janice Streib; m. Lynn C. Sametz, Mar. 29, 1978; children: Noah, Jessi. BS in Indsl. Enging., Auburn U., 1966; JD, Ind. U., Bloomington, 1970. Bar: Ind. 1970, U.S. Supreme Ct. 1987. Rsch. assoc., scientist Inst. Rsch. Pub. Safety Ind. U., Bloomington, 1970-72, asst. to assoc. prof. dept. forensic studies, 1972-78; assoc. prof. law New Eng. Sch. Law, Boston, 1978-80; prof., assoc. dean coll. of law Cleve. State U., 1980-96; prof. law Ohio No. U., Ada, 1996—, dean, 1996—2000. Vis. prof. law U. San Diego, 1983-84, Mich. State U., 2001-02; vis. fellow Assn. Am. Law Schs., Washington, 1993-94; mem. adv. bd. Ctr. Capital Punishment Studies U. Westminster, London, 1996—. Author: Juvenile Justice in America., 1978, Death Penalty for Juveniles, 1987, Death Penalty in a Nutshell, 2003; editor: Capital Punishment Anthology, 1993, Law Deanship Manual, 1993. Mem. ABA (site evaluator 1991-2000), North Ctrl. Assn. (cons. evaluator 1990-2001). Avocation: physical fitness. Office: Ohio No U Coll Law 525 S Main St Ada OH 45810-6000

STREIFF, ARLYNE BASTUNAS, business owner, educator; b. Sacramento, Calif., Nov. 04; d. Peter James and Isabel (Gemnas) Bastunas; children: Peter Joshua, Joshua Gus. BS, U. Nev., 1965; postgrad., U. Calif., Davis, 1965-68, Calif. State U., Chico, 1968, 71. Cert. elem. tchr., Calif., Nev., cert. in English-specially designed lang. acad. instrn. devel. in English. Tchr. reading, lang. and kindergarten Enterprise Elem. Sch. Dist., Redding, Calif., 1965-98, tchr. kindergarten, 1988-98; owner, pres. Arlyne's Svcs., Redding, Calif., 1990—. Author: Niko and His Friends, 1989, Niko The Black Rottweiler, 1995, Color-Talk-Spell. Mem. Rep. Women, Five County Labor Coun., Redding, 1976-93, Calif. Labor Fedn., 1974-97, AFL-CIO, 1974-97. Named Tchr. of Yr., Enterprise Sch. Dist., 1969. Mem. AAUW, Am. Fedn. Tchrs., Calif. Tchrs. Assn. (bargaining spokesperson 1968-72, exec. bd. dirs.), United Tchrs. Enterprise (pres. 1979-80, chmn. lang. com.), Calif. Reading Assn., Enterprise Fedn. Tchrs. (pres. 1974, pres.-elect 1995-97), Calif. State Fedn. Tchrs. (v.p. 1974-75, exec. bd. 1995-97), Redding C. of C., Women of Moose, Elks. Avocations: home interior design, real estate, construction, creative writing, educational advancement. Office: Arlynes Svcs 1468 Benton Dr Redding CA 96003-3116

STREIT, KAREN CROSSNO, secondary school educator, curriculum writer; b. Memphis, Apr. 1, 1956; d. John Franklin, Jr. and Claudette (Windham) Crossno; m. David Streit, June 2, 1979. BA in Journalism/Theatre, U. Miss., 1978, MA in Journalism, 1981. Cert. tchr., Miss. Reporter, photographer Evening Times, W. Memphis, Ark., 1978-79; editor St. Joha Valley Times, Madawaska, Maine, 1979-80; instr. U. Maine, Ft. Kent, 1980; editor-in-chief Presque Isle (Maine) Star Herald, 1980; instr. Miss. U. Women, Columbus, 1980-82; soc. editor Delta Democrat-Times, Greenville, Miss., 1982-87; tchr. Greenville Christian Sch., 1987-89, N.W. Rankin Attendance Ctr., Brandon, Miss., 1989—. Dir. Delta Music Assn., Miss. dvsn. Am. Cancer Soc., Delta Ctr. Stage Community Theatre, Ray Furr Comm. Workshop, Columbus, 1982; mem. adv. bd. 4-H; key person United Way; state bd. sec. March of Dimes; leader Explorer Post Boy Scouts Am.; field dir. Miss Miss. U.S.A. and Miss Teen U.S.A., Greenville, 1987-89. Scholar Miss. Coll., 1992. Mem. AAUW, ASCD, Nat. Fedn. Press Women, Nat. League Am. Pen Women, Bus. and Profl. Women, Miss. Press Assn., Maine Press Assn., Ark. Press Assn. Methodist. Avocations: choir, dance, dramatic performance, community theatre, golf. Home: 941 Tenby Dr Brandon MS 39047-8179 Office: NW Rankin Attendance Ctr Highway 25 Brandon MS 39042

STREITMAN, JEFFREY BRUCE, education administrator; b. Bronx, N.Y., Aug. 5, 1951; s. Milton and Marcia (Helfant) S.; m. Brenda Penny, July 4, 1974; 1 child, Jesse. BA cum laude, CUNY, 1974, MS, 1976; EdD, Fordham U., 1990. Guidance counselor Horizon Sch., Levitown, N.Y., 1976-80, asst. prin., 1980-84; guidance chmn. Lawrence (N.Y.) Pub. Schs., 1984-88, supr. student svcs., 1988-90; asst. supt. schs. Syosset (N.Y.) Cen. Sch. Dist., 1990-94; dep. supt. schs. Syosset Cen. Sch. Dist., 1994—. Mem. ASCD, N.Y. State Pers. Adminstrs., L.I. Pers. Adminstrs. Office: Syosset Cen Sch Dist Pell Ln Syosset NY 11791

STREJCEK, ELIZABETH GEIERMAN, reading specialist, educator; b. Chgo., Dec. 7, 1948; d. Aloysius Herman and Lillian Elizabeth (Cowan) Geierman; m. George Joseph Strejcek, Jan. 27, 1971; children: James Edwin, Theodore Eliot. BA in History, U. Ill., Chgo., 1971, MA in Ednl. Leadership, 1981. Cert. reading specialist, Ill. Subs. tchr. pub. schs., Berwyn, Ill., 1972-74; tchr. reading grades 5-8 South Berwyn Pub. Sch., Berwyn, 1974-77; tchr. reading lab. grades 9-12 Bolinbrook (Ill.) High Sch., 1979-83; tchr. reading grades 7-8 Westview Mid. Sch., Romeoville, Ill., 1983-84, tchr. grades 6-8, 1984-85; chpt. I reading tchr. grades K-5 Northview Elem. Sch., Bolingbrook, 1985-91; tchr. grades 9-10 Morton East H.S., Cicero, 1991—, tchr. spl. program on attendance, chpt. I-title I tchr., 1991, 94, tchr. truancy and attendance program, 1993—, mem. various coms., 1991—. Presenter lectures, demonstrations on reading and writing and using technology in classroom, 1989—, Title I Summer Sch. Curriculum (reading and writing), 1997. Mem. AAUW, Internat. Reading Assn., Ill. Reading Coun. (bd. dirs. 1994-95), Ill. Computing Educators, Nat. Coun. Tchrs. English, Czech Cache, Secondary Reading League (pres. 1993-95, 99-2002), Ill. Title 1 Assn. (pres. 2001-2002). Avocations: pottery/ceramics, computer applications, reading, drawing. Office: 2423 S Austin Blvd Cicero IL 60804-2616

STREKOWSKI, LUCJAN, chemistry educator; b. Grabowo, Poland, June 21, 1945; came to U.S., 1981; s. Antoni and Janina (Chrapowicz) S.; m. Alewtina Smirnova, Oct. 14, 1967; children: Rafal, Anna. BS in Polymer Chemistry with distinction, Mendeleev Inst. Chemistry, Moscow, 1967; PhD in Organic Chemistry, Polish Acad. Scis., 1972; DSc in Chemistry, Adam Mickiewicz U., Poznan, Poland, 1976. Instr. organic chemistry Adam Mickiewicz U., Poznan, 1971-72, asst. prof. dept. chemistry, 1972-78, assoc. prof. dept. chemistry, 1978-81; rsch. assoc. dept. chemistry U. Fla., Gainesville, 1981-84; asst. prof. dept. chemistry Ga. State U., Atlanta, 1984-89, assoc. prof. dept. chemistry, 1989-96, prof. dept. chem., 1996—. Vis. prof. U. Fla., Gainesville, 1979-80, 81, Australian Nat. U., 1980, U. Kans., Lawrence, 1972-73. Editor: Pyridine-Metal Complexes, Vol. 14, Part 6, 1985; N.Am. editor Heterocyclic Comms.; mem. editl. bd. Arkivoc; contbr. more than 210 articles to profl. jours.; patentee in field. Recipient award, Polish Ministry Sci., 1997, Polish Chem. Soc., 1973, Polish Acad. Scis., 1972, Ga. State U., 1993; grantee Am. Chem. Soc.-Petroleum Rsch. Fund, 1985—, Solvay Pharms., 1992—93, Nat. Diagnostics, 1991—93, NIAID/NIMH, 1988—89, Rohm and Hass Co., 1988, Am. Cancer Soc., 1987—89, Rsch. Corp., 1985—94, Milheim Found. Cancer Rsch., 1985—86, DuPont Co., 1996—2000, Small Bus. Innovation Rsch. Program, 2000—02, Coley Pharms., 2003—. Mem. Am. Chem. Soc., Internat. Soc. Heterocyclic Chemistry, Internat. Acad. Scis. of Nature and Soc. (mem. presidium). Avocation: classical music. Office: Ga State Univ Dept Chemistry Atlanta GA 30303 E-mail: lucjan@gsu.edu.

STRENG, WILLIAM HAROLD, chemist, researcher, educator; b. Milw., Mar. 6, 1944; s. W. Harold and Helen C. (Wedemeyer) S.; m. Barbara L. York, Dec. 16, 1969; children: Karen, William. BS, Carroll Coll., 1966; MS, Mich. Tech. U., 1968, PhD, 1971. Postdoctoral rsch. assoc. Clark U., Worcester, Mass., 1971-73; sr. chemist Richardson Merrell Pharm., Cin., 1973-81; sr. rsch. chemist Merrell Dow Pharm., Cin., 1981-90, Marion Merrell Dow, Cin., 1990-92, rsch. scientist, group leader Kansas City, Mo., 1992-94; rsch. scientist Hoechst Marion Roussel, Kansas City, 1994-98, Quintiles, Kansas City, 1999—. Adj. asst. prof. pharmaceutics dept. U. Cin. Sch. of Pharmacy, 1984-99. Contbr. articles to profl. jours. Mem. Loveland (Ohio) Schs. Planning Commn., 1988-92, chmn., 1990, tchr. GED program, 1987-92. Mem. Am. Chem. Soc., Am. Assn. Pharm. Sci. Avocations: camping, fishing, woodworking, reading. Office: Quintiles PO Box 9627 Kansas City MO 64134-0627

STRENGTH, DANNA ELLIOTT, retired nursing educator; b. Texarkana, Ark., Aug. 20, 1937; d. Clyde Olin and Willie (Stephens) Elliott; m. Vernon E. Strength, Dec. 27, 1960; 1 child, Van E. BSN, Tex. Christian U., 1959; MSN, Washington U., 1968; DNSc, Cath. U. of Am., 1986. Instr. The Cath. Univ. of Am., Washington, 1976-84; asst. prof. Georgetown Univ., Washington, 1984-87; assoc. prof. Tex. Christian Univ., Fort Worth, 1987-2000, ret., 2000. Edn. leader Profl. Seminars Internat.; edn. cons. Transcultural Edn. Corp.; med. com. Ft. Worth Sister Cities Internat., Budapest, Hungary, and Bandung, Indonesia. Contbr. articles to profl. jours. Recipient Edn. in a Global Soc. award to study health care in Indonesia and Scandinavia, 1992-94. Mem. ANA, Tex. Nurses' Assn., Am. Assn. for History of Nursing (chairperson nominating com., bylaws com.), Lucy Harris Linn Inst. (treas.), Sigma Theta Tau (Beta Alpha rsch. award). Home: 305 Birchwood Ln Fort Worth TX 76108-4601

STRENGTH, JANIS GRACE, management executive, educator; b. Ozark, Ala., Jan. 31, 1934; d. James Marion and Mary Belle (Riley) Grace; m. Robert Samuel Strength, Sept. 12, 1954; children: Stewart A., James Houston (dec.), Robert David (dec.), James Steven (dec.) BS in Home Econs. and Edn., Auburn U., 1956; MA in Edn., Washington U., St. Louis, 1978, MA in Adminstrn., 1980. Home economist Gulf Power Co., Pensacola, Fla., 1956-59; tchr. sci. Northside Jr. High Sch., Greenwood, S.C., 1961-68; tchrs. home econs. Greenwood High Sch., 1968-70; chairperson dept. sci. Parkway West Jr. High Sch., Chesterfield, Mo., 1975-82; tchr. sci. Parkway West High Sch., Chesterfield, 1982-88; v.p.-sec. Product Safety Mgmt. Inc., Gulf Breeze, Fla., 1989—2001; ret., 2001. Chairperson dist. Phys. Scis. Curriculum Com., 1978-85, Sci. Fair Placement Com., 1978-82, Gifted Edn., 1983-84; leader Phys. Sci. Summer Workshops, Safety Sci. Lab. Workshop; sponsor Nat. Jr. Honor Soc., Parkway West Jr. Class. Supt. youth dept. Sunday sch. Greentrails Meth. Ch., sponsor summer camp; vol. fundraiser March of Dimes, Cerebral Palsy, Multiple Schlorosis, Cancer funds; judge Parkway/Monsanto/St. Louis Post Dispatch Sci. Fairs, 1978—; mem. citizens action com. Parkway Sch. Bd., 1980-84; v.p. United Meth. Women, 2000. Mem. NEA, Nat. Sci. Tchrs. Assn., Ladies Golf Assn. (sec. 1998-99, 2003—), Santa Rosa Women's Club (pres. 1998-2000), Tiger Point Country Club (Gulf Breeze), Raintree Country Club (Hillsboro, Mo.). Republican. Methodist.

STREVER, MARTHA MAY, mathematics educator; b. Rhinebeck, N.Y., Oct. 27, 1939; d. Louis Grant and Marguerite Hazel (Irwin) S. BS, New Paltz (N.Y.) State U., 1961, MS, 1966. Cert. tchr. math. and sci., N.Y. Tchr. math. and sci. Red Hook (N.Y.) Ctrl. Sch., 1961-72, tchr. math., 1961—, chairperson dept. math., 1972—, jr. high computer coord., 1984-92, math/computer instrn. dept. chair, 1992—. Mem. choir, sec.-treas. Rhinebeck (N.Y.) Ref. Ch., 1974—, deacon and elder, 1976-80, Women's Guild edn. chmn., various yrs., pres., 1984-86, 89-90, 92-95, sec., 1996—. Summer Math and Sci. scholar New Paltz State U., 1962. Mem. ASCD, N.Y. State United Tchrs., Dutchess County Math. Tchrs. Assn., Nat. Coun. Tchrs. Math., N.Y. Assn. Math. Suprs., Assn. of Math. Tchrs. N.Y. State, Agonian Alumni Assn., Internat. Soc. for Tech. in Edn., N.Y. State Assn. for Computers and Tech. in Edn., Kappa Delta Pi, Delta Kappa Gamma, Alpha Zeta (1st v.p. 1978-80, pres. 1980-82, music chmn. 1982—). Avocations: playing electronic keyboard, accordion and organ, spoon collecting, stamp collecting, postcard collecting, photography. Home: 940 NY Route 9G Hyde Park NY 12538 Office: Red Hook Ctrl H S 63 W Market St # H S Red Hook NY 12571-1533

STRIBLIN, LORI ANN, critical care nurse, Medicare coordinator, nursing educator; b. Valley, Ala., Sept. 23, 1962; d. James Author and Dorothy Jane (Cole) Burt; m. Thomas Edward Striblin, Oct. 26, 1984; children: Natalie Nicole, Crystal Danielle. AAS in Nursing, So. Union State Jr. Coll., Valley, Ala., 1992. RN, Ala.; cert. ACLS, BLS, in fitness nutrition ICS. Surg. staff nurse East Ala. Med. Ctr., Opelika, 1992-93, surg. charge nurse, 1993-95, critical care ICU staff nurse, 1993-95; nurse case mgr. East Ala. Home Care, Opelika, 1995-96; staff devel. coord., medicare coord. Lanett (Ala.) Geriatric Ctr., 1996-97; case mgr. Lanier Home Health Svcs., Valley, Ala., 1996-97; med. advisor Nu Image Weight Loss Ctr., Opelika, Ala., 1996-97, nurse case mgr. weight loss ctr., counselor, diet educator, 1996-98; nurse case mgr. Chattahoochee Hospice, Valley, Ala., 1998; case mgr. Chattahoochiee Hospice, 1998; critical care nurse cardiovasc. ICU and telementry unit East Ala. Med. Ctr., Opelika, 1999—2002, dialysis staff nurse renal unit, 2003—; dialysis nurse Frecinus Dialysis Corp., Valley, Ala., 2002. Clin. instr. educator So. Union C.C., Valley, 1994-97. Mem. AACN, Ala. State Nurses Assn. Baptist. Avocations: crafts, horseback riding, hiking, swimming, reading, arts. Home: 1608 31st St Valley AL 36854 Office: East Ala Med Ctr Med Ctr Valley AL 36854

STRICK, CYNTHIA LEE, elementary education educator; b. Dennison, Ohio, Jan. 15, 1962; d. John Lee and Donna Elaine (Ross) Kilpatrick; m. Thomas Stephen Strick, Dec. 28, 1985; children: Curtis Russell, Victoria Lynn. BS in Edn., Akron U., 1984; M of Curriculum Instrn., Ashland U., 1995. Day care tchr./aide U. Akron, 1980-84; developmentally handicapped tchr. Lorain (Ohio) City Schs., 1984-90, 6th grade tchr., 1990—. Mem. Internat. Reading Assn. Roman Catholic. Avocations: sports, crafts, camping, working with people. Home: 212 Moorewood Ave Avon Lake OH 44012-1418 Office: Longfellow Elem Sch 1800 Cleveland Blvd Lorain OH 44052-2328

STRICKLAND, ANITA MAURINE, retired business educator, librarian; b. Groom, Tex., Sept. 24, 1923; d. Oliver Austin and Thelma May (Slay) Pool; m. LeRoy Graham Mashburn, Aug. 12, 1945 (dec. Mar. 1977); 1 child, Ronald Gene; m. Reid Strickland, May 27, 1978. BBA, West Tex. State U., 1962, MEd, 1965; postgrad. in library sci., Tex. Women's U., 1970. Cert. tchr., Tex.; cert. librarian. Employment interviewer Douglas Aircraft Co., Oklahoma City, 1942-45; cashier, bookkeeper Southwestern Pub. Services, Groom and Panhandle, Tex., 1950-58; acct. Gen. Motors Outlet, Groom, 1958-62; tchr. bus., lang. arts Groom Pub. Schs., 1962-68; bus. tchr., librarian Amarillo (Tex.) Pub. Schs., 1968-81. Vol. Amarillo Symphony, 1980—, Amarillo Rep. Com., 1981—, Lone Star Ballet, 1981-92; docent Amarillo Mus. Art, 1987—, sec., 1987-90, 93-94, treas., 1987-91; sec. Amarillo Art Alliance, 1989-90. Mem. AAUW (legis. com. 1986-88, sec. 1989-90, bd. dirs. 1989-91), Amarillo C. of C. (vol. women's divsn. 1981-86), Amarillo Christian Women's Club (asst. prayer advisor 1989-90, treas. 1995-96). Baptist. Avocations: piano, reading, swimming, tennis. Home: 6513 Roxton Dr Amarillo TX 79109-5120

STRICKLAND, DOROTHY, education educator; BS, Newark State Coll.; MA, PhD, NYU. Elem. sch. tchr. N.J. pub. sch. sys., reading cons., learning disabilities specialist; prof. edn. Rutgers U., New Brunswick, NJ, 1985—, Samuel DeWitt Proctor Prof. Edn., 2002—. Active in numerous state and nat. adv. bds. Author: Language Literacy and the Child, Process Reading and Writing: A Literature Based Approach, The Administration and Supervision of Reading Programs, Educating Black Children: America's Challenge, Family Storybook Reading, Listen Children: An Anthology of Black Literature, Families: An Anthology of Poetry for Young Children, Teaching Phonics Today, 1998, Beginning Reading and Writing, 2000, Supporting Struggling Readers and Writers, 2002, Preparing Our Teachers, 2002, (Language Arts) Preparing Our Tchr., 2003, Learning & Tchg., 2004. Inducted into the Reading Hall of Fame, pres., 1997-98. Mem. Nat. Coun. Tchrs. English (Rewey Belle Inglis award for Outstanding Woman in English Education Annual Conv., rsch. award, Outstanding Educator in Lang. Arts award 1998), Internat. Reading Assn. (past pres., Outstanding Tchr. Educator of reading award). Home: 131 Coccio Dr West Orange NJ 07052-4121 Office: Rutgers U Dept Edn Grad Sch Edn New Brunswick NJ 08903

STRICKLAND, SANDRA JEAN HEINRICH, nursing educator; b. Tucson, Sept. 18, 1943; d. Henry and Ada (Schmidt) Heinrich; BS, U. Tex. Sch. Nursing, 1965; MS in Nursing (fellow), U. Md., 1969; DrPH, U. Tex., 1978; m. William C. Strickland, Aug. 18, 1973; children: William Henry, Angela Lee. Clin. instr. U. Tex. Sch. Nursing, Galveston, 1965-66; staff nurse Hidalgo County Health Dept., Edinburg, Tex., 1966-67; supr. nursing Tex. Dept. Health Tb Control, Austin, 1969-70; instr. St. Luke's Hosp. Sch. Nursing, Houston, 1971-72, Tex. Women's U. Sch. Nursing, Houston and Dallas, 1972-73; dir. nursing Dallas City Health Dept., 1974-80; assoc. prof. community health nursing grad. program Tex. Woman's U., Dallas, 1980-87, U. Incarnate Word, 1987—; mem. profl. adv. com. Dallas Vis. Nurse Assn., 1978-83, Santa Rosa Home Health Agy., 1991-94; mem. health adv. bd. Dallas Ind. Sch. Dist., 1976-84; chmn. nursing and health services Dallas chpt. ARC, 1984-86, bd. dirs. San Antonio chpt., 1990; Tex. Lung Assn., 1991-97, bd. dirs. San Antonio Chpt., Tex. Public Health Assn. fellow, 1977. Mem. APHA, Tex. Public Health Assn., Sigma Theta Tau. Methodist. Home: 508 Us Highway 90 E Castroville TX 78009-5230

STRICKLIN, REBECCA ELLEN, chemistry educator; b. New Albany, Ind., Feb. 4, 1954; d. Ernest and Mary Ellen (Burnett) S. BS in Chemistry, Ohio U., 1974, MS in Inorganic Chemistry, 1976, EdD in Sci. Edn., 1993. Grad. asst. Ohio U., Athens, 1974-76; quality control lab. technician Procter and Gamble, Cin., 1978; chemistry tchr. Oak Hills High Sch., Cin., 1976—; chemistry instr. Cin. Tech. Coll., 1978-82. Vis. instr. chemistry Miami U., Middletown, Ohio, 1989, Hamilton, 1989—; presenter in field; mem. Sci. Com. Greater Cin., 1980-86, chair tchrs. resources and safety com. 1980-82. Author News for the Classroom column Am. Chem. Soc. Newsletter. Mem. curriculum coun. Ohio U., 1975-76, mem. individual course subcom., 1975-76; advisor Future Tchrs. Am., 1976-79; v.p. local PTA, 1977-79. Tandy Tech. scholar, 1995; grantee Dreyfus Outreach, 1986; Woodrow Wilson Found. fellow, 1985; recipient Catalyst award Chem. Mfrs. Assn., 1995, Outstanding Alumnus award Ohio U., 1996, Ch. and Soc. award 1999. Mem. NEA, ASCD, AAAS, Am. Chem. Soc. (high sch. planning com. Cin. sect., scholarships and grants com. 1987, ednl. svc. chair 1989—), Am. Inst. Chemists, Am. Nuclear Soc., Cin. Hist. Soc., Nat. Sci. Tchrs. Assn. (sci. edn. coun. Ohio), Ohio Acad. Sci. (v.p. sci. ednl. sect. 1989-90, chair coun. S.W. Ohio dist. 1989-92), Ohio Edn. Assn., Southwestern Ohio Edn. Assn., Oak Hills Edn. Assn., World Wildlife Fedn. Democrat. Office: Oak Hills High Sch 3200 Ebenezer Rd Cincinnati OH 45248-4099

STRIDE, JUNE, special education educator, author; b. Meadville, Pa., Dec. 10, 1940; d. Victor Hugo and Ethel May (Clark) Martin; m. Robert Francis Barry, Nov. 8, 1963 (div. Aug. 1984); children: April Elizabeth Barry, Patricia Dawn Barry); m. William A. Stride, Feb. 16, 1993. BS, SUNY, Cortland, 1962; MEd, North Ga. Coll., 1978; EdD, Nova Southeastern U., Ft. Lauderdale, Fla., 1996. Tchr., grades 4-6 Dade County Bd. Edn., Miami, Fla., 1969-71, tchr., gifted grades K-6, 1971-74; acad. dir. residential sch. for exceptional citizens Mountainview Devel. Program, Inc., Clarkesville, Ga., 1974-76; tchr. spokesperson, elem. and jr. high gifted program Habersham County Bd. of Edn., Clarkesville, 1976-80; remedial math. tchr. Dept. Offender Rehab., Alto, Ga., 1980-81; spl. edn. tchr., grades 9-12 Freeport (N.Y.) Union Free Sch. Dist., N.Y., 1981-96, chairperson spl. edn., 1996—2001. Author:Practical Strategies for Responsible High School Inclusion: Special Focus on Students with Behavioral Disabilities, 2003; co-author: Images: Changes, Images: Choices, Images: Challenges, 1994 (Healthy Living award, What's New in Home Econs., 1994), Street Smarts, 1999. Mem. N.Y. State Parent and Tchr. Inc. (hon., life). Avocations: writing, reading, outdoor activities. Home: Apt 302 921 Seagrape Dr Marco Island FL 34145-6241

STRIFLER, PETE, secondary education educator; b. Kennenburg, Germany, Apr. 6, 1949; came to U.S., 1956; s. Karl and Emma Elsa (Agner) S. BS, Ill. State U., 1971, postgrad., 1976-92, No. Ill. U., 1992, Aurora U., 1992; MA, St. Xavier U., 1999. Mem. faculty Sauk Valley Jr. Coll., Dixon, Ill., 1972-73; tchr. social sci. Tremont (Ill.) Community Jr.-Sr. High Sch., 1973—. Lutheran. Avocations: travel, collecting soapstone, photography. Home: 2203 Sunset Dr Pekin IL 61554-5364

STRIKER, CECIL LEOPOLD, archaeologist, educator; b. Cin., July 15, 1932; s. Cecil and Delia (Workum) S.; m. Ute Stephan, Apr. 27, 1968. BA, Oberlin Coll., 1956; MA, NYU, 1960, PhD, 1968; MA (hon.), U. Pa., 1972. From instr. to asst. prof. Vassar Coll., 1962-68; assoc. prof. U. Pa., Phila., 1968-78, prof. history of art, 1978—, chmn. dept. history of art, 1980-87; field archaeologist Dumbarton Oaks Center for Byzantine Studies, 1966-80, fellow, 1972-73. Adj. prof. Sabanci U., 1999—; dir. survey and excavation, Myrelaion, Istanbul, 1965-66; co-dir. Kalenderhane Archaeol. Project, Istanbul, 1966-78, Aegean Dendrochronology Project, 1977-88; gen. archaeol. cons. Istanbul Metro and Bosphorus Tunnel Project, 1985-87; dir. Archtl. Dendrochronology Project, 1988—; cons. Integrated Study of Hagia Sophia Structure, 1991-95. Mem. editorial bd. Architectura: Zeitschrift für Geschichte der Architektur, 1986—. Adv. bd. Ctr. for Advanced Study in the Visual Arts, 1986-88, Samuel H. Kress Found. Art History Fellowship Program, 1986-87. With U.S. Army, 1954-57. Fulbright grant in Germany, 1960-62, NEH grant, 1985-86; art historian in residence Am. Acad. in Rome, 1973. Mem. Archaeol. Inst. Am., Coll. Art Assn., Am. Rsch. Inst. in Turkey (fellow 1965-66, pres. 1978-84, hon. dir. 2002), Coun. Am. Overseas Rsch. Ctr. (chmn. 1980-84), Soc. Archtl. Historians, Turkish Studies Assn., U.S. Nat. Com. for Byzantine Studies, Koldewey Gesellschaft, German Archaeol. Inst. (corr.). E-mail: cstriker@sas.upenn.edu.

STRINGER, PATRICIA ANNE, retired secondary educator; b. Mpls., Mar. 17, 1935; d. Raphael Clarence and Marie Christine (Kwakenat) S. BS, U. Minn., 1960, MA, 1967. Cert. tchr., Minn. Tchr. Sunrise Park Jr. High Sch., White Bear Lake, Minn., 1960-72; tchr., coach Mariner High Sch., White Bear Lake, 1972-84, White Bear Lake High Sch., 1984-91. Mem. adv. bd. Minn. State High Sch. League, 1973-77; cons. in phys. edn., Minn., Wis., Mont., 1978-82; dept. chair White Bear Lake Schs., 1962-91, athletic coord., 1972-82; mem. Minn. State Coaching Cert. Com., 1980. Contbr. articles to profl. jours. Named to Minn. Softball Coaches Hall of Fame, 1992, Regional Coach of Yr., 1980, 90, Minn. Softball Hall of Fame Amateur Softball Assn. Am., 1982. Mem. AAHPERD, Minn. Assn. Health, Phys. Edn., Recreation and Dance (Secondary Phys. Edn. Tchr. of Yr. 1990), Ctrl. Dist. Assn. for Health, Phys. Edn., Recreation and Dance (Secondary Phys. Edn. Tchr. of Yr. 1991), Nat. Assn. for Sports and Phys. Edn., U. Minn. Womens Physical Edn. Alumni Assn. (v.p. 1991-92, pres. 1992-97). Avocations: golf, fishing, travel. Home: 24338 Dawnridge Ct Eden Valley MN 55329-9266

STRINGER, REBECCA HUGGINS, secondary education educator; b. Tuscaloosa, Ala., Jan. 31, 1947; d. Paul and Sarah (Glover) Huggins; m. Seth Phillip Stringer, Aug. 18, 1968 (div. Jan. 1992); children: Seth Prentice, Jenny Rebecca, Simeon Paul, Sarah Sue Annie. BS, U. Montevallo, 1968; MA, U. Ala., 1982. Cert. tchr., Ala. Home econs. tchr. Conecuh County Bd. Edn., Evergreen, Ala., 1968-69; sci. tchr. Coffeeville (Ala.) High Sch., 1970-71; elem. sci. tchr. Coffeeville Elem. Sch., 1971-78; vocat. home econs. tchr. Coffeeville High Sch., 1978—2003; ret. Ecology dir. Boy Scouts Am., Jackson, Ala., 1991-92; active PTA, Coffeeville, 1968-92; dir. ARC, Grove Hill, Ala., 1972-74; active in fundraising drives for St. Jude's Hosp., Kidney Found., Heart Assn., 1970—. Mem. Am. Edn. Assn., Am. Vocat. Assn., Ala. Farmers Fedn. (state women's com. 1981), Order of Ea. Star., Jackson Singles Club. Democrat. Baptist. Avocations: reading, swimming, dancing, walking, cooking. Home: PO Box 661 Jackson AL 36545-0661

STRINGER, WILLIAM JEREMY, university official; b. Oakland, Calif., Nov. 8, 1944; s. William Duane and Mildred May (Andrus) S.; m. Susan Lee Hildebrand; children: Shannon Lee, Kelly Erin, Courtney Elizabeth. BA in English, So. Meth. U., 1966; MA in English, U. Wis., 1968, PhD in Ednl. Adminstrn., 1973. Dir. men's housing Southwestern U., Georgetown, Tex., 1968-69; asst. dir. housing U. Wis., Madison, 1969-73; dir. residential life, assoc. dean student life, adj. prof. Pacific Luth., Tacoma, 1973-78; dir. residential life U. So. Calif., 1978-79, asst. v.p., 1979-84, asst. prof. higher and post-secondary edn., 1980-84; v.p. student life Seattle U., 1984-89, v.p. student devel., 1989-92, assoc. provost, 1989-95, assoc. prof. edn., 1990—, chair ednl. leadership, 1994—97, chair strategic planning, 1997—2000, chair profl. studies, 2001—. Author: How to Survive as a Single Student, 1972, The Role of the Assistant in Higher Education, 1973. Bd. dirs. N.W. Area Luth. Social Svcs. of Wash. and Idaho, pres.-elect, 1989, pres., 1990-91; bd. dirs. Seattle Coalition Ednl. Equity. Recipient John Hubbard Leadership award, 1984; Danforth Found. grantee, 1976-77. Mem. AAUP, Am. Assn. Higher Edn., Nat. Assn. Student Pers. Adminstrs. (bd. dirs. region V 1985-97, mem. editl. bd. Jour. 1995-2001, Disting. Svc. to Profession award 2000, faculty fellow 2002-), Am. Coll. Pers. Assn., Phi Eta Sigma, Sigma Tau Delta, Phi Alpha Theta, Lambda Chi Alpha. Lutheran. Home: 4553 169th Ave SE Bellevue WA 98006-6505 Office: Seattle U Dept Edn Seattle WA 98122 E-mail: stringer@seattleu.edu.

STRINGFELLOW, GERALD B. engineering educator; b. Salt Lake City, Apr. 26, 1942; s. Paul Bennion and Jean (Barton) S.; m. Barbara Farr, June 9, 1962; children: Anne, Heather, Michael. BS, U. Utah, 1964; PhD, Stanford U., 1968. Staff scientist Hewlett Packard Labs., Palo Alto, Calif., 1967-70, group mgr., 1970-80; disting. prof. elec. engring., materials sci. U. Utah, Salt Lake City, 1980—, chmn., 1994-98, adj. prof. physics, 1988—, dean Coll. of Engring., 1998—. Cons. Tex. Instruments, Dallas, 1995-97, AT&T-Bell Labs., Holmdel, N.J., 1986-90, Brit. Telecom., London, 1989-92; editor-in-chief Phase Diagrams for Ceramics, Vol. IX. Author: Organometallic Vapor Phase Epitaxy, 1989, 2d edit., 1999; editor: Metal Organic Vapor Phase Epitaxy, 1986, American Crystal Growth, 1987, Alloy Semiconductor Physics and Electronics, 1989, Phase Equilibria Diagrams-Semiconductors and Chalcogenides, 1991, High Brightness LEDs, 1997; prin. editor Jour. Crystal Growth; letters editor Jour. Electronic Materials, 1992-99; contbr. over 360 articles to profl. jours. Recipient U.S. Sr. Scientist award Alexander von Humboldt Soc., Bonn, Germany, 1979, Gov.'s Sci. Tech. medal State of Utah, 1997; guest fellow Royal Soc., London, 1990. Fellow IEEE, Japan Soc. Promotion of Sci.; mem. Am. Phys. Soc., Electronic Materials Com. (pres. 1985-87), Nat. Acad. Engring. (John Bardeen award, TMS, 2003). Achievements include pioneering development of organometallic vapor phase epitaxy, development of theories of thermodynamic properties of alloy semiconductors; discovery of phenomenon of compositional latching in alloy semiconductor layers grown by epitaxial techniques. Office: U Utah Coll Engring 1495 E 100 S Salt Lake City UT 84112-1109 E-mail: stringfellow@coe.utah.edu.

STRINGILE, MARIE ELIZABETH, educational administrator; b. Bayonne, N.J., May 13, 1954; d. Orlando Salvatore and Amelia Mary (Prisco) S. BA in edn., Jersey State Coll., 1976; MA in adminstrn., St. Peter's Coll., 1988; PhD in Edn. Adminstrn., 1976. Cert. elem. tchr., prin./supr., sch. adminstr., N.J. Tchr. St. James Sch., Newark, N.J., 1976-79; remedial math tchr. Ind. Child Study Teams, Jersey City, N.J., 1979-88, assoc. dir., 1988-90, adminstr., 1990—97, dir. ednl. programs, rsch. and evaluation mgr., 1997—2000; edn. program devel. specialist N.J. Dept. Edn., 2000—. Data documentation monitor Ind. Child Study Teams, Jersey City, 1990—, testing and curriculum specialist, 1990—, staff inservices, 1990—, data collection on all eligible remedial students, 1990—; cons. Devel. Remedial Math. Curriculum, 1993, resource room, 1985-88. Bd. dirs. O.L. Assumption Sch. Bd., 1991-93. Mem. ASCD, Sisters of St. Joseph of Peace (assoc.), Nat. Coun. Tchrs. Math., Internat. Reading Assn., Disabled Vets. Am., Medic Alert Found., Handyman Club Am., Black Seal Boiler Operator, Phi Delta Kappa. Avocations: carpentry, gardening, reading, mechanics, educational research. Home: 133 W 25th St Bayonne NJ 07002-1715 Office: NJ State Dept Edn Program Improvement 240 S Harrison St South Orange NJ

STRIP, CAROL ANN, gifted education specialist, educator; b. Jackson, Mich., July 3, 1945; d. Harold Don and Marion Estelle (Diemer) Gillespie; m. Asriel Strip, June 15, 1978 (div. Dec. 1992). BS, Western Mich. U., 1966, MA, 1969; PhD, Ohio State U, 1994. Cert. elem. prin., Mich.; cert. supr., ednl. specialist, Ohio. Kindergarten tchr. Kalamazoo (Mich.) Pub. Schs., 1967-74, primary tchr., 1974-75, 76-78, title 1-B adminstr., 1975-76; 4th grade tchr. Westerville (Ohio) City Schs., 1978-83; enrichment specialist Dublin (Ohio) City Schs., 1983-88, gifted edn. coord., 1988-94, gifted edn. specialist, 1988-94, gifted edn. specialist, tchr., 1994—; tchr. edn. Ohio State U., 1999—. Adv. bd. mem. Ohio Wesleyan Jr. League, Delaware, 1987—, Dublin Arts Coun., 1989—; workshop presenter, spkr. in field; adj. prof. Ohio State U., Ashley U. Pub. Roeper Rev. Instr. Jour.; author: Helping Gifted Children Soar, 2000; contbr. articles to profl. jours. Bd. dirs. Friends of the Libr., Columbus, 1978-83; com. mem. Ohio State Fair Orphans Day Com., Columbus, 1983-90. Recipient Master of Comms. award Ednl. Facilities Ctr., 1975, Golden Apple Achiever award Ashland Oil, 1993, Silver Anvil award AMA, 1972; named Ctrl. Mich. Tchr. of Yr., 1976. Fellow ASCD, Ohio Assn. Supervision Curriculum Devel., Sch. Study Coun. of Ohio, Ctrl. Ohio Coord. of Gifted, Alpha Chi Omega; mem. NEA, Ohio Ednl. Assn., Nat. Ret. Tchrs. Assn., Ohio Assn. of Gifted Children (regional rep. 1994, Outstanding Educator of Yr. 1994), Gifted

Coord. of Ctrl. Ohio (pres. 1992-93), Alpha Delta Kappa. Republican. Avocations: reading, travel, music, theatre, museums. Home: 8929 Turin Hill Ct N Dublin OH 43017-9414 Office: Arrowhead Elem Sch 2385 Hollenback Rd Lewis Center OH 43035-9043 Fax: (740) 549-1756. E-mail: DocCarolOH@aol.com.

STROBER, MYRA HOFFENBERG, education educator, consultant; b. N.Y.C., Mar. 28, 1941; d. Julius William Hoffenberg and Regina Scharer; m. Samuel Strober, June 23, 1963 (div. Dec. 1983); children: Jason M., Elizabeth A.; m. Jay M. Jackman, Oct. 21, 1990. BS in Indsl. Rels., Cornell U., 1962; MA in Econs., Tufts U., 1965; PhD in Econs., MIT, 1969. Lectr., asst. prof. dept. econs. U. Md., College Park, 1967-70; lectr. U. Calif., Berkeley, 1970-72; asst. prof. grad. sch. bus. Stanford (Calif.) U., 1972-86, assoc. prof. sch. edn., 1979-90, prof. edn., 1990—, assoc. dean acad. affairs, 1993-95, interim dean, 1994; program officer in higher edn. Atlantic Philanthropic Svcs., Ithaca, N.Y., 1998-2000. Organizer Stanford Bus. Conf. Women Mgmt., 1974; founding dir. ctr. rsch. women Stanford U., 1974-76, 79-84, dir. edn. policy inst., 1984-86, dean alumni coll., 1992, mem. policy and planning bd., 1992-93, chair program edn. adminstrn. and policy analysis, 1991-93, chair provost's com. recruitment and retention women faculty, 1992-93, chair faculty senate com. on coms., 1992-93; mem. adv. bd. State of Calif. Office Econ. Policy Planning and Rsch., 1978-80; mem. Coll. Bd. Com. Develop Advanced Placement Exam. Econs., 1987-88; faculty advisor Rutgers Women's Leadership Program, 1991-93. Author: (with others) Industrial Relations, 1972, 1990, Sex, Discrimination and the Division of Labor, 1975, Changing Roles of Men and Women, 1976, Women in the Labor Market, 1979, Educational Policy and Management: Sex Differentials, 1981, Women in the Workplace, 1982, Sex Segregation in the Workplace: Trends, Explanations, Remedies, 1984, The New Palgrave: A Dictionary of Economic Theory and Doctrine, 1987, Computer Chips and Paper Clips: Technology and Women's Employment, Vol. II, 1987, Gender in the Workplace, 1987, Challenge to Human Capital Theory: Implications for the HR Manager, American Economic Review, 1995, Rethinking Economics Through a Feminist Lens, Feminist Economics, 1995, Making and Correcting Errors in Economic Analyses: An Examination of Videotapes, (with Agnes M.K. Chan) the Road Winds Uphill All the Way: Gender, Work, and Family in the U.S. and Japan, 1999, (with Jay M. Jackman) Fear of Feedback, 2003; editor (with Francine E. Gordon) Bringing Women Into Management, 1975, (with others) Women and Poverty, 1986, Industrial Relations, 1990, Challenges to Human Capitol Theory: Implications for HR Managers, 1995, (with Sanford M. Dornbusch) Feminism, Children and the New Families, 1988, Rethinking Economics Through a Feminist Lens, 1995, (with Agnes M.K. Chan) The Road Winds Uphill All The Way: Gender, Work and Family in the U.S. and Japan, 1999, (with Jay M. Jackman) fear of Feedback, 2003; mem. bd. editors Signs: Jour. Women Culture and Soc., 1975-89, assoc. editor, 1980-85; mem. bd. editors Sage Ann. Rev. Women and Work, 1984—; mem. editorial adv. bd. U.S.-Japan Women's Jour., 1991—; assoc. editor Jour. Econ. Edn., 1991—; contbr. chpt. to book, articles to profl. jours. Mem. rsch. adv. task force YWCA, 1989—; chair exec. bd. Stanford Hillel, 1990-92; bd. dirs. Resource Ctr. Women, Palo Alto, Calif., 1983-84; pres. bd. dirs. Kaider Found., Mountain View, Calif., 1990-96. Fellow Stanford U., 1975-77, Schiff House Resident fellow, 85-87. Mem.: NOW (bd. dirs. legal def. and edn. fund 1993—98), Ctr. Gender Equality (bd. dirs. 2000—), Internat. Assn. Feminist Econs. (assoc. editor Feminist Econs. 1994—, pres. 1997), Indsl. Rels. Rsch. Assn., Am. Ednl. Rsch. Assn., Am. Econ. Assn. (mem. com. status of women in profession 1972—75). Office: Stanford U School Edn Stanford CA 94305 E-mail: myra.strober@stanford.edu.

STROCK, GERALD E. school system administrator; Supt. Hatboro-Horsham (Pa.) Sch. Dist., 1986—. State finalist Nat. Supt. Yr., 1993. Office: Hatboro-Horsham Sch Dist 229 Meetinghouse Rd Horsham PA 19044-2192

STROEMPLE, RUTH MARY THOMAS, social welfare administrator; b. Cleve., Jan. 31, 1923; d. Daniel William and Jeanette Alexandria (Webb) Thomas; m. Robert Theodore Stroemple, July 27, 1944 (dec. July 1991); children: Susan, George, Janet, Gayle. BA in Child Devel., Marylhurst Coll., 1981. Specialist infant care Oreg. Health Scis. U., Portland, 1976-85, Emanuel Hosp., Portland, 1986-87; mem. failure to thrive rsch. team Doernbecher Hosp., Portland, 1978-85; founder, dir. Newborn Connection, Portland, 1986-90; founder, dir. Med. Foster Parent Program Childrens' Svcs. Divsn., Portland, 1976-94; specialist infant assessment Foster Parent Program, Childrens' Svcs. Divsn., Portland, 1990-94, cons., trainer, 1991-94. Team leader sensory stimulation program Infant Dystrophy Ctr., Romania; cons. in field. Author: (booklet) Infant Sensory Stimulation, 1986, (manual) Newborn Connection Hospital, 1986, (tng. manual) Medical Foster Parent Handbook, 1990. Ctr. Child Abuse & Neglect grantee, 1991; recipient Golden Rule award J.C. Penny, Portland, 1993. Mem. Infant Devel. Edn. Assn. (cert. instr.), Infant Massage Assn. (cert. instr.), Foster Parent Assn. Avocations: gardening, reading, hiking, family activities. Home: 12535 SW Tooze Rd Sherwood OR 97140-8442

STROH, ROBERT CARL, SR., university official; b. Flint, Mich., July 23, 1937; s. Herbert Chandler and Margaret (LaHive) S.; m. Kelly Ann Pascal, Aug. 8, 1979; children: Robert Carl, Ryan Christopher, Kerry Alexandra; 1 child by previous marriage, Jayme Lynn. BS, Pa. State U., 1959, MS, 1961, PhD, 1964. Sr. staff cons. Auto-Biometrics, State Coll., Pa., 1964-65; programmer, analyst Vitro Labs., Silver Spring, Md., 1965-73; v.p. Applied Urbanetics, Washington, 1973-79; dir. info. and tech. transfer Nat. Assn. Home Builders Nat. Rsch. Ctr., Upper Marlboro, Md., 1979-89; dir. Shimberg Ctr. for Affordable Housing, U. Fla., Gainesville, 1989—. Adj. prof. Montgomery Coll., Rockville, Md., 1981-89. Editor: Wood-Frame House Construction, 1988. Mem. Sigma Xi. Home: 8611 SW 23d Pl Gainesville FL 32607-3461 Office: U Fla Shimberg Ctr Affordable Housing PO Box 115703 Gainesville FL 32611-5703

STROHBEHN, JOHN WALTER, engineering science educator; b. San Diego, Nov. 21, 1936; s. Walter William and Gertrude (Powell) S.; children from previous marriage: Jo, Kris, Carolyn; m. Barbara Ann Brungard, Aug. 30, 1980 BS, Stanford U., 1958, MS, 1959, PhD in Elec. Engring., 1964. Assoc. prof. engring. sci. Dartmouth Coll., Hanover, N.H., 1968-73, prof., 1973-94, assoc. dean, 1976-81, adj. prof. medicine, 1979-90, Sherman Fairchild prof., 1983-91, acting provost, 1987-89, provost, 1989-93; pro-vost, prof. biomed. engring. Duke U., Durham, N.C., 1994-99. Disting. lectr. IEEE Antennas and Propagation Soc., 1979-82; vis. fellow Princeton (N.J.) U., 1993-94. Editor: Laser Propagation in the Clear Atmosphere, 1978; assoc. editor Trans. Ant and Propagation, 1969-71, Trans. Biomed. Engring., 1981-87; contbr. articles to profl. jours. Scoutmaster Boy Scouts Am., Norwich, Vt., 1971-73; bd. dirs. Norwich Recreation and Conservation Council. Fellow AAAS, IEEE, Optical Soc. Am., Am. Inst. Med. Biol. Engring. (founding); mem. Radiation Rsch. Soc., Bioelectromagnetics Soc. (bd. dirs. 1982-85), N.Am. Hyperthermia Group (pres. 1986). Avocations: jogging, hiking, skiing. Office: Duke U Provost's Office PO Box 90005 Durham NC 27708-0005 Home: 10 Whitburn Pl Durham NC 27705-5586

STROHMAIER, THOMAS EDWARD, designer, educator, photographer; b. Cin., Aug. 26, 1943; s. Charles Edward and Margaret Mary (Meyers) S.; m. Margaret Ann Haglage, June 7, 1980; children: Paige Maura, Edward Michael, Phoebe Greer, Michael Thomas. BFA, U. Cin., 1969, MFA, 1973. Asst. prof. design U. Cin., 1973—; City Outreach Program, 1975-76; instr. in design U. Dayton, Ohio, 1976-80, asst. prof. design, 1980-83; pres. Strohmaier Design, Cin., 1983—. Cons. City Arts Corp., Cin., 1977-78, City Beautiful Program, Dayton, 1982; adj. prof. design U. Cin., 1983—, mem. lecture outreach program, 1995, developed digital design program in photography, 1999-2000. Designer urban wall projects Ohio Arts Council, Columbus, 1974, Corbet award, Cin., 1977; patentee in field. U. Dayton grantee, 1980. Mem. Contemporary Arts Ctr., Design, Architecture, Art and Planning Alumni Com., Internat. Freelance Photographers Orgn., Associated Photographers Internat., U. Cin. Decade Club. Clubs: Decade. Republican. Roman Catholic. Avocations: running, cycling. Home: 7311 Redondo Ct Cincinnati OH 45243-1247 Office: Strohmaier Design 5274 Ridge Ave Cincinnati OH 45213-2542 E-mail: tesmah80@aol.com., strohmaier@queencity.com.

STROHSCHEIN, HELEN FRANCES, educational administrator; b. Omaha, Feb. 10, 1954; d. William Francis and Mary Frances (Carson) S. AA summa cum laude, Tyler (Tex.) Jr. Coll., 1974; BS summa cum laude, Stephen F. Austin, 1976, ME, 1984. Tchr. Slack Elem. Sch., Lufkin, Tex., 1977-78, Jr. High West, Lufkin, 1978-86, asst. prin., 1986-87; prin. Anderson Elem. Sch., Lufkin, 1987-91, Jr. High West, Lufkin, 1991-98; dir. for instrn. Dunbar Edn. Ctr., Lufkin, 1998—. Com. mem. So. Assn., Lufkin, 1979-80; chairperson Evaluation Team, Nacogdoches, Tex., 1986; cons. Region VII Svc. Ctr., Kilgore, Tex., 1981-82, 86; workshop facilitator Lufkin Ind. Sch. Dist., 1981, 87—; peer evaluator Tex. Sch. Improvement Initiative, 1996—. Bd. dirs. Angelina County Boys and Girls Club, Lufkin; facilitator Nacogdoches Edn. Summit, 1990. Recipient Spl. Friend award Lufkin Ind. Sch. Dist., 1989. Mem. ASCD, PTA, Tex. Staff Devel. Coun., Tex. Assn. Sch. Adminstrs., Delta Kappa Gamma, Phi Delta Kappa (rsch. rep. 1987-88, newsletter editor 1988-89, 1st v.p. 1989-90, Adminstr. of Yr. 1990). Avocations: reading, walking, skiing, jogging, travel. Home: 3000 S 1st St Apt 920 Lufkin TX 75901-7160 Office: Dunbar Edn Ctr 1806 Martin Luther King Bvd Lufkin TX 75904-3939

STROIK, DUNCAN GREGORY, architect, architectural design educator; b. Phila., Jan. 14, 1962; s. John Stephen and Mary Eugenia (Dorsey) S.; m. Ruth Valeira Engelhardt, Aug. 29, 1987; children: Gabrielle Marie, Raffaella Maria, Giovanni Battista, Pietro Francesco. BS in Architecture, U. Va., 1984; MArch, Yale U., 1987. Registered arch., Ill., Ind., Conn., Ariz., Ala., Ga., Wis., Minn. Tchg. asst. Yale U. Sch. Architecture, New Haven, Conn., 1985-87; arch. Allan Greenberg, Arch., Washington, 1987-90; assoc. prof. U. Notre Dame (Ind.) Sch. Architecture, 1990—; arch. Duncan Stroik, Arch., South Bend, Ind., 1990—. Chmn. lectr. com. U. Notre Dame, Ind., 1990—, mem. undergrad. com., 1992—, com. on internat. studies, 1993-94; chmn. jury Ind. Concrete Masonry Assn., Ind., 1994. Arch., author Building Classical, 1993; exhibitions include U. Steubenville, 1995, N.Y. Acad. of Art, 1994, Yale U. Sch. Architecture, 1995, Chgo. Cultural Ctr., 1995, others; editor: Sacred Arch. Mag., Reconquering Sacred Space, 2000; contbr. articles to profl. jours.; appeared on Bob Vila's In Search of Palladio, 1998. With East Rock Pavilion-Design and Constrn., Yale U. Sch. Architecture, New Haven, 1985; active Habitat for Humanity, New Haven, 1987, U. Notre Dame chpt. faculty adv.; mem. faculty senate U. Notre Dame, 1998—. Palladio and Vitruvius grantee Graham Found. for Advanced Studies, 1991, Student Rsch. grantee Promote Women and Minorities Grad. Studies, U. Notre, Dame, 1993; C.L.V. Meeks Meml. scholar Yale U., New Haven, 1987; Sacred Architecure grantee Homeland Found., 1996; recipient Ind. award, AIA, 1998. Mem.: Inst. for Classical Architecture, Assn. Collegiate Schs. Architecture, Nat. Trust for Hist. Preservation, Classical Am. Roman Catholic. Avocations: classical music, philosophy, travel, painting. Home: 52488 Briarcliff Ln South Bend IN 46635-1104 Office: Univ Notre Dame Sch Architecture Notre Dame IN 46556

STROKE, HINKO HENRY, physicist, educator; b. Zagreb, Croatia, June 16, 1927; came to U.S., 1943, naturalized, 1949; s. Elias and Edith (Mechner) S.; m. Norma Bilchick, Jan. 14, 1956; children: Ilana Lucy, Marija Tamar. BEE, N.J. Inst. Tech., 1949; MS, MIT, 1952, PhD, 1955. From rsch. asst. to rsch. assoc. Princeton (N.J.) U., 1954-57; rsch. staff lab. electronics, lectr. dept. physics MIT, 1957-63; assoc. prof. physics NYU, N.Y.C., 1963-68, prof., 1968—. Dept. chmn. NYU, 1988-91; prof. associé. U. Paris, 1969-70, Ecole Normale Supérieure, 1976; vis. scientist Max Planck Inst. für Quantenoptik, Garching, U. Munich, 1977-78, 81-82, 93; cons. Atomic Instrument Co., MIT Sci. Translation Svc., Tech. Rsch. Group, Cambridge Air Force Rsch. Ctr., Am. Optical Corp., ITT Fed. Labs., NASA, others; mem. com. on line spectra of elements NAS-NRC, 1976-82; sci. assoc. CERN, Geneva, 1983—. Contbg. author: Nuclear Physics, 1963, Atomic Physics, 1969, Hyperfine Interactions in Excited Nuclei, 1971, Francis Bitter: Selected Papers, 1969, Atomic Physics 3, 1973, Nuclear Moments and Nuclear Structure, 1973, A Perspective of Physics, Vol. 1, 1977, Atomic Physics 8, 1983, Lasers in Atomic, Molecular, and Nuclear Physics, 1989—, Symposium on Probing Luminous and Dark Matter, 2000; editor: Comments on Atomic, Molecular and Optical Physics, The Physical Review-The First Hundred Years. Mem. Chorus Pro Musica, 1951—54, 1957—63, Münchener Bach-Chor, Munich, 1977—82, 1992; Choeur pro Arte Lausanne, 1983—; mem. Collegiate Chorale, NY, 1964—94, Dessoff Choirs, 1994—2001, Westchester Oratorio Soc., 2001—. Recipient Sr. U.S. Scientist award Alexander von Humboldt Found., 1977; NATO sr. fellow in sci., 1975 Fellow Am. Phys. Soc. (publs. oversight com. 1991-93), Optical Soc. Am., AAAS; mem. IEEE, European Phys. Soc., Soc. Fraçaise de Physique, Sigma Xi, Tau Beta Pi, Omicron Delta Kappa. Office: NYU Dept Physics 4 Washington Pl New York NY 10003-6621 E-mail: henry.stroke@nyu.edu.

STROLL, BEVERLY MARIE, elementary school principal; b. Akron, Ohio, Aug. 22, 1936; d. Michael Dzatko, William DeVille (stepfather) and Marie Elizabeth (Stock) Dzatko-DeVille; m. Harold E. Stroll, Aug. 22, 1959; 1 child, James. BS, Kent State, 1958, MEd, 1980, Ednl. Specialist, 1988. Cert. elem. principal, elem. supr., tchr. Elem. edn. tchr. Cleve. Pub. Schs., 1958-59, Akron (Ohio) Pub. Schs., 1959-80, chpt. I math tchr., 1980-85, curriculum specialist, 1985-87, program specialist, 1987-91; prin. Zion Christian Sch., Akron, 1991—. Bd. mem. Zion Christian Sch., 1983—, State Supt. Adv. Bd., 1984-89. Co-chair vol. com. Nat. Inventors Hall of Fame, 1990. Named Jennings scholar Martha Holden Jennings Found., 1978-79. Mem. ASCD, Assn. Luth. Devel. Execs., Coalition Ohio Luth. Devel., Greater Clevel. Luth. Prins. Assn., Ohio Assn. Adminstrs. of State and Fed. Programs (exec. bd. 1989-91), Akron Women Adminstrs. (sec. 1988-90), Zion Lutheran Ch. (sec. 1988-96). Avocations: boating, water sports, traveling, bible study. Office: Zion Christian Sch 139 S High St Akron OH 44308-1410

STROM, BRIAN LESLIE, internist, educator; b. N.Y.C., N.Y., Dec. 8, 1949; s. Martin and Edith (Singer) S.; m. Elaine Marilyn Moskowitz, June 4, 1978; children: Shayna Lee, Jordan Blair. BS, Yale U., 1971; MD, Johns Hopkins U., 1975; MPH, U. Calif., Berkeley, 1980. Diplomate Am. Bd. Internal Medicine, Am. Bd. Epidemiology. Intern in medicine U. Calif., San Francisco, 1975-76, resident in medicine, 1976-78, research fellow in clinical pharmacology, 1978-80; from asst. prof. to assoc. prof. medicine and pharmacology U. Pa., Phila., 1980-93, prof. medicine, 1993—, prof. biostatistics & epidemiology, 1995—. Adj. asst. prof. clin. pharmacy Phila. Coll. of Pharmacy and Sci., 1981-90, adj. assoc. prof., 1990-93, adj. prof., 1993—; mem. U. Pa. Cancer Ctr., 1981—; attending staff Hosp. U. Pa., 1980—, co-dir Clin. Epidemiology Unit, 1980-91, dir., 1991-2001; dir. Clin. Pharmacology Cons. Svc., 1981-82; dir. Ctr. for Clin. Epidemiology and Biostats., 1993—, chair dept. biostats. and epidemiology, 1995—; lectr. in field; George S. prod. pub. health and preventive medicine, 2002—; cons. CDC, 1981, Coun. for Internat. Orgn. of Med. Scis., Geneva, Switzerland, 1981-83, Office of Tech. Assessment, Congress of U.S., 1980-81, Aging Rev. Com., Nat. Inst. Aging, 1982, Ministry of Pub. Health, State of Kuwait, 1982, Royal Tropical Inst., Amsterdam, 1983, others. Editl. cons. Johns Hopkins U. Press, J.B. Lippincott; referee Annals of Internal Medicine, Archives of Internal Medicine, Clin. Pharmacology and Therapeutics, Digestive Diseases and Sci., Internat. Jour. Cardiology, Internat. Jour. Epidemiology, Jour. AMA, Jour. Gen. Internal Medicine, Med. Care, Primary Care Tech., Sci.; editor Pharmaepidemiology and Drug Safety; mem. editl. bd. 7 jours.; contbr. numerous articles to profl. jours. Nat. Acad. Scis. grantee, Rockefeller Found. grantee, NIH grantee, many others. Fellow ACP, Am. Coll. Epidemiology, Am. Epidemiology Soc.; mem. Am. Fedn. Med. Rsch., Am. Pub. Health Assn., Am. Soc. Clin. Pharmacology and Therapeutics, Am. Soc. Clin. Investigation, Am. Assn. Physicians, Internat. Soc. Pharmacoepidemiology, Internat. Epideliol. Assn., Soc. for Epidemiologic Rsch., Soc. Gen. Internal Medicine, Inst. Medicine, Inst. Medicine. Democrat. Jewish. Avocations: hiking, biking, camping, skiing. Home: 332 Hidden River Rd Narberth PA 19072-1111

STROM, CARLA CASTALDO, elementary education educator; b. Rahway, N.J., Aug. 11; d. Neil and Loretta (Gleason) Castaldo; m. George Pendleton Strom, Aug. 11, 1962; children: Karen Kimberly, Steven Karl. BS in Edn. cum laude, Syracuse U., 1961; MS in Edn. magna cum laude, U. Bridgeport, 1962; postgrad., Brown U., 1982-89, Sacred Heart U. Cert. tchr., N.Y., N.J., R.I. Tchr. Livingston Elem. Sch., Cranford, N.J., 1962-63, Sherman Sch., Cranford, 1963-65; supplementary instr. Cranford Bd. Edn., 1974-79; tutor remedial students, home instr. R.I. East Greenwich Sch. Com., 1980-83; tchr. Holy Name Sch., Providence, 1983-86, St. Thomas Regional Sch., Providence, 1986-89; tchr. sci., social studies St. Mary Sch., Bethel, Conn., 1989—; with Profl. Learning Ctr. Jupiter (Fla.) Acad., 1995-97; coord. youth ministry St. Jude, Tequestra, Fla., 1997—. Sci. fair coord.; Danbury, Conn., 1991—; participant Here's Looking at You in the Year 2001-Drug Free America. Tchr. confraternity of Christian doctrine, 1972—, Eucharistic min. St. Mary Ch., Bethel, 1991-95; neighborhood leader East Greenwich Tanglewood Assn., 1982-84; Rep. committee-woman, Cranford, 1979-81. Recipient Drug-Free Sch. award Providence Journal, 1987. Mem. Nat. Cath. Tchrs. Assn., Nat. Sci. Tchrs. Assn., Religious Educators Am., Phi Kappa Phi, Kappa Kappa Gamma. Home: Bldg 200 Unit 301 200 Ocean Trail Way Ofc 200 Jupiter FL 33477-5550

STROME, MARSHALL, otolaryngologist, educator; b. Lynn, Mass., Apr. 27, 1940; s. David and Rose (Cantor) S.; m. Deena Lazarov, Sept. 23, 1962; children: Scott Eric, Randall Alan. Degree, U. Mich., 1960, MD, 1964, MS, 1970. Resident in otolaryngology U. Mich., Ann Arbor, 1966-70; asst. prof. U. Conn., Hartford, 1971, Beth Israel-Harvard, Boston, 1972-77, chief otolaryngology, 1977-93; prof., chmn. otolaryngology Cleve. Clinic Found., 1993—. Sr. surgeon Brigham & Women's Hosp., Boston, 1982-93; assoc. prof. harvard Med. Sch., Boston, 1989-93, Longwood ORL coord., 1982-90; mem. cons. bd. Xomed Treace Corp., Jacksonville, Fla., 1987-90; advisor SLT Laser Corp., Oaks, Pa., 1994—; dir. Great Comebacks, Gresham, Oreg.; prof. otolaryngology Cleve. Clinic Found. Health Scis. Ctr. Ohio State U., 1994; hon. guest, prin. spkr. Turkish Otolaryngol. Soc., 1997; Qgura lectr., 2000; mem. sci. adv. bd. Somnus Corp.; pres. Soc. Univ. Otolaryngologists, 2002—. Mem. editl. bd. Harvard Health News Letter, 1976-85; author: Differential Diagnoses in Pediatric ORL, 1975; editor: Manual of Otolaryngology, 1985, Complications of Laser Surgery of the Head and Neck, 1986; transplanted 1st total human larynx, 1998. Mem. fund raising com. Belmont Hill (Mass.) Sch., 1984. Capt. U.S. Army, 1965-71. Recipient Medal City of Paris, 1987, Sword of Saudi Arabia, 1991, Cert. of Appreciation, Ministry of Health-Singapore, 1995, Presdl. citation Coll. Physicians and Surgeons of Pakistan, Classic Telly award, 1999; named One of Best Doctors in Cleve., Cleve. Mag., 1995—, One of Best Drs. in Am., 1996—, Outstanding People of 20th Century, 1999, Medical Hero Guiness Book of World Records, 2000. Mem.: Triological Soc. (v.p. 1990—91), Cartesian Soc. (pres. 1999), Soc. Univ. Otolaryngologists (pres. 2003), Am. Soc. Head and Neck Surgery, Am. Acad. Otolaryngology (Honor award 1987, one of nine recognized for conbtn. to medicine in last 250 years 1999, Internat. Scientist of Yr. 2002), Am. Acad. Facial Plastic Reconstructive Surgery (Medallion of Honor 1989), U. Mich. Med. Ctr. Alumni Soc. (coord. New Eng. Fund. Raising 1992, chair bd. govs. 1992—93, Cleve. Clinic tchr. of yr. 2002). Avocations: cycling, skiing, sculling, sea kyacking, tennis. Office: Cleve Clinic Found 9500 Euclid Ave Cleveland OH 44195-0001

STROMMEN, CLIFFORD H. headmaster; b. Gilby, N.D., May 2, 1935; m. Bette Ann Freeman, Dec. 22, 1963; children: Clint K., Emily A. BS in English, Moorhead State U., 1958; MEd in Ednl. Administrn., U. Houston, 1975, EdD in Ednl. Administrn., 1981. Cert. Eng. tchr., superintendent, dist. administr., N.Y., tchr. English, Phys. Edn., Calif. Tchr. English various sr. and jr. high schs., 1958-70; dir. athletics Seaside High Sch., Monterey, Calif., 1968; dir. dormitories Am. Internat. Sch., New Delhi, India, 1970-72, vice-prin., 1971-72; dir. Am. Embassy Sch. (formerly Am. Internat. Sch.), New Delhi, India, 1972-74; supt. Internat. Sch. Lusaka, Zambia, 1976-84, Escola Graduada de São Paulo, Brazil, 1984-90; headmaster Internat. Sch. Nido de Aguilas, Santiago, Chile, 1990—. Recipient Nat. Superintendent of the Yr. awd., Overseas, Am. Assn. of School Administrators, 1993. Mem. Assn. Am. Sch. Administrs. (Internat. Superintendent of Yr. 1993), Assn. Advancement of Internat. Edn. (bd. dirs. 1983-84, 87-89, v.p. 1991-92, pres. 1993-94), Assn. Am. Schs. Brazil (treas. 1984-88, pres. 1989-90), Assn. Am. Schs. S.Am.(treas. 1985-86, v.p. 1986-87, pres. 1987-88), So. Assn. Colls. and Schs. (Latin Am. com. 1993), Assn. Internat. Schs. Africa (v.p. 1976, pres. 1976-78). Office: Internat Sch Nido de Aguilas Casilla 16211 Correo 9 Santiago Chile

STRONACH, CAREY ELLIOTT, physicist, educator; b. Boston, Aug. 8, 1940; s. Ralph Howard and Frances Burns (Maynard) S.; m. Joan Alice Louise Venner, Aug. 20, 1966; children: John Maynard, Howard Stanley. BS, U. Richmond, Va., 1961; MS, U. Va., 1963; PhD, Coll. William and Mary, 1976. Instr. physics Va. State U., Petersburg, 1965-66, asst. prof., 1966—76, assoc. prof., 1976—80, prof., 1980—. Dir. Muon Spin Rotation Rsch. Program, 1977—, Superconducting Materials Rsch. Program, 1988-97, Nanostructured Materials Rsch. Program, 1997-2001, Galactic Cosmic Radiation Rsch. Program, 1993-97, U.S.-France Joint Muon Spin Rotation Rsch. Program, 1985-91, Magnetic Materials Lab. Devel. Program, 1999-2001, Ctr. Interactive Micromagnetics, 2001—; radiation safety officer Solid State Physics Rsch. Inst., 1983-87; dir. Ctr. Interactive Micromagnetics, 2001—; vis. assoc. prof. U. Alta, 1978-79; guest scientist Brookhaven Nat. Lab.; organizing com. Internat. Symposium on the Electronic Structure and Properties of Hydrogen in Metals, 1982, Internat. Symposium on the Physics and Chemistry of Small Clusters, 1986, From Clusters to Crystals, 1991, Sci. and Tech. Atomically Engineered Materials, 1995, Internat. Symposium on Cluster and Nanostructure Interfaces, 1999, Internat. Symposium Clusters and Nano-Assemblies: From Physical to Life Sciences, 2003; adv. com. Internat. Conf. on Muon Spin Rotation, 1996-99; sci. adv. com. European Workshop on the Spectroscopy of Subatomic Species in Non-Metallic Solids, 1985, govs. com. on Superconducting Supercollider, 1987; TV physics lectr., 1991-94; chair adv. com. Internat. Conf. on Muon Spin Rotation, 1999-2002; founding dir. Ctr. on Interactive Micromagnetics, Va. State U. Contbr. numerous articles to publs. in field; playwright. Pres. Petersburg area chpt. Va. Coun. Human Rels., 1965—67; active Petersburg Commn. Cmty. Rels. Affairs, 1974—77; long-range transp. adv. com. City of Petersburg, 1994—98; steering com. Gilmore for Gov., 1997; active Dramatists Guild; sec. adv. coun. bds. and commns. Commonwealth Coun., 1998—2002; active Richmond Playwrights Forum, 1999—, Virginians for Warner, 2001; corr. sec. Petersburg Dem. Com., 1974—77, active, 1972—85, vice chmn., 1981—85. Fellow duPont Corp., 1961-63, NSF, 1971-72, NASA, 1976; recipient Patrick Henry award Va. Gov. James C. Gilmore III, 2001. Mem.: AAUP (chpt. pres. 1968—70), AAAS, Air Force Assn., Internat. Soc. on Muon Spectroscopy (founding mem.), WWII Meml. Soc. (charter), Sci. Nitlinks Adv. Bd., N.Y. Acad. Scis., Planetary Soc., High Speed Rail/Maglev Assn. (govt. rels. com. 1992—97, Maglev task force 1994—97), Va. Assn. Scholars (bd. govs. 1999—), Southeastern Univs. Rsch. Assn. (site sel. com. 1980—81, materials sci. com. 1983—86, trustee 1983—98, sci. and tech. com. 1986—88, rules com. 1988—92, edn. com. 1992—94, new projects com. 1994—95, Jefferson Lab. com. 1995—98), Va. Acad. Sci. (sec. astronomy, math. and physics sect 1983—84, chmn. 1984—85), Nat. Assn. Scholars, Am. Assn. Physics Tchrs., Am. Phys. Soc., Tri-univ. Meson Facility Users Group, Coun.

Secular Humanism (assoc.), Richmond Area Free Thinkers, Pi Mu Epsilon, Sigma Pi Sigma, Sigma Xi (chpt. sec. 1977—78, chpt. pres. 1980—84, 1987—88), Phi Beta Kappa. Achievements include co-devel. of low-energy muon beam line at the AGS of Brookhaven Nat. Lab.; rsch. in pion-nucleus interactions, heavy-ion reactions, muon spin rotation studies of high-temperature superconductors and related materials, fullerenes, heavy-fermion materials, ferromagnetic metals, metal hydrides, fatigue in metals and other materials; participation in the establishment of the Southeastern Universities Research Association and the Thomas Jefferson Nat. Accelerator Facility; discovery of formation of muonium and muonated radicals in Buckminsterfullerene; discovery of simultaneous high-temp. superconductivity and magnetic ordering in strontium yttrium ruthenate. Home: 2241 Buckner St Petersburg VA 23805-2207 Office: Va State U PO Box 9325 Petersburg VA 23806-0001 E-mail: cstronac@vsu.edu.

STRONG, CAROL JOAN, speech professional, researcher; b. Portland, Oreg., Dec. 26, 1942; d. Orval I. and Marian T. (Lewis) Dunlap; m. William J. Strong, Oct. 20, 1961; children: Kristin, Eric. BS, Utah State U., 1971, EdD, 1989; MA, U. Ill., 1972. Clinician Champaign (Ill.) Sch. Dist., 1972-73; trustee prof., assoc. dean rsch. Utah State U., Logan, 1973—. Rsch. dir. Ski*Hi Inst., Logan, 1989—92. Fellow, Utah State U., 1983; grantee, ASHA Found., 1989. Mem.: AAUW (State of Utah Emerging scholar 1991), Nat. Coun. Tchrs. English, Internat. Reading Assn., Utah Speech, Lang. and Hearing Assn., Nat. Assn. Edn. Young Children, Coun. Exceptional Children, Am. Speech, Lang. and Hearing Assn. Avocations: gardening, motorcycling, walking, reading.

STRONG, JAMES THOMPSON, management, security, human resources consultant; b. Boca Raton, Fla., Oct. 26, 1945; s. Earl William and Mary Joe (Thompson) S.; m. Lenore Jean Stager, Feb. 2, 1974; 1 child, Daria Nicole. BA in Polit. Sci., U. Calif., Riverside, 1973; MS in Strategic Intelligence, Def. Intelligence Coll., Washington, 1982. Factoring specialist. Commd. USAF, 1968, advaned through grades to maj., ret., 1990; faculty Def. Intelligence Coll., Washington, 1982-86; dir. translations USAF, 1986-88, dir. info. svcs., 1988-90; proprietary security mgr. McDonnell-Douglas Technologies, San Diego, 1990-92; owner Employment Svcs. for Bus., San Diego, 1995-97. Adj. prof. internat. rels. U.S. Internat. U., 1996—, internat. bus. Palomar Coll., 1997—. Author: The Basic Industrial Counter-Espionage Cookbook, 1993, The Government Contractor's OPSEC Cookbook, 1993; co-author: The Military Intelligence Community, 1985; mem. editl. bd. Internat. Jour. Intelligence and Counterintelligence, 1986-98; contbr. articles to profl. jours. Recipient Disting. EEO award USAF, 1987, Def. Meritorious Svc. medal 1986, Meritorious Svc. medal, 1981, 90, Joint Svc. Commendation medal Def. Intelligence Agy./NATO, 1982, 85. Mem. Nat. Mil. Intelligence Assn. (bd. dirs. 1984-99, chpt. pres. 1989, 94), Ops. Security Profls. Soc. (chpt. chair 1993, 94-96), Nat. Cargo Security Coun., San Diego Roundtable (exec. coord. 1994, 95), Assn. Former Intelligence Officers (nat. scholarship adminstr. 1994-2002), Am. Soc. for Indsl. Security, Air Force Assn., San Diego Soc. for Human Resource Mgmt. Republican. Avocations: bridge, golf, reading. Home and Office: 1142 Miramonte Gln Escondido CA 92026-1724 E-mail: norejt@cox.net.

STRONG, JOHN SCOTT, finance educator; b. Phila., Aug. 28, 1956; s. John S. and Thelma J. (Willard) S. BS, Washington & Lee U., 1978; M of Pub. Policy, Harvard U., 1981, PhD in Bus. Econs., 1986. Rsch. fellow Harvard U., Cambridge, Mass., 1983-85, 89-90, 93, vis. asst. prof. econs., 1989-90; prof. fin. Coll. William and Mary, Williamsburg, Va., 1985—. Cons. on econs. and fin. Republic of Indonesia, 1987—, MITI, Japan, 1988-89, European Bank for Reconstruction and Devel., 1993-95, Govt. of Bolivia, 1994, Govt. of Russia, 1996, Govts. of Brazil, Argentina and Uruguay, 1997, Govt. of Peru, 1998, World Bank, 1997—. Author: Why Airplanes Crash: Aviation Safety in a Changing World, 1992, Moving to Market: Restructuring Transport in the Former Soviet Union, 1996; co-author 2 books on airline deregulation; contbr. articles to profl. jours. Fulbright scholar, 1978-79; grad. fellow NSF, 1979-82.

STRONG, JUDITH ANN, chemist, educator; b. June 19, 1941; d. Philip Furnald and Hilda Bernice (Hulbert) S.. BS cum laude, SUNY, Albany, 1963; MA, Brandeis U., 1966, PhD, 1970. Asst. prof. chemistry Moorhead State U., Minn., 1969—73, assoc. prof., 1973—81, prof., 1981—, chmn. chemistry dept., 1984—86, dean social and natural scis., 1986—97, assoc. v.p. acad. affairs, 1997—. Recipient Gov.'s Acts of Kindness Vol. award, 1997; fellow, NSF, 1965—67. Mem.: Minn. Acad. Sci., Assn. Women in Sci., Am. Chem. Soc., Soroptimist Internat. (gov. North Ctrl. region 2002—), Sigma Xi. Home: 1209 12th St S Moorhead MN 56560-3707 Office: Minn State U Moorhead Academic Affairs Moorhead MN 56563-0001

STRONG, KARIN HJORT, artist, educator; b. N.Y.C., Jan. 30, 1956; d. Corrin Peter and Mette Hjort (Matthiesen) S. BA, Boston U., 1981; AA, Pratt U., 1985. Art tutor Hampshire Coll., Amherst, Mass., 1977; co-founder, mgr., tchr. Poland Springs (Maine) Cmty. Program, 1977-79; tchr. Southampton Cultural Ctr., 1989-96; tchg. asst. master workshop on art L.I. Univ., Southampton, N.Y., 1990. Bd. mem. Catharine Lorillard Wolfe Art Club, Inc., N.Y.C., 1989-96; painting judge Pen and Brush Club, Inc., N.Y.C., 1995; art show judge J.L.C. Art Ctr., Inc., Stony Brook, N.Y., 1995. Artist represented by Gallery East, Images Gallery, Lizan Tops Gallery, others. Vol. coord. Appalachian Mountain Club, Boston, 1981; monkey trainer to aid quadriplegics Boston U., 1981; spkr., event M.C. CLWAC, Nat. Arts Club, N.Y.C., 1992-95; spkr., lectr. Jimmy Ernst Artist Alliance, East Hampton, N.Y., 1993, Southampton Artists, 1994. Mem. Soc. Animal Artists, Southampton Artists (bd. mem., exhbn. chair, publicity com. 1988-90), Catharine Lorillard Wolfe Art Club, Inc. (pres. 1992-95). Avocations: music, playing guitar, flute and dulcimer, sports, writing.

STRONG, MARCELLA LEE, music specialist, educator; b. East Liverpool, Ohio, Oct. 16, 1954; d. Carl and Ruth I. (White) Hinkle; m. David Lee Strong, Feb 19, 1977. BA magna cum laude, U. Toledo, 1976; MA in Early Childhood Edn., Kent State U., 1982. Cert. music, elem. tchr., Ohio. Music instr. Cardinal Local Schs., Parkman and Huntsburg, Ohio, 1977—. Choir dir. G.V. Nazarene Ch., Orwell, Ohio 1981-83; organist, mem. bd. deacons and stewardship com., sr. choir, jr. choir and ch. band dir. Huntsburg Congl. Ch., 1985—; mem., officer Orwell Farm Bur.; band dir. Kent State U. Coll. for Kids, 1995—. Mem. Cardinal Edn. Assn. (negotiator 1982, 84, 87, 90, 93, 96, 99, 2002, sec. 1983-84, treas. 1984-85, pres. 1985-86, 89-91, 1997-2002), Ohio Music Educators Assn., Kappa Delta Pi, Mu Phi Epsilon, Delta Kappa Gamma. Democrat. Avocations: spectator sports, traveling, reading, chess, member international trivia team. Home: 78 Chaffee Dr Orwell OH 44076-9526 E-mail: dlsmls@yahoo.com.

STRONG, MAYDA NEL, psychologist, educator; b. Albuquerque, May 6, 1942; d. Floyd Samuel and Wanda Christmas (Martin) Strong; 1 child, Robert Allen Willingham. BA in Speech-Theatre cum laude, Tex. Western Coll., 1963; EdM, U. Tex., Austin, 1972, PhD in Counseling Psychology, 1978. Diplomate Am. Bd. Disability Analysts, Am. Bd. Psycol. Specialties, Am. Bd. Forensic Examiners; lic. clin. psychologist, Colo., Kans.; nat. master addiction counselor. Asst. instr. in edn1. psychology U. Tex., Austin, 1974-78; instr. psychology Austin C.C., 1974—78, Otero Jr. Coll., La Junta, Colo., 1979-89; dir. outpatient and emergency svcs. S.E. Colo. Family Guidance and Mental Health Ctr., Inc., La Junta, 1978—81; pvt. practice psychol. therapy La Junta, 1981—2002; supervising psychologist state security program Larned (Kans.) State Hosp., 2002—. Exec. dir. Pathfinders Chem. Dependency program, 1985—94, clin. cons., 1994—2000, adv. bd., 1995—99; clin. psychologist Inst. Forensic Psychiatry, Colo. Mental Health Inst., Pueblo, 1989—94; adj. faculty Adams State Coll., 1992; dir. Revisions Behavior Mgmt. Program, 1996—2002. Dir.: Picketwine Ctr. for Performing Arts, 1980—99, Otero Jr. Coll. Bd. dirs. Picketwire Players, 1995—98; dir. Brighton Beach Memoirs. AAUW fellow, 1974-76. Mem. Kans. Psychol. Assn., Colo. Psychol. Assn. (legis. chmn. for dist. 1978-2002), Am. Contract Bridge League. Home: 1216 W 7th St Larned KS 67550 Office: Larned State Hosp State Security Program RR 3 Larned KS 67550

STRONG, ROBERT THOMAS, former mayor, middle school educator; b. N.Y.C., June 16, 1936; s. Joseph A. and Pauline R. (Manger) S.; m. Evelyn Ann Repasky, Aug. 23, 1958; children: Robyn, Robert Jr. BS, SUNY, Oswego, 1958; MLS, SUNY, Stony Brook, 1976. Social studies tchr. South Country Sch. Dist., Bellport, N.Y., 1958-66, asst. prin. middle sch., 1966-72, tchr., chmn. social studies dept., 1972-91. Student coun. adviser Bellport Middle Sch., 1968-91; prin. Infant Jesus Religious Sch., Port Jefferson, 1966-68. Trustee Village of Port Jefferson, 1991-95, code commr., 1991-99, dep. mayor, 1993-95, mayor, 1995-99; mem., chmn. Zoning Bd. Appeals, Port Jefferson, 1978-91; liaison to pub. safety adv. bd. Village of Port Jefferson, 1991-95; charter mem. Friends of St. Charles Hospice; grad. Suffolk County Citizens Police Acad.; 2d v.p. Suffolk County Village Ofcls., 1998-99; mem. Port Jefferson Harbor Complex Harbor Mgmt. Group; founder, pres. Suffolk County Citizens Police Alumni Assn.; chmn. Village of Port Jefferson Harbor Front Com.; bd. dirs. Port Jefferson Civic Assn. Mem. N.Y. State Tchrs. Assn., Bellport Tchrs. Assn. (treas. 1974-76, bldg. rep. 1989-91), L.I. Coun. for Social Studies, South Country Ret. Educators Assn. (founder, v.p. 1996—), Moose, Kiwanis, S.C.C. Pa. Alumni Assn. (pres.). Roman Catholic. Avocations: skiing, travel, ice skating. Home: 8 Shady Tree Ln Port Jefferson NY 11777

STRONG, ROGER LEE, retired mathematics educator; b. Sturgis, Mich., May 22, 1936; s. Ronald George and Mildred (Hamacher) S.; m. Shirley Anne Knight, Apr. 20, 1958 (div. Apr. 1984); children: Rachelle, Kevin, Todd, David; m. Beverly Ann Stoops, July, 1984. BA, Eastern Mich. U., 1961; MA, U. Mich., 1964, PhD, 1975. Cert. secondary tchr., Mich. Tchr. high sch. math. Livonia (Mich.) Pub. Schs., 1961-88; assoc. prof. math. Francis Marion U., Florence, S.C., 1988—; ret. Adj. asst. prof. math. U. Mich., Dearborn, 1984-88; cons. Sumter (S.C.) Pub. Schs., 1990, Darlington (S.C.) Pub. Schs., 1992, Mullins (S.C.) Pub. Schs., 1997. Author: Numerical Trigonometry, 1969. With USMC, 1956-58. Named Golf Coach of Yr., Mich., 1985, Florence Educator of Yr., Optimist Club, 1993; NSF fellow, 1968-69. Mem. Math. Assn. Am., Nat. Coun. Tchrs. Math., S.C. Coun. Tchrs. Math., Country Club S.C. Episcopalian. Avocations: golf, gardening, bird watching. Office: Francis Marion U Dept Math Florence SC 29501 Home: 7540 W Fairview Ct Crystal River FL 34429-7900

STRONG, VIRGINIA WILKERSON, freelance writer, former educator; b. Vernal, Utah, Mar. 19, 1935; d. Arbun C. and Mildred (Wyman) Wilkerson; m. David Smith, Oct. 6, 1950 (div. Jan. 1960); children: Anna Smith Blyton, Dorothy Smith Wolf, Wendell Lee Smith, Ava Smith Eatman, Karen Smith Ritter; m. Lawrence D. Strong, June 1961 (div. May 1973); children: Lawrence D. Jr., Jeffrey A. BA, U. Miss., 1970, MEd, 1972; PhD, Ohio U., 1985. Cert. elem. edn. tchr., spl. edn. K-12 tchr., ednl. adminstrn. Rsch. asst. U. Miss., University, 1968-70, Utah State U., Logan, 1974-78; tchr. spl. edn. various schs., nr. Oxford, Miss., 1969-74; instr. spl. edn., project coord., rsch. asst. Ohio U., Athens, 1978-82; supr. spl. edn. Meigs County Bd. Edn., Pomeroy, Ohio, 1982-84; tchr. spl. edn., dept. chmn. L.A. Unified Sch. Dist., 1986-93, co-faciliator alcohol drug abuse, 1990-93; freelance writer, owner, mgr. Fenix Devel., Long Beach, Calif., 1990—. Early childhood adv. Utah Bd. Edn., Salt Lake City, 1976, evaluator edn. programs, Salt Lake City and Logan, 1976-77; acting dir. edn., cons. North Miss. Retardation Ctr., Oxford, 1993-94; curriculum developer Meigs County, 1982-84; dir. gifted edn. workshop Ohio U., 1980. Author: The Role of the Special Education Supervisor, 1985, (screenplays) To See the Elephant, Dark Encounters; contbr. articles to newspapers. Elector Dem. Party, Logan, 1976; religious instr. LDS Ch., various locations, 1953-97. U.S. Dept. Edn. grantee Utah State U., 1976. Mem. ASCD, Kappa Delta Pi, Phi Delta Kappa. Avocations: genealogy, gemology, photography, history buff, travel.

STROOCK, DANIEL WYLER, mathematician, educator; b. N.Y.C., Mar. 20, 1940; s. Alan Maxwell and Katherine (Wyler) S.; m. Lucy Barber, Nov. 21, 1962; children: Benjamin, Abraham. AB, Harvard Coll., 1962; PhD, Rockefeller U., 1966. Vis. mem. Courant Inst., N.Y. U., 1966-69, asst. prof., 1969-72; asso. prof. math. U. Colo., Boulder, 1972-75, prof., 1975-84, chmn. dept. math, 1979-81; prof. math. MIT, 1984—. Adj. prof. U. Colo., Beijing Normal U. Author: (with S.R.S. Vanadhan) Multidimensional Diffusion Processes, 1979, (with J.D. Deutschel) Large Deviations, 1989, Probability Theory, An Analytic View, 1993; editor Math. Zeitschrift, 1992-2000, Ill. Jour. Math., 1976-82, Transactions of Am. Math. Soc., 1974-80, Annals of Probability, 1988-93, Advances in Math., 1995—, Jour. Functional Analysis, 1994—; contbr. articles on probability theory to profl. jours. Guggenheim fellow, 1978-79 Mem. Am. Acad. Arts and Scis., Nat. Acad. Scis. Democrat. Jewish. Home: 55 Frost St Cambridge MA 02140-2247 Office: MIT Dept Math Cambridge MA 02139 E-mail: dws@math.mit.edu.

STROUD, NANCY IREDELL, retired secondary school educator, freelance writer, editor; b. Raleigh, N.C., Apr. 10, 1943; d. John Johnson and Neffie (Mitchiner) Iredell. BA in English, Morgan State U., Balt., 1964; MEd in Adult and C.C. Edn., N.C. State U., 1976; postgrad., The Am. U., 1985. Tchr. history and English Pleasant grove Sch., Sampson County, N.C., 1964-65; social rsch. asst. N.C. State U., 1970; tchr. English Garner Consol. Sch., Wake County, N.C., 1965-67, Calumet H.S., Chgo., 1967-69, LeRoy Martin Jr. H.S., Raleigh, 1971-79, Needham B. Broughton H.S., Raleigh, 1979-84, The Chelsea Sch., Silver Spring, Md., 1984-85, Gaithersburg H.S., Montgomery County, Md., 1985-98; exec. editor Cypher mag., 1998-99. Former mem. adminstrv. bd. Trinity United Meth. Ch., mem. coun. on ministries, past chmn. ch. growth, former head liturgist worship com.; mem. United Meth. Women, Libr. Congress, Smithsonian Instn., Nat. Mus. women in the Arts, U.S. Holocaust Meml. Mus., Dem. Nat. Com., The Kennedy Ctr. Recognized as Outstanding Vol., Trinity United Meth. Ch., Germantown, Md., 1986-87. Mem. AAUW, ASCD, NEA, Md. Coun. of Tchrs. of English Lang. Arts, Md. State Tchrs. Assn., Montgomery County Debate League, Montgomery County Edn. Assn., Nat. Coun. Tchrs. English, Nat. Fedn. Interscholastic Speech and Debate Assn., Nat. Ret. Tchrs. Assn., Morgan State U. Alumni Assn., N.C. State U. Alumni Assn., Tchrs. of English in Montgomery County. Avocations: genealogy, classical and jazz music, reading, writing. Home: Unit 2 20317 Beaconfield Ter Germantown MD 20874-3907

STROUD, RHODA M. elementary education educator; Tchr. Webster Magnet Elem. Sch., St. Paul. Apptd. mem. Minn. Bd. Edn. for State of Minn. Recipient State Tchr. of Yr. Elem. award Minn., 1992. Office: Webster Magnet Elem Sch 707 Holly Ave Saint Paul MN 55104-7126

STROUP, SALLY, federal agency administrator; b. Harrisburg, Pa. Grad., Ind. U. Pa., Loyola U. From staff atty. to sr. v.p. legal svcs. and chief counsel Pa. Higher Edn. Agy.; mem. profl. staff com. on edn. and the workforce U.S. Ho. of Reps.; 1993—2001; dir. industry and govt. affairs Apollo Group Inc./U. Phoenix; asst. sec. postsecondary edn. Dept. Edn., Washington, 2001—. Office: Dept Edn Office Postsecondary Edn 1990 K St NW Washington DC 20006*

STROVINK, MARK WILLIAM, physics educator; b. Santa Monica, Calif., July 22, 1944; s. William George and Barbara (Marsh) S.; m. Joyce Catharine Hodgson, Dec. 22, 1965 (div. June 1988); children: Kurt Gregory, Karl William; m. Linda Margaret Cooper, July 5, 1991. BS, MIT, 1965; PhD, Princeton U., 1970. Instr. Princeton (N.J.) U., 1970-71, asst. prof., 1970-73, U. Calif., Berkeley, 1973-76, assoc. prof., 1976-81, prof., 1981—. Vis. asst. prof. Cornell U., Ithaca, N.Y., 1971-72; chmn. physics adv. com. Stanford Linear Accelerator Ctr., Stanford, Calif., 1985-86, Fermilab, Batavia, Ill., 1988-90; mem. high energy physics adv. panel U.S. Dept. Energy, Washington, 1988-92. Contbr. articles to profl. jours. Fellow Am. Phys. Soc. Office: Univ Calif 366 Le Conte Hall Berkeley CA 94720-7303

STROZESKI, MICHAEL WAYNE, director research; b. McKinney, Tex., Aug. 19, 1944; s. Edwin Guy and Margaret K. (Orr) Parchman; m. Sandra Samples, June 9, 1967. BS, U. North Tex., 1966, MEd, 1970, PhD, 1980. Cert. tchr. sci. secondary, prin., supt. Tchr. sci. Grapevine (Tex.) Ind. Sch. Dist., 1966-70; tchr. physics and biology Ft. Worth Country Day Sch., 1970-78; tchg. fellow U. North Tex., Denton, 1978-79; evaluator, exec. dir. planning, research and evaluation Garland (Tex.) Ind. Sch. Dist., 1979—. Adv. mem. grad. program U. North Tex., Denton, 1985—99; dir., CEO Strozeski Enterprises Consulting, Garland, 1985—. LEA rep. Nat. Ctr. for Ednl. Stats., Washington, 1998—; bd. dirs. Garland YMCA; pres. Tex. Statewide Network of Assessment Profls., 2001—. Mem.: Nat. Assn. Test Dirs. (pres. 1988), Nat. Coun. on Measurement in Edn., Am. Assn. Sch. Adminstrs., Am. Edn. Rsch. Assn., Am. evaluation Assn. (charter), Garland Rotary Club (pres. 1993-94, Paul Harris fellow 1994). Avocation: Avocations: camping, climbing, snowmobiling, reading, computers. Home: PO Box 462306 Garland TX 75046-2306 Office: Garland Ind Sch Dist 870 W Buckingham Rd Garland TX 75040-4616

STRUBLE, SANDRA MARIE, reading specialist; b. Paterson, N.J., Oct. 21, 1950; d. Salvatore A. and John H. (Daddow) Adornetto; m. Keith H. Struble, Feb. 17, 1973; 1 child, Samantha. BA, William Paterson Coll., 1972, MA magna cum laude, 1978. Cert. elem. and spl. edn. tchr., N.J. Tchr. grade 4 Butler (N.J.) Pub. Schs., 1972-78, tchr. spl. edn. grades 5th thru 8th, 1979-92, reading specialist, 1992—. Advisor Peg Valley Mental Health Ctr., Pompton Plains, N.J., 1974-78, Drug Abuse Prevention Com., Riverdale, N.J., 1975-78. Butler PTA grantee, 1990-92; recipient Gov.'s Tchr. Recognition Program award, 1992-93. Mem. Assn. for Learning Disabilities, Nat. Coun. Tchrs. English, Internat. Reading Assn. Republican. Methodist. Avocations: ballet, reading. Home: 20 Munson Dr Pompton Plains NJ 07444-1507 Office: Richard Butler Sch 37 Pearl Pl Butler NJ 07405-1442

STRUCHTEMEYER, CAROL SUE, middle school educator; b. Kansas City, Mo., Apr. 21, 1954; d. Olin Carl and Anna Christine (Skou) Brookshier; m. Leland Leonard Struchtemeyer, May 26, 1973; children: Rhonda Sue, Thomas Leland. BS in Edn., Ctrl. Mo. State U., 1975, MS in Edn., 1981; ednl. resource tchr. tng., U. Mo., 1977. Cert. elem. tchr., spl. edn. tchr., Md.; cert. mid. sch. math. tchr., Md. Tchr. elem. Mayview (Mo.) R-7 Sch. Dist., 1975-76; tchr. learning disabilities Odessa (Mo.) R-5 Sch. Dist., 1976-78; tchr. 5th grade Lexington (Mo.) R-5 Sch. Dist., 1978-96, tchr. 7th and 8th grade math, 1997—. Sec. Leslie Bell Intervention Team, Lexington, 1992-94. Mem. Trinity United Ch. of Christ, Lexington, 1990—, Lexington Athletic Boosters, 1992—, Lexington Fine Arts Club, 1992—. Mem. NEA, Nat. Coun. Tchrs. Math., Mo. Edn. Assn., Mo. Coun. Tchrs. Math., Lexington Cmty. Tchrs. Assn. (sec. 1983-84, treas. 1985-86). Avocations: reading, sewing, gardening, walking. Home: PO Box 58 Lexington MO 64067-0058

STRUNK, BETSY ANN WHITENIGHT, education educator; b. Bloomsburg, Pa., May 28, 1942; d. Mathias Clarence and Marianna (Naunas) Whitenight; children: Robert J. Jr., Geoffrey M. BS in Edn., Bloomsburg U., 1964; MEd, West Chester U., 1969; cert. mentally/physically handicapped, Pa. State U., 1981; postgrad., Wilkes U., St. Joseph's U., Drexel U., Western Md. Coll. Cert. elem. edn., spl. edn., single engine pvt. pilot. Tchr. Faust Sch., Bensalem (Pa.) Twp., 1964, Eddystone (Pa.) Elem. Sch., 1964-66, Lima Elem. Sch., Rose Tree Media Sch. Dist., 1966-69, Rose Tree Media (Pa.) Sch. Dist., 1977—; adj. prof. Wilkes Coll., Wilkes-Barre, Pa., 1981-86; instr. Delaware C.C., Media, 1986; instr., dir. ground sch. edn. Brandywine Airport, West Chester, Pa., 1986-88; instr. Drexel U., Phila., 1989—2001, Performance Learning Systems, Inc., Emerson, N.J. and Nevada City, Calif., 1981—2001; rep. FAA, Phila., 1986-88. Spl. edn. resource rm. specialist, tchr. cons. Media Elem. Sch.; spl. edn. supervisory selection com. Rose Tree Media Sch. Dist., spl. edn. resource rm. specialist, tchr. cons.; curriculum designer pvt. pilot ground sch.; instr. and course designer introduction to flying and pilot companion course; chairperson profl. devel. com. Rose Tree Media Sch. Dist., 1992; mem. Insvc. Coun. Delaware County, 1992—2002; mem. educator's adv. com. Phila. Franklin Inst., 1990—92, 1995—; cons. ednl. programs, 1988—; owner, designer Betsy's Belts, Del., N.J., Pa., 1970—74; mem. gov. bd. Southeastern Tchr. Leadership Ctr. West Chester U., Pa.; learning support specialist Glenwood Elem. Sch., Media, Pa., 1994—; educator liaison between sr. citizens and learning support students Lima Estates Retirement Home and Glenwood Elem. Sch., 1994—; tchr. academically gifted program Indian Ln. and Glenwood Elem. Schs., 1998—99; presenter State Pa. Lead Tchr. Conf., 1994, Ind. Sch. Tchrs. Assn., 1995; project dir. video documentary Performance Learning Sys., Calif., 1994; ptnr., owner Whitenight Homestead Partnership, Bloomsburg, Pa. Program dir. video documentaries including : Learning Through Live Events and Teaching Skills for the 21st Century, 1995; editor (chairperson): Deerfield Knoll Quar. Newsletter, 1999—2003; contbr. articles to profl. jours. Mem. Middletown Free Libr. Bd., 1977—79; officer Riddlewood Aux. to Riddle Meml. Hosp., Media, 1973—76; chairperson Lima Christian Nursery Sch., Pa., 1973, March of Dimes, Middletown, 1973; creator Parents of Students with Learning Disabilities Orgn., 1979—82; pres. Roosevelt PTG (Elem. Sch.), Media, 1982; capt. March of Dimes, Media, 1987—91, Diabetes Assn., Media, 1989—91; vol. Tyler Arboretum, Middletown Twp., 1980—82; mem. cmty. rels. com. Deerfield Knoll Homeowner's Assn., 1998—, v.p., bd. dirs., 1999—2002; mem. Wilmington Opera House, Dupont Theatre; founder cmty. orgn. Antique Study Group; chairperson Investment Group, Restaurant Dining Group, 1999—; com. person, v.p. Middletown Twp. Dem. Com., 1974; mem.Vietnamese refugees com. Media Presbyn. Ch., 1975; assoc. mem. Skidaway Presbyn. Ch., Savannah, Ga. Recipient 1st pl. color divsn. Photography award, Pa. Colonial Plantation, 1st pl. color divsn. in Photography, Bloomsburg State Fair, 1994; grantee Fine Arts in Spl. Edn., Pa. Dept. Edn., 1993—94. Mem.: NEA, Media Soc. Performing Arts, Aircraft Owners and Pilots Assn., Nat. Staff Devel. Coun., Pa. State Edn. Assn., Rose Tree Media Edn. Assn. (profl. devel. com. chairperson 1992—93, profl. devel. com. rep. 1990—93, Exceptional Svc. award), Longwood Gardens, Chester County Hist. Soc., Phila. Zoo, Tyler Arboretum, Alpha Delta Kappa. Democrat. Avocations: reading, writing, interior decorating, nature walking, gardening. Home: Willistown Twp 203 Cohasset Ln West Chester PA 19380-6507 Office: Rose Tree Media Sch Dist Glenwood Elem Sch Pennell Rd Media PA 19063 Home (Summer): The Landings on Skidaway Island 7 Franklin Creek Rd South Savannah GA 31411

STRYKER, DANIEL RAY, adult education educator; b. Ruslip, Eng., July 15, 1957; came to U.S., 1959; s. Theodore Ray and Nina Margaret (Bryant) S. BS, Sam Houston State, 1980; MEd, U. Houston, 1988; EdD, Sam Houston State, 1996, MA in History, 2002. Pulmonary functions technician St. Joseph Hosp., Houston, 1981; rschr. U. Tex. Med. Br., Houston, 1981-82; taxpayer svc. rep. IRS, Houston, 1982-85; substitute tchr. Conroe (Tex.) Schs., 1986-88, 91-95; tchr. Aldine Schs., Houston, 1988-90; instr. U. Houston, 1995-96, Western Carolina U., Cullowhee, 1997-98; instr. dept. history and geography Houston C.C., 1998—; instr. dept. history N. Harris Coll., Houston, 1998—. Author: A Cognitive Approach to Teaching History, 1994, Twilight in the City, 1996, Nowhere in the Shadow, 1996, Mirror of Dreams, 1996. Precinct judge Klein Schs., Houston, 1992-96. Athletic scholar, Sam Houston State, Huntsville, 1976. Avocations: reading, writing, camping, mountain climbing. Home: 4135 Swinden Dr Houston TX

77066-3511 Office: Houston CC Dept History and Geography 1550 Foxlake Dr Dept And Houston TX 77084-6029 also: N Harris Coll Dept History 2700 W W Thorne Blvd Houston TX 77073-3410

STRYKER, SHELDON, sociologist, educator; b. St. Paul, May 26, 1924; s. Max and Rose (Moskevitz) S.; m. Alyce Shirley Agranoff, Sept. 7, 1947; children: Robin Sue, Jeffrey, David, Michael, Mark. BA summa cum laude, U. Minn., 1948, MA, 1950, PhD, 1955. Mem. faculty Ind. U., 1951—, prof. sociology, 1964—, disting. prof. sociology, 1985—2002, disting. prof. emeritus, 2002—; dir. Inst. Social Research, 1965-70, 89-94, chmn. dept. sociology, 1969-75; co-dir. Ctr. for Social Rsch., 1989-94. Cons. in field; mem. social scis. research rev. com. NIMH, 1974-79, chmn., 1976-79, mem. research scientist devel. award com., 1981-85 Editor: Sociometry, 1966-69, Rose Monograph Series of Am. Sociol. Assn., 1971-73, Am. Sociol. Rev., 1982-85; assoc. editor: Social Problems, 1957-59; author books, monographs, articles, chpts. in books. Served with AUS, 1943-46. Fellow Social Sci. Research Council, 1959-60, Ctr. Advanced Behavioral Scis., 1986-87; Fulbright research scholar Italy, 1966-67. Mem. Am. Sociol. Assn. (nat. coun. 1965-67, 80-81, chmn. social psychology sect. 1978-79, chmn. publs. com. 1991-93, Cooley-Mead award), Soc. for the Study of Symbolic Interaction (George Herbert Mead award for lifetime scholarship 2000), Ohio Valley Sociol. Soc. (coun. 1965-67), North Ctrl. Sociol. Assn. (pres. 1978-79), Sociol. Rsch. Assn. (coun. 1978-84, pres. 1983-84), Phi Beta Kappa. Home: 3710 Saint Remy Dr Bloomington IN 47401-2418

STUART, ANDREW MICHAEL, education educator; b. Fredericton, Can., Aug. 14, 1957; s. Roy Graham and Jean Mary S.; m. Naomi Joy Shaw, Oct. 25, 1997; 1 child, Joshua Graham. BS, Dalhousie U., Halifax, Can., 1978, MS, 1986, PhD, 1996. Audiologist Children's Hosp. Ea. Ont., Ottawa, Can., 1986-89; rsch. asst. Dalhousie U., Halifax, Can., 1989-92; assoc. prof. East Carolina U., Greenville, N.C., 1996—. Audiology cons. Soc. Care of Handicapped in Gaza Strip, 1994-95. Contbr. articles to profl. jours.; assoc. editor Jour. Speech-Lang.-Pathology and Audiology, 1996-2000; patentee in field. Recipient D.O. Hebb Postgrad. prize, Dalhousie U., 1992; postdoctoral fellow Dalhousie U., 1996; Izaak Walton Killam Meml. Hon. scholar, Dalhousie U., 1992-96. Mem. Am. Speech-Lang.-Hearing Assn., Am. Auditory Soc., Can. Speech-Lang Pathologists and Audiologists. Office: East Carolina U Dept Comm Scis & Disorders Greenville NC 27834

STUART, DABNEY, poet, author, English language educator; b. Richmond, Va., Nov. 4, 1937; s. Walker Dabney Jr. and Martha (vonSchilling) S.; m. Sandra Westcott, Jan. 20, 1983; children: Martha, Nathan vonSchilling, Darren Wynne AB, Davidson Coll., 1960; AM, Harvard U., 1962. Instr. Coll. William and Mary, Williamsburg, Va., 1961-65; prof. English Washington and Lee U., Lexington, Va., 1965—2002, S. Blount Mason Jr. prof. English, 1991—2002. Vis. prof. Middlebury (Vt.) Coll., 1968-69, Ohio U., Athens, 1975, U. Va., Charlottesville, 1981-83. Author: The Diving Bell, 1966, A Particular Place, 1969, The Other Hand, 1974, Friends of Yours, Friends of Mine, 1974, Round and Round, 1976, Nabokov: The Dimensions of Parody, 1978, Rockbridge Poems, 1981, Common Ground, 1982, Don't Look Back, 1987, Narcissus Dreaming, 1990, Sweet Lucy Wine, 1992, Light Years: New and Selected Poems, 1994, Second Sight: Poems for Paintings by Carroll Cloar, 1996, Long Gone, 1996, The Way to Cobbs Creek, 1997, Settlers, 1999, Strains of the Old Man, 1999, No Visible Means of Support, 2001, The Man Who Loves Cezanne, 2003. Recipient Dylan Thomas prize Poetry Soc. Am., 1965, Gov.'s award State of Va., 1979; NEA lit. fellow, 1975, 82, Guggenheim fellow, 1987-88, Individual Artist fellow Va. Commn. for Arts, 1995, resident fellow Rockefeller Study and Conf. Ctr., Bellagio, Italy, 2000. Avocations: food, travel, painting. Home: 30 Edmondson Ave Lexington VA 24450-1904

STUART, EVE LYNNE, elementary education educator; b. Atlantic City, N.J., Nov. 25, 1942; d. Berned Edward and Amelia Louise (Lieteau) Creswell; m. Henry E. Stuart, June 21, 1963 (div. Mar. 1978); children: Lisa Marie, Nanette Cecilia. Student, Cen. State U., Wilberforce, Ohio, 1960-63; BS, Glassboro State U., 1968. Cert. elem. tchr., N.J. Tchr. Head Start, Atlantic City, 1965-66, Atlantic City Pub. Schs., 1967—. Tchr.-cons. N.J. Geog. Alliance, Montclair, N.J., 1990—; mentor tchr. project invest, multicultural tchr., trainer, 1992—; mem. leadership com. N.J. Geographic Alliance, 1992—. Founder, coord. Project Campsite/Summer Breeze, Atlantic City, 1989-90; mem. com. United Negro Coll. Fund, Atlantic City, 1988-89. Recipient Outstanding cert. Nat. Geog. Soc., 1990, Cape May (N.J.) Schs., 1991; Atlantic City Bd. Edn. grantee, 1989-90. Fellow Delta Sigma Theta; mem. NEA, NCCJ, N.J. Coun. for Social Studies (bd. dirs. 1991—), Atlantic City Edn. Assn. (officer 1984-88, award 1985, 86), A.C.C.E.A., A.C.E.A., Phi Delta Kappa (officer 1988-89). Democrat. Roman Catholic. Office: Atlantic City Pub Schs Indiana Ave Sch 117 N Indiana Ave Atlantic City NJ 08401-4209

STUBBS, BARBARA JOAN, secondary education educator; b. Salem, N.J., Apr. 19, 1945; d. Joseph and Mary Eleanor (Conrad) Prochazka; m. William E. Thorp, Sept. 22, 1972 (div. 1981); 1 child, Joanna Denise; m. John L. Stubbs, Feb. 11, 1982; 1 child, Jill L. Washington. BA, Rutgers U., 1967; MA, Rowan Coll., 1995; EdD, U. Sarasota, 1998. With sales dept. Pan Am. World Airways, San Francisco, 1968-70, Phila., 1970-75; owner Eastern Seaboard Stone, Marlton, N.J., 1976-85, Delsea Marble & Granite, Clayton, N.J., 1981-90; tchr. Clearview Regional Sch. Dist., Mullica Hill, N.J., 1990—. Learning cons., N.J. Bd. dirs., treas. Nazarene Ch., Vineland, N.J., 1984-90. Mem. Coun. for Exceptional Children, ASCD. Home: 624 Monroeville Rd Monroeville NJ 08343-2513

STUBBS, DONALD CLARK, retired secondary school educator; b. Providence, Mar. 6, 1935; s. Edward J. and Margaret Eleanor (Clark) S.; m. Lorraine Alice Thivierge, Apr. 3, 1969 (dec. Jan. 1986); 1 child, Derek C.; m. Sarah E. Andrews, Apr. 23, 1999. AB, Cath. U. Am., Washington, 1959, MS, 1966; postgrad., St. John's U., N.Y.C., 1960. Tchr. Bishop Loughlin Meml. High Sch., Bklyn., 1959-61, Bishop Bradley High Sch., Manchester, N.H., 1961-66; tchr., sci. dept. chair LaSalle Mil. Acad., Oakdale, N.Y., 1966-69, Ponaganset Regional High Sch., Glocester, R.I., 1969-2000; ret., 2000. Home: 35 Shove St Woonsocket RI 02895-5741 E-mail: naddad@aol.com.

STUBBS, MARILYN KAY, education administrator; b. Great Bend, Kans., Mar. 21, 1950; d. John Calvin and Rosanna (Edler) Rapp; children: Adam Richard, Anna Elizabeth. BA in English, Kans. State U., 1972. Asst. instr. Kans. State U., Manhattan, 1972; educator All Saints Sch., Kansas City, Kans., 1973-74, Archdiocese of Kansas City, Mo., 1975-78; adminstrv. asst. Sherwood Ctr. for the Exceptional Child, Kansas City, Mo., 1979-89, assoc. dir., 1989—. Cons., trainer NW Mo. Autism Consortium, 1993—98; NW Mo. dist. team leader Positive Behavior Support, Kansas City, 1996—99, Team Tng. Project, Kansas City, 1995—96; trainer Jackson County Bd. Svcs., Kansas City, 1995—. Author (newsletter): Sherwood Chronicle, 1980—86; editor, 1986—2001; contbg. editor, 2001—; editor: Families Addressing Auditory Integration Tng., 1993—95, Bridges, 1997—98. Mem Employment Task Force, 1995—98; spkrs. bur. United Way, Kansas City, 1982—; mem. Assn. United Way Execs., 1989—; adv. com. mem. Nat. Coun. Devel. Disabilities, 1990—94. Named Parent of Yr., Sherwood Parents Assn., 1985. Mem.: TASH (Mo. state bd. dirs.), Am. Assn. on Mental Retardation, Autism Soc. Am. (sec. We. Mo. chpt. 1999, conf. com. mem. 1999, v.p. 2002—), Divers Alert Network, Astron. Soc. Kansas City. Avocations: horseback riding, astronomy, scuba diving, skiing, hunting. Office: Sherwood Center 7938 Chestnut Ave Kansas City MO 64132-3698

STUCK, ROGER DEAN, electrical engineering educator; b. Ventura, Calif., Nov. 6, 1924; s. William Henry and Marian Grace (Ready) S.; m. Opal Christine Phillips, July 25, 1948; children: Dean, Phyllis, Sandra. BSEE, Calif. Inst. Tech., 1947; MSEE, N.C. State U., 1957. Elec. engr. Warren Wilson Coll., Swannanoa, N.C., 1947—, instr. elec. engring. physics, 1948-69, dean students, 1969-72, instr. physics, elec. engr., 1972-86. Author: (charts) The Periodic Table of Physical Concepts, 1977, The Periodic Table of Physical Concepts with Economic Concepts, 1980; (book) The Periodic Table of Physical Concepts Book of Definitions, 1980. Lt. (j.g.) USNR, 1942-46. Mem. Sigma Xi. Republican. Presbyterian. Achievements include identification of gravitational inductance, capacitance and splendor (MVVV) and energy-spread (hc) as a fundamental initial concept of physical creation relating mass and charge which is fundamental to any Grand Unification Theory; the statement of a quantized conservation law for energy-spread to establish an internal and external structure for neutrons, protons, electrons and neutrinos. Home: 65 Green Forest Rd Swannanoa NC 28778-2246

STUCK, WANDA MARIE, special education educator; b. Schoolcraft, Mich. d. Glen Robert and Luella Shearer; m. Paul Stuck; children: Pamela, Lauri, Jeffrey. BS, MA, Western Mich. U. Tchr. spl. edn.; tchr. adult edn. sewing Cunningham Fabrics, Vicksburg, Mich.; tchr. adult edn. computers Edwardsburg (Mich.) Sch., tchr. spl. edn., home econs. Prof. seamstress, Schoolcrest, Mich.; clk. Fields Fabric, Kalamazoo. Bd. dirs. Meth. Ch., Schoolcraft, 1994—; mem. Ladies Libr., Schoolcraft. Mem. AAUW, Coun. Exceptional Children, Learning Disabilities Assn. Mich., Order of Ea. Star. Methodist. Avocations: sewing, reading, quilting.

STUCKEY, HELENJEAN LAUTERBACH, counselor educator; b. Bushnell, Ill., May 17, 1929; d. Edward George and Frances Helen (Simpson) Lauterbach; m. James Dale Stuckey, Sept. 30, 1951; children: Randy Lee, Charles Edward, Beth Ellen. BFA, Ill. Wesleyan U., 1951; MEd, U. Ill., 1969. Cert. art tchr., guidance, psychology instr.; lic. clin. profl. counselor, Ill. Display designer Saks Fifth Ave., Chgo., 1951; interior designer Piper City, Ill., 1953-63; tchr. art Forrest (Ill.)-Strawn-Wing Schs., 1967-68; tchr., counselor Piper City Schs., 1969-74; counselor, tchr. art Ford Cen. Schs., Piper City, 1974-85; psychiat. counselor Community Resource Counseling Ctr., Ford County, Ill., 1985-87; tchr. history, counselor Iroquois West H.S., Gilman, Ill., 1987-88; spl. needs coord. Livingston County Vocat., Pontiac, Ill., 1988-93; ret., 1993; clin. profl. counselor, pvt. practice, 1995—. Substitute tchr., 1993—. Mem. ACA, Ill. Counseling Assn., Ill. Mental Health Counselors Assn., Ill. Ret. Tchrs. (membership chmn.), Delta Kappa Gamma (v.p., sec., program chmn., pres.). Presbyterian. Avocations: skiing, reading, travel, sewing, playing flute. Personal E-mail: hjstuckey@bwsys.net.

STUCKEY, SUSAN JANE, perioperative nurse, consultant; Diploma in nursing, The Polyclinic Med. Ctr., 1971; BBA in Health Care Adminstrn., Pa. State U., 1985; cert., Del. County C.C., Media, Pa., 1988; MBA, Kutztown U., 1996. RN, Pa.; cert. operating rm. nurse; cert. RN first asst. Charge nurse Nightingale Nursing Home, Camp Hill, Pa., 1971-72; clin. educator oper. rm. svcs., staff nurse Harrisburg (Pa.) Hosp., 1972-80; adminstr., nursing coord. Hillcrest Women's Med. Ctr., Harrisburg, 1978-81; office mgr., pvt. scrub nurse Office Dr. Henry Train, Harrisburg, 1979-82; with Kimberly Nurses Med Temps, Cleve., 1982-84; sr. splty. nurse oper. rm. Harrisburg Hosp., 1984-86, splty. supr. surg. svcs. dept., 1986-90; 1st asst. laser/abdominal endoscopy Women's Med. Assocs. P.C., Harrisburg, 1990-96; 1st asst., cons. C.B. Laser Assocs. Inc., Camp Hill, Pa., 1990—96; 1st asst., cons., propr. Peri Operative Care Assocs., Harrisburg, 1996-98; clin. nurse Morton Plant Mease, Dunedin, Fla., 1998-99; clin. nurse, eastern regional clin. mgr. Medtronic Neurol., 1999—. Mem. faculty Pa. Jr. Coll. Med. Arts. Contbr. articles to profl. jours. Mem. Assn. Oper. Rm. Nurses, Am. Assn. Gynecol. Laparoscopists, Am. Soc. for Laser Medicine and Surgery. Office: 301 Lindenwood Dr Ste 217 Malvern PA 19355-1758

STUCKY, NANCY L. special education educator; Tchr. spl. edn. Sandstone Elem., Billings, Mont. Recipient State Tchr. of Yr. Spl. Edn. award Mont., 1992.*

STUDEBAKER, IRVING GLEN, mining engineering consultant; b. Ellensburg, Wash., July 22, 1931; s. Clement Glen and Ruth (Krause) S.; (widowed); children: Ruth, Betty, Raymond, Karl, Donna. BS in Geol. Engring., U. Ariz., 1957, MS in Geology, 1959, PhD in Geol. Engring., 1977. Registered profl. engr., Wash., Nev., Ariz., Colo., Mont. Geophys. engr. Mobil, 1959-61; civil engr. City of Yakima, Wash., 1964-66; instr. Yakima Valley Coll., 1962-67; sr. rsch. geologist Roan Selection Trust, Kalulushi, Zambia, 1967-72; sr. mining engr. Occidental Oil Shale, Grand Junction, Colo., 1974-81; prof. Mont. Coll. Mining Sch., Butte, 1982-96; prof. emeritus, 1996—. Cons. in field. Sgt. U.S. Army, 1951-54, Korea. Mem. N.W. Mining Assn., Geol. Soc. Am., Soc. for Mining and Metall. Engring., Soc. Econ. Geologists, Sigma Xi (pres. Mont. tech. chpt. 1990-91). Avocations: golf, travel. Home and Office: 34222 1st Pl S Apt C Federal Way WA 98003-6537

STUDEBAKER, JOHN MILTON, utilities engineer, consultant, educator; b. Springfield, Ohio, Mar. 31, 1935; s. Frank Milton and Monaruth (Beatty) S.; m. Virginia Ann Van Pelt, Mar. 12, 1960; 1 child, Jacqueline Ann Allcorn. BS in Law, LaSalle U., Chgo., 1969; MS and PhD in Indsl. Engring., Columbia Pacific U., San Rafael, Calif., 1984. Cert. plant engr. Am. Inst. Plant Engrs., profl. cons. Acad. Profl. Cons. & Advisors. Indsl engr. Internat. Harvest Co., 1957-60, supr. indsl. engring., 1960-66, gen. supr. body assembly, 1967-68, mgr. indsl. engring., 1968-70; mgr. manufacturing engring. Lamb Electric Co., 1970—76, Cascade Corp., 1976—78; engring. mgr. Bundy Tubing Corp., Winchester and Cynthia, Ky., 1988—98; chmn. The Studebaker Group, Inc., Alexandria, Va., 1998—; pres. Studebaker Energy Cons., LLC, 1998—. Instr. numerous univs. including Boston U., Clemson U., Cornell U., Harvard U., Duquesne U., U. Ala., U. Ill., U. Wis., Ga. State U., James Madison U., Tex. Tech. U., U. Calif., Calif. State U., Columbia U., Fairleigh Dickinson U., San Francisco State U.; instr. Am. Mgmt. Assn., Rochester Inst. Tech., Ctr. for Profl. Advancement. Author: Slashing Utility Costs Handbook, 1992, Natural Gas Purchasing Handbook, 1994, Electricity Retail Wheeling Handbook, 1995, Electricity Purchasing Handbook, 1996, Utility Negotiation Handbook, 2001, ESCO Handbook, 2001. Mem. NSPE, Am. Inst. Facility Engrs. (cert.), Assn. Energy Engrs. (instr.). Republican. Home and Office: PO Box 708 Winchester KY 40392-0708 E-mail: jstudebaker@studebakerenergy.net.

STUDEBAKER, SALLY JANE, elementary education educator; b. Waukegan, Ill., Sept. 27, 1963; d. Arnold Marcion and Edith Jean (Hire) S.; m. Steve E. Harland, July 27, 1991; 1 child, Gregory James. BA cum laude, Trinity Coll., 1985. Cert. elem. edn. tchr., Ill. Tchr. 3d grade Zion (Ill.) Elem. Sch. Dist., 1985—. Beauty cons. Mary Kay Cosmetics, Dallas, 1989—. Pianist Bonnie Brook Bapt. Ch., 1990—; violinist Zion Chamber Orch. Mem. Zion Edn. Assn. (sec. tchr.'s union 1990—), NEA, Ill. Edn. Assn., Trinity Coll. Alumni Assn. (pres. Deerfield, Ill. chpt. 1987—), Sign Lang. Club (tchr.). Avocations: writing, horseback riding, sports. Office: Shiloh Park Sch 2635 Gabriel Ave Zion IL 60099-2595 Address: Strudbaker %Harland 10235 E Plata Ave Mesa AZ 85212-2396

STUEWE, ISABEL, elementary school educator; BS in English, Concordia U. 5th grade tchr. St. John's Luth. Sch., Orange, Calif. Mem.: Luth. Edn. Assn. (past pres. Luth. elem. tchrs. dept.), Western Assn. Schs. and Colls. (commr.), Nat. Bd. for Profl. Tchg. Stds. (bd. mem. 1992—). Avocations: fishing, camping, reading. Office: St Johns Luth Sch 154 S Shaffer St Orange CA 92866*

STUFFLEBEAM, DANIEL LEROY, education educator; b. Waverly, Iowa, Sept. 19, 1936; s. LeRoy and Melva Stufflebeam; m. Carolyn T. Joseph; children: Kevin D., Tracy Smith, Joseph. BA, State U. Iowa, 1958; MS, Purdue U., 1962, PhD, 1964; postgrad., U. Wis., 1965. Prof., dir. Ohio State U. Evaluation Ctr., Columbus, 1963-73; prof. edn. Western Mich. U. Evaluation Ctr., Kalamazoo, 1973-99, dir., 1973—; Beula McKee prof. edn. Western Mich. U., 1997—2002, disting. univ. prof., 2002—. Author monographs and 15 books; contbr. chpts. to books, articles to profl. jours. Served with U.S. Army, 1960. Recipient Paul Lazersfeld award Evaluation Rsch. Soc., 1985, Jason Millman award Consortium for Rsch. on Ednl. Accountability and Tchr. Evaluation, 1999. Mem.: Am. Evaluation Assn. Baptist. Office: Western Michigan Univ The Evaluation Ctr Kalamazoo MI 49008-5237 Fax: 269-387-5923. E-mail: daniel.stufflebeam@wmich.edu.

STUIVER, MINZE, geological sciences educator; b. Vlagtwedde, Groningen, The Netherlands, Oct. 25, 1929; came to U.S., 1959; m. Annie Hubbelmeyer, July 12, 1956; children: Ingrid, Yolande. D.Sc. in Physics, U. Groningen, 1953, PhD in Biophysics, 1958. Research assoc. Yale U., New Haven, 1959-62, sr. research assoc., dir. Radiocarbon Lab., 1962-69; prof. geol. sci. and zoology U. Wash. Seattle, 1969-82, prof. geol. sci. and quaternary scis., 1982—98, prof. emeritus, 1998—. Editor: Radiocarbon, 1976—88. Named Alexander von Humboldt sr. scientist Fed. Republic Germany, 1983. Office: U Wash Box 351360 Seattle WA 98195-1360

STUKEL, JAMES JOSEPH, academic administrator, mechanical engineering educator; b. Joliet, Ill., Mar. 30, 1937; s. Philip and Julia (Mattivi) S.; m. Mary Joan Helpling, Nov. 27, 1958; children: Catherine, James, David, Paul. BS in Mech. Engring, Purdue U., 1959; MS, U. Ill., Urbana-Champaign, 1963, PhD, 1968. Research engr. W.Va. Pulp and Paper Co., Covington, Va., 1959-61; mem. faculty U. Ill., Urbana-Champaign, 1968—, prof. mech. engring., 1975—, dir. Office Coal Research and Utilization, 1974-76, dir. Office Energy Research, 1976-81, dir. pub. policy program Coll. Engring., 1981-84, assoc. dean Coll. Engring. and dir. Expt. Sta., 1984-85; dean Grad. Coll., vice chancellor for research U. Ill. at Chgo., 1985-86, exec. vice chancellor, vice chancellor academic affairs, 1986-91, interim chancellor, 1990-91, chancellor, 1991-95, pres., 1995—. V.p. Chgo. Tech. Park Corp., 1985-88. pres., 1990-91; exec. sec. midwest Consortium Air Pollution, 1972-73, chmn. bd. dirs., 1973-75; mem. adv. bd. regional studies program Argonne (Ill.) Nat. Lab., 1975-76; adv. com. Energy Resources Commn., 1976; chmn. panel on dispersed electric generating techs. Office Tech. Assessment, U.S. Congress, 1980-81; chmn. rev. adv. bd. tech. rev. dist. heating and combined heat and power systems Internat. Energy Agy, OECD, Paris, 1982-83; cons. in field. Contbr. articles to profl. jours. Pres. parish council Holy Cross Roman Cath. Ch., Urbana, 1967-68. Mem. ASCE (State-of-the-Art of Civil Engring. award 1975), ASME, AAAS, Sigma Xi, Phi Kappa Phi, Pi Tau Sigma. Home: 2650 N Lakeview Ave Apt 1610 Chicago IL 60614-1819 Office: 364 Henry Adm Bldg M/C 346 Urbana IL 61801*

STULL, FRANK WALTER, elementary school educator; b. Easton, Pa., June 4, 1935; s. George Washington and Minnie Elizabeth S.; m. Darlene Joy Hunsicker, Aug. 2, 1958; children: James, Ronald, Wendy. BS, East Stroudsburg State Coll., 1956; MEd, Lehigh U., 1966. Cert. tchr., N.J. Tchr. Korea Heung-Up Bank, Seoul, Korea, 1957-58, Howell Twp. Elem. Sch., Freehold, N.J., 1958-59, Holland Twp. Elem. Sch., Milford, N.J., 1959-91. Bd. dirs., sec., treas., mgr. Hunterdon County Sch. Employees Fed. Credit Union, Phillipsburg, N.J., 1969-87, mem. adv. com., 1995; merit badge counselor Boy Scouts Am., 1970-84, cubmaster, 1971-72; treas., mem. Hist. Preservation Commn. Holland Twp., 1993—; bd. govs. Riegel Ridge Cmty. Ctr., 1997-2000; trustee, scholarship coord. C&E Found., 1997—. Recipient Meritorious Svc. award N.J. Credit Union League, 1988, Tchr. Recognition award State N.J. Gov., 1987, Disting. Achievement award for rsch. and preservation of history of Holland Twp. and surrounding areas; named Outstanding Elem. Tchr. Am., 1972; Experienced Tchr. in Geography fellow Pa. State U., 1967. Mem. NEA, Holland Twp. Edn. Assn., Hunterdon County Edn. Assn., N.J. Edn. Assn., Phi Delta Kappa (chartered mem. Zeta Gamma chpt.). Avocations: photography, travel. Home and Office: 806 Rugby Rd Phillipsburg NJ 08865-2033

STULL, THOMAS JAMES, education educator, coach; b. Dover, Ohio, Dec. 2, 1957; s. James Clyde and Marjorie (Stiffney) S.; children: Casey Marie, Kelly Elizabeth. BS in Mgmt. Sci., Fla. Inst. Tech., Melbourne, 1980; BS in Math. Edn., Eastern Ky. U., 1985; MS in Ednl. Adminstrn., Xavier U., Cinn., 1990. Nat. bd. cert. tchr., cert. math. tchr. AYA. Tchr., basketball coach Holy Trinity Episc. Sch., Melbourne, Fla., 1980-81; asst. baseball coach Eastern Ky. U., Richmond, 1983-85; tchr., coach Ludlow (Ky.) H.S., 1985—. Coach. camp dir. Little League Baseball, Williamsport, Pa., 1978—. Mem. First Presbyn. Ch., Ludlow, Ky., 1987. Named Alumnus of Yr. Lambda Chi Alpha Frat., Melbourne, Fla., 1982, 83. Mem. Nat. Coun. Tchrs. Math., Ky. Edn. Profl. Stds. Bd. Presbyterian. Home: 705 Meadow Wood Dr Apt 8 Crescent Springs KY 41017-4628 Office: Ludlow High School 515 Elm St Ludlow KY 41016-1396 E-mail: tstull@ludlow.k12.ky.us.

STULTZ, NEWELL MAYNARD, retired political science educator; b. Boston, June 13, 1933; s. Irving Washburn and Marjorie May (MacEachern) S.; m. Elizabeth Petronella Olckers, Apr. 6, 1958; children: Elliot Andries, Amy Elizabeth. AB, Dartmouth Coll., 1955; MA, Boston U., 1960, PhD, 1965; MA hon., Brown U., 1968. Fulbright exchange scholar U. Pretoria, South Africa, 1955-56; asst. prof. polit. sci. Northwestern U., Evanston, Ill., 1964-65; asst. prof. to prof. polit. sci. Brown U., Providence, 1965—2003, assoc. grad. dean, 1970-74, assoc. dean of faculty, 1993-98, assoc. provost, 1998-2000; ret., 2003. Vis. fellow Yale U.-South African Research Program, 1977; vis. prof. U. South Africa, Pretoria, 1980; James Gathings lectr. Bucknell U., Lewisburg, Pa., 1980 Author: Afrikaner Politics in South Africa, 1974, Who Goes to Parliament?, 1975, Transkei's Half Loaf, 1979, (bibliography) South Africa, 1989, 2d edit., 1993; co-author: South Africa's Transkei, 1967; co-editor: Governing in Black Africa, 1970, 2d edit., 1986 V.p. World Affairs Council R.I., 1983. Served as lt. (j.g.) USN, 1956-59. Fulbright fellow, 1955-56; NDEA grantee, 1959-62; Ford Found. fellow, 1962-64; Rockefeller Found. fellow, 1976-77 Unitarian Universalist. Home: 371 New Meadow Rd Barrington RI 02806-3729 Office: Brown U Dept Polit Sci PO Box 1844 Providence RI 02912-1844 E-mail: newell_stultz@brown.edu.

STUMP, PAMELA FERRIS, music educator; b. Roanoke, Va., May 1, 1955; d. Leo George and Virginia Belle (Garst) Ferris; m. John Gregg Stump, Sept. 20, 1975; children: John Jr., Matthew Todd, Carrie Michelle. BA in Music, Hollins Coll., 1991, MA, 1996. Cert. music tchr., Va. Pvt. piano tchr., Fincastle, Va., 1976. Organist Wheatland Luth. Ch., Buchanan, Va., 1981—, coun. mem., 1996-97, dir. children's choir, 1993—; pres., part-owner Tinkerview Swim Club Inc., Daleville, Va., 1992—; sec., part-owner Fincastle Motors Inc., 1996—, Fincastle Mulch and Stone, 1996—; instr. in music history Dabney Lancaster C.C., Clifton Forge, Va., 1997—; substitute music tchr. William Clark Middle Sch., Fincastle, 1996. Chmn. Va. Fedn. Music Clubs Festival, Roanoke, 1992-97; bd. dirs. Va. Luth. Homes Aux./Brandon Oaks, Roanoke, 1990-96; chapel and music vol. Brandon Oaks Health Ctr., Roanoke, 1990-96; chmn. ways and means Troutville (Va.) Elem. Sch. PTA, 1994-95. Anne Jett Rogers scholar Roanoke Symphony Assn., 1990, Dorminy Music scholar Hollins Coll.,

1990. Mem. Roanoke Valley Music Tchrs. Assn. (pres. 1987-90), Va. Music Tchrs. Assn. (chmn. high sch. concerto 1990-92), Music Tchrs. Nat. Assn., Thursday Morning Music Club, Order Eastern Star. Avocations: swimming, computers, music. Home: 310 Blue Bird Ln Fincastle VA 24090-3201 Office: Dabney Lancaster CC Clifton Forge VA 24422

STUMP, PATRICIA ANN VERPLOEGH, educator; b. Lovilia, Iowa, Oct. 5, 1930; d. John Henry and Dorcas Benita (White) VerPloegh; m. Bobby H Stump, Oct. 16, 1949; children: Robert Howard, Kirk Duane, Vicki Diane Stump Oswald. AA, Des Moines Area Community Coll, Ankeny, Iowa, 1980; BLS, U. Iowa, 1984; spl. edn. cert., Drake U., 1988. Spl. edn. tchr., jr. high sch. reading tchr. Carlisle (Iowa) Community Sch., 1985-87; spl. edn. tchr. Des Moines Ind. Sch., 1987-88, Pleasantville (Iowa) Community Sch., Pleasantville, Iowa, 1988—95; communications and English tchr. Pleasantville, Iowa, 1989-90; speech coach, 1989—95. Counselor, dir. resource person and worship leader Exceptional Persons Camp, Indianola, Iowa, 1977-95; chmn, Keep Carlisle Beautiful, 2000-2003; elected to Carlisle City Coun., 2001- Mem. NEA, Nat. Coun. Tchrs. English, Des Moines Edn. Assn., Iowa State Edn. Assn., Coun. for Exceptional Children, Learning Disabilities Am. Home: 710 Cole St Carlisle IA 50047-8764

STUMPFF, ROBERT THOMAS, academic administrator; b. Lewistown, Pa., June 25, 1945; s. Harry Clarence and Marjorie Louise (Bossinger) S.; m. Sylvia Simmons, Apr. 22, 1972; children: Robert Dale, Cherie Lynn Stumpff Zimmer. BS, U. Md., 1968; cert., U. Ky., 1978. Asst. dir. athletics U. Md., College Park, 1968-69, asst. dir. Md. student union, 1969-72, assoc. dir. Md. student union, 1973-80, acting dir. Md. student union, 1974-75, bus. mgr. athletics, 1980-81, asst. athletic dir., 1982-88, asst. dir. gen. svcs., facilities mgmt., 1988—. Cons. U.S. Naval Acad. Athletic Assn., Annapolis, Md., 1984; assisting minister St. Paul's Luth. Ch., Fulton, Md., 1996—. Author, editor: Maryland Wrestling, 1964-65, 68-69 (Nation's Best award); asst. editor: Maryland Football Guide, 1965-69, Maryland Basketball, 1964-65, 68-69. Mem. ch. coun. Abiding Savior Lutheran Ch., Columbia, Md., 1986-87; mem. Lutheran campus ministry bd. U. Md., 1995—. Mem. Am. Pub. Works Assn., Solid Waste Assn. N.Am. (cert. mcpl. solid waste mgr., bd. dirs. Mid-Atlantic chpt. 1992-94), Nat. Solid Wastes Mgmt. Assn. Md.-Del. Solid Waste Assn., Md. Recyclers Coalition (bd. dirs. 1997—), Nat. Recycling Coalition, Coll. and U. Recycling Coun., Assn. Phys. Plant Adminstrs., U. Md. Alumni Assn. (life), U. Md. Terrapin Club, U. Md. M Club Found. (life, bd. dirs. 1970—, past pres.), Omicron Delta Kappa (Sigma Chpt. faculty sec.-treas. 1972-76, faculty adviser 1976-91, faculty coord. 1991—). Avocations: reading, sight-seeing. Home: 8206 Bubbling Spring Laurel MD 20723-1079 Office: Univ Md Facilities Mgmt Dept Bldg & Landscape Svcs 1300 Service Building College Park MD 20742-6055 E-mail: rs76@umail.umd.edu.

STUNKARD, ALBERT JAMES, psychiatrist, educator; b. N.Y.C., Feb. 7, 1922; s. Horace Wesley and Frances (Klank) Stunkard. BS, Yale U., 1943; MD, Columbia U., 1945, U. Edinburgh, 1992. Intern in medicine Mass. Gen. Hosp., Boston, 1945—46; resident physician psychiatry Johns Hopkins Hosp., 1948—51, rsch. fellow psychiatry, 1951—52; 1rsch. fellow medicine Columbia U. Svc., Goldwater Meml. Hosp., N.Y.C., 1952—53; Commonwealth rsch. fellow, then asst. prof. medicine Cornell U. Med. Coll., 1953—57; mem. faculty U. Pa., 1957—73, 1976—, prof. psychiatry, 1962—73, 1976—, Kenneth Appel prof. psychiatry, 1968—73, chmn. dept., 1962—73; prof. psychiatry Med. Sch., Stanford U., 1973—76. Contbr. articles on psychol., physiol., sociol., therapeutic and genetic aspects of obesity to profl. jours. Capt. M.C. U.S. Army, 1946—48. Recipient Disting. Svc. award, Am. Psychiat. Assn., 1994, Goldberger award, AMA, 1990, Willendorf award for clin. rsch., Internat. Assn. for Study of Obesity, 1998; fellow, Ctr. for Advanced Study in Behavioral Scis., 1971—72. Mem.: Soc. Behavioral Medicine (past pres.), Assn. Rsch. in Nervous and Mental Diseases (past pres.), Am. Psychosomatic Soc. (past pres.), Acad. Behavioral Medicine Rsch. (past pres.), Am. Assn. of Chmn. of Depts. of Psychiatry (past pres.), Inst. of Medicine of NAS. Achievements include contributions to the behavioral and pharmacological treatment of obesity and to understanding of sociological, physiological, psychological and genetic aspects of the disorder; contributions also to nosology and treatment of the eating disorders. Office: U Pa Sch Medicine Dept Psychiatry 3535 Market St 3rd Flr Philadelphia PA 19104-2641 E-mail: stunkard@mail.med.upenn.edu.

STURDEVANT, WAYNE ALAN, executive management consultant; b. Portland, Oreg., Apr. 3, 1946; s. Hervey Sturdevant and Georgia Bright; m. Helen F. Radbury, Sept. 24, 1976; children: Wayne Jr., Stephen, John, Brian, Daniel. BS in Edn., So. Ill. U., 1980. With USAF, 1964—85, chief on-job-tng. ops., 1982-85; lead engr. McDonnell Douglas Corp., 1985-88; br. mgr. Southeastern Computer Cons., Inc., 1988-2000; pres., COO Apollo Software/eSaba Systems, 2000-01; CEO Sturdevant Assocs., Austin, 2001—. Developed advanced concepts in tech. mgmt., program and media design, and formal quality systems. Contbr. articles to profl. jours. Bishop LDS Ch., 1983-84, 98-2002, stake presidency, 1990-96; exec. bd. Boy Scouts Am., 1986—. Recognized for leadership in multi-nat. programs; recipient Citation of Honor Air Force Assn., 1980, Silver Beaver award Boy Scouts Am., 1998; named Internat. Man of Yr., Internat. Biog. Ctr., 1992. Republican. Avocations: genealogy, camping. Home: 9214 Independence Loop Austin TX 78748-6312 E-mail: sturde1@ev1.net.

STURE, STEIN, civil engineering educator; b. Oslo, Nov. 12, 1947; came to U.S., 1970; s. Alf and Gunnvor (Een) S.; m. Karen J. Marley, June 3, 1989. Student, Schous Inst. Tech., Oslo, 1970; BSCE, U. Colo., 1971, MSCE, 1973, PhD, 1976. Asst. prof. Va. Polytechnic Inst., Blacksburg, 1976-80; rsch. scientist Marshall Space Flight Ctr. NASA, Huntsville, Ala., 1979; from asst. prof. to prof. civil engring. U. Colo., Boulder, 1980—, acting chmn. dept. civil engring., 1990-91, chmn. dept. civil engring., 1994—98, assoc. dean, 2002—. Sr. vis. dept. engring. sci. U. Oxford, Eng., 1985; vis. prof. Norway Inst. Tech., Trondheim, 1985-86. Editor Jour. Engring. Mechanics. Jenkin fellow, 1986. Fellow ASCE (pres. Colo. sect. 1990-91, bd. dirs. 2003—, jour. editor, Walter Huber Civil Engring. Rsch. prize 1990, Richard Torrens award 2000), U.S. Assn. Computational Mechanics; mem. AAAS, Am. Geophys. Union, Am. Soc. Engring. Edn., NASA Ctr. Space Constrn., Internat. Soc. Soil Mech. Found. Engrs., U.S. Nat. Comm./Theoretical and Applied Mechanics. Avocations: skiing, sailing, cross-country skiing, hiking. Home: 1077 Diamond Ct Boulder CO 80303-3244 Office: Univ Colo Dept Civil Engring Boulder CO 80309-0428

STURGES, GLORIA JUNE, learning disabilities educator; b. Ingallas, Kans., Nov. 10, 1937; d. Donald Nathan and Dorothy Ellen (Whaley) Kitch; m. W.G. Bray, Jan. 22, 1960 (div. Apr. 1978); children— Lori Lynn, William Don; m. Sidney James Sturges. B.S. in Edn., Southeastern State U., 1959; M.A. in Edn., Webster U., 1975; postgrad. U. Kans., 1978-84, cert. learning disabilities specialty, 1984. Cert. tchr. elem. edn., Colo., Mo., reading and learning disabilities specialist, Mo. Tchr., Jefferson County Schs., Denver, 1959-60, Briggsdale, Colo., 1960-63, Colo. Sch. for Deaf and Blind, Colorado Springs, 1963-66, Bertha Heid Sch., Thornton, Colo., 1966-70; reading specialist Center Sch. Dist., Kansas City, Mo., 1970-78, learning disabilities specialist, 1985— ; bus. exec. Sturges Co., Independence, Mo., 1982— . Active ARC, 1984—, Nat. Polit. Action, Kansas City, Mo., 1970—. conference presenter Emporia State U. Recipient Excellence in Edn. award ARC, 1984-85; Outstanding Achievement award Colo. for Deaf and Blind, 1963. Mem. Nat. Assn. Females Execs., NEA, Kappa Delta Pi. Republican. Baptist. Avocations: gourmet cooking; tennis; swimming; antiques. Home: 16805 E Cogan Rd Independence MO 64055-2815 Office: Red Bridge Sch 418 E 106th Ter Kansas City MO 64131-4318

STURGES, ROBERT STUART, English language educator; b. Bridgeport, Conn., Apr. 29, 1953; s. Clifford William and Barbara Alice (Mackey) S. BA, U. Bridgeport, 1974; MA, Brown U., 1976, PhD, 1979. Asst. prof. lit. MIT, Cambridge, Mass., 1980-81; asst. prof. English Wesleyan U., Middletown, Conn., 1981-88, U. New Orleans, 1988-91, assoc. prof. English, 1991-96, prof. English, 1996—2002, univ. rsch. prof., 2002—. Mem. editorial bd. Arthuriana, Dallas, 1994—. Author: Medieval Interpretation, 1991, Chaucer's Pardoner and Gender Theory, 2000; mem. editl. bd. Exemplaria, 1998—; contbr. articles to profl. jours. ACLS grantee, 1982; Mellon Found. fellow, 1984-85, Wesleyan Ctr. Humanities Faculty fellow, 1984. Mem. Internat. Arthurian Soc., South Ctrl. Modern Lang. Assn., Southeastern Medieval Assn., MLA Lesbian and Gay Caucus. Democrat. Office: U New Orleans Dept English New Orleans LA 70148-0001

STURGES, SIDNEY JAMES, pharmacist, educator, investment and development company executive; b. Kansas City, Mo., Sept. 29, 1936; s. Sidney Alexander and Lenore Caroline (Lemley) S.; m. Martha Grace Leonard, Nov. 29, 1957 (div. 1979); 1 child, Grace Caroline; m. Gloria June Kitch, Sept. 17, 1983. BS in Pharmacy, U. Mo., 1957, post grad.; MBA in Pharmacy Adminstrn., U. Kans., 1980; PhD in Bus. Adminstrn., Pacific Western U., 1980; cert. in Gerentology, Avila Coll., 1986. Registered pharmacist, Mo., Kans.; registered nursing home adminstr., Mo.; cert. vocat. tchr., Mo. Pharmacist, mgr. Crown Drugs, Kansas City, Mo., 1957-60; pharmacist, owner Sav-On-Drugs and Pharmacy, Kansas City, 1960-62; ptnr. Sam's Bargain Town Drugs, Raytown, Mo., 1961-62; pharmacist, owner Sturges Drugs DBA Barnard Pharmacy, Independence, Mo., 1962—; pres., owner Sturges Med. Corp., Independence, Mo., 1967-1977, Sturgess Investment Corp., Independence, 1967-1978, Sturwood Investment Corp., Independence, 1968—, Sturges Agri-Bus. Co., Independence, 1977—, Sturges Devel. Co., 1984—; bd. dirs. Comprehensive Mental Health Corp., Truman Med. Ctr., 1992; instr. pharmacology Penn Valley C.C., 1976-92; instr., lectr. various clubs and groups. Contbr. articles to profl. jours. Bd. dirs. Independence House, 1981-83; mem. Criminal Justice Adv. Commn., Independence, 1982—. Recipient Outstanding award Kans. City Alcohol and Drug Abuse Council, 1982. Mem. Mo. Sheriffs Assn., Mo. Pharm. Assn. (pharmacy dr. 1981, Pharmacists Against Drug Abuse award 1989), Mo. Found. Pharm. Care, U. Mo. Alumni Assn. Home and Office: Sturges Co 16805 E Cogan Rd Ste B Independence MO 64055-2815

STURLEY, MICHAEL F. law educator; b. Syracuse, N.Y., Feb. 14, 1955; s. Richard Avern and Helen Elizabeth (Fisher) S.; m. Michele Y. Deitch, July 2, 1989; children: Jennifer Diane, Elizabeth Claire. BA, Yale U., 1977, JD, l98l; BA in Jurisprudence, Oxford U., 1980, MA, 1985. Bar: N.Y. l984, U.S. Dist. Ct. (so. and ea. dists.) N.Y. l984, U.S. Supreme Ct. l987. Law clk. to Judge Amalya L. Kearse, U.S. Ct. Appeals for 2d Cir., N.Y.C., l98l-82; law clk. to Justice Lewis F. Powell, Jr. U.S. Supreme Ct., Washington, 1982-83; assoc. Sullivan & Cromwell, N.Y.C., l983-84; asst. prof. law U. Tex. Law Sch., Austin, l984-88, prof., 1988—. Vis. prof. Queen Mary and Westfield Coll., U. London, 1990, advisor Restatement (3d) of Property (servitudes), 1989-2000. Author: (with David W. Robertson and Steven F. Friedell) Admiralty and Maritime Law in the United States, 2001; compiler, editor: The Legislative History of the Carriage of Goods by Sea Act and the Travaux Préparatoires of The Hague Rules, 3 vols., 1990; mem. editl. bd. Jour. Maritime Law and Commerce, 1989—, book rev. editor, 1993—; contbg. author: Benedict on Admiralty, 1990—; contbr. articles to legal jours. Mem. Am. Law Inst., Maritime Law Assn. (proctor), Comité Maritime Internat. (titulary) Office: U Tex Sch Law 727 E Dean Keeton St Austin TX 78705-3224 E-mail: msturley@mail.law.utexas.edu.

STURM, NICHOLAS, biological sciences educator, author; b. Meriden, W.Va., Dec. 19, 1931; s. Henry Earl and Beulah Agnes (Coffman) S. BS, W.Va. Wesleyan Coll., 1952; MS, Purdue U., 1955; postgrad., U. Tex., 1956-59. Head sci. dept. S.W. Tex. Jr. Coll., Uvalde, 1959-61; instr. Amarillo Coll., Tex., 1961-64; asst. prof. Youngstown U., Ohio, 1964-67; prof. biol. scis. Youngstown State U., 1967-95, prof. emeritus, 1995—. Cons. on edn. texts various pubs., 1969-90; field editor various pubs., 1972-86; cons. on computer applications S&S Software, Youngstown, 1986-95, Philippi, 1995—. Author: Exploring Life, 1972, 3d edit., 1986, (computer software) Natural Selection, 1992. Mem. Am. Fern. Soc. (life), Brit. Lichen Soc., Antiquus Mysticusque Orda Rosae Cruris. Avocations: photography, local history, computer programming, multimedia design, nature study. Home: PO Box 69 Philippi WV 26416-0007 Office: Youngstown State U 410 Wick Ave Youngstown OH 44555-0002 E-mail: info@trisware.net., nicksturm@earthlink.net.

STURTEVANT, RUTHANN PATTERSON, anatomy educator; b. Rockford, Ill., Feb. 7, 1927; d. Joseph Hyelmun and Virginia (Wharton) P.; m. Frank Milton Sturtevant Jr., Mar. 18, 1950; children: Barbara (dec.), Jill Sturtevant Rovani, Jan Sturtevant Cassidy. BS, Northwestern U., 1949, MS, 1950; PhD, U. Ark., 1972. Instr. life scis. Ind. State U., Evansville, Ind., 1965—72, asst. prof., 1972—74; asst. prof. anatomy Ind. U. Sch. Medicine, Evansville, 1972—74, U. Evansville, 1972—74; lectr. anatomy Northwestern U., Chgo., 1974—75; asst. prof. anatomy and surgery Loyola U., Maywood, 1975—81; assoc. prof. Loyola U. Sch. Medicine, Maywood, 1981—88, prof., 1988—90, prof. emerita, 1990—. Contbr. articles to profl. jours.; editorial bd. Chronobiology Internat., 1988-90; reviewer numerous profl. jours. Mem. Mayor's Task Force on High Tech. Devel., Chgo., 1983-85; exec. bd. Anatomical Gifts Assn. Ill., Chgo., 1978-89. Grantee, Pott's Found., NIH, others, 1978-88. Mem. Am. Assn. Anatomists, So. Soc. Anatomists (councillor 1978-80), Internat. Soc. Chronobiologists, Am. Soc. Pharmacology and Exptl. Therapeutics, Soc. for Exptl. Biology and Medicine, Am. Assn. Clin. Anatomists, League of Underwater Photographers, Sarasota Scuba Club, Sigma Xi. Avocations: underwater photography, scuba diving, flying, digital imaging. Address: 5760 Midnight Pass Rd Unit 610-D Sarasota FL 34242 E-mail: patty5760@comcast.net.

STURZL, ALICE A. school library administrator; b. Marshfield, Wis., May 22, 1949; d. Aloysius F. and Lorraine R. (Wolk) Beyerl; m. Bruce R. Sturzl, Sr., June 9, 1973; stepchildren: Bruce R., Scott, Daniel, Ann, Todd, Timothy. BA, U. Wis., Oshkosh, 1971. Cert. tchr., Wis. Elem. libr. Sts. Peter and Paul Parish, Oshkosh, 1970-71; libr. Sch. Dist. of Laona, Wis., 1971-73; tchr. math. Our Lady of Perpetual Help, Glendale, Ariz., 1974-75, Most Holy Trinity Parish, Sunnyslope, Ariz., 1975-76; substitute tchr. Sch. Dists. of Laona and Wabeno, Wis., 1976-77; K-12 instructional media specialist Sch. Dist. of Laona, 1977—. Mem. Northeastern Wis. In-Sch. Telecomms. Adv. Bd., Green Bay, 1987-97, pres. 1989-97; trustee, v.p., pres. Wisconsin Valley Libr. Svc. Bd., Wausau, 1984-89, 2000—. Mem. Econ. Devel. Com., Town of Laona, 1987—; mem. parish coun. St. Leonard's Cath. Ch., Laona, intermittently 1983—; active Cmty. Soup and Homecoming/Laona Lions Club, 1983—. Mem. ALA, NEA, Wis. Libr. Assn. (sec. 1993-94, v.p. 1996, pres. 1997, past pres. 1998), Laona Edn. Assn. (sec.-treas.), Wis. Edn. Assn. (No. Tier UniServ), Wis. Ednl. Media Assn., Wis. Libr. Assn. Found. (v.p., sec.). Roman Catholic. Avocations: bowling, reading, travel, helping others, working with numbers. Home: 5170 E Silver Lake Rd Laona WI 54541-9255 Office: Sch Dist of Laona PO Box 100 5216 Forest Ave Laona WI 54541

STYER, ANTOINETTE CARDWELL, middle school administrator; b. Martinsville, Va. d. John E. Cardwell and I. Lois Cardwell Shelton; children: Yvette D., Christopher P. BA in Liberal Arts, Temple U., 1975; MEd in Elem./Secondary Sch. Counseling, Antioch U., Phila., 1980. cert. sec. prin., 1994. Sec. Edward S. Cooper, M.D., Phila., 1960-66; rsch. asst. Temple U., Phila., 1971-73; confidential sec. Sch. Dist. Phila., 1967-71, sec., 1974-76, social worker Child Care Ctr., 1976-86, sch. counselor elem. edn., 1986-89; secondary edn. counselor Sch. Dist. Phila. Roosevelt Mid. Sch., Phila., 1989-97, Germantown Lankenau Motivation H.S., 1997-99; asst. prin. FitzSimons Mid. Sch., Phila., 1999—2000, Grover Washington Jr. H.S., 2000—. Sch. evaluator Mid. States Assn. of Colls. and Schs.; co-organizer Project Exposure: Bus.; chaperone student visit to colls., Atlanta; interviewee Nat. Opinion Rsch. Ctr., Phila., 1971-72; mgmt. trainee GSA, Phila., 1987; del. leader People to People Student Amb. Programs, Australia, 1993, Russia and the Baltic States, 1994, U.K. and Ireland, 1995, South Africa, 1996, 97, France, Italy, Germany, Austria, Switzerland, 1998 (European Discovery). Past chair 75th anniversary com. Pinn Meml. Bapt. Ch., scholarship com., new mem. com., aides to first lady and women's support group; mem. bd. dirs. Day Care Com., bus. devel. com.; ann. vol. United Negro Coll. Fund Telethon, mem. small bus. fundraising com.; bd. dirs. Bus. Devel. Com. Mem. Nat. Coun. Negro Women, Pa. Sch. Counselors Assn., Mid. States Assn. Colls. and Schs., Delta Sigma Theta (life, chpt. journalist, chair May Week, del. to regional conv., mem. scholarship com.), Phi Delta Kappa. Home: 925 E Roumfort Rd Philadelphia PA 19150-3215 Office: 201 E Olney Ave Philadelphia PA 19120

STYLES, TERESA JO, producer, educator; b. Atlanta, Oct. 19, 1950; d. Julian English and Jennie Marine (Sims) S. BA, Spelman Coll., 1972; MA, Northwestern U., 1973; PhD, U. N.C., Chapel Hill, 1998. Rschr. CBS News, N.Y.C., 1975-80, prodr., 1980-85; instr. mass comms. and English Savannah (Ga.) State Coll., 1985-89, asst. prof. English, 1990; asst. prof. mass comm. and women studies dir. Bennett Coll., Greensboro, NC, 1990-93; assoc. prof. mass comm., chmn. journalism and mass comm. N.C. A&T State U., Greensboro, 1993—. Chmn. journalism and mass comm. U. Greensboro, 2001—. Researcher documentary CBS Reports: Teddy, 1979 (Emmy cert.); assoc. producer documentaries for CBS Reports: Blacks: America, 1979 (Columbia Dupont cert. 1979), What Shall We Do About Mother?, 1980 (Emmy cert.), The Defense of the U.S., 1980 (Columbia Dupont cert.). Adv. bd. Greensboro Hist. Mus., Eastern Music Festival, Women's Short Film Project. Mem. Writers Guild Am. (bd. dirs. east 1991-95), Dirs. Guild Am. (bd. dirs. east 1991-95), African Am. Atelier (Greensboro, N.C. bd. dirs.), Eastern Music Festival (bd. dirs.). Avocation: swimming. Home: 4400 Suffolk Trl Greensboro NC 27407-7842 E-mail: teresaj@ncat.edu.

STYNES, BARBARA BILELLO, integrative health professional, educator; b. N.Y.C., Apr. 24, 1951; d. Sylvester Francis and Jacqueline Marie (Giardelli) Bilello; m. Frank Joseph Stynes, Aug. 24, 1969; children: Christopher Francis, Jeremy Scott. BA, Rutgers U., 1976; MA in Health Studies, Antioch U., 1995. Cert. reiki practitioner. Mktg. rep. McNeil Consumer Products Co., Ft. Washington, Pa., 1979-82, Met Path Inc., Des Plaines, Ill., 1982-85; mktg. coord. Life program Meml. Hosp. and YMCA, Chattanooga, 1986-91; mem. Chattanooga Area Wellness Coun., 1986-91, Chattanooga Area Healthcare Coalition, 1986-91; dir. mktg. and comm., met. YMCA, Chattanooga, 1986-91, dir. internat. program, 1989-91, wellness cons., 1992-95; intern Mind/Body Inst., Affiliate Harvard Med. Sch., Deaconess Hosp, Columbus, Ohio, 1995—. Assoc. hospice residential care, 1995; therapeutic touch and presence facilitator, 1995—; lifestyle counselor, 1995—, Reiki practitioner, 1999—; program developer Set for Life, 1996; mindfulness based stress reduction facilitator, 1994—; fiber sculptor, 1975-77; weaver, 1976-79; wellness dir. Carolina Family Medicine & Wellness, Mooresville, N.C., 2000. Vol. comm. com. Am. Heart Assn., 1972-91, Spl. Olympics, Chgo., 1982-84; spkr. Tenn. Safety Belt coalition, 1986-91; clinic leader Am. Lung Assn., Chattanooga, 1986-88, YMCA cert. fitness specialist, 1986—, weight mgmt. specialist, 1987—; chairperson fundraising, trustee Pine Grove Coop. Sch., New Brunswick, N.J., 1977-78; sustaining bd. Choices, 1993-95; bd. dirs. Signal Mountain Newcomers Assn., Tenn., 1985-86; mem. sch. bd. Notre Dame H.S., 1989-91. Mem. NAFE, Omega: Inst. Holistic Studies, Inst. Noetic Scis., Am. Bus. Woman's Network Chattanooga (chair mem.), Fiber Arts Guild, Assn. Profl. Dirs., Kiwanis (chair internat. rels. com. Chattanooga chpt. 1990-91, publicity dir.), Gen. Bd. Newcomers, North Columbus, Sustaining Bd. Choices). Roman Catholic. Avocations: walking, yoga, gardening, travel, music. Home: 2706 Trent Pines Ct Sherrills Ford NC 28673-9132

SU, HUI FANG HUANG, mathematician, educator; b. Taichung, Taiwan, Sept. 7, 1955; came to U.S., 1966; d. Bau-Duan and Chia Mei Huang; m. Tsung-Chow Joe Su, Dec. 26, 1976; children: Julius Tsu-Li, Jonathan Tsu-Wei, Tsu-Te Judith, Jessica Tsu-Yun. BA, CUNY, 1977; MEd, Tex. A&M U., 1978, MS, 1979; EdD, Nova Southeastern U., 1991. Tchr. Pine Grove Elem., Delray Beach, Fla., 1985-98; instrnl. specialist Sch. Dist. Palm Beach County, West Palm Beach, Fla., 1998-99, math. specialist, 1999—2001; program prof. Nova Southeastern U., 2001. Adj. prof. Nova Southeastern U., Ft. Lauderdale, Fla., 1996-2001; presenter in field. Author: Some Ways To...in Mathematics, 1996, Strategies? Tricks? See..., 1997. Bd. dirs. Somerset Neighborhood Charter Sch., 1998—. Recipient NSF Presdl. award, 1998, William T. Dwyer award, Econ. Coun. PBC, 1996; Annenberg Challenge grantee, Fla., 1998—; named one of 50 Most Successful Bus. Women in S. Fla., Fast Track Mag., 2001. Mem. NOW, ASCD, Nat. Coun. Suprs. Math., Nat. Coun. Tchrs. Math., Presdl. Awardees Assn., Nat. Coun., Soroptimist Internat. (Women of Distinction award 1999, Broward County Women of Distinction award 2003). Achievements include development of Math Is Not Difficult (MIND). Home: 2150 Areca Palm Rd Boca Raton FL 33432-7994 Office: 1750 NE 167th St North Miami Beach FL 33162 E-mail: huifangt@aol.com.

SU, TSUNG-CHOW JOE, engineering educator; b. Taipei, Taiwan, Republic of China, July 9, 1947; came to U.S., 1969; s. Chin-shui and Chen-ling (Shih) S.; m. Hui-Fang Angie Huang, Dec. 26, 1976; children: Julius Tsu-Li, Jonathan Tsu-Wei, Judith Tsu-Te, Jessica Tsu-Yun. BS, Nat. Taiwan U., 1968; MS in Aeronautics, Calif. Inst. Technology, 1970, AE, 1973; EngScD, Columbia U., 1974. Registered profl. engr., Fla., Tex. Rsch. teaching asst. Calif. Inst. Technology, Pasadena, 197-72; rsch. asst. Columbia U., N.Y.C., 1972-73; naval architect John J. McMullen Assoc., Inc., N.Y.C., 1974-75; asst. prof. civil engring. Tex. A&M U., College Station, Tex., 1976-82; assoc. prof. ocean engring. Fla. Atlantic U., Boca Raton, 1982-87, prof. ocean engring, 1987-92, prof. mech. engring., 1992—. Contbr. over 80 articles to profl. jours.; assoc. editor Jour. Engring. Mechs., 1991-94. Coord. Calif. Tech. Alumni Fund, South Fla. area, 1987-88. 2d lt. Chinese Army, 1968-69. Grantee in field. Fellow AIAA (assoc.); mem. ASME, ASCE (chmn. fluids com. 1992-94), Am. Acad. Mechanics, Calif. Tech. Alumni Assn., Royal Palm Improvement Assn. Home: 2150 Areca Palm Rd Boca Raton FL 33432-7994 Office: Fla Atlantic U Dept Mech Engring Boca Raton FL 33431 E-mail: su@fau.edu.

SUAREZ, ELISABETH CLEMENCE, counselor educator; b. N.Y.C., Apr. 1, 1960; d. Alfonso Joseph and Maria Cristina (Lacayo) S.; m. June 13, 1959; children: Elisabeth, Christine, Paul, John-Peter. BS in Materials Engring., Rensselaer Poly. Inst., 1982; Cert. of Biblical Studies, Columbia Biblical Sem., 1988; MST in Math., U. N.H., 1989; MA in Counselling, Denver Seminary, 1996; PhD in Counselor Edn. and Supv., U. No. Colo., 2002. Cert. secondary math. educator N.J., lic. profl. counselor Colo. Tchr. math. Timothy Christian Sch., Piscataway, N.J., 1984-87; project coord. Dr. Joan Ferrini-Mundy, U. N.H., Durham, 1988-89; tchr. math. Phillips Exeter (N.H.) Acad., 1989-91; therapist Southwest Counselling Assocs., Littleton, Colo., 1995-97; asst. prof. counseling Denver Seminary, 1997—. Mem. Am. Coun. Assn., Am. Assn. Christian Counselors, Assn. Counselor Edn. Supervision, Christian Assn. Psychol. Studies.

SUAREZ, LUIS EDGARDO, civil engineering educator; b. Jujuy, Argentina, May 14, 1957; came to U.S., 1983; s. Luciano and Maria Mercedes (Colche) S.; m. Rosana Martinez-Cruzado, Dec. 30, 1994. MS in Engring. Mechanics, Va. Poly Inst., 1984, PhD in Engring. Mechanics, 1986. Jr. engr. Atomic Energy Commn. Argentina, Cordoba, 1981; instr. part-time dept. of structures U. Cordoba, 1981-82, asst. prof. grad. programs, 1987-89; rsch.

asst. engring. sci. and mechanics Va. Poly. Inst., Blacksburg, 1983-86, asst. prof. engr. sci. and mechanics dept., 1986-87; asst. prof. gen. engring. dept. U. P.R., Mayaguez, 1989-91, assoc. prof. gen. engring. dept., 1991-96, prof. civil engring., 1996—. Proposal reviewer U.S. Army Rsch. Office, Mayaguez, 1991, NSF, Washington, 1994-95; paper reviewer Jour. Vibration and Acoustics, Jour. Engring. for Industry, Jour. Engring. Structures, Jour. Engring. Mechanics, Jour. Vibration and Control, Mayaguez, AIAA Jour., Jour. of Sound and Vibration, 1992; panelist to select scholarships Battelle, Raleigh, 1991-92; chmn. 5th Pan Am. Congress of Applied Math., 1997. Co-author: Multinational Seismic Design Codes, Handbook, 1992, A Visual Introduction to SAP 2000, 2002; contbr. articles to profl. jours. Cunningham fellow Va. Poly. Inst., 1986, Disting. prof., dept. gen. engring., 1994, Disting. prof. civil engring., 1996, 99; grantee U.S. Army Rsch. Office, 1990, Nat. Ctr. for Earthquake Engring. Rsch., 1992-96, Langley Rsch. Ctr. NASA, 1999, FEMA, 2001-03. Mem. ASCE, ASME, AIAA, Internat. Conf. Bldgs. Offcls., Soc. Exptl. Mechanics, Earthquake Engring. Rsch. Inst., The Vibration Inst., Am. Soc. Engring. Edn., Am. Acad. Mechanics, Sigma Xi (Rsch. award Va. Tech. chpt. 1987). Roman Catholic. Achievements include development of methods for seismic analysis of mechanical equipment that are used in industry, several methods for dynamic analysis of large structural systems. Office: Univ Puerto Rico Ctrl Engring Dept PO Box 9041 Mayaguez PR 00681-9041

SUBLETTE, JULIA WRIGHT, music educator, performer, adjudicator; b. Natural Bridge, Va., Sept. 13, 1929; d. Paul Thomas and Annie Belle (Watkins) Wright; m. Richard Ashmore Sublette, Oct. 18, 1952; children: C. Mark, Carey P., Sylvia S. Bennett, Wright D. BA in Music, Furman U., 1951; MusM, Cin. Conservatory, 1954; postgrad., Chautaugua Inst., N.Y., 1951-52; PhD, Fla. State U., 1993. Ind. piano tchr., 1953—; instr. music and humanities Okaloosa-Walton C.C., Niceville, Fla., 1978—, U. West Fla., Pensacola. Panelist Music Tchr. Nat. Conv., Milw., 1992; instr. art humanities Troy State U., Ala.; featured performer N.W. Fla. Symphony Orch. Editor Fla. Music Tchr., 1991-99; contbr. articles to profl. music jours. Mem. AAUW, Music Tchrs. Nat. Assn. (cert., chmn. so. divsn. jr. high sch. piano/instrumental contests 1986-88), Fla. State Music Tchrs. Assn., So. Assn. Women Historians, Southeastern Hist. Keyboard Soc., Friday Morning Music Club, Colonial Dames of 17th Century Am., Pi Kappa Lambda. Avocations: reading, travel, folk music, herb gardening. Home: 217 Country Club Rd Shalimar FL 32579-2203

SUBRAMANIAN, MARAPPA GOUNDER, reproductive physiologist, educator; b. Sungakkarampatti, Madras, India, Dec. 12, 1938; came to the U.S., 1970; m. Sagunthala Karuppana Subramanian, Aug. 23, 1967; children: Sendhil, Raj. B in Vet. Sci., Vet. Coll., Madras, 1961, M in Vet. Sci., 1967; PhD, Rutgers U., 1974. Cert. lab. dir. Dept. Pub. Health, Mich. Asst. prof. Wayne State U., Detroit, 1981-87, assoc. prof., 1987-92, prof., 1992—. Lab. dir. C.S. Mott Ctr., Detroit, 1977—. Rsch. grantee NIH, 1988—. Mem. Am. Fertility Soc., Soc. for Gynecol. Investigation, Am. Men and Women Sci. Avocations: jogging, racquetball, movies. Office: Wayne State Univ Ob-Gyn Dept 275 E Hancock St Detroit MI 48201-1415

SUBSTAD LOKENSGARD, KATHRYN ANN, small business owner, career consultant; b. Mpls., Dec. 4, 1941; d. Arnold Torger and Ardis Louise (Klanderud) Substad; m. Arvid Luther Lokensgard, Nov. 23, 1963 (div. July 1982); children: Sara Kathryn Lokensgard Dickinson, Sigurd Arvid Lokensgard, Laura Ann Lokensgard. BA, St. Olaf Coll., 1963; postgrad., Pacific Luth. Theol. Sem., 1989. Tchr. Lookout Mountain (Tenn.) Elem. Sch., 1964-66; tchrs. aide Greenvale Elem. Sch., Northfield, Minn., 1974-76; substitute tchr. Inclin Village (Nev.) K-12, 1978-80, asst. libr., 1980-82; fin. aid dir., fgn. student advisor Sierra Nevada Coll., Incline Village, 1982-85, asst. to pres., 1985-89; owner Tahoe Christian Bookstore, Tahoe Vista, Calif., 1993-2000; self-employed in home health svcs., 2000—. Substitute tchr., career cons., 1990-92; liaison to bd. Sierra Nevada Coll., 1985-88. Bd. dirs. ch. coun. Christ the King Luth. Ch., Tahoe City, 1986-89, local pub. TV sta., 1986-89; vol. tchr. ESL, 1991-98; active Nev. Literacy Coalition, 1991-98; bd. dirs. North Tahoe Reading Ctr.; deacon Incline Village Community Presbyn. Ch., 1992-95; trainer, leader Stephen Ministries, 1996-2000. Mem. PEO (social sec. 1988-89), AAUW, C. of C. (bd. dirs. 1988-89, Hospice 1991-98, Citizen of Month 1989). Avocations: tennis, hiking, skiing, sailing, swimming, knitting, porcelain doll-making.

SUCHECKI, LUCY ANNE, elementary education educator; b. East Cleveland, Ohio, May 3, 1945; d. Ben and Adelaide V. (Maneri) Urban; m. Robert K. Suchecki, Aug. 19, 1972. BS, Bowling Green State U., 1967; MA, Oakland U., 1981. Cert. elem. tchr., Mich. Elem. tchr. L'Anse Creuse Pub. Schs., Mt. Clemens, Mich., 1967—. Grade cons. (book) Michigan, 1991. Active Immaculate Conception Ch., 1969—, Anchor Bay Women's Pool League, 1972—. Mem. NEA, MEA, MEA-NEA (local 1), L'Anse Creuse Ednl. Assn. (sec. 1968—), New Baltimore Hist. Soc. Roman Catholic. Avocations: boating, swimming, pool. Home: 8504 Anchor Bay Dr Clay MI 48001-3507 Office: Francis Higgins Elem Sch 29901 24 Mile Rd Chesterfield MI 48051-1760

SUCHY, MARTIN RAYMOND, secondary education educator; b. N.Y.C., Feb. 12, 1946; s. Martin and Helen (Ozimkoski) S.; m. Clarice F. Bauer, Aug. 10, 1968. BS, Fordham U., 1967; MA, Columbia U., 1968. Cert. math. tchr., prin., supr., N.Y., N.J. Tchr. math. North Rockland H.S., Haverstraw, N.Y., 1968-69, Ramsey (N.J.) H.S., 1971—. Tchr. computers Ramsey (N.J.) Adult Sch., 1986-91. Chair parish coun. St. Joseph Ch., Middletown, N.Y., 1991-95, lectr., eucharistic min., 2000—. Served to 1st lt. U.S. Army, 1969-71. Recipient N.J. Gov.'s award for outstanding teaching, 1988. Mem. NEA, Nat. Coun. Tchrs. Math., Assn. Math. Tchrs. N.J., Ramsey Tchrs. Assn., N.J. Edn. Assn., Bergen County Edn. Assn. Roman Catholic. Avocation: gardening. Home: 16 Highview Dr Middletown NY 10941-1039 Office: Ramsey Bd Edn E Main St Ramsey NJ 07446 E-mail: msuchy@ramsey.k12.nj.us.

SUCHY, SUSANNE N. nursing educator; b. Windsor, Ont., Can., Sept. 20, 1945; d. Hartley Joseph and Helen Viola (Derrick) King; m. Richard Andrew Suchy, June 24, 1967; children: Helen Marie, Hartley Andrew, Michael Derrick. Diploma, St. Joseph Sch. Nursing, Flint, Mich., 1966; BSN, Wayne State U., 1969, MSN, 1971. RN, Mich. Afternoon supr., staff nurse oper. and recovery rm. St. John Hosp., Detroit, 1966-70; nursing instr. Henry Ford Community Coll., Dearborn, Mich., 1972—, on leave 1988-90; CNS/case mgr. surg. nursing Harper Hosp., Detroit, 1988-89; CNS case mgr. oncology, 1989—. Mem. Detroit Demonstration Site Team for defining and differentiating ADN/BSN competencies, 1983-87. Contbr. articles to profl. jours. Past bd. dirs., pres. St. Pius Sch. Mem. ANA, AACH, N.Am. Nursing Diagnosis Assn. (by-law com. chmn. 1992-98), Mich. Nursing Diagnosis Assn. (pres. 1987-90, elected by-law chmn. 1991-92, treas. 1993—), NLN, Mich. Nurses Assn. (cabinet nursing practice 1996-98, conv. com. 1996-98), Detroit Dist. Nurses Assn. (past chmn. nominating com., legis. com., sec. 1994-96), Oncology Nursing Soc. (gov. rels. chmn. 1992—, presenter abstract conf. 1991, 95, poster presentations ann. conf. 1991-93, 95, 96, dicussion presenter 1998), Daus. of Isabella (internat. dir. 1992-96, local auditor 1995—, state vice regent 1997—, cir. auditor 1995-97), Wayne State U. Alumni Assn., Sigma Theta Tau (nominating com. 1991-93). Roman Catholic. Home: 12666 Irene St Southgate MI 48195-1765 Office: Henry Ford CC 5101 Evergreen Rd Dearborn MI 48128-2407

SUDOW, THOMAS NISAN, marketing services company executive, broadcaster, chamber of commerce executive; b. Stevens Point, Wis., Nov. 7, 1952; s. Noah and Gertrude (Fein) S.; m. Michele Ross, Aug. 8, 1976; children: Erin, Noah, Nathaniel. Student, U. Wis., 1971, Jerusalem Inst., Israel, 1972; BA, Kent State U., 1976; MSW, Yeshiva U., N.Y.C., 1980. Tchr. Akron (Ohio) Hebrew High Sch., 1976-78; sr. assoc. Jewish Cmty. Fed. of Cleve., 1978-85; exec. dir. Am. Friends of Hebrew U., Beachwood, Ohio, 1986-88; v.p. Cleve. Coll. of Jewish Studies, Beachwood, 1988-93, Solid Sound Rec. Studio, Chgo., 1980-99; pres. T.N.S. and Assocs., 1993—; exec. producer, host Sports Talk for Kids Radio Network, Cleve., 1993—; exec. dir. Beachwood (Ohio) C. of C., 2002—. Instr. Kent (Ohio) State U., 1976-78; radio host Cleve. Hockey Jour. on the Air, Tonight in Baseball, Play by Play, H.S. Hockey Game of the Week; instr. fund raising course Mandel Sch. for Applied Social Sci., Case Western Res. U. Columnist Family Recreation mag., The Cleve. Hockey Jour.; editor Torchlight; host The Cleve. Crunch Coaches Show and playoff, pre-game and half-time shows. Exec. bd. dirs. Kent Sunday Sch., 1976-78; bd. dirs. Park Synagogue, Cleveland Heights, Ohio, 1986-97, pres. Men's Club, 1989-91; bd. dirs. Cleve. Pops Orch.; regional program chair FJMC Conv., v.p. Gt. Lake region, 1992-2000, pres. cabinet, 1995-97 chmn. Cleve. region, 1995-98, internat. exec. com., 1997-99, internat. sec., 1999-2001, internat. v.p. 2001—; founding dir. Congregation Cmty. Inst. Adult Jewish Studies, 1988-93; hon. dir. Bejing Ctr. for Jewish Studies, 1993—; trustee Beachwood C. of C., 1993—, v.p., 1995-99, pres., 1999-2001; exec. com. Beachwood Area Transp. Orgn. Mgmt.; mem. bd. Cleve. Jewish News; vice chair No. Ohio Assn. Chambers Commerce., 2002-03, chair 2003, Ctr. Park Synagogue, 2003. Recipient Young Leadership award, United Jewish Appeal, N.Y.C., 1976, No. Ohio Live award of Achievement Media, 1996, Muiasim Tovim award, FJMC, 2003; named Man of the Yr. Park Synagogue, Cleveland Heights, 1986; Sherman fellow Brandeis U., Waltham, Mass., 1986. Mem. NASW, Conf. Jewish Communal Svc. Workers (chmn. 1986-93), Assn. Jewish Communal Orgn. Profs. (regional chmn. 1981-85), Conf. Alternatives in Jewish Edn., Glass Inst. (chmn. 1986-87), Wahoo Club (pres. 1993-95), Cleve. Indians Heavy Hitters, Nat. Soc. Fundraising Exec., Ohio Fundraising Exec. Coun., Cleve. Cavs Reboudersn (bd. dirs., v.p. 2000, pres. 2001), Sports Media and Mktg. Assn. Ohio, Crohn's and Colts Found. of No. Ohio. Avocations: sports, photography, family, humor. Office: TNS and Assocs 3665 Tolland Rd Cleveland OH 44122-5140

SUELTO, CONSUELO QUILAO, retired nursing educator; b. The Philippines, June 27, 1924; d. Catalina Pamplona; m. Anacleto T. Suelto, Apr. 28, 1952; children: Ramona, Anacleto Q. Jr. Diploma, U. Philippines Sch. Nursing, Manila, 1949; BS in Nursing Edn., Philippine Women's U., Manila, 1955, EdD, 1983; MA in Nursing, U. Philippines, Quezon City, 1960; EdD, P.W. U., 1983. Staff nurse U. Philippines-Philippine Gen. Hosp., 1949-50, instr. Sch. Nursing, 1950-61; adminstrv. officer, asst. dean Philippine Women's U., 1961-68; prin. St. Jude Sch. Nursing, Manila, 1968-73, Lipa City (The Philippines Sch. Nursing, 1976-80; dean Lipa City Coll. Nursing, 1980-84, Golden Gate Coll. Coll. Nursing, Batangas City, The Philippines, 1980-84; coord., instr. St. James Mercy Hosp. Sch. Nursing, Hornell, N.Y., 1973-75, 84-94. Mem. adv. bd. PNA of Fla., 1995. Mem. Philippines Nurses Assn. (life, bd. dirs.), Nurses Assn. of the Am. Assn. of Ob-Gyn. Home: 1623 19th St NE Rochester MN 55906-4339

SUGGARS, CANDICE LOUISE, special education educator; b. Pitts., Jan. 16, 1949; d. Albert Abraham and Patricia Louise (Stepp) S. BS in Elem. Edn., W.Va. U., 1972; MS in Spl. Edn., Johns Hopkins U., 1979, Cert. Advanced Studies, 1986. Clin. supr./head tchr. The Kennedy Kreiger Inst., Balt., 1974-80, inpatient coord., 1980-83, ednl. evaluator, 1980-85, spl. educator/pediatric rehab. team, 1985-86; spl. edn. cons. Charleston County (S.C.) Sch. Dist., 1986-90, spl. edn. pre-sch. tchr., 1990-95; pvt. tutor & cons. children with spl. needs and disabilities Charleston, 1995—; spl. needs cons. U. S.C., 1996—. Mem. adv. bd. S.C. Accelerated Schs. Project, Charleston, 1994-95; parenting instr. Internat. Network of Children and Families, 1999; part-time learning specialist in a pvt. sch., 2000—. Contbg. author: Disadvantaged Pre-School Child, 1979, Leisure Education for the Handicapped Curriculum, 1984. Exhibitor ann. conv. S.C. State Sch. Bd. Assn., 1994. Mem. Coun. for Exceptional Children (hospitality chair 1987-89, publicity chair 1989-90), Nat. Assn. for Edn. of Young Children. Avocations: singing, reading, travel. Home: 29 Savage St Charleston SC 29401-2409

SUGIKI, SHIGEMI, ophthalmologist, educator; b. Wailuku, Hawaii, May 12, 1936; s. Sentaro and Kameno (Matoba) S.; m. Bernice T. Murakami, Dec. 28, 1958; children: Kevin S., Boyd R. AB, Washington U., St. Louis, 1957; MD, Washington U., 1961. Intern St. Luke's Hosp., St. Louis, 1961-62; resident ophthalmology Washington U., St. Louis, 1962-65; chmn. dept. ophthalmology Straub Clinic, Honolulu, 1965-70, Queens Med. Ctr., Honolulu, 1970-73, 80-83, 88-90, 93-2000; clin. prof. ophthalmology Sch. Medicine U. Hawaii, 1997. Maj. M.C., AUS, 1968-70. Decorated Hawaiian NG Commendation medal, 1968. Fellow ACS; mem. Am., Hawaii med. assns., Honolulu County Med. Soc., Am. Acad. Ophthalmology, Contact Lens Assn. Opthalmologists, Pacific Coast Oto-Ophthal. Soc., Pan-Pacific Surg. Assn., Am. Soc. Cataract and Refractive Surgery, Am. Glaucoma Soc., Internat. Assn. Ocular Surgeons, Am. Soc. Contemporary Ophthalmology, Washington U. Eye Alumni Assn., Hawaii Ophthal. Soc., Rsch. To Prevent Blindness. Home: 2398 Aina Lani Pl Honolulu HI 96822-2024 Office: 1380 Lusitana St Ste 714 Honolulu HI 96813-2443

SUGNET, LINDA A'BRUNZO, elementary education educator; b. Elmira, N.Y., Aug. 6, 1949; d. Louis N. and C. Elizabeth (Smith) A'Brunzo. BE, SUNY, Geneseo, 1971; MEd, Elmira Coll., 1976; postgrad., SUNY, Cortland, L.I. U. Cert. elem. tchr., N.Y., Fla. Dir. Gerber Children's Ctr., Jacksonville, Fla., 1980-81; elem. tchr. Monroe County Sch. Bd., Key West, Fla., 1987-88, South Seneca Cen. Sch., Interlaken, N.Y., 1971—. Adj. instr., cons. N.Y. State United Tchrs.; with L.I. U., Albany, Coll. of St. Rose, Albany, Performance Learning Sys., Inc., Nevada City, Calif., 1984—; tchr., mentor, 1995—; mem. Elem. Shared Decision Making Team, 1994-96, mem. curriculum coun., 1996-2000, chair profl. improvement program, 2002—. Recipient Early Childhood Preventive Curriculum grant. Mem. ASCD, Am. Fedn. Tchrs., N.Y. State United Tchrs., South Seneca Tchrs. Assn. (co-pres. 1992-94), Internat. Assn. for the Study of Coop. in Edn., Delta Kappa Gamma. E-mail: lsugnet@southseneca.k12.ny.us.

SULEIMAN, IBRAHIM, computer education educator; b. Argungu, Sokoto, Nigeria, Mar. 7, 1954; came to U.S., 1987; s. Umar and Aisha (Abubakar) S.; m. Hauwa Abubakar, Oct. 24, 1985; children: Muhammad Amin, Aisha. ND in Civil Engring., Kaduna Poly. Inst., Nigeria, 1977; BA/BSc in Stats. and Computers, U. Regina, Sask., Can., 1984; MEd in Urban Edn., Norfolk State U., 1989; EdD, U. Va., 1993. Tech. officer Sokoto State Housing Corp., 1977-88; lectr., head computer sect. Sokoto State Poly. Inst., Brinin Kebbi, 1985-86; part-time tchr., rsch. asst., cons. Norfolk (Va.) State U., 1987-89; computer lab. asst. U. Va., Charlottesville, 1989-90, tech. cons., 1990-91, mgr. multimedia lab., 1991-92; planning and implementation of info. tech., dir. info. tech. Bradford Coll., Mass., 1992—. Cons. U. Sokoto, 1985-86, Norfolk State U., 1987-89. Designer instnl. material in field; developer computer program The Animal Kingdom, 1990. Recipient Nat. Svc. cert. Nat. Youth Svc. Corps., 1986. Fellow U. Regina Alumni Assn., U. Va. Alumni Assn.; mem. Assn. Edn. Comm. Tech., Statis. Assn. Regina. Avocations: reading, soccer, tennis, table tennis, computer conferencing.

SULEIMAN, MICHAEL WADIE, humanities educator; b. Tiberias, Palestine, Feb. 26, 1934; s. Wadie Mikhail Suleiman and Jameeleh Khalil Ailabouni; m. Penelope Ann Powers, Aug. 31, 1963; children: Suad Evans, Gibran. BA, Bradley U., 1960; MS, U. Wis., 1962, PhD, 1965. Asst. prof. Kans. State U., Manhattan, 1965-68, assoc. prof., 1968-72, head dept. polit. sci., 1975-82, prof., 1972—90, Univ. Disting. prof., 1990—. Vis. scholar U. Calif., Berkeley, 1979, U. London, 1969-70; h.s. tchr. Abbotsholme Sch., Rocester, England, 1955-56, The Bishop's Sch., Amman, Jordan, 1953-55. Author: U.S. Policy On Palestine From Wilson to Clinton, 1995, The Arabs in the Mind of America, 1988, American Images of Middle East Peoples, 1977, Political Parties in Lebanon: The Challenge of a Fragmented Political Culture, 1967; author, editor: Arabs in American: Building a New Future, 1999, Arab Americans: Continuity and Change, 1989; co-editor Westview Press series: State, Culture and Society in Arab North Africa, 1989-98; mem. editl. bd. dirs. Jour. Arab Affairs, 1980-93, Arab Jour. Internat. Studies, Internat. Jour. Middle East Studies, 1982-88, Arab Studies Quar., 1979-86, Maghreb Rev., 1988—; contbr. articles to profl. jours., chpts. to books. Pres. Assn. Arab Am. Univ. Grads., Detroit, 1977; scholar, advisor Pub. Affairs TV, Inc., N.Y.C., 1991; bd. dirs. Arab Sociol. Assn., Tunis, Tunisia, 1996-97, Palestinian Am. Rsch. Ctr., 2003—; bd. govs. Am. Rsch. Ctr. in Egypt, N.Y.C., 1991-97; mem. adv. bd. Arab World and Islamic Resources, Berkeley, Calif., Census Info. Ctr., Washington, 2002—, Arab Am. Nat. Mus. and Cultural Ctr., Dearborn, Mich., 2002—, Ctr. for Arab Am. Studies, U. Mich., Dearborn, 2002—. Rsch. fellow Am. Rsch. Ctr., Cairo, 1972-73, Ford Found., 1969-70, U. Wis., 1963-64, Fulbright-Hayes, 1983-84, Inst. Advanced Study, Princeton, N.J., 1994-95; Rsch. grantee NEH, 1989-91, Islamic Civilization grant Ctr. for Internat. Exch. Scholars, 1984. Mem. Am. Polit. Sci. Assn., Middle East Studies Assn. N.Am. (bd. dirs. 1980-82, mem. ethics com. 1992-98), Am. Inst. Maghribi Studies (bd. dirs. 1985-88). Avocations: chess, travel. Office: Kans State U Waters Hall Manhattan KS 66506-4030 Fax: 785-532-2339. E-mail: suleiman@ksu.edu.

SULKIN, HOWARD ALLEN, college president; b. Detroit, Aug. 19, 1941; s. Lewis and Vivian P. (Mandel) S.; m. Constance Annette Adler, Aug. 4, 1963; children— Seth R., Randall K. PhB, Wayne State U., 1963; MBA, U. Chgo., 1965, PhD, 1969; LHD (hon.), De Paul U., 1990. Dir. program rsch., indsl. rels. ctr. U. Chgo., 1964-72; dean Sch. for New Learning, De Paul U., Chgo., 1972-77; v.p. De Paul U., Chgo., 1977-84; pres. Spertus Inst. Jewish Studies, Chgo., 1984—. St. Paul's vis. prof. Rikkyo U., Tokyo, 1970—; cons., evaluator North Central Assn., Chgo., 1975—. Contbr. articles to profl. jours. Sec.-treas. Grant Park Cultural and Ednl. Cmty., Chgo., 1984—; bd. dirs. Chgo. Sinai Congregation, 1972—, pres., 1980-83; bd. dirs. S.E. Chgo. Commn., 1980—, United Way, 1984—, Crusade of Mercy United Way, 1990—; bd. dirs., chmn. Parliament of World's Religions, 1989—. Mem. The Standard Club, Tavern Club. Office: Spertus Inst of Jewish Studies 618 S Michigan Ave Chicago IL 60605-1901

SULLEBARGER, JOHN THOMPSON, internist, cardiologist, educator; b. Plainfield, N.J., May 2, 1957; s. Franklyn Jackson and Joanne Abbott (Aspinall) S.; m. Lorrie Jeanne Miller, June 14, 1980; children: Jeffrey Franklyn, Melissa Jeanne. Student, U. Mainz, 1977; AB, Dartmouth Coll., 1979; MD, Johns Hopkins U., 1983. Intern U. Rochester, N.Y., 1983-84, resident in medicine, 1984-86, fellow in cardiology, 1986-89, from sr. instr. to asst. prof., 1989-92; asst. prof. U. South Fla., Tampa, 1992-96, assoc. prof., 1997-99; dir. CCU Tampa Gen. Hosp., 1997—; dir. interventional cardiology Fla. Cardiovascular Inst., 1999—. Dir. Cardiac Catheterization Lab. James Haley VA Hosp., Tampa, 1992—99; dir. interventional cardiology U. South Fla., 1994—99; attending physician Strong Meml. Hosp., Rochester, 1989—92. Author: (with others) book chapters; contrb. articles to profl. jours. Chmn. Bd. Christian Svc., 1st Bapt. Ch., Rochester, 1991-92. Fellow ACP, 1992, Am. Coll. of Cardiology, 1991, Counc. on Clin. Cardiology of Am. Heart Assn., 1991, N.Y. Cardiological Soc., 1992. Fellow ACP, Soc. Cardiac Angiography and Interventions, Am. Coll. Cardiology, N.Y. Cardiol. Soc.; mem. Am. Heart Assn. (fellow coun. on clin. cardiology). Avocation: music. Office: 508 S Habana Ave Ste 340 Tampa FL 33609-4191

SULLENBERGER, ARA BROOCKS, mathematics educator; b. Amarillo, Tex., Jan. 3, 1933; d. Carl Clarence and Ara Frances (Broocks) Cox; m. Hal Joseph Sullenberger, Nov. 2, 1952; children: Hal Joseph Jr., Ara Broocks Sullenberger Switzer. Student, Randolph-Macon Woman's Coll., 1951—52, So. Meth. U., 1952, U. Tex., Arlington, 1953, Amarillo Coll., 1953—54; BA in Math., Tex. Tech. U., 1955, MA, 1958; postgrad., Tex. Christian U., 1963—67, U. N. Tex., 1969—80, Tarrant County Coll., Fort Worth, Tex., 1972—83. Cert. tchr., Tex. Math. tchr. Tom S. Lubbock (Tex.) High Sch., 1955-56; instr. math. Tex. Tech U., Lubbock, 1956-63; teaching fellow math. Tex. Christian U., Ft. Worth, 1963-64; chmn. dept. math. Ft. Worth Country Day Sch., 1964-67; instr. math. Tarrant County Coll.-South, Ft. Worth, 1967-70, asst. prof. math., 1970-74, assoc. prof. math., 1974-95; prof. emeritus, 1995—; ret., 1995. Cons. Project Change, Ft. Worth, 1967-68; math. scis. advisor Coll. Bd., Princeton, N.J., 1979-83; math. book reviewer for various pub. cos. including Prentice-Hall, McGraw Hill, D.C. Heath, Prindle, Weber & Schmidt, MacMillan, Harcourt, Brace Jovanovich, West, Worth, Saunders, Wadsworth; adj. prof. math. Tex. Christian U., fall 1996. Contbr. article, book revs. to profl. publs.; author book supplement to Intermediate Algebra, 1990. Active Jr. League, Ft. Worth, 1954—73, sustaining mem., 1973—; editor newsletter Crestwood Assn., Ft. Worth, 1984, 1986, 1991, membership sec., 1985, 1990—91, 1995, 1999, pres., 1988—89, 1998—99, crime patrol capt., 1993, 2000—01, v.p., 1993, treas., 1987, 1996, 2003, sec., 1997—98, crime patrol sec., 1999, crime patrol sec.-treas., 2001—. Recipient award for excellence in teaching Gen. Dynamics, 1968. Mem. Math. Assn. Am. (life), Nat. Coun. Tchrs. Math. (life), Am. Math. Assn. Two-Yr. Colls. (life), Tex. Math. Assn. Two-Yr. Colls. (charter, v.p. 1997-99), Tex. Jr. Coll. Tchrs. Assn., Ft. Worth League Neighborhood Assn. (v.p. 1999-2000), Pi Beta Phi. Republican. Episcopalian. Avocations: grandchildren, reading, pets, walking, writing. Home: 600 Eastwood Ave Fort Worth TX 76107-1020 E-mail: halandara@aol.com.

SULLENDER, JOY SHARON, elementary school educator; b. Bloomington, Ind., Apr. 9, 1932; d. Fred Laymond and Edith (Parrish) Medaris. BS, Ind. U., 1959, MS, 1965; postgrad., Ind. U./Purdue U., Indpls., 1991. Cert. tchr. elem. edn. 1-8. Tchr. Monroe Sch., Salem, Ind., 1952-55, Pekin (Ind.) Sch., 1955-61, Highland Park (Ill.) Sch., 1961-62, George Julian Sch. #57, Indpls., 1962—. Mem. prin.'s adv. coun. Indpls. Pub. Schs., 1985-95, supts. adv. coun., 1982-90; state mentor student tchrs., 1969—. Author col.: Let's Be Informed, 1993-95. Class sponsor Best Friends, Indpls., 1990—; vol. Toys for Foster Children, Indpls., 1991—; workshop presenter Alpha Epsilon State, Anderson, South Bend, 1994, 95. NSF grantee, 1971. Mem. PTA (tchr. rep. 1993-95), Ind. Sch. Women's Club (v.p. 1989-91, pres. 1992-94), Delta Kappa Gamma (pres. 1978-80, state com. 1989—, state corr. sec. 1997-99). Office: George Julian School 5435 E Washington St Indianapolis IN 46219-6411 Home: 1310 N Bazil Ave Indianapolis IN 46219-4244

SULLIVAN, CHRISTINE ANNE, secondary school educator; b. Albany, N.Y., June 18, 1956; d. Francis James and Geraldine (Patterson) S. BA summa cum laude, Albertus Magnus Coll., New Haven, Conn., 1978; MS, Ctrl. Conn. State U., New Britain, 1989. Cert. profl. educator Conn., tchr. N.Y. Tchr. Spanish Sacred Heart Acad., Hamden, Conn., 1978—79; adminstrv. asst. Julio Espada, N.Y.C., 1982—83; tchr. Spanish St. Mary's H.S., New Haven, 1983—90; fgn. and internat. rsch./reference asst. Yale U. Law Sch., New Haven, 1990—93; tchr. Spanish Notre Dame H.S., Fairfield, Conn., 1993; tchr. ESL New Haven, 1993—94; tchr. Spanish Jonathan Law H.S., Milford, Conn., 1994—. Adj. prof. Spanish U. Bridgeport (Conn.), 1993—94; dir. religious edn. St. Lawrence Parish, West Haven, Conn., 1985—92. Recipient Honor scholarships, Ctrl. Conn. State U., 1987—88; grantee St. Elizabeth Seton grant, Diocese of Hartford, 1987, 1988, 1989. Mem.: Am. Assn. Tchrs. Spanish and Portuguese (dir. adv. bd. state level 1989—90), Theodore Roosevelt Assn., Sigma Delta Pi. Roman Catholic. Avocations: travel, gardening, Russian history and culture. Home: 52 Richmond Ave West Haven CT 06516 Office: Jonathan Law High Sc 20 Lansdale Ave Milford CT 06460

SULLIVAN, CLAIRE FERGUSON, retired marketing educator; b. Pittsburg, Tex., Sept. 28, 1937; d. Almon Lafayette and Mabel Clara (Williams) Potter; m. Richard Wayne Ferguson, Jan. 31, 1959 (div. Jan. 1980); 1 child, Mark Jeffrey Ferguson; m. David Edward Sullivan, Nov. 2, 1984 BBA, U.

Tex., 1958, MBA, 1961; PhD, U. North Tex., 1973; grad., Harvard Inst. Ednl. Mgmt., 1991. Instr. So. Meth. U., Dallas, 1965-70; asst. prof. U. Utah, Salt Lake City, 1972-74; assoc. prof. U. Ark., Little Rock, 1974-77, U. Tex., Arlington, 1977-80, Ill. State U., Normal, 1980-84; prof., chmn. mktg. Bentley Coll., Waltham, Mass., 1984-89; dean sch. bus. Met. State Coll. Denver, 1989-92, prof. mktg., 1992-97; ret., 1997. Cons. Denver Partnership, 1989-90, Gen. Tel. Co., Irving, Tex., 1983, McKnight Pub. Co., Bloomington, Ill., 1983, dental practitioner, Bloomington, 1982-83, Olympic Fed., Berwyn, Ill., 1982, Denver Partnership Econ. Devel. Adv. Coun., 1989-91; mem. African-Am. Leadership Inst. Gov. Bd. Contbr. mktg. articles to profl. jours. Direct Mktg. Inst. fellow, 1981; Ill. State U. rsch. grantee, 1981-83 Mem. Am. Mktg. Assn. (faculty fellow 1984-85), Beta Gamma Sigma. Republican. Presbyterian. Home: 1502 Canterbury Dr Salt Lake City UT 84108-2833

SULLIVAN, COLLEEN ANNE, physician, educator; b. Lucknow, India, Feb. 11, 1937; came to U.S., 1961; d. Douglas George and Nancy Irene (MacLeod) S.; m. Alexander Walter Gotta, July 17, 1965; 1 child, Nancy Colleen. MB, ChB, U. St. Andrews, Scotland, 1961. Diplomate Am. Bd. Anesthesiology, Am. Coll. Anesthesiologists. Rotating intern Nassau Hosp. (now Winthrop U. Hosp.), Mineola, N.Y., 1961-62; clin. instr. Cornell U., N.Y.C., 1962-64; resident in anesthesiology N.Y. Hosp./Cornell U., 1962-64; fellow in anesthesiology Meml. Sloan-Kettering Cancer Ctr., N.Y.C., 1964-67, asst. prof. Cornell U. Med. Coll., 1978-79; assoc. dir. anesthesia St. Mary's Hosp.-Cath. Med. Ctr., Bklyn., 1968-78; clin. assoc. prof. SUNY, Bklyn., 1979-90, clin. dir. anesthesia, 1990-93, clin. prof. anesthesiology, 1990-97. Clin. dir. anesthesia Kings County Hosp., Bklyn., 1983-90, med. dir. ambulatory surg. unit, 1993-97. Author numerous chpt. in anesthesiology textbooks; contbr. articles to profl. jours. Mem. N.Y. State Soc. Anesthesiologists (mem. ho. of dels. 1983-97, asst. editor Sphere 1990-95, mem. com. sci. program 1990-97), Woman's Club of Great Neck (bd. dirs. 2003). Republican. Roman Catholic. Avocations: reading, cooking.

SULLIVAN, CORNELIUS WAYNE, marine biology educator, university research foundation administrator, government agency administrator; b. Pitts., June 11, 1943; s. John Wayne and Hilda Sullivan; m. Jill Hajjar, Oct. 28, 1966; children: Shane, Preston, Chelsea. BS in Biochemistry, Pa. State U., 1965, MS in Microbiology, 1967; PhD in Marine Biology, U. Calif., San Diego, 1971. Postdoctoral fellow Scripps Inst. Oceanography, La Jolla, Calif., 1971-74; asst. prof. marine biology U. So. Calif., L.A., 1974-80, assoc. prof., 1980-85, prof., 1985—, dir. marine biology sect., 1982-91; dir. Hancock Inst. Marine Studies, L.A., 1991-93; dir. Office of Polar Programs Nat. Sci. Found., Washington, 1993-97. Dir. U.S. Antarctic Program, 1993-97; vice provost rsch. U. So. Calif., 1997—; vis. prof. U. Colo., Boulder, 1981-82, MIT, Cambridge, 1981-82, U.S. Army Cold Regions Rsch. & Engring. Lab., Hanover, 1989, Goddard Space Flight Ctr., Greenbelt, Md., 1990; field team leader Sea Ice Microbial Communities Studies, McMurdo Sound, Antarctica, 1980-86; chief scientist/cruise coord. Antarctic Marine Ecosystem Rsch. at the Ice Edge Zone Project, Weddell Sea, 1983, 86, 88; mem. BIOMASS Working Party on Pack-Ice Zone Studies, 1983-86, ecol. rsch. rev. bd. Dept. Navy, 1982-85; So. Ocean Ecology Group Specialist Sci. Com. on Antarctic Rsch.; chmn. SCOR working group 86 "Sea Ice Ecology" sci. com. on oceanic rsch.; mem. polar rsch. bd. NAS, 1983-86; chmn. com. to evaluate polar rsch. platforms Nat. Rsch. Coun., 1985-88; mem. dir. policy group NSF, 1993-97; bd. dirs., mem. coun. govt. rels. Alfred E. Mann Inst. Biomed. Engring., Washington. Patent in Heat Sensitive Bacterial Alkaline Phosphatase; mem. editl. bd. Jour. Microbiol. Methods, 1982-85, Polar Biology, 1987-98; contbr. over 150 articles to profl. jours. Head of delegation Coun. Mgrs. of Nat. Antarctic Programs, New Zealand, Italy, U.K., 1993-97; mem. consultative meetings U.S. Delegation Antarctic Treaty, 1993-97. Fellow USPHS, 1969-71; recipient Antarctic Svc. medal of U.S., NSF, 1981. Fellow: Calif. Coun. Sci. Tech. (mem. coun.); mem.: AAAS. Office: Univ So Calif University Park Office of the Provost 203 Administration Blgd Los Angeles CA 90089-0001 E-mail: csulliva@usc.edu.

SULLIVAN, DOLORES P. writer, former educator; b. Punxsutawney, Pa., Mar. 16, 1925; AB, Grove City Coll., 1945; postgrad., Columbia U., 1947-49, Sorbonne U., Paris, 1949; MA, Kent State U., 1973. Tchr. Sharpsville Pa. High Sch., 1945-53; advt. copywriter Duane Jones Co., N.Y.C., 1952; mem. editorial staff Winston Pub. Co., Phila., 1953; tchr. Boardman High Sch., Youngstown, Ohio, 1969-92. Author: The History of the Youngstown Vindicator, 1973, William Holmes McGuffey: Schoolmaster to the Nation, 1994, Ten Guidelines for Successful Parenting, 2003; contbr. articles to profl. jours. Home and Office: 204 Forest Park Dr Youngstown OH 44512-1449

SULLIVAN, EDWARD J. fine arts educator; b. N.Y.C., Oct. 26, 1949; BA in Fine Arts and Spanish and Portuguese, NYU, 1971, MA in Spanish and Portuguese, 1972, MA in Fine Arts, 1975, PhD in Fine Arts, 1979. Prof., chmn. fine arts NYU, N.Y.C., 1979—2003. Mem. adv. com. El Museo del Barrio; mem. exhbn. com. Museo de Arte Contemporaneo de Monterrey, Mexico; mem. hon. com. Fundacion Ludwig de Cuba; bd. mem. Mexican Cultural Inst. N.Y. Author: Baroque Painting in Madrid, 1986, Julio Larraz, 1989, Catalogue of the Collection, 1995, Tomas Sanchez, 2003; co-author: Women in Mexico, Modern and Contemporary Art of the Dominican Republic; editor: Latin American Art of the Twentieth Century, 1996, Brazil: Body and Soul, 2001; contbg. editor: Art Nexus. Recipient Victoria Ocampo award, Escuela de Administracion Cultural, Buenos Aires, 1997; fellow, John Simon Guggenheim Meml. Found., 2003, Samuel H. Kress Found., Am. Coun. Learned Socs., Am. Philos. Soc., Program for Cultural Cooperation Between the Ministry of Culture of Spain and N.Am. Univs., Am. Soc. for Hispanic Art Hist. Studies. Mem.: Hispanic Soc. Am. (hon. assoc.), Coll. Art Assn. (bd. dirs.). Office: NYU 100 Washington Sq North New York NY 10003*

SULLIVAN, FAITH HELEN, secondary education educator, writer; b. Pipestone, Minn., Oct. 1, 1933; d. Edgar William Scheid and Helen Florence (Howes) Page; m. Daniel Joseph Sullivan, Oct. 22, 1935; children: Maggie, Ben, Kate. BS, Mankato (Minn.) State U., 1956. English and history tchr., Cambridge, Minn., Evanston, Wyo., Minn., 1956—. Vis. instr. fiction writing Southwest State U., Marshall, Minn.; vis. instr. Split Rock Arts Program, Duluth, Minn., 1998; instr. Loft Literary Ctr., Mpls., 2002-03. Author: Repent, Lanny Merkel, 1981, Watchdog, 1982, Mrs. Demming and The Mythical Beast, 1985, The Cape Ann, 1988, The Empress of One, 1996, What A Woman Must Do, 2000. Mem.: PEN.

SULLIVAN, F(RANK) VICTOR, university administrator, retired educator; b. Wichita, Kans., Mar. 5, 1931; s. Frank Townsend and Olive Mae (Kinseley) S.; m. Mary-Kate Larson, June 2, 1956; children: Mark Kenneth, Olive Louise. BS, Friends U., 1953; MA, U. No. Colo., 1957; EdD, U. Ill., 1964. Tchr. indsl. arts Minneha Pub. Schs., Wichita, 1953-56; instr. indsl. arts Friends U., Wichita, 1956-60; instr. U. Ill. H.S., 1960-63; rsch. assoc. Illini Blind Project, U. Ill., 1963-64; asst. prof. Sch. Tech., Pittsburg (Kans.) State U., 1964-66; assoc. prof. Pittsburg (Kans.) State U., 1966-68; prof. Pittsburg (Kans.) State U., 1968-96, chair dept. tech. studies, 1978-85, interim dean Sch. Tech. and Applied Sci., 1980-82, dean Sch. Tech. and Applied Sci., 1985-96, prof. and dean emeritus, 1996—. Bd. dirs. Am. Inst. Design and Drafting, Bartlesville, Okla., Kans. Tech. Enterprise Corp., Topeka. Exec. dir. Business & Technology Inst. & Ctr. for Design, Develop. & Production, Pittsburgh State U., 1997-98. Bd. trustees Kans. chpt. Nature Conservancy, 1998—. Mem. ESEA (dir./author secondary exploration of tech. Title II project 1971-74, dir. curriculum from contemporary industry summer 1967), Am. Soc. for Engring. Edn. Home: 510 Thomas St Pittsburg KS 66762-6526

SULLIVAN, GREGORY PAUL, secondary education educator; b. Buffalo, June 13, 1957; s. Jerome Patrick and Gloria Mae (Struble) S.; m. Sarah Davis Houston, May 17, 1986; children: Patrick Benjamin, Ryan Christopher. BS in Indsl. Edn., State U. Coll., Oswego, N.Y., 1979; MA in Indsl. Edn., Ball State U., 1983. postgrad. collegiate profl. teaching cert. Grad. asst. mfg. lab. Ball State U., Muncie, Ind., 1982-83; tchr. tech. edn. John Rolfe Mid. Sch., Richmond, Va., 1979-86, Horton Mid. Sch., Pittsboro, N.C., 1986-88, Dunbar Mid. Sch., Lynchburg, Va., 1988-93; supr. career-tech. programs Lynchburg City Schs., 1993—. Coord./judge regional and nat. mfg. contest Tech. Edn. and Collegiate Assn., 1988—; coord. Eisenhower Grant, 1991-92. Asst. dir. Camp Minnehaha, Minnehaha Springs, W.Va., 1979-88. Named Va. Tchr. of Yr., Va. Dept. Edn., 1993. Mem. Soc. Mfg. Engrs. (internat. edn. com. career guidance 1984, 91), Internat. Tech. Edn. Assn. (mem. editl. rev. bd. The Tech. Tchr., delphi com. critical issues and concerns tech. edn. 1992), Coun. Tech. Tchr. Edn. (student svcs. com. 1991), Va. Tech. Edn. Assn. (v.p. 1997, 98), Va. Coun. Tech. Edn. Suprs. (pres. 1997), Phi Delta Kappa, Epsilon Pi Tau, Kappa Delta Pi. Avocations: intramural sports, golf, tennis, running. Home: 724 Sanhill Dr Lynchburg VA 24502-4924 Office: Lynchburg City Schs 10th and Court Sts PO Box 1599 Lynchburg VA 24505-1599

SULLIVAN, J. BRYAN, secondary education educator; b. Worcester, Mass., Sept. 7, 1941; s. William and Sylvia (Sihlman) S.; m. Joan Sundin, Aug. 21, 1965; children: Jeffrey Robert, Kristen Marie. BS in Edn., State Coll. at Worcester, 1965, MEd, 1968. Tchr. math. Hudson (Mass.) Pub. Schs., 1965—. Head math. dept. Hudson Pub. Schs., 1969-75, math. coord., 1975-89. Named to Mass. Math. Hall of Fame, 2002; recipient Spl. Tchrs. are Recognized award, Cornell U., 1994; Tandy scholar, 1993, NSF fellow, U. Del., 1985. Mem.: Worcester County Math. League (pres. 1976, sec. 1993—97), Nat. Coun. Suprs. of Math. (nominations com. 1994, 1995), Mass. Assn. Math. League (pres., pub. rels. chmn.), Nat. Coun. Tchrs. of Math. (conf. chairperson 1988, spkr. various regional, state and nat. confs., rep. 1998—, conf. chairperson 2002), Am. Regions Math. League (exec. bd. 1976—, PSU site dir. 1998—, Founder's award 1993), Assn. Tchrs. of Math. in Mass. (pres. 1985—87, Presdl. award 1983). Democrat. Roman Catholic. Avocations: golf, travel, reading, gardening. Home: 17 Woodside Dr Sterling MA 01564-1416 Office: Hudson H S 69 Brigham St Hudson MA 01749-2785 E-mail: jbsully@earthlink.net.

SULLIVAN, JAMES F. physicist, educator; b. Cin., Mar. 7, 1943; s. James E. and Alma L. (Lienesch) S.; m. Sylvia J. Kasselmann, Aug. 16, 1969; 1 child, Robert L. BS, Xavier U., 1965, MS, 1969. Instr. physics Brebeuf Prep. Sch., Indpls., 1965-67, OMI Coll. Applied Sci., U. Cin., 1968-71, asst. prof. physics, 1971-77, assoc. prof. physics, 1977-88, prof. physics, 1988—; dept. head math., physics, computing tech. U. Cin. OMI Coll. of Applied Sci., 2002. Summer faculty researcher Solar Energy Rsch. Inst., Golden, Colo., 1980; mem. high sch. evaluation team N. Ctrl. Assn., Cin., 1983-85; vis. prof. Arcada Polytechnic Inst., Finland, (Jan-May, 2001). Author: Technical Physics, 1988; Co-author: Laboratory Manual for General Physics, 1973, 83, 90, 92, Physics for Technology Laboratory Manual, 1995, 97. Organizer of events St. Xavier H.S. Alumni, Cin., 1983—; vol. examiner Am. Radio Relay League for U.S. Fed. Comm. Commn., Newington, Conn., 1984—; judge physics category Ohio State Sci. Fair, Delaware, Ohio, 1986—; chief negotiator faculty and librs. U. Cin., 1995. Received John B. Hart award (disting. svc. to Southern Ohio sect. of Am. Assn. of Physics Tchrs.), 2001; named Faculty Mem. of Yr., Gamma Alpha chpt. Tau Alpha Phi, 1983. Fellow Ohio Acad. Sci.; mem. AAUP (v.p. U. Cin. chpt. 1994-96), Am. Assn. Physics Tchrs. (founder, past pres., assoc. sec. So. Ohio sect. 1993—, com. on instrnl. media 1994-98, chief organizer and presenter Fundamentals of Radio workshop Toronto 1985, Columbus, Ohio 1986, Bozeman, Mont. 1987, Orono, Maine 1992, Boise, Idaho 1993, South Bend, Ind. 1994, College Park, Md. 1996, Denver, 1997, com. on metric measurements, 2000-03), Ohio Valley Amateur Radio Assn. (pres. 1997—), Am. Soc. Engring. Edn. Achievements include supervising successful attempt of OMI Coll. Applied Sci. contact of shuttle Challenger during STS-51F mission, 1985. Office: Univ Cin 2220 Victory Pkwy Cincinnati OH 45206-2822

SULLIVAN, KATHLEEN ANN, secondary education educator; b. Palmerton, Pa., Feb. 15, 1946; d. Henry Aloysius and Elizabeth Rose (Pennell) S. AAS, Harriman (N.Y.) Coll., 1966; student, Columbia U., N.Y.C., 1966-69; BS, St. Peter's Coll., Jersey City, 1971. Cert. English educator, N.J. Tchr. 6th grade Immaculate Conception, Bronx, N.Y., 1965-67, tchr. 7th grade, 1967-68; tchr. 8th grade St. Fortunata, Bklyn., 1968-69; tchr. 7th grade St. Augustine, Union City, N.J., 1969-71, tchr. 8th grade, 1971—, vice prin., 1971—. Mem. adv. bd. St. Augustine CYO, Union City, N.J., 1971—, Coll. St. Elizabeth, Morristown, N.J., 1986-92; trustee Weehawken (N.J.) Libr. Bd., 1976-2000. Mem. Natl. Cath. Edn. Assn., Nat. Coun. Tchrs. Math., Assn. Tchrs. Math. N.J. Home: 1400 70th St Apt 1 North Bergen NJ 07047 Office: St Augustine School 3920 New York Ave Union City NJ 07087-4887

SULLIVAN, KATHLEEN M. SKARO, secondary education educator; b. New Ulm, Minn., Mar. 11, 1946; d. Stanford William and Donna Elaine (Arneson) Skaro; m. Nathan Lee Sullivan, Apr. 18, 1965 (div. Dec. 1982); children: Rachel Anne, Rebekah Jean, Scott Michael, Matthew James. BS in English, Mankato State U., 1981, BS in Spanish, 1983, BS in French, 1990, MS in English, 2000. Cert. tchr., Minn. Inventory control clk. 3M Co., New Ulm, 1968-70; distbn. clk. Kraft Foods, New Ulm, 1971-74; tchr. New Ulm Sch. Dist., 1981-83; tchr., coach Gibbon (Minn.) Sch. Dist., 1984-85, Le Sueur (Minn.) Sch. Dist., 1985-86, Sebeka (Minn.) Sch. Dist., 1986-87; tchr. Dassel-Cokato (Minn.) Sch. Dist., 1987; tchr., coach Detroit Lakes (Minn.) Sch. Dist., 1988—95, Blue Earth Area H.S., 1995—2000, Lacqui Parle Valley H.S., 2000—02, Waubun Sch., 2002—. Writer and editor Office of Grants, Mankato (Minn.) State Univ., 1983-84. Mem. Minn. Coun. Teaching Fgn. Langs., Communication and Theater Assn. Minn., Alpha Delta Kappa, Alpha Mu Gamma, Phi Kappa Phi. Avocations: travel, reading, gardening, writing. Office: 1013 Third St Waubun MN 56589

SULLIVAN, KATHRYN ANN, librarian, educator; b. Elmhurst, Ill., Jan. 22, 1954; d. Joseph Terrence and Rose Marie (Wright) S. Student, Triton Jr. Coll., 1972-73; BA, No. Ill. U., 1975, MLS, 1977; D of Sci. in Info. Sci., Nova U., 1991. Chief periodicals clk. No. Ill. U., Dekalb, 1976-77; periodicals librarian West Chgo. (Ill.) Pub. Library, 1977-78, Winona (Minn.) State U., 1978-99, distance learning libr., 2000—. Contbr. articles and short stories to profl. publs. Grantee Winona State U., 1986, 88, 92, 94. Mem.: ALA, Electronically Published Internet Connections, Minn. Libr. Assn. Avocation: writing. Home: 670 Winona St Winona MN 55987-3353

SULLIVAN, LORETTA ROSEANN, elementary education educator; b. Pitts., Jan. 24, 1949; d. Stephen Francis and Loretta (Walz) S. BA, Marymount Coll., Tarrytown, N.Y., 1970; MEd, Duquesne U., 1972. Cert. psychology, elem. edn. and elem. sch. guidance tchr., Pa. Tchr. Colfax Sch., Pitts., 1970—, primary instrnl. team leader, 1997—. Project dir. Common Knowledge, 1997—; math. resource person Pitts. Free Learning Environ. Program, 1972-74; mem. leadership team Reading First, 2002—. Mem. ednl. task force Pitts. Opera, 2000; reading coach Literacy Plus, 2001-03; mem. dist. leadership team Reading First, 2003. Frick Commn. fellow, Pitts., 1972; Tri-State area mini-grantee U. Pitts., 1973; mini-grantee Allegheny Conf. on Community Devel., Pitts., 1980-90; named one of Outstanding Elem. Tchrs. Am., 1974; Pitts. Coun. on Pub. Edn. grantee, 1999. Office: Colfax Sch 2332 Beechwood Blvd Pittsburgh PA 15217-1818

SULLIVAN, LYNN DAVIS, special education educator; b. San Benito, Tex., Sept. 27, 1952; d. Clark Gilbert and Joan Ruth (Cox) Davis; m. Mark W. Sullivan, Mar. 16, 1985. BA, Tex. A&I U., 1973; MEd, Tex. Woman's U., 1982. Cert. elem. tchr., early childhood, handicapped, lang. and learning disabilities; cert. supr. all levels. Ct. liaison Tex. Dept. Human Resources, Fort Worth; specialist spl. edn. Edn. Svc. Ctr., Reg. XI, Fort Worth. Profl. staff coord. Tarrant County Parents United; mem. 1st Tex. Coun. of Camp Fire (Blue Ribbon Vol. award, 1993), Campaign for Children, Child Care Tng. Network, 1990-95; mem. Cmty. Adv. Com. United Cerebral Palsy of Tarrant County, 1994-95. Mem. Assn. Tex. Profl. Educators (local unit pres. 1990-91), Coun. Exceptional Children (state organizing com. divsn. early childhood, sec. Tex. divsn. for early childhood 1987-88, pres. 1994—). Home: 3508 Western Ave Fort Worth TX 76107-6238

SULLIVAN, MARISSA M. elementary school educator; b. Butte, Mont., Nov. 04; d. Walter M. and Gerry T. (Sullivan) S. BA in Biology and Sociology, Gonzaga U., 1984, MA, 1993. Cert. tchr., Wash. 3d grade tchr. Ea. Hoffsetter Sch., Colville, Wash., 1986-87; tchr. grade 2-3 Bemiss, Spokane, 1987-88; kindergarten tchr. Adam Sch., Spokane, Wash., 1988-89; 4th grade tchr. Arlington Elem. Sch., Spokane, Wash., 1989-90, 3d grade tchr., 1990-92, 2d grade tchr., 1992-94, Whitman Elem. Sch., Spokane, 1994—97; kindergarten tchr. Roosevelt Sch., Spokane, 1997-2001, 2003—04. Mem. Dist. 81 Assessment Adv. Com., Spokane, 1992-93, Report Card Rev. Com., Spokane, 1993-94; spkr. N.W. Math. Conf., Victoria, B.C., 1994, Seattle, 1993; mem. site coun. PTO, 2002-03, dept. chmn., prin. selection com., 2002-03. Site coun. rep. Roosevelt Parent Tchr. Orgn. Mem. Nat. Tchrs. Math. Avocations: rubber stamp art, traveling.

SULLIVAN, MARK WHITE, art history educator; b. Lawrence, Mass., Oct. 19, 1949; s. Philip Burdette and Frances P. (White) S.; 1 child, James. BA, Coll. of the Holy Cross, Worcester, Mass., 1971; MA, Bryn Mawr Coll., 1973, PhD, 1981. Instr. Rutgers U., Camden, N.J., 1984, Rosemont (Pa.) Coll., 1985-87; prof. art history Villanova (Pa.) U., 1985—. Author: The Hudson River School: An Annotated Bibliography, 1991. Mem. AAUP (chpt. treas. 1993-95), Assn. for Historians Am. Art, Coll. Art Assn. Avocations: book and art collecting, hiking. Home: 209 Harrogate Rd Wynnewood PA 19096-3129 Office: Villanova Univ Villanova PA 19085 E-mail: mark.sullivan@villanova.edu.

SULLIVAN, MARY JANE, elementary school educator; b. Mason City, Iowa, Nov. 23, 1947; d. Lawrence Wesly and Elizabeth Barbara (Steinbach) Kohler; m. Mark Jay Sullivan, June 26, 1993. BS, Mankato (Minn.) State U., 1970; MS, Iowa State U., 1982. Cert. tchr. K-9, coach K-12, Iowa. Tchr. 5th grade Keokuk (Iowa) Cmty. Sch., 1970-77, West Bend (Iowa) Cmty. Sch., 1977-80; tchr. 6th grade North Mahaska Cmty. Sch., New Sharon, Iowa, 1980—. Author: (poetry teaching book) Poetry Pals, 1982. Mem. Regional telecomms. Coun., Des Moines, 1994—; mem. Iowa Pub. TV, Des Moines, Iowa Heritage Assn., Des Moines. Recipient Excellence in Elem. Sci. award Iowa Acad. Sci., 1998; named County Sci. Tchr. of Yr., Mahaska County Conservation Bd., Oskaloosa, Iowa, 1992; sci. grantee Ctrl. Coll., Iowa Dept. Edn. Mem. NEA, ASCD, Iowa State Edn. Assn. (exec. bd. negotiations), Nat. Staff Devel. Coun. (mem. 1st acad.), Kappa Delta Pi, Phi Delta Kappa (v.p. 1990-91). Roman Catholic. Avocations: reading, cross stitch, walking, gardening. Office: N Mahaska Elem Sch 2163 135th St New Sharon IA 50207-8108

SULLIVAN, MARY JEAN, elementary school educator; b. Cambridge, Mass., May 13, 1956; d. Joseph Leo and Jean Marie (Isaac) S. BA, Flagler Coll., 1978; postgrad., U. No. Fla., 1980—, Fla. State U., 1992, Okla. State U., 1992, U. Fla., 1998, 99, Jacksonville U., 2002—. Cert. elem. educator, Fla. Tchr. grade 2 St. Agnes Sch., St. Augustine, Fla., 1978-79; tchr. grades 1 through 5 Evelyn Hamblen Elem. Sch., St. Augustine, 1979-91; tchr. grade 5 Osceola Elem. Sch., St. Augustine, 1991—, chair math./ sci. Adv. Sci. Club; chairperson, St. John's County Tchr. Edn. Coun., 1985—, SACS Evaluation Team, Duval County Schs., 1988, 89, 90; rep. tchr. edn. coun.; sch. improvement co-chair, 1994-95; trainer coll. intern students; mem. St. John's County Accomplished Practices Acad., 1995, 96; mem. Staff Devel. Coun. for St. John's County, 1997—; state facilitator Project WET; mem. Tchr. Evaluation Renewal Com.; amb. Jet Propulsion Lab., 1999—; amb. Jet Propulsion Ctr., 1999—. Developer tchr. edn. coun. tng. handbook for State of Fla. Active PTO, past pres.; active Cub Scouts Am.; coord. summer recreation Evelyn Hamblen Sch., St. Augustine, 1987—90; dir. tournament Pam Driskell Meml. Paddle Tennis Scholarship Fund, 1986, 1987, 1988, 1989; vol. United Way Olympic Torch Run, summer, 1996, World Golf Hall of Fame, 1998—, Liberty Mut. Legends of Golf, 1998—, First Tee, 2000, Fan Fest, 2000, 2001, Mark Brunell Charity Softball Game, Channel 7 Auction, Let Us Play, Family First, 1999—, 1st Family, 1999, 2000, Joel Smengee Found.; chmn. Gator Bowl Patch Event, 2002; past asst. program dir. Cathedral-Basilica Ch., United Child Care After Sch. Program, 1988—89; mem. Jacksonville Jaguars Booster Club, 1999—; most valuable people capt. Jacksonville Jaguars; escort Tournament Players Championship, 1993—, co-capt., 2001; chmn. spl. events. Liberty Mut. Legends of Golf, 2001. Grantee Fla. Coun. Elem. Edn., 1981-82, Summer Enhancement, 1988-89, Fla. Inst. Oceanography, 1994, St. John's County Horizon award mini-grantee, 1994, 96, 98, Fla. Assn. for Computer Edn., 1994, Fla. Humanities Coun., 1995, Project ARIES, summer 1998; recipient Human Rels. award State of Fla., 1992, NEWEST award, 1992, award Geography Summer Inst., 1992, FPL Horizon Grant award, 2003; named Kiwanis Tchr. of Month, 1993, Evelyn Hamblen Elem. Tchr. of the Yr., 1990, Osceola Elem. Tchr. of the Yr., 1996-97. Mem. NEA, NSTA, Fla. Tchg. Profession, Fla. Assn. Staff Devel. (planning com.), Fla. Geographic Alliance, Fla. Assn. Computer Edn., St. John's Educator Assn., Fla. Assn. for Sci. Tchrs., Solar Sys. Ambs., Jacksonville Jaguars Booster Club (historian, bd. dirs. 2000-02). Office: Osceola Elem Sch 1605 Osceola Elem Sch Rd Saint Augustine FL 32095

SULLIVAN, PATRICIA G. maternal, child and women's health nursing educator; b. Denver, June 26, 1948; d. Dale F. and Wilma (Fritz) Greb; m. Michael T. Sullivan, Sept. 10, 1971; children: Nicholas O., Matthew Alexander, Adam Michael. BS, Loretto Heights Coll., 1971; MS, U. Colo., 1976. Cert. bereavement svcs. counselor. Clin. instr. Loretto Hts. Coll., 1977-81; instr. pathophysiology U. Denver, summers 1983, 84; coord. women's health edn. Swedish Med. Ctr., Englewood, Colo., 1985-86; coord. childbirth edn. Med. Ctr. Hosp., Odessa, Tex., 1986-88; instr. nursing Midland (Tex.) Coll., 1990—; cons. Mosby's Med. Nursing & Allied Health Dictionary. Reviewer: Basic Nursing and Practice, 3d edit., 1995, Women's Health During The Childbearing Years, 2001. Counselor RTS Bereavement Svcs., 1996. Recipient medal for exceptional performance N.I.O.S.D., 2001. Mem. AWHONN, Tex. Nurses Assn., Tex. C.C. Tchrs. Assn., Assn. Reproductive Health Profls., Internat. Soc. Nurses in Genetics, Sigma Theta Tau. Home: 2803 Douglas Ave Midland TX 79701-3831 Office: Midland Coll 3600 N Garfield St # 216 Midland TX 79705-6329 E-mail: psull@midland.cc.tx., durangokid@earthlink.net.

SULLIVAN, ROBERT MARTIN, educational fundraiser; b. Holyoke, Mass., Feb. 12, 1953; s. James John and Emily Mae (Belzarini) S. AB, St. Anselm Coll., 1975; EdM, Harvard U., 1986. Fundraiser Nat. Multiple Sclerosis Soc., N.Y.C., 1976-77; asst. to v.p. devel. St. Anselm Coll., Manchester, N.H., 1977-81, dir. ann. fund, 1981-85, asst. to pres., 1985-91, dir. of devel., 1991—. Mem. Agy. Rels. and Allocations Com., Greater Manchester United Way, 1988—; mem. Common Cause, 1989—; campaign vol. N.H. Cath. Charities, Manchester, 1989-90. Mem. Nat. Soc. Fund Raising Execs., N.H. Coun. on Fund Raising, Am. Assn. Higher Edn., Coun. Advancement and Support of Edn., Rotary. Democrat. Roman Catholic. Office: St Anselm Coll 100 Saint Anselms Dr Manchester NH 03102-1308

SULLIVAN, ROMAINE BRUST, school system administrator; b. Phila., May 10, 1938; d. Raymond W. and Mary E. (Feeley) Brust; m. Francis J.M. Sullivan, mar. 4, 1967; children: Kevin M., Kathleen, M., Kenneth M. BA, Rosemont, 1960; MPH, U. Calif. Berkeley, 1965. Cert. learning handicapped educator, resource specialist, educator in English, Life Sci., Social Studies. Pub. health educator Md. Dept. Health, 1965-70; tchr. Prince Georges County Schs., Oxon Hill, Md., 1972-76; cons. Harcourt Brace Jovanovich Pub., San Francisco, 1980-81; court appointed spl. advocate Voices for Children, San Diego, 1984-86; tchr. Thomas Aquinas High Sch., San Marcos, Calif., 1981-82; dir., edn. therapist RBS Edn. Svcs., Del Mar, Calif., 1985-87; spl. day class tchr. Poway (Calif.) Unified Sch. Dist., 1987-90, resource specialist, 1990—. Counselor first aid merit badge Boy Scouts Am., Solana Beach, 1986-90; instr. first aid ARC, Escondido, Calif., 1988-91. Recipient USPH Traineeship Grant, 1964-65, Grad. Stipend San Diego State U. Foun., 1986-87. Mem. Orton Dyslexia Soc. (pres. San Diego br. 1987-88), Coun. for Exceptional Children. Democrat. Roman Catholic. Avocations: walking, running, reading, choir. Home: 13623 Boquita Dr Del Mar CA 92014-3407

SULLIVAN, SALLY ANNE, secondary education educator; b. Worcester, Mass., Mar. 10, 1947; d. Harold Roland and Anna Elaine (Emerson) Johnson; children: Michael S., Shawn H. BSE, Fitchburg State Coll., 1970, postgrad., Worcester State Coll., U. Ariz., U. Phoenix. Cert. secondary sch. tchr., Mass., Ariz. Tchr. history Hudson (Mass.) Cath. High Sch., 1970-71; tchr. English Hudson (Mass.) High Sch., 1976-78; tchr. English, Spanish, reading, history, writing Lake Havasu Sch. Dist. 1, Havasu City, Ariz., 1981-84; tchr. English, ESL, Spanish, writing Montachusett Regional Vocat. Tech. High Sch., Fitchburg, Mass., 1984—. Presenter writing process program Mt. Wachusett C.C. Conf., 1989, presenter integrating the writing process with Lit., chpt. 1, 25th Anniversary Conf., Hyannis, Mass., 1990; insvc. presenter Whole Lang. approach and establishing a writing ctr. in a classroom K-8, 1992; asst. dir. chpt. 1, 1988—, lead English tchr., English dept. liaison, former chpt. 1 coord. for jr. high level, 1981-84, dir. summer sch., 1993; chairperson reading dept., 1983-84; initiator of one of the first writing labs. in Mass. for chpt. 1 at the H.S. level; curriculum writer for English Lit., Multicultural Lit., Chpt. 1 Writing, Spanish I and II, applied com. and English Mechanics; summer sch. dir. Montachusett Regional Vocat. Tech., 1993. Recipient Horace Mann grant, 1988-89, for writing Integrating Literature and Mechanics with the Writing Process, citation for Excellence in Classroom Commonwealth Mass., 1991; named Outstanding Tchr. of Yr. Montachusett Regional Vocat.-Tech High Sch., 1991-92. Mem. NEA, Nat. Coun. Tchrs. English, Mass. Tchrs. Assn., Montachusett Regional Tchrs. Assn. (pres. elect 1989-90, pres. 1990-91). Home: PO Box 844 Westminster MA 01473-0844 Office: Montachusett Regional Vocat Tech High Sch 1050 Westminster St Fitchburg MA 01420-4649

SULLIVAN, SARAH LOUISE, management and technology consultant; b. Wilmington, Del., Sept. 24, 1954; d. Frederick William III and Ruth (Swavely) S. BS, Bowling Green U., 1975; MS, Ill. Inst. Tech., 1986, PhD, 1990. Programmer Computer Sci. Corp., Langley AFB, Va., 1975-77; sr. systems programmer JPLRCC, Perrysburg, Ohio, 1977-80; sr. systems engr. Kraft Inc., Glenview, Ill., 1980-83; project leader Siemens Gammasonics, Des Plaines, Ill., 1983-85; sect. mgr. Zenith Electronics, Glenview, Ill., 1985; mem. tech. staff AT&T Bell Labs., Naperville, Ill., 1986-87; cons., trainer Sarah L. Sullivan & Assocs., Morton Grove, Ill., 1987-90; instr. Ill. Inst. Tech., Chgo., 1988; asst. prof. dept. computer sci. North Cen. Coll., Naperville, 1988-89, Ind.-Purdue U., Ft. Wayne, 1990-94; prin. engr. Boeing Info. Svcs., Dayton, Ohio, 1995-96, Rockwell Collins, Cedar Rapids, Iowa, 1996-97; with Motorola, Schaumburg, Ill., 1997-98, Sys. Assessment Re-Engring. & Assurance Help, Columbus, Ohio, 1999—. Presenter in field. Mem. IEEE, Assn. for Computing Machinery, Oasis Ctr. for Human Potential.

SULLIVAN, TERESA ANN, law and sociology educator, academic administrator; b. Kewanee, Ill., July 9, 1949; d. Gordon Hager and Mary Elizabeth (Finnegan) S.; m. H. Douglas Laycock, June 14, 1971; children: Joseph Peter, John Patrick. BA, Mich. State U., 1970; MA, U. Chgo., 1972, PhD, 1975. Asst. prof. sociology U. Tex., Austin, 1975-76, assoc. prof. sociology, 1981-87, dir. women's studies, 1985-87, prof. sociology, 1987—, prof. law, 1988—, assoc. dean grad. sch., 1989-90, 1992-95, chair dept. sociology, 1990-92, vice provost, 1994-95, v.p., grad. dean, 1995—2002; asst. prof. sociology U. Chgo., 1977-81; exec. vice-chancellor for acad. affairs U. Tex. System, 2002—. Pres. Southwestern Sociol. Assn., 1988-89; mem. faculty adv. bd. Hogg Found. Mental Health, 1989-92; mem. sociology panel NSF, 1983-85. Author: Marginal Workers Marginal Jobs, 1978; co-author: As We Forgive Our Debtors, 1989 (Silver Gavel 1990), Social Organization of Work, 1990, 2d edit. 1995; co-author: The Fragile Middle Class, 2000; contbr. articles and chpts. to profl. jours. Bd. dirs. Calvert Found., Chgo., 1978, CARA, Inc., Washington, 1985; mem. U.S. Census Bur. Adv. Com., 1989-95, chmn., 1991-92; mem. sociology panel NSF, 1983-85; trustee St. Michael's Acad., 1996-2001. Leadership Tex. 1994. Fellow AAAS (liaison to Population Assn. Am. 1989-91, chair sect. K 1996), Sociol. Rsch. Assn., Am. Sociol. Assn. (sec. 1995—, editor Rose Monograph Series 1988-92), Philos. Soc. Tex., Soc. Study of Social Problems (chair fin. com. 1986-87), Population Assn. Am. (bd. dirs. 1989-91, chair fin. com. 1990-91), Assn. Grad. Schs. (pres. 2001-2002). Roman Catholic. Avocations: volkssporting, sci. fiction. Office: U Tex System 601 Colorado Ste 305 Austin TX 78701

SULLIVAN, THOMAS PATRICK, academic administrator; b. Detroit, July 8, 1947; s. Walter James and Helen Rose (Polosky) S.; m. Barbara Jean Fournier, Aug. 9, 1968; children: Colleen, Brendan. BA in English, U. Dayton, 1969; M. Edn. and Adminstrn., Kent State U., 1971; postgrad., U. Mich., 1988. Tchr. Resurrection Elem. Sch., Dayton, Ohio, 1968-69; administr. residence hall Kent (Ohio) State U., 1969-71; program mgr. residence hall Ea. Mich. U., Ypsilanti, 1971-73, adminstrv. assoc., 1973-76, dir. housing, 1976-83; assoc. provost Wayne County Community Coll., Belleville, Mich., 1983-84, dir. budget and mgmt. devel. Detroit, 1984-85, sr. v.p. acad. affairs, acting provost, 1985-86, acting exec. dean Belleville, 1986-88, dir. budget and mgmt. devel. Detroit, 1988-89; pres. Cleary Univ., Ypsilanti, 1989—. Part-time instr. English and math. Schoolcraft Coll., Livonia, Mich., 1980-90. Home: 9835 Whisperwood Ln Brighton MI 48116-8859 Office: Cleary Univ 3601 Plymouth Rd Ann Arbor MI 48105-2659

SULLIVAN, TIMOTHY JACKSON, law educator, academic administrator; b. Ravenna, Ohio, Apr. 15, 1944; s. Ernest Tulio and Margaret Elizabeth (Caris) Sullivan; m. Anne Doubet Klare, Jan. 21, 1973. AB, Coll. William and Mary, 1966; JD, Harvard U., 1969; LLD (hon.), U. Aberdeen, Scotland, 1993. Asst. prof. law Coll. William and Mary, Williamsburg, Va., 1972—75, assoc. prof., 1975—78, prof., 1978—85, Bryan prof. law, dean, 1985—92, pres., 1992—; exec. asst. for policy Office of Gov. Charles S. Robb, Richmond, Va., 1982—85; atty. Freeman, Drapers' Co., London, 1992. Vis. prof. law U. Va., Charlottesville, 1981; exec. dir. Gov.'s Commn. on Va.'s Future, Richmond, 1982—84; vice-chmn. Gov.'s Commn. on Fed. Spending, Richmond, 1986; mem. Gov.'s Fellows Selection Com., 1985—90, Gov.'s Commn. on Sexual Assault and Substance Abuse on the Coll. Campus (chmn. enforcement subcom.), 1991—92; counsel Commn. on Future of Va.'s Jud. Sys., 1987—89; mem. Livery Drapers Co., 2003. Mem. Va. State Bd. Edn., Richmond, 1987—92; chair Gov.'s Task Force on Intercollegiate Athletics, 1992—93. Decorated Bronze Star; named Outstanding Virginian, Va. 4-H Found., 1999. Fellow: Va. Bar Fedn., Am. Bar Fedn.; mem.: ABA, Va. Bar Assn., Va. State Bar, Am. Arbitration Assn. (bd. dirs. 2000—), Cosmos Club, Univ. Club (N.Y.C., Washington), Bull and Bear Club, Omicron Delta Kappa, Phi Beta Kappa. Democrat. Avocations: wine, swimming, reading, golf. Home: Pres House Williamsburg VA 23185 Office: Coll William & Mary PO Box 8795 Williamsburg VA 23187-8795

SULLIVAN, VIRGINIA L. public affairs educator, consultant; b. Brookhaven, Miss., Oct. 12, 1950; d. Ernest and Loraine Headrick; children: Angelea, Sara. BS in Indsl. Tech., So. Ill. U., 1982; MA in Journalism, U. Colo., 1990. Enlisted USAF, 1975, advanced through grades to maj., 1995, pub. affairs officer, 1975-82, Colorado Springs, 1983-88, Montgomery, Ala., 1990-92, Ankara, Turkey, 1992-93, pub. affairs officer The Pentagon Washington, 1993-96, ret., 1996; pub. rels. instr. Ark. State U., Jonesboro, 1996—. Editor The Leader, 1991. Bd. dirs. Crowley Ridge Girls Scouts USA Coun., Jonesboro, 1997. Mem. Pub. Rels Coun. Ala. (student activities dir. 1991-92), Turkish Am. Assn. (ESL instr. 1993), Assn. Educators in Journalism and Mass. Comm., Pub. Rels. Soc. Am., Lions Club. Republican. Baptist. Avocations: tennis, writing poetry. Office: Ark State U Dept Journalism PO Box 1930 Jonesboro AR 72403-1930

SULLIVAN, WALTER LAURENCE, writer, educator; b. Nashville, Jan. 4, 1924; s. Walter Laurence and Aline (Armstrong) S.; m. Jane Harrison, Aug. 30, 1947; children: Pamela Sullivan Chenery, Walter Laurence, John Harrison. BA, Vanderbilt U., 1947; MFA, U. Iowa, 1949; Litt.D., Episc. Theol. Sem., Lexington, Ky., 1973. Instr. dept. English Vanderbilt U., Nashville, 1949-52, asst. prof., 1952-57, assoc. prof., 1957-63, prof., 1963—2001, prof. emeritus, 2001—. Lectr. on pub. TV. Author: Sojourn of a Stranger, 1957, The Long, Long Love, 1959, Death by Melancholy: Essays on Modern Southern Fiction, 1972, A Requiem for the Renascence: The State of Fiction in the Modern South, 1976, In Praise of Blood Sports and Other Essays, 1990, Allen Tate: A Recollection, 1988, A Time to Dance, 1995, The War the Women Lived, 1995; co-author: Southern Fiction Today: Renascence and Beyond, 1969, Southern Literary Study: Problems and Possibilities, 1975, Writing From the Inside, 1983; writer, narrator film for pub. TV; contbr. articles to publs. 1st lt. USMC, 1943-46. Ford Found. fiction fellow, 1951-52; Rockefeller Found. fiction fellow, 1957-58. Mem. Fellowship of So. Writers. (vice chancellor 1997-99, chancellor, 1999—). Roman Catholic. Home: 6104 Chickering Ct Nashville TN 37215-5002

SULLIVAN, WOODRUFF TURNER, III, astronomy educator, science historian, researcher, astrobiologist, gnomonicist; b. Colorado Springs, Colo., June 17, 1944; s. Woodruff Turner Jr. and Virginia Lucille (Ward) S.; m. Barbara Jean Phillips, June 8, 1968; children: Rachel, Sarah. SB in Physics, MIT, 1966; PhD in Astronomy, U. Md., 1971. Astronomer Naval Research Lab., Washington, 1969-71; postdoctoral fellow U. Groningen, The Netherlands, 1971-73; mem. faculty U. Wash., Seattle, 1973—, prof. astronomy, 1986—. Mem. NASA Search of Extraterrestrial Intelligence Group, Ames Rsch. Ctr., Calif., 1980-94. Editor: Classics in Radio Astronomy, 1982, The Early Years of Radio Astronomy, 1984, Preserving the Astronomical Sky, 2001; contbr. articles to profl. jours. Grantee NSF, NASA. Mem. Internat. Astron. Union, Am. Astron. Soc., History of Sci. Soc. Clubs: Astron. Unit (Seattle). Avocations: hiking, softball, pardating, Scrabble.

SULLIVAN, ZOHREH T. English educator; b. Tehran, Dec. 18, 1941; d. Ali and Zahra (Nowkhiz) Tawakuli; children: Taimur, Kamran. PhD, U. Ill., 1971. Instr. Webster Coll., St. Louis, 1969-70; prof. Damavand Coll., Tehran, 1970—72, U. Ill., Urbana, 1972—. Author: Narratives of Empire, 1993, Exiled Memories: Stories of Iranian Diaspora, 2001, Norton Critical Edition of Rudyard Kipling's Kim, 2002; contbr. articles to profl. jours. Mem. MLA, Mid. East Studies Assn. Democrat. Office: Univ Ill 608 S Wright St Urbana IL 61801-3630

SUMMAR, SHARON KAY, elementary school educator; b. Decatur, Ill, Jan. 27, 1948; d. Robert Dean and Leola (Warren) S. BS in Edn., Ill. State U., 1970, MS in Math., 1988. Tchr., computer coord. Green Valley Grade Sch., Ill., 1970-91; tchr. Midwest Cent. Primary Sch., 1991—. Tchr. asst. U. Ill., Urbana, 1986. Mem. Nat. Coun. Tchr. Math., Ill. Coun. Tchr. Math. Avocations: computer programming, stamp collecting, reading. Office: Midwest Cen Primary Sch 450 Southmoor St Manito IL 61546-9198 E-mail: summar@midwestcentral.org.

SUMMERS, CLYDE WILSON, law educator; b. Grass Range, Mont., Nov. 21, 1918; s. Carl Douglas and Anna Lois (Yontz) S.; m. Evelyn Marie Wahlgren, Aug. 30, 1947; children: Mark, Erica, Craig, Lisa. BS, U. Ill., 1939, JD, 1942, LLD, 1998; LLM, Columbia U., 1946, JSD, 1952; LL.D., U. Leuven, Belgium, 1967, U. Stockholm, 1978, U. Ill., 1998. Bar: N.Y. 1951. Mem. law faculty U. Toledo, 1942-49, U. Buffalo, 1949-56; prof. law Yale U., New Haven, Conn., 1956-66, Garver prof. law, 1966-75; Jefferson B. Fordham prof. law U. Pa., 1975-90, prof. emeritus, 1990—. Hearing examiner Conn. Commn. on Civil Rights, 1963-71 Co-author: Labor Cases and Material, 1968, 1982, Rights of Union Members, 1979, Legal Protection for the Individual Employee, 1989, 1996, 2002; co-editor: Labor Relations and the Law, 1953, Employment Relations and the Law, 1959, Comparative Labor Law Jour., 1984—97. Chmn. Gov.'s Com. on Improper Union Mgmt. Practices N.Y. State, 1957-58; chmn. Conn. Adv. Council on Unemployment Ins. and Employment Service, 1960-72; mem. Conn. Labor Relations Bd., 1966-70, Conn. Bd. Mediation and Arbitration, 1964-72. Guggenheim fellow, 1955-56; Ford fellow, 1963-64; German-Marshall fellow, 1977-78; NEH fellow, 1977-78, Fullbright fellow, 1984-85. Mem. Nat. Acad. Arbitrators (pres. elect), Internat. Soc. Labor Law and Social Legislation. Congregationalist. Home: 753 N 26th St Philadelphia PA 19130-2429 Office: U Pa Sch Law 3400 Chestnut St Philadelphia PA 19104-6204 E-mail: csummers@law.upenn.edu.

SUMMERS, DALE EDWARDS, school system administrator, education educator; b. Hershey, Pa., Oct. 19, 1949; s. Charles Edward and Phyllis Elaine (Risser) S.; m. Linda Louise Lashbrook, Sept. 12, 1950; children: Shannon Robert, Shelby Louise. BS, Ball State U., 1971, MA, 1973, EdD, 1977. Tchr. of emotionally disturbed Muncie (Ind.) Community Schs., 1971-76; asst. elem. prin. Derry Twp. Sch. Dist., Hershey, Pa., 1977-84, asst. high sch. prin., 1985-89; supr. secondary spl. edn. West Shore Sch. Dist., Lemoyne, Pa., 1989-90; prin. Highland Elem. Sch., Camp Hill, Pa., 1990—; asst. prof. edn. Lebanon Valley Coll., Annville, Pa., 1990—. Bd. dirs. The Children's Sch., Lebanon, Pa. Contbr. articles to profl. jours. Bd. dirs. Leadership Lebanon Valley, mem. edn. com. Lebanon C. of C.; asst. coach Hershey (Pa.) Baseball Assn., 1987—; soccer coach Palmyra (Pa.) Recreation Assn., 1987—; bd. dirs. South Cen. Second Mile. Mem. Am. Assn. Secondary Sch. Prins. Republican. Methodist. Avocations: weight lifting, muo duk kwan karate. Home: 24 S Center Ave Palmyra PA 17078-2001

SUMMERS, JANIE I. elementary school principal; b. Spartanburg County, S.C., July 22; d. Earl Dean and Bertha L. Willie (Miller) Irby; m. Johnnie W. Summers, Jr., July 3, 1958; children: Amile Lemoin, Amy Renee. AB, Benedict Coll., 1954; MEd, S.C. State Coll., 1969; postgrad., U. Chgo., U. S.C., U. Nebr., Appalachian State U. Cert. elem. tchr., elem. guidance counselor, elem. prin; cert. A.P.T. observer, P.E.T. trnr. Adult edn. tchr., tchr. in migrant program, counselor Spartanburg Dist. One Schs., Campobello, S.C., prin. Mem. steering com. S.C. Sch. Improvement Council, Spartanburg County Concensus Project; bd. dirs. Spartanburg Educator's Fed. Credit Union; deaconess Mt. Pleasant Bapt. Ch.; mem. S.C. State Supt.'s Prins. Adv. Com., Spartanburg County Sheriff's Citizens Adv. Named Tchr. of Yr., Optimist Club, 1989, Prin. of Yr., Dist. XII PTA. Mem. NEA, S.C. Edn. Assn., S.C. PTA (life hon.), Internat. Reading Assn., S.C. Assn. Elem. and Middle Sch. Prins., Assn. for Supervision and Curriculum Devel., Nat. Assn. of Sec. Prin.'s (assessor), Kappa Delta Pi (chair incentive com.). Avocations: reading, travel. Home: PO Box 513 100 Summers St Inman SC 29349-9205 Office: O P Earle Elem Sch 100 Redland Rd Landrum SC 29356-1717

SUMMERS, LAWRENCE, former government official, academic administrator; b. New Haven, 1954; 2 daughters (twins), 1 son. SB, MIT, 1975; PhD, Harvard U., 1982. Mem. faculty MIT, 1979-82; domestic policy economist Pres'. Com. Econ. Advisors, 1982-83; v.p. devel. econs., chief economist World Bank, 1991-93; prof. econs. Harvard U., Cambridge, Mass., 1983-93, Nathaniel Ropes prof. polit. economy, 1987, pres., 2001—; under sec. for internat. affairs U.S. Dept. Treasury, Washington, 1993-95, dep. sec., 1995-99, sec., 1999-2001. Author Understanding Unemployment; co-author Reform in Eastern Europe; editor series Tax Policy and the Economy; contbr. numerous articles to profl. jours. Recipient John Bates Clark medal, 1993, Alan Waterman award NSF, 1987, disting. achievement award Boys' & Girls' Club Greater Washington, 2000, disting. svc. award Golden Slipper Club & Charities 2000, economic patriot award Concord Coalition, 2000, Stephen P. Guggan award Inst. Internat. Edn., 2000. Fellow NAS, Econometric Soc., Am. Acad. Arts and Scis., Brookhaven Sci. Assocs. (bd. dirs.), Nat. Acad. Sci. Office: Harvard U Office of the President Massachusetts Hall Cambridge MA 02138

SUMMERS, ROBERT SAMUEL, lawyer, author, educator; b. Halfway, Oreg., Sept. 19, 1933; s. Orson William and Estella Bell (Robertson) S.; m. Dorothy Millicent Kopp, June 14, 1955; children: Brent, William, Thomas, Elizabeth, Robert. BS in Polit. Sci., U. Oreg., 1955; postgrad. (Fulbright scholar), U. Southampton, Eng., 1955-56; LLB, Harvard U., 1959; postgrad. rsch., Oxford U., 1964-65, 74-75, 81-82, 88-89; LLD (hon.), U. Helsinki, Finland, 1990, U. Göttingen, Germany, 1994. Bar: Oreg. 1959, N.Y. 1974. Asso. King, Miller, Anderson, Nash and Yerke, Portland, Oreg., 1959-60; asst. prof. law U. Oreg., 1960-63, asso. prof., 1964-68; vis. asso. prof. law Stanford U., 1963-64; prof. U. Oreg., 1968-69, Cornell U., 1969-76, McRoberts rsch. prof. law, 1976—. Summer vis. prof. Ind. U., 1969, U. Mich., 1974, U. Warwick, Eng., 1975, Australia Nat. U., U. Sydney, Australia, 1977; vis. Fulbright prof. U. Vienna, Austria, 1985; Goodhart vis. prof. Cambridge U., Eng., 1991-92; H. Hurst Eminent vis. scholar U. Fla., 1995; rsch. fellow Merton Coll., oxford U., 1981-82, Exeter Coll., Oxford U., 1988-89; cons. Cornell Law Project in publ. schs., N.Y., 1969-74, Law in Am. Soc. project Chgo. Bd. Edn., 1968-69; instr. Nat. Acad. Jud. Edn., 1976—; mem. faculty Salzburg Seminar in Am. Studies, 1990; ofcl. advisor Drafting commn. on New Civil Code for Russian Fedn., 1994-96. Author: Law, Its Nature, Functions and Limits, 1986; (with Hubbard and Campbell) Justice and Order Through Law, 1973; (with Bozzone and Campbell) The American Legal System, 1973; (with Speidel and White) Teaching Materials on Commercial Transactions, 1987, Collective Bargaining and Public Benefit Conferral-A Jurisprudential Critique, 1976, The Uniform Commercial Code, 1988, 4th edit., 1995; (with White) Het Pramatisch Instrumentalisme, 1981, Instrumentalism and American Legal Theory, 1982, Lon L. Fuller-Life and Work, 1984; (with Atiyah) Form and Substance in Anglo-American Law, 1987; (with Hillman) Contract and Related Obligation, 1987; (with MacCormick and others) Interpreting Statutes-A Comparative Study, 1991, Nature of Law and Legal Reasoning, 1993; contbr. book revs. and articles to profl. jours.; editor: Essays in Legal Philosophy, vol. 1, 1968, vol. 2, 1971. Social Sci. Research Council fellow, 1964-65 Mem. Am. Law Inst., Assn. Am. Law Schs. (chmn. sect. jurisprudence 1972-73), Am. Soc. Polit. and Legal Philosophy (v.p. 1976-78), Internat. Acad. Comp. Law, Internat. Assn. of Legal and Social Philosophy Am. Soc. (pres. 1989-91), Austrian Acad. of Scis., Phi Beta Kappa. Republican. Congregationalist. Office: Cornell U Sch Law Myron Taylor Hall Ithaca NY 14853

SUMMERS, TONY EDWARD, academic administrator; b. Pitts., May 26, 1952; s. William Edward and Bertha (Wilson) S.; m. Martha L. Kelly, June 29, 1980; children: Kalen M., Edward A. AA, Community Coll. Allegheny County, 1973; B in Polit. Sci., Duquesne U., 1975; MEd, U. Pitts., 1981. Admissions counselor LaRoche Coll., Allison Park, Pa., 1976-77; asst. dir. fin. aid Community Coll. Allegheny County, Pitts., 1977-81, dir. fin. aid, 1981-87; dir. minority recruitment, retention and transfer program Community Coll. Allegheny Coll., Pitts., 1987—. Adj. instr. Community Coll. Allegheny County, Pitts., 1983—; cons. faculty trainer Pa. Fin. Aid Adminstrs. Tng. Program, 1984-87; cons. instr. Internat. Inst. Tng. and Orgnl. Devel., U. Pitts., 1983—; coach track and cross country Community Coll. Allegheny County, Monroeville, 1984-85. Committeeman 25th Ward Dems., 1979; bd. advisors Upward Bound Program LaRoche Coll., 1980; co-chmn. community council Am. Cancer Soc., Pitts, 1984; mem. Adult Literacy Task Force, Com. of 100 Carnegie Inst., Pitts., 1985—. Named One of Outstanding Young Men Am., 1980, 83; fellow Kellogg Found. 1992-93. Mem. Assn. of Supervision and Curriculum Devel., Pa. Assn. Fin. Aid Adminstrs., Nat. Student Devel. Counsel, Pa. Coll. Personnel Assn. Office: Community Coll Allegheny County 800 Allegheny Ave Pittsburgh PA 15233-1804

SUMMERS, TRACY YVONNE, assistant principal; b. Raymond, Miss., Aug. 12, 1961; d. Neil and Bessie (Christian) S.; divorced, Feb. 1982; 1 child, Shundria Anntawnette. BS in Bus. Edn., Jackson State U., 1985, M in Bus. and Math. Edn., 1988, specialist in sch. adminstrn., 1990; postgrad., U. Miss., 1990-91, Miss. State U., 1993—. Cert. tchr., secondary supr., secondary prin., vocat. dir., Miss. Clk. dept. pers. City of Jackson, Miss., 1978-85; tchr. math. Brinkley Jr. High Sch., Jackson Pub. Sch. Dist., 1985-91; asst. prin. Brinkley Mid. Sch., Jackson Pub. Sch. Dist., 1991-94, Hardy Middle Sch., 1994-95. Cheerleading sponsor Brinkley Jr. High Sch., 1986-90. Dir. singles ministry College Hill Bapt. Ch. Edn. Found. Trust co-grantee, 1990-91, 91-92, 92-93; Entergy Corp. grantee, 1990-91. Mem. ASCD, South Edni. Rsch. Assn., Phi Delta Kappa. Home: 1456 Dewey St Jackson MS 39209-4410 Office: Hardy Middle School 545 Ellis Ave Jackson MS 39209-6202

SUMMERTREE, KATONAH See WINDSOR, PATRICIA

SUMMERVILLE, RICHARD M. mathematician, academic administrator; Provost Christopher Newport U. Office: Christopher Newport U Office of the Provost 1 University Pl Newport News VA 23606-2998 E-mail: rsummer@cnu.edu.

SUMNER, MARGARET ELIZABETH, elementary school educator; b. Clarksdale, Miss., Mar. 17, 1952; d. John Franklin and Julia Myrtle (Hopson) Sullivan; m. David Edwin Sumner, June 3, 1972; children: Julia Dawn, Oakley Raymond. BS in Edn., Delta State U., 1974. Cert. elem. tchr., Miss. Bridal cons. Hancock Fabric, Tupelo, Miss., 1974; mem. prodn. staff Arvin Inc., Verona, Miss., 1976; kindergarten tchr. Bissell (Miss.) Day Care, 1976-77; sec. Borden's Inc., Tupelo, 1977-79; tchr. 3rd grade Verona Jr. High Sch., 1979-80, kindergarten tchr., 1991, tchr. chpt. I remedial reading and math., 1991—; 4th grade tchr. Presbyn. Day Sch., Clarksdale, Miss., 1981-83; 1st grade tchr. Clarksdale Pub. Sch., 1984-90, Tupelo Pub. Sch., 1990, 9th-12th grade tchr. specific learning disability, 1992-93; tchr. developmentally disabled class West Amory (Miss.) Elem. Sch., 1991-92; home econ., computer tchr. Jumpertown Sch. and Wheeler Attendance Ctr., 1993-94; math, lang. arts spl. edn. tchr. Guntown (Miss.) Mid. Sch., 1994-95; tchr. spl. edn. for TMR, developmentally disabled DD, traumatic brain injury, TBI, severe/profound, SP Noxapater Sch., Miss., 1995—99; kindergarten tchr. Noxapater Attendance Ctr., 1999—. Presenter to workshops in field; evaluator Miss. Tchr. Assessment Instrument, 1986—. Mem.: Miss. Assn. Children Under Six, Miss. Profl. Educators. Baptist. Home: PO Box 100 Noxapater MS 39346-0100

SUMNER, WILLIAM MARVIN, anthropology and archaeology educator; b. Detroit, Sept. 8, 1928; s. William Pulford Jr. and Virginia Friel (Umberger) S.; m. Frances Wilson Morton, June 21, 1952 (div. 1975); children: Jane Cassell, William Morton; m. Kathleen A. MacLean, Apr. 7, 1989. Student, Va. Mil. Inst., 1947-48; BS, U.S. Naval Acad., 1952; PhD, U. Pa., 1972. Dir. Am. Inst. Iranian Studies, Tehran, Iran, 1969-71; asst. prof. Ohio State U., Columbus, 1971-73, assoc. prof., 1974-80, prof. anthropology, 1981-89, prof. emeritus, 1989—; dir. Oriental Inst., prof. Near Eastern langs. and civilizations U. Chgo., 1989-98. Dir. excavations at Tal-e Malyan (site of Elamite Anshan) sponsored by Univ. Mus., U. Pa.,

1971— ; v.p. Am. Inst. Iranian Studies, 1983-86. Contbr. chpts. to books, articles and essays to profl. jours. Served to lt. comdr. USN, 1952-64. Grantee NSF, 1975, 76, 79, NEH, 1988. Office: Univ Chgo Oriental Inst 1155 E 58th St Chicago IL 60637-1540 E-mail: sumner.1@osu.edu.

SUMPTER, MARIA ELVIRA, secondary school educator; b. Eagle Pass, Tex., Mar. 15, 1948; d. Jesse Asberry and Trinidad (Cardenas) Sumpter; m. José Victor Villarreal; 1 child, Kira. BA, Tex. Woman's U., 1970; MA, Tex. A&I U., 1979; postgrad., Sul Ross State U. Asst. prin., secondary curriculum coord. Eagle Pass Ind. Sch. Dist., 1986—. Developer Summer Sch. Now! program and in-sch. JTPA. Contbr. articles to local jours.; presenter at Hispanic Conf., 1993. Mem. ASCD, NEA, Tex. State Tchrs. Assn., Phi Sigma Iota. Home: 1265 N Bibb Ave Eagle Pass TX 78852-3803

SUMPTER, SONJA KAY, elementary school educator; b. Weston, W.Va., Aug. 12, 1948; d. Glen A. and Sarah R. (White) Wade; m. Charles Fredrick Sumpter, Mar. 25, 1967; children: Lisa Marie Sumpter Pethtel, Charles Fredrick II. BS in Elem. Edn., Glenville (W.Va.) State Coll., 1984; MS in Edn., W.Va. Wesleyan Coll., 1993; postgrad., W.Va. U., 1994. Cert. tchr. elem. edn. 1-6, math. 5-8. Tchr. Weston (W.Va.) Jr. H.S., 1984-92, Robert Bland Mid. Sch., Weston, 1992—, team leader, 1992-94. Mem. Nat. Coun. Tchrs. Math., Order Ea. Star. Republican. Baptist. Avocations: singing, walking, macrame. Home: RR 4 Box 297 Weston WV 26452-9517 Office: Robert Bland Middle School 358 Court Ave Weston WV 26452-2008

SUN, HAIYIN, optical engineer, educator; b. Kunming, Yunnan, China, July 27, 1958; came to the U.S., 1990; s. Qiyuan Sun and Shouzheng Wang; m. Nan Yang, Oct. 3, 1987; children: Tobias Y., Christina N. BS in Physics, Shanghai (China) Tchrs. U., 1982; MS in Photonics, Shanghai (China) Inst. Optics, and Fine Mechanics, 1985; PhD in Photonics, U. Ark., 1994. Instr. Shanghai Tchr.'s U., 1982; asst. prof. Shanghai Inst. Optics and Fine Mechanics, 1986-88; vis. scientist Telecom. Network Rsch. Ctr. of Germany's Post, Darmstadt, 1988-90; optical engr. Power Tech., Inc., Little Rock, 1994-96; sr. optical engr. Coherent Inc., Auburn, Calif., 1996—. Adj. prof. U. Ark., Little Rock, 1996—; prin. investigator various projects; editor Jour. Optical Comm. Contbr. chpt. to book and numerous articles to profl. jours.; inventor several optical devices. Named Outstanding Rschr., The Justice Dept. USA Govt., 1995; rsch. grantee Ark. Sci. & Engring. Authority, 1993. Avocations: classical music, watching tv movies and sports, cooking. Home: 3 Oakhurst Circle Pittsburgh PA 15215

SUN, LI-TEH, economics educator; b. Hong Kong, Dec. 5, 1939; s. Beh-Yu and Ruey-Jeng (Wang) S.; m. Ping Zhong, June 1, 1991. BA in Econs., Chung Hsing U., Taipei, Taiwan, 1962; MS in Econs., Okla. State U., 1968, PhD in Econs., 1972. Rsch. assoc. U. Mont., Missoula, 1969-70; lectr. Humboldt State U., Arcata, Calif., 1972-75; acad. resource specialist Chancelor's Office Calif. State U. and Colls., Long Beach, Calif., 1975-77; assoc. prof., prof. econ. Nat. Chung Hsing U., Taipei, 1977-81, chair dept. pub. fin., 1978-82; prof. econ. Moorhead State U., Minn., 1982-96. Coord. China programs Moorhead State U., 1987-89. Contbr. articles to profl. jours. Mem. adv. bd. Centre of Humanomics, 1985-96; mem. Mid-Am. Cons. Internat., 1993—. Named Prof. of Yr., Humboldt State U., Arcata, Calif., 1974. Mem. Moorhead Cen. Lions (newsletter editor 1990-93, bd. dirs. 1983-96, pres. 1987-88, Lion of Yr. 1984, 85, 90, 91). Avocations: walking, karaoke, travel. Home: 7312 Charlesborough Ct Lorton VA 22079-1538

SUN, MINGHE, business educator; b. Shouguang, China, Mar. 11, 1954; s. Fulu Sun and Meiying Wang; m. Xingqi Sun, July 10, 1954; children: Shining, Andrew. BS, Northeastern U., Shenyang, China, 1982; MBA, Chinese U. Hong Kong, 1987; PhD, U. Ga., 1992. Asst. prof. U. Tex., San Antonio, 1992—98, assoc. prof., 1998—2003, prof., 2003—. Contbr. articles to profl. jours. Recipient Outstanding Dissertation award Decisoin Scis. Inst., 1993, Outstanding Paper award So. Mgmt. Assn., 1998, Outstanding Tchg. award U. Tex. Sys., 1999, Outstanding Svc. as the Local Arrangements Chair award Prodn. Ops. Soc., 2000. Mem. Inst. Ops. Rsch. and Mgmt. Scis., Decision Sci. Inst. Home: 14107 Soapberry Cove San Antonio TX 78249 Office: U Tex Coll Bus San Antonio TX 78249 Home Fax: 210-558-7861; Office Fax: 210-458-6350. E-mail: msun@utsa.edu.

SUN, TUNG-TIEN, medical science educator; b. Chung King, Szechuan, People's Republic of China, Feb. 20, 1947; s. Chung-Yu and Wen (Lin) S.; m. Brenda Shih-Ying Bao, Aug. 14, 1971; children: I-Hsing, I-Fong. BS in Agrl. Chemistry, Nat. Taiwan U., Taipei, 1967; PhD in Biochemistry, U. Calif., Davis, 1974. Rsch. assoc. dept. biology MIT, Cambridge, 1974-78; asst. prof. depts. dermatology, cell biology and anatomy Johns Hopkins Med. Sch., Balt., 1978-81, assoc. prof. dept. cell biology and anatomy, dermatology, ophthalmology, 1981-82; assoc. prof. depts. dermatology and pharmacology NYU Med. Sch., NYC, 1982-86, prof., 1986-90, Rudolf L. Baer prof., 1990—, prof. dept. urology, 1996—, assoc. dir. Skin Disease Rsch. Ctr., 1989-93, dean's lectr., 2000. William W. Scott Meml. lectr. Johns Hopkins Med. Sch., 2001; adj. prof. Coll. Life Sci. Peking U., 1998—; hon. prof. Third Mil. Med. U., Chung King, China, 1998— Mem. editl. bd. Differentiation, 1984—, Epithelial Cell Biology, 1990-93; assoc. editor Jour. Investigative Dermatology, 1990—, Jour. Dermatol. Sci., 1992-2003; US mng. editor Molecular Biology Report, 1994-96. Recipient Career Devel. award Nat. Eye Inst., 1978-82, Monique Neill-Caulier Career Scientist award, 1984-89, Alcon award in vision rsch., 1993, Wu Jieping Urololgy Found. award Chinese Med. Assn., 1998. Fellow AAAS; mem. Academia Sinica, Am. Soc. Biol. Chemists, Am. Soc. for Cell Biology, Internat. Soc. Differentiation (bd. dir. 1985-88), Nat. Inst. Arthiritis and Musculoskeletal and Skin Diseases (bd. sci. counselors), Soc. Investigative Dermatology (Montagna lectr. 1989, bd. dir. 1993-98), Assn. Rsch. in Vision Sci. and Ophthalmology. Office: NYU Med Sch Dept Dermatology 560 1st Ave New York NY 10016-6402

SUNDBERG, MARSHALL DAVID, biology educator; b. Apr. 18, 1949; m. Sara Jane Brooks, Aug. 1, 1977; children: Marshall Isaac, Adam, Emma. BA in Biology, Carleton Coll., 1971; MA in Botany, U. Minn., 1973, PhD in Botany, 1978. Lab. technician Carleton Coll., Minn., 1973-74; teaching asst. U. Minn., Mpls., 1974-76, rsch. asst., 1976-77; adj. asst. prof. Biology U. Wis., Eau Claire, 1978-85, mem. faculty summer sci. inst., 1982-85; instr. La. State U., Baton Rouge, 1985-88, asst. prof. Biology, 1988-91, coord. dept. Biology, 1988-93, assoc. prof. Biology, 1991-97; prof., chair dept. biol. scis. Emporia State U., 1997—. Author: General Botany Laboratory Workbook, 5th revision, 1984, General Botany 1001 Laboratory Manual, 1986, General Botany 1002 Laboratory Manual, 1987, Biology 1002 Correspondence Study Guide, 1987, Boty 1202: General Botany Laboratory Manual, 1988, Biol 1208: Biology for Science Majors Laboratory Manual, 1988, 2d edit., 1989, Instructor's Manual for J. Mauseth, Introductory Botany, 1991; contbr. articles to profl. jours. Brand fellow U. Minn., 1976-77, Faculty Grants scholar U. Wis., 1984-85. Fellow Linnaean Soc. London; mem. NSTA, AAAS, Am. Inst. Biol. Scis. (coun. mem. at large 1992-95, edn. com. 1994-95, 98-2002), Nat. Sci. Tchrs. Assn., Assn. Biology Lab. Edn., Bot. Soc. Am. (chmn. tchg. sect. 1985-86, workshop com. tchg. sect. 1983-84, slide exch./lab. exch. tchg. sect. 1980-89, edn. com. 1991, 92, Charles H. Bessey award 1992, editor Plant Sci. Bull. 2000—), Internat. Soc. Plant Morphologists, Nat. Assn. Biology Tchrs. (Outstanding 4-Yr. Coll. Tchr. award 1997, 2003), Soc. Econ. Botany, The Nature Conservancy, Sigma Xi (chpt. sec. 1982-84, 93-95, 2000-02, v.p. 1984-85, 96-97, pres. 1996, 99). Home: 1912 Briarcliff Ln Emporia KS 66801-5404 Office: Emporia State U Dept Biol Scis 1200 Commercial St Emporia KS 66801-5087

SUNDBERG, RUTH DOROTHY, physician, educator; b. Chgo., July 29, 1915; d. Carl William and Ruth (Chalbeck) S.; m. Robert H. Reiff, Dec. 24, 1941 (div. 1945). Student, U. Chgo., 1932-34; BS, U. Minn., 1937, MA, 1939, PhD, 1943, MD, 1953. Diplomate: Am. Bd. Pathology. Instr., asst. prof. anatomy U. Minn., 1939-53, assoc. prof., 1953-60, prof., 1960-63, prof. of lab. medicine and anatomy, 1963-73, prof. lab. medicine, pathology and anatomy, 1973-84, emeritus prof., 1984—; hematologist, dir. Hematology Labs., 1945-74, hematologist, co. dir., 1974-84. Editorial bd.: Soc. Exptl. Biology and Medicine, until 1975; mem. editorial bd.: Blood, 1960-67; assoc. editor, 1967-69. Recipient Lucretia Wilder award for research in anatomy, 1939 Mem.: European Soc. Hematology, Sigma Xi. Home: 1255 Shenandoah Ct Marco Island FL 34145-5023

SUNDEM, GARY LEWIS, accounting educator; b. Montevideo, Minn., Nov. 8, 1944; s. Clifford Leroy and Sylvia Edna (Larson) Sundem; m. Elizabeth Sundem; children: Garth Clifford, Jens Lewis. BA, Carleton Coll., 1967; MBA, Stanford U., 1969, PhD, 1971. Asst. prof. U. Wash., Seattle, 1971—74, assoc. prof., 1974—80, prof., 1980—, acctg. dept. chmn., 1978—82, 1988—89, 1996—99, assoc. dean, 1992—95, 1999—2002. Vis. prof. Norwegian Sch. Econs., Bergen, 1974—75; vis. assoc. prof. Cornell U., Ithaca, NY, 1977—78; vis. prof. INSEAD, Fontainebleau, France, 1987; exec. dir. Acctg. Edn. Change Commn., 1989—91; cons. in field; Shaw Found. vis. prof. Nanyang Bus. Sch., Singapore, 2002—03. Author: Introduction to Financial Accounting, 1987, 8th edit., 2002, Introduction to Management Accounting, 1987, 12th edit., 2002; editor: The Acctg. Rev., 1982—86; contbr. articles to profl. jours. Mem.: Nat. Assn. Accts. (nat. bd. dirs. 1986—88, 1999—2002), Fin. Execs. Inst., Am. Acctg. Assn. (exec. com. 1982—85, dist. internat. lectr. 1989, pres. 1991—92). Home: 489 39th Ave E Seattle WA 98112 Office: U Wash Bus Sch PO Box 353200 Seattle WA 98195-3200 E-mail: glsundem@u.washington.edu.

SUNDERLAND, JACKLYN GILES, former alumni affairs director; b. Corpus Christi, Tex., Oct. 21, 1937; d. Elbert Jackson and Mary Kathryn (Garrett) Giles; m. Joseph Alan MacInnis, Nov. 24, 1963 (div. Feb. 1982); children: Mary Kendall Brady, Jackson Alan MacInnis; m. Lane Von Sunderland, June 12, 1988. BA, U. Tex., Austin, 1960. Editor's asst. House & Garden mag., N.Y.C., 1962; reporter Corpus Christi Caller-Times, 1960, 69, Home Furnishings Daily, Fairchild Publs., N.Y.C., 1961, Houston Post, 1963; writer, rschr. Saudi Press Agy., Washington, 1980; writer/rschr. for V.P. U.S. White House, Washington, 1982-84; dir. pub. affairs President's Com. on Mental Retardation, Washington, 1984-85; dir. speakers bur. Commn. on Bicentennial U.S. Constn., Washington, 1985-87; speechwriter Sec. of HHS, Washington, 1987-88, U.S. Sec. of Labor, Washington, 1989; dir. alumni affairs Knox Coll., Galesburg, Ill., 1990-92. Campaign chmn. Am. Cancer Soc., Corpus Christi, 1961; liaison Am. Embassy, Copenhagen, 1965-68; docent, tchr. art Nat. Gallery and Smithsonian Mus., Washington, 1970-73; vestrywoman Grace Episcopal Ch., Galesburg, 1991; mem. Jr. League Washington, 1963-2003; vol. Hospice, 1996-97. Recipient Continental Marine citation for community svc., Camp Pendleton, Calif., 1977. Republican. Home: 185 Park Ln Galesburg IL 61401

SUNDERLAND, NORMAN RAY (NORM SUNDERLAND), health physicist, nuclear engineer educator; b. Lone Wolf, Okla., Aug. 1, 1933; s. Alva Franklin and Octava Pearl (Purcell) S.; m. Marilyn NMN Stanworth, Aug. 27, 1970; children: Melody, Larry, Derreck, Toni, James, Jo Lynn, Stacie, Thomas. BS, Okla. State U., 1960; MEd, U. Nev., Las Vegas, 1973; PhD, Columbia-Pacific U., 1985. Registered radiation protection technologist. Tchr. Ft. Morgan (Colo.) HS, 1960—61, Paxton (Nebr.) HS, 1961—66; asst. dir. environ. sci. REECO (Nev. Test Site), Mercury, Nev., 1966—77; univ. sys. radiation safety officer U. Mo., Columbia, 1977—80; prof. N.E. Mo. State, Kirksville, 1978—84; dir. environ. health, safety U. Mo., Columbia, 1980—82; nuc. power cons. AWC, Inc., Cedar Rapids, Iowa, 1982—85; asst. dir. nuc. assessment divsn. EPA, Las Vegas, 1985—91; dir. environ. health, safety Utah State U., Logan, 1991—98; dir. Envirocare of Tex., Andrews, 1998—. Chair radiation control, Utah, 1987-1992; EPA rep. to Ea. Europe (Poland, Russia), 1989-96; cons. French AEC.; lectr. Ft. Morgan (Colo.) HS, 1960-61, Paxton (Nebr.) HS, 1961-66, U. Mo., Columbia, 1977-80, 78-84, N.E. Mo. State U. and Utah State U., 1991-96. Author: Bio-Physics of Radiation, 1997; co-author: Rad Emergency Response Operations, 1968, (Jour.) Transfer of Radiocesium to Grass, 1993, Transfer of Radiocesium to Soil, 1994; patentee in field. Pres. Mo. Higher Ednl. Assoc., Columbia, 1980-81; bishop LDS Ch., Cedar Rapids, Iowa, 1982-85. With combat engring. U.S. Army, 1953-56, Alaska. Fellow Nat. Health Physics Soc. (pres. MidAm. chpt. 1981-82, Lake Mead chpt. 1988-89, Great Salt Lake chpt. 1994-95, chmn. bd., mem. membership com. 1998—), Nat. Registry Radiation Protection Technicians (sec., mem. nat. bd. 1975-98, emeritus 1992, Arthur Humm Jr. Meml. award 1998); mem. Jaycees. Republican, Democrat. Mem. LDS Ch. Achievements include TRUclean process patent which removes radioactive material from soil (now owned by Lockeed Internat.). Home: 1851 N 1600 E North Logan UT 84341-2114

SUNDERLAND, RAY THOBURN, education educator, administrator; b. Newton Hamilton, Pa., May 13, 1932; s. Thoburn C. and Margaret Ann (Black) S.; m. Marjorie Mae Hatchell, June 17, 1956; children: Scott David, Amy Jean. BS, Shippensburg U., 1954; MEd, Western Md. Coll., 1958; PhD, The Union Inst., 1979. Cert. tchr., prin., Pa. Tchr. Hamilton Elem. Sch., Harrisburg, Pa., 1954-56, Stevens Elem. Sch., Carlisle, Pa., 1956-58, Moreland Elem. Sch., Carlisle, 1958-60; prin. Wilson Elem. Sch., Carlisle, 1960-62; asst. prof. edn. Campus Sch. Bloomsburg (Pa.) U., 1962-66; assoc. prof. edn., coll. supr. Kutztown (Pa.) U., 1966-72, assoc. prof. dir. student teaching, 1972-79, prof., dir. student teaching, 1980—, prof., dir. student teaching and cert., 1989—. Dir. Student Teaching Abroad-England, 1974-93; ednl. specialist Career Coll. Assn., Washington, 1987—. Contbr. articles to profl. jours. Scouting coord. St. John's Luth. Ch., Boy Scouts Am., Kutztown, 1974—, local chair Hawk Mt. Coun. Leadership Dinner, Reading, Pa., 1988—, dist. chair Scouting for Food Hawk Mt. Coun., 1990—; campaign leader The Good Shepherd Home, Allentown, Pa., 1991, 92, fundraiser, 1991; organizer Take Pride in Pa., Kutztown, 1988, 89. With USN, 1951-55. Recipient Wood Badge award Boy Scouts Am., 1984, LAMB award Luth. Ch. Youth Ministries, 1992, Silver Beaver award Boy Scouts Am., 1994. Mem. NEA (life), ASCD, Pa. Assn. Colls. for Tchr. Educators (treas. 1980-90, bd. dirs., Disting. Svc. award 1990), Pa. Assn. Tchr. Educators (sec., treas. 1966-80), Assn. Tchr. Educators (life, chair nat. field dirs. forum 1982-83, Pres.'s award for mem. 1990, 91, dist. mem. award 1993), Pa. State Edn. Assn. (life), Student Pa. State Edn. Assn. (mem. state com. 1984-93, advisor 1979-93, Field Dir. Svc. award 1995), Phi Delta Kappa (life, Kutztown Delta Upsilon chpt. v.p. 1983-84, pres.-elect 1984-85, pres. 1985-86). Avocations: travel, woodworking, gardening, collecting royal doulton character mugs, trailing rv. Home: 16 Curtis Rd Kutztown PA 19530-9205 Office: Kutztown U Beekey Edn Ctr Kutztown PA 19530

SUNDERMAN, DEBORAH ANN, apparel executive, fashion and business educator; b. Detroit, Feb. 21, 1955; d. Eugene Wayne Sunderman and Nancy May (Reams) Sunderman-Elert. BS magna cum laude, No. Mich. U., 1978. Ordained min. Universal Life Ch., 1995; cert. ind. Reiki master, 1995. Design instr. Newbury Coll., Boston, 1978-82, 92-93; asst. to designers Clothware, Boston, 1978-82; designer, ptnr. Toute Nue Swimwear, Boston, 1982; designer Mast Industries, The Limited, Woburn, Mass., 1982-83; designer, founder Deborah Mann & Co., Boston, 1983-98; instr. fashion Mt. Ida Coll., Newton, Mass., 1991, 2001—; owner, designer, buyer Deborah Mann Atelier, 1997-00. Fashion instr. Framingham State Coll., 2001, Lasell Coll., Newton, Mass., 2001, Sch. Fashion Design, Boston, 2001, Mass. Coll. Art, Boston, 2001. Designer garment The Fiberarts Design Book, 1980. Organizer Neighborhood Crime Watch Group, Rossmore Rd., Boston, 1989-90. Recipient 2d Pl. award Peter White Art Exhibit, Marquette, Mich., 1978, Fresh Start award Self Mag., Washington, 1985; named one of Boston's Most Interesting Women, Boston Woman Mag., 1990. Avocations: swimming, reading, walking, music, travel, sewing. E-mail: Sunderwoman@worldnet.att.net.

SUNDQUIST, LEAH RENATA, physical education specialist; b. El Paso, Tex., July 22, 1963; d. Dominic Joseph and Patricia Ann (Manley) Bernardi; m. David Curtis Sundquist, June 23, 1990. AA, N.Mex. Mil. Inst., 1983; BS, U. Tex., El Paso, 1986; MEd in Curriculum and Instrn., City U., Bellevue, Wash., 1996. Field exec. Rio Grande Girl Scout Coun., El Paso, 1983-84; customer teller M-Bank, El Paso, 1984-85; soccer coach St. Clements Sch., El Paso, 1985; substitute tchr. El Paso Sch. Dist., 1986; commd. 2nd lt. U.S. Army, 1983, advanced through grades to maj., 1997, plans/exercise officer, 1990, ops. officer, 1990-1991; comdr. hdqs. Hdqs. Co. 141st Support Bn. U.S. Army N.G., 1996-97; dir. Childrens World Learning Ctr., Federal Way, Wash., 1992-94; phys. edn. specialist, tchr. K-6 Kent (Wash.) Elem. Sch., 1994-2001; health fitness tchr. Camas (Wash.) Mid. Sch., 2001—; ops. and tng. officer Bn S3, 1997-99; exec. officer, 1999—. Coord. NCCJ, El Paso, 1979-81; v.p. Jr. Achievement, El Paso, 1980-81; adult tng. vol. Girl Scout Coun., bd. dirs. Pacific Peaks coun., 1993-99, chair nominating com., 1996, jr. troop leater Totem coun. Girl Scouts U.S., 1996, chair program policies rev. com., 1997, trainer instrn. of adults, tng. coord. team mem., 1997—; bd. dirs. Jr. League Tacoma, 1993, 94, staff devel. coun. mem., 1997-2000, design com., 1998—. 3rd Res. Officer Tng. Corps scholar, 1981-83, H.P. Saunder scholar, 1982; recipient Humanitarian Svc. medal Great Fires of Yellowstone, U.S. Army, 1988, Gold award Girl Scouts U.S.A., 1981; decorated Nat. Def. Svc. medal Desert Storm; meritorius Svc. medal, 1991. Mem. NEA, Wash. Edn. Assn., Assn. U.S. Army, Oreg. Army Nat. Guard Assn., Assn. U.S. Army, Air Def. Artillery Assn., Zeta Tau Alpha (sec. 1983-85, house mgr. 1984-86). Republican. Roman Catholic. Avocations: soccer, fishing, hunting, skydiving, rafting. Home: 3609 NW Endicott St Camas WA 98607

SUNDSTROM, AILEEN LOIS, speech educator; b. Detroit, Mar. 2, 1925; d. Raymond and Gertrude B. (Meyer) Richard; m. Arthur E. Sundstrom, July 10, 1954. BA, Wayne State U., 1946, MA, 1947, PhD, 1964, postgrad., 1977. Tchr. speech, radio Highland Park (Mich.) High, 1947-48; English tchr. Denby High, 1948-49, Barbour Jr. High, 1949-50, Jefferson Jr. High, 1950-52, Denby High, 1952-53, Northwestern High, 1953-56, Cass Tech. High, 1957-65; asst. prof. Mercy Coll., Detroit, 1965-67; instr. performing arts dept. Henry Ford C.C., Dearborn, Mich., 1967—. Dept. spokesperson Henry Ford C.C., 1980-82, chair, 1982-88; speaker in field; text book reviewer; dir., evaluator Interpretative Reading Festival Workshops; chair various coms. Henry Ford C.C.; participant NEH, summer 1994. Contbr. articles to profl. jours. Recipient Ford Found. scholarship, 1961-62. Mem. Assn. Speech Communication, Am. Forensic Assn., Am. Assn. Univ. Women Ednl. Found., Academically Gifted and Talented, Excellence in Interpretative Reading, Mich. Assn. of Speech Communication (pres. 1985-86, presenter, chair confs. 1967—, Disting. Svc. award for festivals 1992, 93), Mich. Intercollegiate Speech League (bd. dirs. Oral Interpretation Festival/Workshops 1977—, pres. 1993-94), Speech Comm. Assn. (presenter, chair conf. programs 1967-90), Ctrl. States Speech Assn. (presenter, chair conf. programs 1978-90, participant NEH summer seminar 1994), Mich. High Sch. Forensic Assn., Beta Sigma Phi, Alpha Beta Pi.

SUNG, DAE DONG, chemist, educator, dean; b. Sichunmyon, Kyung Nam, Republic of Korea, June 17, 1945; s. Cha and Soon Agh (Ha) Sung; m. Byung Hee Yoon, Apr. 13, 1975; children: Myo Ya, Yun Duck. BS, Dong-A U., Pusan, Republic of Korea, 1969, MS, 1977, DSc, 1981. Lectr. Pusan Nat. U., 1977-78, Kyung Nam Tech. Coll., Pusan, 1978-79, Dong-A U., Pusan, 1979-81, from asst. prof. to assoc. prof., 1981-90, prof., 1990—, head lab. basic scis., 1982-83, head Basic Sci. Inst., 1989-91, dean Coll. Natural Scis., 1997—. Rschr. Princeton (N.J.) U., 1983; rsch. fellow Liverpool (Eng.) U., 1997; lectr., spkr. in field. Contbr. articles to profl. jours. Recipient Tchr.'s Day prize, Prime Min. Republic of Korea, 2000; grantee, Republic of Korea Sci. and Engring. Found., 1984, 1987, 1988, 1990, 1993, 1994—98, 2000—02. Fellow: Engring. Royal Soc. United Kingdom (rschr. 1989); mem.: Am. Chem. Soc., Korean Chem. Soc. (Mendeleev Comms. 2000). Avocation: swimming. Office: Dong-A U Dept Chemistry Saha-Gu Pusan 604-714 Republic of Korea E-mail: ddsung@mail.donga.ac.kr.

SUNTRA, CHARLES RATAPOL, surgeon, educator; b. Detroit, Dec. 4, 1968; s. Sathien and Malee Suntra. BA summa cum laude, St. Louis U., 1991, MD cum laude, 1995. Diplomate Am. Bd. Otolaryngology, bd. eligible Am. Bd. Facial Plastic and Reconstructive Surgery. Intern gen. surgery Boston U. Sch. Medicine/Boston Med. Ctr., 1995—96; resident otolaryngology-head and neck surgery Boston U. Sch. Medicine, 1996—2000; chief resident Boston Med. Ctr./Boston U., 1999—2000; fellow facial plastic and reconstructive surgery Park Ctrl. Inst./Forest Park Hosp., St. Louis, 2000—01; med. staff Forest Pk. Hosp., St. Louis, 2000—01, Sutter Gould Med. Found., Modesto, Calif., 2001—, Doctors Med. Ctr., Modesto, 2001; asst. clin. prof. Sch. Medicine U. Calif., Davis. Presenter in field. Contbr. articles to profl. jours. Fellow: ACS, Am. Bd. Otolaryngology; mem.: Thai Physicians Assn. Am., Am. Rhinologic Soc., Am. Acad. Facial Plastic and Reconstructive Surgery, Am. Acad. Otolaryngology-Head and Neck Surgery, Phi Eta Sigma, Alpha Epsilon Delta, Beta Beta Beta, Alpha Sigma Nu, Phi Beta Kappa, Alpha Omega Alpha. Office: Gould Medical Group 600 Coffee Rd Modesto CA 95355 Business E-Mail: suntrac@sutterhealth.org.

SUPANVANIJ, JANIKAN, finance educator; b. Bangkok, Aug. 6, 1971; arrived in U.S., 1993; d. Vitaya and Sopha Supanvanij. BBA, Thammasat U., Bangkok, 1993; MFN in Fin., St. Louis U., 1995, MBA in Fin. and Econs., 1996, postgrad., 1997—. Cert. tchg. skills. Internat. banking facility fgn. exch. dealer The Thai Mil. Bank, Ltd., Bangkok, 1993; instr. St. Louis U., 1997—. Contbr. articles to profl. jours. Mem.: St. Louis U. Grad. Student Assn. (webmaster 1997—2002, GSA rsch. symposium program co-chair 2001—02, pres. 2002—03), Alpha Epsilon Lambda. Office: St Louis U 3674 Lindell Blvd Saint Louis MO 63108

SUPPA-FRIEDMAN, JANICE DESTEFANO, secondary school educator, consultant; b. Morristown, NJ, Apr. 27, 1943; d. Eugene Arthur and Isabella Vienna (Bottiglia) DeS.; m. Dennis Suppa, June 28, 1964 (div. May 1994); children: Julie Ann, Chad Dennis; m. Michael Jac Friedman, Oct. 7, 1995. BS in Edn., Bowling Green State U., 1964; MA in Edn., Va. Poly. Inst. & State U., 1977, cert. advanced grad. study, 1990. Cert. secondary tchr., Va. Tchr. English and reading Northwood (Ohio) Jr. High Sch., 1964—66; tchr. English and history Canaseraga (N.Y.) Ctrl. Schs., 1966—67; tchr. English and reading Marstellar Jr. High Sch., Manassas, Va., 1967—72; tchr. English Taylor Jr. High sch., Warrenton, Va., 1973—74; tchr. English and reading, lang. arts specialist, dept. head, lead tchr. Brentsville Dist. Mid.-Sr. High Sch., Nokesville, Va., 1975—99; reading specialist Graham Park Middle Sch., Dumfries, Va., 1999—2000; ednl. cons., 2000—. Ednl. cons. So. Region Coll. Bd., 2001—; reader for advanced placement literature and composition exam, 1996, 1998-2003; adj. prof. Old Dominion U., 1999, No. Va. C.C., 1992-94; forensics finals judge State of Va., 2000-02; presenter if field. Editor newsletter Spinning Wheel, 1991-94; contbr. articles to profl. jours. Va. English Bull. Tour guide George Washington Fredericksburg Found. at Kenmore Mansion and Plantation, Ferry Farms, Va., 2001—; officer of election Stafford County, 2001—03. Grantee Va. Comm. of the Arts, 1994-95, 2000, Prince William Edn. Found., 1996, 2000, Greater Washington Reading Coun., 1999, 2000, Va. Opera Assn., 2000, So. States Southland Corp., 2000. Mem. NATE (pres. 1992-1994), Nat. Coun. Tchrs. English (coord. Va. state Achievement in Writing awards 1995-2001, Va. state liaison 2001, judge Va. state forensics finals 2000-2003, judge Va. state excellence in lit. mags. 1998-2003), Va. Assn. Tchrs. English (exec. bd. 1992—, v.p. 2001-02, pres.-elect 2002-03, Svc. award 1993), Phi Delta Kappa. Avocations: reading, music, hiking, swimming, biking.

SUPPES, PATRICK, philosophy, statistics, psychology educator and education; b. Tulsa, Mar. 17, 1922; s. George Biddle and Ann (Costello) Suppes; m. Joan Farmer, Apr. 16, 1946 (div. 1970); children: Patricia, Deborah, John Biddle; m. Joan Sieber, Mar. 29, 1970 (div. 1973); m. Christine Johnson, May 26, 1979; children: Alexandra Christine, Michael Patrick. BS, U. Chgo., 1943; PhD (Wendell T. Bush fellow), Columbia U., 1950; LLD, U. Nijmegen, Netherlands, 1979; Dr. honoris causa (hon.), U. Rene Descartes, Paris, 1982, U. Regensburg, Germany, 1999, U. Bologna, Italy, 1999. Instr., Stanford U., 1950—52, asst. prof., 1952—55, assoc. prof., 1955—59, prof. philosophy, statistics, psychology and edn., 1959—92, prof. emeritus. Founder, CEO Computer Curriculum Corp., 1967—90. Author: Introduction to Logic, 1957, Axiomatic Set Theory, 1960, Sets and Numbers, books 1-6, 1966, Studies in the Methodology and Foundations of Science, 1969, A Probabilistic Theory of Causality, 1970, Logique du Probable, 1981, Probabilistic Metaphysics, 1984, Estudios de Filosofia y Metodologí de la Ciencia, 1988, Language for Humans and Robots, 1991, Models and Methods in the Philosophy of Science, 1993, Representation and Invariance of Scientific Structures, 2002; author: (with Davidson and Siegel) Decision Making, 1957; author: (with Richard C. Atkinson) Markov Learning Models for Multiperson Interactions, 1960; author: (with Shirley Hill) First Course in Mathematical Logic, 1964; author: (with Edward J. Crothers) Experiments on Second-Language Learning, 1967; author: (with Max Jerman and Dow Brian) Computer-assisted Instruction, 1965—66, Stanford Arithmetic Program, 1968; author: (with D. Krantz, R.D. Luce and A. Tversky) Foundations of Measurement, Vol. 1, 1971, Vol. 2, 1989, Vol. 3, 1990; author: (with M. Morningstar) Computer-Assisted Instruction at Stanford, 1966-68, 1972; author: (with B. Searle and J. Friend) The Radio Mathematics Project: Nicaragua, 1974-75, 1976; author: (with Colleen Crangle) Language and Learning for Robots, 1994; author: (with Mario Zanotti) Foundations of Probability with Applications, 1996. Served to capt. USAAF, 1942-46. Recipient Nicholas Murray Butler Silver medal, Columbia U., 1965, Disting. Sci. Contbr. award, APA, 1972, Tchrs. Coll. medal for disting. svc., 1978, Nat. medal Sci., NSF, 1990; fellow, Ctr. for Advanced Study Behavioral Scis., 1955—56, NSF, 1957—58. Fellow: APA, AAAS, Assn. Computing Machinery, Am. Acad. Arts and Scis.; mem.: NAS, Chilean Acad. Scis., European Acad. Scis. and Arts, Norwegian Acad. Sci. and Letters (fgn.), Russian Acad. Edn. (fgn.), Am. Ednl. Rsch. Assn. (pres. 1973—74), Internat. Union History and Philosophy of Sci. (pres. divsn. logic, methodology and philosophy of sci. 1975—79), Finnish Acad. Sci. and Letters, Internat. Inst. Philosophy, Croatian Acad. Scis. (corr.), Nat. Acad. Edn. (pres. 1973—77), Acad. Internat. de Philosophie des Scis. (titular), Am. Math. Soc., Assn. Symbolic Logic, Am. Philos. Soc., Am. Philos. Assn., Math. Assn. Am., Sigma Xi. E-mail: psuppes@cstanford.edu.

SUPPLE, JEROME H. academic administrator; b. Boston, Apr. 27, 1936; m. Catherine Evans; 3 children. BS in Chemistry, Boston Coll., 1957, MS in Organic Chemistry, 1959; PhD in Organic Chemistry, U. New Hampshire, 1963. Asst. prof. chemistry SUNY Coll., Fredonia, 1964-69, assoc. prof., 1969-76, prof., 1976-78, acting dept. chair, 1975-76, assoc. dean for arts and scis., 1972-73, assoc. v.p. for acad. affairs, 1973-78, acting v.p. for acad. affairs, 1977, dean for gen. and spl. studies, 1977-78; assoc. provost for undergrad. edn. SUNY Cen. Adminstrn., 1974-75; prof. chemistry, v.p. for acad. affairs SUNY Coll., Plattsburgh, acting pres., 1978-89, on leave 1988-89, acting provost, v.p. for acad. affairs Postsdam, 1988-89; prof. chemistry, pres. S.W. Tex. State U., San Marcos, 1989—. Faculty fellow NSF, vis. rsch. faculty U. East Anglia, Norwich, Eng., 1970-71. Author books; contbr. numerous articles to profl. jours. Mem. Tex. Gov.'s total quality mgmt. steering com. Eastman Kodak rsch. fellow. Mem. AAAS, NCAA (pres. commn.), Am. Chem. Soc., Am. Assn. Higher Edn., Am. Assn. State Colls. and Univs. (bd. dirs.), Am. Coun. on Edn. (mem. commn. on govtl. rels.), So. Assn. Colls. and Schs. Commn. on Colls., Tex. Coun. on Econ. Edn. (bd. dirs.), Tex. Coun. Pub. Univ. Pres. and Chancellors (state affairs and exec. com.), Tex. Assn. Coll. Tchrs., Tex. Higher Edn. Master Plan Adv. Com., San Marcos C. of C. Econ. Devel. Coun., San Marcos Rotary, Golden Key, Sigma Xi (past pres. Fredonia club), Phi Eta Sigma (hon.), Omicron Delta Kappa (hon.). Office: SW Tex State U Office of Pres 1020 J C Kellam Bldg San Marcos TX 78666

SURBECK-HARRIS, JOYCE ANNETTE, special education administrator; b. Jacksonville, Ill., July 21, 1947; d. Myrl Guy and Audrey G. (Black) Surbeck; m. Andrew O. Harris. BS in Edn., Ill. State U., 1974, EdD, 1992; MS in Edn., So. Ill. U., 1976. Cert. tchr.and adminstr., Ill. Program specialist 4 Rivers Spl. Edn., Jacksonville, 1976-79; instr. MacMurray Coll., Jacksonville, 1979-80; program coord. Macon-Piatt Spl. Edn., Decatur, Ill., 1981-83; tchr. Jacksonville Pub. Schs., 1983-84; edn. coord. Family Svcs. and Vis. Nurses Assn. Project Head Start, Alton, Ill., 1984-87; mgr. Ill. State Bd. Edn., Springfield, Ill., 1987-88; state coord. deaf-blind Minn. Dept. of Edn., St. Paul, 1989—, cons., 1990—. Adj. prof. Ill. Coll., Jacksonville, 1980-87; owner Surbeck & Assocs., St. Paul, 1987—; cons. in field. Author: Implemting SLD Criteria, 1992; co-author: Behavior Disorders in Ealry Childhood, 1986; producer tng. video tapes. Developer various parent support programs, Ill, 1973—, Children Linking Families, Minn., 1990. U.S. Office of Edn. grantee, 1989, 90, 91, 92. Mem. Coun. for Exceptional Children, Coun. for Admisntrs. Spl. Edn. Avocations: horse showing and riding, target shooting.

SURBER, JOE ROBERT, assistant superintendent; b. Pawhuska, Okla., Apr. 11, 1942; s. Hugh Richard and Odema (Harris) S.; m. Jo Del Novak; children: Robert Brian, Karrie Jo. BA in Edn., Northeastern State U., 1964; MS in Edn., Okla. State U., 1969, EdD, 1974. Cert. supt., sch. psychologist, sch. counselor. High sch. prin. Unity Bd. Govs., Ponca City, Okla., 1970-71; sch. psychologist Bi-State Mental Health Found., Ponca City, 1971-74; adj. prof. Okla. State U., Ponca City, 1976-84; asst. supt. Ponca City Pub. Schs., 1984—. Pub. The Blue Book of Counseling: Concrete Tools and Techniques, 1976. Past dir. ARC, Ponca City Crime Stoppers, Kay County Youth Shelter, Okla. Assn. Schs. with Impacted Svcs. Staff sgt. USAR, 1966-72. Named One of 3 Outstanding Oklahomans, 1976; recipient Disting. Svc. award, 1973, Outstanding Educator award, 1972. Pres. Okla. Dirs. Spl. Svcs. (past pres.), Okla. Sch. Psychol. Assn. (v.p.). Home: 1308 Desoto Ponca City OK 74604 E-mail: joejo@cableone.net.

SURBER, REGINA BRAMMELL, early childhood education educator, administrator; b. Grayson, Ky., Apr. 3, 1952; d. Jack D. and Opal (Mullins) Brammell; m. Thomas Jerry Surber, Dec. 18, 1976; 1 child, Jerry David. BA in Elem. Edn., Berea Coll., 1974; MA in Early Childhood Edn., Ea. Ky. U., 1975; PhD in Child Care Administrn., Hamilton U., 1998. Cert. K-8 grade tchr., ky., Tenn. Kindergarten tchr. Carter County Bd. Edn., Grayson, Ky.; presch. tchr. Oak Ridge Nursery Sch., Tenn.; elem. tchr. Anderson County Bd. Edn., Clinton, Tenn.; dir. daycare Roane State Community Coll., Harriman, Tenn., 1989-90; exec. dir. Knox Assn. on Young Children, Knoxville, Tenn., 1993-98, Tenn. Assn. for Edn. of Young Children, Nashville, 1999—. Dir. weekday sch. programs 1st Meth. Ch., Oak Ridge, 1990-93. Mem. ASCD, Nat. Assn. for Edn. Young Children, Tenn. Assn. on Young Children, Anderson Area Assn. on Young Children, So. Early Childhood Assn.

SURECK, KAREN EILEEN, special education educator; b. Evansville, Ind., Dec. 8, 1949; d. Paul Edwin and Joyce Eileen (Marshall) Hachmeister; m. Gregory John Sureck, Apr. 18, 1981; children: John Gregory, Kate Elizabeth. BS, Murray State U., 1971; MA, U. Evansville, 1975. Lic. profl. educator. Tchr. spl. edn. Warrick County Sch. Corp., Boonville, Ind., 1971—. Dist. pres. United Meth. Women, Evansville, 1995—. Recipient Outstanding Young Educator award Jaycees, 1974, Outstanding Young Woman of Am. award, 1983. Mem. NEA, AAUW, Ind. State Tchrs. Assn., Warrick County Tchrs. Assn. Republican. Avocations: travel, reading, community involvement. Home: 766 S Rockport Rd Boonville IN 47601-9739 Office: Oakdale Elem Sch 802 S 8th St Boonville IN 47601-2000

SURERUS, DOROTHEA KAE, elementary education educator; b. Brocket, ND, May 22, 1938; d. Stanley Gustave and Alma (Kalliokoski) Berg; married, June 3, 1961 (div., Jan. 1979); children: Kristene, Kelly, Kory. BS, Mayville State U., 1961. Tchr. third grade Beulah (ND) Pub. Sch., 1958-59; tchr. fourth grade Cavalier (ND) Pub. Sch., 1959-60; tchr. second and fourth grade Neche (ND) Pub. Sch., 1962; tchr. basic skills Moorhead (Minn.) Pub. Sch., 1969-70; tchr. elem. edn. Cooperstown (ND) Pub. Sch., 1970—99; tutor Griggs County (ND) Ctrl. Pub. Sch., 1999—2003. Mem. ASCD, NEA, N.D. Edn. Assn., Cooperstown Edn. Assn. (pres. 7 yrs.). Home: PO Box 624 1417 Roberts Ave NE Cooperstown ND 58425-7149 Office: Cooperstown Elem Sch Cooperstown ND 58425

SURMA, JANE ANN, secondary education educator; b. Chgo., Dec. 11, 1947; d. John James and Genevieve (Buettner) S. BS, Barry U., Miami, Fla., 1969; MST, U. Ill., 1974. Tchr. phys. edn. Little Flower H.S., Chgo., 1969-72; tchr. English, phys. edn. and health, coach Oak Lawn (Ill.) Cmty. H.S., 1974—. Named Coach of Yr. Southtown Economist, 1992, Boy's Volleyball Ill. State Championship Coach, 1994, Fred Parks Coach of Yr., 1995. Mem. AAHPERD, Ill. H.S. Coaches Assn., Ill. H.S. Assn., Nat. Coun. Tchrs. English. Roman Catholic.

SURPRENANT, FAITH ELSIE, parochial school educator; b. Webster, Mass., July 7, 1949; d. Conrad H. and Betty A. (Stamp) Redlitz; m. Ronald J. Surprenant, Aug. 3, 1991. BA, Concordia Tchrs. Coll., River Forest, Ill., 1971; MEd, Trenton (N.Y.) State Coll., 1979. Tchr. grades 1-2 Trinity Luth. Sch., Niagara Falls, N.Y., 1971-74; tchr. grades 3-6 Hope Luth. Sch., Levittown, Pa., 1974-81; tchr. grades 4-6 Faith Luth. Sch., Whittier, Calif., 1981-86; prin. St. John's Luth. Sch., S.I., N.Y., 1986-91; tchr. grades 7-8 Hephatha Luth. Sch., Anaheim, Calif., 1991—, asst. prin., 2000—. Tchr. rep. Dist. Elem. Cabinet, Luth. Schs., Irvine, Calif., 1992-96. Mem. Luth. Edn. Assn., Nat. Coun. Tchrs. Math., Eli Home Aux. Lutheran. Avocations: reading, crafts, embroidery. Home: 219 N Wanda Dr Fullerton CA 92833-2645 Office: Hephatha Lutheran School 5900 E Santa Ana Canyon Rd Anaheim CA 92807-3201

SUSKIND, DIANA LEE, education educator; b. Syracuse, N.Y., June 30, 1947; d. Philip and Ida (Landau) S.; m. Mitchell G. Roth, Aug. 5, 1979 (div. Aug. 1989). BS in Elem. Edn., SUNY, Brockport, 1969; postgrad., Syracuse U., 1970, Harvard U., 1994, Emmi Pikler Inst., Budapest, Hungary, 1992; MS in Early Childhood Edn., 1973; EdD in Early Childhood Edn., U. Ill., 1979. Tchr. Earlington Heights Elem. Sch., Miami, Fla., 1969-71; reading specialist Syracuse (N.Y.) Sch. Dist., 1971-72; English tchr., dir. Parent Coop. Nursery Sch. Am. U. Assn., Chaing Mai, Thailand, 1972; childcare giver Kibbutz Beeri, Negev, Israel, 1973; lectr. Fitchburg (Mass.) State Coll., 1973-75; grad. asst. dept. elem. and early childhood edn. U. Ill., Urbana, 1975-79; asst. prof., supr. tchr. tng. Sch. Edn. Calif. State U., L.A., 1980-81; lectr. continuing edn. dept. U. Alaska, Fairbanks, 1984-89; edn. specialist coord. Child Devel. Svcs., Ft. Wainwright Army Base, Alaska, 1985-88, edn. specialist, 1988-89; lead edn. specialist Child Devel. Svcs. Smiley Barracks, Karlsruhe, Germany, 1988-91; asst. prof. edn. Fitchburg State Coll., 1991-99, assoc. prof. edn., 1999—. Head tchr. Pacific Oaks Children's Sch., Pasadena, Calif., summer 1981; vis. faculty mem. dept. psychology U. Alaska, Anchorage, 1981-82, art instr. Fine Arts Camp, 1985; coord. State Wide Early Childhood Conf., Fairbanks, 1985-86; lead presch. tchr. New Eng. Dance Camp, Poland Spring, Maine, 1993, lead infant-toddler tchr., 1994-95; trainer European Edn. Specialists, Germany, 1991; vis. acad. Ctr. for Applied Studies, Queensland U. Tech., Brisbane, Australia, fall 1998; participant NEH Faculty Devel. Workshop for Infusing African and Asian Studies into the Undergrad. Curriculum, 2000, Whispering Woods Conf., Olive Branch, Miss; guest prof. U. Udine, Italy, 2001; spkr. in field; presenter in field; Fulbright sr. specialist N.Z. Child Care Assn., 2003, Tetari Puna Ora o Aotearoa, 2003; keynote spkr. Fairbanks Assn. Young Children, 2003. Contbr. articles to profl. publs.; art exhibited in one woman shows at Karlsruhe, 1987-89; exhibited work at Palace, Haiti, 1994, Leominster Art Assn., 1997 (1st prize, 3d prize, 2d prize Gardner Art Assn. 1998); columnist Anchorage Times, Fairbanks Daily News Miner, 1981-87. Mem. Mayor's Task Force on Families and Children, Fairbanks, 1988-89, vocat. Adv. Coun., Fairbanks North Star Borough Sch. Dist., 1987-88, mem. alternative elem. com., 1986-87; mem. CCREE State Task Force on Early Childhood Edn., 1981-83; bd. dirs. Tanina Child Devel. Ctr., Anchorage, 1981-82. Grantee Fitchburg State Coll. Alumni Assn., 1974, State of Alaska Dept. Cmty. and Regional Affairs, 1988, Project Palms, 1993, A-Tip Alumni Assn., 1974, 93, 96, Marion and Jasper Whiting Found., 1996; fellow Resource for Infant Educarers, 1988—; Fulbright Sr. scholar specialist New Zealand Child Care Assn., 2003. Mem Fairbanks Assn. for Edn. Young Children (v.p. 1985), Kappa Delta Pi, Pi Delta Kappa. Home: 20 Main St 5th Fl Apt O Leominster MA 01453-5530

SUSKIND, SIGMUND RICHARD, microbiology educator; b. N.Y.C., June 19, 1926; s. Seymour and Nina Phillips S.; m. Ann Parker, July 1, 1951; children: Richard, Mark, Steven. AB, NYU, 1948; PhD, Yale U., 1954. Research asst. biology div. Oak Ridge Nat. Lab., 1948-50; USPHS fellow NYU Med. Sch., N.Y.C., 1954-56; mem. faculty Johns Hopkins U., Balt., 1956—, prof. biology, 1965-96, univ. prof., 1983-96, prof. emeritus, 1996—, Univ. ombudsman, 1988-91, dean grad. and undergrad. studies, 1971-78, dean Sch. Arts and Scis., 1978-83. Head molecular biology sect. NSF, 1970-71; cons. NIH, 1966-70, Coun. Grad. Schs., Mid States Assn. Colls. and Secondary Schs., 1973—, NSF, 1986; vis. scientist Weizmann Inst. of Sci., Israel, 1985; trustee Balt. Hebrew U., 1985-93; mem. adv. bd. La. Geriatric Ctr., 1990—. Author: (with P.E. Hartman) Gene Action, 1964, 69, (with P.E. Hartman and T. Wright) Principles of Genetics Laboratory Manual, 1965; editor: (with P.E. Hartman) Foundations of Modern Genetics series, 1964, 69; mem. sci. editorial bd. Johns Hopkins U. Press, 1973-76, 88-91. With USNR, 1944-46. NIH grantee, 1957-76 Fellow AAAS; mem. Am. Soc. Microbiology, Genetics Soc. Am., Am. Assn. Immunology, Am. Soc. Biol. Chemistry and Molecular Biology, Coun. Grad Schs., Assn. Grad. Schs., Northeastern Assn. Grad. Schs. (exec. com. 1975-76, pres. 1977-78). Avocation: research in microbial biochemical genetics and immunogenetics. Office: Johns Hopkins U Dept Biology and McCollum-Pratt Inst 34th and Charles Sts Baltimore MD 21218

SUSKO, CAROL LYNNE, lawyer, accountant; b. Washington, Dec. 5, 1955; d. Frank and Helen Louise (Davis) S. BS in Econs. and Acctg., George Mason U., 1979; JD, Cath. U., 1982; LLM in Taxation, Georgetown U., 1992. Bar: Pa. 1989, D.C. 1990; CPA, Va., Md. Tax acct. Reznick Fedder & Silverman, P.C., Bethesda, Md., 1984-85; sr. tax acct. Pannell Kerr Forster, Alexandria, Va., 1985; tax specialist Coopers & Lybrand, Washington, 1985-87; supervisory tax sr. Frank & Co., McLean, Va., 1987-88; mem. editl. staff Tax Notes Mag., Arlington, Va., 1989-90; adj. faculty Am. U., Washington, 1989—; tax atty. Marriott Corp., Washington, 1993-94; sr. tax mgr. Host Marriott Inc., Washington, 1994-99, KPMG LLP, McLean, Va., 1999—. Mem. ABA, AICPAs, Va. Soc. CPAs, D.C. Soc. CPAs, D.C. Bar Assn. Office: KPMG LLP Ste 3064 1660 International Dr Mc Lean VA 22102-4832 E-mail: csusko@kpmg.com.

SUSSKIND, LAWRENCE ELLIOTT, urban and environmental planner, educator, public dispute mediator; b. N.Y.C., Jan. 12, 1947; s. David J. and Marjorie H. (Friedman) S.; m. Miriam Mason, June 8, 1968 (div. Dec. 1982); m. Leslie Webster Tuttle, Dec. 12, 1982; children: Noah Gates, Lily Webster. AB in Sociology, Columbia U., 1968; M.C.P., MIT, 1970, PhD in Urban Planning, 1973. Asst. prof. urban and environ. planning MIT, Cambridge, 1971-74, assoc. prof., 1974-82, prof., 1982-95, Ford prof., 1995—, head dept., 1978-82, dir. MIT-Harvard Pub. Disputes Program, 1980—; exec. dir. program on negotiation Harvard Law Sch., 1984-87, visiting prof. law, 2001—. Pres. Consensus Bldg. Inst., 1993—. Author: Paternalism, Conflict and Co-Production, 1983, Proposition 1 1/2; Its Impact on Massachusetts, 1983, Resolving Environmental Regulatory Disputes, 1983, Breaking the Impasse, 1987, Environmental Diplomacy, 1994, Reinventing Congress for the 21st Century, 1995, Dealing With an Angry Public, 1996, Consensus Building Handbook, 1999, Negotiating on Behalf of Others, 1999, Negotiating Environmental Agreements, 1999, Better Environmental Policy Studies, 2001, Transboundary Environmental Negotiation, 2002; sr. editor, founder Environ. Impact Assessment Rev., 1980-96; editl. policy bd. Negotiation Jour., 1984—. Mem. Am. Inst. Cert. Planners, Assn. for Conflict Resolution. Jewish. Home: 32 Jericho Hill Rd Southborough MA 01772-1007 Office: MIT 9-330 Cambridge MA 02139 E-mail: susskind@mit.edu.

SUSSMAN, BEVERLY KALL, elementary education educator; b. Bklyn. BA, CUNY, 1962, MEd, 1969. Cert. tchr. N.Y. State, Ill. Tchr. grades kindergarten through 8 N.Y.C. Bd. Edn., Bklyn., 1962-70; tchr. sci. grade 6, unit leader Kildeer Sch. Dist. 96, Buffalo Grove, Ill., 1977—. Instr. Nat. Louis U., Evanston, Ill., 1989—; pres. AIM Bus. Printers, Buffalo Grove; participant NASA workshop; condr. workshops in field. Contbr. articles to profl. jours. Organizer Adopt-A-Whale Program, Buffalo Grove; judge Ill. Jr. Acad. Scis., Buffalo Grove, 1983—. Recipient NASA Edn. Workshop award for elem. sch. tchrs., 1988; named Outstanding Tchr. of Sci. in Ill., NSF, 1989, 90, 91. Mem. NEA, AAAS, AAUW, ASCD, Ill. Edn. Assn., Nat. Sci. Tchrs. Assn. (Presidental award for excellence in sci. tchg. 1994), Ill. Sci. Tchrs. Assn. (award of excellence in secondary sci. tchg. 1993), Coun. for Elem. Sci. Internat. Avocations: sewing, photography, writing. Home: 861 Indian Spring Ln Buffalo Grove IL 60089-1326

SUSSMAN, SHARON ANN, art educator; b. Long Beach, Calif., Mar. 2, 1951; d. Martin and Hazel Edna (Sorenson) S.; children: Sebriano, Django, Eric. BA, U. Calif., Santa Cruz, 1978; postgrad., San Jose State U. Prof. U. Calif., Santa Cruz, 1979—96; visual interface designer Apple Computer, Inc., Sunnyvale, Calif., 1994—95; digital developer DreamWorks Feature Animation, 1996—2002; instr. Kapi'olani C.C., 2002—. Elizabeth Greenshields Found. grantee for painting, 1982, art rsch. grantee Daniel Smith, Inc., 1989, art grantee Santa Cruz Arts Coun., 1993. Mem. Internat. Interactive Comm. Soc. Home: 3532 Sierra Dr Honolulu HI 96818

SUTER, BRUCE WILSEY, electrical engineering educator, researcher; b. Paterson, N.J., Sept. 15, 1949; s. Paul LaBarrer and Susan Robertson (Wilsey) S.; m. Deborah Sue Boudinet, Oct. 4, 1974. BSEE, MSEE, U.South Fla., 1972, PhD in Computer Sci., 1988. Design engr. Honeywell, Inc., St. Petersburg, Fla., 1972-77; sr. design engr. Litton Industries, Woodland Hills, Calif., 1977-80; research asst. U. South Fla., Tampa, 1980-85; instr. computer sci. U. Ala. Birmingham, 1985-88, asst. prof., 1988-89; asst. prof. computer sci. Air Force Inst. Tech., Wright-Patterson AFB, Ohio, 1989-91, assoc. prof. computer sci., 1991-95, assoc. prof. elec. engring., 1995-97, prof. elec. engring., 1997-98; prin. electronics engr. Air Force Rsch. Lab., Rome, N.Y., 1998—. Dir. Air Force Rsch. Lab. Ctr. of Excellence for Integrated Transmission and Exploitation, 2000—; vis. prof. computer sci. Harvard U., 2003—. Assoc. editor IEEE Trans. on Signal Processing, 1994-96; contbr. numerous articles to profl. jours. U. South Fla. Grad. Sch. fellow, 1984-85. Mem. IEEE (Regional award 1999, Gen. Ronald W. Yates award for excellence in tech. transfer 2000, Arthur S. Fleming award, 2001), KC, Eta Kappa Nu, Tau Beta Pi. Democrat. Roman Catholic. Home: c/o Residence Inn 6 Cambridge Ctr Cambridge MA 02142 Office: Air Force Rsch Lab AFRL/IFGC 525 Brooks Rd Rome NY 13441-4505 E-mail: bruce.suter@rl.af.mil.

SUTER, JON MICHAEL, academic library director, educator; b. Holdenville, Okla., Oct. 30, 1941; s. Franklin Hyatt and Erma (Abee) S. BA cum laude, East Cen. State Coll., 1963; MLS, U. Okla., 1964; PhD, Ind. U., 1973. Asst. libr. East Cen. State Coll., Ada, Okla., 1964-76; assoc. libr. East Cen. U., Ada, Okla., 1976-84; dir. librs. Houston Bapt. U., 1984—. Chmn. Libr. Edn. Div. Okla. Libr. Assn., 1981, Coll. Rsch. Libr. Div., Okla., 1982. Contbr. articles to profl. jours. Pres. Ada Camp Gideons Internat., 1980-82. Higher Edn. Act fellow Ind. U., 1969-71. Mem. Popular Culture Assn., Richard III Socl., Med. Acad., Renaissance Soc., Patristics Soc. Republican. Baptist. Avocations: comic books, medieval history. Home: 8271 Wednesbury Ln Houston TX 77074-2918 Office: Houston Bapt U - Moody Libr 7502 Fondren Rd Houston TX 77074-3204 E-mail: jsuter@hbu.edu.

SUTHERLAND, BERRY, geologist, educator; b. Pleasanton, Tex., Feb. 10, 1932; s. John Wesley and Georgia Elizabeth (Savage) S.; m. Betty Jeanne Thompson, Aug. 23, 1961; children: Cathy, Dianne. BS in Geology, U. Tex., 1961; MS, U. Houston, 1968, EdD, 1970. Geol. engr. Caran Engring. Corp., San Antonio, 1961-63; instr. U. Houston, 1963-69; petroleum geologist Getty Oil Co., Houston, 1967-69; asst. prof. U. Fla., Gainesville, 1969-71; mgr. curriculum devel. RCA Corp., Dallas, 1971-72; from asst. prof. to prof. U. Tex., San Antonio, 1972—. Author: Focus on Earth Science, vols. 1-13, 1976-89, La Ciencia de la Tierra y del Espacio, 1985; contbr. articles to profl. jours. Sci. fair dir. Alamo Acad. Sci. & Engring., San Antonio, 1985-97; mem. Action Coalition on Crime Mex. Am. Legal Def. & Edn. Fund, San Antonio, 1978. Served in USN, 1950-54, Guam, Korea. Mem. Geol. Soc. Am., Nat. Street Rod Assn., Sigma Xi, Phi Delta Kappa. Avocations: antique automobiles, hiking, fishing, rock and mineral collecting. Home: 10050 Axis Dr Boerne TX 78006-5122 Office: U Tex 6900 N Loop 1604 W San Antonio TX 78249-1130

SUTRO, EDMUND J. secondary school educator, consultant; b. L.A., Aug. 4, 1946; s. Paul and Ethelwyn (Ziegler) S. AA, L.A. Valley Coll., Van Nuys, 1966; AB, U. So. Calif., L.A., 1969, MSc, 1971; PhD, Stanford U., 1979. Cert. tchr., Calif. Tchr. Pasadena (Calif.) H.S., 1969-92, Arcadia (Calif.) H.S., 1992—. Commr. Calif. Commn. on Tchg. Credentials, Sacramento, 1992-95; mem. adv. bd. Occidental Coll., L.A., 1990—, L.A. Times, 1971-72; reviewer Dept. Edn., Washington; guest lectr. U. So. Calif., Calif. State Coll., L.A., Calif. Inst. Tech., Stanford U.; spkr. Pasadena Star News; acad. cons., L.A.; manuscript reviewer Social Edn. Contbr. articles to profl. jours. Co-chair Calif. chpt. Bush-Quayle '92, 1992; trustee Flintridge Prep. Sch., La Canada, Calif., 1992—, Pilgrim Sch., L.A., 1990—; bd. dirs. L.A. Bach. Festival, Pasadena Chamber Orch.; prodn. chair, bd. dirs., mem. adv. bd. Hollywood Bowl Easter Sunrise Svc.; vol. Head Start, Bell Gardens/Montebello; vol. fundraiser Sta. KCET Channel 28, L.A.; charter mem. Greater L.A. Zoo Assn. Mem. ASCD, Ednl. Excellence Network, Nat. Coun. for the Social Studies, Calif. Coun. for the Social Studies, Phi Delta Kappa, Tau Kappa Epsilon (pres., past pledge trainer). Republican.

SUTTER, BARTON E. literature educator, writer; b. Mpls., Dec. 15, 1949; s. Harold Edwin and Virginia Mae (Eastman) Sutter; m. Dorothea Stowell Diver, Aug. 28, 1994; children: Liselotte D. Stuecher, Bettina J. Stuecher; m. Annette Marie Atkins, 1981 (div. 1991). BA, S.W. State U., Marshall, Minn., 1972; MA, Syracuse U., 1975. Typesetter Composing Rm. New Eng., Boston, 1972—73, Typographic Arts, Mpls., 1976—85; lectr. U. Minn., Mpls., 1986—90, Duluth, 1988—98; from lectr. to sr. lectr. U. Wis., Superior, 1998—. Bd. dirs. Spirit Lake Poetry Series, Duluth. Author: My Father's War, 1991, The Book of Names, 1993, Cold Comfort, 1998. Recipient Minn. Book award for fiction, 1992, Minn. Book award for poetry, 1994, Minn. Book award for creative non-fiction, 1999. Mem.: Assn. Univ. Wis. Profls., Acad. Am. Poets (assoc.). Democrat. Mem. Soc. Of Friends. Avocations: canoeing, fishing, camping, cross country skiing. Home: 1321 E 8th St Duluth MN 55805 Office: Univ Wis Belknap & Catlin Superior WI 54880

SUTTER, MARK ROBERT, school administrator; b. Akron, Ohio, Jan. 15, 1962; s. Robert Roy and Barbara Jean (Hayes) S. BSc in Edn., Kent State U., 1984, MEd, 1988, PhD, 1994. Cert. tchr., adminstr., Ohio. Tchr. Barberton (Ohio) City Schs., 1984-85, Cleveland Heights (Ohio)/University Heights City Schs., 1985-90; jr. high sch. asst. prin. Strongsville (Ohio) City Schs., 1990-94; prin. Willetts Mid. Sch., Brunswick, Ohio, 1994—. Vol. Big Bros./Big Sisters Greater Akron, 1988—. Mem. ASCD, Nat. Assn. Secondary Sch. Adminstrs., Ohio Assn. Secondary Sch. Adminstrs., Kappa Delta Pi. Republican. Methodist. Avocations: foreign travel, scuba diving. Office: Willetts Mid Sch 1045 Hadcock Rd Brunswick OH 44212-2757

SUTTERFIELD, DEBORAH KAY, special education educator; b. Amarillo, Tex., Apr. 22, 1956; d. Gail DeWayne and Esther Jane (Rogge) Quine; m. Thomas Wayne Sutterfield, Dec. 6, 1980; 1 child, Tristan Thomas. AD, Amarillo Jr. Coll., 1976; BS, Tex. Woman's U., 1978. Cert. in spl. edn., elem. edn. Jr. high resource tchr. Dumas (Tex.) Ind. Schs., 1978-80; substitute tchr. Amarillo Ind. Schs., 1980-81, secondary multiple handicapped tchr., 1981-95, functional living instr., 1995—. Pvt. tutor, Amarillo, 1988-94. Vol. Vol. Action Ctr., Amarillo, 1991-94; active Boy Scouts Am., 1989—99 Mem. Coun. for Exceptional Children, Assn. Tex. Profl. Educators (region v.p. 2002—), Friends of Amarillo (Tex.) Libr. Methodist. Avocations: counted cross-stitch, reading, table games. Home: 1909 Beech St Amarillo TX 79106-4505 E-mail: debbie.sutterfield@ama.isd.org.

SUTTERLIN, JAMES SMYRL, political science educator, researcher; b. Frankfort, Ky., Mar. 15, 1922; s. Frederick J. and Agnes (Douglas) S.; m. Betty C. Berven, June 24, 1950 (dec. Jan. 1989); children: Rose E., Sabrina, Jamie Ann, James E.; m. Renate Craine, Dec. 27, 1997. BA, Haverford Coll., 1943; postgrad., Harvard U., 1949, 67; hon. degree in jurisprudence, Kyung Hee U., Seoul, Korea, 1973. Vice-consul U.S. Fgn. Svc., Berlin, 1946-48; polit. officer U.S. Mission, Berlin, 1951-54; 1st sec. U.S. Embassy, Tel Aviv, 1954-56; desk officer U.S. State Dept., Washington, 1956-60; 1st sec. U.S. Embassy, Tokyo, 1960-63, counselor Bonn, 1963-68; dir. U.S. Dept. State, Washington, 1969-72, insp.-gen., 1972-74; dir. UN, N.Y.C., 1974-87; dir. rsch. L.I. U., Bklyn., 1985-87, adj. prof., 1985—; fellow/lectr. Yale U., New Haven, 1988—. Author: Berlin—Symbol of Confrontation, 1989, UN and the Maintenance of Security, 1995, The United Nations in Iraq: Defanging the Viper, 2003. Elder Presbyn. Ch., Port Chester, N.Y., 1976-96; chmn. Samaritan House, White Plains, N.Y., 1990-95; pres. Wainwright House, Rye, 1995-96; chmn. acad. coun. on the UN Brown U., 1995-97. 1st lt. U.S. Army, 1945-46. Recipient Grosse Verdienstkreuz, Fed. Republic of Germany, 1974. Mem. UN Assn. of U.S.A., Am. Coun. on Germany, Coun. Fgn. Rels., Phi Beta Kappa. Avocation: gardening. Home: 17 N Chatsworth Ave Apt 6k-l Larchmont NY 10538-2126 Office: Yale U 34 Hillhouse Ave New Haven CT 06511-3704 E-mail: jsutter729@aol.com.

SUTTLE, HELEN JAYSON, retired education educator; b. Plattsburgh, N.Y., Dec. 13, 1925; d. Harold Lincoln Jayson and Blanche Rabideau Jayson Woods; widowed, 1993; 1 child, Adolphia Helen Suttle Blanton. BA in Edn., Limestone Coll., 1961; MA in Edn., Winthrop U., 1973. Cert. tchr., S.C. Tchr. Madden Elem. Sch., Spartanburg, S.C., 1961-71, West Jr. High Sch., Gaffney, S.C., 1971-81, L.L. Vaughn Elem. Sch., Gaffney, S.C., 1981-88; substitute tchr. Gaffney Dis. 1, 1988—. Vol. SC Budget Control Bd., Upstate Carolina Med. Ctr., Meals on Wheels, Literacy Assn., local soup kitchen; chmn. Cherokee County Rep. Com.; v.p. Ch. Women's Guild, pres., 1998—; dir. religious edn. Sacred Heart Ch., 2001—; pres. Sacred Heart Sr. Citizens Club; treas. ch. com. Greenville Deanery; pres.-elect Piedmont Deanery, 2002—; Eucharistic min., lector; mem. exec. bd. SC Coun. Cath. Ch. Women, 1998—, chair family commn., 1998—; pres. Piedmont Deanery, 2002—03; trustee Limestone Coll. Named woman of Yr., S.C. Coun. Cath. Women Greenville Deanery, 1996. Fellow Internat. Biog. Assn. (life, dep. gov. Am. chpt.), Limestone Coll. Alumni Assn. (pres., chpt. pres.), Fountain Club (charter mem.), Kalosophia Honor Soc. Roman Catholic. Avocations: writing, art, gardening, crafts. Home: 201 Trenton Rd Gaffney SC 29340-3626

SUTTLES, DONALD ROLAND, retired academic administrator, business educator; b. Coldsprings, Ky., Nov. 14, 1929; s. Noah Elseworth and Bertha Viola (Seward) S.; m. Phyllis JoAnn McMullen, Dec. 12, 1952; children: Daniel, Ruth, Jonathan, Donna, Joanna, Stephen. Student, U. Md., 1949-50, U.S. Naval Acad., 1951-52; BBA, U. Cin., 1959; MBA, Xavier U., 1966; EdD, U. N.C.-Greensboro, 1977. Cert. mgmt. acct., internal auditor. With Procter & Gamble Co., Cin., 1952-73, supr., 1959-60, indsl. engr., 1960-63, cost engr., 1963-64, mgr. prodn. planning, 1965-68, asst. security coord., 1968-70, dept. mgr., 1970-73; dir. bus. affairs Piedmont Bible Coll., Winston-Salem, N.C., 1973-80, v.p. adminstrn., faculty, 1990-98; ret., 1998; assoc. prof. bus. Winston-Salem State U., 1978-87; prof. acctg. Catawba Coll., Salisbury, N.C., 1987-91. Bus. cons. Deacon, trustee, tchr. Bible sch. Salem Bapt. Ch.; vol. chaplain, Novant Med. Group. Served with USAF, 1948-51. Mem.: Gideons Internat. Home: 2300 Denise Ln Winston Salem NC 27127-8764

SUTTON, BETTY SHERIFF, elementary education educator; b. Orangeburg, S.C., Jan. 16, 1933; d. Luther Doyle and Mattie (White) Sheriff; m. William Bryan Nunn, June 19, 1954; 1 child, Lisbeth Sheriff Nunn (Mrs. William Reid Clark); m. James Carlton Sutton, Dec. 28, 1979 (dec., 1998). Student, Columbia Coll., 1949-52; BS, U. S.C., 1953. Tchr. grade 4 State of S.C. Pub. Sch., Blackville, 1953-54; tchr. grade 2 Dream Lake Elem. Sch., Apopka, Fla., 1954-64; tchr. spl. edn. Leon County Sch., Tallahassee, Fla., 1965-66; page mother Fla. Ho. Reps., Tallahassee, 1966-67; tchr. grade 3 Timberlane Elem. Sch./Leon County Schs., Tallahassee, 1967-71; tchr. grades 3 and 4 Golfview Elem. Sch./Brevard County Schs., Rockledge, Fla., 1972-86; tchr. grade 1 Cambridge Elem. Sch./Brevard County Schs., Cocoa, Fla., 1987-98; ret., 1998. Pres. Bits of Brevard, Inc., Rockledge. Chmn. Democrats for Conner, 1988, Keep Brevard Beautiful, 1990; active Brevard Symphony Orch. Guild, Brevard Mus. Guild, 1973—, Brevard Heritage Coun., Inc., Episcopal, St. Marks Guild. Recipient S.C. Forestry award State of S.C. Forestry Commn., 1977; ART grantee J. Paul Getty Ctr. for Edn. in the Arts, 1990. Mem. AAUW (pres. 1968-70), Apopka Woman's Club (pres. 1960-62), Apopka Garden Club, Brevard Reading Coun. (v.p. 1980-82), Am. Mothers, Inc., Columbia Coll. Column Club, Columbia Coll. Alumni Club. Ctrl. Fla., U. S.C. Alumni Club (life), Country Club of Rockledge, Delta Kappa Gamma (pres. 1992-94). Avocations: volunteering, reading, swimming, travel, farming. Home: 2201 Royal Oaks Dr Rockledge FL 32955-5440

SUTTON, JOE PERRY, special education educator; b. La Grange, N.C., Feb. 25, 1956; s. Wesley Allen and Shirley Arlene (Ferrell) S.; m. Connie Sue Jett, July 15, 1978; children: Jeremy Donald, Jason Wesley, Jared Paul. BS in Math. Edn., Bob Jones U., 1978; MAEd in Sch. Adminstrn., East Carolina U., 1985, MAEd in Spl. Edn., 1986; PhD in Spl. Edn., U. Va., 1989. Cert. tchr. math., sci., spl. edn., adminstrn., N.C., ednl. diagnostician, spl. edn. tchr., Wyo. Tchr. math. Goldsboro (N.C.) Christian Sch., 1978-79; asst. prin., tchr. math. and sci. Grace Christian Sch., Kinston, N.C., 1979-83; tchr. spl. edn. Dobbs Correctional Sch., Kinston, 1983-86; doctoral fellow U. Va., Charlottesville, 1986-89; prof., chair spl. edn. divsn. Bob Jones U., Greenville, S.C., 1989—. Pres. Exceptional Diagnostics, Simpsonville, S.C., 1991—; mem. S.C. Adv. Coun. on Edn. of Individuals with Disabilities, Columbia, S.C., 1994-2000; mem. bd. dirs. Hidden Treasure Christian Sch., Greenville, 1992—. Co-author: Strategies for Struggling Learners: A Guide for the Teaching Parent, 1995, 97; editor: Special Education: A Biblical Approach; mem. adv. panel Rsch. on Christian Edn. Jour., 1992—; cons./guest editor Assessment for Effective Intervention, 2000—; editor The Palmetto newsletter SCCEC, 1998-99, Selected News of SCTED, 1998-00. Mem. exec. bd. Coun. for Ednl. Diagnostic Svcs., 1997—, treas., 2000—, S.C. Fedn. Coun. Exceptional Children, 1997—, subdivsn. liaison, 1999—. Grantee Va. Dept. Edn., 1987-90, Interstate Maintenance Corp., 1993, Nat. Ctr. for Home Edn. Mem. Coun. Exceptional Children (divsn. learning disabilities, coun. for children with behavioral disorders, divsn. for rsch., coun. for ednl. diagnostic svcs., tchr. edn. divsn., exec. bd. dirs. S.C. subdivsn. tchg. edn. divsn. 1996—, v.p. 1996-97, pres. 1997-98), Children and Adults with Attention Deficit Disorder, Phi Delta Kappa. Home: 220 Douglas Dr Simpsonville SC 29681-6010 Office: Bob Jones Univ 1700 Wade Hampton Blvd Greenville SC 29614-0001 E-mail: sutton@edtesting.com.

SUTTON, JULIA ZEIGLER, retired special education educator; b. Greenville, Ala, July 24, 1935; d. Floyd Millard and Edith Nettles Zeigler; m. William G. Sutton, June 16, 1956; children: William F., Joseph S., Julia N., John M. BS in Edn., 1958. Cert. spl. edn./mental retardation tchr., Ala. Tchr., DIAL III vol. Huntsville City Sch., Ala., 1966, spl. edn. tchr., 1973—98; tchr. Christian Women's Job Corps, Huntsville, 1999—. Mem. adv. bd. Coll. Edn., U. Ala., Tuscaloosa, 2001—. Mem. Civic Club Coun., Huntsville, 1967—68, Huntsville Hosp. Aux., 1965—73, pres., 1967—68; mem./ choir and various positions First United Meth. Ch., Huntsville, 1975—; life mem. Huntsville Hosp. Angel; chmn. Spl. Ministries FUM Ch., 1982—85; vol. DIAL III readiness testing in city and county sch., 2000—. Named one of Outstanding Young Women of Am., 1968; recipient Listed in Who's Who of Am. Women, 2002—03. Mem.: DAR (Twickenham Town chpt. 1st vice regent 2002—), Organizing mem. of Hunts./Madison Co. Panhellenic, Huntsville Alpha Gamma Delta Alumnae Club (past pres. 1962), Coll. of Edn. Capstone Soc., Camellia Soc. (organizing pres. 2001—02), Huntsville Bot. Garden and Garden Guild, Early Works Soc. (chmn. mem. event 1998—), Twickenham Hist. Preservation (bd. dir. 1975—2000, dist. assn. sec. 1985—2000). Methodist. Avocations: cooking British tea foods, heraldry-painting coats of arms, aerobics, community volunteering, collecting teapots and tea china.

SUTTON, PHILIP D(IETRICH), psychologist, educator; b. June 20, 1952; s. Clifton C. and Ida-Lois (Dietrich) S.; m. Kathleen E. Duffy, June 17, 1973; children: Heather, Shivonne. BA, So. Ill. U., 1974; MA, U. Chgo., 1975; PhD, U. Utah, 1979. Lic. psychologist, Colo. Psychologist VA Hosp., Salt Lake City, 1975-76; psychology intern Salt Lake Cmty. Mental Health Ctr., Salt Lake City, 1976-78; counselor, instr. Counseling Ctr., U. Utah, Salt Lake City, 1976-78; counselor, acting dir. spl. svcs. program Met. State Coll., Denver, 1978-80; staff psychologist Kaiser-Permanente Health Plan, Denver, 1980—83; pvt. practice Boulder, Colo., 1983—. Adj. prof. U. Colo., 1979-83; cons. spl. program for disacvantaged students in higher edn. Hew, 1980. Mem. APA, Biofeedback Soc., Am. Soc. Behavioral Medicine. Office: Box 1781 Nederland CO 80466 E-mail: pdsphd@aol.com.

SUTTON, SAMUEL J. lawyer, educator, engineer; b. Chgo., July 21, 1941; s. Samuel J. and Elaine (Blossom) S.; m. Anne V. Sutton, Aug. 28, 1965; children: Paige, Jean, Leah, Jepson. BA in History and Philosophy, U. Ariz., 1964, BSEE, 1967; JD, George Washington U., 1969. Bar: Ariz. 1969, D.C. 1970, U.S. Ct. Appeals (fed. cir.) 1983. Patent atty. Gen. Electric Co., Washington, Phoenix, 1967-70; ptnr. Cahill, Sutton & Thomas, Phoenix, 1970-95, of counsel, 1995—. Prof. law Ariz. State U., Tempe, 1975—; expert witness Fed. Dist. Cts., 1983—; trial cons. to numerous lawyers, 1972—; arbitrator Am. Arbitration Assn., Phoenix, 1971—. Author: Patent Preparation, 1976, Intellectual Property, 1978, Art Law, 1988, Law, Science and Technology, 1991, Licensing Intangible Property, 1994, Commercial Torts, 1995, Patent Litigation, 1996, 120-hr. multimedia series on intellectual property, 1999—, http://lawtech.law.asu.edu, —; pub. sculptures installed at Tanner Sq., Phoenix, Tucson Art Inst., Mobil Corp., Mesa, Ariz., Cox Devel. Co., Tempe, Ariz., Downtown Phoenix, Desert Bot. Garden, Phoenix, Gateway Ctr., Sedona Sculpture Garden, Construct Gallery, Phoenix. Chmn. air pollution hearing bd. City of Phoenix, Maracopa County, 1970-85. Recipient Patent prize Patent Resources Group, 1979, Publ. award IEEE, 1967, Genematus award U. Ariz., 1964, Disting. Achievement award Ariz. State U., 1980, Construct Sculpture prize, 1989. Avocation: large scale steel sculpture. Office: PO Box 32694 Phoenix AZ 85064-2694 E-mail: sam.sutton@asu.edu.

SUTTON, SHARON EGRETTA, architect, educator, artist, musician; b. Cin., Feb. 18, 1941; d. Booker and Egretta (Sutton) Johnson. Student, Manhattan Sch. Music, 1959-62; MusB, U. Hartford, Conn., 1963; postgrad., Parson's Sch. Design, N.Y.C., 1967-69; MArch, Columbia U., 1973; PhM, CUNY, 1981, MA, PhD in Psychology, 1982. Registered architect, N.Y., Wash. Pvt. practice, N.Y.C. and Dexter, Mich., 1976-97. Vis. asst. prof. Pratt Inst., Bklyn., 1975-81; adj. asst. prof. Columbia U., N.Y.C., 1981-82; asst. prof. U. Cin., 1982-84; assoc. prof. U. Mich., Ann Arbor, 1984-94, prof., 1994-97; prof., dir. ctr. environment, edn., and design studies U. Wash., Seattle, 1998—; architect-in-residence NEA, N.Y.C., 1978-82; keynote spkr., lectr. colls. and profl. meetings. One-woman shows include Nat. Urban League, N.Y.C., 1980, Your Heritage House, Detroit, 1986, June Kelly Gallery, N.Y.C., 1987, exhibited in group shows at Studio Mus., 1979, U. Mich. Mus. Art, Ann Arbor, 1988, Art-in-Gen. Gallery, Soho, N.Y.C., 1990, Represented in permanent collections Mint Mus., Charlotte, N.C., Wadsworth Atheneum, Hartford, Conn., Balt. Mus. Art; author: Learning Through the Built Environment, 1985, Weaving a Tapestry of Resistance, 1996; mem. editl. bd.: Jour. Archtl. Edn., 1984—87, 2002—, mem. founding editl. bd.: Jour. Cmty. Svc. Learning, 1996—, mem. founding editl. adv. bd.: Jour. of Children, Youth and Environments, 2002—; contbr. articles to profl. jours.; musician: Man of La Mancha original cast and album, 1967—69; musician: (performed with) orchs. of Bolshoi, Leningrad, and Moiseiyeu, Ballt Cos., Man of La Mancha original cast and album, New World Symphony, Music Makers, Phoenix Woodwind quintet, others. Coord. The Urban Network-an urban design program for youth funded by NEA Design Cities Program Kellogg Found., U. Mich., 1988-97; mem. Seattle Design Commn. 2000—; bd. dirs. Seattle Parks Found., 2003—. Recipient Postbaccalaureate award Danforth Found., 1977-81, Design Rsch. award NEA, 1983, Edn. award Am. Planning Assn., 1991, Regents award for disting. pub. svc. U. Mich., 1992, Mich. Humanities award, 1995, Disting. Prof. award Assn. Collegiate Schs. Architecture, 1996, Life Achievement award Mich. Women's Hall of Fame, 1997; grantee NEA, 1988-90; W.K. Kellogg Found. fellow, 1986-89. Fellow AIA; mem. APA, Am. Ednl. Rsch. Assn., Nat. Archtl. Accreditation Bd. (bd. dirs. 1995-98, pres. 1997-98), Seattle Parks Found. (bd. dirs. 2003—). Democrat. Home: 1017 Minor Ave Apt 504 Seattle WA 98104-1304 Office: Dept Architecture Box 355720 U Wash Seattle WA 98195-5720 E-mail: sesut@u.washington.edu.

SUUBERG, ERIC MICHAEL, chemical engineering educator; b. N.Y.C., Nov. 23, 1951; s. Michael and Aino (Berg) S.; m. Ina Inara Vatvars, Apr. 26, 1987; 1 child, Alessandra Anna. BSChemE, MSChemE, BS in Bus. Mgmt., MIT, 1974, MS in Bus. Mgmt., 1976, ScD in Chem. Engring., 1978. Asst. prof. chem. engring. Carnegie-Mellon U., Pitts., 1977-81; asst. prof. engring. Brown U., Providence, 1981-84, assoc. prof. engring., 1984-90, prof. engring., 1990—, rep. exec. com. fluids, thermal and chem. processes group, 1991—97, assoc. dean faculty, 2003—. Vis. scientist Centre National de la Recherche Scientifique, Mulhouse, France, 1988; invited lectr. Ministry Edn., Monbusho, Japan, 1991, 93, 2003; vis. prof. Tallinn Tech. U., 2001. Mem. internat. editl. bd. Fuel, 1988—, mem. editl. adv. bd. Energy and Fuels, 1990—93, 1998—2000, Americas editor Fuel, 2000—, contbr. over 100 articles to profl. jours. Elected mem. Estonian Am. Nat. Coun., N.Y.C., 1984-99, v.p. 1996-99, bd. dirs. 2002—. Vice Chancellor's Rsch. Best Practice fellow U. Newcastle, Australia, 1995; Fulbright scholar, 2000-01. Mem. AIChE, Combustion Inst., Am. Chem. Soc. (chmn. divsn. fuel chemistry 1991, bd. dirs.-at-large 1995-97, trustee 2002—, H.H. Storch award in fuel chemistry Am. Chem. Soc.. 1999). Office: Brown Univ Divsn Engring Box D Providence RI 02912 E-mail: eric_suuberg@brown.edu.

SUZUKI, JON BYRON, medical educator, periodontist, microbiologist; b. San Antonio, July 22, 1946; s. George K. and Ruby Suzuki. BA in Biology, Ill. Wesleyan U., 1968; PhD in Microbiology magna cum laude, Ill. Inst. Tech., 1971; DDS magna cum laude, Loyola U., 1978. Med. technologist Ill. Masonic Hosp. and Med. Ctr., Chgo., 1966-67; instr. lab. in histology and parasitology Ill. Wesleyan U., Bloomington, 1967-68; med. technologist Augustana Hosp., Chgo., 1968-69; rsch. assoc., instr. microbiology Ill. Inst. Tech., Chgo., 1968-71; clin. rsch. assoc. U. Chgo. Hosps., 1970-71; clin. microbiologist St. Luke's Hosp., Columbia Coll., Physicians and Surgeons, N.Y.C., 1971-73; assoc. med. dir. Paramed Tng. and Registry, Vancouver, B.C., Can., 1973-74; dir. clin. labs. Registry of Hawaii, 1973-74; chmn. clin. labs. edn. Kapiolany Cmty. Coll., U. Hawaii, Honolulu, 1974; lectr. periodontics, oral pathology Loyola U. Med. Ctr., Maywood, Ill., 1974-90; lectr. stomatology Northwestern U. Dental Sch., Chgo., 1982-90; NIH rsch. fellow depts. pathology and periodontics Ctr. for Rsch. in Oral Biology, U. Wash., Seattle, 1978—80; prof. dept. periodontics and microbiology U. Md. Coll. Dental Surgery, Balt., 1980-90; attending faculty divsn. dentistry and oral and maxillofacial surgery Johns Hopkins Med. Inst., Balt., 1985—96; practice specializing in periodontics Balt. and Pitts.; prof., dean Sch. Dental Medicine U. Pitts., 1989—2000, prof., dir. periodontics residency program, 2002—. Cons. Dentsply Internat., York, Pa., U.S. Army, Walter Reed Med. Ctr., Washington, U.S. Army, Ft. Gordon, Ga., USN, Nat. Naval Med. Command, Bethesda, The NutraSweet Col, Chgo., FDA, Rockville, Md., 1990—, Phillips Oral Health Care, Snoqualmie, Wash.; biology/medicine study sect. NIH, Bethesda, 1985-90; nat. adv. dental rsch. coun. NIH/NIDR, Bethesda, 1994-98; vis. scientist Moscow State U., USSR, 1972, NASA, Houston, 1976-92; lectr. Internat. Congress allergology, Tokyo, 1973; lab. dir. Hawaii Dept. Health. Author: Clinical Laboratory Methods for the Medical Assistant, 1974; mem. editl. bd. Jour. Clinical Dentistry, Jour. Practical Hygiene; contbr. articles on rsch. in microbiology, immunology and dentistry to profl. jours. Instr. water safety ARC, Honolulu, 1973-90. Recipient Pres.'s medallion Loyola U., Chgo., 1977; named Alumnus of Yr., Ill. Wesleyan U., 1977, Loyola U., Chgo., 1997. Fellow Acad. Dentistry Internat., Am. Coll. Dentists, Internat. Coll. Dentists, Am. Coll. Stomatognathic Surgeons; mem. ADA (chair coun. sci. affairs 1998), AAUP, Am. Acad. Periodontology (diplomate), Am. Dental Edn. Assn., Am. Inst. Biol. Scis., Internat. Soc. Biophysics, Internat. Soc. Endocrinologists, Ill. Acad. Sci., Am. Internat. Assn. Dental Rsch. (pres. Md. chpt.), Am. Coll. Microbiology (diplomate, examiner), N.Y. Acad. Scis., Sigma Xi, Omicron Kappa Upsilon (past nat. pres., exec. sec.), Beta Beta Beta. Home: Univ Pitts Dental 3501 Terrace St Pittsburgh PA 15261 Office: U Pitts Sch Dental Medicine B100 Salk Hall Pittsburgh PA 15261 Fax: 412-648-8427.

SVAGER, THYRSA ANNE FRAZIER, university administrator, retired educator; b. Wilberforce, Ohio, July 16; d. G. Thurston and E. Anne Frazier; m. Aleksandar Svager. AB, Antioch Coll., Yellow Springs, Ohio, 1951; MA, Ohio State U., 1952, PhD, 1965. Statist. analyst Wright Patterson AFB (Ohio), 1952-53; instr. Tex. So. U., Houston, 1953-54; from asst. to assoc. prof. Ctrl. State U., Wilberforce, 1954-66, prof., chmn., 1966-85, v.p. acad. affairs, 1985-89, exec. v.p., provost, 1989—. Adj. faculty Antioch Coll., 1964; vis. prof. Nat. Sci. Found. Inst., 1966-67; vis. faculty MIT, 1969; cons. in field. Author: Essential Mathematics, 1976, rev. edit., 1983, Compact Facts-Calculus, 1980, (workbook) Modern Elementary Algebra, 1969. NSF grantee, 1969-71, 76-79; recipient Svc. award Jack and Jill Am., 1985, Edn. award Green County Women's Hall of Fame, 1986, Edn. award Top Ladies of Distinction Wilberforce chpt., 1985, Svc. award Challenge 95 Human Needs Task Force, 1992. Mem. NAACP, Nat. Urban League, Math. Assn. Am., Nat. Assn. Math., Nat. Coun. Tchrs. of Math., Assn. Computing Machinery, Assn. Study Afro-Am. Life and History, Phi Mu Epsilon, Beta Kappa Chi, Alpha Kappa Mu, Alpha Kappa Alpha (life). Avocations: travel, tournament bridge, antique glass. Office: Ctrl State U PO Box 174 Wilberforce OH 45384-0174

SVALDI, KATHLEEN ALICE, elementary education educator; b. Chgo., Sept. 14, 1946; d. Albert Fred and Phyllis (Tworkowski) Sodin; m. Livio Svaldi, June 27, 1981; children: Jeffrey, Melissa, Edward. BS in Edn., Loyola U., 1968; postgrad., Nat. Louis U. Cert. Chgo. Bd. of Edn., cert. tchr., Ill., cert. archdiocese of Chgo. Cath. edn. Intermediate tchr. St. Wenceslaus Sch., Chgo., 1968-72, St. Viator Sch., Chgo., 1973-74; primary tchr. St. Wenceslaus Sch., Chgo., 1974-80; intermediate tchr. St. Joan of Arc Sch., Skokie, Ill., 1980-82; primary tchr. St. Peter Sch., Skokie, 1987—. Primary unit leader St. Wenceslaus Sch., Chgo., 1975-79. Mem. ASCD.

SVENSSON, BENGT ANDERS, engineering educator; b. Märserum, Blekinge, Sweden, Mar. 25, 1947; came to the U.S., 1990; s. Gösta Sigfrid and Alva Signhild (Olsson) S.; m. Natalia Nikolaeff, Jan. 20, 1980; children: Andrej, Alexej, Kristina, Paulina. Filosofie magister, U. Lund, Sweden, 1971; tchg. diploma, Lärarhögskolan, Linköping, Sweden, 1974; MSEE, San Jose State U., 1981; single subject tchg. credential, San Francisco State U., 1992. Tchr. math. and physics Väggaskolan, Karlshamn, Sweden, 1974-75, Galanos Secondary Sch., Tanga, Tanzania, 1975-78, AMU, Gothenburg, Sweden, 1978-79; engr. Systron Donner Corp., Sunnyvale, Calif., 1981-82, FFV Underhåll, Arboga, Sweden, 1982-86; computer programmer Televerket Radio, Stockholm, 1986-90; instr. engring. dept. City Coll. San Francisco, Calif., 1991—. Avocations: travel, writing. Home: 135 6th Ave San Francisco CA 94118-1325 Office: City Coll San Francisco 50 Phelan Ave San Francisco CA 94112-1821 E-mail: svensson@exppii.net.

SVETS, GAYLE ANN, elementary education educator; b. Cleve., June 8, 1942; d. William J. McFarlane; children: Michael, Robert. BS in Edn., St. John Coll., Cleve., 1964; MS in Edn., Lake Erie Coll., 1977; MA in Edn. Adminstrn., Vrsuline Coll., 2000. Cert. tchr., Ohio. Tchr. elem. sch. Diocese of Cleve., Cleveland Heights, Ohio, 1964-66, Shaker Heights (Ohio) Bd. Edn., 1966-69; tchr., sci. coord. Phillips-Osborne Sch., Painesville, Ohio, 1972—96; sci. coord. Gilmour Acad., Gates Mills, Ohio, 1996—. Participant watershed watch of Grand River, Lake County Soil and Water Conservation Dist. Producer lesson packet on ecological awareness, 1991. Named Environ. Tchr. of Yr., Lake County, 1991; grantee, Martha Holden Jennings Found., 1989, Ptnrs. in Sci., 1992, in Food Sci, FDA, 2002. Mem. NSTA, Sci. Edn. Coun. Ohio. Office: Gilmour Acad 34001 Cedar Rd Gates Mills OH 44040

SWAIM, RUTH CAROLYN, secondary education educator; b. Oklahoma City, May 3, 1940; d. G. Dale and Helen H. (Meister) Arbuckle; children: Stanley Kent, Sharon Gay. BS in Edn., U. Okla., 1965. Cert. secondary edn. tchr., Calif., Okla. Math. substitute tchr. USN Mil. Dependent, Sangley Pt., Philippines, 1961-63; math. tchr. Norman (Okla.) Pub. Schs., 1963, Bartlesville (Okla.) Pub. Schs., 1963-65, Dewey (Okla.) Pub. Schs., 1965-67; math. lab. instr. L.A. City Schs., 1975-83, math. tchr., 1984—. Chair math dept. All Sch. Tutorial Program Taft High Sch., 1998—; sponsor SADD Taft High Sch. Instr. first Aid ARC, 1961-67; trustee Woodland Hills Community Ch., 1989—; sponsor INTERACT. Recipient Cert. Merit ARC, 1965, hon. svc. award PTA, 1980; named Outstanding Math. Tchr. Tandy, 1989-90; Outstanding Tchr. Los Angeles Classrooms Teachers Math., 1999. Mem. Nat. Coun. Tchrs. Math., NEA, Calif. Tchrs. Assn., Kappa Delta Pi. Home: 4555 San Feliciano Dr Woodland Hills CA 91364-5037 Office: Taft High Sch 5461 Winnetka Ave Woodland Hills CA 91364-2592

SWAIN, DONALD CHRISTIE, retired university president, history educator; b. Des Moines, Oct. 14, 1931; s. G. Christie and Irene L. (Alsop) S.; m. Lavinia Kathryn Lesh, Mar. 5, 1955; children: Alan Christie, Cynthia Catherine. BA, U. Dubuque, 1953; MA in History, U. Calif., Berkeley, 1958, PhD, 1961; D (hon.), U. Louisville, 1995, Bellarmine Coll., 1995. Asst. rsch. historian U. Calif., Berkeley, 1961-63, mem. faculty Davis, 1963-81, prof. history, 1970-81, acad. asst. to chancellor, 1967-68, asst. vice chancellor acad. affairs, 1971, vice chancellor acad. affairs, 1972-75; acad. v.p. U. Calif. System, Berkeley, 1975-81; pres. U. Louisville, 1981-95, pres. emeritus, 1995—, prof. history, 1981-95; ret., 1995. Author: Federal Conservation Policy, 1921-33, 1963, Wilderness Defender: Horace M. Albright and Conservation, 1970; co-editor: The Politics of American Science 1939 to the Present, 1965. Recipient William B. Hellestine award Wis. State Hist. Soc., 1967, Disting. Tchg. award U. Calif., Davis, 1972, Wilson Wyatt award U. Louisville Alumni Assn., 1995; named Louisvillian of Yr., 1995. Democrat. Presbyterian. Office: U Louisville Alumni Ctr Louisville KY 40292-0001 E-mail: dcsandlls@aol.com.

SWAIN, MELINDA SUSAN, elementary education educator; b. Sacramento, Oct. 30, 1944; d. William A. and Maxine (Wickberg) S. BA, Aurora U., 1967; MA, U. N.Mex., 1981. Cert. early adolescence/generalist Nat. Bd. Profl. Tchg. Standards, 1995. Tchr. 1st grade Crownpoint (N.Mex.) Elem. Sch., 1968-69, tchr. English as second lang., 1969-71, Church Rock (N.Mex.) Elem. Sch., 1971-72; tchr. kindergarten Sky City Elem. Sch., Gallup, N.Mex., 1972-73; program specialist Gallup-McKinley County Schs., 1973-82; tchr. 5th grade Lincoln Elem. Sch., Gallup, 1982-96; office for civil rights program compliance officer Gallup-McKinley County Schs., 1996-98; tchr.-in-residence Nat. Bd. Profl. Tchg. Stds., Southfield, Mich., 1998—2000; clin. supr. U. N.Mex., Gallup, 2000—. Mem. Dist. Task Force, Gallup, 1989-96. Columnist N.Mex. Jour. Reading, 1991-97. Recipient N.Mex. World Class Tchrs. Project award, 1994-95. Mem. N.Mex. Coun. Internat. Reading Assn. (pres. 1984, state coord. 1991-97), Four Corners Literacy Coun. of Internat. Reading Assn. (pres., membership dir. 1977—). Avocations: mountain biking, reading, computers, rv-ing. Home: 1000 S Country Club Dr Gallup NM 87301-5929

SWAIN, VIRGINIA M. executive mentor, conflict resolution, reconciliation and peace education consultant, educator; b. Buffalo, N.Y., June 8, 1943; d. Robert Burrough and Joan (Wood) S.; m. Thomas Edward Cone III, May 20, 1964 (div. 1974); 1 child, Thomas Edward Cone IV; m. Joseph Preston Baratta, Jan. 1, 1995. AA, Colby Sawyer Coll., New London, N.H., 1963; MA in Cmty. Bldg. in Orgns., Lesley U., 1993. Tchr. U.S. Peace Corps, West Africa, 1964-66; personnel mgr. Pepperidge Farm Mail Order Co., Clinton, Conn., 1975-81; sales coord. Internat. Salt, Essex, Conn., 1981-84; dir. mktg. Mercy Ctr., Madison, Conn., 1984-86; dir. pub. rels., mktg. Wainwright House, Rye, N.Y., 1986; ind. cons. internat. peacemaking and conflict resolution Old Lyme, Conn., 1986—; co-founder Ctr. for Global Cmty. & World Law, 1993—. Rep. non-govtl. orgn. to UN, N.Y.C., 1991, Global Mediation and Reconciliation Svc., 1992—; mem. Comms. Coord com., Congress for a More Dem. UN, 1991; del. Earth Summit, UN Conf. on Environ. and Devel., Rio de Janeiro, 1992; rep. Assn. World Citizens at the UN; del. UN World Social Summit, Copenhagen, 1995; founder, dir. Inst. for Global Leadership, 2001; founder Global Mediation and Reconciliation Svc., 2003. Author: A Mantle of Roses: A Woman's Journey Home to Peace, 2003; co-author: The Gift of Peace, 1989. Facilitator, cons. Am. Cancer Soc., New London, Conn., 1991; mem. exec. com. Coalition for Strong UN, Boston, 1993-98. Mem. ACA, Inst. for Global Leadership, 2000, Transcend Network Internat. Peace Rsch. Assn., Women in Foreign Policy, Peace Studies Assn., NY Orgnl. Devel. Network, New Eng. Holistic Counselors Assn. Episcopalian. Unitarian. Avocations: tennis, walking, travel, reading, bicycling. E-mail: vswain@global-leader.org.

SWALLEY, GARY WILLIAM, history educator; b. Nov. 22, 1951; s. William Carter and Janiece Lucille (Roustio) S. BA, So. Ill. U., 1974. Tchg. intern Edwardsville (Ill.) Sch. Dist., 1976; substitute tchr. Edwardsville Jr. H.S., 1977; tchr. English, social studies jr. h.s., 1977—. Cons. Ill. State Bd. Edn., 1998; bd. dirs. Nat. Social Studies Coun. Recipient Tchrs. medal Valley Forge, 1982, Thanks to Tchrs. Nat. award, 1990, Profl. Best award Learning mag., 1990, Am. Hero in Edn. award Reader's Digest, 1992, Outstanding Tchr. History award DAR, 1993, Am. Hero award Maxwell House, 1993, Tchr. of Yr. award Nat. Mid. Sch. Social Studies, 1993, Kimmel Comty. Svc. award So. Ill. U., 1995, Ill. History Tchr. of Yr., 1997; Valley Forge Freedoms Found. scholar, 1979; fellow Kezai Koho, 1987 Fulbright Found. 1990; inducted Nat. Tchrs. Hall of Fame, 1996. Mem. Nat. Coun. Social Studies, Edwardsville Edn. Assn., Rotary Fellowship Group Study Exch. Methodist. Office: Edwardsville Jr High Sch 59 S State Route 157 Edwardsville IL 62025-3851

SWAN, ALAN CHARLES, law educator; b. Kalimpong, West Bengal, India, Dec. 29, 1933; came to U.S., 1945; s. Charles Lundeen and Kathleen Vivian (Doucette) S.; m. Mary Joe Smith, Aug. 28, 1954; children—Kathleen Jeanette, Amalie Christine, Alan Charles. B.A., Albion Coll., 1954; J.D., U. Chgo., 1957. Bar: N.Y. 1958. Assoc. Milbank, Tweed, Hadley & McCloy, N.Y.C., 1957-61; asst. gen. counsel AID, Washington, 1961-66; asst. v.p. U. Chgo., professorial lectr. Grad. Sch. Bus., 1966-72; prof. law U. Miami, Coral Gables, Fla., 1972— ; mem. Nat. Lawyers Com. for Soviet Jewry, 1971-80. Author: The Regulation of International Business and Economic Relations, 2d edit., 2001; contbr. articles to profl. jours. Trustee Plymouth Congregational Ch., Miami, 1998-2001; mem. Miami Com. on Fgn. Relations, 1976—, sec. of state adv. com. on pvt. internat. law, 1995—. Mem. Am. Law Inst, ABA, Am. Soc. Internat. Law, Internat. Law Assn., Fla. Bar Assn. Democrat. Home: 14901 SW 82nd Ave Miami FL 33158-1906 Office: U Miami Sch Law Coral Gables FL 33124 E-mail: aswan@law.miami.edu.

SWAN, GEORGE STEVEN, law educator; b. St. Louis; BA, Ohio State U., 1970; JD, U. Notre Dame, 1974; LLM, U. Toronto, 1976, SJD, 1983. Bar: Ohio 1974, U.S. Dist. Ct. (so. dist.) Ohio 1975, U.S. Supreme Ct. 1987, U.S. Ct. Appeals (6th and 11th cirs.) 1993, U.S. Ct. Appeals (10th cir.) 1994, D.C. 1997, Ga. 1997, U.S. Dist. Ct. (no. dist.) Ga. 1997, Fla. 1997, Minn. 1998, Nebr. 1998, N.D. 1998, U.S. Ct. Appeals (7th cir.) 1998, La. 1999, Mass. 1999; ChFC, CLU, CFP. Asst. atty. gen. State of Ohio, Columbus, 1974-75; jud. clk. Supreme Ct. Ohio, Columbus, 1976-78; asst. prof. Del. Law Sch., Wilmington, 1980-83, assoc. prof., 1983-84; prof. law St. Thomas U. Law Sch., Miami, Fla., 1984-88; jud. clk. U.S. Ct. Appeals (7th cir.), Chgo., 1988-89; assoc. prof. N.C. Agrl. & Tech. State U., Greensboro, 1989—. Vis. prof. John Marshall Law Sch., Atlanta, 1996—97, 2000—01. Contbr. articles to law jours. Mem. Ohio State Bar Assn., D.C. Bar, State Bar Ga., Fla. Bar, Mass. Bar Assn., Nebr. State Bar Assn., La. State Bar Assn., N.D. State Bar Assn., Soc. of Fin. Svc. Profls., Fin. Planning Assn., Am. Polit. Sci. Assn. Office: Merrick Hall 1601 E Market St Greensboro NC 27411

SWANN, BRIAN, writer, humanities educator; b. Wallsend, Northumberland, Eng., Aug. 13, 1940; came to U.S., 1963, naturalized, 1980; s. Stanley Frank and Lilyan Mary (Booth) S.; m. Roberta Metz. BA, Queens Coll., Cambridge U., 1962, MA, 1965; PhD, Princeton U., 1970. Instr. Princeton U., 1964-65, lectr., 1968-70, asst. prof., 1970-72; instr. Rutgers U., 1965-66; asst. prof. humanities Cooper Union for Advancement Sci. and Art, N.Y.C., 1972-75, assoc. prof., 1975-80, prof., 1980—, acting dean, 1990-91. Dir. Bennington Writing Workshops, 1988-91. Author: (poetry) The Middle of the Journey, 1982, Song of The Sky: Versions of Native American Song-Poems, 1993, Wearing the Morning Star: Native American Song-Poems, 1996, (children's books) A Basket Full of White Eggs, 1988, The House With No Door, 1998, other books of fiction, translations: editor: Smoothing The Ground: Essays of Native American Oral Literature, 1983; (with Arnold Krupat) Recovering the Word, 1987, I Tell You Now: Autobiographical Essays by Native American Writers, 1987, Coming to Light: Contemporary Translations of the Native American Literatures, 1992, (with Krupat) Here First: Autobiographical Essays by Contemporary Native American Writers, 2000, Voices from Four Directions: Contemporary Translations of the Native Literatures of North America, 2003; editor The Smithsonian Series of Essays on Native American Literatures, 1990-98. NEA fellow, 1981; Creative Arts in Pub. Service grantee, 1982. Office: Cooper Union Adv Sci & Art Faculty Humanities & Social Sci Cooper Sq New York NY 10003

SWANN, LOIS LORRAINE, writer, editor, educator; b. N.Y.C., Nov. 17, 1944; d. Peter J. and Edith M. (De Rose) Riso; m. Terrence Garth Swann, Aug. 15, 1964 (div. 1979); children: Peter Burgess, Polly Loraine; m. Kenneth E. Arndt, Sept. 3, 1988. BA, Marquette U., 1966. Editor Peat, Marwick, Mitchell & Co., N.Y.C., 1980-81; publs. cons. Mfrs. Hanover Trust, N.Y.C., 1981-88. Cons. bus. writing, 1988—; tchr. West H.E.L.P., Mt. Vernon, NY, 1991; tchr. nontraditonal age students writing; founder, reader Calliope's Chamber, 1995—. Author: (novels) The Mists of Manittoo, 1976 (Ohioana Libr. award for 1st novel, 1976), Torn Covenants, 1981; contbr. articles to mags. Election insp. Dem. Party, Bronxville, NY, 1990—. Mem.: Poets and Writers, Authors Guild. Avocation: interior design. Home and Office: 270 Bronxville Rd Bronxville NY 10708

SWANSBURG, RUSSELL CHESTER, medical administrator educator; b. Cambridge, Mass., Aug. 6, 1928; s. William W. and Mary A. (Pierce) S.; m. Laurel Clark, Sept. 1951; children: Philip Wayne, Michael Gary, Richard Jeffrey. Diploma, N.S. Hosp. Sch. Nursing, 1950; BSN, Western Res. U., 1952; MA in Nursing Edn., Columbia U., 1961; PhD, U. Miss., 1984. CNAA. Asst. adminstr. U. of S. Ala. Med. Ctr., Mobile; v.p. U. South Ala., Mobile; prof. Auburn U., Montgomery, Ala., Med. Coll. of Ga., Augusta; instr. Univ. of the Incarnate Word, San Antonio, 1998—. Mil. cons. USAF Surgeon Gen., 1972; sr. med. svc. cons., 1973-76; nurse cons. VA Med. Ctr., Tuskegee, Ala., 1987-88; mem. editl. adv. bd. Nursing Adminstrn. Manual. Author: Team Nursing: A Programmed Learning Experience, 1968, Inservice Education, 1968, The Measurement of Vital Signs, 1970, The Team Plan, 1971, Management of Patient Care Services, 1976, Strategic Career Planning and Development, 1984, The Nurse Manager's Guide to Financial Management, 1988, Management and Leadership for Nurse Managers, 1990 (Book of Yr. Selection, Am. Jour. Nursing 1990), 3d edit., 2002 (Book of Yr. Selection, Am. Jour. Nursing 2002), Introductory Management and Leadership for Clinical Nurses, 1993, 2d edit., 1999 (Book of the Yr. Selection, Am. Jour. Nursing 1999), Staff Development: A Component of Human Resource Development, 1994, Budgeting and Financial Management for Nurse Managers, 1997, (audiovisual course) Nurses & Patients: An Introduction to Nursing Management, 1980; contbr. articles to profl. publs. Bd. dirs. Air Force Village Found., Alzheimer's Care and Research Found. Col. USAF, 1956-76. Decorated Air Medal with oak leaf clusters, Legion of Merit; recipient award for outstanding work in hosp. adminstrn. Ala. State Nurses' Assn., 1985, Outstanding Nursing Svc. Adminstrn. award, 1981, Outstanding Nurse Rschr. 1984, Disting. Svc. award Air Force Village Found., 1999. Fellow AONE, Ala. Orgn. Nurse Exec's. (past state pres.); mem. Council Grad. Edn. Adminstrn. in Nursing (sec.), Ala. Acad. Sci., Sigma Xi, Phi Kappa Phi, Sigma Theta Tau. Home and Office: 4917 Ravenswood Dr Apt 1711 San Antonio TX 78227-4356

SWANSON, AUGUST GEORGE, physician, retired association executive; b. Kearney, Nebr., Aug. 25, 1925; s. Oscar Valderman and Elnora Wilhelmina Emma (Block) Swanson; m. Ellyn Constance Weinel, June 28, 1947; children: Eric, Rebecca, Margaret, Emilie, Jennifer, August. BA, Westminster Coll., Fulton, Mo., 1951; MD, Harvard U., 1949; DSc (hon.), U. Nebr., 1979. Intern King County Hosp., Seattle, 1949—50; resident in internal medicine U. Wash. Affiliated Hosp., 1953—55, neurology, 1955—57; resident in neurology Boston City Hosp., 1958; dir. pediatric neurology, then dir. divsn. neurology U. Wash. Med. Sch., Seattle, 1958—67, assoc. dean acad. affairs, 1967—71; v.p. acad. affairs Assn. Am. Med. Colls., Washington, 1971—89, v.p. grad. med. edn., exec. dir. nat. resident matching program, 1989—91; ret., 1991. Vis. fellow physiology Oxford (Eng.) U., 1963—64; cons. in field. Contbr. articles to profl. jours. With USNR, 1943—46, with USNR, 1950—53. Recipient Abraham Flexner award for distinguished svc. to medical edn., Assn. of Am. Medical Coll., 1992; scholar Markle scholar medicine, 1959—64. Mem.: Am. Neurol. Assn., Inst. Medicine NAS. Achievements include research in brain function, physician edn., med. manpower. Home: 3146 Portage Bay Pl E Apt H Seattle WA 98102-3847 E-mail: gusellyn@comcast.net.

SWANSON, AUSTIN DELAIN, educational administration educator; b. Jamestown, N.Y., June 11, 1930; s. Manley Moris and Beulah Marjorie (Waite) S.; m. Marilyn Jean Peterson, Mar. 31, 1956; children: Paul Delain, Karin Lorine Swanson Daun. BS, Allegheny Coll., 1952; MS, Columbia U., 1955, EdD, 1960. Tchr. Ramapo Cen. High Sch., Suffern, N.Y., 1955-58; rsch. assoc. Tchrs. Coll. Columbia U., N.Y.C., 1958-63; prof. emeritus ednl. adminstrn. SUNY, Buffalo, 1963—, chair dept. ednl. orgn. adminstrn. and policy, 1991-97. Vis. scholar Inst. Edn. U. London, 1979, 93, Zold Inst., Israel, 1988, U. Melbourne, 1999. Author: Modernizing the Little Red School House, 1979, School Finance: Its Economics and Politics, 1991, 2d edit., 1997, 3d edit., 2003, Fundamental Concepts of Educational Leadership, 1995, 2d edit., 2001; contbr. articles to profl. jours. WiTh U.S. Army, 1952-54. Fellow Stanford U., 1969-70; Fulbright scholar U. Melbourne, Australia, 1986. Mem. Am. Ednl. Rsch. Assn., Am. Edn. Fin. Assn., Politics of Edn. Assn., Phi Delta Kappa. Republican. Lutheran. Office: SUNY Grad Sch Edn Buffalo NY 14260-1000

SWANSON, CHRISTINE MASON, art educator; b. Worcester, Mass., Jan. 23, 1950; d. Stanley and Lillian (Price) Mason; m. Peter N. Swanson, 1983; 1 child, Adam. BS in Edn., Plymouth State Coll., 1972. Cert. in art edn. Art tchr. Spencer (Mass.)/East Brookfield Schs., 1972—. Remedial tchr. "Project Me" summer sch., Spencer, 1974-79. Co-prodr. film, 1983. Mem. Leicester (Mass.) Cultural Coun., 1999—. Grantee Mass. Arts Lottery, 1983, Local Cultural Coun., 1993, 94, Alliance for Edn., 1995, 95, 96. Mem. NEA, Mass. Tchrs. Assn., Mass. Art Edn. Assn. (mem. youth art month com. 1990—).

SWANSON, DARLENE MARIE CARLSON, speech therapist, educator, speaker, writer; b. Boone, Iowa, Aug. 8, 1925; d. Arvid Wilhelm and Edith Marie (Peterson) Carlson; m. Reuben Theodore Swanson, Aug. 8, 1948; children: Conrad T., Joyce Marie Swanson Jobson. BA, Augustana Coll., 1947; postgrad., U. Chgo., 1949, Creighton U., 1972; student, Joslyn Art Mus., Omaha, 1975. Cert. tchr., Ill., Nebr. Speech therapist Rock Island and Rockford (Ill.) Pub. Sch. System, 1946-51, Omaha (Nebr.) Pub. Sch. System, 1963-64; ch. organist Calvary Luth. Ch., Moline, Ill., 1944-46; asst. organist Augustana Luth. Ch., Omaha, 1956-63; mortuary organist Swanson-Golden Mortuary, Omaha, 1956-63; freelance lectr., 1960—. Freelance writer, 1960—; chalk artist lectr. and pub. speaker, retreat leader; observer Luth. World Fedn. Assembly, Budapest, Hungary, 1984. Sunday sch. tchr. Kountze Mem. Luth. Ch., Omaha, 1964-74; Sunday sch. supr. St. Andrew's Luth. Ch., West Hemstead, N.Y., 1951-54; sec. Omaha PTA, 1968-70; mem. adv. coun. Cen. High Sch., Omaha, 1971-74, Omaha Pub. Schs., 1971-74; bd. dirs., sec. Luth. Music Program, Inc., 1990—; active Met. Opera Guild, 1986-90, Omaha Opera Guild, 1990—, Omaha Symphony Guild, 1990—; bd. dirs. Bethpage Gt. Britain, 1994—, Omaha Symphony Assn., 1996-99. Named Vol. of Yr. Omaha Head Start Program, 1965. Mem. Omaha Symphony Assn. (bd. dirs. 1996-99), Alumni Assn. Augustana Coll. (bd. dirs. 2000—). Avocations: painting in oils and watercolors, world travel, music. Address: 17475 Frances St Apt 3016 Omaha NE 68130-2354

SWANSON, FERN ROSE, retired elementary education educator; b. Kalmar Twp., Minn. d. Henry E. and Susie (Hastings) Rose; m. Walter E. Swanson, June 24, 1928. Student, Winona (Minn.) Normal Coll., 1918—20; BS, St. Cloud (Minn.) State Coll., 1955, MS, 1958. Tchr. h.s. English, Latin, Eyota, Minn., 1920—21; tchr. jr. h.s. English Appleton, Minn., 1921—22; tchr. elem. schs. Harmony, Minn., 1922—23; tchr. h.s. English, Latin Augusta, Wis., 1923—24, South Haven, Minn., 1927—41, 1943—51, Silver Creek, Minn., 1941—43; tchr. elem. schs. Annandale, Minn., 1951—53; prin., 1953—67; tchr. elem. reading Belgrade, 1967—71. Organizer South Haven coun. Girl Scouts U.S., 1927, leader, 1927—30. Mem.: DAR (charter 50 Yr. Club), Ctrl. Minn. Reading Coun. (past dir.), Minn. Edn. Assn., Ret. Educators Assn. Minn., Minn. Elem. Sch. Prins. Assn. (charter mem. 25 Yr. Club), Rebekah, Ladies of Grand Army Rep. (registrar Lookout Cir., dept. pres. Minn. 1974—77), Betsy Ross Club (nat. pres. 1978, nat. historian 1980—89, nat. patriotic instr. 1981—84, nat. jr. v.p. 1984—85, nat. coun. adminstrn. 1985—88), Delta Kappa Gamma (past chpt. pres., Minn. Woman of Achievement award 1982). Episcopalian And Lutheran. Home: 200 Park Ln Buffalo MN 55313-1336

SWANSON, GORDON IRA, former educational administrator; b. Zimmerman, Minn., Aug. 7, 1920; s. Charles Henry and Alma Hermenia (Collins) S.; m. Dorothy Evangeline Hanson, Jan. 13, 1946; children: Dale Gordon, Dean Edward, Janet Marie, Charles Alan. BS, U. Minn., 1942, MS, 1949, PhD, 1954. Secondary sch. tchr. Alexandria (Minn.) Pub. Schs., 1942-43, 46-49; prof. vocat. edn. U. Minn., St. Paul, 1951-92; program officer UNESCO, Paris, 1959-61; assoc. dir. Nat. Ctr. for Rsch. in Vocat. Edn., Berkeley, Calif., 1989-92; ret., 1992. Spkr., cons. in field, 1965-92. Author: Old Breed News - The High Road, 1993, Memorial Day - Its Meaning, 1993; contbr. articles to profl. jours. Cub master Boy Scouts Am., St. Paul; moderator St. Anthony Park United Ch. of Christ, St. Paul, 1968-69; pres. Am. Swedish Inst., Mpls.; mem. White House Conf. on Edn., Children and Youth. Maj. USMC, 1942-46. Recipient Prosser award Dunwoody Inst., 1992, Outstanding Educator award U. Minn. Coll. Edn., 1994; hon. mem. Ret. Officers Assn. Ireland, 1978. Mem. AAAS, Am. Vocat. Assn. (pres. 1978—), Rural Edn. Assn. (pres.), VFW (life), Svenska Sallskapet, Royal Order of North Star, Phi Delta Kappa (pres. 1964-65). Avocations: writing, collecting and repairing clocks, woodworking. Home: 1440 Raymond Ave Saint Paul MN 55108-1428

SWANSON, LAUREN A. consultant, entrepreneur, educator, researcher; b. Apr. 17, 1951; BS, U. Wyo., 1973; MS, 1974; postgrad., Wheaton Coll., 1977; PhD, U. Ga., 1983. Instr. mktg. U. Wyo., Laramie, 1974-76; grad. instr. mktg., mgmt. sci. U. Ga., Athens, 1978-79; vis. prof. mktg. Grad. Sch. Bus. Adminstrn. Atlanta U., 1980-81; asst. prof. mktg. U. Mass., Boston, 1981-86; rsch. cons. Hill-Holliday-Connors-Cosmopulos Inc., Boston, 1983-86; assoc. in rsch. Fairbank Ctr. for East Asian Rsch. Harvard U., Cambridge, Mass., 1986—; fgn. expert, prof. mktg. and econs. U. Internat. Bus. and Econs., Beijing, 1986-87; assoc. prof. mktg. Chinese U. Hong Kong, 1987-98, assoc. dir. MBA programs, 1991-96; v.p. Dalton (Nebr.) Telecom, 1998-99; cons. in mktg. and telecomms. Dalton, 1999—. Cons. to industry; examiner Hong Kong Quality Award, 1991-95. Guest editor: Internat. Jour. Advtsg.; contbr. numerous articles to profl. jours.

SWANSON, MARY CATHERINE, educational reform program founder; b. Kingsburg, Calif., Sept. 3, 1944; d. Edwin Elmore and Corrine (Miller) Jacobs; m. Thomas Edward Swanson, Aug. 27, 1966; 1 child, Thomas Jacobs. BA in English and Journalism, Calif. State U., San Francisco, 1966; standard teaching credential in secondary edn., U. Calif., 1966; MA in Edn., U. Redlands, 1977; DHL (hon.), U. San Diego, 2002, U. LaVerne, 2003. Svc. adminstrv. credential, Calif.; specialist learning handicapped, Calif.; gifted cert., Calif. Tchr. English and journalism Woodland (Calif.) High Sch., 1966-67, Armijo High Sch., Fairfield, Calif., 1967-69, Moreno Valley High Sch., Sunnymead, Calif., 1969-70, Clairemont High Sch., San Diego, 1970-86; coord. San Diego County Office Edn., 1986-90, dir. AVID project, 1990-92; founder, exec. dir. AVID Ctr., 1992—. Newspaper and yearbook advisor Moreno Valley High Sch., Moreno Valley Sch. Dist., 1969-70; reading program coord. Clairemont High Sch., 1974-80, project English coord. and site plan coord., 1975-80, English dept. chairperson, 1978-86, coord. Advancement Via Individual Determination and WASC accreditation, 1980-86, in-sch. resource tchr., 1982-86; mem. numerous positions and coms. San Diego City Schs., 1974-91; mem. com. univ. and coll. opportunities commn. Calif. State Dept. Edn., 1981-82; mem. adv. com. tchr. edn. program Pt. Loma Coll., 1982-83, tchr. English methods course for tchrs. secondary edn., 1986-87; mem. accreditation vis. com. WASC, 1983, integration monitoring team Crawford High Sch., 1984, adv. com. San Diego Area Writing Project, 1987—; developer numerous curricular programs, 1967—. Community leader Olivenhain Valley 4-H Club, 1981-90; founder Olivenhain Valley Soccer Club, 1982; coord. Clairemont High Sch./Sea World Adopt-A-Sch., 1982-84. Named Headliner of Yr.-Edn./Creative Tchg., San Diego Press Club, 1991, Headline of Yr.-Cmty. Activist, 2002, Woman of Vision, LWV-San Diego, 1992, Nat. Educator of Yr., McGraw Hill, 2001, America's Best Tchr., Time Mag. and CNN, 2001; named to Pres.'s Forum on Tchg. as a Profession, Am. Assn. Higher Edn., 1991; recipient EXCEL award for excellence in tchg., 1985, Exemplary Program award, Nat. Coun. States on Insvc. Edn., 1990, Pioneering Achievement in Edn. award, Charles A. Dana Found., 1991; grantee, BankAmerica Found., 1980, UCSD Acad. Support Svcs., 1980, San Diego Gas and Elec. Found., 1984. Mem. Nat. Coun. Tchrs. English (Nat. Ctr. Excellence award 1985-87), Calif. Coun. Tchrs. English, Calif. Assn. Gifted Edn., Golden Key Nat. Honor Soc. (hon. mem.), Phi Kappa Phi. Office: San Diego County Office Edn 6401 Linda Vista Rd Rm 623 San Diego CA 92111-7319 also: AVID Ctr 5120 Shoreham Pl Ste 120 San Diego CA 92122 E-mail: mcswanson@avidcenter.org.

SWANSON, PEGGY EUBANKS, finance educator; b. Ivanhoe, Tex., Dec. 29, 1936; d. Leslie Samuel and Mary Lee (Reid) Eubanks; m. B. Marc Sommers, Nov. 10, 1993. BBA, U. North Tex., 1957, M. Bus. Edn., 1965; MA in Econs., So. Meth. U., 1967, PhD in Econs., 1978. Instr. El Centro Coll., Dallas, 1967-69, 71-78, bus. div. chmn., 1969-71; asst. prof. econs. U. Tex., Arlington, 1978-79, asst. prof. fin., 1979-84, assoc. prof., 1984-86, chmn. dept. fin. and real estate, 1986-88, prof. fin., 1987—, interim dean Coll. Bus. Adminstrn., 1999—. Expert witness various law firms, primarily Tex. and Calif., 1978—; cons. Internat. Edn. Program, 1992-99; curriculum cons. U. Monterrey, Mexico, 1995, New Saudi Arabia U., 1999. Contbr. articles to acad. profl. jours. Vol. Am. Cancer Soc., Dallas, Arlington, 1981—, Meals on Wheels, Arlington, 1989—; mem. adv. bd. Ryan/Reilly Ctr. for Urban Land Utilization, Arlington, 1986-88. Mem. Fin. Exec. Inst. (chmn. acad. rels. 1987-88), Internat. Bus. Steering Com. (chmn. 1989-91), Am. Fin. Assn., Am. Econ. Assn., Fin. Mgmt. Assn. (hon. faculty mem. Nat. Honor Soc. 1985-86, program com. 1998-99), Southwestern Fin. Assn. (program com. 1987-88, 96), Midwest Fin. Assn. (program com. 1997-98, 98-99), Acad. of Internat. Bus. (program com. 1992-95), Acad. Disting. Tchrs., Phi Beta Delta (membership com. 1987-89). Republican. Episcopalian. Avocations: tennis, gardening. Home: 4921 Bridgewater Dr Arlington TX 76017-2729 Office: U Tex at Arlington PO Box 19449 Arlington TX 76019-0001 E-mail: swanson@uta.edu.

SWANSON, ROBERT LAWRENCE, oceanographer, academic program administrator; b. Balt., Oct. 11, 1938; s. Lawrence Wilbur and Hazel Ruth Swanson; m. Dana Lamont, Sept. 12, 1963; children: Lawrence Daniel, Michael Nathan. BSCE, Lehigh U., 1960; MS in Oceanography, Oreg. State U., 1965, PhD in Oceanography, 1971. Cert. hydrographer. Commd. ensign U.S. Coast and Geodetic Survey (now NOAA), 1960, advanced through grades to capt., 1978; ops. officer U.S. Pathfinder, 1965; comdg. officer U.S. Marmer, 1966; chief oceanographic divsn. Nat. Ocean Survey, NOAA, Rockville, Md., 1969-72; mgr. Marine Ecosys. Analysis, N.Y. Bight project, Stony Brook, 1973—78; dir. Office Marine Pollution Assessment NOAA, Rockville, 1978—83, rsch. assoc. Sea Grant Stony Brook, 1983—84; comdg. officer U.S. Researcher, Miami, 1984—86; chief internat. activities group NOAA, Rockville, 1986, exed. dir. Office Oceanic and Atmospheric Rsch., 1986—87; dir. Waste Reduction and Mgmt. Inst. SUNY, Stony Brook, 1987—, assoc. dean Marine Scis. Rsch. Ctr., 2003—. Adj. prof. Marine Scis. Rsch. Ctr., SUNY, Stony Brook, 1976—; mem. Suffolk

County Coun. Environ. Quality, 1988—, vice chair, 1996—; mem. N.Y. State Oversight Com. on Brookhaven Nat. Lab., 1996—, Coastal Mgmt. Commn. Villages Head-of-the-Harbor and Nissequogue, 1994—2002; chmn. Coastal Mgmt. Commn. Villages Head Harbor and Nissequogue, 1995—97, 1999—2001; trustee Three Village Hist. Soc., 1994—2002; co-chair L.I. Environ. Econ. Roundtable, 1995—; adv. bd. Evan L. Lit Meml. Fund, 1998—; trustee Village of Head of the Harbor, 2002—; cons. in field. Co-author, co-editor: Oxygen Depletion and Associated Benthic Mortalities in N.Y. Bight, 1979; co-editor: Floatable Wastes and the Region's Beaches; mem. editl. bd. N.Y. Bight Monograph Series, 1973-81, Chemistry and Ecology, 1995-2003; co-pub. Waste Mgmt. Rsch. Report, 1988-95; mem. adv. bd. L.I. Hist. Jour., 1995-2003. Recipient Karo award Am. Soc. Mil. Engrs., 1972; Silver medal Dept. Commerce, 1973; Program and Adminstrn. Mgmt. award NOAA, 1975, Unit citation, 1981; sr. exec. fellow John F. Kennedy Sch. Govt., Harvard U., 1983, Spl. Achievement award, 1987, NOAA Corps. Commendations, 1987; named Man of Yr. for environment Three Village Times, 1998. Mem. Am. Mil. Engrs., N.Y. Acad. Scis., ASCE (chmn. hydrography and oceanography com. 1972-74), AAAS, Am. Geophys. Union, Marine Tech. Soc. (chmn. marine pollution com. 1982-92), Cosmos Club, Sigma Xi (pres. SUNYSB chpt. 1998—). Presbyterian. Home: 46 Harbor Hill Rd Saint James NY 11780-1217 Office: SUNY Waste Reduction And Mgmt Ins Stony Brook NY 11794-5000 Office Fax: 631-632-8064. E-mail: lswanson@notes.cc.sunysb.edu.

SWANSON, ROY ARTHUR, classicist, educator; b. St. Paul, Apr. 7, 1925; s. Roy Benjamin and Gertrude (Larson) S.; m. Vivian May Vitous, Mar. 30, 1946; children: Lynn Marie (Mrs. Gerald A. Snider) Robin Lillian, Robert Roy (dec.), Dyack Tyler, Dana Miriam (Mrs. Jon Butts). BA, U. Minn., 1948, BS, 1949, MA, 1951; PhD, U. Ill., 1954. Prin. Maplewood Elementary Sch., St. Paul, 1949-51; instr. U. Ill., 1952-53, Ind. U., 1954-57; asst. prof. U. Minn., Mpls., 1957-61, assoc. prof., 1961-64, acting chmn. classics, 1963-64, prof. classics, chmn. comparative lit., 1964-65; prof. English Macalester Coll., St. Paul, 1965-67, coord. humanities program, 1966-67; prof. comparative lit. and classics U. Wis.-Milw., 1967—, prof. English, 1990-96, prof. emeritus, 2003—, chmn. classics dept., 1967-70, 86-89, chmn. comparative lit., 1970-73, 76-83, coord. Scandinavian studies program, 1982-96. Cons. St. Paul Tchrs. Sr. High Sch. English, 1964 Author: Odi et Amo: The Complete Poetry of Catullus, 1959, Heart of Reason: Introductory Essays in Modern-World Humanities, 1963, Pindar's Odes, 1974, Greek and Latin Word Elements, 1981, The Love Songs of the Carmina Burana, 1987, Pär Lagerkvist: Five Early Works, 1989; editor Minn. Rev., 1963-67; Classical Jour., 1966-72; contbr. articles to profl. jours. With AUS, 1944-46. Decorated Bronze Star; recipient Disting. Teaching award U. Minn., 1962, Disting. Teaching award U. Wis.-Milw., 1974, 91, 99. Home: 11618 N Bobolink Ln Mequon WI 53092-2804 Office: U Wis French/Italian/Comp Lit PO Box 413 Milwaukee WI 53201-0413 E-mail: rexroy333@aol.com., rexcy@uwm.edu.

SWANSON, STEPHEN OLNEY, minister, retired English educator; b. Mpls., Aug. 31, 1932; s. Carl R. and Dorothy Olney Swanson; m. Judith Seleen Swanson, June 10, 1956; children: Scott, Shelley, Noel, Kim, Brian. BA, St. Olaf Coll., 1954; grad. in theology, Luther Theol. Sem., St. Paul, 1958, BD, 1960; MA, U. Oreg., 1964, ArtsD, 1970. Ordained to ministry Evang. Luth. Ch. Am., 1958. Instr. theology Augustana Coll., Sioux Falls, SD, 1957; instr. writing U. Oreg., Eugene, 1964—66; asst. prof. English and writing Tex. Luth. Coll., Seguin, 1966—70; assoc. prof. English and writing Camrose (Alta.) Univ. Coll., 1970—73; prof. writing St. Olaf Coll., Northfield, Minn., 1976—99. Parish pastor Luth. congregations, Minn., 1958-61, Oreg., 1962-65, Sask., 1973-74; interim pastor 31 congregations, Minn., Iowa, Wis., Alta., Sask., 1956—; dir. creative writing Tex. Luth. Coll., 1966-70, Camrose Univ. Coll., 1970-73; coach wrestling, football, volleyball, hockey, Tex., Can., Minn.; co-owner Nine-Ten Press, Northfield, 1997—. Author 26 books for adults, teens and children, including Is There Life After High Sch., 1991, The Earthkeeper Mystery Series, 4 vols., 1994, Moving Out on Your Own, 1995, The First Fall: Ytteroe Hall, 1946, 1997; playwright 6 plays; contbr. articles to jours.; columnist Now and Then, 1998-99; metal sculpture exhbns. include Thirvent Fin. Corp. Gallery, Mpls., 1992, 94, 98, Waldorf Coll., Forest City, Iowa, 1999, Luther Coll., Decorah, Iowa, 2002, Art Ctr. of St. Peter, Minn., 2003, Thrivent Fin. Corp. Gallery, Mpls., 2003, St. Olaf Coll., Northfield, Minn., 2003. Recipient award Minn. Arts Bd., 1987, Blandin Found., Grand Rapids, Minn., 1988-89; fellow NDEA, Washington, 1968-69. Avocations: metal sculpture, fishing, Volvo repair. Home: 910 St Olaf Ave Northfield MN 55057

SWANSON-SCHONES, KRIS MARGIT, developmental adapted physical education educator; b. Mpls., Mar. 22, 1950; d. Donald Theodore Swanson and Alice Alida (Swanson) Suhl; m. Gary Wallace Suhl, Apr. 6, 1974 (div. Aug. 1985); m. Gregory Edward Schones, Dec. 30, 1989. BA, Augsburg Coll., 1972. Cert. devel. adapted phys. edn. tchr., phys. edn. tchr., health tchr., coach/corrective therapist. Devel. adapted phys. edn. tchr. St. Paul Schs., 1972—, adapted athletic dir., 1989—. Mem. adapted athletics adv. bd. Minn. State H.S. League, 1992—. Author: On the Move, 1979. Chmn. hospitality Tanbark Club, Lakeville, Minn., 1992—, mem. show cmty., 1991—; mem. outreach com. Spl. Olympics, Minn., 1989-94. Recipient Nutrition Edn. grant Fed. Govt., 1978-79, Christmas Album grant Spl. Olympics, 1989, Internat. Spl. Olympics Coach award Minn. Spl. Olympics, 1991. Mem. NEA, AAHPERD, Minn. Edn. Assn., Minn. Assn. Adapted Athletics (exec. bd. 1989—, sec. exec. bd. 1990—, Outstanding Svc. award Minn. State H.S. League 2001). Avocations: showing horses and dogs, gardening, fishing. Home: 16280 Webster Ct Prior Lake MN 55372-9772 Office: Humboldt Jr High Sch 640 Humboldt Ave Saint Paul MN 55107-2996

SWAP, WALTER CHARLES, academic dean, psychology educator; b. Seattle, Jan. 23, 1943; s. Clifford Lloyd and Edna Frances (Hastings) S.; m. Susan Webster McAllister, June 25, 1966 (dec.); m. Dorothy André Leonard, May 3, 1997; children: Clifford John, Alison Frances. BA, Harvard U., 1965; PhD, U. Mich., 1970. Prof. psychology Tufts U., Medford, Mass., 1971-95, chmn. psychology dept., 1983-89, dean undergrad. edn., 1990-94; dean colls., 1994—99. Editor, author: Group Decision Making, 1984, When Sparks Fly: Igniting Creativity in Groups (with Dorothy Leonard), 1999; contbr. articles to scholarly jours. Mem. Soc. for Exptl. Social Psychology. Democrat. Unitarian-Universalist. Avocations: competitive road running, musical performing, organic gardening. Home: 7 Wainwright Rd Apt 110 Winchester MA 01890-2394 Office: Tufts U Ballou Hall Medford MA 02155

SWARTLING, DANIEL JOSEPH, chemistry educator, researcher; b. Black Falls, Wis., Sept. 3, 1960; s. Ronald James Swartling and Jean Marie (Welda) Trester. BS, Winona State U., 1985; PhD, U. N.D., 1989. Rsch. asst. Purdue U., West Lafayette, Ind., 1989-90; rsch. assoc. U. Chgo., 1990-92; teaching fellow S. Meth. U., Dallas, 1992-94; asst. prof. chemistry Tenn. Tech. U., Cookeville, 1994—. Cons. ARCH Rsch. Corp., Chgo., 1992—. Contbr. chpt. to book; contbr. articles to prof. jours. Mem. Am. Chem. Soc., Am. Scientific Glassblowers Soc., Am. Orchid Soc., Am. soc. Biochemists and Molecular Biologists, Sigma Xi. Avocations: radio, gardening, cycling, sports, music. Office: Tenn Tech U PO Box 5055 Cookeville TN 38505-0001

SWARTWOUT, JOSEPH RODOLPH, obstetrics and gynecology educator, administrator; b. Pascagoula, Miss., June 17, 1925; s. Thomas Roswell and Marshall (Coleman) S.; m. Brandon C. Leftwich, Jan. 23, 1989. Student, Miss. Coll., 1943-44; MD, Tulane U., 1951. Intern Touro Infirmary, New Orleans, 1951-52; asst. in obstetrics and medicine Tulane U., 1952-53, instr., 1955-60; Nat. Found. fellow Harvard U., 1953-55; asst. in medicine Peter Bent Brigham Hosp., Boston, 1953-55; assoc. in obstetric rsch. Boston Lying-In-Hosp., 1953-55; asst. prof. U. Pitts., 1960-61; assoc. prof. Emory U., Atlanta, 1961-66; assoc. prof. ob-gyn. U. Chgo., 1967-80; chief ob-gyn. at Prime Health, also clin. assoc. prof. U. Kans. Sch. Medicine, 1978-80; prof. dept. ob-gyn. Mercer U. Sch. Medicine, Macon, Ga., 1980-95, prof. emeritus, 1995; dist. health dir. Dist. 5-2, Macon, Ga., 1996—; dist. dir. Ga. Divsn. Pub. Health, Macon, 1996—. Mem. Ga. State Coun. on Maternal and Infant Health. Fellow Am. Coll. Obstetricians and Gynecologists; mem. AMA, APHA, Med. Assn. Ga., Bibb County Med. Soc. Home: 4384 Peach Pkwy Fort Valley GA 31030-8155

SWARTZ, CAROL I. academic administrator; b. Providence, Dec. 15, 1950; d. Leo L. and Lillian (Gordon) S. BA, U. R.I., 1973; MSW, Portland State U., 1977. Cert. social Worker, 1978. Social worker Children's Friend and Svcs., Providence, 1973-75; counselor S.E. Youth Svcs. Ctr., Portland, Oreg., 1975-77; dir. treatment Mt. Hood Treatment Ctr., Sandy, Oreg., 1977-79; coord. child devel. svcs. Corbett (Oreg.) Sch. Dist., 1978-80; clinician Homer (Alaska) Cmty. Mental Health Ctr., 1980-82; adj. instr. psychology and sociology U. Alaska, Kachemak Bay Campus, Homer, 1984-86; dir. U. Alaska, Kachemak Bay campus, Homer, 1986—. Founding dir. So. Peninsula Women's Svcs., Homer, 1981-83; mgmt. cons. 1984-86; Alaska guardian ad litem, 1984-86. Trustee Homer Found., 1993—; mem. Homer Sister City Assn., 1992—; bd. dirs. Pratt Mus., Homer, 1992-94, Homer Coun. of Arts, 1993-95. Mem. Nat. Assn. of Higher Edn., Nat. Assn. Women in Edn., Nat. Assn. Women in C.C., Rotary Internat., Homer C. of C. (Citizen of Yr. nominee 1983, 86). Avocations: travel, reading, camping, sailing, hiking. Home: PO Box 2748 Homer AK 99603-2748

SWARTZ, JAMES EDWARD, chemistry educator, dean, university administrator; b. Washington, June 12, 1951; s. Donald M. and Geneva R. (Henderson) S.; m. Louanne L. Curtis, June 6, 1980 (dec. 1986); m. Cynthea Mosier, Apr. 1, 1988. BS in Chemistry, Stanislaus State Coll., Turlock, Calif., 1973; PhD in Chemistry, U. Calif., Santa Cruz, 1978. Instr. U. Calif., Santa Cruz, 1978; rsch. fellow Calif. Inst. Tech., Pasadena, 1978-80; asst. prof. Grinnell (Iowa) Coll., 1980-86, assoc. prof. chemistry, 1986-93, prof., 1993—, v.p. acad. affairs, dean, 1998—. Vis. prof. U. Minn., Mpls., 1986—87; mem. adv. coun. Iowa Energy Ctr.; cons.-evaluator Commn. Higher Edn., N. Cent. Assn., 1995—; bd. dirs. Am. Conf. Acad. Deans, 2000—. Contbr. articles to profl. jours. Grantee Petroelum Rsch. Fund, 1981-83, Rsch. Corp., 1981-83, 84-86, 86-88, NSF, 1982-84, 90-93, 91-94. Mem. AAAS, Am. Chem. Soc., Iowa Acad. Scis., Am. Wind Energy Assn. Home: 1233 Summer St Grinnell IA 50112-1547 Office: Grinnell Coll Office of Dean Grinnell IA 50112-1690

SWARTZ, MELVIN JAY, lawyer, writer; b. Boston, July 21, 1930; s. Jack M. and Rose (Rosenberg) S.; children: Julianne, Jonathan Samuel. BA, Syracuse U., 1953; LLB, Boston U., 1957. Bar: N.Y. 1959, Ariz. 1961. Assoc. Alfred S. Julian, N.Y.C., 1957-59; ptnr. Finks & Swartz, Youngtown, Sun City, Phoenix, 1961-70, Swartz & Jeckel, P.C., Sun City, Youngtown, Scottsdale, Ariz., 1971-82. Author: Don't Die Broke, A Guide to Secure Retirement, 1974, rev. edit., 2000, (book and cassettes) Keep What You Own, 1989, rev. edit., 2000, Retire Without Fear, 1995; columnist News-Sun, Sun City, 1979-83; author column Swartz on Aging. Bd. dirs. Valley of the Sun Sch. for Retarded Children, 1975-79. Mem. ABA, Ariz. Bar Assn., N.Y. Bar Assn., Maricopa County Bar Assn., Scottsdale Bar Assn., Ctrl. Ariz. Estate Planning Coun., Masons (Phoenix). Jewish. Office: 3416 N 44th St Unit 22 Phoenix AZ 85018-6044 E-mail: swartzmj@worldnet.att.net.

SWARTZ, THOMAS R. economist, educator; b. Phila., Aug. 31, 1937; s. Henry Jr. and Elizabeth (Thomas) S.; m. Jeanne Marie Jourdan, Aug. 12, 1961; children: Mary Butler, Karen Miller, Jennifer, Anne, Rebecca. BA, LaSalle U., 1960; MA, Ohio U., 1962; PhD, Ind. U., 1965. Asst. prof. U. Notre Dame, Ind., 1965-70, assoc. dept. chair, 1968-70, assoc. prof., 1970-78, acting dir. grad. studies, 1977-78, prof. econs., 1978—, dir. program econ. policy, 1982-85; resident dir. U. Notre Dame London Program, 1990-91, U. Notre Dame Austraulia Program, Fremantle, 1996. Vis. prof. U. Notre Dame London Program 1982, 85, 90-91, 2001—; fellow Inst. for Ednl. Initiatives, 1997—; dir. London Summer Program, 2001—; fiscal cons. Ind. Commn. State Tax, Indpls., 1965-68, also spl. tax cons., 1971-81, City of South Bend, Ind., 1972-75. Co-editor: The Supply Side, 1983, Changing Face of Fiscal Federalism, 1990, Urban Finance Under Siege, 1993, Taking Sides, 11th edit., 2004, America's Working Poor, 1995; contbr. articles to profl. jours. Bd. dirs. Forever Learning Inst., South Bend, Ind., 1988-93; mem. steering com. Mayor's Housing Forum, South Bend, 1989-95; chair Com. Svcs. Block Grant, South Bend, 1985-90, Econ. Devel. Task Force, South Bend, 1985. Rsch. fellow Nat. Ctr. Urban Ethnic Affairs, 1979-85; recipient Danforth Assoc. award Danforth Found., 1972-86, Tchg. award Kanzajian Found., 1974; rsch. grantee Mellon Found., 1998—. Fellow Inst. Ednl. Initiatives. Democrat. Roman Catholic. Avocations: racquetball, golf. Office: U Notre Dame Dept Econs 414 Decio Hall Notre Dame IN 46556-5644 E-mail: swartz.1@nd.edu.

SWARTZ, WILLIAM RICK, school psychologist; b. Buffalo, Dec. 27, 1951; s. William Wallace and Ruth Mae (Williams) S.; m. Saundra Kay Hess, June 21, 1980. BS in Edn., Bucknell U., Lewisburg, Pa., 1974; MS in Edn., Bucknell U., 1976; MEd, Shippensburg (Pa.) State U., 1982. Sch. psychologist Waynesboro (Pa.) Area Sch. Dist., 1976—. Ednl. cons. Mont Alto Campus, Pa. State U., 1990-93. Mem. Assn. of Sch. Psychologists of Pa., Coun. for Exceptional Children. Avocations: theater, music, art. Office: Waynesboro Area Sch Dist 210 Clayton Ave Waynesboro PA 17268-2014

SWARTZENDRUBER, CALVIN FREDERICK, chemistry educator, chemical health official; b. Goshen, Ind., June 14, 1971; s. Sanford Calvin and Carolyn Esther (Martin) S.; m. Karen Lynn LeFevre, Aug. 6, 1993; children: Logan Nicol, Madison Elizabeth, Michaela Lynn. AA, Hesston Coll., 1991; BA, Goshen Coll., 1993; postgrad., U. Notre Dame, 1994-98; MS, Purdue U., 2002. Cert. tchr., Ind. Sci. tchr. South Bend (Ind.) Cmty. Schs., 1993-94, Elkhart (Ind.) Cmty. Schs., 1994—; Chem. Hygiene Officer Goshen (Ind.) Coll., 1994—, mem. safety com., 1995—. Cons., developer CFS Web Designs, Goshen, 1996—. Mem. Radio Amateur Civil Emergency Svc., Goshen, 1985—; mem. adv. bd. Elkhart County SKYWARN, Goshen, 1995—. Mem. Am. Chem. Soc., Ind. Alliance Chem. Tchrs., Hoosier Assn. Sci. Tchrs. Mennonite. Achievements include rsch. in the devel. of streptogramin antibiotics. Office: Goshen Coll 1700 S Main St Goshen IN 46526-4724

SWARTZLANDER, EARL EUGENE, JR., engineering educator, former electronics company executive; b. San Antonio, Feb. 1, 1945; s. Earl Eugene and Jane (Nicholas) S.; m. Joan Vickery, June 9, 1968. BSEE, Purdue U., 1967; MSEE, U. Colo., 1969; PhD, U. So. Calif., 1972. Registered profl. engr., Ala., Calif., Colo., Tex. Devel. engr. Ball Bros. Rsch. Corp., Boulder, Colo., 1967-69; Hughes fellow, mem. tech. staff Hughes Aircraft Co., Culver City, Calif., 1969-73; mem. rsch. staff Tech. Svc. Co., Santa Monica, Calif., 1973-74; chief engr. Geophys. Systems Corp., Pasadena, Calif., 1974-75, staff engr. to sr. staff engr., 1975-79, project mgr., 1979-84, lab. mgr., 1985-87; dir. ind. R&D TRW Inc., Redondo Beach, Calif., 1987-90; Schlumberger Centennial prof. engring. dept. elec. and computer engring. U. Tex., Austin, 1990—; mem. tech. adv. bd. Automatic Parallel Designs. Gen. chmn. Internat. Conf. Wafer Scale Integration, 1989, Internat. Conf. Application Specific Array Processors, 1990, 94, 11th Internat. Symposium on Computer Arithmetic, 1992, 31st Ann. Asilomar Conf. on Signals, Sys., and Computers, 1997, others; chmn. 3d Internat. Conf. Parallel and Distributed Sys., Taiwan, 1993, 12th Internat. Conf. on Application-Specific Systems, Architectures and Processors, 2000; mem. tech. adv. bd. Automatic Parallel Designs. Author: VLSI Signal Processing Systems, 1986; editor: Computer Design Development, 1976, Systolic Signal Processing Systems, 1987, Wafer Scale Integration, 1989, Computer Arithmetic Vol. 1 and 2, 1990, Application Specific Processors, 1996; editor-in-chief Jour. of VLSI Signal Processing, 1989-95, IEEE Transactions on Computers, 1991-94, IEEE Transactions on Signal Processing, 1995; editor: IEEE Transactions on Computers, 1982-86, IEEE Transactions on Parallel and Distributed Systems, 1989-90; hardware area editor ACM Computing Revs., 1985—; assoc. editor: IEEE Jour. Solid-State Circuits, 1984-88; contbr. more than 300 articles to profl. jours. and tech. conf. procs. Bd. dirs. Casiano Estates Homeowners Assn., Bel Air, Calif., 1976-78, pres., 1978-80; bd. dirs. Benedict Hills Estates Homeowners Assn., Beverly Hills, Calif., 1984—, pres., 1990-95. Recipient Disting. Engring. Alumnus award Purdue U., 1989, U. Colo., 1997, Outstanding Elec. Engr. award Purdue U., 1992, knight Imperial Russian Order St. John of Jerusalem (Knights of Malta), 1993. Fellow: IEEE (hist. com. 1996—, fellows com. 2000—, 3d Millennium medal 2000); mem.: IEEE Solid-State Cirs. Coun. (sec. 1992—93, treas. 1994—97), IEEE Signal Proc. Soc. (bd. govs. 1992—94), IEEE Computer Soc. (bd. govs. 1987—91, Golden Core award 1996), Omicron Delta Kappa, Sigma Tau, Eta Kappa Nu. Office: U Tex Austin Dept Elec Computer Engring Austin TX 78712

SWEARER, DONALD KEENEY, Asian religions educator, writer; b. Wichita, Kans., Aug. 2, 1934; s. Edward Mays and Elloise Catherine (Keeney) S.; m. Nancy Chester; children: Susan Marie, Stephen Edward. AB cum laude, Princeton U., 1956, MA, 1965, PhD, 1967; BD, Yale U., 1962, STM, 1963. Instr. English dept. Bangkok Christian Coll., 1957-60; adminstrv. asst. Edward W. Hazen Found., New Haven, 1961-63; instr., then asst. prof. Oberlin (Ohio) Coll., 1965-70; assoc. prof. Swarthmore (Pa.) Coll., 1970-75, prof. Asian religions, 1975—, Eugene M. Lang Rsch. prof., 1987-92, Charles and Harriet Cox McDowell prof., 1993—, chair dept. religion, 1986-91; Numata prof. Buddhist studies U. Hawaii, 1993; Hershey vis. prof. Buddhist studies Harvard Div. Sch., 2000—01. Adj. prof. U. Pa., Phila., 1979-93, Temple U., Phila., 1991—; film. cons. ABC, 1972, BBC, 1977, WGBH, 1991-93; lectr. Smithsonian Instn., 1982—, Asia Soc. N.Y., 1982—; bd. advisors Religious Pluralism Project, 1998—, Forum on Religion and Ecology, 1998—. Author: Wat Haripunjaya, 1976, Dialogue. The Key to Understanding Other Religions, 1977, Buddhism and Society in Southeast Asia, 1981; co-author: For the Sake of the World. The Spirit of Buddhist and Christian Monasticism, 1989, Becoming the Buddha: The Ritual of Image Consecration in Thailand, 2004; co-editor: Ethics, Wealth and Salvation. A Study in Buddhist Social Ethics, 1989, Me-and-Mine, Selected Essays of Bhikkhu Buddhadasa, 1989, The Buddhist World of Southeast Asia, 1995, The Legend of Queen Cama, 1998, The State of Buddhist Studies in the World, 1972-1977, 2000; mem. editl. bd. Jour. Religious Ethics, 1978-93, Jour. Ecumenical Studies, 1983—; asst. editor Jour. Asian Studies, 1978-80; book rev. editor S.E. Asia Religious Studies Rev., 1985-93; contbr. articles to various publs. Mem. adult edn. com. Swarthmore Presbyn. Ch., 1985-87, 92-93, 97-98. Recipient Henry Luce Found. award, 2001—; Asian religions study fellow Soc. Religion in Higher Edn., Sri Lanka, Thailand, Japan, 1967-68, NEH sr. fellow Thailand, 1972-73, Rockefeller Found. humanities fellow, Thailand, 1985-86, Guggenheim fellow, 1994, Fulbright fellow Dept. Edn., 1994, NEH fellow, 1998-99; sr. rsch. scholar Fulbright Found., 1989-90, 94; NEH transl. grantee, 1990-91. Mem. AAUP, Assn. Asian Studies (bd. dirs. 1977-80), Am. Acad. Religion (v.p. mid-Atlantic region 1971-72), Am. Soc. Study of Religion, Soc. Buddhist-Christian Studies (bd. dirs. 1995-98), Phi Beta Kappa. Democrat. Home: 109 Columbia Ave Swarthmore PA 19081-1615 Office: Swarthmore Coll Dept Religion 500 College Ave Ste 2 Swarthmore PA 19081-1306

SWEAT, LYNDA SUE, cooking instructor, catering company owner, deaconess; b. Phoenix, Apr. 5, 1949; d. Troy Eugene and Patricia June (Tignor) Lauchner; m. Doyle Dwayne Sweat, Feb. 7, 1976; children: Shannon Sue, Derek Dwayne. BA in Am. Studies, Ariz. State U, 2001, M in Religious Studies, Diploma Barrett Honors Coll., Ariz. State U, 2002. Leasing sec. Coldwell, Banker, Phoenix, 1968-74; exec. sec. Santa Anita Devel., Phoenix, 1974-78; prin., owner Tummy Yummy's, Phoenix, 1989—. Instr., Women's Seminars for Chs. on Christian Hospitality, 1984—; deaconess Palmcroft Bapt. Ch., Phoenix, 1989—, dir. fellowship com., editor and writer newsletter. Mem. Ariz. Bar Assn. Women's Aux., Maricopa County Bar Assn. Women's Aux., Southwestern Bible Coll. Women's Aux., Women in Food and Wine in Ariz. Club, Piecemakers (pres.). Republican. Avocations: crafting, quilting, porcelain doll making. Home: 19937 N Denaro Dr Glendale AZ 85308-5648

SWEAT, NORA ELLEN, home economics educator; b. Glendale, Ky., July 11, 1948; d. Joseph Francis and Juanita Gertrude (Boarman) Vaillancourt; m. Michael Francis Sweat, July 21, 1973; 1 child, Joseph William. BS, We. Ky. U., 1970, MA, 1977. Cert. tchr., Ky. Tchr. home econs. West Hardin High Sch., Stephensburg, Ky., 1970-90, Cen. Hardin High Sch., Cecilia, Ky., 1990—2000. Sec. Hardin County Schs. Performing Arts Ctr., 2001—. Mem. Am. Vocat. Assn. (Region II Vocat. Edn. Tchr. of Yr. 1992), Ky. Vocat. Assn. (v.p. 1987-91, Vocat. Edn. Tchr. of Yr. 1992), Ky. Future Homemakers (hon.), Ky. Home Econs. Tchrs. Assn. Democrat. Roman Catholic. Avocations: cooking, entertaining, piano. Home and Office: 2862 Shepherdsville Rd Elizabethtown KY 42701-9539

SWEATLOCK, SUZANNE MARIE, primary education educator; b. Huntington, Pa., Apr. 28, 1957; d. Rudy A. and Margaret A. (Mickley) S. BS, Juniata Coll., 1979; MEd, cert. spl. edn., Millersville U., 1985. Head tchr. Huntington (Pa.) County Child Devel. Inc., 1979; child devel. specialist Lebanon (Pa.) County Head Start, 1979-80; tchr. Pa. Migrant Program, Lebanon, 1980, Gov. Mifflin Sch. Dist., Shillington, Pa., 1980—. Resident dir. Albright Coll., Reading, Pa., 1982-92; adv. bd. mem, 1983-92. Bldg. rep., mem. negotiations com. Gov. Mifflin Edn. Assn., 1980—; mem. Cumru PTO, 1980—. Recipient Salute to Teaching award Pa. Acad. for the Profession of Teaching, 1990. Roman Catholic. Avocations: reading, bike riding, fittness walking. Home: 2024 Hale Ct Wyomissing PA 19610-1430 Office: Gov Mifflin Sch Dist 10 S Waverly St Shillington PA 19607-2642

SWEDA, LINDA IRENE, elementary school educator; b. Elyria, Ohio, June 16, 1951; d. Charles R. and Hattie M. (Nolan) Rogers; m. Robert D. Winningham, Jan. 29, 19071 (div. Mar. 1988); 1 child, Ryan D.; m. Paul G. Sweda, July 2, 1993. BS in Edn. summa cum laude, Ohio U., 1976; MA in Edn. and Supervision, Ashland U., 1989. Cert. tchr., Ohio. Psychiat. technician Licking County Meml. Hosp., Newark, Ohio, 1971-72; psychiat. technician, house parent Nelsonville (Ohio) Children's Ctr., 1972-73; tchr. Elyria City Schs., 1977—, mem. tchr. mentorship com., 1990—, mem. math. coun. adv., 1991—, mem. tchr. camp intervention program, 1991—, mem. venture capital grant rsch. Jefferson Elem. Sch., 1992—. Insvc. facilitator Math Manipulatives, 1993-94; spkr. Sch. Levy, Elyria, 1987, 89. Scriptwriter (video) Math Matters, 1993. Mem. adv. bd., participant Cleve. Children's Mus., 1989-91; campaign worker coun., mayors, judges, senate, house, 1994—; participant, rschr. Polit. Discussion Group, Elyria, 1989—; mem. Earth Island Inst., San Francisco, 1994; mentor Lorain County Ctr. for Leadership, 1990—. Named Martha Holden Jennings scholar, 1979. Mem. NEA, Ohio Edn. Assn., Elyria Edn. Assn. Avocations: reading, decorating, painting, swimming. Home: 989 Gulf Rd Elyria OH 44035-2961 Office: Jefferson Elem Sch 615 Foster Ave Elyria OH 44035-3328

SWEEN, JOYCE ANN, psychologist, evaluation methodologist; b. N.Y.C. d. Sigfried Joseph Ellmer and Julie (Hollins) Ellmer Hutchins; children: Terri Lynn, James Michael. BS in Math., Antioch Coll., 1960; MS in Exptl. Psychology, Northwestern U., 1965, PhD Social Psychology/Evaluation Rsch., 1971. Univ. fellow Northwestern U., Evanston, Ill., 1960-63, dir. compuer ops. Inst. Met. Studies, 1965-70; asst. prof. sociology DePaul U., Chgo., 1971-74, assoc. prof., 1974-80, prof., 1980-83, prof. sociology and pub. svcs., 1983—. Cons. Nat. Commn. on Violence, 1968; evaluator Office Adolescent Pregnancy Programs, 1988-92, Office of Substance Abuse Prevention, 1988-93, Office of Treament Improvement, 1988-93, dropout prevention program Aspira of Ill., 1984-88, Dept. of Edn., 1989-95, AIDS prevention program, Ctrs. for Disease Ctrl., 1992, Chgo. Dept. Health, 1993-95, Ctr. for Substance Abuse Treatment, 1995-2001, AIDS Found., 1997—; cons. in field. Author articles on fertility, African polygyny, childlessness, teen pregnancy, urbanization, social effects of assassination, evaluation methodology, exptl. regression designs, sch. dropout prevention, survery rsch., AIDS prevention, bilingual edn., violence. NIH grantee, 1971-75, 78-81; NSF grantee, 1979-82; AMA grantee, 1991. Mem. AAAS, APA, Internat. Sociol. Assn., Am. Sociol. Assn., Am. Evaluation Assn., Midwest Sociol. Assn., Sigma Xi. Office: DePaul U Dept Sociology 990 W Fullerton Ave Chicago IL 60614-3298

SWEENEY, GARNETTE GRINNELL, elementary education educator; b. Pensacola, Fla., Oct. 5, 1964; d. Robert Orlando and Diane (Dodge) Grinnell; m. John William Sweeney, Feb. 21, 1988. AD, Ctrl. Va. C.C., Lynchburg, 1985; BS, Radford U., 1987; M in Adminstrn. and Supervision, Va. Tech., 1994. Tchr. elem. Bedford (Va.) County Schs., 1989-94, tchr. mid. sch., 1994—. Coach Odyssey of the Mind, Lynchburg, Va., 1991-93, 94-95, trainer, problem chpt., state judge, 1994. Named Conservation Educator of Yr. Peaks of Otter Soil and Conservation Dist., 1991-92; recipient Environ. award Jr. Women's Club Va., 1991, Hon. Mention Newsweek and Amway Environ. Awareness, 1992. Mem. ASCD, Fraternal Order Police. Republican. Avocations: skiing, travel, hiking, canoeing, reading. Office: Bedford County Pub Schs PO Box 748 Bedford VA 24523-0748

SWEENEY, JUDITH KIERNAN, secondary education educator; Tchr. science grades 8-12 Lincoln (R.I.) Jr.-Sr. High Sch., 1994; curator of edn. Mus. Natural History, Providence, 1994. Named State Tchr. of Yr. Science award R.I., 1992. Office: Mus Natural History Roger William Park Providence RI 02905

SWEENY, STEPHEN JUDE, academic administrator; b. N.Y.C., Sept. 15, 1943; s. Herbert Vincent and Isabel Mary (Dolan) S.; m. Barbara Mary Stasz, Aug. 7, 1976. BA in Spanish, Cath. U., 1966; MA in Theology, Manhattan Coll., 1971, MA in Counseling Psychology, 1976; PhD, NYU, 1991. Prin. Incarnation Elem. and Jr. High Sch., N.Y.C., 1969-73; dir. campus ministry Manhattan Coll., N.Y.C., 1973-76; asst. to provost Coll. of New Rochelle, N.Y., 1976-78, mem. edn. dept., 1976—, exec. asst. to pres., 1978-80, v.p. for planning, 1980-81, sr. v.p., 1981-97, pres., 1997—. Bd. trustees exec. com., com. on fin. and adminstrn. Commn. Ind. Colls. and Univs.; bd. trustees, chmn. acad. affairs com., chmn., student affairs com. Coll. St. Elizabeth; bd. trustees strategic planning com., mem. com. LaSalle Acad., Network of Sacred Heart Schs.; membership com. Network of Sacred Heart Schs.; bd. dirs. Neylan Commn. Colls. and Univs., Cardinal McCloskey Svcs., Women's Coll. Coalition. Mem.: Soc. Friendly Sons St. Patrick (N.Y.C.), Soc. Friendly Sons of St. Patrick (Westchester), Sovereign Mil. Order of Malta (med. com.), Knights of the Holy Sepulchre. Roman Catholic. Office: The College of New Rochelle 29 Castle Pl New Rochelle NY 10805-2338

SWEET, JOHANNA MAE, secondary school educator; b. Little Falls, N.Y., Aug. 28, 1956; d. Eugene Harvey and Catherine Marlene (Livingston) Clemons; m. Donald Charles Sweet, Aug. 19, 1978; children: Crystal Morgan, Mallory Lynn, Kyle Eugene. BS in Secondary Social Sci., SUNY, Oneonta, 1978, MS in Edn., 1981. Cert. tchr., N.Y. Reading tchr. Oppenheim-Ephratah Ctrl. Sch., St. Johnsville, N.Y., 1978—, social studies tchr., 1989—, mem. compact dist. com., 1992—; Coll. Now instr. Herkimer County C.C., Herkimer, NY, 2002—. Sunday sch. tchr. United Meth. Ch., Lassellsville, N.Y., 1989-90. Mem. DAR (chmn. Am. history essay com. St. Johnsville chpt. 1991—). Republican. Avocations: knitting, crocheting, camping, cross-country skiing. Office: Oppenheim-Ephratah Ctrl Sch 6486 State Highway 29 Saint Johnsville NY 13452-2799 Home: 5475 State Highway 29 Saint Johnsville NY 13452-2119 E-mail: djsweet@telenet.net.

SWEETSER, RUTH EMILIE ZIEMANN, academic administrator; b. Milw., July 26, 1945; d. Theodore William and Ottilia Loretta (Brandt) Ziemann; m. Steven Gary Sweetser, Aug. 22, 1970; children: Daniel Seth, Douglas William Alden. BA, Hope Coll., 1967; postgrad., Standford U.; MA, U. Chgo., 1972; postgrad. seminar, Ill. State U., 1975. Tchr. Barrington (Ill.) Consolidated High Sch., 1968-75; asst. bus. mgr. Midwest Coll. Engring., Lombard, Ill., 1983-84, bus. and adminstrn. dir., 1984-86; facilities mgr. Ill. Inst. Tech., Glen Ellyn, 1986-89, assoc. dir. Wheaton, Ill., 1989—. Mktg./comms. chair Ill. R&D Corridor Coun., DuPage County, 1988-91, project dir., 1991-92; mem. Corridor Group, Met. Econ. Devel. Alliance, Chg./DuPage County, DuKane Valley Coun., 1989—, bd. dirs., 1993-95; achievement award judge Women in Mgmt., 1986. Dir. enrichment support group German for Kids YMCA, PALS, Lombard, 1980-86; chmn. DuPage Ares Engr.'s Week Program, DuPage County, 1985—; co-chair Glenbard Citizens for Quality Edn., DuPage County, 1989—; active Lombard Hist. Soc., 1986—, Am. Cancer Soc., Lombard, 1988-92, Friends of the Libr., Lombard, 1988—, Village of Lombard Plan Commn., 1990—, strategic plan com. Glenbard East High Sch., 1990—, Glenbard East Citizens Adv. Coun., mem. 1990—, pres., 1992-94, steering com. Sch. Dist. 44 Referendum Effort, Lombard, 1991—, traveling exhibit chair DuPage County Sesquicentennial Steering Com., 1988-89, higher edn. symposium com., 1989; past pres., mem. community EXPO steering com. Lombard Community Leaders; elder Community Presbyn. Ch., 1990-92, blood drive chair, 1984-92, accompanist, 1975—; founder ambassadors program Glenbard East Citizens Adv. Coun., 1992—. Fellow U. Chgo., 1967. Mem. AAUW (Ill. task force 1991—, nat. membership com. 1989-93, membership v.p. Ill. div. 1986-90, Ill. pres. 1995—, Highest Membership Growth award 1988, chair nominating com., Named Gift honoree 1983, Agt. of Change award 1991), Ill. Women's Agenda (pres. 1990-91), DuPage Area Assn. Bus. and Industry (nominating com. 1991, chair liaison com. 1992—). Avocations: professional piano accompanist, scuba diving, volleyball. Office: Ill Inst Tech 201 E Loop Rd Wheaton IL 60187-8488

SWEEZY, MELANIE ELIZABETH, elementary school educator; b. Orlando, Fla., Nov. 16, 1952; d. Henry Marvin Goldman Jr. and Shirley Elizabeth (Daugherty) Reid. BA in Elem. Edn., U. Ctrl. Fla., 1987; M of Adminstrn. and Supervision, George Washington U., 1995. Cert. tchr., Md. Acctg. mgr. Optimum Systems, Inc., Rockville, Md., 1972-83; elem. educator Orange County Bd. Edn., Orlando, 1987, Dept. Def. Schs., Naples, Italy, 1987-90, Charles County Bd. Edn., Waldorf, Md., 1990—. Cons., task writer Md. Dept. Edn., Balt., 1990-94, 96-98; staff developer Charles County Bd. Edn., Waldorf, 1991-94 (Outstanding Sttaff Developer award 1994, Exemplary Tchr. award 1994); com., advisor PreK-4 Integrated Curriculum Project, Washington, 1992-94; mem. Charles County Curriculum Framework Com., 1994—. Mem. Rockville Chpt. Jaycees, 1981-83; regional and state judge Odyssey of the Mind, Waldorf, Balt., 1993—. Mem. NEA, ASCD, Nat. Coun. Social Studies, Md. Alliance of Geography. Republican. Lutheran. Avocations: golf, arts and crafts, walking, sewing.

SWENSON, JAMES REED, physician, educator; b. Utah, Nov. 18, 1933; s. Reed K. and Ruth (Freebairn) S.; m. Sharon Coray, Aug. 21, 1953; children— Richard, Karen, Leslie, David, Julie. Student, Weber Coll., 1952-54; MD, U. Utah, 1959. Intern, then resident in phys. medicine and rehab.; mem. faculty div. phys. medicine and rehab. U. Utah Sch. Medicine, Salt Lake City, chmn. div., 1965—2001, asso. prof., 1970-85, prof., 1985—2002. Chmn. bd. trustees U. Utah Sch. Alcoholism and Other Drug Dependencies; founder Miss Wheelchair Utah Pageant. Served to capt. M.C. U.S. Army, 1960-62. Mem. AMA, Utah State Med. Assn., Am. Acad. Phys. Medicine and Rehab., Assn. Acad. Physiatrists, Am. Spinal Injury Assn., Utah Soc. Phys. Medicine & Rehab., Am. Med. Soc. Alcoholism.

SWERDLOFF, RONALD S. medical educator, researcher; b. Pomona, Calif., Feb. 18, 1938; s. Julius Lewis and Eva (Kelman) S.; m. Christina Wang; children: Jonathan Nicolai, Peter Loren, Paul Im, Michael Im. BS, U. Calif., 1959, MD, 1962. Diplomate Am. Bd. Internal Medicine, Am. Bd. Endocrinology. Intern U. Wash., Seattle, 1962-63, resident, 1963-64; rsch. assoc. NIH, Bethesda, Md., 1964-66; resident UCLA Sch. Medicine, 1966-67; rsch. fellow Harbor-UCLA Med. Ctr., Torrance, Calif., 1967-69, asst. prof., 1969-72, assoc. prof. divsn. Endocrinology, 1972-78, chief divsn. Endocrinology, 1973—, prof., 1978—, assoc. chair dept. medicine, 1997—; dir. UCLA Population Rsch. Ctr., Torrance, 1986-92, Mellon Found. Ctr. in Reproductive Medicine, 1997—. Dir. WHO Collaborating Ctr. Reprodn., Torrance; cons. WHO Geneva, 1982-90, NIH, Bethesda, 1982—, UN Fertility Planning Assn., Geneva, 1983—, Am. Bd. Internal Medicine, Phila., 1989—; inaugural lectr. Australian Soc. Reproductive Biology, Perth, 1990; mem. tech. adv. com. Contraceptive R&D Agy. (CONRAD, AID), 1992—. Editor 3 books; contbr. 100 chpts. to books, 250 articles to profl. jours. Bd. dirs., vice chair Harbor-UCLA Rsch. and Edn. Inst. Fellow: ACP; mem.: We. Soc. Clin. Rsch. (pres. 1983—84, UCLA Sherman Mellinkoff award, Mayo Soley award 2000), Endocrinology Soc., Pacific Coast Fertility (pres. 1984, Squibb award, Outstanding Rsch. award 1976, 1984, Wyeth award 1984), Am. Soc. Clin. Rsch. (pres. we. sect. 1972—73), Am. Assn. Physicians, Am. Soc. Andrology (pres. 1992—93, Serono award 1986). Office: Harbor UCLA Med Ctr Divsn Endocrinology 1000 W Carson St Torrance CA 90502-2004 E-mail: swerdloff@gcrc.rei.edu.

SWERDLOW, MARTIN ABRAHAM, physician, pathologist, educator; b. Chgo., July 7, 1923; s. Sol Hyman and Rose (Lasky) Swerdlow; m. Marion Levin, May 19, 1945; children: Steven Howard, Gary Bruce. Student, Herzl Jr. Coll., 1941-42; BS, U. Ill., 1945; MD, U. Ill., Chgo., 1947. Diplomate Am Bd Pathology. Intern Michael Reese Hosp. and Med. Center, Chgo., 1947-48, resident, 1948-50, 51-52, mem. staff, 1974—, chmn. dept. pathology, v.p. acad. affairs, 1974-90; pathologist Menorah Med Ctr, Kansas City, Mo., 1954—57. Asst prof, pathologist Univ Ill Col Med, Chicago, 1957—59, assoc prof, 1959—60, clin prof, 1960—64, prof, pathologist, 1966—72, assoc dean, prof pathology, 1970—72; prof pathology, chmn Univ Mo, Kansas City, 1972—74; prof pathology Univ Chicago, 1975—89, Geever prof, head pathology emeritus, 1993—; mem comt standards Chicago Health Sys Agency, 1976—. With MC U.S. Army, 1944—45. Recipient Alumnus of the Yr Award, Univ Ill Col Med, 1973, Instructorship Award, Univ Ill, 1960, 1965, 1968, 1971, 1972. Mem.: Inst Med, Am Soc Dermatopathology, Am Acad Dermatology, Int Acad Pathology, Col Am Pathologists, Am Soc Clin Pathologists, Chicago Pathology Soc (pres 1980—). Jewish. Office: U Ill Coll Medicine Dept Pathology 1819 W Polk St Chicago IL 60612-7331 E-mail: maswerdl@uic.edu.

SWETMAN, GLENN ROBERT, English language educator, poet; b. May 20, 1936; s. Glenn Lyle and June (Read) S.; m. Margarita Ortiz, Feb. 8, 1964 (div. 1979); children: Margarita June, Glenn Lyle Maximilian, Glenda Louise. BS, U. So. Miss., 1957, MA, 1959; PhD, Tulane U., 1966. Instr. U. So. Miss., 1957-58, asst. prof., 1964-66; instr. Ark. State U., 1958-59, McNeese U., 1959-61; instr. English Univ. Coll. Tulane U., 1961-64, spl. asst. dept. elec. engring., 1961-64; assoc. prof. La. Inst. Tech., 1966-67; prof., head dept. langs. Nicholls State Coll., Thibodaux, La., 1967-69, head dept. English, 1969-71, prof., 1971-91; prof. emeritus William Carey Coll., Gulfport, Miss., 1991—. Writer in residence, prof. English William Carey Coll., Gulfport, 1991—; ptnr. Breeland Pl., Biloxi, 1960—; stringer, corr. Shreveport (La.) Times, 1966—; ptnr. Ormuba, Inc., 1975—; cons. tech. writing Union Carbide Corp., Am. Fedn. Tchrs. State v.p. Nat. Com. to Resist Attacks on Tenure, 1974—. Book reviewer Jackson (Miss.) State Times, 1961; contbr. poetry to various publs. including Poet, Prairie Schooner, Trace, Ball State U. Forum, Film Quar., Poetry Australia, numerous others worldwide; author: (books of poems) Tunel de Amor, 1973, Deka #1, 1973, Deka #2, 1979, Shards, 1979, Concerning Carpenters, 1980, Son of Igor, 1982, Poems of the Fantastic, 1990; contbr. numerous articles to encys.; cons. editor (poetry) Paon Press, 1974—, Scott-Foresman, 1975; mem. editl. bd. Scholar and Educator, 1980—. Subdivsn. coord. Rep. Party, Hattiesburg, Miss., 1964. With AUS, 1957. Recipient Poetry awards KQUE Haiku contest, 1964, Coll. Arts contest, L.A., 1966, Black Ship Festival, Yoqosuka, Japan, 1967, Green World Brief Forms award Green World Poetry Editors, 1965. Mem. MLA, S. Cen. MLA, So. Literary Festival Assn. (v.p. 1975-76, 82-83, pres. 1984-85), Coll. Writers Soc. La. (pres. 1971-72, exec. dir. 1983—), IEEE, Am. Assn. Engring. Edn., La. Poetry Soc. (pres. 1971-74, 86—), Internat. Boswellian Inst., Nat. Fedn. State Poetry Socs. (2d v.p., nat. membership chmn. 1972-74, pres. 1976-77), Nat. Soc. Scholars and Educators (bd. dirs. 1982—, sec. exec. bd. 1986—, sec. bd. dirs. 1968—, sec. soc. 1989—, exec. edn. 2001-), Am. Fedn. Tchrs. (chpt. pres. 1973-78), Nat. Fedn. State Poetry Socs. (1st v.p. 1975-76, exec. bd. 1972—), Phi Eta Sigma, Omicron Delta Kappa. Home: PO Box 146 Biloxi MS 39533-0146 Office: William Carey Coll 1856 Beach Dr Gulfport MS 39507-1508

SWETT, STEPHEN FREDERICK, JR., artist, educator; b. Englewood, N.J., Sept. 14, 1935; s. Stephen Frederick and Frances (Gulotta) S.; m. Annette Palazzolo, Nov. 18, 1961; children: Susan, Kimberly Ann, Stephen Laurence. BA, Montclair State Coll., 1959, MA, 1965; EdD in Ednl. Adminstrn., Rutgers U., 1976; grad., North Light Art Sch., 1995. Tchr. Long Branch (N.J.) H.S., 1961-62, Roselle Park (N.J.) H.S., 1962-73; rsch. asst. Rutgers U., New Brunswick, N.J., 1973-74; instrnl. supr. Elmwood Park (N.J.) Schs., 1974-76, Morris Hills Regional Schs., Denville, N.J., 1976-77; asst. prin. Lawrence H.S., Lawrenceville, N.J., 1977-79; prin. Stafford Intermediate Sch., Manahawkin, N.J., 1979-94; recreation and art cons., 1994—. Participant NSF Inst. in physics, chemistry and math. Seton Hall U., 1964, Newark Coll. Engring., 1965, Stevens Inst. Tech., summers 1966-68; rschr. sch. fin. Exhibited in group shows at Sheldon Meml. Art Gallery, 1998, Period Gallery, Omaha, 1998, 99, Montserrat Gallery, N.Y.C., 2000, The Looking Glass Art Gallery, Hawley, Pa., 2000. With AUS, 1959-61. Mem. Roselle Park Edn. Assn. (pres. 1971-73), Nat. Soc. Study Edn., Am. Assn. Physics Tchrs., Am. Inst. Physics, Am. Assn. Sch. Adminstrs., N.J. Assn. Sch. Adminstrs., Nat. Assn. Elem. and Mid. Sch. Adminstrs., N.J. Assn. Elem. and Mid. Sch. Adminstrs., Nat. Assn. Secondary Sch. Prins., Phi Delta Kappa (sec. Rutgers chpt. 1977-80, v.p. 1980-82, pres. 1983-84). Home: 306 Tenth Ave Belmar NJ 07719-2313

SWIBINSKI, EDWARD THOMAS, physician, educator; b. Jersey City, Jan. 26, 1950; s. Stanley Adolph and Celina Frances (Szymanski) S. BA, Rutgers U., 1972; MD, N.Y. Med. Coll., 1975. Diplomate Am. Bd. Internal Medicine, Am. Bd. Endocrinology and Metabolism. Resident in medicine N.Y. Med. Coll., N.Y.C., 1975-78; gen. internist Nat. Health Svcs. Corp., Camden, N.J., 1978-79; fellow in endocrinology Hosp. of U. Pa., Phila., 1979-80, Robert Wood Johnson Med. Sch., Piscataway, N.J., 1980-81; assoc. clin. prof. medicine U. Medicine and Dentistry N.J.-R.W. Johnson Med. Sch.; divsn. chief endocrinology Our Lady of Lourdes Ctr. Mem. ACP, Phila. Endocrinology Soc. (v.p. 1993-94, bd. dirs. 1991-96, pres. 1994-95), Camden County Med. Soc., Phi Beta Kappa, Alpha Omega Alpha. Roman Catholic. Office: 1210 Brace Rd Cherry Hill NJ 08034-3213

SWIENER, RITA ROCHELLE, psychologist, educator; b. Pitts., July 31, 1941; d. Julius D. and Rose (Sheinbein) Swiener; 1 child, Samuel L. Schuff. BA, U. Mo., St. Louis, 1970; MA in Psychology, So. Ill. U., Edwardsville, 1973. Prof. Psychology State Cmty. Coll., East St. Louis, Ill., 1972-96; pvt. practice St. Louis, 1972—. Adj. faculty St. Louis C.C., Meramac, 1993—; pres. Ill. C.C. Faculty Assn., 1979-80; trustee State Univs. Retirement Sys., 1990; pres. local 3912 IFT-AFT, East St. Louis, 1983-92; chairperson social and behavior panel Ill. C.C. Bd. and Bd. of Higher Edn. Articulation Initiative, 1992-96. Pres. Call-for-Help, Inc., Edgemont, Ill., 1990-92, 94-97; pres. and founder Santa's Helpers, Inc., St. Louis, 1966—; mem., founder Joy E. Whitener scholarship com. U. Mo. at St. Louis, 1990—. Recipient Outstanding C.C. Faculty Mem. award Ill. C.C. Trustees Assn., 1985, David Erikson award for Outstanding Leadership Ill. C.C. Faculty Assn., 1988, Hometown Hero award KPLR-TV, Suburban Jour., Hardees, St. Louis, 1994, Christmas Spirit award KSD-TV, John Pertzborn, St. Louis, 1990. Mem. APA, U. Mo. St. Louis Psychology Alumni Assn. (treas. 1989-91, Disting. Alumni award 1992), St. Louis Women Psychologist, Mo. Psychol. Assn. Jewish. Avocations: boating, travel, reading. Home: 7832 Balson Ave Saint Louis MO 63130-3624 E-mail: stlri@aol.com.

SWIFT, JILL ANNE, industrial engineer, educator; b. Memphis, Nov. 12, 1959; d. Gary Green and Sharon (Willoughby) Brown; m. Fredrick Wallace Swift, June 12, 1987; children: Andrew, Samantha. BS, Memphis State U., 1981, MS, 1982; PhD, Okla. State U., 1987. Registered profl. engr., Fla.; cert. quality mgr., quality engr. Design engr. DuPont Co., Glasgow, Del., 1982-83; head dept. physics Coll. Boca Raton, Fla., 1983-87; asst. prof. indsl. engring. U. Miami, Coral Gables, Fla., 1987-96; quality cons., 1996—; dir. quality assurance Cubic Transp. Systems, Tullahoma, Tenn., 1997—. Vis. scholar Air Force Inst. Tech., Wright-Patterson AFB, Ohio, 1988; cons. A.T. Kearney, Amman, Jordan, 1990; quality liaison U. Miami Inst. Study of Quality in Mfg. and Svc., 1988—; cons., spkr. in field. Author: Introduction to Modern Statistical Quality Control and Management, 1995, Principles of Total Quality Control, 1996; co-author: Principles of Total Quality, 1997; contbr. articles to profl. publs. Mem. IIE (chpt. dir. 1988-90, Christmas toy dr. coord. 1989, 90), Am. Soc. Engring. Edn., Am. Soc. Quality Control, Phi Kappa Phi, Alpha Pi Mu (faculty adviser 1988-96), Tau Beta Pi. Republican. Avocations: cross-stitch, reading. E-mail: drj@classicnet.net.

SWIFT, RONNI, special education educator; b. Bklyn., Oct. 11, 1950; d. Milton and Lillian (Siegel) S. BA, C.W. Post Coll., L.I. U., 1972, MS in Spl. Edn., 1976, profl. diploma in ednl. adminstrn., 1999. Cert. sch. adminstr./supr., sch. dist. adminstr., transitional svcs. adminstr. Tchr. vocat. tng. div. Bklyn. Sch. for Spl. Children, 1973-74, tchr. day sch. div., 1975-76, tchr. nursery sch. div., 1976-78; tchr. Ednl. Ctr. Assn. for Help of Retarded Children, Brookville, N.Y., 1978-80, art tchr., 1980—, tchr. transitional workshop tng., 1993—, spl. edn. adminstr., pre-sch. evaluator, 2003—. Com. mem. Very Spl. Arts Festival, Nassau County, L.I. Mem. ASCD, Assn. for the Help of Retarded Children (Nassau County chpt.), Phi Delta Kappa. Office: AHRC Ednl Ctr The Silver Bldg 189 Wheatley Rd Glen Head NY 11545-2699

SWINNEY, CAROL JOYCE, secondary education educator; Langs. tchr. Hugoton (Kans.) High Sch., 1972-98; dir. distance learning S.W. Plains Regional Svcs. Ctr., Kans., 1998—. Named Kans. Tchr. of Yr., Disney for Lang. Tchr. of Yr., 1993, Milken Nat. Educator, 1992. Office: PO Drawer 1010 Sublette KS 67877-1010

SWINNEY, HARRY LEONARD, physics educator; b. Opelousas, La., Apr. 10, 1939; s. Leonard Robert and Ethel Ruth (Bertheaud) S.; m. Gloria Luyas, Oct. 21, 1967 (dec. Oct. 1997); 1 child, Brent Luyas (dec.); m. Lizabeth Kelley, Aug. 12, 2000. BS in Physics, Rhodes Coll., 1961; PhD in Physics, Johns Hopkins U., 1968. Vis. asst. prof. Johns Hopkins U., 1970-71; asst. prof. physics NYU, 1971-73; assoc. prof. CCNY, 1973-77, prof., 1978; prof. physics U. Tex., Austin, 1978—, Trull Centennial prof., 1984-90, Sid Richardson Found. regents chair, 1990—, dir. Ctr. Nonlinear Dynamics, 1985—. Morris Loeb lectr. Harvard U., 1982. Editor: Hydrodynamic Instabilities and the Transition to Turbulence, 1985; contbr. articles to profl. jours. Regents chair Sid Richardson Found., 1990—. Grantee NSF, Dept. Energy, NASA, Office Naval Rsch., Welch, others; Guggenheim fellow, 1982-83. Fellow AAAS, Am. Phys. Soc. (exec. bd. 1992-94, Fluid Dynamics prize 1996); mem. NAS, Am. Acad. Arts and Scis., Am. Assn. Physics Tchrs. Democrat. Methodist. Office: U Tex Dept Physics Ctr Nonlinear Dynamics Austin TX 78712 E-mail: Swinney@physics.utexas.edu.

SWINNEY, PHYLLIS MARIE, elementary education educator; b. Weimar, Tex., Oct. 27, 1950; d. Albert Frederick and Mary Ann (Potthast) Janecka; m. William Albert Swinney Jr., June 28, 1975; 1 child, Sarah Noelle. BS, U. Tex., 1973; M in Curriculum & Instrn., reading specialist cert., U. Tex., San Antonio, 1983; bilingual cert., Trinity U., San Antonio, 1976. Cert. elem. edn., bilingual edn., supervision and curriculum, reading specialist. Elem. tchr. Austin (Tex.) Ind. Sch. Dist., 1973-75, San Antonio (Tex.) Ind. Sch. Dist., 1975-77, Comal Ind. Sch. Dist., Bulverde, Tex., 1977-80, substitute tchr., 1980-83; reading specialist St. Mary's Hall, San Antonio, 1983—. Dir. Summer Reading Camp, San Antonio, 1988-95; instr. U. Tex., San Antonio, 1991, 92; instr. Spring at the Hall, Scottish Rite Dyslexia tng. program. Sunday sch. tchr. St. Joseph's Ch., Bulverde; vol. Raul Jimenez Thanksgiving Dinner for Srs., San Antonio, 1994; vol. various polit. campaigns; chairperson Battered Women's Shelter Project. Grantee Holt-Dupont Co., San Antonio, 1985, 87, 89, 95, 01. Mem. Internat. Reading Assn., Tex. State Reading Assn., Alamo Reading Coun. (vol. Reading in the Mall 1983-92), Neuropsychol. Issues Group, Parents and Reading (com. sect., treas., chairperson). Avocations: reading, psychology, gardening, computer technology, photography. Office: St Marys Hall 9401 Starcrest Dr San Antonio TX 78217-4199 E-mail: pswinney@smhall.org.

SWINSON, SUE WHITLOW, secondary education educator; b. Rocky Mount, Va., Apr. 14, 1939; d. Homer P. and Etholene R. (Ramsey) Whitlow; m. Arthur Pitt Burgess, 1961 (div. 1975); 1 child, Robert A.; m. William Edward Swinson, Jr., Sept. 7, 1979. AB, Coll. of William & Mary, 1961; MEd, Ga. State U., 1978. Cert. lifetime profl. DT-5. Tchr. Latin Chesterfield (Va.) County Bd. Edn., 1961-62; Army tchr. USAF I, Augsburg, Germany, 1962-64; tchr. Latin Henrico County Bd. Edn., Richmond, Va., 1965-68; tchr. Latin, English, history DeKalb County Bd. Edn., Decatur, Ga., 1974-92; tchr. Latin and English Randolph County Bd. Edn., Cuthbert, Ga., 1992—, ret., 1977; dental asst. Book selection com. DeKalb County Bd. Edn., Decatur, 1983-84. Co-author, editor quar. bull. The Georgia Classicist, 1985-86; co-author: (resource guide) Ga. Advanced Latin State Dept. Resource, 1992-93; co-author: (curriculum guide) Latin Curriculum Guides. Named Ga. Latin Tchr. of Yr., Ga. Classical Assn., 1986, 92, recipient Student-Tchr. Achievement Recognition award, 1991-92, 96-97. Mem. Am. Classical League, Ga. Classical Assn. (co-editor state paper 1985-86), Fgn. Lang. Assn. of Ga., Profl. Assn. Ga. Educators. Republican. Methodist. Avocations: reading, golf, fishing, gardening, bridge. Home: RR 2 Box 254-d Georgetown GA 31754-9579

SWINTON, GWENDOLYN DELORES, secondary education educator; b. L.A., Mar. 20, 1930; d. Victor David and Ellise (Shelly) Parris; m. Edward Lawson Swinton, Sept. 9, 1950; 1 child, Dedra Kaye Swinton Tyree. BS, Wiley Coll., Marshall, Tex., 1951; MS, Tchrs. Coll., N.Y.C., 1966; MA, Prairie View A&M Coll., 1974; student, So. Meth. U., 1964-65. Tchr. sci. and phys. edn., girls coach Barnett High Sch., Terrell, Tex., 1953-55; counselor Dallas County Boys Home, Hutchins, Tex., 1956-57; tchr. health and phys. edn., girls coach Dalworth High Sch., Grand Prairie, Tex., 1960-66; tchr. gen. sci. and phys. edn. Robert E. Lee Jr. High Sch., Grand Prairie, 1966-69; tchr. phys. edn. and health sci. elem. and secondary schs., Dallas, 1969-79; tchr. sci., phys. edn. and social studies John XXIII Cath. Sch., Dallas, 1989—. Mem. Sigma Gamma Rho. Home: 1807 Meadow Valley Ln Dallas TX 75232-2753

SWINTON, JANET RUTH (PETERSON), English language educator; b. Laramie, Wyo., May 8, 1948; d. George W. Peterson and Myrtle R. (Mason) Forney; m. Duane M. Swinton, Aug. 9, 1975; children: Jennifer, Nathan. BA, U. Wyoming, 1970; postgrad., U. Colo., 1971-72, U. Iowa, 1977; MEd,

Ea. Wash. U., 1983. Tchr. Coronado Hills Jr. High Sch., Denver, 1970-72; tchr. sr. high Dept. Def. Overseas Schs., Kaiserslautern, Germany, 1972-75; instr. and staff developer Kirkwood Community Coll., Cedar Rapids, Iowa, 1975-77; instr. English Spokane (Wash.) Falls Community Coll., 1983—, dir. Communication Learning Ctr., 1983-89. Faculty rep. to bd. trustees C.C.s of Spokane, 1985-90, faculty devel. coord., 1991—. Co-author: Read and Respond, 1988, 2d edit., 1992, 3d edit., 1994. Named Outstanding Tchr., Burlington No., 1986. Mem. Wash. Assn. for Devel. Edn. (pres. 1987-88), Wash. Coll. Reading and Learning Assn. (pres. 1990-91). Democrat. Presbyterian. Avocations: snow skiing, reading, soccer. Office: Spokane Falls Community Coll 3410 W Fort George Wright Dr Spokane WA 99224-5284

SWINYARD, SHARON JOAN, language professional, educator, administrator; b. Salt Lake City, July 20, 1943; d. Chester Allan and Vivian (Redford) S. BA in Spanish with honors, NYU, 1965, MA, 1966; PhD, Stanford U., 1972. Program asst. NYU and U. Madrid, 1965; teaching, rsch. asst. Stanford (Calif.) U., 1966-68, 72; assoc. in Spanish U. Calif., Santa Barbara, 1970-72; prof., chmn. Hispanic studies dept. St. Joseph's Coll., Mountain View, Calif., 1974-84, asst. to pres., 1981-84; prof., chmn. Hispanic studies dept. St. Patrick's Sem., Menlo Park, Calif., 1979-84; dir. ann. giving, assoc. dir., exec. dir. Children's Hosp. San Francisco Found., 1984-86; campaign dir. Lucile Packard Children's Hosp./Med. Devel. Stanford U., 1986-89; dir. devel. Menlo Sch. and Coll., Atherton, Calif., 1989-90; fundraising cons., 1990—. Bd. dir. humanities program Antaeus Group, 1975—. Translator: El Niño con espina bifida, 4th edit., 1984. Recipient cert. del rector U. Madrid y del Pres. de NYU, 1964, 66, diploma Iberoamericana de Miembro de Honor del com. Directive de la Revista Iberoamericana de Rehab. M. dica, 1966; N.Y. State Regents scholar NYU, 1965, NYU cholar, 1965-66; Stanford U. grantee 1969-70; recipient Silver medal Coun. for Advancement and Support of Edn., 1988.

SWIRE, EDITH WYPLER, music educator, musician, violist, violinist; b. Boston, Feb. 16, 1943; d. Alfred R. Wypler Jr. and Frances (Glenn) Emery Wypler; m. James Bennett Swire, June 11, 1965; 1 child, Elizabeth Swire Falker. BA, Wellesley (Mass.) Coll., 1965; MFA, Sarah Lawrence Coll., Bronxville, N.Y., 1983; postgrad., Coll. of New Rochelle, 1984-85; student prof. studies master prog. in health advocacy, Sarah Lawrence Coll. Tchr. instrumental music, viola, violin The Windsor Sch., Boston, 1965-66; tchr., dir. The Lenox Sch., N.Y.C., 1967-76; music curriculum devel. The Nightingale-Bamford Sch., N.Y.C., 1968-69; head of fine arts dept. The Lenox Sch., N.Y.C., 1976-78, head of instrumental music, 1978-80; founder, dir., tchr. of string sch. Serpentine String Sch., Larchmont, 1981—96. Mem. founding com. Inter Sch. Orch., N.Y.C., 1972, trustee, 1976—; panelist Nat. Assn. Ind. Sch. Conf., N.Y.C., 1977. Mem. music and worship com., Larchmont Ave. Ch., 1978-82, 88. Mem. Westchester Musicians Guild, N.Y. State Music Tchrs. Assn., Music Tchrs. Nat. Assn., Music Tchrs. Coun. Westchester (program com.), Violin Soc. Am., Wellesley in Westchester, Am. String Tchrs. Assn., The Viola Soc. of N.Y. Avocations: study of Alexander Technique, chamber music. Home and Office: 11 Serpentine Trail Larchmont NY 10538-2618

SWIRNOFF, LOIS, artist, color theorist; b. Bklyn., May 9, 1931; d. Harold and Fannie (Goldstein) Swirnoff; m. Richard Boyce (dec.); 1 child, Dr. Joshua Avram Boyce. Cert. of graduation, Cooper Union Art Sch., N.Y.C., 1951; BFA, Yale U., 1953, MFA summa cum laude, 1956. Instr. art Wellesley (Mass.) Coll., 1954-58; asst. prof. UCLA, 1965-68, vis. lectr., 1981-86, assoc. prof., 1986-90, prof. emerita, 1990—; lectr. Harvard U., Cambridge, Mass., 1968-75; assoc. prof., chmn. art dept. Skidmore Coll., Saratoga Springs, N.Y., 1977-81; guest artist Cooper Union Art Sch., 1990-91, adj. prof., 1991—; Feltman Chair The Cooper Union, N.Y., 2001—02. Author: Dimensional Color, 1989, 2d edit., 2003, Van Nostrand Reinhold, 1992, The Color of Cities, 2000; one-woman shows include Farnsworth Mus., 1958, Swetoff Gallery, Boston, 1962, Inst. Internat. Edn., N.Y.C., 1978—79, NAS, Washington, 1982—83, The Woman's Bldg., L.A., Bradford Coll. Laura Knott Gallery, 1988, Wellesley Coll., Gallery BAI, N.Y.C., 1996, N.Y. Sch. of Interior Design, 2000—01, exhibited in group shows at City Art Mus., St. Louis, 1951, Bklyn. Mus., 1951, Munson-Williams Proctor Inst., Unica, N.Y., 1956, Swetzoff Gallery, 1963—65, Inst. Contemporary Art, Boston, 1961, LaJolla (Calif.) Mus., 1968, L.A. County Mus., 1968, Represented in permanent collections Addison Gallery Am. Art at Andover, Wellesley Coll., Mary I. Bunting Inst., Radcliffe Coll, UCLA, also pvt.collections. Recipient merit award Art Dirs. Club N.Y., 1979; Fulbright fellow, Florence, Italy, 1951-52, Yale-Norfolk summer fellow, 1953, fellow Mary I. Bunting Inst., Radcliffe Coll., 1961-63, Yaddo fellow, 1985-86; Mellon faculty grantee Skidmore Coll., 1981, grantee Graham Found., 1988, 98. Studio: 80 Monmouth St Brookline MA 02446-5607 E-mail: swirnoff@aol.com.

SWITZER, CAROLYN JOAN, artist, educator; b. Petoskey, Mich., Apr. 20, 1931; d. Eugene Constant and Burnis Hazel (Lower) S. Student, Wayne State U., 1954-55, St. John's Coll., Santa Fe, N.Mex., 1993; BA, Mich. State U., 1953, MA, 1964. Cert. tchr., Mich. Art tchr. Ferndale Bd. of Edn., 1953-56, Birmingham Bd. of Edn., Mich., 1956-96; pvt. tchr. drawing and painting. Exhbns. include state and local shows, galleries and pvt. collections. Cons. Girl Scouts U.S., Birmingham, Petoskey, Mich.; mem. Crooked Tree Arts Coun., Petoskey Recipient recognition award for svc. to community, Birmingham Edn. Assn. Coun., 1967, Outstanding Sr. Woman Lantern Night MSU, 1953. Mem. AAUW (scholar, Mich. State U., 1962), Nat. Art Edn. Assn., Mich. Art Edn. Assn., Mich. Edn. Assn., Detroit Inst. Art, Nat. Mus. for Women in Arts, Mich. Coun. for Arts, Art Study Club of Petoskey, Zonta Internat., Crooked Tree Arts Ctr. Petoskey. Avocations: music/singing, reading, exercise class, walking, photography. Home: 805 Lindell Ave Petoskey MI 49770-3159

SWITZER, JO YOUNG, academic administrator, dean; b. Huntington, Ind., Mar. 4, 1948; d. John Frederick and Miriam Lucile (Kindy) Young; children: Sarah Kate Keller, John Christian Keller. BA, Manchester Coll., 1969; MA, U. Kans., 1977, PhD, 1980; postdoctoral, Ind. U., 1983, Harvard U., 1995. English tchr., Dearborn Heights, Mich., 1969-70, Fenton High Sch., Bensenville, Ill., 1970-73; asst. instr. U. Kans., Lawrence, 1977-79; asst. prof. Ind. U.-Purdue, Ft. Wayne, Ind., 1979-82; assoc. prof. Manchester Coll., North Manchester, Ind., 1982-87, Ind. U.-Purdue, Ft. Wayne, Ind., 1987-93; v.p., dean for acad. affairs and prof. comm. studies Manchester Coll., 1993—. Recipient E. C. Buehler award U. Kans., 1978; grantee NEH, 1983. Mem. Central States Comm. Assn. (Outstanding Young Educator award 1982), Coun. of Ind. Colls., Am. Coun. on Edn., Am. Assn. Colls. and Univs. Home: 3069 E 1200 N Roanoke IN 46783 Office: Manchester Coll Office Acad Affairs 604 E College Ave North Manchester IN 46962-1276 Fax: 260-982-5042. E-mail: jyswitzer@manchester.edu.

SWITZER, PAUL, statistics educator; b. St. Boniface, Man., Can., Mar. 4, 1939; BA with honors, U. Man., 1961; AM, Harvard U., 1963, PhD, 1965. Mem. faculty Stanford (Calif.) U., 1965—, now prof. stats. and earth scis., chmn. dept. stats., 1979-82. Fellow Internat. Statis. Inst., Am. Statis. Assn. (editor jour. 1986-88), Inst. Math. Stats. (editor jour. 1995-97).

SWITZER, ROBERT LEE, biochemistry educator; b. Clinton, Iowa, Aug. 26, 1940; s. Stephen and Elva Delila (Allison) S.; m. Bonnie George, June 13, 1965; children: Brian, Stephanie. BS, U. Ill., 1961; PhD, U. Calif., Berkeley, 1966. Research fellow Lab. Biochemistry, Nat. Heart Inst., Bethesda, Md., 1966-68; asst. prof. biochemistry U. Ill., Urbana, 1968—73, assoc. prof., 1973—78, prof. biochemistry and basic med. scis., 1978—2002, prof. emeritus, 2002—, dept. head, 1988—93. Mem. biochemistry study sect. NIH, 1985-89, chmn., 1987-89; guest prof. U. Copenhagen, 1995; mem. microbial physiology and genetics study sect., NIH, 1998-2000. Author: (with Liam F. Garrity) Experimental Biochemistry, 3rd rev. edit., 1999; mem. bd. editors Jour. Bacteriology, 1977-82, 1985—2002, Archives Biochemistry and Biophysics, 1977-98, Jour. Biol. Chemistry, 1980-85; contbr. articles to profl. jours. NSF predoctoral fellow, 1961-66; NIH postdoctoral fellow, 1966-68; Guggenheim fellow, 1975 Mem. Am. Soc. for Biochemistry and Molecular Biology, Am. Soc. Microbiology, Am. Chem. Soc., AAAS, Sigma Xi. Home: 404 W Michigan Ave Urbana IL 61801-4948 Office: U Ill Dept Biochemistry 600 S Mathews Ave Urbana IL 61801-3602

SWYGERT, HAYWOOD PATRICK, university president, law educator; b. Phila., Mar. 17, 1943; s. LeRoy and Gustina (Rogers) Huzzy; m. Sonja Branson, Aug. 22, 1969; children: Haywood Patrick, Michael Branson. AB in History, Howard U., 1965, JD cum laude, 1968. Bar: D.C. 1968, Pa. 1970, N.Y. 1970. Law clk. to chief judge U.S. Ct. Appeals (3d cir.), Phila., 1968—69; assoc. Debevoise, Plimpton, Lyons & Gates, N.Y.C., 1969—70; adminstrv. asst. to Congressman Charles B. Rangel NY, 1971—72; spl. asst. dist. atty., 1973; from asst. prof. to prof. law Temple U., 1972—90, v.p. adminstrn., 1982—88, exec. v.p., 1988—90; pres. SUNY, Albany, 1990—95, Howard U., Washington, 1995—. Bd. dirs. United Tech. Corp., Hartford Fin. Svcs. Group. Gov.'s rep. Southeastern Pa. Transp. Authority, 1987—90; bd. trustees Inst. Pub. Adminstrn., 1992—99; exec. com. Pub. Law Ctr., Phila., 1980—88; bd. dirs. NY State Coun. on Humanities, 1991—95; chmn. ednl. structure, policies and practices NY State Spl. Commn., 1993—95; co-chmn. joint task force grad. edn. Nat. Assn. State Univs. and Land Grant Colls./Am. Assn. State Coll. and Univs., 1993—95; Bd. dirs. New Community Devel. Corp., HUD, 1980—82; bd. dirs. Nat. Pub. Radio, 1995—96. Mem.: ABA, Victory Funds (trustee 1994—2002), Middle States Assn. Colls. and Schs. (commn. on higher edn. 1992—95). Home: 3119 Arizona Ave NW Washington DC 20016-3420 Office: Howard U Office of Pres 2400 6th St NW Ste 402 Washington DC 20059-0002

SYCHTERZ, TERESA A. education educator; b. Reading, Pa., May 26, 1952; d. Chester F. and Dorothy (Andrejansky) S. BS in Elem. Edn., Kutztown (Pa.) U., 1974; cert. pastoral ministry, Allentown Coll. St. Francis, 1981; MS in Elem. Adminstrn., U. Scranton, 1991; PhD in Curriculum and Instrn., Pa. State U., 1999. Tchr. St. Catharine of Siena Sch., Reading, 1974—98; prof. Kutztown (Pa.) U., 1998—. Facilitator Fatima Renewal Ctr., Dalton, Pa., 1980-91; presenter in field; cons. Glenside Elem. Sch., Reading, 2003—. Author: The Bible and Me, 1986; contbr. articles to profl. jours. Spkr. at ch. groups, colls., schs., various cities in Pa., 1980-90; mem. adv. bd. Student Best program of Learning Mag.; mem. profl. devel. com. Diocese of Allentown; mem. edn. com. Reading Mus., 2001—; mem. strategic plan com., Act 48 com. Brandywine Heights Sch. Dist.. Named vol. of the yr. Our Lady of Fatima Ctr., Scranton, 1984. Mem. Nat. Coun. Tchrs. English, Internat. Reading Assn., Children's Lit. Assn., Sacred Dance Guild (pres. Ea. chpt. 1986-88), Phi Delta Kappa. Roman Catholic. Avocations: skiing, singing. Office: Kutztown U 201 Beekey Kutztown PA 19530

SYED, IBRAHIM BIJLI, medical educator and physicist, author, philosopher, theologist, public speaker, writer; b. Bellary, India, Mar. 16, 1939; came to U.S., 1969, naturalized, 1975; s. Ahmed Bijli and Mumtaz Begum (Maniyar) S.; m. Sajida Shariff, Nov. 29, 1964; children: Mubin, Zafrin. BS with honors, Veerasaiva Coll., Bellary U., Mysore, 1960; MS with honors and distinction, Bangalore U., Mysore, 1962; diploma, U. Bombay, 1964; DSc, Johns Hopkins U., 1972; PhD (hon.), Malta, 1985. Cert. hazard control officer, 1980, internat. health care safety profl., 1980; diplomate Am. Bd. Radiology, Am. Bd. Health Physics. Lectr. physics Veerasaiva Coll., Bellary U., Mysore, 1962-63; med. physicist, radiation safety officer Victoria Hosp., India, 1964-67, Bowring and Lady Curz on Hosp. & Postgrad. Med. Rsch. Inst., Bangalore, India, 1964-67; cons. med. physicist, radiation safety officer Ministry of Health, Govt. of Karnataka, India, 1964-67, Bangalore Nursing Home, India, 1964-67; med. physicist, radiation safety officer Baystate Med. Ctr., Springfield, Mass., 1973-79; assoc. prof. Springfield Tech. C.C.; also adj. prof. radiology Holyoke (Mass.) C.C., 1973-79; asst. clin. prof. nuclear medicine U. Conn. Sch. Medicine, Farmington, 1975-79; cons. med. physicist Mercy Hosp., Springfield, 1973-79, Wing Meml. Hosp., Palmer, Mass., 1973-79; med. physicist, radiation safety officer VAMC, Louisville, 1979—, exec. officer radiation safety com., 1979—; prof. medicine U. Louisville Sch. Medicine, 1979—, dir. nuclear med. scis., 1980—; mem. Instl. Review Bd. Veterans Admin. Medical Ctr., Louisville, 2000—. Guest lectr. religious studies program U. Louisville, 1979—; vis. prof. Bangalore U., 1987—88, Gulbarga U., India, 1987—88; vis. scientist Bhabha Atomic Rsch. Ctr., Bombay; invited spkr. Veerasaiva Coll., Bellary, India, 1996, Vijayanagar Coll., Hospet, 1996, Vajayanagar Inst. Med. Scis., Bellary, 1996, Deccan Coll. Med. Scis., Hyderabad, India, Bhabha Atomic Rsch. Ctr., Bombay, 1997, 15th Ann. Islamic Conf. New Eng., Islamic Coun. New Eng., 1999, Coun. for a Parliament of the World's Religions, Cape Town, South Africa, 1999, Garden City Coll. Bangalore, 2000, Veerasaiva Coll., Bellary, 2000, Islamic Rsch. Found., Mumbai, India, 2001, Islamic Assn. of Essex, England, 2001, Assn. Muslim Social Scientists, Detroit, 2001, Islamic Orgn. Med. Scis., Cairo, 2002; PhD thesis examiner Allahabad U., 1996—; course dir. licensing for nuclear cardiologists U. Louisville, 1980—, mem. admissions com. nuclear medicine program, 1980—; guest relief examiner Am. Bd. Radiology, 1991; examiner in radiol physics, 95, 97, 98, 2000; examiner in radiol. physics, 03; mem. panel of examiners Am. Bd. Health Physics; PhD thesis examiner U. Delhi, Internat. Inst. for Advanced Study, Clayton, Mo., 1985—, Allahabad (India) U., 1996—; faculty mem. Med. Physicists of India Ann. Meeting, 1987; IAEA tchr. expert in nuclear medicine on mission to People's Republic of Bangladesh, 86; to Guatemala, 94; founder, pres. Islamic Rsch. Found. Internat., Louisville, 1988—; convener Internat. Conf. on Islamic Renaissance: Action Plan for the 21st Century, Chgo., 1995; cons. Coun. Sci. and Indsl. Rsch., Govt. India, 0809—, Am. Coun. Sci. and Health, 1980—; cons. gastroenterology and urology divsn. FDA, HHS, 1988—, cons. radiopharm. divsn., 1989—; cons. Govt. India in nuclear medicine, diagnostic radiol. physics, therapeutic radiol. physics and radiation safety, 1992; cons. radiol. and med. nuc. physics Govt. India, Un Devel. Program, 1992; convenor Internat. Conf. on Islamic Renaissance, Chgo., 1995; guest spkr. Muslim Cmty. Ctr., Chgo., 1988; invited spkr. objective studies and Islamic voice, Bangalore, 96, Parliament of World Religions, Chgo., 1993, Cape Town, South Africa, 99, Cooper Mosque, Mississauga, Ont., Canada, 2002. Author: Radiation Safety for Allied Health Professionals, Radiation Safety Manual, 1979, Intellectual Achievements of Muslims, 2002; contbg. editor Jour. of Islamic Food and Nutrition Coun. of Am., 1986—, health and sci. column Muslim Jour., 1989—; freelance writer Minaret Biweekly, N.Y.C., 1975—, Islamic Voice, India, 1988—, Al-Balaagh, Lenasia, South Africa, 1989—, AL'FURQAN Internat., Norcross, Ga., 1990, Message Internat., Jamaica, N.Y., 1990, Minaret Monthly Mag., L.A., 1995—, The Message, London, 1998—, The Minaret, Botswana, 1998—; editor: Science and Technology for the Developing World, 1988; mem. editl. bd. Jour. Islamic Med. Assn., 1981—; regular contbr. Pres.'s Page; manuscript reviewer for sci. and med. jours., 1973; assoc. editor AAlim, 1998—; contbr. more than 100 articles to sci. jours.; pub. internat. more than 110 articles on various topics of Islam in jours. and mags. Moderator fgn. policy workshop U.S. Dept. State, Louisville, 2000; spkr. Dayton (Ohio) Islamic Ctr., 2000, Muslim Student Assn. U. Cin., 2000; spkr.. Muslim Cmty. Ctr., Chgo., 2001; invited spkr. Muslim Assn. of Cleveland East, Cleve., 2002. Recipient Disting. Cmty. Svc. award India Cmty. Found., 1982, Hind Rattan Jewel of India Title award Govt. India, 1994; WHO fellow, Govt. India scholar Bhabha Atomic Rsch. Ctr., Bombay, 1963-64; USPHS fellow Johns Hopkins U., 1969-72. Fellow Inst. Physics (U.K.), Am. Inst. Chemists, Royal Soc. Health, Am. Coll. Radiology, Internat. Acad. Med. Physics; mem. Am. Assn. Physicists in Medicine, Am. Coll. Nuclear Medicine, Health Physics Soc., Am. Acad. Health Physics, Soc. Nuclear Medicine (faculty mem. ann. meeting 1987, convenor internat. conf. 1995), Nat. Assn. Ams. of Asian Indian Descent (chmn. state pub. rels. com. 1982—), Islamic Med. Assn. N.Am. (life, faculty 1994, 96, 98), Internat. Inst. Islamic Medicine (faculty Orlando, Fla. 1996, 97, Birmingham, U.K. 1998), Islamic Soc. N.Am. (faculty Chgo. 1998), Islamic Soc. Balt. (founding mem.), Islamic Cultural Ctr., Louisville, Islamic Assn. Maritime Provinces Can., Halifax, N.S. (asst. sec. 1967-69), Health Physics Soc. (chmn. med. health physics com. 1989—, affirmative action com. 1984—), Am. Assn. Physicists in Medicine (biol. effects com.), Assn. Muslim Scientists and Engrs. N.Am. (program chmn. ann. conf. 1987, treas. 1987-88, sec. 1988—), AAUP, Soc. Nuclear Medicine India (life, faculty mem. ann. meeting 1987, invited spkr. and faculty ann. meeting 1996), Assn. Med. Physicists India (life, invited spkr. and faculty ann. meeting Madras 1996), Med. and Biol. Physics (divsn. Can.) Assn. Physicists, Hosp. Physicists Assn., N.Y. Acad. Scis., Islamic Assn. Maritime Provinces of Can., Ky. Med. Assn., Jefferson County Med. Soc. (assoc.), Sigma Xi. Islamic. Home: 7102 W Shefford Ln Louisville KY 40242-6462 Office: 800 Zorn Ave Louisville KY 40206-1433 E-mail: irfi@iname.com.

SYKES, BRIAN DOUGLAS, biochemistry educator, researcher; b. Montreal, Que., Aug. 30, 1943; s. Douglas Lehman and Mary (Anber) S.; m. Nancy Lynne Sengelaub, May 25, 1968; children: David, Michael. B.Sc., U. Alta., 1965; PhD, Stanford U., 1969. Asst. prof. chemistry Harvard U., Cambridge, Mass., 1969-74, assoc. prof., 1974-75; assoc. prof. biochemistry U. Alta. (Can.), Edmonton, 1975-80, prof., 1980—, McCalla rsch. prof., 1994-95, prof., 1997—, now univ. prof. Assoc. editor Jour. Biomolecular NMR, 1991—. Recipient Steacie prize Nat. Sci. Engring. Rsch. Coun., 1982, Kaplan Rsch. award, 1992, Herzberg award 1998; Woodrow Wilson fellow, 1965, Alfred P. Sloan fellow, 1971. Fellow Royal Soc. of Can., Royal Soc. Can.; mem. Can. Biochem. Soc. (pres., Ayerst award 1982), Biophys. Soc. (councillor 1989-92), Am. Chem. Soc., Protein Soc. Home: 11312 37th Ave Edmonton AB Canada T6J 0H5

SYKES, LYNN RAY, geologist, educator; b. Pitts., Apr. 16, 1937; s. Lloyd Ascutney and Margaret (Woodburn) S.; m. Kathleen Mahoney, April 19, 1998. BS, MS, MIT, 1960; PhD in Geology, Columbia U., 1964. Phys. sci. aide geophys. lab. U.S. Geol. Survey, Silver Spring, Md., summer 1956; participant summer coop. program Geophys. Svc. Inc., Dallas, 1958; Summer Rsch. fellow Woods Hole (Mass.) Oceanographic Inst., 1959; rsch. asst. Lamont-Doherty Earth Obs.-Columbia U., 1961-64, rsch. assoc. in seismology, 1964-66, adj. asst. prof. geology, 1966-68, asst. prof., 1968-69, assoc. prof., 1969-73, prof., 1973-78, Higgins prof. earth and environ. scis., 1978—, mem. univ. com. on acad. priorities, 1977-79. Research geophysicist earth scis. labs. U.S. Dept. Commerce, 1966-68; Mem. panel polar geophysics Nat. Acad. Scis., 1968; adv. com. to ESSA Rsch. Labs., 1968-69; mem. subcom. geodesy and cartography applications steering com. NASA, 1968-70; mem. com. on world-wide standardized network Nat. Acad. Scis./NRC, 1969, com. seismology, 1972-73, panel earthquake prediction, 1973-75; organizing sec. Internat. Symposium Mech. Properties and Processes of Mantle of Internat. Upper Mantle Com., 1970; mem. panel on deep crustal drilling in marine areas JOIDES, 1970-71; advisor N.Y. State Geol. Survey and N.Y. State Environ. Protection Agy., 1970-80; mem. U.S. Geodynamics Panel on Mid-Atlantic Ridge, 1971-72; mem. working group U.S./USSR Joint Program for Earthquake Prediction, 1973-77; mem. U.S. Del. on Earthquake Prediction to USSR, fall, 1973; mem. adv. com. on proposals for earthquake prediction U.S. Geol. Survey, 1974, adv. panel earthquake hazards program, 1977-82; mem. U.S. Tech. Del. for talks on treaty on Threshold Limitations Underground Nuclear Explosions, Moscow, USSR, summer, 1974; mem. rev. panel earth scis. NSF, 1974-77; mem. study groups on plate interiors and Cocos and Caribbean plates U.S. Geodynamics Com.; mem. U.S. Seismology Group to People's Republic of China, fall, 1974; vis. prof. Earthquake Rsch. Inst. of Tokyo (Japan) U., fall 1974; Fairchild vis. scholar Calif. Inst. Tech., 1981; vis. fellow Clare Hall, Cambridge U., 1982; chmn. nat. earthquake prediction evaluation coun., U.S. Geol. Survey, 1984-88; mem. com. acad. priorities Columbia U., 1977-78, Columbia U. Arms Control Seminar, 1984-93, mem. external rev. com. Nat. Earthquake Hazards Reduction Program, 1987-88; mem. com. on verification of nuclear testing, treaties, Office Tech. Assessment, U.S. Congress, 1986-87; participant Belmont (Md.) Conf. on Nuclear Test Ban Policy, 1988; U.S. com. for decade of natural hazards reduction NRC, 1989-90; participant on TV show NOVA. Contbg. author: History of the Earth's Crust, 1968, Geodynamics of Iceland and the North Atlantic Area, 1974, Encounter with the Earth, 1975; Assoc. editor: Jour. Geophys. Research, 1968-70; Contbr. numerous articles to profl. jours. Pres. Far West 77th St. Block Assn., N.Y.C., 1973-74. Recipient H. O. Wood award in seismology Carnegie Instn. of Washington, 1967-70, Edward John Noble Leadership award during first three years grad. study, Pub. Service award Fedn. Am. Scientists, 1986, John Wesley Powell award U.S. Geol. Survey, 1991, G. Unger Vetlesen prize, Columbia U., 2000; Sloan fellow, 1969-71; grantee NSF, AEC, Air Force Office Sci. Rsch., NASA, N.Y. State Sci. and Tech. Found., N.Y. State Atomic and Space Devel. Authority, U.S. Geol. Survey, Sloan Found., John D. and Catherine T. MacArthur Found., Carnegie Corp., 1988-89; Guggenheim fellow, 1988-89; Proctor & Gamble scholar. Fellow Am. Geophys. Union (Macelwave award to Outstanding Young Geophysicist for 1970, Walter H. Bucher medal for original contbns. to basic knowledge of Earth's crust 1975, pres. sect. tectonophysics 1972-74, pres. sect. on seismology 1982-84), Seismol. Soc. Am. (Medal 1998), Geol. Soc. Am., Geol. Soc. London; mem. Nat. Acad. Scis., Am. Acad. Arts. and Scis., Royal Astron. Soc., N.Y. Acad. Scis. (pres. geol. sect. 1970-71) Achievements include research includes maj. contbns. on plate tectonics, earthquake prediction and discrimination of underground nuclear explosions from earthquakes, arms control. Office: Columbia U PO Box 1000 Lamont-Doherty Earth Obs Rm 230C Palisades NY 10964-1000

SYKES, MARY LOU STRAIN, retired reading educator; b. Lancaster, Tex., Jan. 28, 1941; d. Ellis White and Ruth Clark Strain; m. Donald Ray Sykes, Nov. 25, 1965; children: Donna Ruth, Debra Renee. AA, Tyler Jr. Coll., 1961; B of Music Edn., U. North Tex., 1963, MusM, 1969; EdD, Tex. Woman's U., 1990. Cert. reading, mid-mgmt., supervision, elem., lang. disabled and music. Music tchr. grades 3-7 Dallas Ind. Sch. Dist., 1963-72; tchr. pvt. piano lessons Lancaster, 1972-75; tchr. reading and music Dean Learning Ctr., Dallas, 1975-76, Shelton Sch., Dallas, 1976-79; tchr. reading and 1st grade Lancaster Ind. Sch. Dist., 1979-85; tchr. reading Waxahachie (Tex.) H.S., 1985-92, Tex. Woman's U., Denton, 1985-92, Garland (Tex.) Ind. Sch. Dist., 1992—; tchr. reading and elem. edn. East Tex. State U., Commerce, 1993—2002, ret., 2002. Pres. Friends of the Libr., Lancaster, 1991-92; mem. Lancaster Tomorrow, 1991-92, 96—. Mem. Internat. Reading Assn., Tex. Reading Assn. (treas. 1985, Literacy award 1996), Tex. Secondary Reading Coun. (treas. 1987-91, pres. 1991-93), Tex. Joint Coun. Edn., South Dallas/Ellis Reading Coun. (pres. 1983-85, 91-92), Phi Delta Kappa. Home: Box 616 525 E Belt Line Rd Lancaster TX 75146-3625

SYKES, RUTH L. special education educator; b. Fairfield, Tex., Dec. 19, 1941; d. F. W. and LaKatie (Jordan) McIlveen; m. Alexander Sykes, Sept. 15, 1963; children: Lajourka, Jennifer, Dorothy, Reneé. Student, Prairie View, 1960-62; BS, Bishop Coll., 1965; postgrad., Tex. State U., 1980. Cert. elem., special edn., Tex. Tchr. reading Fairfield (Tex.) Ind. Sch. Dist., 1965-66, parochial schs., Houston, 1968-70; substitute tchr. Houston Ind. Sch. Dist., 1972-75, tchr. special edn., 1975-87, tchr. 3d grade, 1987-88, tchr. 5th grade, 1988-89, coord., 1989-90, tchr. functional special edn., 1990-91, tchr. special edn. resource, 1991—. Tchr. Career Ladder, Houston, 1987—; chair promotion/retention referral com., Highland Hgts. Sch., 1975-82, 89-90. Troop 336 leader Boy Scouts Am., Houston, 1975-80. Mem. Houston Tchrs. Assn., Charity Ch. (souvenir book 1992). Democrat. Baptist. Avocations: reading, travel, sports, church. Home: 6635 Brownie Campbell St Houston TX 77086-1904

SYLLA, RICHARD EUGENE, economics educator; b. Harvey, Ill., Jan. 16, 1940; s. Benedict Andrew and Mary Gladys (Curran) S.; m. Edith Anne Dudley, June 22, 1963; children: Anne Curran, Margaret Dudley. BA, Harvard U., 1962, MA, 1965, PhD, 1969. Prof. econs. and bus. N.C. State U., Raleigh, 1968-90; Henry Kaufman prof. history fin. insts. and markets NYU, N.Y.C., 1990—, prof. econs., 1990—, acting chmn. dept. econs., 2002—03. Cons. Citibank NA, N.Y.C., 1979-82, Chase Manhattan Bank, N.Y.C., 1983-85; vis. prof. U. Pa., Phila., 1983, U. N.C., Chapel Hill, 1988; rsch. assoc. Nat. Bur. of Econ. Rsch., 1983—; trustee Mus. Am. Fin. History, 2002-. Author: The American Capital Market, 1975; co-author: Evolution of the American Economy, 1980, 2d edit., 1993, A History of Interest Rates, 1991, rev. edit., 1996; co-editor: Patterns of European Industrialization, 1991, Anglo-American Financial Systems, 1995, The State, The Financial System, and Economic Modernization, 1999; editor Jour. Econ. History, 1978-84. Trustee Mus. Am. Fin. History, 2002—. Study fellow NEH, 1975-76; Rsch. grantee NSF, 1985-94, 98-02, Sloan Found., 1995-97. Mem. Am. Econs. Assn., Econ. History Assn. (v.p. 1987-88, trustee 1977-88, Arthur H. Cole prize 1970, pres. 2000-2001), Bus. History Conf. (trustee 1991-94, 2002—), So. Econ. Assn. (v.p. 1981-82), Cliometrics Soc. (trustee 1997-2000, trustee chair 1998-2000). Avocations: golf, hiking, stamp collecting, arts. Home: 110 Bleecker St Apt 23D New York NY 10012-2106 Office: NYU 44 W 4th St New York NY 10012-1106 E-mail: rsylla@stern.nyu.edu.

SYLVERS, ARLENE MARDER, clinical psychologist; b. Bklyn., June 2, 1938; d. Harry Isadore and Helen (Yurkowitz) Marder; m. Schuyler Sylvers, June 2, 1957 (div. 1970); children: Steven Eric, Lee Alan. BA in Psychology, Calif. State U., Northridge, 1972, MA in Psychology, 1974; PhD in Clin. Psychology, Internat. Coll., 1984. Lic. marriage, family and child counselor, Calif.; cert. adminstrv. svc. credential, std. designated svc. credential, pupil pers. svcs., sch. psychology, psych. ccmty. coll. tchg., Calif.; lic. psychologist, Calif. Tchr. spl. edn. Eleby Hall, 1972; dist. psychologist Newhall (Calif.) Sch. Dist., 1974-81, coord. spl. svcs., 1978-81, dir. spl. svcs. dept., 1981-98; pvt. practice marriage, family and child therapy, 1980—. Chmn. dirs. coun. Spl. Edn. Local Plan Area, Santa Clarita, Calif., 1976—; instr. dept. edn. Calif. Luth. Coll., part-time 1976-80; presenter in field to cmty. adv. couns. and univs. Pub. spkr. for various parent and cmty. groups. Mem. Am. Assn. Marriage and Family Therapists, Assn. Calif. Sch. Adminstrs., Calif. Assn. Marriage and Family Therapists, Alpha Gamma Sigma, Sigma Tau Simga, Psi Chi, Phi Delta Kappa. Avocations: writing poetry, travel, yoga, theater, opera. Office: 23550 Lyons Ave Ste 207 Newhall CA 91321-5756

SYLVESTER, NANCY KATHERINE, management consultant; b. Evansville, Ind., July 17, 1947; d. Leonard Nicholas and Marjorie (Moore) Jochim; m. James Andrew Sylvester, Aug 21, 1971; children: Marcy Dee, Holly Nicole. BS, Ind. State U., 1969; MA, U. Mich., 1970. Registered profl. parliamentarian; cert. prof. parliamentarian; leadership/team/meeting mgmt. specialist; cert. tchr. of parliamentary procedure. Prof. speech Rock Valley Coll., Rockford, Ill., 1970-2001, prof. emeritus speech, 2001—. Chmn. bd. First Fed. Savs. Bank, Belvidere, Ill., 1996-98. Author: Handbook for Effective Meetings, 1993, Basics of Parliamentary Procedure, 1997, Complete Idiots Guide to Parliamentary Procedure, 2004; contbr. articles to profl. jours. Bd. dirs. Jr. League Rockford, 1974-78, Rock River Homeowners Assn., 1990-91; pres. Children's Devel. Ctr. Aux. Bd., Rockford, 1984-85; parliamentarian Winnebago County Dem. Caucus, 1991; vice-chmn. Commn. on Am. Parliamentary Practice, 1989-90, chmn., 1990-91; nat. parliamentarian Girl Scouts U.S., 1996-97, bd. dirs. Rock River coun., 1979-81. Recipient Jardene medal Ind. State U., 1969, RVC Faculty of Yr. award, 1994, Athena award Rockford Area C. of C., 1999, Alta Hulett award for the professions YWCA, 2001; Rockham scholar U. Mich., 1969-70. Mem.: Royal Neighbors of Am. (parliamentarian 2001—), Am. Speech-Lang.-Hearing Assn. (parliamentarian 1994—), Info. Sys. Audit and Control Assn. (parliamentarian 1994—98), Ind. Accts. Assn. Ill. (parliamentarian 1990—2000), Am. Soc. Pain Mgmt. Nurses (nat. parliamentarian 1994—97), Phi Rho Pi (region 4 v.p. 1972—73, nat. v.p. 1973—74), Rockford C. of C. (ex-officer bd. dirs., Athena award 1999), Nat. League Nursing (parliamentarian 1995), Coun. Better Bus. Burs. (parliamentarian 1993), Speech Commn. Assn., Nat. Assn. Parliamentarians (chmn. nat. nominating com. 1997—99, bd. dirs. 1997—, chmn. bylaws com. 1999—2001, nat. parliamentarian 2001—03), Nat. Assn. Ins. Women (parliamentarian 1983—91), Am. Assn. Nurse Anesthetists (parliamentarian 2000—), Ill. Assn. Parliamentarians, Am. Vet. Med. Assn. (parliamentarian 1998—), Nat. Coun. State Bds. Nursing (parliamentarian 1992—99), Am. Women Soc. CPAs (parliamentarian 1991—96), Am. Soc. Women Accts. (parliamentarian 1980—), Am. Inst. Parliamentarians, Am. Bowling Congress (parliamentarian 2003—), Women's Internat. Bowling Congress (parliamentarian 2003—). Home and Office: 4826 River Bluff Ct Loves Park IL 61111-5836 Fax: 815-877-5290. E-mail: nancy@nancysylvester.com.

SYMANK, OLETA MARLENE, elementary school educator; b. Elkins, W.Va., Aug. 24, 1957; d. Odis Milton and Oleta Frances (Owen) McNeill; m. Clarence Theodore Symank, May 3, 1986. BS in Edn., Baylor U., 1980. Cert. tchr., Tex. Tchr. kindergarten St. Mary's Cath. Sch., Waco, Tex., 1980-85; tchr. H.O. Whitehurst Elem. Sch., Groesbeck, Tex., 1985-92, Provident Heights Elem., Waco, Tex., 1992—99, Meadowbrook Elem. Sch., Waco, Tex., 1999—. Mem. Assn. Tex. Profl. Tchr., Assn. Tex. Profl. Educators. Republican. Presbyterian. Avocations: sewing, reading. Home: 176 Hazelwood Dr Waco TX 76712-2717

SYMONDS, PAUL SOUTHWORTH, mechanical engineering educator, researcher; b. Manila, Aug. 20, 1916; came to U.S., 1917; s. George R.B. and Claire Louise (Southworth) S.; m. Ilese Powell, Jan. 23, 1943; children: Alan Powell, Robin Peter. BS, Rensselaer Poly. Inst., 1938; MS, Cornell U., 1941, PhD, 1943; Docteur en Sciences Appliquées (hon.), Faculté Polytechnique de Mons, Belgium, 1988. Instr. mechanics Cornell U., Ithaca, N.Y., 1941-43; physicist Naval Research Lab., Washington, 1943-47; asst. prof. engring. Brown U., Providence, 1947-51, assoc. prof., 1951-54, prof., 1954-83, prof. engring. rsch. emeritus, 1983—, chmn. div. engring., 1959-62. Mem. editl. bd. Quar. Applied Math., 1965—; mem. editl. adv. bd. Internat. Jour. Impact Engring., 1983—; also numerous papers in tech. jours. Recipient Fulbright award 1949-50, 57-58; fellow Imperial Chem. Industries, Cambridge, U.K., 1950-51; Guggenheim fellow Swansea, Wales, 1957-58; NSF sr. postdoctoral fellow Oxford, Eng., 1964-65. Fellow ASME, ASCE, Am. Acad. Mechanics; mem. Internat. Assn. Bridge and Structural Engring. Home: 229 Medway St Apt 110 Providence RI 02906-5300 Office: Brown U Divsn Enging Providence RI 02912-0001 E-mail: paul_symonds@brown.edu.

SYMS, HELEN MAKSYM, educational administrator; b. Wilkes Barre, Pa., Nov. 12, 1918; d. Walter and Anna (Kowalewski) Maksym; m. Louis Harold Syms, Aug. 16, 1947; children: Harold Edward, Robert Louis. BA, Hunter Coll., 1941; MS, Columbia U., 1947; teaching credentials, Calif. State U., Northridge, 1964. Statis. clk. McGraw Hill Pub. Co., N.Y.C., 1941-42; acct. Flexpansion Corp., N.Y.C., 1943-47, Oliver Wellington & Co., N.Y.C., 1947-48, Broadcast Measurement Bur., N.Y.C., 1948-51; tchr. Calif. State U., Northridge, 1964, Burbank (Calif.) Unified Sch. Dist., 1964-79; chmn. bus. edn. dept. Burbank H.S., 1974-79; docent, acct. arts coun. Calif. State U., Northridge, 1979—; tchr. MEND-Meet Each Need with Dignity Learning Ctr., Pacoima, Calif., 1987-89; assoc. dir. M.E.N.D. (Meet Each Need with Dignity) Learning Ctr., Pacoima, Calif., 1989-96. Mem. Phi Beta Kappa, Delta Kappa Gamma (pres. 1972-74, treas. Xi chpt. 1982-90, 92-2002, treas. area IX 1975-78). Home: 9219 Whitaker Ave Northridge CA 91343-3538

SYNNOTT, MARCIA GRAHAM, history educator; b. Camden, N.J., July 4, 1939; d. Thomas Whitney and Beatrice Adelaide (Colby) S.; m. William Edwin Sharp, June 16, 1979; children: Willard William Sharp, Laurel Beth Sharp. AB, Radcliffe Coll., 1961; MA, Brown U., 1964; PhD, U. Mass., 1974. History tchr. MacDuffie Sch., Springfield, Mass., 1963-68; instr. U. S.C., Columbia, 1972-74, asst. prof., 1974-79, assoc. prof. history, 1979-97, dir. grad. studies history dept., 1990-92, prof. history, 1997—. Author: The Half-Opened Door, 1979; contbr. essays to books. Active university-wide cmty. svc. projects. Fulbright scholar, 1988; Am. Coun. Learned Socs. grantee, 1981. Mem. Am. Hist. Assn., So. Hist. Assn., Orgn. Am. Historians (membership com. 1990-93), S.C. Hist. Assn. (pres. 1994-95), History of Edn. Soc. (mem. editl. bd. 1996, 97, 98, bd. dirs. 2000-02). Avocations: historic sites and museums, snow skiing, walking. Office: U SC Dept History Columbia SC 29208-0001

SYPHERS, MARY FRANCES, music educator; b. Floresville, Tex., Sept. 26, 1912; d. Little Fleming and Lillian Frances (Herrington) Spruce; m. Ansel James Syphers, July 23, 1959 (dec. 1972). BA in English, U. Tex., 1938; MEd, So. Meth. U., Dallas, 1950; studied voice with Dr. Wilcox, studied composition with Roy Harris,, 1947, studied Music Edn. with Augustus Zansig. Cert. high sch. music tchr., cert. elem. tchr., Tex. Tchr. music Ehlers Country Sch., Poth, Tex., 1931-35, Poth Ind. Sch. Dist., 1936-40, Sinton (Tex.) Ind. Sch. Dist., 1941, Stephen J. Hay Sch., Dallas, 1942-50, Alamo Sch., Dallas, 1951—, Edwin J. Kiest Sch., Dallas, 1955—, Lakewood Elem., Dallas, 1976-81. Voice, drama tchr. Poth Ind. Sch. dist., 1936-40. Contbg. author: New England To Texas, 1986. Choir dir. 1st Meth. Ch., Sinton, Tex., 1941-42; soloist, jr. choir dir. Oaklawn Meth. Ch., Dallas, 1942-43; soloist 1st Presbyn. Ch., Dallas, 1943-46, Highland Park Presbyn. Ch., Dallas, 1946-47; symphony chorus Dallas Music Staff, 1944-60; mem. choir St. Michael and All Angels Episocpal Ch., Dallas, 1949-91; organizer jr. female vols. USO, Dallas, 1960-70, coordinator jr. female vols. anniversary celebration, Dallas, 1966; mem. publicity com. So. Meml. Assn., Dallas, 1981; life mem. PTA; mem. Shakespeare Study Club. Recipient Citation as member of concert choir Am. Culture and Lang. Ctr., Salzburg, Austria, 1987. Mem. New Eng. Women (pres. Tex. chpt. 1985-87), Dallas Coun. World Affairs, Dallas Inst. Humanities (sponser), Buckland Hist. Soc. (life), Nat. Soc. Colonial Dames (chmn. 1981-90), DAR (Jane Douglas chpt.), Standard Club Dallas (recreation sec. 1981-91), Delta Kappa Gamma (pres. Epsilon chpt. 1960-62). Democrat. Episcopalian. Avocations: genealogy, book binding, picture taking, reading, family history. Home: 2729 Laurel Oaks Dr Garland TX 75044-6939

SYROPOULOS, MIKE, retired school system director; b. Kato Hora, Navpactos, Greece, Jan. 18, 1934; came to U.S., 1951; s. Polykarpos Dimitri and Constantoula P. (Konstantinopoulos) S.; m. Sandra Francis Flick, Jan. 3, 1942; children: Pericles, Connie, Tina. BS, Wayne State U., 1960, MEd, 1965, EdD, 1971. Cert. secondary tchr., Mich. Tchr. Detroit Pub. Schs., 1960-66, dept. head, 1966-67, acting supr., 1967-69, rsch. asst., 1969-74, program assoc., 1976-97; asst. dir. Wayne (Mich.) County Intermediate Dist., 1974-76; pres. Rsch. & Evaluation Specialists Inc., Clinton Twp., Mich., 1997—. Pres. Rsch. & Evaluation Specialists Inc., Clinton Twp., Mich., 1997—. Contbr. articles to reports. V.p. St. John Greek Orthodox Ch., Sterling Heights, Mich., 1987, pres., 1988; bd. dirs. U. Mich. Modern Greek Studies, 2000—; external v.p. Hellenic Soc. Paedeia Mich., 2001—; chmn. AHEPA Edn. Found., 2002-2004; apptd. Hellenic Cultural Commn.; bd. visitors Liberal Arts Coll., Wayne State U., 2003—. With U.S. Army, 1956-58. Mem.: Nat. Edn. Found., Mich. Edn. Rsch. Assn., Mich. Assn. Supervision Curriculum (bd. dirs. 1994—), Am. Hellenic Edn. Progressive Assn. (athletic dir. 1992, treas. 1994, sec. 1995, lt. gov. 1996, gov. 1997, supreme gov. 1998—2000, bd. dirs. Nat. Edn. Found., chmn. Nat. Edn. Foun. 2003—), ASCD. Greek Orthodox. Avocation: golfing. Home: 46602 Red River Dr Macomb MI 48044-5442 Office: Rsch & Evaluation Specialists Inc PO Box 380102 Clinton Township MI 48038-0060 E-mail: msyropou@aol.com.

SYSTER, CHERYL LU, special education administrator; b. Des Moines, July 11, 1943; d. George Albert and Vernal Louise (Stutsman) Martin; m. Albert Roy Syster, June 26, 1965; children Christina Lynn, David Albert. BS in Elem. Edn., Ind. (Pa.) U., 1965, M in Elem. Edn., 1967; spl. edn. cert., Kent (Ohio) State U., 1980. Cert. prin., 1994. 3rd grade tchr. Hempfield (Pa.) Area Schs., 1965-68; substitute and homebound tchr. Derry (Pa.) Area Schs., 1968-77; learning disabilities tutor Mentor (Ohio) Schs., 1978-82, Newbury (Ohio) Schs., 1982-83; behavior handicap tchr. Painesville (Ohio) Sch., 1983-84; educable mental handicap tchr. Blairsville/Saltsburg Schs., 1985; resource rm. tchr. Ligonier (Pa.) Valley Schs., 1985-87; trainable mental handicap tchr. Wake County Schs., Raleigh, NC, 1987-91, dept. chair exceptional children, 1991—97, sr. adminstr. h.s. spl. edn., 1997—. Participant Christopher Columbus Consortium, Raleigh, 1990—. Vol. Life Experiences, Raleigh, 1988—, Assn. Retarded Citizens, Raleigh, 1988—. Grant U. Pa., 1986; named Tchr. of Yr. Assn. for Retarded Citizens, 1990. Mem. NEA, ASCD, Coun. for Exceptional Children (v.p., editor, program chair, Educator of Yr. 1997), Wake County Coun. for Exceptional Children (pres.), Ea. Star (chaplain 1975-77), N.C. Assn. Educators. Republican. Methodist. Avocations: boating, water skiing, swimming, reading, painting, tennis. Home: 1824 Lodestar Dr Raleigh NC 27615-2602 Office: Wake County Pub Sch Sys 4401 Atlantic Ave Raleigh NC 27604

SZABO, ALBERT, architect, educator; b. N.Y.C., Nov. 7, 1925; s. Benjamin and Jane (Margolies) S.; m. Brenda Dyer, Dec. 26, 1951; children: Ellen Bryna Szabo, Stephen, Rebecca Szabo Salvadori, Jeannette. Student, Bklyn. Coll., 1942-47, Inst. Design, Chgo., 1947-48; MArch, Harvard U., 1952. Apprentice Marcel Breuer Architect, 1947-48; instr. Inst. Design, Chgo., 1951-53; prof. architecture Grad. Sch. Design Harvard U., Cambridge, Mass., 1954-96; prof. emeritus, 1996—; chmn. dept. archtl. scis. Harvard U., Cambridge, Mass., 1964-68, assoc. chmn., head tutor dept. visual and environ. studies, 1968-70, prof. visual and environ. studies, chmn. dept. visual and environ. studies, 1970-72, sec. faculty design, 1964-74, prof. visual and environ. studies, 1970-91; archtl. design practice with Brenda Dyer Szabo, Chgo. and Cambridge, 1953—; ptnr. Soltan/Szabo Assocs., Inc., Cambridge, 1967-71. Vis. prof. Rensselaer Poly. Inst., 1967-68; Fulbright cons. to municipality of Tehran, Iran; Fulbright Hayes lectr. in architecture, Tehran, 1972, Kabul U. Afghanistan, 1974-76; cons. U.S. AID, Afghanistan, 1974-76, Govt. Afghanistan, 1974-76; acting curator Loeb Fellowship in Advanced Environ. Studies, 1974, cons. King Faisal U. Coll. Architecture and Planning, 1983; mem. edn. com. Boston Archtl. Ctr. Sch. Architecture, 1981-90; Osgood Hooker prof. visual art Faculty of Arts and Scis., 1991-96, prof. emeritus, 1996—. Author: (with others) The Shape of Our Cities, 1957; editor: (with others) Housing generated by User Needs, 1972, (with B.D. Szabo) Preliminary Notes on Indigenous Architecture of Afghanistan, 1978, (with T.J. Barfield) Afghanistan: An Atlas of Indigenous Domestic Architecture, 1991 (Outstanding Acad. Book award ALA 1992). Served with USAAF, 1944-45. Recipient Alpha Rho Chi medal Harvard U., 1952; Wheelwright travelling fellow Harvard U., 1963, Nat. Endowment for Arts fellow, 1980; Tozier Fund rsch. grantee Harvard U., 1963, Milton Fund rsch. grantee, 1966, 72, 77, 84, 87, Faculty rsch. grantee, 1978, The Aga Khan Program Islamic Architecture grantee, 1988, Faculty of Arts and Scis. Clark Fund Rsch. grantee, 1997; 1st One Man Show, Carpenter Center for the Visual Arts, 2001. Mem. Assn. Collegiate Schs. Architecture (N.E. regional dir. 1969-70). Office: Harvard U Carpenter Ctr 19 Prescott St Cambridge MA 02138-3902 E-mail: szabo@fas.harvard.edu.

SZABO, BARNA ALADAR, mechanical engineering educator, mining engineer; b. Martonvasar, Hungary, Sept. 21, 1935; came to U.S., 1967, naturalized, 1974; s. Jozsef and Gizella (Ivanyi) S.; m. Magdalin Gerstmayer, July 23, 1960; children: Mark, Nicholas. BASc., U. Toronto, Ont., Can., 1962; MS, SUNY, Buffalo, 1966, PhD, 1968; D. honoris causa, U. of Miskolc, Hungary, 1998. Registered profl. engr., Mo. Mining engr. Internat. Nickel Co. Can., 1960-62; engr. Acres Cons. Services Ltd., Niagara Falls, Can., 1962-66; instr. SUNY, Buffalo, 1966-68; mem. faculty Washington U., St. Louis, 1968—, prof. mech. engring., 1974—, Albert P. and Blanche Y. Greensfelder prof., 1975—, dir. Ctr. Computational Mechanics, 1977-92; chmn. engring. software Rsch. and Devel., Inc., St. Louis, 1989—. Author: (with Ivo Babuska) Finite Element Analysis, 1991; contbr. articles to profl. jours. Fellow U.S. Assn. Computational Mechanics (founding mem.); mem. ASME, Hungarian Acad. Sci., Soc. Engring. Sci. Home: 48 Crestwood Dr Clayton MO 63105-3033 Office: PO Box 1129 Saint Louis MO 63188-1129 E-mail: szabo@me.wustl.edu.

SZAREK, WALTER ANTHONY, chemist, educator; b. St. Catharines, Ont., Can., Apr. 19, 1938; s. Anthony and Sophia (Kania) S. BSc, McMaster U., 1960, MSc, 1962; PhD, Queen's U., 1964. Postdoctoral fellow in chemistry Ohio State U., Columbus, 1964-65; asst. prof. biochemistry Rutgers U., New Brunswick, N.J., 1965-67; asst. prof. chemistry Queen's U., Kingston, Ont., 1967-71, assoc. prof., 1971-76, prof., 1976—, dir. Carbohydrate Research Inst., 1976-85; founding mem., prin. investigator Neurochem, Inc., 1993—. Cons. to govt. and industry; mem. Premier's Coun. Tech. Fund. Mem. editl. adv. bd. Carbohydrate Rsch. jour., 1973-97, Jour. of Carbohydrate Chemistry, 1994-2001; contbr. articles to profl. jours. Recipient Tchg. Excellence award Queen's U. Arts and Sci. Undergrad. Soc., 1988-89, Tchg. Excellence in Chemistry award, 1993, 2000, 2002. Fellow Chem. Inst. Can.; mem. AAAS, Am. Chem. Soc. (chmn. divsn. carbohydrate chemistry 1982-83, councilor 2002—, Claude S. Hudson award in carbohydrate chemistry 1989, Melville L. Wolfrom award 1992), Inst. Theol. Encounter with Sci. and Tech. (Newman bd. dirs.), Royal Soc. Chemistry, N.Y. Acad. Scis., Soc. Glycobiology. Roman Catholic. Office: Dept Chemistry Queens Univ Kingston ON Canada K7L 3N6 Fax: 613-533-6532. E-mail: szarekw@chem.queensu.ca.

SZKODY, PAULA, astronomy educator, researcher; b. Detroit, July 17, 1948; d. Julian and Pauline (Wolski) S.; m. Donald E. Brownlee, Mar. 19, 1976; children: Allison, Carson. BS in Astrophysics, Mich. State U., 1970; MS in Astronomy, U. Wash., 1972, PhD in Astronomy, 1975. Rsch. asst. Observatoire de Geneve, 1969, Kitt Peak Nat. Obs., 1970; rsch., teaching asst. U. Wash., Seattle, 1970-75, rsch. assoc., lectr., 1975-82, sr. rsch. assoc., 1982-83, rsch. assoc. prof., 1983-91, rsch. prof., 1991-93, prof., 1993—. Part-time mem. faculty Seattle U., 1974-75, 82, Bellevue Coll., 1975-77; vis. scientist Kitt Peak Nat. Obs., 1976; vis. instr. UCLA, 1977, adj. asst. prof., 1980, 81; vis. asst. prof. U. Hawaii, 1978; vis. assoc. prof. Calif. Inst. Tech., 1978-79, 80, mem. XTE users com., 1996-99; mem. users com. Internat. Ultraviolet Explorer, 1983-85, 93-97; mem. A.J. Cannon adv. com. AAUW, 1986-91, chmn. 1988-90; mem. mgmt. ops. working group on Ultraviolet/Visual/Relativity, NASA, 1988-91. Contbr. numerous articles to profl. jours. Recipient Annie J. Cannon award, 1978. Fellow AAAS (mem. nominating com. 1990-93, chairperson 1993, mem.-at-large 1995-99); mem. Am. Assn. Variable Star Observers, Am. Astron. Soc. (councilor 1996-99), Internat. Astron. Union; mem. commn. 42 organizing com. 1991-97, v.p. 1997-00, pres. 2000—), Astron. Soc. Pacific (bd. dirs. 1988-92), Phi Beta Kappa. Office: U Wash Dept Astronomy PO Box 351580 Seattle WA 98195-1580 E-mail: szkody@astro.washington.edu.

SZOLNOKI, JOHN FRANK, special education educator, administrator; b. N.Y.C., Apr. 16, 1956; s. Jacob and Anna (Reinwald) S.; m. Judy Lynn Gitterman, June 7, 1981; children: Melissa Beth, David Jacob. BS, Manhattan Coll., 1978; MS, Coll New Rochelle, 1981; MEd, Columbia U., 1983, EdD, 1988. Cert. tchr. spl. edn., sch. adminstr., supr., dist. adminstr., N.Y. Therapy aide Office Mental Health, N.Y. State Bronx Psychiat. Ctr., 1978; tchr. sci. 6th-8th grades Sts. Philip and James Sch., Archdiocese of N.Y., 1978-79; program supr. occpl. edn. classes St. Mary's Habibilitation Inst. Inst. Applied Human Dynamics, Bronx, N.Y., 1979-83; sch. supr. Assn. for Help of Retarded Children Bronx Habilitation Ctr., N.Y.C., 1983-87; spl. educator Mt. Pleasant-Blythedale Union Free Sch. Dist., Valhalla, N.Y., 1987-88; spl. edn. educator Bd. Coop. Ednl. Svcs. So. Westchester, White Plains, NY, 1988—2003, Dobbs Ferry (N.Y.) H.S., 1995-96, Harrison (N.Y.) H.S., 1996-97, Hommocks Mid. Sch., Larchmont, NY, 2002—. Adj. prof. Western Conn. State U., Danbury, 1988-89, St. Thomas Aquinas Coll., Sparkill, N.Y., 1990, 91, Coll. New Rochelle, N.Y., 2001-03, CUNY Hunter, 1994-99; team leader Bd. Coop. Ednl. Svcs., So. Westchester, 1989-93, site coord. extended sch. yr. program Rye Lake campus, 1991-95; presenter in field; Ctr. Spl. Edn. and Tng. Resource Ctr., workshop presenter supts. day, 1995. Vol. firefighter, sec. hook & ladder Harrison (N.Y.) Fire Dept., 1993-95, lt., 1996-97 capt., 1998-99 (Firefighter of Yr. 1990); mem. com. Very Spl. Arts,White Plains, N.Y., 1990; parent rep. exec. bd. Harrison Children's Ctr., 1991-93, 95—; lector, tchr. catechism St. Gregory the Gt. Roman Cath. Ch., 1994-95; EMT vol. Harrison Ambulance Corps, 1993-94; aux. police officer N.Y.C. Police Dept., 1975-77; mem. Ctrl. Westchester Vicariate Coun., Archdiocese of N.Y., 1998—; mem. parish coun. St. Gregory the Great, 1998—; panel mem. surrogate decision making com. N.Y. State Commn. on Quality Care for the Mentally Disabled, 1999—. Grantee: Readers Digest Found., Westchester Edn. Coalition, 1990, Innovation Network, Westchester, Rockland Impact II, Adaptor award, 1991, 92, 93, 94, 95, 97, 98, 2000 Mem. Am. Assn. on Mental Retardation (rsch. project norming examiner adaptive behavior scale 1991), Internat. Reading Assn., Coun. for Exceptional Children (pres. Hunter Coll. chpt. 1997-2000, regional rep. to bd. dirs. N.Y. State Fedn. 1990-93, treas. 1993-96, exec. bd. dirs. 1993-96, del. Nat. conv. 1998, co-chair N.Y. state conv. 1997, sec. 2002—, co-chmn. promotion/publicity subcom. local arrangements com. ann. conv. 2002), Kappa Delta Pi, Phi Delta Kappa. Avocation: marathon runner (finisher N.Y.C. 1989, 92, 93). Home: 127 Webster Ave Harrison NY 10528-2913 Office: Bd Coop Ednl Svcs So Westchester 1606 Old Orchard St White Plains NY 10604-1049

SZTANDERA, LES MARK, computer science educator; b. Zabrze, Poland, Dec. 19, 1961; came to U.S., 1989; s. Felix and Regina (Sowa) S.; m. Wanda Monica Wietrzycka, Apr. 5, 1986; 1 child, Claudia Sabrina. Diploma, Cambridge (Eng.) U., 1989; MS, U. Mo., 1990; PhD, U. Toledo, Ohio, 1993. Rsch., tchg. asst. U. Mo., Columbia, 1989-90, U. Toledo, 1991-93; asst. prof. Phila. U., 1993-98, assoc. prof., 1998—, head computer sci. dept., 1997—. Reviewer coll. textbooks Prentice Hall Co., Englewood Cliffs, N.J., 1993—, McGraw-Hill Co., N.Y.C., 1993—, profl. jours. in field; organizer, mem. coms., chmn. various internat. confs. Contbr. numerous articles to profl. jours. Rsch. grantee Am. Heart Assn., Washington, 1991, Cray-Pitts. Supercomputing Ctr., 1992, 94, 96, NSF, Washington, 1996, Nat. Textile Ctr., Wilmington, 1998-2002, Dept. Commerce, Washington, 1998-2002. Mem. Assn. for Computing Machinery, N. Am. Fuzzy Info. Processing Soc., Can. Soc. for Fuzzy Info. and Neural Systems. Achievements include development of fuzzy neural trees, contributions to fuzzy set theory. Office: Phila Univ Computer Info Sys Philadelphia PA 19144 E-mail: sztanderal@philau.edu.

SZWED, BERYL J. school system administrator, mathematics educator; b. Bklyn., Mar. 21, 1948; d. Jules and Bertha (Dlugash) Cooper; m. Joseph Szwed, May 28, 1970; children: Nissa, Rory, Joshua. BS in Elem. Edn., SUNY, Cortland, 1970; MS in Guidance, Counseling, Tex. A and I U., 1973; postgrad, SUNY, Oswego; postgrad., U. N.H. Cert. elem. tchr. K-6 perm., Math. secondary 7-12. Guidance counselor, test dist. coord. Cato-Meridian Sch. Dist., NY; test adminstr. Fed. Correctional Inst., Raybrook, NY; remedial math. specialist, Title I coord. Lake Placid (N.Y.) Schs., dist. testing coord., acad. intervention svcs. Adj. instr. math. North Country C.C., Saranac Lake, N.Y.; math. cons.; coordinating mentor N.Y. State Elem. Math. Mentors, 1993-97; mem. Mid. Sch. Mathline, 1994-97; master tchr. Internat. Tchr. Tng. Inst., Montreal, 1997-98; natl. presenter in field. Creator Pamper Your Child With Math program; contbr. articles to profl. jours. Area staff devel. com., vice chmn. Instructional TV Sch. Svc. com. WCFE,

Plattsburgh, N.Y.; coord., chmn. scholarship com. Adirondack Festival Am. Music; sec., treas., grant writer Adirondack Singers; chair Messiah Sing-In; sec. Town Hall Players; sports chair Saranac Lake (N.Y.) Winter Carnival, 1996-2003, queen, 2000; mem. Saranac Lake (N.Y.) High Sch. Parent, Teacher, Student Assn. 1994-97; v.p. Saranac Lake Women's Civic Chamber, 2000-03, mem. bd. dirs., 2003-. Grantee Adirondack Tchr. Ctr., 1988, 89, 96, NYSACE, 1989, 95, Mathematics in the 21st Century, 1990, NSF Leadership Network, 1991-93. Mem. ASCD (assoc.), Nat. Coun. Tchrs. Math. (rep. 2001-), N.Y. State Assn. Math. Suprs. (v.p., spring conf. coord. 2000, pres. 2000-2001), Assn. Math. tchrs. N.Y. State (dist. rep. Essex, Hamilton, Clinton, and Franklin counties), elem. rep. exec. bd. 1993-95, rec. sec. to exec. bd. 1995-96, external affairs com. chmn., summer conf. coord. 1998, ednl. materials chair 1997-99, summer site coord. 1998—), N.Y. State Assn. Comprehensive Educators, Delta Kappa Gamma (Beta Mu chpt. treas. 1993-97, pres. 1998-2002, state conf. chmn. 2003, Pi state exec. sec. 2003—). Home: 157 Kiwassa Rd Saranac Lake NY 12983-2319

SZYMANSKI, EDNA MORA, dean; b. Caracas, Venezuela, Mar. 19, 1952; came to U.S., 1952; d. José Angel and Helen Adele (McHugh) Mora; m. Michael Bernard, Mar. 30, 1973. BS, Rensselaer Poly. Inst., 1972; MS, U. Scranton, 1974; PhD, U. Tex., 1988. Cert. rehab. counselor. Vocat. evaluator Mohawk Valley Workshop, Utica, N.Y., 1974-75; vocat. rehab. counselor N.Y. State Office Vocat. Rehab., Utica, 1975-80, sr. vocat. rehab. counselor, 1980-87; rsch. assoc. U. Tex., Austin, 1988-89; asst. prof. U. Wis., Madison, 1989-91, assoc. prof., 1991-93, assoc. dean sch. edn., 1993-97, dir. rehab. rsch. and tng. ctr., 1993-96, prof. rehab. psychology and spl. edn., 1997—99, chair dept. rehab. psychology and spl. edn., 1997-99, fellow tchg. acad., 1997; dean Coll. Edn. U. Md., College Park, 1999—. Cons. Rsch. Assocs. Syracuse, N.Y., 1988-90. Co-author various book chpts.; co-editor: Rehabilitation Counseling Basics and Beyond, 1992, 98; co-editor Work and Disability, 1996, 2003, Rehabilitation Counseling Bull., 1994-2000; contbr. articles to profl. jours. Mem. Pres.'s Com. on Employment of People with Disabilities, Washington, 1987-97. Recipient Rsch. award Am. Assn. Counselor Edn. and Supr., 1991. Mem. ACA (chair rsch. com. 1992-94, Rsch. awards 1990, 93, 95), Am. Rehab. Counseling Assn. (pres. 1985-86, rsch. award 1989, 94, Disting. Profl. award 1997, James F. Garrett award for disting. career in rehab. rsch. 1999), Coun. Rehab. Edn. (chair rsch. com. 1990-95, v.p. 1993-95, 97), Nat. Coun. Rehab. Edn. (chair rsch. com. 1992-99, Rehab. Edn. Rschr. of Yr. 1993, New Career in Rehab. Edn. award 1990). Office: U Md Coll Edn 3119 Benjamin Bldg College Park MD 20742-1100 E-mail: ednas@umd.edu.

TAAKE, KAREN RENEÉ, secondary education educator; b. Tuscola, Ill., Aug. 12, 1946; d. Howard Allen and June E. (Davis) Tope; m. Richard Everett Taake, June 26, 1971; children: Katy Reneé. BS in Art Edn., So. Ill. U., Edwardsville, 1969; MEd, Maryville U., St. Louis, 1995. Cert. elem., secondary tchr., Ill. Art tchr. Grant Jr. H.S., Fairview Heights, Ill., 1969-70; art tchr. Collinsville (Ill.) Sr. H.S., 1970—. Mem. NEA, Ill. Edn. Assn., Nat. Art Edn. Assn., Ill. Art Edn. Assn., Madison County Art Edn. Assn., Phi Delta Kappa. Home: 112 Bridle Ridge Rd Collinsville IL 62234-4322 Office: Collinsville Sr High Sch 2201 S Morrison Ave Collinsville IL 62234-1449

TABANDERA, KATHLYNN ROSEMARY, secondary education educator; b. Honolulu, Aug. 6, 1960; d. William Fernandez and Sakae Sandra (Shibata) Rosa; m. Russell Takao Tabandera, Dec. 24, 1979 (div. 2000); children: Tiffany Nohelani, Christine Lei, Angela Nani, Nicole Ku'ulei, Ricky William Kanaina. BA in Psychology, BA in Econs., BBA in Bus. Adminstrn., Tchr. Edn. Program, U. Hawaii, Hilo, 1988, Profl. Edn. Program, 1989, Natural Sci. Certificate Program, 1994; MEd, Almeda Coll. and U., 2002. Profl. cert. secondary educator, Hawaii; cert. paralegal. Adminstr. Tabandera Fishing Co., Hilo, Hawaii, 1980-85; realtor assoc. Ala Kai Realty Inc., Hilo, Hawaii, 1985—; owner Tracks Enterprises, Hilo, Hawaii, 1985—; tchr. Kohala High Sch. Alternative Learning Ctr., 1989-91; social studies tchr. Honoka'a High Sch., 1991-92; real estate appraiser Hilo, 1992. Tchr. Hilo H.S. Alt. Learning Ctr., 1992-94, Waiakea H.S., 1994-2001, social studies tcht. Kea'au H.S., 2001—; mentor, tutor Kamehameha Schs. Talent Search, 1993-94; commr. on mayor's com. on people with disabilities, 1993-96; sales dir. Amerivox, 1995-97; adminstrv. asst. Newmans Nursery, 1995-97. Named to Dean's List, U. Hawaii, 1985-88. Mem. AAUW, NEA, NAFE, ASCD, Am. Soc. Profl. Appraisers, Hawaii Island Bd. Realtors, Hawaii Assn. Realtors, Nat. Assn. Realtors, Hawaii State Tchrs. Assn., Adminstrn. of Justice. Avocations: animal breeding and raising, ornamental horticulture, reading.

TABATZNIK, BERNARD, retired physician, educator; b. Mir, Poland, Jan. 8, 1927; came to U.S., 1959, naturalized, 1966; s. Max and Fay (Ginsberg) T.; m. Marjorie Turner, Jan. 8, 1956; children: Darron Mark, Keith Donald, Ilana Wendy; m. Charline Edwards Harmon, Aug. 7, 1992. BSc, U. Witwatersrand, South Africa, 1945, MB, BChir, 1949. Intern Baragwanath Hosp., Johannesburg, South Africa, 1950-51, Hillingdon Hosp., Ashford Hosp., also research unit Canadian Red Cross Meml. Hosp., Taplow, Eng., 1951-54; med. registrar Ashford Hosp., 1954-56, Johannesburg Gen. Hosp., 1956-58; physician Baragwanath Hosp., 1956-59; fellow in medicine Sch. Medicine Johns Hopkins U., Balt., 1959-60, fellow in cardiology, 1960-61, asst. prof. medicine, 1966-97, ret., 1997; head cardiopulmonary divsn. Sinai Hosp., Balt., 1961-72, assoc. chief medicine, 1964-72; chief cardiology dept. North Charles Gen. Hosp., Balt., 1972; also dir. med. edn., dir. Postgrad. Inst., coord. ambulatory svcs.; med. dir. Nurse Practitioner-Physician Asst. Program, Ch. Hosp., Balt., 1987-90. Contbr. articles to profl. jours. Recipient Save-A-Heart Humanitarian award, 1977, Maimonides award, 1983, Shaarei Zion Humanitarian award, 1987. Fellow Royal Coll. Physicians (London); mem. South African Cardiac Soc., Am. Heart Assn., Md. Heart Assn. (chmn. health careers 1964-66), Laennec Cardiovasc. Sound Group. Home: HC 3 Box 180 Monterey VA 24465-9313 E-mail: btabatznik@aol.com.

TABOR, BEVERLY ANN, retired elementary school educator; b. Dallas, Feb. 12, 1943; m. Charles W. Tabor, Aug. 22, 1964; children: Shawn, Josh. BS in Edn., U. N. Tex., 1964, MEd in Guidance, Counseling, 1970. Cert. tchr. elem. art, guidance and counseling, supr., Tex. Elem. tchr. Ft. Davis (Tex.) Ind. Sch. Dist., 1964-65, Mesquite (Tex.) Ind. Sch. Dist., 1965-69, 71-97; counselor Amarillo (Tex.) Ind. Sch. Dist., 1970-71; ret. Mem. ins. adv. com. Tchr. Retirement Sys. of Tex., Austin, 1986-97; chmn. site based mgmt. com. Tosch Elem. Sch., Mesquite, 1992-94, mentor for new tchrs., student tchrs., H.S. students considering the tchg. profession. Life mem. Tosch Elem. PTA, 1985—. Named to Apple Corps, 1995. Mem. Tex. State Tchrs. Assn. (life), Mesquite Edn. Assn., Alpha Delta Kappa (past pres. Mesquite). Avocation: arts and crafts. Home: 271 County Road 2504 Mineola TX 75773-3143

TABOR, CURTIS HAROLD, JR., librarian, minister; b. Atlanta, July 3, 1936; s. Curtis Harold and Gerturde Olive (Casey) Tabor; m. Dorothy May Corbin, June 30, 1957 (dec. June 1996); m. Paulene C Pennington, July 12, 1997; children: Timothy M, John M. AA, Fla. Coll., Temple Terrace, 1957; BA, Harding Coll., 1960; MA, Butler U., 1969; MDiv, Bapt. Missionary Assn. Theol. Sem., Jacksonville, Tex., 1974; MLS, Tex. Woman's U., 1977. Min. Ch. of Christ, Bowling Green, Ky., 1960-61, Hamilton, Ont., Can., 1961-64, Indpls., 1964-67, Nacogdoches, Tex., 1967-75, Dallas, 1976-77, Columbus, Miss., 1977-79, Tampa, Fla., 1993-97, Maryville, Tenn., 1997—; reference libr. Blount County Pub. Libr., 1998—. Teacher Great Lakes Christian Col, Beamville, Ont, Canada, 1961—64; bible chair dir Stephen F Austin State Univ, Nacogdoches, 1967—75; participated archeological excavations, Tell Gezer, Israel, 1969, Tell Lachish, Israel, 80; profl libr sci Fla Col, Temple Terrace, 1979—85, libr dir, 1985—97. Author (with others): (book) Resurrection, 1973, Biblical Authority, 1974, The Lord of Glory, 1980, Making A Difference: Florida College, the First Fifty Years, 1996. Cub master Boy Scouts Am, Nacogdoches, 1970—75; pres Nacogdoches Baseball Asn, 1974—75; vol driving instr 55 Alive AARP, 1998—2001. Recipient Scouters Key, Cub Scouts Ams, 1975. Mem.: SAR, Tampa Bay Libr. Consortium (treas 1986—89), Beta Phi Mu, Eta Beta Rho. Republican. Mem. Ch. Of Christ. Avocations: amateur radio (KC4XS), locksmithing. Home: 1906 Raulston View Dr Maryville TN 37803-2868 E-mail: haltabor@yahoo.com.

TACKER, WILLIS ARNOLD, JR., medical educator, researcher; b. Tyler, Tex., May 24, 1942; s. Willis Arnold and Willie Mae (Massey) T.; m. Martha J. McClelland, Mar. 18, 1967; children: Sarah Mae, Betsy Jane, Katherine Ann. BS, Baylor U., 1964, MD, PhD, 1970. Lic. physician, Ind., Alaska, Tex. Intern Mayo Grad. Sch. Medicine Mayo Clinic, Rochester, Minn., 1970-71; pvt. practice Prudhoe Bay, Alaska, 1971; instr. dept. physiology Baylor Coll. Medicine, Houston, 1971-73, asst. prof. dept. physiology, 1973-74; clin. prof. family medicine Ind. U. Sch. Medicine, West Lafayette, Ind., 1981—; vis. asst. prof. Biomed. Engring. Ctr., Purdue U., West Lafayette, 1974-76, assoc. prof. Sch. Vet. Medicine, 1976-79; assoc. dir. William A. Hillenbrand Biomed. Engring. Ctr., Purdue U., West Lafayette, 1980-93, prof. Sch. Vet. Medicine, 1979—, acting dir., 1991-93; exec. dir. Hillenbrand Biomed. Engring. Ctr., 1993-95. Vis. rsch. fellow Sch. Aerospace Medicine, Brooks AFB, San Antonio, 1982; with Corp. Sci. and Tech., State of Ind., 1985-88; presenter, cons. in field. Author: Some Advice on Getting Grants, 1991; co-author: Electrical Defibrillation, 1980; author: (with others) Handbook of Engineering and Medicine and Biology, 1980, Implantable Sensors for Closed-Loop Prosthetic Systems, 1985, Encyclopedia of Medical Devices and Instrumentation, 1988, (with others) Defibrillation of the Heart, 1994; contbr. numerous articles to profl. jours. Chmn. bd. dirs. Assn. Advancemnt Med. Instrumentation Found., Arlington, Va., 1987-95. Mem. Am. Heart Assn. (bd. dirs. Ind. affiliate 1975-81, med. edn. com. 1975-81, pub. health edn. com. 1975-81, chmn. ad hoc com. CPR tng. for physicians 1976-77, rsch. review com. 1988-90), Am. Physiol. Soc., Ind. State Med. Assn., Tippecanoe County Med. Soc., Assn. Advancement Med. Instrumentation (chmn. various coms., bd. dirs. 1981-84, pres. 1985-86), Am. Men and Women Sci., Alpha Epsilon Delta, Beta Beta Beta, Soc. Sigma Xi. Achievements include research in biomedical engineering, cardiovascular physiology, medical education, emergency cardiovascular care, motor evoked potentials, skeletal muscle ventricle; patents for an apparatus and method for measurement and control of blood pressure, electrode system and method for implantable defibrillators, pressure mapping system with capacitive measuring pad. Office: Purdue U Lynn Hall West Lafayette IN 47907 E-mail: tacker@vet.purdue.edu.

TACKETT, STEPHEN DOUGLAS, education services specialist; b. Waverly, Ohio, Apr. 27, 1939; s. James Elbert and Zelma Iola (Manahan) T.; m. Magdalena Schneider, Jan. 4, 1958; children: Doris, Janice, Jerry, Suzanne. AA, El Paso C.C., 1974; BS, SUNY, Albany, 1976; MA, Ball State U., 1979. Nat. cert. counselor; lic. profl. clin. counselor. Enlisted U.S. Army, 1955, advanced through grades to Command Sgt. Maj., 1973, retired, 1982; instr. Mt. Wachusett C.C., Gardner, Mass., 1979-81; asst. dir. Evaluation U.S. Army Sgts. Maj. Acad., Ft. Bliss, Tex., 1981-82; dir. substance abuse treatment Sun Valley Hosp., El Paso, Tex., 1982-84; from guidance counselor to ednl. svcs. officer U.S. Army, Germany, 1984-86, 88-90; edn. advisor U.S. Army Sgts. Maj. Acad., Fort Bliss, 1990-92; edn. svcs. specialist Mil. Entrance Processing Sta., El Paso, 1992—. Mem. adv. bd. for Counselor Edn. U. Tex., El Paso, 1983. Cubmaster Boy Scouts Am., Ft. Leonard Wood, Mo., 1970-71, com. mem., Frankfurt, Germany, 1972-73, asst. scoutmaster, Kaiserslautern, Germany, 1976-79. Mem. ACA, Assn. for Career and Tech. Edn., Nat. Assn. Secondary Sch. Prins., Tex. Assn. Secondary Sch. Prins., Tex. Counseling Assn. Office: Mil Entrance Processing Sta Ste E 6380 Morgan Ave El Paso TX 79906-4610

TACKETT, WILLIAM EDWARD, school system administrator; b. Salem, N.J., Aug. 26, 1957; s. Bill and Beverly Ruth (Appleby) T. B in Religious Edn., Valley Forge Christian Coll., 1976; MEd, Temple U., 1984; MA, Glassboro State U., 1992; postgrad., LaSalle U., Phila. Tchr. Pennsville (N.J.) Christian Acad., 1980-82; prin. Cumberland Christian Sch., Vineland, N.J., 1982-86; tchr., asst. prin. Elsonboro (N.J.) Twp. Sch., 1986-92; prin. Salem (N.J.) County Spl. Svcs., 1992-93; adminstrv. pool Brandywine Sch. Dist., Wilmington, Del., 1993-94; asst. prin. Alloway (N.J.) Twp. Sch., 1994-97; prin. Cooper Elem. Sch., Cherry Hill, N.J., 1997—. Dir. Pennsville Day Camp, 1980-86; asst. pastor Pennsville Assembly of God, 1980-84, 1986-88; assoc. pastor First Assembly of God, Carney's Point, N.J., 1990—. Mem. adv. bd. Drug Awareness, Pennsville, N.J., 1990, BIg Brother, Big Sister bd., Salem County, N.J., 1991. Named Tchr. of Yr., N.J. Dept. Edn., Elsinboro, N.J., 1988. Avocations: canoeing, sailing, hiking, camping, bicycling. Home: 1840 Frontage Rd Apt 804 Cherry Hill NJ 08034-2203 Office: Cooper Sch Greentree Rd Cherry Hill NJ 08001

TACKI, BERNADETTE SUSAN, principal; b. Kenosha, Wis., Oct. 21, 1913; d. Peter Frank and Anna (Rathke) T. BS in Edn., Dominican Coll., 1952; MA in Edn., Northwestern U., 1958. Tchr. Whitley Sch., Brighton Twp., Wis., 1932-33, Highland Sch., Pleasant Prairie, Wis., 1933-41, Victory Sch., Pleasant Prairie, 1941-47, Paris (Wis.) Consol. Sch., 1947-53, Southport Sch., Kenosha, 1953-61; prin. Harvey Sch., Kenosha, 1961-80; tchr. St. Casimir, Kenosha, 1983-93, vol. tchr. part-time, 1983—. Pres. Kenosha County Hist. Soc., 1985-89, St. James Parish Coun., Kenosha, 1975-89. Recipient Disting. Svc. award Wis. State Dept., 1980. Mem. AAUW, PTA, Ret. Tchrs. Assn., Kenosha County Tchrs. Assn. (past pres.), Kenosha Edn. Assn. (past pres.), Schubert Club, Quota Club, Delta Kappa Gamma (past pres.). Republican. Roman Catholic. Avocations: reading, traveling. Home: 4401 32nd Ave Kenosha WI 53144-1917

TADDEI, EDWARD P. school system administrator; b. Jenkintown, Pa., Dec. 19, 1930; s. Vincent J. and Josephine (Ronciglione) T.; m. Joan Marie Heffernan, Aug. 25, 1956; children: Joanne, Edward Jr., Barbara Joan, Gerard. BS in Secondary Edn., Temple U., 1952, MEd, 1956. Math. tchr. Upper Dublin Jr./Sr. High Sch., Ft. Washington, Pa., 1954-64, chmn. math. dept., 1957-64; asst. prin. Upper Dublin Jr. High Sch., Ft. Washington, 1964-67; dir. mid. sch. Upper Dublin Sch. Dist., Ft. Washington, 1976-78, pers. asst. to supt., 1978-89, asst. supt., 1989-93, ret., 1993. Varsity basketball coach Upper Dublin High Sch., 1960-67; adj. prof. math. Montgomery County C.C., Blue Bell, Pa., 1984—. Bd. dirs. Northwestern Corp. drug and alcohol prevention program, Ambler, Pa., 1989—; basketball official Pa. Interscholastic Athletic Assn., 1948-78. Cpl. U.S. Army, 1952-54. Decorated Legion of Honor. Mem. St. Alphonsus Men's Club, Oak Terr. Country Club, Rotary. Republican. Roman Catholic. Avocations: golf, travel, coaching basketball. Home: 1530 Temple Dr Maple Glen PA 19002-3318

TADYCH, RENITA, English eduator; b. Manitowoc, Wis., Aug. 5, 1934; d. Zenon S. and Anita (Broecker) T. BA, Silver Lake Coll., Manitowoc, Wis., 1960; MA, U. Dayton, 1972; PhD, Indiana U. of Pa., 1992. Life cert. tchr., Wis.; joined Franciscan Sisters of Christian Charity, 1948. Elem. tchr. Dioceses of Steubenville (Ohio), Green Bay & LaCrosse (Wis.), Dioceses of Gaylord (Mich.) and L.A., 1952-66; secondary tchr. Dioceses of Chgo., Omaha, Milw. and Green Bay, 1967—83; prof. Silver Lake Coll., Diocese of Green Bay, Manitowoc, Wis., 1983. Mem. adv. bd. Collegiate Press, Alta Loma, Calif., 1994-95; supr. honors program Roncalli H.S., Manitowoc, 1984-99, Mishicot H.S., Washington H.S. Two Rivers. Mem. Nat. Coun. Tchrs. English, Wis. Coun. Tchrs. English (coll. and univ. com. 1993-96). Roman Catholic. Avocations: reading, knitting, crocheting, walking. Home and Office: Silver Lake Coll 2406 S Alverno Rd Manitowoc WI 54220-9319 E-mail: srt@silver.sl.edu.

TAFLOVE, ALLEN, electrical engineer, educator, researcher, consultant; b. Chgo., June 14, 1949; s. Harry and Leah T.; m. Sylvia Hinda Friedman, Nov. 6, 1977; children: Michael Lee, Nathan Brent. BS with highest distinction, Northwestern U., 1971, MS, 1972, PhD, 1975. Assoc. engr. IIT Rsch. Inst., Chgo., 1975-78, rsch. engr., 1978-81, sr. engr., 1981-84; assoc. prof. Northwestern U., Evanston, Ill., 1984-88, prof., 1988—, Charles Deering McCormick prof., 2000—03; master Lindgren/Slivka Residential Coll. Sci. & Engring., 2000—. Author: Computational Electrodynamics: The Finite-Difference Time-Domain Method, 1995; co-author: Computational Electromagnetics: Integral Equation Approach, 1993, Computational Electrodynamics: The Finite-Difference Time-Domain Method, 2d edit., 2000; editor: Advances in Computational Electrodynamics: The Finite-Difference Time-Domain Method, 1998; contbr. 20 book chpts., over 80 articles to profl. jours.and mags. Fellow: IEEE. Achievements include listed on ISI HighlyCited.com; first to pioneer of finite-difference time-domain method in computational electrodynamics. Office: Northwestern U Dept Elec and Comp Engring 2145 Sheridan Rd Evanston IL 60208-0834 E-mail: taflove@ece.northwestern.edu.

TAFOYA, JOE, school system administrator; BA, MA, San Diego State U.; D, Northern Ariz. U., 1983. Various San Diego City Schools, 1969—90; asst. supt. Santa Ana Unified Sch. Dist., 1990—94, dep. supt. of curriculum, 1994—99; dir. Dept. Def. Edn. Activity, 2000—. Recipient Exceptional Civilian Svc. award, Office of Sec. of Def., 2001. Office: Dept of Def Edn Activity 4040 N Fairfax Dr Arlington VA 22203

TAFT, WILLIAM HOWARD, journalism educator; b. Mexico, Mo., Oct. 24, 1915; s. Raymond E. and Ferrie (Dains) T.; m. Myrtle Marie Adams, Jan. 18, 1941; children: Marie, William Howard, Alice. AB, Westminster Coll., 1937; B in Journalism, U. Mo., 1938, MA, 1939; PhD, Western Res. U., 1951. Dir. pub. rels. Hiram (Ohio) Coll., 1939-40, 47-48; asst. prof. journalism Youngstown (Ohio) Coll., 1946-48; prof. Defiance (Ohio) Coll., 1948-50; assoc. prof. Memphis State Coll., 1950-56; prof. U. Mo., Columbia, 1956-81, assoc. dean grad. programs, 1980-81. Yearbook cons., 1957—. Author: Let's Publish That Top-Rated Yearbook, 1961, (with others) Modern Journalism, 1962, Missouri Newspapers, 1964, Missouri Newspapers, When and Where, 1808-1962, 1964, American Journalism History, 1968, rev. edit., 1977, Newspapers as Tools for Historians, 1970, (with others) Mass Media and the National Experience, 1971, Donrey Media; A Low Profile Group, 1976, Magazines for the Eighties, 1981, Encyclopedia of 20th Century Journalists, 1986, Missouri Newspapers and the Missouri Press Association, 125 Years of Service, 1867-1992, 1992, Wit and Wisdom of Country Editors, 1996, Show-Me Journalists: The First 200 Years, 2003; contbr. articles to profl. jours. and encys. With USAAF, 1941-45. Recipient Faculty-Alumni citation U. Mo., 1979, Alumni Achievement award Westminster Coll., 1987; rsch. fellow Washington Journalism Ctr., 1967; inducted into Mo. Newspaper Hall of Fame, 2001. Mem. Assn. Edn. Journalism and Mass. Comm. (Presdl. award 1991), Boone County Hist. Soc. (past pres.), Kiwanis (life; past pres., Churchman of Yr. 1987, Kiwanian of Yr. 1993, Tablet of Honor 1997, George F. Hixson award), Delta Tau Delta (life), Pi Delta Epsilon, Kappa Tau Alpha (nat. treas., exec. dir. 1962-91). Republican. Methodist. Home: 107 Sondra Ave Columbia MO 65202-1416 E-mail: whtpenny@aol.com.

TAGGART, HELEN M. nurse; b. Savannah, Ga., Dec. 6, 1946; d. Thomas Anthony and Ruth Elizabeth (Sisson) McKenzie; m. Thomas Robert Taggart, Mar. 9, 1968; children: Kathleen Taggart Swanner, Thomas Robert Jr. BSN, Armstrong State Coll., 1978; MSN, Ga. So. U., 1992; postgrad., U. Ala., Birmingham, 1995—. Staff nurse St. Joseph's Hosp., Savannah, 1967-68, 77-89, head nurse, 1971-74, St. Mary's Hosp., Athens, Ga., 1968-71; instr. Armstrong State Coll., Savannah, 1989-92; asst. prof. Armstrong Atlantic State U., Savannah, 1992—. Profl. adv. com. Nat. Multiple Sclerosis Soc., Atlanta, 1992-96; bd. mem. Ga. Bd. Nursing, Atlanta, 1994—; mem. Clin. Simulation Task Force Nat. Coun. State Bds. Nursing, Chgo., 1996-99. Editor, contbr.: Adult Nursing in Acute Community, 1998; contbr. articles to profl. jours. and chpts. to books. Counselor Multiple Sclerosis Support Group, Savannah, 1989-97. Nat. Assn. Orthop. Nurses rsch. grantee, 1996, U. Ala. (Birmingham) traineeship grantee, 1997, Armstrong Atlantic State U. rsch. grantee, 1997-98. Mem. Nat. League Nurses (exec. bd. 1996-98), Assn. Bus. Women Am. (exec. bd. 1994-96), Nat. Assn. Orthop. Nurses (rsch. com. 1995-99), Ga. Nurses Assn. (exec. bd. 1992-96). Avocations: gardening, swimming, snow skiing. Home: 6 Mulberry Bluff Dr Savannah GA 31406-3226 Office: Armstrong Atlantic State University 11935 Abercorn St Savannah GA 31419-1989

TAGGETTE, DEBORAH JEAN, special education educator; b. Dover Foxcroft, Maine, Sept. 24, 1952; d. Ernest Lyford and Arlene Elizabeth (Dority) Fairbrother; m. Berton Louis Taggette, July 19, 1975; children: Angela Beth, Chad Berton. BS in Edn., U. Maine, Fort Kent, 1975. Asst. tchr. spl. edn. Community High Sch., Fort Kent, 1978-79, substitute tchr. spl. edn., 1980, tchr. severly handicapped, 1984-92, resource rm. tchr., 1992-94, self contained tchr., 1994—. Transistion team of disabled students Community High Sch., 1993. Tchr. religious edn. St. Charles Parish; foster parent. Mem. DAV (life mem.), Order of Ea. Star (Miriam 140), Order of Rainbow for Girls (worthy advisor chpt. 17 1970-71), Grand Assembly (Grand Cross of Colors 1970), Vet. Meml. Fund of St. Francis. Avocations: reading, sewing, snowmobiling, boating, camping. Home: 1033 Main St Saint Francis ME 04774-9701 Office: SAD 27 Community High Sch Pleasant St Fort Kent ME 04743-1240

TAGUCHI, AILEEN TAKAYO, special education educator; b. Lahaina, Hawaii, Apr. 16, 1943; d. Robert Tamotsu and Asako (Michikami) Tanaka; m. Donald Earl Taguchi, Aug. 21, 1965; children: Wendy Takae, Kara Keiko, Kristie Kiyoko. BS, Ind. U., 1965; MA, Calif. Luth. U., 1989. Spl. edn. tchr., elem. tchr., coord. early childhood edn. Bandini St. Sch., La., 1965-77; tchr. learning disabled group L.A. Unified Sch. Dist., 1977-79, itinerant tchr. of physically handicapped, 1979-80, resource specialist tchr. 156th St. Sch., 1980-85, program specialist, 1985-89, coordinating specialist spl. edn., 1989-94, specialist, divsn. spl. edn., 1994—. Home: 16903 Betty Ave Cerritos CA 90703-1437

TAI, WEI-HUA, mechanics scientist, educator; b. Fengxiang, Shaanxi, China, Jan. 16, 1959; s. Feng-Tang Tai and Yan Zhang; m. Xin-Qiao Wang, July 18, 1987; 1 child, Yu. BS, Northwestern Inst. Light Inds., China, 1981; MS, Huazhong U. Sci. Tech., Wuhan, China, 1984; PhD, Beijing U. Aero. Astro., 1988. Tchg. asst. U. Sci. Tech. Beijing, 1988-89, lectr., 1989-91, assoc. prof., 1991-95; rsch. assoc. Hong Kong Poly. U., 1995-96; vis. scientist U. Mich., Dearborn, 1996—. Dir. computer lab. U. Sci. Tech. Beijing, 1989-95, dir. material lab., 1991-95. Author: Handbook of Engineering Mechanics, 1994; contbr. articles to profl. jours. including Engring. Fract. Mechanics, Internat. Jour. Solids. Named Excellent Young Tchr., Internat. Edn. and Tech. Found., 1994, Excellent Young Leading Scholar in Beijing, Beijing Govt., 1993. Fellow Chinese Soc. Modern Des.; mem. ASME, Soc. Automobile Engrs., Soc. Mfg. Engrs. (sr.), Chinese Soc. Mechanics, Chinese Soc. Metals. Office: Intro Tech Inc Ste 320 1700 W Big Beaver Troy MI 48084

TAINATONGA, ROSIE R. director; b. Guam; BS in Bus. Adminstrn., U. Guam. Dir. of edn. Coun. of Chief State Sch. Officers, Washington, 1999—. Office: Coun of Chief State Sch Officers Ste 700 One Massachusetts Ave NW Washington DC 20001-1431

TAIT, PATRICIA ANN, secondary education educator; b. Sacramento, Calif., Nov. 26, 1942; d. Frank Scott and Anna Mae (Chubbey) Smith; m. Arthur Fitzwilliam Tait, Jr., Dec. 27, 1968; children: Arthur Fitzwilliam III, Lauryn Kristine. BS in Edn., Tex. Western Coll., 1965; BA in English, U.

Tex., El Paso, 1966, MA in English, 1974. Cert. secondary educator, English, ESOL, Fla., Tex. Tchr. English Cheyenne Mountain High Sch., Colorado Springs, 1966-69; tchr. English, dept. chairperson Christ the King Internat. Sch., Okinawa, Japan, 1970-71; pres. Accurate Secretarial and Typing Svc., 1971—; tchr. English Forest High Sch., Ocala, Fla., 1979—, co-chair Eng. dept., 1990—. Cons. Fla. Writing Project, Gainesville, 1984—; presenter Marion County Tchrs. English, Ocala, 1985—. Author: Joseph Conrad: The Development of Character in the Jungle, 1974. Named Master Tchr., State of Fla., 1983-84, 84-85. Mem. NEA, Nat. Coun. Tchrs. English, Fla. Coun. Tchrs. English, Marion County Tchrs. English, Marion County Edn. Assn., Fla. Tchrs. Profl. Edn. Assn. Democrat. Episcopalian. Avocation: equine activities. Home: 5109 SE 4th St Ocala FL 34471-3304 Office: Forest High Sch 1614 SE Fort King St Ocala FL 34471-2599

TAKACS, KRISTY B. educator; b. Anaheim, Calif., Jan. 30, 1968; d. John A. and Karen A. T. BA in English, UCLA, 1990; MA in Secondary Edn., Loyola Marymount U., 1995. Tchr. independent study, ESL Fullerton (Calif.) Unified H.S. Dist., 1991-93; tchr. English Don Bosco Tech. Inst., Rosemead, Calif., 1993-97; tchr. English, reading, journalism, softball coach Walker Jr. H.S., 1997-99; tchr. English, journalism Cypress (Calif.) H.S., 1999—, chmn. dept. E.L.D. L.A. Archdiocese grantee, 1994. E-mail: takacs_k@auhsd.k12.ca.us.

TAKACS, WENDY EMERY, economics educator; b. Wayne, N.J., Aug. 3, 1947; d. Wendell Sherwin and Louise Marie Emery. BA, Douglass Coll., 1969; MA in Internat. Rels., John Hopkins U., 1971, MA in Econs., 1973, PhD in Econs., 1976. Rsch. asst. Pres.' Commn. on Internat. Trade and Investment Policy, Washington, 1970-71; economist Internat. Fin. Div. Bd. Govs. Fed. Res. System, Washington, 1975-76; from asst. prof. to prof. U. Md., Balt., 1976—; profl. lectr. John Hopkins SAIS, Washington, 1976—. Rsch. fellow The Brookings Instn., Washington, 1973-74; vis. fellow dept. econs. U. Bristol, Eng., 1984-87, Inst. for Internat. Econs., Washington, 1986-87, Inst. for Internat. Econ. Studies, Stockholm, Sweden, 1987; cons. The World Bank, Washington, 1988—; co-dir. UNDP/World Bank Trade Expansion program, 1993-95. Co-author Auction Quotas and U.S. Trade Policy, 1987; contbr. articles to profl. jours. Mem. Am. Econ. Assn., Can. Econ. Assn., Internat. Trade and Fin. Assn. (bd. dirs. 1991-93, 2000-03,, v.p. 1997, pres. 1999), Western Econ. Assn., Md. Combined Tng. Assn. (sec. 1980-82). Avocations: dressage and combined training, long distance walking. Office: UMBC Dept Econs Baltimore MD 21250 Home: 1900 Long Corner Rd Mount Airy MD 21771-3738

TAKANISHI, LILLIAN K. elementary school educator; b. Koloa, Hawaii, May 19, 1935; d. Saburo and Ayano (Ishida) Kunioka; m. Kenso Takanishi, July 11, 1959; children: Kendra Shizuyo, Kendace Tami. BS in Edn., N.E. Mo. State Tchrs. Coll., 1956; postgrad., U. Hawaii. Cert. profl. edn. Tchr. grade 4 Eleele (Hawaii) Sch., ret., 1990, site coord. After Sch. Plus Program, 1990-97, facilitator parent cmty. network ctr., 1990-97. Facilitator parent community network ctr., Eleele Sch., 199-97; asst. dir. Eleele/Kamehameha Summer Sch., 1991, 92, 93; tchr. Waimea/Kamehameha Summer Sch., 1994. Adv. jr. Girl Scouts of the U.S., sr. 4H Club, jr. Y-Teens, Civil Air Patrol. Recipient Kauai Dist.'s Dept. of Edn. Sustained Superior Performance and Employee of Yr. award, 1992-93. Mem. Hawaii State Tchrs. Assn. (v.p., sec., treas. Kauai chpt.), Parent Teacher Student Assn. (treas., grade level chmn.), Kau Ele Pepe Safety Action Team, Nana's House (bd. dirs. 1997—), Ho'o Lokahi, Delta Kappa Gamma (2d v.p. Eta chpt., sec.). Home: PO Box 396 Eleele HI 96705-0396

TAKASHIMA, SHIRO, biophysics educator; b. Tokyo, May 12, 1923; s. Atsuharu and Yoshie (Miyoshi) T.; m. Yuki Morita, June 26, 1953; children: Nozomi L., Makoto D. BS, U. Tokyo, 1947, PhD, 1955. Assoc. prof. Osaka U., Japan, 1959-63; rsch. scientist Walter Reed Med. Ctr., Washington, 1963-64; asst. prof. U. Pa., Phila., 1964-70, assoc. prof., 1970-76, prof. bioengring., 1976-92; prof. emeritus, 1993—. Mem. editorial bd. J. Biol. Physics., The Netherlands, 1977-97. Author: Electrical Properties of Biopolymers and Membrane, 1989; (book chpt.) Principles and Technics of Protein Chemistry, 1968; contbr. articles to profl. jours.; organizer internat. confs. Bd. dirs. Japanese Assn. of Greater Phila., 1983-90. Recipient Vis. Prof. grants Ministry of Edn., Italy, 1984, Japan Soc. of Sci., 1977, Yamada Found., 1990, Disting. Svc. award overseas Japanese Edn., Kensho-Kai, Japan, 1997; decorated for disting. achievements in sci. and edn., Japanese Govt., 1997. Mem. IEEE, Biophysical Soc., N.Y. Acad. Scis. Democrat. Methodist. Achievements include rsch. into dielectric relaxation of biopolymers, electrical properties of excitable mempranes from nerves and muscles. Home: 659 Niblick Ln Wallingford PA 19086-6675 Office: U Pa Dept Bioengring Philadelphia PA 19104-6392 E-mail: Stakashima@earthlink.net., Takashim@seas.upenn.edu.

TAKEMOTO, CORY NOBORU, mathematics educator; b. Honolulu, June 29, 1962; s. Nobuo and Ritsuko Takemoto; m. Karen Noriko Hara, Aug. 25, 1990. BS, U. Hawaii, 1985, profl. diploma, 1986, MA, 1990. Tchr. Kailua (Hawaii) High Sch., 1986-87; substitute tchr. Punahou Sch., Honolulu, 1990-91; lectr. math. Honolulu C.C., 1991-92, instr. math., 1993-94, Leeward C.C., Pearl City, Hawaii, 1994—. Mem. Math. Assn. Am. Avocations: singing, bicycling. Office: Leeward CC 46-045 Ala Ike Pearl City HI 96782

TAKEO, MAKOTO, physics education educator; b. Yamagata, Japan, Apr. 6, 1920; came to U.S., 1950; s. Yasuji and Tada (Sasaki) T.; m. Nov. 11, 1946; children: Osami, Yuko, Hiroshi. Rigakushi, Tohoku U., Sendai, Japan, 1943; MS in Physics, U. Oregon, 1951, PhD, 1953. Rsch. staff Naval Inst. Tech., Tokyo, 1944-45; asst. prof. Def. Acad., Yokosuka, Japan, 1953-56; from asst. prof. physics to prof. emeritus Portland (Oreg.) State U., 1956—, chair physics dept., 1988-90; asst. prof. math. U. Calgary, Can., 1959-62. Cons. Sandia Corp., Albuquerque, 1957-62, U. Oreg., Eugene, 1956-59, Mitshbishi Heavy Industries, Hiroshima, Japan. Referee Revs. of Modern Physics, Phys. Rev. Jour. Applied Physics, Jour. Colloid and Interface Sci., Ency. Applied Physics, Advance in Phys. Sci. USSR, Jour. Quantitative Spectroscopy Radiation Transfer; author: (book) Disperse Systems, 1998 (citation by editor of Revs. of Modern Physics 1989); contbr. articles to profl. jours. Recipient rsch. grants U. Oreg., 1957-74, U.S. Army Rsch. Office, 1984-88. Mem. Am. Phys. Soc., Phys. Soc. Japan. Home: 6510 SW 33rd Pl Portland OR 97239 Office: Portland State U Physics Dept PO Box 751 Portland OR 97207-0751

TALBOT, EMILE JOSEPH, French language educator; b. Brunswick, Maine, Apr. 12, 1941; s. Joseph Emile and Flora Talbot; m. Elizabeth Mullen, Aug. 6, 1966; children: Marc, Paul. BA, St. Francis Coll., Biddeford, Maine, 1963; MA, Brown U., 1965, PhD, 1968. From instr. French to prof. U. Ill., Urbana, 1967—86, prof., 1986—, head dept. French, 1988-94. Author: (book) Stendhal and Romantic Esthetics, 1985, Stendhal Revisited, 1993, Reading Nelligan, 2002; editor: La Critique Stendhalienne, 1979; rev. editor: The French Rev., 1979—82, Quebec Studies, 1988—93, mem. editl. bd.: Nineteenth-Century French Studies, 1986—2003, La Revue Francophone, 1990—96, Quebec Studies, 1993—96; mem. editl. bd. Quebec Studies, 2003—; mem. editl. bd.: Etudes Francophones, 1996—. Decorated chevalier Ordre des Palmes Académiques (France); fellow, Ctr. Advanced Study U. Ill., 1973, Assoc., 1988, NEH, 1973—74, Camargo Found., France, 1976. Mem.: MLA, Am. Coun. Quebec Studies (v.p. 1995—97, pres. 1997—99), Assn. Can. Studies in U.S., Am. Assn. Tchrs. French. Roman Catholic. Office: U Illinois Dept French 707 S Mathews Ave Urbana IL 61801-3625 E-mail: ejtalbot@uiuc.edu.

TALBOT, KATHLEEN MARY, elementary education educator; b. Lansdown, Pa., Apr. 11, 1944; d. Bernard Lawrence and Kathleen T. (Fleck) T. BS, Chestnut Hill Coll., 1971; MEd, Kutztown U., 1980. Cert. elem. tchr., Pa., Del. Tchr. elem. schs. Archdiocese of Phila., 1965-83, 83-86, Diocese of Wilmington (Del.), 1983-85, Garnet Valley Sch. Dist., Concordville, Pa., 1985—. Co-chairperson mid. states evaluation, Drexel Hill, Pa., 1979-81; adj. prof. Chestnut Hill Coll., Phila. 1980-91; coord. math. curriculum Garnet Valley Sch. Dist., Corcordsville, 1991—; mem. strategic planning steering com., 1994—. Author: Voices of the Valley, 1994. Grantee Impact Ptnrs. in Edn., 1989, Garnet Valley Sch. Dist., 1992, Gif of Time award, 1994. Mem. NEA, ASCD, Nat. Coun. Tchrs. Math., Pa. Edn. Assn., Chester County Reading Assn., Garnet Valley Edn. Assn. (mem. negotiating team 1992-93). Democrat. Roman Catholic. Avocations: gardening, walking, golf, tennis, skiing.

TALBOT, LEE MERRIAM, ecologist, educator, foundation administrator; b. New Bedford, Mass., Aug. 2, 1930; s. Murrell Williams and Zenaida (Merriam) T.; m. Martha Walcott Hayne, May 16, 1959; children: Lawrence Hayne, Russell Merriam. BA, U. Calif., Berkeley, 1953, MA, PhD, U. Calif., Berkeley, 1963. Biologist Arctic Research Lab., Point Barrow, Alaska, 1951; staff ecologist Internat. Union for Conservation, Brussels, 1954-56; ecologist, dir. East African ecol. research project Nat. Acad. Scis., Govts. of Kenya and Tanzania, 1959-63; wildlife advisor UN Spl. Fund, Africa, 1963-64; dir. S.E. Asia project Internat. Union for Conservation, 1964-65; resident ecologist, field rep. for internat. affairs Smithsonian Instn., Washington, 1966-70; sr. scientist, dir. internat. activities Pres.'s Council on Environ. Quality, Washington, 1970-78; sr. sci. advisor Internat. Council Sci. Unions, Paris, 1978-83; dir. conservation, spl. sci. advisor World Wildlife Fund Internat., Switzerland, 1978-80; dir. gen. Internat. Union for Conservation of Nature and Natural Resources, Gland, Switzerland, 1980-83; research fellow Environ. and Policy Inst., East West Ctr., 1983-87; vis. fellow World Resources Inst., Washington, 1984-89; sr. environ. advisor World Bank, 1984—; pres. Lee Talbot Assocs. Internat., 1991—; sr. prof. environ. scis., internat. affairs and pub. policy George Mason U., Va., 1994—. Cons. UNESCO, World Bank, Asian Devel. Bank, Nat. Geog. Soc., Inter-Am. Devel. Bank, The Nature Conservancy, U.S. Govt., U. Calif., UN Spl. Fund, WHO, UN Environment Program, UN Univ., UN Devel. Programme Govts. Laos, People's Republic China, Bhutan; conservation coord. Internat. Biol. Program, 1965-70; bd. dirs., chmn. bd. Ecologically Sustainable Devel., Inc., Inst. Ecosys. Studies, World Found. for Environ. and Devel.; mem. corp. N.Y. Bot. Gardens. Author 17 books and monographs; contbr. articles to profl. jours. Active Boy Scouts Am., Geneva, 1980-82, Washington, 1987-95. With USMC, 1953-54. Decorated officer Order of Lion (Senegal); recipient Fgn. Field Rsch. award Nat. Acad. Scis., 1959, CINE Golden Eagle award, 1969, Albert Schweitzer medal, 1975, Regents Lectureship award U. Calif.-Santa Barbara, 1986, Pierre Chaleur prize for lit. French Acad. Scis., 1993; finalist Univ.-Wide Tchg. Excellence award George Mason U., 1997, Festschrift Career Achievement in Environ. Sci. and Policy award George Mason U., 2003. Fellow Royal Geog. Soc., Royal Soc. Arts, AAAS, N.Y. Zool. Soc.; mem. Am. Inst. Biol. Scis. (Disting. Svc. award 1979), Acad. Medicine, World Conservation Union (hon.), Am. Assn. for Club of Rome, Am. Soc. Mammalogists, Ecol. Soc., Wildlife Soc. (Outstanding Publ. award 1963), Soc. for Conservation Biology, Internat. Soc. for Ecol. Econs., Boone and Crockett Club (N.Y.C.), Explorers Club (N.Y.C.), Cosmos Club (Washington), Sigma Xi, Phi Kappa Sigma. Achievements include incorporation of ecological principles in international development; development of new principles for management of wild resources; biodiversity conservation; definition of ecosystem dynamics of tropical savannahs including role of fire, feeding habits and migrations of wild herbivores; development and negotiation of national legislation and international agreements for environmental protection. Home: 6656 Chilton Ct Mc Lean VA 22101-4422

TALBOT, MARY LEE, minister; b. Cleve., Apr. 18, 1953; d. Richard William and Mary Helen (Jacobs) T. BA, Coll. Wooster, 1975; MDiv, Andover-Newton Theol. Sch., 1979; MPhil, Tchrs. Coll. Columbia U., 1990; PhD, Columbia U., 1997. Qrdained to ministry Presbyterian Ch. (U.S.A.), 1981. Asst. in ministry Grace Congl. Ch., Framingham, Mass., 1975-78; resources coord. Women's Theol. Coalition, Boston, 1977-79; assoc. editor Youth Mag., Phila., 1979-80; co-dir. youth and young adult program Presbyn. Ch. U.S.A., N.Y.C., 1981-88; cons. in religious edn. N.Y.C., 1988-90; dir. continuing edn. Pitts. Theol. Sem., Pitts., 1990—2001; interim pastor Hebron U.P. Ch., Clinton, 2002—. Bd. dirs. Christian Assn., U. Pa., 1979-81; mem. religion com. Chautauqua Inst., 1988-91. Author, editor: (program resource) Suicide and Youth, 1981, (newsletter) Trackings, 1986-88; editor: Racism and Anti-Racism, 1982, One Fantastic Book, 1982, My Identity: A Gift from God, 1987, A Guidebook for Presbyterian Youth Ministry, 1988, God's Gift of Sexuality, 1989, Celebrate Bible Study, 1990; contbr. articles to Youth Mag., Alert, Chautauquan Daily, others. Bd. dirs. Christian Assn., U. Pa., 1979-81. Recipient English award Bus. and Profl. Women, 1971. Mem. Assn. Presbyn. Ch. Educators, Assn. Presbyn. Clergywomen, Religious Edn. Assn. (bd. dirs. 1986-91), History of Edn. Soc., Kappa Delta Pi. Democrat. Office: 1767 Rte 30 Clinton PA 15026

TALBOT, SUSAN ANDERSON, French language educator; b. Madison, Wis., Oct. 15, 1930; d. Donald Wells and Florence (Aitken) Anderson; m. John Talbot, July 15, 1952; children: Peter W., Deborah M. Talbot Frandsen. BA, Radcliffe U., 1952; MA, U. Mont., 1980. Tchr. French Ea. Mont. Coll., Billings, 1967-70, sr. high sch., Billings, 1968, Hellgate High Sch., Missoula, Mont., 1977-79. Chair Youth Homes Bd., Missoula, 1981-83, United Way Campaign, Missoula, 1986-87, Mont. Arts Coun., 1984-89, Mont. Community Found., 1991—. Recipient "George" award Missoula C. of C., 1986, Silver Achievement award YWCA, 1987; co-recipient Gov.'s award for arts, 1994. Mem. Internat. Women's Forum. Episcopalian. Home: 11 Greenbrier Dr Missoula MT 59802-3353

TALBOTT, MARY ANN BRITT, secondary education educator; b. Augusta, Ga., Nov. 29, 1945; d. Charles Hubert and Mary Ann (Day) Britt; m. Lonnie Loyd Talbott, Oct. 20, 1978. AB, U. Ga., 1967, EdS, 1981, Cert. in Adminstrn./Supervision, 1989; MEd, Augusta Coll., 1975. Cert. tchr. support specialist. Tchr. English Hilsman Jr. H.S., Athens, Ga., 1967-68; tchr. English, chmn. dept. Tubman Jr. H.S., Augusta, Ga., 1969-73, Aquinas H.S., Augusta, 1973-79; tchr. English Winder (Ga.)-Barrow H.S., 1979-82; tchr. remedial writing/reading/math, career planning, Latin Morrow (Ga.) H.S., 1982-91, tchr. English, 1982-93, Brunswick (Ga.) H.S., 1993—, mem. discipline task force, 1995-96. Instr. English Clayton State Coll., Morrow, 1991-92, Ga. Mil. Coll., Ft. Gordon, 1975-77; instr. staff devel. Clayton County Bd. Edn., Jonesboro, Ga., 1985-91. Elder Stockbridge (Ga.) Presbyn. Ch., 1989-92; active Am. Cancer Soc., Augusta Choral Soc., Athens Choral Soc.; mem. Evangel. Luth. Ch. Resurrection, Augusta, Ga., 1995—. Recipient Psi Achievment award, 1979-81. Mem. Delta Kappa Gamma (pres. 1978-80, chmn. music com. 1985-87, 89-91, chair Psi State Achievement Award Com. 1979-81, dist. dir. 1981-83, scholar 1980, 87, Golden Gift award 1984), Alpha Lambda Delta, Kappa Delta Sigma, Phi Delta Kappa (Tchr. of Yr. 1989). Lutheran. Avocations: reading, travel, fine arts, computers. Office: Brunswick High Sch Habersham St Brunswick GA 31520

TALBOTT, NANCY COSTIGAN, science educator; b. Hutchinson, Kans., July 26, 1941; d. Loyd L. and Dorothy I. (Scheele) McQuilliam; m. James I. Costigan (dec. May 1991); children: James T. Costigan, Jayne Costigan Inlow, Jeanne Costigan, Jennifer Costigan Burr; m. William C. Talbott, Sept. 24, 1994. BS in Edn., Ft. Hays Kans. State U., 1963, MS in Comm., 1991. Tchr. Unified Sch. Dist. 489, Hays, Kans., 1963-64, 77—. Keynote spkr. Phi Delta Kappa, Kans., 1992-96; state leadership team Operation Phys. Sci., Kans., 1992—; nat. leadership team Operation Primary Phys. Sci., 1993—; assembly presenter Physics Is Fun, Kans., Okla. and Colo., 1990—. Bd. dirs., pres. Parish Coun., Immaculate Heart of Mary, 1991—; emcee Gov.'s Scholars Award Program, Topeka, 1994; state leadership team Kans. Excellence in Edn., Topeka, 1994—. Named Milken Nat. Educator, Milken Family Found., 1993, Kans. Tchr. of Yr., Kans. Bd. of Edn., 1994; recipient Ann. Award for Excellence in Tchg., Nancy Landon Kassebaum, 1993; Christa McAuliffe fellow, 1990-91; Eisenhower grantee, 1991, 92, 96. Mem. NEA, (nat. rep. local and state chpts. 1980—), Kans. Assn. Tchrs. of Sci. (bd. dirs., dist. rep. 1989-95), Univ. Alumni Assn. (bd. dirs. 1991—), Phi Kappa Phi. Roman Catholic. Avocations: golf, traveling, reading, bridge. Office: Kennedy Mid Sch 1309 Fort St Hays KS 67601-3742

TALEFF, MICHAEL JAMES, chemical dependency educator, consultant; b. Pitts., Apr. 10, 1945; s. Michael Elo and Stella Taleff; m. Audrey Elaine Cole, Aug. 7, 1971; children: Stephanie Dawn, Joseph Michael. BA in Clin. Psychology, Ind. U. of Pa., 1972, MA in Counselor Edn., 1974; PhD in Counselor Edn., U. Pitts., 1987. Registered instr. Office Drug & Alcohol Programs, Pa. Therapist Community Mental Health Ctr. Beaver County, 1974-76, Gateway Rehab. Ctr., Aliquippa, Pa., 1976-84; clin. dir. Roxbury Treatment Ctr., Shippensburg, Pa., 1984, Cove Forge Treatment Ctr., Williamsburg, Pa., 1984-87, Ligonier (Pa.) Valley Treatment Ctr., 1987-88; cons., instr., condr. workshops Edn. & Cons. Svc., 1988—; asst. prof., coord. chem. dependency counselor tng. program Pa. State U., University Park, 1992-93, coord. master's program in chem. dependency, 1993—2001. Part-time instr. Pa. State U., 1985-2001; coord. Ctr. Substance Abuse U. Hawaii, 2001—; ctrl. Pa. rep. Pa. Drug and Alcohol Cert. Bd., 1981-87; condr. workshops Rutgers Sch. Alcohol Studies, 1989, 90, 91, 92, 93, 94, 95, 96, 97, 98, 99, ACA Conf. 1998, 99, NAAOAC Conf., 1998, 99, The Meadows Psychiat. Ctr., 1990; editor Jour. of Teaching in Addictions, 2001-. Contbr. articles to profl. jours. Sgt. USAF, 1965-69. Mem. ACA, Nat. Assn. Cert. Chem. Dependency Counselors, Nat. Assn. Alcoholism and Drug Abuse Counselors, Hawaii Cert. Substance Abuse Counselor, Planetary Soc., Incase Internat. (pres. 1997-98, 2003-), Avocation: astronomy.

TALIAFERRO, JAMES HUBERT, JR., communications educator; b. Chattanooga, Feb. 21, 1924; s. James Hubert and Ida Estelle (Gilbert) T. Student, Davidson Coll., 1942-43; BS, U. Denver, 1948; MS, Columbia U., 1949; PhD, NYU, 1976. Advt. exec. McCann-Erickson Inc., N.Y.C., 1951-53, Grey Advt. Agy., N.Y.C., 1953-55, Kenyon & Eckhardt, Inc., N.Y.C., 1955-61, Sullivan Stauffer Colwell & Bayles, N.Y.C., 1961-68; instr. speech Bklyn. Coll., CUNY, N.Y.C., 1968-75, asst. prof., 1975-82, dep. chmn. dept. speech, 1980-82; prof. dept. communications Rutgers U., New Brunswick, N.J., 1982—; ptnr. Lifestory, Inc., 1985-94. Vis. prof. Fashion Inst. Tech., N.Y.C., 1987-90; ptnr. Taliaferro/Grau & Assocs., Ltd.; cons. in field; assoc. producer New Am. Playwright Series, 1970; assoc. dir. Reading for Blind, Bklyn. Coll., 1976-80; drama critic Housatonic Valley Pub. Co. newspapers, 1973-85. Author plays: Inside Out, 1963; Tour de Force, 1963; also articles, papers. Chmn. Foun. for Mus. of Am. Theatre, 1974-80; trustee Rahway Landmarks Assn. (N.J.), 1983-85; bd. dirs. 320 E 57th St. Corp., 1982-86; bd. dirs., dir. pub. rels. Health House, Chattanooga; bd. dirs. Chattanooga Cares; mem. vestry Christ Ch., Chattanooga. With U.S. Army, 1943-45. Mem. Am. Soc. Theatre Rsch., Internat. Communication Assn., Speech Communication Assn., Eastern Communication Assn., Huguenot Soc. Am., SAR Democrat. Episcopalian. Home: 249 Sunset Dr Rising Fawn GA 30738-4120 Office: Rutgers U Dept Comm Sch Comm Info Libr Sci New Brunswick NJ 08903

TALLEY, DORIS LANIER, instructional technology specialist; b. Asheboro, N.C., Aug. 21, 1949; d. James Wayne and Edith (Dunning) L.; m. Wayne F. Talley, Nov. 15, 1970; children: A. Suzanne Talley Hawkins, Elizabeth Crystal Talley. BS in Elem. Edn., Appalachian State U., 1971; MLS, U. N.C., Greensboro, 1979. Cert. tchr., media specialist, N.C. Classroom tchr. Randolph County Schs., Asheboro, N.C., 1971-83, media coord., 1983-99, instrnl. tech. specialist, 1999—. In-service instr. for Asheboro City and Randolph County tchrs., 1990-95; instr. in computer operation, Randolph C.C., Asheboro, N.C., 1996-97. Story Teller Seagrove (N.C.) Country Days, 1996, Randolph County (N.C.) Pub. Libr., various civic events, Asheboro, 1995-96. Mem. N.C. Assn. for Ednl. Comms. and Tech. (conf. presenter 1995), N.C. Libr. Assn. (conf. presenter 1988, 98), Delta Kappa Gamma (Delta Nu chpt.). Democrat. Methodist. Avocations: reading, story telling, exercise and fitness, travel. Home: 2695 Hickory Dr Asheboro NC 27205-1669 Office: 2222 S Fayetteville St Ste C Asheboro NC 27205-7368

TALLEY, MELVIN GARY, academic administrator; b. West Chester, Pa., Feb. 26, 1945; s. Melvin G. and Alberta M. (Faddis) T.; m. Jolene Keller (div.); children: Kristin Jolene, Mark Gary. BS, Pa. State U., 1967; D (hon.), Bristol (Tenn.) Coll., 1988; MBA, U. Mo., 1998. Registered rep. DeHaven & Townsend, Phila., 1967-68; dir. Brown Mackie Coll., Salina and Overland Park, Kans., 1968-72, pres., 1972—94, also bd. dirs.; mng. ptnr. ETG, LP, 2002—. Pres. Realty Mgmt. Investment Co., Salina, 1976—94; advisor region VI HEW, 1976-86, chmn. Region VII Adv. Proprietary Coun., 1989; mem. adv. bd. U.S. Office of Edn., 1988; chmn. region VII Coun. for Pvt. Career Colls. and Schs., 1989. Author: Reassessing Values in Postsecondary Edn., 1977. Bd. dirs. St. Francis Boys Home, Salina, 1975. Mem. Pvt. Edn. Research Council, Inner Circle, Assn. Ind. Colls. and Schs. (bd. dirs. Washington chpt. 1968-78), Cheyenne Savings and Loan Assn. (bd. dirs.). Home: 4609 W 113th Terr Brittany Ct Leawood KS 66211 Office: Brown Mackie Coll 126 S Santa Fe Ave Salina KS 67401-2810

TALLMAN, CLIFFORD WAYNE, retired school system administrator, consultant; b. Columbus, Ohio, June 13, 1932; s. Frank Albert and Ella Louise (Ott) T.; m. Ruth Anne Fletcher, Apr. 6, 1958; children: Martin, David, Kathryn Haines. BS in Edn., Capital U., 1954; MA, Ohio State U., 1960; EdS, Bowling Green U., 1965. Cert. supt., Ohio, Ill., Mich., Ky., Pa., N.Y. Tchr. Southwestern City Schs., Grove City, Ohio, 1954-60; supt. Republic (Ohio) Local Schs., 1960-63, Columbus Grove Schs., Grove City, 1963-65, Jackson Local Schs., Massillon, Ohio, 1965-73, Brecksville (Ohio) City Schs., 1973-78, Kent County Schs., Independence, Ky., 1978-80, Otsego Local Schs., Tontogany, Ohio, 1980-86; prof. Bowling Green (Ohio) U., 1980-86; supt. Coloma (Mich.) Community Schs., 1986—94; pres. Tallman Ednl. Cons., 1993—2003. Prof. Southwestern C.C., 1996-97; ednl. cons. AMA, Chgo., 1963; commr. Right to Read, Washington, 1973; cons. Am. Arbitratioin Assn., Tech. Adv. Svcs. for Attys.; speaker at local, state and nat. edn. profl. orgns. Contbr. articles to profl. jours. Active Berrien County Hist. Assn., Coloma, Selective Svc. Bd., Washington; newsletter editor Rotary Club, Coloma, 1986-90. With USNR, 1951-54, USA, 1954-56. I/D/E/A scholar, 1969; Found. for Econ. Edn. scholar, 1971; named to Honorable Order Ky. Cols. Mem. Ohio Edn. Assn., Mich. Assn. Sch. Bds., Berrien Assn. Sch. Adminstrs., Am. Assn. Sch. Adminstrs., Mich. Assn. Sch. Adminstrs., Buckeye Assn. Sch. Adminstrs., Coloma C. of C., Bowling Green U. Alumni Assn., Rotary, Lions, Phi Delta Kappa. Lutheran. Avocations: gardening, computers, organ music, chess, traveling. Home: 5540 Red Arrow Hwy Coloma MI 49038-8943 Office: PO Box 550 Coloma MI 49038-0550

TALMADGE, MARY CHRISTINE, nursing educator; b. Monticello, Ga., Nov. 6, 1940; d. Herbert Pope and Margaret (Allen) T.; m. Larry Benson, Aug. 10, 1962 (div. 1975). Diploma, Crawford W. Long Hosp. Sch. of Nursing, Atlanta, 1961; BSN, U. Dayton, 1966; MPH, U. Hawaii, 1971, PhD, 1989. RN; cert. Family Life Edn. Staff charge nurse Crawford W. Long Hosp., Atlanta, 1961-62; instr. LPN program Dayton (Ohio) Bd. Edn., 1963-66; instr. Miami Valley Hosp. Sch. of Nursing, Dayton, 1967-69; clin. nurse specialist Hawaii State Hosp., Kaneohe, 1970-77, dir. nursing, 1978-80; adminstrv. asst. to dir. health Hawaii State Dept. of Health, Honolulu, 1977-78; clin. nurse specialist Windward Community Counseling Ctr., Kaneohe, 1980-83; asst. prof. U. Hawaii, 1983-85; assoc. prof. Hawaii Loa Coll., Kaneohe, 1987-89; assoc. prof., acting dept. head Ga. So. U., Statesboro, 1990-93; prof., chair dept. nursing Calif. State U., Long

Beach, 1993—. Cons. Tokyo Women's Med. Coll. Sch. of Nursing, 1988-90; local and internat. healthcare orgns. Sec., mem. Gov.'s Commn. on Mental Health and Criminal Justice, Honolulu, 1978-80; mem., chmn. Windward Oahu Svc. Area Bd. on Mental Health and Substance Abuse, Honolulu, 1985-86; candidate Neighborhood Bd. Kaneohe, 1988; bd. dirs. New Beginnings for Children; chair nursing task force, health com. Statesboro C. of C. Recipient Cmty. Svc. award African-Am. Caucus, Ga. So. U., 1993. Mem. Nat. League Nursing, Sigma Theta Tau, Phi Kappa Phi (faculty 1995). Democrat. Methodist. Avocation: breeder and handler of miniature schnauzers. Office: Calif State U Nursing Bldg Rm 17 Long Beach CA 90802

TALMAGE, LISA BIRNSTEIN, music educator; b. Riverhead, N.Y., 1966; d. Alfred Rudolf and Edith Laviny Birnstein; m. Douglas Talmage, July 22, 1989; 2 children. MusB in Flute Performance, New England Conservatory, 1988; MS in Edn., C.W. Post Coll./L.I. U., 1991. Cert. tchr. music K-12. Flute instr. Foxborough (Mass.) H.S., 1987-88; chamber music instr. N.E. Conservatory Prep. Div., Boston, 1987-88; flute instr. The Music Box, Riverhead, 1988-89, Ea. Suffolk Sch. Music, Riverhead, 1988-89; choral instr. Riverhead Mid. Sch., 1991—99; band instr. grades 5-6 Pulaski St. Elem. Sch., 1999—; band instr. grade 4 Riley Ave. Elem. Sch., 1990—; pvt. flute instr., 1990—. Choir dir. Our Redeemer Luth. Ch., Aquebogue, N.Y., 1990-91, First Congl. Ch., Riverhead, 1992-93. Named winner club competition N.Y. Flute Club, 1987, C.W. Post Concerto Competition, 1990. Mem. NY State Band Assn., Music Educators Nat. Conf., N.Y. State Sch. Music Assn., Suffolk County Music Educators Assn. (exec. bd. dirs. 1992-94, choral festival chair 1992-94), Mu Phi Epsilon (N.Y.C. alumni chpt.). Office: Pulaski St Elem Sch 300 Pulaski St Riverhead NY 11901 Home: 2916 Sound Ave Riverhead NY 11901-1113

TAM, FRANCIS MAN KEI, physics educator; b. Macao, Asia, Dec. 7, 1938; came to U.S., 1960; naturalized, 1974; s. Anthony Wai Chiu and Agatha (Yeung) Tam; m. Margaret McGann, Oct. 28, 1978; children: Mary Christina, Peter Anthony, Matthew Philip. Gen. cert. edn., U. London, 1959; cert. of matriculation, U. Hong Kong, 1959; BA, U. Calif., Berkeley, 1963; MS, U. Minn., 1967. Reader U. Calif., Berkeley, 1962-63; teaching asst. U. Minn., Mpls., 1963-65, rsch. asst., 1965-67; asst. prof. physics Frostburg (Md.) State U., 1967-95, assoc. prof. physics, 1995. Cons. sci. fair projects Regional Edn. Svc. of Appalachia, Cumberland, Md., 1989-96. Author: Thunderstorm Electrification, 1972; reviewer textbooks in field; contbr. articles to profl. publs. Pastoral leader Mary, Servant of the Lord Prayer Community, St. Peter and Paul's Cath. Ch., Cumberland, 1977-80; advisor Dem. Club, Frostburg State Coll., 1969-70. Westinghouse Corp. grantee, 1990; recipient Outstanding Alumnus award Yuet Wah Coll., 1970. Mem. Am. Phys. Soc., Am. Geophys. Union, Am. Meteorol. Soc., Am. Assn. Physics Tchrs. (Disting. Svc. award Appalachian sect. 1991, sect. rep. 1991—, sec.-treas. 1981-91, pres. 1978-79, chmn. com. on minorities in physics edn. 1989-91, mem. com. on profl. concerns 1991-94, membership and benefits com., 1994-97, nominating com. 1997-98, com. on history and philosophy 1999-02, mem. and benefits com., 2003—). Roman Catholic. Avocations: collecting chinese antiques, table tennis, tai chi. Home: 33 Teaberry Ln Frostburg MD 21532-2301 Office: Frostburg State U Physics Dept Frostburg MD 21532 E-mail: ftam@frostburg.edu.

TAMAREN, MICHELE CAROL, special education educator; b. Hartford, Conn., Aug. 2, 1947; d. Herman Harold and Betty (Leavitt) Liss; m. David Stephen Tamaren, June 8, 1968; 1 child, Scott. BS in Elem. Edn., U. Conn., 1969; MA in Spl. Edn., St. Joseph Coll., West Hartford, Conn., 1976. Cert. elem. and spl. edn. tchr. Conn., Mass. Tchr. N.Y. Inst. Spl. Edn., Bronx, 1971-74; ednl. cons. Renbrook Sch., West Hartford, 1975-78; grad. instr. St. Joseph Coll., 1978; elem. tchr. Acton (Mass.) Pub. Schs., 1969-70, tchr. spl. edn., 1978-94, inclusion and behavioral specialist, 1996-2000; learning specialist and writer Educators Pub. Svc., Cambridge, Mass., 1994-96. Ednl. cons. to schs., parents, orgns., pubs., 1980—2000. Author: (book) I Make a Difference, 1992; contbr. articles to profl. jours. Bd. dirs. United Way, Acton-Boxborough, 1996—99. Grantee, Mass. Gov.'s Alliance Against Drugs, 1992; Horace Mann grantee, Mass. Dept. Edn., 1987, 1988. Mem.: Kappa Delta Pi, Phi Kappa Phi. Avocations: travel, writing, reading, distance walking. Home and Office: 34 Constitution Way Apt D Marblehead MA 01945-4652 E-mail: mtamaren@aol.com.

TAMBORLANE, WILLIAM V., JR., physician, biomedical researcher, pediatrics educator; b. N.Y.C., Aug. 25, 1946; s. William and Eleanor (Bernabo) T.; m. Kathleen Mary Blinn, Dec. 27, 1969; children: Melissa, Amy, James. BS, Georgetown U., 1968, MD, 1972. Diplomate Am. Bd. Pediatrics, Am. Bd. Pediatric Endocrinology. Attending physician Yale New Haven Hosp., 1977—. Asst. prof. pediatrics Yale U., New Haven, 1977-81, dir. Children's Diabetes Ctr., 1977—; assoc. prof. pediatrics Sch. Medicine, New Haven, 1982-83; chief pediatric endocrinology and diabetes Yale Sch. Medicine, 1985—, prof. prdiatrics, 1986—; program dir. Yale Children's Clin. Rsch. Ctr., N.H., Conn., 1986—; chmn. Lawson Wilkens Diabetes Com., 1988-89; dir. Yale Pediatric Pharmacology Rsch. Unit, 1999—; chair steering com. Diabetes Rsch. Children Network, 2001—. Editor: Yale Guide to Children's Nutrition, 1997. Recipient Jonathan May award, Charles Best award Am. Diabetes Assn., 1979, Clin. Investigator award NIH, 1979-82. Mem. Am. Fedn. Clin. Rsch., Am. Soc. Clin. Investigation, Endocrine Soc., Soc. Pediatric Rsch., Phi Beta Kappa. Office: Yale U Sch Med Children's Clin Rsch Ctr 333 Cedar St New Haven CT 06510-3289

TAMBURRO, BARBARA BOSCAINO, educator; b. Newark, Sept. 15, 1954; d. Michael Archangel and Marion (Alfano) Boscaino; m. Ronald R. Tamburro, June 5, 1982. BA in Music Edn., Montclair State U., 1976; MA in Music, Jersey City State Coll., 1978; DLitt, Drew U., 2002. Tchr., conductor Livingston (N.J.) Pub. Schs., 1979—; pres., founder Encore Strings, Inc., Verona, N.J., 1995—. Performer (violin) Encore String Quartet, 1986—; rec. artist Fox, Vangelder & Mini Sound Studios; author: The Corda Collection; contbg. editor Maestronet Pub. Mem. NEA, Am. String Tchrs. Assn., Music Educators Nat. Conf. Avocation: travel. Home: 123 Crescent Rd Florham Park NJ 07932 Office: Livingston High Sch 30 Robert Harp Dr Livingston NJ 07039

TAMBURRO, PETER JAMES, JR., secondary school educator; b. Hoboken, N.J., Jan. 20, 1947; s. Peter James and Rose Catherine (Verta) Tamburro; m. Andrea Everitt Huber, Aug. 21, 1976 (div. 1998); children: Peter James III, Christopher Harding, Matthew Everitt. BA in Polit. Sci, Dickinson Coll., 1969; MAT in Social Studies, Trenton State Coll., 1973. Cert. secondary sch. tchr., social studies N.J. Tchr. Morris Sch. Dist., Morristown, N.J., 1973-76, Hanover Park Regional H.S. Dist., East Hanover, NJ, 1976—. Cross country coach Hanover Park H.S., East Hanover, 1983—2003, volleyball coach, 1990—98, asst. basketball coach, 1994—2001; judge Bicentennial Com., NJ; asst. basketball coach Caldwell (N.J.) Coll., 1989—93; cons. Hist. Commn., East Hanover, 1989—92; cons. for developing Advanced Placement history programs, reader Advanced Placement exams ETS; mem. hist. com. Washington Twp., 1994—97, curriculum adv. com., 1996—97; adj. prof. William Paterson U., NJ, 1999—; spkr. in field. Author: (book) Gateway to Morris, 1993, Learn Chess from the Greats, 2000; editor (with Dale Brandreth): The Chess Diary of Rudolph Spielmann; editor: Atlantic Chess News, 1973—76, 2000—02; contbr. articles to chess mags.; nationally syndicated columnist: U.S. Chess Fedn., 1994—2001, columnist: Chessmates, Newark Star Ledger, 1997—; host internet radio show Openings for Amateurs, www.chess.fm. Mem. Hist. Commn., Washington Twp., NJ, 1994—96; scoutmaster Boy Scouts Am., 1994—97; team capt. Rep. Nat. Conv., 2000; Rep. County Committeeman Hanover Twp., NJ, 1984—88; legis. aide Assemblyman Robert Martin, Trenton, 1985—89; Rep. County Committeeman Morristown, NJ, 2002—03. Named N.J.'s Outstanding Tchr. History, DAR, 1990, Cross Country State Section Champions, 1987, 2000, 2001, 2002, Morris County Coach of the Yr., Cross Country, 2000; fellow Taft Inst. Two Party Govt., Fairleigh Dickinson U., 1984, Woodrow Wilson Found., 1991, Nat., Coun. Basic Edn., Washington, 1993; grantee, NSF, 1978, Dodge Found., Madison, N.J., 1987. Mem.: Chess Journalists Am. (v.p. 1990—99, pres. 1999—, awards 1995, 1996, 1997, 2002, 2003), U.S. Chess Fedn. (nat. chmn. hist. com. 1994—99), N.J. Edn. Assn., Hanover Park Regional Ednl. Assn. (v.p. 1994—95, pres. 1995—2001), Morris County Hist. Soc., Nat. Coun. Social Studies. Avocations: rare books, chess. Home: 22 Budd St Morristown NJ 07960-5304 Office: Hanover Park High Sch 63 Mount Pleasant Ave East Hanover NJ 07936-2601

TAMEZ GUERRA, REYES S. secretary of public education for Mexico; b. Monterrey, Nuevo León, Mex., Apr. 18, 1953; BS in Parasitological Bacteriological Chemistry, U. Nuevo León; MS, DS, Nat.Sch. Biol. Scis., Nat. Polytech. Inst. Asst. prof. Nat. Polytech Inst.; assoc. prof. Zaragosa Nat. Sch. Profl. Studies of UNAM; prof. Immunology and Chemoimmunity Autonomous U. Nueva León, Mexico, pres.; sec. of public edn. México, Mex. City, 2000—. Mem. appraisal com. for scholarships and rsch. projects Asst. Directorate of Sci. Devel. CONACyT; lectr. to sci. groups Various world wide.; mem. com. coop. and study Univs. of Latin Am.; chmn. of northeastern regional coun., mem. nat coun. ANUIES; alt v.p. Am. Univ. Orgn. Author: books; contbr. articles. Office: Office Pub Edn de Orgentina de Gonzalez Obregon # 28 06029 Mexico City Mexico

TAMORI, DAVID ISAMU, secondary education educator; b. Oakland, Calif., Sept. 20, 1949; s. Shoji Masaharu and Shizu (Akiyama) T.; m. Carolee Jean Zoff, Feb. 14; children: Tina Maria Tamori Riggs, Leanna Gean Lundfords, Mesha Lynn Bowers. AA, Diablo Valley Coll., 1969; BA, Chico State Coll., 1970, secondary tchg. credential, 1971. Cert. in art for early adolescence through young adulthood. Art tchr., chmn. dept. visual and performing arts Oroville (Calif.) High Sch., 1973—, head coach wrestling, 1973—. Staff mem. Calif. Art Project, Calif. State U., Humboldt, Walker Creek and Chico, 1989—; art panelist Calif. Commn. Tchr. Credentialling, Sacramento, 1990-92; art panelist Ednl. Testing Svc., Princeton, N.J., 1990—; mem. Nat. Bd. for Profl. Teaching Stds./Far West Lab. for Ednl. R&D Art Assessment, 1994—; mem. bias rev. commn. Nat. Evaluation Sys., Inc., 1994—. Devel. team mgr., scorer trainer Sensei Concord/Oroville Judo Club, 1973—, yodan 4 degree black belt. Mem. Nat. Art Edn. Assn. (Pacific Region Secondary Art Educator of Yr. 1999), Calif. Arts Edn. Assn. (North Area past pres., Secondary Art Educator of Yr. 1992-93), Calif. Tchrs. Assn., Oroville Secondary Tchrs. Assn., Calif. Arts Project. Avocations: middle-east drumming, ceramics, jewelry design, computer videographics. Home: 111 Putnam Dr Oroville CA 95966-9244 E-mail: dtamori@cncnet.com.

TAMPLIN, MARY RANKE, secondary education educator; b. Boston, July 12, 1954; d. Robert Alexander and Sarah Helen (Johnsen) Ranke; m. James Alan Tamplin, May 6, 1989. MusB in Edn., Peabody Conservatory, 1976, BA, 1978, MusM, 1979. Sr. mem. staff Peabody Prep. Sch., Balt., 1975—. Founder, coord. Peabody Prep Br. Md. Hall Creative Arts, Annapolis, 1982-83; supervising tchr., cons. Harbour Sch., Annapolis, 1992-94. Author: (with others) Dr. Edward Gordon's Book on Learning Theory, 1987. Mem. St. John the Evangelist Ch., Severna Pk., Md., 1971-82, dir. music, 1979-82, organist, substitute choir dir., children's choir dir., 2003—; com. mem. music divsn., Archdiocese Balt., 1981-83; vol. Md. Hall Creative Arts, Annapolis, 1984—. Md. State Senatorial scholar, 1972-76; recipient Three Arts Club of Homeland award, 1973. Mem. Music Tchrs. Nat. Assn., Md. State Music Tchrs. Assn., Anne Arundel County Music Tchrs. Assn. (sec. 1997—), Am. Liszt Soc., Coll. Music Soc., Mu Phi Epsilon (pres., achievement award, 1975). Roman Catholic. Avocations: sailing, crafts, reading. Home: 24 Baldridge Rd Annapolis MD 21401-2241 Office: Peabody Preparatory Sch 21 E Mount Vernon Pl Baltimore MD 21202-2308 E-mail: mtamplin@peabody.jnu.edu.

TAN, COLLEEN WOO, communications educator; b. San Francisco, May 6, 1923; d. Mr. and Mrs. S.H. Nq Quinn; m. Lawrence K.J. Tan; children: Lawrence L., Lance C. BA in English/Am. Lit., Ind. U., 1950, MA in English, 1952; MA in Speech Arts, Whittier Coll., 1972; postgrad., U. Calif. Berkeley, 1952-53. Cert. secondary edn. tchr., K-12, community coll., Calif. Tchng. aide English U. Calif., Berkeley, 1952-53; tchr. English and Social Studies Whittier (Calif.) High Sch., 1957-60; prof. speech comms. Mt. San Antonio Coll., Walnut, Calif., 1960-94; dir. forensics, 1969-80; sen. acad. senate Mt. San Antonio Coll., Walnut, Calif., 1982-90, faculty rep., 1990—. Recipient Woman of Achievement Edn. award San Gabriel Valley, Calif. YWCA, 1995; named Outstanding Prof. Emeritus, Mt. San Antonio Coll. Found., 1994. Mem. AAUW (pres. Whittier Br. 1982, cultural interests chair Calif. state divsn. 1985-87, Fellowship award 1973-74, Las Distinguidas award 1992), Calif. Asian-Am. Faculty Assn., Delta Kappa Gamma, Phi Beta Kappa (Outstanding Educator of Am. award 1972). Roman Catholic. Avocations: creative writing, reading fiction, attending theater, music, dance. Home: 13724 Sunrise Dr Whittier CA 90602-2547 Office: Mt San Antonio 1100 N Grand Ave Walnut CA 91789-1341

TAN, HUI QIAN, computer science and civil engineering educator; b. Tsingtao, China, June 12, 1948; s. Dumen Tan and Ruifan Rao; m. Ren Zhong, June 16, 1994; children: William W., Danny D. BA, Oberlin Coll., 1982; MS, Kent State U., 1984, PhD, 1986. Asst. prof. computer sci. and civil engring. U. Akron, Ohio, 1986-89, assoc., 1990—; rsch. prof. Kent (Ohio) State U., 1987. Contbr. articles to profl. jours. Grantee NASA, 1987—, 91—, NSF, 1988-92. Mem. IEEE Computer Soc., Assn. for Computing Machinery, SIGSAM Assn. for Computing Machinery, Phi Beta Kappa. Avocations: classical music, history, literature, swimming, cycling.

TAN, WAI-YUAN, statistics educator, researcher; b. China, Aug. 14, 1934; came to U.S., 1969; m. Shiow-Jen Lin, Dec. 12, 1964; children: Emy, Eden. MS in Math., U. Wis., 1963, PhD in Stats., 1964. Assoc. prof. Wash. State U., Pullman, 1972-75; prof. Memphis State U., 1975-90, rsch. prof., 1990—. Cancer expert NCI/NIH, Bethesda, Md., 1984-85, IPA, 1986-87; vis. scientist CIIT, Research Triangle Park, N.C., 1988; math. statist. Ctrs. for Disease Control, Atlanta, 1990; vis. prof. Emory U., Atlanta, 1990; AIDS study sect. NIH, Bethesda, 1989—. Author: Robust Inferences, 1986, Stochastic Models of Carcinogenesis, 1991, Sampling Distributions of Laguerre Polynomials and Applications, 1998, Stochastic Models of AIDS Epidemiology and HIV Pathogenesis, 2000, Stochastic Models with Applications to Genetics, Cancers, AIDS and Other Biomedical Systems, 2002; contbr. over 185 articles to profl. jours. Grantee Oak Ridge Nat. Lab., 1980, NSF, 1982-84, EPA, 1989-95, NIH, 1993-99, ASA, 1995—. Fellow: Am. Statis. Assn.; mem.: Chinese Statis. Assoc., Biometric Soc., Internat. Statis. Inst. Home: 8031 Brooxie Cv Memphis TN 38138-8102 Office: U Memphis Dept Math Scis Memphis TN 38152-0001

TANAKA, KAY, genetics educator; b. Osaka, Japan, Mar. 2, 1929; came to U.S., 1969; d. Kumaji and Fusa (Nakamae) T.; m. Tomoko Hasegawa, Nov. 5, 1954; children: Atau, Elly Margaret. MD, U. Tokyo, 1956, Dr. Med. Sci., 1961; MA (hon.), Yale U., 1983. Asst. prof. medicine Harvard Med. Sch., Boston, 1969-73; sr. rsch. scientist Yale U., New Haven, Conn., 1973-82, prof. genetics, 1983-94, prof. emeritus, 1995—. Mem. biochemistry study sect. NIH, Bethesda, Md., 1983-84. Contbr. numerous articles to sci. jours., chpts. to books. Grantee NIH, 1971-95, March of Dimes, 1974-92. Mem. Am. Soc. Biol. Chemistry, Am. Soc. Human Genetics, Soc. Inborn Metabolic Disorders. Office: Yale U Dept Genetics 333 Cedar St New Haven CT 06510-3289

TANDON, RAJIV, psychiatrist, educator; b. Kanpur, India, Aug. 3, 1956; came to U.S., 1984; s. Bhagwan Sarup and Usha (Mehrotra) T.; m. Chanchal Nammi Vohra; children: Neeraj, Anisha, Gitanjali. Student, St. Xavier's Coll., Bombay, India, 1974; BS, All India Inst., New Delhi, 1980; MD, Nat. Inst. of MH, India, 1983. Sr. resident Mental Health and Neuro-Scis., India, 1983-84; resident U. Mich. Hosps., Ann Arbor, 1984-87, attending psychiatrist, 1987-2000. Dir. schizophrenia program, dir. hosp. svcs. divsn. U. Mich., Ann Arbor, 1987—2000, assoc. prof., 1993—99, prof., 1999—; cons. Lenawee County Cmty. Mental Health, Adrian, Mich., 1985—99. Author: Biochemical Parameters of Mixed Affective States; Negative Schizophrenic Symptoms: Pathophysiology and Clinical Implications; contbr. more than 120 articles to profl. jours. Recipient Young Scientist's award Biennial Winter workshop on Schizophrenia, 1990, 92, Travel award Am. Coll. Neuropsychopharmacology/Mead, 1990, Rsch. Excellence award Am. Assn. Psychiatrists from India, 1993, Sci. award, Best Drs. in Am. award, 1994-98, Gerald Klerman award for outstanding rsch. by a Nat. Alliance for Rsch. in Schizophrenia and Depression young investigator, 1995, FuturPsych award CINP, 1997. Mem. Am. Psychiat. Assn. (Wisniewski Young Psychiatrist Rschr. award 1993), World Fedn. Mental Health, Soc. for Neurosci., N.Y. Acad. Scis., Soc. Biol. Psychiatry, Mich. Psychiat. Soc. Democrat. Hindu. Office: U Mich Med Ctr Dept Psychiatry Box 0120 1500 E Medical Center Dr # 9C Ann Arbor MI 48109-0005

TANELLA, VALERIE CAGIANO, elementary school educator; b. Hopatcong, N.J., July 25, 1936; d. Valentine and Rosalie (Balzano) Cagiano; m. Anthony F. Tanella, Sept. 5, 1969; children: Christine, Robert, Dean. BS in Elem. Edn., William Paterson Coll., 1969; MA, Marywood Coll, 1981; post grad. studies, Jersey City Coll, 1981-83. 2d grade tchr. Mt. Olive (N.J.) Bd. Edn., 1967-69; tchr. Hopatcong (N.J.) Bd. of Edn., 1970—98; ret. Named Sussex County Tchr. of Yr, 1983-84, Sussex County Supt.'s Assn., Hopatcong Tchr. of Influence, Hopatcong H.S. Nat. Honor Soc., 1990, 92. Mem. Sussex County Tchrs. of Yr., 1991—. Roman Catholic. Avocations: reading, swimming, family, travel. Office: Hopatcong Middle Sch PO Box 1029 Hopatcong NJ 07843-0829 Home: PO Box 2103 Tarpon Springs FL 34688-2103

TANENBAUM, BASIL SAMUEL, engineering educator; b. Providence, Dec. 1, 1934; s. Harry Milton and Rena Ada (Herr) Tanenbaum; m. Carol Binder, Aug. 26, 1956; children: Laurie, Stephen, David. BS summa cum laude, Brown U., 1956; MS, Yale U., 1957, PhD in Physics, 1960. Staff physicist Raytheon Co., Waltham, Mass., 1960-63; prof. engring. Case Western Res. U., Cleve., 1963-75; prof. Harvey Mudd Coll., Claremont, Calif., 1975—, Norman F. Sprague, Jr. prof. life scis., 1996—, dean faculty, 1975-93. Vis. scientist Arecibo (P.R.) Obs. Cornell U., 1968—69; vis. assoc. prof. Northwestern U., Evanston, Ill., 1970; mem. sci. adv. com. Nat. Astronomy and Ionosphere Ctr., 1972—77; dir. Minority Engrs. Indsl. Opportunity Program, 1973—75; mem. sci. adv. com. Calif. Poly. Inst., Pomona, 1976—87; mem. engring. and sci. adv. com. Calif. State U., Fullerton, 1976—87; dir. summer sci. program Thacher Sch., Ojai, Calif., 1977—82; vis. scholar Laser Inst. U. Calif., Irvine, Calif., 1993—94, Irvine, 1998, Irvine, 2000—, mem. biomedical engring. adv. com., 2000—; mem. nat. adv. com. Rowan Coll., Glassboro, NJ, 1993—2000; mem. Eisenhower adv. com. Calif. Postsecondary Edn. Com., 1993—97; pres.'s adv. coun. Olin Coll. Engring., Needham, Mass., 2001—, vice chmn., 2001, chmn., 02; interim assoc. dean joint sci. dept. The Claremont Colls., 2003—; cons. in field. Author: (book) Plasma Physics, 1967. Trustee Western U. Health Scis., Pomona, 1997—. Recipient Tchg. award, Case Western Res. U., 1974; fellow Woods Hole Oceanog. Inst. fellow, 1959, NSF fellow, Yale U., 1956—60, Sr. Sterling fellow, 1959. Mem.: AAUP, IEEE, AAAS, Am. Soc. Engring. Edn., Am. Phys. Soc., Sigma Xi (Rsch. award 1969). Home: 611 W Delaware Dr Claremont CA 91711-3458 Office: Harvey Mudd Coll 301 E 12th St Claremont CA 91711-5901 E-mail: sam_tanenbaum@hmc.edu.

TANG, DEBBY TSENG, counselor; b. Taichung, Taiwan, Aug. 20, 1956; came to U.S., 1979 MS, Purdue U., 1980, PhD, 1984. Nat. cert. counselor and career counselor; lic. profl. counselor, Mich.; lic. clin. profl. counselor, Ill. Counselor Purdue U., West Lafayette, Ind., 1981-84; oranizational cons. U. Mich., Ann Arbor, 1984-86; counselor Wayne State U., Detroit, 1987-95, pvt. practice, 1996—. Mem. faculty Ea. Mich. U., Ysilanti, 1989—. Named Counselor of Yr., Mich. Minority Women's Network, 1989. Mem. ACCA (exec. coun. 1995-97), ACA, AAUP (Wayne State chpt. chair acad. staff steering com. 1989-90), Mich. Coll. Pers. Assn. (pres. 1993-94, editor newsletter 1989-91), Phi Kappa Phi. Home: 1337 Green Trails Dr Naperville IL 60540-7032

TANG, IRVING CHE-HONG, mathematician, educator; b. Macau, China, Dec. 29, 1931; came to U.S., 1948; s. Man-yan and Susie Wei-chun (Chung) T. BS, U. Calif., Berkeley, 1952; MS, U. Ill., 1953; DS, Washington U., St. Louis, 1965. Chartered engr., Brit. Engring. Coun. Design engr. Friden Calculators, San Leandro, Calif., 1955-56; staff engr. IBM Corp., San Jose, Calif., 1956-66; postdoctoral fellow U. Oslo, 1966-68; head math. dept. NSW Inst. Tech., Sydney, Australia, 1969-76, Hong Kong Poly., 1977-89; prof. math. Phillips U., Enid, Okla., 1989-91, Oklahoma City C.C., Rose State Coll., 1991-94, Okla. State U., Oklahoma City, 1994-97, 99—, Ednl. Testing Svc., Princeton, N.J., 1997-99. Contbr. articles to profl. jours. Fellow Brit. Computer Soc.; mem. Math. Assn. Am., Hong Kong Math. Soc. (pres. 1977-81), Sigma Xi, Tau Beta Pi, Eta Kappa Nu. Office: Okla State U Math Dept Oklahoma City OK 73107 E-mail: ictang@osuokc.edu., tangic@cal.berkeley.edu.

TANG, PAUL CHI LUNG, philosophy educator; b. Vancouver, B.C., Can., Jan. 23, 1944; came to U.S., 1971; s. Pei-sung and Violet (Wong) T. BSc with high distinction, U. B.C., 1966; MA in Edn., Simon Fraser U., Vancouver, 1971; MA, Washington U., St. Louis, 1975, PhD, 1982; cert. in bioethics, Kennedy Inst. Ethics, 1983; diploma in piano, Royal Conservatory Music, Toronto, 1962. Teaching asst. philosophy of edn. Simon Fraser U., 1969-71; instr. philosophy St. Louis C.C. at Meramec, Kirkwood, Mo., 1975-82; instr., lectr. philosophy Washington U., 1972-76; adj. asst. prof. Harris-Stowe State Coll., St. Louis, 1980-82; asst. prof. philosophy Grinnell (Iowa) Coll., 1982-85; asst. prof. to assoc. prof. to prof. dept. philosophy Calif. State U., Long Beach, 1985—, chmn. dept. philosophy, 1988-94, acting chmn., 1998. Vis. lectr. philosophy So. Ill. U., Edwardsville, 1978-79. Editor: Philosophy of Sci. Assn. Newsletter, 1985—90; asst. editor: Philosophy of Sci. acad. jour., 1972—75, dep. editor: The Social Sci. Jour., 1999—; contbr. articles to profl. publs., revs. to profl. publs. Senator Internat. Parliament for Safety and Peace, Palermo, Italy. Decorated knight Templar Order of Jerusalem, knight Order Holy Cross of Jerusalem, knight comdr. Lofsenic Ursinius Order, chevalier Grand Croix de Milice du St. Sepulcre; recipient cert. of merit Student Philosophy Assn., 1988-90, 93-94, spl. award, 1992, Calif. State Senate Recognition award for commitment to edn., 1997; named faculty advisor of yr. Assoc. Students, 1987, 90, 91, 95, Highland Lord of Camster, Scotland, 1995; Paul Tang prize in philosophy named in his honor, 1996-99; fellow Washington U., 1971, summer rsch. fellow Calif. State U., 1988, 96, NEH fellow Harvard U., 1988, NEH Summer Seminar fellow, 1988; internat. scholar Phi Beta Delta, interdisciplinary scholar Phi Kappa Phi, 1993, Phi Beta Kappa, 2000, Phi Sigma Tau; grantee vis. philosophers program Coun. for Philos. Studies, 1987, 91, 92; Disting. Vis. Scholars and Artists Fund, Calif. State U., 1988, 89, rsch. grantee, 1995, 97, 99. Fellow: World Lit. Acad.; mem.: Maison Internat. des Intellectuels de l'Acad. Francaise, Soc. Philosophy and Psychology, Brit. Soc. Philosophy of Sci., Iowa Philos. Soc. (pres. 1985—86), Hastings Ctr., Kennedy Inst. Ethics, History of Sci. Soc., Philosophy of Sci. Assn., Am. Philos. Assn. (Excellence in Tchg. award 1995, 1997), numerous others, Order Internat. Fellowship (Eng.), Companion of Honour (Eng.), Golden Key Internat. Hon. Soc. (Internat. Man of Yr. 1995—96), Internat. Order Merit (Eng.). Avocations: hiking, tennis, chess, music, travel. Home: 5050 E Garford St Apt 228 Long Beach CA 90815-2859 Office: Calif State U Dept Philosophy 1250 N Bellflower Blvd Long Beach CA 90840-0006 E-mail: pcltang@csulb.edu.

TANG, YINGCHAN EDWIN, marketing educator; b. Taipei, Taiwan, Apr. 1, 1953; came to U.S., 1981; s. Shiu-Yuan Shih; m. Chih-Ping Wang; children: James Devon, Deborah Charlotte. BA, BS, Nat. Chengchi U., Taiwan, 1976; MS in Bus. Adminstrn., Tex. Tech. U., 1984; PhD in Mgmt. Sci., U. Tex., Dallas, 1989. Rsch. asst. Nat. Chengchi U., Taiwan, 1974-76, U. Tex., Dallas, 1984-88, teaching fellow, 1987-88; vis. asst. prof. N. C. State U., 1988-91; asst. prof. mktg. N.C. State U., Raleigh, 1992-94; assoc. prof. Chinese U. of Hong Kong, 1994-96. Adv. bd. N.C. Taiwanese Found., 1990—; chair N.C. chpt. Taiwanese Am. Assn., 1994. With Chinese Marine Corps, 1976-78. Recipient Grad. Student scholarship U. Tex., Dallas, 1984-88, Best Rsch. Paper award Sixth Ann. Southwestern Doctoral Symposium on Doctoral Rsch. in Mktg., U. Houston, 1987, Southwestern Doctoral Consortium fellow, 1987. Mem. Am. Mktg. Assn. (Best of Track paper award 1996), Am. Statis. Assn., Acad. Mgmt., The Inst. of Mgmt. Sci., TIMS Mktg. Coll. Avocations: fishing, biking. Office: Marketing Dept Chinese Univ of Hong Kong Shatin Hong Kong

TANGHERLINI, TIMOTHY R. literature educator; b. Durham, N.C., Oct. 2, 1963; AB magna cum laude, Harvard U., 1985; MA in Scandinavian Studies, U. Calif., Berkeley, 1986, PhD, 1992. Cert. in Modern Icelandic, Korean lang. Video producer/editor Harvard-Danforth Ctr. for Teaching and Learning/Harvard U., Cambridge, Mass., 1981-85; rsch. asst. U. Calif., Berkeley, 1987, teaching asst. in Danish, 1986-91; vis. asst. prof. Scandinavian sect. Program in Folklore/Myth UCLA, 1991—. Contbr. articles to profl. jours. John Harvard scholar, 1984, Luce scholar, 1987-88, Bernard Osher Found. fellow, Am. Scandinavian Found. fellow, 1990, Regents fellow U. Calif., Berkeley, 1985, 91; recipient other grants and awards. Mem. MLA, Am. Anthrop. Assn., Am. Folklore Soc., Assn. Asian Studies, Foreningen Danmarks Folkeminder, Internat. Soc. for Folk Narrative Rsch., Nordic Inst. Folklore, Soc. for Advancement of Scandinavian Study. Office: UCLA Scandinavian Sect 332 Royce Hall Los Angeles CA 90024

TANICK, MARSHALL HOWARD, lawyer, law educator; b. Mpls., May 9, 1947; s. Jack and Esther (Kohn) T.; m. Cathy E. Gorlin, Feb. 20, 1982; children: Lauren, Ross. BA, U. Minn., 1969; JD, Stanford U., 1973. Bar: Calif. 1973, Minn. 1974. Law clk. to presiding justice U.S. Dist. Ct., Mpls., 1973-74; assoc. Robins, Davis & Lyons, Mpls., 1974-76; ptnr. Tanick & Heins, P.A., Mpls., 1976-89, Mansfield & Tanick, Mpls., 1989—. Prof. constrn., real estate and media law U. Minn., Mpls., 1983—, Hamline U., St. Paul, 1982—; prof. constl. law William Mitchell Coll. Law, 1994. Editor: Hennepin Lawyer, Bench, Bar and Litigation mag.; contbr. articles to mags. Avocation: writing. Home: 1230 Angelo Dr Minneapolis MN 55422-4710 Office: Mansfield & Tanick 900 2nd Ave S Ste 1560 Minneapolis MN 55402-3383

TANIS, JAMES ROBERT, library director, history educator, clergyman; b. Phillipsburg, N.J., June 26, 1928; s. John Christian and Bertha Marie (Tobiasson) T.; m. Florence Borgmann, June 26, 1963; children— Marjorie Martha, James Tobiasson. BA, Yale, 1951; B.D., Union Theol. Sem., N.Y.C., 1954; Dr. Theol., U. Utrecht, Netherlands, 1967; LittD (hon.), Dickinson Coll., Carlisle, Pa., 1994. Ordained to ministry Presbyn. Ch., 1954. Co-pastor Greystone Presbyn. Ch., Elizabeth, N.J., 1954-55; librarian, mem. faculty Harvard Div. Sch., 1956-65; univ. librarian Yale U., 1965-68; mem. faculty Yale Div. Sch., 1968-69; dir. libraries, prof. history Bryn Mawr (Pa.) Coll., 1969-97; guest curator Phila. Mus. Art, 1997—2002; parish assoc. Valley Forge Presbyn. Ch., King of Prussia, Pa., 1973—. Author: Calvinistic Pietism in the Middle Colonies, 1967; co-author: Bookbinding in America, 1983, Images of Discord/De Tweedracht Verbeeld, 1993, Fantasy and Fashion, 1996, Leaves of Gold: Manuscript Illumination from Philadelphia Collections, 2001. Decorated officer Order Orange-Nassau. Home: 11302 Shannondell Dr Audubon PA 19403 E-mail: jrtanis@sdlifestyle.com.

TANKARD, JAMES WILLIAM, JR., journalism educator, writer; b. Newport News, Va., June 20, 1941; s. James William and Eileen (Looney) T.; m. Sara Elaine Fuller, July 21, 1973; children: Amy Elizabeth, Jessica Hope, Margaret Elaine. BS, Va. Poly. Inst., 1963; MA, U. N.C., 1965; PhD, Stanford U., 1970. Newswriter AP, Charlotte, N.C., 1965; reporter The Raleigh (N.C.) Times, 1965-66; vis. asst. prof. U. Tex., Austin, 1970, U. Wis., Madison, 1970-71; asst. prof. Temple U., Phila., 1971-72, U. Tex., Austin, 1972-76, assoc. prof., 1976-82, prof., 1982—, Jesse Jones prof. in journalism, 1989—. Author: The Statistical Pioneers, 1984; co-author: Basic News Reporting, 1977, Communication Theories, 1979, 5th edit., 2001, Mass Media in the Information Age, 1990; editor Journalism Monographs, 1988-94. Mem. AAUP, Assn. for Edn. in Journalism and Mass Communication (chair rsch. com. 1987-88), Internat. Communication Assn., Soc. Profl. Journalists. Avocations: hiking, bicycling, songwriting. Home: 3300 Jamesborough St Austin TX 78703-1132 Office: U Tex Sch Journalism Austin TX 78712

TANKERSLEY, MELISSA MAUPIN, educational administrator; b. Jesup, Ga., Nov. 29, 1948; d. Elwin Courtney and Betrie Glenn (Hatcher) Maupin; m. William Little Tankersley, Apr. 19, 1968; children: Tracey, Will, Shane. BA in Elem. Edn., Furman U., 1970. Cert. tchr., N.C. 0cons. summer activities program, 1990—; tchr. Person County Schs., Roxboro, N.C., 1971-75, Greensboro (N.C.) City Schs., 1975-77; computer cons. Gail Fox Systems, Greensboro, 1987-89; computer coord. Greensboro Day Sch., 1989—, dept. chmn., 1993—. Community rep. for grantsmanship Greensboro Youth Coun., 1983; bd. dirs. Jr. League Greensboro, 1981, McIver Sch. PTA, Greensboro, 1988, Page High Sch. Booster Club; pres. Assn. for Retarded Citizens, Greensboro, 1990; mem. Greensboro Symphony Guild. Mem. ASCD, Internat. Soc. for Tech. in Edn. Democrat. Avocations: reading, water skiing.

TANKIN, RICHARD SAMUEL, fluid dynamics engineer, educator; b. Balt., July 14, 1924; s. Harry Jacob and Bertha (Haberer) T.; m. Anne Raudelunas, Dec. 2, 1956; children: Roberta, David, John. BA, Johns Hopkins U., 1948, BS, 1950; MS, MIT, 1954; PhD, Harvard U., 1960. Asst. prof. U. Del., 1960-61; mem. faculty Northwestern U., 1961—, prof. fluid dynamics, 1968—, chmn. dept. mech. engring. and astronautical scis., 1973-78. Served with AUS, 1943-44; Served with USNR, 1944-45. Mem. ASME, AIAA, Am. Geophys. Union, Tau Beta Pi. Home: 820 Ridge Ter Evanston IL 60201-2430

TANNEHILL, DARCY ANITA BARTINS, academic administrator; b. Pitts., May 14, 1958; d. Paul Joseph and Ileane Anita (Yearman) Bartins; m. Gary Edward Mack, Oct. 28, 1979 (div. Apr. 1989); 1 child, Courtney Anita; m. Norman Bruce Tannehill Jr., Feb. 14, 1991; stepchildren: Andrea, Bruce. BA, Duquesne U., 1978, MSEd, 1986; postgrad., U. Pitts., 1993—. Rsch. asst. U. Pitts., 1979-81; adult edn. tchr. Allegheny Intermediate Unit, Pitts., 1985-86, counselor, statistician, 1986-90; coord. evening programs Robert Morris U., Moon Twp., Pa., 1990—92, asst. dir. academic svcs., 1992—93, assoc. dir. academic svcs., 1993—94, assoc. dean admissions, 1994—96, assoc. dean of enrollment mgmt. adult and cont. edn., 1996—97, assoc. dean student affairs and enrollment mgmt., 1997—99, dean Pitts. Ctr., 1999—2002, dean Sch. Adult and Continuing Edn., 2002—. Mem. AAHE, Nat. Assn. Women in Edn., Pa. Am. Coun. on Edn., Nat. Identification Program, Nat. Assn. Coll. Admissions Counselors, Continuing Edn. Assn., Am. Coun. on Adult and Experiential Learning, Exec. Women Internat. Republican. Presbyterian. Avocations: reading, music. Home: 4482 Battleridge Rd Mc Donald PA 15057-2587 Office: Robert Morris U 6001 University Blvd Moon Township PA 15108 E-mail: tannehill@rmu.edu.

TANNEHILL, JOHN C. aerospace engineer, educator; b. Salem, Ill., Oct. 14, 1943; s. John Bell and Pearl Hanna (Trulin) T.; m. Marcia Kay George, Jan. 28, 1967; children: Michelle, Johnny. BS, Iowa State U., 1965, MS, 1967, PhD, 1969. Aerospace engr. NASA Flight Rsch. Ctr., Edwards, Calif., 1965; mem. tech. staff Aerospace Cor., El Segundo, Calif., 1967; NASA-ASEE fellow NASA Ames Rsch. Ctr., Moffett Field, Calif., 1970-71; asst. prof. aerospace engring. Iowa State U., Ames, 1969-74, assoc. prof., 1974-79, prof., 1979—, mgr. Computational Fluid Dynamics Ctr., 1984—. Chmn. bd. Engring. Analysis, Inc., Ames, 1976—. Co-author: Computational Fluid Mechanics and Heat Transfer, 1984, 2d edit., 1997, Handbook of Numerical Heat Transfer, 1988; contbr. articles to profl. jours. NSF trainee, 1965-68; Iowa State U. Rsch. Found. fellow, 1968-69; NASA fellow, 1970-71. Fellow AIAA (chmn. Iowa sect. 1989-91); mem. Am. Soc. Engring. Edn., Sigma Xi, Sigma Gamma Tau, Tau Beta Pi. Home: 3214 Greenwood Cir Ames IA 50014-4570 Office: Iowa State U Dept Aerospace Engring Ames IA 50011-2271

TANNEN, RICKI LEWIS, lawyer, depth psychologist, educator; b. N.Y.C., Apr. 29, 1952; d. Paul and Lillian (Singer) Lewis; m. Marc Jay Tannen, Aug. 25, 1972; children: Laine Amy, Adam Jesse. BA in Social Scis., U. Fla., 1975, MEd in Psycholinguistics, JD with honors, U. Fla., 1981; LLM, Harvard U., 1991; PhD, Pacifica Grad. Inst., 2002. Bar: Fla. 1982. Tchr., guidance counselor Oak Hall Pvt. Sch., Gainesville, Fla., 1976-79; atty., jud. clk. U.S. Dist. Cts., Miami, Fla., 1981-82; rep. assoc. Ft. Lauderdale (Fla.) News, Sun-Sentinel newspaper, Ferrero, Middlebrooks, Strickland & Fischer, 1982-88; of counsel Klein & Tannen, Hollywood, Fla., 1990-91; mem., 1992—. Mem. gender bias study commn. Fla. Supreme Ct., 1986, apptd. commr., reporter, 1987—; adj. prof. women and the law, media law, rhetoric, comm. law Fla. Atlantic U., 1984-88, 1995—; mem. faculty Chautauqua Instn., 1995-98; co-chmn. Fla. Bar Media Law Conf., 1996; rsch. coord. Ctr. for Govtl. Responsibility, Gainesville, 1979-81. Editor: Elderly Law in Florida, 1982; author: Report of the Florida Supreme Court Gender Bias Commn.; contbr. articles to profl. jours. Bd. dirs. C.G. Jung Inst. South Fla., 1996—; dir. Inner Work Studies Program, 1995—; dir. Communitas. Mem. APA, ABA, AAUW, NOW, Nat. Coun. Jewish Women, Fla. Bar Assn. (com. on equal opportunity 1988—), Fla. Assn. women Lawyers, Assn. Psychol. Type, Assn. Transpersonal Psychology. Office: 1007 S North Lake Dr Hollywood FL 33019-1314 E-mail: rtannen@gate.net.

TANNENWALD, LESLIE KEITER, rabbi, justice of peace, educational administrator, chaplain; b. Boston, May 5, 1949; d. Irving Jules and Barbara June (Caplan) Keiter; m. Robert Tannenwald. BA, Brandeis U., 1971, MA, 1976; MA in Edn. and Counseling, Simmons Coll., Boston, 1972. Cert. social worker, tchr., Mass.; justice of the peace. Sr. assoc. Combined Jewish Philanthropies of Greater Boston, 1977-84; ednl. cons. Bur. Jewish Edn., Boston, 1985-87; ednl. dir. Congregation Shalom Emeth, Burlington, Mass., 1987-92; religious sch. dir. Falmouth (Mass.) Jewish Congregation, 1993-99; pres. Jewish Life Svcs., Newton, Mass., 1993—; rabbi Temple Emmanuel, Chelsea, 2001—. Cons. Selected Ednl. Orgns., Boston, 1972; chaplain, rabbi to local nursing home facilities. Author: Curriculum, Male and Female, 1979 (Honors award 1971), Understanding the Holocaust, 1990, Awakening: Alternative Creative Learning Techniques, 1995. Officer, bd. dirs. Combined Jewish Philantropies of Greater Boston, 1972—; mem. Am. Jewish Congress, Boston, 1976—; rabbi, religious leader Sherborn Congregation, 1995—97, Congregation Agudath Achim (Medway), 1999—2001; title of damsel Imperial Order St. John Ecumenical Found. Recipient Leadership award Inst. Leadership Devel. and Fund Raising Mem. Nat. Alliance Profl. & Exec. Women, Alumni Assn. Benjamin S. Hornstein Program of Jewish Communal Svc., Assn. Jewish Community Personnel. Democrat. Avocations: swimming, watercolor painting, music. Home: 6 Clifton Rd Newton MA 02459-3147 E-mail: rabbiles18@aol.com.

TANNER, DANIEL, curriculum theory educator; b. N.Y.C., Sept. 22, 1926; s. Jack and Lillian (Jupiter) T.; m. Laurel Nan Jacobson, July 11, 1948 (div. 1988). BS with honors, Mich. State U., 1949, MS, 1952; PhD, Ohio State U., 1955. Asst. prof. edn. San Francisco State Coll., 1955-60; assoc. prof. edn., coord. Midwest program on airborne TV instrn. Purdue U., 1960-62; assoc. prof. edn., assoc. dir. internat. program for edn. leaders Northwestern U., 1962-64; assoc. prof. rsch. divsn. tchr. edn. CUNY, 1964-66; prof. edn., dir. Ctr. for Urban Edn., U. Wis.-Milw. Sch. Edn., 1966-67; prof. edn., dir. grad. programs in curriculum theory and devel. Grad. Sch. Edn., Rutgers U., New Brunswick, N.J., 1967—, chmn. dept. curriculum and instrn., 1969-72, faculty rsch. fellow, 1974-75, 88-89. Vis. lectr. U. Kansas City, summer 1956, Tchrs. Coll. Columbia, summer 1966; vis. prof. Emory U., summer 1968, SUNY, Binghamton, winter 1968, U. London, 1975, King Abdulaziz U., Saudi Arabia, winter 1992, U. Iowa, summer 1996; disting. lectr. ASCD, 1985, 86, Dewey Meml. lectr., 1984, Raths Meml. lectr., SUNY, 1984; Leadership Inst. lectr. U. Del., summer 1990; disting. lectr. Rider U., 1996; vis. scholar U. London Inst. Edn., 1974-75; mem. rev. bd. coll. work-study program U.S. Office Edn., 1965; mem. symposium on comparative curriculum history Inst. Sci. Edn. Kiel U., Fed. Republic Germany, 1989; del. leader Citizen Amb. Program, People-to-People Internat., Republic of South Africa, 1996, China, 1997, Dem. Citizenship Project Czech Republic, USIA, 1996-98; cons. U. Tex. Med. Ctr., 1961-62, Chgo. Sch. Survey, 1964-65, ctr. Urban Edn., N.Y.C., 1964-65, West Chgo. Sch. Survey, 1963-64, Nat. Ednl. TV Ctr., N.Y.C., 1963, Campbell County (Va.) Sch. Survey, 1970, Memphis Schs., 1977-78, Perth Amboy (NJ) Schs., 1996-97; ASCD Commn. on Gen. Edn., 1980-81, West Orange, N.J., Curriculum Study, 1984, ASCD Commn. on Secondary Sch. Practices, 1985, ASCD Ednl. Policy Task Force, 1985, NASSP Curriculum Coun., 1985-95; SUNY Buffalo External Evaluation, 1988; dir. Nat. Curriculum Inst., Washington, 1987; delivered Founder's Day address Delaware Valley Coll., 1985' keynote address Nat. Conf. Citizen Edn., Palacky U., Czech Rep., 1998. Author: Schools for Youth: Change and Challenge in Secondary Education, 1965, Secondary Curriculum: Theory and Development, 1971, Secondary Education: Perspectives and Prospects, 1972, Using Behavioral Objectives in the Classroom, 1972, Curriculum Development: Theory into Practice, 3rd edit., 1995, Supervision in Education, 1987, History of the School Curriculum, 1991, Crusade for Democracy: Progressive Education at the Crossroads, 1991, 2002; founding editor, contbg. author: Rsch. Rev. for Sch. Leaders, 1996, 98, 00, Philosophy of Edn. Ency., 1996, Ency. of Education, 2d edit., 2003, Curriculum Issues, 87th Yearbook NSSE, 1988, 98th Yearbook, 1999, Ency. of Ednl. Rsch., 5th edit., 1982, Readings in Education Psychology, 1965, Yearbook of the Association for Student Teaching, 1962, The Great Debate, Our Schools in Crisis, 1959, Educational Issues in a Changing Society, 1964, Programs, Teachers and Machines, 1964, Views on American Schooling, 1964, The Training of America's Teachers, 1975, Curriculum and Instruction, 1981; co-author: Teen Talk: Curriculum Materials in Communications, 1971; co-editor: Improving the School Curriculum, 1988, Restructuring for an Interdisciplinary Curriculum, 1992, Curriculum Issues and the New Century, 1995; contbg. editor: Ednl. Leadership, 1969-74; mem. editl. bd. Tex. Tech. Jour. Edn., 1984-89, Tchg. Edn., 1986-90, Jour. Curriculum Supervision; editorial cons.: Ency. of Ednl. Rsch., 5th edit., 1982, Ency. of Edn., 2d edit., 2003, Jour. Ednl. Psychology; founding editor Rev. of Rsch. for Sch. Leaders; contbr. Atlantic Monthly, Bull. of Atomic Scientists and other nat. mags., ednl. jours. Trustee Delaware Valley Coll., Doylestown, Pa., 1981-95; bd. dirs. Ohio State Alumni Assn. N.J., 1990-96. Recipient Excellence award Edn. Press Am., 1989, Distinguished Educator award Rider U., 1996; Univ. scholar Ohio State U., 1955. Fellow AAAS, John Dewey Soc. (bd. dirs. 1985-88, archivist 1989-, chmn. lectrs. commn. 1999-, pres. 2001-03); mem. AAUP, Am. Ednl. Rsch. Assn., N.Y. Acad. Scis., Am. Polit. Sci. Assn., Am. Ednl. Studies Assn., Nat. Soc. Study Edn., Phi Kappa Phi, Phi Delta Kappa (Svc. award 1957). Home: Highwood Rd Somerset NJ 08873 Office: Grad Sch Edn Rutgers U New Brunswick NJ 08901-1183 Fax: 732-732-6803.

TANNER, DEBBIE STIVLAND, elementary education educator; b. Racine, Wis., Oct. 12, 1962; d. Gary Henry and Judith Eleanor (Halstead) Stivland; m. Walter Martin Tanner, May 9, 1987. BA, Lenoir-Rhyne Coll., 1984; M in Ednl. Change and Technol. Innovation, Walden U., 1999. Cert. elem. tchr., Fla. Tchr. Luth. Parish Sch., St. Thomas, V.I., 1985-87, West Yadkin Sch., Yadkinville, N.C., 1987-89, Calusa Elem. Sch., Palm Beach County Sch., Boca Raton, Fla., 1989-98; tech. coord. Pine Grove Elem. Sch. of Arts Palm Beach (Fla.) County Sch., 1998-99, tchr. Coral Reef Elem., 1999—. Office: Coral Reef Elem 6151 Hagen Ranch Rd Lake Worth FL 33467 E-mail: imtanner@earthlink.net.

TANNER, JANE, mathematics educator; b. Syracuse, N.Y., Aug. 20, 1956; d. Francis Duane and Barbara Ann (Zimmerman) Tanner; m. David Allen Covillion, Apr. 18, 1980 (dec. Sept. 1996); m. Andrew Rowe, June 30, 2001. AB, Cornell U., 1978; MS, SUNY, Oswego, 1982; postgrad., SUNY, Syracuse, 1983-86. Cert. elem. and math. tchr., N.Y. Math. tchr. 7th grade Ray Jr. High Sch., Baldwinsville, N.Y., 1978-79; math. tchr. 6th/7th grades Zogg Mid. Sch., Liverpool, N.Y., 1979-81; tchr. math. Liverpool High Sch., 1981-82; prof. Onondaga C.C., Syracuse, 1982—; tchr. math. Lafayette (N.Y.) H.S., 1986. Text reviewer in field. Co-author: Mathematics Teacher, 1978; contbr. articles to profl. jours. Mem. planning com. Syracuse Sci. Fair, 1982-96. N.Y. State Regents scholar, 1974, James L. Sears Found. scholar, 1974. Mem. AAUW, Nat. Coun. Tchrs. Math., Assn. Math. Tchrs. N.Y. State, Math. Assn. Am., Assn. for Women in Math., N.Y. State United Tchrs., Am. Fedn. Tchrs., Onondaga County Math. Tchrs., N.Y. State Assn. Two-Yr. Colls., N.Y. State Math. Assn. Two-Yr. Colls. (pres., state scholarship chair), Am. Math. Assn. Two-Yr. Colls (prodn. mgr. AMATYC Rev.), Onondaga C.C. Fedn. Tchrs. (sec. 1987-2001, del.-at-large 2001—), Embroiderers Guild Am., Am. Needlepoint Guild (v.p.), Delta Kappa Gamma (rec. sec., pres. Beta Kappa chpt., state exec. sec., state pres.), Alpha Phi (house corp. bd. Delta chpt., sec., pres. Fingerlakes alumnae chpt., N.E. region human resources coord.). Republican. Avocations: traveling, crossword puzzles, reading, crafts. Home: 231 Searles Rd Parish NY 13131 Office: Onondaga Community Coll Math Dept Syracuse NY 13215 E-mail: tannerj@aurora.sunyocc.edu.

TANNER, JOHN DOUGLAS, JR., history educator, writer; b. Quantico, Va., Oct. 2, 1943; s. John Douglas and Dorothy Lucille (Walker) T.; m. Jo Ann Boyd, Jan. 1964 (div. Aug. 1966); 1 child, Lorena Desiree; m. Laurel Jean Selfridge, Dec. 19, 1967 (div. Oct. 1987); children: John DouglasIII, Stephen Douglas, Elizabeth Jane; m. Karen H. Olson, Apr. 16, 1988. BA, Pomona Coll., 1966; MA, Claremont Grad. U., 1968; postgrad., U. Calif., Riverside, 1976, 84-86, U. Calif., San Diego, 1984-87, U. Pacific, 1993. Cert. tchr. Calif. Asst. swimming, water polo coach Pomona Coll., 1966-69; rsch. asst. history dept. Claremont Grad. U., 1967-69; prof. history Palomar Coll., San Marcos, Calif., 1969—, pres. faculty, 1970-71, v.p. faculty senate, 1971-72. Author: Olaf Swenson and his Siberian Imports jour., 1978 (Dog Writers Assn. Am. Best Series award 1979), Campaign for Los Angeles, 1846-47, 69, Alaskan Trails, Siberian Dogs, 1998; co-author: Last of the Old-Time Outlaws: The George West Musgrave Story, 2002; co-editor: Don Juan Forster, 1970; contbr. articles to profl. jours. Citizens com. Fallbrook (Calif.) San. Dist., 1980; merit badge counselor Boy Scouts Am., 1975-85; Martin County Hist. Soc., Morgan County Hist. Soc., Fallbrook Hist. Soc., San Diego Opera Guild, San Diego Classical Music Soc., Opera Pacific Guild. Chautauqua fellow NSF, 1979. Mem. Nat. Assn. for Outlaw and Lawman History, Inc., Western Outlaw-Lawman History Assn. (adv. bd., editl. bd.), Custer Battlefield Hist. and Mus. Assn. (life), Western Writers Am., Old Trail Drivers Assn. Tex., The Westerners, So. Calif. Siberian Husky Assn. (pres. 1972-79), U.S. Shooting Team (Inner Circle), Sons of the Rep. of Tex., Western History Assn., Ariz. Hist. Soc., N.Mex. Hist. Soc., Siberian Husky Club Am. (bd. dirs. 1974-78, 1st v.p. 1978-79). Republican. Episcopalian. Avocations: collecting S.W. Indian art, backpacking, wine making, writing, opera. Home: 2308 Willow Glen Rd Fallbrook CA 92028-8605 Office: Palomar Coll 1140 W Mission Rd San Marcos CA 92069-1415

TANNER, LAUREL NAN, education educator; b. Detroit, Feb. 16, 1929; d. Howard Nicholas and Celia (Solovich) Jacobson; m. Daniel Tanner, July 11, 1948; m. Kenneth J. Rehage, Nov. 25, 1989. BS in Social Sci, Mich. State U., 1949, MA in Edn., 1953; EdD, Columbia U., 1967. Pub. sch. tchr., 1950-64; instr. tchr. edn. Hunter Coll., 1964-66, asst. prof., 1967-69; supr. Milw. Pub. Schs., 1966-67; mem. faculty Temple U., Phila., 1969—, prof. edn., 1974-89, prof. emerita, 1993—; prof. edn. U. Houston, 1989-96. Vis. professorial scholar U. London Inst. Edn., 1974-75; vis. scholar Stanford U., 1984-85, U. Chgo., 1988-89; curriculum cons., 1969—; disting. vis. prof. San Francisco State U., 1987. Author: Classroom Discipline for Effective Teaching and Learning, 1978, La Disciplina en la enseñanza y el Aprendizaje, 1980, Dewey's Laboratory School: Lessons for Today, 1997 ; co-author: Classroom Teaching and Learning, 1971, Curriculum Development: Theory into Practice, 1975, 3d edit., 1995, Supervision in Education: Problems and Practices, 1987, (with Daniel Tanner) History of the School Curriculum, 1990; editor Nat. Soc. Study Edn. Critical Issues in Curriculum, 87th yearbook, part 1, 1988. Faculty rsch. fellow Temple U., 1970, 80, 81; recipient John Dewey Rsch. award, 1981-82, Rsch. Excellence award U. Houston, 1992, Outstanding Writing award Am. Assn. Colls. Tchr. Edn., 1998; Spencer Found. rsch. grantee, 1992. Mem. ASCD (dir. 1982-84), Soc. Study Curriculum History (founder, 1st pres. 1978-79), Am. Edn. Rsch. Assn. (com. on role and status of women in edn. R & D 1994-97), Profs. Curriculum Assn. (Factotum 1983-84, chair membership com. 1994-95), Am. Ednl. Studies Assn., John Dewey Soc. (bd. dirs. 1989-91, pres. 2000-01), Alumni Coun. Tchrs. Coll. Columbia U.

TANNER, MERRILEE, special education educator; b. Kansas City, Mo., Aug. 13, 1950; BA in English, French, Washington U., St. Louis, 1972; MEd in Learning Disabilities, U. Mo., 1979, MEd in Ednl. Adminstrn., 1984; PhD in Ednl. Adminstrn., Columbia Pacific U., 1985. Cert. tchr., prin., supt., spl. edn. adminstr., Mo. Resource tchr. St. Louis Pub. Schs., 1978-81, placement specialist, 1981-85, de-segregation coord., 1985-88; tchr. of mentally retarded Spl. Sch. Dist. St. Louis County, St. Louis, 1990, tchr. spl. edn. reading, 1990—. Adj. faculty Webster U., St. Louis, 1990—; spl. edn. cons. Essex (Vt.) Town Sch. Dist., 1989. Mem. Coun. Exceptional Children (chpt. sec. 1990-91, pres.-elect 1989-90). E-mail: DrMerrilee@aol.com.

TANZI, RONALD THOMAS, artist, educator; b. Brookline, Mass., Mar. 3, 1949; s. Henry Francis and Jennie (Vicenza) T.; m. Patricia Marie Morrill, Mar. 16, 1974 (div. Apr. 1990); children: Jenni Grace, Jacob Thomas. Student, Chapman Coll., Orange, Calif., 1968-70, Ea. Wash. U., Cheney, 1970-72; BFA magna cum laude, U. Wash., 1984; MFA, U. Cin., 1986. Artist self-employed, Spokane, Boston, Seattle, 1970—; art editor Contbr.'s Copy Quar., Spokane, 1970-73; instr., lectr. U. Cin., 1984-86; instr. U. Wash., Seattle, 1986-87, Seattle Cmty. Colls. (North and Ctrl. campuses), 1987—, Edmonds (Wash.) C.C., 1992—, Bellevue (Wash.) C.C., 1993—. Dir. R's Studio Gallery, Cheney, 1971-73; visual advisor Masque Theater Co., Everett, Wash., 1987-88; lectr. Seattle Art Mus., 1991, Seattle Art League, 1992, Bellevue Art Mus., 1995. Exhibited paintings in shows including Spokane City Arts, 1971, Pacific Northwest Annual, 1976, N.W. Traditions: A Retrospective, 1987, King County Arts Commn., 1988, Faculty Art Shows, North Seattle C.C. and Bellevue C.C., 1994, 95, 96, 97, 98, 99, Philip Howe Gallery, 1998; artist, pub. commn. Metro Bus Shelter Mural Program, 1991, Harborview Med. Ctr. Mural, 1995; represented in pvt. collections in U.S., Japan, Germany, Finland. Instr. City Arts Program, Lynnwood, Wash., 1987-93, Pike Place Sr. Ctr., Seattle, 1992-94, S.E. Seattle Sr. Ctr., 1993-94, Creative Retirement Ctr., Seattle, 1993-94. Sgt. USAF, 1966-70, Vietnam. U. Cin. Grad. scholar, 1984, 85, 86. Mem. Coll.

Art Assn., Am. Fedn. Tchrs., Wash. State Fedn. Tchrs., Seattle Art Mus., Phi Beta Kappa. Avocations: swimming, hiking, travel. Office: 8820 Corliss Ave N Seattle WA 98103-4137 E-mail: rtanzi@sccd.ctc.edu.

TAO, MARIANO, biochemistry educator; b. Davao, Philippines, Mar. 3, 1938; came to U.S., 1963; s. Bong-Hua and Siu-Hua (Co) T.; m. Pearl Koh, June 3, 1967; children: Stephen, Kevin. BSChemE, Cheng Kung U., Tainan, Taiwan, 1962; PhD in Biochemistry, U. Wash., 1967. Sr. fellow U. Wash., Seattle, 1967-68; guest investigator Rockefeller U., N.Y.C., 1968-70; asst. prof. U. Ill., Chgo., 1970-74, assoc. prof., 1974-78, prof. dept. biochemistry and molecular biology, 1978-98, prof. emeritus, 1998—, acting head, 1979-80. Biochemistry study sect. NIH, 1985-89; established investigator Am. Heart Assn., 1973-78. Mem. Am. Soc. Biochemistry and Molecular Biology, Am. Chem. Soc. Achievements include membrane abnormality and diseases I and II. Home: 1305 Darien Club Dr Darien IL 60561-3671 Office: U Ill Chicago 1853 W Polk St Chicago IL 60612-4316

TAO, RONGJIA, physicist, educator; b. Shanghai, Jan. 28, 1947; came to U.S., 1979; s. Yun Tao and Xiao-Mei Zou; m. Weiying Duanmu, Dec. 22, 1976; children: Han, Jing. MA, Columbia U., 1980, PhD, 1982. Rsch. assoc. U. Wash., Seattle, 1982-84; rsch. fellow U. Cambridge, Eng., 1984; rsch. asst. prof. U. So. Calif., L.A., 1984-85; asst. prof. physics Northeastern U., Boston, 1985-89, So. Ill. U., Carbondale, 1989-91, assoc. prof. physics, 1991-92, prof. physics, 1993-2000, chmn. dept. physics, 1994-99; prof. physics Temple U., Phila., 2000—. Cons. UN Developing Program, N.Y. and China, 1992—; chair Internat. Conf. on Electrorheological Fluids, Carbondale, 1991, Feldkirch, Austria, 1993, Internat. Conf. on Electrorheological Fluids and Magneto-Rheological Suspension, Honolulu, 1999. Editor, author: Electrorheological Fluids, 1992, Electrorheological Fluids, Mechanism, Properties, Materials and Applications, 1994, Electrorheological Fluids and Magnetorheological Suspensions, 2000; contbr. articles to profl. jours. Grantee Office of Naval Rsch. 1990, 92, 97, 2000, NSF, 1996, 2000; recipient award Omni mag., 1987. Mem. Am. Phys. Soc. Achievements include discovery that electric-field induced solidification is the physical mechanism of electrorheological fluids, the crystalline structure of electrorheological fluids is a body-centered tetragonal lattice, high temperature superconducting granular particles aggregate together into a ball in a strong electric field. Office: Temple U Dept Physics Philadelphia PA 19112

TAPLEY, PHILIP ALLEN, language educator, literature educator; b. Blackwell, Okla., June 11, 1938; s. Robert G. Sr. and Valena M. (Simmons) Tapley; m. Mary Stringer, Aug. 10, 1974; children: Mary Margaret, Laura Katherine. BA, U. North Tex., 1960, MA, 1962; PhD, La. State U., 1974; cert. in Victorian lit., U. London, 1966; postdoc., U. Miss., 1989. Cert. secondary tchr. Tex. Tchg. asst. U. North Tex., Denton, 1960-61, La. State U., Baton Rouge, 1961-65, 68-69, instr., 1965-68; from asst. prof. to assoc. prof. La. Coll., Pineville, 1969-80, prof. dept. English, journalism and langs., 1980—, acting chmn. dept. English, journalism and langs., 1980, sr. faculty marshall, 2001—. Tchr. Karamay U. Liberal Arts and Scis., China, 1998, China, 2001; condr. study tour from La. Coll. to Ireland, 1999; maj. scholar, presenter La. Endowment Humanities, Alexandria, 1977—; vis. cons. Ctrl. La. Electric Co., Pineville, 1989—95; mem. faculty coun. La. Coll., 1998—2000, vice chmn. faculty, 1999—2000. Author: (book) A History of First United Methodist, 1976, 2d edit., 1989; author: (with others) Proceedings of the Red River Symposium, 1987, 2d edit., 1991; co-author: Issues and Identities in Literature, 1997, Critical Survey of Short Fiction, 2d rev. edit., 2000, Survey of Long Fiction, 2d rev. edit., 2001; contbr. articles to profl. jours. Pres. Friends Rapides Libr., Alexandria, 1985—86, 1997, bd. dirs., 1996—99; mem. adv. bd. Arna Bontemps Mus., 1995—; lay eucharistic min. Episc. Ch., 1997—; aux. del. ann. conv. western La. Diocese Episcopal Ch., 2000—02; dir. Inst. Adult Edn., mem. rector search com. St. James Episcopal Parish, 2002—03. Recipient 30-Yr. Svc. award, La. Coll., 1999; Mellon Found. fellow, 1982, 1988, Ford Found. fellow, 1989. Mem.: AAUP, MLA, Hist. Assn. Ctrl. La. (pres. 1978—80, bd. dirs. 1978—98), La. Folklore Soc. (v.p. 1977—78, pres. 1978—79), South Ctrl. MLA (program chair so. lit. 1979), Sigma Delta Chi, Omicron Delta Kappa (faculty sec., chief sponsor 1997—2000), Sigma Tau Delta (mem. nat. scholarships and awards com. 2001—03, 25 Yr. award as local chpt. faculty sponsor), Alpha Chi, Phi Kappa Phi. Democrat. Episcopalian. Avocations: reading, music, historic preservation, folklore collecting. Home: 1721 Polk St Alexandria LA 71301-6334 Office: La Coll English Dept 1140 College Dr Pineville LA 71360-5122

TAPP, ANNE RENEE GOSS, education educator; b. Saginaw, Mich., Sept. 13, 1967; d. Donald Joseph and Deanna E. (Degen) Goss. BS in Edn. cum laude, Cen. Mich. U., 1990; MAT summa cum laude, Oakland U., 1993; EdD in Curriculum and Instn., Wayne State U., 1999. Tchr. Mt. Clemens (Mich.) Cmty. Schs., 1990, Davison (Mich.) Cmty. Schs., 1990—99; mentor tchr. JASON Found. for Edn., 1991—99; dir. Challenger Ctr. for Space Sci. Edn.; STARDUST educator fellow, 1998—; asst. prof. Saginaw Valley State U., University Center, Mich., 2002—. Pres. Student Adv. Coun., 1989—90; rep. Ctrl. Mich. Univs. Counseling and Spl. Edn. Dept., 1989—90; tchr. GAMSTC Task Force, 1995—99; tchr. argonaut JASON VIII Jason Found. Edn., 1997; presenter in field. Co-author: Unit 1 JASON VI and VII Curriculums; author: computer programs; contbr. articles to profl. jours. Vol. Spl. Olympics, 1986—, Adopt-a-Grandparent, 1986—89. Named Genessee County Tchr. of the Yr., 1993; recipient Adult Good Samaritan, ARC, 1999. Mem.: ASCD, Internat. Reading Assn., Assn. Tchr. Educators, Nat. Sci. Tchrs. Assn.

TAPP, MAMIE PEARL, educational association administration; b. Aiken, S.C., July 20, 1955; d. Willie Lee and Nancy (Madison) Garrett; m. Anthony Karl Tapp, Aug. 13, 1983; children: Anthony K. II, Barry Garrett, Myles Jarvis. BA, CUNY, 1977; MA, New Sch. for Social Rsch., 1984; postgrad., Nova Southeastern U., 1994—. Flight attendant Capitol Airlines, Jamaica, N.Y., 1976-81; pers. assoc. Cmty. Svc. Soc., N.Y.C., 1982-83; pers. specialist Marriott Hotel, Tampa, Fla., 1983-84; dir. placement Tampa Coll., 1984-86, facility coord., 1986-87, compliance officer, 1987-88; career counselor Alpha House, Tampa, 1988-91; career specialist U. Tampa, 1991-96, adj. prof., 1992-93; career specialist Jr. Achievement Greater Tampa, Inc., Tampa, 1996—, tchr. asst. program adv. com. mem., 1996-98. Tchr. asst. program adv. com. Hillsborough H.S., 1996-97; sr. edn. svc. mgr. Jr. Achievement, 1997—. Author: (novels) Resumes, 1992, Cover Letters, 1991, Thank You Letters, 1992, (poetry) Inner Peace, 1999; co-editor: I Cried, 2001, Life, 2002. Bd. dirs. Children's Mus. Tampa, 1992-94; com. mem. United Way, Tampa, 1994-95; mem. bd. St. Peter Claver Cath. Sch., Tampa, 1995-99, exec. com. Glee Club, 1995; vol. Scout troop leader, 1997-98. Recipient Outstanding Bus. Woman award Am. Bus. Women's Assn., Tampa, 1987, Cmty. Svc. award Tampa Connections, 1993, Editor's Choice award Internat. Libr. of Poetry, 1999. Mem.: AAUW, Fla. Assn. Women in Edn., Am. Vocat. Assn. Roman Catholic. Avocations: reading, sewing. Office: Jr Achievement Central Maryland Inc 10711 Red Run Blvd Ste 110 Owings Mills MD 21117 E-mail: tapptbjpt@earthlink.net.

TAPPER, LANCE HOWARD, secondary education educator; b. Encino, Calif., Apr. 11, 1961; s. Lloyd Edward and Dorothy Charlotte (Silvers) T. BA in History, UCLA, 1983. Lic. tchr., Calif.; lic. Hazzan Commn., Cantors Assembly, N.Y. Cantor Verdugo Hills Hebrew Ctr., Tujunga, Calif., 1979-81, Temple Ner Tamid, Simi Valley, Calif., 1981-82; Hazzan Hazzan, Downey, Calif., 1983—; tchr. Birmingham High Sch., Van Nuys, Calif., 1984-90, Taft High Sch., Woodland Hills, Calif., 1990—. Madelyn Hunter teaching fellow Grad. Sch. Edn., UCLA, 1985; recipient Outstanding Secondary Student Teaching award Grad. Sch. Edn., UCLA, 1985. Mem. United Tchrs. L.A. (mem.-at-large 1986-87), Cantors Assembly (western region chair 1992-94, nat. exec. coun. 1993-96), Guild Temple Musicians, L.A. Sertoma Club (freedom award in gen. edn. 1994). Democrat. Jewish. Avocations: music, singing, reading, swimming. Office: Taft High Sch 5461 Winnetka Ave Woodland Hills CA 91364-2592

TAQQU, MURAD SALMAN, mathematics educator; b. Mar. 21, 1942; Diploma in physics, Inst. Tech., Lausanne, Switzerland, 1965; licence in math., U. Lausanne, 1966; MA, Columbia U., 1969, PhD, 1972. Lectr. math. Hebrew U., Jerusalem, 1972-73; postdoctorate rsch. fellow Weizmann Inst., Rehovot, Israel, 1973-74; asst. prof. Cornell U., Ithaca, N.Y., 1974-81, assoc. prof., 1981-85, prof., 1985-86, Boston U., 1985—. Vis. assoc. prof. Stanford (Calif.) U., 1981-82; vis. rsch. scientist Courant Inst., NYU, N.Y.C., 1985; vis. scholar Harvard Coll., Cambridge, Mass., 1987-88; organizer profl. confs.; cons. sci. reviewer. Author: Stable Non-Gaussian Random Processes: Stochastic Models with Infinite Variance, 1994; editor: Dependence in Probability and Statistics, 1986, Statistical Techniques and Applications, 1998, Theory and Application of Long-range Dependence, 2003; contbr. articles to profl. publs. Recipient William J. Bennett award IEEE Comms. Soc., 1995, W.R.G. Baker prize award IEEE, 1996, Best Paper award Eur. Assn. Signal Processing, 2002; John Simon Guggenheim fellow, 1987. Fellow Inst. Math. Stats., Am. Math. Soc., Internat. Statis. Inst., Bernoulli Soc., Bachelier Fin. Soc. Office: Boston U Dept Math 111 Cummington St Boston MA 02215-2411

TARAN, LEONARDO, classicist, educator; b. Galarza, Argentina, Feb. 22, 1933; came to U.S., 1958, naturalized, 1976; s. Miguel and Liuba Taran; m. Judit Sofia Lida, Dec. 10, 1971; 1 child, Gabriel Andrew. Legal degree, U. Buenos Aires, 1958; PhD in Classics, Princeton U., 1962. Jr. fellow Inst. Research in Humanities, U. Wis., 1962-63, Center Hellenic Studies, Washington, 1963-64; asst. prof. classics U. Calif., Los Angeles, 1964-67; mem. faculty Columbia U., 1967—, prof. Greek and Latin, 1971—, Jay prof. Greek and Latin, 1987—, chmn. dept., 1976-79. Mem. Inst. Advanced Study, Princeton, N.J., 1966-67, 78-79; trustee Assn. Mems. Inst. Advanced Study, 1974-79; mem. mng. com. Am. Sch. Classical Studies, 1976— Author: Parmenides, 1965, Asclepius of Tralles, Commentary to Nicomachus' Introduction to Arithmetic, 1969, Plato, Philip of Opus and the Pseudo-Platonic Epinomis, 1975, Anonymous Commentary on Aristotle's De Interpretatione, 1978, Speusippus of Athens, 1981, Collected Papers (1962-1999), 2001; co-author: Eraclito: Testimonianze e imitazioni, 1972; Editorial bd.: Columbia Studies in the Classical Tradition, 1976-80. Am. Coun. Learned Socs. fellow, 1966-67, 71-72, Guggenheim Found. fellow, 1975, NEH fellow, 1986-87; grantee Am. Philos. Soc., 1963, 71, 75, Am. Coun. Learned Socs., 1968, 72, NEH, 1985-87, 88-89. Mem. Am. Philol. Assn., Classical Assn. Atlantic States, Soc. Ancient Greek Philosophy, Assn. Guillaume Budé. Home: 39 Claremont Ave New York NY 10027-6802 Office: Columbia U 615 Hamilton Hall New York NY 10027 E-mail: lt1@columbia.edu.

TARANIK, JAMES VLADIMIR, geologist, educator; b. Los Angeles, Apr. 23, 1940; s. Vladimir James and Jeanette Downing (Smith) T.; m. Colleen Sue Glessner, Dec. 4, 1971; children: Debra Lynn, Danny Lee. BSc in Geology, Stanford U., 1964; PhD, Colo. Sch. Mines, 1974. Chief remote sensing Iowa Geol. Survey, Iowa City, 1971-74; prin. remote sensing scientist Earth Resources Observation Systems Data Ctr., U.S. Geol. Survey, Sioux Falls, S.D., 1975-79; chief non-renewable resources br., resource observation div. Office of Space and Terrestrial Applications, NASA Hdqrs., Washington, 1979-82; dean mines Mackay Sch. Mines U. Nev., Reno, 1982-87, prof. of geology and geophysics, 1982—, Arthur Brant chair of geophysics, 1996—; pres. Desert Research Inst., Univ. and C.C. Sys. Nev., 1987-98; Regents's prof. and pres. emeritus Desert Rsch. Inst., Univ. and C.C. Sys. Nev., 1998—2003; adj. prof. geology U. Iowa, 1971-79; vis. prof. civil engring. Iowa State U., 1972-74; adj. prof. earth sci. U. S.D., 1976-79; program scientist for space shuttle large format camera expt. for heat capacity mapping mission, liaison Geol. Scis. Bd., Nat. Acad. Scis., 1981-82; dir. NOAA Coop. Inst. Aerospace Sci. & Terrestrial Applications, 1986-94; program dir. NASA Space Grant consortium Univ. and C.C. Sys. Nev., Reno, 1991—, dir. NASA EPSCOR program, 1998—, acting dean Mackay Sch. of Mines, 2003—; dir. Great Basin Ctr. Geothermal Energy, 2000—03; acting dean Mackay Sch. Mines, 2003—. Team mem. Shuttle Imaging Radar-B Sci. Team NASA, 1983-88, mem. space applications adv. com., 1986-88; chmn. remote sensing subcom. SAAC, 1986-88; chmn. working group on civil space commercialization Dept. Commerce, 1982-84, mem. civil operational remote sensing satellite com., 1983-84; bd. dirs. Earth Satellite Corp., 1994-2002, Newmont Mining Corp.; mem. adv. com. NASA Space Sci. and Applications Com., 1988-90, Nat. Def. Exec. Res., 1986-94, AF studies bd., com. on strategic relocatable targets, 1989-91; mem. pre-launch rev. bd., NASA, Space Radar Lab., 1993-94; mem. fed. lab. rev. task force, NASA, 1994-96; prin. investigator Japanese Earth Resources Satellite, 1991-94; mem. environ. task force MEDEA, Mitre Corp., McLean, Va., 1993-98; mem. mapping scis. com. Nat. Rsch. Coun., 2001—; cons. Jet Propulsion Lab., Calif., Hughes Aircraft Corp., Lockheed-Marietta Corp., Mitre Corp., TRW; developer remote sensing program and remote sensing lab. for State of Iowa, ednl. program in remote sensing for Iowa univs. and U. Nev., Reno; program scientist for 2d space shuttle flight Office Space and Terrestrial Applications Program; mem. terrestrial geol. applications program NASA, 1981-82; co-investigator Can. Radarsat Program, 1995—; program dir. NASA Space Grant and NASA EPSCOR, Nev., 1998—; mem. mapping scis. com. Nat. Rsch. Coun., 2001—. Contbr. to profl. jours. Bd. dirs. Mountain States Legal Found., 2000-. Served with C.E. U.S. Army, 1965-67; mil. intelligence officer Res. Decorated Bronze Star medal; recipient Spl. Achievement award U.S. Geol. Survey, 1978, Exceptional Sci. Achievement medal NASA, 1982, NASA Group Achievement award Shuttle imaging radar, 1990, NASA Johnson Space Ctr. Group Achievement award for large format camera, 1985; NASA prin. investigator, 1973, 83-88, prin. investigator French Spot-1 Program to Evaluate Spot 1986-88; NDEA fellow, 1968-71. Fellow: AAAS, Am. Soc. Photogrammetry Remote Sensing, Explorers Club, Geol. Soc. Am.; mem.: AIAA (sr.), IEEE (sr.), Soc. Econ. Geologists, Am. Geol. Inst. Found. (trustee 1999—), Am. Inst. Metall. Engrs., Am. Astron. Soc. (sr.), Soc. Mining Engrs. Am., Am. Assn. Petroleum Geologists (chmn. rsch. com. 2000—), Am. Geophys. Union, Soc. Exploration Geophysicists, Internat. Acad. Astronautics, Bohemian Club San Francisco. Home: PO Box 7175 Reno NV 89510-7175 E-mail: jtaranik@mines.unr.edu.

TARAS, RAYMOND CASIMER, political science educator; b. Montreal, Quebec, Can., Nov. 6, 1946; came to U.S., 1982; s. Mieczyslaw Alexander and Stella (Pacewicz) T.; m. Malgorzata Maria Kacprzyk, May 29, 1982; children: Michael, Krzysztof. BA, U. Montreal, 1967; MA, Sussex U., Eng., 1968; MPhil, Essex U., Eng., 1972; PhD, U. Warsaw, Poland, 1982. Lectr. Coventry Poly., Eng., 1972-76; steward, freighter MS Mona Star, West Africa, 1977; translator Europe, 1978-80; rsch. assoc. Concordia U., Can, 1981-82; asst. prof. U. Mich., 1982-83, U. Ky., 1983-84; assoc. prof. Tulane U., New Orleans, 1984—. Polit. analyst, local TV sta., New Orleans, 1989—; cons. Local Democracy Poland, Rutgers, N.J., 1990. Author: Ideology in a Socialist State, 1984, Poland: Socialist State, Rebellious Nation, 1986, Consolidating Democracy in Poland, 1995; co-author: Le Debat Linguistique au Quebec, 1987, Political Culture & Foreign Policy in Latin America, 1990; editor: Leadership Change in Communist States, 1989, The Road to Disillusion: From Critical Marxism to Postcommunism, 1992, Handbook of Political Science Research on the USSR and Eastern Europe, 1992, Nations and Politics in the Soviet Successor States, 1993. Can. Coun. fellow U. Warsaw, 1978-81, Nat. fellow Hoover Inst., 1990-91. Mem. Am. Polit. Sci. Assn., Am. Assn. Advancement Slavic Studies, Internat. Polit. Sci. Assn., Acad. Polit. Sci., Union des Ecrivains Quebecois, Brit. Assn. for Slavic and East European Studies. Home: 3322 Annunciation St New Orleans LA 70115-1202 Office: Tulane U Dept Polit Sci New Orleans LA 70118

TARBI, WILLIAM RHEINLANDER, secondary education educator, curriculum consultant, educational technology researcher; b. San Bernardino, Calif., Feb. 23, 1949; s. William Metro and Sue (Rheinlander) T.; m. Jenny Workman, Apr. 10, 1980 (div. 1985); m. Michele Hastings, July 4, 1990; children: Amy, Melissa. AA, Santa Barbara City Coll., 1969; BA in History, U. Calif., Santa Barbara, 1976; MA, U. Redlands, 1992. Cert. secondary edn. social studies tchr., Calif. Reporter AP, Santa Barbara, Calif., 1976-80, UPI, Seattle, 1980-85, Golden West Radio Network, Seattle, 1980-85; tchr. Redlands (Calif.) Unified Sch. Dist., 1986—. Cons. IMCOM, Redlands, 1985—. Mrm. E Clampus Vitus, Phi Delta Kappa. Avocations: painting, photography, writing, gardening, fencing.

TARDONA, DANIEL RICHARD, cognitive ethologist, writer, park ranger, educator; b. Bklyn., Nov. 9, 1953; s. Felix Carmine and Patricia Ann (Tynan) Tardona. BA, Monmouth Coll., 1976; MA, Cen. Mich. U., 1981. Cert. sch. psychologist N.J. Pediat. psychologist Montclair (N.J.) State Coll., 1982-83; radiation/hazardous substances safety asst. Cytogen Corp., Princeton, N.J., 1984-85; park naturalist Frozen Head State Natural Area, Wartburg, Tenn., 1986; park ranger Cape Hatteras Nat. Seashore, Manteo, N.C., 1987, Great Smoky Mtns. Nat. Pk., Gatlinburg, Tenn., 1987-90, asst. dist. supr., 1990-92; west dist. supr. Timucuan Ecological and Hist. Preserve, Jacksonville, Fla., 1992—. Adj. prof. dept. psychology U. North Fla., Jacksonville, 2001—. Mem. editl. rev. bd.: Infant Mental Health Jour., 1982—85, guest reviewer: Edn. and Treatment of Children, 1980, 1981; contbr. articles to profl. jours. Mem. Fla. Audobon Soc., 1992—. Trustees Scholar, Rider Coll., 1983—84. Mem.: Internat. Wildlife Rehab. Coun., Wildlife Soc., Animal Behavior Mgmt. Alliance, Animal Behavior Soc., Internat. Primatol. Soc., Psi Chi, Phi Delta Kappa, Sigma Gamma Epsilon. Achievements include research in animal learning and behavior, captive animal behavioral enrichment, evolution and anthrozoology, wildlife behavior and conservation. Home and Office: Timucuan Ecol and Hist Preserve 13165 Mt Pleasant Rd Jacksonville FL 32225-1240 E-mail: Daniel_Tardona@nps.gov.

TARGOWSKI, ANDREW STANISLAW, computer information educator, consultant; b. Warsaw, Oct. 9, 1937; came to US, 1980; s. Stanislaw Adam and Halina (Krzyzanska) T.; m. Alicja Kowalczyk, Jan. 22, 1966 (div. 1977); 1 child, Stanislaw; m. Irmina Dura, Mar. 11, 1978; children: Agnieszka, Kubas, John. MS in Indsl. Engring., M in Indsl., Warsaw Poly., 1961, PhD in Computer Sci., 1968. Head dept. systems design Inst. Orgn. and Machinery Industry, Warsaw, 1961-64; pres. Warsaw Computer Svc. Ctr., 1965-71; sr. v.p. Bur. for Info. Tech., 1971-74; assoc. prof. Hamilton Coll., Clinton, NY, 1974-75; cons. Machinery Industry Ministry, Warsaw, 1976-79; prof. computer info. systems Western Mich. U., Kalamazoo, 1980-82, 85—; prof. Hofstra U., Hempstead, NY, 1982-84, Ea. Ky. U., Richmond, 1984-85; chmn., chief exec. officer Semantex, Systems Architects, Inc., 1988—. Chmn. Greater Kalamazoo Telecity USA Project. Author: Organization of Computer Centers, 1971, Organization of Data processing Process, 1975, Informatics, Models of Systems and Devel, 1980, Red Fascism, 1982, The Architecture and Planning of Enterprise-wide Info. Mgmt. Systems, 1990, The Momentary End of History, 1991, In the Pursuit of Time, 1993, Defense of Poland, 1993, Vision of Poland, 1995, Global Information Infrastructure, 1996, Enterprise Information Infrastructure, 2000, Fate of Poland and World, 2000, Informatics Without Illusion-Memoirs, 2001, Electronic Enterprise, 2003, Civilization and Information, 2003. Pres. Polish Tennis Assn., Warsaw, 1971-72; chair planning com. Polish Study Ctr.; chmn. steering com. Kalamazoo Telecity; bd. dir. Polish Am. Congress, 2001; pres. World Rsch. Coun. of Poles Living Abroad, 2001; pres. Colleagues Internat., 2000-01. Mem. Assn. Info. Resources Mgmt. (v.p.), Polish Inst. Arts and Sci., U.S. Tennis Assn., YMCA. Roman Catholic. Avocations: tennis, sailing, skiing, reading. Home: 5485 Saddle Club Dr Kalamazoo MI 49009-9774 Office: Western Mich U Dept Bus Info Systems Kalamazoo MI 49008

TARJAN, ROBERT ENDRE, computer scientist, educator; b. Pomona, Calif., Apr. 30, 1948; s. George and Helen Emma (Blome) T.; m. Gail Maria Zawacki, Apr. 22, 1978 (div. June 1992); children: Alice Marisha, Zosia Emma Zawacki, Lily Maxine. BS, Calif. Inst. Tech., 1969; MS, Stanford U., 1971, PhD, 1972. Asst. prof. Cornell U., Ithaca, N.Y., 1972-73; Miller fellow U. Calif., Berkeley, 1973-75; asst. prof. Stanford U., Palo Alto, Calif., 1975-77, assoc. prof., 1977-80; mem. tech. staff AT&T Bell Labs., Murray Hill, N.J., 1980-90; adj. prof. NYU, 1981-85; James S. McDonnell Disting. U. prof. Princeton (N.J.) U., 1985—. Adj. fellow NEC Rsch. Inst., Princeton, 1969-97; co-dir. DIMACS Princeton U. and Rutgers U., 1989-94; chief scientist Inter Trust Technologies, Inc., Sunnyvale, Calif., 1997-2002, Hewlett Packard, Palo, Alto, Calif., 2002—. Author: Data Structures and Network Algorithms, 1983; (with G. Polya and D. Woods) Notes on Introductory Combinatorics, 1983. Recipient Nevanlinna prize Internat. Meth. Union, 1983; Guggenheim fellow, 1978. Fellow AAAS, Am. Acad. Arts and Scis.; mem. NAS, NAE, Am. Philos. Soc., Assn. Computing Machinery (A.M. Turing award 1986), Soc. Indsl. and Applied Math. Office: Princeton U Dept Computer Sci Princeton NJ 08544-0001

TARLEY, JOANNA JANE, elementary school educator; b. Fairmont, W. Va., Sept. 19, 1960; d. Jospeh and Margaret Madeline (Plymale) T. BA in Elem. Edn., Fairmont State Coll., 1981; MA Reading Specialist, W. Va. U., 1988. Cert. tchr., W. Va. Tchr. Mingo County Bd. Edn. Dingess Grade Sch., Williamson, W. Va., 1982-86; tchr. chpt. 1 Mannington (W. Va.) Middle Sch., 1989—. Active Calvary Temple Assembly of God Ch. Mem. W. Va. Edn. Assn., Marion County Reading Coun. Avocations: reading, ceramics, music, needlepoint, gardening. Home: RR 1 Box 151 Fairmont WV 26554-9727

TARNOW, FREDRIC HERMAN, science educator; b. Chgo., Jan. 6, 1933; s. Harold B. and Maria (Kropp) T.; m. Beverly L. Weber, Dec. 5, 1953; children: Lillian Marie, Fredric H., LaVerne A. Kind. BS in Secondary Edn., Biology, Northeastern Ill. U., 1972; MA in Ednl. Adminstrn., Northern Ill. u., 1974. Tchr. Sch. Dist. # 54, Schaumburg, Ill., 1972-78, 85-87, chmn. sci., 1978-85; ednl. cons. North Cook Ednl. Svc. Ctr., Glenview, Ill., 1987-93; instr. Govs. State U., University Ctr., Ill., 1980—, Aurora (Ill.) U., 1990—. Adj. prof., Nat. Coll., Evanston, Ill., 1986—, vis. lectr., instructor Northeastern U., Chgo., 1989—. Contbr. articles to profl. jours. With U.S. Army, 1954-56, res., 1956-89. Recipient Presdl. award State of Ill., 1986, 87. Mem. ASCD, Nat. Biology Tchrs. Assn. (elem. chmn. 1985-88), Nat. Sci. Tchrs. Assn., Nat. Coun. Tchrs. Math., Nat. Sci. Supr. Assn., Ill. Sci. Tchrs. Assn. (regional dir. 1985-87). Home: 3657 N St Louis Ave Chicago IL 60618-4225 Office: Hands-On Minds-On Learning 3657 N Saint Louis Ave Chicago IL 60618-4225

TARPLEY, JAMES DOUGLAS, journalism educator, magazine editor; b. Los Angeles, May 2, 1946; Cert. tchr., Mo. BS in Edn., S.W. Mo. U., 1968, MA in English, 1972; MA in Mass Comm., Ctrl. Mo. U., 1976; PhD in Journalism, So. Ill. U., 1983. Prof. journalism Evangel Coll., Springfield, Mo., 1976-87; chmn. Sch. of Journalism Regent U. (formerly Christian Broadcasting Network U.), Virginia Beach, Va., 1987—; dir. The Wash. Grad. Journalism Ctr. Guest lectr. Cen. Mo. U., S.W. Mo. U., So. Ill. U., U. Ohio summer journalism workshops, 1976—. Youth page editor Eldon Advertiser, 1972-76, mng. editor Home Free, 1988-90, High Adventure, 1983-87, Criminal Justice Management, 1978-81, editor Ranger News, 1979-81, design and layout editor Vision Mag., 1984-87; free-lance writer, contbr. biog. entries to profl. publs.; free-lance photographer; graphic artist, copywriter Disco-Fair advt. dept., 1964-68. Exec. com. Eldon PTA, 1971-74; youth dir. Eldon Assembly of God, 1968-75; Sunday sch. supt. Cen. Assembly of God, Springfield, Mo., 1978-82; mem. Sch. Effectiveness Evaluation Team Springfield Pub. Schs., 1985-86, 86-87. Recipient Mo. Journalism Tchr. Yr. award, 1976, Cert. of Merit Columbia U., 1984, Gold Medal of Merit Columbia U. Scholastic Press Assn., 1984, Ruritan Gov.'s award, 1997, Ruritan of Yr. award Great Bridge Ruritans, 1998, 99; named Outstanding Grad., Dept. Mass Communication Cen. Mo. U. 1976; fellow U. Pa. and Freedom Found. project on press freedom, 1984, Nat. Newspaper Fund Fellow Dow Jones and U. Mo., 1975; named fellow of Scripps-Howard CCCU Washington D.C. Capstone proj., 1995, 2002, Am. Press Inst. fellow, 1995, 2002. Mem. Assn. Christian Collegiate Media (nat. exec. dir. 1995—), Coll. Media Advisers (bd. dirs., chmn. various coms., pres. citation 1981, 84-89), Soc. Coll. Journalists (pres. 1992—, exec. dir. 1983-92, pres. citation 1981, 85, 87, 90), Assn. Christian Collegiate Media (exec. dir. 1995—), Assn. Edn. in Journalism and Mass Comm., Nat. Conf. Editl. Writers (com. scholarly rsch. 1985), Soc. Newspaper Design (edn. com. 1986-88), Broadcast Edn. Assn. (intern. com. 1984), Assn. Journalism Historials, Inst. Cert. Photographers, Mo. Tchrs. Assn., Evang. Press Assn., Ruritan Outstanding Club Pres. award Holland dist. 1999), Pi Delta Kappa. Republican. Avocations: writing, photography, painting. Office: Washington Grad Journ Ctr Regent U No Va 1650 Diagonal Rd Alexandria VA 22314 Home: 42843 Shaler St Chantilly VA 20152-3921 E-mail: Doc44685@aol.com., dougtar@regent.edu.

TARQUINIO, ANTOINETTE CAMILLE, special education educator; b. Pitts., June 13, 1956; d. Edythe Marie Tarquinio. BS in Edn., Calif. U. Pa., 1993. Merchandising asst. Wetterau Inc., Belle Vernon, Pa., 1979-91; pvt. tutor Monessen, Pa., 1991-93; devel. specialist Early Intervention, Monessen, 1994—, Diversified Human Svcs., Monessen, 1994—. Residential program worker community living arrangements Diversified Human Svcs., Monessen, 1991-93. Choir dir. Epiphany of Our Lord Ch., Monessen, 1990—. Named All Am. Scholar, 1993; recipient Nat. Collegiate award U.S. Achievement Acad., 1991, 93. Mem. Coun. for Exceptional Children, Sigma Pi Epsilon Delta, Kappa Delta Pi. Democrat. Roman Catholic. Avocations: camping, hiking, reading, wildlife preservation, animal protection, music, sports. Home and Office: 26 Overhill Dr Monessen PA 15062-2506

TARRY, (JIMMIE) PATRICIA, real estate broker, retired elementary education educator; b. Palestine, Tex., July 6, 1928; d. Ralph Stanley and Grace Wynona (Henry) Radford; m. George D. Tarry Jr., Sept. 2, 1950; 1 child, Radford George Tarry. BA, Rice U., 1949; MEd, U. Houston, 1954; postgrad., U. Tex., Tyler, 1970-80, East Tex. State U., Commerce, 1970-80. Cert. tchr. Tex.; lic. real estate broker. Pers. clk. Am. Republic Oil Co., Houston, 1945-49; elem. tchr. Galena Park (Tex.) Elem. Sch., 1950-52; pers. clk. Shell Oil Co., Houston, 1953; elem. tchr. Houston Ind. Sch. Dist., 1952-56, Tyler Ind. Sch. Dist., 1961-81; real estate broker Tarry Real Estate, Tyler, 1981—. Bd. dirs. Tarry Allied Van Lines, Tyler; chmn. Tyler Ind. Sch. Dist. Reading Guide, Tyler, 1970; pilot reading tchr. Am. Book Co., Tyler, 1974; cons. Weekly Reader, Middletown, Conn., 1978-81. Contbr. articles to mags. Mem. Tyler Woman's Forum, 1960-90; pres. Chapel Class of Marvin, Tyler, 1962, 72; sec. Marvin Meth. Women Soc., Tyler, 1960. Recipient Disting. Svc. award Tex. State Tchrs. Assn., 1969. Mem. Nat. Edn. Soc. (life), Tyler State Tchrs. Assn., Classroom Tchrs. Assn., East Tex. Genealogy Soc. (life), Hollytree Country Club, Tyler Tennis and Swim Club, Eastern Star, Daus. of Nile, Delta Kappa Gamma Internat. (v.p. 1980-90, sec. Kappa Pi chpt.), Delta Kappa Gamma (Achievement award 1987), Kappa Delta Pi. Home: 1819 Easy St Tyler TX 75703-1610

TARTE, TERESA MICHELLE, elementary education educator; b. Prince George's County, Md., May 13, 1959; d. Alfred S. and Edith C. (Burch) Lamoureux; m. Michael Earl Tarte, Nov. 29, 1980; children: Kristin Michelle, Jennifer Courtney. BA, U. Tex., San Antonio, 1980. Cert. tchr., Tex. Tchr. Southwest Ind. Sch. Dist., San Antonio, 1980—, grade level facilitator, 1986-91, sci. instrnl. coord., 1991-95, assessment instrnl. coord., 1992-93, site-based mgmt. trainer, 1992-94. Mem. Dist.-Wide Improvement Coun., 1991—, coord. sci. fair, 1992, trainer writing team, 1993-94. Author curriculum materials. Cultural arts coord. Big Country Elem. Sch. PTA, San Antonio, 1987—; mem. Christian Evers Elem. PTA, San Antonio, 1992; mem. Jack Jordan Mid. Sch. PTA. Named Disting. Educator in San Antonio, Trinity U., 1986. Mem. Assn. Childhood Edn. Internat., San Antonio Literacy Network, Sci. Tchrs. Assn. Tex., Tex. Coun. Tchrs. Math., Alamo Dist. Coun. Tchrs. Math., Assn. Tex. Profl. Educators. Roman Catholic. Avocations: reading, piano, travel. Home: 9026 Deer Park San Antonio TX 78251-2959

TASKER, GRETA SUE, English as second language educator; b. Wichita, Kans., May 29, 1944; d. Cecil Tipton Gray and Neva Nancy (Rounds) Gray-Jones; m. David Byron Tasker, Dec. 19, 1964; children: Jack Weston, Richard Wade. BS in Edn., Emporia State U., 1966; MA, U. Kans., 1984. Spanish tchr. Hawaii State Dept. Edn., Honolulu, 1967-70; ESL tchr. Olathe (Kans.) Dist. Schs., 1981—, coord., 1981-98. Named Kans. Bilingual Tchr. of Yr. Kans. Assn. Bilingual Edn., 1989-90. Mem. TESOL, Kans. TESOL. Avocations: travel, biking, hiking, pets, rollerblading.

TATA, XERXES RAMYAR, physicist, educator; b. Bombay, Apr. 27, 1954; came to U.S., 1976; s. Ramyar Dadabhoy and Hira Tata. BSc, Bombay U., 1974; MSc, Indian Inst. Technology, Bombay, 1976; PhD, U. Tex., 1981. Lectr., rsch. assoc. U. Tex., Austin, 1981-83; rsch. assoc. U. Oreg., Eugene, 1983-86; asst. scientist U. Wis., Madison, 1986-88; from assoc. prof. to prof. U. Hawaii, Honolulu, 1988—. Sci. assoc. CERN, Geneva, Switzerland, 1984-85; vis. scientist KEK, Japanese Lab. for High Energy Physics, 1987-88. Fellow: Am. Phys. Soc. Office: U Hawaii Dept Physics 2505 Correa Rd Honolulu HI 96822-2219

TATE, MICHAEL LYNN, history educator; b. Big Spring, Tex., Jan. 24, 1947; s. Richard A. and Ruby L. (Harrell) T.; m. Carol Janet Castleberry, June 19, 1971; children: Kerin S., Shannon L. BA, Austin Coll., Sherman, Tex., 1969; MA, U. Toledo, 1970, PhD, 1974. Asst. prof. history U. Nebr., Omaha, 1974-78, assoc. prof., 1978-83, prof., 1983—. Author: The Indians of Texas: An Annotated Research Bibliography, 1986, The Upstream People: An Annotated Research Bibliography of the Omaha Tribe, 1991, Nebr. History: An Annotated Bibliography, 1995, The Frontier Army in the Settlement of the West, 1999; contbg. editor Am. Indian Quar., 1975-81; exec. editor for history Govt. Pubs. Rev., 1981—; abstractor America: History and Life, 1978—; contbr. articles to profl. jours. Office: U Nebr at Omaha Dept History Omaha NE 68182-0001

TATEL, DAVID STEPHEN, federal judge; b. Washington, Mar. 16, 1942; s. Howard Edwin and Molly (Abramowitz) Tatel; m. Edith Sara Bassichis, Aug. 29, 1965; children: Rebecca, Stephanie, Joshua, Emily. BA, U. Mich., 1963; JD, U. Chgo., 1966. Bar: Ill. 1966. Instr. U. Mich., Ann Arbor, 1966—67; assoc. Sidley & Austin, Chgo. and Washington, 1967—69, 1970—72; dir. Chgo. Lawyer's Com., 1969—70, Nat. Lawyers Comm. for Civil Rights Under Law, Washington, 1972—74; dir. Office for Civil Rights HEW, Washington, 1977—79; assoc., ptnr. Hogan & Hartson, Washington, 1974—77, ptnr., 1979—94; cir. judge U.S. Ct. Appeals (D.C. cir.), Washington, 1994—. Lectr. Stanford U. Law Sch., 1991—92; co-chmn. Nat. Lawyers Com. for Civil Rights Under Law, Washington, 1989—91; chmn., bd. dirs. Spencer Found., Chgo., 1990—97. Bd. dirs. Carnegie Found. for Advancement in Tchg., Stanford, Calif., 1997—. Office: US Ct Appeals 333 Constitution Ave NW US Courthouse Washington DC 20001-2866*

TATNALL, ANN WESLAGER, reading educator; b. Uniontown, Pa., June 1, 1935; d. Clinton Alfred and Ruth Georgia (Hurst) Weslager; m. George Gress Tatnall, Oct. 8, 1954; children: Peggy Ann, George Richardson. BS in Edn., U. Del., 1967; MA in Edn., Glassboro State Coll., 1978. Cert. reading specialist, cert. supr., cert. elem. tchr., N.J. Tchr. reading Oldmans Twp. Bd. of Edn., Pedricktown, N.J., 1972-78, reading specialist, 1978-95, reading supr., 1981-95. Mem. N.J. Dept. of Edn. Minimum Basic Skills Test Devel. Com., Trenton, N.J., 1981-82; mem. Quad-Dist. Reading Coordination Com., Salem County, N.J., 1987-95; chairperson Adminstrv. Com. of Oldmans Twp. Schs., Pedricktown, N.J., 1993-95. Chair Woodstown (NJ) Candlelight House Tour, 1983-99, homes chair, 2000—; pres. Pilesgrove-Woodstown Hist. Soc., 1994-99, v.p., 1999-2001, pres. 2002-03, trustee, 2003; v.p. Pilesgrove Libr. Assn., 1994-2002, pres., 2003; sec. Hist. Preservation Commn., Woodstown, 1989—; mem. jr. bd. Wilmington (Del.) Med. Ctr., 1969—, treas. Thrift Shop, 1970-75; trustee United Way of Salem County, 1997-99; mem. Salem County Cultural and Heritage Commn., 1997—. Recipient Gov.'s Tchr. Recognition Program award Gov. of N.J., 1988; selected Hands Across the Water, Russian/USA Tchr. Exchange, 1990-91; named Salem County Woman of Achievement, 1998. Mem. AAUW, Internat. Reading Assn., N.J. Reading Assn., Woman's Club of Woodstown. Avocations: travel, reading, Univ. of Del. football, restoration of historic houses, granddaughters. Home: 209 N Main St Woodstown NJ 08098-1227

TATUM, JOAN GLENNALYN JOHN, secondary school educator; b. Scottsbluff, Nebr., Jan. 5, 1934; d. Glenn Edwin and Blanche Constance (Dundon) John; m. William Earl Tatum, Apr. 6, 1954 (div. Apr. 1988); children: Cherie Elizabeth Tatum Love, Michele Tatum Brackett, John William, Amy Denise Tatum Stanton. AA, U. Fla., 1954; BA, U. South Fla., 1969, MA, 1971. Cert. tchr., Fla. Substitute tchr. Pub. Sch. Dist., Sarasota, Fla., 1966-67; bus., vocat. edn. tchr. Riverview High Sch., Sarasota, 1969-96, Sarasota Tech. Inst., 1969—. Curriculum coord. bus.-vocat. edn. dept. Riverview H.S., 1990—, instructional tech. facilitator, 1996—; adj. prof. St. Francis Coll. (name now U. St. Francis), Joliet, Ill., 1988, 91, 93, 94, 98; computer health course instr. Nat.- Louis U., 1998-99; state and dist. textbook evaluation teams Fla. Dept. Edn., Sarasota, sch. to dist. tech. rep., 1985—; chmn. Riverview Tech. Com., 1987—; assoc. master tchr. State Fla. Bd. Edn., 1984-87; coun. chair Dist. Sch. Based Mgmt., Sarasota, 1991-93; chmn. Riverview Sch. Based Mgmt., 1991-93; project coord. Riverview Sr. Acad. Integrated Studies, 1991-95; dance tchr. various studios, Sarasota, 1949-67; sec. and office staff various govtl., cmty. and dance studios, Sarasota, 1951-59. Supervisory com. Sarasota Coastal Credit Union, 1985-98. Senate Edn. scholar Sarasota High/Fla. Legislature, 1951; named Tchr. of Yr. Riverview High Sch., 1991-92. Mem. Internat. Soc. Bus. Educators, Nat. Bus. Edn. Assn., Am. Vocat. Assn., So. Bus. Edn. Assn., Fla. Bus. Edn. Assn., Fla. Vocat. Assn., Sarasota County Vocat. Adult Assn. (pres. 1989-90), Fla. Assn. for Computers in Edn., Internat. Soc. for Tech. in Edn., Order of Rainbow (mem. adv. bd. 1977—, Grand Cross Color award 1949), Order Ea. Star, Kappa Delta Pi, Delta Pi Epsilon, Alpha Delta Kappa (chpt. treas. 1982-86, chpt. pres. 1986-88, chmn. state ad hoc com. 1989-90, chmn. state candidate qualifications com. 1994-96, chmn. state budget com. 1996-98, dist. treas. 1987-92, dist. chmn. 1992-94, state rec. sec. 1998—, State Honoris Causa award 1992). Presbyterian. Avocations: theatre, choreography, dance, family, walking. Home: 4152 Moss Oak Pl Sarasota FL 34231-2934 Office: Riverview HS One Ram Way Sarasota FL 34231

TAUB, LARRY STEVEN, education administrator; b. N.Y.C., Dec. 28, 1952; s. Marvin and Blanche (Schweitzer) T. BA, Hofstra U., 1975; MA, NYU, 1976; Ed.D., Columbia Univ., 2002. Cert. social studies tchr., N.Y. Tchr. N.Y. Sch. for the Deaf, White Plains, N.Y., 1976-92, ednl. administrator, 1992—. Mem. Conf. Educational Admin. Schs. for the Deaf. Mem. Am. Deafness and Rehab. Assn., N.Y. State Educators of the Deaf. Office: Gov Baxter Sch for the Deaf Mackworth Island Falmouth ME 04105

TAUBER, ROSALYN, educational therapist, learning consultant; b. Newark, Sept. 25, 1930; d. Schlomo and Clara (Berman) Tauber; m. Saul Scheidlinger, May 26, 1974. BA, Kean Coll., Union, N.J., 1951; MA, Columbia U., 1956; postgrad., CCNY, 1962, Montclair (N.J.) State Coll., 1965. Cert. speech pathologist, tchr. spl. edn. and hearing handicapped, N.Y.; cert. learning disabilities tchr., cons., speech defective and hearing handicapped, N.J. Primary grade tchr. Pub. Sch., Newark, 1951-58, coord. speech and hearing svcs. Livingston, N.J., 1958-61; speech and hearing clinician Columbia Presbyn. Med. Ctr., N.Y.C., 1962; adj. lectr. CCNY, 1971-74; learning cons. Pub. Sch., Summit, NJ, 1962-86, Horace Mann Sch., Bronx, NY, 1983-88, 93-95; pvt. practice as learning cons., Mamaroneck, NY, 1982—. Cons. Young & Rubicam, N.Y.C., 1971, NIH, 1970; mem. adv. bd. Found. for Devel. Disabled Children in Israel, 1990. Editor: Study Skills Textbook, 1969; contbr. articles to profl. jours. Vol., The Jewish Mus., N.Y.C. Mem. Am. Speech, Hearing, and Lang. Assn., Assn. Tchrs. in Ind. Schs., Orton Dyslexia Soc., Westchester Speech and Hearing Assn. (mentor).

TAUC, JAN, physics educator; b. Pardubice, Czechoslovakia, Apr. 15, 1922; came to U.S., 1969, naturalized, 1978; s. Jan and Josefa (Semonska) T.; m. Vera Koubelova, Oct. 18, 1947; children: Elena (Mrs. Milan Kokta), Jan. Ing.Dr. in Elec. Engring., Tech. U. Prague, 1949; RNDr., Charles U., 1956; Dr.Sc. in Physics, Czechoslovak Acad. Scis., 1956. Scientist microwave research Sci. and Tech. Research Inst., Tanvald and Prague, 1949-52; head semiconductor dept. Inst. Solid State Physics, Czechoslovak Acad. Scis., 1953-69; prof. exptl. physics Charles U., 1964-69, dir. Inst. Physics, 1968-69; mem. tech. staff Bell Telephone Labs., Murray Hill, N.J., 1969-70; prof. engring. and physics Brown U., 1970-83, L. Herbert Ballou prof. engring. and physics, 1983-92, L. Herbert Ballou prof. emeritus, 1992—, dir. material research lab., 1983-88. Dir. E. Fermi Summer Sch., Varenna, Italy, 1965; vis. prof. U. Paris, 1969, Stanford U., 1977, Max Planck Inst. Solid State Research, Stuttgart, Germany, 1982; UNESCO fellow, Harvard, 1961-62 Author: Photo and Thermoelectric Effects in Semiconductors, 1962, also numerous articles; editor: The Optical Properties of Solids, 1966, Amorphous and Liquid Semiconductors, 1974; co-editor: Solid State Communications, 1963-92. Recipient Nat. prize Czechoslovak Govt., 1955, 69; Sr. U.S. Scientist award Humboldt Found., 1981, Silver medal Union of Czechoslovak Mathematicians and Physicists, 1992; Jan Tauc Grad. Fellowship in Engring. at Brown U. in his honor, 2003; de Scientia et Humanitate Optime Meritis medal, 2003. Fellow AAAS, Am. Phys. Soc. (Frank Isakson prize 1982, David Adler award 1988); mem. NAS, European Phys. Soc. (founding), Czechoslovak Acad. Scis. (corr. 1963-71, 90-91, fgn. 1991-92, Hlavka medal 1992, de Scientia et Humanitate Optime Meritus medal 2003), Czech Learned Soc. (hon.). Office: Brown U Divsn Engring Providence RI 02912-0001

TAVERAS, JUAN MANUEL, physician, educator; b. Dominican Republic, Sept. 27, 1919; came to U.S., 1944, naturalized, 1950; s. Marcos M. and Ana L. (Rodriguez) T.; m. Bernice Helen McGonigle, June 12, 1947 (dec. 1990); children: Angela Forbes Summers, Louisa Helen Taveras Koranda, Jeffrey Lawrence; m. Mariana Margarita Bucher, Mar. 18, 1991. BS, Normal Sch. Santiago, Dominican Republic, 1937; MD, U. Santo Domingo, Dominican Republic, 1943, U. Pa., 1949; MS honoris causa, Harvard Med. Sch., 1971; Dr. honoris causa, Univ. Nacional Pedro Henriquez Ureña, Dominican Republic, 1987; Doctor Honoris Causa, U. Catolica Madre Y Maestra, Santiago, Dominican Republic, 1992. Diplomate: Am. Bd. Radiology. Instr. anatomy U. Santo Domingo, 1943-44; fellow radiology Grad. Hosp. U. Pa., 1945-48; rotating intern Misericordia Hosp., Phila., 1949-50; asst. radiologist Presbyn. Hosp., N.Y.C., 1950-52, asst. attending radiologist, 1953-56, assoc. attending radiologist, 1956-60, attending radiologist, 1960-65; dir. radiology Neurol. Inst., N.Y.C., 1952-65; cons. USPHS Hosp., S.I., N.Y., 1952-65, Morristown (N.J.) Meml. Hosp., 1957-65, St. Barnabas Hosp., N.Y.C., 1959-65, VA Hosp., Bronx, N.Y., 1960-65; asst. instr. radiology U. Pa. Sch. Medicine, 1947-48; faculty Columbia Coll. Phys. and Surg., 1950-65, prof. radiology, 1959-65; prof. radiology, chmn. dept., dir. Mallinckrodt Inst. Radiology, Washington U. Sch. Medicine, St. Louis, 1965-71; radiologist-in-chief Barnes and Allied Hosps., St. Louis, 1965-71; cons. neuroradiology service Unit 1 St. Louis City Hosp., 1966-71; cons. radiology Jewish Hosp., St. Louis, 1966-71; prof. radiology Harvard Med. Sch., 1971-89, prof. radiology emeritus, 1989—; radiologist-in-chief Mass. Gen. Hosp., Boston, 1971-88. Pres. VII Symposium Neuroradiologieum, 1964; hon. prof. U. Chile, 1978, Peruvian U. Cayetano Heredia, 1994; founder, cons. Diagnosis and Advanced Medicine Ctr. in Juan M. Taveras Health Plaza, Santo Domingo, Dominican Republic, 1997—. Author: Neuroradiology, 1996; (with Ross Golden) Roentgenology of the Abdomen, 1961, (with Ernest H. Wood) Diagnostic Neuroradiology, 1964, 2d edit., 1976, (with Norman Leeds) Dynamic Factors in Diagnosis of Supratentorial Brain Tumors by Cerebral Angiography, 1969, (with F. Morello) Normal Neuroradiology, 1979, (with James Provenzale) Clinical Cases in Neuroradiology, 1994, (with Laszlo Szlavy) Noncoronary Angioplasty, 1994; editor: (with others) Recent Advances in the Study of Cerebral Circulation, 1970, Cysticercosis of the Central Nervous System, 1983, Radiology: Diagnosis, Imaging, Intervention, 1986, Radiologia e Imagen, Diagnostica y Terapeutica, 1998, 99; chief editor: Am. Jour. Neuroradiology, 1980-89; contbr. numerous articles to profl. jours. Bd. dirs. Edward Mallinckrodt, Jr. Found., 1980-96. Decorated knight Order of Duarte Sanchez y Mella (Dominican Republic) 1972; Juan M. Taveras professorship established in his honor Harvard Med. Sch., 1988. Fellow: Am. Coll. Radiology (gold medal 1985); mem.: AMA, Japan Radiol. Soc., Hungarian Radiologic Soc., Radiol. Assn. Ctrl. Am. an dPanama, Tex. Radiol. Soc., Rocky Mountain Radiol. Soc., Radiol. Soc. Venezuela, Iberrian Latin Am. Soc. Neuroradiology (pres. 1988—91, pres. IC congress 1992), New Eng. Roentgen Ray Soc., Brazilian Radiol. Soc., Colombia Neurol. Soc., Costa Rica Soc. Radiology, Mass. Radiol. Soc., Assn. U. Radiologists (gold mdeal 1985), Nat. Acads. Practice, N.Y. Acad. Scis., Am. Soc. Neuroradiology (pres. 1962—64, gold medal 1995), World Fedn. Neurology, Am. Assn. Neurol. Surgeons (assoc.), Phila. Roentgen Ray Soc. (hon.), European Soc. Neuroradiology (hon.), Mexican Neuroradiology Soc. (hon. prize of merit award), Inter-Am. Coll. Radiology, Mass. Med. Soc., Radiol. Soc. N.Am. (gold medal 1981), Am. Roentgen Ray Soc. (gold medal 1988), Am. Neurol. Assn., Alpha Omega Alpha. Republican. Home: 85 E India Row Apt 40F Boston MA 02110-3394 Office: Mass Gen Hosp 55 Fruit St Boston MA 02114-2696

TAVOSSI, HASSON M. physics and engineering educator, consultant; b. Kermanshah, Iran, Oct. 22, 1948; s. Mohammad and Ashraf-el-Sadat Tavossi. BSc, U. Essex, Colchester, Eng., 1973; MS, U. Paris, 1981, PhD, 1984. Cert. process engr., French Ministry Higher Edn. and Rsch., Commn. Energy and Process Engring. Instr. Telecom France, Paris, 1985; postdoctoral and instr. U. Paris XII and VII, 1986-94; instr. Pa. Coll. Tech., Williamsport, 1994; prof. Lycoming Coll., Williamsport, 1995; instr. Pa. State U., State College, 1995—2000; prof. Mesa State Coll., 2000—. Rschr. France Atomic Energy Commn., Val-de-Marne Lab., 1982-86; cons. Lockheed Martin Tactical Def., University Park, 1996—. Contbr. chpt. to book, articles to profl. jours. and conf. procs., including Atmospheric Pollution Jour., Chem. Soc. Am. Jour., Ultrasonics and Acoustics. Instr. Continuing and Distance Edn., Pa. State U., 1996-97. Recipient Northampton (Eng.) County Coun. scholarship, 1970-73, Assn. Contamination Prevention prize, Paris, 1984. Mem. IEEE, AAAS, ASME, Am. Phys. Soc., Acoustical Soc. Am., Sigma Xi. Achievements include development of new technique for air pollution control of submicron particles using high-intensity acoustic waves; contribution to advancement of theory of wave propagation in porous and granular materials. Office: Mesa State Coll 1100 North Ave Grand Junction CO 81501-3122 Home: 463 Margi Ct Grand Junction CO 81504-2611 E-mail: htavossi@mesastate.edu.

TAWYEA, EDWARD WAYNE, university administrator, librarian; b. Detroit, Apr. 29, 1950; s. Wayne J. and Florence Tawyea. BA, U. Detroit, 1972; MS in Libr. Sci., Wayne State U., 1978. Assoc. dir. Northwestern U. Med. Libr., Chgo., 1978-88; dir. acad. info. svcs. and rsch., univ. libr. Thomas Jefferson U., Phila., 1988—. Cons. N.E. Ohio U. Coll. Medicine, Rootstown, Ohio, 1994, N.Y. Med. Coll., Valhalla, 1994; bd. dirs. Chgo. Access Corp. Mem. Assn. Acad. Health Scis. Librs. (bd. dirs. 1989-92, pres. 1996-97), Beta Phi Mu. Office: Thomas Jefferson U 310 Scott 1020 Walnut St Philadelphia PA 19107-5567

TAYLER, IRENE, English literature educator; b. Abilene, Tex., July 13, 1934; d. B. Brown Smith and Madeline (Bowron); m. Edward W. Tayler, June 3, 1961 (div. 1971); children: Edward Jr., Jesse; m. Saul Touster, Jan. 14, 1978. BA in Philosophy, Stanford U., 1956, MA in Am. Lit., 1961, PhD in English Lit., 1968. Tchr. Breadloaf Sch. of Eng., Middlebury, Vt., 1970, 71, 75, 76; teaching asst. Stanford U., Calif., 1958-60; lectr. Columbia U., N.Y., 1961-71; asst. prof. CUNY, 1971-73, assoc. prof., 1973-76, MIT, Cambridge, 1976-82, prof., 1982-96, sec. of the faculty, 1993-95, retired, 1996. Chair gov. com. The English Inst., 1981. Author: Blake's Illustrations to the Poems of Gray, 1971, Holy Ghosts: The Male Muses of Emily and Charlotte Bronte, 1990; contbr. articles to profl. jours. Internat. Inst. Edn. fellow U. Munich, 1957-58; Wilson fellow Stanford U., 1961-62; ACLS study grantee, 1968-69; Faculty Rsch. Found. grantee CUNY, 1972-73; NEH sr. scholar fellow, 1980; Mac Vicar faculty fellow MIT, 1993-2003. Mem.: St. Botolph Club (Boston) (pres. 2000—03). E-mail: itayler@mit.edu.

TAYLOR, ALTON LEE, education educator; b. Kannapolis, N.C., Aug. 8, 1936; s. Robert Lee and Elizabeth Rose (Pitts) T.; m. Ann Paige Gill, July 31, 1964; children: Shannon Leigh, Hunter Page (dec.). BA, Pfeiffer Coll., 1958; MEd, U. Va., 1962, EdD, 1965. Tchr. Morehead City (N.C.) High Sch., 1958-60, Newport News (Va.) High Sch., 1960-61; rsch. supr. Dept. Edn., Richmond, Va., 1965-67; prof., adminstr. U. Va., Charlottesville, 1967—2003. Editor: Individual Privacy, 1977; co-author several books; contbr. articles to profl. jours. Mem. sch. bd. Albemarle County, Va., Charlottesville, 1972-75; bd. dirs. Appalachian Regional Lab., Charleston, W.Va., 1966-67. Fellow AAAS; mem. Assn. Instnl. Rsch. (treas. 1974-77, Outstanding Svc. award 1990), Assn. Univ. Summer Session (pres. 1985-86), Assn. Study Higher Edn., Kappa Delta Pi, Omicron Delta Kappa, Phi Delta Kappa, Raven Soc. Presbyterian. Home: 2601 Bennington Rd Charlottesville VA 22901-2210 Office: U Va Summer Session PO Box 400161 Charlottesville VA 22904-4161

TAYLOR, ANN, human resources specialist, educator; b. Gordonville, Pa., Feb. 28, 1940; d. Gideon S. and Elizabeth L. Stoltzfus; m. James R. Taylor III, Feb. 18, 1983 (dec. Sept. 1995). BA, Ea. Mennonite U., 1966; MEd, Millersville (Pa.) U., 1979; EdD, Temple U., 1995. Caseworker Lancaster (Pa.) Welfare Dept., 1969-72, Lancaster County Probation Parole Dept., 1967-69; parole agent Pa. Bd. Probation, Parole, Harrisburg, 1972-85; human resource cons., trainer Taylor Assocs., Lancaster, 1985—. Adj. prof. bus. mgmt. Pa. State U., Lancaster, 1979-2000; spkr. in field; free lance trainer Hamilton Bank, Lancaster, 1985-91, Armstrong World Industries, Lancaster, 1987, 91; adv. com. staff trainer Vantage Drug and Alcohol Facility, Lancaster, 1983-85. Co-author: Fire Up Your Brilliance; co-author articles to profl. jours. Vol. Lancaster County Mental Health Ctr., 1983-94; seminar leader Fulton County (Pa.) C. of C., 1985-86, York County (Pa.) C. of C., 1985-86, Lancaster County C. of C., 1985-88. Mem. Internat. Coaching Fedn. Democrat. Episcopalian. Avocations: travel, reading, gardening, hiking. Office: 214 E King St Lancaster PA 17602 E-mail: brilliance@comcast.net.

TAYLOR, AUBREY ELMO, physiologist, educator; b. El Paso, Tex., June 4, 1933; s. Virgil T. and Mildred (Maher) Taylor; m. Mary Jane Davis, Apr. 4, 1953; children: Audrey Jane Hildebrand, Lenda Sue Taylor Brown, Mary Ann. BA in Math. and Psychology, Tex. Christian U., 1960; PhD in Physiology, U. Miss., 1964. Fellow biophysics lab. Harvard U. Med. Sch., Boston, 1965-67; from asst. prof. to prof. dept. physiology U. Miss. Coll. Medicine, Jackson, 1967-77; prof., chmn. dept. physiology U. South Ala. Coll. Medicine, Mobile, 1977—2002, Louise Lenoir Locke eminent scholar disting. prof. emeritus, 2002—. Pulmonary score com. mem. Nat. Heart,

Lung and Blood Inst., 1976; with Surgery and Anesthesiology, 1979—82, Manpower Com., 1985—95; chmn. RAP, 1983. Mem. editl. bd.: Jour. Applied Physiology, 1994—, Critical Care Medicine, 1991—97, Circulation Rsch., Am. Jour. Physiology, Internat. Pathophysiology, Microcirculatory and Lymphatic Rsch., Chinese Jour. Physiology, Microcirculation, Jour. Biomed. Sci., Am. Rev. Resp. and Critical Care Jour., Internat. Soc. Pathology, author 9 books: ; contbr. chapters to books, over 730 articles to profl. jours.; N.Am. editor: Clin. Scis., 1998—. With U.S. Army, 1953—55. Named Disting. Physiologist Am. Coll. Chest Physicians, 1994; recipient Lederle Faculty award, 1967—70, Philip Dow award, U. Ga., 1984, NIH Merit award, 1987—97, Lucian award, McGill U., 1988, John Whitney award, U. Ark., 1990, Gelen award, Intestinal Shock Soc., 1991, Arthur C. Guyton award, U. Miss Coll. Medicine, 1993, Disting. Alumnus award, Tex. Christian U., 1998, Disting Svc. award, USA med. Alumni Assn., 2000, Myerson-De Luzio Lectr., Tulane Sch. Medicine, 1997, Disting. Lectr., La State U., Shreveport, 1997, Abreu Meml. Keynote Spkr., U. Tex. Sch. Medicine, Galveston, 1998, Med. Student Rsch. Conf., 1998, Wu-Ho-Su Meml. Symposium Spl. Lectr., chmn. med. student rsch. award com., Am. Heart Assn., 1992—, Wiggers award, Am. Physiol. Soc., 1987, Eugene Landis Rsch. award, Micro Circulatory Soc., 1985, State Rsch. award, Acad. Scis, 1988, award, N.Y. Acad. Scis., 1988; grantee NIH, 1964—. Fellow: Royal Soc. Medicine (bd. dirs.), Am. Heart Assn. (So. regional rev. com. 1977—81, cardiopulmonary, critical care coun. 1977—, chmn. 1979—81, EIA Rev. Com. 1986—95, pulmonary and devel. rev. com. 1987—95, nat. rsch. com. 1990—95, del. assembly 1990—99, chmn. 1993—98, chmn. grant/rev.com 1994—95, coun. affairs com. 1994—98, nominating com. 1998—99, basic sci. com. 1998—, circulation coun., chmn., AALAC bd. trustees rep., Bronze award Miss. AHA 1976, Dickinson W. Richards award 1988, Outstanding Ala. AHA program 1993, Sci. Coun. Achievement award 1995, Disting. Svc. award 1995, Rsch. Achievement award 1997, So. Ala. Dist. Achievement award 2000, Gala honoree 2000, Hall of Fame Spring Hill Hosp. Heart Assn. 2001), AAAS; mem.: European Respiratory Soc. (sec. lung injury group), Am. Thoracic Soc., Fedn. Am. Socs. for Exptl. Biology (bd. dirs. 1988—90, reorganizing com.), Biophys. Soc., N.Y. Acad. Scis., Internat. Pathophysiology Soc. (v.p. 1991—99), N. Am. Soc. Lymphology (pres. 1988—90, Cecil Drinker Rsch. award 1988), Internat. Lymphology Soc., Ala. Acad. Scis. (Ann. State Rsch. award 1988), Micro Circulatory Soc. (coun. 1977—81, pres. 1981—83, Eugene Landis Rsch. award 1985), Assn. Dept. Chairs of Physiology (exec. com. 1996—2001, sec. treas. 1998—2002), Am. Physiol. Soc. (coun. 1984—87, chmn. mem. com. 1985—87, pres. 1987—90, hon. com., chmn. 1993—96, chmn. Perkins fellow com. 1996—98, Cannon lectr. 1999, Wiggers award 1987, Achievement award 2002), NAS (com. for Internat. Union Physiol. Sci.), Sigma Xi, Alpha Omega Alpha. Democrat. Presbyterian. Achievements include research in in cardio-pulmonary physiology, fluid balance, edema, microcirculation and capillary exchange of solute and water and inflammatory processes in the lung. Home: 11 Audubon Pl Mobile AL 36606-1907

TAYLOR, BARBARA ANN OLIN, writer, educational consultant; b. St. Louis, Feb. 8, 1933; d. Spencer Truman and Ann Amelia (Whitney) Olin; m. F. Morgan Taylor Jr., Apr. 5, 1954; children: Frederick M. III, Spencer O., James W., John F. AB, Smith Coll., 1954; M in Mgmt., Northwestern U., 1978, PhD, 1984; LHD, U. New Haven, 1995. Mem. faculty Hamden (Conn.) Hall Country Day Sch., 1972-74; cons. Booz, Allen & Hamilton, Inc., Chgo., 1979; program assoc. Northwestern U., Evanston, Ill., 1982; co-founder, exec. dir. Nat. Ctr. Effective Schs. R&D, Okemos, Mich., 1986-89, rsch. assoc., 1987; chmn. Nat. Ctr. for Effective Schs. Resource and Devel. Found., 2002—; cons. on effective schs. rsch. and reform Nat. Ctr. Effective Schs. R&D U. Wis., Madison, 1990-96; pres. Excelsior! Found., Chgo., 1994—. Mem. exec. com. Hudson Inst., New Am. Schs. Devel. Corp. Design Team, 1990-94; Danforth Disting. lectr. U. Nebr., Omaha, 1993. Co-author: Making School Reform Happen, 1993, Keepers of the Dream, 1994, The Revolution Revisited: Effective Schools and Systemic Reform, 1995; editor: Case Studies in Effective Schools Research, 1990; contbr. articles to profl. jours. Pres. Jr. League of New Haven, 1967-69; pres. NCCJ, New Haven, 1971-73; co-chair Coalition Housing and Human Resources, Hartford-New Haven, 1970-73; co-chair steering com. Day Care Conn., Hartford, 1971-73; trustee U. New Haven, 1961-71, Smith Coll., Northampton, Mass., 1984-90, Choate Rosemary Hall Sch., 1973-78, Lake Forest Coll., 1996—, Hudson Inst., 1989-97, Northwestern U., 1998-2002. Recipient Humanitarian award Mt. Calvary Bapt. Ch., 1988, Outstanding Alumna award John Burroughs Sch., 1994, Pres.'s award U. New Haven. Mem. ASCD, Nat. Commn. Citizens Edn. (bd. dirs. 1980-86), Nat. Staff Devel. Coun., Phi Delta Kappa (Internat. award for Outstanding Svc. 2000). Episcopalian. Office: Nat Ctr Effective Schs Rsch & Devel 222 E Wisconsin Ave Ste 301 Lake Forest IL 60045-1723

TAYLOR, BEVERLY LACY, musician, educator, stringed instrument restorer; b. Denver, Mar. 1, 1928; d. Frederick Thurlow and Ruth (Rogers) Lacy; m. Arthur D. Taylor, Mar. 18, 1967. BA, Wheaton Coll., Norton, Mass., 1949; postgrad., U. Denver, 1951-53, U. Colo., 1953. Scene designer, tech. dir. Piper Players, Idaho Springs, Colo., 1949-51; art instr. Denver Art Mus., 1952; craft and speech instr. Wallace Sch., Denver, 1953; illustrator dept. native art Denver Art Mus., 1954-56; designer, owner The Art Studio, Santa Fe, 1956-58; instr., owner Classic Guitar Studio, Santa Fe, 1959—; instr. classical guitar Santa Fe Conservatory of Music, 1966-67, Coll. Sante Fe, 1971-72; stringed instrument restorer Lacy Taylor Studio, Santa Fe, 1967—. One-woman shows of mosaic panels include Mus. N.Mex., Santa Fe, 1959; exhibited in group shows at Mus. New Mex., 1962, 63; executed mosaic panels Denver Art Mus. Bd. mem. Renesan, Elderhostel Inst. Network. Recipient Miriam Carpenter Art prize Wheaton Coll., 1949, prize N.Mex. State Fair, 1959, 61. Mem. Guild Am. Luthiers, Assn. String Instrument Artisans. Avocations: drawing, gardening, dog training, horse therapy programs for handicapped adults and children. Home: 1210 Canyon Rd Santa Fe NM 87501-6128

TAYLOR, BILLIE WESLEY, retired secondary education educator, investor; b. Charleston, W.Va, Aug. 14, 1940; s. Billie W and Effie (Adams) T.; m. Elisabeth Julia Coler, Jan. 27, 1960; 1 child, Rose Letitia Taylor Allen. BA, Wilmington Coll., 1961; MA, Ohio State U., 1963; PhD, Columbia Pacific U., 1993. Cert. secondary tchr., prin., Ohio. Tchr. Columbus (Ohio) Pub. Schs., 1961-64; records, forms officer U.S. Army, Battle Creek, Mich., 1964-65; prodn. planner Hoover Ball & Bearing Co., Ann Arbor, Mich., 1965-66; dist. exec. Boy Scouts Am., Detroit, 1966-72; sales tng. Standard Register Co., Dayton, Ohio, 1972-74; tchr. Dayton Pub. Schs., 1974-95, curriculum specialist for computer tech., 1989-93. Spkr. in field. Author: History of the D-MC Park District, 1988, Classroom Discipline, 1987. Pres., Johnson Sch. PTA, Taylor, Mich., 1966-67; dist. chmn., Boy Scouts Am., Dayton, 1974-79; mem. S.E. Dayton Priority Bd., Dayton, 1976-77. Recipient Pres. trophy Boy Scouts of Am., 1970; Jenning's scholar Martha Holden Jennings Found., 1980-81. Mem. Nat. Geographic Soc. (life), Nat. Audubon Soc., Smithsonian Nat. Assocs. (charter mem.), Libr. of Congress Assocs. (charter), Nat. Mus. of the Am. Indian (charter), Am. Birding Assn., The Nature Conservancy (life), Am. Assn. Individual Investors (life), Masons. Avocations: birding, motorhoming, foreign travel, reading. Home: 131 Snow Hill Ave Kettering OH 45429-1705

TAYLOR, CAROLYN KAY, music educator; b. Protection, Kans., Mar. 30, 1938; d. Thomas George and Ruby D. Boone; m. Joseph Taylor; children: Corinne K. Maloch, Holly D. Peter, Daren K. Degree in Liberal Studies, Calif. State U., Chico, 1981. Life credential in music Calif. C.C., 1976, cert. multiple subject K-8 Calif., 1991. Instr. Butte C.C., Oroville, Calif., 1976—98; fine arts and music specialist Chico Unified Sch. Dist., Calif., 1985—. Handbell choir dir. First Christian Ch., Chico, 1976—94; choir and handbell choir dir. Bidwell Meml. Presbyn. Ch., Chico, 1979—81; choir dir. Aldersgate United Meth. Ch., 1998—. Musician: Touring Handbell Choir, 1980. Grantee, Kappa Delta Pi, Calif. State U., Chico, 1981. Mem.: Calif. Music Educators' Assn. (treas. .exec. bd. 1994—98, sec. exec. bd. 1998—2001), Am. Orff-Schulwerk Assn. (pres. 1987—89, sec. 1999—2001), Mt. Lassen Chapter, American Orff-Schulwerk Association, California Music Educators' Association, Northern Section. Methodist. Avocation: music. Office: Chapman Sch 1071 E 16th St Chico CA 95928 Office Fax: 530-891-3294.

TAYLOR, DEBORAH ANN, education educator; b. Knoxville, Tenn., Sept. 1, 1951; AB, Cornell U., 1972; MS, Rutgers U., 1974, PhD, 1976. Asst./assoc. prof. Colby-Sawyer Coll., New London, N.H., 1976-86, v.p. student devel., 1986-90, prof., chair psychology, 1992—2001, academic dean, 2001—. Cons. Capital Region Healthcare Corp., Concord, 1994—. Office: Colby-Sawyer Coll 541 Main St New London NH 03257

TAYLOR, DONNA LYNNE, adult training coordinator; b. Balt., July 1, 1944; d. Noel Leroy and Dorothy Anna (Henry) Welsh; 1 child, Tom A., Jr. BS, Okla. State U., 1965, EdD, 1992; MS, Phillips U., 1984. Cert. vocat. bus. and trade and indsl. edn. tchr., prin., supt., vocat. adminstr., Okla. Retail sales, Tulsa, 1961-62; secretary Okla. State U. Coop. Extension Svc., Stillwater, 1965-67; secondary instr. social studies Waller Jr. High, Enid, Okla., 1967-69; substitute instr. Autry Tech. Ctr., Enid, 1971-78, instr. vocat. bus. part-time, 1978-84, instr. vocat. bus. full time, 1984-94, coord. adult edn., 1994—; small bus. owner Lynne's Country Crafts, Enid, 1975-85; coord. adult edn. Autry Tech. Ctr., Enid, 1994—; adult educator Sch. Continuing Edn., Enid, 1981-85. Mem. strategic planning com. and policy and procedures com. Staff Devel. Affirmative Action, Enid, 1989—; presenter ann. confs. and meetings Okla. State Dept. Vocat. Tech., Stillwater, 1991-92; coord., chair Articulation Agreement Com., Enid, 1991-93; advisor FBLA/Phi Beta Lambda, Enid, 1990-94; mem. North Ctrl. Accreditation Steering Com., 1992-93, staff devel. chair, 1993-94. Bd. dirs. Sch. Continuing Edn., Enid, 1975-85; mem. vol. YWCA, March of Dimes, Am. Heart Assn., MS Soc., Am. Diabetes Assn., Enid Art Assn., 1985—; deacon Christian Ch., Enid, 1986-88, elder, 1988-92, 95-96, bd. dirs. 1998—; bd. dirs., mem. steering com. Leadership Greater Enid. Recipient Women of Achievement award March of Dimes, 1992; named Okla. Bus. Tchr. of Yr., 1994. Mem. Am. Vocat. Assn., Okla Vocat. Assn., Enid C. of C. (edn. com. 1991-92), Phi Delta Kappa (sec. 1992—), PEO Sisterhood. Republican. Avocations: art, volunteering, reading. Home: 2110 Appomattox Enid OK 73703-2008 Office: Autry Tech Ctr 1201 W Willow Rd Enid OK 73703-2506

TAYLOR, EDWARD CURTIS, chemistry educator; b. Springfield, Mass., Aug. 3, 1923; s. Edward Curtis and Margaret Louise (Anderson) T.; m. Virginia Dion Crouse, June 29, 1946; children: Edward Newton, Susan Raines. Student, Hamilton Coll., 1942-44, DSc (hon.), 1969; AB, Cornell U., 1946, PhD, 1949. Postdoctoral fellow Nat. Acad. Scis., Zurich, Switzerland, 1949-50; DuPont postdoctoral fellow chemistry U. Ill., 1950-51, faculty, 1951-54, asst. prof. organic chemistry, 1952-54; faculty Princeton U., 1954—, prof. chemistry, 1964—, A. Barton Hepburn prof. organic chemistry, 1966—, A. Barton Hepburn prof. organic chemistry emeritus, 1997—, chmn. dept. chemistry, 1974-79, sr. rsch. scientist, 1997—. Vis. prof. Technische Hochschule, Stuttgart, Fed. Republic Germany, 1960, U. East Anglia, 1969, 71; Disting. vis. prof. U. Buffalo, 1968, U. Wyo., 1977; Backer lectr. U. Groningen, Holland, 1969; mem. chemistry adv. com. Office Sci. Research, USAF, 1962-73, Cancer Chemotherapy Nat. Service Ctr., 1958-62; mem. internat. adv. bd. Ctr. Medicinal Chemistry, Bar-Ilan U., Israel, 1994—; cons. rsch. divs. Procter & Gamble, 1953-80, Eastman Kodak Co., 1965-83, Tenn. Eastman Co., 1968-83, Eli Lilly & Co., 1960-2002, Burroughs Wellcome Co., 1983-95, E.I. duPont de Nemours & Co., 1986-90, Polaroid Corp., 1986-2001, Dow Elanco Co., 1989-96, DuPont Merck Pharm. Co., 1990-97, Dow AgroScis., 1997-2003, DuPont Pharms. Co., 1997-2001. Author: (with McKillop) Chemistry of Cyclic Enaminonitriles and o-Aminonitriles, 1970, Principles of Heterocyclic Chemistry: film and audio courses, 1974; editor (with Raphael and Wynberg) Advances in Organic Chemistry, vols I-V, 1960-65, (with Wynberg) Vol VI, 1969, vols. VII-IX, 1970-79 (with W. Pfleiderer) Pteridine Chemistry, 1964, The Chemistry of Heterocyclic Compounds, 1968—, General Heterocyclic Chemistry, 1968—; organic chemistry editl. advisor John Wiley & Sons, Inc., 1968—; mem. editl. adv. bd. Jour. Medicinal Chemistry, 1962-66, Jour. Organic Chemistry, 1971-75, Synthetic Communications, 1971—, Heterocycles, 1973—, Chm. Substructure Index, 1971—, Advances in Heterocyclic Chemistry, 1983—, Pteridines, 1989—. Recipient rsch. awards SmithKline and French Found., 1955, Hoffmann-LaRoche Foun., 1964-65, Ciba Found., 1971, Disting. Hamilton award, 1977, U.S. Sr. Scientist prize Alexander von Humboldt Found., 1983, Disting. Alumni medal Hamilton Coll., 1990, F. Gowland Hopkins medal, 1993; sr. faculty fellow Harvard U., 1959; Guggenheim fellow, 1979-80. Fellow N.Y. Acad. Scis., Am. Inst. Chemists; mem. Am. Chem. Soc. (award for creative work in synthetic organic chemistry, 1974, chmn. organic chemistry div. 1976-77, Arthur C. Cope scholar award 1994), German Chem. Soc., Royal Soc. London, Internat. Soc. Heterocyclic Chemistry (5th Internat.. award 1989), Phi Beta Kappa, Sigma Xi, Phi Kappa Phi. Home: 288 Western Way Princeton NJ 08540-5337 E-mail: etaylor@princeton.edu.

TAYLOR, ELISABETH COLER, retired secondary school educator; b. N.Y.C., Jan. 24, 1942; d. Gerhard Helmut and Judith Coler; m. Billie Wesley Taylor II, Jan. 27, 1960; children: Letitia Rose, Billie Albert. Student, Wilmington Coll., 1959-60; BS, Wayne State U., Detroit, 1969; MS, The Ohio State U., 1980; postgrad., Wright State U., Dayton, Ohio, 1989—. Cert. home economist. H.s. tchr. home econs., computer sci., lang. arts Dayton (Ohio) City Schs., 1972-99. Bd. dirs. Camp Fire Girls, 1970-71, vol. Detroit Mus. of Art, 1970-71, group leader Camp Fire Girls, Boy Scouts, Dayton, 1968-74. Mem. AAUW (life), Am. Mensa Ltd. (life). Avocations: birding, travelling, needlework. Home: 131 Snow Hill Ave Dayton OH 45429-1705

TAYLOR, FANNIE TURNBULL, social education and arts administration educator; b. Kansas City, Mo., Sept. 11, 1913; d. Henry King and Fannie Elizabeth (Sills) Turnbull; m. Robert Taylor, Dec. 2, 1938 (div. 1974); children: Kathleen Muir Taylor Isaacs, Anne Kingston Taylor Wadsack. BA, U. Wis., 1938; LHD (hon.), Buena Vista Coll., Storm Lake, Iowa, 1975. Mem. faculty U. Wis., Madison, 1941—, prof. social edn., 1949—, emerita, 1979—. Dir. Wis. Union Theater, 1946-66, coord. univ. systems arts coun., 1967-70, assoc. dir. Ctr. Arts Adminstrn., 1970-72, coord. Consortium for Arts, 1976-84; cons. in field. Author: The Arts at a New Frontier: The National Endowment for the Arts, Wisconsin Union Theater: Fifty Golden Years (Book award of Merit, State Hist. Soc. Wis. 1990); contbr. articles to profl. jours. Program dir. music Nat. Endowment Arts, 1966-67, program info. dir., 1972-76; bd. dirs. Wis. Arts Coun., 1964-72, Wis. Found. Arts, 1976-91, Madison Civic Music Assn., 1976-84, Madison Children's Mus., 1983-96, Elvehjem Mus. Art Coun., 1976—, chair 1983-86; Madison Civic Ctr. Found., 1981-94; hon. chair Wis. Union Theater Program Endowment Fund, 1985—; bd. dirs. Wis. chpt. Nature Conservancy, 1963-84, chmn. 1976-77; bd. dirs. Shorewood Hills Found., 1976—, pres., 1976-81. Recipient Oak Leaf award Nature Conservancy, 1981, Wis. Gov.'s award in Support of the Arts, 1992, Madison Cmty. Found. Asset Builders Leadership award, 2002; named Woman of Distinction, Madison YWCA, 1994. Fellow Wis. Acad. Scis., Arts and Letters; mem. Assn. Performing Arts Presenters (founder, exec. dir. 1957-72, 1st recipient Fannie Taylor award 1972), Am. Assn. Dance Cos. (bd. dirs. 1967-72), Nat. Assn. Regional Ballet (bd. dirs. 1975-77), Nat. Guild Cmty. Music Schs. Arts (bd. dirs. 1977-80), Women in Comm. (Writers' Cup 1980), U. Wis. Found., U. Wis. Alumni Assn. (Disting. Svc. award 1979), Madison Civics Club (pres. 1969-70), Univ. Club (pres. 1982-85), Blackhawk Club. Home: 8301 Old Sauk Rd Apt 303 Middleton WI 53562-4393 E-mail: ftaylor@facstaff.wisc.edu.

TAYLOR, G. DON, industrial engineering educator; b. Anchorage, Alaska, Mar. 25, 1960; s. Gaylon Don and Rita M. (Eudy) T.; m. Jo Ellen Gibson, June 6, 1987; children: Daniel Alexander, Caroline Frances. BS in Indsl. Engring., U. Tex., Arlington, 1983, MS in Indsl. Engring., 1985; PhD, U. Mass., 1990. Registered profl. engr., Ark. Mfg. engr., supr. Tex. Instruments Inc., Lewisville, 1983-86; process engr. Digital Equipment Corp., Enfield, Conn., 1987-89; asst. prof. U. Ark., Fayetteville, 1990-94, assoc. prof. indsl. engring., 1994-98; prof., dir. The Logistics Inst., 1998—99; Mary Lee and George F. Duthie Chair in Engring. Logistics U. Louisville, 2000—. Dir. Ctr. for Engring Logistics and Distbn, U. Louisville, Ky., 2001—. Contbr. more than 160 articles to tech. pubs. Mem. Am. Soc. Engring. Edn., Inst. Indsl. Engrs. (sr. mem., faculty advisor 1992-93), Sigma Xi, Tau Beta Pi. Achievements include principal investigator on research grants totaling more than $4 million. Home: 2909 Pin Oak Dr La Grange KY 40031-9490 Office: U Louisville Dept Indsl Engring Louisville KY 40292

TAYLOR, HUGH PETTINGILL, JR., geologist, educator; b. Holbrook, Ariz., Dec. 27, 1932; s. Hugh Pettingill and Genevieve (Fillerup) T.; m. Candis E. Hoffman, 1982. BS, Calif. Inst. Tech., 1954; A.M., Harvard U., 1955; PhD, Calif. Inst. Tech., 1959. Asst. prof. geochemistry Pa. State U., 1960-62; mem. faculty div. geol. and planetary scis. Calif. Inst. Tech., 1962—, now prof. geology, Robert P. Sharp prof., 1981. Crosby vis. prof. M.I.T., 1978; vis. prof. Stanford U., 1981; William Smith lectr. Geol. Soc. London, 1976; Hofmann lectr. Harvard U., 1980; Cloos lectr. Johns Hopkins U., 1986; with U.S. Geol. Survey, Saudi Arabia, 1980-81 Author: The Oxygen Isotope Geochemistry of Igneous Rocks, 1968, Stable Isotopes in High Temperature Geological Processes, 1986, Stable Isotope Geochemistry, 1991; assoc. editor Bull. Geol. Soc. Am, 1969-71, Geochimica Cosmochimica Acta, 1971-76; editor Chem. Geology, 1985-91. Recipient Day medal Geol. Soc. Am., Urey medal European Assn. Geochem., 1995. Fellow NAS, Soc. Econ. Geol., Geol. Soc. Am., Am. Geophys. Union, Mineral. Soc. Am. (councillor), Am. Acad. Arts and Scis.; mem. Geochem. Soc. (councillor). Republican.

TAYLOR, JAMES SHEPPARD, communications educator; b. Montgomery, Ala., Dec. 15, 1943; s. Elbert Ruppert and Mary Pinckard (Bryan) T.; m. Mary Ann Luck, Mar. 30, 1972; children: John Brinson Overstreet, Laura Luck Biering. BA in Speech, Auburn U., 1965, MA in Speech, 1966; PhD in Rhetoric and Pub. Address, Fla. State U., 1968. Grad. asst. Auburn (Ala.) U., 1965-66, asst. prof. speech, 1969-73; grad. asst. Fla. State U., Tallahassee, 1966-68; asst. prof. speech N.C. State U., Raleigh, 1968-69; assoc. prof., chair comms. Houston Bapt. U., 1973-94, prof., chair comms., assoc. dean arts and humanities, 1994-98, dean arts and humanities, 1998—. Editl. assoc. So. Speech Jour., 1967-68; mem. editl. bd. N.C. Jour. Speech, 1966-69; news and notions editor So. Speech Comm. Jour., 1972-75. Recipient Tchg. Excellence and Campus Leadership award Sears-Roebuck Found., 1989-90. Mem. Tex. Speech Comm. Assn., So. States Comm. Assn., Speech Comm. Assn. (ERIC evaluator 1973-76), Phi Kappa Phi, Phi Delta Kappa, Kappa Delta Pi, Omicron Delta Kappa. Democrat. Methodist. Avocations: golf, running, tennis, hiking, reading. Office: Houston Bapt U 7502 Fondren Rd Houston TX 77074-3298 E-mail: jtaylor@hbu.edu., jsheppardtaylor@msn.com.

TAYLOR, JANE ELLEN, elementary educator; b. Port Clinton, Ohio, Feb. 2, 1955; d. Santo Thomas and Martha Zelma (Finefrock) Cipti; m. William Michael Taylor, Apr. 30, 1976; children: Aaron, Molly. BS in Edn., Ohio State U., 1979; MEd in Curriculum and Instrn., Ashland U., 1995. Paralegal cert. Am. Paralegal Assn. Mid. sch. team leader Discovery Sch., Mansfield, Ohio, 1979-82; tchr. 3rd/4th grade St. Edward's Sch., Ashland, Ohio, 1984-86; tchr. 4th grade St. Joseph's Sch., Libertyville, Ill., 1987-88; tchr. 2nd grade South Jordan (Utah) Elem. Sch., 1990-91; tchr. 1st grade Bataan Elem. Sch., Port Clinton, 1995-96, tchr. 2nd grade intervention class, 1996—, tchr. 3rd grade, 1997-98, tchr. 1st grade, 1998-99, tchr. 2nd grade, 1999—. Com. mem. Blue Ribon Com., Port Clinton, 1996—. Author: Mrs. T. and the Can-Do Kids, 1997. Active Bataan Parent/Tchr. Orgn., Bataan Sch., 1997—. Recipient Wal-Mart Tchr. of the Yr. award, 1997. Mem. Future Educators Am. (co-advisor 1996—), Port Clinton Athletic Boosters, Port Clinton Music Boosters, Port Clinton Acad. Boosters. Republican. Roman Catholic. Avocations: reading, swimming, computers, home decorating, family activities. Office: Bataan Elem W 6th St Port Clinton OH 43452

TAYLOR, JANET WINONA MILLS, secondary school educator; b. Shelby, N.C., Aug. 3, 1948; d. Robert Lee Sr. and Janet Elizabeth (Plair) Mills; m. Bernard D. Taylor, Dec. 31, 1983; 1 child, Adam Jason. BS in Health Edn., Morgan State Coll., 1974; MS in Ednl. Leadership, Morgan State U., 1986, EdD in Ednl. Adminstrn., 1994. Md. State Dept. Edn. Advanced Profl. cert. for supt., supr., secondary prin., health and gen. sci. tchr. grades 5-12. Tchr. Baltimore (Md.) City Pub. Schs., 1973-78; health educator Morgan State Coll., Balt., 1978-79; tchr. Montgomery County Pub. Schs., Rockville, 1979—. Tech. writer, cons. The Assignment Group, Rockville, Md., 1990—; rsch. cons., rsch. assoc. Inst. for Urban Rsch., Morgan State U., 1992-93; libr. adv. bd. mem. Morgan State U., Balt., 1993—; grant cons. United Missionary Bapt., Inc., Balt., 1993—; GED test adminstr. Md. State Dept. Edn., Balt., 1993-94; co-dir. for grants and proposals United Missionary Bapt. Devel. Corp. Md., Balt., 1993—; mem. selection and evaluation adv. com. Montgomery County Pub. Schs., Rockville, 1993—. Editor (monthly jour.) The Doorkeeper, 1987-88. Dir. youth ministry Mt. Hebron Bapt. Ch., Balt., 1990-94; co-dir. children's ministry Bapt. Congress Christian Edn., Balt., 1992-94; corr. sec. Bapt. Congress Christian Edn., Balt., 1993—. Sgt. USAR, 1975-80. Mem. AERA, Zeta Phi Beta. Baptist. Avocations: reading, traveling, playing computer games and chess. Home: 3401 Southern Ave Baltimore MD 21214-3025

TAYLOR, JEAN MULL, home economics educator, secondary educator; b. Clover, Va., Feb. 18, 1953; d. Albert Herman and Helen (Jones) Mull; m. Derek Lester, June 28, 1975; children: Jennifer, Brian. BS, Longwood Coll., 1975; postgrad., Clemson U., 1984, U. S.C., 1986, U. Va., 1991; MS, Va. Poly. and Tech. U., Blacksburg, 1995. Cert. tchr., nutritionist, Va., S.C. Tchr. home econs. Bluestone Sr. High Sch., Skipwith, Va., 1975, Whitlock Jr. High Sch., Spartanburg, S.C., 1976-80, McCracken Jr. High Sch., 1984-85, James F. Byrnes High Sch., 1985-87; tchr. occupl. home econs. Park View Sr. High Sch., South Hill, Va., 1987—96; tchr. home econs. Cape Hatteras Sch. Career Devel. Ctr., Buxton, NC, 1996—. State officer advisor, master advisor FHA/HERO, Va., 1990-94, advisor mentor, 1992-93; cons. home econs.; mem. adv. bd. Va. Assn. Future Homemakers Am.-Home Econs. Related Occupations, Richmond, Va., 1989—; journalist cmty. newspaper, Spartanburg, 1983-87. Pres. Upsy Daisy Garden Club, Spartanburg, 1980; moderator Presbyn. Women, Chase City, Va., 1989-91; enabler Presbyn. Women, Presbytery of the James, 1991-95; lead tchr., coord. Cmty. of Caring. Student Body Nutrition Edn. grantee Va. Dept. Edn., 1991-92. Mem. Va. Home Econs. Tchr. Assn. (pres. elect 1992-93, South Ctrl. Tchr. of Yr. 1991, pres. 1993-94, Tchr. of Yr. 1993), Am. Vocat. Assn., Va. Vocat. Assn., Am. Home Econs. Assn., Va. Home Econs. Assn., N.C. Spl. Needs Assn., N.C. Assn. for Career and Tech. Edn. (tchr., mentor Dare County Schs.), N.C. Vocat. Assn. (spl. pops and guidance divsn.), Garden Clubs S.C. (life), Nat. Fedn. of Garden Clubs, Kiwanis Club (pres. 2002—).. Avocations: boating, gardening, collecting books and antiques, cooking. Home: PO Box 283 Frisco NC 27936-0283 Office: Park View Sr High Sch RR 1 Box 118 South Hill VA 23970-9506 also: Cape Hatteras Sch Career Devel Ctr PO Box 948 Buxton NC 27920-0948

TAYLOR, JEFFREY LEE, political science educator, author; b. Spencer, Iowa, Jan. 30, 1961; s. James Lee and Judith Lane (Crowder) Taylor; m. Shirley Jean Bentz, Dec. 29, 1990; 1 child, William Taylor (dec.). BA magna cum laude, Northwestern Coll., 1983; MA, U. Iowa, 1985; PhD, U. Mo., 1997. Libr., instr. No. State U., Aberdeen, S.D., 1985-90; libr. Lincoln U., Jefferson City, Mo., 1994-95, Univ. Ctr. Rochester, Minn., 1997—; instr. polit. sci. Rochester Cmty. and Tech. Coll., 1999—. Instr. S.D. Pub. Library Tng. Inst., Pierre, 1987, Southea. Libraries Coop., Rochester, 1997-98. Author: From Radical to Respectable, 1997. Chair Boone County Green Party, Columbia, Mo., 1994-96, Mo. Green Party, 1996; chair Olmsted County Green Party, Rochester, 2001-02; co-mgr. McGaa for Senate, 2002. State of Iowa scholar, 1979. Mem. Am. Polit. Sci. Assn., Acad. Polit. Sci., Minn. Libr. Assn. Mem. Soc. of Friends. Office: Univ Ctr Rochester 851 30th Ave SE Rochester MN 55904

TAYLOR, JOHN W. mycologist, educator; BA in Ecology, U. Calif., Berkeley, Calif., 1972; MS in Mycology, U. Calif., Davis, Calif., 1974, PhD in Botany, 1978. Tchr. mycology U. Calif., prof. Dept. Plant Biology. Contbr. numerous articles to scientific jours. Recipient William H. Weston award, 1994. Office: Dept of Plant Biology 321 Koshland Hall Univ Calif Berkeley CA 94720*

TAYLOR, KAREN MARIE, education educator; b. Batavia, N.Y., June 15, 1961; d. Francis Edward and Barbara (Kearney) Dyrbala; m. Kenneth Douglas Taylor, July 3, 1992; 1 child, Kyle. AS, Genesee Community Coll., 1982; BS, Utah State U., 1984; MS, Nazareth Coll., 1991. Cert. tchr., N.Y., Ark. Reading coord. Genesee-Wyoming BOCES, Batavia, N.Y., 1985; secondary English educator Penn Yan (N.Y.) Acad., 1985-92, alternative edn. tchr., 1987-88; instr. TESOL Hobart Coll., Geneva, N.Y., 1991; adj. instr. English Genesee Cmty. Coll., Batavia, N.Y., 1993-97, instr. English/TESOL, 1997—. Class advisor Penn Yan Acad., 1986-89, drug free schs. mem., 1989-90, student coun. advisor, 1989-92, coord. natural helpers, 1990-92; vis. lectr. English Ark. Tech. U., Russellville, Ark., 1992-93; TESOL instr. Genesee Valley BOCES, 1993-97. Author: (poetry) A Child's World, 1985 (Honorable Mention 1985), Always: A Vilanelle, 1985 (Honorable Mention 1985), You, 1985 (Honorable Mention 1985), The American Flag, 1986 (Honorable Mention 1986). Mem. Assn. Sch. Curriculum and Design, Nat. Coun. Tchrs. English. Democrat. Roman Catholic. Avocations: creative writing, canoeing, fishing, hiking, attending cultural events. Home: 15 Favor St Attica NY 14011-1201

TAYLOR, KENNETH DOUGLAS, stockbroker, finance and computer consultant, educator; b. Topeka, Nov. 21, 1942; s. Olin Orlando and Lola Louise (Conley) T.; AB, George Washington U., 1964, MS in Stats., 1966; MS in Computer Sci. SUNY, 1990, PhD in Math. Eurotech, 1992, (univ. fellow); student of Peter Hilton; postgrad., McGill U., 1975, Bowdoin Coll., U. Montreal; m. Joy Ellen Rice, May 25, 1973 (div. Nov. 1981); m. Elizabeth Flanagan Brunner, May 6, 1995. Registered rep./stockbroker, options principal. Sr. programmer C-E-I-R, Inc., 1963, 69; instr. Army Map Svc., 1964-65; student instr. McGill U., 1966-71; rsch. assoc. U. Va. Med. Sch., 1972; fin. and computer cons., Plymouth, N.Y., 1973-87; computer scientist USAF, 1989-90; broker Russell Hawkes Assoc./Linsco/Pvt. Ledger, 1993-94, LESKO Fin Svcs, 1994—; sec. Richmond (Va.) Computer Club, 1977. Contbr. articles to profl. jours. Summer grantee NSF, Can. Research Council. Mem. ASTM, Am. Math. Soc. Home: PO Box 288 Montrose PA 18801-0288 Office: LESKO Fin Svcs Centre Plz 53 Chenango St Binghamton NY 13901-2820

TAYLOR, KENNETH LAPHAM, history and science educator; b. LA, Calif., May 16, 1941; s. Angus Ellis and Mary Kathleen (Lapham) T.; m. Melva Lee Johnson, Aug. 28, 1969; children: Melissa, Benjamin, Nathaniel. AB, Harvard U., 1962, AM, 1965, PhD, 1968. Asst. prof. U. Okla., Norman, Okla., 1967-72, assoc. prof., 1972-86, dept. chair history sci., 1979-92, 99, prof., 1986—. Hudson/Torchmark Presidential Prof., 2002-, Contbr. early history geology articles to profl. jours. Posdoctoral Rsch. fellow Centre Nat. de la Recherche Scientifique, Paris, 1973-74, Visiting Scholar, Ecole des Hautes Etudes en Sciences Sociales, Paris, 2001. Mem. Internat. Commn. for History Geol. Scis., US Nat. Com. for History Geology (chair 1990-93), History of Earth Scis. Soc. (pres. 1997-98), History of Sci. Soc. (vis. lectr. 1990-92), Geol. Soc. Am. (chair Hist. Geology divsn. 1999), Geol. Soc. London (Sue Tyler Friedman medal 1998). Home: 718 W Timberdell Rd Norman OK 73072-6323 Office: U Okla Dept History Sci Norman OK 73019-3106 E-mail: ktaylor@ou.edu.

TAYLOR, LEIGH HERBERT, college dean; b. Chgo., Oct. 23, 1941; s. Herbert and Leona Taylor; m. Nancy E. Young; children: Jennifer, Jeremiah. BA, U. Tulsa, 1964, JD, 1966; LLM, NYU, 1969. Bar: Okla. 1966, Ill. 1976. Trial atty. Civil Rights div. Dept. Justice, Washington, 1966-68; prof. DePaul U. Coll. Law, Chgo., 1969-77, asst. dean, 1972-73, assoc. dean, 1973-77; dean Coll. Law, Ohio No. U., Ada, 1977-78, Sch. Law Southwestern U., L.A., 1978—. Mem. adv. bd. 1st Woman's Bank of L.A., 1981-85; dir. Law Sch. Admissions Svcs., Inc., 1982-86; chmn. audit com. Law Sch. Admissions Coun., 1989-91, trustee, 1991-98, chair-elect, 1994-95, chair, 1995-97; mem. bd. trustees Coun. on Legal Edn. Opportunity, 1993-96, NALP Found., 1999—, chair-elect, 2002—. Editor-in-chief Tulsa Law Jour., 1966; author: Strategies for Law-Focused Education, 1977; (with others) Law in a New Land, 1972; mem. editorial bd. Family Law Quarterly, 1977-78. Bd. dirs. Criminal Def. Consortium Cook County (Ill.), Inc., 1975-77, L.A. Press Club Found., NALP Found., 1999—. With AUS, 1959. Fellow Am. Bar Found.; mem. ABA (accreditation com. 1991-95), Law in Am. Soc. Found., Ill. Bar Assn., Chgo. Bar Assn. (rec. sec.), L.A. County Bar Assn., Okla. Bar Assn. Office: Southwestern U Sch Law Office of Dean 675 S Westmoreland Ave Los Angeles CA 90005-3905 E-mail: ltaylor@swlaw.edu.

TAYLOR, LESLI ANN, pediatric surgery educator; b. N.Y.C., Mar. 2, 1953; d. Charles Vincent Taylor and Valene Patricia (Blake) Garfield. BFA, Boston U., 1975; MD, Johns Hopkins U., 1981. Diplomate Am. Bd. Surgery. Surg. resident Beth Israel Hosp., Boston, 1981-88; rsch. fellow Pediatric Rsch. Lab. Mass. Gen. Hosp., Boston, 1984-86; fellow pediatric surgery Children's Hosp. of Phila., Phila., 1988-90; asst. prof. pediatric surgery U. N.C., Chapel Hill, 1990-97, assoc. prof. pediat. surgery, 1997—. Author: (booklet) Think Twice: The Medical Effects of Physical Punishment, 1985. Recipient Nat. Rsch. Svc. award NIH, 1984-86. Fellow Am. Coll. Surgeons; mem. AMA, Am. Acad. Pediatrics, Am. Pediat. Surg. Assn. Achievements include research on organ preservation for pediatric liver transplantation and short bowel syndrome. E-mail: lataylor@med.unc.edu.

TAYLOR, LYNDA DORA, school administrator, principal; b. Chgo., Sept. 11, 1951; d. Dock and Earnestine (Mims) Yancey; m. Robert Taylor, Aug. 4, 1973; children: Robert Jamal, Kyla Nichelle, Shavon Lynn, Lisa Michelle, Joshua Andrew. BS, No. Ill. U., 1973, MS, 1975. Cert. adminstr., elem. tchr., spl. edn. tchr., tchr. of physically handicapped, Ill. Tchr. Ill. Children's Hosp. Sch., 1973; cons., coord. Ill. Office Edn., DeKalb, 1976-77; tchr. Valley View Sch.-Salek Elem., Bolingbrook, Ill., 1980, Mesa (Ariz.) Pub. Schs., Valley View Schs.-Northview, Bolingbrook, assoc. prin., 1988-90, Valley View Schs.-Tibbott, Bolingbrook, 1990-94; prin. Maercker Elem. Sch., Westmont, Ill., 1994—. Cons. Knutson Cons. Firm, Chgo., 1988-89. Creator vol. program, writing program, others. Emergency food chair FISH, Bolingbrook, 1989—; leader Girl Scouts U.S., Bolingbrook, 1991—; chair Family Life Conf.-Ill., Little Rock, 1989—. Recipient various awards. Mem. ASCD, Nat. Prins. Assn., Ill. Reading Assn., Ill. Prins. Assn., Phi Delta Kappa, Delta Sigma Theta. Baptist. Avocations: reading, skating, exercise. Office: Valley View Schs-Tibbott 520 Gary Dr Bolingbrook IL 60440-2400

TAYLOR, MARGARET WISCHMEYER, retired language educator; b. Terre Haute, Ind., Aug. 5, 1920; d. Carl and Grace (Riehle) Wischmeyer; m. John Edward Taylor, Sept. 5, 1942 (dec. 1988); children: Deborah Ann, Tobin Edward (dec. 2002), Mary Leesa. BA magna cum laude, Duke U., 1941; MA, John Carroll U., Cleve., 1973. Feature writer Dayton (Ohio) Daily News, 1945-53; freelance writer Cleve., 1953—; asst. to Dr. Joseph B. Rhine Duke U. Parapsychology Lab., Durham, NC, 1941; asst. prof. English and journalism Ea. Campus, Cuyahoga CC, Cleve., 1973-92, prof. emeritus, 1992—, advisor campus newspaper, 1973-84, dir. Writers Conf., 1975-90. Writing cons., editor various cos. and pubs., Cleve., 1973—; founder, operator Grammar Hot Line, 1987-92. Author: Crystal Lake Reflections, 1985, English 101 Can Be Fun, 1991, The Basic English Handbook, 1995. Recipient top state honors Ohio Newspaper Women's Assn., 1947, award for best ednl., best overall stories Am. Heart Assn., 1970, Besse award for tchg. excellence, 1980, Profl. Excellence award, 1985, Provost's Pride award, 1987, Nat. Tchg. Excellence award Coun. for Advancement and Support of Edn., 1989; named Ohio Outstanding Citizen, Ohio Ho. Reps., 1987, 89, Innovator of Yr., League for Innovations in C.C.s, 1988, Pres.'s award Cuyahoga C.C., 1992. Mem. Mensa, Phi Beta Kappa, Pi Beta Phi. Presbyterian. Avocations: grammar consulting, reading, writing. Home: 27900 Fairmount Blvd Cleveland OH 44124-4616 E-mail: taylorstock@ameritech.net.

TAYLOR, MARGARET TURNER, clothing designer, architectural designer, economist, writer, planner; b. Wilmington, N.C., May 7, 1944. A.B. in Econs., Smith Coll., 1966; M.A. in Econ. History, U. Pa., 1970, now Ph.D. candidate in City and Regional Planning. Tchr. Jefferson Jr. High Sch., New Orleans, 1966-69; instr. econs. U. Tex.-El Paso, 1974-75; adj. prof. econs., Salisbury State U., Md., 1976-78; prin. mgr., designer Margaret Norriss, women's clothing, Salisbury, Md., 1980-95; owner Functional Design Ideas, Inc., 1995—; planner at Wharton Ctr. Applied Research, Phila., 1985-86; planning cons., writer.

TAYLOR, MARK ALAN, academic administrator; b. Mt. Vernon, Ill., Apr. 10, 1959; s. Roy Jr. and Lora Kathleen (Ashby) T.; m. Kimberly June Weldon, June 15, 1996. BS, Ariz. State U., 1981; PhD, Purdue U., 1986. Rsch. scientist Purdue U., West Lafayette, Ind., 1986-87; faculty assoc. Ariz. State U. West, Tempe, 1987-90; asst. prof. Grand Canyon U., Phoenix, 1987-92, assoc. prof., 1992-94, asst. v.p., 1990-92, prof., 1994—, v.p. program devel., 1992—. Lectr. Agrl. Coll., Urumchi, China, summer 1988; adj. assoc. prof., coord. med. edn. Kirksville (Mo.) Coll. Osteo. Medicine/S.W. Ctr., 1990-94, assoc. dean for adminstrv. affairs, 1994-95, asst. to pres., 1995—; acad. liaison and design cons. Alcyone Group Inc., 1995—; mem. Ariz. Advanced Placement Bd., Phoenix, 1987—, Ariz. Biology Conf., Phoenix, 1988—, Ariz. Alliance Sci. and Tech. Edn., Phoenix, 1987—. Author: Biochemistry of the Cell, 1989, Genetics: A Human and Molecular Approach, 1990, Microbiology: A Medical Frontier, 1989, Biology: Cell Structure and Function, 1989, 2d edit., 1991, Developmental Biology, 1991, Cell Biology, 1992, 96, 98, Careers in Health Care and Medicine, 1992, 94, 98; contbr. numerous articles to profl. jours. Mem. adv. coun. Salvation Army, Phoenix, 1990-93. Recipient James S. Mountain Meml. award, Founder's award Woods Hole Oceanographic Inst., 1984. Mem. AAAS, Soc. Devel. Biology, Am. Soc. Cell Biology, Am. Inst. Biol. Scis., N.Y. Acad. Sci., Ariz.-Nev. Acad. Sci., Sigma Xi, Phi Beta Kappa, Phi Kappa Phi. Republican. Methodist. Achievements include research in the regulation of translation and meiotic maturation in Xenopus laevis; development of health care education programs and consortiums. Office: Grand Canyon Univ 3300 W Camelback Rd Phoenix AZ 85017-1097

TAYLOR, MARY KATHLEEN, school system administrator; b. Lincoln, Ill., Dec. 6, 1948; d. Ward Wailynn and Helen Louise (Twomey) T. BS in Edn., Ea. Ill. U., 1970; MS in Phys. Edn., U. N.C., 1977; MS in Edn., Ill. State U., 1986, postgrad. Tchr. various sch. dists., Ill., 1970-81; asst. dir. Tha Huong Refugee Program, Peoria, Ill., 1981-82; asst. prin. GA adminstrn. Metcalf Lab. Sch., Normal, Ill., 1985-86; prin. Blue Ridge CUSD #18, Farmer City, Ill., 1986-87, Woodland CUSD #5, Streator, Ill., 1987-89; supr. Ill. State Bd. Edn., Springfield, 1990—. Author, editor, pub. Sportswoman Mag., 1977-79; author jour. Midwest Comparative Edn. Assn., 1989. USFHA del. U.S. Olympic Co. Ho. of Del., 1980-84. Mem. NOW, AAUW, United Meth. Women, Nat. Assn. Female Execs., Nat. Soc. Colonial Daus. of 17th Century, Nat. Assn. Coun. for Citizens against Govt. Waste, Nat. Abortion Rights Action League, Greenpeace, Nat. Wildlife Fedn., World Wildlife Fund, Nat. Parks & Conservations Assn., Nat. Conservancy, Nat. Audubon Soc., Smithsonian, Am. Mus. Nat. Hist., Assn. Supervision and Curriculum Devel., Ill. Assn. Supervision and Curriculum Devel., Ill. Prins. Assn., Am. Assn. Health, Phys. Edn., Recreation and Dance, Ill. Assn. Health, Phys. Edn., Recreation and Dance, U.S. Field Hockey Assn. (exec. com. 1976-86, adminstrv. coun. 1976-87), Midwest Field Hockey Assn., Ctrl. Ill. Field Hockey Assn. Avocations: music, backpacking, gardening. Office: Ill State Bd Edn 100 N 1st St Springfield IL 62702-5042

TAYLOR, MARY LEE, retired college administrator; b. Amarillo, Tex., Nov. 13, 1931; d. David Kelly and Bessie F. (Peck) McGehee; m. Lindsey Taylor, Sept. 13, 1950 (dec. Aug. 1985); children: Gary, Kent, Ronald. BS, W. Tex. State U., 1959; MEd, Tex. Tech U., 1975. Tchr. Mesquite (Tex.) Pub. Schs., 1961-63; resource tchr. Amarillo Pub. Schs., 1971-79, supr., 1979-80; reading instr. Amarillo Coll., 1981-88, asst. prof. reading, 1988-93, assoc. prof., 1994-95. Project dir. Tex. Edn. Agy., Austin, 1984-85, 85-86, Amarillo Coll., 1988-89. Instr. GED Ctr. for Neighborhood Ministries, Phoenix, 2001—02. Mem. Tex. Assn. for Children with Learning Disabilities (meritorious svc. award 1985), Coll. Reading and Learning Assn. (spl. interest group leader 1987-89, cert. 1988, editor newsletter 1987-89), Am. Assn. Cmty. and Jr. Colls., North Plains Assn. for Learning Disabilities (pres. 1987-88, coord. accessibility svcs. 1993—), Tex. Assn. Developmental Educators (membership chmn. 1992-93), Assn. of Higher Edn. and Disabled Students. Avocations: camping, hiking. E-mail: mlltaylor@aol.com.

TAYLOR, MARYANN COURTNEY, elementary education educator; b. Lynn, Mass., May 6, 1948; d. Wilfred Rosario and Mary Evelyn (Brennan) LaFrance; m. Leonard Dwelley Taylor, Apr, 19, 1969; 1 child, Leonard Dwelley III. BS, Bridgewater State Coll., 1970, MEd, 1972; cert. in paralegal studies, Northea. U., Boston, 1987; postgrad., New England Sch. Law, 1987-88, Oxford (Eng.) U., 1989, Fairfield U., Boston U., Lesley Coll., Boston Archtl. Ctr., 1980—. Cert. tchr., Mass. Tchr. Plymouth (Mass.) Pub. Schs., 1970—. Retail lumber sales Taylor Lumber Co., Inc., Marshfield, Mass., 1981-94; owner, pres. Taylor Forest Products, Inc., 1993—. Editor newsletter Cub Scout Pack 212, 1979-83. Vol. South Shore Sci. Ctr., Norwell, Mass., 1980-81, March of Dimes, Marshfield, 1982-85. Mem. NEA, Mass. Tchrs. Assn., Edn. Assn. Plymouth-Carver (union rep. 1989—), Better Bus. Bur. (vol.). Avocation: extensive travel. Home: PO Box 1206 124 Ferry St Marshfield MA 02050-2417 Office: Plymouth Pub Sch System Lincoln St Plymouth MA 02360

TAYLOR, MICHAEL BROOKS, economist, educator; b. Ann Arbor, Mich., Mar. 18, 1944; s. William Brooks and Roma G. (Sims) T.; m. Cynthia Wieboldt, Sept. 26, 1972 (div.); children: William B., Catherine Hallie. BA, Carleton Coll., 1966; PhD, Harvard U., 1976; MBA, Ohio U., 1984. Asst. prof. Occidental Coll., L.A., 1974-76, Berea (Ky.) Coll., 1976-77, Marietta (Ohio) Coll., 1977-86, assoc. prof., 1986-94, prof., 1994—, McCoy Disting. prof., 1994—99. Vis. assoc. prof. mgmt. Southwestern U. Fin. and Econs, China, 1986-87; vis. prof. Fgn. Affairs Coll., China, 1996. Co-author: Pictorial Guide to America Spinning Wheels, 1975, Spinning Wheels and Their Accessories, 2003; author (book chpt.): Ready for the Real World, 1994. Avocations: spinning wheel historian, golf, tennis, motorcycling. Office: Marietta College 102 Thomas Hall Marietta OH 45750

TAYLOR, MILLICENT RUTH, elementary school educator; b. Kingston, Jamaica, Nov. 18, 1944; came to U.S., 1981; m. Henry Taylor; children: T'ousant, Howard, Annette, Kerry-Ann. BE, U. West Indies, 1981; MS, U. Miami, 1991. Cert. elem. edn. tchr., secondary social sci. tchr., Fla. Chairperson dept. history Mays Middle Sch., Miami, Fla., 1987—, peer tchr., 1987—; clin. tchr., 1990—; seminar presenter Mays Middle Sch., Miami, Fla., 1987-88, clin. tchr., 1990—. Leader, trainer Global Edn., Miami, Fla. 1989, sponsor History Bee, Miami, 1988-90, Geography Bee, 1988-90, 2003. Recipient State award for tchg. econs. Dade County Sch., 1992, Nat. award for tchg. econs. Joint Coun. Econ. Edn., 1991, State award for Gov. Awards for Excellence, 1995, Nat. award for tchg. econs. Nat. Coun. Econ. Edn., 1995. Mem. ASCD, Seventh Day Adventist. Avocations: reading, travel, sewing, photography. Home: 19834 SW 118th Ave Miami FL 33177-4435 Office: Mays Middle Sch Goulds FL 33170

TAYLOR, MORRIS ANTHONY, chemistry educator; b. St. Louis, July 10, 1922; s. Henry Clay Nathaniel and Georgia Lee Anna (Kenner) T.; m. Millie Betty Fudge, July 17, 1948 (dec. Jan. 1969); children: Carla Maria, Morris Jr.; m. Veonnia Joyce McDonald, Aug. 4, 1973; children: Dorcas Lynnea, Demetrius Sirrom. BS in Chemistry, St. Louis U., 1952. Rsch. chemist Universal Match Corp., Ferguson, Mo., 1952-54; mfg. chemist Sigma Chem., St. Louis, 1954; clin. chemist 5th Army Area Med. Lab., St. Louis, 1955-56; analytical chemist U.S. Dept. Agr.-Agrl. Rsch. Svc. Meat & Poultry Inspection, St. Louis, 1956-67; supervisory chemist U.S. Dept. Agr.-Food Safety and Quality Svc., St. Louis, 1967-76, chemist in charge, 1976-79; adj. prof. chemistry St. Louis Community Coll., from 1981. Rating panel mem. Bd. CSC, St. Louis, 1969-79; reviewer Assn. Ofcl. Analytical Chemists, St. Louis, 1969-79; collaborator FDA Labs. on Analytical Methods, St. Louis, 1969-79. Bd. mem. Draft Bd. III, St. Louis, 1970-76. With U.S. Army, 1942-46. Fellow Am. Inst. Chemists; mem. Am. Chem. Soc., Internat. Union Pure and Applied Chemistry, St. Louis U. Alumni Chemists (Pioneer award 1994). Roman Catholic. Home: Saint Louis, Mo. Died Apr. 21, 2001.

TAYLOR, NORMAN FLOYD, computer educator, administrator; b. Dover, Ohio, Oct. 29, 1932; s. James Benton and Lela Augusta T.; m. Peggy Ann Cox, Sept. 7, 1952; children: Norman Dudley, Steven Dexter, Gregory Dennis. BS, U. Houston, 1954; MEd, Kent State U., 1963, EdS, 1977. Band dir. Ashtabula (Ohio) Area City Schs., 1958-70, prin., 1970-74, Shaker Heights (Ohio) City Schs., 1974-81, Perry (Ohio) Local Schs., 1981-85; treas. Jos. Badger Local Schs., Kinsman, Ohio, 1987-89; supr. computer instrn. support svcs. Ashtabula (Ohio) Area City Schs., 1989-93, computer instr., 1993-99, Lakeland C.C., Kirtland, Ohio, 1999—. Asst. prof. computer sci. Kent State U., Burton, Ohio, 1982-86, Ashtabula, 1987-88, adj. prof., Burton, 1999—, Cleve. State U., 2003—. Contbr. articles to profl. jours. Dir. Ashtabula Ch. Choir, 1958-78; mem. Ludlow Community Assn., Shaker Heights, 1974-81. Mem. NEA, Ohio Edn. Assn., Ohio Assn. Elem. Sch. Adminstrs., Shaker Heights Elem. Prins. Assn. (pres. 1980-81), Ashtabula Mid. Mgmt. Assn. (pres. 1973-74), Kiwanis Club, Phi Delta Kappa. Presbyterian. Avocations: music, golf, skiing. Home: 2501 Southwood Drive Painesville OH 44077-4956

TAYLOR, PATRICIA LEE, special education educator; b. Cadillac, Mich., Dec. 2, 1946; d. Leo Arthur and Betty Jean (Norden) Dunbar; m. Thomas Taylor, Dec. 26, 1974 (div. Oct. 1985); children: David, Christopher, Taryn. BA, Mich. State U., 1971, MA, 1973; MEd, U. Ctrl. Fla., 1993. Cert. elem. tchr., spl. edn. tchr., tchr. mentally handicapped and emotionally impaired. Tchr. primary emotionally handicapped Ctr. for Adjustive Edn., Sarasota, Fla., 1971-72, Roosevelt Jr. High Sch., Cocoa Beach, Fla., 1973-76, Edgewood Jr. High Sch., Merritt Island, Fla., 1973-76; tchr. varying exceptionalities Cadillac Sr. High Sch., 1976-77, tchr., 1982-89; tchr. pre-sch. Tom Thumb Coop. Nursery, Cadillac, 1979-81; tchr. devel. kindergarten Kenwood Elem. Sch., Cadillac, 1981-82; tchr. exceptional edn. on-the-job tng. Maynard Evans High Sch., Orlando, Fla., 1989-94; asst. prin. Magnolia Sch., Orlando, Fla., 1994—. Faculty rep., exec. bd. Classroom Tchrs. Assn., Cadillac, 1985-87; coach disabled sports team, Orlando, 1989-90; mem. com. Standards for Student Support Svcs. Mich. State Bd. Edn., Lansing, 1987-88; mentor gifted/talented Cadillac H.S., 1988-89; mem. Hospitality, Health and Industry Tng. Adv. Coun.; Cmty. Based Instrn. Com., Orlando, 1990-91; participant Four Seasons project Nat. Center for Restructuring Edn., Schs., Tchg., 1993. Author: Students Do the Job, 1991; editor: Feelings, Reflections, 1988, The Writer's Grip, 1989; editor yearbook, 1977. Mem. Mercy Hosp. Aux. Guild, Cadillac, 1976-81; troop leader Girl Scouts U.S., Cadillac, 1986-87; den mother Boy Scouts Am., Cadillac, 1986-87. Recipient Innovative Classroom Practices award Found. for Orange County Pub. Schs./Walt Disney World, 1991, Teacher-ific award Found. for Orange County Pub. Schs./Walt Disney World, 1992. Mem. NEA, ASCD, Nat. Assn. Realtors Coun. for Exceptional Children (mini-grantee 1991), Mich. Assn. Children with Learning Disabilities, Fla. Edn. Assn., Mich. Edn. Assn., Nat. Urban Alliance/Foxfire, Coun. for Exceptional Children (chpt. 155 pres. 1995—), Assn. Univ. Women, Coun. Adminstrs. Exceptional Children, Phi Delta Kappa, Kappa Delta Phi. Democrat. Presbyterian. Avocations: painting, creative writing, scuba diving, flying, tennis. Home: 7112 Caloosa Ct Orlando FL 32819-5041 Office: Magnolia Sch 1900 Matterhorn Dr Orlando FL 32818-5899

TAYLOR, PAUL FRANKLIN, college dean; b. Portsmouth, Ohio, Oct. 28, 1946; s. Frank Claude and Geneva Ruth (Jones) T.; m. Kimberly Kay Manes, Oct. 5, 2002; children: Victoria Carol, Matthew Winston, Kate Franklin. BA, U. Ky., 1970; MA, Gerogetown (Ky.) Coll., 1972. Sports writer Lexigton (Ky.) Herald-Leader, 1970-71; dir. admissions and fin. aid Shawnee State U., Portsmouth, Ohio, 1971-73; guidance counselor Cen. Ky. State Vocat. Tech. Sch., Lexington, 1973-74; dir. training Bluegrass Employment and Training Program, Lexington, 1974-76; career counselor Lexington Tech. Inst., 1976-77; asst. dir. student svcs. Lexington C.C., 1977-86, dean enrollment mgmt. and student affairs, 1986—. Mem. Am. Assn. Collegiate Registrars and Admissions Officers (bd. dirs., v.p. admissions and enrollment mgmt. 1999-2002, pres. 2003), So. Assn. Collegiate Admissions Ofcrs. and Registrars (exec. com. 1990-91, v.p. for profl. devel. 1992-94, v.p. for membership states and regionals 1994-96, pres. 1997), Ky. Assn. Collegiate Admissions Ofcrs. and Registrars (v.p. admissions 1984-86, pres. 1987-88), Ky. Assn. for Promotion Coll. Admissions (pres. 1983-84), Ky. Assn. Collegiate Admissions Counselors. Democrat. Avocations: snow skiing, golf, volleyball, softball, running. Office: Lexington Community College Cooper Dr Lexington KY 40506-0235 E-mail: pault@uky.edu.

TAYLOR, RAYMOND ELLORY, engineering executive; b. Ames, Iowa, Oct. 19, 1929; s. Alva A. and Maude Marguerite (Crowe) T.; m. Elfa M. Shaffer, Apr. 22, 1952; children, Wayne, David. BS in Chem. Tech., Iowa State U., 1951; MS in Phys. Chemistry, U. Idaho, 1956; PhD in Solid State Tech., Pa. State U., 1967. Chemist, supr. GE, Richland, Wash., 1951-56; sr. rsch. engr. Atomics Internat., Canoga Park, Calif., 1957-64; assoc. sr. rschr. Thermophysical Properties Rsch. Lab/Purdue U., West Lafayette, Ind., 1967-75, dir., 1975-95; pres. Thermophysical Properties Rsch. Lab., West Lafayette, Ind., 1996—. Cons. Ordinance Enrging. Assocs., GE, Sandia Nat. Labs., Lockheed Missle and Space Co., Atomic Energy Commn. Can., Bendix Brake Divsn., Theta Industries, Technometrics, Air Force Materials Lab., Combustion Engrng. Co., Supertemp Co., Argonne Nat. Lab., GM, Office Naval Rsch., Pennwalt Corp., Vesuvius Crucible Co., Gibson Electric Co., Proctor and Gamble, ALCOA, Corning Glass Co., Dept. Energy, Naval Surface Weapons Ctr., Bethlehem Steel, Cohart Refractories Co., Corp., Roll Mfrs. Inst., Carborundum Co., Areospace Corp., Sandvik Corp., Cummings Engine Corp., Travenol Labs., Sloan Kettering, Dana Perfect Circle, Teledyne Energy Systems, Pfizer Inc., Hughes Aircraft, Allegheny Ludlum Steel Co., CMW Inc., We. Electric Co., Reliance Universal Inc., AMP Inc., Kock Rsch. and Tech. Ctr., Ctrl. Inst. Indsl. Rsch., Semi-Alloys,

Gen. Scis. Inc., Carpenter Techs., Hercules Aerospace Co., Bush-Wellman, Brunswick Corp., North Am. Refractories, Zicar Corp., Hayes Internat., E. I. DuPont, Ferro Corp., Storgae Techs., CTS, IBM Inc., Sci. Applications, Outboard Marine Corp.; presenter in field. Editor Review Sci. Instruments; contbr. numerous articles and reports to sci. jours.; co-inventor direct heating flash diffusivity apparatus, device and techniques to measure thermal diffusivity/conductivity of thin films; research in transport properties at high tempuratures, diffusivity of composite materials, transport properites, multiproperty measurements, thermophotovoltaic energy conservation work, computer applications in the laboratory, high tempurature thermal conductivity reference standards, sonic measurements of insulations; inventor automatic non-destructive aircraft brake discs. Mem. ASTM (governing bd.), North Am. Thermal Analysis Soc., Internat. Thermal Expansion Symposium (governing bd., by-laws com.), Sigma Xi, Phi Lambda Upsilon, Phi Eta Sigma, Phi Kappa Phi. Home: 1700 Lindberg Rd Apt 226 West Lafayette IN 47906-7321

TAYLOR, ROBERT LEE, financial services and sales executive, information systems account executive, educator; b. Adrian, Mich., Jan. 9, 1944; s. Jack Raleigh and Virginia Dixon (Oakes) T.; m. Janice Grace George, Dec. 9, 1961; children: Robin, Lynne, David. AA, Siena Heights Coll., 1974; BA, 1976. Fellow Life Underwriting Tng. Coun.; with computer ops. Gen. Parts divsn. Ford Motor Co., Rawsonville, Mich., 1965-66; prodn. monitoring supr. Saline Plant, Mich., 1966-75; methods and sys. analyst Ypsilanti Plant, Mich., 1975-77; data processing supr. Milan Plant, Mich., 1977-82; sr. sys. analyst Plastics, Paint and Vinyl divsn., Wixom, Mich., 1982-85; sys. engr. Electronic Data Sys., Warren, Mich., 1985-86; sys. engr. mgr. Romulus (Mich.) Parts Distbn. Ctr. Plant, 1986-87; customer svc. mgr. Toledo, 1987-88; project mgr. Computer Task Group, Southfield, Mich., 1988-89; tech. svcs. mgr., 1989-92; spl. agent Prudential, Tecumseh, Mich., 1992-94; instr. data processing Siena Heights Coll., Adrian, 1985-86; bd. dirs. Lenawee Area Life Underwriters, 1993—, pub. chmn., 1993, nat. committeeman, 1994, 1998—2001, pres-elect, 1995, pres., 1996, 2002; fin. advisorAIG/VALIC, 1994—. Commr. Tecumseh Planning Commn., Mich., 1976-80, vice-chmn., 1981-82; trustee Tecumseh Bd. Edn., 1981-82, sec., 1983-84, chmn. citizens adv. com., 1983, chmn. computer adv. com., 1984, chmn. policy com., 1983-84; chmn. Tecumseh Area Laymen's Assn., 1983; mem. exec. com. Lenawee County Rep. Party, 1982-88, prcinct del., 1982-88, chmn. computer com., 1984-86; state del. State of Mich., 1983-85, 87; founding advisor Evang. Free Ch. Adrian-Tecumseh, 1984-85, elder, 1986-88, 90-92, 94-98, Sunday Sch. supt., 1984-87, 89-90, chmn. Christian edn., 1986-89, 90-91, chmn. planning-bldg. com., 1987-93; asst. Sunday Sch. supt. Berean Bapt. Ch., Adrian, 1980-83; tchr. mentally impaired, 1977-83; deacon Sunday sch. supt. Grace Bible Ch., Tecumseh, 1973-76; chmn. bd. deacons First Bapt. Ch., Tecumseh, 1970-71, youth advisor, 1968-71, Layman of Yr., 1970; vice-chmn. Tecumseh Area Crusade for Christ, 1973, facilities chmn. Lenawee County Crusade for Christ, 1986; chmn. Life Action Crusade, 1987; men's divsn. chmn. Lenawee Area Celebration, 1996. Served with USAF, 1961-65. Mem. Computer & Automated sys. Assn. (sr.) Mfg. Automation Protocol, Lenawee Assn. Life Underwriter, Nat. Assn. Life Underwriters, Mich. Assn. Life Undrewriters, Soc. Mfg. Engrs. Avocations: golf, genealogy. Office: VALIC 601 Outer Dr Tecumseh MI 49286-1446 E-mail: robert_taylor@aigvalic.com.

TAYLOR, RONALD LEE, academic administrator; b. Urbana, Ill., Nov. 11, 1943; s. Lee R. and Katherine L. (Becker) Taylor; m. Patricia D. Fitzimmons, Mar. 10, 1973; children: Jamie, Lara, Meredith, Dana. AB, Harvard U., 1966; MBA, Stanford U., 1971. Asst. contr. Bell & Howell, Chgo., 1971-73; pres., co-CEO DeVry Inc., Chgo., 1973—. Bd. dirs. La Petite Acad., Inc.; trustee Higher Learning Commn., North Ctrl. Assn. Colls. and Schs., 2003—. Com. chmn. Ill. Bd. Higher Edn., Springfield, 1985—; mem. mgmt. bd. Stanford U. Sch. Bus. Office: DeVry Inc 1 Tower Ln Ste 1000 Hinsdale IL 60181-4663 E-mail: rtaylor@devry.com.

TAYLOR, ROWAN SHAW, music educator, composer, conductor; b. Ogden, Utah, June 1, 1927; s. Hugh Taylor and Lucille (Olsen) Gaenger; m. Dorothy Foulger, June 26, 1946 (div. 1953); children: Kathleen, Scott; m. Priscilla Pulliam, Aug. 29, 1957; children: Mark, Dianne, Paul, John (dec.), Eric, Brent, Charlotte. BA, Brigham Young U., 1952, MA, 1957. Tchr. San Juan Sch. Dist., Blanding, Utah, 1948-50; with C.F. Braun Engring. Firm, 1950-58; tchr. L.A. Unified Dist., 1958-64; from instr. to prof. L.A. C.C., Woodland Hills, Calif., 1964—. Condr., composer numerous symphonies and mus. works. With U.S. Army, 1955-56, Korea. Republican. Mem. Ch. Jesus Christ of LDS. Avocation: collecting cologne bottles. Home: 22544 Tiara St Woodland Hills CA 91367-3335

TAYLOR, ROY LEWIS, botanist, educator; b. Olds, Alta., Can., Apr. 12, 1932; s. Martin Gilbert and Crystal (Thomas) T. B.Sc., Sir George Williams U., Montreal, Que., Can., 1957; PhD, U. Calif. at Berkeley, 1962; DSc (hon.), U. B.C., Vancouver, Can., 1997. Pub. sch. tchr. Olds Sch. Div., 1949-52; jr. high sch. tchr. Calgary Sch. Bd., Alta., 1953-55; chief taxonomy sect., research br. Can. Agrl. Dept., Ottawa, Ont., 1962-68; dir. Bot. Garden, prof. botany, prof. plant scis. U. B.C., Vancouver, 1968-85; pres., CEO Chgo. Hort. Soc., 1985-94; dir. Chgo. Bot. Garden, Glencoe, Ill., 1985-94; exec. dir. Rancho Santa Ana Bot. Garden, Claremont, Calif., 1994-99; prof. botany, chmn. botany program Claremont Grad. U., 1994-99, dir. emeritus, 1999. Pres. Western Bot. Svcs. Ltd. Author: The Evolution of Canada's Flora, 1966, Flora of the Queen Charlotte Islands, Vols. I and II, 1968, Vascular Plants of British Columbia: A Descriptive Resource Inventory, 1977; The Rare Plants of British Columbia, 1985; assoc. editor Pacific Horticulture, 2001—. Mem. State of Ill. Bd. Natural Resources and Conservation, 1987-94; trustee Nature Ill. Found., 1990-94, Elisabeth C. Miller Bot. Garden Trust, Seattle, 1994—, Elisabeth C. Miller Bot. Garden Endowment, 2001—, The Arbor Fund, Seattle, 1997—, chmn., 2002—; bd. dirs. Milner Gardens and Woodland Soc., Qualicum Beach, B.C., Can., 2000—, chmn., 2002—. Fellow Linnean Soc. London (hon.); mem. Can. Bot. Assn. (pres. 1967-68), Biol. Coun. Can. (pres. 1973-74), Am. Assn. Mus. (accreditation com. 1980-85, chmn. 1985-91, chmn. ethics commn. 1991-93), Am. Assn. Bot. Gardens and Arboreta (hon. life; pres. 1976, 77, award of merit 1987), Am. Soc. Bot. Artists (bd. dirs. 1997—), Claremont C. of C. (bd. dirs. 1995-98), Ottawa Valley Curling Assn. (pres. 1968-69), Miner Gardens and Woodland Soc. (bd. dirs. 2000—, chmn. 2002—), B.C. Soc. Landscape Archs. (hon.), U. B.C. Bot. Garden (hon.), Chgo. Hort Soc. (life, medal 1994), Gov. Gen.'s Curling Club Can. (life). E-mail: taylor.rl@shaw.ca.

TAYLOR, RUTH ARLEEN LESHER, marketing educator; b. Riverton, Iowa, Mar. 7, 1941; d. Clyde Almond and Bernice Emogene (Graves) Lesher; m. Leslie (Milburn) Taylor, Aug. 10, 1963; children: Treg Anthony, John Leslie II. BS in Home Econs. Edn. magna cum laude, U. Houston, 1975; MEd, Tex. Christian U., 1977; PhD, U. N. Tex., 1981. Prof. mktg. Tarrant County C.C., Ft. Worth, 1977-78, North Tex. State U., Denton, 1978-81, Southwestern U., Georgetown, Tex., 1982-87, S.W. Tex. State U., San Marcos, 1981-82, 87—. Dir. travel to China, Japan, Hong Kong, Costa Rica, Morocco, Europe, Eng., Mex., Dominican Republic, Venezuela, Chile, Peru; faculty intern Tex. Dept. Econ. Devel. and Tex. Sec. of State Office; collaborator STAT-USA and Internat. Catalog Exhbn. U.S. Dept. Commerce. Author: Text Maps Study Guides, 1994—; contbg. author: The Psychology of Fashion, 1985, Ethics in Accounting, 1994; contbr. articles to profl. jours. Mem. Lost Creek Garden Club, Austin, Tex., 1985—, v.p.; vol. Bob Bullock State Hist. Mus. Grantee Merrick Found., 1991. Mem.: DAR, Am. Soc. for Competitiveness, Winthrop Soc., French Huguenot Soc., Colonial Dames, Internat. Hospitality Coun. (bd. dirs.), Mayflower Soc., Mktg. Mgmt. Assn., Western Mktg. Educators Assn., Am. Mktg. Assn., Alpha Mu Alpha, Alpha Kappa Psi, Phi Delta Kappa, Phi Epsilon Omicron, Beta Gamma Sigma. Avocations: travel, gardening, reading, entertaining. Office: Texas State University 601 University Dr San Marcos TX 78666-4685

TAYLOR, SHAREN RAE (SHAREN MCCALL), special education educator; b. Springfield, Ill., Feb. 26, 1946; d. Robert Jr. and Marie Elizabeth (Motley) McCall; m. Robert Lawrence Taylor, Aug. 13, 1966; children: Rhett Alan, Ryan Andrew, Raegan Alyssa. BS in Elem. Edn., Ill. State U., 1968; MA in Spl. Edn., Northeastern Ill. U., 1990. Cert. trainable mentally handicapped, children and adolescent tchr., Ill. Tchr. 1st grade Argenta (Ill.) Oreanna Schs., 1968; tchr. 3d grade Auburn (Ill.) Pub. Schs., 1968-69, substitute tchr., 1970-73; substitute tutor Virden (Ill.) Pub. Schs., 1970-73, Warrensburg (Ill.) Pub. Schs., 1974-75; tchr. kindergarten Peppermint Stick Pre-Sch., Grayslake, Ill., 1981-84; tchr.'s asst. Laremont Sch., Gages Lake, Ill., 1984-86, job coach, 1986-87, substitute tchr., 2003—; tchr. trainable mentally handicapped Laremont Satellite Class, Mundelein, Ill., 1987-91, Oak Grove Sch, Libertyville, Ill., 1991-95, O'Plaine Sch., Gurnee, Ill., 1995-98, Viking Sch., Gurnee, 1998—2003. Fin. sec. Faith Bapt. Ch., Grayslake, 1985—88, 2003—, deaconess, 1989—91. Republican. Avocations: reading, music, movies, theatre. Home: 2514 Lippizan Ln Grayslake IL 60030

TAYLOR, SHARON KAY, elementary school counselor; b. Ft. Worth, Oct. 13, 1954; d. Cecil James and Mary Evelyn (Careathers) Owens; m. Kenneth Carroll Taylor, May 21, 1977; children: Anna Marie, Scott Owens. BS, Howard Payne U., 1976; MEd, North Tex. State, 1986. Tchr. Elem. Pub. Sch., Belton, Tex., 1979-89; counselor Kelley Elem. Sch., Denver City, Tex., 1989—. Mem. Tex. Assn. Counseling and Devel., Tex. Sch. Counselors Assn., Assn. for Play Therapy, Beta Sigma Phi. Democrat. Baptist. Avocations: compiling scrapbooks, gardening. Home: PO Box 486 Denver City TX 79323-0486 Office: Kelley Elementary School 500 N Soland Ave Denver City TX 79323-2824

TAYLOR, SHERRILL RUTH, management educator; b. Endwell, N.Y., July 9, 1943; d. Wallace Bixby and Lillie Mary (Sprague) Ingalls; m. William Leon Taylor, July 18, 1964; children: Mark William, Tammie Ann. BBA, Tex. Women's U., 1983, MBA, 1986. Cert. sr. profl. human resources. Pers. rep. Tex. Women's U., Denton, Tex., 1986-87; fleet upgrade coord. Xerox Corp., Oakland, Calif., 1987-88; with Sun Diamond Growers, Pleasanton, Calif., 1988-90; mgmt. lectr. Tex. Women's U., Denton, 1990—, dir. Small Bus. Inst., 1993—; co-fellow Sam Walton Students In Free Enterprise. Named Disting. Alumna, dept. bus. and econs. Tex. Woman's U., 1999, Human Resource S.W. Educator of Yr., 1999. Mem. Denton Human Resource Assn., Small Bus. Inst. Dirs. Assn. (nat. v.p. publs. 1997-98, nat. v.p. case competition 1998—), Assn. Small Businesses and Entrepreneurship, Internat. Credit Assn. Denton County (sec. 1995-97), Dallas Human Resource Mgmt. Assn., Inc. Methodist. Avocation: sweet adelines chorus. Office: Tex Women's U Dept Bus PO Box 425738 Denton TX 76204-5738

TAYLOR, TIMOTHY LEON, college dean; b. Danville, Ill., May 7, 1963; s. Howard L. and A. Jane (Pate) T.; m. Melisa Sue Swenny, May 25, 1991. AAS in Electronics Tech., Danville Area C.C., 1985, AAS in Indsl. Maintenance, 1986; BS in Electronics Mgmt., So. Ill. U., 1989, MS Ed. in Vocat. Edn., 1991. Store mgr. Marty K Restaurant, Danville, 1979-86; owner, operator Tayco Sys., Pekin, Ill., 1986-87; mgr. Gatsby's Bar & Billiards, Carbondale, Ill., 1988-91; machine operator Ambrosia Chocolate Co., Milw., 1991-92; dir. electronics MBTI Bus. Tng. Inst., Milw., 1992-94; assoc. dean indsl. occupations, agr. and apprenticeship Blackhawk Tech. Coll., Janesville, Wis., 1994—. Cons., owner Taylor Info. Mgmt. Sys., Stoughton, Wis., 1991—. Recipient Curriculum Devel. award Accrediting Coun. Indpendent Colls. and Schs., 1993. Mem. ASCD. Baptist. Avocations: music performance, basketball, baseball, football. Office: Blackhawk Tech Coll 6004 Prairie Ave Janesville WI 53547

TAYLOR, VESTA FISK, real estate broker, educator; b. Ottawa County, Okla., July 15, 1917; d. Ira Sylvester and Judie Maude (Garman) Fisk; m. George E. Taylor, Aug. 17, 1957 (dec. Oct. 1963); stepchildren: Joyce, Jean, Luther. AA, Northea. Okla. A&M, 1936; BA, N.E. State U., Tahlequah, Okla., 1937; MA, Okla. State U., 1942. Life cert. Spanish, English, history, elem. Tchr. rural sch. grades 1-4, Ottawa County, Okla., 1931-33; tchr. rural sch. grades 1-8, 1933-38; tchr. H.S. Spanish, English Wyandotte, Okla., 1938-42; tchr. H.S. Spanish, English, math. Miami, Okla., 1942-57; tchr. H.S. Spanish Jacksonville, Ill., 1960-65; tchr. H.S. Spanish, English Miami, 1965-79; owner, broker First Lady Realty, Miami, 1979—; tchr. real estate for licensing N.E. Okla. Vocat.-Tech., Afton, 1980-94. Radio spellmaster weekly-county groups Coleman Theater Stage, 1954-57; radio program weekly 4-H, Miami, 1953-57; weekly radio program telling story of Pilot Club Internat., Jacksonville, Ill., 1960-61. Author: (poem) The Country School, 1994. Vol. sec. Ottawa County Seniors' Ctr., 1993—; mem. restoration com. Friends of Theater, 1993—; mem. Friends of the Libr., 1994—. Named Outstanding Coach Ottawa County 4-H Clubs, Miami, 1955, 67, Outstanding Alumnus All Yrs. H.S. Reunion, Wyandotte, Okla., 1992, Champion Speller N.E. Okla. Retirees, Oklahoma City, 1991. Mem. AAUW (pres. 1978-80, treas. 1994-98), Ottawa Coutny Ret. Educators (treas. 1990-95, corr. sec. 1995—), Miami Classroom Tchr. (v.p. 1973-77), Tri-state Travel Club (purser 1989-95), Kappa Kappa Iota (pres. 1988-92, treas. 1986-88). Democrat. Baptist. Avocations: gardening, reading, travel, volunteering. Home: 821 Jefferson Blvd Miami OK 74354-4910 Office: First Lady Realty 821 Jefferson St Miami OK 74354-4910

TAYLOR, WILLIAM MALCOLM, environmentalist, educator, executive recruiter; b. South Hiram, Maine, June 18, 1933; s. William Myers and Gladys Marie (Weldy) T.; stepmother Edna (Tyson) Taylor; m. Carrie Mae Fiedler, Aug. 31, 1957 (div. Sept. 1980); children: William Stephan, Alyson Marie, Eric Fiedler; m. Elizabeth Van Horn, June 18, 1983. Student, George Sch., 1948-50; BA in Liberal Arts, Pa. State U., 1956; MEd, U. N.C., 1962. Instr. ESL Anatolia Coll., Am. Lang. Ctr., Salonica, Greece, 1956-58; tchr. biology-chemistry Coral Shores H.S., Tavernier, Fla., 1961-62; pk. naturalist Everglades Nat. Pk., Fla., 1962-65; tech. editor Nat. Pk. Svc., Washington, 1965-67; chief interpretation Canyonlands Nat. Pk., Utah, 1967-71; environ. edn. specialist western regional office Nat. Pk. Svc., Calif., 1971-77; dir. program devel. Living History Ctr., Novato, Calif., 1981-83; exec. recruiter, ptnr. Van Horn, Taylor & Assocs, Biotech-Biomed. Rsch., Calif., 1983-95, 98—. Mem. 2d World Conf. on Nat. Parks and Equivalent Reserves, 10th Internat. Seminar on Nat. Parks, U.S., Can., Mex. Author: The Strands Walk, Exercises in Guided Inquiry for Children; founder, developer ednl. program Environ. Living Program, 1973 (Calif. Bicentennial Commn. award 1974, Don Perryman award Calif. Social Studies Coun., 1975, Nat. Bicentennial Adminstrn. sponsorship 1976). Bd. dirs. Novato Environ. Quality Com., 1973-76; mem. Calif. Conservation Com., 1973-76; mem. Utah Environ. Com., 1968-71; vol. Ariz. Symphony Orch. Assn. Mem. Civil Air Patrol. Mem.: Big Industries Orgn. So. Ariz. (chmn. membership), Mensa (pres. Tucson chpt.). Avocations: amateur magic, illusions, birding, history. Home: 1644 N Woodland Ave Tucson AZ 85712-4147

TAYLOR CLAUD, ANDREA, educational consultant; b. Warrenton, Va., Nov. 5, 1952; d. Andrew Earl and Catherine (Dennis) Taylor; m. Maurice J. Claud. BS, Norfolk State U., 1974, MA, 1983; postgrad., Old Dominion U., 1975-76, 89; MA in Cmty. Counseling, Regent U., 2000. Profl. collegiate cert. in learning disabilities, mentally handicapped and emotionally handicapped. Classrm. tchr. Facquier County Sch. System, Warrenton, Va., 1974-75; child devel. specialist, team leader Norfolk Pub. Schs., Norfolk, Va., 1976-82, ednl. diagnostician, 1982-87; ednl. cons. Va. State Dept. Edn., Norfolk, 1987—; v.p. M.A. Trucking, Inc. and MAC Leasing, Inc. V.p. DECAA Enterprises, Norfolk, 1983—. Mem. Nat. Kidney Found. of Va., Hampton Rds., Lindenwood Civic League, Norfolk, Pleasant Grovet Bapt. Ch., Va. Beach; troop leader Girl Scouts U.S.A., Norfolk, 1977-79. Named Dubutante, Norfolk Med. Soc. Aux., 1969, Outstanding Young Women of Am., 1983; recipient Apple for Tchr. award, 1997, Outstanding Renal Healthcare Profl. Yr. award, 1998. Mem. NAFE, NEA, Va. Edn. Assn., Norfolk Edn. Assn., Coun. Exceptional Children, Assn. Supervision and Curriculum Devel., Delta Sigma Theta. Democrat. Avocations: traveling, reading, listening to music, fishing. Office: Children's Hosp of King's Daus Hosp Edn Program 601 Childrens Ln Norfolk VA 23507-1910

TAYMOR, BETTY, political science educator; b. Balt., Mar. 22, 1921; d. William and Tillie (Blum) Bernstein; m. Melvin Lester Taymor, June 7, 1942; children; Michael, Laurie, Julie. AB, Goucher Coll., 1942; MA in Am. Govt., Boston U., 1967; LHD (hon.), Goucher Coll., 2001. Dir. program for women in politics and govt. Boston Coll., 1970-92; instr. in govt. Northeastern U., Boston, 1969-71; cons. office of pres. U. Mass., Boston, 1973-74; instr. MA in Urban Affairs program Boston U., 1967-68; instr. in politics & govt. McCormack Inst., Boston, 1973-92; coord. Boston Network for Women in Politics & Govt. U. Mass.-Boston, 1992-94; dir. spl. projects Ctr. for Women in Politics & Pub. Policy U. Mass.-Boston, 1992—. Author: Running Against the Wind: The Struggle of Women in Massachusettes Politics, 2000. State committeewoman Dem. State Com., Boston, 1956-92, nat. committeewoman, Washington, 1976-96; mem. U.S. nat. commn. UNESCO, 1966; bd. dirs. Univ. Hosp., boston, 1989-91; mem. New Eng. Bd. Higher Edn., 1985-89; mem. adv. com. John F. Kennedy Libr. Elizabeth King Ellicott fellow Goucher Coll., 1959-60; recipient Abigail Adams award Mass. Women's Polit. Caucus, 1989. Avocations: tennis, reading, theatre. Home: 975 Memorial Dr Apt 601A Cambridge MA 02138-5803 Business E-Mail: akahn@massmed.org.

TAYS, GLENNY MAE, retired secondary education educator, adult education educator; b. Presho, SD, Mar. 12, 1933; d. Glen Harold and Grayce Agnes (LaVelle) Trimble; m. Richard Ray Tays, May 29, 1954; children: Robert Glen, Thomas Gene. BA, Dakota Wesleyan U., 1956; MEd, U. Mont., 1961. Cert. secondary sch. tchr. and prin. Bus. tchr. Kimball (S.D.) H.S., 1956-58; English/bus. tchr. Burke (S.D.) H.S., 1962-65; Bus. Inst. dept. head DesMoines Area C.C., Boone, Iowa, 1966-78; English/journalism tchr. St. Martin's Acad., Rapid City, S.D., 1979-82; English tchr., dept. head Todd County H.S., Mission, S.D., 1982-95; sch. dist. media specialist C EB, Eagle Butte, S.D., 1995-99; ret., 1999. Pres. Des Moines Area C.C. Faculty Assn., Boone, 1968-70; pres.-elect Iowa Bus. Edn. Assn., State of Iowa, 1972-73, pres., 1973-74; editor North Ctrl. Bus. Edn. Conv. Bull., Des Moines, 1972; tchr. Bus. Inst., Black Hills State U. Br. Campus, Rapid City, S.D., 1981-82, Sinte Gleska U., Mission, S.D., 1983-84. Pres. Burke Women's Club, SD, 1961—63; vol. ARC, Easter Seals, United Fund, Boone, Iowa, 1965; coord. Country Club Jr. Golf Program, Boone, 1968—74; golf mother Booster Club Boone HS, Iowa, 1972—73; spl. projects chmn. Soroptimist Club Internat., Boone, 1973, March of Dimes, 2001; pres.-elect alumni bd. Wesleyan U., 2001, v.p. alumni bd., 2003. Named Outstanding Young Women in Am., 1970, Outstanding Educator, Dakota Wesleyan U., 1978. Mem. ASCD, NEA, AAUW, Nat. Coun. Tchrs. English, Cath. Daus. Am., ProLiteracy America, Delta Kappa Gamma (historian 2000-01, corr. sec. 2003-2004). Democrat. Roman Catholic. Avocations: reading, writing, antiquing, collecting pre-1900 books, golfing. Home: 4206 Foothill Dr Rapid City SD 57702-7015 E-mail: gtays@aol.com.

TCHAKAROVA, BOGDANA, retired radiologist, educator; b. Bulgaria, 1931; MD, Pavlov Higher Inst. Medicine, 1955. Diplomate Am. Bd. Radiology. Intern Miriam Hosp., Providence, R.I., 1969-70; resident in radiology Boston City Hosp., 1971-74; fellow R.I. Hosp., Providence, 1974-75; staff VAMC Hosp., West Roxbury, Mass., ret., 1995; clin. instr. radiology Harvard U., 1987-96. Mem. Am. Coll. Radiology.

TCHOUNWOU, PAUL BERNARD, environmental health specialist, toxicologist, educator; b. Bangou, Cameroon, Aug. 14, 1960; came to U.S., 1985; s. Maurice and Christine (Kouanang) Seumo; m. Martha Namondo Mondoa, Aug. 3, 1990; children: Christine K., Hervey M., Solange S. BSc, U. Yaounde, Cameroon, 1983, MSc, 1984; MS in Pub. Health, Tulane U., 1986, ScD, 1990. Cert. toxicologist Nat. Environ. Health Assn.; registered sanitarian La. State Bd. Examiners for Sanitarians. Tchg. asst. Tulane Sch. Pub. Health, New Orleans, 1988—90; med. rschr. Inst. Med. Rsch., Yaounde, 1991—94; asst. prof. Faculty Medicine, Yaounde, 1992—94; rsch. assoc. Xavier & Tulane Univs., New Orleans, 1994—96; assoc. prof., dir. environ. sci. PhD program Jackson State U., 1996—; adj. assoc. prof. sch. pub. health Tulane U., 1999—; prof., dir. environ. sci. doctoral program Jackson State U., 2001—; dep. dir. Ctr. for Environ. Health, Jackson State U., 2003—. Adj. assoc. prof. Tulane U. Sch. Pub. Health, 1999—; environ. health cons. Orstom & UNICEF, Yaounde, 1992-93, U.S. AID, Kaele, 1991-93; rsch. supr. Tulane Sch. Pub. Health, New Orleans, 1994—; tng. and rsch. fellow U.S. AID, Washington, 1985-90; adj. assoc. prof. environ. health scis. Tulane U. Sch. Pub. Health and Tropical Medicine, 1999—; dep. dir. Ctr. Environ. Health Jackson State U., 2003—. Editor-in-chief: Internat. Jour. of Environ. Rsch. and Pub. Health, 2003—, mem. editl. bd.: Internat. Jour. Environ. Toxicology and Water Quality, 1994—, guest editor: Internat. Jour. Molecular Scis., 2002—, regional editor: USA-Environ. Toxicology, 2002—, mem. overseas editl. bd.: Jour. Environ. Biology, 2002—; contbr. articles to profl. jours. Grantee, Internat. Devel. Rsch. Ctr., 1992—93, Nat. Aeronautics and Space Adminstrn., 1977—99, NIH, 1998—, Nat. Oceanic and Atmospheric Adminstrn., 2001—, Dept. Army, 2002—03. Mem. APHA, AAUP, AAAS, Am. Assn. Cancer Rsch., Water Environ. Fedn., Cameroon Bioscis. Soc., Cameroon Assn. Epidemiology, Nat. Environ. Health Assn., N.Y. Acad. Scis., Soc. Environ. Toxicology and Chemistry, Soc. Toxicology, Delta Omega. Roman Catholic. Avocations: travel, playing tennis, watching tv sport programs. Home: 230 Clark Farms Rd Madison MS 39110-8112 Office: Jackson State U Sch Sci & Tech PO Box 18540 Jackson MS 39217

TEABO-SANDOE, GLENDA PATTERSON, elementary education educator; b. Otisville, N.Y., Sept. 21, 1939; d. Glenn R. and Edna (Cuddeback) Patterson; children: Geoffrey, Laura, Eric. BS in Elem. Edn., Seton Hall U., South Orange, N.J., 1970; MS in Edn., Canisius Coll., Buffalo, 1977. Tchr. 5th grade Minisink Valley Cen. Sch., Slate Hill, N.Y., 1973-74, tchr. 1st grade, 1974-95; retired, 1995. Com. rep. for gifted, effective schs. rep., grade level chmn., reading coun. Minisink Valley Cen. Schs. Sunday sch. tchr., dir. summer Bible sch., dir. Christmas pageants, deacon Otisville-Mt. Hope Presbyn. Ch. Mem. AARP, Consumers Union (life), ABC Reading Coun., N.Y. State Reading Assn. (mini-grantee 1990), Minisink Valley Tchrs. Assn. Avocations: piano, volunteer work, biking, knitting, reading. Home: 162 South St Middletown NY 10940-6524

TEAGUE, DEBORAH GANT, elementary school educator; b. Mankato, Minn., Jan. 23, 1952; d. Dorsett H. and Gwynlyn (Himmelman) Gant; m. William Lial Teague, June 7, 1991. AA, Meramec C.C., Kirkwood, Mo., 1972; BS, U. Mo., 1974, Edn. Specialist, 1989; MS, U. Minn., 1982. Tchr. Mexico (Mo.) Pub. Sch., 1977—. Recipient Presdl. Award in Excellence in Math. and Sci., NSF and Nat. Sci. Tchr. Assn., 1993; Fulbright Exch. fellow, 1985; Mo. State Incentive grantee Mo. State Dept. Edn., 1987, 88. Mem. Nat. Sci. Tchrs. Assn., Coun. of Elem. Sci. Teaching Internat., Assn. Presdl. Awardee Sci. Tchrs., Mo. Sci. Tchrs. Assn., N.E. Mo. State Tchrs. Assn. (exec. com. 1992-94), Phi Delta Kappa. Avocations: walking, swimming, travel. Home: 701 Ringo St Mexico MO 65265-1220 Office: Mexico Public Sch 1250 W Curtis St Mexico MO 65265-1855

TEARE, BERNICE ADELINE, elementary school educator, reading specialist; b. Camden, N.J., May 31, 1942; d. Harry Kenneth and Lorraine

P. (Blazer) Schwab; m. Paul A. Teare, Aug. 19, 1967; 1 child, Paul Brian. BA, Glassboro State Coll., 1964, MA, 1967; cert. prin./supr., Trenton State Coll., 1977, MEd, cert. reading specialist, Trenton State Coll., 1979. Cert. tchr., N.J.; cert. reading specialist, N.J. Elem. tchr. Cherry Hill (N.J.) Pub. Schs., 1964-86, reading specialist, 1986—. Conf. presenter West Jersey Reading Coun., Marlton, 1992-94, Reading Coun. South Jersey, Marlton, 1992-94, ASCD, 1993, 97, Internat. Reading Assn., Toronto, 1994, Anaheim, Calif., 1995, New Orleans, 1996, Atlanta, 1997, Orlando, 1998, San Diego, 1999; staff devel. trainer Cherry Hill Sch. Dist., 1991-2001. Author: Update '93 Resource Book, 1992, First Grade Resource Book, 1993, Second Grade Resource Book, 1994, Primary '94 Resource Book, 1994, Kindergarten Resource Book, 1996; contbr. articles to profl. jours. Mem. ASCD, Internat. Reading Assn., N.J. Reading Assn., Reading Coun. South Jersey, West Jersey Reading Coun., Kappa Delta Pi. Avocations: reading, travel, teddy bear collecting, children's literature, computers. Office: Kingston Sch Kingston Rd Cherry Hill NJ 08034

TEBBEN, SHARON LEE, education educator; b. Fairfield, Iowa, Oct. 15, 1943; d. Richard Paul and Arline Marie (Sires) Brandt; m. E. Marvin Tebben, Sept. 7, 1963; children: Laurel Ann, Leslie Kay, Paul Marvin. BS, Mankato State U., 1965; MS, U. Wyo., 1973; EdD, U. St. Thomas, 1992. Tchr. chemistry San Diego City Schs., 1965-68, Alhambra City Schs., Calif., 1968-70; tchg. asst. U. Wyo., Laramie, 1970-73; mem. faculty Presentation Coll., Aberdeen, S.D., 1974-92, chmn. dept. chemistry, 1975-92; asst. prof. edn. Northern State U., Aberdeen, 1992-95, assoc. prof., 1995—, assoc. dean sch. of edn., dir. grad. studies, 1995, dean of edn., 1999—; NCA cons./evaluator, 1990—. NDEA fellow, 1971-73. Mem. AAUW, ASCD, Higher Learning Commn. (cons., evaluator, mem. accreditation review coun.), Phi Kappa Phi, Alpha Lambda Delta, Phi Delta Kappa. Office: Northern State U 1200 S Jay St Aberdeen SD 57401-7155

TEBBS, CAROL ANN, secondary education educator, academic administrator; b. Columbus, Ohio, Sept. 9, 1939; d. John Arthur and Ann Laurie (Wickham) Williams; m. Ronald Daniel Tebbs, Mar. 31, 1957; children: Kimberly Ann, Ronald Dan. BA in English, Whittier Coll., 1963, MA in English and Edn., 1972. Cert. tchr. K-adult Calif. Tchr. art and English Hacienda La Puente Unified Sch. Dist., Hacienda Heights, Calif., 1963-84; tchr. advanced placement English, acad. decathlon advisor, yearbook advisor Glen A. Wilson H.S., Hacienda Heights, 1984—2000. Mentor tchr. Hacienda La Puente Sch. Dist., Hacienda Heights, 1988—2000; reader, tchr. trainer advanced placement English Coll. Bd., 2000—; bd. dirs. Kepler Coll., pres., 2003—; bd. dirs., tchr. Online Coll., 2000—. Author (e-books): Beyond Basics: Moving the Chart in Time, Beyond Basics: Tools for the Consulting Astrologer; writer (jour.) Kosmos, Mountain Astrologer, 1995—. Named Tchr. of the Yr., Nat. Walmart Stores Found., 1998; recipient D. Fedderson Cmty. Svc. award, PTA, 1970, Teacher of the Year, 1971, Glen A. Wilson Faculty Tchr. of Yr. award, 1999—2000. Mem.: United Astrology Congress (program chair 1986, 1989, 1992, coord. 1995, bd. chmn. 1995—99, co-founder), Internat. Soc. Astrol. Rsch. (pres. 1988—95, bd. dirs.), Delta Kappa Gamma. Methodist. Home and Office: 56870 Jack Nicklaus Blvd La Quinta CA 92253-5074

TEDDER, DANIEL WILLIAM, chemical engineering educator; b. Orlando, Fla., Apr. 13, 1946; s. Daniel Webster and Adelaide Katheryn (Bruechert) T.; m. Wendy Elizabeth Widhelm, Aug. 3, 1968; children: Lisa Christine, Rachel Marie. Student, Kenyon Coll., 1964-67; B Chem. Engring. with highest honors, Ga. Inst. Tech., 1972; MS, U. Wis., 1973, PhD, 1975. Registered profl. engr., Tenn., Ga. Lab. technician Agrico Chem. Co., Pierce, Fla., 1965-67, Puritan Chem. Co., Atlanta, 1967-68; engr. Humble Oil and Refining Co., Baytown, Tex., summer 1972; staff engr. Oak Ridge (Tenn.) Nat. Lab., 1975-79; asst. prof. chem. engring. Ga. Inst. Tech., Atlanta, 1979-84, assoc. prof., 1984—. Organizer symposia Emerging Techs. for Hazardous Waste Mgmt.; conf. presenter in field, 1977—; engring. cons. BCM Techs., Inc., Amherstberg, Ont., Can., 1985, Nat. Bur. Standards, U.S. Dept. Commerce, 1986—, Thermax Inc., Atlanta, 1987-88, Exxon R & D Lab., Baton Rouge, 1989—, Waste Policy Inst., Blacksburg, Va., 1992—, Geotech ChemNuclear, Golden, Colo., 1992—, Martin Marietta, Oak Ridge, 1992—, Resource Preservation Corp., Union City, Ga., 1992—; reviewer Jour. Phys. Chemistry, 1993—; others. Sr. series editor: Radioactive Waste Management Handbook; exec. editor Toxic and Hazardous Substance Control; assoc. editor Solvent Extraction and Ion Exchange; editor: (with F.G. Pohland) Emerging Technologies in Hazardous Waste Management, 1989, I, 1990, II, 1991, III, 1993, IV, 1994, V, 1995; contbr. numerous articles to profl. jours., chpts. to books. Mem. AIChE (pub. awareness com. Knoxville 1978-79), Am. Chem. Soc. (symposium chmn. I&EC divsn. 1989—), Am. Nuclear Soc., Water Pollution Control Fedn. Achievements include patents in process producing absolute ethanol by solvent extraction and vacuum distillation, fractional distillation of C2/C3 hydrocarbon at optimum pressures, others. Office: Ga Inst Tech Sch Chem Engring 778 Atlantic Dr Atlanta GA 30332-0001

TEDESCO, FRANCIS JOSEPH, university administrator; b. Derby, Conn., Mar. 8, 1944; s. Lena (Tufano) Tedesco; m. Luann Lee Ekern, Aug. 1, 1970; 1 child, Jennifer Nicole. BS cum laude, Fairfield U., 1965; MD cum laude, St. Louis U., 1969. Asst. instr. Hosp. of U. Pa., Phila., 1971-72; asst. prof. Washington U. Sch. Medicine, St. Louis, 1974-75, U. Miami (Fla.) Sch. Medicine, 1975-77, co-dir. clin. research, 1976-78, assoc. prof., 1977-78, Med. Coll. Ga., Augusta, 1978-81, chief of gastroenterology dept., 1978-88, prof., 1981—, acting v.p. clin. activities, 1984, v.p. for clin. activities, 1984-88, Interim dean Sch. of Medicine, 1986-88, pres., 1988—2001, pres. emeritus, 2001—. Cons. Med.-Letter/AMA divsn. drugs, Dwight D. Eisenhower Army Med. Ctr., Ft. Gordon, Ga., VA Med. Ctr., Augusta, Walter Reed Army Med. Ctr., Washington; mem. gastroenterology spl. study sect. NIH, Washington, 1982—, mem. nat. digestive disease adv. bd., 1985-88, vice chmn., 1986-87, chmn., 1987-88; mem. Ty Cobb Found. Scholarship Bd., 1998—. Contbr. numerous articles to profl. jours. Bd. dirs. Augusta Country Day Sch., 1981-83, Am. Cancer Soc., Augusta, 1985—, v.p., 1986—; bd. dirs., exec. com. Ga. Coalition for Health, 1995-2002; chmn. Gov.'s Health Strategies Coun., 1992-2002; bd. visitors CDC, 1998—; nat. adv. bd. Ga. Acad. Sci., Math. and Engring., 1998—; mem. Ty Cobb Fedn. Bd., 1998—. Recipient Eddie Palmer award for gastrointestinal endoscopy, 1983, cert. of appreciation Am. Cancer Soc., 1986, Outstanding Faculty award Med. Coll. Ga. Sch. Medicine, 1988, Profl. Achievement award Fairfield U., 1993, alumni merit award St. Louis U. Sch. Medicine, 1996; Avalon Found. scholar St. Louis U., 1968-69, Paul Harris fellow Rotary, 1990, Spirit of Ga. award Ga. Econ. Devel. Assn., 1998. Fellow ACP, Am. Fedn. Clin. Investigation, Am. Gastroent. Assn., Am. Soc. Gastrointestinal Endoscopy (treas. 1981-84, pres.-elect 1984-85, pres. 1985-86, Rudolph Schindler award 1993); mem. Am. Coll. Gastroenterology, So. Soc. Clin. Investigation, Richmond County Med. Soc., Med. Assn. Ga. Roman Catholic. Avocations: reading, swimming. Home: 2810 Peachtree Pl Augusta GA 30909 Office: Med Coll Ga Office Pres 1120 15th St Augusta GA 30912-0006

TEDESCO, PAUL HERBERT, humanities educator; b. Nashua, N.H., Dec. 28, 1928; s. Steven R. and Ruth (Weaver) T.; m. Eleanor Martha Hollis, Jan. 24, 1953; children: Steven Anthony, Sara Adams Tagget, James Beattie. AB in History, Harvard Coll., 1952; AM in History, Boston U., 1955, PhD in History, 1970; CAGS in Adminstrn., Northeastern U., Boston, 1974. Instr. humanities Mich. State U., East Lansing, 1955-60; tchr. history Great Neck (N.Y.) North H.S., 1960-62; chmn. dept. social studies Canton (Mass.) H.S., 1962-65; prof., chmn. edn. Northeastern U., Boston, 1965-87; Fulbright prof. history Peking U., Beijing, China, 1988-89; historian-in-residence City of Haverhill, Mass., 1989-90; lectr. bus., history, govt. edn. Asian divsn. U. Md., Korea, Japan, Guam, 1990-94; team leader, lectr. Joint Siberian-Am. Faculty, Irkutsk State U., Siberia, 1994-95; edn. coord. Asian divsn. U. Md., 1995-97; lectr. U. Md. European divsn., 1997—. Nat. dir. BHelp (Bus., History and Econ. Life Program), Boston, 1968—; cons. in field. Author: Teaching with Case Studies, 1978, A New England City: Haverhill Massachusetts, 1987, Attleboro, Massachusetts: The Hub of the Jewelry Industry, 1979, Protection, Patriotism and Prosperity: James M. Swank, the AISA, and the Tariff, 1872-1913, 1985; author, editor: The Creative Social Science Teacher, 1970, The Thunder of the Mills, 1981, Dover, Mass., 2000. Mem. Town Fin. Com., Canton, Mass., 1966-68. With U.S. Army, 1952-54. Recipient FEI Nat. collegiate award, 1985, Freedoms Found. George Washington medal for econ. edn., 1984. Mem. New Eng. History Tchrs. Assn. (past pres., Kidger award 1975), Dover Hist. Soc. (pres.).

TEDROS, THEODORE ZAKI, real estate broker, appraiser, educator; b. Cairo, June 25, 1910; Naturalized, 1966; s. Zaki and Faika (Lotfi) T.; married 1962; 1 child, Samuel N. BA in Math., Tex. Christian U., 1957, MEd with honors, 1958; postgrad., Fla. State U., 1961. Tchr. pub. schs., Addis Ababa, Ethiopia, 1947-56, The American Inst., Addis Ababa, Ethiopia, 1952-56; instr. math. Fla. State U., Tallahassee, 1958-59; tchr. math. Fla. Mil. Sch. and Coll., Deland, Fla., 1961-64; tchr. Volusia County Bd. Instrn., Deland, 1964-75; real estate broker Daytona Beach, Fla., 1975-98; appraiser, 1978-92. Prof. ednl. sociology U. Man., Winnipeg, Can., summers 1962-64. Sunday sch. tchr., Fla.; mem. Nat. Coun. Math. Tchrs., 1959-75, Phi Delta Kappa, 1960-80. Mem. Nat. Assn. Master Appraisers (v.p. 1985-86), Fla. Assn. Realtors, Daytona Beach Area Bd. Realtors, Nat. Assn. Realtors (cert. 1978-90). Democrat. Home: 611 E Tall Pine Ter Deland FL 32724-7122

TEELEY, KEVIN, educational association administrator; b. Detroit, 1954; BA in Sociology and Elem. Edn., U. Wash., 1978. Tchr. 5th and 6th grade gifted students Lake Washington Sch. Dist., Redmond, Wash., 1978—91, curriculum/staff devel. specialist, 1994—95; pres. Lake Washington Edn. Assn., Redmond, 1991—94, 1996—. Mem.: NEA (mem. profl. stds. and practice com. 1996—2002, rep. goodwill mission to Russia 2000, del. Edn. Internat. World Congress 1998, 2001), Nat. Bd. for Profl. Tchg. Stds. (bd. mem.). Office: Lake Washington Edn Assn 7300 208th Ave NE Redmond WA 98053

TEETS, WALTER RALPH, accounting educator; b. Boulder, Colo., Oct. 1, 1950; s. Otis E. and Elsie (Purchase) T.; m. Mary Anne Clougherty; stepchildren: Katherine Wierman, Elizabeth Wierman. B in Music Edn., U. Colo., 1973; MMus, U. Wis., Madison, 1976; MS in Edn., U. Wis., Whitewater, 1981, MS in Acctg., 1985; PhD, U. Chgo., 1989. Asst. prof. Wash. U., St. Louis, 1986-89, U. Ill., Urbana-Champaign, Ill., 1989-94, Gonzaga U., Spokane, Wash., 1994-99, assoc. prof., 1999—. Continuing profl. edn. spkr. Gonzaga U., 1996—2003, Wash. Soc. CPAs, numerous others; vis. assoc. prof. U. Notre Dame, 2000. Editor Fin. Reporting Jour., 1998—02; spl. guest editor Issues in Acctg. Edn., 2001-03; contbr. articles to profl. jours. Recipient Outstanding Acctg. Educator award Wash. Soc. CPAs, 1998-99; Acad. acctg. fellow Office of Chief Acct., U.S. SEC, 1997-98. Mem. Am. Acctg. Assn. (editor Fin. Reporting Jour. newsletter Fin. Acctg. and Reporting sect. 1998—02), Wash. Soc. CPAs (bd. dirs. Spokane chpt.), K.C. (fin. sec. 1990-93, 99-2003). Avocations: music, cross-country skiing, four-wheeling. Office: Gonzaga Univ 502 E Boone Ave Spokane WA 99258-0001 Fax: 509-323-5811. E-mail: teets@gem.gonzaga.edu.

TEGOVICH, ELAINE A. elementary education educator; b. Woonsocket, R.I., May 29, 1958; d. Kosta Stereo and Ida Anastasia (Steve) T. Student, Columbus Internat. Coll., Sevilla, Spain, 1979; BS in Edn., Worcester (Mass.) State Coll., 1980; MA in Lang., Reading and Culture, U. Ariz., 1991, EdS in Lang., Reading and Culture, 1993. Cert. elem., bilingual tchr., Mass., elem., bilingual tchr., reading specialist, Ariz. English as 2d lang./bilingual tchr. West Boylston (Mass.) Schs., 1980-81; elem. tchr. Sahuarita (Ariz.) Schs., 1981-93; reading specialist Gilbert (Ariz.) Schs., 1993—. Grad. instr. reading edn. No. Ariz. U., 2000—. Contbr. articles to profl. jours. State treas. Ariz. Edn. Assn. Women's Caucus, 1992-95; membership co-chair Gilbert Edn. Assn., 1993-97, co-pres., 1997-99; bldg. rep. Sahuarita Edn. Assn., 1981-93; coach Am. Youth Soccer Orgn., Amado, Ariz., 1981-83. Recipient Fulbright Meml. Fund scholar, 1998; fellow Korea Soc., 2000. Mem. AAUW (Eleanor Roosevelt fellowship 1990-91), Internat. Reading Assn., Phi Delta Kappa, Delta Kappa Gamma. Eastern Orthodox. Avocations: reading, travel, skiing, bicycling, photography. Home: 2331 E Stottler Dr Gilbert AZ 85296-3922 Office: Mesquite Elem 1000 E Mesquite St Gilbert AZ 85296-1814

TEGUH, COLLIN, physician, educator; b. Medan, Indonesia, Aug. 25, 1957; s. Tonga and Tsit Wati (Salim) T.; m. Lisa Hom; children: Justen W., Branden C., Brittany Lisa. BA, U. Calif. San Diego, 1983; DO, U. Osteo. Medicine Des Moines, 1991. Diplomate Am. Acad. Family Physicians, Am. Acad. Ambulatory Care. Rsch. asst. Scripp Meml. and Whittier Inst. for Endocrinology & Diabetes, LaJolla, Calif., 1983-87, U. Osteo. Medicine and Health Scis., Des Moines, 1988-90; intern, resident San Bernardino (Calif.) County Med. Ctr., 1991-93; clin. rsch. investigator, pvt. practice San Diego, 1999—. Asst. clin. prof. U. Calif. San Diego, LaJolla, 1995—, Coll. Osteo. Medicine, Pomona, Calif., 1995—; mem. pharmacy and therapeutic com. Cmty. Health Care Group, San Diego. Contbr. articles to profl. jours. Pharmacy and therapeutic com. mem. for Cmty. Health Group. Fellow: Am. Acad. Family Physician (diplomate); mem.: Am. Tropical Medicine and Hygiene, San Diego Acad. Family Physicians, San Diego Osteo. Med. Assn. (exec. bd.), Am. Acad. Ambulatory Care (diplomate), U. Osteo Medicine and Health Scis. Alumni Assn., U. Calif. San Diego Alumni Assn. Avocations: snorkeling, hiking, reading, horticulture, travel. Office: North Park Med Ctr 3780 El Cajon Blvd San Diego CA 92105-1033

TEHRANI, FLEUR TAHER, electrical engineer, educator, researcher; b. Tehran, Iran, Feb. 16, 1956; came to U.S., 1984; d. Hassan and Pourandokht (Monfared) T.; m. Akbar E. Torbat, June 16, 1997. BS in Elec. Engring., Arya-Mehr U. of Tech., Tehran, 1975; DIC in Comm. Engring., Imperial Coll. Sci. and Tech., London, 1977; MSc in Comm. Engring., U. London, 1977, PhD in Elec. Engring., 1981. Registered profl. engr., Calif. Comm. engr. Planning Orgn. of Iran, Tehran, 1977-78; lectr. A elec. engring. Robert Gordon's Inst. Tech., Aberdeen, U.K., 1982-83; lectr. II elec. engring. South Bank U., London, England, 1983—84; asst. prof. elec. engring. Calif. State U., Fullerton, 1985-91, assoc. prof. elec. engring., 1991-94, prof. elec. engring., 1994—, dir. pharm. engring. program, 1999-2001. Vis. assoc. prof. elec. engring. Drexel U., Phila., 1987-88; sys. cons. Telebit Corp., Cupertino. Calif., 1985; engring. cons. PRD, Inc., Dresher, Pa., 1989-92; mem. NASA/Am. Soc. Engring. Edn. summer faculty Jet Propulsion Lab., Calif. Inst. Tech., Pasadena, 1995, 96. Contbr. articles to profl. jours.; patentee in field. Recipient Best Rsch. Manuscript award Assn. for the Advancement of Med. Instrumentation, 1993, NASA/Am. Soc. Engring. Edn. Recognition award for rsch. contbns., 1995, 96. Fellow Inst. for Advancement of Engring.; mem. IEEE, Women in Sci. and Engring. (chair Calif. State U. chpt. 1990-91), Assn. Profs. and Scholars of Iranian Heritage (pres. 1991-92), Sigma Delta Epsilon. Avocations: music, literature, poetry, stamp collecting. Office: Calif State U Coll Engring & Computer Sci 800 N State College Blvd Fullerton CA 92831-3547 E-mail: ftehrani@fullerton.edu.

TEHRANIAN, MAJID, political economy and communications educator; b. Iran, Mar. 22, 1937; m. Katharine Kia; children: Terrence, Yalda, John, Maryam. BA in Govt., Dartmouth Coll., 1959; MA in Middle Eastern Studies, Harvard U., 1961, PhD in Polit. Economy and Govt., 1969. Asst. prof. econs. Lesley Coll., 1964-69; assoc. prof. polit. sci. New Coll. U. South Fla., 1969-71; dir. social planning Plan Orgn. of Iran, 1971-72; sr. analyst, dir. rsch. Indsl. Mgmt. Inst., 1972-74; dir. prospective planning project Nat. Iranian Radio & TV, 1974-75; prof., founding dir. Iran Communications & Devel. Inst., 1976-78; program specialist communication planning and studies Div. Devel. of Communication Systems UNESCO, Paris, 1979-80; fellow Communication Inst., East West Ctr., 1981-82; chair dept. communication U. Hawaii, Manoa, 1986-88, prof. dept. communication, 1981—, dir. Matsunaga Inst. Peace, 1990-92, dir. Toda Inst. Global Peace Policy Rsch., 1996—. Vis. scholar Inst. for Communication Rsch., Stanford U., 1977; vis. fellow St. Anthony's Coll., Oxford U., 1978-79; vis. scholar Ctr. for Internat. Affairs MIT, 1980-81, Can., U.S. and USSR universities, 1988; rsch. affiliate Ctr. for Middle Eastern Studies, Harvard U., 1980-81; vis. prof. dept. govt. Harvard Summer Sch., 1989-90; dir.-elect and dir. Inst. for Peace, U. Hawaii, coun. and exec. com., 1986—; rsch. fellow Social Sci. Rsch. Inst., U. Hawaii, Manoa, 1982-83, 84-86; lectr. in field. Author: Towards a Systematic Theory of National Development, 1974, Socio-Economic and Communications Indicators in Development Planning, 1981, Technologies of Power, 1990; co-author: The Middle East: Its Government and Politics, 1972, The Global Context of the Formation of Domestic Communications Policies, 1975, Policy Towards Social Sciences in Asia and Oceania, 1978, Worlds Apart: Human Securityand Global Goverance, 1999, Asia Peace: Security and Goverance in the Asia Pacific Region, 1999, Global Communication and World Politics, 1999, Global Civilization (in Japanese, English, Persian), 2000-2003, Dialogue of Civilizations, 2002; editor: Communications Policy for Development, 1977, Letters from Jerusalem, 1990, Deconstructing Paradise: Dependency, Development and Discourse in Hawaii, 1990, Peace and Policy, Bridging a Gulf: Peacebuilding in West Asia, 2003; co-editor: Restructuring for World Peace: On the Threshold of the 21st Century, 1992, Toward Democratic Governance 2000, Choose Dialogue, 2000 (in Japanese), (with David W. Chappell) Dialogue of Civilizations: A New Peace Agenda for the New Millenium, 2002, (with Michael Intriligator and Alexander Nikitin) Eurasia: A New Peace Agenda, 2003; contbr. articles to profl. jours.; reviewer in field. Scholar Dartmouth Coll., 1955-59, Fujio Matsuda scholar, 1990-91; Jane Addams Peace Found. fellow, 1961, Ford Found. fellow Harvard U., 1959-61, fellow St. Anthony's Coll., Oxford, 1978-79, fellow East West Ctr. Communication Isnt., 1977, 81, 82; rsch. grantee Social Sci. Rsch. Inst., U. Hawaii, Manoa, 1982-85, UNESCO rsch. grantee, 1983-84, Can. Studies Faculty Enrichment grantee, 1988, Hawaii Interactive TV System Curriculum Devel. grantee, 1989; recipient Dartmouth Colby & Grimez Prizes, 1959, Excellence in Teaching award 1989, Soka U. award of highest honor, Disting. Svc. award Assn. Edn. in Journalism and Mass Communication, 1998. Fellow World Acad. Art & Sci.; mem. Internat. Inst. Comm. (bd. trustees 1979-81), Internat. Comm. Assn. (conf. theme chair for Asia 1989), Pacific Telecomm. Coun., Middle East Studies Assn. N.Am., Middle East Econs. Assn. (nat. adv. bd.), Soc. for Iranian Studies (founding exec. sec. 1967-71), Worldview Internat. Found. Avocations: swimming, tennis, chess, poetry. Home: 2627 Manoa Rd Honolulu HI 96822-1767 Office: U Hawaii Sch of Communication Honolulu HI 96822 also: Toda Inst 1600 Kapiolani Blvd Ste 1111 Honolulu HI 96814-3806 Fax: 808 955-6476.

TEICH, ALAN HARVEY, psychology educator, clinical psychologist; b. East Meadow, N.Y., May 29, 1955; s. Robert and Sonia (Kahan) T.; m. Diane Lees; children: Sarah, Daniel, Jim, Tracey, Meghan. BS, SUNY, Brockport, 1977; MA, SUNY, Geneseo, 1979; PhD, U. Miami, 1987. Lic. psychologist, Pa. Asst. lab. instr. U. Pitts., Johnstown, Pa., 1979-82; tchg./rsch. asst. U. Miami, Coral Gables, Fla., 1982-87; asst. prof. U. Pitts., Johnstown, 1987-94, assoc. prof., 1995—, interim chair natural scis. divsn., 1997-98, chmn. natural scis. divsn., 1998—2003. Presenter in field. Contbr. articles to profl. jours. Bd. dirs. Victim Svcs., Johnstown, 1992—, Johnstown Concert Ballet, 1995-2003. Mem. APA, Pa. Soc. Behavioral Medicine, Laurel Mountain Psychol. Assn. (exec. bd. dirs., pres. 1993-95). Home: 2240 Spear Ave Johnstown PA 15905-1646 Office: U Pitts Johnstown 113A Krebs Hall Johnstown PA 15904

TEICH, MALVIN CARL, electrical engineering educator; b. N.Y.C., May 4, 1939; s. Sidney R. and Loretta K. Teich SB in Physics, MIT, 1961; MSEE, Stanford U., 1962; PhD in Quantum Electronics, Cornell U., 1966. Research scientist MIT Lincoln Lab., Lexington, Mass., 1966-67; prof. engring. sci. Columbia U., 1967-96, prof. emeritus, 1996—, chmn. dept. elec. engring., 1978-80, mem. Columbia Radiation Lab., faculty applied physics dept.; prof. elec. computer engring., biomed. engring., physics Boston U., 1995—. Mem. Photonics Ctr., Boston U., also Ctr. Adaptive Sys., Hearing Rsch. Ctr.; mem. sci. bd. Inst. Physics, Czech Acad. Scis., Prague. Author: (with B.E.A. Saleh) Fundamentals of Photonics, 1991; dep. editor Quantum Optics, 1988-92; bd. editors Jour. Visual Comm. and Image Representation, 1989-92, Jemná Mechanika a Optika, 1994—; contbr. articles to profl. jours.; patentee in field. Recipient Citation Classic award Inst. for Sci. Info., 1981; Meml. Gold medal of Palacky U., Czech Republic, 1992; Guggenheim Meml. Found. fellow, 1973. Fellow AAAS, IEEE (Browder J. Thompson Meml. prize 1969, Morris E. Leeds award 1997), Optical Soc. Am. (editl. adv. panel Optics Letters 1977-79), Am. Phys. Soc., Acoustical Soc. Am.; mem. Sigma Xi, Tau Beta Pi. Office: Boston U Dept Elec and Computer Engr 8 Saint Mary's St Boston MA 02215-2421 E-mail: teich@bu.edu.

TEICHMAN, EVELYN, antiques appraiser, educator, estate liquidator; b. N.Y.C., Mar. 13, 1929; d. Bernard and Minnie (Goldenberg) Mensch; m. Milton Teichman, Jan. 16, 1949; children: David, Jeb, Sondra. Student, CUNY, 1946-49. Tchr. Bergen County Adult Schs., N.J., 1976—; freelance appraiser Paramus, N.J., 1978—; house contents and estate sale coord. Home: 56 Bush Pl Paramus NJ 07652-4004 Fax: 201-262-9552. E-mail: yonkiel@cs.com.

TEITELBAUM, HARRY, English educator; b. Leipzig, Germany, Sept. 23, 1930; came to U.S., 1939; s. Simon and Rencia (Spindel) T.; m. Marilyn L. Nober, Nov. 7, 1953; children: Mark, David, Deborah. BA, Bkyn. Coll., 1952, MA, 1953; ABD, NYU, 1968. Cert. tchr. English, math., supr. secondary edn., N.Y.; cmty. coll. instr. liberal arts, Calif. Teaching fellow Bklyn. Coll., 1953; instr. U.S. Armed Forces Inst., Germany, 1954-55; substitute tchr. N.Y.C. High Schs., Bklyn., 1955; tchr. English Elmont (N.Y.) Meml. High Sch., 1955-60; tutor SAT Plainview, N.Y., 1963-68; English tchr. Plainview-Old Bethpage Sch. Dist., 1960-85; dept. chmn. John F. Kennedy High Sch., Plainview, 1966-70; adj. prof. Hofstra U., Hempstead, N.Y., 1958-74, Suffolk County C.C., Selden, N.Y., 1974-87, Saddleback Coll., Mission Viejo, Calif., 1988—2001. Judge various writing and speaking contests, L.I., N.Y., 1964-85; scholar-lectr. Orange County Calif. Librs., 1989. Author: How to Write a Thesis, 1964, 75, 94, 98, How to Write Book Reports, 1975, 89, 95, 98; co-author: How to Write Themes and Essays, rev. edit., 1994; contbr. articles to profl. jours. and newspapers. Cpl. U.S. Army, 1953-55. Recipient Disting. Tchr. award Alpha Sigma Lambda Hofstra U., 1969, John F. Kennedy High Sch., 1979. Avocations: skiing, tennis, woodworking, jogging. Home: 29562 Avante Laguna Niguel CA 92677-7949

TEITELBAUM, MARILYN LEAH, special education educator; b. Bklyn., June 12, 1930; d. Abraham and Fay (Ingis) Nober; m. Harry Teitelbaum, Nov. 7, 1953; children: Mark, David, Deborah. BA, Bklyn. Coll., 1953; MS, Queens Coll., 1968, L.I. U., 1982. Cert. tchr., N.Y. Elem. and spl. edn. tchr., Franklin Square, N.Y., 1955-57; elem. tchr. Manetto Hill Sch., Plainview, N.Y., 1968-70, Northport (N.Y.) Sch. Dist., 1970-78, spl. edn. tchr., 1978-87; pvt. spl. edn. tchr. Laguna Niguel, Calif., 1988—2002. Author: Teachers as Consumers-What They Should Know About the Hearing Impaired Child, 1981. V.p. Friends of Libr., Laguna Niguel Pub. Libr., 1988—. Recipient outstanding tchr. award Northport PTA, 1987. Mem. NEA, Coun. Exceptional Children, United Tchrs. Northport, Orange County Dyslexic Soc. Avocations: reading, travel, painting, piano. Home: 29562 Avante Laguna Niguel CA 92677-7949

TEIXEIRA, ARTHUR ALVES, food engineer, educator, consultant; b. Fall River, Mass., Jan. 30, 1944; s. Arthur Araujo and Emelia (Alves) T.; m. Jean E. Lamb, Dec. 26, 1966 (dec. Dec. 1983); children: A. Allan, Scott C.; m. Marjorie St. John, June 28, 1986; 1 stepchild, Craig St. John. PhD, U. Mass., 1971. Registered profl. engr., Fla., Mass. Rsch. engr. Ross Labs., Columbus, Ohio, 1971-73, R&D group leader, 1973-77; sr. cons. Arthur D. Little, Inc., Cambridge, Mass., 1977-82; assoc. prof. U. Fla., Gainesville, 1982-89, prof., 1989—. Sci. advisor Escola Superior de Biotecnologia, Porto, Portugal, 1991-96, FMC Corp., Santa Clara, Calif., 1989-92; internat. cons., Brazil, Chile, Cuba, France, Hungary, Indonesia, Israel, Ireland, Kenya, Poland, Portugal, Peru, Romania, Bulgaria; reviewer USDA, Washington, 1991—. Author: Computerized Food Processing Operations, 1989; contbr. 8 chpts. to books, 50 articles to profl. jours. Judge Internat. Sci. Fair, Orlando, Fla., 1991. Recipient Golden Retort Award of Merit (IFTPS), 1994, Fulbright scholar award, Portugal, 1990—91, Peru, 2000, Disting. Food Engr. award, IAFIS/FPEI/ASAE, 2001, Sr. Faculty award, U. Fla. chpt. Gamma Sigma Delta, 1996, Tchr. of Yr. award, U. Fla. Coll. Engring., 1996; fellow, NATO, 1988—89. Fellow Am. Soc. Agrl. Engrs. (dir. 1988-90, Paper awards 1988-89, 2001, assoc. editor Transactions of ASAE 1985—); mem. AIChE, ASAE, Inst. Food Technologists (mem. editl. bd. 1980-83, 2003—), Am. Soc. Engring. Edn., Inst. Thermal Process Specialists, Coun. on Agrl. Sci. and Tech., R & D Assocs., Gamma Sigma Delta (chpt. pres. U. Fla. 1999-2000), Sigma Xi, Alpha Epsilon, Tau Beta Pi. Roman Catholic. Achievements include design of on-line process control system to assure safety of sterilized canned foods; tech. and econ. feasiblity for radiation sterilization of disposable feeding devices; research in computer optimization and control of food sterilization processes and mathematical modelling of bacterial spore population dynamics in processed foods. Office: U Fla Rogers Hall Gainesville FL 32611-0570 E-mail: aateixeira@mail.ifas.ufl.edu.

TEJA, AMYN SADRUDIN, chemical engineering educator, consultant; b. Zanzibar, Tanzania, May 11, 1946; came to U.S., 1980; s. Sadrudin N. and Amina T.; m. Carole Rosina Thurlow, July 3, 1971; children: Kerima Amy, Adam Riaz. BSc in Engring., U. London, London, 1968; PhD, U. London, 1972. Intern Warren Springs Lab., Stevenage, England, 1966, Brit. Gas Corp., London, 1968; rsch. fellow in chem. engring. Loughborough U. Tech., England, 1971-74, chem. engring. lectr., 1974-80; assoc. prof. chem. engring. Ga. Inst. Tech., Atlanta, 1980-83, prof., 1984-90, dir. Fluid Properties Rsch. Inst., 1985—, regents prof. Sch. Chem. Engring., 1990—, regents prof. Woodruff Sch. Mech. Engring., 1991—2001, co-dir. Specialty Separations Ctr., 1992—, assoc. chair grad. studies, 1994—. Cons. Laporte Chems., England, 1971; vis. assoc. prof. chem. engring. U. Del., Newark, 1978—79; cons. Mobil Rsch. and Devel. Co., NJ, 1979; vis. assoc. prof. chem. engring. Ohio State U., 1980; cons. Conoco Ltd., Humberside Refinery, England, 1980, Milliken Chem. Co., Spartanburg, SC, 1981—83, Hoechst Celanese Corp., Corpus Christi, Tex., 1984, Philip Morris U.S.A., Richmond, Va., 1984—87, DuPont Co., 1988, Shell Oil Co., 1989—93, Union Carbide Corp., South Charleston, W.Va., 1989—96, Hoechst Celanese Corp., Charlotte, 1992; presenter in field, reviewer various jours. Editor: Chemical Engineering and the Environment, 1981; mem. editl. bd. Reports on the Progress of Applied Chemistry, 1972-76, Critical Reports on Applied Chemistry, 1976-80, Jour. Chem. and Engring. Data, 1991-96, Chem. Engring. Rsch. Compendium, 1990—, Jour. Supercritical Fluids, 1990—; assoc. editor The Chem. Engring. Jour., 1973-2003; contbr. more than 200 articles to profl. jour. Recipient Hinchley medal Instn. Chem. Engrs., 1968, IBM Rsch. scholarship, 1968-71, Gas Coun. Rsch. scholarship, 1968-71, Brit. Coun. Younger Rsch. Workers award, 1977, Outstanding Tchr. award Omega Chi Epsilon, 1990. Fellow AIChE (pub. com. 1992—, jour. rev., Inst. Award for Excellence in Indsl. Gases Tech. 2002); mem. Am. Soc. Engring. Edn., Am. Chem. Soc., Sigma Xi (v.p. Ga. Tech. chpt. 1991-92. pres. 1992-93, Supr. Outstanding MS Thesis in Engring. 1984, 90, Supr. Outstanding PhD Thesis 1993, 96, Sustained Rsch. award 1987). Avocations: tennis, science fiction. Home: 6282 Indian Field Norcross GA 30092-1372 Office: Ga Inst Tech Sch Chem Engring Atlanta GA 30332-0100 E-mail: amyn.teja@che.gatech.edu.

TELANG, NITIN T. cancer biologist, educator; b. Bombay, July 3, 1943; came to U.S., 1976; s. Trimbak Pandharinath and Madhumalati (Kanitkar) T. BSc, U. Poona, India, 1963, MSc, 1966, PhD, 1974. Assoc. rsch. scientist Tata Meml. Hosp. Cancer Rsch., Bombay, 1974-76; rsch. assoc. U. Nebr., Lincoln, 1976-78; staff fellow Am. Health Found., Valhalla, N.Y., 1978-81; rsch. assoc. Sloan-Kettering Inst., N.Y.C., 1981-85; asst. attending biochemist Meml. Sloan-Ketering Cancer Ctr., N.Y.C., 1985-91; assoc. prof. Cornell U. Med. Coll., N.Y.C., 1991—; dir. divsn. carcinogenesis & prevention Strang-Cornell Cancer Rsch. Lab., N.Y.C., 1991-95, dir. carcinogenesis and nutrition core lab., 1991—; dir. divsn. carcinogenesis and prevention Strang Cancer Rsch. Lab., The Rockefeller U., 1995—, sr. scientist, head Julian H. Robertson Jr. Chemoprevention Rsch. Lab., Strang Cancer Prevention Ctr., 1998—. Vis. investigator The Rockefeller U., N.Y.C., 1985-89. Contbr. numerous articles to profl. jours. Mem. Am. Assn. Cancer Rsch., Am. Soc. Cell Biology, Am. Inst. Nutrition, European Assn. Cancer Rsch. Office: Strang Cancer Rsch Lab Rockefeller Univ 1230 York Ave New York NY 10021-6307

TELENCIO, GLORIA JEAN, elementary education educator; b. Trenton, N.J., Sept. 3, 1955; d. John and Anne (Tymoch) T. BA cum laude, Georgian Ct. Coll., 1977. Cert. elem. edn. Math and sci. tchr. grade 8 St. Anthony's Grammar Sch., Trenton, 1977-78; elem. tchr. grade 7 St. Mary's Assumption Sch., Trenton, 1978-79; elem. tchr. grade 2 Hamilton Twp. Bd. Edn., Trenton, 1979-85, elem. tchr. grade 1, 1985—. Sch. coord. Regional Curriculum Svc. Unit, Learning Resource Ctr.-Ctrl., 1990-95. Tech. rep., exec. bd. PTA, 1981-91, 1994-97. Recipient State of N.J. Gov.'s Tchr. Recognition award State of N.J., 1991, Resolution of Commendation, Town Coun. of the Twp. of Hamilton, 1991; named Tchr. of Yr., Hamilton Twp. Dist., 1999-00; mini-grantee Bd. Edn., 1987-88, McDonald's Classroom grantee, 1999. Mem. NEA, N.J. Edn. Assn., Hamilton Edn. Assn., Sunnybrae PTA (tchr. rep. exec. bd. 1981-91, co-chair PTA 25th Anniversary com. 1990-91), Kappa Delta Pi, Sigma Tau Delta, Pi Delta Phi, Delta Tau Kappa. Republican. Byzantine Catholic. Avocations: reading, theatre, music. Home: 31 Newkirk Ave Trenton NJ 08629-1429 Office: Sunnybrae Elem Sch 166 Elton Ave Trenton NJ 08620-1622

TELICZAN, CASIMIR JOSEPH, secondary school educator; b. Grand Rapids, Mich., Sept. 12, 1953; s. Edmund Raphael Teliczan (dec.) and Marjorie Ann VanTuinen; m. Michelle Marie Teliczan, Jan. 29, 1983; children: Sean (dec.), Cheri, Gregory. AA in Mgmt., L.A. C.C., 1979; AAS in Interpreting and Translating, C.C. of AF, 1985, AAS in tech. instructing, 1986; BS in Liberal Studies, Excelcior Coll., Albany, 1989; MEd in Secondary and Adult Edn., Grand Valley State U., 1999; PhD of Alternative Edn., Concordia U., 2001. Cert. tchr., Mich. Enlisted USAF, 1973, advanced through grades to sr. master sgt., linguist, 1973-78, counselor, 1979-82, chief collection mgr. Hahn AB, Germany, 1983-86, chief European tng. Goodfellow AFB, Tex., 1987-91, supt., 1991-92, exec. officer, 1992-93, ret., 1993; sci. tchr., head dept. River Valley Acad., Rockford, Mich., 1994—, tech. liaison, 2000—, summer sch. dir., 2000—. Rugby coach Hahn AB, 1983-86, Goodfellow AFB, 1987-93, Cedar Springs, Rockford, 1997-98; rugby officiator, 1983-2002; treas. NCO Acad. Grads. Assn., 1991. Edn. grantee Rockford Edn. Found., 1998-2003. Mem. Air Force Assn. (life), Mich. Alternative Edn. Orgn., Rockford Edn. Assn. Avocations: fishing, rugby, hunting, Karate. Office: River Valley Acad 350 N Main St Rockford MI 49341-1020 E-mail: cteliczan@rockford.k12.mi.us.

TELLER, DOUGLAS H. artist, educator; b. Battle Creek, Mich., June 1, 1933; s. Harold Isaac and Irene Margarite (Bailey) T. BA, Western Mich. U., 1956; MFA, George Washington U., 1962. Tchr. art Montgomery County Pub. Schs., Silver Spring, Md., 1958-62; prof. fine arts George Washington U., Washington, 1963-96, prof. emeritus, 1996—. Dealer, exhibitor Serendipity Gallery, Boca Grande, Fla.; workshop instr. Boca Grande Art Alliance, Englewood Art Ctr. One-person show Corcoran Gallery of Art, 1965, Cosmos Club, Washington, 1986, Airlie Found., 1992, Arts Club Washington, 1998; represented in permanent collections Corcoran Gallery of Art, George Washington U., U.S. Art in Embassies Program; represented in pvt. collections, U.S, S.Am., and Europe. 1st lt. USAR, 1955-63. Mem. Fla. Watercolor Soc., So. Watercolor Soc., Suncoast Water Color Soc., Fla. Artists Group, Inc., Sarasota Visual Art Ctr. Democrat. Avocations: music, reading, gardening. Home and Office: 5719 Pierrimac Dr Sarasota FL 34231

TELLER, LORRAINE HELEN, reading specialist and basic skills educator; b. Jersey City, Mar. 17, 1945; d. David Harry Teller and Josephine May (Goodman) Teller Lieberman; m. Robert A. Dickson, Nov. 27, 1966 (div. Jan. 1988); children: Davide Rya, Ian Marshall, Sascha Michael. BA, U. Calif., Chico, 1968; MA, Montclair State Coll., 1976; postgrad., Rutgers U. Tchr. Pleasant Valley High Sch., Chico, Calif., 1967-68, Zama Am. High Sch., Camp Zama, Japan, 1968-70; tchr. then reading specialist Lakewood (N.J.) High Sch., 1971-81; reading specialist Lacey Twp. High Sch., Lanoka Harbor, N.J., 1981-89; programs coord. Harrington Discovery Ctr., Amarillo, 1989-91; from reading specialist to basic skills supr. Essex County Vo-Tech High Sch., Newark, N.J., 1991—. Dir. Ctr. for READ, Toms River, N.J., 1976—; cons. Fgn. Lang. Inst., Tokyo, 1968-70, Toms River Adult Sch., 1970-76; storyteller Lakewood Community Sch., 1978-83; lectr. in field; health sci. educator, Don Harrington Discovery Ctr., Amarillo, Tex., supr. lang. arts, reading, fgn. lang. Pinelands Regional Jr. Sr. High Sch., Tuckerton, N.J., 1987-88. Recipient Texstar/Gaspar award Am. Cancer Soc. Mem. NEA, N.J. Edn. Assn., Nat. Council Tchrs. English, N.J. Council Tchrs. English, Internat. Reading Assn., N.J. Reading Assn., Assn. Supervision and Curriculum Devel., Nat. Assn. Female Execs., Hadassah, Phi Delta Kappa. Home: 134 Ravine Ave West Caldwell NJ 07006-7609 Office: Essex County Vo-Tech Sch 68 S Harrison St East Orange NJ 07018-1703

TEMARES, M. LEWIS, university dean, academic administrator; b. N.Y.C., Feb. 5, 1941; s. Nathan and Gertrude (Weiss) T.; m. Eleanor Liebman, Dec. 8, 1962 (div. Mar. 1975); m. Louise Cortinovis Delphus, Jan. 1, 1989; children: Scott, Stacy, Christy, Jennifer. BBA, MBA; MS, Columbia U.; PhD. V.p. and dean engring. U. Miami, Fla. Office: Univ of Miami Info Tech Miami FL 33146

TEMIN, PETER, economist, educator; b. Phila., Dec. 17, 1937; s. Henry and Annette T.; m. Charlotte Brucar Fox, Aug. 21, 1966; children: Elizabeth Sara, Melanie Wynn. BA, Swarthmore Coll., 1959; PhD, MIT, 1964. Mem. faculty MIT, 1965—, prof. econs., 1970—. Author: Iron and Steel in Nineteenth Century America, 1964, The Jacksonian Economy, 1969, Causal Factors in American Economic Growth in the 19th Century, 1975, Did Monetary Forces Cause the Great Depression?, 1976, Taking Your Medicine: Drug Regulation in the United States, 1980, The Fall of the Bell System, 1987, Lessons from the Great Depression, 1989, Inside the Business Enterprise, 1991, (with C. Feinstein and G. Toniolo) The European Economy Between The Wars, 1997, Engines of Enterprise: An Economic History of New England, 2000. Mem. Am. Econ. Assn., Econ. History Assn., Econ. History Soc., Phi Beta Kappa. Home: 15 Channing St Cambridge MA 02138-4713 Office: MIT Dept Econs Cambridge MA 02139

TEMKIN, JUDITH CELIA, elementary school educator; b. N.Y.C., July 16, 1943; d. Samuel and Lucy Clara (Bogage) Olchak; m. Samuel Temkin, June 20, 1965; children: David, Michael. BA magna cum laude, Queens Coll., 1964. Cert. elem. tchr., N.Y., N.J., R.I. Tchr. Providence Pub. Schs., 1965-66, Highland Park (N.J.) Pub. Schs., 1967-68, 77-78; adult basic edn. tchr. Bound Brook (N.J.) Pub. Schs., 1972-74; kindergarten tchr. Rutgers Prep. Sch., Somerset, N.J., 1976-77; gifted tchr. Milltown (N.J.) Sch. Dist., 1978-83, elem. tchr., 1983—, early childhood edn. leader tchr., 1993-94. Presenter workshops on techniques for tchg. gifted, Office of the County Supt., Middlesex County, N.J., 1979-82, Getting Children to Write, 1984. Chairperson desegregation com. Highland Park Bd. Edn., 1978-79, mem. long-range planning com., 1972-74; pres. Highland Park chpt. LWV, 1976-77, chairperson edn. com., 1967-74. Recipient Gov.'s Tchr. Recognition award, 1995-96. Mem. Internat. Reading Assn., N.J. Sci. Tchrs. Assn., Phi Beta Kappa. Home: 113 Graham St Highland Park NJ 08904-2131 Office: Parkview Sch Violet Ter Milltown NJ 08850

TEMKIN, LARRY SCOTT, philosopher, educator; b. Milw., May 29, 1954; s. Blair Huntly and Leah Dahlia (Sigman) T.; m. Margaret Ellen Grimm, May 26, 1975; children: Daniel Eric, Andrea Beth, Rebecca Leigh. BA-Honors degree in Philosophy, U. Wis., 1975; student, Oxford U., Eng., 1978-79; PhD, Princeton U., 1983. Instr. philosophy Rice U., Houston, 1980-83, asst. prof., 1983-89, assoc. prof., 1989-95, prof., 1995—; prof. philosophy Rutgers U., 2000—. Vis. appointment U. Pitts., 1986; vis. fellow All Souls Coll., Oxford U.; speaker in field. Author: Inequality; contbr. articles to profl. jours. Recipient Phi Beta Kappa Outstanding Tchr. award, George R. Brown awards for superior teaching, George R. Brown awards for excellence in teaching, Nicholas Salgo Outstanding Tchr. award; Danforth fellow, Nat. Humanities Ctr. fellow, Weiner fellow, Harvard fellow for Program in Ethics and the Professions. Mem. Am. Philos. Assn., Phi Beta Kappa. Avocations: camping, sports. Home: 30 Buckingham Dr East Brunswick NJ 08816-3349 Office: Rice U Dept Philosophy MS 14 6100 Main St Houston TX 77005-1892

TEMKIN, TERRIE CHARLENE, professional non-profit administrator, educator; b. Milw., June 6, 1950; d. Blair Huntley and Leah Dahlia (Sigman) T. BS in Communication, Ohio U., 1971; MA, U. Ill., 1972; EdS, U. Wis., Milw., 1976; PhD, U. Okla., 1984. Dir. spl. programs B'nai B'rith Youth Orgn., Milw., 1972-73; speech comm. specialist Alverno Coll., Milw., 1973-75; tng. and devel. specialist pvt. practice San Diego, 1975-78; fundraiser Am. Heart Assn., L.A., 1978-80; mgmt. cons. Hosp. Learning Ctrs., L.A., 1980-84; exec. dir. Women's Am. ORT, Hallandale, Fla., 1985-94; pres. Nonprofit Mgmt. Solutions, Inc., Hollywood, Fla., 1994—. Adj. prof. Nova U., Ft. Lauderdale, Fla., 1989-2000, Barry U., North Miami, Fla., 1995—, Fla. Atlantic U., 2002—. Editor Nonprofit Mgmt. Solutions, 1995-97; contbr. chpts. in books, articles to profl. jours. Co-chair edn. com. Bus. Vols. for Arts, Miami, Fla., 1985-87; bd. dirs. Bridge Theater, Miami, 1985-89, Am. Cancer Soc., 1995-2001; mem. adv. com. Single Parent/Displaced Homemaker Program, Broward County, Fla., 1987-88; chair pub. info. com. Fla. Edn. and Employment Coun. for Women and Girls, 1991-94; pres. Core Strategies for Non Profits, 2002—. Named Outstanding Young Woman of Am., 1982, Woman of Yr. Nonprofit Comm., 2002; NDEA fellow, 1972. Mem. Soc. for Nonprofit Mgmt., Alliance for Nonprofit Mgmt. Assn. of vol. Adminstrs., Assn. Profl. Fundraisers, Fla. Assn. Nonprofit Orgns., Assn. for Rsch. on Nonprofit Orgns. and vol. Action. Dirs. of Vol. Svcs., B'nai B'rith Youth Orgn. (pres. adult bd. 1989-2001), Bus. and Profl. Women's Network (co-chair 1987-89), Women's Am. Orgn. for Rehab. through Tng. (life), Jewish Women Internat. (life), Hadassah (life). Jewish. Avocations: art collecting, traveling.

TEMONEY, VERNEDA DANIELS, elementary education educator; b. Timmonsville, S.C., Mar. 29, 1949; d. Burin Theodore Daniels and Mary Elizabeth (Jackson) Daniels-Cusaac; m. Ronn Temoney, Aug. 21, 1987; children: Wanda Deneise Brown-Joe, Ezra DeShaun Brown. Dental asst. diploma, Florence Darlington Tech., 1968; BS, Francis Marion Coll., 1981, postgrad., 1981—, U. S.C., Aiken, 1988-89. Cert. elem. tchr., dental asst., S.C. Dental asst. G. A. Williams, DDS, Florence, S.C., 1968-69; substitute tchr. Florence Dist. I Schs., 1970-72, tchr.'s asst., 1973-74; elem. tchr. Florence, Dillon, Aiken, Darlington, and Richmond County Pub. Schs., S.C. and Ga., 1981—; pvt. tchr. music Williams Community Sch., Florence, 1970-72. Tutor, instr. music Temoney's Music and Tutorial Inst., Dillon, Florence, Timmonsville and Aiken, S.C., Augusta, Ga., 1990-92; instr. 4th grade C.T. Walker adopter Richmond County Pub. Schs., Augusta, 1990-92; coord. nat. geography bee East Aiken Elem., C.T. Walker and West Hortsville Elem.; field tester Nat. Bd. Profl. Teaching Stds., 1993. Editor: (manual) Let's Practice, Practice, Practice, 1991. Tchr. Edn. Plus Savannah Grove Bapt. Ch., Effingham, S.C., music dir., Bible tchr. Olive Grove Bapt. Ch., Effingham Bapt. Ch., Center Bapt. Ch., Mt. Carmel Black History Choir; speaker various chs. Mem. NEA, Nat. Edn. Rep. Assembly (del. 1985, 86), Nat. Coun. Negro Women, S.C. Edn. Assn. (pres. local chpt. 1986-87), Florence-Dist. I Edn. Assn. (chair Upper Pee Dee Uniserve adv. coun. 1986-87), S.C. Sci. Coun. Avocations: playing and listening to gospel and contemporary music, creating hands-on learning projects, writing poetry. Home and Office: 4019 Jackie Proctor Rd PO Box 718 Timmonsville SC 29161-0718

TEMPELIS, CONSTANTINE HARRY, immunologist, educator; b. Superior, Wis., Aug. 27, 1927; s. Harry and Thelma Marie (Hoff) T.; m. Nancy Louise Foster, Aug. 27, 1955; children: William H., Daniel S. BS, U. Wis.-Superior, 1950; MS, U. Wis.-Madison, 1953, PhD, 1955. Project assoc. immunology U. Wis., Madison, 1955-57; instr. immunology U. W.Va., Morgantown, 1957-58; asst. rsch. immunologist U. Calif., Berkeley, 1958-66, assoc. prof. immunology, 1966-72, prof., 1972-95, prof. emeritus, 1995—, prof. grad. sch., 1996—. Vis. scientist Wellcome Rsch. Labs., Beckenham, Kent, Eng., 1977-78, U. Innsbruck, Austria, 1985, 90, 91; cons. in field. Contbr. articles to profl. jours. Served with USNR, 1945-46. Recipient Rsch. Career Devel. award, 1965-70; Fogarty sr. internat. fellow NIH, 1977-78 Mem. AAAS, Am. Assn. Immunologists, Fedn. Am. Soc. Exptl. Biology, Sigma Xi. Office: U Calif Sch Pub Health Berkeley CA 94720-0001 E-mail: chtemp@uclink4.berkeley.edu.

TEMPLE, JACK DONALD, JR., physician, medical educator; b. Miami, July 30, 1952; s. Jack Donald and Helen (Underhill) T.; m. Regina Ann Kramer, Jan. 14, 1984; children: Laura, Kathleen, Elizabeth. AA, Miami-Dade C.C., 1972; BS in Chemistry, U. Miami, 1974, MD, 1978. Diplomate Nat. Bd. Med. Examiners. Med. intern Jackson Meml. Hosp., Miami, 1978-79, med. resident, 1978-81, clin. fellow, 1981-85, attending physician, 1985—, dir. hematology clinic, 1985-92; clin. instr. U. Miami, 1981-82, asst. prof., 1985-91, assoc. prof., 1991—. Chief med. svc. U. Miami Hosp., 1993—; dir. Harrington Lat. Am. Tng. Programs, Miami, 1992—. Contbr. chpt. to book, articles to med. jours. Named Dr. of Yr. S. Fla. Mag., 1991. Mem. AAAS, Leukemia Soc. Am. (bd. trustees S. Fla. 1992—), U. Miami Alumni Assn. (pres. medicine 1991-94). Achievements include development of new treatments for sickle cell anemia and lymphomatoid granulomatosis. Office: U Miami Sch Medicine Sylvester Cancer Ctr 1475 NW 12th Ave Miami FL 33136-1002 E-mail: jtemple@med.miami.edu.

TENENBAUM, BERNARD HIRSH, entrepreneur, educator; b. Long Beach, N.Y., Dec. 23, 1954; s. Abraham Benjamin and Helen Pearl (Wahrhaft) T. BA, Columbia Coll., 1976; postgrad., Stanford U., 1976-77; MBA, U. Pa., 1981. Mgr. Lido Beach (N.Y.) Hotel, 1976-77; gen. mgr. Sound Spectrum, Huntington, N.Y., 1977-78; dir. Small Bus. Ctr., Phila., 1980-84; asst. dir. Entre Ctr., Phila., 1984-85, assoc. dir., 1986-88; prof. entrepreneurial studies, dir. Fairleigh Dickinson U., Madison, N.J., 1988-93; v.p. corp. devel. Russ Berrie & Co., Inc., 1993-97; pres. Children's Leisure Products Group, The Jordan Co., N.Y.C., 1997—2003. Cons. Phila. Phillies, 1984-85; ret. bd. dirs. WPI Group, Inc., Ogontz Ave. Redevel. Corp., West Phila. Ptnership; ret. dir. Russ Berrie & Co. Del. Securities Exchange Commn. on Small Bus. Capital Formation, 1984-86; vice chmn. Small Bus. Devel. Ctr. adv. bd., Phila., 1983—; bd. dirs. Pvt. Industry Council, Phila., 1983-88; chmn. Small Bus. Fair, Phila., 1983-88. Mem. Phila. C. of C. (vice chmn. small bus. coun. 1982-86, chmn. 1986-88), Venture Assn. N.J. (v.p.). Democrat. Jewish. Avocations: swimming, sports cars, music, literature, film. Office: Chldns Leisure Products LLC 71 Tamarack Cir Skillman NJ 08558 E-mail: bernie@btenenbaum.com.

TENENBAUM, INEZ MOORE, superintendent of education; b. Hawkinsville, GA; m. Samuel J. Tenenbaum. Bsc, U. Ga., 1972, MEd, 1974; JD, U. S.C., 1986. Tchr. Elementary Sch.; dir. rsch. S.C. House Reps., 1977-83; attorney Sinkler & Boye, P.A., 1986-92; supt. edn. S.C. Dept. Edn., Columbia, 1999—. Founder S.C. Ctr. Family Policy. Office: South Carolina Dept Edn Rutledge Bldg 1429 Senate St Columbia SC 29201-3730*

TENENBAUM, JEFFREY MARK, academic librarian; b. Phila., Apr. 10, 1945; s. Paul and Hansi (Barber) T. BA, Pa. State U., 1966; MLS, McGill U., 1968. Documents librarian, then reference librarian U. Toronto (Ont., Can.) Library, 1968-72; reference librarian U. Mass. Library, Amherst, 1973—. Vis. ref. libr. McGill U., Montreal, 1984, Nat. Libr. Can., Ottawa, Ont., 1999; mem. Info. Access Co. Acad. Libr. Product Adv. Bd., Foster City, Calif., 1992-94. Mem. Amherst Pub. Art Commn., 1994-2000. Mem. ALA, Assn. Can. Studies in U.S., Am. Coun. Que. Studies, Mid-Atlantic and New Eng. Conf. for Can. Studies (sec. 1992-96), Pioneer Valley Assn. Acad. Librs. (pres. 1989-90), Assn. Coll. and Rsch. Librs., Beta Phi Mu, Phi Alpha Theta, Pi Gamma Mu. Jewish. Home: 27 Montague Rd Apt 48 Amherst MA 01002-1043 Office: U Mass U Libr 154 Hicks Way Amherst MA 01003-9275 E-mail: jmt@library.umass.edu.

TENER, CAROL JOAN, retired secondary education educator; b. Cleve., Feb. 10, 1935; d. Peter Paul and Mamie Christine (Dombrowski) Manusack; m. Dale Keith Tener, Feb. 13, 1958 (div. Aug. 1991); children: Dean Robert, Susan Dawn Tener Belair. Student, Cleve. Mus. Art, 1948-53, Cleve. Art Inst., 1953-54; BS in Edn. cum laude, Kent State U., 1957; MS in Supervision, Akron U., 1974; postgrad., Kent State U., 1964, 81, 88-90, Akron U., 1975, 79, John Carroll U., 1982, 83, 85-86, Ohio U., 1987, Baldwin Wallace Coll., 1989. Cert. permanent K-12 tchr., Ohio; cert. vol. counselor for Ohio sr. health ins. Ohio Dept. Ins. Stenographer Equitable Life Iowa, Cleve., 1953-54; tchr. elem. art Cuyahoga Falls (Ohio) Bd. Edn., 1957-58, 62-63, 65-68, tchr. jr. high sch., 1968-69; tchr. high sch. Brecksville (Ohio)-Broadview Heights Sch. Dist., 1969-94; chmn. dept. art Brecksville-Broadview Heights (Ohio) H.S., 1979-94, chmn. curriculum devel., 1982, 89; ret., 1994. Instr. for children Kent State U., 1956; advisor, prodr. cmty. svc. in art Brecksville Broadview Heights Bd. of Edn., 1969-94; former tchr. recreation and adult art edn. City of Cuyahoga Falls, 1967-68; com. mem. North Ctrl. evaluation com. Nordonia H.S., Nordonia City, Ohio, 1978, Solon H.S., Solon City, Ohio, 1989; chmn. north ctrl. evaluation com. Garfield Heights H.S., 1991; chair pilot program curriculum devel. com. in art/econs. Brecksville-Broadview Heights H.S., 1985-86, 86-87. Contbr. articles to newspapers, brochures, mags.; commd. artist for mural Brecksville City's Kids Quarters, 1994, Christopher Columbus/John Glen portraits in relief commemorating Columbus Day, 1961, Wooster (Ohio) Products Co.; editor Greater Cleve. chpt. Ohio Ret. Tchrs. Assn., 1998-2002; contbr. to Resources for You, 2003, Ohio Sr. Health Ins. Info. Program, Ohio Dept. Ins. Chmn. Artmart Invitational Exhibit PTA, 1982-94; active Meals on Wheels program in Brecksville and Broadview Hts., 1995-98, Heart Disease collection, 1995, Stow-Glen Assisted Living Visitations, 1994-95, NCR Assisted Living transp. provision to hosps. and dr. in neighboring county; trustee, sec. Gettysburg Devel. Block Group Parma, 1995-96, Kids Quarters, 1994; Med Save fraud vol. Cuyahoga County Dept. Sr. and Adult Svcs., 2000-2002, spkrs. bur.; sr. health ins. info. program, cert. vol. counselor of OSHIIP under the Dept. of Insurance, Ohio Dept. Ins., 2001—. Recipient Ohio Coun. on Econ. Edn. award, 1985-86, award for significant svc. to cmty. Ret. and Sr. Vol. Program of USA, 1996, Svc. award Greater Cleve. Chpt./Ohio Ret. Tchrs. Assn., 1998, Outstanding Svc. award Sr. Medicare Patrol Projects, Cert. of Appreciation, U.S. Dept. Health and Human Svcs. Adminstrn. on Aging, 2002; Pres.'s scholar Kent State U., 1954-57; Resolution to thank a Med-Save Project Vol. signed by Cuyahoga County Commrs. Tim McCormack, pres., Jimmy Dimora, v.p., and Peter Lawson Jones, commr. Mem.: NAFE, ASCD, NEA (life), AAUW, S.W. Area Ret. Educators (co-chair 1996—98, program chair 1996—98, program coord. 1999—2000), Nat. Mus. Women in Arts, Cleve. Mus. Art, Acad. Econ. Edn., Brecksville Edn. Assn., Internat. Platform Assn., Nat. Art Edn. Assn., Ohio Ret. Tchrs. Assn. (life; registration chair 1997—98, pres.-elect Cleve. chpt. 1998, program chair 1998, interim editor 1998, circulation mgr. 1998—2002, chpt. pres. 1999, editor 1999—2002, trustee 2000, guest spkr. on newsletter writing and pub. 2000, nominating chair 2000—01, by-law chair 2000—01, bylaw chair 2000—01, Pub. Rels. awards 1999—2002), Phi Delta Kappa Pi. Roman Catholic. Avocations: european and american museum tours, photography, collecting books on architecture, painting. Home: 7301 Sagamore Rd Parma OH 44134-5732

TENNIES, ROBERT HUNTER, headmaster; b. Bogotá, Colombia, Aug. 19, 1952; s. Leo C. and Ruth (Winston) T.; m. Ruth Ellen Fischer, June 14, 1975; children: Debbie, Julie. BS, Wheaton (Ill.) Coll., 1973; MA, U. South Fla., 1975; EdS, Fla. Atlantic U., 1978, EdD, 1982. Sci. tchr. Cypress Lake Middle Sch., Ft. Myers, Fla., 1973-77, Boca Raton (Fla.) Christian Sch., 1977-78, asst. adminstr., 1978-84, headmaster, 1984—, min. of children, 1984-90; interim. min. of edn., 1991-93. Spkr. Internat. Conf. Religious Edn., Petrozavodsk, Russia; mem. Nat. Rev. Panel Blue Ribbon Schs., 1999. Recipient Excellence in Edn. award Nat. Assn. Elem. Prins., 1990, 97. Mem. Nat. Sci. Tchrs. Assn., Assn. of Christian Schs. Internat. (accreditation commn.), Nat. Assn. Elem. Sch. Prins. Avocation: camping. Home: 2415 NW 30th Rd Boca Raton FL 33431-6214 Office: Boca Raton Christian Sch 315 NW 4th St Boca Raton FL 33432-3739 E-mail: Tennies_r@popmail.firn.edu., bocachristian@bocachristian.org.

TEPLY, MARK LAWRENCE, mathematics educator; b. Lincoln, Nebr., Jan. 11, 1942; s. Lawrence Joseph and Gertrude M. (Kupfer) T.; m. Kathleen K. McGrayel, Aug. 1968 (div. 1978); 1 child, David; m. Nancy Lee Wilkowske, Mar. 12, 1983; children: Stephanie, Andrew, Grant. BA, U. Nebr., 1963, MA, 1965, PhD, 1968. Instr. U. So. Calif., L.A., 1967-68; asst. prof. U. Fla., Gainesville, 1968-73, assoc. prof., 1973-81, prof., 1981-85, U. Wis., Milw., 1985—. Editor: Communications in Algebra, 1982—; editor 2 book series by Marcel Dekker, 1983—; author: Finiteness Conditions on Torsion Theories, 1984, A History of the Singular Splitting Problem, 1984, Semicocritical Modules, 1987; contbr. 70 articles to profl. jours. NSF grantee U. Fla., 1973, 77-78, U.S. Dept. Edn. grantee U. Wis., Milw., 1990—. Mem. Am. Math. Soc., Math. Assn. Am. Lutheran. Office: U Wis Dept Math Milwaukee WI 53201-0413

TEPPER, MARCY ELIZABETH, drug education director; b. Salt Lake City, Aug. 22, 1949; d. Warren Roswell and Rosemary Tepper. PhD, U. Ariz., Tucson, Ariz., 1983; MEd, U. Utah, Salt Lake City, Utah, 1972; Filosfia Y Letras, U. Valencia, Valencia, Spain, 1971; BA, San Francisco Coll. for Women, San Francisco, Calif., 1971. Cert. principal, mathematics, spanish tchr. 1990. Adjunct asst. prof. U. Arizona, Tucson, 1983—86; dir., owner 1.2.1 Tutoring, Tucson, 1984—90; counselor Teton County Sch. Dist., Jackson, Wyo., 1990—94; lectr. Ariz. State U., Tempe, Ariz., 1995—98; tchr. Santa Fe Public Schools, Santa Fe, 1998—99; coun. Safe Sch. Healthy Students Grant, Ethete, Wyo., 1999—2001; mid. sch. coord. Fremont County Schools #14, Ethete, Wyo., 2001—. Bd. mem. Ariz. Women Mathematics Sci., Tempe, 1997—98. Recipient Nat. Outdoor Leadership Sch. (NOLS) scholarship, 2003. Mem.: Interagy. Coord. Coalition (v.p. 2000—01, pres. 2001—03), Teton County Task Force (bd. 1992—94). Office: Wyoming Indian Sch 638 Blue Sky Highway Ethete WY 82520 Office Fax: 307-335-7318. Personal E-mail: marcyet@mail.trib.com. Business E-Mail: marcyt@fremont14.k12.wy.us.

TER-ABRAMYANTS, LALA ABRAMOVNA, artist, educator; b. Myaundzha, Kolyma, USSR, Aug. 4, 1956; d. Abram Moiseevitch and Valentina Vasilevna (Shestakova) T.-A.; m. Vitaliy Alexandrovich Osminin, July 8, 1980 (div. Sept. 1988); 1 child, Veronika Osminina; m. Alex Korsunsky, Jan. 5, 1991; 1 child, Abram Korsunsky. Student, Art Inst. Moscow, 1990. Photo retoucher Armavir (Russia) Photo Studio, 1974-75; artist designer Rwy. Sta. Dept., Moscow, 1975-80; archivist Art Inst. Moscow, 1983-86; graphic artist Newspaper Pub. House, Moscow, 1986-87; visual artist Factory of Art Prodn., Moscow, 1987-90, silk painter, 1990-92; pvt. tchr. drawing and painting Bronx, N.Y., 1994—; instr. painting on silk Riverdale YM-YWHA, N.Y.C., 1995. Batic textile artist OUS Co. Inc., 1993—. Exhibited in group shows at Moscow Textile Fabrics, Oslo, Norway, 1991, Ctrl. House of Painters, Moscow, 1992, Princeton, N.Y., 1992, Madison Sq., N.Y.C., 1992, NYANA, N.Y.C., 1993, L.I., N.Y., 1994, Lincoln Sq., N.Y.C., 1996. Avocations: theater, cinema, music, reading, cooking. Home: 3871 Sedgwick Ave Apt 6J Bronx NY 10463-4467

TERAN, SISTER MARY INEZ, retired nun, educator; b. Austin, Tex., Nov. 15, 1924; d. Jose Julian and Petra (Meza) T. BA, Our Lady of the Lake U., 1960; MDE, Cath. U. Am., 1965. Joined Congregation Sisters of Divine Providence, Roman Cath. Ch., 1941. Coord. religious edn. Archdiocese San Antonio, 1966-71; dir. religious edn. Dolores Ch., Austin, 1971-74, St. Henry's Ch., San Antonio, 1974-78, St. Margaret Mary Ch., San Antonio, 1978-82, St. John Berchmans Ch., San Antonio, 1982-84, St. Cyril and Methodius Ch., Granger, Tex., 1986-88, Sacred Heart Ch., Von Ormy, Tex., 1988-94; ret., 1994. Vol. St. Jude Ch., San Antonio, 1994—2003. Mex.-Am. Cultural Ctr. scholar, San Antonio, 1985-86. Home: 603 SW 24th St San Antonio TX 78207-4621

TERBORG-PENN, ROSALYN MARIAN, historian, educator; b. Bklyn., Oct. 22, 1941; d. Jacques Arnold Sr. and Jeanne (Van Horn) Terborg; 1 dau., Jeanna Carolyn Terborg Penn. BA in History, Queens Coll. CUNY, 1963; MA in History, George Washington U., 1967; PhD in Afro-Am. History, Howard U., 1978. Daycare tchr. Friendship House Assn., Washington, 1964-66; program dir. Southwest House Assn., Washington, 1966-69; adj. prof. U. Md.-Balt. County, Catonsville, 1977-78, Howard C.C., Columbia, Md., 1970-74; prof. history Morgan State U., Balt., 1969—, project dir. oral history project, 1978-79, coord. grad. programs in history, 1986—. Project dir. Assn. Black Women Hist. Rsch. Conf., Washington, 1982-83. Author: (with Thomas Holt and Cassandra Smith-Parker) A Special Mission: the Story of Freedman's Hospital, 1862-1962, 1975, African American Women in the Struggle for the Vote, 1850-1920, 1998; editor: (with Sharon Harley) The Afro-American Woman: Struggles and Images, 1978, 81, 97, (with Darlene Clark Hine and Elsa Barkley Brown) Black Women in America: An Historical Encyclopedia, 1993, 94, (with Sharon Harley and Andrea Benton Rushing) Women in Africa, 1987, (with Andrea Benton Rushing) Women in Africa and the African Diaspora: A Reader, 1996, (with Janice Sumler-Edmond) Black Women's History at the Intersection of Knowledge and Power, 2000; history editor Feminist Studies, 1984-89; mem. editl. bd. Md. Hist. Mag., 1988-94. Founding mem. Howard County Commn. for Women. Ford Found. fellow, 1980-81, Smithsonian Instn. fellow, 1982, 94-95; Howard U. grad. fellow in history, 1973-74, recipient Rayford W. Logan Grad. Essay award Howard U., 1973, Letitia Woods Brown Meml. prize for best article, 1988, Anna Julia Cooper award for disting. scholarship Sage Women's Ednl. Press, 1993, Letitia Woods Brown Meml. Book prize, 1998, Disting. Black Marylander in Edn. award, Towson Univ., 2003. Mem. Assn. Black Women Historians (co-founder, 1st nat. dir. 1980-82, nat. treas. 1982-84, cert. outstanding achievement 1981, Lorraine A. Williams Leadership award 1998), Am. Hist. Assn. (mem. com. on women historians 1978-81, Joan Kelly Prize com. 1984-86, chair com. on women historians 1991-94), Orgn. Am. Historians (mem. black women's history project adv. com. 1980-81), Alpha Kappa Alpha (mem. Internat. Archives and Heritage com. 1994-96). Office: Morgan State U 1700 E Cold Spring Ln Baltimore MD 21251-0002

TERHUNE, JANE HOWELL, legal assistant, educator; b. Newark, June 8, 1932; d. Charles Edwin and Audrey L. (Rogers) Howell; m. Richard N. Terhune, Dec. 22, 1951 (div. 1980); children: Richard C., Susan J., Carolyn A. Cert., Katherine Gibbs Sch., 1951. cert. legal asst. specialist, civil litigation. Legal sec. Howell, Kirby, et al, Jacksonville, Fla., 1954-56, Bidwell Adam, Gulfport, Miss., 1962-63; legal asst. Sinkler Gibbs & Simons, Charleston, S.C., 1963-77; sr. legal asst. Hall, Estill, Hardwick, Gable, Golden & Nelson, P.C., Tulsa, Okla., 1977-97; ret., 1997. Adv. com. to legal asst. com. ABA, Chgo., 1978-85; adj. instr. legal asst. program Tulsa C.C., 1978-97; trustee Okla. Sinfonia, Inc., Tulsa, 1984-92; speaker/faculty Cert. Legal Asst. Short Course, 1986-97. Contbr. articles to profl. jours.; seminar speaker in field. Mem. Nat. Assn. Legal Assts. (founder, charter pres. 1975-77, chmn. certifying bd. 1977-80, parl. 1988-90). Republican. Presbyterian. Avocations: golf, gardening, reading, walking, music. Home: 1706 Oak St Georgetown SC 29440-4038

TERILLI, JOSEPH ANTHONY, secondary education educator; b. Winthrop, Mass., June 14, 1948; s. Joseph Anthony and Mary Grace (Colontuoni) T.; m. Carol Ann Saccardo, Oct. 8, 1971; 1 child, Joseph Anthony III. BS, Boston Coll., 1970, MEd, 1973. Tchr., adminstr. Boston Pub. Schs., 1972-77; tchr. Coolidge Jr. H.S., Reading, Mass., 1977-84, Reading Meml. H.S., 1984—, mentor tchr., 1988—. Pres., CEO Terilli Enterprises Devel. Corp., Aruba, 1986—; mem. Profl. Devel. Com., Reading, 1988-92. Author: Blood on the Chalkboard, How Children Succeed, also newspaper articles, booklets, monographs and mock trial; pub. (newsletter) Political Action Network (PAN). Mem. exec. bd., Mass. state chair Dem. Party (New Dems.). Mem. C. of C., Kiwanis (past sec.). Roman Catholic. Avocations: politics, travel, writing, collecing comic books. Home: 27 Lawndale Rd Stoneham MA 02180-1014 Office: Reading Meml HS 62 Oakland Rd Reading MA 01867-1613

TERMINELLA, LUIGI, critical care physician, educator; b. Catania, Italy, Nov. 15, 1960; came to U.S., 1961; s. Roberto and Josephine (Bartolotta) T. MD summa cum laude, U. Catania, 1986. Pathology asst. Brotman Med. Ctr., Culver City, Calif., 1987-89; transitional resident Miriam Hosp./Brown U., Providence, 1989-90; resident in internal medicine U. Hawaii, Honolulu, 1990-92; tng. in critical care/internal medicine U. Hawaii/Queen's Med. Ctr., Honolulu, 1992-93; transfusion svc. physician Blood Bank of Hawaii, Honolulu, 1992-93; internal medicine physician Hawaii Physician Svcs., Honolulu, 1993—; critical care physician Queen's Med. Ctr., Honolulu, 1993—. Mem. clin. faculty John H. Burns Sch. Medicine, U. Hawaii, Honolulu, 1994—; pres. Pualani Family Health, SRL, Corp., Honolulu. Recipient Clementi award U. Catania, 1986, others. Mem. ACP, AMA, Am. Soc. Internal Medicine, Hawaiian Soc. Critical Care, Soc. Critical Care Medicine. Avocations: photography, law, architecture. Office: Queen's Med Ctr 1301 Punchbowl St # 4B Honolulu HI 96813-2413

TERMINI, OLGA ASCHER, music educator, educator; b. Hamburg, Germany, May 19, 1930; came to U.S., 1952; d. Viktor and Martha M. (Schuett) Ascher; married, Nov. 20, 1955 (dec. July 1979). MusB, U. So. Calif., 1954, MusM, 1957, PhD, 1970. Instr. music Stevenson Jr. H.S., L.A., 1954-57, Fairfax H.S., L.A., 1957-72; asst. prof. music Calif. State U., L.A., 1972-76, assoc.prof. music, 1976-81, prof. music, 1981-96, part-time prof. music, 1996—, prof. emeritus, 1997—. Instr. voice classes L.A. City Coll., 1957-64; instr. music history and theory Pasadena (Calif.) City Coll., 1973-76; vis. prof. musicology Claremont (Calif.) Grad. Sch., 1986, 95, 98, 2002, Pomona Coll., 2003. Contbr. articles to music revs. and profl. publs.; translator various German-English articles for profl. jours. Mem. edit. bd. Jour. of the Arnold Schoenberg Inst., 1974-81; bd. dirs. Glendale (Calif.) Chamber Orch., 1985-89, CSULA Friends of Music, pres., 1997—; vp. bd. dirs. Pacific Contemporary Music Ctr., 1987-96, newsletter editor, 1988-96; substitute soloist 1st Ch. Christian Scientist, Alhambra, Calif., 1990-2001; bd. dirs. Neighborhood Music Sch. Music scholar Ebell Club, 1953-54, Fulbright grantee, Venice, Italy, 1966-67, Calif. State U. Instnl. grantee, 1974-75, 75-76; recipient Trustees' Outstanding Prof. award Calif. State U. Sys., 1990. Mem. NEA, Am. Musicol. Soc. (Pacific S.W. chpt. sec. 1981-83, v.p. 1984-86, pres. 1986-88, elective counselor 1990-92), Coll. Music Soc. (life), Calif. Music Tchrs. Assn., Am. Handel Soc., Music Tchrs. Assn. Calif. (Glendale br.), Friends of Music Calif. State U. L.A. (pres. 1997—), Phi Kappa Phi, Phi Kappa Lambda. Democrat. Avocations: concerts, operas, museums. Home: 4278 Sea View Ln Los Angeles CA 90065-3350 Office: Calif State U dept Music 5151 State University Dr Los Angeles CA 90032-4226

TERMINI, ROSEANN BRIDGET, law educator; b. Phila., Feb. 2, 1953; d. Vincent James and Bridget (Marano) Termini. BS magna cum laude, Drexel U., 1975; MEd, Temple U., 1979, JD, 1985, grad. in food and pharmacy law, 1998. Bar: Pa. 1985, U.S. Dist. Ct. (ea. dist.) Pa. 1985, DC 1986. Jud. clk. Superior Ct. Pa., Allentown, 1985-86; atty. Pa. Power & Light Co., Allentown, 1986-87; corp. counsel food and drug law Lemmon Co., Sellersville, Pa., 1987-88; sr. dep. atty. bur. consumer protection plain lang. law Office of Atty. Gen., Harrisburg, Pa., 1988-96; prof. Villanova U. Sch. Law, 1996-2000; prof. food and drug law Temple U. Sch. Pharmacy, Phila., 1998—, St. Joseph U., 2000—. Spkr. continuing legal edn.-plain lang. laws, eviron. conf.; adj. prof. Widener U. Sch. Law, 1993—, Dickinson Sch. Law; specialized food, drug, cosmetic and med. device law course dir. pres.'s coun. Immaculata Coll.; mem. on-line distance learning legal issues pharmacy promotion and legal environ. bus. St. Joseph U., 2002; instr. online exec. MBA program Drexel U., 2002—. Author: (book) Food, Drug and Medical Device Law: Topics and Cases, 2001, (manual) Health Law: Federal Regulation of Drugs, Biologies, Medical Devices, Foods and Dietary Supplements, 2003; contbr. articles to profl. jours., law revs. Active Sr. Citizens Project Outreach, Hospice, 1986—; mem. St. Thomas More Law Bd. Mem.: ABA (mem. various coms.), Pa. Bar Assn. (ethics, exceptional children and environ. sects., Plain English award 1999), Bar Assn. DC, Drexel U. Alumni Assn., Temple U. Law Alumni Assn., Phi Alpha Delta, Omicron Nu. Avocations: tap dancing, hiking, cross-country skiing. E-mail: rtermini@attorney.com., info@foetipublications.com.

TERMUENDE, EDWIN ARTHUR, retired chemistry educator; b. Joliet, Ill., Oct. 16, 1941; s. Gustav John Jr. and Alice Emily (Stienfatt) T.; m. Eileen Rose Greges, Aug. 5, 1967; children: Dawn Lynn Fokken, Amy Leigh. BS, So. Ill. U., 1965; MEd in Adminstn. and Supervision, Loyola U., 1972; MA, Govs. State U., 1976. Sci. tchr. Dwight D. Eisenhower H.S., 1966-68, Harold L. Richards H.S., 1968-75, Alan B. Shepard H.S., 1975-93; chemistry tchr. Polaris Sch. for Individual Edn., 1993-98. Mem. sch. improvement com. Polaris Sch. for Individual Edn., 1993-98, mem. dirs. coun., 1994-95; mem. NCA sch. and community evaluation com. Alan B. Shepard H.S., 1991-92, co-chair NCA evaluation com., 1976-77; advisor CHSD 218 spl. edn. tchrs. for 2 yr. spl. edn. sci. curriculum, 1991-92; reviewer textbooks Delmar Pubs., 1991-94; sr. reviewer Quality Sch. Revs. Ill. State Bd. Edn., 1997—; presenter in field. Asst. leader Peotone Pep Pushers 4-H Club, 1982-94; bd. dirs. Ill. 4-H Found., 1990-98; mem. state 4-H conf. com., Ill., 1989; chaperone for Ill. del. Nat. 4-H Congress, 1990, vol. coord., 1990, 91; mem. authoring com. Ill. 4-H Awards Application, 1992-93. Recipient Ill. 4-H Alumni award U. Ill., 1990. Mem. AAAS, ASCD, Nat. Sci. Tchrs. Assn., Ill. Sci. Tchrs. Assn., Ill. Assn. of Chemistry Tchrs., Am. Chem. Soc., Assn. Am. Educators. Avocations: photography, 4-h leader. Home: PO Box 1283 Beecher IL 60401-1283

TERNUS, JEAN ANN, nursing educator; b. Columbus, Nebr., Feb. 29, 1944; d. Maurice Henry and Marcella (Huntemer) T. BS in Nursing, Mt. Marty Coll., 1966; MS, Kans. State U., 1977. RN Kans., Mo., Nebr. Staff nurse Brian Meml. Hosp., Lincoln, Nebr., 1966-67, VA Hosp., Milw., 1967-69, Kans. City, Mo., 1969-72; nursing instr. Kans. City Comm. Coll., Kans., 1973—; cardiovasc. nurse specialist Meth. Hosp., Houston, 1973. Mem. AAUW, NEA, AACN, Kans. State Nurses Assn.(pres. dist. II 1980-82, 2002-2004, chair dist. newsletter 1980-2000, edit newsletter 1980-82, Dist. 2 bd. dirs. 2001—, 2d v.p. 1986-90, 1st v.p. 1990-92, sec. dist. II 1993—, v.p. 1993-95), NLN, Gerontol. Nurses Assn., Kans. Nurses Found. (bd. dirs. 1990-91, sec. 1992—, pres.-elect 1995—, pres. 1997-2002, bd. trustees 2002—), Sigma Theta Tau, Delta Kappa Gamma. Democrat. Roman Catholic. Home: 5342 Juniper Dr Shawnee Mission KS 66205-2225 Office: Kansas City CC 7250 State Ave Kansas City KS 66112-3003 E-mail: jternus@toto.net.

TERPENING, ALICE MARGARET, elementary school educator; b. Galesburg, Ill., Jan. 26, 1955; d. Harold L. and Nancy Louise (Manchester) T. BS, Faith Bapt. Bible Coll., 1978; MEd, Pensacola Christian Coll., 1984. Cert. elem. education educator, Iowa, Ill. Elem. tchr. Calvary Bapt. Sch., Menomonee Falls, Wis., 1978-81, Mill Rd Christian Sch., Evansville, Ind., 1981-86, 88-89, Fortelaza (Brazil) Acad., 1986-88, Grandview Park Bapt. Sch., Des Moines, 1989-96, Galesburg (Ill.) Christian Sch., 1996—. Coop. tchr. Faith Bapt. Bible Coll., Ankeny, Iowa, 1989-96. Active Grandview Park Bapt. Ch., Des Moines, 1989-96, Colonial Bapt. Ch., Galesburg, 1996-2003, Faith Bapt. Ch., Galesburg, 2003—. Avocations: traveling, sewing, crafts, reading, rubber stamping.

TERRELL, NATALIE DORETHEA, contractor; b. Norfolk, Va., Mar. 11, 1959; d. Louis Smith Sr. and Rosia Lee (Little) T. BBA in Bus. Mgmt., Ea. Mich. U., 1983; MS in Instnl. Tech., Ga. State U., 1994. Cert. tchr., Ga. Sr. tax examiner, trainer IRS, Chamblee, Ga., 1985-88; tchr. bus. edn. DeKalb County Bd. Edn., Decatur, Ga., 1988-92, 1994—95; ednl. instrn. specialist EduQuest--An IBM Co., Atlanta, 1992—94. Tax cons. Terrell Cons. Svc., Decatur, 1991—. Recipient Nat. Commemorative Cert. US Achievement Acad., 1988. Mem. Nat. Bus. Edn. Assn., Internat. Soc. Performance Inst., Assn. Supervision and Curriculum Devel., Project Mgmt. Inst. Avocations: ceramic, brass and crystal owl collecting. Home: 6431 Pinebark Way Morrow GA 30260-1767

TERRILL, JULIA ANN, elementary education educator; b. St. Joseph, Mo., Nov. 24, 1954; d. Jule Holmes and Beverly Jean (Brown) T. BS in Elem. Edn., N.W. Mo. State U., 1976, MEd, 1980. Tchr. learning disabilities Nodaway-Holt, Maitland, Mo., 1976-79, Lexington (Mo.) R-V, 1979-84, classroom tchr., 1984—. Mem. Young Citizens for Jerry Litton, Chillicothe, Mo., 1972, 76; mem. PTO, 1984—, historian, 1993-94, 94-95, 95-96; mem. Leslie Bell Tchr. Support Team, 1995-96, 96-97, Level II Math. Com., 1984—. Mem. Mo. State Tchrs. Assn., Comty. Tchrs. Assn. (sec. 1992-93), Order Ea. Star, Delta Kappa Gamma (chair personal growth and svcs. com. 1996-98, 2d v.p. 1998—). Baptist. Avocations: reading, playing piano and giving lessons, swimming, walking, traveling. Office: Lexington R-V Sch Leslie Bell 400 S 20th St Lexington MO 64067-1844

TERRILL, ROSS GLADWIN, writer, educator; b. Melbourne, Australia; arrived in U.S., 1965, naturalized, 1979; s. Frank and Muriel (Lloyd) Terrill. BA with honors, U. Melbourne; PhD, Harvard U., 1970. Tutor in polit. sci. U. Melbourne, 1962-63; staff sec. Australian Student Christian Movement, 1964-65; tchg. fellow Harvard U., 1968-70, lectr. govt., 1970-73, assoc. prof., 1974-78, rsch. assoc. E. Asian studies, 1970—, dir. student programs Ctr. Internat. Affairs, 1974-78; contbg. editor Atlantic Monthly, 1970-84; rsch. fellow Asia Soc., 1977—79. Vis. prof. U. Tex., Austin, 1999—. Author: China Profile, 1969, China and Ourselves, 1971, 800,000,000: The Real China, 1972, R. H. Tawney and His Times, 1973, Flowers on an Iron Tree, 1975, The Future of China, 1978, The China Difference, 1979, Mao: A Biography, 1980, rev., 2000, White-Boned Demon, 1984, The Australians, 1987, Madam Mao, 1992, rev., 1999, China in Our Time, 1992, The Australians: How We Live Now, 2000, The New Chinese Empire, 2003; contbr. articles to profl. jours. Recipient Nat. Mag. award, 1972, George Polk Meml. award outstanding mag. reporting, 1972, Sumner prize, 1970. Mem.: PEN, Authors Guild, Harvard Club (N.Y.C.). Home: 87 Gainsborough St Boston MA 02115-4911 E-mail: terr@compuserve.com.

TERRY, ALICE REBECCA, educational consultant; b. Detroit; d. Henry Christian and Phyllis Ireen (Greene) Beams; children: Crescent Lynn Terry, Angela Anne Terry; m. Edward Smith Lynn, July 5, 1985. BA, Azusa Pacific U., 1969; MA, LaVerne U., 1981. Cert. early childhood edn., std. elem. edn., reading specialist, adminstrv. svcs. Tchr. staff devel. specialist Orange (Calif.) Unified Sch. Dist., 1974-85; educational cons., dir. More LIFE Through Mgmt., La Mirada, Calif., 1985—. Staff devel. com. mem. Assn. Calif. Sch. Adminstrs., Sacramento, 1981—. Author: Classroom Management, 1989, Alternative To Worksheets, 1992. Vol. advisor Sunday Nite Group Svc. Divsn., 1976—. Recipient Outstanding Svc. to Students award City of Orange. Mem. ASTD, Assn. Calif. Sch. Adminstrs., Assn. Supervision & Curriculum Devel., Assn. Psychol. Type. Republican. Avocations: reading, music, camping, hiking, skiing. Office: More LIFE Through Mgmt 15936 Dalmatian Ave La Mirada CA 90638-5718

TERRY, GEORGE MARSHALL, vocational studies educator; b. Aulander, N.C., Jan. 19, 1944; s. Godfrey Jackson and Virginia Elizabeth (Burden) T.; m. Judith Elaine Bland, June 12, 1964; children: Randy, Jeffrey, Michelle, Cynthia. AS, Mt. Olive Coll., 1982. Cert. tchr., N.C. Vocat. tchr. Bertie Jr. H.S., Windsor, N.C., 1970-72; home builder various locations, 1967—; tchr. carpentry Lakewood H.S., Roseboro, N.C., 1984-93; vocat. testing coord. Sampson County Schs., 1993-95; tchr. constrn. tech. Midway H.S., Dunn, N.C., 1995—. Curriculum carpentry team leader N.C. Trade and Indsl. Dept. Edn., Raleigh, 1989-93; trade and industry adv. bd. N.C. Dept. Pub. Edn., Raleigh, 1989-93. Pastor Weldon (N.C.) Pentecostal Holiness Ch., Mt. Olive, N.C., 1979-82, Sharon Pentecostal Holiness Ch., Clinton, N.C., 1982-94. Mem. NEA, ASCD, Am. Vocat. Assn., Nat. Assn. Trade and Indsl. Educators, N.C. Vocat. Assn., Associated Gen. Contractors Am. (cert. master residential carpenter), Millenium/Aulander Lions Club (pres. 1970-71). Republican. Home: PO Box 603 Salemburg NC 28385-0603 Office: Sampson County Schs PO Box 439 Clinton NC 28329-0439

TERRY, LEON CASS, neurologist, educator; b. Dec. 22, 1940; s. Leon Herbert and Zella Irene (Boyd) T.; m. Suzanne Martinson, June 27, 1964; children: Kristin, Sean. Pharm. D., U. Mich., 1964; MD, Marquette U., 1969; PhD, McGill U., 1982; MBA, U.D. Fla., 1994. Diplomate Am. Bd. Psychiatry and Neurology, Am. Bd. Med. Mgmt. Intern U. Rochester, N.Y., 1969-70; staff assoc. NIH, 1970-72; resident in neurology McGill U., Montreal, Que., Can., 1972-75; MRC fellow, 1975-78; assoc. prof. U. Tenn., Memphis, 1978-81; prof. neurology U. Mich., Ann Arbor, 1981-89; assoc. prof. physiology, 1982-89; asst. chief neurology VA Med. Ctr., Ann Arbor, 1982-89; chmn. dept. neurology Med. Coll. of Wis., Milw., 1989—2000, prof. neurology and physiology, 1989—. Dir. clin neurosci. ctr. and multiple sclerosis clinic, Med. Coll. Wis.; assoc. dean for amb. care, 1996-98; vice chief of staff Froedtert Hosp., 1994-97; chief of staff, 1997-98; chief med. officer cenegenics, 1997-98. Contbr. articles to profl. jours, chpts. to books. Served to lt. comdr. USPHS, 1970-72. NIH grantee, 1981-92; VA grantee, 1980-92; VA Clin. Investigator award, 1980-81. Mem. AMA, Am. Soc. Clin. Investigation, Cen. Soc. Clin. Investigation, Am. Neurol. Assn., Am. Coll. Physician Execs. (vice chmn. academic health ctr. soc. 1994-95, chair, 1995-98, leader forum health care delivery 1995-98), Am. Coll. Healthcare Execs., Endocrine Soc., Am. Acad. Neurology, Internat. Soc. Neuroendocrinilogy, Internat. Soc. Psychoeuroendocrinilogy, Soc. Neurosci., Soc. Rsch. Biol. Rhythms, Milw. Acad. Physicians, Wis. Neurol. Assn., Wis. State Med. Soc. (del.-elect 1995-96), Med. Soc. Milw. County, Milw. Neuropsychiatric Soc. (pres.-elect.). Avocations: pilot, skiing, scuba diving, computers. Office: Med Coll Wis Dept Neurology Froedtert Hosp 9200 W Watertown Plank Rd Milwaukee WI 53226-3557 E-mail: cass@cass-terry.com., cass@megapathdsl.com.

TERRY, MARGARET SMOOT, special education educator; b. Elkin, N.C., July 5, 1945; d. Claude Dennis and Eula (Powell) Smoot; div.; 1 child, Susan Leigh. BEd, Fla. Atlantic U., 1966, MEd, 1969; Edn. Specialist, U. South Fla., 1985. Cert. tchr., Fla. Tchr. Wynnebrook Elem. Sch., West Palm Beach, Fla., 1967-73; tchr. spl. edn. Boca Raton (Fla.) Elem. Sch., 1973-75, J.C. Mitchell Elem. Sch., Boca Raton, 1975-83, Loggers Run Mid. Sch., Boca Raton, 1983-84; computer specialist Palm Beach County Schs., West Palm Beach, 1984-89; coord. exceptional student edn. Addison Mizner Elem. Sch., Boca Raton, 1989-92, Del Prado Elem. Sch., Boca Raton, 1992—. Adj. prof. Fla. Atlantic U., Boca Raton, 1987-89; computer trainer Palm Beach County Schs., 1984-89, tech. trainer, 1991-92; cons. Weiss Sch. for Gifted, West Palm Beach, 1988-89; presenter program at computer conf., Palvia, Bulgaria, 1984. Mem. Fla. Assn. Sci. Tchrs., Fla. Assn. Gifted, Phi Beta Kappa, Delta Kappa Gamma (pres. Alpha Omega chpt. 1988-90). Democrat. Home: 735 Heron Dr Delray Beach FL 33444-1923 Office: Del Prado Elem Sch Del Prado Cir Delray Beach FL 33483

TERRY, ROBERT MEREDITH, foreign language educator; b. Danville, Va., Dec. 16, 1939; s. Willard Terry and Martha Willeford; m. Anne Reynolds Beggarly, Jan. 30, 1965; children: Michael Reynolds, Christopher Robert, Meredith Anne. BA in French, Randolph-Macon Coll., Ashland, Va., 1962; PhD in Romance Langs., Duke U., Durham. N.C., 1966. Asst. prof. French U. Fla., Gainesville, Fla., 1966-68; assoc. prof. U. Richmond, Richmond, Va., 1968-83, prof., 1983—. Pres. Am. Coun. on Tchg. Fgn. Langs., 1994, mem. exec. coun., 1983-85, 2000—. Co-author: Accent: Conversational French I, 1980, Vous Y Etes!, 1990, Intersections, 1991; editor Dimension, So. Conf. on Lang. Tchg., 1991-97; assoc. editor ACTFL Foreign Language Education Series, 1994, 96, 98, 99, 2000; editor N.E. Conf. Report, 2000; articles editor NECTFL Rev.; contbr. articles to profl. jours. Recipient Stephen A. Freeman award N.E. Conf. on Teaching Fgn. Lang., 1990, Robert J. Ludwig Nat. Fgn. Lang. Leadership award, 1995. Mem. Am. Coun. on Tchg. Fgn. Langs., Fgn. Lang. Assn. Va., Am. Assn. Tchrs. French, So. Conf. on Lang. Tchg. Home: 1504 Cloister Dr Richmond VA 23233-4035 Office: Univ Richmond PO Box 25 28 Westhampton Way Richmond VA 23173-0025 E-mail: rterry@richmond.edu.

TERVO, DENISE ANN, psychologist, educator; b. Denver, Aug. 28, 1950; d. John Collin and Irene Geraldine (Schueth) T.; m. Paul Saenger, June 2, 1973 (div. June 1981); m. Michael Craig Clemmens, Aug. 7, 1982; children: Lindsey, Brenden. Student, U. Ga., 1968-70; BA in Sociology, U. N.C., 1972, MEd, 1975; PhD in Counseling, U. Pitts., 1988. Lic. in psychology, lic. counselor. Ednl. cons. Ky. River Foothills Devel. Coun. Headstart Area Program, Richmond, Ky., 1976-80; liaison ednl. counselor Cen. Ky. Re-Edn. Program, Lexington, 1976-80; child devel. specialist Childrens Hosp., Pitts., 1980-84; ednl. cons., psychotherapist Comty. Human Svcs., Pitts., 1984-86; intern in psychology Psychol. Specialists Inc., Pitts., 1984-89; pvt. practice psycyology Pitts., 1989—. Mem. faculty Gestalt Inst. Cleve., 1994—, mem. assoc. staff, 1997—, co-chair Working with Psychol. Process Track-GIC; cons. Madison County Interagy. Group for Parents Anonymous, Richmond, 1978-80; adj. prof. Sch. Social Work Ea. Ky. U., Richmond, 1977-79. Mem. Pitts. Ctr. for Arts, 1994—, Pitts. Ballet, 1989—, Nat. History and Sci. Mus., Pitts., 1987-94. Mem. NAFE, APA, ACA, NOW, Ky. Coun. Children with Behavioral Disorders (pres., state coord. 1978-79), Hampton Alliance for Ednl. Excellence, Alpha Lambda Delta, Phi Beta Kappa. Avocations: running, swimming, hiking, camping, dancing. Office: 401 Shady Ave Apt 104A Pittsburgh PA 15206-4457

TESFARMARIAM, BERNICE JEFFERSON, school administrator, counselor; b. Pitts., Nov. 29, 1940; q. Felix A. and Geraldine (Conner) Bell. MS in Edn., Duquesne U., 1991; postgrad., John Jay Coll., Duquesne U., 1993—. Libr. tech. asst. N.Y. Pub. Libr., N.Y.C., 1968-79; law clk. U.S. Steel, Pitts., 1979-86; resident advisor Transitional Svcs., Pitts., 1987-89; primary case mgr. adolescent impatient unit, prevention specialist Mercy Ctr., Pitts., 1989-92; project coord. Bd. of Edn., Pitts., 1993—; pvt. practice counselor Bernice Tesfarmariam & Assocs., Pitts., 1991—. Com. mem. Youth Employment Alliance, Pitts., 1994—; v.p. Ciloets USX, Pitts., 1985-86; presenter, cons. and group facilitator on motivation, empowerment, addiction, prevention, intervention and self esteem. Author brochures, tng. manuals in field. Bd. dirs. Beltzhoover Neighborhood Cmty., Pitts., 1994; adv. bd. Literacy Coun., Pitts., 1984, McGovern Ctr., Pitts., 1992; v.p. Local 1930 Newspaper Guild, N.Y.C., 1977-79. Recipient Cert. of Appreciation, Dist. Wide chpt. 1, 1994, MA/MR/D&A Allegheny County, 1992, Am. Heart Assn., 1986; Literacy Coun. grantee USS Corp., 1986. Mem. Phi Delta Kappa, Chi Sigma Iota (life). Democrat. Baptist. Avocations: collecting african art, opera, theatre, museum, writing. Home: 400 Chalfont St Pittsburgh PA 15210-1421 Office: Pitts Pub Schs Office Pupil Affairs 341 S Bellefield Ave Pittsburgh PA 15213-3552

TESSIER-LAVIGNE, MARC TREVOR, neurobiologist, researcher; b. Trenton, Ont., Can., Dec. 18, 1959; came to U.S., l987; s. Yves Jacques and Sheila Christine (Midgley) Tessier-L.; m. Mary Alanna Hynes, Feb. 4, 1989; children: Christian, Kyle, Ella. BSc, McGill U., l980; BA, Oxford U., l982; PhD, U. London, 1986. Exec. dir. Can. Student Pugwash Orgn., Ottawa, Ont., 1982-83; rsch. fellow devel. neurobiology unit Med. Rsch. Coun., London, l986-87; rsch. fellow Ctr. for Neurobiology, Columbia U., N.Y.C., 1987-91; asst. prof. dept. anatomy U. Calif., San Francisco, 1991-95, assoc. prof. dept. anatomy, 1995-97, prof. dept. anatomy and dept. biochemistry and biophysics, 1997—2000; Susan B. Ford prof. dept. biol. scis. Sch. Humanities and Scis. Stanford U., 2000—. Asst. investigator Howard Hughes Med. Inst., 1994-97; investigator Howard Hughes Med. Inst., 1997—. Contbr. articles on neurobiology to profl. jours. Recipient McKnight Investigator award, 1994, Karl Judson Herrick award for comparative neurology Am. Assn. Anatomists, 1994, Ameritec prize for significant contbn. in basic rsch. towards cure for paralysis, 1995, Ipsen prize for neuronal plasticity, 1996, Viktor Hamburger award in devel. neurobiology Internat. Jour. Devel. Neurosci., Young Investigator award Soc. for Neurosci., 1997, Wakeman award, 1998, Rober Dow award, 2003; Rhodes scholar, 1980, Commonwealth scholar, 1983, Markey scholar, 1989, Searle scholar, 1991, McKnight scholar, 1991; Klingenstein fellow, 1992. Fellow: AAAS, Royal Soc. of Can., The Royal Soc. (London); mem.: Soc. for Neuroscience (nominating com. 2000—02). Office: Stanford Univ Sch of Humanities/Scis Dept Biol Scis Stanford CA 94305-5020 Home: 361 Ridgeway Rd Woodside CA 94062-2343

TETHERLY, JONATHAN COLLIESON, chaplain, educator; b. Boston, Nov. 12, 1944; s. Edgar Osborne and Margaret Rena (Collieson) T.; m. Katsuyo Handa, Nov. 4, 1972; children: Christine Yuriko Tetherly-Lewis, Naomi Collieson. BS cum laude, U. N.H., 1966; MS, U. Minn., 1971; MDiv, Andover Newton Theol. Sch., 1974. Ordained min. United Ch. of Christ. Instr. biology Assumption Coll., Richardton, N.D., 1968-71; min. Congl. United Ch. of Christ and United Ch. Christ, Willsboro and Wadhams, N.Y., 1974-79, Federated Ch., Chicopee, Mass., 1979-90; comty. min. Coun. of Chs. of Greater Springfield, Mass., 1990; chaplain Hampden County Sheriff's Dept. and Correctional Ctr., Ludlow, Mass., 1988—. Substitute tchr. Springfield, West Springfield, South Hadley, Holyoke, and Ludlow pub. schs., 1990—; mem. Coun. for Mission Outreach and Social Responsibility, Mass. Conf. United Ch. of Christ, Framingham, Mass., 1983-87, founder, chair Criminal Justice Task Force, Mass. Conf. United Ch. of Christ, 1987-90; chair Hampden Assn. United Ch. of Christ missions, Hampden County, Mass., 1981-87, 89-96; steward United Food and Comml. Workers Union Local 1459, 1999—; track coach Minnechaug Regional H.S., Wilbraham, Mass., 2003—; western Mass. track and field ofcl., 1993—. Pres. Champlain Valley Housing Assn., Pt. Henry, NY, 1975-79; mem.-at-large Chicopee Sch. Com., 1986-91; rep. Ward 5 Chicopee Sch. com., 2000—; adv. bd. Title XX, Elizabethtown, NY, 1976-79; legis. com. Mass. Assn. Sch. Coms., Boston, 1990-91, 2001—; bd. dirs. Union Cmty. Fund Pioneer Valley, Mass. Citizens Against the Death Penalty, 1982—; track and field official, Western Mass., 1993-2002; asst. coach boys' track and field team Minnechang Regl. H.S., 2003. Recipient Comty. Svc. award Valley Opportunity Coun., 1982, Haystack cert. of recognition Mass. Conf. of United Ch. Christ, 1995, recognition award Mass. Citizens Against Death Penalty, 1991. Mem. Mass. Assn. Profl. Substitute Tchrs. (pres.), Chicopee Clergy Assn., Greater Springfield Harriers, Arise for Social Justice, Critical Resistance. Democrat. Avocations: track, distance running, making maple syrup. Home: 29 Arlington St Chicopee MA 01020-2503 Office: Hampden County Correct Ctr 627 Randall Rd Ludlow MA 01056-1080

TETREAULT, LOUIS N. art educator; b. Pawtucket, R.I., Dec. 21, 1949; s. Lorenzo A. and Evelyn M. (Proulx) T.; 1 child, Lisa. BS in Edn., R.I. Coll., 1972; M in Art Edn., R.I. Sch. of Design, 1980. Cert. primary/secondary tchr., R.I. Art tchr. Pawtucket (R.I.) Sch. Dept., 1972—; instr. R.I. Sch. of Design, Providence, 1980—. Vol. Pawtucket Arts Coun., 1987—. Prin. works include pub. rels. design Pawtucket Teachers Alliance, 1992 (First Pl. award), team logo Pawtucket Parks and Recreation Dept., 1985; represented in R.I. Sch. of Design Woods-Gerry Gallery, Providence, Pawtucket City Hall Gallery, Pawtucket Pub. Libr. Mem. Le Foyer Club, Pawtucket, 1972; vol. mayoral candidate, Pawtucket, 1991. Recipient Best of Show award Reis Gallery, 1981. Mem. Nat. Art Edn. Assn., R.I. Art Tchrs. Assn., Pawtucket Tchrs. Alliance, R.I. Sch. of Design Alumni Assn. Roman Catholic. Avocations: painting, photography, reading, theatre, health club. Home: PO Box 3105 Pawtucket RI 02861-0950

TETTEGAH, SHARON YVONNE, education educator; b. Wichita Falls, Tex., Jan. 14, 1956; d. Lawrence Guice and Doris Jean (Leak) Oliver; 1 child, Tandra Ainsworth; m. Joseph Miller Zangai, Dec. 22, 1978 (div. 1983); 1 child, Tonia Monjay Zangai; m. George Tettegah, Apr. 28, 1989; children: Nicole Jennifer, Michael Scott. AA, Coll. Alameda, 1985; BA, U. Calif., Davis, 1988, teaching cert., 1989, MA, 1991; PhD in Ednl. Psychology, U. Calif., Santa Barbara, 1997. Cert. elem. tchr., Calif., Online web-based tchg. and learning, Calif. State U., Hayward. Clk. II Alameda County Mcpl. Ct., Oakland, Calif., 1976-77; acct. clk. Alameda County Social Svcs., Oakland, 1977-78, eligibility technician, 1978-82; supervising clk. Alameda County Health Care Svcs., Oakland, 1982-84; tchr. Davis (Calif.) Joint Unified Sch. Dist., 1988-89, L.A. Unified Schs., L.A., 1990-92, Oakland Unified Sch. Dist., Oakland, 1992—, tchr. sci. mentor, 1993—; teaching asst. U. Calif., Santa Barbara, 1993-94; adminstrv. intern Oxnard Unified Sch. Dist., 1994, U. Calif. Cultural Awareness Program, Santa Barbara, 1994—; rsch. cons. to vice chancellor students affairs, cons. tchr. edn. program, facilitor registrar's office U. Calif., Santa Barbara, 1995-96, rsch. asst. Grad. Sch. Edn., 1996—; asst. prof. tchr. edn. Calif. State U., Hayward, 1998—, cons. Cal Teach, Office of the Chancellor, 1999. Cons. U. Calif., Davis, 1988-89, Montessori Ctr. Sch., Santa Barbara, Calif., 1996, Oakland-Hayward Sch. Partnership, Oakland, 1998-99, Cal Teach, Office of the Chancellor, 1999; multicultural cons. Davis Unified Sch. Dist., 1988-89; edn. cons. Ednl. Testing Svc., Emeryville, Calif., 1994; cons., dir., 2000—; chair diversity com. of Santa Barbara Village Charter Sch.; mem. academic senate com. undergrad enrollment and admissions U. Calif. Santa Barbara, 1995, tchr. cross-cultural interactions course, summer, 1995; mem. academic affairs affirmative action com. U. Calif. Santa Barbara, 1995-96, grad. sch. of edn., grad. affairs and affirmative action comms. U. Calif. Santa Barbara, 1995-96; rsch. cons. Oakland Unified Sch. Dist., 1998-99, African Am. Literacy and Culture Project, Oakland Pub. Schs., Oakland, 1998—; gubernatorial appointee to State Interagy. Coord. Coun., 1999—; chmn. Com. on Rsch., Calif. State U., 2000-01, mem. Academic Senate, Hayward; faculty Univ. Ill., Urbana-Champaign, 2001. Contbr. articles to profl. jours. Mem. U. Calif. Santa Barbara Acad. Senate Bd. Undergraduate Admissions and Records; co-chair Diversity Com. Montecito-Santa Barbara Charter Sch.; pres. African-Am. Grad. and Profl. Students Orgn., Davis, 1988-89; gubernatorial appointee State Interagy. Coordinating Coun., Calif., 1999; commissioned Calif. Policy Makers Inst. Health & Poverty, Lt. Gov., 2001. Recipient Charlene Richardson Acad. Honors award Coll. Alameda, 1985; Calif. State Acad. fellow, 1989-91, Grad. Opportunity Acad. Excellence fellow, 1994-95, Vice Chancellors Acad. Achievement fellowship U. Calif. Santa Barbara, 1995-96, Vice Chancellors Acad. Fellowship Grad. Divsn., 1995-96, 96-97. Mem. APA, Am. Ednl. Researchers Assn., Calif. Sci. Tchrs. Assn., Calif. Advocacy for Math and Sci., Calif. Tchrs. Assn., Calif. Media Libr. Educators Assn., PTA, Multicultural Curriculum Assn., Supervision and Curriculum Leadership Assn., Bay Area Sci. and Tech. Educators Corsortium, Pan-African Students Assn., Kappa Delta Pi. Avocations: travelling, reading, preparing gourmet foods, tennis. Office: U Calif Santa Barbara Sch Edn/Ednl Psychology Santa Barbara CA 93106

TEWHEY, KAREN MARIE, special education and mental health administrator; b. Cambridge, Mass., Nov. 21, 1949; d. John Richard and Alice (Smith) Donovan; m. James Richard Tewhey, Feb. 18, 1981; children: Katherine Michaela, James Allyn Tripoli. BA, Simmons Coll., Boston, 1971; MA, Lesley Coll., Cambridge, 1976. Cert. tchr., prin., Mass. Spl. edn. tchr. Krebs Sch., Lexington, Mass., 1976-79, Judge Baker Guidance Clinic, Boston, 1979-80; coord. Hampshire Collaborative, Northampton, Mass., 1980-81; therapeutic tchr. Amherst (Mass.) Elem. Schs., 1985-86; coord. Amherst Alternative High Sch., 1981-85; prin. Mass. Migrant Edn., Holyoke, 1986; edn. specialist Dept. Edn., Boston, 1987-88; spl. edn./mental health adminstr. ABCD Head Start, Boston, 1988—. Adj. faculty Urban Coll., Boston, 1990-94, Lesley Coll., 1988-90. Mem. Coun. for Exceptional Children (div. early childhood). Office: ABCD Head Start 178 Tremont St Boston MA 02111-1093

TEXLEY, TAMERA SUE, musician, educator; b. Broken Bow, Nebr., Feb. 13, 1965; d. Dennis A. and Faith M. (Stahl) Tyson; m. Darrell A. Texley, Apr. 14, 1990; 1 child, Andrew. BFA in Music Edn., Peru State Coll., 1987; MA in Cirriculm and Instruction with ESL endorsement, Wayne State Coll., 2003. Music tchr. Orleans (Nebr.) H.S., 1987-88; asst. mgr. Godfathers Pizza, Hastings, Nebr., 1988-89; music tchr. Spalding (Nebr.) Acad., 1989-91; parent tchr. Christian Heritage Children's Home, Hickman, Nebr., 1991-95; owner, tchr. The Music Studio, Albion, Nebr., 1996—2000; tchr. K-6 music Newman Grove Pub. Sch., Newman Grove, Nebr., 1998—2003; tchr. St. Michael's Sch., 2003—. Dir. Albion Area Arts Coun., 1999-2003. Mem. Albion C. of C. (bd. dirs. 1997-99), Music Tchrs. Nat. Assn., Albion Woman's Club, PEO. Mem. Assembly of God Ch. Home: 2944 200th St Albion NE 68620-9607 Office: 2944 200th St Albion NE 68620-1231 E-mail: datt@frontiernet.net.

TEZAK, EDWARD GEORGE, mechanics educator; b. Steelton, Pa., Oct. 16, 1940; s. John Frank and Mary Cecilia (Shiprak) T.; m. Martha Katherine Leyko, Sept. 10, 1966; children: Christine Louise, Edward Scott. BS, U.S. Mil. Acad., 1963; MS in Astrodynamics, UCLA, 1967; PhD in Engring. Mechanics, Va. Poly. Inst. and State U., 1979. Commd. 2d lt. U.S. Army, 1963, advanced through grades to col., 1985; co. comdr., XO B Co. 13th Engr. Battalion, Camp Casey, Korea, 1964-65; engr. battalion advisor 6th ARVN Engr. Group, QuiNhon and DaNang, Vietnam, 1967-68; instr., then asst. prof. dept. mechanics U.S. Mil. Acad., West Point, N.Y., 1969-72; plans officer U.S. Army Engr. Group, Saigon, Vietnam, 1972-73; USMA fellow Army War Coll., Carlisle, Pa., 1982-83; group dir. dept. mechanics U.S. Mil. Acad., 1976-88, dep. head dept. mechanics, 1988, assoc. dean, 1989-93; ret. U.S. Army, 1993; dean Sch. Info. Sys. and Engring. Tech. SUNY, Utica, 1993-97, dean Coll. Tech. Alfred State, 1998-99; assoc. prof. Alfred State Coll., 1999-2000, prof. mechanics, 2000—; sec., treas. Coun. for Engring. Tech. N.Y. State (CETNYS), 2000—. Mem. adv. bd. dept. math. U.S. Mil. Acad., 1993-97, mem. adv. bd. dept. civil and mech. engring., 2002—. Mem. Cmty. Counsel, Utica, 1994-97. Decorated Legion of Merit. Mem. ASME, Am. Soc. Engring. Edn. (bd. dirs., chair PIC III 1993-95, exec. com. mech. divsn., program chair, divsn. chair 1989-93, vice program chair engrng. tech. divsn. 2001-02, program chair 2002-03, Outstanding Campus Liaison Rep. award Mid. Atlantic sect. 1991, Outstanding Tchr./Educator of Yr award St. Lawrence sect. 2001), NY State Engring. Tech. Assn. (exec. com. 2000—), Phi Kappa Phi. Roman Catholic. Avocations: bowling, golf, skiing. Home: 450 N Main St Wellsville NY 14895-1042 E-mail: tezakeg@alfredstate.edu.

TEZLA, ALBERT, English educator; b. S. Bend, Ind., Dec. 13, 1915; s. Mihály and Lucza (Szénási) Tezla; m. Olive Anna Fox, July 26, 1941; children: Michael William, Kathy Elaine. BA, U. Chgo., 1941, MA, 1947, PhD, 1952. Instr. Ind. U. Ext., S. Bend, 1946-48; from instr. to assoc. prof. U. Minn., Duluth, 1949-61, prof., 1961-82, prof. emeritus, 1982—. Vis. prof. Hungarian lit. Columbia U., N.Y.C., 1966, cons., 1967-71, 77-81, vis. scholar, 1975; cons. U. Minn., Mpls., 1968-83; project reviewer NEH, Washington, 1979-82; vis. prof. Hungarian lit. U. Minn., Duluth, 1998. Author: An Introductory Bibliography to the Study of Hungarian Literature, 1964, Hungarian Authors: A Bibliographical Handbook, 1970, The Hazardous Quest: Hungarian Immigrants in the United States, 1895-1920, 1993; co-author: Academic American Encyclopedia, 1980, World Authors, 1975-80, 1985, Benét's Readers Encyclopedia, 1987, World Authors, 1980-85, 1991; editor, contbg. translator: Ocean at the Window: Hungarian Prose and Poetry since 1945, 1980, Three Contemporary Hungarian Plays, 1992; contbg. translator: Hungarian Short Stories, 1983, The Kiss: 20th Century Hungarian Short Stories, 1993; translator: God in the Wagon: Ten Short Stories (Ferenc Sánta), 1985 (Hungarian Pubs. award 1985), The Fifth Seal (Ferenc Sánta), 1986 (Hungarian Pubs. award 1986), Somewhere in a Distant Fabled Land: American Hungarians, 1895-1920, 1987, On the Balcony: Selected Short Stories (Iván Mándy), 1988 (Hungarian Pubs. award 1988), Hungary: A Brief History (István Lázár), 1990, An Illustrated History of Hungary (István Lázár), 1992, Memoir of Hungary, 1944-48 (Sándor Márai), 1996, Once There Was a Central Europe: Selected Short Stories and Other Writings (Miklós Mészoly), 1997, A Wartime Memoir, Hungary, 1944-45 (Alaine Polcz), 1998, Authoring, Barbering and Other Occupations, 2002; editl. cons. Holmes and Meier Pubs., 1998. Lt. (s.g.) USN, 1942-46, PTO. Recipient Diplome d'honeur, Inst. Cultural Rels., Hungary, 1970, Commemorative medal, 1970, Endre Ady Medallion, Presidium Hungarian PEN Ctr., 1986, Pro Cultura Hungarica award, Rep. Hungary, 1996, Abraham Lincoln award, Am. Hungarian Found., 1998; fellow Fulbright Rsch. fellow, Associated Bd. Rsch. Coun., 1959—60, Rsch. fellow, Internat. Co. Traveling Grants, 1963—64, Internat. Rsch. and Exchs. Bd., 1978; grantee Rsch. grantee, Am. Coun. Learned Socs., 1961, 1968, NEH, 1978—82. Mem. Internat. Assn. Hungarian Studies (mem. exec. com. 1978-83, John Lotz Meml. award 1986), Am. Hungarian Educators' Assn., Fulbright Assn. Democrat. Avocations: gardening, physical fitness, reading, classical films. Home: 5412 London Rd Duluth MN 55804-2511

THACHER, BARBARA AUCHINCLOSS, history educator; b. Oyster Bay, N.Y., July 27, 1918; d. Hugh and Frances Coverdale (Newlands) Auchincloss; m. Thomas Thacher, Aug. 4, 1942; children: Barbara Burrall Thacher Plimpton, Elizabeth Coverdale Thacher Hawn, Thomas Day II, Hugh Auchincloss, Peter Anthony, Andrew. BA cum laude, Bryn Mawr Coll., 1940; MA in History, Columbia U., 1965. Editl. rschr. Newsweek, N.Y.C., 1940-41, 44; writer N.Y. Times Sunday Mag., News of Week Rev., N.Y.C., 1941-43; co-editor Christmas Booklist for Children Harper's Mag., N.Y.C., 1957-59; asst. history dept. Barnard Coll., N.Y.C., 1964-65; rsch. asst. Ctr. Urban Edn., N.Y.C., 1966. Bd. dirs. Bryn Mawr Coll., 1966-88, chair bd. trustees, 1980-87, emeritus, 1988—, City Univ. of N.Y., trustee, 1970-73, WNET-TV-Channel 13, trustee, 1978-88; active Sheltering Arms Children's Svc., Istanbul Women's Coll., Leake & Watts Children's Home Svcs., Yonkers and N.Y.C., 1961-83, emeritus, 1983—, N.Y.C. Park Assn., Riverdale Girls Sch.; trustee Tchrs. Coll. Columbia U. Mem. Cosmopolitan Club (gov.), North Haven Casino. Democrat. Presbyterian. Home: Apt 311 88 Notch Hill Rd North Branford CT 06471-1852

THACKER, JANICE DEE, parochial school art educator; b. Nashville, Dec. 14, 1945; d. James Watt and Mildred J. (Nichols) Brown; m. John Stephen Thacker, Aug. 16, 1968 (div. 1983); 1 child, James Aaron. Student, George Peabody Coll., 1963-65; BS in Edn., U. Tenn., 1968. Art tchr. Tyson Jr. High Sch., Knoxville, Tenn., 1969-72, Cumberland Middle Sch., Nashville, 1972-73, Bearden Middle Sch., Knoxville, 1973-74, Lincoln Middle Sch., Catasauqua, Pa., 1974-75, St. John's Sch., Olean, N.Y., 1975-78, Holy Innocents' Episcopal Sch., Atlanta, 1978—. Art instr., artist, juror Women's Coun. for the Arts, Atlanta, 1990. Group exhbn. The Community Arts Collection of Ga., Athens, 1993. Extended ministries bd. Holy Innocents' Episcopal Ch., Atlanta, 1992—, summer camp artist, tchr., 1989—; art tchr., fundraiser Egleston Childrens Hosp., Atlanta, 1989—; artist Habitat for Humanity, Atlanta, 1991—. Mem. Nat. Art Edn. Assn., Ga. Art Edn. Assn. Republican. Episcopalian. Avocations: painting, mono printmaking, tennis, roller skating, bridge. Home: 4400 Old Mabry Rd Roswell GA 30075-1939

THACKER, JERRY LYNN, school administrator; b. Mishawaka, Ind., July 7, 1950; s. Burl Willis and Azzie Dell (Davidson) T.; m. Donna Lee, Aug. 11, 1973. BA, Bethel Coll., Mishawaka, Ind., 1972; MS, Ind. U., S. Bend, 1975; EdD, Andrews U., Berrien Springs, Mich., 1987. Tchr., individually guided edn. team leader Penn-Harris Madison Sch. Corp., Osceola, Ind., 1972-85; elem. prin. Twin lakes Sch. Corp., Monticello, Ind., 1985-89; dir. curriculum Saginaw (Mich.) Ind. Sch. Dist., 1989-90; dir. elem. edn. MSD Lawrence Twp., Indpl., 1990-96, asst. supt. for Human Resources, 1996-98; supt. of schs. Logansport (Ind.) Cmty. Sch. Corp., 1998—. Presenter in field; contbr. numerous articles to profl. publs. Recipient various grants; recipient Award for Svc. to Profession, Ind. Assn. Curriculum Devel., others. Mem. ASCD, Nat. Assn. Elem. Prins., IAEMSP (pres.), AASA, Internat Reading Assn., Pi Lambda Theta, Phi Delta Kappa. Home: 831 Meadowview Dr Logansport IN 46947-1333

THACKRAY, ARNOLD WILFRID, historian, foundation executive; b. Eng., July 30, 1939; came to U.S., 1967, naturalized, 1982; s. Wilfrid Cecil and Mary (Clarke) T.; m. Barbara Hughes, 1964 (div. 1990); children: Helen Mary, Gillian Winifrid, Timothy Arnold; m. Diana Schueler, 1994; 1 stepchild, Gregory Jordan. B.Sc., Bristol (Eng.) U., 1960; MA, Cambridge (Eng.) U., 1965, PhD, 1966. Research chemist Robert Dempster and Co., Yorkshire, Eng., 1960-61; research fellow Churchill Coll., Cambridge U., 1965-68; prof. history and sociology of sci. U. Pa., Phila., 1968-96, Joseph Priestley prof. emeritus history/sociology of sci., 1996—, chmn. dept., 1970-77, dir. Beckman Ctr. for History of Chemistry, 1982-96; prof. history, prof. chemistry, dean grad. studies and research U. Md., 1985-86. Exec. dir., libr. Chem. Heritage Found., 1987-96, pres., 1996—; vis. lectr. Harvard U., 1967-68; vis. fellow All Souls Coll., Oxford, Eng., 1977-78; mem. Inst. Advanced Study, 1980. Editor: Isis, an Internat. Rev. of History of Science and its Cultural Influences, 1978-85, Osiris, 1985-94, Science After '40, 1992, Constructing Knowledge in the History of Science, 1995, Private Science, 1998, (with others) Science and Values, 1974, Toward a Metric of Science, 1978; author: Atoms and Powers, 1970, John Dalton, 1972, (with others) Gentlemen of Science, 1981-82, Chemistry in America, 1985, (with others) Arnold O. Beckman, 2000; contbr. articles to profl. jours. Recipient Gladstone Essay prize, also pub. speaking prize Churchill Coll., Cambridge U.; Guggenheim fellow, 1971-72, 85-86; Ctr. for Advanced Study in Behavioral Scis. fellow, 1973-74, 83-84 Fellow AAAS, Am. Acad. Arts and Scis., Royal Hist. Soc., Royal Chem. Soc.; mem. Am. Chem. Soc. (Dexter award 1983), Am. Hist. Assn., Manchester LIt. and Philos. Soc. (corr.), History of Sci. Soc., Am. Coun. Learned Socs. (bd. dirs., treas. 1985-96), Soc. for Social Studies of Sci. (pres. 1981-83), Am. Coun. on Edn. (bd. dirs. 1987), Société Chimie (bd. dirs. 1997—), Cosmos Club (Washington). Episcopalian. E-mail: athackray@chemheritage.org.

THADANI, UDHO, physician, cardiologist; b. Hyderabad, India, Apr. 1, 1941; came to U.S., 1980; s. Vensimal Mulchand and Gopi Thadani; m. Dorothy Ann Thadani, 1974; 1 child, Emma Sarala. MBBS, All India Inst. Med. Scis., New Delhi, 1964. Lic. physician, Okla., Ont., Can., Eng., India; cert. internal medicine, U.K., Can.; cert. cardiology, Can.; diplomate in internal medicine and cardiovasc. diseases Am. Bd. Internal Medicine. Intern All India Inst. Med. Scis., New Delhi, 1964-65, house physician, surgeon, 1965-66; house physician in medicine Joyce Green Hosp., Dartford, Kent, Eng., 1966-67; sr. house physician in medicine Kingston Gen. Hosp., Hull, Eng., 1967-69, registrar, rsch. fellow in medicine and cardiology, 1969-71, U. Leeds (Eng.), The Gen. Infirmary at Leeds, 1971-75; sr. rsch. fellow, clin. asst. medicine Queen's U., Kingston Gen. Hosp., Ont., Can., 1975-78; asst. prof. medicine Queen's U., Kingston, 1978-80; staff physician Kingston Gen. Hosp., 1978-80; assoc. prof. medicine U. Okla. Health Scis. Ctr., Oklahoma City, 1980-83; prof. medicine Okla. U. Health Scis. Ctr., Oklahoma City, 1983—2001, prof. emeritus medicine, 2001, mem. cardiology fellowship com., 1980-82; dir. clin. cardiology Okla. U. Health Scis. Ctr. and VA Med. Ctr., Oklahoma City, 1980-87, vice chief cardiovascular sect., 1981-99, dir. clin. rsch., 1987-99. Vice-chmn. rsch. and devel. com. VA Med. Ctr., Oklahoma City, 1989-92, chmn. physiology-pharmacology categorical rev. com., 1989-94, chmn. rsch. and devel. com., VA Med. Ctr. Oklahoma City, 1992-94, 2003—; sr. rsch. fellow Ont. Heart Found., 1978-80, rsch. fellow, 1976-78; rsch. fellow dept. medicine Queen's U., Kingston, Ont., 1975-76; rsch. fellow U. Leeds, Pub. Health and Ciba Found., dept. medicine and cardiovascular sect. Leeds Gen. Infirmary, 1971-75. Editor: Medical Therapy of Ischemic Heart Disease, 1992, Nitrates Updated, 1996; mem. editl. bd. panel Cardiology Drug Facts and Comparison, 1989; contbg. rev. panel Drug Facts and Comparisons, 1989—; mem. editl. bd. Internat. Jour. Cardiology, 1987-93, Cardiovascular Drugs and Therapy, 1987—, Heart Diseases, 1999-, Am. Jour. Pharmacology, 2000-; reviewer Circulation, Jour. Am. Coll. Cardiology, Am. Jour. Cardiology, Brit. Heart Jour., Internat. Jour. Cardiology, Can. Jour. Cardiology, European Heart Jour., Annals of Internal Medicine, New Eng. Jour. Medicine, Archives of Internal Medicine, Cardiovascular Drugs and Therapy, Drugs, European Jour. Pharmacology, Clin. Pharmacology and Therapeutics; contbr. over 200 articles to profl. jours., chpts. to books. Fellow: Royal Coll. Physicians and Surgeons Can., Coun. Clin. Cardiology Am. Heart Assn. (coun. rep. Okla. 1989—2000), Am. Coll. Cardiology (mem. cardiovasc. drug com. 1990—94), Royal Soc. Medicine London, Royal Coll. Physicians Can.; mem.: Can. Cardiovasc. Soc., Royal Coll. Phycisians U.K., Phi Kappa Phi (mem. FDA cardiovasc. and renal drugs adv. com. 1995—99). Avocations: gardening, tennis, travel. Office: Okla U Health Sci Ctr Cardiology Sect 920 SL Young WP 3120 Oklahoma City OK 73104 E-mail: udho-thadani@ouhsc.edu.

THALL, RICHARD VINCENT, school system administrator; b. San Francisco, Sept. 12, 1940; s. Albert Vincent and Alice Stella (O'Brien) T.; m. Ellyn Marie Wisherop, June 15, 1963; children: Kristen Ellyn, Richard Vincent Jr. AA, City Coll. San Francisco, 1961; BA, San Francisco State Coll., 1964; MA, San Francisco State U., 1971. Cert. elem. tchr., Calif.; cert. secondary tchr., Calif.; cert. community coll. tchr., Calif. Tchr. biology San Francisco Unified Sch. Dist., 1965-66, Mt. Diablo Unified Sch. Dist., Concord, Calif., 1966-79, program dir. water environ. studies program, 1979—. Ranger/naturalist State of Calif., Brannan Island, 1973-78; naturalist Adventure Internat., Oakland, Calif., 1979-81; lectr. Princess Cruise Lines, 1982—, Sea Goddess, 1986—, Sun Lines, 1987, Sitmar Lines, 1989, Royal Caribbean Internat., 1989—; lectr. naturalist Posh Talks, Inc., 1982—; spkr. commencements U. Calif., Berkeley, 1989. Author: Ecological Sampling of the Sacramento-San Joaquin Delta, 1976; Water Environment Studies Program, 1986; co-author: Project MER Laboratory Manual, 1982. Mem. Contra Costa County (Calif.) Natural Resources Commn., 1975-78, vice-chmn., 1977-78; active Save Mt. Diablo, Concord, 1969-76, v.p., 1974-75; mem. citizens com. Assn. Bay Area Govt. Water Quality, 1979-82, vice-chmn., 1980-82; active John Marsh Home Restoration Com., Martinez, Calif., 1977-78; troop com. chmn. Boy Scouts Am., Concord, 1984-86, asst. scoutmaster, 1985-87. Recipient Recognition and Excellence cert. Assn. Calif. Sch. Adminstrs., 1984, Wood Badge award Boy Scouts Am., 1986; grantee State Calif., 1982, 84, San Francisco Estuary Project, 1992, EPA, 1992, Shell Oil Co., 1993. Mem. AAAS, Nat. Assn. Biology Tchrs., Nat., Audubon Soc., Am. Mus. Natural Hist., Nat. Geog. Soc., Smithsonian Instn. (assoc.). Republican. Roman Catholic. Avocations: skiing, jogging, reading, hiking, photography. Home: 1712 Lindenwood Dr Concord CA 94521-1109 Office: Mt Diablo Unified Sch Dist 1936 Carlotta Dr Concord CA 94519-1358 E-mail: rothall@aol.com.

THARNEY, LEONARD JOHN, education educator, consultant; b. New Haven, Nov. 6, 1929; s. Lillian A. Batey; m. Denise A. Gauvin, June 20, 1981; children: Karen L., Linda L. BS, Trenton (N.J.) State Coll., 1954; MEd, Rutgers U., 1959; postgrad., Lehigh U., Bethlehem, Pa., 1963-70, Columbia U.; grad., Command & Gen. Staff Coll., Ft. Leavenworth, Kans., 1972. Cert. secondary math. and sci. tchr., elem. tchr. Tchr. (elem. demonstration) Trenton State Coll., NJ, 1954-60; tchr. (jr. high demonstration) Ewing Twp. Sch., NJ, 1960-63; cons., evaluator Am. Coun. on Edn., Washington, 1975-95, field coord., 1995—; cons., evaluator Mid. States Assn., Phila., 1987—; prof. Trenton State Coll., 1963-92, prof. emeritus, 1993—, dept. chmn., 1988-92. Cons. to internat. sch. for curriculum or sci. edn., Monrovia, Accra, Athens, Mogadishu, Cairo, Alexandria, Aleppo, Damascus, 1975—; tchr. grad. courses in curriculum and ednl. rsch. at overseas sites, Spain, Cyprus, Saudi Arabia, Syria, 1981—; exch. prof. Worcester Coll. Higher Edn., Eng., 1984-85; presenter sci. edn. workshops, AISA Internat. Conf., Nairobi, 1987; rep. from Coll. to Prins. Tng. Ctr., London, 1994; bd. dir. Trenton, NJ chpt. People to People Internat., 1995-98, chpt. pres., 1998—; NJ del. Worldwide Conf. of People to People Internat., Chester, Eng., 1998, Hong Kong, 2000, Aalborg, Denmark, 2001, Kansas City, Mo., 2002, Ronam, Romania, 2003; internat. trustee, 2000; 15th World Wide Conf. del., Kansas City, Mo., 2002, mem. Accrediting Commn. of the Distance Education and training Council, Wash., DC, 2000—. Co-author 7 manuals for uniform constrn. codes. Col. AUS, 1947-81. Recipient ACE award for outstanding svc. in mil. evaluations, 1987, cert. of appreciation, presdl. citation, 1989, spl. plaque award, others, Outstanding Svc. and Support award 112th FA Assn., 1998; decorated meritorious svc. medal U.S. Army, 1981. Mem.: ASCD, Nat. Coun. Social Studies, Assn. for Edn. Tchrs. in Sci., Assn. Tchr. Educators, Am. Air Mus. in Britain (founding mem.), Trenton Club (pres. 2002—03), Torch Club Internat. (bd. dir., founding mem. 1998—2001, v.p. 2001—02). Home: 20 Lawrenceville-Penning Rd Lawrenceville NJ 08648-1648

THATCHER, BLYTHE DARLYN, assistant principal; b. Kansas City, Mo., Aug. 15, 1947; d. Aubria DeVille and Irene Lois (Cowan) Thatcher. AA, Ricks Coll., Rexburg, Idaho, 1967; BS, Brigham Young U., 1971, MEd, 1983, EdS, 1985. Cert. elem., spl. edn., adminstr., Utah. Spl. edn. tchr. K-6 J. Allen Axson Sch. #8, Jacksonville, Fla., 1971-72; resource tchr., dept. chair Westland Elem. Sch., Sandy, Utah, 1972-78; resource English tchr. Mt. Jordan Mid. Sch., Sandy, Utah, 1978-80; resource tchr., dept. chair Butler Mid. Sch., Sandy, Utah, 1980-87, tchr. specialist/English tchr., 1987-89, adminstrv. asst./English tchr., 1989-90; asst. prin. Bonneville Jr. H.S., Salt Lake City, 1990-93, Granger H.S., Salt Lake City, 1993-96, Olympus H.S., 1996-98, Plymouth Elem. and Westbrook Elem. Schs., 1998—. Presenter, instr. state-wide writing confs., workshops, 1987-89, 99. Editor, contbg. author: Heroines of the Restoration, 1997; contbg. author: (poetry book) Where Feelings Flower, 1992, LDS Women's Treasury, 1997; editor The Am. Mother Mag., 1994-95; editor: A Fruitful Season, 1988; contbg. editor: A Singular Life, 1987; editl. asst. The Legacy Remembered and Renewed 1914-70, 1982; chmn. nat. editl. bd. Am. Mothers, Inc., 1994-95; exec. editor: Mother Love, 1995. Mem. Utah Office of Edn. Quality Indicates in Utah Schs. Task Force, Salt Lake City, 1989-90; county del. Utah Rep. Party, Salt Lake City, 1978; vol. Am. Cancer Soc., Utah Heart Assn., Detention Ctr., 1977-79. Fellow Utah Prins. Acad.; mem. Granite Assn. of Sch. Adminstrs. (bd. dirs. 1992-94, editor Adminstrv. Advantage 1992-94), Granite Assn. Jr. High Asst. Prins. (pres. 1992-93), Jordan Edn. Assn. (editor, originator Good Apples newsletter 1984-85), Utah Assn. of Women (chpt. and region pres. 1978-79), Parent Tchr. Student Assn. (2nd v.p. 1987-88), Utah Found., Utah Women's Ednl. Adminstrs. Assn. (secondary dist. rep., exec. bd. mem. 1995—, newsletter editor 1997—), Utah Days of '47 (sub-com. chair Pioneer of Progress awards 1995—), Granite Assn. Elem. Sch. Prins. Mem. Lds Ch. Avocations: writing, editing, poetry, speech writer. Home: 1254 Cove Park Cir Murray UT 84123-7954 Office: Granite Sch Dist 340 E 3545 S Salt Lake City UT 84115-4697

THATCHER, JANET SOLVERSON, financial advisor, writer; b. Sept. 24, 1946; m. John G. Thatcher, Mar. 20. 1976. BA, U. Wis., 1968, MBA, 1976, PhD, 1979. Svc. rep. Wis. Telephone Co., Beloit, 1968-71; trust dept. Baraboo (Wis.) Nat. Bank, 1971-73; pension, profit sharing trust dept. Firstar, Madison, 1973-74; asst. prof. fin. Va. Tech., Blacksburg, 1978-82, Clarkson U., Potsdam, N.Y., 1982-86; prof. U. Wis., Whitewater, 1986—2001. Contbr. articles to profl. jours. Home: 4546 Wavertree St San Luis Obispo CA 93401-7831

THATCHER, MURIEL BURGER, mathematics education educator, consultant; b. Newark, June 26, 1940; d. Arthur Frederick and Maynessa (Main) Burger; m. Glenn Michael Thatcher, Oct. 4, 1975; children: Laura, Scott. BA in Math. Edn., Montclair State Coll., 1962, MA in Pure and Applied Math., 1971; D in Math. Edn., Rutgers U., 1995. Cert. tchr., supr., N.J. Tchr. math. Park Jr. H.S., Scotch Plains-Fanwood, N.J., 1962-68; sys. programmer AT&T Bell Labs., Murray Hill, N.J., 1968-70; tchr. math., math. supr., computer coord. Scotch Plains Fanwood H.S., 1970-87; ednl. specialist math. N.J. Dept. Edn., Old Bridge, 1987-91; pvt. practice as math. cons. Basking Ridge, N.J., 1991-92, Pine Knoll Shores, N.C., 1992—. Adj. prof. Kean Coll., Union, N.J., 1982-87; mem. steering com., pub. rels. N.J. Math. Coalition, 1990-92. Editl. advisor Computer Literacy, 1985; creator 3 badges for Girl Scouts U.S., 1980; video tapes for instructovision for Nat. Assn. Elem. Sch. Prins., 1995; co-author (K-8 textbook series) Math Advantage, 1998. Asst. Cub troop leader Boy Scouts Am.; mem. Brownie troop com. Girl Scouts U.S., 1997—; troop leader Girl Scouts U.S., Maplewood, N.J., 1958-72, asst. leader internat. conf., Mexico, 1965, leadership trainer, Micronesia, 1970; leader, founder Community Coordinating Coun., Scotch Plains, 1963-67. Recipient Disting. Svc. award Grad. Sch. Edn., Rutgers U., 1997, Disting. Math. Alumna award Montclair State Coll., 1992, Thanks badge Girl Scouts U.S., 1960. Mem. ASCD, Nat. Coun. Tchrs. Math. (N.J. rep. 1989-92), Nat. Coun. Suprs. Math., Assn. Math. Tchrs. N.J. (exec. coun. rep. Nat. Coun. Tchrs. Math. 1989-92), N.C. Coun. Tchrs. of Math. Republican. Presbyterian. Avocations: travel, swimming, camping, skiing, antiquing. Home and Office: 136 Lagoon Ln Pine Knoll Shores NC 28512-6305

THATCHER, SHARON LOUISE, medical educator; b. Seattle, Feb. 17, 1942; d. Ralph McDonald and Audra Joy (Clauson) Thatcher. AB, Ga. State Coll., Milledgeville, 1964; degree in med. tech., Spartanburg Gen. Hosp., 1965; MEd, Ga. State U., 1981, EdS, 1987. Technologist chemistry dept. Greenville (S.C.) Gen. Hosp., 1965-66, Emory U. Hosp., Atlanta, 1966; hematology and bone marrow technologist Office of Dr. Spencer Brewer Jr., Atlanta, 1966-67; asst. lab. supr. chemistry dept. Grady Hosp., Atlanta, 1967-69; lab. technologist Ga. Mental Health Inst., Atlanta, 1969-70; chief lab. technologist Habersham County Hosp., Clarksville, Ga., 1970-72; survey officer Ga. Dept. Human Resources, 1972-74; part owner, gen. mgr. Nolan Biology Labs., Stone Mountain, Ga., 1974-75; bacteriology dept. technologist Northside Hosp., Atlanta, 1975-76; sales rep. Curtin Mathison Sci. Products, Atlanta, 1976-78; night supr. labs. Decatur (Ga.) Hosp., 1978; dir., ednl. coord. med. lab. tech. and phlebotomy tech. programs DeKalb Tech. Inst., Clarkston, Ga., 1978—, chairperson dept. allied health, 1980-86. Cons. Med. Lab. Cons., Atlanta, 1987—; mem. site survey team Nat. Accrediting Agy. for Clin. Lab. Scis., Chgo., 1980, 85, 91, site survey team coord., 1993, 94, 95, 96; speaker and presenter in field. Named Outstanding Speaker Am. Soc. for Phlebotomy Technicians, 1986. Mem. Am Soc. for Clin. Lab. Scientists (exhibit chair region III 1971-72), Am. Microbiology Soc., Ga. Soc. for Clin. Lab. Scientists (chair membership 1970-71, exhibit chair 1971-72, pres.-elect 1974-75, pres. 1975-76, bd. dirs. 1976-77, convention chair ann. state meeting 1989-90, Omicron Sigma award 1990, Gloria F. Gilbert achievement award 1993), Kappa Delta Pi. Avocations: ceramics, cross-stitch, 5k walks, gardening. Office: DeKalb Tech Inst 495 N Indian Creek Dr Clarkston GA 30021-2359

THAYER, MICHAEL J. secondary education educator; Tchr. Las Cruces (N.Mex.) Mid. Sch., 1972-94, Las Cruces H.S., 1994—. Named N.Mex. Tchr. of Yr., 1992. Office: Las Cruces HS 1755 El Paseo St Las Cruces NM 88001-6011

THÉ, HOANG-DINH, middle school educator; b. Thua-Thien, Vietnam, Mar. 12, 1943; BS, Lincoln U., 1966, MA, 1973; cert. in edn., U. San Francisco, 1979; MA, San Diego State U., 1980; D Naturopathy, Internat. U., 1993. Cert. tchr., Calif. Instr. Def. Lang. Inst., Monterey, Calif., 1966-71; social worker Internat. Inst. of San Francisco, 1975-78; spl. asst. to the dean Lincoln U., San Francisco, 1971-73; tchr. social studies, math. and scis. Francisco Mid. Sch., San Francisco, 1980—. Cons. Ctr. for Internat. Communication and Devel., Long Beach, Calif., 1988—. Mem. Nat. Geographic Soc., Internat. Phonetic Assn., Internat. Soc. of Naturopathy. Avocations: reading, writing, stamp collector, tai-chi. Home: PO Box 42-5386 San Francisco CA 94142-5386

THEEB, JUDITH ANN, elementary school educator; b. Torrington, Conn., Mar. 23, 1949; d. John Joseph and Florence (Pastore) Vedovelli; m. Maurice John Theeb Jr., June 28, 1985; 1 child, Wendy Ann. BA, Cen. Conn. State U., 1978, MA, 1984; postgrad., So. Conn. State U., 1990. Cert. adminstr. and supr., Conn. Chpt. I tchr. Torrington (Conn.) Bd. Edn., 1978-79, elem. tchr., 1979—2000, instrnl. supr., asst. prin., 2000—. Nat. trainer Talents Unltd. of Mobile, Ala., Torrington, 1989—. Co-author: (handbook) Principals Guide to New Teacher Orientation, 1987, (curriculum guide) Remedial Literature Based K-5 Reading Program, 1989. Mem. NEA, Conn. Edn. Assn., Conn. Assn. Supervision and Curriculum Devel., EMSPAC, Alpha Delta Kappa. Democrat. Roman Catholic. Avocations: crafts, snow skiing, poetry, walking, cooking. Home: 89 Castlewood Dr Torrington CT 06790-5945

THEISS, PATRICIA KELLEY, public health researcher, educator; b. Atlanta, Dec. 12, 1934; d. Charles Henry and Susie Carlota (Tate) Kelley; m. Erich Albert Theiss (div. Aug. 1996). BA, Wellesley Coll., 1956; MS, Howard U., 1958, Cert. in Secondary Edn., 1959. Rsch. asst. Armed Forces Inst. Pathology, Washington, 1959-61; heath edn. phone coord. Howard U. Cancer Ctr., Washington, 1977-81; program assoc. D.C. Lung Assn., Washington, 1981-85; co-project dir. Know Your Body Evaluation Project Georgetown U. Sch. Medicine, Washington, 1985-87; coord. minority health grant for cancer coalition Commn. Pub. Health, Washington, 1988-89, coord. data-based intervention rsch., 1989-93, protocol coord. immunization protocol NIH-DC initiative, 1994-97; pub. health advisor Dept. Health State Ctr. Health Stats. Inst. Minority Health Statistics Initiative, Washington, 1997—; coord. D.C. Healthy People 2010 Plan Initiative, 1998—; state contact U.S. Office Minority Health, Washington, 1999—. Mem. task force for substance abuse use Abuse Edn. for D.C. Pub. Schs., 1984-85; mem. Health Mothers/Health Babies Coalition, 1985-89. Contbr. articles to profl. jours. Chair health and welfare com. D.C. PTA, 1986-89; coord. AIDS awareness edn. State PTA, D.C., 1987-89. Recipient Cmty. Svc. award D.C. Assn. Health, Recreation and Dance, 1987. Mem. APHA, Met. Washington Pub. Health Assn. (pres. 1987-88). Democrat. Congregationalist. Avocations: oil painting, horseback riding. Home: 2501 Calvert St NW #902 Washington DC 20008 Office: DC Dept Health SCHS 825 N Capitol St NE Washington DC 20002-4210 E-mail: patricia.theiss@dc.gov.

THELIN, JOHN ROBERT, academic administrator, education educator, historian; b. West Newton, Mass., Oct. 15, 1947; s. George Willard and Rozalija Katherine (Komarec) T.; m. Anna Sharon Blackburn, June 24, 1978. AB cum laude, Brown U., 1969; MA, U. Calif., Berkeley, 1972, PhD, 1973. Rsch. asst. Brown U., Providence, 1968-69; researcher, lectr. U. Calif., Berkeley, 1972-74; asst. prof. U. Ky., Lexington, 1974-77; asst. dean Pomona Coll., Claremont, Calif., 1977-79; from asst. dir. to rsch. dir. Assn. Ind. Calif. Colls. and Univs., Santa Ana, 1979-81; chancellor prof. Coll. William and Mary, Williamsburg, Va., 1981-93, pres. faculty assembly, 1990-91; prof. higher edn. & philanthropy Ind. U., Bloomington, 1993-96; prof. ednl. policy and history U. Ky., Lexington, 1996—, disting. univ. rsch. prof., 2001—. Vis. prof. grad. sch. Claremont U., 1978—81; vis. scholar U. Calif., Berkeley, 1995; curator Marquandia Soc., 1971—2003; essay rev. editor Rev. of Higher Edn., 1979—91; rsch. cons. NSF, Washington, 1991; mem. faculty senate U. Ky., 1997—; guest faculty Coll. Bus. Mgmt. Inst., summer, 1998, 99, 2000, 01, 02, 03; mem., chair social sci. com. Grad. Coun., U.K., 1998—2001; keynote spkr. Sesquicentennial of Harvard Athletics Assn., Harvard U., 2002. Author: Higher Education and Its Useful Past, 1982, The Cultivation of Ivy, 1976, Higher Education and Public Policy, 1991, Games Colleges Play, 1994, A History of American Higher Education, 2004; author: (with others) The Old College Try, 1989, One Hundred Classic Books About Higher Education, 2001; assoc. editor (jour.) Higher Edn.: Theory and Rsch., 1983—91, guest columnist Lexington Herald-Leader, 2001. Pres., bd. dirs. United Way, Williamsburg, 1987-89; pres. Friends of Williamsburg Libr., 1989. Rsch. grantee Spencer Found., 1989-91, 99-2001; Regents fellow U. Calif., 1972; named to Order of Ky. Cols., 1998; recipient Outstanding Faculty Rsch. award Coll. of Edn., U. Ky., 2000. Mem. Assn. for Study of Higher Edn. (bd. dirs. 1988-90, keynote spkr. 1994, pres. 1999-2000), History of Edn. Soc. (editl. bd. 1988-91), Phi Beta Kappa (Faculty award for advancement of scholarship Alpha of Va. 1986, Alpha of R.I. 1969), Omicron Delta Kappa. Avocations: long-distance running, history of Los Angeles and California, sports history. Home: 1745 Richmond Rd Lexington KY 40502 Office: U Ky Edn Policy Studies Lexington KY 40506-1 E-mail: JThelin@uky.edu.

THEODORE, CRYSTAL, artist, retired educator; b. Greenville, S.C., July 27, 1917; d. James Voutsas and Florence Gertrude (Bell) T. AB magna cum laude, Winthrop Coll., 1938; MA, Columbia U., 1942, EdD, 1953; postgrad., U. Ga., 1947. Instr. art Winthrop Coll., 1938-43; prof. art, head dept. Huntingdon (Ala.) Coll., 1946-52, E. Tenn. State U., 1953-57, Madison Coll., 1957-68; vis. prof. art World Campus Afloat Chapman Coll., Calif., 1967; prof. art James Madison U., Harrisonburg, Va., 1968-83, prof. emeritus. Contbr. articles to profl. jours.; paintings in regional and nat. art exhbns. Bd. dirs. Rockingham Fine Arts Assn., 1980—85, 1989, Citizens for the Downtown, 1989, Women's Coop. Coun. Harrisonburg and Rockingham County, 1976—79, Valley Coun. of the Arts, 1998—99, Shenandoah Coun. of the Arts, 1996—, pres., 1996—2002; founder OASIS Co-op Gallery, 2000. Served with USMC, 1944—46. Gen. Edn. Bd. of Rockefeller Found. fellow, 1952-53; recipient award Carnegie Found. Advancement of Tchg., 1947, 48, 49, 50; Ednl. Found. Program grantee AAUW, 1981-82; rsch. grantee Ednl. Radio and TV Ctr., 1956. Mem.: AAUW (cultural interests rep., nat. dir. 1980—82), Va. Mus., Va. Watercolor Soc., Mensa, Pi Lambda Theta, Eta Sigma Phi, Kappa Pi. Democrat. Lutheran. Home: 150 Bear Wallow Ln Harrisonburg VA 22802-4822

THEODORIDIS, GEORGE CONSTANTIN, biomedical engineering educator, researcher; b. Braila, Romania, Dec. 3, 1935; came to U.S., 1959; s. Constantin George and Anastasia (Haritopoulos) T.; m. Lilly Kate Hyman, Sept. 20, 1975; 1 child, Alexander. BS in Mechanical and Elec. Engring., Nat. Tech. U. Athens, 1959; DSc, MIT, Cambridge, Mass., 1964. Rsch. assoc. MIT, Cambridge, Mass., 1964; sr. scientist Am. Sci. Engring., Cambridge, Mass., 1964-68; assoc. prof. in residence U. Calif., Berkeley, 1968-70; biomedical engring. U. Va., Charlottesville, 1970—; prof. elec. engring. U. Patras, Greece, 1976-83. Cons. Food and Drug Adminstrn., Washington, 1975-76, Applied Physics Lab, Columbia, Md., 1978-79. Author: Applied Math, 1983; contbr. articles to profl. jours. Den leader Boy Scouts Am., Charlottesville, Va., 1984-85. Fulbright fellow U.S. Govt., MIT, 1959-60; Nato fellow NATO, MIT, 1961-64; Spl. fellow NIH, U. Calif., 1968-70; recipient teaching award GE, MIT, 1963. Mem. Inst. Elec. and Electronics Engrs., Sigma Xi. Greek Orthodox. Avocations: history, travel. Home: 1817 Fendall Ave Charlottesville VA 22903-1613 Office: U Va Dept Biomed Enging PO Box 377 Charlottesville VA 22902-0377

THEOHARIDES, THEOHARIS CONSTANTIN, pharmacologist, physician, educator; b. Thessaloniki, Macedonia, Greece, Feb. 11, 1950; s. Constantin A. and Marika (Krava) T.; m. Efthalia I. Triarhou, July 10, 1981; children: Niove, Konstantinos. Diploma with honors, Anatolia Coll., 1968; BA in Biology, History of Sci. and Med., Yale U., 1972, MS in Immunology, MPhil in Endocrinology, Yale U., 1975, PhD in Pharmacology, 1978; postgrad., Tufts U., Harvard U. Asst. in rsch. biology Yale U., New Haven, 1968—71, asst. in rsch. pharmacology, 1973—78, spl. instr. modern Greek, 1974, 77, exec. sec. univ. senate, 1976—78, rsch. assoc. faculty clin. immunology, 1978—83; asst. prof. biochemistry and pharmacology Tufts U., Boston, 1983—88, co-dir. med. pharmacology curriculum, 1983—85, 1983—85, dir. med. pharmacology, 1985—93, assoc. prof. pharmacology, biochemistry and psychiatry, 1989—94, dir. grad. pharmacology, 1994—2000, prof. pharmacology and internal medicine, 1995—, prof. biochemistry, 2002—. Vis. faculty Aristotelian U. Sch. Medicine, Thessaloniki, 1979; trustee Anatolia Coll., 1984-85; clin. pharmacologist Commonwealth Mass. Drug Formulary Commn., 1985—; co-chmn. neuroimmunology 2d and 3d World Conf. on Inflammation, Monte Carlo, 1986, 89; mem. internat. adv. bd. 4th, 5th, 6th and 7th World Conf. on Inflammation, Geneva, 1991, 93, 95, 97; spl. cons. Min. of Health, Greece, 1993-95; mem. supreme spl. sci. health coun. Hellenic Republic, 1998—; chmn. Internat. Com. to Upgrade Med. Edn. in Greece, 1994; bd. dirs., spl. cons. Inst. Pharm. Rsch. & Tech., Athens, 1994—; mem. supreme health bd. Hellenic Inst. Social Welfare, 1999—. Author books on pharmacology; mem. editorial bd. numerous jours.; contbr. articles to profl. jours.; patentee in field. Bd. dirs., v.p. for rels. with Greece, Krikos, 1978-79; sec. Assn. Greeks to Yale, 1974-79, pres., 1982-83; mem. supreme sci. health coun. Hellenic Republic, 1997-2000, mem. supreme health care bd. Ministry of Labor, 1999-2002; bd. trustees, exec. bd. Hellenic Coll., 2000-02. Recipient Theodore Buyler award, Yale U., 1972, George Papanicoalou Grad. award, 1977, Med. award, Hellenic Med. Soc. N.Y., 1979, 1983, M.C. Winternitz prize in pathology, Yale U., 1980, Disting Svc. award, Tufts U. Alumni Assn., 1986, Spl. Faculty Recognition award, Tufts U. Med. Sch., 1987, 1988, Boston Mayor Menino Cmty. Svc. award, 1998, Oliver Smith award, 1999, Archon of Ecunemical Patriarchate of Christian Orthodox Ch., 2000. Mem. AMA, AAUP, AAAS, Hellenic Biochem. and Biophys. Soc., N.Y. Acad. Scis., Am. Inst. History Pharmacy, Soc. Health and Human Values, Am. Assn. History Medicine, Am. Soc. Cell Biology, Soc. Neurosci., Am. Fedn. Clin. Rsch., Conn. Acad. Arts and Scis., Am. Soc. Pharmacology and Exptl. Therapeutics, Hellenic Soc. Cancer Rsch., Hellenic Soc. Med. Chemistry, Internat. Soc. Immunopharmacology, Am. Soc. Microbiology, Am. Assn. Immunologists, Internat. Soc. History of Medicine, Mass. Med. Soc., N.E. Hellenic Med. Soc. (sec. 1984-85, v.p. 1985-86, 94-96, pres. 1986-87), Hellenic Sci. Assn. Boston (bd. dirs. 1985), Internat. Anatolia Alumni Assn. (sec. 1984-85), Alpha Omega Alpha, Sigma Xi. Achievements include research on mechanisms of release of secretory products: immunopharmacology membrane functions of polyamines; pathophysiology of mast cells in neuroimmunoendocrine diseases exacerbated by stress such as irritable bowel syndrome, interstitial cystitis, migraines and multiple sclerosis. Home: 14 Parkman St Apt 2 Brookline MA 02446-3802 Office: Tufts U Sch Med 136 Harrison Ave Boston MA 02111-1817

THEOPOLD, KLAUS HELLMUT, chemistry educator; b. Berlin, Apr. 18, 1954; came to U.S., 1978; s. Arnold and Gudula (Henjes) T.; children: Beatine Elise, Jessica Gudula, Nikolas McGeary, Karl Arnold. Vordiplom, U. Hamburg, Germany, 1977; PhD in Inorganic Chem., U. Calif.-Berkeley, 1982. Postdoctoral assoc. MIT, Cambridge, 1982-83; asst. prof. inorganic chem. Cornell U., Ithaca, N.Y., 1983-90; assoc. prof. inorganic chem. U. Del., 1990-95, prof. inorganic chem., 1995—, joint appointment in chem. engring., 1993. Vis. scientist inorganic chem., Oxford U., 1994; cons. Chevron Chem. Co., Kingwood, Tex., 1991-2001, Chevron Phillips Chem. Co., Bartlesville, Okla., 2001—; vis. prof. U. B.C., 2001—. Contbr. articles to profl. jours. Served with German Army, 1974-75. Recipient Newly Appointed Young Faculty in Chemistry award Camille and Henry Dreyfus Fund, 1983, Presdl. Young Investigator award NSF, 1985; Alfred P. Sloan Rsch. fellow, 1992. Fellow AAAS; mem. Am. Chem. Soc., Gesellschaft Deutscher Chemiker, Sigma Xi. Office: U Del Dept Chemistry Biochem Newark DE 19716 E-mail: theopold@udel.edu.

THERNSTROM, ABIGAIL (MANN), political scientist; b. N.Y.C., Sept. 14, 1936; d. Ferdinand and Helen (Robison) Mann; m. Stephan Thernstrom, Jan. 3, 1959; children: Melanie, Samuel. BA, Barnard Coll., N.Y.C., 1958; MA, Harvard U., 1961; PhD, 1975. Lectr. Harvard U., Cambridge, Mass., 1975-78; project dir. The Twentieth Century Fund, N.Y.C., 1981-86; vis. lectr. Harvard U., Cambridge, Mass., 1988-89, Boston Coll., 1990; stringer The Economist, London, 1988-92; adjunct prof. Sch. Edn. Boston U., 1991-97; sr. fellow The Manhattan Inst., N.Y.C., 1993—. Mem. domestic strategy group Aspen (Colo.) Inst., 1992-97; mem. edn. policy com. Hudson Inst., 1994-97; mem. bd. dirs. Inst. for Justice, Washington, 1993—; mem. adv. bd. Am. Friends of the Inst. for Justice, London, 1993-2003; mem. Mass. State Bd. of Edn., 1995—; commr. U.S. Commn. on Civil Rights, 2001—. Author: Whose Votes Count?: Affirmative Action and Minority Voting Rights, 1987, School Choice in Massachusetts, 1991; co-author: (with Stephan Thernstrom) America in Black and White: One Nation Indivisible, 1997, No Excuses: Closing the Racial Gap in Learning, 2003; editor: A Democracy Reader, 1992; co-editor: Beyond the Color Line: New Perspectives on Race and Ethnicity in America, 2002; contbr. articles to profl. jours. Mem. Citizen's Initiative on Race and Ethnicity, 1998-2002. Recipient Anisfield Wolf Book award, 1987, Am. Bar Assn. cert. merit, 1988, Best Policy Book award Polit. Studies Orgn., 1987, Benchmark Book award Ctr. for Judicial Studies, 1987. Am. Polit. Sci. Assn. Home and Office: 1445 Massachusetts Ave Lexington MA 02420-3810 E-mail: thernstr@fas.harvard.edu.

THERNSTROM, STEPHAN, historian, educator; b. Port Huron, Mich., Nov. 5, 1934; s. Albert George and Bernadene (Robbins) T.; m. Abigail Mann, Jan. 3, 1959; children— Melanie Rachel, Samuel Altgeld. BS, Northwestern U., 1956; A.M., Harvard, 1958, PhD, 1962. Instr. history Harvard U., Cambridge, Mass., 1962-66, asst. prof., 1966-67, prof., 1973-81, Winthrop prof., 1981—, chmn. com. on higher degrees in history of Am. civilization, 1985-92; prof. Brandeis U., 1967-69, UCLA, 1969-73; Pitt. prof. Am. history and instns. Cambridge U., 1978-79; dir. Charles Warren Ctr. for Research in Am. History, 1980-83. Author: Poverty and Progress, 1964, Poverty, Planning and Politics in the New Boston, 1969, The Other Bostonians, 1973, History of the American People, 1984, 88; co-author: America in Black and White, 1997, Reflections on The Shape of the River, 1999, No Excuses: Closing the Racial Gap in Learning, 2003; editor: Harvard Ency. Am. Ethnic Groups; co-editor: Harvard Studies in Urban History; Cambridge Interdisciplinary Perspectives on Modern History Series, Beyond the Color Line, 2001. Recipient Bancroft prize, R.R. Hawkins award, Faculty prize Harvard U. Press, Waldo G. Leland prize; Guggenheim fellow, John M. Olin fellow, ACLS fellow, sr. fellow Manhattan inst., 1998—, Nat. Humanities Coun., 2003—, Nat. Coun. for the Humanities, 2003—. Office: Harvard U Robinson Hall Cambridge MA 02138

THERRIEN, ANITA AURORE, elementary school educator; b. Lewiston, Maine, Apr. 1, 1937; d. Albert Leo and Florence (Clukey) T. Diploma, Ecole Pratique de Langue Francaise, Paris, 1957, diploma, 1963; BS in Edn., U. Maine, 1970, MEd, 1975. Cert. tchr., adminstr., Maine. Tchr. kindergarten St. Dominic Inst., Brookline, Mass., 1957-58; tchr. 1st and 3d grades St. Rita's Sch., Staten Island, N.Y., 1958-63; tchr. 1st and 4th grades Sabattus (Maine) Elem. Sch., 1967-92; ret., 1992. Scorer Maine Ednl. Assessment, Hinckley, 1988, mem. support team, 1988. Singer Holy Family Choir, Lewiston, 1984-88, Magic Pops Chorus, Lewiston, 1988-95. Honorable mention Alliance Francaise, 1958. Mem. Nat. Coun. Tchrs. of English, NEA (life), N.E. Coalition Ednl. Leaders, Sabattus Tchrs. Assn. (treas., chief negotiator 1967—), Maine Tchrs. Assn. Republican. Roman Catholic. Avocations: piano, singing, fishing, cross-country skiing, cycling.

THEVENET, PATRICIA CONFREY, social studies educator; b. Norwich, Conn., Apr. 16, 1924; d. John George and Gertrude Pauline (Doolittle) Confrey; m. Rubén Thevenet, Dec. 15, 1945 (dec. Mar. 1983); chldren: Susanne, Gregory, Richard, R. James. BS, U. Conn., 1944; AM, U. Chgo., 1945; EdM, Columbia U., 1992, EdD, 1994. Cert. elem. tchr., N.J. Counselor testing and guidance U. Chgo., 1945; home economist Western Mass. Electric Co., Pittsfield, 1946; tchr. Unquowa Sch., Fairfield, Conn., 1950-53, Alpine (N.J.) Sch., 1968-86; program asst. soc. studies Tchrs. Coll. Columbia U., N.Y.C., 1987-93; ret., 1993. Historian Borough Northvale, N.J., 1987-94; participant summer seminar Smithsonian Instn., Washington, 1984. Del. 2d dist. rep. Town Mtg., Trumbull, Conn., 1954-56; pres., trustee Northvale Pub. Libr. Assn., 1957-63; trustee Northvale Bd. Edn., 1963-72, pres. Northvale Bd. Edn., 1969-70; exec. bd. dirs. Bergen County (N.J.) County Bds. Edn., 1965-72; mem. Evening Sch. Comm. No. Valley Regional Dist., Bergen County, 1976-83; trustee Voluntown Libr., 1997-2001. Mem. AAUW, Voluntown Hist. Soc., Friends of Slater Mus., DAR. Home: 88 N Shore Rd # B Voluntown CT 06384-1719

THIBADEAU, EUGENE FRANCIS, education educator, consultant; b. NYC, May 18, 1933; s. Eugene Servanis and Lillian (Archer) T.; 1 child, Christine. BA, NYU, 1959, MA, 1967, MA, 1968, PhD, 1973. Instr. NYU, N.Y.C., 1968; lectr. in philosophy Dowling Coll., Oakdale, N.Y., 1968-70; prof. edn. Indiana U. of Pa., Indiana, Pa., 1970—. Vis. assoc. prof. Adelphi U., Garden City, N.Y., 1974-75; vis. scholar NYU, N.Y.C., 1984-85; vis. prof. Hofstra U., Hempstead, N.Y., 1974-75, 84, 86, Fudan U., Shanghai, China, 2000; cons. Central Bur. of Ednl. Visits, London, 1980-81, Commonwealth Speakers Bur., Harrisburg, Pa., 1983-85, U.S. Dept. Edn., Washington, 1983-85, Pa. Dept. Edn., Harrisburg, 1988—. Author: Opening Up Education-In Theory and Practice, 1976, Curriculum Theory, 1988, Existentialism in the Classroom, 1994; rev. editor: Focus on Learning, 1973-77, editor, 1977-84; contbg. editor: International Encyclopedia of Education, 2d edit., International Encyclopedia of Teaching and Teacher Education, 2nd edit., International Encyclopedia of Social and Behavioral Sciences; contbr. articles to profl. jours. Active United Way, Indiana, Pa., 1980—, NAACP, Indiana, 1985—, Red Cross, Indiana, 1985—. Fulbright sr. lectr. Thames Polytechnic, London, 1978-79, Fulbright sr. scholar Janus Pannonius U., Peces, Hungary, 1990-91; foreign expert Shanghai (China) Tchrs. U., 1988; designated faculty rsch. assoc. Inst. for Applied Rsch. and Pub. Policy, Indiana U. Pa., 1989; named Commonwealth Teaching fellow and Cert. Excellence in Teaching, Pa. State Colls. and Univ. Disting. Faculty Awards Com., 1976; recipient Founder's Day award, NYU, 1973, Outstanding Prof. award Ind. U. Pa.-Pa. State Edn. Assn., 1993. Fellow Am. Philosophy Edn. Soc.; mem. Am. Ednl. Studies Assn., AAUP, The S.W. Philosophy Edn. Soc., ASCD. Avocations: traveling, skiing, tennis, reading, chess. Home: 534 Chestnut Ridge Rd Penn Run PA 15765 Office: Indiana Univ Pa 131 Stouffer Hall Indiana PA 15705

THIBODEAU, GARY A. academic administrator; b. Sioux City, Iowa, Sept. 26, 1938; m. Emogene J. McCarville, Aug. 1, 1964; children: Douglas James, Beth Ann. BS, Creighton U., 1962; MS, S.D. State U., 1967, MS, 1970, PhD, 1971. Profl. service rep. Baxter Lab., Inc., Deerfield, Ill., 1963-65; tchr., researcher dept. biology S.D. State U., Brookings, 1965-76, asst. to v.p. for acad. affairs, 1976-80, v.p. for adminstrn., 1980-85; chancellor U. Wis., River Falls, 1985-2000; sr. v.p. acad. affairs U. Wis. Sys., 2000—01. Mem. investment com. U. Wis., River Falls Found.; trustee W. Cen. Wis. Consortium U. Wis. System; bd. dirs. U. Wis. at River Falls Found.; mem. Phi Kappa Phi nat. budget rev. and adv. comm., Phi Kappa Phi Found. investment comm., comm. on Agrl. and Rural Devel., steering commn. Coun. of Rural Colls. and Univs., Joint Coun. on Food and Agrl. Scis., USDA. Author: Basic Concepts in Anatomy and Physiology, 1983, Athletic Injury Assessment, 1994, Structure and Function of the Body, 1996, The Human Body in Health and Disease, 1996, Textbook of Anatomy and Physiology, 1996. Mem. AAAS, Am. Assn. Anatomists, Human Anatomy and Physiology Soc., Sigma Xi, Phi Kappa Phi, Gamma Sigma Delta, Gamma Alpha. Office: U Wis 116 N Hall River Falls WI 54022

THIE, GENEVIEVE ANN ROBINSON, retired secondary school educator; b. Aledo, Ill., Sept. 4, 1939; d. Leroy James and Wilma Elizabeth (Wood) Robinson; m. Irvin Emil Thie, Sept. 9, 1977; children: Vyona Ann, Daryl Irvin. BA, Iowa State Tchrs. Coll., Cedar Falls, 1961; MA, U. No. Iowa, Cedar Falls, 1969. Tchr. Cedar Rapids (Iowa) Sch. Bd., 1961-64, New Hartford (Iowa) Sch. Bd., 1965-68, Holmes Jr. High Sch., Cedar Falls, 1968-77; tchr. East Bay High Sch. Hillsborough County Sch. Bd., Tampa, Fla., 1979-84, tchr. Armwood High Sch., 1984-97, ret., 1997. Editor Iowa Coun. Tchrs. Math. Jour., 1975-78. Mem. NEA, Nat. Coun. Tchrs. Math., Math. Assn. Am., Fla. Coun. Tchrs. Math., Hillsborough County Tchrs. Math., Phi Delta Kappa. Episcopalian. Avocations: reading, golfing, traveling. Home: 265 Fairway Dr Spearfish SD 57783-3111

THIEDE, RICHARD WESLEY, retired communications educator; b. Detroit, Mar. 30, 1936; s. Harold Victor and Blanche May (Gross) T. BS, Ea. Mich. U., 1961; MA, U. Ill., 1963; PhD, U. Mo., 1977. Tchg. asst. U. Ill., Urbana, 1961-62; tchr. Ctrl. H.S., Battle Creek, Mich., 1962-63, Shafer H.S., Southgate, Mich., 1963-64, Chadsey H.S., Detroit, 1964-68, Stevenson H.S., Livonia, Mich., 1968-71; teaching/tech. asst. U. Mo., Columbia, 1971-74; instr. Ottumwa Hts. Coll., Iowa, 1975-76, Midland Luth. Coll., Fremont, Nebr., 1976-77; prof. comm. arts Defiance (Ohio) Coll., 1978-97, prof. emeritus, 1997—, instr., 1999, 2003; substitute tchr. Wayne Trace H.S., Ohio, 2002—03. Tchr. summer sch. Southwestern H.S., Detroit, 1966, Cody H.S., Detroit, 1967-68; tchr. evening sch. Chadsey H.S., 1965-67, Stevenson H.S., 1969-70, numerous others; adj. instr. Northwest State C.C., Archbold, Ohio, fall 1997. Mem. AARP, Eagles, Alpha Psi Omega, Kappa Delta Pi, Tau Kappa Epsilon (hon.). Democrat. Achievements include specializing in applications of machine systems control theory to problems of social and educational measurement. Home: 615 W Sycamore St Columbus Grove OH 45830-1023

THIEL, PHILIP, design educator; b. Bklyn., Dec. 20, 1920; s. Philip and Alma Theone (Meyer) T.; m. Midori Kono, 1955; children: Philip Kenji, Nancy Tamiko, Susan Akiko, Peter Akira (dec.). BSc, Webb Inst. Naval Architecture, 1943; MSc, U. Mich., 1948; BArch, MIT, 1952. Registered arch., Wash. Instr. naval architecture MIT, Cambridge, 1949-50; instr. architecture U. Calif., Berkeley, 1954-56, asst. prof., 1956-60; assoc. prof. U. Wash., Seattle, 1961-66, prof. visual design and experiential notation, 1966-91; guest prof. Tokyo Inst. Tech., 1976-78; vis. prof. Sapporo (Japan) Sch. of Arts, 1992-98. Lectr., U.S., Can. Japan, Norway, Denmark, Sweden, Eng., Austria, Switzerland, Peru, Bolivia, Korea; cons. FAO, Rome, 1952; co-founder Environment and Behavior, 1969; founder Ctr. for Experiential Notation, Seattle, 1981. Author: Freehand Drawing, 1965, Visual Awareness and Design, 1981, People, Paths and Purposes, 1997; patentee in field. Soc. Naval Architects and Marine Engrs. scholar, 1947; Rehmann scholar AIA, 1960; NIMH grantee, 1967, Nat. Endowment for Arts, 1969, Graham Found., 1995. Mem. Soc. Naval Architects and Marine Engrs. (assoc.), Phi Beta Kappa, Sigma Xi.

THIEME, GEORGIA LEE, special education educator; b. Urbana, Ohio, Feb. 12, 1952; d. Howard Carroll and Marion Irene (Teague) Odum; m. Leslie Ralph Thieme, Apr. 10, 1970; children: Jacquelene, Tracy, Frank, Jennifer, Bryan, Benjamin. AA, Glen Oaks Community Coll., Centreville, Mich., 1988; BS, Western Mich. U., 1990; MA, 1993. Tchr. spl. edn. White Pigeon (Mich.) Comty. Schs., 1990—. Part-time instr. Western Mich. U., 1994—; mem. St. Joe County (Mich.) Intermediate Sch. Dist. Past bd. dirs. St. Joe County Domestic Assault Shelter, Three Rivers, Mich.; mem. Three Rivers Community Players, Adoption and Foster Parents Mich. Assn., Lansing; family St. Joe County Foster Parents, Centreville, Mich., 1984-91. Zora Ellsworth scholar Western Mich. Edn. Dept., Kalamazoo, 1989-90, presdl. scholar Spl. Edn. Dept., 1990. Mem. AAUW, Student Coun. for Exceptional Children (bd. govs. 1989-90), Mich. Edn. Assn., Golden Key Honor Soc., Phi Kappa Phi, Beta Sigma Phi. Avocations: community theatre, reading sci. fiction, needle work, gardening. Home: 22660 Williams Landing Rd Sturgis MI 49091-9218

THIER, SAMUEL OSIAH, physician, educator; b. Bklyn., June 23, 1937; s. Sidney and May Henrietta Thier; m. Paula Dell Finkelstein, June 28, 1958; children: Audrey Lauren, Stephanie Ellen, Sara Leslie. Student, Cornell U., 1953—56; MD, SUNY, Syracuse, 1960, DSc (hon.), 1987, Tufts U., 1988, George Washington U., 1988, Mt. Sinai Sch. Med., 1989, Hahnemann U., 1989; DSc (hon.), U. Pa., 1994, Dartmouth Coll., 1996; LHD (hon.), Rush U., 1988, Va. Commonwealth U., 1992, Med. Coll. Pa., 1992; LHD (hon.), Brandeis U., 1994. Diplomate Am. Bd. Internal Medicine. Intern Mass. Gen. Hosp., Boston, 1960—61, asst. resident, 1961—62, sr. resident, 1964—65, clin. and research fellow, 1965, chief resident, 1966; clin. asso. Nat. Inst. Arthritis and Metabolic Diseases, 1962—64; from instr. to asst. prof. medicine Harvard U. Med. Sch., 1967—69; prof. medicine, health care policy Harvard Med. Sch., 1994—; asst. in medicine, chief renal unit Mass. Gen. Hosp., Boston, 1967—69; asso. prof., then prof. medicine U. Pa. Med. Sch., 1969—72, vice chmn. dept., 1971—74; assoc. dir. med. svcs. Hosp. U. Pa., 1969—71; David Paige Smith prof. medicine Yale U. Sch. Medicine, 1978—81, Sterling prof. medicine, 1981—85, chmn. dept., 1975—85; pres. Inst. Medicine NAS, Washington, 1985—91; pres., Univ. prof. Brandeis U., Waltham, Mass., 1991—94; pres. Mass. Gen. Hosp., Boston, 1994—97, Ptnrs. HealthCare Sys., Inc., Boston, 1994—96, 1997—2002, CEO, 1996—2002. Chief medicine Yale-New Haven Hosp., 1975—85, trustee, 1978—85; bd. dirs. Conn. Hospice, Inc., 1976—82; dir. Am. Bd. Internal Medicine, 1977—85, exec. com., 1981—85, chmn., 1984—85. Mem. editl. bd.: New Eng. Jour. Medicine, 1978—81; contbr. articles to med. jours. Mem. adv. com. to the dir. NIH, 1980—85. With USPHS, 1962—64. Recipient Christian R. and Mary F. Lindback Found. Disting. Tchg. award, 1971. Mem.: ACP (bd. regents 1982—85), Interurban Clin. Club, Assn. Am. Physicians, Assn. Profs. Medicine, Internat. Soc. Nephrology, Am. Physiol. Soc., Am. Soc. Nephrology, Am. Fedn. Clin. Rsch. (pres. 1976—77), John Morgan Soc., Assn. Am. Med. Colls. (adminstrv. bd. coun. acad. socs.), Alpha Omega Alpha. Home: 99-20 Florence St Apt 4B Chestnut Hill MA 02467-1927

THIES, LYNN WAPINSKI, elementary education educator; b. Pottsville, Pa., Aug. 11, 1946; d. Stanley Walter and Mary Etta (Stevens) Wapinski; m. Wynn Gerrard, June 14, 1969; children: Heather Anne, Kevin Leonard. BA in Edn., Assoc. Libr. Sci., U. S.C., 1968. Tchr. 5th grade Ft. Jackson (S.C.) Elem. Sch., 1968-70; tchr. 4th and 5th grades Groner Elem. Sch., Scholls, Oreg., 1970-72; tchr. 1st grade Welches (Oreg.) Elem., 1980; tchr. 6th grade Sandy (Oreg.) Elem. Sch. Dist. 46, 1983-87, tchr. 3rd grade, 1987-94, tchr. mixed-age class, ages 7 and 8, 1994-96, 2nd grade tchr., 1996—. Mem. lang. arts curriculum com. Firwood Elem. Sch., Sandy Elem. Sch. Dist. 46, 1986-87, mem. 21st Century S.I.T.E. com., 1994-97, sci. curriculum com., 1995—; active Oreg. Consortium Quality Sci., Portland, 1985-87, Oreg. Cadre Quality Sci. Edn., Sandy, 1987-89, Sci. Curriculum Consortium, Sandy, 1989-92. Leader, mem. Day Camp core staff Girl Scouts U.S., mem. hist. re-enactment group, vol. Columbia River Girl Scout coun., Portland, 1972-92; mem. Oreg. Dept. Edn. Eisenhower grantee, 1994, 95, 96, 97, Oregon Dept. Edn. Primary Math Project grantee, 1996-97. Mem. NEA, ASCD, Internat. Reading Assn., Oreg. State Tchrs. Assn., Oreg. Consortium for Quality in Sci. Edn., Oreg. Cadre for Assistance to Tchrs. Sci., Oreg. Sci. Tchrs. Assn., Clackamas County Sci. Tchrs. Assn., Barlow Trail Long Rifles. Democrat. Roman Catholic. Avocations: historical reinactment, percussion rifle competitions, historical memorabilia, research into american history. Home: 51956 E Terra Fern Dr Sandy OR 97055-6478

THIGPEN, LEWIS, engineering educator; b. Quincy, Fla., Aug. 29, 1938; s. Alonzo and Emma (Ray) T. BS in Mech. Engring. magna cum laude, Howard U., 1964; MS, Ill. Inst. Tech., 1967, PhD, 1970. Profl. engr., D.C. Tech. staff mem. Sandia Nat. Labs., Albuquerque, 1969-73; asst. prof. Lowell (Mass.) Technol. Inst., 1973-75; from physicist to group leader Lawrence Livermore Lab., Livermore, Calif., 1975-88; chmn. mech. engring. Howard U., Washington, 1988—. Adv. com. mechanics NSF, Washington, 1990-91; program evaluator Mass. Higher Edn. Coord. Coun., Boston, 1991. Asst. leader Boy Scouts Am., Chgo., 1967-69; Served in U.S. Army, 1955-58, Germany. NASA fellow, 1964-67. Fellow ASME (region III com. chair 1996-98, accreditation bd. engring. and tech. evaluator 1991-98, vice-chair nat. dept. heads com. 1999-2000, chair nat. dept. heads com. 2000-01); mem. AIAA, Am. Soc. Engring. Edn. (fellowship rev. panel 1990-94), Math. Throughout the Curriculum (adv. bd. 1996—), N.Y. Acad. Scis., Sigma Xi. Achievements include patent in field and research in earth penetrating projectiles, constitutive modelling of geologic materials and theoretical seismology. Office: Howard U Dept Mech Engring 2300 6th St NW Washington DC 20001-2323 E-mail: thigpen@scs.howard.edu.

THISTLE, ANNA, youth services and post-secondary education minister; Sr. level positions at various branches Canadian Imperial Bank of Commerce, Canada; mgr. Nfld. and Labrador Credit Union, GrandFalls-Windsor, Canada, 1977—96, mem. legis. assembly St. John's, Canada, 1996—; pres. treasury bd. Nfld.-Labrador Parliament, 1996—2001, min. dept labor, 2001—03, min. youth services and post-secondary education, 2003—. Bd, dirs. Provincial Govt. Adv. Coun. on Economy; mem. Royal Commn. on Edn. Adv. Com. Fund raiser Heart and Stroke Assn.; vol Exploits Disabled Assn.; bd. dirs. South and Ctrl. Health Found., Exploits Valley Devel. Assn. Office: PO Box 8700 St John's NL A1B 4J6 Canada Office Fax: 709-729-7481.

THOERING, ROBERT CHARLES, elementary education educator; b. Huntington, N.Y., Jan. 3, 1964; s. Robert Theodore and Mary Agnes Thoering. BA, St. John's U., 1986, MEd, 1991; prof. diploma, Fordham U., 2003. Cert. tchr. reading, social studies, N.Y. Assoc. tchr. Holy Cross H.S., Flushing, N.Y., 1985; prin. Our Lady of Refuge Sch., Bklyn., 1986—2002. Editor: Hope's Treasure, 1991—2000. Founder, dir. St. Anne's Mission Bd., Middle Village, 1997-2002; mem. Greater Ridgewood (N.Y.) Hist. Soc., Queens Genealogy Workshop, Ridgewood, Irish Family History Forum, Hempstead, N.Y. Mem. ASCD, Nat. Cath. Edn. Assn., Nat. Assn. Student Activity Advisers, Nat. Coun. Tchrs. English, Internat. Reading Assn., N.Y. State English Coun. Republican. Roman Catholic. Avocations: gardening, travel, literature. Home: 7207 66th Rd Middle Village NY 11379-2115 Office: Our Lady of Refuge Sch 1087 Ocean Ave Brooklyn NY 11230

THOMAE, MARY JOAN PANGBORN, special education educator; b. Sheboygan, Wis, July 19, 1958; d. Donald Rumsey and Joan Ruth (Thompson) Pangborn; m. Michael Jay Thomae, Oct. 27, 1990; 1 child, Zachary John. BA, Carthage Coll., Kenosha, Wis., 1981; MS in Edn., U. Wis., Whitewater, 1988. Cert. elem. tchr., learning disabled and emotionally disturbed edn., Wis. Tchr. learning disabled pub. sch., De Forest, Wis., 1981-85; tchr. asst. spl. edn. dept. U. Wis., Madison, 1985-86; tchr. learning disabled and emotionally disturbed pub. sch., Cambridge, Wis., 1985-86, Oak Creek, Wis., 1986—. Coord. designated vocat. instr. program Family and Consumer Edn. Dept., 1992-2002; active New Tchr. Mentor program, 2002—. Mem. Coun. for Exceptional Child., Oak Creek Tchr. Union (bldg. rep. 1987-89, 90-91, renaissance steering com. 1990—, chair new faculty recognition com., 1994—). Avocations: aerobics, cooking, homemaking. Office: Oak Creek High Sch 340 E Puetz Rd Oak Creek WI 53154-3200

THOMAN, MARY E. business and marketing educator, rancher; b. Kemmerer, Wyo., Sept. 14, 1949; d. William J. and Mary A. (Ferentchak) T. AA, Western Wyo. C.C., Rock Springs, 1970; BS in Bus., U. Wyo., 1972; MEd in Mktg., Colo. State U., 1978, PhD in Vocat./Secondary Adminstrn., 1981. Profl. Teaching Cert., Wyo. Bus. edn. Green River (Wyo.) H.S., 1972-75; part time bus. and mktg. instr. Western Wyo. C.C., Green River, 1972-77, Rock Springs, Wyo., 1972-80, Kemmerer, Wyo., 1983—; mktg. and coop. educator Green River H.S., 1975-77; asst. dir. Nev. St. Coun. on Vocat. Edn., Carson City, Nev., 1977; exec. dir. Mont. St. Coun. on Vocat. Edn., Helena, Mont., 1981-82; cattle/sheep rancher Kemmerer, 1981—; sr. sales dir. Mary Kay Cosmetics, Kemmerer, Wyo., 1988—. Ednl. cons. past chair Wyo. St. Coun. on Vocat. Edn., Cheyenne, 1984-93; bus. cons. Western Wyo. Coll., Rock Springs, 1983—; sch.-to-work, S.W. Wyo. Collaberative Team; edn. cons. Kemmerer Sch. Dist., 1993—, chair voc/tech prep bus. curriculum com.; mem. Wyo. Agr. in Classroom, 1992-96; mem. Wyo. Task Force on Fed. Lands Policy, 1998—, Wyo. State Treasurer's Spl. Adv. Coun. on State Investing, 1999, exec. com., co-chair Fed. Lands Policy Wyo. Woolgrowers Assn., 1998—. Active western range issues; testifier on Range Reform Hearings; mem. Cumberland Allotment Coordinated Resource Mgmt. Team Bur. Land Mgmt.; mem. S.W. Wyo. Resource Rendezvous Steering Com.; dist. supr. Big Sandy Conservation Dist., 1999—; appointee Wyo. Fed. Lands Task Force, 1998—. Ednl./Profl. Devel. Act fellow, 1977-78, Grad. Leadership Devel. awardee, 1978-81. Mem. Kemmerer C. of C. (edn. com., bd. dirs. 1992—). Roman Catholic. Avocations: flying, skiing, gardening, dancing, traveling. Home: PO Box 146 Green River WY 82935-0146

THOMAS, ALTA PARKER, retired secondary school educator; b. Butte, Mont., Sept. 18, 1940; d. Charles Clayton and Sarah Elizabeth (Bennett) Parker Hopkins; m. Vivian William Thomas Jr., Aug. 19, 1962; children: Christine Michelle Thomas Wentland, Tracy Ann Thomas, Lisa Janine Thomas Julson. BS, Mont. State U., 1962; MEd, Walla Walla Coll., 1991. Cert. tchr., Wash. Rsch. chemist Dow Chem. Co., Midland, Mich., 1962-64; tchr. Granite Sch. Dist., Salt Lake City, 1964-65; home and hosp. tchr. Richland (Wash.) Schs., 1975-77; sci. tchr. Kennewick (Wash.) Sch. Dist., 1977-84, high sch. biology tchr., 1994—2000, sci. dept. chair, 1992-94. Coord. Internat. Baccalaureate Kennewick Sch. Dist., 1994-2000, chmn. sci. curriculum com., 1987-89, rep. dist. circle com., 1991-93; coach sci. olympiad team Kennewick H.S., 1988-94, mem. staff devel. com., 1985-91, site coun., 1995. Patented oven cleaner formula; editor: Curnutt Family Cookbook, 1986. Founder acad. booster club Kennewick High Sch., 1985. REST fellow Battelle Pacific N.W. Lab., 1988. Mem. Nat. Assn. Biology Tchrs., NEA, Wash. Edn. Assn., Kennewick Edn. Assn. (rep., negotiator 1977—), Wash. Sci. Tchr. Assn., Delta Kappa Gamma (membership chair, polit. affairs chair 1984—). Presbyterian. Avocations: birding, hiking, cross stitch, quilting, reading. Home: 4029 S Cascade St Kennewick WA 99337-5185 Office: Kennewick High Sch 500 S Dayton St Kennewick WA 99336-5674

THOMAS, BARBARA WAYNE, elementary school educator; b. Bristol, Va., Feb. 13, 1942; d. John Christopher and Theda Gaynelle (Fleenor) T. AA, Va. Intermont Coll., 1962; BS, East Tenn. State U., 1965. Tchr. St. Ann's Sch., Bristol, Va., 1965-72, Weaver Elem. Sch., Bristol, Tenn., 1975—. Mem. NEA, Tenn. Edn. Assn., Sullivan County Dem. Women, Bristol Woman's Club, Pilot Internat. Club, Delta Kappa Gamma, Beta Sigma Phi Sorority. Presbyterian. Avocations: reading, traveling, playing cards. Home: 2009 Edgemont Ave Bristol TN 37620-4723 Office: Weaver School 3441 Weaver Pk Bristol TN 37620

THOMAS, BESSIE, primary education educator; b. Shreveport, La., Nov. 30, 1943; d. Fleen and Tommie Lee (Anderson) Myles; m. Jesse Thomas, May 11, 1968 (dec. 1995). BS, Grambling Coll., 1966; MS, Grambling State U., 1976; postgrad., various colls. and univs., 1967-79. Cert. primary and elem. tchr., La. 1st grade tchr. Pine St. Sch., Hamburg, Ark., 1966-67, Pine Grove Elem. Sch., Shreveport, 1967-70, Mooringsport (La.) Sch., 1970-81; early childhood edn. tchr. Fairfield Elem. Sch., Shreveport, 1981-2000, Mooretown Elem. Sch. Ctr., 2001—03. Active Word of Faith Ch. Internat. Grantee Caddo Pub. Edn. Found., 1995—. Mem. NEA. Democrat. Avocations: inspirational reading, travel, interacting with children, viewing works of art. Home: 2831 Abbie St Shreveport LA 71103-2130 E-mail: blmt@bellsouth.net.

THOMAS, BEVERLY IRENE, special education educator, educational diagnostician, substance abuse counselor; b. Del Rio, Tex., Nov. 12, 1939; d. Clyde and Eve Whistler; m. James Thomas, Jan. 28, 1972; children: Kenneth (dec.), Wade, Robert, Darcy, Betty Kay, James III, Debra, Brenda, Michael. BM summa cum laude, Sul Ross State U., 1972, MEd, 1976, MEd in Counseling, 1992, MEd in Mid. Mgmt., 1996. Cert. music, elem. edn., music edn., learning disabilities, spl. edn. generic, ednl. diagnosis, ednl. counseling, spl. edn. counseling and mid. mgmt. Tchr. Pecos-Barstow-Toyah Ind. Sch. Dist., 1974—92, 1999—; edn. diagnostician West Tex. State Sch., Tex. Youth Commn., ret., 1999; tchr. spl. edn. and enhanced 5th grade Pecos-Barstow-Toyah Ind. Sch. Dist., 1999-2000; youth counselor Tex. Workforce Ctr., Pecos, 2000; substance abuse counselor Reeves County Detention Ctr., 2001—. Gifted-talented coordinator 5th grade, Pecos-Barstow-Toyah Ind. Sch. Dist., 1999-2000. Mem. AAUW, ASCD, NEA, MENSA, Assn. for Children with Learning Disabilities (local sec. 1974), Tex. State Tchrs. Assn. (treas. 1991-94), Tex. Ednl. Diagnosticians Assn., Tex. Profl. Ednl. Diagnosticians, Reeves County Assn. of Children with Learning Disabilities, Nat. Coun. Tchrs. of Maths., Nat. Coun. Tchrs. English, Learning Disabilities Assn., Nat. Coun. for Geog. Edn., Learning Disabilities Assoc., Tex., Coun. for Exceptional Children, Tex. Counseling Assn., Am. Correctional Assn., Alpha Chi, Kappa Delta Pi, Chi Sigma Iota.

THOMAS, CAROL F. educational association administrator; MA in Ednl. Psychology, San Francisco State U.; PhD in Edn., U. Calif., Berkeley. Sr. program dir. S.W. Regional Lab., Los Alamitos, Calif., 1989—95; assoc. exec. dir. N.W. Regional Edn. Lab., Portland, Oreg., 1995—2001, CEO, 2001—. Office: NW Regional Ednl Lab Ste 500 101 SW Main St Portland OR 97204*

THOMAS, CAROLYN HARPER, elementary educator; b. Villa Ridge, Ill., June 24, 1950; d. John Nathan Sr and Walterene (Carter) Harper. BS in Edn., Ind. U., Gary, 1977; M in Early Childhood Edn., Edinboro (Pa.) State Coll., 1980. Lic. tchr., Ohio, Ind. Tchr. Ashtabula (Ohio) Area City Schs., 1978-91; program coord. Project Have Hope Mary Chatman Community Ctr., Ashtabula, 1987-90; coord. summer recreation program Ashtabula City Schs. & Job Tng. Partnership Act, summer 1989, 90; tchr. Gary Community Sch. Corp., 1991—; lead tchr. Kids Enrichment Program, Gary, 1992—. Program coord. I Can-Tutorial and Enrichment, 1995—; mem. Kneely Mae Fleming Scholarship Selection Com., Ashtabula, 1989-91. Mem. allocations com. United Way, Ashtabula, 1989-90. Mem. Gary Reading Coun., N.W. Ind. Assn. Black Sch. Educators. Pentecostal. also: Kuny Elem Sch 5050 Vermont St Gary IN 46409-2961

THOMAS, CLAUDEWELL SIDNEY, psychiatry educator; b. N.Y.C., Oct. 5, 1932; s. Humphrey Sidney and Frances Elizabeth (Collins) T.; m. Carolyn Pauline Rozansky, Sept. 6, 1958; children: Jeffrey Evan, Julie-Anne Elizabeth, Jessica Edith. BA, Columbia U., 1952; MD, SUNY, Downstate Med. Ctr., 1956; MPH, Yale U., 1964. Diplomate Nat. Bd. Med. Examiners, Am. Bd. Psychiatry, Am. Bd. Forensic Medicine, Am. Bd. Psychol. Specialties. From instr. to assoc. prof. Yale U., New Haven, 1963-68, dir. Yale tng. program in social community psychiatry, 1967-70; dir. div. mental health service programs NIMH, Washington, 1970-73; chmn. dept. psychiatry U.M.D.N.J., Newark, 1973-83; prof. dept. psychiatry Drew Med. Sch., 1983—, chmn. dept. psychiatry, 1983-93; prof. dept. psychiatry UCLA, 1983-94, vice chmn. dept. psychiatry, 1983-93, prof. emeritus dept. psychiatry, 1994—; med. dir. Tokanui Hosp., TeAwamutu, N.Z., 1996. Cons. A.K. Rice Inst., Washington, 1978—80, SAMSA/PHS Cons., 1991—99, L.A. County Homeless Outreach Program, 2001—; mem. LA County Superior Ct. Psychol. Panel, 1991—97; cons. psychiatrist L.A. County AB2034 Homeless Outreach Program (Skid Row Dual Diagnoses), 2001—. Author: (with B. Bergen) Issues and Problems in Social Psychiatry, 1966; editor (with R. Bryce LaPorte) Alienation in Contemporary Society, 1976, (with J. Lindenthal) Psychiatry and Mental Health Science Handbook; mem. editl. bd. Internat. Jour. Mental Health, Adminstrn. In Mental Health. Bd. dirs. Bay Area Found., 1987—. Served to capt. USAF, 1959-61. Fellow APHA, Am. Psychoanalytic Assn. (hon.), Am. Psychiat. Assn. (disting. life), Royal Soc. Health, N.Y. Acad. Sci., N.Y. Acad. Medicine; mem. Am. Sociol. Assn., Am. Coll. Mental Health Adminstrs., Am. Coll. Forensic Examiners, Am. Coll. Psychiatrists, Sigma Xi. Avocations: tennis, racquetball, violin, piano. Office: 30676 Palos Verdes Dr E Palos Verdes Peninsula CA 90275-6354 also: 500 Pacific Coast Hwy Ste 208 Seal Beach CA 90740 E-mail: cysid32@ucla.edu.

THOMAS, DAVID ANSELL, retired university dean; b. Holliday, Tex., July 5, 1917; s. John Calvin Mitchell and Alice (Willet) T.; m. Mary Elizabeth Smith, May 18, 1946; 1 dau., Ann Elizabeth. BA, Tex. Tech. Coll., 1937; MBA, Tex. Christian U., 1948; PhD, U. Mich., 1956. C.P.A., Tex. Accountant Texaco, Inc., 1937-42; asso. prof. Tex. Christian U., 1946-49; lectr. U. Mich., 1949-53; prof. accounting Cornell U., Ithaca, N.Y., 1953-84; assoc. dean Cornell U. Grad. Sch. Mgmt., 1962-79; acting dean Cornell U. Grad. Sch. Bus. and Pub. Adminstrn., 1979-81; dean Samuel Curtis Johnson Grad. Sch. Mgmt. Cornell U., 1981-84. Author: Accelerated Amortization of Defense Facilities, 1958, Accounting for Home Builders, 1952; Contbr. numerous articles to publs.; Editor: Fed. Accountant, 1956-58. Pres. Exec. Investors, Inc.; exec. dir. Charles E. Merrill Family Found., 1954-57, Robert A. Magowan Found., 1957-60; adminstr. Charles E. Merrill Trust, 1957-81, Ithaca Growth Fund.; Bd. dirs. Ithaca Opera Assn., Cornell Student Agys. Served to capt. USAAF, 1942-46, PTO. Mem. Tex. Soc. C.P.A.'s, Nat. Assn. Accountants, Am. Accounting Assn., Phi Beta Kappa, Beta Alpha Psi. Clubs: Cornell of N.Y, University, Statler (pres., dir.). Home: Devenshire Park 1560 Jasper Ct Venice FL 34292-4336

THOMAS, DOROTHY WORTHY, English educator; b. Charlotte, N.C., Dec. 13, 1940; d. Utah Worthy and Myrtle Lee (Harvey) Kirkpatrick; m. Leon R. Thomas, Dec. 15, 1963; children: Tonya Monique, Tracy Michele, Tecla Mionne, Tasha Monette. BA in English, Bennett Coll., 1963; MA in French, Hampton U., 1973; Cert. in Advanced Studies in Ednl. Adminstrn., Coll. of William and Mary, 1982; postgrad., Ind. U. of Pa., 1993—; PhD candidate. Cert. tchr., Va. French and English tchr. Irwin Ave. Jr. High Sch., Charlotte, 1963-65, Huntington High Sch., Newport News, Va., 1966-71, Warwick High Sch., Newport News, 1971-88; English tchr. Booker T. Washington High Sch., Reidsville, N.C., 1965-66; staff devel. specialist Newport News Pub. Schs., 1988-91; asst. prof. English Hampton (Va.) U., 1991—. Cons. Newport News Pub. Schs., 1988-91. Author brochure Program for Effective Teaching, 1990. Fellow ASCD, Va. Assn. Tchrs. of English, Nat. Coun. Tchrs. of English, Jack & Jill of Am., Inc., Kappa Delta Pi, Alpha Kappa Alpha (Epistoleus 1992—). Democrat. Presbyterian. Avocations: aerobics, reading, travel, bowling. Home: 1232 Patrick Ln Newport News VA 23608-2428

THOMAS, ELLEN LOUISE, school system administrator; b. Doylestown, Pa., Nov. 30, 1940; d. Edward Martin and Evelyn Graham (Axenroth) Happ; m. Eugene Greene Leffever, June 30, 1963 (dec. Nov. 1978); children: Eugene Greene II, Jeanette Ellen Dellaripa; m. William Dewey Thomas, Sept. 15, 1981; 1 child, Jeremiah David. BA in Edn., Immaculata (Pa.) Coll., 1962; postgrad., Pa. State U., 1962-67. Pvt. practice tutor, Doylestown, 1958-65; tchr. Cen. Bucks Sch. System, Doylestown, 1962-65; adminstr. The Curiosity Shoppe, Doylestown, 1965—. The Toddler Ctr., Doylestown, 1979—; exec. dir. Camp Curiosity, Doylestown, 1984—, Thomas Lea Equestrian Ctr., Doylestown, 1988—. Tchr. trainer Confortunity of Christian Doctrine, Doylestown, 1965-78; cons. early childhood Am. Sch. in Hong Kong, 1981-84; lectr. in early childhood Bucks County Community Ctr., Newtown, Pa., 1978-90; workshop facilitator Head Start, Phila., 1990; cons. day care Cen. Bucks C. of C., Doylestown, 1989-90; ednl. coord. Forest Grove Presbyn. Ch., 1984-90. Mem. U.S. C. of C., Washington, Bucks County C. of C., Doylestown, Nat. Fedn. of Ind. Bus., Washington; children's ministry coord. Jesus Focus Ministry, 1995—; trainer Pa. Child Care, 1995—; pres. Pa. Day Camp Assn., 1998-2000; Sunday sch. tchr. Hilltown Bapt. Ch., 1995-2000; mem. Am. Camping Assn., 1994-, Plumstead Christian Sch. Bd., 1995-2001; varsity tennis coach, Plumstead Christian Sch.-boys, 1998-2003, girls, 2001-03; children's chmn. Central Bucks Village Fair, 2001-03. Mem. ASCD, Assn. for Childhood Edn. Internat., United Pvt. Acad. Schs. Assn., Bucks County Assn. Edn. Young Children (pres. 1974-78). Office: The Curiosity Shoppe 4425 Landisville Rd Doylestown PA 18901-1134 E-mail: FaxThomdew@aol.com.

THOMAS, ENOLIA, nutritionist, educator; b. Little Rock, Ark., June 1, 1938; d. Calvin - and Bernice Thomas. BS, Lincoln U., Jefferson City, Mo., 1960. Hosp. dietician Dept. Health, Christiansted, Saint Croix, Virgin Islands, 1969—72; chief nutritionist Dept. Social Welfare, St Croix. Virgin Islands, 1972—83; hosp. dietician Vets Adminstrn., Kerrville, Tex., 1984—85; rsch. dietician King Fasial Specialist Hosp. and Rsch. Ctr., Riyadh, Saudi Arabia, 1985—96; nutritionist Denver Dept. Human Svcs., 1996—. Contbr. articles to profl. jours. Vol. libr. docent Denver Pub. Libr., 1997—. Major USAF, 1960—69. Recipient Title 7 Older Americans Act/ Virgin Islands Elderly Nutrition Program, Commission On Aging, 1973 - 1983. Mem.: Nat. Assn. Commodity Supplemental Food Program (bd. dirs. 1999—2001), Am. Dietetic Assn., Stiles African Am. Heritage Ctr. (bd. dirs. 2001—04), Girl Scouts of Am. (life; troop leader 1962—83), Toastmasters Internat. (Toastmaster of the Yr. 1995), Alpha Kappa Alpha, Inc. (life; pres. 1978—82, Outstanding Woman in the Field of Nutrition). Home: 2298 S Kenton Way Aurora CO 80014 Office: Denver Food Assistance Program 80 South Santa Fe Dr Denver CO 80223 Office Fax: (720) 944-3418. Business E-Mail: enolia.thomas@dhs.co.denver.co.us.

THOMAS, ESTHER MERLENE, elementary and adult education educator; b. San Diego, Oct. 16, 1945; d. Merton Alfred and Nellie Lida (Von Pilz) T. AA with honors, Grossmont Coll., 1966; BA with honors, San Diego State U., 1969; MA, U. Redlands, 1977. Cert. elem. and adult edn. tchr. Tchr. Cajon Valley Union Sch. Dist., El Cajon, 1969—; sci. fair coord. Flying Hills Sch. Tchr. Hopi and Navajo Native Americans, Ariz., Utah, 1964-74, Goose and Gander Nursery Sch., Lakeside, Calif., 1964-66; dir., supt. Bible and Sunday schs. various chs., Lakeside, 1961-87; mem. sci. com., math. coun. Cajon Valley Union Sch. Dist., 1990-91, libr. com., 1997-98. Author: Individualized Curriculum in the Affective Domain, co-author Campbell County, The Treasured Years, Legends of the Lakeside; songwriter: songs Never Trouble Trouble, Old Glory, Jesus Is Our Lord, Daniel's Prayer, There Lay Jesus, God's Hands, Washing Machine Charlie, Playmates, The Kid in the Hall, Spring Time on the Blue Ridge, Christ's DNA, If You Need Me, Chances, Blame, The Star of Bethlehem, Where the Eagle Flies, Born to Win, Happy Birthday Dear Jesus, Christmas Lights, Walk the Line, You Don't Know What Repentance Is, I'm Asking You, Clear the Path Lord, Aqua Forte, In the Volume of the Book, Home is Where the Heart Is, You Don't Even Know Who I Am, No Place to Cry, To Walk With God, Ixnay, If You Never Loved Me, for Columbine Records Corp., Life of A Single Woman, Take This Pain Away, We Can Keep In Touch, Let Me Know; contbr. articles to profl. jours., newspapers, chpts. to books. Tem. U.S. Senatorial Club, Washington, 1984—, Conservative Caucus, Inc., Washington, 1988—, Ronald Reagan Presdl. Found., Ronald Reagan Rep. Ctr., 1988, Rep. Presdl. Citizen's Adv. Commn., 1989—, Rep. Platform Planning Com., Calif., 1992, at-large del. representing dist. #45, Lakeside, Calif., 1992, 1995—, Am. Security Coun., Washington, 1994, Congressman Hunter's Off Road Adv. Coun., El Cajon, Calif., 1994, Century Club, San Diego Rep. Century Club, 1995; mem. health articulation com. project AIDS, Cajon Valley Union Sch. Dist., 1988—, Recruit Depot Hist. Mus., San Diego, 1989, Citizen's Drug Free Am., Calif., 1989—, The Heritage Found., 1988—; charter mem. Marine Corps Mus.; mem. Lakeside Centennial Com., 1985-86; hon. mem. Rep. Presdl. Task Force, Washington, 1986; del. Calif. Rep. Senatorial Mid-Term Conv., Washington, 1994; mus. curator Lakeside Hist. Soc., 1992-93; mem. Rep. Nat. Com., Washingotn, 2003 Recipient Outstanding Svc. award PTA, 1972-74, Outstanding Tchr. award KYXY Radio, San Diego, 1999; recognized for various contbns. Commdg. Post Gen., San Diego Bd. Edn., 1989. Mem. NRA, Tchrs. Assn., Calif. Tchrs. Assn., Cajon Valley Educators Assn. (faculty advisor, rep. 1980-82, 84-86, 87-88), Nat. Trust for Hist. Preservation, Christian Bus. and Profl. Women, Trust for Hist. Preservation, Ridgecrest Golden Terrace Park Assn. (pres. 1998-99), Nashville Songwriters Assn., Capitol Hill Women's Club, Am. Ctr. for Law and Justice, Internat. Christian Women's Club (Christian amb. to Taiwan, Korea, 1974), Paul Revere Soc. Republican. Avocations: travel, vocal music, piano, guitar. Home: 13594 Hwy 8 # 3 Lakeside CA 92040-5235 Office: Flying Hills Elem Sch 1251 Finch St El Cajon CA 92020-1433

THOMAS, ETHEL COLVIN NICHOLS (MRS. LEWIS VICTOR THOMAS), counselor, educator; b. Cranston, R.I., Mar. 31, 1913; d. Charles Russell and Mabel Maria (Colvin) Nichols; Ph.B., Pembroke Coll. in Brown U., 1934; M.A., Brown U., 1938; Ed.D., Rutgers U., 1979; m. Lewis Victor Thomas, July 26, 1945 (dec. Oct. 1965); 1 child, Glenn Nichols. Tchr. English, Cranston High Sch., 1934-39; social dir. and adviser to freshmen, Fox Hall, Boston U., 1939-40; instr. to asst. prof. English Am. Coll. for Girls, Istanbul, Turkey, 1940-44; dean freshman, dir. admission Women's Coll. of Middlebury, Vt., 1944-45; tchr. English, Robert Coll., Istanbul, 1945-46; instr. English, Rider Coll., Trenton, N.J., 1950-51; tchr. English, Princeton (N.J.) High Sch., 1951-61, counselor, 1960-62, 72-83, coll. counselor, 1962-72, sr. peer counselor, 1986—. Mem. NEA, AAUW, Nat. Assn. Women Deans Adminstrs. and Counselors, Am. Assn. Counseling and Devel., Bus. and Profl. Women's Club (named Woman of Yr., Princeton chpt. 1977), Met. Mus. Art, Phi Delta Kappa, Kappa Delta Pi. Presbyn. Clubs: Brown University (N.Y.C.); Nassau.

THOMAS, FAYE EVELYN J. elementary and secondary school educator; b. Summerfield, La., Aug. 3, 1933; d. Reginald Felton and Atlee (Hunter) Johnson; m. Archie Taylor Thomas, Sept. 8, 1960; 1 child, Dwayne Andre. BA, So. U., 1954; student, Tuskegee Inst., 1958, student, 1969, U. Detroit, 1961, student, 1962, student, 1963, Ctrl. Mich. U., 1965; MS, U. Ctrl. Ark., 1971, Cleve. State U., 1979. Tchr. Cullen (La.) Elem. Sch., 1957; tchr. English and social studies Charles Brown H.S., Springhill, La., 1957—70; tchr. English, Upward Bound Program, Grambling State U., 1968; tchr. English, Springhill H.S., 1970; elem. intermediate tchr. Riveredge Elem. Sch., Berea, Ohio, 1971—93; tchr. 7th grade English, Ford Mid. Sch., 1993—94. Tchr. asst. elem. coun. curriculum and instrn. Berea Sch. Dist., 1984—85. Author: When the Time Is Right, Move On, A Journey to the Mountain Top. Grantee, EDPA, 1970—71, Internat. Paper Found., 1958, 1960, NDEA, 1965; scholar Martha Holden Jennings scholar, 1984—85. Mem.: NEA, Assn. Supervision and Curriculum Devel., N.E. Ohio Tchrs. Assn., Berea Edn. Assn., Ohio Edn. Assn., Ohio Motorists Assn., Charles Brown Soc. Orgn. (trustee 1984—), Black Caucus NEA, People United to Save Humanity, Toastmasters, Order Eastern Star. Democrat. Baptist. Home: 19353 Bagley Rd Cleveland OH 44130-3319

THOMAS, FRANCES MARGUERITE LAKE, retired elementary school educator; b. Detroit, July 27, 1939; d. F. Albert and Marguerite J. Lake; m. William Joseph Thomas, Feb. 10, 1973; stepchildren: Cynthia Thomas Van de Wetering, Karen Thomas Johnson. BS, Ctrl. Mich. U., 1961, tchg. cert., 1961. Lang. devel. specialist cert. Calif. Tchr. Meadowbrook Elem. Sch., Rochester, Mich., 1961-63, Chambers Elem. Sch., Kingston, N.Y., 1963-64, Ridgecrest Elem. Sch., Huntsville, Ala., 1964-65; tchr. Dept. Def.-Overseas Dependent Schs. Baumholder (Germany) Elem., 1965-66, Tyler Primary Naha, Naha AFB, Okinawa, Japan, 1966-68; tchr. Cassell Elem. Sch., Alum Rock Union Sch. Dist., San Jose, Calif., 1968-97; ret., 1997. Mem.: AAUW (v.p. membership 1998—2001, v.p. edn. found. 2002—), Rep. Women, Delta Kappa Gamma. Avocations: gardening, quilting, photography. Home: 13495 Bass Trl Grass Valley CA 95945-9506

THOMAS, HAZEL BEATRICE, state official; b. Franklin, Tenn. d. William Henry Fuller and Mattie Betty (Covington) Fuller Young; m. Charles B. Thomas (dec. 1969); children; Charles Bradford Jr., Deborah Carlotta (dec.). BA, Fisk U., 1946; MA, Tenn. State U., 1972. Cert. elem. and secondary tchr., Tenn. Tchr. elem. Met.-Nashville Sch., 1954-87; rsch. assoc. Johns Hopkins U., Balt., 1978-79, Marquette U., Milw., 1979-86; exec. asst. to commr. edn. Tenn. Dept. Edn., Nashville, 1987—. Cons. Peer Mediated Learning System, Nashville, 1980-82; instr. Met. Sch. Tchr. Ctr., Nasvhville, 1985-87; mem. tech. assistance team for high sch. that work, So. Regional Edn. Bd., 1998-99; nat. disseminator student team learning rsch. project, Johns Hopkins U., 1978-1979. Author training modules Substitute Teaching, Tchr. Aides. Pres. Davidson County Dem. Women, Nashville, 1985-87; v.p. Tenn. Fedn. Dem. Women, 1989-91, pres., 2001—; pres. elect Nashville Women's Polit. Caucus, 1991—; pres. Tenn. Women's Polit. Caucus, 1994-95; mem. adminstrv. com. of bd. Nat. Women's Polit. Caucus, 1993-95, v.p., 1995—, v.p. edn. and tng., 2001—; mem. Tenn. Leadership, Inc., 1992—; spkr., polit. trainer US Info. Agy., Nairobi, Kenya, 1997; mem. exec. bd. Citizen's Com. for Ann. Gov.'s Prayer Breakfast, 1992—; mem. exec. com. Tenn. Dem. Party, 2001—; chmn. edn. com. Bellevue C. of C.; pres. Tenn. Fedn. Dem. Women, 2001-03; v.p. Nat. Fedn. Dem. Women, 2002—; mem. pub. edn. and govt. com. Metro. Govt. Nashville, Tenn., 2002-03. Recipient Svc. to Edn. and Teaching Profession award Nat. Coun. Negro Women, 1988; Nat. Def. Edn. Act scholar, 1965, 67. Mem. Am. Bus. Womens Assn. (charter), Tenn. Edn. Assn. (pres. dept. classroom tchr. 1974-75, state dept. affiliate, pres. 1988-Ed. c90), Bellevue C. of C. (bd. govs. 1990-91, edn. chair 2002-03), Assn. Classroom Tchr. (pres. S.E. region 1975-76), Met. Nashville Edn. Assn. (exec. bd. 1971-77), Bellevue Sertoma Club (life, pres. 1990-91), Nat. Women's Polit. Caucus (v.p. 1995—), Nat. Assn. Dem. Women (v.p., 2003-05, named Woman of Distinction for Tenn., 2002, 03), Nat. Fedn. Dem. Women (v.p. 2003). Democrat. Baptist. Avocations: reading, bridge. Office: Tenn Dept Edn Andrew Johnson Tower 710 James Robertson Pkwy Nashville TN 37243-1219 E-mail: hthomas@mail.state.tn.us.

THOMAS, JACQUELYN MAY, librarian; b. Mechanicsburg, Pa., Jan. 26, 1932; d. William John and Gladys Elizabeth (Warren) Harvey; m. David Edward Thomas, Aug. 28, 1954; children: Lesley J., Courtenay J., Hilary A. BA summa cum laude, Gettysburg Coll., 1954; student, U. N.C., 1969; MEd, U. N.H., 1971. Libr. Phillips Exeter Acad., Exeter, N.H., 1971-77, acad. libr., 1977—. Chair governing bd. Child Care Ctr., 1987-91; chair Com. to Enhance Status of Women, Exeter, 1981-84; chair Loewenstein Com., Exeter, 1982—; pres. Cum Laude Soc., Exeter, 1984-86; James H. Ottaway Jr. prof., 1990—; mem. bldg. com. Exeter Pub. Libr., 1986-88; chair No. New Eng., Coun. for Women in Ind. Schs., 1985-87; chmn. Lamont Poetry Program, Exeter, 1984-86. Editor: The Design of the Library: A Guide to Sources of Information, 1981, Rarities of Our Time: The Special Collections of the Phillips Exeter Academy Library; pub.: Memorial Minutes, Phillips Exeter Academy, 1936-2002. Libr. trustee, treas. Exeter Day Sch., 1965-69; bd. Exeter Hosp. Vols., 1954-59; mem. Exeter Hosp. Corp., 1978—; bd. dirs. Greater Portsmouth Cmty. Found., 1990—; active AAC&U, On Campus with Women, Wellesley Coll. Ctr. for Rsch. on Women; mem. People to People Amb. Program, sch. and youth svcs. libr. del. to People's Rep. China, 1998. Grantee N.H. Coun. for Humanities, 1981-82, NEH, 1982; recipient Lillian Radford trust award, 1989. Mem. ALA, Internat. Assn. Sch. Librs., New Eng. Libr. Assn., N.J., Ednl. Media Assn., New Eng. Assn. Ind. Sch. Librs., Am. Assn. Sch. Librs. (chmn. non-pub. sch. sect.), Phi Beta Kappa. Home: 17 Eagle Dr Newmarket NH 03857 Office: Class of 1945 Libr Phillips Exeter Acad 20 Main St Exeter NH 03833-2460 Fax: 603-777-4389. E-mail: jthomas@exeter.edu.

THOMAS, JAMES BERT, JR., government official; b. Tallahassee, Mar. 16, 1935; s. James Bert and Stella E. (Lewis) T.; m. Sharon Mae Kelly, June 16, 1962; children: James Bert III, Mary Elizabeth, John Christopher. BS, Fla. State U., 1957. C.P.A., Fla. Spl. auditor Office State Comptroller, Jacksonville, Fla., 1958; jr. auditor J.D.A. Holley & Co., C.P.A.'s, Tallahassee, 1959; sr. auditor Office of the State Auditor, Tallahassee, 1959-60; trainee, audit dir. HUD audit div., Washington, 1960-71; asst. dir. Bur. Accounts ICC, Washington, 1972-75, dir. Bur. Accounts, 1977-80; inspector gen. U.S. Dept. HUD, Washington, 1975-77, U.S. Dept. Edn., Washington, 1980-95; dir. auditing Office of the Gov., State of Fla., Tallahassee, 1995—. Mem. Pres.'s Coun. Integrity and Efficiency, chmn. audit stds. subcom., 1984-95, chmn. audit com., 1989-90. Mem. AICPA (strategic planning com. 1987-90, chmn. govt. auditing standards adv. coun. 1991—), Inst. Internal Auditors (trustee Rsch. Found. 1991-92), Assn. Govt. Accts. (chmn. fin. mgmt. standards bd. 1985-86), Accts. Roundtable. Roman Catholic. Home: 4737 Tory Sound Ln Unit 601 Tallahassee FL 32309-2266 Office: Exec Office of Governor Rm 2107 The Capitol Tallahassee FL 32399-0001

THOMAS, JAMES PATRICK, special education educator; b. Chgo., Sept. 24, 1946; s. Jacque Anthony and Dorothy Lucille (Brown) T.; m. Cathy E. Hanks, Sept. 29, 1979 (div. Aug. 1990); 1 child, Nicholas Jacque. BA in History and Polit. Sci., Drake U., 1973; MS in Pub. Adminstrn., Troy State U., 1983; MS in Spl. Edn., cert. advanced grad. studies, Johns Hopkins U., 1994. cert. spl. educator. Commd. 2nd lt. USAF, 1973, advanced through grades to maj., 1985; missile launch officer, instr., crew comdr., contr. 91st Strategic Missile Wing, Minot, N.D., 1974-78; exec. officer, asst. ops. officer, resource advisor 6916th Electronic Security Squadron, Hellenikon Air Base, Greece, 1978-81; chief programs br. 6940th Electronic Security Wing, Ft. Meade, Md., 1981-82; program mgr. USAF Ops. Security Hq USAF/XOEO Directorate of Electronic Combat, Washington, 1982-85; intelligence collection activities mgr./chief Hdqrs. U.S. European Command, Stuttgart, Germany, 1986-88; signals intelligence planning staff officer Nat. Security Agy., Ft. Meade, 1988-90; cons. spl. edn. Balt., 1991—. Adj. faculty mem. Catonsville (Md.) C.C., 1991—; spl. educator Howard County Sch. System, Columbia, 1992-94, Boonsborro (Md.) Middle Sch., 1994-96, Hiatt Mid. Sch., Des Moines, 1996-98, Johnston (Iowa) Mid. Sch., 1998-99, Johnston High Sch., 1999-2000, Variety Sch., Las Vegas, Nev., 2000—. Author: (pamphlet) Your Rights to Legal Advice, 1994; co-author: The Outcome of a Services Evaluation for Families of Vietnam Vets. with Children with Disabilities in the Balt. Met. Area, 1995. Pres. Cath. Men Parish Athens, Greece, 1979—81, 1975—78. With USN, 1964—73. Decorated Purple Heart, 2 Def. Meritorious Svc.

medals, Meritorious Svc. medals, Air Force Commendation medal, Air medal, Air Force Achievement medal, Navy Combat Action Ribbon, Vietnam Gallantry Cross. Mem.: KC, VFW (life), Swiftboat Sailors Assn. Inc. (pres. 1995—2002), Am. Legion China Post 1, Disabled Am. Vets. (life), Air Force Assn. (life), Ret. Officers Assn. (life), Mil. Order Purple Heart (life), Navy League (life), Vets. Vietnam War (life), Phoenix Soc., Soaring Assn. Am., Phi Delta Gamma. Roman Catholic. Avocations: pilot of sailplanes, sailing, snorkeling, golf, running, photography. Home: 1929 High Mesa Dr Henderson NV 89012-6182

THOMAS, JANEY SUE, elementary school principal; b. Clarksville, Tenn., Feb. 10, 1949; d. James Ernest and Ethel Mae (Evans) Kirkland; m. Tony Lee Thomas, Oct. 9, 1965; children: Jeff, Kelli. BS in Elem. Edn., Austin Peay State U., 1979, MA in Elem. Edn. Adminstrn., 1982, postgrad., 1987-89. Tchr. Charlotte (Tenn.) Jr. High Sch., 1979-86; prin. Vanleer (Tenn.) Elem. Sch., 1986-91, Oakmont Elem. Sch., Dickson, Tenn., 1991—. Ednl. rep. Concerned Citizens for Edn., Dickson County, 1988; mem. com. United Way Med. Tenn., Dickson County, 1990-91, bd. dirs., 1992-93. Recipient Nat. Sch. of Recognition award U.S. Dept. Edn., 1990. Mem. NAESP (Excellence in Edn. award 1989-90), Tenn. Assn. Elem. Sch. Prins. (Nat. Exemplary Sch. award 1989-90), Dickson County Edn. Assn. (pres. 1989-90). Baptist. Avocations: reading, traveling, shopping. Home: 226 Druid Hills Dr Dickson TN 37055-3331 Office: Oakmont Elem Sch 630 Highway 46 S Dickson TN 37055-2552

THOMAS, JEAN-JACQUES ROBERT, Romance languages educator; b. Mirecourt, Vosges, France, Jan. 20, 1948; s. Jean-Robert and Yvonne Marie-Rose (Ladner) T.; m. Mary Lorene Hammial, Aug. 21, 1976; children: Dominick, Robert. Lic., U. Lille, France, 1968, M, 1969; diplome in lang. Orientales, PhD, U. Paris, France, 1972. Teaching asst. U. Paris, 1969-71, asst. researcher, 1971-72; lectr. U. Mich., 1972-75; asst. prof. Columbia U., N.Y.C., 1975-81; assoc. prof. Duke U., Durham, N.C., 1981-87, prof., 1989—, chmn. romance studies, 1989-94; pres. Educo, Paris, 1988-89, 95-96; dir. Institute French Studies U. Calif., Santa Barbara, 1991—. Bd. dirs. Studies in Twenty-Century Lit., Lincoln, Nebr., Palmes Académiques, 1994. Author: Lire Leiris, 1972, La Langue la Poésie, 1987, La Langue Volée, 1988; co-author: Poétique Générative, 1978, Poética Generativa, 1983, 89; translator:Sémiotique de la Poésie, 1983; assoc. editor: Sub-Stance, 1975—, Poetics Today, 1980—. Grantee Rackham Found., 1973, IBM, 1984, Sloan Found., 1985. Mem. MLA (chmn. divsn. 1980-81, 86-87, 93-95), N.E. MLA (chmn. sect. 1982-83), Semiotic Soc. Am. Home: 26 Porchlight Ct Durham NC 27707-2442 Office: Duke U Dept Romance Studies Durham NC 27706

THOMAS, JOAB LANGSTON, retired university president, biology educator; b. Holt, Ala., Feb. 14, 1933; s. Ralph Cage and Chamintney Elizabeth (Stovall) Thomas; m. Marly A. Dukes, Dec. 22, 1954; children: Catherine, David, Jennifer, Frances. AB, Harvard U., 1955, MA, 1957, PhD, 1959; DSc (hon.), U. Ala., 1981; LLD (hon.), Stillman Coll., 1987; LHD (hon.), Tri-State U., 1994; LHD (hon.), N.C. State U., 1998. Cytotaxonomist Arnold Aboretum, Harvard, 1959—61; prof. biology U. Ala., University, 1966—76, 1988—91, asst. dean Coll. Arts and Scis., 1964—65, 1969, dean for student devel., 1969—74, v.p., 1974—76, dir. Herbarium, 1961—76, dir. Arboretum, 1964—69, pres. Tuscaloosa, 1981—88; chancellor N.C. State U., Raleigh, 1976—81; pres. Pa. State U., University Park, 1990—95, pres. emeritus, 1995. Bd. dirs. Mellon Corp.; intern acad. adminstrn. Am. Coun. on Edn., 1971. Author: A Monographic Study of the Cyrillaceae, 1960, Wildflowers of Alabama and Adjoining States, 1973, The Rising South, 1976, Poisonous Plants and Venomous Animals of Alabama and Adjoining States, 1990. Bd. dirs. Internat. Potato Ctr., 1977—83, chmn., 1982—83; bd. dirs. Internat. Svc. for Nat. Agrl. Rsch., 1985—91. Named Citizen of Yr., City of Tuscaloosa, 1987; recipient Ala. Acad. Honor, 1983, Palmer Mus. Art medal, Coll. Pres.'s award, All-Am. Football Found., 1997, Spl. Recognition award, Assn. for Continuing Higher Edn., 1998. Mem.: Golden Key, Phi Kappa Phi, Omicron Delta Kappa (Laurel Crowned Circle award 2001), Sigma Xi, Phi Beta Kappa. Office: Univ Ala 413 Sci Collections Bldg Tuscaloosa AL 35487-0001 E-mail: jlthomas@dbtech.net.

THOMAS, JOHN EDWIN, retired academic administrator; b. Fort Worth, Tex., Apr. 23, 1931; s. John L. and Dorothy F. T.; m. Janice Paula Winzinek, Jan. 29, 1967; children— John L., Christa T., Scott A., Brandon F. BSEE, U. Kans., 1953; JD, U. Mo., Kansas City, 1961; MS, Fla. State U., 1965, DBA, 1970. With Wagner Electric Corp., St. Louis, 1955-63, mgr. elec. apparatus div. Atlanta, 1961-63; with NASA, Cape Kennedy, Fla., 1963-70, chief requirements and resources office, dir. tech. support, 1966-70; prof., head gen. bus. dept. East Tex. State U., 1970-72; dean (Coll. Scis. and Tech.), 1972-74; vice chancellor for acad. affairs Appalachian State U., Boone, N.C., 1974-79, chancellor, 1979-93; ret. N.C. Utilities Commn., Raleigh, 1993; spl. advisor for sci., tech. & higher edn. Gov. State of N.C., Raleigh, 1994, ret., 1994. Chair N.C. Utilities Commn., 1993-94; spl. advisor to Gov. of State of N.C. on sci./tech. and higher edn., 1994; edn./comm. cons. and chancellor emeritus, Appalachian State U., 1994—. Mem. N.C. Agy. for Pub. Telecommunications. Served with USN, 1949-50, USMC, 1953-55. NDEA fellow, 1968 Mem. Fed. Bar Assn., Soc. Advancement Mgmt., So. Mgmt. Assn., Phi Delta Kappa, Pi Sigma Epsilon, Delta Gamma Sigma., Phi Kappa Phi Clubs: Kiwanis. Methodist. Home: 342 Wildwood Run Daisy Ridge Banner Elk NC 28604

THOMAS, JONATHAN WAYNE, engineering educator; b. Henderson, Ky., Dec. 12, 1950; s. Wayne and Mary (Browning) T.; m. Rhonda G. Thomas, Sept. 20, 1975; children: Rachel, Jarod. AAS, Rend Lake Jr. Coll., 1971; BS, Ind. State U., 1973, MSS, 1974. Chmn. transp. tech. Vocat. Tech. Coll., Evansville, Ind., 1977-80, chmn. tech. divsn., 1980-83, dir. instrn. Sellersburg, Ind., 1983—, exec. dean, 1986-95, Ivy Tech. State Coll., Madison, Ind., 1995—2001; pres. Prysm Consulting Svcs., Nashville, 2001—. Contbr. articles to profl. jours. Mem. Am. Tech. Edn. Assn., Soc. Automotive Engrs., Soc. Human Resource Mgmt., Ind. Vocat. Assn., Ind. Vocat. Post-Secondary Edn. Assn. (v.p. 1984—), Epsilon Pi Tau. Avocations: fishing, camping, flying, spelunking, dune buggies. Home: 424 Rembrandt Dr Old Hickory TN 37138-1719 E-mail: jthomas@vol.com.

THOMAS, JUDITH LYNN, retired secondary school educator; b. Grand Rapids, Mich., July 27, 1940; d. L. Ford and Jenniemae (Lull) Stephens; m. Mac Barton Thomas, June 16, 1962; children: Lisa Rae, James Ian. AA, Grand Rapids Jr. Coll., 1960; BA, Western Mich. U., 1962; postgrad., Mich. State U., 1963-64, Western Mich. U., 1963-64, 90-94. Cert. tchr., Mich. Tchr. jr. high Lakeshore Pub. Schs., Stevensville, Mich., 1962-65, Rockford (Mich.) Pub. Schs., 1965-73; adult edn. instr. Rockford (Mich.) Community Edn., 1974-79, Northview Community Edn., Grand Rapids, Mich., 1973-78; substitute tchr. Centerville (Ohio) Schs., 1978-81, East China Schs., Marine City, Mich., 1981-86; alternative tchr. Algonac Alternative Learning Ctr., Marine City, Mich., 1983-85; tchr. Howell (Mich.) Adult Edn., 1987-88; alternative tchr. Enterprise High Sch., Fowlerville, Mich., 1988-95; tchr. Lowell Jr. H.S., 1996; tchr., acad. adminstr. Creative Techs. Charter Acad., Cedar Springs, Mich., 1998—2001, ret., 2001—. Bd. dirs. Single Parents Program, Howell, 1989-92. Vol. Grand Rapids Symphony, 1960-62; officer, worthy matron Order of the Eastern Star, Rockford, 1976-77. Recipient Tchr. Mini-Grant, State of Mich., 1989. Mem. NEA, Mich. Edn. Assn., Mich. Coun. Tchrs. English, Mich. Reading Assn., Mich. Secondary Reading Interests, Mich. Alternative Edn. Assn. (spring conf. planning com. 1991, 93), Mich. Assn. of Am. Avocations: reading, family, camping, hiking, boating, swimming, travel, sewing. Home: 6851 12 Mile Rd NE Rockford MI 49341-9706 Office: Creative Techs Schs Charter Acad 350 Pine St Cedar Springs MI 49319-8680

THOMAS, KATHERINE CAROL, special education educator; b. Alice, Tex., June 15, 1943; d. Charles Anthony Sr. and elvira (Garcia) Rogers; m. Richard Harold Jr. Thomas, Aug. 9, 1980; 1 child, Rhonda Crystal. BS in Edn., Tex. A&I U., 1965; MS in Edn., Anticoch U., 1975. Tchr. Salazar Elem. Sch., Alice, Tex., 1965-73; supr. Alice Indetification and Referral System, 1975-78; supr. bilingual edn. Alice (Tex.) Sch. Dist., 1978-80, tchr., supr. migrant edn., 1980-83, tchr. spl. edn., 1983—. Sec.-treas. Slazar PTA, 1965-75; mem. com. Water Authority Commn., Alice, 1981. Mem. Tex. Tchrs. Assn., NEA, Am. Tchrs. Prins. Assn., Childhood Edn. Assn. (treas. 1968-74), AAUP, Spl. Edn. Assn. Democratic. Roman Catholic. Home: PO Box 3132 Alice TX 78333-3132

THOMAS, LARRY WAYNE, secondary school educator; b. Kansas City, Mo., Mar. 25, 1936; s. Carl K. and Violette V. (Leonard) T.; m. Charlotte S. Hamilton, July 25, 1959; children: Mark W., Lori Sue, Lisa Jane. BS in Edn., Cen. Mo. State U., 1958; MA in Am. History, U. Mo., Kansas City, 1968; postgrad., Vanderbilt U., 1964, U. Mo., Kansas City, 1970-90. Cert. social studies tchr., Mo. Tchr. Pattonville Sch. Dist., Bridgeton, Mo., 1959-64; part-time tchr. Penn Valley Community Coll., Kansas City, 1968-70; tchr. social studies Kansas City Sch. Dist., 1964—. Tchr. liaison Law Sch., U. Mo.-Kansas City, 1987—, Kansas City Bar (Young Lawyers), 1987—, Metro. Bar (Young Lawyers), Jackson County Bar Assn., 1991—; Mo. rep. Law and Constl. Democracy Inst., Vanderbilt U., summer 1964; del. Mo. Bar Assn. tchr. conv., 1978, 81, 87, 92; dept., law related resource tchr., 1986—; cp-presenter Mo. Bar Assn. tchrs. meeting, 1993; steering com. Kansas City Met. Bar Assn. Summer Intern program, 1993. N.E. coord. Nat. Youth Svcs. Rally, 1993. Recipient Kansas City Pub. Svc. award The Lawyers Assn. (Young Lawyers sect.), 1991. Mem. ABA (youth edn.), Mo. Bar Assn. (E.A. Richter Group award for citizenship edn. 1994), Nat. Coun. Social Studies, Mo. Hist. Soc., Constl. Rights Found., Mo. Coun. Social Studies. Republican. Baptist. Avocations: golf, travel, reading. Home: 11313 Cleveland Ave Kansas City MO 64137-2332 Office: NE Law & Pub Svc Magnet Sch 415 Van Brunt Blvd Kansas City MO 64124-2130

THOMAS, LAWRENCE ELDON, mathematics educator; b. Columbus, Ohio, Mar. 15, 1942; s. Bertram D. and Glorian (Butler) T.; m. Rebecca Nolan, June 13, 1970; children: David Nolan, Kathleen Rebecca. BS, U. Mich., 1964; PhD, Yale U., 1970. Rsch. asst. math. dept. Swiss Fed. Inst. Tech., Zurich, 1970-72; rsch. asst. physics dept. U. Geneva, 1972-74; asst. prof. math. U. Va., Charlottesville, 1974-76, assoc. prof., 1976-82, prof., 1982—, chmn. dept., 1989-93. Contbr. articles on theory of Schrodinger operators, statis. mechanics and stochastic processes to profl. jours. Mem. Am. Math. Soc., Am. Physics Soc., Internat. Nat. Math. Physics, Phi Beta Kappa. Avocations: sailing, tennis. Home: 2308 Glenn Ct Charlottesville VA 22901-2913 Office: U Va Dept Math Cabell Dr Charlottesville VA 22903

THOMAS, LEONA MARLENE, health information educator; b. Rock Springs, Wyo., Jan. 15, 1933; d. Leonard H. and Opal (Wright) Francis; children: Peter, Paul, Patrick, Alexis. BA, Govs. State U., 1982, MHS, 1986; cert. med. records adminstrn., U. Colo., 1954. Staff assoc. Am. Med. Records Assn., Chgo., 1972-77, asst. editor, 1979-81; statistician Westlake Hosp., Melrose Park, Ill., 1982-84; asst. prof. Chgo. State U., 1984—, acting dir. health info. adminstrn. program, 1991-92; acting dir. health info. Internat. Coll., Naples, Fla., 1994; dir. health info. adminstrn. program Chgo. State U., 1994—. Mem. adv. com. Wellness Ctr., mem. adv. com. occupl. therapy program Chgo. State U. Mem. Assembly on Edn., Am. Health Info. Mgmt. Assn., APHA, Chgo. and Vicinity Med. Records Assn., Ill. Assn. Allied Health Profls., Gov.'s State Alumni Assn. Democrat. Methodist. Home: 6340 Americana Dr Apt 1101 Willowbrook IL 60527 Office: Chgo State U Coll Health Scis 95th at King Dr Chicago IL 60628

THOMAS, LINDSEY KAY, JR., research ecology biologist, educator, consultant; b. Salt Lake City, Apr. 16, 1931; s. Lindsey Kay and Naomi Lurie (Biesinger) T.; m. Nancy Ruth Van Dyke, Aug. 24, 1956; children: Elizabeth Nan Thomas Cardinale, David Lindsey, Wayne Hal, Dorothy Ann Thomas Brown. BS, Utah State Agrl. Coll., 1953; MS, Brigham Young U., 1958; PhD, Duke U., 1974. Park naturalist Nat. Capital Pks., Nat. Pk. Svc., Washington, 1957—62, pk. naturalist and rschr. Region 6, 1962—63, rsch. pk. naturalist Nat. Capital Region, 1963—66; rsch. biologist S.E. Temperate Forest Pk. Areas, Washington, 1966, Durham, NC, 1966—67, Great Falls, Md., 1967—71, Nat. Capital Pks., Great Falls, 1971—74, Nat. Capital Region, Triangle, Va., 1974—93, Washington, 1985—93, Nat. Biol. Svc., Washington, Triangle, 1993—96; resource mgmt. specialist Balt.-Washington Pkwy., Greenbelt, Md., 1996, Nat. Capital Parks-East, 1996—98; rsch. ecologist emeritus and cons. Nat. Capital Region, Nat. Park Svc., 1998—. Bd. dirs. Prince William County (Va.) Svc. Authority, 1996—; adj. prof. George Mason U., Fairfax, Va., 1988—, George Washington U., Washington, 1992-98; instr. Dept. Agr. Grad. Sch., 1964-66; aquatic ecol. cons. Fairfax County (Va.) Fedn. Citizens Assns., 1970-71; guest lectr. Washington Tech. Inst. (now U. D.C.), 1976. Contbr. articles to profl. jours. Wildlife mgmt. cons. Girl Scouts Am., Loudoun County, Va., 1958; asst. scoutmaster, scoutmaster, merit badges counselor Boy Scouts Am., 1958—, Scouters Tng. award, 1961. Recipient incentive awards Nat. Park Svc., 1962, Superior Performance award, 1989; rsch. grantee Washington Biologists' Field Club, 1977, 82. Mem.: AAAS, Nat. Trust for Historic Preservation, Washington Biologists' Field Club, So. Appalachian Bot. Soc., Soc. for Early Hist. Archaeology, The Nature Conservancy, George Wright Soc., Ecol. Soc. Am., Bot. Soc. Washington, Sigma Xi. Mem. Lds Ch. Home: 13854 Delaney Rd Woodbridge VA 22193-4654 Office: Balt-Washingtn Pky 6565 Greenbelt Rd Greenbelt MD 20770-3207 also: Prince William Forest Park 18100 Park Hdqs Rd Triangle VA 22172

THOMAS, LISA FRANCINE, secondary school educator, assistant principal; b. New Haven, Feb. 15, 1966; d. Fred and Elaine Carolyn (Webb) McCauley; married, Apr. 22, 2001. AA, Mt. Sacred Heart Coll., Hamden, Conn., 1988; BA in History, So. Conn. State U., 1989, MS in History, 1992, 6th yr. cert. advanced grad. studies, 1998. Cert. secondary edn. grades 7-12, Conn. Tchr. St. Lawrence Sch., West Haven, Conn., 1989-95, Wilbur Cross H.S., New Haven, 1996-2001; asst. prin. East Lyme (Conn.) H.S., 2001—. Adj. prof. So. Conn. State U., New Haven, 1993-2001. Vol. Conn. Spl. Olympics, New Haven, 1989—; dist. coord. Nat. History Day, Conn. Hist. Soc., Hartford, 1993-98. Recipient cert. for dedicated svcs. and encouragement of student participation Conn. Hist. Soc., Hartford, 1992, cert. appreciation Jr. Achievement, Wallingford, Conn., 1992; named Outstanding Tchr. of Merit Conn. Hist. Soc., 1997, Best Beginning Educator Support Tchr., 2000. Mem. AAUP, ASCD, Am. Assn. Sch. Adminstrs., Nat. Cath. Edn. Assn., Conn. Coun. for the Social Studies, Conn. and New Haven Hist. Socs., Conn. Geographic Alliance, Conn. Humanities Coun. Congregationalist. Avocations: musician, reading. Home: 81 Main St # 47 Branford CT 06405 E-mail: lisa.thomas@eastlymeschools.org.

THOMAS, LLOYD BREWSTER, economics educator; b. Columbia, Mo., Oct. 22, 1941; s. Lloyd B. and Marianne (Moon) T.; m. Sally Leach, Aug. 11, 1963; 1 child, Elizabeth. AB, U. Mo., 1963, AM, 1964; PhD, Northwestern U., 1970. Instr. Northwestern U., Evanston, Ill., 1966-68; asst. prof. econs. Kan. State U., Manhattan, 1968-72, assoc. prof., 1974-81, prof., 1983—; asst. prof. Fla. State U., Tallahassee, 1973-74. Vis. prof. U. Calif., Berkeley, 1981-82, U. Del., 1993, U. Ind., Bloomington, 1997-98, Adelaide U., 2002; prof., chair dept. econs. U. Idaho, 1989. Author: Money, Banking and Economic Activity, 3d edit., 1986, Principles of Economics, 2d edit, 1993, Principles of Macroeconomics, 2d edit,, 1993, Principles of Microeconomics, 2d edit, 1993, Money, Banking and Financial Markets, 1997; contbr. articles to profl. jours. Mem. Am. Econs. Assn., Midwest Econs. Assn., So. Econs. Assn., Western Econs. Assn., Phi Kappa Phi. Avocations: tennis, classical music. Home: 1501 N 10th St Manhattan KS 66502-4607 E-mail: lbt@ksu.edu.

THOMAS, MARCELLA ELAINE, elementary education educator; b. Blythe, Calif., July 20, 1946; d. Will H. and Carrie E. (Mack) Ector Sr.; m. George Walter Thomas, July 10, 1982; 1 child, Danielle Elaine. AA, Palo Verde Community Coll., 1966; BA, Calif. State U., L.A., 1970; MA, Azusa Pacific U., 1972; postgrad., U. Calif. at Riverside. Cert. tchr., Calif. Mentor tchr. 5th grade Palo Verde Unified Sch. Dist., Blythe, Calif. Named to Delta Kappa Gamma Internat. Soc. (past pres.); recipient Tchr. of Yr. award. Mem. Nat. Tchrs. Assn., Calif. Tchrs. Assn., Palo Verde Tchrs. Assn. Home: 331 Bristlecone Ave Blythe CA 92225-2415

THOMAS, MARGARET ANN, educational administrator, art educator; b. Waukesha, Wis., June 19, 1951; d. Melvin Michael and Elizabeth (Brewer) T.; m. Bruce Fiedler; 1 child, James. BA in Art Edn., Beloit Coll., 1974; MA in Art, U. Wis., Whitewater, 1981, MA in Ednl. Psychology, 1985; MS in Ednl. Adminstrn., U. Wis., 1995, PhD in Ednl. Adminstrn., Ednl. Psychology. Cert. K-12 art tchr., Wis., elem. and H.S. prin., curriculum dir. K-12, supt. Tchr. art Beloit (Wis.) Pub. Schs., 1974—; adj. prof. Beloit Coll., 1992—; prin. Mclenegan Elem. Sch., Beloit, 1999—2001, adminstr. grants, 2001—02, adminstr. acad. reporting sys., 2002—; adminstr. Synectics Mid. Charter Schs., 2003—. Muralist instr. Beloit Coll., summers, 1985-91, adj. prof., 1993—; adj. prof. Nat. Louis U., 1994—; adminstr. Charter Schs., 2003. Author: Effective Teachers; Effective Schools, 1989; contbr. articles to profl. jours. Bd. dirs. Wis.-Gate Found., 1985-87, Wis. Racquetball Assn., 1986-87, Wis. Future Problem Solving, 1986-87; pres. bd. dirs. YWCA, 1987-91; dir. Beloit and Vicinity Art Show, Beloit Coll., 1982-84, Rock Prairie Showcase Festival; founder Summer Explorers Beloit Coll. Mem. Wis. Coun. for Gifted and Talented (bd. dirs. 1984-87, v.p. 1985-86, pres. 1986-87). Home: 4421 Ruger Ave Janesville WI 53546-9780 E-mail: mathomas@sdb.k12.wi.us.

THOMAS, MARIANNE GREGORY, school psychologist; b. N.Y.C., Dec. 10, 1945; BS, U. Conn., 1985; MS, So. Conn. State U., 1987; cert. advanced studies, ednl. adminstrn., NYU, 1998. Cert. sch psychologist Conn, NY. Sch. psychology intern Greenwich (Conn.) Pub. Schs., 1986-87; sch. psychologist Hawthorne (N.Y.)-Cedar Knolls, U.F.S.D., 1987-88, Darien (Conn.) Pub. Schs., 1988—. Adj. instr. Coll. New Rochelle, 2002. Mem.: APA, NASP (cert), Conn Asn Sch Psychologists, Kappa Delta Pi, Phi Delta Kappa. Home: 154 Indian Rock Rd New Canaan CT 06840-3117

THOMAS, OUIDA POWER, music educator; b. Louisville, Miss., Nov. 25, 1939; d. Robert Alvin and Mavis (Simpson) Power; m. Charles Victor Thomas, Aug. 4, 1962; children: Karla Victoria, Sylvia Katharine Thomas White, Charles Gregory. BS in Bus. Edn. with highest honors, Miss. State U., Starkville, 1963; M Music Edn., Delta State U., 1993; postgrad., U. Memphis, 1996—. Nat. cert. tchr. of music. Ind. music tchr. piano and organ, Grenada, Miss., 1963—; classroom gen. music tchr. Kirk Acad., Grenada, 1977-87. Adjudicator auditions Federated Music Clubs, Oxford, Miss., 1990—. Accompanist musical prodns. Grenada Fine Arts Playhouse, 1979-81; organist, choirmaster All Saints' Episcopal Ch., Grenada, 1977—; mem. music and liturgy com. Episcopal Diocese of Miss., 1996-99. Mem. Am. Guild Organists, Nat. Guild Piano Tchrs. (chmn. local auditions 1977—, adjudicator auditions 1993—), Music Tchrs. Nat. Assn. (cert. in piano and organ), Miss. Music Tchrs. Assn. (cert. in piano and organ, exec. bd. 1993-94, state chair pre-coll. student activities 1995-96, chair state cert. 1999-2000, adjudicator auditions 1993—), Grenada Area Music Tchrs. Assn. (v.p. 1995—). Avocations: gardening, needlework. Home: 1985 Wooded Dr Grenada MS 38901-4073

THOMAS, PAMELA ADRIENNE, special education educator; b. St. Louis, Oct. 28, 1940; d. Charles Seraphin Fernandez and Adrienne Louise (O'Brien) Fernandez Reeg; divorced, 1977; m. Alvertis T. Thomas, July 22, 1981. BA in Spanish and EdS, Maryville U., 1962; Cert. EdS, U. Ky., 1966-67; MA in Edn., St. Louis U., 1974. Cert. learning disabilities, behavior disorders, educable mentally retarded, Spanish, Mo. Tchr. Pawnee Rock Kans. Sch., 1963-64; diagnostic tchr. Frankfort State Hosp. Sch., Ky., 1964-67; spl. edn. tchr. St. Louis City Pub. Schs., 1968-71, itinerant tchr., 1971-73, ednl. strategist, 1973-74, elem. level resource tchr., 1974-78, secondary resource tchr., dept. head, 1978—, head dept. spl. edn., 1978—, resource tchr., 1998—, dept. head, 1998; ret., 2000. Co-author: Sophomore English Resource for Credit Curriculum Handbook, 1991. Co-author: Teaching Foreign Language to Handicapped Secondary Students, 1990. Pres. Council for Exceptional Children, local chpt. #103, 1982-83, Mo. Division of Mentally Retarded, 1985-87. Mem. Alpha Delta Kappa (St. Louis chpt. pres. 1982-84). Avocations: traveling, reading, swimming, theatre, handicrafts. Home: 4534 Ohio Ave Saint Louis MO 63111-1324

THOMAS, PEARL ELIZABETH, English educator; b. N.Y.C., Feb. 22, 1928; d. Humphrey S. and Frances (Collins) T. BS, CCNY, 1948, MA, 1952; PhD, Columbia U., 1977; postgrad., Union Grad. Sch. Chmn. English dept. N.Y.C. secondary schs.; asst. prof. CUNY, N.Y.C., 1977-83; prin. A.P. Randolph High Sch.; adj. prof. U. Calif., Irvine, 1983—, L.A. Coll., 1988-91. Author: (series) Adventures in Literature, 1980-90, College Video on Native Son, 1991. Recipient awards for Contbn. to Edn. 1976-83. Mem. MLA, Am. Tchrs. English, Global Network in Edn. Address: 30676 Palos Verdes Dr E Rancho Palos Verdes CA 90275-6354

THOMAS, PETER CHARLES, psychologist, educator; b. Houston, Sept. 24, 1947; s. Stephen and Eileen S. (Steyn) T.; m. Beverly J. Call, Aug. 30, 1969; children: Jonathan, Stephen, Katherine. BA in Psychology, Emory U., 1969; MEd in Sch. Psychology, Ga. State U., 1970, PhD in Sch. Psychology, 1978. Instr. Ga. State U., Atlanta, 1970-72; cons. Ga. Dept. Edn., Atlanta, 1972-73; field coord. U.S. Office Edn.: Exemplary Racial Discrimation Project, N.C., 1974; psychologist Dekalb County Sch. System, Atlanta, 1973-82; pvt. practice Atlanta, 1982—. Cons. Decatur City Sch. Sys., 1982-86, Ga. Spl. Olympics Program, Atlanta, 1987, Fulton County Sch. Sys., 1984-87; mem. adv. bd. Village of St. Joseph, Gables Acad., 1981-94, AIDS and Drug adv. bd. Met. Regional Ednl. Svc. Agy., Atlanta, The Howard Schs.; bd. dirs. Profl. Acad. Custody Evaluators, Doylestown Borough, Pa., 1993—. Bd. dirs. Briarcliff Woods Civic Assn., Atlanta, 1982-84, North Atlanta Parents Coun., 1990—; bd. dirs., pres. Briarcliff Woods Beach Club, Atlanta, 1980-82, 85-87. Recipient Service award Down Syndrome Assn. of Atlanta, 1986. Fellow Ga. Psychol. Assn. (Divsn. G chmn. 1985-87, 96-97, treas. 1996-99, mem. ethics com. 2000—; Cert. of Merit for Outstanding Contbn. to Profession of Psychology, 1987, Pres. award 1999); mem. APA, Nat. Acad. Neuropsychology, Soc. Personality Assessment, Assn. Children with Learning Disabilities, Ga. Assn. Sch. Psychologists (bd. mem. 1982-83). Avocations: swimming, ballroom dancing, home remodeling. Home: 1821 Morris Landers Dr NE Atlanta GA 30345-4103 Office: 2900 Paces Ferry Rd SE Ste C100 Atlanta GA 30339-5773

THOMAS, RHONDA ROBBINS, marketing educator, consultant; b. Houston, Dec. 15, 1958; d. George B. and Barbara (Lillich) R.; m. Fred Holt Thomas, Aug. 22, 1981 (div. 1991); children: Brian P., Paige A.; m. Michael G. Florimbi, Oct. 18, 1997; 1 child, Allegra F. BA, U. Tex., 1980; MBA, So. Meth. U., 1989; PhD, U. Tex., Arlington, 1994. Profl. interior designer. Pres., CEO Design Austin, Tex., 1984-90; pres. Denova, Austin, 1988-93; prin. MarketShare Cons., 1993-95; asst. prof. mktg. Suffolk U., Boston, 1996-98; vis. prof. mktg. Sellinger Sch. Bus. Loyola Coll., Balt., 1998—; sr. mgr. e-bus. Deloitte Consulting, 2000—. Cons. SABRE Decision Techs., 1995-98; vis. asst. prof. mktg. U. Tex. Arlington, 1990-95, Loyola Coll., Balt., 1998-99; adj. mem. mktg. faculty Cox Sch. So. Meth. U., 1993-95. Bd. dirs. Children's Cancer Ctr., Austin, 1987-88, Dallas Mus. Art, 1990-94. Lester Johnson Grad. fellow Inst. Bus. Designers Found., 1990, Lakawanna Leather fellow, 1991. Mem. DAR, Am. Soc. Interior Designers (Design Excellence award 1985, 87, 88), Inst. Bus. Designers, Austin C. of C.

THOMAS, RONALD ROBERT, English literature educator, writer; b. Orange, N.J., Jan. 29, 1949; s. Robert Louis and Doris Josephine (Rambo) T.; m. Mary Domingo Rosenstock, June 15, 1991. BA in English, Wheaton Coll., 1971; MA in English and Am. Lit., Brandeis U., 1978, PhD in English and Am. Lit., 1983. Asst. prof. English lit. U. Chgo., 1982-90; assoc. prof. Trinity Coll., Hartford, Conn., 1990—2003, chmn. dept. English, 1993—2003, chief of staff, v.p., 1998—2001, acting pres., 2001—02; pres. Univ. Puget Sound, Tacoma, 2003—. Author: Dreams of Authority: Freud and the Fictions of the Unconscious, 1990; contbr. articles to profl. jours., chpt. to Columbia History of Brit. Novel. Andrew Mellon fellow Harvard U., 1991-92. Mem. MLA, Dickens Soc., Soc. for Study of Narrative Lit., N.E. Victorian Assn., Interdisciplinary 19th-Century Studies Assn. Office: Univ Puget Sound 1500 North Warner Tacoma WA 98416*

THOMAS, SANDRA MARIE, training company executive; b. N.Y.C., Mar. 4, 1939; d. Dudley George and Helen Claire (Pitt) T. Student, Coll. of V.I., 1963-64, New Sch. for Social Rsch., N.Y.C., 1970-74, Art Students League, 1974-76, Fordham U., 1980-82, N.Y.U., 1984-85. Mgr. Cutlass Shop, St. Thomas, V.I., 1964-67; rate analyst, in house trainer TWA, N.Y.C., 1968-85; seminar leader Big Body Work Shop, Orlando, Fla., 1986-87; pres., exec. dir. Leisure Learning Labs., Inc., Orlando, 1988-90; owner Skills Link, Orlando, 1992—. Human resource devel. cons.; speaker, workshop leader on cultural diversity; coord. Frank Covino Portrait Painters workshops, 1993. Editor Orange County Dem., 1994; contbr. articles to profl. publs. Recipient awards for paintings. Mem. Am. Soc. for Tng. and Devel. (multi-cultural chair Cen. Fla. chpt. 1988-91), Fla. Freelance Writers Assn. Avocations: water sports, writing, painting, needlework, travel. Office: Skills Link 4524 Curry Ford Rd Ste 629 Orlando FL 32812-2711

THOMAS, SARAH ELAINE, elementary music educator; b. Little Rock, Aug. 8, 1947; d. William and Madie Murle (Stout) Collins; m. Gary Wayne Thomas Aug. 8, 1970 (dec. Nov. 1991). MusB in Edn., U. N. Tex., 1970; M in Ednl. Adminstrn., Dallas Bapt. U., 1997. Cert. tchr.-all-levels, Tex. Music tchr. Winnetka Elem., Dallas, 1970-82, L. K. Hall Elem., Dallas, 1982-94, Kleberg Elem., Dallas, 1994—2001, Pleasant Grove (Tex.) Elem., 2001—. Staff. devel. presenter Dallas Ind. Sch. Dist., 1977-97, 97-2003; workshop presenter Tex. Arts Coun., Austin, 1990-94. Bd. dirs. Dallas PTA, 1980-82; bd. dirs. Dallas All-City Elem. Choir, chair, 1991—, dir., 1999-2003. Named Class Act Teacher, Sta. KDFW-TV, Dallas, 1992. Mem. PTA (life), Am. Fedn. Tchrs., Tex. Music Educators Assn., Dallas Music Educators Assn. (v.p. 1992), Am. Orff-Schulwerk Assn., Music Educators Nat. Conf., Rotary (Svc. Above Self award 2003). Avocations: cooking, sewing, gardening, travel. Home: 2407 Norwich Ct Arlington TX 76015-3262 Office: Pleasant Grove Elem 1614 N St Dallas TX 75217

THOMAS, SHARYN LEE, elementary education educator; b. Springfield, Mass., Nov. 6, 1948; d. John H. and Meta L. (Postell) T. BFA, U. Mass. at Amherst, 1974; MEd, Springfield Coll., 1980; postgrad. in Spanish, Worcester State Coll., Am. Internat. Coll.; postgrad., Our Lady of Elms Coll., Anna Maria Coll., 1990, Fitchburg State Coll., 1994. Cert. elem. educator K-8, Mass., art educator K-12, Mass. Classroom tchr. Springfield (Mass.) Pub. Schs., 1980-83, tchr. K-4 FLES/Spanish, art and art appreciation, 1983-88, tchr. grades 5 and 6, 1988-91, tchr. 3rd grade, 1991—. Tchr. tng. task force Springfield Coll., 1993. Recipient Dept. Edn. Bd. Edn. Citation Merit for Exemplary Ednl. Program, 1986, Springfield Edn. Fund Mini-Grant, 1986. Mem. Mass. Fgn. Lang. Assn., Am. Assn. Tchrs. Spanish and Portuguese, Mass. Tchrs. Assn., Springfield Edn. Assn.

THOMAS, SHIRLEY, author, educator, business executive; b. Glendale, Calif. d. Oscar Miller and Ruby (Thomas) Annis; m. W. White, Feb. 22, 1949 (div. June 1952); m. William C. Perkins, Oct. 24, 1969. BA in Modern Lit., U. Sussex, Eng., 1960, PhD in Comm., 1967; diploma, Russian Fedn. Cosmonautics, 1995. Actress, writer, producer, dir. numerous radio and TV stas., 1942-46; v.p. Commodore Prodns., Hollywood, Calif., 1946-52; pres. Annis & Thomas, Inc., Hollywood, 1952—; prof. technical writing U. So. Calif., L.A., 1975—. Hollywood corr. NBC, 1952-56; editor motion pictures CBS, Hollywood, 1956-58; corr. Voice of Am., 1958-59; now free lance writer; cons. biol. scis. communication project George Washington U., 1965-66; cons. Stanford Rsch. Inst., 1967-68, Jet Propulsion Lab., 1969-70. Author: Men of Space vols. 1-8, 1960-68, Spanish trans., 1961, Italian, 1962; Space Tracking Facilities, 1963, Computers: Their History, Present Applications and Future, 1965; The Book of Diets, 1974. Organizer, chmn. City of L.A. Space Adv. Com., 1964-73, Women's Space Symposia, 1962-73; founder, chmn. Aerospace Hist. Soc. Inc.; chmn. Theodore von Karman Postage Stamp Com., 1965—, stamp issued 1992; bd. dirs. World Children's Transplant Fund, 1993—, Achievement Rewards for Coll. Scients. Recipient Aerospace Excellence award Calif. Mus. Found. 1991, Nat. Medal Honor DAR, 1992, Yuri Gagarin Medal Honor, 1995. Fellow Brit. Interplanetary Soc.; mem. AIAA, AAAS, Internat. Acad. Astronautics, Internat. Soc. Aviation Writers, Air Force Assn. (Airpower Arts and Letters award 1961), Internat. Acad. Astronautics, Nat. Aero. Assn., Nat. Asn. Sci. Writers, Soc. for Tech. Communications, Am. Astronautical Soc., Nat. Geog. Soc., Am. Soc. Pub. Adminstrn. (sci. and tech. in govt. com. 1972—), Achievement Awards for Coll. Scientists, Theta Sigma Phi, Phi Beta. Home: 8027 Hollywood Blvd Los Angeles CA 90046-2510 Office: U So Calif Profl Writing Program University Park Waite Phillips Hall 404 Los Angeles CA 90089-0001 E-mail: snowtech@pacbell.net.

THOMAS, SUZANNE WARD, public relations executive, communications educator, radio personality; b. Akron, Ohio, Sept. 21, 1954; d. Kendall Kramer and Margaret Ann (Owen) Ward; m. James Michael Thomas, Oct. 20, 1980; children: Seth Evin, James Kendall. BS in Edn., Miami U., Oxford, Ohio, 1977; MA in Comm., Regent U., Virginia Beach, Va., 1980. Writer, prodr. Sta. WVIZ, PBS, Cleve., 1980-82; dir. pub. rels. Sta. WOAC-TV, Canton, Ohio, 1982-83, hostess children's show, 1982-84; v.p. Thomas Video Prodns., Canal Fulton, Ohio, 1987-90; dir. pub. rels., instr. comm. Malone Coll., Canton, 1990—, editor The Malone Mag., 1990—; co-host morning radio show Sta. WNPQ-FM, 2001—. Co-hose morning radio program 95.9 FM-WNPQ, 2001—, host radio cmty. affairs program, 2001—. Author: (children's book) The Miracles of Jesus, 1991, also manuals. Hostess pub. affairs program Community TV Consortium, Canton, 1987; subcom. chmn. Govt. Day, Leadership Canton, 1987; v.p. Right to Life Ednl. Found., Canton, 1990; chmn. pub. rels. Jr. League Canton, 1986-87, rec. sec., 1987-88; bd. dirs. PTO, 1989-90; mgmt. assistance program United Way, 1998-99. Recipient Sparkler award Jr. League Canton, 1986, Pub. Rels. award, 1987, Addy awards Canton Advt. Club, 1992, 96. Mem. Sales and Mktg. Execs. (bd. dirs. Stark County chpt. 1989), Assn. Jr. Leagues Internat., Pub. Rels. Soc. Am. (accredited in pub. rels. 1995, bd. dirs.). Republican. Avocations: reading, tennis, aerobics, golf, writing. Office: Malone Coll 515 25th St NW Canton OH 44709-3823

THOMAS, TERESA ANN, microbiologist, educator; b. Wilkes-Barre, Pa., Oct. 17, 1939; d. Sam Charles and Edna Grace T. BS cum laude, Coll. Misericordia, 1961; MS in Biology, Am. U., Beirut, 1965; MS in Microbiology, U. So. Calif., 1973; cert. in ednl. tech., U. Calif., San Diego, 1998. Tchr., sci. supr., curriculum coord. Meyers HS, Wilkes-Barre, 1962-64, Wilkes-Barre Area Public Schs., 1961-66; rsch. assoc. Proctor Found. Rsch. in Ophthalmology U. Calif. Med. Ctr., San Francisco, 1966-68; instr. Robert Coll. of Istanbul, Turkey, 1968-71, Am. Edn. in Luxembourg, 1971-72, Bosco Tech. Inst., Rosemead, Calif., 1973-74, San Diego C.C. Dist., 1974-80; prof. microbiology and ecology Sch. Math Sci. and Engring. Southwestern Coll., Chula Vista, Calif., 1980—; mem. Vecinos Baja Studies EcoMundo team internat. program Southwestern Coll., mem. staff devel. com., 2001—. Pres. acad. senate, 1984-85, del., 1986-89; chmn., coord., steering com. project Cultural Rsch. Ednl. and Trade Exch., 1991-2000, Southwestern Coll.-Shanghai Inst. Fgn. Trade; coord. Southwestern Coll. Great Teaching Seminar, 1987, 88, 89, coord. scholars program, 1988-90; steering com. Southwestern Coll.; exec. com. Acad. Senate for Calif. C.C.s, 1985-86, Chancellor of Calif. C.C.s Adv. and Rev. Coun. Fund for Instrnl. Improvement, 1984-86; co-project dir. statewide, coord. So. Calif. Biotech. Edn. Consortium, 1993-95, steering com., 1993-98; adj. asst. prof. Chapman Coll., San Diego, 1974-83, San Diego State U., 1977-79; chmn. Am. Colls. Istanbul Sci. Week, 1969-71; adv. bd. Chapman Coll. Cmty. Ctr., 1979-80; cons. sci. curriculum Calif. Dept. Edn., 1986-89; pres. Internat. Rels. Club, 1959-61; mem. San Francisco World Affairs Coun., 1966-68, San Diego World Affairs Coun., 1992—; v.p. Palomar Palace Estates Home Owners Assn., 1983-85, pres., 1994-99, v.p., 1999—; mem. Rsch. Conf. on Undergrad. Microbiology Edn., Conn. Coll., 1999; bd. dir. US Orgn. Med. Ednl. Needs, US Internat. Boundary and Water Commn. Citizens Forum; presenter in field. NSTA Jour. of Coll. Sci. Tchg. Life mem. Chula Vista Nature Ctr.; mem. Internat. Friendship Commn., Chula Vista, 1985-95, vice chmn., 1989-90, chmn., 1990-92; mem. US-Mex. Sister Cities Assn., nat. bd. dir., 1992-94, gen. chair 30th nat. conv., 1993; active City of Chula Vista Resource Conservation Commn., 1996—, chmn. 2002—; active Chula Vista Bd. Ethics, 1999-2000; co-organizer Chula Vista People-to-People Sister City Dels. to Odawara City, Japan, 1991, 94, 99; cmty. adv. com. San Diego Mus. Man, 2000—; mem. County San Diego Solid Waste Hearing Panel, 2000—; citizens forum bd. US Internat. Boundary and Water Commn., 2002-; steering com. Chula Vista Gen. Plan Update, 2002—; hon. coach SWC Jaguars Basketball Team, 2003; com. mem. Chula Vista Environ., Open Space and Sustainable Devel., 2002—. Rsch. grant Pa. Heart Assn., 1962; NSF fellow, 1965, USPHS fellow, 1972-73; recipient Nat. Tchg. Excellence award Nat. Inst. Staff and Orgnl. Devel., 1989; named Southwestern Coll. Woman of Distinction, 1987; Hon. Coach Southwestern Coll. Ladies Basketball Aces, 2001. Mem.: NEA, NIH (mentor Bridges to the Future program Southwestern Coll. and San Diego 1993—98, steering com.), Faculty Assn. Calif. C.C.s (state policy com. 2003—), Am. Assn. Cmty. and Jr. Colls., Calif. Tchrs. Assn., Nat. Sci. Tchrs. Assn. (coord. internat. honors exch. lectr. competition 1986, internat. com.), Am. Soc. Microbiology (So. Calif. Microbe Discovery Team 1995—99), Calif. Sci. Tchrs. Assn. (life), Nat. Assn. Biology Tchrs. (life), Chula Vista-Odawara (Japan) Sister Cities Assn. (founding pres. 1994—), Am. U. Beirut Alumni and Friends of San Diego (1st v.p. 1984—91), San Diego Zool. Soc., Japan Soc. San Diego and Tijuana (life), Japanese Hist. Soc. San Diego (life), Am.-Lebanese Assn. San Diego (1st v.p. 1984—91, pres. 1988—93, chmn. scholarship com.), Am. Lebanese Syrian Ladies Club (pres. 1982—83), Lions Internat. (bull. editor 1991—93, 2d v.p. 1992—93, 1st v.p. 1993—94, editor Roaring Times Newsletter 1993—94, chmn. dist. internat. rels. and cooperations com. 1993—95, pres. S.W. San Diego County chpt. 1994—95, Sweetwater Zone chmn. dist. 4-L6 1996—97, pub. rels. 1997—98, Best Bull. award 1992—93, named S.W. San Diego County Lion of Yr. 2000), Delta Kappa Gamma (Outstanding Pub. Svc. award Gamma Omicron chpt. 2003), Phi Theta Kappa, Sigma Phi Sigma, Kappa Gamma Pi (pres. Wilkes-Barre chpt. 1963—64, pres. San Francisco chpt. 1967—68), Alpha Pi Epsilon (life; advisor Southwestern Coll. chpt. 1989—90, founder).

THOMAS, THERESA BROWN, middle school educator; b. Birmingham, Ala., Apr. 9, 1947; d. William Brown and Helen Margaret Smith Cunningham; divorced; 1 child, David Patrick Farmer. BA, U. Ala., 1970, MA, 1975; M in Pub. and Pvt. Mgmt., Birmingham So. Coll., 1992. Cert. prin., tchr., Ala. Tchr. Am. history Pizitz Middle Sch., Birmingham, 1970-93, chair dept. social studies, 1989-93; asst. prin. Smith Middle Sch., Birmingham, 1993—. Supr. Ala. Gas Co., Birmingham, summers 1988-90; dir. assembly program Pizitz Middle Sch., 1978—, sch. budget chairperson, 1990-92, project bus. coord., 1988-93; reader/evaluator So. Asns. Colls. and Schs., Birmingham, 1991, cons., Troy, Ala., 1990. Coord. Bessemer (Ala.) Centennial Commn., 1986; bd. dirs. Green Isle Civic League, Bessemer, 1976—, City of Bessemer Civic Ctr., 1994—; mem. Concerned Citizens of Bessemer, 1984; mem. Birmingham alumni coun. United Negro Coll. Fund, 1993—. Named to Outstanding Young Women of Am., 1981; recipient Second Mile award Parents of Exceptional Children, 1992; Hearst Found. scholar, 1989-91; Nat. Black MBA Assn. scholar, 1989. Mem. NEA, Ala. Edn. Assn. (del. 1984-85), Vestavia Hills Edn. Assn. (sec. 1972, pres. 1984), Nat. Black MBA Assn., Nat Coun. Social Studies, Nat. Geog. Alliance, Rho Nu Tau (pres., Soror of Yr. 1986). Baptist. Avocations: speed walking, meditation, flower gardening, the arts. Home: 12 Varin Way Bessemer AL 35022-5326 Office: Smith Middle Sch 1124 Five Mile Rd Birmingham AL 35215-7216

THOMAS, TOM ELDON, corrections educator; b. Bakersfield, Calif., Apr. 21, 1937; s. John E. and Grace Mae T.; children: Tammie, Wayne. BA, Calif. State U., 1961, MA, 1966; PhD, U. Oreg., 1972. Cert. secondary tchr., Calif., Oreg., Hawaii; cert. in sch. adminstrn., Guam, Calif. Sr. program assoc. Northwest Regional Ednl. Lab., Portland, Oreg., 1972-77; assoc. prof. U. Hawaii, Honolulu, 1980-85, Portland State U., 1985-89; acad. v.p. No. Marianas Coll., Saipan, 1989-91; curriculum dir. Fairfax Sch. Dist., 1991-95; corrections educator Calif. Dept. Corrections, 1996—2002. Contbr. articles to profl. jours. With U.S. Army, 1954-57. Fulbright fellow, India. Mem. ASCD, Nat. Coun. Social Studies, Phi Delta Kappa. Home: 2521 20th St Bakersfield CA 93301-3415

THOMAS, YVONNE SHIREY, family and consumer science educator; b. Jenner Cross Roads, Pa., Dec. 1, 1938; d. Edward Merle and Orphabel (Shaffer) Shirey; m. William Edward Thomas, Dec. 23, 1961; children: Scott Forrest, Matthew David. BS, Indiana U. of Pa., 1960; MS, Hood Coll., 1987. Home econs. educator Bristol (Pa.) Jr. Sr. High Sch., 1960-64; elem. educator Barbers Point Elem. Sch., Ewa Beach, Hawaii, 1964-65; guidance counselor Workman Jr. High Sch., Pensacola, Fla., 1966-68; mid. sch. educator Broadfording Christian Acad., Hagerstown, Md., 1973-76; home econs. educator Hancock (Md.) Jr. Sr. High Sch., 1986-88, Springfield Middle Sch., Williamsport, Md., 1988—; ret., 2001. Consumer affairs intern Citicorp Credit Svcs., Inc, Hagerstown, 1986; career day coord. Springfield Middle Sch., Williamsport, 1988-92. Bd. mem. Washington County Commn. for Women, Hagerstown, 1989-96, Cedar Ridge Ministries, Hagerstown, 1990-95, 96-2002. Recipient Judith Ruchkin Rsch. award Md. ASCD, Balt., 1987, award Md. Nutrition Adv. Coun., 1997-99; named Washington County Home Econs. Tchr. of Yr., Md. Home Econs. Assn., Hagerstown, 1989, Women-on-the-Move, The Herald Mail Co., Hagerstown, 1991; winner Md. Nutritional Adv. Coun. State, 1998-99, Mid Atlantic Nutrition Adv. Coun., 2000-01. Mem. AAUW (chair edn. fund 1989-90, v.p. membership 1990-92, grant 1992, pres.-elect 1992-93, pres. 1993-94, grantee 1994, chair Md. state edn. fund 1990-92, ednl. equity chair 1994-2000), NEA, Md. Tchrs. Assn. (Dorothy Lloyd Women's Rights award 1996), Am. Assn. Family and Consumer Scis. (cert. family life educator 1990-98), Soroptimist Internat. (Women of Distinction award 1996, Regional Woman of Distinction 1996), Delta Zeta (pres. 1959-60). Republican. Grace Brethren. Avocations: watercolor painting, quilting, hiking, traveling. Home: 19001 Rock Maple Dr Hagerstown MD 21742-2458

THOMASON, DEBORAH LEE, kindergarten educator; b. Commerce, Tex., Aug. 23, 1956; d. Carlos Ray and Gladys Lou (Moses) Presley; m. Tommy George Thomason, Dec. 31, 1976; 1 child, Joshua Adam. AAS, Mountain View Coll., Dallas, 1989; B of gen. studies, Tex. Christian U., 1992. Pre-sch. tchr. Americare, Mesquite, Tex., 1977-79, Busy Bee Child Devel. Ctr., Lynchburg, Va., 1980; nursery coord. First Bapt. Ch., Commerce, 1981-82; asst. dir. La Petite Academy, Grand Prairie, Tex., 1982-83; pre-kindergarten tchr. Children's World, Grand Prairie, 1983-87; pre-sch. tchr. Rocking Horse Acad., Arlington, Tex., 1988-91, kindergarten tchr., 1993—2002; child devel. specialist Child Card Mgmt. Svcs., Ft. Worth, 2002—. Conf. coord. Internat. Inst. Lit. Learning, Commerce, summers 1993, 94, 95; nat. workshop presenter Pathways to Literacy Confs., 2000. Vol. Tarrant County Food Bank, Ft. Worth, 1991. Mem. Internat. Reading Assn., Nat. Coun. Tchrs. English, Kindergarten Tchrs. Tex., Whole Lang. Umbrella. Home: 6006 Ashcreek Ct Arlington TX 76018-3000 Office: Child Care Mgmt Svc 2804 Race St Fort Worth TX 76111

THOMPSON, ADRIENNE, secondary school educator; Tchr. advanced placement art history Sch. for Creative and Performing Arts, Cin. Mem. arts assessment steering com. Ohio Art Coun. Named Music Educator of the Yr., Ohio Art Edn. Assn. Mus. Divsn., 2000; recipient Ohio Govs. award for excellence in tchg., 1998, Outstanding Excellence award, Cin. Pub. Schs., 1999. Mem.: Nat. Bd. for Profl. Tchg. Stds. (bd. mem.). Office: Sch for Creative and Performing Arts 1310 Sycamore St Cincinnati OH 45202*

THOMPSON, ALICE MAE BROUSSARD, special education administrator; b. Opelousas, La., May 15, 1950; d. Melvin and Roseanna (Joseph) Broussard; m. Samuel Joe Thompson; 1 child, Tameka Rose Thompson. BS in Vocat. Home Econs., McNeese State U., 1973; MEd in Spl. Edn., U. Mo., St. Louis, 1993; cert. in mid-mgmt., Tex. So. U., 1993; student, Harvard U., 1995—2001; D in Ednl. Adminstrn., Strassford U., 2002. Food svc. supr. Parkland Meml. Hosp., Dallas, 1982-83; tchr. home econs. Milw. pub. schs., 1984-85, Epworth Pvt. Sch., Webster Grove, Mo., 1988-91; tchr. career lab. Ft. Bend Ind. Sch. Dist., Sugarland, Tex., 1985-87, tchr. resource math., 1991-92, coord. spl. edn., 1993—; pres. Thompson & Assoc. Edn. Resources. Cons. Inclusion, Tex., 1993; coord. Inclusion Adv. Bd., Sugarland, 1993—; mem. Inclusion Works Adv. Bd., Austin, 1994—. Mem. NAFE, ASCD, Coun. for Exceptional Children, Nat. Assn. Black Educators, Alpha Kappa Alpha (v.p. chpt.). Avocations: reading, tennis, traveling. Home: 2811 Plantation Wood Ln Missouri City TX 77459-4253 Office: Ft Bend Ind Sch Dist PO Box 1004 Sugar Land TX 77487-1004

THOMPSON, ANA CALZADA, secondary education educator, mathematician; b. Sanderson, Tex., Nov. 29, 1940; d. Leopoldo G. and Maria Deo Gracia (Sandoval) Calzada; m. Tommy Salinas Thompson, July 1, 1962; children: Tommy Michael, Anthony Jude, Ana Marie. BS, Sul Ross State U., Alpine, Tex., 1966; MEd, S.W. Tex. State U., 1980. Tchr. Poteet (Tex.) Ind. Sch. Dist., 1965-67, Northside Ind. Sch. Dist., San Antonio, 1967-68; tchr. math. N.E. Ind. Sch. Dist., San Antonio, 1968-97, chmn. dept., 1976-97. Prof. math. St. Philips Coll., San Antonio, 1986—; mem. Region 20 Tchr. Ctr., San Antonio, 1978-82; pres. S.W. Tchr. Ctr., San Marcos, Tex., 1970-82. Contbg. author: Graphing Power, 1995. Sec., La Vernia (Tex.) Ind. Sch. Dist., 1977-87, mem. bd., 1978-87; del. Tex. Dem. Conv., Houston, 1988, Ft. Worth, 1992, Dallas, 1996, El Paso, 2002; del. Guadalupe County Dem. Com., Seguin, Tex., 1988, 92, 96, 2002. Mem. NEA, Nat. Coun. Tchrs. Math., Tex. Tchrs. Assn., Alamo Dist. Coun. Tchrs. Math. Roman Catholic. Avocations: reading, knitting, travel, gardening.

THOMPSON, ANDREW ERNEST, secondary school educator; b. Springfield, Mass., Oct. 17, 1947; s. Richard Ernest and Virginia Laurie (Knight) T.; children: Stephanie Anne, Elizabeth Clare, Adam Richard. BA in Maths., Bridgewater State Coll., 1969; M in Maths., Worcester Polytech. Inst., 1988; postgrad., Harvard U., 1988, Mich. State U., 1989-90. Cert. math., secondary edn. and social studies tchr., secondary adminstrn. Test engr. Pratt & Whitney Aircraft Co., 1968; tchr. math. Whitman (Mass.) Pub. Schs., 1969-91, Whitman-Hanson Regl. Sch. Dist., 1991-2001, Wareham (Mass.) Pub. Schs., 2001—; sr. mem. faculty Cambridge (Mass.) Coll., 2000—. Mgr. Dairy Queen Ice Cream, 1976-77; curriculum coord. Horace Mann, 1986-88; curriculum cons. Bridgewater (Mass.) Pub. Schs., 1987-89; scorer Mass. Ednl. Assessment Program, 1990, 92; sr. faculty Cambridge Coll., Mass. Mem. Bridgewater Sch. Com., 1992-95; supt. Ctrl. Sq. Congl. Ch., 1989-90, 92-94; cubmaster Boy Scouts Am., Bridgewater, 1988-92, troop com., 1992-95; mem. Bridgewater-Raynham Sch. Com., 1999-2001. Recipient Harvard U. Practitioner award, 1988; NSF grantee, 1989-90. Mem. ASCD, Am. Math. Soc., Assn. Tchrs. Math. in Mass., Nat. Coun. Tchrs. Math., Math. Assn. Am., Mass. Tchrs. Assn., Plymouth County Edn. Assn. (bd. dirs. 1977-84, chmn. county negotiating com. 1981-83), Whitman Edn. Assn. (pres.-elect 1981, 83, pres. 1982-84, chmn. negotiating com. 1977-80, 90-92), Whitman Hanson Edn. Assn. (pres. 1992-2001). Home: PO Box 419 Bridgewater MA 02324-0419

THOMPSON, ANNIE LAURA (ANNE), foreign language educator; b. Henderson, Tenn., July 8, 1937; d. Wesley Sylvester and Letha Irene (Jones) T.; m. Edward L. Patterson, June 7, 1980. BA, U. Ala., 1959; MA, Duke U., 1961; PhD, Tulane U., 1973. Instr. Spanish lang. U. Miss., Oxford, 1960-64; instr. Auburn (Ala.) U., 1964-66; tchg. asst. Tulane U., New Orleans, 1966-70; prof. Spanish lang. Delgado C.C., New Orleans, 1970—. Instr. Spanish for Physicians and Med. Persons Tulane U., La. State U. Med. Eye Ctr., Ochsner Clinic and Hosp. Author: Religious Elements in the Quijote, 1960, The Attempt of Spanish Intellectuals to Create a New Spain, 1930-36, 1973, The Generation of 1898: Intellectual Politicians; asst. editor The Crusader, 1961-64. Rep. candidate for gov. State of La., 1991, 95, for 1st Dist. U.S. Congress, 1992; alt. mem. La. Coastal Commn., 1984—; del. Women's State Rep. Conv., 1987, La. State Rep. Conv., 1990, 93, La. Coastal Adv. Coun., 1988, Pan Am. Commn., 1992-95; v.p. pub. rels. Alliance for Good Govt., 1990; candidate State Senate La., 1994; mem. DAR (Vieux Carré chpt.), 2000. Recipient Outstanding Tchr. award Delgado Coll. Student Govt. Assn., 1974; Woodoow Wilson fellow, 1959-60, NDEA fellow, 1968-69. Mem. AAUP, DAR, Pachyderm Club, Women's Rep. Club, Phi Beta Kappa, Phi Alpha Theta, Sigma Delta Pi. Republican. Mem. Ch. of Christ. Home: PO Box 24399 New Orleans LA 70184-4399

THOMPSON, ARLENE RITA, nursing educator; b. Yakima, Wash., May 17, 1933; d. Paul James and Esther Margaret (Danroth) T. BS in Nursing, U. Wash., 1966, Masters in Nursing, 1970, postgrad., 1982—. Staff nurse Univ. Teaching Hosp., Seattle, 1966-69; mem. nursing faculty U. Wash. Sch. Nurses, Seattle, 1971-73; critical care nurse Virginia Mason Hosp., Seattle, 1973—; educator Seattle Pacific U. Sch. Nursing, 1981—. Nurse legal cons. nursing edn., critical care nurse. Contbr. articles to profl. jours. USPHS grantee, 1969; nursing scholar Virginia Mason Hosp., 1965. Mem. Am. Assn. Critical Care Nurses (cert.), Am. Nurses Assn., Am. Heart Assn., Nat. League Nursing, Sigma Theta Tau, Alpha Tau Omega. Republican. Presbyterian. Avocations: sewing, swimming, jogging, bicycle riding, hiking. Home: 2320 W Newton St Seattle WA 98199-4115 Office: Seattle Pacific U 3307 3rd Ave W Seattle WA 98119-1997

THOMPSON, BERNIDA LAMERLE, principal, consultant, educator; b. Tuskeegee, Ala., July 5, 1946; d. Berry James Sr. and Doris LaMerle (Askey) T.; m. Rolando Amerson, June 15, 1968 (div. Aug. 1988); children: Afriye Amerson, Mwando Amerson. BS in Elem. Edn., Cen. State U., 1968; MEd in Adminstrn. and Curriculum, Miami U., Oxford, Ohio, 1971; EdD in Early and Mid. Childhood Edn., Nova U., 1992. Classroom elem. sch. tchr. Dayton Pub. Schs.; asst. prin., intern St. James Cath. Sch., Dayton, Ohio; tchr. St. Augustine Cath. Sch., Washington; sci. resource tchr. D.C. Pub. Schs., Washington; founding tchr., prin. Roots Activity Learning Ctr., Washington, 1977—, Roots Pub. Charter Sch., 1999—. Multicultural advisor HBJ 1992 Reading Textbook. Author: Black Madonnas and Young Lions a Rite of Passage for African American Adolescents, 1992, rev. edit., 1998, Africentric Interdisciplinary Multi-Level Hands On Science, 1994, rev. edit., 2001; contbr. articles to profl. jours. Mem. Nat. Assn. Edn. Young Children, World Coun. Curriculum Instrn., Coun Ind. Black Inst., Inst. Ind. Edn., Nat. Black Child Devel. Inst. Office: Roots Pub Charter Sch 15 Kennedy St NW Washington DC 20011-5201

THOMPSON, BERTHA BOYA, retired education educator, antique dealer and appraiser; b. New Castle, Pa., Jan. 31, 1917; d. Frank L. and Kathryn Belle (Park) Boya; m. John L. Thompson, Mar. 27, 1942; children: Kay Lynn Thompson Koolage, Scott McClain. BS in Elem. & Secondary

Edn., Slippery Rock State Coll., 1940; MA in Geography and History, Miami U., 1954; EdD, Ind. U., 1961. Cert. elem. and secondary edn. tchr. Elem. tchr., reading specialist New Castle (Pa.) Sch. System, 1940-45; tchr., chmn. social studies Talawanda Sch. System, Oxford, Ohio, 1954-63; assoc. prof. psychology and geography, chair edn. dept. Western Coll. for Women, Oxford, 1963-74; assoc. prof. edn., reading clinic Miami U., Oxford, 1974-78, prof. emeritus, 1978—; pvt. antique dealer, appraiser Oxford, 1978—. Contbr. articles to profl. jours. Mem. folk art com. Miami U. Art Mus., Oxford, 1974-76; mem. adv. com. Smith libr., Oxford Pub. Libr., 1978-81. Mem. AAUP, Nat. Coun. Geographic Edn. (exec. bd. dirs. 1966-69), Nat. Soc. for Study Edn., Assn. Am. Geographers, Soc. Women Geographers, Nat. Coun. for the Social Studies, Pi Lambda Theta, Zeta Tau Alpha, Pi Gamma Mu, Gamma Theta Upsilon, Kappa Delta Pi. Avocations: antique collecting, reading, travel, tennis. Home: 6073 Contreras Rd Oxford OH 45056-9708

THOMPSON, BONNIE RANSA, education consultant; b. Charleroi, Pa., Oct. 12, 1940; d. William Edward and Edith Lorraine Ransa; m. Joel E. Thompson, June 15, 1963 (div. Dec. 1980). BA, Seton Hill Coll., Greensburg, Pa., 1963; MEd, Ariz. State U., 1979, postgrad. Cert. in secondary chemistry, anthropology, and gifted edn., Ariz. Tchr. chemistry Scotch Plains (N.J.)-Fanwood High Sch., 1963—74; tchr. chemistry and anthropology Tolleson (Ariz.) Union High Sch., 1974—93; tchr. chemistry Westview High Sch., Phoenix, 1992—2002; owner Driven Solutions, Inc.-Material Handling Systems, 1996—2000; cons. Del E. Webb Sch. Constrn., Ariz. State U., 2002. Instr. anthropology and archaeology Rio Salado CC, Sun City, Ariz., 1981—88; instr. chemistry Glendale (Ariz.) C.C., 1988—2002; mem. Ariz. Reagent and Task Force on Lab. Sci., Tempe, 1987; instr. chemistry Estrella Mt. C.C., 1996—98; pres. Brite Ednl. Programs, Ltd., Phoenix, 1988—91; tchr., cons. Pitts. SuperComputer Project, Tolleson, Ariz., 1992—; amb. People to People Sci. Exchange summer program, Russia, 1989—90, Australia, 1991—92, New Zealand, 1991—92; rsch. partnership HS/Coll. Flinn Found. Rsch. Corp., 1988—91. Editor: Starting at Ground Zero, 1988, others; editor: Energy Education Kits, 1985; contbr. articles to mags. V.p. Villa Casitas Townhouse Assn., Phoenix, 1991—92, pres., 1993—. Woodrow Wilson fellow, 1983; recipient Golden Bell award Ariz. Sch. Bd. Assn., 1985, 88; recipient Growth Incentives for Tchrs. award GTE Corp., 1987, Tech. Scholar award Tandy Corp., 1990, Excellence in Constrn. Innovative Edn. award Am. Subcontractors Assn. Ariz., 2000; named Outstanding High Sch. Sci. Tchr. Ariz. Coun. for Engring. and Scientific Assocs., 1993. Mem. NEA, Ariz. Edn. Assn., Tolleson Edn. Assn. (pres. 1981-83), Nat. Sci. Tchrs. Assn., Ariz. Sci. Tchrs. Assn., Ariz. Alliance for Math., Sci. and Tech., S.W. Archeol. Team. Avocations: reading, touring motorcycles. Address: 5638 S 42 Ave Phoenix AZ 85041 E-mail: brtefg@msn.com.

THOMPSON, CARLA JO HORN, mathematics educator; b. Oklahoma City, Feb. 10, 1951; d. Hubert Henry and Gilleen Cora (Hall) Horn; m. Michael J. Thompson, Aug. 4, 1973 (div. 1986); 1 child, Emily Jane. BS, U. Tulsa, 1972, MTA, 1973, EdD, 1980; postgrad, Okla. State U., 1975-77; dist. math. coord., Tulsa Pub. Schs., 1995-96. Tchr. math. Sapulpa (Okla.) pub. schs., 1973-79; research asst. U. Tulsa, 1979-80; asst. prof. math. and statistics Tulsa Jr. Coll., 1980—; research statistician Social & Edn. Research Assocs., Tulsa, 1987—. Vis. adj. prof. U. Tulsa, 1989—, Univ. Ctr. at Tulsa, 1989—; reviewer Harcourt/Brace & Javonovich, Tulsa, 1988-89; cons. Little Brown Pubrs., Tulsa, 1984-86; evaluator Random House Pubrs., Tulsa, 1982-84. Contbr. articles to profl. jours.; author test manual: Basic Mathematics, 1989. Vol. Tulsa pub. schs., 1988—; co-leader Brownie troop Girl Scouts U.S., Tulsa, 1988—. Named Tchr. of the Yr., Sapulpa Pub Schs., 1979, Okla. Prof. of Yr., Carnegie Found., 1995. U. Tulsa grantee, 1980. Mem. Okla. Council Tchrs. Math. (coll. rep., exec. bd. 1983—), Am. Math. Assn. Two-Yr. Colls. (editorial bd. 1985—), Nat. Council Tchrs. Math., Phi Delta Kappa, Kappa Delta Pi. Democrat. Avocations: piano, dance, ballet, bicycling, flying. Office: Tulsa Community College 3727 E Apache St Tulsa OK 74115-3150 E-mail: cthompso2@tulsa.cc.ok.us.

THOMPSON, CATHERINE RUSH, physical therapist, educator; b. Kansas City, Mo., Feb. 26, 1954; d. John Adams and Jacqueline (Richard) Rush; m. Gerald Lathen Thompson, Aug. 4, 1979 (dec. July 2003); children: Richard Lathen, Eric Rush. BS in Phys. Therapy with distinction, U. Colo., Denver, 1976; MS in Spl. Edn. with distinction, U. Kans., 1981; PhD in Psychology and Edn., U. Mo.Kansas City, 2001. Cert. phys. therapist, Kans., Mo. Sch. phys. therapist Easter Seal Soc., Miami, Fla., 1976, Taylor Rehab. Ctr., Cedar Rapids, Iowa, 1977-79; cons. B.W. Shepard State Schs., Kansas City, Mo., 1979-86; pediatric phys. therapist Consol. Sch. Dist. 1, Kansas City, Mo., 1986-94, Spina Bifida Clinic-U. Kans. Med. Ctr., Kansas City, Kans., 1991-94; instr. phys. therapy U. Kans. Med. Ctr., Kansas City, Kans., 1990-96, Rockhurst Coll., 1997—. Phys. therapy cons. Lakemary Ctr., Paola, Kans., 1991—1995; pediat. phys. therapist, early intervention for Johnson Co. and Leavenworth Co., 2002-; mem. desegregation monitoring com. Kansas City (Mo.) Sch. Dist., 1991—1993; chair Kansas City (Mo.) Pediatric Alliance, 1981-84; adv. com. Ctr. for Devel. Disabled, Kansas City, Mo., 1982-85; pres. Rush Assocs., Inc., 1980-85; spkr. in field. Festival chair Hyde Park Neighborhood Assn., Kansas City, Mo., 1985; parent rep. sch. adv. com. Faxon Montessori Sch., Kansas City, Mo., 1987; summer tchr. Trinity United Meth. Ch., Kansas City, Mo., 1991; grants chair sch. adv. com. Ecole Longan, Kansas City, Mo., 1991. Arthur Mag fellow U. Mo., 1989. Mem. Am. Phys. Therapy Assn. (abstract editor pediatric sect. 1981-83), Kans. Phys. Therapy Assn. (rsch. com. 1989-94), Spina Bifida Assn., Kansas City Soc. Neurosci., Ind. Therapy Svcs. (pres. 1982-86). Avocations: wellness, historic preservation, gardening, poetry. Home: 711 Manheim Rd Kansas City MO 64109-2633 Office: Rockhurst Univ Dept Phys Therapy Edn 108 Van Ackeran Kansas City MO 64110-2561

THOMPSON, CHERYL ANN, special education educator; b. Berlin, Sept. 15, 1967; d. Edward Joseph and Kathleen (Snay) T. BS in Spl. Edn., Westfield (Mass.) State Coll., 1989; MEd, R.I. Coll., 1994. Spl. edn. tchr. Behavior Rsch. Inst., Providence, R.I., 1989-92, Boston Ctr. for Blind Children, 1993-94, Barnstable Pub. Schs., Hyannis, Mass., 1996—; day program supr. Residential Rehab. Ctrs. Inc., Brewster, Mass., 1994-96; spl. edn. tchr. Barnstable Pub. Schs., Hyannis, Mass., 1996—. Mem. Assn. for Persons with Severe Handicaps, Am. Assn. on Mental Retardation, Prader-Willi Syndrome Assn. Democrat. Roman Catholic. Avocations: collecting clowns, reading, softball, animals. Home: 365 Rt 6 15 Locust St # A South Yarmouth MA 02664-5617

THOMPSON, DEBORAH CARPENTER, private school educator; b. Rutland, Vt., Feb. 22, 1943; d. Edwards Shinville and Frances (Howley) Carpenter; m. Hall Thompson, Sept. 4, 1965; children: Anne, Joel. BA, U. Vt., 1965; MEd, Boston U., 1968. Pres. Gtr. Portland (Maine) Childbirth Edn. Assn., 1973-78; assoc. in parish adminstrn. Congregational Ch. Cumberland (Maine), 1980-87; tutor English, history North Yarmouth Acad., Yarmouth, Maine, 1988—. Mem. Congregational Ch. Cumberland, 1976—. Mem. Maine Audubon Soc., Portland (Maine) Mus. Art, Portland Country Club, Val Halla Golf Course (chair bd. trustees 1987-93, greens com. 1997—). Avocations: golf, gardening, cross country skiing, politics, art. Home: 240 Greely Rd Cumberland Center ME 04021-9379

THOMPSON, DENISSE R. mathematics educator; b. Keesler AFB, Miss., Aug. 26, 1954; BA, BS, U. South Fla., 1976, MA, 1980; PhD, U. Chgo., 1992. Cert. tchr., Fla. Tchr. Hernando County Schs., Brooksville, Fla., 1977-82; instr. maths. Manatee C.C., Bradenton, Fla., 1982-87; asst. prof. U. South Fla., Tampa, 1991-97, assoc. prof., 1997—2003, prof., 2003—. Cons. in field. Author: Fundamental Skills of Mathematics, 1987, Advanced Algebra, 1990, 2d edit., 1996, (with others) Precalculus and Discrete Mathematics, 1992, Nat. Coun. Tchrs. of Math. Yearbook, 1991, 93, 94, 95, 2002; co-editor: Standards-Based School Mathematics: What Are They? What do Students Learn?; contbr. articles to profl. jours. Recipient Carolyn Hoefer Meml. award Pi Lambda Theta, 1988. Mem. ASCD, Math. Assn. Am., Nat. Coun. Tchrs. Math., Nat. Coun. Suprs. Math., Assn. Women in Math., Phi Delta Kappa, Phi Kappa Phi. Office: U South Fla College of Edn EDU162 Tampa FL 33620

THOMPSON, DOROTHY BARNARD, elementary school educator; b. Flushing, NY, Aug. 14, 1933; d. Henry Clay and Cecelia Minnie Theresa (La Pardo) Barnard; m. Norman Earl Thompson, Aug. 12, 1956 (dec.); children: Greg, Scot, Henry, Marc (dec.), Matthew. BSEd, SUNY, New Paltz, 1953; MS, Hofstra U., 1984. Cert. elem. tchr. K-6th grades, reading specialist K-12th grades, NY. Adjunct prof. Suffolk Community Coll., Brentwood, NY, 1987—; adj. prof. Nassau Cmty. Coll., Uniondale, NY, 1986—; adj. prof., instr. Ctr. for Acad. Achievement Long Isl. U., Greenvale, NY, 1984-92; tchr. reading, 1st and 2nd grades Long Beach Pub. Sch., NY, 1988—. Mem. founding group Parent/Tchr., The Learning Tree, Garden City, NY, 1971; founder parent coop. Happy Day Nursery Sch., Bellmore, NY, 1975; parent-tchr. Commonwealth Sch., Bay Shore, Oakdale, 1976-82. Office: 456 Neptune Blvd Long Beach NY 11561-2400 E-mail: anetco01@aol.com.

THOMPSON, DOROTHY MAE, school system administrator, real estate manager; b. Idaho, Ohio, Jan. 10, 1932; d. Sanford M. and Elizabeth (Smith) Williams; m. Robert D. Van Meter, Sept. 27, 1957 (dec. 1974); children: Carmen, Lois, Holly; m. Charles Thompson, Jan. 18, 1977. Student, Ohio U., 1957-60; BS in Edn., Rio Grande Coll., 1965; MS in Ednl. Adminstrn., Xavier U., 1968, MS in Pupil Pers., 1969. Elem. tchr. Pike County Schs., Piketon, Ohio, 1959-69; guidance counselor Piketon High Sch., 1971-73; coord. spl. edn. Waverly (Ohio) City Schs., 1969-71, elem. supr., 1973-79, asst. supt., 1979-81; mgr. personal real estate New Smyrna Beach, Fla., 1982-90; farm mgr. Abbeville, S.C., 1990—. Mem. AAUW, Delta Kappa Gamma (v.p.). Methodist. Avocations: gardening, cooking, sewing. Address: PO Box 565 Bainbridge OH 45612-0565

THOMPSON, EDWARD IVINS BRADBRIDGE, biological chemistry and genetics educator, molecular endocrinologist, department chairman; b. Burlington, Iowa, Dec. 20, 1933; s. Edward Bills and Lois Elizabeth (Bradbridge) T.; m. Lynn Taylor Parsons; children: Elizabeth Lynn, Edward Ernest Bradbridge. BA with distinction, Rice U., 1955; postgrad., Cambridge U., 1957-58; MD, Harvard U., 1960. Intern The Presbyn. Hosp., N.Y.C., 1960-61, asst. resident internal medicine, 1961-62; rsch. assoc. Nat. Inst. Mental Health, NIH, Bethesda, Md., 1962-64; rsch. scientist Nat. Inst. Arthritis and Metabolic Diseases, NIH, Bethesda, Md., 1964-68, Lab of Biochemistry, Nat. Cancer Inst., NIH, Bethesda, Md., 1968-73, sect. chief, 1973-84; I.H. Kempner prof. U. Tex. Med. Br., Galveston, 1984, prof., chmn. dept. human biol. chemistry and genetics, 1984—, prof. internal medicine, 1984—, interim dir. Sealy Ctr. for Molecular Sci., 1996—. Attending physician Nat. Naval Med. Ctr., Bethesda, 1978-80; chmn. hormones and cancer task force NIH, Bethesda, 1978-80; co-chmn. Gordon Research Conf., 1980; mem. adv. com. on Biochem. & Chem. Carcinogenesis, Am. Cancer Soc., 1982-86; mem. revision com. Endocrinology adv. panel U.S. Pharmacopoeial Conv., Inc., 1980-85; mem. council for clin. investigation and research awds., Am. Cancer Soc., 1989-93; bd. scientific overseers Pennington Nutrition Rsch. Ctr. La. State U., 199-98—; Fulbright prof., Marburg, Germany. 1992-93; vis. prof. Bristol U., U.K., 1998; vis. prof. U. Bristol, U.K., 1998; mem. edn. bd. Am. Med. and Grad. Depts. Biochemistry, 1999—. Co-editor Gene Expression and Carcinogenesis in Cultured Liver, 1975, Steroid Receptors and the Management of Cancer, 1979, DNA: Protein Interactions and Gene Regulation, other vols. in field; assoc. editor Cancer Rsch. jour., 1976-86; corr. editor Jour. Steroid Biochemistry, 1977-85; founding editor-in-chief Molecular Endocrinology Jour., 1985-92; editor-in-chief Endocrine Reviews,, 2001—; mem. editl. bd. Steroids & WWW Jour. Biology, 1995—, Molecular Endocrinology, 1998; contbr. over 200 sci. articles to profl. jours. Mem. troop com. Girl Scouts U.S., Rockville, Md., 1970-76; mem. PTA, Rockville, 1967-77, Wilderness Soc., Washington, 1964-75; initiator sci. edn. liaison program Galveston Pub. Schs., 1991; mem. pres.'s cabinet U. Tex. Med. Br. Served as med. dir. USPHS, 1962-84. Grantee NIH, Walls Rsch., Nat. Inst. Diabetes and Digestive and Kidney Diseases, Nat. Cancer Inst.; Am. Cancer Soc. scholar, 1992-93; Fulbright scholar; recipient J.G. Sinclair award Sigma Xi, 1997. Mem. Am. Soc. Cell Biology, Am. Assn. Cancer Rsch., Am. Soc. Biol. Chemists, Endocrine Soc. (mem. history com. 1999), Am. Soc. Microbiology, Am. Coll. Med. Genetics (affiliate), S.W. Ennviron. Mutagen Soc., The Yacht Club, Raquet Club, Harvard Club, Pres.'s Clubs of Rice U. and U. Tex. Med. Br., Phi Beta Kappa, Alpha Omega Alpha. Achievements include patent on anti-tumor activity of a modified fragment of glucocorticoid receptor. Office: U Tex Med Br Dept Human Biol Chem & Gene Galveston TX 77555-0001 E-mail: bthompso@utmb.edu.

THOMPSON, ELLEN ANN, elementary education educator; b. Newton, Mass., Mar. 23, 1955; d. Arthur Malachi and Eva Louise (Harris) T.; m. John A. Rasys, Nov. 30, 1980 (div. Apr. 1987); 1 child, Christopher Michael Rasys; m. James E. Holzschuh, July 1, 1995. BS in Edn., U. Vt., 1977, MEd, 1986, postgrad. Cert. elem. tchr., spl. edn. tchr., Vt.; nat. bd. cert. tchr. early childhood generalist. Title I tchr. remedial reading grades 1-3 Colchester (Vt.) Sch. Dist., 1977-78; title I readiness rm. tchr. Union Meml Sch., Colchester, 1978-79, tchr. grade 2 transitional grade, 1979-81, classroom tchr. grades 1-3 multiage, 1981-99; adj. instr. dept. grad. edn. U. Vt., Burlington, 1987—; adj. instr. undergrad. edn. program Trinity Coll., Burlington, 1992-94. Presenter N.E. Whole Lang. Conf., Johnson (Vt.) State Coll., 1987-97, resource agt. tchr. insvc. programs Vt. Dept. Edn., 1988—, resource cons. Vt. Writing Portfolio Assessment Program, 1990—, network leader # 16, 1991-95; conf. presenter, adj. instr. Am. Inst. for Creative Edn., Augusta, Maine, 1988-92; art cons. Within the Forest, Sci. Rsch. Assocs., 1991—; ednl. cons., presenter Soc. for Devel. Edn., Peterborough, N.H.; teaching fellow regional lab. Rural Small Sch. Network, 1991-92; pres. Ellen A. Thompson, Inc., 1999—; reading lang. arts cons., Vt. Dept. Edn., 1999-2000; adj. prof. U. Vt., Undergrad. Sch. Edn., literacy cons. Reading Excellence Award Grant Program, Winooski, Vt., Gloucester, Mass., 2000—. Author: (videos) The Nuts and Bolts of Multiage Classrooms, 1994, How to Teach in a Multiage Classroom, 1994, (book) I Teach First Grade!, 2001. Recipient State Teacher of the Yr. awd., Vermont, Coun. of Chief State School Offices, 1993. Mem. ASCD, Nat. Coun. Tchrs. English (presenter 1991, 92), Internat. Reading Assn. (presenter annual conf. 1991, Leaders of Readers award 1990), Vt. Coun. on Reading (newsletter editor and conf. presenter 1988—, pres. 1991-92), Vt. Tchrs. Applying Whole Lang., Colchester Edn. Assn. (internal newsletter 1987-89, newsletter editor 1988-89, 96-98), Phi Delta Kappa. Home: 89 East Shore Rd South Hero VT 05486-4911

THOMPSON, EWA M. foreign language educator; b. Kaunas, Lithuania; came to U.S., 1963; d. Jozef and Maria Majewski; m. James R. Thompson. BA in English and Russian, U. Warsaw, Poland, 1963; MFA in Piano, Sopot Conservatory Music, 1963; MA in English, Ohio U., 1964; PhD in Comparative Lit., Vanderbilt U., 1967. Instr. Vanderbilt U., Nashville, Tenn., 1964-67; asst. prof. Ind. State U., Terre Haute, 1967-68, Ind. U., 1968-70, Rice U., Houston, 1967-73, assoc. prof., 1974-79, prof., 1979—, chair, 1987-90; assoc. prof. U. Va., Charlottesville, 1973-74. Cons. NEH, 1973—, The John D. and Catherine T. MacArthur Found., The John Simon Guggenheim Found., U.S. Dept. Edn.; vis. cons. Tex. A&M U.; seminar dir. NEH Summer Inst., Southeastern La. U., 1990; chair Russian lit. conf. Rice U., 1989; lectr. various colls. and univs. Author: Russian Formalism and Anglo-American New Criticism: A Comparative Study, 1971, Witold Gombrowicz, 1979, Polish transl., 2002, Understanding Russia: The Holy Fool in Russian Culture, 1987 (Chinese transl. 1995, 2nd Chinese edit. 1998), The Search for Self-Definition in Russian Literature, 1991, Imperial Knowledge: Russian Literature and Colonialism, 2000, Polish transl., 2000; editor the Sarmatian Rev., (www.ruf.rice.edu/[]sarmatia) 1988—; contbr. articles to profl. jours., chpts. to books. Mellon grant, 1990, Rice U. grant 1990, Internat. Rsch. and Exchanges Sr. Scholar grant, 1991; Hoover Inst. fellow, 1988; scholar Vanderbilt U., 1964-67; recipient Silver Thistle award Houston's Scottish Heritage Found., 1988. Roman Catholic. Home: 142 Stoney Creek Houston TX 77024 Office: Rice University 6100 S Main St MS 32 Houston TX 77005-1892 E-mail: ethomp@rice.edu.

THOMPSON, GREGORY LEE, social sciences educator; b. Huntington Park, Calif., June 14, 1946; s. Karl Windsor and Virginia Alice (Hanna) T. AB in Geography, U. Calif., Davis, 1968; M of City Planning, U. Calif., Berkeley, 1970; PhD in Social Scis., U. Calif., Irvine, 1987. Transp. planner City of Edmonton (Alberta) Transit Sys., 1970-72; transp. analyst Can. Transport Commn., Ottawa, Ontario, 1972-73; transp. coord. City of Berkeley (Calif.) Planning Dept., 1973-74; sr. transp. planner San Diego County, 1974-77, Met. Transp. Devel. Bd., San Diego, 1977-80; sr. cons. Mass Transit, Calif. Assembly, Sacramento, 1980-81; rsch. fellow Hagley Mus. & Libr., Wilmington, Del., 1987-88; asst. prof. Fla. State U., Tallahassee, 1988-94, assoc. prof., 1994—2003, prof., 2003—. Author: The Passenger Train in the Motor Age: California 1910-1941, 1993; contbr. articles to profl. jours. Organizer, pres. Citizens of Rail Calif., San Diego, 1976-80. Named Advanced Rsch. fellow Andrew W. Mellon/NEH, 1987-88, Disting. Student scholar Sch. Engring. U. Calif., Irvine, 1983. Mem. Am. Planning Assn. (sect. dir. San Diego), Soc. for History of Technology, Econ. History Assn., Bus. History Assn., Planning History Assn., Am. Inst. Cert. Planners. Democrat. Avocations: photography, swimming. Home: 2635 Lucerne Dr Tallahassee FL 32303-2261 Office: Fla State U Dept Urban Regional Pl Tallahassee FL 32306

THOMPSON, HUGH LEE, academic administrator; b. Martinsburg, W.Va., Mar. 25, 1934; s. Frank Leslie and Althea T.; m. Patricia Smith; children: Cheri, Linda, Tempe, Vicki. BS, BA in English and Secondary Edn, Shepherd Coll., Shepherdstown, W.Va., 1956; MS, Pa. State U., 1958; PhD in Higher Edn. Adminstrn, Case Western Res. U., 1969. Mem. faculty Pa. State U., 1957-60, Akron (Ohio) U., 1960-62, Baldwin-Wallace Coll., Berea, Ohio, 1962-70, asst. to pres., 1966-69, dir. instl. planning, asst. to pres., 1969-70; coord. Associated Colls., Cleve., 1970-71; pres. Siena Heights U., Adrian, Mich., 1971-77, Detroit Inst. Tech., 1977-80; chancellor Ind. U., Kokomo, 1980-90; pres. Washburn U., Topeka, 1990-97, Higher Edn. Assocs., Merritt Island, Fla., 1997—; interim v.p. for acad. affairs Clarke Coll., 1999-2000. Former mem. pres.'s adv. coun. Assn. Governing Bds. Univs. and Colls.; Fulbright scholar to China, 1998, to Bulgaria, 2001, to Cyprus, 2002, to Trinidad, 2003. Mem. Am. Assn. State Colls. and Univs. (coun. of state reps., steering com. urban and met. univs. coun.), North Ctrl. Assn. (evaluator, cons.). Home and Office: 225 S Tropical Trail Merritt Island FL 32052 E-mail: hughthompson@worldnet.att.net.

THOMPSON, JEANIE WALLER, secondary school educator; b. DeWitt, Ark., Nov. 30, 1954; d. Homer Clifford and Ruby Imogene (McAdams) Waller; m. Frank Augustus Thompson, Jr., Oct. 1, 1983; children: Jennifer Christen, Trev Franklin; stepchildren, Frank Thompson III (dec.), Joe Bob Thompson. BFA, U. Tex., Tyler, 1984, MA, 1988. Cert. elem. tchr. Tex. Tchr. Trinity Day Sch., Longview, Tex., 1982-84; tchr. music, choir Hallsville (Tex.) Ind. Sch. Dist., 1985-95; tchr. music, choir, bilingual tchr. Pine Tree Ind. Sch. Dist., Longview, Tex., 1995—. Mem. Tex. Music Educators Assn., Tex. Choral Dirs. Assn., Assn. Tex. Profl. Educators, Beta Sigma Phi. Home: 1207 Briarwood Ln Longview TX 75604-3507 Office: Pine Tree Ind Sch Dist PO Box 5878 Longview TX 75608-5878

THOMPSON, JOHN TILYNN, ophthalmologist, educator; b. Ann Arbor, Mich., June 8, 1956; s. John Morgan and Dorothy Georgene (Kinne) T.; m. Mary Ann Serpi; children: Lauren Alexis, John Michael. Student, Oberlin Coll., 1973-75; BA cum laude, Johns Hopkins U., 1977, MD, 1980. Diplomate Am. Bd. Ophthalmology, 1985. Intern Cedars-Sinai Med. Ctr., L.A., 1980-81; resident Wilmer Ophthalmologic Inst., Balt., 1981-84, asst. chief svc., 1986; asst. prof. Yale U., New Haven, 1986-90, assoc. prof., 1990-91; assoc. clin. prof. U. Md., Balt., 1993—; ptnr. The Retina Inst. Md., Balt., 1991-96, Retina Specialists, Balt., 1996—; asst. prof. The Wilmer Inst., Johns Hopkins U. Dir. retina sect. Yale U., 1986-91. Contbr. articles to profl. jours. Grantee Conn. Lions Eye Found., 1986-91, The Hearst Found., 1989-90; Wilmer Ophthalmologic Inst. fellow, 1984-85, Heed Found. fellow, 1984; recipient Lamport award Biomed. Rsch. Johns Hopkins U., 1978. Fellow Am. Acad. Ophthalmology (honor award 1988); mem. AMA, Assn. Rsch. in Vision & Ophthalmology, The Retina Soc., The Macula Soc., The Vitreous Soc., Phi Beta Kappa. Avocations: tennis, classical piano, computer programming. Office: Retina Specialists 6569 N Charles St Ste 605 Towson MD 21204-6833

THOMPSON, JOYCE ANN, education consultant; b. Little Rock, Mar. 31, 1948; d. James Willie and Mattie Lee (Swope) Wallace; m. Lonnie Thompson, July 24, 1974; children: Nelieta Manoi, Kayle Ayo, Toyin Jean. BA, Okla. Bapt. U., 1970; MA, Calif. State U., Bakersfield, 1983. Cert. secondary tchr., adminstv. svcs. Tchr. bus. edn. Kern High Sch. Dist., Bakersfield, 1970-72, 77-78, 85-87, GED lang. instr., 1987-90, Outreach cons., 1990—; acctg. inst. Santa Barbara Bus. Coll., 1983-85; typing tchr. Greenfield Jr. High Sch., Bakersfield, 1978-83. Mem. adv. coun. Foothill High Sch., Bakersfield, 1990—, hearing panel Kern High Sch. Dist., 1991—. Author: Graduation Requires Attendance Daily, 1990, Parent Partners, 1990. Mem. NEA, Kern High Faculty Assn., Kern High Counseling Assn., Calif. Tchrs. Assn., Bus. and Profl. Persons Orgn., Young Women's Christian Coun. Mem. Ch. of God in Christ. Avocations: creative writing, reading. Home: PO Box 10072 Bakersfield CA 93389-0072 Office: Foothill High Sch 501 Park Dr Bakersfield CA 93306-6099

THOMPSON, KENNETH W(INIFRED), educational association administrator, writer, editor, social sciences educator; b. Des Moines, Aug. 29, 1921; s. Thor Carlyle and Agnes (Rorbeck) T.; m. Betty Bergquist (dec.); m. Beverly Bourret (dec.); children: Kenneth Caryle, Paul Andrew, James David, Carolyn Cordry. AB, Augustana Coll., 1943, LHD (hon.), LLD, Augustana Coll., 1986; MA, U. Chgo., 1948, PhD, 1950; LLD, U. Notre Dame, 1964, Bowdoin Coll., 1972, St. Michael's Coll., 1973, St. Olaf Coll., 1974, U. Denver, 1983; L.H.D., W.Va. Wesleyan U., 1970; LHD, Nebr. Wesleyan Coll., 1971. Lectr. social scis. U. Chgo., 1948, asst. prof. polit. sci., 1951-53; from asst. prof. to assoc. prof. polit. sci. Northwestern U., 1949-55, chmn. internat. relations com., 1951-55; asst. dir. social scis Rockefeller Found., 1955-57, from assoc. dir. social scis. to v.p., 1957-73; dir. higher edn. for devel. Internat. Council for Ednl. Devel., 1974-76; Commonwealth prof. govt. and fgn. affairs U. Va., 1975-78, White Burkett Miller prof. govt. and fgn. affairs, 1979-86; J. Wilson Newman prof. govt. and fgn. affairs, 1986—; dir. White Burkett Miller Ctr. Pub. Affairs, 1978-98; dir. emeritus Miller Ctr., 1999—. Riverside Meml. lectr. Riverside Ch., N.Y.C., 1958; Lilly lectr. Duke, 1959; James Stokes lectr. N.Y.U., 1962; Rockwell lectr. Rice U., 1965; Ernest Griffith lectr. Am. U.; Andrew Cecil lectr. U. Tex., 1983; Stuber lectr. U. Rochester, 1984; Morgenthau Meml. lectr., N.Y.C., Mike Mansfield Ctr. lectr., U. Mont.; dir. Inst. Study World Politics, N.Y.C., 1975-01; cons. in field. Author, editor: Principles and Problems of International Politics, 1951, 82, Man and Modern Society, 1953, Christian Ethics and the Dilemmas of Foreign Policy, 1959, 81, Conflict and Cooperation Among Nations, 1960, Political Realism and the Crisis of World Politics, 1960, 82, American Diplomacy and Emergent Problems, 1962, 82, Foreign Policies in a World of Change, 1964, The Moral Issue in Statecraft, 1966, Reconstituting the Human Community, 1972, Foreign Assistance: A View From Private Sector, 1972, 82, Higher Education for National Development, 1972, Understanding World Politics, 1975, Higher Edn. and Social Change, 1976, World Politics, 1976, Truth and Tragedy, 1977, Ethics and Foreign Policy, 1978, Interpreters and Critics of the Cold War, 1978, Foreign Policy and the Democratic Process, 1978, Ethics, Functionalism and Power, 1979, Morality and Foreign Policy, 1980, Masters of International Thought, 1980, The Virginia Papers, vols. 1-30, 1979-96, The President and the Public Philosophy, 1981, Cold War Theories: World Polarization, 1944-53, Vol. I, 1981,91. Winston S. Churchill's World View, 1983, 89, Toynbees's World Politics and History, 1985, Moralism and Morality, 1985, Ethics and International Relations, 1985, Theory and Practice of International Relations, 1987, Arms Control and Foreign Policy, 1990, Traditions and Values in Politics and Diplomacy, 1992, Fathers of International Thought, 1994, Schools of Thought in International Relations, 1996; editor: Am. Values Series, Vols. I-XX, Presdl. Nominating Process, Vols. I-IV, Portraits of American Presidents, Vols. I-IX, Herbert Butterfield: The Ethics of History; The American Presidency, Vols. I-XVI, 1982-83, Ethics and International Relations, 1985, Moral Dimensions of American Foreign Policy, 1985, 94, The Credibility of Leadership and Institutions, Vols. I-XX, 1983-86, Rhetoric and Political Discourse, Vols.I-XX, Governance, Vols. I-VII, 1990-97, Constitutionalism, Vols. I-VII, 1989-91, Presidency and Science Advising, Vols. I-VIII, 1986-90, Political Transitions and Foreign Policy, Vols. I-IX, 1985-91, A World in Change, Vols. I-XI, 1989-96, Presidential Disability, Vols. I-IV, 1989-96, A New World Order, Vols. I-VI, 1991-97, Great American Presidents, 1994, Defeated Presidential Candidates, 1994, Statesmen Who Were Never President, 1996; bd. editors Society, Ethics and International Affairs, Interpretation, The Rev. of Politics; contbr. articles to profl. jours. Pres. Dist. of Scarsdale and Mamaroneck (N.Y.) Bd. Edn., 1965-68; trustee Union Theol. Sem., 1967-71, Dillard U., 1975-96, Social Sci. Found., U. Denver, 1974-94, Compton Found., 1975-98. 1st lt. AUS, 1943-46. Named Va. laureate, 1981; recipient Phi Beta Kappa and Va. Coll. Stores prizes, Va. Social Sci. Assn. ann. award, English Speaking Union award.Spl. Edward Weintal prize Georgetown U. Acad. Diplomacy, 1999. Fellow Soc. Religion Higher Edn., Am. Acad. Arts and Scis.; mem. Century Club, Scarsdale Town Club, Raven Soc. (ann. award U. Va.), Phi Beta Kappa (pres.), Omicron Delta Phi. Office: Univ Va Miller Ctr PO Box 400406 Charlottesville VA 22904-4406

THOMPSON, LARRY JAMES, retired gifted education educator; b. Savannah, Ga., May 14, 1948; s. James Howell and Dorothy (Hendley) T. BA, Armstrong Atlantic State U., 1970; MAT, Tulane U., 1974; EdD, U. Ga., 1986. Cert. tchr., instrnl. supr., adminstr., Ga. Tchr. social studies Chatham County Bd. Edn., Savannah, 1970-71, 75-87, adminstrv. coord. social studies, 1987-97, gifted, talented educator, 1997-2001; ret., 2001. With USNR, 1971-73. Mem. Nat. Coun. Social Studies, Ga. Coun. Social Studies, Profl. Assn. Ga. Educators, Ga. Hist. Soc., Nat. Trust for Hist. Preservation. Home: 18 E Deerwood Rd Savannah GA 31410-3171

THOMPSON, LAVERNE ELIZABETH THOMAS, college official; b. Bklyn., July 17, 1945; d. Roscoe Lee and Mary Elizabeth (Blackwell) Thomas (dec.). BA in English, Bluffton Coll., 1967; MS in Ednl. Adminstrn./Supervision, U. Dayton, 1977; PhD in Higher Edn., U. Toledo, 1991. Cert. sch. prin., secondary sch. supr., realtor, Ohio. Tchr. English and speech Piqua (Ohio) Ctrl. H.S., 1967—68; instr. Lima (Ohio) Sr. H.S., 1968—77, Shawnee H.S., Lima, 1977—86; grad. asst. U. Toledo, 1986—91, interim counselor, adminstr. student support svcs., 1989, interim adminstrv. asst. multicultural student devel., 1990; dir. pre-svc. edn./urban tchr. program Wayne County C.C., Detroit, 1996—2002; chief acad. officer N.W. campus Wayne County C.C. Dist., Detroit, 2002—. Real estate agt. Alberta Lee Realty, Lima, Ohio, 1978-82, Slonaker Realty, Lima, 1982-84, Gooding Co., Lima, 1985-90; substitute English tchr., Maumee (Ohio) City Schs., 1996; adj. prof., acad. coord. alternative edn. Spring Arbor Coll., Lambertville, Mich., 1995-96; reviewer Eisenhower Grants for Higher Edn., Mich. Dept. Edn., 1997, 98, 99, 2000, 01; stakeholder Skillman Found. project Child Care Coord. Coun. Greater Detroit, Wayne County, 1998-2001; mem. exec. bd. Young Educators Soc. Mich., 1999—. Editor Higher Edn. newsletter, 1987. Participant 17th ann. Nat. Conf. on Citizenship, Washington, 1962; co-chair Brotherhood Dinner Sr. H.S., Lima, 1976; bd. dirs. Lima YWCA, 1971. Mem. Va. Assn. New Homemakers Am. (state pres. 1962, nat. pres. 1963), All God's Children Collectors' Club, Belleek Collectors' Internat. Soc., Harmony Kingdom Collectors Club, Boyd's Bears Friends Collectors Club. Avocations: periodical reading, writing, walking. Home: 13851 Sibley Rd Riverview MI 48192-7759

THOMPSON, LOLA MAY, music educator, volunteer; b. Mpls., Mar. 10, 1931; d. Jens Christian and Lydia Mathilda (Ronsberg) Jensen; m. Wayne Leo Thompson, July 27, 1957; children: Mark Wayne, Scott Christopher. BS, U. Minn., 1953, postgrad., 1953—54. Nationally cert. tchr. of music. Music supr. Little Falls (Minn.) Pub. Schs., 1954-57; music coord. Bloomington (Minn.) Pub. Schs., 1957-61; tchr., owner Thompson Piano Studio, St. Paul, 1961—. Sr. choir dir. Holy Trinity Ch., Mpls., 1953-54, 1st English Luth. Ch., Little Falls, Minn., 1954-57, dir. Jr. Sunday Sch. Choir Cen. Luth. Ch., Mpls., 1970—; benefit co-chmn. Dale Warland Singers, 1989, 95, benefit chmn., 1989-90, benefit honorary chair, 1991; bd. dirs. Friends of Dale Warland Singers; chmn. Thursday Mus. 100th Anniverssary, 1992; organist specializing in wedding music, 1950—. Author: Haarstad, 1992; editor nat. Haarstad newsletter; composer numerous children's songs, choir piece Twenty-Seventh Psalm, 1949 (received award). Pres. Friends of St. Paul Chamber Orch., 1974—77, coun., 1977—; benefit chmn., 1978—80, 1988; gen. chmn. Minn. Orch. and Women's Assn. for Young Artist Competition, 1982—84, repertoire chmn., 1984—; advisor Women's Assn. Minn. Orch., 1986—; benefit chmn. U. Minn. Found., 1984—85; mem. com. for gala opening U. Minn. Mann Performing Arts Ctr., 1993; mem. Minn. Hist. Soc. Women's Orgn.; accompanist Mpls. Choraliers, 1950—54; mem. 1006 Avenue Soc. of Minn. Gov.'s Residence; spl. events advisor Hamline U., 1990; chmn. 100th Anniversary of Thursday Musical, 35th Anniversary Celebration of The St. Paul Chamber Orch., 1993; co-chair Dale Warland Singers Gala, 1989—90, 1996—2001. Recipient Good Neighbor award Sta. WCCO, 1985, Ultimate Friend award Friends of the St. Paul Chamber Orch., 1999. Mem. AAUW, Music Tchrs. Nat. Assn., Minn. Music Tchrs. Assn. (state chair Student Achievement Fund, grants and funding), Minn. Opera Assn., Sigma Alpha Iota (nat. province v.p. 1979-82, pres. St. Paul-Mpls. chpt. 1969-72, 83-85, Sword of Honor 1969, Rose of Honor 1970, 50 Yr. award 2001) Republican. Lutheran. Avocations: needlepoint, boating, swimming, travel, family history.

THOMPSON, LULA AVERHART, retired educator; b. Farmersville, Ala. d. Frank and Octavia (Reese) Averhart; m. Oscar Lee Thompson. AB cum laude, Paine Coll., 1939; postgrad., U. Ala., 1942, Western Res. U., 1950; MEd, Ala. State Coll., 1959; tchr. trainer cert., Fla. State U., 1966; EdS, Auburn U., 1972, double AA profl. tchg. cert., 1973. Tchr. home econs. Fairfield Bd. Edn., 1939-49, tchr. math., 1950-63, tchr. social studies, 1963-73. Life mem., Sunday sch. tchr., former sec. Sunday sch., former dir. youth programs Mars Hill Bapt. Ch., Democrat. Avocations: ceramics, designing and making personal clothing and hats, reading, traveling. Home: 4500 Mcclain St Bessemer AL 35020-1848

THOMPSON, LYNN KATHRYN SINGER, educational administrator; b. Ames, Iowa, Nov. 30, 1947; d. William Andrew and Virginia Preston (Russell) Singer. BA, Cornell Coll., Mt. Vernon, Iowa, 1970; MA in Edn., Ariz. State U., 1980; EdD, No. Ariz. U., 1990. Cert. tchr. and adminstr., Ariz. Tchr. Crane Elem. Dist., Yuma, Ariz., 1970-81, 86-90; coord. fed. programs Crane Elem Dist., Yuma, Ariz., 1981-83, asst. prin., 1983-85, dir. lang. acquisition and fed. programs, 1990-99, prin., 1999-2001, assoc. supt., 2001—. Bd. dirs. Yuma Fine Arts Assn., 1982-84; mem. Ariz. State Com. Practitioners, Phoenix, 1994—. Recipient Golden Bell award Ariz. Sch. Bds. Assn., 1992; Delta Kappa Gamma scholar, 1987, 89. Mem. PEO Internat., Delta Kappa Gamma (pres. 1988-90), Phi Delta Kappa (bd. dirs., rsch. chair 1991-95), ZONTA Internat. (bd. dirs. Yuma 1991, pres. 1996-97, 98). Avocations: home restoration, camping, antiques, reading. Office: Yuma Elem Dist 1 450 W 6th St Yuma AZ 85364 E-mail: d1_thompson@yumaed.org.

THOMPSON, MARCIA SLONE, choral director, educator; b. Ary, Ky., June 30, 1959; d. Ray and Wevena (Hall) Slone; m. Randall C. Thompson, Sept. 22, 1979; children: Tiffany, Ashley, Brittany, Alicia, Jessica, Matthew. B in Music Edn., Pikeville Coll., 1981; M in Secondary Edn., Morehead State U., 1985. Cert. Rank I supervision, music edn. tchr. with endorsement, grades K-12. Guitarist Slone Family Band, 1970-77; pvt. practice Hindman, Ky., 1977-93; band, choral dir. Pike County Bd. Edn., Pikeville, Ky., 1981-82, Floyd County Bd. Edn., Eastern, Ky., 1982-87; choral dir. Knott County Bd. Edn., Hindman, 1987—, Knott County Central High, Hindman, Ky, 1987—. Piano instr. guitar instr., Upward Bound program Pikeville Coll., Hindman, 1977. Albums include Appalachian Bluegrass, 1972, Ramblin' Round with Slone Family, 1977; appeared on the Grand Ole Opry, 1976. Band conductor jr. high divsn. Pike County All-County Festival, Pikeville, 1981; music chair Red White Blue Festival, Martin, Ky., 1982; music judge Floyd County All-County Band, Prestonsburg, Ky., 1982-87; band dir. Ky. Derby Festival Parade, Louisville, 1985; piano accompanist choir 1st Bapt. Ch., Hindman, 1990-91, nursery asst., 1990-93, dir. youth choir, 1992, choral dir. music makers (children's music), 1994, Bapt. young women's hospitality officer, 1995, mem. sch. com.; performer Senator Benny Bailey Salute, Prestonsburg, 1991, Gingerbread Festival, Hindman, 1992-95; active Bapt. Young Women, 1993-95; co-founder Knott County Fine Arts Day Celebration, 1992—, hospitality officer Hindman Baptist Ch. Young Women's Group, 1995. Mem. Nat. Educators Assn., Am. Choral Dirs. Assn., Ky. Educators Assn., Ky. Music Educators. Democrat. Avocations: arranging music, playing piano, guitar, skating, reading. Home: 186 Sky Light Dr Hindman KY 41822-8647 Office: Knott County Ctrl High Sch Hindman KY 41822

THOMPSON, MARGIE JANE, retired elementary school educator; b. Peoria, Ill. d. Andrew Dean and Hilda Martha (Sinn) Dilkey; m. Patrick Perry Thompson, June 25, 1961; children: Kelli Jo, Marci Lynn (dec). BE, Ill. State U., 1961. Cons. Regional Office of Edn., Rockford, Ill., 1979, 80, 81, dir., 1981-83, Abilities Ctr., Rockford, 1983-84; educator Kellar Sch. Dist., Peoria, 1961-65, Rockford Pub. Schs., 1984—98; ret., 1998. Mem. AAUW (v.p. 1974-76, pres. 1976-78). Home: 3468 N Trainer Rd Rockford IL 61114-8156

THOMPSON, NANCY JO, special education educator, elementary education educator, consultant; b. Crawfordsville, Ind., Apr. 17, 1950; BE, Manchester Coll., 1971; MEd, Ind. U., South Bend, 1978. Cert. elem. tchr., tchr. emotionally disturbed K-12, Ind. Tchr. 6th grade Boone County Sch. Corp., Dover, Ind., 1971-72; lead tchr. N. Manchester (Ind.) Day Care Ctr., 1972-73; processor H & R Block, Elkhart, Ind., 1973; dept. head, sales Grinnell's Music Store, Elkhart, Ind., 1974-75; adminstrv. asst. Oaklawn Psychiat. Ctr., Elkhart, 1975-76; tchr. emotionally handicapped Treehouse-Day Treatment Program Oaklawn Psychiat., Elkhart, 1976-78; tchr. emotionally handicapped Elkhart Community Schs., 1978-85, resource team cons., 1985-94; tchr. diagnostic class EH Diagnostic Day Sch., Elkhart, 1994—. State trainer Ind. Dept. Edn., Indpls., 1987-89; bd. dirs. Loveway, Inc., Therapeutic Horseback Riding. Treas. Hively Ave. Nursery Sch., Elkhart, 1974; band mem. Elkhart Mcpl. Band, 1974-77; youth adv. Hively Ave. Mennonite Ch., Elkhart, 1980-84. Mem. NEA, Coun. Exceptional Children (cert. excellence profl. standards, practices Tri-County Coun. 1984), Coun. Children with Behavioral Disorders, Nat. Coun. Autistic Citizens, Ind. State Tchrs. Assn. Avocations: traveling, music, theater, handi-crafts, cross-country skiing. Office: Elkhart Community Schools Eastwood Elem Sch Dept Diagnostic 53215 County Road 15 Elkhart IN 46514-8583

THOMPSON, NOVELLA WOODRUM, college administrator, psychotherapist; b. Frankfurt, Germany, Apr. 24, 1968; d. Gary Lynn and Kaye Yvonne (Hickman) Woodrum; m. Philip Drew Thompson, Nov. 12, 1994. BA, W.Va. Wesleyan Coll., Buckhannon, 1992; MA, W.Va. Grad. Coll., Institute, 1994. Counselor, parent educator The Family Ctr., Inc., Beckley, W.Va., 1993; counselor Women's Resource Ctr., Beckley, 1993-94; psychotherapist The Family Inst. of W.Va., Beckley, 1994-95; dean Sch. Acad. Enrichment & Lifelong Learning Coll. W.Va., Beckley, 1995—. Guest lectr. W.Va. Grad. Coll., 1994-95; vol. counselor Women's Resource Ctr., Beckley, 1992-93; cons. non-traditional programs Coll. WVa., Beckley, 1995; parent educator & lectr. The Family Ctr. Raleigh County Cmty. Alliance Assn., 1994—. Author: Prior Learning Assessment (PLA), 1996; editor: Experience Counts, 1995. Mem. bd. dirs. The Family Ctr., Beckley, 1993; panelist, speaker Stop Child Abuse Now (SCAN), Beckley, 1994. Recognized for Comty. Svc., Register-Herald "A Celebration of Women." Mem. ACA, W.Va. Counseling Assn., W.Va. Assn. for Specialists in Group Work, Coun. for Adult and Exptl. Learning (state rep. 1996). Avocations: reading, gardening, cross-stitch, decorating, crafts, golf. Office: Coll WVa PO Box Ag Beckley WV 25802-2830 Home: 1944 Belleville Rd SW Roanoke VA 24015-2710

THOMPSON, PHYLLIS DARLENE, retired elementary school educator; b. West Milton, Ohio, May 21, 1934; d. Howard Luther and Dorothy Mae (Heisey) Yount; m. Joel Kent Thompson, Aug. 22, 1954 (div. Feb. 1981); children: George Kevin, Jolanna Renee, Howard Kraig. BS in Edn., Manchester Coll., 1956; MEd, LaVerne U., 1977. Cert. tchr., Ill. Tchr. Dist. 83, North Lake, Ill., 1956-59; missionary, tchr. Ambon (Indonesia) U., 1961-62; tchr. Dist. Unit 46, Elgin, Ill., 1969—2000. Organizer Mother Goose Day Care Ctr., Elgin, 1970s. Choir mem. Highland Ave Ch. of the Brethren, Elgin, 1964—, bd. chair, 1980-83, ch. bd., 1997-98. Recipient Ednl. Excellence award State of Ill., 1978, Disting. Educator award Kane County, 1978. Mem. NEA, Ill. Edn. Assn., Elgin Tchrs. Assn. (bldg. rep. 1994-96), Alpha Delta Kappa (pres., v.p., sec. 1972—). Democrat. Avocations: letter writing, reading, cross stitching, walking. Home: 11 Kensington Loop Elgin IL 60123-2720

THOMPSON, RAHMONA ANN, plant taxonomist; b. Oklahoma City, June 17, 1953; d. Raymond D. and Marilyn Frances (Strong) James; m. Ronald K. Thompson, Aug. 2, 1971. BS in Botany, Okla. U., 1978, MS in Botany, 1981; PhD in Botany, Okla. State U., 1988. Rsch. assoc. Okla. Biol. Survey, Norman, 1988-90; interim curator Robert Bebb Herbarium, Norman, 1990-91; prof. East Ctrl. U., Ada, Okla., 1991—. Taxon editor Flora of N.Am., St. Louis, 1990-2002; bd. dirs. Flora of Okla. Project, Stillwater. Contbr. articles to profl. jours. Bd. dirs. Environ. Control Adv. Bd., Norman, 1991—. Mem.: Nat. Assn. Biology Tchrs., Bot. Soc. Am., Am. Soc. Plant Taxonomists. Democrat. Achievements include research on taxonomic problems in Poaceae, especially generic boundries in Paniceae, spikelet anatomy and science education. Office: East Central U Biology Dept Ada OK 74820

THOMPSON, RAYMOND EUGENE, JR., education educator; b. Merrilville, Ind., Apr. 19, 1958; s. Mary A. (Be) Thompson. AA, Purdue U., 1979, BS, 1980, MS, 1985. Flight instr. Culver (Ind.) Mil. Acad., 1978; asst. prof. Lewis U., Romeoville, Ill., 1980-81; maintenance supr. Aviation Svcs. FBO, Romeoville, 1981; teaching asst. Purdue U., West Lafayette, Ind., 1979-80, asst. prof. edn., 1982-92, assoc. prof., 1993—. Cons. E. G. Composites, Indpls., 1989—, Am. Trans Air, Indpls., 1990—, Am. Corp. Mfg. Learning Ctr., Stuart, Fla., 1992—; aero. tech. curriculum chair Purdue U., 1997-2003, coord. student svcs. dept. aviation tech., 1998—, asst. head dept. Aviation Tech., 2003-. Author: Applied Composite Technology, 1992; editor book chpt.; author curriculum in field. Named Outstanding Maintenance Inst., Aviation Tech. Edn. Coun., 1993. Mem. ASM Internat., Great Lake Aviation Tech. Edn. Coun., Soc. for Advancement of Material and Process Engring., Soc. Mfg. Engrs., Am. Soc. Non-Destructive Testing, Profl. Aircraft Maintenance Assn. Avocations: flying, drama, music, outdoor activities.

THOMPSON, REX ALLEN, school business administrator; b. Hodgenville, Ky., Oct. 20, 1936; s. Veachil Ira and Lucille Mae (Higgason) T.; m. Elizabeth Ann Wolfe, July 10, 1960; 1 child, Jill Ann Thompson Miller. BSBA, Murray State U., 1958, MBA, 1968, cert. rank I, 1981. Commd. 2d lt. U.S. Army, 1958, advanced through grades to capt., 1964; supr. sch. dist. fin. Ky. Dept. of Edn., Frankfort, 1961-62; bus. mgr., asst. to v.p. Murray (Ky.) State U., 1962-79; sch. bus. adminstr. Paducah (Ky.) Bd. of Edn., 1979-91; v.p. bus. and adminstrv. svcs. Bapt. Meml. Coll. Health Scis., Memphis, 1995—. Advisory dir. Republic Bank, Paducah, 1987-95. Bd. dirs., treas. Ky. Bapt. Healthcare Found., Louisville, 1984-94. Mem. Murray State U. Alumni Assn. (past pres.), Paducah Lions Club, Murray Lions Club (past pres.). Democrat. Southern Baptist. Avocation: coin collecting. Home: 6607 Willow Break Dr Bartlett TN 38135-3075 Office: Bapt Meml Coll Hlth Scis Memphis TN 38104 E-mail: rex.thompson@bchs.edu., tho9133@aol.com.

THOMPSON, SANDRA JANE, secondary school educator; b. Clarion, Pa., Nov. 21, 1953; d. Robert Stewart and Dorothy Jean (Wishart) T. BS, Clarion U., 1975. Cert. secondary tchr., Idaho. Tchr. 8th grade sci. Edgewood (Md.) Mid. Sch., 1975-80; tchr. 9th grade math. Idaho Sch. Dist. #60, Shelley, Idaho, 1980-92, tchr. 10th-12th grades math. and AP calculus and stats., 1992—. Pvt. tutor, Shelley, 1983—; girls basketball coach, Shelley, 1984-88; mentor tchr. Idaho Sch. Dist. 60, Shelley, 1989-91; math./sci. cons. Scantron Corp., 1999—. Pres., bd. dirs. Dogs N Stuff Found., Inc., 1997-2002. Mem. NEA, Idaho Edn. Assn., Shelley Edn. Assn. Avocations: reading, leathercraft, hiking, wildlife photography, equine activities. Home: 1173 East 1400 North Shelley ID 83274-5146 Office: Shelley High Sch 570 W Fir St Shelley ID 83274-1449

THOMPSON, THEODORE ROBERT, pediatric educator; b. Dayton, Ohio, July 18, 1943; s. Theodore Roosevelt and Helen (Casey) J.;m. Lynette Joanne Shenk; 1 child, S. Beth. BS, Wittenberg U., 1965; MD, U. Pa., 1969. Diplomate Am. Bd. Pediatrics (Neonatal, Perinatal Medicine). Resident in pediat. U. Minn. Hosp., Mpls., 1969-72, chief resident in pediat., 1971-72, fellow neonatal, perinatal, 1974-75, asst. prof., 1975-80, dir. divsn. neonatology and newborn intensive care unit, 1977-80, assoc. prof., 1980-85, prof., 1985—, co-dir. Med. Outreach, 1988-91, med. dir. med. outreach, 1991-00, assoc. chief of pediat., 1988—2003, assoc. head pediat. edn. and cmty. health, 2003—; med. dir. outreach, sec. bd. dirs. and exec. com. U. Minn. Physicians, 1992—, dir. clin. edn. med. students, 1999—. Exec. com. Fairview U. Med. Ctr., 2002—, assoc. chief affairs dept. pediat., 1991—2003, assoc. head edn. and cmty. affairs dept. pediat., 2003—. Editor: Newborn Intensive Care: A Practical Manual, 1983. Bd. dirs. Life Link III, St. Paul, 1987—; cons. Maternal and Child Health, Minn. Bd. Health, 1975-94; bd. dirs. Minn. Med. Found., 1995-99. With USPHS. 1972-74. Recipient Avocacy award, U. Minn. Med. Sch. Fellow: Am. Acad. Pediats.; mem.: Gt. Plains Orgn. for Perinatal Health Care (Sioux Falls, SD Kunshe award 1989). Lutheran. Office: MMC 39 420 Delaware St SE Minneapolis MN 55455-0374 E-mail: thomp005@umn.edu.

THOMPSON, THOMAS ADRIAN, sculptor; b. Sidney, Mont., Aug. 28, 1944; s. Vernon Eugene and Helen Alice (Torstenson) T.; m. M. Aileen Braun, June 7, 1968; children: Blair C., Meghann C. BA, Concordia Coll., 1966; postgrad., Mich. State U., 1968-69, Oakland U., 1970-72. Art tchr. Carman Ainsworth Sch. Dist., Flint, Mich., 1966-98; ret., 1998. Chmn. Flint Art Curriculum Com., 1980. Mem. adv. bd. Mich. Equine Artists; mem. Gand Blanc Arts Coun. Mem. NEA, Nat. Art. Edn. Assn., Mich. Art Edn. Assn. (liaison mem.), Internat. Arabian Horse Assn., Arabian Horse Registry. Lutheran. Avocations: painting, scuplture, golf. Home: 1409 Kings Carriage Grand Blanc MI 48439-1622 E-mail: tathomps@msn.com.

THOMPSON, TOMMY GEORGE, secretary of health and human services, former governor; b. Elroy, Wis., Nov. 19, 1941; s. Allan and Julia (Dutton) T.; m. Sue Ann Mashak, 1969; children: Kelli Sue, Tommi, Jason. BS in Polit. Sci. and History, U. Wis., 1963, JD, 1966. Polit. intern U.S. Rep. Thomson, 1963; legis. messenger Wis. State Senate, 1964-66; sole practice Elroy and Mauston, Wis., 1966-87; mem. Dist. 87 Wis. State Assembly, 1966-87, asst. minority leader, 1972-81, floor leader, 1981-87; self-employed real estate broker Mauston, 1970—; gov. State of Wis., 1987-2001; sec. U.S. Dept. Health & Human Svcs., Washington, 2001—. Alt. del. Rep. Nat. Conv., 1976; chmn. Intergovtl. Policy Adv. Commn. to U.S. Trade Rep.; chmn. Natl. Govs. Assn., 1995-96, mem. nat. govs. assn. exec. com.; chmn. bd. dirs., Amtrak, 1998-99. Served with USAR. Recipient med. award for Legis. Wis. Acad. Gen. Practice, Thomas Jefferson Freedon award Am. Legis. Exchange Coun., 1991, Most Valuable Pub. Official award City and State Mag., 1991, Governance award Free Congress Found., 1992, Governing Mag. Public Ofcl. of the Year, 1997, recipient Horatio Alger Awd., 1998, USA Mex. C of C, Good Neighbor Awd., 1999. Mem. ABA, Wis. Bar Assn., Rep. Govs. Assn., Phi Delta Phi. Republican. Roman Catholic. Office: Dept HHS Office of the Secy 200 Independence Ave SW Washington DC 20201-0004 Office Fax: 202-690-7203.*

THOMPSON, TRACY MARIE, social studies educator; b. Elkton, Md., Oct. 14, 1969; d. Gene Allen Thompson and Dorothy Ann (Loper) Newton. BS in Edn., U. Md., 1991. Cert. tchr., Md. Social studies tchr. Cecil County Bd. Edn., Perryville, Md., 1991—. Mem. Nat. Geog. Soc., ASCD, Nat. Coun. Social Studies. Avocations: field hockey, softball, music, reading. Office: Cecil County Bd Edn 850 Aiken Ave Perryville MD 21903-2738

THOMPSON, VETTA LYNN SANDERS, psychologist, educator; b. Birmingham, Ala., Sept. 7, 1959; d. Grover and Vera Lee (King) S.; m. Cavelli Andre Thompson, May 27, 1990; children: Olajuwon, Malik Rashad, Kimberlyn, Assata Iyana. BA, Harvard U., 1981; MA, Duke U., 1984, PhD, 1988. Cert. psychologist and health svc. provider, State of Mo. Com. Psychologists. Psychology intern Malcolm Bliss Mental Health Ctr., St. Louis, 1985-86; psychotherapist, testing coord. Washington U. Child Guidance Clinic, St. Louis, 1986-87; psychologist, treatment team coord. Hawthorn Children's Psychiatric Hosp., St. Louis, 1987-89; asst. prof. U. Mo., St. Louis, 1989-95, assoc. prof., coord. black studies, 1995—. Tchg. asst. Duke U., Durham, N.C., 1982-84, rsch. asst., 1984-85; chair monitoring com. crisis access sys. Ea. Regional Adv. Coun. Dept. Mental Health, St. Louis, 1995-97; chair African Am. Task Force on Mental Health, Jefferson City, Mo., 1995-97; chair budget and planning com. Ea. Regional Adv. Coun., Dept. Mental Health, St. Louis, 1996-97, pres. Ea. Regional Adv. Coun., 1997-99; mem. children's mental health planning group St. Louis Mental Health Bd., 1996-97. Mem. editl. adv. bd. A Turbulent Voyage: Readings in African American Studies, 1995-96; mem. bd. editl. advisors Gt. Plains Rsch.; contbr. articles to profl. jours. Mem. adv. com. on violence prevention and investment in youth Mo. House, Jefferson City, 1995; mem. managed care steering com. Dept. Mental Health, Jefferson City, 1995—96, mem. strategic planning adv. coun., 1997; mem. Mo. Bd. for Respiratory Care, 1997; mem. state com. for psychologists Mo., 1997—; chair, 2000—02; sec., chair discipline com., 1999—2000; bd. dirs. St. Louis Mental Health Assn., sec., 2000—02, chair planning com., 2002, 2d v.p., 2002, pres., 2003. Kellogg Found.-Mo. Youth Initiative fellow, 1991-93; Ctr. for Great Plains Studies fellow U. Nebr., 1995—; recipient Disting. Svc. award Mental Health Assn. St. Louis, 1998, 99. Mem. APA (divsns. 1, 45), Assn. Black Psychologists, Am. Orthopsychiat. Assn. Methodist. Avocations: aerobics, walking, jazz. Office: U Mo 8001 Natural Bridge Rd Saint Louis MO 63121-4401

THOMPSON, VICKI LYN, elementary school educator; b. Miles City, Mont., Aug. 16, 1969; d. Herbert John and LaVonne Darlene (Myrhe) Sackman; m. David Lee Thompson, June 27, 1992. BS, Mont. State U., 1991. Cert. tchr., N.D. 3d grade classroom tchr. Natrona County Pub. Schs., Casper, Wyo., 1991-93; learning resource ctr. tchr. Dubuque (Iowa) Cmty. Pub. Schs., 1993-96; 6th grade classroom tchr. Wash. Elem. Sch., Jamestown, N.D., 1997—. Youth group leader First Presbyn. Chs., Casper, Dubuque and Jamestown, 1991—; summer camp dir. Presbytery of Wyo., 1992-93. Recipient First Yr. Tchr. award Sallie Mae, 1992. Mem. Internat. Reading Assn., Iowa Talented and Gifted Assn., Iowa Coun. Math., Phi Delta Kappa. Avocations: reading, biking, riding horse, playing sports. Home: 1704 2nd Pl NE Jamestown ND 58401-3915

THOMPSON, VIRIGINA A. elementary education educator; b. Logan, Ohio, May 4, 1940; d. Charles Frederick and Margaret Frances (Shelton) Wilcoxen; m. Paul Calvin Reed, Sept. 24, 1958 (div. Jan. 1974); children: P. Bradley, John C., Thomas G.; m. James Willard Thompson, Jr., June 11, 1976. BS in Elem. Edn., Ohio State U., 1977; MS in Sch. Counseling, U. Dayton, Ohio, 1990. Cert. in elem. edn. 1-8, elem. guidance and counseling, Ohio. Classroom tchr. Anna (Ohio) Local Schs., 1977—. Chair Old Trails Uniserv Coun., Piqua, Ohio, 1982-86. Chair bd. trustees Shelby County Mental Health, Sidney, Ohio, 1989-94; mem. Dem. Ctr. Com. of Shelby County, Sidney, 1992—; mem. com. Black Achievers Scholarship, Sidney, 1988—; treas. Botkins (Ohio) Hist. Soc., 1987—. Recipient Bus. Adv. Coun. Tchr. Yr. award C. of C., Sidney, 1992, Pres.'s Award univ. scholar Ohio State Univ., 1976. Mem. Ohio Edn. Assn. (voting del.), Anna Local Tchrs. Assn. (pres. 1978, 85, 91-94), Ohio State Alumni Assn., Phi Kappa Phi, Delta Kappa Gamma. Democrat. Methodist. Avocations: travel, antiques, theatre. Home: 106 W State St Botkins OH 45306 Office: Anna Local Sch Dist 204 N 2d St Anna OH 45302

THOMPSON, WADE S. artist, art and design educator, administrator; b. Moorhead, Minn., July 30, 1946; s. Roy S. and Nora A. (Hanson) T.; m. Maureen Larkey, June 14, 1975; children: Mora Eileen, Sarah Maria. BA in Art with distinction, Macalaster Coll., 1968; MA, MFA, Bowling Green U., 1972; postgrad., Pratt Inst., 1985. Graphic designer Assoc. Design, St. Paul, 1969-70; asst. prof. art Temple U., Phila., 1972-79; prof. art and design S.W. Mo. State U., Springfield, Mo., 1979—, asst. head dept. art and design, 1999—2001; acting head S.W. Mo. State Univ., Springfield, 2002—03. Lectr. U. Art and Design Helsinki, 1994; vis. prof. U. Minn., Mpls., 1995; organizing chair 1998 Williamsburg Conf.,, 1996—; organizing chair Color and Design: 21st Century Tech. and Creativity Conf., 1998; organizing chair, moderator Artist and Digital Media Symposium, AIC Color, Rochester, NY, 2001; spkr., presenter in field. Contbr. articles to profl. jour.; one or two person shows include Alnico Gallery, NYC, 1977, Nat. Art Ctr., NYC, 1980, Jan Weiner Gallery, Kansas City, Mo., 1986, Peter Drew Galleries, Boca Raton, Fla., 1988, Mary Bell Galleries, Chgo., 1989, Still-Zinsel Contemporary Art, New Orleans, 1990, Aaron Gallery, Washington, 1990, Alexandre Hogue Gallery U. Tulsa, Okla., 1991, The Parthenon Mus., Nashville, 1995, Jack Meier Gallery, Houston, 1997, numerous others; group exhibn. include Provincetown (Mass.) Art Assn., 1976, Portsmouth (Va.) Art Ctr., 1976, The Smithsonian Traveling Exhibn., 1977-79, J.B. Speed Mus., Louisville, Ky., 1981, 84, The Nelson Gallery Atkins Mus., Kansas City, Mo., 1982, George Walter Vincent Smith Art Mus./Mus. Fine Arts, Springfield, Mass., 1984, 86, West Surrey Coll. Art and Design, Farnham, Surrey, Eng., 1984, Lamar Dodd Art Ctr., LaGrange, Ga., 1985, Arlington (Tex.) Mus. Art, 1989, Still-Zinsel Contemporary Fine Art, New Orleans, 1992, The Watkins Gallery Am. U., Washington, 1993, Elliot Smith Gallery, St. Louis, 1996, Keyes Gallery, Springfield, Mo., 1998, Malton Gallery, Cin., 2001, numerous others; featured in Am. Artist mag., catalog Color Archive Collections U. Art and Design Helsinki, The Oak Ridger, New Orleans Art Rev., New Art Examiner, The Kans. City Star, numerous others. Disting. scholar S.W. Mo. State U., 1992; recipient award for acrylic Chautauqua Nat. Exhbn., 1984, Color Archive Collection award U. Art and Design, Helsinki, Finland, 1997; grantee visual arts program Mo. Arts Coun., 1998. Mem. Inter-Soc. Color Coun. (nat. bd. dir. 1995-98, vice chair art, design, psychology interest group 1992-94, chair art, design, psychology interest group 1994-96). Home: 1910 E Cardinal St Springfield MO 65804-4329 Office: SW Mo State U Dept Art and Design 901 S National Ave Springfield MO 65804-0088

THOMPSON, WALLACE REEVES, III, physical education educator; b. Atlanta, Oct. 17, 1950; s. Wallace Reeves II and Annie Mae (Neal) T.; m. Sherrilyn Winkfield, Aug. 19, 1976 (div. 1985); 1 child, Sherrilyn M. m. Sandra Hicks, Feb. 28, 1994; 3 children: Garry C., Keneisha R., Ira. BA, Morehouse Coll., 1973. Cert. phys. edn. tchr., Ga. Phys. edn. tchr. Atlanta Pub. Schs., 1974—. Coach Saturday Sch. for the Arts, Atlanta, 1979-81. Vol. Nat. Black Arts Festival, Atlanta, 1990—, Ga. State Games, Atlanta, 1992—; coach Butler St. YMCA, Atlanta, 1982-85, AAU-Jr. Olympics, Atlanta, 1977-82, Centennial Olympics, Sports Video Viewing Room, Atlanta, 1996. Mem. AAHPERD. Baptist. Home: 119 Anderson Ave NW Atlanta GA 30314-1852 Office: Anderson Park Elem Sch 2050 Tiger Flowers Dr NW Atlanta GA 30314-1326

THOMPSON, WILLIAM, JR., engineering educator; b. Hyannis, Mass., Dec. 4, 1936; s. William and Dinella Helen (Szeliga) T.; m. Martha Marion Cate, July 4, 1959; children: Melanie A., Sharon E., Jennifer L., Keith W. SB, MIT, 1958; MS, Northeastern U., 1963; PhD, Pa. State U., 1971. Staff engr. Raytheon Co., Wayland, Mass., 1958-60; sr. engr. Cambridge (Mass.) Acoustical Assocs., 1960-66; rsch. asst. Applied Rsch. Lab., State College, Pa., 1966-72; asst. prof. engring. sci. Pa. State U., University Park, 1972-78, assoc. prof., 1978-85, prof., 1985-2001, prof. emeritus, 2001—. Head transducer group Applied Rsch. Lab., State College, 1971-80; sabbatic leave Naval Rsch. Lab., Orlando, Fla., 1988-89; chairperson IBM Master Tchrs. Team, 1997-98. Contbr. articles to profl. jours.; patentee in field. Bd. dirs., treas., past pres. Nittany Mountain chpt. Am. Diabetes Assn., State College, 1979-92; bd. dirs., asst. treas., treas. Mid-Pa. affiliate, Bethlehem, 1980-90; bd. dirs. Sight-Loss Support Group of Ctrl. Pa., 1999—, treas. 2000. Recipient Disting. Svc. citation Mid-Pa. Affiliate Am. Diabetes Assn., 1981, and Affiliate Svc. award, 1988, J.R. Cardenuto award, Sight-loss Support Group of Ctrl. Pa., 1998. Fellow Acoustical Soc. Am. (patent reviewer of soc. jour. 1990—); mem. Soc. Engring. Sci., Lions (pres. State College 1981-82, 89-90, sec.-treas. 1984-88, 90-92, treas. 1992—, dist. diabetes chmn. 1983-88, 94—, chmn. Ctr. Lions Foresight Commn. 1992—, Melvin Jones fellow 1991, internat. leadership award 1998, dist. chmn. Habitat for Humanity, 2001—), Cen. Pa. Ballroom Dancers Assn. (pres.-elect 1997-98, pres. 1998-99). Republican. Avocations: sports, reading, photography, ballroom dancing. Home: 1245-62 Westerly Pky State College PA 16801 Office: Pa State U Dept of Engring Sci and Mechanics 212 Earth and Engring Scis University Park PA 16802-6812 E-mail: W1TESM@engr.psu.edu.

THOMPSON, WILLIAM ANCKER, intramural-recreational sports director, educator; b. Syracuse, N.Y., Apr. 26, 1931; s. Frederick Howe Thompson and Ellen (Ensten) Ancker; m. Sally Whitmer; children: Cary, Paige. BS, Springfield (Mass.) Coll., 1953; MA, Calif. State U., Long Beach, 1960; postgrad., U. So. Calif., L.A., 1961-62. Phys. dir. Wendell P. Clark Meml., Winchendon, Mass., 1956-57; dir. intramural/recreational sports Long Beach City Coll., 1958-96, dir. intramural/recreational sports emeritus, 1996—; with promotion and sales div. Calif. Sports, Inc. (L.A. Lakers, Kings), L.A. and Inglewood, 1960-76, v.p. sales L.A. and Englewood, 1970-71. Co-author: Modern Sports Officiating, 1974, 5th rev. edit., 1993. 1st lt. USMC, 1954-56, Korea. Mem. Nat. Intramural-Recreational Sports Assn. (v.p. 1974-76, pres. 1976-77, Honor award 1980), Old Ranch Country Club. Avocations: swimming, golf, writing, reading, avocado grower. Office: Long Beach City Coll 4901 E Carson St Long Beach CA 90808-1706

THOMPSON, WILLIAM JOSEPH, secondary school educator, coach; b. Sedalia, Mo., Jan. 4, 1953; s. Robert Clark and Maxine Flavia (Pettyjohn) T.; m. Deborah Ann St. Germaine, Dec. 21, 1992; children: Bleys Kueck, Jordan Kueck, Seth Thompson. BA in History, Okla. State U., 1975; MA in History, U. Mo., 1981. Cert. tchr.Colo., Mo. Grad. tchg. asst. history U. Mo., Columbia, 1975-79; social studies tchr. Rampart H.S., Colorado Springs, Colo., 1983—, sch. writing assessment com., 1991-93, mem. sch. accountability com., 1993-94. Named Coach of Yr., Gazette Telegraph, 1986. Mem. Nat. Coun. for the Social Studies, Colo. H.S. Activities Assn., Nat. Soccer Coaches Assn. Am., Phi Delta Kappa. Office: Rampart HS 8250 Lexington Dr Colorado Springs CO 80920-4301

THOMPSON, WILLIAM TALIAFERRO, JR., internist, educator; b. Petersburg, Va., May 26, 1913; s. William Taliaferro and Anne C. (McIlwaine) T.; m. Jessie G. Baker, June 21, 1941; children— William Taliaferro III, Addison Baker, Jessie Ball. AB, Davidson Coll., 1934, Sc.D. (hon.), 1975; MD, Med. Coll. Va., 1938. Diplomate Am. Bd. Internal Medicine. Intern 4th med. service Boston City Hosp., 1938-40; asst. resident Mass. Gen. Hosp., 1940-41; resident Med. Coll. Va., Richmond, 1941, mem. faculty, 1946—, William Branch Porter prof., chmn. dept. medicine, also chief med. services hosps., 1959-73, prof., 1959-75, emeritus prof., 1975—, W.T. Thompson Jr. prof., 1978; mem. staff McGuire Clinic-St. Luke's Hosp., 1946-54; chief medicine service McGuire VA Hosp., 1954-59; med. dir. Westminister-Canterbury House, Richmond, 1975-87. Editor Va. Med. Monthly, 1976-82; contbr. to med. jours. Chmn. bd. mgrs., mem. med. adv. bd. Alfred I. DuPont Inst. and Nemours Found., 1962-78; med. adv. bd. Greenbrier Clinic; pres. Va. Assn. Mental Health, 1955-57, Richmond Bd. Housing and Hygiene, 1952-59; bd. dirs. Meml. Guidance Clinic, 1950-59, Maymont Found., Richmond, 1975-78; bd. dirs. Med. Coll. Va. Found., 1981— ; trustee Collegiate Sch., 1952-69, pres., 1965-67; trustee Davidson Coll., 1965-73, 78-80, bd. visitors, 1981— ; bd. visitors Longwood Coll., 1982-84; trustee, Union Theol. Sem., Richmond, 1960-70, 78—, Crippled Childrens' Hosp., 1975—, Westminster Canterbury House, 1982-86, St. Luke's Hosp., 1981-85, Westminster Canterbury Found., 1987—. Served to maj. M.C. AUS, 1941-46. Recipient cert. of disting. svc. Med. Soc. Va., 1982, Outstanding Tchr. award Med. Coll. Va., 1985, Outstanding Med. Alumnus award, 1986, Disting. Svc. to Medicine award Med. Coll. Va., 1986, Lettie Pate Evans/Whitehead Evans award Westminster Canterbury House. Mem. ACP (master, chmn. Va. sect. 1961, gov. for Va. 1971-75, Laureate award Va. chpt. 1986), Am. Clin. and Climatological Assn., N.Y. Acad. Scis., Am. Fedn. Clin. Research, So. Soc. Clin. Investigation, Richmond Acad. Medicine (pres. 1972), Davidson Coll. Nat. Alumni Assn. (pres. 1979-80), Phi Beta Kappa, Alpha Omega Alpha, Omicron Delta Kappa, Kappa Sigma. Presbyterian (deacon, elder). Clubs: Country of Va. (Richmond), Commonwealth (Richmond). Home: Richmond, Va. Died Feb. 19, 2002.

THOMPSON-CAGER-STRAND, CHEZIA, literature educator, writer, performance artist; b. St. Louis, Sept. 8, 1951; d. James Henry and Emma Jean Thompson; m. Lawrence Chris Cager Jr., May 19, 1984 (div. 1995); 1 child, Chezia; m. Mark Strand, 1999; 1 stepchild, Stephan. BA, Washington U., St. Louis, 1973, MA, 1975; ArtsD, Carnegie-Mellon U., 1984. Tchg. asst. Washington U., 1973-76; instr., asst. prof. St. Louis C.C., 1975-79; asst. prof. Clarion (Pa.) State U., 1980-82, U. Md., Catonsville, 1982-86; assoc. prof. Smith Coll., Northampton, Mass., 1986-89; vis. assoc. prof. Bowie (Md.) State U., 1989-90; sr. v.p. Park Heights Devel. Corp., Balt., 1990-92; cons. Balt. City Pub. Sch., Inst. Div., 1992-94; prof. lang. & lit. Md. Inst. Coll. Art, Balt., 1993—. Disting. scholar in residence U. Pa. Dept. Theatre, University Park, 1989; project dir. poetry enrichment program U. City Pub. Sch., 1972; performance artist Artscape, 1996, exhibit curator, 1997; curator In Celebration of Maryland Artists, Govt. House, Annapolis, 1998; exhibit curator Through The Fire To the Limit: African Am. Artists in Md. Govt. House, Annapolis, 1999, Eye of Carl Clark, Photographer Md. Art Place, 2000. Author: Jumpin' Rope on the Axis, 1986, Power Objects, 1996 (Artscape Poetry Competition award 1996), The Presence of Things Unseen, 1996, Praise Song for Katherine Dunham Artscape, 1996, numerous poems; dir. dramatic works including Narrator Vachel Lindsay's Congo Visits Langston Hughes, 1989, Jestina's Calypso, 1988, 7 Principles: or how I got ova, 1987, Tribute to Martin Luther King, 1985; contbr. poetry to Catch a Fire!!!: Across Generational Anthology of Contemporary African-American Poetry, 1998, Dark Eros: Black Erotic Writings, 1997, International Dimensions of Black Women's Writing*Vol. I, 1995; contbg. editor: Maryland Poetry Review, Baltimore Review, Word Wrights, LINK: A Jour. of the Arts in Balt. and Beyond; contbr. lit. criticisms, articles to profl. jours, freelance for St. Louis Am. News., Pitts. Courier News, Balt. Sun News. Mem. adv. bd. Sexual Assault Recovery Ctr., Balt., 1989-93; site proj. evaluator Nat. Endowment Arts, Washington, 1984; mem. Heritage Art panel Md. State Coun. Arts, 1990-94; cons. Balt. Arrabers Documentation Project, 1992; bd. dirs. Md. Art Place, 1990-2000. Recipient Paul Robeson Black Artist award Washington U., 1972, W.E.B. DuBois Svc. award, 1973, Merit for Poetry award Mo. State Coun. Arts, 1974, Mayor's Citizen Citation Poetry award, 1996, Resolution for Literacy award City Coun. Balt., 1996, Md. State Arts Coun. Individual Artist award in poetry, 1999, Disting. Black Marylander award, 2000; named Oyo Traditions Pan-African Cultural Innovator, 1996. Mem. Nat. Women Studies Assn., Nat. Assn. Tchrs. English, Nat. Black Theater Network, African Lit. Assn., Coll. Art Assn. Office: Md Inst Coll Art Dept Lang and Lit 1300 W Mount Royal Ave Baltimore MD 21217-4134

THOMPSON PYBAS, JOYCE ELIZABETH, retired state education official; b. Pearson, Okla., Nov. 22, 1929; d. Walter Samuel and Clara Gertrude (Davis) T.; m. Gordon Pybas, May 22, 1989. BS, Okla. State U., 1951; M in Home Econs., Okla. U., 1974. Cert. vocat. and gen. home econs., Okla. Home econs. tchr. Wister (Okla.) High Sch., 1951-55, Tishomingo (Okla.) High Sch., 1955-56, Wilson (Okla.) High Sch., 1956-67, Konawa (Okla.) High Sch., 1967-71; dist. supr. State Dept. of Vo-Tech., Oklahoma City, 1971-80, state supr. Stillwater, Okla., 1980-88; ret., 1988. Mem. adv. com. Future Homemakers Am., Oklahoma City, 1961-68; treas. Nat. Assn. State Suprs., Washington, 1983-87; advisor Nat. Assn. Vocat. Home Econs. Tchrs., Washington, 1986-87. Chairperson Okla. Home Econs. Legis. Network, Stillwater, 1984; mem. fin. com. Wes Watkins for Gov., Stillwater, 1988-90. Named Tchr. of Yr. Ancient Free and Accepted Masons, Wilson, 1960, 65; recipient Grand Cross of Colors, Internat. Order of Rainbow, Wilson, 1964, Hon. membership Future Homemakers of Am., Oklahoma City, 1976, Young Homemakers of Okla., Oklahoma City, 1977, Spl. award of merit Nat. Assn. Vocat. Home Econs. Tchrs., Washington, 1986. Mem. Am. Vocat. Assn. (life mem., membership chair 1981-84), Okla. Vocat. Assn. (life mem., v.p. 1965), Am. Legion Aux., Order Ea. Star. Democrat. Mem. Church of Christ. Avocations: reading, sewing, vol. work, cooking, water skiing. Home: 7 E Janice Apt 101 Yukon OK 73099

THOMPSON-STANTON, MARY JEAN, secondary educator; b. Kirksville, Mo., Feb. 19, 1959; d. Perley and Letha L. (Pinson) Thompson; m. Larry Stanton, June 14, 1981 (div. 1991); children: Lucas, Caitlin. BA in English/Speech-Theatre, N.E. Mo. State U., 1980; MA in Communication Studies, U. Iowa, 1990. Cert. secondary sch. tchr., Mo., Iowa. Secondary lang. arts tchr., Brashear, Mo., 1980-81; substitute tchr., tutor Iowa City Sch. System, 1981-83; long term substitute tchr. S.E. Jr. High Sch., Iowa City, 1984-85; presch. tchr. Montessori Sch. Iowa City, 1985-86; speech/theatre tchr. Muscatine (Iowa) Community Coll., 1987-88; grad. instr. dept. rhetoric U. Iowa, 1988-89, grad. instr. dept. communication studies, 1989-90; instr. English, dir. acad. devel. Mt. Mercy Coll., Cedar Rapids, Iowa, 1990—. Author: (poetry) Epiphany, Radiant Resurrection, Distance. Mem. Ctrl. States Communication Assn., Iowa Devel. Edn. Assn., Midwest Coll. Learning Ctr. Assn., Nat. Assn. for Devel. Edn., Speech Communication Assn., Sigma Tau Delta. Home: 412 3rd Ave S Mount Vernon IA 52314-1715 Office: Mount Mercy Coll 1330 Elmhurst Dr NE Cedar Rapids IA 52402-4763

THOMSON, MABEL AMELIA, retired elementary school educator; b. Lancaster, Minn., Oct. 28, 1910; d. Ernest R. and Sophie Olinda (Rotert) Poore; m. Robert John Thomson, June 20, 1936; children: James Robert, William John. BS, U. Ill., 1933; MEd, Steven F. Austin Coll., Nacogdoches, Tex., 1959. Tchr. La Harpe (Ill.) Sch. Dist., 1930, Scotland (Ill.) Sch. Dist., 1934, Washburn (Ill.) Sch. Dist., 1935-36, Tyler (Tex.) Ind. Sch. Dist., 1959-76; ret., 1976. Substitute tchr. Tyler (Tex.) Ind. Sch. Dist., 1976-86 Past pres. Woman's Soc. Christian Svc. of local Meth. Ch. Mem. AAUW (pres. Tyler chpt. 1947-48), Am. Childhood Edn. (pres. 1960-61), Alpha Delta Kappa (charter Tyler br.), Phi Mu (life). Republican. Methodist. Avocations: reading, gardening, bridge.

THOMSON, MARJORIE BELLE ANDERSON, sociology educator, consultant; b. Topeka, Dec. 4, 1921; d. Roy John and Bessie Margaret (Knarr) Anderson; m. John Whitner Thomson, Jan. 4, 1952 (div. June 9, 1963); 1 child, John Coe. Diploma hostess, Trans World Airlines, 1945; diploma, U.Saltillo, Mex., 1945; BS, Butler U., 1957; MS, Ft. Hays Kans. State U., 1966; postgrad., U. Calif., Santa Barbara, 1968, Kans. State U., 1972-73, Kans. U., 1973. Cert. elem. tchr., Calif., Colo., Ind., Kans., jr. coll. tchr. Tech. libr. N.Am. Aviation, Dallas, 1944-45; flight attendant TWA, Kansas City, Mo., 1945-50; recreation dir. U.S. Govt., Ft. Carson, Colo., 1951-52; elem. tchr. Indpls. Pub. Schs., 1954-57; jr. high tchr. Cheyenne County Schs., Cheyenne Wells, Colo., 1958-59; elem. tchr. Sherman County Schs., Goodland, Kans., 1961-62; lectr. Calif. Luth. U., Thousand Oaks, 1967-69; instr. Ft. Hays Kans. State U., 1969-71; dir. HeadStart Kans. Coun. of Agrl. Workers and Low Income Families, Inc., Goodland, 1971-72; supr. U.S. Govt. Manpower Devel. Programs, Plainville, Kans., 1972-74; bilingual counselor Kans. Dept. Human Resources, Goodland, 1975-82. Leader trainee Expt. in Internat. Living, Brattleboro, Vt., 1967-71; cons. M. Anderson & Co., Lakewood, Colo., 1982—; participant Internat. Peace Walk, Moscow to Archangel, Russia, 1991, N.Am. Conf. on Ecology and the Soviet Save Peace and Nature Ecol. Collective, Russia, 1992, Liberators-The Holocaust Awareness Inst., Denver, 1992; amb. internat. Friendship Force, Tiblisi, Republic of Georgia, 1991, Republic South Africa, 1995, Republic of Turkey, 1996, Republic of Egypt, 1999, Republic of Israel-Kfar Blum Kibbutz, 1999, Republic of Austria, 1999; presenter State Conv. AAUW, Aurora, Colo., 1992, presenter nat. conv. Am. Acad. Audiology, Denver, 1992; cons. Gov.'s Conf. in Libr. and Info. Svc., Vail, Colo., 1992; presenter annual conf. Nat. Emergency Number 911 Assn., Denver, 1996. Docent Colo. Gallery of the Arts, Littleton, 1989; spkr. Internat. Self Help for Hard of Hearing People, Inc., 1990—, mem. state recreation resource com. for Self Help for Hard of Hearing People Internat. Conv., Denver, 1991; mem. Denver Deaf and Hard of Hearing Access Com., 1991—; spkr. Ret. Sr. Vol. Program, Denver, 1992—; dir. Holiday Project, Denver, 1992; mem. Lakewood Access Com., 1994—, Arvada Ctr.'s Women's Voices com., 1995; participant women readers com. Rocky Mountain News, Denver, 1995; trustee Internat. Self Help for Hard of Hearing People, Inc., Bethesda, Md., 1995-98; Deaf Panel spkr. for Deaf Awareness Week, Denver, 1995-98; program co-chair Lakewood Woman's Club, 1996, 97; mem. access adv. com. Arvada Ctr. for Arts and Humanities, 1997; commr. Denver Commn. for People with Disabilities, 1997-98; mem. Colo. State Rehab. Adv. Coun., 1997—, 98, Gov.'s Adv. Coun. for People with Disabilities, 1998—; mem. Lakewood Citizen Police Acad. XIX, 1999; participant Funding Assistive Technology: Where to Turn in Colo. and When, Denver, 1999, Sr. Transp. Summit, Denver, 2000; mem. program com. Wisdom Keepers, Lakewood, 1999-2000; participant Aurora 5 States Assistive Tech. Conf. for Disabled, 1999-2000; mem. Colo. State Sr. Drug Abuse Task Force, 2000-02; apptd. mem. Lakewood Sr. Citizen's Adv. Commn., 2000-. Recipient Svc. award, Mayor of Lakewood, 1995, Honorable Mention Four Who Dare, Colo. Bus. and Profl. Women and KCNC Channel 4, 1995, J.C. Penney Nat. Golden Rule award for cmty. vol. svc., 1996, Cmty. Svc. award, Mayor Denver, 1996, City and County of Denver Proclamation for Marjorie Thomson Day, Mayor Wellington E. Webb, Apr. 8, 1997, Svc. Recognition award, Oticon Co., 1997, Worker of Yr. Recognition award, Dickie Co., 1997, coll. scholarship presented in her name, Alpha Sigma Alpha, 2000; grantee, NSF, 1970, 1971. Mem. AAUW (life; v.p., program chairperson Lakewood br. 1996, Trailblazer award Denver br. 1997, mem. diversity com. Colo. 1997-98), AARP (pres. Denver-Grandview chpt. 1994), VFW Aux. (life), Sociologists for Women in Soc. (participant Gullah Culture, Charleston, S.C. 1997), Bus. and Profl. Woman's Club, Internat. Peace Walkers, Spellbinders, Denver Press Club (Wheat Ridge Grange # 155 1993-98), Lakewood Woman's Club, TWA Internat. Clipped Wings (cert.), Mile High Wings, Order Ea. Star (life), Sons of Norway, UNESCO, Bus. and Profl. Women's Club (com. for Ms. Golden Bus. and Profl. Woman of Yr. 1999), Confederate Air Force (hon. col.), Toastmasters, PHAMALy, Pi Gamma Mu, Alpha Sigma Alpha (life, participant Centennial Conv., Alumni Star). Democrat. Presbyterian. Avocations: photography, traveling, whitewater rafting, storytelling, writing.

THOMSON, SONDRA K. secondary school educator; b. Audubon, Iowa, Aug. 24, 1940; d. Merlyn Franklyn and Leona Marie Peterson; m. Alan Richard Thomson, Sept. 3, 1989; children from previous marriage: Paul Spiegel, Joni Spiegel, Steve Spiegel. BA magna cum laude, Calif. State U., Hayward, 1988; MA in Spl. Edn., Chapman U., 2000. Cert. resource specialist, learning handicapped credential, social sci. credential. Co founder, assoc. editor Am. Remnant Mission, Pleasant Hill, Calif., 1977—84; substitute tchr. Mt. Diablo Sch. Dist., Concord, Calif., 1985—90; spl. day class tchr. Antioch Sch. Dist., Antioch, Calif., 1997—99; resource specialist Deer Valley HS, Antioch, Calif., 1999—, mem. adv. coun., 2002—03. Adv. coun. Deer Valley HS, 2002, 2003—. Contbr. articles to mags. Office: Deer Valley HS 4700 Lone Tree Way Antioch CA 94509

THOMSON, VIRGINIA WINBOURN, humanities educator, writer; b. Oakland, California, Aug. 6, 1930; d. Harry Linn and Jennie Cook (Vineyard) Thomson. AA, San Mateo Coll., 1949; BA, San Jose State Coll., 1951; MA, U. Calif., Berkeley, 1952. Cert. secondary tchr. Calif. Social sci. tchr. Capuchino HS, San Bruno, Calif., 1952—54, Watsonville HS, Calif., 1954—87. Saleswoman, storyteller Home Interiors, San Mateo, 1963—64. Author: The Lion Desk, 1965, Short Talks Around the Lord's Table, 1985, numerous poems, Lawson's Castle, 2001. Mem.: AAUW (licentiate), Nat. Geog. Soc. (life), Calif. Alumni Assn. (life), Calif. Writer's Club (life), Homer Honor Soc. Internat. Poets, Phi Alpha Theta. Republican.

THORBURN, JAMES ALEXANDER, retired humanities educator; b. Martins Ferry, Ohio, Aug. 24, 1923; s. Charles David and Mary Edna (Ruble) Thorburn; m. Lois McElroy, July 3, 1954; children: Alexander Maurice, Melissa Rachel; m. June Yingling O'Leary, Apr. 18, 1981. BA, Ohio State U., 1949, MA, 1951; postgrad., U. Mo., 1954—55; PhD, La. State U., 1977. Head English dept. high sch., Sheridan, Mich., 1951—52; instr. English U. Mo., Columbia, 1952—55, Monmouth (Ill.) Coll., 1955—56, U. Tex., El Paso, 1956—60, U. Mo., St. Louis, 1960—61, La. State U., Baton Rouge, 1961—70; prof. Southeastern La. U., Hammond, 1970—89, prof. emeritus English and linguistics; ret. Testing and cert. examiner English Lang. Inst., U. Mich., 1969—; participant Southeastern Conf. on Linguistics; mem. Conf. Christianity and Lit. Contbg. author Exercises in English, 1955, also poetry, short stories, book rev. editor Experiment, 1958—87; editor: Innisfree, 1984—89. With F.A. AUS, 1943—46. Mem.: MLA, La. Ret. Tchrs. Assn., La. Assn. for Coll. Composition, Am. Dialect Soc., Linguistic Soc. Am., Avalon World Arts Acad., Linguistic Assn. S.W., Sociedad Nacional Hispánica, Internat.

Poetry Soc., Phi Kappa Phi (named emeritus life), Phi Mu Alpha Sinfonia, Sigma Delta Pi. Republican. Presbyterian. Home: 602 Susan Dr Hammond LA 70403-3444 Office: Southeastern La U # 739 Hammond LA 70402-0001

THORNBURGH, DANIEL ESTON, retired university administrator, journalism educator; b. Terre Haute, Ind., Sept. 17, 1930; s. Lester D. and Dorothy (Green) T.; m. Adrianne Ames, Aug. 11, 1956; children: Debra Kay Thornburgh Considine, Stewart Beckett, Malcolm Noble. BS, Ind. State U., 1952; MA, U. Iowa, 1957; EdD, Ind. U., 1980. Reporter Terre Haute Star, 1952; publicity dir. Simpson Coll., Indianola, Iowa, 1955-57; info. dir. Marshall U., Huntington, W.Va., 1957-59, Eastern Ill. U., Charleston, 1959-65, chmn., prof. journalism, 1965-84, dir. univ. rels., 1984-92. Vis. prof. U. Hawaii, 1982—83, U. Fla., 1993—94, Millikin U., 1996; mem. Gov.'s Coun. Health and Phys. Fitness, 1987—2003; pub. Casey Banner Times, Ill., 1967—69. Editor: (with others) Interpretative Reporting Workbook, 1982. Mem. Charleston City Coun., 1973-77; active Ill. Recreation Coun., Springfield, 1979-85; pres. Coles Hist. Soc., Charleston, 1972-74, 92; pres., trustee Five Mile House Found., 1998—; trustee Lincoln and Sargent Farm Found., 1999—; chmn. higher edn. and campus min. com. Meth. Ch., 2000-02. With U.S. Army, 1952—54. Named Outstanding Advisor, Coun. Coll. Publs. Advisors, 1971. Mem. Charleston C. of C. (area man of yr. award 1971), Assn. Edn. Journalism and Mass Comm., Pub. Rels. Soc. Am., Soc. Profl. Journalists, Coun. Advancement and Support Edn. (EIU PRSSA chpt.), Assn. Preservation Hist. Coles County (Merit award 2003), Masons (Cmty. Builder award 1997), Elks, Rotary (pres. Charleston 1976-77, dist. gov. 6490 2000-01). Methodist. Avocations: tennis, writing. Home: 1405 Buchanan Ave Charleston IL 61920-2924

THORNBURY, JOHN ROUSSEAU, radiologist, physician; b. Cleve., Mar. 16, 1929; s. Purla Lee and Gertrude (Glidden) T.; m. Julia Lee McGregor, Mar. 20, 1955; children: Lee Allison, John McGregor. AB cum laude, Miami U., Oxford, Ohio, 1950; MD, Ohio State U., 1955. Diplomate: Am. Bd. Radiology. Intern Hurley Hosp., Flint, Mich., 1955-56; resident U. Iowa Hosps., Iowa City, 1958-61; instr., asst. prof. radiology U. Colo. Med. Center, Denver, 1962-63; practice medicine specializing in radiology Denver, 1962-63, Iowa City, 1963-66, Seattle, 1966-68, Ann Arbor, Mich., 1968-79, Albuquerque, 1979-84, Rochester, N.Y., 1984-89, Madison, Wis., 1989-94. Mem. staff U. Wisconsin Hosp., Madison; prof. radiology, chief sect. of body imaging, U. Wis. Med. Sch., 1989-94, prof. emeritus, 1994—; asst. prof. radiology U. Iowa Hosps., 1963-66, U. Wash. Hosp., Seattle, 1966-68; assoc. prof. radiology U. Mich. Med. Ctr., 1968-71, prof., 1971-79, chief uroradiology section, 1971-79; prof. radiology, chief divsn. diagnostic radiology Sch. Medicine, U. N.Mex., 1979-84; prof. radiology U. Rochester Sch. Medicine, 1984-89, acting chmn., 1985-87; chmn. sci. com. on efficacy studies Nat. Coun. on Radiation Protection, 1980-95; rapporteur/mem. sci. group on indications/limitations of x-ray diagnostic procedures WHO, 1983; cons. com. on efficacy of magnetic resonance nat. health tech. adv. panel Australian Inst. Health, 1986; invited U.S. cons. MRI program, Nijmegen, The Netherlands, 1992; mem. planning group Low Back Pain Collaboratives and Nat. Congress, Inst. for Health Care Improvement, 1997-98; mem. methodologic rsch. issues working group NIH and Pub. Health Svc.-Office of Women's Health, 1998; cons., spkr. Royal Australasian Coll. Radiologists, Melbourne, Australia, 1997; cons. tech. assessment and outcomes rsch., 1994—; cons. to Am. Soc. Neuroradiology, 1995-2000; lectr. in field. Co-author/cons. Clin. Efficacy Assessment Project, Am. Coll. Physicians, 1986-89; assoc. editor: Yearbook of Radiology, 1971-82; mem. editl. bd.: Contemporary Diagnostic Radiology, 1977-84, Urologic Radiology, 1977-84 Bd. dirs. Sally Jobe Found., Denver, 1996—. Capt., M.C. USAF, 1956-58. Recipient Dist. Svc. award Am. Bd. Radiology, 2000, Alumni Achievement award Ohio State U. Coll. Medicine, 2000, Gold medal Assn. Univ. Radiologists, 2002; grantee Agy. Health Care Policy and Rsch., 1986-91, U. Rochester, 1986-89, U. Wis., Madison, 1989-91. Fellow Am. Coll. Radiology (mem. emeritus); mem. Am. Coll. Radiology Imaging Network (outcomes and quality of life subcom., urology com., NIH, 1999-2002), Soc. Uroradiology (pres. 1976-77, dir. 1977-79), Assn. Univ. Radiologists (pres. 1980-81), Radiol. Soc. N.Am., Am. Roentgen Ray Soc. (Caldwell medal 1993), Soc. for Health Svcs. Rsch. in Radiology (adv. com. to bd. dirs. 1998—), Colo. Radiol. Soc., Phi Beta Kappa, Delta Tau Delta, Omicron Delta Kappa, Phi Chi. Republican. Lutheran. Home: 185 Morgan Pl Castle Rock CO 80108

THORNE, BARBARA LOCKWOOD, guidance counselor, secondary education educator; b. Rochester, N.Y., Nov. 12, 1938; d. Harvey J. and Clara (Lee) Lockwood; m. Marc E. Thorne, July 21, 1962; children: John, Andrew. BA, Westminster Coll., 1960; postgrad., Cornell U., 1961; MS, U. Bridgeport, 1987, 6th Yr. Cert., 1991. Cert. tchr., N.Y.; lic. prof. counselor, Conn.; nat. bd. cert. counselor. Tchr. social studies Greece Olympia High Sch., Rochester, N.Y., 1961-63, East High Sch., Rochester, 1963-64; tchr. recreation Fairfield (Conn.) YMCA, 1965-70; tutor, substitute tchr. Needham (Mass.) Alternate High Sch., 1970-78; tchr. social studies Alternate Learning Program Darien (Conn.) High Sch., 1978-88, team leader, 1982-88, guidance counselor, 1988—, coord. student assistance team, 1991—. Locat advisor A Better Chance, Darien, 1989—. Chmn. Youth Commn., Darien, 1982-85; mem. Park and Recreation Commn., Darien, 1985-97, chmn., 1991-97; elected to Bd. Selectmen, Darien, 1997—. Recipient Vol. Svc. award Community Coun., Darien, 1977, 2003. Mem. ASCD, AAUW, NEA, LWV (pres., bd. dirs. 1975-85, Sears Found. award 1963, Vol. in Govt. award 1993), Assn. Secondary Sch. Adminstrn., Am. Assn. Counseling and Devel., Nat. Coun. Social Studies, New England Assn. Coll. Admission Counseling, Jr. League Stamford/Norwalk. Democrat. Congregationalist. Avocations: reading, tennis, cross-country skiing. E-mail: bthorne@optonline.net.

THORNE, JOYE HOLLEY, special education administrator; b. Shreveport, La., Jan. 4, 1933; d. Lockett Beecher and A. Irene (McWilliams) Holley; m. Michael S. Thorne, July 24, 1953; 1 child, Michael S. Jr. BS, Centenary Coll., 1954; MEd, U. Houston, 1969, EdD, 1974. Cert. tchr., Tex. Tchr. Aldine Ind. Sch. Dist., Houston, 1959-66, curriculum cons., 1966-69, dir. spl. edn., 1969—. Adj. prof. U. Houston, Clear Lake, Tex., 1974-83, U. St. Thomas, Houston, 1993—; spl. edn. specialist Dept. Def. Dependent Schs., Washington, 1983-84. Recipient Pres.'s award Gulf Coast chpt. Coun. Exceptional Children, Austin, Tex., 1980. Mem. Coun. Exceptional Children (pres. Gulf Coast chpt. 1976-77, pres. Tex. fedn. 1982-83, Pres.'s award 1980), Tex. Coun. Adminstrs. Spl. Edn. (pres. 1985-86, Dir. of Yr. award 1993). Republican. Methodist. Avocations: needlework, quilting, travel. Office: Aldine Ind Sch Dist 1617 Lauder Rd Houston TX 77039-3025

THORNE, KIP STEPHEN, physicist, educator; b. Logan, Utah, June 1, 1940; s. David Wynne and Alison (Comish) T.; m. Linda Jeanne Peterson, Sept. 12, 1960 (div. 1977); children: Kares Anne, Bret Carter; m. Carolee Joyce Winstein, July 7, 1984. BS in Physics, Calif. Inst. Tech., 1962; A.M. in Physics (Woodrow Wilson fellow, Danforth Found. fellow), Princeton U., 1963, PhD in Physics (Danforth Found. fellow, NSF fellow), 1965, postgrad. (NSF postdoctoral fellow), 1965-66; D.Sc. (hon.), Ill. Coll., 1979; Dr.h.c., Moscow U., 1981; D.Sc. (hon.), Utah State U., 2000, U. Glasgow, 2001; D.H.L. (hon.), Claremont Grad. U., 2002. Research fellow Calif. Inst. Tech., 1966-67, assoc. prof. theoretical physics, 1967-70, prof., 1970—, William R. Kenan, Jr. prof., 1981-91, Feynman prof. theoretical physics, 1991—. Fulbright lectr., France, 1966; vis. assoc. prof. U. Chgo., 1968; vis. prof. Moscow U., 1969, 75, 78, 82, 83, 86, 88, 90, 98; vis. sr. rsch. assoc. Cornell U., 1977, A.D. White prof.-at-large, 1968-92; adj. prof. U. Utah, 1971-98; mem. Internat. Com. on Gen. Relativity and Gravitation, 1971-80, 92-01, Com. on U.S.-USSR Coop. in Physics, 1978-79, Space Sci. Bd., NASA, 1980-83; co-founder, chair steering com. LIGO, 1984-87. Co-author: Gravitation Theory and Gravitational Collapse, 1965, Gravitation, 1973, Black Holes: The Membrane Paradigm, 1986, Black Holes and Time Warps: Einstein's Outrageous Legacy, 1994. Alfred P. Sloan Found. Rsch. fellow, 1966-68; John Simon Guggenheim fellow, 1967; recipient Sci. Writing award in physics and astronomy Am. Inst. Physics, 1969, 94, P.A.M. Dirac Meml. lectureship Cambridge U., 1995, Karl Schwarzschild medal Astron. Soc. Germany, 1996, J. Robert Oppenheimer Meml. lectureship U. Calif., 1999, Charles Darwin Meml. Lectureship Royal Astron. Soc., 2000, Arthur Holly Compton Meml. lectureship Washington U., 2001, Herzberg Meml. Lectureship Can. Assn. Physicists, 2001; Robinson Prize in Cosmology, U. Newcastle, 2002. Fellow Am. Phys. Soc. (Julius Edgar Lilienfeld prize 1996, chair topical group in gravity 1997-98); mem. Am. Philosophical Soc., Nat. Acad. Scis., Am. Acad. Arts and Scis., Am. Astron. Soc., Internat. Astron. Union, AAAS, Russian Acad. Scis., Sigma Xi, Tau Beta Pi. Office: California Inst Tech 130-33 Theoretical Astrophysics 1200 E California Blvd Pasadena CA 91106

THORNTON, J. RONALD, technology consultant; b. Fayetteville, Tenn., Aug. 19, 1939; s. James Alanda and Thelma White (McGee) T.; m. Mary Beth Packard, June 14, 1964 (div. Apr. 1975); 1 child, Nancy Carole; m. Martha Klemann, Jan. 23, 1976 (div. Apr. 1982); 1 child, Trey; m. Bernice McKinney, Feb. 14, 1986; 1 child, Paul Leon. BS in Physics and Math., Berry Coll., 1961; MA in Physics, Wake Forest Coll., 1964; postgrad., U. Ala., 1965-66, Rollins Coll., 1970. Rsch. physicist Brown Engring. Co., Huntsville, Ala., 1963-66; sr. staff engr. Martin Marietta Corp., Orlando, Fla., 1966-75; dep. dir. NASA, Washington, 1976-77; exec. asst. Congressman Louis Frey, Jr., Orlando, 1978; pres. Tens Tec, Inc., Orlando, 1978-79; dir. So. Tech. Applications Ctr. U. Fla., Gainesville, Fla., 1979—2002. Bd. dirs., treas. North Fla. Tech. Innovation Ctr., 1994—; mem. light wave tech. com. Fla. High Tech. and Indsl. Coun., Tallahassee, 1986—93, NASA Tech. Transfer Exec. Com., Washington, 1987—, Javits Fellowship Bd., Washington, 1986—91, Gov.'s New Porduct Award Com., Tallahassee, 1988—94, Fla. K-12 Math., Sci. and Computer Sci. Edn. Quality Improvement Adv. Coun., 1989—94, Fla. Sci. Edn. Improvement Adv.Com., 1991—92; bd. dirs. North Fla. Enterprise Corp., 2001—. Pres. Orange County Young Rep. Club, Orlando, 1970-71; treas. Fla. Fedn. Young Reps., Orlando, 1971-72; chmn. Fla. Fedn. Young Reps., Orlando, 1972-74; pres. Gainesville Area Innovation Network, 1988-89. Named Engr. Exhibiting Tech. Excellence and Accomplishment cen. Fla. chpt. Fla. Engring. Soc., 1975, Achievement award NASA, 1977. Mem. IEEE, Soc. Mfg. Engrs., Tech. Transfer Soc. (pres. 1999, bd. dirs. 1996—2001, Thomas Jefferson award 1999), Nat. Assn. Mgmt. and Tech. Assistance Ctrs. (bd. dirs. 1988, pres. 1992). Republican. Avocations: music, travel, reading, golf. Home and Office: 17829 NW 20th Ave Newberry FL 32669-2143 E-mail: ronthornton@cox.net.

THORNTON, MAURICE, retired academic administrator; b. Birmingham, Ala., Dec. 31, 1930; s. William Cullen and Alberta (Jones) T.; m. Elizabeth Ann McDonald, Apr. 15, 1961; children: Karen, Susan, Christopher. BS, Ala. State U., 1952; MEd, Cleve. State U., 1973; EdD, Nova-Southeastern U., 1981; golden diploma (hon.), Ala. State U., 2002. Investigative caseworker, supr. title V Cuyahoga County Welfare Dept., Cleve., 1958-67, coord. neighborhood youth corps, asst. dir. pers. dept., 1958-67; equal employment officer, minority recruiter Cuyahoga C.C., Cleve., 1967-82, dir. equal opportunity, 1967-82; dir. affirmative action compliance SUNY, Albany, 1982—; dir. affirmative action program SUNY Sys. Adminstrn., Albany, 1982-97. Sec. Capital Dist. Human Rights Adv. Com., Albany; N.Y. mid-Hudson coord. Am. Assn. Affirmative Action Officers, Albany; univ. coord. Capital Dist. Black and Puerto Rican Caucus, Albany; participant Leadership Devel. Program, Cleve. and Albany; adj. prof. SUNY, Albany, 1998—. Contbr. articles to profl. jours. Active NAACP; fundraiser United Negro Coll. Fund, Albany and Cleve.; loaned exec. program United Way, Albany and Cleve.; exec. adv. bd. Boy Scouts Am.; deacon Westminster Presbyn. Ch. Scholar State of Ala., State of Ohio. Mem. Vets. Assn. (nat. v.p. 369th), 100 Black Men (charter, adv. com. on restoration and display of N.Y. State's mil. battle flags-commn.), Omega Psi Phi, Sigma Pi Phi (charter). Avocations: walking, reading, golf, traveling, history buff. Home: 7 Keith Rd Delmar NY 12054-4006 Office: SUNY State University Albany Albany NY 12203 E-mail: maurice@empireone.net.

THORNTON, RONALD, physicist, educator; Prof. rsch. edn. physics dept. Tufts U., Medford, Mass., prof., dir. sci. math tchgs. ctr., 1993—. Recipient Disting. Svc. citation award, 1993. Office: Tufts Univ Ctr for Sci Math Teaching 4 Colby St Medford MA 02155-6013

THORNTON, SPENCER P. ophthalmologist, educator; b. West Palm Beach, Fla., Sept. 16, 1929; s. Ray Spencer and Mae (Phillips) T.; m. Annie Glenn Cooper, Oct. 6, 1956; children: Steven Pitts, David Spencer, Ray Cooper, Beth Ellen. BS, Wake Forest Coll., 1951, MD, 1954. Diplomate: Am. Bd. Ophthalmology. Intern Ga. Bapt. Hosp., Atlanta, 1954-55; resident gen. surgery U. Ala. Med. Center, 1955-56; resident ophthalmology Vanderbilt U. Sch. Medicine, 1960-63; practice medicine specializing in ophthalmic surgery Nashville, 1960—; med. dir. Thornton Eye Ctr., 1995-99; clin. prof. ophthalmology U. Tenn., Memphis, 2002. Disting. vis. prof. dept. ophthalmology U. Tenn., 2001; mem. staff Bapt. Hosp., chief ophthalmology svc., 1982-87; guest prof., vis. lectr. U. Toronto, 1990-92, U. Paris, 1989, Rothchilds Inst., Paris, 1992, 94, U. Pretoria, 1991, 93, others; instr. Moscow Inst. Eye Microsurgery, 1981; instr. ophthalmic surgery Am. Acad. Ophthalmology Ann. Courses; lectr. lens implant symposiums Eng., Spain, Australia, Switzerland, Can., Sweden, Greece, Germany, France, Republic of South Africa, Japan; Berzelius lectr. U. Lund, Sweden, 1992; P.J. Hay Gold medal lectr., North of Eng. Ophthal. Soc., Scarborough, 1992; pres. Biosyntrx Inc., 2002—. King Features syndicated newspaper columnist, 1959-60, feature writer, NBC radio and TV, 1958-60; author, co-author textbooks on cataract and refractive surgery; mem. editl. bd. Jour. Refractive and Corneal Surgery, Jour. Cataract and Refractive Surgery, Video Jour. Ophthalmology, Ocular Surgery News (Ophthalmologist of Yr. 1996), Ophthalmic Practice (Can.), Eye Care Tech. Mag. (Lifetime Achievement award 1996); contbr. articles to profl. jours.; inventor instruments and devices for refractive and lens implant surgery. Named one of 100 Best Ophthalmologists in Am., Ophthalmology Times mag., 1996, Outstanding Young Men of Yr., U.S. Jaycees, 1965; recipient Honor award Can. Implant Assn., 1993, Outstanding Achievement award Bowman Gray Sch. Medicine, 1995. Fellow: ACS (life), Am. Coll. Nutritional Medicine (pres. 2000—), Am. Acad. Ophthalmology (honor award 1995); mem.: Am. Soc. Cataract and Refractive Surgery (pres. 1997—99), Can. Implant Soc. (life), South African Intraocular Implant Soc. (life), Am. Med. Soc. Vienna (life), Internat. Refractive Surgery Club (v.p. 1994), Delta Kappa Alpha, Phi Rho Sigma. Baptist. Home and Office: 5070 Villa Crest Dr Nashville TN 37220-1425 E-mail: spthornton@biosyntrx.com.

THORSON-HOUCK, JANICE HARGREAVES, speech, language pathologist; b. Birmingham, Ala., Oct. 22, 1943; d. Harold Trevelyn and Johnnie Lou (Phillips) Hargreaves; m. William Gerald Thorson, July 4, 1974 (dec. 1984); children: Alice, William, Laura, Elizabeth, Ronald, John; m. Lawrence Clifton Houck, June 25, 1994. BA in Speech/Lang. Pathology, U. Ala., 1969, MA, 1974. Cert. speech/lang. pathologist. Speech/lang. pathologist S.E. Ala. Rehab. Ctr., Dothan, 1969-71, Birmingham City Schs., 1974-90, Midfield (Ala.) City Schs., 1990-95, Birmingham City Schs., 1995—. Cub scout den leader Boy Scouts Am., Birmingham, 1978-79; trustee Nat. Reye's Syndrome Found., Bryan, Ohio, 1985—, nat. sec., 1983-84, pres. Ala. region, 1981-85. Recipient John Dieckman Disting. Svc. award Nat. Reye's Syndrome Found., 1986. Mem. Am. Speech-Lang.-Hearing Assn., Speech and Hearing Assn. Ala. (chair sch. affairs com. 1991-95, Cert. of Appreciation 1986, 90), Pub. Sch. Caucus (sec. 1993-94), Phi Beta Kappa, Delta Kappa Gamma (2d v.p. 1994-96, sec. 1996—). Presbyterian. Avocations: handcrafts, water sports, boating. Home: 3905 Rock Creek Dr Birmingham AL 35223-1683 Office: Birmingham Pub Schs 417 29th St S Birmingham AL 35233-2823

THOULESS, DAVID JAMES, retired physicist, educator; b. Bearsden, Scotland, Sept. 21, 1934; arrived in U.S., 1979, naturalized, 1994; s. Robert Henry and Priscilla (Gorton) T.; m. Margaret Elizabeth Scrase, July 26, 1958; children: Michael, Christopher, Helen. BA, U. Cambridge, Eng., 1955, ScD, 1986; PhD, Cornell U., 1958. Physicist Lawrence Berkeley Lab., Calif., 1958-59; rsch. fellow U. Birmingham, England, 1959—61, prof. math. physics, 1965—78; lectr., fellow Churchill Coll. U. Cambridge, England, 1961—65; prof. physics Queen's U., Kingston, Ont., Can., 1978; prof. applied sci. Yale U., New Haven, 1979-80; prof. physics U. Wash., Seattle, 1980—2003; ret. Author: Quantum Mechanics of Many Body Systems, 2d edit., 1972, Topological Quantum Numbers in Nonrelativistic Physics, 1998. Recipient Maxwell medal Inst. Physics, 1973, Holweck prize Soc. Francaise de Physique-Inst. Physics, 1980, Fritz London award for Low temperature physics, Fritz London Meml. Fund, 1984, Wolf prize in physics, 1990, Paul Dirac medal Inst. Physics, 1993, Lars Onsager prize Am. Phys. Soc., 2000; Edwin Uehling disting. scholar U. Wash., 1988-98. Fellow: Royal Soc.; mem.: NAS. Office: U Wash PO Box 351560 Seattle WA 98195-1560 E-mail: Thouless@phys.washington.edu.

THRIFT, JULIANNE STILL, academic administrator; b. Barnwell, S.C. m. Ashley Ormand Thrift; children: Lindsay, Laura. BA, MEd, U. S.C.; PhD in Pub. Policy, George Washington U. Formerly asst. exec. dir. Nat. Assn. Coll. and Univ. Attys.; ombudsman U. S.C.; exec. dir. Nat. Inst. Ind. Colls. and Univs., 1982-88; exec. v.p. Nat. Assn. Ind. Colls. and Univs., Washington, 1988-91; pres. Salem Acad. and Coll., Winston-Salem, N.C., 1991—. Office: Salem Coll Office of the President Winston Salem NC 27108-0548

THRIFT, SHARRON WOODARD, director; b. Waycross, Ga., July 18, 1962; d. Lawrence Marvin and Evon Mattie (Lee) Woodard; m. Gary Wayne Thrift, July 5, 1987; children: Dustin Wayne, Zachary Lawrence. BS in Edn., U. Ga., 1983; MEd, Valdosta State Coll., 1987, EdS, 1993. Cert. bus. edn. tchr. Night sch. keyboarding instr. Waycross-Ware Tech., 1984-87; bus. edn. instr. Brantley County HS, Nahunta, Ga., 1984-85, data processing coord., 1985-93, CBE coord., 1993—. Projects chairperson Blackshear (Ga.) Pilot Club, 1988—89. Mem.: Profl. Assn. Ga. Educators, Ga. Bus. Edn. Assn., Nat. Bus. Edn. Assn. Republican. Baptist. Avocations: crafts, reading. Office: Brantley County HS RR 1 Box 4 Nahunta GA 31553-9710

THUEME, WILLIAM HAROLD, secondary school educator, travel coordinator; b. St. Clair, Mich., Sept. 4, 1945; s. Harold Arthur and Delphine Betty (Buhl) Thueme; m. Katheen Koning, May 8, 1971; children: Benjamin William, Rebecca Kathleen, Jeffery William, Sarah Kathleen; m. Nora Thueme (div. Sept. 1993). Student, Port Huron Jr. Coll., 1963-64; BA, Mich. State U., 1967, MA, 1969; PhD in Counseling, Progressive Universal Life Ch., 1993, PhD in Motivation, PhD in Paranormal Psychology, Progressive Universal Life Ch., 1997, PhD in Psychometrics, 1999; postgrad., Oakland U., 1971, San Francisco State U., 1975, U. Hawaii, 1975; student, Spring Arbor Coll., 1968; PhD in Reading Edn., U. Mich., 1977; PhD (hon.), Aspen U., 2003. Cert. tchr., Mich. Ordained min. Universal Life Ch. Tchr. pub. schs., Charlotte, Mich., 1967-69, Ann Arbor, Mich., 1969—. Fgn. travel coord.-Ambs. Abroad Program, Amsterdam, The Netherlands, 1968—; regional driver coord. for Southeastern Mich. Avis Rent-a-Car, 1983—. Active UN Children's Found., Mich. Sheriffs Ednl. Found., Woods Rd. Assn., Normal Pk. Neighborhood Assn., U.S. Legal Found., Found. for Nicaraguan Democracy, Habitat for Humanity Internat. (charter), Carter Ctr., Nat. Coun. Better Edn., participant Skyhook II Project; elections coord. Eaton County (Mich.) Rep. Party, 1968, mem. nat. com., 1968—, mem. nat. senatorial com.; mem. troop com. Coun. Boy Scouts Am., Ypsilanti, counselor for reading, 1988-89; cub scout summer camp instr. Inventor's Assistance League, Internat., Incorp. (Life mem.). Shore Nat. Network of Poet's Soc. Wolverne Coun., 1987, merit badge counselor, 1988-89; coach of the angels Ypsilanti Am. Little League, 1988, (life mem.) Inventors Assistance League, Shore Nat. Network of Poets Soc.; parent adv. bd. The Childrens Devel. Lab. Ea. Mich. U., 1988-89; active Mich. United Conservation Clubs, Big Bros. Am., Charlotte, Mich., Human Rights Watch, Nat. Security Caucus U.S., 1988—, Heritage Found., 1988—, ofcl. sponsor Mandate for Leadership III, Policy Strategies for 1990's Project, Project Save Our Schs., 1988—, Citizens United for Better Edn., World Awareness, Inc., Group 61 Amnesty Internat., Legal Affairs Coun., Coun. for Inter-Am. Security, Nicaraguan Resistance Edn. Found., Nat. Right to Work Legal Def. Found., Citizens Against Govt. Waste, Citizens Commn. for Ethics in Govt., Citizens for Decency Through Law, Inc., Participating Parents for Progress in Ypsilanti Pub. Schs.; parents adv. bd. Chapelle Elem. Sch., Ypsilanti, 1989-90, West Mid. Sch., Ypsilanti, 1991-92, Ypsilanti Pub. Schs., 1990—, Ypsilanti H.S.; charter sponsor Victory over Communism Project; nominated charter mem. Presdl. Task Force; participant The Imperial Congress: Crisis in the Separation of Powers Project, line-item veto project The Heritage Found., 1989, campaign to revise medicare catastrophic coverage law project Nat. Assn. Uniformed Svcs., 1989, repeal of catastrophic coverage act program Conservative Caucus Inc., 1989, Srs. Coal. Against the Tax, 1989; nat. adv. coun. Citizens Com. for Right to Bear Arms; jr. and sr. choir, Sunday sch. tchr. St. Paul's Luth. Ch., 1959-64 (Perfect Attendance award 8 yrs.), Marine city, Mich., 1960-63; youth Sunday sch. tchr., dir. youth min. coun. Lawrence Ave. Meth. Ch., Charlotte, Mich., 1967-69, life ELCA Evang. Luth. Ch. in Am., Treas. St. Paul's Luther League, 1960; mem. Second Amendment Sisters (assoc. mem. for Gentlemen of All Ages), 2003, World Peace and Diplomacy Forum (founding cabinet, life mem.), 2003, World Nations Congress (senator seat for lifetime term). Recipient Spl. Recognition award Richard Nixon, 1968-79, Gerald Ford, 1974-76, Ronald Reagan, 1971-88, George Bush, 1988-92, Spl. Recognition award Reagan Presdl. Campaign, 1981, Bush Presdl. Campaign, 1988, Citizen of Yr. award Citizens Com. for Right to Bear Arms, 1988, cert. recognition U.S. Justice Found., 1991, Hale Found., Am. Security Coun. 30th Anniversary Spl. Recognition cert., cert. appreciation award 2d Amendment Found., 1988, Appreciation of Devoted and Valuable Svc. award Chapelle Elem. Sch., 1988-89, Merit Badge, Wolverine Coun.; Internat. Peace prize, United Cultural Conv., 2002, One Thousand Great Ams., Internat. Biographical Ctr., England, 2002, Lifetime Achievement award, 2001, Teaching Intellectuals of the World, Am. Biog. Inst.,2001, Outstanding contributions to Literacy, Edn., Humanitarians and Peace, 2002; named One of Most Outstanding People of 20th Century, IBC, Cambridge, Eng., 1997, Internat. Man of Yr., IBC, 1998, Outstanding Intellectuals of 21st Century, award letters from First Lady Nancy Regan, Mich. Gov. John Engler, Nelson Mandella, award from The Am. Biog. Inst. for Literacy and Peace Contbn., 2001, Worldwide Honors List in appreciation of outstanding contbn. to peace through understanding Internat. Biog. Ctr., Cambridge, Eng., 2003, Presdl. Seal of Honor for contbns. to peace through understanding Am. Biog. Inst., 2003, 21st Century award for achievements in the field of peace through understanding Internat. Biog. Ctr., 2003, Tchg. Excellence award, Cmty. Svc. award, Global Relations award, 2002, numerous others. Mem. NEA, NRA (life, endowment), The Lincoln Inst. for Rsch. Edn., United Conservatives of Am. (participant citizens against the catastrophic health act tax 1989), Mich. Edn. Assn., Internat. Reading Assn., Mich. Sheriffs Assn. (assoc.), Police Marksmanship Assn., Washtenaw Reading Coun., Southeastern Mich. Reading Assn., Mich. Reading Assn., Mich. Assn. for Supervision and Curriculum Devel., Ann Arbor Edn. Assn., Am. Security Coun., Am. Def. Inst., Found. for Christian Living, Am. Family Assn., Nat. Geog. Soc., Am. Film Inst., Internat. Freelance Photographers Orgn. (life), Taxpayers Edn. Lobby, Gun Owners Am., Nat. Assn. Federally Lic. Firearms Dealers, Conservative Caucus, Inc., Ams. for Freedom, Tri-County Sportsman League, Mich. United Conservation Clubs, Mich. State

U. Alumni Assn. (Blue Water chpt.), Mich. State U. Coll. Comm. Arts Alumni Assn., Mich. State U. Coll. Social Sci. Alumni Assn., Ft. Gratiot, Lions Club (v.p. 1998—), Lions Club Internat., Washtenaw Sportsmen's Club (Ypsilanti), Internat. Optimist Club (v.p., bd. dirs. 1975-78) (Ann Arbor), Port Huron Noon Optimist Club, Judo Black Belt Fedn. Am., Sigma Alpha Eta. Lutheran.

THUESEN, GERALD JORGEN, industrial engineer, educator; b. Oklahoma City, July 20, 1938; s. Holger G. and Helen S. T.; m. Harriett M. Thuesen; children: Karen E., Dyan T. Jacobus. BS, Stanford U., 1960, MS, 1961, PhD, 1968. Engr. Pacific Tel. Co., San Francisco, 1961-62, Atlantic Richfield Co., Dallas, 1962-63; asst. prof. indsl. engring. U. Tex., Arlington, 1963, 67-68; assoc. prof. indsl. and sys. engring. Ga. Inst. Tech., Atlanta, 1968-76, prof., 1976-96, prof. emeritus, 1996—. Author: Engineering Economy, 4th edit., 1971, 5th edit., 1977, 6th edit., 1984, 7th edit., 1989, 8th edit., 1993, 9th edit., 2001, Economic Decision Analysis, 1974, 2nd edit., 1980, 3rd edit., 1998; assoc. editor: The Engring. Economist, 1974-80, editor, 1981-91. NASA/Am. Soc. Engring. Edn. summer faculty fellow, 1970 Fellow Inst. Indsl. Engrs. (dept. editor Trans. 1976-80, v.p. publs. 1979-80, divsn. dir. 1978-80, Wellington award 1989, Publs. award 1990, bd. trustees 1979-87), Am. Soc. Engring. Edn. (bd. dirs. 1977-79, Eugene L. Grant award 1977, 91); mem. Sigma Xi. Office: Ga Inst Tech Sch Indsl & System Engring Atlanta GA 30332-0205

THURBER, BARTON DENNISON, English literature educator, writer; b. Pasadena, Calif., Mar. 7, 1948; s. Richard Barton and Gay (Breitinger) T.; m. Beatrix Ann Durfee; 1 child, Jessica Durfee. BA, Stanford U., 1970; AM, Harvard U., 1974, PhD, 1978. Asst. prof. English U. San Diego, 1978-81, assoc. prof., 1981-85, prof., 1985—, chair dept. English, 1980-86, dir. Ctr. for Rsch. in Interactive Techs., 1986-91. Lectr. San Diego Hist. Soc., 1982, Athenaeum Mus. and Arts Libr., 1990-94, San Diego Children's Mus., 1988, others. Author: In Our Own Image, 1985, (play) The Situation is This, 1984, (play) Man Made, 1998, (computer programs) Warsaw 1939, 1989, The Newbook Editor, 1989; also essays. Office: U San Diego 5998 Alcala Park San Diego CA 92110-2476 E-mail: bthurbe1@san.rr.com., thurber@sandiego.edu.

THURSTON, JOHN THOMAS, university advancement official; b. Lockport, N.Y., Oct. 24, 1948; s. John Henry and Helen Lenore (Shaffert) Mahar. BA in English and Journalism, So. Ark. U., 1971. Ednl. affairs writer SUNY, Buffalo, 1972-74, sci. editor, 1974-76, news editor, 1976-77, assoc. dir. Univ. New Burs., 1977-78, dir., 1979-83, assoc. dir. pub. affairs, 1983-86, staff assoc. Univ. Rels., 1987-92, budget and pers. officer dept.Univ. Advancement and Devel., 1992-99, grant writer, 2000—. Communications instr., freelance writer, cons. Hockey coach, ofcl., youth baseball, basketball and football, pres. Western N.Y. High Sch. Club, 1983-85; pres. Lockport Tigers Youth Hockey Assn., 1996—. Recipient nat. award Coun. Advancement and Support of Edn., 1975, 78; named Lockport Sportsman of Yr., 1984. Mem. Coun. Advancement and Support Higher Edn., Nat. Assn. Sci. Writers, Constrn. Writers Am., Pub. Rels. Soc. Am., USA Hockey, Prof. Com. Western N.Y. Republican. Roman Catholic. Home: 4 Rogers Ave Lockport NY 14094-2520 Office: SUNY 318 Wende Hall Buffalo NY 14214 E-mail: jtt13@adelphia.net.

THYSEN, BENJAMIN, biochemist, health science facility administrator, researcher; b. N.Y.C., July 27, 1932; s. Bernard and Clara (Linietsky) Tissenbaum; children: Julie Ann. BS, CCNY, 1954; MS, U. Mo., 1963; PhD, St. Louis U. Med. Sch., 1967. Instr. biochemistry and ob-gyn. depts. St. Louis U. Med. Sch., 1967-68; sr. rsch. scientist Technicon Instrument Corp., Ardsly, N.Y., 1968-69, group leader Tarrytown, N.Y., 1969-70; asst. prof. lab., med., and ob-gyn depts. Albert Einstein Coll. Medicine, Bronx, N.Y., 1971-86, assoc. prof. lab. med. and ob-gyn depts., 1986-2001, assoc. prof. epidemioogy and ob-gyn. depts., 2001—, dir. endocrine labs., 1971-2001, dir. andrology labs., 1997-2001; lab. dir. Park Ave. Fertility, N.Y.C., 2001—. Cons. Technicon Instrument Corp., Tarrytown, 1979-81; mem. spl. study sect. Nat. Inst. Environ. Health Sci., 1986. Contbr. articles to profl. jours. Served with U.S. Army, 1956-58. Recipient Cancer Rsch. award St. Louis U., 1967-68; NIH fellow, 1963-66; E.A. Doisy sr. fellow, 1966-67. Mem. AAAS, Fed. Am. Socs. Exptl. Biology, Assn. Clin. Scientists, Soc. Study of Reprodn., Endocrine Soc., Sigma Xi. Office: Albert Einstein Coll Med 1300 Morris Park Ave Bronx NY 10461-2659 E-mail: thysen@aecom.yu.edu.

TIA, MANG, civil engineering educator; b. Phnom-Penh, Cambodia, Aug. 31, 1953; came to U.S., 1972; s. Chhay and You (Khou) T.; m. Liang Tsi Maria Mao, May 25, 1980; children: Samuel Q., Luke L., Timothy J. BSCE, BSME, MIT, 1976; MSCE, Purdue U., 1978, PhD in Civil Engring., 1982. Registered profl. engr., Fla. Vis. asst. prof. La. Tech. U., Ruston, La., 1982; vis. rsch. assoc. prof. Nat. Ctrl. U., Taiwan, 1989-90; asst. prof. U. Fla., Gainesville, 1982-87, assoc. prof., 1987-92, prof. civil engring., 1992—. Cons. in field. Contbr. articles to Jour. Asphalt Paving Technologists, ACI Material Jours., ASCE Transp. Jour., Transp. Rsch. Record. Deacon Gainesville Chinese Christian Ch., 1990—. Mem. ASCE, ASTM, Am. Concrete Inst., Am. Soc. Engring. Edn., Assn. Asphalt Paving Technologists, Transp. Rsch. Bd. Achievements include patent for Field Permeability Test Apparatus for Concrete. Home: 8214 NW 63rd Pl Gainesville FL 32653-6806

TIAN, FEI-RAN, mathematician, educator; BS in Math., Jinan U., China, 1984; MS in Math., Clarkson U., 1987; PhD in Math., Courant Inst., 1991. Assoc. prof. math. Ohio State U., 2002—; Dicikson instr. math. U. Chgo., 1991—93; postdoctoral staff MSRI, 1993—94; vis. mem. Courant Inst., 1994—95; asst. prof. math. Ohio State U., 1995—2002, assoc. prof. math., 2002—. Fellow, John Simon Guggenheim Meml. Found., 2003. Office: Ohio State Univ Dept Math 231 W 18th Ave Columbus OH 43210*

TIBBITTS, THEODORE WILLIAM, horticulturist, researcher; b. La Crosse, Wis., Apr. 10, 1929; s. John Wilson and Vivian Sophia (Elver) T.; m. Allison Lou Mahan, Aug. 25, 1956 (dec. June 1975); children: Scott, Tia Anne; m. Mary Florence Olmsted, June 22, 1985 (dec. June 1999); m. Mary Hall Bond, July 21, 2001. BS, U. Wis., 1950, MS, 1952, PhD, 1953. Asst prof., assoc. prof., and prof. U. Wis., Madison, 1955-96, emeritus prof., 1996—, dir. Biotron, 1987-92; sr. rsch. engr. N.Am. Aviation, L.A., 1965-66. Cons. Johnson Space Ctr., Manned Spaceflight Ctr., Apollo Flights, 1969-70; vis. prof. U. Guelph, Ont., Can., 1981; mem. NASA Controlled Ecol. Life Support System Discipline Working Group, Washington, 1989-94. Author: Controlled Environment Guidelines for Plant Research, 1979; co-author: Growth Chamber Manual, 1978, 1997; contbr. articles to sci. jours. Elder Covenant Presbyn. Ch:, Madison, 1961-65. With U.S. Army, 1953-55. Recipient Rsch. award Dept. Sci. and Indsl. Rsch., New Zealand, 1981. Fellow Am. Soc. Hort. Sci. (assoc. editor, Marion Meadows award); mem. AAAS, Am. Inst. Biol. Sci., Internat. Hort. Soc., Potato Assn. Am., Am. Soc. Gravitational and Space Biology (bd. dirs.), Am. Soc. Plant Physiologists, Internat. Commn. of Illumination (CIE). Achievements include development of guidelines for controlled environment research, optimizing growth of potatoes for life support in space, patent for use of light-emitting diodes for irradiation of plants; establishment of causal factors for physiological disorders in vegetable species; plant experiment on Biosatellite flights 1966-67, growth chamber experiments on shuttle flight, 1992, 93, 94; first successful crop production in space (potatoes), 1995. Office: U Wis Dept Hort Madison WI 53706

TICE, CAROL HOFF, intergenerational specialist, consultant; b. Ashville, N.C., Oct. 6, 1931; d. Amos H. and Fern (Irvin) Hoff; m. (div.); children: Karin E., Jonathan H. BS, Manchester Coll., North Manchester, Ind., 1954; MEd, Cornell U., 1955. Cert. tchr., Mich., N.Y., N.J. Tchr. Princeton (N.J.) Schs., 1955-60; tchr. Ann Arbor (Mich.) Schs., 1964—; dir. intergenerational programs Inst. for Study Children and Families Eastern Mich. U., Ypsilanti, 1985-96. Founder, pres. Lifespan Resources, Inc., Ann Arbor, 1979—; presdl. appointee to U.S. Nat. Commn. Internat. Yr. of the Child, Washington, 1979-81; del. to White House Conf. on Aging, Washington, 1995. Innovator; program, Tch. Learning Intergenerational Communities, 1971; author: Guide Books and articles, Community of Caring, 1980; co-producer, Film, What We Have, 1976 (award, Milan, Italy Film Festival 1982). Trustee Blue Lake Fine Arts Camp, Twin Lake, Mich., 1975—; dir. Visual Arts Colony, 1990—. Recipient Program Innovation award, Mich. Dept. Edn., 1974—80, C.S. Mott Found. award, 1982, Nat. Found. Improvement in Edn. award, Washington, 1986, Disting. Alumni award, Manchester Coll., 1979, A+ Break the Mold award, U.S. Sec. of Edn., 1992, Ann Arbor Sch. Supts. Golden Apple award, 1999, Disting. Svc. award, Mich. Art Edn. Assn., 2001; fellow Ford Found. fellow, Ithaca, N.Y., 1955. Mem. AAUW (agt. 1979, Agent of Change award), Generations United (hon. com. for Margaret Mead Centennial 2001, 1998—, Pioneer award 1989), Mich. Edn. Assn. (hon. mention Program Innovation 2000), Optimist Club (Humanitarian award). Democrat. Presbyterian. Office: Scarlett MS 3300 Lorraine St Ann Arbor MI 48108-1970

TIDBALL, CHARLES STANLEY, computer scientist, educator; b. Geneva, Apr. 15, 1928; (parents Am. citizens); s. Charles Taylor and Adele (Desmaison) T.; m. Mary Elizabeth Peters, Oct. 25, 1952. BA, Wesleyan U., 1950; MS (Univ. scholar), U. Rochester, 1952; PhD, U. Wis., Madison, 1955; MD (Shattuck fellow, Van Noyes scholar), U. Chgo., 1958; LHD (hon.), Wilson Coll., 1994; DSc (hon.), Hood Coll., 1999. Rotating intern Madison (Wis.) Gen. Hosp., 1958-59; physician I Mendota State Hosp., Madison, 1959; asst. research prof. physiology dept. George Washington U. Med. Center, Washington, 1959-63, USPHS spl. fellow, 1960-61, asso. prof., acting chmn. dept., 1963-64, prof., 1964-65, chmn. dept., 1964-71, Henry D. Fry prof., 1965-84, research prof. med., 1972-80; dir. Office Computer Assisted Edn. George Washington U. Med. Ctr., 1973-75, dir. Office Computer Assisted Edn. and Svcs., 1975-78; Lucie Stern disting. vis. prof. natural scis. Mills Coll., 1980; prof. edn. George Washington U., 1982-84, dir. ednl. computing tech. program Sch. Edn., 1982-84, prof. computer medicine Med. Ctr., 1984-92, prof. emeritus computer medicine, 1992, prof. neurol. surgery, 1990-92, prof. emeritus neurol. surgery, 1992; civil surgeon Immigration and Naturalization Svc., Dept. Justice, Washington, 1986-89; disting. rsch. scholar, co-dir. Tidball Ctr. for Study Ednl. Environments Hood Coll., Frederick, Md., 1994—. Trustee in residence Skidmore Coll., 1995. Author: (with others) Consolidated Index to For Thy Great Glory, 1993, (with others) Taking Women Seriously, 1999; editor: (with M. C. Shelesnyak) Frontiers in the Teaching of Physiology: Computer Literacy and Simulation, 1981; mem. editorial bd.: Jour. Applied Physiology, 1966-69, Jour. Computer-Based Instrn., 1974-89, Am. Jour. Physiology; assoc. editor physiology tchr. sect.; The Physiologist, 1979-85; contbr. articles to profl. jours. Trustee Cathedral Choral Soc., 1976-79, Wilson Coll., 1983-92, Everitt-Pomeroy, 1993-96, Population Reference Bur., 1987-94, 1996-2002, chmn. bd. trustees, 1992-94, sec., 1994-97; lay reader St. Albans Parish, 1965-67, Washington Nat. Cathedral, 1967-94, lay eucharist minister, 1994—, clergy asst., 1968—, homilist, 1977—, info. sys. specialist, 1986-93, vol. mgr. info. sys. program, 1993—; mem. commn. Episcopal Diocese Washington, 1976-78; mem. com. mgmt. YMCA Camp Letts, 1968-96, chmn., 1972-75, dir., chmn. Endowment Fund, 1977-96; bd. dirs. Met. YMCA, Washington, 1972-84, trustees coun., 1984-91, fin. com., 1972-93, v.p. internat. program, 1974-75, asst. treas., 1975-77, v.p., treas., 1977-79, vice chmn., 1979-80, chmn., 1980-82, pres. of found., 1991-93; bd. dirs., treas. Woodley Ensemble, 1993-2003; bd. dirs. Mid-Atlantic Region YMCA, 1974-83; bd. dirs., vice-chmn. Cathedral West Condo., 1983-84, chmn., 1984-87, 91-93, fin. com., 1979-94; bd. dirs. Buckingham's Choice Residents' Assn., 2000-02, chmn. resident svcs. com. Recipient award Washington Acad. Scis., 1967, Leader of Yr. award Met. YMCA, Washington, 1974, Red Triangle award, 1976, Service award, 1979; Dakota Indian name Am. Youth Found., 1976; Research Career Devel. award USPHS, 1961-63 Mem. Am. Physiol. Soc. (emeritus). Home: 3200 Baker Cir #I-235 Adamstown MD 21710 E-mail: ctidball@gwu.edu.

TIDD, JOYCE CARTER, etiquette educator; b. Chipley, FL, May 29, 1932; d. Brown Carter and Gussie Gurtrude Tiller; m. Matthew Heywood Tidd, Jan. 27, 1951; 1 child, Michael Heywood. Diploma, U. Ext. Conservatory, Chgo., 1971. Ch. choir dir. Hamp Stevens Meth. Ch., Columbus, Ga., 1949—50; co-chmn. of music Morningside Presbyn., Columbus, Ga., 1965—72; founder, owner Joyce Tidd Music Studio, Columbus, Ga., 1956—2001; founder, tchr. Sherwood Etiquette Sch., Columbus, Ga., 1996—2001. Home: 5846 Eula Ave Columbus GA 31909

TIDWELL, BETTY DAVENPORT, special education educator; b. Birmingham, Ala., Feb. 15, 1953; d. William Harry and Edna Earl (Staggs) Davenport; m. Michael J. Tidwell; children: David, Daniel. Dental technician, Carrer Acad., Atlanta, 1973; BS in Spl. Edn. with honors, Auburn U., Montgomery, 1992, M in Mild Learning Handicapped, 1994. Cert. spl. edn. tchr., Ala. Dental technician Clanton (Ala.) Dental Lab., 1973-86; tchr. asst. Clanton Elem. Sch., 1988—, tchr. spl. edn., 1992—; tchr. emotionally conflicted Children's Harbor (Ala.) Sch.; edn. coord. Cmty. Intensive Treatment for Youth, Clanton, Ala., 1994—. Sec. Thorsby (Ala.) Band Boosters, 1989-91; parade organizer Thorsby Swedish Heritage Com., 1992-93. Mem. NEA, Ala. Edn. Assn., Coun. for Exceptional Children, Kappa Delta Phi, Phi Kappa Phi. Baptist. Avocations: crafts, playing piano, singing, special olympics. Home: PO Box 1 Jones AL 36749-0001

TIEDEMANN, RUTH ELIZABETH FULTON (SUNNYE TIEDEMANN), writer, educator; b. Knoxville, Tenn., Aug. 27, 1935; d. Frank Keene and Ruth Almeda (McConnell) Fulton; m. Herbert Allen Tiedemann, Sept. 3, 1955; children: Ruth Patten, Keene Fulton, Melvin John (dec.), Herbert Allen Jr. Student, U. Tenn., 1953-56; cert. in real estate, U. Md., 1976, cert. appraiser, 1977; student, U. Okla., 1983-84. Mgr. Corbin Co. Realtors, Bartlesville, Okla., 1977-80; legal document analyst Phillips Petroleum Co., Bartlesville, 1980-84; indexer, legal analyst, 1996; columnist Bartlesville Examiner-Enterprise, 1984-94, 96—; pres. Pens and Lens, Bartlesville, 1985—; book columnist The Bartlesville Times, 1994-95. Contemporary books editor Rave Revs. Mag., N.Y.C., 1987-89; publicity dir. Okla. Mozart Internat. Festival, Bartlesville, 1988; adj. prof. Bartlesville Wesleyan Coll., 1990-96; tchr. creative writing Tri-County Vocat. Tech. Contbr. articles to comml. mags. and profl. jours. and newspapers. Co-founder Bartlesville Compassionate Friends, 1979—; developer libr. Creative Writing Contest. Mem. Women's Coun. Realtors, Okla. Writers Fedn. (Creative Writing award 1987, 89, 92, 93, 95), Nat. Book Critics Cir., Sisters in Crime (nat. newsletter editor 1997-98), Bartlesville WordWeavers (pres. 1991-92), Tulsa Nightwriters, Okla. Ctr. for the Book (bd. dirs.), Delta Delta Delta. Republican. Presbyterian. Home: 316 Brannon Dr Murray NE 68409-2073

TIEMANN, BARBARA JEAN, special education educator; b. Gothenberg, Nebr., Jan. 22, 1955; d. Thurl L. Rogge and Betty R. (Kent) Van Eperen; m. Robert L. Tiemann, June 3, 1977; children: Erich, Hans, Robin (dec.) BS in Elem. Edn., U. Nebr., 1987, MEd, 2000, MEd with severe/profound endorsement. Cert. tchr. Nebr., Fla. Kindergarten tchr. Ft. Pierce (Fla.) Elem. Sch., 1988-89, devel. kindergarten tchr., 1989; psychol. svcs. asst. Beatrice State Devel. Ctr., 1993—2000; resource tchr. Lincoln (Nebr.) Schs., 2000—. Mem. Creighton Parents Assn., Humanities Coun. Mem. NEA, Eastern Star, Lincoln Edn. Assn., Nebraska Edn. Assn., After 5, U. Nebraska Alumni, Compassionate Friends.

TIEN, CHANG-LIN, b. Wuhan, China; arrived in U.S., 1956; m. Di-Hwa Tien; children: Norman, Phyllis, Christine. Bachelor's, Nat. Taiwan U.; master's, U. Louisville, 1957; MA, PhD, Princeton U., 1959; numerous doctoral degrees (hon.), univs. in U.S. and abroad. With faculty mech. engring. U. Calif., Berkeley, 1959—88, 1990—, prof. mech. engring., A. Martin Berlin Chair prof. mech. engring., vice chancellor rsch., 1983—85, exec. vice chancellor, UCI disting. prof. Irvine, 1988—90, univ. prof. emeritus, NEC disting. prof. engring. Berkeley. Chmn. Chief Exec.'s Commn. on Innovation and Tech., Hong Kong, 1980; mem. U.S. Nat. Sci. Bd., U.S. Nat. Commn. on Math. and Sci. Tchg. for 21st Century; sr. advisor to numerous high-tech venture funds and cos.; co-chair Nat. Commn. on Asia in schs.; bd. dirs. Wells Fargo Bank, Kaiser Permanente, Shanghai Comml. Bank. Author one book, editor numerous vols., three internat. jours.; contbr. articles to profl. jours. Active cmty. rels. activities and ednl. reform programs.; active cmty. rels. activities and ednl. reform programs. Recipient Max Jakob Meml. award, 1981, steroid named in his honor Tien Chang-Lin Star, Internat. Astron. Union, 1999, mega oil tanker named in his honor Chang-Lin Tien, 2000. Fellow: AAAS; mem.: NAE, San Francisco Bay Area Econ. Forum (chmn.), Asia Found. (chmn.), Coun. Fgn. Rels., Pacific Coun. on Internat. Policy. Achievements include research in microscale heat transfer; effects of short length scales; short time scales; the material microstructure on thermophysical phenomena; themal radiation. Office: Dept Mech Engring U Calif 6101 Etcheverry Hall Berkeley CA 94720-1740 Fax: 510-643-3887. E-mail: nancie@me.berkeley.edu.

TIENDA, MARTA, demographer, educator; b. Tex. PhD in Sociology, U. Tex., 1977. From asst. prof. to prof. rural sociology U. Wis., Madison, 1976—87; vis. prof. Stanford U., 1987; Ralph Lewis prof. sociology U. Chgo., 1994—97, chmn. dept. sociology, 1994—96; prof. sociology and pub. affairs Princeton U., NJ, 1997—, dir. office population rsch., 1998—2002, Maruice P. During '22 prof. demographic studies, 1999—. Rsch. assoc. office population rsch. Princeton U., 1997—; rsch. assoc. Ogburn-Stouffer Ctr. Co-author: Hispanics in the U.S. Economy, 1985, Hispanic Population of the United States, 1987, Divided Opportunities, 1988, The Color of Opportunity, 2001, Youth in Cities, 2002; contbr. articles to profl. jours. Trustee Kaiser Family Found., Carnegie Corp.; mem. bd. Fed. Res. Bank N.Y. N.Y. Guggenheim fellow. Fellow: AAAS, Ctr. Advanced Study Behavioral Scis.; mem.: Internat. Union for Sci. Study of Population, Population Assn. Am., Am. Econ. Assn., Am. Sociol. Assn. Office: Office Population Rsch Princeton U 247 Wallace Hall Princeton NJ 08544-2091

TIERNO, PHILIP MARIO, JR., microbiologist, educator, researcher; b. Bklyn., June 5, 1943; s. Philip M. and Phyllis (Tringone) T.; m. Josephine Martinez, Apr. 2, 1967; children: Alexandra Lorraine, Meredith Anne. BS, LI U., 1965; MS, NYU, 1974, PhD, 1977. Microbiologist Luth. Med. Ctr., Bklyn., 1965-66; chief rsch. microbiologist hemodialysis unit VA Hosp., Bronx, N.Y., 1966-70; dir. microbiology divsn. NYU Med. Ctr. Goldwater Meml. Hosp., F.D. Roosevelt Island, N.Y., 1970-81; assoc. and cons. microbiologist Maimonides Med. Ctr., Bklyn., 1970-79; dir. microbiology dept. Tisch-Univ. Hosp., NYU Med. Ctr., 1981—. Adj. asst. prof. CUNY, 1974—76, Bloomfield (N.J.) Coll., 1975—82; assoc. prof. microbiology and pathology NYU Med. Sch., 1981—; cons. Office Atty. Gen. N.Y. State, NIH, Coll. of Am. Pathologists, Dept. Health City of New York, 1981—; mem. Mayoral Task Force on Bioterrorism, N.Y.C. Author: The Secret Life of Germs: Observations and Lessons from a Microbe Hunter, 2001, Protect Yourself Against Bioterrorism, 2002, Nuclear, Chemical and Biological Terrorism: Emergency Response and Public Protection, 2003; contbr. articles to profl. jours., chapters to books. Pres. Flushing Taxpayers Assn., 1973-77; bd. dirs. Comprehensive Health Planning Agy. City N.Y., 1974-75, Norwood Bd. Adjustment, N.J., 1978-83, 86-98, Norwood Bd. Edn., 1983-86; chmn. Norwood Environ. Commn., 1986-98; co-founder, bd. dirs. Found. Sci. Rsch. in Pub. Interest, S.I., N.Y., 1985—. Mem. AAAS, N.Y. Acad. Scis., Am. Acad. Microbiology, Am. Pub. Health Assn., Am. Soc. Microbiology, Optimists (v.p. Norwood 1978-95), Knights of Malta (Knighthood). Home: 102 Harbor Cove Piermont NY 10968 Office: Tisch Hosp-Microbiology Dept NYU Med Ctr 560 1st Ave New York NY 10016-6402

TIGAR, MICHAEL EDWARD, law educator; b. Glendale, Calif., Jan. 18, 1941; s. Charles Henry and Margaret Elizabeth (Lang) T.; m. Pamet Ayer Jones, Sept. 21, 1961 (div. Mar. 1973); children: Jon Steven, Katherine Ayer; m. Amanda G. Birrell, Feb. 16, 1980 (div. Aug. 1996); 1 child, Elizabeth Torrey; m. Jane E. Blanksteen, Aug. 22, 1996. BA in Polit. Sci., U. Calif., Berkeley, 1962, JD, 1966. Bar: D.C. 1967, U.S. Ct. Appeals (2d, 4th, 5th, 6th, 7th, 8th, 9th, 10th, 11th, fed. and D.C. cirs.), U.S. Tax Ct., U.S. Supreme Ct. 1972, N.Y. 1993. Assoc. Williams & Connolly, Washington, 1966-69; editor-in-chief Selective Svc. Law Reporter, Washington, 1967-69; acting prof. law UCLA, 1969-71; pvt. practice law Grasse, France, 1972-74; assoc. William & Connolly, Washington, 1974, ptnr., 1975-77, Tigar & Buffone, Washington, 1977-84; prof. law U. Tex., Austin, 1984-87, Joseph D. Jamail Centennial prof. law, 1987-98; of counsel Haddon, Morgan & Foreman, Denver, 1996-98; prof. law, and Edwin A. Mooers, Sr., Scholar Am. U. Washington Coll. Law, Washington, 1998—. Reporter 5th Cir. Pattern Jury Instrns., Austin, 1988-90. Author: Practice Manual Selective Service Law Reporter, 1968, Law and the Rise of Capitalism, 1977, (with Jane B. Tigar) Federal Appeals: Jurisdiction and Practice, 3d edit., 1999, Examining Witnesses, 1993, Persuasion: The Litigator's Art, 1999; contbr. articles to profl. jours. Mem. ABA (vice chair 1987-88, chair elect 1988-89, chair 1989-90 sect. litigation). Avocations: sailing, cooking. Office: Washington Coll Law 4801 Massachusetts Ave NW Washington DC 20016-8196

TIGER, LIONEL, social scientist, anthropology consultant; b. Montreal, Que., Can., Feb. 5, 1937; s. Martin and Lillian (Schneider) T.; m. Virginia Conner, Aug. 19, 1964; 1 child, Sebastian Benjamin. BA, McGill U., 1957, MA, 1959; PhD, U. London, 1963. Instr. anthropology U. Ghana, Accra, 1960; asst. prof. dept. anthropology and sociology U. B.C., Vancouver, Canada, 1963—68; assoc. prof. anthropology Rutgers U., New Brunswick, NJ, 1969—74, prof. anthropology, 1974—, Charles Darwin prof. anthropology, 1990—. Cons., rsch. dir. Harry F. Guggenheim Found., N.Y.C., 1972-84; chmn. bd. social scientists U.S. News and World Report, 1986-88; sci. adv. bd. Am. Wine Inst., San Francisco; sr. rsch. assoc. Nat. Inst. Pub. Policy. Author: Men in Groups, 1969, 2d edit., 1987, (with Robin Rox) The Imperial Animal, 1971, 3d edit., 1998, (with Joseph Shepher) Women in the Kibbutz, 1975, Optimism: The Biology of Hope, 1979, 2d edit., 1994, China's Food, 1985, The Manufacture of Evil: Ethics, Evolution and the Industrial System, 1987; editor: Female Hierarchies, 1978, (with Michael Robinson) Man and Beast Revisited, 1992, The Pursuit of Pleasure, 1992, 2d edit., 2000, The Decline of Males, 1999, The Apes of New York, 2003; mem. editl. bd. Social Sci. Info., Ethology and Sociobiology jour., Jour. of Social Distress and the Homeless. Bd. advisors David R. Graham Found., Toronto; cultural laureate N.Y.C. Landmarks Found., 1999. Recipient W.I. Susman award for excellence in tchg., 1985, McNaughton prize for creative writing; Guggenheim fellow, 1969, rsch. fellow ASDA Found., 1985, Can. Coun., fgn. area tng. fellow Ford Found., Can. Coun.-Killam fellow for interdisciplinary rsch., Rockefeller fellow Aspen Inst., 1979, H.F. Guggenheim Found, fellow, 1988-891 Inst. for Law and Behavioral Rsch. fellow. Mem. PEN (mem. exec. bd., treas. 1988-91, v.p. 1991-94), Am. Anthrop. Assn., Internat. Humanist Assn. (humanist laureate), Can. Humanists Assn. (hon.), Soc. for Study of Evolution, Century Assn. Home: 248 W 23rd St Fl 4 New York NY 10011-2304 also: RR 2 Millbrook NY 12545-9802 E-mail: Rutgers U 131 George St New Brunswick NJ 08901-1414 E-mail: ltiger@rcl.rutgers.edu.

TIGNOR, GEORGE, school system administrator; BA in Biology, St. Mary of Plains Coll., 1969; MA in Botany, Kans. U., Lawrence, 1972; postgrad., Emporia State U., 1974-76. Sci. instr. Rosedale H.S., Kansas City, Kans., 1969-71, Washington H.S., Kansas City, 1973-74, F.L. Schlagle H.S., Kansas City, 1974-76; asst. prin., athletic dir. Wyandotte H.S., Kansas

City, 1976-80; prin. Rosedale Mid. Sch., Kansas City, 1980-81, Parsons (Kans.) H.S., 1981-97, Goddard (Kans.) HS, asst. supt. Named Prin. of Yr., Nat. Assn. Secondary Sch. Prins, 1995, Kans. Prin. of Yr., Kans. Assn. Secondary Sch. Prins., 1995.*

TIGUE, WILLIAM BERNARD, adult education educator; b. Wilkes-Barre, Pa., Aug. 20, 1945; s. Joseph Francis and Susanna Agatha (Opet) T.; m. Faye Gage Cox, Dec. 10, 1977 (div. 1980); m. Dolores Cruz Arriaga, Apr. 17, 1993. BA, Kings Coll., 1967; MA, East Tenn. State U., 1969; TESOL cert., UCLA, 1997. Reporter Johnson City (Tenn.) Press-Chronicle and Knoxville Jour., 1968—72; dir. pub. rels. Beech Mountain, NC, 1972—76, Bellemead Devel. Corp., Fla., 1976—80; account exec. Carl Byoir & Assocs., San Francisco, 1980—82; editor internal publs. Crocker Nat. Bank, San Francisco, 1983—84; copywriter acct. exec. Doremus & Co., San Francisco; assoc. publ., sales mgr. Calif. Bicyclist Yellow Jersey Enterprises, San Francisco, 1988; tchr. English, L.A. County C.C. Dist., 1988—; tchr. adult edn. L.A. Unified Sch. Dist., 1988—. Mem. Women Educators of So. Calif. Democrat. Roman Catholic. Avocations: reading, cooking, AAA profl. baseball. Home: 329 California Ave Apt 8 Santa Monica CA 90403-5014 Office: LA County Sch Dist 329 California Ave Unit 8 Santa Monica CA 90403 E-mail: billtigue@excite.com.

TIJERINA, RAUL MARTIN, physics and mathematics educator; b. Brownsville, Tex., Dec. 10, 1962; s. Gregorio and Maria Olivia (Reyes) T. BS in Physics, U. North Tex., 1987; Cert. in Teaching, U. Tex., Brownsville, 1989. Cert. tchr., Tex. Math., physics tchr. U. Tex., Brownsville, 1988—; math., algebra tchr. Brownsville Ind. Sch. Dist., 1988—. Mem. Nat. Coun. Tchrs. Math., Math. Assn. Am., Am. Inst. Physics. Roman Catholic. Avocations: computers, racquetball, softball. Office: Perkins Mid Sch 4750 Austin Rd Brownsville TX 78521-5455

TILAAR, HENRY A.R. social planner educator; b. Tondano, Indonesia, June 16, 1932; s. Kilala and Engelien (Mamuaya) T.; m. Martha Handana, Jan. 12, 1964; children: Bryan, Pingkan, Wulan, Kilala. MA in Edn., U. Indonesia, Jakarta, 1961; MSc in Edn., Ind. U., 1967, EdD, 1969. Prof. State U. of Tchrs. Coll., Jakarta, 1969-97; asst. min. Nat. Devel. Office (Bappenas), Jakarta, 1986-93; prof. U. Jakarta, 1987-98, prof. emeritus, 1997—. Dir. Inst. Ednl. Mgmt. Devel., Jakarta, 1991—; cons. in field. Author: Education in National Development, 1990, National Education Management, 1992, Indonesian Education Development, 1945-1995, A Policy Study, 1995, Human Resources Development, Vision and Mission for 2020, 1997, Agenda for Education Reform for 21st Century, 1998, Education, Culture, and Civil Society, 1999, New Paradigms of National Education, 2000, National Education Reconstruction, 2001, Social Change and Education, A Transformative Pedagogy for Indonesia, 2002, Power and Education, A Cultural Studies Perspective, 2003. Chmn. bd. advisors Cath. U., Jakarta, 1995-99; mem. bd. advisors Acad. Mgmt., Jakarta, 1996. Recipient Grand medal of merit Republic of Indonesia, 1998. Mem. Nat. Rsch. Coun., Indonesian Edn. Assn., Indonesian Soc. for Advancement of Social Scis., Indonesian Lectrs. Assn. Mem. Democratic Party. Roman Catholic. Avocations: gardening, jogging, watching soccer. Home: Jl Patra Kuningan Utara Blok L-VII No 4 Jakarta Indonesia Office: LPMP State U Jakarta Jl Rawamangun Muka Jakarta DKI Indonesia E-mail: hartilaar@marthatilaar.net.

TILDEN, SAMUEL JOSEPH, pediatrician, educator; b. New Orleans, Feb. 1, 1950; s. Melvin Howard and Anastasie (Abadie) T.; m. Marsha B. Tilden, July 30, 1977; children: S. Grey, Katherine B. BS, Tulane U., 1971, MD, 1977; MS, U. Calif. Berkeley, 1973; JD, Birmingham Sch. Law, 1999. Bar: Ala. 1999. Dir. PICU St. Joseph's Hosp./ Children's Health Ctr., Phoenix, 1983-88; assoc. prof. U. Ala. Birmingham, 1988-93, prof., 1993—. Rshc. compliance officer U. Ala., Birmingham, 2002—. Office: AB 880 1530 3rd Ave S Birmingham AL 35294-0108 E-mail: stilden@uab.edu.

TILGER, JUSTINE THARP, research director; b. New Point, Ind., Sept. 11, 1931; d. Joseph Riley and Marcella Lorene (King) Tharp; m. Clarence A. Tilger II, Aug. 22, 1959 (div. Nov. 1972); children: Evelyn Mary, Clarence Arthur III, Joseph Thomas. AB, U. Chgo., 1951; BA, St. Mary's Coll., Notre Dame, Ind., 1954; MA, Ind. U., 1962, PhD, 1971. Mem. Sisters of the Holy Cross, Notre Dame, 1954-58; teaching fellow Ind. U., Bloomington, 1959-61; asst. editor Ind. Mag. History, Bloomington, 1962-64; bookkeeper Touche Ross, Boston, 1974-77; mgr. account services Harvard U., Cambridge, Mass., 1977-81; dir. research and records Bentley Coll., Waltham, Mass., 1982-84; dir. support services Sta. WGBH-TV, Boston, 1985; dir. research Tufts U., Medford, Mass., 1986—. Cons. Laduke Assocs., Framingham, Mass., 1972-74, New Eng. Ballet, Sudbury, Mass., 1981-82. V.p. Potter Rd. Sch. Assn., Framingham, 1968-69; chmn. vols. St. Anselm's, Sudbury, 1970-71. Mem. Coun. for Advancement and Support Edn., Assn. Records Mgmt. Adminstrs., Am. Prospect Rsch. Assn., New Eng. Devel. Rsch. Assn., Mass. Bus. and Profl. Women (sec. 1981-82), Mensa. Roman Catholic. Avocations: dramatics, travel. Home: 142 Maynard Rd Apt 303B Framingham MA 01701-2512 Office: Tufts U Dept of Research Pachard Hall Medford MA 02155

TILGHMAN, SHIRLEY MARIE, academic administrator, biology educator; PhD in biochemistry, Temple U., 1975. Prof. molecular biology Princeton (N.J.) U., 1986—, Howard A. Prior prof. in life scis., pres., 2001—. Investigator Howard Hughes Med. Inst., bd. dirs., Brookhaven Sci. Lab. Co-editor: Gene Expression & Its Control, 1991, Genes & Phenotypes, 1991, Genetic & Physical Mapping, 1991, Genome Maps & Neurological Disorders, 1993, Genome Rearrangement & Stability, 1993, Regional Physical Mapping, 1993. Mem.: Inst. of Medicine, Nat. Acad. Sci., Am. Philos. Soc. Office: Princeton U One Nassau Hall Princeton NJ 08544-0001

TILL, FRANKLIN L. school system administrator; b. San Diego, Jan. 20, 1947; s. Franklin L. Sr. and Luella Jane (Krough) T.; m. Barbara Jane Till, May 1, 1971; children: Marlo, Jeffrey. BA, San Diego State U., 1969, MA, 1973; EdD, U. So. Calif., 1981. Vice prin. secondary schs. San Diego United Sch. Dist., ops. mgr., prin. mid. level, dep. supt. Contbr. articles to profl. jours. Bd. dirs. YMCA, Urban Corps, Tough Tennis, Vol. Ctr., United Way; mem. exec. bd. ACSA Sch. to Career. Recipient three PTA Hon. Svc. awards. Mem. Assn. of Calif. Sch. Adminstrs. (Disting. Leaders award), Adminstrs. Assn. Home: 1150 NW 120th Ave Plantation FL 33323-2528

TILLAPAUGH, THOMAS ALLAN, school administrator; b. Britton, S.D., Dec. 30, 1953; s. Herbert Allan and Betty Ann (Wellman) T.; m. Yvonne Marie Groleau, July 10, 1976; children: Cherie, Rebecca, Richard, Neil. BS, Oral Roberts U., 1976, MA in Edn., 1986; teaching cert., Henderson State U., 1978; postgrad., Denver U., 1991—. Tchr. sci. and math. Webbers Falls (Okla.) Pub. Sch., 1978-80; adminstr. Calvary Temple Christian Acad., Broken Arrow, Okla., 1980-84; tchr. sci. and math. Cedarwood Christian Acad., Denver, 1984-86; founder, adminstr. Denver St. Sch., 1985—. Named a Tchr. Who Makes a Difference, Rocky Mountain News/Sta. KCNC-TV, NBC, Denver, 1986. Mem. ASCD. Avocations: basketball, softball, travel, map collecting, hiking. Home: 9996 W Cornell Pl Lakewood CO 80227-4353 Office: Denver St Sch 1567 Marion St Denver CO 80218-1512

TILLAR, AIMEE CAMPBELL, early childhood professional; b. Bay Village, Ohio, May 23, 1960; d. James Hamilton and Eleanore (Kirk) C.; children: Shannon Nicole, Rebecca Brianne. AA in Early Childhood Edn., Diablo Valley Coll., 1979; cert. in Montessori edn., U. Puget Sound, 1982. Cert. child ctr. oper., Calif.; lic. family day care provider, Wash. Tchr. Contra Costa Head Start, Antioch, Calif., 1979-81; child care specialist Evergreen State Coll., Olympia, Wash., 1981-82; owner, dir. Day Care Home, Lacey, Wash., 1982-84; edn. coord. No. Ky. Head Start, Newport, 1986-87; dir. Toddler Inn St. Elizabeth Med. Ctr., Covington, Ky., 1987—. Bd. dirs. svc. effectiveness com. New Perceptions, Inc., 1988-90; mem. child care adv. bd. No. Ky. Vocat.-Tech. Sch., 1992—. Mem. Nat. Assn. Edn. Young Children (accreditation validator 1991—), Comprehensive Cmty. Child Care (cons. 1993—), Nat. Assn. Hosp.-Affiliated Child Care Programs, So. Assn. Children Under Six, No. Ky. C. of C. (bd. dirs. child care com. 1988-89), Ky. Assn. Children Under Six (Marion B. Hamilton Meml. grantee 1990). Office: Saint Elizabeth Med Ctr 401 E 20th St Covington KY 41014-1583

TILLEY, SUZANNE DENISE, education specialist; b. Corpus Christi, Tex., Sept. 14, 1963; d. Franklin Roosevelt and Sharie Jerilyn Tilley. BA in Early Childhood Edn., U. Guam, 1984; MEd, Tex. Tech. U., 1994, postgrad., 1994—. Cert. elem. tchr., Tex. Kindergarten tchr. San Angelo (Tex.) Ind. Sch. Dist., 1985-91; edn. coord. South Plains Head Start, Levelland, Tex., 1992-93; disability coord. SHAPES Head Start, Levelland, 1993-94, edn. specialist, 1994—. Co-owner Opening a World of Learning for All Children, Littlefield, Tex., 1993—; presenter profl. confs., 1993-94. CPR, first aid instr. ARC, Lubbock, Tex., 1992—. Capt. USAR, 1985—. Mem. Tex. Head Start Assn., Nat. Assn. for Edn. Young Children, South Plains Assn. Edn. Young Children. Avocations: reading, creating educational activities. Home: 1031 W 7th St Littlefield TX 79339-3703 Office: SHAPES Head Start 1301 Houston St Levelland TX 79336-3313

TILLMAN, JOHN LEE, principal; b. Mesa, Ariz., Jan. 31, 1947; s. W.L. and Juanita (Johnson) T.; m. Judith Ann Tuxhorn, May 31, 1980; children Matthew Lee, Andrew Lee. BA, Adams State Coll., 1969, MA, 1975. Cert. tchr., Colo., Va.; cert. adminstr., Colo. Music tchr. Mountain Valley Sch., Saguache, Colo., 1969-70; dir. music Hargrave Mil. Acad., Chatham, Va., 1970-76; music tchr. Sargent Sch. Dist., Monte Vista, Colo., 1976-82, secondary prin., 1982-95, dir. devel., 1995—. Bd. control Colo. H.S. Activities Assn., Denver, 1990-93; alumni bd. dirs. Adams State Coll., Alamosa, Colo., 1990-93. Music dir. Calvary Bapt. Ch., Monte Vista, 1976—. Mem. Am. Assn. Sch. Adminstrs., Colo. Assn. Sch. Execs., Colo. Music Educators Nat. Conf., Phi Delta Kappa. Baptist. Avocations: computers, music, electronics, woodworking. Office: Sargent Sch Dist 7090 N County Road 2 E Monte Vista CO 81144-9756

TILLMAN, MARY NORMAN, urban affairs consultant; b. Atlanta, Jan. 31, 1926; d. Mary Nellie Shehee; m. James A. Tillman Jr., Apr. 11, 1952; children: James A., Gina G. BA, Morris Brown Coll., 1947; postgrad., U. Minn., 1964, Old Dominion U., 1975—. Asst. bus. mgr. Morris Brown Coll., Atlanta, 1947-53; race rels. and urban affairs cons. Tillman Assocs. Cons. Social Engrs., Atlanta and Syracuse, N.Y., 1963—, sr. ptnr., treas., from 1965, now pres. Bd. dirs. The Tillman Inst. of Human Rels., Inc.; clin. prof. United Theol. Sem., New Brighton, Minn.; adj. prof. Gordon-Conwell Theol. Sem., South Hamilton, Mass. Author: What is Your Racism Quotient?, 1964, A Common Sense Approach to Racism and Other Exclusivities, 1998, (with James A. Tillman, Jr.) Why America Needs Racism and Poverty, 1972, Black Intellectuals, White Liberals and Race Relations: An Analytic Overview, 1973; What is your Exclusivity Quotient, 1978, A Common Sense Approach to Racism and Other Exclusivities, 2001; also articles. Mem. adv. coun. to urban ministries dept. So. Bapt. Conv., Cmty. Rels. Commn., Atlanta; bd. dirs. Christian Coun. Met. Atlanta, Tillman Inst. Human Rels. Mem. Tidewater Assn. Pub. Adminstrs. (dir.), Am. Acad. Cons., Nat. Black Writers Consortium (v.p.), Joint Ctr. for Polit. Studies. Office: 1765 Glenview Dr SW Atlanta GA 30331-2307

TILSON, DANIEL, elementary education educator; Tchr. Eastwood Elem. Sch., Roseburg, Oreg., 1985—. Recipient Excellence in Sci. Tchg. award, 1990, Milken Nat. Edn. award, 1992, State Tchr. of Yr. elem. award Oreg., 1992; Christa McAuliffe fellow, 1988. Office: Eastwood Elem Sch 2550 SE Waldon Ave Roseburg OR 97470-3805 E-mail: dtilson@roseburg.k12.or.us.

TILSTRA, SALLY ANN, computer information systems educator, clinical laboratory scientist; b. Rapid City, S.D., Jan. 26, 1958; d. George Orland and Virginia Katherine (French) Kaubisch; m. Ronald Gary Tilstra, July 12, 1980; 1 child, Kara Renae. BS in Med. Tech., U. S.D., 1980, MBA in Mgmt. Info. Sys., 1994. Cert. specialist in hematology. Med. tech. generalist Sioux Valley Hosp., Sioux Falls, S.D., 1980-82, med. tech. hematology, 1982-89, med. tech. instr., 1989-95; outreach mgr. lab. Weiner Meml. Med. Ctr., Marshall, Minn., 1995-97; instr. computer info. syss. S.E. Tech. Inst., Sioux Falls, S.D., 1997—. Active mem. First United Meth. Ch., Sioux Falls. Mem. Am. Soc. for Clin. Pathology, Am. Soc. for Clin. Lab. Sci., Nat. Cert. Agy., Bus. Soc., Assn. Info. Tech. Profls., Beta Gamma Sigma. Avocations: reading, camping, fishing, cross-stitching, walking. Home: 6512 Cheyenne Dr Sioux Falls SD 57106-1646

TIMCENKO, LYDIA TEODORA, biochemist, chemist; b. Beograd, Yugoslavia, July 4, 1951; arrived in U.S., 1975; d. Teodor Pavle and Branislava (Spasojevic) Timcenko; m. Ghazi Youssef, June 16, 1980 (div. Oct. 1989); children: Ali Alexander Youssef, Kareem Misha Youssef; m. Peter Porzio, Mar. 11, 1996. BS in Chemistry, U. Belgrade, Yugoslavia, 1975; MS, Wayne State U., 1977, PhD, 1984. Grad. asst. Wayne State U., Detroit, 1976-78, 81-84, rsch. assoc., 1986-88, lectr. in chemistry, 1989; postdoctoral fellow Mich. Cancer Found., Detroit, 1985; postdoctoral fellow Sch. Medicine Wayne State U., 1986-88; lectr. in chemistry Lawrence Tech. U., Southfield, Mich., 1989, 90-91; biochemist Strohtech, Inc., Detroit, 1990-91; prof. chemistry Sussex County Coll., Newton, NJ, 1997—99; asst. prof. chemistry N.Y. Techol. Coll., City U. Bklyn., 1999—; sci. tchr. New Milford (NJ) H.S., 2002, Newton (N.J.) H.S., 2002—. Prin. investigator, rsch. scientist ICN Galenika Inst., Clin. Ctr. Serbia, Belgrade, 1991—96; rsch. scientist, mktg. cons. Huet Biol., Birmingham, Mich., 1987—91; adj. prof. chemistry Kean Coll.; adj. prof. dept. chemistry and chem. biology Stevens Inst. Tech., Castle Point on Hudson, Hoboken, NJ; adj. assoc. prof. organic chemistry Pace U., N.Y.C., 2002. Contbr. articles to profl. jours. Mem.: Am. Chem. Soc., Am. Soc. Microbiology, Phi Lambda Upsilon. Achievements include research in in shigella toxin in shigella and E. coli; mitoch GPO in advenal cortex; liberation of labile sufur from ferredoxins; adhesion shigella to HCTH and HELA; localization of GST and GP in adrenal. Home: 306 State Route 94 Columbia NJ 07832-2771

TIMME, KATHRYN PEARL, secondary education educator; b. Houston, Feb. 15, 1934; d. William Emil and Neoma Leila (Harvey) T. BA, Rice U., 1956; MA, U. Houston, 1965. Cert. secondary tchr., Tex. Tchr. Houston Ind. Sch. Dist., 1956—. Rsch. fellow Houston Maths. and Sci. Consortium, 1986-87. Author: Horticultural Chemistry, 1976, Chemistry of The Sea, 1977, Textile Chemistry, 1978, Geochemistry, 1982, Exploring Electrolytes, 1987. Grantee NSF, 1970, 72, Houston Bus. Com., 1987, Impact II, 1989. Mem. Am. Chem. Soc., Phi Beta Kappa (Rice chpt.), Phi Alpha Theta. Episcopalian. Avocation: animal rights projects. Office: Robert E Lee High Sch 6529 Beverlyhill St Houston TX 77057-6499

TIMMERHAUS, KLAUS DIETER, chemical engineering educator; b. Mpls., Sept. 10, 1924; s. Paul P. and Elsa L. (Bever) T.; m. Jean L. Mevis, Aug. 3, 1952; 1 dau., Carol Jane. BS in Chem. Engring, U. Ill., 1948, MS, 1949, PhD, 1951. Registered prof. engr., Colo. Process design engr. Calif. Rsch. Corp., Richmond, Calif., 1952-53; extension lectr. U. Calif., Berkeley, Calif., 1952; mem. faculty U. Colo., Boulder, Colo., 1953-95, prof. chem. engring., 1963—86, asso. dean engring., 1963—86, dir. engring. rsch. ctr. coll. engring., 1963-86, chmn. aerospace dept., 1986—89, chmn. chem. engring. dept., 1986-89, Patten Chair Disting. prof., 1986-89, presdl. tchg. scholar, 1989—. Chem. engr. cryogenics lab. Nat. Bur. Standards, Boulder, summers 1955,57,59,61; lectr. U. Calif. at L.A., 1961-62; sect. head engring. div. NSF, 1972-73; cons. in field. Bd. dirs. Colo. Engring. Expt. Sta., Inc., Engring. Measurements Co., both Boulder Editor: Advances in Cryogenic Engineering, vols. 1-25, 1954-80; co-editor: Internat. Cryogenic Monograph Series, 1965— . Served with USNR, 1944-46. Recipient Disting. Svc. award Dept. Commerce, 1957, Samuel C. Collins award for outstanding contbns. to cyrogenic tech., 1967, Meritorious Svc. award Cryogenic Engring. Conf., 1987, Disting. Pub. Svc. award NSF, 1984; named CASE Colo. Prof. of Yr., 1993, Disting. Lectr., L-T Fan, 2001. Fellow AAAS (v.p. 1985, pres. 1986, Southwestern and Rocky Mountain divsn. Pres.'s award 1989), Internat. Inst. Refrigeration (v.p. 1979-87, pres. 1987-95, US nat. commn. 1983—, pres. 1983-86, W.T. Pentzer award 1989), AIChE (v.p. 1975, pres. 1976, Alpha Chi Sigma award for chem. engring. rsch., 1968, Founders award 1978, Eminent Chem. Engr. award 1983, W.K. Lewis award 1987, F.J. Van Antwerpen award 1991, Inst. Lecture award 1995), Am. Soc. for Engring. Edn. (bd. dirs. 1986-88, George Westinghouse award 1968, 3M Chem. Engring. divsn. award 1980, Engring. Rsch. Coun. award 1990, Delos Svc. award 1991); mem. NAE, Am. Astron. Soc., Austrian Acad. Sci., Cryogenic Engring. Conf. (chmn. 1956-67, bd. dirs. 1967—), Internat. Cryocooler Conf. (bd. dirs. 1980—), Soc. Automotive Engrs. (Ralph Teetor award 1991), Sigma Xi (v.p. 1986-87, pres. 1987-88, bd. dirs. 1981-89), Verein Deitscher Ingenieure, Cryogenic Soc. Am., Sigma Tau, Tau Beta Pi, Phi Lambda Upsilon. Home: 905 Brooklawn Dr Boulder CO 80303-2708 E-mail: klaus.timmerhaus@colorado.edu.

TIMMONS, SHARON L. retired elementary education educator; b. South Kansas City, Mo., July 25, 1949; d. Clyde George and Sarah Ethyl (Thrift) Manley; m. Joseph D. Timmons, June 6, 1970; children: Stacia, Matt. BSE, U. Kans., 1972; MA, U. Mo., Kansas City, 1980. Cert. elem., jr. high tchr., Mo; elem. tchr., Kans. Elem. team tchr. Loretto Acad., Kansas City, Mo., 1976-80; team tchr. 8th grade Ctr. Sch. Dist. 58, Kansas City, Mo., 1980-94; ret., 1994. Author: (Title II grants) For Indivdualized Math Program, Kansas City Rep. for Scientific Literacy. Mem. Sigma Kappa.

TIMMRECK, THOMAS C. health sciences and health administration educator; b. Montpelier, Idaho, June 15, 1946; s. Archie Carl and Janone (Jensen) T.; m. Ellen Prusse, Jan. 27, 1971; children: Chad Thomas, Benjamin Brian, Julie Anne. AA, Ricks Coll., 1968; BS, Brigham Young U., 1971; MEd, Oreg. State U., 1972; MA, No. Ariz. U., 1981; PhD, U. Utah, 1976. Program dir. Cache County Aging Program, Logan, Utah, 1972-73; asst. prof. div. health edn. Tex. Tech U., Lubbock, 1976-77; asst. prof. dept. health care adminstrn. Idaho State U., Pocatello, 1977-78; dept. chair, asst. prof. health services program No. Ariz. U., Flagstaff, 1978-84; cons., dir. grants Beth Israel Hosp., Denver, 1985; prof. dept. health scis. and human ecology, coordinator grad. studies, coordinator health adminstrn. and planning Calif. State U., San Bernardino, 1985—2002; ret., 2002; pres. Health Care Mgmt. Assocs., 1985—2000. Presenter at nat. confs.; dept. chair health and wellness dept., faculty Loretto Heights Coll., Denver; adj. faculty Dept. Mgmt. U. Denver, Dept. Mgmt. and Health Adminstrn. U. Colo., Denver, dept. bus. adminstrn. U. Redlands (Calif.), U. So. Calif., L.A., Chapman U. Author: Dictionary of Health Services Management, rev. 2d edit., 1987, Health Services Cyclopedic Dictionary, 3d edit., An Introduction to Epidemiology, 1994, 2d edit., 1998, Planning and Program Development and Evaluation: A Handbook for Health Promotion, Aging, and Health Services, 1995; mem. editl. bd. Jour. Health Values, 1986—, Basic Epidemiological Methods and Biostats., Dictionary of Epidemiology and Public Health, 1996; contbr. numerous articles on health care adminstrn., behavioral health, gerontology and health edn. to profl. jours. Chmn., bd. dirs. Inland Counties Health System Agy.; mem. strategic planning com. chmn. Vis. Nurses Assn. of Inland Counties; bd. dirs. health svc. orgns. With U.S. Army, 1966-72, Vietnam. Mem. Assn. Advancement of Health Edn., Am. Acad. Mgmt., Assn. Univ. Programs in Health Care Adminstrn., Healthcare Forum. Republican. Mem. Lds Ch.

TIMPANE, PHILIP MICHAEL, education educator, policy analyst; b. Troy, N.Y., Nov. 27, 1934; s. Philip Thomas and Rita (Killeen) T.; m. Genevieve LaGrua, Nov. 30, 1957; children: Michael J., Joseph T., Paul J., David A. AB, Cath. U. Am., 1956, MA, 1964, LLD (hon.), 1991; MPA, Harvard U., 1970; LittD (hon.), Wagner Coll., 1986. Historian Joint Chiefs of Staff Dept. Def., 1961-65; spl. asst. civil rights Office of Sec. Def., 1965-68; edn. policy planner HEW, 1968-72; sr. fellow Brookings Instn., 1972-74; dir. edn. policy ctr. RAND Corp., 1974-77; dep. dir. Nat. Inst. Edn., Washington, 1977-80, dir., 1980-81; prof. edn. Columbia U. Tchrs. Coll., N.Y.C., 1981—, dean, 1981-84, pres., 1984-94; mem. Aspen Inst. Edn. Program, 1974-77, 87—; v.p. and sr. scholar Carnegie Found. for Advancement Tchg., Princeton, N.J., 1994-97; sr. adv. for edn. policy RAND, Washington, 1997—. Author: Corporate Interest in Public Education in the Cities, 1982; co-author: Youth Policy in Transition, 1976, Business Impact on Education and Child Development Reform, 1991, Rhetoric Versus Reality: What We Know and What We Need to Know about Vouchers and Charter Schools, 2001, Options for Restructuring the Safe and Drug-Free Schools and Communities Act, 2001; co-editor: Planned Variation in Education, 1975, Work Incentives and Income Guarantees, 1975, Ethical and Legal Issues in Social Experimentation, 1975, Higher Education and School Reform, 1998, Rediscovering the Democratic Purposes of Education, 2000; editor: Federal Interest in Financing Schooling, 1978. Mem. Arlington (Va.) Sch. Bd., 1972—76, chmn., 1973—74; bd. dirs. Children's TV Workshop, 1989—99, Jobs for the Future, 1995—2002, Inst. Ednl. Leadership, 1999—, So. Edn. Found., 1995—2003. Democrat. Roman Catholic. Office: Aspen Inst Edn Program 1 Dupont Cir Ste 700 Washington DC 20036 E-mail: mike.timpane@aspeninst.org.

TINCHER, BARBARA JEAN, university official; b. Shawano, Wis., June 9, 1963; d. George William and Phyllis Jean (Albrecht) T. Student, Ripon Coll., 1983-84; BA, U. Minn., 1988. Cert. theatre adminstrn. Artistic and gen. adminstrv. asst. Pepsico Internat. Performing Arts Festival, Purchase, N.Y., 1986; programming and press asst. Riverside Studios, Hammersmith, England, 1987; club coord. Guthrie Theater, Mpls., 1986-88; devel. assoc. Huntington Theatre Co., Boston, 1988-89, coord. ann. fund, 1989-90; mgr. ann. fund L.A. (Calif.) Theatre Ctr., 1990, dir. devel., 1991; ind. fund raising cons. L.A., 1991; bd. devel. specialist AIDS Project L.A., Calif., 1991-94, dir. bd. rels., 1994-95; dir. leadership gifts Lawrence U., Appleton, Wis., 1995—. Mem. Women in Devel. Greater Boston, 1989-90; del. Conf. About Vols. Regional Theatres, Milw., 1990; participant fall fund raising day Nat. Soc. Fund Raising Execs., L.A., 1990, Non-Profit Mgmt. Inst. Bd. Devel. Tng., San Diego, 1992, Nat. Ctr. for Non-Profit Bds. Annual Conf., 1994. Guest panelist AIDS Vision Cable Show, 1992, John Brown Planned Giving Conf., 1996, Conrad Teitell Philanthropy Tax Inst., 1996, Nat. Conf. on Planned Giving, New Orleans, 1997. Bd. dirs. Attic Theatre, 1996—, chmn. devel. com., 1999—. Mem. Alpha Xi Delta. Methodist. Avocations: cultural activities, animals, dogs. Home: 731 S Lynndale Dr Appleton WI 54914-4402 Office: Lawrence U PO Box 599 Appleton WI 54912-0599

TINCK, ELIZABETH ANN, special education educator; b. Cleve., July 29, 1955; d. William T. and Mary Kathern (Hartley) T. BS in Edn., Yougstown State Coll., 1979. Spl. tutor math. Madison (Ohio) Schs., 1979-83, tutor learning disabilities, 1980-81, adult educator, 1980-83, home bound educator, 1980-87; severe behavior educator Ashtabula (Ohio) County Schs., 1987—98, educator children with behavioral disorders, 1998—99; tutor L.D. Kirtland Schs. L.D., 1999—2000; sub. tchr. Painsville Township Schs., 2000—; tchr. 2d grade Archbishop Lyke Elem. Sch., Cleve., 2003—; tchr. spl. edn. Hope Acads. Chapleside, Cleve., 2003—. Mem. Coun. Children with Behavioral Disorders, Soc. Roller Skating Tchrs. Assn. Avocations: roller skating, camping. Home: 63 Wailele Dr Madison OH 44057-2737 E-mail: lizsk@ncweb.com.

TING, SAMUEL CHAO CHUNG, physicist, educator; b. Ann Arbor, Mich., Jan. 27, 1936; s. Kuan H. and Jeanne (Wong) Ting; m. Susan Carol Marks, Apr. 28, 1985; children: Jeanne Min, Amy Min, Christopher M. BS in Engring., U. Mich., 1959, MS, 1960, PhD in Physics, 1962, ScD (hon.), 1978, Chinese U. Hong Kong, 1987, U. Bologna, Italy, 1988, Columbia U., 1990, U. Sci. and Tech., China, 1990, Moscow State U., 1991, U. Bucharest, Romania, 1993, Nat. Tsinghua U., Taiwan, 2002, Nat. Jiaotong U., 2003. Ford Found. fellow CERN (European Orgn. Nuc. Rsch.), Geneva, 1963; instr. physics Columbia U., 1964, asst. prof., 1965—67; group leader Deutsches Elektronen-Synchrotron, Hamburg, Germany, 1966; assoc. prof. physics MIT, Cambridge, 1967—68, prof., 1969—; Thomas Dudley Cabot Inst. prof. M.I.T., 1977—. Program cons. divsn. particles and fields Am. Phys. Soc., 1970; hon. prof. Beijing Normal Coll., 1987, Jiatong U., Shanghai, 1987, U. Bologna, Italy, 1988. Assoc. editor Nuc. Physics B, 1970, editl. bd. Nuc. Instruments and Methods, Mathematical Modeling; contbr. articles to profl. jours. Recipient Nobel prize in Physics, 1976, De Gasperi prize in Sci., Italian Republic, 1988, Ernest Orlando Lawrence award, U.S. Govt., 1976, Gold medal in Sci., City of Brescia, Italy, 1988, Golden Leopard award, Town of Taormina, 1988, Forum Engelberg prize, 1966, Pub. Svc. medal, NASA, 2001; fellow Am. Acad. Arts and Scis., 1975. Mem.: NAS, Deutsche Acad. Naturforscher Leopoldina, Russian Acad. Sci., Acad. Sinica, Pakistani Acad. Sci. Office: MIT Dept Physics 51 Vassar St Cambridge MA 02139-4308

TINGUS, STEVEN JAMES, physiologist researcher, educator; b. Sacramento, Calif., Aug. 19, 1963; s. James George and Joanne Fotene (Kamilos) T. BS in Biol. Sci., U. Calif., Davis, 1985, MS in Physiology, 1990, C.Phil. in Physiology, 1994. Dir. US dept. edn. Nat. Inst. on Disability and Rehab. Rsch., Wash., 2001—. Mem.: AAAS, Am. Coll. Healthcare Execs. Republican. Greek Orthodox. Home: Apt 1101 2250 Clarendon Blvd Arlington VA 22201-3341 Office: Dir Nat Inst on Disability and Rehab US Dept Edn 400 Maryland Ave SW Washington DC 20202*

TINKER, AVERILL FAITH, special education educator; b. Rochester, N.Y., May 7, 1953; d. George Douglas and Adele (Page) M.; m. William Dean, Sept. 17, 1977 (div. Dec. 1989); children: Paul, David. B in Music Edn., Baldwin-Wallace Coll., 1975; M in Music Therapy, So. Meth. U., 1978; cert. in spl. edn., Tex. Women's U., 1984; postgrad., Notre Dame Coll., 1996. Cert. spl. edn. Music therapist Terrell (Tex.) State Hosp., 1978-79, Ft. Worth State Sch., 1979-84, spl. edn. tchr., 1985-86, Sch. Adminstrv. Unit 43, Newport, N.H., 1986-93, Hartford High Sch., White River Junction, Vt., 1993-94, Dothan Brook Elem. Sch., White River Junction, 1994—. Organist, choir dir. St. Paul's Episc. Ch., White River Junction, Vt., 1988-99, organist West Lebanon Congregational Ch., 1999—; vol. Spl. Olympics, N.H., 1987-88; den mother Cub Scouts, Vt., 1988. Mem. Coun. for Exceptional Children, Am. Guild Organists, Am. Guild English Handbell Ringers, Kappa Delta Pi, Mu Phi Epsilon. Democrat. Avocations: swimming, hiking, attending concerts. E-mial. Home: 6 College Ave Lebanon NH 03766-2504 E-mail: averill.tinker@valley.net.

TINKER, THOMAS EATON, headmaster; b. Providence, May 24, 1941; s. George Milan and Ruth (Eaton) T.; m. Rosalyn May Stillman, Dec. 21, 1968. BA, Columbia U., 1963; MA, Brown U., 1968. English instr. Tabor Acad., Marion, Mass., 1964-66; history instr. Wheeler Sch., Providence, 1967-77; headmaster Broadmeadow Sch., Middletown, Del., 1977-82, St. Paul's Sch., Garden City, N.Y., 1982-89, The Barnard Sch., N.Y.C., 1989-93; assoc. head sch. Trevor Day Sch., N.Y.C., 1993—. Evaluator Mid. State Assn. Colls. and Schs., Phila., 1978—. Trustee Barnard Sch. Found., 1993—; bd. dirs. Univ. Club L.I., 1984-86. With USAR, 1963-69. Mem. Nat. Assn. Ind. Schs., N.Y. State Assn. Ind. Schs., L.I. Episcopal Sch. Assn. (v.p./treas. 1984-89), Del. Assn. Ind. Schs. (sec. 1978-82). Episcopalian. Avocation: sailing. Home: 137 James St Rochelle Park NJ 07662-3422 Office: Trevor Day Sch 4 E 90th St New York NY 10128-0603

TINKHAM, MICHAEL, physicist, educator; b. Green Lake County, Wis., Feb. 23, 1928; s. Clayton Harold and LaVerna (Krause) T.; m. Mary Stephanie Merin, June 24, 1961; children: Jeffrey Michael, Christopher Gillespie. AB, Ripon (Wis.) Coll., 1951, Sc.D. (hon.), 1976; MS, MIT, 1951; PhD, 1954; MA (hon.), Harvard, 1966; DSc (hon), ETH Zurich, 1997. NSF postdoctoral fellow at Clarendon Lab., Oxford (Eng.) U., 1954-55; successively research physicist, lectr., asst. prof., asso. prof., prof. physics U. Calif. at Berkeley, 1955-66; Gordon McKay prof. applied physics Harvard U., 1966—, prof. physics, 1966-80, Rumford prof. physics, 1980—, chmn. physics dept., 1975-78. Cons. to industry, 1958—; participant internat. seminars and confs.; mem. commn. on very low temperatures Internat. Union Pure and applied Physics, 1972-78; vis. Miller rsch. prof. U. Calif.-Berkeley, 1987; vis. prof. Technical Univ., Delft, The Netherlands, 1993. Author: Group Theory and Quantum Mechanics, 1964, Superconductivity, 1965, Introduction to Superconductivity, 1975, 2d edit., 1996; contbr. articles to profl. jours. Served USNR, 1945-46. Recipient award Alexander von Humboldt Found. U. Karlsruhe, W. Ger., 1978-79; NSF sr. postdoctoral fellow Cavendish lab.; vis. fellow Clare Hall Cambridge (Eng.) U., 1971-72; Guggenheim fellow, 1963-64 Fellow Am. Phys. Soc. (chmn. div. solid state physics 1966-67, Buckley prize 1974, Richtmyer lectr. 1977), AAAS; mem. Am. Acad. Arts and Scis., Nat. Acad. Scis. Home: 98 Rutledge Rd Belmont MA 02478-2633 Office: Harvard Univ Physics Dept Lyman Lab of Physics 326 Cambridge MA 02138 E-mail: tinkham@RSJ.harvard.edu.

TIPPECONNIC, JOHN W., III, director, educator; BS in Secondary Edn., Okla. State U.; MEd in Ednl. Adminstrn., Pa. State U., 1971, PhD in Ednl. Adminstrn., 1975. Dir. Office of Indian Edn. Programs Dept. of the Interior, Washington, 1990—95; prof. leadership and policy studies Ariz. State U., 1995—96; prof. edn. Pa. State U., U. Pk., Pa., 1996—, dir. Am. Indian Leadership Program, 1996—. Office: Pa State Univ 0301 Rackley Bldg University Park PA 16802*

TIPPING, SHARON RUTLEDGE, elementary school educator; b. Odessa, Tex., Jan. 24, 1948; d. L.D. Rutledge and Hazel (Simpson) Smithee; m. Eldon Tipping Jr., Dec. 21, 1968; 1 child, Teresa Lynn. BA magna cum laude, Baylor U., 1969; MEd, Tex. A&M U., 1973. Cert. provisional elem. tchr., profl. counselor, provisional lang. and learning disabilities. Tchr. Oakdale Elem. Sch., Springlake, N.C., 1969-70, Hamilton Park Elem. Sch., Richardson Ind. Sch. Dist., Dallas, 1979-90, Brentfield Elem. Sch., Richardson Ind. Sch. Dist., Dallas, 1990-92; ednl. cons. Jostens Learning, 1992-94, nat. curriculum and instrn. specialist, 1994-97, regional mktg. mgr., 1997—. Cons. REgion X Svc. Ctr., 1988-90. Chmn. Mother's March of Dimes, Richardson, Tex., 1976, 77, 78; vol. caseworker Family Outreach, Richardson, 1975-79; pres. Hamilton Park Elem. PTA. Mem. ASCD, Nat. Staff Devel. Coun., Nat. Coun. Tchrs. Math., Assn. Tex. Profl. Educators, N. Tex. Reading Coun., Richardson Edn. Assn., Phi Delta Kappa. Home and Office: 3700 Nightingale Ct Plano TX 75093-7525

TIPTON, KAREN, middle school educator; b. Junction City, Kans., Aug. 29, 1935; d. Clarence Calvert and Olive Ann (Bennett) T.; m. Merle Francis Channel, July 5, 1951 (div. Mar. 1983); children: Gloria Jeane Channel McKim, Steven Blair, Michael Curtis, Patrick Rock Channel. BS in Math., U. So. Colo., 1972; MA in Edn., Lesley Coll., 1990. Cert. tchr., Colo. Tchr. Pueblo (Colo.) Sch. Dist. 70, 1973—. Mem. NEA, AAUW, Pueblo County Tchrs. Assn., Colo. State Hist. Soc., Elks, Eagles. Home: 316 W 21st St Pueblo CO 81003-2516

TIRELLA, THERESA MARY, special education educator; b. Worcester, Mass., Apr. 22, 1963; d. Samuel Louis and Cecilia Barbara (Trczinski) T. BS, Northeastern U., 1986, MEd, 1989. Acting supr., childcare worker Dr. Franklin Perkins Sch., Lancaster, Mass., 1983-84; sr. recreational counselor Friendly House Inc., Worcester, 1985; adult edn. educator Action for Boston Community Devel., 1986-87; spl. edn. educator Cotting Sch., Lexington, Mass., 1987—. Cons. United Cerebral Palsy, Watertown, Mass., 1993, Spl. Needs Advocacy Network Newton, Mass., 1991-93; corrd, bd. dirs. Access Now, Boston, 1991-93. Vol. mem. program planning com. Ptnrs. for Disabled Youth, Boston, 1991-94; vol. tutor Bethel Bapt. Ch., Roxbury, Mass., 1991-92, mem. youth com., 1991-92, mem. choir, 1991-92. Mem. Assn. for Suprevision and Curriculum Devel., Northeastern Univj. Women's Alumni Club, Northeastern U. Alumni Assn. Avocations: reading, graphic arts, crafts, arts, basketball. Home: 17 Seaverns Ave Jamaica Plain MA 02130-2874

TIRRO, FRANK PASCALE, music educator, author, composer; b. Omaha, Sept. 20, 1935; s. Frank and Mary Carmela (Spensieri) T.; m. Charlene Rae Whitney, Aug. 16, 1961; children: John Andrew, Cynthia Anne. B.M.E., U. Nebr., 1960; M.M., Northwestern U., 1961; PhD, U. Chgo., 1974. Chmn. lab. sch. U. Chgo., Ill., 1961—70; fellow of Villa I Tatti Harvard U., Florence, Italy, 1971—72; lectr. U. Kans., Lawrence, Kans., 1972—73; asst. prof. music Duke U., Durham, NC, 1973—74; dir. Southeastern Inst. Medieval and Renaissance Studies, Durham, NC, 1978—80; chmn., assoc. prof. music Duke U., Durham, NC, 1973—80; prof. Yale U., New Haven, 1980—, dean, 1980—89. Reader, cons. several univ. presses; jurist Parisot Internat. Cello Competition, Sao Paolo, Brazil, 1981. Author: Historia del Jazz Clásico, 2001, Historia del Jazz Moderno, 2001, Jazz: A History, 1977, rev. edit., 1993, Renaissance Choirbooks in the Archive of San Petronio in Bologna, 1986, Living With Jazz, 1996, (with others) The Humanities: Cultural Roots and Continuities, 1980, 6th edit., 2000; editor: Medieval and Renaissance Studies No. 9, 1982; mem. editl. bd. Wittenberg Rev.; composer American Jazz Mass, 1960; assoc. editor Am. Nat. Biography, 1994—. Bd. dirs. New Haven Symphony, 1980-89, Neighborhood Music Sch., New Haven, 1982-89, Chamber Orch. New Eng., 1980-82, Ctr. for Black Music Rsch., 1985-91. Recipient Standard Composer award Am. Soc. Composers, Authors and Pubs., 1966, 99, 2000, 01, Gustavus Fine Arts medal, 1988, Duke Ellington Fellow medal, 1989; travel grantee Am. Coun. Learned Socs., 1967; rsch. grantee Duke U., 1978; named to Omaha Ctrl. H.S. Hall of Fame, 2002. Mem. Am. Musicol. Soc. (council 1978-80), Coll. Music Soc. (council 1980-82, mem. exec. bd. 1984-86), Nat. Assn. Schs. of Music, Internat. Soc. Jazz Research, Renaissance Soc. Am., Mory's Club, Yale Club (NYC). Republican. Lutheran. Office: Yale U Sch Music PO Box 208246 New Haven CT 06520-8246 E-mail: frank.tirro@yale.edu.

TIRYAKIAN, EDWARD ASHOD, sociology educator; b. Bronxville, N.Y., Aug. 6, 1929; s. Ashod Haroutioun and Keghinee (Agathon) T.; m. Josefina Cintron, Sept. 5, 1953; children: Edmund Carlos, Edwyn Ashod. BA summa cum laude, Princeton U., 1952; MA, Harvard U., 1954, PhD, 1956; PhD (hon.), U. Rene Descartes, Paris, 1987. Instr. Princeton U., 1956-57, asst. prof., 1957-62; lectr. Harvard U., 1962-65; assoc. prof. Duke U., Durham, N.C., 1965-67, prof., 1967—, chmn. dept. sociology and anthropology, 1969-72, dir. internat. studies, 1988-91. Vis. lectr. U. Philippines, 1954-55, Bryn Mawr Coll., 1957-59; vis. scientist program Am. Sociol. Assn., 1967-70; vis. prof.-Laval U., Quebec City, Que., Can., 1978, Inst. Polit. Studies, Paris, 1992, Free U., Berlin, 1996; summer seminar dir. NEH, 1978, 80, 93, 89, 91, 96; lectr. Kyoto Am. Studies Summer Seminar, 1985, project leader Fulbright New Cent. Scholars Program, 2002-03. Author: Sociologism and Existentialism, 1962; Editor: Sociological Theory, Values and Sociocultural Change: Essays in Honor of P.A. Sorokin, 1963, The Phenomenon of Sociology, 1971, On the Margin of the Visible: Sociology, the Esoteric, and the Occult, 1974, The Global Crisis: Sociological Analyses and Responses, 1984; co-editor: Theoretical Sociology: Perspectives and Developments, 1970; New Nationalisms of the Developed West, 1985. Fellow Ctr. for Advanced Study in Behavioral Scis., 1997-98; recipient Fulbright rsch. award, 1955; Ford faculty rsch. fellow, 1971-72, fellow Ctr. for Advanced Study in Behavioral Scis., 1997-98, Disting. New Century scholar Fulbright Scholar Program, 2002-03. Mem. Am. Sociol. Assn., African Studies Assn., Am. Soc. for Study Religion (co uncil 1975-78, pres. 1981-84), Assn. Internationale des Sociologues de Langue Française (v.p. 1985-88, pres. 1988-92), Soc. for Phenomenology and Existential Philosophy, Phi Beta Kappa. Clubs: Princeton, Century Assn. (N.Y.C.). Home: 16 Pascal Way Durham NC 27705-4924

TISCHFIELD, JAY ARNOLD, genetics educator; b. N.Y.C., June 15, 1946; s. Max and Ethel Barbara (Smith) T.; m. Donna Marie Mitchell, Aug. 29, 1978; children: Max Alexander, Samuel Eli, David James. BS, Bklyn. Coll., 1967; MPH, Yale U., 1969, PhD, 1973. Diplomate Am. Bd. Med. Genetics. Asst. prof. Case Western Reserve U., Cleve., 1972-78; assoc. prof., prof. Med. Coll. of Ga., Augusta, 1978-87; prof., dir. div. molecular genetics Ind. U. Sch. Medicine, Indpls., 1987—98; MacMillan prof. and chair, dept. of Genetics Rutgers U., 1998—. Prof. of Pediat. and Psychiatry Robert Wood Johnson Med. Sch., 1998—; mem., Sci. Adv. Bd. Genome Inst. of Singapore. Contbr. articles to profl. jours. Named Disting. Alumnus, Bklyn. Coll., 1990; NIH postdoctoral fellow, 1967-72; grantee NIH, 1972—, NSF, 1983-85. Mem. Am. Soc. for Human Genetics, Am. Soc. for Microbiology, AAAS, Sigma Xi, Yale Club of Ind. Achievements include patents in field. Office: Rutgers U Dept Genetics 604 Allison Rd Piscataway NJ 08854-8000

TISCHLER, HENRY LUDWIG, sociology educator; b. Shanghai, Sept. 3, 1945; s. Helmut and Alice (Muller) T.; m. Linda Carol Hayes, Aug. 5, 1973; children: Melissa Lauren, Benjamin Hayes. BA in Psychology, Temple U., 1967; MA in Sociology, Northeastern U., Boston, 1969, PhD in Sociology, 1976. Sr. lectr. Northeastern U., 1969-82; prof. sociology Framingham (Mass.) State Coll., 1969—; assoc. in edn. Harvard U. Grad. Sch. of Edn., Cambridge, Mass., 1980-82. Vis. prof. sociology Tufts U., Medford, Mass., 1993, Montclair State U., Upper Montclair, N.J. Producer/host: (nat. pub. radio show) Cover to Cover, WGBH-FM/WICN-FM, Boston, 1992—; author: (books) Race and Ethnic Relations, 1978, Introduction to Sociology, 1st-8th edit., 1983-, Debating Points: Race and Ethnic Relations, 1999, Debating Points: Crime and Corrections, 2001, Debating Points: Marriage and Family Issues, 2001. Office: Framingham State Coll State St Framingham MA 01701 E-mail: htischl@frc.mass.edu.

TISDALE, JAMES EDWARD, pharmacy educator, pharmacotherapy researcher; b. Winnipeg, Man., Can., Apr. 23, 1960; arrived in US, 1986; s. Charles Edward Murray and Helen Joan (Millar) T. BSc in Pharmacy, U. Man., 1983; PharmD, SUNY, Buffalo, 1988. Bd. cert. pharmacotherapy specialist. Pharmacist Health Scis. Ctr., Winnipeg, 1984-86; fellow cardiovascular therapeutics Hartford (Conn.) Hosp., 1988-90; clin. asst. prof. U. Conn., Storrs, 1988-90; adj. clin. instr. Mass. Coll. Pharmacy and Allied Health Scis., Springfield, 1988-90; asst. prof. Coll. Pharmacy and Health Scis. Wayne State U., Detroit, 1990-96, assoc. prof. Coll. Pharmacy and Health Scis., 1996—2002; coord. edn. and tng. dept. pharmacy Henry Ford Hosp., Detroit, 1990—2002; assoc. prof. Sch. Pharmacy and Pharm. Sci., Purdue U., Indpls., 2002—. Contbr. articles to profl. jours., chpts. to books. Mem.: Am. Soc. Health-Sys. Pharmacists, Am. Pharm. Assn., Am. Soc. Clin. Pharmacology and Therapeutics, Am. Heart Assn. Mich. (chmn. profl. edn. com. 1993—95, mem. clin. cardiology coun. 1994—), Am. Coll. Clin. Pharmacy (chmn. publs. com. 1993—94, chmn. rsch. affairs com. 1995—97, chmn. ann. meeting program com. 1997—99, chmn. constn. and bylaws com. 1999—2000, bd. regents 2001—). Achievements include research in antiarrhythmic drug pharmacokinetics and pharmacotherapy, drug therapy of atrial fibrillation and cardiac arrhythmias induced by drugs. Office: Purdue Univ Dept of Pharmacy Practice Sch Pharm W7555 Myers Bldg WHS 1001 W 10th St Indianapolis IN 46202 E-mail: jtisdale@iupui.edu.

TISHNER, KERI LYNN, visual art education consultant; b. Santa Ana, Calif., June 1, 1964; d. Albert John, Jr. and Barbara Ann (Milner) Geverink; m. David Jackson Tishner, Apr. 27, 1985. BA in Art with distinction, Calif. State U., Long Beach, 1988, tchg. credentials, 1991; postgrad., Calif. State U., San Bernardino, 1994—99. State D coaching license Calif. Youth Soccer Assn. Art tchr. Apple Valley (Calif.) H.S., 1991—99, Granite Hills H.S., Apple Valley, 1999—2002, dept. chair visual and performing arts, 1999—2002; visual art edn. cons. DrawPaintCreate.com, 2002—. Mentor tchr., 1998—2000. Presenter in field of art. Participant Calif. Arts Project, San Bernardino, 1995. Mem. NEA, Nat. Art Edn. Assn., Calif. Tchrs. Assn., Calif. Art Edn. Assn., Los Angeles County Mus. Art, Norton Simon Mus. Art, Apple Valley Unified Tchrs. Assn. Avocations: inline skating, ski boarding, art, computers, skiing. E-mail: keri@drawpaintcreate.com.

TISSUE, MIKE, medical educator, respiratory therapist; b. Garfield, Wash., Aug. 24, 1941; s. Altha Lester and Fern Adeline (Willard) T.; m. Marjorie Lena Atkinson, Feb. 24, 1961 (div. June 1991); children: Sue Tipton, Pam Kromholtz, Paul, Donna; m. Mary Emma Napier, Aug. 24, 1998. AAS (4 degrees) with honors, Spokane (Wash.) C.C., 1985; BS in Respiratory Therapy cum laude, Loma Linda (Calif.) U., 1987; MS in Respiratory Care, Ga. State U., 1999. Registered cardiovasc. invasive specialist, cardiac sonographer Nat. Soc. Cardiopulmonary Technol./Cardiovasc. Credentialing Internat.; registered respiratory therapist, pulmonary function technologist, neonatal pediat. specialist NBRC; registered respiratory care practitioner, Ga.; diplomate sr. disability analyst Am. Bd. Disability Analysts. Respiratory intern, Level III NICU Therapist Loma Linda (Calif.) U. Med. Ctr., 1985-87; educator, therapist Riyadh (Saudi Arabia) Armed Forces Hosp., 1987-91; dept. head respiratory care Security Forces Hosp., Riyadh, 1991-93; asst. prof., dir. clin. edn. respiratory therapy program Morehead (Ky.) State U., 1993-94; program dir. assoc. degree respiratory therapy Chattahoochee Tech. Coll., Marietta, Ga., 1994—98; clin. instr. Ga. State U., Atlanta, 1999-2001; dir. respiratory therapy program Nat. Inst. Tech., Atlanta, 2001—. Pres., founder Riyadh Cardiorespiratory Soc., 1988-93; rschr. Loma Linda U., 1987, Riyadh Armed Forces Hosp., 1988; instr. and affiliate faculty ACLS Wash. State Heart Assn., 1983-85, Calif. Heart Assn., 1985-87, Saudi Heart Assn., 1985-87, Ky. Heart Assn., 1993-94, Ga. affiliate, 1994—; instr. and affiliate faculty pediatric advanced life support Saudi Heart Assn., 1987-93; instr. and affiliate faculty basic life support/CPR Wash. State, 1974-85, Calif., 1985-87, Saudi Heart Assn., 1987-93, Ky. Heart Assn., 1993-94, Ga. affiliate, 1994—; cons. ARC, Tacoma, Wash., 1984, instr. advanced 1st aid, standard 1st aid, CPR, 1975—, Inland Empire Chpt., Spokane, Wash., 1975-94, San Bernardino/Redlands Svc. Ctr., Loma Linda, 1985-87, Am. Cmty. Svcs. U.S. Embassy, Riyadh, 1991-93, U.S. Mil. Operation Desert Storm, Riyadh, 1991-93, Ga. affiliate Cobb County chpt., Marietta, 1994—; instr. Freedom From Smoking Clinic Program Am. Lung Assn., Calif., 1985-87, Saudi Arabia, 1987-93, Smyrna, Ga., 1994-96; mem. Instl. Effectiveness Com., Campus Computer Com. Chattahoochee Tech. Coll., 1994-98. Contbr. articles to profl. jours. Bd. dirs. Am. Heart Assn., Spokane, 1976-83, chair fin. com., 1981-83; chair spkrs. bur. ARC, Inland Empire Chpt., Spokane, 1982-85, chair pub. rels., 1983-85; mem. Calif. affiliate San Bernardino Chpt., Loma Linda, 1985-87, Ga. affiliate Cobb County Chpt., Marietta, 1994—; chair programming and spkrs. bur. Am. Lung Assn., Smyrna, Ga., 1994-98, chmn. bd. dirs., 1995-96; sec. Cobb County Cmty. Coun., Marietta, 1995-96, spkr., 1995, v.p., 1996, pres. 1997; vol. Ga. Internat. Cultural Exch., 1995; registry exam. sr. proctor Cardiovascular Credentialing Internat./Nat. Bd. Cardiovascular Technologists, Riyadh, 1987-90; commr. Boy Scouts Am., Spokane, 1973-82, wood badge, 1977, commrs. key, 1977, scouters key, 1979. Named Citizen of Day KGA Radio, Spokane, 1983. Mem. AAUP (legislature com. Atlanta 1995-96), Am. Assn. Respiratory Care (therapist driven protocol rev. com. 1994, ad hoc com. on patient-driven-protocol rev. com. 1996, ad hoc com. for sects. rev. 1995-96, job analysis, neonatal pedit. specialist 2002), Applied Measurement Profls., Alliance of Cardiovas. Profls., Ga. Soc. Respiratory Care (chmn. cardiopulmonary com. 1994-95, edn. com., smoking and health com.), Phi Delta Kappa (Alpha Nu chpt. Morehead, Ky. 1993-94, Kennesaw Mountain chpt. Atlanta 1994—, pub. rels. Com. 1995-96). Roman Catholic. Avocations: photography, travel. Home: 1881 Arnold Dr SW Austell GA 30106-2907 Office: Nat Inst Tech Respiratory Therapy Program 1706 Northeast Pkwy Atlanta GA 30329 E-mail: miketissue@juno.com.

TITE, JOHN GREGORY, secondary school educator; b. Southbridge, Mass., Sept. 20, 1941; s. Gregory Louca and Androniq (Zhidro) T. BS, U. Mass., 1963; MEd, Worcester (Mass.) State Coll., 1966; MS, Clarkson Coll. Tech., 1971. Instr. math. Grafton (Mass.) Pub. Schs., 1963-67, math. dept. chairperson, calculus instr., 1967—. Adj. prof. calculus Anna Maria Coll., Paxton, Mass., 1986-88; in-svc. instr. metrics for h.s. and elem. tchrs., 1974-76; spkr. in field. Grantee NSF, 1965, 67, 75, Computer Assisted Math Project grant U. Mass., 1985-86. Mem. Assn. of Tchrs. of Math. in Mass. (pres., exhibits chmn. 1970), Nat. Coun. Suprs. of Math., Nat. Coun. of Tchrs. of Math. (chmn. films and filmstrips com. 1973, chmn. sales of materials 1976), Neighborhood Assn. of Math. Dept. Heads (bd. dirs. 1976-79). Avocations: reading, traveling, walking. Home: 12 Arrowhead Ave Auburn MA 01501-2302 Office: Grafton Pub Schs 24 Providence Rd Grafton MA 01519-1178

TITSWORTH, TOBIE RICHARD, III, academic administrator; b. Henryetta, Okla., May 13, 1945; s. Tobie Richard II and Thelma Edith (Stephens) T.; m. Laura Jeanne Barnes, Dec. 24, 1966; children: Scottie Richard, Stephanie Ann Titsworth Alves. BS, Okla. State U., 1967, MS, 1973, EdD, 1976. Cert. tchr., supt., Okla. Vocat. agriculture instr. Miami (Okla.) Pub. Schs., 1971-74; grad. rsch. asst. Okla. State U., Stillwater, 1974-75; asst. prof. Tex. A&M U., College Station, 1975-79; v.p. continuing and tech. edn. Rogers State Coll., Claremore, Okla., 1979-90, v.p. for academics, 1990-92; advisor USAFR, Wright-Patterson AFB, Ohio, 1992-95; sr. systems engr. Electronic Data Systems Corp., 1995; v.p. for acad. affairs Okla. State U., Okmulgee, 1995-98; asst. supt. bus. and industry svcs. Northeast Tech. Ctrs., Pryor, Okla., 1998-2000, dept. supt., 2000—. Adj. faculty Wright State U., Dayton, Ohio, 1993-95; mem. adv. com. Sinclair C.C., Dayton, 1992-95; vis. lectr., cons. Air Force Inst. Tech., Wright-Patterson AFB, 1993-95. Contbr. chpt. to book and articles to profl. jours. Chair, vice chair Clarmore Park Bd. Commrs., 1988-90; vice chair, bd. dirs. Claremore Area United Way, 1989-91; bd. dirs., divsn. v.p. Claremont Area C. of C.; bd. dirs. Pryor Area C. of C., v.p., 1998—; leadership Pryor grad., 1999; leadership Vo-Tech III, 2000; deacon, tchr. Adult Bible Study, Faith Bapt. Ch. With USAF, 1968-71, ret., col. USAFR, 1998—. Named to Hall of Fame Muskogee Svc. League, 1991. Mem. ASCD, Okla. Assn. Cmty. and Jr. Colls. (pres. 1987-88), Okla. Tech. Soc. (pres. 1986-87, pres. instrnl. adminstrn. 1986-87), Am. Tech. Edn. Assn., Okla. Vocational Assn., Assn. Career and Tech. Edn. Baptist. Avocations: woodworking, collecting, reading, walking, racquetball. Office: Northeast Tech Ctr PO Box 487 Pryor OK 74362 E-mail: titsworth@netechcenters.com.

TITUS, ROBERT C. geologist, educator; b. Paterson, N.J., Aug. 9, 1946; s. John Lorimer and Hattie Mae (Seiwell) T. BS, Rutgers U., 1968; AM, Boston U., 1971, PhD, 1974. Asst. prof. Windham Coll., Putney, Vt., 1973-74; from asst. prof. to prof. and chmn. dept. geology Hartwick Coll., Oneonta, N.Y., 1974—. Author: The Catskills: A Geological Guide, 1993, 2d edit., 1998, The Catskills in the Ice Age, 1996, 2d edit., 2003; contbr. numerous articles to profl. jours. and popular mags.; columnist Kaatskill Life Mag., 1991—, Woodstock Times, 1996-2001, Greenville Press, 1999—, Columbia County Ind., 2002—. Recipient Sears-Roebuck award, 1990. Mem. Geol. Soc. Am., Paleontological Soc. (N.E. sect. pres. 1993), Sigma Xi. Avocation: hiking.

TOALE, THOMAS EDWARD, school system administrator, priest; b. Independence, Iowa, Aug. 30, 1953; s. Francis Mark and Clara R. (DePaepe) T. BS in Biology, Loras Coll., 1975, MA in Ednl. Adminstrn., 1986; MA in Theology, St. Paul Sem., 1980; PhD in Ednl. Adminstrn., U. Iowa, 1988. Ordained priest Roman Cath. Ch., 1981; cert. tchr., prin., supt., Iowa. Tchr. St. Joseph Key West, Dubuque, Iowa, 1975-77, Marquette High Sch., Bellevue, Iowa, 1981-84, prin., 1984-86; assoc. supt. Archdiocese of Dubuque, 1986-87, supt. schs., 1987—. Assoc. pastor St. Joseph Ch., Bellevue, 1981-84; pastor Sts. Peter and Paul Ch., Springbrook, Iowa, 1984-86, St. Peter, Temple Hill, Cascade, Iowa, 1986—. Mem. Nat. Cath. Edn. Assn. (pres., chief adminstrn. Cath. edn.). Office: Archdiocese of Dubuque 1229 Mount Loretta Ave Dubuque IA 52003-7826

TOBBEN, LARRY JOHN, elementary education educator; b. Washington, Oct. 14, 1948; s. James Virgil and Dorothy Ann (Peters) T. BEd, N.E. Mo. State U., 1972; MEd, Nat. Louis U., 1974. Cert. elem. tchr., Mo. Tchr. Immaculate Conception Sch., Union, Mo., 1972-74; tchr. elem. art Washington (Mo.) Pub. Schs., 1974—, chairperson coms., 1986—. Mem. NEA, Nat. Art Edn. Assn., Mid-Mo. Fine Arts Soc., Washington Community Tchrs. Assn. (pres. 1990-91, 92-93), St. Louis Region Art Tchrs. Assn., Friends of St. Louis Art Mus., KC, Elks, St. Gertrude Men's Soc. (pres. 1974-75). Democrat. Roman Catholic. Avocations: reading, water sports, interior design, fine arts, high school sports. Home: 1800 Pottery Rd Washington MO 63090-4192

TOBIA, SUSAN J. reading educator; b. Providence, Nov. 21, 1946; d. Salvino Paul and Gertrude C. (LaRochelle) T. BA, Newton Coll. Sacred Heart, Mass., 1968; MEd, Temple U., 1970, PhD, 1988. Cert. in spl. edn., Pa. Tchr. educable retarded Phila. Pub. Schs., 1968-71; learning disabilities tchr. Nat. Regional Resource Ctr., King of Prussia, Pa., 1971-73, DeKalb County Schs., Decatur, Ga., 1973-74, Clarke County Schs., Athens, Ga., 1974-75, Mayfield City Schs., Cleve., 1975-77; reading instr. Temple U., Phila., 1977-80; reading specialist coord., program dir. Met. Collegiate Ctr., Phila., 1980-84; prof. reading/study skills C.C. Phila., 1984-93, coord. collaborative learning cmty., 1993-2000, dir. welfare to work through higher edn. program, 2000—02, acting asst. dean ednl. support svcs., 2002, acting dir. N.E. Regional Ctr., 2003—. Curriculum design cons. Phila. Electric Co., 1985-87, Fellowship Commn., Phila., 1990, 92, 94; instr. Beaver Coll., Glenside, Pa., 1988; curriculum cons. Concerned Black Men, Phila., 1991-92. Author: (curriculum) Private Industry Council Transition Program, 1992; contbr. chpt. to book. Exec. officer Citizens Com. on Pub. Edn. in Phila., 1985-94; exec. team City Coun. Campaign, Phila., 1990-91, mem. team, 1994; co-chair student readiness work team Phila. Edn. Summit, 1997-98; mem. Mayor's Commn. on Literacy, 2002—; bd. dirs. Cmty. Women's Edn. Project, 2003—; mem. Edn. First Compact, 2003—. Recipient Outstanding Contbn. to Spl. Programs and Support Svcs. award C.C. Phila., 1987, Excellence in Tchg. award C.C. Phila., 1996. Mem. Internat. Reading Assn., Delaware Valley Reading Assn., Nat. Assn. for Devel. Educators, Pa. Assn. for Devel. Educators. Avocations: tennis, skating, reading, movies, photography. Office: CC of Phila 1700 Spring Garden St Philadelphia PA 19130-3936 E-mail: stobia@ccp.cc.pa.us.

TOBIAS, JUDY, university development executive; b. Pitts. d. Saul Albert Landau and Bess (Previn) Kurzman; m. Seth Tobias (dec. May 1983); children: Stephen Frederic, Andrew Previn; m. Lewis F. Davis, 1990. Student, Silvermine Artists Guild, 1951-55; BA (hon.) (hon.), New Coll. of Calif., 1989. Art cons. Westchester Mental Health Asn., White Plains, N.Y., 1968-69; cons. sch. social work NYU, 1973-74, devel. exec., 1976—. Conf. coord. Today's Family: Implications for the Future, N.Y.C., 1974-75; cons. Playschools, Inc., N.Y.C., 1975; majority counsel mem. Emily's List, 1991—. Mem. Gov.'s Commn. on Continuing Edn., Albany, N.Y., 1968-70, Nat. Coun. on Children and Youth, Washington, 1974-75, Manhattan Inter-Hosp. Group on Child Abuse, 1975-76; chmn. N.Y. met. com. for UNICEF, 1976-77; mem. exec. com. Town Hall Found., N.Y.C., 1979—, vice chmn., 1986-90; founder, bd. dirs. N.Y. chpt. WAIF, Inc., 1961-99, nat. pres., 1978-82, nat. bd. dirs., 1978—; pres. emeritus, 1993-99; bd. dirs. Citizen's Com. for Children, City of N.Y., 1975—, v.p., 1983-90, 97-99; bd. dirs. Am. br. Internat. Social Svc., 1965-80; bd. dirs. Andrew Glover Youth Program, 1986-89, mem. adv. coun., 1989—; bd. dirs. Goddard Riverside Cmty. Ctr., 1985—, Dance Mag. Found., 1986-92, St. John's Place Family Ctr., 1987-93, Capitol Hall Preservation Corp., 1989-93, chmn. bd. Inst. for Cultural Diversity, steering com., The Leadership Connection, 1992—. Recipient Nat. Humanitarian award, WAIF, 1990, Millennium Honoree award, NYU Sch. Social Work, 2000. Mem. Child Study Assn. Am. (bd. dirs. 1963-71, pres. 1969-71, bd. dirs. Wel-Met Inc. 1972-85), Brookings Instn. (coun. mem. 1998—), Emily's List (majority coun. 1990—). E-mail: ajtdavis@aol.com.

TOBIAS, RICHARD CHARLES, retired secondary educator, consultant; b. Chgo., Sept. 12, 1937; s. Joseph and Genevieve (Stwora) T.; m. Marian Jeanette Johnson, June 4, 1966; children: Timothy Richard, Denise Marie BS in Edn., U. Wis., River Falls, 1959, MS in Edn., 1968; DArts, U. No. Colo., 1976. Cert. tchr., Minn., Wis. Tchr. sci. Webster (Wis.) Sr. H.S., 1962-66, Burnsville (Minn.) Sr. H.S., 1966-97, chmn. dept., 1985—88; ret., 1997. Cons. product devel. 3M, St. Paul, 1980-84, mem. steering com. North Ctrl. Assn. Cmty. Schs., 1974-78, chmn., 1981-84. Contbr. articles to profl. jours. Active Indianhead coun. Boy Scouts Am., 1980-87. With U.S. Army, 1960-62. Recipient tchr. intern program award St. Paul C. of C., 1991. Mem. NEA (life), Am. Soc. Parasitologists, Assn. Biology Tchrs., Minn. Sci. Tchrs. Assn., Minn. Acad. Sci., Minn. Edn. Assn., Sigma Xi. Democrat. Roman Catholic. Home: 4337 Onyx Dr Saint Paul MN 55122-2019

TOBIAS, SHEILA, writer, educator; b. N.Y., Apr. 26, 1935; d. Paul Jay and Rose (Steinberger) Tobias; m. Carlos Stern, Oct. 11, 1970 (div. 1982); m. Carl T. Tomizuka, Dec. 16, 1987. BA, Harvard Radcliffe U., 1957; MA, Columbia U., 1961, MPhil, 1974; PhD (hon.), Drury Coll., 1994, Wheelock Coll., 1995; PhD (hon.), SUNY, Potsdam, 1996, Mich. State U., 2000, Worcester Polytech, 2002. Journalist, W. Germany, U.S. and Fed. Republic Germany, 1957-65; lect. in history C.C.N.Y., N.Y.C., 1965-67; univ. adminstr. Cornell U., Wesleyan U., 1967-78; lect. in women's studies U. Calif., San Diego, 1985-92; lect. in war, peace studies U. So. Calif., 1985-88. Cons. sci. and bus. U. Amsterdam, Leiden, Netherlands, 1995—98; pres. Outreach Coord. Sci. Master's Initiative, 1997—; vis. prof. U. Amsterdam, U. Leiden, 1994—97. Author: Overcoming Math Anxiety, 1978, rev. edit., 1994, Succeed with Math, 1987, Revitalizing Undergraduate Science: Why Some Things Work and Most Don't, 1992, Science as a Career: Perceptions and Realities, 1995; co-author: The People's Guide to National Defense, 1982, Women, Militarism and War, 1987, They're Not Dumb, They're Different, 1990, (with Carl T. Tomizuka) Breaking the Science Barrier, 1992, Rethinking Science as a Career, 1995, (with Jacqueline Raphael) The Hidden Curriculum, 1997, Faces of Feminism, 1997. Fellow AAAS; mem. Am. Assn. Higher Edn. (bd. dirs. 1993-97), Coll. Sci. Tchrs. Assn., Nat. Women's Studies Assn., Phi Beta Kappa. Avocations: outdoor hiking, skiing. E-mail: Sheila@SheilaTobias.com.

TOBIAS, TOM, JR., retired elementary school educator; b. July 22, 1932; s. Thomas N. Sr. and Mary A. (Hanton) T.; m. Kathleen A. Black, May 28, 1964; 1 child, Amy. BA, Ea. Mich. U., 1965, MA, 1966; postgrad., Mich. State U., U. Nev. Cert. elem./secondary tchr., Mich. Tchr. Ypsilanti (Mich.) Pub. Schs., 1965—. Vis. lectr. Ea. Mich. U., Ypsilanti, 1980-90; former mem. edit. bd. Scholastic Pub. Co., N.Y.C. Cartoonist, Mich. Reading Jours.; author teaching materials. Vice pres. Ypsilanti Hist. Soc.; bd. dirs. Ypsilanti Heritage Found. With USAF, 1951-55. Recipient Outstanding Alumnus award Ea. Mich. U., 1985. Mem. Ypsilanti Edn. Assn. (past pres.).

TOBIASSEN, BARBARA SUE, systems analyst consultant, educator, Peace Corps volunteer; b. Bklyn., Feb. 22, 1950; d. Vincent and Esther Alice (Hansen) M. BA in Math Edn., Rider Coll., 1972; postgrad., Montclair State U., 1973. Cert. secondary tchr., N.J. Math tchr. Westwood (N.J.) H.S., 1973-80; programmer Prudential Ins. Co., Roseland, N.J., 1980-81; programmer, analyst Grand Union, Paramus, N.J., 1981-82; cons. Five Techs., Montvale, N.J., 1987-90; project mgr. Info. Sci., Inc., Montvale, 1982-84, cons., project mgr., 1987-90; pres. B. Maxwell Assoc., Inc., Westwood, N.J., 1990—; vol. Peace Corps; mem. Peace Corps., 2001—02; tchr. St. Paul's Luth., Accra, Ghana, 2002—. Guest spkr. Info. Sci., Best of Am., Computer Assocs. B.A.C.; educator, Ghana W. Africa, 2002-. Contbr. articles to profl. jours. Vol. Peace Corps, 2001—02. Mem.: APA (v.p. N.J. chpt. 1996), NAFE, Am. Payroll Assn., N.J. Info., Westwood Heritage Soc. Republican. Lutheran. Avocations: travel, reading, gardening, hiking. E-mail: btobiassen2003@yahoo.com.

TOBIN, AILEEN WEBB, educational administrator; b. Milford, Del., July 9, 1949; d. Wilson Webster Webb and Dorothy Marie (Benson) Rust; m. Thomas Joseph Tobin, Jr., July 31, 1971. BA cum laude, U. Del., 1971, MEd, 1975, PhD, 1981. Cert. tchr. secondary edn., cert. reading specialist, cert. reading cons., Del. Dir. Del. Tutoring Ctr., Wilmington, 1971-74; grad. teaching asst. U. Del., Newark, 1974-81, instr. Coll. Edn., 1978-82; ednl. specialist U.S. Army Ordnance Ctr. & Sch., Aberdeen Proving Ground, Md., 1982-85, chief internal eval. br., 1985-88, chief evaluation divsn., 1988, chief standardization and analysis div., 1988-90, dir. quality assurance, 1990-94, dir. tactical support equipment dept., 1994-98, dir. command planning office, 1998—. Cons. Dorchester County Sch. Dist., Dorchester County, Md., 1977-80; rsch. assoc., Ctr. for Ednl. Leadership, Newark, 1981-82; staff assoc., Rsch. for Better Schs., Inc., Phila., 1981-84. Author: (book chpt.) Approaches Informal Eval. of Reading, 1982, Dialogues in Literary Research, 1988, Cognitive & Social Perspectives for Literary Research & Instruction, 1989; contbr. articles to profl. jours. Recipient Silver award Fed. Exec. Bd., 1992, Comdr.'s award for Civil Svc. Dept. Army, 1994, 96, Order of Samuel Sharpe award Ordnance Corps Assn., 1994, Superior Civil Svc. award Dept. Army, 1995, 98. Mem. Internat. Reading Assn., Nat. Reading Conf., Am. Ednl. Rsch. Assn., Am. Evaluation Assn., Ordnance Corps Assn., Kappa Delta Pi. Methodist. Avocations: travel, reading, tennis, sailing. Home: 4839 Plum Run Ct Wilmington DE 19808-1715 Office: US Army Ordnance Ctr & Sch ATSL CP Aberdeen Proving Ground MD 21005

TOBIN, DANIEL EUGENE, poet, English language educator; b. Bklyn., Jan. 13, 1958; s. Gerard Daniel Tobin and Helen Teresa Ruane; m. Christine Casson. BA summa cum laude, Iona Coll., 1980; MTS, Harvard U., 1983; PhD, U. Va., 1991; MFA (hon.), Warren Wilson Coll., 1990. Assoc. prof. and chair of dept. Emerson Coll., Boston, 1991—. Presenter, reader in field. Author: (poetry book) Where the World Is Made, 1999 (Bakeless prize in poetry), (critical book) Passage to the Center: Imagination and The Sacrea in the Poetry of Seamus Heaney; contbr. poetry to anthologies, also essays and revs. Recipient Discovery/The Nation award Unterberg Poetry Ctr., 1995, Internat. Merit award The Atlanta Rev., 1996, Greensboro Rev. prize in poetry, Donn Godwin Poetry award, 2000, Yankee Mag. Poetry award, 2001, Robert Penn Warren award Winner, 2002; grantee Harvard U., 1981-83, faculty devel. grantee Carthage Coll., 1992-97; Dupont fellow U. Va., 1985-86, Marchant fellow U. Va., 1986-87, Commonwealth fellow U. Va., 1987-88, Rotary Internat. fellow Univ. Coll. Dublin, Ireland, 1988-89, dissertation fellow U. Va., 1989-90, creative writing fellow Nat. Endowment for Arts, 1996, Ali Dor-Ner fellow in poetry Friends of Writers, 1997, Vt. Studio Ctr. fellow in poetry, 1998, fellow Irish Am. Cultural Inst., 1999, Robert Frost fellow Breadloaf Writers Conf.; Breadloaf scholar Breadloaf Writers Conf., 1995, 99. Mem. MLA, Acad. Am. Poets, Am. Acad. Religion, Associated Writing Programs. Office: Emerson Coll 120 Boylston St Boston MA 02124-1929

TOBIN, ILONA LINES, psychologist, marriage and family counselor, educator, media consultant; b. Trenton, Mich., Apr. 15, 1943; d. Frank John and Marjorie Cathalean (Lines) Kotyuk; m. Roger Lee Tobin, Aug. 20, 1966. BA, Ea. Mich. U., 1965, MA, 1968, Mich. State U., 1975; EdD, Wayne State U., 1978. Diplomate Am. Bd. Sexology, lic. marriage & family therapist, cert. sex educator & counselor, sex therapist, lic. psychologist. Tchr., counselor Willow Run Pub. Schs., Ypsilanti, Mich., 1966-72; prof. Macomb County C.C., Mt. Clemens, Mich., 1974-79; psychotherapist Identity Ctr., Inc., Mt. Clemens, 1974-79; dir. treatment Alternative Lifestyles, Inc., Orchard Lake, Mich., 1979-80; psychologist Profl. Psychotherapy and Counseling Ctr., Farmington Hills, Mich., 1980-83; pvt. practice clin. psychology Birmingham, Mich., 1983—. Lectr. Wayne State U., Detroit, 1977—88; tchr. med. edn. St. Jospeh's Hosp., Pontiac, Mich., 1993—98; recruitment dir. Upward Bound Ea. Mich. U., Ypsilanti, Mich., 1969—72. Creator Doc's Dolls. Co-chmn. Birmingham Families in Action, 1982—83; mem. exec. bd., v.p. pres. Birmingham Cmty. Women's Ctr., 1984—85, also bd. dirs.; mem. adv. bd. Woodside Med. Ctr. for Chemically Dependent Women, 1984—86; mem. Rep. Presdl. Round Table, 2001; bd. dirs. HAVEN-Oakland County's Phys. and Sexual Abuse Ctr. and Oakland Area Counselors Assn., 1984—85. NIMH fellow, 1976-78; Wayne State U. scholar, 1976-78. Mem. ASCD, APA, Mich. Psychol. Assn. (mass media cons. 1983—, mem. crisis intervention network, legis. com. 1992-94), Am. Assn. Sex Educators, Counselors and Therapists, Pi Lambda Theta, Phi Delta Kappa. Jewish.

TOBON, HECTOR, gynecologic pathologist, educator; b. Aranzazu, Colombia, Sept. 20, 1934; came to U.S., 1962; MD, Univ. de Caldas, S.Am. Diplomate Am. Bd. Pathology. Intern Hosp. San Juan de Dios Armenia; resident Inst. Nat. Cancer, Hosp. San Juan de Dios Bogota; resident in pathology Meml. Hosp., Danville, Va., 1962-65, Presbyn. U. Hosp./U. Pitts. Med. Ctr., 1965-66; assoc. prof. pathology U. Pitts., 1967—2000, prof. emeritus, Sch. Medicine, 2000—. Assoc. chief pathology Magee Womens Hosp., Pitts., 1986-99 Office: Magee Womens Hosp 300 Halket St Ofc 4420 Pittsburgh PA 15213-3180

TOBUREN, LARRY HOWARD, physicist, educator; b. Clay Center, Kans., July 9, 1940; s. Howard H. and Beulah (Boyd) T.; m. Lana L. Henry, June 16, 1962; children: Debra L., Tina L. BA, Emporia State U., 1962; PhD, Vanderbilt U., 1968. Research scientist Battelle Northwest Lab., Richland, Wash., 1967-80, staff scientist, mgr. radiation physics and chemistry sect., 1980-93; sr. program officer NRC/NAS, Washington, 1993-95; prof. physics East Carolina U., Greenville, NC, 1995—, dir. Accelerator Lab., 1995—2002, dir. grad. studies in physics, 2000—. Affiliate asst. prof. radiological physics U. Wash., 1982-91, affiliate assoc. prof. environ. health, 1991-94; adj. lectr. environ. scis. Wash. State U., 1991-94. Contbr. articles to profl. jours. Fellow Am. Phys. Soc.; mem. AAAS, Radiation Research Soc., Internat. Radiation Physics Soc., Health Physics Soc. Office: East Carolina Univ Dept of Physics Greenville NC 27858-4353 Home: 1405 Warwick Cir Winterville NC 28590-9227

TODD, JOAN ABERNATHY, secondary school educator; b. Roanoke Rapids, N.C., June 14, 1947; d. Benjamin Cornelius and Mildred Lee (Davis) Abernathy; m. Douglas Felton Todd, Dec. 16, 1973 (dec. Aug. 1988); 1 child, Jason Douglas. BS, East Carolina U., Greenville, N.C., 1969. Cert. tchr., N.C. Tchr. Youngsville H.S., NC, 1969, Greensville County, Emporia, Va., 1969—72, Northwest H.S., Littleton, NC, 1972—82; tchr. home econs. Eastman Middle Sch., Enfield, NC, 1982—96, Northwest H.S., Littleton, 1996—2001; ret., 2001. Instr. N.C. League of Middle Schs., Charlotte, 1990, Halifax C.C., Weldon, N.C., 1990-91; mentor tchr. Eastman Middle Sch., 1987-96; condr. workshops. Pres., treas. Sunshine Ext. Club, Roanoke Rapids, 1988-90, sec., 1995—; pres. Parents Without Ptnrs., Roanoke Rapids, 1992, Heritage Crafters, Halifax, 1992-96; vol. N.C. Coop. Ext. Mem. NEA (bldg. rep. 1980-94), N.C. Edn. Assn. (dist. 12 sec. 1995-96, Halifax County Edn. Assn. (sec. 1990-93, pres. 1994-95, 96-97), N.C. Home Econs. Assn. (pres. 1999-2000), Delta Kappa Gamma (2d v.p. 1995-96, 1st v.p. 1996, pres. 1996—). Avocations: reading, needlework, sewing, crafts.

TODD, SHIRLEY ANN, school system administrator; b. May 23, 1935; d. William Leonard and Margaret Judy (Simmons) Brown; m. Thomas Byron Todd, July 7, 1962 (dec. July 1977). BS in Edn., Madison Coll., 1956; MEd, U. Va., 1971. Cert. tchr. Va. Elem. tchr. Fairfax County Sch. Bd., Fairfax, Va., 1966—71; guidance counselor James F. Cooper Mid. Sch., McLean, Va., 1971—88, dir. guidance, 1988—96; chmn. mktg. Lake Anne Joint Venture, Falls Church, Va., 1979—81, mng. ptnr., 1980—82. Editor (newsletter): Vintage Ladies No. Va., 2002—03. Newsletter editdor Vintage Ladies of No. Va., 2002—03; del. Fairfax County Rep. Conv., 1985. Fellow: Fairfax Edn. Assn. (bd. dirs. 1968—70, profl. rights and responsibilities commn. 1970—72); mem.: ASCD, NEA, Va. Sch. Counselors Assn., Va. Counselors Assn., Va. Counselors Assn. (exec. com. 1987), No. Va. Counselors Assn. (exec. bd. 1982—83, hospitality and social chmn.), Va. Edn. Assn. (state com. on local assns. and urban affairs 1969—70), Vintage Ladies of No. Va. (newsletter editor 2002—03), Women's Golf Assn. (pres. 1997—98, 2002—), Welcome Club of No. Va. (pres. 2003—04), Chantilly Nat. Golf and Country Club (v.p. social 1981—82). Baptist. Avocations: golf, tennis. Home: 6543 Bay Tree Ct Falls Church VA 22041-1001

TODD, WILLIAM ERIC, secondary school educator; b. L.A., Apr. 5, 1941; s. William Hugh and Eleanor F. T.; children: Erica, David. BS, Calif. Polytech. State U., 1969, MA, 1973. Automotive technician pvt. practice, Bakersfield, Calif., 1969—; tchr. Kern H.S., Bakersfield, 1969—2003; automotive, sci. cons., 2003—. Advisor Auto Club, Bakersfield, 1971-93; chmn. Auto Tech Adv. Com., Bakersfield, 1984—. Scout master Boy Scouts Am., Bakersfield, 1978-80. With U.S. Army, 1960-63. Named Master Auto Technician Nat. Inst. for Auto Svc. Excellence, 1985, 89, 94. Mem. NEA, Nat. Sci. Tchr. Assn., Calif. Auto Tchrs., Calif. Tchrs. Assn., Calif. Sci. Tchr. Assn.

TOEWS, CHARLOTTE LOUISE, secondary school educator; b. Enid, Okla., Jan. 19, 1953; d. Burle and Dona (La Porte) Milbers; m. Jason Toews, July 28, 1973; children: Justin, Ginger. BS in Edn., Okla. State U., 1975; MEd, Phillips U., 1985; postgrad., Okla. State U., 1991. Acctg. clk. Farmers Grain Co., Ames, Okla., 1976-77, Johnston Grain Co., Enid, 1977-78; head bookkeeper Meth. Golden Age Home, Enid, 1981—; tchr. bus. Chisholm High Sch., Enid, Okla., 1981—. Mem. NEA, Nat. Bus. Edn. Assn., Okla. Bus. Edn. Assn., Okla. Edn. Assn., Chisholm Edn. Assn. (treas., v.p., mem. negotiations com., parliamentarian, pres.). Home: 3614 Willow Ln Enid OK 73703

TOFLE, RUTH BRENT, design educator, researcher, educator; b. Washington, Mo., Sept. 11, 1951; d. Clarence Frank and Dorothy May (Horstick) Stumpe; m. Edward Everett Brent, May 14, 1972 (div. Mar. 1999); 2 children; m. Marvin Tofle, Nov. 17, 2001. BS cum laude, U. Mo., 1972; MA, U. Minn., 1974, PhD, 1978. Cert. of qualification Nat. Coun. Interior Design Qualification; registered comml. interior designer, Mo., 2000. Postdoctoral fellow in socio-clin. geriatrics NIMH, 1978-79; asst. prof. U. Mo., Columbia, 1981-86, assoc. prof. design, 1986-92, prof., 1992—, acting dept. chair, 1984-85, chair environ. design dept., 1985—. Project dir. Adminstrn. on Aging Grant, 1979-81; v.p. Idea Works, Inc., Columbia, 1981-99; chair campus planning com. for facilities and grounds, U. Mo., Columbia, 1993—. Co-author: (computer software) Home-Safe-Home, 1989; co-editor: Popular American Housing, 1995, Aging, Autonomy and Architecture: Advances in Assisted Living, 1999; dep. editor: Jour. Housing for Elderly; assoc. editor: Jour. Archtl. and Planning Rsch.; contbr. articles to profl. jours. Active Mayor's Task Force, Columbia Low-Income Housing, 1984-85; mem. Main St. adv. coun. dept. econ. devel. State of Mo., 1989-90; regional chairperson dists. 84 and 85 United Way, Columbia, 1989, 90, 98, 99, 2000, 2001; mem. adv. bd. Pub. Housing Authority, Columbia, 1984-85; chairperson North Cen. Region-54 Agrl. Expt. Sta. Rsch., 1989-91; mem. Columbia Regional Home Health and Hospice Adv. Bd., Columbia Regional Hosp., 1993-2000; mem. pub. bldg. devel. and fin. com. City of Columbia, 2000—; bd. trustees The Mo. 4-H Found., 1997—, co-chair mktg. and pub. rels. com.; chair campus planning com. for facilities and grounds U. Mo., 1993—. Grantee Adminstrn. on Aging, 1979-81, VA, 1981, Am. Home Econs. Assn., 1981-82, 2 Joel Polsky Found. Interior Design Rsch. grantee, 1986, 87; recipient Fulbright award Chinese History and Culture, 1988, exch. faculty award Prince of Sonkla U., Thailand, 1990, Chonnam U., Korea, 1992; Fulbright fellow to Morocco and Tunisia, 1993. Mem. Am. Home Econs. Assn. (chmn. art/design sect. 1984-87, New Achievers award 1987), Am. Assn. Housing Educators, Am. Soc. Interior Designers (allied mem., chmn. position papers com. 1988-90, Presdl. citation 1990), Interior Design Educators Coun., Nat. Coun. for Interior Design (cert.), Environ. Design Rsch. Assn., Illuminating Engring. Soc. (participant workshop for tchrs.), Gerontol. Assn., Mo. Fulbright Alumni Assn. (membership chmn. 1989-90, v.p. 1990-92, pres. 1992-94), Univ. Club Inc. (pres. 1991-92, bd. dirs., sec. 1993-95, U. Mo. faculty alumni award 1992), Gamma Sigma Delta (pres. 1993-94, Disting. Adminstrn. award 1997), Omicron Nu, Phi Upsilon Omicron. Home: 1805 Cliff Dr Columbia MO 65201 Office: U Mo Dept Environ Design 137 Stanley Hall Columbia MO 65211-7700 E-mail: TofleR@missouri.edu.

TOFT, THELMA MARILYN, secondary school educator; b. Balt., Sept. 15, 1943; d. George Edward and Thelma Iola (Smith) Trageser; m. Ronald Harry Toft, Aug. 27, 1966 (div. 1998); 1 child, Joanna Lynn. BS in Med. Tech., Mt. St. Agnes Coll., Balt., 1965; BSE, Coll. Notre Dame, Balt., 1972; MEd, Pa. State U., 1983. Recreation dir. Villa Maria, Balt., 1961-65; blood bank supr. Wayman Park NIH, Balt., 1965-68; tchr. Sacred Heart, St. Mary's Govan's, Balt., 1968-74, Lincoln Intermediate Unit # 12, Adams County, Pa., 1979-80, York (Pa.) City Sch. Dist., 1980—; curriculum dir. M.O.E.S.T. Pa. State U., 1991-93. Mem. Pa. State Consortium-Pa. Team for Improving Math. and Sc.; grant writer, spkr. in field; writer Project Connections curriculum. Active Girl Scouts USA, Hanover, 1988-92, leader, 1984-87; mgmt. bd. Agrl. Indsl. Mus. Mem. ASCD, AAUW, Nat. Ptnrs. in Edn., Am. Bus. Women's Assn. (edn. com. 1992, sec. 1993, Chpt. Woman of Yr. 1994, York County Woman of Yr 1995), Phi Delta Kappa. Democrat. Roman Catholic. Avocations: writing, marketing. Home: 30 Panther Dr Hanover PA 17331-8888

TOKAR, BETTE LEWIS, economics educator; b. Mar. 26, 1935; d. Howard H. and Irma Rhodes (Pixton) Lewis; m. Jacob John Tokar, Oct. 1, 1955; children: Teresa, Bonnie, Michael, Robert. Student, Ursinus Coll., 1953—55; BA in Polit. Economy, Holy Family U., 1967; MA in Econs., Temple U., 1973, EdD, 1993. Lectr. Holy Family U., Phila., 1972—75, instr., 1975—78, asst. prof., 1978—82, dept. chair, 1977—85, assoc. prof., 1982—96, prof., 1986—. Lectr. La Salle Coll., Phila., 1977, Cmty. Coll. Phila., 1986—96; assessor CLEO, Phila., 1979—85. Bd. dirs. St. Andrews-in-the-Field; candidate for auditor Lower Southampton Township, Bucks County, Pa., 1967, 1969, dem. committeewoman, 1968; treas. Dem. Club Lower Township, Bucks County, 1968; bd. dirs Chapel of Four Chaplins, 1994—2002, Pine Tree Farms Assoc., Feasterville, Pa., 1968. Mem.: MENSA, Fin. Mgmt. Assn., Internat. Trade & Fin. Assn., Am. Mgmt. Assn., Am. Econ. Assn., Am. Acctg. Assn., Nat. Bus. Edn. Assn., Assn. Social Edn., Acad. Internat. Bus., Pi Gamma Mu, Delta Pi Epsilon. Episcopalian. Office: Holy Family Univ Grant And Frankford Ave Philadelphia PA 19114-2094

TOLAN, VICKI IRVENA, physical education educator; b. Vancouver, B.C., Can., Apr. 8, 1949; d. James R. and Adah St. C. (Holmes) Butchart; m. John C. Tolan, Mar. 26, 1988; children: Shauna, Jeffrey, Julie, Kelcie. BA in Edn., Western Wash. U., 1971, postgrad., 1972; M of Sports Sci.,

U.S. Sports Acad., 1988. Cert. tchr., Wash., Calif. Tchr. Pt. Garden Mid. Sch., Everett, Wash., 1971-74; tchr. phys. edn. Deaconnes Children's Home, Everett, 1972; tchr. phys. edn., health, social studies Mid. Sch., Everett, 1971-74; subs. tchr. Everett and Marysville, Wash., 1974-76, Lakewood, Wash., 1976-77; tchr. ESL Pt. Angeles (Calif.) Sch. Dist., 1983-86, tchr. photography, swimming, health, phys. edn., aerobics, 1986-87, phys. edn. and health specialist, 1987-89; tchr. Alta Loma (Calif.) Sch. Dist., 1989—. Student tchr. phys. edn., Lynnwood, Wash., 1971, Bellingham, Wash., 1971; soccer coach youth teams. Pt. Angeles Sch. Dist., 1972—, mem. AIDS/drugs curriculum com., 1986—; cheerleader advisor, 1988, 89, tchr. elem. summer sch., 1986, 87; owner Kits Camera, Pt. Angeles, 1974-83; dist. chair phys. edn. dept. Alta Loma Jr. High Sch., 1989—, chmn. phys. edn. dept., 1992-93. Instr. swimming, Kenmore, 1965-72; founder, coord., pres. Olympic Peninsula Women's Soccer League, 1979-86; bd. dirs. Womanfest, 1985, 86; coord. Jump Rope for Heart, Pt. Angeles, 1989. Named Mother of Yr. Pt. Angeles, 1983, 84, Sports Woman of Yr. Pt. Angeles, 1986; recipient State Phys. Fitness award Pres.'s Challenge, 1988, Nat. Phys. Fitness award Pres.'s Challenge, 1988. Mem. AAHPERD, AAUW, Internat. Pageant Assn., Calif. Assn. Health, Phys. Edn., Recreation and Dance, Delta Kappa Gamma. Republican. Roman Catholic. Avocations: photography, reading, soccer, tennis. Office: Alta Loma Jr High Sch 9000 Lemon Ave Alta Loma CA 91701-3357

TOLIAS, LINDA PUROFF, music educator; b. Dearborn, Mich., Nov. 26, 1954; d. Nick Puroff and Milka Stoycheff; m. Peter Elias Tolias, June 26, 1988. MusB in Music Edn. with honors, U. Mich., 1976; MusM in Music Performance, Wayne State U., 1992. Tchr. music El Dorado (Ark.) Pub. Schs., 1976-77, Ferndale (Mich.) Pub. Schs., 1979-83; tchr. bands and orch. Dearborn Pub. Schs., 1983—. Founder, condr. El Dorado Youth Symphony, 1976-77; instr. Oakland U. Summer Music Camp, Rochester, Mich., 1982-84; condr., string clinician Oakland U. Youth Orch., Rochester, 1982-84; string clinician Dearborn Pub. Schs., 1983-96, Farmington Pub. Schs., 1994-96; music performer Detroit Symphony Orch., 1978-83, Mich. Opera Theatre, 1977-90; prin. violinist U. Mich. Philharm. Orch., 1975-77, South Ark. Symphony, 1976-77, Detroit Symphony Civic Orch., 1977-79; mem. Las Palmas Internat. Opera Orch. '76 Tour; mem. Internat. Musicians Local 5, 1978. Sponsor City Beautiful Commn., Dearborn, 1983—. Fellowship U. Mich., 1975-76; recipient Roberta Siegel award for Opera, 1975-76, Music Educator of Yr. award 1998. Mem. NOW, Mich. Educator's Nat. Conf., U. Mich. Alumni Assn., Am. String Tchrs. of Am. Democrat. Greek Orthodox. Avocations: music, reading, dancing, cooking. Home: 32267 Auburn Dr Beverly Hills MI 48025-4234

TOLINO, ARLENE BECENTI, elementary education educator; b. Crownpoint, N.Mex., Dec. 26, 1942; d. Little Billie and Mary (Arviso) Becenti; m. Albert Ray Tolino, Nov. 23, 1963; children: Adrian, Nathaniel Ray, Bryan. BS, U. N.Mex., 1977; MA, No. Ariz. U., 1984. Cert. elem. tchr., N.Mex. Ednl. aide Bur. Ind. Affairs Ea. Agy., Crownpoint, 1966-77, elem. tchr. Mariano Lake, N.Mex., 1977-79, Crownpoint, 1979—, adult edn. tchr., summer 1988. Sch. curriculum trainer BeautyWay curriculum Navajo Tribe, Crownpoint, 1989; computer tchr. Crownpoint Community Sch., 1988-89; site coord. pilot project ICON, Crownpoint, 1986-87; mem. com., tutor Gifted and Talented Program, Crownpoint, 1989-91. Sch. coord. Girl Scouts Am., 1977-79; sec. Navajo Nation Chpt. Officers, Crownpoint, 1983-86; mem. St. Paul Parish Coun., Crownpoint, 1982—, sec., 1992—, chairperson edn. com. 1992—; pres. Crownpoint Community Sch. Staff Assn., 1992—. Recipient Appreciation award Chaparral coun. Girl Scouts U.S.A., 1978, Title I Outstanding Tchr. award Crownpoint Community Sch. Parent Action Com., 1981, Ea. Navajo Coun., 1988. Mem. Ea. Navajo Agy. Tchrs. (sch. rep. 1987-88). Democrat. Roman Catholic. Avocations: reading, computers, crocheting, ceramics, sewing. Home: PO Box 344 Crownpoint NM 87313-0344 Office: Crownpoint Community PO Box Drawer H Crownpoint NM 87313

TOLIYAT, HAMID ABOLHASANI, electrical engineer, educator; b. Mashhad, Iran, Apr. 26, 1957; came to U.S., 1984; s. Javad Abolhasani and Fatemeh (Nazemian) T.; m. Mina Mashhadi Rahimian, Aug. 1, 1982; children: Amir-Hossein Abolhasani, Mohammad Abolhasani. BS, Sharif U. Tech., 1982; MSc, W.Va. U., 1986; PhD, U. Wis., 1991. Engr. Ministry Energy, Teran, Iran, 1980-81; lead engr. Khorasan Regional Electric Co., Mashhad, 1982-83; engr. Allen Bradley Co., Milw., 1988-89; asst. prof. Ferdowsi U., Mashhad, 1991-94, Tex. A&M U., College Station, 1994—. Lectr. U. Wis., Madison, 1987-91; v.p. MINTEC, College Station, 1996—. Patentee in field. Mem. IEEE (sr., contbr. jour.), Sigma Xi. Avocations: soccer, basketball, swimming. Office: Dept Elec Engring Texas A&M Univ College Station TX 77843-0001

TOLL, JOHN SAMPSON, university president, physics educator; b. Denver, Oct. 25, 1923; s. Oliver Wolcott and Merle d'Aubigne (Sampson) T.; m. Deborah Ann Taintor, Oct. 24, 1970; children: Dacia Merle Sampson, Caroline Taintor. BS with honors, Yale U., 1944; AM, Princeton U., 1948, PhD, 1952; DSc (hon.), U. Md., 1973, U. Wroclaw, Poland, 1975; LLD (hon.), Adelphi U., 1978; PhD (hon.), Fudan U., Peoples Republic China, 1987; LHD (hon.), SUNY, Stony Brook, 1990; LLD (hon.), U. Md., Eastern Shore, 1993. Mng. editor, acting chmn. Yale Sci. mag., 1943-44; with Princeton U., 1946-49, proctor fellow, 1948-49; Friends of Elementary Particle Theory Research grantee for study in France, 1950; theoretical physicist Los Alamos Sci. Lab., 1950-51; staff mem., assoc. dir. Project Matterhorn, Forrestal Rsch. Ctr., Princeton U., 1951-53; prof., chmn. physics and astronomy U. Md., 1953-65; pres., prof. physics SUNY, Stony Brook, 1965-78, U. Md., 1978-88, chancellor, 1988-89, chancellor emeritus, prof. physics, 1989—; pres. Univs. Rsch. Assn., Washington, 1989-94, Washington Coll., Chestertown, Md., 1995—. 1st dir. chancellor's panel on univ. pruposes SUNY, 1970; physics cons. to editl. staff Nat. Sci. Tchrs. Assn., 1957—61; U.S. del., head scientist, secretariat Internat. Conf. High Energy Physics, 1960; mem.-at-large U.S. nat. com. Internat. Union Pure and Applied Physics, 1960—63; chmn. rsch. adv. com. on electrophysics NASA, 1961—65; mem. gov. Md. Sci. Resources Adv. Bd., 1963—65; mem., chmn. adv. panel for physics NSF, 1964—67; mem. N.Y. Gov.'s Adv. Com. Atomic Energy, 1966—70; mem. commn. plans and objectives higher edn. Am. Coun. Edn., 1966—69; mem. Hall of Records Commn., 1979—88; mem., chmn. adv. coun. Princeton Plasma Physics Lab., 1979—85; mem. adv. coun. pres.'s Assn. Governing Bds., 1980—88, So. Regional Edn. Bd., 1980—90; mem. exec. com. Washington/Balt. Regional Assn., 1980—89, Nat. Assn. State Univs. and Land Grant Colls., 1980—88, Ctr. Study of the Presidency, 1983—84; mem. univ. programs panel of energy rsch. bd. Dept. Energy, 1982—83; mem. adv. com. SBHE, 1983—89, Md. Gov.'s Chesapeake Bay Coun., 1985; mem. resource com. state trade policy coun. Gov.'s high tech roundtable Md. Dept. Econ. Devel., 1986—89; chmn. marine divsn. NASULGC, 1986; bd. trustees Aspen Inst. Humanities, 1987—89; mem. commn. higher edn. Middle States Assn. Colls. and Schs., 1987; chmn. adv. panel on tech. risks and opportunities for U.S. energy supply and demand U.S. Office Tech. Assessment, 1987—91, chmn. adv. panel on internat. collaboration in def. tech., 1989—91; mem. Sea Grant rev. panel U.S. Dept. Commerce, 1992—, chair, 1996—97; mem. com. financing higher edn. Nat. Assn. Ind. Colls. and Univs., 1996—98; bd. govs. Chesapeake Bay Maritime Mus., 1996—; dir. Md. Gov.'s Blue Ribbon Citizens Pfiesteria Action Commn., 1997; mem. governing coun. Wye Faculty Seminar, 1997—; dir. Eastern Shore Assn. Coll. Pres., 1998—; mem. bd. dirs. Md. Ctr. Agro-Ecology, Inc., 1999—; vis. prof. Nordic Inst. Theoretical Physics, Niels Bohr Inst., Denmark, U. Lund, Sweden, 1975—76; mem. math. scis. edn. bd. NAS; mem. Higher Edn. Heritage Action Com., 2002—. Contbr. articles to profl. jours. Mem. adv. coun. Del-Mar-Va coun. Boy Scouts Am., 1999—; mem. Higher Edn. Heritage Action Com., 2002—; bd. dirs. Hodson Scholarship Found., 1996, Mid-Shore Cmty. Found., 2002—. Recipient Benjamin Barge prize in math. Yale U., 1943, George Beckwith medal for Proficiency in Astronomy, 1944, Outstanding Citizen award City of Denver, 1958, Outstanding Tchr. award U. Md. Men's League, 1965, Copernicus award govt. of Poland, 1973; Stony Brook Found. award for disting. contbns. to edn., 1979, Disting. Svc. award State of Md., 1981, Silver medal Sci. U. Tokyo, 1994, Internat. Landmark award U. Md., 1994, first recipient Lifetime Achievement award Md. Assn. for Higher Edn., 2000, Chief Exec. Leadership award Coun. for Advancement and Support Edn., 2000; named Washingtonian of Yr., 1985, Citizen of Yr. Chestertown Optimist Club, 1997, John S. Toll Physics Bldg., Univ. Md., 2001; John Simon Guggenheim Meml. Found. fellow Inst. Theoretical Physics U. Copenhagen, U. Lund, Sweden, 1958-59. Fellow AAAS, Am. Phys. Soc., Washington Acad. Scis. (pres. 1995-96), N.Y. Acad. Scis.; mem. NSTA, Am. Coun. Edn. (bd. dirs. 1986-89, NAACP (life), Am. Assn. Physics Tchrs., Fedn. Am. Scientists (chmn. 1961-62), Philos. Soc. Washington, Assn. Higher Edn., Yale U. Sci. and Engring. Assn. (award for disting. contbns. 1996), Cosmos Club, Hamilton St. Club, Baltimore, Univ. Club (Washington and N.Y.), Phi Beta Kappa, Phi Kappa Phi (disting., Marylander of Yr. 2000 award), Sigma Xi (Sci. Achievement award 1965), Omicron Delta Kappa (hon.), Sigma Pi Sigma. Achievements include research on elementary particle theory, scattering. Office: U Md Dept Physics College Park MD 20742-4111 also: Washington Coll Pres's Office Chestertown MD 21620 E-mail: johntoll@physics.umd.edu., jtoll2@washcoll.edu.

TOLLESON, NANETTE BRITTAIN, realtor, educator; b. Gadsden, Ala., Dec. 20, 1954; d. Lee Ray and Edna Earle (Lee) Brittain; m. David William Tolleson, Jan. 20, 1996. BS, Jacksonville (Ala.) State U., 1986; MBA, Tenn. State U., 1992. Prodn. Goodyear Tire Co., Gadsden, 1977-87; asst. dir. Tenn Ctr. Lab. Mgmt. Rels., Nashville, 1987-96; sales agent Susie Weems Real Estate, Gadsden, 1997—98; pres. Betty Lane Bow Co., Inc., Rainbow City, Ala., 1999—2000; mng. broker First Village Realty, Fla., 2000—. Instr. Gadsden State C.C., 1996—2000. Pres. Dem. Women, 1996. Avocations: antiques, golf, sports. Home: PO Box 1886 Lady Lake FL 32158

TOLLIVER, EDITH CATHERINE, retired educator; b. Greenup, Ky., Sept. 6, 1925; d. Reece Madison and Nancy Elizabeth (Knipp) Bowling; m. Homer Tolliver, May 4, 1949 (dec. Nov. 1987); children: Gary M., Rodney D., James C., William H.; m. Robert O. Hutchins, July 7, 1990. BA, Morehead (Ky.) U., 1960; MA, Calif. State U., 1990. Cert. elem. tchr., Calif., Ky.; cert. reading specialist, Calif. Tchr. Fleming County Schs., Flemingsburg, Ky., 1943-48; factory worker Ecorse, Mich., 1948-49; tchr. Greenup County Schs., 1953-54, Carter County Schs., Olive Hill, Ky., 1954-62; 1st grade tchr. San Jacinto (Calif.) Elem. Sch., 1963-68, 72-87, mentor tchr., 1987-90; reading specialist Hyatt Elem., San Jacinto, 1968-72; 1 st grade tchr. DeAnza Elem., San Jacinto, 1987-95; ret., 1995; substitute tchr., 1995-96. Named Tchr. of Yr. San Jacinto Elem. Sch., 1982, 85. Mem. NEA, Calif. Tchrs. Assn., San Jacinto Tchrs. Assn. (sec. 1972, v.p. 1985, treas. 1995), Delta Kappa Gamma. Republican. Southern Baptist. Home: 26032 Amy Ln Hemet CA 92544-6230

TOLLMAN, THOMAS ANDREW, librarian; b. Omaha, Mar. 14, 1939; s. James Perry and Elizabeth (McVey) T.; m. Teresa Ramírez, Jan. 4, 1964; children: James Daniel, Lisa Maria. BA, Carleton Coll., 1960; MA, U. Chgo., 1965, U. Minn., 1974; postgrad., U. Ariz., 1977-79. Admissions counselor Carleton Coll., Northfield, Minn., 1960-62, asst. dean of coll., 1968-73; assoc. prof., reference libr. N.W. Mo. State U., Maryville, 1974-77; adj. instr. U. Ariz., Tucson, 1977-79; chair libr. reference dept. U. Nebr., Omaha, 1979-88, reference libr., 1988—, prof., 1997—. Sr. lectr. Fulbright Commn., Quito, Ecuador, 1991. Contbr. articles to profl. jours. Mem. ALA, Nebr. Libr. Assn., Spl. Librs. Assn., Assn. Coll. and Rsch. Librs., Reference and Adult Svcs. Div., Reforma, Nebr. Libr. Assn. (disting. svc. award, 1995). Mem. ALA, Nebr. Libr. Assn. (Disting. Svc. award 1995), Spl. Librs. Assn., Assn. Coll. and Rsch. Librs., Reference and Adult Svcs. Divsn., Reforma. Avocations: running, bicycling. Home: 12380 196th Cir NW Elk River MN 55330-2157 Office: Reference Libr U Nebr Omaha NE 68182-0001

TOLLNER, ERNEST WILLIAM, agricultural engineering educator, agricultural radiology consultant; b. Maysville, Ky., July 14, 1949; s. Ernest Edward and Ruby Geneva (Henderson) T.; m. Caren Gayle Crane, Sept. 27, 1987. BS, U. Ky., 1972; PhD, Auburn (Ala.) U., 1981. Registered profl. engr., Ga. Rsch. specialist U. Ky., Lexington, 1972-74, rsch. engr., 1974-76; teaching asst. Tex. A&M U., College Station, 1976-77; rsch. specialist Auburn U., 1977-80; asst. prof. U. Ga., Griffin, 1980-85, assoc. prof., 1985-90, prof., 1990—, grad. coord., 2000—. Chmn. Coll. Faculty Coun., U. Ga., chmn. Coll. Agr. Faculty Coun., 1998; cons. to govtl. agys. and pvt. indusry; mem. Ga. State Acad. Panel addressing stream sediment transport issues. Author: Introduction to Natural Resource Engineering; contbr. 70 articles to profl. jours. Treas. Condominium Assn., Peachtree City, 1988-91. Mem. Am. Soc. Agrl. Engrs., Am. Soc. Engring. Edn., Sigma Xi (pres. U. Ga. chpt. 1997-98, grad. program coord. 1999). Achievements include first to use an x-ray tomographic scanner devoted solely to agricultural research tasks; pioneered research into the use of vegetative filterstrips for sediment control; pioneered alternative, nonaerobic composting process for farm and municipal wastes; coordinated bioconversion laboratory construction at University of Georgia; lectr. strategic planning workshop on Bayesian statistics, 2003; development in water resource work in Africa and Ctrl. Am. Home: 1010 Rogers Rd Bogart GA 30622-2723 Office: U Ga Dept Biology and Agrl Engring Driftmier Engring Ctr Athens GA 30602 E-mail: btollner@engr.uga.edu.

TOLMAN, RICHARD ROBINS, zoology educator; b. Ogden, Utah, Dec. 1, 1937; s. Dale Richards and Dorothy (Robins) T.; m. Bonnie Bjornn, Aug. 18, 1964; children: David, Alicia, Brett, Matthew. BS, U. Utah, 1963, MSEd, 1964; PhD, Oreg. State U., 1969. Tchr. sci. Davis County Sch. Dist., Bountiful, Utah, 1964-66; instr. Mt. Hood C.C., Gresham, Oreg., 1968-69; staff assoc., project dir. Biol. Scis. Curriculum Study, Boulder, Colo., 1969-82; prof. zoology Brigham Young U., Provo, Utah, 1982—, chair dept. of zoology, 1994-98, assoc. dean Coll. Biology and Agrl., 1998—2001, clin. dept. physiology & develop. biology, 2001—. Contbr. articles to profl. jours. Scoutmaster Boy Scouts Am., Orem, Utah, 1992. With USAR, 1956-63. Alcuin fellow Brigham Young U., 1991. Mem. Nat. Sci. Tchrs. Assn., Utah Sci. Tchrs. Assn. (exec. sec. 1991—), Nat. Assn. for Rsch. in Sci. Teaching, Nat. Assn. of Biology Tchrs. Mem. Ch. of LDS. Avocations: whitewater rafting, hunting, fishing, hiking. Home: 174 E 1825 S Orem UT 84058-7836 Office: Brigham Young Univ Dept Zoology Provo UT 84602 E-mail: richard_tolman@byu.edu.

TOMA, RAMSES BARSOUM, food science and nutrition educator; b. Cairo, Nov. 9, 1938; came to U.S., 1968; s. Barsoum Toma Khalil and Fieka (Ibrahim) Gabriel; m. Rosette Toma; children: Narmer, Kamy. BS in Agr., Ain Shams U., Cairo, 1959, MS in Food Tech., 1965; PhD in Food Sci., La. State U., 1971; MPH, U. Minn., 1980. Food inspector Ministry of Food Supplies, Egypt, 1960-67; chemist Crystal Foods, New Orleans, 1968; from asst. prof. to prof. U. N.D., Grand Fork, 1972-84; prof. Calif. State U., Long Beach, 1984—. Mem. trade mission to Mid. East countries for N.D., 1976; cons. to food industries, Long Beach, 1984—; vis. prof. Cairo U., Mansora U.; adj. prof. Ain Shams U., Cairo; bd. dirs. Internat. Cmty. Coun. Contbr. more than 71 rsch. articles to profl. and sci. jours. Mem. Rep. Com., Orange County, Calif., 1984; bd. dirs. St. George Ch.; mem. adv. bd. Orange Coast Coll., Calif. Named Disting. Prof., Calif. State U., 1991, Best Advisor of the Yr., 2001. Fellow Am. Inst. Chemists, Am. Chem. Soc.; mem. Am. Dietitian Assn., Inst. food Tech., Am. Assn. Cereal Chemists, Am. Inst. Nutrition, Internat. Cmty. Coun., Egypt Am. Scholars U.S.A. (v.p. 2002—), Sigma Xi, Phi Kappa Phi, Phi Beta Delta. Republican. Mem. Christian Ch. Christian Orthodox. Avocations: swimming, fishing. Office: Calif State U 1250 N Bellflower Blvd Long Beach CA 90840-0001

TOMAR, RUSSELL HERMAN, pathologist, educator, researcher; b. Phila., Oct. 19, 1937; s. Julius and Ethel (Weinreb) T.; m. Karen J. Kent, Aug. 29, 1965; children: Elizabeth, David. BA in Journalism, George Washington U., 1959, MD, 1963. Diplomate Am. Bd. Pathology, Am. Bd. Allergy and Immunology, Am. Bd. Pathology, Immunopathology. Intern Barnes Hosp., Washington U. Sch. Medicine, 1963-64, resident in medicine, 1964-65; asst. prof. medicine SUNY, Syracuse, 1971-79, assoc. prof., 1979-88, assoc. prof. microbiology, 1980-84, prof., 1984-88, asst. prof. pathology, 1974-76, assoc. prof., 1976-83, prof., 1983-88, dir. immunopathology, 1974-88, attending physician immunodeficiency clinic, 1982-88, acting dir. microbiology, 1977-78, 82-83, interim dir. clin. pathology, 1986-87; prof. pathology and lab. medicine U. Wis. Ctr. for Health Scis., Madison, 1988—; dir. div. lab medicine U. Wis., Madison, 1988-95, dir. immunopathology and diagnostic immunology, 1995-98, prof. preventive medicine, 1999—; chair dept. pathology Stroger Hosp. Cook County, Chgo., 1999—; prof. pathology Rush U., 1999—. Past mem. numerous coms. SUNY, Syracuse, U. Wis., Madison; mem. exec. com., chair and med. cons. AIDS Task Force Cen. N.Y., 1983-88. Assoc. editor Jour. Clin. Lab. Analysis; contbr. articles, rev. to profl. jours. Mem. pub. health com. Onondaga County Med. Soc., 1987-88. Lt. comdr. USPHS, 1965-67. Allergy and Immunology Div. fellow U. Pa. Fellow Coll. Am. Pathologists (diagnostics immunology rsch. com. 1993-2003, stds. com. 1995-97, commn. on clin. pathology 1997-2003), Am. Soc. Clin. Pathology (com. on continuing edn. immunopathology 1985-91, pathology data presentation com. 1976-79), Am. Acad. Allergy (penicillin hypersensitivity com. 1973-77); mem. AAAS, Am. Assn. Immunologists, Am. Assn. Pathology, Acad. Clin. Lab. Physicians and Scientists (com. on rsch. 1979-81, chairperson immunology 1979), Clin. Immunology Soc. (clin. lab. immunology com., chair coun. 1991-96). Office: Stroger Cook County Dept Pathology 1901 W Harrison St Chicago IL 60612 Fax: 312-864-9493. E-mail: russell.tomar@hektoen.org.

TOMASSO, BERNARD GERARD, library media specialist; b. Rochester, N.Y., Mar. 28, 1950; s. Louis Joseph and Margaret Mary (Huether) T.; m. Margaret Rose Baglione, Aug. 25, 1973; children: Laura S., Christina L., Brian S. BA, St. Bonaventure U., 1973; MLS, Syracuse U., 1988, postgrad., 1989—. Cert. sch. libr. media specialist, elem. tchr., N.Y. Lang. Arts tchr. Holy Family Sch., Rochester, 1973-75; English tchr. Ellicottville (N.Y.) Ctrl. Sch., 1975-76; reading specialist Seneca Nation of Indians, Salamanca, N.Y., 1976-78; reading, Lang. Arts tchr. Port Byron (N.Y.) Ctrl. Sch., 1978-88, libr. media specialist, 1988—, computer, info. tech. coord., 1989—. Chairperson Sch. Libr. System Coun., Auburn, N.Y., 1991-92; treas. Syracuse U. Sch. Info. Studies Alumni Assn., 1988-90. Active commn. on ecumenism and interreligious affairs Roman Cath. Diocese Rochester, N.Y. Named Educator Yr. Syracuse newspapers, 1992; Manwaring scholar Syracuse U. Sch. Edn., 1990-91. Mem. ASCD, N.Y. Libr. Assn. (audio-visual chmn. sch. libr. media sect. 1993 conf.), Internat. Soc. Tech. Educators, Internat. Assn. Sch. Librarianship, Am. Fedn. Tchrs., N.Y. State Computer and Tech. Educators, Assn. Ednl. Comm. and Tech., Beta Phi Mu. Avocations: writing, walking. Office: Port Byron Ctrl Sch Maple Ave Port Byron NY 13140-9647

TOMAZIC, TERRY JOHN, research methodology educator, statistical consultant; b. Melbourne, Fla., Jan. 18, 1947; s. John F. and Marion V. (Ballare) T.; m. Gretchen Sue Phillips, May 19, 1973; 1 child, Nicholas Philip. BA, MA, U. Detroit, 1971; PhD, N.C. State U., 1981. Instr. Belmont (N.C.) Abbey Coll., 1972-75; tchg. asst. N.C. State U., Raleigh, 1975-81; asst. prof. Mid. Tenn. State U., Murfreesboro, 1981-85, U. Ala., Huntsville, 1985-86, St. Louis (Mo.) U., 1986-89, assoc. prof., 1989-95, prof., 1995—, chmn. dept. of rsch. methodology, 1997—. Cons. McDonnell-Douglas Corp., St. Louis, 1990-91, Spl. Sch. Dist., St. Louis, 1992-93, Mehlville Sch. Dist., St. Louis, 1995—, Regional Justice Info. Svc., St. Louis, 1996—. Contbr. articles to profl. jours. Mem. Am. Statis. Assn., So. Sociol. Soc., Internat. Folk Dance Assn. (pres. 1989-95). Democrat. Roman Catholic. Avocation: international folk dancing. Office: St Louis Univ 3750 Lindell Blvd Saint Louis MO 63108-3412

TOMEK, WILLIAM GOODRICH, agricultural economist; b. Table Rock, Nebr., Sept. 20, 1932; s. John and Ruth Genevieve (Goodrich) T. BS, U. Nebr., 1956, MA, 1957; PhD, U. Minn., 1961. Asst. prof. Cornell U., Ithaca, N.Y., 1961-66, NSF fellow, 1965, assoc. prof. agrl. econs., 1966-70, prof., 1970-99, grad. sch. prof., 2000—, chmn. dept. agrl. econs., 1988-93. Vis. econ. USDA, 1978-79; vis. fellow Stanford U., 1968-69, U. New Eng., Australia, 1988; mem. adv. panel Rev. Agrl. Econs., 1996-98. Author: Agricultural Product Prices, 2003; editor: Am. Jour. Agrl. Econs., 1975-77; co-editor: Chgo. Bd. Trade Rsch. Symposia, 1993-2001; mem. editl. bd. Jour. Futures Markets, 1992-95; contbr. articles to profl. jours. Served with U.S. Army, 1953-55. Recipient Earl Combs Jr. award Chgo. Bd. Trade Found. Mem. Am. Agrl. Econs. Assn. (pres. 1985-86), Am. Econ. Assn., Econometric Soc., Northeastern Agrl. Econs. Assn., Am. Agrl. Econs. Assn. (awards 1981, 89, 97, fellow), Gamma Sigma Delta (rsch. award 1994). Democrat. Methodist. Office: Cornell U Warren Hall Ithaca NY 14853-7801 E-mail: wgt1@cornell.edu.

TOMICH-BOLOGNESI, VERA, secondary school educator; b. L.A. d. Peter S. and Yovanka (Ivanovich) T.; m. Gino Bolognesi, July 12, 1969. AA, John Muir Jr. Coll., Pasadena, Calif., 1951; BA in Polit. Sci., UCLA, 1953, MEd, 1955, EdD, 1960. Cert. secondary tchr., Calif.; cert. secondary sch. adminstrn., Calif.; cert. jr. coll. tchr., Calif. Tchg. asst. dept. edn. UCLA, 1956; tchr., dept. chmn. Culver City (Calif.) Unified Sch. Dist., 1956-91; rschr., writer U.S. Dept. Edn., Washington, 1961, del. to Yugoslavia, 1965; co-owner, exec. Metrocolor Engring., San Gabriel, Calif., 1973—. Cons., Continental Culture Specialists, Inc., Glendale, Calif., 1985-92; rsch. asst. Law Firm of Driscoll & Tomich, San Marino, Calif., 1989—. Author: Education in Yugoslavia and the New Reform, 1963, Higher Education and Teacher Training in Yugoslavia, 1967; screenplay editor 1996—. Bd. trustees St. Sava Serbian Orthodox Ch., San Gabriel, 1975—, mem., 1960—. Named an Outstanding Young Women of Am., 1966; recipient Episcopal Gramata, Serbian Orthodox Ch. of Western Am., 1996, 2002. Mem. NEA (life), Calif. Tchrs. Assn., UCLA Alumni Assn., Alpha Gamma Sigma, Pi Lambda Theta. Home: 100 E Roses Rd San Gabriel CA 91775-2343 Office: Metrocolor Engring 5110 Walnut Grove Ave San Gabriel CA 91776-2026

TOMITA, TATSUO, pathologist, educator, diabetes researcher; b. Tokyo, Apr. 20, 1939; came to U.S., 1970; s. Tatsusaburo and Haru (Hiraga) T. MD, Tokyo Med. and Dental U., 1965; PhD, Yokohama (Japan) City U., 1970. Diplomate Am. Bd. Pathology. Asst. resident Barnes Hosp. and Washington U., St. Louis, 1970-73; resident Jewish Hosp. St. Louis, 1973-74; fellow Med. Ctr. U. Kans., Kansas City, 1974-75, asst. prof., 1975-80, assoc. prof., 1980-85, prof., 1985—2002, Tex. Tech. Med. Ctr., El Paso, 2002—. Mem. editorial bd. Internat. Assn. Pancreatology, Omaha, 1985-88; contbr. articles to Diabetes, Endocrinology, Am. Jour. Pathology, Diabetologia. Grantee NIH, 1979-84, Am. Heart Assn., 1985-87, 89-91. Mem. AAAS, Am. Assn. Pathologists, Am. Diabetes Assn. (grantee 1983-85), Sigma Xi. Achievements include in vitro analysis on diabetogenic effects of alloxan, pancreatic polypeptide producing islet cell tumors of the pancreas, pancreatic polypeptide secretion in exptl. diabetes. Home: 625 Moondale Dr El Paso TX 79912 Office: Tex Tech Med Ctr 4801 Alberta Ave El Paso TX 79912

TOMIZUKA, MASAYOSHI, mechanical engineering educator, researcher; b. Tokyo, Mar. 31, 1946; came to U.S., 1970; s. Makoto and Shizuko (Nagatome) T.; m. Miwako Tomizawa, Sept. 5, 1971; children: Lica, Yumi. MS, Keio U., Japan, 1970; PhD, MIT, 1974. Rsch. assoc. Keio U., 1974; asst. prof. U. Calif., Berkeley, 1974-80, assoc. prof., 1980-86, prof., 1986—, Roscoe and Elizabeth Hughes prof., 1996-97, Cheryl and John Neerhout Jr. disting. prof., 1998—. Assoc. editor: Internat. Fedn.

Automation Control Automatica, 1993-2000; contbr. more than 150 articles to profl. jours. NSF grantee, 1976-78, 81-83, 86-89, 93—, State of Calif. grantee, 1984-86, 88-93. Fellow ASME (chmn. dynamic systems and control divsn. 1986-87, tech. editor Jour. Dynamic Systems Measurement and Control, 1988-93), IEEE (assoc. editor IEEE control sys. mag. 1986-88, editor-in-chief IEEE/ASME Transactions on Mechatronics 1997-99), Soc. Mfg. Engrs. (mem. sci. com. 1993—). Office: U Calif Dept Mech Engring Berkeley CA 94720-1740 E-mail: tomizuka@me.berkeley.edu.

TOMKEWITZ, MARIE ADELE, elementary school educator; b. San Antonio, Feb. 26, 1965; d. David Eugene and Marie Frances (Sergi) Tomkewitz. BS in Elem. Edn., S.W. Tex. State U., 1988. Tchr. 2nd grade Sinclair Elem. Sch. East Ctrl. Ind. Sch. Dist., San Antonio, 1990—, chmn. 2nd grade, 1992-93, tchr. 2nd grade Sinclair Elem. Sch. Mem. Holy Spirit Cath. Ch., San Antonio, 1965—. Mem. Kappa Delta Pi, Alpha Phi. Avocations: reading, tennis. Home: 1119 Melissa Dr San Antonio TX 78213-2028 Office: Sinclair Elem Sch 6126 Sinclair Rd San Antonio TX 78222-2400

TOMKINS, JOANNE KARK, health physicist, educator; b. Newark, Sept. 18, 1953; d. Jon Joseph and Anna Rose (Peters) Kark; m. Robert Norton McVey, Mar. 24, 1979 (div. Apr. 1980); m. Robin Joseph Tomkins, Mar. 6, 1992. BS, Villanova U., 1975; postgrad., Colo. State U., 1984-85. Cert. nuclear medicine technologist. Analytical chemistry technician SpectroChem Labs., Inc., Franklin Lakes, N.J., 1976-77; nuclear medicine technologist Albert Einstein Med. Ctr., Phila., 1977-79; biol. technician Oak Ridge (Tenn.) Nat. Lab., 1979-81, radiol. technician, 1981-84; nuclear safety health physicist Ill. Dept. Nuclear Safety, Glen Ellyn, 1986—. Instr. radiation safety Oakton C.C., Des Plaines, Ill., 1989-91. Contbr. articles to profl. jours. Recipient program cert. of appreciation Suburban Bldg. Ofcls. Conf., 1988. Mem. Soc. Nuclear Medicine (assoc.), Health Physics Soc. (plenary treas. Midwest chpt. 1989, pub. info. com. 1989-92, chmn. legis. com. 1990-92). Roman Catholic. Avocations: reading, tennis, horseback riding, scuba diving, playing piano. Office: Ill Dept Nuclear Safety 800 Roosevelt Rd Ste 200 Glen Ellyn IL 60137-5839

TOMKINS, SUSAN GAIL, secondary education educator; b. Gallatin, Tenn., Feb. 15, 1957; d. Raymond James Moredock and Ann P. Nunley; m. William Richard Tomkins, Jan. 6, 1979; children: William Richard Jr., Charles Augustus Lewis. BS, George Peabody Coll. Tchrs., 1978; MEd, Tenn. State U., 1998. Lic. profl. tchr., Tenn. Tchr. White Ho. (Tenn.) H.S. Yearbook advisor White Ho. H.S., 1979-95, key club advisor, 1996-99. Recipient Golden Apple award McDonald's, 1995. Office: White Ho HS 508 Tyree Springs Rd S White House TN 37188-5432 Fax: 615-672-6406.

TOMKOVICZ, JAMES JOSEPH, law educator; b. L.A., Oct. 10, 1951; s. Anthony Edward and Vivian Marion (Coory) T.; m. Nancy Louise Abboud, June 27, 1987; children: Vivian Rose, Michelle Evelene, Henry James. BA, U. So. Calif., 1973; JD, UCLA, 1976. Bar: Calif. 1976, U.S. Dist. Ct. (so. dist.) Calif., U.S. Ct. Appeals (9th and 10th cirs.), U.S. Supreme Ct. Law clk. to Hon. Edward J. Schwartz, San Diego, 1976-77; law clk. to Hon. John M. Ferren Washington, 1977-78; atty. U.S. Dept. Justice, Washington, 1979-80; assoc. prof. law U. Iowa, Iowa City, 1982-86, prof., 1986—. Vis. prof. U. Iowa, Iowa City, 1981, U. Mich., Ann Arbor, 1992; adj. prof. UCLA, 1981-82. Author: (casebook) Criminal Procedure, 4th edit. (with W. White), 2001, (book) The Right to the Assistance of Counsel, 2002; (outline) Criminal Procedure, 1997; contbr. articles to profl. jours. Mem. Order of Coif, Phi Beta Kappa. Democrat. Roman Catholic. Avocations: running, softball, creative writing. Office: U Iowa Coll Law Melrose & Byngton Iowa City IA 52242 E-mail: james-tomkovicz@uiowa.edu.

TOMLINSON, BRUCE LLOYD, biology educator, researcher; b. Toronto, Ont., Can., Dec. 15, 1950; s. Wilbur Harvey and Betty Joan (Greenslade) T.; m. Donna Elaine Massie, June 18, 1977. MSc, U. Waterloo, Waterloo, Ont., 1978, PhD, 1983. Postdoctoral fellow Ohio State U., Columbus, 1983-84, rsch. assoc., 1984-88; asst. prof. SUNY, Fredonia, 1988-93, assoc. prof. and chair dept. biology, 1993-99. Contbr. articles to profl. jours. Ont. Grad. scholar, Ont. Gov.; Rsch. grantee Cottrell Rsch. Found., 1989. Mem. AAAS, Soc. Devel. Biology, Sigma Xi. Office: SUNY Dept Biology Jewett Ha Fredonia NY 14063

TOMLINSON, FEROL MARTIN, reading and learning center media specialist; b. Woodstock, Ill., Sept. 21, 1931; d. Clinton E. and Minnie Ada (Tremere) Martin; m. Henry Sawyer Tomlinson, June 27, 1953; children: Lynn Tomlinson Lenker, Lee Eleanor Baseley. BS, U. Ill., 1953; cert. reading specialist, Nat. Coll. Edn., 1966. Cert. learning ctr. media specialist, 1977. Tchr. McHenry (Ill.) Sch. Dist., 1953-55, Johnsburg Sch. Dist. 12, 1958-91, tchr. remedial reading, 1965-67, dir. learning ctr., 1970-83; head tchr. Ringwood (Ill.) Sch., 1977-91; dir. Dist. 12 Summer Sch., 1965-68. Active McHenry Choral Club, 1953-72, 4-H; sec.-treas.; assoc. Milk Producers Ill., 1967-75; sec.-treas. McHenry County Lamb and Wool Prodrs., 1978-81; trustee Ringwood Meth. Ch., 1990-98, Ringwood Cmty. Cemetary, 1990-97. Named Outstanding Delta Zeta Alumnae U. Ill. 1968; recipient Svc. award Assoc. Milk Prodrs. Ill., 1974; named Dist. 12 Tchr. of Yr., 1978, Disting. grad. McHenry Cmty. H.S., 1989, Ringwood Sch. Libr. dedicated as Ferol M. Tomlinson Learning Ctr., 1991. Mem. U. Ill. Alumnae Assn., NEA, Ill. Edn. Assn., Johnsburg Tchr. Assn. (past officer), DAR (Becky Thatcher award Ill. DAR), Order Eastern Star, Delta Kappa Gamma (sec. 1972-76, v.p. 1980-82, pres. 1986-88, Ill. Achievement award 1988), Delta Zeta (past chpt. pres. 1951-53). Republican. Methodist. Office: 4700 School Rd Ringwood IL 60072-9606 Home: 2501 N Martin Rd Mchenry IL 60050-9001

TOMLINSON, JULIETTE SHELL, elementary school educator; b. Atlanta, July 31, 1943; d. Robert Harold and Dorothy Anne (Johnson) Shell; m. John Arthur Tomlinson, June 6, 1964; children: Robert Tyler, Ashley Shell. BA, Trenton State Coll., 1965, MA, 1967. Tchr. Lawrenceville (N.J.) Schs., 1965-67, Cen. Bucks (Pa.) Schs., 1967—, acting prin., 1990, prin., 1993—. Social studies curriculum developer, 1990-92; organizer math. workshops, Doylestown, 1989-91. Pres. Am. Field Svc., Doylestown, Pa., 1978-85; troop leader Girl Scouts U.S.A., Doylestown, 1981-82; mem. adv. bd. Civil War Svc. Assn.; chmn. pub. rels., tres. Ctrl. Bucks Edn. Assn.; active Holistic Writing Process Leader, Instrnl.Support Team, Strategic Planning Steering Comm., Performance Appraisal Task Force. Mem. NEA, Pa. State Edn. Aassn., Central Bucks Edn. Assn. Republican. Presbyterian. Home: 191 Cherry Ln Doylestown PA 18901-3136 Office: Simon Butler Elem Sch 200 Brittany Dr Chalfont PA 18914-2306

TOMLINSON, LINDA SUE, special education educator; b. Elkart, Ind., Mar. 20, 1951; d. Forrest and Myrtle L. (Mitchell) Skaggs; m. Donald Alan Tomlinson, Feb. 14, 1980; 1 child, Richard Shane; 1 stepchild, Randall Alan. BS, Mid. Tenn. State U., 1985, MS, 1987; MEd, Vanderbilt U., 1993. Cert. tchr., Tenn. Tchr. 4th grade Bedford County Sch. Dist., Shelbyville, Tenn., 1986; tchr. 4th and 6th grades Cheatham County Sch. Dist., Pegram, Tenn., 1987-89; tchr. 5th grade Greater Nashville Jr. Acad., 1989-90; spl. edn. tchr. Hickman County Sch. System, Lyles, Tenn., 1992-93; tchr. spl. edn., vision Riverside Elem., Columbia, Tenn., 1993—. Instr. Spl. Riders Program, Franklin, Tenn, summer, 1991; grad. teaching asst. Mid. Tenn. state U., Murfreesboro, 1986-87. Faculty fellow Vanderbilt U., 1991-92. Mem. Coun. for Exceptional Children (divsn. vision and learning disabilities). Avocations: training show dogs, horseback riding, swimming, water skiing, camping. Home: PO Box 416 Townsend TN 37882-0416

TOMLINSON, SUSAN WINGFIELD, social studies educator; b. Indpls., Apr. 11, 1956; d. George Emerson and Janet Wingfield (Murphy) Carlisle; m. Charles Everett Tomlinson, Aug. 14, 1976. BS, Ball State U., 1977, MA in Edn., 1982; cert. in gifted edn., Purdue U., 1985, 86. Cert. tchr. social studies and gifted edn., Ind. Tchr. social studies Justice Jr. H.S., Marion, Ind., 1977-79, Storer Mid. Sch., Muncie, Ind., 1979-80; lectr. global futures Burris Lab. Sch. Ball State U., Muncie, 1982-86; talented and gifted specialist Mannheim (Germany) Mid. & H.S., 1986-91; tchr. social studies Park Tudor Schs., Indpls., 1992; tchr. geography Franklin Twp. Mid. Sch., Indpls., 1992—2002; tchr. history, geography Franklin Ctrl. H.S., Indpls., 2002—. Mem. adv. com. Germany and the New Europe, Ohio Dept. Edn., Columbus, 1993-94; chair adv. com. Franklin Twp. Mid. Sch., Indpls., 1993-94, mem. behavior mgmt. com., 1995-98, mem. tech. cadre com., 1999-2002, Africa Celebration '98 edn. subcom.; mem. tchr. adv. coun. Ind. Hist. Soc., 2002—; participant Geog. Educators Network Ind. Falls Ohio summer workshop, 1997. Contbr. articles to ednl. jours. Fulbright summer fellow People's Republic of China, 1990; Jane Lowery Bacon Tchr. grantee, 2000, 03. Mem. Nat. Assn. for Gifted Children Germany (pres.-elect, pres., past pres. 1988-91), Ind. Coun. for Social Studies (presenter ann. convs. 1993-2003, bd. dirs. 1996-98, 2001-03, newsletter editor 2002—), Nat. Coun. Geog. Edn. (conv. presenter 1998), Nat. Coun. Social Studies (rep. ho. dels. 1997). Avocations: horseback riding, travel, writing, reading, painting. Office: Franklin Ctrl HS 6215 S Franklin Rd Indianapolis IN 46259-1398 E-mail: stomlins@scican.net.

TOMLINSON, WILLIAM HOLMES, management educator, retired army officer; b. Thornton, Ark., Apr. 12, 1922; s. Hugh Oscar and Lucy Gray (Holmes) T.; m. Dorothy Payne, June 10, 1947 (dec.); children: Jane Axtell, Lucy Gray, William Payne; m. Florence Mood Smith, May 1, 1969 (div.); m. Suzanne Scollard Gill, Mar. 16, 1977. Student, Centenary Coll., 1938-39; BS, U.S. Mil. Acad., 1943; grad., Field Arty. Sch., 1951, Air Command Staff Coll., 1958; MBA, U. Ala., 1960; MS in Internat. Affairs, George Washington U., 1966; grad., U.S. Army War Coll., 1966, Indsl. Coll. Armed Forces, 1968; PhD in Bus. Adminstrn., Am. U., 1974; grad. Advanced Mgmt. Program, Harvard U., 1968, 69. Commd. 2d lt. U.S. Army, 1943, advanced through grades to col., field arty., 1966; combat svc. in Leyte and Cebu Philippines 246 Field Arty. Bn. Americal Divsn., 1945; aide de camp to comdg. gen. Robert Eichelberger 8th U.S. Army, Japan, 1945-48; exec. officer 34 FA Bn, ops. officer 9th Divsn. Arty. Germany and Ft. Carson, Colo., 1954-57; with ODCSPER, 1960—61, Office of Undersec. Army, The Pentagon, Washington, 1961-64; comdr. 2d Bn. 8th Arty. and 7th Divsn. Arty. UN Comd. South Korea, 1964-65; faculty Indsl. Coll. Armed Forces, Ft. McNair, Washington, 1966-72, U. North Fla., Jacksonville, 1972—2002, prof. mgmt., 1993—2002, prof. emeritus, 2003—. Vis. prof. U. Glasgow, Scotland, 1987; vis. lectr. Moscow Linguistics U., Plekhanov Econ. U., Ulyanovsk U., Russia, 1993; mem. Nat. Def. Exec. Res., Fed. Emergency Mgmt. Agy., 1976—. Author: Assessment of the National Defense Executive Reserve, 1974; co-author: International Business, Theory and Practice, 1991, Business Policy and Strategy, 2000; contbr. articles to profl. jours. Mem. exec. bd. Jacksonville Campus Ministry, 1991—, pres., 2002-. Decorated Bronze Star, Legion of Merit, Philippine Liberation medal, Japanese Occupation, Asiatic Pacific with Invasion Arrow; recipient Freedom Found. award, 1967-71, Sr. Profl. in Human Resources, Tchg. Incentive award State Univ. Sys., 1994-95. Mem. SAR, Sons Confederate Vets., Soc. Human Resource Mgmt., Acad. Mgmt., Indsl. Rels. Rsch. Assn., Acad. Internat. Bus., European Internat. Bus. Assn., Internat. Trade and Fin. Assn., Exec. Svc. Corp. Bd., Co. Mil. Historians, Nat. Eagle Scout Assn., N.E. Fla. Employee Svcs. Mgmt. Assn. (charter pres. 1987-89), West Point Soc. North Fla. (pres. 1976-77), Mil. Order Stars and Bars (comdr. 1980-90), Army Navy Club, Fla. Yacht Club, Masons, Shriners, Rotary, Beta Gamma Sigma (pres. 1988-89), Kappa Alpha. Presbyterian (elder). Home: 1890 Shadowlawn St Jacksonville FL 32205-9430 Office: 1890 Shadowlawn St Jacksonville FL 32205-9430 E-mail: wtomlins@attbi.com.

TOMOVIC, MILETA MILOS, mechanical engineer, educator; b. Belgrade, Yugoslavia, Dec. 29, 1955; came to U.S., 1979; naturalized, 1995; s. Milos Nedeljko and Danica Dane (Lemaic) T.; m. Cynthia Lou Bell, Apr. 15, 1994; children: Adriane, Milos, Senja. BS, U. Belgrade, 1979; MS, MIT, 1981; PhD, U. Mich., 1991. Rsch. asst. MIT, Cambridge, Mass., 1979-81, 83-85; design engr. Foundry Belgrade, 1982-83; sys. engr. Energoproject, Belgrade, 1985-86; assoc. prof. Purdue U., West Lafayette, Ind., 1991—2003, W.C. Furnas prof., 2003—; v.p. Metalcasting Engring., Inc., 1996—. Cons. Tech. Assistance Program, 1993—; mem. adv. bd. Engineered Casting Solutions. Assoc. editor Foundry, 1995—, also conf. procs. in field; author textbook on materials and mfg. processes. Named Key prof., Foundry Edn. Found., 1991—, Ind. Rep. of Yr., 2002; recipient Rep. Gold medal, 2002, 2003, Dir.'s award, Am. Metal Casting Consortium, 2002, Outstanding Faculty, 1967, 2001; grantee, Purdue Rsch. Found., 1994—95. Mem.: ASME (chpt. bd. dirs. 1993—95), Am. Foundrymen Soc. (chpt. bd. dirs. 1995—), Am. Soc. Engring. Educators, Am. Soc. Metals (chpt. chmn. 1994—95). Christian Orthodox. Achievements include patents in areas of metalcasting refiner plates for pulp and paper industry, mill balls for cement and metal extraction industry; research on wear and impact resistant materials, new metalcasting technologies, welding processes. Home: 3344 Dubois St West Lafayette IN 47906-1199 Office: Purdue U MET Dept Knoy Hall West Lafayette IN 47907

TOMPKINS, CURTIS JOHNSTON, academic administrator; b. Roanoke, Va., July 14, 1942; s. Joseph Buford and Rebecca (Johnston) T.; m. Mary Katherine Hasle, Sept. 5, 1964; children: Robert, Joseph, Rebecca. BS, Va. Poly. Inst., 1965, MS, 1967; PhD, Ga. Inst. Tech., 1971. Indsl. engr. E.I. DuPont de Nemours, Richmond, Va., 1965-67; instr. Sch. Indsl. and Systems Engring., Ga. Inst. Tech., Atlanta, 1968-71; assoc. prof. Colgate Darden Grad. Sch. Bus. Adminstrn., U. Va., Charlottesville, 1971-77; prof., chmn. dept. indsl. engring. W.Va. U., Morgantown, 1977-80, dean Coll. Engring., 1980-91; pres. Mich. Technol. U., Houghton, 1991—, also bd. dirs. Mem. engring. accreditation commn. Accreditation Bd. for Engring. and Tech., 1981-86; mem. exec. bd. Engring. Deans Coun., 1985-89, vice chmn., 1987-89; mem. engring. adv. com., chmn. of planning com. NSF, 1988-91, chm. Mich. Univs. pres. coun., 1996-98; Pres. Coun. Assn. Governing bds. 1996—, Gov's. Workforce Commn., 1996-2002; mem. engring. adv. bd. U. Cin., 1996-99 Author: (with L.E. Grayson) Management of Public Sector and Nonprofit Organizations, 1983, (with others) Maynard's Industrial Engineering Handbook, 1992; contbr. chpt. to Ency. of Profl. Mgmt, 1978, 83. Co-chmn. W.Va. Gov.'s Coun. on Econ. Devel.; bd. dirs. Pub. Land Corp. W.Va., 1980-89, Mich. C. of C., 1997—, vice chmn., 2002—; mem. faculty Nat. Acad. Voluntarism, United Way Am., 1976-91; mem. Morgantown Water Commn., 1981-87, Morgantown Utility Bd., 1987-91, steering com. W.Va. Conf. on Environ., 1985-89, Coun. on Competitiveness, 1998—, Mich. Higher Edn. Assistance Authority, The Mich. Higher Edn. Student Loan Authority, 2002—; chmn. Monogalia County United Way, 1989-90; campaign chmn. Copper Country United Way, 1995-96. Named to Com. of 100 Va. Tech. Coll., Disting. Alumni Acad. dept. indsl. engring; recipient Frank and Lillian Gilbreth Indsl. Engring. award Inst. Indsl. Engrs., 1998. Fellow Inst. Indsl. Engrs. (life mem., trustee 1983-90, pres. 1988-89), Nat. Soc. Profl. Engrs., Am. Soc. Engring. Edn. (pres. 1990-91), Mich. Soc. Profl. Engrs.; mem. Am. Assn. Engring. Soc. (bd. govs. 1987-90, exec. com. 1987-90, sec.-treas. 1989-90), Jr. Engring. Tech. Soc. (bd. dirs. 1988-91), Nat. Soc. for Sci., Tech. and Society (bd. dirs. 1991-94), Internat. Hall of Fame of Sci. and Engring. (hon. trustee), Ga. Tech. Coll. Engring. Disting. Alumni Acad., Ga. Tech. Sch. Indsl. and Sys. Engring. Disting. Alumni Acad., W.Va. U. Dept. Indsl. Engring. Disting. Alumni Acad. (hon.), Mich. C. of C. (bd. dirs 1997—), Blue Key (hon.), Sigma Xi, Phi Kappa Phi, Tau Beta Pi, Alpha Pi Mu. Methodist. Home: 21680 Woodland Rd Houghton MI 49931-9746 Office: MI Tech U 1400 Townsend Dr Houghton MI 49931-1200 E-mail: curt@mtu.edu.

TOMPKINS, JAMES RICHARD, special education educator; b. Camden, N.J., Jan. 17, 1935; s. Leo Joseph and Cecelia Nichols; children: Tim, Mark. BA cum laude, Mt. St. Mary's Coll., 1959; postgrad., U. Mich., 1960; MA, Niagara U., 1961; PhD, Cath. U., 1971. Coord. unit on edn. of emotionally disturbed Bur. Edn. Handicapped-USOE, Washington, 1966-71; asst. prof. U. N.C., Chapel Hill, 1971-72; exec. dir. N.C. Govs. Advocacy Commn., Raleigh, 1972-74; prof. spl. edn. Appalachian State U., Boone, N.C., 1974—. Cons. edn. of disturbed children N.C. Dept. Human Resources. Contbr. articles to profl. jours. Mem. Coun. Exceptional Children, Coun. Children with Behavior Disorders, Coun. Career Devel., Give Youth a Chance Inc., Arts and Humanities for the Handicapped, N.C. Tchr. Preparation Programs for Emotionally Disturbed Children. Home: 117 Meadowbrook Ln Deep Gap NC 28618-9688

TOMPKINS, JEANNIE KAY, special education educator; b. Portage, Wis., Feb. 8, 1944; d. Matt and Ivy (Lee) Keiller; m. Robert Jay Tompkins, June 18, 1967; children: Troy M., Lee M. BA, U. Ariz., 1966, MEd, 1970. Tchr. spl. edn. Moreno Valley Sch. Dist., Sunnymead, Calif., 1966-67; tchr. educationally handicapped Centralia Sch. Dist., Buena Park, Calif., 1967-68; pupil appraisal rm. tchr. Tucson Unified Sch. Dist., 1968-69, learning disabilities resource tchr., 1969-70; learning disabilities tchr., diagnostician Grace Christian Sch., Tucson, 1979-89; special edn. resource tchr. Vail Sch. Dist. # 20, 1989—. Organizer, dir. Attention Deficit Disorders Support Group for Parents, Tucson, 1988. Mem. task force for presch. handicapped Ariz. State Dept. Edn.; precinct committeeman Pima County. Govt. scholar, 1970. Mem. Ariz. Coun. for Learning Disabilities, Coun. for Exceptional Children. Republican. Avocations: country crafts, reading, testing. Home: 600 S Avenida Los Reyes Tucson AZ 85748-6835

TOMPKINS, JOHN ANDY, commissioner of education; BA in English, East Ctrl. State U., Ada, Okla., 1969; MS in Ednl. Adminstrn., Emporia State U., 1973; EdD, U.Kans., 1977. Tchr. English Pauls Valley H.S., Okla., 1969—70, Hugoton H.S., Kans., 1970—72; prin Pomona H.S., Kans., 1973—76; supt. Satanta Pub. Schs., Kans., 1977—79, El Dorado Pub. Schs., Kans., 1979—87, Salina Pub. Schs., Kans., 1987—94; chmn, dept. spl. svcs. and adminstrv. studies Pittsburg State U., Kans., 1994—95, interim dean Sch. of Edn., 1995—96; commr. edn. State of Kans., Topeka, 1996—. Mem. leadership Kans. Class of 1980; Kans. rep. Kans. Bd. Edn. Coun. for Policy Rsch. in Edn., 1990—92. Named Kansas Supt. of Yr., 1991—92. Mem.: Coun. of Supts. (chmn. redesign com. dist. leadership lic. 1994—95, chmn. taskforce on spl. edn. class size/case load 1986), United Sch. Adminstrs. of Kansas, Kansas Assn. Sch. Adminstrs. (bd. dirs. 1982—85, pres. 1983—84, bd. dirs. 1989—93), Am. Assn. Sch. Adminstrs. Office: Kans State Dept Edn 120 SE 10th Ave Topeka KS 66612-1182 E-mail: atompkins@ksde.org.

TOMPKINS, SHARON LEE, primary education educator; b. Catskill, N.Y., Oct. 27, 1961; d. Harold Emory and Joan (Phillips) T. BA in Theatre and English, Potsdam Coll. Arts and Scis., 1983; cert. in edn., Potsdam Coll., 1985; MS in Edn., Cortland Coll., 1990. Cert. primary edn. tchr., N.Y. Kindergarten educator Camden (N.Y.) Cen. Schs., 1985-89; pre 1st grade educator Catskill (N.Y.) Ctrl. Schs., 1989-94, modified 1st grade educator, 1994-95, 1st grade educator, 1995—99, 2002—, 2nd grade educator, 1999—2002. Mem. Greene County (N.Y.) Ladies Aux., 1985—; mem. Hose Co. 1 Ladies Aux., Catskill, 1979—, sec., 1990-94; pres. Catskill Rescue Squad, 1994-95, 1st lt., 1995-96, treas. 1996-98; vice chair bd. dirs. Catskill Valley EMS, Inc., 2001-02. Mem. Catskill Tchrs. Assn. (sec. 1990-93, pres. 1993-99, bldg. rep. 2001-03), DAR, Order of Eastern Star, Gamma Sigma Sigma (nat. v.p. 1989-91, chpt. pres. 1990, nat. pres. 1991-93, dist. 3 dir. 1995-97, mem. Empire Alumnae Chap., nat. parliamentarian 1999). Democrat. Methodist. Avocations: travel, reading, computer and desk top publishing, crafts. Home: 134 Park Ln Leeds NY 12451-1624 Office: Catskill Ctrl Schs Irving 1 Academy St Catskill NY 12414-1304 E-mail: sltomp@aol.com.

TONACK, DELORIS, elementary school educator; Elem. tchr. math. and sci. Goodrich Jr. High Sch., 1996—. Recipient Nebr. State Tchr. of Yr. award math./sci., 1992. Office: Sci Focus Program 1222 S 27th St Lincoln NE 68502-1832

TONAY, VERONICA KATHERINE, psychology educator; b. LaJolla, Calif., Mar. 28, 1960; BA with honors, U. Calif., Santa Cruz, 1985; MA, U. Calif., Berkeley, 1988, PhD, 1993. Lic. clin. psychologist. Teaching asst. U. Calif.-Berkeley, U. Calif.-Santa Cruz, 1985-88; psychology intern Family Svcs. Assn., Santa Cruz, 1989-90; lectr. psychology U. Calif., Santa Cruz, 1989—, Berkeley, 1992-94; psychology intern Santa Cruz County Children's Mental Health, 1994-95, registered Psychological asst., 1995-97; dir. Psychology Field Study Program U. Calif., Santa Cruz, 1994-97. Clin. psychologist, rschr., Santa Cruz. Author: The Creative Dreamer, 1995, The Creative Dreamer's Journal and Workbook, 1997, (video) Subconscious Journeys, 1997, Every Dream Interpreted, 2003. Fellow State of Calif., 1985-89. Mem. APA (program chmn. div. 32 1989-90), Assn. for Study of Dreams (conf. organizer 1987-88, 91-92, 98-99, 2000-2001). Avocations: writing, painting, gardening. Office: U Calif Psychology Dept Santa Cruz CA 95064 E-mail: VKtonay@cats.ucsc.edu.

TONDOWIDJOJO, JOHN VINCENT, communication educator, priest; b. Ngawi, Indonesia, Sept. 27, 1934; s. Kanjeng Raden Mas Tumenggung Tondowidjojo and Raden Ayu Soetiretno. BPhil, Inst. Philosophy, Surabaya, Indonesia, 1958; strata II theology, Coll. Brignole Sale, Genoa, Italy, 1963; bacc-strata III, Pontificia U. Urbaniana, Rome, 1988. Specialization in composition & dirigent Centro Della Cultura, Venice, Italy, 1961, comm., art & media Trinity & All Saints Coll., U.K., 1979, pub. rels. & interpersonal comm. Niagara U., 1985, mgmt. for mgrs. U. Minn., 1985; priest of Congregation of the Mission. Lectr. Cath. U., Surabaya, 1963-85, Inst. Theology & Philosophy, Malang, Indonesia, 1980—; dir. nat. comm. tng. ctr. Sanggar Bina Tama, Surabaya, 1979—; lectr. Cath. U. Atma Jaya, Yogyakarta, Indonesia, 1998—. Chmn. Found. Widya Sasana Inst., Malang, 1989-93, Found. Widya Yuwana Inst., Madiun, Indonesia, 1994—, Catechetical Commn. Diocese, Surabaya, 1974084, Social Comm. Commn. Diocese, Surabaya, 1976—, Interreligious Commn. Diocese, Surabaya, 1988-96; dir. diocese Pastoral Tng. Ctr., Madiun, 1997—; moderator Diocese Cath. Profls., Surabaya, 1979—; inventor in field. Editor, author books & bull. Sanggar Bina Tama Comm. Tng. Ctr.; author: Menapak Jejak Misionaris Lazaris 5 vols., 1995, Ethnology in Indonesia 5 vols., 1993, Pertumbuhan dan perkembangan St. Cornelius, Madiun, 1897-1998, 1998, Sejarah perkembangan Keuskupan Surabaya, 1800-2000, 12 vols. Recipient CTC Sanggar Bina Tama appreciation award Pontifical Commn. Comm. Social, The Vatican, 1982, Man of Yr. award, 1998; named Outstanding Man of 20th Century, 2000. Mem. ASTD, IFTDO, IPRA, UCIP (amb. journalism), WACC, AMIC, Inst. Tng. Devel., Ctr. Bus. Ethics. Roman Catholic. Avocations: music, public relations, writing. Home and Office: Jalan Residen Sudirman No 3 Surabaya 60136 Indonesia Fax: 62-31-5684004. E-mail: tondo@stts.edu.

TONEY, BARBARA CHADWICK, elementary education educator; b. Summit, N.J., July 13, 1945; d. Frank J. and Eunice (Riotte) Chadwick; m. Roger Charlesworth Toney, Aug. 5, 1967; children: Tracey, Ryan. AB, Muhlenberg, 1967; MEd, Tex. Women's U., 1986. Educator U.S. Armed Forces Sch., Stuttgart, Germany, 1968-69, Boyden Sch., Walpole, Mass., 1970, Plano (Tex.) Ind. Sch. Dist., 1981—. Cons. Region 10, Dallas, 1988.

Named One of 100 Terrific Tchrs. PTA, 1984; recipient Perot award for Excellence in Teaching. Fellow Delta Kappa Gamma (rsch. 1986-88, courtesy 1990—), PTA (life). Lutheran. Avocations: golfing, snow skiing, traveling, crafts, reading. Home: 3408 Seltzer Dr Plano TX 75023-5804

TONG, ROSEMARIE, medical humanities and philosophy educator, consultant and researcher; b. Chgo., July 19, 1947; d. Joseph John and Lillian (Nedued) Behensky; m. Paul Ki-King Tong, Aug. 15, 1971 (dec. Apr. 1988); children: Paul Shih-Mien Tong, John Joseph Tong; m. Jeremiah Putnam, Aug. 1, 1992. BA, Marygrove Coll., 1970; MA, Cath. U., 1971; PhD, Temple U., 1978; LLD (hon.), Marygrove Coll., 1987; LHD (hon.), SUNY, Oneonta, 1993. Asst. and assoc. prof. philosophy Williams Coll., Williamstown, Mass., 1978-88; vis. disting. prof. humanities Davidson (N.C.) Coll., 1988-89, Thatcher Prof. in med. humanities and philosophy, 1989-99; prof. humanities and philosophy U. N.C., Charlotte, 1999—; dir. Ctr. for Profl. and Applied Ethics, Charlotte, 2002—. L. Stacy Davidson vis. chair in liberal arts U. Miss., Oxford, 1998; Louise M. Olmstead vis. prof. philosophy and women's studies, Lafayette Coll., Easton, Pa., 1993; disting. prof. health care ethics U. N.C., Charlotte, 1999—; manuscript reviewer Wadsworth Pub. Co., 1985-92; curriculum reviewer philosophy dept. Carlton and Bowdoin Colls., 1986; honors examiner Hobart and William Smith Colls., 1990; dissertation dir., adj. faculty The Union Inst., 1992-93; cons., judge, panelist, organizer and speaker in field; mem. numerous U. coms. Author: Women, Sex and the Law, 1984, Ethics in Policy Analysis, 1985, Feminist Thought: A Comprehensive Introduction, 1989, Feminist Philosophies: Problems, Theories, and Applications, 1991, Feminine and Feminist Ethics, 1993, Feminist Thought: A More Comprehensive Introduction, 1998, (with Larry Kaplan) Controlling Our Reproductive Destiny, 1994, Feminist Philosophy: Essential Readings in Theory, Reinterpretation and Application, 1994, Feminist Bioethics, 1997, Feminist Thought: A More Comprehensive Ethics, 1998, Globalizing Feminist Bioethics: Crosscultural Perspectives, 2000; contbr. numerous articles to profl. jours.; mem. various editl. bds. Project reviewer Annenberg/CPB Project, Washington, 1986; policy writer dvsn. health svcs. rsch. and policy U. Minn., 1988, Frank Graham Porter Early Childhood Ctr., U. N.C. Chapel Hill, 1988; mem. Charlotte task force Congl. Task Force Health Care, Congressman Alex McMillan, 1991, standards and ethics com. Hospice N.C., 1991, resource and ethics coms. McMillan-Spratt Task Force Health Care Policy, 1992, pastoral care com. Carolinas Med. Ctr., 1990—, ethics com. Presbyn. Hosp., 1990—, N.E. Regional Hosp., 1991, Nat. Adv. Bd. Ethics in Reproduction, Washington, 1993; active Hastings Ctr. Project Undergrad. Values Edn., Briarcliff Manor, N.Y., 1993, N.C. Found. Humanities and Pub. Policy; mem. bioethics Resource Group, 1992—; mem. feminist approaches to bioethics network, 1996—; dir. med. humanities program Davidson Coll., 1988-98. Named Prof. of Yr., Carnegie Found. and Coun. Advancement and Support of Edn., 1986. Mem. Internat. Assn. for Feminist Approaches to Bioethics Network (coord. 1999—), Internat. Assn. Bioethics (chair 2003—), Am. Assn. for Bioethics and Humanities, Am. Cath. Philos. Assn., Am. Philos. Assn. (ad hoc com. computers, pub. and role of Am. Philos. Assn. 1984, adv. com. to program com. 1986-88, nomination com. 1989-91, nat. com. on status of women 1989-93, 2003—), Am. Legal Studies and Assn., Am. Soc. Pol. and Legal Philosophy, Am. Soc. Law and Medicine, Nat. Coun. Rsch. on Women, Nat. Women Studies Assn., Internat. Assn. Philosophy Law and Social Philosophy, Assn. Practical and Profl. Ethics, Society Christian Ethics, Soc. Women in Philosophy, Soc. Philosophy and Tech., Soc. Philosophy and Pub. Affairs, Soc. Study of Women Philosophers, Network Feminist Approaches to Bioethics, The Hastings Ctr., Triangle Bioethics Group, So. Soc. Philosophy and Psychology. Avocations: aerobics, boating, hiking.

TONJES, MARIAN JEANNETTE BENTON, education educator; b. Rockville Center, NY, Feb. 16, 1929; d. Millard Warren and Felicia E. (Tyler) Benton; m. Charles F. Tonjes (div. 1965); children: Jeffrey Charles, Kenneth Warren. BA, U. N.Mex., 1951, cert., 1966, MA, 1969; EdD, U. Miami, 1975. Dir. recreation Stuyvesant Town Housing Project, N.Y.C., 1951-53; tchr. music., phys. edn. Sunset Mesa Day Sch., Albuquerque, 1953-54; tchr. remedial reading Zia Elem. Sch., Albuquerque, 1965-67; tchr. secondary devel. reading Rio Grande High Sch., Albuquerque, 1967-69; rsch. asst. reading Southwestern Coop. Ednl. Lab., Albuquerque, 1969-71; assoc. dir., vis. instr. Fla. Ctr. Tchr. Tng. Materials U. Miami, 1971-72; asst. prof. U.S. Internat. U., San Diego, 1972-75; prof. edn. Western Wash. U., Bellingham, 1975-94, prof. emerita, 1994—; dir. summer study at Oriel Coll. Oxford (Eng.) U., 1976—93. Adj. prof. U. N.Mex., Albuquerque, 1995—, reading supr. Manzanita Ctr., 1968; vis. prof. adult edn. Palomar (Calif.) Jr. Coll., 1974; vis. prof. U. Guam, Mangilao, 1989-90; invited guest Russian Reading Assn., Moscow, 1992; internat. travel adv. Vantage Deluxe Travel, 2002—; spkr. European Conf. reading, Tallinn, Estonia, 2003; cons. in field. Author: (with Miles V. Zintz) Teaching Reading/Thinking Study Skills in Content Classroom, 3rd edit., Secondary Reading, Writing and Learning, 1991, (with Roy Wolpow and Miles Zintz) Integrated Content Literacy, 1999. Trustee The White Mountain Sch., 2000—; tour assoc. In the Footsteps of Dickens, England, 2001; mem. read by three com. Albuquerque Bus. and Edn. Compact. Tng. Tchr. Trainers grantee, 1975; NDEA fellow Okla. State U., 1969. Mem.: Am. Reading Forum, Internat. Reading Assn., PEO (past chpt. pres.), World Congress in Reading Buenos Aires, European Coun. Internat. Schs., European Conf. in Reading (spkr., Estonia 2003), UK Reading Assn., Internat. Reading Assn. (non-print media and reading com. 1980—83, workshop dir. S.W. regional confs. 1982, travel, interchange and study tours com. 1984—86, mem. com. internat. devel. N.Am. 1991—96, Outstanding Tchr. Educator award 1981—2003), Am. Reading Forum (chmn. bd. dirs. 1983—85), Albuquerque Tennis Club, Internat. Soc. Rwy. Travelers, Delta Delta Delta. Presbyterian. Avocations: miniatures, tennis, bridge, art, travel.

TONKIN, HUMPHREY RICHARD, academic administrator, educator; b. Truro, Cornwall, Eng., Dec. 2, 1939; came to U.S., 1962; s. George Leslie and Lorna Winifred (Sandry) T.; m. Sandra Julie Winberg, Mar. 9, 1968 (div. 1981); m. Jane Spencer Edwards, Oct. 1, 1983; 1 child, Sebastian George. BA, St. John's Coll., Cambridge, Eng., 1962, MA, 1966; AM, PhD, Harvard U., 1966; DLitt (hon.), U. Hartford, 1999. Asst. prof. English U. Pa., Phila., 1966-71, assoc. prof., 1971-80, prof., 1980-83, vice-provost undergrad. studies, 1971-75, coord. internat. programs, 1977-83, master Stouffer Coll. House, 1980-83; pres. State Univ. Coll., Potsdam, N.Y., 1983-88, U. Hartford, Conn., 1989-98, prof. humanities, pres. emeritus, 1998—; vis. fellow Whitney Humanities Ctr. Yale U., 1998-99. Vis. prof. English Columbia U., N.Y.C., 1980-81; exec. dir. Ctr. Rsch. and Documentation on World Lang. Problems, Rotterdam and Hartford, 1974—. Editor: Language Problems and Language Planning; author: (bibliography) Sir Walter Raleigh, 1971, Esperanto and International Language Problems, 4th edit., 1977, Spenser's Courteous Pastoral, 1972; author: (with Jane Edwards) The World in the Curriculum, 1981, The Faerie Queene, 1989; editor (with Allison Keef): Language in Religion, 1989, Esperanto, Interlinguistics and Planned Language, 1997; editor: (with Timothy Reagan) Language in the 21st Century, 2003; editor, translator Esperanto: Language, Literature and Community (Pierre Janton), 1993, Maskerado: Dancing Around Death in Nazi Hungary (Tivadar Soros), 2000; contbr. articles to profl. jours. Pres. Pa. Coun. Internat. Edn., 1980-81; bd. dirs. World Affairs Coun. Phila., 1979-83, Zamenhof Found., 1987-94, Hartford Symphony Orch., 1989-98, World Affairs Coun. Conn., 1989—, Greater Hartford Arts Coun., 1989-99, Can.-U.S. Found. Ednl. Exchange, 1997—, chmn. 1999-2000; bd. dirs. World Learning, 1998—; chmn. Coun. Internat. Exch. Scholars, 1988-94, Esperantic Studies Found., 1991—, Partnership for Svc.-Learning, 1991-96, v.p., 2001—; bd. dirs. Am. Forum, 1985—, chmn., 1998—. Recipient Lindback award for disting. teaching, 1970; Frank Knox fellow Harvard U., 1962-66; Guggenheim fellow, 1974 Fellow Acad. Esperanto; mem. Universal Esperanto Assn. (pres. 1974-80, 86-89, rep. to UN 1974-83, hon. com. 1995—), Spenser Soc. (pres. 1983-84, former dir.), Internat. Acad. Scis. San Marino, Conn. Acad. Arts and Scis., Cosmos Club. Home: 279 Ridgewood Rd West Hartford CT 06107-3542 Office: U Hartford Mortensen Libr 200 Bloomfield Ave West Hartford CT 06117-1599 E-mail: tonkin@hartford.edu.

TONKONOGY, JOSEPH MOSES, physician, neuropsychiatrist, researcher; b. Belaya Tserkov, Kiev, Ukraine, Oct. 22, 1925; cmae to U.S., 1979, naturalized, 1985; s. Moysey Iosifovich and Beyla (Gdalievna (Schvachkina) T.; married; children: Vitaly, Milla, Bella. MD, Military Med. Acad., Leningrad, USSR, 1947; PhD, All Union Acad. Med. Sci., Moscow, 1956; DSc, 1st Med. Inst., Leningrad, 1966. From asst. to prof. The Bechterev Inst., Leningrad, 1956-66, prof., chmn., 1966-78; assoc. Boston U. Sch. Medicine, 1980-81; physician VA Med. Ctr., Northampton, Mass., 1981-87; assoc. prof. U. Mass. Med. Ctr., Worcester, 1987-95, prof., 1995—. Dir. neuropsychiatry svc. Worcester State Hosp., Mass., 1989—. Author: Introduction to Clinical Neuropsychology, 1973, Vascular Aphasia, 1986, The Brief Neuropsychological Cognitive Examination, 1997; editor: Problems of Contemporary Psychoneurology, 1966, Psychological Experiment in Psychiatry and Neurology, 1969, Mathematical Methods in Psychiatry and Neurology, 1971, Current Problems of Clinical Psychology, 1975; cons. (book) Soviet Military Psychiatry, 1986; contbr. numerous articles to profl. jours. Capt. Med. Corps, Germany, 1947-48. Recipient The Bechterev Prize, All Union Acad. Med. Scis., Moscow, 1974. Fellow: The Royal Soc. Medicine (U.K.); mem.: Internet Psychogeriatric Soc., Soc. Neurosci., Internat. Neuropsychol. Soc., Am. Acad. Neurology, Am. Neuropsychiat. Assn. Jewish. Office: U Mass Med Ctr Dept of Psychiatry 55 Lake Ave N Worcester MA 01655-0002

TOOLE, JAMES FRANCIS, medical educator; b. Atlanta, Mar. 22, 1925; s. Walter O'Brien and Helen (Whitehurst) T.; m. Patricia Anne Wooldridge, Oct. 25, 1952; children: William, Anne, James, Douglas Sean, Lauren, Robert, Dean Tyler, Kyle, Kaitlin, Grace. BA, Princeton U., 1947; MD, Cornell U., 1949; LLB, LaSalle Extension U., 1963; Dr. Honoris Causa, U. Targu Mures, Romania, 1998. Intern, then resident internal medicine and neurology U. Pa. Hosp., London, 1949—55, Nat. Hosp., London, 1955—56; mem. faculty U. Pa. Sch. Medicine, 1959—61; prof. neurology, chmn. dept. Bowman Gray Sch. Medicine Wake Forest U., 1962—83. Vis. prof. neuroscis. U. Calif., San Diego, 1969—70; vis. scholar Oxford U., 1989; mem. Nat. Bd. Med. Examiners, 1970—76; mem. task force arteriosclerosis Nat. Heart Lung & Blood Inst., 1970—81; chmn. 6th and 7th Princeton confs. cerebrovascular diseases; cons. epidemiology WHO, Japan, 1972, 73, 93, USSR, 68, Switzerland, 74, Côte d'Ivoire, 77; mem. Lasker Awards com., 1976—77; chmn. neuropharmacologic drugs com. FDA, 1979; chair Commn. on Presdl. Disability, 1994—97; cons. NASA, 1966. Author: Cerebrovascular Diseases, 5th edit., 1999; editor: Current Concepts in Cerebrovascular Disease, 1969—73, Jour. Neurol. Sci., 1990—97; mem. editl. bd. Annals Internal Medicine, 1968—75, Stroke, 1972—74; mem. editl. bd. Jour. AMA, 1975—77; mem. editl. bd. Ann. Neurology, 1980—86, Jour. of Neurology, 1985—89. Pres. N.C. Heart Assn., 1976-77. Served with AUS, 1950-51; flight surgeon USNR, 1951-53. Decorated Bronze Star with V, Combat Med. badge. Master: ACP (licentiate); fellow: Royal Coll. Physicians, AAAS (life); mem.: AMA, Soc. for Neurosci., Hungarian Neurol. Soc., Polish Neurol. Soc., N.C. Stroke Assn. (pres. 1999—2001), Nat. Stroke Assn. (bd. dirs. 1993—, exec. com. 1994—, chmn. Commn. on U.S. Presdl. Disability 1994—), Internat. Stroke Soc. (exec. com. 1989—97, program chmn. 1992, pres. 2000—), Irish Neurol. Assn. (hon.), Am. Clin. and Climatol Assn. (life), Assn. Brit. Neurologists (hon.), German Neurol. Soc. (hon.), Austrian Soc. Neurology (hon.), Russian Acad. Neurology (hon.), Am. Soc. Neuroimaging (pres. 1992—94), Am. Acad. Neurology, World Fedn. Neurology (sec.-treas. 1982—89, mgmt. com. 1990—98, pres. 1998—2001, chmn. Rsch. and Edn. Found. 1999—), Am. Neurol. Assn. (sec.-treas. 1978—82, pres. 1984—85, historian 1988—, archivist), Am. Physiol. Soc., Am. Heart Assn. (chmn. com. ethics 1970—75). Home: 1836 Virginia Rd Winston Salem NC 27104-2316 E-mail: jtoole@wfubmc.edu.

TOOMBS, CATHY WEST, assistant principal; b. Lafayette, Tenn., Dec. 9, 1954; d. Frank and Eudrice Estelle (Russell) West; m. Paul E. Toombs, Jr., June 18, 1977. BS, Mid. Tenn. State U., 1975, MEd, 1986, EdS, 1991; EdD, Tenn. State U., 2000. Cert. tchr. English, speech, adminstrn., supervision, Tenn. Tchr. spl. edn. Eastside Elem. Sch., McMinnville, Tenn., 1975-76; tchr. English, speech, drama Mt. Juliet (Tenn.) H.S., 1976-90; dir. continuing studies Mid. Tenn. State U., Murfreesboro, 1990-94; asst. prin. Lebanon (Tenn.) H.S., 1994—2001, Mt. Juliet (Tenn.) H.S., 2001—. Mem.: ASCD, Tenn. Assn. Supervision and Curriculum Devel., Phi Kappa Delta, Phi Kappa Phi, Alpha Delta Kappa. Home: PO Box 595 Mount Juliet TN 37121-0595 Office: Lebanon HS 415 Harding Dr Lebanon TN 37087-3978 E-mail: toombsc@hotmail.com.

TOOMEY, BEVERLY GUELLA, social work educator; b. Cleve., Aug. 8, 1940; d. Fred John and Frances (Sutkowy) Guella; m. Rickard S. Toomey, Jr., Oct. 6, 1962 (div. Sept. 1981); children: Rickard S. III, A. Katherine; m. Richard J. First, Jan. 4, 1985. BA cum laude, Miami U., 1962; MSW, Ohio State U., 1974, PhD, 1977. Lic. ind. social worker. Asst. prof. Ohio State U., Columbus, 1977-81, assoc. prof., 1981-90, prof., 1990—; acting dean Coll. of Social Work, 1993-94. Mem. Ohio State U. Acad. of Teaching, Columbus, 1993—; chmn. Panel on Breakup of Family Commn. Interprofl. Edn., Columbus, 1987-89. Author: Practice Focused Research, 1985; author, editor: Mentally Ill Offenders and the Criminal Justice System, 1979; editor: Social Work in the 1980's, 1981; reviewer NIMH, Washington, 1982-86; contbr. over 40 articles to profl. jours. Mem. Ohio Hunger Task Force, Columbus, 1991; bd. dirs. Friends of Homeless, Columbus, 1985-89, YWCA, Columbus, 1989—; evaluation com. United Way, Columbus, 1988-90. Rural homelessness grantee NIMH, 1989-92. Mem. NASW (Social Worker of Yr. 1989), Coun. Social Work Edn., Nat. Women's Studies Assn., Am. Evaluation Assn., Phi Beta Kappa, Alpha Delta Mu. Office: Ohio State Univ 1947 N College Rd Columbus OH 43210-1123

TOOMEY, PAULA KATHLEEN, special education educator, educational technologist, consultant; b. Framingham, Mass., July 15, 1959; d. Paul Joseph and Mary Theresa (Coronella) T. AB in Econs., Boston Coll., 1984; postgrad., Harvard U., 1993—; MS in Edn., Simmons Coll., 1998. Office supr. ADIA, Cambridge, Mass., 1985-87; accounts receivable coord. WGBH Ednl. Found., Boston, 1987-88; fin. analyst Sta. WGBH-TV, Boston, 1988-91; unit mgr. Descriptive Video Svc. WGBH Ednl. Found., Boston, 1991-96; tchr. Franciscan's Children's Hosp.--Kennedy Day Sch. Cons. accessible technologies specialist. Vol. cons. Grow Golphybhangyang, Nepal, 1993-95; vol. tchr. Jr. Achievement, Boston, 1987; vol. master's swim coach YMCA, Brighton, Mass., 1990-93; vol. Franciscan Children's Hosp., Brighton, 1991-93; active NOW. Mem. AAUW. Roman Catholic. Avocations: creative writing, photography, trekking, swimming, cycling.

TOOP, GILLIAN V. retired secondary school educator; b. Taunton, Somerset, England, Apr. 15, 1946; came to U.S., 1953, naturalized; d. Gilbert Harry and Vera Yard; m. George C. Toop Jr., June 24, 1967; 1 child, Kevin George. BA, Marietta Coll., 1967; MS in Edn., U. Pa., 1971; postgrad., U. Va. and George Mason U., 1989-90. Cert. elem. and secondary tchr. Spanish, English, French, N.J., Pa. Tchr. Pa. Pub. Schs., 1967-70, 1971-73, Big Spring (Tex.) Ind. Schs., 1970-71, Voorhees (N.J.) Twp. Schs., 1974-76; tchr., team leader Fairfax County Pub. Schs., Reston, Va., 1981—2001; ret., 2001. Part time cons. tchr. Fairfax County Schs., 1991; mem. Dogwood Ednl. Task Force, Fairfax County Schs., 1989-96. Contbr. articles to profl. jours. V.p., pub., editor Women of Alluvium, Voorhees, 1976-78; chmn. Lakeside Cluster Assn., Reston, Va.; mem. exec. bd. PTA, Reston, 1985—. Grantee Honeywell Corp., 1987, 88, 89, Impact II, 1992. Mem. NEA, Smithsonian Assocs., Sigma Delta Pi, Sigma Kappa Nat. Sorority (v.p. scholarship 1965-67).

TOOR, RUTH, librarian, consultant; b. Vienna, Nov. 24, 1933; came to U.S., 1938; d. John and Frieda Arak; m. Jay W. Toor, June 21, 1953; children: Mark S., Cary N. BA, U. Del., 1953; MLS, Rutgers U., 1972. Libr. Southern Blvd. Sch., Chatham, NJ, 1972—2001; cons., 2001—. Adj. prof. Rutgers U.; del. Nat. Forum for History Standards, 1992; speaker in field. Author: Media Skills Puzzlers, 1984, Sharks, Ships & Potato Chips, 1986, Stars, States & Historic Dates, 1987, Reasons, Roles & Realities, 1989, At Your Finger Tips, 1992, Learning, Linking and Critical Thinking, 1994, Raising Readers, 1997, Puzzles, Patterns & Problem Solving, 1999; editor: Sch. Libr.'s Workshop Jour., 1980—. Mem. ALA (joint children's book coun. 1987-91, 1998-2002, com. on legis. 1994-97, pay equity com. 1999-2001, coun. at large 1997-2000), Am. Assn. Sch. Librs. (intellectual freedom com. 1988-91, chair flexible scheduling task force 1989-91, exec. com., bd. dirs. 1991-94, pres. 1992-93, mem. guidelines implementation com. 1994-97, chair nominating com. 1998-99, chair conf. program planning com. 2000-02, nat. sch. libr. media program of Yr. com. 2002), Assn. for Libr. Svc. to Children (chair scholarships com. 1983-87, priority cons. 1987-91, bd. dirs. 1990-91, mem. 1995 Caldecott award com., legis. com. 2001-03), Ednl. Media Assn. N.J. (pres. 1984-85, profl. devel. rsch. chair 1986-91). Avocations: travel, theatre, jazz, reading.

TOOTHE, KAREN LEE, elementary and secondary school educator; b. Seattle, Dec. 13, 1957; d. Russell Minor and Donna Jean (Drolet) McGraw; m. Edward Frank Toothe, Aug. 6, 1983; 1 child, Kendall Erin. BA in Psychology with high honors, U. Fla., 1977, MEd in Emotional Handicaps and Learning Disabilities, 1979. Cert. behavior analysis Fla. Dept. Profl. Regulation, behavior analyst Nat. Behavior Analyst Bd. Alternative edn. self-contained tchr. grades 2 and 3 Gainesville Acad., Micanopy, Fla., 1979; emotional handicaps self-contained tchr. Ctr. Sch. Alternative Sch., Gainesville, Fla., 1979-80; learning disabilities resource tchr. grades 2 and 3 Galaxy Elem. Sch., Boynton Beach, Fla., 1980-81, learning disabilities self-contained tchr. grades 1-3, 1981, varying exceptionalities self-contained tchr. grades 3-5, 1981-83, chpt. one remedial reading tchr. grades 3 and 4, 1982-83; sec. and visual display unit operator Manpower, London, 1983-84; dir. sci./geography/social studies program Fairley House Sch., London, 1984-86, specific learning difficulties self-contained tchr. ages 8-12, dir. computing program, 1984-89; specific learning difficulties resource tchr. ages 8-16 Dyslexia Inst., Sutton Coldfield, Eng., 1990; behavior specialist, head Exceptional Student Edn. dept. Gateway High Sch., Kissimmee, Fla., 1990, behavior specialist, head ESE dept., 1991, resource compliance specialist, head ESE dept., 1991-93, tchr. summer youth tng. and enrichment program, 1993, Osceola High Sch., Kissimmee, 1992; resource compliance specialist, program specialist for mentally handicapped, physically impaired, occupational and phys. therapy programs St. Cloud (Fla.) Mid. Sch., 1993-96, local augmentative/assistive tech. specialist, 1995—; resource compliance specialist, program specialist physically impaired occupl./phys. therapy programs, local augmentative/assistive tech. specialist Hickory Tree Elem. Sch., 1996-97, program specialist assistive tech., occpl., and phys. therapy, physically impaired programs, 1997-99, program specialist assistive tech., 1999—. Sch. rep. CREATE, Alachua County, Fla., 1979-80, Palm Beach County South Area Tchr. Edn. Ctr. Coun., 1980-83, chmn., 1982-83; mem. writing team Title IV-C Ednl. Improvement Grant, Palm Beach County, Fla., 1981; mem. math. curriculum writing team Palm Beach County (Fla.) Schs., 1983; mem., co-dir. Fairley House Rsch. Com., 1984-90; co-founder, dir. Rsch. Database, London, 1984-89; co-chmn. computer and behavior/social aspects writing teams Dyslexia Inst. Math., Staines, Eng., 1990; lectr., course tutor Brit. Dyslexia Assn., Crewe, Eng., 1990; mem. Vocat.-Exceptional Com., 1991-93; mem. Osceola Reading Coun., 1991-98; mem. sch. adv. com. Gateway High Sch., 1991-93, St. Cloud Mid. Sch., 1993-96; mem. sch. adv. com. Hickory Tree Elem. Sch., 1999-2000, Ctr. for Ind. Living Assitance for Tech. Divsn.; presenter in field. Mem. bd. assistive tech. divsn. Ctr. for Ind. Living. Named Mid. Sch. Profl. of Yr. Osceola chpt. Coun. Exceptional Children, 1995, 96, Profl. Recognized Spl. Educator, 1997; winner Disney's Teacherific Spl. Judges award, 1997; recipient Outstanding Svcs. to CEC award, 2002, 2003, Outstanding Related Svcs. Tchr. of Yr., 2003, Outstanding Support Svcs. award, 2003. Mem. CEC (named local chpt. Mid. Sch. Profl. of Yr. 1995, 96, exec. com. 1997—, C.A.N. rep. 1997-99, pres.-elect 1999-2000, pres. 2000-01, Outstanding Svcs. to CEC award 2002, 03, Outstanding Related Svcs. Tchr. of Yr. 2003, Outstanding Support Svcs. award 2003), Fla. Soc. for Augmentative and Alt. Comm., Phi Beta Kappa. Avocations: traveling, reading, physical fitness, scuba diving, arts and crafts. Home: 2175 James Dr Saint Cloud FL 34771-8830 Office: Osceola Dist Schs ESE Adminstrv Annex 805 Bill Beck Blvd Kissimmee FL 34744-4492 E-mail: toothek@osceola.k12.fl.us.

TOPAZIO, LAWRENCE PETER, special education educator; b. Waterbury, Conn., Apr. 6, 1948; s. Nicholas Angelo and Stella Veronica (Lagownik) T.; m. Maureen Ellen Hanlon; children: Nicholas, Michael. BS in Elem. Edn., So. Conn. State U., New Haven, 1971; MS in Spl. Edn., So. Conn. State U., 1978. Cert. tchr. learning disabilities K-12. Tchr., spl. edn. tchr. Stadley Roush Sch., Danbury, Conn., 1972-83; tchr. resource rm. Danbury H.S., 1983—. Pres. Wolcott (Conn.) Spl. Edn. PTA, 1993—. Mem. NEA, Coun. Exceptional Children, Conn. Assn. Children with Learning Disabilities, Conn. State PTA, Conn. Parent Advocacy Ctr. Home: 62 Woodward Dr Wolcott CT 06716-2823

TOPETZES, FAY KALAFAT, retired school guidance counselor; b. Auburn, Ind., July 13, 1923; d. Alexander Christ and Andromache Basiliou Kalafat; m. Nick John Topetzes, Jan. 31, 1953; children: Andrea Topetzes Mann, John Nick, Sophia Angela. BS in Acctg. and English, Ind. U., 1945; cert. tchr., Marquette U., 1969, MS in Guidance and Counseling, 1973. Cert. tchr., Wis. Acct. Dana Corp., Auburn, Ind., 1945-47; mgr. theaters Kalafat Bros., Ind., 1947-53; tchr. Univ. Sch. of Milw., 1962-64, Spencerian Bus. Coll., Milw., 1959-62, Milw. Pub. Schs., 1962-69; counselor, dir. guidance West Allis (Wis.) Ctrl. H.S., 1969-86; ret., 1986. Charter pres., mem. Ind. U. of Greek Am. Student Assn., 1942-45; bd. dirs. Gov.'s Tourism Coun. of Wis., Milw., 1990—, FLW Heritage Bd., Madison, Wis., 1990—; vol. for many charitable orgns.; active in ch., ednl., cultural and art orgns. Mem. APA, AAUW (past pres., pub. policy chairperson, Nat. award 1994-95), Wis. Pers. and Guidance Assn., Wis. Assn. Sch. Counselors, Milw. Found. for Women, Daus. of Penelope (dist. gov. 2 dists., nat. chmn. various coms. 1994-96, Penelope of Yr. award), numerous Hellenic orgns. Home: 9119 N White Oak Ln Bayside WI 53217-6203

TOPOLSKI, CATHERINE, science educator; b. Bridgeport, Conn., Feb. 23, 1948; d. Edward Joseph and Jean (Skierski) Topolski; m. Richard A. Hoffman, Feb. 1970 (div. June 1981); children: Alan Hoffman, Alexandria Hoffman, Aaron Hoffman. BS, Sacred Heart U., Fairfield, Conn., 1984; MS, So. Conn. State U., 1993. Sci. tchr. Emmett O'Brien Vocat. Tech. H.S., Ansonia, Conn., 1985—2002, Bullard Havens Vocat. Tech. H.S., Bridgeport, Conn., 2002—. Class advisor, ski club advisor, student assistance team peer mediator Emmett O'Brien Vocat. Tech. H.S., 1987—. Organizer Emmett O'Brien River Cleanup Naugatuck River Watershed Assn., Conn., 1994—. Mem.: Conn. Sci. Tchrs. Assn., New Eng. Sci. Tchrs. Assn., Sacred Heart Alumni Assn. Roman Catholic. Avocations: reading, exploring nature, volleyball.

TOPP, JANICE, mental health and clinical nurse specialist, educator; b. New Rockford, ND, Apr. 23, 1943; d. Vernon and Leona (Grager) Topp; 1 child, Victor. BS, S.D. State U., 1965; MS in Nursing, Purdue U., Hammond, Ind., 1986. Resource nurse Meth. Hosps., Merrillville, Ind.; asst prof. nursing Purdue U., Westville, Ind. Mem. Am. Psychiat. Nurses Assn., Internat. Women in Aviation, Aircraft Owners and Pilots Assn., 99's Internat. Women's Pilots Assn., Sigma Theta Tau. Home: 531 E Greening Rd Westville IN 46391-9451

TORABI, MOHAMMAD R. healthcare educator; b. Nahavard, Iran, Feb. 19, 1951; s. Mohammad Ibrahim Torabi and Malous Malekey; children: Ali, Amir. BS, Tehran U., 1975, MSPH, 1978; PhD, Purdue U., 1982; MPH, Ind. U., 1984. Teaching asst. Purdue U., West Lafayette, Ind., 1980-82; postdoctoral fellow Ind. U., Bloomington, 1982-84, asst. prof. Health Edn., 1984-89, assoc. prof. Health Edn., 1989-93, prof., 1993—, chancellors prof., 1997—, chair dept. applied health sci., 1999—. Co-author: Healthy Lifestyle Education, 1984; editor Health Education Monograph series; contbr. articles to profl. jours. Bd. dirs. Am. Cancer Soc., Bloomington, 1984-86, Assn. Advancement Health Edn., 1992-1995; pres.-elect, Am. Acad. Health Behavior, 2002—; pres. Am. Lung Assn./Ind., 1990-91. Recipient Disting. Tchg. award Ind. U., 1993, Disting. Svc. award, 1996, Disting. Alumnus award Purdue U., Auerbach medal Lung Assn., Scholar award Am. Assn. for Health Edn., 2000, Profl. Svc. to Health Edn. award, 2003. Mem. APHA, Am. Sch. Health Assn. (chair rsch. coun. 1990-91, bd. dirs. 1993-1996, Howe award 2001), Phi Delta Kappa (Ind. U. pres. 1989-90). Office: Ind U 116 Hper Bloomington IN 47404 E-mail: torabi@indiana.edu.

TORBAT, AKBAR ESFAHANI, investment advisor, economics educator, researcher; b. Esfahan, Iran, Nov. 29, 1945; came to U.S., 1972; s. Ali and Gohar Soltan Torbat E.; m. Fleur Taher Tehrani, June 16, 1997. MS in Engring., Tehran Poly., 1969; MS in Indsl. Engring., U. Tex., Arlington, 1974; MA in Polit. Economy, U. Tex., Dallas, 1980, PhD in Polit. Economy, 1987. Registered investment advisor. Indsl. engr. Long Star Gas Co., Dallas, 1974-77; lectr. Richland Coll., Dallas, 1987-88, UCLA, L.A., 1990, Calif. State U., L.A., 1989-97, Northridge, 1994-97, U. So. Calif., L.A., 1996-97, Calif. State U. Dominguez Hills, Carson, 1998—; pres. Investek Co., Anaheim, Calif., 2000—01. Cons. in field; lectr. Calif. State U., Fullerton, 2000-01. Contbr. articles to profl. jours. Mem. Am. Econ. Assn., Network Iranian Profl. Orange County, Internat. Studies Assn., Western Econ. Assn., Internat. Mid. East Studies Assn., Mid. East Econ. Assn., Ctr. for Iranian Rsch. and Analysis. Avocation: chess. Home: 6066 E Butterfield Ln Anaheim CA 92807-4844

TORDIFF, HAZEL MIDGLEY, education director; b. Columbia Station, Ohio, Sept. 24, 1920; d. Joseph and Mary Ceclia (Vitovec) Midgley; m. Joseph F. Tordiff, Nov. 13, 1946; children: Cathy, Joseph F. Tordiff Jr., John C. BS, Kent State U., 1942; student, U. Va., 1968, Catholic U., 1975. Instr. Warren (Ohio) Bus. Coll., 1942-44; exec. sec. to plant mgr. GE, Warren, 1943-44; adminstrv. asst. Fgn. Svc., Dept. State, and Am. Embassy, Stockholm and Lisbon, Portugal, 1947-52; dir. tng. Washington Bus. Sch., Vienna, Va., 1969—2000; ret., 2000. Leader Girls Scouts U.S., Bonn, Germany, 1960—64; den mother Cub Scouts Am., Bonn, 1962—66; scorekeeper Little League Baseball, Bonn, Vienna, 1960—70. Sgt. WAC U.S. Army, 1944—47. Named Outstanding Bus. Tchr. in U.S., Assn. Ind. Schs. and Colls., 1984. Mem.: Profl. Secs. Internat. (faculty sponsor 1981—84). Avocations: bowling, gardening, sports spectator. Home: 1302 Ross Dr SW Vienna VA 22180-6724

TORGERSEN, PAUL ERNEST, academic administrator, educator; b. N.Y.C., Oct. 13, 1931; s. Einar and Frances (Hansen) T.; m. Dorothea Hildegarde Zuschlag, Sept. 11, 1954; children: Karen Elizabeth, Janis Elaine, James Einar. BS, Lehigh U., 1953, DEng, 1994; MS, Ohio State U., 1956, PhD, 1959. Grad. tchg. asst. Ohio State U., Columbus, 1957, instr., 1957-59; asst. to assoc. prof. Okla. State U., Stillwater, 1959-66; prof., dept. head, dean Coll. Engring. Va. Tech, Blacksburg, 1967-93, pres., 1993-2000, John W. Hancock chair of engring. Dir. Roanoke (Va.) Electric Steel, 1986-2001, Luna Innovations, 2000—, EDD, 1996—. Author 5 books. Mem. Gov. Mark Warner's Commn. on Bd. of Visitor Appts., Richmond, Va., 2002--; So.State Energy Bd., Richmond, 1986-90. 1st lt. USAF, 1953-55. Fellow Am. Soc. Engring. Edn. (Lamme medal 1994), Inst. Indsl. Engring (Frank and Lillian Gibreth award 2001); mem. Nat. Acad. Engring. (coun. 1999--). Avocation: tennis. Office: Va Tech 302A Whittemore Blacksburg VA 24061-0118

TORKPO, BETTYE JEWELL, kindergarten educator; b. Dumas, Ark. d. Etherine (Jackson) James; m. George K. Torkpo, Apr. 19, 1977. Cert. group tchr., Essex County Coll., Newark, N.J., 1985, AA, 1993; diploma, Phillips Bus. Sch., East Orange, N.J., 1990. Student tchr. Mattie Jackson D.C. pre-sch., Okla. City, 1976; housekeeper Holiday Inn, Livingston, N.J., 1977-78; subst. tchr. State of N.J. C.D.C., East Orange, 1978; tchr.'s aide Orange (N.J.) Daycare, 1978-79; housekeeper Rsorts Hotel-Casino, Atlantic City, N.J., 1979-82; tchr. Mustard Seed C.C., Newark, 1986-89, The Urban League of Essex County, Newark, 1989-90, kindergarten tchr., 1992; tchr.'s asst. Newark Pre-Sch. Coun., 1991-92. Head usher, pres. fellowship com. Imani Bapt. Ch. of Christ Inc. Democrat. Baptist. Avocations: reading, teaching, writing, poetry, church, security investigation. Home: 410 Prospect St East Orange NJ 07017-3311

TORMA, DENISE M. assistant principal; b. Bethlehem, Pa. BA, Moravian Coll., 1977; MS in Ednl. Sci. with distinction, Temple U., 1985; student, East Stroudsburg U., 1990-91. Cert. secondary tchr., Pa., N.J., N.Y.; cert. elem. and secondary adminstr., Pa. Tchr. S.S. Simon and Jude Sch., Bethlehem, 1980-86, Phillipsburg (N.J.) High Sch., 1986-88, East Stroudsburg (Pa.) High Sch., 1988-91; asst. prin. Eyer Jr. High Sch., Macungie, Pa., 1991-93, Emmaus (Pa.) High Sch., 1993—. Mem. NASSP, Nat. Assn. Secondary Sch. Prins., Pa. Assn. Secondary Sch. Prins., Moravian Coll. Alumni Assn., Phi Delta Kappa. Office: Emmaus High Sch 851 North St Unit 1 Emmaus PA 18049-2296

TORNETTA, FRANK JOSEPH, anesthesiologist, educator, consultant; b. Norristown, Pa., Jan. 22, 1916; s. Joseph F. and Maria (Ciaccio) T.; m. Edith Galullo, Nov. 21, 1941 (dec. 1952); m. Norma Zollers, July 16, 1957; children: Frank Jr., David A., Mark A. BS, Ursinus Coll., 1938; MA, U. Pa., 1940; PhD, NYU, 1943; MD, Hahnemann Med. Coll., 1946. Diplomate Am. Bd. Anesthesiology, 1953. Instr. U. Md., College Park, 1940, Hofstra Coll., Hempstead, N.Y., 1941; teaching fellow NYU, N.Y.C., 1941-43; asst. instr. Med. Sch. U. Pa., Phila., 1949-50; dir. dept. anesthesiology. dir. Sch. Anesthesia, founder Montgomery Hosp. Med. Ctr., Norristown, Pa., 1950-91; clin. assoc. prof. Sch. Medicine Temple U., Phila., 1985-91. Lectr. Grad. Sch. St. Joseph's U., Phila., 1987-91. Contbr. articles to profl. jours. Chmn. task force Montgomery County Health Dept., Norristown, 1989-91; active Valley Forge chpt. Boy Scouts Am., Norristown, 1982. Lt. USN, 1943-50. Fellow Am. Coll. Chest Physicians, Am. Coll. Anesthesiologists, Coll. Physicians Phila.; mem. Pa. Soc. Anesthesiologists (pres. 1970), Montgomery County Med. Soc. (pres. 1969), Montgomery Hosp. Med. Staff Assn. (pres. 1960), Hahnemann Med. Coll. Alumni Assn. (v.p. 1982), KC. Republican. Roman Catholic. Home: 307 Anthony Dr Plymouth Meeting PA 19462-1109 Office: Montgomery Hosp Med Ctr 1300 Powell St Norristown PA 19401-3324

TORQUATO, SALVATORE, materials science and chemistry educator; b. Falerna, Calabria, Italy, Feb. 10, 1954; came to U.S., 1955; s. Vincent and Palma (Vaccaro) T.; m. Kim Tracey Hoberock, Nov. 8, 1975; children: Michelle, Lisa. BSME, Syracuse U., 1975; MSME, SUNY, Stony Brook, 1977, PhD in Mech. Engring., 1980. Rsch. engr. Grumman Aerospace Corp., Bethpage, N.Y., 1975-78; rsch. asst. dept. mech. engring. SUNY, Stony Brook, 1978-80; asst. prof. dept. mech. engring. GM Inst., Flint, Mich., 1981-82; from asst. to assoc. prof. depts. mech., aerospace & chem. engring. N.C. State U., Raleigh, 1982-90, prof. depts. mech., aerospace & chem. engring., 1991-92; prof. Civil Engring. Princeton (N.J.) U., 1992-99, prof. chemistry, 2000—. Vis. prof. Courant Inst. Math. Scis., N.Y.C., 1990-91; cons. Eastman Kodak, Rochester, N.Y., 1989—; mem. Inst. Advanced Study, 1998-99. Contbr. articles to profl. jours. Grumman Masters fellow, 1975-77; fellow Guggenheim, 1998; grantee NSF, 1982—, U.S. Dept. Energy, 1986—; recipient Engring. Rsch. Achievement award Alcoa Co., 1987, Disting. Engring. Rsch. award, 1989, Gustus L. Larson Meml. award, 1994. Fellow ASME; mem. Am. Inst. Chem. Engrs., Am. Phys. Soc., Soc. Engring. Sci., Soc. for Indsl. and Applied Math. Avocations: racquetball, reading, music. Office: Princeton U Princeton Materials Inst Dept Chemistry Princeton NJ 08544-0001

TORRENCE, ROSETTA (PHILLIPS), educational consultant; b. New Rochelle, N.Y., Nov. 3, 1948; d. Stanley Livinston and Evelyn Ann Phillips; m. John Wesley Torrence, Sept. 14, 1981. BA in Edn. cum laude, Bklyn. Coll., 1974. Instr. Dept. Def.-Kadena Air Base, Okinawa, Japan, 1984-86, Halifax C.C., Weldon, N.C., 1986-88; dir. The Ednl. Workshop, Richmond, Va., 1989—; ednl. cons. Philip Morris, USA (EDTC), Richmond, 1989—, Juvenile and Domestic Rels. Dist. Ct., Richmond, 1993—, Jack & Jill, Inc., Richmond, 1994—; dir. Sound-It-Out The Easy Way, Inc., 1995—. Author: (booklet, cassette) Sound-It-Out The Easy Way Phonics Program, 1989, (workbook, cassette) Sound-It-Out The Easy Way Pre-Phonics Workbook, 1993, Sound-It-Out The Easy Way: The Syllables Workbook, 1993, Sound-It-Out The Easy Way Phonics Readers, 1993. Spokesperson Concerned Business & Residents of South Side Community Group, Richmond, 1993. Baptist. Avocations: reading, writing, teaching, swimming, yoga. Home and Office: The Ednl Workshop 1818 Stockton St Richmond VA 23224-3762

TORRENS, PEGGY JEAN, technical school coordinator; b. El Dorado, Kans., Oct. 7, 1952; d. Wayne E. and Evelyn M. (Hornbostel) Clark; m. Dennis L. Torrens, May 3, 1975; children: Jason L., Jennifer L. BS in Edn., Emporia State U., 1974, MS, 1975. Cert. secondary tchr., Kans. Instr. reading Burlington (Kans.) High Sch., 1974-75, Lowther Mid. Sch., Emporia, Kans., 1975-76; coord. resouce ctr., tech. prep coord. Flint Hills Tech. Coll., Emporia, Kans., 1976—, TQM team leader. Mem., chairperson Profl. Devel. Coun., Emporia, Kans., 1990—, applied curriculum inservice presenter; inservice presenter Nat. Tech. Prep., 1996, State Tech. Prep., 1997. Author software programs; reviewer workbook Modern Reading, 1982. Community leader Lyon County 4-H, Emporia, 1988—. Mem. NEA, Emporia Women's Golf Assn. (v.p.). Democrat. Lutheran. Avocations: reading, crafts, quilting, golf. Office: Flint Hills Tech Coll 3301 W 18th Ave Emporia KS 66801-5957

TORRES, GILBERT VINCENT, retired elementary education educator; b. Trinidad, Colo., Mar. 3, 1944; s. Vincent and Lucy (Griego) T.; m. Anna Mae Perea, June 20, 1964; children: Gilbert V. Jr., Carol Lynn. AA, Trinidad State Jr. Coll., 1965; BA, Adams State Coll., 1967; MA, N.Mex. Highlands U., 1972. Elem. sch. math. tchr. Santa Fe (N.Mex.) Pub. Schs., 1967—2002. Recipient Tchr. Who Inspires award, 1999. Mem. Nat. Edn. Assn., Nat. Coun. Tchrs. Math. Democrat. Roman Catholic. Home: 1233 San Felipe Ave Santa Fe NM 87505-3396

TORTOLANI, ANTHONY JOHN, surgeon, educator; b. Eastchester, N.Y., Oct. 15, 1943; s. Salvatore Paul and Yolanda (Vecciarelli) T.; m. Beth Callahan, Dec. 15, 1967 (dec. Oct. 1993); children: Julia Sue, Paul Justin; m. Katherine Gormley, Sept. 25, 1999. BS, Fordham U., 1965; MD, George Washington Sch. Medicine, 1969. Diplomate Am. Bd. Surgery, Am. Bd. Thoracic Surgery. Chief divsn. cardiovascular & thoracic surgery North Shore U. Hosp., Manhasset, N.Y., 1978-90, chmn. dept. surgery, 1988-96, chmn. med. bd., 1994-96, chmn. dept. surgery Glen Cove, N.Y., 1990-96; John D. Mountain chair surgery North Shore U. Hosp.- Cornell U. Med. Coll., Manhasset, 1989-96, program dir. surg. residency program, 1992-96; prof. surgery Cornell U. Med. Coll., N.Y.C., 1993-97, prof. cardiothoracic surgery, 1997-99; mem. staff N.Y. Hosp., N.Y.C., 1997-99; dir., prof. cardiothoracic surgery Jack D. Weiler Hosp./Montefiore Med. Ctr. Albert Einstein Coll. of Medicine, N.Y.C., 1999-2001; prof. clin. cardiothoracic surgery Weill Med. Coll. Cornell U., 2002—. Vice chmn. N.Y. Presbyn. Cornell Cardiothoracic Surgery Network. Active Columbus Citizens Found., N.Y.C. Maj. USAF, 1974-76. Roman Catholic. Avocation: breeding arabian horses. Office: NY Presbyn Hosp 525 E 68th St Rm M-404 New York NY 10021

TOSSETT, GLORIA VAY, educator, administrator; b. Hamar, N.D., Jan. 31, 1926; d. Oscar and Lena Bernice (Ellingson) Tossett; m. Arthur Andrew Borstad, Dec. 29, 1946 (dec.); children: Stafne Tossett Borstad, Ivy Vay Borstad. BS in Edn. and Religion, Concordia Coll., Moorhead, Minn., 1968; MS in Ednl. Adminstrn., N.D. State U., Fargo, 1972; degree in bus. adminstrn., Jamestown (N.D.) Coll., 1982. Sch. coord. Harding County Schs., Buffalo, S.D., 1972-73; pub. sch. supt. Balfour (N.D.) Sch., 1975-76, Flaxton (N.D.) Sch., 1978-79; pub. sch. supt., prin. and bus. tchr. Buchanan (N.D.) Pub. Sch., 1981-82; tchr., curriculum coord. Little Hoop C.C., Ft. Totten, N.D., 1983-84; bilingual curriculum coord., adminstr., instr. art and music Trenton, N.D., 1986-89. Mem. Spl. Edn. Bd., Burke County, N.D., 1978-79, Stutsman County, N.D., 1981-82. Author: (children's lit.) Angel Album, 1989, Twuddleville Mouse, 1989. Candidate for state supt. of pub. instrn., N.D., 1984. Mem. Am. Assn. Ret. Persons, Order Eastern Star (officer). Avocations: organ, philately, piano, reading, collecting books. Home: PO Box 115 Sheyenne ND 58374-0115

TOSSI, ALICE LOUISE, special education educator; b. St. Augustine, Fla., Feb. 25, 1941; d. Hubert Parker and Marie Francis (Mecca) Hahn; m. Donald Joseph Tossi, Feb. 19, 1966; children: Kevin, Craig, Raymond. BA, Rollins Coll., 1978. Cert. elem. tchr., Fla. Sec. Diocese of St. Augustine, Fla., 1958-59, Fla. East Coast Ry., St. Augustine, 1959-60; legal sec. Mahon & Stratford, Jacksonville, Fla., 1960-61; sec. comptroller's dept. Esso Standard Oil S. A., Ltd., Coral Gables, Fla., 1962-63; sec. Kelly Temporary, Maitland, Fla., 1976-78; tchr. All Souls Elem., Sanford, Fla., 1979-81, Harbor Elem., Maitland, 1981-82; sec., tech. asst. physically impaired Seminole County Sch. Bd., Sanford, 1983—; chorus pars profl. Sweet Adelines show Lakeview Mid. Sch., 1957—2003; asst. Highlands Elem. Sch., Winter Springs, Fla. Bd. dirs. Seminole County Dem. Assn., 1983. Mem. Coun. of Exceptional Edn. (sec. 1986-90, Placque 1987), Seminole County Sch. Bd. Assn. (sec. polit. action com.). Roman Catholic. Home: 114 W Woodland Dr Sanford FL 32773-5706

TOSTE, ANTHONY PAIM, chemistry educator, researcher; b. Mountain View, Calif., June 26, 1948; BS in Chemistry with honors, Santa Clara (Calif.) U., 1970; PhD in Biochemistry and Chemistry, U. Calif., Berkeley, 1976. Rsch. fellow Cardiovascular Rsch. Inst., San Francisco, 1977-79; rsch. scientist Battelle Meml. Inst. Pacific N.W. Nat. Lab., Richland, Wash., 1980-88; asst. prof. S.W. Mo. State U., Springfield, 1988-94, assoc. prof., 1994-99, full prof., 1999—. Cons. Mitsubishi Metal Corp., Tokyo, 1984-87, Dow Chem., Tex., 1994-96; presenter in field. Contbr. articles to jours. in field, cmty. svc. presentations. Bd. dirs. Mid Columbia Arts Coun., Richland, 1987-88, Bot. Soc. S.W. Mo., Springfield, 1997-2002; pres. bd. dirs. Springfield Sister Cities Assn., 1993-96; co-founder, leader Internat. Friendship Delegations to Japan, 1996, 99, 2001, 03. Rsch./equipment grantee NSF, 1990; recipient Diverse Cmty. award Sister Cities Internat., Boston, 1996. Mem. Am. Chem. Soc. (treas. Ozark sect. 1989-91, chmn.-elect 2000, chmn. 2000-01), Am. Nuc. Soc. (Best Poster award 1987), Assn. Ofcl. Analytical Chemists (program chair 1986, 90), Mo. Acad. Sci. (program chair 1997, 2002). Avocations: picture framing, collecting fine art, woodworking, reading, cinema. Home: 2113 E Woodhaven Pl Springfield MO 65804-6767 Office: SW Mo State U Dept Chemistry 901 S National Ave Springfield MO 65804-0088 E-mail: anthonytoste@smsu.edu.

TOSTI, SALLY T. artist, educator; b. Scranton, Pa., Jan. 21, 1946; d. Ivan and Helen (Odell) Thompson; m. Robert Matthew Tosti, May 3, 1974; 1 child, Jennifer Marie. BS in Art Edn., Ind. (Pa.) U., 1967; postgrad., Tyler Sch. Art, 1969-70; MFA in Drawing and Painting, Marywood Coll., 1985. Art tchr. Bristol Twp. Schs., Levittown, Pa., 1967-69, Ctrl. Bucks Schs., Doylestown, Pa., 1971. Adj. faculty Marywood Coll., Scranton, Pa., 1986-87; art coord. Keystone Coll., LaPlume, Pa., 1991-96, adj. faculty, 1995—. Exhbns. include San Diego Art Inst., 1993-94, Allentown (Pa.) Art Mus., Abercombie Gallerie, 1994, Lakeview Mus., 1995, U. Tex., Tyler, 1995-96, Linder Art Gallery, 1994—, Haggin Mus., Stockton, Calif., 1996, Fla. Printmakers Soc. Traveling Exhbn., 1995-97, So. Graphics Traveling Exbhn., 1996—, Elon Coll., N.C., 1997, Moss-Thorns Gallery Art, 1997, others. Active Countryside Conservancy, Waverly, Pa. Grantee Pa. Coun. Arts, 1995; F. Lammot Belin Arts scholar, 1996. Mem. Waverly Womans Club, Print Ctr. Phila., So. Graphics Coun., Am. Print Alliance, Womens Studio Workshop, Everhart Mus. Democrat. Home: PO Box 776 Waverly PA 18471-0776

TOTTEN, ANDREA LEE, elementary education educator; b. Reno, Nev., Apr. 10, 1947; d. Andrew Vance and Shirley Lee (Boyce) Anderson; m. Donald Edward Totten, July 24, 1982; children: Laura Ann, Dana Marie. BS in Secondary Edn., U. Nev., 1970, BS in Elem. Edn., 1971, reading specialist, 1991. Cert. tchr., Nev. Tchr. elem. grades Washoe County Sch. Dist., Reno, 1979—. Sec. bd. dirs. His Little Sch., Sparks, Nev., 1988-92. Named Tchr. of Week, Reno (Nev.)-Gazette Jour., Neighbors Sparks Edition, 1989. Mem. Internat. Reading Assn., Nev. Edn. Assn., Washoe County Tchrs. Assn. (Disting. Performance award 1992). Republican. Baptist. Avocations: reading, gardening, camping, bicycling, hiking. Home: 14175 Saddlebow Dr Reno NV 89511-6730 Office: Washoe County Sch Dist Reno NV 89509

TOTZ, SUE ROSENE, secondary school educator; b. Rockford, Ill., June 13, 1954; d. Wendell O. and Irene Rose (Suski) Rosene; m. Ronald R. Totz, June 28, 1975. BSEd, Rockford Coll., 1980; MSEd, No. Ill. U., 1987; student, Nat. Coll. of Edn., Lombard, Ill.; cert. in Libr. Media, U. Moscow, Idaho, 1995. Cert. tchr. reading, k-12, Ill. Instr. Rockford (Ill.) Coll., Rock Valley Coll., Rockford; tchr. 4th grade Christian Life Ctr. Sch., Rockford; tchr. middle sch. reading Woodstock (Ill.) Sch. Dist., 1987-97, dir. Learning Resource Ctr., 1997—. Regional rep. to state bd. Ill. Assn. MId. Schs., 1989—; presenter Assn. Ill. Mid. Sch. Conf., 1988, 91-97. Recipient award Those Who Excel award of merit Ill. State Bd. Edn.; named Sch. Dist. Tchr. of Yr., 1990--. Mem. ALA, Ill. Sch. Libr. Media Assn., Internat. Reading Assn., Ill. Reading Coun., No. Ill. Reading Coun., Nat. Mid. Sch. Assn. (presenter 1994, 95, 98), Alpha Delta Kappa. Office: 2121 N Seminary Ave Woodstock IL 60098-2641

TOULOUSE, MARK GENE, religion educator; b. Des Moines, Feb. 1, 1952; s. O. J. and Joan (VanDeventer) T.; m. Jeffica L. Smith, July 31, 1976; children: Joshua Aaron, Marcie JoAnn, Cara Lynn. BA, Howard Payne U., 1974; MDiv, Southwestern Bapt. Theol. Sem., 1977; PhD, U. Chgo., 1984. Instr. Ill. Benedictine Coll., Lisle, 1980-82, asst. prof., 1982-84, Grad. Sem., Phillips U., Enid, Okla., 1984-86; prof. Tex. Christian U., Ft. Worth, 1986—, dean, 1991—2002. Author: The Transformation of John Foster Dulles, 1985, Joined in Discipleship: The Maturing of an American Religious Movement, 1992, Joined in Discipleship: The Shaping of Contemporary Disciples Identity, 1997; co-editor: Makers of Christian Theology in America, 1997, Sources of Christian Theology in America, 1999; editor: Walter Scott: A Nineteenth Century Evangelical, 1999; contbr. articles to religious jours. Henry Luce III fellow Theol., 1997-98; Theol. scholar, rsch. award Assn. Theol. Schs., 1990-91. Mem. Am. Acad. Religion (jr. scholar S.W. region 1990-91), Am. Soc. Ch. History. Home: 136 Crown Ridge Ct Azle TX 76020 Office: Brite Divinity Sch TCU Box 298130 Fort Worth TX 76129-0001 E-mail: m.toulouse@tcu.edu.

TOURETZKY, MURIEL WALTER, nursing educator; b. Elizabeth, N.J., Jan. 9, 1944; d. Robert Harry and Marian Elizabeth (Bannan) Walter; m. Simeon Jacob Touretzky, Jan. 24, 1982. BS in Med. Tech., Rutgers U., 1966; MS in Biology, U. Mo., St. Louis, 1977; BSN, Rutgers U., 1986. RN, N.J.; cert. tchr., N.J., cert. health edn. specialist, cert. sch. nurse ANA, cert. sch. nurse, N.J. Lead nurse pediatric unit St. Michael's Med. Ctr., Newark, 1986-89; instnl. supr. Woodbridge (N.J.) Devel. Ctr., 1989; sch. nurse Regional Sch. Union Campus, Scotch Plains, N.J., 1989—; part-time instr. scis. practical nursing program Middlesex County Vocat. and Tech. Schs., East Brunswick, N.J., 1989—. Mem. ANA, Am. Sch. Health Assn. (sch. nurse com.), Nat. Assn. Sch. Nurses, Am. Assn. Blood Banks, Sigma Theta Tau. Home: 592 Madison Dr # B Monroe Township NJ 08831-4330 Office: 1524 Terrill Rd Scotch Plains NJ 07076-2914

TOWLE, ALEXIS CHARLES (LEX TOWLE), education advocate; b. Newburyport, Mass., Mar. 23, 1946; s. Sidney Norwood and Nancy Lois (Roberts) Towle; m. Maryellen Foote, Oct. 19, 1991; children: Ian, Devon. BA, Oundle Coll., Northants, Eng., 1964, Yale U., 1968. V.p., trust officer Nat. Shawmut Bank, Boston, 1973-78; v.p., fin. cons. Merrill Lynch & Co., Boston, 1979-82, Kidder, Peabody & Co., Boston, 1983-88; v.p., investment banker Boston Bay Capital, Inc., Boston, 1988-93; dir. devel., campaign Boston Renaissance Charter Sch., 1994-95; pres. Appletree Inst. Edn. Innovation, Washington, D.C., 1995—. Treas., chmn. fin. com., trustee Stoneridge Montessori Sch., Beverly Mass., 1994-2003; co-founder, trustee Cesar Chavez Charter Sch., Washington, 1998-99, Washington Math Sci. Charter Sch., 1998-2001, Paul Jr. High Charter Sch., Washington, 1999-2000, founder Apple Early Literacy Presch., Washington, 2001. Author (with others) amendments to D.C. School Reform Act of 1995. Leadership gifts com. Kent Sch., Conn. Lt. USMC, 1968-71, Vietnam. Mem. Nat. Soc. Fundraising Execs. (edn. com.), Planned Giving Group New England (edn. com.). Republican. Episcopalian. Avocations: skiing, ice hockey, gardening. Home: 21 Fellows Rd Ipswich MA 01938-2710 Office: Appletree Inst Edn Innovation 907 Sixth St SW Ste 615 Washington DC 20024 Fax: 202-488-3991. E-mail: lextowle@aol.com.

TOWLE, LEX See TOWLE, ALEXIS

TOWNE, KATHLEEN DUGAN, counselor, educator; b. Brockton, Mass., June 14, 1947; d. Kastanter Julius and Alice Lucy (Nevitt) Dugan; m. Stephen Burrows Dates, June 17, 1967 (div. 1981); children: Carrie D. Dates, Liza D. Dates, S. MacDonald Dates; m. Bruce Gene Towne, Aug. 21, 1981; 1 child, M. Schuyler Littlefield. BA in English, U. Vt., 1969, MEd in Counseling, 1971; MEd in Gifted Edn., Johnson State Coll., 1983, MEd in Adminstrn., 1988. Cert. tchr., counselor, prin., Vt. Tchr. Westford (Vt.) Elem. Sch., 1969-70; tchr., acting dir. Renhen Presch., Essex, Vt., 1970-71; real estate broker Riddell Assocs., Burlington, Vt., 1974-78; aide, coach Burlington High Sch., 1980-81; assoc. prof. Champlain Coll., Burlington, 1981-87; counselor Fairfax (Vt.) Pub. Sch. Dist., 1987-88; gifted coord. Montpelier (Vt.) Pub. Sch. Dist., 1988-90; counselor Milton (Vt.) Pub. Sch. Dist., 1990-92, coord. adminstrv. svcs., 1992—. Bd. dirs. Vt. Coun. for Gifted Edn., pres., 1989-91; co-founder, presenter Project All Resources Combined, Milton, 1990—; coord. Drug/Alcohol Super Team, Milton, 1991—; co-founder, dir. Connect Through Communication-Conflict Mediation, Milton, 1990—. Co-author: I Am Not Feeling Too Good About This War, 1991. Justice of the Peace, State of Vt., 1987—; bd. of civil authority Town of Colchester, Vt., 1987—, sch. bd., 1987-88; trustee Burnham Meml. Libr., Colchester, 1983-85; chmn. Cemetery Commn., Colchester, 1981-82. Named Outstanding Young Woman of Am., 1980. Mem. AACD, AAUW, Vt. Counseling Assn. Avocations: collecting antiques, painting/design, jewelry making.

TOWNSEND, BARBARA LOUISE, reading specialist, elementary school educator; b. Elkhart Lake, Wis., Aug. 21, 1956; d. Ronald Ernst and Valeria Louise (Horneck) Mauk; m. Thomas Charles Townsend, Oct. 6, 1979; children: Evan Thomas, Eric Louis. BSE in Elem. Edn., U. Wis., Whitewater, 1978, MSE in Reading, 1983. Transp. coord., driver for disabled U. Wis., Whitewater, 1976-78; libr. Traver Grade Sch., Lake Geneva, Wis., 1978-90, tchr. grades 1 and 2, 1978-90; reading specialist Elkhorn (Wis.) Area Sch. Dist., 1990—. Mem. strategic planning com. Elkhorn Area Sch. Dist., 1994, mem. strategic plan action team, 1994-95, mentor tchr., 2000-01; coach Battle of Books, 1996—. Coun. mem., Sunday Sch. tchr., choir 1st Congl. United Ch. of Christ, Elkhorn, 1978—; leader CHAMPS, West Side Sch., Elkhorn, 1994-00, leader PRIDE, West Side Sch., 2001—. Named Outstanding Leader in Edn. AAUW, Lake Geneva br., 1992, Tchr. of Yr., Kiwanis, 2002-03. Mem. Internat. Reading Assn., Wis. State Reading Assn., So. Lakes Reading Coun. Avocations: reading, gardening, music, needlework. E-mail: townba#elkhorn.k12.wi.us. Home: 1309 Robincrest Ln Elkhorn WI 53121-9483 Office: West Side Elem Sch 222 Sunset Dr Elkhorn WI 53121-1220

TOWNSEND, BRENDA S. educational association administrator; Dir. profl. devel. Internat. Reading Assn., Newark, Del., 1992—, dir. con. and affiliate svcs. Mem. adv. bd. The Gooding Inst. Rsch. in Family Literacy. Office: Internat Reading Assn 800 Barksdale Rd PO Box 8139 Newark DE 19714-8139*

TOWNSEND, CHARLES EDWARD, Slavic languages educator; b. New Rochelle, N.Y., Sept. 29, 1932; s. Charles Edward and Lois (Fukushima) T.; m. Janet Linner, Sept. 18, 1957; children: Erica, Sylvia, Louise. BA, Yale U., 1954; MA, Harvard U., 1960, PhD, 1962. Instr., then asst. prof. Harvard U., 1962-66; mem. faculty Princeton U., 1966—2002, dir. Critical Langs. Program, 1968-70, prof. Slavic langs., 1971—2002, chmn. dept., prof. emeritus, 2002—. Author: Russian Word Formation, 1968, Continuing With Russian, 1970, Memoirs of Princess Natalja Borisovna Dolgorukaja, 1977, Czech Through Russian, 1981, A Description of Spoken Prague Czech, 1990, Russian Readings for Close Analysis, 1993, Common and Comparative Slavic, 1996. Served with U.S. Army, 1955-58. IREX grantee, 1968, 89; Fulbright grantee, 1954-55, 71, 83, 88; Ford Found. fellow, 1958-60; NDEA fellow, 1960-62 Mem. Am. Coun. Tchrs. Russian, Am. Assn. Tchrs. Slavic and East European Langs. (Disting. Contbn. to Profession award), N.Am. Assn. Tchrs. Czech (pres. 1992-94), Am. Assn. Advancement Slavic Studies, Linguistic Soc. Czech Republic (hon.), Czechoslovak Soc. Arts. and Scis., Phi Beta Kappa. Home: 145 Hickory Ct Princeton NJ 08540-3434 Office: Princeton U Dept Slavic Langs 238 E Pyne Princeton NJ 08544-0001

TOWNSEND, FRANK MARION, pathology educator; b. Stamford, Tex., Oct. 29, 1914; s. Frank M. and Beatrice (House) T.; m. Gerda Eberlein, 1940 (dec. div. 1944); 1 son, Frank M.; m. Ann Graf, Aug. 25, 1951; 1 son, Robert N. Student, San Antonio Coll., 1931-32, U. Tex., 1932-34; MD, Tulane U., 1938. Diplomate: Am. Bd. Pathology. Intern Polyclinic Hosp., N.Y.C., 1939-40; commd. 1st lt. M.C., U.S. Army, 1940, advanced through grades to lt. col., 1946; resident instr. pathology Washington U., 1945-47; trans. to USAF, 1949, advanced through grades to col., 1956; instr. pathology Coll. Medicine, U. Nebr., 1947-48; asso. pathologist Scott and White Clinic, Temple, Tex., 1948-49; asso. prof. pathology Med. Br. U. Tex., Galveston, 1949-59; flight surgeon USAF, 1950-65; dir. labs. USAF Hosp. (now Wilford Hall USAF Hosp.), Lackland AFB, Tex., 1950-54; cons. pathology Office of Surgeon Gen. Hdqrs. USAF, Washington, 1954-63, chief cons. group Office of Surgeon Gen. Hdqrs., 1954-55; dep. dir. Armed Forces Inst. Pathology, Washington, 1955-59, dir., 1959-63; vice comdr. aerospace med. divsn. Air Force Systems Command, 1963-65, ret., 1965; practice medicine specializing in pathology San Antonio, 1965—; dir. labs. San Antonio State Chest Hosp.; consulting pathologist Tex. Dept. Health hosps., 1965-72; clin. prof. pathology U. Tex. Med. Sch., San Antonio, 1969-72, prof., chmn. dept. pathology Health Sci. Ctr., 1972-86, emeritus chmn., prof., 1986—2001. Cons. U. Tex. Cancer Ctr.-M.D. Anderson Hosp., 1966-80, NASA, 1967-75; mem. adv. bd. cancer WHO, 1958-75; mem. Armed Forces Epidemiology Bd., 1983-91; bd. govs. Armed Forces Inst. Pathology, 1984-95. Mem. editorial bd. Tex. Med. Jour., 1978-86; contbr. articles to med. jours. Mem. adv. coun. Civil War Centennial Commn., 1960-65; bd. dirs. Alamo Area Sci. Fair, 1967-73. Decorated D.S.M., Legion of Merit; recipient Founders medal Assn. Mil. Surgeons, 1961, medal of honor DAR, 1997; recipient Comdr.'s award Armed Forces Epidemiol. Bd., 1990; F.M. Townsend Chair of Pathology endowed in his honor by faculty of Dept. Pathology, U. Tex. Health Sci. Ctr., 1987, The Annual Frank M. Townsend M.D. lectr. endowed in hist honor by faculty dept. pathology U. Tex. Health Sci. Ctr., San Antonio, 1999. Fellow ACP, Coll. Am. Pathologists (edn. advisor on accreditation, commr. lab. accreditation South Ctrl. States region 1971-84), Am. Soc. Clin. Pathologists (Ward Burdick award 1983), Aerospace Med. Assn. (H.G. Mosely award 1962); mem. AMA, AAAS, Tex. Med. Assn., Internat. Acad. Aviation and Space Medicine, Tex. Soc. Pathologists (Caldwell award 1971), Am. Assn. Pathologists, Internat. Acad. Pathology, Acad. Clin. Lab. Physicians and Scientists, Soc. Med. Cons. to Armed Forces, Torch Club. Home: Harwood, Tex. Died Oct. 31, 2001.

TOWNSEND, LEROY B. chemistry educator, university administrator, researcher; b. Lubbock, Tex., Dec. 20, 1933; s. L.B. and Ocie Mae (McBride) T.; m. Sammy Beames, Sept. 15, 1953; children: Lisa Loree, LeRoy Byron. BA in Chemistry and Math., N.Mex. Highlands U.-Las Vegas, 1955, MS, 1957; PhD, Ariz. State U.-Tempe, 1965; DSc. (hon.), U. Nebr. Assoc. prof. medicinal chemistry U. Utah, Salt Lake City, 1971-75, prof., 1975-78, adj. prof. chemistry, 1975-78; prof. medicinal chemistry U. Mich., Ann Arbor, 1979—, Albert B. Prescott prof. medicinal chemistry, 1985—, prof. chemistry, 1979—, chmn., dir. interdept. grad. program in medicinal chemistry, 1979—99. Chmn. drug discovery and devel. program Comprehensive Cancer Ctr.; mem. cancer rsch. com. Nat. Cancer Inst., 1979—99, mem. com. on devel. treatments for rare genetic disease dept. human genetics; mem. nat. adv. com. on AIDS to NIAID; mem. steering com. on chemotherapy of malaria WHO; mem. study sect. on chemotherapy of cancer Nat. Am. Cancer Soc.; mem. Am. Cancer Soc. study sect. drug devel. hematology and pathology; mem. various ad hoc site visit teams Nat. Cancer Inst.; chmn. purines and pyrimidines Gordon Rsch. Conf.; chmn. Nat. Medicinal Chemistry Symposium; pres. Internat. Congress Heterocyclic Chemistry; participant symposia in field; lectr. various nat. and internat. sci. congresses. Contbr. articles to profl. jours.; assoc. editor Internat. Jour. Heterocyclic Chemistry; mem. editorial bd. Jour. Carbohydrates, Nucleosides, Nucleotides, Jour. Nucleosides and Nucleotides, Jour. Chinese Pharm. Soc., Jour. Medicinal Chemistry. Recipient Smissman-Bristol Myers-Squibb award in medicinal chemistry, Taito O. Soine Meml. award; various grants; named Disting. prof. MAGB. Fellow AAAS; mem. Am. Chem. Soc. (chmn., counsilor medicinal chemistry div.), Internat. Soc. Heterocyclic Chemistry (treas., pres. 1973-79), Nat. Am. Chem. Soc. (chmn. divsn. of medicinal chemistry), Sigma Xi, Phi Kappa Phi. Office: U Mich Coll Pharmacy Coll Pharmacy 4569 Pharmacy CC Little Bldg Ann Arbor MI 48109-1065 Home: 2721 Winter Garden Ct Ann Arbor MI 48105-1567

TOWNSEND, LUCY FORSYTH, historian, educator; b. Pikeville, Ky., Sept. 16, 1944; d. Frank J. and Lucy Dolores (Webber) Forsyth; m. James Arthur Townsend, Jan. 1, 1972. BA, Mich. State U., 1966; MA, Memphis State U., 1970, Fuller Theol. Sem., Pasadena, Calif., 1979; PhD, Loyola U., Chgo., 1985. Tchr. McKenzie (Tenn.) Jr. H.S., 1967-68; adj. prof. Crighton Coll., Memphis, 1969-74; tchr. (part time) Evangelical Christian Sch., Memphis, 1970-73; tchr. Village Christian Sch., Sun Valley, Calif., 1975-77; dir. children's Christian edn. La Crescenta (Calif.) Presbyn. Ch., 1977-79; adj. prof. Azusa (Calif.) Pacific U., 1978-79; adj. instr. Elgin (Ill.) C.C., 1980-84; from asst. prof. to full prof. history of edn. No. Ill. U., De Kalb, 1987—, prof., 1999—; archivist Blackwell History of Edn. Mus. and Rsch. Collection, No. Ill. U., DeKalb, 1994-96; curator Blackwell History of Edn. Rsch. Collection, No. Ill. U., DeKalb, 1996—2001. Free lance writer, cons., editor David C. Cook Publ. Co., Elgin, 1979-86. Author: (biography) The Best Helpers of One Another, 1988, (children's book) Learning About Hidden Treasures, 1987; co-author: Creative Dramatics for Young Children, 1986; co-editor: A Meere Scholler: Cross-Cultural Perspectives on Our Educational Heritage, 1996, Women: A Global Perspective, 2002; editor: Vitae Scholasticae, 1987—88, 1996—98; co-editor, 1998—2000. Recipient Hon. Mention Children's Poem, Evangelical Press Assn., 1987. Mem. Internat. Soc. for Ednl. Biography (pres. 1994-95), Midwest History of Edn. Soc. (v.p. 1994-95, pres. 1995-96), Am. Ednl. Studies Assn. (sec. 1996-2000), Am. Ednl. Rsch. Assn., History of Edn. Soc., Thresholds in Edn. Found. (mem. exec. bd. 1992—), Coun. Learned Socs. Edn. (bd. examiners Nat. Coun. Accreditation Tchr. Edn. 1995-1999). Avocations: drama, music, biking. Office: No Ill University EPF Dept Dekalb IL 60115 E-mail: etownsend@niu.edu.

TOWNSEND, MILES AVERILL, aerospace and mechanical engineering educator; b. Buffalo, N.Y., Apr. 16, 1935; s. Francis Devere and Sylvia (Wolpa) T.; children: Kathleen Townsend Hastings, Melissa, Stephen, Joel, Philip. BA, Stanford U., 1955; BS MechE, U. Mich., 1958; advanced cert., U. Ill., 1963, MS in Theoretical and Applied Mechanics, 1967; PhD, U. Wis., 1971. Registered profl. engr., Ill., Wis., Tenn., Ont. Project engr. Sundstrand, Rockford, Ill., 1959-63, Twin Disc Inc., Rockford, 1963-65, 67-68; sr. engr. Westinghouse Electric Corp., Sunnyvale, Calif., 1965-67; instr., fellow U. Wis., Madison, 1968-71; assoc. prof. U. Toronto, Ont., Can., 1971-74; prof. mech. engring. Vanderbilt U., Nashville, 1974-81; Wilson prof. mech. and aerospace engring. U. Va., Charlottesville, 1981—, chmn. dept., 1981-91. Ptnr., v.p. Endev Ltd., Can. and U.S., 1972—; cons. in field. Contbr. numerous articles on dynamics, design dynamical systems, controls and optimization to profl. jours.; 7 patents in field. Recipient numerous research grants and contracts. Fellow ASME, AAAS; mem. N.Y. Acad. Scis., Sigma Xi, Phi Kappa Phi, Pi Tau Sigma. Avocations: running, reading, music. Home: 212 Alderman Rd Charlottesville VA 22903-1704 Office: U Va Dept Mech and Aerospace Engring Thornton Hall Charlottesville VA 22903-2442 E-mail: mat@virginia.edu.

TOWNSEND, SUSAN LOUISE, elementary school administrator; b. Denver, Apr. 16, 1951; d. Calvin William and Roselyn Louise (Wilder) Scheidler; m. John Richard Townsend, July 28, 1973; children: Jeffrey, Kristen. BA in Elem. Edn., U. No. Colo., 1973, MA in Ednl. Adminstrn., 1990. Cert. tchr. elem. edn., adminstr., Colo. Tchr. Arlington Elem. Sch., Greeley, Colo., 1973-75, Meeker Elem. Sch., Greeley, 1975-77; adminstr. Child Devel. Ctr., Billings, Mont., 1982-84; tchr. Cameron Elem. Sch., Greeley, 1984-88, Scott Elem. Sch., Greeley, 1988-89, spl. adminstrv. assignment, 1989-91, adminstr., 1991-94; curriculum coord. Weld Sch. Dist. 6, 1994—; auditor PDK Internat. Curriculum Mgmt. Audit Ctr., 1996—. Cons. Weld Sch. Dist. 6, Greeley, 1988—; presenter on edn. and classroom mgmt., Greeley, 1988—. Author: (learning programs) Jump Start, 1989—, Fast Track, 1990—, Read, Write and Launch, 1991—, Parent Power Plus, 1991 (Gov.'s Creativity Initiative award 1991). Named United Meth. Woman of Yr. United Meth. Ch., 1982; nominated for Colo. Excellence in Edn. award, 1993, Phi Delta Kappa Outstanding Educator award, 1994. Fellow Danforth Assn.; mem. NEA, ASCD, Colo. Assn. Sch. Execs., Colo. Edn. Assn., Greeley Educators Assn., Phi Delta Kappa, Alpha Delta Kappa (sec. 1976—). Avocations: reading, crafts, family activities, decorating, woodworking. Office: Weld Sch Dist 6 Ednl Svcs Bldg Greeley CO 80631-4304

TOWNSEND-BUTTERWORTH, DIANA BARNARD, educational consultant, author; b. Albany, N.Y., Dec. 12; d. Barnard and Marjorie (Bradley) Townsend; m. J. Warner Butterworth, Jan. 23, 1969; children: James, Diana. AB, Harvard-Radcliffe Coll., 1960; MA, Tchrs. Coll., Columbia U., 1971. Tchr. St. Bernard's Sch., N.Y.C., 1963-78, head of lower sch. English, 1965-71, head of jr. sch., 1971-78; assoc. dir. Early Care Ctr., N.Y.C., 1984-87; acad. advisor Columbia Coll., N.Y.C., 1987-88; ednl. cons., lectr. N.Y.C., 1988—. Dir. parent involvement initiative Ctr. Ednl. Outreach & Innovation, Tchrs. Coll., Columbia U., 1996, chmn. devel. com. alumni coun. Tchrs. Coll., 1994-98; chmn. sub-com. Harvard schs. com. Harvard Coll., Cambridge, Mass., 1975—. Author: Preschool and Your Child: What You Should Know, 1995, Your Child's First School, 1992 (Parent's Choice award 1992), (book chpt.) Handbook of Clinical Assessment of Children and Adolescents; contbr. articles to ednl. publs. and jours. Mem. women's health symposium steering com. N.Y. Hosp., N.Y.C., 1988—. Mem. Assn. Lower Sch. Heads (co-founder 1975), Alumni Coun. Tchrs. Coll. (com. chair 1993-98), Harvard Faculty Club. Avocations: skiing, hiking, swimming, theatre, reading. Home: 1170 5th Ave New York NY 10029-6527

TOWNSLEY, LISA GAIL, mathematics educator; b. Honolulu, June 25, 1960; d. Sidney Joseph and Mary Irmhild (Fuss) Townsley. BS, Santa Clara (Calif.) U., 1981; MS, Northwestern U., 1983, PhD, 1988. Prof. math. Benedictine U., Lisle, Ill., 1987—. Exam. reader, table leader AP/ETS, Clemson, S.C., 1991—. Author: The DERIVE Calculus Workbook, 1994, Cohomology Rings of Finite Groups, 2003; contbr. articles to profl. jours.; performer Chgo. Festival Ballet Co. Named to Faculty All Stars, Chgo. Tribune, 1994; grantee, NSF, 1993, 2001. Mem. Math. Assn. Am., Assn. for Women in Math., Am. Math. Soc., Phi Beta Kappa, Kappa Mu Epsilon, Alpha Sigma Nu. Democrat. Office: Benedictine U 5700 College Rd Lisle IL 60532-2851

TOYAMA, HIROSHI, radiologist, educator; b. Nagoya, Aichi, Japan, Apr. 24, 1958; s. Naohiko and Teruko (Hibino) T.; m. Masako Suzumura, Oct. 10, 1988; children: Yutaka, Yoko. BM, Fujita Health U., Toyoake, Japan, 1984, D Med. Sci., 1990. Resident Fujita Health U. Hosp., 1984-86, radiologist, 1986-90; postdoctoral fellow dept. radiology Fujita Health U., 1990-91, asst. prof. dept. radiology, 1992—; rsch. fellow dept. radiology U. Toronto, 1991—92. Vis. scientist molecular imaging br. NIMH, NIH, 2001—03. Contbr. articles to profl. jours. Recipient Best Sci. Exhibit award, 7th Asia and Oceania Congress Nuclear Medicine and Biology, 4th Internat. Congress Nuclear Oncology, 2000; grantee, Yoshida Found. for Sci. and Tech., 1991. Fellow: Japan-N.Am. Med. Exch. Found. (grantee 1991); mem.: Japanese Soc. Nuc. Medicine (councilor), Japan Radiol. Soc., Soc. Nuc. Medicine (bd. dirs. councilor brain imaging coun. 2001—). Avocations: travel, art museums, baseball. Office: 1-98 Dengakugakubo Kutsukake Toyoake Aichi 470-1192 Japan E-mail: htoyama@fujita-hu.ac.jp.

TOYAMA, JEWEL B.C. elementary school educator, physical education educator; b. Honolulu, Sept. 9, 1955; d. Lawrence K.K. and Karen O.L. (Young) Mun; m. Gerald Masami Toyama, June 19, 1982; children: Brandee Lei, Troy Kosuke, Lacee. BEd, U. Hawaii, 1977, profl. diploma in edn., 1978; MEd, Bowling Green State U., 1988. Cert. elem. tchr., Hawaii. Phys. edn. workshop resource tchr. Honolulu Dist. Dept. Edn., 1976-78; phys. edn. resource tchr. State of Hawaii Dept. Edn., Maui, 1978-80; tchr. phys. edn. Hanahauoli Sch., Honolulu, 1980—. Instr. BYU-Hawaii, Laie, summer 1991, HPER Inst. U. Hawaii, summer 1992; cons. Early Edn. Ctr., Honolulu, spring 1991; workshop presentor Hawaii Assn. for Educating Young Children, Honolulu, spring 1991. Volleyball instr. YWCA, Honolulu, 1976—; mem. United Ch. of Christ, Honolulu. Mem. Am. Assn. Phys. Edn., Recreation and Dance (life, S.W. Dist. Elem. Phys. Edn. Tchr. of Yr. 1992), Hawaii Assn. for Health, Physical Edn., Recreation, and Dance (pres. 1993-94, life, elem. chair elect 1982-83, elem. div. chair 1983-84, 89-90, sec. 1998-2000, conv. mgr. s.w. dist. 1995, 2000, Elem. Phys. Edn. Tchr. of Yr. 1992). Avocations: volleyball, swimming, tennis, sewing, outdoor education. Office: Hanahauoli Sch 1922 Makiki St Honolulu HI 96822-2099

TOZER, WILLIAM EVANS, entomologist, educator; b. Binghamton, N.Y., July 7, 1947; s. William Evans and Gertrude Genevieve (Lewis) T. BS in Natural Sci., Niagara U., 1969; MS in Biology, Ball State U., 1979; PhD in Entomology, U. Calif., Berkeley, 1986. Cert. C.C. biology and zoology tchr. Calif. Jr. H.S. sci. and English tchr. St. Patricks Sch., Corning, N.Y., 1969-71; tchg. asst. biology Ball State U., Muncie, Ind., 1974-76; pvt. practice biol. eviron. cons. Berkeley, Calif., 1976-79, 86-88; rsch. asst. U. Calf., Berkeley, 1979-86; dept. head edn. and tng. USN Disease Vector Ecology and Control Ctr., Poulsbo, Wash., 1988—. Mem., acting chmn. San Francisco Bay Area Mosquito Control Coun., Alameda, 1988-96; chmn. com., mem. Armed Forces Pest Mgmt. Bd., Washington, 1994—; bd. dirs. Cert. and Tng. Assessment Group, EPA/USDA, 2001--. Editor (field handbook) Navy Environmental Health Center, 1994; contbr. articles to profl. jours. With U.S. Army, 1971-73. Mem. Am. Entomol. Soc., Sigma Xi. Achievements include first to publish evidence for underwater behavioral thermoregulation in adult insects. Home: 1407 NW Santa Fe Ln Apt 304 Silverdale WA 98383-7915 Office: USN Disease Vector Ecol Control Ctr 2850 Thresher Ave Silverdale WA 98315- E-mail: William.tozer@ndvecc.navy.mil.

TRABILSY, DAVID MITCHELL, academic administrator; b. Plainfield, N.J., Jan. 24, 1948; s. Mitchell and Helen Frances (McGinley) T.; m. Connie Jo Manley, July 2, 1971; children: Jessica Anne, Christopher Mitchell. BA in History, Rutgers Coll., 1970, EdM, 1973, EdS in Ednl. Theory, 1982; cert., Oxford (Eng.) U., 1969. Social studies tchr. New Brunswick (N.J.) H.S., 1970-72, 74-75; asst. and acting dir. admissions Rutgers U., Camden, N.J., 1978-82; dir. admissions Robert Wood Johnson Med. Sch., Piscataway, N.J., 1982-87; asst. dean, dir. admissions Sch. Medicine Johns Hopkins U., Balt., 1987-2000, founder, dir. post-baccalaureate premed. program, 2000—. Part-time instr. Rutgers U., 1976-87; tchg. asst. Douglass Coll., New Brunswick, 1977-78; mem. com. Coll. Bd. Sponsored Scholarship Program, 1994. Vestry Sunday sch. supt. St. Mark's Ch., Highland, Md., 1990-93; mem. curriculum com. Jackson Twp. Bd. Edn., 1981-87, mem. rent levelling bd., 1984-85; chair, treas. New Brunswick Episcopal Urban Work Com., 1970-78. Named one of Outstanding Young Men in Am., Jaycees, 1982, 83, N.J. Statesman award, 1986, Internat. Senator award, 1987. Mem. N.E. Admissions Com. (vice chair 1990-93), Assn. Am. Med. Coll. (chair 1993-96), Consortium Med. Schs. and Women's Colls. (treas.), N.E. Assn. Advisors Health Professions (exec. com. 2001—). Avocations: travel, sports, music. Office: Johns Hopkins U 3003 N Charles St Baltimore MD 21218 E-mail: dmtrab@jhu.edu.

TRACANNA, KIM, elementary and secondary physical education educator; b. Washington, Pa., Nov. 3, 1960; d. Frank and Mary Lou (Nardi) T. BSEd in Health and PE, Slippery Rock U., 1982; MS, U. N.C., 1985. Cert. health and physical edn. tchr. K-12, Fla., CPR, Advanced First Aid, ARC. Instr. PE Young World, Inc., Greensboro, N.C.; instr. PE and Health Beth-Ctr. Elem. Sch., Fredericktown, Pa.; rsch. asst. Physical Edn. Dept. U. N.C., Greensboro; instr. phys. edn., health coord. Lakeside Elem. Sch., Orange Park, Fla., 1986—. Mem. exec. bd. dirs. Fla. Striders CORE Team Curriculum Coun. Active in civic orgns., bd. dirs. Clay County Tchrs. Acad. Excellence, 1994—. Recipient World Fellowship award for Outstanding Young Scholar, 1987, cert. of Outstanding Achievment in Elem. PE, 1987, Supt.'s Cert. of Achievement Clay County Sch. Bd., 1987, Gov.'s Leadership award, 1988, Unsung Hero of Yr. award, Jacksonville Track Club, 1989; named to Young Profl. Hall of Fame, 1987: named Tchr. of Yr. Lakeside Elem. Sch., 1995, Fla. Phys. Edn. Tchr. of Yr., 1999-2000, Model Phys. Edn. Program of Yr., Fla., 2000; dist finalist for Tchr. of Yr., Clay County Schs., 1995. Mem. AAHPERD, Fla. Alliance for Health, Phys. Edn., Recreation and Dance (Profl. Recognition awards 1995, 2001), Am. Running and Fitness Assn., Clay County Reading Coun., Clay County Edn. Assn., Nat. Assn. for Edn. of Young Children, Nat. Assn. for Sports and Phys. Edn., Nat. Assn. for Girls and Women in Sports, Phi Epsilon Kappa (Outstanding PE Major award 1982), Sigma Sigma Kappa. Office: Lakeside Elem Sch 2752 Moody Rd Orange Park FL 32073

TRACEY, TERENCE JOHN, psychology educator; b. Washington, Mar. 2, 1952; s. Gerald A. and Virginia R. Tracey; m. Cheelan Bo Linn, Aug. 11, 1979 (div. 1990; children: Beilee, Erin, Cameron; m. Cynthia Glidden, Jan. 1, 1995; 1 child, Trevor. BA, Cornell U., 1974; MS in Edn., U. Kans., 1977; PhD, U. Md., 1981. Registered psychologist, Ill., N.Y. Psychologist SUNY, Buffalo, 1981-83; prof. ednl. psychology and psychology U. Ill., Champaign, 1983-99, acting assoc. chair dept. ednl. psychology, 1986-89, assoc. chair, dept. ednl. psychology, 1995-97, dir. tng. divsn. counseling psychology, 1988-91, 98-99; prof., dir. tng. counseling psychology, inerim assoc. dean Coll. Edn., Ariz. State U., 1999—. Therapist Psychol. Clinic, Champaign, 1984-99; cons. VA Med. Ctr., Danville, ill., 1985-99. Assoc. editor Jour. Counseling Psychology; contbr. over 100 articles to profl. jours., chpts. to books. Fellow APA, Am. Psychol. Soc., Am. Assn. Applied and Preventative Psychology; mem. Am. Ednl. Rsch. Assn. (com. chair 1987-89, Outstanding Rsch. award 1989, 97). Avocation: squash. Office: Ariz State U PO Box 870611 Tempe AZ 85287-0611

TRACEY, VALERIE LEWIS, special education educator; b. N.Y.C., Dec. 20, 1953; d. Alvin Walter and Vida Arlene (Davies) Lewis; m. Steven William Tracey, Aug. 15, 1981; children: Sean Michael, Heather Brianna. BS, So. Conn. State U., 1975, MS, 1981. Cert. tchr. spl. edn., phys. edn. Tchr. phys. edn. Danbury (Conn.) Pub. Schs., 1975-79, tchr. spl. edn., 1980—. Recipient Recognition award Coun. Exceptional Children, 1991. Mem. ASCD, Phi Delta Kappa. Home: 13 Hawthorne Hill Rd Newtown CT 06470-1404 Office: Rogers Park Mid Sch 21 Memorial Dr Danbury CT 06810-8005

TRACHTENBERG, STEPHEN JOEL, university president; b. Bklyn., Dec. 14, 1937; s. Oscar M. and Shoshana G. (Weinstock) Trachtenberg; m. Francine Zorn, June 24, 1971; children: Adam Maccabee, Ben-Lev. BA, Columbia U., 1959; JD, Yale U., 1962; M in Pub. Adminstrn., Harvard U., 1966; LHD (hon.), Trinity Coll., 1986; HHD (hon.), U. Hartford, 1989; LLD (hon.), Hanyang U., Seoul, 1990; DPA (hon.), Kyonggi U., Seoul, 1994; LLD (hon.), Richmond Coll., London, 1995; MD (hon.), Odessa State Med. U., Ukraine, 1996; LLD (hon.), Mount Vernon Coll., 1997; LHD (hon.), Boston U., 1999, Gratz Coll., 1999; LLD (hon.), So. Conn. State U., 2001, U. New Haven, 2002. Bar: N.Y. 1964, U.S. Supreme Ct. 1967. Atty. AEC, 1962—65; legis. asst. to Congressman John Brademas of Ind., Washington, 1965; tutor law Harvard Coll.; tchg. fellow edn. and pub. policy J.F. Kennedy Grad. Sch. Govt., Harvard U., 1965—66; spl. asst. to U.S. edn. commr. Office of Edn., HEW, Washington, 1966—68; assoc. prof. polit. sci. Boston U., 1969—77, assoc. dean, 1969—70, dean, 1970—74, v.p. acad. svcs., 1976—77, assoc. v.p., co-counsel, 1974—76; pres., prof. pub. adminstrn. U. Hartford, Conn., 1977—88, George Washington U., Washington, 1988—. Adv. bd. The Presidency; mem. Fed. City Coun.; bd. dirs. Consortium of Univs. Washington Met. Area, Riggs Bank, Greater Washington Bd. Trade, Nat. Edn. Telecom. Orgn., Washington Rsch. Libr. Consortium, DC Com. to Promote Washington; exec. adv. coun. SCT Edn. Sys. Contbr. articles to profl. jours. Trustee Al-Akhawayn U., Morocco, Com. for Econ. Devel.; active 2001 U.S. Savs. Bonds Vol. Com.; chmn. Md./DC Selection Com., 1998—2003, Rhodes Scholarships; active D.C. Mayor's Bus. Adv. Coun.; exec. panel Chief Naval Ops.; bd. overseers List Coll. Jewish Theol. Sem. Am.; bd. dirs. Urban League, Washington; chair, bd. dirs. D.C. C. of C.; chair, pres. council Atlantic 10 Conf.; mem. bd. dirs. Chiang Indsl. Charity Found., Hong Kong. Decorated Grand Officier du Wissam Al Alaoui King Mohammed VI of Morocco; named Outstanding Young Person, Boston Jr. C. of C., 1970, Alumnus of Yr., James Madison H.S., Bklyn., 1982, Washingtonian of Yr., Washingtonian Mag., 2000, Jan. 22, 1998 Stephen Joel Trachtenberg Day, D.C. City Council, Feb. 2, 1999 Stephen Joel Trachtenberg Day, Mayor of San Francisco; named one of 100 Young Leaders, Acad. Am. Council Learning, 1978, Fifty Outstanding

Alumni Problem Solvers, Harvard's John F. Kennedy Sch. Govt., 1987, "The 2002 Forty Foward" Annual List 40 Most Influential People in Town, Wash. Bus. Forward mag., 2002; recipient Myrtle Wreath award, Hadassah, 1982, Scopus award, Am. Friends of Hebrew U., 1984, Human Rels. award, NCCJ, 1987, NAACP award, 1988, Conn. Bar Assn. citation, 1988, Univ. medal of highest honor, Kyung Hee U., Korea, 1990, Martin Luther King, Jr. Internat. Salute award, 1992, Hannah G. Solomon award, Nat. Coun. Jewish Women, 1992, Father of Yr. award, Washington Urban League, 1993, Univ. Pres. medal, Kyonggi U., Korea, 1993, Merit award, Am. Czech and Slovak Assn., 1993, John Jay award, Columbia U., 1995, Spirit of Democracy award, Am. Jewish Congress, 1995, Newcomen Soc. award, 1995, Disting. Achievement medal, Greenberg Ctr. for Judaic Studies U. Hartford, 1995, Humanitarian award, B'nai B'rith, 1996, Disting. Pub. Svc. award, U.S. Dept. of State Sec.'s Open Forum, 1997, Tree of Life award, Jewish Nat. Fund, 1999, High Twelve Internat. Founders award, 2000, Key of Life award, Egypt's Internat. Econ. Forum, 2001, medal of merit, U.S. Dept. Treasury, 2001, Father Yr. award, Am. Diabetes Assn., 2002, Humanitarian award, The Albert B. Sabin Vaccine Inst., 2003; fellow Winston Churchill, Eng., 1969, Hon. Wolcott fellow, 1999, Morse Coll. Yale U. Fellow: Am. Acad. Arts and Scis.; mem.: Bus.-Higher Edn. Forum, Ind. Retail Cattleman's Assn. (adv. coun.), Sr. Soc. Sachems, Coun. Fgn. Rels., Newcomen Soc. U.S. (life; trustee), Am. Coun. Learned Soc. (assoc.), Internat. Assn. Univ. Pres. (N.Am. coun.), N.Y. Acad. Scis., Am. Assn. Univ. Adminstrs. (pres. 1998—2000, Disting. Svc. award 1996), Council for the United Nations U. (vice chair), Hannibal Club, Nat. Press Club, Cosmos Club, Harvard Club, Tumble Brook Country Club, Univ. Club, George Washington U. Club, Masons (33d degree, Grand Cross award), Phi Beta Kappa. Office: George Washington U Office of Pres 2121 Eye St N W Rm 802 Washington DC 20052-0001

TRACHUK, LILLIAN ELIZABETH, music educator; b. Monroe, Wis., July 28, 1921; d. William John Blair and Stella Mae Harness-Blair; m. Max A. Trachuk, Dec. 21, 1949 (dec. Sept. 1983); children: Thomas Max, William Anton. Piano tchr., Newport News, Va., 1964—. Home: 101 Burnham Pl Newport News VA 23606

TRACI, KATHLEEN FRANCES, library media specialist; b. Chgo., Jan. 13, 1943; d. William Henry and Mary Teresa (O'Connor) Kammien; m. Paul A. Traci, Nov. 25, 1965; children: Sean, Meg, Beth, Patricia. MLS, U. Wis., 1975; EdS, Butler U., 1991; EdD, Ind. U., 1998. Libr. media specialist Waukesha (Wis.) Elem. Sch., 1976-84, Butler Middle Sch., Waukesha, 1984-86; libr. Marian Coll., Indpls., 1987-88; libr. media specialist Noblesville (Ind.) Middle Sch., 1990-91, Decatur Ctrl. High Sch., Indpls., 1991—98; dir. libr. media svcs. Rockford (Ill.) Pub. Schs. #205, 1999—. Pres. Friends of Hussey-Mayfield Libr., Zionsville, Ind.; bd. dirs. Rock Valley C.C. Libr., Rockford Pub. Libr. Found. Mem. ALA, ASCD, Am. Assn. Sch. Librs., Ill. Sch. Libr. Media Assn., Ind. U. Sch. Adminstrs. Assn. Avocations: swimming, exercising, reading, storytelling, fishing. Home: 2640 Saddlebrook Dr Naperville IL 60564-4623 Office: Libr Media Svcs Dept/Sterling Holley Ctr Rockford Pub Schs 2000 Christina St Rockford IL 61104 E-mail: tracik@rps205.com.

TRACY, CHRISTINA L. secondary school educator; b. Marshall, Ill., June 12, 1942; d. Lawrence and Kathryn (Setzer) Goekler; m. Darrell M. Tracy, Nov. 28, 1964; children: Lawrence, Melissa, Melanie, Megan, Mynda. BS in Edn., Ea. Ill. U., 1964; postgrad., Ill. State U. Cert. secondary chemistry, math., physics, computer edn. tchr., Ill. Chemistry, physics, computer, biology, environ. sci. and math. tchr. Arcola (Ill.) High Sch., 1964-65, Rossville (Ill.)-Alvin High Sch., 1966—. State student advisor Ill. Jr. Acad. Sci., 1985-2000. Leader 4-H Club, Rossville, 1966-91; pres. Rossville Jr. Women's Club, 1971; pres., trustee Vermilion County Conservation Dist., Danville, Ill., 1980-89. Recipient Rsch. Sci. Tchr. award Sigma Xi, 1991, Golden Apple award, 1996. Mem. Ill. Beta Clubs (state pres. 1997-99). Office: Rossville-Alvin High Sch 350 N Chicago St Rossville IL 60963-9700

TRACY, PATRICIA ANN KOOP, secondary school educator; b. Chickasaw, Ala., Sept. 28, 1947; d. Augustus Galloway Koop and Mildred (Willingham) Koop Conlon; m. Charles Gerald Tracy, Jan. 24, 1970; children: Charles Gerald Jr., William Todd, Michael Patrick. BS in Edn., U. Ala., Tuscaloosa, 1970; postgrad., Ala. State U., Montgomery, 1988, Troy State U., 1989, U. Ala., Huntsville, 1989, Ala. State U., 1995, Auburn U., Montgomery, 1994. Cert. secondary sci. tchr., elem. tchr. Tchr. sci. St. Bede Sch., Montgomery, Ala., 1986-90, coord. Sci. Fair, head dept. sci., 1986-90; libr., media specialist Our Lady Queen Mercy Sch., 1992-93, libr., media specialist, computer tchr., 1993-94, mem. libr. and media, earth sci. tchr., 1994-98; tchr. Wetumpka Jr. H.S., 1998—. Chair sci. dept. Wetumpka Jr. H.S., 2001—; sponsor Ala. Math. & Sci. Bowl Competition, Bayer/NSF Cmty. Grant, sci. club; established reading program for grades K-8 involving parents of K-2 and computers in grades 3-8; developed hands-on approach in media with filmstrip, book tapes, computer games and other games involving cognitive skills; sci. fair co-coord., 1994—. Mem.: Ala. Sci. Tchrs. Assn., Nat. Cath. Edn. Assn., Ala. Edn. Assn., Wetumpka H.S. PTO, Ala. Alumni Assn., Montgomery Cath. H.S. PTO, Ala. Conservancy, Ala. Mus. Natural History, Delta Kappa Gamma, Alpha Xi Delta. Roman Catholic. Avocations: crafts, water sports, reading, gardening, work for cleaner environment. Home: 2424 Trotters Trl Wetumpka AL 36093-2311 Office: 170 S Ann Electric Eclectic AL 36024

TRACY, ROBERT (ROBERT EDWARD TRACY), English language educator, poetry translator; b. Woburn, Mass., Nov. 23, 1928; s. Hubert William and Vera Mary (Hurley) T.; m. Rebecca Garrison, Aug. 26, 1956; children: Jessica Janes, Hugh Garrison, Dominick O'Donovan. AB in Greek with honors, Boston Coll., 1950; MA, Harvard U., 1954, PhD, 1960. Teaching fellow Harvard U., Cambridge, Mass., 1954-58; instr. Carleton Coll., Northfield, Minn., 1958-60; from asst. prof. English, to assoc. prof., then prof. U. Calif., Berkeley, 1960-89, prof. English and Celtic Studies, 1989—, assoc. dir. Dickens Project, 1994-95. Vis. prof., Bruern fellow in Am. studies U. Leeds, Eng., 1965-66; vis. prof., Leverhulme fellow Trinity Coll., Dublin, 1971-72; vis. Kathryn W. Davis prof. slavic studies Wellesley (Mass.) Coll., 1979; Charles Mills Gayley lectr. U. Calif., Berkeley, 1989-90; vis. prof. Anglo-Irish lit. Trinity Coll., 1995-96. Author: Trollope's Later Novels, 1978, The Unappeasable Host: Studies in Irish Identities, 1998; translator (poems by Osip Mandelstam): Stone, 1981, 2d edit., 1991; editor J.M Synge's The Aran Islands, 1962, The Way We Live Now (Anthony Trollope), 1974, The Macdermots of Ballycloran (Anthony Trollope), 1989, Nina Balatka and Linda Tressel (Anthony Trollope), 1991, In A Glass Darkly (Sheridan Le Fanu) 1993, Rhapsody in Stephen's Green (Flann O'Brien), 1994; adv. editor The Recorder, 1985—, LIT (Lit., Interpretation, Theory), 1989—, Dickens Studies Annual, 2001—; contbr. articles and revs. to numerous jours. including Shakespeare Quarterly, So. Rev., Nineteenth-Century Fiction, Irish Univ. Rev., Eire-Ireland, Irish Literary Supplement, others; poetry translations in New Orleans Rev., Poetry, N.Y. Rev. of Books, Ploughshares, others. Appointed mem. cultural panel San Francisco-Cork Sister City Com. Fulbright travel grantee, 1965-66; recipient humanities research fellowships U. Calif., Berkeley, 1962, 69, 78, 81, 86, 92; Guggenheim fellow, 1981-82. Mem. MLA, Philol. Assn. Pacific Coast, Am. Conf. for Irish Studies, Internat. Assn. for Study of Irish Lit. Avocation: exploring western Ireland and no. Calif. Office: U Calif Dept English Berkeley CA 94720-1030

TRACY, TRACY FAIRCLOTH, special education educator; b. Washington, Aug. 22, 1961; d. James Claybert and Esther (Harrell) Faircloth; m. Charles Randall Tracy, Aug. 16, 1986; children: James Wren, Corissa Estelle. BS in Spl. Edn.-Mental Retardation, Old Dominion U., 1983. Tchr. Newport News (Va.) Pub. Schs., 1983—, cmty.-based instrn. specialist, 1992—2000, cmty.-based program adminstr., 2001—. Leader Camp Fire, Inc., Newport News, 1983—92; vol. Newport News Spl. Olympics, 1984—, treas., 1987—; active Va. PTA, Nat. PTA. Named to Outstanding Young Women Am., 1988; recipient Outstanding Svc. award, Newport News Spl. Olympics, 1986, 1988, 1990, Citizenship award, Denbigh Kiwanis, 1988, Appreciation award, Hampton-Newport News Cmty. Svcs. Bd., 1989, included in Am. Registry of Outstanding Profl. Mem.: Student Coun. Exceptional Children (pres. 1982—83), Coun. Exceptional Children, Assn. Retarded Citizens, Alpha Chi, Kappa Delta Pi (Nu Eta chpt.). Democrat. Methodist. Avocations: arts and crafts, swimming, walking. Home: 4708 Harlequin Way Chesapeake VA 23321-1247 Office: Enterprise Acad 813 Diligence Dr Ste 110 Newport News VA 23606-4237 E-mail: ctracywin@cox.net.

TRAFALIS, THEODOROS VASSILIOS, industrial engineering educator; b. Athens, Attica, Greece, Sept. 17, 1959; came to U.S., 1982; s. Vassilios and Joanna (Demesticha) T.; m. Irini Iordani Nerantzopoulou, Aug. 17, 1987. BS in Maths., U. Athens, 1982; MS in Maths., Purdue U., West LaFayette, Ind., 1984, MS in Indsl. Engring., 1987, PhD in Ops. Rsch., 1989. Instr. dept. maths. Purdue U., West Lafayette, 1982-89, vis. asst. prof. indsl. engring., 1989-90; asst. prof. indsl. engring. U. Okla., Norman, 1991-97, assoc. prof. indsl. engring., 1997—2002, prof. indsl. engring., 2002—. Vis. asst. prof. CUST, U. Blaise Pascal, France, 1998; vis. assoc. prof. Tech. U. Crete, Greece, 1998; invited lectr. XIV Sys. Engring. Meeting, Santiago, Chile, 1989; spkr. in field. Contbr. articles to profl. jours. Pres. Hellenic Student Assn. Purdue U., 1987-89, faculty advisor, 1989-90. With Greek Navy, 1990. Recipient Rsch. Initiation award NSF, others, 1991—; U. Athens scholar, 1978-82; Purdue U. fellow, 1982, David Ross Found. fellow, 1988, 89; Kerr McGee Disting. lectr. U. Okla., 1995; Pres.'s fellow U. Okla., 1996; Rsch. fellow Delft Tech. U., 1996, Akita Perfectural U., Japan, 2001. Mem. Ops. Rsch. Soc. Am., Hellenic Operational Soc., Soc. Indsl. and Applied Maths., Engring. Edn., Internat. Soc. Multiple Criteria Decision Making, Inst. Indsl. Engrs., Internat. Soc. Neural Networks, Omega Rho. Avocations: swimming, tennis, photography. Office: 202 W Boyd Rm 124 Norman OK 73019

TRAINA, RICHARD PAUL, academic administrator; b. San Francisco, June 3, 1937; s. Frank Ignatius and Isabelle (Thomas) T.; m. Margaret Bradley Warner, June 6, 1959; children: Cristina Traina Hutchison, Michelle Traina Riecke, Matthew Warner, Michael Derek BA, U. Santa Clara, 1958; MA, U. Calif., Berkeley, 1960, PhD, 1964. Instr. history Wabash Coll., Crawfordsville, Ind., 1963-64, asst. prof., 1964-68, assoc. prof., 1968-74, dean, 1969-74; dean, prof. Franklin & Marshall Coll., Lancaster, Pa., 1974-81, acad. v.p., dean, 1981-84; pres. Clark U., Worcester, Mass., 1984-2000. Author: American Diplomacy and the Spanish Civil War, 1968; co-editor: (with A. Rappaport) Present in the Past, 1972 Bd. dirs. Alden Trust, 2001—. Mem. Orgns. of Am. Historians, Soc. for Values in Higher Edn. Democrat. Roman Catholic. Home: 50 Salisbury St Unit 44 Worcester MA 01609-3130

TRAINES, ROSE WUNDERBAUM, sculptor, educator; b. Monroeville, Ind., Sept. 13, 1928; d. Louis and Leah (Fogel) Wunderbaum; m. Robert Jacob Traines, June 25, 1949; children: Claudia Denise Traines Lang, Monica Rae Traines Martin. Student, Ind. State Tchr.'s Coll., 1946—48, Mich. State U., 1948—49; BS, Ctrl. Mich. U., 1951. Lectr. in field. One person shows include Ctrl. Mich. U., Mt. Pleasant, 1964, Alma Artmobile, Mich., 1972, Ctrl. Mich. Homecoming, Mount Pleasant, Mich., 1982, Internat. Inst. Scrap Iron and Steel, Inc., Washington, 1983, Fontainebleau Hotel, Miami Beach, Fla., 1983, Elliott Mus. Art Gallery, Stuart, Fla., 1988, 98, Walt Kuhn Gallery, Cape Neddick, Maine, 1988, Coll. Club of Boston, 1990, Brass Latch Gallery, Montpelier, Ind., 1991, 96, 98, Vero Beach Ctr. for the Arts, Fla., 1992, Maritime and Yachting Mus., Stuart, Fla., 1997, Mid-Mich. Regional Med. Ctr., Healing Arts Gallery, Midland, 1997, Northwood Gallery, Midland, Mich., Commerca Bank Art Series, Palm Beach Gardens, 2002, Gallery Five, Tequesta, Fla., 2002, Michigan U. Park Libr. Gallery, 2002, Art Reach of Mid. Mich., Mt. Pleasant, 2002; two-person shows include Gallery One, North Palm Beach, 1973, Midland Ctr. for the Arts, Mich., 1976, Springfield Art Mart, Ohio, 1977, Hillel Student Ctr. Gallery-U. Cin., 1993, others; exhibited in group shows including Saginaw Mus. Art, Mich., 1965, Grand Rapids Mus., Mich., 1966, Kalamazoo Mus., Mich., 1967, Kellogg/Kresge Art Ctr., Mich. State U., East Lansing, 1967, Art Reach Mid-Mich., Mount Pleasant Mich., 1987, Salmagundi Club, N.Y.C., 1988, 91-92, 96, Copley Soc., Boston, 1990, 95, Allied Artists of Am., Inc., N.Y.C., 1995-96, Self Family Arts Ctr., Hilton Head Island, S.C., 1996-97, Palm Beach Gardens Fla. City Hall, 2003, Palm Beach Gardens Cmty. Ctr., 2003, others; represented in permanent collections at Dow-Corning Corp. Collection, Midland Ctr. for the Arts, Elliott Mus., Stuart, Fla., Walt Kuhn Gallery, Maine, Pullen Elem. Sch., Isabella Bank and Trust Co., Ctrl. Mich. U., Blake Libr, Stuart, Fla., La Belle Mgmt. Corp., Morey Bandit Industries, Mich., Ctrl. Mich. Cmty. Hosp., Northwood U., The Vets. Meml. Libr., Brass Latch Gallery, others. Tchr. Jewish Sunday Sch., Mt. Pleasant, 1955-70; officer Child and Youth Study Clubs, Mt. Pleasant, 1963-73; mem. City Recreation Commn., Mt. Pleasant, 1963-73, Area Health Planning Coun., Mt. Pleasant, 1974-80; pres., vol. Hosp. Aux. Med. Care, Red Cross Blood Bank, United Fund Cancer Dr., Mt. Pleasant, 1960-80; storyteller pub. libr., Mt. Pleasant, 1957-79. Recipient Northwood U. Artist award, Midland Ctr. for Arts, Mich., 2002. Mem.: Brass Latch Gallery, Art Reach of Mid-Mich., Hilton Head Art League S.C. (Lifetime of Creative Excellence award 1998), Copley Soc. Boston (signature mem.), Allied Artists of Am. (Mems. award of merit 1996, Raymond H. Brumer Meml. award 1999), Nat. Mus. of Women in Arts (charter), Salmagundi Club (Philip Isenberg award 1993, Pamela Singleton award 1997, Elliot Liskin Meml. award 1998, Anonymous award 1998, Peters Sculpture Materials award 2001, Alphaeus P. Cole Meml. award 2001, Mems. Meml. award 2003). Jewish. Avocations: lecturing, community work, tennis, presenting humorous programs, drums. Home: 1217 North Dr Mount Pleasant MI 48858-3226

TRAINOR, JERRY ALLEN, vocational education professional; b. Pablo, Mont., May 19, 1937; s. Harry Frances and Eva Grace (Simonis) T.; m. Joyce Evelyn Rice, July 2, 1962 (div. 1970); 1 child, Darryn Sean; m. Helen Elizabeth Wahl, Aug. 29, 1974; children: Hillary Gay, Erin Lane Estein. BS in Edn., U. Idaho, 1987, MEd, 1989. Asst. prof. welding tech. Lewis and Clark State Coll., Lewiston, Idaho, 1983-89; coord. Cen. Idaho Vocat. Edn. Consortium, Lapwai, 1989-91; vocat. counselor Alaska Tech. Ctr., Kotzebue, 1991-93; career counselor, job devel. specialist Arctic Sivunmun Ilisagvik Coll., Barrow, Alaska. Bd. dirs. Profl. Devel. for Educators, State of Idaho, 1987; presenter at profl. confs. Contbr. articles to profl. publs; author curriculum materials. Mem. Winter Carnival com., Prince George, B.C., Can., 1975; regional rep. Libertarian Party Idaho, 1986. Winner various ice racing and hill climbing competitions Can. Auto Sports Club; named New Vocat. Educator of Yr. State of Idaho, 1986. Mem. NEA, ASCD, Am. Vocat. Assn., Phi Delta Kappa. Nazarene. Avocations: automobile racing, snowmachine touring, hunting, photography. Office: Arctic Sivunmun Ilisagvik Coll PO Box 749 Barrow AK 99723-0749

TRAINOR, JOHN FELIX, retired economics educator; b. Mpls., Dec. 1, 1921; s. James Patrick and Myra Catherine (Pauly) T.; m. Margaret Dolores Pudenz, July 3, 1965 (dec. 1977); children: John Anthony, Patrick James. BA cum laude, Coll. St. Thomas, 1943; MA, U. Minn., 1950; PhD, Wash. State U., 1970. Instr. high sch., Mpls., 1946-47; instr. Coll. St. Thomas, 1949-50; v.p. Trainor Candy Co., Mpls., 1949-56; instr., asst. prof. econs. Rockhurst Coll., Kansas City, Mo., 1956-62; instr. Wash. State U., Pullman, 1966-67; asst. prof. Minn. State U., Moorhead, 1967—70, assoc. prof. econs., 1971-87, prof. econ., 1988-89, chmn. dept. econs., 1981-89; prof. emeritus, 1989—. Pres. Minn. Econs. Assn., 1976—77. Author: (with Frank J. Kottke) The Nursing Home Industry in the State of Washington, 1968. Ensign to Lt. (j.g.) USNR, 1943-46, ETO. Mem. Assn. Social Econs., Omicron Delta Epsilon. Roman Catholic. Avocations: hiking, reading, solving and constructing crossword puzzles. Home: 1333 4th Ave S Moorhead MN 56560-2971

TRAN, NAM VAN, health education specialist; b. Saigon, Vietnam, July 29, 1943; came to U.S., 1983; s. Giap Van Tran and Thai Thi Nguyen; m. Hien Quy Pham; children: Kelly, Peter, Linda. MD, U. Saigon, 1969; MPH, U. Hawaii, 1987. Instr. U. Saigon Sch. Medicine, 1968-70; attending physician, chief dermatology dept. Naval Hosp., Saigon, South Vietnam, 1970-75; attending physician, dermatology Venereology Hosp., Ho Chi Minh City, 1977-83; asst. project dir. Health is Gold U. Calif., San Francisco, 1988-90; health edn. specialist Santa Clara Valley Health and Hosp. Sys., San Jose, Calif., 1990—. Pub. health cons. Asian Am. Cmty. Involvement, San Jose, Calif., 1990-94, Alexian Brothers Hosp., San Jose, 1992—. Author: How to Stop Smoking, 1990, How to Protect Your Health, 1992, Delivery: Easily & Pleasantly, 1995, Health is Gold, 1996. Recipient commendation City of San Jose, 1990. Mem. APHA, Vietnamese Physicians Assn. No. Calif. (bd. dirs. 1992-96, award 1994, 1996), Vietnamese Physicians Assn. of Free World, Vietnamese Physicians Assn. of USA. Avocations: reading, listening to music. Home: 884 Coventry Way Milpitas CA 95035-3587 Office: Santa Clara Valley Health and Hosp Sys 595 Millich Dr Ste 100 Campbell CA 95008-0550

TRANI, EUGENE PAUL, university president, educator; b. Bklyn., Nov. 2, 1939; s. Frank Joseph and Rose Gertrude (Kelly) T.; m. Lois Elizabeth Quigley, June 2, 1962; children: Anne Chapman, Frank. BA in History with honors, U. Notre Dame, 1961; MA, Ind. U., 1963, PhD, 1966. Instr. history Ohio State U., Columbus, 1965-67; asst. prof. So. Ill. U., Carbondale, 1967-71, assoc. prof., 1971-75, prof., 1975-76; asst. v.p. acad. affairs, prof. U. Nebr., 1976-80; prof., vice chancellor acad. affairs U. Mo. Kansas City, 1980-86; prof., v.p. acad. affairs U. Wis. System, 1986-90; pres. Va. Commonwealth U., 1990—; pres. bd. dirs. Va. Biotech Rsch. Park, 1992-97, chmn., 1997—; pres., chmn. VCU Health Sys., 2000—. Vis. asst. prof. U. Wis., Milw., 1969; bd. dirs. Met. Richmond SunTrust Mid-Atlantic Bank, SunTrust Mid-Atlantic Bank, Universal Corp., LandAm. Fin. Group, Inc.; mem. commn. Internat. Edn. Am. Coun. Ed., 1991—; bd. gov. Ctr. Russian Am. Bus., Washington, 1993-98; adv. coun. on Grad. Studies and Rsch., U. Notre Dame, 1994—, NASULGC, 1980—, chair commn. on internat. affairs, 1993-94; vis. prof. Univ. Coll., Dublin, 2002; bd. advisors Inst. for U.S. Studies, U. London, 1993-99; cons. in field. Author, editor: Concerns of a Conservative Democrat, 1968, The Treaty of Portsmouth: An Adventure in American Diplomacy, 1969, (with Donald E. Davis) The First Cold War, 2002; The Secretaries of the Department of the Interior, 1849-69, 1975, (with David Wilson) The Presidency of Warren G. Harding, 3d edit., 1989; contbr. articles to profl. jours., newspapers; book reviewer. Permanent mem. Coun. Fgn. Rels., N.Y.C., 1979—; bd. dirs. Richmond Ballet, 1991-96, NCCJ, Richmond, 1991-94, Va. Spl. Olympics, 1991-96, YMCA of Greater Richmond, 1992—, Richmond Renaissance, 1992-96, 2001—, chmn., 2001—; bd. dirs. Met. Bus. Found., 1992-98; mem. U.S. Savs. Bond Vol. Com., chmn. higher edn. area, 1992-93; adv. bd. Greater Richmond chpt. ARC, 1992—; mem. Gov.'s Commn. Info. Tech. in Va., 1998-2000; bd. dirs. Collegiate Sch., 1998—; adv. bd. Black History Archives Project, 1992-96; bd. dirs. Va. Ctr. for Innovative Tech., 1990-96, Capital Area Assembly, 1990-93, Richmond Symphony, 1991-94, Richmond Symphony Coun., 1995—; mem. coun. advisors Christian Children's Fund, 1992-95; mem. Ctrl. Richmond Assn., 1992-96; bd. trustees Va. Hist. Soc., 1994-96, Theatre Va., 1994-97, Richmond Children's Mus., 1994—, World Affairs Coun. of Greater Richmond, 1999-2003; bd. dirs. Sci. Mus. of Va. Found., 1994—; mem. Gov.'s Biotech. Initiative Adv. Bd., 2002—; bd. dirs. Qatar Found. for Edn. Sci. Comm. Devel. Fellow Russian and East European Inst., 1964-65, Nat. Hist. Publs. Commn., 1969-70, Woodrow Wilson Internat. Ctr. Scholars, 1972-73, So. Ill. U. Sabbatical Leave, 1975-76, Coun. Internat. Exchange Scholars, 1981, U. Mo. Faculty, 1981; grantee U.S. Dept. Interior Rsch., 1965-66, So. Ill. U. Office Rsch. and Projects, 1967-74, Am. Philos. Soc., 1968, 72, So. Ill U. Summer Rsch. 1970, 72, 75, Lilly Endowment, 1975-76, Sloan Commn. Govt. and Higher Edn., 1978, USIA Am. Participants Program, 1984-86, 88, 90; Inst. for U.S. Studies fellow U. London, 1995, fellow commoner St. John's Coll., Cambridge, 1998; recipient Younger Humanist award NEH, 1972-73, Leadership and Achievement award Ctrl. Richmond Assn., 1992, Biotech. Leadership award Va. Biotech. Assn., 1999; recipient Disting. Leadership award, Nat. Assn. Cmty. Leaders, 1994, Richmond Humanitarian award, NCCJ, 1995, Flame Bearer of Edn. award Coll. Fund/UNCF, 1998, Richmond Joint Engrs. Coun. Cmty. Svc. award, 2002; named Style Mag. Richmonder of Yr., 1998, Hope award, Nat. MS Soc., 2003, others. Mem. Internat. Inst. Strategic Studies, Am. Assn. Advancement Slavic Studies, Orgn. Am. Historians, Soc. Historians Am. Fgn. Rels., Greater Richmond C. of C. (bd. dirs. 1991-96, chmn. 1997-98), Phi Kappa Phi. Roman Catholic. Avocations: reading, travel, basketball, golf. Office: Va Commonwealth U Box 842512 910 W Franklin St Richmond VA 23284-2512 E-mail: etrani@vcu.edu.

TRAPASSO, JOSEPH ANGELO, secondary school educator, coach; b. Albany, N.Y., July 17, 1951; s. Joseph Angelo and Patricia Mary (Vennard) T.; m. Darcie Jo Turner, Apr. 16, 1993; 1 child, Stephanie Anne. BA in Bus. Econs., LeMoyne Coll., 1973; postgrad., U. Albany, 1974-75, St. Rose Coll., 1975-76. Phys. edn. tchr. Cathedral Acad., Albany, N.Y., 1974-75; bus. tchr., jr. varsity basketball coach Cardinal McCloskey H.S., Albany, N.Y., 1975-76; bus. tchr., dept. chmn. Cath. Ctrl. H.S., Troy, N.Y., 1976—, varsity tennis coach, 1977-79, head and asst. basketball coach, 1978, 80, 82, bus. dept. chairperson, 1984—, N.Y. State mock trial tchr., coach, 1985—, acad. sports advisor, 1990-91, 92, faculty senate pres., 1994—. Asst. tennis coach U. Albany, 1994—; co-owner The Darcie Trapasso Summer Tennis Camp, 1993—. Basketball coach Cathedral Acad., Albany, 1974-75; head tennis coach Siena Coll., Loudonville, N.Y., 1979-94; trustee Guilderland (N.Y.) Town Libr., 1987-88; tennis dir. Guilderland Parks and Recreation, summers 1980, 81, 82; tournament dir. women's tennis N.Y. State Divsn. III Athletic Assn., 1984, 85, 86. Named Mock Trial County Champion, Rensalaer N.Y. Bar Assn., 1980s, 90s. Mem. NCAA, Nat. Bus. Educator Assn. Am., Bus. and Mktg. Educators Assn. Capital Dist., Intercollegiate Tennis Assn., U.S. Tennis Assn. Avocations: tennis, jogging, writing poetry, listening to music, reading short stories. Home and Office: 25 Parkwood St Albany NY 12203-3625

TRAPHAN, BERNARD RICHARD, computer scientist, educator; b. Stamford, Conn., Feb. 7, 1967; s. Bernard Richard and Elizabeth (Biagiotti) T. BS in Computer Sci., Fla. State U., 1990, EdS in Coll. Teaching, 1991, MS in Computer Sci., MBA, 1993, postgrad., 1993—. Pres., CEO MicroSonic Software, Tallahassee, Fla., 1983—; teaching asst. dept. computer sci., rsch. asst. ednl. rsch. Fla. State U., Tallahassee, 1990-91; computer analyst Fla. Ho. of Reps., Tallahassee, 1990-91; fin. analyst Dept. of Air Force, Washington, 1992—; internat. pres. Student Advocate Assembly, Tallahassee, 1991—. Chair Fla. Congress of Grad. Students, Tallahassee, 1993—. Contbr. articles to profl. pubs. Candidate for sch. supt. Leon County Schs., Fla., 1992. Mem. Assn. Computing Machinery (vice-chair 1989-91), Mortar Bd., Mensa, Phi Beta Kappa, Phi Kappa Phi. Avocations: basketball, baseball, piano, guitar, bass. Office: Student Advocate Assembly 619 S Woodward Ave Ste 20528 Tallahassee FL 32304-4339

TRAUB, J(OSEPH) F(REDERICK), computer scientist, educator; b. June 24, 1932; m. Pamela Ann McCorduck, Dec. 6, 1969; children: Claudia Renee, Hillary Anne. BS, CCNY, 1954; PhD, Columbia U., 1959; DSc (hon.), U. Cen. Fla., 2001. Tech. staff Bell Labs., Murray Hill, N.J., 1959-70; prof. computer sci. and math., head dept. computer sci. Carnegie-Mellon U., Pitts., 1971-79; Edwin Howard Armstrong prof. computer sci., chmn. dept., prof. math. Columbia U., 1979-86; prof. computer sci.

Princeton (N.J.) U., 1986-87; pres. John Von Neumann Nat. Supercomputer Ctr., Consortium for Sci. Computing, Princeton, 1986-87; Edwin Howard Armstrong prof., chmn. dept. computer sci., prof. math. Columbia U., N.Y.C., 1987-89, Edwin Howard Armstrong prof. computer sci., math., 1989—; external prof. Santa Fe Inst., 1995-98; fellow Biosgroup, 1998—2003. Dir. N.Y. State Ctr. Computers and Info. Systems, 1982-88; disting. lectr. MIT, 1977; vis. Mackay prof. U. Calif., Berkeley, 1978-79; cons. Hewlett-Packard, 1982, IBM, 1984, Schlumberger, 1986, Signet Bank, 1994, Lucent Techs., 1996, Bios Group, 1998—; mem. pres.'s adv. com. computer sci. Stanford U., 1972-75, chmn., 1975-76; adv. com. Fed. Jud. Center; mem. sci. council I.R.I.A., Paris, 1976-80; central steering com., computing sci. and engring. research study NSF, also liaison to panel on theoretical computer sci. and panel on numerical comp., 1974-80; mem. adv. com. Carnegie-Mellon Inst. Research, 1978-79; mem. applied math. div. rev. com. Argonne Nat. Lab., 1973-75; mem. adv. com. math. and computer sci. NSF, 1978-80; chmn. computer sci. and tech. bd. NRC, 1986-90; chmn. computer sci. and telecommunications bd. NRC, 1990-92; trustee Columbia U. Press, 1983-85; founding chair Spl. Interest Group on Numerical Math., 1965-71. Author: Iterative Methods for the Solution of Equations, 1964, Russian edit., 1985; (with H. Wozniakowski) A General Theory of Optimal Algorithms, 1980, Russian edit., 1983, Chelsea, 1998; (with G. Wasilkowski and H. Wozniakowski) Information, Uncertainty, Complexity, 1983, Information-Based Complexity, 1988; (with A.G. Werschulz) Complexity and Information, 1998; editor: Complexity of Sequential and Parallel Numerical Algorithms, 1973, Analytic Computational Complexity, 1976, Algorithms and Complexity: New Directions and Recent Results, 1976, Jour. Assn. Computing Machinery, 1970-76, Transactions on Math. Software, 1974-76, Jour. Computer and Sys. Scis., 1973-86, Internat. Jour. on Computers and Math. with Applications, 1974—, Cohabiting With Computers, 1985; (with P. Hut and D. Ruelle) Fundamental Sources of Unpredictability, 1997; founding editor Jour. Complexity, 1985—, Ann. Rev. Computer Sci., 1986-92; assoc. editor Complexity, 1995—. Sherman Fairchild Disting. scholar Calif. Inst. Tech., 1991, 92; recipient Award for Disting. Svc. to Computing Rsch. Computer Rsch. Assn., 1992, Lezione Lincee Acad. Nazionale dei Lincei, 1993, Sr. Scientist award Alexander Von Humboldt Found., 1992-98, City of N.Y. Mayor's award for excellence in sci. and tech., 1999. Fellow AAAS (coun. 1971-74), ACM (chmn. award com. 1974-76), N.Y. Acad. Scis.; mem. IEEE (Emanuel R. Piore Gold medal 1991), NAE (membership com. for computer sci., elec. engring. and control 1986-87, membership com. for computer sci. and engring. 1987-91, presdl. search com. 1993-94), Conf. Bd. Math. Scis. (coun. 1971-74), Soc. Indsl. and Applied Math., Am. Math. Soc. Office: Columbia University Dept Computer Sci 1214 Amsterdam Ave #MC0401 New York NY 10027-7003 E-mail: traub@cs.columbia.edu.

TRAUGH, DONALD GEORGE, III, secondary education educator; b. Tucson, Aug. 5, 1950; s. Donald G. Jr. and Leatrice (Rhodes) Traugh-Long; m. Brenda Kay Kreischer, June 14, 1975; children: Jonathan P., Brandon M. AB in Edn., Fairmont (W.Va.) State U., 1974; MEd in Social Studies, Bloomsburg (Pa.) State U., 1980. Cert. tchr., Pa. Tchr. social studies Bloomsburg Area Sch. Dist., 1974—, chmn. dept. social studies, 1978—. Adj. prof. Bloomsburg U., 1999—; co-chair social studies curriculum staff Bloomsburg Area Sch. Dist., 1984—. Vol. firefighter Catawissa (Pa.) Hose Co. 1, 1969—, chief dept., 1987—; mem. Catawissa Borough Coun., 1977-89, v.p., 1987-89. Mem. NEA, Pa. Edn. Assn., Bloomsburg Area Edn. Assn., Nat. Coun. Social Studies, Mid. States Assn. Social Studies, Pa. Coun. Social Studies, Internat. Assn. Fire Chiefs, Nat. Fire Prevention Assn., Nat. Fire Protection Assn., Keystone State Fire Chiefs Assn., Pi Gamma Mu, Delta Sigma Phi. Democrat. Lutheran. Avocations: coaching football, hunting, fishing, scouting, gardening. Home: 503 E Main St Catawissa PA 17820-1030 Office: Bloomsburg HS 1200 Railroad St Bloomsburg PA 17815-3613 E-mail: dtraugh@bloomhs.k12.pa., firewalk@ptdprolog.net.

TRAUTMANN, PATRICIA ANN, communications educator, storyteller; b. Hot Springs, SD, Jan. 6, 1932; d.. Forest Houston and Clara Ruth (Allen) Doling; m. Robert D. Trautmann, Aug. 11, 1954; children: Kurt, Elaine, Sarah, Cynthia, Gretchen. BA, Jamestown Coll., 1954; MA, U. No. Colo., 1962; PhD, Vanderbilt U., 1984; post grad., Ga. So. U., 1992-93. Tchr. various sch., Colo., ND, Mich., 1954-67; part-time instr. English Kans. State Coll., Pitts., 1967-70; part-time instr. English, children's lit. Baldwin-Wallace Coll., Berea, Parma, Ohio, 1970-73; part-time instr. children's lit., reading, lang. arts U. Tenn., Nashville, 1973-78; English instr. Valdosta H.S., Ga., 1978-82; assoc. prof. English, Speech, Lang., asst. dir. programs Ga. Mil. Coll., Milledgeville, 1982-86; assoc. prof. English, art, humanities, lang. South Ga. Coll., Douglas, 1986-94, chair humanities and art history, 1988-94, prof. art history, 1989; assoc. prof. English, comm. skills Isothermal C.C., Spindale, NC, 1995—, prof. art appreciation and history, 1996—. Cons. for reading, children's books in schs. and other instns., Kans., Ohio, Tenn., Ga., N.C., 1964—. Storyteller, spkr., internat. lore, poetry, children's lit., world mythology, 1967—. Recipient Humanities award South Ga. Coll., 1993. Mem. AAUW, Music Club. Democrat. Avocations: drawing, painting, singing, gardening, hiking. Home: 257 N Washington St Rutherfordton NC 28139-2405 Office: Isothermal C C Dept English nd Comm Skills Spindale NC 28139 E-mail: ptrautma@isothermal.cc.nc.us.

TRAUTMANN, THOMAS ROGER, history and anthropology educator; b. Madison, Wis., May 27, 1940; s. Milton and Esther Florence (Trachte) T.; m. Marcella Hauolilani Choy, Sept. 25, 1962; children: Theodore William, Robert Arthur. BA, Beloit Coll., 1962; PhD, U. London, 1968. Lectr. in history Sch. Oriental and African Studies, U. London, 1965-68; asst. prof. history U. Mich., Ann Arbor, 1968-71, assoc. prof., 1971-77, prof., 1977—, Richard Hudson rsch. prof., 1979, prof. history and anthropology, 1984—, chmn. dept. history, 1987-90, Steelcase rsch. prof., 1993-94, dir. Inst. Humanities, Mary Fair Croushore prof. humanities, 1997—2002, Marshall D. Sahlins coll. prof. history and anthropology, 1997—. Author: Kautilya and the Arthasastra, 1971, Dravidian Kinship, 1981, Lewis Henry Morgan and the Invention of Kinship, 1987; author: (with K.S. Kabelac) The Library of Lewis Henry Morgan, 1994; author: (edit. with Diane Owen Hughes) Time: Histories and Ethnologies, 1995, Aryans and British India, 1997; author: (edit. with Maurice Godelier and Franklin Tjon Sie Fat) Transformations of Kinship, 1999; editor: Comparative Studies in Society and History, 1997—; contbr. articles on India, kinship and history of anthropology. Sr. Humanist fellow NEH, 1984. Mem. Am. Anthrop. Assn., Assn. Asian Studies, Am. Inst. Indian Studies (mem. exec. com. trustee, sr. rsch. fellow in India 1985, 97), Phi Beta Kappa. Office: U Mich Dept History Ann Arbor MI 48109-1003

TRAUTWEIN, GEORGE WILLIAM, conductor, educator; b. Chgo., Aug. 5, 1927; s. William Jacob and Hilda (Martin) T.; m. Barbara Wilson, Jan. 20, 1955; children: Paul Martin, Matthew Richard. MusB, Oberlin Conservatory, Ohio, 1951; MusM, Cleve. Inst. Music, 1955; MusD, Ind. U., 1961. Mem. faculty U. Minn., U. Tex., Austin, Armstrong (Ga.) State Coll.; arts cons. Nat. Endowment Arts; dir. internat. study program for Wake Forest U. at Tokai U., Japan, 1995. Violinist Indpls. Symphony Orch., 1947-48, Balt. Symphony Orch., 1951-52, Nat. Symphony Orch., Washington, 1952-53, Cleve. Orch., 1953-57, Chautauqua Symphony Orch., N.Y., 1953-59, Camerata Acad., Salzburg, 1957-58, Mozarteum Orch., Salzburg, 1958 (Fulbright grantee 1958), assoc. condr. Dallas Symphony Orch., 1962-66, Mpls. Symphony, 1966-73; music dir. S.D. Symphony, 1971-75, Internat. Congress Strings, Ohio, 1973-75; music dir., condr. Savannah (Ga.) Symphony Orch., 1974-77; music adv., prin. guest condr. Evansville (Ind.) Philharm., 1979-80; music dir., condr. RIAS Edn. Network, Berlin, 1979, Tucson Symphony Orch., 1977-81; artistic dir., condr. Piedmont Chamber Orch.; prin. condr. Internat. Music program; dir. orchestral programs, N.C. Sch. of Arts, 1981-83; dir. instrumental ensembles, Wake Forest U., 1983-96, dir. Artists series, 1985-98; guest appearances with orchs., U.S., Germany, Sweden, France, Rumania, Jugoslavia, Portugal, Hong Kong, India, P.R., Mex. Adv. bd. Avery Fisher Found., N.Y.C. Served with USN, 1948-49. Recipient Orpheus award Phi Mu Alpha, 1971, ASCAP award, 1979, 82, World Peace award Ministry of World Harmony, 1983; Fulbright grantee Mozarteum, Salzburg, 1958; Sr. Fulbright lectr., India, 1989-90. Mem. Am. Fedn. Musicians, Chamber Music Soc. Am., Sir Thomas Beecham Soc., Erich Wolfgang Korngold Soc., Literacy Initiative Assn., Condrs. Guild Am. Avocations: string quartet, art reproduction, British cuisine, W.B. Yeats, James Joyce. Office: Wake Forest U PO Box 7411 Winston Salem NC 27109-7411

TRAVER, ROBERT WILLIAM, SR., management consultant, author, lecturer, engineer; b. Waterbury, Conn., Oct. 13, 1930; s. Alfred Matthew Sr. and Dorothy Viola (Thomson) T.; m. Eleanor Jean Finnemore (div. Feb. 1963); children: Robert William Jr., Jeffrey Matthew, Elizabeth; m. Valarie Jane Mason. B in Mech. Engring., Clarkson U., 1955; MBA, U. Mass., 1963. Registered profl. engr., N.Y. Quality control engr. Gen. Electric Co., Pittsfield, Mass., 1955-62; mgr. reliability and quality assurance Tansitor Electronics, Inc., Bennington, Vt., 1962-65; sr. cons. Rath & Strong, Inc., Lexington, Mass., 1965-70; regional mgr. TAC, Inc., Albany, N.Y., 1970-72; dist. mgr. IDS, Inc., Albany, 1972-81; v.p. Reddy, Traver & Woods, Inc., Lexington, 1981-96; owner Traver Assocs., Averill Pk., N.Y., 1996—. Participant in ednl. exch. with Peoples Republic of China, 1985, Australia and New Zealand, 1986. Author: Manufacturing Solutions for Consistent Quality and Reliability; contbr. articles to profl. jours. Chmn. lake com. Crooked Lake Improvement Assn., Averill Park, N.Y., 1973-74; v.p. Sand Lake (N.Y.) Businessmen's Assn., 1974-76. With U.S. Army, 1950. Fellow Am. Soc. for Quality; mem. Trout Unltd. Republican. Congregationalist. Avocations: fishing, gardening. Home and Office: 184 Eastern Union Tpke Averill Park NY 12018-9563 E-mail: rwtraver@aol.com.

TRAVERS, CAROL, mathematics educator; b. Oil City, Pa., July 10, 1941; d. Philip Patrick and Frances Mary (McNamara) Healy; divorced; children: William. Joseph, Bruce, Rose. BS in Elem. Edn., State U. Pa., 1962; MS in Elem. Edn., SUNY, Brockport, 1977. Tchr. elem. sch. Lincoln-Garfield Sch., New Castle, Pa., 1962-64; tchr. Mohawk Area Schs., Mt. Jackson, Pa., 1964-65; tchr. nursery sch. Learn 'N' Play Sch., Middleport, N.Y., 1970-77; tchr. remedial reading Royalton-Hartland, Middleport, N.Y., 1977-80; tchr. remedial reading, remedial math Middleport Elem. Sch., 1980—. Co-chair bldg. team Sch. Bldg. Team, Middleport, 1989-91, 94-95; mem. computer coun. Roy-Hart Dist., Middleport, 1981—, chmn. prof. coun.; rep. Math. Standards Support Group, Lockport, N.Y., 1990—. Co-author/editor:)booklet) Child Study Team, 1989. Mem. Nat. Coun. Math. Tchrs., N.Y. State Maths. Tchrs., Assn. Compensatory Educators, PTA. Democrat. Roman Catholic. Avocations: model railroading, travel, sewing, home remodeling. Office: Middleport Elem Sch State St Middleport NY 14105-1196

TRAVERSE, ALFRED, palynology educator, clergyman; b. Port Hill, P.E.I., Can., Sept. 7, 1925; s. Alfred Freeman and Pearle (Akerley) T.; m. Elizabeth Jane Insley, June 30, 1951; children: Paul, Martha, John, Celia. SB, Harvard U., 1946, AM, 1948, PhD, 1951; cert. in botany, Kings Coll., Cambridge, Eng., 1947; MDiv, Episcopal Theol. Sem. S.W., 1965. Tchg. fellow Harvard U., 1947-51; coal technologist U.S. Bur. Mines, Grand Forks, N.D., 1951-55; head Fuels Microscopy Lab., Denver, 1955; palynologist Shell Devel. Co., Houston, 1955-62; cons. palynologist Austin, Tex., 1962-65; asst. prof. geology U. Tex., Austin, 1965-66; assoc. prof. geology and biology Pa. State U., University Park, 1966-70, prof. palynology, 1970-96, prof. emeritus, 1996—; ordained to ministry Episcopal Ch., 1965; asst. priest St. Matthew's Ch., Austin, 1965-66, St. Paul's Ch., Philipsburg, Pa., 1966-75, Christuskirche (Old Cath.), Zurich, Switzerland, 1980-81; vicar St. John's Ch., Huntingdon, Pa., 1975-80. Adj. prof. geobiology Juniata Coll., 1977-82; guest prof. Geol. Inst., Swiss Fed. Tech. Inst., Zurich, 1980-81; councillor Internat. Commn. Palynology, 1973-77, 80—, pres., 1977-80, archivist, historian, 1986—; on-bd. scientist Glomar Challenger, 1975; Fulbright prof. Senckenberg Rsch. Inst., Frankfurt, 1992. Author: Paleopalynology, 1988, Sedimentation of Organic Particles, 1994; mem. editl. bd. Catalog Fossil Spores and Pollen, 1957-66, editor-in-chief, 1966-76; palynological editor: Palaeontographica, 1989-95. Recipient Internat. prize Palaeobot. Soc. India, 1990-91, Korrespondierendes Mitglied, Senckenbergische Naturforschende Gesellschaft, 1992—; Rsch. grant NSF, 1966-87. Fellow AAAS, Geol. Soc. Am.; mem. Bot. Soc. Am. (sec.-treas. paleobot. sect. 1957-60, chmn. sect. 1960-61), Internat. Assn. Plant Taxonomists (sec. com. fossil plants 1969-93), Am. Assn. Stratigraphic Palynologists (sec.-treas. 1967-70, pres. 1970-71, chmn. type collections com. 1989-91, Excellence in Edn. medal 2000), Internat. Fedn. Palynol. Soc. (pres. 1976-80, archivist 1980—). Home: Rd 2 Box 390 Huntingdon PA 16652-9209 Office: 406 Deike Bldg University Park PA 16802-2713

TRAVIS, LAURA ROSE, elementary education educator; b. Waynesburg, Pa., Jan. 23, 1944; d. Isaac Jesse and Violet Rae (Hixenbaugh) Ammons; m. Bobby Dale Jones, July 20, 1963 (div. Aug. 1982); children: Bernard, Marvin, Tonya; m. Harold Dean Travis, June 21, 1990. BA in Edn., Glenville (W.Va.) State Coll., 1983; postgrad., W.Va. Grad. Coll., 1992-94. Tchr. Glade Elem. Sch., Cowen, W.Va., 1984-90; substitute tchr. Putnum County Sch. Bd., Winfield, W.Va., 1990-94; tchr. Rock Branch Elem. Sch., Nitro, W.Va., 1994—. Coord. for sch. age East Nitro Christian Educare, 1991-94. Pres. Cowen Woman's Club, 1977-80; sec. Cowen Garden Club, 1978-81, chairperson for Sch. Improvement com., 1995-97, faculty senate pres., 1997-99, social studies coord., 1997—, lead tchr. for 4th and 5th grade tchrs., 1999—. Named Tchr. of Yr., Rock Branch Elem. Sch., 2001—02. Mem. Order Ea. Star, Kappa Delta Pi, Alpha Delta Kappa. Democrat. Avocations: sewing, cooking, reading, grandchildren. E-mail: lartravis@aol.com.

TRAVISANO, THOMAS JOSEPH, English language educator; b. Livingston, N.J., Dec. 14, 1951; s. Frank Peter and Nancy (Drees) T.; m. Elsa Kathryn Thompson, May 23, 1981; children: Michael Coulliette, Emily Claire. BA, Haverford Coll., 1973; MA, U. Va., 1975, PhD, 1981. Asst. prof. English Coll. of William and Mary, 1980-82, Hartwick Coll., Oneonta, NY, 1982-86, assoc. prof. English, 1987-94, prof. English, 1994—, Cora A. Babcock prof. English, 1995-98, acting chair dept. English and theatre arts, 2002—03. Lectr. The Am. Century, Oneonta, 1992-97; dir. Am. Century Project N.Y., 1995-97; lectr. in field. Author: Elizabeth Bishop: Her Artistic Development, 1988—97, Midcentury Quartet: Bishop, Lowell, Jarrell, Berryman and the Making of a Postmodern Aesthetic, 1999; editor: Elizabeth Bishop Bull., 1991—97; co-editor: Gendered Modernisms: American Women Poets and Their Readers, 1996, The New Anthology of American Poetry: Vol. One, Beginnings to 1900, 2003; contbg. editor: Listener mag., 1995—2000; contbr. articles. NEH grantee 1983, 88, 94, 2000, Hartwick Coll. grantee 1983, 85, 87, 89, 92, 96-97, 2000-2001; Win Wandersee Scholar in Residence, 1999-2000; Dupont fellow, 1976-79; Hartwick Coll. faculty rsch. summer fellow, 1989. Mem. MLA, ALA, Elizabeth Bishop Soc. (mem. organizing com. 1991—, editor newsletter 1992—, pres. 1997—), MUG One: Macintosh Users Group of Oneonta (pres. 1991-94). Avocation: classical music. Home: 28 State St Oneonta NY 13820-1311 Office: Hartwick Coll 218 Clark Hall Oneonta NY 13820

TRAVIS-JASPERING, MARGARET ROSE, artist, educator; b. St. Louis, Dec. 1, 1950; d. George Thomas and Margaret Lina (Black) Travis; m. Richard W. Jaspering, Jan. 31, 1989; children: Wendy E., Mandy E., Sarah M., Chloe K., Jo Anne Urian. BFA, Lindenwood Coll., 1980, postgrad., 1981, U. Mo., St. Louis, 1980, U. Mo., Columbia, 1981. Cert. art edn. tchr. K-12. Tchr. Public Schs. St. Charles, Lincoln, Warren Counties, Mo., 1978-90; represented by Bournstein's Art Exchange, St. Louis, 1992-98. Instr. adult art painting workshops, 1976-90. Exhibited in group shows at Harry Henderson Gallery, Lindenwood Colls., 1976-80, Grand Gallery South, Belleville Ceramic Show, 1987 (Best of Show, 4 1st pl. awards), Internat. Ceramic Conv. and Show, 1988 (Best of Show, Best of Category, 5 1st pl. awards), Greater St. Louis Ceramic Assn. Show, 1988 (Best of Show, 1st pl. award), 76th Ann. Sculpture and Fine Crafts, 1989, Black and White Show, 1989, U. Mo., Chancellor's Residence, 1988-90, St. Charles Artists Guild, 1989 (Best of Show), Nat. Invitational of Am. Contemporary Art, Boston, 1993, Art St. Louis, Women's Cauces for Art, The New England Fine Arts Inst., Fine Arts Fair & Wine Fest, Washington, Mo., 1993, St. Charles Artists Guild, St. Louis Artists Guild, O'Fallon Art & Wine Gala, Creve Couer 50th Anniversary Art Celebration, 1999, 2 murals for St. Mary's Ch., Hawkpoint, Mo., 1998—, Craft Alliance Gallery, 2000, 4th O'Fallon Art & Wine Gala, 2000, The Sheldon Gallery, St. Louis, 2000 ; contbr. catalog, mags; represented in pvt. and comml. collections. Organizer Art for Animals fundraiser Animal Welfare Assn., Warren Co., Mo., 1991-93; active St. Charles Artists Guild, 1987-89. Dept. scholar in art Lindenwood Colls., 1976-80, nat. art exhbn., Scholastic Mag., 1967, 69. Mem. Art St. Louis, St. Louis Artists Guild & Craft Alliance. Roman Catholic. Avocations: gardening, swimming. Office: Jasmar Studios and Gallery PO Box 147 980 Archer Rd Foristell MO 63348-0147

TRAYLOR, JOYCE ELAINE, adult education educator; b. Rantoul, Ill., Sept. 22, 1955; d. August Charles and Peggy Joyce (Baker) Oberbeck; m. Gregory Lee Traylor (div. July 1991); 1 child, Janell Amelia. BSEd, S.W. Mo. State U., 1977, MSEd, 1993. High sch. tchr. Forsyth (Mo.) Pub. Schs., 1977-79; postsecondary tchr. Graff Vocat. Tech. Sch., Springfield, Mo., 1979-81; tng. coord. to prodn. control clk. Paul Mueller Co. Inc., Springfield, 1981-85; seminar leader, adminstrv. asst. Mgmt. Devel. Inst. S.W. Mo. State U., Springfield, 1982-85, program coord., 1985-93; owner Traylor Tng. Svcs., Springfield, Mo., 1993—2003; Midwest regional mgr. ITC, 1994—96; rsch. analyst Granit Broadcasting, NY, 1996—2000; sr. rsch. analyst Market Source Rsch. Ctr., Springfield, 2000—; instr. Coll. of Bus. Adminstrn. Southwest Mo. State Univ., 2001—. Pres. Ozarks Soc. Tng. and Devel., Springfield, 1994, also bd. dirs.; interim instr. dept. mgmt. Southwest Mo. State U., 2001—. Bd. mem. Bus./Industry Edn. Alliance, Springfield, 1990. Mem. Springfield Area C. of C. (bd. mem. 1991—, bd. mem. profl. devel. div. 1990—, pres. profl. devel. div. 1991), Mo. Vocat. Assn., Mo. Bus. Edn. Assn., Delta Phi Epsilon (charter Ozarks chpt.). Democrat. Methodist. Avocations: horsemanship, creative writing, ballroom dancing. Office: 1729 Garland Ct Republic MO 65738-9142

TRAYNOR, BARBARA MARY, school system administrator; b. Somerset, Mass., May 1, 1935; d. Joseph Chadwick and Ivah Helene (Richardson) T. BA in Music Edn., Syracuse (N.Y.) U., 1957; cert., Calvin Coolidge Coll., 1958, Bridgewater (Mass.) State Coll, 1959; MEd in Guidance and Counseling, U. Va., 1963; postgrad., Ithaca Coll., 1959, U. Md., Loyola U., Balt., Bowie State Coll. Asst. supr. elem. music New Bedford (Mass.) Pub. Schs., 1957-59; supr. vocal music Swansea (Mass.) Pub. Schs., 1959-60, 60-61; guidance counselor jr. high Prince Georges County Pub. Schs., Upper Marlboro, Md., 1963-64, 64-65, guidance counselor sr. high, 1965-68, pupil pers. worker, 1969-73, coord. student transfer desegregation, 1973-74, 84-85, supr. student transfer and records, 1985-86, 94-95. Student records cons. Records Rights, Responsibilities, Inc., Md. and D.C., 1981-94. Author: (manual) Student Records Guidelines, 1983. Fin. supporter Capitol Hill Arts Workshop, Washington, 1981-94; violinist Annapolis (Md.) Symphony Orch., 1963-67; singer Paul Hill Chorale, Takoma Park, Md., 1979-81. Mem. Am. Pers. Guidance Assn., Internat. Assn. Pupil Pers. Workers, Orton Dyslexia Soc., Kappa Delta Pi. Republican. Avocations: painting, sculpture, music, ballet, sports. Home: 2121 Jamieson Ave Unit 701 Alexandria VA 22314-5710 Office: Prince George County Pub Sch 14201 School Ln Upper Marlboro MD 20772-2866

TREACY, SANDRA JOANNE PRATT, art educator, artist; b. New Haven, Aug. 5, 1934; d. Willis Hadley Jr. and Gladys May (Gell) P.; m. Gillette van Nuyse, Aug. 27, 1955; 1 child, Jonathan Todd. BFA, R.I. Sch. Design, 1956; student, William Paterson Coll., 1973-74. Cert. elem. and secondary tchr., N.J. Tchr. art and music Pkwy. Christian Ch., Ft. Lauderdale, Fla., 1964-66; developer Pequannock Twp. Bd. of Edn., Pompton Plains, N.J., 1970-72, tchr. art, 1972-76; vol. art tchr. Person County Bd. of Edn., Roxboro, N.C., 1978-80, tchr. art, 1980-91, So. Jr. High Sch., Roxboro, 1989-91, Woodland Elem. Sch., Roxboro, 1989-93; tchr. Helena Elem. Sch., Timberlake, N.C., 1991-93. Tchr. elem. art Bethel Hill Sch., Roxboro, 1974-79, vol. art tchr., 1979-80; tchr. basic art, vol. all elem. schs. Person County, Roxboro, 1977-80; tchr. arts and crafts, summers 1981-882; tchr. art home sch. So. Mid. Sch., 1993—, Person H.S., 1993-94. Artist, illustrator. Mem. Roxboro EMTs, 1979-81; bd. dirs. Person County Arts Coun., 1980--81, 93-95, pres., 1981-82; piano and organ choir accompanist Concord United Meth. Ch., 1981—; leader Morgan Trotters, 1992-94, asst. dir., 1993-96, bd. dirs.; coach, horseback riding for handicapped. Mem. NEA, Nat. Mus. of Women in the Arts (continuing charter), Smithsonian Assocs., N.C. Assn. Arts Edn., N.C. Assn. Educators, N.C. Art Soc. Mus. of Art, Internat. Platform Assn., Womans Club (tchr. Pompton Plains chpt. 1974-79), Person County Saddle Club (rec. sec. 1981-84), Puddingston Pony Club (dist. sec. 1974-75 Montville Twp. chpt.), Roxboro Garden Club (continuing, commr. 1980-82, pres. 1982-84, 87—, sec. 1993-94, 97-98, v.p. 1993-95, pres. 1995—), Roxboro Woman's Club (arts dept.). Republican. Avocations: horseback riding, swimming, sailing, reading, playing piano and organ. Home: 1345 Kelly Brewer Rd Leasburg NC 27291-9622

TREADWAY, WILLIAM JACK, JR., biochemistry and chemistry educator; b. Johnson City, Tenn., Feb. 22, 1949; s. William Jack and Amelia T.; children: Corrie, Christen, Kyle. BS, U. Ill., 1972; PhD, Loyola U., 1976. Tchg. asst. Loyola U., 1971-73, rsch. asst., 1973-75; rsch. assoc. Thomas Jefferson U., Phila., 1975-77, Temple U., 1977-78; asst. prof. Wake Forest U., 1978-81; prof. biochemistry Parkland Coll., Champaign, Ill., 1981—. Recipient Sci. award Bausch and Lomb Co., 1967, Postdoctoral Tng. award NIH. Mem. NISOD (Teaching Excellence award 1993). Office: Parkland Coll Nat Sci 2400 W Bradley Ave Champaign IL 61821-1806 Home: 1005 W Charles St Champaign IL 61821

TREESE, LISA MAUREEN, deaf educator; b. Chgo., Apr. 15, 1963; d. Robert James and Mary Elyse (Ziegler) Doyle; m. Randy William Treese, Aug. 3, 1985; 1 child, Timothy Charles. BS, Indiana U. Pa., 1985. Cert. tchr., Pa., S.C. Substitute tchr. Meyersdale (Pa.) Area Sch. Dist., 1986-87; itinerant tchr. of hearing handicapped students Horry County Sch. Dist., Conway, S.C., 1987-88; tchr. of mentally handicapped students Conway Mid. Sch., 1988-90, tchr. of hearing handicapped students, 1990-91, Whittemore Park Mid. Sch., Conway, 1991—. Staff devel. chair Strategic Planning Tact Team. Instr. Sunday sch. St. James Cath. Ch., Conway, 1991—, chair family com. ladies guild, 1992; team mem. Worldwide Marriage Encounter, Conway, 1992-94. Mem. Am. Sign Lang. Tchrs. Orgn., Conv. Am. Instrs. Deaf, S.C. Edn. Assn., Horry County Coun. Exceptional Children (v.p. 1991-92), S.C. Assn. of Deaf, Sunshine Coastal Assn. of Deaf, CAID. Democrat. Roman Catholic. Avocations: gardening, needlepoint, crochet, reading, antiques. Home: 802 Berrywood Ct Myrtle Beach SC 29588-8800

TREFTS, JOAN LANDENBERGER, retired educator, administrator; b. Pitts., Jan. 31, 1930; d. William Henry III and Eleanore (Campbell) Landenberger;m. Albert Sharpe Trefts Sr., June 20, 1952 (dec.); children: Dorothy, Albert Jr., William, Deborah, Elizabeth. AB, Western Coll. for Women, 1952; M, John Carroll U., 1982, M, 1984. Lic. and cert. home economist, cert. prin., N.Y., Ohio, supr., biol. sci., econs., voact. edn., pre-kindergarten edn. Summer sch. prin. John Adams H.S., Collinwood and South High, Cleve., 1972-95. Cons. Cleve. Partnership Program. Trustee Chautauqua Literacy and Sci. Cir., Presbyn. Assn. Chautauqua, NY. Named Tchr. of Yr., Cleve., 1994. Mem.: DAR (state officer 2000—), Ohio Vocat.

Assn. (bd. dirs.), Am. Vocat. Assn. (nat. com.), Am. Home Econs. Assn., Presbyn. Assn. (trustee), Dames of Ct. of Honor (pres. gen. 2001—), Colonial Daus. of 17th Century (nat. officer), Daus. Am. Colonists (state officer), Nat. Officers Colonial Clergy (nat. officer, chancellor), Colonial Dames Am. (pres. chpt. 18, nat. officer ct. honor), U.S. Daus. of 1912, Colonial Dames of XVII Century, New Eng. Soc. of Western Res. (pres.), Clearwater Country Club, Cleve. Skating Club, Union Clubs. Republican. Presbyterian. Avocations: curling, rug hooking, needlepoint. Home: 20101 Malvern Rd Shaker Heights OH 44122-2825

TREGLE, LINDA MARIE, dance educator; b. Fort Sill, Okla., Sept. 8, 1947; d. Franklin and Helen Marie (Diggs) T. BA, Mills Coll., Stockton, Calif., 1970, MA, 1974; life credential, U. Calif., 1974. Founder, dir., choreographer Internat. Studios, Inc., Stockton, 1970—; dance instr. San Joaquin Delta Coll., Stockton, 1970—; program cons., choreographer Alpha Kappa Alpha, Stockton, 1984—, choreographer SDW Motion Pictures, Stockton, 1983—; advisor Internat. Dance Club San Joaquin, 1970—; founder, dir. Tregles Internat. Dance Co., 1970—; mem. Ruth Beckford's Dance Studio. Directed and choreographed numerous dance prodn. videos. Mem. NAACP, Black Employment Trends (community rep. 1988—), Calif. Tchrs. Assn., Alpha Kappa Alpha. Avocations: creative writing, table sports, drama, arts, dance. Home: 2411 Arden Ln Stockton CA 95210-3256 Office: San Joaquin Delta Coll 5151 Pacific Ave Stockton CA 95207-6304

TREJOS, CHARLOTTE MARIE, humanities educator, consultant; b. Trout Lake, Mich., July 5, 1920; d. Charles Floyd and Lula May (Force) Draper; m. J. Mario Trejos, Jan. 8, 1961; 1 child, J. Mario Jr. Tchg. credentials, State of Calif., 1989; MA, Hawthorne Coll., 1975; DD, Min. Salvation Ch., 1986. Tchr. English El Colegio Anglo-Am., Cochabamba, Bolivia, 1965-66; tchr. Hawthorne (Calif.) Christian Sch., 1966-75; owner Trejos Literary Cons., Carson, Calif., 1976—. Author: My Carson, Your Carson, 1987, Variegated Verse, 1973, Yesterday Was Sunday, 1994; contbr. articles to profl. jours. Voter registerer Democrats. With U.S. Army, 1942-43. Named Poet of Yr. Nat. Poetry Pub. Assn., 1974; recipient Golden Poet award World of Poetry, 1993. Mem. Soc. Ibero-Am. Escritores de Los Estados Unidos Am. (pres. 1985—, Cert. Recognition 1986). Avocations: music, tap dancing, art, gardening. Home and Office: 510 Copper Basin Rd Lot 15 Prescott AZ 86303-4637

TRELFA, EUGENIA MARIE, elementary school educator; b. San Francisco, May 29, 1946; d. Samuel Eugene and Mildred Marie (Adkins) Henderson; m. Tim Trelfa, Nov. 21, 1981; children: Natasha Alexandra, Danielle Marie. BA, U. Calif., Davis, 1967; MA, U. No. Colo., 1975; cert., San Francisco State U., 1969. Cert. tchr., life, Calif., tchr. developmental reading, Colo. Dance instr. Walnut Creek (Calif.) Parks and Recreation; tchr. Santa Clara (Calif.) Schs., Douglas County Schs., Castle Rock, Colo., Cherry Creek Schs., Englewood, Colo. Contbr. rsch. to profl. jours. Recipient Dist. grant. Mem. NEA, Colo. Edn. Assn., Cherry Creek Tchrs. Assn., Nat. Coun. Tchrs. Math.

TRELSTAD, ROBERT LAURENCE, pathology educator, cell biologist; b. Redding, Calif., June 16, 1940; s. Bertram Laurence and Dorothy (Axt) T.; m. Barbara Stanton Henken, Aug. 27, 1961; children: Derek, Graham, Brian, Jeremy. BA, Columbia U., 1961; MD, Harvard U., 1966. From asst. to assoc. prof. Harvard Med. Sch., Boston, 1972-81; chief pathology Shriners Burns Inst., Boston, 1975-81; staff pathologist Mass. Gen. Hosp., Boston, 1972-81; prof., chair pathology Robert Wood Johnson Med. Sch., Piscataway/New Brunswick, N.J., 1981-98; acting dir. Child Health Inst. of N.J., 1998—. Paz chair devel. biology, 1999—. Mem. study sect. NIH, Bethesda, Md., 1971-75, 86-90; mem. adv. coun. Nat. Inst. Child Health and Human Devel., 1993-97; chmn. health professions adv. com. Princeton U., 2002—. Co-founder, editor-in-chief: Keyboard Publishing, Inc., 1990; past mem. editorial bd. various profl. jours. including Jour. Cell Biology, Am. Jour. Pathology, Devel. Biology, Devel. Dynamics. Lt. comdr. USPHS, 1967—69. Helen Hay Whitney Found. fellow, 1969-72; recipient Rsch. Faculty award Am. Cancer Soc., 1972-76, Disting. Tchr. in Basic Scis. award Alpha Omega Alpha and Assn. Am. Med. Colls., 1992. Mem. Am. Soc. Cell Biology (sec. 1982-88), Soc. Devel. Biology (pres. 1983). Home: 35 Westcott Rd Princeton NJ 08540-3038 Office: Robert Wood Johnson Med Sch Child Health Inst New Brunswick NJ 08901

TREMAIN, RICHARD DEAN, vocational educator; b. Pittsburg, Kans., Sept. 18, 1954; s. Gerald Dean and Shirley Nell (Dye) T.; m. Judy Elaine Weathers, Dec. 23, 1972; children: Curtis Shane, Kimberly Jane. BS, Pittsburg State U., 1987, MS, 1992. Cert. tchr. secondary, post-secondary welding; cert. welding inspector, cert. bldg. adminstrn. Welder Poli-Tron, Inc., Pittsburg, 1972-73, Atlas Steel, Oswego, Kans., 1973-74, Sauder Tank & Tower, Emporia, Kans., 1974-75, Pittsburg Steel, 1975-77; instr. Kans. State Sch. for Deaf, Olathe, 1977-87, Johnson County Area Vocat. Sch., Olathe, 1987—; asst. dir. Johnson County Tech. Edn. Ctr., 1996—. Mem. Kans. N.G., 1972-94; mem. adv. com. Johnson County C.C., Overland Park, Kans., 1993—. Recipient Erickson Trophy, N.G. Bur., 1984, Disting. Grad. award N.G. Assn. Kans., 1984; decorated Army Commendation medal (2). Mem. NEA, Kans. Edn. Assn., Nat. Vocat. Assn., Kans. Vocat. Assn. (dist. v.p. 1990-91), Am. Welding Soc. (scholarship com. 1993—), Kans. Sch. for Deaf Edn. Assn. (pres. 1984-85), Masons (3d degree), Kappa Delta Pi. Republican. Avocations: hunting, fishing, water skiing, snow skiing, softball. Home: 2325 W Post Oak Rd Olathe KS 66061-5064 Office: Johnson County Tech Edn Ctr 311 E Park St Olathe KS 66061-5407

TREMBA, LEATRICE JOY, special education educator; d. Harvey Adolph and Agnes Barbara (Bambousek) Eiben; m. Michael Henry Tremba, Jr., Feb. 2, 1963; children: Marilynda Dione, Michael David. BSED, Ohio U., 1960; MSED, Kent State U., 1961. Cert. elem. tchr., Ohio, spl. edn. tchr., Ohio. Tchr. Cleve. Pub. Schs., 1958-63; specialist language arts Community Action for Youth, Cleve., 1963-64; tchr. spl. edn. Tuscarawas Valley Schs., Bolivar and Mineral, Ohio, 1983—; tchr. ABE ABLE Buckeye Joint Vocat., New Philadelphia, Ohio, 1983—. Consortium reading speaker Buckeye Joint Vocat., New Philadelphia, Ohio, 1989-91; tchr. coll. for kids Kent State U., summer 1993. Co-author: (handbook) Selected Bibliography on Human Relations, 1964, Phonetic Guide, 1992; author (radio commls.) Literacy Awareness, 1989, EPA Awareness, 1991; (TV lit. series) Adult Reading Series, 1990, (enrichment unit) Career Program for DH, 1991. Supt. Vacation Bible Summer Sch.; mem. Tuscarawas Philharm. Chorus. Mem. Coun. for Exceptional Children (program dir. 1987, 89), Kappa Delta Pi (v.p. 1959-60). Avocations: reading, gardening, church soloist, accordionist. Home: 2870 State Route 800 NE Dover OH 44622-7993

TREMBATH, MARJORIE FAYE, elementary school educator; b. Fosston, Minn., July 4, 1949; d. Alvin G. and Margith E. (Hagen) Modin; m. Glen H. Trembath, June 9, 1973; children: Eric, Corey. BS, Bemidji State Coll., 1971; MA, U. St. Thomas, St. Paul, 1995. Tchr. 3rd grade Warren (Minn.) Pub. Sch., 1971-77; tchr. 2nd grade East Grand Forks (Minn.) Pub. Sch., 1977-81, tchr. 1st grade, 1981-84, tchr. 2nd grade, 1984-98, tchr. 3rd grade, 1998—. Mem. libr. bd. Our Saviors Luth. Ch., East Grand Forks, 1975-88, confirmation instr., 1988-93. Mem. North Star Reading Coun. Democrat. Lutheran. Avocations: sewing, painting, gardening. Home: 29 Garden Ct NW East Grand Forks MN 56721-1237 E-mail: mtrembath@egf.k12.mn.us.

TREMBLAY, MARC ADÉLARD, anthropologist, educator; b. Les Eboulements, Que., Can., Apr. 24, 1922; s. Willie and Laurette (Tremblay) T.; m. Jacqueline Cyr, Dec. 27, 1949; children: Geneviève, Lorraine, Marc, Colette, Dominique, Suzanne. AB, U. Montreal, 1944, L.S.A., 1948; MA, Laval U., 1950; PhD, Cornell U., 1954; PhD (hon.), Ottawa U., 1982, Guelph U., 1983, U. N. B.C., 1994, Carleton U., 1995, U. Ste. Anne, 1997, McGill U., 1998. Research asso. Cornell U., 1953-56; mem. faculty Laval U., 1956-93, prof. anthropology, 1963-68, 81-93, prof. emeritus, 1994, vice dean social scis., 1968-71, dean Grad. Sch., 1971-79, also mem. univ. council.; pres. Quebec Coun. Social Rsch., 1987-91. Dir. Inuit and Circupolar Study Group Laval U., 1991—93; mem. Nunavik Commn., 1999—2001. Author 25 books and monographs in social scis., about 200 articles. Decorated officer Order of Can., gt. officer Order of Que.; recipient Que. Lit. prize, 1965, Innis-Gerin prize Royal Soc. Can., 1979, Molson prize Can. Coun., 1987, Prix Marcel Vincent ACFAS, 1988, Contbn. exceptionnelle Societé de sociologie et d'anthropolotie, 1990, Esdras Minville award Soc. St.-Jean Baptiste, 1991; named to Internat. Order of Merit, Internat. Biog. Inst., Cambridge, Eng., 1990. Mem. Royal Soc. Can. (pres. 1981-84), Acad. des Scis. Morales et Politiques (sec.), Rsch. Inst. Pub. Policy, Am. Anthrop. Assn. (past fellow), Am. Sociology Soc. (past fellow), Can. Soc. Applied Anthropology, Can. Sociology and Anthropology Assn. (founding pres.), Can. Ethnology Soc. (past pres.), Assn. Can. Univs. for Northern Studies (past pres.), Assn. Internat. Sociology, Societe des savants et sci. Can. (v.p., pres. nat. order Quebec 1998-2000). Home: 835 N Orléans St Sainte Foy QC Canada G1X 3J4 Office: Laval Univ Dept Anthropology Quebec QC Canada G1K 7P4 Fax: (418) 653-9865. E-mail: matremgt@globetrotter.net.

TREMBLAY, MARY DENISE, administrator, educator; b. Lowell, Mass., Aug. 29, 1951; d. Romeo D. and Marion A. (Metivier) Martel; m. Richard J. Tremblay; children: Richard Jr., Christopher, Miriam. BA in Edn., U. Mass., 1973; MEd, Rivier Coll., 1990. Instr. U. Mass., Lowell, Spl. Needs Program, Lowell, asst. dir., dir.; tchr. St. Joseph's Sch., Lowell; dir. PMA Devel. Ctr., Hudson, N.H., Chapel Sch., Nashua, N.H. Mem. adv. bd. Chapel Sch., N.H. Tech. Inst., Nashua, Child Care Network, Nashua. Mem. Nat. Assn. Edn. Young Children, N.H. Assn. Edn. Young Children (bd. sec. 1994-95, mem. adv. bd.), Assn. Childhood Edn. Internat. Avocations: painting, crafts, archery, antiques, music. Office: Chapel Sch 3 Lutheran Dr Nashua NH 03063-2909

TREMBLAY, WILLIAM ANDREW, English language educator, writer; b. Southbridge, Mass., June 9, 1940; s. Arthur Achille and Irene (Fontaine) T.; m. Cynthia Ann Crooks, Sept. 28, 1962; children: William Crooks, Benjamin Philip, John Fontaine. BA, Clark U., 1962, MA, 1969; MFA in Poetry, U. Mass., 1972. English tchr. Southbridge (Mass.) High Sch., 1962-63, Sutton (Mass.) High Sch., 1963-65, Tantasqua Regional High Sch., Sturbridge, Mass., 1965-67; asst. prof. Leicester (Mass.) Jr. Coll., 1967-70; teaching asst. U. Mass., Amherst, 1970-72; instr. Springfield (Mass.) Coll., 1972-73; prof. English Colo. State U., Fort Collins, 1973—, dir. MFA program in creative writing. Fulbright-Hays lectureship, Lisbon, Portugal, 1979, NEH summer program, 1981; mem. program dirs. coun. Associated Writing Programs, 1984-86. Author: The June Rise: The Apocryphal Letters of Antoine Janis, 1994, (poetry) Shooting Script: Door of Fire, 2003, Rainstorm Over the Alphabet, 2001, Duhamel: Ideas of Order in Little Canada, 1986, Second Sun: New and Selected Poems, 1985, Home Front, 1978, The Anarchist Heart, 1977, Crying in the Cheap Seats, 1971; editor-in-chief: Colo. Rev., 1983-91. Nat. Endowment for the Humanities, 1981, Summer writing fellow Corp. of Yaddo, 1989, Creative Writing fellow Nat. Endowment for Arts, 1985; recipient Pushcart prize Pushcart Prize Anthology, 1987, Best Am. Poetry, 2003. Mem.: Puerto del Sol (bd. advisors, John F. Stern Dist. Prof. award 2002), Am. Acad. Poetry, Poudre Wilderness Vol. Home: 3412 Lancaster Dr Fort Collins CO 80525-2817 Office: Colo State U Dept English Fort Collins CO 80523-0001

TREMMEL, LYNN ALISON, elementary education educator; b. Chgo., Sept. 23, 1957; d. Herbert and Annette (Finn) Froehlich; m. Friedrich Tremmel, July 8, 1984; children: Michael, Gina. BA in Edn., Nat. Coll. Edn., Evanston, Ill., 1979, MEd, 1982. Cert. elem. tchr. Ill. Tchr. 6th grade math. Daniel Wright Mid. Sch., Sch. Dist. 103, Lake Forest, Ill., 1979-89; advanced math. tchr. grades 7-8 Transfiguration Sch., Wauconda, Ill., 1998—2000, St. Joseph Sch., Libertyville, Ill., 2001—. Sec. Local Tchrs. Assn., Lake Forest. Article reviewer Ill. Coun. Tchrs. Math. Jour., 1992—. Parent adv. bd. Family Cir., Libertyville, Ill., 1992—94; Sunday sch. tchr. United Meth. Ch., Libertyville, Ill., 1993—95, youth coun., 2000—. Mem. Nat. Coun. Tchrs. Math., Ill. Coun. Tchrs. Math. Home: 328 Butterfield Ln Libertyville IL 60048-1718

TRENARY, MICHAEL, chemist, educator; b. L.A., July 8, 1956; s. Bernard Elroy and Jean Ann (Morris) Trenary; m. Wendy Greenhouse, June 10, 1984; children: Eleanor Jane, Russell Jack. BS, U. Calif., Berkeley, 1978; PhD, MIT, 1982. Rsch. asst. prof. U. Pitts., 1982-84; asst. prof. U. Ill., Chgo., 1984-89, assoc. prof., 1989-92, prof., 1992—. Contbr. articles to sci. jours. Scholar, U. Ill. Found., 1990; Dreyfus Tchr. scholar, Henry and Camille Dreyfus Found., 1989. Fellow: Am. Vacuum Soc.; mem.: Am. Phys. Soc., Am. Chem. Soc. Office: U Ill at Chgo Dept Chemistry 845 W Taylor St Chicago IL 60607-7056 Business E-Mail: mtrenary.uic.edu.

TRENERY, MARY ELLEN, librarian; b. Conran, Mo., Jan. 10, 1939; d. John Herman and Stella Cecelia (Durbin) Hulshof; m. Frank E. Trenery, June 10, 1967 (dec. Dec. 25, 1999). BA in Classics, Coll. New Rochelle, 1962; MALS, Rosary Coll., River Forest, Ill., 1966; postgrad., Fla. Atlantic U., Boca Raton, 1986-89. Tchr. grades 6, 8 Archdiocesan Sch. System, St. Louis, 1962-64; serials and acquisition libr. U. Ill., Chgo., 1966-69; acquisitions, circulation and cataloging libr. Rosary Coll., River Forest, Ill., 1964-66, 70-72; libr. media specialist St. Coleman Cath. Sch., Pompano Beach, Fla., 1973-94. Coord. for self study St. Coleman Schs., 1982, 83, 89, 90; cons. Pompano Beach City Libr. Author: Policies and Procedures for School Libraries, 1976, UICC Call Number (founding editor), 1967-68, NIUCLA Newsletter (editor 1969-72). Fed. Funding liaison with Broward County Sch. Bd., 1974-94. Mem. Ill. Libr. Assn. (sch. and tech. svcs. div. chair 1967-69), Cath. Libr. Assn. (No. Ill. unit chair, sec. 1969-72).

TRENNEPOHL, GARY LEE, university administrator, finance educator; b. Detroit, Dec. 6, 1946; s. Leo Donald and Wilma Mae (Tiesnvold) T.; m. Sandra K. Yeager, June 9, 1968; children: Paige E., Adrienne A. BS, U. Tulsa, 1968; MBA, Utah State U., 1971; PhD, Tex. Tech U., 1976. Asst. prof. aero studies Tex. Tech. U., Lubbock, 1972-74; asst./assoc. prof. fin. Ariz. State U., Tempe, 1977—82; prof. U. Mo., Columbia, 1982-86, dir. Sch. Bus., 1984-86; prof., head dept. fin. Tex. A&M U., College Station, 1986-91, assoc. dean Coll. Bus., 1991-93, Peters prof. fin., 1992-95, exec. assoc. dean, 1994-95; dean Coll. Bus. Okla. State U., Stillwater, 1995-99; pres. Okla. State U.-Tulsa, 1999—. Mem. faculty Options Inst., Chgo. Bd. Options Exch., 1987—. Author: An Introduction to Financial Management, 1984, Investment Management, 1993; assoc. editor Jour. Fin. Rsch., 1983-96; contr. chpts. Encyclopedia of Investments, Options: Essential Concepts; contbr. articles to profl. jours. Capt. USAF, 1968-72. Decorated Commendation medal with oak leaf cluster, Vietnam Svc. medal. Mem. Fin. Mgmt. Assn. (v.p. program 1993, pres. 1993-94), So. Fin. Assn., Southwestern Fin. Assn. (bd. dirs. 1983-84, pres. 1986), Midwest Fin. Assn. (bd. dirs. 1985-89). Lutheran. Office: Okla State U Tulsa 700 N Greenwood Ave Tulsa OK 74106-0702 E-mail: garyt@osu-tulsa.okstate.edu.

TRENT, ROBERT HAROLD, retired business educator; b. Norfolk, Va., Aug. 3, 1933; s. Floyd Murton and Myrtle Eugenia (White) T.; m. Joanne Bell, Aug. 17, 1951; 1 child, John Thomas BS, U. Richmond, 1963; PhD, U. N.C., 1968. Asst. prof. U. N.C., Chapel Hill, 1968-69; assoc. prof. commerce McIntire Sch. Commerce U. Va., Charlottesville, 1970-74, prof. commerce, 1975-84, Ralph A. Beeton prof. free enterprise, 1985-91; C. & P. Telephone Co. prof. commerce U. Va., Charlottesville, 1991-98, prof. commerce emeritus, 1998—. Co-author: Marketing Decision Making, 1976, 4th edit., 1988; editor: Developments in Management Information Systems, 1974 Mem. Beta Gamma Sigma, Omicron Delta Kappa.

TRESCOTT, PAUL BARTON, economics educator; b. Bloomsburg, Pa., Nov. 22, 1925; s. Paul Henry and Stella Henrietta (Potts) T.; children by previous marriage: Jeffrey A., Jill V., Andrew B. (dec.); m. Kathleen Colcord, Aug. 15, 1982. BA, Swarthmore Coll., 1949; MA, Princeton U., 1951, PhD, 1954. Reporter Evening Bulletin, Phila., 1948; instr. in econ. Princeton (N.J.) U., 1952-54; asst. assoc. prof. Kenyon Coll., Gambier, Ohio, 1954-67; prof. in econs. Miami U., Oxford, Ohio, 1967-69; prof. in econs., history So. Meth. U., Dallas, 1969-76; prof. in econs. So. Ill. U., Carbondale, 1976—. Vis. prof. in econs. Thammassat U., Bangkok, 1965-67, People's U., Beijing, 1992; vis. prof. in fin. U. Ill., Champaign and Urbana, 1981; acad. adv. commn. to Thailand U.S. Dept. State, Washington, 1968-70. Authors: Money, Banking and Economic Welfare, 1960, 2d edit., 1965, Financing American Enterprise, 1963, rep., 1982, The Logic of the Price System, 1970, Thailand's Monetary Experience, 1971. Sgt. U.S. Army, 1944-46. Rsch. grantee Brookings Inst., Washington, 1961-62; Fulbright scholar U.S. Govt., Peking U., China, 1983-84, Tech. U., Czestochowa, Poland, 1996. Mem. Am. Econs. Assn., History Econs. Soc. Avocations: music, traveling. Office: So Ill U Dept Econs Carbondale IL 62901

TRETHEWEY, NATASHA, poet, literature educator; b. Gulfport, Miss., 1966; BA in English, U. Ga.; MA in English and Creative Writing, Hollins U.; MFA in Poetry, U. Mass. Instr. Auburn U.; poet, assoc. prof. English Emory U., Atlanta, 2001—. Author: Domestic Work, 2000 (Cave Canem Poetry prize, 1999, Miss. Inst. of Arts and Letters Book prize, 2001, Lillian Smith award for peotry, 2001), Bellocq's Ophelia; contbr. poetry to publs. Recipient Disting. Young Alumna award, U. Mass., Julia Peterkin award, Converse Coll., Grolier Poetry prize, Grolier Bookstore, Cambridge, Mass., Margaret Walker award for poetry, Poets and Writers mag. and QBR: The Black Book Rev., Jessica Nobel-Maxwell Meml. award for poetry, Am. Poetry Rev.; fellow, John Simon Guggenheim Meml. Found., 2003, Nat. Endowment for the Arts, Ala. State Coun. on the Arts, Money for Women/Barbara Deming Meml. Fund; Bunting fellow, Radcliffe Inst. for Advanced Study, Radcliffe U., 2000—01. Office: Emory Univ Creative Writing Program 537 Kilgo Cir Atlanta GA 30322*

TREVINO, JERRY ROSALEZ, retired secondary school principal; b. Bee County, Tex., July 9, 1943; s. Geronimo R. and Hilaria (Rosalez) T.; m. Juanita Escalante, Jan. 1, 1985; 1 child, John-Michael. BA, U. Houston, 1967, MEd, 1974; PhD, Kennedy-Western U., 1988; postgrad., U. Tex., Permian Basin, 1988-92. Cert. tchr., adminstr., supt., Tex. Tchr. N.E. Houston Sch. Dist., 1966-70, pub. rels. officer, 1970-72, asst. prin., 1972-76; tchr. Harris County Dept. Edn., Houston, 1968-72, Austin (Tex.) Ind. Sch. Dist., 1977-87; asst. prin. Tex. Youth Commn., Pyote, 1987-91, prin., 1991-96, ret., 1996. Chair edn. seminar, 24th Internat. Congress, Oxford (Eng.) U., 1997; reader, U.S. Dept. Edn., 1996-97; mentor Austin Ind. Sch. Dist., 1996-98; Title VII project dir. U.S. Dept. Edn., Pyote, 1988-96; instr. Austin C.C., 1980-84, chair, Prin. Coun. for Edn. of Lang. Minority Students, S.W. Ednl. Devel. Lab., Austin, 1994-96; rschr. and ednl. cons. Bentiva Co., 2002—. Editor newsletter The Flyer, 1970-72; contbr. articles to profl. publs. Mem. Community Adv. Coun., Pyote, 1987-96; mem. Tex. Children's Mental Health Plan, Monahans, Tex., 1991-96; mem. planning com. Permian Basin Quality Work Force, Midland, Tex., 1992-96; mem. Supt.'s Coun., Pyote, 1987-96. Named Outstanding Adminstr. of Permian Basin (Golden Apple award) Permian Basin Private Industry Coun., 1994. Mem. ASCD, Nat. Assn. for Bilingual Edn., Order Internat. Ambs., Tex. Assn. Secondary Sch. Prins., Civil Air Patrol, Soc. of Leading Intellectuals of the World. Presbyterian. Avocations: flying, travel, reading, landscaping. Address: PO Box 299 Paige TX 78659

TREVOR, LESLIE JEAN, special education educator; b. Texas City, Tex., Mar. 22, 1957; d. William Giles and Betty Jo (Langhammer) Hill; m. Stephen Lynn Trevor, June 11, 1988. BS in Elem. Edn., U. Tex., 1979. Tchr. reading Wiederstein Elem. Sch., Cibolo, Tex., 1979-82; tchr. compensatory Olympia Elem. Sch., Universal City, Tex., 1992—, lead tchr., dept. head spl. educators, 1996-97. Decision making team Olympia Elem., 1994-97. Chmn. Jr. League San Antonio, 1994—; vol. Botanical Gardens Childrens Saturday Classes, 1996-97. Mem. Assn. Tex. Profl. Educators, U. Tex. Austin Alumni Assn. (life), No. Hills Country Club, Gamma Phi Beta (pres. 1979-80), Gamma Phi. Republican. Lutheran. Home: 8646 Park Olympia Universal City TX 78148-3262 Office: Olympia Elem Sch 8439 Athenian Dr Universal City TX 78148-2601

TREZZA, ALPHONSE FIORE, librarian, educator; b. Phila., Dec. 27, 1920; s. Vincent and Amalia (Ferrara) T.; m. Mildred Di Pietro, May 19, 1945; children: Carol Ann Trezza Johnston, Alphonse Fiore. BS, U. Pa., 1948, MS, 1950, postgrad.; LHD (hon.), Rosary Coll., 1997. Page Free Library, Phila., 1940-41, 45-48, library asst., 1948-49; cataloger, asst. reference librarian Villanova U., 1949-50, instr., 1956-60; head circulation dept. U. Pa. Library, 1950-56; lectr. Drexel Inst. Sch. Library Sci., 1951-60; editor Cath. Library world, 1956-60; exec. sec. Cath. Library Assn., 1956-60; assoc. exec. dir. ALA, exec. sec. library adminstrn. div., 1960-67, assoc. dir. adminstrv. services, 1967-69; dir. Ill. State Library, Springfield, 1969-74; lectr. Grad. Sch. Library and Info. Sci., Cath. U., 1975-82; exec. dir. Nat. Commn. on Libraries and Info. Scis., Washington, 1974-80; dir. intergovt. library Cooperation Project Fed. Library Com./Library of Congress, Washington, 1980-82; assoc. prof. Sch. Library and Info. Studies Fla. State U., Tallahassee, 1982-87, prof., 1987-93, emeritus prof., 1993—. Mem. Ill. Library LSCA TITLE I-II Adv. Commn., 1963-69; mem. network devel. com. Library of Congress, 1977-82; bd. visitors Sch. Library and Info. Sci., U. Pitts., 1977-80; cons. Becker & Hayes, Inc., 1980-84, King Research, Inc., 1981-82; mem. planning com and steering com. Fla. Gov.'s Conf. on Library and Info. Svcs., 1988-91. Nat. chmn. Cath. Book Week, 1954—56; pres. Joliet Diocesan Bd. Edn., 1966—68; auditor Borough of Norwood, Pa., 1958—60; mem. patron's bd. Fla. State U. Sch. Theater, 2000—; bd. mem. Lafayette Oaks Home Assn., 2002—; Dem. committeeman Lombard, Ill., 1961—69; Eucharistic min. Blessed Sacramento Cath. Ch., 1984—, mem. parish coun., 2000—. 1st lt. USAF, 1942—45. Decorated Air medal; recipient Ofcl. commendation White House Conf. on Libr. and Info. Svc., 1979, citation State Libr. Agys., 1994, Silver award Commn. Libr. Info. Sci., 1996. Mem. ALA (coun. 1973-82, 88-92, mem. exec. bd. 1974-79, chmn. stats. coordinating com. 1970-74, mem. pub. com. 1975-78, 81-83, 87-89, chmn. adv. com. interface, 1979-83, chmn. membership com. 1983-84, chmn. nominating com. 1988-89, mem. legis. com. 1989-91, adv. bd. ALA Yearbook 1976-91, Assn. Specialized and Coop. Library Agys. legis. com., 1987-89, ad hoc com. White House Conf. on Libr. and Info. Svcs. 1989-91, chmn. awards com. 1990-92, Exceptional Achievement award 1981, J.B. Lippincott award 1989), Cath. Library Assn. (life, adv. coun. 1960—), Ill. Library Assn. (chmn. legis.-library devel. com. 1964-69, mem. exec. bd., libr's. citation 1974), Fla. Library Assn. (bd. dirs. 1987-93, pres. 1991-92, intellectual freedom com., chmn. com. on Fla. Librs. publ., editor, publ. com., planning com., 1991, site com.), Continuing Libr. Edn. Network and Exchange (pres. 1982-83), Internat. Fedn. Library Assns. and Institutions (statistics standing com. 1976-85, planning com.), Coun. Nat. Library Assns. (chmn. 1959-61), Assn. Coll. and Research Librarians (pres. Phila. chpt. 1953-55), Drexel Inst. Library Sch. Alumni Assn. (pres. 1955-56, exec. bd. 1956-60, chmn. chief officers State Library Agys. 1973-74), Chgo. Library Club (pres. 1969), Assn. Library and Info. Sci. Edn. (govt. relation com. 1985-87), Drexel U. Alumni Assn. (Outstanding Alumnus award 1963), Kappa Phi Kappa (chpt. pres. 1948), Beta Phi Mu (hon.). Lodges: K.C. E-mail: atrezza@mailer.fsu.edu.

TRIANTAFYLLOU, MICHAEL STEFANOS, ocean engineering educator; b. Athens, Greece, Oct. 27, 1951; came to U.S., 1974; s. Stefanos M. and Penelopi I. (Koutras) T.; m. Joan L. Kimball, Sept. 22, 1985; children: Stefanos R., Kimon K. MS in Ocean Engring., MSME, MIT, 1977, ScD, 1979. Rsch. assoc. MIT, Cambridge, Mass., 1978-79, asst. prof., 1979-83, assoc. prof., 1983-86, tenured assoc. prof., 1986-90, prof., dir. ocean engrng. testing tank, 1990—. Vis. scientist Woods Hole (Mass.) Oceanographic Inst., 1990—; com. chair MIT/Woods Hole Joint Program in Oceanography. Featured cover Scientific American; contbr. articles to profl. jours. Rsch. grantee OFfice NAval Rsch., Office Naval Tech., NSF, Doherty Found. Dept. Commerce, 1979—. Mem. Internat. Soc. Offshore and Polar Engrs. (founding mem.), Soc. Naval Architects and Marine Engrs. (papers com., vice chmn. OC-2 com.), Am. Phys. Soc. Office: MIT 77 Massachusetts Ave Rm 5-323 Cambridge MA 02139-4307

TRICE, MARY SUE WILLIAMS, guidance counselor; b. Marietta, Ga., Aug. 9, 1950; d. Pembroke Whitfield and Virginia Swanson Williams; m. Richard Alan Trice, Dec. 15, 1972; 1 child, Mary Katherine. BA in Art Edn., West Ga. Coll., 1971, MEd, 1972. Guidance counselor, art tchr. Monroe Acad., Forsyth, Ga., 1975-78; art tchr. Gwin Oaks Elem. Sch., Lawrenceville, Ga., 1978-79; h.s. counselor Ctrl. Gwinnett H.S., Lawrenceville, Ga., 1979-89, Berkmar H.S., Lilburn, Ga., 1989—. Bd. dirs. Ga. Edn. Articulation Com., Atlanta. Girl Scout leader Northwest Ga. Girl Scouts, Suwanee, 1981-2002, svc. unit dir., 1997-2002. Mem. Am. Sch. Counselor Assn., Girl Scouts Am. (life), Ga. Sch. Counselors Assn., Atlanta Yacht Club. Home: 5155 Meadowbrook Cir Suwanee GA 30024-1964

TRICHEL, MARY LYDIA, middle school educator; b. Rosenberg, Tex., Feb. 2, 1957; d. Henry John and Henrietta (Jurek) Pavlicek; m. Keith Trichel, Aug. 8, 1981; children: Daniel, Nicholas. BS cum laude, Tex. A & M U., 1980. Cert. tchr., Tex. Social studies tchr. grades 6, 7 and 8 St. Francis de Sales, Houston, 1980-81; English tchr. grades 7 and 8 Dean Morgan Jr. High, Casper, Wyo., 1983-86; English and journalism tchr. grades 9 and 11 Tecumseh (Okla.) High Sch., 1987; English tchr. grade 6 Christa McAuliffe Middle Sch., Houston, 1988-92; tchr. Tex. history grade 7, journalism grade 8 Lake Olympia Middle Sch., Missouri City, Tex., 1991-92; tchr. social studies 6th grade Lake Olympia Mid. Sch. Ft. Bend Ind. Sch. Dist., 1993-96; tchr. social studies 6th grade Atascocita Mid. Sch. Humble Ind. Sch. Dist., 1997—. Recipient teaching awards. Mem. Nat. Coun. Tchrs. English, Nat. Coun. Tchrs. Social Studies, Am. Fedn. Tchrs. Avocations: desktop publishing, scuba diving, traveling. Home: 14306 Hartshill Dr Houston TX 77044-5066

TRIESCHMANN, ELIZABETH SUZANNE, elementary school educator; b. Hot Springs, Ark., Mar. 16, 1960; d. Willian Douglas II and Anna Sue (Looper) McCoy; m. John Cypert Treischmann, Dec. 20, 1980; children: John Benjamin. BS in Edn., Henderson State U., 1982. Cert. tchr. Ark., N.C. Substitute tchr. Hot Springs (Ark.) City Schs., 1982; tchr. Greehouse Pre-Sch., Yuma, Ariz., 1983-84, Stone St. Elem. Sch., Camp LeJeune, N.C., 1985-86, Hot Springs City Schs., 1990-91, St. Francis of Assisi Sch., Jacksonville, N.C., 1986-90, 91-93. Mem. Internat. Reading Assn. (Onslow county), Beta Sigma Phi (Gamma Theta chpt., sec. 1992-93). Methodist. Avocations: reading, swimming, cross stitch. Home: 108 Alta Vista St Hot Springs National Park AR 71913-6909

TRIGG, GLYN RAY, guidance counselor, educational administrator, customer service representative; b. Canton, Miss., Apr. 21, 1964; s. Bruce L. and Eunice W. (Davis) T. BS in Social and Rehabilitative Svcs., U. So. Miss., 1991. Alcohol-drug counselor, intervention-prevention counselor S.W. Miss. Mental Health, McComb, 1992-93; guidance counselor, tchr. phys. edn., coach Porter's Chapel Acad., Vicksburg, Miss., 1993-95, interim headmaster, 1994—. Bell ringer Salvation Army, Vicksburg, 1993; organizer, activities chmn. Eagle Fest, Porter's Chapel Patron's Club, 1994. Named Jaycee of Month, Hattiesburg Jaycees, 1991, recipient cert. of merit, Jacke Eckerd svc. award. Mem. Jackson Jaycees (2d dir. 1990-92, Jaycee of Month 1992), Kiwanis (faculty advisor Key Club 1993-94). Baptist. Home: 6675 Old Canton Rd Apt 2047 Ridgeland MS 39157-1334 Office: Skyte 1 Comms 3450 Highway 80 W Jackson MS 39209-7201

TRILLING, GEORGE HENRY, physicist, educator; b. Bialystok, Poland, Sept. 18, 1930; came to U.S., 1941; s. Max and Eugenie (Walfisz) T.; m. Madeleine Alice Monic, June 26, 1955; children: Stephen, Yvonne, David. BS, Calif. Inst. Tech., Pasadena, 1951, PhD, 1955. Research fellow Calif. Inst. Tech., Pasadena, 1955-56; Fulbright post-doctoral fellow Ecole Polytechnique, Paris, 1956-57; asst. to assoc. prof. U. Mich., Ann Arbor, 1957-60; assoc. to prof. dept. physics U. Calif., Berkeley, 1960-94, prof. emeritus, 1994—. Fellow Am. Phys. Soc., Am. Acad. Arts and Scis.; mem. NAS. Achievements include: research in high energy physics. Office: Lawrence Berkeley Nat Lab Berkeley CA 94720-0001

TRILLING, LEON, aeronautical engineering educator; b. Bialystok, Poland, July 15, 1924; came to U.S., 1940, naturalized, 1946; s. Oswald and Regina (Zakhejm) T.; m. Edna Yuval, Feb. 17, 1946; children: Alex R., Roger S. BS, Calif. Inst. Tech., 1944, MS, 1946, PhD, 1948. Research fellow Calif. Inst. Tech., 1948- 50; Fulbright scholar U. Paris, 1950-51, vis. prof., 1963-64; mem. faculty MIT, Cambridge, 1951—, prof. aeros. and astronautics, 1962-94, prof. emeritus, 1994—, mem. coun. on primary and secondary edn., 1992—. Mem. Program in Sci. Tech. and Society, Engrng. Edn. Mission to Soviet Union, 1958; vis. prof. Delft Tech. U., 1974-75; vis. prof. engrng. Carleton Coll., 1987 Pres. Met. Com. Ednl. Opportunity, 1967-70, Council for Understanding of Tech. in Human Affairs, 1984— Guggenheim fellow, 1963-64 Fellow AAAS. Home: 180 Beacon St Boston MA 02116-1408 Office: MIT 77 Massachusetts Ave Cambridge MA 02139-4307

TRIMARCHI, RUTH ELLEN, educator, researcher, community activist; b. Adams, Mass., Jan. 9, 1954; d. Anthony Rocco and Millicent June (Brimmer) T.; m. David Wayne Miller, Sept. 17, 1981; children: Eliot, Jacob. BA in Biology, Vassar Coll., 1978; MEd, U. Mass., 1993. Cert. tchr., Mass. Rsch. asst. U. Ghent (Belgium), 1978-79, Harvard U., Cambridge, Mass., 1980-81; tchr. sci. Amherst (Mass.) Regional H.S., 1994—. Fund raiser Abortion Rights Fund of Western Mass., Amherst, 1989—; mem. Amherst Town Meeting, 1999—; bd. dirs. A Better Chance House, Amherst, 2001—, LWV, Amherst, 1991—93; mem. adv. com. Children's Svcs. Dept., Amherst, 1990—93. Mem. Phi Delta Kappa. Avocations: children and women's rights, science, education. Office: Amherst Regional HS 22 Matoon St Amherst MA 01002-2139

TRIMBLE, GARNET O'CULL, retired elementary music educator; b. Maysville, Ky., Aug. 18, 1945; d. George and Grace (Thomas) O'Cull; m. Shelby C. Trimble; children: Shelby Scott, Bryant Keith. B of Music Edn., Morehead State U., 1970, MEd, 1974. Tchr. grade 5 May's Lick (Ky.) Elem. Sch., 1965-66; tchr. vocal music K-8 and h.s. chorus Ripley (Ohio)-Union-Lewis Schs., 1966-93; tchr. elem. vocal music Ripley Elem. Sch., 1993—2001; part-time prof. music Maysville C.C. Dist. XVI rep. for Ohio, Music in Our Schs. Month, Nat. Educators Nat. Conf., 1966—; mem. Best Effort Superior Team, Ripley Schs., 1993-94. Contbr. to mus. publs. and profl. jours. Leader 4-H Club, Orangeburg, Ky., 1990-94; past mem. Mason-Maysville Arts Commn., 1991-93; chmn. Cmty. Resource Night. Mem. NEA, Ohio Music Educators, Ripley-Union-Lewis Huntington Edn. Assn. (bldg. rep. 1993, 94, v.p. 1995), Orangeburg Lioness Club (sec., past pres. 1993—). Republican. Avocations: quilting, singing, playing piano, helping others. Home: 7421 Mount Carmel Rd Maysville KY 41056-9496 Office: Maysville CC US 68-1855 Maysville KY 41056

TRIMBLE, ROBERT BOGUE, research biologist; b. Balt., July 2, 1943; s. George Simpson and Janet Anna (Bogue) T.; m. Kathleen Marie Davis, May 17, 1969 (dec. Aug. 1988); 1 child, Alison Bogue; m. Elizabeth Gould Belden, Dec. 3, 1994. BS in Biology, Rensselaer Poly. Inst., 1965, MS in Biology, 1967, PhD in Biology, 1969. From rsch. scientist I to rsch. scientist V N.Y. State Dept. Health Wadsworth Ctr., Albany, 1970-93, rsch. scientist VI, 1993—; dep. dir. Wadsworth Ctr. Office of Rsch., 2002—, dir., 2003—; prof. biomed. sci. SUNY Sch. Pub. Health, Albany, 1989—; assoc. chmn. grad. studies exec. com. dept. biomed. sci. Albany Med. Coll., 1998—2003. Mem. USPHS Cell Biology and Physiol. I Study Sect., Bethesda, Md., 1985-89, Am. Cancer Soc. Personnel Rev. Group, Atlanta, 1991-96, USPHS Rev. Res. Panel, Bethesda, 1989-93. Mem. editl. bd. Jour. Biol. Chemistry, 1992-97, Glycobiology, 1996—, Analytical Biochemistry, 1997—; contbr. over 70 articles to profl. jours., chpts. to books. Grantee Nat. Inst. Aging, 1977-81, Nat. Inst. Gen. Med. Sci., 1977—; recipient Recognition award N.Y. State Health Commr., 2003. Mem. Am. Soc. for Biochemistry and Molecular Biology, Soc. for Glycobiology (exec. bd. 1995-98), Am. Soc. for Microbiology, AAAS, Sigma Xi. Episcopalian. Office: NY State Dept Health Wadsworth Ctr C-547 Albany NY 12201-0509 E-mail: trimble@wadsworth.org.

TRINKUS, LAIMA MARY, special education educator; b. Chgo., Mar. 6, 1950; d. Steven and Antonia (Ambrasas) Trinkus. BS in Sociology, Daemen Coll., Buffalo, 1974; MS in Behavioral Sci. Spl. Edn., SUNY, Buffalo, 1987. Cert. spl. edn. tchr., N.Y. Tchr. aide Cantalician Ctr. for Learning, Buffalo, 1975-78, tchr. spl. edn., 1978-85, Erie I Bd. Coop. Edn. Svcs., Lancaster, N.Y., 1985—. Vol. Spl. Olympics, Buffalo, 1976—. Home: 9821 Greiner Rd Clarence NY 14031-1237

TRIPOLE, MARTIN R. religion educator, priest; b. Penn Yan, N.Y., June 14, 1935; s. James and Mary T. BA, Fordham U., 1957, MPhil, 1963; postgrad., Syracuse U., 1957-58; ThM, Woodstock Coll., 1968; STD, Inst. Catholique de Paris, 1972. Joined S.J., Roman Cath. Ch., 1958, ordained priest, 1967. Instr. Bellarmine Coll., Plattsburg, N.Y., 1957-58, Le Moyne Coll., Syracuse, N.Y., 1962-64; asst. prof. Marquette U., Milw., 1974-75; assoc. prof. St. Joseph's U., Phila., 1972—. Instr. St. Agnes Coll., Balt., 1967. Author: Jesus Event and Our Response, 1980, Faith Beyond Justice: Widening the Perspective, 1994; contbr. articles to profl. jours. Mem. Am. Acad. Religion, Cath. Theol. Soc. Am., Coll. Theol. Soc. Roman Catholic. Home: 5600 City Ave Philadelphia PA 19131-1308 Office: 5600 City Line Ave Philadelphia PA 19131-1308

TRIPOLITIS, ANTONIA, religion, classics and comparative literature educator; b. Phila. PhD, U. Pa., 1971. Rsch. assoc. Inst. for Antiquity and Christianity, Claremont, Calif., 1971—; asst. dean acad. affairs Rutgers U., New Brunswick, N.J., 1975-76, assoc. dean acad. affairs, 1976-79, chair, grad. dir. classical studies, 1979-87, assoc. prof. classics, comparative lit. and religion, 1987—2003, dir. modern Greek Studies, 1995—, prof., 2002—. Author: Doctrine of Soul in Thought of Plotinus and Origen, 1978, Origen: A Critical Reading, 1985, Kassia: The Legend, The Woman, and Her Work, 1991, Religions of the Hellenistic-Roman Age, 2001; contbr. numerous articles to profl. jours. Nat. Geographic Soc. grantee, 1968-69. Mem. AAUW (fellowship 1969-70), Am. Literary Translators Assn., Am. Soc. Ch. History, Am. Acad. Religion, Soc. Bibl. Lit., Soc. for Neoplatonic Studies, N.Am. Patristic Soc. Office: Rutgers U Dept Modern Greek Studies Livingston Campus B313 Lucy Stone Hall New Brunswick NJ 08901

TRIPP, APRIL, special education services professional; BS, Calif. State U., Fullerton, Calif., 1981; MA with hons., Calif. State U., Long Beach, Calif., 1985; MS, Johns Hopkins U., 1994; PhD with hons., Tex. Woman's U., 1989. 1st coord. adapted physical edn. Balt. County Pub. Schs.; assoc. prof. U. Ill., Urbana-Champaign, Ill. Chmn. adapted physical edn. section Md. AHPERD; mem. Nat. Cert. for Adapted Physical Edn. Standards Com., Spl. Olympics. Recipient Excellence in Edn. award-Spl. Tchr. of Yr. Balt. County, Mabel Lee award Am. Alliance Health, Phys. Edn., Recreation and Dance, 1994; grantee Nat. Handicapped Sports. Mem. Nat. PTA (hon. life award 1993), ARAPCS (mem. adapted physical activity coun. exec. com.) Office: Dept Kinesiology Univ Ill Louise Freer Hall 906 S Goodwin Ave Urbana IL 61801 Office Fax: 217-244-7322. E-mail: atripp3@uiuc.edu.*

TRIPP, LUKE SAMUEL, educator; b. Atoka, Tenn., Feb. 6, 1941; s. Luke Samuel and Dorothy Mae (Watson) T.; m. Hedwidge Mary Bruyns, Aug. 21, 1989; children: Ruth, Azania, Comrade. BS, Wayne State U., 1966; MA, U. Mich., 1974, PhD, 1980. Computer programmer No. Elec. Co., Montreal, Que., Can., 1966-68; tchr. elem. sch. math. Santa Maria Edn. Ctr., Detroit, 1969-70; instr. black studies Wayne County C.C., Detroit, 1971-72; tchr. secondary sch. sci. Cmty. Skills Ctr., Ann Arbor, Mich., 1971-73; dir. grad. rsch. U. Mich., Ann Arbor, 1977-80; asst. prof. U. Ill., Champaign, 1981-82, So. Ill. U., Carbondale, 1982-89; from asst. prof. to prof. social sci. St. Cloud (Minn.) State U., 1989-95, prof., 1995—2003; chmn. Dept. of Cmty. Studies, 2003. Co-founder, coord. Faculty/Staff Color Caucus, St. Cloud, 1989—; founder, dir. Human Rights Coputhon, St. Cloud, 1989-91, So. Ill. Anti-Aparthied Coalition, Carbondale, 1984-87. Dir. polit. edn. Nat. Black Ind. Polit. Party, Ann Arbor, 1980-81; co-founder, mem. exec. bd. Labor Defense League, Detroit, 1970-71, League Revolutionary Black Workers, Detroit, 1968-70; coord. Nat. Black Econ. Devel. Conf., Detroit, 1969-70; student activist SNCC, Detroit, 1960-65. Mem. Nat. Coun. Black Studies, Assn. Study Afro-Am. Life and History. Office: St Cloud State U 720 4th Ave S Saint Cloud MN 56301-4498 E-mail: ltripp@stcloudstate.edu.

TRITTEN, JAMES JOHN, national security educator; b. Yonkers, N.Y., Oct. 3, 1945; s. James Hanley and Jennie (Szucs) Tritten; m. Kathleen Brattesani (div. 1983); children: Kimberly, James John Jr.; m. Jasmine Clark, Dec. 29, 1990. BA in Internat. Studies, Am. U., 1971; MA in Internat. Affairs, Fla. State U., 1978; AM in Internat. Rels., U. So. Calif., L.A., 1982, PhD in Internat. Rels., 1984. Commd. officer USN, 1967, advanced through grades to commdr., 1981; joint strategic plans officer Office of the Chief of Naval Ops., Washington, 1984-85; asst. dir. net assessment Office of the Sec. of Def., Washington, 1985-86; chmn. dept. nat. security affairs Naval Postgrad. Sch., Monterey, Calif., 1986-89; ret. USN, 1989; assoc. prof. nat. security affairs Naval Postgrad. Sch., Monterey, 1989-93; spl. asst. to comdr. Naval Doctrine Command, Norfolk, Va., 1993-96; chief policy and plan divsn. U.S. Joint Forces Command, Suffolk, Va., 1996-01, mem. joint doctrine divsn., 2001—02; chief tng. and inspections divsn. Def. Threat Reduction Agy., Albuquerque, 2002—, asst. chief staff, 2002—. Cons. Rand Corp., Santa Monica, Calif., 1982—84; with Nat. Security Rsch., Fairfax, Va., 1992, Amerlnd, Alexandria, Va., 1996. Author: (book) Soviet Naval Forces and Nuclear Warfare, 1986, Our New National Security Strategy, 1992 (George Washington Honor medal, 1991), A Doctrine Reader, 1996; contbr. chapters to books, articles to profl. jours. Mem. Adv. Bd. on Alcohol Related Problems, Monterey, 1987—90; bd. dirs., officer Leadership Monterey Peninsula, 1989—92, Carmel Valley (Calif.) Property Owners Assn., 1989—91; commr. Airport Land Use Commn., Monterey County, 1990—93. Decorated Def. Superior Svc. medal Sec. Def., Washington, Meritorious Svc. medal Sec. Navy, Navy Civillian Supr. Svc. medal; recipient Joint Meritorious Civilian Svc. award, Chmn. Joint Chiefs Staff, 1998, Alfred Thayer Mahan award for literary achievement, Navy League U.S., 1986. Mem.: Mil. Ops. Rsch. Soc. (v.p. 1990—91), U.S. Naval Inst. (Silver and Bronze medals), Naval Order U.S., Pi Gamma Mu, Pi Sigma Alpha. Republican. Presbyterian. Avocations: hiking, writing. Office: Def Threat Reduction Agy-CST 1680 Texas St SE Kirtland Afb NM 87117 E-mail: james.tritten@ao.dtra.mil.

TRITTON, THOMAS RICHARD, academic administrator, biologist, educator; b. Lakewood, Ohio, Dec. 20, 1947; s. William Frank and Margie Jean (Galbraith) Tritton; m. Louise Meschter Tritton; children: Lara, Christiana. BA, Ohio Wesleyan U., 1969; PhD, Boston U., 1973. Asst. prof. Yale Med. Sch., New Haven, 1975—80; assoc. prof. Yale U., 1980—85; prof. U. Vt., Burlington, 1985—97, vice provost, 1991—97; pres. Haverford Coll., Pa., 1997—. Mem. NIH Exptl. Therapeutics Study Sect., 1988—92. Editor books; mem. editl. bd.: various profl. jours.; contbr. scientific papers to profl. jours. Mem.: Am. Soc. Biol. Chemists, Am. Assn. Cancer Rsch. (com. mem.). Mem. Soc. Of Friends. Avocations: music, tennis. Office: Haverford Coll 370 Lancaster Ave Haverford PA 19041-1336 E-mail: ttritton@haverford.edu.

TRIULZI, DANIEL ALBERT, classical and modern languages educator, priest; b. Alexandria, Egypt, May 21, 1947; s. Eugene W. and Pauline Arlette (De La Rayna) T. Certificat d'Etudes, Music Conservatory, Fribourg, Switzerland, 1965; BA in Classical and Fgn. Langs., St. Mary's U., San Antonio, 1970; postgrad.Biblical and Cognate Lit., U. Toronto, Ont., Can., 1977-78; postgrad., U. Fribourg, Switzerland, 1978-83, Middlebury (Vt.) Coll., 1978; postgrad. in Early Christian Literature, U. Dayton, 1991—. Cert. secondary French, Spanish and Latin tchr., Mo., Tex.; ordained priest, Roman Cath. Ch. 1981. Tchr. fgn. langs. Vianney High Sch., St. Louis, 1970-71; instr. English and religion Colegio Santa Maria, Lima, Peru, 1971-73, prin. mid. sch., 1973-75; vice prin. Colegio San Jose, Trujillo, Peru, 1975-76; instr. music history Trujillo Conservatory Music, 1975-76; tchr. music Spanish Embassy High Sch., Fribourg, Switzerland, 1980-82; tchr. fng. langs., chaplain, counselor Nolan High Sch., Ft. Worth, 1984-90, dir. gifted students program, 1984-86. Instr. N.T. grad. theology program St. Mary's U., San Antonio, 1985; presenter in field. Papers read before profl. orgns. Life mem. Chamber Orch. Trujillo, 1976—. Fellow NEH, 1985. Mem. Cath. Bibl. Assn., Soc. Bibl. Lit., Am. Acad. Religion, Am. Soc. Papyrologists, Delta Epsilon Sigma. Avocations: chamber music, greco-roman numismatics. Home: 57 Woodland Ave Dayton OH 45409-2853 Office: U Dayton Internat Marian Rsch Inst Dayton OH 45469

TROESTER, DENNIS LEE, physical education educator; b. McCook, N.C., June 28, 1948; s. Carl Christopher and Maria Anna (Carolina) Troester. BA in Edn., Kearney State, 1971. Physical edn. educator Rep. Valley Schs., Indianola, Nebr., 1971—, athletic dir., 2003—. Recipient Women's Coach of Yr. award, State Farm Ins., 1998, Regional Coach of Yr. award, Nat. Coaches Assn., 2002—03. Mem.: NEA, Nebr. Schs. Interscholastic Activities Athletic Assn., Nebr. Coaches Assn. (adv. com. volleyball 1996—, Nebr. volleyball coach of yr. award 1998, Friend to Volleyball award 2001), Nebr. Edn. Assn. Republican. Lutheran. Avocations: hunting, fishing. Home: RR1 Box 140 Indianola NE 69034 Office: Republican Valley Schools Box 80 A Indianola NE 69034 Fax: 308-364-2508. E-mail: dtroeste@esu15.org.

TROJAHN, LYNN, academic administrator; b. Ft. Smith, Mar. 30, 1962; m. Craig William Trojahn, May 25, 1989; 1 child, Rachel. B of Internat. Rels. & Spanish, Colgate U.; MBA, Am. Grad. Sch. Internat. Mgmt., 1986. Devel. Breakthrough Found., San Francisco, 1984-91, Emergency Housing, San Jose, Calif., 1991-92, U. N.Mex. Gen. Libr., Albuquerque, 1993—. Author Libr. Devel. mag., 1997. Mem. Nat. Soc. Fundraising Execs. (v.p. 1993—), Acad. Libr. Advancement & Devel. Network (founder), Kiwanis, Phi Eta Sigma. Avocations: reading, golf, volunteering, public speaking, horseback riding. Office: U N Mex Zimmerman Libr Tale At Roma Albuquerque NM 87131-0001

TROJAN, PENELOPE ANN, physical education educator; b. Lansford, Pa., July 18, 1944; d. Chester John and Marie Louise (DeMarco) T. BS, E. Stroudsburg U., 1966, MEd, 1968. Cert. tchr. Pa., N.Y. Tchr. Panther Valley Ctrl. Schs., Lansford, Pa., 1966-67; grad. asst. E. Stroudsburg (Pa.) U., 1967-68; from instr. to assoc. prof. Mohawk Valley C.C., Utica, N.Y., 1968-92, prof., 1992—. Cons. Ctr. State Tchr. Ctr., New Hartford, N.Y., 1982—. Mem. AAHPERD, Nat. Jr. Coll. Athletic Assn. Region III Tennis Coaches Assn. (sec. 1989—, asst. dir. 1979-82), Utica Bd. Ofcls. for Women's Sports (pres. 1974—), Utica Bd. Ofcls. for Women's Basketball (pres. 1976-81, cert., svc. award 1981), Utica Bd. Ofcls. for Women's Softball (pres. 1977-79, cert., Svc. award 1992), Utica Bd. Ofcls. for Volleyball (cert.), N.Y. State Girls Basketball Ofcls. Assn. (pres. 1983-85, clinician 1987—. Avocations: racquetball, jogging, cross-country skiing, camping, tennis. Office: Mohawk Valley C C 1101 Sherman Dr Utica NY 13501-5308

TROLL, RALPH, biology educator; b. Reinheim, Hesse, Germany, Oct. 8, 1932; came to U.S., 1947; s. Johann Christian and Nelly (Bentheim) T.; m. Loretta Frieda Glaser, June 28, 1958; children: Michael B., Karen N., Krista A. BS, U. Ill., 1957, MS, 1958; PhD, U. Minn., 1965. Instr. biology Augustana Coll., Rock Island, Ill., 1959-63, asst. prof., 1963-66, assoc. prof., 1966-72, prof., 1972—99, prof. emeritus, 1999—. Author: Life of Marcello Malphigi, 1989; contbr. articles to profl. jours. With U.S. Army, 1952-54, Japan. Recipient NSF summer fellow, U. Ariz., 1959, Duke U., 1960, U. Minn., 1961, Oreg. State U., 1966. Mem. Ill. State Acad. Sci.

TROMBLEY, DONALD B. academic administrator; BS, SUNY, Plattsburgh, 1970; MA, U. Mo., Kansas City, 1980, PhD, 1984. Supt. Dryden (N.Y.) Cen. Sch. Dist., 1988—98, Corning City Sch. Dist., Painted Post, NY, 1999—. Mem. Am. Assn. Sch. Adminstrs./NSBA Joint Com. for Devel. of Key Work of School Bds. publ., 2000. Mem.: N.Y. State Staff Devel. Coun. (pres. 1993—94), N.Y. State Coun. Sch. Supts. (pres. 2000—01), Am. Assn. Sch. Adminstrs. (small/rural schs. adv. com. 1998—2001, suburban schs. adv. com. 2001—04, adv. coun. for N.Y. State Assn. 2001—04, mem. Century Club 2001). Office: Corning-Painted Post Area Sch Dist 165 Charles St Painted Post NY 14870-1331*

TROPMAN, JOHN ELMER, social sciences educator; b. Syracuse, NY, Sept. 14, 1939; s. Elmer and Elizabeth (Overfield) T.; m. Penelope Savino, June 20, 1964; children: Sarah, Jessica, Matthew. AB, Oberlin U., 1961; AM, U. Chgo., 1963; PhD, U. Mich., 1967. Asst. prof. U. Mich., Ann Arbor, 1965-70, assoc. prof., 1970-76, prof. social work and social sci., 1976—. Author: Policy Management, 1984, American Values and Social Welfare, 1989, Entrepreneurial Systems, 1989, Catholic Ethic in American Society, 1996, Catholic Ethic and the Spirit of Community, 2002, Making Meetings Work, 1996, 2002, Successful Community Leadership, 1997. Recipient Monsignour O'Grady award Catholic U., Washington, 1986. Mem. Mich. Soc. Fellows (chair 1988-89). Avocation: fly fishing. Home: 3568 River Pines Dr Ann Arbor MI 48103-9516

TROST, BARRY MARTIN, chemist, educator; b. Phila., June 13, 1941; s. Joseph and Esther T.; m. Susan Paula Shapiro, Nov. 25, 1967; children: Aaron David, Carey Daniel. BA cum laude, U. Pa., 1962; PhD, MIT, 1965; D (hon.), U. Claude Bernard, Lyons, France, 1994, Technion, Israel, 1997. Mem. faculty U. Wis., Madison, 1965—, prof., chemistry, 1969—, Evan P. and Marion Helfaer prof. chemistry, from 1976, Vilas rsch. prof. chemistry; prof. chemistry Stanford U., 1987—, Tamaki prof. humanities and scis., 1990, chmn. dept., 1996—2002; Lord Todd vis. prof. Cambridge U., England, 2002—. Cons. Merck, Sharp & Dohme, E.I. duPont de Nemours.; Chem. Soc. centenary lectr., 1982 Author: Problems in Spectroscopy, 1967, Sulfur Ylides, 1975; editor-in-chief Comprehensive Organic Synthesis, 1991—, ChemTracts/Organic Chemistry, 1993—; editor: Structure and Reactivity Concepts in Organic Chemistry series, 1972—; assoc. editor Jour. Am. Chem. Soc., 1974-80; mem. editl. bd. Organic Reactions Series, 1971—, Chemistry A European Jour., 1995—. Sci. of Synthesis, Houben-Weyl Methods of Molecular Transformations, 1995—; contbr. numerous articles to profl. jours. Named Chem. Pioneer, Am. Inst. Chemists, 1983; recipient Dreyfus Found. Tech.-Scholar award, 1970, 1977, Creative Work in Synthetic Organic Chemistry award, 1981, Baekland medal, 1981, Alexander von Humboldt award, 1984, Guenther award, 1990, Janssen prize, 1990, Roger Adams award, Am. Chem. Soc., 1995, Presdl. Green Univ. Challenge award, 1998, Nicholas medal, 2000, Yamada prize, 2001, Yamada Prize, 2001, ACS Nobel Laureate Signature award, Graduate Ed. Chemistry, 2002; fellow, NSF, 1963—65, Sloan Found., 1967—69, Am. Swiss Found., 1975—, Zencca, 1997; scholar Cope scholar, 1989. Mem.: NAS, AAAS, Chem. Soc. London, Am. Acad. Arts and Scis., Am. Chem.

Soc. (award in pure chemistry 1977, Roger Adams award 1995, Herbert C. Brown award for creative rsch. in synthetic methods 1999, Nobel Laureate Signature award for grad. edn. in chemistry 2002, Arthur C. Lope award 2004). Office: Stanford U Dept Chemistry Stanford CA 94305

TROTTER, BETTY LOU, retired secondary school educator; b. Junction City, Kans., Mar. 20, 1925; d. Claude Frank and Mertie (Ware) Short; m. James Brown Trotter, June 4, 1946; children: James B., Jay M., Mark R., Lee R.F. AA, Stephens Coll., 1945; BA cum laude, U. N.Mex., 1948; MA, U. Mo., Kansas City, 1972. Cert. music and secondary English tchr., Mo. Substitute tchr. Denver Pub. Schs., 1960—63; tchr. English, Consol. Sch. Dist. 2, Raytown, Mo., 1966—85; ret., 1985; sales assoc. Jones Store Co., Kansas City, 1987—99. Vice pres. Independence (Mo.) Neighborhood Coun., 1985-89, 91-92. Recipient outstanding svc. award Nat. Coun. Tchrs. English, 1979. Mem. AAUW (pres. Raytown 1980-82), Raytown Arts Coun. (sec.), Mortar Bd., Phi Kappa Phi, Pi Lambda Theta, Sigma Alpha Iota (pres. Denver 1960-62). Democrat. Mem. Ch. of Christ. Avocations: reading, quilting, embroidery, crocheting. Home: 11833 E 47th Ter Kansas City MO 64133-2487

TROTTER, F(REDERICK) THOMAS, retired academic administrator; b. L.A., Apr. 17, 1926; s. Fred B. and Hazel (Thomas) T.; m. Gania Demaree, June 27, 1953; children— Ruth Elizabeth, Paula Anne (dec.), Tania, Mary. AB, Occidental Coll., 1950, DD, 1968; STB, Boston U., 1953, PhD, 1958; LHD, Ill. Wesleyan U., 1974, Cornell Coll., 1985, Westmar Coll., 1987; LLD, U. Pacific, 1978, Wesleyan Coll., 1981; EdD, Columbia Coll., 1984; LittD, Alaska Pacific U., 1987. Exec. sec. Boston U. Student Christian Assn., 1951-54; ordained elder Calif.-Pacific, Methodist Ch., 1953; pastor Montclair (Calif.) Meth. Ch., 1956-59; lectr. So. Calif. Sch. Theology at Claremont, 1957-59, instr., 1959-60, asst. prof., 1960-63, assoc. prof., 1963-66, prof., 1966, dean, 1961; prof. religion and arts, dean Sch. Theology Claremont, 1961-73; mem. Bd. Higher Edn. and Ministry, United Meth. Ch., 1972-73, gen. sec., 1973-87; pres. Alaska Pacific U., Anchorage, 1988-95; ret., 1995. Dir. Inst. for Antiquity and Christianity at Claremont. Author: Jesus and the Historian, 1968, Loving God with One's Mind, 1987, God Is with Us, 1997, Politics, Morality, and Higher Education, 1997, weekly column local newspapers; editor-at-large: Christian Century, 1969-84. Trustee Dillard U. Served with USAAF, 1944-46. Kent fellow Soc. for Values in Higher Edn., 1954; Dempster fellow Meth. Ch., 1954 Mem. Rotary Internat. (Anchorage Downtown), Commonwealth North. Home: 75-136 Kiowa Dr Indian Wells CA 92210

TROTTER, GWENDOLYN DIANE NELSON, choral and vocal educator, music publisher; b. Little Rock, Nov. 13, 1950; d. Milton Donaghey and Dora Elizabeth (Gillespie) N. BBA, U. Ark., 1972; MBA, Calif. State U., Dominguez Hills, 1979, postgrad. in voice/piano, 1980-81; postgrad. in audio recording, Calif. State U., Dominguez Hills, 1993-96; postgrad. in acctg., UCLA, 1973-84. Adminstrv. asst. Ark. Plan, Inc., Little Rock, 1969-73; acct. Hughes Aircraft Co., L.A., 1973-80, ops. auditor, 1986-90, property mgmt. specialist, 1990-93; dir. music dept. Baldwin Hills Baptist Ch., L.A., 1979-94; choral, vocal instr. Crossroads Acad. Arts and Sci., 1994-97; with By Faith Cons. & Pub., Inglewood, Calif., 1997—; music specialist L.A. Unified Sch. Dist., 1996—. Auditor Baldwin Hills Baptist Ch., 1983-96; cons. LAUSO Saturday Fine Arts Conservatory, 1995-97; Internet mktg. cons.; moderator for Urban Black Gospel E-mail Discussion List. Author music: (Christian mus. drama) Wings Like Eagles, 1988, mus. dir., L.A., 1988-89; playwright: Dissin' Your Body, 1993; invited speaker seminars and workshops; vocal dir. Guys and Dolls Washington High Performing Art Magnet; clinician conducting music workshops to promote multicultural understanding. Founder, exec. dir. Christian Action Now Is Good Econs., a visual and performing arts orgn. for at-risk youth, 1993; founder, pres. By Faith Cons. and Publishing, 1993; exec. dir. Change, performing arts orgn. for at-risk youth; moderator Urban Black Gospel E-Mail Discussion list. Named Outstanding Tchr. of Yr., ECLA, 2001. Mem. Am. Choral Dirs. Assn., Heritage Music Found., Mu Phi Epsilon, Alpha Kappa Alpha (grad. advisor 1978-79, del. 1980-81). Home: 14563 Saddle Peak Ct Fontana CA 92336

TROUPE, MARILYN KAY, educational administrator; b. Tulsa, Sept. 30, 1945; d. Ernest Robinson and Lucille (Andrew) T. BA in History, Okla. State U., 1967, MA in History, 1976, EdD, 1993; lic. in cosmetology, Troupe's Beauty Sch., 1970. Cert. tchr. Okla., Tenn. Tchr. social studies Maragret Hudson Prog., Tulsa, 1969-81; tutor Tulsa Indian Youth, 1971-72; instr. cosmetology McLain-Tulsa Pub. Schs., 1982-94; instrnl. devel. specialist Okla. Dept. Vocat. and Tech. Edn., Stillwater, 1987-94; asst. prof., coord. tchr. prep. prog. chair divsn. liberal studies and edn. Lane Coll., Jackson, Tenn., 1995-97; dir. divsn. educator preparation Ky. Edn. Profl. Stds. Bd., Frankfort, 1997—. Vis. lectr. Okla. State U., 1980-81; cons., lectr. cosmetology. Bd. dirs., mem. adv. bd. Stillwater Park and Recreation, Stillwater Cmty. Rels. and Fair Housing, 1991-94; bd. dirs. Adult Day Care Ctr., 1990-94, Early Childhood Profl. Devel. Coun.; v.p. Okla. Recreation and Park Soc., 1994; judge Okla. Sch. Sci. and Math., 1994; mem. Leadership Stillwater, 1990; vol. Spl. Olympics State Games, Meals on Wheels, United Way, Frankfort Soup Kitchen; mem. women's adv. coun. Jackson Regional Hosp.; mem. adv. com. Okla. Task Force: Goals for Tomorrow, Roman Cath. Ch., Tulsa, 1985-86; mem. Ky. Early Childhood Profl. Devel. Coun.; grad. Leadership Ky., 2001; mem. Ky. Literacy Partnership. Recipient numerous awards for profl. and civic contbns. including Woman of the Yr. award Zeta Phi Beta, 1985, Salute award Gov. Okla., 1985, Outstanding Cmty. Svc. cert. WomenFest, 1985. Mem. AAUW, ASCD, Nat. Coun. Accredition Tchr. Edn. (bd. examiners), Okla. Assn. Advancement of Black Ams. in Vocat. Edn. (Golden Torch award 1994), Ky. Assn. Black Sch. Educators, Vocat. Indsl. Clubs Am. (dist. adv. 1985-86, Appreciation award 1985), Am. Vocat. Assn., Okla. Vocat. Assn., Okla. State Beauty Culturalists League (pres. 1979-85, Outstanding Svc. award 1985), Nat. Assn. Bus. and Profl. Women's Club (charter mem., past pres.), Stillwater C. of C. (bd. dirs.), Langston Alumni Assn., Frankfort-Lexington Links, Cath. Daus. Am., Phi Alpha Theta, Theta Nu Sigma, Alpha Kappa Alpha (Soror of the Yr. 1993), Iota Lambda Sigma, Phi Delta Kappa, Alpha Kappa Alpha. Democrat. Avocations: travel, reading, collecting antiques, volunteer work, shopping.

TROUT, CHARLES HATHAWAY, historian, educator; b. Seattle, Nov. 3, 1935; s. Charles Whyron and Elizabeth (Hathaway) T.; m. Margot Stevens, Dec. 30, 1961 (div. 1983); children: Nicholas H., Benjamin C.; m. Katherine Taylor Griffiths, Oct. 6, 1984. BA, Amherst Coll., 1957; MA, Columbia U., 1961, PhD, 1972. History instr. Hill Sch., Pottstown, Pa., 1958-59, Philips Exeter Acad., (N.H.), 1960-69; prof. history Mt. Holyoke Coll., South Hadley, Mass., 1969-80; provost, dean faculty Colgate U., Hamilton, N.Y., 1980-90; pres. Washington Coll., Chestertown, Md., 1990-95; tchr. Tchr. for Africa, Korongoi, Litein, Kenya, 1996-97. Vis. prof. U. Mass. Labor Rels. and Rsch. Ctr., 1974-80; interim pres., Harcum Coll., Bryn Mawr, Pa., 2002-03, pres., 2003—. Author: Boston, The Great Depression, and the New Deal. Chmn. bd. World Edn. Inc.; trustee Sultana Projects, Inc. Columbia U. Pres.'s scholar, 1959-60; NEH rsch. fellow, 1975-76; Charles Warren fellow Harvard U., 1978-79. Democrat. Episcopalian. Home: 211 N Queen St Chestertown MD 21620-1627 Office: Harcum Coll Office of President Bryn Mawr PA 19010

TROUTNER, JOANNE JOHNSON, school technology administrator, educator, administrator, consultant; b. Muncie, Ind., Sept. 9, 1952; d. Donal Russel and Lois Vivian (Hicks) Johnson; m. Lary William Troutner, May 17, 1975. BA in Media and English, Purdue U., 1974; MS in Edn., 1976. Media spls. Lafayette (Ind.) Sch. Corp., 1974-77, 81-83; computer resource tchr., 1983-84; media splst. Tippecanoe Sch. Corp., Lafayette, Ind., 1984-85; ednl. support, 1985-87; coord. instrl. support, 1988-94; dir. tech. and media, tchr. English Minot (N.D.) Pub. Schs., 1978-79, 1994—; media splst., 1979-81. Vis. prof. cont. edn. U. S.C., Columbia, summer 1983, U. N.D.; instr. Purdue U., West Lafayette; software selector Elem. Sch. Libr. Collection. Author: The Media Specialist, The Microcomputer and the Curriculum, 1983, World Desk-Classroom Internet Guide, 1998, The Internet: A Curriculum Oriented Guide, 1998, 03, Using the Internet and Technology to Strengthen Learning in English/Language Arts and Social Studies, 1999, Integrating Technology and the Internet into English and Social Studies Classrooms, 1999, Strengthening Your Social Studies Classroom, 2002; contbr. Deans Adv. Coun., Sch. Edn. Purdue U., 2003-. Dist. Alumni, Sch Edn. Purdue U., 2003. materials rev. column Sch. Libr., Media Quar.; computer literacy columnist Jour. Computers in Math. and Sci. Tchg.; computer software columnist Tchr. Libr., 1989—, internet columnist, 1995—; editor newsletter Ind. Computer Educators. Active Greater Lafayette Leadership Acad. Alumni Group, 1983—; mem. dean's adv. coun. Purdue U.; bd. dirs. Tippecanoe County Pub. Libr., pres., 1994—95, trustee, 1990—2000; bd. dirs. Lafayette Family Svc. Agy., 1987—89. Recipient Disting. Alumni award, Purdue U. Sch. Edn., 2003. Mem. ALA, Ind. Assn. Media Educators (chmn. computer div. 1982-84), Am. Assn. Sch. Librarians (sec. 1983-84, 2nd v.p. 1985-86), Internat. Coun. for Computers in Edn. (interactive video spl. interest group newsletter editor 1986-87), Ind. Computer Educators (bd. dirs. 1986-92, pres. 1990-91), Internat. Soc. Tech. Educators, Assn. Supr. and Curriculum Devel., Phi Beta Kappa, Kappa Delta Gamma, Phi Delta Kappa (v.p. programs 1987-88, v.p. memberships 1988-89, pres. 1989-90). Home: 4001 Penny Packers Mill Rd Lafayette IN 47909-3557 Office: Tippecanoe Sch Corp 21 Elston Rd Lafayette IN 47909-2899 E-mail: troutner@mindspring.com.

TROUTT, WILLIAM EARL, academic administrator; b. Bolivar, Tenn., June 13, 1949; s. Jack and Earline (Shearin) Troutt; m. Carole Pearson, Nov. 26, 1970; children: Carole Anne, Jack. BA, Union U., Jackson, Tenn., 1971; MA, U. Louisville, 1972; PhD, Vanderbilt U., 1978. Admissions counselor Union U., 1973—75; asst. dir. Tenn. Higher Edn. Commn., Nashville, 1975—78; sr. assoc. McManis Assocs. Inc., Washington, 1978—80; exec. v.p. Belmont Coll., Nashville, 1981—82, pres., 1982—99, Rhodes Coll., Memphis, 1999—. Active Leadership Nashville, Mayors Com. on Excellence; sec. Tenn. Student Assistance Corp., 1986—. Named one of Nations Most Effective Coll. Pres., Exxon Found. Study, 1986; scholar Luther Rice Scholar, So. Bapt. Theol. Sem., 1971. Mem.: So. Assn. Colls. and Schs. (commnr. commn. colls. 1986—), Tenn. Ind. Colls. Fund (sec.-treas. 1986—), Tenn. Coun. Pvt. Colls. (chmn. 1985—), Nashville Area C. of C. (bd. dirs. 1985—), Rotary. Office: Office of the Pres 2000 N Pkwy Memphis TN 38112-1690

TROVATO-CANTORI, LORRAINE MARIA, art educator; b. Bklyn., Aug. 19, 1965; d. Joseph Charles and Frances Grace (Palma) Trovato; m. Chris D. Cantori, Sept. 20, 1992; 1 child, Ceasar-Augustus. BFA, Sch. Visual Arts, N.Y.C., 1987; MFA, Lehman Coll., 1992. Cert. tchr. fine art, N.Y. Art educator N.Y.C. Dept. Parks and Recreation, 1985-87, P.S. 33 N.Y.C. Bd. Edn., 1988-91, Middle Sch. 45 N.Y.C. Bd. Edn., 1991—. Art edn. cons. Bronx (N.Y.) Coun. on Arts, 1991—; mus. educator N.Y.C. Bd. Edn./Met. Mus. Art, 1991—. Exhibited eight paintings Greenburgh Pub. Libr., 1995-96. Grantee Bronx Coun. on Arts, 1991, N.Y.C. Dept. Edn., 1992. Mem. Forum Italian Am. Educators. Roman Catholic. Office: Middle Sch 45 2502 Lorillard Pl Bronx NY 10458-5997

TROXCLAIR, DEBRA ANN, gifted education educator; b. New Orleans, Jan. 29, 1953; d. Richard Joseph and Joyce Marie (Braud) Troxclair; divorced; 1 child, Christopher Richard Pinner. BA, U. New Orleans, 1976, MEd, 1989; PhD, U. So. Miss., 1997. Cert. edn. 4th grade tchr. Laurel Elem. Sch., New Orleans, 1977; 2d grade tchr. St. Frances Cabrini Elem., New Orleans, 1977-80; 1st grade tchr. St. Joseph Sch., Gretna, La., 1982-83; kindergarden tchr. Lake Castle Pvt. Sch., New Orleans, 1983-84; libr. St. Frances Cabrini, New Orleans, 1984-85; 3d grade tchr. Abney Elem. Sch., Slidell, La., 1985-89; gifted resource tchr. Little Oak Elem., Slidell, 1989-97; instr. Delgado C.C., Slidell, 1991-94; asst. prof. spl. edn. Gifted U. S. Ala., 1998-99; 6th grade gifted tchr. Alief Ind. Sch. Dist., 2000—01. Cons. St. Tammany Parish Schs., Slidell, 1988-89, 90-91; adj. prof. Houston Bapt. U., 2002, U. St. Thomas, 2002-03; presenter at numerous confs.; vis. asst. prof. tchr. edn. Southeastern La. U.; academic dean Summer Inst. for Gifted, Bryn Mawr, Pa., 2003. Mem. Westminster Presbyn. Ch., Houston, Tex. Recipient Disting. Teaching awrd Northwestern State U., 1996; Grad. Student scholar U. So. Miss., 1995-96; La. Assn. for Gifted and Talented grantee, 1996. Mem. Internat. Reading Assn., Coun. for Exceptional Children, Nat. Assn. for Gifted Children (chair computers and tech. divsn.), Tex. Assn. For Gifted Tchrs., Kappa Delta Pi, Phi Delta Kappa (pres. St. Tammany Parish 1991). Presbyterian. Avocations: jazzercize, painting, computers, sewing.

TROXEL, DONALD EUGENE, electrical engineering educator; b. Trenton, N.J., Mar. 11, 1934; s. Shirley Monroe and Emma Ruth Troxel; m. Eileen Millicent Cronk, Aug. 23, 1963; children: Gregory, Jocelyn, Andrea. BS, Rutgers U., 1956; SM, MIT, 1960, PhD, 1962. Ford Found. postdoctoral fellow, asst. prof. MIT, Cambridge, Mass., 1962-64, asst. prof. dept. elec. engring., 1964-67, assoc. prof., 1967-85, prof. elec. engring., 1985—; asst. prof. Tufts U., Medford, Mass., 1963. Bd. dirs. ECRM, Inc., Tewksbury, Mass. 1st lt. U.S. Army, 1956-58. Mem. IEEE (sr. mem., Leonard G. Abraham Prize Paper award 1971), Assn. for Computing Machinery, Sigma Xi, Tau Beta Pi, Eta Kappa Nu, Pi Mu Epsilon. Home: 4 Madison St Belmont MA 02478-3536 Office: MIT 77 Massachusetts Ave # 36-287 Cambridge MA 02139-4307

TROXEL, STEVEN RICHARD, communication studies educator; b. Oklahoma City, Sept. 18, 1951; s. Richard Maloy and Noma Lee (Renfro) T.; m. Rosana Faye Schmucker, June 21, 1981; children: S. Michael, Ariel. BA, Okla. Bapt. U., Shawnee, 1974; postgrad., So. Bapt. Theol. Sem., Louisville, 1974-75; MA, Wheaton Coll., 1977; PhD, U. Va., 1996. Radio announcer WIVE-FM, Ashland, Va., 1977-78; asst. to dir. media svcs. Union Theol. Sem. in Va., Richmond, 1978-80; dir. media ministries Grove Ave. Bapt. Ch., Richmond, 1980-85; prof. comm. studies Liberty U., Lynchburg, Va., 1985—. Fund raising cons., 1983-88; chmn. elect Lynchburg Aquatic League, 1995, chmn., 1995-96; owner Oak Crest Resources, 1996—; CFO Yappy Dog Prodns., Inc., 1997-99. Author: (computer program) Writing Broadcast Leads, 1992, (booklet) Timing a Video System, 1991, (multi-media program), Join in the Singing; Join in the Song, 1984; co-author: (booklet) Bone Marrow Transplantation, 1993, (computer program) Notable Norman, 1993; contbr. articles to profl. jours.; exec. prodr. weekly TV show Ctrl. Va. News Rev., 1992. Cert. ofcl. U.S. Swimming, Va., 1992-96, swimming ofcl. YMCA, 1991-96; maj. supporting actor The Living Christmas Tree, Lynchburg, 1990. Mem. Mensa (exec. com. Ctr. Va. chpt. 1992-96). Republican. Baptist. Avocations: swimming, flying, home remodeling, history. Office: Liberty U 1971 University Blvd Lynchburg VA 24502-2213

TROXELL, RAYMOND ROBERT, JR., college administrator; b. Easton, Pa., July 11, 1932; s. Raymond Robert and Mary Jane (Cooney) T.; m. Barbara Lou Foulk, Aug. 11, 1955; children: Gayle L., Pamella A., Lynn R. BA in Polit. Sci., Lafayette Coll., 1956; MA in Internat. Rel., Lehigh U., 1960, MS in Adminstrn., 1964; PhD in Adminstrn., Southwestern U., 1974. Tchr./prin., curriculum coord. Easton (Pa.) Area High Sch., 1956-66; asst. supt. West York Area, York, Pa., 1966-67, supt., 1967-79, Windber (Pa.) Schs., 1979-82; gen. edn. coord., life experience coord., dean grad. sch., mgmt. coord., prof. Tampa (Fla.) Coll., 1982—. Vis. prof. Western Md. Coll., Westminster, 1967-82; model schs. dir. Pa. Consortium, 1975-82; cons. in field; evaluator U.S. Office Edn., Washington, 1973—; lectr. in field; conductor workshops/seminars in field; participant edn. seminar in eastern Europe, Siberia, USSR. Author: Administrative Accountability, 1977, Successful Negotiations, 1979, New Trends in Supervision, 1981, Performance Based Curriculum, 1982, Institutional Effectiveness; contbr. articles to profl. jours. Active various charitable orgns. Mott Found. grantee, Ford Found. grantee; recipient Valley Forge Freedoms Found. award, Am. Educators medal, Outstanding Tchrs. award. Mem. Am. Assn. Sch. Adminstrs., Assn. for Supervision and Curriculum Devel., Coun. on Basic Edn., Am. Acad. Polit. and Social Sci., Ctr. for Study of the Presidency, Nat. Assn. Secondary Sch. Prins., Nat. Sch. Bds. Assn., Am. Judicature Soc., Am. Mgmt. Assn., Coun. for Adult Experiential Learning, U.S. Office of Edn. Fund for the Improvement of Postsecondary Edn., Lehigh Valley Grad. Sch. Edn. Alumni coun., Soc. Ednl. Adminstrs. of Lehigh U., Kappa Phi Kappa, Phi Delta Kappa. Lutheran. Avocations: golf, swimming, writing, hiking, travel. Home: 2311 Mountain View Dr Dover PA 17315-3516 Office: Tampa College 3319 W Hillsborough Ave Tampa FL 33614-5801 Address: 2311 Mountain View Dr Dover PA 17315-3516

TROY, CHARLES DAVID, secondary social studies educator; b. Bronx, N.Y., Nov. 8, 1951; s. JOhn and Ralisue (Evans) T. BA in Sociology and History, Warren Wilson Coll., Swannanoa, N.C., 1974; MA in Social Studies Edn., Columbia U., 1982, EdM in Social Studies Edn., 1985; postgrad. Social worker Alexander Schs., Inc., Union Mills, N.C., 1974; tchr. 8th grade English and social studies Tabernacle Jr. High Sch., Maysville, N.C., 1974-78; tchr. English and Math. Peace Corps/Ghana, Washington, 1978-80; substitute tchr. high sch. social studies A.P. Randolph Campus High Sch., N.Y.C., 1984, Graphic Communications Arts High Sch., N.Y.C., 1985; tchr. 9th and 10th social studies St. Nicholas, Bronx, N.Y., 1982, tchr. 7th English and social studies, 1983; tchr. 8th grade social studies N.Y.C. Bd. Edn., Satellite East Jr. High Sch., Bklyn., 1986—; lectr. world history Empire State Coll., N.Y.C., 1988—. Recipient Excellence in Teaching award Bronx Re-entry Program, 1988. Mem. Kappa Delta Pi, Phi Delta Kappa. Democrat. Avocations: chess, writing poetry, tennis, horseback riding. Office: Satellite East Jr High Sch 50 Jefferson Ave Brooklyn NY 11216-1609

TROY, CHERRYL APRIL, secondary education educator; b. Chgo., Apr. 3, 1947; d. Harold Axel and Marilynn Joanne (Becker) Karlberg; children: Cary David, Rebecca Sarah. BA, So. Ill. U., 1972; MA, Loyola U., 1987. Cert. secondary edn. tchr., Ill., yoga and stress mgmt. educator. Adminstrv. asst. FSC Paper Co., Alsip, Ill., 1985-91, William Blair & Co., Chgo., 1985-87; part-time instr. Spanish Moraine Valley C.C., Palos Hills, Ill., 1987—; advanced placement tchr. Spanish and French Comm. High Sch. Dist. # 218, Oaklawn, Ill., 1991—. Mem. survivor com. Susan Komen Breast Cancer Found., Chgo., 1998—. Mem. Am. Assn. Tchrs. Spanish, AAUW, MLA, Ill. Assn. Tchrs. Spanish, Assn. Yoga Therapists, Phi Delta Kappa. Avocations: yoga, stress management, opera, travel, writing. Home: 13321 Ash Ct Palos Heights IL 60463 Office: Dwight Eisenhower High Sch 12700 Sacramento Ave Blue Island IL 60406-1822

TROZZOLO, ANTHONY MARION, chemistry educator; b. Chgo., Jan. 11, 1930; s. Pasquale and Francesca (Vercillo) T.; m. Doris C. Stoffregen, Oct. 8, 1955; children: Thomas, Susan, Patricia, Michael, Lisa, Laura. BS, Ill. Inst. Tech., 1950; MS, U. Chgo., 1957, PhD, 1960. Asst. chemist Chgo. Midway Labs., 1952-53; assoc. chemist Armour Rsch. Found., Chgo., 1953-56; tech. staff Bell Labs., Murray Hill, N.J., 1959-75; Charles L. Huisking prof. chemistry U. Notre Dame, 1975-92, Charles L. Huisking prof. emeritus, 1992—; asst. dean U. Notre Dame Coll. Sci., 1993-98; P.C. Reilly lectr. U. Notre Dame, 1972, Hesburgh Alumni lectr., 1986, Disting. lectr. sci., 1986. Vis. prof. Columbia U., N.Y.C., 1971, U. Colo., 1981, Katholieke U. Leuven, Belgium, 1983, Max Planck Inst. für Strahlenchemie, Mülheim/Ruhr, Fed. Republic Germany, 1990; vis. lectr. Academia Sinica, 1984, 85; Phillips lectr. U. Okla., 1971; C.L. Brown lectr. Rutgers U., 1975; Sigma Xi lectr. Bowling Green U., 1976, Abbott Labs., 1978; M. Faraday lectr. No. Ill. U., 1976; F.O. Butler lectr. S.D. State U., 1978; Chevron lectr. U. Nev., Reno, 1983; J. Crano lectr. U. Akron, 2000; plenary lectr. various internat. confs.; founder, chmn. Gordon Conf. on Organic Photochemistry, 1964; trustee Gordon Rsch. Confs., 1988-92; cons. in field. Assoc. editor Jour. Am. Chem. Soc., 1975-76; editor Chem. Revs., 1977-84; editorial adv. bd. Accounts of Chem. Rsch., 1977-85; cons. editor Encyclopedia of Science and Technology, 1982-92; contbr. articles to profl. jours.; patentee in field. Fellow AEC, 1951, NSF, 1957-59; named Hon. Citizen of Castrolibero, Italy, 1997; recipient Pietro Bucci prize U. Calabria/Italian Chem. Soc., 1997. Fellow: AAAS, Inter-Am. Photochem. Soc., N.Y. Acad. Scis. (chmn. chem. scis. sect. 1969—70, Halpern award in photochemistry 1980), Am. Inst. Chemists (Student award 1950); mem.: Am. Chem. Soc. (lectr., Tex. lectr. 1975, Disting. Svc. award St. Joseph Valley sect. 1979, Coronado lectr. 1980, Pacific Coast lectr. 1981, Coronado lectr. 1993, N.Y. State lectr. 1993, Hoosier lectr. 1995, Ozark lectr. 1995, Coronado lectr. 1998, Osage lectr. 1998, Rocky Mountain lectr. 1996, 2002), Sigma Xi. Roman Catholic. Home: 1329 E Washington St South Bend IN 46617-3340 Office: U Notre Dame Dept Chemistry-Biochemistry Notre Dame IN 46556-5670 E-mail: trozzolo.4@nd.edu.

TRPIS, MILAN, vector biologist, scientist, educator; b. Mojsova Lucka, Slovakia, Dec. 20, 1930; came to U.S., 1971, naturalized, 1977; s. Gaspar and Anna (Sevcikova) T.; m. Ludmila Tonkovic, Dec. 15, 1956; children: Martin, Peter, Katarina. MS, Comenius U., Bratislava, 1956; PhD, Charles U., Prague, 1960. Research asst. Slovak Acad. Sci., Bratislava, 1953-56, sci. asst., 1956-60, scientist, 1960-62, ind. scientist, 1962-69; ecologist-entomologist East Africa-Aedes Rsch. Unit WHO, Dar es Salaam, Tanzania, 1969-71; asst. faculty fellow dept. biology U. Notre Dame, 1971-73, assoc. faculty fellow, 1973-74; assoc. prof. med. entomology Johns Hopkins U. Sch. Hygiene and Pub. Health, 1974-78, prof., 1978—, dir. labs. med. entomology. Med. entomology; rsch. assoc. U. Ill., Urbana, 1966-67, Can. Dept. Agr., Lethbridge, Alta., 1967-68; dir. Biol. Rsch. Inst. Am., 1971-79; external dir. rsch. Liberiran Inst. Biomed. Rsch., 1981-89; dir. AID project on transmission of river blindness in areas of Liberia, Sierra Leone, and Cote d'Ivoire; dir. WHO rsch. grant; tech. adv. com. AID Vector Biology and Control Project, 1986-91; dir. Johns Hopkins U./Fed. U. Tech. Akure Onchocerciasis Project in Nigeria, 1991-94, Johns Hopkins U./Organisation de Coordination et de Cooperation pour la Lutte les Grandes Endemies-Pierre Richet Inst. Onchocerciasis Project, Bouakè, Ivory Coast, 1993-96; dir. Johns Hopkins U./Pierre Richet Inst./ORSTOM onchocerciasis project in Ivory Coast, 1993-96; prof.-advisor doctoral students, Africa, Asia, Cen. Am., 1979—. Editor: Jour. Biologia, 1956-71, Jour. Entomol. Problems, 1960-72; zool. sect.: Jour. Biol. Works, 1960-71; Contbr. articles to profl. jours. Dir. WHO project on prophylactic drugs for river blindness, Liberia, 1985-87. Recipient Slovak Acad. Sci., 1st prize for research project. Mem. AAUP, AAAS, Am. Inst. Biol. Soci., Am. Mosquito Control Assn., Am. Soc. Parasitologists, Helminthol. Soc. Washington, Am. Soc. Tropical Medicine and Hygiene, Entomol. Soc. Am., Am. Genetic Assn., Soc. of Vector Ecology, N.Y. Acad. Scis., Johns Hopkins U. Tropical Medicine Club, Smithsonian Assocs., Royal Soc. Tropical Medicine and Hygiene, Royal Entomol. Soc. of London, Sigma Xi, Delta Omega (Alpha chpt.). Home: 1504 Ivy Hill Rd Cockeysville MD 21030-1418 Office: Johns Hopkins U 615 N Wolfe St Baltimore MD 21205-2103 E-mail: mtrpis@jhsph.edu.

TRUAX, DENNIS DALE, civil engineer, educator, consultant; b. Hagerstown, Md., July 25, 1953; s. Bernard James and Dorothy Hilda Truax; m. Jeanie Ann Knable, Aug. 20, 1977. BSCE, Va. Poly. Inst. and State U., 1976; MS, Miss. State U., 1978, PhD, 1986. Registered profl. engr., Miss.; diplomate Environ. Engring. Asst. dep. constrn. mgr. Fairfax County, Va., 1972-74; design engr. Washington County, Md., 1976; instr. Miss. State U., Starkville, 1980-86, asst. prof. civil engring., 1986-91, assoc. prof., 1991-96, prof., 1996—. Prin. corp. pres. ASD, LLC, 1997-2000; prin., v.p. engring. ATi, Inc., 2000—; environ. engring. cons. Mem. editl. bd. ASCE/NSPE Profl. Issues Jour., 1999—. Lay leader Aldersgate United Meth. Ch., Starkville, 1982-85, chmn. pastor/parish rels., 1985-86, chmn.

coun. on ministries, 1986-90, chmn. adminstrv. bd., 1990-92, chmn. fin. com., 1992-94, 2001-2003, chmn. bd. trustees, 1996-97; adviser Triangle Fraternity, Starkville, Alumni Bd. Dirs. treas., 1989-96; bd. dirs. Meth. Student Ctr., Miss. State U., 1983-90, chmn. pastor/parish rels., 1984-86, v.p. bd., 1986, pres., 1987-89, treas., 1990-91; del. to ann. conf. Miss. Conf. United Meth. Ch., also vice chmn. com. on higher edn.; active Starkville dist. lay coun. Miss. State Herrin-Hess Prof., 1993-94, 94-95, 95-96. Recipient Golden Key Outstanding Faculty award Golden Key Nat. Honor Soc., 1994, Miss. Outstanding Civil Engr. of Yr., ASCE Miss. sect., 1995; named Outstanding Young Man Am., U.S. Jaycees, 1983. Fellow ASCE (chair student svcs. com. 1995-96, vice chair 1996-97, adv. Miss. State student chpt. 1981—, chair career guidance com. 1991-92, sec. 1990-91, Miss. sect. pres.-elect 1990-91, pres. 1991-92, chmn. student svc. com. 1995-96, scholarship com. 1998—, chair scholarship com. 2000-01, No. Miss. br. pres. 2000-2001, dist. 14 dir. 2001--, fin. com., com. on diversity and women in civil engring.); mem. NSPE, Am. Water Works Assn. (Ala.-Miss. 41 chpt. scholarship bd. dirs. 1994—, bd. sec.-treas. 1998—), Miss. Engring. Soc. (pres., pres.-elect region 3 v.p., bd. dirs., Tombigbee chpt. pres., chpt. pres.-elect, Engring. educator 1995, Educator of the Yr. award 1995), Water Environ. Fedn. (rsch. com.), Sigma Xi (sec., pres.-elect, pres. Miss. State chpt.), Tau Beta Pi, Chi Epsilon. Democrat. Home: 1054 Southgate Dr Starkville MS 39759-8810 Office: Miss State U PO Box 9546 Mississippi State MS 39762-9546

TRUESDELL, TIMOTHY L. private investor; b. Niles, Mich., Oct. 8, 1951; s. Patrick Daniel and LaVonne Marie (Fries) T. BA, U. Notre Dame, 1974. Asst. to exec. dir. Notre Dame U. Alumni Assn., 1974-77, asst. dir., 1977-79; alumni editor Notre Dame mag., 1979-83; v.p. Truesdell Real Estate Investment, Sacramento, 1983-85; dir. devel. rsch. U. Notre Dame, 1985-99; portfolio mgr. Kamm Partnership, South Bend, Ind., 1999—. Devel. cons. Am. Acad. Neurology, 1991-92, Harvest Devel., Ponte Vedra, Fla., 1999—, Hospice of St. Joseph County, South Bend, Ind., 1992-93, U. St. Thomas, Mpls., Xavier U., Cin., 1993-94, Niles Comty. Libr., 1993-97, St. Joseph Mishawaka (Ind.) Health Svcs., 1995-96, Berrien County ARC, 1996, Advancement Ptnrs., Inc., Columbus, 1996—, Little Flower Cath. Ch., South Bend, Ind., 1997-98, No. Ind. Ctr. for History, South Bend, 1998-2000; bd. dirs. Women's Care Ctr., Mishawaka, Ind., 1999-2000. Councilman City of Niles, 1983-91; pres. St. Mary's Sch Bd. Edn., Niles, 1981-82; chmn. S.W. Mich. Comty. Ambulance, Niles, 1985-89; mem. Berrien County (Mich.) Reps.; pres. Fernwood Bot. Garden, Niles, 1997-98. Mem. Am. Assn. Individual Investors, Assn. Profl. Rschrs. for Advancement, Optimists (sec. 1983-84), Knights of Malta, Notre Dame Club of St. Joseph Valley, Notre Dame Club of Kalamazoo. Republican. Roman Catholic. Avocations: golf, antique collecting. Office: 11185 Elizabeth Dr Three Rivers MI 49093 E-mail: timothy.truesdell@verizon.net.

TRUETT, DALE BRIAN, economics/finance educator, consultant; b. Gary, Ind., July 25, 1940; s. Louis Theodore and Flora (Toma) T.; m. Lila Jean Matile, Apr. 4, 1977; children: Katherine, Patrick. BA, Purdue U., 1962; MA, U. Tex., 1964, PhD, 1967. Asst. prof. U. Fla., Gainesville, 1967-71; assoc. prof., chmn. econ. Fla. Internat. U., Miami, 1971-73; prof., dir. econ./fin. U. Tex., San Antonio, 1973-75, prof., 1976—, Ashbel Smith prof. econs., 1997—2002. Cons. City Pub. Svc. of San Antonio, 2000—, Southwestern Bell Publs., St. Louis, 1990-99, Ctrl. de Servicios de Carga, Mex., 1994-95, Continental Floral Greens, San Antonio, 1987-88, AHMSA Steel Internat., Mex., 1981. Author: Managerial Economics, 7th edit., 2001; contbr. articles to profl. jours. Rsch. grantee U. Tex., San Antonio, 1993, 94, 95, 96, 2001, 02, 03, U.S. Dept. Edn., 1991-92; recipient Rsch. award U. Tex., San Antonio, 1994, 97. Mem. Am. Econ. Assn., So. Econ. Assn., Western Econ. Assn., Congress of Polit. Economists, Internat. Avocations: international travel, photography. Home: 16402 NW Military Hwy San Antonio TX 78231-1224 Office: Univ Tex Dept Econs 6900 N Loop 1604 W San Antonio TX 78249-1130

TRUETT, LILA FLORY, economics educator; b. Emporia, Kans., June 30, 1947; d. Ulysses Earl and Ursula Mabel (Schwindt) Matile; m. Donald Gene Flory, May 26, 1967 (div. 1973); m. Dale Brian Truett, Apr. 4, 1977; stepchildren: Katherine, Patrick. BA in Math., Kans. State U., 1968; MA in Econs., U. Iowa, 1971, PhD in Econs., 1972. Teaching asst., then part-time instr. U. Iowa, Iowa City, 1969-71; asst. prof. Iowa Wesleyan Coll., Mt. Pleasant, 1971-73, Appalachian State U., Boone, N.C., 1973-75; from asst. prof. to prof. econs. U. Tex., San Antonio, 1975—81, prof. econs., 1981—. Outside reviewer dept. econs., Colo. State U., Colorado Springs, 1988, S.W. Tex. State U., San Marcos, Tex., 2001. Co-author: Intermediate Microeconomics, 1984, Economics, 1987, Managerial Economics, 7th edit., 2001; contbr. numerous articles to profl. jours. Mem. Fin. Execs. Inst., Fin. Mgmt. Assn., Am. Econ. Assn., So. Econ. Assn., Ea. Fin. Assn., Midwest Fin. Assn., Western Econs. Assn., Ea. Econs. Assn., Omicron Delta Epsilon, Beta Gamma Sigma. Brethren. Avocations: reading, music, travel, gardening. Home: 16402 NW Military Hwy San Antonio TX 78231-1224 Office: U Tex Dept EconS San Antonio TX 78249-0633

TRUHLAR, DONALD GENE, chemist, educator; b. Chgo., Feb. 27, 1944; s. John Joseph and Lucille Marie (Vancura) T.; m. Jane Teresa Gust, Aug. 28, 1965; children: Sara Elizabeth, Stephanie Marie. BA in Chemistry summa cum laude, St. Mary's Coll., Winona, Minn., 1965; PhD in Chemistry, Calif. Inst. Tech., 1970. Asst. prof. chemistry and chem. physics U. Minn., Mpls., 1969—72, assoc. prof., 1972—76, prof., 1976—93, Inst. of Tech. prof., 1993—98, Inst. of Tech. disting. prof., 1998—, Lloyd H. Reyerson prof., 2002—. Cons. Los Alamos Sci. Lab.; vis. fellow Joint Inst. for Lab. Astrophysics, 1975-76; sci. dir. Minn. Supercomputer Inst., 1987-88, dir., 1988—. Editor Theoretical Chemistry Accounts (Theoretica Chemica Acta), 1985—98, Computer Physics Comms., 1986—, Topics Phys. Chemistry, 1992—99, Understanding Chem. Reactivity, 1990—92, editl. bd. Jour. Chem. Physics, 1978—80, Chem. Physics Letters, 1982—, Jour. Phys. Chemistry, 1985—87, Understanding Chem. Reactivity, 1993—, Advances in Chem. Physics, 1993—, Internat. Jour. Modern Physics C., 1994—, IEEE Computational Sci. and Engring., 1994—98, Internat. Jour. Quantum Chemistry, 1996—2000, Computing in Sci. and Engring., 1999—, assoc. editor Theoretical Chemistry Accounts, 1998—2001, chief adv. editor, 2002—. Fellow, Alfred P. Sloan Found., 1973—77; grantee, NSF, 1971—, NASA, 1987—95, U.S. Dept. Energy, 1979—, NIST, 1995—98, Dept. of Def., 2001—; scholar, Ruhland Walzer Meml. scholar, 1961—62; John Stauffer fellow, 1965—66, NDEA fellow, 1966—68. Fellow AAAS, Am. Phys. Soc.; mem. Am. Chem. Soc. (sec.-treas. theoretical chemistry subdivsn. 1980-89, councilor 1985-87, assoc. editor jour. 1984—, Award for computers in chem. and pharm. rsch. 2000). Achievements include research, numerous publications in field. Home: 5033 Thomas Ave S Minneapolis MN 55410-2240 Office: U Minn 207 Pleasant St SE Minneapolis MN 55455-0431 E-mail: truhlar@umn.edu.

TRUITT, SHIRLEY ANN BOWDLE, middle school educator; b. Cambridge, Md., July 14, 1933; d. Thomas Woodrow and Sarah Virginia (Corkran) Bowdle; m. Herman James Truitt, June 19, 1955; children: Jennie Ann Knapp, Thomas Lee, Sarah Jane. BS, Salisbury (Md.) State Coll., 1955, MEd, 1977. Cert. reading specialist, elem. tchr., Md., Del. Tchr. North Salisbury Elem. Sch., Salisbury, 1955-57, Selbyville (Del.) Elem. Sch., 1963-64, Whaleyville (Md.) Elem. Sch., 1965-67, Phillip C. Showell Sch., Selbyville, 1970-73; reading specialist Selbyville Mid. Sch., 1974-91; lang. arts and math. tchr. Sussex Ctrl. Mid. Sch., Millsboro, Del., 1991—. Cooperating tchr. Wilmington Coll., 1996, adv. bd., 1995—. Sec. Worcester County Recreation and Parks Commn., 1972-84; pres. United Meth. Ch., Whaleyville; troop leader Girl Scouts U.S., Berlin, Md., 1968-73; mem. adv. com. Wilmington Coll. Named Tchr. of Yr., Indian River Sch. Dist., 1973, 94, recipient Supts. award, 1993. Mem. AAUW (pres. Salisbury 1988—), Nat. Assn. Secondary Sch. Prins., Del. State Reading Assn. (pres. 1980-81), Sussex Country Orgn. Reading (pres. 1977, 86), Alpha Delta Kappa (pres. 1986), Phi Delta Kappa (charter mem. eastern shore chpt.). Avocations: collecting clocks, growing orchids. Home: 11517 Dale Rd Whaleyville MD 21872-2026

TRUITT, WILLIAM HARVEY, private school educator; b. Alton, Ill., May 27, 1935; s. Howard Earl and Mary Margaret (Haper) T.; m. Janetha Mitchell, Aug. 5, 1961; children: Joy Elizabeth, Janita Ann. BA, Principia Coll., 1957; MA, So. Ill. U., 1964. Headmaster Forman Schs., Litchfield, Conn.; prin. upper and lower sch. The Principia, St. Louis, headmaster. Mem. NASSP, Mo. Assn. Secondary Prins., St. Louis Ind. Sch. Heads, Mo. Ind. Schs. (pres. 1983-84), Am. Coun. for Am. Pvt. Edn. (v.p. 1983-84), North Cen. Accrediting Assn. (exec. bd. dirs. 1988-91). Home: 13201 Clayton Rd Saint Louis MO 63131-1002

TRUJILLO, LORENZO A. lawyer, educator; b. Denver, Aug. 10, 1951; s. Filbert G. and Marie O. Trujillo; m. Ellen Alires; children: Javier Antonio, Lorenzo Feliciano, Kristina Alires. BA, U. Colo., 1972, MA, 1974, postgrad.; EdD, U. San Francisco, 1979; JD, U. Colo., 1993. Bar: Colo. 1994, U.S. Dist. Ct. Colo. 1994, U.S. Ct. Appeals (10th cir.) 1994, U.S. Supreme Ct. 1999; cert. edn. tchr., prin., supt., Colo. Exec. assoc. Inter-Am. Rsch. Assocs., Rosslyn, Va., 1980-82; exec. dir. humanities Jefferson County Pub. Schs., Golden, Colo., 1982-89; pvt. practice edn. cons. Lakewood, Colo., 1989-93; gen. corp. counsel Am. Achievement Schs., Inc., Lakewood, Colo., 1994-96; atty. Frie, Arndt & Trujillo Law Firm, Arvada, Colo., 1994-96, ptnr., 1995-97; dist. hearing officer, dir. of instrn. Adams County Sch. Dist. 14, 1996—97, dir. human resources, 1998-99, dist. attendance officer/legal counsel, prin. H.S., 1999—. Co-chair Mellon fellowships The Coll. Bd., N.Y.C., 1987-93; cons. U.S.I.A. Fulbright Tchr. Exch. Program, Washington, 1987-93; editl. advisor Harcourt, Brace, Jovanovich Pub., Orlando, Fla., 1988-93; mem. Colo. Supreme Ct. Multicultural Commn., 1996-98, 99—; mem. Colo. Supreme Ct. Families in the Cts. Commn., 2001-02; mem. 17th Jud. Dist. Nominating Com., 2002—; adj. prof. law U. Denver Sch. Law, 2002. Contbr. numerous articles to profl. jours. Mem. panel of arbitrators Am. Arbitration Assn., 1994-present; panelist, evaluator Nat. Endowment for the Arts, 1976—. Recipient Legal Aid Clinic Acad. award Colo. Bar Assn., 1993, Pro Bono award, 1993, Loyola U. Acad. award, 1993, Gov.'s award for excellence in the arts State of Colo., 1996, others. Mem. Am. Assn. Tchrs. of Spanish and Portuguese (pres. Colo. chpt. 1985-88), Colo. Hispanic Bar Assn. (bd. dirs. 2001-, pres.-elect 2003), Am. Immigration Lawyers Assn., Nat. Sch. Bds. Coun. Sch. Attys., Nat. Assn. Judiciary Interpreters and Translators, Colo. Bar Assn. (probate and trust sect., grievance policy com. 1995-97, ethics com. 1995-96), U. San Francisco Alumni Assn. (founder, pres. 1987-90), Phi Delta Kappa (chair internat. edn. com. 1988-89), Phi Alpha Delta. Avocation: violinist. Office: Adams County Sch Dist 14 6500 E 72d Ave Commerce City CO 80022-2380

TRUJILLO, MICHAEL JOSEPH, elementary school principal; b. L.A., May 14, 1939; s. Damacio and Helen (Rubalcava) T.; m. Yolanda Flores, June 23, 1973; children: Roberto Miguel, Antonio Miguel. BA in Spanish, Iona Coll., 1961; MA in Counseling Psychology, Santa Clara U., 1973. Cert. tchr., adminstr., supr., pupil pers., Calif. Tchr. St. Laurence H.S., Chgo., 1961-62, Christian Bros. H.S., Butte, Mont., 1962-64, Damien Meml. H.S., Honolulu, 1964-68, St. Patrick's H.S., Vallejo, Calif., 1968-71; jr. H.S. tchr., elem. sch. counselor, vice prin. jr. H.S. Pajaro Valley Unified Sch. Dist., Watsonville, Calif., 1971-77; elem. sch. prin. Natividad Sch. Salinas (Calif.) City Sch. Dist., Salinas, 1977-96, elem. sch. prin. Loma Vista Sch., 1996—. Cons., presenter in planning for year round edn. Bd. dirs. North Monterey Unified Sch. Dist., Moss Landing, Calif., 1983-91. Recipient Cert. of Recognition, Calif. Senator Henry Mello, 1992. Mem. ASCD, NAESP, Calif. Assn. Yr. Round Edn. (pres. 1994-95), Assn. Calif. Sch. Adminstrs. Democrat. Roman Catholic. Home: 14597 Charter Oak Blvd Salinas CA 93907-1015 Office: Loma Vista Sch 757 Sausal Dr Salinas CA 93906-2242

TRUMBLE, RICHARD DWAIN, superintendent, consultant; b. Laona, Wis., June 6, 1937; BA, U. Minn., 1963; MA, U. Wis., 1967, PhD, 1970. Cert. tchr., prin., supt., Minn., W.Va., Va., Wis. Park dir. Bd. Park Commrs., Mpls., 1959-63; tchr. Madison (Wis.) Pub. Schs., 1963-67; teaching asst. U. Wis., Madison, 1967-69; asst. supt. Oswego (Ill.) Pub. Schs., 1969-70, Waukesha (Wis.) Pub. Schs., 1970-74; supt. Austin (Minn.) Pub. Schs., 1974-80, South Washington County Pub. Schs., Cottage Grove, Minn., 1980-86, Kanawha County Pub. Schs., Charleston, W.Va., 1986-90, Portsmouth (Va.) Pub. Schs., 1990—. Bd. dirs. Portsmouth Pub. Schs. Found., 1990—, ACCESS, scholarship found., Norfolk, Va., 1990—; mem. edn. com. Urban League, Norfolk, 1992—. With USNR, 1956-59. Named Disting. West Virginian, Gov. of Va., 1989, Person of Yr., Va. Pilot-Ledger Star, 1991, productivity award U.S. Senate, 1992. Mem. Am. Assn. Sch. Adminstrs., Va. Assn. Sch. Adminstrs., Portsmouth C. of C. (bd. dirs. 1990—), Rotary, Phi Delta Kappa. Avocations: travel, skiing. Office: Portsmouth Pub Schs 801 Crawford St Portsmouth VA 23704-3822

TRUNK, JAMES FRANCIS, secondary school educator; b. Cleve., Feb. 23, 1943; s. Frank A. and Dorothy A. (McCann) T.; m. Catalina Delgado, Oct. 30, 1965; children: Maria, Sean. BA, St. Edward U., 1965; MA, U. Mid-Fla., 1973. Cert. secondary sch. English tchr., Fla. 7th grade tchr. St. Mary Sch., Chardon, Ohio, 1965-66; 9th-12th grade English tchr. St. Frederick H.S., Monroe, La., 1966-67; 5th and 6th grade English and reading tchr. St. John Vianney Sch., Orlando, Fla., 1974-75, St. Andrew Sch., Orlando, 1975-98, Robinswood Mid. Sch., Orlando, 1998-2000, Annunciation Sch., Albuquerque, 2000—. Part-time English grammar tchr. Orlando Coll., 1975-84. Mem. Nat. Coun. Tchrs. English, Assn. Tchrs. in Cath. Schs. in Orlando Diocese (founder). Avocation: photography. Home: 1804 Dartmouth Dr NE Albuquerque NM 87106-1744

TRUOG, DEAN-DANIEL WESLEY, educator, consultant; b. Denver, Apr. 1, 1938; s. George Calvin and Zelma Elizabeth (Bennett) T.; m. Dorothy Anne Harding, May 31, 1961; children: David Robert, Denise Dawne. Student, Bethel Coll., 1960-61, L'Abri Fellowship Found., Switzerland, 1967-68; diploma in Bible and Leadership Devel., The Navigators Internat. Tng. Inst., 1968; BA in History, U. Colo., 1971; Diploma in Gen. Univ. Studies in French Civilization, U. Strasbourg, France, 1977; MA in Liberal Edn., St. John's Coll., 1986; M of Liberal Arts in History of Sci., Harvard U., 1987; postgrad., Boston U., 1987-93. Sr. resident adv. U. Colo., Boulder, 1964-65; rep., tutor, lectr. biblical studies and practical christianity The Navigators, 1965-93; rep. for greater Washington area, 1965-67; training asst. The Navigators, Colorado Springs, Colo., 1968, rep. at U. Colo. Boulder, 1968-70, No. Colo. dir., 1970-71, spl. adv. Birmingham, Eng., 1971-72, rep. at large Boulder, Colo., 1979-80; founding dir., pres. Les Navigateurs, France, 1972-84, v.p., 1984-85, rep. to U. Strasbourg, 1973-79, rep. to U. Grenoble, 1980-85; sr. teaching fellow in nondeptmental studies Harvard U., Cambridge, Mass., 1987-90; founding pres., life mgmt. cons./counselor Cornerstone Inst. for Values and Relationships, 1990—; v.p. U.S.-Bulgaria Inst., Cambridge, 1991—; spl. cons. to mems. U.S. Congress, 1993—. Tutor North House, Harvard U., 1987-91; founding chmn. Harvard Christian Assocs., 1987-92; spkr., tchr. profl. confs.; designer, dir. leadership devel. programs, Boston, Washington, Colo., Austria, France, Switzerland. With USN, 1958-59. Mem. AAAS, History of Sci. Soc., Am. Sci. Affiliation, Soc. Christian Philosophers, Assn. for Religion and Intellectual Llife, Inst. on Religion in Age of Sci., Ctr. for Theology and Natural Scis., Nat. Assn. Scholars, Rotary. Presbyterian. Avocations: cycling, gardening, skiing, tennis, swimming. Home and Office: 15 Sheridan Rd Swampscott MA 01907-2046

TRUSDELL, MARY LOUISE CANTRELL, retired state educational administrator; b. Chandler, Okla., Oct. 24, 1921; d. George Herbert and Lois Elizabeth (Bruce) Cantrell; m. Robert William Trusdell, Jan. 7, 1943; children— Timothy Lee, Laurence Michael. BA, Ga. So. Coll., 1965; MEd, U. Va., 1974. Dir. specific learning disabilities program Savannah Country Day Sch., Ga., 1960-65; learning disabilities tchr. Richmond pub. schs., Va., 1966-73; dir. New Community Sch., Richmond, 1974-75; dir. Fed. Learning Disabilities Project, Dept HEW, Mid. Peninsula, Va., 1975-76; supr. programs for learning disabled Va. Dept. Edn., Richmond, 1976-86; bd. dirs. Learning Disabilities Council, Richmond, Very Spl. Arts- Va., 1986-91; mem. adv. com. Learning Disabilities Research and Devel. Project, Woodrow Wilson Rehab. Ctr., Fisherville, Va., 1983. Co-editor: Understanding Learning Disabilities: A Parent Guide and Workbook, 1989, 3d edit., 2002. Bd. dirs. Savannah Assn. Retarded Children, 1957-60, Meml. Guidance Clinic, Richmond, 1966-69. Named Tchr. of Yr., Learning Disabilities Ctr., Richmond, 1972. Mem. Orton Dyslexia Soc. (pres. capital area br. 1968-70, nat. bd. dirs. 1970-72, Va. br. 1986-91), Alliance for the Mentally Ill. Cen. Va. (pres. 1991-93). Presbyterian. Avocations: travel, theater, reading.

TRYBUL, THEODORE NICHOLAS, engineering educator; b. Chgo., Apr. 12, 1935; s. Theodore and Sophie Trybul; children: Adrienne, Barbie, Cathy, Diane, Elizabeth, Teddy. BS summa cum laude, U.-Ill., 1957; MS summa cum laude, U. N.Mex., 1963; DSc summa cum laude, George Washington U., 1976. Registered profl. engr., D.C. Dir. Sr. Exec. Svc., ES-IV Fed. Govt., Washington, 1966-83; prof. George Washington U., Washington, 1983-94, Tex. Grad. Sch., Corpus Christi, Tex., 1994—98; prof. and dir. Natl. U., Grad. Sch. Bus. and Tech., Sacramento, 1998—. Cons. NSF, Advanced Rsch. Projects Agy., U.S. Dept. Edn., NIH, Advanced Material Concepts Agy., Surgeon Gen.'s Office, Natl. Acad. Scis., IBM, Intel, Microsoft, GTSI; adv. bd. NSF, NIH, Natl. Acad. Engring., Surgeon Gen.'s Office. Contbr. articles to profl. jours. Officer Corpus Christi C. of C., Neuces Club, Millionaires Club, CC Town Club. Col. U.S. Army, 1957. Fellow ASME, Soc. for Computer Simulation, Health Care Execs., Sir Isaac Walton, Audubonn Soc., Sierra Club; mem. Pi Tau Sigma, Phi Betta Kappa, Kappa Mu Epsilon, Sigma Xi, Am. Assn. U. Prof.'s and Adminstr.'s, Soc. Computer Simulation, Am. Mgmt. Assn. Avocations: golf, tennis, fishing, mountain climbing. Office: Auburn Lake Trails CC 2418 Westville Trail Cool CA 95614 E-mail: ttrybul@hotmail.com.

TRYBUS, RAYMOND J. higher education executive, psychologist; b. Chgo., Jan. 9, 1944; s. Fred and Cecilia (Liszka) T.; m. Sandra A. Noone, Aug. 19, 1967; children: David, Nicole. BS, St. Louis U., 1965, MS, 1970, PhD, 1971. Lic. psychologist, Md., D.C., Calif. Dir. demographic studies Gallaudet U., Washington, 1974-78, dean grad. studies and rsch., 1978-88; academic dean Calif. Sch. Profl. Psychology, San Diego, 1988—90, chancellor, 1990—99; exec. v.p. Alliant U. Found., San Diego, 1999—2001; assoc. provost and dean Grad. Studies Nat. U., La Jolla, Calif., 2002, provost & v.p. acad. affairs, 2002—. Dir. Rehab. Rsch. and Tng. Ctr., 1994—2003; adminstr. Project ESSEA (Ethiopia, Somalia, Sudan and Eritrea in Africa), 2000—. Mem. sci. rev. bd. Dept. Vets. Affairs Rehab. Rsch. and Devel. Program, 1991—; cons. Mental Health Ctr. for Deaf, Lanham, Md., 1982-88, Congl. Rsch. Svc., 1982-84, McGill U. Nat. Study Hearing Impairment in Can., 1984-88. Grantee, NIMH, Nat. Inst. Disability and Rehab. Rsch., Spencer Found., Tex. Edn. Agy., W.K. Kellogg Found., Robert Wood Johnson Found., The Calif. Endowment, Alliance Healthcare Found. Mem.: APA, Am. Assn. Higher Edn., Am. Deafness and Rehab. Assn., San Diego Psychol. Assn., Calif. Psychol. Assn. (pres. divsn. edn. and tng. 1990—92). Roman Catholic. Home: 6342 Cibola Rd San Diego CA 92120-2124 Office: Nat U 11255 N Torrey Pines Rd La Jolla CA 92037-1011

TRYGESTAD, JOANN CAROL, secondary education educator; b. Mpls., Feb. 11, 1950; d. Harvey Oscar and Frances Anne (Libera) T. BS, U. Minn., 1972, MEd, 1983, PhD, 1997. Cert. tchr. social studies, history, English, Minn. Tchr. Sch. Dist. 742, St. Cloud, Minn., 1973-77, Sch. Dist. 196, Rosemount, Minn., 1977—. Grad. asst. U. Minn., Mpls., 1988-90; adj. instr. Hamline U., St. Paul, 1987-90, asst. prof., 1999—; steering com. mem. Alliance for Geography, St. Paul, 1988—; cons. in field. Contbr. articles to profl. jours. Mem. Nat. Coun. for Social Studies, Nat. Coun. for Geog. Edn., Am. Ednl. Rsch. Assn. Home: 4133 Arbor Ln Eagan MN 55122-2895 Office: Rosemount Sch Dist 14445 Diamond Path W Rosemount MN 55068-4143

TRZYNA, CHRIS, physical education educator; b. Chgo. d. Edward and Helen Trzyna. BS, No. Ill. U., 1976, MS, 1983, C.A.S. in Adminstrn. and Supervision, 1991. Cert. tchr. Ill. Tchr., asst. athletic dir. Libertyville HS, 1976—; girls volleyball coach Libertyville HS, 1987—. Recipient Volleyball Coach of the Yr., Libertyville HS, 2000. Mem.: AAHPERD, Ill. Athletic Dirs. Assn., Ill. High Sch. Assn. (soccer adv. com.), Ill. Assn. Health, Phys. Edn. Recreation and Dance, Delta Psi Kappa (v.p. 1975—76). Office: Libertyville High School 708 W Park Ave Libertyville IL 60048-2604 Business E-Mail: chris.trzyna@district128.org.

TSAI, BOR-SHENG, educator; b. Kaohsiung, Taiwan, China, Apr. 8, 1950; came to U.S., 1978; s. Yu-shiu and Huo-chu T.; m. Shiu-hwa Yu; 1 child, Shengdar. BA in Libr. Sci., Fu-jen Cath. U., 1974; MS in Info. Sci., Case Western Reserve U., 1979, PhD in Info. Sci., 1987. Intern Libr. Plastics Techs., Kaohsiung, 1973; acquisitions libr. Nat. Cen. Libr., Taiwan, 1976-77; reference libr. Case Western Reserve U., Cleve., 1981; instr., designer CATS, bilingual/multicultural program Cleve. Pub. Schs., 1985-86; asst. prof. libr. and info. sci. program Wayne State U., Detroit, 1987-97; assoc. prof. Sch. Info. and Libr. Sci., Pratt Inst., N.Y.C., 1997—. Cons. in field. Mem. ALA, AAUP, Am. Soc. Info. Sci. and Tech. (chpt. rep. 1992-93, info. sci. commn., Continuing Edn. Commn. 1993-95, mem. com. 2000—, mem. Watson Davis award com. 2000—, mem, ISI Citation Award com. 2002—), Chinese-Am. Librs. Assn. (coord., chmn. E-Mail com. 1991-94, chmn. E-Pub. com. 1994-95, pub. com. 1990-93, 94, scholarship com. 1996-97, editor E-Jour. 1992-95), Mich. Libr. Assn., Assn. Libr. and Info. Sci. Edn., Internat. Soc. Scientometrics & Infometrics. Avocations: painting, soccer, chess, writing, sightseeing. Office: Pratt Inst Sch Info and Libr Sci 144 W 14th St New York NY 10011

TSCHERNISCH, SERGEI P. academic administrator; BA, San Francisco State U.; MFA in Theatre, Stanford U.; student, San Francisco Actors' Workshop, Stanford Repertory Theatre. Founding mem. Calif. Inst. of Arts, 1969, mem. faculty, assoc. dean Sch. Theatre, dir., 1969-80; prof. dept. theatre U. Md., College Park, 1980-82; dir. divsn. performing and visual arts Northeastern U., Boston, 1982-92; dean Coll. of Comm. and Fine Arts Loyola Marymount U., L.A., 1992-94; pres. Cornish Coll. of Arts, Seattle, 1994—. Advisor NEA; mem. com. USIA; cons. to many festivals. Office: Cornish Coll Arts 710 E Roy St Seattle WA 98102-4604*

TSCHETTER, LOIS JEAN, retired elementary education educator; b. Algona, Iowa, Nov. 21, 1936; d. Clifford Wayne and Floy Faye (Eckstein) Riebhoff; m. Calvin Joe Tschetter, June 13, 1956; children: Scott, Susan Tschetter Grandgeorge. BS in Elem. Edn., U. No. Iowa, 1978; MS in Elem. Adminstrn., Drake U., 1991. Kindergarten tchr. Kalona schs., Iowa, 1956-58; title I tchr. Eagle Grove Cmty. Schs., 1967-69, 2d grade tchr., 1969-85, chair for curriculum coms., 1980—95, 1st grade tchr., 1985-95, co-facilitator of sch. improvement team, 1994-95, curriculum dir., at-risk coord., 1995—99. Cert. tchr., trainer for Growing Healthy Nat. Ctr. for Health Edn., San Bruno, CAlif., 1981—. Mem. NEA, Iowa State Edn. Assn., Internat. Reading Assn., Iowa Reading Assn., Iowa Coun. Tchrs. of Math., Alpha Delta Kappa (treas. 1992—), Beta Sigma Phi (pres. 1987-88). Republican. Meth. Avocations: bridge, fishing, boating, music. Office: Eagle Grove Cmty Schs 216 N Commercial Ave Eagle Grove IA 50533-1722

TSCHUMY, FREDA COFFING, artist, educator; b. Danville, Ill., Mar. 18, 1939; d. Frederick Winfield and Minnie Isabelle (Buck) Coffing; m. William Edward Tschumy, Jr., June 17, 1967; 1 child, William Coffing. BA, Vassar Coll., 1961; postgrad., Art Students' League N.Y., 1961-63, Accademia di Belli Arti, Rome, 1963; MFA, U. Miami, 1990. Instr. art Miami (Fla.) Fine Arts Conservatory, 1968; instr. ceramics Grove House, Coconut Grove, Fla., summer 1970; instr. sculpture Upstairs Gallery, Miami Beach, 1971, Continuum Gallery, Miami Beach, 1972-73; instr. painting Barry Coll., Miami, fall 1974; instr. sculpture Met. Mus. Sch., Coral Gables, Fla., 1980-89, Bass Mus. Sch., Miami Beach, 1989-92; teaching asst. U. Miami, Coral Gables, 1988-90, lectr. sculpture, pres., 1991—, dir. foundry, 1992—. Pres. founding mem. Continuum Gallery, Miami Beach, 1971-75, treas. 1975-83; treas. The Gallery at Mayfair, Coconut Grove, 1982-83, pres., 1983-84; artist in residence Hawaii Sch. for Girls, Honolulu, 1987; founding dir. Foundry Guild, U. Miami, Coral Gables, 1993—. Prin. works include sculptures at Dade Metrorail Univ. Sta., Melbourne (Fla.) Libr.; traveling exhbn. various colls., Miami. Mem. Tropical Audubon Soc., Miami, 1975—, Fla. Conservation Found., 1978—, Fla. Pub. Interest Rsch. Group, 1986—, Fla. Abortion Rights Action League, 1985—. Recipient Excellence award, Sculptors Fla. 1972, Fine Art Achievement award Binney & Smith, 1990, award of Excellence, Art in the Downtown Downtown Devel. Authority, Ft. Lauderdale, Fla.; grantee Posey Found., 1989. Mem. Am. Foundryman's Soc., Womens Caucus Art (1st v.p. local chpt. 1981-86, bd. dirs. 1980-91, nat. bd. dirs. 1982-85), Internat. Sculpture Ctr. Avocations: travel, reading, swimming, cycling. Studio: 3610 Bayview Rd Miami FL 33133-6503

TSE, HARLEY Y. immunologist, educator; b. China, July 17, 1947; s. Ton-Cheuk and Hou-Ying (Choy) T.; m. Kwai-Fong Chui, Jan. 13, 1979; children: Kevin Y., Alan C., Leslie W. BS with honors, Calif. Inst. Tech., 1972; PhD, U. Calif., San Diego, 1977; MBA, Rutgers U., 1986. Fellow Arthritis Found., NIH, Bethesda, Md., 1977-80; sr. rsch. immunologist Merck Sharp & Dohme Rsch. Lab., Rahway, N.J., 1980-83, rsch. fellow, 1983-86; adj. asst. prof. Columbia U., 1981-84; assoc. prof. Wayne State U. Sch. Medicine, Detroit, 1986—. Mem. immunol. sci. study sect. NIH, 1995-99. Contbr. articles to profl. jours. Bd. dirs. Chinese Social Svc. Ctr., San Diego, 1975. Recipient NIH Rsch. Career Devel. award, 1992-97; Calif. Biochem. Rsch. fellow, 1975; Arthritis Found. fellow, 1977-80; NIH grantee; Nat. Multiple Sclerosis Soc. grantee, 1988—. Mem. Am. Assn. Immunologists, Chinese Student Assn. (pres. 1974-76), Soc. Chinese Bioscientists in Am., Detroit Immunol. Soc. (pres. 1989-91). Roman Catholic. Home: 5393 Tequesta Dr West Bloomfield MI 48323-2351 Office: Wayne State U Sch Medicine 540 E Canfield St Detroit MI 48201-1928 E-mail: htse@wayne.edu.

TSE, MAN-CHUN MARINA, educational association administrator; b. Kai-Ping, China, Dec. 14, 1948; came to U.S., 1972; d. Sun-Poo and Su-ling Cheung. BA in English, U. Chinese Culture, Taipei, Taiwan, 1970; MS in Spl. Edn., U. So. Calif., 1974; leadership program diploma, Harvard U., 2003. Cert. tchr., spl. edn. tchr., Calif. Rsch. asst. lit. U. Chinese Culture, 1970-72; English tchr. Tang-Suede Mid. Sch., Taiwan, 1970-72; instr. Willing Workers, Adult Handicapped Program L.A. Sch. Dist., 1976-77; instr. ESL Evans Adult Sch., L.A., 1977—82; instr. ESL and polit. sci. Lincoln Adult Sch., L.A., 1986—94; spl. edn. tchr. Duarte (Calif.) Unified Sch. Dist., 1977—2000; prin. assoc. under sec. Office of English Lang. Acquisition, Lang. Enhancement and Acad. Achievement for Limited English Proficient Students U.S. Dept. Edn., 2000—. Commr., program co-chair Calif. Spl. Edn. Adv. Commn., Sacramento, 1994-96; mem. Calif. State Bd. Edn., 1996-99; mem. Calif. State Summer Sch. for the Arts, 1998-99; coun. mem. L.A. County Children Planning Coun., 1995—; com. mem. L.A. County Sci. & Engring. Fair Com., 1993—; hon. adv. bd. Asian Youth Ctr., San Gabriel City, Calif., 1992—; exec. bd. Pres. Com. on Employment of People with Disabilities (U.S.), 1997—; com. mem. tchr. devel. project Nat. Assn. State Bd. Edn., 1977—; mem. Calif. State Supts. Art Task Force, 1997-98; advisor Calif. Coun. Tech., 1996-99; mem. Calif. Rehab. Coun. Appeared on numerous TV and radio programs. Bd. trustee Bruggemeyer Libr., Monterey Park, Calif., 1993-99; pres. L.A. County Coun. Reps., 1994—; mem. Calif. Statewide Focus Group Diversity, Sacramento, 1995-97; chair Chinese Am. Edn. Assn., 1993—; co-chair, co-founder Multi-Cultural Cmty. Assn., 1992—; bd. dirs. Rosemead-Taipei Sister City, 1993—, San Gabriel Valley Charity Night Com., 1992—; chmn. Los Angeles County-Taipei County Friendship Com., 1996—. Recipient Recognition cert. Duarte Edn. Found., 1990, Calif. Legis. Assembly, 1993, cert. Valley View Sch., 1991, award State Calif., 1991, Appreciation award City Rosemead, 1992, Commendation cert. Alhambra Sch. Dist., 1992-93, Edn. award Asian Youth Ctr., 1992, 1992, Commendation cert. City L.A., 1992, commendation County L.A., 1992, award U.S. Congress, 1993, Proclamation City Alhambra, 1993, Chinese Am. PTA award, 1993, John Anson Ford award L.A. County Human Rels. Com., 1993, Appreciation cert. Chinese Consolidated Benevolent Assn., 1994, City Monterey Park, 1995, Recognition cert. Calif. State Senate, 1994, Spl. Achievement award Calif. Spl. Edn. Adv. Commn., 1997, Duarte United Edn. Ctr., 1997, Outstanding Comm. Svc. award City of Duarte, Calif., 1997, Disting. Woman of Yr. award Calif. 24th Dist. Sen.'s Office, 1997, Svc. award Calif. Fedn. Exceptional Children Coun., 1998, Calif. Sanitorial award, 1999, L.A. County Bd. Suprs. Outstanding Svc. award, 1999, Monterey Park City award, 1999. Mem. Calif. Tchr. Assn., Chinese Edn. Assn., Internat. Platform Assn., Nat. Assn. State Bds. Edn. Office: US Dept Edn Mary Switzer Bldg 330 C St SW Rm 5082 Washington DC 20202-6510

TSENG, HOWARD SHIH CHANG, business and economics educator, investment company executive; b. Tainan, Taiwan, Jan. 14, 1935; came to U.S., 1963; s. Picheng and Chaoliu (Wang) T.; m. Evelina M. Young, Dec. 25, 1965; 1 child, Elaine Evelina. BA, Nat. Taiwan U., Taipei, 1957, MA, 1963; PhD, U. Okla., 1972. Chief economist Cooperative Bank Taiwan, Taipei, 1959-61; dir. tax services Bur. Taxation, Govt. Taiwan, Republic China, Taipei, 1961-63; instr. U. Okla., Norman, 1968; asst. prof. Ga. So. U., Statosboro, 1968-71; prof. bus. and econs. Catawba Coll., Salisbury, 1971—2001; adj. prof. San Francisco State U., 2002—, 2002—. Pres. Am. Prudential Investments, Salisbury, 1981-89; pres. Tsengs Investments, 1990—. Author: Investments, 1982; contbr. articles to profl. jours. Coordinator, supporter study mathematically precocious youth Johns Hopkins U., Balt., 1982—; ptnr. World Vision, Calif., 1986-92. Academic research grantee Academia Sinica, Taipei, 1962; Ford Found. fellow, Taipei, 1963. Mem. AAUP, Ea. Econ. Assn., Am. Econ. Assn., Am. Assn. Individual Investors, Taiwan Investment (organizer 1986—), Taiwanese-Am. Assn. Greater Charlotte (pres. 1994-96), Nat. Travel Club. Avocations: antique collector, traveling, reading. Home: 316 Bethel Dr Salisbury NC 28144-2808 Office: Catawba Coll W Innes St Salisbury NC 28144 Fax: 704-637-5724. E-mail: stseng@catawba.edu., stsengs@hotmail.com.

TSIN, ANDREW TSANG CHEUNG, cell biology and biochemistry researcher; b. Hong Kong, July 19, 1950; came to U.S., 1979; m. Wendy L. Wickstrom, Jan. 20, 1979; 1 child, Cathy Mei. BS in Biology, Dalhousie U., Halifax, N.S., Can., 1973; MS in Zoology, U. Alberta, Edmonton, Alta., Can., 1976, PhD in Zoology, 1979; postgrad., Baylor Coll. Medicine, 1979-81. Prof. biochemistry and cell biology U. Tex., San Antonio, 1990—; prof. ophthalmology U. Tex. Health Sci. Ctr., San Antonio, 1990—, minority biomed. rsch. support program dir., 1991—. Cons. Alcon Lab., Ft. Worth, 1989-90; adminstrv. officer radiation and laser safety U. Tex., San Antonio, 1985-92, dir. divsn. life sci., 1994-95; sci. advisor, cons. NIH, Bethesda, Md., 1987—, NSF, Washington, 1987—. Contbr. articles to profl. jours. Named postgrad. scholar Nation Rsch. Coun. of Can., 1977-78, postdoctoral fellow Med. Rsch. Coun. Can., 1979-82, Alta. Heritage Found. Med. Rsch. fellow, 1981-82. Mem. AAAS, Am. Soc. Biochemistry and Molecular Biology, Assn. for Rsch. in Vision and Ophthalmology, Am. Physiol. Soc., Soc. for Neurosci. Achievements include research in cell biology of the retina, biochemistry of membrane proteins, metabolism of retinoids, comparative animal physiology, and environmental and evolutionary biology. Office: U Tex San Antonio Dept Biology San Antonio TX 78249 E-mail: atsin@utsa.edu.

TSOHANTARIDIS, TIMOTHEOS, minister, religion educator; b. Katerini, Greece, Feb. 7, 1954; came to U.S., 1967; s. Ioannis and Parthena (Karipidis) T.; m. Valerie Ann Hoffman, July 11, 1977; children: Demetrius, Thaddeus. BA, Barrington Coll., 1977; MDiv, Gordon-Conwell, 1980; MA, Ashland Theol. Sem., 1985; PhD, 2002. Ordained to ministry Evang. Friends Ch., 1986. Ch. planter Ea. region Evang. Friends Ch., North Ridgeville, Ohio, 1980-85; prof. religion, Greek, dir. Christian life, soccer coach George Fox Coll., Newberg, Oreg., 1985—90; prof. Biblical studies George Fox U., 1993—. Author: (in Greek) Greek Evangelicals: Pontus to Katerini, 1985. Mem. Am. Acad. Religion, Soc. Bibl. Lit., Nat. Soccer Coaches Athletic Assn. (soccer coach, Nat. Coach of Yr. 1989). Home: 414 N Meridian St Newberg OR 97132-2625 Office: George Fox Coll 414 N Meridian St Newberg OR 97132-2625

TSUBAKI, ANDREW TAKAHISA, theater director, educator; b. Chiyoda-ku, Tokyo, Japan, Nov. 29, 1931; s. Ken and Yasu (Oyama) T.; m. Lilly Yuri, Aug. 3, 1963; children: Arthur Yuichi, Philip Takeshi. BA in English, Tokyo Gakugei U., Tokyo, Japan, 1954; postgrad. in Drama, U. Saskatchewan, Saskatoon, Canada, 1958-59; MFA in Theatre Arts, Tex. Christian U., 1961; PhD in Speech & Drama, U. Ill., 1967. Tchr. Bunkyo-ku 4th Jr. High Sch., Tokyo, 1954—58; instr., scene designer Bowling Green (Ohio) State U., 1964—68; asst. prof. speech & drama U. Kans., Lawrence, 1968—73, assoc. prof., 1973—79; vis. assoc. prof. Carleton Coll., Northfield, Minn., 1974; lectr. Tsuda U., Tokyo, 1975; vis. assoc. prof. theatre Tel-Aviv (Israel) U., 1975—76; vis. prof. theatre Mo. Repertory Theatre, Kansas City, Mo., 1976, Nat. Sch. Drama, New Delhi, 1983; prof. theatre, film, east Asian Languages and Cultures U. Kans., Lawrence, 1979—2000, prof. emeritus, 2000—. Dir. Internat. Theatre Studies Ctr., U. Kans., Lawrence, 1971-2000, Operation Internat. Classical Theatre, 1988—; Benedict disting. vis. prof. Asian studies Carleton Coll., 1993; area editor Asian Theatre Jour., U. Hawaii, Honolulu, 1982-94; chmn. East Asian Langs. and Cultures, U. Kans., Lawrence, 1983-90; mem. editl. bd. Studies in Am. Drama, Oxford, Miss., 1985-88. Dir. plays Kanjincho, 1973, Rashomon, 1976, 96, King Lear, 1985, Fujito and Shimizu, 1985, Hippolytus, 1990, Busu and the Missing Lamb (Japan) 1992, Suehirogari and Sumidagawa, 1992, 93, Tea, 1995; choreographed Antigone (Greece), 1987, Hamlet (Germany), 1989, The Resistible Rise of Arturo Ui, 1991, Man and the Masses (Germany), 1993, The Children of Fate (Hungary), 1994, The Great Theatre of the World (Germany); editor Theatre Companies of the World, 1986; contbg. author to Indian Theatre: Traditions of Performance, 1990; contbr. 7 entries in Japanese Traditional plays to the Internat. Dictionary of Theatre, vol. 1, 1992, vol. 2, 1994. Recipient World Univ. Svc. Scholarship U. Saskatchewan, 1958-59, University fellow U. Ill., 1961-62, Rsch. fellow The Japan Found., 1974-75, 90, Rsch. Fulbright grantee, 1983. Fellow Coll. Am. Theatre (elected 2002); mem. Am. Theatre Assn., Asian Theatre Program (chair 1976-79), Assn. for Asian Studies, Assn. Kans. Theatres., Assn. Kans. Theatres U/C Div. (chmn. 1980-82), Assn. for Theatre in Higher Edn., Assn. for Asian Performance. Democrat. Buddhist. Avocations: ki-aikido (4th dan), photography, travel. Home: 924 Holiday Dr Lawrence KS 66049-3005 E-mail: atsubaki@ku.edu.

TSUI, SOO HING, educational research consultant; b. Hong Kong, Aug. 2, 1959; came to U.S., 1985; d. Sik Tin and Yuk Kam (Cheung) T. BSW cum laude, Nat. Taiwan U., 1983; MSW cum laude, Columbua U., 1987, postgrad., 1992—. Cert. social worker, N.Y. Dir. cmty. handicapped ctr., Taipei, Taiwan, 1983-85; dir. youth recreational program, 1986; social work dept. supr. St. Margaret's House, N.Y.C., 1987-89; chief bilingual sch. social work N.Y.C. Bd. Edn., 1990—, rsch. cons., 1993—; rschr. Columbia U., N.Y.C., 1991-95; chief rsch. cons. N.Y.C. Dept. Transp., 1993-96; cheif rschr. immigrant social svcs. N.Y.C. Bd. Edn., 1996—. Bilingual social worker Nat. Assn. Asian/Am. Edn., 1989—; union social work regional rep. N.Y.C. Bd. Edn., 1990-93, citywide bilingual social work rep., 1991-93, citywide social work budget allocation comms. rep., 1992-93; mem. conf. planning com. bd. Amb. For Christ, Boston, 1991-93; coord. doctoral colloquial com. bd., 1991-93, Scholarships Coun. Social Work Edn., Columbia U., N.Y.C., 1992-94; mem. planning com. social work bd. Asian Am. Comms., N.Y.C., 1991-95; exec. dir. alumni bd. Columbia U. Sch. Social Work, 1995—, exec. dir. bd. Columbia newsletters Columbia U. Sch. Social Work, 1996—; exec. bd. dirs. Chinese for Christ, 1993-95. Recipient Nat. Acad. award, 1979-83; Nat. Acad. scholar, 1987-88; Nat. Rsch. fellow Sch. Coun. on Social Work Edn., 1992-94. Home: 65-38 Booth St Apt 2B Rego Park NY 11374

TSUMURA, YUMIKO, Japanese language and culture educator, consultant; b. Gobo City, Wakayama, Japan, Mar. 8, 1939; came to the U.S., 1972; s. Yoshio and Masako (Moriguchi) T.; m. Motoi Umano, Apr. 13, 1961 (dec. Apr. 1962); 1 child, Junko; m. Samuel B. Grolmes, Mar. 2, 1969. BA, Kwansei Gakuin U., Nishinomiya, Japan, 1961, MA, 1965, postgrad., 1965-66; MFA, U. Iowa, 1968. Lectr. Baika Women's Coll., Osaka, Japan, 1970-72, Calif. State U., San Jose, 1973-74, U. Santa Clara, Calif., 1975-77, West Valley Coll., Saratoga, Calif., 1974-79; assoc. prof. Foothill Coll., Los Altos Hills, Calif., 1974—; asst. prof. Coll. San Mateo, Calif., 1975—; asst. prof. Japanese lang. and culture, shodo Cañada Coll., Redwood City, Calif., 1974—. U.S.-Japan intercultural cons. Apple Computer, Inc., Cupertino, Calif., 1984—, NASA Ames Rsch. Ctr., Mountain View, Calif., 1987-93, Hewlett Packard Co., Santa Clara, 1992—, Kobe Steel U.S.A., Inc., San Jose, 1992— Co-translator: (with Sam Grolmes) Poetry of Kyuichi Tamura, 1998, Tamura Ryuichi Poens 1946-1998, 2000, Let Those Who Appear, 2002, (Japanese poetry and fiction) New Directions Annual, 1970-74; contbr. poetry to lit. jours., 1967—. Artist rep. Junko Tsumura, Igor Scedrov piano cello duo Cultural Comm. and Cons., Palo Alto, 1988—; lectr. and demonstrator on Shodo Galerija Foruma Mladih, Varazdin, Croatia, 1993; bd. dirs. Japanese Cultural Ctr., Foothill Coll., 1994. Honor scholar Kwansei Gakuin U., Nishinomiya, 1958-59; Travel grantee Fulbright-Hayes Commn., Tokyo, 1966, Internat. Peace Scholarship grantee P.E.O. Internat. Peace Fund, Des Moines, 1967-68. Mem. No. Calif. Tchrs. Assn. Avocations: poetry, shodo ink brush art, classical music, dance, cooking. Home: 723 Torreya Ct Palo Alto CA 94303-4160 Office: Foothill Coll 4000 Middlefield Rd Palo Alto CA 94303-4739

TUBBS, STEPHEN WALTER, social studies educator; b. Waverly, N.Y., Nov. 13, 1951; s. Walter Wilbur and Edith (Kline) T.; m. Julia Ann Lamb, Dec. 11, 1976. BS Secondary Edn., SUNY, Geneseo, 1972; MS Secondary Edn., Elmira Coll., 1975. Cert. social studies tchr., N.Y., Pa. Social studies instr., 9-12 Athens (Pa.) High Sch., 1976-80, SRU High Sch., East Smithfield, Pa., 1980-89, chmn. social studies dept., 1983-89; social studies instr., 9-12 Athens Area High Sch., 1989—, chmn. social studies dept., 1989—. Fireman Hook and Ladder Vol Fir Co., 1971—. NEH summer scholar, SUNY, Brockport, 1986. Avocation: developing and building high end loudspeaker systems. Home: 39 Warren St Sayre PA 18840-2927

TUBIS, ARNOLD, physics educator; b. Pottstown, Pa., Mar. 28, 1932; s. Joseph and Rose (Nemiroff) T.; m. Charlotte Ida Litman, June 14, 1959; children: Cheryl Lynne Tubis Brown, Eliot Jason. BS in Physics, MIT, 1954, PhD in Physics, 1959. Asst. prof. dept. physics Worcester (Mass.) Poly. Inst., 1958-60; rsch. assoc. Purdue U., West Lafayette, Ind., 1960-62, asst. prof. physics, 1962-64, assoc. prof., 1964-69, prof. physics, 1969—2000, asst. head dept. physics, 1966-73, head dept. physics, 1988-97, prof. emeritus, 2000—. Chmn. tech. com. Internat. Workshop on Mechanics of Hearing, Boston, 1985; cons. in field. Editor conf. procs.; contbr. numerous articles to refereed jours. Pres. Congregation Sons of Abraham Synagogue, Lafayette, Ind., 1976-78. Am. Phys. Soc. fellow, 1977; grantee AEC, Deafness Rsch. Found., Dept. Energy, Energy Rsch. and Devel. Adminstrn., NIH, NSF, Office Naval Rsch.; vis. scholar Inst. Nonlinear Sci., U. Calif. San Diego, La Jolla, 2000—. Fellow Acoustical Soc. Am. (tech. com. mem. musical acoustics 1984-89, physiol. and psychol. acoustics 1992-97); mem. AAAS, AAUP, Am. Assn. Physics Tchrs., Am. Phys. Soc., Assn. Rsch. on Otolaryngology, Catgut Acoustical Soc., N.Y. Acad. Scis., Sigma Xi, Sigma Pi Sigma. Jewish. Avocations: hiking, music, reading, puzzles, origami.

TUCCERI, CLIVE KNOWLES, science writer and educator, consultant; b. Bryn Mawr, Pa., Apr. 20, 1953; d. William Henry and Clive Ellis (Knowles) Hulick; m. Eugene Angelo Tucceri, Sept. 1, 1984 (div. Nov. 1991); 1 child, Clive Edna. BA in Geology, Williams Coll., 1975; MS in Coastal Geology, Boston Coll., 1982. Head sci. dept. Stuart Hall Sch., Staunton, Va., 1975-77; mem. sci. faculty William Penn Charter Sch., Phila., 1977-79, Tower Sch., Marblehead, Mass., 1982-86, Bentley Coll., Waltham, Mass., 1986-88; adminstrv. dir., co-founder Stout Aquatic Libr. Nat. Marine and Aquatic Edn. Resource Ctr., Wakefield, R.I., 1982-89; mem. sci. faculty Mabelle B. Avery Sch., Somers, Conn., 1989-90; mem. faculty, head sci. dept. MacDuffie Sch., Springfield, Mass., 1992-93; mem. sci. faculty East Hampton (Conn.) Middle Sch., 1993—, sci. team leader, 1994-95, sci. chairperson grades K-12, 1995—, 8th grade advisor, 2000—01. Cons. Longmeadow (Mass.) Pub. Schs., 1989-94, Addison-Wesley Pub. Co., Menlo Prk, Calif., 1986-94; cons., freelance writer Prentice-Hall Inc., Needham, Mass., 1991. Co-head class agt. Williams Coll. Alumni Fund, 2000—, vice chair, 2003—; admissions rep. Williams Coll., 2001—; vol. The Bushnell Ctr. for Performing Arts, 2001—; mem. search com. Christ Ch., Middle Haddam, Conn., 2000—01, mem. vestry, 2002—; bd. dirs. People Against Rape, Staunton, 1976—77. Mem.: AAUW (bd. dirs., br. pres.-elect 1975—77, v.p. 1985—86, sec. 1986—87), NEA, NSTA, Cousteau Soc., Conn. Edn. Assn., Conn. Sci Tchrs. Assn., Conn. Sci. Suprs. Assn., Mass. Environ. Edn. Soc. (bd. dirs. 1985—88), Mass. Marine Educators (pres. 1987—89, bd. dirs. 1983—91, editor Flotsam and Jetsam MA Marine Educators newsletter 1991—97), Southeastern New Eng. Marine Educators (publs. chair Nat. Conf. com.), Nat. Mid. Level Sci. Tchrs. Assn., Nat. Marine Edn. Assn. (sec. 1986—87, chpt. rep. 1987 1989), Sigma Xi. Episcopalian. Avocations: renovating old homes, sailing, gardening, reading. Home: 12 Birchwood Dr East Hampton CT 06424-1312

TUCK, CAROLYN WEAVER, middle school educator; b. Petersburg, Va., Nov. 18, 1947; d. Fred William Weaver and Virginia Evelyn (Fick) Lang; m. Michael Lewis Jones, Dec. 27, 1969 (div. 1991); children: Kristen Michelle Jones, Kara Denise Jones; m. Richard Harper Tuck, July 30, 1994. BS, Radford U., 1970, MS, 1971; adminstrv. cert., William and Mary Coll., 1991, George Washington U., 1991. Cert. secondary sch. prin., English and history tchr., Va. English tchr. Galax (Va.) City Schs., 1971-72, Waynesville (N.C.) Schs., 1973-75; circulation libr. Western Carolina U., Cullowhee, N.C., 1972-73; English and history tchr. Poquoson (Va.) City Schs., 1975—81, 1985—2002; acting asst. prin. Poquoson (Va.) Mid. Schs., 1989; libr. media specialist Poquoson (Va.) Mid. Sch., 2002—. Rep. to state MS conf. Va. Bd. Edn., Poquoson, 1991. Writer advanced social studies/English curriculum; contbr. articles to profl. jours. Solicitor Am. Cancer Soc., Poquoson, 1992—, Mother's March of Dimes, 1996—; bible sch. tchr. Tabernacle Meth. Ch., Poquoson, 1994—. Mem. NEA, Va. Edn. Assn., Poquoson Edn. Assn. (v.p. 2000—), Nat. Mid. Sch. Assn., Pi Gamma Mu, Sigma Tau Delta. Avocations: bridge, travel, doll collecting, genealogy. Home: 105 Shallow Lagoon Yorktown VA 23693-4111 Office: Poquoson Mid Sch 985 Poquoson Ave Poquoson VA 23662-1799

TUCKER, ALAN CURTISS, mathematics educator; b. Princeton, N.J., July 6, 1943; s. Albert William and Alice Judson (Curtiss) W.; m. Amanda Almira Zeisler, Aug. 31, 1968 (div. 1997); children: Lisa, Kathryn, Edward; m. Ann K. Hong, Feb. 16, 1997. BA, Harvard U., 1965; MS, Stanford U., 1967, PhD, 1969. Asst. prof. applied math. SUNY, Stony Brook, 1970-73, assoc. prof. applied math., 1973-78, prof. applied math., chmn., 1978-89, SUNY Disting. Teaching prof., 1989—. Vis. asst. prof. math. U. Wis., Madison, 1969-70; vis. assoc. prof. computer sci. U. Calif., San Diego, 1976-77; vis. prof. ops. research Stanford U., 1983-84; cons. Sloan Found., 1981-85; acad. cons. 40 colls. and univs. Author: Applied Combinatorics, 1980, Unified Introduction to Linear Algebra, 1987, Linear Algebra, 1993; assoc. editor Math. Monthly, 1996—, Applied Maths. Letters, 1986—; contbr. 45 rsch. articles to profl. jours. Ga. U. Consortium Disting. Visitor, 1982; NSF grantee, 1972-86. Mem. Math. Assn. Am. (chmn. publs. 1982-86, editor Studies in Math. series 1979-86, v.p. 1988-90, chmn. ednl. coun. 1990-96, Disting. Tchr. award 1994, Trevor Evans award 1996), U.S. Commn. Math. Instrn., Am. Math. Soc., Ops. Rsch. Soc. Am., Soc. Indsl. Applied Maths., Sigma Xi (chpt. pres. 1987—). Home: 19 Crosby Place Cold Spring Harbor NY 11724-2404 Office: SUNY At Stony Brook Dept Of Applied Math Stony Brook NY 11794-3600 E-mail: atucker@notes.sunysb.edu.

TUCKER, AUBREY STEPHEN, composer, music industry consultant; b. Pine Bluff, Ark., Mar. 3, 1945; s. Aubrey Sylvester and Marcelle Eugenia (Landreth) T.; m. Edythe Latrell Arnold, Nov. 27, 1965 (div. Sept. 1974); children: Stephanie Latrell, Jennifer Leigh; m. Marjorie Ellen Clifton, Dec. 27, 1979; children: Aubrey Clifton, Emily Lucille. BA, U. Houston, 1972; MusM, Rice U., 1989, postgrad., 1989—. Owner Aubrey Tucker Music Prodns. and Consulting, Houston, 1967—; instr., music arranger U.S. Army Element Sch. Music, Norfolk, Va., 1969-71; trombonist, arranger Woody Herman Herd, 1971; trombonist Johnny Haig Orch., Las Vegas, Nev., 1974-78, Lido de Paris-Stardust Hotel, Las Vegas, 1978-81; TV producer and dir. Studio I, Galveston, Tex., 1983-84; audio producer and engr. Limelight Rec. Studio, Dickinson, Tex., 1984-85; dept. head music Houston Community Coll., 1985—. Musician Buddy Kirk Orch., Galveston, 1983-85, 89—; leader Aubrey Tucker's Uptown Orch., Houston, 1985-89; music dir. Houston Community Orch., 1988-89; exec. food and beverage ops. Flagship Hotel, Galveston, Tex., 1991-92. Dir., producer opera Back Home, 1989; composer chamber music Liaisons/Voyage II, 1990, Tropopause to Illinois for 9 percussion, 1992, 4 Canons for Violin and Viola, 1993, 4 Canons for Two Trombones, 1993, Big Bands Are Back! For Electronic Tape, 1993, 4 Cantigas for Flute, Bass Trombone and 2 Percussion, 1993; recording (CD, casette) Buddy Kirk featuring Aubrey Tucker, 1993; trombonist, arranger Ill. Jacquet Big Band, N.Y.C., 1990-92; principle trombone, Am. Pops Orchestra, 1993—. Music dir. Spring Br. Christian Ch., Houston, 1992-93. With U.S. Army, 1969-71. Recipient Best Orch. award Las Vegas Entertainment Awards, 1974, 75, 76, 77, 78; downbeat Mag. scholar, 1971; fellow U. Houston, 1972-73, Rice U., 1988-89. Democrat. Christian. Avocations: films, history, american civil war. Home: 14702 Mauna Loa Ln Houston TX 77040-1406 Office: Houston Community Coll 5514 Clara Rd Houston TX 77041-7204

TUCKER, CALANTHIA RALLINGS, school administrator; b. Chgo., Oct. 22, 1946; d. Donnell and Exie Bernettia (Williams) Rallings; m. Joseph Tuckerm June 25, 1967; children: La Canas Yvette, Tahirah Michelle Tucker Elliott. BS, Tenn. State U., 1968; MS, Va. Poly. and State U., 1978; EdD, Vanderbilt U., 1992. Tchr. Fairfax County Pub. Sch., Alexandria, Va., 1969-72, 1976-82, human rels. specialist, 1982-85; asst. prin. Robert E. Lee H.S., Springfield, Va., 1985-90; prin. Mt. Vernon H.S., Alexandria, 1990—; adminstrv. officer Fairfax County Pub. Schs. Supts. Office, 1999—. Cons. U. Va., 1984, Red Clay Sch. Dist., Wilmington, Del., 1997; guest lectr. George Washington U., Washington, 1996-98; mem. nat. safety focus group on sch. violence U.S. Dept. Edn., Calif., 1993. Exec. bd. mem. Gum Spring Cmty. Corp, Alexandria, 1994; mem. Mt. Vernon Cmty. Coalition, Alexandria, 1993—. Recipient Disting. Edn. Leadership award Washington Post, 1996-97, E.L. Patterson Cmty. Svc. award Urban League, Inc., 1997, Edn. award NAACP, Va., 1997; named Prin. of the Yr. Fairfax County Pub. Schs., 1996-97, Minority Achievement Prin. of the Yr., 1996. Mem. ASCD,

Am. Assn. Sch. Adminstrs., Fairfax County H.S. Prins. Assn., Black Women United Action (Among Most Admired Women 1996), Phi Delta Kappa (historian), Delta Kappa Gamma. Democrat. Church of Christ. Avocations: art, reading, jogging. Home: 11106 Lakenheath Way Oakton VA 22124-1912 Office: Burkholder Adminstrv Ctr 10700 Page Ave Fairfax VA 22030-4006 E-mail: ctucker@burkholder.fcps.K12.va.us.

TUCKER, DAVID WAYNE, elementary school educator, antique dealer; b. Eldorado, Ill., Oct. 13, 1953; s. Donnie G. and Rosalie (Grant) T.; m. Kay S. Gritmacker, May 21, 1977. BS, So. Ill. U., 1984, MS in Edn., 1993, postgrad., 1993—. Cert. tchr., Ill. Grad. asst. So. Ill. U., Edwardsville, 1984-85; 5th grade tchr. Belle Valley Elem. Dist., Belleville, Ill., 1985-86; 7th grade tchr. Ritenour Sch. Dist., St. Anne, Mo., 1986-87; 5th grade tchr. Roxana (Ill.) Cmty. Schs., 1987—. Mem. alumni bd. dirs. Blackburn Coll., Carlinville, Ill., 1993-98. Mem. Ill. Coun. Tchrs. Math., Ill. Sci. Tchrs. Assn. Avocations: basketball, bowling, chess, reading, collecting depression era glass. Office: Roxana Sch Dist N Chaffer Ave Roxana IL 62084 E-mail: tuckant@charter.net.

TUCKER, EDWIN WALLACE, law educator; b. N.Y.C., Feb. 25, 1927; s. Benjamin and May Tucker; m. Gladys Lipschutz, Sept. 14, 1952; children: Sherwin M., Pamela A. BA, NYU, 1948; LLB, Harvard U., 1951; LLM, N.Y. Law Sch., 1963, JSD, 1964; MA, Trinity Coll., Hartford, Conn., 1967. Bar: N.Y. 1955, U.S. Dist. Ct. (ea. and so. dists.) N.Y. 1958, U.S. Ct. Appeals (2d cir.) 1958, U.S. Supreme Ct. 1960. Pvt. practice, N.Y.C., 1955-63; Disting. Alumni prof. and prof. bus. law U. Conn., Storrs, 1963—, mem. bd. editors occasional paper and monograph series, 1966-70. Author: Adjudication of Social Issues, 1971, 2d edit., 1977, Legal Regulation of the Environment, 1972, Administrative Agencies, Regulation of Enterprise, and Individual Liberties, 1975, CPA Law Review, 1985; co-author: The Legal and Ethical Environment of Business, 1992; book rev. editor Am. Bus. Law Jour., 1964-65, adv. editor, 1974—; co-editor Am. Bus. Jour., 1965-73; mem. editl. bd. Am. Jour. Small Bus., 1979-86; editor Jour. Legal Studies Edn., 1983-85, editor-in-chief, 1985-87, adv. editor, 1987—; mem. bd. editors North Atlantic Regional Bus. Law Rev., 1984—. With USAF, 1951-55. Recipient medal of excellence Am. Bus. Law Assn., 1979. Mem. Acad. Legal Studies in Bus., North Atlantic Regional Bus. Law Assn. Home: 11 Eastwood Rd Storrs Mansfield CT 06268-2401

TUCKER, EUNICE JONES, retired secondary education educator; b. Abbeville, Ala., Jan. 17, 1930; d. Drew and Emma Lee Jones; m. Percy Lee Ashford, Dec. 24, 1954 (div. Aug. 1976); 1 child, Randall Alonzo; m. Willie Zdvie Tucker, Nov. 18, 1985. BS, Ala. A&M U., 1954, MS, 1969. Tchr. biology Dixon Mills (Ala.) H.S., 1954-57; clk. Ala. A&M U., Normal, 1958-66; adminstr. Drake Tech. Coll., Normal, 1966-67; tchr. reading Moulton (Ala.) H.S., 1967-70; tchr. English Edd White Mid. Sch., Huntsville, Ala., 1970-71; tchr. sci. Whitesburg Mid. Sch., Huntsville, 1971-79, Stone Mid. Sch., Huntsville, 1979-92. Mem. Ala. Dem. Conf., Huntsville, 1993-96; mem. women's coalition Equality for Women, Huntsville, 1991—. Named to Nat. Women's Hall of Fame, 1994. Mem. AAUW (bd. dirs. 1994—), Nat. Libr. of Congress Assocs. (charter). Apostolic Holiness. Avocations: reading, decorating, basketball, walking, church work. Home: 2126 Pisgah Dr Huntsville AL 35810

TUCKER, GARY WILSON, nursing educator; b. Oct. 2, 1956; s. Clayton Wilson Jr. and Jewell (Shelton) T. AAS, Cleveland (Tenn.) State Community Coll., 1980; BSW, Lamar U., Beaumont, Tex., 1991; MPH, U. Tex. Sch. Pub. Health, 1996; BSN, Lamar U., 1999. Nurse, relief shift supr. Moccasin Bend Mental Health Inst., Chattanooga, 1980-81; staff nurse pediat. ICU Thompson Childrens', Chattanooga, 1981-83; nurse, cons. King Fahad Hosp., Riyadh, Saudi Arabia, 1983; staff nurse ICU/ CCU Beaumont (Tex.) Med.-Surg. Hosp., 1984-88; charge nurse CCU, hemodialysis Bapt. Hosp., Beaumont, 1988-93, cardio-vascular nurse educator, 1993-96, dept. head, staff devel. and continuing edn. nurse, 1996-99; rsch. technican U. Tex., Houston Health Sci. Ctr., 1998-99; nursing instr. Lamar U., Beaumont, Tex., 1999—. Mem.: ANA, Tex. Assn. Coll. Tchrs., Am. Assembly Men in Nursing, Tex. Nurses Assn., Sigma Theta Tau. Home: 601 22nd St Beaumont TX 77706-4915 Office: Lamar U Dept Nursing PO Box 10081 Beaumont TX 77710-0081 E-mail: tuckergw@hal.lamar.edu.

TUCKER, JAMES RAYMOND, primary education educator; b. Pueblo, Colo., Apr. 18, 1944; s. James George and Pauline F. (Sena) T.; m. Kathie Owens; 1 child, Brittany. BA, U. So. Colo., 1966; MA, U. No. Colo., 1990, postgrad., 1991. Tchr. Sinclair Mid. Sch., Englewood, Colo., 1971-93, Denver Pub. Schs., 1993—. Co-dir. Nick Bolleteri Tennis Acad., Boulder, Colo., 1986; head tennis coach Englewood High Sch., 1971—. Sgt. U.S. Army, 1967-70. Mem. NEA, U.S. Profl. Tennis Assn., U.S. Profl. Tennis Registry, Internat. Platform Assn., Colo. Edn. Assn., Meadow Creek Tennis and Fitness, Colo. H.S. Coaches Assn. (Achievement award 1989, 92, Tchr. of Yr. 1973, 78, 86, Coach of Yr. 1986, 87, 90, 96, 97, Franklin award 1988, 89). Home: 2316 S Harlan Ct Lakewood CO 80227-3962

TUCKER, JANET GRACE, university educator, researcher; b. Danbury, Conn., July 14, 1942; d. Julius F. and Rose Alta Fine; m. William Frederick Tucker, Aug. 26, 1967; 1 child, Robert Eliot. AB, Ind. U., 1963, MA, 1965, PhD, 1973. Prof. U. Ark., Fayetteville, 1990—96, assoc. prof., 1996—. Author: Revolution Betrayed, 1996; editor: Against the Grain.

TUCKER, JOHN AVERY, retired academic administrator, electrical engineer; b. Milton, Mass, Jan. 28, 1924; s. Seth Davenport and Ruth Lincoln (Avery) T. BSEE cum laude, Northeastern U., 1949; M. of Engring., Yale U., 1950. Registered profl. engr., Mass. Mem. tech. staff Bell Tel. Labs., Inc., NYC, 1950; engr. New Eng. Tel & Tel. Co., Boston, 1951-56; instr. elec. engring., Lincoln Inst. Northeastern U., Boston, 1955; with dept. elec. engring. and computer sci. MIT, Cambridge, Mass., 1956—2002, 1st adminstrv. officer, 1963, dir. VI-A internship program in elec. engring./computer sci., 1969-87, spl. asst. to dept. head, 1987-89, emeritus dir. VI-A program, lectr., 1989—2002; ret., 2002. Deacon emeritus Wellesley Hills Congl. Ch., mem., 1936—; bd. dirs. Wellesley chpt. ARC, 1978; chief of staff Wellesley Vets. Parade, 1996. Sgt. U.S. Army Signal Corps, 1943-46, PTO. Recipient Outstanding Alumnus in Edn. award Northeastern U., 1994, G. Y Billard award MIT, 1981. Mem.: AARP (bd. dir. MIT/Cambridge chpt. 1990—97), IEEE (life), IEEE (sr.), Am. Soc. Engring. Edn. (life), Wellesley Hist. Soc. (bd. dir. 1993—, 1st v.p. 1995—98, 2000), MIT Alumni Assoc. (hon.; Hon. mem. 1985), Appalachian Mountain Club, Tau Beta Pi Assn. (v.p. NU chpt. 1949, chief advisor 1971—, Nat. Outstanding Advisor award 1998), Eta Kappa Nu (founder Northeastern U. chpt. 1950, faculty advisor MIT 1956—74, nat. bd. dir. 1959—61, faculty advisor MIT 1989—, Outstanding Svc. award 2000, Disting. Svc. Award 2002). Avocation: photography. Home: 153 Brook St Wellesley MA 02482-6641

TUCKER, JOHN CURTIS, school system administrator; b. Tullahoma, Tenn., Mar. 6, 1946; s. J.C. and Jewel Virgie (Tuggle) T.; m. Carol Anne Bryan, June 14, 1975. BSBA, Mid. Tenn. State U., 1968; MEd in Administrn., Supervision, U. South Fla., 1981. Cert. tchr., Fla. Tchr. Hernando County Sch. Bd., Brooksville, Fla., 1968-81, purchasing dir., 1981-88, 90—, secondary supr., 1988-90. Mem. Brooksville Health Adv. Bd., 1991—; vis. com. So. Assn. Colls. and Schs., 1992; mem. Florida delegation to Russia Nat. Inst. Gov. Purchasing. Mayor, councilman City of Brooksville, 1987—, v.p. city pers. bd., 1984-86; founder, adviser Hernando County Community Alliance, 1990; pres. Brooksville Jaycees, 1979-80. Recipient Speak-Up award Fla. Jaycees, 1978, Human Improvement award, 1980, Key Man award Brooksville Jaycees, 1979; recipient Brotherhood-Sisterhood award Brotherhood-Sisterhood Assn., Brooksville, 1991. Mem. Fla. Assn. Sch. Adminstrs., Hernando County Sch. Adminstrs. Assn. (v.p. 1987-90, pres. 1993—), Lions (bd. dirs. 1991—). Avocations: baseball cards, travel, civic affairs. Home: 15173 Willowood Ln Brooksville FL 34604-8162 Office: Sch Bd Hernando County 919 N Broad St Brooksville FL 34601-2397

TUCKER, JOSEPH, clergyman, former dean; b. Columbus, Ga., Mar. 5, 1920; s. John Joseph and Irene (Blakely) T.; m. Vivian Theodosia Hampton, Feb. 8, 1948; 1 child, Joy Celeste. BA, Fisk U., 1950; MDiv, Union Theol. Sem., 1953; MS in Libr. Svc., Columbia U., 1970; postgrad., Colgate Rochester Divinity Sch., 1987; DD (hon.), Va. Sem. and Coll., 1988. Asst. dean of men, basic coll. dir. Fisk U., Nashville, 1953-54; periodicals libr. Union Theol. Sem. Libr., N.Y.C., 1959-70; pastoral counselor Harlem Interfaith Counseling Svc., N.Y.C., 1967-68; reference libr. Hofstra U. Libr., Hempstead, N.Y., 1970-74; tchr. N.Y. Theol. Sem., N.Y.C., 1977; dean, tchr. Va. Sem. and Coll. N.Y. Extension, Queens Village, N.Y., 1988-91; founder, pres. Lamplighter's Sch. Religious Studies, Hempstead, 1992; founder, pastor Joyful Heart Bapt. Ch., Hempstead, 1969—. Radio bible tchr., 1996—; co-chmn. L.I. Men of Integrity Task Force, 1997—. Mem. Bapt. Ministers' Conf. N.Y. and Vicinity (com. chmn. 1990—), Bapt. Ministers' Conf. Greater N.Y. and Vicinity. Home: 76 E Marshall St Hempstead NY 11550-7406 Office: Joyful Heart Bapt Ch 101 Greenwich St Hempstead NY 11550-5626

TUCKER, RICHARD LEE, civil engineer, educator; b. Wichita Falls, Tex., July 19, 1935; s. Floyd Alfred and Zula Florence (Morris) T.; m. Shirley Sue Tucker, Sept. 1, 1956; children: Bryan Alfred, Karen Leigh. BCE, U. Tex., 1958, MCE, 1960, PhDCE, 1963. Registered profl. engr., Tex. Instr. civil engring. U. Tex., 1960-62, from asst. prof. to prof., 1962-74, assoc. dean engring., 1963-74; v.p Luther Hill & Assoc., Inc., Dallas, 1974-76; Joe C. Walter chair in engring. U. Tex., Austin, 1976—, dir. Constrn. Industry Inst., 1983-98, dir. Ctr. Constrn. Industry Studies, 1998—. Pres. Tucker and Tucker Cons., Inc., Austin, 1976—. Contbr. numerous articles and papers to profl. jours. Recipient Erwin C. Perry award, Coll. Engring., U. Tex., 1978, Faculty Excellence award, 1986, Joe J. King Profl. Engring. Achievement award, 1990, Disting. Engring. Grad., 1994; Ronald Reagan award for Individual Initiative, Constrn. Industry Inst., 1991; named Outstanding Young Engr., Tex. Soc. Profl. Engrs., 1965, Outstanding Young Man, City of Arlington, 1967; Michael Scott Endowed Rsch. fellow Inst. for Constructive Capitalism, 1990-91. Fellow ASCE (R.L. Peurifoy award 1986, Thomas Fitch Rowland prize 1987, Tex. sect. award of honor 1990); mem. NSPE (Constrn. Engring. Educator award of the Profl. Engrs. in Constrn. 1993), NAE, NRC, Soc. Am. Mil. Engrs., The Moles (hon.). Baptist. Office: Univ Tex Coll Engring Constrn Industry Inst ECJ5 2 Austin TX 78712

TUCKER, RUTH M. elementary education educator; b. Glendale, Ky., Apr. 7, 1937; d. Lloyd and Rosie (Stewart) Thomas; m. Raymond B. Tucker, June 25, 1960 (dec. June 16, 1984); children: Rennard, Raelynn. BS, Eastern Mich. U., 1959; MA, U. Mich., 1963. Cert. tchr., Mich. Tchr. Detroit Bd. of Edn., 1959—. Workshop leader Detroit Bd. of Edn., 1988. Active Met. Detroit Reading Coun. Recipient Prin's. and Educators Achievement award State of Mich./Booker T. Washington Bus. Assn., 1991. Mem. ASCD, NAACP, Jack and Jill of Am., Inc., Oakland County, Inc. (charter), Detroit Fed. Tchrs., Alpha Kappa Alpha. Avocations: singing, reading, travelling, playing the piano.

TUCKER, WILLIAM EDWARD, academic administrator, minister; b. Charlotte, N.C., June 22, 1932; s. Cecil Edward and Ethel Elizabeth (Godley) T.; m. Ruby Jean Jones, Apr. 8, 1955; children: Janet Sue, William Edward, Gordon Vance. BA, Barton Coll., Wilson, N.C., 1953, LLD (hon.), 1978; BD, Tex. Christian U., 1956; MA, Yale U., 1958, PhD, 1960; LHD (hon.), Chapman Univ., 1981; DH (hon.), Bethany Coll., 1982; DD (hon.), Austin Coll., 1985; LHD (hon.), Kentucky Wesleyan Coll., 1989. Ordained to ministry Disciples of Christ Ch., 1956; prof. Barton Coll., 1959-66, chmn. dept. religion and philosophy, 1961-66; mem. faculty Brite Div. Sch., Tex. Christian U., 1966-76, prof. ch. history, 1969-76, dean, 1971-76, chancellor, 1979-98, chancellor emeritus, 1998—. Pres. Bethany (W.Va.) Coll., 1976-79; dir. RadioShack Corp., 1985-2003, Brown and Lupton Found.; mem. gen. bd. Christian Ch. (Disciples of Christ), 1971-74, 75-87, adminstrv. com., 1975-81, chmn. theol. edn. commn., 1972-73, mem. exec. com., chmn. bd. higher edn., 1975-77; dir. Christian Ch. Found., 1980-83; moderator Christian Ch. (Disciples of Christ), 1983-85 Author: J.H. Garrison and Disciples of Christ, 1964, (with others) Journey in Faith: A History of the Christian Church (Disciples of Christ), 1975; also articles. Bd. dirs. Van Cliburn Found., 1981—, Amon Carter Mus. Mem. Exch. Club, Phi Beta Kappa. Home: 2337 Colonial Pky Fort Worth TX 76109-1030 Office: 100 Throckmorton St Ste 416 Fort Worth TX 76102-2870 E-mail: w.tucker@tcu.edu.

TUCKMAN, BRUCE WAYNE, educational psychologist, educator, researcher; b. N.Y.C., Nov. 24, 1938; s. Jack Stanley and Sophie Sylvia (Goldberg) T.; children: Blair Z., Bret A. BS, Rensselaer Poly. Inst., 1960; MA, Princeton U., 1962, PhD, 1963. Rsch. assoc. Princeton (N.J.) U., 1963; rsch. psychologist Naval Med. Rsch. Inst., Bethesda, Md., 1963-65; assoc. prof. edn. Rutgers U., New Brunswick, N.J., 1965-70; prof., 1970-78; dir. Bur. Rsch. and Devel.-Rutgers U., New Brunswick, 1975-78; dean Coll. Edn. Baruch Coll., CUNY, 1978-82; sr. rsch. fellow CUNY, 1982-83; dean Coll. Edn. Fla. State U., Tallahassee, 1983-86, prof., 1983—98; prof. dir. acad. learning lab. Ohio State U., Columbus, 1998—. Author: Preparing to Teach the Disadvantaged, 1969 (N.J. Assn. Tchrs. of English Author's award 1969), Conducting Educational Research, 1972, 5th rev. edit., 1999 (Phi Delta Kappa Rsch. award 1973), Evaluating Instructional Programs, 1979, 2d rev. edit., 1985, Analyzing and Designing Educational Research, 1979, Effective College Management, 1987, Testing for Teachers, 1988; (novel) Long Road to Boston, 1988, Educational Psychology: From Theory to Application, 1992, 96, 98, 2002, Learning and Motivation Strategies: Your Guide to Success, 2002. Rsch. dir. Task Force on Competency Stds. Trenton, N.J., 1976. N.Y. State Regents scholar, 1956; Kappa Nu grad. scholar, 1960; NIMH predoctoral fellow, 1961, 62; Rutgers U. faculty study fellow, 1974-75 Fellow: APA; mem.: Am. Ednl. Rsch. Assn. Office: 250B Younkin Success Ctr 1640 Neil Ave Columbus OH 43201-2333

TUDOR, MARY LOUISE DRUMMOND, retired elementary school educator; b. Long Beach, Calif., Nov. 9, 1937; d. Wesley Carlton and Dora Elizabeth (Blankenbeckler) Drummond; m. Gary Albert Tudor, June 18, 1960 (div. May 1980); children: Tamara Lynn, Michelle Denise Tudor Chapman. BS in Edn., U. So. Calif., 1959, MS in Edn., 1964; MS in Counseling Psychology, Calif. State U., Long Beach, 1984. Cert. elem. adminstr., pupil pers. in counseling, lang. devel. specialist Calif. Tchr. L.A. Unified Sch. Dist., 1959-68, Long Beach Unified Sch. Dist., 1968-95; ret., 1995. Substitute tchr. Lake Havasu (Ariz.) Unified Sch. Dist., 1998—. Mem. Lake Havasu Cmty. Choir, Lake Havasu City Charter Com., 1998. Nat. Meth. Bd. scholar, 1955. Mem.: DAR (Lake Havasu chpt.), AAUW (pres. Lake Havasu chpt. 2003—), NEA, Women's Bowling Assn. (past v.p., pres. Tues. ladies bowling league), Internat. Soc. Poets, London Bridge Assn. Rep. Women (3d v.p.), U. So. Calif. Alumni, Long Beach City Coll. Found. Friends of Langs., Rt. 66 Assn., Lake Havasu Elkettes (past v.p.), Order Ea. Star, Delta Delta Delta (founder Saddleback Valley alumnae 1973—75, past pres. 1973—75, pres. and founder Colorado River alumnae 1996—), Psi Chi, Phi Delta Gamma, Kappa Delta Pi, Phi Delta Kappa. Republican. Methodist. Avocations: genealogy, bowling, reading, travel, swimming. E-mail: mlthavasu@redrivernet.com.

TUFTS, ROBERT B. academic administrator; b. Cleve., Nov. 5, 1940; s. Robert L. and Dora Mae (Yingling) T.; m. Nancy Intihar, June 22, 1968 (div. Feb. 1990); children: Therese, Kevin R.; m. Ellen Sanders, May 29, 1998. BA cum laude, Cleve. State U., 1967; MA, Case Western Res. U., 1972; postgrad., U. Akron, 1973-76. Admissions counselor Cleve. State U., 1967-69, asst. registrar, 1969-70, Youngstown (Ohio) State U., 1970-73, U. Akron (Ohio), 1973-75, assoc. registrar, 1975-78; registrar Portland (Oreg.) State U., 1978-2000, The Art Inst. of Portland, 2000—. Com. mem. Park Recreation Adv. Bd., W. Linn., Oreg., 1981-84; presenter on fraudulent credentials, 1987—. Contbr. articles to profl. jours. With U.S. Army, 1959-62, Korea. Mem. Oreg. Assn. Registrars and Admissions Officers (sec.-treas. 1988-90), Pacific Assn. Collegiate Registrars and Admissions Officers (mem. program com. 1986-87, exec. bd., chair local arrangement 64th Ann. Mtg., Portland 1990, chair facilities com. 73d annual mtg., 1999), Am. Assn. Collegiate Registrars and Admissions Officers (local arrangements com., chair pub. com. 82nd Ann. Mtg., Reno, 1996, mem. facilities planning mgmt. com. 1975-78, chmn. of com. 1977-78), Nat. Assn. Coll. and Univ. Bus. Officers, Theta Rho. Democrat. Mem. Unitarian Ch. Avocations: mountaineering, camping, home projects. Home: 4981 Prospect St West Linn OR 97068-3116 Office: The Art Inst of Portland 1122 NW Davis St Portland OR 97209-2911 E-mail: tuftsr@aii.edu.

TUKE, ROBERT DUDLEY, lawyer, educator; b. Rochester, NY, Dec. 5, 1947; s. Theodore Robert and Doris Jean (Smith) T.; m. Susan Devereux Cummins, June 21, 1969; children: Andrew, Sarah. BA with distinction, U. Va., 1969; JD, Vanderbilt U., 1976. Bar: Tenn. 1976, U.S. Dist. Ct. (mid. dist.) Tenn. 1976, U.S. Ct. Appeals (6th cir.) 1976, U.S. Ct. Appeals (4th cir.) 1978, U.S. Ct. Appeals (fed. cir.) 1993, U.S. Supreme Ct. 1986, U.S. Ct. Internat. Trade 1993. Assoc. Farris, Warfield & Kanaday, Nashville, 1976—79, ptnr., 1980—94, Tuke Yopp & Sweeney, Nashville, 1994—99, Trauger, Ney & Tuke, Nashville, 2000—. Adj. prof. law Vanderbilt U. Law Sch., Nashville; faculty PLI, 1995—; mem. AMA Drs.' Adv. Network. Author: (with others) Tennessee Practice, 1992—; editor-in-chief Vanderbilt Law Rev.; contbr. articles to profl. jours. Mem. Tenn. Adoption Law Study Commn., 1993-96, Metro CATV Com. Capt. USMC, 1969-73. Decorated Cross of Gallantry; Patrick Wilson Merit scholar. Mem. ABA, Am. Health Law Assn., Nat. Assn. Bond Lawyers, Am. Acad. Adoption Attys. (trustee), Tenn. Bar Assn., Nashville Bar Assn., Order of Coif. Democrat. Episcopalian. Avocations: rowing, running, cycling, hiking, travel. Office: 222 4th Ave N Nashville TN 37219-2115 E-mail: rtuke@tntlaw.net.

TUKEY, HAROLD BRADFORD, JR., horticulture educator; b. Geneva, N.Y., May 29, 1934; s. Harold Bradford and Ruth (Schweigert) T.; m. Helen Dunbar Parker, June 25, 1955; children: Ruth Thurbon, Carol Tukey Schwartz, Harold Bradford. BS, Mich. State U., 1955, MS, 1956, PhD, 1958. Research asst. South Haven Expt. Sta., Mich., 1955; AEC grad. research asst. Mich. State U., 1955-58; NSF fellow Calif. Inst. Tech, 1958-59; asst. prof. dept. floriculture and ornamental horticulture Cornell U., Ithaca, N.Y., 1959-64, assoc. prof., 1964-70, prof., 1970-80; prof. urban horticulture U. Wash., Seattle, 1980-97, prof. emeritus, 1997—, dir. Arboreta, 1980-92, dir. Ctr. Urban Horticulture, 1980-92. Cons. Internat. Bonsai mag., Electric Power Rsch. Inst., P.R. Nuclear Ctr., 1965-66; mem. adv. com. Seattle-U. Wash. Arboretum and Bot. Garden, 1980-92, vice chmn., 1982, chmn., 1986-87; vis. scholar U. Nebr., 1982, 98; vis. prof. U. Calif., Davis, 1973; lectr. U. Western Sydney-Hawkesburg U. Melbourne, Victoria Coll. Agrl. and Horticulture, 1995, Massey U., 1996; Hill prof. U. Minn., 1996; mem. various coms. Nat. Acad. Scis.-NRC; bd. dirs. Arbor Fund Bloedel Res., 1980-92, pres., 1983-84. Mem. editorial bd. Jour. Environ. Horticulture, Arboretum Bull. Mem. nat. adv. com. USDA, 1990—; pres. Ithaca PTA; troop advisor Boy Scouts Am., Ithaca. Lt. U.S. Army, 1958. Recipient B.Y. Morrison award USDA, 1987; NSF fellow, 1958-59; named to Lansing (Mich.) Sports Hall of Fame, 1987; grantee NSF, 1962, 75, Bot. Soc. Am., 1964; hon. dr. Portuguese Soc. Hort., 1985. Fellow Am. Soc. Hort. Sci. (dir. 1970-71); mem. Internat. Soc. Hort. Sci. (U.S. del. to coun. 1971-90, chmn. commn. for amateur horticulture 1974-83, exec. com. 1974-90, v.p. 1978-82, pres. 1982-86, past pres. 1986-90, chmn. comm. Urban Horticulture 1990-94, hon. mem. 1994), Wash. State Nursery and Landscape Assn. (hon. mem. 1995), Internat. Plant Propagators Soc. (hon., ea. region dir. 1969-71, v.p. 1972, pres. 1973, internat. pres. 1976), Am. Hort. Soc. (dir. 1972-81, exec. com. 1974-81, v.p. 1978-80, citation of merit 1981), Royal Hort. Soc. (London) (v.p. hon. 1993—), Bot. Soc. Am., N.W. Horticulture Soc. (dir. 1980-92), Arboretum Found. (dir. 1980-92), Rotary, Sigma Xi, Alpha Zeta, Phi Kappa Phi, Pi Alpha Xi, Xi Sigma Pi. Presbyterian. Home: 3300 E St Andrews Way Seattle WA 98112-3750 Office: U Wash Ctr Urban Horticulture PO Box 354115 Seattle WA 98195-4115 E-mail: tukeyhb@email.msn.com.

TULE, SHARON BURCHARD, school system administrator; b. Norritown, Pa., Oct. 4, 1950; m. James O. Tule III, June 17, 1972; children: Jenifer Lyn, Sarah Elizabeth. BS, E. Carolina U., 1978, MEd, 1983. Cert. tchr., adminstr. (mid.). Classroom tchr. S. Lenoir High Sch., Deep Run, N.C., 1978-83; reading tchr. Warren (Tex.) Ind. Sch. Dist., 1984-86; classroom tchr. Woodville (Tex.) Ind. Sch. Dist., 1986-88; ednl. specialist Region V Edn. Svc. Ctr., Beaumont, Tex., 1988-91, cons., 1989—; asst. supt. Hardin Jefferson Ind. Sch. Dist., Sour Lake, Tex., 1991—. Author: (parent handbook) Preparing Your Student for the Competency Test, 1979. Recipient Outstanding Educator award Deep Run Jaycees, 1982. Mem. ASCD, Tex. Assn. for Gifted and Talented, Am. Bus. Women's Assn., Internat. Reading Assn., Alpha Delta Kappa (treas.), Tex. Aggie Moms. Methodist. Avocations: camping, sewing, needlework. Home: PO Box 355 Fayetteville TX 78940-0355 Office: Hardin Jefferson Ind Sch Dist PO Box 490 Sour Lake TX 77659-0490

TULL, STEVEN GERALD, secondary education educator; b. Peoria, Ill., Dec. 18, 1954; s. Ralph Gerald Tull and Maella Christean (Daugherty) Bridgeman; m. Virginia Marie Kimmet, July 30, 1983. BA, So. Ill. U., 1981; postgrad., Coll. Great Falls, 1983-90; MA, San Diego State U., 1996. Cert. tchr., Mont. Commd. officer USAF, 1973, advanced through grades to 1st lt., translator, 1973-79; intelligence specialist Ill. Air N.G., Springfield, 1979-80; missile launch comdr. USAF, Great Falls, Mont., 1982-86; English educator Superior (Mont.) Sch. Dist. #3, 1990—. Cmty. rep. Acad. Yr. U.S.A. Internat., San Francisco, 1994—. Fellow Christa McAuliffe fellow, 2001. Mem. ASCD, NEA, Nat. Coun. Tchrs. English, Internat. Reading Assn., Superior Edn. Assn. (local pres. 1996-97), Mt. Assn. of Tchrs. of English/Lang. Arts (v.p. 1998-99, pres. 1999-2000, Disting. Educator award 2002). Avocations: writing, cycling, educational research, reading, language study. Home: 639 4th Ave East Superior MT 59872 Office: Superior High Sch 410 Arizona Ave Superior MT 59872 E-mail: stull@bigsky.net.

TULL, TRENT ASHLEY, college administrator; b. Mar. 16, 1972; BS, U. So. Miss., 1994, MEd, 1995. Southeastern regional dir. Golden Key Natl. Hon. Soc., Atlanta, 1995-97; dir. student activities Middle Ga. Coll., Cochran, 1997-98; dir. student life Floyd Coll., Rome, Ga., 1998—, coord. Inst. Coll. Student Vaules, 2001—. Office: 3310 John Hancock Dr Tallahassee FL 32312-1535 E-mail: ashleytull@aol.com.

TULL, WILLIS CLAYTON, JR., librarian; b. Crisfield, Md., Feb. 22, 1931; s. Willis Clayton and Agnes Virginia (Milbourne) T.; m. Taeko Itoi, Dec. 18, 1952. Student, U. Balt., 1948, Johns Hopkins U., 1956; BS, Towson (Md.) State Coll., 1957; MLS, Rutgers U., 1962; postgrad., Miami U., Oxford, Ohio, 1979. Editl. clk. 500th Mil. Intelligence Svc. Group, 1952-53; tchr. Hereford Jr.-Sr. H.S., Parkton, Md., 1957-59; aide Enoch Pratt Free Libr., Balt., 1959-61, profl. asst., 1962-64; coord. adult svcs. Washington County Free Libr., Hagerstown, Md., 1964-67; asst. regional libr. Eastern Shore Regional Libr., Salisbury, Md., 1967; br. libr. Balt. County Pub. Libr., Pikesville, Md., 1968-71, asst. area br. libr. Essex, Md., 1971-72, sr. info. specialist Catonsville, Md., 1972-87, on-line supr. Towson, Md., 1988-89, sr. info. specialist Reisterstown, Md., 1989-90; exec. dir. Milbourne and Tull Rsch. Ctr., 1991—2002. Contbr. to profl. and geneal. jours. Mem. Rep. Ctrl. Com. Baltimore County, 1971-72. With U.S. Army, 1949-52. Fellow Nat. Congress Patriotic Orgns.; mem. Freedom To Read Found., Md. Libr. Assn. (chmn. intellectual freedom com. 1969-70), Friends Johns Hopkins U. Librs., Md. Assn. for Adult Edn. (coord. Western Md. region 1965-67), Am. Coun. Trustees and Alumni, Am. Acad. Religion, Ctr. for Theology and the Natural Scis., Metaphys. Soc. Am., Nat. Assn. Scholars, Woodrow Wilson Internat. Ctr. for Scholars, Assn. for Asian Studies, World Future Soc., Freedom House, Internat. Rescue Com., Nature Conservancy, Unitarian and Universalist Geneal. Soc. (founder, bd. dirs. 1971-87), Md. Geneal. Soc., Royal Soc. St. George, Sons and Daus. Pilgrims, Descs. Early Quakers, SAR, Soc. War of 1812, Ancient and Hon. Mech. Co. Balt., Rutgers Club, Kappa Delta Pi. Home: 800 Southerly Rd Apt 414 Towson MD 21286-8407 E-mail: tullito1@msn.com.

TULLER, HARRY LOUIS, materials science and engineering educator; BS, Columbia U., 1966, MS, 1967, DSc in Engring., 1973. Rsch. assoc. physics Technion, Haifa, Israel, 1974-75; from asst. to assoc. prof. materials sci. and engring. MIT, Cambridge, 1975-81, prof. materials sci. and engring., 1981—; dir. Crystal Physics and Electroceramics Lab., Cambridge, 1985—. Vis. prof. U. Pierre et Marie Curie, Paris, 1990; faculty chair Sumitomo Electric Industries, 1992-98. Co-editor: High Temperature Superconductors, 1988, Electroceramics and Solid State Ionics, 1988, Science and Technology of Fast Ion Conductors, 1989, Sold State Ionics, 1992, Interfacially Controlled Functional Materials: Electrical and Chemical Properties, 2000, Oxygen Ion and Mixed Conductors and Their Technological Applications, 2000; series editor: Electronic Materials: Science and Technology; editor-in-chief Jour. Electroceramics. Fulbright travel grantee, 1990, Alexander von Humboldt fellow, 1997. Fellow Am. Ceramic Soc. (N.E. chair 1983); mem. IEEE, Electrochem. Soc. (co-organizer 1st, 2d and 3d internat. symposium ionic and mixed conducting ceramics 1991, 94, 97, co-organizer 1997 NATO/ASI Oxygen Ion & Mixed Conductors Summer Sch.), Materials Rsch. Soc. Jewish. Avocations: photography, gardening. Office: MIT 77 Massachusetts Ave Rm 13-3126 Cambridge MA 02139-4307

TULLY, HUGH MICHAEL, music educator; b. N.Y.C., Sept. 21, 1947; s. Hugh Joseph and Grace Esther (Glynn) T.; children: Andrea Clare, Alexander Clayton. BS, Western Conn. State U., 1969; MS, U. N.H., 1980; EdD, Boston U., 1989. Dir. music Ashford (Conn.) Elem. Sch., 1969-72, Berlin (N.H.) Regional Cath. Sch., 1972-77; band dir. Somersworth (N.H.) H.S., 1977—. Founder, liaison Somersworth Music Boosters, 1980—; spokesperson Consortium Chamber Singers, Brookfield, N.H., 1989-91. Mem. Mensa. Avocation: writing children's stories. Home: 204 Wentworth Rd Brookfield NH 03872-7104 Office: Somersworth HS Memorial Dr Somersworth NH 03878

TULY, CHARLES A. mathematics and computer science educator; b. N.Y.C., Feb. 17, 1947; s. Bernard and Ruth (Rimler) T.; m. Eileen Aida, Nov. 22, 1969; children: Beth, Benay. BS in Edn., Buffalo State, 1967; MS, Yeshiva U., 1971. Perm. cert., N.Y. Tchr. Yonkers (N.Y.) High Sch., 1967-85, Rockland C.C., Suffern, N.Y., 1980-83, Charles E. Gorton High Sch., Yonkers, 1985—. Mgr. H. & R. Block, Pearl River, N.Y., 1975-83. Mem. Nat. Coun. Tchrs. Math., Assn. Math. Tchrs. N.Y., Yonkers Fedn. Tchrs. (rep. to edn. 2000 steering com.). Avocations: fantasy baseball, telecommunications. Home: 19 Oakwood Ter Spring Valley NY 10977-1504 Office: Shonnard Pl Yonkers NY 10703

TUMAN, WALTER VLADIMIR, Russian language educator, researcher; b. Heidelberg, Germany, Jan. 21, 1946; came to U.S., 1949; s. Val Alexander Tuman and Valida (Zedins) Grasis; m. Helena Eugenia Makarowsky, June 6, 1970; children: Gregory Vladimir, Larissa Alexandra. BA, Fordham U., 1967; MS in Russian, Linguistics, Georgetown U., 1970, PhD in Russian, 1975. Supr. Russian dept. Def. Lang. Inst., Washington, 1972-75, developer course-curriculum Monterey, Calif., 1975-78; asst. prof. Russian Hollins (Va.) Coll., 1978-84; dir. fgn. lang. lab. La. State U., Baton Rouge, 1984-90; assoc. prof., coord. Russian program Thunderbird Campus Am. Grad. Sch. Internat. Mgmt., Glendale, Ariz., 1990-95, prof., 1995—2001; prof. emeritus, 2001. Cons. various univs.; grant participant, cons. US AID Consortia Am. Buss., NIS, 1993—, U.S. Commerce Dept., Nizhny Novgorod, Volgograd, Am. Bus. Ctrs., 1994—; cons. Cisco Sys., 2000—. Author: Think Russian: Level I, 1993; editor: A Bibliography of Computer-Aided Language Learning, 1986; contbg. editor Jour. Ednl. Techniques and Techs., 1987-91; mem. editl. bd.: Jour. Lang. in Internat. Bus.; author book revs., computer programs, conf. presentations; contbr. articles to profl. jours. Georgetown U. fellow, 1969; recipient Prof.'s Exch. award Internat. Rsch. and Exchs. Bd. (USSR), 1979; Mednick Meml. Fund grantee Va. Found. for Ind. Colls. (Australia), 1983, Apple Computer grantee, 1989, U.S. Dept. Edn. grantee Ctr. Internat. Bus. Edn. and Rsch., 1993—. Mem. Am. Assn. Tchrs. Slavic and East European Langs. (v.p. 1981-84, founder Monterey, Calif. chpt.), Am. Coun. on the Teaching Fgn. Langs., Am. Coun. Tchrs. Russian (bd. dirs. 1992-98), Internat. Assn. Learning Lab. Dirs., Assn. Internat. Linguistique Appliquée. Russian Orthodox. Office: Am Grad Sch Internat Mgmt 15249 N 59th Ave Glendale AZ 85306-3236 E-mail: tumanw@t-bird.edu.

TUNG, FRANK YAO-TSUNG, microbiologist educator; b. Tainan, Taiwan, Republic of China, Feb. 6, 1958; came to U.S., 1984; m. Man-Hwa Do, July 10, 1982; children: Kuang-Tsung, Jack. BS, Tunghai U., Taichung, Taiwan, Republic of China, 1980; MS, Nat. Yangming U., Taipei, Taiwan, 1984; PhD, U. Tenn., 1987. Postdoctoral fellow Harvard U., Boston, 1988-90; asst. prof. U. Fla., Gainesville, 1990-94, U. Pitts., 1994—. Contbr. articles to profl. jours. Recipient Rsch. awards NIH, 1991—, Am. Cancer Soc., 1994-95. Mem. Am. Soc. Microbiology. Office: U Pittsburgh 130 Desoto St Rm 439 Pittsburgh PA 15213-2535

TUNG, ROSALIE LAM, business educator, consultant; b. Shanghai, Dec. 2, 1948; came to U.S., 1975; d. Andrew Yan-Fu and Pauline Wai-Kam Lam; m. Byron Poon-Yang Tung, June 17, 1972; 1 chlid, Michele Christine. BA, York U., 1972; MBA, U. B.C., 1974, PhD in Bus. Adminstrn., 1977. Lectr. diploma divsn. U. B.C., 1975, lectr. exec. devel. program, 1975; asst. prof. mgmt. Grad. Sch. Mgmt., U. Oreg., Eugene, 1977-80; assoc. prof. U. Pa., Phila., 1981-86; prof., dir. internat. bus. ctr. U. Wis., Milw., 1986-90; endowed chaired prof. Simon Fraser U., 1991—. Fgn. expert Fgn. Investment Commn., China; vis. scholar U. Manchester (Eng.) Sci. and Tech., 1980; vis. prof. UCLA, 1981, Harvard U., 1988, Copenhagen Bus. Sch., 1995, 97, Chinese U. Hong Kong, 1997, Peking U., 2001; Wis. disting. prof. U. Wis. Sys., 1988-90, Ming and Stella Wong chair in internat. bus., 1991—. Author: Management Practices in China, 1980, U.S.-China Trade Negotiations, 1982, Chinese Industrial Society After Mao, 1982, Business Negotiations with the Japanese, 1984, Key to Japan's Economic Strength: Human Power, 1984, The New Expatriates: Managing Human Resources Abroad, 1988; editor: Strategic Management in the U.S. and Japan, 1987, International Management in International Library of Business and Management Series, 1994, Internat. Ency. Bus. and Mgmt., 1996, IEBM Handbook of International Business, 1998, Learning from World Class Companies, 2001. Recipient Leonore Rowe Williams award U. Pa., 1990, U. B.C. Alumni 75th Anniversary award, 1990, Advanced Global Competitiveness Rsch. award, 1997, Woman of Distinction in the Professions, Mgmt. and Trades award YWCA, Vancouver, 1998; York U. scholar, 1972; Univ. fellow, Seagram Bus. fellow, H.R. MacMillan Family fellow; Oppenheimer Bros. Found. fellow, 1973-74, U. B.C. fellow, 1974-75, H.R. Macmillan Found. fellow, 1975-77. Fellow Royal Soc. Can., Acad. Mgmt. (bd. govs. 1987-89, v.p. 2001-02, pres. 2002—), Internat. Acad. Cultural Rsch. (founding), Acad. Internat. Bus. (mem. exec. bd., treas. 1985-86); mem. Internat. Assn. Applied Psychology, Am. Arbitration Assn. (comml. panel arbitrators). Roman Catholic. Avocation: creative writing. Office: Simon Fraser U Faculty Bus Adminstrn Burnaby BC Canada V5A 1S6

TUNHEIM, JERALD ARDEN, academic administrator, physics educator; b. Claremont, S.D., Sept. 3, 1940; s. Johannes and Annie Tunheim; children: Jon, Angie, Alec. BS in Engring. Physics, S.D. State U., 1962, MS in Physics, 1964; PhD in Physics, Okla. State U., 1968. Vis. scientist Sandia Corp., Albuquerque, 1970-71, Ames (Iowa) AEC Labs., 1972; asst. prof. S.D. State U., Brookings, 1968-73, assoc. prof., 1973-78, prof., 1978-80, prof., head physics dept., 1980-85; dean Ea. Wash. U., Cheney, 1985-87; pres. Dakota State U., Madison, S.D., 1987—. Bd. dirs. Nat. Skill Stds. Bd., 1998—. Co-author: Elementary Particles and Unitary Symmetry, 1966, Quantum Field Theory, 1966; contbr. articles to profl.jours. Bd. dirs. Lake Area Improvement Corp. Grantee USDA, 1987-88, S.D. Govt. Office Edn. Devel., 1988-89, U.S. Dept. Edn., Eisenhower Program, 1985-86, 87-90, 92-93, 95-96, U.S. Dept. Edn. Math. and Sci. Program, 1989-92; named Tchr. of Yr. S.D. State U., 1972. Mem. NSPE, Am. Phys. Soc., Am. Assn. Physics Tchrs., Madison C. of C. (bd. dirs. 1990—), Rotary. Republican. Lutheran. Office: Dakota State U Office of President 820 N Washington Ave Madison SD 57042-1799 E-mail: Jerald.Tunheim@dsu.edu.

TUNNELL, MICHAEL O'GRADY, education educator; b. Nocona, Tex., June 14, 1950; s. Grady Tolan and Trudy (Müller) Chupp; m. Glenna Maurine Henry, June 12, 1972; children: Heather Anne Wall, Holly Lyne Argyle, Nikki Leigh, Quincy Michael. BA, U. Utah, 1973; MEd, Utah State U., 1978; EdD, Brigham Young U., 1986. Cert. tchr., Utah. Tchr. Uintah Sch. Dist., Vernal, Utah, 1973-75; tchr., libr. media specialist Wasatch Sch. Dist., Heber City, Utah, 1976-85; asst. prof. Ark. State U., Jonesboro, 1985-87, No. Ill. U., DeKalb, 1987-92; assoc. prof., prof. Brigham Young U., Provo, Utah, 1992—. Author: Chinook! (Am. Booksellers Pick of the Lists), 1993, The Joke's on George (Assn. Mormon Letters award in Children's Lit., 1993), 1993, Beauty and the Beastly Children (Am. Booksellers Pick of the Lists), 1993, The Children of Topaz (Carter G. Woodson Honor Book, Parents' Choice award, 1997 Notable Children's Book in the Field of Social Studies), 1996, Mailing May (ALA Notable Book, Parent's Choice award, 1998 Tchr.'s Choices Book), 1997, School Spirits (1998 Parent's Choice Recommended Story Book), 1997, Halloween Pie, 1999, Brothers in Valor (Jr. Libr. Guild selection, 2002 Notable Book for a Global Soc.), 2001, Children's Literature, Briefly, 1996, 2000-, The Story of Ourselves: Teaching History Through Children's Literature, 1993, The Prydain Companion, 1989, 2003, Lloyd Alexander: A Biobibliography, 1991, Children's Literature: Engaging Teachers and Children in Good Books, 2002; contbr. to children's mags., profl. jours. Mem. ALA, Nat. Coun. Tchrs. English (bd. dirs. 1995-97), Internat. Reading Assn., Soc. Children's Book Writers and Illustrators. Democrat. Mem. Lds Ch. Avocations: reading, photography. Office: Brigham Young U Dept Tchr Edn 201K McKay Bldg Provo UT 84602

TUNSTALL, DOROTHY FIEBRICH, early childhood educator; b. Elizabeth City, Va., Sept. 18, 1939; d. Louie Ludwig and Nancy Julia (Drafts) Fiebrich; m. Frank S. Clark Jr., June 11, 1961 (div. 1970); children: Sherri Ann D'Alessio, Debra Sue Pate, Frank S. Clark III; m. Jim Tunstall, June 1995 (div.). BA in Elem. Edn., Stetson U., 1961, MA in Edn., 1963; Ed. Spec. in Edn. Adminstrn., U. S.C., 1991, PhD in Early Childhood, 1993. Cert. tchr. Fla., S.C. Substitute tchr. Broward County Schs., Ft. Lauderdale, Fla., 1963-70, EABE tchr., 1972-80; title I, tchr. for fed. govt. South Fla. State Hosp., Pembroke Pines, Fla., 1970-72; tchr. spl. edn. Richland Sch. Dist. #2, Columbia, S.C., 1980-81; COBOL programmer Comptr. Gen.'s Office, Columbia, 1982-85; tchr. spl. edn. Calhoun County Schs., St. Matthews, S.C., 1985-88; tchr. kindergarten Fairfield County Schs., Winnsboro, S.C., 1989-92; dir. St. Paul's Child Care Ministry, Columbia, SC, 1997—2000, Good Shepherd Day Sch., Columbia, 2001—. Adj. prof. U. S.C., Columbia, 1994—. Active Lexington County Adolescent Pregnancy Prevention Bd., 1999—, Lexington County First Steps Bd., 2001—03; v.p. unit 7 Am. Legion Aux., 2000—02, pres. unit 7, 2002—. Mem.: AAUW (pres. 1998—2002), Mental Health Assn. in Mid-Carolina (v.p. 1992—93, bd. dirs., Pres. award 1993), Lexington County Arts Assn. (pres. 1992—93, Newcomer's award 1981), Wildlife Action Inc. (pres. 1991—93), Beta Sigma Phi (Girl of Yr. 1967). Avocations: reading, gardening. Home: 159 Corley Mill Rd Lexington SC 29072-7600 Office: Good Shepherd Day Sch 3909 Forest Dr Columbia SC 29204

TUOVINEN, OLLI HEIKKI, microbiology educator; b. Helsinki, Apr. 8, 1944; m. Manel Yapa, Jan. 8, 1972; children: Henrikki, Katariina, Karoliina. PhD, U. London, 1973. Mem. faculty Ohio State U., Columbus, 1978—. Contbr. articles to profl. jours. Mem.: Soc. Gen. Microbiology, Internat. Soc. Limnology, Am. Soc. Microbiology. Office: Ohio State U Dept Microbiology 484 W 12th Ave Columbus OH 43210-1214 Fax: 614-292-8120. Business E-Mail: tuovinen.1@osu.edu.

TURCK, MARSHA ANN, physical education educator; b. Celina, Ohio, June 22, 1954; d. Lloyd John and Alice H. Yaney; m. Lauris F. Turck, June 30, 1979; 1 child, Grant. BS, Ohio State U., 1976; MS, Xavier U., 1982. Cert. educator, Ohio. Tchr. phys. edn. West Clermont Local Schs., Amelia, Ohio, 1976—. Sec. Madeira (Ohio) Recreation Bd., 1984-90. Bd. dirs. YMCA, Blue Ash, Ohio, 1979-83. Mem. AAHPERD, NEA, Ohio Assn. Health, Phys. Edn., Recreation and Dance, Cin. Nature Ctr., Nature Conservancy, Nat. Pks. Avocations: scuba diving, travel, bicycling, walking, hiking. Home: 6429 Kenwood Rd Cincinnati OH 45243-2313

TURCO, ALFRED, JR., English language educator; b. Providence, 1940; s. Alfred and Delia Maria Turco; m. Elizabeth Nora Davis, 1969 (div. 1981); children— Ellen, Jeffrey AB, Brown U., 1962; A.M., Harvard U., 1963, PhD, 1969; MA ad eundem gradum (hon.), Wesleyan U., 1981. Instr. English Wesleyan U., Middletown, Conn., 1967-69, asst. prof., 1969-74, assoc. prof., 1974-80, prof., 1980—; vis. assoc. prof. Cornell U., Ithaca, N.Y., 1980. Cons. Cornell U. Press, Hartford Stage Co., Hackett Pub. Co. Author: Shaw's Moral Vision, 1976; guest editor: Shaw's Neglected Plays (Shaw: Vol. 7), 1987; contbr. articles on Scandinavian lit. to profl. jours.; mem. editorial bd. Ann. of Bernard Shaw Studies, 1985—. Danforth Found. fellow, 1963-67; Woodrow Wilson Found. hon. fellow, 1963 Mem. Phi Beta Kappa Avocation: gourmet cooking. Home: 58 Prospect St Portland CT 06480-1131 Office: Wesleyan U Middletown CT 06457

TUREKIAN, KARL KAREKIN, geochemistry educator; b. NYC, Oct. 25, 1927; s. Vaughan Thomas and Victoria (Guleserian) T.; m. Arax Roxanne Hagopian, Apr. 22, 1962; children: Karla Ann, Vaughan Charles. AB, Wheaton (Ill.) Coll., 1949; MA, Columbia U., 1951, PhD, 1955; DSc (hon.), SUNY, Stony Brook, 1989. Lectr. geology Columbia U., 1953-54, rsch. assoc. Lamont-Doherty Earth Obs., 1954-56; faculty, asst. prof. Yale U., 1956-61, assoc. prof., 1961-65, prof. geology and geophysics, 1965-72, Henry Barnard Davis prof. geology and geophysics, 1972-85, Benjamin Silliman prof., 1985—2003, Sterling prof., 2003—, chmn. dept., 1982-88; curator meteorites and planetary sci., archaeology coun., dir. Yale U. Ctr. for the Study of Global Change; chmn. studies in the environment, 1992-93; dir. Yale Inst. for Biospheric Studies, 1999—2003. Cons. Pres.'s Commn. Marine Sci. Engring. and Resources, 1967-68; oceanography panel NSF, 1968-70; NASA exobiology panel Am. Inst. Biol. Scientists, 1966-69; mem. NAS-NRC climate rsch. bd., 1977-80, ocean sci. bd., 1979-82, ocean studies bd., 1989-92, 98-2000, bd. on global change, 1992-95, Commn. Phys. Scis., Math. Resources, 1986-90, Commn. Geoscis., Environment, Resources, 1990-92, Com. Global Change Rsch., 1994-98; mem. com. on techs. for cleanup of subsurface contamination DOE Weapons Complex, 1997-98; mem. group experts sci. aspects Marine Pollution UN, 1971-73. Author: Oceans, 1968, 2d edit., 1976, Chemistry of the Earth, 1972, (with B.J. Skinner) Man and the Ocean, 1973, (with C.K. Drake, J. Imbrie and J.A. Knauss) Oceanography, 1978, Global Environmental Change, 1996; editor: (with J. Steele and S. Thorpe) Encyclopedia of Ocean Sciences, 2001; editor Jour. Geophys. Resource, 1969-75, Earth and Planetary Sci. Letters, 1975-89, Global Biogeochemical Cycles, 1990-95, Geochim. Cosmochim. Acta, 1997-99. Served with USNR, 1945-46. Guggenheim fellow Cambridge U., 1962-63; Fairchild Disting. scholar Calif. Inst. Tech., 1988; recipient Wollaston medal, The Geol. Soc. London, 1998. Fellow AAAS, Geol. Soc. Am., Meteoritical Soc., Am. Geophys. Union (Maurice Ewing medal 1997), Am. Acad. Arts and Scis.; mem. NAS, Am. Chem. Soc., Geochem. Soc. (pres. 1975-76, V.M. Goldschmidt medal 1989), Sigma Xi (pres. Yale chpt. 1961-62). Home: 555 Skiff St North Haven CT 06473-3013 Office: Yale U Dept Geology and Geophysics PO Box 208109 New Haven CT 06520-8109 E-mail: karl.turekian@yale.edu.

TURINO, GERARD MICHAEL, physician, medical scientist, educator; b. N.Y.C., May 16, 1924; s. Michael and Lucy (Arciero) T.; m. Dorothy Estes, Aug. 25, 1951; children: Peter, Phillip, James. AB, Princeton U., 1945; MD, Columbia U., 1948. Diplomate: Am. Bd. Internal Medicine. Intern Columbia U., Bellevue Hosp., 1948-49, asst. resident in medicine, 1949-50; resident in medicine New Haven Hosp., 1950-51; chief resident in medicine Columbia U. div. Bellevue Hosp., 1953-54; sr. fellow N.Y. Heart Assn., 1956-60; career investigator Health Research Council City of N.Y., 1961-71; asst. prof. medicine Columbia U., 1960-67, assoc. prof., 1967-72, prof. medicine, 1973-83, John H. Keating prof. medicine, 1983—; mem. staff Presbyn. Hosp., N.Y.C., 1960—, attending physician, 1983—; dir. med. svcs. St. Lukes-Roosevelt Hosp., N.Y.C., 1983-92; dir. St. Lukes-Roosevelt Hosp. James P. Mara Ctr, 1997. Cons. on sci. affairs Am. Thoracic Soc., 1992—; mem. sci. adv. com. Nat. Heart, Lung, and Blood Inst., Am. Lung Assn., Am. Heart Assn., N.Y. Lung Assn., N.Y. Heart Assn.; mem. staff divsn. med. sci. Nat. Rsch. Coun., Washington;mem. Sci. Adv. Coun. Alpha, Antitrypsin Found. cons. VA Hosp., East Orange, N.J., 1962-67; cons. in medicine Englewood (N.J.) Hosp., Hackensack (N.J.) Hosp., pres.-elect Am. Bur. Med. Advancement in China, 1994, pres., 1994-2001, chmn., 2001-. Contbr. articles to med. jours. Mem. Bd. Edn., Alpine, N.J., 1960-67. Served to capt. USAF, 1951-53. Recipient Joseph Mather Smith prize Columbia U., 1965, Alumni medal, 1983, Silver medal Alumni Assn. Coll. Physicians and Surgeons Columbia U., 1979, gold medal, 1986, Edward Livingston Trudeau medal Am. Lung Assn., 2003, Fellow AAAS; mem. Assn. Am. Physicians, Am. Soc. Clin. Investigation, Harvey Soc., Am. Thoracic Soc. (pres. 1987-88, Edward Livingston Trudeau prize 2003), Am. Fedn. Clin. Rsch., Am. Physiol. Soc. (chmn. steering com. respiration sect.), Am. Heart Assn. (award of merit 1980, Disting. Achievement award 1989, bd. dirs.), N.Y. Heart Assn. (pres. 1981-83, dir.), N.Y. Lung Assn. (dir.), N.Y. Med.-Surg. Soc. (pres. 1995), N.Y. Clin. Soc., Princeton Club (N.Y.C.), Maidstone Club, Devon Yacht Club, Century Assn. Club. Home: 66 E 79th St New York NY 10021-0244 Office: St Lukes Roosevelt Hosp 1000 10th Ave New York NY 10019-1192 E-mail: GMT1@Columbia.edu.

TURK, AUSTIN THEODORE, sociology educator; b. Gainesville, Ga., May 28, 1934; s. Hollis Theodore and Ruth (Vandiver) T.; m. Janet Stuart Irving, Oct. 4, 1957 (div. 1977); children: Catherine, Jennifer; m. Ruth-Ellen Marie Grimes, July 27, 1985. BA cum laude, U. Ga., 1956; MA, U. Ky., 1959; PhD, U. Wis., 1962. Acting instr. sociology U. Wis., Madison, 1961-62; from instr. to prof. sociology Ind. U., Bloomington, 1962-74; prof. U. Toronto, Can., 1974-88, U. Calif., Riverside, 1988—, chmn. dept. sociology, 1989-94; interim dir. Robert B. Presley Ctr. for Crime and Justice Studies, 1994-95. Author: Criminality and Legal Order, 1969, Political Criminality, 1982; gen. editor crime and justice series SUNY Press, Albany, 1990—; contbr. articles to jours. in field. Mem. Calif. Mus. Photography, 1988—, Citizens Univ. Com., 1990—. Recipient Paul Tappan award Western Soc. Criminology, 1989. Fellow Am. Soc. Criminology (pres. 1984-85); mem. Am. Sociol. Assn. (chair criminology sect. 1975-76), Law and Soc. Assn. (trustee 1982-85), Acad. Criminal Justice Scis. Democrat. Avocations: gardening, reading, swimming, tennis. Office: Dept Sociology U Calif Riverside Riverside CA 92521-0001 E-mail: austin.turk@ucr.edu.

TURK, ELEANOR LOUISE, history educator; b. Charlottesville, Va., Sept. 9, 1935; d. Alan P. and Louise H. (Goodman) Fort; divorced; 1 child, Andrew Kittridge. BA, Ohio Wesleyan U., 1957; MA, U. Ill., 1970; PhD, U. Wis., 1975. Asst. dean Coll. Arts and Scis. U. Kans., Lawrence, 1977-78; asst. dean Sch. Humanities and Social Scis. Ithaca (N.Y.) Coll., 1978-83; from assoc. prof. to prof. history Ind. U. East, Richmond, 1983—2003, prof. history emeritus, 2003—, chmn. divsn. Humanities and Social Scis., 1983-87, asst. vice chancellor for assessment, 1993-97, faculty colloquim on excellence in teaching, 1991—, chmn. instnl. self-study com., 1990-92. Author: The History of Germany, 1999 (Choice Outstanding Acad. Title award, 1999). Bd. dirs., dep. chair Inst. for Advanced Studies, Ind. U., Bloomington, 1991-92, chair, 1992-94; mem. pres.'s coun. for internat. programs, 1984—; pres. Sister Cities of Richmond, Inc., 1987-90, bd. dirs., 1987-92, 95—; del., panel chair USSR/USA Sister Cities Conf., Tashkent, 1989; bd. dirs., treas. Wayne County Arts Consortium, Richmond, 1986-89. Recipient Excellence in Writing award Kans. State Hist. Soc., 1983, Cmty. Leadership award Richmond YWCA, 1989, John W. Ryan award for Disting. Contbns. to Internat. Programs and Studies Ind. U., 1995; Fulbright scholar Kiel U., Germany, 1957-58, German Landeskunde, 1992. Mem. Assn. for German Studies, Ctrl. European History Assn., Soc. for German-Am. Studies, Ind. Assn. Historians, World History Assn., Kans. State Hist. Soc. (life), Phi Beta Kappa, Phi Alpha Theta, Pi Sigma Alpha. Democrat. Unitarian Universalist. Office: Ind U East 2325 Chester Blvd Richmond IN 47374-1220

TURK, ELIZABETH ANN, music educator; b. N.Y.C., July 10, 1957; d. William Robert Turk, Elizabeth Ann Brittingham. BA in Music and History, Dowling Coll.; MA in German Lang. and Lit., Hofstra U.; MA in European History, SUNY Stony Brook; MA in Music Libr. Sci., Columbia U. Tchg. asst SUNY, Stony Brook, 1986—88; lectr. music Dowling Coll., Oakdale, NY, 1988—91; tchr. music Amityville Pub. Schs., Amityville, NY, 1991—; dir. theater arts and music dir. Miller Pl. H.S.; music dir. Amityville H.S., Commack H.S. South, Carriage House Players, Kids for Kids Theater, Inc. Tchr. vocal music Miller Place Pub. Sch., Miller Place, NY, Hewlett Woodmere Pub. Sch., Hewlett, NY; pvt. tchr. and vocal coach, Massapequa, NY. Singer (soloist): Rome Opera Festival, 1989, 1990; performer: Tchaikovsky Competition, 1978, 1982, 1986, Minn. Opera, 1979, 1980, 1981, L.I. Youth Orch. Summer Tours; dir.: Sleeping Beauty, Sound of Music, Fiddler on the Roof, Little Shop of Horrors, Cinderella, Oliver, numerous others; choreographer Fiddler on the Roof, Sound of Music, Little Shop of Horrors, Oliver, Grease. Recipient award for further study, Met. Opera, 1981—90, Herald award for choreography and music dir. Mem.: Suffolk County Music Educator's Assn., Music Educators Nat. Conf., Suffolk County Wrestling Assn. (tournament dir. league V 1974—, numerous awards), White Star Triangle (Beloved Queen 1973—74), Order Ea. Star (various offices, assoc. condr.). Home: 90 Clock Blvd Massapequa NY 11758

TURKO, ALEXANDER ANTHONY, biology educator, hypnotherapist; b. Bridgeport, Conn., Aug. 19, 1943; s. Alexander I. and Elizabeth K. (Kulcsar) T.; m. Nancy Bally Hoinacky, Dec. 30, 1967; children: Michelle Lynn, Mark A. BA, So. Conn. State U., 1965, MS, 1967, postgrad., 1976. Cert. hypnotherapist, cert. master hypnotherapist. Assoc. prof. So. Conn. State U., New Haven, 1965—, coord. nurse anesthesia program. Mem.: AAUP, Nat. Guild Hypnotists. Home: 634 Popes Island Rd Milford CT 06460-1742 Business E-Mail: turkoa1@southernct.edu.

TURKUS-WORKMAN, CAROL ANN, elementary school educator; b. Balt., Nov. 12, 1946; d. Stanley Phillip and Catherine Anna (Koppleman) Turkus; m. William Thomas Workman, Apr. 23, 1973 (div. 1983); children: Devin Thomas, Timothy Michael. BA in History, Calif. State U., Long Beach, 1969; spl. cert. classroom mgmt., Centralia Sch. Dist., 1980; M in Adminstrn. Mgmt., U. La Verne, 1997. Cert. crosscultural lang. and acad. devel.; cert. adminstrv. credential. Educator Centralia Sch. Dist., Buena Park, Calif., 1970—, ednl. tech., 1986—. Cons. U. Sch.-Space Sci. Acad.,

Cleve., 1991. Unit commr. Boy Scouts Am., Orange County Coun., 1989-96; co. systems officer Starfleet Bulletin Bd. System, Long Beach, 1990-94; life mem. PTA, Buena Park. Recipient Gold Leaf, PTA Nat., 1991, Woodbadge Beads, Boy Scouts Am., 1991. Mem. AAUW, Computer Using Educators, Order of Arrow, Kappa Delta Pi. Republican. Roman Catholic. Avocations: sailing, camping, reading, writing. Office: Centralia Sch Dist 6215 San Rolando Way Buena Park CA 90620-3635 Address: 11762 Argyle Dr Los Alamitos CA 90720-4226 E-mail: homego@earthlink.net.

TURLEY, KATHY ELAINE, elementary school educator; b. Albertville, Ala., Sept. 28, 1956; d. Walter Lester and Melba (Mays) Smith; m. Aubrey Dale Turley, Jan. 3, 1975; children: Keri LeeAnn, Johnna Katherine. BS, Jacksonville (Ala.) State U., 1984; MA, U. ala., 1986, AA, 1990. Cert. tchr., Ala. Bookkeeper, teller Albertville Nat. Bank, 1974-78; spl. edn. aide Marshall County Schs., Guntersville, Ala., 1978-79, spl. edn. sec., 1979-85, tchr. 6th grade, 1985-86, Albertville City Schs., 1986—. Mem. NEA, Assn. Supr. Curriculum, Ala. Edn. Assn., Ala. Sci. Tchrs. Assn., Kappa Kappa Iota. Avocations: music, reading, sewing, horseback riding. Office: Albertville City Schs 901 W McKinney Ave Albertville AL 35950-1300

TURNBULL, H. RUTHERFORD, III, law educator, lawyer; b. NYC, Sept. 22, 1937; s. Henry R. and Ruth (White) T.; m. Mary M. Slingluff, Apr. 4, 1964 (div. 1972); m. Ann Patterson, Mar. 23, 1974; children: Jay, Amy, Katherine. Grad., The Kent (Conn.) Sch., 1955; BA, Johns Hopkins U., 1959; LLB with hon., U. Md., 1964; LLM, Harvard U., 1969. Bar: Md., N.C. Law clerk to Hon. Emory H. Niles Supreme Bench Balt. City, 1959-60; law clerk to Hon. Roszel C. Thomsen U.S. Dist. Ct. Md., 1962-63; assoc. Piper & Marbury, Balt., 1964-67; prof. Inst. Govt. U. N.C., Chapel Hill, 1969-80, U. Kans., Lawrence, 1980—. Prof. spl. edn., courtesy prof. law U. Kans. Editor-in-chief Md. Law Review. Cons., author, lectr., co-dir. Beach Ctr. on Disability, U. Kans.; pres. Full Citizenship Inc., Lawrence, 1987-93; spl. staff-fellow U.S. Senate subcom. on disability policy, Washington, 1987-88; bd. dirs. Camphill Assn. N.Am., Inc., 1985-87; trustee Judge David L. Bazelon Ctr. Mental Health Law, 1993—, chmn., 1999—. With U.S. Army, 1960-65. Recipient Nat. Leadership award Nat. Assn. Pvt. Residential Resources, 1988, Internat. Coun. for Exceptional Children, 1996, Am. Assn. on Mental Retardation, 1997, Century award Nat. Trust for Hist. Preservation in Mental Retardation, 1999, Nat. Advocate award Am. Music Therapy Assn., 2002; named Nat. Educator of Yr., ARC, 1982; Public Policy fellow Joseph P. Kennedy, Jr. Found., 1987-88. Fellow Am. Assn. on Mental Retardation (pres. 1985-86, bd. dirs. 1980-86); mem. ABA (chmn. disability law commn. 1991-95), U.S.A. As sn. for Retarded Citizens (sec. and dir. 1981-83), Assn. for Persons with Severe Handicaps (treas. 1988, bd. dirs. 1987-90), Nat. Assn. Rehab. Rsch. and Tng. Ctrs. (chair govt. affairs com. 1990-93), Internat. Assn. Scientific Study of Mental Deficiency, Internat. League of Assns. for Persons with Mental Handicaps, Johns Hopkins U. Alumni Assn. (pres. N.C. chpt. 1977-79). Democrat. Episcopalian. Home: 1636 Alvamar Dr Lawrence KS 66047-1714 Office: U Kans 3111 Haworth Hall 1200 Sunnyside Ave Lawrence KS 66045-7534 E-mail: Rud@ku.edu.

TURNBULL, R. CRAIG, secondary school educator; b. Detroit, Apr. 13, 1951; s. Bruce and Rita Turnbull; m. Karen Turnbull, Aug. 20, 1983; children: Steven, Douglas. BS in Edn., Ctrl. Mich. U., 1981. Cert. secondary tchr., Mich. Mgr. Mt. Pleasant (Mich.) Food Co-op., 1974-76, Wheatland Music Co-op., Remus, Mich., 1974-79; house painter Lake, Mich., 1972-84; tchr. Inland Lakes Schs., Indian River, Mich., 1982; tchr., coach Chippewa Hills Shcs., Remus, 1983—. Organizer Youth in Govt., Remus, 1984-95; mem. social studies project Phi Delta Kappa, Big Rapids, 1992; mem. project Mich. Law Related Edn., East Lansing, 1988-95; tchr. cons. Mich. Geog. Alliance, Mt. Pleasant, 1990-95. Pres. Diamond Lake Assn., Barryton, Mich., 1991-95; mem. Barryton Sch. PTA, 1991-95, Mecosta County for the Healing of Racism, 1993-95; founder, sponsor Culture Coun., Remus, 1992-95; mem. Com. Mid. Mich. Free Concerts, 1974-95; mem. U.S. China Friendship Assn., 1976-80; v.p. Sherman City Union Ch. Restoration, 1976—. Recipient County Basketball Coach of Yr. award Mt. Pleasant Morning Sun newspaper, 1990, Curriculum Frameworks award Mich. Partnership for New Edn., 1994; named Area Softball Coach of Yr. Big Rapids Pioneer newspaper, 1992. Mem. ASCD, Mich. Lake and Streams Assn. Avocations: gardening, backpacking, biking, travel, cross-country skiing. Home: 5732 Harding Rd Barryton MI 49305-9754 Office: Chippewa Hills Sch 3664 Arthur Rd Remus MI 49340-9350

TURNBULL, VERNONA HARMSEN, retired residence counselor, education educator; b. Teeds Grove, Iowa, Dec. 6, 1916; d. Henry Ferdinand and Ida Amelia (Dohrmann) Harmsen; m. Alexander Turnbull, Oct. 12, 1961. BA, Cornell Coll., Mt. Vernon, Iowa, 1939; MEd, U. Colo., Boulder, 1947, profl. cert. edn., 1955. Cert. secondary and h.s. tchr. Tchr. English, Latin and phys. edn. Winslow (Ill.) H.S., 1939-45; dir. women's activities, instr. Trinidad (Colo.) State Jr. Coll., 1947-53; counselor women, assoc. prof. edn. Western State Coll., Gunnison, Colo., 1953-54; instr., residence counselor Stephens Coll., Columbia, Mo., 1955-61; ret., 1961. Active Salvation Army Aux. Mem. AAUW, Am. Assn. Ret. Persons (corr. sec. 1986-87), Kena Kampers Camping Club. Avocations: photography, camping, art, dancing, baking.

TURNDORF, HERMAN, anesthesiologist, educator; b. Paterson, N.J., Dec. 22, 1930; s. Charles R. and Ruth (Blumberg) T.; m. Sietske Huisman, Nov. 24, 1957; children: David, Michael Pieter. AB, Oberlin Coll., 1952; MD, U. Pa., 1956. Diplomate Am. Bd. Anesthesiology. Instr. anesthesiology U. Pa. Hosp., 1957-59; asst. anesthetist med. sch. Harvard U., Mass. Gen. Hosp., Boston, 1961-63; assoc. attending anesthesiologist, asst. dir. dept. anesthesiology Mt. Sinai Hosp., N.Y.C., 1963-70, clin. prof. anesthesiology, 1966-70; prof., chmn. dept. anesthesiology W.Va. U. Sch. Medicine and Med. Ctr., Morgantown, 1970-74, NYU Sch. Medicine, 1974—2000; dir. anesthesiology NYU Tisch Hosp., Bellevue Hosp. Ctr., 1974—2000; pres. med. bd., med. dir. Bellevue Hosp. Med. Ctr., 1990—91, 1997; ret., 2000. Co-author: Anesthesia and Neurosurgery, 2nd edit., 1986, Trauma, Anesthesia and Intensive Care, 1990; contbr. over 200 articles to profl. jours. Lt. M.C., USNR, 1959-61. Fellow Am. Coll. Chest Physicians, Am. Coll. Anesthesiologists (mem. bd. govs. 1977-85, chmn. bd. govs. 1984), N.Y. Acad. Medicine; mem. AMA, Am. Soc. Anesthesiologists, Assn. Univ. Anesthetists, Internat. Soc. Study of Pain, Soc. Acad. Anesthesia Chairmen, Soc. Critical Care Medicine, Soc. Neurosurg. Anesthesia and Neurologic Supportive Care, N.Y. Acad. Scis., N.Y. State Soc. Anesthesiologists.

TURNER, ANN COFFEEN, reading specialist educator; b. Evanston, Ill., Oct. 16, 1930; d. Carl Roy and Louise Glatz (Groser) Coffeen; m. Harvey Stewart Turner, Sept. 7, 1952; children: Catharine Whitford, Victoria Louise. BA, Cornell U., 1952; MAT, Seton Hall U., S. Orange, N.J., 1980; MA, Kean Coll., Union, N.J., 1984; cert., Montclair State Coll., 1985. Reading tchr. Pediatric Lang. Disorder Clinic/Columbia Med. Ctr., N.Y.C., 1955-57, Far Brook Sch., Short Hills, N.J., 1963-77; reading specialist Gill St. Bernard's Sch., Bernardsville, N.J., 1978—; learning disabilities tchr., cons. Author: (ednl. materials) Packets Game, 1999, Spelling With Clues, 1999, Mnemonic-Picture Game, 1999, Trading Game, 1999, Color Code, 1999, Nine Retold Tales, 1999. Past singer Morris Chorale, Morristown, NJ, Masterwork Chorus. Cornell U. nat. scholar, 1948-52. Mem. Orton Dyslexia Soc., Kappa Delta Pi. Home: 211 Mountainside Rd Mendham NJ 07945-1100 Office: Gill St Bernards Sch PO Box 604 Gladstone NJ 07934-0604

TURNER, BILLIE LEE, botanist, educator; b. Yoakum, Tex., Feb. 22, 1925; s. James Madison and Julia Irene (Harper) T.; m. Virginia Ruth Mathis, Sept. 27, 1944 (div. Feb. 1968); children: Billie Lee, Matt Warnock; m. Pauline Henderson, Oct. 22, 1969 (div. Jan. 1975); m. Gayle Langford, Apr. 18, 1980; children (adopted): Roy P., Robert L. BS, Sul Ross State Coll., 1949; MS, So. Meth. U., 1950; PhD, Wash. State U., 1953. Teaching asst. botany dept. Wash. State U., 1951-53; instr. botany dept. U. Tex., Austin, 1953, asst. prof., 1954-58, assoc. prof., 1958-61, prof., 1961-2000, now S.F. Blake prof. botany, chmn., 1967-75, dir. Plant Resources Ctr., 1957—, emeritus prof., 2000—. Asso. investigator ecol. study vegetation of, Africa, U. Ariz., Office Naval Research, 1956-57; vis. prof. U. Mont., summers 1971, 73, U. Mass., 1974 Author: Vegetational Changes in Africa Over a Third of a Century, 1959, Leguminosae of Texas, 1960, Biochemical Systematics, 1963, Chemotaxonomy of Leguminosae, 1972, Biology and Chemistry of Compositae, 1977, Plant Chemosystematics, 1984; assoc. editor: Southwestern Naturalist, 1959—. Served to 1st lt. USAAF, 1943-47. NSF postdoctoral fellow U. Liverpool, 1965-66. Mem. Bot. Soc. Am. (sec. 1958-59, 60-64, v.p. 1969), Tex. Acad. Sci., Southwestern Assn. Naturalists (pres. 1967, gov.), Am. Soc. Plant Taxonomists (Asa Gray award 1991), Internat. Assn. Plant Taxonomists, Soc. Study Evolution, Phi Beta Kappa, Sigma Xi. Office: U Tex Plant Resources Ctr Main Bldg 228 Austin TX 78712

TURNER, BONESE COLLINS, artist, educator; b. Abilene, Kans. d. Paul Edwin and Ruby (Seybold) Collins; m. Glenn E. Turner; 1 child, Craig Collins. BS in Edn., MEd, U. Idaho; MA, Calif. State U., Northridge, 1974. Instr. art L.A. Pierce Coll., Woodland Hills, Calif., 1964—. Prof. art Calif. State U., Northridge, 1986-89; art instr. L.A. Valley Coll., Van Nuys, 1987-89, Moorpark (Calif.) Coll., 1988-98, Arrowmont Coll. Arts & Crafts, Gatlinburg, Tenn., 1995-96; advisor Coll. Art and Arch. U. Idaho, 1988—; juror for art exhbns. including Nat. Watercolor Soc., 1980, 91, San Diego Art Inst., Brand Nat. Watermedia Exhbn., 1980, 96-97, prin. gallery Orlando Gallery, Tarzana, Calif. Represented in permanent collections Smithsonian Inst., Olympic Arts Festival, L.A.; one-woman shows include Angel's Gate Gallery, San Pedro, Calif., 1989, Art Store Gallery, Studio City, Calif., 1988, L.A. Pierce Coll. Gallery, 1988, Brand Art Gallery, Glendale, Calif., 1988, 93, 2000, Coos (Oreg.) Art Mus., 1988, U. Nev., 1987, Orlando Gallery, Sherman Oaks, Calif., 1993, 98, 2002, Burbank (Calif.) Creative Arts Ctr., 2000, Village Sq. Gallery, Montrose, Calif., 2002; prin. works in pub. collections The Smithsonian Inst., Hartung Performing Arts Ctr., Moscow, Idaho, Robert V. Fulton Mus. Art, Calif. State U., San Bernardino, Calif., Home Savs. and Loan, San Bernardino Sun Telegram Newspapers, Oreg. Coun. for the Arts, Newport, Oreg. Pub. Librs., Brand Libr., Glendale, Calif., Lincoln (Nebr.) Pub. Lib., Indsl. Tile Corp., Lincoln, Nebr. Recipient Springfield (Mo.) Art Mus. award, 1989, 2002, 1st prize Brand XXVIII, 1998, Glendale, Calif., Butler Art Inst. award, 1989, 1st award in graphics Diamond Jubilee Exhibit/Pasadena Soc. Artists, 2002, Nat. award Acrylic Painters Assn. Eng. and U.S.A., 1996. Mem. Nat. Acrylic Painters Assn. of Eng. (award 1996), Nat. Mortar Bd. Soc., Nat. Watercolor Soc. (life, past pres., Purchase prize 1979), Watercolor U.S.A. Honor Soc. (award), Watercolor West. Avocations: bicycling, music, singing.

TURNER, CATHERINE MCDONALD, middle school principal; b. Washington, Sept. 6, 1951; d. Maurice John and Winona Catherine (Wedlake) McDonald; m. Paul McArthur Brooks (div. Mar. 1984); children: Amanda Gale, Paul McArthur Jr.; m. Gilbert Eugene Turner, Aug. 2, 1985. BA in English and Edn., Lenoir Rhyne Coll., 1974; MEd in Secondary Sch. Adminstrn., The Citadel, 1994. Cert. secondary tchr., secondary adminstr., S.C. Tchr. English Carver High Sch., Winston-Salem, N.C., 1974-79, head English dept., 1978-79; tchr. English Coastal Acad., Myrtle Beach, S.C., 1979-85, head English dept., 1983-85; tchr. secondary English Walterboro (S.C.) High Sch., 1985—. Presnter workshops. Recipient Award of Excellence in Teaching, S.C. Gov.'s Sch. for Sci. and Maths., 1991; named S.C. State Asst. Prin. of Yr., NAASP and McDonalds Corp., 2000. Mem. NEA, ASCD, Nat. Mid. Sch. Assn., S.C. Assn. Secondary Adminstrs., S.C. Edn. Assn., S.C. Coun. Tchrs. English, Nat. Coun. Tchrs. English, Colleton County Edn. Assn. (sec. 1989-92), Speakers Bur. Roman Catholic. Avocations: horse-back riding, writing, reading, boating, fishing. Home: 114 Sharon Dr Walterboro SC 29488-2854 Office: Colleton Mid Sch 603 Colleton Loop Walterboro SC 29488

TURNER, DANIEL SHELTON, civil engineering educator; b. Montgomery, Ala., Dec. 9, 1945; s. Daniel H. and Emma Augusta (Nelson) T.; m. Peggy Joyce Eads McDaniel, Nov. 12, 1965 (div. 1976); children: Daniel Johnathan, David Jerome; m. Linda C. Sharpe, Dec. 30, 1978. BCE, U. Ala., 1968, MCE, 1970; PhD in Civil Engring., Tex. A&M U., 1980. Registered profl. engr. and land surveyor. Asst. prof. civil engring. tech. Ga. So. Coll., Statesboro, 1973—76, U. Ala., Tuscaloosa, 1976—81; asst. rsch. engr. Tex. Transp. Inst., College Station, 1980; acting dir. engring. tech. program dept. civil engring. U. Ala., Tuscaloosa, 1981—84, prof., head dept. civil and environ. engring., 1984—2001, dir. univ. transp. rsch. ctr., 2001—. Bd. dirs., sect. chair transp. rsch. bd. Accreditation Bd. for Engrs. and Tech. Contbr. over 275 articles to profl. jours. Bd. dirs. Am. Cancer Soc., Bulloch County, Ga., 1976; oversight com. Bapt. Student Union, U. Ala., 1985-89; dir. Bapt. HS Bapt. Young Men., Tuscaloosa County, 1987-91; exec. subcom. Gov.'s Task Force Against Drunk Driving, Ala., 1983-85; treas. Coun. U. Transp. Ctrs., 2003—. Capt. USAF, 1969-73. Mem. ASCE (state pres. 1988-89, nat. bd. dirs. 1992-95, chair tech. activities 1995-96, nat. treas. 1996-97, nat. pres. 1998—), Inst. Transp. Engrs. (state pres. 1987-88, dist. pres. 1994, chair edn. coun. 1991-92, chair legis. com. 1996, Hensley award as Outstanding Transp. Engr. in So. U.S. 1991), Nat. Safety Coun. (traffic records com., roadway environ. com.), Capstone Engring. Soc. Office: U Ala Civil Engring Dept PO Box 870205 Tuscaloosa AL 35487-0154

TURNER, ELIZABETH ROBINSON, secondary education educator; b. Madison, Wis., Feb. 19, 1946; d. Elbert Elden and Elva Esther (Miller) Robinson; m. William John Turner, Mar. 10, 1990; 1 child, Ian Elbert Robinson. BS in English edn. with honors, U. Wis., 1968; MS, No. Ill. U., 1972. Lic. tchr. high sch., Social Emotional Disorders/Learning Disabilities, Ill. English tchr. E.G. Kromrey Jr. High Sch., Middleton, Wis., 1968-69, Addison (Ill.) Trail High Sch., 1969-70; tchr. severe emotionally disturbed Larkin Home for Children, Elgin, Ill., 1976-84; tchr. primary diagnostic Davis Elem. Sch. Dist. 303, St. Charles, Ill., 1984-87; tchr. trainer/cons. N.W. Suburban Spl. Edn. Orgn., Palatine, Ill., 1987-89; spl. edn. cons. Keystone Area Edn. Agy. # 1, Dubuque, Iowa, 1989-90; 6th grade tchr. Haines Jr. High Sch. Dist. 303, St. Charles, 1990—. Cons. various sch. dists. and schs., Ill., Iowa, Wis., 1987—. Recipient Kane County Disting. Educator award Kane County Edn. Region, 1986. Mem. Assn. Ill. Mid. Schs., Ill. Reading Coun., Delta Kappa Gamma, Phi Delta Kappa. Avocations: storytelling, swimming, wild flowers, reading, writing.

TURNER, ELNORA CRANKFIELD, special education educator and administrator; b. Anniston, Ala., June 16, 1953; d. Willie B. Watts and Elmira (Turnre) Crankfield Watts; m. Edward Ell Turner; children: Joseph Hawkins Jr., Nicholas (dec.), Quincy, Demetrius. BS, Jacksonville (Ala.) State U., 1975, MS, 1983, EdS, 1994, adminstrv. cert., 1995. Tchr.'s aide Anniston City Schs., 1978-83, tchr., 1983-95, supr. spl. edn., 1995—, dir. parent support group, 1996—. Pub. spkr. Bapt. Ch. Avocations: working with children, sewing, speaking, church. Home: PO Box 1082 Anniston AL 36202-1082

TURNER, ELVIN L. retired educational administrator; b. Springfield, Ohio, Jan. 9, 1938; s. Willie and Jinada (Lawson) T.; m. Betty Jo Breckinridge, June 11, 1966 (div. Jan. 1972); 1 child, Anthony; m. Carrie Johnson, Aug. 3, 1972; 1 child, Brenetta Bell. BS in Biology and Chemistry, Knoxville (Tenn.) Coll., 1962; MEd, U. Cin., 1968; postgrad., Nova U., Ft. Lauderdale, Fla., 1973, Kensington U., Glendale, Calif., 1993—. Cert. secondary prin., tchr., Ohio. Spl. edn. tchr. Cin. Pub. Schs., 1965-69, coord. spl. edn., 1969-72, asst. prin., 1972-78, prin., 1978-90, asst. prin., 1990-93. Part-time adj. prof. Mt. St. Joseph (Ohio) Coll., 1987—88; mem. adv. com. Millcreek Psychiat. Ctr. for Children, Cin., 1988—89; bus driver Bristol Village Retirement Cmty., 1997—99; ombudsman Pro-Srs., Cin., 1993—96, Waverly, Ohio, 1997—; vol. ombudsman rep. Area Agy. on Aging Dist. Seven, Inc., Portsmouth, Ohio; sec. Bristol Village Residents Assn., 1997. Vol. Ohio Dept Aging, Columbus, 2002—; asst. feeding program Visiting The Sick Ministries; master of ceremonies Black History Month Soul Food Luncheon; elected sec. exec. adv. coun. Bristol Village Nat. Ch. Residencies, Waverly, 1997; mem. bd. deacons New Hope Bapt. Ch., Hamilton, Ohio, 1993; Sunday sch. tchr. Bethel AME Ch., Lebanon, Ohio, 1996; active Pilgrim Missionary Bapt. Ch., Columbus, Ohio, 2000—; chmn. sick com. Usher Bd.; mem. Templeaire Choir; Bible study course instr. Asbury North United Meth. Ch., Columbus, 2000—01, instr. Vacation Bible Sch., 2000; bd. dirs. Big Bros./Big Sisters, Cin., 1973. Recipient plaques and grants, including plaque for statewide outstanding sr. vol. radio, TV and newspaper coverage, Independence, Ohio, 2001. Mem. Nat. Assn. for Secondary Sch. Prins., Prins. Assn. Secondary Sch. Adminstrs., Knoxville Coll. Alumni Assn., Phi Delta Kappa, Alpha Phi Alpha. Avocations: bowling, golf, reading, travel. Home: PO Box 13617 Columbus OH 43213-0617 Office: 923 Findlay St Portsmouth OH 45662

TURNER, FAITH MOSSEAU, special education educator; b. Herkimer, N.Y., Dec. 9, 1959; d. Richard Allen and Bea Elisabeth (Olmstead) Mosseau; m. David G. Turner, June 30, 1990; children: Courtney, Claire. BS, Roberts Wesleyan, 1982; MS, U. Albany, 1987. Tchr. Kenwood Child Devel. Ctr., Albany, NY, 1987—; parenting instr. Alight Care ctr., Troy, NY, 2003—. Pianist, choir mem. Victorious Life Christian Ch. Recipient Fellowship award Rsch. Found., 1986-87. Mem. Coun. for Exceptional Children. Avocations: reading, performing piano and voice, camping, hiking. Home: 6 Corina Ct Watervliet NY 12189-1135 Office: Kenwood Child Devel Ctr 799 S Pearl St Albany NY 12202-1027

TURNER, GWENDOLYN YVONNE, education educator; b. Little Rock, Sept. 17, 1951; d. Thomas Edward and Pearl Ellen (Hamilton) T. BA, Ark. State U., Jonesboro, 1973; MEd, U. Ark., Fayetteville, 1978, EdD, 1983. Cert. reading specialist, adult edn. and social studies tchr., Ark. Tchr. Ft. Smith (Ark.) Public Schs., 1978-79; reading specialist U. Central Ark., 1979-80; instr. U. Ark., Fayetteville, 1980-83, asst. prof., 1983-86, Okla. State U., Stillwater, 1986-89; assoc. prof. U. Mo., St. Louis, 1989—. Cons. Okla. Pub. Schs., Oklahoma City, Edmond, Tulsa, 1986-89, Augusta (Ark.) Pub. Schs., 1988; family literacy cons.; mem. profl. devel. schs. collaborative Regional Ednl. Partnership, 1993, Commn. on Tchrs. in Diverse Settings, 1991—; literacy place adv. bd. Scholastic Pub. Co., 1993-95. Reviewer: Free Inquiry in Creative Sociology, 1989—, Reading Rsch. and Instruction, 1993; co-author: Making Schools a Place of Peace; contbr. articles to profl. jours. Bd. dirs. St. Louis Literacy Coun., 1990—, LWV, Fayetteville, Ark., 1986; mem. State Evaluation Team for Certification of Colls. of Edn. Inst. on Writing, Reading and Civic Education grantee, Harvard U., 1990; recipient Achafoa Apple for Teacher award Mortar Board, Okla. State U., 1989-90, Cert. of Appreciation Laubach Literacy Internat., 1990, Wilson award Ark. Bus. & Profl. Women's Club, Mo. NEA Spl. Svc. award, 1991, Cert. of Honor Ctr. for Community Edn. Okla. State U., 1989; Gerald Howard Read Internat. Seminar Scholar People's Republic China, 1985; Modern Curriculum Acad. Rsch. Scholarship. Mem. ASCD, Am. Assn. Colls. for Tchr. Edn. (instl. rep.), Internat. Reading Assn. (sch. rev. team 1990), Coll. Reading Assn. (monography rev. bd. 1989, adult learning divsn. 1990-92), Assn. Tchr. Educators (monograph rev. bd. 1989, com. mem. 1989-92, cert. of appreciation 1990), Am. Ednl. Rsch. Assn., Phi Kappa Phi. Avocations: reading, traveling, collecting ethnic art. Office: U Mo 8001 Natural Bridge Rd Saint Louis MO 63121-4401

TURNER, HAZEL M. adult education educator; b. Birmingham, Ala., Mar. 1, 1926; d. Will and Georgia Ann (Beard) McCarter; m. Victor Caesar Turner Jr., Nov. 28, 1957; children: Victor C. III, Michael David. BS in Elem. Edn., Tuskegee U., 1950; MA in Guidance and Counseling, NYU, 1952, EdD in Student Pers. Adminstrn., 1960. Dean of women Alcorn Coll., Lorman, Miss., 1950-53; dir. student svcs. Tuskegee (Ala.) U., 1955-58; dir. youth programs Lansing (Mich.) YWCA, 1960-61; dir. spl. edn. Lansing Pub. Schs., 1961-66; dir. student pers. svcs. Ann Arbor (Mich.) Pub. Schs., 1966-85; vis. lectr. Ea. Mich. U., Ypsilanti, 1985-96. Mem. from Mich. State Dept. Pub. Instrn. to seminar Harvard U., 1968. Co-chair fundraising Ann Arbor Cmty. Ctr., 1972-74; vol. United Way, Lansing and Ann Arbor, 1970-74; mem. divsnl. bd. Catherine McAuley Health Ctr., Mission Health, Ann Arbor, 1980-85; chair Ret. Sr. Vol. Program, Ann Arbor, 1988—, mem. adv. com. 1993-95; co-chair pers. com. Housing Bur. for Srs., 1990-94. Named Outstanding Female Educator, Delta Kappa Gamma, 1978, Citizen of Yr. Ann Arbor News, 1997; recipient Founder's Day award NYU, 1971. Mem. AAUW, Mich. Assn. Tchr. Educators, the Links, Inc. (v.p., pres. 1985-87, rep. to UN Decade of Women Conf., Nairobi, Kenya 1985), Alpha Kappa Alpha. Avocations: computers, reading, travel, spectator sports, bridge. Home: 1219 Ardmoor Ave Ann Arbor MI 48103-5345

TURNER, MARY ALICE, elementary school educator; b. Birmingham, Ala., Aug. 8, 1946; d. Henry and Elzona (Griffin) Johnson; m. Raymond Carver Turner, July 6, 1968; 1 child, Taunya Nicole. BS in Edn., Ala. A&M U., 1968, MEd, 1992. Cert. tchr. home econs. edn., elem. edn., early childhood edn. Elem. tchr. Huntsville (Ala.) City Schs., 1969—. Mem. Parent/Sch./Tchr. adv. bd. Ridgecrest Elem. Sch., Huntsville, 1978; tchr. rep. PTA, Rolling Hills Elem. Sch., Huntsville, 1988-93. Recipient Award for Dedicated Svc. Rolling Hills PTA, 1988. Mem. ASCD, NEA, Ala. Edn. Assn., Huntsville Edn. Assn. (sch. rep. 1969-96, mem. budget com., rule and regulations com. review), Ala. Reading Assn., Alpha Kappa Alpha. Democrat. Baptist. Avocations: needlepoint, sewing, reading, public speaking. Home: 213 Lake Carmel Ct Huntsville AL 35811-8005 Office: Rolling Hills Elem Sch 2901 Hilltop Ter NW Huntsville AL 35810-1862

TURNER, MARY JANE, educational administrator; b. Colorado Springs, Colo., June 1, 1923; d. David Edward and Ina Mabel (Campbell) Nickelson; m. Harold Adair Turner, Feb. 15, 1945 (dec.); children: Mary Ann, Harold Adair III. BA in Polit. Sci., U. Colo., 1947, MPA in Pub. Adminstrn., 1968, PhD in Polit. Sci., 1978. Secondary tchr. Canon City (Colo.) Sch. Dist., 1950-53; tchr. assoc. in polit. sci. U. Colo., Denver, 1968-70, Boulder, 1970-71; rsch. asst. Social Sci. Edn. Consortium, Boulder, 1971, staff assoc., 1972-77; dir. Colo. Legal Edn. Program, Boulder, 1977-84; assoc. dir. Ctr. for Civic Edn., Calabasas, Calif., 1984-88; dir. Close Up Found., Alexandria, Va., 1988-92, sr. edn. advisor Arlington, Va., 1992—. Author: Political Science in the New Social Studies, 1972; co-author: American Government: Principles and Practices, 1983, 4th edit., 1996, Law in the Classroom, 1984, Civics: Citizens in Action, 1986, 2d edit., 1991, U.S. Government Resource Book, 1989; contbg. author: Internat. Ency. Dictionary of Edn., 2000. Chair curriculum com. Idaho State Bar Found., 2000—. Recipient Isadore Starr award for spl. achievement in law-related edn. ABA, 1997. Mem. Nat. Coun. for Social Studies (chair nominations 1983-84, chair bicentennial com. 1986), Social Sci. Edn. Consortium (pres. 1986-87, bd. dirs. 1984-87, 99—), Pi Lambda Theta, Pi Sigma Alpha. Democrat. Presbyterian. Office: Close Up Found 44 Canal Center Plz Alexandria VA 22314-1592 E-mail: turnermj@my180.net.

TURNER, ROBERT GERALD, university president; b. Atlanta, Tex., Nov. 25, 1945; s. Robert B. and Oreta Lois (Porter) T.; m. Gail Oliver, Dec. 21, 1968; children: Angela Jan, Jessica Diane AA, Lubbock Christian Coll., 1966, LLD (hon.), 1985, Pepperdine U., 1989; BS, Abilene Christian U., 1968; MA, U. Tex., 1970, PhD, 1975. Tchr. Weatherford High Sch., Tex., 1968-69; tchr. Lanier High Sch., Austin, Tex., 1969-70; instr. psychology San Antonio Coll., 1970-72; instr. Prairie View A & M U., Tex., 1973-75; asst. prof. psychology Pepperdine U., Malibu, Calif., 1975-78, assoc. prof. psychology, 1978-79, dir. testing, 1975-76, chmn. social sci. div., 1976-78, assoc. v.p. univ. affairs, 1979; assoc. prof. psychology U. Okla., Norman,

1979-84, exec. asst. to pres., 1979-81, acting provost, 1982, v.p. exec. affairs, 1981-84; chancellor U. Miss., University, 1984-95; pres. So. Meth. U., Dallas, 1995—. Pres. Southeastern Conf., 1985-87; trustee Pepperdine U., 1994-95; mem. Pres.'s Commn., NCAA, 1989-92, chmn., 1991-92; mem. Knight Commn. on Intercollegiate Athletics, 1991-2003; chmn. pres. coun. Miss. Assn. Colls., 1985-86; mem. def. adv. com. Svc. Acad. Athletic Programs, 1992—; bd. dirs. J.C. Penney, Am. Advantage Funds. Author: (with L. Willerman) Readings About Individual and Group Differences, 1979. Contbr. articles to profl. jours. Recipient Outstanding Alumni award Abilene Christian U., 1989; inducted New Boston H.S. Athletic Hall of Fame, 1993. Mem. Young Pres. Orgn., Sigma Xi, Beta Alpha Psi, Phi Theta Kappa, Alpha Chi, Phi Kappa Phi. Mem. Ch. of Christ. Avocations: tennis; golf; reading; traveling. Office: So Meth Univ Office Of The Pres Dallas TX 75275-0001

TURNER, SADIE LEE, elementary educator; b. Utica, Miss., Apr. 8, 1939; d. Albert Lee and Sadie (Green) Lee Jordan; m. Isaac Turner Jr., Jan. 1, 1965; 1 child, Sharvonne. BS in Elem. Edn., Jackson State Coll., 1963; MA in Edn., Governors State U., 1981; postgrad., Chgo. State U., 1982. Cert. tchr., Ill. Tchr. 3d grade Carver Elem. Sch., Picayune, Miss., 1963-64; substitute tchr. Forrestville Elem. Sch., Chgo., 1965; tchr. elem. grades Carter Woodson North Sch., Chgo., 1965-89, instr. computer lab., 1989—. Tchr. rep. local sch. coun., Chgo., 1989-91; sec. profl. problems com., Chgo., 1990-92, asst. sec. courtesy com., 1990-92. Solicitor United Negro Coll. Fund, 1985-92, United Way, 1989-92, Children's Aid Soc., 1989-92. Recipient Svc. award Washington Park Community, chgo., 1983. Mem. Jackson State Alumni Assn., Governor State U. Alumni Assn., Ladies Knights Peter Claver (election com. 1992—, Svc. award 1991). Democrat. Roman Catholic. Avocations: reading, sewing. Home: 8829 S Harper Ave Chicago IL 60619-7148

TURNER, STEVEN CORNELL, agricultural economics educator; b. Atlanta, Dec. 4, 1953; s. Arthur Cleaborn and Charlotte Elizabeth (Cornell) T.; m. Virginia Louise Bond, Aug. 27, 1988. BA, Mercer U., 1975; MS, U. Ga., 1981; PhD, Va. Tech., 1986. Asst. prof. U. Ga., Athens, Ga., 1986-92, assoc. prof., 1993—2003, prof., 2003—. Mem. Am. Agrl. Econ. Assn., So. Agrl. Econ. Assn., Western Agrl. Econ. Assn. Mem. Ch. of Christ. Home: 234 Greystone Ter Athens GA 30606-4461 Office: U Ga Conner Hall Athens GA 30602

TURNER, V(ERAS) DEAN, dean; b. Tompkinsville, Ky., Oct. 19, 1925; s. Hubert B. and Hazel Pearl (Craig) T.; m. Maxine H. Henson, June 30, 1946; children: Sharon Kay, Ruth Diane. BS, Northwestern U., 1946; MA, U. Ill., 1949; PhD, U. Okla., 1968. Instr. dept. math. Moark Bapt. Coll., West Plains, Mo., 1949-51; instr. chair of math. dept. Champaign (Ill.) Jr. H.S., 1953-56; spl. instr. math. U. Okla., Norman, 1965-66; prof. Mankato (Minn.) State U., 1956-73, chairperson, dept. math., 1973-77, dean, 1977-89, dean emeritus, Coll. of Natural Scis., Math, Home Econs., 1989—. Chairperson external affairs subcom. on internat. math. edn. Upper Midwest Danforth Found., 1974-77; cons. Haldingford (Minn.) Sch., Assn. of Math. Tchrs. in Mex., Toluca; faculty senate, fiscal affairs com. Mankato State U., Sch. Arts and Scis. exec. com., curriculum com., dean selection com., chmn. task force on consolidation; mem. Study Group to Peoples Republic of China, 1980; mem. Minn. Coun. of Engring. Deans; mem. State U. Systems task force on admissions requirements. Co-author: Introduction to Mathematics, 1972, Principles of Mathematics, 1972. Comdr. USN, 1944, WWII, Korean War. Mem. Nat. Coun. of Tchrs. of Math., Math. Assn. of Am., Minn. Coun. of Tchrs. of Math., Sch. Sci. and Math. Assn., Phi Delta Kappa (pres. Mankato State U. chpt. 1984-85), Sigma Xi. Republican. Baptist. Home: 1034 Siena Oaks Cir W Palm Beach Gardens FL 33410-5122

TUROCK, BETTY JANE, library and information science educator; b. Scranton, Pa., June 12; d. David and Ruth Carolyn (Sweetser) Argust; m. Frank M. Turock, June 16, 1956; children: David L., B. Drew. BA magna cum laude (Charles Weston scholar), Syracuse U., 1955; postgrad. (scholar), U. Pa., 1956; MLS, Rutgers U., 1970, PhD, 1981. Library and materials coordinator Holmdel (N.J.) Public Schs., 1963-65; story-teller Wheaton (Ill.) Public Library, 1965-67; ednl. media specialist Alhambra Public Sch., Phoenix, 1967-70; br. librarian, area librarian, head extension service Forsyth County Public Library System, Winston-Salem, NC, 1970—73; asst. dir., dir. Montclair (N.J.) Public Library, 1973—76; asst. dir. Monroe County Library System, Rochester, N.Y., 1978-81; asst. prof. Rutgers U. Sch. Comms., Info. and Libr. Studies, 1981-87; assoc. prof. Rutgers U. Sch. Comm. Info and Libr. Studies, 1987-93, prof., 1994—, dept. chair, 1989-95, dir. MLS program, 1990-95, assoc. dean, 2002—. Vis. prof. Rutgers U. Grad. Sch. Library and Info. Studies, 1980-81; adviser U.S. Dept. Edn. Office of Libr. Programs, 1988-89. Author: Serving Older Adults, 1983, Creating a Financial Plan, 1992; editor: The Bottom Line, 1984-90; contbr. articles to profl. jours. Trustee Raritan Twp. (N.J.) Pub. Libr., 1961—62, Keystone Coll., 1991—, Freedom to Read Found., 1994—97, Librs. for the Future, 1994—97, Fund for Am.'s Librs., 1995, Trejo Found., 1995—; trustee Bd. Am. Libr., Paris, 1999—; mem. Bd. Edn. Raritan Twp., 1962—66; ALA coord. Task Force on Women, 1978—80; mem. action coun.; treas. Social Responsibilities Round Table, 1978—82. Charles Weston scholar Syracuse U., 1955; recipient N.J. Libr. Leadership award, 1994; named Woman of Yr. Raritan-Holmdel Woman's Club, 1975. Mem. AAUP, Am. Soc. Info. Sci., Assn. Libr. and Info. Sci Edn., Am. Libr. Assn. (pres. 1995-96, pres.-elect 1994-95, exec. bd. 1991-97, coun. 1988-97, equality award 1998), Rutgers U. Grad. Sch. Library and Info. Studies Alumni Assn. (pres. 1977-78, Disting. Alumni award 1994, Extraordinary Libr. Advocate of 20th Century award 2000), Phi Beta Kappa, Psi Chi, Beta Phi Mu, Pi Beta Phi. Unitarian Universalist. Home: 39 Highwood Rd Somerset NJ 08873-1834 Office: Rutgers U 4 Huntington St New Brunswick NJ 08901-1071 E-mail: bturock@scils.rutgers.edu.

TURPIN, CALVIN COOLIDGE, retired university administrator, educator; b. Granite City, Ill., Nov. 8, 1924; s. Golden and Gertrude (West) T.; m. Eudell Coody, June 29, 1944; children: Susan Turpin Jones, John Thomas. BA, Baylor U., 1949, MA, 1952; BD, So. Bapt. Theol. Sem., 1955, M of Religious Edn., 1958; MA, Vanderbilt U., 1962; MDiv, So. Bapt. Theol. Sem., 1973; DSc in Theology, Golden Gate Bapt. Theol. Sem., 1967. Prof. history and Greek Jacksonville Coll., Tex., 1950-52; prof. religion Belmont Coll., Nashville, 1955-56, Austin-Peay State U., Clarksville, Tenn., 1956-57; assoc. libr. Inst. of Old Testament Golden Gate Bapt. Theol. Sem., Mill Valley, Calif., 1961-66; dir. librs., prof. libr. sci. Minot (N.D.) State Coll., 1966-67; dir. librs., prof. religion Judson Coll., Marion, Ala., 1967-70; prof. religion, dir. librs. Hardin-Simmons U., Abilene, Tex., 1970-77. Vis. prof. Tex. Woman's U., Denton, 1974-75. Author: Beyond My Dreams: Memories and Interpretations, 1992, Writings and a Selected Bibliography of Calvin C. Turpin, 1995, 50 Years of Ministry: Challenges and Changes, 1997; co-author: Rupert N. Richardson: The Man and His Works, 1971, History of the First Baptist Church, Gilroy, California, 1995; contbr. numerous articles to profl. publs. Nat. dep. chief chaplains CAP-USAF Aux., 1990-92; Calif. dept. chaplain Am. Legion, San Francisco, 1990-92, 94-95; nat. chaplain, Am. Legion, Indpls., 2000-01; vets. pk. commr. San Benito County, Hollister, Calif., 1990-92; rent control commr. City of Hollister, 1993-95. Brigadier gen. USSC, 1992—. Named San Benito County LULAC Vet. of the Yr., 2001; named to, Ark. Boys State Hall of Fame, 2001; Lilly Endowment scholar, Lilly Found., 1962. Mem. Rotary Club, Lions Club, Beta Phi Mu, Phi Delta Kappa, Gamma Iota. Republican. Baptist. Avocations: volunteer chaplaincy, writing, authentic cowboy cooking. Home: 188 Elm Dr Hollister CA 95023-3430

TURPIN, JOSEPH OVILA, counselor, educator; b. Rockford, Ill., July 11, 1943; s. D. John and Mona Belle (Albright) T.; m. Hester R. Thompson, June 26, 1969; children: Matthew, Michael. AB in Sociology, Ind. U., 1965, MS in Mental Retardation, 1966, postgrad., 1966-67; PhD in Rehab. Psychology, U. Wis., 1986. Rsch. assoc. Ind. U., Bloomington, 1966-67; instr. U. Wis. Parkside Ext., Kenosha, 1967-71; tchr. Kenosha Unified Sch. Dist., 1967-71; coord. Racine area Gov.'s Com. on Spl. Learning State of Wis. Dept. Adminstrn., 1971-73; dir. Racine County Comprehensive Mental Health, Mental Retardation, Alcohol and Other Drug Abuse Svc. Bd, 1973-78; vocat. cons., counselor supr. Industrial Injury Clinic, Neenah, Wis., 1978-83; owner, vocat. expert Vocat. Counseling Svc., Inc., Madison, Wis., 1983-88; teaching intern, counseling supr., student tchr. supr. U. Wis., Madison, 1983-86; asst. prof. rehab. counselor edn. Ohio U., Athens, 1986-89; assoc. prof. rehab. counseling program Calif. State U., San Bernardino, 1989-94, prof. rehab. counseling program, 1994—, coord. rehab. counseling program, 1990-94, 2000—. Mem. sch. psychologist exam. com. Dept. Edn. State of Ohio, 1989; rschr., presenter, cons. in field. Contbr. articles to profl. publs. Bd. dir. United Cerebral Palsy of Racine County, 1969-73, Children's House, Inc., Racine, 1971-73, Ctrl. Ohio Regional Coun. on Alcoholism, 1987-89, Ctr. for Cmty. Counseling and Edn., 1993-99, pres., 1998; bd. dir. Inland Caregivers Resource Ctr., 1993-99, Health and Hosp. Planning Com. of Racine County, 1976; treas. Cub Scout Pack # 68, Boy Scouts Am., Neenah, 1981-83, Whitcomb Village Assn., Inc., 1984; bd. dir. Aquinas HS, 1992-94, pres. 1994; HS liaison West Point Parents Club of Inland Empire, 1992-94; budget rev. com. United Fund Racine County, 1975. Grantee Rehab. Svcs. Adminstrn., 1985-88, Ohio U., 1987-88, Ohio U. Coll. Osteo. Medicine and Coll. Edn., 1989, Office Spl. Edn. and Rehab., 1989-92, Inland Reg. Ctr., 1999. Mem. ACA (pub. policy and legis. com. 1992-94, various subcoms.), APA, Assn. Counselor Educators and Supr. (we. region legis. chair 1996-98), Am. Rehab. Counseling Assn. (exec. coun. 1992-94, ethics com. 1990-91, chair coun. on profl. preparation and stds. 1992-94), Nat. Rehab. Counseling Assn. (bd. dirs. 1993-94, chmn. grievance com., pres. 1997), Nat. Rehab. Assn. (bd. dir. 1998), Nat. Rehab. Assoc. Pacific Region, (Bd. dir., 2002; pres-elect. 2002) Alliance Rehab. Counseling (bd. dir. 1996-98, co-chair 1998). Office: Calif State U 5500 University Pkwy San Bernardino CA 92407-2318 Business E-Mail: jturpin@csusb.edu. E-mail: rx300xx@aol.com.

TURRO, NICHOLAS JOHN, chemistry educator; b. Middletown, Conn., May 18, 1938; s. Nicholas John and Philomena (Russo) T.; m. Sandra Jean Misenti, Aug. 6, 1960; children: Cynthia Suzanne, Claire Melinda. BA, Wesleyan U., 1960, DSc (hon.), 1984; PhD, Calif. Inst. Tech., 1963. Instr. chemistry Columbia U., N.Y.C., 1964-65, asst. prof., 1965-67, assoc. prof., 1967-69, prof. chemistry, 1969—, William P. Schweitzer prof. chemistry, 1982—, chmn. chemistry dept., 1981-84, co-chmn. dept. chem. engring. and applied chemistry, 1997-2000, prof. earth and environ. engring., 1998—. Author: Molecular Photochemistry, 1965; author: (with A.A. Lamola) Energy Transfer and Organic Photochemistry, 1971; author: Modern Molecular Photochemistry, 1978; mem. editl. bd.: Jour. Reactive Intermediates. Recipient Eastman Kodak award for excellence in grad. rsch. pure chemistry, 1973, award, E.O. Lawrence U.S. Dept. Energy, 1983, Porter medal, European Photochem. Soc., Inter-Am. Photochem. Soc., 1994, Havinga medal, Leiden, The Netherlands, 1994, Disting. Alumnus award, Calif. Inst. Tech., 1996, Strahlenchemie preis, Max-Planck-Inst., Mülheim, Germany, 1998, Dir's. award for Tchr.-Scholar, NSF, 2002; fellow NSF, Alfred P. Sloan Found., Guggenheim fellow, Oxford U., 1985. Mem.: AAAS, NAS (editl. bd. Procs. NAS 2002—), European Photo-Chem. Assn. (Porter medal), Inter-Am. Photochemistry Soc. (award 1991, 1994), N.Y. Acad. Scis. (Freda and Gregory Halpern award in photochemistry 1977), Am. Chem. Soc. (mem. editl. bd. jour. 1984—87, Fresenius award 1973, award for pure chemistry 1974, Harrison Howe award Rochester, N.Y. sect. 1986, Arthur C. Cope award 1986, James Flack Norris award 1987, award in colloid and surface chemistry 1999, Gibbs medal award Chgo. sect. 2000), Sigma Xi, Phi Beta Kappa. Office: Columbia U 3000 Broadway New York NY 10027-6941

TUSHNET, MARK VICTOR, law educator; b. Newark, N.J., Nov. 18, 1945; s. Leonard and Fannie (Brandchaft) T.; m. Elizabeth Alexander, Aug. 23, 1969; children: Rebecca, Laura. BA magna cum laude, Harvard U., 1967; JD, MA in History, Yale U., 1971. Law clk. Judge George Edwards, Detroit, 1971-72, Justice Thurgood Marshall, Washington, 1972-73; prof. U. Wis. Law Sch., 1973-81, Georgetown U. Law Ctr., Washington, 1981—, assoc. dean rsch. and scholarship, 1992-96, Carmack Waterhouse prof. constl. law, 1996—. Vis. prof. U. Tex., 1977-78, U. So. Calif., 1989, U. Chgo., 1994, Columbia U., 1999-2000. Author: (with Stone, Seidman and Sunstein) Constitutional Law, 1986, 3d edit., 1996, (with Fink) Federal Jurisdiction: Policy and Practice, 1984, 2d edit., 1987, (with Fink, Mullenix and Rowe) Federal Courts in the 21st Century, 1996, The American Law of Slavery, 1981, The NAACP's Legal Strategy Against Segregated Education 1925-1950, 1987 (Littleton-Griswold prize Am. Hist. Assn.), Red, White, and Blue: A Critical Analysis of Constitutional Law, 1988, (with Jackson) Comparative Constitutional Law, 1999; editor: Comparative Constitutional Federalism: Europe and America, 1990, Making Civil Rights Law: Thurgood Marshall and the Supreme Court, 1936-61, 1994, (with Seidman) Remnants of Beliefs: Contemporary Constitutional Issues, 1996, Making Constitutional Law: Thurgood Marshall and the Supreme Court, 1961-1991, 1997, Taking the Constitution Away from the Courts, 1999, (with V. Jackson) Defining the Field of Comparative Constitutional Law, 2002, The New Constitutional Order, 2003; contbr. articles to profl. jours. Fellow: Am. Acad. Arts and Sci.; mem.: Assn. Am. Law Schs. (pres. 2003). Jewish. Office: Georgetown U Law Ctr 600 New Jersey Ave NW Washington DC 20001-2022 E-mail: tushnet@law.georgetown.edu.

TUSSING, LEWIS BENTON, III, (TONY TUSSING), secondary education educator, coach; b. Columbus, Ohio, May 23, 1943; s. Lewis Benton and Dorothy (Schueller) T.; m. Monica Kane, Nov. 23, 1974; children: Leith Benton, Ethan Kane. BA, Stetson U., 1966. Cert. educator, Fla., track and field ofcl. Tchr. geography Volusia County Sch. Bd., Deland, Fla., 1966-97; dir. Camp Sparta, Sebring, Fla., 1967-79; adminstrv. asst. Volusia County Schs., Deland, 1983-88. Asst. football coach, head track and swim coach, asst. athletic dir. Deland H.S.; dept. chair Southwestern Mid. Sch., Deltona Mid. Sch., Deland. Mem. mid. sch. task force Volusia County Sch. Sys., Deland, 1997; v.p., pres. Glenwood (Fla.) Civic Assn.; vol. Deland Recreation Dept.; adv. coun. Southwestern Sch., 1997—, sec., 2000—; adv. coun. Deland H.S., 1999—, v.p., 2000-2002, pres. 2003—. Recipient Race Rels. award Greater Union 1st Bapt., Deland, 1990, Svc. award Volusia Coun. Social Studies, Deland, 1993, Vol. of Yr. award United Way, 1998, Vols. in Pub. Schs. (V.I.P.S.), 1999; named Tchr. of Yr., Deltona Mid. Sch., 1994, Southwestern Mid. Sch., 1998. Mem. NEA (ret.), U.S. Geog. Educators, Fla. Geog. Educators, Fla. Edn. Assn., Volusia County Edn. Assn., Jaycees (v.p.), Lake Eustis Sailing Club (sec. 2001—, flying scots bd. 2002—), Optimists (v.p., pres.), Kiwanis (hon., dir. jr. olympics 1962-97). Republican. Roman Catholic. Avocations: sailing, stamp collecting, youth work, volunteer work, geography.

TUTKO, ROBERT JOSEPH, law enforcement officer, radiology administrator; b. Buffalo, Nov. 18, 1955; s. Robert Edward and Agatha (Pagliaccio) T.; m. Susan Joy Biddle, Oct. 29, 1976; children: Suzan Denise, Nicola Marie. Student, SUNY, Brockport, 1973-74; AAS, Trocaire Coll., 1982; BS, Pacific Western U., 1992, MS, 1995, PhD, 1998; postgrad. in nursing, SUNY, 1997. Dir. X-ray svcs. Fla. Ctr. for Knee Surgery, Clearwater, 1985-86; surgery X-ray technologist St. Joseph's Hosp., Tampa, Fla., 1986-90; dir. radiology Met. Gen. Hosp., Pinellas Park, Fla., 1990-91; dir. med. imaging Univ. Gen. Hosp. and Women's Med. Ctr., Seminole, Fla., 1991-92; program dir. Sch. Radiology St. Joseph Hosp., Memphis, 1992-94; physician asst. DeSoto Family Practice, Olive Branch, Miss., 1995-96; mem. med. staff Klein Internal Medicine, Germantown, Tenn., 1996-98; police officer Memphis Police Dept., Memphis, Tenn., 1998—. Founder, dir. continuing edn. TCB Med. Edn., Palm Harbor, Fla., 1985-91, pres., CEO, Germantown, Tenn., 1992—; tchr. Hillsborough County Schs., Tampa, 1989-92; lectr. profl. confs.; nat. radiology specialist Concorde Career Colls., Inc., Kansas City, Mo., 1994-95; advisor U. Memphis Rsch. Project, 1997-98. Author: (curriculum) Limited X-Ray, 1995, Limited Basic Medical Assistant, 1996, Occupational Burnout in Healthcare Workers, 1996; pub. MPD Centurion, 2000—; contbr. articles to profl. jours. County chmn. radiology group Pinellas County Non-Profit Hosp. Venture Group, 1990-91; lectr. Pinellas County Sch. System, 1984-91; vol. Shelby County Sheriff's Dept. Tng. Acad., 1997; mem. MPD Crisis Intervention Team. Sgt. U.S. Army, 1974-75. Recipient commendation letter Pinellas Park Police Dept., 1991. Mem. Am. Legion, Am. Educators Radiol. Scis., Am. Soc. Radiol. Technologists, Tenn. Soc. Radiol. Technologists, Fla. Soc. Radiol. Technologists, Ga. Soc. Radiol. Technologists, Colo. Soc. Radiol. Technologists, Am. Healthcare Radiology Adminstrs., Fraternal Order of Police, Tenn. Law Enforcement Assn., KC (treas. 1989-91, Knight of Month Dec. 1989), Memphis Police Assn. (bd. dirs. 2001—). Democrat. Roman Catholic. Avocations: cooking, sports, cars, golf, music. Home: 3265 Foxbriar Dr Memphis TN 38115-3107 Office: Memphis Police Dept N Precinct 3633 New Allen Rd Memphis TN 38128 E-mail: mpdphd29@midsouth.rr.com.

TUTTLE, DONNA LYNN, secondary school educator; b. Tallahassee, May 1, 1956; d. Richard M. and Juanita M. (Schubert) T.; children: William Kenneth Packard, Heather Ruth Packard. Cert., U. St. Andrews, Scotland, 1973; student, Tex. Woman's U., 1974-77; BA, North Tex. State U., 1979; MS, Fla. State U., 1988. Cert. math. tchr., Fla. Savs. rep. II, individual retirement account specialist Gibraltar Savs. & Loan, Healdsburg, Calif., 1980-84; tchr. math. Aucilla Christian Acad., Monticello, Fla., 1985; computer trainer, data entry clk. Taylor County Sch. Bd., Perry, Fla., 1988-89, tchr. math., 1988—, head Dept. Math., 2003. Computer cons., Perry, 1988. Leader/co-leader Girl Scouts U.S., 1992-2003; Awana leader, 1990-93; dir., tchr. Sunday sch. 1st Bapt. Ch., Perry, 1990-91, 94-96. Avocations: sewing, needlecrafts, calligraphy, scrapbooking. Home: 1104 E Julia St Perry FL 32347-2919 Office: Taylor County H S 900 N Johnson Stripling Rd Perry FL 32347-2109

TUTTLE, LAURA SHIVE, healthcare educator, administrator; b. Morristown, N.J., Nov. 19, 1962; d. Richard Byron and Patricia (Butler) Shive; m. Richard Lawrence Tuttle, Dec. 15, 1984; 1 child, Marissa Lynn. BSN, Skidmore Coll., 1984; postgrad., Northeastern U., 1992-93, U. Colo., 1998—. RN. Pub. health nurse Navy Relief Vis. Nurse, San Diego, 1985-86; home health nurse Trend Home Health, San Diego, 1986-87, Scripps Home Health Care, San Diego, 1987, Community Health and Counseling Svcs., Bangor, Maine, 1988-89; clin. svcs. coord. Bangor Dist. Nursing Assn., 1989-91; clin. supr. Spl. Care Home Health Svcs., Woburn, Mass., 1991, br. dir. Quincy, Mass., 1991-92; founder, dir. Career Visions, Inc., Brockton, Mass., 1992-98, dir. Attleboro, Mass., 1998—. Nursing instr. Eastern Maine Tech. Coll., Bangor, 1988-89; pub. speaker Maine Vets. Homes, Augusta, 1991, Bangor Dist. Nursing Assn., 1990-91. Co-author: Clinical Care of the Geriatric Patient, 1991. Mem. NAFE, Prof. Ski Instrs. Assn. (cert. 1982). Avocations: skiing, sailing, traveling.

TUUL, JOHANNES, physics educator, researcher; b. Tarvastu, Viljandi, Estonia, May 23, 1922; came to U.S., 1956, naturalized, 1962; s. Johan and Emilie (Tulf) T.; m. Marjatta Murtoniemi, July 14, 1957 (div. Aug. 1971); children: Melinda, Melissa; m. Sonia Esmeralda Manosalva, Sept. 15, 1976; 1 child, Johannes. Elem. Tchg. Credential, Tartu Normal Sch., Estonia, 1941; diploma in Elec. Engring., Stockholm Tech. Inst., 1947; BS, U. Stockholm, 1955, MA, 1956; ScM, Brown U., 1957, PhD, 1960. Tchr. Valuste Elem. Sch., 1941-43; escaped to Finland December, 1943; after Finland surrendered to Russia escaped to Sweden, 1944; instr. Stockholm Tech. Inst., 1947-49; lab. engr. Electrical Prospecting Co., Stockholm, 1949-53; elec. engr. LM Ericsson Telephone Co., Stockholm, 1954-55; rsch. physicist Am. Cyanamid Co., Stamford, Conn., 1960-62; sr. rsch. physicist Bell & Howell Rsch. Ctr., Pasadena, Calif., 1962-65; from asst. to assoc. prof. Calif. State Poly. U., Pomona, 1965-68, chmn. physics and earth scis. dept., 1971-75, prof. physics, 1975-91; prof. emeritus, 1992—. Vis. prof. Pahlavi U., Shiraz, Iran, 1968-70; cons. Bell & Howell Rsch. Ctr., Pasadena, Calif., 1965, Teledyne Co., Pasadena, Calif., 1968; guest researcher Naval Weapons Ctr., China Lake, Calif., 1967, 72; resident dir. Calif. State U. Internat. Programs in Sweden and Denmark, 1977-78. Author: Physics Made Easy, 1974; contbr. articles to profl. jours. Pres. Group Against Smoking Pollution, Pomona Valley, Calif., 1976; foster parent Foster Parents Plan, Inc., Warwick, R.I., 1964-2003; block capt. Neighborhood Watch, West Covina, Calif., 1982-84; citizen amb. People to People Internat., 1990—; mem. Physics Edn. Del. to Peoples Rep. China, 1990; mem. Baltic Assist Delegation, 1992; mem. Industry and Sci. Initiative 1 Delegation to Cuba, 2000; mem. Mission in Understanding to Iceland and Greenland, 2002. Fellow Brown U., 1957-58; rsch. grantee U. Namur (Belgium), 1978, Ctr. Nat. Recherche Scientifique, France, 1979; recipient Humanitarian Fellowship award Save the Children Fedn., 1968, spl. award Travelers' Century Club, 1998. Mem. AAAS (life), N.Y. Acad. Scis., Am. Phys. Soc. Republican. Roman Catholic. Achievements include research in energy conservation and new energy technologies.

TWOMEY, ELIZABETH ANN MOLLOY, education educator; b. Lynn, Mass. d. Hugh E. and Theresa A. (Callahan) Molloy; children: Ann, Paula, Charles. AB, Emmanuel Coll., 1959; MEd, Mass. State Coll., 1964; EdD, Boston Coll., 1982; LLB (hon.), Notre Dame, Manchester, N.H., 1984; LHL (hon.), Emmanuel Coll., 1998. Elem. sch. tchr. Lynn (Mass.) Pub. Schs., 1959-63; English tchr. Reading (Mass.) Pub. Schs., 1973-75, prin., 1975-81, vice prin., 1981-82; supt. Lincoln (Mass.) Pub. Schs., 1982-88; assoc. commr. Dept. Edn., Quincy, Mass., 1988-92, dep. commr. Concord, N.H., 1992-94, commr., 1994—2000. Adj. prof. Lynch Sch. Edn. Boston Coll., 2000—. Trustee Emmanuel Coll., Boston, 1975-85, U. N.H., Durham, 1994—. Recipient Disting. Alumni award Emmanuel Coll., 1984. Avocations: walking, reading, gardening. Office: Lynch Sch Education Boston Coll Concord NH 02467*

TWYMAN, NITA (VENITA TWYMAN), music educator; b. Beloit, Wis., July 14, 1948; d. W.R. and Geneva L. (Goodman) Corvin; m. Dennis D. Twyman, Aug. 16, 1969; children: Christopher Grant, Kevin Scott. AA with honors, Southwestern Coll., Oklahoma City, 1968; B Music Edn. cum laude, So. Nazarene U., 1971; postgrad., U. Okla., 1970-71, 91-94; MMus, Oklahoma City U., 1975. Piano instr. Oklahoma City Southwestern Coll., 1968-70; pvt. music instr. Twyman Piano Studio, Oklahoma City, 1968—. Adj. faculty mem. Redlands C.C., El Reno, Okla., 1995—; creative cons. Great Start in Music ednl. music video; choir dir. Ctrl. Ch., Oklahoma City, 1989; staff accompanist Oklahoma City First Pentecostal Holiness Ch., 1966-68. Solo performances at local churches. Mem. Nat. Guild Piano Tchrs. (nat. tchr. cert., nat. adjudicator), Music Tchrs. Nat. Assn. (nat. cert. in piano and music theory, Piano Technicians Guild grantee 1991), Okla. Music Tchrs. Assn. (adjudicator), Ctrl. Okla. Music Tchrs. Assn. (sec., parliamentarian, treas., mem. various coms.), Okla. Fedn. Music Clubs (adjudicator), Oklahoma City Pianists Club (performer), Phi Kappa Lambda. Avocations: scuba diving, bicycling, water skiing, snow skiing. Office: Nita Twyman Piano Studio 5915 NW 23rd St Ste 107 Oklahoma City OK 73127-1254

TYAU, GAYLORE CHOY YEN, business educator; b. Honolulu, May 13, 1934; d. Moses M.F. and Bessie (Amana) T. BS, U. Calif., Berkeley, 1956, MBA, 1959; student, San Francisco State U., 1956-58. Cert. bus. tchr., instr., C.C. supervision credential, Calif. Tchr. bus. Harry Ellis H.S., Richmond, Calif., 1959-64, Westmoor H.S., Daly City, Calif., 1964-89; instr. bus. City Coll. San Francisco, 1978-87, 88—. Office mgr. P.F. Freytag Assocs., San Francisco, 1978-86. Coordinator Pacific Telephone Co.'s Adopt-a-Sch. Program, Colma, Calif, 1987. Grantee Bechtel Corp., 1983.

Mem. ASCD, Nat. Bus. Edn. Assn., Calif. Bus. Assn. (chairperson program com. 1979, mem. program com. 1981-82, Pacific Bell contract edn. grantee 1989), Calif. Bus. Educatos Assn. (co-chair exec. bd. Bay sect. 1994—), Assn. for Career and Tech. Edn., Western Bus. and Info. Tech. Educators, Internat. Soc. for Bus. Edn., City Coll. Faculty Assn., Jefferson Union High Sch. Dist. Tchrs. Assn., Commonwealth Club of Calif., Beta Phi Gamma. Republican. Episcopalian. Avocations: travel, volunteer work with senior citizens, consulting, tutoring. Home: 4050 17th St Apt 1 San Francisco CA 94114-4202

TYGIEL, MARTI (MARTHA TYGIEL), instrumental music educator; b. Bklyn., June 28, 1940; d. Gustave and Rose (Gross) T. MusB, Manhattan Sch. Music, 1960, MusM, 1961. Lic. music tchr., N.Y.; lic. tchr. orchestral music, N.Y.C. Tchr. orchestral music N.Y.C. Bd. Edn., 1961-66; dir. promotion Carl Fischer, Inc., N.Y.C., 1966-67, dir. edn., 1979-81; ind. tchr. violin N.Y.C., 1961—; dir. instrumental music, orch., condr., band condr. Horace Mann Sch., Riverdale, N.Y., 1986—. Mem. Music Educators Nat. Conf., Am. String Tchrs. Assn., N.Y. State Sch. Music Assn., Chamber Music Assocs. Home: 600 W 246th St Apt 1102 Bronx NY 10471-3624 Office: Horace Mann Sch 4440 Tibbett Ave Bronx NY 10471-3416

TYKOT, ROBERT HOWARD, social sciences educator, archaeologist; b. N.Y.C., June 30, 1961; s. Howard Benson Tykot and Joan Florence Spitaleri; m. Cynthia Armstrong Grant, Apr. 29, 1989; children: Jeffrey Nathan, Matthew William. BS in Chemistry & Archaeology, Tufts U., 1983, MA in Classical Archaeology, 1984; PhD in Anthropology, Harvard U., 1995. Tchg. and rsch. asst. Tufts U., 1982-84; tchg. fellow Harvard U., 1987-94, mgr. Archaeometry Lab., 1990-96; lectr. anthropology U. Mass., Boston, 1995-96; asst. prof. U. South Fla., Tampa, 1996-2001, assoc. prof., dep. chmn., 2001—03. Field dir., asst. project dir. Excavations at Santa Barbara, Sardinia, Italy, 1987-91; prin. investigator Field Survey of Monte Arci, Sardinia, 1987-90, Lipari, Palmarola and Pantelleria, 2000-2003, evacuations at Sennixeddu, Sardinia, 2002—. Editor: Sardinia in the Mediterranean: A Footprint in the Sea, 1992, Sardinian and Aegean Chronology, 1998, Social Dynamics of the Central Mediterranean, 1999; contbr. articles to profl. jours. Rsch. grantee Sigma Xi, 1991, Nat. Sci. Found., 2000—2003, grantee Wenner-Gren Found., 1995; travel grantee Am. Coun. Learned Socs., Italy, 1996, S.H. Kress Found., France, 1995, Italy, 2000, Pres. Faculty Excellence award, 2003. Mem. Soc. Archaeol. Scis. (bull. editor 1997—), Archaeol. Inst. Am. (pres. Boston chpt. 1993-96, v.p. Tampa chpt. 1998—), Harvard Archaeol. Soc. (pres. 1987-90), Soc. Am. Archaeology. Avocations: photography, golf, model rocketry. Office: U South Fla Dept Anthropol 4202 E Fowler Ave Soc107 Tampa FL 33620-8100 E-mail: rtykot@cas.usf.edu.

TYLER, PRISCILLA, retired English language and education educator; b. Cleve., Oct. 23, 1908; d. Ralph Sargent and Alice Lorraine (Campbell) T. BA in Latin and Greek, Radcliffe Coll., 1932; MA in Edn., Case Western Res. U., 1934, PhD in English, 1953; LLD (hon.), Carleton U., Ottawa, Ont., Can., 1993. Parole officer, case worker Cleve. Sch. for Girls, 1934-35; tchr. English, Latin and French Cleveland Heights (Ohio) Pub. Schs., 1935-45; instr. to asst. prof. English Flora Stone Mather Coll., Cleve., 1945-59; asst. dean Flora Stone Mather Coll. Western Reserve U., Cleve., 1957-59; asst. prof. edn., head dept. English Sch. of Edn. Harvard U., Cambridge, Mass., 1959-63; assoc. prof. English, U. Ill., Champaign-Urbana, 1963-67, dir. freshman rhetoric, 1966-67; prof. English and edn. U. Mo., Kansas City, 1967-78, prof. emeritus, 1978—. Instr. N.S. (Can.) Dept. Edn., Halifax, summers 1972-73; condr. numerous seminars; former lectr. U. Calif., Berkeley, U. Chgo., Purdue U., U. Mo., Columbia, U. Nebr., Emory U., Fresno State U., Calif. State U., Hayward, San Jose State Coll., Mills Coll., Ala., Tift Coll., Ga., Va. Poly. Inst. and Midwestern U., Tex. Editor: Harpers Modern Classics, 19 vols., 1963, Writers the Other Side of the Horizon, 1964; co-author (intro. with and Maree Brooks), co-editor: (with Maree Brooks) Inupiat Paitot, 1974, co-editor (with Maree Brooks) Sevukakmet, Ways of Life on St. Lawrence Island (Helen Slwooko Carius), 1979, The Epic of Qayaq (Lela Kiana Oman), 1995, World Literature Written in English, 1965-69; interviewed authors, Jan Carew, Wilson Harris, Guyana, George Lamming, Barbados, Christopher Okigbo and Chinua Achebe, Nigeria, Derek Wolcott, St. Lucia, Andrew Salkey, Jamaica; also articles. Mem. Ohio Gov.'s Com. on Employment of Physically Handicapped, 1957; mem. Friends of Art of Carleton U., Nelson Atkins Mus. Art, Kansas City, Ottawa (Kans.) Art Gallery, Friends of Libr., Ottawa, Kansas. Recipient Outstanding Achievement and Contbns. in Field of Edn. award Western Res. U., 1962, Disting. Alumna award Laurel Sch., Cleve., 1994; Priscilla Tyler Endowment Fund named in her honor Case Western Res. U., 1980. Mem. MLA, NEA, Archaeol. Inst. Am., Nat. Coun. Tchrs. English (v.p. 1963, mem. com. on history of the profession 1965-68, Commn. on Composition 1968-71, trustee Rsch. Found. 1970-78, Disting. Svc. award 1978), Conf. on Coll. Composition and Comm. (pres. 1963), Arctic Inst. N.Am., Inuit Art Found., Franklin County (Kansas) Hist. Assn., Calif. Assn. Tchrs. English (hon.. Curriculum Commn. Ctrl. Calif.), Delta Kappa Gamma (pres. Upsilon chpt. 1950-52). Democrat. Presbyterian. Avocations: collecting rare books of american and english grammar, inuit art, history and culture, travel. Home: 4213 Kentucky Ter Ottawa KS 66067-8715

TYLER, RICHARD JAMES, personal and professional development educator; b. Warwick, R.I., June 16, 1957; s. Virginia (Campanella) Tyler. Gen. mgr. Gem Exch., Charlotte, N.C., 1977; nat. sales mgr. So. Merchandising, Charlotte, 1978; pres. Direct Import Distributing, New Orleans, 1981; nat. territorty dir. TV Fanfare Pub., 1982; v.p. ARC Pub., New Orleans, 1983; exec. v.p., gen. mgr. Superior Bedrooms, Inc., 1984; CEO Richard Tyler Internat., Inc., Houston, Internat. Bus. Inst., Inc., Houston, Tyler Internat. Rsch. Inst., Inc., Houston, Shopportunities, Houston, Richard Tyler Investments Ltd., 2000. Mem. adv. bd. Sales and Mktg. Mag., N.Y.C., 1991—; founder Leadership of Tomorrow program; profl. speaker, cons. in field. Author: Creating Excellence in Quality and Service, 1991, The Science and Art of Excellent Selling, 1993, Richard Tyler's Guide to Entrepreneurial Excellence, 1993, Richard Tyler's Smart Business Strategies: The Guide to Small Business Marketing Excellence, 1996, The Power of Professional Selling Program, 2002; pub. newsletter Richard Tyler's Excellence Edge, 1992, Entrepreneur Cover Story, 1999; contbr. articles to profl. publs. Mem. Rep.-Senatorial Inner Cir., Washington, 1991; mem. presdl. victory team Rep. Nat. Com., 2002, Tex. rep. pres. club, 2002; bd. dirs. Be An Angel Fund Charity, 2002. Mem. ASTD, Soc. Human Resource Mgmt., Nat. Speakers Assn., Internat. Platform Assn., Internat. Assn. Entrepreneurs. Avocations: sports, theater, deep sea fishing, amateur wrestling. E-mail: richardtyler@richardtyler.com.

TYLER, RONNIE CURTIS, historian; b. Temple, Tex., Dec. 29, 1941; s. Jasper J. and Melba Curtis (James) T.; m. Paula Eyrich, Aug. 24, 1974. BSE, Abilene (Tex.) Christian Coll., 1964; MA, Tex. Christian U., 1966, PhD (Univ. fellow), 1968; DHL, Austin Coll., 1986. Instr. history Austin Coll., Sherman, Tex., 1967-68, asst. prof., 1968-69; asst. dir. collections and programs Amon Carter Mus., Ft. Worth, 1969-86; dir. Tex. State Hist. Assn., 1986—; prof. history U. Tex., Austin, 1986—. Adj. prof. history Tex. Christian U., 1971-72; cons. visual materials Western. Am. art. Author: Santiago Vidaurri and the Confederacy, 1973, The Big Bend: The Last Texas Frontier, 1975, The Image of America in Caricature and Cartoon, 1975, The Cowboy, 1975, The Mexican War: A Lithographic Record, 1974, The Rodeo Photographs of John Addison Stryker, 1978, Visions of America: Pioneer Artists in a New Land, 1983, Views of Texas: The Watercolors of Sarah Ann Hardinge, 1852-56, 1988, Nature's Classics: John James Audubon's Birds and Animals, 1992, Audubon's Great National Work: The Royal Octavo Edition of the Birds of America, 1993, Prints of the West, 1994, Alfred Jacob Miller: Artist as Explorer, 1999; (with Paula Eyrich Tyler) Texas Museums: A Guidebook, 1983; editor: (with Lawrence R. Murphy) The Slave Narratives of Texas, 1974, Posada's Mexico, 1979, Alfred Jacob Miller: Artist on the Oregon, 1982, Wanderings in the Southwest in 1855 (J.D.B. Stillman), 1990, Prints and Printmakers of Texas, 1997. Pres. Tarrant County (Tex.) Hist. Soc., 1975-77. Good Neighbor Commn. scholar Instituto Tecnologico Monterrey, Mex., 1967; Am. Philos. Soc. grantee, 1970-71; recipient H. Bailey Carroll award, 1974; Coral H. Tullis award, 1976 Mem. Am. Antiquarian Soc., Tex. Inst. Letters (Friends of Dallas Pub. Libr. award), Philos. Soc. Tex. (sec. 1990—), Phi Beta Kappa. Home: 4400 Balcones Dr Austin TX 78731-5710 Office: Ctr Studies Tex Hist 2/306 Richardson Hall University Tex Austin TX 78712 E-mail: rtyler@mail.utexas.edu.

TYNDALL, GAYE LYNN, secondary education educator; b. Reno, Apr. 21, 1953; d. Chris H. and Ellen (Hutchinson) Gansberg; m. Dave Tyndall, Mar. 17, 1973; children: Jody, Dave. BS, U. Nev., Reno, 1987, postgrad. Cert. secondary tchr. Tchr. math, sci. Douglas High Sch., Minden, Nev., 1987—. Treas. Nev. Sci. Project, Reno, 1990—; presenter Reading and Writing in the Math Classroom Internat. Reading Assn., Nat. Sci. Tchrs., Assn., 1990-92. Recipient Nev. State Tchr. of Yr. award Nev. Bd. Edn., 1993. Mem. Nat. Coun. Tchrs. Math., Calif. Math Coun. Avocations: momming, rodeo, family activities. Office: Douglas High Sch PO Box 1888 Minden NV 89423-1888

TYNES, THEODORE ARCHIBALD, educational administrator; b. Portsmouth, Va., Sept. 24, 1932; s. Theodore Archibald and Mildred Antonette (Lee) T.; m. Bettye Clayton, June, 1955 (div. June 1970); children: Karen A. Culbert, David Lee, Tammy Alecia Simpers; m. Cassandra Washington, Nov. 17, 1989; 1 child, Jordan Alexandria. BS in Edn., W.Va. State Coll., 1954; postgrad., Calif. State U., L.A., 1959, Mt. San Antonio Coll. 1962, Chaffey Coll., 1962, Azusa Pacific Coll., 1967; MA in Edn1. Adminstrn., U. Calif., Berkeley, 1969; PhD in Adminstrn. and Mgmt., Columbia Pacific U., 1989. Tchr., athletic dir., coach Walker Grant High Sch., Fredericksburg, Va., 1958-59; dir. programs and aquatics L.A. Times Boys Club, L.A., 1959-62; tchr., dir. recreation, acting edn. supr. youth tng. sch. Calif. Youth Authority, Chino, 1962-68; tchr., dir. drug abuse program Benjamin Franklin Jr. High Sch., San Francisco, 1968-70; asst. prin. Pomona (Calif.) High Sch., 1970-72; prin. Garey High Sch., Pomona, 1972-75; adminstrv. asst. to supt. Bd. Edn., East Orange, N.J.; asst. to commr. U.S. Dept. Edn., Washington; Rockefeller fellow, supt. adminstrv. intern Rockefeller Found., N.Y.C., 1975-76; supervising state coord. sch. programs Office Essex County Supt. N.J. State Dept. Edn., East Orange, 1976-77; rsch. asst., dir. tech. assistance career info. system U. Oreg., Eugene, 1977-79; dir. ednl. placement U. Calif., Irvine, 1979; prin. edn. svcs. Woodrow Wilson Rehab. Ctr., Fisherville, Va., 1980-87; med. courier Urology Inc., Richmond, Va., 1988-90; vice prin. Ithaca (N.Y.) H.S., 1991-94; asst. prin. Wyandanch (N.Y.) Meml. High Sch., 1996-97. Cons. Fielder and Assocs., Berkeley, 1969-80, Jefferson High Sch., Portland, Oreg., 1970, U. Calif., Berkeley, 1972, U. Calif., Riverside, 1972, Calif. Luth. Coll., 1972, Compton Unified Sch. Dist., 1973, Goleta Unified Schs., 1973, Rialto Sch. Dist., 1973, Grant Union Sch. Dist., Sacramento, Calif., 1973-75, San Mateo Sch. Dist., Tri Dist. Drug Abuse project, 1973, North Ward Cultural Ctr., Newark, N.J., 1976, Nat. Career Conf., Denver, 1978, Opportunities Indulstrialization Ctrs. Am., Phila., Bklyn., Detroit, Poughkeepsie, N.Y., 1980, Tynes & Assocs., 1988; lectr. seminar San Francisco City Coll., 1968-69. Author various curricula, monitoring procedures, grants. 1965—. City commr. Human Rels., Pomona, Calif., 1972-74; pres. San Antonio League, Calif., 1972-75; exec. bd. dirs. Augusta-Waynesboro Boys and Girls Clubs of Am., 1998-99, corp. v.p. resource & devel., 1998-99. With USAF, 1954-57. Named Coach of Yr. L.A. Times Boys Club, 1959; fellow Rockefeller Found., 1975; recipient Adminstrv. award for Excellence Woodrow Wilson Rehab., 1987 Mem. NAACP, Am. Assn. Sch. Adminstrs., Nat. Assn. Secondary Sch. Prins., Nat Alliance Black Sch. Adminstrs., Assn. Supervision and Career Devel., Assn. Ednl. Data Systems., Assn. Calif. Sch. Adminstrs., Va. Govtl. Employees Assn., Va. Rehab. Assn., South Bay Pers. Guidance Assn., Pomona Adminstrs. Assn., Ithaca Prins. Assn., Wyandancg Strategic Planning Assn., Wyandanch Adminstrn. Assn., Fisherville Ruritan, Phi Delta Kappa, Omega Psi Phi (Basilius Pi Rho chpt. 1965). Democrat. Episcopalian. Avocations: video and still photogrpahy, music, art, sports. Home: 18 King Richard Rd Waynesboro VA 22980-9246

TYRER, JOHN LLOYD, retired headmaster; b. Brockton, Mass., Jan. 16, 1928; s. Lloyd Perkins and Dorothy (Nicholson) T.; m. Jeanne Irene Dunning, June 7, 1952; children: Alison Jane, John Lloyd, David Dunning, Jill Anne. AB, Bowdoin Coll., 1949; MA, Middlebury (Vt.) Coll., 1959. Tchr. Wilbraham (Mass.) Acad., 1949-53; tchr., adminstr. Hill Sch., Pottstown, Pa., 1953-64; headmaster Asheville (N.C.) Sch., 1964-92; headmaster emeritus, 1994—. Cons. Ind. Ednl. Svcs., 1994-97; mem. adv. bd. Warren Wilson Coll., 1972-87. Bd. dirs. Asheville Cmty. Concert Assn., 1970-93, chmn., 1988-90; bd. dirs. Asheville Country Day Sch., 1965-68, A Better Chance, 1988-92, St. Genevieve/Gibbons Hall Sch., 1970-77, Webb Sch., Tenn., 1986-89, Ind. Ednl. Svcs., 1970-75, Coun. Religion in Ind. Schs., 1969-78, ASSIST, 1991—, chmn., 1996—; bd. dirs. Ft. Myers Cmty. Concert Assn., 1993—, also sec.; bd. dirs. Lit. Vols. of Am., Lee County, Fla., 1995-2002. With U.S. Army, 1946-47. Mem. Nat. Assn. Ind. Schs. (bd. dirs., chmn. com. on boarding schs., chmn. membership com.), So. Assn. Ind. Schs. (pres., bd. dirs.), Mid.-South Assn. Ind. Schs. (bd. dirs.), N.C. Assn. Ind. Schs. (pres., bd. dirs.), Headmasters Assn., So. Headmasters Assn., English-Speaking Union (bd. dirs., pres. Asheville br., chmn. secondary sch. exchange com.), Theta Delta Chi. Episcopalian. Home: 1353 Kingswood Ct Fort Myers FL 33919-1927

TYRER-FERRARO, POLLY ANN, music instructor, software developer; b. St. Louis, Mo., Aug. 25, 1964; d. Jack Harold and Elizabeth (Neff) Tyrer; m. Joseph Scott Ferraro, Aug. 12, 1994; 1 child, Maria Ann Ferraro. BM, Cen. Meth. Coll., 1986; MM, Southern Meth. Univ., 1988. Ind. piano tchr., Dallas, 1988—; ptnr., owner Concert Master, Dallas, 1993—; owner Keynote Studio. Adv. bd. Dallas Southwest MTA, De Soto, Tex., 1990-97, Jr. Pianist Guild, Dallas, 1996-97, Dallas Music Tchr., 1990-92; mem. tchr.'s evaluation panel Hal Leonard, Milw., 1996; presenter Tex. Music Tchr. Conv., 1994. Author; Technique TIme, 1997; composer (music): Various Ensembles, 1995-97; arranger various Technique Disks, 1994-97; contbr. articles to profl. jours. Active Downwinders, Dallas, 1996—, Planned Parenthood, Dallas, 1992—. Recipient Nat. Honor Roll award Nat. Guild Music Tchrs., 1994. Mem. Dallas Southwest Music Tchrs. (pres. 1991-92, treas. 1997-98), Jr. Pianist Guild (v.p. 1996-98), World of Music Com. Avocations: cats, music, doll houses. Home: 1308 Carriage Creek Desoto TX 75115-3637 Office: The Keynote Studio 1308 Carriage Creek Dr Desoto TX 75115-3637

TYRL, PAUL, mathematics educator, researcher, consultant; b. Prague, Czech Rep., Dec. 24, 1951; came to U.S., 1970, naturalized, 1978; s. Vladimir Tyrl and Marta Kocian. BA with honors, N.J. City U., 1977, MA, 1980; EdD, Rutgers U., 1987. Cert. tchr. secondary edn., higher edn. N.J. quality controller Agfa-Perutz, Munich, 1969-70; technician AT&T, Kearny, N.J., 1970-73; acquisition librarian N.J. City U., 1973-74, post office supr., 1974-76, dir. math. lab., instr. math., 1976-80; instr. math. Hudson County C.C., N.J., 1980-82, assoc. prof., coord. math., 1982-84; prof., chmn. math., acad. coord., curriculum dir. Sch. New Resources-New Rochelle Coll., N.Y.C., 1984—. Rschr. Rutgers U., New Brunswick, N.J., 1980—; cons. Jersey City Bd. Edn., N.J., 1982—. Contbr. articles to profl. jours. Recipient Commemorative medal of honor, 1986. Mem. AAAS, ASCD, Nat. Coun. Tchrs. Math. (reviewer and referee), N.Y. Acad. Scis., Am. Ednl. Rsch. Assn., Math. Assn. Am., Am. Math. Assn. 2-Yr. Colls., Am. Math. Soc., Am. Mus. Natural History, Nat. Geog. Soc., Nat. Wildlife Fedn., Smithsonian Instn. Roman Catholic. Achievements include research in mathematics anxiety and mathematics problem solving.

TYSON, CARLA LEA, director; b. Scott AFB, Ill., Sept. 20, 1959; d. Carl Lee Tyson, Odell Tyson. BS, Incarnate Word U., 1982; Masters Health Care Adminstrn., Tex. Woman's U., 1990; D Higher Edn. Adminstrn., Tex. So. U., 1999. Registered health info. adminstr. 1982. Tng. coord. Tex. Dept. Health, Austin, 1982—83; mgr. med. recs. VA Med. Ctr., Houston, 1983—84; mgr. rec. processing Jefferson Davis Hosp., 1984—86; regional rec. adminstr. Tex. Dept. Criminal Justice, Huntsville, 1986—92; chair dept. health info. tech. Houston C.C. System, 1992—. Pres. Sounds of Success, Inc., Houston, 1999—; v.p. Houston Area Health Info. Mgmt. Assn, 1993—95. Author: (interactive CD) Numbering and Filing Systems, 1996, (6 cassette audio recording and workbook) Audio Review Series for Health Information, 2000. Vol. Lee Brown for Mayor, Houston, 1996—96, Ada Edwards for City Council, 2001—01. Fellow, Houston C.C. System, 1996. Mem.: Am. Health Info. Mgmt. Assn. (item writer 2001—). Avocations: aerobics, weight lifting. Office: Houston CC System 1900 Galen Houston TX 77030 Office Fax: 713.718.7401. Business E-Mail: carla.tyson@hccs.edu.

TYSON, CYNTHIA HALDENBY, academic administrator; b. Scunthorpe, Lincolnshire, Eng., July 2, 1937; came to U.S., 1959; d. Frederick and Florence Edna (Stacey) Haldenby; children: Marcus James, Alexandra Elizabeth. BA, U. Leeds, Eng., 1958, MA, 1959, PhD, 1971; DHL (hon.), Mary Baldwin Coll., 2003. Lectr. Brit. Council, Leeds, 1959; faculty U. Tenn., Knoxville, 1959-60, Seton Hall U., South Orange, N.J., 1963-69; faculty, v.p. Queens Coll., Charlotte, N.C., 1969-85; pres. Mary Baldwin Coll., Staunton, Va., 1985—2003, pres. emerita, 2003—; pres. Robert Haywood Morrison Found., 2002—. Contbr. articles to profl. jours. Mem. Va. Internat. Trade Commn., Richmond, 1987; trustee Am. Frontier Culture Mus., Va.; mem. Va. Lottery Bd., 1987-94; chair selection com. State of Va. Rhodes Scholarship Competition, 1993-97; bd. dirs. Cmty. Found. Staunton, Augusta County and Waynesboro, 1993-98. Fulbright scholar, 1959; Ford Found. grantee Harvard U., 1981; Shell Oil scholar Harvard U., 1982. Mem.: Assn. Presbyn. Colls. and Univs. (bd. dirs. 1998), So. Assn. Colls. and Schs. (vice chair 1998, pres.-elect 2001, pres. 2002), Assn. Va. Colls. and Univs. (pres. 1997—98), So. Assn. Colls. for Women (pres. 1980—81), Mary Baldwin Coll. (hon.), Phi Beta Kappa. Republican. Office: Robert Haywood Morrison Found 1373 East Morehead St Ste 2 Charlotte NC 28204-2979 E-mail: chtyson@mbc.edu.

TYSVAER, CYNTHIA KAY, social studies educator; b. N.Y.C., Dec. 18, 1955; d. George Y. and Marcelle Kay; m. Svein B. Tysvaer, Aug. 15, 1981; children: Kyle, Zachary. AAS, Rockland C.C., 1976; BS, Mercy Coll., 1978; MA in Adminstrn., SDA, 1990; MS in Edn., L.I. U., 1993. Cert. social studies 7-12. Social worker St. Dominic's Home, Blauvelt, N.Y., 1978-82; tchr. East Ramapo Cen. Sch., Spring Valley, N.Y., 1986—, dean of students, 1998—, facilitator for smaller learning cmtys., 2001—02. Mem. P.I.N.S. Reform Advocacy of NY. Author, mem. pilot project in tech., 1992—. Com. chmn. Boy Scouts Am., Ft. Montgomery, 1991-92, den mother, 1992-93; liaison Parents, Tchrs. & Friends, Ft. Montgomery, 1994-95. Mem. ASCD. Avocations: traveling, cooking. Home: 3 Lori Ln Chester NY 10918-4714 E-mail: ctysvaer@ercsd.k12.ny.us.

TYUNAITIS, PATRICIA ANN, elementary school educator; b. Kenosha, Wis., Feb. 15, 1942; d. John Anton and Antoinette (Tunkieicz) T. BS, Alverno U., 1966; MAT, Webster U., 1982; postgrad., Walden U., 1994—. Cert. elem., secondary tchr., Wis. Tchr. St. John the Bapt. Sch., Johnsburg, Wis., 1964—67, St. Matthew's Sch., Campbellsport, Wis., 1967—68, St. Monica's Sch., Whitefish Bay, Wis., 1968—71; math. tchr. New Holstein (Wis.) Elem. Sch., 1971—, mem. sch. restructuring com., 1994; owner Miss T's Learning Ctr., Pipe Village, 2000—. Adj. prof. Silver Lake Coll., Manitowoc, Wis., 1993—, Marian Coll., Fond du Lac, Wis., 1993—98; tchr. U.Wis., Oshkosh, 1995—, St. Mary's U., 1995—; math. instr. Cleveland Tech. Coll., 2002. Mem. performance assessment tng. team Dept. Pub. Instrn., Madison, Wis., 1992—. Recipient Herb Kohl award for excellence in teaching State of Wis., 1996, Wis. Presdl. award for excellence in tchg. math., Wisc. Disting. Math. Tchr. Yr., 1999. Mem. ASCD, Nat. Coun. Tchrs. Math., Math. Assn. Am., Nat. Assn. Tchrs. Am., New Holstein Edn. Assn., Wis. Math. Coun., Optimist Club (coord. local forensic contest 1991—, sch. coach Odyssey of the Mind 1986—, sch. coord. Odyssey of the Mind 1992, regional dir. Stevens Point chpt. 1992—). Home: N10335 Hwy 151 Malone WI 53049-1225 E-mail: tyunaitis@cs.com.

TZAGOURNIS, MANUEL, physician, educator, university administrator; b. Youngstown, Ohio, Oct. 20, 1934; s. Adam and Argiro T.; m. Madeline Jean Kalos, Aug. 30, 1958; children: Adam, Alice, Ellen, Jack, George. BS, Ohio State U., 1956, MD, 1960, MS, 1967. Intern Phila. Gen. Hosp., 1960-61; resident Ohio State U., Columbus, 1961-63, chief med. resident, 1966-67, instr., 1967-68, asst. prof., 1968-70, assoc. prof., 1970-74, prof., 1974—, asst. dean Coll. Medicine, 1973-75, assoc. dean, med. dirs. hosps., 1975-80, v.p. health svcs., dean of medicine, 1981-95, v.p. health scis., 1995-99; pvt. practice endocrinology Columbus, 1967—; dean emeritus Coll. medicine Ohio State U., Columbus, v.p. health scis. emeritus, 2001—; mem. staff Ohio State U. Hosps./James Cancer Hosp. & Rsch. Ctr. Contbg. author: textbook Endocrinology, 1974, Clinical Diabetes: Modern Management, 1980; co-author: Diabetes Mellitus, 1983, 88; contbr. chpts. to books. Citation Ohio State Senate Resolution No. 984, 1989. Capt. U.S. Army, 1962-64; bd. trustees Hellenic Coll./Holy Cross. Recipient Homeric Order of Ahepa Cleve. chpt., 1976, Phys. of Yr. award Hellenic Med. Soc. N.Y., 1989; citations Ohio State Senate and Ho. of Reps., 1975, 83 Mem. AMA, Am. Red Cross (past chair, bd. dirs. ctrl. Ohio 1996—), Assn. Am. Med. Colls., Columbus Med. Assn., Deans' Coun. Mem. Greek Orthodox Ch. Home: 4335 Sawmill Rd Columbus OH 43220-2243 Office: Ohio State U Coll Medicine 1024 Cramblett Hall 456 W 10th Ave Columbus OH 43210-1238

TZIMOPOULOS, NICHOLAS D. educational administrator; b. Eptachorion, Greece, Feb. 19, 1941; came to U.S., 1956; s. Demetrius and Soultana (Davos) T. BA in Chemistry and Math., U. N.H., 1965; MS in Analytical Chemistry, Boston Coll., 1967, PhD in Phys. Chemistry, 1971. Dir. rsch. So. N.H. Services, Manchester, 1978-80; prof. phys. chemistry U. Northern Fla., Jacksonville, 1981-82; chmn. math and sci. The Bartram Sch., Jacksonville, Fla., 1980-83; prof. chemistry Valencia C.C., Orlando, Fla., 1983-84; dir. sci. edn. Schs. of the Tarrytowns, North Tarrytown, N.Y., 1984-91; dir. sci., math. and tech. Lexington (Mass.) Pub. Schs., 1989—2002; pres. Omega Pub., 2002—. Adj. prof. sci. edn. Boston U., 1993—; nat. acad. advisor The Tesseract Group, Inc., 1997—. Author: Modified Null-Point Potentiometry, 1967, Irreversible Processes, 1971, mathematics-Science Curricula, 1982, Modern Chemistry, 1990, 93, Life, Earth, Physical Sciences, 1987, 90, General Sciences Books 1 and 2, 1987, 90, The Next Generation: Teachers Resources Curriculum Guide, 1993, The Stuff of Dreams: Teachers Resource Curriculum Guide, 1993. N.H. rep. N.E. Metric Action Council, 1978-80; Tufts U. del. New Eng. Energy Congress, 1978; liaison Kiwanis Regional Sci. and Engring. Fair, Jacksonville, 1983; founder N.H. Legis. Acad. Sci. and Tech., Concord, 1980; mem. operating com. Mass. Sci. Fair, 1990—. Recipient Outstanding commendations in sci. achievement Internat. Sci. and Engring. Fair, 1986, CMA Catalyst award, 1987, N.Y. State Presdl. award for excellence in sci. and math., 1989. Fellow: Signa Xi (exec. bd. Harvard U. chpt. 1998); mem.: NSTA (coordination and superision sci. edn. com. 2001—), ASCD, AAAS, Nat. Sci. Tchrs. Assn., Fla. Acad. Sci., N.Y. Acad. Sci., Am. Chem. Soc. (Fla. congl. del. 1984, treas. Fla. sect. 1983, 1984, chmn. Jacksonville sect. 1982—83, dir. Westchester County, N.Y. sub-sect. 1986—, high sch. esams. com. 1982—86, Outstanding Chem. Tchr. Fla. 1982, S F U.S. 1983, Nichols award 1986), Greek Orthodox Youth Assn. (pres. Manchester, N.H. 1963—65), Rotary Internat. Democrat. Avocations: photography, classical music, guitar, travel, soccer.

UCLES, MAUREEN ELLEN, bilingual educator; b. Portsmouth, Ohio, Dec. 7, 1966; d. Harold Edwin and Betty Rosemary (Scherer) Stamper; m. Jose Armando Ucles, May 17, 1993. BS in Elem. Edn., Franciscan U., Steubenville, Ohio, 1989; bilingual endorsement, U. Tex., El Paso, 1993. Cert. bilingual, ESL 1-12 elem, 6-12 history secondary tchr. Jr. high volleyball and basketball coach Aquinas Elem. Sch., Steubenville, 1987-90; tchr. 8th grade Holy Rosary Elem. Sch., Steubenville, 1990; tchr. 5th, 6th, 7th and 8th grade St. Agnes Elem. Sch., Mingo Junction, Ohio, 1990; varsity volleyball coach Notre Dame H.S., Portsmouth, Ohio, 1990; day camp dir. Portsmouth YMCA, 1990; vol., tchr.-trainer U.S. Peace Corps, Honduras, Ctrl. Am., 1990-92; tchr. 1st grade New Orleans Pub. Sch., 1992-93; tchr. 3rd grade bilingual Ysleta Ind. Sch. Dist., El Paso, 1993—. Peace Corps fellow U. Tex., El Paso, 1993-94. Mem. Assn. Tex. Profl. Educators. Roman Catholic. Avocations: poetry, dancing, travel, sports, music. Office: Dolphin Ter Elem Sch 9790 Pickerel Dr El Paso TX 79924-5699

UDAGAWA, TAKESHI, physicist, educator; b. Tokyo, May 3, 1932; came to U.S., 1970; s. Saheiji Udagawa and Teruko (Yamazaki) Urayama; m. Yukiko Amano, Mar. 20, 1960 (dec. Oct. 1989); children: Yoichi, Taturo; m. Mami Eto, Apr. 15, 1991. BS, Tokyo Inst. Sci., 1957; MS, Tokyo U. of Edn., 1959, PhD, 1962. Instr. Tokyo Inst. Tech., 1962-64; rsch. assoc. Fla. State U., Tallahassee, 1964-66; rsch. fellow Niels Bohn Inst., Copenhagen, 1966-68; assoc. prof. Kyoto (Japan) U., 1968-70; prof. dept. physics U. Tex., Austin, 1970—. Rsch. fellow Kernforschungsanlage, Juelich, Germany, 1981-95. Contbr. articles to profl. jours. Rsch. grantee Dept. Energy, Washington, 1970-96. Mem. Am. Phys. Soc., Japanese Phys. Soc. Achievements include contbns. to various aspects of nuclear reaction theories. Home: 4018 Amy Cir Austin TX 78759-8146 Office: U Tex Dept Physics Austin TX 78712 E-mail: udagawa@physics.utexas.edu.

UDDIN, WAHEED, civil engineer, educator; b. Karachi, Pakistan, Feb. 8, 1949; came to U.S., 1981; s. Hameed and Amjadi (Begum) U.; m. Rukhsana Tayyab, July 1, 1978; children: Omar W., Usman W., Asad W. BSCE, U. Karachi, 1970; MS in Geotech. Engring., Asian Inst. Tech., Bangkok, 1975; PhD in Transp. Engring., U. Tex., 1984. Registered profl. engr., Tex. Lab. engr. Airport Devel. Agy., Ltd., Pakistan, 1971-73; materials engr. Netherlands Airport cons., Jeddah, Saudi Arabia, 1975-78; asst. rsch. engr. U. Petroleum and Minerals Rsch. Inst., Dhahran, Saudi Arabia, 1978-81; rsc. engr. Austin (Tex.) Rsch. Engrs., Inc., 1984-87; pavement/materials engr. Tex. R&D Found., Riverdale, Md., 1987-89; UN pavement expert UNCHS/Dubai Municipality, Dubai, 1989-91; assoc. prof. U. Miss., University, 1993—. Founder, infrastructure cons. Engring. Mgmt. Applications, Inc., Silver Spring, Md., 1992—; liaison officer for Saudi Arabia and UAE Asian Geotech. Info. Ctr., Bangkok, 1976-81; numerous conf. presentations in field. Co-author: Infrastructure Management, 1997; co-founder, editor Internat. Jour. Pavements, 2002; contbr. over 60 articles to profl. jours. M Engring. scholar Govt. of U.K., 1973-75. Mem. ASCE, ASTM, Internat. Soc. Asphalt Pavements (founder), Chi Epsilon. Achievements include patent for highway pavement nondestructive testing and analysis methodology, infrastructure maintenance methodology, road user cost and benefit analysis software. Office: U Miss Dept Civil Engring University MS 38677

UDVARHELYI, GEORGE BELA, neurosurgery educator emeritus, cultural affairs administrator; b. Budapest, Hungary, May 14, 1920; came to U.S., 1955; s. Bela and Margaret (Bakacs) U.; m. Elspeth Mary Campbell, July 24, 1956; children: Ian Steven, Susan Margaret, Jane Elizabeth. BS, St. Stephen Coll., 1938; MD, U. Budapest, 1944, U. Buenos Aires, 1952; D honoris causa, Semmelweis Med. Sch., Budapest, 1988, Western Md. Coll., 1997. Diplomate Am. Bd. Neurol. Surgery. Intern resident in surgery Red Cross Hosp./11th Mil. Hosp., Budapest, 1942-44; asst. resident Neurol. Univ. Clinic, Budapest, 1944-46; postdoctoral fellow U. Vienna, Austria, 1946-47; fgn. asst. Psychiat. Clinic, U. Berne, Switzerland, 1947-48; asst. resident in neurosurgery Hosp. Espanol, Cordoba, Argentina, 1948-50; resident neurosurgeon Inst. Neurosurgery, U. Buenos Aires, 1950-53; asst. Neurolsurgical Clinic, U. Cologne, Fed. Republic Germany, 1953-54; registrar Royal Infirmary, Edinburgh, Scotland, 1954-55; from fellow to full prof. Johns Hopkins U., Balt., 1955-84, prof. emeritus, dir. cultural affairs, 1984-92, assoc. prof. radiology, 1963-84, Phi Beta Kappa lectr., 1980. Neurosurg. cons. Social Security Adminstrn., Balt., 1962-89, Disability Determination Svc., Balt., 1991-93; vis. prof., guest lectr. U. Va., Charlottesville, 1977, Children's Hosp. Ea. Ont., Ottawa, Can., 1977, U. Salzburg, Austria, 1981, U. Vienna, Austria, 1983, Mayo Clinic, Rochester, Minn., 1983, U. Cape Town, Republic of South Africa, 1984, U. Porto, Portugal, 1985; vis. prof. Temple U., Phila., 1979, U. Vt., Burlington, 1980, Aukland (New Zealand) Gen. Hosp., 1989, George Washington U., 1991, U. Mainz, Fed. Republic Germany, 1991, numerous others; lectr. in field. Contbr. numerous articles to profl. jours., book chpts. Mem. program com. Balt. Symphony Orch., 1972-80, edn. com. Walters Art Gallery, Balt., 1985-88. Recipient Lincoln award Am. Hungarian Found., 1980, Eisenberg award Humanities, 1996; Humanities grantee NEH, 1984-91. Fellow ACS; mem. AAUP, Am. Assn. Neurol. Surgeons (life, Humanitarian award 1991), Congress Neurol. Surgeons (sr.), Am. Assn. Neuropathologists, Pan-Am. Med. Assn., Soc. Brit. Neurol. Surgeons (corr.), Pavlovian Soc. N.Am., German Neurol. Soc. (corr.), Internat. Soc. Pediatric Neurosurgery (founding), Hungarian Neurosurg. Soc. (corr.), Argentine Acad. Sci. (corr.), Am. Soc. for Laser Medicine and Surgery (charter), Johns Hopkins Med. Assn., Johns Hopkins Faculty Club, 14 West Hamilton Club (chair steering com. 1977-83), Cosmos Club (chair program subcom. 1991—), Landsdowne Club (London), Alpha Omega Alpha. Roman Catholic. Avocations: music, literature, travel, chess. Home and Office: 111 Hamlet Hill Rd Apt 303 Baltimore MD 21210-1518

UDWADIA, FIRDAUS ERACH, engineering educator, consultant; b. Bombay, Aug. 28, 1947; came to U.S., 1968. s. Erach Rustam and Perin P. (Lentin) U.; m. Farida Gagrat, Jan. 6, 1977; children: Shanaira, Zubin. BS, Indian Inst. Tech., Bombay, 1968; MS, Calif. Inst. Tech., 1969, PhD, 1972; MBA, U. So. Calif., 1985. Mem. faculty Calif. Inst. Tech., Pasadena, 1972-74; asst. prof. engring. U. So. Calif., Los Angeles, 1974-77, assoc. prof. mech., civil, and aerospace engring. and bus. adminstrn., 1977-83, prof. mech. engring., civil engring. and bus. adminstrn., 1983-86, prof. engring, bus. adminstrn., maths., 1986—, prof. engring., bus. adminstrn., math., 1999—; also bd. dirs. Structural Identification Computing Facility, U. So. Calif. Cons. Jet Propulsion Lab., Pasadena, 1978—, Argonne Nat. Lab., 1982-83, Air Force Rocket Lab., Edwards AFB. Calif., 1984—; vis. prof. applied mechanics and mech. engring. Calif. Inst. Tech., Pasadena, 1993. Editor (assoc.): (jour.) Applied Math. and Computation, Jour. Optimization Theory and Applications, Jour. Franklin Inst., Jour. Differential Equations and Dynamical Sys., Nonlinear Studies, Jour. Math. Analysis and Applications, Jour. Math. Problems in Engring.; editor: Jour. of Aerospace Engring.; author: (book) Analytical Dynamics, A New Approach, 1996; mem. adv. bd.: jour. Jour. Tech. Forecasting and Social Change; editor: Advances in Dynamics and Control, 2000; contbr. articles to profl. jours. Bd. dirs. Crisis Mgmt. Ctr., U. So. Calif. NSF grantee, 1976—; recipient Golden Poet award, 1990. Mem. AIAA, ASCE, Am. Acad. Mechanics, Soc. Indsl. and Applied Math., Seismological Soc. Am., Sigma Xi (Earthquake Engring. Research Inst., 1971, 74, 84). Achievements include patents for in field. Avocations: writing poetry, piano, chess. Home: 2100 S Santa Anita Ave Arcadia CA 91006-4611 Office: U So Calif 430K Olin Hall University Park Los Angeles CA 90007 E-mail: fudwadia@usc.edu.

UDZIELA, LORETTA ANN, elementary education educator; b. Blue Island, Ill., July 30, 1933; d. John Joseph and Stephanie Matilda (Parzygnot) U. BA, De Paul U., 1963; MS, U. Wis., Milw., 1971, reading specialist lic., 1973. Elem. tchr. Archdiocese of Chgo., 1952-66, Milw. Pub. Schs., 1966-76, reading clinician, 1976-82, pod coord. grade 4, 1982-92, intermediate unit coord., 1992-93, sch. safety cadet advisor, 1992-93, peer mediation coord., 1991-93. Cooperating tchr. Alverno Coll., Milw., 1969-74, Marquette U., Milw., 1982-83, U. Wis., Milw., 1988-92. Tchr. rep. Jeremiah Curtin Sch. PTA, Milw., 1972-74; mem. Intergroup Coun. for Women, Milw., 1978-80; coord. Stamp Club, 21st St. Sch., Milw., 1984-92; vol. food distbr. Marquette U. HS, Milw., 1986-92; mem. adult choir St. Charles Borromeo Ch., 1976-2000, catechist mentor CCD program, 1993-, sec., Human Concerns Commn., 2002—; adminstrn. asst. Creative Custom Homes, 1994-99, Nat. Office of Post-Abortion Reconciliation and Healing, 1999—; coord. Wis. Area Felician Assoc., 2001—. Mem. Internat. Reading Assn. (membership com. 1972-78), Disabled Reading Assn., Delta Kappa Gamma (2d v.p. 1978-80), Phi Delta Kappa (scholarship com. 1986-87), Pi Lambda Theta. Roman Cath. Avocations: reading, travel, contests, volunteer work. Home: 10373 S Mockingbird Ln Oak Creek WI 53154-6315

UEHLING, BARBARA STANER, educational administrator; b. Wichita, Kans., June 12, 1932; d. Roy W. and Mary Elizabeth (Hilt) Staner; children: Jeffrey Steven, David Edward. BA, U. Wichita, 1954; MA, Northwestern U., 1956, PhD, 1958; hon. degree, Drury Coll., 1978; LLD (hon.), Ohio State U., 1980. Mem. psychology faculty Oglethorpe U., Atlanta, 1959-64, Emory U., Atlanta, 1966-69; adj. prof. U. R.I., Kingston, 1970-72; dean Roger Williams Coll., Bristol, R.I., 1972-74; dean arts scis. Ill. State U., Normal, 1974-76; provost U. Okla., Norman, 1976-78; chancellor U. Mo.-Columbia, 1978-86, U. Calif., Santa Barbara, 1987-94; sr. vis. fellow Am. Council Edn., 1987; mem. Pacific Rim Pub. U. Pres. Conf., 1990-92; exec. dir. Bus. and Higher Edn. Forum, Washington, 1995-97. Cons. North Ctr. Accreditation Assn., 1974-86; mem. nat. educator adv. com. to Compt. Gen. of U.S., 1978-79; mem. Commn. on Mil.-Higher Edn. Rels., 1978-79, Am.Coun. on Edn., bd. dirs. 1979-83, treas., 1982-83, mem. Bus.-Higher Edn. Forum, 1980-94, exec. com. 1991-94; Commn. on Internat. Edn., 1992-94, vice chair 1993; bd. dirs. Coun. of Postsecondary Edn., 1986-87, 90-93, Meredith Corp., 1980-99; mem. Transatlantic Dialogue, PEW Found., 1991-93. Author: Women in Academe: Steps to Greater Equality, 1979; editorial bd. Jour. Higher Edn. Mgmt., 1986-95; contbr. articles to profl. jours. Bd. dirs., chmn. Nat. Ctr. Higher Edn. Mgmt. Sys., 1977-80; trustee Carnegie Found. for Advancement of Teaching, 1980-86, Santa Barbara Med. Found. Clinic, 1989-94; bd. dirs. Resources for the Future, 1985-94; mem. select com. on athletics NCAA, 1983-84, also mem. presdl. commn.; mem. Nat. Coun. on Edn. Rsch., 1980-82. Social Sci. Research Council fellow, 1954-55; NSF fellow, 1956-57; NIMH postdoctoral research fellow, 1964-67; named one of 100 Young Leaders of Acad. Change Mag. and ACE, 1978; recipient Alumni Achievement award Wichita State U., 1978, Alumnae award Northwestern U., 1985, Excellence in Edn. award Pi Lambda Theta, 1989. Mem. Am. Assn. Higher Edn. (bd. dirs. 1974-77, pres. 1977-78), Western Coll. Assn. (pres.-elect 1988-89,k pres. 1990-92), Golden Key, Sigma Xi. E-mail: bcharlton3@hotmail.com.

UGWU, DAVID EGBO, academic director, consulting company executive; b. Enugu, Anambra, Nigeria, Dec. 6, 1950; came to U.S., 1974; s. Ugwu Nwamba Enyiduru and Ujo (Nnaji) Ugwu; m. Patricia Ifeoma, Jan. 5, 1979; children: Chiugo, Adaeze, Oguejiofor, Chidiebere. BS in Chem. Engring., Mich. Tech. U., 1978; MBA, Gov.'s State U., 1981; PhD in Higher Edn., So. Ill. U., 1985, MS in Mech. Engring., MSME, So. Ill. U., 1991. Chem. analyst Nigerian Cement Co., Nkalagu, 1971-74; sales rep. Southwest Pub. Co., Nashville, 1975-76, Dumbo Enterprises, Inc., Detroit, 1977-78; plant engr., project engr. Linde div. Union Carbide Corp., East Chicago, Ind., 1978-83; rsch. devel. specialist Coal Rsch. Ctr./So. Ill. U., Carbondale, 1983-85; rschr. dept. mech. engring. So. Ill. U., Carbondale, 1985-87; dir. rsch. and grants Ariz. Western Coll., Yuma, 1987-89; dir. Inst. Planning and Rsch. Lorain County C.C., Elyria, Ohio, 1990—; asst. pres. Galveston (Tex.) Coll. Pres. Eagle Consulting and Contracting Svcs. Co., Elyria, 1990—; cons. U.S. Dept. Edn., Washington, 1990—. Co-author: Chemical Desulfurization of Coal, 1987; contbr. to profl. jours. Fellow Post Doctoral Acad. Higher Edn.; mem. Am. Inst. Chem. Engring., Assn. Instl. Researchers, Toastmasters Internat., Kappa Delta Pi. Avocations: tennis, soccer. Home: 14107 Village Birch St Houston TX 77062-2076 Office: Lorain County 1005 N Abbe Rd Elyria OH 44035-1691

UHLIG, RUTH ANGUS, secondary school educator; b. Prattsburg, N.Y. d. Austin K. Angus and Genevieve (Allen) Morris; m. Robert A. Uhlig, Apr. 5, 1958; children: Robert, Richard. BS, Adelphi U., 1952; MS, Iowa State U., 1954. Cert. permanent secondary math. tchr., N.Y. Home extension agt. Nassau County Coop. Extension, Mineola, N.Y., 1955-59; tchr. math. Lyme Cen. Sch., Chaumont, N.Y., 1976-95. Chmn. Nassau County Nutrition Coun., 1963-65. Chmn. vision com. Cape Vincent, N.Y. Devel. Coun., 1990—93; bd. dirs. Land Trust Ontario Bay Initiative, 2000—; organizer Owners Hist. Stone House Group. Grantee Tchrs. Ctr. Jefferson-Lewis County, 1988. Mem. AAUW, N.Y. State Math. Tchrs. Assn. (dist. rep. Jefferson and Oswego counties chpt. 1988-95), Coll. Women's Club Jefferson County (Watertown pres. 1988-90), Vincent C. of C. (dir. 1995-2001), Cape Vincent Garden Club (pres. 1995—), Sigma Delta Epsilon, Iota Sigma Pi, Alpha Delta Kappa. Republican. Presbyterian. Avocations: quilting, collecting and refinishing antiques, painting, skiing, swimming. Home: PO Box 326 Cape Vincent NY 13618-0326 also: 301 S Harbour Oaks Saint Simons Island GA 31522

UHRIG, ROBERT EUGENE, nuclear engineer, educator; b. Raymond, Ill., Aug. 6, 1928; s. John Matthew and Anna LaDonna (Fireman) U.; m. Paula Margaret Schnepf, Nov. 27, 1954; children: Robert John, Joseph Charles, Mary Catherine, Charles William, Jean Marie, Thomas Paul, Fredrick James. BS with honors, U. Ill., 1948; MS Iowa State U, 1950, PhD, 1954; grad. Advanced Mgmt. Program, Harvard U., 1976. Registered profl. engr., Iowa, Fla. Instr. engring. mechanics Iowa State U., 1948-51; assoc. engr., research asst. Inst. Atomic Research (at univ.), 1951-54, assoc. prof. engring. mechanics and nuclear engring., also group leader, 1956-60; prof. nuclear engring., chmn. dept. U. Fla., Gainesville, 1960-68, on leave, 1967-68, dean Coll. Engring., 1968-73; dean emeritus, 1989—; dep. asst. dir. research Dept. Def., Washington, 1967-68; dir. nuclear affairs Fla. Power & Light Co., Miami, 1973-74, v.p. for nuclear affairs, 1974-75, v.p. nuclear and gen. engring., 1976-78, v.p. advanced systems and tech., 1978-86; disting. prof. engring. U. Tenn., Knoxville, 1986—2002, disting. prof. engring. emeritus, 2003—; disting. scientist Oak Ridge Nat. Lab., 1986—2002, disting. scientist emeritus, 2003—. Rep. Dept. Def. to com. on acad. sci. and engring. Fed. Council Sci. and Tech., 1967; chmn. engring. adv. com. NSF, 1972-73; bd. dirs. Engring. Council Profl. Devel., 1968-72; mem. commn. edn. for engring. profession Nat. Assn. State Univs. and Land Grant Colls., 1969-72; apptd. mem. adv. com. on reactor safeguards U.S. Nuc. Regulatory Commn., 1997-2001. Author: Random Noise Techniques in Nuclear Reactor Systems, 1970, trans. into Russian, 1974; co-author: (with Lefteri H. Tsoukalas) Fuzzy and Neural Approaches in Engineering, 1997—. Served to 1st lt. USAF; instr. engring. mechanics U.S. Mil. Acad. 1954-56. Recipient Sec. of Def. Civilian Service award, 1968, Outstanding Alumni award U. Ill. Coll. Engring., 1970, Alumni Profl. Achievement award Iowa State U., 1972, President's medallion U. Fla., 1973; Disting. Achievement citation Iowa State U. Alumni Assn., 1980, Glenn Murphy awd., Am. Soc. for Engineering Education, 1992. Fellow ASME (life, Richards Meml. award 1969), AAAS, Am. Nuclear Soc. (chmn. edn. com. 1962-64, chmn. tech. group for edn. 1964-66, bd. dirs. 1965-68, exec. com. bd. 1966-68); mem. Am. Soc. Engring. Edn. (pres. S.E. sect. 1972-73, chmn. nuclear engring. divsn. 1966-67, 88-89, rsch. award S.E. sect. 1962, Glenn Murphy award as Outstanding Educator 1992), John Henry Newman Honor Soc., Sigma Xi, Tau Beta Pi, Phi Mu Epsilon, Pi Tau Sigma, Phi Kappa Phi (Disting. Mem. award 1997). Home: 5221 NW 44th Pl Gainesville FL 32606-4328 Office: U Tenn Pasqua Nuclear Engring Bldg Knoxville TN 37996-2300 E-mail: ruhrig@utk.edu.

UKEN, MARCILE RENA, music educator; b. Avon, S.D., Sept. 16, 1931; d. Martin Andrew and Helen (Janssen) Bertus; m. Emil Jaden Uken, Dec. 8, 1953 (dec. 1990). BS, Southern State Coll., 1952. Cert. secondary sch. tchr., Nebr. Tchr. pub. sch., Delmont, S.D., 1952-53, Carroll (Nebr.) Pub. Sch., 1954-56; spl. edn. tchr. State of Nebr., Wayne, 1953-60; piano tchr. pvt. studio, Wayne, 1955. Co-chairperson Am. Cancer Soc., Wayne, 1964-76; mem. Federated Women's Club, Wayne. Fellow Nat. Fedn. Music Clubs, Music Tchrs. Nat. Assn., Nebr. Music Tchrs., Siouxland Music Tchrs.; mem. Bus. and Profl. Women. Avocations: exercise group, bible studies, music concerts, Nebr. Huskers football, working with youth groups.

UKOHA, OZURU OCHU, surgeon, educator; MD, U. Mo., 1987. Diplomate Am. Bd. Surgery, Am. Bd. Thoracic Surgery. Intern St. Vincents Med. Ctr., Bridgeport, Conn., 1987-88; resident in surgery Beth Israel Med. Ctr., N.Y.C., 1988-90, Meml. Sloan Kettering Cancer Ctr., N.Y.C., 1990-91, St. Mary's Hosp., Waterbury, Conn., 1991-93; fellow in thoracic surgery Yale U. Sch. Medicine, New Haven, 1993-98; clin. asst. prof. cardiothoracic surgery W.Va. U. Sch. Medicine, Charleston, 1998—. Mem. AMA, ACS, Am. Coll. Cardiology, Soc. Thoracic Surgeons, Internat. Soc. for Heart and Lung Transplantation. Office: WVa U Sch Medicine 3100 Maccorkle Ave Charleston WV 25304-1223

UKPONMWAN, LUCY, elementary education educator; BA, U. Ife, Nigeria, 1981; MPA, Suffolk U., 1985. Tchr. EDO Coll., Benin, Nigeria, 1981-82; substitute tchr. Yonkers (NY) Bd. Edn., 1985-89, tchr. sixth grade, 1997—, N.Y.C. Bd. Edn., 1990—97. Vol. Bronx Mcpl. Hosp., 1989. Mem. ASCD. Office: CES 64X 1425 Walton Ave Bronx NY 10452-6901

ULABY, FAWWAZ TAYSSIR, electrical engineering and computer science educator, research center administrator; b. Damascus, Syria, Feb. 4, 1943; came to U.S. 1964; s. Tayssir Kamel and Makram (Ard) U.; children: Neda, Aziza, Laith. BS in Physics, Am. U. Beirut, 1964; MSEE, U. Tex., 1966, PhDEE, 1968. Asst. prof. elec. and computer engring. U. Kans., Lawrence, 1968-71, assoc. prof., 1971-76, prof., 1976-84; prof. elec. engring. and computer sci. U. Mich., Ann Arbor, 1984—, dir. NASA Ctr. for Space Terahertz Tech., 1988—, Williams Disting. prof., 1993—, v.p. for rsch., 1999—. Author: Microwave Remote Sensing, Vol. 1, 1981, Vol. 2, 1982, Vol. 3, 1986, Radar Polarimetry, 1990. Recipient Kuwait prize in applied scis. Govt. of Kuwait, 1987, NASA Group Achievement award, 1990. Fellow IEEE (gen. chmn. internat. symposium 1981, Disting. Achievement award 1983, Centennial medal 1984); mem. IEEE Geosci. and Remote Sensing Soc. (exec. editor jour., pres. 1979-81), Internat. Union Radio Sci., Nat. Acad. Engring. Avocations: flying kites, racketball. Office: U Mich 3228 EECS 1301 Beal Ave Ann Arbor MI 48109-2122

ULEN, GENE ELDRIDGE, elementary school educator; b. Detroit, June 13, 1939; d. James Swan and Dorothy Benson Eldridge; m. Ian Paul Ulen, Aug. 10, 1933; children: Heather Jean, Lori Dorothy. BA in Edn., Mich. State U., 1960, MA in Edn., 1961; adminstrv. credential, Point Loma U., 1987. 2nd grade tchr. San Diego Unified Schs., San Diego, 1962—70; 6th grade tchr. Crown Pointe Elem. Sch., San Diego, 1971—86; 4th-5th gifted class tchr. Cadman Elem. Sch., San Diego, 1987—2000; substitute tchr. All Saints Sch., San Diego, 2000—. Active San Diego Nat. Women Polit. Group, 1995—2000; sec. LaJolla (Calif.) Dem. Club, 2000—02. Mem.: LWV, LaJolla Book Club, Phi Delta Kappa (bd. mem. 1986—2000). Episcopalian. Avocations: roses, sailing, bridge, tennis. Home: 5840 Cozzens St San Diego CA 92122

ULLMAN, JEFFREY DAVID, computer scientist, educator; b. N.Y.C., Nov. 22, 1942; s. Seymour and Nedra L. (Hart) Ullman; m. Holly E. Ullman, Nov. 19, 1967; children: Peter, Scott, Jonathan. BS, Columbia U., 1963; PhD, Princeton U., 1966, U. Brussels, 1975, U. Paris-Dauphine, 1992. Mem. tech. staff Bell Labs., Murray Hill, NJ, 1966-69, cons., 1969-89; prof. elec. engring., computer sci. Princeton (N.J.) U., 1969-79; prof. computer sci. Stanford (Calif.) U., 1979—2003, prof. emeritus, 2003—. Mem. computer sci. adv. panel NSF, 1974—77, mem. info., robotics and intelligent sys. adv. panel, 1986—88; mem. exam. com. computer sci. grad. record exam. Endl. Testing Svc., 1978—86; chmn. doctoral rating com. computer sci. N.Y. State Regents, 1989—93, 1998—99; mem. tech. adv. bd. Google, 1998—, Viquity, 1999—2002, Surromed, 1999—, Whizbang Labs, 1999—2002, Quiq, 1999—2002; adv. bd. World Wide Web Consortium, 1998—99; bd. dirs. Junglee, 1996—98, Kirusa, 2001—03, Enosys software, 2000—01, 2002—03. Author: (book) Principles of Database and Knowledge-Base Systems, 1988, 1989; author: (with A. V. Aho and J. E. Hopcroft) Data Structures and Algorithms, 1983; author: (with A. V. Aho and R. Sethi) Compilers: Principles, Techniques and Tools, 1986; author: (with A. V. Aho) Foundations of Computer Science, 1992, Elements of ML Programming, 1994, 1998; author: (with J. Widom) A First Course in Database Systems, 1997, 2002; author: (with J. E. Hopcroft and R. Motwani) Intro. to Automata, Languages, and Computation, 2001; author: (with H. Garcia-Molina and J. Widom) The Complete Book of Database Systems, 2002. Fellow Guggenheim, 1989. Fellow: Assn. Computing Machinery (coun. 1978—80, Spl. Interest Group Mgmt. Data Contbns. award 1996, Outstanding Educator award 1998, Knuth prize 2000); mem.: NAE, Spl. Interest Group Mgmt. Data (vice chmn. 1983—95), Computing Rsch. Assn. (bd. dirs. 1994—2001), Spl. Interest Group Automata and Computability Theory (sec.-treas. 1973—75). Home: 1023 Cathcart Way Palo Alto CA 94305-1048 Office: Stanford U Dept Computer Sci 433 Gates Hall 4A-Wing Stanford CA 94305-9040 E-mail: Ullman@cs.stanford.edu.

ULLMAN, RICHARD HENRY, political science educator; b. Balt., Dec. 12, 1933; s. Jerome E. and Frances (Oppenheimer) U.; m. Margaret Yoma Crosfield, July 4, 1959 (div.); children: Claire Frances, Jennifer Margaret; m. Susan Sorrell, May 6, 1977 (div.); m. Gail Marie Morgan, Dec. 24, 1983. AB, Harvard U., 1955; BPhil, Oxford (Eng.) U., 1957, DPhil, 1960. Rsch. fellow European history and politics St. Antony's Coll., Oxford U., 1958-59; from instr. govt. to asst. prof. Harvard U., 1960-65; assoc. prof. politics and internat. affairs Princeton (N.J.) U., 1965-69, prof., 1969-77, 79—, David K.E. Bruce prof. internat. affairs, 1988—. George Eastman vis. prof. Oxford U., 1991-92; mem. policy planning staff Office Asst. Sec. Def., 1967-68; mem. staff Nat. Security Coun., Exec. Office Pres., 1967; dir. studies Coun. Fgn. Rels., 1973-76, dir. 1980's project, 1974-77, editor fgn. policy, 1978-80; mem. policy planning staff Dept. of State, 1999-2000. Author: Intervention and the War, 1961, Britain and the Russian Civil War, November 1918-January 1920, 1968, The Anglo-Soviet Accord, 1972, vols. I, II and III Anglo-Soviet Relations, 1917-21, Securing Europe, 1991; editor, contbr. Fgn. Policy Jour., 1978-80, Western Europe and the Crisis in U.S.-Soviet Relations, 1987, The World and Yugoslavia's Wars, 1996, (with others) Theory and Policy in International Relations, 1972; mem. editorial bd. N.Y. Times, 1977-78; contbr. articles to profl. jours. Chmn. bd. trustees World Peace Found., Boston, 1980-84, 95—. Rhodes scholar, 1955-58; recipient George Louis Beer prize Am. Hist. Assn., 1969 Fellow Am. Acad. Arts and Scis.; mem. Coun. Fgn. Rels., Internat. Inst. Strategic Studies. Home: 12 Maple St Princeton NJ 08542-3852 Office: Ctr Internat Studies Bendheim Hall Princeton Univ Hl Princeton NJ 08544-0001

ULLOA, JUSTO CELSO, Spanish educator; b. Havana, Cuba, Oct. 20, 1942; came to U.S., 1960; s. Derby Celso Ulloa and Margo (Hernandez) Usame; m. Leonor Rosario Alvarez, July 17, 1971; children: Sandra Leonor, Justin Alfonso. BS, Fla. State U., 1966; MA, U. Ga., 1969; PhD, U. Ky., 1973. With Va. Poly. Inst. and State U., Blacksburg, 1972-74, asst. prof., 1974-79, prof., 1987—. Vis. prof. U. Ky., Lexington, Spring 1989. Author: Graded Spanish Reader: Segunda Etapa, 1982, 5th edit., 1966, Lezama Lima y sus Lectores: guia y compendio bibliografico, 1987, Graded Spanish Reader: Primera Etapa, Alternate, 1987, 3d edit., 1996; assoc. editor, book rev. editor Critica Hispanica, 1979—; editor-in-chief Cuban Literary

Studies, 1990—. Recipient Acad. Teaching Excellence, Va. Tech., 1992, Alumni Teaching award, 1992. Mem. South Atlantic MLA (exec. com. 1996-99, v.p. 2003—), Mountain Interstate Fgn. Lang. Conf. (v.p. 1975-76, 82-83, 90-91, 97-98, pres. 1976-77, 83-84, 92-93, 98-99), Order of the Discoverers, Phi Kappa Phi, Sigma Delta Pi (state dir. 1976-80, 96-99, v.p. 1986-90). Office: Va Poly Inst and State U Dept Fgn Lang Lit Blacksburg VA 24061-0225

ULLRICH, ROXIE ANN, special education educator; b. Ft. Dodge, Iowa, Nov. 10, 1951; d. Rocco William and Mary Veronica (Casady) Jackowell; m. Thomas Earl Ullrich, Aug. 10, 1974; children: Holly Ann, Anthony Joseph. BA, Creighton U., 1973; MA in Teaching, Morningside Coll., 1991. Cert. tchr. Iowa, cons. in spl. edn. Iowa. Tchr. Corpus Christi Sch., Ft. Dodge, Iowa, 1973-74, Westwood Community Schs., Sloan, Iowa, 1974-80, Sioux City Community Schs., 1987—. Cert. judge Iowa High Sch. Speech Assn., Des Moines, 1975—; supt. Woodbury County Fair; leader 4H Club; mem. Westwood Cmty. Sch. Bd., Sloan, Iowa. Mem. Am. Paint Horse Assn., Am. Quarter Horse Assn., Sioux City Hist. Assn., Sioux City Art Ctr., M.I. Hummel Club, Red Hat Soc., Phi Delta Kappa. Avocations: doll collector, plate collector, horse-back riding. Home: PO Box W 819 Brown St Sloan IA 51055

ULMAN, LLOYD, retired social sciences educator; b. NYC, Apr. 22, 1920; s. Harry Richmond Ulman and Ruth Joanna Langer; m. Lassie Agoos Finck, July 4, 1948. AB, Columbia Coll., 1940; AM, U. Wis., 1941; PhD, Harvard U., 1950. Asst. prof. econ. U. Minn., Mpls., 1950—52, assoc. prof. econ., 1952—56, prof. econ., 1956—58; prof. econ. and indsl. rels. U. Calif., Berkeley, Calif., 1958—90, dir. Inst. Indsl. Rels., 1963—81. Sr. labor economist Coun. Econ. Advisors, Washington, 1961—62; cons. Fed. Res. Bd., Washington, 1966—67; mem. Pres. Pay Adv. Com., Washington, 1979—80. Author: The Rise of the Nat. Trade Union, 1955; co-author: Unionism, Econ. Stblzn. and Incomes Policies, 1983, Work and Pay in the United States and Japan, 1997. Active City of Berkeley Personnel Bd., 1980. Lt. USN, 1942—46, PTO, Africa. Named to Order of the Northern Star, King of Sweden, 1979; fellow vis. fellow, All Souls Coll. Oxford U., 1973—74. Mem.: New Coll. Oxford Univ. (Berkeley Citation 1990), Am. Econ. Assn., Indsl. Rels. Rsch. Assn. (pres. 1985—86). Achievements include research in in devel. of labor institutions and their impact on economic stabilization policies. Avocations: tennis, gardening. Home: 776 Creston Rd Berkeley CA 94708-1254 Office: Dept Econ U Calif Berkeley Berkeley CA 94720

ULOSEVICH, STEVEN NILS, social scientist, management consultant, educator, trainer; b. Tampa, Fla., Nov. 19, 1947; s. Steven Anthony and Coragene (Paulson) U.; m. Pamela Elmeda Locke, June 27, 1970; children: Christina, Garrett. BA, U. N.C., Greensboro, 1969; MBA, Webster U., 1981; EdD, U. So. Calif., 1990; SPHR Cert., Human Resources Inst., 2002. Commd. 2d lt. USAF, 1970, advanced through grades to maj., ret., 1992; sr. assoc. JWK Internat., Inc., Universal City, Tex., 1992-93; owner, prin. cons. Ulosevich & Assocs., China Grove, Tex., 1993—; sr. scientist, program mgr. Gen. Dynamics, San Antonio, 1995-98, sr. cons., 1999—; dir. cons. and tng. svcs. Holt Cons. Svcs., Inc., San Antonio, 1998-99; dir. tng. and orgnl. devel. So. Steel Co., San Antonio, 2000—02. Asst. prof. Embry-Riddle Aero U., Honolulu, 1988-91, San Antonio, 1992—; prof. Troy State U. Sch. Edn., Honolulu, 1990-91, Webster U., San Antonio, 1992—, U. of Incarnate Word, San Antonio, 1996-97; with San Antonio New Schs. Devel. Found., 1991-95, San Antonio 2000; bd. dirs. Alamo Tech Prep Consortium, chmn., 2002—; bd. govs. Character Edn. Inst., 1996-99. Contbr. articles to profl. jours. Educare scholar, U. So. Calif., 1989. Mem. ASTD, Soc. for Human Resource Mgmt., Survival and Flight Equipment Assn. (chpt. pres. 1986-88), Human Factors and Ergonomics Soc., Air Force Assn., Order of Daedalians, Phi Delta Kappa, Delta Epsilon. Avocations: gardening, golf, music, photography, reading.

ULTAN, LLOYD, historian, educator; b. Bronx, N.Y., Feb. 16, 1938; s. Louis and Sophie U. BA cum laude, Hunter Coll., 1959; MA, Columbia U., 1960. Assoc. Edward Williams Coll., Fairleigh Dickinson U., Hackensack, NJ, 1964-74, asst. prof. history, 1974-75, assoc. prof., 1975-83, prof., 1983—. Cons. in field. Editor Bronx County Hist. Soc. Jour., 1964—, Bronx County Hist. Soc. Press, 1981—; author: The Beautiful Bronx, 1920-50, 1979, Legacy of the Revolution: The Valentine-Varian House, 1983, The Bronx in the Innocent Years, 1890-1925, 1985, The Presidents of the United States, 1989, The Bronx in the Frontier Era: From the Beginning to 1696, 1993, The Bronx: It Was Only Yesterday, 1935-65, 1993, Roots of the Republic, Vol. VI, 1996, The Bronx Cookbook, 1997, Bronx Accent: A Literary and Pictorial History of the Borough, 2000, The Birth of The Bronx, 1609-1900, 2000; contbr. Ency. N.Y. City, 1995. Gen. sec. Bronx Civic League, 1964—67; v.p. bd. trustees Bronx County Hist. Soc., 1965—67, 1977—84, curator, 1968—71, pres., 1971—76, historian, 1986—; founding mem., bd. dirs. Bronx Coun. on Arts, 1968—71; chmn. Bronx County Bicentennial Commn., 1973—76, Bronx Borough Pres.'s Bicentennial Adv. Com., 1974—76; vice chmn. Commn. Celebrating 350 Yrs. of the Bronx, 1989; mem. program guidelines com. N.Y.C. Dept. Cultural Affairs, 1976—77; mem. N.Y.C. Com. on Cultural Concerns, 1982—88, N.Y.C. Mayor's Task Force on Spontaneous Memls., 2002; bd. sponsors Historic Preservation com. St. Ann's Ch. Morrisania, 1987—; ofcl. historian Bronx Borough, NY, 1996—; bd. dirs. Nat. Shrine Bill of Rights, Mt. Vernon, NY, 1983—, 91 Van Cortlandt Owners Corp., 1986—. Recipient Fairleigh Dickinson U. 15-Yr. award, 1979, 20-Yr. award, 1984, 25-Yr. award, 1989, 30-Yr. award, 1994, 35-Yr. award, 1999, Outstanding Tchr. of Yr. award, 1994; named N.Y.C. Centennial Historian, 1999, N.Y.C. Book award for borough history N.Y. Soc. Libr., 2001; named to Hunter Coll. Alumni Hall of Fame, 1974; N.Y. State Regents Coll. tchg. fellow, 1959. Mem.: AAUP (v.p. Teaneck chpt. 1992—93, sec. coun. of FDU chpts. 1992—93), N.Y. Hist. Soc., Am. Hist. Assn., Sigma Lambda, Alpha Chi Alpha, Phi Alpha Theta. Home and Office: 91 Van Cortlandt Ave W Bronx NY 10463-2712

UMBDENSTOCK, JUDY JEAN, physical education educator, real estate agent, farmer, entrepreneur; b. Aurora, Ill., Feb. 12, 1952; d. Alfred Alloyuisious and Mary Emma (Orha) U. AA, Elgin (Ill.) Community Coll., 1972, AS, 1973; BA, Aurora U., 1977; grad., Robert Allens Wealth Tng. 2000, 1991; grad. real estate course, Profl. Edn. Inst., 1991. Cert. phys. edn. tchr., secondary edn. tchr.; lic. real estate salesperson, Ill. Tchr. phys. edn., varsity head coach volleyball and track St. Laurence Sch., Elgin, 1970-75; asst. coach varsity basketball East Aurora High Sch., 1976-77; jr. varsity coach softball St. Charles (Ill.) High Sch., 1978-79, phys. edn. tchr., 1978-79; head coach volleyball/basketball, tchr. algebra and geometry Canton Jr. H.S., Streamwood, Ill., 1979-82; varsity coach volleyball and softball Elgin High Sch., 1982-85, phys. edn. tchr., 1982-86, jr. varsity basketball coach, 1983-84; tchr. elem. phys. edn. Sch. Dist. U-46 Heritage Elem. Sch., Streamwood, 1986—, Parkwood Elem. Sch., Hanover Park, Ill., 1986—. Substitute tchr. Elgin, St. Charles and Burlington (Ill.) H.S., 1977-78; Ill. H.S. rated sports referee Elgin and St. Charles Area H.S., 1970-85; cons. Draft and Carriage Horse Assn., Kane County, 1981—; owner Umbdenstock Country Feed & Seed Store, Elgin, 1988-94; owner/ptnr. Jud Enterprises, 1992—; real estate agent Century 21 New Heritage Inc., 1994—. Leader, youth counselor 4-H (farming and animal husbandry), Northern Ill. area, 1970—; campaign supporter state and local Reps. for re-election, Kane county, 1974-86. Served with U.S. Army, 1976-77, with USNR, 1981-87. Scholar Elgin Panhellenic Soc., 1972. Mem. NEA, NAFE, Ill. Edn. Assn., Nat. Farmers Orgn. (pub. relations 1967-80), Airplane Owners and Pilots Assn., Am. Assn. Health, Phys. Edn. and Recreation, Elgin Tchrs. Assn., South Elgin Bus. Assn., Elgin Assn. Realtors, Nat. Wildlife Assn., Nat. Audubon Soc., Disabled Am. Vet. Comdr. Club, People for the Ethnic Treatment Animals, Ill. Coaches Orgn., Am. Draft Horse Assn., Kane County Tchrs. Credit Union, Kane County Farm Bureau. Clubs: Barrington (Ill.) Carriage, 99's Women's Pilot Assn. Home: 8n129 Umbdenstock Rd Elgin IL 60123-8828 Office: Sch Dist U-46 E Chicago St Elgin IL 60120-5522 also: Century 21 New Heritage Inc 41 N Mclean Blvd Elgin IL 60123-5140

UMEH, MARIE ARLENE, English language educator; b. Bklyn., Aug. 29, 1947; d. Rudolph Vasper and Erma Eunice (Hinds) Linton; m. Davidson C. Umeh, Jan. 7, 1976; children: Ikechukwu, Uchenna, Chizoba, Ugochukwu. BA, St. John's U., Jamaica, N.Y., 1970; MS, Syracuse U., 1972; MPS, Cornell U., 1977; MA, U. Wis., 1980, PhD, 1981. Instr. SUNY, Brockport, 1972-74, Oneonta, 1974-75; asst. instr. Cornell U., Ithaca, N.Y., 1976-77; prin. lectr. Anambra State Coll., Awka, Nigeria, 1982-89; substitute assoc. prof. Medgar Evers Coll., CUNY, Bklyn., 1989; adj. prof. Hostos C.C., CUNY, Bronx, 1990—2003, Queens Coll., CUNY, Flushing, N.Y., 1990; assoc. prof. English John Jay Coll., CUNY, 1990—, faculty advisor, 1989—. Adj. prof. SUNY, Stony Brook, 2000—. Editor: Flora Nwapa, 1998, Buchi Emecheta, 1996; editor Rsch. in African Lit., 1995, Who's Who Among American Teachers, 1998; contbg. editor: Who's Who in Contemporary Women's Writing, 2001. Recipient Africademic award, John Jay Coll. African Students Assn., 1996, Dominican Students award, 1993, PSC-CUNY award, 1998, 1999, Gender Studies award, John Jay Coll-.,CUNY, 2001; fellow, NEH, 1991, Summer Tchrs. Workshop, 2003. Mem.: AAUW, MLA (African Lit. Divsn. exec. 1999—2001), Virginia Woolf Soc., N.Y. African Studies Assn., African Lit. Assn. Avocations: reading, writing, aerobics, jazz. Office: CUNY John Jay CollCriminal Justice Dept English 445 W 59th St New York NY 10019-1104 E-mail: msumeh@aol.com.

UMFLEET, LLOYD TRUMAN, electrical engineering technology educator; b. Grangeville, Idaho, June 2, 1944; s. Lloyd Truman Sr. and Bessie Viola (MacKay) U.; m. Ruth Ann Strickland, Oct. 26, 1968. BSEE, U. Mo., 1966; MSIM, Poly. Inst. Bklyn., 1971; M in Engring., U. Colo., 1988. Registered profl. engr., Tex. Asst. engr. Union Electric, St. Louis, 1966; elec. engr. Power Authority State of N.Y., N.Y.C., 1967-68, Consol. Edison, N.Y.C., 1968-71; ind. engring. cons. Toledo, 1971-76; chief elec. engr. Goldston Engring., Inc., Corpus Christi, Tex., 1976-80; mgr. elec. engring. Berry Engring., Inc., Corpus Christi, 1980-84; instr. elec. tech. Bee County C.C., Beeville, Tex., 1984-86; asst. prof. Del Mar Coll., Corpus Christi, 1988—. Cons. engring. Ctrl. Power and Light, Corpus Christi, 1991, 92, INDTECH, Inc., Corpus Christi, 1994, 95, Schneider Engring. Inc., Boerne, Tex., 1996. Mem. IEEE (sr.), Am. Soc. Engring. Edn., Instrument Soc. Am., Rockport Sailing Club (commodore 1982). Achievements include development of universal power circle for educational purposes. Office: Del Mar Coll 101 Baldwin Blvd Corpus Christi TX 78404-3805

UMHOEFER, AURAL M. retired dean, educational consultant; b. Wausau, Wis., May 11, 1942; d. Mark John Vladick, Alice Marion Vladick; m. Paul Anthony Umhoefer. MS, U. Wis., 1965; BA in French, Rosary Coll., 1964—64. Head libr. Green Bay ctr. U. Wis., 1965—68, dir. learning resource ctr., 1968—80, dean, campus exec. officer Sauk county campus, 1980—2002, ret., 2002; cons. U. Wis. Sys., 2003—. Bd. dirs. Wells Fargo, Baraboo; bd. dirs. Hist. Sites Found. Circus World Mus., Baraboo, 1984—90; bd. dirs. Wis. Correctional Ednl. Assn., 1990—98. Bd. dirs. Boy Scouts Am., Madison, 1985—97; mem. devel. coun. St. Clare Hosp., Baraboo, 1993—97. Named Outstanding Young Women of Am., 1975, Aural M. Umhoefer bldg. in her honor, U. Wis., Green Bay, 2002; recipient Outstanding Alumni award, Newman H.S. - Wausau, Wis., 1992, Citation from Senate, State of Wis., 1991, Pub. Svc. award, Fed. Bur. Prisons, 1991, Appreciation award, Circus World Mus., 1986. Mem.: AAUW (corp. rep. 1985—97, Wis. Women Leaders in Edn. award 1986, 1989), Wis. Correctional Edn. Assn. (v.p., pres. 1994—98), U. Wis. Alumni Assn. (pres. 1984—86, Spark Plug award 1992), Rotary Internat. (vocat. chair). Avocations: cooking, reading, travel, gardening. Home: 700 Effinger Rd Baraboo WI 53913 Office: University of Wisconsin 1006 Connie Rd Baraboo WI 53913 Fax: 608-356-4074. Personal E-mail: pauralum@jvlnet.com. Business E-Mail: aumhoefe@uwc.edu.

UMLAUF, KAREN ELIZABETH, educator; b. Oak Park, Illinois, June 7, 1946; d. Paul F. and Ann Elizabeth (Schwaigert) Boehne; m. Gerhardt E. Umlauf, July 2, 1972; 1 child, Robert Gerhardt. BA, Valparaiso U., Ind., 1968; post grad., Ohio State U., 1970-71, U. Ill., Chgo., 1974-76; MA, Wheaton Coll., Ill., 1990. Cert. ILL., secondary edn. tchr. English tchr. LaPorte Jr. High Sch., LaPorte, Ind., 1968-70; grad. teaching asst. Ohio State U., Columbus, 1970-71; adminstrv. asst. Am. Assn. Dental Sch., Chgo., 1971; tchr. English, journalism Oak Pk. River Forest High Sch., Oak Pk., Ill., 1971-74; English tchr. Elk Grove High Sch. Dist. 214, Elk Grove, Ill., 1974-76; realtor Bundy Morgan Realty, Medinah, Ill., 1978-80; mktg. dir. First Nat. Bank, Hoffman Estates, Ill., 1980-83; travel coord. Journeys Internat., Bloomingdale, Ill., 1983-84; tchr. English Lake Pk. High Sch. Dist. 108, Roselle, Ill., 1984—. Sec. bd. edn. Trinity Luth. Ch., Roselle, 1978-83; yrbook. adviser Oak Park-River Forest High Sch., Oak Park, 1971-74; asst. swim coach Elk Grove High Sch., Dist. 214, 1974-76. Contbg. articles to profl. jour.; freelance reporter LaPorte Herald Argus, 1968-70; newspaper adviser Lake Park High Sch. Dist. 108, Roselle, Ill., 1984-86; reporter Bloomingdale Almanac, 1978-80. Juvenile counselor LaPorte County, Ind., 1969-70. Recipient: Gallup Award; Adviser Quill and Scholl (Nat.). Mem. Nat. Coun. English Teachers; Lake Pk. Edn. Assn.; Ill. Edn. Assn.; NEA. Republican. Lutheran. Office: Lake Pk High Sch Dist 108 600 Medinah Rd Roselle IL 60172-2598

UMMINGER, BRUCE LYNN, government official, scientist, educator; b. Dayton, Ohio, Apr. 10, 1941; s. Frederick William and Elnora Mae (Waltemathe) U.; m. Judith Lackey Bryant, Dec. 17, 1966; children: Alison Grace, April Lynn BS magna cum laude with honors in biology, Yale U., 1963, MS, 1966, MPhil, 1968, PhD, 1969; postgrad., U. Calif., Berkeley, 1963-64; cert. univ. adminstrv./mgmt. tng. program, U. Cin., 1975; cert., Fed. Exec. Inst., 1984. Asst. prof. dept. biol. scis. U. Cin., 1969-73, assoc. prof. dept. biol. scis., 1973-75, acting head dept. biol. scis., 1973-75, prof. dept. biol. scis., 1975-81, dir. grad. affairs, 1978-79; program dir. regulatory biology program NSF, Washington, 1979-84, dept. dir. cellular bioscis. divsn., 1984-89, mem. sr. exec. svc., 1984—, acting divsn. dir., 1985-87, 88-89, divsn. dir. cellular bioscis. divsn., 1989-91, divsn. dir. integrative biology and neuroscience, 1991—99, sr. scientist office integrative activities, office of dir., 1999—; sr. advisor on health policy Office of Internat. Health Policy Dept. State, Washington, 1988; sr. advisor on biodiversity Smithsonian Instn., 1993-94. Exec. sec. Nat. Sci. Bd. Com. on Ctrs. and Individual Investigator Awards, 1986-88; mem. NSF rev. panel Exptl. Program to Stimulate Competitive Rsch., 1989, Rsch. Improvement in Minority Instns., 1986, 87, U.S.-India Coop. Rsch. Program, 1981-82, U.S.-India Exch. of Scholars Program, 1979-81; vice chmn. biotech. rsch. subcom. Fed. Coord. Coun. on Sci. Engring. and Tech., Office Sci. and Tech. Policy, 1991-94; exec. sec. subcom. biodiversity and ecosystem dynamics, com. on environment and natural resources Nat. Sci. and Tech. Coun., 1994, mem. interagy. working group on rsch. misconduct policy implementation, 2000—; mem. group nat. experts on safety in biotech., OECD, 1988-89; mem. sr. exec. panel Exec. Potential Program, Office Pers. Mgmt., 1988-89; mem. space shuttle proposal rev. panel in life scis. NASA, 1978, rsch. assocs. in space biology award com., 1985-91, chmn. cell and devel. biology discipline working group, space biology program, 1990-91, chmn. gravitational biology panel, NASA Specialized Ctrs. Rsch. and Tng., 1990, chmn. NASA specialized ctrs. rsch. and tng. peer rev. panel, 1995, mem. exec. steering com. in life scis., 1991, mem. gravitational biology facility sci. working group, 1992-95, mem. space sta. biol. rsch. project sci. working group, 1995-96, mem. NASA neurolab. steering com., 1993; mem. panel study biol. diversity, Bd. Sci. and Tech. Internat. Devel. NRC, 1989; exec. sec. adv. planning bd. Nat. Biodiversity Info. Ctr., Smithsonian Instn., 1993-94; mem. adv. screening com. in life scis. Coun. for Internat. Exchange of Scholars, 1978-81; liaison rep. nat. heart, lung and blood adv. coun. NIH, 1979-87, nat. adv. child health and human devel. coun., 1990-99; recombinant DNA adv. com., 1988; liaison representative agrl. biotech. Rsch. Adv. com., USDA, 1989-94; mem. Interagy. Rsch. animal com., 1984-88; Interagency working group on Internat. Biotech., 1988-94; chmn. proposal panel in biology Sci. Found. Ireland, 2002, Human Proteomics Site Visit, 2003. Author book chpts. and contbr. articles to profl. jours.; assoc. editor Jour. Exptl. Zoology, 1977-79; editorial adv. bd. Gen. and Comparative Endocrinology, 1982 Mem. world mission com. Ch. of the Redeemer, New Haven, 1967-68; Sunday Sch. steering com. Calvary Episcopal Ch., Cin., 1972-73, sr. acolyte, 1972-77, adult edn. com., 1975-76; deacon Faith Presbyn. Ch., Springfield, Va., 1996-99; adv. com. mem. Wakefield H.S., 1991-92, PTA exec. bd., 1991-92; sci. adv. com. Arlington Pub. Schs., 1987-92, adv. coun. on instrn., 1991-92; adv. bd. mem. Campbell Comml. Coll., Cin., 1977-79. Recipient George Rieveschl, Jr. Rsch. award U. Cin., 1973, Presdl. Rank Meritorious Exec. award NSF, 1992; U. Cin. Grad. Sch. fellow 1977—, NSF fellow 1964; rsch. grantee NSF 1971-79. Fellow AAAS (coun. 1980-83, 89-90, mem. program com. for 1989 ann. meeting 1988, chairperson-elect sect. G-Biol. Scis. 1987-88, chairperson 1988-89, ret. 1989-90), N.Y. Acad. Scis.; mem. Am. Soc. Zoologists (sec., mem. exec. com. 1979-81, chmn. nominating com. 1981, sec. divsn. of comparative physiology and biochemistry 1976-77, chmn. Congl. Sci. Fellow Program com. 1986-89, mem. 1991-93), Soc. for Integrative and Comparative Biology, Am. Physiol. Soc. (program adv. com. 1978-81, program exec. com., 1983-86, mem. steering com., comparative physiology sect. 1978-81, sec. Am. Physiol. Soc.-Am. Soc. Zoologists Task Force on Comparative Physiology 1977-78), Am. Inst. Biol. Scis. (chmn. selection com., congl. sci. fellow zool. scis. 1987, mem. congl. fellow liaisons com. 1991), Sr. Execs. Assn., Assn. of Yale Alumni (del. 1990-93), Mory's Assn., Yale Club (Washington), Masons (32 degree), Shriners, Sigma Xi (Disting. Rsch. award U. Cin. chpt. 1973, pres. U. Cin. chpt. 1977-79), Mensa. Episcopalian. Home: 4087B S Four Mile Run Dr Arlington VA 22204-5604 Office: NSF Ofc Integrative Activities 4201 Wilson Blvd Rm 1270 Arlington VA 22230-0001 E-mail: bumminge@nsf.gov.

UMPIERRE, LUZ MARIA, women studies educator, foreign language educator; b. Santurce, P.R., Oct. 15, 1947; d. Eduardo Umpierre-Pulzoni and Providencia (Herrera) Umpierre. BA, Sagrado Corazón, Santurce, 1970; MA, Bryn Mawr Coll., 1976, PhD, 1978; postgrad., U. Kans., 1981-82, New Sch. for Social Rsch., 1995-96. Asst. prof. Rutgers U., New Brunswick, N.j., 1978-84, assoc. prof., 1984-89; prof., head dept. Western Ky. U., Bowling Green, 1989-91; prof., chair dept. SUNY, Brockport, 1991-94, sr. lectr. Cortland, 1996-97. Vis. asst. prof. Ithaca (N.Y.) Coll., 1997-98; assoc. prof. Bates Coll., Maine, 1998-2000. Author: (poems) In Wonderland, 1982, ...And Other Misfortunes, 1985, The Margarita Poems, 1987, For Christine, 1995; mem. editl. bd. Third Woman Press, 1990—, The Américas Rev., 1989-94. Guest spkr. AIDS Mass., Boston, 1990; sec. N.J. Voters for Civil Liberty, 1984. Named Woman of Yr. Western Ky. U., 1990, Outstanding Woman of Maine U.S. Congress Proclamation, 2002; recipient Lifetime Achievement award Coalition of Gay & Lesbian Orgn. in N.J., 1990; Ford Found. fellow, 1981. Mem. MLA (del. 1978), Mujeres, Feministas Unidas. Avocations: writing, reading, lobbying. Home: PO Box 568 Auburn ME 04212-0568 E-mail: LUmpierre@aol.com.

UNDERDOWN, DAVID EDWARD, historian, educator; b. Wells, Eng., Aug. 19, 1925; s. John Percival and Ethel Mary (Gell) U. BA, U. Oxford, 1950, MA, 1951, Yale U., 1952; B.Litt., U. Oxford, 1953; D.Litt. hon., U. of South, 1981. Asst. prof. U. of South, Sewanee, Tenn., 1953-58, assoc. prof., 1958-62; then assoc. prof. U. Va., Charlottesville, 1962-68; prof. Brown U., Providence, 1968-85, Munro-Goodwin Wilkinson prof., 1978-85; vis. prof. Yale U., New Haven, 1979, prof., 1986-94, George Burton Adams prof., 1994-96, emeritus, 1996—. Dir. Yale Ctr. Parliamentary History, 1985-96; vis. Mellon prof. Inst. for Advanced Study, 1988-89; vis. fellow All Souls Coll., Oxford, 1992; Ford's lectr. Oxford U., 1992. Author: Royalist Conspiracy in England, 1960, Pride's Purge, 1971, Somerset in the Civil War and Interregnum, 1973, Revel, Riot and Rebellion, 1985, Fire from Heaven, 1992, A Freeborn People, 1996, Start of Play, 2000. Guggenheim fellow, 1964-65, 91-92, fellow Am. Coun. Learned Socs., 1973-74, NEH fellow, 1980-81. Fellow Royal Hist. Soc., Brit. Acad. (corrs.); mem. Am. Hist. Assn., Conf. Brit. Studies. Office: Yale U Dept History New Haven CT 06520 E-mail: dunderd@attglobal.net.

UNDERDUE, MARILYN ROSETTA, special education educator; b. Washington, Apr. 20, 1944; d. Houston Cohen Green and Rosetta Virginia (Blackwell) Green Mitchell; m. Hollowell Shields Jones, May 10, 1969 (div. Apr. 1976); 1 child, Alia Michele; m. William Henry Underdue, May 29, 1982. BS, D.C. Tchrs. Coll., 1967. Cert. tchr., D.C. Tchr. 3d grade Washington Pub. Schs., 1967-69; tchr. spl. edn. Dept. of Edn., Wahiawa, Hawaii, 1969-71; tchr. spl. edn. resource D.C. Pub. Schs., Washington, 1972—. Mem. Coun. for Exceptional Children, Blackwell Family Assn. (recording sec. 1973-90, corres. sec. 1990-92, scholarship co-chair 1990-92), P.G. Jack and Jill Am. (fin. sec. 1984-86, treas. 1986-88, Svc. award 1984, 86, 89, 90), Phi Delta Kappa. Democrat. Episcopalian. Avocations: shopping, reading, gardening, cooking, walking. Home: 11306 White House Rd Upper Marlboro MD 20774-2337

UNDERHILL, GLENN MORIS, physics educator, consultant; b. Trenton, Nebr., Oct. 30, 1925; s. George Frederick and Anna Mabel (Jackson) U.; student McCook Jr. Coll., 1942-44; B.S., Kearney State Coll., 1955; M.A. in Physics, U. Nebr., 1957, Ph.D., 1963; m. F. Susan Ann Day, Dec. 27, 1958; children: G. Mark, Rachel S. Underhill Lueck, Sterling D., Gretchen E. Underhill Hinkle, Cynthia A. Underhill Hanus, Enoch M. Head tchr. Gordon (Nebr.) Indian Sch., 1950-53; grad. asst. U. Nebr., Lincoln, 1955-59, instr., 1960-62; assoc. prof. Kearney (Nebr.) State Coll., 1963-67, planetarium dir., 1966-91, prof. physics, 1967-91, head dept. physics and phys. sci., 1971-77; cons.; vis. lectr. various schs.; lectr. in field. Mem. Riverdale (Nebr.) Village Bd., 1978—, chmn. bd., 1978— . Recipient Council of Deans Service award Kearney State Coll., 1983, Nebr. Admirals award. Mem. Am. Phys. Soc., Am. Assn. Physics Tchrs., Nebr. Acad. Sci., AAAS, Sigma Xi, Lambda Delta Lambda, Sigma Tau Delta, Kappa Delta Pi. Republican. Mem. Ch. of God. Contbr. articles to profl. jours. Home: PO Box 70 Riverdale NE 68870-0070 Office: U Nebr-Kearney Kearney NE 68849

UNDERWOOD, DEANNA KAY, librarian; b. Medicine Lodge, Kans., Oct. 2, 1962; d. Kenneth Edward and Janet Sue (Hammond) Winters; m. Roger Alan Underwood, Aug. 2, 1986; children: Lane Alan, Lindsey Kay. BS in Elem. Edn., Sterling (Kans.) Coll., 1984. Tchr. 4th grade White Rock Elem. Sch., Burr Oak, Kans., 1984-86, tchr. kindergarten Esbon, Kans., 1986-87; libr. aide mid. and high schs. White Rock Schs., Esbon and Burr Oak, 1987-91, K-12 libr., 1992—. Chmn. reading com., mem. ednl. leadership team com. Unified Sch. Dist. 104, Esbon and Burr Oak, 1993—. Chmn. adminstrv. coun. United Meth. Ch., Esbon, 1989—, trustee coun., 1993—. Mem.: Kans. Assn. Sch. Librs. Republican. Avocations: reading, cooking, cross-stitch. Home: RR 1 Box 14 Esbon KS 66941-9703 Office: White Rock HS PO Box 345 633 Main St Burr Oak KS 66936-9738

UNDERWOOD, MARTHA JANE MENKE, artist, educator; b. Quincy, Ill., Nov. 28, 1934; d. Francis Norman Menke and Ruth Rosemary (Wells) Zoller; divorced; children: Leslie, Stephen. BA, Scripps Coll., 1956; MFA, Otis Art Inst., 1958. Cert. adult edn. and post secondary tchr. Designer staineglass windows Wallis-Wiley Studio, Pasadena, Calif., 1959-60; mural asst., designer Millard Sheets Murals, Inc., Claremont, Calif., 1960-68; art instr. adult edn. Monrovia, Pomona and Claremont Sch. Dists., Calif., 1967-69; prof. art Chaffey C.C., Alta Loma, Calif., 1970-96; ret., 1996; free lance illustrator, 1975—; watercolorist, 1970—. Lectr. and demonstrator in field; judge many art competitions, 2000-2002; watercolor demonstrator to various art assns., Southern Calif. Contbr. photographs to: How to Create Your Own Designs, 1968, Weaving Without Loom, 1969; illustrator: Opening a Can of Words, 1994, coloring books about baseball team mascots, 1995, 96, 98; contbr. illustrations to Wayfarers Jour. Co-chmn. Recording for the Blind Art Fundraiser, Upland, Calif., 1995-2002; bd. dirs. Scripps Fine Arts Found, co-pres. 1999-2002; art fundraiser RCFB, 2003. Recipient Strathmore award, 1985, Grumbacher awards Assoc. Artists of Upland, Calif., 1990, 92, 95, 96, 2000, Assoc. Artists of Inland Empire, Grumbacher award, 2001, Daniel Smith award Assoc. Artists Open Show, 2002; Faculty Initiated Projects Program grantee, 1991-92. Mem. Assoc. Artists, Pomona Valley Art Assn., Chaffey Cmty. Art Assn. (bd. dirs., exhbn. chmn. 2000), L.A. County Fair Assn. (Millard Sheets gallery com.), Assoc. Art Assn. (chmn. 2003). Avocations: travel, languages, history, golf.

UNGAR, ROSELVA MAY, primary and elementary educator; b. Detroit, Oct. 31, 1926; d. John and Elva Rushton; m. Kenneth Sawyer Goodman, Dec. 26, 1946 (div. 1950); m. Fred Ungar, June 22, 1952 (div. 1977); children: Daniel Brian, Carol Leslie, Lisa Maya. Student, U. Mich., 1946-48; BA, UCLA; MA, Pacific Oaks Coll. Cert. elem. tchr.; cert. early childhood; bilingual cert. of competency in Spanish. Recreation dir. Detroit City Parks and Recreation, 1946-50, L.A. Unified Sch. Dist., 1950-52, tchr., 1984—2001, mentor tchr. elem. edn., 1988-94, ret., 2001; tchr. head start Found. Early Childhood Edn., L.A., 1965-73; staff organizer Early Childhood Fedn. Local 1475 AFT, L.A., 1973-79; staff rep. Calif. Fedn. Tchrs., L.A., 1979-83. Contbr. articles to profl. jours. Mem. Gov.'s Adv. Com. Child Care, L.A., 1980-83; mem. Sierra Club, 1978—; mem. So. Calif. Libr. Social Studies, L.A., 1989—; charter mem. Mus. Am. Indian Smithsonian Inst., 1994—; Nat. Ctr. Early Childhood Workforce, Children's Def. Fund, Womens Internat. League for Peace and Freedom, ACLU, So. Poverty Law Ctr., Food First, Meiklejohn Civil Liberties Inst.; bd. dirs., pres. Found. for Early Childhood Edn., 1997—, Coalition Progressive L.A. Mem. Nat. Assn. Multicultural Edn. Adv. Bd. (teach L.A., UCLA Ctr.), Calif. Assn. Bilingual Edn., So. Calif. Assn., Edn. Young Children, Early Childhood Fedn. (pres. emeritus 1979—), United Tchrs. L.A. (chpt. chair 1984-96, east area dir. and UTLA bd. dirs. 1996-99), L.A. Coalition Labor Union Women (charter; bd. dirs. 1980-86). Avocations: guitar, folk songs, hiking. Home: 20349 Jay Carroll Dr Santa Clarita CA 91350-1959 E-mail: roselvau@yahoo.com.

UNGER, ROBERTA MARIE, special education educator; b. Oakland, Calif., Apr. 22, 1944; d. Lowber and Roberta June (Hedrick) Randolph; m. William Mitchell Unger, Jr., June 29, 1970; 1 child by previous marriage, Diana Marie Holt; 1 child, William Mitchell III. BA in Edn., San Francisco State U., 1965; postgrad., Utah State U., 1967, 73, Frostburg (Md.) State U., 1973, 84, Lamar U., 1991; MA in Ednl. Adminstrn., W.Va. U., 1984. Cert. tchr., Calif., Utah, Md., W.Va.; cert. elem. tchr., supervising tchr., tchr. edn. assoc. elem. edn./mentally retarded, English tchr., gifted edn., learning disabilities, behavior disorders, pre-sch. tchr., mentally retarded, W.Va. Tchr. 2d grade North Park Elem. Sch., Box Elder County, Utah, 1965-67; tchr. spl. edn. emotionally disturbed grades 5-8 Centre St. Sch., Allegany County, Md., 1967-68; tchr. 3rd grade Dennett Rd. Elem. Sch., Garrett County, Md., 1968-69; tchr. 2d & 3rd grades Grantsville Elem. Sch., Garrett County, Md., 1969-70; tchr. 1-high sch. grades spl. and regular edn. Short Gap Elem. Sch., Mineral County, W.Va., 1970-77; supervising tchr. W.Va. U., Morgantown, 1973-76; tchr. summer satellite program gifted edn. Frostburg State U., 1985; tchr. spl. edn. Frankfort H.S., Ridgeley, W.Va., 1977—, collaborative and consulting spl. edn. tchr., 1983—, mentor tchr., 1991-92, 96-97. Former vol. San Francisco Hosp.; past usher Oakland Civic Light Opera Assn.; mem. Cmty. Concert Assn., Allied Arts Coun., St. Thomas Woman's Study Group, No. Maidu Tribe Calif. Native Ams., Frostburg Cmty. Orch., 1968; dir. youth programs grades 7-12 Emmanuel Episcopal Ch., Cumberland (Md.) Sunday Sch. tchr.; coach Odyssey of the Mind, 1987—; club sponsor Ski Club, AFS, Classic Club. Grantee W.Va. Dept. Edn., 1986, 87, 89-91; Match Free Competitive grantee W.Va. Dept. Edn., 1990-91. Mem. NEA, W.Va. Edn. Assn., Mineral County Edn. Assn. (past bldg. rep., past dept. chair spl. edn., past county chair mentally impaired, past chair county secondary integrative collaboration com., county chair integrative collaboration spl. edn. svc. ages 6-12), Nat. Coun. for Exceptional Children (nat. conv. presenter 1989, 92, 93, 95, 97), W.Va. State Coun. for Exceptional Children (Mem. of Yr. award 1991, state conf. presenter 1984—, sec. 1990, 91, 92, v.p. 1993, pres.-elect 1994, pres. 1995-96, newsletter editor 1992—, subdivsn. mental retardation developmental disabilities organizing chair 1992-93, pres. divsn. mental retardation 1994-95, pres., chair state conv. 1993—, coun. exceptional children Nat. MRDD membership com. 1995—, coun. exceptional children Nat. DLD multicultural com., 1995—), Coun. for Exceptional Children (v.p. W.Va. divsn. learning disabilities 1988, membership chmn. 1988-89, pres. 1990, newsletter editor divsn. learning disabilities 1991—, sec. Coun. Exceptional Children Am. Indian caucus 1989—, del. nat. conv. 1990—), Am. Indian Soc. Washington, Allegany County Hist. Soc., Mineral County Hist. Soc., Mooretown Maidu Rancheria. Episcopalian. Avocations: playing piano and cello, skiing, painting and sewing, operating farmette, collecting antiques. Office: Frankfort High Sch RR 3 Box 169 Ridgeley WV 26753-9510

UNSWORTH, MICHAEL EDWARD, university librarian; b. Indpls., July 10, 1950; s. Cecil Walker and Dorothy Louise (Wolf) U.; m. Lynn Maria Kaczor, Feb. 12, 1977 (div. Sept. 1981). BA, Ind. U.-Purdue U., Indpls., 1973; MLS, Ind. U., Bloomington, 1974; MA, U. Notre Dame, 1978. Libr. U. Notre Dame, Ind., 1974-79, Colo. State U., Ft. Collins, 1979-84, Mich. State U., East Lansing, 1984—. Cons. Chadwyk-Healey, Inc., Alexandria, Va., 1988—; intern Inst. for Editing of Hist. Documents, Madison, Wis., 1993; asst. dir. Can. Studies Ctr. Mich. State U., 1999—. Co-author: Future War Novels, 1984; editor: Military Periodicals, 1990; mem. editl. bd. Mich. State U. Press, 1994—; contbr. articles to profl. publs. Mem. faculty coun. U. Notre Dame, 1978; mem. Mich. Freedom of Info. Com.; bd. dirs. Greater Lansing Hist. Soc., 1991-93. Recipient Faculty Rsch. grant Can. Embassy, 1997. Mem. Assn. for Bibliography of History, Soc. for Mil. History, Hist. Soc. Mich., Mich. Oral History Soc. Avocations: hiking, backpacking, cross-country skiing. Home: PO Box 6253 East Lansing MI 48826-6253 Office: Mich State Univ Libraries East Lansing MI 48824

UNWIN, CYNTHIA GIRARD, secondary education educator; b. Littleton, Colo., May 3, 1964; d. Larry J. and Judith S. (Smiley) Girard; m. Brian K. Unwin, Aug. 10, 1985; children: Kelly Marie, Emily Elizabeth. BA Psychology, U. Colo., 1985; MEd, Auburn U., 1989, PhD, 1993. Cert. tchr., Ga. Classroom tchr. Holy Cross Sch., Garrett Park, Md., 1986-88; grad. tchg. asst. Auburn (Ala.) U., 1988-93, instr., 1994, Columbus (Ga.) Coll., 1992-94; chpt. I tchr. Harlem (Ga.) Mid. Sch., 1994-97; asst. prof. reading edn. Augusta (Ga.) State U., 1997—99; reading tchr. Killeen (Tex.) Ind. Sch. Dist., 1999—2002; reading cons., children's author, 2002—. Youth ministry vol. Holy Cross Ch., Garrett Park, 1986-88, St. Anne Ch., Columbus, 1988-94. Mem. Internat. Reading Assn. (coun. pres. 1992-94, 2000—), Nat. Coun. Tchrs. English, Assembly on Lit. for Adolescents/NCTE, Phi Delta Kappa (Outstanding Dissertation award Auburn chpt. 1994), Phi Beta Kappa. Roman Catholic. Avocations: reading, gardening, photography. Home: 2109 Grizzly Trl Harker Heights TX 76548-5657

UPCHURCH, SALLY ANN, school counselor; b. Owensboro, Ky., July 16, 1951; d. Ezekiel Thomas and Anna Myrl (Duncan) Allen; m. Gary Allen Upchurch, Aug. 5, 1972; children: Jeffrey Allen, Gregory Wayne, Michael Shane. BA in English Lang. and Lit. Edn., Ky. Wesleyan Coll., 1974; MA in Guidance and Counseling Edn., Western Ky. U., 1979, postgrad., 1984—. Cert. English tchr., guidance and counseling, Ky. English tchr. Fordsville (Ky.) High Sch., 1974-76; lang. arts tchr. Ohio County Mid. Sch., Hartford, Ky., 1976-90; guidance counselor Ohio County Schs., Hartford, 1990—. Pres. Central City Bus. and Profl. Women, 1989-91, del. nat. conv., 1989, del. Ky. conv., 1988-90, bd. dirs. S.W. region, 1991, bd. dirs. Ky., 1989-91. Named Woman of Yr., Central City Bus. and Profl. Women, 1988, Appreciation award, Central City Bus. and Profl. Women, 1990; named Ky. Col., State of Ky., 1990. Mem. Ky. Counseling Assn., Ky. Sch. Counselors Assn., Am. Counseling Assn., Daviess/McLean Bapt. Assn. (child care com. 1989-93). Baptist. Avocations: church librarian, reading, singing, music, cooking. Home: 1644 Hamlin Chapel Rd Hartford KY 42347-9712 Office: Fordsville Sch 359 W Main St Fordsville KY 42343-9763

UPHAM, STEADMAN, anthropology educator, university dean, academic administrator; b. Denver, Apr. 4, 1949; s. Albert Tyler and Jane Catherine (Steadman) U; m. Margaret Anne Cooper, Aug. 21, 1971; children: Erin Cooper, Nathan Steadman. BA, U. Redlands, 1971; MA, Ariz. State U., 1977, PhD, 1980. Dist. sales mgr. Ind. News Co. Inc., Los Angeles, 1971-72; regional sales mgr. Petersen Pub. Co, Los Angeles, 1972-74; archeologist, researcher Bur. Land Mgmt., Phoenix, 1979; research asst. Ariz. State U., Tempe, 1979-80; chief archeologist Soil Sytems Inc., Phoenix, 1980-81, N.Mex. State U., Las Cruces, N.Mex., 1981-85, asst. prof. to assoc. prof., 1982-87, assoc. dean, 1987-90; prof. anthropology, vice provost for rsch., grad. dean U. Oreg., Eugene, 1990—. Inerim dir. Cultural Resources Mgmt. divsn. N.Mex. State U., Las Cruces, 1988; mem. exec. com. Assn. Grad. Schs., 1994—; bd. dirs. Coun. Grad. Schs., 1995—. Author: Polities and Power, 1982, A Hopi Social History, 1992; editor: Computer Graphics in Archaeology, 1979, Mogollon Variability, 1986, The Sociopolitical Structure of Prehistoric Southwest Societies, 1989, The Evolution of Political Systems, 1990; also articles. Advanced seminar grantee Sch. of Am. Research, 1987, research grantee NSF, 1979, 1984-85, Hist. Preservation grantee State of N.Mex., 1982-84, 1991, 92, Ford Found. 1991-92, U.S. Dept. Edn. 1991-93. Fellow Am. Anthropol. Assn.; mem. Nat. Phys. Sci. Consortium (pres. 1992-95), We. Assn. Grad. Schs. (pres. 1994-95), Assn. Grad. Schs. (exec. com. 1995—), Coun. Grad. Schs. (bd. dirs. 1995—). Office: U Oreg Office Acad Affairs 207 Johnson Hall Eugene OR 97403

UPSHUR, CAROLE CHRISTOFK, psychologist, educator; b. Des Moines, Oct. 18, 1948; d. Robert Richard and Margaret (Davis) Chistofk; 1 child, Emily. AB, U. So. Calif., 1969; EdM, Harvard U., 1970, EdD, 1975. Lic. psychologist, Mass. Planner Mass. Com. on Criminal Justice, Boston, 1970-73; licensing specialist, planner, policy specialist Mass. Office for Children, Boston, 1973-76; asst. prof. Coll. Pub. and Cmty. Svc. U. Mass., Boston, 1976-81, assoc. prof., 1982-93, prof., 1993-2001, chmn. Ctr. for Cmty. Planning, 1979—81, 1984—86, 1995—96. Sr. rsch. fellow Maurice Gaston Inst. Latino Pub. Policy, 1993—, Ctr. Social Devel. & Edn., 1991-2001, Gerontology Inst., 1996-2001, McCormack Inst. for Pub. Affairs, dir. PhD in Pub. Policy program, 1995-2001; cons. to govt. and cmty. agencies; assoc. in pediatrics, sr. rsch. assoc. U. Mass. Med. Sch., 1983-94; adj. prof. Heller Sch. Social Welfare, Brandeis U., 1985-98; vis. prof. family medicine and cmty. health U. Mass. Med. Sch. and Meml. Health Care, 2001—. Contbr. articles to profl. jours. Mem. Brookline Human Rels.-Youth Resources Commn., 1988-91, Gov.'s Commn. on Facility Consolidation, 1991-92, Mass. Healthcare Adv. Com., 1993—. Fellow Mass. Psychol. Assn.; mem. APA, APHA, Soc. Tchrs. of Family Medicine. Office: U Mass Med Sch Dept Family Med 55 Lake Ave N Worcester MA 01655

UPTON, LORRAINE FRANCES, elementary education educator; b. Balt., Dec. 26, 1947; d. Meyer and Adeline (Kanstor) Cohen; m. Michael K. Upton, Sept. 25, 1970; 1 child, Matthew Colin. BS, Boston U., 1969; MEd, Temple U., 1974. Cert. elem. tchr., reading specialist, Pa. VISTA employee, Brighton, Mass., 1968; tchr. Boston Pub. Sch. Dist., 1969-70, tchr. 3d grade, 1971-94; tchr. 4th grade Neshaminy Sch. Dist., Langhorne, Pa., 1995—. Instr. The Learning Mag., The Reading Teaching. Contbr. articles to profl. jours. Active social outreach programs; minority inspector during polit. elections, Yardley, Pa.; instr. Learning Mag., The Reading Tchr. Recipient Gift of Time tribute Am. Family Inst. Pa., 1992; Harold C. Case scholar Boston U., 1969. Mem. Internat. Reading Assn., Internat. Platform Assn. Office: Samuel Everett Elem Sch Forsythia Dr Levittown PA 19056 Home: 3 Herrada Way Santa Fe NM 87508-8206

URBAN, PATRICIA A. former elementary school educator; b. Chgo., Oct. 15, 1932; d. Clifford and Caroline (Viegi) Brocken; m. Francis C. Urban, Oct. 20, 1956; children: Jim, David, Anthony, Mary Joan, Barbara, Margaret, Judy, Sharon, Jennifer. BA, Rosary Coll., River Forest, Ill., 1954; MS in Edn., Chgo. State U., 1979; MEd, Loyola U., Chgo., 1986. Cert. tchr., reading tchr., Ill. Tchr. St. Joseph Ch. Sch., Summit, Ill., 1954-56; profl. reading tutor Loyola U., 1987-90; tchr. social studies and reading Dist. 104 Schs., Summit, 1974-94; ret., 1994. Named. Dist. 104 Tchr. of Yr., 1987. Home: 1019 Walter St Lemont IL 60439-3920

URBANSKI, HENRY, foreign language educator; b. Mosciska, Poland, Oct. 9, 1937; s. Marian Urbanski and Anna Klang; m. Dorota Urbanski, Sept. 17, 1963; children: Andre, Ania. BS, St. John Fisher Coll., 1963; MA, Fordham U., 1965; PhD, NYU, 1972, Tashkent State Econ. U., Uzbekistan, 1997. Dist. svc. prof. SUNY, New Paltz, 1965—. Dir. Lang. Immersion Inst., New Paltz, 1981—. Author: Chekhov as Viewed by His Russian Contemporaries, 1979. Recipient Disting. Tchr. award N.Y. State Assn. Fgn. Lang. Tchrs., 1986, Internat. Trade award Hudson Valley C. of C., 1998. Avocations: chess, reading. Office: SUNY New Paltz NY 12561 E-mail: lll@newpaltz.edu.

URCIOLO, JOHN RAPHAEL, II, real estate developer, real estate and finance educator; b. Washington, June 29, 1947; s. Joseph John and Phillie Marie (Petrone) U.; m. Jean Marie Manning, Jan. 2, 1972 (dec. Jan. 1990); m. Andrea Zedalis, Mar. 9, 2002. BBA, Am. U., 1969, MS in real estate, 1971. Cert. real estate broker, appraiser. Rschr. Homer Hoyt Inst., Washington, 1967-69; econ. Nat. Assn. Home Builders, Washington, 1971-75; lectr., assoc. prof. Montgomery Coll., Rockville, Md., 1971-72; assoc. prof. U. Md., College Park, 1972-79; property mgr. Urciolo Realty Co., Washington, 1976-79; comml. broker Urciolo & Urciolo, Washington, 1980-82; real estate developer Urciolo Properties, LLC, Takoma Park, Md., 1982—. Cons. Nat. Ski Area Assn., Hartford, 1978-79, Montgomery County Govt., Rockville, 1980-81; adj. prof. Am. U., Washington, 1980-91; court expert Superior Ct. for D.C., Civil and Criminal divsns.; lectr. to various orgns. Author: Real Estate Manual, 1976; co-author: The White Book of Ski Areas (U.S. and Can.), 1977-79, Industry Edition-The White Book, 1978, The Housing Fact Book, 1976, Housing Component Costs, 1975, 2d edit., 1976, Material Usage in Housing, 1970; co-editor: Labor Wage Rate Bulletin, 1976. Co-chair bd. dirs. Liz Lerman Dance Exch., Takoma Park, Md., 1997—; chmn. facade adv. bd. and Econ. Devel. Com., City of Takoma Park; chmn. bd. Lido Civic Club of Washington. Fellow Urban Mass Transp. Assn., 1969, Am. U., 1970; Soc. Real Estate Appraisers scholar, 1968. Mem. Cert. Real Estate Appraisers, Am. Planning Assn., Am. Univ. Real Estate Assn. (charter, v.p. edn., v.p. award 1983), Rho Epsilon (editor newsletter 1969). Republican. Roman Catholic. Avocations: skiing, golf. Office: Urciolo & Urciolo 6935 Laurel Ave Ste 100 Takoma Park MD 20912-4413

URESTI, RONDA VEVERKA, elementary bilingual education educator; b. Newton, Iowa, May 23, 1963; d. Terry Joe and Carol Jean VeVerka; m. Eulalio Uresti, Dec. 18, 1993; 1 child, Wyatt. BA in Elem. Edn., Ctrl. U., 1994. Cert. tchr. gifted and talented. Instr. mentally challenged adults Progress Ind., Newton, 1989-94; bilingual tchr. San Carlos Elem. Sch., Edinburg, Tex., 1994—. Mem. adv. bd. J & E Corp., Edcouch, Tex., 1989-98; 1st grade curriculum writer, Edinburg Sch. Dist., 1995, 96, mem. assessment adv. com., 1996, mem. tech. com., 1996; G.T. curriculum writer, 1996-97, alignment com. chair, 1996-98. Grantee Jasper Charter Am. Bus. Women's Assn., Newton, 1992, 93. Mem. Ind. Order of Odd Fellows Rebekah Lodge (sec. 1992—), Phi Kappa Phi. Mem. Church of Christ. Avocations: quarter horses, hunting, fishing. Home: Apt C 640 E Fairground St Marion OH 43302-2662

URIBE, JENNIE ANN, elementary school educator; b. National City, Calif., Apr. 17, 1958; d. Robert and Alice (Packard) U. BA, San Diego State U., 1981, cert. teacher, 1982; MB, Nat. Univ., 2000. Tchr. Langdon Ave. Sch., L.A. Unified Sch. Dist., Sepulveda, Calif., 1984-94, tchr. potentally gifted students class, 1987-94; tchr. Spreckels Elem. Sch., San Diego City Schs., 1994—97, Rosa Elem., 1997—. Tchr./advisor for student govt., 1987-93; guide tchr., 1997—; prof. deve. advisor, 1997—. Mem. adv. coun. Sch. Site, 1992-1997. Avocations: tennis, music, movies, reading. Home: 2259 Peach Tree Ln Spring Valley CA 91977-7046 Office: Rosa Parks Elem Sch 4510 Landis St San Diego CA 92103

URISTA, DIANE JEAN, music educator, researcher; b. Mpls., Mar. 28, 1957; d. Joseph and Jean Helen (Sanzenbach) U.; m. Peter John Quehl, June 1, 1985 (div. Sept. 1994); m. Jonathan Jaye Niefeld, July 6, 1996. MusB, Concordia Coll., Moorhead, Minn., 1979; MusM, Northwestern U., 1990; MPhil, Columbia U., 1996. Coord. Children's Music Program Am. Conservatory Music, Chgo., 1986-90; instr. music humanities Columbia U., N.Y.C., 1993—; instr. music theory NYU, N.Y.C., 1997—. Foster parent, Plan Internat., Honduras, 1985— Mellon fellow Columbia U., 1993-97. Mem. AAUW (Am. Dissertation fellow 1997), Coll. Music Soc., Soc. Music Theory, Mu Phi Epsilon. Avocations: reading, poetry, ice skating, movies.

URQUHART, SALLY ANN, environmental scientist, chemist, educator; b. Omaha, June 8, 1946; d. Howard E. and Mary Josephine (Johnson) Lee; m. Henry O. Urquhart, July 31, 1968; children: Mary L. Urquhart Kelly, Andrew L. BS in Chemistry, U. Tex., Arlington, 1968; MS in Environ. Scis., U. Tex., Dallas, 1986. Cert. chemistry and composite H.S. sci., Tex.; lic. asbestos mgmt. planner, Tex. Rsch. asst. U. Tex. Dallas, Richardson, 1980-82; high sch. sci. tchr. Allen (Tex.) Ind. Sch. Dist., 1983-87; hazardous materials specialist Dallas Area Rapid Transit, 1987-90, environ. compliance officer, 1990-94, environmental compliance coordination officer, 1994-95; pres. Comprehensive Environ. Svcs. Inc., Dallas, 1995—2000; tchr. chemistry Richardard Tex. Ind. Sch. Dist., 1998—, tchr. advanced placement chemistry, 2000—. Contbr. articles to Tech. Tchr. Pres. Beacon Sunday Sch. Spring Valley United Meth. Ch., Dallas, 1987, adminstrv. bd. dirs., 1989, com. status and role of women, 1992; vol. Tex. Natural Resource Conservation commn. EnviroMentor Program, 1997-2000. Scholar Richardson (Tex.) Br. AAUW, 1980; recipient dir.'s award Soc. Tex. Environ. Profls., 1997. Mem. Assn. Chemistry Tchrs. Tex., Sci. Tchrs. Assn. Tex., Assn. Tex. Profl. Educators., U. Tex.-Dallas Alumnae Assn. (com. 1992-94). Avocations: jewelry design, counted cross stitching. Home: 310 Sallie Cir Richardson TX 75081-4229

URQUHART, TONY, artist, educator; b. Niagara Falls, Ont., Can., Apr. 9, 1934; s. Archer Marsh and Maryon Louise (Morse) U.; m. Madeline Mary Jennings, July 1958 (div. 1976); children: Allyson, Robin, Marsh, Aidan; m. Mary Jane Carter Keele, May 1976; 1 dau., Emily. B.F.A., U. Buffalo, 1958. Artist-in-residence U. Western Ont., London, 1960-63, 64-65, asst. prof. fine arts, 1967-70, assoc. prof., 1970-72; prof. fine art U. Waterloo, Ont., 1972-99, chmn. dept., 1977-79, 82-85, 94-96, ret., 1999; lectr. McMaster U., Hamilton, Ont., 1966-67. One-man shows Winnipeg Art Gallery, 1959, Walker Art Gallery, Mpls., 1960, Richard Demarco Gallery, Edinburgh, Scotland, 1975, Power of Invention: Drawings from seven decades, Nat. Gallery Can., 2003; group shows, Pitts. Biennial, 1958, Guggenheim Internat., N.Y.C., 1958, Art of the Ams. and Spain, Madrid, Barcelona, Rome, Paris, 1964, Nat. Gallery Can., Toronto, 1972, Mus. Modern Art, Paris, 1976; represented permanent collections, Nat. Gallery Can., Art Gallery, Ont., Fed. Art Bank of Ottawa, Montreal Mus., Vancouver Art Gallery, Mus. Modern Art, Victoria and Albert Mus., London, Museo Civico, Lugano, Switzerland, Hirshhorn Mus., Washington, Bibliotec Nat., Paris; chmn., Jack Chambers Meml. Found., 1978-85; resident artist, Kitchener-Waterloo Art Gallery, Kitchener, Ont., 1981-83; illustrator: The Broken Ark: A Book of Beasts, 1969, I Am Walking in the Garden of His Imaginary Palace by Jane Urquhart, 1982, False Shuffles by Jane Urquhart, 1982, (50 drawings) Cells of Ourselves (text G.M. Dault), 1989, Memories of a Governor General's Daughter, 1990, Warbrain: poems by Stuart MacKinnon, 1994, Walking to the Saints, by Anne McPherson, 2000. Decorated Order of Can.; recipient Edits, I Arts Coun., Ont., 1974, Kilchener Waterloo Visual Arts award, 1994; winner Nat. Outdoor Sculpture Competition MacDonald Stewart Art Ctr., 1987, Outdoor Sculpture competition, Rim Park, Waterloo, 2002; grantee Can. Coun. award, 1963, 79, travel grantee, 1967, 69, 70, 74, 75, 76, 88, 91, project cost grantee, 1981, 82, short-term grantee, 1991, All Can. Coun. Mem. Can. Artists Representation (1 of 3 founding mem.'s, sec. 1968-71, life 1999), Nat. Gallery of Can. (life), Art Gallery of Ont. (life), London Reginal Art Gallery (life), MacDonald Stewart Art Centre Gallery Stratford (life). Office: Dept Fine Arts U Waterloo Waterloo ON Canada N2L 3G1

URSPRUNG, DEBORAH LYNN, special education educator, counselor; b. Liberty, Tex., Sept. 10, 1952; d. Norman Arnold and Roberta Starr (Gay) U.; m. Ernest Fredrick Fritzsching, July 14, 1979 (div. Dec. 1982). Grad., Sam Houston State U., Huntsville, Tex., 1975; MEd, Lamar U., 1999. Cert. tchr., elem. tchr., psychology, spl. edn. tchr., Tex. Elem. tchr. psychology, tchr. spl. edn. Aldine Ind. Sch. Dist., Houston, 1976-79; secondary tchr. spl. edn. Tarkington (Tex.) Ind. Sch. Dist., 1982-85, Vidor (Tex.) Ind. Sch. Dist., 1985-93, Hull Daisetta (Tex.) Ind. Sch. Dist., 1994—; resource counselor Channelview (Tex.) Ind. Sch. Dist., 2000—. Mem. support staff Channelview Ind. Sch. Dist. Mem. ASCD, AAUW, Am. Counseling Assn., Assn. Spiritual, Ethical and Religious Values in Counseling, Tex. Assn. Classroom Tchrs., Archaeology Inst. Am., Alpha Delta Kappa (sec. 1996—). Republican. Roman Catholic. Avocations: southwest art and jewelry, needlework, travel, archaeology, natural history. Home: PO Box 725 Rye TX 77369-0725 Office: Channelview Ind Sch Dist 1403 Sheldon Rd Channelview TX 77530-2603

USEEM, MICHAEL, management consultant educator; b. Nov. 6, 1942; s. John Herald and Ruth (Hill) U.; m. Elizabeth Livingston, June 15, 1968; children: Jerry, Andrea, Susan. BS in Physics, U. Mich., 1964; MA in Physics, Harvard U., 1966, PhD in Sociology, 1970. Prof. mgmt. U. Pa., Phila., 1990—. Dir. Wharton Ctr. for Leadership and Change Mgmt.; cons. in field. Author: The Inner Circle, 1984, Liberal Education and the Corporation, 1989, Executive Defense, 1993, Investor Capitalism, 1996, The Leadership Moment, 1998, Leading Up, 2001; co-author: Upward Bound, 2003. Office: U Pa Wharton Sch Mgmt Dept Philadelphia PA 19104-6370 E-mail: useem@wharton.upenn.edu.

USELTON, DARRELL BRENT, social sciences educator, researcher; b. Union City, Tenn., Mar. 17, 1954; s. James Edward Uselton and Nancy Eleanor Sawyer; m. Rebecca Gail Barnett, Mar. 9, 1974 (div.); m. Mary Beth Doty, May 8, 1982. BA, U. Memphis, 1995; grad., Mil. Police Sch., Ft. Gordon, Ga., 1973, Tenn. Law Enforcement Tng. Acad., Nashville, 1977; MA, U. Memphis, 1997. Legal investigator, bus. mgr. Gerber & Gerber law firm, Memphis, 1979—83; exec. adminstr. Fogelman Properties, Inc., Memphis, 1983—84; sales adminstr., asst. v.p. Union Planters Investment Ganking Group, Memphis, 1984—88; regoinal mgr., asst. v.p. Storage USA, Inc., Memphis, 1988—89; asst. mgr. ednl. coord. Mississippi River Mus., Memphis, 1995; history instr. U. Memphis, 1998—; social scis. instr. Mid-South C.C., West Memphis, Ark., 1998—2003, Strayer U., 2003—; rsch. assoc. Ctr. for Rsch. and Ednl. Policy U. Memphis, 2003—.

Bd. dirs. Sales and Mktg. Execs. of Memphis, Inc., 1989; faculty advisor Phi Theta Kappa Nat. Honors Soc., 1999—. Contbr. articles to profl. jours. Coord. Citizens for Better Govt. PAC, Memphis, 1983—84. Mem.: Phi Alpha Theta.

USHER, CHARLES LINDSEY, social work educator, public policy analyst; b. Portsmouth, Va., Aug. 12, 1949; s. Henry George and Lottie Frances (Dickens) U.; m. Janan Bailey, Aug. 14, 1971; children: Lindsay Erin, Ellen Ashley. BA in Polit. Sci., Old Dominion U., 1971, M in Urban Studies, 1974; postgrad., U. Mich., 1975; PhD in Polit. Sci., Emory U., 1976. Asst. prof. polit. sci. Miami U. of Ohio, Oxford, 1976-78, U. N.C., Charlotte, 1978-80; policy analyst, sr. policy analyst Rsch. Triangle Inst., Rsch. Triangle Park, N.C., 1980-84, dir. Ctr. for Policy Studies, 1985-92; exec. dir. Northeastern N.C. Tomorrow, Inc., Elizabeth City, 1984-85; Wallace H. Kuralt Sr. prof. pub. welfare policy/adminstrn. U. N.C., Chapel Hill, 1993—. Presenter in field. Assoc. editor Evaluation Rev., 1987-89; contbr. articles to profl. jours. Grantee Annie E. Casey Found., 1992—, Edna McConnel Clark Found., 1995-96. Mem. ASPA, Am. Evaluation Assn., Am. Pub. Human Svcs. Home: 4215 Swarthmore Rd Durham NC 27707-5389 Office: U NC Sch Social Work 301 Pittsboro St Chapel Hill NC 27599-3550

USHER, MARY MARGARET, special education educator; b. Chgo., July 5, 1949; d. Earl Raymond and Rebecca Patricia (McElroy) Asher; m. James Lee Usher; children: Sherri, Michael, Lori. BS in Edn., U. North Tex., 1971; cert. in behaviorally disorder, Harris Stowe State Coll., 1991. Cert. tchr., Mo.; cert. tchr. learning disabled, mentally handicapped. Substitute tchr. Fox Sch. Dist., Arnold, Mo., 1986-87, 89—, Windsor Sch. Dist., Imperial, Mo., 1985-87, 89—, Spl. Svcs. Co-op., Imperial, 1987, 89—; paraprofessional physically impaired class Pevely Elem., 1992—; juvenile detention ctr. tchr. Jefferson County Children's Home, Mo., 1993-96; spl. edn. tchr. Mo. Eastern Correctional Ctr., Pacific, 1997-2000, Windsor H.S., Imperial, Mo., 2000—01; substitute tchr. Spl. Sch. Dist. St. Louis County, St. Louis, 2001—02, Mehlville Sch. Dist., St. Louis, 2001—02; spl. edn. tchr. Hawthorn Children's Psychiatric Hosp., 2002—. V.p. bd. dirs. Imperial Khoury League, 1987—89, chmn. ways and means com., 1989—90; dist. sec. United Meth. Women, 1993—96; United Meth. Women mem. nominations com. Gateway Ctrl. dist., 2003—; pres. New Hope United Meth. Ch., 1990—91, sec., 1998—99, coord. for interpretation of edn. in mission, nominating com., pres., 2002, New Hope United Meth. Women, 2001—. Mem. Coun. for Exceptional Children (pres. 1991, v.p. Jefferson County chpt. 1994-95, pres. Jefferson County chpt. 1995-96), St. Louis Zoo Friends Assn., Friends of Jefferson County Libr., Kappa Delta. Avocations: reading, crossword puzzles, travel, country western dancing. Home: 5125 Darkmoor Ln Imperial MO 63052-3032 E-mail: mmu1949@hotmail.com.

USHER, NANCY SPEAR, retired language arts educator; b. Malden, Mass., Mar. 13, 1938; d. George Alonzo and Mary Elizabeth (York) Spear; m. Walter Lansley Whitlock, June 13, 1959 (div. Oct. 1961); m. Frederic Laurence Usher, Apr. 19, 1970 (dec. April 1998). BS in Edn., U. So. Maine, 1960; postgrad., Boston U., Salem State Coll., 1964-68. 5th grade tchr. Melrose (Mass.) Sch. Dept., 1961-63, 7th grade English tchr., 1963-65, 71-97, 7th grade spl. needs tchr., 1965-70; ret., 1997. Freshman girls' basketball coach Melrose High Athletic Dept., 1973-77. Mem. U. So. Maine Alumni Assn. Avocations: golf, boating, reading. E-mail: nusher38@aol.com.

USRY, JANA PRIVETTE, special education educator; b. Richmond, Va., Oct. 23, 1943; d. Millard Due and Dorothy (Daneman) Privette; m. David Page Usry, Feb. 5, 1972 (dec. Sept. 1975); 1 stepchild, Stephanie Page Usry. BA in Psychology, Mary Washington Coll.; MEd in Spl. Edn., U. Va.; postgrad., Va. Commonwealth U., 1984. Cert. tchr. psychology, and spl. edn.; cert. spl. edn. supr., elem. and secondary prin., secondary sch. adminstr. and supr. Tchr. emotionally disturbed Va. Treatment Ctr. for Children, summer 1966; program cons. Va. Soc. for Prevention of Blindness, Inc., 1966-67; tchr. emotionally disturbed, intermediate and self-contained Henrico County Pub. Schs., 1967-70; tchr. emotionally disturbed and learning disabled The Learning Ctr., St. Joseph's Villa, 1971-73; ednl. cons., tchr. dept. pediatrics, adolescent unit Med. Coll. of Va., 1973-74; spl. edn. tchr. Albert Hill Mid. Sch./Richmond Pub. Schs., 1974-78, Thomas Jefferson High Sch./Richmond Pub. Schs., 1978-86, United Meth. Family Svcs., 1986-87, Monacan High Sch., Chesterfield County, 1987-88, Higland Springs High Sch./Henrico County Pub. Schs., 1988-93; tchr. Henrico Juvenile Detention Home, Richmond, Va., 1993-95; tchr., adminstrv. asst. Henrico H.S., Richmond, 1995—. Organizer learning disabilities workshop Supt.'s Sch. for the Gifted, 1980; condr. workshops and state convs. for learning disabled youth Va. Assn. for Children with Learning Disabilities, 1980, 81; condr. in-svc. workshop fgn. lang. tchrs. City of Richmond, 1982-83; participant learning disabilities workshop Va. State Dept. of Spl. Edn., Lynchburg, 1983; condr. learning disabilities workshops Richmond Pub. Schs., spring 1983; mem. com. on permanent records for exceptional edn. Richmond Pub. Schs., 1984, sponsor cheerleaders, pep club, other extra-curricular activities; mem. spl. edn. curriculum task force Learning Disabilities Sect. Henrico County Pub. Schs., 1989-90; mem. leadership team, faculty trainer Highland Springs High Sch. Moving Up Project, 1989-90, 90-91; guest speaker Found. for Dyslexia, 1991. Member Westhampton Jr. Woman's Club, Richmond, 1967-71, Women's Com. of Richmond Symphony, 1971-78, Va. Mus. of Fine Arts, Richmond, 1967-78, Richmond Symphony Chorus, 1991—. Mem. NEA, ASCD, Va. Edn. Assn., Learning Disability Assn. Va., Learning Disability Assn. Richmond, Henrico Edn. Assn., Orton Dyslexia Soc., Coun. for Exceptional Children (past treas. state unit devel. com., past del. assembly Nat. Conv.), Learning Disabilities Assn., Richmond Jazz Soc., U. Va. Alumni Assn., Mary Washington Coll. Alumni Assn. (class agt., past pres. Richmond chpt.), Mu Phi Epsilon, Phi Delta Kappa. Avocations: ballet, modern dance, classical piano, snow skiing, gourmet cooking. Home: PO Box 25692 Richmond VA 23260-5692

UTKU, SENOL, civil engineer, computer science educator; b. Suruc, Turkey, Nov. 23, 1931; s. Sukru and Sukufe (Gumus) U.; m. Bisulay Bereket, May 9, 1964; children: Ayda, Sinan. Diploma in engring., Istanbul Tech. U., 1954; MS, MIT, 1959, ScD, 1960. Civil engr., Istanbul, Turkey. Rsch. engr. IBM, 1959-60; asst. prof. structural engring MIT, 1960-62; assoc. prof. Middle East Tech U., Ankara, Turkey, 1962-63; exec. dir. Computation Ctr., Istanbul Tech. U., 1963-65; tech. staff Jet Propulsion Lab., Pasadena, Calif., 1965-70; assoc. prof. civil engring Duke U., Durham, N.C., 1970-72, prof., 1972-79, prof. civil engring., prof. computer sci., 1979—2001, dir. undergrad. studies, 1980-87, dir. grad. studies, 1987-89, prof. emeritus civil engring. and computer sci., 2002—; prof. emetirus engring. scis. Istanbul Tech. U., 1994—. Sr. Fulbright lectr., Turkey, 1998. Author: ELAS Software, 1968, Elementary Structural Analysis, 4th edit., 1991, Linear Analysis of Discrete Structures, 1991, Theory of Adaptive Structures, 1998; co-author: Dynamics of Offshore Structures, 1984, Finite Element Handbook, 1987, Parallel Processing in Computational Mechanics, 1992, Intelligent Structural Systems, 1992; contbr. articles to profl. jours. Fulbright scholar, Turkey, 1957; recipient Pres.'s Fund award Calif. Inst. Tech., 1981, NASA award, 1969, 71, 77, 84, 86-87, Internat. Joint Rsch. award NSF, 1991-92. Fellow ASCE; mem. AAUP, Am. Acad. Mechanics, Fulbright Assn., Am. Soc. for Engring. Edn., Structural Engring. Inst. (charter), Sigma Xi, Chi Epsilon. Office: Duke U 121 Hudson Hall Durham NC 27708-0287 E-mail: bsutku@ttnet.net.tr., senol.utku@duke.edu.

UTLEY, F. KNOWLTON, library director, educator; b. Northampton, Mass., May 4, 1935; s. Frederick K. and Florence E. (Moore) Utley; m. Faith E. Green, July 2, 1960; children: Richard F., Stephen R., David E. BS, Castleton State Coll., 1960; MA, U. Conn., 1967; EdD, Boston U., 1979; MLS, U. Ala., 1993. Tchr. indsl. arts Montpelier (Vt.) High Sch., 1960-61, Southwick (Mass.) High Sch., 1961-63; tchr., drafting instr. Putnam (Conn.) High Sch., 1963-68; media specialist Cen. Conn. State U., New Britain, 1968-69, dir. media svcs., 1969-72; doctoral teaching fellow Boston U., 1972-73; dir. libr., media svcs. Manchester (Mass.) Pub. Schs., 1973-79; assoc. prof. libr. scis. U. Maine, Farmington, 1979-80; dir. grad. program libr. media Livingston (Ala.) U., 1980-83; dir. libr. media svcs. Am. Internat. Coll., Springfield, Mass., 1983—. Pres. C/W Mars-Ctrl. and We. Mass. Auto Res., 1987—88; chmn. bd. dirs. Cooperating Librs. of Great Springfield, 1988—89, We. Mass. Media Coun., 1991—93; founder, headmaster Hampshire Christian Acad., South Hadley, Mass., 1996—2002. Mem. Belchertown Housing Authority, 2000—; trustee Clapp Meml. Libr., Belchertown, Mass., 2003—. Mem.: ALA, Mass. Libr. Assn., Mass. Sch. Libr. Media Assn., New Eng. Libr. Assn., New Eng. Edn. Media Assn., Assn. Edn. Comm. and Tech., Am. Christian Schs. Internat., Phi Delta Kappa. Home: 11 Canal Dr Belchertown MA 01007-9224 Office: Am Internat Coll 1000 State St Springfield MA 01109-3151 E-mail: kutley@cwmars.org.

UTLEY, ROSE, nursing educator and researcher; b. Broken Arrow, Okla., Aug. 31, 1953; d. Reuben D. and Margie B. (Hudson) U. ADN, Rochester C.C., Minn., 1976; BSN, U. Minn., 1981, MS, 1985; PhD, Wayne State U. RN, N.D., Mich.; CEN. Staff nurse emergency dept. Fairview Community Hosp., Mpls., 1979-86; instr. nursing U. N.D., Grand Forks, 1985-87, U. Mich., Ann Arbor, 1987-91; staff nurse emergency dept. Saratoga Hosp., Detroit, 1991-97. Contbr. articles to profl. jours. Mem. AACCN, Emergency Nurses Assn., Sigma Theta. Home: 6504 S Farm Road 189 Rogersville MO 65742-8257

UTTAL, WILLIAM R(EICHENSTEIN), psychology and engineering educator, research scientist; b. Mineola, N.Y., Mar. 24, 1931; s. Joseph and Claire (Reichenstein) U.; m. Michiye Nishimura, Dec. 20, 1954; children: Taneil, Lynet, Lisa. Student, Miami U. Oxford, Ohio, 1947-48; BS in Physics, U. Cin., 1951; PhD in Exptl. Psychology and Biophysics, Ohio State U., 1957. Staff Psychologist, mgr. behavioral sci. group IBM Rsch. Ctr., Yorktown Heights, NY, 1957-63; assoc. prof. U. Mich., Ann Arbor, 1963-68, prof. psychology, 1968-86, rsch. scientist, 1963-86, prof. emeritus, 1986—; grad. affiliate faculty dept. psychology U. Hawaii, 1986-88; rsch. scientist Naval Ocean Systems Ctr.-Hawaii Lab., Kailua, 1985-88; prof., chmn. dept. psychology Ariz. State U., Tempe, 1988—90, prof. dept. indsl. engring., 1992—99, affiliated prof., Dept. of Computer Sci. and Engring., 1993-98, prof. emeritus, 1999—. Vis. prof. Kyoto (Japan) Prefectural Med. U., 1965-66, Sensory Sci. Lab., U. Hawaii, 1968, 73, 2003, U. Western Australia, 1970-71, U. Hawaii, 1978-79, 80-81, U. Auckland, 1996, U. Freiburg, 1997, U. Sydney, 1999; pres. Nat. Conf. on On-Line Uses Computers in Psychology, 1974. Author: Real Time Computers: Techniques and Applications in the Psychological Sciences, 1968, Generative Computer Assisted Instruction in Analytic Geometry, 1972, The Psychobiology of Sensory Coding, 1973, Cellular Neurophysiology and Integration: An Interpretive Introduction, 1975, An Autocorrelation Theory of Visual Form Detection, 1975, The Psychobiology of Mind, 1978, A Taxonomy of Visual Processes, 1981, Visual Form Detection in Three Dimensional Space, 1983, Principles of Psychobiology, 1983, The Detection of Nonplanar Surfaces in Visual Space, 1985, The Perception of Dotted Forms, 1987, On Seeing Forms, 1988, The Swimmer: A Computational Model of a Perceptual Motor System, 1992, Toward a New Behaviorism: The Case Against Perceptual Reductionism, 1998, A Computational Model of Vision: The Role of Combination, 1999, The War Between Mentalism and Behaviorism, 2000, The New Phrenology: Limits on the Localization of Cognitive Processes in the Brain, 2001, A Behaviorist Looks at Form Recognition, 2002, Psychomythics, 2003, also numerous articles; editor: Readings in Sensory Coding, 1972; assoc. editor Readings in Sensory Coding, 1972, Behavioral Rsch. Method and Instrn., 1968—90, Computing: Archives for Electronic Computing, 1963—75, Jour. Exptl. Psychology, Perception and Performance, 1974—79, cons. editor Jour. Exptl. Psychology: Applied, 1994—97, patentee in field. Served to 2d lt. USAF, 1951-53. USPHS spl. postdoctoral fellow, 1965-66; NIMH research scientist award, 1971-76 Fellow AAAS, Am. Psychol. Assn., Am. Psychol. Soc. (charter), Soc. Exptl. Psychologists (chmn. 1994-95); mem. Psychonomics Soc. Office: Ariz State U Dept Indsl Engring Tempe AZ 85287-1104 E-mail: aowru@asu.edu.

UTTER, DONALD L. music educator; b. Poughkeepsie, N.Y., Apr. 18, 1951; s. Clarence and Marion (Cobb) U. BS, Susquehanna U., 1974; MusM, Ind. U., 1979. Cert. tchr. music K-12 N.Y. Music educator Webutuck Ctrl. Sch., Anenia, N.Y., 1979-84, Pawling (N.Y.) High Sch., 1984—. Rep. N.Y. State Sch. Music, Pawling, 1995-98; solo festival judge N.Y., 1990—; past v.p. Tchrs. Assn., 1993-94. Bd. dirs. Pawling (N.Y.) Concert Series, 1988—, County Farm Bur., Millbrook, N.Y., 1991-95; bd. dirs. Rep. Party, Pawling, 1993, chmn., 2000-03; varsity golf coach Pawling H.S. Named Coach of the Yr., Pawling High Sch., 1994. Mem. Dutchess County Music Educators (chmn. All-County Music Festival 1993-95), Music Educators Nat. Conf., Am. Fedn. Musicians Local 85. Republican. Methodist. Avocations: golf, skiing, reading. Home: 93 Harmony Rd Pawling NY 12564-0089 Office: Pawling HS Reservoir Rd Pawling NY 12564

UYEHARA, CATHERINE FAY TAKAKO (CATHERINE YAMAUCHI), physiologist, educator, pharmacologist; b. Honolulu, Dec. 20, 1959; d. Thomas Takashi and Eiko (Haraguchi) Uyehara; m. Alan Hisao Yamauchi, Feb. 17, 1990. BS, Yale U., 1981; PhD in Physiology, U. Hawaii, Honolulu, 1987. Postdoctoral fellow SmithKline Beecham Pharms., King of Prussia, Pa., 1987-89; mem. grad. faculty in pediatrics U. Hawaii John Burns Sch. Medicine, Honolulu, 1991—; rsch. pharmacologist Kapiolani Med. Ctr. for Women and Children, Honolulu, 1990-91. Statis. cons. Tripler Army Med. Ctr., Honolulu, 1984-87, 89—, chief rsch. pharmacology, 1991—, dir. collaborative rsch. program, 1995—; mem. grad. faculty in pharmacology U. Hawaii John A. Burns Sch. Medicine, 1993—; grad. faculty Interdisciplinary Biomed. Sci. program, 1995-98, Cell and Molecular Biology program, 1998-2002, mem. grad. faculty in physiology, 1999-2002. Contbr. articles to profl. jours. Mem. Am. Fedn. for Med. Rsch., Am. Physiol. Soc., Am. Heart Assn., Soc. Uniformed Endocrinologists, Endocrine Soc., We. Soc. Pediatric Rsch., N.Y. Acad. Scis., Hawaii Acad. Sci., Sigma Xi. Democrat. Mem. Christian Ch. Avocations: swimming, diving, crafts, horticulture, music. Office: Dept Clin Investigation 1 Jarrett White Rd Bldg 40 Tamc HI 96859

UYEHARA, HARRY YOSHIMI, library educator; b. Honolulu, Jan. 6, 1934; s. Saburo and Uto (Yamashiro) U. BEd, U. Hawaii, 1958; AMLS, U. Mich., 1965; MA, Columbia U., 1970, EdD, 1978. Cert. sch. libr., media specialist. Tchr., libr. Waiakea-Kai Elem. & Intermediate Sch., Hilo, Hawaii, 1960-61; libr. Wahiawa (Hawaii) Intermediate Sch., 1961-66; program specialist Hawaii State Dept. of Edn., Honolulu, 1966-76; asst. prof. library studies U. Hawaii, Honolulu, 1976-83; dean learning resources U. Guam, Mangilao, 1983-89; assoc. prof. libr. and info. studies U. Hawaii, Honolulu, 1989-91; assoc. prof. Edn. U. Guam, Mangilao, 1991-93; prof. libr. faculty Guam C.C., Mangilao, 1994-96, ret., 1997; ednl. and libr. cons., 1998—. Mem. in-svc. adv. coun. Hawaii State Dept. of Edn., Honolulu, 1977-80, adv. coun. of librs. Guam Pub. Libr., Agana, 1983-89. Editor (jours.) HLA Jour., 1978, The Golden Key, 1981, 82. With U.S. Army, 1958-60. Mem. Hawaii Libr. Assn. (pres. 1977-78), Hawaii Assn. Sch. Librs. (pres. 1982-83), Guam Libr. Assn. (pres. 1984-85), Phi Delta Kappa, Kappa Delta Pi. Home: 99-723 Aiea Heights Dr Aiea HI 96701-3502

UYENO, LANI AKEMI, education educator; b. Wahiawa, Hawaii, Apr. 4, 1954; d. Gilbert Kenichi and Tomoyo (Imura) Yuruki; m. Kenneth Akira Uyeno, May 6, 1978; children: Julie Masako, Joy Hiromi. BEd, U. Hawaii, 1976, MEd, 1977. Cert. tchr., Hawaii. Tchr. Kapiolani C.C., Honolulu, 1977-85; asst. prof. Leeward C.C., Pearl City, Hawaii, 1977—. Mem. adv. bd. Hawaii Writing Project, Honolulu, 1991—, co-dir., 1991. Contbr. articles, short stories to profl. publs. Buddhist. Avocations: reading, research. Office: Leeward CC 96-045 Ala Ike St Pearl City HI 96782-3366

UYGUR, MUSTAFA ETI, materials and mechanical engineering educator; b. Kayseri, Turkey, Jan. 22, 1941; s. Ali and Mumine (Oktay) U.; m. Selime Kobakci, Dec. 16, 1971; children: Ayse, Esra, Zeynep, Ali. BSME, Mid. East Tech. U., Ankara, Turkey, 1963, MSc in Mech. Engring., 1964; MSc in Engring., Purdue U., 1967; PhD in Materials Sci. and Engring., Mid. East Tech. U., Ankara, Turkey, 1971. Rsch. assoc. Am. Oil Co. Rsch. Labs., Whiting, Ind., 1967; instr. Mid. East Tech. U., Ankara, Turkey, 1967-71, asst. prof., 1971-77, assoc. prof., 1977-84; prof. Gazi U., Ankara, Turkey, 1984-90; prof. mech. engring. dept. King Saud U., Riyadh, Saudi Arabia, 1990—. Asst. chmn. materials sci. and engring. dept. Mid. East Tech. U., Ankara, 1977-80; dep. dean faculty tech. edn. Gazi U., Ankara, 1984-86, mem. coll. coun., grad. coll. coun., univ. senate, 1984-90; tech. & sci. advisor to dep. Min. of Nat. Def., Def. Industries Devel. Adminstrn., Ankara, 1987-90. Author: Dynamic NDT of Materials, 1976, 83, Glossary of Powder Metallurgy Terms, 1982, X-Ray Crystallography, 1983, Materials Science and Engineering, 1997, 2d edit., 2002, Laboratory Manual for Materials Science and Engineering, 1997, 2d edit., 2002, CD-Materials Sci & Engring., 1997, 4th edit., 2002, CD-Laboratory for Materials Science and Engineering, 1998, 3d edit., 2002; editor-in-chief: Science-Research-Technology Five-Year Main Plan, 1988; contbr. over 100 articles to profl. jours.; supr. for devel. of many ednl. computer programs. Specialization com. on nonferrous materials State Planning Orgn., Ankara, 1982, chmn. specialization com. on transfer of high tech. and employment, 1987-88, specialization com. on sci. rsch., tech., 1987-88, chmn. editl. com. on sci., rsch., tech., 1988. Lt. (engr.) Turkish Army Tech. Svc.-Weapons Dept., 1973-74. Scholar Turkish Iron-Steel Works, 1963-64; rsch. grantee Turkish Sci. Rsch. Coun., 1971-73. Mem. Internat. Plansee Soc. Powder Metallurgy, Internat. Soc. Crystallographers, Am. Powder Metallurgy Inst. Internat., Am. Soc. for Metals Internat., Am. Soc. for Metals Internat.-Metall. Soc., Materials Rsch. Soc., Turkish Assn. for Powder Metallurgy (founder). Avocations: reading, music, computers, swimming, bowling. E-mail: mustafauygur@hotmail.com.

UZSOY, PATRICIA J. nursing educator and administrator; b. Corning, Ark. m. Namik K. Diploma, Mo. Bapt. Hosp. Sch. Nursing, St. Louis, 1960; BSN, Washington U., St. Louis, 1962; MEd, Lynchburg Coll., 1977, EdS, 1981; MS in Nursing, U. Va., 1987. RN, Va. Dean Schs. of Nursing Lynchburg (Va.) Gen. Hosp. Mem. ANA, NLN, Va. Nurses Assn. (Nurse of Yr. dist. III 1987).

VACCARO, MARTHA WALSH, secondary school educator; b. Centerville, Mass., July 26, 1930; d. Edwin Arnold and Anne (Molony) Walsh; m. Ralph Francis Vaccaro, Apr. 19, 1955; children: Christopher, Adelaide, John, Mark, Thomas (dec.), Peter. BS, Trinity Coll., Burlington, Vt., 1952; postgrad., Southeastern Mass. U., 1983, Bridgewater State U., 1987-88. Cert. math., sch., biology secondary tchr., Mass. Rsch. asst. Woods Hole (Mass.) Oceanographic Inst., 1952-58; substitute tchr. Falmouth (Mass.) Pub. Schs., 1981-87, math. tchr., 1987—2000; math. instr. Mass. Maritime Acad., Buzzards Bay, 2001—. Pvt. math. tutor, 1958-81. Mem. Falmouth Town Fin. Com., 1970-81; chmn. Falmouth Sewer Adv. Com., 1980-86; mem. Falmouth Human Svcs. Com., 1971-86; rep. Falmouth Town Meeting, 1981—; new tchrs. mentor Falmouth Sch. Sys., 2001—. Recipient Marian medal Diocese of Fall River, 1971. Mem. Nat. Coun. Tchrs. Math., Birthright. Republican. Roman Catholic. Avocations: gardening, knitting, sewing, books, religious education teaching. Home: Box 245 25 Hidden Village Rd West Falmouth MA 02574

VACCARO, NICHOLAS CARMINE, English language and media educator; b. Bklyn., July 16, 1942; s. Joseph Anthony Vaccaro and Carmela (Tallarico) Chicorelli; m. Jane Elizabeth Forgiel, July 7, 1973; children: Stephen Nicholas, Christopher Joseph. BA in English, St. John's U., 1964, MS in Edn., 1966, Profl. Diploma in Adminstrn., 1978. Tchr. English South Huntington (N.Y.) Schs., 1965-68, Elwood Schs., East Northport, N.Y., 1968-69; tchr. English and media Massapequa (N.Y.) Schs., 1969—; novelist Sterling Lord-Literistic Lit. Agy., N.Y.C., 1984—; screenwriter Sterlinglord-Literistic Literary Agy., N.Y.C., 1984—. Curriculum rsch. & program devel. Massapequa Schs., 1971-72, 78, 82, 84, 88; drama club dir. Berner and Massapequa High Schs., 1970-73, 78-82, 91, creative writing advisor, 1982-93; in-svc. educator Tchr. Effectiveness Inst. Contbr. articles to profl. jours. Mgr. Little League Baseball, Northport, 1984-91, Youth Ctr. Soccer, 1989. Recipient Nat. Tchrs. award NBC and Carnegie Found. for Advancement of Teaching, 1990, NEH and Coun. for Basic Edn. fellow, 1991. Mem. Mensa, Nat. Coun. Tchrs. English, Massapequa Fedn. Tchrs., Phi Delta Kappa. Roman Catholic. Avocations: textbook writing, novelist, screenwriter, directing theatre productions. Home: 208 Highland Ave Northport NY 11768-1657 Office: Massapequa High Sch 4925 Merrick Rd Massapequa NY 11758-6297

VACCARO, NICK ANTHONY, principal; b. New Orleans, July 17, 1944; s. Nick A. Sr. and Rose (Giovingo) V.; m. Linda L. Lavigne, Jan. 21, 1968; 1 child, David A. BS, Southeastern La. U., 1969, MEd, 1975, postgrad., 1986. Cert. secondary tchr., La. Tchr. sci. Independence (La.) Boys Sch., 1969-78, Independence High Sch., 1978-91, asst. prin., 1991—, acting prin., 1994-95. Head sci. dept. Independence High Sch., 1978-91; vol. VISTA Office Econ. Opportunity, Washington, 1966-67; chmn. steering Com. for Accreditation, So. Assn., 1984-85. Mem. zoning com. Town of Independence, 1977-78, planning bd., 1985-86; pres., mem. Mater Dolorosa Sch. Bd., Independence, 1984-90. Mem. NEA, La. Assn. Edn., La. Assn. Sch. Execs., Tangipahoa Assn. Edn. Democrat. Avocations: reading, home repairs. Home: PO Box 376 Independence LA 70443-0376

VADASZ, PETER, engineering educator, consultant; b. Bucharest, Romania, Jan. 5, 1951; s. Johan and Aurelia (Bercov) V.; m. Alisa Sol Levy, May 28, 1980; children: John Johnathan, Nataly Imbar, Gabriel Stephen. BS in Mech. Engring., TECHNION-Israel Inst. Tech., Haifa, Israel, 1979; MS in Mech. Engring., TECHNION-Israel Inst. Tech., 1983, DSc., 1988. Registered profl. engr., Israel, South Africa. Devel. engr. Poper Engring. Ltd., Haifa, 1979-80; indsl. R&D and project engr. Israel Electric Corp. Ltd., Haifa, 1980-86, project mgr., 1986-88, head, energy storage sect., 1988-90; asst. prof. Mech. Engring. U. Durban-Westville, Durban, South Africa, 1991-92, prof., head dept. Mech. Engring., 1992-98; prof., chair dept. mech. engring. No. Ariz. U., Flagstaff, 2002—. Consulting engr.; mem. editl. adv. bd. Internat. Jour. Applied Thermodynamics, SAIMechE R&D Jour., Referees, Jour. Fluid Mechs., Jour. Heat Transfer; Transport in Porous Media, Kluwer Dordrecht, The Netherlands, Internat. Jour. Heat Mass Transfer; lectr. in field. Author: (with A. Bejan, D.G. Kröger) Energy and the Environment, 1999; contbr. 8 chpts. to profl. books, 87 articles to profl. jours. or conf. procs. Fellow U. Durban-Westville, 1997; recipient FRD core rolling grant Found. for R&D, Pretoria, South Africa, 1994-96, "A" rating award as world leader in sci. and engring. NRF; rsch. grantee U.D.W., Westville, 1993, 94. Fellow ASME (Bd. Govs. award 1994-95), South African Inst. Mech. Engrs., South African Inst. Energy. Avocations: ice skating, tennis, chess, music, computers. Office: Dept Mech Engring Northern Ariz U PO Box 15600 Flagstaff AZ 86011-5600 Home: Apt 2082 Bldg 26 4343 E Soliere Ave Flagstaff AZ 86004 E-mail: peter.vadasz@nau.edu.

VAGT, ROBERT F. academic administrator; m. Ruth Anne Vagt, 1968; children: Ashley, Lindsey. BA in Psychology, Davidson Coll., 1969; MDiv, Duke U. Ordained to ministry Presbyn. Ch. Dir. clin. programs N.W. Ala. Mental Health Ctr.; exec. dir. Mcpl. Assistance Corp., N.Y.C., 1979—80; chmn., pres., COO Seagull Energy Corp.; pres. Davidson Coll., 1997—. Bd.

dirs. Cornell Cos., Inc. Bd. vis. Davidson Coll., 1992—, mem. Ultra Soc., nat. leader Ann. Fund, 1993—95. Recipient Alumni Svc. award, Davidson Coll., 1996. Office: Pres's Office Davidson Coll PO Box 1719 Davidson NC 28036-1719

VAHSEN, FAUSTENA F. (PENNY), elementary education educator; b. San Diego, June 19, 1932; d. John Ernest and Faustena (Roberts) Fradd; m. George Martin Vahsen, June 10, 1952 (dec. July 1980); children: David, Cathleen, Sharon, Steve, James. BA, Hood Coll., 1953; MEd, Loyola Coll., Balt., 1984. Cert. elem. tchr., Md. Longterm substitute tchr. elem. schs., various locations, 1971-84; tchr. sci. Magothy River Middle Sch., Arnold, Md., 1985-97; tutor Bd. Edn., Annapolis, Md., 1998—. Author: workbook and tchrs. manual.; contbr. Naval Inst. Procs. Mag. Docent, Dept. Natural Resources, Annapolis, 1998—; mem. design team Anne Arundel Partnership on Edn.; mem. Md. Partnership for Tchg. and Learning K-16; judge Bayer/NSF awards for innovative projects. Recipient Grand prize tchg. team award Prentice Hall/NMSAT, 1995, Nat. Educator award Milken Family Found., 1995-96; named Tchr. of Yr., Anne Arundel County Bd. Edn., 1988, hon. grad. U.S. Naval Acad., 2000; grantee GTE, 1993. Mem. Caritas of St. Johns Coll. Republican. Avocation: sponsoring USNA midshipmen. Home: 313 Halsey Rd Annapolis MD 21401-3218

VAIDYA, KIRIT RAMESHCHANDRA, anesthesiologist, educator; b. Sihor, India, Feb. 20, 1937; came to U.S., 1971; s. Rameshchandra Harilal Vaidya and Kanta Bachubhai Mulani; m. Rashmi Kirit Vaidya; children: Kaushal, Sujal. BSc, Gujrat U., India, 1959; MB BS, Karnatak U., India, 1965. Intern St. Joseph Hosp., Providence, 1971-72; resident in anesthesiology R.I. Hosp., Providence, 1973, Boston City Hosp., 1974-76; clin. instr. anesthesiology Boston U. Sch. Medicine, 1977-79; staff anesthesiologist Bridgeport (Conn.) Hosp., 1979—; asst. clin. prof. anesthesiology U. Conn. Med. Ctr., Farmington, 1987—. Mem. Am. Assn. Physicians from India, Conn. Assn. Physicians from India (pres. 2000-2002), Fairfield County Med. Assn., Conn. State Soc. Medicine, Conn. State Soc. Anesthesiologists, Am. Soc. Anesthesiologists, Internat. Anesthesiology Assn. Hindu. Home: 54 Quail Trl Trumbull CT 06611-5259 Office: Bridgeport Anesthesia Assocs 965 White Plains Rd Ste 301 Trumbull CT 06611-4566 E-mail: kvaidya@pol.net.

VALAKIS, M. LOIS, retired elementary school educator; b. Phila., Jan. 25, 1939; d. John Demosthenes and Blanche Antoinette Marquis Valakis. BS in Edn., Framingham (Mass.) State Tchrs. Coll., 1959. Elem. edn. tchr. Town of Framingham, 1959—98. Mem. ESEA Title III project, Framingham, 1969—70. Avocations: reading, music, photography. Home: 2 Concord Ter Framingham MA 01702

VALDATA, PATRICIA, English language educator, aviation writer; b. New Brunswick, N.J., Oct. 16, 1952; d. William Rudolph and Ethel Ann (Kovacs) V.; m. Robert W. Schreiber, Apr. 21, 1979. BA, Douglass Coll., 1974; BA with honors, Rutgers U. Coll., 1977; MFA, Goddard Coll., 1991. Supr. AT&T Long Lines, Bedminster, N.J., 1979-81; mgr. info. svcs. N.J. Ednl. Computer Network, Edison, 1981-83; tech. writer on contract to Bell Comm. Rsch., Piscataway, N.J., 1983-86; v.p. Computer System Design & Mgmt. Inc., Annandale, N.J., 1986-88; adj. instr. Del. Tech. and C.C., Wilmington, 1989-90, Cecil C.C., Elkton, Md., 1990—95; adj. instr. dept. English, U. Del., Newark, 1991—93, asst. prof., 1993—97; project mgr. Zeneca Pharms., 1997—2000; pres. Cloudstreet Comm., 2000—; asst. prof. Neumann Coll., Aston, Pa., 2002—. Faculty cons. Ednl. Testing Svc., 1993-97; presenter 3d Nat. Women in Aviation Conf., 1992, 98. Author: Crosswind, Looking for Bivalve. Mem. Women Soaring Pilots Assn. (co-founder, sec. 1986-96, pres. 1997-2001), Atlantic Soaring Club (co-founder, pres. 1992). Office: Neumann Coll One Neumann Dr Aston PA 19014-1298

VALDEZ, DIANNA MARIE, language educator, consultant; b. Santa Fe, N.Mex., July 13, 1949; d. Delfino Julian and Margaret Erlinda Valdez. BSc, U. N.Mex., 1971, MA, 1981. Cert. Reading Tchr. N.Mex., 76, English as Second Lang. & Bilingual Tchr. N.Mex., 96. From classroom tchr. to instl. coach Albuquerque Pub. Sch., Albuquerque, 1971—2002, instl. coach, 2002—. Adj. instr. Lesley Coll., Cambridge, Mass., 1986—90; writing cons. San Felipe Elem. Sch., San Felipe Pueblo, N.Mex., 1998. Author, editor: Curriculum Integration Guide, 1984. Mem. ctrl. coord. coun. Title I Homeless Project, Albuquerque, 1998—2001; active supporter All Faith's Receiving Home, Albuquerque, 1995—2001. Recipient Achievement award, Theta State, 2001. Fellow: Nat. Writing Project-Rio Grande; mem.: Internat. Reading Assn. (pres. Camino Real coun. 1999—2000, Mem. of Yr. award 2001), Delta Kappa Gamma (state 1st v.p. 1982—2002, State Achievement award 2001). Republican. Roman Catholic. Avocations: needlecrafts, reading, writing, multimedia technology, trout fishing. Home: PO Box 1071 Corrales NM 87048 Office: Albuquerque Pub Schs Griegos Elem 4040 San Isidro NW Albuquerque NM 87107

VALDEZ, FELICIA M. special education educator; b. Washington, Feb. 24, 1948; d. Joseph Alvin and Bettye Mae (Weaver); children: Ronald Nathaniel Tabor II, Tracye Thomas. B, Antioch U., 1976, M, 1978; D, George Washington U., 1992. Tchr. Children's Inn, Washington, D.C., 1976-77; early childhood specialist Children's Hosp., Washington, D.C., 1977-86, coord. edn. svcs., 1986-92, dir. early intervention inst., 1992—. Cons. Valdez & Assocs., Washington, 1993—, Mayor's Transition Team, Washington, 1990. Contbr. chpt. to book. Chair. Interagency Coordinating Coun., Washington, 1989-90; chairperson Devel. Disabilities Coun., Washington., 1990—; mem. President's Commn. Mental Retardation, 1991, state adv. panel Spl. Edn., Washington, 1988-89. Mem. Coun. for Exceptional Children, Am. Speech & Hearing Assn., Nat. Assn. Edn. Young Children, Assn. Supervision & Curriculum, Phi Beta Gamma, Phi Delta Kappa. Roman Catholic. Avocations: interior decorating, interior design, golfing, reading. Home: 312 Buchanan St NW Washington DC 20011-4726 Office: Children's Hosp PO Box 90575 Washington DC 20090-0575

VALDEZ, MARIA DEL ROSARIO, perinatal nurse, educator; b. San Antonio, Nov. 4, 1955; d. Guadalupe Garza and Beatrice Consuelo (Martinez) V. BS in Nursing, BA in Psychology, Incarnate Word Coll., San Antonio, 1978; MSN, U. Tex. Health Sci. Ctr., San Antonio, 1986; PhD in Nursing, Tex. Woman's U., 1999; postgrad., U. Calif.-San Francisco, 2001—02. RN, Tex., Wash. Nurse, team leader Santa Rosa Med. Ctr., San Antonio, 1979-81, Met. Gen. Hosp., San Antonio, 1981-85; childbirth educator Santa Rosa Hosp., 1985-87, obstetrics clin. educator, 1987-94; instr. nursing Incarnate Word Coll., 1989-94; part-time perinatal staff nurse several nursing agys., Houston, 1994-99; staff nurse North Ctrl. Bapt. Hosp., San Antonio, 1995-98; asst. prof. Wash. State U., Spokane, 1999—; postdoc. fellow HIV prevention and edn. U. Calif., San Francisco, 2001—02. Instr. in Basic Life Support/CPR, Am. Heart Assn., 1985-95, Prepared Childbirth, Coun. of Childbirth Edn. Specialists, 1985, instr. neonatal resucitation, 1989, instr.; mem. adv. bd. Hispanic Nurse Practice in Medically Underprivileged Areas, Ctr. for Health Policy Devel., San Antonio, 1989-91, Tex. Works Together program United Way, San Antonio, 1990—. Mem. ANA, NAACOG, Tex. Nurses' Assn., Nat. Assn. Hispanic Nurses, Am. Soc. Psychoprophy Obstets., Internat. Childbirth Edn. Assn., Coun. Childbirth Edn. Specialists, Sigma Theta Tau. Roman Catholic. Avocations: reading, bowling, crochet, needlepoint, cross-stitch. Home: 6012 W Wind River Dr Spokane WA 99208

VALENTA, JANET ANNE, substance abuse professional; b. Cleve., Sept. 22, 1948; d. Frank A. and Ann (Kogoy) Shenk; m. Mario Valenta, May 22, 1971. BA, Cleve. State U., 1970; postgrad., Rutgers U., 1973, U. Cin., 1976-84. Cert. prevention cons. Ohio, Nat. Inst. for trauma and loss sch. specialist. Purchasing clk./typist Restaurant div. Stouffer Foods Corp., Cleve., 1967-71; cmty. info. specialist Trumbull Warren Office of Econ. Opportunity, Warren, Ohio, 1972; edn. dir. Trumbull County Coun. on Alcoholism, Warren, 1973-78; rehab. counselor Trumbull County Bur. Vocat. Rehab., Niles, Ohio, 1979-80; owner, operator Ironsmith, Niles, 1978-79; cons., trainer Ohio Network Tng. and Assistance to Schs. and Cmty., Youngstown, Ohio, 1987—; prevention edn. coord. Cmty. Recovery Resource Ctr., Youngstown, 1979-94; prevention coord. Neil Kennedy Recovery Clinic, Youngstown, 1994—. Ohio tng. coord. Babesworld Home, Inc., Detroit, 1986-99; nat. chair pub. health caucus Nat. Assn. Prevention Profls., Chgo., 1976-77. Publicity chair Trumbull Art Guild, Warren, 1974—76; policy coun. Youngstown Cmty. Action, Headstart, 1988—90; active Summer Arts Butler Art Mus., 1997—2002, Ohio Violence Prevention Process, 2002; bd. dirs. Ebony Life Support Group, Inc., Youngstown, 1992. Named Woman of Yr., Warren Bus. and Profl. Women's Assn., 1978. Mem. Alcohol and Drug Abuse Prevention Assn. Ohio. Office: Neil Kennedy Recovery Clinic 2151 Rush Blvd Youngstown OH 44507-1535

VALENTI, BETTY JANET, resource specialist, educator; b. Detroit, Apr. 12, 1956; d. Beverly Rex and Mary Gracia (Nelson) McMinn; m. Nick Jonathon Valenti, Dec. 29, 1990; 1 child, Lindsay Elizabeth. Student, U. Calif., Irvine, 1985, credential resource specialist, 1991; BS in Spl. Edn., Ea. Mich. U., 1979. Specialty physically handicapped Capistrano (Calif.) Unified Sch. Dist., 1980-90; spl. day tchr. Pasadena (Calif.) Unified Sch. Dist., 1990-91; resource specialist Kepple Union Sch. Dist., Pearblossom, Calif., 1991-92; early interventionist Palmdale (Calif.) Sch. Dist., 1996-97, resource specialist, 1994—. Parent cons. Nat. Parent to Parent Support and Info. Sys., Inc., Blue Ridge, Ga., Hemihypertrophy, Blue Ridge, 1996-97; spl. edn. rep. Sch. Site Coun.-Rep. Tumbleweed Sch., Palmdale, 1995-97; coord. Coordinated Compliance Rev., 1991-97. Educator specialist Coun. Adv. Com. for Spl. Edn. Antelope Valley Local Plan, Palmdale, 1996; Spl. Olympics coach Richard Henry Dana Sch., Dana Point, Calif., 1984, 85. Mem. AAUW, Calif. Assn. Resource Specialists, Nat. Parent to Parent Support and Info. Sys. Republican. Presbyterian. Avocations: drawing, reading, computer software research, swimming, traveling. Home: 39522 Rowan Ct Palmdale CA 93551-4073

VALENTI, PAULA ANNE (PELAK), art educator, assistant principal; b. Danville, Pa., Feb. 2, 1956; d. Daniel Timothy and Marie Vincenzia (Folger) Pelak. BA, Kean U., 1978, MA, 1983; supr. cert., Montclair U., 1998; postgrad. exec. doctoral program, Seton Hall U., 2001—. Cert. supr. art, art educator grades K-12, elem. educator with specialty in gifted and talented. Art tchr. Montclair (N.J.) Pub. Schs., 1978-84, Dumont (N.J.) H.S., 1984-86, Ridgewood (N.J.) Pub. Schs., 1986-99; supr. art Newark Pub. Schs., 1999—2001; supr. visual and performing arts Englewood (N.J.) Pub. Schs., 2001; asst. prin. Dwight Morrow H.S., Englewood, NJ, 2002—. Founding mem. Hands and Minds Inst./Art Edn. N.J., 1991—; curriculum cons. Yavneh Acad., Paramus, N.J., 1998-99. Exhibited in group shows Kean Coll., 1977, 78, Faculty Show, Ridgewood, N.J., 1987, 92, Priory, Newark, 2000, 2001, Univ. Coun. for Art Edn., Bklyn., 2001; juried shows include St. John's, Newark, 2000. Recipient Govs. award State N.J., State Museum, 1993, 96, 2003; grantee N.J. State Coun. Arts, Trenton, 1989. Mem. Nat. Art Edn. Assn. (ea. region rep. 1994-96, profl. materials com. 1998—, Ea. Region Elem. Art Educator of Yr. 1993), Art Educators N.J. (pres. 1991-92, Disting. Achievement award 1995, fellow, 2002), Phi Delta Kappa. Democrat. Roman Catholic. Home: 80 Lincoln Pl Waldwick NJ 07463-2115 Office: Dwight Morrow HS 274 Knickerbocker Rd Englewood NJ 07631 E-mail: pells@verizon.net.

VALENTIN, JOAN MARIE, secondary school educator; b. Gettysburg, Pa., Aug. 14, 1960; d. Joseph Leroy Hess and Anna Jane (Wetzel) Hess Bucher; m. Javier Valentin, Oct. 17, 1987; children: Andrea Leigh, Samuel Brody. BS in Math. Edn., Shippensburg U., 1981, MA, 1987. Cert. secondary sch. tchr., Pa.; cert. math supr. Math. tchr. Downingtown (Pa.) Sr. High Sch., 1982—. Mem. Nat. Coun. Tchrs. of Math., Pa. Coun. Tchrs. Math., Ctrl. Pa. Assn. Tchrs. Math. Republican. Roman Catholic. Avocations: reading, crafts. Home: 142 Carriage House Dr Willow Street PA 17584-9025 Office: Downingtown High Sch West 445 Manor Ave Downingtown PA 19335-1725

VALENTINE, CHARLES FRANCIS, educational administrator; b. Vineland, N.J., May 17, 1934; s. Quinton and Mary V.; m. Anne Marie Williams. BS, Glassboro State Coll., 1956, MA, 1965; EdD, Nova U., 1980. Cert. sch. adminstr., N.J. Tchr. Vineland Bd. Edn., 1956-65, prin., supr., 1965-77, dir. thorough and efficient edn. and supplementary programs, 1977-84, asst. supt. mandated, aux. and fed. programs, 1984-93; supt., 1993—97. Adj. instr. Glassboro (N.J.) State Coll., 1974, Jersey City State Coll., 1981; audio-visual commr. Cumberland County, 1993—; bd. dirs. Vineland Libr., 1993-97. Scoutmaster Vineland area Boy Scouts Am., 1956-62, committeeman, 1962—, mem. exec. com. So. N.J. couns., 1978—, co-chmn. Atlantic So. N.J. com., 1990; past pres., exec. com., bd. dirs. Greater Vineland United Fund; chmn. Combined Health and Human Campaign for Cumberland County, 1987-97; past pres. So. N.J. chpt. Exceptional Children, 1984-85; mem. Cumberland County Pvt. Industry Coun., 1979-82, Vineland Edn. Found., 1985-97, South Jersey Employer Edn. Consortium, 1985—; mem. Cumberland County Coll. Student Devel. Adv. Bd., 1981-2002; mem. Cumberland County Coll. Retirement Coll., 2001—; commentator St. Isidore Ch., Vineland, 1966—, mem. pastoral planning com., 1973-76, parish coun., 1982-85; bd. dirs. Vineland YMCA, 1975-99, devel. chmn., 1977-78; adv. bd. N.J. Hist. Soc.; bd. dirs. Cumberland unit Am. Cancer Soc., 198-97—, chmn. bd. dirs., 1984-85; commr. Vinland Environmental, 1978-99; bd. mem. Vineland Svc. Club Coun., 1991—; bd. trustees Vineland Devel. Ctr., 1991—; chmn. Vineland Teen Adv. Partnership, 2002—; edn. chmn. Cumberland County Human Rels. Commn., 2002—; dir. Cumberland County PTA Dist., 1993—, legis. chmn., 2001—; citizen mem. Sch. Mgmt. Teams Johnston and Landis Schs., 1998—; v.p. Alzheimer's Support Group of Cumberland County, 2002—; vice chmn. Cumberland County Profl. Devel. Bd., 2000—; mem. Rowan U. Tchrs. Edn. Adv. Coun., 1993—. Mem. NEA (life), Nat. Assn. Elem. Sch. Prins. (Life), N.J. Edn. Assn. (life), Glassboro State Coll. Alumni Assn. (life), Vineland Hist. and Antiquarian Soc. (life), N.J. Folklore Soc. (life), Alliance N.J. Environ. Edn., N.J. Assn. Sch. Adminstrs. (life, diplomate 1988), Urban Tech. Alliance, South Jersey Schoolmen's Assn. (pres.), Friends of Vineland Pub. Libr. (life), N.J. Congress Parents and Tchrs. (life), Atlantic City Art Ctr. (life), Phi Delta Kappa (life), Kappa Delta Pi (life).

VALENTINE, GORDON CARLTON, retired secondary school educator; b. Norwich, N.Y., Nov. 18, 1946; s. Carlton Everett and Helen Janet (Thompson) V.; m. Deborah Lee Preston, Oct. 15, 1977; children: Heather, Megan, Matthew. BA, SUNY, Cortland, 1968, MS in Edn., 1970. Cert. tchr., N.Y. Tchr. Sherburne-Earlville Ctrl. Sch., Sherburne, N.Y., 1968-70, Marathon (N.Y.) Ctrl. Sch., 1970-87; social welfare examiner Dept. Social Svcs., Cortland, 1988; tchr. Homer (N.Y.) Ctrl. Sch., 1989—2003; ret., 2003—. Adj. instr. Tompkins-Cortland C.C., Dryden, N.Y., 1982—; mem. profl. staff devel. and supportive supervision model Homer Ctrl. Sch., 1989-92, asst. varsity cross country coach, jr. high track coach, varsity track coach, 1972-87, jr. high soccer coach, 1972-86, jr. varsity girls' soccer coach, 1989-90. Recipient Christa McAliffe Tchr.'s award, 1991, Yearbook Dedication, 1983. Mem. ASCD, Homer Tchrs. Assn., NYSUT, AFT, Challenger Ctr. of NASA, Ctrl. N.Y. State Coun. for Social Studies, Nat. Coun. Social Studies, SUNY Cortland Alumni Assn. (bd. dirs. 1993—, mem. admissions com., mem. mktg. com., mem. rsch. devel. com., nom. and by-law com., young alumni com., exec. com., rec. sec. 1998-2002, asst. treas. 2002-03). Democrat. Avocations: running, reading, volunteer coaching. Home: 4024 Collegeview Dr Cortland NY 13045-1501

VALENTINE, JAMES WILLIAM, paleobiology educator, writer; b. LA, Nov. 10, 1926; s. Adelbert Cuthbert and Isabel (Davis) V.; m. Grace Evelyn Whysner, Dec. 21, 1957 (div. 1972); children— Anita, Ian; m. Cathryn Alice Campbell, Sept. 10, 1978 (div. 1986); 1 child, Geoffrey; m. Diane Mondragon, Mar. 16, 1987. BA, Phillips U., 1951; MA, UCLA, 1954, PhD, 1958. From asst. prof. to assoc. prof. U. Mo., Columbia, 1958-64; from assoc. prof. to prof. U. Calif., Davis, 1964-77, prof. geol. scis. Santa Barbara, 1977-90, prof. integrative biology Berkeley, 1990-93, emeritus, 1993—. Author: Evolutionary Paleoecology of the Marine Biosphere, 1973; editor: Phanerozoic Diversity, 1985; co-author: Evolution, 1977, Evolving, 1979; contbr. articles to profl. jours. Served with USNR, 1944-46, PTO. Fulbright research scholar, Australia, 1962-63; Guggenheim fellow Yale U., Oxford U., Eng., 1968-69; Rockefeller Found. scholar in residence, Bellagio, Italy, summer 1974; grantee NSF, NASA Fellow Am. Acad. Arts and Scis., Geol. Soc. Am.; mem. NAS, AAAS, Paleontol. Soc. (pres. 1974-75, medal 1996). Avocation: collecting works of charles darwin. Home: 1351 Glendale Ave Berkeley CA 94708-2025 Office: U Calif Dept Integrative Biology Berkeley CA 94720-0001 E-mail: jwvsossi@socrates.berkeley.edu.

VALENTINE, PHYLLIS LOUISE, counseling administrator; d. Harold Gray and Velma Eura Long; m. Samuel L. Valentine, Dec. 30, 1995. BA, St. Augustine's Coll., 1970; MEd, Bowie State U., 1992; student, Trinity Coll., 1974—77, Georgetown U., 1989, U. D.C., 1974—88. Cert. sch. counselor K-12, reading tchr. K-12. Evening reading reacher Loton Reformatory Youth Ctr. II PSI Assocs., Washington, 1984—86; chpt. 1 reading/math. lab tchr. D.C. Pub. Schs., 1986—92, chpt. 1 resource asst., 1992—93; chpt. 1 CAI lab tchr./team coord. C.W. Harris Elem. Sch., Washington, 1992—95; sch. counselor J.C. Nalle Elem. Sch., Washington, 1995—. Mem. tchr. adv. bd. Ctr. for Artistry in Tchg., Washington, 1999—; dir., presenter J.C. Nalle Sch. Extended Day, 1998. V.p. Brandywine Sta. Townhouse Assn., Upper Marlboro, Md., 1990—97. Recipient Letter of Commendation, Exec. Dir. Chpt. 1 program, 1987, AIMs Pilot, Bryan Elem. Sch., 1984, HOST Corp., 1994, DCPS Parent Ctr. Incentive, 1997. Mem.: D.C. Sch. Counseling Assn., Am. Sch. Counseling Assn., Am. Counseling Assn., Tots & Teens Inc. (pres. 1985—93, corr. sec. 1985—93, youth leader 1987—91, D.C. chpt., award 1990—91), D.C. Counseling Assn. (pres.-elect 2001—02, pres. 2002, dedicated svc. plaque 1993), Phi Delta Kappa (mem. Beta chpt.), Nat. Sorority Phi Delta Kappa (Beta chpt.), Sigma Gamma Rho (recording sec., anti-basilus 1971—78). Avocations: gardening, listening to jazz music, dancing. Business E-Mail: phyllis.valentine@k12.us.

VALENTINE, TARA E. early childhood educator; b. Chester, N.Y., Nov. 10, 1969; BA, N.C. State U., Raleigh, 1991; MA, Rutgers U., 1998. Presch. handicapped tchr. Allegro, Cedar Knolls, N.J., 1991-94, South Orange and Maplewood (N.J.) Sch. Dist., 1995-96; autism tchr. Douglass Devel. Ctr., New Brunswick, N.J., 1994-95, tchr. milti-age early childhood educator, spl. educator, 1996-98; ednl. dir. Renaissance Learning Ctr., Palm Beach Gardens, Fla., 1999—. Behavioral cons., parent trainer cons. Ctr. Outreach Svcs. Autism Cmty.; presenter Ctr. Outreach Svcs. for Autism Cmty. Conf., 1998. Active U.S. Master Swimming, 1993—, N.Y.C. Marathon, 1995, Half-Ironman Triathlon, 1997. Recipient 1st Place 1 Mile Swim award Seaside Heights (N.J.) Dept. Recreation, 1995. Mem. Coun. Exceptional Children (divsn. early childhood), Nat. Assn. Edn. Young Children. Avocation: swimming. Home: 1202 Sandpiper Ln Lantana FL 33462-4214

VALENTINI, ANNA MARIA, elementary education educator, reading specialist; b. Cortlandt Manor, N.Y., June 11, 1959; d. Rudolph and Rosa (DiPietro) V. AS in Liberal Arts, Westchester C.C., Valhalla, N.Y., 1979, acctg. cert., 1980; BS, SUNY, Oneonta, 1982; MS, Fordham U., 1986. Cert. elem. edn., N.Y.; cert. reading specialization grades K-12, N.Y. Child care MOPS, Oneonta, N.Y., 1981-82; vol. tchr. pre-kindergarten Bugbee-Migrant Children, Oneonta, 1982; substitute tchr. grades K-8 various sch. dists., N.Y., 1982-84; tchr. grade 3 St. Joseph Sch., Yonkers, N.Y., 1984-85; tchr. pre-kindergarten Immaculate Conception Sch., Irvington, N.Y., 1985-88; tchr. grade 4 St. Elizabeth Ann Seton Sch., Shrub Oak, N.Y., 1988-89; sec., substitute tchr. grades K-8 Peekskill (N.Y.) Ctrl. Schs., 1989-90; tchr. grades 6-8 St. Theresa Sch., Briarcliff Manor, N.Y., 1990—. Skin care mgr. Salon Royale, Peekskill, 1975-90; mem. discipline com. St. Joseph, Yonkers, 1984-85; cheerleading coach Immaculate Conception, Irvington, 1985-88; make-up coord. St. Theresa Drama Club, Briarcliff, 1990—; afterschool staff St. Theresa, Briarcliff, 1991-92, tchr. adult edn. Italian I. Nutrition grantee Archdiocese of N.Y., 1993. Avocations: arts and crafts, fundraising, piano, photography, cooking. Home: 10 Woodland Blvd Cortlandt Manor NY 10567-1041

VALENTINI, JOSE ESTEBAN, chemical engineering director, scientist, educator; b. Cordoba, Argentina, May 10, 1950; came to U.S., 1980; s. Cesar Santiago and Irma Judith (Drehock) V.; m. Silvia Dolores Castillo, Apr. 16, 1979; children: Bryan Esteban, Romina Natalia. MS, U. Buenos Aires, 1973; DSc, U. La Plata, Argentina, 1977; MS, U. Pitts., 1981; postgrad., Duke U., 1981-84. Postdoctoral fellow Duke U., Durham, N.C., 1981-84; prof. NYU Med. Ctr., N.Y.C., 1984—; sr. scientist E.I. DuPont ExP STA Inkjet Ink. SBU, 1984—; dir., scientist surface rheology group Rutgers U., N.J., 1985—. Mem. adv. bd. dept. chem. enging. Rutgers U., N.J., 1986-91. Contbr. articles to profl. jours. Leader ARC, Argentina, 1973-74; mem. Rotary, Argentina, 1975, Jaycees, N.C., 1984-85. NIH grantee, 1982, 84; Ministry of Edn. scholar Argentina, 1979; recipient Presdl. award Pres. of Argentina, 1968. Mem. N.Y. Acad. Sci., Soc. of Spectroscopy, Am. Chem. Soc. (Polymer Rsch. award 1999), Sigma Xi. Achievements include patents in coating technology; research in surface science, coating, cancer research, toxicology and rheology. Office: EI DuPont ExP Station H Clay & Rt 141 Bldg 402/21251 Wilmington DE 19880 E-mail: jose-esteban.valentini@usa.dupont.com.

VALERO, HERNANDO, statistics educator; b. Girardot, Colombia, July 24, 1954; came to U.S., 1979; s. Pablo Jose and Zoila Rosa (Melgarejo) V.; m. Patricia M. Correal, Oct. 24, 1977 (div. 1987); children: Hernando, Miguel; m. Damaris Diaz, Nov. 24, 1988; children: Pablo Jose, Damaris Rosaura. BS in Statistics, Nat. U., Bogota, 1979; MS in Statist. Computing, U. Ctrl. Fla., 1984; postgrad., Oreg. State U., 1992. Tchr. Am. Coll. High Sch., Girardot, 1971-72; instr. Universidad Externado de Colombia, Bogota, 1979, Universidad Jorge Tadeo Lozano, Bogota, 1979; grad. asst. U. Ctrl. Fla., Orlando, 1984; asst. prof. Universidad Pedagogica y Tecnologica de Colombia, Tunja, 1985-86; instr. U. P.R., Ponce, 1988-89; asst. prof. Inter Am. U., Ponce, 1986—. Vis. instr. U. Ctrl. Fla., 1985 Author study guides, data analysis, others in field. Mem. Math. Assn. of Am., Am. Statis. Assn. Avocation: soccer. Home: PO Box 324 Alta Vista Santa Isabel PR 00757-0324 Office: InterAm U Carr # 1 Mercedita Ponce PR 00715

VALESIO, PAOLO, Italian language and literature educator, writer; b. Bologna, Italy, Oct. 14, 1939; came to U.S., 1963; s. Germano and Maria (Galletti) V.; 1 child, Sara. Dottorato in Lettere, U. Bologna, 1961, Libera Docenza in Glottologia, 1969; MA (hon.), Yale U., 1976. Lectr. Istituto di Glottologia, U. Bologna, 1961-62, 67-68; teaching fellow dept. Romance langs. and lit. Harvard U., Cambridge, Mass., 1965-66, lectr., 1969-70, assoc. prof., 1970-73; assoc. prof. Italian, dir. grad. studies dept. French and Italian NYU, 1973-75; prof. Italian, chmn. dept. Yale U., New Haven, 1976-88, dir. grad. studies dept. Italian, 1989-94, chmn. dept. Italian, 1995—2001. Author: Novantiqua, 1980, Ascoltare il Silenzio, 1986, Gabriele d'Annunzio: The Dark Flame, 1992, (novel) Il Regno Doloroso, 1983, (poems) La Rosa Verde, 1987, Le Isole del Lago, 1990, Analogia del Mondo, 1992, Nightchant, 1995, (stories) S'Incontrano Gli Amanti, 1993; co-editor: Vocabolario Zingarelli, Bologna, 1970; Am. corr. mag. Poesia, Milan, 1992—. Recipient first prize Nat. Poetry Competition San Vito,

1992, Lit. prize Am. Assn. Italian Studies, 1993; named Cavaliere Ufficiale, Order of Merit of The Republic of Italy, 1994. Roman Catholic. Office: Yale Univ Dept Italian PO Box 208311 New Haven CT 06520-8311

VALETTE, REBECCA MARIANNE, Romance languages educator; b. N.Y.C., Dec. 21, 1938; d. Gerhard and Ruth Adelgunde (Bischoff) Loose; m. Jean-Paul Valette, Aug. 6, 1959; children: Jean-Michel, Nathalie, Pierre. BA, Mt. Holyoke Coll., 1959, LHD (hon.), 1974; PhD, U. Colo., 1963. Instr., examiner in French and German U. So. Fla., 1961-63; instr. NATO Def. Coll., Paris, 1963-64, Wellesley Coll., 1964-65; asst. prof. Romance Langs. Boston Coll., 1965-68, assoc., 1968-73, prof., 1973—2003, prof. emeritus, 2003—. Lectr., cons. fgn. lang. pedagogy; Fulbright sr. lectr., Germany, 1974; Am. Council on Edn. fellow in acad. adminstrn., 1976-77. Author: Modern Language Testing, 1967, rev. edit., 1977, French for Mastery, 1975, rev. edit., 1988, Contacts, 1976, rev. edit., 1993, 97, 2001, C'est Comme Ça, 1978, rev. edit., 1986, Spanish for Mastery, 1980, rev. edit., 1989, 94, Album: Cuentos del Mundo Hispanico, 1984, rev. edit., 1992, French for Fluency, 1985, Situations, 1988, rev. edit., 1994, Discovering French, 1994, 97, 2001, 2001, A votre tour, 1995, Ventanas Uno, 1998, Images 1, 2, 3, 1999, Reflections on the Connolly Book of Hours, 1999, Weaving the Dance, 2000, Discovering French Nouveau, 2004; contbr. articles to fgn. lang. pedagogy and Native Am. art publs. Decorated officer Palmes Académiques, chevalier Ordre Nat. du Mérite (France). Mem. MLA (chmn. div. on tchg. of lang. 1980-81), Am. Coun. on Tchg. Fgn. Langs., Am. Assn. Tchrs. French (v.p. 1980-86, pres. 1992-94), Alliance Francaise of Boston and Cambridge (pres. 2002—), Phi Beta Kappa, Alpha Sigma Nu, Pi Delta Phi. Home: 16 Mount Alvernia Rd Chestnut Hill MA 02467-1019 Office: Boston Coll Lyons 304 Chestnut Hill MA 02467-3804 E-mail: valette@bc.edu.

VALLAT, LOUISE MARIE, elementary school educator, poet; b. Bklyn., Jan. 13, 1945; d. Joseph Anthony and Marie (Curcio) DeRiggi; m. Bruce Robert Vallat, Sept. 3, 1966; children: Anthony Joseph, Deborah Maria. BA, CUNY-Queens Coll., 1976, MS in Elem. Edn., 1991. Cert. elem. tchr., elem. English tchr., N.Y. Tchr. Bd. Edn., N.Y.C. Pub. Schs., Bklyn., 1990—. Author: (poetry) From Kindergarten to Graduate School, 1992; contbr. poetry to Am. Poetry Anthologies, 1990. Named Poet of Merit, finalist Poet of Yr. contest Am. Poetry Assn., Santa Cruz, Calif., 1990; recipient Editor's Choice award Nat. Libr. Congress, 1993. Mem. Nat. Writing Project. Avocations: writing, painting, organ and guitar, storytelling, poetry.

VALLBONA, RIMA-GRETEL ROTHE, foreign language educator, writer; b. San Jose, Costa Rica, Mar. 15, 1931; d. Ferdinand Hermann and Emilia (Strassburger) Rothe; m. Carlos Vallbona, Dec. 26, 1956; children: Rima-Nuri, Carlos-Fernando, Maria-Teresa, Maria-Luisa. BA/BS, Colegio Superior de Senoritas, San Jose, Costa Rica, 1948; diploma, U. Paris, 1953; diploma in Spanish Philology, U. Salamanca, Spain, 1954; MA, U. Costa Rica, 1962; D in Modern Langs., Middlebury Coll., 1981. Tchr. Liceo J.J. Vargas Calvo, Costa Rica, 1955-56; faculty U. St. Thomas, Houston, 1964-95, prof. Spanish, 1978-95, Cullen Found. prof. Spanish, 1989, head Spanish dept., 1966-71, chmn. dept. modern fgn. lang. 5, 1978-80, prof. emeritus, 1995—. Vis. prof. U. Houston, 1975-76, Rice U., 1974, 80-83, 95, U. St. Thomas, Argentina, 1972; vis. prof. U. St. Thomas, Merida program, 1987-95. Author: Noche en Vela, 1968, Yolanda Oreamuno, 1972, La Obra en Prosa de Eunice Odio, 1981, Baraja de Soledades, Las Sombras que Perseguimos, 1983, Polvo del Camino, 1972, La Salamandra Rosada, 1979, Mujeres y Agonias, 1982, Cosecha de Pecadores, 1988, El arcangel del perdon, 1990, Mundo, demonio y mujer, 1991, Los infiernos de la mujer y algo mas, 1992, (crit. edit.) Vida i sucesos de la Monja Alferez, 1992, Flowering Inferno-Tales of Sinking Hearts, 1994, La narrativa de Yolanda Oreamuno, 1996, Tormy, la Prodigiosa Gata de Donaldito, 1997, Tejedoras de sueñnos versus realidad, 2003; mem. (editl. bd.) Letras Femeninas, 1984—98, Alba de America, U.S., sec. (culture) Inst. Literario y Cultural Hispanico; co-dir.: Foro Literario, 1987—89; contbg. editor: The Americas Rev., 1989—95; contbr. numerous articles and short stories to lit. mags. Mem. scholarship com. Inst. Hispanic Culture, 1978, 79, 88, 91, chmn., 1979, bd. dirs., 1974-76, 88-89, 91-92, chmn. cultural activities, 1979, 80, 85, 88-89; bd. dirs. Houstoh Pub. Libr., 1984-86; bd. dirs. Cultural Arts Coun. Houston, 1991-92. Recipient Aquileo J. Echeverria Novel prize, 1968, Jorge Luis Borges Short Story prize, Argentina, 1977, Agripina Montes del Valle Novel prize, 1978, Constantin Found. grant for rsch., U. St. Thomas, 1981, Lit. award, S.W. Conf. Latin Am. Studies, 1982, Ancora Lit. award, Costa Rica, 1984, Civil Merit award, King Juan Carlos I of Spain, 1989, Children's Book award, Bay Area Writers League, 2003. Mem.: Nat. Writers Assn., Inst. Lit. y Cultural Hispanico, Casa Argentina de Houston, Inst. Hispanic Culture Houston, Latin Am. Writers Assn. Costa Rica, Inst. Internat. de Lit. Iberoam., Latin Am. Studies Assn., Academia Norteamericana de la Lengua Espanola (elected), S.W. Conf. Orgn. Latin Am Studies, South Ctrl. MLA, Houston Area Tchrs. Fgn. Lang., Houston Area Tchrs. Spanish and Portuguese, Am. Assn. Tchrs. Spanish and Portuguese, Sigma Delta Pi, Phi Sigma Iota. Roman Catholic. Home: 3706 Lake St Houston TX 77098-5522 E-mail: rvallbona@aol.com.

VALLEE, MARIE LYDIA, library media specialist; b. St. Charles, Mo., Aug. 15, 1948; d. Leroy William and Lillian Irene Strack; m. James L. Vallee, Aug. 2, 1969; children: David, Ken. BS in Edn., U. Mo., 1969; MLS, Kans. State Tchrs. Coll., 1973. Cert. K-12 sch. libr., Mo. Libr. Blue Springs Jr.-Sr. HS, Mo., 1969-70, Harrisonville Sr. HS, Mo., 1970-94, libr. media specialist, 1994—. Mem. Harrisonville Cass R-IX Schs. Long-Range Planning Core Team, 1994-95, mem. technology planning com., 1997, fin. com., 1999-2000; mem. strategic planning com. Cass County Pub. Libr., 1999. V.p. Harrisonville Cmty. Tchrs. Assn., 1974-75, pres., 1975-76. Named Educator of Yr., Harrisonville C. of C., 1991, Harrisonville MNEA Svc. Excellence Award, 2001. Mem. ALA, NEA, Mo. Edn. Assn., Harrisonville Edn. Assn., Am. Assn. Sch. Librs., Mo. Assn. Sch. Librs., Beta Sigma Phi (Girl of Yr. award). Avocation: reading. Home: 105 S Price Ave Harrisonville MO 64701-2011 Office: Harrisonville Sr HS 1504 E Elm St Harrisonville MO 64701-2022

VALLENTYNE, PETER LLOYD, philosophy educator; b. New Haven, Mar. 25, 1952; s. John Ruben and Ann Vera (Tracy) V.; m. Marie Helene Pastides, June 26, 1981. BA, McGill U., Montreal, Que., Can., 1978; MA, U. Pitts., 1981, PhD, 1984. Actuarial supr. Great West Life Assurance Co., Winnipeg, Man., Can., 1973-75; asst. prof. U. Western Ont., London, 1984-88, Va. Commonwealth U., Richmond, 1988-90, assoc. prof. philosophy, 1990-2000, prof. philosophy, 2000—03. Editor: Contractarianism and Rational Choice: Essays on Gauthier, 1991, The Origin of Left-Libertarianism, 2000, Left-Libertarianism and Its Critics, 2000; assoc. editor: Politics, Philosophy and Economics, 2000, Desert and Justice, 6 vols., 2003; mem. editl. bd. Utilitas, 1994—, Econs. and Philosophy, 1998-2003, editor, 2003—, Ethics, 2003—. Mem. Am. Philos. Assn., Can. Philos. Assn., So. Soc. Philosophy and Psychology, Va. PHilos. Assn. (pres. 1994-95). Avocations: piano, ballroom dance, art films. Office: Dept Philosophy U Missouri Columbia Columbia MO 65211 Business E-Mail: Vallentynep@missouri.edu.

VALSARAJ, KALLIAT THAZHATHUVEETIL, chemical engineering educator; b. Tellichery, Kerala, India, Oct. 2, 1957; came to U.S., 1980; s. Mundayat B. Nambiar and Kalliat T. Bhanumathy; m. Nisha Valsaraj, Dec. 24, 1990; children: Viveca, Vinay. MS, Indian Inst. Tech., Madras, India, 1980; PhD, Vanderbilt U., 1983. Affiliate faculty U. Ark., Fayetteville, 1983-86; sr. rsch. assoc. Hazardous Waste Rsch. Ctr. La. State U., Baton Rouge, 1986-90, asst. prof., 1990-93, assoc. prof., 1994-99, Ike East prof. chem. engring., 1999—, dept. chem. engring. Mem. panel directions in separations NSF, 1989-90; cons. Balsam Engr. Cons., Salem, N.H., 1990-91, Vicksburg (Miss.) Chems., Borden Chems. and Plastics, La.; presenter in field. Author: Elements of Environmental Engineering: Thermodynamics and Kinetics, 1995, 2nd edit., 2000; contbr. numerous articles to profl. jours. Grantee Dept. Def., 1986-89, NSF, 1989, 92-95, 2001—, EPA, 1989-92, 93-97, 97-98, U.S. Army, 1998—. Mem. Am. Chem. Soc., Am. Inst. Chem. Engrs., Nat. Geographic Soc., Air and Waste Mgmt. Assn. Achievements include patent for innovative groundwater treatment; patent for subsurface NAPL treatment. Home: 6348 Hope Estates Dr Baton Rouge LA 70820 Office: La State U Dept Chem Engring Baton Rouge LA 70803-0001 E-mail: valsaraj@che.lsu.edu.

VAMOS, IGOR, art educator; MFA, U. Calif., San Diego. Instr. Calif. Inst. for the Arts; asst. prof. electronic art Rensselaer Poly. Inst., 1998—. Dir. media resources The Ctr. for Land Use Interpretation, L.A. Fellow, John Simon Guggenheim Meml. Found., 2003. Office: Rensselaer Poly Inst 110 8th St Troy NY 12180*

VAN ALMEN, KAREN, art educator; b. Cleve., Oct. 13, 1940; d. Richard Earl and Arla Marie (Northam) Van A.; m. Ken Connell 1963 (div. 1981); children: Korby Matthew, Kathren Diane, Kevin Andrew; m. Ronald Sackett, Feb. 14, 1985. BA, Baldwin-Wallace Coll., 1962; MA, Ohio State U., 1977. Cert. tchr. art edn., social studies, K-12, Mich. Art tchr. jr. high Bay Village (Ohio) City Schs., 1962-63; art tchr. H.S. Westchester County Schs., Hamilton, Ohio, 1963-64; art tchr. elem. Whitehall City Schs., Columbus, Ohio, 1964-66; tchr. Pennfield City Schs., Battle Creek, Mich., 1984-95. Med. art work purchased by Mich. State U. Med. Sch., East Lansing, 1990; participant Summer Tchr. Inst. on Latino Art and Culture in U.S., at Nat. Mus. Am. Art-Smithsonian Instn., 1995; tchr. art sr. citizens. Exhibited in group shows at Traverse City (Mich.) Resort, 1987, Stouffer's Battle Creek MAEA Exhibit, 1988, Tecumseh (Mich.) Radison Resort, 1989, Downtown Gallery, Grand Rapids, 1990, Noble Schuler's Gallery, Albion, Mich., 1990, Internat. Art and Galleries, Grand Rapids, 1990, Western Mich. U. Adminstrn. Bldg., Med. Art Exhbt., Kalamazoo, 1991, MAEA Exhibit, Battle Creek, 1991, Access Vision, Battle Creek, 1992, Fife Lake (Mich.) Gallery, 1994, Kalamazoo Area Shows, 1996, 98, Pub. Tea Ceremony, 1996, 98, Kalamazoo Art Inst. Area Show, 1996-98, S.W. Mich. Watercolors Artist Assn. Show, Sturgis, 1998, Burnham Brook, Battle Creek, Mich., 2003, others; pub. Teen Tour...Chicago's Sculptures, 1995, The Gallery, Battle Creek, Mich., 1999-2000, Art Ctr. Gallery at Commerce Point, Battle Creek, 2000-01, Art Works, Big Rapids, Mich., 2001; exhbt. med. art Bronson Hosp., Kalamazoo, Mich., 2001-2002, Med. Art on Tour Med. Hosps., 2002-, S.W. Mich. Watercolor Soc. exhibit, Kalamazoo, 2002. Amb. to Japan-Tchr. Exch., 1991. Recipient Outstanding Educator award W.K. Kellogg Found., Battle Creek, 1992. Mem. NEA, Nat. Art Edn. Assn., Mich. Art Edn. Assn. (coun. mem. liaison 1995-96), Mich. Edn. Assn., Pennfield Edn. Assn., S.W. Mich. Watercolor Soc. Avocations: canoeing to remote areas for photography and painting of wild life, creating art surrounding history of old towns in mich. Home: Westlake Woods Studio 55 Hickory Nut Ln Battle Creek MI 49015-1325 Studio: Little Manatee Springs Studio 3012 N Lemon Lime Dr Wimauma FL 33598 E-mail: kvanalmen@hotmail.com.

VAN ALSTYNE, JUDITH STURGES, retired language educator; b. Columbus, Ohio, June 9, 1934; d. Rexford Leland and Wilma Irene (Styan) Van Alstyne; m. Dan C. Duckham (div. 1964); children: Kenton Leland, Jeffrey Clarke. BA, Miami U., Oxford, Ohio, 1956; MEd, Fla. Atlantic U., 1967. Sr. prof. Broward CC, Ft. Lauderdale, Fla., 1967-88, spl. asst. women's affairs, 1972—88, dir. cmty. svcs., 1973—74, dir. cultural affairs, 1974—75; ret., 1988. Spkr., cons. Malaysian Coll., 1984; ednl. travel group tour guide, 1984—88; v.p., ptnr. Downtown Travel Ctr., Ft. Lauderdale, 1993—. Author: (book) Write It Right, 1980, Professional and Technical Writing Strategies, 5th edit., 2002; freelance writer travel articles: ; contbr. articles and poetry to profl. jours. Bd. dirs. Broward CC Found., Inc., Fla., 1973—, Broward Friends of Libr., Fla., 1994—98, Broward Friends Miami (Fla.) City Ballet, 1994—98, 2001—03; active Sister cities/People to People, Ft. Lauderdale, 1988—99; docent Ft. Lauderdale Mus. Art, 1988—, docent coun., 1999—2002, docent pres., 2001—03; officer, mem. Friends Mus., Ft. Lauderdale, 1992—, Broward Pub. Libr. Found., Fla., 1998. Recipient award of achievement, Soc. Tech. Comm., 1986, award of distinction, Fla. Soc. Tech. Comm. Mem.: English-Speaking Union (bd. dirs. 1984—89), Travelers Century Club. Democrat. Episcopalian. Home and Office: # 265 1688 S Ocean Ln Fort Lauderdale FL 33316-3346 E-mail: ladyvanj@aol.com., judithvanalstyne@aol.com.

VAN ALTENA, ALICIA MORA, language educator; b. San Juan, Argentina, May 31, 1945; came to U.S., 1986; d. Francisco and Pilar (Garcia) Mora; m. William Foster van Altena, June 2, 1986. MA in Edn., Nat. U., San Juan, 1978. Prof. 2d lang. state colls. and high schs., San Juan, 1971-80; asst. prof. State U., San Juan, 1981-86; teaching asst. So. Conn. State U., New Haven, 1987-88; lectr. Yale U., New Haven, 1987-91, dir .beginners, 1992-94, lang. coord., 1993-94, sr. lectr., 1993—. Bd. dirs. Fedn. of Tchrs. of English, Argentina, 1983-86. Roman Catholic. Avocations: travel, photography, gardening. Home: 105 Swarthmore St Hamden CT 06517-1916 Office: Yale U Yale Spanish Dept 82 Wall St # 90 New Haven CT 06511-6605

VAN AMBURGH, (BRENDA) ELIZABETH, principal; b. Dallas, July 22, 1963; d. Sam Wheeler Jr. and Brenda B. (Brock) Folsom; m. Michael Betts Van Amburgh, Dec. 19, 1987; children: Rachel, Hannah. BA in English, BA in Elem. Edn., U. Tex., Arlington, 1985; MEd, Tex. Woman's U., 1990. Cert. in reading, early childhood edn., gifted edn., supervision and adminstrn., Tex. Tchr. Plummer Elem., Cedar Hill, 1983-85; tchr. K-4th grade, 1985—; tchr. High Pointe Elem., Cedar Hill, 1985-87, Highlands Elem., Cedar Hill, 1987-97; tchr. grades 6-8 Midlothian (Tex.) Mid. Sch., 1997—99; prin. Longbranch Elem., Midlothian, 1999—. Presenter in field. Author: Have the HOTS for Reading!, 1991, Analogies, 1993. Mem. ASCD, Internat. Reading Assn., Tex. Assn. for Improvement of Reading, Tex. Elem. Prins., Phi Kappa Phi, Delta Kappa Gamma. Methodist. Avocations: musical and theatrical pursuits, needlecrafts, reading, writing. Home: 1440 Honeysuckle Ridge Ct Midlothian TX 76065-5680 E-mail: Beth_Van_Amburgh@midlothian-isd.net.

VAN AMBURGH, ROBERT JOSEPH, school system administrator; b. Albany, N.Y., Apr. 23, 1947; s. Roy Francis and Evelyn (Houting) Van A.; m. Barbara Ann McAteer, June 28, 1970; children: Brian, Amy. BA, Providence Coll., 1969; MA, Coll. of St. Rose, 1973. Cert. adminstr., N.Y. Tchr. City Sch. Dist. of Albany, 1969-77, supr. social studies, 1977—, prin. Albany evening H.S., 1979-85, prin. Albany summer sch., 1986—. Cons. N.Y. State Edn. Dept., Albany, 1983-86, Houghton Mifflin Pub., 1985. Mem. Albany Common Coun., 1983—, Albany County Dem. Com., 1973—, Capitalize Albany Commn., 1994—. Mem. Albany Pub. Schs. Adminstrs. Assn. (pres. 1989), N.Y. State Social Studies Supervisory Assn. (v.p. 1984-86, Supr. of Yr. 1994), Providence Coll. Alumni Assn. (pres. 1991-93, Disting. Svc. award 1994). Democrat. Roman Catholic. Avocations: basketball, politics, local history. Home: 34 Cambridge Rd Albany NY 12203-3002 Office: City Sch Dist of Albany 700 Washington Ave Albany NY 12203-1404

VAN APPLEDORN, MARY JEANNE, composer, music educator, pianist; b. Holland, Mich., Oct. 2, 1927; d. John and Elizabeth (Rinck) van A. MusB with distinction, Eastman Sch. Music, 1948, MusM, 1950, PhD in Music, 1966; postgrad., MIT, 1982. Chmn. music theory and music composition Tex. Tech. Univ., Lubbock, 1950—, chmn., founder symposium of contemporary music, 1951-82, chmn. grad. studies in music, 1970-81, Paul Whitfield Horn prof., 1989—. Mem. Ann. ASCAP Std. Panel AWards, 1980—2003. Author: Keyboard Singing and Dictation Manual, 1968; composer: Suite for Carillon (1st prize World Carillon Fedn. 1980), 1980, Cacophony for Band (Va. Coll. Band Dirs. Nat. Assn. award 1981), Lux: Legend of Sankta Lucia for Band, 1982, Liquid Gold for Saxophone and Tape (Premio Ancona award 1986), 1986, Four Duos for Viola and Cello (1st prize Tex. Composers Guild), 1987, Set of Seven (N.Y.C. Ballet), 1988, Sonatine for Clarinet and Piano, Weill Recital Hall, N.Y.C., 1988, 7th World Congress Women in Music, 1991, Concerto for Trumpet and Band, 1990, Festival a Kerkrade, Cantata: Rising Night After Night, 1990; music recorded by Vienna Modern Masters, Slovak Radio Orch. and Chorus, Bratislava, Czechoslovakia; composer: Terrestrial Music, a double concerto for violin and piano with string orch., 1997, Cycles of Moons and Tides for concert band, 1995, Rhapsody for Violin and Orch. recorded by Polish Radio Orch., 1997, Les hommes vides (T.S. Eliot's "The Hollow Men" in French translation by Pierre Leyris) for unaccompanied SATB choir, 1996, Symphony for Percussion Orchestra, 2000, Opus One CD177: Cycles of Moons and Tides for Symphonic Band, 1995, Passages (Brit. Trombone Assn. award 1996), Music of Enchantment for Native Am. flute, strings and percussion, 1997, Gestures for clarinet quartet, 1999, Miniatures for Trombone Quartet, 2000, Songs without Words for 2 coloratura sopranos and piano, 2000, Meliora, fanfare for orchestra, 2000, Symphony of Celebration, 2002, Soundscapes for bassoon and strings, 2002, Passages III for clarinet, violoncello and piano, 2003, A Symphony of Celebration for Orchestra, 2003. Commd. for carillon work Skybells Crystal Cath. Carillon, 1991. Recipient Internat. Trumpet Guild Brass Trio Competition award for Trio Italiano, 1996, Rhapsody for Violin and Orch., 1996, Incantations for Oboe and Piano, 1998, Five Psalms for Trumpet, Tenor Voice and Piano, 1998, Galilean Galaxies for Flute, Bassoon and Piano, 1998, Symphony for Percussion Orch., 2000, Festive Fanfare and Postlude for Trumpets, Snare Drums and Cymbals, 2000, A Symphony of Celebration, 2002, Meliora Symphony for Winds and Percussion, 2003; faculty rsch. grantee Tex. Tech. U ., 1982, MIT, 1982. Mem. ASCAP (mem. ann. std. panel awards 1980-2003), Soc. Composers Inc., Internat. League Women Composers, Delta Kappa Gamma (internat. scholar 1959-60), Mu Phi Epsilon, Alpha Chi Omega, Kappa Kappa Psi, Tau Beta Sigma. Home: 1629 16th St Apt 216 Lubbock TX 79401-4703 Office: Tex Tech U PO Box 42033 Lubbock TX 79409-2033 E-mail: mvanappl@ttacs.ttu.edu.

VAN ARENDONK, SUSAN CAROLE, elementary school educator; b. Marshalltown, Iowa, Feb. 16, 1954; d. Ernest Jerome and Alice Marjorie (Harmon) Groff; m. Wayne Alan Van Arendonk, Aug. 14, 1994. BS, Iowa State U., 1976; MS in Edn., U. Kans., 1981; EdS, U. Iowa, 2001. Professionally recognized spl. educator Coun. for Exception Children, 1999; nat. bd. cert. tchr. exceptional needs. Resource rm. aide Pinckney Elem., Lawrence, Kans., 1976-77; tchr. spl. edn. Booth Elem. Sch., Wichita, Kans., 1977-78; tchr. resource rm. Clinton (Iowa) Cmty. Schs., 1978-80; tchr. spl. edn. Henry Sabin Elem. Sch., Clinton, 1980-83; edn. specialist U. Iowa, 1984; cons. No. Trails Area Edn. Agy., Clear Lake, Iowa, 1984-86; tchr. resource rm. Tomiyasu Elem. Sch., Las Vegas, 1986-88, 90-92, tchr. 3d grade, 1988-90, 92-94; tchr. lang. arts, spl. edn. Haysville (Kans.) Mid. Sch., 1996-97; tchr. behavior disorders Heartspring, Wichita, Kans., 1997-98; tchr. spl. edn. Gammon Elem., Wichita, 1998-2000, Curtis Mid. Sch., Wichita, 2000—. Edn. specialist, student tchr. supr. U. Iowa, 1983, grad. asst. 1984; cons. Heartland Area Edn. Agy., Johnston, Iowa, 1994-96. Treas. State Rep. Campaign, Iowa, 1974, publicity chmn., 1974. Mem. Coun. Exceptional Children, Iowa State Alumni Assn. (life), U. Iowa Alumni Assn. (life), Humane Soc. Am., U. Kans. Alumni Assn., Phi Lambda Theta. Democrat. Jewish. Home: 2359 N Parkridge Ct Wichita KS 67205-2002 Office: Curtis Mid Sch 1031 S Edgemoor Wichita KS 67218 E-mail: wvonarendonk@cox.net.

VANARNHEM, SYLVIA, elementary education educator; b. Atlanta, Oct. 18, 1949; d. Arthur J. and Eva L. (Sadowsky) Frey; m. John Charles VanArnhem, Sept. 4, 1971; children: Chad Matthew, Jay Bradley. BS in Edn., Bowling Green State U., 1971; MA in Edn., Cleve. State U., 1991. Tchr. elem. sch. Montgomery County Schs., Blacksburg, Va., 1972-79, Willoughby (Ohio) - Eastlake Schs., 1984—. Leader student coun. Royalview Elem. Sch., Willowick, Ohio, 1987—, conflict mediation, 1988—, chair 4th grade, 1992—. Treas. Willowick Baseball League, 1986-92, coach, 1982-92. Named TV 8 Tchr. of Week, 1995, Tchr. of Yr., PTA, 1994; W-E Schs. Sci. grantee, 1989. Mem. NEA, Ohio Edn. Assn., Willoughby-Eastlake Tchrs. Assn. Republican. Lutheran. Avocations: softball, reading, traveling. Home: 8470 Mansion Blvd Mentor OH 44060-4142 Office: Royalview Elem Sch 31500 Royalview Dr Willowick OH 44095-4266 E-mail: we_vanarnhem@lgca.org.

VAN ARSDALE, STEPHANIE KAY LORENZ, cardiovascular clinical specialist, nursing educator, researcher; b. Butte, Mont., June 20, 1952; d. Hubert Nelson and Pauline Anna (Tebo) Lorenz; m. Roy Burbank Van Arsdale, June 18, 1978; children: Christopher, Erica. Diploma, St. Johns McNamara, Sch. Nursing, 1975; BSN cum laude, U. Utah, 1978, MSN, 1979; EdD, U. Ark., 1993. RN, Tenn.; cert. ACLS instr., Am. Heart Assn.; cert. BLS instr.-trainer, Am. Heart Assn. Staff nurse cardiovascular surg. ICU Presbyn. Hosp. Ctr., Albuquerque, 1975-76; staff nurse surg. ICU and CCU U. Utah Med. Ctr., Salt Lake City, 1976-78; clin. specialist residency LDS Hosp., Salt Lake City, 1979; asst. prof. dept. Baccalaureate Nursing Ea. Ky. U., Richmond, 1980-84; staff nurse critical care unit Pattie A. Clay Hosp., Richmond, 1981-83; med. clinician Washington Regional Med. Ctr., Fayetteville, Ark., 1985; cardiovascular clin. specialist VA Med. Ctr., Fayetteville, 1985-93; assoc. prof. U. Memphis, 1993-96; asst. prof. U. Ark. for Med. Scis., Little Rock, 1996-98; prof. Bapt. Coll. Health Scis., Memphis, 1998—2003; clinical educator perioperative svcs. LeBonheur Children's Hosp., Memphis, 2003—. CPR instr. in cmty., Fayetteville and Richmond, 1980-93; mem. adj. faculty div. nursing Northeastern State U., Tahlequah, Okla., 1986-93, U. Ark., Fayetteville, 1989-93; mem. adj. clin. faculty U. Ark. for Med. Scis. Coll. Nursing, Little Rock, 1988-93; charter mem., spkr. N.W. Ark. Critical Care Consortium, Area Health Edn. Ctr., Fayetteville, 1989-93; presenter in field. Contbr. articles to profl. jours. Coord., vol. Home Meals Delivery Program, Richmond, Ky., 1981-84; adminstrv. bd., Sunday sch. tchr., sec. adult forum Ctrl. United Meth. Ch., Fayetteville, 1986-87; troop leader Girl Scouts Am. NOARK Coun., Fayetteville, 1987-90; sound sys. operator Christ United Meth. Ch., 1993-96, choir mem. Recipient Nurse of Yr. award for excellence in nursing practice, Dist. 9, Ark. State Nurses Assn., 1987, Loewenberg Sch. of Nursing Uotstanding Faculty award, U. Memphis, 1995; grantee, Ctrl. U.S. Earthquake Consortium, 1993, U.S. Geologic Survey, 1994, Miss. Emergency Mgmt. Agy., 1996, Ill. Emergency Mgmt. Agy., 1998, Ind. Emergency Mgmt. Agy., 1998, USGS, 1996, 1999. Mem.: AACN (CCRN, bd. dirs., chpt. sec. program com. 1994—96, pres.-elect 1998, pres. 1998—2000), ANA (v.p. Dist. 9 1985—86, pres. 1987—88, mem. image com. 1990—93, chmn. program com. 1986—87, state 2d v.p. 1988—90, clin. nurse specialist coun. 1991—93), Nat. League for Nursing (mem. nominating com. Ky. 1984—85), Sigma Theta Tau. Methodist. Avocations: skiing, crafts. Home: 8872 Farmoor Rd Germantown TN 38139 Office: LeBonheur Childrens Hosp 50 N Dunlap Memphis TN 38103

VANARSDALL, ROBERT LEE, JR., orthodontist, educator; b. Crewe, Va., Feb. 7, 1940; s. Robert Lee Sr. and Margie Mae (Jenkins) V.; m. Sandra E. Hoffman, Aug. 11, 1962; children: Robert Lee III, Lesley, Ashley. BA in Econs., Coll. William and Mary, 1962; DDS, Med. Coll. Va., 1970; cert. Orthodontics and Periodontics, U. Pa., 1973. Diplomate Am. Acad. Periodontology, Am. Bd. Orthodontics. Staff Children's Hosp., Phila., 1973—; prof. orthodontics, chmn. dept. orthodontics U. Pa., Phila., 1981—; prof. dentistry, chmn. Med. Coll. Pa., Phila., 1989—. K.G. prof. orthodontics U. Sydney, Australia, 2001; bd. dir. Nat. Dental Ins. Co., Denver. Editor: Internat. Jour. Adult Orthodontics and Orthognathic Surgery, 1986-2003, Orthodontoics: Current Principles and Techniques, 2d edit., 1994, 3d edit., 2000; editl. bd. profl. jours.; contbr. articles to profl. jours. Bd. dirs. Phila. Soc. William and Mary Alumni Assn. Lt. USNR, 1962-65. Fellow Coll. Physicians of Phila. 1978, Am. Coll. Dentistry 1980. Mem. ADA, Am. Assn. Orthodontists, Stomatological Club Phila., Angle Soc. Orthodontists (v.p. ea. component), Phila. Soc. Orthodontists (pres. 1989, chmn. sci. affairs coun. 1990—), Internat. Coll. of Dentists. Roman Catholic. Avocations: antiques, architecture. Home: 208 Ashwood Rd Villanova PA 19085-1504 Office: Penn Dental Curtis Ctr 625 Walnut St Philadelphia PA 19106 Office Fax: 215-625-2430.

VANAUKER, LANA, recreational therapist, educator; b. Youngstown, Ohio, Sept. 19, 1949; d. William Marshall and Joanne Norma (Kimmel) Speece; m. Dwight Edward VanAuker, Mar. 16, 1969 (div. 1976); 1 child, Heidi. BS in Edn. cum laude, Kent (Ohio) State U., 1974; MS in Edn., Youngstown (Ohio) U., 1989. Cert. tchr., Ohio; nat. cert. activity cons. Phys. edn. instr. St. Joseph Sch., Campbell, Ohio, 1973-75; program dir. YWCA, Youngstown, 1975-85; exercise technician Youngstown State U., 1985—86; health educator Park Vista Retirement Ctr., Youngstown, 1986-87; sch. tchr. Salem (Ohio) City Sch., 1987-88; recreational therapist Trumbull Meml. Hosp., Warren, Ohio, 1988—. Activity cons. Mahoning/Trumbull Nursing Homes, Warren, 1990-92; adv. bd. rep. Ohio State Bur. Health Promotion Phys. Fitness, 1996—; mem. adv. bd. Ohio State Executive Physical Fitness Dept. Health, 1996; tchr. Mohican Youth Ctr., Loudonville, Ohio, 1998-99. Producer chair exercise sr. video Exercise is the Fountain of Youth, 1993; photographer, choreographer; cover photography feature Mahoning County Med. Soc. Bull., 2000; exhibited in group show Forum Health, 1999. Vol. Am. Cancer Soc., 1980—, Am. Heart Assn., 1986—, Dance for Heart, 1980-86; mem. State of Ohio Phys. Fitness Adv. Bd., 1996-97. Youngstown State U. scholar, 1986-89; recipient 1st pl. Kodak Internat. Newspaper Snapshot award, 1998-99, 1st Place Internat. Libr. Photography, 2000. Mem.: AAHPERD, U.S. Amateur Ballroom Dance Assn. (v.p. 2002—03), Pa. Activity Profl. Assn. (pres., spkr. 2001), Resident Activity Profl. Assn. (pres. 1994—96, 2001—03), Youngstown Camera Club (social chair 1989—90, pres. 1993—95), Kappa Delta Pi. Democrat. Presbyterian. Avocations: photography, international dance, volleyball, aerobics, travel. Home: 5764 S Turner Rd Canfield OH 44406-8737 Office: 4N Unit Forum Health 1350 E Market St Warren OH 44483-6608

VAN BRACKLE, ANITA SHORT, early childhood education educator; b. Alexandria, Va., Aug. 17, 1947; d. Verlon and Wilma (Moore) Short; m. Lewis N. Van Brackle III; 1 child, Robert Michael. BS in Elem. Edn., Radford U., 1969; MEd in Learning Disabilities, Va. Poly. Inst. and State U., 1977, EdD in Curriculum and Instrn., 1991. Tchr. grades 1-7, spl. edn., Radford, Va., 1970-72, Chatham, N.J., 1972-78, Roanoke, Va., 1978-79, Atlanta, 1979-88; instr. math. methods Va. Poly. Inst. and State U., Blacksburg, 1988-91; asst. prof. West Ga. Coll., Carrollton, 1991—. Faculty advisor Student Ga. Assn. of Educators, West Ga. Coll., 1991-93; presenter in field. Editor (newsletter) News & Notes, 1990-91, (jour.) Teachers Talking to Teachers: Putting Science in the Hands of Children, 1992-93. Rsch. grantee examining areas of stress West Ga. Coll., 1991-92, rsch. grantee the lang. of math. West Ga. Coll., 1991-92. Mem. Nat. Coun. Tchrs. of Math., Ga. Assn. Edn., NEA, Assn. of Curriculum and Devel., Assn. for Childhood Edn. Internat., Phi Kappa Phi, Phi Delta Kappa. Home: 1200 Cedarstone Dr Dallas GA 30132-4538 Office: Education Complex West Ga Coll Carrollton GA 30118

VAN BRUMMELEN, HARRO WALTER, education educator; b. The Hague, The Netherlands, Jan. 7, 1942; arrived in Can., 1953; s. Henry William and Nancy (Ryksen) Van B.; m. Wilma P. Demoor, Oct. 24, 1942; children: Glen, Timothy, Yolanda. BSc, McGill U., Montreal, Que., Can., 1963; MEd, U. Toronto, Ont., Can., 1972; EdD, U. B.C., Vancouver, 1984. Tchr. math. King City (Ont.) Secondary Sch., 1963-65, Toronto Dist. Christian H.S., Woodbridge, 1965-69; tchr., prin. Edmonton (Alta., Can.) Christian H.S., 1969-77; edn. coord. Soc. Christian Schs. B.C., Surrey, 1977-86; chair edn. dept. Trinity Western U., Langley, Canada, 1986-94, dean faculty social scis. and edn., 1991—97, dean undergrad. studies, 1997—2001, dean. Sch. Edn., 2001—. Mem. quality assessment bd. Govt. of B.C., 2003—. Author: Telling the Next Generation, 1986, Walking With God in the Classroom, 1988, 2d edit., 1998, Steppingstones to Curriculum, 1995, 2d edit., 2002; co-author: Vision With a Task, 1993; editor: Nurturing Christians as Reflective Educators, 1997. Bd. dirs. Inst. Christian Studies, Toronto, 1989-92; chair ch. coun. Christian Reformed Ch., Langley, B.C., Can., 1992-95, 2001—; mem. adv. bd. Tchrs. Christian Fellowship, Montreal, Que., 1992-95; mem. task force on edn. Evang. Fellowship Can., Markham, Ont., 1994-98; pres., Derby Reach Regional Park Assn., 1996-99; mem. B.C. Degree Quality Assessment Bd. Recipient award of recognition Min. Edn., Govt. B.C., Victoria, 1992, Award for Exceptional Contbns., Christian Schs. Internat., 1995. Mem. ASCD, Can. Soc. Study Edn., Can. Assn. Deans of Edn., B.C. Deans of Edn., Can. Assn. Curriculum Studies, Christian Tchrs. Assn. B.C. (hon.), Internat. Assn. for Promotion of Christian Higher Edn. Office: Trinity Western U 7600 Glover Rd Langley BC Canada V2Y 1Y1 E-mail: vanbrumm@twu.ca.

VANBRUNT-KRAMER, KAREN, business administration educator; b. Milw., May 1, 1934; D. Roy Charles and Viola Marguerita (Yerges) VanBrunt; m. Allen Lloyd Weitermann (div. 1963); 1 child, Tera Lee Johnson; m. Keith Kramer (div. 1979); children: Holden Jon, Stafford James. BS, U. Wis., 1956; MA, NYU, 1976; PhD, Ohio State U., 1992. Owner Design By Karen Lee, Larchmont, N.Y., 1975-82; interior designer Maurice Vallency Design, N.Y.C., 1976-79; grad. rsch. assoc. Ctr. on Edn. and Tng. for Employment, Columbus, Ohio, 1987-92; assoc. prof. bus. adminstrn. St. Joseph Coll., West Hartford, Conn., 1992-99. Lectr. and curriculum developer entrepreneurship state vocat. schs., high schs., colls., and univs. throughout U.S. and Ea. Europe, 1987-92; instr. Berkeley Sch., White Plains, N.Y., 1968-82; adj. prof. N.Y.C. C.C., 1979-83, Milw. Area Tech. Coll., 1983-85, Columbus (Ohio) State C.C., 1986-90, Capital U., Columbus, 1998, U. Wis. Milw., Mt. Mary Coll., Milw.; participant Women in Soc. Citizen Amb. Program to China, 1997, leader Women in Exec. Mgmt. Bus., 1998; mem. Inst. World Affairs, U. Wis., Milw., 1999—. Mem. Wadsworth Atheneum, Hartford, 1992—99, West Hartford Art League, 1993—99; vol. U. Conn. Health Ctr., Farmington, Little Sisters of the Poor, St. Joseph Residence, Enfield, Conn., 1989—92, Milw. Art Mus.; docent Columbus Symphony Orch., 1986—92; mem. women's guild First Cmty. Ch., Columbus, 1985—92. Mem. AAUP (membership chair 1993-97), AAUW (past social chair Wis. br.), NAFE, World Affairs Coun., Am. Vocat. Assn., Ohio Vocat. Assn., Coalition for Effective Orgns., Am. Mktg. Assn., Am. Mgmt. Assn., Nat. Edn. Ctr. for Women in Bus., World Federalist Assn. (Milw. sec./treas. 2001—), Phi Beta Kappa, Phi Kappa Phi, Phi Lambda Theta, Phi Delta Kappa, Delta Pi Epsilon, Omicron Tau Theta. Avocations: theatre, art, music, photography, ice dancing. Home: 125 N University Dr Unit 322S West Bend WI 53095-2954

VAN BULCK, MARGARET WEST, financial planner, educator; b. Chgo., Nov. 25, 1955; d. Lee Allen and Margaret Ellen (Sauls) West; m. Hendrikus E.J.M.L. van Bulck, Aug. 7, 1976; children: Marcel Allen, Sydney Josette. BS in Mktg., U. S.C., 1978; MA in Econs., Clemson U., 1981. CPA, S.C. Econs. instr. St. Andrews Presbyn. Coll., Laurinburg, N.C., 1980-82; staff acct. L. Allen West, CPA, Sumter, S.C., 1982-84; ptnr. West & Van Bulck, CPAs, Sumter, 1984-88, Van Bulck & Co., CPA's, Sumter, 1989—. Part time instr. U. S.C., Sumter, 1985-87, mem. full time faculty, 1989-92. Contbr. articles to profl. jours. Treas. Make-A-Wish Found., Sumter, 1985-87, wish granting chmn. 1987-88; edn. found. chmn. Laurinburg/Scotland County chpt. AAUW, 1981-83; treas. Friends Sumter County Library, 1986-88, Sumter Gallery of Art, 1989-91; mem. Jr. Welfare League, Sumter; Circle Bible leader, Sunday Sch. tchr., hospice vol., 1990-92; deacon First Presbyn. Ch., 1994-97; den leader pack 86 Boy Scouts of Am., 1992-95, troop com. mem., advancement chair, 1998-2001, troop com. treas., 2000-. Recipient Sirrine Found. award, Clemson U., 1978, 79; grantee U.S. Dept. Labor, 1979-80. Mem. AICPA, S.C. Assn. CPAs, Internat. Assn. Fin. Planning, Sumter Estate Planning Coun. (past treas.), Trian Club (treas. 1998—), Carolinian Club, Omicron Delta Epsilon. Presbyterian. Home: 234 Haynsworth St PO Box 1327 Sumter SC 29151-1327 Office: Van Bulck & Co CPAs PO Box 1327 Sumter SC 29151-1327 E-mail: margaretvb@sc.rr.com., margaret@vanbulckCPAs.com.

VAN BUREN, PHYLLIS EILEEN, Spanish and German language educator; b. Montevideo, Minn., June 4, 1947; d. Helge Thorfin and Alice Lillian (Johnsrud) Goulson; m. Barry Redmond Van Buren, Apr. 4, 1970; children: Priscila Victoria Princesa, Barry Redmond Barón. Student, Escuela de Bellas Artes, Guadalajara, Mex., 1968; BS, St. Cloud (Minn.) State U., 1969, MS, 1976; postgrad., Goethe Inst., Mannheim, West Germany, 1984, U. Costa Rica, 1989; PhD, The Union Inst., Cin., 1992. Instr. in Spanish Red Wing (Minn.) Pub. Schs., 1969-70; instr. in Spanish and German St. Cloud Pub. Schs., 1970-80; prof. foreign lang. edn., German and Spanish St. Cloud State U., 1975, 79—. Advanced placement reader Ednl. Testing Svcs., Princeton, N.J., 1987—; translator in field; mem. Cen. State Adv. Bd. Contbr. articles to El Noticiero, Minn. Lang. Rev., Hispania; textbook reviewer. Coord. children's programs St. Cloud, 1970—; vol. ELS instr. St. Cloud Community, 1973—; reviewer St. Cloud Pub. Schs., 1985-89. Dept. Def. fellow, 1969, Goethe Inst. fellow, 1983; grantee N.W. Area Found., 1985-86, Bush Found., 1986, Fund for the Improvement of Postsecondary Edn./NEH, 1993-97. Mem. AAUW (exec. bd. 1988-92, grantee Minn. Internat. AR 1992), ASCD, MLA, Am. Assn. Tchrs. Spanish and Portuguese, Am. Assn. Tchrs. German, Am. Coun. Tchg. Fgn. Langs. (tester 1989—), Minn. Coun. Tchg. Fgn. Langs. (exec. bd.), Nat. Network for Early Lang. Learning, Phi Kappa Phi (pres.-elect 1991-92, pres. 1992-93), Sigma Delta Pi, Delta Kappa Gamma, Delta Phi Alpha. Republican. Lutheran. Avocations: family, camping, cross-country skiing, swimming, crafts. Home: 3001 County Rd # 146 Clearwater MN 55320-1405 Office: St Cloud State U 720 4th Ave S Saint Cloud MN 56301-4498

VAN CAMP, DIANA J. music educator; b. Washington, Oct. 24, 1946; d. Gordon Ashley and Gabrielle Marie-Anne Van Camp. B in Music Edn., Ind. U., 1969; MusM, Fla. State U., 1976; PhD in Music Edn., Ohio State U., 1989. Cert. tchr. music K-12 Ohio. Orch. tchr. Gainesville (Fla.) City Schs., 1969—72; orch. tchr., profl. violinist Memphis Symphony and Schs., 1975—79; music edn. and orch. tchr. Otterbein Coll., Westerville, Ohio, 1979—82; tchg. assoc. music edn. Ohio State U., Columbus, 1982—85; orch. dir. Bexley (Ohio) City Schs., 1985—86, Newark (Ohio) City Schs., 1987—. Pvt. violin studio, Newark, 1990—. Violinist: Southea. Ohio Symphony, 1992—, Welsh Hills Symphony, 1990—, Land of Legend Philharmonic, 1995—, Ctrl. Ohio Symphony, 2000—. Grantee, Nat. Endowment for the Arts, 1975—79. Mem.: Ohio Music Educators Assn., Music Educators Nat. Conf., Sigma Alpha Iota. Avocations: walking, hiking, swimming, church work. Home: 125 Beechtree Rd Whitehall OH 43213

VANCE, CYNTHIA LYNN, psychology educator; b. Norwalk, Calif., Mar. 31, 1960; d. Dennis Keith and Donna Kay (Harryman) V. BS, U. Oreg., 1982; MS, U. Wis., Milw., 1987, PhD, 1991. Tchg. asst. U. Wis., Milw., 1983-89; computer graphics mgr. Montgomery Media, Inc., Milw., 1987-92; asst. prof. Cardinal Stritch Coll., Milw., 1992-93, Piedmont Coll., Demorest, Ga., 1993-99, assoc. prof., 1999—. Contbr. articles to profl. jours. Mem. bd. advisors North Ga. Tech. Inst., 1997-99; vol. Dunwoody (Ga.)-DeKalb Kiwanis Club, 1993—. Ga. Gov.'s Tchr. fellow, 2000-01. Mem. AAUP, APA, Assn. Women in Psychology, S.E. Psychol. Assn., Am. Psychol. Soc., Am. Assn. Higher Edn. Office: Piedmont Coll PO Box 10 Demorest GA 30535-0010

VANCE, DAVID A. information systems educator; b. Anchorage, 1948; s. Alvin V. and Mary Vance; m. Nancy Niemann; children: John, Emily, Ryan. AA, Grossmont Coll., 1976; BBA, Nat. U., 1982, MBA, 1984, postgrad., 1985; PhD, So. Ill. U., 2000. Ordained to ministry United Christian Faith Ministries, 2002. Tech. supr. USN, San Diego, 1970-74; engr., project mgr. Wavetek Data Communications, San Diego, 1975-79; v.p. ops. Specialized Systems, Inc., San Diego, 1979-81; prin. Sunhill R&D, San Diego, 1981-84; exec. dir. Brunswick Inst. Tech., San Diego, 1985; tech. staff mem. Veda, Inc., Orlando, Fla. and San Diego, 1985-88; tng. analyst Eagle Tech., Inc., Winter Park, Fla., 1988-89; prof. mgmt. Fla. So. Coll., Orlando, 1988-94; tchr., student mgmt. doctoral program So. Ill. U., Carbondale, 1994-99; asst. prof. Miss. State U., 1999—2000, prof., 2000—. Prin. DA Vance & Assocs., Winter Park, 1986-94; adj. prof. mgmt. Webster U., 1991-94, Fla. So. Coll., 1988-94; vis. asst. prof. So. Ill. U., 1991-94; lectr. in field. Rep. precinct committeeman, Orange County, Fla., 1988, del. state conv., 1988; chmn. svc. com. CSO, Inc., 1991. Recipient Achievement award ACCESS, San Diego, 1980; Worthy scholar Woodrow Wilson Found., 1966, Leadership scholar Nat. U., San Diego, 1984. Mem. Am. MENSA, Ltd., Internat. Platform Assn., Info. Resources Mgmt. Assn., Computer Profls. for Social Responsibility. Avocations: outdoor sports, music. Office: Miss State U Dept Mgmt and IS PO Box 9581 Mississippi State MS 39762-9581

VANCE, ELBRIDGE PUTNAM, mathematics educator; b. Cin., Feb. 7, 1915; s. Selby Frame and Jeannie (Putnam) V.; m. Margaret Gertrude Stoffel, Aug. 5, 1939 (div. 1975); children: Susan (Mrs. Timothy Griffin), Peter Selby, Douglas Putnam, Emily (Mrs. Charles Harold Beynon III); m. Jean Haigh, Jan. 1975. Student, Haverford Coll., 1932-33; AB, Coll. Wooster, 1936; MA, U. Mich., 1937, PhD, 1939. Asst. U. Mich., 1937-39; instr. U. Nev., 1939-41, asst. prof., 1941-43; vis. lectr. Oberlin (Ohio) Coll., 1943-46, asst. prof., 1946-50, asso. prof., 1950-54, prof., 1954-83, prof. emeritus, 1983—, chmn. dept., 1948-77, acting dean Coll. Arts and Scis., 2d semester, 1965-66, 1st semester, 1970-71. Chmn. advanced placement com. Coll. Entrance Exam. Bd., 1961-65, chief reader, 1956-61; chmn. com. examiners math. Comprehensive Coll. Tests, Ednl. Testing Service, 1965-67 Author: Trigonometry, 2d edit, 1969, Unified Algebra and Trigonometry, 1955, Fundamentals of Mathematics, 1960, Modern College Algebra, 3d edit, 1973, Modern Algebra and Trigonometry, 3d edit, 1973, An Introduction to Modern Mathematics, 2d edit, 1968, Mathematics 12, 1968, Solution Manual for Mathematics 12, 1968; Book review editor: Am. Math. Monthly, 1949-57; asso. editor, 1964-67. Mem. Oberlin Sch. Bd., 1952-60, pres., 1957-60. NSF Faculty fellow, 1960-61 Mem. Math. Assn. Am., Nat. Council Tchrs. of Math., Am. Math. Soc., Phi Beta Kappa, Sigma Xi, Phi Kappa Phi. Home: 315 Yorktown Pl Apt D4 Vermilion OH 44089-2104

VANCE, ELIZABETH ANN, retired elementary school educator; b. Macon, Ga., Aug. 30, 1947; d. William Poole and Frances Irene (Cooner) V. AB in English, Mercer U., 1969, MEd in Elem. Edn., 1972, EdS in Early Childhood Edn., 1991. Cert. tchr., Ga. Tchr. 1st grade Eugenia Hamilton Sch.-Bibb County, Macon, 1969-70; tchr. Danforth Primary-Bibb County, Macon, 1970—2000; intervention program tchr. Florence Bernd Sch.-Bibb County, Macon, 2001—02. Mem. Macon Jr. Woman's Club, 1984-96, sec. 1986, 88, 92; MJW Club rep. to the Mus. of Arts Scis. Bd. Dirs.; mem. Prof. Aux. of Mus. of Arts and Scis., Macon, 1979-91; chmn., 1985-87. Mem. ASCD, Profl. Assn. Ga. Educators, Internat. Reading Assn., Macon Symphony Guild, Mus. Guild Inc. of Mus. Arts and Scis. (sec. 1993—), Macon 2000 Ptnrship, Middle Ga. Hist. Soc., Phi Delta Kappa, Delta Kappa Gamma (sec. 1992-96, pres. 1996-98), Alpha Delta Kappa (sec. 1984-86, v.p. 1992-94, pres. 1994-96). Presbyterian. Avocation: gardening. Home: 797 Boulevard Macon GA 31211-1404 Office: Danforth Primary Sch Bibb County 1301 Shurling Dr Macon GA 31211-2194

VANCE, PAUL L. school system administrator; b. Phila. From tchr. to adminstr. Phila. Sch. System, 1961—72; intern supt. Balt. Pub. Schs., 1972—73, Washington Pub. Schs., DC, 1973; dep. supt. Balt. Schs., 1973—77; area assoc. supt. Montgomery County Schs., 1977—87, dep. supt., 1987—91, supt., 1991—99; ret., 1999; supt. D.C. Pub. Schs., Washington, 2000—. Office: DC Pub Schs 825 N Capitol St Srte 900 Washington DC 20002

VANCE, PHOEBE AVALON, educator; b. Chattanooga, Tenn., May 27, 1949; d; Thomas Byrd and Ava Lee (McCullough) V. BS, U. Tenn., 1973, MS, 1974, EdD, 1978. Lic. profl. counselor, Tenn.; nat. cert. counselor; cert. cognitive-behavioral therapist, level 1 trained in eye movement desensitization and reprocessing. Securities broker Henderson, Few & Co., Knoxville, Tenn., 1978; owner, oper. Vance Furniture Co., Jasper, Tenn., 1980-88; mem. grad. faculty, asst. prof. U. Tenn., Chattanooga, 1989—. Mem. career adv. bd. Stephens Coll., Columbia, Mo., 1993—; mem. srs. adv. bd. Chattanooga State Tech. C.C., 1992-94; spkr., presenter in field. Mem. AAUP, ACA, Tenn. Counseling Assn., Tenn. Assn. Marriage and Family Counselors (charter), Tenn. Assn. Counselor Edn. and Supervision (sec. 1993-95), Internat. Assn. Marriage and Family Therapists, Tenn. Mental Health Counselors Assn. Avocations: travel, scuba diving. Home: 6755 Hickory Brook Rd Chattanooga TN 37421-1773 Office: U Tenn Chattanooga 615 Mccallie Ave Chattanooga TN 37403-2504

VANCE, SANDRA JOHNSON, secondary school educator; b. Parkersburg, W Va, Oct. 23, 1945; d. Maurice Aubrey and Louise Mindwell (Price) Johnson; m. Larry Wayne Vance, June 24, 1970; children: Edward Maurice, James Allen. BS in Phys. Edn., W.Va. U., 1969; MEd, Ga. State U., 1972, EdS, 1985. Cert. mental retardation, career, phys. edn. and health, gen. sci., vocat. edn., instrnl. supervision. Tchr. interrelated resource Birney Elem. Sch., Cobb, Ga., 1969-80; tchr. MIMH Tapp Mid. Sch., Cobb, Ga., 1980-85; related vocat. instruct. specialist Pebblebrook HS, Cobb, Ga., 1980-83; related vocat. instrn. specialist Douglas County HS, Douglasville, Ga., 1983—2002, advisor for related vocat. instrn., head dept. spl. edn., 1999—2002. Treas. Related Vocat. Instrn. Enrichment Camp, 1985-93; advisor related vocat. instrn. Douglas County H.S. Club, Douglas County Student Coun. for Exceptional Children, 1988-95; instr. for staff devel. on computers, 1995—; mem. spl. edn. adv. panel Ga. Dept. Edn., 1997-99. Mem. Tech. Com.; instr. ARC; com. treas. Troop 749 Boy Scouts Am., Mableton, 1993-95. Mem. NEA, Ga. Assn. Career and Tech. Ed., Coun. for Exceptional Children, Ga. Fedn. Coun. for Exceptional Children (treas. 1989-91), Ga. Edn. Assn., Douglas County Assn. Educators, Douglas County Coun. for Exceptional Children (pres. 1986), Metro Atlanta Coun. for Exceptional Children (pres. 1987), Kappa Delta Pi. Home: 4636 Rodney Pl Austell GA 30106-1938

VANCE, TAMMY RENA, special education educator; b. Ogden, Utah, July 1, 1966; d. James Carl Andre and Virginia Nell (Betts) Camp; m. Steven Allen Vance Sr., June 24, 1983; children: Steven Allen Jr., Jennifer Lauren. AAS, East Ark. C.C., 1986; BS in Edn., Ark. State U., Jonesboro, 1988, postgrad., 1989. Cert. tchr. early childhood and elem. sch. tchr., cert. tchr. mid. sch. English, Ark. Tchr. 1st grade Lee Acad., Marianna, Ark., 1988-89, Wheatly (Ark.) Elem. Sch., 1989-90; substitute tchr. Wynne (Ark.) Pub. Schs., 1990-91, paraprofl. 1st grade, 1991-93; substitute tchr. Wynne Intermediate Sch., 1993, spl. edn. tchr. 3rd grade, 1994—. Dir. day care facility Tiny Town, Wynne, 1990. Active Christian Coalition, 1992—; treas. Women's Missionary Union; tchr., pianist, children's dir. East Bapt. Ch., 1987—. Mem. Gamma Beta Phi. Republican. Avocations: church activities, playing piano, song writing, camping, activities with family and friends. Home: 702 N Terry St Wynne AR 72396-2244 Office: Wynne Intermediate Sch Bridges St Wynne AR 72396

VANDAM, LEROY DAVID, anesthesiologist, educator; b. N.Y.C., Jan. 19, 1914; s. Albert Herman and Esther Henrietta (Cahan) V.; m. Regina Phyllis Rutherford, Nov. 30, 1939; children: Albert Rutherford, Samuel Whiting. PhB magna cum laude, Brown U., 1934; MD, NYU, 1938; MA, Harvard U., 1967. Diplomate Am. Bd. Anesthesiology. Resident surgeon Beth Israel Hosp., Boston, 1942-43; fellow in surgery Johns Hopkins Hosp., Balt., 1945-47; asst. prof. anesthesia U. Pa. Med. Sch., Phila., 1951-54; instr. in anesthesia WHO, Copenhagen, 1953; surgeon Peter Bent Prigham Hosp., Boston, 1954-69; prof. of anaesthesia Harvard Med. Sch., Boston, 1967-80, prof. emeritus, 1980—. Mem. com. on revision U.S. Pharmacopoeia, Washington, 1970-75. Editor-in-chief Jour. Anesthesiology, 1962-70; mem. editorial bd. New Eng. Jour. Medicine, 1976-80; author texts: (with others) Introduction to Anesthesia, 1967—, To Make the Patient Ready for Anesthesia, 1980, 2d edit., 1984, The Genesis of Contemporary Anesthesia, 1982; contbr. over 250 articles, revs. to profl. publs., chpts. to books. 1st lt. Med. Corps, AUS, 1943-73. Fellow Am. Coll. Cardiology; mem. Assn. Univ. Anesthesiologists (pres. 1964-65, Disting. Svc. award 1967), Halsted Surg. Soc., Aesculapian Club, Phi Beta Kappa, Sigma Xi, Alpha Omega Alpha. Home: 10 Longwood Dr Apt 268 Westwood MA 02090-1141 Office: Brigham & Women's Hosp 75 Francis St Boston MA 02115-6106

VANDAMENT, WILLIAM EUGENE, retired academic administrator; b. Hannibal, Mo., Sept. 6, 1931; s. Alva E. and Ruth Alice (Mahood) V.; m. Margery Vandament, Feb. 2, 1952; children: Jane Louise, Lisa Ann. BA, Quincy Coll., 1952; MS, So. Ill. U., 1953; MS in Psychology, U. Mass., 1963, PhD, 1964; LittD, No. Mich. U., 1997. Psychologist Bacon Clinic, Racine, Wis., 1954-61; NDEA fellow U. Mass., Amherst, 1961-64; asst. prof. SUNY, Binghamton, 1964-69, univ. examiner and dir. instl. research, 1969-73, asst. v.p. planning, instl. research, 1972-76; exec. asst. to pres., dir. budget and resources Ohio State U., Columbus, 1976-79, v.p. fin. and planning, 1979-81; sr. v.p. adminstrn. NYU, N.Y.C., 1981-83; provost, vice chancellor acad. affairs Calif. State U. System, Long Beach, 1983-87; Trustees prof. Calif. State U., Fullerton, 1987-92; pres. No. Mich. U., 1991-97, ret., 1997. Contbr. articles to psychol. jours. and books on higher edn. Office: 2662 E 20th St Apt 310 Signal Hill CA 90755 E-mail: vandament@aol.com.

VAN DEBURG, WILLIAM LLOYD, educator; b. Kalamazoo, May 8, 1948; s. Lloyd E. and Cora E. Van Deburg; m. Alice Honeywell, July 1, 1967 (div. Feb. 1988); children: Marcie, Theodore; m. Diane Sommers, June 17, 1989. BA, We. Mich. U., 1970; MA, Mich. State U., 1971, PhD, 1973. Asst. prof. U. Wis., Madison, 1973-79, assoc. prof., 1979-85, prof., 1985—. Author: The Slave Drivers, 1979, Slavery and Race in American Popular Culture, 1984, New Day in Babylon, 1992 (Gustavus Myers Ctr. Outstanding Book award 1993), Black Camelot, 1997; editor: Modern Black Nationalism, 1997. Nat. Def. Edn. Act fellow U.S. Govt., 1970-73, Penrose Fund grantee Am. Philos. Soc., 1974, grantee Alfred P. Sloan Found., 1975, fellow Danforth Found., 1975-81, grantee Spencer Found., 1979, rsch. associateship William F. Vilas Trust, 1986-88, Evjue-Bascom professorship, 2003. Mem. Orgn. Am. Historians. Office: U Wis 4141 HC White Hall 600 N Park St Madison WI 53706-1403 E-mail: wlvandeb@facstaff.wisc.edu.

VANDEN, HARRY EDWIN, political science educator; b. Wilmington, Del., Sept. 29, 1943; s. Harry Edwin Sr. and Rena Baker (Van Zandt) V.; m. Vera Esther Ballin, Sept. 3, 1967 (div. Feb. 1995); children: David Jeffrey, Jonathan Harry. Diploma, U. Madrid, 1965; BA, Albright Coll., 1966; MA, Cert. in L.Am. Studies, Syracuse U., 1969; PhD, New Sch. Social Rsch., 1976. Field rsch. coord. Nat. Opinion Rsch. Ctr., N.Y.C., 1969-70; adj. asst. prof. Richmond Coll., CUNY, N.Y.C., 1971; Fulbright scholar U.S. Govt., Lima, Peru, 1973-74; tech. expert Inst. Nacional Administración Pública, Lima, 1974-75; from asst. prof. to prof. U. South Fla., Tampa, 1975—, dir. Caribbean and L.Am. Ctr., 1993-97. Author: Mariátegui: influencias en su formación ideológica, 1975, National Marxism in Latin America, 1986, A Bibliography of Latin American Marxism, 1991; co-author: Democracy and Socialism in Sandinista Nicaragua, 1993, Latin America: The Power Game, 2002; co-editor: The Undermining of the Sandinista Revolution, 1997; contbr. articles to profl. jours., chpts. to books. V.p. bd. dirs. WMNF Cmty.

Radio, Tampa, 1990-96; bd. dirs. Hispanic Svcs. Coun., Tampa, 1996-2003; internal. election observator with Jimmy Carter/Carter Ctr., Venezuela, 1998, Nicaragua, 2001. NEH grantee, 1980. Mem. Soc. for Iberian and L.Am. Thought (pres. 1983-85), Southeastern Coun. on L.Am. Studies (pres. 1988-89), L.Am. Studies Assn. (co-chair Ctrl. Am. sect. 1997-2000), Am. Polit. Sci. Assn., Am. Soc. Internat Law. Democrat. Avocations: Judo, swimming, sailing. Office: U South Fla Dept Govt 4202 E Fowler Ave Tampa FL 33620-8100 E-mail: vanden@chuma1.cas.usf.edu.

VANDENBERG, DONALD, retired education educator, philosopher; b. Milw., Wis., Aug. 4, 1931; arrived in Australia, 1976; s. Richard Albert and Elsie Eleanor Dorothy (Sheamann) V.; m. Erma Jean Pinkston, May 19, 1955; children: Marta, Donald Jr., Sara Ellen. BA cum laude, Maryville Coll., 1958; MA, U. Wis., 1961; PhD, U. Ill., 1966. Cert. high school English tchr., philosopher of edn. at tertiary level. English tchr. Whitehall (Mich.) Sr. H.S., 1960-62; philosopher of edn. U. Calgary, Alta., Can., 1965-68, 72-73, Pa. State U., State College, 1968-72, UCLA, 1973-76; reader in edn. U. Queensland, Brisbane, Australia, 1976-96, ret., 1996. Author: Being and Education, 1971, Human Rights in Education, 1983, Education as a Human Right, 1990; editor: Teaching and Learning, 1969, Theory of Knowledge and Problems of Education, 1969, Phenomenology and Educational Discourse, 1997; contbr. articles to profl. jours. With USN, 1949-53. Coe fellow in Am. studies, U. Wyoming, Laramie, 1958-59; recipient GTA award U. Ill., Urbana, 1962-65. Fellow Philosophy of Edn. Soc. (program com. 1971-72). Avocations: running, swimming, gardening, housekeeping. Home: 737 W Broad St Eufaula AL 36027-1913 E-mail: dvanden1@earthlink.net.

VANDERGRIFF, SUSAN ELLEN, special education educator; b. Bklyn., June 10, 1951; d. Rudolph and Estelle (Gruber) Schiffman; m. John Oliver Vandergriff, Apr. 2, 1977; children: Remington Wyatt; stepchildren: Debbie, Nita, John, Jim. AA, Kingsboro C.C., Bklyn., 1971; BA in Psychology, CUNY, 1974; MEd, U. Ariz., 1981. Cert. tchr. Ariz., Mo. Presch. tchr. Children's Learning Ctr., Bklyn., 1974-75; remedial math. tchr. Laquey (Mo.) Elem. Sch., 1977-80; spl. edn. tchr. Tucson United Sch. Dist., 1982-97, Camdenton (Mo.) R-111 Sch. Dist., 1997—. Mem. NEA, CEC, Internat. Reading Assn., Learning Disability Assn. Avocations: gardening, home food canning. Office: Camdenton R-111 Oak Ridge Elem Sch PO Box 1409 Camdenton MO 65020-1409

VANDERHOEF, LARRY NEIL, academic administrator; b. Perham, Minn., Mar. 20, 1941; s. Wilmar James and Ida Lucille (Wothe) Vanderhoef; m. Rosalie Suzanne Slifka, Aug. 31, 1963; children: Susan Marie, Jonathan Lee. BS, U. Wis., Milw., 1964, MS, 1965; PhD, Purdue U., 1969, Doctorate (hon.), 2000, Inje U. Korea, 2002. Postdoctorate U. Wis., Madison, 1969—70; asst. prof. biology U. Ill., Urbana, 1970-74, assoc. prof., 1974—77, prof., 1977—80, head dept. plant biology, 1977—80; provost Agrl. and Life Scis., U. Md., College Park, 1980—84; exec. vice chancellor U. Calif., Davis, 1984—91, exec. vice chancellor, provost, 1991—94; chancellor, 1994—. Rsch. assoc. U. Wis., 1970—72; vis. investigator Carnegie Inst., 1976—77, Edinburgh (Scotland) U., 1978; cons. in field. Fellow, NRC, 1969—70, Eisenhower fellow, 1987; grantee Dimond Travel grantee, 1975, NSF, 1972, 1974, 1976—79, NATO, 1980. Mem.: AAAS, Nat. Assn. State Univ. and Land Grant Colls. (exec. com. 2000—), Am. Soc. Plant Physiology (bd. editors 1977—82, trustee, exec. com., treas. 1982—88, chmn. bd. trustees 1994—97). Home: 16 College Park Davis CA 95616-3607 Office: U Calif Davis Office Chancellor Davis CA 95616

VANDERHOOFT, JAN ERIC, orthopedic surgeon, educator; b. Salt Lake City, May 16, 1962; s. Gerard F. and Else-Marie Vanderhooft; m. Sheryll Jo Vanderhooft, Mar. 25, 1984; children: Peter, Lauren. BS, Stanford (Calif.) U., 1984; MD, U. Utah, 1988. Cert. Am. Bd. Orthopaedic Surgeons, added qualification in hand surgery. Resident, fellow U. Wash., Seattle, 1988-94; attending physician Salt Lake Orthopedic Clinic, 1994—; clin. dir. orthop. rotation St. Mark's Hosp. U. Utah, 1998—; clin. dir. family medicine residency orthop. rotation Columbia St. Mark's, 1998—. Clin. instr. U. Wash., 1993-94; asst. clin. prof. dept. orthopedics U. Utah. Contbr. articles to profl. jours. and chpts. to textbooks. Bd. dirs. Turn Cmty. Svcs., Salt Lake City, 1996—, chmn. bd., 2000—. Recipient: Family Medicine Res. award for excellene in tchg., 1995, 96, 98, 99. Fellow Am. Acad. Orthopaedic Surgeons; mem. Western Musculoskeletal Assn. (bd. dirs. 1995-96), Am. Soc. for Surgery of Hand, Utah Med. Assn., Western Orthop. Assn., Utah Orthopedic Soc., Alpha Omega Alpha. Office: Salt Lake Orthopedic Clinic 1160 E 3900 S Ste 5000 Salt Lake City UT 84124-1275

VAN DER PLUIJM, BERNARDUS ADRIANUS (BEN VAN DER PLUIJM), geologist, educator; b. Enschede, The Netherlands, Sept. 30, 1955; arrived in U.S., 1985; m. Elisabeth H. Quint; children: Wouter, Robert. MS, U. Leiden, 1981; PhD, U. New Brunswick, 1984. Asst. prof. U. Mich., Ann Arbor, 1985-91, assoc. prof., 1991-96, prof. geol. sci., 1996—, prof. environ., 2003—, dir. global change program, 2000—. Office: U Mich Dept Geological Sciences Ann Arbor MI 48109 E-mail: vdpluijm@umich.edu.

VAN DER SPIEGEL, JAN, engineering educator; b. Aalst, Belgium, Apr. 12, 1951; arrived in U.S., 1980; s. Robert and Celestine Van der Spiegel. BSEE, U. Leuven, 1971, MSEE, 1974, PhD in Elec. Engring., 1979; M of Arts and Sci., U. Pa., 1988. 2d lt. Belgian Air Force, 1979—80; asst. prof. elec. engring. U. Pa., Phila., 1981-87, assoc. prof., 1987-95, prof. elec. engring., 1995—, dir. Ctr. Sensor Tech., 1989-98, chmn. dep. elec. engring., 1998—2002, interim chmn. dept. elec. and sys. engring., 2002—. Patentee integ. ambient sensing, radiation sens. retina sens., gen prupost neural comp., novel ferroelectric sensors, background calibration for pipelined analog-digital converters; editor Sensors and Actuators, 1986—. Postdoctoral fellow U. Pa., 1980-81; named Presdl. Young Investigator The White House, 1984. Fellow IEEE; mem. Neural Network Soc., Tau Beta Pi. Office: U Pa Ctr Sensor Techs Moore Sch Elec Engring 200 S 33d St Rm 203 Philadelphia PA 19104-6314

VANDERSYPEN, RITA DEBONA, guidance counselor, academic administrator; d. Sam S. and Myrtle (Genova) DeBona; m. Robert Louis Vandersypen, Aug. 17, 1974; children: Regina Marie, Ryan Matthew. BA summa cum laude, La. Coll., 1975; MEd, La. State U., 1980, postgrad., 1982; EdS, Northwestern State U., Natchitoches, La., 1993. Eligibility worker Rapides Parish Office Family Svcs., Alexandria, 1975-78; welfare social worker Rapides Parish Foster Care Svcs., Alexandria, 1978-79; tchr. A. Wettermark High Sch., Boyce, La., 1979-84; tchr. English English Alexandria Sr. High Sch., 1984-92, guidance counselor, 1992-2000; asst. prin., curriculum coord. Brame Jr. H.S., Alexandria, La., 2000—. Contbr. to handbook and curriculum guide. Sponsor Future Voters Am. Club, 1984-89, 4-H Club, 1988-97. Mem. Rapides Assn. Principals, Rapides Fedn. Tchrs., La. Assn. Principals, La. Vocat. Assn., La. Mid. Sch. Assn., Rapides Livestock Club, Belgian-Am. Club, Am. Quarter Horse Assn., Phi Kappa Phi, Kappa Delta Pi. Roman Catholic. Office: Brame Jr HS 4800 Dawn St Alexandria LA 71301-3301

VAN DER TUIN, MARY BRAMSON, headmistress; b. Tiquisate, Guatemala, Dec. 28, 1939; came to U.S., 1957; d. George Peabody Jr. and Edelgard (Kohkemper-Meza) Hamlin; (div.); children: Rachel Bramson, Ruth Bramson. BA, Wellesley Coll., 1961; cert. tchr., Swarthmore Coll., 1981; MA in Ednl. Adminstrn., Mich. State U., 1992. Tchr.'s aide Wellesley (Mass.) Coll. Nursery Sch., 1960; recreation aide Judge Baker Guidance Clinic, Boston, 1961; tchr. English and history St. Dunstan's Episcopal Sch., Christiansted, U.S.V.I., 1964-65; tchr. history Marple-Newtown (Pa.) Sr. H.S., 1967-74, Springside Sch., Chestnut Hill, Pa., 1976-84, dir. upper sch., 1975-80; headmistress Kingswood Sch. Cranbrook, Bloomfield Hills, Mich., 1980-85, Eton Acad., Birmingham, Mich., 1986—2003. Evaluator Ind. Schs. Assn. of Ctrl. States, 1984—2003, North Ctrl. Assn. Colls. and Schs., Ann Arbor, Mich., 1990—2003, cons. Eton Acad., 2003-. Pres. Assn. Ind. Mich. Schs., 1982-85, 2001-03; bd. dirs. Overseas Edn. Fund, Washington, 1978-80, Ind. Ednl. Svcs., Princeton, N.J., 1982-85, Henry Ford Med. Ctr., West Bloomfield, 1990-96, Arts Found. of Mich., Detroit, 1992-96, Reading to Reduce Recidivism, 1994-99, The Friends' Sch., Detroit, 1997-2000; mem. sch. bd. Wallingford-Swarthmore (Pa.) Sch. Dist., 1975-78; pres. Birmingham Cmty. Coalition, 2000-03, bd. mem. Kingsbury Sch., 2003-, Edn. Freedom Fund, 2003-. Mary Bramson Faculty Devel. Fund created in her honor, Cranbrook Schs., Kingswood Sch. Alumnae, 1985; Klingenstein Vis. fellow Tchrs.' Coll., Columbia U., N.Y.C., 1997; recipient Athena award Birmingham C. of C., 2002. Mem. Mich. Assn. Learning Disabilities Educators, Assn. Ind. Mich. Schs. (pres. 2000-2003). Avocations: learning, reading in spanish and english, volunteering for latino agendas, arts, gardening.

VANDERVEEN, JOSEPH RICHARD, special education administrator; b. Muskegon, Mich., June 12, 1937; s. J. Barnie and M. Gertrude (Dwyer) V.; m. Hollee Beadle, Feb. 1962 (div. Feb. 1989); children: Joseph, Heather, Patrick; m. Rosemary Whittington, Jul.1, 2002. BA, Western Mich. U., 1960, MA, 1965, EdS, 1971. Cert. secondary sch. tchr., sch. psychologist, adminstr., Mich. Tchr., coach Ravenna (Mich.) Schs., 1960-63, Springfield (Mich.) Pub. Schs., 1963-65; sch. psychologist St. Joseph Intermediate Sch. Dist., Centreville, Mich., 1965-67; dir. psychol. svcs. Kent Intermediate Sch. Dist., Grand Rapids, Mich., 1967-76, regional dir. spl. edn., 1984-90; dir. spl. edn. Forest Hills Pub. Schs., Grand Rapids, 1976-84; regional dir. spl. edn. Kentwood (Mich.) Pub. Schs., 1990-96; ret., 1996. Clin. psychologist Psychiat. Cons. Svcs., Grand Rapids, 1976-85; adj. prof. Mich. State U., Lansing, 1975-77, Grand Valley State U., Allendale, Mich., 1978-90. Author: Handbook for School Psychologists, 1974, also curriculum materials. Mem. exec. bd. Kent County Spl. Olympics, Grand Rapids, 1971-76; advisor Kent County Community Mental Health Bd., Grand Rapids, 1974-76. Mem. Coun. for Exceptional Children (pres. Grand Rapids chpt. 1990-93), West Mich. Pers. and Guidance Assn. (pres. 1980-81), Grand Rapids Area Psychol. Assn. (sec. 1973-79), Mich. Assn. Sch. Psychologists (pres. 1976), Nat. Assn. Sch. Psychologists (del. 1978-81), Mich. Assn. Soc. Spl. Edn. Adminstrs., KC, Phi Delta Kappa (sec. 1991-96). Roman Catholic. Avocations: tennis, basketball, softball, furniture refinishing, golf. Home: 1559 E Westchester Dr Chandler AZ 85249

VANDER VELDE, WALLACE EARL, aeronautical and astronautical educator; b. Jamestown, Mich., June 4, 1929; s. Peter Nelson and Janet (Keizer) Vander V.; m. Winifred Helen Bunai, Aug. 29, 1954; children: Susan Jane, Peter Russell. BS in Aero Engring, Purdue U., 1951; Sc.D., Mass. Inst. Tech., 1956. Dir. applications engring. GPS Instrument Co., Inc., Newton, Mass., 1956-57; mem. faculty Mass. Inst. Tech., 1957—, prof. aero. and astronautics, 1965—. Cons. to industry, 1958— Author: Flight Vehicle Control Systems, Part VII of Space Navigation, Guidance and Control, 1966, (with Arthur Gelb) Multiple-Input Describing Functions, 1968; also papers. Served to 1st lt. USAF, 1951-53. Recipient Edn. award Am. Automatic Control Coun., 1988. Fellow AIAA; mem. IEEE. Home: 50 High St Winchester MA 01890-3314 Office: MIT Rm 9-335 Dept Aero and Astronautics Cambridge MA 02139

VANDER WEG, PHILLIP DALE, art educator, academic administrator, sculptor; b. Benton Harbor, Mich., Aug. 16, 1943; s. Sam Dirk and Trena (Poort) Vander W.; m. Judith Greville, Dec. 15, 1966; 1 child, Kara Sue. BS in Design, U. Mich., 1965, MFA, 1968. Art instr., prof. art Mid. Tenn. State U., Murfreesboro, 1968-89, acting head Mufreesboro, 1983-85, 88-89; chair dept. art, prof. art We. Mich. U., Kalamazoo, 1989-97, 00—, prof. art, 1998—. Cons., editl. reviewer Prentice-Hall Pubs., Englewood Cliffs, N.J., 1978-90; mem. region 5 adv. panel Mich. Artist Program, Detroit Inst. Art, 1990-92; mem. rev. panel Tenn. Art Commn. Visual Arts, Nashville, 1986-89. Prin. works include Columbia State U., 1979, Vanderbilt U., Nashville, 1987, Tenn. Arts Commn., 1988. Mem. Kalamazoo Pub. Art Commn., 1992—. Mem. Nat. Assn. Schs. of Art and Design, Nat. Coun. Art Adminstrs., Founds. in Art Theory and Edn. (founder, bd. dirs. 1976-84). Home: 6791 Penny Ln Kalamazoo MI 49009-8539 Office: Western Mich U Dept Art Oliver St Kalamazoo MI 49008

VANDERWERF, MARY ANN, elementary school educator, consultant; b. Buffalo, N.Y., Aug. 18, 1938; d. Richard and Petronella Gertruida (Hell) V.; m. Malcolm Donald Brutman, Apr. 30, 1989; 1 child, Susan Still. BS in Edn., SUNY, Buffalo, 1970, MA in English, 1971, PhD in Rsch. and Evaluation in Edn., 1981. Cert. tchr., N.Y. Legal sec. Hetzelt & Watson, Buffalo, 1957-64; exec. sec. Bell Aerospace Corp., Wheatfield, N.Y., 1964-69; tchr. Amherst (N.Y.) Ctrl. Schs., 1972-94; instr. SUNY, Buffalo, 1979, 85-86, children's lit. cons., 1980-92; pres., cons., facilitator The Synergy Advantage, Inc., Amherst, 1994-99; collaborator U.S. Space and Rocket Ctr./U.S. Space Acad., Huntsville, Ala., 1995-97. Presenter Williamsville Ctrl. Schs., Internat. Reading Assn., Ireland, 1982, Anaheim, Calif., 1983, New Orleans, 1985, 89, Toronto, Ont., Can., 1988, N.Y. State English Coun., Amherst, 1984, St. Bonaventure U., 1984, Amherst Ctrl. Sch. Dist., 1986, 92, 94, Creative Problem Solving Inst., Buffalo, 1986—, Early Childhood Edn. Conf., 1988, Early Childhood Edn. Coun. Western N.Y., Buffalo, 1990, U. Nev., Las Vegas, 1991; book reviewer Harper Collins Children's Books, 1991; adj. prof. tchg. strategies Canisius Coll., Buffalo, 1997-99. Author: (with others) Science and Technology in Fact and Fiction/Children's, 1989, Science and Technology in Fact and Fiction: Young Adult, 1990, Teacher to Teacher: Strategies for the Elementary Classroom, 1993; contbr. articles to profl. jours. Advisor child life dept. Children's Hosp., Buffalo, 1984-85. Mem. Am. Fedn. Tchrs., Internat. Reading Assn. (cons. Niagara Frontier Reading Coun.), Creative Edn. Found., N.Y. State Coun. Tchrs. English (presenter), Children's Lit. Assn., Hans Christian Andersen Soc., Pi Lambda Theta (Alpha Nu chpt.). Avocations: sailing, reading, grandparenting, traveling. Home: 1860 N Forest Rd Williamsville NY 14221-1321 also: 3933 Cape Cole Blvd Punta Gorda FL 33955-3818

VANDEVENDER, BARBARA JEWELL, elementary education educator, farmer; b. Trenton, Mo., Dec. 4, 1929; d. Raleigh Leon and Rose Rea (Dryer) S.; m. Delbert Lyle Vandevender, Aug. 15, 1948; children: Lyle Gail, James R. BS, N.E. Mo. State U., 1971, MA, 1973. Elem. tchr. Williams Sch., Spickard, Mo., 1948-49; reading specialist Spikard R-2 Sch., 1971-74, Princeton (Mo.) R-5 Sch., 1974—. Mem. ad hoc com. State Dept. Edn., Jefferson City, Mo., 1994-95; speaker in field. Pres. Spickard PTA, 1963-64, Women's Ext. Club, Galt, Mo.; foster mother Family Svcs., Trenton, Mi., 1972-79; mem. ad hoc com. State Dept. of Edn., Jefferson City, Mo., 1994-95. Pres. Spickard PTA, 1963-64, Women's Ext. Club, Galt, Mo.; foster mother Family Svcs., Trenton, Mo., 1972-79; mem. ad hoc com. State Dept. Edn., Jefferson City, Mo., 1994-95. Recipient Mo. State Conservation award Goodyear Tire Co., Akron, Ohio, 1972, Balanced Farming award Gulf Oil Co., N.Y.C., 1972, Mo. State Farming award Kansas City C. of C., 1974, FHA State Farming award, Jefferson City, Mo., 1974, Outstanding Leadership Mo. U., Columbia, 1976, Ednl. Leadership award MSTA, Columbia, 1984, Outstanding Contbn. to Internat. Reading Assn., Newark, Del., 1988, Mo. Senate Resolution of Achievement, 1998. Mem. Internat. Reading Assn. (pres. North Ctrl. coun. 1985-86). Republican. Baptist.

VANDEVERE, JOYCE RYDER, retired educator, activist; b. Alameda, Calif., Feb. 17, 1927; d. Loren Lincoln and Isabel (Snyder) Ryder; m. Judson Eells Vandevere, Aug. 15, 1956; children: Keith Ryder, Gwyn Shelley. BA magna cum laude, Pomona Coll., 1948; MA in Psychology, Stanford U., 1951. Prin. Presidio Hill Nursery Sch., San Francisco, 1951-53; tchr. Aid to Retarded Children Nursery Sch., San Francisco, 1953-56, Head Start, Seaside, Calif., 1969; kindergarten & elem. tchr. The Learning Community sch. Monterey (Calif.) Peninsula Unified Sch. Dist., 1971-88; ret., 1988. Pres. Women's Internat. League for Peace & Freedom, Monterey, 1990—92; treas. Coalition of Minority Orgns., Monterey, 1991—; chair Peace Coalition of Monterey County, 1991—92, 1995—2001; mem. Monterey County Commn. on the Status of Women, 2000—, vice-chair, 2002—. Recipient Ralph Atkinson Civil Liberties award, Monterey County ACLU, 2000, Pearl Ross Feminist Activist award, 2002. Mem. Phi Beta Kappa, Sigma Xi. Home: 93 Via Ventura Monterey CA 93940-4340

VAN DE WALLE, ETIENNE, demographer; b. Namur, Belgium, Apr. 29, 1932; came to U.S., 1961; s. Arnould and Yolande (Blommaert) Van De W.; m. Francine Robyns de Schneidauer, Aug. 24, 1955; children: Dominique, Nicolas, Jean-Francois, Patrice. Dr. in Law, U. Louvain, Belgium, 1956, MA in Econs., 1957, PhD in Demography, 1973. Researcher Irsac, Rwanda, Burundi, 1957-61; rsch. assoc. Princeton (N.J.) U., 1962-64, rsch. staff, 1964-67, rsch. demographer, 1967-72; vis. lectr. U. Calif., Berkeley, 1971-72; prof. U. Pa., Phila., 1972—. Dir. Population Studies Ctr., U. Pa., 1976-82; sr. assoc. The Population Coun., Bamako, Mali, 1982. Author: The Female Population of France, 1974; co-author: The Demography of Tropical Africa, 1968. Fellowship Woodrow Wilson Ctr. for Scholars, 1976. Mem. Internat. Union for Scientific Study of Population, Population Assn. of Am. (pres. 1992). Home: 261 Sycamore Ave Merion Station PA 19066-1545 Office: Population Studies Ctr 3718 Locust Walk Philadelphia PA 19104-6209 E-mail: etiennev@pop.upenn.edu.

VANDIVER, FRANK EVERSON, institute administrator, former university president, author, educator; b. Austin, Tex., Dec. 9, 1925; s. Harry Shultz and Maude Folmsbee (Everson) V.; m. Carol Sue Smith, Apr. 19, 1952 (dec. 1979); children: Nita, Nancy, Frank Alexander; m. Renée Aubry, Mar. 21, 1980. Rockefeller fellow in humanities, U. Tex., 1946-47, Rockefeller fellow in Am. Studies, 1947-48, MA, 1949; PhD, Tulane U., 1951; MA (by decree), Oxford (Eng.) U., 1963; HHD (hon.), Austin Coll., 1977; DHL (hon.), Lincoln Coll., 1989, BA (hon.), 1994. Apptd. historian Army Service Forces Depot, Civil Service, San Antonio, 1944-45, Air U., 1951; prof. history La. State U., summers 1953-57; asst. prof. history Washington U., St. Louis, 1952-55, Rice U., Houston, 1955-56, assoc. prof., 1956-58, prof., 1958-65, Harris Masterson Jr. prof. history, 1965-79, chmn. dept. history and polit. sci., 1962-63, dept. history, 1968-69, acting pres., 1969-70, provost, 1970-79, v.p., 1975-79; pres., chancellor N. Tex. State U., Denton and Tex. Coll. Osteo. Medicine, 1979-81; pres. Tex. A&M U., College Station, 1981-88, pres. emeritus, disting. U. prof., 1988—; founding pres. Acad. Marshall Plan, 1992; Sara and John Lindsey chair in humanities, 1988. Harmsworth prof. Am. history Oxford U., 1963-64; vis. prof. history U. Ariz., summer 1961; master Margarett Root Brown Coll., Rice U., 1964-66; Harmon lectr. Air Force Acad., 1963; Keese lectr. U. Chattanooga, 1967; Fortenbaugh lectr. Gettysburg Coll., 1974; Phi Beta Kappa assoc. lectr., 1970— ; vis. prof. mil. history U.S. Mil. Acad., 1973-74; hon. pres. Occidental U., St. Louis, 1975-80; chmn. bd. Am. U. Cairo, 1992-97, acting pres., 1997-98. Editor: The Civil War Diary of General Josiah Gorgas, 1947, Confederate Blockade Running Through Bermuda, 1981-65: Letters and Cargo Manifests, 1947, Proceedings of First Confederate Congress, 4th Session, 1953, Proceedings of Second Confederate Congress, 1959, A Collection of Louisiana Confederate Letters; new edit., J.E. Johnston's Narrative of Military Operations; new edit., J.A. Early's Civil War Memoirs, The Idea of the South, 1964, Battlefields and Landmarks of the Civil War, 1996; author: Ploughshares Into Swords: Josiah Gorgas and Confederate Ordnance, 1952, Rebel Brass: the Confederate Command System, 1956, Mighty Stonewall, 1957, Fields of Glory, (with W.H. Nelson), 1960, Jubal's Raid, 1960, Basic History of the Confederacy, 1962, Jefferson Davis and the Confederate State, 1964, Their Tattered Flags: The Epic of the Confederacy, 1970, The Southwest: South or West?, 1975, Black Jack: The Life and Times of John J. Pershing, 1977 (Nat. Book Award finalist 1978), (address) The Long Loom of Lincoln, 1986, Blood Brothers: A Short History of the Civil War, 1992, Shadows of Vietnam: Lyndon Johnson's Wars, 1997, 1001 Things Everyone Should Know About the Civil War, 1999, 1001 Things Everyone Should Know About World War II, 2002; also hist. articles, mem. bd. editors: U.S. Grant Papers, 1973—. Mem. bd. trustees Am. U. in Cairo, 1988, chmn., 1992-97. Recipient Laureate Lincoln Acad., Ill., 1973, Carr P. Collins prize Tex. Inst. Letters, 1958, Harry S. Truman award Kansas City Civil War Round Table, Jefferson Davis award Confederate Meml. Lit. Soc., 1970, Fletcher Pratt award N.Y. Civil War Round Table, 1970, Outstanding Civilian Svc. medal Dept. Army, 1974, Nevins-Freeman award Chgo. Civil War Round Table, 1982, T. Harry Williams Meml. award, 1985, Pres. medal Am. U. in Cairo, 1999; named Hon. Knight San Jacinto, 1993, Hon. Mem. Sons of Republic of Tex., 1986; rsch. grantee Am. Philos. Soc., 1953, 54, 60, Huntington Libr. rsch. grantee, 1961; Guggenheim fellow, 1955-56. Fellow Tex. Hist. Assn.; mem. Am. Hist. Assn., So. Hist. Assn. (assoc. editor jour. 1959-62, pres. 1975-76), Tex. Inst. Letters (past pres.), Jefferson Davis Assn. (pres., chmn. adv. bd. editors of papers), Soc. Am. Historians (councillor), Tex. Philos. Soc. (pres. 1978), Civil War Round Table (Houston), Orgn. Am. Historians, Phi Beta Kappa. Clubs: Cosmos, Army and Navy (Washington); Briarcrest Country (College Station). Achievements include originating idea of Coll. space grant program. Office: The Mosher Inst for Internat Policy Studies Texas A&M U 2400 TAMU Blocker Bldg College Station TX 77843-2400 E-mail: smaxwell@tamu.edu.

VAN DOMELEN, JOHN EMORY, retired English studies educator, gemstone dealer; b. Macon, Ga., Dec. 5, 1935; s. John Bouwens and Margaret Lucinda Van Domelen; m. Paula Joyce Van Domelen, Aug. 25, 1962; children: John Paul, Elizabeth Dawn, Clifford Bruce. BA, Calvin Coll., 1957; MA, U. Mich., 1960; PhD, Mich. State U., 1964. Asst. prof. English Wis. State U., Platteville, 1963-67; assoc. prof. English U. No. Iowa, Cedar Falls, 1967-70; prof. English Tex. A&M U, College Station, 1970-96. Propr. The Carat Patch, College Station, 1990-2003. Author: Tarzan of Athens, 1987, Bibliography: John Heath-Stubbs, 1987, The Haunted Heart, 1993. Bd. dirs. Mus. Natural History, Bryan, Tex., 1974-75. Fulbright scholar, 1990-91. Republican. Methodist. Avocations: reading, travel, gardening. Home: 310 Lee Ave College Station TX 77840-3149 E-mail: carat310@juno.com.

VAN DOMMELEN, DAVID B. artist, educator; b. Grand Rapids, Mich., Aug. 21, 1929; s. Henry and Thelma (Brown) Van D.; m. Michal Bohnstedt; children: Erica, Dorn. Diploma in interior design, Harrington Inst., Chgo., 1951; BA, Mich. State U., 1956, MA, 1957. Art cons. Warren (Mich.) Schs., 1957-59; instr. home art Pa. State U., State College, 1959-62, assoc. prof. interiors, 1964-73, prof. art edn., 1973-87, prof. emeritus, 1987—. Asst. prof. design, U. Maine, Orono, 1962-64; instr., Haystack Mountain Crafts Schs., Deer Isle, Maine, 1963, 64, 74, Arrowmont Arts and Crafts, Gatlinburg, Tenn., 1971-82; vis. prof., U. Iowa, Iowa City, 1967, 68, 70. Author: Decorative Wall Hangings: Art with Fabric, 1962, Walls: Enrichment & Ornamentation, 1965, Designing & Decorating Interiors, 1965, New Uses for Old Cannonballs, 1966, Doughboy Letters, 1977, North to the Past, 1997, Allen Eaton: Dean of American Crafts, 2003; contbr. articles to profl. jours.; represented in numerous art exhbns. Cpl. U.S. Army, 1952—54. Grantee for craft rsch., Ford Found., 1972, OAS, 1976, Pa. State U., 1986; recipient Eleanor Fishborn award, Ednl. Press. Am., 1973. Mem. Am. Craft Coun., Am. Home Econs. Assn. (bd. dirs. 1966-71), Pa. Home Econs. Assn. (pres. 1970), Am.-Scandinavian Found., Internat. Fedn. Home Econs., Lions. Avocation: stamp collecting. Home: RR 1 Box 631 Petersburg PA 16669-9248 Office: Pa State U 207 Arts Coll University Park PA 16802

VAN DOVER, KAREN, middle and elementary school educator, curriculum consultant, language arts specialist, lecturer; b. Astoria, N.Y. d. Frederick A. and Frances L. (Thomas) Van D. BA, CUNY; MALS, SUNY, Stony Brook; postgrad., St. John's U., Jamaica, N.Y. Cert. permanent N-6 tchr., art tchr. K-12, sch. adminstr., supr., N.Y. Tchr., sch. dist. adminstr. St. James (N.Y.) Elem. Sch.; tchr. Nesaquake Intermediate Sch., St. James, lead tchr. English, 1984-92, Smithtown Mid Sch., St. James, 1992-93, curriculum specialist, 1993—. Leader staff devel. and curriculum devel. workshops Smithtown Sch. Dist., 1984—, mem. supt.'s adv. com. for gifted and talented, mem. supt. adv. com. for lang. arts assessment, mem. textbook selection coms. site-based mgmt. team, 1994—, chair 1996-99, master tchr. bd. Prentice Hall, Englewood Cliffs, N.J., 1990—, chair ELA com. for curriculum and the stds., 2000. Contbg. author: Prentice Hall Literature Copper, 1991, 94. Corr. sec. Yaphank Taxpayers and Civic Assn., 1984-86, Nesaquake Sch. PTA, 1990-91, mem., 1977-92; mem. Smithtown Mid. Sch. PTA, 1992—. Mem. ASCD, Am. Ednl. Rsch. Assn., Nat. Assn. Secondary Sch. Prins., Nat. Assn. Elem. Sch. Prins., L.I. Lang. Arts Coun., Nat. Coun. Tchrs. English, Internat. Reading Assn., Nat. Middle Schs. Assn., N.Y. State English Coun., Internat. Platform Assn., Phi Delta Kappa. Home: 8 Penn Commons Yaphank NY 11980-2025 Office: Smithtown Middle Sch 10 School St Saint James NY 11780-1800 E-mail: kvandover@smithtown.k12.ny.us.

VAN DUSEN, DONNA BAYNE, communications consultant, educator, researcher; b. Phila., Apr. 21, 1949; d. John Culbertson and Evelyn Gertrude (Godfrey) Bayne; m. David William Van Dusen, Nov. 30, 1968 (div. Dec. 1989); children: Heather, James. BA, Temple U., 1984, MA, 1986, PhD, 1993. Instr. Kutztown (Pa.) U., 1986—87, Ursinus Coll., Collegeville, Pa., 1987—96; cons., rschr. Comm. Rsch. Assoc., Valley Forge, Pa., 1993—96; assoc. prof. MS in Mgmt. program Regis U., Denver, 1998—. Rschr. Fox Chase Cancer Ctr., Phila., 1985-86; adj. faculty Temple U. Law Sch., 1994-97, LaSalle U., 1994-96, Wharton Sch., U. Pa., 1994-95; asst. prof. Beaver Coll., Glenside, Pa., 1995-96; faculty Jones Internat. U., 1996-99, Metro State U., Denver, 1997-99; cons. Human Comm. Resources and Solutions, 1997—, acad. coun. chair, 2002-. Writer Mountain Connection, 1998—. Vol. Friends in Transition; vol. mediator Victim Offender Reconciliation Program. Recipient Excellence in Tchg. award, 2003. Mem.: Nat. Comm. Assn. Avocations: oil painting, creative writing, sailing, gardening, reading. Home: 2589 Alkire St Golden CO 80401 E-mail: dvanduse@regis.edu.

VAN DUSEN, LANI MARIE, psychologist; b. Alexandria, Va., July 23, 1960; d. Arthur Ellsworth and Ann Marie (Brennan) Van D. BS magna cum laude, U. Ga., 1982, MS, 1985, PhD, 1988. Cert. secondary tchr., Ga. Tchr. Henry County Sch. Sys., McDonough, Ga., 1982-83; rsch. psychologist Metrica Inc., Bryan, Tex., 1988; asst. prof. psychology U. Ga., Athens, 1988-89, chmn. Conf. for Behavioral Scis., 1987; assoc. prof. psychology Utah State U., Logan, 1989—. Cons. Western Inst. for rsch. and Evaluation, Logan, 1990—; bd. dirs. Human Learrning Clinic, Logan, 1990—, Ctr. for Sch. of Future; reviewer William C. Brown Pubs., 1990, Dushkin Pub. Group Inc., 1990-91. Contbr. articles to profl. jours. Fellow Menninger Found.; mem. APA, Psychonomic Soc., Am. Ednl. Rsch. Assn., AAUP, ASCD. Republican. Avocations: hiking, tennis, skiing, knitting, swimming. Home: 1633 N 1200 E North Logan UT 84341-2102 Office: Utah State U Dept Psychology Umc 2810 Old Main Hill Logan UT 84322-0001

VANEK, JAROSLAV, economist, educator; b. Prague, Czechoslovakia, Apr. 20, 1930; came to U.S., 1955, naturalized, 1960; s. Josef and Jaroslava (Tucek) V.; m. Wilda M. Marraffino, Dec. 26, 1959; children: Joseph, Francis, Rosemarie, Steven, Teresa. Degree in stats., Sorbonne, Paris, 1951; license in econ., U. Geneva, 1954; PhD, MIT, 1957. Instr., then asst. prof. Harvard U., 1957-63; adviser AID, 1964; mem. faculty Cornell U., 1964-96, prof. econs., 1966-96, Carl Marks prof. internat. studies, 1969-96, dir. program comparative econ. devel., 1968-73, dir. program participation and labor-managed systems, 1969-96, prof. emeritus, 1996—. Mem. nat. adv. bd. econs. NSF, 1969-70; founder, pres. S.T.E.V.E.N. Found. (Solar Tech. and Energy for Vital Econ. Needs), 1985—. Author: International Trade: Theory and Economic Policy, 1962, The Balance of Payments, Level of Economic Activity and the Value of Currency, 1962, The Natural Resource Content of United States Foreign Trade, 1870-1955, 1963, General Equilibrium of International Discrimination, 1965, Estimating Foreign Resource Needs for Economic Development, 1966, Maximal Economic Growth, 1968, The General Theory of Labor-Managed Market Economies, 1970, The Participatory Economy, 1971, Self-Management: Economic Liberation of Man, 1975, The Labor-Managed Economy, 1977, Crisis and Reform: East and West: Essays in Social Economy, 1989, Toward Full Democracy, Political and Economic, In Russia, 1993; also manuscripts on solar tech., contbr. to Advances in the Economic Analysis of Participatory and Labor-Managed Firms, Vol. 2, 1987, Vol. 7, 2003, Destructive International Trade from Justice for Labour to Global Strategy, 1998, inventor several solar tech. designs, including solar steam engines, pumps, refrigerators, cookers, holder 1 patent. Roman Catholic. Home: 414 Triphammer Rd Ithaca NY 14850-2521 Office: Cornell U Econs Dept 462 Uris Hall Ithaca NY 14853-7601 E-mail: jv19@cornell.edu.

VAN HOOSER, PATRICIA LOU SCOTT, art educator; b. Springfield, Mo., Oct. 4, 1934; d. Arthur Irving and Isoline Elizabeth (Jones) Scott; m. Buckley Blaine Van Hooser, Mar. 28, 1956 (div.); children: Buckley Blaine II, Craig Alan. BA, Drury U., 1956; MS in Art, Pittsburg (Kans.) State U., 1968. Society writer Springfield News & Leader & Press, 1955—56; hostess radio program Sta. KSEK, Pittsburg, Kans., 1962—63; tchr. art and home econs. Hurley (Mo.) HS, 1956—57; art supr. elem. sch. Mountain Grove, Mo., 1960; tchr. art Hickory Hills Sch., Springfield, 1960—61; tchr art and English jr. and sr. schs., Baxter Springs, Kans., 1965—75; art coord. Joplin (Mo.) Elem. Sch. Dist., 1975—. Lectr. in field; chmn. for S.W. Mo., Nat. Youth Art Month. Bd. dirs. Spiva Art Ctr.; sec. Parents without Ptnrs., CV & FE Credit Union; bd. recorder S.W. Mo. Credit Unions. Mem.: ASCD, NEA, AAUW (2d v.p. Joplin br.), Epsilon Sigma Alpha, Pittsburg State U. Alumni Assn. (sec., pres. Joplin br.), Joplin Cmty. Concert Assn., S.W. Mo. Mus. Assn., Mo. Edn. Assn., S.W. Mo. Dist. Art Tchrs., Mo. Art Edn. Assn., Nat. Art Edn. Assn., Assn. Childhood Edn. Internat. (pres. Joplin br., pres. Mo. state), Writers of Six Bulls, Joplin Writer's Guild, Cafe au Lait Club. Methodist. E-mail: Pvanhooser6@cs.com.

VAN HOOSIER, JUDY ANN, elementary education educator; b. Huntingburg, Ind. d. Victor John and Jean M. (Lichlyter) Fleck; m. Gary Wayne Van Hoosier, Oct. 21, 1967; children: Matthew, Michael. BS in Elem. Edn., St. Benedict Coll., 1967; MA in Elem. Edn., U. Evansville, 1978; MA in Supervision and Adminstrn., Ind. State U., 2000. Tchr. 3d grade Holy Redeemer Sch., Evansville, Ind., 1967-68; tchr. 2d grade Good Shepherd Sch., Evansville, 1969-71, 75-98, prin., 1998—. Mem. textbook adoption com. Evansville Diocesan Schs., 1983-84, 88-89, 96-97, 2002-03; mem. liturgy commn. St. Clement Ch., Boonville, Ind., 1994-96, edn. com., 1980-83; mem. VFW Aux., 1973-96; mem. Literacy Coalition, 1997—. Mem. Internat. Reading Assn., Ind. State Reading Assn., Nat. Cath. Ednl. Assn., Evansville Area Reading Coun. (membership chmn. 1991-93, v.p. 1995-96, pres.-elect 1996—, pres. 1997-98, reading tchr. of yr. 1991, bd. dirs. 1985-87, 94—, bldg. rep. 1981-97, outstanding educator award 1995), Delta Kappa Gamma (sec. 1994-96, 2d v.p. 1996—, v.p. 1996-98, pres. 1998—). Roman Catholic. Avocations: cooking, children's literature. Office: Good Shepherd Sch 2301 N Stockwell Rd Evansville IN 47715-1800

VAN HORN, RICHARD LINLEY, academic administrator; b. Chgo., Nov. 2, 1932; s. Richard Linley and Mildred Dorothy (Wright) Van H.; m. Susan Householder, May 29, 1954 (dec.); children: Susan Elizabeth, Patricia Suzanne, Lynda Sue; m. Betty Pfefferbaum, May 29, 1988. BS with highest honors, Yale U., 1954; MS, MIT, 1956; PhD, Carnegie-Mellon U., 1976; D of Bus. (hon.), Reitsumeikan U., Kyoto, Japan, 1991. Asst. dir. Army EDP Project, MIT, Cambridge, 1956-57; research staff Rand Corp., Santa Monica, Calif., 1957-60, head mgmt. systems group, 1960-67; dir., prof. mgmt. systems European Inst. Advanced Studies in Mgmt., Brussels, 1971-73; asso. dean Grad. Sch. Indsl. Adminstrn., Carnegie-Mellon U., Pitts., 1967-71, dir. budget and planning, 1973-74, v.p. for bus. affairs, 1974-77, v.p. for mgmt., 1977-80, provost and prof. mgmt., 1980-83; chancellor U. Houston, 1983-86, pres., 1986-89, U. Okla., 1989-94; pres. emeritus and regent's prof. Coll. of Bus. U. Okla., Norman, 1994—; Clarence E. Page prof. aviation U. Okla., Norman, 1995—; dir. mgmt. info. sys. divsn. Coll. Bus. U Okla., 1997—2000. Author: (with Robert H. Gregory) Automatic Data Processing Systems, 1960, 2nd edit. 1963, (with R.H. Gregory) Business Data Processing and Programming, 1963, (with C.H. Kriebel and J.T. Heames) Management Information Systems: Progress and Perspectives, 1971; contbr. articles to profl. jours.; asso. editor: Jour. Inst. Mgmt. Scis, 1964-78 Bd. dirs. Last Frontier coun. Boy Scouts Am., Kirkpatrick Ctr., Nelson-Atkins Art Mus., Truman Libr. Inst., State Fair Okla., Okla. Futures Commn., Okla. Health Scis. Ctr. Found., Inc., Okla. Ednl. TV Authority. Mem. Inst. Mgmt. Sci. (nat. council mem. 1963-65, sec.-treas. 1964), Assn. for Computing Machinery (nat. lectr. 1969-70), Council on Govt. Relations (bd. dirs. 1981-83) Avocation: commercial pilot. Office: U Okla Coll Of Bus Norman OK 73019-0001 Home: 3900 N Harvey Pkwy Oklahoma City OK 73118

VAN HORNE, JAMES CARTER, economist, educator; b. South Bend, Ind., Aug. 6, 1935; s. Ralph and Helen (McCarter) Van H.; m. Mary A. Roth, Aug. 27, 1960; children: Drew, Stuart, Stephen. AB, De Pauw U., 1957, DSc (hon.), 1986; MBA, Northwestern U., 1961, PhD, 1964. Comml. lending rep. Continental Ill. Nat. Bank, Chgo., 1958-62; prof. fin. Stanford U. Grad. Sch. Bus., 1965-75, A.P. Giannini prof. fin., 1976—, assoc. dean, 1973-75, 76-80; dep. asst. sec. Dept. Treasury, 1975-76. Bd. dirs. BB&K Fund Group, Suntron Corp.; chmn. Montgomery St. Income Securities; commr. workers compensation Rate Making Study Commn., State of Calif., 1990-92. Author: Function and Analysis of Capital Market Rates, 1970, Financial Market Rates and Flows, 2001; co-author: Fundamentals of Financial Management, 2001, Financial Management and Policy, 2002; assoc. editor Jour. fin. and Quantitative Analysis, 1969-85, Jour. Fin., 1971-73, Jour. Fixed Income, 1990—. Mem. bd. trustees DePauw U., 1989-96. With AUS, 1957. Mem. Am. Fin. Assn. (past pres., dir.), Western Fin. Assn. (past pres., dir.), Fin. Mgmt. Assn. Home: 2000 Webster St Palo Alto CA 94301-4049 Office: Stanford U Grad Sch Bus Stanford CA 94305

VAN KIRK, ROBERT JOHN, nursing case manager, educator; b. Jersey City, Sept. 18, 1944; s. Robert and Doris V.; m. Marjorie Ann Carroll, Mar. 23, 1968 (div. Nov. 30, 1993); children: Walter, Michael, Robert Jr., Peggy; m. Nancy A. Fix, Aug. 31, 1996. BA cum laude, U. Conn., 1974; MEd, Kent State U., 1983; D of Nursing, Case Western Reserve U., 1986. RN Ohio. Sales mgr. Nutmeg Home Protection, Middlebury, Conn., 1972-74; theater mgr. SBC Mgmt. Corp., Boston, 1974; dist. supr. Selected Theatres Mgmt. Corp., Lyndhurst, Ohio, 1974-86; nat. sales mgr. ZBS Video, Inc., Lyndhurst, 1981-82; staff nurse Cleve. Clinic Found., 1986-87, clin. instr., 1987-88, head nurse, 1988-93, case mgr., 1993—, diabetes educator, 2002—; asst. clin. prof. Case Western Reserve U., Frances Payne Bolton Sch. Nursing, Cleve., 1990—; case mgr. Cleve. Clin. Home Care, 1993—2002; CEO Lifelong Learning, Inc., Chagrin Falls, Ohio, 2002—. Health officer Lake County (Ohio) Bd. Alcohol, Drug Addiction and Mental Health Svcs., 1991—; co-chmn. United Way, Cleve., 1991-93. Staff sgt. U.S. Army, 1964—71, Vietnam. Recipient Achievement award Greater Cleve. Nurses Assn., 1986. Mem. AACN, Am. Assn. Tchrs. German, Am. Assn. Tchrs. Portuguese and Spanish, Assn. Specialists in Aging, Frances Payne Bolton Sch. Nursing Alumni Assn. (pres. 1992-93), Kappa Delta Pi, Sigma Theta Tau. Avocations: pocket billards, furniture making. Home: 495 Bell Rd Chagrin Falls OH 44022-4160 Office: Cleve Clinic Found 6801 Brecksville Rd Ste 10 Independence OH 44131 also: Lifelong Learning Inc PMB 132 46 Shopping Plz Chagrin Falls OH 44022-3022 E-mail: drbobvankirk@adelphia.net.

VAN KLEEK, LAURENCE MCKEE (LAURIE VAN KLEEK), minister, librarian, educator; b. Vancouver, B.C., Can., Dec. 14, 1944; m. Darlene H. Van Kleek, May 11, 1974; children: Lineke E., Kyle L., Benjamin C. ThB diploma, Western Pentecostal Bible Coll., 1969; BA, Wilfrid Laurier U., 1971; MDiv, Waterloo Luth. Sem., 1972; MA, Assemblies of God Theol. Sem., 1977; libr. technician diploma, U. Coll. of Fraser Valley, 1984; MLS, U. B.C., 1988. Ordained to ministry Pentecostal Assemblies Can., 1975. Lectr. Western Pentecostal Assemblies Can., 1975, Western Pentecostal Bible Coll., Abbotsford, B.C., 1972-76, libr., 1978—, libr., asst. prof., 1978-90, adminstr., 1990—. Supply chaplain Regional Psychiat. Centre, Abbotsford, B.C., 1978-85. Vol. in prison ministry Regional Psychiat. Centre, 1975-77. Gale-Beitel Meml. scholar, 1965. Mem. Assn. Christian Librs., Northwest Assn. Christian Librs. (pres. 1994-96). Home: 32216 Mouat Dr Abbotsford (Clearbrook) BC Canada V2T 4H9 Office: Western Pentecostal Bible Coll 35235 Straiton Rd Clayburn BC Canada also: PO Box 1700 Abbotsford BC Canada V2S 7E7

VAN KLEY, HAROLD, chemistry educator; b. Chgo., Mar. 7, 1932; s. Jacob and Dora (Dekker) Van K.; m. Helen Priscilla Hawks, Sept. 12, 1959; children: Cynthia, Michael. Student, U. Ill., Chgo., 1949-50; AB, Calvin Coll., 1953; MS, U. Wis., 1955, PhD, 1958. Instr. in biochemistry St. Louis U. Sch. Medicine, 1958-59, sr. instr., 1959-61, asst. prof., 1961-82; dir. biochemistry rsch. St. Mary's Health Ctr., St. Louis, 1967-82; prof. chemistry Trinity Christian Coll., Palos Hts., Ill., 1982—97, prof. emeritus chemistry, 1997—. Spl. faculty Argonne (Ill.) Nat. Lab., 1983-92, sabbatical leave 1994-95; analytical chemist. Chem. Waste Mgmt., Riverdale, Ill., 1989-91. Contbr. articles to profl. jours. Sec. bd. trustees Covenant Theol. Sem., St. Louis, 1962-84; bd. dirs. Ref. Presbyn. Found., St. Louis, 1977-81. NIH fellow, 1957, grantee, 1961-68. Mem. AAAS, Am. Chem. Soc., Am. Soc. Biochemistry and Molecular Biology, Sigma Xi (exec. com. 1973). Mem. Christian Reformed Ch. Office: Trinity Christian Coll 6601 W College Dr Palos Heights IL 60463-0929

VAN KOUWENBERG, MARTHA NESTER, secondary education educator; b. Allentown, Pa., Aug. 29, 1946; d. Franklin George and Jean Elizabeth (Schleicher) Nester; children: Beverly, Matthew. BS, Moravian Coll., Bethlehem, Pa., 1968; postgrad., Lehigh U., 1968-71; MEd, Pa. State U., 1997. Cert. math. tchr., N.J., Pa. Asst. treas. Upper Dublin Twp., Fort Washington, Pa., 1965-68; math. tchr. Salisbury Twp. High Sch., Allentown, 1968-70, New Phila. (Ohio) High Sch., 1970-71; coll. preparatory instr. St. Louis High Sch., Seoul, Korea, 1975; math. instr. Burlington County C.C., Ft. Dix, NJ, 1976-79; GED instr. Temple U., Mainz, Germany, 1980-82; math. tchr. Ephrata (Pa.) High Sch., 1984-85, Red Lion (Pa.) Area High Sch., 1985—2002. Mem. Lancaster Found. for Ednl. Enrichment. Named one of People Who Made a Difference USA Today, 1988; recipient award Pa. Dept. Edn. and Assn. Elem. and Secondary Prins., 1990. Mem. NEA, ASCD, Red Lion Area Edn. Assn. (treas. 1991-94, pres. 1995-2001), Pa. State Edn. Assn. (prof. ethics, chair so. region), Pa. Coun. Tchrs. Math., Nat. Coun. Tchrs. Math., Phi Delta Kappa. Home: 746 E Chestnut St Lancaster PA 17602-3126 Office: Red Lion Area Sch Dist 200 Horace Mann Ave Red Lion PA 17356-2403 E-mail: mlnvk@aol.com.

VAN LEER, JERILYN MOSHER, library media specialist; b. Franklin, N.H., July 15, 1954; d. Bruce Rodney and Beverly Colleen (Remick) Mosher; m. Eric Preston Van Leer, June 5, 1976; children: Meredith Lynn, Justin Curtis. BS, So. Conn. State U., 1976, MLS, 1982, diploma in adminstrn. and supervision, 1989. Libr. media specialist, intermediate adminstr., Conn. Libr. media specialist Har-Bur Mid. Sch., Regional Sch. Dist. # 10, Burlington, Conn., 1977-85; dir. libr. media svcs. Litchfield (Conn.) Pub Schs., 1985-88; asst. instrnl. leader libr. media svcs. West Hartford (Conn.) Pub. Schs., 1988-90; libr. media specialist Sedgwick Mid. Sch., West Hartford, 1990-92; libr. media svcs. coord. West Hartford Pub. Schs., 1993—. Bd. dirs. region 1 Coop. Libr. Svc. Unit, Waterbury, Conn., 1985, Capitol Region Libr. Coun., 1997; co-chair Sch. Libr. Media Specialist Roundtable, 1986, mem. planning com. Capitol Region Libr. Coun., 1989; mem. Com. Revising Libr. Media and Computer Guidelines, Dept. Edn., 1988; learning resources and tech. facilitator West Hartford Pub. Schs., 1990—. Libr. sci. and instrnl. tech. scholar So. Conn. State U., New Haven, 1982; recipient Outstanding Libr. award Conn. Libr. Assn., 1984. Mem. NEA, ALA, Assn. for Ednl. Comms. and Tech., Am. Assn. Sch. Librs., Conn. Edn. Assn., Conn. Ednl. Media Assn. (bd. dirs. 1996), New Eng. Ednl. Media Assn., Beta Phi Mu. Avocations: horseback riding, snowshoeing. Home: 213 Cotton Hill Rd New Hartford CT 06057-3417 Office: West Hartford Pub Schs 28 S Main St Hartford CT 06107-2406

VANMARCKE, ERIK HECTOR, civil engineer, educator; b. Menen, Belgium, Aug. 6, 1941; arrived in U.S., 1965, naturalized, 1976; s. Louis Eugene and Rachel Louisa (van Hollebeke) Vanmarcke; m. Margaret Marie Delesie, May 25, 1965 (div. Feb. 22, 1999); children: Lieven Vanmarcke, Ann Vanmarcke, Kristien Vanmarcke; m. Marilyn Durkee, July 14, 2001. BS, U. Leuven, Belgium, 1965; MS, U. Del., 1967; PhD in Civil Engring, MIT, 1970. From instr. to prof. civil engring. MIT, Cambridge, 1969-85, Gilbert W. Winslow Career Devel. prof., 1974-77, dir. civil engring. sys. group, 1976-80; prof. civil engring. and ops. rsch. Princeton (N.J.) U., 1985—, affiliated faculty mem. Bendheim Ctr. Fin., 1998—, dir. grad. studies civil engring. and ops. rsch., 1990—. Cons. Office Sci. and Tech. Policy, 1978—80, Nat. Inst. Stds. and Tech., 2003, various govt. agys. and engring. firms; vis. scholar in engring. Harvard U., 1984—85; Shimizu Corp. vis. prof. Stanford U., 1991; mem. exec. com. Princeton Materials Inst., 1991—93; mem. Princeton Environ. Inst., 1996—; mem. com. vulnerability critical infrastructure Nat. Res. Coun., 1999—2001. Author: (book) Random Fields: Analysis and Synthesis, 1983, Quantum Origins of Cosmic Structure, 1997; editor: Internat. Jour. Structural Safety, 1981—91. Named Disting. Probabilistic Methods Educator, Soc. Automotive Engrs., 2002; recipient Sr. Scientist award, Japan Soc. Promotion Sci., 1991, Disting. Engring. Alumnus award, U. Del., 1994. Mem.: ASCE (chair com. risk assessment and mgmt. Geo-Inst. 1996—, chair com. risk and vulnerability Coun. Natural Disaster Reduction 1998—, chair exec. com. Coun. Infrastructure Reliability and Security 2003—, Raymond C. Reese Rsch. award 1975, Walter L. Huber Rsch. prize 1984), Royal Acad. Arts and Scis. Belgium (fgn.), Internat. Soc. Soil Mechanics and Geotech. Engring. (chair com. TC32 risk assessment and mgmt. 1998—2001), Seismol. Soc. Am., Am. Geophys. Union. Home: 578 Province Line Rd Hopewell NJ 08525-3104 E-mail: evm@princeton.edu.

VAN MIDDLESWORTH, LESTER, physiology, biophysics and medicine educator; b. Washington, Jan. 13, 1919; s. Lester and Hazel Lucile (Brandt) VanM.; m. Nellie Rue Franklin, June 29, 1948; children: Linda V. Anderson, Jane V. Norman, Frank L., Paul E. BS in Chemistry, U. Va., 1940, MS in Chemistry, 1942, MS in Physiology, 1944; PhD in Physiology, U. Calif., Berkeley, 1946; MD, U. Tenn., 1951. Teaching asst. dept. physiology U. Va., 1944, U. Calif., Berkeley, 1944—45; instr. U. Tenn. Med. Units, Memphis, 1946—52, instr. in medicine, 1953—57, asst. prof. physiology, 1952—54, assoc. prof., 1954—59, prof., 1959—89, prof. emeritus physiology and biophysics, 1989—, asst. prof. medicine, 1957—61, assoc. prof., 1961—72, prof. medicine, 1972—89, prof. medicine emeritus, 1989, Disting. prof. physiology and medicine, 1986—. Rotating intern City of Memphis Hosps., 1951-52; cons. chief chemist Piedmont Apple Products Corp., Charlottesville, Va., 1940-46, Crocker Radiation Lab., U. Calif., Berkeley, 1946-47, Oak Ridge Inst. Nuclear Studies, 1950-54; guest co-investigator Endocrine Labs. Tufts Med. Coll., Boston, summers 1954, 55, 56, 59, 61, 64, 66, 69, Scripps Clinic and Rsch. Found., La Jolla, Calif., 1957; guest investigator in endocrinology Harbor Gen. Hosp., UCLA, 1971, Frederick Joliot Hosp., Orsay, France, 1972, Lawrence Livermore Radiation Lab. U. Calif., 1970; staff mem. clinic for med. thyroid disease patients, City of Memphis and U., Tenn., 1951—; mem. internat. com., 1990-2002. Author 145 publs. in profl. jours., 186 abstracts and oral presentations; work on permanent display Smithsonian Nat. Mus. Am. History, Washington, D.C. Recipient Disting. Svc. award, 1985, Disting. Alumnus award U. Tenn. Coll. Medicine, 1989; USPHS career rsch. grantee, 1962-89. Mem. Am. Chem. Soc., Am. Physiol. Soc., AAAS, Soc. Exptl. Biology and Medicine, Am. Soc. Clin. Investigation, So. Soc. Clin. Investigation, Health Physics Soc., Endocrine Soc., Am. Thyroid Assn. (Disting. Svc. award 1988), Sigma Xi (rsch. award 1944, 86, nat. lectr. 1989-91), Alpha Chi Sigma Achievements include research in audiogenic siezures and worldwide radioiodine fallout. Home: 1950 Lyndale Ave Memphis TN 38107-5109 Office: U Tenn Health Sci Ctr 894 Union Ave Memphis TN 38163-3514

VANN, JOHN DANIEL, III, library consultant, historian; b. Raleigh, N.C., June 14, 1935; s. John Daniel Jr. and Sybil Dean (Wilson) V.; m. Ellen Jane Rogers, June 21, 1969; children: John Daniel IV, Justin Fitz Patrick. BA with honors, U. N.C., 1957; MA, Yale U., 1959, PhD, 1965; M in Librarianship, Emory U., 1971; postgrad., Columbia U., 1962-63, Stanford U., 1977-78. Ordained deacon, elder Presbyn. Ch., commd. temporary supply preacher Northumberland Presbytery. Assoc. prof. history Campbell Coll., Buie's Creek, N.C., 1961-63; bibliographer European history and lit. Newberry Libr., Chgo., 1963-65, asst. reference librarian, 1963-65; prof. history Calif. Bapt. Coll., Riverside, 1965-66; dir. libr., prof. history Bapt. Coll. at Charleston, S.C., 1966-69; libr. Keuka Coll., Keuka Park, N.Y., 1969-71; chief libr., prof. libr., chmn. libr. dept. S.I. Community Coll. CUNY, 1971-76; prof. libr. Coll. S.I. CUNY, 1976-79; head libr. Lockwood Libr./SUNY, Buffalo, 1979-80; asst. dir. for planning, univ. librs. SUNY, Buffalo, 1980-81; exec. dir. librs. and learning resources, prof. U. Wis., Oshkosh, 1981-87; dir. libr. svcs. Bloomsburg U. Pa., 1987-89, dean libr. svcs., 1989-98; spl. asst. to vice chancellor for info. technology Pa. State Sys. Higher Edn., 1999; prin. J. Daniel Vann Consulting, 2000—; interim dir., adj. prof. of bibliography Union Theol. Sem. and Presbyn. Sch. of Christian Edn., 2003—. Resident planner, cons. on libr. bldgs. and collection devel.; bd. dirs. Coun. Wis. Librs., 1983-86, Susquehanna Libr. Coop., 1987-98, sec./treas., 1993-95. Mem. internat. editl. bd. Libr. Times Internat., 1984—; contbr. chpts. to books, articles to profl. jours. Trustee Maplewood (N.J.) Meml. Libr., 1977-79, v.p., 1979; bd. dirs. Coun. Wis. Librs., 1983-86, Midwest Rotary Multi-Dist. Short Term Internat. Youth Exch., 1987, Oshkosh (Wis.) Symphony Assn., 1986-87, Protestant campus ministry Bloomsburg U., 1999—2002, United Cerebral Palsy of Winnebagoland, Oshkosh, 1986-87; active coms. Winnebago Presbytery, Presbyn. Ch., 1984-87; com. on min. Northumberland Prsbytery, Presbyn. Ch., 1992-96, com. on preparation for ministry, 1996—2002, coun., 1999—2002; commr. Synod of Trinity Presbyn. Ch. (USA), 1999—2003, exec. com., 2002—2003. Acad. Libr. Mgmt. intern Coun. on Libr. Resources Stanford U., 1977-78. Mem. ALA (com. mem.), Am. Hist. Assn., Archons of Colophon, Assn. for Libr. Collections and Tech. Svcs., Assn. Coll. and Rsch. Librs. (com. chmn., sec. chmn. 1977-78, editl. bd., bd. dirs. 1976-78), Bibliog. Soc. Am., Libr. Adminstrn. and Mgmt. Assn. (com. mem.), Libr. and Info. Tech. Assn., Reference and User Svcs. Assn., Medieval Acad. Am., Pa. Libr. Assn. (coun., sect. dir., mem. coun., Round Table chair), Bloomsburg Rotary Club (Paul Harris fellow), Beta Phi Mu, Phi Alpha Theta. Republican. Home: 810 E 2nd St Bloomsburg PA 17815-2011 also: 1216 Rennie Ave Richmond VA 23227-4723

VANN, LORA JANE, reading educator, retired; b. Chgo. d. Amos Alva and Mary Prudie (Ellery) V. BA, Marian Coll., Indpls., 1958; MA, Ball State U., 1963, EdD, 1985. Cert. life tchr., reading specialist, supr., Ind. Elem. tchr., asst. prin. Indpls. Pub. Schs., 1959-71; instr. dept. edn. William Woods Coll., Fulton, Mo., 1972-73; tchr. reading, supr. Washington Twp. Schs., Indpls., 1973—2002; ret., 2002. Teaching fellow Ball State U., Muncie, Ind., l980-8l; cons. Advanced Tech., Inc., Indpls., l987; vis. cons. North Cen. Assn., Bloomington, Ind., 1988, Peace Pole Project Ideas, 2001. Author: Self-Concept and Parochial School Children, 1985, Sigma's Outstanding Women of the 20th Century, 3 vols., l986, 88, 25th Anniversary (1965-90) History of the Life Membership (NAACP) Committee, 1990; co-author: Multi-Cultural Global Awareness African-American Resources, 1992; editor newsletters Reading Timely Topics, l974-80, AS News, l985-2002. Pres. St. Rita Bd. Edn., Indpls., l987-89; founder Afro-Am. Children's Theatre, 1987. Cath. Interracial Coun. scholar, 1954; NDEA grantee, 1964, 65, Fulbright grantee, Birmingham, Eng., 1967-68, Ball State U. grantee, l980-8l. Mem Internat. Reading Assn., Nat. Coun. Negro Women (charter, sec. Cen. Ind. sect. 198l-84), Washington Twp. Edn. Assn. (chmn. polit. action com. 1987-88, co-chmn. 1988-89), AAUW, Fulbright Assn., Kappa Delta Pi, Phi Delta Kappa, Sigma Gamma Rho (treas. cen. region 1981-86, chpt. pres. 1986-90, 96-2000, trustee nat. edn. found.). Roman Catholic. Avocations: reading, walking, playing piano. Home: 2801 Hillside Ave Indianapolis IN 46218

VAN NESS, JOHN WINSLOW, mathematics educator; b. McLean, Ill., Aug. 16, 1936; s. Winslow John and Nora Ada (Williams) Van N.; m. Nancy Mae Clark, June 6, 1964; children: Karen, Julia, David. BS, Northwestern U., 1959; PhD, Brown U., 1964. Asst. prof. U. Wash., Seattle, 1966-71; assoc. prof. Carnegie-Mellon U., Pitts., 1971-73; prof. U. Tex.-Dallas, Richardson, 1973—, program head in math. scis., 1973-92, assoc. dean Sch. Natural Scis., 1978-83. Vis. asst. prof. Stanford (Calif.) U., 1964-66. Author: Statistical Regression with Measurement Error, 1999; assoc. editor Jou. Am. Statis. Assn., 1976-79, Pattern Recognition, 1994—; contbr. articles to profl. jours. Grantee NSF, 1967-69, 69-70, 70-73, 73-74, 74-75, 75-76, 76-77, 77-79, 79-81, 92-94, State of Tex., 1976-77, 79-80, 82-83, 86-87. Fellow Inst. Math. Statistics, Am. Statis. Assn.; mem. Pattern Recognition Soc., Classification Soc., Sigma Xi, Tau Beta Pi. Avocations: painting, collecting fossils, racquetball. Office: U Tex Dallas Program Math Scis PO Box 830688 Richardson TX 75083-0688

VAN NESS, PATRICIA WOOD, religious studies educator, consultant, author; b. Peterborough, NH, Sept. 12, 1925; d. Leslie Townsend and Bernice E. (Coburn) Wood; m. John Hasbrouck Van Ness, June 13, 1953; children: Peter Wood, Stephen Hasbrouck, Timothy Coburn. BA, U. Wash., 1947; MA, Inst. Transpersonal Psychology, Palo Alto, Calif., 1993. Leader various workshops and retreats, 1979—; records mgr. dept. pub. rels. Std. Oil Co. (now Exxon Corp.), NJ, 1948-50; sec. pub. rels. dept. Std. Oil Co., NJ, 1951; sec. law dept. Johnson & Johnson, New Brunswick, NJ, 1953-54; reporter Hudson Valley Newspapers, Highland, NY, 1972-74; acting assoc. dir. office of pub. rels. SUNY, New Paltz, 1974; ednl. cons. Ulster County Assn. for Mental Health, Kingston, NY, 1973-76; Christian educator Meth. Ch., New Paltz, NY, 1976—78, White Plains Presbyn. Ch., NY, 1978—81; adminstrv. asst. Ctr. for Cont. Edn. Calif. Econ., Palo Alto, Calif., 1983-84; profl. rep. pvt. practice Palo Alto, 1984; adminstrv. asst. Inventory Transfer Systems Inc., Palo Alto, 1984-85; Christian Educator Bedford Presbyn. Ch., NH, 1986—88; coord. pub. rels., adminstrv. asst. Inst. Transpersonal Psychology, Menlo Pk., NJ, 1981-83. Workshop leader and cons. Author: Transforming Bible Study with Children, 1991; assoc. editor and writer Bible Workbench, 1993—; contbr. numerous articles to profl. jours. Trustee Peterborough (NH) Players, 1998—2001. Mem. Assn. Presbyn. Ch. Educators. Avocations: swimming, reading, contra dancing, theater. Home: 11 Jaquith Rd Jaffrey NH 03452-6406 E-mail: pwvn@monad.net.

VAN NOORD, DIANE C. artist, educator; b. Muskegon, Mich., Dec. 12, 1950; d. Ernest Raymond and Judith Ann Olsen; m. Calvin G. Van Noord, Sept. 26, 1981; children: Tawn Star, Brian Calvin, Timothy John. BA, Hope Coll., 1991; MA, Western Mich. U., 1994. Artist, Holland, Mich., 1989—; substitute tchr. Holland (Mich.) Christian Schs., 1996—99; pvt. art tchr. Holland, 2000—. Guest lectr. Counterpart Assn., Grand Haven, Mich., 1997, Lakeland Painters, Grand Haven, 1997, Traverse City (Mich.) Art Assn., 1997, Holland Christian Schs., 1998, 99, 2000. Exhbns. include Neville Pub. Mus., Green Bay, Wis., 1994, Carillon Gallery, Ft. Worth, 1995, 97, Sedona (Ariz.) Arts Ctr., 1995, 96, 99, Holland Area Arts Coun., 1995, Pitts. Ctr. for the Arts, 1995, Miss. Mus. Art, Jackson, 1995, Unitarian Universalist Ch., Phoenix, 1996, Lakeland Painters, Grand Haven, Mich., 1996, Sun Cities Mus. Art, Sun City, Ariz., 1997, Art Inst. Phoenix, 1998, Hill Country Arts Found., Ingram, Tex., 1998, Mus. Tex. Tech. U., Lubbock, 1998, Dunton Gallery, Arlington Heights, Ill., 2000, Internat. Mus. Art, El Paso, 2000, among others; one-woman shows include Gallery Upstairs, Grand Haven, 1996, Moynihan Gallery, Holland, 1997, Trinity Presbyn. Ch., Denton, 1997, Show Sabbatical, 1998, 99, Freedom Village, Holland, 2000, Acad. Artists Assn., Springfield, Mass., 2001, Hilton Head Art League, 2001, Oil Painters Am., Chgo., 2002, Audubon Artists N.Y., 2002, Magnum Opus XIV, Sacramento, 2002, Am. Artists Profl. League, N.Y.C., 2002, Celebration of Western Art, San Francisco, 2002, Hilton Head Art League, 2003, Oil Painters Am., Taos, N.Mex., 2003, others; permanent collections in Fla., Ariz., Mich., Nebr., Ind.; contbr. articles to profl. jours. Recipient Merchant's award Lakeland Painters, 1996, No. Ariz. Watercolor Soc., Sedona Arts Ctr., 1999, Diane Parssinen Meml. awrd No. Ariz. Watercolor Soc., 2001, 2d prize Internat. Artist Mag., 2002, Hon. Mention, Artists Mag., 2002. Mem. Ariz. Watercolor Assn., No. Ariz. Watercolor Assn., Oil Painters Am. (assoc.), Nat. Watercolor Soc. (assoc.), Allied Artists (assoc.), Am. Women Artists (assoc.). Republican. Home: 6418 Oakridge Dr Holland MI 49423-8999 E-mail: dvn@dianevannoord.com.

VAN ORDEN, PHYLLIS JEANNE, librarian, educator; b. Adrian, Mich., July 7, 1932; d. Warren Philip and Mabel A. Nancy (Russell) Van O. BS, Ea. Mich. U., 1954; AMLS, U. Mich., 1958; EdD, Wayne State U., 1970. Sch. librarian East Detroit (Mich.) Pub. Schs., 1954-57; librarian San Diego Pub. Library, 1958-60; media specialist Royal Oak (Mich.) Pub. Schs., 1960-64; librarian Oakland U., Rochester, Mich., 1964-66; instr. Wayne State U., Detroit, 1966-70; asst. prof. Rutgers U., New Brunswick, N.J., 1970-76; prof. library science Fla. State U., Tallahassee, 1977-91, assoc. dean for instrn., 1988-91; prof. libr. sci. program Wayne State U., Detroit, 1991-93; dir. Grad. Sch. of Libr. and Info. Sci. U. Wash., Seattle, 1993-96; cons. in field, 1996—. Editor: Elementary School Library Collection, 1974-77; author: Collection Program in Schools, 2001, Library Service to Children, 1992, Selecting Books for the Elementary School Library Media Center, 2000. Fla. State Libr. grantee, 1984, 86, 88; Lillian Bradshaw scholar Tex. Woman's U., 1993. Mem.: ALA (libr. resources and tech. svcs. divsn., Blackwell/N.Am. scholarship award 1983), Assn. for Libr. and Info. Sci. Edn. (pres. 1990, Svc. award 1997), Assn. Libr. Svc. to Children (past pres., Dist. Svc. award 2002), Pi Lambda Theta. Avocations: music, knitting, physical fitness, cooking, travel. E-mail: vanordp@u.washington.edu.

VAN PATTEN, BILL, foreign language educator; BA, U. Santa Clara; MA, PhD, U. Tex. Asst. prof. of Spanish Mich. State Univ., Univ. Ill., Urbana-Champaign, 1985-89, assoc. prof., 1989—95, prof. Spanish and Second Lang. Acquisition, 1995—. Mem. adv. com. for Studies in Second Lang. Aquisition; dir. Grad. Studies in Spanish, Italian and Portuguese. Chief designer of PBS series: Destinos: An Introduction to Spanish, 1992. Recipient Nelson Brooks award Excellence in the Teaching of Culture, Tchr. Scholar award. Office: Univ Ill at Chgo 601 S Morgan MC 315 Chicago IL 60667-7117*

VAN PATTEN, JAMES JEFFERS, education educator; b. North Rose, N.Y., Sept. 8, 1925; s. Earl F. and Dorothy (Jeffers) Van P.; married. BA, Syracuse U., 1949; ME, Tex. Western Coll., 1959; PhD, U. Tex., Austin, 1962. Asst. prof. philosophy and edn. Central Mo. State U., Warrensburg, 1962-64, assoc. prof., 1964-69; assoc. prof. fis. overseas U. Okla., Norman, 1969-71; prof. edn. U. Ark., Fayetteville, 1971-99, prof. emeritus, 1999—. Visiting scholar, U. Mich., 1981, UCLA, 1987, U. Tex., Austin, 1987; vis. prof./scholar U. Fla., Gainesville, 1994; adj. Fla. Atlantic U., 2000-03. Editor: Conflict, Permanency and Change in Education, 1976, Philosophy, Social Science and Education, 1989, College Teaching and Higher Education Leadership, 1990, Social-Cultural Foundations of Educational Policy in the U.S., 1991, Watersheds in Higher Education, 1997, Challenges and Opportunities For a New Millennium, 1998, Challenges and Opportunities for Education in the 21st Century, 1999, Higher Education Culture, Case Studies For A New Century, 2000, A New Century In Retrospect and Prospect, 2000; Author: Academic Profiles in Higher Education, 1992, The Many Faces of the Culture of Higher Education, 1993, The Culture of Higher Education: A Case Study Approach, 1996, What's Really Happening in Education: A Case Study Approach, 1997; Co-author: (with G. Chen and George C. Stone) Individual and Collective Contributions to Humaneness In Our Time, 1997, (with John Pulliam) History of Education in America, 8th edit., 2003, (with Timothy J. Bergen) A Case Study Approach to a Multi-Cultural Mosaic for Education, 2003; contbr. articles to profl. jours. including Futures Rsch. Quar.; founder Jour. of Thought, Educational Systems for the 21st Century, Futures Rsch. Quarterly, summer 2000. Served with inf. U.S. Army, 1944-45. Decorated Purple Heart. Mem. Am. Ednl. Studies Assn., Southern Future Soc., World Future Soc., Am. Philosophy Assn., Southwestern Philosophy of Edn. Soc. (pres. 1970), Am. Ednl. Rsch. Assn., Edn. Law Assn., Nat. Assn. Legal Assts., Kiwanis, Phi Delta Kappa (pres. chpt. U. Ark. 1976-77). Home: 434 W Hawthorn St Fayetteville AR 72701-1934 E-mail: jvanpatt@aol.com.

VAN PATTEN, MURIEL MAY, educational consultant; b. Quincy, Mich., Apr. 27, 1932; d. Lloyd Delmar and Edwina Weaver (Parsons) Van P. BS, Ea. Mich. U., 1954, MA, 1962; postgrad., Wayne State U., 1967. Art tchr. Fenton (Mich.) Pub. Schs., 1954-56; arts and crafts instr. Chgo. Park Dist., 1955-56; tchr. Wayne (Mich.) Cmty. Sch. Dist., 1956-60, dir. art, 1960-65, elem. sch. prin., 1965-74, learning cons., 1974-75; accountability liaison specialist Mich. State Dept. Edn., Lansing, 1975-77, supr. instrnl. specialist program, 1977-79, dir. sch. program svcs., 1979-84; cons. Detroit Pub. Schs., 1988-89, Kent County Intermediate Sch. Dist., Lansing, 1989-90; cons. in field, 1985—. Dir. secondary edn., coord. student tchrs. Ea. Mich. U., 1962; vis. guest lectr. edn., art depts. Editor, author: (policy book) Michigan Core Curriculum, 1989-90; contbr. chpt. to book. Sch. liaison Soc. for Entertainment and Arts Devel., Charlotte County, Fla., 1987-88; v.p. Friends of Music, Charlotte County, 1987-88; grants co-chair Arts Coun., Charlotte County, 1988-89; local govt. chair LWV, Charlotte County, 1989; pres. Friends of Music of Charlotte County, Inc., 1998—. Mem. NEA, Nat. Art Edn. Assn., Mich. Art Edn. Assn., MIch. Dirs. Pub. Sch. Art Edn. (chmn. 1966-67), Mich. Assn. Supervision and Curriculum Devel., Mich. Assn. Elem. Prins., Coun. for Dem. and Secular Humanism, Inst. for Ojectivist Studies, Cato Inst., Phi Delta Kappa, Sigma Nu Phi (v.p. 1954), Soroptimist Fedn. Am., Soroptimist of Wayne (rec. sec. 1967). Avocation: visual artist. Home: 533 Skylark Ln NW Port Charlotte FL 33952-6529

VAN PELT, ARNOLD FRANCIS, JR., biologist, educator, researcher; b. Orange, N.J., Sept. 24, 1924; s. Arnold Francis and Fredericka Emma (Kleiber) Van P.; m. Gladys Mae Smith, June 24, 1947; children: Stephen Arnold, Susan Frances. BA, Swarthmore Coll., 1945; MS, U. Fla., 1947, PhD, 1950. Assoc. prof. biology Appalachian State U., Boone, N.C., 1950-54; prof. Tusculum Coll., Greeneville, Tenn., 1954-63, Greensboro (N.C.) Coll., 1963—89, chmn. dept. sci. and math., 1963—74, 1975—89, chmn. divsn. sci. math., 1964—71, chmn. divsn. sci. and math., 1982—83, dir. Allied Health programs, 1975—89, Moore prof. biology, 1980-88, Moore disting. prof. emeritus, 1988—. Cons. entomology and ecology, Tex., Greensboro, 1989—; adj. faculty mem. nursing U. N.C., Greensboro, 1974, Moses H. Cone Meml. Hosp., Greensboro, 1975, 77, 83-89, Forsyth Meml. Hosp., Winston-Salem, 1972-89; cons., rschr. Big Bend Nat. Pk., 1982-95, Nat. Pk. Sys., 1996—. Contbr. articles to profl. jours. Grantee NSF, Rsch. Corp., N.Y., Big Bend (Tex.) Nat. History Assn., Piedmont U. Ctr., Winston-Salem, Oak Ridge Nat. Lab., Savannah River Ecology Lab., S.C., Greensboro Coll.; recipient Alpha Chi award, 1987; Arnold Van Pelt Best Biology Sr. award established in his honor Greensboro Coll., 1991. Mem. AAAS, Entomol. Soc. Am., S.W. Assn. Naturalists, S.W. Entomol. Soc., Sigma Xi (treas. Greensboro chpt. 1978-79, sec. 1980-81, pres. 1983). Mem. Soc. Of Friends. Home: 203 Howell Pl Greensboro NC 27455-1712 E-mail: avanpelt@aol.com.

VAN PILSUM, JOHN FRANKLIN, biochemist, educator; b. Prairie City, Iowa, Jan. 28, 1922; s. John Peter and Vera Elisabeth (Moore) Van P.; m. Shirley Elaine Newsom, Oct. 14, 1958; children: John Robert, Patricia Mona, Barbara Joyce, Mary Ann, Elizabeth Joan, William Franklin. BS, State U. Iowa, 1943, PhD, 1949. Instr. L.I. Coll. Medicine, Bklyn., 1949-51; asst. prof. coll. medicine U. Utah, Salt Lake City, 1951-54; asst. prof. biochemistry U. Minn., Mpls., 1954-63, assoc. prof. biochemistry, 1963-71, prof. biochemistry, 1971-94, prof. biochemistry emeritus, 1994—. Contbr. articles to profl. jours. Lt. USN, 1944-46. Recipient numerous grants NIH. Mem. Am. Soc. Biochemistry and Molecular Biology, Am. Inst. Nutrition, Histochem. Soc. Achievements include work with Guanidinium compound metabolism. Home: 4356 Leander Ln Columbia Heights MN 55421-3067 Office: U Minn Dept Biochem Molecular Biolog & Biophysics 1479 Gartner Ave Saint Paul MN 55108

VANPOOL, CYNTHIA PAULA, special education educator, special services consultant; b. San Antonio, Dec. 8, 1946; d. Walter Foye and Pauline (Karger) Phillips; m. Darrell William Vanpool, Feb. 3, 1968; children: George Karger, William Davies. AB in English, Drury Coll., 1968; MS in Spl. Edn. Tchg., Pittsburg (Kans.) State U., 1987. Cert. tchr., Kans., Mo., Okla.; cert. instr. in Quest Skills for Adolescents. Tchr. lang. arts and journalism Miami (Okla.) Pub. Schs., 1968-69; dir. Christian edn./outreach ministries First Assembly of God, Miami, 1981-83; substitute tchr. Miami Pub. Sch. Dist., 1983-85, learning disabilities specialist, journalism sponsor/advisor, 1985-93, spl. svcs. cons., 1993—. Chair spl. edn. dept. Will Rogers Jr. H.S./Mid. Sch., Miami, 1988-94, nat. jr. honor soc. advisor, 1993-94; homebound instr.; cooperating educator for student tchr. practicum student supervision, supr. resident tchr.; cons., tutor, presenter in field; pvt. practice ednl. cons.; chairperson adv. bd. Joyful Learning Ctr. Child Care Sch. Recipient Cert. of Appreciation, Miami Evening Lions Club, 1987, Disting. Svc. award Okla. Lions Clubs, 1988, Internat. Presdl. Cert. of Appreciation for Humanitarian Svc., Lions Internat., 1988; Miami Pub. Sch. Enrichment Found. grantee, 1995, 97. Mem. Coun. for Exceptional Children, Divsn. for Learning Disabilities, Coun. for Children with Behavior Disorders, Phi Kappa Phi. Mem. Assembly of God. Ch. Avocations: reading, writing, entertaining, movies, music. Home: 6996 S 590 Rd Miami OK 74354-4500 Office: Miami Pub Schs 1930 B St NE Miami OK 74354-2117

VAN RAALTE, POLLY ANN, reading and writing specialist, photojournalist; b. N.Y.C., Sept. 22, 1951; d. Byron Emmanuel and Enid (Godnick) Van R. Student, U. London, 1972; BA, Beaver Coll., 1973; MS in Edn., U. Pa., 1974, EdD, 1994, West Chester State Coll., 1977. Title I reading tchr. Oakview Sch., West Deptford Twp. Sch. Dist., Woodbury, N.J., 1974-75, title I reading supr., 1975 summer; lang. arts coord. Main Line Day Sch., Mitchell Sch., Haverford, Pa., 1975-76; reading supr. Salvation Army, Phila., summer 1976; reading Huntingdon Jr. H.S., Abington (Pa.) Sch. Dist., 1976-78; reading specialist No. 2 Sch., Lawrence Pub. Sch., Inwood, N.Y., 1978-87; high sch. reading specialist Cedarhurst, N.Y., 1988-93, Lawrence (N.Y.) H.S., 1988-93; elem. reading specialist No. 5 Sch., 1992—; reading specialist Hewlett (N.Y.) Elem. Sch., Hewlett-Woodmere Pub. Sch., 1987-88, Lawrence Mid. Sch., 1993-95; instr. reading and spl. edn. dept. Adelphi U., 1979—. Columnist South Shore Record, featured columnist, 1992—; columnist Boulevard Mag., 1995-97; photojournalist Manhattan Reports, 1997-2002; feature columnist www.15minutesmagazine.com. Bd. dirs., mem. exec. bd. Five Towns Cmty. Ctr., 1991-93, co-chmn. ednl. youth svcs. edn. com., 1991-93; cons. to sch. dists.; advisor Am. Biog. Inst., Inc.; coord. Five Towns Young Voter Registration, Hewlett, N.Y., summer 1971; chmn. class fund Beaver Coll., also mem. internat. rels. com. U. Pa. scholar, 1977-78; mem. assoc. divsn. Jewish Guild for Blind; mem. N.Y. City Sports Commn.; co-chair youth svcs. com. Mem. Internat. Reading Assn., Wis. Reading Assn., Nat. Coun. Tchrs. English, Nassau Reading Coun., N.Y. Reading Assn., Coun. Exceptional Children, Coun. for a Beautiful Israel, Nat. Assn. Gifted Children, Am. Assn. of the Gifted, Nat./State Leadership Tng. Inst. on the Gifted and Talented, Children's Lit. Assembly, N.Y. State English Coun., Assn. Curriculum Devel., Am. Israel Pub. Affairs Com., New Leadership Com. of Jewish Nat. Fund, State of Israel Bonds New Leadership, Simon Wiesenthal New Leadership Soc., Nat. Polit. Action Com., Am. Friends of Hebrew U. (torch com.), Technion Soc., Am. Friends David Yellin Tchr.'s Coll., Am. Friends Israel Philharm., Am. Friends of Tel Aviv U., Am. Israel Cultural Found., Hadassah, Film Soc. Lincoln Ctr., U.S. Olympic Soc., Friends of N.Y.C. Sports Commn., Cooper-Hewitt Mus., Mus. Modern Art, Met. Mus. Art, Whitney Mus., Phila. Mus. Art, Smithsonian Inst., Friends of Carnegie-Hall, Friends of Am. Ballet Theatre, Friends of Am. Theatre Wing, Women's Am. Orgn. for Rehab. Through Tng. (citi women divsn. N.Y.C.), U. Pa. Alumni Assn. N.Y.C., Dorot Soc., Human Rels. Club (sec.), Actors'Fund, Pi Lambda Theta, Kappa Delta Pi (sec., Internat. Tennis Hall of Fame). Home: 26 Meadow Ln Lawrence NY 11559-1828 Office: #5 Sch Cedarhurst Ave Cedarhurst NY 11516

VAN RIPER, CHARLES, III, biology educator; b. Mahopac, N.Y., Sept. 24, 1943; s. Charles II and Dorothy (Wilson) van R.; m. Sandra Jean Guest, June 4, 1977; children: Charles IV, Jacqueline, Kimberly, Carena. BS, Colo. State U., 1966, MS, 1967; PhD, U. Hawaii, 1978. Unit leader Nat. Park Svc., Davis, Calif., 1979-87, rsch. scientist, 1987-89, unit leader Flagstaff, Ariz., 1989-94; sta. leader U.S. Geol. Soc./Biol. Resources divsn. Colorado Plateau Rsch. Sta., Flagstaff, 1994—. Asst. adj. prof. dept. zoology U. Calif., Davis, 1980-85; assoc. adj. prof. Dept. Wildlife/Fisheries Biology, Davis, 1985-89; prof. biol. sci. No. Ariz. U., Flagstaff, 1990—; team mem. Western U.S. Peregrine Falcon Recovery Team, 1982—. Contbr. articles to profl. jours. Bd. dirs. Coconino County 4-H Livestock, Flagstaff, 1990—, Co-op Extension Ariz., Tucson, 1980—, Coconino County Fair, Flagstaff, 1995—. Recipient Spl. Merit award Nat. Biol. Svc., 1995, Dir.'s award for rsch. Nat. Park Svc., 1991, Western Region award for sci. Nat. Park Svc., 1991. Fellow Am. Ornithologists Union (chmn. 1990-96); mem. Cooper Ornithol. Soc. (bd. dirs. 1983-86, honoree 1993), George Wright Soc., Hawaii Audubon Soc. (v.p. 1974-79). Achievements include work with preservation of endangered species in Hawaii, California and Arizona. Office: Colorado Plateau Rsch Sta PO Box 5614 Flagstaff AZ 86011-0001

VAN RY, GINGER LEE, school psychologist; b. Alexandria, Va., June 26, 1953; d. Ray Ellsworth Hensley and Bernice Anne (Weidel) Wolter; m. Willem Hendrik Van Ry, Aug 23, 1986; 1 child, Anika Claire. AA, U. Nev., Las Vegas, 1973; BA, U. Wash., 1983, MEd, 1985. Cert. sch. psychologist (nationally). Psychometrist The Mason Clinic, Seattle, 1980-84, supr., psychology lab., 1984-86; sch. psychologist Everett (Wash.) Sch. Dist., 1986—. Mem. profl. ednl. adv. bd. U. Wash. Sch. Psychology, Seattle, 1995—; mem. early childhood devel. del. to China, 2000. Author: (with others) Wash. State Assn. of Sch. Psychologists Best Practice Handbook, 1993. Co-pres. Lake Cavanaugh Hghts. Assn., Seattle, 1994-95, chmn. long-range planning com., 1995—. Mem. AAUW, NEA, NASP (nationally cert. sch. psychologist), Wash. State Assn. Sch. Psychologists (chair profl. devel. com. 1995-2001), Wash. State Edn. Assn., U. Wash. Alumni Assn. Democrat. Avocations: reading, travel, fgn. cultures, woodworking, horticulture. Office: The Everett Sch Dist PO Box 2098 Everett WA 98203-0098

VAN SCODER, LINDA I. medical educator, department chairman; b. Defiance, Ohio, Mar. 20, 1953; d. Robert Allen Van Scoder and Esther Irene (Miller) Blair. BS in Respiratory Therapy, U. Cin., 1975; MS in Allied Health Edn., Ind. U., 1979, EdD in Adult Edn., 1985. Registered respiratory therapist. Respiratory crit. care supr. Meth. Hosp., Indpls., 1975-76, chief of pediatric respiratory therapy, 1976-78, dir. clin. edn., 1978-79, Butler Univ./Meth. Hosp., Indpls., 1979-85; asst. prof. gen. studies DePauw U., Greencastle, Ind., 1989-92; program dir. Ball State U./Meth. Hosp., Indpls., 1985-99; assoc. prof. Ind. U., 1999—2002; program dir. Clarian health and Aff. Univs., 2002—. Adj. prof. Ball State U., 1985-99. Co-author: Advanced Emergency Care for Paramedic Practice, 1992, (proceedings) Delineating the Education Direction for the Future, 1992, Year 2001: An Action Agenda, 1993; editor: Respiratory Care Edn. Ann., 1994—. Pub. health educator DePauw U., Puno, Peru, 1986, coord. health worker tng., Mactan, Philippines, 1987, Bo, Sierra Leone, 1989, Las Matas de Farfan, Dominican Rep., 1991. Mem. Am. Assn. Respiratory Care (bd. dirs. 1998-02, Educator of Yr. 1993, editl. bd. 1992-94, cons. to com. on accreditation 1993, chair edn. com. 1997-98), Ind. Soc. Respiratory Care (v.p. 1979), Ind. Allied Health Assn. (bd. dirs. 1990-91), Am. Thoracic Soc., Respiratory Care Accreditation Bd. (rep., pres.-elect 1995, pres. 1996). Avocations: travel, theater. Home: 225 N Arsenal Ave Indianapolis IN 46201-3801 E-mail: lvanscod@iupui.edu.

VANSTROM, MARILYN JUNE CHRISTENSEN, retired elementary education educator; b. Mpls., June 10, 1924; d. Harry Clifford and Myrtle Agnes (Hagland) Christensen; m. Reginald Earl Vanstrom, Mar. 20, 1948; children: Gary Alan, Kathryn June Vanstrom Marinello. AA, U. Minn., 1943, BS, 1946. Cert. elem. tchr., N.Y., Ill. Tchr. Pub. Sch., St. Louis Park, Minn., 1946-47, Deephaven, Minn., 1947-50, Chicago Heights, Ill., 1950-52, Steger, Ill., 1964, substitute tchr. Dobbs Ferry, N.Y., 1965-72, Yonkers, N.Y., 1965-92. Mem. Ch. Women, Christ Meml. Luth. Ch. Mem. AAUW (life, pres. So. Westchester br. 1988-90, Ednl. Found. award 1990), Morning Book Club, Evening Book Club (Met. West br. Minn., So. Westchester br. N.Y.), Yonkers Fedn. Tchrs., U. Minn. Alumni Assn. Democrat. Avocations: painting, sketching, choir, piano, travel. Home: 12300 Marion Ln W Apt 2105 Minnetonka MN 55305-1317

VAN STRYLAND, ERIC WILLIAM, physics educator, consultant; b. South Bend, Ind., June 3, 1947; s. Robert Gerritt and Nancy Jean (Coggan) Van S.; m. Barbara Van Strylan, Dec. 31, 1987. BS in Physics, Humboldt State U., 1970; MS in Physics, U. Ariz., 1975, PhD in Physics, 1976. Tchg. asst. in physics U. Ariz., Tucson, 1970-72, rsch. asst. Optical Scis. Ctr., 1972-73, rsch. assoc. Optical Scis. Ctr., 1973-76; rsch. scientist Ctr. for Laser Studies U. So. Calif., 1976-78; asst. prof. physics U. North Tex., 1978-82, assoc. prof. physics, 1982-86, chmn. Ctr. for Applied Quantum Electronics, Physics, 1983-85, prof. physics, 1986-87, disting. rsch. prof., 1987, adj. prof., 1987-92; prof. physics and elec. engring. CREOL U. Ctrl. Fla., Orlando, 1987—, dir. sch. optics, 1999—. Vis. prof. physics Heriot-Watt U., Edinburgh, Scotland, 1985; hon. prof. Sch. Physics and Astronomy, U. St. Andrews, Scotland, 1995-96; presenter IEEE Conf. Laser Engring. and Applications, San Diego, 1978, Lasers 83, San Francisco, 1983, S.W. Conf. on Optics, Albuquerque, 1985, SPIE 1985 L.A. Tech. Symposium on Optical and Electo-Optical Engring., L.A., 1985, Optical Properties of Liquid Crystals Conf., Naples, Italy, 1986, Cetraro, Italy, 1990, Laser 87, Lake Tahoe, Nev., 1987, Internat. Conf. on Nonlinear Optics, Ashford Castle, Ireland, 1988, Optical Soc. Am., Santa Clara, Calif., 1988, Orlando, Fla., 1989, Kirtland AFB, 1989, Interdisciplinary Laser Sci. conf., Stanford, Calif., 1989, Lasers 89, New Orleans, 1989, Conf. on Nonlinear Optics, Kauai, Hawaii, 1990, Lasers 90, San Diego, 1990, Program on Eye Protection against the Battlefield Laser Threat, Washington, 1990, Nonlinear Optics 1991, Adelaide, Australia, 1991, Workshop on Liquid Cell Power Limiters, Washington, 1991, Am. Ceramic Soc., Crystal City, Va., 1991, 4th Conf. on Crystal Growth, Atlantic City, N.J., 1991, XIV Internat. Conf. on Coherent and Nonlinear Optics, Leningrad, 1991, 22nd Winter Colloquium on Quantum Electronics, Snowbird, Utah, 1992, 23th Winter Colloquium, 1993, Internat. Sch. on Nonlinear Photonics and Optical Physics, Capri, Italy, 1992, IQEC, Vienna, 1992, Gordon Rsch.

Conf. on Crystal Growth, Oxnard, Calif., 1993. Author: (with others) Optical Materials, 1994, Nonlinear Optics of Organic Molecular and Polymeric Materials, 1995, Novel Optical Materials and Applications, 1995, among others; assoc. editor: The Handbook of Optics, 1994; topical editor Optics Letters, 1995—; mem. editl. bd. Rev. Sci. Instruments, 1978-81, Nonlinear Optics, 1991—; contbr. more than 100 articles to profl. jours. including IEEE Jour. Quantum Electronics, Phys. Rev., Optics Letters, Molecular Crystal Liquid, Jour. Chem. Physics, among others. Grantee NSF, 1981-83, 83-87, 87-91, 92-95, 94—, Rsch. Corp., 1979, 82-86, Naval Weapons Ctr., 1979-80, Office Naval Rsch., 1981-84, Robert A. Welch Found., 1981-84, Def. Advanced Rsch. Projects Agy., 1983-89, U.S. Army Night Vision Lab., 1984-86, 88-92, Night Vision-Electro-Optics Ctr., 1986-87, Battelle Columbus Labs., 1987-88, 92, Gen. Dynamics, 1987-88, Fla. High Tech. and Indsl. Coun., 1988, 89, 90, 91, McDonnell Douglas, 1988-89, Jet Propulsion Lab., 1988-89, Army Rsch. Office, 1990, SBIR with Schwartz E-O, 1991, Air Force Office Sci. Rsch., 1991—, Hughes Rsch. Labs., 1992, Dept. Sponsored Rsch. UCF, 1991—, Joint Svcs. Program Naval Air Warfare Ctr., 1993-97, NATO, 1994-96, 96-97, Jet Process Corp., 1994-96, DURIP, 1994-95, Rocketdyne Divsn., Rockwell Internat., 1994-95, among others. Fellow Optical Soc. Am. (edn. coun., laser safety stds. com., advisor Fla. student sect., chair nonlinear optics sect. tech. coun. 1993, quantum electronics divsn. tech. coun. 1994—, chair Fla. fundraising for educator's day ann. meeting Orlando, physics judge for 1991 Internat. Sci. and Engring. Fair Orlando); mem. IEEE (sr., ultrafast subcom.), Soc. Photo-Optical Instrumentation Engrs., Materials Rsch. Soc., Am. Phys. Soc., Laser Inst. Am. (bd. govs.), Phi Kappa Phi, Sigma Pi Sigma. Achievements include rsch. in characterization of the nonlinear optical properties of materials (particularly semiconductors), multiphoton absorption and associated nonlinear refraction, laser induced damage, measurement of ultrashort relaxation times, ultrashot pulse prodn., and ultrasensitive detection of nonlinear optical properties. Office: U Ctrl Fla Ctr for Rsch Optics & Lasers 4000 Central Florida Blvd Orlando FL 32816-8005

VAN SWOL, NOEL WARREN, secondary education educator and administrator; b. N.Y.C., Dec. 30, 1941; s. Erwin Anton and Hildegard Van S. BA, Am. U., 1964; MA, Columbia U., 1967; MS, Syracuse U., 1972. Asst. underwriter Comml. Union Ins. Group Ltd., N.Y.C., 1964-66; tchr. social studies jr. high sch., Bklyn., 1966-67, Liberty (N.Y.) Ctrl. H.S., 1967-69; instr. student pers. Sullivan County (N.Y.) C.C., 1969-70; tchr. social studies East Syracuse-Minoa (N.Y.) H.S., 1970—, coord. social studies, 1976—. Adj. prof. history and govt. Columbia Coll. Residence Edn. Ctr., 1990—; adj. instr. pub. affairs Syracuse U., 1990—, adj. instr. econ., 1992—; cons. to trainer of tchr. trainers project Syracuse U., 1971-74. Contbr. articles to profl. jours. V.p. Fremont (N.Y.) Taxpayers and Civic Assn., 1971; mem. Town of Fremont Rep. Vacancy Com., 1967, 73, 74, 78, 80, 81, 83; bd. dirs. Project Legal, 1983-84; candidate Tchr. in Space Project. Tchr. Leadership Devel. fellow, 1971; Freedom Founds. fellow, 1986, 87. Mem. ASCD, Am. Hist. Assn., N.Y. State Hist. Assn., Am. Polit. Sci. Assn., Ind. Landholders Assn. (v.p. 1992-96, pres. 1996—), N.Y. State Coun. Social Studies, Ctrl. N.Y. Coun. Social Studies, N.Y. State Social Studies Suprs. Assn., Orgn. Am. Historians, Soc. for History Edn., Upper Delaware Scenic River Assn., Upper Delaware Coalition Concerned Citizens, Nat. Inholders Assn., Am. Landrights Assn., Upper Delaware Citizens Alliance, Western Sullivan County Taxpayers Assn. Home: 91 Viaduct Rd Long Eddy NY 12760-5633

VAN TASSEL-BASKA, JOYCE LENORE, education educator; b. Toledo, July 28, 1944; d. Robert Rae and Eleanor Jane (Kenyon) Sloan; m. Thomas Harold Van Tassel, May 21, 1964 (div. 1975); m. Leland Karl Baska, July 25, 1980; 1 child, Ariel Sloan. BEd cum laude, U. Toledo, 1966, MA, MEd, 1969, EdD, 1981. Tchr. Toledo Pub. Schs., 1965-72, coord. gifted programs, 1973-76; dir. Ill. gifted program Ill. State Bd. Edn., Springfield, 1976-79; dir., area svc. ctr. Matteson (Ill.) Sch. Dist., 1979-82; dir. Ctr. for Talent Devel. Northwestern U., Evanston, Ill., 1982-87; Smith prof. edn. Coll. William and Mary, Williamsburg, Va., 1987—, dir. Ctr. for Gifted Edn., 1988—2002, exec. dir. Ctr. for Gifted Edn., 2002—. Mem. Va. Adv. Bd. on Gifted and Talented, 1988-2000; mem. State Ohio Adv. Bd. Gifted and Talented, 1975-76; mem. edn. coun. Nat. Bus. Consortium, 1981-84. Mem. editorial bd. Roeper Rev., 1980-82; pub. Talent Devel. Quar., 1983-87; manuscript rev. editor Jour. Edn. of Gifted, 1981—; mem. editorial adv. bd. Critical Issues in Gifted Edn. series; mem. editorial bd. Gifted Child Quar., 1984-97, Jour. Advanced Devel.; column editor Understanding the Gifted Newsletter, 1984-90: editor Gifted and Talented Internat., 1997—; book review ed., Gifted Child Quarterly, author 12 books; contbr. chpts. and over 260 articles to profl. jours. Bd. trustees Lourdes High Sch., Chgo., 1985-86. Recipient Outstanding Faculty award State Coun. Higher Edn. Va., 1993, 97; grantee U.S. Office Edn., 1977-78, 78-79, Ill. State Bd. Edn., 1979-82, 84-91, R ichardson Found., 1986, 89, Fry Found., 1987-90, Va. State Coun. Higher Edn., 1987-89, 90-91, 93-95, Bur. Indian Affairs, 1989, Hughes Found., 1989-94, Va. State Libr., 1989-90, Va. State Dept. Edn., 1990-93, 93-95, Funding Agy. U.S. Dept. Edn., 1989, 90-93, 93-95, 96-99, 2000-02, 02—; eminent scholar Coll. William and Mary, 1987—, Nat. Ednl. policy fellow U.S. Office Edn., 1979-80, Paul Witty fellow in gifted edn., 1979, Outstanding Rsch. Paper award Mensa, 1995, Phi Beta Kappa Fac. Awd., 1995, Dist. Scholar, Nat. Assoc. Gifted Children, 1997. Mem. ASCD, Nat. Assn. Gifted Children (bd. dirs. 1984-90, Disting. Scholar award 1997), Coun. Exceptional Children, Assn. for Gifted (pres. 1980-81), World Coun. on Gifted, Am. Ednl. Rsch. Assn., Phi Beta Kappa, Phi Delta Kappa (pres. Northwestern chpt. 1986-87). Avocations: photography, tennis, writing. Home: 128 Harriet Cir Williamsburg VA 23185-5115 Office: Coll William and Mary Jones Hall Williamsburg VA 23185

VAN TIL, JON, sociology educator; b. Columbus, Ohio, May 15, 1939; m. Trudy Heller, Jan. 2, 1976; children: Ross, Claire. B.A., Swarthmore Coll., 1961; M.A., U.N.C., 1963; Ph.D., U. Calif.-Berkeley, 1970. Instr. sociology Purdue U., West Lafayette, Ind., 1965-66; instr. Swarthmore (Pa.) Coll., 1966-69, asst. prof., 1969-72; rsch. assoc. Brookings Inst., Washington, 1970-71; exec. dir. Pa. Law and Justice Inst., Phila., 1972-74; prof. dept. urban studies and community devel. Rutgers U., Camden, N.J., 1974—. Author: Mapping the Third Sector, 1988, Critical Issues in American Philanthropy, 1990, Growing Civil Society, 2000; contbr. articles to profl. jours.; editor-in-chief: Nonprofit and Voluntary Sector Quarterly, 1979-92. Mem. Phi Beta Kappa. Office: Rutgers U Coll Arts and Scis Camden NJ 08102

VAN TIL, WILLIAM, education educator, writer; b. Corona, NY, Jan. 8, 1911; s. William Joseph and Florence Alberta (MacLean) Van T.; m. Beatrice Barbara Blaha, Aug. 24, 1935; children: Jon, Barbara, Roy. BA, Columbia U., 1933; MA, Tchrs. Coll., 1935; PhD, Ohio State U., 1946. Tchr. N.Y. State Tng. Sch. for Boys, 1933-34; instr. dept. univ. schs. Coll. Edn., Ohio State U., 1934-36, asst. prof., 1936-43, on leave, 1943-45; researchist, writer Consumer Edn. Study NEA, 1943-44; dir. learning materials Bur. Intercultural Edn., 1944-47; prof. edn. U. Ill., 1947-51; prof. edn., chmn. div. curriculum and teaching George Peabody Coll. Tchrs., Nashville, 1951-57; prof. edn., chmn. dept. secondary edn. N.Y. U., 1957-66, head div. secondary and higher edn., 1966-67; Coffman disting. prof. edn. Ind. State U., Terre Haute, 1967-77, prof. emeritus, 1977; dir. univ. workshops Writing for Profl. Publs., 1978—; founder Lake Lure Press, 1983. Author: The Danube Flows Through Fascism, Economic Roads for American Democracy, The Making of a Modern Educator, Modern Education for the Junior High School Years, The Year 2000: Teacher Education, One Way of Looking At It, Education: A Beginning, Another Way of Looking At It, Van Til on Education, Secondary Education: School and Community, Writing for Professional Publication, rev., 1986; autobiography My Way of Looking At It, 1983, expanded 2d edit., 1996; Sketches, 1989, Admonitions and Challenges, 2002; editor: Forces Affecting American Education, Curriculum: Quest for Relevance, ASCD in Retrospect, 1986, Critique on Work Teaching Education, 1993; author: Teachers and Mentors: Profiles of Distinguished Twentieth Century Professors of Education, 1996, U. S.C. dissertation, William Van Til: Pub. Intellectual, 2002; co-editor: Democratic Human Relations, Intercultural Attitudes in the Making, Education in American Life; adv. editor Houghton Mifflin, 1964-70; interviewed in Social Education, 1989, Preface to the Eight Year Study Revisited, 1998; contbr. articles to profl. jours., popular mags. including Saturday Rev., Woman's Day, Parents; columnist: Ednl. Leadership, Contemporary Edn., Kappan; adv. bd. Profl. Educator, 1984-95. Mem. Ill. Interracial Commn., 1949-51; moderator Nashville Sch. desegregation meetings, 1955-57; mem. adv. bd. Jour. Tchr. Edn., 1956-59; co-organizer Nashville Community Rels. Conf., 1956; cons. Phelps-Stokes Fund project, 1958-62; mem. staff P.R. Edn. Survey, 1958-59, Iran Tchr. Edn. Survey, 1962, V.I. Edn. Survey, 1964; lectr. abroad, 1974; mem. staff U. Ind. Phi Delta Kappa Inst., 1984-90; 1st Ann. Van Til lectr. Ind. State U., 1989. Recipient Centennial Achievement award, Ohio State U., 1970; awards N.J. Collegiate Press Assn., 1962; N.J. Assn. Tchrs. English, 1962; named to Edn. Hall of Fame, Ohio State U., 1989; Annual Van Til Lectr. Series, Ind. State U., est. 1989, est. Annual Van Til Writing award, 1989, award of recognition Spring conf., 1999. Mem. John Dewey Soc. (v.p. 1957-60, acting pres. 1958-59, pres. 1964-66, award 1977, 86, Outstanding Achievement award 1991), Assn. Supervision and Curriculum Devel. (dir. 1951-54, 57-60, pres. 1961-62, chmn. rev. council 1972-73, resolutions com. 1982-85), United Educators (chmn. bd. educators 1969-77), Nat. Soc. Coll. Tchrs. Edn. (pres. 1967-68), Am. Edn. Studies Assn. (editorial bd. 1970-77), Asso. Orgn. Tchr. Edn. (adv. council 1967-73, chmn. issues tchr. edn. 1972-73), Nat. Soc. Study Edn. (editor Yearbook Issues in Secondary Edn. 1976), Kappa Delta Pi (laureate 1980—, chmn. book-of-yr. com. 1984-86, contbr. Honor in Teaching Reflections 1990). Home: 1120 E Davis Dr Terre Haute IN 47802-4065

VAN UMMERSEN, CLAIRE A(NN), academic administrator, biologist, educator; b. Chelsea, Mass., July 28, 1935; d. George and Catherine (Courtovich); m. Frank Van Ummersen, June 7, 1958; children: Lynn, Scott. BS, Tufts U., 1957, MS, 1960, PhD, 1963; DSc (hon.), U. Mass., 1988, U. Maine, 1991. Rsch. asst. Tufts U., 1957-60, 60-67, grad. asst. in embryology, 1962, postdoctoral tchg. asst., 1963-66, lectr. in biology, 1967-68; asst. prof. biology U. Mass., Boston, 1968-74, assoc. prof., 1974—86, assoc. dean acad. affairs, 1975-76, assoc. vice chancellor acad. affairs, 1976-78, chancellor, 1978-79, dir. Environ. Sci. Ctr., 1980-82; assoc. vice chancellor acad. affairs Mass. Bd. Regents for Higher Edn., 1982-85, vice chancellor for mgmt. systems and telecommunications, 1985-86; chancellor Univ. System N.H., Durham, 1986-92; sr. fellow New Eng. Bd. Higher Edn., 1992-93; sr. fellow New Eng. Resource Ctr. Higher Edn. U. Mass., 1992-93; pres. Cleve. (Ohio) State U., 1993—2001; v.p., dir. Office of Women Am. Coun. Edn., 2001—. Cons. Mass. Bd. Regents, 1981-82, AGB, 1992—, Kuwait U., 1992-93; asst. Lancaster Course in Ophthalmology, Mass. Eye. and Ear Infirmary, 1962-69, lectr., 1970-93, also coord.; reviewer HEW; mem. rsch. team which established safety stds. for exposure to microwave radiation, 1958-65; participant Leadership Am. program, 1992-93; bd. dirs. Nat. Coun. Sci. Environment, 1998- . Active N.H. Ct. Systems Rev. Task Force, 1989-90, Leadership Cleve. Class '95, Gov.'s Coun. on Sci. and Tech., 1996-98, Strategy Coun. Cleve. Pub. Schs., 1996-98, Cleve. Sports Commn., 1999-2001, Cleve. Mcpl. Sch. Dist. Bd., 1999-2001; New Eng. Bd. Higher Edn., 1986-92, exec. com., 1989-92, N.H. adv. coun., 1990-92; chair Rhodes Scholarship Selection Com., 1986-91; bd. dirs. N.H. Bus. and Industry Assn., 1987-93; governing bd. N.H. Math. Coalition, 1991-92; exec. com. 21st Century Learning Cmty., 1992-93; state panelist N.H. Women in Higher Edn., 1986-93; bd. dirs. Urban League Greater Cleve., 1993-2001, strategic planning com., chair edn. com., 1996-99, sec., exec. com., 1997-99; bd. dirs. Great Lakes Sci. and Tech. Ctr., 1993-2001, edn. com., 1995-2001; bd. dirs. Greater Cleve. Growth Assn., 1994-2001, Civic Vision 2000 and Beyond, Cleve., 1997-98; bd. dirs., exec. com. Sci. and Tech. Coun. Cleve. Tomorrow, 1998-99; rep. N.E. Ohio Tech. Coalition, 1999-2001; trustee Ohio Aerospace Inst., 1993-2001, exec. com., 1996-2001; strategic planning com. United Way, 1996-2000, chair environ. scan subcom. 1996-2001; leadership devel. com. ACE, 1995-98, women's commn., 1999-2001; bd. dirs. United Way, 1995-2001; co-chair Pub. Sector Campaign, 1997-98; bd. dirs. NCAA, divsn. 1, exec. com., 1999-2001; mem. AGB Ctr. for Pub. Higher Edn. Trusteeship and Goverance, 2001-03; adv. com. Assn. Liaison Officers Adv. Com., 1998-2001. Recipient Disting. Svc. medal U. Mass., 1979, Woman of the Yr. Achievement award YWCA, 1998; Am. Cancer Soc. grantee Tufts U., 1960. Mem. Am. Coun. on Edn. (com. on self-regulation 1987-91), Nat. Conf. Cmty. and Justice (program com. 1996-2001), State Higher Exec. Officers (fed. rels. com., 1986-92, cost accountability task force, exec. com. 1990-92), ACE (com. leadership devel.), Nat. Assn. Sys. Heads (exec. com. 1990-92), Nat. Ctr. for Edn. Stats. (network adv. com. 1989-92), Am. Assn. State Colls. and Univs. (comn. on urban agenda 1996-2001), New Eng. Assn. Schs. and Colls. (commn. on higher edn. 1990-93), North Ctrl. Assn. Schs. and Colls. (evaluator 1993-2001, chair accreditation teams 1986-90), Greater Cleve. Round Table (bd. dirs. 1993-2001, exec. com. 1995-2001), Cleve. Playhouse (trustee 1994-2001), Nat. Assn. State Univs. and Land Grant Colls. (exec. com. on urban agenda, mem. commn. tech. transfer, state rep. Am. Assn. State Colls. and Univs. (bd. dirs. 1996-99, mem. emerging issues task force 1996-98), Phi Beta Kappa, Sigma Xi. Office: American Coun on Edn One DuPont Cir NW Washington DC 20036-1193 E-mail: claire_van_ummersen@ace.nche.edu.

VAN VALIN, SHARON FRANCES, secondary school educator; b. Twin Falls, Idaho, Dec. 16, 1939; d. Frank and Bessie (Broyles) Zlatnik; m. Victor van Valin, June 26, 1964 (div. 1984); children: Vanessa, Jonathan. MusB, Whitman Coll., 1962; degree, U. Wash., Seattle, 1963; MPA, Seattle U., 1985. Tchr. Cascade Jr. High Sch., Seattle, 1963-65; pvt. practice tchr. Seattle, 1965—; tchr. Canyon Pk. Jr. High Sch., Bothell, Wash., 1966-68; job line coord., counselor State Employment Security Dept., Bothell, 1968-69. Judge Bainbridge Island Mus. Arts Competition, 1999-2001; presenter, spkr. in field. Recipient Nat. Composition award Music Tchrs. Nat. Assn., 1993. Mem. Wash. State Music Tchrs. Assn. (program chmn. Eastside chpt. 1982, v.p. 1983, workshop instr. 1980—, clinician for conv. 1993, panel conv. 1995, workshops for tchrs. in original composition, 1996, 1997, 1998, 2000), Nat. Guild Piano Tchrs. (piano and composition adjudicator 1988—), Nat. Fedn. Music Clubs (piano performance adjudicator 1993—), Bellevue Philharmonic Guild (featured speaker, 2002). Avocations: tennis, golf, reading, museums, travel. Home: 3312 81st Pl SE # B Mercer Island WA 98040-3034

VANVLIET, MARY LYNNE, English language educator, photography assistant; b. Frankfort, N.Y., Jan. 21, 1949; d. Nicholas Luke and Madeline (Cobb) Chuff; m. Douglas VanVliet, Sept. 4, 1982; children: Bryan, Timothy. BA in English Edn., SUNY, Albany, 1970, MA in English Edn., 1975. Cert. tchr. English 7-12, gen. edn., N.Y. Tchr. English grade 10, New Hartford, NY, 1970-72; tchr. English grade 12 Ctrl. Sq. (N.Y.) Ctrl. Sch., 1972-73; tchr. English grades 10 and 12 Averill Pk. (N.Y.) H.S., 1973-86; tchr. English grades 9, 10, pub. speaking and debate Maple Hill H.S., Castleton, NY, 1993—. Advisor Class of 1998, sch. newspaper advisor Odyssey of the Mind Coach, mem. discipline com. Maple Hill H.S., 1995—. Mem. Schodock Bus. Adv. Bd., Character Edn. Com., MHHS; com. woman Poestenkill (N.Y.) Dems., 1979. Career Day grantee Capital Dist. Tchrs. Ctr., Schodack, 1995. Mem. Nat. Coun. Tchrs. of English. Avocations: writing poetry, travel, reading. Home: 1524 Maple Crest Dr Castleton On Hudson NY 12033-1608 Office: Maple Hill H S Maple Hill Rd Castleton On Hudson NY 12033

VAN WAGNER, ELLEN, lawyer, law educator; b. Chgo., Dec. 10, 1942; d. Paul David and Eleanor (Sullivan) Van W.; m. Burton Neal Genda, Mar. 27, 1964 (div.); children: Kevin Paul, Kelly Elan. BA, U. Ariz., 1964; MA, Calif. State U., L.A., 1971; JD, U. La Verne, 1984. Bar: Calif. 1984, U.S. Dist. Ct. (cen. dist.) Calif. 1985, U.S. Ct. Appeals (9th cir.) 1985. Tchr., adminstr. Baldwin Park (Calif.) Sch. Dist., 1965-81; ptnr. Rose, Klein & Marias, Pomona, Calif., 1985-94. Prof. U. La Verne (Calif.) Coll. Law, 1987—. Writer, asst. editor U. La Verne Law Rev., 1981-83, editor-in-chief, 1983-84. Chmn. youth activities commn. City of Baldwin Park, 1971-81. Recipient Humanitarian and Svc. awards L.A. Human Rels. Commn., 1976, 77. Mem. Calif. Bar Assn., L.A. County Bar Assn., Ea. County Bar Assn., Phi Delta Theta. Avocations: traveling, sports. Home: PO Box 351 Blue Jay CA 92317-0351 Office: Law Offices Ellen Van Wagner 12474 Central Ave Ste B Chino CA 91710-2664

VAN WIE, PAUL DAVID, secondary school educator, historian, educator; b. Manhasset, N.Y., Sept. 29, 1956; s. Joseph Paul and Florence Elizabeth (Wagner) van W.; m. Ellen Mary van Wie, June 25, 1983; children: Mary Ellen, Elisabeth, Paul David, Joseph. BA, C.W. Post Coll., 1978, MA, 1987; PhD, CUNY, 1989. Cert. secondary edn. Tchr. Spackenkill High Sch., Poughkeepsie, N.Y., 1981-82, Schreiber High Sch., Port Washington, N.Y., 1982-84, Wheatley Sch., Old Westbury, N.Y., 1984—; adj. prof. N.Y. Inst. Tech., Old Westbury, 1987-92, Hofstra U., Hempstead, N.Y., 1992—. Mem. dean's adv. com. L.I. U., Old Brookville, N.Y., 1992-96. Author: The Way it Was, 1994, Image, History and Politics, 1998. Historian Village of Franklin Square, N.Y., 1979—, libr. trustee, 1989—; landmarks commr. Town of Hempstead, 1989—; pres. Franklin Square Hist. Soc.; v.p. Franklin Square Cmty. League, 1990-96. Nat. Humanities fellow U.S. Govt., 1988, Fulbright scholar U.S. Govt., 1990, Coun. Basic Edn. fellow, 1996; recipient Leadership award Nat. Soc. Daughters of Am. Revolution, 1982, N.Y. State Tchr. of Yr. award N.Y. Dept. Edn., 1992. Mem. Am. Hist. Assn., L.I. Coun. Social Studies, Franklin Square Hist. Soc. (pres.). Office: The Wheatley Sch 11 Bacon Rd Old Westbury NY 11568-1502

VAN ZANT, SUSAN LUCILLE, principal; b. Torrance, Calif., Apr. 29, 1942; d. Paul McHenry and Lucille Eileen (McQuarrie) Mansfield; m. Jerry Brian Van Zant, Oct. 27, 1960; children: Steven Brian, Karen Daphne Van Zant Hosaka. BA in History and Social Sci., Calif. State U., Long Beach, 1966; MA in Curriculum, No. Ariz. U., 1974; EdD in Adminstrn., U.S. Internat. U., 1982. Cert. elem. tchr., kindergarten and secondary sch. adminstr., Calif. Tchr. Borrego Springs (Calif.) Unified Sch., 1967-69, Poway (Calif.) Unified Sch. Dist., 1969-76, prin., 1976—. Instr. community rels., law and fin. Nat. U., San Diego, 1987-92. Author: (with others) The Principal as Chief Executive, 1991; contbr. articles to profl. jours. Named Calif. Educator of Yr. Calif. State Dept. of Edn./Milken Found., 1989, Blue Ribbon Sch., U.S. Dept. of Edn., 1994; recipient Educator's award Freedom's Found., 1990. Mem. Nat. Assn. Elem. Sch. Prins. (bd. dirs., state leader, Disting. Prin. award 1988), Calif. Alliance for Edn. (coord.), Assn. Calif. Sch. Adminstrs. (chair elem. adminstrn.), Poway Assn. Sch. Mgrs. (pres. 1982), San Diego/Imperial County Adminstrs. (pres. 1993-94), Delta Kappa Gamma (pres. 1990-92). Baptist. Home: 16204 Quail Rock Rd Ramona CA 92065-7214 E-mail: suvanzant@aol.com.

VAN ZANTEN, DAVID THEODORE, humanities educator; b. Aug. 31, 1943; BA, Princeton U., 1965; MA, Harvard U., 1966, PhD, 1970. Asst. prof. McGill U., Montreal, 1970-71; from asst. to assoc. prof. U. Pa., Phila., 1971-79; from assoc. prof. to prof. Northwestern U., Evanston, Ill., 1979—. Office: Northwestern U 244 Kresge Hall Evanston IL 60208-2208 E-mail: d-van@northwestern.edu.

VAN ZILE, PHILIP TAYLOR, III, lawyer, educator; b. Detroit, Feb. 17, 1945; s. Philip Taylor II and Ruth (Butzel) Van Z.; m. Susan Jones, Sept. 12, 1981; children: Caroline Sage, Philip Taylor IV. BA, Oberlin Coll., 1968; MDiv, Union Theol. Sem., 1971; JD, Mich. State U., 1975. Bar: Mich. 1976, D.C. 1976, U.S. Dist. Ct. (ea. dist.) Mich. 1976, U.S. Ct. Appeals (6th cir.) 1976, U.S. Supreme Ct. 1977, Pa. 1981. Law clk. Mich. Ct. Appeals, Detroit, 1976-78, Mich. Supreme Ct., Detroit and Lansing, Mich., 1978-80; asst. corp. counsel Office of Corp. Counsel, Washington, 1980-87; assoc. Killian & Gephart, Harrisburg, Pa., 1987-89; prin. Law Office of Philip T. Van Zile, Harrisburg, 1989-91; assoc. coun. Office Chief Coun. Pa. Dept. Conservation and Natural Resources, Harrisburg, 1991—; assoc. realtor M.C. Walker Realty, Mechanicsburg, Pa., 1997—. Teaching fellow Detroit Coll. Law, 1976-80; teaching asst. Detroit Gen. Hosp., 1978-80; teaching assoc. Acad. Med. Arts and Bus., Harrisburg, 1990-91. Contbr. articles to profl. jours. Ordained elder Mechanicsburg Presbyn. Ch., 1995—, chmn. vol. ministries, 1995, chmn. peacemaking, 1996, chmn. staff, 1997—. Mem. ABA, Kenwood Club (Chevy Chase, Md.). Office: Pa Dept Conservation/Natural Resources Office Chief Counsel 400 Market St Harrisburg PA 17101-2301

VARADARAJAN, KALATHOOR, mathmatics educator, researcher; b. Bezwada, India, Apr. 13, 1935; parents Kalathoor Soundara and Parimalavalli (Parimalavalli) Rajan; m. Pattu Varadarajan, June 22, 1961; children: Suchitra, Srinivasan. BA with honors, Loyola Coll., Madras, India, 1955; PhD, Columbia U., 1960. Rsch. fellow Tata Inst. Fundamental Rsch., Bombay, 1960-61, fellow, 1961-67; vis. assoc. prof. U. Ill., Urbana, 1967-69; reader Tata Inst. Fundamental Rsch., Bombay, 1969-71; assoc. prof. U. Calgary, Alta., Can., 1971-73, prof., 1973—. Nat. bd. vis. prof. Nat. Bd. Higher Math, India, 1986, 91; vis. prof. Univ. Sydney, Australia, 1984. Author: The Finiteness Obstruction of C.T.C. Wall, 1989; contbr. more than 100 articles to profl. jours. Home: 5944 Dalridge Hill NW Calgary AB Canada T3A1L9 Office: U Calgary Dept Math 2500 Univ Dr NW Calgary AB Canada T2N1N4 E-mail: varadara@math.ucalgary.ca.

VARGA, DEBORAH TRIGG, music educator, entertainment company owner; b. Dayton, Ohio, Dec. 15, 1955; d. Ernest Cushman and Phyllis Ann (Martz) Trigg; m. Ali M. Abadi, Dec. 30, 1980 (div. July 1987); 1 child, Darren Vincent; m. Richard Charles Varga, June 25, 1994; 1 child, Kathryn Lenore. B of Music Edn. in Violin Performance, Converse Coll., Spartanburg, S.C., 1977. Music educator Seminole County Sch. Bd., Sanford, Fla., 1978-92, Howard County Pub. Schs., Ellicott City, Md., 1993—. Co-founder, co-owner Gold Star Entertainement, Inc., Orlando, Fla., 1984-86, Ctr. Stage Entertainment, Inc., Maitland, Fla., 1986-92; owner Varga Music Entertainement, Highland, Md., 1993—, Composer children's songs, 1990—, Martin Luther King Tribute, Human Rights Commn., Howard County, 1997-00. Mem. Am. Fedn. Musicians, Music Educators Nat. Conf., Am. String. Tchrs. Assn., Nat. Orch. Assn. Avocations: waterskiing, whitewater rafting, tennis, golf, reading. Home: 13464 Allnutt Ln Highland MD 20777-9743

VARGAS, JULIE S. behaviorologist, educator; b. Mpls., Apr. 28, 1938; d. d. Burrhus Frederic and Eve (Blue) S.; m. Ernest A. Vargas, June 30, 1962; children: Lisa Kristina, Justine. AB in Music, Harvard U., 1960; MA in Music Edn., Columbia U., 1962; PhD in Ednl. Rsch., U. Pitts., 1969. Tchr. third grade Spense Sch., N.Y.C., 1960-61; tchr. fourth grade Monroeville (Pa.) Area Schs., 1961-62; prof. ednl. psychology W.Va. U., Morgantown, 1966—. Pres. B.F. Skinner Found., Cambridge, Mass., 1988—; cons. New Century Edn. Corp., Piscataway, N.J., 1975-88. Author: Writing Worthwhile Behavioral Objectives, 1973, Behavioral Psychology for Teachers, 1977; co-author: Teaching Behavior to Infants, 1990; author: (software tutorial) Something to Think About (Reading), 1986; chief editor: The Behavioral Analyst jour., 1979-81. Vis. scholar Harvard U., 1994. Mem. Assn. for Behavior Analysis (pres. 1989-90), Internat. Soc. for Behaviorology (sec. 1992-95, chmn. bd. publs. 1995—). Democrat. Avocations: classical guitar playing, violist with W.Va. U. orchestra, sailing. Home: 519 Park St Morgantown WV 26501-6617 Office: W Va Univ PO Box 6122 Morgantown WV 26506-6122 E-mail: julie.vargas@mail.wvu.edu.

VARGAS, TERESA MARIE BRADLEY, elementary school educator; b. Blackfoot, Idaho, June 3, 1958; d. Dal Gene and Helen Marie (Walton) Bradley; m. Leonardo Almira Vargas, 1987; 3 children. AA, Ricks Coll., 1978; BA, Idaho State U., 1985; MEd in Ednl. Leadership, U. Idaho, 2000. First grade tchr. Minidoka County Sch. Dist 331, Heyburn, Idaho. Mem.: NEA, Idaho Edn. Assn., Phi Kappa Phi. Home: 1559 Malta Ave Burley ID 83318-1945

VARGAS-ALCARO, JUANA AMADA, elementary education educator; b. Tenares, Dominican Republic, Mar. 30, 1952; came to U.S., 1968; d. Jorge Ramon and Virginia (Rojas) Vargas; m. Sidney Feldman, Aug. 9, 1976 (div. 1979); m. Elizardo de Jesus Pèrez, Apr. 7, 1982 (dec. Sept. 1992); children: Steven Louis Feldman, Sylvester Ely; m. Jack D. Alcaro, Feb. 14, 1994. BA in Fgn. Lang., Gordon Coll., Wenham, Mass., 1976; MEd in Adminstrn., U. Mass., Lowell, 1988; MEd and Computers, Lesley Coll., 1988; postgrad., Nova Southeastern U. Bilingual tchr. Lawrence (Mass.) Pub. Schs., 1976-77, bilingual and ESL tchr., 1982-85, tchr. computers, 1985-90; tchr. Spanish, Carol Morgan Sch. Santo Domingo, Dominican Republic, 1978-82; tchr. lit. Am. Sch. Santo Domingo, 1990-92; tchr. Spanish, Dade County Pub. Schs., Miami, Fla., 1992-93, tchr. computers, 1993—. Mem. grant writing team Allapattah Elem. Sch., Miami, 1993—. Avocations: reading, computers, antiques, music, art. Office: Allapattah Elem Sch 4700 NW 12th Ave Miami FL 33127-2214 Address: 1364 SW 181st Ave Pembroke Pines FL 33029-4903

VARIAN, HAL RONALD, economics educator; b. Wooster, Ohio, Mar. 18, 1947; s. Max Ronald and Elaine Catherine (Shultzman) V.; m. Carol Johnston, Nov. 1986. S.B., MIT, 1969; MA, PhD (NSF fellow), U. Calif.-Berkeley, 1973. Asst. prof. econs. MIT, 1973-77; prof. U. Mich., 1977-95, prof. fin., 1983-95, Reuben Kempf prof. econs., 1984-95; prof. sch. bus., dean sch. info. mgmt. and sys. U. Calif., Berkeley, 1995—, Class of 1944 prof., 1996—. Siena chair in econs., U. Siena, Italy, 1990. Author: Microeconomic Analysis, 1978, Intermediate Microeconomics, 1987, Information Rules, 1998; co-editor Am. Econ. Rev., 1987-90. Guggenheim fellow, 1979-80; Fulbright scholar, 1990 Fellow AAAS, Econometric Soc.; mem. Am. Econ. Soc. Home: 1198 Estates Dr Lafayette CA 94549-2749 Office: U Calif Sims 102 South Hl Berkeley CA 94720-0001

VARMA, AMIY, civil engineer, educator; b. Patna, Bihar, India, Apr. 14, 1963; came to U.S., 1986; s. Devendra Prasad and Bimal (Prasad) V.; m. Jaya Johari, Mar. 2, 1994; children: Ashish, Anurag. BTech. in Civil Engring., Indian Inst. Tech., Bombay, 1985; MSCE, Vanderbilt U., 1987; PhD, Purdue U., 1993. Registered profl. engr., N.D. Planning engr. Tata Electric Cos., Bombay, 1985-86; rsch. asst. Vanderbilt U., Nashville, 1986-87, Purdue U., West Lafayette, Ind., 1987-90; asst. prof. N.D. State U., Fargo, 1990-96, assoc. prof., 1996—. Contbr. articles to Tranp. Rsch., Transport Revs., Trasnp. Rsch. Record, others. S.D. Dept. Transp. rsch. grantee, 1994, 99, N.D. State U. grantee, 1994, 96, NSF, 1995, NSF EPSCOR grantee, 1996, 98. Mem. ASCE, Am. Inst. Cert. Planners, Inst. Transp. Engring. (various couns.), World Conf. Transp. Rsch. Soc., Chi Epsilon. Achievements include expertise in sustainable transportation and transportation financing and economics; research experience in infrastructure management, transportation systems, airport planning and design, traffic engineering and computer-aided design. Home: 1 S 2d St Apg 5-303 Fargo ND 58103 Office: ND State U Dept Civil Engring Fargo ND 58105

VARNER, CHARLEEN LAVERNE MCCLANAHAN (MRS. ROBERT B. VARNER), nutritionist, educator, administrator, dietitian; b. Alba, Mo., Aug. 28, 1931; d. Roy Calvin and Lela Ruhama (Smith) McClanahan; student Joplin (Mo.) Jr. Coll., 1949-51; BS in Edn., Kans. State Coll. Pittsburg, 1953; MS, U. Ark., 1958; PhD, Tex. Woman's U. 1966; postgrad. Mich. State U., summer, 1955, U. Mo., summer 1962; m. Robert Bernard Varner, July 4, 1953. Apprentice county home agt. U. Mo., summer 1952; tchr. Ferry Pass Sch., Escambia County, Fla., 1953-54; tchr. biology, home econs. Joplin Sr. H.S., 1954-59; instr. home econs. Kans. State Coll., Pittsburg, 1959-63; lectr. foods, nutrition Coll. Household Arts and Scis., Tex. Woman's U., 1963-64, rsch. asst. NASA grant, 1964-66; assoc. prof. home econs. Central Mo. State U., Warrensburg, 1966-70, adviser to Colhecon, 1966-70, adviser to Alpha Sigma Alpha, 1967-70, 72, mem. bd. advisers Honors Group, 1967-70; prof., head dept. home econs. Kans. State Tchrs. Coll., Emporia, 1970-73; prof., chmn. dept. home econs. Benedictine Coll., Atchison, Kans., 1973-74; prof., chmn. dept. home econs. Baker U., Baldwin City, Kans., 1974-75; owner, operator Diet-Con Dietary Cons. Enterprises, cons. dietitian, 1973—, Home-Con Cons. Enterprises. Mem. Joplin Little Theater, 1956-60. Mem. NEA, Mo., Kans. state tchrs. assns., AAUW, Am., Mo., Kans. dietetics assns., Am., Mo., Kans. home econs. assns., Mo. Acad. Scis., AAUP, U. Ark. Alumni Assn., Alumni Assn. Kans. State Coll. of Pittsburg, Am. Vocat. Assn., Assn. Edn. Young Children, Sigma Xi, Beta Sigma Phi, Beta Beta Beta, Alpha Sigma Alpha, Delta Kappa Gamma, Kappa Kappa Iota, Phi Upsilon Omicron, Theta Alpha Pi, Kappa Phi. Methodist (organist). Home: PO Box 1009 Topeka KS 66601-1009

VARNER, VANCE SIEBER, science educator; b. Lewistown, Pa., Aug. 8, 1967; s. George Thomas and Kay (Sieber) V. BS, Pa. State U., 1991. Earth sci., geosci. and environ. tchr. Upper Dauphin Area High Sch., Elizabethville, Pa., 1991—. Varsity soccer coach Upper Dauphin High Sch., 1991—, asst. varsity wrestling coach, 1991—. Recipient Nat. Sallie Mae Tchr. award Student Loan Mktg. Assn., 1992. Mem. Pa. Sci. Tchr. Assn., Harrisburg Area Geol. Soc. Avocations: fishing, outdoors. Home: RR 3 Box 255 Mifflintown PA 17059-9803 Office: RR 3 Box 255 Mifflintown PA 17059-9803

VARNER, WILLIAM HENRY, music educator; b. Chanute, Kans., May 30, 1953; s. George W. and Zelda Mae (Weber) V.; m. Vicci Kara Ervin, June 21, 1975 (div. Jan. 1995); children: Isaac George, Joshua Lloyd. AA, Independence Cmty. Jr. Coll., 1973; B of Music Edn., Friends U., 1976; M of Music Edn., Holy Names Coll., 1981. Cert. all-level music educator; endorsed trainer in Edn. Through Movement: Building the Foundation, Tex. Elem. music educator Humboldt (Kans.) Elem. Sch., 1976-78, Kayenta (Ariz.) Elem. Sch., 1978-80; elem., secondary music educator Ingalls (Kans.) Ind. Sch. Dist., 1981-82, Refugio (Tex.) Ind. Sch. Dist., 1982-86; elem. educator Tuleso/Midway Ind. Sch. Dist., Corpus Christi, Tex., 1986-88, Flour Bluff Ind. Sch. Dist., Corpus Christi, Tex., 1988-89, Richardson (Tex.) Ind. Sch. Dist., 1989—. Adj. prof. Corpus Christi State U., 1988; clinician Edn. Through Movement: Building the Found., Clinton, Mich., 1988—. Contbr. articles to S.W. Musician, 1993-95. Mem. Turtle Creek Chorale, Dallas, 1993—2000; dir. music First Christian Ch., Richardson, 1994—2001, Irving, 2001—. Mem. Kodaly Educators of Tex., Tex. Music Educators (elem. chair 1982-86, state elem. chair 1993-95). Republican. Avocations: cmty. theatre, baking, movies, composing music. Home: 129 Cimarron Trl # 2185 Irving TX 75063 Office: Hamilton Pk Pacesetter Magnet Sch 8301 Towns Dallas TX 75243 E-mail: will.varner@risd.org.

VARNON, SUZANNE, speech language pathologist; b. Dallas, Nov. 23, 1948; d. Howard A. and Mable Anne (Jacobsen) Muhm; m. Charles D. Varnon, Nov. 13, 1971; 1 child, Justin C. BA, Baylor U., 1970; deaf edn. cert., Tex. Woman's U., 1974; postgrad., East Tex. State U., 1991-95; MS, U. North Tex., 1978. Cert. speech lang. pathologist, diagnotician, spl. edn. Speech lang. pathologist Richardson (Tex.) Ind. Sch. Dist., 1970-78; tchr. mother's day out Park Cities Bapt. Ch., Dallas, 1979-81; pvt. practice speech lang. pathologist Dallas, 1979-81; speech lang. pathologist Garland (Tex.) Ind. Sch. Dist., 1981—. Supr. clin. fellowship year Garland (Tex.) Ind. Sch. Dist., 1982—; medicaid supr., 1993—. Participant vacation bible sch. Lake Highlands Bapt. Ch., Dallas, summer 1979—; sec.-treas. woman's missionary union, 1980-92; life mem. PTA, 1995—. Lic. speech lang. pathology, Tex. Mem. Am. Speech Hearing Assn. (cert. clin. competence), Tex. Speech Hearing Assn., Speech Pathologists Assn. Near Dallas, Kappa Kappa Gamma, Phi Delta Kappa. Republican. Baptist. Avocation: aerobics. Home: 10407 Chesterton Dr Dallas TX 75238-2205 Office: Garland Ind Sch Dist Toler Elem 3520 Guthrie Rd Garland TX 75043-6220

VARNUM, ROBIN RANELLE, English language professional, educator; b. Pasadena, Calif., May 8, 1950; d. George W. Varnum and Rosemary (Purdy) Vaughan; m. Juris Zagarins, May 28, 1978; children: Sofija E. Zagarins, Marija S. Zagarins. AB, William Jewell Coll., 1971; MA, U. Wash., 1977; EdD, U. Mass., 1992. English tchr. U.S. Peace Corps, Afghanistan, 1971-73; libr. technician U. Wash. Libr., Seattle, 1974-77; instr. Western New England Coll., Springfield, Mass., 1978-90, Holyoke (Mass.) C.C., 1991-92; assoc. fellow Inst. for Advanced Study U. Mass., Amherst, 1992—; instr. Am. Internat. Coll., Springfield, Mass., 1993—. Author: Fencing with Words: A History of Writing Instruction at Amherst College During the Era of Theodore Biard, 1938-1966, 1996; co-editor (with Christina T. Gibbons): The Language of Comics: Word and Image, 2001; contbr. articles to profl. jours. Publicity apprentice Seattle Opera, 1977; freelance writer Springfield Mag., 1978; publicity asst. Stage West Theater, Springfield, 1978-79; newsletter editor Massasoit Montessori Sch., Springfield, 1982-83; mem. McKnight Neighborhood Coun., Springfield, 1978-90, Spl. Com. on Racial Balance, Springfield, 1982-83, MAgnet Sch. Adv. Com., Springfield, 1986-87; clk. of vestry St. Peter's Episcopal Ch., Springfield, 1995—. Mem. Nat. Coun. Tchrs. English, Appalachian Mountain Club. Democrat. Anglican. Avocations: hiking, sewing. Home: 121 Harvard St Springfield MA 01109-3821 Office: Am Internat Coll Lee Hall # 22 1000 State St Springfield MA 01109-3151

VASILAKI, LINDA BOOZER, music educator; b. Grand Rapids, Mich., Jan. 2, 1949; d. Gordon and Dianne (Demmon) Boozer; m. Yuri G. Vasilaki, Sept. 29, 1979; children: Camilla Dianne, Andrew Alten, Maria Demmon. BMus in Edn., Mich. State U., 1971; MFA, U. Iowa, 1973; EdD in Curriculum and Instrn., Argosy U., Sarasota, Fla., 2003. Cert. kindergarten-12 music tchr., 7-8 all subjects tchr., Mich., Fla.; cert. Orff, Level 1. Kindergarten-6 music cons. Grand Rapids (Mich.) Pub. Schs., 1973-75; tchr., founder Suzuki violin program Grand Rapids Bd. Edn., 1976-80; tchr. violin Nat. Music Camp, Interlochen, Mich., 1981, 82; chair music dept., orch. dir. Out of Door Acad., Sarasota, Fla., 1983—; founder, dir. Encore Fine Arts Program, Sarasota, Fla., 1988—. Tchr. viola Blue Lake Fine Arts Camp, Muskegon, 1973; violist Fla. West Coast Symphony, Sarasota, 1982—; mem. Grand Rapids Symphony, 1973-80; tchr. Suzuki Assn. Am., Sarasota, 1976—; adj. music/viola faculty Hope Coll., Grand Valley State Coll. Author: Music Lovers' Cookbook, 1983, Symbol of Liberty, 1985; editor: Out of Door Academy Cuisine, 1983; contbr. articles to profl. jours. Counselor, music therapist Indian Trails Camp for the Phys. Handicapped, Grand Rapids, 1968-69; violist Venice (Fla.) Symphony, 1991-92; former mem. faculty New Eng. Music Camp. Scholar New Coll. Music Festival, 1971, Lenox String Quartet Seminar, 1971, Banff (Can.) Centre-Fine Arts String Quartet Seminar, 1972, U. Iowa, 1972-73; Fla. Humanities grantee, summer 1995. Mem. Phi Kappa Lambda, Kappa Alpha Theta, Delta Omicron (pres. 1971), Delta Kappa Gamma. Avocations: music, reading, writing. Home: 3341 Bougainvillea St Sarasota FL 34239-5704 E-mail: lvasilaki@oda.edu.

VASILEIADIS, SAVVAS, chemical engineer, environmental engineer, materials engineer, educator; b. Thessaloniki, Greece, Apr. 18, 1963; arrived in US, 1988, naturalized, 2000; m. Zoe Dimitrios Ziaka; children: Eugenia-Melina, Artemis-Dimitria. Diploma in Chem. Engring., Aristotle U., Thessaloniki, Greece, 1987; MS in Chem. and Materials Engring., Syracuse U., 1990; PhD in Chem. Engring., U. So. Calif., 1994. Registered profl. engr. Rsch. engr. Chem. Industries of No. Greece, Thessaloniki, 1985—86; rsch. assoc. chem. engring. and materials sci. Syracuse U., NY, 1988-90; rsch. assoc. U. So. Calif., L.A., 1990-94; rsch. fellow in chem. engring. Loker Hydrocarbon Rsch. Inst. U. So. Calif., LA, 1994—96, faculty, 1997—. R&D dir., prin. officer ZIVATECH, L.A., 1994—; activities coord. grad. student orgn., U. So. Calif., 1993; tech. com. IASTED, 2002—, chmn., 2003. Contbr. articles to profl. jours. Recipient paper award R.J. Kokes, 1993, 95, AIChE, 1993, 95-96, Materials Rsch. Soc., 1994, U. So. Calif. Pres.' award, 1996; fellow Norwegian Ednl. Coun., 1987; several R&D innovation and process devel. awards and grants. Mem. AIChE, Materials Rsch. Soc., N.Am. Catalysis Soc., Am. Chem. Soc., N.Y. Acad. Scis. Ea. Orthodox. Achievements include novel reactor, permreactor process designs and experiments for methane-steam reforming, methane-CO2 reforming, water gas shift, and alkane dehydration reactions with applications in methanol and chemical synthesis, in power generation cycles and fuel cells; research on reaction and separation chem. processes, chem. kinetics and catalysis, materials and polymers sci. and engring, chem. processing and engring.; patentee in field. Home: 15549 Dearborn St North Hills CA 91343-3267 Office: Univ So Calif Sch Engring Kap 230C Los Angeles CA 90089-0001

VASILOPOULOS, ATHANASIOS V. engineering educator; b. Mavranei, Grevena, Greece, May 25, 1937; came to U.S., 1955; s. Vasilios and Ekaterini Vasilopoulos; m. Paraskevi Tsiotas, Feb. 5, 1961; children: Basil John, Katherine, Pamela. BEE, NYU, 1962, MEE, 1965, PhD in Ops. Rsch., 1974. Computer technician Atomic Energy Commn., NYU, N.Y.C., 1957-59; asst. engr. Am. Electric Power Co., N.Y.C., 1959-62; staff engr. Grumman Aerospace, Bethpage, N.Y., 1962-78; assoc. prof. ops. rsch. St. John's U., Jamaica, N.Y., 1978—. Adj. prof. math. SUNY at Farmingdale, 1974-78; vis. prof. U. Crete, Greece, 1980; cons. State of N.Y., Albany and Syracuse, summer 1982, AT&T, N.Y.C., summer 1985, Grumman Aerospace, 1980-91, Blue Bay Shipping, N.Y.C., 1983-84. Referee ASME Jour. Engring. for Industry, 1984, Jour. Collegiate Microcomputer, Terre Haute, Ind., 1984-87; contbr. articles to Jour. Quality Tech., Jour. Collegiate Microcomputer, Jour. Bus. Forecasting, others. Mem. coun. Boy Scouts Am., Commack, N.Y., 1970-75; soccer coach Huntington (N.Y.) Boys Club, 1974-75; v.p. St. Paraskevi Greek Orthodox Ch., Greenlawn, N.Y., 1976-78, chmn. edn. com., 1968-85. Recipient Patriarch Athenagoras medallion Greek Orthodox Archdiocese N.Y.C., 1981. Mem. IEEE (sr.), N.Y. Acad. Scis., Ops. Rsch. Soc. Am., Inst. of Mgmt. Scis. Achievements include development of method for analyzing generalized quality control data, method for generating correlated random variables for quality control applications, use of extended input-output methodology for forecasting purposes; proposal of methodology to use computer to generate density functions for sums of independent random variables; use of computer to demonstrate validity of central limit theorem and law of large numbers in statistics. Office: St John's Univ Grand Central And Utopia Pkwy Jamaica NY 11439-0001

VASILY, JOHN TIMOTHY, information systems executive, state government official; b. Everett, Mass., Feb. 5, 1961; s. Andrew and Catherine Agnes (Coyne) V. BA, U. Mass., 1983; MBA, Suffolk U., 1992. Data analyst Higher Edn. Coord. Coun., Boston, 1984-92; sr. programmer, analyst Babson Coll., Babson Park, Mass., 1992-96; dir. new sys. devel. Mass. Dept. Youth Svcs., Boston, 1996-2000; chief info. officer Mass. Dept. Mental Retardation, Boston, 2000—. Adj. instr. Newbury Coll., Brookline, Mass., 1992—, Suffolk U., Boston, 2001—. Co-author: Massachusetts Integrated Post Secondary Education Data System, 1990; author: 1986-87 Completions Supplement, 1989. Recipient Citation for Outstanding Performance Commonwealth of Mass., 1998. Mem. IEEE, Delta Mu Delta, Omicron Delta Epsilon. Avocations: bowling, fishing, hiking, golf, photography. E-mail: John.Vasily@dmr.state.ma.us.

VASQUES, VICTORIA L. federal agency administrator; m. Fabrice Vasques; 1 child, Alex. BS, Calif. State U., Fullerton; tchg. credentials, U. Calif., Irvine. Dir., Indian Edn. US Dept. Edn., Wash., 2002—; dir., Indian affairs US Dept. Energy, Wash.; edn. program spec. Off Indian Edn., Indian Reservation Econ., Wash., Pres. Commn. HIV Epidemic, Wash.; tech. asst. spec. Nat. Congress of Am. Indians; tribal liaison Com. for 50th Pres. Inaugural. Named Am. Indian Woman of Yr., 1986. Mem.: Decade Soc. Office: US Dept Edn Indian Edn 400 Maryland Ave SW FOB-6 Rm 3W205 Washington DC 20202 E-mail: victoria.vasques@ed.gov.*

VASQUEZ, WILLIAM LEROY, business educator, consultant; b. Austin, Tex., Mar. 9, 1944; s. Eliseo M. and Janie (Garcia) V. BS with distinction, Nova Southeastern U., 1983, MBA, 1985, DBA, 1992. Cert. Inst. Cert. Profl. Mgrs., 1990, Inst. Cert. Computing Profls., 1993. Svc. mgr. Data Gen. Corp., various, Latin Am., 1972-80; product mgr. Gould, Inc., Ft. Lauderdale, Fla., 1980—84, Tektronix Inc., Portland, Oreg., 1984—86, Racal-Milgo, Ft. Lauderdale, 1988—90, Citibank Internat., Ft. Lauderdale, 1991—2001; ret., 2001. Instr. City U., Portland campus, 1987-88; Maryhurst Coll., 1985-88, Nova Southeastern U. (domestic and internat.), 1988—, pres. internat. alumni assn.; instr. St. Thomas U., 1989—, Fla. Atlantic U., 1993—. Mem. VFW, Nat. Bus. Edn. Assn., U.S. Submarine Vets., Inc., Mensa. Republican. Presbyterian. Avocations: guitar, model trains, fine arts. Home: 9788 NW 18th St Coral Springs FL 33071-5824 Office: Fla Met Univ Grad Sch Business 1040 Bayview Dr Fort Lauderdale FL 33304

VASSAR, JOHN DIXIE, JR., technical consultant, military aviator; b. Portsmouth, Va., Dec. 10, 1953; s. John Dixie and Hazell Marrie (Barr) V.; m. Karen Patricia Schad, May 6, 1990; 1 child, Kathryn Schad. BS in Biology/Nuclear Sci., Va. Tech., 1976, postgrad., 1981-83, Johns Hopkins U., 1984-88; MA in Mgmt., U.S. Army Command/Gen. Staff Coll., 1991; MS in Technology Mgmt., U. Md., 1998, postgrad., 1998—2001, U. Phoenix, 2001—. Radiol. technician Va. Power, Surry, 1976; asst. atomic reactor supr. Va. Tech., Blacksburg, Va., 1982-83; project mgr. Westinghouse, Columbia, Md., 1983-87; CWO, aviator Del. Army Nat. Guard, 1995—; tech. cons. Eldon Enterprises, Columbia, Md., 1987—. Indsl. advisor Va. Tech. Nuclear Sci. Engring. Program, Blacksburg, Va., 1983-84; fin. cons., registered rep. Waddell and Reed Fin. Svcs., Columbia, Md., 1992; tech. cons. Jaycor, Vienna, Va., 1993-96; data mgr. Dyncorp Corp., Columbia, Md., 1997-98; prof. info. sys., campus coll. chmn. tech. U. Phoenix, 2001—; acad. accreditation reviewer Am. Coun. Higher Edn., 2002—. Contbr. articles to profl. jours. Mem. Sound Money Assn., Cocoa Beach, Fla., 1981-90; pastoral cons. South Columbia Bapt. Ch. Capt. USAFR, 1976-88, capt. USAR, 1988-90, CWO, USAR, 1990-95 with Del. Army N.G., 1995—. Mem. Am. Nuclear Soc. (sec. Va. Tech. chpt. 1982-83), Health Physics Soc. (v.p. Va. Tech. chpt. 1975-76), Am. Assn. Fin. Profls., Nat. Assn. Securities Dealers, Va. Tech. Alumni and Athletic Assn., Highty Tighty Alumni Assn., Va. Tech. Corps. of Cadets Alumni Assn., Sierra Club, Hazardous Materials Controls Rsch. Inst., Environ. Mgmt. Assn., Nat. Guard Assn., Masons. Republican. Baptist. Avocations: music, horticulture, investing, reading, fitness. Home and Office: 6205 Ashton Park Ct Columbia MD 21044-3947 E-mail: jvassar639@aol.com.

VASSAR, WILLIAM GERALD, gifted and talented education educator; b. Springfield, Mass., Oct. 5, 1925; s. William Walter and Mary Ellen (Burns) V.; m. Barbara Ellen Benhard, June 21, 1952; children: William G., James P., Richard G., Carol A. Vassar Pettit. BA in History magna cum laude, Am. Internat. Coll., Springfield, 1950; MEd, Springfield Coll., 1951; cert. of advanced grad. study, U. Mass., 1967, postgrad., 1962-70. Elem. tchr. West Springfield (Mass.) Pub. Schs., 1950-53, jr. high tchr., 1953-55, secondary sch. prin., 1955-65, dir. program for gifted, 1955-65; sr. supr. academically talented Mass. State Dept. Edn., Boston, 1965-66; state dir. programs for gifted and talented Conn. State Dept. Edn., Hartford, 1966-86; coord. gifted edn., dept. spl. edn. Cen. Conn. State U., New Britain, 1968-86, asst. to dean Sch. Edn., 1986-88; spl. cons. advanced placement program The Coll. Bd., N.Y.C., 1986—; prodr. interactive satellite confs. on Advanced Placement, 1992—. Coord. White House Task Force Gifted and Talented, Washington, 1967-68, U.S. Dept. Edn. Congl. Study Gifted and Talented, Washington, 1969-71, Capitol Region Edn. Coun. Info. and Resource Ctr., Windsor, Conn., 1992—; cons. gifted and talented U.S. Dept. Edn., 1967-85, Nat. Assn. State Bds. Edn., 1978-84, George Washington U. Edn. Policy Fellowship Program, 1978-84; spl. cons. gifted and talented legislation Staff of Senate subcom. on Edn., 1967-85; vis. lectr. U. Conn., 1966-83, So. Conn. State U., 1970-84, Sacred Heart U., 1986—, others. Contbg. editor The Gifted Child Quar., Jour. Talented and Gifted; author monographs; contbr. numerous articles to profl. jours. Mem. exec. bd. Mass. Commn. on Children and Youth, Boston, 1959-65, Nat. Commn. Orgn. and Children and Youth, Washington, 1964-68; mem. Conn. Commn. on Youth Svcs., Hartford, 1966-70; mem. Mass. Hwy. Safety Commn., Boston, 1957-63; baseball scout San Francisco Giants, 1957-70. With USN, 1943-46, PTO. Named Disting. Educator U.S. Dept. Edn. Office Gifted, Washington, 1974, Disting. Educator, Conn. State Legislature, Hartford, 1986; recipient Disting. Svc. award Mass. Commn. on Children and Youth, Boston, 1966, Gold Pass award Mass. Baseball Umpires Assn., 1997. Mem. ASCD, Internat. Coun. Exceptional Children (pres. Assn. Gifted divsn. 1970-71, chmn. regionals 1969-78, Disting. Svc. award 1972), Nat. Assn. Gifted Children (life, pres. 1965-68, bd. dirs. 1960-68, Disting. Svc. award 1974, Pres.' award for lifetime significant contbn. 1998), Coun. State Dirs. Gifted (pres. 1977-80), Conn. Assn. Gifted, Conn. Assn. Pub. Sch. Supts. (ret.), Nat. Football Hall of Fame Found., Eastern Assn. Intercollegiate Football Ofcls., Indian Hill Country Club, Eastern Coll. Athletic Conf., Phi Delta Kappa. Democrat. Roman Catholic. Avocations: reading, golf, football. Home: 47 Dowd St Newington CT 06111-2611

VASSIL, PAMELA, graphic designer, writer, administrator; b. N.Y.C., Nov. 29, 1943; d. George Peter and Lenora (Zabludofsky) Vassilopoulos; 1 child, Sadye Lee. BS in Art Edn., Hofstra U., 1965; MA in Art Edn., NYU, 1968. Designer Columbia Records, N.Y.C., 1970-72; assoc. art dir. Harper's Bazaar, N.Y.C., 1972-74; designer, mech. artist Album Graphics Inc., N.Y.C., 1974-75; free-lance designer, mech. artist; prodn. dir. Push Pin Studios, N.Y.C., 1975-77; art dir. OpEd and editl. pages N.Y. Times, N.Y.C., 1977-79, art dir. Arts and Leisure sect., 1982-87, art dir. Living sect., 1987; free-lance designer/art dir./mech. artist, 1979-82; instr. production, graphic design and illustration Parsons Sch. Design, N.Y.C., 1974—; instr. illustration Sch. Visual Arts, 1981; features art dir. The Daily News, N.Y.C., 1987; sr. art dir. Wells, Rich, Greene Inc., N.Y.C., 1987-88; free-lance graphic designer/art dir., 1988-89; design dir. Roger Black Inc., N.Y.C., 1989-90, McCall's mag., N.Y.C., 1990-91, freelance art dir., 1991-92; dir. continuing edn. Parson's Sch. Design, 1992-99; nat. membership dir. Hadassah, 1999-2000, nat. comm. dir., 2000—. Assoc. editor and designer: (book) Images of Labor, 1981; contbr., co-editor: Jews. Mag.; contbr. articles to 60 Gramercy Park Newsletter, N.Y. Times, Big Apple Parent, Mondo Greco.

VASSILOPOULOU-SELLIN, RENA, clinician investigator; b. Dec. 29, 1949; MD, Albert Einstein Coll. Medicine, 1974. Resident Montefiore Hosp., Bronx, 1974-77; fellow Northwestern U., Chgo., 1977-80; prof. Univ. Tex., Houston, 1980—. Fellow ACP, Am. Assn. Clin. Endocrinol.; mem. AAAS, AMA, Am. Soc. Bone and Mineral Rsch., Am. Diabetes Assn., Am. Soc. Clin. Oncology, Endo Soc. Office: Anderson Cancer Ctr 1515 Holcombe Blvd # 15 Houston TX 77030-4009

VASWANI, SHEILA ANN, secondary education educator; b. N.Y.C., Feb. 27, 1948; d. Elwood Stanley and Julia Zita (Sullivan) Kent; m. A. N. Vaswani; 1 child, Neela. BA in Asian Studies and Eurasian History, Hofstra U., 1972; MA in Chinese Studies, St. John's U., Jamacia, N.Y., 1977. Mng. editor County Weekly, Vt., 1979-80; secondary social studies tchr. Babylon (N.Y.) H.S., 1984—. Co-organizer adv. program Babylon (N.Y.) H.S., 1991-94, mem. middle states evaluation com., 1991-92, mem. human rels. seventh grade coms., 1993-94; presenter in field. Advisor Babylon (N.Y.) H.S. chpt. Nat. Honor Soc., 1989—, Home Econ. Club, Babylon, 1980—; v.p. Parents, Tchrs., Students Assn., Babylon, 1994—. Nominee Tchr. of

Month award, Channel 12, 1994; named Friend of Fgn. Lang., 2003, Friend of Home Econs., 1997, Diplomate of N.Y. State Acad. Tchg. and Learning, 2000; recipient LILT award, 2003. Mem.: Registry of Outstanding Profls., L.I. Coun. for Social Studies, Nat. Coun. for Social Studies. Avocations: art, religion, philosophy, ethnic cooking, travel. Office: Babylon High Sch 50 Railroad Ave Babylon NY 11702-2221

VATANDOOST, NOSSI MALEK, art school administrator; b. May 22, 1935; d. Adullah Goodar and Mahtaban (Goodar) Malek; m. Ira Varandoost, May 30, 1964; children: Debbie, Cyrus. BA, Western Ky. U., 1970. Art tchr. Met.-Davidson County Sch. Sys., Nashville, 1970-71; dir., owner Nossi Coll. Art, Goodlettsville, Tenn., 1973—. Dir Tenn. Proprietary Bus. Sch. Assn., Inc., pres. Crimson Corp.; treas. Malek & Assos. Inc., 1976; dir. EXCEL Edn. Corp., 1980-86; vis. lectr., cons. EXCEL Bus. Inst., 1980-86. Active mem. Nat. Trust for Hist. Preservation. Mem.: NAFE, Internat. Coun. Design Schs. (pres. 1997—98), Art Inst. Nashville (founder, CEO), Career Coll. Assn., Art Resources of Tenn. (pres. 2000—01), Nat. Assn. of Schs. of Art and Design, Nat. Mus. Women in the Arts (charter), Hendersonville Art Guild, Hendersonville Art Coun. (com. chmn.). Club: Soroptimists (Upper Cumberland Valley, Tenn.). Home: 104 Whirlaway Ct Hendersonville TN 37075 Office: 907 Two Mile Pky Goodlettsville TN 37072-2324

VAUGHAN, ALDEN TRUE, history educator; b. Providence, Jan. 23, 1929; s. Dana Prescott and Muriel Louise (True) V.; m. Lauraine A. Freethy, June 1, 1956 (div. 1981); children: Jeffrey Alden, Lynn Elizabeth; m. Virginia Mason Carr, July 16, 1983. BA, Amherst Coll., 1950; MEd, Columbia U., 1956, MA in History, 1958, PhD, 1964. Tchr. Hackley Sch., Tarrytown, N.Y., 1950-51, A.B. Davis High Sch., Mt. Vernon, N.Y., 1956-60; From history instr. to prof. Columbia U., N.Y.C., 1961—, prof. emeritus, 1994. Editor Polit. Sci. Quar., N.Y., 1970-71; gen. editor Early Am. Indian Documents, Univ. Pubs. of Am., 1977—; assoc. editor Ency. of the N.Am. Colonies, Scribners, N.Y., 1993; vis. adj. prof. CUNY, Lehman Coll., N.Y.C., 1971; vis. prof. Clark U., Worcester, Mass., 1987. Author: New England Frontier, 1965, rev. edit., 1979, 3d edit., 1995, American Genesis, 1975, Shakespeare's Caliban, 1991, Roots of American Racism, 1995, others; co-editor: Arden Shakespeare's The Tempest, 1999; contbr. articles to Am. Heritage, Am. Hist. Rev., New Eng. Quar., others. Lt. (j.g.) USNR, 1951-55. Recipient fellowship Guggenheim Found., 1973, Sr. fellowship Folger Shakespeare Libr., 1977, 89, Sr. fellowship Am. Antiquarian Soc., 1983. Mem. Am. Antiquarian Soc. (sr. fellowship), Am. Soc. for Ethnohistory, Shakespeare Assn. Am., Soc. Am. Historians (exec. sec., treas. 1965-70), Orgn. Am. Historians (program chmn. 1976), Inst. Early Am. History and Culture (coun. mem. 1985-87), Colonial Soc. Mass., Mass. Hist. Soc. Home: 50 Howland Ter Worcester MA 01602-2631

VAUGHAN, EMMETT JOHN, academic dean, insurance educator; b. Omaha, Dec. 1, 1934; s. Leo William and Mary (Simones) V.; m. Lonne Kay Smith, July 2, 1955; children: Therese, Timothy, Mary, Joan, Thomas, Michael, Emmett (dec.). BA in Econs., Creighton U., 1960; MA in Econs. and Ins., U. Nebr., 1962, PhD in Econs. and Ins., 1964. Asst. prof. U. Iowa, Iowa City, 1963-65, assoc. prof., 1965-68, Partington Disting. prof. ins., 1968—, dean Div. Continuing Edn., 1986-2000. Author: Fundamentals of Risk and Insurance, 1972, 7th edit., 1996, Risk Management, 1997; contbr. numerous articles to profl. jours. Participated in assessment of war damages in Kuwait UN Commn. on Compensation, 1992. Capt. USAR, 1955-75. Named to Iowa Ins. Hall of Fame, 1997. Mem. Japan Risk Mgmt. Soc. (hon.) Office: U Iowa 116 Internat Ctr Inst Ins Edn & Rsch Iowa City IA 52242

VAUGHAN, JOSEPH LEE, JR., education educator, consultant; b. Charlottesville, Va., Dec. 31, 1942; s. Joseph Lee and Ann (Doner) V.; m. Linda Marie De Silva; children: Leigh Ann, Kelley, Stephen, Kathleen. BA, U. Va., 1964, MEd, 1968, EdD, 1974. Tchr. Madison (Va.) High Sch., 1965-67, Darlington Sch., Rome, Ga., 1967-69, Woodberry Forest (Va.) Sch., 1969-74; asst. prof. edn. U. Ariz., Tucson, 1974-80; prof. Tex. A&M U.-Commerce, Mesquite, 1980—, dir. programs in reading edn., 1980-86, 91-92. Dir. programs in reading edn. East Tex. State U., 1980—86; dir. Tex. Ctr. Learning Styles, 1989—95; exec. dir. Children's Inst. of Literacy Devel., Inc., 1995—; dean of faculty St. Alban's Episc. Sch., Arlington, Tex., 2001—02. Co-author: Reading and Learning in Content Classrooms, 1978, 2d rev. edit., 1985, Reading and Reasoning Beyond The Primary Grades, 1986. Bd. govs. Sancta Sophia Sem., 1991-98. Mem. ASCD, Nat. Reading Conf., Internat. Reading Assn., Soc. Effective Affective Learning. Unitarian Universalist. Avocations: golf, travel, reading, antiques. Home: 447 Ridgemont Dr Heath TX 75126 Office: Tex A&M U-Commerce 2600 Motley Dr Mesquite TX 75150-3840

VAUGHAN, OTHA H., JR., retired aerospace engineer; b. Anderson, SC, July 1, 1929; s. Otha H. and Ethel (Mayfield) Vaughan; m. Betty Frances McCoy; children: Thera Virginia, Leslie, Frances. BSME, Clemson U., 1951, MSME, 1959; postgrad., U. Tenn. Space Inst., Tullahoma, 1975-81, U. Ala., Huntsville, 1974-75. Registered profl. engr., Ala. Commd. 2nd lt. USAF, 1951, advanced through grades to lt. col., 1972; mem. Von Braun R&D group Army Ballistic Missile Agy. (ABMA), Redstone Arsenal, Ala., 1956-60; retired USAF, 1979; rsch. engr., charter mem. NASA Marshall Space Flight Ctr., Huntsville, 1960-99; ret., 1999. Contbr. articles to profl. jours. Named to Thomas Green Clemson Acad. Engrs. and Scientists, Clemson U., 2001. Fellow: AIAA (assoc. Herman Oberth award Ala.-Miss. sect. 1999 1999); mem.: SAR, Res. Officers Assn. (life), Air Force Assn. (life; past v.p. Huntsville chpt.), Exptl. Aircraft Assn., Antique Aircraft Assn. (life), Blackbirds Assn., Minute Man Soc. Ala., Interplanetary Free Floaters (zero-gravity flights in NASA KC-135 aircraft), 8th Air Force Hist. Soc., Nat. Space Club, Shriners, Masons, Aviation Hall of Fame (chartered mem.). Achievements include patents for lunar communications receiver and transmitter for lunar surface missions; participation in design of rocket and space vehicle systems; development of Redstone, Jupiter, Jupiter C, Juno, Saturn I, Saturn IB, and Saturn V, Skylab and Apollo program, and the Space Shuttle launch vehicle systems; design of design criteria for lunar surface operations and mobility for lunar rover program; research in environmental design criteria for lunar and planetary exploration vehicles; zero-g atomospheric cloud physics; atmospheric electricity. Home: 10102 Westleigh Dr SE Huntsville AL 35803-1647 E-mail: skeetv@knology.net.

VAUGHN, EULALIA COBB, retired science educator, mathematician; b. Smithville, Tenn., Aug. 1, 1926; d. Luther Leonidas Fuson and Allie Pearl Redmon; m. Lewis Latane Cobb, Aug. 14, 1944 (dec. 1980); children: Carl Cobb, Luther Fuson Cobb, Lewis Cobb Jr., James Cobb, David R. Cobb, John Winston Cobb; m. Floyce Vaughn, 1983. BS, Mid. Tenn. State U., 1946, MEd, 1980. Tchr. Secondary Sch., Tulahoma, Tenn., 1946, sci. and math. tchr., 1947, 1948, Pine Bluff, Ark., 1959, Birmingham, Ala., 1965, Nashville, 1965—91; ret. Chair dept. various schs., Tenn., 1967—91; pres. Dekalb County Ret. Tchrs. Assn., 1992—98; tchr. mission sch., 1996—; sponsor Sci. Olympiad Glencliff H.S., Nashville (state winner). Author: Poetry Book, 2001; contbr. articles to Nashville Tennesean. Voter registration Dem. Party, Smithville, 1995—2001, mem. steering com.; women's leader United Meth. Women, Cookeville, Tenn., 1991—2001, sec. comm., dist. pres., 1992—. Mem.: Family Cmty. Edn. (pres.). Democrat. Methodist. Avocation: family. Home: PO Box 132 1161 S Mountain St Smithville TN 37166

VAUGHN, JOHN CARROLL, minister, educator; b. Louisville, Sept. 22, 1948; s. Harold D. and Morel (Johnson) V.; m. Brenda Joyce Lyttle, June 17, 1968; children: Deborah, John, Rebecca, Daniel, Joseph. BA, Bob Jones U., 1977, MMin, 1991, DD, 1989. Ordained to ministry Bapt. Ch., 1978. Sr. pastor Faith Baptist Ch., Greenville, S.C., 1977—; founder/adminstr. Hidden Treasure Christian Sch., Greenville, S.C., 1980-84; founder Iglesia Bautista de la Fe, Greenville, S.C., 1981-93. Founder/dir. Hidden Treasure Ministries, Greenville, 1981-; exec. bd. Associated Gospel Chs., Hopewell, Va., 1987-93; chaplain Greenville Police Dept., 1987—. Editor: (instrnl. video) Sufficient Grace, 1987, Frontline Mag., 1997—; author: (textbook) Special Education: A Biblical Approach, 1991, (biography) More Precious Than Gold, 1994. Chmn. Greenville County Human Rels. Commn., 1986-89; counselor Greenville County Crisis Response Team, 1987-91; co-chmn. Greenville County Sex Edn. Adv. Com., 1988-91; mem. exec. bd. dirs. Fundamental Bapt. Fellowship, 1988-98, exec. dir., 1997-1998, exec. v.p. 1998-2003, pres. 2003-; mem. exec. bd. dirs. The Wilds, 1992—, Internat. Bapt. Missions, 1993—, Christians for Religious Freedom, 1993-98; cooperating bd. Bob Jones U., 2003. Mem. SAR, Internat. Conf. Police Chaplains, Am. Assn. Christian Schs. (exec. bd. dirs. 1992-98), ACFT Owners and Pilots Assn., Am. Legion, S.C. Assn. Christian Schs. (pres. 1988—). Republican. Avocations: flying, golf, gardening, reading, history, writing. Home: 117 Frontline Dr Taylors SC 29687-2675 Office: Faith Bapt Ch 500 W Lee Rd Taylors SC 29687-2513

VAUGHN, LISA DAWN, physician, educator; b. Ashland, Ky., May 10, 1961; d. Charles Clinton and Mildred Darlene (Cantrell) V. AS in Biology, U. Ky., 1981, BS in Zoology, 1983; DO, W.Va. Sch. Osteo. Medicine, 1988. Diplomate Nat. Osteo. Med. Bd.; cert. Am. Assn. Med. Rev. officer, 1996. Gen. intern Doctors Hosp. Inc., Massillon, Ohio, 1988-89, family practice resident, 1989-91; emergency room physician Coastal Emergency Svcs., Snowpark, Ohio, 1989-90; urgent care physician Acute Care Specialists, Akron, Ohio, 1991; physician Portage Family Practice Clinic, North Canton, Ohio, 1991-95, First Care Family Health & Immediate Care Ctr., Canton, Ohio, 1995-95; dir. occupl. medicine First Care, Canton, 1996, med. dir. urgent care sys., 1996-97; physician Mercy Health Ctr. Jackson, Ohio, 1997—. Clin. asst. faculty Ohio U. Coll. Medicine, Athens, 1990-91, adj. clin. faculty, 1992—; asst. dir. family practice residency Ohio U. Coll. Medicine-Doctors Hosp. Inc., Massillon, 1992-95; urgent CARE physician First Care, Canton, Ohio, 1995—; med. dir. family home health svc. Doctors Hosp., 1992-94, chmn. dept. family medicine, 1994-95; med. dir. Riczo and Co. Managed Care Orgn., 1997—;med. adv. to Canton City Schools, Med. Assisting Program; med. advisor Boy Scouts Med. Explorers, Massillon, 1989-90; med. career advisor Girl Scouts Career Day, Canton, 1990; affiliate physician Cleve. Clinic, 1991—; med. advisor Canton City Sch. Med. Assisting Program, 2002—. Contbr. poems. Col. Ky. Cols. Assn., Ashland, 1989—; vol. United Way of Stark County, 1990-91. Mem. Cleve. Clinic Found. (affiliate physician), AMA, Am. Coll. Osteo. Family Physicians, Am. Osteo. Assn. (cert.), Ohio State Med. Assn., W.Va. Soc. Osteo. Medicine, Stark County Med. Soc., Sigma Sigma Phi (sec. 1985-86). Democrat. Avocations: writing, horseback riding, poetry. Office: Statcare of Jackson 7452 Fulton Dr NW Massillon OH 44646-9393

VAUGHN, MICHAEL THAYER, physicist, educator; b. Chgo., Aug. 6, 1936; s. Charles Le Clair and Kathleen Inez (Thayer) V; m. Gudrun Royek, Sept. 11, 1971 (dec. May 1984); m. Penelope Eve Reader, July 15, 1988. AB, Columbia U., 1955; PhD, Purdue U., 1960. Grad. asst. Purdue U., West Lafayette, Ind., 1955-59; rsch. assoc., instr. U. Pa., Phila., 1959-62; asst. prof. Ind. U., Bloomington, 1962-64; assoc. prof. Northeastern U., Boston, 1964-73, prof., 1973—. Vis. scientist Argonne (Ill.) Nat. Lab., 1967, U. Vienna, Austria, 1970-71, Internat. Ctr. for Theoretical Physics, Trieste, Italy, 1971, U. Southampton, Eng., 1979, 86, 93. Contbr. more than 50 articles to profl. jours. Sci. Rsch. Coun. Eng. fellow, 1979, Sci. & Engring. Rsch. Coun. Eng. fellow, 1986. Mem. AAAS, Am. Phys. Soc. Achievements include research in calculation of two-loop beta functions for renormalization of general quantum field theory, Z=0 criterion for compositeness. Office: Northeastern U Physics Dept 111 DA Boston MA 02115

VAUGHN, VICKI LYNN, education educator; b. New Castle, Ind., Nov. 10, 1947; d. Robert Allen and Geneva Aileen (Bishop) Fulton; m. Virgil Encil Vaughn, Jr., Aug. 26, 1967; children: Joshua Allen, Jordan Tanner. BS, Ball State U., Muncie, Ind., 1969, MA, 1973; PhD, Purdue U., 1991. Elem. tchr. New Castle (Ind.) Cmty. Sch. Corp., 1969-86; gifted/talented tchr. Marion (Ind.) Cmty. Sch. Corp., 1986-88, Lafayette (Ind.) Sch. Corp., 1988-93; dept. chair, asst. prof. Ball State U., Muncie, 1993-96; lectr. grad. courses Purdue U., West Lafayette, Ind., 1991—; prin. Vinton Elem. Sch., Lafayette, 1993—; Challenge coord. Lafayette Sch. Corp., 1996—. Assoc. Ctr. for Gifted Studies and Talent Devel., Munice, 1993—, Ctr. for Creative Learning, Sarasota, Fla., 1994—; cons. Ind. schs., 1993—; G/T coord. Lafayette Sch. Corp., Lafayette, 1993-96. Co-editor Nat. Assn. Labs. Schs. Jour.; reviewer articles Jour. Secondary Gifted Edn., Tchr. Educator, others; contbr. articles to profl. jours. Ind. Dept. Edn. learning grantee, 1993, 4Rs grantee, 1994. Mem. ASCD (assoc.), Nat. Assn. for Gifted Children, Nat. Assn. for Lab. Schs., Ind. Assn. for Gifted (rsch. com. 1988—), Phi Delta Kappa, Phi Kappa Phi. Avocations: reading, dancing, travel. Home: 2114 S 6th St Lafayette IN 47905-2142 Office: Vinton Elem Sch 3101 Elmwood Ave Lafayette IN 47904-1709

VAVALA, DOMENIC ANTHONY, medical scientist, retired military officer; b. Providence, Feb. 1, 1925; s. Salvatore and Maria (Grenci) V. Certificate basic engring., Yale U. Army Specialized Training Program, 1944; BA, Brown U., 1947; MS, U. R.I., 1950; MA, Trinity U., San Antonio, 1954; PhD in Physiology, Accademia di Studi Superiori "Minerva", Italy, 1957; MEd, U. Houston, 1958; DSc (hon.), Nobile Accademia di Santa Teodora Imperatrice, Rome, 1966, DMS (hon.), 1970; DPH (hon.), Nobile Accademia di Santa Teodora Imperatrice, 1983; D Pedagogy (hon.), Studiorum Universitas Constantiniana of Sovrano Ordine Constantiniano di San Giorgio, Rome, 1966; EdD (hon.), Imperiale Accademia di San Cirillo, Pomezia, Italy, 1977; LittD, Univ. Internazionale Sveva "Frederick II", Bergamo, Italy, 1979; D Health Scis. (hon.), Johnson & Wales U., 1993; LLD (hon.), Fridericus II U., Capua, Italy, 1997; MD (hon.), Frederick II U., Providence, Rhode Island, 1999. Research asst. tumor research U. R.I., also asst. entomol. research, 1950; research asst. pharmacology Boston U. Sch. Medicine, 1950-51; commd. 2d lt. med. service USAF, 1951, advanced through grades to lt. col., 1968; physiologist cold injury research team Army Med. Research Lab., Osaka (Japan) Army Hosp., 1951-52; research aviation physiologist USAF Sch. Aviation Medicine, Randolph AFB, Tex., 1952-54, 3605th USAF Hosp., Ellington AFB, Tex., 1955-57, chief physiol. tng., 1957; cons. aviation physiology, film prodn. dept. U. Houston, 1956; research aviation physiologist, head acad. sect. dept. physiol. tng. USAF Hosp., Lackland AFB, Tex., 1957-58; vis. prof. physiology Incarnate Word Coll., San Antonio, 1958; research aviation physiologist, chief physiol. tng. comdr. 832d Physiol. Tng. Flight, 832d Tactical Hosp., Cannon AFB, N.Mex., 1958-65; adj. faculty mem. Eastern N.Mex. U., Portales, 1959-64; instr. adult edn. divsn. Clovis (N.Mex.) mcpl. schs., 1960; research aviation physiologist, comdr. 15th Physiol. Tng. Flight, 824th USAF Dispensary, Kadena Air Base, Okinawa, 1965-66; research scientist, directorate fgn. tech., aerospace med. div. Brooks AFB, Tex., 1966-68; chief R & D support and interface div., dep. dir. for fgn. tech., 1968-70; adj. instr. Johnson & Wales U., Providence, 1973-74; instr. humanities Johnson and Wales U., Providence, 1974-75, asst. prof. humanities, 1975-77, prof. health scis. and nutrition, 1977-93, prof. emeritus, 1993—, coord. biomed. and behavioral scis. Day Coll. divsn., 1973-75, psychology coord. vets. div. Coll. Continuing Edn., 1974-76, assoc. dean adj. faculty, 1975, dean faculty, 1975-77, coord. acad. devel., 1977-78, dir. mus. series, 1990—, curator Chapel Empress St. Theodora, 1992—. Pres. corp., chmn. bd. dirs. Sovereign Constantinian Order of St. George, Inc., R.I., 1986—; pres. corp., chmn. bd. dirs. The Noble Acad. of Empress St. Theodora of R.I., Inc., 1988—; instr. anatomy, physiology and med. terminology R.I. Hosp., Providence, R.I., 1987-90. Writer, producer: (TV Series) Your Body in Flight, Sta. KUHT, Houston, 1956; (TV series) Highway to Health, Okinawa, 1965; editor-in-chief: NADUS Jour., 1963-85; compiled and edited: Fifty Years of Progress of Soviet Medicine, 1917-67; abstractor, translator in medicine Chem. Abstracts Svc., Am. Chem. Soc., Ohio State U., 1963-74; editor: (Cath. parish newspaper) The Logos, Kadena Air Base, Okinawa, 1965-66 (1st pl. 5th Air Force chapel printed news contest); contbr. articles to profl. jours. Trustee, Gov. Ctr. Sch., Providence, 1979-85; mem. scholarship com. St. Sahag and, St. Mesrob Armenian Apostolic Ch., Providence; choir master, music dir. Cannon AFB, N.Mex. Cath. Parish, 1958-65. Served with AUS, 1943-44. Recipient Disting. Svc. award Clovis (N.Mex.) Jaycees, 1959, Acad. Palms Gold medal Accademia Studi Superiori "Minerva", 1960, citation, chief chaplains USAF, 1970, commendation medal USAF, 1970, chief biomed. scientist insignia, biomed. scis. corps USAF Med. Svc., 1970, spl. faculty citation Johnson and Wales U., 1981, contbn. awd. doctoral program ednl. leadership Alan Feinstein Grad. Sch., Johnson and Wales U., Providence, RI, 1999; academician divsn. scis. Accademia di Studi Superiori "Minerva", 1960; Min. Plenipotentiary for U.S. of Nobile Accademia di Santa Teodora Imperatrice, Rome, 1967, rector pro tempore, 1980; decorated knight grand officer Merit Class, Sovereign Constantinian Order St. George, Rome, 1969, Knight of Grand Cross with Constantinian neckchain, Justice Class, Sovereign Constantinian Order St. George, 1969, Knight of Grand Cross Justice Class, Order St. John of Jerusalem, Knights of Malta, Bari, Italy, 1984, Knight of Grand Cross Justice Class, Order St. John of Jerusalem, Knights of Cyprus, Rhodes and Malta, Bari, 1984, Knight of Grand Cordon Justice Class, Order Teutonic Knights, Sao Paulo, 1986, Knight of Grand Cross Justice Class, Mil. Order St. Gereon, Sao Paulo, 1986, Knight of Grand Cross Justice Class, Mil. and Hospitalier Order St Jean d'Acre and St. Thomas, Capua, Italy, 1987, Knight of Grand Cross Justice Class, Mil. and Hospitalier Order St. Mary of Bethlehem, Capua, 1987; recipient Ednl. Professionalism award Domei Toastmasters Internat., 1965; named Magnificent Rector and Pres., The Constantinian U. (Studiorum Universitas Constantiniana), Italy, 1970, Marquis of Royal Throne of Swabia of Hohenstaufen Dynasty, Prince Jean von Schwaben, Bergamo, Italy, 1984, Duke of the New Rome of Imperial Dynasty of Amorium by His Imperial Highness Prince Don Francesco Amoroso d'Aragona, Capua, 2000. Fellow AAAS (emeritus), Tex. Acad. Sci., Royal Soc. Health (London; emeritus), Am. Inst. Chemists (emeritus); mem. Assn. Mil. Surgeons U.S. (life), Nat. Assn. Doctors U.S. (founder 1958, sec.-treas. 1958-85, editor-in-chief The NADUS Jour. 1963-68), Accademia di San Cirillo Italy (hon.), N.Y. Acad. Scis., Phi Sigma, Kappa Delta Pi, Phi Kappa Phi, Alpha Beta Kappa (charter mem., pres. R.I. Alpha chpt. Johnson & Wales U. 1984-92). Home: 30 Oaklawn Ave Apt 219 Cranston RI 02920-9319

VAYNMAN, SEMYON, materials scientist, educator; b. Odessa, USSR, Oct. 2, 1949; came to U.S., 1980; s. Kelman and Esther (Potashnik) V.; m. Dora Skladman, Nov. 18, 1977; children: Ethel, Alexander. MS in Chemistry, Odessa U., 1973; PhD in Materials Sci., Northwestern U., 1986. Rsch. scientist Rsch. Inst. Foundry Tech., Odessa, 1973-77, Rsch. Inst. Power Industry, Lvov, USSR, 1977-80, GARD, Niles, Ill., 1981-84; rsch. prof. Northwestern U., Evanston, Ill., 1986—. Reviewer Jour. Electronic Packaging, 1989, IEEE publ., 1988—; mem. adv. bd. sci. com. for solder joints reliability Dept. Def., Washington, 1989-90. Contbr. sci. papers to profl. publs., chpts. to books. Mem. Am. Soc. Metals, Mineral, Metals and Materials Soc. (electronic packaging and interconnection materials com. 1989—). Achievements include 2 patents in foundry technology. Office: Northwestern U 1801 Maple Ave Evanston IL 60208-0001

VAZQUEZ, JOSÉ ANTONIO, education educator; b. San Germ(á)n, P.R., Nov. 30, 1936; came to U.S., 1957; s. José and Montserrate (Faria) V. BA, Inter-Am. U., P.R., 1956; MA, Columbia U., 1959. Bilingual tchr. in sch. and community rels. N.Y.C. Bd. Edn., 1957-65, supr., bilingual tchrs. in sch. and community rels., 1965-68, dir., bilingual tchrs. in sch. and community rels., 1968-71; prof. CUNY (Hunter Coll.), 1971—. Div. dir. Project BEST, Hunter Coll. component of N.Y.C. Consortium for Bilingual Edn., 1971-75; chief, bilingual/multicultural div. Nat. Inst. Edn., Washington, 1976-77; dir. Hunter-C.W. Post Bilingual Edn. Svc. Ctr., N.Y.C., 1981-83; prin. investigator Significant Bilingual Instrn. Features Study, 1981-83; dir. N.Y.C. Bilingual Edn. Multifunctional Support Ctr., 1983-86; co-dir. Ford Found. Dropout Prevention Collaboratives Program, 1986-87; dir. N.Y.C. Multifunctional Resource Ctr., 1987—. Author: El Espanol: Eslabon Cultural, 1978. Mem. N.Y. State Commr. of Edn.'s Adv. Coun. on Bilingual Edn., 1971—, chair, 1971-74; chmn. Fed. Task Force on the Assessment of Ednl. Needs of Puerto Rican Children and Youth in N.Y. State (HEW), 1972-73. Recipient Cuban Nat. Planning Coun. award, 1986, Gladys Correa Meml. award N.Y. State Assn. for Bilingual Edn., 1982, Am. Heritage award John F. Kennedy Lib. for Minorities, 1974. Mem. Nat. Assn. Bilingual Edn., Am. Ednl. Rsch. Assn., N.Y. State Assn. for Bilingual Edn., Tchrs. of English to Speakers of Other Languages. Office: CUNY Hunter Coll 695 Park Ave Rm 925W New York NY 10021-5024

VAZQUEZ-CAMUÑAS, MARIBEL, elementary school educator, educator; b. San Juan, Dec. 13, 1956; d. Carlos A. and María I. (Camuñas) Vázquez-Santoni; children: Carlos S. Ramírez, Nellie M. Ramírez. BA cum laude, U. P.R., 1975-79, MPH in Edn., 1979-80. Lic. tchr. Health educator mem. Com. Continuing Health Edn. Hosp. Regional, Bayamon, P.R., 1980-81; 4th and 5th grades math and sci. tchr., 5th grade English tchr. Colegio Mater Salvatoris, 1981-86; 4th and 5th grades math and sci., 5th and 6th grades math tchr., chairperson math dept. Academia Perpetuo Socorro, San Juan, 1986-93. Mem. Nat. Coun. Tchrs. of Math., Liga Puertorriqueña de Ayuda a Niños con Problemas de Aprendizaje. Roman Catholic. Avocations: reading, painting, watercolors. Home: 1301 Ave Magdalena Apt 203 San Juan PR 00907-1932

VAZSONYI, ALEXANDER THOMAS, education educator; b. Traverse City, Mich., Oct. 16, 1964; AA, Northwestern Mich. Coll., 1987; BS, Grand Valley State U., 1989; MS, U. Ariz., 1993, PhD, 1995. Program coord. The U. of Ariz., Tucson, 1994—95; asst. rsch. scientist U. Ariz., 1995—96; asst. prof. Auburn U., Ala., 1996—2000, assoc. prof., 2000—. Cons. U. Ala., Tuscaloosa, 2001—, Kent State U., Ohio, 1999—2000. Editor: Jour. of Early Adolescence; contbr. articles to profl. jours. Faculty advisor Grad. Student Orgn., Auburn U., 2001—02. Nominee Disting. Alumna/Alumnus award, Grand Valley State U., 2000. Mem.: Soc. for Rsch. on Adolescence, Am. Soc. Criminology, Ctr. for the Advancement of Youth Health. Avocation: photography, music, travel. Office: Auburn Univ Dept Human Devel and Family Studies 284 Spidle Hall Auburn AL 36849

VAZSONYI, NICHOLAS, foreign languages educator; b. Traverse City, Mich., May 31, 1963; s. Balint and Barbara (Whittington) V.; m. Agnes Mueller, Mar. 1, 1996; 1 child, Leah. BA summa cum laude, Ind. U., 1982; MA, UCLA, 1988, PhD, 1993. Legal asst. Barnes & Thornburg, Indpls., 1982-84; artistic dir. Telemusic Inc., Bloomington, Ind., 1984-86, 88-90; instr. UCLA, 1993-94; asst. prof. German Vanderbilt U., Nashville, 1994-97; assoc. prof. German U. S.C., Columbia, 1997—. Mng. editor New German Review, L.A., 1990-93. Author: Lukacs Reads Goethe: From Aestheticism to Stalinism, 1997; author, editor: Searching for Common Ground: Diskurse zur deutschen Identitat 1750-1871, 2000, Wagner's Meistersinger: Performance, History, Representation, 2003; contbr. numerous articles to profl. jours. Mem. MLA, Am. Assn. Tchrs. of German, Goethe Soc. N.Am., German Studies Assn., Phi Beta Kappa. Office: U SC German Studies Program Columbia SC 29208-0001 E-mail: vazsonyi@sc.edu.

VEACH, PATRICIA J. music educator; b. Belleville, Kans., Apr. 25, 1948; d. Kenneth D. and Marcella L. (Sterba) Holmes; m. Robert E. Veach, May 25, 1991; children: Tony, Tonya. B Music Edn., Marymount Coll., 1970; MS, Kans. State U., 1983. K-12 vocal instr. Unified Sch. Dist. # 393, Solomon, Kans., 1970-94; owner Stitches & More, 1995—. Mem. Music Educators Nat. Conf. Avocations: reading, golf, crafts, word games. Home: 1 Ludford Cir Bella Vista AR 72714

VEACO, LELIA, retired education educator; b. San Francisco, Sept. 14, 1923; d. Arthur Hamilton McCain and Eleonore McWalter; m. Robert G. Veaco, Feb. 29, 1944; children: Kristina, Constance V. Dilts, Nicolas S. BA in Psychology, U. Calif., Berkeley, 1945; MA, Calif. State U., Fresno, 1969; EdD, U. of the Pacific, 1973. Cert. tchr. (life), Calif. Tchr. elem. edn., Central Valley, Calif., 1946-69; prof. Calif. Sch. Profl. Psychology, Fresno, 1973-97, prof. emerita, 1997—. Contbr. articles to profl. jours. Bd. dirs. Assoc. Ctr. for Therapy, Fresno, 1979-96. Mem. Phi Delta Kappa (bd. dirs.). Democrat. Unitarian Universalist. Avocations: gardening, cooking, reading. Home: 3756 Portage Cir S Stockton CA 95219-3836 Office: Calif Sch Profl Psychology 5130 E Clinton Way Fresno CA 93727-2014

VEAL, LAURA, secondary school educator; b. Houston, Aug. 12, 1975; d. Robert Leslie and Becki (Lynn) Veal. BA, Baylor U., Waco, Tex., 1996. Cert. Secondary Sch. tchr.Latin Tex., 1999. Tchr. Latin, English Garland (Tex.) Ind. Sch. Dist., 1997—2000; Latin tchr. Plano (Tex.)Ind. Sch. Dist., 2000—. Member Nat. Charity League Golden Corridor chpt., Plano, 1987—93. Mem.: CAMWS, Am. Classical League, Tex. Classical Association. Personal E-mail: LatTchr@aol.com.

VEASEL, WALTER, minister, educator; b. Balt., Apr. 11, 1925; s. William Edward Veasel and Mary Lula (Boyd-Veasel) Ebert; m. Helen Ilene Gank; children: William, Holly, Bradley, Heide. ThB, Holmes Coll. of the Bible, 1947; BS in Elem. Edn., Towson State U., 1970; M in Ministries, Zion Sem., 1986. Ordained to ministry Pentecostal Holiness Ch., 1947; cert. tchr. Md. Tchr. Balt. City Schs., 1959-84; pastor Mid Atlantic Conf. Pentecostal Holiness Ch., 1948-54, 1960-70, St. Catherines and London, Canada, 1955-59; founder, pastor Cmty. Ch., 1970-90; pastor emeritus Woodbridge Valley Ch. of God, 1990-94; prin. Tabernacle Christian Sch., Balt., 1988-94. Conf. Sunday sch. sec./treas.; conf. youth v.p.; conf. sec/treas., bd. dirs., 1950—70; instr. Tabernacle Bible Inst., 1970—75, Faith Sch. Theology, 1993. Co-editor: Veasel Genealogy 1813-1999. Deacon, trustee Full Gospel Pentecostal Ch., Ellicott City, 1999—; vol. nursing homes, reform schs. and prisons, 1948—; mem. adv. bd. Evangel Christian Acad., Balt., 1996—. Recipient Vols. cert., Ho. of Corrections, 1975—, Frederick Villa Nursing Home, 1980—. Republican. Home: 5025 Montgomery Rd Ellicott City MD 21043-6750 also: 638 Clark Lohr Rd Swanton MD 21561-2255

VEATCH, ROBERT MARLIN, philosophy educator, medical ethics researcher; b. Utica, N.Y., Jan. 22, 1939; s. Cecil Ross and Regina (Braddock) V.; m. Laurelyn Kay Lovett, June 17, 1961 (div. Oct. 1986); children: Paul Martin, Carlton Elliot; m. Ann Bender Pastore, May 23, 1987. BS, Purdue U., 1961; MS, U. Calif. at San Francisco, 1962; BD, Harvard U., 1964, MA, 1970, PhD, 1971; D Humanities (hon.), Creighton U., 1999. Teaching fellow Harvard U., 1968-70; research assoc. in medicine Coll. Physicians and Surgeons, Columbia U., 1971-72; assoc. for med. ethics Inst. of Society, Ethics and Life Scis., Hastings-on-Hudson, N.Y., 1970-75, sr. assoc., 1975-79; prof. med. ethics Kennedy Inst. Ethics Georgetown U., 1979—, prof. philosophy, 1981—, dir., 1989-96; adj. prof. depts. community and family medicine and ob/gyn, 1984—. Mem. vis. faculty various colls. and univs.; mem. gov. bd. Washington Regional Transplant Consortium, 1988—; bd. dirs. Hospice Care D.C., 1989-96, 97-99, pres., 1993-95; active United Network Organ Sharing Ethics Com., 1989-95. Author: Value-Freedom in Science and Technology, 1976, Death, Dying and the Biological Revolution, 1976, rev. edit., 1989, Case Studies in Medical Ethics, 1977, A Theory of Medical Ethics, 1981, The Foundations of Justice, 1987, The Patient as Partner, 1987; (with Sarah T. Fry) Case Studies in Nursing Ethics, 1987, rev. edit., 2000, The Patient-Physician Relationship: The Patient as Partner, Part 2, 1991; (with James T. Rule) Ethical Questions in Dentistry, 1993, (with Harley Flack) Case Studies in Allied Health Ethics, 1997, (with Paul DeVries and Lisa Newton) Ethics Applied, 2d. edit., 1999, (with Amy Haddad) Case Studies in Pharmacy Ethics, 1999, The Basics of Bioethics, 2000, 2d edit., 2003, Transplantation Ethics, 2000; editor or co-editor: Bibliography of Society, Ethics and the Life Sciences, 1973, rev. edit., 1978, The Teaching of Medical Ethics, 1973, Death Inside Out, 1975, Ethics and Health Policy, 1976, Teaching of Bioethics, 1976, Population Policy and Ethics, 1977, Life Span: Values and Life Extending Technologies, 1979, Cases in Bioethics From the Hastings Center Report, 1982, Medical Ethics, 1989, 2d edit., 1997, Cross Cultural Perspectives in Medical Ethics, 1989, rev. edit., 2000; (with Edmund D. Pellegrino and John P. Langan) Ethics, Trust, and the Professions, 1991; (with Tom L. Beauchamp) Ethical Issues in Death and Dying, 1996, (with Hans-Martin Sass and Rihito Kimura) Advance Directives and Surrogate Decision Making in Health Care: United States, Germany, and Japan, 1998, (with Albert R. Jonsen and LeRoy Walters) Source Book in Bioethics: A Documentary History, 1998; assoc. editor Encyclopedia of Bioethics, 1998; editl. bd. Jour. AMA, 1976-86, Jour. Medicine and Philosophy, 1980—, Harvard Theol. Rev., 1975—, Jour. Religious Ethics, 1981—; editl. adv. bd. Forum on Medicine, 1977-81; contbg. editor Hosp. Physician, 1975-85, Am. Jour. Hosp. Pharmacy, 1989-99; sr. editor Kennedy Inst. Ethics Jour., 1991—; contbr. articles to profl. jours. Mem. Soc. Christian Ethics. Office: Georgetown U Kennedy Inst Of Ethics Washington DC 20057-0001 E-mail: veatchr@georgetown.edu.

VECCHIO, ROBERT PETER, business management educator; b. Chgo., June 29, 1950; s. Dominick C. and Angeline V.; m. Betty Ann Vecchio; Aug. 21, 1974; children: Julie, Mark. BS summa cum laude, DePaul U., 1972; MA, U. Ill., 1974, PhD, 1976. Instr. U. Ill., Urbana, 1973-76; mem. faculty dept. mgmt. U. Notre Dame, 1976—, dept. chmn., 1983-90, Franklin D. Schurz Prof. Mgmt., 1986—. Editor Jour. of Mgmt., 1995-2000. Fellow: SMA, APA, Am. Psychol. Soc., Soc. for Indsl. and Orgnl. Psychology; mem.: Midwest Psychol. Assn., Midwest Acad. Mgmt., Decision Scis. Inst., Acad. of Mgmt., Phi Eta Sigma, Delta Epsilon Sigma, Phi Kappa Phi. Home: 16856 Hampton Dr Granger IN 46530-6907 Office: U Notre Dame Dept Mgmt Notre Dame IN 46556

VEECH, LYNDA ANNE, musician, educator; b. Montclair, N.J., July 19, 1969; d. Robert Gerald, Sr. and Josephine Veech. B in Music Edn., Rutgers U., New Brunswick, 1991, MA in Music History, 1995; MusM in Piano Performance and Pedagogy, Westminster Choir Coll., Princeton, N.J., 1998. Cert. tchr. N.J. Faculty mem. Westminster Conservatory, Princeton, 1995—2000; pvt. studio dir. Studio of Lynda A. Veech, Verona, NJ, 1995—; faculty mem. Essex County Coll., Woodbridge, NJ, 1996—98, Caldwell (N.J.) Coll., 2000—01; choral dir. Caldwell and West Caldwell Pub. Schs., 2000—02; music tchr. Bartle Elem. Sch., Highland Park, NJ, 2002—03, Morris Cath. HS, Denville, NJ, 2003—. Cons. freelance work, Verona, NJ, 1995—2002; participant Hands Across the Water Internat. Tchr. Exch. Program, Australia, 2002. Performer Ameropa Internat. Music Festival, Prague, Czech Republic, 2001. Bd. dirs. Music and More Booster Club, Caldwell, NJ, 2001—02; ch. musician 1st Bapt. Ch., Montclair, 2000—01; organist, choir dir. Calvary Luth. Ch., 2003—; vocalist Canticle AIDS Benefit Ensemble, NJ, 1999—2000. Grantee, Rutgers U., 1991—95, Westminster Choir Coll., 1995—97. Mem.: Music Edn. Assn. (co-founder 2000—), Nat. Conf. Piano Pedagogy, Piano Tchrs. Guild, N.J. Edn. Assn., Am. Choral Dir.'s Assn., Music Educator's Nat. Conf. (treas. 1987, v.p. 1991). Roman Catholic. Avocations: reading, swimming, ballet, writing poetry, playing music in sacred and secular settings. Home: 124 Sunset Ave Verona NJ 07044 Office: Morris Cath High Sch 200 Morris Ave Denville NJ 07834-1360 Personal E-mail: notenut@aol.com.

VEEDER, NANCY WALKER, social work educator; b. Albany, N.Y., Mar. 17, 1937; d. Harold Gerit and Alice (Walker) V. AB, Smith Coll., Northampton, Mass., 1959; MS, Simmons Sch. Social Work, Boston, 1963; PhD, Brandeis U., 1974; MBA, Boston Coll., 1990. Prof., grad. sch. social work Boston Coll., Chestnut Hill, 1968—. Home: 53 Lake Ave Newton Center MA 02459-2110 E-mail: veeder@bc.edu.

VEILLE, JEAN-CLAUDE, maternal-fetal medicine physician, educator; b. France; came to U.S., 1982; m. Ann Veille; children: Olivier, Xavier, Patrique, Robert. BS, McGill U., 1971; MD, U. Montpellier, France, 1977. Fellow in maternal-fetal medicine Oreg. Health Scis., Portland, 1982-84; from asst. prof. to assoc. prof. Case Western Res. U., Cleve., 1984-90; chief maternal, fetal medicine Case Western Reserve U., Cleve., 1989-90; assoc. prof., dir. maternal-fetal med. fellowship program Wake Forest U. Sch. Medicine, Winston-Salem, N.C., 1990-95, prof., 1995—, chief maternal-fetal medicine sect., 1997—2002; chmn. dept. ob-gyn. Albany (N.Y.) Med. Ctr., 2002—. Contbr. articles to profl. jours. Grantee NIH, 1991-2002. Office: 47 New Scotland Ave Albany NY E-mail: veillej@mail.amc.edu.

VELARDO, JOSEPH THOMAS, molecular biology and endocrinology educator; b. Newark, Jan. 27, 1923; s. Michael Arthur and Antoinette (I.) V.; m. Forresta M.-M. Power, Aug. 12, 1948 (dec. July 1976). AB, U. No. Colo., 1948; SM, Miami U., Oxford, Ohio, 1949; PhD, Harvard U., 1952. Rsch. fellow in biology and endocrinology Harvard U., Cambridge, Mass., 1952-53; rsch. assoc. in pathology, ob-gyn. and surgery Harvard U. Sch. Medicine, Boston, 1953-55; asst. in surgery Peter Bent Brigham and Women's Hosp., Boston, 1954-55; asst. prof. anatomy and endocrinology Sch. Medicine, Yale U., New Haven, 1955-61; prof. anatomy, chmn. dept. N.Y. Med. Coll., N.Y.C., 1961-62; cons. N.Y. Fertility Inst., 1961-62; dir. Inst. for Study Human Reprodn., Cleve., 1962-67; prof. biology John Carroll U., Cleve., 1962-67; mem. rsch. and edn. divs. St. Ann Ob-Gyn. Hosp., Cleve., 1962-67, head dept. rsch., 1964-67; prof. anatomy Stritch Sch. Medicine Loyola U., Chgo., 1967-88, chmn. dept. anatomy Stritch Sch. of Medicine, 1967-73; v.p. Universal Rsch. Systems, Warren, Ohio, 1975—; pres. University Rsch. Systems, Lombard, 1979—. Internat. Basic and Biol.-Biomed. Curricula, Lombard, Ill., 1979—. Course moderator laparoscopy Brazil-Israel Congress on Fertility and Sterility, Brazil Soc. of Human Reprodn., Rio de Janeiro, 1973; mem. curriculum com. Yale U. Sch. Medicine, 1956—61, dir. exptl. mammalian labs., 1956—61; organizer, chmn. symposia in field; initial charter founder, mem. U. Sacramento, 2003. Author: (with others) Annual Reviews Physiology, Reproduction, 1961, Histochemistry of Enzymes in the Female Genital System, 1963, The Ovary, 1963, The Ureter, 1967, rev. edit., 1981; editor, contbr.: Endocrinology of Reproduction, 1958, The Essentials of Human Reproduction, 1958; cons. editor, co-author: The Uterus, 1959; contbr. Progestational Substances, 1958, Trophoblast and Its Tumors, 1959, The Vagina, 1959, Hormonal Steroids, Biochemistry, Pharmacology and Therapeutics, 1964, Human Reproduction, 1973; co-editor, contbr.: Biology of Reproduction, Basic and Clinical Studies, 1973; contbr. articles to profl. jours.; live broadcasts on major radio and TV networks on subjects of bioscis., biomed. careers and biomed. subjects; co-author, co-dir. med. movie on human reprodn. The Soft Anvil; life history and research highlights chronicled in The Endocrinologist, vol II, 2001, Initial Charter Founder Member, University of Sacramento, 2003. Apptd. U.S. del. to Vatican, 1964; charter mem. U.S. Rep. Presdl. Task Force, 1988—; charter mem. U.S. Rep. Nat. Senatorial Com., 1988—, Rep. Nat. Com. Victory Team, 2003; mem. Rep. Senate Adv. Coun., 1997—; rep. U.S. Senate Inner Circle, 1988—, U.S. Rep. Senatorial Commn., 1991—. With USAAF, World War II, 1943-45. Decorated Presdl. Unit citation, 2 Bronze Stars; recipient award Lederle Med. Faculty Awards Com., 1955-58, Cert. of Achievement U.S. Rep. Nat. Senatorial Com., 1999; Disting. Alumni award, The William R. Ross award in sci., U. No. Colo., 1999; named hon. citizen City of Sao Paulo, Brazil, 1972; U.S. del. to Vatican, 1964. Fellow AAAS, N.Y. Acad. Scis. (co-organizer, chmn., consulting editor internat. symposium The Uterus), Gerontol. Soc., Pacific Coast Fertility Soc. (hon.); mem. French Nat. Soc. for Study of Sterility and Fertility (exec. hon. pres. IVth World Congress on Fertility and Sterility 1962), Am. Assn. Anatomists, Am. Soc. Zoologists, Soc. for Integrative and Comparative Biology (organizer symposium The Uterus), Am. Physiol. Soc. (vis. prof. 1962), Endocrine Soc., Soc. Endocrinology (Gt. Britain), Soc. Exptl. Biology and Medicine, Am. Soc. Study Sterility (Rubin award 1954), Internat. Fertility Assn., Pan Am. Assn. Anatomy (co-organizer symposium Reproduction 1972), Midwestern Soc. Anatomists (pres. 1973-74), Mexican Soc. Anatomy (hon.), Harvard Club, Sigma Xi, Kappa Delta Pi, Phi Sigma, Gamma Alpha, Alpha Epsilon Delta. Roman Catholic. Achievements include extensive original research and publications on the physiology and development of decidual tissue (experimental equivalent of the maternal portion of the placenta) in the rat; biological investigation of eighteen human adenohypophyses (anterior lobes of the human pituitary glands); induction of ovulation utilizing highly purified adenohypophyseal gonadotropic hormones in mammals; the pacemaker action of ovarian sex steroid hormones in reproductive processes; and the interaction of steroids in reproductive mechanisms. Office: 607 E Wilson Ave Lombard IL 60148-4062

VELAZQUEZ, JOSEPH, management and mathematics educator; b. N.Y.C., Dec. 3, 1938; m. Geraldine Khaner, Aug. 31, 1963; children: Mark, Brenda. BA, Hunter Coll., 1966; MSEE, N.J. Inst. Tech., 1977; MBA, Monmouth Coll., 1972; EdD, Temple U., 1989. Physicist Columbia U., N.Y.C., 1962-65; instr. Montclair Coll., Upper Montclair, N.J., 1973-74; instr. distance learning and accelerated courses Georgian Court Coll., Lakewood, NJ, 1987—2003; program mgr., engr. Terrestrial Space Program Mgmt. Office, Monmouth, N.J., 1993-95; prof. mgmt. Bekeley Coll., N.J., 2000—. Mem. AICEA, IEEE, Langly AFB Aero Club, Phi Delta Kappa. Avocation: flying (instrument and private pilot's license).

VÉLEZ-JUARBE, LUIS ANTONIO, industrial pharmacy educator; b. Utuado, P.R., June 9, 1947; s. Bonafacio and Luz E. (Juarbe) V.; m. Nayda I. Santiago, Mar. 4, 1988; children: Luis M., Antonio L., Eileen, Luis A., Krystal A. BS in Pharmacy, U. Puerto Rico, 1971; PhD in Indsl. Pharmacy, Purdue U., 1977. Prof. U. Puerto Rico, San Juan, 1971-85; pharm. tech. mgr. Warner Lambert, Inc., Vega Baja, P.R., 1986-89; mfg. mgr. Parmax Divsn. Baxter, Aguada, P.R., 1989-92; tech. svc. mgr. Dade Diagnostics of P.R., Inc., Aguada, 1992-96. Indsl. cons. mfg., mktg., P.R., Mex., U.S., 1976-85; chairmn. adv. bd. Econ. Devel. Adminstrn., San Juan, 1977-86; v.p. Bioequivalence Bd., San Juan, 1982-86 Editor P.R. Health Sci. Jour., 1982-86, P.R. Pharm. Assn. Jour., 1983-84 (award 1983). Mem. internal review bd. U. Puerto Rico, 1976-86, cons. on indsl. affairs, 1994—; evaluator PR2000 Indsl. Excellence, P.R., 1992—. Recipient cert. Puerto Rico Pharm. Assn., San Juan, 1982-83; named Rschr. of Yr., U. Puerto Rico, 1985. Mem. Am. Assn. Pharm. Scientists, Puerto Rico Mfg. Assn. (1st v.p.), Am. Chem. Soc., Am. Soc. Quality Control, Rho Chi, Rho Pi Phi. Roman Catholic. Achievements include development of bioadheside polymers /co-polymer for controlled release drug delivery system; a industrial validation group for PRMA/FDA Organization 1976-95; project mgr. for technology transfer for Warner Lambert, Inc. and Paramax, division of Baxter; comparative study of Maxide and Diazide as consultant. Avocations: tennis, jogging, music, meditation, weightlifting. Office: Dade Diagnostics of PR Inc Rd 115 Km 22 6 PO Box 865 Aguada PR 00602 Address: Cond Parque De Loyola 500 Ave Jesus T Pinero Apt 303 San Juan PR 00918-4051

VELICER, JANET SCHAFBUCH, retired elementary school educator; b. Cedar Rapids, Iowa, Aug. 27, 1941; d. Allan J. and Geraldine Frances (Stuart) Schafbuch; m. Leland Frank Velicer, Aug. 17, 1963 (dec. Dec. 2000); children: Mark Allan, Gregory Jon, Daniel James. BS, Iowa State U., 1963, MS, 1966; cert. Elem. Edn., Mich. State U., 1976. Tchr. chemistry Prendergast High Sch., Upper Darby, Pa., 1964-65; tchr. home econs. Cardinal O'Hara High Sch., Springfield, Pa., 1965-66; substitute tchr. Pa., Mich., 1967-76; elem. tchr. Winans Elem. Sch., Waverly, Mich., 1976-78, Wardcliff Elem. Sch., Okemos, Mich., 1978-94; tchr. gifted and talented alternative program grades 4 and 5 Hiawatha Elem. Sch., Okemos, 1994-95; tchr. grade 4 Wardcliff Elem. Sch., 1995-2001; ret., 2001. Computer coord., Great Books coord.; dist. com. mem. math, computer, substance abuse, cable TV, evaluation revision Okemos Pub. Schs., Instrnl. Coun.; del. Mich. Edn. Exch. Opportunity Program, Germany, 1999. Author: (video) Wardcliff School Documentary, 1982, The Integrated Arts Program of the Okemos Elementary Schools, 1983. Citizens adv. com. to develop a five-yr. plan, 1982-83, bldg. utilization adv. com., 1983-84, cmty. use of schs. adv. com., 1984-85, strategic planning steering com., 1989-90, taking our schs. into tomorrow com., 1990-91, bonding election steering com., 1991; chmn. wellness com. Okemos Pub. Schs., 1993-95; bd. dirs. Okemos Music Patrons, 1981-86, pres., 1984-86; faculty rep. PTO; leadership coun. Nat. Inst. Clin. Application Behavioral Medicine, 1998—; chaperone Okemos HS German Club Exch., 1987, Benton Cmty. HS Spanish Club Exch., Mex., 1995, Costa Rica, 1999, Spain, 2001, 03. Recipient Classrooms of Tomorrow Tchr. award Mich. Dept. Edn., 1990. Mem. NEA, NAFE, AARP, Nat. Ret. Tchrs. Assn., Mich. Edn. Assn., Inst. Noetic Scis., Okemos Edn. Assn. (exec. coun.), Lansing Womens Club, Phi Kappa Phi, Mich. Coun. Tchrs. Math., Omicron Nu, Iota Sigma Pi. Democrat. Avocations: swimming, reading, hiking, travel, cultural events. Home: 2678 Blue Haven Ct East Lansing MI 48823-3804 E-mail: jvelicer@msu.edu.

VELLA, SANDRA RACHAEL, principal; b. Springfield, Mass., Jan. 19, 1946; d. Joseph James and Josephine Anna (DiMonaco) V. BA, Coll. of Our Lady Of Elms, 1967; MA, Westfield State Coll., 1974, postgrad., 1975. Cert. elem. sch. tchr., prin. Tchr. elem. sch. Samuel Bowles Sch., Springfield, Mass., 1967-86, prin. elem. sch., 1986—. Historian Italian Cultural Ctr., 1988—; bd. dirs. Springfield Preservation Trust, 1988-94; coord. Com. Di Monaco for Mayor, Springfield, 1989-90; co-author drug program Healthy Me Gov. Alliance vs. Drug, 1992-94; bd. dirs. Forest Park Civic Assn., 1990-92; bd. dirs. New Eng. Puppetry Theatre, 1984-92; mem. adv. coun. Springfield Cmty. Police sector, E. Springfield, 1995—; grad. Citizen's Police Acad.; numerous ednl. and altruistic civic sub. coms. Recipient Serviam award Italian Cultural Ctr. Western Mass., 1992, Mass. Gov.'s Alliance vs. Drugs award, 1988-90. Mem. Springfield Elem. Prins. Assn., Alpha Delta Kappa (Kappa pres. 1991-94, state chaplain 1994-96, sgt-at-arms 1992-94, 2002—, historian 1981-85). Democrat. Roman Catholic. Avocations: art, local history, gardening. Home: 99 Appleton St Springfield MA 01108-2949 Office: Samuel Bowles Sch 24 Bowles Park Springfield MA 01104-1510 E-mail: vellas@sps.springfield.ma.us.

VENABLE, DEMETRIUS D. physics educator; b. Powhatan, Va., Oct. 11, 1947; s. James B. and J. Viola (Bell) V.; m. Geri Elizabeth Turner, Nov. 29, 1969; children: Juanita, Jessica. BS, Va. State U., Petersburg, 1970; MS, Am. U., 1972, PhD, 1974. Sr. assoc. engr. IBM, Fishkill, N.Y., 1974-76; asst. prof. physics St. Paul's Coll., Lawrenceville, Va., 1976-78; prof. Hampton (Va.) U., 1978-95; prof. physics Howard U., Washington, 1995—. Mem. adv. com. fusion energy U.S. Dept. Energy, Washington, 1994-96; bd. dirs. Va. Aerospace Bus. Roundtable, Hampton, 1993-95. Recipient Faculty award for excellence in sci. White House Sci. and Tech. Adv. Com., 1988, Disting. Pub. Svc. medal NASA, 1994. Mem. Am. Assn. Physics Tchrs. (com. chair 1985, Disting. Svc. citation 1994), Am. Geophys. Union, Nat. Soc. Black Physicists (bd. dirs., exec. sec. 1998—), Southeastern Univs. Rsch. Assn. (bd. dirs. 1995). Office: Howard U 2355 6th St NW Washington DC 20001-2322

VENDITTI, CLELIA ROSE See PALMER, CHRISTINE

VENDLER, HELEN HENNESSY, literature educator, poetry critic; b. Boston, Mass., Apr. 30, 1933; d. George and Helen (Conway) Hennessy; 1 son, David. AB, Emmanuel Coll., 1954; PhD, Harvard U., 1960; PhD (hon.), U. Oslo, 1981; D.Litt. (hon.), Smith Coll., 1980, Kenyon Coll., 1982; D.Litt. (hon.), U. Hartford, 1985; DLitt (hon.), Union Coll., 1986, Columbia U., 1987, Washington U., 1991; D.Litt. (hon.), Marlboro Coll., 1989, Yale U., 2000; DHL (hon.), Dartmouth Coll., 1992, U. Mass., Amherst, 1992, Bates Coll., 1992, U. Toronto, Ont., Can., 1992, Trinity Coll., Dublin, Ireland, 1993; DHL (hon.), Fitchburg State U., 1990, U. Cambridge, 1997, Nat. U., Ireland, 1998, Wabash Coll., 1998, U. Mass, Dartmouth, 2000, Yale U., 2000, U. Aberdeen, 2000, Tufts U., 2001, Amherst Coll., 2002, Colby Coll., 2003. Instr. Cornell U., Ithaca, N.Y., 1960-63; lectr. Swarthmore (Pa.) Coll. and Haverford (Pa.) Coll., 1963-64; asst. prof. Smith Coll., Northampton, Mass., 1964-66; assoc. prof. Boston U., 1966-68, prof., 1968-85. Fulbright lectr. U. Bordeaux, France, 1968-69; vis. prof. Harvard U., 1981-85, Kenan prof., 1985—, Porter U. prof., 1990—, assoc. acad. dean, 1987-92, sr. fellow Harvard Soc. Fellows, 1981-93; poetry critic New Yorker, 1978-99; mem. ednl. adv. bd. Guggenheim Found., 1991-2001, Pulitzer Prize Bd., 1991-99. Author: Yeats's Vision and the Later Plays, 1963, On Extended Wings: Wallace Stevens' Longer Poems, 1969, The Poetry of George Herbert, 1975, Part of Nature, Part of Us, 1980, The Odes of John Keats, 1983, Wallace Stevens: Words Chosen Out of Desire, 1984; editor: Harvard Book of Contemporary American Poetry, 1985, Voices and Visions: The Poet in America, 1987, The Music of What Happens, 1988, Soul Says, 1995, The Given and the Made, 1995, The Breaking of Style, 1995, Poems, Poets, Poetry, 1995, The Art of Shakespeare's Sonnets, 1997, Seamus Heaney, 1998; Coming of Age as a Poet, 2003. Bd. dirs. Nat. Humanities Ctr., 1989—93. Recipient Lowell prize, 1969, Explicator prize, 1969, award Nat. Inst. Arts and Letters, 1975, Radcliffe Grad. Soc. medal, 1978, Nat. Book Critics award, 1980, Keats-Shelley Assn. award, 1994, Truman Capote award, 1996; Fulbright fellow, 1954, AAUW fellow, 1959, Guggenheim fellow, 1971-72, Am. Coun. Learned Socs. fellow, 1971-72, NEH fellow, 1980, 85, 94, Overseas fellow Churchill Coll., Cambridge, 1980, Charles Stewart Parnell fellow Magdalene Coll., Cambridge, 1996, hon. fellow, 1996—. Mem. MLA (exec. coun. 1972-75, pres. 1980), AAAL, English Inst. (trustee 1977-85), Am. Acad. Arts and Scis. (v.p. 1992-95), Norwegian Acad. Letters and Sci., Am. Philos. Soc. (Jefferson medal 2000), Phi Beta Kappa. Home: 54 Trowbridge St # 2 Cambridge MA 02138-4113 Office: Harvard U Dept English Barker Center Cambridge MA 02138-3929

VENERABLE, SHIRLEY MARIE, gifted education educator; b. Washington, Nov. 12, 1931; d. John Henry and Jessie Josephine (Young) Washington; m. Wendell Grant Venerable, Feb. 15, 1959; children: Angela Elizabeth Maria Venerable-Joyner, Wendell Mark. PhB, Northwestern U., 1963; MA, Roosevelt U., 1976, postgrad., 1985. Cert. in diagnostic and prescriptive reading, gifted edn., finger math., fine arts, Ill. Tchr. Lewis Champlin Sch., 1963-74, John Hay Acad., Chgo., 1975-87, Leslie Lewis Elem. Sch., Chgo., 1988-99, Robert Emmet Sch., Chgo., 1999—. Sponsor Reading Marathon Club, Chgo., 1991—; co-creator Project SMART-Stimulating Math. and Reading Techniques John Hay Acad., Chgo., 1987-90, curriculum coord., 1985-87; creative dance student, tchr. Kathryn Duham Sch., N.Y.C., 1955-56; creative dance tchr. Doris Patterson Dance Sch., Washington, 1953-55; recorder evening divsn. Northwestern U., Chgo., 1956-62; exch. student tchr. Conservatory Dance Movements, Chgo., 1958-59; art cons. Chgo. Pub. Sch., 1967. Author primary activities Let's Act and Chat, 1991-94, Teaching Black History Through Classroom Tours, 1989-90. Solicitor, vol. United Negro Coll. Fund, Chgo., 1994; sponsor Ward Reading Assn. Marathon, Chgo., 1991-94, 99; active St. Giles Coun. Cath. Women, 1985-96; vol. REAC Ctr. Programs Books, Info., Literacy and Learning, 1997-98. Recipient Meritorious award United Negro Coll. Fund, 1990, 94, Recognition award Alderman Percy Giles, Chgo., 1993. Mem.: ASCD (assoc. Recognition of Svcs. award 1989), Internat. Reading Assn., Nat. Women of Achievement Assn. (Chgo. chpt.), Phi Delta Kappa, Sigma Gamma Rho (Delta Sigma grad. chpt. 1963—93, Sigma chpt. 1992, Eta Xi Sigma chpt.), Eta Xi Sigma (Pearl award for excellence in edn. 1997). Roman Catholic. Home: 1108 N Euclid Ave Oak Park IL 60302-1219

VENEZIA, WILLIAM THOMAS, school system administrator, counseling consultant; b. Jersey City, Mar. 20, 1952; s. Thomas Michael and Carmela (Crocamo) V. BA in History, St. Peter's Coll., 1974, postgrad., 1978-79, MA in Adminstrn./Supervision, 1984; postgrad., Jersey City State

Coll., 1988-90. Cert. tchr., prin., supt., N.J.; cert. in student personnel svcs., N.J. Tchr. various schs. Jersey City Bd. Edn., 1976-92; guidance counselor P.S. # 27/Dickinson High Sch., Jersey City, 1990-92; counselor Montclair (N.J.) State Coll., 1991-92; asst. prin. Frelinghuysen Sch., Morristown, NJ, 1992-97; prin. Alexander Hamilton Sch., Morristown, 1997—2002; dir. guidance Morris Sch. Dist., 2001—02; prin. Thomas Jefferson Sch., Morristown, 2002—. Asst. football coach various schs., 1975-89; instr., adminstr. G.E.D. and A.B.E. programs Jersey City Bd. Edn., 1977-82; interim bd. sec., bus. adminstr. Weehawken Bd. Edn., 1984; mem. adv. bd. Cornerstone Sch., Jersey City, 1988-91; counselor Coll. Bound program Jersey City State Coll., 1989-90; pre-coll. counselor UPWARD Bound project Montclair State Coll., 1991; cons. N.J. Devils hockey team, East Rutherford, 1992, D.A.R.E. program Hudson County Prosecutor, Jersey City, 1992. Vol. counselor Giant Steps adolescent substance abuse treatment facility; active Dante Alighieri Soc., Jersey City, 1993, Jersey City Parents' Coun. Mem. ASCD, NEA, Am. Football Coaches Assn., N.J. Edn. Assn., Assn. Adult Edn. in N.J., N.J. Assn. Sch. Bus. Officials, Hudson County Personnel and Guidance Assn., Morris Pub. Schs. Adminstrv. Coun., Iron Bound Execs. Assn., St. Peter's Coll. Grad. Edn. Assn., Hoboken Elks. Avocations: basketball, travel, antiques. Home: 1 Hickory St Clark NJ 07066-1924 Office: Thomas Jefferson Sch 101 James St Morristown NJ 07960

VENEZIANO, DAVID ALEXANDER, parochial school educator; b. Chgo., Apr. 28, 1948; s. Louis and Lillian (Slater) V.; m. Georgia Bobal, Oct. 27, 1972; children: David A, Anthony D. BA, St. Joseph Calumet Coll., 1970; MA, DePaul U., 1972. Cert. tchr., Ind. Tchr. St. Mary Sch., Griffith, Ind., 1973—. Mem. Nat. Cath. Edn. Assn. Roman Catholic.

VENIS, LINDA DIANE, academic administrator, educator; b. Pasadena, Calif., Nov. 15, 1948; d. Ashton Harwood Venis and Grace (Bullock) Miller; m. Gary Arther Berg, Mar. 9, 1991; 1 child, Laura Grace Berg. BA magna cum laude, UCLA, 1970, PhD, 1978. Lectr. English UCLA, 1982-85, adj. asst. prof. Dept. English, 1987-90; lectr. Sch. Fine Arts U. So. Calif., L.A., 1985—; assoc. dir. studies UCLA/London & Cambridge Programs UCLA Extension, 1986-91, head writers program, 1985—, dir. dept. arts, 1992—. Contbr. articles to profl. jours. Recipient Profl. Contbrns. to Continuing Edn. award Continuing Edn. Assn., UCLA Disting. Tchg. award, 1985. Mem. PEN USA/West (bd. dirs. 1993—, adv. bd. 1992-93), Women in Film, Assn. Acad. Women. Office: UCLA Extension The Arts 10995 Le Conte Ave Los Angeles CA 90095-3001

VENRICK, KRISTIE LUND, mathematics educator; b. Longmont, Colo., Oct. 7, 1955; d. Myron Joseph and Christine Lorraine Thompson; m. James Thomas Venrick, Feb. 14, 1986; 1 child, Emily Lund. BS, Bethany Coll., 1977; MA, U. No. Colo., 2002. Tchr. St. Vrain Valley Schs., Longmont, Colo., 1978—2000, math. coord., 2000—. Named Educator of Yr., Longmont C. of C., 1996; recipient Presdl. award for Excellence in Math. and Sci. Tchg., White House and NSF, 2000. Mem.: AAUW, Nat. Coun. Suprs. Math., Nat. Coun. Tchrs. Math., Phi Delta Kappa. Republican. Lutheran. Home: 3567 Columbia Dr Longmont CO 80503 Office: St Vrain Valley Sch Dist 395 S Pratt Pky Longmont CO 80501

VENTRESS, MARY ELLEN, school system administrator; b. Lafayette, La., Feb. 8, 1943; d. James Andrew and Mary Eloise (Pace) Banfield; m. Vernon Mark Ventress Jr., Nov. 20, 1965; children: Mark Andrew, Jennifer Lyle. BA, La. State U., 1965; MEd, U. So. La., 1981. Tchr. East Baton Rouge Parish, 1965-67, Lafayette Parish, 1972-76; asst. prin. Lafayette Parish-Edgar Martin Sch., Lafayette, 1976-86; prin. Lafayette Parish-Broadmoor Elem. Sch., 1986-91, Lafayette Parish-Edgar Martin Mid. Sch., 1991—. Mem. Lafayette Parish Prin.'s Assn. (sec. 1986-87, v.p. 1987-88, pres. 1988-89), La. Assn. Computer Using Educators (Outstanding Computer Educator 1987, Nat. Excellence award 1989-90). Home: 103 Berwick Cir Lafayette LA 70508-6439 Office: Edgar Martin Mid Sch 401 Broadmoor Blvd Lafayette LA 70503-5201

VENTSEL, EDUARD SERGEEVICH, engineering mechanics educator; b. Kharkov, Russia, Sept. 28, 1937; came to U.S., 1992; s. Sergei Veniaminovich and Maria Osipovna (Streltsina) V.; m. Liliya Borisovna Lumer, July 4, 1963; 1 child, Irina Vinarski. MS, Civil Engring. Inst., Kharkov, Ukraine, 1960, candidate of sci., 1967; DS, Civil Engring. Inst., Moscow, 1985. Head aviation structures Mil. Aviation Engring. Higher Coll., Kharkov, 1966-76; prof., head applied mechanics Civil Engring. Inst., 1985-92; prof. engring. sci. and mechanics Pa. State U., State College, 1992—. Vis. prof. civil engring. U. Southampton, U.K., 1990; vis. prof. structural mechanics Sivil Engring. Inst., Cottbus, Germany, 1989., Author textbooks and monographs in solid mechanics. Mem. specialized couns. in defense of dissertations Kiev (USSR) Civil Engring., 1986-92, Poltava Civil Engring. Structures, Poltava, 1986-92. Recipient State award for sci. activity in mechanics Ukraine Republic, 1982. Office: Engring Sci and Mechanics Dept Pa State Univ 203B Earth & Enging Sci Bldg University Park PA 16802-6812 Home: 357 Mcbath St State College PA 16801-2762 Office: 205 A Earth and Engring Sci Bldg University Park PA 16802

VENTURACCI, TONI MARIE, artist, substitute educator; b. Battle Mountain, N.V., Nov. 19, 1958; d. Tony Simone Ancho and Deanna Paul; m. Steven Louie Venturacci, July 28, 1979; children: Daniel Steven, Kassi Marie. A in Bus., W.N.C.C., Fallon, N.V., 1999. Substitute educator Churchill County Sch. Dist., Fallon, Nev., 1998—2001; pvt. art tchr. Nev., 2000—01. Organizer fundraisers Nev. State H.S. Rodeo, 1998—2001. Mem.: Am. Paint Horse Assn. (accomplished painter), Am. Qtr. Horse Assn. (accomplished breeder). Republican. Roman Catholic. Avocations: horses, art work, sewing, cooking, rodeoing. Home: 445 Venturacci Ln Fallon NV 89406

VENUTI, RUTH LOUISE, secondary school educator, counselor; b. Spokane, Wash., July 1, 1957; d. Louis Jesse and Ruth Virginia (Mussetter) V. BA, Fla. So. Coll., 1979; MA in Counseling, Liberty U., Lynchburg, Va., 1990; specialist degree, Stetson U., 1992. Cert. elem., mid. sch. math. and secondary Spanish tchr., Fla. Elem. tchr. Polk County Sch. Bd., Auburndale, Fla., 1979, Bartow, Fla., 1979-84; jr. high sch. tchr. Volusia County Sch. Bd., Deltona, Fla., 1984-88, mid. sch. tchr., 1988—, NEAT observer, 1982, peer tchr., 1988-92, hosp./home bound program tutor, 1997. Tutor Fla. Sheriff's Girls' Villa, Bartow, 1979-80, Fla. United Meth. Children's Home, Enterprise, 1984; ednl. dir. Rohr House, abuse shelter, Bartow, 1980-81. Recipient Cert. of Commendation from Pres. Nixon, 1974, Apple pin Volusia County Sch. Bd., 1988. Mem. Nat. Coun. Tchrs. Math., Kappa Delta Pi. Avocations: creative writing, music, sign language, church activities, computers. Home: 2536 Marsh Rd Deland FL 32724-9026 Office: Galaxy Mid Sch 2400 Eustace Ave Deltona FL 32725-1786

VERBEKE, KAREN ANN, education educator; b. Clearfield, Pa., Mar. 31, 1948; d. Maurice George and Evelyn (Czarnecki) V. BA, Pa. State U., 1970; MEd, U. Md., 1971; postgrad., U. Colo., 1974; PhD, U. Md., 1982. Cert. elem. edn., spl. edn. Tchr. emotionally handicapped Dade County Pub. Schs., Miami, Fla., 1971-72; tchr. learning disabled, gifted, math. Howard County Pub. Schs., Ellicott City, Md., 1972-82; faculty rsch. assoc. U. Md., College Park, 1982-85; asst. prof. Beaver Coll., Glenside, Pa., 1985-90; assoc. prof., coord. of spl. edn., dept. edn. assoc. prof. dept. edn. and coord. spl. edn., Princess Anne, 1990—; faculty fellow Beaver Coll., Glenside, Pa., 1988-89; clin. prof. Profl. Devel. Sch., 1997—2000, acting chair dept. edn., acting dir. tchr. edn. Adj. instr. Va. Commonwealth U., Richmond, 1979-80; instr. The Cath. U. Am., Washington, 1983; lectr. Howard U., Washington, 1984-85; hearing officer Dept. Spl. Edn., Md. State Dept. Edn., Balt., 1983-96; apptd. mem. Md. State Adv. Com. on Spl. Edn., 1994-97; bd. dirs. Odyssey of the Mind, Inc., Glassboro, N.J., scholarship chmn., 1988-91. Editor: Md. Coun. for Tchrs. of Math. Jour., 1982-84; contbr. articles to profl. jours. Mem. appointed Md. state (adv. com. on spl. edn. 1994, task force on gifted edn. 1994-95, awarded Regional Staff Devel. Ctr. for Gifted/Talented grant Dept. of Edn. and Nat. Security Agency). Recipient Lindback award for Disting. Teaching, Christian and Mary Lindback Found., Beaver Coll., 1987, Sam Kirk Educator of Yr. in Learning Disabilities award, 1994-95, Pres.'s Tchr.-Scholar award U. Md. Ea. Shore, 1994, Beaver Coll. Phi Delta Kappa Educator of the Yr., 1994; Retraining Tchrs. grantee Pa. Dept. Edn., Harrisburg, 1989; Md. Higher Edn Commn. grantee, 1991-92, Md. Dept. Edn./Nat. Security Agy. grantee for Regional Staff Devel. Ctr. for Gifted/Talented; Policy fellow Inst. Ednl. Leadership George Washington U., 1977-78; Eisenhower grantee. Mem. Rsch. Coun. for Diagnostic and Prescriptive Math. (mem. coord. 1987-93), Pa. Fedn. Coun. for Exceptional Children (pres. tchr. edn. divsn. 1988-90), Pa. State U. Alumni Assn., U. Md. Alumni Assn., Zonta Internat., Phila. Club (svc. chmn. 1988-90, v.p. 1990), Phi Delta Kappa (v.p. programs 1994-95, v.p. membership 1995-96, pres. 1996-97), Kappa Delta Pi (convocation com.). Home: 419 Rolling Rd Salisbury MD 21801-7115 E-mail: kaverkee@mail.umes.edu.

VERBISH, DEBORAH LOUISE, elementary school educator; b. Hammond, Ind., Apr. 24, 1948; d. Frank E. and Hazel J. (Beck) Jutkus; m. George D. Verbish, Nov. 23, 1974; children: Jennifer E., Michelle K. B in Elem. Edn., Ind. U., Gary, 1971; M in Elem. Edn., Purdue U., Calumet, Ind., 1975. Cert. tchr. elem. sch., Ind. Tchr. grade 3 McKinley Elem. Sch., East Chgo., Ind., 1971-79, tchr. grade 1, 1979. Bd. trustees Holy Ghost Orthodox Ch., East Chgo., tchr. ch. sch., 1981—, Ladies Altar Soc. Mem. Am. Fedn. Tchrs., Am. Carpathian Russian Youth Orgn., Ind. Spina Bifida Soc., East Chgo. Credit Union (bd. dirs., sec., v.p 1971-91). Avocations: reading, crafts, needle work, crocheting.

VERBURG, JOANN, artist, photography educator; b. Summit, N.J., June 9, 1950; d. Robert Martin and Jane Carol Verburg; m. James McConaughy Moore, July 21, 1984. BA, Ohio Wesleyan U., 1972; MFA, Rochester Inst. Tech., 1977. Coord. spl. events The Phila. (Pa.) Mus. Art, 1972-74; exhbn. curator, rschr. Internat. Mus. Photography, Rochester, N.Y., 1974-77; photographer, rsch. coord. The Rephotographic Survey Project, Breckenridge, Colo., 1977-83; artist liaison Polaroid Corp., Cambridge, Mass., 1978-81; photography vis. artist The Colo. Coll., Colorado Springs, Colo., 1984-94; adj. prof. photography Hamline U., St. Paul, 1989—. Critic dept. photography Yale Sch. Art, 1994; vis. artist Minn. Coll. Art and Design, Mpls., 1981-83, 2001. Author: Second View: A Rephotographic Survey, 1984; artist: (catalog) Robert Wilson's Knee Plays, 1984, (book/exhbn. catalog) Pleasures and Terrors of Domestic Comfort, 1991; exhbns. include Robert Mann Gallery, N.Y.C, 1995, Pace/MacGill Gallery, N.Y.C., 1993, Mus. of Modern Art, N.Y.C., 1990, Light Gallery, N.Y.C., 1985, Mpls. Inst. of Arts, Mpls., 2001, G.Gibson Gallery, Seattle, 2000. Artist fellow Guggenheim Found., N.Y.C., 1986, McKnight Found., Mpls., 1988, Bush Found., St. Paul, 1993-94.

VERBY, JOHN EDWARD, JR., physician, educator; b. St. Paul, May 24, 1923; s. John E. and Amy (Martinson) V.; m. Jane Verby, June 15, 1946; children: John E. III, Steve, Ruth, Karl. BA, Carleton Coll., Northfield, Minn., 1944; BS, U. Minn., 1946, MB, 1947, MD, 1948. Diplomate Am. Bd. Family Practice. Intern Hennepin County Gen. Hosp., Mpls., 1947-49; pvt. family practice Litchfield, Minn., 1949-51, 53-54; ptnr. Olmsted Med.-Surg. Group, Rochester, Minn., 1954-69; assoc. prof. U. Minn., Mpls., 1969-73, acting head family practice/community medicine, asst. head, 1970-71, 71-72, mem. Grad. Sch. faculty, 1971—; dir. Rural Physician Assoc. Program, Mpls., 1971—; prof. Dept. Family Practice/Community Health, U. Minn., 1973—. Cons. and lectr. in field; vis. prof. Welsh Nat. Sch. Medicine, Cardiff, Wales, 1977-78, N.Y. State U., Syracuse, 1988-89; developer Rural Physician Assoc. Program W.Va. Med. Sch., 1989-90. Author: Medical Examination Book in Family Practice,1st edit., 1972, 2nd. edit., 1973, 3rd. edit., 1978, 4th edit., 1983; co-author: How to Talk to Doctors; contbr. articles to profl. jours. Lay liturgist Hillcrest United Mth. Ch., 1980—. With USN, 1942-45; 1st lt. U.S.Army, 1951-53. Grantee U. Minn. Hosps. and Clinics, 1985-89, Minn. Med. Found., 1980, 84, Fed. Health Professions Project, 1972-76, others; recipient Cert. Appreciation U. Minn. Bd. Regents, 1992. Fellow Am. Acad. Family Physicians (charter, Thomas W. Johnson award 1991), Am. Geriatric Soc.; mem. AMA (Physicians Recognition award 1969-85), Am. Rural Health Assn. (award 1981), Minn. Acad. Family Physicians (Tchr. of Yr. award 1988, John E. Verby award 1987), Internat. Soc. Gen. Medicine (bd. dirs., assoc. mem.), Hennepin County Med. Soc. Home: 9609 Washburn Ave S Minneapolis MN 55431-2460

VERDU, SERGIO, engineering educator; b. Barcelona, Aug. 15, 1958; came to U.S., 1980; s. Tomas Verdu and Visitacion Lucas; m. Mercedes Paratje, Jan. 19, 1982; 1 child, Ariana. Diploma telecomm. engr., Polytech. U. Barcelona, 1980; MS, U. Ill., 1982, PhD, 1984. Asst. prof. Princeton (N.J.) U., 1984-89, assoc. prof., 1989-92, prof., 1993—. Prin. investigator U.S. Office Naval Rsch., N.J. Dept. Higher Edn., U. S. Army Rsch. Office, N.J. Commn. Sci. and Tech., NSF, U.S.-Israel Binational Sci. Found.; vis. prof. U. Calif., Berkeley, 1998; vis. rsch. prof., Math. Sci. Rsch. Inst., 2002. Author: Multiuser Detection, 1998, Information Theory: Fifty Years of Discovery, 1999; mem. editl. bd. Transactions on Info. Theory, 1990-94; ; editor-in-chief Foundations and Trends in Comm. and Info. Theory, 2003—; contbr. numerous articles to profl. jours, book chpts. Recipient Nat. U. prize Ministry Edn., Spain, 1982, Presdl. Young Invesitgator award NSF, 1988, Frederick E. Terman award Am. Soc. Engring. Edn., 2000. Fellow: IEEE (Outstanding Paper award 1998, Millennium medal 2000); mem.: Info. Theory Soc. (bd. govs. 1989—99, v.p. 1995, pres. 1997, Golden Jubilee Paper award 1998, Leonard G. Abraham Paper award 2002). Office: Princeton U Dept Elec Engring Princeton NJ 08544-0001 E-mail: verdu@princeton.edu.

VERELINE, CATHERINE, elementary school educator, administrator; b. Queens, N.Y., Nov. 7, 1953; d. Joseph F. and Anne M. (Parkin) V. BA, John F. Kennedy Coll., 1975; MALS, SUNY, Stony Brook, 1987; Profl. dip., C. W. Post L.I. U., 1992. Tchr. St. John of God, Central Islip, N.Y., 1975-81; sch. dist. transp. adminstr. Port Bus, Port Jefferson, N.Y., 1981-84; tchr. Sachem Sch., Holtville, N.Y., 1984-86, Half Hollow Hills Sch., Dix Hills, N.Y., 1986-88, Amityville (N.Y.) Sch., 1988-89, Central Islip Pub. Schs., 1989-91. Avocation: music. Home: 118 Harper St Patchogue NY 11772-2460 Office: Central Islip Pub Schs Wheeler Rd Central Islip NY 11722

VERGASON, GLENN A. special education educator, researcher; b. Bartow, Fla., Jan. 19, 1930; s. Alvin Lavern and Lonnie Mae (O'Cain) V.; m. Barbara Jean Ross, Sept. 12, 1951; children: Linda Campbell, Lee (dec.), Ralph, Lynne Moeder. BS, Fla. State U., 1953, MS, 1954; EdD, George Peabody Coll., 1962. Tchr. orthopedically handicapped, sch. psychometrist Thomasville (Ga.) City Schs., 1954-55, instr., supr., and spl. edn. dir., 1955-57; cons. Ga. State Dept. Edn., Atlanta, 1957-60; assoc. prof. U. Ala., Tuscaloosa, 1962—64, prof., 1964—65, chmn. dept. spl. edn., 1965-76; prof. Ga. State U., Atlanta, 1976-92, prof. emeritus, 1993—, coord. vision program, 1968-92, coord. spl. edn. adminstrn., 1982-92; pres. Vergason & Assocs., Inc., Lithonia, Ga., 1992-95. Author books and monographs; assoc. editor Exceptional Children, 1963-77, Focus on Exceptional Children, 1969—99, Tchr. Edn. and Spl. Edn., 1986-93, Tchg. Exceptional Children, 1986-89, B.C. Jour. Spl. Edn., 1988-91, Internat. Jour. Spl. Edn. and Rehab., 1992-95, Remedial and Spl. Edn., 1992—99, Issues in Spl. Edn. Rehab., 1993-94; also numerous articles. Trustee Care Trust Found., Atlanta, 1990-93, Davison Sch., Decatur, Ga. Fellow Am. Assn. Mental Retardation (life mem.); mem. Ga. Fedn. Coun. Exceptional Children (bd. govs. 1983-84, 87-90, 91-93, gov. pioneer divsn. 1993-96, President's award 1987, 89, Burton Blatt Humanitarian award 1993, Romaine Mackie Leadership award 1995), Internat. Coun. Exceptional Children (bd. govs.-at-large 1978-81), Found. Exceptional Children (pres.-elect, pres. 1984-88), Atlanta Coun. Exceptional Children (pres.-elect, pres. 1967-69, Outstanding Mem. award 1972). Methodist. Avocations: golf, fishing. Home and Office: 521 77th St Holmes Beach FL 34217-1009 E-mail: gvghorse@gbronline.com.

VERGNAUD, JEAN-MAURICE, science educator, researcher; b. Audincourt, Doubs, France, Dec. 3, 1932; s. Joseph and Marie-Louise (Buthod-Ruffier) V.; m. Michele Trouin, Dec. 20, 1979. MS, U. Lyon, France, 1956; PhD in Catalysis, U. Dijon, France, 1960; PhD in Chromatography, U. Lyon, 1965. Engr. CEA, Paris, 1959, Progil, Lyon, 1960-68; prof. U. Algiers, Algeria, 1968-71, U. St. Etienne, France, 1972—. Referee Am. Assn. Pharm. Sci. Author: Drying of Polymeric and Solid Materials, 1992, Cure of Thermosetting Resins, 1992, Dosage Forms for Controlled Release with Polymers, 1993, Liquid Transport Processes in Polymeric Materials, 1994; mem. editl. adv. bd. Polymer Testing, Rubber Plastics and Composites, Polymer and Polymer Composites, Jour. Polymer Engring., Jour. Drying Tech.; referee 7 jours. on polymers and 2 jours. on pharmacy. Pres. French Chem. Soc. of Lyon, 1963-68; v.p. U. St. Etienne, 1972-75. Recipient French Indsl. Soc. award, Paris, 1965, French Acad. Scis. award, Paris, 1977. Mem. Am. Chem. Soc. (George S. Whitby award 1998). Avocations: skiing, tennis, piano. Home: Rte de Chavanne Chemin de Grange Bruyas 42400 Saint Chamond France Office: Univ St Etienne 23 Dr P Michelon 42023 Saint Etienne France E-mail: Vergnaud.Jean-Maurice@wanadoo.fr.

VERINK, ELLIS DANIEL, JR., metallurgical engineering educator, consultant; b. Peking, China, Feb. 9, 1920; s. Ellis Daniel and Phoebe Elizabeth (Smith) V.; m. Martha Eulala Owens, July 4, 1942; children: Barbara Ann, Wendy Susan. BS, Purdue U., 1941; MS, Ohio State U., 1963, PhD, 1965. Registered profl. engr., Fla., Pa., Calif. Mgr. chem. sect., sales devel. divsn. Alcoa, New Kensington, Pa., 1946-59, mgr. chem. and petroleum indsl. sales Pitts., 1959-62; assoc. prof. metall. engring. U. Fla., Gainesville, 1965-68, prof. materials sci. and engring., 1968—, disting. svc. prof., 1984-91, prof. emeritus, 1991—; pres. Materials Cons., Inc., 1970—. Cons. Aluminum Assn., Washington, 1966-84; mem. U.S. nuclear waste tech. rev. bd., 1989-97. Author: Corrosion Testing Made Easy, The Basics, 1993; editor: Methods of Materials Selections, 1968, Material Stability and Environmental Degradation, 1988; contbr. articles to profl. jours. Pres. Gainesville YMCA, 1977. Recipient Sam Tour award ASTM, 1979, Donald E. Marlowe award Am. Soc. Engring. Edn., 1991; recipient Disting. Alumnus award Ohio State U., 1982, Disting. Faculty award Fla. Blue Key, 1983; named Tchr.-Scholar of Year U. Fla., 1979 Fellow Metall. Soc. of AIME (pres. 1984, Educator of Yr. award 1988), Am. Soc. Materials Internat., Nat. Assn. Corrosion Engrs. Internat. (bd. dirs. 1984-87, Willis Rodney Whitney award; mem. Masons, Shriners, Kiwanis, Sigma Xi, Tau Beta Pi. Republican. Presbyterian. Office: U Fla Dept Materials Sci Eng Gainesville FL 32611 Home: Apt M224 7805 NW 28th Pl Gainesville FL 32606-8659

VERMILYEA, STANLEY GEORGE, prosthodontist, educator; b. Portland, Oreg., Jan. 29, 1946; s. Stanley Edmonds and Hattie Willamina (Bittner) V.; m. Barbara Jean Koester Ternus, June 23, 1967 (div. Dec. 1979); 1 child, Sheryl Eileen; m. Ileana Esther Villamarzo, July 3, 1980; 1 child, Michael Enrique. BS, Portland State Coll., 1970; DMD, U. Oreg., Portland, 1971; MS in Dental Materials, U. Mich., 1976; cert. in prosthodontics, Walter Reed Army Med. Ctr., Washington, 1985. Diplomate Am. Bd. Prosthodontics. Commd. 2d lt. U.S. Army, 1971, advanced through grades to col., 1985, dentist, 1971-76; rschr. dental materials U.S. Army Inst. Dental Rsch., Washington, 1976-80, chief dental materials rsch., 1980-83; prosthodontist U.S. Army, various locations, 1983-89, co-dir. residency in prosthodontics Washington, 1989-92, ret., 1992; asst. prof. Coll. Dentistry Ohio State U., Columbus, 1992-95, chmn. primary care, 1996—, assoc. dean clin. affairs, 2001—. Contbr. chpt. to book and articles to profl. jours. Fellow Am. Coll. Prosthodontists, Acad. Gen. Dentistry; mem. Internat. Assn. Dental Rsch. Achievements include research on the corrosion characteristics of dental alloys as well as the compositions and microstructural features of dental materials. Office: Ohio State U Coll Dentistry 305 W 12th Ave Columbus OH 43210-1267 E-mail: vermilyea.1@osu.edu.

VERNON, ARTHUR, educational administrator; b. N.Y.C., May 31, 1947; s. Chester M. and Lillian (Rosenfeld) V.; m. Michele Hope Levinthal, June 8, 1969; children: Ari, Devora, Shamar, Ronit. AB, Hunter Coll., 1968; BHL, Hebrew Union Coll./Jewish Inst. Religion, 1972; MA, HUC-JIR, 1973, DD, 1998. Prin. Solomon Schecter Day Sch., Teaneck, N.J., 1974-76; cons. Bd. Jewish Edn., Washington, 1976-78; asst. dir. Bur. Jewish Edn., Cleve., 1978-85, exec. dir. Houston, 1985-89; dept. dir. Jewish Edn. Svc. N.Am., N.Y.C., 1989-2000. Mem. adv. bd. Am. Jewish com. Petschek Ctr., N.Y.C., 1989—; mem. ednl. adv. com. Jewish Nat. Fund, N.Y.C., 1991-98. Author curriculum pamphlet AIDS: A Jewish Response, 1990; editor mag. Pedagogic Reporter, 1991-92, Agenda: Jewish Education, 1992—. Bd. dirs. Open Congregation, Inc., N.Y.C., 1989—, treas., 1993-95, pres. 1996-98; vice chmn. nat. Jewish Com. on Scouting, Irving, Tex., 1991—. Mem. Coun. for Jewish Edn. (v.p. 1991-95, treas. 1995-96, pres. 1996-99), Religious Edn. Assn., Coalition for Advancement of Jewish Edn. Home: 22 Mountain Way West Orange NJ 07052-3717 Office: Jewish Edn Svc N Am 22 Mountain Way West Orange NJ 07052-3717

VERO, RADU, freelance medical and scientific illustrator, educator, writer, consultant; b. Bucharest, Romania, Oct. 20, 1926; came to U.S., 1973; s. Leon and Bella Sylvia (Spiegler) V.; m. Susan Ezpeleta D'Aste. BA, Inst. Architecture, Bucharest, 1951. Freelance illustrator, Bucharest, 1952-61, 1961-73, 1973—. Mem. faculty Fashion Inst. Tech., N.Y.C., 1982—; discoverer novel set of curves (cubals) in analytic geometry. Author: Understanding Perspective, 1980, Airbrush, 1982, Airbrush 2, 1984. Recipient illustration award N.Y. Acad. Scis., 1975, Vargas award, 1997. Mem. N.Y. Acad. Scis.

VERONA, MONICA J. concert pianist, educator; b. Milw., July 2, 1956; d. Emanuel A. and Winifred M. V. BA in Italian and Art History, U. Wis., Milw., 1982; MusM, Manhattan Sch. Music, 1984; Performer's Cert. Degree, No. Ill. U., 1987; doctoral student, Manhattan Sch. Music, 1985-92. Teaching asst. piano and chamber music No. Ill. U., DeKalb, 1984-85; piano faculty The Fleming Sch., N.Y.C., 1987-90, The Calhoun Sch., N.Y.C., 1989—, Bklyn. Coll. Preparatory Ctr. for the Performing Arts, 1992—, The Trevor Day Sch., 1996—, Bloomingdale Sch. of Music, 1999—. Sub. tchr. in solo and duo piano lit. Manhattan Sch. of Music Preparatory Divsn., 1987. Author: J.S. Bach's Chromatic Fantasy and Fugue: A Study of Virtuoso Keyboard Forms From the 16th to 18th Centuries, 1995; solo performances include: Met. Mus. Art, Salzburg Festival, Ravinia Festival, U.S. Dept. Interior/Am. Landmarks Festival, New Rochelle Pub. Libr. Series, Manhattan Sch. Music, Steinway Hall, N.Y.C., Klavierhaus, N.Y.C., Nicholas Roerich Mus., Tenri Cultural Inst., N.Y.C., Bklyn. Coll., No. Ill. U., PBS TV Milw., U. Wis., Goeth Inst. Milw., Park Ave. Christian Ch. Recital Series, N.Y.C., St. Paul's Recital Series, Nyack, N.Y., St. Peter's Concert Series at Citicorp, N.Y.C., Milw. Cath. Symphony Orch., Donnell N.Y. Pub. Lib. Series, Charles Allis Art Mus., Milw., Katonah Village Recital Series, Villa Terrace Mus., Milw.; chamber music performances include: Manhattan Sch. Music, No. Ill. U., Goethe Inst., Met. Mus. of Art, N.Y., Tenri Cultural Inst., N.Y.C., others; participant numerous music festivals. Recipient numerous scholarships, 1975-87, first prize Nat. Fedn. Music Clubs Competition, 1976, third prize Mu Phi Epsilon Scholarship Competition, 1977, first prize Ida Schroeder Found.

Scholarship Competition, 1978. Mem. Mu Phi Epsilon (prs. N.Y.C. 1998—). Roman Catholic. Avocations: gardening, drawing. Home and Office: 45 Tiemann Pl Apt 5M New York NY 10027-3327

VERONIS, GEORGE, geophysics educator; b. New Brunswick, N.J., June 6, 1926; s. Nicholas Emmanuel and Angeliki (Efthimakis) V.; m. Anna Margareta Olsson, Nov. 8, 1963; m. Catherine Elizabeth, Jan. 29, 1949 (div. Nov. 1962); children— Melissa, Benjamin. A.B., Lafayette Coll., 1950; Ph.D., Brown U., 1954; M.A. (hon.), Yale U., 1966; DSc (hon.) Lafayette Coll. 1997. Staff meteorologist Inst. Advanced Study, Princeton, 1953-56; staff mathematician Woods Hole Oceanographic Inst., Mass., 1956-64, mem. staff, dir. geophys. fluid dynamics summer program, 1959—, assoc. prof. MIT, Cambridge, 1961-64, research oceanographer, 1964-66; prof. geophysics and applied sci. Yale U., New Haven, 1966—, Henry Barnard Davis prof., 1985—, chmn. geology and geophysics, 1976-79, dir. applied math, 1979-93. Editor Jour. Marine Rsch., 1973—; contbr. articles to profl. jours. Served with USN, 1943-46. Fellow Am. Acad. Arts and Scis., Am. Geophys. Union; mem. NAS, Norwegian Acad. Scis. (Robert L. and Bettie P. Cody award 1989, Henry Stommel Rsch. award 1997). Greek Orthodox. E-mail: george.veronis@yale.edu.

VERPLOEGEN, LORRAINE JEAN, elementary school educator; b. Havre, Mont., Mar. 15, 1950; d. Edwin Edgar and Donna Lee (Perry) Larson; m. Frank Edward Verploegen, Nov. 17, 1973; children: Eric James, Erin Jean. BS in Edn., Mont. State U., Billings, 1972; MEd, Mont. State U., Havre, 1991. Remedial reading tchr. Huntley Project, Worden, Mont., 1972; primary resource tchr. Havre Pub. Schs., 1972-75, 78-79, 1991-92, intermediate resource tchr., 1989-91, tchr. grades 1, 2 and 3, 1976-79, 79-80, reading recovery tchr. leader, 1992—; itinerant resource tchr. Bear Paw Coop, Chinook, Mont., 1988; primary resource tchr. Rocky Boy Elem. Sch., Box Elder, Mont., 1988; tchr. K-6 Cottonwood Country Sch., Havre, 1982-86. 4-H leader Hill County 4-H, Havre, 1984-94. Mont. State Reading Coun. Tchr. Project grantee, 1993-94. Mem. NEA, Tri-County Reading Coun. (pres., v.p.), Mont. State Reading Coun. (state chair 1982-92, Leadership award 1991), Havre Edn. Assn. (pres.), Internat. Reading Assn. Avocations: reading, cross-stitch, crocheting, music. Home: HC 30 Box 79B Havre MT 59501-9706

VERRILL, KATHLEEN WILLS, special education educator; b. Tucson, Jan. 4, 1938; d. William Oscar Wills and Helen Louise (Boswell) Perry; m. Thomas Anthony Verrill, July 30, 1966; 1 child, Nathan Anthony. AA, Monterey Peninsula Coll., 1958; BA, San Francisco State U., 1963, MA, 1965. Tchr. educable mentally retarded Albany (Calif.) Unified Schs., 1963-70, Sch. Dist. # 49, Fairfield, Maine, 1970-73; resource tchr. Indpls. Schs., 1973-75; tchr. learning handicapped Phila. Sch. Dist., 1975-77, ednl. evaluator, 1977-79, instructional advisor, 1979-81; resource specialist San Francisco Unified Schs., 1981-82, Alameda (Calif.) Unified Sch. Dist., 1982—. Author Food Centered Curriculum for Learning Disabled, 1965. Rep. Sch. Dist. Affirmative Action com., Alameda, 1988-90. Recipient PTA Calif. Hon. Svc. award Lum Sch., 1991; named Tchr. of Yr. Alameda Sch. Dist., 1986; Crown Zellerbach Found. fellowship, 1964, edn. grant Alameda County Schs., 1964. Mem. NEA, Coun. Exceptional Children, Alameda Edn. Assn. (rep. 1989-90), Calif. Tchrs. Assn., Delta Kappa Gamma (chmn. rsch. 1988-89, pres. Delta Zeta chpt. 1992-94, exec. bd. 1994—). Avocations: travel, classical music, reading, cooking, study of artists. Office: Alameda Unified Sch Dist 1801 Sandcreek Way Alameda CA 94501-6024

VERSTEGEN, DEBORAH A. policy and finance educator; b. Neenah, Wis., Oct. 27, 1946; d. Gerald C. and Margaret A. (Lamers) V. BA, Loretto Heights Coll., 1969; EdM, U. Rochester, 1972; MS, U. Wis., 1981, PhD, 1983. Adminstr. Iditarod Area Sch. Dist., McGrath, Alaska, 1976-79; rsch. asst. Wis. Ctr. for Edn. Rsch., 1981-84; dir. asst. prof. mid-mgmt. program U. Tex., Austin, 1984-86; asst. prof. edn. in policy and finance U. Va., Charlottesville, 1986-91, assoc. prof. edn. in policy and finance, 1992-99, prof., 2000—. Assoc. rsch. fellow Oxford U., Eng., 1991; adv. bd. U.S. Dept. Edn., 1989-92. Author over 200 books, reports, chpts., articles and revs., latest being The Impacts of Litigation and Legislation on Public School Finance, 1990, Spheres of Justice in Education, 1991; editor Jour. Edn. Fin., 1990-93, editor edn. policy, 1993—. Treas. LVW, 1986, mem. Va. state bd., 1995—97, Va. edn. chair, 1993—2001. Recipient Disting. Achievement award, U. Wis., Madison, 1997. Mem.: AAUP (exec. bd. Va. 1999—, pres.-elect 2003, pres. 2003, 2003—), U. Coun. on Ednl. Adminstrn. (adv. bd. fin. ctr. 1991—, disting. svc. award 1991), Women Edn. Leaders Va. (chair 1988, pres. 1999—2000, founder), Am. Ednl. Rsch. Assn. (SIG chair fiscal issues and policy 2002—), Am. Ednl. Fin. Assn. (bd. dirs., 1986—89, disting. svc. award 1989), Phi Kappa Phi, Phi Delta Kappa. Home: 2156 Timber Mdws Charlottesville VA 22911-7231 Office: U Va Curry Sch Edn Ruffner Hall 405 Emmet St S Charlottesville VA 22903-2424 E-mail: dav3e@virginia.edu.

VERSTEGEN, JOHN P.L. theriogenologist, educator; b. Duren, Germany, May 16, 1956; Degree in Vet. Medicine, U. Liege, Belgium, 1980, PhD, 1986; M in Biostats., U. Paris, 1983; M in Informatics, U. Brussels, 1984. Asst. U. Liege, 1980-86, agregg. 1980-91; prof. small animal theriogenology Diplomate ECAR. Cons. pharm. co., Belgium, France, Germany, U.K. and Italy; bd. dirs. Sperm Bank in Canine, Belgium; bd. dirs. Belgium Coun. for Lab. Animal Sci., FELASA, ECAR, EVSSAR. Author: Adrenergic Agents, 1993; editor: Fertility and Infertility, 1993-97. Mem. Soc. Study Reprodn., Soc. for Theriogenology, Assn. for the Study of Animal Reprodn. (v.p.), Assn. Vet. Anesthesiologist, European Soc. Cellular Biology, European Soc. for Study of Small Animal Reprodn. (founding mem.). Avocations: climbing, squash, swimming. Office: Univ of Liege Copa B44 BD Colonster 20 Liege 4000 Belgium

VERTS, LITA JEANNE, university administrator; b. Jonesboro, Ark., Apr. 13, 1935; d. William Gus and Lolita Josephine (Peeler) Nash; m. B. J. Verts, Aug. 29, 1954 (div. 1975); 1 child, William Trigg. BA, Oreg. State U., 1973; MA in Lingustics, U. Oreg., 1974; postgrad., U. Hawaii, 1977. Librarian Forest Research Lab., Corvallis, Oreg., 1966-69; instr. English Lang. Inst., Corvallis, 1974-80; dir. spl. svcs. Oreg. State U., Corvallis, 1980-96, faculty senator, 1988-96; ret., 1996. Editor ann. book: Trio Achievers, 1986, 87, 88; contbr. articles to profl. jours. Precinct com. Rep. Party, Corvallis, 1977-80; adminstrv. bd. 1st United Meth. Ch., Corvallis, 1987-89, mem. fin. com., 1987-93, tchr. Bible, 1978—; bd. dirs. Westminster Ho., United Campus Ministries, 1994-95; adv. coun. Disabilities Svc., Linn, Benton, Lincoln Counties, 1990-99, vice-chmn., 1992-93, chmn. 1993-94; citizen adv. bd. on Transit, 1998—, intercity steering com., 1999—, Corvallis Downtown Parking Commn., 1999—; Oreg. Longterm Care Ombudsman, 1999—. Mem. N.W. Assn. Spl. Programs (pres. 1985-86), Nat. Coun. Ednl. Opportunities Assn. (bd. dirs. 1984-87), Nat. Gardening Assn., Alpha Phi (mem. corp. bd. Beta Upsilon chpt. 1990-96). Republican. Methodist. Avocations: gardening, photography, golf. Home: 530 SE Mayberry Ave Corvallis OR 97333-1866 Office: Spl Svcs Project Waldo 337 OSU Corvallis OR 97331 E-mail: l.verts@attbi.com.

VESPER, REBECCA HESSICK, child development specialist, special education and parent educator; b. Monroe, La., Nov. 20, 1963; d. Carl Samuel and Myrra (Flanigan) Hessick; m. Richard Kent Vesper, Aug. 3, 1985; children: Kaitlin Rebecca, Morgan Paige. BA in English Edn., BS in Psychology, U. La., Lafayette, 1986; postgrad., Northwestern State U. La., U. Ark. Cert. tchr., La., Ark., Tex. Dir. presch. class 1st Bapt. Ch. Nursery, Lafayette, La., 1982-84; tchr. English, Captain Shreve High Sch., Shreveport, La., 1986-87; dir. Christian edn. Kings Highway Christian Ch., Shreveport, 1987-88; tchr. kindergarten, at-risk pre-kindergarten Lakeshore Elem. Sch., Shreveport, 1988-91; tchr. non-categorical presch. handicapped 81st St. Early Childhood Edn. Ctr., Shreveport, La., 1991-92; tchr. spl. edn. Bates Elem. Sch., Fayetteville, Ark., 1992-95; child devel. specialist Northwest Ark. Edn. Svcs. Coop., 1995—98; tchr. spl. edn. Asbell Elem. Sch., Fayetteville, 1998—99, Washington Elem. Sch., Fayetteville, 1999—; owner, faux finish artisan, trainer Decorative Effects Studio, 1997—. Owner, cons. Parenting Resources, 1994—. Esther Cooley Meml. grad. scholar Northwestern State U., 1989, T.H. Harris scholar, 1981, Wanda Bedell scholar, 1981. Mem. La Leche Internat., La. Assn. Children Under Six (bd. dirs., rec. sec.), So. Early Childhood Assn., Coun. on Exceptional Children (mem. divsn. early childhood), U. La. Lafayette Alumni Assn., Order of Omega, Chi Omega (pres., vice pres., pres.) Republican. Baptist. Avocations: music, theater, dance, skiing, artwork. Home: 409 N 39th St Rogers AR 72756-1886

VEST, CHARLES MARSTILLER, academic administrator; b. Morgantown, W.Va., Sept. 9, 1941; s. Marvin Lewis and Winifred Louise (Buzzard) V.; m. Rebecca Ann McCue, June 8, 1963; children: Ann Kemper, John Andrew. BSME, W.Va. U., 1963; MSME, U. Mich., 1964, PhD, 1967; DEng (hon.), Mich. Tech. U., 1992, W.Va. U., 1994, Ill. Inst. Tech., 1998, U. Notre Dame, 1998, Musashi Inst. Tech., 1999, NC State U., 2002. Asst. prof., then assoc. prof. U. Mich., Ann Arbor, 1968—77, prof. mech. engring., 1977—90, assoc. dean acad. affairs Coll. Engring., 1981—86, dean Coll. Engring., 1986—89, provost, v.p. acad. affairs, 1989—90; pres. MIT, Cambridge, 1990—. Bd. dirs. E.I. du Pont de Nemours and Co., IBM, Blanchette Rockefeller Neurosci. Inst.; vis. assoc. prof. Stanford (Calif.) U., 1974-75. Author: Holographic Interferometry, 1979; assoc. editor Jour. Optical Soc. Am., 1982-83; contbr. articles to profl. jours. Trustee Woods Hole Oceanographic Inst., Univ. Corp. for Advanced Internet Devel., WGBH Ednl. Found.; adv. trustee TIAX adv. bd., Environ. Rsch. Inst. Mich. Recipient Excellence in Rsch. award U. Mich., 1980, Disting. Svc. award, 1972, Disting. Visitor award U. La Plata, Argentina, 1979, Centennial medal Am Soc. Engring. Edn., 1993, Arthur M. Bueche award Nat. Acad. Engring., 2000, Nat. Leadership award Phi Kappa Psi, 1999., Pres.' award Accrediation Bd. for Engring. and Tech., 2002. Fellow AAAS, Am. Acad. Arts and Scis., Optical Soc. Am., ASME; mem. NAE, Assn. Women in Sci., Sigma Xi, Tau Beta Pi, Pi Tau Sigma. Presbyterian. Office: MIT 77 Massachusetts Ave Cambridge MA 02139-4307

VEST, JAMES MURRAY, foreign language and literature educator; b. Roanoke, Va., Mar. 27, 1947; s. Eddie Lewis and Irene (Cannaday) V.; m. Nancy Foltz, June 6, 1970; 1 child, Cecelia. BA, Davidson (N.C.) Coll., 1969; MA, Duke U., 1971, PhD, 1973. From asst. to assoc. prof. Rhodes Coll., Memphis, 1973-91, chmn. French dept., 1983-98, prof., 1991—, head French program, 1984-98. Adminstr. Rhodes in Paris Program, France, 1978-87; organizer faculty teaching seminars, 1988—. Author: The French Face of Ophelia, 1989, The Poetic Works of Maurice de Guérin, 1991, Hitchcock and France, 2003; contbr. articles to profl. jours. Chmn. Urban Outreach Commn., Memphis, 1978-81; leader youth groups, 1983—. Capt. U.S. Army Res., 1973—. Recipient campus svc. award Sears-Roebuck, 1990, Outstanding Teaching award Clarence Day Found., Memphis, 1984, Am. Assn. Higher Edn., 1988; Woodrow Wilson fellow, 1971, NDEA Title IV fellow, 1969. Mem. MLA, So. Atlantic Modern Lang. Assn., Am. Assn. of Tchrs. of French, Am. Coun. Teaching Fgn. Lang. Avocations: cinema, hiking. Office: 2000 N Pkwy Rhodes C Memphis TN 38112 Address: 633 East Dr Memphis TN 38112

VEST, ROSEMARIE LYNN TORRES, secondary school educator; b. Pueblo, Colo., Jan. 16, 1958; d. Onesimo Bernabe and Maria Bersabe (Lucero) Torres; m. Donald R. Vest, May 1, 1982. BA, U. So. Colo., 1979, BS, 1991; cert. travel agt., Travel Trade Sch., Pueblo, 1986. Cert. secondary tchr., Colo.; lic. local pastor United Meth. Ch. Tutor U. So. Colo., Pueblo, 1977-79; sales rep. Intermountain Prodns., Colorado Springs, Colo., 1979-80; tutor, Pueblo, 1980-82, 84-85; travel agt. So. Colo. Travel, Pueblo, 1986-88; children's program facilitator El Mesias Family Support Program, Pueblo, 1987-88; substitute tchr. social studies Sch. Dist. 60, Pueblo, 1990—, Freed Mid. Sch., Pueblo, 1991, 92. Chpt. 1 Summer Reading Program, 1992, 93, 94, 95; instr. Travel and Tourism Dept. Pueblo C.C., 1994-95, Dept Social Studies, 1996-97. Tchr. Sunday sch., chairperson adminstrv. bd. cert. lay spkr., lay rep. to ann. conf. Ch. Evangelism, co-chmn. Trinity United Meth. Ch., Pueblo, 1989-94, parish coun. rep. to Trinity/Bethel Coop. Parish; sponsor United Meth. Youth United Meth. Ch.; tchr. Sunday Sch., co-coord. vacation Bible sch., edn. chairperson, 1994—, cert. lay spkr., ministerial program asst., lay leader Bethel United Meth. Ch., 1994—; craft facilitator Integrated Health Svcs., Pueblo, 1991—; spiritual devotions/worship leader Pueblo Manor Nursing Home, 1993—; vol. resident svcs. Pueblo County Bd. for Developmental Disabilities, 1989—; mem. conf. leadership team, parliamentarian Rocky Mountain Conf. United Meth. Ch., 1995, dist. rep., 1997—; ministerial candidate United Meth. Ch.; conf. rep. Rocky Mountain Conf. Coun. on Fin. and Adminstrn., 1996—. Recipient Excellence in Tchg. award Freed Mid. Sch., 1992, Vol. of Yr. award IHS of Pueblo, 1995. Mem. Assn. Am. Geographers, Nat. Oceanog. Soc., Nat. Geog. Soc. Democrat. Avocations: crafts, photography, reading, cross-stitch, listening to music. Home: 125 W Grant Apt C Pueblo CO 81004-2000

VESTAL, THELMA SHAW, history educator; b. Spring Hill, Tenn., Apr. 19, 1946; d. Ester Lena McKissack; m. Danny Vestal, June 28, 1976; children: Danny La'Brian, Felecia De'Lece. BS, Tenn. State U., 1969, MS, 1972. Sec. Tenn. State U., Nashville, 1969-72, counselor, 1972-76; substitute tchr. Metro Pub. Schs., Nashville, 1977-85; U.S. history tchr. Dupont-Tyler Mid. Sch., Hermitage, Tenn., 1985—. Mem. Operation C.A.N., Nashville, 1985—. Active ARC, Nashville, 1988—. Named Educator of Yr., Nashville Mid. Sch. Assn., 1992-93; recipient Outstanding Christian award Schrader Lane Ch. of Christ, Nashville, 1989-90, Golden Apple award, 1996. Mem. Nat. Geographic Soc., Metro Nashville Coun. for Social Studies, Tenn. Edn. Assn., NEA, Nat. Coun. for Social Studies. Democrat. Ch. of Christ. Avocations: reading, bowling, music, dancing.

VETERE, LAURA ANN, school system administrator, educator; b. Elizabeth, N.J., Nov. 17, 1958; d. Robert and Pearl V. BS magne cum laude, East Stroudsburg U., 1980; M in edn. adminstrn., Kean Coll., 1994. Cert. elem. edn. tchr., secondary edn. tchr. Tchr. Elizabeth (N.J.) H.S., 1980-88, Colonia (N.J.) H.S., 1988-94; v.p. Newbury Sch., Howell, N.J., 1994—. Registered Holistic scorer Hunterdon County Edn. Svcs. commn., Flemington, N.J., 1990—. Recipient Commendation award Kean-Comprehensive Examiners, 1994. Mem. Phi Delta Kappa. Avocations: reading, body shaping. Office: 179 Newbury Rd Howell NJ 07731-1813

VETTERLING, MARY-ANNE, Spanish language and literature educator; b. Cleve., Aug. 7, 1948; d. Thomas James and Catherine (Manning) Lee; m. William Thomas Vetterling, Aug. 18, 1973. BA magna cum laude, Smith Coll., 1970; AM, Harvard U., 1971, PhD, 1977. Teaching fellow Harvard U., Cambridge, Mass., 1972-76; instr. Northeastern U., Boston, 1976-77, asst. prof. Spanish & Portuguese, 1977-83; tchr. Spanish Buckingham Browne & Nichols, Cambridge, 1983-84; asst. prof. Spanish Regis Coll., Weston, Mass., 1984-88, assoc. prof. Spanish, 1988-95, prof. Spanish, 1995—. Editor MaFLA Newsletter; author bibliography, articles. Sec. Paint Rock Pool, Lexington, Mass., 1989-92. Recipient honor Woodrow Wilson Found., 1970, Alfonso X the Wise award, 1998. Mem. MLA (divsn. Medieval Spanish lit.), Am. Assn. Tchrs. Spanish & Portuguese (chpt. treas., editor, pres., sec. bd. dirs. 1977-, exec. coun. 1997-99, 2002-, nat. v.p. 2002, pres. 2003), Phi Beta Kappa. Avocations: stamp collecting, amateur radio. Office: Regis College Dept Spanish 235 Wellesley St Weston MA 02493-1571 E-mail: mav@regiscollege.edu.

VEVERKA, RUTH TONRY, retired secondary school educator; b. Martinsburg, W.Va., June 24, 1918; d. James Charles and May Elizabeth (Matthews) Tonry; m. Rudolph Edward Veverka, Sept. 18, 1948; 1 child, Karen Elizabeth. BS in Home Econs., W.Va. U., 1940; MA, U. Nebr., 1950; postgrad., U. Nebr., Omaha, 1970. Cert. tchr., W.Va., Nebr. Tchr. Ft. Ashby (W.Va.) High Sch., 1940-41, Bunker Hill (W.Va.) High Sch., 1941-42; cryptanalyst USN, Washington, 1946-48; libr. sci. worker Westside Community Schs., Omaha, 1970-88. Mem. ARC, Arlington, Va., 1953-56, Navy Relief Soc., San Diego, 1959-61. Lt. USN, 1942-46. Mem. AAUW, Home Economists in Homemaking, Women Accepted for Vol. Emegency Svc., Feminine Vets. World War II, Order Ea. Star, 1918 Club, Phi Upsilon Omicron, Kappa Delta Pi, Pi Lambda Theta, Pi Mu Epsilon, Alpha Xi Delta. Republican. Lutheran. Avocations: reading, swimming, needlepoint.

VEZERIDIS, MICHAEL PANAGIOTIS, surgeon, educator; b. Thessaloniki, Greece, Dec. 16, 1943; came to U.S., 1974; s. Panagiotis and Sofia (Avramidis) V.; m. Therese Mary Statz; children: Peter Statz, Alexander Michael. MD, U. Athens, 1967; MA (hon) ad eundem, Brown U., 1989. Diplomate Am. Bd. Surgery. Fellow surg. rsch. Harvard Med. Sch./Mass. Gen. Hosp., Boston, 1974-77; resident U. Mass., Worcester, 1977-80; fellow in surg. oncology Roswell Park Meml. Inst., Buffalo, 1980-81, attending surgeon, 1981-82; staff surgeon VA Med. Ctr., Providence, 1982-84; asst. prof. surgery Brown U., Providence, 1982-88; chief surg. oncology VA Med. Ctr., Providence, 1984—, assoc. chief surgery, 1986-98, chief surgery, 1998—; cons. in surgery R.I. Hosp., Providence, 1987—; surg. oncologist Roger Williams Med. Ctr., Providence, 1989—; assoc. dir. div. surg. oncology Brown U., Providence, 1989—, assoc. prof. surgery, 1988-94, prof., 1994—; prof. surgery Boston U. Sch. Medicine, 1999—. Chmn. profl. edn. com. R.I. divsn. Am. Cancer Soc., Providence, 1987-89, pres.-elect 1989-91, pres. 1991-93, del. dir. to nat. bd. dirs., 1993-96, mem. Nat. Assembly of the Am. Cancer Soc., 1997—, bd. dirs. New Eng. divsn., 1997-2001, chief med. officer New. Eng. divsn., 1999-2001; chmn. R.I. State Cancer Liaison Program ACS, 1999—; vis. prof. U. Patras (Greece) Med. Sch., 1988; mem. sci. adv. com. Clin. Rsch. Ctr., Brown U., Providence, 1989-91. Contbr. articles to profl. jours. and chpts. in med. books. Mem. parish coun. Ch. of Annunciation, Cranston, R.I., 1985-91; v.p. Hellenic Cultural Soc. Southeastern New Eng., Providence, 1987-89. Decorated Navy Commendation medal; named Profl. Fed. Employee of Yr., R.I. Fed. Exec. Coun., 1987; recipient St. George medal Am. Cancer Soc.; Merit Rev. Cancer Rsch. grantee VA, 1983-89. Fellow ACS (treas. R.I. chpt. 1996-2000, pres.-elect 2000-2002, pres. 2002-); mem. Soc. Surg. Oncology, Assn. for Acad. Surgery, Am. Soc. Clin. Oncology, N.Y. Acad. Scis. (life), Soc. for Surgery Alimentary Tract, Am. Assn. for Cancer Rsch., Collegium Internat. Chirurgiae Digestivae, Assn. Mil. Surgeons U.S., Soc. for Metastasis Rsch., New Eng. Cancer Soc., New Eng. Surg. Soc., Quidnessett Country Club. Greek Orthodox. Avocations: classical music, reading, fencing, tennis, squash, cross-country skiing. Home: 50 Limerock Dr East Greenwich RI 02818-1643 Office: Univ Surg Assocs Ste 470 Two Dudley St Providence RI 02905

VEZINA, VICKY LYNNE, middle school educator; b. Cheyenne, Wyo., June 3, 1950; d. Charles James and Wanda Louise (Byers) Seidl; m. Gary Edward Vezina, June 30, 1968; children: Jeffrey James, Michelle Annette. AS in Elem. Edn., Parkland Jr. Coll., Champaign, Ill., 1989; BS in Edn., Ea. Ill. U., 1991. Cert. tchr. K-9 in social sci. arts, gen. sci., social sci. Food demonstrator Beatrice Foods, Cheyenne, 1967; chambermaid Home Ranch Motel, Cheyenne, 1968; dog bather/groomer Shellhart's Boarding Kennels & Grooming, Cheyenne, 1968-69; parent vol. Bement (Ill.) Grad Sch., 1985-87; substitute tchr. Bement, Monticello and Cerro Gordo (Ill.) Pub. Schs., 1991—. Home bound tutor Bement H.S., 1992, 93; truancy tutor Bement Grade Sch., 1993, 94, summer tutor, 1998—; presch. tester Bement Sch. Dist., 1986-87. Chmn. membership com. Bement PTA, 1986—87; vol. Bement Sch. Dist # 5, 1985—87; tchr. Sunday sch./Bible sch. Christian Ch., Bement, 1973—79; co-chair Christian Edn. Com. 1st Presbyn. Ch., Monticello, 1998—, chmn. Christian Edn. Com., 2002, 2003, mem. Christian Clown Troupe, 2000—, elected elder, 2001, mem. adult choir, 1998—. Named Vol. of the Yr., Bement Sch. Dist. #5, 1987. Mem. VFW Aux., Kappa Delta Pi, Alpha Sigma Lambda, Alpha Omega. Democrat. Presbyterian. Avocations: reading, crocheting, word search puzzles, bowling, sight seeing. Home: 432 W Shumway St Bement IL 61813-1342

VIANDS, DONALD REX, plant breeder and educator; b. Riverdale, Md., Apr. 1, 1952; s. Walter Leroy and Lydia (Zeh) V.; m. Janice Ann Ruppelt, Aug. 7, 1976; children: Jamie Christopher, April Suzanne. BS in Agronomy, U. Md., 1974; MS in Plant Breeding, U. Minn., 1977, PhD in Plant Breeding, 1979. Undergrad. rsch. asst. U. Md., College Park, 1969-74; grad. rsch. asst. U. Minn., St. Paul, 1974-79; asst. prof. Cornell U., Ithaca, NY, 1979-85, assoc. prof., 1985-92, prof., 1992—, assoc. dir. acad. programs, 1995—2002, assoc. dean, dir. acad. programs, 2003—. Mem. adv. com. biotech. sci. adv. com. EPA, Washington, 1987-95; mem. steering com. N.Y. State North Country Devel. Program, 1990-99; adv. N.Y. State Forage and Grassland Coun., 1984-90, Alfalfa Crop Adv. Com., 1984-92. Contbr. articles to profl. jours., chpts. to books. Sunday sch. tchr. People's Bapt. Ch., Newfield, N.Y., 1988-2000, deacon, 1988-90, 93-98, Awana comdr., 1993-2000. Named Most Influential Faculty Mem. for Merrill Presdl. Scholar, Cornell U., 1991. Mem. Am. Soc. Agronomy (N.E. regional coord. mem. com. 1998-99), Crop Sci. Soc. Am., Am. Seed Trade Assn. (mem. minimum distance com. 1988-94), N.Am. Alfalfa Improvement Conf. (sec. 1984-86, v.p. 1986-88, pres. 1988-90), Ea. Forage Improvement Conf., Am. Forage and Grassland Coun. Republican. Achievements include development of 11 alfalfa varieties and 1 birdsfoot trefoil variety. Office: Cornell Univ Office Acad Programs 151 Roberts Hall Ithaca NY 14853-5905 E-mail: drv3@cornell.edu.

VICK, SUSAN, playwright, educator, director, actress; b. Raleigh, NC, Nov. 4, 1945; d. Thomas B. Jr. and Merle (Hayes) V. MFA, So. Meth. U., 1969; PhD, U. Ill., 1979. Prof. drama/theatre and dir. theatre Worcester (Mass.) Poly. Inst., 1981—; playwright Excuse Me For Living Prodns., Cambridge, Mass., 1989—, Festival Fringe, Edinburgh, 1989—. Playwright Ensemble Studio Theatre, N.Y.C., 1981-83; founder WPI Ann. New Voices Festival of Original Plays, 1982. Editor: (2 vols.) Playwrights Press, Amherst, 1988—; playwright: When I Was Your Age, 1982, Ord-Way Ames-Gay, 1982, Investments, 1985, Half Naked, 1989, Quandary, 1983, Meat Selection, 1984, Give My Love to Everyone But, 1989; appeared in plays including Rip Van Winkle, 1979, Why I Live at The P.O., 1982, The Play Group, 1984-85, Present Stage, 1985, Sister Mary Ignatius Explain It All, 1986, Wipeout, 1988, Bogus Joan, 1992-93; dir. play Give My Love to Everyone But, 1990 (Edinburgh Festival); theatre editor: Sojourner The Women's Forum, 1995-98; dramatist, script cons. Clyde Unity Theatre, Glasgow, Scotland, 1992-93, 1999-2000. Dir., Women's Community Theatre, Amherst, 1981-84, Upstart, Wis., 1994. Faculty fellow U. Ill., 1976-77, Bd. of Trustees Award for Outstanding Tchg., Worcester Poly. Inst., 1997. Mem. U.S. Inst. for Theatre Tech., Nat. Assn. Schs. Theatre, New Eng. Theatre Conf., Inc., Drama League, Dramatists Guild (assoc.), Soc. Stage Dirs. and Choreographers (assoc.), U.S. Inst. Theatre Tech., New England Theatre Conf., Nat. Assn. Schs. Theatre, Alpha Phi Omega (Svc. to Students award 1996). Avocations: puppets, frogs, travel. Office: Worcester Poly Tech Inst 100 Institute Rd Worcester MA 01609-2247

VICKERS, MARK STEPHEN, business educator, travel industry executive, sculptor, painter; b. Vallego, Calif., Sept. 11, 1957; s. John Frederick and Anna Ruth (Boschell) V. BA in Bus. Adminstrn., Azusa Pacific U., 1979; grad. studies, U. Bourgogne, Dijon, France, 1986-87. Dir. public relations Azusa Pacific div. Bus., 1977-78; copywriter Pennington, Inc., Fullerton, Calif., 1978; dir. communications Glendora (Calif.) C. of C., 1979; asst. mgr., dir. public relations Burbank (Calif.) C. of C., 1979-82, exec. dir., 1982-84; v.p. Astra Tours and Travel, Los Angeles, 1984-86; custom group cons. Marquis Tours, Vallejo, 1987—; bus. instr. St. Patrick's High Sch., Vallejo, 1987—; pres. US Sportsmarque, 1987—. Author: Selling Art on the Internet, 2000, Right-Brained Guide to a Left-Brained Industry, 2002; columnist, poet and contbg. editor Calif. Chamber Execs.

Assn. Newsletter and Burbank Bus. Today mag. Coordinator Burbank Trade Fair Festival. Recipient Eagle Scout award Boy Scouts Am., 1971; Bus. award Bank of Am., 1975; Outstanding Young Man of Am. award U.S. Jaycees, 1982; Calif. State Senate Resolution award, 1984. Mem. Am. Chamber Execs. Assn., Calif. Chamber Execs. Assn., Los Angeles Public Interest Radio and TV Ednl. Soc. Clubs: Toastmasters (Burbank); San Fernando Valley Press (pres.).

VICKERS, NANCY J. academic administrator; BA, Mt. Holyoke Coll., 1967, LHD (hon.), 1999; MA, Yale U., 1971, PhD, 1976. Prof. French and Italian Dartmouth Coll., 1973—87; prof. French, Italian, and comparative literature U. Southern Calif., 1987—97, dean curriculum and instrn. Coll. Letters, Arts and Scis., 1994—97; pres. Bryn Mawr Coll., 1997—. Vis. prof. Harvard U., U. Pa., UCLA; bd. dirs. Bryn Mawr Bank Corp.; bd. govs. U. Calif. Humanities Rsch. Inst., Coun. Dante Soc. Am. Recipient Presdl. medal Outstanding Leadership and Achievement, Dartmouth Coll., 1991; fellow vis. fellow, Princeton U. Office: Bryn Mawr Coll 101 N Merion Ave Bryn Mawr PA 19010-2899

VICKMAN, PATRICIA ANN, preschool educator; b. Green Bay, Wis., Nov. 3, 1951; d. Orville A. and Hyacinth C. (Rueckl) Van Laanen; m. Patrick John Vickman, Oct. 20, 1972; children: Sarah Anne, John Edward. BS in Growth and Devel., U. Wis., Green Bay, 1972; postgrad., Minot State Coll., 1975-76. Cert pre-kindergarten and kindergarten tchr., Minn. Head start instr. Hazel Green (Wis.) Pub. Schs., 1973; head tchr. Noah's Ark, St. Paul, 1973-74, Golden Hours Day Care, Eagan, Minn., 1974; tchr. asst. Cathedral of the Sacred Heart, Winona, Minn., 1981-82, pre-sch. tchr., 1982-86, Winona Area Cath. Schs., 1986—. Leader River Trails coun. Girl Scouts U.S.A., Winona, 1985-89; mem. adult choir Cathedral of Sacred Heart, Winona, 1984—, eucharistic min., 1990; sec. St. Stan's Band Boosters, 1988-90. Mem. Assn. for Childhood Edn. Internat., Nat. Cath. Edn. Assn., River City Rascals Winona Clown Club. Roman Catholic. Avocations: clowning, reading for self and children, travel, music. Home: 880 Hickory Ln Winona MN 55987-4160 Office: Winona Area Cath Schs Saint Marys Sch 1315 W Broadway St Winona MN 55987-2327

VIDAL, MAUREEN ERIS, theater educator, actress; b. Bklyn., Mar. 18, 1956; d. Louis and Lillian (Kaplan) Hendelman; m. Juan Vidal, June 25, 1974 (div. Sept. 1981); m. Guillermo Eduardo Uriarte, Dec. 22, 1986. BA, Bklyn. Coll., 1976, MS, 1981. From english tchr. to drama tchr. N.Y.C. Bd. Edn., 1976—2002, dean, 1997—, drama tchr., 2002—, chair women's history dept., 2003—. Mem PETA Humane Soc. Mem.: AFTRA, Gorilla Soc., Nat. Anti-Vivisection Soc. (mem. physicians' com. for responsible medicine), Heights Players Theater Co. (arranger theatrical performance for residents of homeless shelters 1986—, exec. bd., sec. 1993—, actress), Doris Day Animal League, Delta Psi Omega. Avocations: travel, white-water rafting, scuba diving, skydiving, theater. Home: 3380 Nostrand Ave Brooklyn NY 11229-4056 Office: I S 318 101 Walton St Brooklyn NY 11206-4311 also: Heights Players 26 Willow Pl Brooklyn NY 11201-4513 E-mail: MVidal4942@aol.com.

VIDERGAR, TERESA, music educator, musician; b. San Barnardino, Calif., Oct. 9, 1963; d. John August and Frances Vidergar. MusB in Piano Performance, Calif. State U., Fullerton, 1986; MusM in Piano Performance, Eastman Sch. Music, 1990. Piano instr. Teresa Vidergar Piano Studio, Fontana, Calif., 1981—; staff accompanist Temple Beth Israel Synagogue, Pomona, Calif., 1984—87, St. Anne Cath. Ch., San Bernardino, 1986—87, accompanist San Barnardino, Calif., 1991—96; accompanist for diocese Holy Rosary Cathedral, San Bernardino, 1986—87; piano accompanist CCD Congress, Cath. Convention, Anaheim, Calif., 1987; piano soloist, recitalist city colls. and recital series, Calif. and NY, 1986—94; piano instr. Music Maker Music Sch., Anaheim, 1996—. Piano adjudicator South Western Youth Music Festival, Southern Calif., 2000—. Bd. dirs., chmn. regional festival So. Calif. Jr. Bach Festival, 2001—. Recipient 3d prize, Joanna Hodges Internat. Piano Competition, 1985, Cert. of Merit, So. Calif. Jr. Bach Festival. Mem.: Music Tchrs. Assn. Calif. (state adjudicator chmn. for Composers Today program 2001—, 2d v.p. San Bernardino br. 1997—, award for Young Artist Debut Concert 1985, award for performance at state conv. 1985, Cert. of Merit Piano Exams), Music Tchrs. Nat. Assn. Office: Music Maker Music Sch 5701 E Santa Ana Canyon Rd Anaheim CA 92807

VIEL, DORI MICHELE, secondary education educator; b. Denver, Sept. 14, 1953; d. James Russell and Thelma Jean (Tirrill) Davee; m. Timothy John Viel, June 20, 1982; children: Tyeler Michele, Jasmin Marie, Lisan Mikel. Student, San Diego State U., 1973-74; BA, U. Calif., Irvine, 1978; student, Chico (Calif.) State U., 1989-90. Mem. health curriculum revied guide Orange Unified Sch. Dist., 1976-77; vol. Peace Corps, 1978-80; tchr. Crow Indian Reservation, Mont., 1980-81, Hayfork (Calif.) High Sch., 1981-82, Twin Fall (Idaho) Sch. Dist., 1983-86, Mountain Valley Unified Sch. Dist., Hayfork, 1986—. Presenter confs. Recipient CTA Outstanding Tchr. award, 1991, Tchr. of Yr. award Trinity County, 1992. Mem. Calif. Assessment Program, Calif. Arts Edn. Assn., Calif. Art Project (county team, region II), Mountain Valley Tchrs. Assn. (exec. coun.), Trinity County Arts Coun., Arts Ptnrs. Office: Mountain Valley Unified Sch Dist Oak St Hayfork CA 96041

VIERK, JANICE MARIE, English educator; b. Grand Island, Nebr., Sept. 16, 1950; d. Glen Albert and Winifred Ruth (Donigan) V.; m. Dennis Anthony Bagley, Oct. 16, 1971 (div. 1981); children: Daniel Anthony, Daemon Andrew; m. Ronald Francis Mimick, Oct. 2, 1998. BA in Edn., U. Nebr., 1971, MA, 1980, PhD, 1997. Instr. Bergan H.S., Fremont, Nebr., 1974-81, Bennington (Nebr.) H.S., 1990-93, Coll. of St. Mary, Omaha, 1990-95, Bellevue (Nebr.) U., 1994—99, Iowa Western C.C., Council Bluffs, 1997-99, Met. C.C., Omaha, 1981—99, prof., 1999—. English dept. head Bennington H.S., 1990-93, Bergan H.S., Fremont, Nebr., 1974-81. Coord. Hillary Rodham Clinton Fan Club, Nebr., 1995-98. Faculty devel. grant Coll. of St. Mary, 1994, 95. Mem. Nat. Coun. Tchrs. of English, Assn. of Theatre in English Edn., Phi Theta Kappa. Avocations: writing, fitness, theatre, movies. Home: 4304 Hickory St Omaha NE 68105-2411 Office: Met Cmty Coll PO Box 3777 Omaha NE 68103-0777 E-mail: jvierk@cox.net., jvierk@metrop.muneb.edu.

VIGEN, KATHRYN L. VOSS, nursing administrator, educator; b. Lakefield, Minn., Sept. 24, 1934; d. Edward Stanley and Bertha C. (Richter) Voss; m. David C. Vigen, June 23, 1956 (div. 1977); children: Eric. E., Amy Vigen Hemstad, Aana Marie. BS in Nursing magna cum laude, St. Olaf Coll., 1956; MEd, S.D. State U., 1975; MS, Rush U., 1980; PhD, U. Minn., 1987. RN. Staff nurse various hosps., Mpls, Boston, Chgo., 1956-68; nursing instr. S.E.A. Sch. Practical Nursing, Sioux Falls, S.D., 1969-74; statewide coord. upward mobility in nursing Augustana Coll., Sioux Falls, S.D., 1974-78; cons./researcher S.D. Commn. Higher Edn., 1974-79; gov. appointed bd. mem. S.D. Bd. Nursing, 1975-79; RN upward mobility project dir., chair/dir. div. of nursing Huron Coll. S.D. State U., 1978-79, mobility project dir., 1980-84; head dept. nursing, assoc. prof. Luther Coll., Decorah, Iowa, 1984-94; prof. nursing Graceland Coll., Independence, Mo., 1994-2001; dir., dean Sch. Nursing, North Park U., Chgo., 2001—. Cons. in field; developer outreach MSN programs Graceland Coll.; governing bd. mem. Midwest Alliance in Nursing, S.D. and Iowa, 1984-92, Mo., 1998—; founder Soc. for Advancement of Nursing, Malta, 1992; developer Health Care in the Mediterranean Study Abroad Program, Greece and Malta, 1994, 96, 98; developer summer internship for Maltese nursing students Mayo Med. Ctr. and Luther Coll.; presenter on internat. collaboration with Malta for nursing leadership 2d Internat. Acad. Congress on Nursing, Kansas City, 1996; presenter in field. Author: Role of a Dean in a Private Liberal Arts College, 1992; devel. and initiated 3 nursing programs in S.D., 1974-84 (named Women of Yr., 1982). Lobbyist Nursing Schs. in S.D., 1974-79; task force mem. Sen. Tom Harkin's Nurse's Adv. Com., 1986-94. Fellow to rep. U.S.A. ANA cand. in internat. coun. nursing 3M, St. Paul, 1978; recipient Leadership award Bush Found., St. Paul, 1979; Faculty fellow Minn. Area Geriatric Edn. Ctr. U. Minn., 1990-91; Fulbright scholar to Malta, 1992; recipient Fulbright award Malta Coun. Internat. Exch. of Scholars, Washington, 1992—; named Disting. Alumna, St. Olaf Coll., 2003. Mem. AAUW, ANA, AACN (hon. mem.), Am. Assn. Colls. Nursing (hon., exec. devel. subcom. 1990—, Hon. Mem. award), Internat. Assn. Human Caring, Iowa Nurse's Assn. (bd. dirs. 1989-92, mem. nursing edn. com. 1989—, co-pres. 1989—), Midwest Alliance in Nursing (gov. bd. rep. Iowa 1989-92, chair membership com. 1989-92, Mo., 1998—, S.D. gov. bd. rep. 1984-86, Rozella Schlotfeldt Leadership award 1993), Iowa Acad. Sci., Iowa Assn. Colls. Nursing Soc., Gerontol. Soc. Am., Am. Assn. Colls. Mich., Rotary, Sigma Theta Tau. Democrat. Lutheran. Avocations: singing, travel and other cultures, meeting people, sailing, reading. Home: 5360 N Lowell Ave # 412 Chicago IL 60630 Office: North Park U 3225 W Foster Ave Chicago IL 60625

VIGIL, DANIEL AGUSTIN, academic administrator; b. Denver, Feb. 13, 1947; s. Agustin and Rachel (Naranjo) V.; m. Claudia Cartier. BA in History, U. Colo., Denver, 1978, JD, 1982. Bar: Colo. 1982, U.S. Dist. Ct. Colo. 1983. Project mgr. Mathematics Policy Rsch., Denver, 1978; law clk. Denver Dist. Ct., 1982-83; ptnr. Vigil and Bley, Denver, 1983-85; asst. dean sch. law U. Colo., Boulder, 1983-89, assoc. dean sch. law, 1989—. Apptd. by chief justice of Colo. Supreme Ct. to serve on Colo. Supreme Ct. Ad Hoc Com. on miniority participation in legal profession, 1988-94; adj. prof. U. Colo. Sch. Law; mem. Gov. Colo. Lottery Commn., 1990-97; mem. Colo. Supreme Ct. Hearing Bd., 1998-2002; mem. atty. regulatory adv. com. Colo. Supreme Ct., 2002—; vis. law prof. U. Denver Law Coll., 2003—. Editor (newsletter) Class Action, 1987-88; co-editor (ethics com. column) Colo. Lawyer, 1995-97. Bd. dirs. Legal Aid Soc. Met. Denver, 1986-99, chmn. bd. dirs., 1998-99; past v.p. Colo. Minority Scholarhip Consortium, pres. 1990-91; bd. trustees Colo. Atty.'s Fund for Client Protection, 2001—; bd. trustees Boulder Bar Found., 2000-, pres. 2003; mem. Task Force on Cmty. Race Rels., Boulder, 1989-94; past mem. jud. nomination rev. com. U.S. Senator Tim Wirth; chmn. bd. dirs. Colo. Legal Svcs., 2000-. Mem. Colo. Bar Assn. (mem. legal edn. and admissions com. 1989-94, chmn. 1989-91, bd. govs. 1991, 97—), Hispanic Nat. Bar Assn. (chmn. scholarship com. 1990-95), Colo Hispanic Bar Assn. (bd. dirs. 1985-89, pres. 1990), Denver Bar Assn. (joint com. on minorities in the legal profession 1993-95), Boulder County Bar Assn. (ex-officio mem., trustee), Inns of Ct. (Penfield Tate chpt.), Phi Delta Phi (faculty sponsor). Roman Catholic. Avocations: skiing, cosmology. Home: 2550 Winding River Dr 0-4 Broomfield CO 80020 Office: U Colo Sch Law PO Box 401 Boulder CO 80303 E-mail: daniel.vigil@colorado.edu.

VIGNA, DEAN JOSEPH, social studies educator; b. Joliet, Ill., July 9, 1961; s. Bernard C. Jr. and Lois G. Vigna; m. Melissa J. Pfeifer, Aug. 6, 1983; 1 child, Allison Marie. BA, Eureka Coll., 1983. Tchr. 6th grade social studies Coal City (Ill.) Mid. Sch., 1983-85; tchr. social studies Coal City H.S., 1985—, basketball coach, 1983-89, baseball coach, 1986-93. Mentor tchr. for younger educators Coal City Sch. Dist., 1992—, chair social studies curriculum, 1993—; all state acad. selection team Chgo. Tribune, 2001-03. V.p., pres. coun. United Luth. Ch., Gardner, Ill., 1993—. Named Tchr. of Yr., Wal-Mart, 2003; named one of Those Who Excel, Ill. State Bd. Edn., 2001. Mem.: ASCD. Avocations: golf, reading, collecting autographs. Home: 792 Quail Run Coal City IL 60416-2420 Office: Coal City H S 655 W Division St Coal City IL 60416-1454 E-mail: dvigna@uti.com.

VILARDEBO, ANGIE MARIE, management consultant, parochial school educator; b. Tampa, Fla., July 15, 1938; d. Vincent and Antonina (Fazio) Noto; m. Charles Kenneth Vilardebo, June 26, 1960; children: Charles, Kenneth, Michele, Melanie. BA, Notre Dame Md., 1960; post-grad., Rollins Coll., 1980. Cert. tchr., Fla. Tchr. Sea Park Elem. Sch., Satellite Beach, Fla., 1960-61; office mgr. Computer Systems Enterprises, Satellite Beach, 1973-76; artist Satellite Beach, 1976-79; employment counselor Career Cons., Melbourne, Fla., 1979-80; tchr. Our Lady of Lourdes Parochial Sch., Melbourne, 1980-89, 93-98; pres. Consol. Ventures, Inc., Satellite Beach, 1989—, Versatile Suppliers, Inc., Satellite Beach, 1989-93. Prin. search com. Diocese of Orlando, Fla., 1989-90. Patentee personal grading machine. V.p. Jaycees, Satellite Beach, 1976-77, pres., 1977-78. Recipient 1st Place Art award Fla. Fedn. Woman's Clubs, 1978, 2nd Place Art award, 1979, Honorable Mention, 1980. Mem. Satellite Beach Woman's Club, Paper Chaser's Investment Club, Brevard Arts Ctr. & Mus., Space Coast Art League (social chmn. 1987—), CompuVest Investment Club. Roman Catholic. Avocations: bridge, writing, reading, oil painting, entrepreneurship. Home and Office: 100 Riverside Dr Apt 706 Cocoa FL 32922-7866

VILE, SANDRA JANE, leadership training educator; b. Oceanside, N.Y., Oct. 4, 1939; d. John Oliver and Roberta May (Wood) Ryan; m. Joseph Charles Vile, June 27, 1964; children: Jonathan Charles, Susan Jane. BS in Christian Edn. cum laude, Nyack Coll., 1961; MS in Edn., SUNY, Oneonta, 1963; diploma, Childrens Ministries Inst., Warrenton, Mo., 1974; Cert. in Visual Comm., Faith Venture Visuals, Inc., Lititz, Pa., 1979. Cert. elem. tchr., N.Y. Tchr. Hudson (N.Y.) City Sch. Dist., 1961-64, South Orangetown Ctrl. Sch. Dist., Orangeburg, N.Y., 1964-67; local dir. Child Evangelism Fellowship of Empire State, Afton, N.Y., 1972-88, state tng. instr., 1988-92; leadership tng. instr. Child Evangelism Fellowship, Inc., Warrenton, 1992—2002, vol. leadership tng. instr., 2002—. Vis. lectr. Nyack (N.Y.) Coll., 1967; tng. cons. Faith Venture Visuals, Inc., 1980-96. Contbr.: Children's Ministry Resource Bible, 1993. Lay leader Teen Missions, Inc., Merritt Island, Fla., 1982. Recipient Alumna of Yr. award Faith Venture Visuals, Inc., 1993. Mem. Pro Merito Soc., Logicians Soc. Avocations: computers, travel, counted cross-stitch. Home and Office: 270 Route 27B Hudson NY 12534-3919

VILLANUEVA, E. GARY, internist, educator; b. Lipa City, Philippines, Dec. 27; s. Engracio Kalaw Villanueva and Rosario Cuenca; m. Imelda Garcia Villanueva, May 4, 1982; children: Donna-Mae Villanueva-Dry, Elaine Villanueva-Jones, Gerald, Paul, Joseph. MD, U. Santo Tomas, Philippines, 1958; ScD (hon.), John Dewey U.; LLD (hon.), Adam Smith U. Diplomate Am. Bd. Ambulatory Medicine, Am. Bd. Disability Analyst. Profl. lectr., mem. faculty pharmacy, medicine, biochemistry U. St. Tomas, Manila, Philippines, 1967—70; dir. medicine Luth. Hosp. Bklyn., 1973—79; attending physician internal medicine Cath. Med. Ctr. Bklyn. and Queens St. Mary's Hosp., Bklyn., 1979—98; asst. prof. medicine SUNY Health Sci. Ctr., Bklyn., 1997—2003; attending physician internal medicine Jamaica Hosp. Med. Ctr., Medisys ENY, Bklyn. Exec. dir. Royal Pontifical UST Med. Alumni Assn. in the State of N.Y., N.Y.C.; pres. N.Y.-N.J. chpt. Am. Coll. Internat. Physician, 1983—90; pres. med. bd. St. Mary's Hosp., Bklyn., 1990—91. Author: (book) Intermediary Metabolism, Procedure Manual, 1968 (Academic Textbook, 1969); composer: Ode of the PMAA, 1980; editor: (newsletter) ACIP News Bull.; contbr. scientific papers to confs. and sci. jours., essays and editorials to profl. jours. Named Parade Grand Marshal, Philippine Independence Day Parade, 1995, knight of Malta, St. John of Jerusalem; Melvin Jones fellow, Internat. Assn. Lions Clubs, 1988. Fellow: ACP, Am. Acad. Ambulatory Medicine; mem.: Lions (gov. dist. 20-K1 N.Y. and Bermuda 2001—02, Grand Master Key award 1990). Roman Catholic. Avocation: travel. Home: 738 Hylan Blvd Staten Island NY 10305

VILLARREAL, SHARON MARIE, elementary education educator; b. Ventura, Calif., Mar. 26, 1961; d. José G. and Sharon N. (Kay) V.; 1 child, Elizabeth Maribel. BA in Spanish, U. Calif., Davis, 1985; bilingual cert. competence in Spanish, Calif. State U., Dominguez Hills, 1988, multiple subject tchg. credential, 1993; MA in Edn. Adminstrn., Calif. State U., L.A. Cert. multiple subject tchr. with bilingual emphasis, Calif. Tchr. Nevin Avenue Elem. Sch., L.A. Unified Sch. Dist., 1985—, categorical program coord., 1989-93, mem. sch. leadership coun., 1991. Mem. Booster Club, St. Andrew Sch., Pasadena, Calif., 1993-96; tchr. religious edn. St. Andrew Parish, 1994-96. Mem. NEA, Am. Fedn. Tchrs., Union Tchrs. L.A., Calif. Aggie Alumni Assn. Democrat. Avocations: camping, basketball, Spanish literature, volleyball, poetry. Office: Nevin Avenue Elem Sch 1569 E 32nd St Los Angeles CA 90011-2213

VILLELLA, EDWARD JOSEPH, ballet dancer, educator, choreographer, artistic director, performing arts administrator; b. L.I., N.Y., Oct. 1, 1936; s. Joseph and Mildred (DeGiovanni) Villella; m. Janet Greschler (div.); 1 child, Roddy; m. Linda Carbonetta; children: Christa Francesca, Lauren. BS in Marine Transp., N.Y. State Maritime Coll., 1957; LHD (hon.), Boston Conservatory, 1985, hon. degree, Union Coll., Schenectady, N.Y., 1991; DHL (hon.), St. Thomas U., Miami, Fla., 1994, U. S.C., 1997; DFA (hon.), SUNY Maritime Coll., Bronx, 1998; Doctor (hon.), Fla. Atlantic U., 2000, U. N.C., Asheville, 2002, Coll. Charleston, 2002. Mem. N.Y.C. Ballet, 1957, soloist, 1958-60, prin. soloist, 1960-83; artistic dir. Ballet Okla., Oklahoma City, 1983-86; founding artistic dir., CEO Miami (Fla.) City Ballet, 1985—. Vis. artist U.S. Mil. Acad., West Point, 1981—82; vis. artist Salute to Balanchine residency Harvard U., 1999—2000; vis. prof. dance U. Iowa, 1981; resident Heritage chair arts and cultural criticism George Mason U.; Dorthy F. Schmidt artist-in-residence Coll. of Arts and Letters, 2000—01. Dancer Symphony C., Scotch Symphony, We. Symphony, Donizetti Variations, Swan Lake, La Source, The Nutcracker, Agon, Stars and Stripes, The Prodigal Son, The Figure in the Carpet, 1960, Electronics, 1961, A Midsummer Night's Dream, 1962, Bugaku, 1963, Tarantella, 1964, Harlequinade, 1965, The Brahms-Schoenberg Quartet, 1966, Jewels, 1967, Symphony in Three Movements, 1972, Schéhérazade, 1975, choreographer Narkissas, 1966, Shostakovitch Ballet Suite, 1972, Shenandoah, 1975, Gayane Pas de Deux, 1972, Salute to Cole, 1973, Sea Chanties, 1974, Prelude, Riffs and Fugues, 1980, dancer TV The Ed Sullivan Show, Bell Telephone Hour, Mike Douglas Show, TV spl. Harlequin, 1975 (Emmy award); co-author (autobiography): Prodigal Son, 1991. Mem. Nat. Coun. Arts, 1968—74; chmn. Commn. for Cultural Affairs, N.Y.C., 1978; bd. visitors N.C. Sch. for Arts; mem. adv. panel Nat. Endowment for Arts; trustee Wolf Trap Found. for Arts; miracle maker Big Bros.-Big Sisters, Miami-Dade County, Fla., 2003. Named Miamian of Yr., UNICO Nat., 1993, Miracle Maker, Big Bros. Big Sisters of Greater Miami, 2003; named to Fla. Artists Hall of Fame, 1997; recipient Dance Mag. award, 1964, Lions of Performing Arts award, N.Y. Pub. Libr., 1987, Capezio Dance award, 1989, Gold medal, Nat. Soc. Arts and Letters, 1990, William G. Anderson Merit award, AAHPERD, 1991, Nat. Medal of Arts award, 1997, Kennedy Ctr. Honors, 1997, Cultural Soc. award, Bklyn. Ctr. for Performing Arts at Bklyn. Coll., 1998, Am. Irreplaceable Dance Treasures: The First 100; Robert J.H. Kiphuth fellow, Yale U., 2001, Hon. Theater Arts Br. fellow, U.S. Imperial Soc. Tchrs. Dancing, 2003.

VILLEMAIRE, DIANE DAVIS, adult education educator; b. Burlington, Vt., Nov. 21, 1946; d. Ellsworth Quinlan and Elizabeth Charlotte (Galvin) Davis; m. Bernard Philip Villemaire, Aug. 16, 1969; 1 child, Emily Jane. BS, U. Vt., 1968, MA, 1994; PhD, McGill U., Montreal, Que., Can., 1999. Cert. secondary sch. tchr., Vt. Rsch. asst. U. Vt., Burlington, 1965-68; tchr. biology Burlington H.S., 1968-71, Harwood Union H.S., Moretown, Vt., 1971—. Adj. faculty U. Vt., 1998—; equity specialist Harwood Union HS, Duxbury, Vt., 2002—. Author: E.A. Burtt, Historian and Philosopher, A Biography of the author of the Metaphysical Foundations of Modern Physical Science, 2002. Mem. NEA, AAUW (discussion leader), Am. Assn. Biology Tchrs. (Outstanding Biology Tchr. award 1978), Soc. for Advancement of Am. Philosophy, Phi Alpha Theta. Democrat. Avocations: antique flowers, art, travel, science and scientific advancements. Office: Harwood Union HS Vt Rt 100 South Duxbury VT 05660-9404

VILLENA-ALVAREZ, JUANITA I. language educator, consultant; b. Baguio, Philippines, Aug. 27; arrived in France, 1987, Spain, 1986; came to U.S., 1988; d. Juan J. V. and Milagros M. Ibarra; m. Beda E. Alvarez, Jr., June 27, 1992; 1 child, Natalie Noelle. BA magna cum laude, U. Philippines, Quezon City, 1986; Magistère French Civilization, U. Paris, 1988; MA in French Lit., U. Cin., 1989, PhD in French Lit., 1994. Instr. French, Spanish U. Philippines, Quezon, 1986; grad. tchg. asst. U. Cin., 1988-93; instr. French Miami U., Oxford, Ohio, 1993; assoc. prof. U. S.C., Beaufort, 1994—, dir. liberal studies, 2003—. Lang. cons. Software Clearing House, Cin., 1989-90, EGlobe2B, Beaufort, 2000; material devel. Judith Muyskens, Cin., 1988-90. Author: The Allegory of Literary Representation, 1997, Instructor Resources and Student Resources for Exito comml., 2001; creator more than 100 websites on teaching; contbr. article to profl. jour. Charles Phelps Taft fellow, 1993-94; recipient Rotary Amb. Goodwill Rotary Internat., 1987-88. Mem. MLA, Am. Assn. French Tchrs., S.C. Assn. Fgn. Lang. Tchrs., Alliance Française (Cin., lang. cons. 1993), French Circle (Beaufort, lang. coord. 1994—), Phi Kappa Phi. Avocations: writing, travel, translations. Home: 2 Quail Ridge Loop Beaufort SC 29906 Office: U SC 801 Carteret St Beaufort SC 29902-4601

VINCENSI, AVIS A. sales executive, medical educator; b. Hazardville, Conn., July 10, 1949; d. George P. Vincensi and Hilda G. (Boucher) Vincensi(dec.). AS in Bus., Holyoke (Mass.) CC, 1987. Registered diagnostic med. sonographer, radiologic tech., radiography, mammography. Xray technologist Baystate Med. Ctr., Springfield, Mass., 1969—73, Colley Dickinson Hosp., Holyoke, Mass., 1969—73, Holyoke Hosp., 1969—87, sonographer, 1973—82; sonographer, supr. Providence Hosp., Holyoke, 1982—87; sonographer Diagnostic Imaging, Springfield, Mass., 1987—90; product specialist/product mktg. sales Corometrics Med. Sys., Wallingford, Conn., 1991—96; diagnostic reagent rep. Sigma Diagnostics, St. Louis, 1996—2002; clin. adj. prof. Springfield Tech. CC, 1999—2002, assoc. prof., 2002—, bd. dirs., 1999—, assoc. prof., dept. chair diagnostic med. sonography, 2002—. Recipient 2 Gold medals and 1 Silver medal Tai Chi competition, 2002. Mem.: Am. Inst. Ultrasonic Medicine, Am. Registry Diagnostic Med. Sonographers. Home: 101 Acushnet Ave Springfield MA 01105-2218 Fax: 413-731-8908. E-mail: avincensi@stcc.edu.

VINCENT, PHYLLIS MATTINGLY, secondary music educator; b. Springfield, Ky., Nov. 21, 1946; d. J. B. and Mattie Francis (Boswell) Mattingly; m. Joe E. Vincent, June 17, 1972; children: Jennifer Jo, Kevin Edward. B Music Edn., Georgetown (Ky.) U., 1969; M Music Edn., Ea. Ky. U., Richmond, 1973; Rank I in Music Edn., U. Ky., 1991, PhD in Music Edn., 1997. Cert. tchr. Choral dir., organist Harrodsburg (Ky.) Meth. Ch., 1967-69; choral/vocal music tchr. Western High Sch., Louisville, 1970-73, Myers Middle Sch., Louisville, 1974-75; pianist 1st Bapt. Ch., Frankfort, Ky., 1982-95; choral/vocal music tchr. Western Hills High Sch., Frankfort, Ky., 1980—2000; asst. prof. music edn. No. Ky. U., 2000—01, Lexington (Ky.) Traditional Magnet Sch., 2001—03, Bondurant Mid. Sch., 2003—. Mem. Am. Choral Dirs. Assn., Ky. Music Educators Assn. (accompanist All-State Chorus 1986, Tchr. of Yr. award dist. 7-11, 1987, 96, H.S. Tchr. of Yr. 1996, pres. 1997-99, pres. dist. 7-11, 1991-93, mem. all-acad. honor faculty 1985, 86, 89, 92, 95, Disting. Svc. award 2001), Alpha Delta Kappa, Phi Delta Kappa. Baptist. Avocations: swimming, golf, photography, flowers. Home: 207 Esperanza Dr Frankfort KY 40601-4626 Fax: 502-695-7727. E-mail: pmvincent@dcr.net.

VINCENT, SHIRLEY JONES, secondary education educator; b. Plainfield, N.J., Nov. 23, 1947; d. Norman Eby and Muriel Audrey (Gustafson) Jones; m. Reginald P. Vincent, Feb. 2, 1974; children: David L., Sarah C. BA, Susquehanna U., 1969; MA, SUNY, Albany, 1979. English tchr. North Plainfield (N.J.) H.S., 1969-72, Marple Newtown Jr. H.S., Newtown Square, Pa., 1972-74, South Glens Falls (N.Y.) H.S., 1975-76, Lenox (Mass.) Meml. H.S., 1978—. Co-presenter workshops, 1994. Author, editor: Grandfather, 1996; editor Timshel, creative writing publ., 1992—;

co-presenter 5 TV shows, Sta. MCET, Cambridge, Mass., 1996; featured (TV show) Chronicle, Boston, 1994. Mem. NEA, Nat. Coun. Tchrs. Englishd, Mass. Tchrs. Assn. Home: 43 Birchwood Ln Lenox MA 01240-2105 Office: Lenox Meml High Sch 197 East St Lenox MA 01240-2206

VINES, DIANE WELCH, psychotherapist, educator; b. Rochester, Minn., Apr. 3, 1945; d. Howard Henshel and Edna (Steck) Welch; children: Juan Antonio, Michael. AA, St. Petersburg Jr. Coll., 1964; BS magna cum laude, Vanderbilt U., 1967; MA with honors, NYU, 1973; PhD in Sociology, Boston U., 1986. Cert. psychiat nurse, pscychotherapist, Mass.; cert, secondary sch. tchr., Pa. Staff nurse Mercy Hops., St. Petersburg, 1964-65; instr. Suncoast Hosp., Largo, Fla., 1965; coord. emotionally disturbed children unit state hosp., Phila., 1967-68; instr. nursing Mt. Sinai Hosp. Sch. Nursing, N.Y.C., 1968-69; asst. dir. nursing Vista Hill Psychiat. Hosp., Chula Vista, Calif., 1969-70; instr. Grossmont (Calif.) Vocat. Nursing Sch., 1970; chmn. dept. New Rochelle (N.Y.) Hosp. Sch. Nursing, 1970-71; part-time staff nurse Manhattan Bowery Project, N.Y.C., 1971-72; evening supr. emotionally disturbed children and adolescents Bronx State Hosp., 1972-73; psychotherapist Albert Einstein Med. Ctr., Bronx, 1973-74; instr. Faulkner Hosp. Sch. Nursing, Boston, 1974-75; instr., fgn. nurse grad. program Health and Hosps., Boston, 1974-75; pvt. practice psychotheraphy, co-founder Beacon Assocs., Brookline, Mass., 1976-82; dir. ambulatory nursing Boston Children's Hosp. Med. Ctr., 1975-78; asst. prof. grad. program psychiat. Cmty. Mental Health Nursing, Boston, 1978-82; instr., lectr. Boston U., N.E. U., 1980-81; White House fellow, spl. asst. to sec. edn. Washington, 1982-83; dir. Nat. Adult Literacy Initiative U.S. Dept. Edn., 1983-85; dir. spl. programs Calif. State U., 1985-90; dean Sch. Health Calif. State U., Dominguez Hills, 1990-94; pvt. practice psychotherapy West L.A., 1986—; v.p. Calif. State U. Inst., 1994—; chief acad. officer Calif. Virtual U. Design/Planning, 1997—. Mem. adv. com. Mass. Bd. Registration in Nursing, 1980-82; co-founder sexual abuse program Children's Hosp. Med. Ctr., Boston, 1977, cons., 1978; psychiat. nurse cons. Criminal victimology Cons., Inc., Boston, 1978; exec. prodr. pub. svc. campaigns; instr. in field; guest lectr. seminars. Contbr. articles to profl. jours. and chpt. in textbooks. Active YMCA, Germantown, Pa.; vol. activities dir. Boys' Club, Nat. City, Calif.; bd. pres. Project Litearcy, L.A., 1990; chair edn. com. Calif. Art Coun., 1987-88; mem. White House fellows regionalselection panel, 1989, 90, 91, 92; mem. arts edn. adv. com. Calif. State Dept. Edn., 1988-89, mem. adult edn. adv. com., 1989; literacy advisor Southport Inst., 1988-89; cons. Times Mirror, 1985-86, L.A. 2000, 1988-90; vice-chmn. Calif. State Coun. on Vocat. Edn., 1995—; vice-chmnm., chmn. elect Western Interstae Commn. on Higher Edn., 1996—; prin. investigator The Calif. Arts Project, 1995—. Recipient Nat. Rsch. Svc. award, 1981. Mem. ANA, State Nurses Assn., Nurses Ind. Practice, Women Health Washington, Calif. Alliance for Literacy, Nurses Wash. Roundtable, Am. Orhtopsychiat. Assn., Nurses United for Reimbursement of Svcs., Advanced Coun. Psychiat. Mental Health Nursing (Am. Nurses Assn.), advs. Child Psychiat. Nursing, Am. Sociol. Assn., Calif. Nurses Assn., Sigma Theta TAu, Phi Theta Kappa. Home: 7101 SE 36th Ave Portland OR 97202-8327 Office: Oregon U Sys PO Box 751 Portland OR 97207

VINSON, JACK ROGER, mechanical engineer, educator; b. Kansas City, Nov. 10, 1929; s. Harry Roger and Myrtle (Kiple) V.; m. Gertrude (Trudy) Hovey, June 11, 1955 (dec. Sept. 1977); children: Jack R. Jr., Stephen Scott, Jeffrey Alan, Christopher Lee; m. Mildred (Midge) Cohen, June 25, 1983. BME, Cornell U., 1952; PhD, U. Pa., 1961. Engr. student Black & Veatch Consulting Engrs., Kansas City, 1947-52; functional engr. GE, Phila., 1956-61; v.p. Dyna/Structures, Inc., Drexel Hill, Pa., 1961-65; ptnr. Structural Mechanics Assocs., Penn Valley, Pa., 1965—; from assoc. prof. to H. Fletcher Brown prof. U. Del., Newark, 1964—. Author: The Behavior of Thin Walled Structures, 1989, Structural Mechanics: The Behavior of Plates and Shells, 1974, The Behavior of Shells Composed of Isotropic and Composite Materials, 1993, The Behavior of Sandwich Structures of Isotropic and Composite Materials, 1999; co-author: Composite Materials and Their Use in Structures, 1975, 2d edit., 2002, The Behavior of Structures Composed of Composite Materials, 1985; editor-in-chief Jour. of Sandwich Sturctures and Materials. 1st Lt. USAF, 1954-56. Fellow AIAA (Award in Structural Mechanics 1977), ASME (life, chmn. aerospace divsn. 1980-81, Centennial medal 1981), Am. Soc. for Composites (v.p. 1996-97, pres. 1998-99, Techmonic award 1998, mem. internat. conf. on composite materials exec. com., region 3 v.p. 1999-2001). Episcopalian. Home: 1433 Sandy Cir Narberth PA 19072-1121 Office: U Del Dept Mech Engring Newark DE 19716

VINSON, JAMES SPANGLER, academic administrator; b. Chambersburg, Pa., May 17, 1941; s. Wilbur S. and Anna M. (Spangler) V.; m. Susan Alexander, Apr. 8, 1967; children: Suzannah, Elizabeth. BA, Gettysburg Coll., 1963; MS, U. Va., 1965, PhD, 1967. Asst. prof. physics MacMurray Coll., Jacksonville, Ill., 1967-71; assoc. prof. physics U. N.C., Asheville, 1971-78, prof. physics, 1974-78, chmn. dept. physics, dir. acad. computing, 1974-78; prof. physics, dean Coll. Arts and Scis. U. Hartford (Conn.), 1978-83; v.p. acad. affairs Trinity U., San Antonio, 1983-87; pres. U. Evansville, Ind., 1987-2001, pres. emeritus, 2001—; pres. Nat. Sci. Ctr. Found., Augusta, Ga., 2002—. Computer cons. Contbr. articles to profl. jours. Mem. Am. Phys. Soc., World Future Soc., AAAS, Am. Assn. for Advancement of Humanities, Am. Assn. for Higher Edn., Am. Assn. Physics Tchrs., Phi Beta Kappa, Sigma Xi, Phi Sigma Kappa. Methodist.

VINSON, MARK ALAN, English language and literature educator; b. Murray, Ky., July 14, 1958; s. C.D. Jr. and Betty Sue (Outland) V.; m. Lisa Carole Fennell, July 16, 1994. Student, Murray State U., 1976-79; BA, BSE, U. Memphis, 1981, MA, 1983; Specialist of Arts in English, U. Miss., 1987. Ordained to ministry Bapt. Ch. as deacon, 1989. Teaching asst. U. Memphis, 1982-83, instr. English, 1987-90; teaching asst. U. Miss., Oxford, 1984; instr. English N.W. Miss. Jr. Coll., Oxford, 1984-87, Shelby State C.C., Memphis, 1989, State Tech. Inst., Memphis, 1989; asst. prof. English Union U., Memphis, 1990-95, Crichton Coll., Memphis, 1995—. Named one of Outstanding Young Men of Am., 1988, 92, 96. Mem. Am. Dialect Soc., Am. Cut Glass Assn. (life), Conf. on Christianity and Lit., Sigma Tau Delta (charter mem., program chmn. 1981-83), Modern Lang. Assn. Republican. Southern Baptist. Avocations: collecting american brilliant cut glass, fossils, william faulkner memorabilia. Home: 191 Perkins Extd Memphis TN 38117 Office: Crichton Coll 6655 Winchester Rd Memphis TN 38115-4335

VINSON, VICTORIA DEAN, middle school educator; b. Cedartown, Ga., June 19, 1952; d. BennieDean Vinson and Katherine Louise (Green) Easterwood; m. Richard E. Wright, July 23, 1994. BSEd, U. Ga., 1975; postgrad., Valdosta State U., 1976-78, Berry Coll., 1980-81, U. Maryland, Lakenheath, Eng., 1982-84, W. Ga. Coll., 1991. Cert. K-12 gifted tchr., Ga. Tchr. Tift County High Sch., Tifton, Ga., 1976-79, Elm St. Mid. Sch., Rockmart, Ga., 1980-81, 85-89, tchr. of gifted, 1991—; tchr. RAF Feltwell (Eng.)-Lakenheath Mid. Sch., 1981-84. Instr. aerobics Floyd Med. Ctr., Rome, Ga., 1985-89; tchr./asst. Baird Ballet Co., Rome, 1984-88; tchr., choreographer Rome City Ballet, 198991, Acad. Performing Arts, Cedartown, 1992-93. Mem. ASCD, NEA, Ga. Edn. Assn., Polk Edn. Assn., Nat. Coun. Tchrs. English, Ga. Supporters for Gifted, Profl. Dance Tchrs. Assn., Nat. Dance Exercise Inst. Tng. Assn., Beta Sigma Phi. Republican. Home: 99 Seab Green Rd Cedartown GA 30125-4637 Office: Elm St Mid Sch 100 Morgan Valley Rd Rockmart GA 30153-1610

VIOLA, MARY JO, art history educator; b. Yonkers, N.Y., July 25, 1941; d. William F. and May (Cleary) O'Connor; m. Jerome Joseph Viola, June 21, 1967 (dec. Feb. 1990). BA in Fine Arts, Coll. of Mt. St. Vincent, 1963; MA in Art History, NYU, 1966; MPhil in Art History, CUNY, 1983, PhD in Art History, 1992. Art history tchr. Georgian Ct. Coll., N.J., 1965-66, Hollins Coll., Roanoke, Va., 1966-67, Marymount Coll., Tarrytown, N.Y., 1967-71, Baruch Coll., CUNY, N.Y.C., 1974-97, Bklyn. Coll., 1990-97, Parsons Sch. of Design, N.Y.C., 1991-93, Rutgers U., 1993-95, Bronx C.C. CUNY, 1997—. Curator exhbns. Baruch Coll. Gallery, N.Y.C., 1987-88. Editor: A World View of Art History, 1985; art exhibited at Tribes Gallery, N.Y.C., 1996; creater ednl. videos. Rschr. for ethnic festivals, N.Y.C., 1993—. Fellow Nat. Trust for Hist. Preservation, 1964, Marymount Coll., 1970, Boston Mus. Fine Arts/CUNY, 1978, Luce Found., 1988. Mem. Coll. Art Assn., Historians of Am. Art, City Lore. Avocations: tai chi, argentine tango, ballroom dance. Home and Office: 37 Roosevelt St Yonkers NY 10701-5823

VIOLAND-SANCHEZ, EMMA NATIVIDAD, school administrator, educator; b. Cochabamba, Bolivia, Nov. 5, 1944; came to U.S., 1961; d. Adalberto Violand and Emma Sanchez; children: James, Julia. BS, Radford U., 1966, MS, 1968; EdD, George Washington U., 1987. Postgrad. profl. lic. Tchr., counselor Am. Coop. Sch., La Paz, Bolivia, 1963, 71-76; instr. Ariz. Western Coll., Yuma, 1967-68; tchr., counselor St. Andrews Sch., La Paz, 1968-71; rschr. Instituto Boliviano Estudio Accion Social, La Paz, 1968-71; bilingual resource specialist Arlington (Va.) Pub. Schs., 1976-78, secondary project coord. Title VII, 1978-80, supr. ESOL, 1980—. Adj. prof. U. Catolica, La Paz, 1974-75, George Mason U., Fairfax, Va., 1986-94, George Washington U., Washington, 1988-97, Georgetown U., 1997—; cons. sch. dists., univs., Ministry of Edn. in Bolivia, 1976—, in El Salvador, 1996, in Escuela, Americana, San Salvador, Ministry of Devel. in Bolivia, 1996. Author: Vocational and Professional Handbook for Bolivia, 1971; contbg. author: Learning Styles in the ESL/EFL Classroom, 1995, Understanding Learning Styles in the Second Language Classroom, 1998, (monographs) Ministry of Education, 1988, National Clearinghouse for Bilingual Education, 1990, 91. Founder, pres. coun. 4606 LULAC, Arlington, 1987-96; founder chair Immigration Rights Task Force, Arlington, 1989-92; bd. trustees United Way Nat. Capital Area, Washington, 1989-94; exec. bd. Com. of 100, Arlington, 1994-95. Named one of Notable Women of Arlington, Arlington County, 1993; recipient Outstanding Dissertation award Nat. Assn. Bilingual Edn., 1988, Award Arlington County Dept. of Human Svcs., 1996; Am. fellow AAUW, 1986-87; Fulbright Sr. scholar, 1995-96. Mem. ASCD, TESOL (rsch. bd. 1979—). Avocations: travel, research, hispanic/latin american issues, consulting, sports. Office: Arlington Pub Schs 1426 N Quincy St Arlington VA 22207-3646

VIOLENUS, AGNES A. retired school system administrator; b. N.Y.C., May 17, 1931; d. Antonio and Constance Violenus. BA, Hunter Coll., 1952; MA, Columbia U., 1958; EdD, Nova U., 1990. Tchr. N.Y. State Day Care, N.Y.C., 1952-53, N.Y.C. Bd. Edn., 1953-66; asst. prin. N.Y.C. Elem. and Jr. H.S., 1966-91; student tchr. supr. dept. edn., adj. lectr. CCNY, 1997—. Adj. instr. computer dept. continuing edn. divsn. York Coll., N.Y.C., 1985-88, Hunter Coll., N.Y.C., 1998—; adj. instr. tchr. mentor program grad. edn. divsn. CCNY, 1990-91; reviewer ednl. and instrnl. films; judge news and documentary Emmy awards NATAS, 1995, 97, 2000, 2002. Co-author: LOGO: K-12, 1980; contbr. articles to profl. jours. Mem. mid-Manhattan br. NAACP, mem. com. on Afro-Am. acad., cultural, and tech. olympics; life mem. Girl Scouts U.S., N.Y.C.; bd. visitors Manhattan Psychiat. Ctr., 1995, pres., 2000, chair 1999—; vol. advisor math., sci., computers Workshop Ctr., CCNY, 1995-97; bd. dirs. Hunter Coll. Scholarship and Welfare Fund. Recipient Dedicated Svc. award Coun. Suprs. and Adminstrs., Appreciation award Aerospace Edn. Assn., 1985, Significant Contbn. award Am. Soc. for Aerospace Edn., 1985, Leaders' Day Cert. of Appreciation, Girl Scouts U.S., 1997. Mem. ASCE, AAUW, Am. Ednl. Rsch. Assn., Assn. Advancement of Computing in Edn., Assn. Computers in Math. and Sci. Tchg., Soc. for Info. Tech. and Tchr. Edn., Assn. for Women in Sci., Nat. Tech. Assn., N.Y. Acad. Scis. (scientists in schs. program 1995), Nat. Assn. Negro Bus. and Profl. Women's Clubs (scholarship com. 1989—, family math. com. 1995, rec. sec. 1994-95, profl. award 1997), Nat. Black Child Devel. Inst. (bd. dirs. 1991—, sci. exhibit com. 1995, v.p. 1999, co-chair entering coll. zone program 1999, 2000, pub. policy com. 1991—, Bridge Bldr.'s award 1995), Schomburg Ctr. Rsch. in Black Culture Schomburg Corp. (vols. adv. com. 1992—, bd. trustee, co-chair corp. task force on African-Am. in math., sci. and tech. 1992—, pres. 1995-98, treas. 1999-2000), Doctorate Assn. N.Y. Educators, N.Y. Alliance Black Sch. Educators, Hunter Coll. Alumni Assn. (bd. dirs. 1993—, rec. sec. 1996-99, treas. 1999—2002, named to Hall of Fame 1998), Bank St. Alumni Coun. Greater N.Y. (asst. sect. 1991-93), Wistarians Alumni Hunter Coll. (exec. com. 1990—, pres. 1990-94). Democrat. Roman Catholic. Avocations: aeronautics and space science, music, collecting black education memorabilia, instructing survival strategies and techniques for women and children, family genealogy.

VIROSTKO, JOAN, elementry school educator; b. Jackson Heights, N.Y., Feb. 6; d. John and Dorothy Veronica (Eckert) Virostko. Cert. of Studies, Oxford U., 1972, 73; B.S., St. John's U., 1968, M.S., 1970, P.D., 1972, 85, M.B.A., 1980, Ph.D., 1983, SAS, SDA, 1985. Cert. elem. tchr., N.Y.; cert. sch. bldg. adminstr., sch. dist. adminstr., N.Y. Educator Half Hollow Hills Paumanok Sch., Dix Hills, N.Y.; instr. Oxford U., England, summer 1985, 86; instr., 1987—. Contbr. Ellis Island Found, 1984-86; lector Sacred Heart Cath. Ch., Glendale, N.Y., 1986-87; sustaining mem. Rep. Nat. Com., 1980—, sponsor 1980— . Recipient Disting. Dissertation award, 1983; named Educator of Yr., N.Y. State Assn. Tchrs., 1985, 92, 95, 99, 2001. Mem. N.Y. State United Tchrs. Assn., Kappa Delta Pi, Phi Delta Kappa, Alpha Sigma Alpha, Delta Sigma Chi. Republican. Avocations: traveling, music, water and snow skiing, water sports. Office: Half Hollow Hills Paumanok Sch 1 Seamans Neck Rd Dix Hills NY 11746-7114 Address: 5731 69th Ln Maspeth NY 11378-1918

VIS, MARY A. MURGA, elementary education educator; b. East Chicago, Ind., Nov. 25, 1932; d. John and Rose (Cheranko) Murga; m. Ira Vis, Sept. 5, 1970; 1 child, Douglas. Diploma, Nat. Inst. Practical Nursing, Chgo., 1955; BS cum laude, St. Joseph's Coll., East Chicago, 1968; MS, Purdue U., Hammond, Ind., 1974, reading specialist endorsement, 1991. Elem. tchr. Gary Sch. Diocese, Hammond, 1968-70; tchr. spl. edn. Hammond Sch. System, 1986-87; elem. tchr. East Chicago Sch. System, 1987—. Author: East Chicago My Hometown, 1993. Mem. Hammond Area Reading Coun., AAUW, Delta Epsilon Sigma. Office: 2400 Cardinal Dr East Chicago IN 46312-3185

VISCUSI, W(ILLIAM) G. KIP, economics educator; b. Trenton, N.J., Oct. 3, 1949; s. William Edward and Evelyn (Martin) V.; m. Catherine Makdisi, Sep. 26, 1972 (div.); children: Kira Margaret, Michael Kip; m. Joni Hersch, Jan. 18, 1998. AB summa cum laude, Harvard U., 1971, MPP, 1973, AM, 1974, PhD, 1976. Prof. econs. Northwestern U., Evanston, Ill., 1976-80, 85-88; dep. dir. White House Council on Wage and Price Stability, Washington, 1979-81; prof. econs. Duke U., Durham, N.C., 1981-85; John M. Olin prof. econs. U. Chgo., 1985-86; George G. Allen prof. econs. Duke U., Durham, N.C., 1988-96; John M. Olin prof. law and econs. Harvard Law Sch., 1995, John F. Cogan Jr. prof. law and econs., 1996—. Rsch. assoc. Nat. Bur. Econ. Rsch., 1978—, Nat. Commn. for Employment Policy, 1981; mem. EPA Sci. Adv. Bd., 1986—, econs. bd., 1992—, Clean Air Act, 1992—, Nat. Acad. Sci. Panel, 1978-79; cons. U.S. Gen. Acctg. Office, 1981-85, Dept. Justice, 1986-87, 89-91, U.S. Office Mgmt. and Budget, 1983; assoc. reporter Am. Law Inst., 1986-91; adj. fellow in civil justice Manhattan Inst., 1987—; inaugural spkr. Geneva Risk Econ. Lectrs., Geneva Assn. Risk and Ins., 1989; John R. Commons lectr. U. Wis., 1990; Ayne Ryde lectr. Lund U., Sweden. Author: Employment Hazards, 1979 (Wells prize 1977), Risk by Choice, 1983, Reforming Products Liability, 1991, Fatal Tradeoffs, 1992, Smoking, 1992, Rational Risk Policy, 1998, Smoke-filled Rooms: A Post-mortem on the Tobacco Deal, 2002; editor Jour. Risk and Uncertainty; contbg. editor Regulation mag.; assoc. editor Internat. Rev. of Law Econs., Geneva Papers on Risk and Ins. Theory, Jour. Regulatory Econs., Jour. Environ. Econs. and Mgmt., J Risk and Ins., Rev. Econs. and Stats., Am. Econ. Rev., Managerial and Decision Econs., Contemporary Econ. Policy. Recipient Article of the Yr. award Econ. Inquiry, 1988, Royal Econ. Soc., 1999; Book of the Yr. awards Am. Risk and Ins. Assn., 1992, 93, 94, 2000, Article award Am. Risk and Ins. Assn., 1999. Mem. Am. Econs. Assn., Econometric Soc., Assn. Environ. and Resource Economists, Assn. for Pub. Policy Analysis and Mgmt., So. Econs. Assn. We. Econs. Assn., Managerials and Decision Econs. Roman Catholic. Office: Harvard Law Sch Hauser 302 Cambridge MA 02138

VITAGLIANO, KATHLEEN ALYCE FULLER, secondary education educator; b. Oneida, N.Y., May 3, 1949; d. Allen Herbert and Phyllis Ann (Fearon) Fuller; m. Gene Angelo Vitagliano, Feb. 10, 1973 (div. 1998); children: Marissa Ariana, Marc Anthony, Michael Allen. BA in English, SUNY, Buffalo, 1971, EdM in English Education, 1973; cert. creative studies, SUC, Buffalo, 1990. Cert. secondary English tchr. N.Y., sch. dist. adminstr., N.Y. Tchr. English grades 7-12 Buffalo Pub. Schs., N.Y., 1972-93, 95-97, tchr. of gifted grades 5-8, 1992-97; magnet sch. tchr. specialist Campus West Sch., Buffalo, 1993-95; asst. prin. Kensington H.S., Buffalo, 1997—2001, Grover Cleveland H.S., Buffalo, 2001—02; mid. sch. prin. Buffalo, 2002—. Facilitator Creative Problem Solving, 1990—; workshop presenter Buffalo Tchr. Ctr., 1992—; bd. dirs Parent, Tchr. and Student Cmty. Orgn of City Honors Sch., 1993—97, v.p., 1994—97; mem. Ednl. Leadership Buffalo, 1998, Supt. Adv. Com., 2000—02, Harvard Prin. Leadership Inst., 2003; lectr. in field. Singer Buffalo Philharm. Chorus, N.Y., 1973—, bd. dirs., 2002—; mem. Just Buffalo Literary Ctr., 1991—; del. Buffalo Tchrs. Fedn., 1992-97; choir Westminster Presbyn. Ch., 1998—; mem. Harvard Prins. Ctr. Leadership Inst., 2003. Grantee NEH, 1985; recipient Pathfinders award for sch./bus. partnership, 1995; Western N.Y. Writing Project fellow Canisius Coll., 1990, 95, 99; poetry collection editor 1995, 2002. Mem.: ASCD, Elem. Prins. Assn., Secondary Asst. Prins. Assn. (sec. 1998—2001), Coun. Tchrs. English, N.Y. State English Coun. (Tchr. of Excellence award 1991), Internat. Creativity Network, Creative Edn. Found., Creative Studies Alumni Assn. State U. Coll. Buffalo (newsletter editor 1991—95, v.p. 1992—96), Grad. Sch. Edn. Alumni Assn. SUNY Buffalo, Phi Delta Kappa. Avocations: singing, writing poetry, drama, reading. Home: 343 Sanders Rd Buffalo NY 14216-1420 Office: WEB # 71 Mid Sch 1409 E Delavan Ave Buffalo NY 14215 E-mail: kvitagliano@buffalo.k12.ny.us.

VITALE, FRANCIS M. preschool director; b. Bronx, N.Y., Dec. 26, 1937; d. Peter Robert and Vitina (Incandella) DiPaola; m. Anthony Joseph Vitale, Apr. 26, 1970; children: Stephanie Maria, Jeffrey Anthony. BA, Coll. of New Rochelle, 1991. Founder, dir. The Caring Place, Inc., New Rochelle, N.Y. Mem. Westchester Assn. for Edn. of Young Children, Child Care Coun. Westchester, New Rochelle C. of C. Home: 36 Robbins Rd New Rochelle NY 10801-1115

VITEK, VICTORIA LYNN, speech-language pathologist; b. St. Louis, Aug. 27, 1967; d. Ronald Vernon Vincent and Carol Marie (McCoy) Anderson; m. Scott Allen Vitek, Nov. 24, 1990. BS in Speech/Lang. Pathology, Ctrl. Mo. State U., Warrensburg, 1989, MS in Speech/Lang. Pathology, 1990; M in Regular and Spl. Edn. Adminstrn., U. Mo., Kansas City, 2002. Speech./lang. pathologist Kansas City (Kans.) Pub. Schs., 1990-97, Liberty (Mo.) Pub. Schs., 1997-99, Kearney (Mo.) Pub. Schs., 1999—. Lutheran. Home: 113 Lakeland Dr Smithville MO 64089-8878

VITZ, PAUL CLAYTON, psychologist, educator; b. Toledo, Aug. 27, 1935; m. Evelyn Birge; 6 children. BA high honors in Psychology, U. Mich., 1953; PhD, Stanford U., 1962. Instr. psychology Pomona (Calif.) Coll., 1962-64; asst. prof. NYU, 1965-70, assoc. prof., 1970-85, dir. psychology dept. undergrad. program, 1973-79, prof., 1985—, acting dir. master's program, 1988-89, 90-91, acting dir. grad. program, 1989-90. Adj. prof. John Paul II Inst. on Marriage and Family, Washington, 1990-2003, Internat. Acad. Philosophy, 1994-98, Inst. for Psychol. Scis., 2000—; lectr. in field. Author: Psychology as Religion: The Cult of Self-Worship, 1977, 2d edit., 1994, (with A.B. Glimcher) Modern Art and Modern Science: The Parallel Analysis of Vision, 1984, Censorship: Evidence of Bias in Our Children's Textbooks, 1986, Sigmund Freud's Christian Unconscious, 1988, Faith of the Fatherless: The Psychology of Atheism, 1999; editor: (with S. Krason) Defending the Family: A Sourcebook, 1998; contbr. articles to profl. jours., chpts. to books. Rsch. grantee Nat. Inst. Mental Health, 1963-64, 64-66, 66-67, Nat. Inst. Neurol. Diseases and Blindness grantee, 1970-73, 73-74, Shalom Found. grantee, 1974-78, Nat. Inst. Edn. grantee, 1983, 84-85, Dept. Edn. grantee, 1986-87. Office: NYU Dept Psychology New York NY 10003

VIVARELLI, DANIEL GEORGE, SR., special education and learning disabilities educator, consultant; b. Vineland, N.J., May 25, 1947; s. Daniel Thomas and Lillian Rachel (Johnson) V.; m. Judith Alice Moses, July 12, 1969; children: Cara Marie, Daniel George Jr. BA in Spl. Edn., Trenton State Coll., 1969; MEd in Learning Disabilities, Glassboro (N.J.) State Coll., 1972, postgrad., 1986. Cert. prin./supr., N.J.; cert. tchr. of handicapped, N.J., learning disabilities tchr./cons., N.J. Tchr. of handicapped Vineland Pub. Schs., 1969-72, learning disabilities tchr., cons., 1972-75, Camden County Tech. Schs., Sicklerville, NJ, 1975—2003, chmn. child study team, 1978—2003. Mem. Cumberland County Tech. Edn. Ctr. Bd. Edn. Mem. Collegiate Basketball Ofcls. Assn., Vocat. Indsl. Clubs Am. Lutheran. Home: 114 Sycamore Ln Vineland NJ 08361-2953 E-mail: vivmom@aol.com.

VIVELO, JACQUELINE JEAN, author, English language educator; b. Lumberton, Miss., Jan. 23, 1943; d. Jack and Virginia Olivia (Bond) Jones; m. Frank Robert Vivelo, June 19, 1965; 1 child, Alexandra J. BA, U. Tenn., Knoxville, 1965, MA, 1970. Caseworker N.Y.C. Dept. Welfare, 1965-66; instr. reading Knoxville Coll., 1968-70; instr. English Middlesex County Coll., Edison, N.J., 1970-72, U. Mo., Rolla, 1975-77, Middlesex County Coll., Edison, 1978-80, Lebanon Valley Coll., Annville, Pa., 1981-87, asst. prof. English, 1987-91. Author: Super Sleuth, 1985 (Best Book award), Beagle in Trouble, 1986, A Trick of the Light, 1987, Super Sleuth and the Bare Bones, 1988, Writing Fiction: A Handbook for Creative Writing, 1993, Reading to Matthew, 1993 (Best Book award), Mr. Scatter's Magic Spell, 1993, Chills Run Down My Spine, 1994, Have You Lost Your Kangaroo?, 1995, Chills in the Night, 1997, Miss Topple Walks on Air, 1998; editor: College Education Achievement Project's Handbook for College Reading Teachers, 1969; co-editor: American Indian Prose and Poetry, 1974: contbr. articles/short stories to various publs. Recipient Best Book award Am. Child Study Assn., 1985, Young Book Trust, U.K., 1994, Pa. Coun. of the Arts Fellowship award for Lit., 1992; NIMH grantee, 1969-70. Mem. Children's Lit. Coun. Pa. (v.p. 1991), Soc. Children's Book Writers, Mystery Writers Am., Sigma Tau Delta (sponsor Omicron Omicron chpt. 1988-90), Pi Lambda Theta. Home: 3205 Rinconada Cir Santa Fe NM 87507

VIZZINI, CAROL REDFIELD, symphony musician, music educator; b. San Diego, Jan. 3, 1946; d. Ernest Sylvester and Eleanor Diana (Soneson) Redfield; m. Edward Tracy Browning (div. 1981); children: Victor, Charlotte; m. Joseph Russell Vizzini, Apr. 12, 1997. MusB, Phila. Musical Acad., 1968. Prin. cellist Somerset Hills Symphony, Basking Ridge, N.J., 1971-81, New Philharm. of N.W. N.J., Morristown, 1978-87; asst. prin. cellist Princeton (N.J.) Chamber Symphony, 1985-95; prin. cellist Orch. St. Peter-by-the-Sea, Point Pleasant, N.J., 1987-92; instr. in cello Westminster Conservatory, Rider U., Princeton, 1987—, head string dept., 1992—. Chamber music coach Vt. Music and Arts Ctr., Lyndonville, 1980-81; coach Greater Princeton Youth Orch., 1989-92; chamber music coach N.J. Youth Symphonies, Summit, 1989—; chamber music coord. Westminster Conservatory, 1991-98. Author: Cello Scales, Volume One (One and Two Octave Scales), 1997, Cello Scales, Volume Two (Three and Four Octave Scales), 2000. Mem. Am. String Tchrs. Assn., Am. Fedn. Musicians, Music Tchrs. Nat. Assn. (string coord. 1989-93). Avocations: gardening, fly fishing, travel. Office: Westminster Conservatory of Music Rider Univ 101 Walnut Ln Princeton NJ 08540-3819 E-mail: cjvizzini@earthlink.net.

VLACH, ROSE ANNE, elementary school teacher; b. Michigan City, Ind., Oct. 18, 1960; d. Joseph W. Jr. and Rose E. (May) P. BA, Purdue U., 1982; MEd, U. Houston, 1987. Cert. ednl. diagnostician, Tex. 1988; cert. elem. tchr. Tex, 1984, spl. edn. Tex., 1984. Resource room tchr. Dodson Elem. Sch., Houston, 1983-90, generic spl. edn. tchr., 1990-94; life skills tchr. Piney Point Elem. Sch., Houston, 1994—99; ednl. diagnostician Cobb Elem., Channelview, Tex., 2001—. Mem. Reading is Fundamental Com., Houston, 1988-94. Author: (computer software) What's the Weather?, 1983. Mem. Rite of Christian Initiation of Adults Team St. Francis de Sales, Houston, 1992-95, lector, 1994-99; vol. income tax assistance IRS, Houston, 1994-97. Recipient Spl. Edn. Tchr. of Yr. award, Houston, 1997. Roman Catholic. Home: 14330 Long Shadow Dr Houston TX 77015-1735 Office: Cobb Elem 915 Dell Dale Channelview TX 77530

VLADUTIU, ADRIAN O. physician, educator; b. Bucharest, Romania, Aug. 5, 1940; came to U.S., 1969, naturalized 1974; s. Octavian and Veturia (Chirescu) V.; m. Georgirene D. Therrien; children: Christina Lynn, Catherine Joy. MD, Sch. Medicine, Bucharest, 1962; PhD in Immunopathology, Sch. Medicine, Jassy, Romania, 1968. Diplomate Am. Bd. Pathology. Asst. prof. physiopathology Sch. Medicine, Bucharest, 1968-71; assoc. prof. pathology SUNY Sch. Medicine, Buffalo, 1978-81, prof. pathology, 1981—; pathologist Buffalo Gen. Hosp., 1974—, dir. clin. labs., 1982—2001, prof. microbiology, 1982—, prof. medicine, 1985—. Cons. Niagara Falls (N.Y.) Meml. Hosp., 1976—82, Tri-County Hosp., Gowanda, NY, 1991—93; acting head dept. pathology Buffalo Gen. Hosp, 1985—86; dir. lab. Deaconess Hosp. Buffalo, 1982—91, Columbus Meml., Buffalo, 1996—98. Author: Pleural Effusion, 1986; contbr. chapters to books, articles to profl. jours. Med. Rsch. Coun. Can. fellow, 1968, Buswell fellow, 1969; recipient rsch. award Ministry Edn. Romania, 1965, rsch. award NIH, 1985. Fellow: ACP, Nat. Acad. Clin. Biochemistry, Coll. Am. Pathologists; mem.: Soc. Exptl. Biol. Medicine, Am. Soc. Investigative Pathology, Assn. Am. Immunologists. Achievements include first demonstration of the association of autoimmunity with major histocompability antigens. Home: 80 Oakview Dr Buffalo NY 14221-1420

VOCE, JOAN A. CIFONELLI, retired elementary school educator; b. Utica, N.Y., Mar. 22, 1936; d. Albert and Theresa (Buono) Cifonelli; m. Eugene R. Voce Sr., Aug. 16, 1958; children: Eugene R. Jr., Lisa V. Stewart, Mark L., Daniel A. BS in Elem. Edn., Coll. St. Rose, Albany, N.Y., 1958; MS in Elem. Edn., SUNY, Cortland, 1981. Elem. tchr. Utica (N.Y.) Pub. Schs., 1958-59, 61-62, 64-67; tchr. Deerfield Elem. Sch., Whitesboro (N.Y.) Ctrl. Sch. Dist., 1968-91. Vol. Presbyn. Home for Ctrl. N.Y.; mem. St. Anne's Ch., Whitesboro, NY, Our Lady of Hope Ch., Port Orange, Fla. Mem. AAUW (Mohawk Valley br.), N.Y. State United Tchrs., Whitesboro Ret. Tchrs. Assn., Am. Assn. Ret. Persons, Oneida County Ret. Tchrs. Assn. (sec.), N.Y. State Ret. Tchrs. Assn., Coll. of St. Rose Alumni Assn., Utica Symphony League, Mohawk Valley Performing Arts, Pelican Bay Country Club (Daytona Beach, Fla.), Skenandoa Golf and Country Club (Clinton, NY), Alpha Delta Kappa (v.p. 1974-76, pres. 1976-78, corr. sec. 1972-74, rec. sec. 1986-88, 90-91). Avocations: reading, travel, golf, gourmet cooking, theatre. Home: 109 Birchwood Ln Whitesboro NY 13492-2517 Address: 201 Surf Scooter Dr Daytona Beach FL 32119 E-mail: jcvoce@webtv.net.

VODYANOY, VITALY JACOB, biophysicist, educator; b. Kiev, Ukraine, USSR, June 2, 1941; came to U.S., 1979; s. Jacob and Vera (Reznik) V.; m. Galina Rubin, Apr. 22, 1967; 1 child, Valerie. MS in Physics, Moscow Physical Engring. Inst., 1964; PhD in Biophysics, Agrophysical Rsch. Inst., Leningrad, USSR, 1973. Asst. prof. Inst. of Semiconductors, Leningrad, USSR, 1965-72; assoc. prof. A.F. Ioffe Physicotech. U., Leningrad, 1972-78; sr. rsch. scientist NYU, 1979-82; rsch. assoc. U. Calif., Irvine, 1982-89; assoc. prof. Auburn (Ala.) U., 1989-93, prof., 1993—. Ad hoc reviewer NSF, Washington, 1985—; dir. Biosensor Lab. of Inst. for Biol. Detection Sys. Author: (with others) Membrane Biophysics, 1971, Physics of Solid State and Neutron Scattering, 1974, Receptors Events and Transduction Mechanisms in Taste and Olfaction, 1989, Molecular Electronics: Biosensors and Biocomputers, 1989, Central Nervous System Neurotransmitters and Neuromodulators, 1994; contbr. more than 80 articles to profl. jours.; inventor device for film deposition, methods for forming monolayers. Grantee NSF-U. Calif., 1982-85, 85-88, U.S. Army Rsch. Office, 1985-88, U. Calif., 1986-88, 88-92, U. Calif., FAA, 1993-97, 2001—, Battelle, 1997-2000, NSF, 1998-2000, Def. Advanced Rsch. Projects Agy., Auburn U., 2000—, Tech. Support Working Group, 2002—, others; recipient Animal Health award Pfizer, 2000. Mem. AAAS, Am. Phys. Soc., Biophys. Soc., Fedn. Am. Socs. for Exptl. Biology, Soc. for Neurosci., Phi Beta Delta, Phi Zeta. Republican. Jewish. Avocation: medical herbs. Office: Auburn U Coll of Vet Medicine 212 Greene Hall Auburn AL 36849-6121 E-mail: vodyavi@vetmed.auburn.edu.

VOEGTLIN-ANDERSON, MARY MARGARET, secondary school educator, music educator; b. Seattle, Wash. d. Joseph Walter and Veronica Margaret (Conroy) Voegtlin; m. Terry Lee Anderson, Mar. 19, 1977 (div. July 20, 1982). BA cum laude, Marylhurst U., 1963; postgrad., U. Wash., 1963—65, Oakland U., 1968, Seattle Pacific U., 1982—84. Cert. std. tchg. grades K-12 Wash. Profl. cellist Oreg. Symphony, Portland, 1962—63; tchr. music and humanities Chinook Middle Sch., Seattle, 1963—89, gifted edn. specialist, 1983—89; tchr. music, music dept. chair Highline H.S., Seattle, 1989—, tchr. honors English, 1989—. Contralto soloist Mt. Baker Pk. Presbyn. Ch., 1966—68, U. Congl. Ch., Seattle, 1968—73; profl. singer Seattle Opera Co., 1968—70; vocal coach, advisor Highline Jazz Ensemble, Seattle, 1990—2003; pvt. piano and voice tchr., Seattle, 1991—; astronomy club advisor Highline H.S., Seattle, 1998—2003; dir. Highline Dist. Youth Orch., 2003, Burien Sr. Choir, 2003; trustee Sunlight Waters Corp., 2002—. Contbr. articles to profl. jours. Officer, sec. 46th Legis. Dist. Dem. Party, Seattle, 1974—78, chairperson Initiative 314 Campaign, 1975; Wash. state conv. del. Dem. Party, Olympia, 1976, Dem. precinct chairperson Seattle, 1976—77. Grantee Fulbright Scholarship grant, Nat. Tchrs. Performance Inst., Oberlin Coll., Ohio, 1970. Mem.: NEA, Nat. Coun. Tchrs. English, Seattle Astron. Soc., Music Educators' Nat. Conf. Roman Catholic. Avocations: astronomy, reading, bicycling, writing, hiking. Office: Highline HS 225 S 152nd St Seattle WA 98148 E-mail: mvanderson@aol.com., Mvanderson03@aol.com.

VOGEL, DIANE OSCHERWITZ, primary education educator; b. Cin., Nov. 1, 1951; d. Louis and Florence (Small) Oscherwitz; m. Edward Herschel Vogel, Nov. 30, 1975; children: Steven, Ross. BS in Edn., Miami U., Oxford, Ohio, 1973; MEd, Ga. State U., 1975. Cert. tchr., Ga. Tchr. spl. edn. DeKalb County Schs., Decatur, Ga., 1973-82; primary tchr. Hebrew Acad., Atlanta, 1982-85, Bibb County Bd. Edn., Macon, Ga., 1986—. Sundy sch. prin. Congregation Sherah Israel, Macon, 1989-94; host family Ga. Jr. Miss State Program, Macon, 1989—. Mem. Profl. Assn. Ga. Educators, Mid. Ga. Reading Coun., Hadassah (life). Avocation: prodigy computer network. Home: 527 Commanche Dr Macon GA 31210-4204 Office: Redding Elem Sch 8062 Eisenhower Pkwy Lizella GA 31052-3202

VOGEL, GLORIA JEAN HILTS, secondary school educator; b. Detroit, Mar. 24, 1947; d. Roy Ellis and Helen Amanda (Ludwig) Hilts; m. Charles Orville Vogel, Oct. 6, 1973; children: Mark Robert, Amanda Jean. BA in English and History, Mich. State U., 1969; MA Tchg. in English, Fitchburg State U., 1978. English tchr. Woodbury Sch., Salem, NH, 1969-73, No. Mid. Sch., Westford, Mass., 1973-76, Westford Acad., 1976—98, Leominster HS, 1998—. Dealer 19th century Am. art, Townsend, Mass., 1973—. Webelos leader Boy Scouts Am., Townsend, 1989-91; mem. choir Townsend Congl. Ch.; founding mem. Wall of Tolerance, Nat. Campaign for Tolerance, 2002, Nat. Women's History Mus., 2002. Recipient Excellence in Tchr. award, Acad. Devel. Ctr., 2000. Mem. AAUW, NEA, Nat. Coun. Tchrs. English, Mass. Tchrs. Assn., Westford Edn. Assn., Nat. Women's History Mus., Leominster Edn. Assn. Democrat. Home: 3 Sycamore Dr Townsend MA 01469-1312 Office: Leominster High Sch 122 Granite St Leominster MA 01453

VOGEL, H. VICTORIA, psychotherapist, trauma, post-traumatic stress disorder and addiction recovery counselor and educator, author; BA, U. Md., 1968; MA, NYU, 1970, 75; MEd, Columbia U., 1982, postgrad., 1982—; cert., Am. Projective Drawing Inst., 1983; CASAC, New Sch. U. for Social Rsch., 2000. Diplomate Am. Acad. Experts in Traumatic Stress; cert. addiction recovery counselor, expert in traumatic stress, alcohol and substance abuse counselor, addictions treatment, addiction counseling alcohol and substance abuse. Art therapist Childville, Bklyn., 1962-64; tchr. Montgomery County (Md.) Jr. H.S., 1968-69; with H.S. divsn. N.Y.C. Bd. Edn., 1970—; guidance counselor, instr., psychotherapist in pvt. practice. Guidance counselor, instr., psychotherapist in pvt. practice; clin. counseling cons. psychodiagnosis and devel. studies, art/play therapy The Modern Sch., 1984—; art/play therapist Hosp. Ctr. for Neuromuscular Disease and Devel. Disorders, 1986—; employment counselor-adminstr. N.Y. State Dept. Labor Concentrated Employment Program, 1971-72; intern psychotherapy and psychoanalysis psychiat. divsn. Ctrl. Islip Hosp., 1973-75, Calif. Grad. Inst., L.A.; intern psychol. counseling and rehab. N.J. Coll. Medicine, Newark, 1979. Author: The Never Ending Story of Alcohol, Drugs and Other Substance Abuse, 1992, Variant Sexual Behavior and the Aesthetic Modern Nudes, 1992, Psychological Science of School Behavior Intervention, 1993, Joycean Conceptual Modernism: Relationships and Deviant Sexuality, 1995, Electronic Evil Eyes, 1995 (U.S. Cert. of Recognition, 1996), Psychological Paradigms of Alcohol Violence Suicide Trauma Addiction Variant Pathologies PTSD and Schizophrenia, 1999. Mem. com. for spl. events NYU, 1989; participant clin. and artistic perspectives Am. Acad. Psychoanalysis Conf., 1990, participant clin. postmodernism and psychoanalysis, 1996; aux. police officer N.Y. Police Dept., 1994—; chair bylaws com. Columbia U., 1995—. Mem.: ACA, AAAS, APA, Tchrs. Coll. Adminstrv. Women in Edn., Assn. Humanistic Psychology (exec. sec. 1981), Art/Play Therapy, N.Y. Art Tchrs. Assn., Am. Acad. Experts Traumatic Stress (diplomate in expert traumatic stress), Am. Soc. Group Psychotherapy and Psychodrama (publs. com. 1984—), Am. Orthopsychiat. Assn., Am. Psychol. Soc., Phi Delta Kappa (editor chpt. newsletter 1981—84, exec. sec. Columbia U. chpt. 1984—, chmn. nominating com. for chpt. officers 1986—, rsch. rep. 1986—, pub. rels. exec. bd. dirs. 1991, NYU chpt. v.p. programs 1994—).

VOGEL, RUTH ANNE, retired elementary school educator; b. Dayton, Ohio, Sept. 26, 1938; d. William Luther and Orpha May (Albright) Gaugh; m. Aug. 13, 1960 (div. Feb. 1973). BS in Edn., Otterbein Coll., 1961; postgrad., Ind. U., 1964, Otterbein Coll., 1976, Ohio State U., 1990, postgrad., 1998, Ohio U., 1998. Cert. elem. tchr., Ohio. Tchr. Bath (Ohio)-Richfield Bd. Edn., 1961, Lorain (Ohio) Bd. Edn., 1961-63, South Bend (Ind.) Bd. Edn., 1963-66, Columbus (Ohio) Bd. Edn., 1978-99; ret., 1999. 5th and 6th grade phys. edn. South Bend Bd. Edn., 1963-66, adult phys. edn., 1963-66; choral dir. Gladstone Elem., Columbus Bd. Edn., 1978-80; profl. devel. Starling Middle Sch. and Ohio State U., Columbus, 1992-93; chpt. 1 sch. wide project Staring Middle Sch., Columbus, 1994. Author: (manuscript) The Franklinton Spirit, 1999. Vol. Cancer Soc., Columbus, 1988—, Heart Fund, 1988—; leader Together Against Panic, 1990—. Mem.: NEA, Columbus Edn. Assn., Ind. Edn. Assn., Ohio Edn. Assn. Avocations: music, reading, needlework, gardening, camping.

VOGEL, SALLY THOMAS, psychologist, social worker, educator; b. Joplin, Mo., July 3, 1925; d. Clyde Albert Thomas and Kathryn (Waite) Thompson; m. F. Lincoln Vogel, Sept. 4, 1946; children: Kathryn Duchin, Linda, Robert L. BA, Beaver Coll., 1947; MEd, North Adams State Coll., 1969; EdS, Seton Hall U., 1995. Case worker Pa. Dept. Welfare, Phila., 1947-48; high sch. tchr. Downington High Sch., Coatesville, Pa., 1969-71; sch. social worker Delaware Valley High Sch., Frenchtown, N.J., 1970-84; study team coord. Holland Twp. Sch., Milford, N.J., 1975-85, sch. social worker, 1975-90, guidance counselor, 1990-94; sch. psychologist Lake Shore Sch. Dist., St. Clair Shores, Mich., 1998—2002. Instr. in Parent Effectiveness and Tchr. Effectiveness, Hunt County Adult Edn., N.J., 1975-84; advanced trainee Edn. Tng. Inst., Calif., 1984-89; presenter in field. Acting exec. dir. Big Bros./Big Sisters (founder), Hunterdon County, N.J., 1976. Recipient Ed Kiley Svc. award Big Bros./Big Sisters, 1978. Mem.: AAUW, NASP, MASP. Office: Lake Shore Sch Dist Violet Sch 22020 Violet Saint Clair Shores MI 48081

VOGEL, VICTOR GERALD, medical educator, researcher; b. Bethlehem, Pa., Mar. 14, 1952; s. Victor Gerald Jr. and Margaret Moser (Smith) V.; m. Saralyn Sue Schaffner, June 25, 1977; children: Heather Marie, Christiaan Keith. Diplomate Am. Bd. Internal Medicine, Am. Bd. Preventive Medicine, Nat. Bd. Med. Examiners. Resident in internal medicine Balt. City Hosps., 1978-81; fellow in med. oncology Johns Hopkins Oncology Ctr., Balt., 1983-86; Andrew W. Mellon fellow Johns Hopkins Sch. Hygiene Pub. Health, Balt., 1984-86; asst. prof. medicine and epidemiology U. Tex./M.D. Anderson Cancer Ctr., Houston, 1986-93, assoc. prof. clin. cancer prevention, 1993-95; asst. prof. epidemiology U. Tex. Sch. Pub. Health, Houston, 1987-95; prof. medicine and epidemiology U. Pitts. Cancer Inst./Magee-Womens Hosp., 1996—, dir. MAGEE/UPCI breast cancer program, 1996—2002, dir. MAGEE/UPCI breast cancer prevention program, 2003—. Epidemiologist Tex. breast screening project Am. Cancer Soc., 1986-93; mem. data and safety monitoring bd. Women's Health Initiative, NIH, 1994—; bd. dirs. Nat. Surg. Adjuvant Breast and Bowel Project Found., Inc., 1997—, AMC Cancer Ctr., Denver, 1996-99; protocol chmn. Nat. Cancer Inst. Study of Tamoxifen and Raloxifene. Contbr. articles to profl. jours. Founding mem. Nat. Surg. adjuvant Breast and Bowel Project Found., Inc. Served with USPHS, 1981-83. Named Med. Vol. of Yr., Am. Cancer Soc., 1983, award 1987, career devel. award, 1990-93; fellow Susan G. Komen Breast Cancer Found., 1990-93. Fellow Am. Coll. Preventive Medicine, ACP; mem. Am. Soc. Clin. Oncology, Am. Soc. Preventive Oncology, Christian Med. and Dental Assn., Am. Assn. Cancer Rsch. Republican. Presbyterian. Avocation: flying. Office: University of Pittsburgh Cancer Inst Magee-Womens Hosp 300 Halket St Rm 3524 Pittsburgh PA 15213-3108 E-mail: vvogel@mail.magee.edu.

VOGELEY, CLYDE EICHER, JR., engineering educator, artist, consultant; b. Pitts., Oct. 19, 1917; s. Clyde Eicher and Eva May (Reynolds) V.; m. Blanche Wormington Peters, Dec. 15, 1947; children: Eva Anne, Susan Elizabeth Steele. BFA in Art Edn., Carnegie Mellon U., 1940; BS in Engring. Physics, U. Pitts., 1944, PhD in Math., 1949. Art supr. Pub. Sch. System, Spingdale, Pa., 1940-41; rsch. engr. Westinghouse Rsch. Labs., East Pitts., Pa., 1944-54; adj. prof. math. U. Pitts., 1954-64; sr. scientist Bettis Atomic Power Lab., West Mifflin, Pa., 1956-59, supr. tech. tng., 1959-71; mgr. Bettis Reactor Engring. Sch., West Mifflin, 1971-77, dir., 1977-92; cons. U.S. Dept. Energy, Washington, 1992-95. Cons. Bettis Atomic Power Lab., W. Mifflin, 1954-56; U.S. Navy Nuclear Power Schs., Mare Island, Calif., Bainbridge, Md., 1959-69. Author: (grad. sch. course) Non-linear Differential Equations, 1954; (rev. text) Ordinary Differential Equations, Rev. edit. 5, Shock and Vibration Problems, Rev. Edit. 6, 1991; rsch. report distributed to Brit., Can. and U.S. Govts. for use in design of airborne radar systems, 1944; oil painting represented in permanent Latrobe collection; acrylics, water colors and Christmas card designs in several pvt. collections; oil painting included in Barbara H. Nakle's A Unique Vision of Art, 1997, water color included in collection Superior Ct. of Pa. 1999. Pres., trustee Whitehall (Pa.) Pub. Libr., 1985. Recipient letter of commendation naval reactors br. USN, 1992. Mem. IEEE (life), Am. Phys. Soc., Assoc. Artists Pitts. (hon.), Pitts. Watercolor Soc., Sigma Xi, Sigma Pi Sigma, Sigma Tau. Presbyterian. Achievements include patents for Automatic Continuous Wave Radar Tracking System, Modulating Signals Passing Along Ridged Waveguides, Ridged Waveguide Matching Device, Method for Joining Several Ridged Waveguides, Antenna Feed Modulation Unit, others. Home: c/o Susan Steele 102 Appletree Dr Beaver PA 15009

VOGELMAN, LAWRENCE ALLEN, law educator. lawyer; b. Bklyn., Feb. 24, 1949; s. Herman and Gertrude (Wohl) V.; m. Deborah Malka, Jan. 24, 1971 (div. Aug. 1980); m. Marcia Sikowitz, Mar. 3, 1985 (div. Nov. 1999). BA, Bklyn. Coll., 1970; JD, Bklyn. Law Sch., 1973. Bar: N.Y. 1974, U.S. Dist. Ct. (so. and ea. dists.) N.Y. 1975, U.S. Ct. Appeals (2d cir.) 1975, U.S. Ct. Appeals (3d cir.) 1983, U.S. Supreme Ct. 1983, N.H. 1994, U.S. Dist. Ct. N.H. 1994, U.S. Ct. Appeals (1st cir.) 2001. Trial atty. Legal Aid Soc., NYC, 1973-77; assoc. appellate counsel Criminal Appeals Bur., NYC, 1977-78; clin. prof. law Yeshiva U. Benjamin N. Cardozo Sch. Law, NYC, 1979-93; dep. dir. NH Pub. Defender, Concord, NH, 1993-97; ptnr. Shuchman, Krause & Vogelman, PLLC, 1997—. Adj. prof. law Franklin Pierce Law Ctr., 1994-98; faculty Inst. for Criminal Def. Advocacy, 1995—; program dir. Max Freund Litigation Ctr., 1984—; team leader Emory U. Trial Techniques Program, Atlanta, 1981-89, NJ region, Nat. Inst. Trial Advocacy, 1997—; faculty N.E. region, Nat. Inst. Trial Advocacy, 1985—, Tom C. Clark Ctr. for Advocacy, Hofstra U. Sch. Law, 1985—, Legal Aid Soc. Trial Advocacy Program, 1986-89, Widener U. Law Sch. Intensive Trial Program, 1987-91, U. San Francisco Intensive Trial Advocacy Program, 1991—; mem. indigent's assigned counsel panel, appellate div. First Dept., NYC, 1979-94; crminal justice act panel US Dist. Ct. (so. and ea. dist.) NY, 1985-94, dist. NH, 1997—; adminstrv. law judge NYC Environ. Control Bd., 1980-81. Author, editor: Cases and Materials on Clinical Legal Education, 1979; editor revisions to Eyewitness Identification. Pres. bd. trustees Woodward Park Sch., 1990—94; bd. dirs., legal coun. N.H. Civil Liberties Union. Fellow: Am. Bd. Criminal Lawyers; mem.: ATLA (exec. com. civil rights sect.), N.H. Trial Lawyers Assn., N.Y. State Defenders Assn., N.H. Bar Assn. (ethics com. 1995—, dispute resolution com. 1999—, bd. law examiners 1999—, fed. ct. adv. com. 2002—, sec. fed. practice sect. 2003—), N.H. Assn. Criminal Defense Lawyers, Nat. Assn. Criminal Defense Lawyers, Soc. Am. Law Tchrs., Assn. Legal Aid Attys. (chmn. bargaining com. 1974—79, exec. v.p. 1977—78, exec. com. 1984—86), Assn. of Bar of City of N.Y., Fortune Soc. (exec. com., bd. dirs.), Am. Inns of Ct. (master Daniel Webster Inn), Order of Barristers. Democrat. Jewish. Achievements include notable cases such as: People vs. Joel Steinberg, represented co-defendant, Hedda Nussbaum in homicide death Lisa Steinberg; US vs. Falvey, in which Irish Rep. Army supporters were acquitted of gun running because of knowledge and approval of CIA; Bell vs. Coughlin, which involved highly publicized homicide of 2 NY police officers; People vs. Roche, which established agy. def. to drug sale in State of NY highest ct.; US vs. Joseph, which appealed convictions in Brinks case. Home: 22 Cedar Point Rd Durham NH 03824 Office: Shuchman Krause & Vogelman PLLC PO Box 220 Exeter NH 03833-0220 E-mail: lav@sisna.com., larryvpd@aol.com.

VOGES, ALICE FURBY, retired secondary school educator, real estate agent; b. Brush, Colo., Jan. 14, 1930; d. Ross Andrew and Marie Margaret (Dreith) Furby; m. Kenneth O. Voges, Sept. 1, 1949; children: Jan Marie Voges Reaver, James Kenneth. BA in Speech Edn., Pacific U., 1952. Grad. Realtor Inst. Tchr. Shumway Jr. H.S., Vancouver, Wash., 1952-54, Banks (Oreg.) H.S., 1955-57, Tillamook (Oreg.) H.S., 1960-88, speech coach, 1964-88; realtor Schmidt Real Estate, Tillamook, 1979-82, Pete Anderson Realty, Inc., Tillamook, 1982—. Bd. dirs. Tillamook Sch. Dist. 9, 1989—, Habitat for Humanity, 1999—, Guideon Auxiliary, 2002—; mem. Oreg. Sch. Bds. Assn. Dist. 5, 1993; pres. Aid Assn. of Luths., Trivent Fraternal for Lutherans, Br. 1553, 1993-96; mem. ch. choir, 1990—. Named to Speech Coach Hall of Fame, Oreg. H.S. Speech League, 1990. Mem. AAUW, Nat. Sch. Bds. Assn. (del. conv. Anaheim, Calif. 1993, San Francisco, 1995, Orlando, Fla. 1996), Delta Kappa Gamma (v.p. Alpha Gamma chpt. 1994). Republican. Lutheran. Avocations: bridge, traveling, grandchildren. Office: Pete Anderson Realty Inc Advantage Real Estate Network 709 Pacific Ave Tillamook OR 97141-3823

VOGLER, DIANE CLARK, elementary school principal; b. McGehee, Ark., Jan. 11, 1945; d. Stuart Emerson and Mamye Tompye (Campbell) Clark; m. Richard Joseph Vogler, June 16, 1968 (dec. Nov. 1979); children: Amy Diane, Jodi Leigh. BSE, Ark. A&M Coll., 1966; MSE, U. Ark., 1975, EdS, 1983. Cert. elem. adminstr., Ark. Tchr. 6th grade McGehee Pub. Schs., 1966-67; tchr. 5th grade North Little Rock (Ark.) Schs., 1967-68, tchr. 6th grade, 1970-73, tchr. math. grades 1-6, 1975-80; tchr. 6th grade Manhattan (Kans.) Pub. Schs., 1968-70; tchr. 1st grade Pulaski County Spl. Schs., North Little Rock, 1980-85, prin., 1985—, Sylvan Hills Elem., Pulaski County Special Sch. Dist., Sherwood, Ark., 1990—. Mem., dean West Gulf Regional Sch. of Christian Mission United Meth. Women, North Little Rock, 1980—; del. Ark. Dems., Little Rock, 1988; active Sylvan Hills Elem. PTA; dir women's divsn. of the gen. bd. Global Ministries United Meth. Ch., 1996—. Recipient Tchr. of Yr. award Ark. PTA Coun., 1985, Ednl. Excellence award Greater Little Rock C. of C., 1985; named Elem. Prin. of Yr. Pulaski County Spl. Sch. Dist., 1994. Mem. ASCD, Internat. Reading Assn., Nat. Assn. Elem. Sch. Prins., Ctrl. Ark. Reading Coun., Ark. Assn. Elem. Prins. (zone dir. 1990-93), Pulaski County Adminstrs. Assn. (pres. 1989-90), Pulaski County Elem. Prins.' Forum (pres. 1993-94), Sherwood Rotary Club, Delta Kappa Gamma (pres. 1981-82), Phi Delta Kappa. Democrat. Avocations: music, needlework, travel. Office: Pulaski County Spl Sch Dist 402 Dee Jay Hudson Dr Sherwood AR 72120-2302

VOGT, ROCHUS EUGEN, physicist, educator; b. Neckarelz, Germany, Dec. 21, 1929; came to U.S., 1953; s. Heinrich and Paula (Schaefer) V.; m. Micheline Alice Yvonne Bauduin, Sept. 6, 1958; children: Michele, Nicole. Student, U. Karlsruhe, Germany, 1950-52, U. Heidelberg, 1952-53; SM, U. Chgo., 1957, PhD, 1961. Asst. prof. physics Calif. Inst. Tech., Pasadena, 1962-65, assoc. prof., 1965-70, prof., 1970—2002, R. Stanton Avery disting. svc. prof., 1982—2002, R. Stanton Avery disting. svc. prof. and prof. physics emeritus, 2002—, chmn. faculty, 1975-77, chief scientist Jet Propulsion Lab., 1977-78, chmn. div. physics, math. and astronomy, 1978-83, acting dir. Owens Valley Radio Obs., 1980-81, v.p. and provost, 1983-87. Vis. prof. physics MIT, 1988-94; dir. Caltech/MIT Laser Interferometer Gravitational Wave Observatory Project, 1987-94. Author: Cosmic Rays (in World Book Ency.), 1978, (with R.B. Leighton) Exercises in Introductory Physics, 1969; contbr. articles to profl. jours. Fulbright fellow, 1953-54; recipient Exceptional Sci. Achievement medal NASA, 1981, Profl. Achievement award U. Chgo. Alumni Assn., 1981. Fellow AAAS, A. Phys. Soc. Achievements include research in astrophysics and gravitation. Office: Calif Inst Tech Dept Physics 103-33 Pasadena CA 91125-0001 E-mail: vogt@caltech.edu.

VOGT, SHARON MADONNA, writer, educator; b. St. Ann, Mo., June 12, 1963; d. Ralph Paul and Jane Louise (Sandberg) V. BS in Edn., Northeast Mo. State U., 1985; MAT, Webster U., 1989. Cert. tchr., Mo. Tchr., coord. math. St. Cletus Sch., St. Charles, Mo., 1986-88; writer, math. editor Ligature, Inc., St. Louis, 1989-90; tchr., math. adviser Pattonville Adult Edn., St. Ann, Mo., 1991-93; dir., cons. math. ednl. svcs. Vogt Cons., Madison, Wis., 1991—. Author: Math Review, 1991, Math Journal Writing and Problem Solving, 1991, vol. 2, 1995, Linking Math and Literature, 1992, Graphing, 1992, Money Fun, 1993, Multicultural Math., 1995, Middle School Multicultural Math. Activities, 1995, Geometry Activities, 1995, Middle School Journal Writing, 1995, Pre-Algebra, 1996, Geometry, 1996, Algebra, 1996, Problem Solving Test Bank, 1996, Multicultural Algebra Activities, 1996, Olympic Math., 1996. Mem. Nat. Coun. Tchrs. Math., Alpha Phi Sigma. Avocations: music, nature walks, racquetball, crafts. Home and Office: 513 Seven Nations Dr Madison WI 53713-3389 E-mail: smvogt@mathwriter.com., ashleyshea@earthlink.net.

VOIGHT, MICHAEL LEE, physical education educator; b. Missoula, Mont., July 27, 1959; s. Robin Lee and Elaine Susan (Johnson) Voight; m. Cissy Margie Irving, May 9, 1992. BS, Portland (Oreg.)State U., 1981; MEd, U. Va., Charlottesville, 1982; DHSc, U. St. Augustine, Fla., 1995. Dir. Sportsmedicine Sports Clinic, Miami, Fla., 1984—89; chief sports medicine STAR Sportsmedicine, Miami, 1989—91; nat. dir. sportsmedicine Sports PT, Bryn Mawr, Pa., 1991—93; dir. Berkshire Inst., Reading, Pa., 1993—98; asst. prof. U. Miami Sch. of Medicine, Miami, 1985—2000; prof. Belmont U. Sch. of Phys. Tng., Nashville, 1998—. Cons. phys. therapist Miami (Fla.) Heat Basketball, 1988—93; Cons. phys. therapist Miami Dolphins Football Club, 1989—91; phys. therapist Pan Am Games, Havana, Cuba, 1991; phys. therapist Olympic Games, Atlanta, 1996; bd. dirs. Jour. Orthopedic Sports, 2000—. Author (editor): (Book) Orthopedic Rehabilitation Techniques, 2001; contbr. chapters to books, 2000. Mem.: Internat. Fedn. Sports Amsterdam (sec. 2000—), Internat. Soc. for Arthroscopy, Knee Surgery and Orthopedic Sports Medicine, Am. Orthop. Soc. for Sports Medicine, Nat. Athletic Tng. Assn. (cert. athletic trainer), Am. Phys. Therapy Assn. (treas. sports. phys. therapy sect. 1990—95, v.p. sports phys.therapy sect. 2000—, cert. sports phys. therapist, cert. orthopedic phys. therapist). Avocations: skiing, sailing, travel. Office: Belmont Univ 1900 Belmont Blvd Nashville TN 37212

VOITLE, ROBERT ALLEN, college dean, physiologist; b. Parkersburg, W.Va., May 12, 1938; s. Ray Christian and Ruby Virginia (Hannaman) V.; m. Linda Ellen Loveday, Dec. 5, 1975; children: Robert Allen, Elizabeth Anne, Christian Blair, Vanessa Virginia. BS, W.Va. U., 1962; MS, W.Va., 1965; PhD, U. Tenn., 1969. Asst. in poultry U. Tenn., Knoxville, 1965-69; asst. prof. physiology U. Fla., Gainesville, 1969-75, assoc. prof., 1975-79; prof., head dept. poultry Calif. Poly. State U., San Luis Obispo, 1979-81; dean Coll. Agr., Auburn U., Ala., 1981—2000, prof. poultry sci., 2000—. Cons. Columbia Bank for Coops., S.C., 1972 Contbr. articles to sci. jours. Pres., other offices Alachua County Fair Assn., Gainesville, 1969-79. Recipient Pub. Service award Alachua County Commn., 1975; recipient Tchr. of Yr. award U. Fla., 1977, Golden Feather award Calif. Poly. Inst., 1982 Mem. Poultry Sci. Assn., So. Poultry Sci. Assn., Gainesville Jaycees (JCI senatorship), Sigma Xi, Gamma Sigma Delta Clubs: Elks. Episcopalian. Home: 2247 Longwood Dr Auburn AL 36830-7105 Office: Auburn U Coll Agr Auburn AL 36849 E-mail: rvoitle@ag.auburn.edu.

VOLK, CECILIA ANN, elementary education educator; b. Greensburg, Ind., Mar. 8, 1956; d. Paul George and Ruth (Martin) Volk. BS, Purdue U., 1978; MA in Edn., Ball State U., 1984. Cert. K-Primary tchr., Ind. Tchr. spl. edn. Greensburg Cmty. Schs., 1978-79; tchr. Decatur County Day Care, Greensburg, 1979-81; tchr. 1st grade St. Louis Sch., Batesville, Ind., 1983-91, kindergarten tchr., 1991—. tchr. kindergarten, 1991—. Mem. ASCD, Am. Assn. Family and Consumer Scis., Nat. Assn. Edn. Young Children, Ind. Assn. Edn. Young Chidren, Nat. Coun. Tchrs. Math., Ind. Home Econs. Assn., Nat. Cath. Ednl. Assn., Purdue Alumni Assn., Delta Kappa Gamma. Home: 1035 N Broadway St Greensburg IN 47240-1309 Office: St Louis Sch 17 E Saint Louis Pl Batesville IN 47006-1397

VOLKERING, MARY JOE, special education educator; b. Covington, Ky., Mar. 13, 1936; d. Everett Thomas and Edna Mae (Bohmer) Foley; m. Jack Lawrence Volkering, Aug. 19, 1961 (dec. Jan. 11, 1989); 1 child, Tara. BA, Thomas More Coll, 1961; MEd, U. Cin., 1977. Cert. educator of mentally handicapped, Ohio, Ky. Asst. engr. AT&T Co., Cin., 1956-63; tchr. severe & profound Comprehensive Care, Covington, Ky., 1970-76; tchr. mentally retarded Riverside Good Counsel Sch., Ft. Mitchell, Ky., 1976-79; tchr. trainable handicapped Covington (Ky.) Ind. Sch., 1979-99, spl. edn. cons., 1999—. Bd. dirs. No. Ky. Assn. for Retarded, Covington, 1980—; adj. prof. No. Ky. U., Highland Heights, 1987-88. Leader Girl Scout Troop, Ft. Wright, Ky., 1973. Named John Bauer Spl. Edn. Tchr. of the Yr. North Ky. Assn. Retarded, 1979, Tchr. of the Yr. G.O. Swing Sch., Covington Ind. Schs., 1986, Golden Apple Nominee Tchr., Ky. Post and Jaycees, 1988. Mem. No. Ky. Assn. Retarded (treas. 1984-86, sec. 1980-82). Democrat. Roman Catholic.

VOLKMAN, ALVIN, physician, research scientist, educator, retired; b. Bklyn., June 10, 1926; s. Henry Phillip and Sarah Lucille (Silverstein) V.; m. Winifred Joan Grinnell, June 12, 1947 (div. Aug. 1967); children: Karl Frederick, Nicholas James, Rebecca Jane Evans, Margaret Rose Werrell, Deborah Ann Falls; m. Carol Ann Fishel, Jan 26, 1973 (dec. Sept. 1992); 1 child, Natalie Fishel; 1 stepchild, Jeffrey C. Moore; m. A. Suzanne Hiss, Oct. 6, 1997. BS, Union Coll., 1947; MD, U. Buffalo, 1951; D in Philosophy, U. Oxford, Eng., 1963. Diplomate Nat. Bd. Med. Examiners, Am. Bd. Pathology. Intern Mt. Sinai Hosp., Cleve., 1951-52; rsch. fellow dept. anatomy Western Res. U. Sch. Medicine, 1952-54; resident, then sr. resident, then asst. in pathology Peter Bent Brigham Hosp., Boston, 1956-60; asst. prof. pathology Columbia U. Coll. Physicians and Surgeons, 1960-66; asst. mem., then assoc. mem. Trudeau Inst., Saranac Lake, N.Y., 1966-67; prof. dept. pathology East Carolina U. Sch. Medicine, Greenville, N.C., 1977—, acting chmn. dept. pathology, 1989-90, asoc. dean for rsch. and grad. studies, 1989-95, prof. emeritus, 1995—, ret., 1999. Mem. NIH study sect. immunological scis., 1975-79, chmn., 1977-79. Contbr. articles to sci. jours. Served to lt. USNR, 1954-56. Am. Cancer Soc. scholar, 1961-63, Arth and Rheumat Found. fellow, 1952-54. Mem. AAAS, Am. Soc. Investigative Pathology, Am. Assn. Immunologists, Am. Soc. Hematology, Reticuloendothelial Soc., Am. Soc. Microbiologists, N.Y. Acad. Scis., Soc., Leukocyte Biology (hon. life). E-mail: alphavic@earthlink.net.

VOLL, JOHN OBERT, history educator; b. Hudson, Wis., Apr. 20, 1936; s. Obert Frank and Ruth Olivia (Seaberg) V.; m. Sarah Lynne Potts, June 12, 1965; children: Sarah Layla, Michael Obert. AB summa cum laude, Dartmouth Coll., 1958, PhD (Ford Found. fellow), 1969; AM (Danforth fellow), Harvard U., 1960. Instr. history U. N.H., Durham, 1965-69, asst. prof., 1969-74, assoc. prof., 1974-82, prof., 1982-95, chair dept., 1988-91; prof. Georgetown U., Washington, 1995—, dep. dir. Ctr. for Muslim-Christian Understanding, 1996—. Mem. history and social scis. adv. com. Coll. Bd. 1983-86, chmn. European history and world cultures achievement test com., 1985-88; tchg. fellow Harvard U., 1969. Harvard Ctr. for Middle Eastern, Studies Vist. Com., 2003-. Author: Historical Dictionary of the Sudan, 1978, 2nd edit., 1992, Islam Continuity and Change in the Modern World, 2nd edit., 1994; (with others) The Sudan: Unity and Diversity, 1985, Eighteenth Century Renewal and Reform in Islam, 1987, Sudan: State and Society in Crisis, 1991, Islam and Democracy, 1996, Makers of Contemporary Islam, 2001; contbr. articles to profl. jours. Mem. bd. Ecumenical Ministry U. N.H., 1974-78, pres., 1975-77; chmn. social action Durham Cmty. Ch., 1974-75, mem. ch. coun., 1977-78, deacon, 1986—. Sheldon traveling fellow, 1960-61, U. N.H. summer fellow, 1969, 89, NEH fellow, 1971-72, Fulbright faculty rsch. abroad fellow, 1978-79, Inst. Advanced Studies fellow Hebrew U., 1984-85; recipient Egyptian Presdl. medal, 1991. Mem. Am. Coun. Learned Socs. (del. 1989-96, del. exec. com. 1989-92, bd. dirs. 1990-92), New England Hist. Assn. (sec. 1975-78, v.p. 1981, pres. 1982), Sudan Studies Assn. (bd. dirs. 1981-82, co-exec. dir. 1990-94), N.H. Coun. on World Affairs (bd. dirs. 1978-95), Am. Hist. Assn. (chmn. program com. 1999), Mid. East Studies Assn. (bd. dirs. 1987-89, pres. 1992-93), Am. Coun. for Study of Islamic Socs. (bd. dirs. 1989—, v.p. 1989-91), N.H. Humanities Coun. (bd. dirs. 1991-95). Mem. United Ch. of Christ. Home: 4000 Cathedral Ave NW Apt 652B Washington DC 20016-5205 Office: Ctr Muslim Christian Understanding Georgetown U Washington DC 20057-0001 E-mail: vollj@georgetown.edu.

VOLLAN, RODNEY R. mathmatics educator, coach; b. Sioux Falls, S.D., Dec. 31, 1959; s. Clare Ordell and Carolyn Rae Vollan. BA, Augustana Coll., 1981; MA, U. S.D., 1992. Math. tchr. Montrose (S.D.) Sch. Dist., 1981—84; adj. instr. Augustana Coll., 1984—85; math. tchr. Chaparral H.S., Las Vegas, 1985—91, Cimarron Meml. H.S., Las Vegas, 1991—, math. dept. chair. Mem. Nat. Coun. Tchrs. of Math. Democrat. E-mail: rvollan@aol.com.

VOLLBRECHT, EDWARD ALAN, school superintendent; b. Freeport, N.Y., July 22, 1941; s. Edward Chester and Lillian Elizabeth (Heinecke) V.; m. Catherine Ann Salgado, Dec. 2, 1977; 1 child, Matthew Grayson. BS, SUNY, New Paltz, 1963; MS, Hofstra U., 1968; PhD, Walden U., Naples, Fla., 1973. Adminstrv. asst. Pearl River (N.Y.) Sch. Dist., 1968-70, asst. prin., 1970-71; prin. Mark Twain Mid. Sch., Yonkers, N.Y., 1971-73; asst. dir. mid. schs. Yonkers Pub. Schs., 1973-74, dir. secondary edn., 1974-75; asst. supt. Bethlehem (Pa.) Area Sch. Dist., 1975-78; supt. schs. South Williamsport (Pa.) Area Sch. Dist., 1978-84, N.W. Area Sch. Dist., Shickshinny, Pa., 1984-88, Everett (Pa.) Area Sch. Dist., 1988—. Cons. New Eng. Sch. Devel. Coun., Boston, 1973-75; adj. prof. Manhattan Coll., N.Y.C., 1975-76, Lehigh U., Bethlehem, 1978-79. Mem. Everett Area Indsl. Devel. Corp., 1988—, Wet Providence Indsl. Devel. Authority, Bedford County Devel. Authority, Bedford County Devel. Assn., Bedford County Planning Commn.; exec. bd. Shippensburg Sch. Study Coun., Pa. State Sch. Study Coun. Educator of Yr., 1998, Svc. for Youth award YMCA, Yonkers, 1975. Mem. ASCD, Am. Assn. Sch. Adminstrs., Pa. Assn. Sch. Adminstrs., Pa. Assn. Rural and Small Schs. (exec. bd.), Pa. Sch. Bds. Assn., Bedford County Ednl. Found., Allegany C.C. Found., Lions, Rotary, Naurashank, Phi Delta Kappa. Republican. Roman Catholic. Home: 415 Locust Ct Everett PA 15537

VOLPE, ANGELO ANTHONY, former university president, chemistry educator; b. Nov. 8, 1938; s. Bernard Charles and Serafina (Martorana) V.; m. Jennette Murray, May 15, 1965. BS, Bklyn. Coll., 1959; MS, U. Md., 1962, PhD, 1966; M in Engring. (hons.), Stevens Inst. Tech., 1975. Rsch. chemist USN Ordnance Lab., Silver Spring, Md., 1961-66; from asst. prof. to prof. chemistry Stevens Inst. Tech., Hoboken, N.J., 1966-77; chmn. dept. chemistry East Carolina U., Greenville, N.C., 1977-80, dean Coll. Arts and Scis., 1980-83, vice chancellor for acad. affairs, 1983-87; pres. Tenn. Technol. U., Cookeville, 1987-2000, pres. emeritus, 2000—. Adj. prof. textile chem. N.C. State U., Raleigh, 1978-82; guest lect. Plastics Inst. Am., Hoboken, 1967-82. Contbr. articles to profl. jours. Recipient Ednl. Svc. award Plastics Inst. Am., 1973; named Freygang Outstanding Tchr., Stevens Inst. Tech., 1975. Mem. Am. Chem. Soc., Tenn. Acad. Scis., Sigma Xi, Phi Kappa Phi. Democrat. Roman Catholic. Avocations: golf, reading. Home: 734 Loweland Rd Cookeville TN 38501-2888 E-mail: avolpe@tntech.edu.

VOLPE, EDMOND L(ORIS), college president; b. New Haven, Nov. 16, 1922; s. Joseph D. and Rose (Maisano) V.; m. Rose Conte, May 20, 1950; children: Rosalind, Lisa. AB, U. Mich., 1943; MA, Columbia U., 1947, PhD, 1954. Instr. N.Y. U., 1949-54; mem. faculty City Coll. N.Y., 1954-74, prof. English, 1968-74, chmn. dept., 1964-70; pres. Richmond Coll., 1974-76, Coll. S.I., 1976-94. Fulbright prof. Am. lit., France, 1960-61 Author: A Reader's Guide to William Faulkner, 1964, The Comprehensive College, 2001; also anthologies and coll. text books.; Co-editor: Eleven Modern Short Novels. Bd. dirs. Staten Island United Way, 1975—, S.I. council Boy Scouts Am., 1977-84, S.I. Doctors Hosp., 1977-78, Snug Harbor Cultural Ctr., 1978-83, St. Vincent's Hosp., 1979—; mem. N.Y.C. Mayor's Commn. on Bias, 1986-88. With AUS, 1943-46. Recipient Commendatore Order of Merit, Republic of Italy, Cmty. Svc. award Italian Club S.I., Humanitarian award S.I. Jewish Found. Sch., Mills G. Skinner award S.I. br. N.Y. Urban League, Christopher Columbus award Columbian Assn. Bd. Edn., Disting. Cmty. Svc. award YMCA, Cmty. Svc. award S.I. Women's divsn. Am. Com. on Italian Migration, Outstanding Achievement award Guiseppe Mazzini Lodge of Sons of Italy; named Educator of Yr. Am. Legion Richmond County. Mem. MLA, Am. Studies Assn., Assn. Dept. English (exec. com. 1969-71), Am. Assn. State Colls. and Univs. (task force ednl. opportunites for the aging, research and liason com., com. internat. programs, health affairs com.), Am. Assn. Higher Edn., Am. Assn. Colls. for Tchr. Edn., Am. Assn. Univ. Profs., Am. Council Edn., Am. Studies Assn., Assn. Colls. and Univs. N.Y., Assn. Depts. of English (nat. exec. com.), Coll. English Assn. (nat. bd. dirs.), Consortium Internat. Programs, Inst. Internat. Edn., Inc., Middle States Assn. Colls. and Schs. Clubs: Andiron N.Y. (pres. 1972-75).

VOLPE, EILEEN RAE, retired special education educator; b. Fort Morgan, Colo., Aug. 23, 1942; d. Earl Lester and Ellen Ada (Hearting) Moore; m. David P. Volpe, July 28, 1965 (div. 1980); children: David P. Jr., Christina Marie. BA, U. No. Colo., 1964, MA, 1978. Cert. fine art tchr., learning handicapped specialist, resource specialist. 5th grade tchr. Meml. Elem. Sch., Milford, Mass., 1967-68; fine arts jr./sr. high tchr. Nipmuc Regional Jr. Sr. H.S., Mendon, Mass., 1968-69; spl. edn. tchr. Saugus (Calif.) H.S., 1979—98, Valencia (Calif.) H.S., 1998—2003; ret., 2003. Publicity dir. Sacred Heart Ch. Sch., Milford, Mass., 1974-75, float coord. bicentennial parade, 1975. Author: (poetry) Seasons to Come, 1994, Best Poems of 1997, The Other Side of Midnight, 1997, Best of 2001 Poems; contbr. to Best of Millennium Poetry, 1999-2000, Best of 2002 Poems. Mem. Calif. Tchr. Assn., Coun. for Exceptional Children, DAR, Phi Delta Kappa, Kappa Delta Pi. Republican. Avocations: arts and crafts, photography, travel, doll collecting and creation.

VOLPE, ELLEN MARIE, secondary school educator; b. Bronx, N.Y., Aug. 2, 1949; d. George Thomas and Mary (Popadinecz) Soloweyko; m. Ronald Edward Volpe, May 22, 1971; children: Keith, Daniel, Christopher, Stephanie. BBA, Pace U., 1971; MA in Teaching, Sacred Heart U., 1986. Tchr. Conn. Bus. Inst., Stratford, 1979-80, Katherine Gibbs Sch., Norwalk, Conn., 1980-89; adj. instr. So. Cen. Community Coll., New Haven, 1986-87, Salt Lake C. C., Phillips Jr. Coll., Salt Lake City, 1992-93; instr. Bryman Sch., Salt Lake City, 1990-92; tchr. Indian Hills Mid. Sch., Sandy, Utah, 1993-99, vocational dept. chmn.; tchr. MaST Cmty. Charter Sch., Phila., 1999-2001. Bus. team leader reaccreditation and tech. coms. Indian Hills Mid. Sch., 1996, vocat. dept. chair; mem. curriculum rev. com. Katharine Gibbs Sch., 1989-90. Avocations: ceramics, gardening. Home: 51 West St Warwick NY 10990-1432 E-mail: compteach50@hotmail.com.

VOLZ, ANNABELLE WEKAR, learning disabilities educator, consultant; b. Niagara Falls, N.Y., May 24, 1926; d. Fred Wekar and Margaret Eleanor (McGillivray) Wekar Treadwell; m. William Mount Volz, May 9, 1958; children: Amy D., William M. Jr. BA, Seton Hill Coll., 1948; MS in Elem. Edn., N.Y. State Univ. Coll., 1956. Cert. learning disabilities cons. N.J. Georgian Ct. Coll., 1981. Lab. technician Moore Bus. Forms Inc., Niagara Falls, 1948-50, Niagara Falls Health Dept., 1950-53; tchr. Niagara Falls Bd. Edn., 1953-56, Am. Dependent Sch., Ashiya, Japan, 1956-58, Mehlville Bd. Edn., St. Louis County, Mo., 1968-70, U.S. Dependent Schs. European Theatre, Weisbaden, Fed. Republic of Germany, 1970-74; paraprofl. Medford (N.J.) Bd. Edn., 1978-81; learning disabilities tchr., cons. Southampton Bd. Edn., Vincentown, N.J., 1981-91. Mem. Womens Fin. Info. Program, Burlington County, 1990-91. Mem. LWV (N.C. chpt., Winston-Salem chpt. 1993-99, sec. 1994-96, mem. chair 199 6-99, voter's guide chair 1996, 98, LWV Piedmont chpt.), AAUW (N.J. chpt. Medford chpt. 1982-91, N.C. Winston Salem chpt. 1992—, treas. 1993-2000), Nat. Retired Edn. Assn., N.J. Retired Edn. Assn., Assn. Learning Cons., Seton Hill Alumnae Assn., Kappa Delta Pi. Home: 5080 Mountain View Rd Winston Salem NC 27104-5110

VOLZ, WILLIAM HARRY, law educator, administrator; b. Sandusky, Mich., Dec. 28, 1946; s. Harry Bender and Belva Geneva (Riehl) V. BA, Mich. State U., 1968; MA, U. Mich., 1972; MBA, Harvard U., 1978; JD, Wayne State U., 1975. Bar: mich. 1975. Atty. pvt. practice, Detroit, 1975-77; mgmt. analyst Office of Gen. Counsel, HEW, Woodlawn, Md., 1977; from asst. to dean Wayne State U., Detroit, 1978—86, dean, 1986—95; dir. Ctr. for Legal Studies Wayne State U. Law Sch., 1996-97. Cons. Merrill Lynch, Pierce, Fenner & Smith, N.Y.C., 1980-93, City of Detroit Law Dept., 1982, Mich. Supreme Ct., Detroit, 1981; ptnr. Mich. CPA Rev., Southfield, 1983-85; expert witness in product liability, comml. law and bus. ethics; pres. Wedgewood Group. Author: Managing a Trial, 1982; contbr. articles to legal jours.; mem. editl. bds. of bus. and law jours. Internat. adv. bd. Inst. Mgmt., I. L'viv, Ukraine, Legal counsel Free Legal Aid Clinic, Inc., Detroitm 1976—, Shared Ministries, Detroit, 1981, Sino-Am. Tech. Exch. coun., China, 1982; chair advt. rev. panel BBB, Detroit, 1988-90; pres. Mich. Acad. Sci., Arts and Letters, 1995-96, 98-2000, bd. dirs.; pres. Common Ground, PLAYERS; bd. dirs. Greater Detroit Alliance Bus., Olde Custodian Fund. Mem.: ABA, The Wedgewood Group (pres.), Players, Amateur Medicant Soc. (commissionaire 1981—85), Harvard Bus. Sch. Club Detroitm, Econ. Club Detroit, Detroit Athletic Club, Beta Alpha Psu, Alpha Kappa Psi, Golden Key. Mem. Reorganized Lds Ch. Home: 3846 Wedgewood Dr Bloomfield Hills MI 48301-3949 Office: Wayne State U Sch Bus Adminstrn Cass Ave Detroit MI 48202 E-mail: w.h.volz@wayne.edu.

VOMACKA, JILL ELIZABETH, adapted physical education specialist; b. Franklin Square, N.Y., July 30, 1954; d. John William and Elizabeth Jane (Kettel) V. BS, Cortland U., 1976; MA, Adelphi U., 1981. Cert. phys. edn. tchr., adapted phys. edn. specialist, N.Y. Water safety instr. ARC, Mineola, N.Y., 1976—, adapted aquatics instr., 1989—; physical edn. tchr. Franklin Square (N.Y.) Sch. Dist., 1977—, adapted phys. edn. specialist, coordinator, 1977—; instr. N.Y. State Park Games for the Physically Challenged, L.I., 1986—. Adapted phys. edn. coord., specialist, cons., Franklin Square Sch. Dist. 1976—; adapted phys. edn. specialist Hofstra U., Hempstead, N.Y., 1980—; adj. prof. adapted phys. edn. Hofstra U., Hempstead, N.Y., 1980—; swimming coord. N.Y. State Games for the Physically Challenged, 1991—. Asst. leader Girl Scouts of U.S., Floral Park, N.Y., 1976-78; first aid instr. ARC, Mineola, 1976-78. Recipient PTA award Franklin Square Schs., 1974, 76, 93, Svc. award award N.Y. State Parks Games for the Physically Challenged, 1991, 95. Mem. N.Y. State Assn. for Health, Phys. Edn., Recreation and Dance (pres.-elect adapted phys. activity 1995-97). Avocations: outdoor edn., camping, fishing, playing guitar, photography. Office: John St Elem Sch Nassau Blvd Franklin Square NY 11010

VOM SAAL, WALTER, psychology educator; b. NYC, Nov. 29, 1944; s. W. Rudolf and Jane (Towle) vom S.; children: Daniel, Laura, Jeffrey. BA, Columbia U., 1966; MA, McMaster U., 1967, PhD, 1969. Asst. prof. psychology Princeton (N.J.) U., 1969-74; assoc. prof. Millersville (Pa.) U., 1974-79, prof. psychology, 1979-86, assoc. v.p., 1986-89; provost and v.p. acad. affairs SUNY, Oneonta, 1989-94, acting pres. Plattsburgh, 1993-94, prof. psychology, 1989—. Named Disting. tchg. fellow Commonwealth of Pa., 1979, Disting. Tchg. chair, 1979. Mem. Phi Beta Kappa. Home: 103 Elm St Oneonta NY 13820 Office: SUNY 502 Fitzelle Hall Oneonta NY 13820

VON BERNUTH, ROBERT DEAN, agricultural engineering educator, consultant; b. Del Norte, Colo., Apr. 14, 1946; s. John Daniel and Bernice H. (Dunlap) von B.; m. Judy M. Wehrman, Dec. 27, 1969; children: Jeanie, Suzie BSE, Colo. State U., 1968; MS, U. Idaho, 1970; MBA, Claremont (Calif.) Grad. Sch., 1980; PhD in Engring., U. Nebr., 1982. Registered profl. engr., Calif., Nebr. Agrl. product mgr. Rain Bird Sprinkler Mfg., Glendora, Calif., 1974-80; instr. agrl. engring. U. Nebr., Lincoln, 1980-82; from assoc. prof. to prof. U. Tenn., Knoxville, 1982-90; prof. Mich. State U., East Lansing, 1990—, chmn., 1992-96. V.p. Von-Sol Cons., Lincoln, 1980-82; prin. Von Bernuth Agrl. cons., Knoxville, East Lansing, 1982—. Patentee in field. With USNR, 1970—98, Vietnam. Decorated DFC (2); recipient Disting. Naval Grad. award USN Flight Program, Pensacola, Fla., 1970. Fellow Am. Soc. Agrl. Engrs.; mem. ASCE, Irrigation Assn. (Person of Yr. 1994), Naval Res. Assn. Avocations: flying, skiing, antique tractors. Office: Mich State U Sch of Constrn Mgmt 213 Farrall Hall East Lansing MI 48824-1323

VON BURG, FREDERICK E., SR., secondary school educator, writer; b. Biel, Switzerland, Feb. 22, 1934; arrived in U.S., 1942; s. Emil and Frieda Von Burg; m. Loretta Sauls, Aug. 25, 1962; children: Gregory, Paul, Frederick Jr. BS in Edn., St. John's U., 1961, MS in Edn., 1965. Cert. secondary sch. prin., supr., English tchr. N.Y., 1965. English tchr. Levittown (N.Y.) Schs., 1961—64, Sch. Dist. #13, S. Huntington, NY, 1964—66, Levittown (N.Y.) Schs., 1966—92; Tutor Creative Tutoring, Plainview, NY, 1992—95. Camp counselor and supr. Various camps, NY, 1952—79. Author: Raising Your Future, 2000, Keep My White Sneakers, Kit Carson, 2002, States of the Mind, 2003. Achievements include development of new names for Jean Piaget's Periods of Development. Avocations: canoeing, hiking, skiing.

VON DASSANOWSKY, ELFI (ELFRIEDE MARIA VON DASSANOWSKY), film producer, educator, opera singer; b. Vienna, Feb. 2, 1924; d. Franz Leopold and Anna (Grünwald-Esterhazy) von Dass.; 3 children. Diploma, Hochschule für Musik und darstellende Kunst, Vienna, 1944; vocal studies with Paula Mark-Neusser, piano studies with Emil von Sauer. Actress in Austrian theater and film, 1946—53; broadcast announcer Forces Broadcasting, Central Europe, Vienna, BBC, Vienna; co-founder, prodr. Belvedere Film Studio, Austria, 1946; adminstr., casting dir. Phoebus Internat. Film, Germany, 1951; pres. Belvedere Film Productions, L.A., 1999—. Various business activities, 1968-90, music coach for film dir. Karl Hartl and actor Curd Jurgens, 1941-42; vocal coach, piano classes, N.Y., Hollywood, 1955-67; faculty mem., cons. numerous internat. acads. and cultural orgns.; star contract UFA Studios, Berlin, 1944. Opera debut as Susanne in Le Nozze di Figaro, St. Pölten, 1946; guest appearances in Vienna, St. Pölten, Hamburg, Flensburg, Munich, 1946-53; prin. roles soprano and mezzo include Agathe in Freischütz, Mimi in Boheme, Hansel and Gretel, Lola in Cavalleria Rusticana, Orlofsky in Fledermaus; numerous leading roles in Viennese operetta; spl. vocal and piano recitals for Allied high Command Europe, 1947-49; European radio performances as singer and pianist, Co-Producer: Die Glücksmühle, 1947, Wer küsst Wen?,1947, Der Leberfleck, 1948, Dr. Rosin, 1949, Märchen vom Glück, 1949; exec. prodr. Semmelweis, 2001, Wilson Chance, 2003. Decorated Chevalier, Ordre des Arts et des Lettres, France, 2001, Order of Merit in Gold, City of Vienna, 2002; recipient Accademica Honoris Causa Accademia Culturale d'Europe, 1990, Order of Merit in Gold, Austria, 1991, Gold Medallion City of Vienna, 1996, Honor City of L.A., 1996, Mozart medal UNESCO, 1997, medal of honor Austrian Film Archives, 1998; named Elfriede von Dassanowsky Day Calif. State Senate, 1996; granted title of Prof. by Austrian Pres., 1998, Women's Internat. Ctr. Living Legacy award, 2000. Mem. Austrian Am. Film Assn., Assn. Austrian Film Producers, Women's Internat. Ctr., U.S. National Women's Hall of Fame, Friends of L.A. Philharm. Roman Catholic. Home and Office: 13052 Moorpark St Ste 203 Studio City CA 91604-5003 E-mail: Belvederefilm@yahoo.com.

VONDEREMBSE, MARK ANTHONY, management educator; b. Lima, Ohio, Nov. 5, 1948; s. Paul Edward and Ruth Mary (Beck) V.; m. Sandra S. Scott, Aug. 26, 1972 (div. Dec. 1994); children: Anthony Joseph, Elaine Mary; m. Gayle C. Swartz, June 21, 1997; stepchildren: Leisje Christine, Tosje Elizabeth, Vanessa Nicole, Talia Ranae, Maryke Justine. BSCE, U. Toledo, 1971; MBA, U. Pa., 1973; PhD in Bus. Adminstrn., U. Mich., 1979. Instr. U. Toledo, 1973-75, prof., 1977—. Dir. chmn. info. sys. and ops. mgmt. dept. U. Toledo, 1983-85, 87-91, MS and PhD in mfg. mgmt., 1994-2001. Contbr. articles to profl. jours. Pres., bd. dirs. Lott Industries, Toledo, 1986—. Mem. Decision Scis. Inst. (regional v.p. 1988-90), Beta Gamma Sigma, Phi Kappa Phi, Tau Beta Pi. Roman Catholic. Avocation: officiating college football. Office: U Toledo 2801 W Bancroft St Toledo OH 43606-3328

VON DER MEHDEN, FRED R. political science educator; b. San Francisco, Dec. 1, 1927; s. Fred G. and Margaret (de Valasco) von der M.; m. Audrey Eleanor Whitehead, Dec. 27, 1954; children: Laura Davis, Victoria Margaret Fredrickson. BA, U. of Pacific, 1948; MA, Claremont Grad. Sch., 1950; PhD, U. Calif. Berkeley, 1957. Mem. faculty U. Wis. Madison, 1957-68; chmn. East Asian studies U. Wis.-Madison, 1963-65, 67-68; Albert Thomas prof. polit. sci. Rice U., 1968—2000, dir. Center for Research, 1969-70, chmn. dept., 1975-78, dir. program devel. studies, 1978-83; editor Rice U. Press, 1982-95; Albert Thomas prof. emeritus Rice U., 2000—. Cons. AID, 1967-78 Author: Politics of the Developing Nations, 1964, 2d edit., 1969, Religion and Nationalism in Southeast Asia, 1963, Comparative Political Violence, 1973; co-author: Issues of Political Development, 1967, The Military and Politics of Five Developing Nations, 1970, Southeast Asia 1930-1970, 1974, Religion and Modernization in Southeast Asia, 1986, Two Worlds of Islam, 1993; editor: (with R. Soligo) Issues on Income Distribution, 1975, Ethnic Groups of Houston, 1984. Mem. Mid-West Conf. Asian Affairs (pres. 1968-69), Assn. Asian Studies, Am. Polit. Sci. Assn., S.W. Conf. Asian Affairs (pres. 1976-77) Home: 12530 Mossycup Dr Houston TX 77024-4937

VON GONTEN, KEVIN PAUL, priest, liturgist, theologian; b. Bklyn., Mar. 21, 1949; s. Joseph William and Marion Von G. BA in Religious Studies, St. Francis Coll., Bklyn., 1979; AM in Hist. Theology, Fordham U., 1982; STM in Liturgy, Gen. Theol. Sem., NYC, 1987. Ordained to ministry Episcopal Ch. as deacon, 1987, as priest, 1987. Prof. St. Francis Coll., Bklyn., 1982-87; asst. pastor St. Gregory's Ch., Parsippany, N.J., 1985-87; assoc. rector St. Stephen's Ch., Port Washington, N.Y., 1987-89; vicar All Souls Ch., Stony Brook, NY, 1989—2002. Prof. George Mercer Sch. Theology, Garden City, N.Y.; chmn. Diocesan Commn. on Liturgy, 1989-99; dir. exploration of ministry program Diocese of L.I., 1987-2000; asst. sec. trustees Diocese of L.I., 1995-98; pres. bd. mgrs. Camp DeWolfe, 1995-97; sec. of conv. Diocese of L.I., 1993-99, chair dept. mission, 1998-2002. Author: The Great Vigil of Easter. Active N.Y. State Firefighter. Mem. Am. Acad. Religion, Nat. Assn. for the Catechumenate, Coll. Theology Soc., Theta Alpha Kappa. E-mail: frkpv@optonline.net.

VON HIPPEL, FRANK NIELS, public and international affairs educator; b. Cambridge, Mass., Dec. 26, 1937; s. Arthur Robert and Dagmar (Franck) von H.; m. Patricia Bardi, June, 1987; 1 child from previous marriage, Paul Thomas. S.B., MIT, 1959; PhD, Oxford U., 1962. Rsch. assoc. U. Chgo., 1962-64, Cornell U., Ithaca, N.Y., 1964-66; asst. prof. Stanford U., Calif., 1966-69; assoc. physicist Argonne Nat. Lab., Ill., 1970-73; research physicist Princeton U., N.J., 1974-83, prof. pub. and internat. affairs, 1983-93, 95—; asst. dir. for nat. security Pres.'s Office of Sci. and Tech. Policy, Washington, N.J., 1993-94. Bd. dirs. Bull. of Atomic Scientists, Chgo., 1983-86, mem. editl. bd., 1996—, chmn. editl. bd., 1991-93. Author: Advice and Dissent, 1974, Citizen Scientist, 1991; chmn. editl. bd. Sci. and Global Security, 1989—; contbr. articles to profl. jours. Rhodes scholar, 1959-62; McArthur Found. Prize fellow, 1993-98. Fellow AAAS (bd. dirs. 1987-88, Hilliard Roderick prize in Sci., Arms Control and Internat. Security 1994); mem. Fedn. Am. Scientists (chmn. 1979-84, Pub. Svc. award 1989), Fedn. Am. Scientists Fund (chmn. 1986-93, 96—). Home: 3 University Way Princeton Junction NJ 08550-1617 Office: Princeton Univ Woodrow Wilson Sch Princeton NJ 08544-0001

VON HIPPEL, PETER HANS, chemistry educator, molecular biology researcher; b. Goettingen, Germany, Mar. 13, 1931; came to U.S., 1937, naturalized, 1942; s. Arthur Robert and Dagmar (franck) von H.; m. Josephine Baron Raskind, June 20, 1954; children: David F., James A., Benjamin J. BS, MIT, 1952, MS, 1953, PhD, 1955. Phys. biochemist Naval Med. Research Inst., Bethesda, Md., 1956-59; from asst. prof. to assoc. prof. biochemistry Med. Sch. Dartmouth Coll., 1959-67; prof. chemistry, mem. Inst. Molecular Biology U. Oreg., 1967-79, dir. Inst. Molecular Biology, 1969-80, chmn. dept. chemistry, 1980-87; rsch. prof. chemistry Am. Cancer Soc., 1989—. Chmn. biopolymers Gordon Conf., 1968; mem. trustees vis. com. biology dept. MIT, 1973-76; mem. bd. sci. counsellors Nat. Inst. Arthritis, Metabolic and Digestive Diseases, NIH, 1974-78, mem. coun. Nat. Inst. Gen. Med. Scis., 1982-86, mem. dir.'s adv. com., 1987-92; mem. sci. and tech. ctrs. adv. com. NSF, 1987-89; bd. dirs. Fedn. Am. Socs. for Exptl. Biology, 1994-98; mem. NIH-CSR panel on boundaries for sci. rev., 1998—. Mem. editl. bd. Jour. Biol. Chemistry, 1967-73, 76-82, Biochem. Biophys. Acta, 1965-70, Physiol. Revs., 1972-77, Biochemistry, 1977-80, Trends in Biochem. Soc., 1987—, Protein Sci., 1990-95; editor Jour. Molecular Biology, 1986-94; contbr. articles to profl. jours., chpts. to books. Lt. M.S.C. USNR, 1956-59. Recipient Merck award Am. Soc. Biochem. and Molecular Biology, 2000; NSF predoctoral fellow, 1953-55; NIH postdoctoral fellow, 1955-56; NIH sr. fellow, 1959-67; Guggenheim fellow, 1973-74 Fellow Am. Acad. Arts and Scis.; mem. AAAS, Am. Chem. Soc., Am. Soc. Biol. Chemists, Biophys. Soc. (mem. coun. 1970-73, pres. 1973-74), Nat. Acad. Scis., Fedn. Biochem. and Molecular Biology, Am. Scientists, Sigma Xi. Home: 1900 Crest Dr Eugene OR 97405-1753

VON MEHREN, ARTHUR TAYLOR, lawyer, educator; b. Albert Lea, Minn., Aug. 10, 1922; s. Sigurd Anders and Eulalia Marion (Anderson) von M.; m. Joan Elizabeth Moore, Oct. 11, 1947; children— George Moore, Peter Anders, Philip Taylor S.B., Harvard U., 1942, LL.B., 1945, PhD, 1946; Faculty of Law, U. Zurich, 1946-47; Faculte de Droit, U. Paris, 1948-49; Doctor iuris (h.c.), Katholieke U., Leuven, 1985, U. Pantheon-Assas (Paris II), 2000. Bar: Mass. 1950, U.S. Dist. Ct. Mass. 1980. Law clk. U.S. Ct. Appeals (1st cir.), 1945-46; asst. prof. law Harvard U., 1946-53, prof., 1953-76, Story prof., 1976-93, prof. emeritus, 1993—, dir. East Asian legal studies program, 1981-83; acting chief legislation br., legal div. Occupation Mil. Govt. U.S.,Germany, 1947-48, cons. legal div., 1949. Tchr. Salzburg Seminar in Am. Studies, summers 1953, 54; Fulbright research prof. U. Tokyo, Japan, 1956-57, Rome, Italy, 1968-69; cons. legal studies Ford Found., New Delhi, 1962-63; vis. prof. U. Frankfurt, summer 1967, City Univ. Hong Kong, 1995; Ford vis. prof. Inst. Advanced Legal Studies, U. London, 1976; assoc. prof. U. Paris, 1977; Goodhart prof. legal sci. U. Cambridge, 1983-84, fellow Downing Coll., 1983-84, hon. fellow, 1984—; fellow Wissenschaftskolleg zu Berlin, 1990-91. Author: The Civil Law System: An Introduction to the Comparative Study of Law, 1957, 2d edit. (with J. Gordley), 1977, Law in the United States: A General and Comparative View, 1988, (with D.T. Trautman) The Law of Multistate Problems: Cases and Materials on the Conflict of Laws, 1965, (with S. Symeonides and W. Perdue) Conflict of Laws: American, Comparative, International, 1998, International Commercial Arbitration, 1999, (with J. Varady, J. Barcelo) 2d edit., 2002; mem. editl. bd. Am. Jour. Comparative Law, 1952-86; contbr. articles to profl. jours.; editor: Law in Japan-The Legal Order in a Changing Soc., 1963; mem. editl. com. Internat. Ency. Comparative Law, 1969—. Mem. U.S. Del. Hague Conf. pvt. internat. law, 1966, 68, 76, 80, 85, 93, 96, 2001. Named to Order of the Rising Sun, golden rays Japanese Govt., 1989; Guggenheim fellow, 1968-69; inst. fellow Sackler Inst. Advanced Studies, 1986-87. Mem. ABA (Leonard J. Theberge Award for Pvt. Internat. Law 1997, Sect. of Internat. Law and Practice), Am. Acad. Arts and Scis., Internat. Acad. Comparative Law (Can. prize 2002), Institut de Droit Internat., Japanese Am. Soc. Legal Studies, Am. Soc. Comparative Law (bd. dirs., former pres.), Am. Soc. Polit. and Legal Philosophy, Institut Grand-Duchal (corr.), Phi Beta Kappa. Office: Harvard Law Sch/ AR-231 1545 Massachusetts Ave Cambridge MA 02138-2903 E-mail: vonmehre@law.harvard.edu.

VON MERING, OTTO OSWALD, anthropology educator; b. Berlin, Oct. 21, 1922; came to Switzerland, 1933, to U.S., 1939, naturalized, 1954; s. Otto O. and Henriette (Troeger) von M.; m. Shirley Ruth Brook, Sept. 11, 1954; children: Gretchen, Karin, Gregory, Hilary, Celia. Grad., Belmont Hill Sch., 1940; BA in History, Williams Coll., 1944; PhD in Social Anthropology, Harvard U., 1956. Instr. Belmont Hill Sch., Belmont, Mass., 1945-47, Boston U., 1947-48, Cambridge Jr. Coll., 1948-49; rsch. asst. lab. social rels. Harvard U., 1950-51, Boston Psychopathic Hosp., 1951-53; Russell Sage Found. fellow N.Y.C., 1953-55; asst. prof. social anthropology U. Pitts. Coll. Medicine, 1955-60, assoc. prof., 1960-65, prof. social anthropology, 1965-71; prof. child devel. and child care U. Pitts. Coll. Allied Health Professions, 1969-71; prof. anthropology and family medicine U. Fla., 1971-76, prof. anthropology in ob-gyn, 1979-84, prof. anthropology and gerontology, 1986-96, prof. anthropology and gerontology emeritus, 1998, joint prof. dept. medicine, coll. medicine, 1994-96. Lectr. Sigmund Freud Inst., Frankfurt, Germany, 1962-64, Pitts. Psychoanalytical Inst., 1960--71, Interuniv. Forum, 1967-71; tech. adviser Maurice Falk Med. Fund, 1964-75; Fulbright vis. lectr., 1962-63; Richard-Merton guest prof. Heidelberg U., Germany, 1962-63; vis. prof. Dartmouth, 1970-71; vis. lectr. continuing edn. Med. Coll. of Pa., 1990-92, vis. lectr. U. Sheffield, Eng., Fall, 1995, U. Liverpool, 1995, U. Augsburg, 1997, U. Heidelberg, fall 1997; hon. vis. prof. U. Coll. London Med. Sch., fall 1997; bd. dirs. Tech. Assistance Resource Assocs., U. Fla., 1979-84; supr. grad. study program Ctr. Gerontologic Studies, U. Fla., 1983-85, assoc. dir. 1985-86, dir. 1986-96, prof. emeritus 1998; mem. coordinating com. Geriatric Edn. Ctr., Coll. of Medicine, U. Fla., 1986-96; mem. med. selection com. Coll. Medicine U. Fla., 2000—; mem. adv. bd. nursing programs Santa Fe C.C., 2001—; mem. nat. tech. expert panel on long-term care Health Care Financing Adminstrn., Washington; chair, mem. adv. bd. Internat. Exchange Ctr. on Gerontology State U. System of Fla., 1987-92; adv. bd. Second Season Broadcasting Network, Palm Beach, Fla., 1989-92, Fla. Policy Exch. Ctr. on Aging, State U. System Fla., 1991-95, Assoc. Health Industries of Fla., Inc., Nat. Shared Housing Resource Ctr., Balt.; cons. mental hosps. Author: Remotivating the Mental Patient, 1957, A Grammar of Human Values, 1961, (with Mitscherlich and Brocher) Der Kranke in der Modernen Gesellschaft, 1967, (with Kasdan) Anthropology in the Behavioral and Health Sciences, 1970, (with Maria Alvarez) Aging, Demography and Well-Being in Latin America, 1989; (with R. Binstock and L. Cluff) The Future of Long Term Care, 1996; also articles; commentary editor: Human Organization, 1974-76; corr. editor Jour. Geriatric Psychiatry, 1990-98; mem. editl. bd. Med. Anthropology, 1976-84, Ednl. Gerontology, 1990-2002, Australasian Leisure for Pleasure Jour., 1995-2000, Jour. Cross-Cultural Gerontology, 1996-2002. Mem. nat. adv. bd. Nat. Shared Housing Resource Ctr., 1994-95; pres. Dedicated Alt. Resources for the Elderly, 1996-98; mem., bd. dirs. No. Ctrl. Fla. chpt. Alzheimer's Assn., 1996—2002; bd. dirs. Shepherd's Ctrs. Am., Gainesville, 1998-2000; adv. bd. nursing programs, Santa Fe Cmty. Coll., Gainesville, 2001—, bd. dirs., 2000—. Recipient Fulbright-Hayes Travel award, 1962-63; grantee Wenner-Gren Found., N.Y., 1962-63, Am. Philos. Soc., 1962-63, Maurice Falk Med. Fund, 1970-71, US-DHHS, 1979-83, Walter Reed Army Inst. Rsch., 1987-91. US-ADA/Fla. Dept. of Elder Affairs, 1993-94; spl. fellow NIMH, 1971-72. Fellow AAAS, Am. Anthrop. Assn. (mem. James Mooney award com. 1978-81, vis. lectr. 1961,-62, 71-74, 91-92), Am. Gerontol. Soc., Royal Soc. Health, Acad. Psychosomatic Medicine, Am. Ethnological Soc., Soc. Applied Anthropology, Royal Anthrop. Inst.; mem. Assn. Am. Med. Colls., Assn. Anthrop. Gerontol. (pres.-elect 1991-92, pres. 1992-93), Am. Fedn. Clin. Research, Am. Public Health Assn., Canadian Assn. Gerontology, British Soc. Gerontology, Med. Group Mgmt. Assn., World Fedn. Mental Health, Internat. Assn. Social Psychiatry (regional counselor 1973-81), Internat. Hosp. Fedn., Help Age Internat. (London). Home: 818 NW 21st St Gainesville FL 32603-1027 Office: U Fla Dept Anthropology and Gerontology Turlington Hall Gainesville FL 32611

VON MOSCH, WANDA GAIL, middle school educator; b. Richmond, Va., Jan. 21, 1952; d. Jesse James Sr. and Thelma Arleen (Bruce) Perdue; m. Carl Allan Von Mosch, June 24, 1978; children: Carl Allan Jr., Sarah Ashley, Katie Danielle. BS, Longwood Coll., 1974; postgrad., Old Dominion U., 1991—. Tchr. pub. schs. City of Hampton, Va., 1974-77, City of Virginia Beach, Va., 1977—. Mem. planning coun. and faculty coun. Great Neck Mid. Sch., also coord. ptnrs. in edn. and comm. liaison; coord., coach Odyssey of Mind. Mem. adminstrv. bd. Francis Asbury United Meth. Ch., Virginia Beach, 1986—, supt., 1991; Bethel Bible grad. and tchr. Va. Marine Sci. Mus., Virginia Beach, 1990—, Sunday sch. tchr., 1983—; Great Neck coord. and team coach Odyssey of Mind, 1997-98, participant, Malcolm Baldridge TQM procedure, US Congress for independent learning. Recipient PTA award for Disting. Svc., 1990; named Tchr. of Yr., Walmart, 2000, Great Neck, 2002. Mem. NEA, PTA, Va. Edn. Assn., Virginia Beach Edn. Assn., Va. Reading Coun., Va. Math. League, Virginia Beach Reading Coun., Va. Beach Tchr. Forum. Republican. Avocations: reading, cooking, music, board games, golf. Office: Great Neck Middle Sch North Great Neck Rd Virginia Beach VA 23454-1112

VON ROSENBERG, GARY MARCUS, JR., parochial school educator; b. Baumholder, Federal Republic of Germany, Feb. 22, 1956; s. Gary Marcus and Maria Gwendolyn (Pickett) Von R. BA, Cleve. State U., 1979; BS, U. Tex., 1991. Jr. high sch. sci. tchr. St. Andrew's Sch., Ft. Worth, 1982-86; math. tchr., coach, moderator Monsignor Nolan High Sch., Ft. Worth, 1986—. Creator jr. high Sci. Fair program. Capt. U.S. Army field artillery, 1979-82. Recipient Sci. Fair Tchr. award Ft. Worth Regional Sci. Fair, 1985, runner-up, 1984. Mem. ASCD, Nat. Coun. Tchrs. Math., The Math. Assn. Am., The Nat. Sci. Tchrs. Assn. Home: 1525 Lincolnshire Way Fort Worth TX 76134-5583

VONSCHULZE-DELITZSCH, MARILYN WANDLING (LADY VONSCHULZE-DELITZSCH), artist, writer; b. Alton, Ill., May 16, 1932; d. Ralph Marion and Mary Mildred (Branson) W.; m. Sir Georg W.W. Herzog VonSchulze-Delitzsch; children: Jeffrey, Douglas, Pamela. Student, Monticello Coll., Godfrey, Ill, 1950-51, U. Ill., 1951-53; BA in Art, Webster U., St. Louis, 1968; MA Edn. in Art Edn., Washington U., St. Louis, 1975. Cert. tchr. art Kindergarten-Grade 12, Mo. 4th grade tchr. Alton (Ill.) Pub. Schs., 1961-62; art. buying dept. Gardner Advt. Co. Inc., St. Louis, 1962-63; art tchr. mid. sch. Lindbergh Sch. Dist., St. Louis, 1968-75; cons., designer V.P. Fair, Inc., St. Louis, 1982; adminstrv. asst. to headmaster, coll. counseling dept. John Burroughs Sch., St. Louis, 1979-82; dir. pub. rels. and advt. Dance St. Louis, 1983-85; freelance art and design St. Louis, 1970—; tchr. art mid. sch. St. Louis Pub. Schs., 1987-90, tchr. art Elem. Magnet Sch. for Visual and Performing Arts, 1990-98. Tchr. drawing and painting Summer Arts Inst., St. Louis Pub. Schs., 1992, graphic arts designer, cons. comty. affairs divsn., 1985-96, sch. vol. divsn., 1990-92, Webster Groves (Mo.) Sch. Dist., 1989-90, Pub. Sch. Retirement Sys., St. Louis, 1991; implementer classroom multi-cultural art edn. projects, 1987-98; summer participant Improving Visual Arts Edn., Getty Ctr. for Edn. in Arts, 1990; book illustrator-McGraw Hill Inter-Americana de Mexico, Mexico City, 1994-95, Simon & Schuster, Mexico City. Designer (cover and icons) English Language Teaching Text, 1996; designer Centennial Logo for St. Louis Pub. Schs. Sesquicentennial, 1988; painter, designer murals for Ctrl. Presbyn. Ch. Nursery, 1978-79, St. Nicholas Greek Orthodox Ch., 1980; designer two outdoor villages VP Fair, Arch Grounds, St. Louis, 1982; published writer. Patron St. Louis Symphony Orch. Recipient merit and honor awards Nat. Sch. Pub. Rels. Assn., 1990, 91, 92, 93, 95, Mo. Sch. Pub. Rels. Assn., 1989-90, 91, 92, 93. Mem. St. Louis Art Mus., PEO Sisterhood, Nat. Soc. DAR, Colonial Dames of 17th Cent., United Daus. of Confederacy, Chi Omega Alumnae. Avocations: Native American arts and culture, paintings, drawings, portraits. E-mail: tulipsaintlouis@earthlink.net.

VON SCHWARZ, CAROLYN M. GEIGER, psychotherapist, educator; b. Greenville, Mich., May 16, 1949; d. Raymond Lavern and Bernice Clara (Schoenborn) Geiger; m. Jeffrey George von Schwarz, Apr. 25, 1970 (div. Sept. 1979); children: Sean Raymond, Laura Elizabeth. BA, Wayne State U., 1988, MEd, 1992. Lic. profl. counselor. Counselor Edn. Tng. Rsch. Found., 1986-89; dir., therapist von Schwarz Assocs., Grosse Pointe Farms, Mich., 1989—; pvt. practice Boysville, Mich., 1996—. Spkr. in field. Vol. therapist, COO Grateful Home, Homeless Shelter, Treatment Shelter, Detroit, 1991-93; vol. Sacred Heart Ctr., Detroit, 1978—, SAC2, Grosse Pointe Farms, 1985—; cons. Treehouse Players, Grosse Pointe Woods. Mem. Psi Chi. Republican. Roman Catholic. Avocations: fitness, home restoration/renovation, traveling.

VONTUR, RUTH POTH, retired elementary school educator; b. Beeville, Tex., Sept. 10, 1944; d. Robert Bennal and Ruth (Matejek) Poth; m. Robert F. Vontur, Aug. 8, 1964; children: Catherine Anne, Craig Robert, Cynthia Anne. BS in Edn., Southwest Tex. State U., 1966. Cert. health and phys. edn. tchr., biology tchr. Tex. Tchg. asst. Blessed Sacrament Confraternity Christian Doctrine, Poth, Tex., 1958-64; phys. edn. tchr. Judson Ind. Sch. Dist., Converse, Tex., 1966-68, St. Monica's Altar Soc. (Coun. of Cath. Women), Converse, Tex., 1974-96; substitute tchr. St. Monica's Confraternity Christian Doctrine, Converse, Tex., 1971—2003, Judson Ind. Sch. Dist., San Antonio, 1972-75, 80-81, phys. edn. tchr. Converse, 1966-68, 81-2000; ret., 2000. County adv. bd. Am. Heart Assn., San Antonio, Tex., 1985-88, jump rope for heart coord., 1984-2000, heart ptnr., 1992-2000 (recognized Tex. Jump Rope for Heart Pioneer, 1999); mentor Converse Elem. Sch., 1998-2003, outstanding mentor, 2000-01. Pres. St. Monica's Altar Soc., Converse, 1975; mem. St. Monica's Altar Soc., 1974-96; mem. fin. com. St. Monica's Cath. Ch., 2003; sponsor Young Astronauts, 1993-2000, Hall Patrol, 1990-93, 96-2000, Flag Patrol, 1996-2000; contact person elem. phys. edn. Judson ISD, 1982-96; Eucharistic minister. Recipient award Tex. Pioneer Jump Rope for Heart, AHA, 1999. Mem.: Tex. Ret. Tchrs. Assn., Randolph Area Ret. Educators, Cath. Daus. Am. Roman Catholic. Avocations: oil painting, tee shirt painting, sewing, home decorating, gardening. Home: 587 Co Rd 221 Floresville TX 78147 E-mail: ruthv3000@aol.com.

VOORHEES, STEPHANIE ROBIN FAUGHT, retired art educator; b. Indpls., Dec. 18, 1951; d. Edward Francis and Dorothy Marie (Teague) Faught; m. James Osborn Voorhees, June 19, 1999. BFA, Montclair (N.J.) State U., 1973, postgrad., 1974-76. Substitute tchr. Woodbridge (N.J.) Twp. Bd. of Edn., 1971-73, elem. art tchr., 1973-84, 85-86; middle sch. art tchr. Colonia (N.J.) Middle Sch., 1984-85; high sch. art tchr. Woodbridge HS, 1986—90; middle sch. art tchr. Avenel (N.J.) Middle Sch., 1990-94; art tchr. John F. Kennedy H.S., Iselin, N.J., 1994-98, ret., 1998. Spkr. Woodbridge River Watch, 1991; pvt. art tchr., 1983-93; yearbook advisor Woodbridge H.S., 1989-90, Avenel Mid. Sch., 1991-94, John F. Kennedy H.S., 1995-98; play set designer, 1989, 94-97. Illustrator: Care of the Lower Back, 1975, Touching All the Bases, 1993; profl. muralist. Campaign vol. Rep. Party, Woodbridge, 1992; sec. to the producer Fgn. Broadcast Svc. Dem./Rep. Nat. Convs., Miami, 1972. Recipient Gov.'s Tchr. Recognition award NJ State Dept. of Edn., 1992, Excellence in Edn. award Woodbridge C. of C., 1992. Mem. AAUW, Woodbridge Twp. Fedn. of Tchrs. (v.p. 1980-83, pres. 1983-95, cert. of merit, 1982), Art Educators of N.J., Met. Mus. of Art, Manatee County Vets. Coun. (sr. v.p.), Ecology Club (advisor 1990-94), Am. Legion Aux. 325 (historian 2000-01, treas. 2001-2003), Am. Legion (sec. 2003-, treas. post 325, sec. post 30), Cabane 880 (historian 2000-01, garde de la port 2001-02, condr. 2003—), VFW Post 10141 Ladies Aux. (sec. 2000, sr. v.p. 2001-03). Baptist. Avocations: singing, playing piano, dancing, writing, cruise travel. Home: 29 River Isles Bradenton FL 34208-9003

VOORHIES, MELINDA J(ACQUE), principal; b. Bunkie, La., Feb. 6, 1951; d. John Huddie and Stella (Moss) V. BS, Northwestern State U., 1973; MS, U. Tenn., 1974; postgrad., La. State U., 1989. Cert. tchr. health, safety and phys. edn., spl. edn. tchr. Asst. prof., basketball coach U. Montevallo, Ala., 1974-79; tchr. phys. edn., basketball coach Woodlawn High Sch., Baton Rouge, 1980-82; tchr. behavior disordered students East Baton Rouge Parish Sch. System, 1982-88, instrnl. specialist behavior disordered programs, 1988—2000; prin. Valley Park Alternative Sch., 2000—. Basketball coach Runnels Sch., Baton Rouge, 1986-88; master facilitator Nat. Crisis Prevention Inst., Brookfield, Wis., 1988—; 1st referee finals women's div. I Volleyball Championships, Nat. Collegiate Athletic Assn., 1990; coord. volleyball officials Southeastern Conf., 2001—. Vol. Baton Rouge Food Bank, 1989—. Recipient Wilbur Park Referee Emeritus award, 2002; named Ea. Conf. Coach of Yr., State Coach of Yr., La. Christian Sch. Athletic Assn., 1988. Mem. NEA, La. Edn. Assn., Coun. Exceptional Children, East Baton Rouge Parish Assn. Educators (polit. action com., tchrs. rights com.), La. Prin. Assn., La. Assn. Sch. Execs., Nat. Assn. Secondary Sch. Prin., Assn. Supr. Curriculum Instruction, U.S.A. Volleyball Assn. (referee 1982—), Profl. Assn. Volleyball Officials, Child and Adolescent Svc. System Program. Avocations: bicycling, weight lifting, skiing, fishing, reading. Home: 15825 Woodwick Ave Baton Rouge LA 70816 Office: Valley Park Alternative Sch 4510 Bawell St Baton Rouge LA 70808-1708

VOORNEVELD, RICHARD BURKE, education educator, college official; b. L.I., N.Y., Nov. 16, 1949; s. Albert Henery and Margaret Rita (Burke) V.; m. Susan Monroe Straus, Aug. 3, 1974; children: Edward Corrie, Margaret Brice. BA in Elem. Edn., St. Leo (Fla.) Coll., 1972; MA in Edn. for Gifted, U. So. Fla., 1973; PhD in Spl. Edn., U. Fla., 1982. Cert. elem. tchr., gifted and talented edn., behavior disorders, adminstrv. supr., Fla. Tchr. gifted child edn. Alachua County Sch. Bd., Gainesville, Fla., 1973-79, chmn. gifted edn. program, 1974-78, coord. community leadership program (gifted), 1979-81; clinic liaison multidisciplinary and tng. program Shands Teaching Hosp., Gainesville, 1981-83; asst. prof. edn. Coll. of Charleston, S.C., 1981—, dir. spl. edn., 1987-88, dir. student devel., 1988-90, dean of students, 1990—; dean of students, dir. Ctr. for Student Wellness, 1994—; asst. head master Mason Prep., Charleston, 1999—. Participant, presenter numerous nat. and internat. workshops, 1972—. Contbr. articles to profl. jours., editor 2 books. Bd. dirs. PUSH, Charlotte, N.C., 1989. Recipient merit award Alachua County Tchrs. of Gifted, 1976; grantee S.C. Commn. on Higher Edn., 1985-86. Mem. Nat. Assn. Student Pers. Adminstrsn., Coun. for Exceptional Children, Am. Coll. Health Assocs., Assn. Frat. Advisors, S.C. Inter-Frat. Coun., St. Leo Coll. Alumni Assn. (treas. bd. dirs. 1989), Pi Kappa Phi, Kappa Delta Pi. Roman Catholic. Avocations: horseback riding, tennis. Office: Mason Prep Halsey Blvd Charleston SC 29401 Home: Unit 204 3 Chisolm St Charleston SC 29401-1838

VORNBERG, JAMES ALVIN, education educator; b. Corpus Christi, Tex., Nov. 23, 1943; s. Hadley F. and Gladys O. (Smith) V.; children: Scott, Mark. BS in Edn., S.E. Mo. State U., 1965; MEd, U. Ariz., 1969, PhD, 1973. Cert. tchr., prin., supt., Mo., Tex., Ariz. Tchr. Pattonville Schs., St. Ann, Mo., 1965-66; asst. to supt. Am. Sch., São Paulo, Brazil, 1971-73; asst. prof. U. Ariz., Tucson, 1973-74; from asst. prof. to assoc. prof. Tex. A&M U.-Commerce, 1974-81, prof., 1981—, head dept., 2001—, dir. Prins. Ctr., 1985—. Co-author: The New School Leader for 21st Century: The Principal, 2002; co-author, editor: Texas Public School Organization and Administration, 1989, 91, 93, 94, 96, 98, 2000. Lt. col. USAFR, 1967-94. Office: Tex A&M U-Commerce Dept Ednl Adminstrn Commerce TX 75429

VOROSCAK, ROBERT ANTHONY, rehabilitation specialist, educator; b. Blakely, Pa., Aug. 1, 1938; s. Stephen Joseph and Theresa Evangeline (DelleDonne) V.; m. Theresa Josephine Paternoster, Aug. 27, 1960; 1 child, Stacey Lydia. BA, U. Conn., 1960; MS, U. Bridgeport, 1962, EdD, 1988; CAGS, NYU, 1974. Tchr. math. Masuk H.S., Monroe, Conn., 1960-66, chmn. dept., 1966-67; sr. counselor Bur. Rehab. Svcs. divsn. Vocat. Rehab. Conn., Norwalk, 1967-73, vocat. rehab. supr. Bridgeport, 1973-75, coord. facilities sect., bur. planning, evaluation and tng. Hartford, 1975-86; coord. planning and program devel. and human resource devel. Orgn. Support, 1986-95; retional tng. coord. rehab cont. edn. prog. cmty. providers U. Hartford, 1995—2001. Mem. adj. faculty, cons. Assumption Coll., Worcester, Mass., U. Hartford.; mem. Hartford Area Rehab. Exec. Com., 1978-82; bd. dirs., corporator CW Group, Inc., CW Resources. Recipient Disting. Svc. award Easter Seal Soc. Conn., 1988, Pres.'s award Conn. State Employees Assn., 1988; named Man. of Yr., Am. Sch. for Deaf, West Hartford, 1978; George Washington U. Inst. Ednl Leadership fellow, 1980-81. Mem. Conn. Assn. Rehab. Facilities (Disting. Svc. award 1986), Conn. Rehab. Assn. (treas. 1989-90, bd. dirs., E.P. Chester award 1985, Robert W. Bain award 1995), Farmington Valley Assn. Retarded and Handicapped (bd. dirs.), Conn. Rehab. Adminstrs. Assn. (bd. dirs.), Nat. Rehab. Assn., Nat. Rehab. Counseling Assn., Conn. Rehab. Counseling Assn., Conn. Rehab. Adminstrsn. Assn., N.E. Rehab. Assn. (conn. coun. on devel. disabilities 1991-96, Meritorious Svc. award 1985). Republican. Roman Catholic. Avocations: skiing, swimming, travel, gardening, reading. Home: 11 Michael Rd Simsbury CT 06070-1921 E-mail: drbob@cshore.com.

VOROUS, MARGARET ESTELLE, primary, middle and secondary school educator; b. Charles Town, W.Va., Feb. 14, 1947; d. Benjamin Welton and Helen Virginia (Owens) Vorous. AA in Pre-Edn. (Laureate Scholar), Potomac State Coll., W.Va. U., 1967; BS in Elem. Edn., James Madison U., 1970, MS in Edn., 1975, postgrad., spring 1978, fall 1979, summer 1979, 81; postgrad. U. Va., summers 1977, 78, fall 1978, 89, 91, James Madison U., fall 1981-82, summer 1979, 81-82; MEd in Media Svcs., East Tenn. State U., 1988, 89. Cert. library sci., cert. adminstrn./supervisory, cert. learning disability and gifted edn. Tchr. 3d-4th grade Highview Sch., Frederick County, Va., 1968-69, 3d grade Kernstown Elem. Sch., Frederick County, 1970-71, E. Wilson Morrison Elem. Sch., Front Royal, Va., 1971-72, Stonewall Elem. Sch., Frederick County, 1972-78; tchr. 4th grade South Jefferson Elem. Sch., Jefferson County (W.Va.) Schs., 1978-79, Emergency Sch. Aid Act reading tchr./reading specialist, 1980-82, reading tchr./specialist Page Jackson Solar Elem. Sch., 1983-87; adult basic edn. tchr. Dowell J. Howard Vocat. Ctr., Winchester, Va., 1984-87, G.E.D. tchr., coordinator, 1985-87; libr., media specialist Powell Valley Middle Sch., 1988-91; ABE/GED/ESL tchr. for JOBS program Berkeley County Schs., 1992-94; libr., media specialist Northwestern Elem., 1994-95, first grade tchr., 1995-97; librarian, media specialist Widmyer Elem., 1997—; tchr. 4th grade Ranson (W.Va.) Elem. Sch., 1979; reading tutor; reading tutor, trainer Laubach Literacy Internat., 1989—; art rep. Creative Arts Festival at Kernstown, 1971, Stonewall elem. schs., 1973-77; mem. cultural task force Frederick County Sch., 1974-75, music task force, 1973-74, textbook adoption com. for reading, writing, 1976-77; GED chief examiner, Morgan County Pub. Schs., 1999-; LDSC tchr., Mill Creek Intermediate, 2001-02, LD Resource tchr., Marlowe/Bedington Elem., 2002-, others. Founder, editor: The Reading Gazette, The Reading Tribune, Emergency Sch. Aid Act Reading Program, South Jefferson Elem. Sch., 1980-81, Shepherdstown Elem. Sch., 1981-82; creator numerous reading games, activities. Vol. fundraiser Am. Cancer Soc., Frederick County, Va., 1981; vol. blood donor Am. Red Cross, 1978—; mem. Frederick County Polit. Action Com., Jefferson County Polit. Action Com.; del. 103-109th Ann. Diocesan Convs., Episc. Ch., registrar of vestry Grace Episc. Ch., Middleway, W.Va., 1980-87, lic. lay reader, 1980-90, lic. chalice bearer, 1983-90; lic. lay reader, lay eucharistic min. St. Pauls's on-the-Hill, Winchester, Va., 1996—, vestry mem., corr. sec., 1997—; del. 203rd, 204th ann. coun. Diocese of Va., 1998, 99; committeeperson Lebanon Dems., 1988-89; commd. mem. Order of Jerusalem, 1985—; VEMA leadership participant, 1989-91, 95; facilitator VEMA Conf., 1994, 97; participant Seven Habits program Covey Leadership Ctr., 1993, Spring Festival Children's Lit., Frostburg (Md.) State U., 1998. Recipient various awards, including being named Miss Alpine Princess, award for Excellence in Adult Basic Edn. Dept. Edn., Charleston, W.Va., 1994, RIF Site Coord. for Honorable mention, 1995, Asst Coord. Pritt for Gov. Campaign (DEM), 1995-96, RIF Nat. Poster contest Storyteller for Chpt. I workshop and Ctrl. Elementary, 1994-96, Sigma Phi Omega, 1967, Postulant, Franciscan Order of the Divine Compassion, 2000-01, others. Mem. Lions Club (various offices), Internat. Reading Assn., NEA, Va. Reading Assn., Shenandoah Valley Reading Council, Assn. Supervision and Curriculum Devel., W.Va. Edn. Assn., NEA. Jefferson County Edn. Assn. (faculty rep.), Fauquier County Edn. Assn., Va. Edn. Assn., W.Va. Adult Edn. Assn., Va. Ednl. Media Assn., South Jefferson PTA, Potomac State Coll. Alumni Assn., James Madison U. Alumni Assn., Frederick County Dem. Women, Morgan County Edn. Assn.; mem. PTO Widmyr Elem., Pleasant View Elem., Kappa Delta Pi, Phi Delta Kappa, Phi Kappa Phi.

VOROUS, PATRICIA ANN MARIE, elementary school educator; b. Cleve., Sept. 12, 1951; d. Leon Jr. and Margaret (Cotter) V. BS Edn. in Elem. Edn., St. John Coll., Cleve., 1973; postgrad., Notre Dame Coll., Cleve., 1988, Baldwin-Wallace Coll., Berea, Ohio, summer 1979, 91, Ashland Coll., 1995. Cert. tchr., Ohio. Intermediate tchr. lang. arts, social studies St. Mel Sch., Cleve., 1973-74; grade 6 tchr. lang. arts, social studies and religion St. James Sch., Lakewood, Ohio, 1975-80; tchr. grades 5 and 6 Our Lady of the Angels Schs., Cleve., 1980—. Supervisory tchr. for elem. edn. students Cleve. State U.; from asst. dir. to dir. Lakewood Recreation Dept. Summer Play Ctr., 1973-94, summer 1995; safety patrol coord. Our Lady of Angels, Cleve., 1985—. Craftsman animals, dolls, 3-D scenes for fall festivals and gifts. Roman Catholic. Avocations: travel, swimming, raising showing and training my arabian gelding, basketball.

VOS, GAIL ANN, talented and gifted educator; b. Dearborn, Mich., Feb. 27, 1956; d. Donald Parker and Marion I. (Brush) Mitchell; m. Bruce Everett Vos, June 26, 1977; children: Bryan Parker Vos, Justin Daniel Vos. BS, Ea. Mich. U., 1977; MEd, Wayne State U., 1995. Middle sch. tchr. Trenton (Mich.) Pub. Schs., 1977-79, 2nd grade tchr., 1979-80, learning disabilities resource tchr., 1980-89, sch. dist. tchr. cons., 1989-93, gifted tchr., 1993—. Sch. dist. rep. Wayne County Parent Adv. Bd., Romulas, Mich., 1987-90. Cub scout com., chairperson, leader Boy Scouts Am., Trenton, 1988-94; elder, Christian edn. chairperson Presbyn. Ch., Allen Park, Mich., 1980-85. Grantee Wayne County Intermediate Sch. Dist., 1989, 92, 94, Electronic Data Sys., 1992; named Outstanding Educator Trenton Jaycees, 1989-90. Mem. ASCD, Mich. Assn. of Learning Disabilities Educators. Avocations: needlework, reading, travel camping, swimming. Office: Anderson Elem 2600 Harrison Ave Trenton MI 48183-2483

VOSKA, KATHRYN CAPLES, consultant, facilitator; b. Berkeley, Calif., Dec. 26, 1942; d. Donald Buxton and Ellen Marion (Smith) Caples; m. David Karl Nehrling, Aug. 15, 1964 (div. Nov. 1980); children: Sandra E. Nehrling, Barbara M. Nehrling, Melissa A. Nehrling-Holmgren; m. James Edward Voska, Aug. 31, 1985. BS, Northwestern U., 1964; MS, Nat.-Louis U., 1989. Cert. teacher, Ill.; cert. career mgmt. fellow practitioner Inst. Career Cert. Internat. Tchr. pub. schs., Northbrook and Evanston, Ill., 1964-65; acting phys. dir. YWCA, Evanston, Ill., 1975; quality control technician Baxter Travenol, Morton Grove, Ill., 1978-80; sr. quality assurance analyst Hollister Inc., Libertyville, Ill., 1980-85; info. ctr. trainer, tech. training mgr. Rand McNally, Skokie, Ill., 1985-92; cons., facilitator Capka & Assocs., Skokie and Kansas City, 1992—; dir. edn. Nat. Office Machine Dealers, 1992-94; career and mgmt. cons. Right Mgmt. Cons., Overland Park, Kans., 1994—. Pvt. practice estate conservator. Telephone worker Contact Chgo. Crisis Hotline, 1989-90; CPR instr. trainer Amer. Heart Assn., Chgo., 1977-89; aquatic dir. YMCA, Evanston, Ill., 1969-80; rep. Alumnae Panhellenic Coun., Evanston, 1969-75; grad. Leadership Overland Park, 1996, mem. 15th anniv. special task force. Mem. ASTD (bd. dirs. Kansas City chpt. 1997-99), ASCD, Soc. Human Resource Mgmt., Midwest Soc. Profl. Cons., Assn. for Mgmt. Orgn. Design, Chgo. Orgn. Data Processing Educators, Chgo. Computer Soc., Info. Ctr. Exch. of Chgo., Assn. Quality and Participation, Am. Soc. for Quality (teller N.E. Ill. sect. 1982-84), Internat. Soc. for Performance Improvement, Assn. Career Profls. Internat. founding pres. Kansas City chpt., nat. bd. dirs. 2000—, nat. bd. v.p., pres. elect 2002—), Learning Resource Network. Presbyterian. Avocations: scuba diving, swimming, hiking, camping, travel. Home: 1001 E 118th Ter Kansas City MO 64131-3828 Office: Right Mgmt Cons 7300 W 110th St Ste 800 Overland Park KS 66210-2387 E-mail: kathy.voska@right.com., kvoska@kc.rr.com.

VOSS, JAMES FREDERICK, psychologist, educator; b. Chgo., Dec. 5, 1930; s. Leo Carl and Lydia (Isreal) V.; m. Marilyn Lydia Timm, June 20, 1953 (dec. Oct. 1982); children: Barbara Lynn, Katherine Ann, Mark Frederick, Carol Jean, David James; m. Deborah Jane Steinbach, Oct. 8, 1988 (div. 1997); 1 child, Regina Lynn. BA, Valparaiso (Ind.) U., 1952; MS, U. Wis., 1954, PhD, 1956. Instr., asst. prof. Wis. State Coll., Eau Claire, 1956-58; asst. prof., asso. prof. Coll. of Wooster, Ohio, 1958-63; asso. prof. U. Pitts., 1963-66, prof., 1966—, chmn. dept. psychology, 1968-70, assoc. dir. Learning Rsch. and Devel. Ctr., 1985-92; prin. investigator Nat. Inst. Child Health and Human Devel., 1956-58, 59-70. Fulbright Disting. prof., lectr., USSR, 1979; NSF fellow Ind. U., 1960; vis. prof. U. Wis., 1964; vis. prof., NIMH spl. fellow U. Calif., Irvine, 1970—; vis. prof. Mershon Ctr., Ohio State U., 1989. Author: Psychology as a Behavioral Science, 1974; editor: Approaches to Thought, 1969, Topics in Human Performance, 1972, Informal Reasoning and Education, 1990; cons. editor: Jour. Exptl. Psychology, 1975-80, Jour. Verbal Learning and Verbal Behavior, 1981-87. Recipient Disting. Alumni award Valparaiso U., 1979 Fellow APA, AAAS; mem. Midwestern Psychol. Assn., Eastern Pychol. Assn., N.Y. Acad. Sci., Psychonomic Soc. (sec.-treas. 1978-80), Am. Diabetes Assn. (chmn. bd. Western Pa. affiliate 1974-77, 173-75), Internat. Soc. Polit. Psychology, Sigma Xi.

VOSS, TERENCE J. human factors scientist, educator; b. Cin., June 29, 1942; s. Harold A. and Marguerite (C.) Voss; m. Charmaine E. Wilson, Sept. 3, 1983. BA, SUNY, Geneseo, 1965; MA, Fla. Atlantic U., 1972; postgrad., U. Mont., 1973-78. Cert. profl.ergonomist. Dept. dir., sr. staff scientist Essex Corp., Alexandria, Va., 1980-88; sr. human factors scientist Advanced Resources Devel. Corp., Columbia, Md., 1988-90; lead human factors scientist, fellow engr. Westinghouse Savannah River Co., Aiken, SC, 1990-97, Washington Safety Mgmt. Solutions, LLC, Aiken, 1997—. Cons. in field; mem. adj. faculty psychology dept. DePaul U., Chgo., 1990; human factors cons. U.S. Dept. Energy, 1990—. Contbr. articles to profl. jours. Mem. Citizens Nuc. Tech. Awareness. Named Citizen Amb., People to People Internat., 1985, 1997. Mem.: IEEE (nuc. power engring. com., chair subcom. human factors, control facilities and reliability), Internat. Ergonomics Assn. (process control tech. com.), Sci. Rsch. Soc. N.Am., Human Factors and Ergonomics Soc., Am. Nuc. Soc., Sigma Xi. Achievements include contributions resulting in improvements to nuclear facilities and national consensus standards therby reducing human error, facilitating human behavior and increasing operator and public safety. Home: 203 Trafalgar St SW Aiken SC 29801-3745 Office: Washington Safety Mgmt Solutions LLC PO Box 5388 Aiken SC 29804-5388

VOSSOUGHI, SHAPOUR, chemical and petroleum engineering educator; b. Siahkal, Gilan, Iran, June 25, 1945; s. Mirza Aghasi and Ghamar Talat (Farahpour) V.; m. Ziba Mani, Nov. 6, 1973; children: Anahita, Sarah, Nadia. Grad. diploma, McGill U., Montreal, Can., 1971; MSc., U. Alta., Edmonton, Can., 1973, PhD, 1976. Instr. Arya-Mehr U., Tehran, Iran, 1967-70; rsch. assoc. U. Kans., Lawrence, 1976-77, asst. scientist, 1977-78; sr. scientist Nat. Iranian Oil Co., Tehran, 1978-79; asst. scientist U. Kans., Lawrence, 1979-81, assoc. scientist, 1981-82, assoc. prof., 1982-94, prof., 1994—. Researcher Shell Rsch. Ctr., Rijswijk, the Netherlands, 1978-79; sabbatical researcher Elf Aquitaine, Pau, France, 1989-90; tech. presenter in field; cons. for UN, Nat. Iranian Oil Co. and U. of Petroleum Industry, Ahwaz, Iran. Contbr. over 30 publs. to profl. jours. including Can. Jour. Chem. Engring., Jour. Can. Petroleum Tech., Soc. Petroleum Engrs. Jour., Jour. Thermal Anal., Indsl. Engring. Chem. Fundamentals, Trans. Soc. Petroleum Engrs., Thermochimica Acta, Chem. Engring. Commun., SPE Reservoir Engring., Jour. Petroleum Sci. and Engring. Faculty fellow EXXON Edn. Found., 1982-85; rsch. grantee Columbian Resources Inc., Topeka, 1989, U. Kans., 1983-89, Dept. of Energy, 1982-84, 92—, Core Labs., 1980-81. Mem. Soc. Petroleum Engrs., Am. Inst. Chem. Engrs., N.Am. Thermal Analysis Soc., Soc. of Rheology, Sigma Xi. Achievements include patent in field. Home: 1035 Lakecrest Rd Lawrence KS 66049-3321 Office: U Kans 4006 Learned Hall Lawrence KS 66045-7526 E-mail: shapour@ku.edu.

VOTAW, JOHN FREDERICK, educational foundation executive, educator; b. Richmond, Va., May 9, 1939; s. Frederick Lee and Katherine (B.) V.; m. Joyce Marie Miller, June 8, 1961; children: Laura, Cynthia, Mary, John Jr. BS, U.S. Mil. Acad., 1961; MA in History, U. Calif., Davis, 1969; grad., U.S. Army Colls., 1970, grad., 1985; PhD in History, Temple U., 1991. Commd. 2d lt. U.S. Army, 1961, advanced through grades to lt. col., 1976; comdr. Company C 1st bn. 69th Armor U.S. Army, Hawaii, 1964-65; comdr. Troop A 1st Squadron 11th ACR U.S. Army, South Vietnam, 1966-67, comdr. C&C Squadron 11th ACR, 1975-77; asst. prof. history U.S. Mil. Acad., West Point, N.Y., 1970-73, asst. dean for plans and programs, 1980-81, asst. prof., 1981-82; dep. dir. U.S. Army Mil. History Inst., Carlisle Barracks, Pa., 1983-86; ret. U.S. Army, 1986; dir. First Divsn. Mus., Wheaton, 1986—; exec. dir. Cantigny First Divsn. Found., Wheaton, 1991—. Adj. asst. prof. history Dominican U. (formerly Rosary Coll.), River Forest, Ill., 1991-98, adj. assoc. prof. history, 1998—; dir. Col. Robt. R. McCormick Rsch. Ctr., Wheaton, 1991-2002; series editor Cantigny Mil. History Series. Contbg. author: The D-Day Encyclopedia, 1993, The Encyclopedia of American Wars - The First World War, 1994, The European Powers in the First World War: An Encyclopedia, 1996, Encyclopedia of the Vietnam War, 3 vols., 1998, A Guide to the Study and Use of Military History, 1979, History in Dispute, vol. 5, Encyclopedia of American Military History, 3 vols., 2003; contbr. articles to profl. jours. Mem. adv. com. Ctr. for the Study of Force and Diplomacy, Temple U., 1996—. Decorated Legion of Merit, Bronze Star with "V" device, Purple Heart (3 awards) and others. Mem. Am. Hist. Assn., Orgn. Am. Historians, Soc. for Mil. History (trustee 2001—), Am. Assn. Mus., U.S. Naval Inst. (life), U.S. Army War Coll. Alumni Assn. (life), Ret. Officers Assn. (life), Disabled Am. Vets., Assn. Grads. U.S. Mil. Acad., U. Calif. Davis Alumni Assn. (life), Am. Vets. (life), Am. Legion (life), Kiwanis (Wheaton club 1986—, pres. 1991-92), Phi Alpha Theta, Phi Kappa Phi (life). Avocations: reading, writing, classical music, golf. Office: First Divsn Mus at Cantigny 1 S 151 Winfield Rd Wheaton IL 60187-6097 E-mail: jvotaw@tribune.com.

VOUGHT, BARBARA BALTZ, secondary school educator; b. Pocahontas, Ark., July 9, 1936; d. George Henry and Margaret Frances (Dust) Baltz; m. Carl David Vought, June 5, 1962; children: Vivian Eugenia Terry, Stewart Lee, Stephanie Vought Ortel. BS, Siena Coll., 1958; student, St. Louis U., 1960-61, La. State U., 1962-63, U. Ala., 1972-74. Cert. secondary tchr., Ala. Rsch. asst. Kennedy VAMTG Hosp., Memphis, 1958-60; tchr. Corning (Ark.) High Sch., 1961-62; grad. asst. La. State U., Baton Rouge, 1962-63; instr. U. Ala., Huntsville, 1965-76; tchr. Lee High Sch., Huntsville, 1976; tchr. sci. Randolph Sch., Huntsville, 1976-83, chmn. sci., 1983—98. Grad. fellow St. Louis U., 1960-61; bd. dirs. Ala. State Sci. Fair, Decatur. Co-contbr. articles to profl. jours. Recipient Excellence in Sci. Teaching award U.S. Army Sci. and Humanities, 1984; named Sci. Tchr. of Yr., Calhoun Found., 1985, 87, Outstanding Faculty Mem., Randolph Sch., 1993. Mem. Botanical Garden Soc., Hist. Huntsville Found., Women's Guild Mus. Art (team capt. art bldg. fund campaign 1993, treas. 2000, fin. chmn. 2001, 2002), Delta Kappa Gamma. Roman Catholic. Avocations: travel, collecting antiques. Office: Randolph Sch 1005 Drake Ave SE Huntsville AL 35802-1099

VREELAND-FLYNN, TRACY LYNN, elementary education educator; b. San Antonio, Oct. 18, 1966; d. James Chester and Mary Lou (Meighan) V.; m. Russell Brian Flynn; 1 child, Brian Russell Flynn. BS in Edn., Shippensburg (Pa.) U., 1989; MEd, St. Francis Coll., Loretto, Pa., 1994. women's and men's varsity asst., swim team coach Altoona Area H.S., 1991-92. Tchr. Altoona (Pa.) Area Sch. Dist., 1990—, tchr. 3d grade, 1990—96, tchr. 4th grade, 1996-98, tchr. 6th grade, 1998-99, tchr. 5th-6th grade, 1999—, webmaster, 1998—. Computer trainer; dist.-wide tech. coord. com. Altoona Area Sch. Dist.; parent-cmty. study team ACT 178 dist. com. Outcomes Bd. Edn.; tchr. computer camps Altoona Area Sch. Dist., 1993-96; instr. in field. Mem. NEA, ASCD, Nat. Reading Assn., Pa. State Edn. Assn., Altoona Area Edn. Assn. Republican. Roman Catholic. Home: 4 Woodland Terrace Duncansville PA 16635 Office: Logan Elem Sch 301 Sycamore St Altoona PA 16602 E-mail: trflynn@pennwoods.net.

VU, JOSEPH DUONG, financial educator; b. Hanoi, Vietnam, Mar. 13, 1952; s. Phuong and Nhan (Trinh) V.; m. Huyen Tran T. Do, July 1, 1978; children: Christine, Daniel. BBA, Ohio U., 1973; MBA, U. Chgo., 1975, PhD in Fin., 1984. Asst. prof. Loyola U., Chgo., 1981-85, U. Ill., Chgo., 1985-88; assoc. prof. fin. DePaul U., Chgo., 1988—. Author: Investment Management, 1993. Mem. Am. Fin. Assn., Vietnamese Assn. Ill. (pres. 1993-98). Avocation: tennis. E-mail: jvu@condor.depaul.edu.

VUJOVIC, MARY JANE, education and employment training planner; b. Huntington, N.Y., Dec. 3, 1951; d. Carl David Brell, Sr. and Alice Lucille (Hanson) B. BS in Psychology cum laude, U. Wash., 1973, postgrad., 1980-84. Spl. edn. tchr. Town of Huntington, 1972; adminstrv. asst. Daishowa Am. Corp., Seattle, 1973-74; with King County Work Tng. Program, Seattle, 1973-85, records sect. mgr., 1977-84, contracts mgr., 1984-85; tech. cons., program mgr. Refugee Ctr. of Clark County, Vancouver, Wash., 1985-87; instr., counselor S.W. Wash. Pvt. Industry Coun., Vancouver, 1986-87; planner Wash. Human Devel., Seattle, 1987, dir. planning and MIS, 1987-94; tech. cons. SJL and Assocs., Seattle, 1990—; dir. prog. devel. and evaluation Yakima Valley Opportunities Industrialization Ctr., 1994-2000; dir. devel. and adminstrn. Snohomish County Workforce Devel. Coun., 2000—. Mem. planning and adv. com. Seattle-King County Pvt. Industry Coun., 1987-94; mem. Partnership for Tng. and Employment Careers, Washington, 1991-94. Bd. dirs. Slavia, Seattle, St. James Refugee Program, Seattle, 1993-95. Mem. Phi Beta Kappa. Avocation: south slavic dance and cultural preservation. Office: Snohomish County Workforce Devel Coun 917 134th St SW Everett WA 98204-9377 E-mail: maryjane@snocowdc.org.

VUNCANNON, DELCIE HOBSON, educator, librarian; b. Glendale, Calif., Apr. 26, 1925; d. Stephen Douglas and Erma Elsie (Hoffman) Hobson; m. James Mervin Parker, July 17, 1946 (div. 1960); children—Stephen, Jamie, Whitney, Michael, Timothy, Kelly. B.A., Pomona Coll., 1946; M.A. in Classics, U. Calif.-Berkeley, 1962, M.L.S., 1964. Reference librarian U. Calif.-Davis, 1964-68; reference librarian Calif. State U.-Sacramento, 1968-70, instr., San Bernardino, 1979-81; asst. prof. Chapman Coll., Palms, Calif., 1974—, Coll. Desert, Palm Desert, Calif., 1973— ; adminstrv. head No. Ariz. City Libraries, Flagstaff, 1970-72; cons. archaeologist. Contbr. articles to profl. jours. Mem. Am. Rock Art Research Assn. (bd. dirs. 1979), Rock Publs., Mus. of Man, Archaeol. Survey Assn. So. Calif. Republican. Home: PO Box 711 Yucca Valley CA 92286-0711

VUNJAK-NOVAKOVIC, GORDANA, chemical engineer, educator; b. Belgrade, Yugoslavia, Aug. 26, 1948; arrived in U.S., 1993; d. Vlajko and Mila (Simeunovic) Vunjak; m. Branko Novakovic, Oct. 27, 1974; 1 child, Stasha Novakovic. BS, U. Belgrade, 1972, MS, 1975, PhD, 1980. From asst. prof. to prof. chem. engring. Belgrade U., 1981—. From rsch. scientist to prin. rsch. scientist MIT, Cambridge, 1992—; adj. prof. Tufts U., Boston, 1994—. Contbr. articles to profl. jours., chapters to books. Fulbright Found. fellow, 1986—87. Fellow: Am. Inst. Med. and Biomed. Engring.; mem.: AIChE, AAAS, Orthop. Rsch. Soc., Soc. for Vitro Biology, Materials Rsch. Soc., Fulbright Scholars. Avocations: literature, classical music, movies, travel. Office: MIT E25-330 77 Massachusetts Ave Cambridge MA 02139-4301 E-mail: gordana@mit.edu.

VUŠKOVIĆ, LEPOSAVA, physicist, educator; b. Lešnica, Yugoslavia, Apr. 23, 1941; d. Djordje and Kristina (Obućina) Jovanović; m. Marko Vušković, Feb. 2, 1964 (div. Oct. 1982); children: Kristina, Ivo; m. Svetozar Popović, July 18, 1987; 1 stepchild, Ljubica Popović. Diploma in Phys. Chemistry, U. Belgrade, Yugoslavia, 1963, MS in Physics, 1968, PhD in Physics, 1972. Rsch. fellow Inst. Physics U. Belgrade, 1964-73, from rsch. scientist to head Atomic Physics Lab., 1973-78; NRC/NASA sr. resident rsch. assoc. Jet Propulsion Lab., Pasadena, Calif., 1978-80; dir. atomic laser and high energy physics div. Inst. Physics U. Belgrade, 1981-85; assoc. prof. U. of Arts, Belgrade, 1973-85; assoc. rsch. prof. dept. physics NYU, N.Y.C., 1985-93; assoc. prof. dept. physics Old Dominion U., Norfolk, Va., 1993—2002, prof., 2002—. Mem. gen. com. Internat. Conf. on Physics of Electronic and Atomic Collisions, 1977—81, 1995—99, mem. organizing com. VIII Conf., 1973, mem. organizing com. VII Symposium on Physics of Ionized Gases, Yugoslavia, 76, Dubrovnik, 82; mem. exec. com. Gaseous Electronic Conf., 1997—, sec.-elect, 1997, sec., 99, chair, 2001—. Author: (textbook) The Physics of Cinematography, 1985, (with others) Metrology of Gaseous Pollutants, 1981, Investigation of Electron-Atom Laser Interactions, 1982. Fellow Am. Phys. Soc. (mem. divsn. atomic, molecular and optical physics, publ. com. 1994-97); mem. Optical Soc. Am., European Phys. Soc., Sigma Xi.

WACHSMANN, ELIZABETH RIDEOUT, reading specialist; b. Richmond, Va., Apr. 28, 1945; d. John Nelson and Lily Smith (Garter) Rideout; m. Marvin Rudolph Wachsmann, Aug. 14, 1966; children: Rebecca W. Campbell, Richard Nelson. BS, James Madison Univ., 1966; MEd in Adminstrn. and Supervision, Va. State U., 1989, MEd in Diagnosit and Remedial Reading, 1994. 1st grade tchr. Sussex (Va.) Pub. Schs., 1966-70; 6th grade tchr. Tidewater Acad., Wakefield, Va., 1978-89; 1st grade tchr. Surry (Va.) County Pub. Schs., 1989-92, reading specialist, 1992—. Named Tchr. of Yr. Daily Press/Newport News Shipbuilders, 1992. Mem. ASCD, Internat. Reading Assn., Richmond Area Reading Assn., Va. Br. ORton Dyslexic Soc., Assn. for Childhood Edn. Internat., Nat. Coun. Tchrs. of English, Va. Br. Orton Dyslexic Soc., Phi Delta Kappa, Kappa Delta Pi. United Methodist. Avocations: reading, handwork, cooking, gardening. Home: 13019 Robinson Rd Stony Creek VA 23882-3737 Office: Surry County Pub Schs PO Box 317 Surry VA 23883-0317

WACHTER-REAM, THERESÉ, elementary school educator, supervisor; b. Altoona, Pa., Mar. 24, 1955; d. Leo J. and Verneda A. Wachter; m. David D. Ream, Aug. 26, 1978. BS in Elem. Edn., St. Francis Coll., Loretto, Pa., 1977, MEd in Edn., 1981, MA in Pastoral Min., 1985; PhD in Curriculum and Instrn., Pa. State U., 1994. Instrnl. II Cert., Pa. Elem. educator Altoona (Pa.) Area Sch. Dist., 1977-79, St. Patrick Sch., Newry, Pa., 1979-86; instr. of edn. St. Francis Coll., Loretto, Pa., 1986-90. Bd. dirs. Penn Alto Bottling Works, Inc., Altoona, Pa., 1977-86, Altoona-Johnstown Family Life Office, Ebensburg, Pa., 1986-88, Leo J. and Verneda A Wachter Found., Altoona, Pa., 1987—. Mem. ASCD, Am. Counseling Assn., Assn. for Psychol. Type, Phi Delta Kappa. Roman Catholic. Home: Umbria RR# 3 Orrick Rd Kirksville MO 63501-9803

WACKER-B. DEBORAH, secondary Spanish and special education educator; b. San Diego, Dec. 22, 1945; d. Robert Eugene and Marion Llewella (Bancroft) Wacker; m. William E. Calvert, Dec. 22, 1966 (div. Aug. 1984); 1 child, William E. Calvert II; m. John Steven Bertram, Mar. 8, 1985 (div. Feb. 2001). BA, Belhaven Coll., Jackson, Miss., 1967. Cert. tchr., Miss., Tex. Mid. sch. spl. edn. tchr. Killeen (Tex.) Ind. Sch. Dist., 1982-85; elem. sch. spl. edn. tchr., tchr. ESL, Mansfield (Tex.) Ind. Sch. Dist., 1985-86; jr. high sch. spl. edn. tchr., head dept. Arlington (Tex.) Ind. Sch. Dist., 1986-90; jr. high sch. spl. edn. tchr. Conroe (Tex.) Ind. Sch. Dist.,

1990-92, high sch. spl. edn. tchr., 1992-93, tchr. Spanish, 1993-97, com. mem. supt.'s tchr. adv. bd., 1991-92, com. mem. prin.'s site-based mgmt. adv. team, 1991-92, mem. health benefits com., 1991-94, mem. benefits com., 1995-96; v.p. Bertram Cons., Inc., 1995—; substitute tchr. Northland Christian Sch., 1997—; Spanish tchr., Klein Intermediate Sch., 2000—. Substitute tchr. several sch. dists., 1997-99. Soprano Montgomery County Choral Soc., Conroe, 1991—94, sect. leader, 1995—96; mem. Campus Site-Based Decision Making Team, 1996—97, Arlington Choral Soc., 1986—89; sponsor Tex. Future Tchrs. Am., 1995—97; mem. Houston Symphony League, 1997—2003, Houston Mus. Fine Arts, 1996—97, 1998—, Houston Mus. Natural Sci.; soprano Houston Choral Soc., 2001—. Mem.: NEA, AAUW, Klein Edn. Assn. (v.p. 2002—03), Am. Coun. Tchrs. Fgn. Lang., Conroe Edn. Assn. (pres.-elect 1990—92, exec. com. 1994—97, pres.-elect 1995—97), Tex. State Tchrs. Assn. (1st pres. 1991, spl. edn. caucus), Tex. Fgn. Lang. Assn., Internat. Club (sponsor 1995—2002). Methodist. Avocations: music, reading, travel, internet, birding. Home: Stonegate Villas # 1615 11111 Grant Rd Cypress TX 77429 E-mail: debbiewb@aol.com.

WADDINGTON, BETTE HOPE (ELIZABETH CROWDER), violinist, educator; b. San Francisco; d. John and Marguerite (Crowder) Waddington. BA in Music, U. Calif., Berkeley, 1945, postgrad., Julliard Sch. Music, 1950, San Jose State Coll., 1955; MA in Music and Art, San Francisco U., 1953; studied with, Joseph Fuchs, Melvin Ritter, Frank Gittelson, Felix Khuner, Daniel Bonsack, D.C. Dounis, Naoum Blinder, Eddy Brown. Cert. gen. elem. and secondary tchr., Calif.; life cert. music and art for jr. coll.; cert. in librarianship for elem. sch. to jr. coll., Calif. Violinist Erie (Pa.) Symphony, 1950-51, Dallas Symphony, 1957-58, St. Louis Symphony, 1958-95. Toured alone and with St. Louis Symphony U.S., Can., Middle East, Japan, China, England, Korea, Europe, Africa; concert master Peninsula Symphony, Redwood City and San Mateo, Calif., Grove Music Soc., N.Y.C.; violinist St. Louis Symphony, 1958-95, violinist emeritus; numerous recs. St. Louis Symphony, 1958—. Julliard Sch. Music scholar 1950, San Jose State Coll. scholar 1955. Mem. Am. String Tchrs. Assn., Am. Musicians Union (life, St. Louis and San Francisco chpts.), U. Calif. Alumnae Assn. (life, Berkeley), San Francisco State U. Alumni Assn. (life), San Jose State U. Alumni Assn. (life), Sierra Club (life), Alpha Beta Alpha. Avocations: travel, art, archeology, history, drawing, painting. Office: St Louis Symphony Orch care Powell Symphony Hall 718 N Grand Blvd Saint Louis MO 63103-1011

WADDINGTON, IRMA JOANN, music teacher; b. Nokomis, Ill., June 7, 1929; d. Albert William and Rose Minnie (Hueschen) Miller; m. Ralph Roger Waddington, Nov. 3, 1946; children: Joann, Janet, Jennifer. Cert. piano, organ Ill. State Music Tchrs. Assn. Music tchr. pvt. studio, Pana, Ill., 1957—; ch. organist, choir dir. St. Paul Luth. Ch., Pana, 1957—; keyboard player Waddington Trio, Pana, 1987—98, 2000—02. Composer: Memories of Kerri, 1983, Rejoice! Rejoice!, 1993, Praise! Praise!, 1993. Organist Rotary Club, Pana, 1985—, sr. citizens, Pana, 1970—, local nursing homes, Pana, 1974—. Named Best Piano Teacher, Decatur (Ill.) Herald & Review, 1987, Member of Yr. Decatur Area Music Tchrs. Assn., 1997. Mem. Am. Fedn. Musicians (pres., 1965-68), Music Tchrs. Nat. Assn., Decatur Area Music Tchrs. Assn. (pres. 1983, 84, 90, 94, 95, clinician, 1979—), Ill. Music Tchrs. Assn. (clinician 1991 conv.). Republican. Lutheran. Avocations: travel, golf. Home: 709A Kitchell Ave Pana IL 62557-1875

WADDY, PATRICIA A. architectural history educator; b. Cannelton, Ind., July 29, 1941; d. Luther and Gertrude Viola (Brandyberry) W. BA, Rice U., 1963; MA, Tulane U., 1965; PhD, NYU, 1973. Vis. lectr. Carnegie-Mellon U., Pitts., 1970-71, asst. prof., 1971-77; assoc. prof. archtl. history Syracuse U., NY, 1977-91, prof., 1991—2002, Disting. prof. architecture, 2002—. Vis. lectr. Cornell U., Ithaca, N.Y., 1977, vis. assoc. prof., 1980. Author: Seventeenth-Century Roman Palaces: Use and The Art of the Plan, 1990 (Alice Davis Hitchcock award 1992); co-author: (with D. DiCastro and A.M. Pedrocchi) Il Palazzo Pallavicini Rospigliosi e la Galleria Pallavicini, 2000; editor Nicodemus Tessin the Younger, Traicté dela decoration interieure (1717), 2002. Fulbright grantee, Rome, 1968-69; fellow Am. Acad. in Rome, 1970, Nat. Humanities Ctr., 1984-85, Samuel H. Kress sr. fellow Nat. Gallery Art, 1994-95, NEH fellow, 1998-99, Guggenheim fellow, 1999-00, Am. Coun. Learned Soc. fellow, 1978. Mem. Soc. Archtl. Historians (book rev. editor Jour. 1985-88, editor 1990-93, 2d v.p. 1993-94, 1st v.p. 1994-96, pres. 1996-98), Coll. Art Assn., Renaissance Soc. Am. Office: Syracuse U Sch Architecture Syracuse NY 13244-1250 E-mail: pwaddy@syr.edu.

WADE, BENNY BERNAR, educational administrator; b. Crisp County, Ga., Oct. 3, 1939; s. Julius D. and Eleanor Eugenia (Boulware) W.; m. Merle Bailey Wade, Nov. 11, 1957; children: Noel, Tara. BS in Edn., Ga. So. Coll., 1964; MEd, U. Ga., 1968, Specialist Edn., 1973, EdD, 1977. Lic. reading specialist gifted, adminstrn. and supervision. Tchr., coach Turner County Bd. Edn., Ashburn, Ga., 1964-67; acad. skills coord. Ga. Southwestern Coll., Americus, 1968-71, asst. prof., 1978; curriculum dir. Dooly County Bd. Edn., Vienna, Ga., 1971-78; dir. edn. svcs. agy. Heart of Ga. Coop. Ednl. Svcs. Agy./Regional Ednl. Svcs. Agy., Eastman, 1979-94; exec. dir. RANREB Learning Enhancement Svcs., Inc., Eastman, Ga., 1994—. Cons. parent edn., Eastman, 1977—; mem. Regional Ednl. Svcs. Agy. stds. task force Ga. Dept. Edn., Atlanta, 1988-91; mentor, coach So. Regional Ednl. Bd., 1993-94; owner Sylvan Learning Ctr., Albany, Ga., 1995-98. Author: Benny's Book of Peruvian Proverbs, 1983; editor newsletter Ga. RESA Dirs., 1992. Organizer Four Dimensional Wellness Club, Eastman, 1991; activist Environ. Concers Agy., Eastman, 1989—. Exp. tchr. fellow U. Ga., Athens, 1967; recipient Alumni award for ednl. leadership Ga. Southwestern Coll., Americus, 1980. Mem. Internat. Reading Assn. (local leadership chairperson 1992-93), Ga. Regional Ednl. Svcs. Agy. Dirs. (pres. 1984-85), Ga. Assn. Ednl. Leaders, Amarathine Runners Alliance of the Cosmos (founder), Eastman Rotary (pres. 1985-86), Phi Delta Kappa. Democrat. Methodist. Avocations: reading, writing, running, ruminating, renewing. Home: PO Box 334 Cordele GA 31010-0334 Office: RANREB Learning Enhancement Svcs Inc PO Box 334 Cordele GA 31010-0334

WADE, JUNE BOOTH, secondary school educator; b. St. Petersburg, Fla., Dec. 24, 1934; d. Monroe Phillippi and Julia Lenoir (Burdett) Booth; m. Charles Wade, Feb. 18, 1956; children: Susan Wade Infanzon, John Eric. BSJM, U. Fla., 1956. Tchr. English and journalism Hillsborough County Schs., Tampa, Fla. Mem. Nat. Coun. Tchrs. English, Fla. Coun. Tchrs. English, Hillsborough Coun. Tchrs. English, Delta Kappa Gamma. West Hillsboraigh Chapter, Ret. Educators of FL.

WADE, LEROY GROVER, JR., chemistry educator; b. Jacksonville, Fla., Oct. 8, 1947; s. Leroy Grover and Margaret Lena (Stevens) W.; m. Sandra Martinez Kooreny; children: Christine Elizabeth, Jennifer Diane. BA summa cum laude, Rice U., 1969; AM, Harvard U., 1970, PhD, 1974. Resident rsch. fellow Du Pont Corp., Wilmington, Del., 1969; tchg. fellow in chemistry Harvard U., Cambridge, Mass., 1969-74, sr. adviser to freshmen, 1971-74; resident sci. tutor Radcliffe Coll., Cambridge, 1970-74; asst. prof. chemistry Colo. State U., Ft. Collins, 1974-80, assoc. prof., 1980-89; prof. chemistry Whitman Coll., Walla Walla, Wash., 1989—. Author: Annual Reports in Organic Synthesis, 1975-82, 8 vols., Compendium of Organic Synthetic Methods, Vols. III, IV, V, 1977, 80, 84, Organic Chemistry, 1987, 5th edit., 2003; contbr. articles to sci. jours.; reviewer profl. jours., textbooks. Mem. AAAS, Am. Chem. Soc., Catgut Acoustical Soc., Am. Acad. Forensic Scis., Phi Beta Kappa (pres. Colo. State U. chpt. 1983-84), Sigma Xi. Home: 1123 Sturm Ave Walla Walla WA 99362-3690 Office: Whitman Coll Chemistry Dept Walla Walla WA 99362 E-mail: wadelg@whitman.edu.

WADE, REBECCA HAYGOOD, education professional; b. Manila, Nov. 27, 1946; d. Wilbon Benfield and Gloria (Atencio) Haygood; m. William Edward Wade, Dec. 6, 1968; 1 child, William Edward, Jr. BA, U. Philippines, Manila, 1972; MA, Ball State U., 1979. Lic. profl. counselor, Nebr.; cert. profl. counselor, Nebr., Tex. Instr. U. Philippines, Clark AFB, 1972-73; testing specialist Zweibruecken AFB, Fed. Republic Germany, 1978-79; guidance counselor Untalan H.S., Barrigada, Guam, 1979-84; social svc. worker ARC, Andersen AFB, Guam, 1982-83, Family Support Ctr., Offutt AFB, Nebr., 1985-86; edn. counselor Edn. Ctr., Offutt AFB, 1986-90, edn. svcs. officer, 1990—. Adj. prof. Met. C.C., Omaha, 1991—. Editor: AF Nathan Althsuler, 1989. Vol. USAF Wives Clubs, Clark AFB, Philippines, Bucks Harbor Air Force Sta., Maine, 1974-77; mem. Altrusa Internat. Club, Bellevue, Nebr., 1987—. Mem. Am. Counseling Assn., Assn. for Counselors and Educators in Govt., Nebr. Counseling Assn., Assn. for Multicultural Counseling and Devel., Nebr. Mental State Bd. (bd. dirs.), Nebr. Counseling and Devel. (bd. dirs. 1990-91, Counselor of Yr. 1990), Nebr. Commn. on Status of Women (Women of Yr. award 1992), Nebr. Assn. Multicultural Counseling and Devel. (pres. 1989-90). Avocations: sports, reading, traveling. Office: 55 Mission Support Squadron Offutt A F B NE 68113

WADE, ROBERT HIRSCH BEARD, international consultant, former government and educational association official; b. Tamaqua, Pa., Oct. 5, 1916; s. Edgar Gerber and Florence Annabelle (Hirsch) W.; m. Eleanor Marguerite Borden, Sept. 14, 1946; 1 son, Gregory Borden. AB magna cum laude, Lafayette Coll., 1937; diplome d'etudes universitaires, Bordeaux U., 1938; PhD, Yale U., 1942. Instr. French Yale U., 1939-42; chief Far Eastern analyst Office Naval Intelligence, 1946-54; asst. Office Nat. Security Coun. Affairs, Dept. Def., Washington, 1954-56, dir., 1956-61; spl. asst. to asst. sec. state for ednl. and cultural affairs, 1962; dir. multilateral and spl. activities Bur. Ednl. and Cultural Affairs, Dept. State, 1962-64; U.S. permanent rep. to UNESCO, with rank of minister, 1964-69; asst. dir. U.S. Arms Control & Disarmament Agy., Washington, 1969-73; exec. dir. Fgn. Student Service Council, Washington, 1974-77; dir. Washington office Am. Assembly Collegiate Schs. Bus., 1977-85; internat. cons., 1986—. Mem. U.S. del. to UNESCO Gen. Confs., 1962, 1964, 1966, 68; dep. U.S. mem. exec. bd. UNESCO, 1964-69; mem. U.S. Nat. Commn. for UNESCO, 1977-83, vice chmn., 1978-79; editor Mulberry Press, 1995—. Author, editor: Management for XXI Century, 1982. Trustee Am. Coll. in Paris, 1967-78, chmn. bd., 1967-69. Served to lt. USNR, 1942-46, PTO. Recipient Merit Citation award, Nat. Civil Svc. League. Fellow Acad. Internat. Bus.; mem. Am. Fgn. Svc. Assn., French Heritage Soc., Union Interalliee (Paris), Racing Club (Paris), Chevy Chase Club (Washington), Phi Beta Kappa, Kappa Delta Rho (Ordo Honorium 1991). Republican. Christian Scientist. Avocations: tennis, swimming, piano. Home and Office: 2700 Virginia Ave NW Apt 301 Washington DC 20037

WADE, SALLY MOSELEY, special education educator; b. Little Rock, Ark., Oct. 12, 1951; d. Thomas Wakefield and Doris Virginia (Willis) M.; m. Rodney Carlton Wade, Aug. 16, 1975; children: Sarah Rachel, Wakefield Carlton. BA, Hendrix Coll., 1973; MEd, U. Ark., 1978. Cert. tchr., Ark., Mo., Fla. Tchr. Mitchell Intermediate Sch., Little Rock, 1973-76; learning disabilities tchr. Granite Mountain Intermediate Sch., Little Rock, 1976-79; tchr. psychiat. treatment program Child Study Ctr. U. Ark. Sch. Med. Scis., Little Rock, 1979-80; tchr. spl. edn. Benton (Ark.) Sr. High Sch., 1980; diagnostic tchr. Project LEARN, coord. ednl.-vocat. programs St. Louis County Juvenile Ct., Clayton, Mo., 1980-85; program specialist diagnostic and learning resources system Fla. Bur. Edn. Exceptional Students, Tallahassee, 1986-87; dir. edn. U. South Fla. Psychiatry Ctr., Tampa, 1987-88; parent resource specialist, exec. dir. Fla. Diagnostic-Learning Resources System Specialized Ctr., Tampa, 1988-92, parent resource specialist, dir. spl. children, spl. care, 1992—. Adj. prof. dept. spl. edn. U. South Fla., 1990—; cons. U. Miami, Fla., 1992; trainer numerous orgns., 1989—; pres. Family Network on Disabilities of Fla., 1990-92. Bd. dirs. Very Spl. Arts Fla., 1988—, Fla. Alliance Info. and Referral Svcs., 1992. Methodist. Avocations: hiking, boating, scuba diving. Home: 2520 Bordeaux Way Lutz FL 33559-4020 Office: Diagnostic Learning System 3500 E Fletcher Ave Tampa FL 33613-4708

WADE, SUSAN KAYE, elementary education educator; b. East St. Louis, Ill., Nov. 29, 1956; d. Floyd Robert and Rosemary (Reichert) W. Postgrad., Ill. State U., 1981, 82, So. Ill. U., Edwardsville, 2001—02. Cert. in elem. edn., elem. reading, teaching visually impaired, Ill. Resource tchr. visually impaired Alta Sita Elem. Sch., East St. Louis, 1978-79; tchr. 3d grade St. Catherine Laboure Sch., Cahokia, Ill., 1979-95; tchr. 2d grade Holy Family Sch., Cahokia, 1995—2001; tchr. 3d grade Corpus Christi Cath. Sch., Cahokia, 2001—. Curriculum writer, textbook reviewer St. Catherine Laboure Sch., 1979-95. Liturgy planner, Eucharistic minister, lector Corpus Christi Cath. Sch. Mem. Nat. Cath. Edn. Assn., Coun. for Exceptional Children. Republican. Roman Catholic. Avocations: creating games, art, writing, reading. Home: 806 St Thomas Ln Cahokia IL 62206-1811 Office: Corpus Christi Cath Sch 116 E 1st St Cahokia IL 62206-1852

WADE, THOMAS EDWARD, electrical engineering educator, university research administrator; b. Jacksonville, Fla., Sept. 14, 1943; s. Wilton Fred and Alice Lucyle (Hedge) W.; m. Ann Elizabeth Chitty, Aug. 6, 1966; children: Amy Renee, Nathan Thomas, Laura Ann. BSEE, U. Fla., Gainesville, 1966, MSEE, 1968, PhD, 1974. Cert. rsch. adminstr., 1992. Interim asst. prof. U. Fla., Gainesville, 1974-76; prof. elec. engring. Miss. State U., Starkville, 1976-85; state-wide dir. microelectronics rsch. lab. Miss., 1978-85; assoc. dean, prof. elec. engring. U. South Fla., Tampa, 1985—. Dir. Engring. Indsl. Experiment Sta., 1986-93, exec. dir. Ctrs. for Engring. R&D, 1985-90, mem. presdl. faculty adv. com. for rsch. and tech. devel., 1986-88, mem. fed. demonstration project com. for contracts and grants, 1986-88; mem. adv. bd. USF Exec. Fellows Program, 1987-91; chmn. evaluation task force applied rsch. grants program High Tech. and Industry Coun. State of Fla., 1988-90, vice chmn. microelectronics and materials subcoms. 1987-93, mem. telecom. subcom., 1988-89, chmn. legis. report com. FHTIC, 1989-90, chmn. U. sabbatical com., 1997-98; vice chmn. subcom. on microelectronics and materials Enterprise Fla. Innovation Partnership, 1993-94, chmn. univ. sabbatical com., 1997-98; mem. Tampa Bay Internat. Super Task Force, 1986-92, vice chmn. edn. com. 1988; dir. Fla. Ctr. for Microelectronics Design and Test, 1986-88; bd. dirs. NASA Ctr. Comml. Devel. of Space Comm. Ctr., Fla., 1990-93; bd. trustees Trinity Coll. Fla., 1997—, exec. com. 1998—, chmn. strategic planning com., 2001-; bd. trustees Toccoa Falls Coll., 2002; bd. dirs. New Tampa YMCA; rev. panel govt.-univ.-industry rsch. round table for fed. demonstration project NAS, 1988; solid state circuit specialist Applied Microcircuits Corp., San Diego, 1981-82; sr. scientist NASA Marshall Space Flight Ctr., Huntsville, Ala., 1983; scientist Trilogy Semiconductor Corp., Santa Clara, Calif., 1984; organizer, chmn. Very Large Scale Integrated/Ultra Large Scale Integrated Multilevel Interconnection Conf., Seminar and Exhbn., editor procs., 1991—; organizer, gen. chmn. Dielectrics for Ultra Large Scale Integrated Multilevel Interconnection Conf., 1995—, Chem.-Mech.-Polish Planarization for Ultra Large Scale Integration, 1996—, Conductors for Ultra Large Scale Integrated Multilevel Interconnection Conf., 2000—; cons. in field. Author: Polyimides for Very Large Scale Integrated Applications, 1984, (U.S. Army handbook) Modern Very Large Scale Integrated Circuit Fabrication Processes, 1984, Photosensitive Polyimides for Very Large Scale Integrated Applications, 1986, Very Large Scale Multilevel Interconnection Advanced Metals Tutorial, 1996—, Very Large Scale Multilevel Interconnection Tutorial, 1987—; contr. chpts. on electronics to World Book encys., 1997; contbr. over 125 articles to profl. jours. Active First Bapt. Ch., Temple Terrace, Fla., vice-chmn. bd. deacons 1989-90, chmn. bd. deacons, 1990-91, 93-94, chmn. pastor search com., 1990-91, vice-chmn. long range planning com., 1989-91, vice-chmn. pastor search com., 1994-95, dir. adult coed III Sunday sch. dept., 1993-94, ch. coun., 1994-95, ch. trustee, 1999—, mem. constn. and bylaws com., 1997-99, trustee, 1999—; treas. Tampa Palms Owners Assn., 1994-95, chmn. home decorating com., 1997; vol., United Fund, Miss. State U., 1983-85. Recipient Outstanding Engring. Tchg. award Coll. Engring. U. Fla., 1976, Outstanding Tchg. Incentive program award State of Fla., 1998, Cert. of Recognition NASA (5 times), 1981-88, Outstanding Rsch. award Sigma Xi, 1984, Outstanding Contbn. to Sci. and Tech. award Fla. Gov., 1989, 90, Outstanding Undergrad. Tchg. award U. South Fla., 1999. Mem. AAAS, NSPE, IEEE (sr. mem., guest editor periodical 1982, gen. chmn. Internat. Very Large Scale Integrated Multilevel Interconnection Conf. annually 1984-90, editor conf. procs., 1984-90, chmn. acad. affairs com. CHMT Soc., 1984-86, gen. chmn. univ./govt./industry microelectronics symposium, 1981, tech. program commn., 1991, bd. dirs. workshop on tungsten and other refractory metals 1987-90), Am. Soc. Engring. Edn. (gen. chmn. engring. rsch. coun. ann. meeting 1987, chmn. engring. rsch. coun. adminstrv. com. 1987-90, chmn. coun., 1990-92, session chmn. ann. meeting 1990, 92, bd. dirs. 1990-92, mem. nominations com. 1992-94, mem. long range planning com. 1992-95, Centennial Cert. 1992, 2d Century Cert. 1993), World Future Soc. Internat. Soc. Hybrid Microelectronics, Assn. U.S. Army (bd. dir. Suncoast chpt. 1991-93), Soc. Photo Optical Instrumentation Engring., Univ. Faculty Senate Assn. of Miss. (organizer 1985), Am. Vacuum Soc., Am. Phs. Soc., Am. Electronics Assn., Am. Inst. Physics, Nat. Coun. Univ. Rsch. Adminstrn., Soc. Rsch. Adminstrs (external rels. com. for SRA 1988-91), Fla. Engring. Soc. (v.p. edn. com. 1987-92, pres. 1989-90, bd. dirs. 1989-90, Fla. engring. found. trustee 1989-90, ann. meeting steering com. 1989-90, Outstanding Svc. to the Profession award 1992), Soc. Am. Mil. Engring., Order of Engrs., 1991, Sigma Xi (v.p. 1985), Tau Beta Pi (Fla. Alpha chpt. pres. 1969, 71, faculty advisor Miss. Alpha chpt. 1977-85, faculty advisor Fla. Gamma chpt. 1986—, Outstanding hon. soc. advisor award 1994), Eta Kappa Nu (pres. U. Fla. chpt. 1968, Org. Charter Chpt. U. South Fla. 1998, faculty adv. Kappa Xi chpt. 1998—, Outstanding Honor Soc. Adv. award 1998-99), Sigma Tau, Omicron Delta Kappa, Soc. Am. Inventors, Fla. Blue Key (v.p. 1972, sec. 1971), Epsilon Lambda Chi (founder 1970, pres. 1971). Club: Downtown Tampa Rotary (Paul Harris fellow 1987,94, 2000, perfect attendance award 1986—, chmn. com. on environ. issues 1990), Rotary Club New Tampa (organizer, charter mem., pres. 1995-96, v.p. 1996-97, mem. exec. com. 1996—, dir. internat. svc. 1997-98, sr. dir. 1998-99, 99-2001). Avocations: collecting antique furniture, carpentry, restoring antique sports cars, basketball. Home: 5316 Witham Ct E Tampa FL 33647-1026

WADLEY, CYNTHIA ANN (CYNDE), elementary school educator; b. Moorhead, Minn., Feb. 27, 1963; d. Donald Stewart and Janice Rae (Pittman) Larson; m. Mark Manning Wadley, June 25, 1988. BS, McMurry Coll., 1988; student, Hardin-Simmons U., 1981-85. Tchr. Hawley (Tex.) Ind. Sch. Dist., 1988-89, Wylie Ind. Sch. Dist., Abilene, Tex., 1988—97, 1999—, Abilene Ind. Sch. Dist., 1997—99. Mem. Assn. Tex. Profl. Educators. Lutheran. Avocations: sewing, scrapbooks, rubberstamping.

WADLEY, SUSAN SNOW, anthropologist; b. Balt., Nov. 18, 1943; d. Chester Page and Ellen Snow (Foster) W.; m. Bruce Woods Derr, Dec. 28, 1971 (div. July 1989); children: Shona Snow, Laura Woods; m. Richard Olanoff, July 4, 1992. BA, Carleton Coll., Northfield, 1965; MA, U. Chgo., 1967, PhD, 1973. Instr. Syracuse U., 1970-73, asst. prof., 1973-76, dir. fgn. and comparative studies program, 1978-83, prof., 1982, dir. So. Asia Ctr., 1985—, Ford-Maxwell prof. South Asian Studies, 1996—, chair anthropology dept., 1990-95, assoc. dean Coll. of Arts and Scis., 2003—. Trustee Am. Inst. Indian Studies, Chgo., 1984-93, exec. com., 1991-94; mem. joint com. South Asia Social Sci. Rsch. Coun., 1982-89. Author: Shakti: Power in the Conceptual Struture of Krimpur Women, 1975. Women in India: Two Perspectives, 1978, revised, 1989, 95, Struggling with Destiny in Karimpur, 1925-84, 1994; editor: Power of Tamil Women, 1980, Oral Epics in India, 1989, Media and the Transformation of Religion in South Asia, 1995. Pres. Edward Smith Parent Tchr. Orgn., Syracuse, 1988-89; pres. bd. dirs. Open Hand Internat. Mask and Puppet Mus., 2000-2003. Grantee NSF, 1967-69, U.S. Dept. Edn., 1983-84, Smithsonian Instn., 1983-84, Am. Inst. Indian Studies, 1989, Social Scis. Rsch. Coun., 1989, NEH, 1995, 98. Mem. Am. Anthropological Soc., Am. Folklore Soc., Assn. for Asian Studies. Home: 302 Carlton Dr Syracuse NY 13214-1906 Office: Syracuse U Maxwell Sch Syracuse NY 13244-0001 Business E-Mail: sswadley@maxwell.syr.edu.

WADLINGTON, WALTER JAMES, law educator; b. Biloxi, Miss., Jan. 17, 1931; s. Walter and Bernice (Taylor) Wadlington; m. Ruth Miller Hardie, Aug. 20, 1955; children: Claire, Charlotte, Ian, Susan, Derek Alan. AB, Duke U., 1951; LLB, Tulane U., 1954. Bar: La. 1954, Va. 1965. Pvt. practice, New Orleans, 1954—55, 1958—59; asst. prof. Tulane U., 1960—62; mem. faculty U. Va., 1962—, prof law, 1964—, James Madison prof., 1970—2002, James Madison prof. emeritus, 2002—, prof. legal medicine Med. Sch., 1979—2002, Harrison Found. rsch. prof., 1990—92. Tutor civil law U. Edinburgh, Scotland, 1959—60; vis. Tazewell Taylor prof. law Coll. William and Mary, 1986; med. malpractice program dir. Robert Wood Johnson, 1985—91, mem. adv. com. clin. scholars program, 1989—97; chmn. nat. adv. bd. Improving Malpractice Prevention and Compensation Sys., 1994—98; Disting. Health Law Tchr. Am. Soc. Law, Medicine and Ethics; trustee-at-large Edn. Commn. Fgn. Med. Grads., 1998—. Author (with O. Brien): Cases and Materials on Domestic Relations, 1970, 5th edit., 2002, Family Law in Perspective, 2001; author: (with Waltz and Dworkin) Cases and Materials on Law and Medicine, 1980; editor-in-chief: Tulane U. Law Rev., 1953—54; author (Davis, Scott, and Whitebread): Children in the Legal System, 2d edit., 1997. Scholar Fulbright scholar, U. Edinburgh, 1959—60. Mem.: Am. Law Inst., Inst. of Medicine of NAS, Found. Advancement Internat. Med. Edn. and Rsch. (bd. mem., sec. 2001—). Home: 1620 Keith Valley Rd Charlottesville VA 22901-3018 Office: U Va Sch Law 580 Massie Rd Charlottesville VA 22903-1738 E-mail: wjw@virginia.edu.

WADLOW, JOAN KRUEGER, academic administrator; b. LeMars, Iowa, Aug. 21, 1932; d. R. John and Norma I. (IhLe) Krueger; m. Richard R. Wadlow, July 27, 1958; children: Dawn, Kit. BA, U. Nebr., Lincoln, 1953; MA (Seacrest Journalism fellow 1953-54), Fletcher Sch. Law and Diplomacy, 1956; PhD (Rotary fellow 1956-57), U. Nebr., Lincoln, 1963; cert., Grad. Inst. Internat. Studies, Geneva, 1957. Mem. faculty U. Nebr., Lincoln, 1966-79, prof. polit. scis., 1964-79, assoc. dean Coll. Arts and Scis., 1972-79; prof. polit. scis., dean Coll. Arts and Scis., U. Wyo., Laramie, 1979-84, v.p. acad. affairs, 1984-86; prof. polit. sci., provost U. Okla., Norman, 1986-91; chancellor U. Alaska, Fairbanks, 1991-99. Cons. on fed. grants; bd. dirs. Alaska Sea Life Ctr., Key Bank Alaska; mem. Commn. Colls. N.W. Assn.; pres. Lan Constrn., Inc., 1999—; bd. dirs. Sanitary Dist., 2002— Author articles in field. Bd. dirs. Nat. Merit Scholarship Corp., 1988-97, Lincoln United Way, 1976-77, Bryan Hosp., Lincoln, 1978-79, Washington Ctr., 1986-99, Key Bank of Alaska, Alaska SeaLife Ctr.; v.p., exec. commr. North Cen. Assn., pres., 1991; univ. pres. mission to Isreal, 1998; pres. adv. bd. Lincoln YWCA, 1970-71; mem. def. adv. com. Women in the Svcs., 1987-89; mem. community adv. bd. Alaska Airlines; mem. Univ. Pres.'s Mission to Israel, 1998; mem. bd. dirs. Netarts Oceanside San. Dist., 2002-. Recipient Mortar Board Teaching award, 1976, Disting. Teaching award U. Nebr., Lincoln, 1979, Alumni Scholar Achievement award Rotary Internat., 1998, Alumni Achievement award U. Nebr., 2003; fellow Conf. Coop. Man, Lund. Sweden, 1956. Mem. NCAA (divsn. II pres. coun. 1997-99), Internat. Studies Assn. (co-editor Internat. Studies Notes 1978-91), Nat. Assn. State Univs. and Land-Grant Colls. (exec. com. coun. acad. affairs 1989-91, chair internat. affairs counsel 1996-97), Western Assn. Africanists (pres. 1980-82), Assn. Western Univs. (pres. 1993), Coun. Colls. Arts and Scis. (pres. 1983-84), Greater Fairbanks C. of C., Gamma Phi Beta. Republican. Congregationalist. Address: Chancellor Emerita PO Box 246 Oceanside OR 97134-0246

WADMAN, WILLIAM WOOD, III, educational director, technical research executive, consulting company executive; b. Oakland, Calif., Nov. 13, 1936; s. William Wood, Jr., and Lula Fay (Raisner) W.; children: Roxanne Alyce Wadman Hubbling, Raymond Alan (dec.), Theresa Hope Wadman Boudreaux; m. Barbara Jean Wadman; stepchildren: Denise Ellen Varine Skrypkar, Brian Ronald Varine. M.A., U. Calif., Irvine, 1978. Cert. program mgr. tng. Radiation safety specialist, accelerator health physicist U. Calif. Lawrence Berkeley Lab., 1957-68; campus radiation safety officer U. Calif., Irvine, 1968-79; dir. ops., radiation safety officer Radiation Sterilizers, Inc., Tustin, Calif., 1979-80; prin., pres. Wm. Wadman & Assocs. Inc., 1980—; mem. operational review team Princeton U. Rsch. Campus TOKOMAK Fusion Test Facility, 1993-94; technical project mgr. for upgrades projects Los Alamos Nat. Lab. 1994-96, tech. project mgr. for 3 projects, 1995—; mem. team No. 1, health physics appraisal program NRC, 1980—, operational readiness review team to Princeton U. Rsch. Campus TOKOMAK Fusion Test Facility, 1993-94; cons. health physicist to industry; lectr. sch. social ecology, 1974-79, dept. community and environ. medicine U. Calif., Irvine, 1979-80, instr. in environ. health and safety, 1968-79, Orange Coast Coll., in radiation exposure reduction design engrng. Iowa Electric Light & Power; trainer Mason & Hanger-Silas Mason Co., Los Alamos Nat. Lab.; instr. in medium energy cyclotron radiation safety UCLBL, lectr. in accelerator health physics, 1966, 67; curriculum developer in field; subject matter expert Los Alamos Nat. Lab., Earth and Environ. Scis., Tech. Support Office. Active Cub Scouts; chief umpire Mission Viejo Little League, 1973. Served with USNR, 1955-63. Recipient award for profl. achievement U. Calif. Alumni Assn., 1972, Outstanding Performance award U. Calif., Irvine, 1973. Mem. Health Physics Soc. (treas. 1979-81, editor proc. 11th symposium, pres. So. Calif. chpt. 1977, Professionalism award 1975), Internat. Radiation Protection Assn. (U.S. del. 4th Congress 1977, 8th Congress 1992), Am. Nuclear Soc., Am. Public Health Assn. (chmn. program 1978, chmn. radiol. health sect. 1979-80), Campus Radiation Safety Officers (chmn. 1975, editor proc. 5th conf. 1975), ASTM, Project Mgmt. Inst. Club: UCI Univ. (dir. 1976, sec. 1977, treas. 1978). Contbr. articles to tech. jours. Achievements include research in radiation protection and environmental sciences; Avocations: sailing, Tae Kwon Do, wood working, numesmantics. Home: 3687 Red Cedar Way Lake Oswego OR 97035-3525 Office: 675 Fairview Dr Ste 246 Carson City NV 89701-5428

WADSWORTH, CHRISTOPHER, school system administrator, director; b. Boston, June 18, 1940; s. Philip Pearson and Elizabeth (Shaffer) W.; m. Lori Dingman, July 27, 1963; children: Benjamin, Thomas Pearson. BA cum laude, Harvard U., 1962, MA, 1965, MA in Teaching, 1969. Adminstr. Harvard Coll., Cambridge, Mass., 1963-69; headmaster Nichols Sch., Buffalo, 1969-79, Belmont (Mass.) Hill Sch., 1979-93; head Robert Coll. of Istanbul, Turkey, 1993—2001; exec. dir. Internat. Boy's Schs. Coalition, Dennis, Mass., 2001—. Trustee White Mountain Sch., Littleton, N.H., 1989-93, Winsor Sch., Boston, 1990-93, Istanbul Internat. Cmty. Sch., Cape Cod Acad., 2003, Cape Cod Mus. Fine Arts, 2002—; mem. com. N.E. area coun. YMCA, 1968-74, 80-87; trustee, v.p. N.Y. State Assn. Ind. Schs., 1971-79. Mem. Country Day Sch. Headmasters Assn. (v.p. 1989-90), Headmasters Assn. (sec. 1990-92), Phi Delta Kappa. Avocations: fly fishing, jazz, banjo, racquet sports. Home and Office: PO Box 117 Dennis MA 02638

WADSWORTH, HARRISON MORTON, JR., industrial engineering educator, consultant; b. Duluth, Minn., Aug. 20, 1924; s. Harrison Morton and Alice English (Densmore) W.; m. Irene Hawkins, Nov. 16, 1950; children: Harrison M. III, Alice E. Wadsworth Lunsford. BS in Indsl. Engring., Ga. Inst. Tech., 1950, MS in Indsl. Engring., 1955; PhD, Case Western Res. U., 1960. Registered profl. engr., Ohio. Quality control engr. Union Carbide Corp., Cleve., 1954-56; asst. prof. indsl. engring. Mich. State U., East Lansing, 1956-57; rsch. assoc. Case Western Res. U., Cleve., 1957-60; vis. prof. Middle East Tech. U., Ankara, Turkey, 1967-68; assoc. prof. Ga. Inst. Tech., Atlanta, 1960-64, prof., 1964-91, prof. emeritus, 1991—; pvt. practice cons. Atlanta, 1960—. Author: (with others) Modern Methods for Quality Control and Improvement, 1986 (Book of the Yr. award 1987), 2d edit., 2002; editor: Jour. Quality Tech. (Appreciation award 1982), 1979-82), Handbook of Statistics, 1985, 98; contbr. articles to profl. jours. With U.S. Army, 1943-46, PTO. Fellow Am. Soc. Quality Control (Brumbaugh award 1970, Austin Bonis award 1985, J.L. Jones medal 1986, Schewhart medal 1988, Freund-Marquardt medal 2002), Inst. Indsl. Engrs. (life); mem. Am. Statis. Assn., Sigma Xi. Home: 660 Valley Green Dr NE Atlanta GA 30342-3434

WAGENAAR, THEODORE CLARENCE, sociology educator; b. Heerhugowaard, The Netherlands, July 19, 1948; came to U.S., 1951, naturalized, 1961; 1 child, Keri. AB, Calvin Coll., Grand Rapids, Mich., 1970; MA, Ohio State U., 1971, PhD, 1975. Cert. elem. sch. tchr., Ohio. Asst. prof. sociology Miami U. of Ohio, Oxford, 1975-78, assoc. prof., 1978-82, prof., 1982—, chmn. dept. sociology and anthropology, 1986-92. Program analyst Nat. Ctr. Edn. Stats., Washington, 1980. Author: Readings for Social Research, 1980, Review Guide-Sociology, 1997, Practicing Social Research, 2000; editor Teaching Sociology, 1986-91. Rsch. fellow Am. Statis. Assn./NSF, 1995—; Nat. Ctr. Edn.-Stats. grantee, 1981-85; recipient Mauksch award Disting. Contbns. to Undergrad. Sociology, 1984; Carnegie scholar, 1999-2000. Mem. Am. Sociol. Assn. (Disting. Contbn. to Undergrad. Edn. award 1992), North Ctrl. Sociol. Assn. (Disting. Contbn. to Undergrad. Edn. award 1992), Midwest Sociol. Soc. Home: 6120 Stephenson Rd Oxford OH 45056-9010 Office: Miami U Dept Sociology Oxford OH 45056 E-mail: wagenate@muohio.edu.

WAGGONER, LAWRENCE WILLIAM, law educator; b. Sidney, Ohio, July 2, 1937; s. William J. and Gladys L. Waggoner; m. Lynne S. Applebaum, Aug. 27, 1963; children: Ellen, Diane. BBA, U. Cin., 1960; JD, U. Mich., 1963; PhD, Oxford (Eng.) U., 1966. Assoc. Cravath, Swaine & Moore, N.Y.C., 1963; prof. law U. Ill., Champaign, 1968-72, U. Va., Charlottesville, 1972—74, U. Mich., Ann Arbor, 1974-84, Lewis M. Simes prof. law, 1987—. Dir. rsch., chief reporter joint editorial bd. for Uniform Trust and Estate Acts, 1986-94, dir. rsch., 1994—, joint editl. bd. uniform trust and estate acts; adviser restatement (2d) of property, 1987-90; reporter restatement (3d) of property, 1990—. Author: Estates in Land and Future Interests in a Nutshell, 1981, 2d edit., 1993, Federal Taxation of Gifts, Trusts, and Estates, 3d edit., 1997, Family Property Law: Wills, Trusts, and Future Interests, 1991, 3d edit., 2002. Served to capt., U.S. Army, 1966-68. Fulbright scholar Oxford U., 1963-65. Mem. Am. Law Inst., Am. Coll. Trust and Estates Counsel, Internat. Acad. Estate and Trust Law. Office: U Mich Law Sch 625 S State St Ann Arbor MI 48109-1215

WAGMAN, MICHAEL MARK, gifted and talented educator; b. Phila., Mar. 10, 1964; s. Marvin Morton and Elaine Judith (Kaplan) W.; m. Janice Ilene Heyderman, Aug. 5, 1990; 1 child, Aaron Seth. BS in Edn., Social Studies, West Chester U., 1986; MS in Tech. in Edn., Chestnut Hill Coll., 1993. Cert. instr. level II, social studies, lifetime, Pa. Asst. dir. Cherokee Day Camp, Bensalem, Pa., 1987-94 summers; tchr. social studies and gifted support Sch. Dist. of Springfield Twp., Oreland, Pa., 1987—; adj. prof. ednl. tech. Chestnut Hill Coll., Phila., 1993—. Faculty advisor Model Orgn. Am. States, Washington, 1987—, World Affairs Coun. of Phila., 1988—, Tchg. in a Nuclear Age, Phila., 1989—; sec., bd. dirs. Global Edn. Motivators, Phila., 1992—; presenter ednl. tech. confs., Pa., 1991—. Prodr. of student local history videos for cmty. cable, 1993—. Campus coord. Commonwealth Assn. of Students, West Chester, Pa., 1982-83; The Friar Soc. Svc. Soc., West Chester Chpt., 1985-86; sch. coord. blood drive ARC, 1989—, faculty advisor Springfield Twp. H.S. Student Coun., Erdenheim, Pa., 1989—; co-chair strategic planning Sch. Dist. Springfield Twp., Oreland, Pa., 1993-94. Mem. ASCD, NEA, Pa. Edn. Assn., Internat. Soc. for Tech. in Edn., Coun. for Exceptional Children, World Future Soc. Avocations: computers, sci. fiction, current events, reading. Office: Sch Dist of Springfield Twp 1901 Paper Mill Rd Oreland PA 19075-2418

WAGNER, CHARLENE BROOK, publishing consultant; b. L.A. d. Edward J. and Eva (Anderson) Brook; children: Gordon, Brook, John. BS, Tex. Christian U., 1952; MEd, Sam Houston U., 1973; postgrad., U. Tex., Austin, 1975, Tex. A&M U., 1977. Sci. educator Spring Branch Ind. Sch. Dist., Houston, 1970-98; ret., 2000; dir. CompuKidZ, Houston, 1998—2000; cons. Scott Foresman, Addison Wesley, Ginn, Houston. Cons. Scott Foresman Pub. Co., Houston, 2000-01; owner Sci. Instrnl. Sys. Co., 1988—; dir. Compukidz. Mem. Houston Symphony League, 1992, Mus. Fine Arts, Mus. of Art of Am. West, Houston, 1989, Mus. Natural Scis., Women's Christian Home, Houston, 1991; mem. Houston Grand Opera Guild, mem. exec. bd. 1999-2000, rec./corr. sec.; social chmn. Encore, 1988; mem. Magic Circle Rep. Women's Club. Mem.: AAUW, NAFE, NEA, Internat. Platform Assn., Spring Branch Edn. Assn., Tex. State Tchrs. Assn., Heather and Thistle Soc., Wellington Soc. for Arts (Houston chpt.), Clan Anderson Soc., Art League Houston, Shepherd Soc., Watercolor Arts Soc. (Houston), Houston Highland Games Assn., Space City Ski Club. Episcopalian. Avocations: painting, watercolor media. Home: 2670 Marilee Ln Apt B54 Houston TX 77057-4264 Office: 2301 Fountain View Dr Apt 85 Houston TX 77057-4620 E-mail: wagner2670@aol.com.

WAGNER, DIANE M(ARGARET), theology educator, chaplain; b. Hancock, Mich., Apr. 22, 1943; d. Benjamin Philip and Eunice Rose (La Mothe) W. BA, Alverno Coll., Milw., 1965; MA, Mundelein Coll., Chgo., 1972; student, Clin. Pastoral Edn., Milw., 1979-80. Cert. advanced standing chaplain, 1982. Tchr. grade 1 St. Peter Sch., Skokie, Ill., 1964-65; tchr. grades 1 and 2 St. Cecelia Sch., Hubbell, Mich., 1965-67; tchr. grades 1, 2, 4-6 St. Joseph Sch., Wilmette, Ill., 1967-71; tchr. grade 5. middle grade coord. St. Mary Sch., Buffalo Grove, Ill., 1971-73; tchr. grade 5 St. Alphonsus Sch., Greendale, Wis., 1973-74; recruiter Sch. Sisters of St. Francis, Milw., 1974-79; chaplain, dir. pastoral care Tau Home Health Care Agy., Milw., 1980-88, dir. vols., 1981-88; chaplain, dir. pastoral care St. Mary's Hill Hosp., Milw., 1988-92; tchr. theology, asoc. chaplain Divine Savior Holy Angels High Sch., Milw., 1993—. Mem. Chaplain Adv. Bd., Milw., 1982-88, pres., 1985-88. Author: (tape) College of Chaplains, 1986. Vice pres bd. dirs. Clare Towers, Inc., Milw., 1981-87. Recipient Cert. Appreciation, Clare Towers, Inc., 1987. Mem. Nat. Assn. Cath. Chaplains (sec. regional bd. dirs. 1986-88), Milw. Area Dirs. Pastroal Care Assn. (pres. 1987-88). Democrat. Roman Catholic. Avocations: reading, camping, golfing. Home: 2619 N 39th St Milwaukee WI 53210-2503 Office: Divine Savior Holy Angels High Sch 4257 N 100th St Milwaukee WI 53222-1313

WAGNER, DOUGLAS ALAN, secondary school educator; b. Washington, June 20, 1957; s. Robert Earl and Bernice (Bittner) W.; m. Linda Sue Tinsley, July 18, 1981; children: John Robert, James Alan. BS in Indsl. Mgmt., Ga. Inst. Tech., 1980; student, N.C. State U., 1975-76; MEd in Math., Ga. State U., 1987, EdS, 1991, PhD in Math. Edn., 1994. Cert. spl. edn. tchr., Ga. Mfrs. rep. Hitachi Corp., Atlanta, 1981; tchr. math., football coach Gwinnett Bd. Edn., Lawrenceville, Ga., 1981-84, 85—, chmn. math. dept., 1995—; prodn. supr. Campbell Soup Co., Maxton, N.C., 1984-85. Asst. varsity football coach Parkview H.S., Lilburn, Ga., 1981-90, head jr. varsity football coach, 1983-88; grad. rsch. asst. Atlanta Math. Project/NSF, 1990-94; steering com. Coll. Mgmt., Ga. Inst. Tech., Atlanta, 1983-84, cons., U.S. Dept. Edn., 1997, Cisco Sys., 2001—. Author curriculum materials; spkr. in field. Tchr. ch. sch. St. Andrews Presbyn. Ch., Tucker, Ga., 1977-80, ordained elder, 1979—, clk. pro-tem, 2001; pres. Westminister Presbyn. Ch. Choir, Snellville, Ga., 1989-90, elem. sch. coord., 1995-96. Recipient, Parkview High Sch. Tchr. of the Yr. Runner-up, 1989-90, Parkview H.S. Tchr. of the Yr. 1992-93, Gwinnett Co. Tchr. of the Yr. Finalist, 1992-93. Mem. NEA, Ga. Assn. Educators, Nat. Coun. Tchrs. Math., Ga. Coun. Tchrs. Math., So. Assn. Colls. and Schs. (steering com. Parkview High Sch. 1988-89, peer rev. team), mem. Gwinnett Co. Curriculum Revision, 1991-94, Gwinnett Co. Textbook Adoption Com., 1999-2000), Nat. Bd. Cert. Candidate, 2002-2003 Republican. Avocations: golf, fishing, hunting, flying. Home: 1995 Pinella Dr Grayson GA 30017-1705 Office: Parkview High Sch 998 Cole Rd SW Lilburn GA 30047-5499

WAGNER, ELLYN S(ANTI), mathematics educator; BS, No. Ariz. U., 1971, MA, 1974; postgrad., George Mason U., 1980-82. Cert. tchr., Va. Tchr. math. Flagstaff (Ariz.) Pub. Schs., 1972-76, head math. dept., 1974-76; asst. prof. math. No. Va. C.C., Annandale, Va., 1976—. Participant Writing Across the Curriculum Workshops, Annandale, 1992-93. Recipient recognition for outstanding contbns. to edn. No. Va. C.C. Alumni Fedn., 1993. Mem. Am. Math. Assn. Two-Yr. Colls., Va. Math. Assn. Two-Yr. Colls. (regional v.p. 1989-91, coord. spring conf. 1992), Phi Kappa Phi. Avocations: classical piano, ballroom dancing. E-mail: ewagner@nv.cc.va.us.

WAGNER, FRANCES RITA, secondary school educator; b. Pasadena, Calif., Feb. 8, 1947; d. Joseph Francis and Reta Clarice (Bell) Inco; m. Danny Eugene Wagner, Aug. 6, 1969; 1 child, Christine Marie Wagner Barth. BA, Calif. State Coll., 1969; Cert. Paralegal Studies, U. La Verne (Calif.), 1991; MA in Tchg., Grand Canyon U., 2001. Cert. instrumental music tchr., English lit. tchr., social scis. tchr. Calif. Tchr. La Canada (Calif.) Unified Sch. Dist., 1984-90, Covina Valley Unified Sch. Dist., Covina, Calif., 1991—, cons., 1996—, splst. at-risk students, 1997. Cons. Pasadena (Calif.) C.C., 1987. Author: poems. Mem. PTA South Hills H.S., Covina, Calif., 1991—. Grantee L.A. Opera Assn., 1997; recipient mini-grant Rotary Club Internat., 1996; named Hon. Life Mem. PTA South Hills H.S., 1996; Winner 1st Place Art PACE Art Found., 1995. Mem. Sigma Alpha Iota, Phi Delta Kappa. Avocations: writing, gardening, embroidery, art, baking. Office: South Hills HS 645 S Barranca St West Covina CA 91791-2943

WAGNER, GERALDINE MARIE, nursing educator, consultant; b. Renton, Wash., Apr. 12, 1948; d. Ernest F. and Vera P. (Temiraeff) W. AA, Pasadena City Coll., 1970; BA cum laude, Calif. State U., Northridge, 1977; BSN, Calif. State U., L.A., 1982; MEd summa cum laude, Azusa Pacific U., 1993. Cert. pub. health nurse, Calif. Dept. Health Svcs. In utilization mgmt. Blue Cross, Woodland Hills, Calif., 1987-88, Healthmarc, Pasadena, Calif., 1988-90; nursing educator, asst. dir. vocat. nursing program Casa Loma Coll., L.A., 1991-92, dir. program planning and devel., and coord. continuing edn. Lake View Terrace, 1992-93; dir. vocat. nursing program Glendale (Calif.) Career Coll., 1994-95; with patient care rev. svcs. U. So. Calif. U. Hosp., L.A., 1996—; med.-legal nurse cons., 2000—. Capt. Nurse Corp, U.S. Army, 1979-84. Mem. Am. Math. Soc., Computer Using Educators, Res. Officers Assn. of U.S., Am. Legion (3d vice comdr.), Army Nurse Corps. Assn., Amvets, Cath. War Vets., Assn. U.S. Army, Nat. Assn. Cath. Nurses, U.S. Naval Inst., Fellowship of Cath. Scholars, Inst. of Religious Life, Mil. Officer Assn. Am., Assn. of Hebrew Catholics, Order of Preachers, Pi Lambda Theta, Sigma Theta Tau. Roman Catholic. Home: 924 Rock Rose Ln Lompoc CA 93436 E-mail: srgmwagnerop@earthlink.net.

WAGNER, GÜNTER PAUL, biologist educator; b. Vienna, May 28, 1954; came to U.S., 1991; s. Otto Karl and Käthe Auguste (Birke) W.; m. Herta Ruttner Brinkmann, Dec. 31, 1978 (div. 1985); 1 child, Susanne Karoline; m. Michaela Sabine Hauser, July 19, 1985; children: Veronika Eszter, Nikolas Frederik. PhD, U. Vienna, Austria, 1979; MA (hon.), Yale U., 1992. Asst. prof. U. Vienna, 1985-90, assoc. prof., 1990-91; prof. biology Yale U., New Haven, 1991—2003, Alison Richard prof., 2003—, chmn. dept. ecology and evolutionary biology, 1996—2001. Bd. dirs. Konrad Lorenz Inst. for Evolution and Cognition Rsch.; vis. prof. Northwestern U., Evanston, Ill., 1987-88, U. Basel, Switzerland, 1991, U. Leiden, The Netherlands, 1995; Gompertz lectr. U. Calif., Berkeley, 1993; disting. lectr. Internat. Inst. for Applied Sys. Analysis, 1995; Sewell Wright lectr. U. Chgo., 1996. Mem. editl. bd.: Theory in the Bioscis., 1998—, Jour. of Theoretical Biology, 1999—2001, Evolution and Devel., 1999—, Biology and Philosophy, 2001—, Am. Naturalist, 2001—, chief editor: Molecular and Devel. Evolution, 1999—, mem. publ. com.: Yale U. Press, 1992—95; contbr. articles to profl. jours. Recipient MacArthur prize MacArthur Found., 1992. Fellow AAAS; mem. European Soc. Evolutionary Biology (editl. bd. 1988-92), Austrian Acad. Scis. (corr.), Soc. for Study of Evolution (assoc. editor 1994-97), Soc. Systematic Biology, Soc. for Integrative and Comparative Biology (chair divsn. evolutionary devel. biology 2000—). Lutheran. Avocations: sailing, canoeing, horseback riding, literature, music. Office: Yale Univ 165 Prospect St New Haven CT 06520-8106 E-mail: gunter.wagner@yale.edu.

WAGNER, HAZEL ANN, primary and elementary school educator; b. Hallock, Minn., July 3, 1953; d. Harold R. and Helen Mattson; m. Ronald D. Wagner, June 9, 1973; children: Angela, Jon. AS, Sauk Valley Jr. Coll., Dixon, Ill., 1973; BS, Idaho State U., Pocatello, 1981. Cert. elem. edn. tchr., Idaho. Kindergarten tchr. Sch. Dist. 25, Pocatello, Idaho, 1981--. Mem. Wilcox leadership com. Sch. Dist. 25, 2002, mem. kindergarten report card com., 2002—03. Ch. coun. Good Shepherd Luth. Ch., Pocatello, 1990-97, sec. 1992-93, christian edn. chmn. 1990-92. Mem. NEA, Idaho Edn. Assn., Pocatello Edn. Assn., Nat. Assn. Edn. Young Children, Pocatello Assn. Edn. Young Children. Avocations: grandchildren, plants, crafts, gardening. Home: 2095 N Inkom Rd Inkom ID 83245-1719

WAGNER, MARILYN FAITH, retired elementary school educator; b. Salinas, Calif. d. Clay Chester and Gladys Edna (Wiley) W. AA, Hartnell Coll., Salinas, 1956; BA, San Jose (Calif.) State U., 1958; MA in Computer Edn., U.S. Internat. U., San Diego, 1987; diploma, Inst. Children's Lit., Redding Ridge, Conn., 1981. Cert. elem. tchr., cross-cultural lang. acad. devel., tech. in edn., Calif. Tchr. Hollister (Calif.) Elem. Sch., 1958—60, Greenfield (Calif.) Schs., 1958—2000, Alum Roc, Union Sch. Dist., San Jose, 1960—2000; ret., 2000; substitute and contract tchr. Alum Roc Union Sch. Dist., San Jose, Calif., 2001—. Mem. Calif. Ret. Tchrs. Assn., Spartan Found., Monterey Bay Aquarium.

WAGNER, MARVIN, general and vascular surgeon, educator; b. Milw., Feb. 20, 1919; s. Benjamin and Ella (Drotman) W.; m. Shirley Semon; children: Terry, Jeffrey, Penny. MD, Marquette U., 1944, MS, 1951. Diplomate Am. Bd. Surgery. Intern Mt. Sinai Med. Ctr., Milw., 1944-45, jr. and sr. resident in surgery, 1945-46, 47-50; pvt. practice Milw., 1950—. Mem. staff Columbia, Milw. Children's, Milwaukee County Gen., St. Joseph's, VA, Froedtery Meml. Luth. hosps., Good Samaritan Med. Ctr., Sinai-Samaritan Ctr.; chmn., chief dept. surgery St. Michael's Hosp., 1965-69, pres. med. staff, 1981-82; vascular cons. Trinity Meml. Hosp., Waukesha (Wis.) Meml. Hosp.; clin. prof. surgery, adj. prof. anatomy Med. Coll. Wis., Milw.; mem. occupational adv. com. Milw. Area Tech. Coll., 1982-83; lectr., condr. workshops, site visitor in field; also others. Author: (with T. Lawson) Segmental Anatomy: Applications to Clinical Medicine, 1982 (Most Outstanding Book in Health Scis. award Assn. Am. Pubs. 1982), Atlas of Chest Imaging; contbr. over 85 articles to med. jours. including Surgery, Wis. Med. Jour., Am. Jour. Obstet. Surg. Gynecology, Modern Medicine, AMA Archives Surgery, Marquette Med. Rev., Am. Jour. Gastroenterology, Surg. Gynecology and Obstetrics, Sci., Transplantation Bull., Angiology, Abdominal Surgery, Am. Jour. Surgery, Archives Surgery, Jour. AMA. Mem. United Way Corp., 1975-78; chmn. physicians div. United Fund, 1972, bd. dirs., 1973-76, chmn. profl. div., 1973, co-chmn. doctor's div., 1977; mem. agy. facilities rev. com. and steering com. Southeastern Wis. Health Systems Agy., 1976-77; mem. adlumni fund raising com. Marquette U., 1971-72; mem. fund rasing com. project 75, Med. Coll. Wis., 1975-76. Recipient Disting. Svc. award Med. Coll. Wis., 1980, Alumnus of Yr. award, 1985, citation Milw. County Bd. Supervisors, 1988; Marvin Wagner endowed chair in anatomy and cellular biology named in his honor, 1988-91; grantee Am. Heart Assn., 1957-59, Milw. Cancer Soc., 1959-60, Wis. Heart Assn., 1960, USPHS, 1960-62, 86-89, NIH, 1960-62, Taitel, 1961, 62, 64, 65, 66, 3M Corp., 1968, Med. Coll. Wis., 1972, Winters Rsch. Found., 1976-80, McMillan Pub. Co., 1979-82, Tisshberg Found., 1985. Fellow ACS (sci. exhibit award 1957, 70); mem. AAUP, AMA (Physician's recognition award 1980-85, 89), Am. Assn. Anatomists, Cen. Surg. Soc., Collegium Internat. Chirurglae Digestivae, Soc. for Surgery Alimentary Tract, Am. Assn. Clin. Anatomists, Milw. Acad. Medicine, Milw. Acad. Surgery (coun. 1973-76), N.Y. Acad. Scis., Western Surg. Assn., Wis. Heart Assn., Wis. Surg. Soc. (coun. 1973-76), Med. Soc. Milwaukee County (pres. 1975, President's citation 1975), Alpha Omega Alpha. Achievements include patent for spandex sutures and prosthesis patches. Office: Med Coll Wis Anatomy and Cellular Biology 8701 W Watertown Plank Rd Milwaukee WI 53226-3548 also: 2350 W Villard Ave Ste 203 Milwaukee WI 53209-5082

WAGNER, PAUL ANTHONY, JR., education educator; b. Pitts., Aug. 28, 1947; s. Paul A. and Mary K. Wagner; children: Nicole S., Eric P., Jason G., Emily Ryanne. BS, N.E. Mo. State U., 1969; MEd, U. Mo., 1972; MA in Philosophy, 1976, PhD in Philosophy of Edn., 1978. Internal expeditor electromotive div. GM, La Grange, Ill., 1970-71; instr. Moberly (Mo.) Jr. Coll., 1972-73, U. Mo., Columbia, 1973-78, acting dir. instl. rsch. and planning, 1990-92, dir. univ. self study, 1991-92; instr. Mo. Mil. Acad., 1978-79; prof. edn. and philosophy U. Houston-Clear Lake, Atrium Ctr. Disting. Rsch. Prof., 1980, Chancellor's Disting. Svc. Prof., 1985, dir. Inst. Logical and Cognitive Studies, 1980—, dir. Project in Profl. Ethics, 1989—, chmn. Dept. Edn. Found., 1989-92; adj. prof. bus. mgmt. U. Houston-Victoria, chmn. edn. dept., 2003—. Judge Sears Intercollegiate Ethics Bowl, Dallas, 1998; pres. Wagner & Assoc. Ednl. Consulting, 1988-93; dir. Tex. Ctr. for Study Profl. Ethics in Tchg., 1988-95; rsch. assoc. Ctr. for Moral Devel., Harvard U., 1985-86; vis. scholar Stanford U., Palo Alto, Calif., 1981; cons. total quality mgmt. Golden Gate U., 1992-93, M.D. Anderson Cancer Ctr. and Hosp., 1992-93, U. Houston-Victoria, 1993; cons. strategic planning Houston Chronicle Newspaper, 1997; chair So. Accreditation of Coll. and Sch. steering com. U. Houston, Clear Lake, 1990-93, pres. faculty senate, 1999-2001; chair planning and budgeting com., chair, Univ. Life com., 2003-2007, Houston Tenneco Marathon, 1992-94; steering com. Trilateral Conf. and Supershow Greater Human Partnership, 1994-95; cons., ethics trainer Am. Leadership Forum, 1995-98; planning com. Tex. Ethics in Govt. Ann. Conf., 1995-98; ; adj. prof. ethical theory U. Houston, 2000—; faculty exec. com. U. Houston Sys., 1999-2001, chair univ. life com., 2003—; cons. in field. Author: (with F. Kierstead) The Ethical Legal and Multicultural Founds. of Teaching, 1992, Understanding Professional Ethics, 1996, Wagner-Kierstead Moral Self-Assessment Protocol, 2d edit., 2002; contbr. articles to profl. jours. on sci. edn., mgmt. theory and philosophy of edn.; Mem. editl. bd. Jour. of Thought, 19815, Focus on Learning, 1982-85; editorial cons. Instrnl. Scis., 1981-83; editorial assoc. Brain and Behavioral Scis., 1985. Vice-chmn. Human Rights Com., Columbia, Mo., 1978-79; Sunday sch. tchr. Mary Queen Cath. Ch., Friendswood, Tex., 1979-85; choir, Queen of Angels Catholic Ch., Dickinson, Tex, founding bd. dir. Bay Area Symphony Soc., 1983-85; capital campaign com. Soc. Prevention Cruelty to Animals, 1989-91; publicity com. Am. Cancer Soc., Houston chpt., 1989-92; cons. in strategic planning M.D. Anderson Cancer Ctr. vol. divsn., 1992-93; steering com. City of Houston Emerging Bus. Conf., 1994-95, Trilateral Conf., Greater Houston Partnership, 1994-95; active Houston Bus. Promise; chair strategic planning com. Leadership Houston, 1996-98; bd. dir. Houston Vol. Ctr., Leanna Spraianno Dance Co., 1999-2002, Baker Inst., 1998-2001, chair, 1999-2001; ann. leadership briefing com. Rice U., 2001-03; mem. Linda Lorelle Scholarship Com., 1995—, Project Grad Coordinating Coun., 1994-96, pres., 1995-96; emcee, expert commentator for pub. TV, Channel 8, Houston, 1989-2002. Sgt. Mo. N.G., 1970-76; mem. choir Queen of Angels Cath. Ch., Dickinson, Tex., 2003--. Recipient Cert. of Appreciation,

City of Columbia, 1978; K.E. Graessle scholar, 1968, Mo. Peace Studies Inst. grantee, 1971. Mem. AAUP, Assn. Applied and Profl. Ethics, Am. Assn. Pub. Adminstrs. (ethics com.), Am. Philos. Assn., Assn. Philosophers in Edn. (exec. bd., v.p.), Philosophy of Edn. Soc. (exec. sec.-treas., hospitality chair 1995-96), Am. Ednl. Studies Assn., Philosophy Sci. Assn., S.W. Philosophy Edn. Soc., Tex. Network for Tchr. Tng. in Philosophy for Children (bd. dirs. 1983-90), Tex. Ctr. for Ethics in Edn. (bd. dirs. 1990-98), Tex. Ednl. Found. Soc. (pres. 1995-98), Tex. Assn. Coll. Tchrs., So. Assn. Colls. Coord., Houston Bar Assn. (steering com. NAFTA Conf. 1993-94), Informal Logic Assn., Leadership Houston, Friends Hermann Pk., Clearlake Cir. (chair 1979-85), Phi Delta Kappa, Kappa Delta Pi. Roman Catholic. Avocations: running, reading, opera, ballet. Home: RR 4 Box 217 Navasota TX 77868-9413 Office: U Houston 2700 Bay Area Blvd Rm 338 Houston TX 77058-1002

WAGNER, PETER EWING, physics and electrical engineering educator; b. Ann Arbor, Mich., July 4, 1929; s. Paul Clark and Charlotta Josephine (Ewing) W.; m. Caryl Jean Veon, June 23, 1951; children: Ann Frances, Stephen Charles. Student, Occidental Coll., 1946-48; AB with honors, U. Calif., Berkeley, 1950, PhD, 1956. Teaching rsch. asst. U. Calif., 1950-56; rsch. physicist Westinghouse Rsch. Labs., Pitts., 1956-59; assoc. prof. elec. engring. Johns Hopkins, 1960-65, prof., 1965-73; dir. Ctr. for Environ. and Estuarine Studies U. Md., 1973-80, prof., 1973-81. Vis. prof. physics U. Ala., Huntsville, 1980-81, prof., 1981; vice chancellor for acad. affairs, prof. physics U. Miss., 1981-84; provost, prof. physics and elec. engring. Utah State U., 1984-89; v.p. acad. affars and provost SUNY, Binghamton, 1989-92, prof. physics and elec. engring., 1989-99, prof. emeritus, 1999—; spl. projects engr. State of Md., 1971-72; mem. Gov.'s Sci. Adv. Coun., 1973-77, Md. Power Plant Siting Adv. Com., 1972-80; cons. in field. Contbr. articles to profl. jours.; patentee in field. Trustee Chesapeake Rsch. Consortium, 1974-80, chmn. bd. trustees, 1979-80. Guggenheim fellow Oxford U., 1966-67 Mem. Nat. Assn. State Univs. and Land Grant Colls. (mem. coun. acad. affairs, mem. affirmative action com. 1986-89, chmn. nominating com. 1988-89, chmn. libr. commn. 1989-92), Ctr. Rsch. Librs. (bd. dirs. 1991-97, mem. budget and fin. com. 1991-93, vice chair 1992-93, chair 1993-94, chair nominating com. 1994-95), Sierra Club (chpt. chair conservation com. 2000—, mem. chpt. exec. com. 2000—), U. Calif. Berkeley Alumni Assn. (life), Blue Key, Gold Key, Phi Beta Kappa, Phi Beta Kappa Fellows (life, bd. dirs. 1995-2001), Sigma Xi (life), Phi Kappa Phi, Eta Kappa Nu. Home: 2650 Maple Ave Morro Bay CA 93442-1726 E-mail: cpwags@charter.net.

WAGNER, ROBERT TODD, university president, sociology educator; b. Sioux Falls, S.D., Oct. 30, 1932; s. Hans Herman and Helen Emilie (Castle) W.; m. Mary Kathryn Mumford, June 23, 1954; children: Christopher, Andrea. BA, Augustana Coll., Sioux Falls, 1954; MDiv, Seabury Western Theol. Sem., 1957, STM, 1970; PhD, S.D. State U., 1972; DHL, Augustana Coll., 1994. Ordained to ministry Episc. Ch., 1957. Staff analyst AMA, Chgo., 1954-57; vicar Ch. of Holy Apostles, Sioux Falls, 1957-64; chaplain All Saints Sch., Sioux Falls, 1962-64; rector Trinity Episcopal Ch., Watertown, S.D., 1964-69; prof. sociology S.D. State U., Brookings, 1971—, acting head dept. sociology, 1978, asst. to v.p. for acad. affairs, 1980-84, pres., 1985-97; v.p. Dakota State U., Madison, S.D., 1984-85. Cons. sociologist Devel. Planning and Research, Manhattan, Kans., 1976-85; bd. dirs. Deuel County Nat. Bank, Clear Lake, S.D., Found. Seed Stock. Bd. dirs. Karl Mundt Found., Prairie Repertory Theatre, REACH, S.D. 4-H Found., S.D. State U. Found., SA Found., Griffith Charitable Trust, F.O. Butler Found., Christian Edn. Camp and Conf. of Episcopal Dioceses of S.D. Arthur Vinning Davis Found. fellow, 1969-70, Episcopal Ch. Found. fellow, 1969-71, Augustana Coll. fellow, 1977. Mem. Nat. Assn. State Univs. and Land Grant Colls., Brookings C. of C., Phi Kappa Phi, Phi Kappa Delta, Pi Gamma Mu, Alpha Kappa Delta, Alpha Lambda Delta, Sigma Gamma Delta. Lodges: Elks, Rotary. Republican. Avocations: railroading, gardening, cooking.*

WAGNER, ROY, anthropology educator, researcher; b. Cleve., Oct. 2, 1938; s. Richard Robert and Florence Helen (Mueller) W.; m. Brenda Sue Geilhausen, June 14, 1968 (div. Dec. 1994); children: Erika Susan, Jonathan Richard. AB, Harvard U., 1961; AM, U. Chgo., 1962, PhD, 1966. Asst. prof. anthropology So. Ill. U., Carbondale, 1966-68; assoc. prof. Northwestern U., Evanston, Ill., 1969-74; prof. U. Va., Charlottesville, 1974—, chmn. dept., 1974-79. Mem. cultural anthropology panel NSF, Washington, 1981-82. Author: (novels) Habu, 1972, The Invention fo Culture, 1975, Lethal Speech, 1978, Symbols That Stand for Themselves, 1986, An Anthropology of the Subject, 2000. Social Sci. Research Council faculty research grantee, 1968; NSF postdoctoral research grantee, 1979. Fellow Am. Anthropol. Assn. Avocation: student hot-air balloon pilot. Home: 726 Cargil Ln Charlottesville VA 22902-4302 Office: U Va Dept Anthropology University Station Charlottesville VA 22906

WAGNER, RUTH JOOS, secondary school educator; b. L.A., June 1, 1933; d. Walter Joos and Ruth McKenzie (Edwards) J.; m. Gerald Dayton Wagner, Dec. 17, 1960; 1 child, Gregory Dayton. BA, UCLA, 1955, MA, 1976. Cert. primary Tchr., Calif. Kindergarten tchr. Inglewood (Calif.) Unified Sch. Dist., 1955—59, 1963—93, Coronado (Calif.) Unified Sch. Dist., 1959-62; pres. Rainbow West Assocs., L.A., 1986—. Ball chmn. League for Crippled Children, L.A., 1984, pres., 1988; bd. trustees L.A. Orthopaedic Hosp. Found., 1996-98; bd. dirs. L.A. Orthopaedic Hosp., 1998—; pres. League for Crippled Children, 2003—. Named Tchr. of Yr., Inglewood Sch. Dist., 1984. Mem. NEA, Calif. Tchrs. Assn, Inglewood Tchrs. Assn., Greater L.A. Zoo Assn., World Affairs Coun., Lake Arrowhead Country Club. Republican. Episcopalian. Avocations: tennis, watercolor painting. Home: 2117 Eric Dr Los Angeles CA 90049-1816

WAGNER, SAMUEL, V, secondary school English language educator, college counselor; b. West Chester, Pa., Dec. 28, 1965; s. Samuel and Mary Ann (Baker) Wagner; m. Allison Lee Lewis, May 25, 1991; children: Samuel Jackson, Spencer Lee. BS in English Lit., Haverford Coll., 1988; MEd, U. New Orleans, 1995. Intern in English, asst. coach Westtown (Pa.) Sch., spring 1989; tchr. upper sch. English Metairie (La.) Pk. Country Day Sch., 1989-97; head upper sch. Hutchison Sch., Memphis, 1997—99; dir. coll. counseling The Miami Valley Sch., Dayton, Ohio, 1999—. Asst. varsity soccer coach Metairie Pk. Country Day Sch., 1989—94; advisor to student senate Metairie Country Day Sch., 1990—95, chairperson headmaster adv. com., 1994—97, coll. counselor, 1995—97; interim upper sch. prin. Miami Valley Sch., 2000—01; presenter ann. conf. Ind. Sch. Assn. of the South, New Orleans, 1992, New Orleans, 96. Mem.: Nat. Assn. Coll. Admissions Counseling, Nat. Coun. Tchrs. English, So. Assn. for Coll. Admissions Counseling, Nat. Assn. Secondary Sch. Prins., Kappa Delta Pi, Phi Delta Kappa, Alpha Theta Epsilon. Republican. Mem. Soc. Of Friends. Home: 5209 Mallet Club Dr Dayton OH 45439-3278 Office: The Miami Valley Sch 5151 Denise Dr Dayton OH 45429

WAGNER, SUSAN ELIZABETH, secondary school educator; b. Shelby, Ohio, Jan. 22, 1951; d. Joseph H. and Patricia A. (Shoup) W. BS, U. Dayton, 1973. Cert. tchr., Tex., Ohio. Tchr. health and phys. edn. Copperas Cove (Tex.) High Sch., 1973—, dept. chairperson, 1979—, head coach cross country and track, 1986—, girls athletic coord., 1994, asst. athletic dir., 1995. Mem. bd. govs. Copperas Cove High Sch., 1993. Mem. AAHPERD, Am. Assn. Health Educators, Tex. Alliance Health, Phys. Edn., Recreation and Dance, Tex. Classroom Tchrs. Assn., Tex. Girls Coaches Assn., Athletic Congress USA (cert. official), Nat. Sports and Phys. Edn. Home: 701 N 19th St Copperas Cove TX 76522-1202 Office: Copperas Cove High Sch 400 S 25th St Copperas Cove TX 76522-2099

WAGNER, WILLIAM GERARD, university dean, physicist, consultant, information scientist, investment manager; b. St. Cloud, Minn., Aug. 22, 1936; s. Gerard C. and Mary V. (Cloone) W.; m. Janet Agatha Rowe, Jan. 30, 1968 (div. 1978); children: Mary, Robert, David, Anne; m. Christiane LeGuen, Feb. 21, 1985 (div. 1989); m. Yvonne Naomi Moussette, Dec. 4, 1995. BS, Calif. Inst. Tech., 1958, PhD (NSF fellow, Howard Hughes fellow), 1962. Cons. Rand Corp., Santa Monica, Calif., 1960-65; sr. staff physicist Hughes Research Lab., Malibu, Calif., 1960-69; lectr. physics Calif. Inst. Tech., Pasadena, 1963-65; asst. prof. physics U. Calif. at Irvine, 1965-66; assoc. prof. physics and elec. engring. U. So. Calif., L.A., 1966-69, prof. depts. physics and elec. engring., 1969—, dean div. natural scis. and math. Coll. Letters, Arts and Scis., 1973-87, dean interdisciplinary studies and developmental activities, 1987-89, spl. asst. automated record services, 1975-81; founder program in neural, informational & behavioral scis., 1982—. Chmn. bd. Malibu Securities Corp., L.A., 1971—; cons. Janus Mgmt. Corp., L.A., 1970-71, Croesus Capital Corp., L.A., 1971-74, Fin. Horizons Inc., Beverly Hills, Calif., 1971—; allied mem. Pacific Stock Exch., 1974-82; fin. and computer cons. Hollywood Reporter, 1979-81; mem. adv. coun. for emerging engring. techs. NSF, 1987-89; cons. Wagner Tech. Solutions, L.A., 2001—. Contbr. articles on physics to sci. publs. Richard Chase Tolman postdoctoral fellow, 1962-65 Mem. Am. Phys. Soc., Nat. Assn. Security Dealers, Sigma Xi. Home: 2828 Patricia Ave Los Angeles CA 90064-4425 Office: U So Calif Hedco Neurosci Bldg Los Angeles CA 90089-0001

WAGNER-SERWIN, DOROTHY ELIZABETH, elementary education educator; b. Wauzeka, Wis., Nov. 19; d. Albert Magnus and Evelyn Cecelia (Degnan) Doll; m. Melvin Herman Wagner, June 30, 1941 (dec. July 1981); m. Robert Carl Serwin, Dec. 26, 1987; children: Diana, Jeannie, Lori, Richard. BA, Dominican Coll., 1974. Tchr. grades 2-4 St. Joseph's Sch., Racine, Wis., 1960-68, 69; tchr. grade 1 St. Lucy's Sch., Racine, 1969; tchr. Learning Ctr. St. John Nepomuk Sch., Racine, 1969-71, tchr. grades 1 and 2, kindergarten, 1971-91, ret., 1991. V.p. St. Vincent de Paul. Mem. AAUW (chmn. publicity com. 1975-94, registration com. 1995-98), Assn. Early Childhood Edn. (sec. 1970-92), Am. Legion Aux., KC, Shoop Park Golf Club (asst. chmn. 1994-95, golf chmn. 1996-97). Avocations: golf, tennis, skiing, skating, swimming.

WAGNESS, LORRAINE MELVA, gifted education educator; b. Bellingham, Wash., June 11, 1933; d. William Barkley and Laura Iola (Starr) Nattrass; m. Lee Wagness, Aug. 24, 1969; 1 child, Kathryn Lorraine. BA, Western Wash. State U., 1955; MA, City U., Seattle, Wash., 1993. Cert. tchr. grades kindergarten through 12, Wash. Tchr. Bellingham Sch. Dist., 1955-57, Eugene (Oreg.) Sch. Dist., 1957-59; tchr. talented and gifted, libr., arts specialist Seattle Pub. Schs., 1959—. Chmn. Science Fair, 1995, 96, Art Show, 1995, 96. Photographer various publs., 1984-90; exhibited batik/paintings area shows (1st pl. Wash. Arts Contest 1990). Vol., demonstrator weaving and spinning Woodland Pk. Zoo Guild, Seattle, 1984—; pres. Sigma Kappa Mothers' Club, U. Wash., 1982-84. Sci. scholar Wash. State Garden Clubs, Seattle, 1960; partnership grantee Lafayette Sch. PTA, Seattle, 1994, 95. Mem. NEA (bldg. rep. 1980-90), Wash. Edn. Assn. (bldg. rep. 1980-90), Seattle Tchrs. Assn. (bldg. rep. 1980-90), AAUW (Outstanding Sr. award 1955), Internat. Reading Assn. (mem. coms. 1990-96), Associated Women Students (pres. 1955), Gen. Fedn. Women's Clubs (sec., treas. 1988-92, Club Woman of Yr. 1986, 90), Evergreen Garden Club (treas., sec. 1985—), Delta Kappa Gamma (v.p. Beta Beta chpt. 1991-96), Pi Lambda Theta (mem. coms. Seattle area chpt. 1988—). Presbyterian. Avocations: international travel, arts and crafts, gardening, reading, photography. Home: 17040 Sylvester Rd SW Seattle WA 98166-3434

WAGONER, GERALDINE VANDER POL, music educator; b. Kankakee, Ill., Sept. 16, 1931; d. Ralph and Josie (Mieras) VanderPol; children: Joel Timothy, Stephanie Anne. BA, Central U. Of Iowa, 1954; MA, Montclair State Coll., 1968; postgrad., Juilliard Sch. Music, 1955-56, 66-67, NYU, Royal Conservatory, Toronto, 1971, Mozarteum, Salzburg, Austria, 1972. Music specialist Bd. Edn., Edison, NJ, 1954—74, Ridgewood, 1975-95; dir. Musical Spheres Co., 1995—. Mem. Amb. to Amb. program Russian Conservatories, 1998. Composer: tonal rhythmic curriculum for assessing children. Trustee, Hudson Symphony Orch., 1965-71; mem. Met. Mus. of Art, Teaching fellow NYU, 1990-91; adj. prof. music William Paterson Coll., Wayne, N.J. Mem. Profl. Music Tchrs. Guild (cert. for highest goals and achievements 1966), Nat. Music Tchrs. Nat. Assn., N.J. Music Tchrs. Assn., Am. Orff Schulwerk Assn., NEA, Music Educators Nat. Conf., Nat. Guild Piano Tchrs. (judge 2003—), Met. Opera Guild, Netherland-Am. Found., Collegiate Chorale N.Y.C. 1995—, Lyceum Soc. of N.Y. Acad. Scis., Netherland Club, Coll. Club. E-mail: wagonerg@optonline.net.

WAGONER, JENNINGS LEE, JR., history educator; b. Winston-Salem, NC, July 26, 1938; s. Jennings Lee and Carolyn Nelme (Phifer) W.; m. Shirley Canady, Aug. 12, 1962; children: David Carroll, Brian Jennings. BA, Wake Forest U., 1960; MAT, Duke U., 1961; PhD, Ohio State U., 1968. Tchr. High Point Pub. Schs., NC, 1960-62; instr. Wake Forest U., 1963-65; tchg. assoc. Ohio State U., Ohio, 1965-68; from asst. prof. to prof. history of edn. U. Va., Charlottesville, Va., 1968—; dir. Ctr. for Study Higher Edn., 1975-85, chmn. leadership and policy studies, 1985-87; disting. prof. Curry Sch. Edn. U Va., Va., 1987, William C. Parrish Jr. Endowed prof., 1994—. Vis. research scholar Harvard U., 1972, U. Calif., Berkeley, 1984; vis. prof. Monash U., Melbourne, Australia, 1992. Author: Thomas Jefferson and the Education of a New Nation, 1976; co-author: American Education: A History, 1996; co-editor: Changing Politics of Education, 1978: editl. bd. History of Edn. Quar., Ednl. Studies jour.; contbr. articles to profl. jours. Recipient Disting. Prof. award Univ. of Va. Alumni Assoc., 1996, Sesquicentennial fellow U. Va., 1972, 84, 90. Mem. History of Edn. Soc. (pres. 1983-85, bd. dirs. 1979-81), Am. Ednl. Rsch. Assn. (v.p. divsn. F 1981-83), Orgn. Am. Historians, Am. Ednl. Studies Assn. (bd. dirs.), Assn. Study Higher Edn., Raven Soc., Outward Bound, Kappa Delta Pi, Phi Delta Kappa, Omicron Delta Kappa (faculty advisor), Golden Key Nat. Honor Soc. Avocatins: hiking, fishing, canoeing. Home: 468 Dry Bridge Rd Charlottesvle VA 22903-7456 Office: U Va 405 Emmet St Charlottesville VA 22903

WAGONER, ROBERT VERNON, astrophysicist, educator; b. Teaneck, N.J., Aug. 6, 1938; s. Robert Vernon and Marie Theresa (Clifford) W.; m. Lynne Ray Moses, Sept. 2, 1963 (div. Feb. 1986); children: Alexa Frances, Shannon Stephanie; m. Stephanie Brewster, June 27, 1987. BME, Cornell U., 1961; MS, Stanford U., 1962, PhD, 1965. Rsch. fellow in physics Calif. Inst. Tech., 1965-68, Sherman Fairchild Disting. scholar, 1976; asst. prof. astronomy Cornell U., 1968-71, assoc. prof., 1971-73; assoc. prof. physics Stanford U., 1973-77, prof., 1977—. George Ellery Hale disting. vis. prof. U. Chgo., 1978; mem. Com. on Space Astronomy and Astrophysics, 1979-82, theory study panel Space Sci. Bd., 1980-82, physics survey com. NRC, 1983-84; grant selection com. NSERC (Can.), 1990-93; active Laser Interferometer Gravitational-Wave Obs. Sci. Collaboration. Contbr. articles on theoretical astrophysics and gravitation to profl. jours., mags.; co-author Cosmic Horizons, 1982; patentee in field. Sloan Found. rsch. fellow, 1969-71; Guggenheim Meml. fellow, 1979; grantee NSF, 1973-90, 2000-03, NASA, 1982-99. Fellow Am. Phys. Soc.; mem. Am. Astron. Soc., Internat. Astron. Union, Tau Beta Pi, Phi Kappa Phi Office: Stanford U Dept Physics Stanford CA 94305-4060 E-mail: wagoner@stanford.edu.

WAIDLER, BEVERLY MAE, music teacher; b. Eau Claire, Wis., Jan. 14, 1941; d. George Hiram and Myrtle Julianna (Gunderson) Gilbertson; m. Brian Edmund Waidler Sr., Aug. 12, 1961; children: Brian Edmund jr., Sonvy Kristina, Heidi Julianna. BS in Elem. Edn., U. Md., 1962, MEd in Music and Piano/Voice, 1976. Cert. elem. and music tchr. Tchr. 5th grade Pub. Schs. Prince George's County, Bladensburg, Md., 1962; GS 5 mortgage notes accts. clk. Fed. Housing Authority, Washington, 1963-64; 4th grade substitute tchr. Amidon Sch., Washington, 1966; music tchr. vocal and gen. Parkland Jr. H.S. Montgomery County Pub. Schs., Rockville, Md., 1966-67; pvt. piano tchr. Rockville, 1966-80; salesperson, then office worker Sears Montomery Mall, Bethesda, 1989-91; substitute tchr. Pub. Schs. D.C. and Montgomery County, Rockville, Gaithersburg, Washington, 1991-95; pvt. piano and voice instr. Rockville, 1995—. Singing recitals include Weisbaden, Germany, 1982, Kaiserslautern, Germany, 1982, Pirmasens, Germany, 1983. Election office worker Dem. gubinatorial race, Wheaton, 1992; unit pres. Ch. Women United, 1976-78, mem. 1997—; lobby participant Internat. Women's Year, 1975. Mem. AAUW, Phi Theta Delta, Friday Morning Music Club. Democrat. Baptist. Avocations: art appreciation, reading biographies, walking, yoga. Home: 7036 Wick Ln Rockville MD 20855-1963

WAITE, DONALD EUGENE, medical educator, consultant; b. Columbus, Ohio, Aug. 25, 1925; s. Sidney B. and Louise Alice (Lipsey) W.; children: David L., Larry R., James A., Steve C., Debra J., Julie A., Craig D., Tracy E., Christopher R. DO in Osteo. Medicine, U. Osteo. Medicine and Health Scis., 1955; MPH, U. Calif., Berkeley, 1979. Intern Doctors Hosp., Columbus, Ohio, 1955-56; pvt. practice Columbus, 1956-72; prof. family medicine Mich. State U., East Lansing, 1972-90, prof. emeritus, 1990—. Cons. Environ. Health Conss., Columbus, East Lansing, 1990—; mem. occupl. health del. to Poland, Hungary and Czechoslovakia, 1992; mem. Aerospace Med. Assn. del. to People's Republic of China, 1993. Author: Your Environment, Your Health and You, 1991, Environmental Health Hazards, 1994, 2d edit., 2002. Med. examiner FAA, East Lansing, 1964-90; asst. scoutmaster Boy Scouts Am., East Lansing, 1980-83. With USN, 1943-45. Mem. Am. Osteo. Assn., Am. Coll. Occupl. Medicine, Aerospace Med. Assn., Ohio Osteo. Assn., Mich. Assn. Osteo. Physicians. Avocations: skiing, fishing, hunting. Home: 117 Agate Way Williamston MI 48895-9434 Office: Mich State U Dept Family Medicine East Lansing MI 48824 E-mail: waited@msu.edu.

WAITE, LEMUEL WARREN, library director; b. Ashland, Ky., July 13, 1955; s. Lemuel Crenshaw and Polly Jane (Davidson) W. BS, U. Ky., 1980, MLS, 1988. Bookkeeper Ky. Geol. Survey, Lexington, 1981-84; libr. asst. Ky. Christian Coll., Grayson, 1986-88, libr., 1988-89, dir. libr., 1989—. Minister Blue Bank Christian Ch., Flemingsburg, Ky., 1988—, Moore's Ferry Christian Ch., Salt Lick, Ky., 1986-88. Author various poems and essays. Mem. ALA, APA, ACD, Am. Theol. Libr. Assn., Disciples of Christ Hist. Soc., Ind. Hist. Soc., Ky. Libr. Assn., Beta Phi Mu. Democrat. Avocations: sculpture, poetry, sketching. Home: 501 Snodgrass Ln Grayson KY 41143-2112 Office: Ky Christian Coll Coll Libr 100 Academic Pkwy Grayson KY 41143-2205

WAITE, WILLIAM MCCASTLINE, electrical engineer educator, consultant; b. N.Y.C., Jan. 14, 1939; s. William Wiley and Grace McCastline (Smith) W.; m. Joanne Lischer Waite, June 18, 1960; 1 child, William Frederick. AB in Physics, Oberlin (Ohio) Coll., 1960; MS in Elec. Engring., Columbia U., N.Y.C., 1962; PhD in Elec. Engring., 1965. Asst. prof. Elec. Engring. U. Colo., Boulder, 1966-70, assoc. prof. Elec. Engring., 1970-74, dept. chair Elec. Engring., 1990-94, prof. Elec.Engring., 1974—. Vis. lectr. Monash U., Clayton, Australia, 1970-71, U. Karlsruhe, Germany, 1973, Melbourne U., Parkville, Australia, 1977, 82, 88, RMIT U., Melbourne, Australia, 2000; dir. Lang. Resources, Boulder, 1979-89; adj. prof. Queensland U. Tech., Brisbane, Australia, 1994, Australian Nat. U., 1996; vis. prof. U Nacional San Luis, Argentina, 1996; guest prof. TU Darmstadt, Germany, 1997. Author: Implementing Software for Non-Numeric Applications, 1973, Software Manual for the Elementary Functions, 1980, Compiler Construction, 1984, Introduction to Compiler Construction, 1993. Vis. fellow Macquarie U., Sydney, 1998, 2000, 03. Griffith U. Brisbane, 2003 Mem. Assn. for Computing Machinery. Avocation: flight instruction. Office: Electrical Engineering University Of Colorado Boulder CO 80309-0425 E-mail: william.waite@colorado.edu.

WAKE, DAVID BURTON, biology educator; b. Webster, S.D., June 8, 1936; s. Thomas B. and Ina H. (Solem) W.; m. Marvalee Hendricks, June 23, 1962; 1 child, Thomas Andrew BA, Pacific Luth. U., 1958; MS, U. So. Calif., 1960, PhD, 1964. Instr. anatomy and biology U. Chgo., 1964-66, asst. prof. anatomy and biology, 1966-69; assoc. prof. zoology U. Calif., Berkeley, 1969-72, prof., 1972-89, John and Margaret Gompertz prof., 1991-97, prof. integrative biology, 1989—2003, prof. emeritus integrative biology, 2003—. Dir. Mus. Vertebrate Zoology U. Calif., Berkeley, 1971-98; curator Herpetology Mus. Vertebrate Zoology, U. Calif., 1969-2003; vis. Alexander Agassiz prof. Mus. Comparative Zoology, Harvard U., 2002. Author: Biology, 1979; co-editor: Functional Vertebrate Morphology, 1985, Complex Organismal Functions: Integration and Evolution in the Vertebrates, 1989. Recipient Quantrell Teaching award U. Chgo., 1967, Outstanding Alumnus award Pacific Luth. U., 1979, Joseph Grinnell medal Mus. Vertebrate Zoology, 1998, Henry S. Fitch award Am. Soc. Ichthyologists and Herpetologists, 1999; grantee NSF, 1965—; Guggenheim fellow, 1982. Fellow AAAS, Am. Acad. Arts and Scis.; mem. NAS, NRC (bd. biology 1986-92), Am. Philos. Soc., Internat. Union for Conservation of Nature and Natural Resources (chair task force on declining amphibian populations 1990-92), Am. Soc. Zoologists (pres. 1992), Am. Soc. Naturalists (pres. 1989), Am. Soc. Ichthyologists and Herpetologists (bd. govs.), Soc. Study Evolution (pres. 1983, editor 1979-81), Soc. Systematic Biology (coun. 1980-84), Herpetologist's League (Disting. Herpetologist 1984). Home: 999 Middlefield Rd Berkeley CA 94708-1509 E-mail: wakelab@uclink4.berkeley.edu.

WAKEMAN, FREDERIC EVANS, JR., historian, educator; b. Kansas City, Kans., Dec. 12, 1937; s. Frederic Evans and Margaret Ruth (Keyes) W.; married He Lea Liang; children: Frederic Evans III, Matthew Clark, Sarah Elizabeth. BA, Harvard Coll., 1959; postgrad., Institut d'Etudes Politiques, U. Paris, 1959-60; MA, U. Calif., Berkeley, 1962, PhD, 1965. Asst. prof. history U. Calif., Berkeley, 1965-67, assoc. prof., 1968-70, prof., 1970-89, Haas prof. Asian Studies, 1989—, dir. Ctr. Chinese Studies, 1972-79; humanities research prof., vis. scholar Corpus Christi Coll., U. Cambridge, Eng., 1976-77, Beijing U., 1980-81, 85. Acad. adviser U.S. Ednl. Del. for Study in China; chmn. Joint Com. Chinese Studies Am. Coun. Learned Socs./Social Sci. Rsch. Coun.; sr. adviser Beijing office NAS; pres. Social Sci. Rsch. Coun., 1986-89, chmn. com. on scholarly comm. with China, 1995-2000; dir. Inst. East Asian Studies, Berkeley, 1990-2001; vis. prof. U. Heidelberg, Germany, 2000; hon. prof. China People's U. Author: Strangers at the Gate, 1966, History and Will, 1973, The Fall of Imperial China, 1975, Conflict and Control in Late Imperial China, 1976, Ming and Qing Historical Studies in the People's Republic of China, 1981, The Great Enterprise, 1986, Shanghai Sojourners, 1992, Policing Shanghai, 1995, Shanghai Badlands, 1996, China's Quest for Modernization, 1997, Reappraising Republican China, 2000, Spymaster, 2003. Harvard Nat. scholar, 1955-59; Tower fellow, 1959-60; Fgn. Area fellow, 1963-65; Am. Coun. Learned Socs. fellow, 1967-68; Guggenheim fellow, 1973-74; NRC fellow, 1985. Mem. Am. Acad. Arts and Scis., Coun. on Fgn. Rels., Am. Hist. Assn. (pres.), Am. Philos. Soc., Shanghai Acad. Social Scis. (fgn.). Home: 501 Delancey St Apt 409 San Francisco CA 94107-1432 Office: U Calif Inst East Asian Studies Berkeley CA 94720-0001 E-mail: jingcha@socrates.berkeley.edu.

WAKS, LEONARD JOSEPH, philosophy and education educator; b. Bklyn., Dec. 21, 1942; s. Meyer and Beatrice (Dichter) W. BA in Philosophy, U. Wis., 1964, PhD in Philosophy, 1968; EdD in Psycho-ednl. Processes, Temple U., 1984. Instr., teaching asst. U. Wis., Madison, 1964-66; asst. prof. philosophy Purdue U., West Lafayette, Ind., 1966-68; asst. prof. philosophy and edn. Stanford (Calif.) U., 1968-71; from assoc. prof. to prof. edn. Temple U., Phila., 1971—, chair ednl. leadership and policy studies dept., 1996—2001. Prof. sci., tech. and soc. Pa. State U., University Park, 1985-92; cons. in field. Author: Technology's School,

1995; contbr. articles to profl. jours. Mem. Am. Edn. Rsch. Assn., Am. Philos. Assn. Avocations: book collecting, photography, traveling. Home: 2341 S Lambert St Philadelphia PA 19145 Office: Temple U Edn Leadership/ Policy Studies Ritter Hall Philadelphia PA 19122 E-mail: lwaks@temple.edu., ljwaks@yahoo.com.

WALBY, SANDRA LEE, principal; b. Detroit, Aug. 10, 1950; d. Glenn Bernard and Laura (Dolan) Titus; m. Brian Richard Walby Sr., Aug. 19, 1978; children: Brian Richard, Michelle Laurén. BS, Eastern Mich. U., 1972, MA, 1977; EdS, Oakland U., Rochester, Mich., 1993. Cert. tchr., adminstr., Mich. Reading tchr. Our Lady Star of the Sea Sch., Grosse Pointe Woods, Mich., 1973-77; reading specialist Allegan (Mich.) Pub. Schs., 1977-78, Anchor Bay Schs., New Baltimore, Mich., 1978-79; tchr. of gifted program Forest Hills Schs., Grand Rapids, Mich., 1979-80, 1st grade tchr., 1981-82, kindergarten tchr., 1979-84; adult edn. tchr. Chippewa Valley Schs., Clinton Twp., Mich., 1984-87, lang. arts. cons., chpt. I dir., 1987-90; at risk coord., cons. Avondale Schs., Auburn Hills, Mich., 1990-95; prin. Plumbrook Elem., Utica Schs., Sterling Heights, Mich., 1995—. Speaker in field. Author: Mentor/Business Partnership, 1991, Implementing and Evaluation a Peer Tutor Program, 1991, Whole Group Instruction, Meeting Individual Needs, 1992. Recipient Leadership award Dow Chem. Co., 1971; Rochester Hills C. of C. grantee, 1991, 95. Mem. ASCD, Mich. Reading Assn., Learning Disabilities Assn., Internat. Reading Assn. Avocations: reading, tennis, dancing, painting, writing. Home: 3705 Heron Ridge Dr Rochester Hills MI 48309-4522 Office: Plumbrook Elem 39660 Spalding Dr Sterling Heights MI 48313-4870 Address: 3705 Heron Ridge Dr Rochester Hills MI 48309-4522

WALCOTT, CHARLES, neurobiology and behavior educator; b. Boston, July 19, 1934; s. Charles Folsom and Susan (Cabot) W.; m. Jane Clayton Taylor, Aug. 14, 1976; children: Thomas Stewart, Samuel Cabot. AB, Harvard U., 1956; PhD, Cornell U., 1959. Asst. prof. div. engring. and applied physics Harvard U., Cambridge, Mass., 1961-65; asst. prof. biology Tufts U., Medford, Mass., 1965-67; assoc. prof. dept. biology SUNY, Stony Brook, 1967-74, prof. dept. biology, 1974-81; prof., exec. dir. Cornell Lab. of Ornithology, Ithaca, N.Y., 1981-93, Louis Agassiz Fuertes dir., 1992-95; prof. neurobiology and behavior Cornell U., 1981—, dir. divsn. biol. scis., 1998-99, assoc. dean of the univ. faculty, 2000—03, dean of univ. faculty, 2003—. Cons., dir. Elem. Sci. Study, Watertown, Mass., 1961-67; dir. 3-2-1- Contact, Children's TV Workshop, N.Y.C., 1978—; dir. L.A. Fuertes. Contbr. many rsch. papers to sci. jours. Dir. sci. TV, Mass. Audubon, Lincoln, 1959-61. Avocations: gardening, sailing, photography. Home: 84 Besemer Hill Rd Ithaca NY 14850-9636 Office: Cornell U Dept Neurobiology Behavior W255 Seeley Mudd Hall Ithaca NY 14853 E-mail: cw38@cornell.edu.

WALCZAK, ANN MARIE, elementary education educator; b. Fernandina Beach, Fla., May 10, 1947; d. Francis L. and Marie (Halter) Artelli; m. Stanley A. Walczak, Aug. 17, 1969; children: Sandra Ann, Christopher, Brian, Heather Marie. BA in Early Childhood Edn., William Paterson Coll., 1969, MA in Reading/Lang. Arts, 1975; postgrad., Seaton Hall U., 1991—. Cert. elem. tchr., prin./supr., N.J.; cert. libr. Elem. tchr. Ridgewood (N.J.) Bd. Edn., 1969—. Dist. coord. Writing to Read, Ridgewood Bd. Edn., 1985-90, spl. programs coord. Instrnl. Svcs., 1986-92, coord. Saturday Programs in Problem Solving, 1986-92, acting dir. curriculum and instrn., 1990-91, intern prin., 1992-93, acting dir. Infant-Toddler Ctr., 1993; IBM Writing to Read tchr. trainer IBM/Ridgewood Pub. Schs., 1986-90; tchr. trainer Mainland Inst., Pa., 1980; cons., adv. bd. Mini-Round Table Consortium, N.J., 1990-92. Curator Travell Children's Mus., 1993; author, editor: Analogy Masters, 1986; author, editor Connections mag., 1989; editor (brochure) Martin Luther King, Jr., 1989; author: Reading and Language Arts Curriculum K-5, 1998. Chairperson scholarship com. Marching Band, Ridgewood, 1995; Cornerstone dir. Holy Trinity Ch., Hackensack, N.J., 1994; parent vol. Girl Scouts Am., Ridgewood, 1990; fundraising New Players, Ridgewood, 1995—. Recipient grant Pub. Edn. Found., 1993. Mem. NEA, ASCD, N.J. Tchrs. Assn., Bergen County Tchrs. Assn., Early Childhood Edn. Assn., Reading Tchrs. Assn., Nat. Coun. Tchrs. Math., Phi Lamba Theta. Roman Catholic. Avocations: dancing (U.S. Ballroom champion 1978-79), boating, skiing, reading, theater. Home: 142 Buckingham Dr Hackensack NJ 07601-1303 Office: Ridgewood Pub Schs 49 Cottage Pl Ridgewood NJ 07450-3813

WALD, FRANCINE JOY WEINTRAUB (MRS. BERNARD J. WALD), physicist, academic administrator; b. Bklyn., Jan. 13, 1938; d. Irving and Minnie (Reisig) Weintraub; m. Bernard J. Wald, FEb. 2, 1964; children: David Evan, Kevin Mitchell. Student, Bklyn. Coll., 1955-57; BEE, CCNY, 1960; MS, Poly. Inst. Bklyn., 1962, PhD, 1969. Engr. Remington Rand Univac divsn. Sperry Rand Corp., Phila., 1960; instr. Poly. Inst. Bklyn., 1962-64, adj. rsch. assoc., 1969-70; lectr. N.Y. C.C., Bklyn., 1969, 70; instr. sci. Friends Sem., N.Y.C., 1975-76, chmn. dept. sci., 1976-94; instr. sci., chmn. dept. sci. Nightingale-Bamford Sch., N.Y.C., 1994-99. Adj. assoc. prof. NYU. NDEA fellow, 1962-64. Mem. AAAS, Am. Phys. Soc., Am. Assn. Physics Tchrs., Assn. Tchrs. in Ind. Schs., N.Y. Acad. Scis., Nat. Sci. Tchrs. Assn., Sigma Xi, Tau Beta Pi, Eta Kappa Nu.

WALD, MARY S. retired risk management and personal finance educator; b. Baker, Oreg., June 17, 1943; d. Paul H. and Mary Elsie (Bartshe) Stoner; m. Lance Albert Wald, June 22, 1968. BA in English, Albertson Coll. of Idaho, Caldwell, 1966; MBA in Fin., Temple U., 1984. Tchr. Salt Lake City Bd. Edn., 1967-74; office mgr. Montgomery County Homemaker-Home Health Aide Svc., Inc., Blue Bell, Pa., 1975-82; adj. instr. risk mgmt. and personal fin. Temple U., Phila., 1984-99, ret., 1999. Co-author: Controlling Your Money, Step By Step, 1987. Named Outstanding Tchr. of Yr., Salt Lake City Bd. Edn., 1973-74. Mem. Am. Risk and Ins. Assn., Gamma Iota Sigma, Golden Key Nat. Honor Soc. (hon. mem.). Republican. E-mail: mwald2@juno.com.

WALDBAUER, GILBERT PETER, entomologist, educator; b. Bridgeport, Conn., Apr. 18, 1928; s. George Henry and Hedwig Martha (Gribisch) W.; m. Stephanie Margot Stiefel, Jan. 2, 1955; children: Gwen Ruth, Susan Martha. Student, U. Conn., 1949-50; BS, U. Mass., 1953; MS, U. Ill., Urbana, 1956, PhD, 1960. Instr. entomology U. Ill., Urbana, 1958-60, asst. prof., 1960-65, assoc. prof., 1965-71, prof., 1971—, prof. agrl. entomology Coll. Agr., 1971—, prof. emeritus, 1995—. Sr. scientist Ill. Natural History Survey; vis. scientist ICA, Palmira, Colombia, 1971; vis. sr. scientist Internat. Rice Rsch. Inst., 1978-79; cons. AID, 1985; vis. prof. U. Philippines, 1978-79. Author: Insects Through the Seasons, 1996, The Handy Bug Answer Book, 1998, The Birder's Bug Book, 1998, Millions of Monarchs, Bunches of Beetles, 2000, What Good Are Bugs?, 2003; contbg. author: Insect and Mite Nutrition, 1972, Introduction to Insect Pest Management, 1975, Evolution of Insect Migration and Diapause, 1978, Sampling Methods in Soybean Entomology, 1980, Mimicry and the Evolutionary Process, 1988, Ann. Rev. Entomology, 1991; contbr. numerous articles to profl. jours. Served with AUS, 1946-47, PTO. Grantee Agrl. Rsch. Svc. USDA, 1966-71, 83-90, Nat. Geog. Soc., 1972-74, NSF, 1976-79, 82-90. Mem. AAAS, Sigma Xi, Phi Kappa Phi. Home: 807A Ramblewood Ct Savoy IL 61874-9568 Office: U Ill Dept Entomology 320 Morrill Hall Urbana IL 61801

WALDEN, ALICE, artist, educator; b. Billings, Mont., June 14, 1943; d. George John and Lilly (Sevick) Martin; m. Dee Edward Walden, June 23, 1962; children: San Dee Walden Russell, Kevin. BA, Mont. State U., 1980. Cert. art tchr., Mont. Bookkeeper 1st State Bank, Livingston, Mont., 1961-62, Gallatin Farmers Co., Bozeman, Mont., 1966-71; acctg. asst. Rowland Thomas & Co., Miles City, Mont., 1972-78, Don Winslow & Assocs., Miles City, 1979-80; home bound tchr. Sch. Dist. # 1, Miles City, 1980-81, gifted edn. tchr., 1981-86, art tchr., 1986—; profl. artist Miles City, 1991—; owner, mgr. Wool House Gallery, Miles City, 1994—. Executed various steel sculptures in pvt. collections, N.D., Wyo., Mont., Wash., Calif. Home: 419 N 7th St Miles City MT 59301-3117

WALDEN, JAMES WILLIAM, accountant, educator; b. Jellico, Tenn., Mar. 5, 1936; s. William Evert and Bertha L. (Faulkner) W.; m. Eva June Selvia, Jan. 16, 1957 (dec. Aug. 1988); 1 child, James William; m. Hattie Nan Lamb, Jan. 6, 1990 (div. June 1992); m. Janet Faulkner, Aug. 12, 1993 (div. May 2001). BS, Miami U., Oxford, Ohio, 1963; MBA, Xavier U., Cin., 1966. CPA, Ohio. Tchr. math. Middletown (Ohio) City Sch. Dist., 1963-67, Fairfield (Ohio) High Sch., 1967-69; instr. accounting Sinclair Community Coll., Dayton, Ohio, 1969-72, asst. prof., 1972-75, assoc. prof., 1975-78, prof., 1978-89, prof. emeritus, 1991—. Cons., public acct.; mem. adj. faculty in acctg. Capital U., 1980—. Group comdr., fin. officer, chief staff Ohio Wing, CAP. Served with USAF, 1954-59. Mem. Butler County Torch Club, Pub. Accts. Soc. Ohio (pres. S.W. chpt. 1985-86), Inst. Mgmt. Accts., Nat. Soc. Pub. Accts., Greater Hamilton Estate Planning Coun., Ohio Soc. CPAs, Springboro C. of C. (bd. dirs., treas.), Am. Legion (life), Rotary Club, Lions Club, Kiwanis Club (pres. Springboro chpt.), Beta Alpha Psi. Home: PO Box 469 Springboro OH 45066-0469 Office: Sinclair C C 265 N Main St Springboro OH 45066-9255

WALDINGER SEFF, MARGARET, special elementary education educator; b. N.Y.C., June 12, 1949; d. Herbert Francis Waldinger and Michelle (Rubin) Cohen; children: Dylan Paul Seff, Cortney Sara Seff, Blake Adam Seff. BA, Hofstra U., 1971; postgrad., NYU, 1971-73; MA, Fairleigh Dickinson U., 1986. Cert. elem. sch. tchr., tchr. of handicapped, learning disability tchr. cons., N.J. Tchr. pub. schs., N.J., N.Y., 1984-88; learning specialist Manchester (Vt.) Elem. Sch., 1988—. Adv., ednl. therapist, N.J., 1983-88. Reading grantee Tuxedo Park Sch., 1986, Bennington Rutland Supervisory Union, 1992. Avocations: sports, reading, home restorations, drawing. Home: RR 1 Box 2291 Manchester Center VT 05255-9738 Office: Manchester Elem Sch Memorial Dr Manchester Center VT 05255

WALDO, CATHERINE RUTH, private school educator; b. Erie, Pa., Nov. 5, 1946; d. James Allen and Ruth Catherine (Rubner) Babcock; m. James Robert Waldo, June, 1968; children; Robert, Ruth Ann. BA in History magna cum laude, Duke U., 1968. Cert. tchr., Okla. Tchr. Shawnee (Okla.) Pub. Schs., 1968-70; tchr., team leader Norman (Okla.) Pub. Schs., 1971-73; tchr., social studies chmn. Westminster Sch., Oklahoma City, Okla., 1990—. Mem. edn. commn. Westminster Presbyn. Ch., Oklahoma City, 1980-93, deacon, 1981-84, coord. early childhood programs, 1988-90, elder, 1990-93; mem. coun. Ward 2 City of Nichols Hills, Okla., 1989-93; bd. dirs. Assn. Ctrl. Okla. Govts., Oklahoma City, 1989-93; vol., planning com. World Neighbors. Recipient Colonial Williamsburg Summer Inst., Okla. Found. for Excellence, 1994. Mem. Nat. Coun. Tchrs. English, Nat. Coun. for Social Studies, Okla. Coun. for Social Studies, Okla. Coun. Tchrs. English. Presbyterian. Avocations: reading, hiking, odyssey of the mind, local political issues. Home: 1100 Tedford Way Oklahoma City OK 73116-6007 Office: Westminster Sch 612 NW 44th St Oklahoma City OK 73118-6699

WALENDOWSKI, GEORGE JERRY, accounting and business educator; b. Han-Minden, Germany, Mar. 25, 1947; came to US, 1949; s. Stefan (dec.) and Eugenia (Lewandowska) W. AA, LA City Coll., 1968; BS, Calif. State U., LA, 1970, MBA, 1972; cert. completion, Inst. Mgmt. Accts., 2000—. Cert. community coll. instr. acctg. and mgmt., Calif. Acct. Unocal (formerly Union Oil Co. Calif.), LA, 1972-76, data control supr., 1976-78, acctg. analyst, 1978-79; sr. fin. analyst Hughes Aircraft Co., El Segundo, Calif., 1979-83, fin. planning specialist, 1983-84, program controls specialist, 1984-86, bus. mgmt. specialist, 1986-92, bus. analyst, 1993-95. Adj. instr. bus. math. L.A. City Coll., 1976-80, acctg., 1980-97, 99—, mem. acctg. adv. com., 1984, 87, 89, 99, acctg. and bus. Pasadena City Coll., 1996-2001, 03; reviewer conf. papers. Contbr. articles to profl. jours. Mem. commn. Rep. Pres. Task Force, 1986. Recipient Medal of Merit, Rep. Presdl. Task Force, 1984, cert. of merit, named registered life mem. commn., 1986, named Honor Roll life mem., 1989; recipient Vice-Presdl. Cert. of Commendation, Rep. Nat. Hall of Honor, 1992, Rep. Congl. cert. of Appreciation, 1993, Rep. Congl. Order of Freedom award Nat. Rep. Congl. Com., 1995, Recognition award LA chpt. Strategic Leadership Forum, 1983. Mem.: Midwest Fin. Assn. (program rev. com. 2002), Ea. Fin. Assn. (program rev. com. 2000), Soc. Advancement Mgmt. (editl. rev. bd. Advanced Mgmt. Jour. 1999—, selection com. mem. Internat. Conf. 2000), Nat. Bus. Edn. Assn., Am. Acctg. Assn. (competitive manuscript com. 1997—98, reviewer tchg. curr. sect. 1998, tchg. and curriculum sect. two-yr. coll. issues com. 1998—99), Inst. Mgmt. Accts. (author's cir. L.A. chpt. 1980, mem. editl. adv. bd. Strategic Fin. and Mgmt. Acctg. Quarterly 2002—, Robert Half author's trophy 1980, cert. of appreciation 1980, 1983), Acad. Mgmt. (reviewer social issues in mgmt. divsn. 1991, mgmt. edn. and devel. divsn. program rev. com. 1998, 1999, reviewer bus. policy and strategy divsn. 2002—03, reviewer for acad. of mngmt. learning & ed. Jour. 2003—), U.S. Chess Fedn., Delta Pi Epsilon, Beta Gamma Sigma. Republican. Roman Catholic. Home: 426 N Citrus Ave Los Angeles CA 90036-2632 Office: LA City Coll 855 N Vermont Ave Los Angeles CA 90029 E-mail: geowalen@msn.com.

WALENSKY, DOROTHY CHARLOTTE, foreign language educator; b. N.Y.C., Mar. 23, 1941; d. Oliver L. and Henny T. (Schlesinger) Marton; m. Ernest Leonard Walensky, Aug. 17, 1968; 1 child. BA, Adelphi U., 1962; MA in Spanish, Middlebury Coll. and U. Madrid, 1963; MA in Teaching, Fairleigh Dickinson U., 1966. Bilingual sec. internat. div. Turner Jones Co., Inc., N.Y.C., 1963-64; prof. Spanish and German, Fairleigh Dickinson U., Teaneck, N.J., 1965—. Mem. AAUP, Am. Assn. Tchrs. of Spanish and Portuguese, Am. Assn. Tchrs. of German, Modern Lang. Assn., Sigma Delta Pi, Delta Phi Alpha. Avocations: travel, photography, stamp collector, tennis, ice skating. Office: Fairleigh Dickinson U 1000 River Rd Teaneck NJ 07666-1996

WALES, PATRICE, school system administrator; b. Washington, Sept. 9, 1935; d. Robert Corning and Bernadette Mary (Dyer) W. BA, Dunbarton Coll. of Holy Cross, 1957; MTS, Cath. U. Am., 1978; PhD, U. Md., 1993. Cert. tchr., supt., Md. Tchr. mid. sch. St. Marys, Laurel, Md., 1960-61; tchr. high sch. St. Vincent Pallotti High Sch., Laurel, Md., 1962-65; instr. nursing sch. St. Mary's Sch. Nursing, Huntington, W.Va., 1965-66; tchr. St. Vincent Pallotti High Sch., Laurel, Md., 1967-76, adminstr., 1976—, chair sci. dept., 1962-80, dean students, 1976-87, sponsorship dir., 1988—. Bd. dirs. St. Vincent Pallotti HS, Laurel; trustee St. Joseph's Hosp., Buckhannon, W.Va., 1990—, v.p. 2003; dir. German Exch. Program, Laurel, Ahlen, Germany, 1976-96, Maesawa H.S. Exch., Japan, 1997; exec. sec. US Nat. Coord. Coun. Senator Sisters Senate Archdiocese of Washington, 1993—, pres., 1998-2001. NSF grantee, 1967, 69, 71. Mem. ASCD, Nat. Cath. Edn. Assn., Nat. Soc. Daughters of Am. Revolution (chaplain Toaping Castle chpt.), Am. Governance and Leadership Group. Roman Catholic. Avocations: walking, biking. Home: 404 8th St Laurel MD 20707-4032 Office: St Vincent Pallotti High Sch 113 Saint Marys Pl Laurel MD 20707-4099

WALFORD, GERALD ALBERT, physical education educator; b. Sudbury, Ont., Can., Aug. 14, 1937; came to the U.S., 1961; s. Gerald E. and Lena (Vitone) W.; divorced; 1 child, Gerald E. BS in Phys. Edn., U. N.D., 1961; MS in Phys. Edn., Ithaca Coll., 1965; PhD in Psychology of Sport, U. Md., 1988. Golf and hockey profl. Dalhousie U., Halifax, N.S., Can., 1965-72; athletic dir., head phys. edn. Ctrl. H.S., Hermitage, Nfld., Can., 1976-79, Warwick (Bermuda) Acad., 1979-83; instr. phys. edn. Prince George's C.C., Largo, Md., 1984-87; coach hockey and golf U. Wis., LaCrosse, 1987-89; head dept. phys. edn. Alice Lloyd Coll., Pippa Passes, Ky., 1989—; golf profl., dir. jr. and adult golf schs. Holiday Valley Resort, Ellicottville, N.Y., 1989—. Coach golf and men's soccer and hockey Dalhousie U., 1969-72; instr. golf No. Va. C.C., U. Md., 1984; golf profl. Hillview Golf Course, LaCrosse, 1986-89; tchr. geography and history, head hockey coach East Grand Forks H.S., 1961-62; tchr. phys. edn. and health, head hockey coach Aurora-Hoyt Lakes H.S., 1962-63; asst. prof., asst. golf coach East Stroudsburg (Pa.) U., 1986-88; dir. intramural hockey, instr. phys. edn. Ohio State U., 1974-76; presenter profl. confs. Author: Ice Hockey: An Illustrated Guide for Coaches, 1971, Hockey Coaching, 1993, Hockey Skills and Drill Book, 1993, Youth Hockey, 1994, The TAO of Teaching, 1995, Physical Education Academic Handbook, 1999; Performance Golf, 2001; contbg. author: Mindset for Winning-A Coaches Manual for Mental Training, 1988; contbr. articles to profl. publs.; appeared in TV prodns., including: (ednl. film) Hockey and Mathematics, CBC; (series of informative talks) Health and Fitness, area Fox affiliate; (instrnl. video) Golf, area Fox affiliate and ind. mktg.; contbr. articles to profl. jours. Mem. PGA, N.Am. Soc. Psychology of Sport and Phys. Activity (presenter conv. 1985), Can. Profl. Golfer's Assn. (class A), Am. Hockey Coaches Assn. (presenter 1967), Can. Hockey Coaches Assn., Golf Coaches Assn. Am., Halifax Centennial Lacrosse Assn., Internat. Soc. for Humor Studies (presenter 1994). Home: ALC Purpose Rd Pippa Passes KY 41844 Office: Alice Lloyd Coll ALC Purpose Rd Pippa Passes KY 41844

WALI, MOHAN KISHEN, environmental science and natural resources educator; b. Kashmir, India, Mar. 1, 1937; came to U.S., 1969, naturalized, 1975; s. Jagan Nath and Somavati (Wattal) W.; m. Sarla Safaya, Sept. 25, 1960; children: Pamela, Promod. BS, U. Jammu and Kashmir, 1957; MS, U. Allahabad, India, 1960; PhD, U. B.C., Can., 1970. Lectr. S.P. Coll., Srinagar, Kashmir, 1963-65; rsch. fellow U. Copenhagen, 1965-66; grad. fellow U. B.C., 1967-69; asst. prof. biology U. N.D., Grand Forks, 1969-73, assoc. prof., 1973-79, prof., 1979-83, Hill rsch. prof., 1973; dir. Forest River Biology Area Field Sta., 1970-79, Project Reclamation, 1975-83; spl. asst. to univ. pres., 1977-82; staff ecologist Grand Forks Energy Rsch. Lab. U.S. Dept. Interior, 1974-75; prof. Coll. Environ. Sci. and Forestry SUNY, Syracuse, 1983-89, dir. grad. program environ. sci., 1983-85, prof. Sch. Natural Resources, 1990—, dir. Sch. Natural Resources, assoc. dean Coll. Agr., 1990-93; dir. Environ. Sci. Grad. program Ohio State U., Columbus, 2001—. Vice chmn. N.D. Air Pollution Adv. Coun., 1981-83; co-chair IV Internat. Congress on Ecology, 1986. Editor: Some Environmental Aspects of Strip-Mining in North Dakota, 1973, Prairie: A Multiple View, 1975, Practices and Problems of Land Reclamation in Western North America, 1975, Ecology and Coal Resource Development, 1979, Ecosystem Rehabilitation-Preamble to Sustainable Development, 1992; co-editor Agriculture and the Environment, 1993; sr. editor Reclamation Rev., 1976-80, chief editor, 1980-81; chief editor Reclamation and Revegetation Rsch., 1982-87; contbr. articles to profl. jours. Recipient B.C. Gamble Disting. Tchg. and Svc. award, 1977. Fellow AAAS, Nat. Acad. Scis. India; mem. Ecol. Soc. Am. (chmn. sect. internat. activities 1980-84), Bot. Ecol. Soc., Can. Bot. Assn. (dir. ecology sect. 1976-79, v.p. 1982-83), Am. Soc. Agronomy, Am. Inst. Biol. Sci. (gen. chmn. 34th ann. meeting), Internat. Assn. Ecolog (co-chmn. IV Internat. Congress Ecology), Internat. Soc. Soil Sci., N.D. Acad. Sci. (chmn. editl. com. 1979-81), Sigma Xi (nat. lectr. 1983-85, pres. Ohio State chpt. 1993-94, pres. Syracuse chpt. 1984-85, Outstanding Rsch. award U. N.D. chpt. 1975). Office: Ohio State U Sch Natural Resources 2021 Coffey Rd Columbus OH 43210-1044

WALINSKY, PAUL, cardiology educator; b. Phila., June 21, 1940; s. Aaron and Bess (Kleiman) W.; m. Stephanie Sosenko, Nov. 27, 1971; children: Shira, Daniel. BA, Temple U., 1961; MD, U. Pa., 1965. Cert. Nat. Bd. Med. Examiners, Am. Bd. Internal Medicine Cardiovascular. Instr. medicine Thomas Jefferson U., Phila., 1973-75, asst. prof. medicine, 1975-79, assoc. prof. medicine, 1979-82, prof. medicine, 1982—. Cons. EP Technologies, Mountain View, Calif., 1991-93, Baxter Edwards, Irvine, Calif., 1988-91, C.R. Bard, Billerica, Mass., 1994, ESP Pharma, 2002. Contbr. articles to profl. jours.; reviewer profl. jours.; inventor method for high frequency ablation, percutaneous microwave catheter angioplasty. Capt. USAF, 1967—69. Fellow Am. Coll. Cardiology, ACP; mem. AMA, Pa. Med. Soc., Phila. County Med. Assn. Achievements include 14 U.S. patents in field of perfusion balloon catheter, microwave aided balloon angioplasty with lumen measurement, intravascular ultrasonic imaging catheter and method for making same, and acoustic catheter with rotary drive. Office: Thomas Jefferson U 111 S 11th St Philadelphia PA 19107-5084 E-mail: Paul.Walinsky@mail.tju.edu.

WALKA, ANNE LAURAINE, English language educator; b. Jersey City, Oct. 16, 1959; d. Felix and Anna (Grocki) Walka; m. Joseph E. Natoli, July 11, 1992 (div. July 1997); children: Timothy Edward (dec.), Kara Krystine. BA, Montclair State Coll., Upper Montclair, N.J., 1982, MA, 1990, NYU, 1984; postgrad., So. Ill. U., 1990—. Cert. English and math. tchr., N.J. Adj. prof. prep. studies dept. County Coll. Morris, Randolph, N.J., 1985-89; adj. prof. basic skills dept. Hudson County Community Coll., Jersey City, 1985-89; adj. prof. English, Jersey City State Coll., 1985-89; instr. academically talented youth program Montclair State U., 1985-97; adj. prof. English Montclair State Coll., 1985-93; grad. asst. English dept. So. Ill. U., Carbondale, 1990-92; substitute tchr. Secaucus (N.J.) Bd. Edn., 1993-94; tchr., drama coach, newspaper/literary mag. advisor Immaculate Conception H.S., Montclair, N.J., 1994-98; tchr. math. Eastside H.S., Paterson, N.J., 1998-99; tchr. math. and English, Secaucus (N.J.) Mid./H.S., 1999—2002; tchr. 8th grade math Robert Waters Sch., Union City, 2003—. Moderator for newspaper, lit. mag., news broadcasts. Contbr. poetry to various publs. Mem. MLA, Nat. Coun. Tchrs. English, Am. Film Inst., Soc. Cinema Studies, Soc. Animation Studies, Popular Culture Assn., Nat. Coun. Tchrs. Math., N.J. Edn. Assn. Home: 719 Irving Pl Secaucus NJ 07094-3218 E-mail: magicshadows@comcast.net.

WALKER, AMY MELISSA, English as second language educator; b. Oct. 17, 1965; Student, U. Madrid, 1985-86; BA in Spanish, Elmira Coll., 1987; MS in Fgn. Lang. Edn., Syracuse U., 1989, MA in Linguistics, 1995. Tchr. Syracuse (N.Y.) City Sch. Dist., 1989-90; instr. English Lang. Inst., Syracuse U., 1990—. Sales assoc. Kaufmann's; beauty cons. Mary Kay Cosmetics. Photography exhibits at The Cmty. Folk Art Gallery, Syracuse, N.Y., 1998, Syracuse U. Cmty. Darkrooms Mems. Show, 1999. Mem. adult edn. com. May Meml. Unitarian Universalist Soc., Syracuse, 1993-99, mem. min.'s adv. com., 1995-96, mem. denominational affairs com., 1997-98. Mem. TESOL. Avocations: photography, writing, asian indian, middle eastern and african cooking, reading. Office: Syracuse U English Lang Inst 700 University Ave Syracuse NY 13210-1719

WALKER, ANNETTE, retired counseling administrator; b. Birmingham, Ala., Sept. 20, 1953; d. Jesse and Luegene (Wright) W. BS in Edn., Huntingdon Coll., 1974; MS in Adminstrn. and Supervision, Troy State U., 1977, 78, MS in Sch. Counseling, 1990, AA in Sch. Adminstrn., 1992; diploma, World Travel Sch., 1990; diploma in Cosmetology, John Patterson Coll., 1992; MEd in higher Edn. Adminstrn., Auburn (Ala.) U., 1995. Cert. tchr., adminstr., Ala.; lic. cosmetologist, Ala.; lic. funeral dir., Ala. Tchr. Montgomery (Ala.) Pub. Sch. System, 1976-89, sch. counselor, 1989—2000; lit. tchr. Fed. Bur. of Justice, 1997—2000; ret., 2000. Tchr. Fed. Govt., 1997—, U.S. Bur. Justice, 1997—; gymnastics tchr. Cleveland Ave. YMCA, 1971-76; girls coach Montgomery Parks and Recreation, 1973-76; summer sch. sci. tchr. grades 7-9, 1977-88; chmn. dept. sci. Bellingrath Sch., 1987-90, courtesy com., 1987-88, sch. discipline com., 1977-84; recreation asst. Gunter AFB, Ala., 1981-83; calligraphy tchr. Gunter Youth Ctr., 1982; program dir. Maxwell AFB, Ala., 1983-89, vol. tchr. Internat. Officer Sch., 1985—, Adult Laubach Reading Prog., Ala. Goodwill Amb., 1985—, day camp dir., 1987, calligraphy tchr., 1988; trainer internat. law for sec. students, Ala., 1995—; leader of workshops in field; sales rep. Ala. World Travel, 1990—; behavior aid Brantwood Children's Home, 1996—; computer tchr. hs diploma program Montgomery County Sch., 1995—; behavior aide Brantwood Children's Home, 1995—;

hotel auditor, 1995—; Am. del. to China, People to People Internat., 1998; acad. advisor C.C. of Air Force, Maxwell AFB, Ala., 2002—. Mem. CAP; tchr. Sunday sch. Beulah Bapt. Ch., Montgomery; vol. zoo activities Tech. Scholarship Program for Ala. Tchrs. Computer Courses, Montgomery, Ala.; bd. dirs. Cleveland Ave. YMCA, 1976-80; sponsor Bell-Howe chpt. Young Astronauts, 1986-90, Pate Howe chpt. Young Astronauts, 1991-92; judge Montgomery County Children Festival Elem. Sci. Fair, 1988-90; bd. dirs. Troy State U. Drug Free Schs., 1992—; chmn. Maxwell AFB Red Cross-Youth, 1986-88; goodwill amb. sponsor to various families (award 1989, 95); State of Ala. rep. P.A.T.C.H.-Internat. Law Inst., 1995; bd. dirs. People to People Internat., 2000. Named Tchr. of the Week, WCOV-TV, 1992, Ala. Tchr. in Space Program, summer, 1989, Local Coord. Young Astronaut Program, 1988, Citizen Amb. to China, People to People Internat., 1999; recipient Outstanding High Sch. Sci./Math. Tchr. award, Sigma Xi, 1989, Most Outstanding Youth Coun. Leader award, Maxwell AFB Youth Ctr., 1987, Outstanding Ala. Goodwill Amb. award, 1989, 1995, Tchr. of Yr. award, Paterson Sch., 1990, Career Infusion award (Most Appreciated Tchr. award), 1987, Montgomery Pub. Sch., 1982, 1984, Earthwatch Ednl. award, Israel, 1997, 20 Class award, Maxwell AFB Internat. Fgn. Officer Program, 25 Class award, 2003; Fulbright scholar, Japan, 1999. Mem. NEA, Internat. Platform Assn., People to People Internat. (founder, bd. trustees, organizer, pres. Ala. chpt. 1998), Nat. Sci. Tchrs. Assn., Ala. Sch. Counselors, Montgomery Sch. Counselors Assn., Montgomery County Ednl. Assn., Space Camp Amb., Huntingdon Alumni Assn. (sec.-treas.), Ala. Goodwill Amb., Montgomery Capital City Club, Young Astronauts, Ea. Star, Japan Friends of Fulbright Meml. Fund Tchr. Prog., Water Watch, Montgomery, AL, Zeta Phi Beta, Chi Delta Phi, Kappa Pi. Avocations: international travel, calligraphy, international food, cruising. Home: 2501 Westwood Dr Montgomery AL 36108 E-mail: awalker2001@yahoo.com.

WALKER, CAROLYN PEYTON, English language educator; b. Charlottesville, Va., Sept. 15, 1942; d. Clay M. and Ruth Peyton. BA with distinction in Am. History/Lit., Sweet Briar Coll., 1965; cert. in French, Alliance Francaise, Paris, 1966; EdM, Tufts U., 1970; MA in Englisn and Am. Lit, Stanford U., 1974, PhD in English Edn., 1977. Tchr. elem. and jr. h.s., Switzerland, 1967-69; tchr. elem. grades Boston Sch. System, 1966-67, 69-70, Newark (Calif) Unified Sch. System, 1970-72; instr. divsn. Humanities Canada Coll., Redwood City, Calif., 1973, 76-78; instr. Sch. Bus. U. San Francisco, 1973-74; evaluation cons. Inst. Profl. Devel., San Jose, Calif., 1975-76; asst. dir. Stanford U. Learning Assistance Ctr., Calif., 1972—77, dir., 1977—84, supr. counselors, tutors and tchrs., 1972-84; lectr., dept. English Stanford U., 1977-84, lectr., Sch. Edn., 1975-84; pvt. practice corp. tng., 1983—; mem. faculty U. Calif., Santa Cruz, Berkeley, 1995—; prof. dept. English San Jose State U., 1984-93, dir. The Writing Ctr. dept. English, 1986—93, dir. Steinbeck Rsch. Ctr., 1986—87; cons. Advanced Micro Devices, Calif., 1996, CellNet Data Sys., 1996—98, Fujitsu, 1997, Proxim, 1997—98, AMP, 1997—98; tech. Comm. Internat., 1997—2002, VISA Internat., 1999—, Inovant, Inc. Condr. reading and writing workshops, 1972—; review Random House Books, 1978-95, Rsch. in the Teaching of English, 1983-95, Course Tech., Inc., 1990; cons. Basic Skills Task Force, U.S. Office Edn., 1977-79, Right to Read, Calif. State Dept. Edn., 1977-85, Program for Gifted and Talented, Fremont (Calif). Unified Sch. Dist., 1981-82; bd. dirs. The Tech Mus. of Innovation, San Jose, 1983-84; head cons. to pres. to evaluate college's writing program, San Jose City Coll., 1985-87, cons. U. Texas, Dallas, 1984; cons. DeAnza Coll., 2000-01; cons. Stanford U., 1977-78, 84; cons., CCNY, 1979, U. Wis., 1980; numerous testing programs; cons. to pres. San Diego State U., 1982; Ednl. Testing Svc., 1985-88; English dept. Writing Ctr., 1986-93; ednl. cons. Sun Microsystems, 2002;— spkr. numerous profl. confs.; cons. in field. Author: Handbook for Teaching Assistants at Stanford University, 1977, Learning Center Courses for Faculty and Staff: Reading, Writing, and Time Management, 1981, How to Succeed as a New Teacher: A Handbook for Teaching Assistants, 1978, ESL Courses for Faculty & Staff: An Additional Opportunity to Serve the Campus Community, 1983, (with Karen Wilson) Tutor Handbook for the Writing Center at San Jose State University, 1989, (with others) Academic Tutoring at the Learning Assistance Center, 1980, Writing Conference Talk: Factors Associated with HIgh and Low Rated Writing Conferences, 1987, Lifeline Mac: A Handbook for Instructors in the Macintosh Computer Classrooms, 1989, Communications with the Faculty: Vital Links for the Success of Writing Centers, 1991, Coming to America, 1993, Teacher Dominance in the Writing Conference, 1992, Instant Curriculum: Just Add Tutors and Students, 1993; editor newsletter Environ. Vols. Inc., Palo Alto, Calif., 1999—; contbr. chpts. to Black American Literature Forum, 1991; contbr. articles to profl. jours. Founding mem. Tech. Mus. of Innovation, San Jose, Calif., 1995; vol. fundraiser Peninsula Ctr. for the Blind, Palo Alto, Calif., 1982—. The Resource Ctr. for Women, Palo Alto, 1975—76, Pathways Hospice, 2002—; vol. Gamble Garden Ctr., 1989—. Recipient Award for Outstanding Contbns., U.S. HEW, 1979, award ASPPIRE (federally funded program), 1985, two awards Student Affirmative Action, 1986, award Western Coll. Reading & Leanring Assn., 1984, founding mem. Tech Museum of Innovation, 1995; numerous other awards and grants. Home: 2350 Waverley St Palo Alto CA 94301-4143 E-mail: wavedd@pacbell.net.

WALKER, CAROLYN SMITH, college services administrator, counselor; b. Atlanta, May 9, 1946; d. George Taft and Lonnie Bell (Bates) Smith; 1 child from previous marriage, Gary Sherard Walker II. BA in Psychology, Clark Coll., Atlanta, 1970; MS in Counseling & Guidance, U. Nebr., Omaha, 1975. Lic. and cert. profl. counselor, Ga. Adult basic edn. instr. Atlanta Pub. Schs., 1970-71, adult basic edn. site coord., 1971; adult basic edn. instr. Omaha-Nebr. Tech. C.C., Omaha, 1971-74, dir. adult basic edn., 1974; guidance counselor Omaha Pub. Schs., 1974-76; recruitment counselor Minority Women Employment Program, Atlanta, 1976-77; career planning and employment preparation instr. Discovery Learning Inc., Job Tng. and Pntrship Act, Atlanta, 1985-86; dir. counseling and testing svcs. Atlanta Met. Coll., 1977—, assoc. v.p. for student affairs, 1998—. Test supr. Ednl. Testing Svc., Princeton, N.J., 1980—, Psychology Corp., San Antonio, 1991-99, Law Sch. Admissions Test, Newtown, Pa., 1991-99; cons. Commn. on Colls., So. Assn. Colls. and Schs., Atlanta, 1978—; jr. c.c. rep. Placement & Coop. Edn., Atlanta, 1987-90. Editor newsletters Romar On-Line, 1997, The Brief, 1984, 85, Guided Studies News, 1974; contbg. author: (manual) AJC Self-Study, 1981, 2000; author: (manual) Policies and Procedures for Coordinated Counseling, 1981, 3d edit., 1999, Policies and Procedures for Learning Disability Services, 1997, 2d edit., 1999, Women's Coalition for Habitat for Humanity in Atlanta, 1993-95, 97. Pres. Atlanta Barristers Wives Inc., 1984, 85; mem. steering com. Atlanta Mayor's Masked Ball, 1987; mem. memberships sales com. Atlanta Arts Festival, 1986, Neighborhood Arts Ctr., 1986; state host Dem. Nat. Conv., Atlanta, 1988; mem. Heritage Valley Cmty. Neighborhood Assn., 1982—. Recipient Outstanding Svc. award Nat. Orientation Dirs. Assn., 1985, 86, Literacy Action, Inc., 1978, Atlanta Met. Coll., 1987, others. Mem. Ga. Coll. Personnel Assn., Ga. Mental Health Counselors Assn., Nat. Coun. Student Devel., Univ. System Counseling Dirs., 100 Women Internat. Inc. (charter mem.), Am. Assn. Community and Jr. Colls., The Links Inc., Ga. Assn. Women Deans, Counselors and Adminstrs., Ga. Coll. Conselors Assn. Democrat. Methodist. Avocations: tennis, travel, horticulture. Home: 3511 Toll House Ln SW Atlanta GA 30331-2330 Office: Atlanta Metro Coll 1630 Metropolitan Pkwy SW Atlanta GA 30310-4448

WALKER, DAVID A(LAN), finance educator, educator; b. York, Pa., Jan. 5, 1941; s. Arthur Benjamin and Alva (Strasbougher) Walker; m. Audrey Thayer, Aug. 21, 1982; children: Matthew Billett, Elizabeth Penniman Bilhartz. BA, Pa. State U., 1962; MS, Iowa State U., 1964, PhD, 1968. Asst. prof. Pa. State U., 1968-70; economist FDIC, 1970-76, 78-80; vis. assoc. prof. Northwestern U., 1976-77; dir. rsch. Office Comptroller of Currency, 1977-78; assoc. prof. fin. Georgetown U., 1980-82, prof., 1982-92, assoc. dean, 1985-87, John A. Largay prof., 1992—. Chair governing bd. Credit Rsch. Ctr., 1997—; dir. Capital Mkts. Rsch. Ctr., 1989—; hon. com. mem. Wall St. Inst., 2002--; advisor U.S. Dept. Treas., U.S. SBA; cons. in field. Co-author textbooks; editor Jour. Fin. Rsch., 1981-87; co-editor Jour. Small Bus. Fin., 1992-95; mem. editl. bd. Jour. Fin. Rsch., Fin. Mgmt., J.F.Q.A., Fin. Rev., Quar. Rev. Econs. and Fin., Jour. Small Bus. Fin.; contbr. articles to profl. jours. NDEA fellow, 1962-64. Mem. Am. Econ. Assn., So. Fin. Assn. (bd. dirs.), Ea. Fin. Assn. (bd. dirs.), Fin. Mgmt. Assn. (v.p. 1990-91, pres. 1994-95, trustee 1995—, chair bd. trustees 1999—), Beta Gamma Sigma. Republican. Home: 4416 Que St NW Washington DC 20007 Office: Georgetown U Sch Bus Washington DC 20057-0001 E-mail: walkerd@msb.edu.

WALKER, DONALD EDWIN, history educator; b. Hammond, Ind., Feb. 6, 1941; s. Carl Thurston and Verla Irene (Cutler) W.; m. Julie Ann Woerpel, Dec. 20, 1960; children: Theodore R., Susan J. Walker. BA, Ind. U., 1963; MA, U. S.D., 1964; postgrad., U. Wyo., 1964-65; PhD, Mich. State U., 1982. Asst. prof. Olivet (Mich.) Coll., 1965-74, assoc. prof., 1974-82, prof., 1982—. Cons. Score Cards, Westport, Conn., 1991. Co-author: Baseball and American Culture, 1995; contbr. articles to profl. jours. City coun. mem. Olivet City Coun., 1977—; police commr. Olivet Police Dept., 1984—; mayor pro tempore City of Olivet, 1983—. Mem. Orgn. of Am. Historians, Western History Assn., Phi Alpha Theta, Phi Kappa Phi, Omicron Delta Kappa, Phi Mu Alpha. Methodist. Avocations: gardening, music, reading, traveling, walking. Home: PO 516 407 Washington Olivet MI 49076-9601 Office: Olivet Coll Dept History Mott Bldg Olivet MI 49076

WALKER, FRANCES MORINE, retired special education educator; b. Bolckow, Mo., Mar. 1, 1931; d. Ralph Ernest and Mabel Marie (Campbell) Dorrel; m. Robert D. Walker (div. 1983); children: Debra (dec.), Denise, David, Diane, Darla, Dennis, Douglas. Student, S.W. Baptist Jr. Coll., Bolivar, Mo., 1949-51; BS, Mo. Western U., 1969; post grad., N.W. Mo. State Coll. Tchr. Whitehall Sch., Bolckow, 1951-53; spl. edn. tchr. Savannah (Mo.) R111 Sch., 1970-95; ret., 1995. Tchr., coach Spl. Olympics, Savannah, 1970-95; ct. apptd. spl. advocate for neglected and abused children, 1995—. Tchr. Sunday sch. classes from nursery to sr. adults; mem. coun. Econ. Opportunity Corp., 1994, Mentoring Moms, 1994-96; ct.-apptd. spl. advocate for neglected and abused children, 1996—; vol. mus., sch., others. Mem. Mo. Tchrs. Assn., Classrooom Tchrs. Assn. (bldg. rep.), Sertoma (pres. Savannah 1988-89, bd. dirs., Svc. to Mankind award 1985). Republican. Baptist. Avocations: reading, volunteering. Home: 302 Dogwood Apt B Savannah MO 64485 also: Savannah Jr High 701 W Chestnut St Savannah MO 64485-1445

WALKER, GEORGE KONTZ, law educator; b. Tuscaloosa, Ala., July 8, 1938; s. Joseph Henry and Catherine Louise (Indorf) W.; m. Phyllis Ann Sherman, July 30, 1966; children: Charles Edward, Mary Neel. BA, U. Ala., 1959; LLB, Vanderbilt U., 1966; AM, Duke U., 1968; LLM, U. Va., 1972; postgrad. (Sterling fellow), Law Sch. Yale U., 1975-76. Bar: Va. 1967, N.C. 1976. Law clk. U.S. Dist. Ct., Richmond, Va., 1966-67; assoc. Hunton, Williams, Gay, Powell & Gibson, Richmond, 1967-70; pvt. practice Charlottesville, Va., 1970-71; asst. prof. Law Sch. Wake Forest U., Winston-Salem, N.C., 1972-73, assoc. prof. Law Sch., 1974-77, prof. Law Sch., 1977—, mem. bd. advisors Divinity Sch., 1991-94; Charles H. Stockton prof. internat. law U.S. Naval War Coll., 1992-93. Vis. prof. Marshall-Wythe Sch. Law, Coll. William and Mary, Williamsburg, Va., 1979-80, U. Ala. Law Sch., 1985; cons. Naval War Coll., 1976—, Nat. Def. Exec. Res., 1991—, Naval War Coll., Internat. Law Dept. Adv. Bd., 1993—. Author: The Tanker War, 1980-88, 2000; contbr. articles to profl. jours. With USN, 1959-62, capt. USNR, ret. Woodrow Wilson fellow, 1962-63; decorated Order of the long Leaf Pine; recipient Joseph Branch Alumni Svc. award, Wake Forest, 1988, Meritorious Unit Commendation, 1992-93; named Hon. Atty. Gen. N.C., 1986. Mem.: ABA, Internat. Inst. Humanitarian Law, Maritime Law Assn., Am. Law Inst., Am. Judicature Soc., Internat. Law Assn. (exec. com. Am. br. 2001—), Am. Soc. Internat. Law (exec. coun. 1988—91), N.C. Bar Assn. (v.p. 1997—98), Va. Bar Assn., Order of Barristers (hon.), Piedmont Club, Phi Delta Phi, Sigma Alpha Epsilon, Phi Beta Kappa, Order of the Coif (hon.). Democrat. Episcopalian. Home: 3321 Pennington Ln Winston Salem NC 27106-5439 Office: Wake Forest U Sch Law PO Box 7206 Winston Salem NC 27109-7206

WALKER, JAMES WILLIAM, secondary education educator, freelance writer; b. Akron, Ohio, Feb. 5, 1947; s. Arthur Hobart and Ella Mae (Slade) W.; 1 child, Michael James. BS, Kent (Ohio) State U., 1973, MEd, 1979. Lic. secondary educator in physics, English, ednl. media, Ohio. Journeyman pipefitter Goodyear Tire & Rubber Co., Akron, 1968-76; tchr. sci., media specialist Jackson Local Schs., Massillon, Ohio, 1976—, curriculum specialist, 1999—. Guest columnist The Canton Repository, 1986—; contbr. articles to profl. jours. Pres. Friends of the North Canton (Ohio) Libr., 1981-82, Unitarian Universalist Congregation of Canton, 1992-94, 2000; bd. dirs. Hunger Task Force of Stark County, Ohio, 1991-95; county organizer Ams. United for Separation of Ch. and State, 1997; chmn., bd. trustees Massillon Mus., 2002-2003. Cameras in the Curriculum grantee Eastman Kodak Corp., Rochester, N.Y., 1984, grantee Martha Holden Jennings Found., Cleve., 1984-85; recipient Acker award Ohio Acad. Sci., Columbus, 1986, Krecker award Battelle Rsch. Inst., Columbus, 1986. Mem. NEA, Jackson Profl. Edn. Assn. (bldg. rep. 1988-89, 98-99). Avocations: motorcycling, art collecting, photography, vintage baseball. Office: Jackson H S 7600 Fulton Dr NW Massillon OH 44646-9393 E-mail: radiochips@hotmail.com.

WALKER, LEANN FOX, special education educator; b. Cookeville, Tenn., July 15, 1970; d. Leland H. and Nancy Welch Fox; m. George Leslie, Aug. 4, 1995; children: Britin Marquette, Mayson Keeley, Daleigh Morgan. BS, Tenn. Tech. U., Cookeville, TN, 1997, MA, 1999. Cert. cosmetologist. Adv. mgr. Roses, Inc, Cookeville, 1988—90; cosmetologist Shear Magic, Cookeville, 1990—91; ednl. diagnostician Jackson County Sch., Gainesboro, 1997—98; spl. educator Jackson County H.S., Gainesboro, Tenn., 1998—. Home: 1147 Pippin Rd Cookeville TN 38501 Office: Jackson County HS 190 Blue Devil Ln Gainesboro TN 38562 Home Fax: 931-268-4067. Personal E-mail: glw5@charter.net. Business E-Mail: walkerl15@k12tn.net.

WALKER, LORENE, retired elementary school educator; b. Clovis, N.Mex., July 27, 1911; d. Jessie H. and Tille Eula (Harlan) Black; m. Carl Westley Walker, June 9, 1934; children: Wesley, Charles. BS, N.Mex. State U., 1933; M Family Life, Cen. Wash. U., 1959, postgrad., 1956-74. Tchr. home econs. Floyd Sch., near Portales, N.Mex., 1933-34, Navajo Meth. Mission, Farmington, N.Mex., 1947-48; home agt. extension svc. Wash. State Coop. Extension Svc., Yakima, 1948-56; family life, counseling tchr. West Valley Sch., Yakima, 1956-71, spl. elem. reading tchr., 1971-75; tour organizer, leader Mission Tour, Yakima, 1966-98; trainer missioners United Meth. Ch., Yakima, Wash., 1998—. Coord. 4-H camps, fairs and programs Wash. Coop. Extension Svc., Yakima, 1950-56. Chairperson Experiment for Internat. Living, Yakima Valley Rep. Women's Club, 1960-67; docent, tour leader Yakima Valley Mus., 1976—; trustee Found. Pacific Northwest United Meth. Ch., 1984—; pres. Columbia River dist. United Meth. Ch., 1987-88, chairperson global missions, 1993-94; chair Tour With a Mission, 1966-2003. Mem. AAUW (treas. 1962-66, bd. dirs., chair internat. rels. 1962-89; spl. honor award 1989), United Meth. Women (pres. 1987-89; spl. recognition 1989), Wesleyan Svc. Guild Meth. Women. (officer 1964-68), Alpha Delta Kappa (pres. 1967-69). Avocations: gardening, travel, needlework, international political and cultural news. Home: 101 N 48th Ave Apt 25A Yakima WA 98908-3179

WALKER, LUCY DORIS, secondary school educator, writer; b. Ridgeway, NC, May 6, 1951; d. Edgerton Verl and Mary Ellen (Williams) Plummer; m. William A. Walker Jr., June 21, 1969 (div. Aug. 1974); 1 child, Lucretia Marie. BA in English Edn., Fairleigh Dickinson U., 1975; MA in Theater Arts, Montclair State U., 1977. Cert. English and theater arts tchr., N.J. Tchr., dir., actor, writer Ctr. Modern Dance Edn., Hackensack, NJ, 1978; writer, dir. Am. Theater Actors, NYC, 1978-79; tchr. multicultural hub Ctr. Internat. Studies, Cultural Events, Teaneck HS, Teaneck, NJ, 1979—; coord. Teaneck Arts Acad. at Teaneck HS, Teaneck, NJ, 2002—. Artistic dir. Teaneck H.S. dance ensemble, 1989—; program coord. African and African-Am. Studies Resource Ctr., 1990—; instructional leader for fine and performing arts, coord. Teaneck Arts Acad.. Writer and choreographer various plays, 1979-95. Recipient Acad. Achievement award Fairleigh Dickinson U. Opportunities Program, 1974, Black Heritage award Nat. Assn. Negro Bus. & Profl. Women's Clubs, 1991. Mem. NEA, NJ Edn. Assn. Democrat. Baptist. Avocations: sewing, gardening, hiking, painting, music. Home: 363 Washington Pl Englewood NJ 07631-3232 Office: Teaneck HS 100 Elizabeth Ave Teaneck NJ 07666-4713 E-mail: walkplum@aol.com.

WALKER, MARIE FULLER, elementary education educator; b. Pa. d. Gladys Fuller; m. Frederick T. Walker; children: Frederick T. Jr., Nicole Marie. BA in History, U. Philippines, 1969; MEd, West Chester U., 1992. Cert. elem. tchr., Calif., Pa., N.C., Okla., Ala.; cert. elem. adminstr., prin., Pa. Tchr. ESL Royal Thai Army Sch. Nursing, Bangkok, Thailand, 1975; tchr. 2d grade Ruam Rudee Internat. Sch., Bangkok, Thailand, 1975-76; tchr. 3d grade St. Adelaide Sch., Highland, Calif., 1976-77; tchr. Midwest City (Okla.) Sch., 1980-82; tchr. 4th grade Rainbow Elem. Sch., Coatesville, Pa., 1989—. Administered vol. programs ARC, Ft. Bragg and Pope AFB, recruited and trained vols., official community spokesperson, nat. cons., Washington, vol. cons., 1984 (Vol. of Yr. award N.C., 1983, Achievements awards 1983, 84, 85, Clara Barton award 1984). Recipient N.C. Outstanding Vol. Adminstr./Coord., Gov., 1984, Gift of Time award Family Inst., 1992, Dir. Edn. Excellence award IST PDE, 1994; grantee Math, 1994, Ecology, 1995, Butterfly Garden, 1995, Arts Spl. Edn., 1995, 96, Arts in Edn., 1995, 96, Math. Lab., 1996, Hist. Rsch. Tech., 1996. Mem. NEA, NAESP, PTA, Pa. Assn. Elem. Sch. Prins., Phi Delta Kappa. Avocations: reading, walking, gardening, travel. Home: 17 Willow Pond Rd Malvern PA 19355-2888 Office: Rainbow Elem Sch 50 Country Club Rd Coatesville PA 19320-1813

WALKER, MARY DIANE, secondary school educator; b. Royal Oak, Mich., Sept. 11, 1955; d. Thomas Walker and Mary Jo Brown Stevenson. BS in Med. Records Adminstrn., U. Ctrl. Fla., 1979; MEd, U. South Fla., 1995, postgrad., 1997—. Registered records adminstr.; cert. secondary sci. and biology tchr., Fla. Tchr. Key Tng. Ctr., Lecanto, Fla., 1982-87; tchr. biology, phys. sci., environ. sci. and gen. sci. Lecanto H.S., 1987—. Tchr. Withlacoochee Environ. Tng. Ctr., 1992, teaching fellow, 1993-98; facilitator Project WILD; computer instr. Withlacoochee Tech. Inst., Inverness, Fla., Ctrl. Fla. C.C., Lecanto, 2000—, Lake Sumter C.C., Sumterville, Fla., 1999. Mem. NEA, Fla. Edn. Assn., Nat. Audubon Soc., League Environ. Educators Fla., Fla. Assn. Sci. Tchrs., Phi Kappa Phi. Methodist. Avocations: music, playing piano, travel, rollerblading, photography. Home: PO Box 1121 Floral City FL 34436-1121 Office: Lecanto High Sch 3810 W Educational Path Lecanto FL 34461-8052

WALKER, MICHAEL JAMES, surgeon, educator; BSc, U. Toronto, Ont., Can., 1968; MD, SUNY, Syracuse, 1972. Diplomate Am. Bd. Med. Examiners, Am. Bd. Surgery. Intern R.I. Hosp., Providence, 1972-73; resident U. Ill. Hosp., Chgo., 1975-82, surgical oncology fellow, 1982-83; instr. surgery U. Ill., Chgo., 1979-82, asst. prof., 1982-88, assoc. prof., 1988-89; assoc. prof. surgery Ohio State U., Columbus, 1989—. Contbr. articles to profl. jours. Am. Cancer Soc. jr. faculty fellow, 1983-86; NIH Physician Investigator, 1984-87. Fellow ACS; mem. Soc. Univ. Surgeons, Cen. Surg. Assn., Soc. of Surg. Oncology, Am. Soc. Clin. Oncology, Soc. for Exptl. Biology and Medicine, Am. Assn. for Cancer Rsch.

WALKER, MICHAEL LEON, education educator; b. Cin., May 17, 1942; s. Degree and Annie (Wynn) W. BA, Wayne State U., 1970, EdD, 1991; MA, U. Detroit, 1978. Asst. prof. La. State U., Shreveport, 1991-92, U. Nebr., Lincoln, 1992-94, SUNY, Plattsburgh, 1994-95, Ea. Mich. U., 1995—. Mem. Martin Luther King Club, Plattsburgh, 1994. Recipient award for Svc. to Children, Salvation Army, Lincoln, 1993, 1994. Mem. Nat. Coun. Tchrs. of English, Internat. Reading Assn., Nat. Reading Conf., Phi Delta Kappa. Democrat. Baptist. Avocations: reading, organ, piano. also: # 468 51 W Hancock St Detroit MI 48201-1303

WALKER, PAULETTE PATRICIA, special education educator; b. Lebanon, Pa., Sept. 30, 1956; d. Paul W. and Alice L. (Eisenhour) Walmer; m. Craig A. Walker, May 30, 1981. BS in Spl. Edn., Bloomsburg (Pa.) State Coll., 1978; MEd, Millersville (Pa.) State Coll., 1981. Cert. mentally and physically handicapped tchr., Pa. House parent Shiloh Family Guidance Ctr., Reading, Pa., 1978-81, Outreach, Harrisburg, Pa., 1981-82; tchr. Brookside Montessori Sch., Carlisle, Pa., 1983-85; supr. Ctr. for Indsl. Tng., Mechanicsburg, Pa., 1985-86; tchr. Capital Area Intermediate Unit, Summerdale, Pa., 1986—. Mentor induction program, mem. steering com. Capital Area Intermediate Unit, 1989-91, chmn. life skills curriculum writing team, summer 1990, mem. specially designed instrn. writing team, summer 1992, mem. multi-disabilities support team, 1993-95, mktg. and new products devel. team, 1993-94. Mem. Coun. for Exceptional Children, Kappa Delta Pi Ednl. Hon. Soc. Avocations: gardening, reading, walking. Home: 640 Alricks St Harrisburg PA 17110-2210

WALKER, RICHARD BRIAN, chemistry educator; b. Quincy, Mass., May 14, 1948; s. George Edgar and Eva Mary (Taylor) W. BS in Biochemistry, U. So. Calif., 1970; PhD in Pharm. Chemistry, U. Calif., San Francisco, 1975. Rsch. assoc. Oreg. State U., Corvallis, 1975-76, U. Wash., Seattle, 1976-78; lectr. U.S. Internat. U., San Diego, 1978-81, Hamdard Sch. Pharmacy, New Delhi, India, 1981-82; rsch. scientist Biophysica Found., San Diego, 1982-83; assoc. prof. chemistry U. Ozarks, Clarksville, Ark., 1983-84; asst. to assoc. prof. chemistry U. Ark., Pine Bluff, 1984-96, prof. chemistry, 1996—. Prin. investigator minority biomed. rsch. support program NIH, Bethesda, Md., 1986—; project dir. Ark. Systemic Sci. Initiative; rev. in field. Contbr. articles to profl. jours. Coord. home Bible fellowship The Way Internat., Pine Bluff, 1984-99; judge Ctrl. Ark. Sci. Fair, Little Rock, 1986—. NIH rsch. grantee, 1986, 89, 93. Mem. Am. Chem. Soc., Ark. Acad. Scis., Am. Assn. Pharm. Scientists, Sigma Xi. Avocations: fishing, golf, skiing. Office: 1200 University Dr Pine Bluff AR 71601-2799 E-mail: walker_r@vx4500.uapb.edu.

WALKER, ROBERT MOWBRAY, physicist, educator; b. Phila., Feb. 6, 1929; s. Robert and Margaret (Seivwright) W.; m. Alice J. Agedal, Sept. 2, 1951 (dec. Oct. 15, 2002); children: Eric, Mark; m. Ghislaine Crozaz, Aug. 24, 1973. BS in Physics, Union Coll., 1950, D.Sc., 1967; MS, Yale U., 1951, PhD, 1954; Dr honoris causa, Université de Clermont-Ferrand, 1975. Physicist Gen. Electric Research Lab., Schenectady, 1954-62, 63-66; McDonnell prof. physics Washington U., St. Louis, 1966—2002, prof. physics, 2002—; dir. McDonnell Center for Space Scis., St. Louis, 1975-99. Vis. prof. U. Paris, 1962—63; adj. prof. metallurgy Rensselaer Poly. Inst., 1958, adj. prof. physics, 1965—66; vis. prof. physics and geology Calif. Inst. Tech., 1972, Phys. Research Lab., Ahmedabad, India, 1981, Institut d'Astrophysique, Paris, 1981; vis. prof. Inst. D'Astrophysique Univ. Libre, Brussels, 2001—; nat. lectr. Sigma Xi, 1984—85; pres. Vols. for Internat. Tech. Assistance, 1960—62, 1965—66, founder, 1960; mem. Lunar Sample Analysis Planning Team, 1968—70; bd. dirs. Univs. Space Rsch. Assn., 1969—71; mem. Lunar Sample Rev. Bd., 1970—72; adv. com. Lunar Sci. Inst., 1972—75; mem. temporary nominating group in planetary scis. Nat. Acad. Scis., 1973—75, bd. on sci. and tech. for internat. devel., 1974—76, com. planetary and lunar exploration, 1977—80, mem. space sci. bd.,

1979—82; mem. organizing com. Com. on Space Research-Internat. Astron. Union, Marseille, France, 1984; mem. task force on sci. uses of space sta. Solar System Exploration Com., 1985—86; mem. Antarctic Meteorite Working Group, 1985—92, NASA Planetary Geosci. Strategy Com., 1986—88, European Sci. Found. Sci. Orgn. Com., Workshop on Analysis of Samples from Solar System Bodies, 1990; chmn. Antarctic Meteorite Working Group, 1990—92; mem. cosmic dust allocation com. NASA, 1998; vis. com. dept. terrestial magnetism Carnegie Instn., 1998; vis. com. Max Planck fur Chemie, Mainz, Germany, 1998. Decorated officer de l'Ordre des Palmes Academiques (France); recipient Disting. Svc. award Am. Nuclear Soc., 1964, Yale Engring. Assn. award for contbn. to basic and applied sci., 1966, Indsl. Rsch. awards, 1964, 65; Exceptional Sci. Achievement award NASA, 1970; E.O. Lawrence award AEC, 1971; Antarctic Svc. medal NSF, 1985; NSF fellow, 1962-63; Asteroid 1985 JWI named in his honor, 1999. Fellow AAAS, Am. Phys. Soc., Meteoritical Soc. (Leonard medal 1993), Am. Geophys. Union, Indian Inst. of Astrophysics (hon.); mem. NAS (mem. polar rsch. bd. com. 1995, J. Lawrence Smith medal 1991), Am. Astron. Soc., St. Louis Acad. Scis. (Peter Raven Lifetime Scientific Achievement award 1997); founder, first pres. Vol. Internat. Tech. Assistance (VITA), 1958. Achievements include research and publs. on cosmic rays, nuclear physics, geophysics, radiation effects in solids, particularly devel. solid state track detectors and their application to geophysics and nuclear physics problems; discovery of fossil particle tracks in terrestrial and extra-terrestrial materials and fission track method of dating; application of phys. scis. to art and archaeology; lab. studies of interplanetary dust and interstellar grains in primitive meteorites. Home: 1143B Appleseed Lane Saint Louis MO 63132

WALKER, ROBERTA SMYTH, school system administrator; b. Tacoma, June 18, 1943; d. Robert Middleton and Maxine (Hartl) Smyth; m. Ronald E. Walker, Apr. 1962 (div. Mar. 1965); 1 child, David M.; m. James R. Hawkins, July 19, 1985 (dec. Sept. 1991). BA, Evergreen State Coll., Olympia, Wash., 1982; MS, Seattle Pacific U., 1989. Pers. analyst Seattle Sch. Dist., 1977-83, dir. staff rels., 1983-86; exec. dir. employee rels. Renton (Wash.) Sch. Dist., 1986—. Adj. faculty Seattle Pacific U., 1989—, Western Wash. U., 1995—. Vol. Crisis Clinic, Seattle, 1993—. Recipient Angel in Seattle award AT&T Wireless and Intiman Theatre, 1995. Mem. Wash. Assn. Sch. Adminstrs., Employee Rels. and Negotiations Network (pres. 1991-92), Sno-King Negotiators. Office: Renton Sch Dist 435 Main Ave S Renton WA 98055-2711

WALKER, SAMMIE LEE, retired elementary education educator; b. Elkhart, Tex., July 10, 1927; d. Samuel and Mary (Pigford) Nathaniel; m. R.L. Walker, Oct. 12, 1952 (dec. 1994); children: Winfred, Frederick, Mary, Pearlene, Gladys, Robert, Ethel. BS, Tex. Coll., 1951; MEd, Tex. So. U., 1979. Cert. tchr., home econs. educator, elem. educator. Seamstress Madonna Guild Factory, Houston, 1958-60; presch. tchr. Project Head Start, Houston, 1961-64; tchr. Houston Ind. Schs., 1964-86. Tchr. Harris County Youth Authority, Clear Lake, Tex., 1985; costume maker CETA program Houston Ind. Sch. Dist., 1984. Tchr. Trinity Garden Ch. of Christ, 1956—; phys. fitness coord. Kashmere Garden Sr. Citizen Club, Houston, 1986-92; home care provider Tex. Home Health Care, Houston, 1988-93. Recipient Friendship award Houston Christian Inst., 1993. Mem. NEA. Avocations: sewing, cooking, travel, volunteer work for local charities and school districts. Home: Houston, Tex. Died Oct. 11, 2000.

WALKER, SHARON LOUISE, gifted education educator; b. St. Paul, Mar. 26, 1944; d. John Franklin and Catherine G. (Keiffer) Corkill; m. David Glenn Smith, June 11, 1964 (div. Feb. 1980); 1 child, Carina Ann Smith; m. William Laurens Walker III, Nov. 10, 1981. BS in Edn., U. Md., 1971; M in Adminstrn. and Supervision, U. Va., 1990. Cert. elem. sch. prin., K-12 tchr. of gifted, 1-7 classroom tchr., K-12 tchr. art, Va. Tchr. 3rd and 4th grades Seat Pleasant (Md.) Elem. Sch., 1971-75; tchr. 4th grade Venable Elem. Sch., Charlottesville, Va., 1975-79; tchr. 3rd and 4th grade gifted edn. Quest program Charlottesville City Schs., 1979-99; gifted resource specialist K-4 Jackson Via Elem. Sch., 1999—. Coord. acad. summer sch. Summer Discovery grades kindergarten through 4 Charlottesville City Schs., 1988-94, mem. various curriculum, staff devel., award coms., 1990—; seminar leader summer enrichment program U. Va., Charlottesville, 1986-89; gifted resource specialist Jackson Via Elem., 1999—. Mem., chairperson placement com. Jr. League, Charlottesville, 1977—; mem. edn. com. Bayly Art Mus., Charlottesville, 1984-89; bd. dirs., devel. chairperson Charlottesville Albemarle Youth Orch., 1991-93; bd. dirs., mem. program com. Madison Ho., U. Va., 1994—, bd. dirs., co-chair, 1996—; mem. women's com. Martha Jefferson Hosp. Devel. Office, 1998—. Mem. Charlottesville Edn. Assn., Phi Delta Kappa (U. Va. chpt.), Delta Kappa Gamma (v.p. 1993-95, chair rsch. com. 1996—, pres. 1998—). Home: 105 Finders Way Charlottesville VA 22901-1916

WALKER, SUZANNAH WOLF, language educator; b. Akron, Ohio, May 3, 1954; d. Robert Patton and Katherine Jane (Guglielmi) Wolf Jr.; m. Timothy Gordon Walker, Dec. 23, 1988 (div. Dec. 21, 1992). BA in Secondary Edn., U. Akron, 1976; MA in Pub. Rels, Kent State U., 1987. Tchr. English, Spanish Cuyahoga Falls (Ohio) City Sch., 1977—96; tchr. English DOD Dependents Sch., Wurzburg, Germany, 1981—82; tchr. English, Spanish Canton (Ohio) City Schs., 1999—. Mem. supt. adv. com. Cuyahoga Falls City Sch., 1995, bldg. rep., 1992—95, Canton City Schs., 2000—03. Pub. rels. intern Ronald McDonald House, Cleve., 1985. Mem.: NEA, Canton Profl. Educators Assn. (mem. exec. com. 2003—), N.E. Ohio Fgn. Lang. Assn., Ohio Fgn. Lang. Assn., Cuyahoga Falls Edn. Assn., Ohio Edn. Assn. Home: 3430 E Prescott Cir Cuyahoga Falls OH 44223

WALKER, VIRGINIA L. art educator; b. Elkridge, W.Va., June 29, 1926; d. William Frank and Margaret Elizabeth (Scott) Birchfield; m. Oynus Robbley Walker, Mar. 13, 1946; 1 child, Elaine Helene Walker Evans. BS, Morris Harvey Coll., 1954; MA, W.Va. U., 1967. Cert. art tchr., K-12, elem. tchr., W.Va. Tchr. Fayette County Bd. Edn., Elkridge, W.Va., Beards Fork, W.Va., Oak Hill and Greenbrier Sch., Crighton, W.Va.; tchr. art 7-12 Kanawna County Schs., Cedar Grove, W.Va., county art supr. Charleston, W.Va.; curriculum devel. specialist W.Va. Dept. Edn., Charleston; painting tchr. Leisure World, Laguna Hills, Calif. Mem. adj. faculty W.Va. State Coll. Artist: (watercolor/acrylic) Through the Glass Darkly (award 1968), Spring (reviewed in Art Rev. jour. 1967), Mama! Mama! the Bridge (Appalachian Corridors 1968); contbr. articles to profl. jours.; exhibitor numerous shows. Past chmn. W.Va. Arts for Handicapped, W.Va. Alliance for Arts Edn. Mem. Nat. Art Edn. Assn., NEA, W.Va. Art Edn. Assn. (pres. 1976-78). Home: 25721 Califia Dr Laguna Hills CA 92653-5111 Office: Leisure World Laguna Hills CA 92653

WALKER, WANDA GAIL, special education educator; b. Montgomery, Ala., June 7, 1946; d. Carter Warren Gamaliel and Ruth Jones (Carter) Walker. BS in Elem. Edn., Campbell U., 1968; MA in Christian Edn., Scarritt Coll., 1970; cert. in tchg. of learning disabled, Pembroke U., 1994. Cert. tchr. class A, N.C. Dir. Christian edn. United Meth. Ch., Roxboro, N.C., 1970-76, diaconal min. Hamlet, N.C., 1976-77, Rockingham, N.C., 1977-85; head teller Montgomery Savs. and Loan, Rockingham, 1985-87; loan officer-credit R.W. Goodman Co., Rockingham, 1987-89; tchr. spl. edn. Richmond County Schs., Hamlet, 1987—. Active Richmond County Reading Coun., Hamlet, 1989—. Bd. dirs. Sandhill Manor Group Home, Hamlet, 1977—. Eisenhower grantee U. N.C., 1994; recipient Mission award United Meth. Women, N.C. Conf., 1990; named Best Working Mem., Women's Club Hamlet, 1991. Mem. Woman's Club Hamlet (treas. 1989-91, 1st v.p. 1992-94). Democrat. Avocations: church activities, reading, volunteer work. Home: 1502 Davis St Jacksonville NC 28540-5013 Office: Richmond County Schs Hamlet Ave Hamlet NC 28345

WALKER, WANDA MEDORA, retired elementary school educator, consultant; b. San Diego, Aug. 28, 1923; d. Bryant Hereford and Anna Genevieve (Barnes) Howard; m. Elmer Manfred Walker, Nov. 23, 1949 (dec. Aug. 1978); children: Kathleen May Stewart (dec.), Mary Ellen Quessenberry, Sydney Edward, Jessie Ann Meacham. BA, San Diego State U., 1947; MA, U. Wash., 1948; PhD, Calif. Western U., 1967. Cert. (life) spl. secondary music tchr., elem. tchr., sch. adminstr. Elem. tchr. Lakeside (Calif.) Elem. Dist., 1948-50, La Mesa (Calif.) Sch. Dist., 1951-53, San Diego City Schs. Dist., 1953-57, cons. gifted, 1957-59, vice prin., 1959-62; prin. San Diego Schs. Dist., 1962-88. Rep. San Diego City Schs. War Against Litter, 1971—76; pres. Assn. Calif. Sch. Adminstrs. Ret., 1992—94. Recipient Am. Educators medal Freedoms Found. Valley Forge, 1973, Woman of Yr. award Pres. Coun. Women's Svc., Bus. & Profl. Clubs San Diego, 1980, Woman of Action award Soroptomists Internat. El Cajon, 1992. Mem.: AAUW (parliamentarian 1989—98, Appreciation award 1992), Sr. Resource Ctr. (adv. bd., vol. 1989—), Assn. Calif. Sch. Adminstrs. (pres.), San Diego City Sch. Adminstrn. Assn. (pres. 1976—77), Calif. Retired Tchrs., Singing Hills Women's Golf Club. Avocations: photography, painting, gardening, golf, music. Home: 13208 Julian Ave Lakeside CA 92040-4312

WALKER, WILBUR GORDON, physician, educator; b. Lena, La, Sept. 18, 1926; s. Daniel Clark and Ettie (Hodnett) W.; m. Betty Couch, Aug. 23, 1947; children: Wilbur Gordon, Martha Jane, Joseph Marshall, Carla Frances. Student, La. State U., 1942-44, 46-47, La. Coll., 1947; MD, Tulane U., 1951. Intern Johns Hopkins Hosp., Balt., 1951-52; resident Charity Hosp., New Orleans, 1952-53; asst. resident Johns Hopkins Hosp., Balt., 1953-54, fellow in medicine, 1954-56, resident physician, 1956-57, physician, 1957—, dir. Clin. Research Center, 1960-88; faculty Johns Hopkins U. Sch. Medicine, 1956—, prof. medicine, 1968—, prof. internat. health, 1990—, chmn. com. on clin. investigation, 1964-71; prof. internat. health Johns Hopkins U. Sch. Med., 1990—; ednl. policy com. Johns Hopkins U. Sch. Medicine, 1976-80; exec. com., dept. med., 1973-79; admissions com. Johns Hopkins U. Sch. Med., 1988-92; dir. renal div. Johns Hopkins U. Sch. Medicine, 1958-88, admissions com., 1988-92. Attending physician Balt. City Hosp., 1960-88; established investigator Am. Heart Assn., 1957-60; dir. dept. rsch. medicine Good Samaritan Hosp., Balt., 1968—; chmn. med. bd., 1972-74; vis. prof. Guys Hosp. Med. Sch., London, 1980; clin., rsch. ctr. com. NIH, 1970-76, renal disease and urology grants com., 1968-76, chmn. clin. rsch. ctr. com., 1975-76; McIlrath prof., hon. cons. physician Royal Prince Alfred Hosp., Sydney, Australia, 1968—; chmn. Coun. on Rsch. Md. Heart Assn., 1963-64; chmn. med. adv. bd. Md. Kidney Found., 1966-68; mem. Md. Gov. Commn. on Kidney Disease, 1970-80, 83-88; chmn. Md. Kidney Commn., 1975-80; chmn. computer com. div. rsch. resources NIH, 1973-75, hypertension and chronic renal failure working group, 1988-90. Editl. adv. bd. Am. Jour. Medicine, 1975-85; editl. bd. Kidney Internat., 1978-82; sec. editor: Principles and Practices of Medicine, 17th-21st edit.; co-editor: Potassium in Cardiovascular and Renal Medicine; contbr. articles to profl. jour. Trustee Md. Heart Assn., Good Samaritan Hosp., 1998—; Served with USNR, 1944-45. Alumni Lifetime Achievement Award Tulane Univ. Sch. of Med.; Lifetime Achievement Award given by consortium for South Eastern Hypertension Control (COSEHC). Fellow ACP; mem. Am. Physiol. Soc. Am. Fdn. Clin. Research, Am. Soc. Clin. Investigation, Am. Soc. Nephrology, Council High Blood Pressure Research, Am. Clin. and Climatol. Assn., Interurban Clin. Club (sec. 1977-81, pres. 1981-82) Clubs: Peripatetic. Home: 3812 Fenchurch Rd Baltimore MD 21218-1824 E-mail: wgordonwalkersr@msn.com.

WALKER, WILLIAM OLIVER, JR., retired theology studies educator, dean; b. Sweetwater, Tex., Dec. 6, 1930; s. William Oliver and Frances Baker (White) W.; m. Mary Scott Daugherty, Dec. 22, 1955 (div. Dec. 1978); children: William Scott, Mary Evan, Michael Neal. BA, Austin Coll., 1953; MDiv, Austin Presbyn. Sem., 1957; MA, U. Tex., 1958; PhD, Duke U., 1962. Instr. religion Austin Coll., Sherman, Tex., 1954-55, Duke U., 1960-62; from asst. to prof. religion Trinity U., San Antonio, 1962—2002; ret., 2002. Chair dept., 1980-88, acting dean divsn. Humanities and Arts, 1988-89, dean, 1989-2002. Editor: The Relationships, 1978, The Harper-Collins Bible Pronunciation Guide, 1994; assoc. editor HarperCollins Bible Dictionary, 1996. Mem. Studiorum Novi Testamenti Soc., Soc. Bibl. Lit. (regional sec.-treas. 1980-86, pres. 1999-2000), Am. Acad. Religion (regional pres. 1966-67), Cath. Bibl. Assn. Am. Democrat. Presbyterian. Avocations: tennis, traveling, photography. Home: 315 Cloverleaf Ave San Antonio TX 78209-3822

WALKER-LAROSE, LINDA WALESKA, elementary education educator; b. New Haven, Conn., June 19, 1952; d. Edward Lawrence and Waleska Katherine (Bussmann) W.; m. Mr. LaRose, Aug. 17, 1996. BS, So. Conn. State Coll., 1974, postgrad., 1979. Tchr. 4th grade Union Sch., West Haven, Conn., 1974-75, tchr. 2d grade, 1975-76; tchr. 3d grade Washington Sch., West Haven, 1976-81; tchr. 1st grade Washington Magnet Sch., West Haven, 1981—. Unit leader Washington Magnet Sch., 1991—; coop. tchr., mentor Conn. Dept. Edn., West Haven, 1987—. Mem. PTA (2d v.p. 1987—), Schooner Inc., New Haven, New Haven Preservation Trust. Mem. Conn. Fedn. Tchrs., Vintage Truck Assn. Avocations: knitting, restoration of Victorian home, making Victorian lampshades, collecting and restoring old cars and trucks. Office: Washington Magnet Sch 369 Washington Ave New Haven CT 06519-9998

WALKER SCHLAGECK, KATHRINE L. museum educational administrator, educator; b. San Jose, Calif., Mar. 12, 1962; d. Paul D. and Barbara (White) W.; m. John L. Schlageck, Jan. 10, 1998; 1 child, Benjamin David. BA with honors, Stanford U., 1984; MA, Coll. William and Mary, 1986; cert. mus. mgmt., U. Colo., 1996. Archaeologist Va. Rsch. Ctr. for Archaelogy, Newport, 1984-85; curatorial asst. Colonial Williamsburg Found., Va., 1985-86; asst. curator, coord. edn. Nantucket (Mass.) Historical Assn., 1986-88; dir. edn. Webb-Deane-Stevens Mus., Wethersfield, Conn., 1988-91, Lyman Allyn Art Mus., New London, Conn., 1991-94, Beach Mus. Art, Kans. State U., Manhattan, 1994—. Mem. Mass. Arts Lottery Coun., Nantucket, 1988-89; chair diversity subcom. Regional Adv. Com. on Edn. Reform, 1994; adv. bd. Manhattan Arts Coun., 1995-96; panelist Kans. Arts Commn., 1995; steering com. Take a Stand Ednl. Collaborative; grant reviewer Inst. Mus. and Libr. Svcs., 1995, 97, 99, 2003. Author: (curriculum) The Outsiders, 1990, The Face in Art, 1994, (gallery guide) From Distaff Side, 1992, Sunflower State Quilts: A guide to publicly held quilt collections in Kansas, 1999; author: (with others) Cultural Diversity in Literature, Art and Music, 1992, The American Collection 1620-1920: Guide to the Palmer Gallery, 1994; author, editor: (curriculum) The Prairie Through New Eyes, 2001; author, curator: Beyond Oz: Children's Book Illustration from the Region, 2002, Beyond Oz/Visual Literacy Curriculum, 2003. Vol. tchr. Nantucket Learning & Resource Ctr., 1988; mem. New London Culture and Tourism Alliance, 1991—; edn. com. Manhattan C. of C., 1996; active Big Brothers, Big Sisters, 1996; fundraiser United Way, 1997. Grantee Inst. Mus. Svcs., Nantucket, 1987, 88, Rockefellor Found./Conn. Humanities Coun., New London, 1991-92; scholar Conn. Humanities Coun., 1989—, Mid Am. Arts Alliance, 1999, Kans. Arts Commn., 2001. Mem. Am. Assn. Mus. (rep. bd. 1990-93, 95—, edn. com. 1988—, Excellence and Equity award) Nat. Art Edn. Assn. (Mus. Educator of Yr. Western divsn. 2000), New Eng. Mus. Assn. (edn. com. 1988-94, chair 1991-94), Mountain Plains Mus. Assn. (chair edn. com. 1995—, sec. 1997-98, program chair 2002), Conn. Art Docents Network (bd. dirs. 1991—), Alliance of Cultural Educators of Hartford, Nat. Art Edn. Assn. (Mus. Educator of the Yr. western divsn.), Kans. Art Edn. Assn. (Mus. Educator of the Yr. 1999-2000), W.A. White Cmty. Partnership (bd. dirs.). Avocations: the arts, multicultural education, skiing, writing. Office: Beach Mus Art 701 Beach Ln Manhattan KS 66506-0600 E-mail: klwalk@ksu.edu.

WALKER-SHIVERS, DAUPHINE, humanities educator; b. Marion, Ark. d. Geoffrey and Myrtle Juanita Walker; m. James Shivers, Aug. 29, 1981 (dec. Apr. 1994). BA, Wayne State U., MA, 1967; PhD, U. Mich., 1980. Newspaper reporter Mich. Chronicle, Detroit, 1953-55; social worker Detroit Dept. Social Svcs., Detroit, 1955-56; tchr. Detroit Pub. Schs., 1956-60, U.S. Overseas Schs., France, 1960-64, Detroit Pub. Schs., 1964-70; prof. Wayne County C.C., Detroit, 1970-76, 81—, dept. chair humanities, speech, philosophy, 1976-81. Pres., CEO Pub. Comm. & Concepts, Detroit, 1984-90. Editor: Detroit NAACP Reporter, 1984. Pres. Top Ladies of Distinction, Detroit, 1984-89, nat. historian, 1986-90; 1st v.p. Consortium Cmty. Orgns., 1995—; pub. local ch. newspapers, Detroit, 1983-88; mem. exec. bd. Fair Housing Ctr. Detroit, 1986—; fundraiser Detroit Inst. Arts, African Art Gallery, 1968-70. Named Top Solicitor Detroit NAACP, 1993, 93, 94; recipient Outstanding Svc. award Detroit NAACP, 1992, Sustained Superior Svc. award U.S. Overseas Schs., U.S. Army, France, 1964. Mem. AAUW, Met. Detroit Alliance Black Educators, Detroit Assn. Black Storytellers. Avocations: reading, interior decorating, travel, growing house plants. Office: Wayne County CC 8551 Greenfield Rd Detroit MI 48228-2224

WALKER-TAYLOR, YVONNE, retired college president; b. New Bedford, Mass., Apr. 17, 1916; d. Dougal Ormonde and Eva Emma (Revallion) Walker; m. Robert Harvey Taylor (dec.) BS, Wilberforce U., 1936; MA, Boston U., 1938; Edn. Specialist, U. Kans., 1964; L.H.D. (hon.), Morris Brown Coll., 1985; Dr. Pedagogy (hon.), Medaille Coll., 1985, Northeastern Coll., 1985. Asst. acad. dean Wilberforce U., Ohio, 1967-68, v.p., acad. dean, 1973-83, provost, 1983-84, pres., 1984-88; Disting. Presdl. prof. Edn. Ctrl. State U., 1990-96. Bd. dirs. Nat. Commn. on Coop. Edn., 1977-82, 83-88, United Way, Xenia, Ohio, 1985-88; chmn. culture planning council Nat. Mus. Afro-Am. History; sec. Greene Oaks Health Ctr., 1983-87; bd. trustees, Dayton Art Inst; v.p. jud. coun. AME Ch.; mem. Ohio Humanities Coun., 1994—, Greene City Violence Bd. Named Woman of Yr., Met. Civic Women's Assn., Dayton, 1984, one of Top Ten Women, Dayton Newspapers-Women's Coalition, Dayton, 1984, Outstanding Woman of Yr., Iota Phi Lambda, Dayton, 1985; recipient Drum Major for Justice award So. Christian Leadership Conf., 1986; named to Greene County Hall of Fame, 1990. Mem. Com. on Ednl. Credit and Credentials of the Am. Council on Edn., Alpha Kappa Alpha, Phi Delta Kappa. African Methodist Episcopalian. Club: Links (past pres.) Avocations: reading, swimming, horseshoes, tennis, bicycling. Home: 1279 Wilberforce-Clifton Rd Wilberforce OH 45384-9999 Office: Wilberforce U Brush Row Rd PO Box 336 Wilberforce OH 45384-0336 E-mail: deonwt@aol.com.

WALKOWITZ, DANIEL JAY, historian, filmmaker, educator; b. Paterson, N.J., Nov. 25, 1942; s. Sol and Selda (Margel) W.; m. Judith Rosenberg, Dec. 26, 1965; 1 child, Rebecca Lara. AB, U. Rochester, 1964, PhD, 1972; postgrad., U. Grenoble, France, 1965. Lectr. in history U. Rochester, N.Y., 1967-69; instr. history Renssalaer Poly. Inst., Troy, N.Y., 1969-71; asst. prof. history Rutgers U., New Brunswick, N.J., 1971-78, NYU, N.Y.C., 1978-81, assoc. prof., 1981-88, co-dir. pub. history program, 1981-89, prof., 1988—, dir. met. studies, 1989—. Ptnr., film producer PastTimes Prodns., N.Y.C., 1982-97; vis. prof. U. Calif. Irvine, 1982, Johns Hopkins U., 1991-92, Stanford U., 2002; editorial sec. Radical History Rev., N.Y.C., 1985-89; bd. dirs. N.Y. Marxist Sch., 1987-90. Author: Worker City, Company Town, 1978, Working With Class, 1999; co-author: Workers of the Donbass Speak, 1995; film project dir. The Molders of Troy, 1980; co-editor: Workers in the Industrial Revolution, 1974, Working-Class America, 1984; video dir., co-prodr., dir., writer: Perestroika From Below, 1990; co-prodr., writer Public History Today. Grantee, Nat. Endowment Humanities, 1976, 78, 82; Affiliate fellow Stanford Humanities Ctr., 2001-02. Mem. Nat. Coun. Pub. History (bd. dirs. 1986-89), Am. Hist. Assn., Orgn. Am. Historians, Oral History Assn. Avocation: international folk dance. Office: NYU Dept Met Study Porgram New York NY 10003 E-mail: daniel.walkowitz@nyu.edu.

WALL, CARLON EARL, secondary education educator; b. Temple, Tex., Mar. 9, 1948; s. C. W. and Carmen C. Wall; m. Avis L. Sugarek, Jan. 2, 1983; 1 child, Emily Kathleen. BA, Howard Payne U., 1970; MA, Sam Houston State U., 1972. Profl. teaching cert., Tex. Tchr. Mt. View State Sch. for Boys, Gatesville, Tex., 1972-73; tchr. h.s. Rio Vista (Tex.) Ind. Sch. Dist., 1973-83, Cleburne (Tex.) Ind. Sch. Dist., 1983—, head social studies dept.; tchr. Hill Jr. Coll., Cleburne, 1985—. Mem. NEA, Nat. Coun. Social Studies, United Educators Assn., Tex. State Tchrs. Assn., Tex. Coun. Social Studies (exec. bd. dirs. 1994-96), Cleburne Educators Assn. (pres. 1990-92), Brazos River Coun. Social Studies (pres. 1994-96). Baptist. Office: 1501 Harlin Dr Cleburne TX 76033-7039 E-mail: earl.wall@cleburne.k12.tx.us.

WALL, DIANE EVE, political science educator; b. Detroit, Nov. 17, 1944; d. Albert George and Jean Carol Bradley. BA in History and Edn., Mich. State U., 1966, MA in History, 1969, MA in Polit. Sci., 1979, PhD in Polit. Sci., 1983. Cert. permanent secondary tchr., Mich. Secondary tchr. Corunna (Mich.) Pub. Schs., 1966-67, N.W. Pub. Schs., Rives Junction, Mich., 1967-73; lectr. Tidewater C.C., Chesapeake, Va., 1974-77; instr. Wayne State U., Detroit, fall 1980, Lansing (Mich.) C.C., 1981-83, Ctrl. Mich. U., Mt. Pleasant, 1982; prof. dept. polit. sci. Miss. State U., 1983—, undergrad. coord., 1993—. Pre-law advisor Miss. State U., 1990—93, chair, 1993—. Co-editor spl. issue Southea. Polit. Rev.; contbr. articles, revs. to profl. jours., chpt. to book, entry to ency. Evaluator Citizen's Task Force, Chesapeake, Va., 1977; panelist flag burning program Ednl. TV, Mississippi State, 1990, prayer in pub. sch., Starkville Cmty. TV, 1995. Recipient Paideia award Miss. State U. Coll. Arts and Scis., 1988, Miss. State U. Outstanding Woman Tchg. Faculty award Pres.'s Commn. on Status of Women, 1994, Acad. Advising award Miss. State U., 1994, Outstanding Advisor award Nat. Acad. Advising Assn. and ACT, 1995, Miss. State U. Upper Level Undergrad. Tchg. award Miss. State U. Alumni Assn., 2000; Grad. Office fellow Mich. State U., 1980; Miss. State U. rsch. grantee, 1984. Mem. ASPA (exec. bd. Sect. for Women 1987-90, Miss. chpt. pres. 1992-93), LWV (Chesapeake charter pres. 1976-77), Miss. Polit. Sci. Assn. (exec. dir. 1991-93), Miss. State U. Soc. Scholars (pres. 1992-93), Miss. State U. Faculty Women's Assn. (v.p. 1985-86, pres. 1986-88, scholar 1987-89), Phi Kappa Phi (v.p. 1985-86, pres. 1986-88), Pi Sigma Alpha (Ann. Chpt. Activities award 1991). Democrat. Methodist. Avocations: dog obedience training, corvette activities, gardening. Office: Miss State U PO Drawer PC Mississippi State MS 39762 E-mail: dew1@ps.msstate.edu .

WALL, HARRIET MARIE, psychology educator; b. St. Louis, Oct. 21, 1942; d. Solomon P. and Charlotte B. (Goldman) Shakofsky; m. Daniel Braunstein, Aug. 5, 1962 (div. Apr., 1978); 1 child, Laura Ruth; m. Vance George Marshall II, Sept. 26, 1988. BS, Purdue U., 1963; MS, San Diego State U., 1965; PhD, U. Rochester, 1971. Rsch. asst. U.S. Navy, San Diego, 1963-65, U. Rochester (N.Y.) Med. Sch., 1965-66; asst. prof. Monroe C.C., Rochester, 1970-71; prof. psychology, dir. rsch., assoc. dean, dean U. Mich., Flint, 1972—, chair, prof. psychology. Home: 10471 S Leelanau Way Traverse City MI 49684 Office: U Mich Dept Psychology Flint MI 48502 E-mail: hwall@umflint.edu.

WALL, JULIA ANN WILHITE, educational administrator, consultant; b. Eros, La., Aug. 6, 1942; d. Walter Elder and Myrtle Lee (Aswell) Wilhite; children: Julia Ann, Lee Barclay, Whitney Leane. BA, Northeast La. State U., Monroe, 1965; MA, La. Tech. U., Ruston, 1969; Adminstr. Cert., Stephen F. Austin U., 1981. Tchr. profoundly handicapped G. B. Cooley Hosp., West Monroe, La., 1966-68; speech pathologist Ouachita Parish Schs., Monroe, La., 1969-71, various independent sch. dists., Tex., 1971-75; coord. lang., speech, hearing Longview (Tex.) Independent Sch. Dist., 1975-79; asst. prin. Longview (Tex.) High Sch., 1979-80; prin. Hudson Prep Sch., Longview, Tex., 1980-83; head of sch. Trinity Sch. Tex.,

Longview, 1983-95, Gaston Day Sch., Gastonia, N.C., 1995—. Bd. dirs. Tex. Assn. Non-Pub. Schs., Austin, 1988-94. Bd. dirs. Zonta Internat., Longview, Tex., 1983-86, Am. Heart Assn., Longview, 1982-86, Vol. Action Coun., Longview, 1982-85, Palmer Drug Abuse Program, Longview, 1988, pres. 1988-89, Gregg County Children's Assn., 1991-95, Longview Opera Repertory Co., 1992-94; vestry mem. Trinity Episc. Ch., Longview, 1980-83; mem. Teen Coalition, Longview, 1990-94; sustainer Jr. League Longview. Recipient First Lady of Longview award Beta Sigma Phi, 1982, Premier Principal award Tex. PTA, Ft. Worth, Tex., 1983. Mem. Tex. Assn. Gifted and Talented, Tex. ASCD, LeTourneau Univ. Assocs., Rotary, Phi Delta Kappa. Republican. Episcopalian. Avocations: gardening, reading, sewing, music, drama.

WALL, ROBERT THOMPSON, secondary school educator; b. Luray, Va., May 31, 1943; s. Robert Alexander and Mary Ann (Coffman) W.; m. Sarah S. Wall, Aug. 19, 1967; children: Melissa Coffman, Jennifer Grey. BA, Va. Poly. Inst. and State U., 1966; MA, Radford (Va.) U., 1971; postgrad., U. Fla., 1978. Tchr. instrumental and choral music Halifax County Schs., Halifax, Va.; tchr. instrumental music Montgomery County Schs., Christiansburg, Va.; chmn. fine arts dept. Christiansburg Middle Sch., 1991—99; fine arts supr. Montgomery County Sch. Dist., 1999—. Judge, clinician and adjudicator for marching and concert bands; curriculum and instrn. clin. affiliate Va. Poly. Inst. and State U., Blacksburg, Radford (Va.) U.; clinician, guest condr. for mid-Atlantic band camps Ferrum Coll., Va.; guest condr. all-dist. bands in Va., N.C., S.C. Composer: Published Windsor Portrait, 1990, Adagio for horn and piano, 1982, Nocturne for flute and piano, 1987, Royal Brigade, 1988, Prelude and tarantelle, 1991, An American Tattoo, 1994, arrangement of Recuerdos de la Alhambra for Marimba and Piano, 2002; compositions commd. by Va. State Symphony Orch., Charlotte (N.C.) Mecklenburg County Schs., Rural Retreat (Va.) H.S., Va. Dist. VI and Dist. V Band Dirs. Assn.; music performed at Va. Music Educators Conf., 1990, 95, 97, Midwest Band Conv., Chgo., 1990, Finland Radio, 1993, Great Britain, 1993, 94, France, 1995, Windsor Portrait rec. by Windsor (Ont., Can.) Mil. Band, 1995. Recipient Young composers award Va. Music Clubs, 1960, Va. Govs. Sch. Presdl. citation, 1990, 92, Teaching award Halifax County Schs., 1972. Mem. ASCAP, Music Educators Nat. Conf., Nat. Band Assn., Va. Music Educators Assn. (exec. bd.), Va. Band and Orch. Dirs. Assn. (instrumental chmn. dist. VI), Modern Music Masters (life, past adv. coun., exec. bd.), Phi Beta Mu, Phi Delta Kappa. Home: 2810 Mt Vernon Ln Blacksburg VA 24060-8121 E-mail: rwall@mail.mcps.org.

WALLACE, ANDREW GROVER, physician, educator, medical school dean; b. Columbus, Ohio, Mar. 22, 1935; s. Richard Homes and Eleanor Bradley (Grover) W.; m. Kathleen Barrick Altvater, June 22, 1957; children: Stephen Andrew, Michael Bradley, Kathleen Claude. BS, Duke U., 1958, MD, 1959. Diplomate Am. Bd. Internal Medicine. Intern medicine Duke U. Hosp., Durham, N.C., 1959-60, asst. resident, 1960-61; fellow NIH, Bethesda, Md., 1961-63; chief resident medicine Duke U., Durham, 1963-64, asst. prof., 1965-67, assoc. prof., 1967-71, chief, divsn. cardiology, 1970-81, prof. medicine, 1971—, Walter Kempner prof. medicine, 1973; vice chancellor health affairs, chief exec. officer Duke U. Hosp., Durham, 1981-87; v.p. health affairs Duke U., 1987-90; dean Dartmouth Med. Sch., Hanover, N.H., 1990-98. V.p. for health affairs Dartmouth Coll., 1990-98; cons. program project com., cardiology adv. com. and pharmacology study sect. Nat. Heart and Lung Inst., cardiovascular merit rev. bd. VA. Co-author: (with R.S. Williams) Biological Effects of Physical Activity, 1989; mem. editl. bd. Am. Jour. of Physiology, 1965-70, Jour. of Pharmacology and Exptl. Therapeutics, 1966-71, Jour. of Molecular and Cellular Cardiology, 1970-75, Jour. of Clin. Investigation, 1973-78. Pres. Durham YMCA Swim Assn., 1975-77; bd. dirs. Durham C. of C.; co-chmn. Nat. Jr. Olympics, 1976. Markle scholar, 1965-70 Mem. AAAS, AAMC, NAS, Inst. of Medicine, Am. Fedn. for Clin. Rsch. (coun.), Am. Soc. Internal Medicine, Am. Soc. Clin. Investigation, Am. Heart Assn. (coun. on clin. cardiology), Am. Physiol. Soc., Biomed. Engring. Soc., Soc. Med. Adminstrs., Assn. Am. Med. Colls. (adv. com. electronic residency 1992-94, generalist initiative 1993-95, mission and orgn. 1994-2000, exec. coun. 1996-98), N.H. Med. Soc., So. Soc. Clin. Investigation. Home: 2112 Faucette Mill Rd Hillsborough NC 27278-7553

WALLACE, BARBARA FAITH, linguistics educator; b. NYC, Dec. 15, 1952; d. Robert Earl and Faith Willi (Jones) Wallace Ringgold; m. Glenn Ronald Gadsden, Feb. 14, 1980 (div. 1982); 1 child, Faith Willi; m. Melvin Wilson Orr, June 8, 1984 (dec. 1989); children: Theodora-Michele Alexandria, Martha Xaviar Underwood. Diploma, U. London, 1977; MA, M Philosophy, CUNY, 1981. Tchr. descriptive linguistics Queens Coll., N.Y.C., 1979-80; tchr. African history John Jay Coll., N.Y.C., 1981-82; tchr. anthropol. linguistics CCNY, 1981-84; tchr. linguistics, math. coord., classroom and sci. Smart Process N.Y.C. Bd. Edn., 1986—, tchr.-in-charge Project Learn, Pub. Sch. 197M, 1990, founder, coord. Girls Intramurals Club, 1992—; chief officer Barbara Co., 2001—. Lang. arts dir. Coll. New Rochelle/Harlem, NYC, 1982-84; prison instr. basic skills, pre-GED and Computer Literacy LaGuardia Community Coll., 1984-85, Higher Edn. Devel. Fund, Bronx, 1984-85; tchr. computer literacy NYU, 1987; mem. NYU Ctr. for Latin Am. and Carribean Studies Summer Seminar, 1986; artist, asst. Faith Ringgold, 1991—; tchr., math. coord. NYC Bd. Edn., 1986—; tutor BELL Found., 1998-2000; co-chair Art with Kids grant selection com., Anyone Can Fly Found., Inc., 2003—. Critic reader math. textbooks Scott, Foresman and Co., 1989; editor: Faith Ringgold Story Quilts and Other Narratives, 2003; exhibitor; contbr. articles to profl. jours. Named Coun. Internat. Edn. Exchange grantee, 1974, Brit. Fedn. U. Women scholar, 1976, fellow CUNY, 1977-81, grant Fund for N.Y.C. Pub. Edn., 1992, grant Women Sports Found., 1993. Mem.: Am. Fedn. Tchr., NY State United Tchr., United Fedn. Tchr., Nat. Coun. Tchr. Math., Assn. Math. Tchr. NY State, Linguistic Soc. Am. (Linguistic Inst. scholar and travel award 1978, travel grantee 1978), Barbara Faith Co. (chief officer and founder), Greenpeace, NY Bot. Soc., Nat. Wildlife Found., Order Eastern Star. Avocations: computer, travel, photography. Home: 10 W 135th St Apt 11S New York NY 10037-2623 Office: John B Russwurm Sch 2230 5th Ave New York NY 10037-2196 also: Barbara Faith Co PO Box 246 New York NY 10037-0246

WALLACE, BETTY JEAN, elementary school educator, lay minister; b. Denison, Tex., Dec. 5, 1927; d. Claude Herman and Pearl Victoria (Freels) Moore; m. Billy Dean McKneely, Sept. 2, 1950 (div. Nov. 1964); children: Rebecca Lynn, Paul King, David Freels, John Walker, Philip Andrew McKneely. Student, Tulane U., 1947; BA, Baylor U., 1949; postgrad., U. Houston, 1949-50, 74, 81, Rocky Mountain Bible Inst., 1959, U. Colo., 1969-70, U. No. Colo., 1965, 68, 72, U. St. Thomas, 1992, Autonomous U. Guadalajara, summer 1993; MEd, Houston Bapt. U., 1985. Cert. life profl. elem., high sch., life profl. reading specialist, secondary field ESL tchr., Tex. Tchr. Galena Park (Tex.) Ind. Sch. Dist., 1949-50, 52-53, 72-98, Corpus Christi (Tex.) Independent Sch. Dist., 1950-51, Denver Pub. Schs., 1953-54, 63-72, Wackenhut Cleveland (Tex.) Correctional Ctr., 1999—. Author: The Holy Spirit Today, 1989, Our God of Infinite Variety, 1991, God Speaks in a Variety of Ways, 1991. Sunday sch. tchr. So. Bapt. Conv. chs., Tex., 1946-50, Denver, 1952-56; tchr. kindergarten Emmanuel Bapt. Ch., Denver, 1956-59, 60-63; missionary, Queretaro, Mex., 1977, 78; mem. Rep. Senatorial Inner Circle, Washington, 1989-91, 2002, Round Table for Ronald Reagan, Washington, 1989-90; mem. Pres.' Club, 2002-03; helper Feed the Poor, Houston, 1983-85; active Suicide Prevention, Houston, 1973-76, Literacy, Houston, 1978-81; rep. NEA, Denver, 1966-72; mem. Retirement Com., Denver, 1970-72; bd. advisors Oliver North, 1994. Recipient Rep. Senatorial medal of freedom, 1994, Rep. Senatorial medal of Victory, Justice, Freedom and Liberty, 2002, Congl. Order of Merit, 2003; grantee, NSF, 1969—70. Mem. Tex. Classroom Tchrs. Assn. (officer rep., pres. Galena Park chpt. 1988-91), Pres.'s Club, Delta Alpha Pi (pres. Waco chpt. 1948-49), Alpha Epsilon Delta. Republican. Avocations: writing, archeology, gardening, reading, gem/jewelry collecting and designing. Home: 14831 Anoka Dr Channelview TX 77530-3201

WALLACE, CLINTON JOHN, middle school educator; b. New Orleans, Mar. 11, 1948; s. Daisy Benoit Wallace; m. Mariette Fung, Aug. 25, 1978. BS in Math., U. Southwestern La., 1970; MA in Teaching, Duke U., Durham, N.C., 1973; postgrad., La. State U., 1985. Cert. secondary math., computer sci. tchr.; cert. in adminstrn./supervision. Tchr. math. Maury H.S., Norfolk, Va., 1972-74, Linear Jr. H.S., Shreveport, La., 1974-82; math./computer sci. tchr. Caddo Mid. Magnet Sch., Shreveport, 1982-83, Herndon Magnet Sch., Belcher, La., 1983—; faculty computer sci. and edn. La. State U., Shreveport, 1990—. Instr. math. project Red River Mid. Sch., Shreveport, 1991; instr., grant writer Primary Math for the 21st Century Project, Shreveport, 1995. Recipient Presd. Award for Excellence in Teaching Math., NSF, 1993; La. Systemic Initiatives Program Primary Edn. grantee, 1995; Woodrow Wilson Found. fellow, 1993. Mem. Nat. Coun. Tchrs. Math., Nat. Coun. Suprs. of Math., N.W. La. Math. Assn. (pres. 1990-91), Phi Delta Kappa. Avocations: reading, tennis. Home: PO Box 78185 Shreveport LA 71137-8185

WALLACE, DON, JR., law educator; b. Vienna, Apr. 23, 1932; s. Don and Julie (Baer) Wallace; m. Daphne Mary Wickham, 1963; children: Alexandra Creed, Sarah Anne, Benjamin James. BA with high honors, Yale U., 1953; LL.B. cum laude, Harvard U., 1957. Bar: N.Y. 1957, D.C. 1978. Assoc. Fleischmann, Jaeckle, Stokes and Hitchcock, N.Y.C., 1959-60, Paul, Weiss, Rifkind, Wharton and Garrison, N.Y.C., 1957-58, 60-62; rsch. asst. to faculty mem. Harvard Law Sch., Cambridge, Mass., 1958-59; regional legal adv. Middle East AID, Dept. State, 1963-65, dep. asst. gen. counsel, 1965-66; assoc. prof. law Georgetown U. Law Ctr., Washington, 1966-71, prof., 1971—2002; chmn. Internat. Law Inst., Washington, 1969—; adj./emeritus prof. Georgetown U. Law Ctr., Washington, 2002—. Cons. AID, 1966-70, UN Centre on Transnat. Corps., 1977-78; counsel Wald, Harkrader & Ross, Washington, 1978-86, Arnold & Porter, 1986-89, Shearman & Sterling, 1989-98, Morgan, Lewis & Bockius, 1998—; legal advisor State of Qatar, 1979-82; chmn. adv. com. on tech. and world trade Office of Tech. Assessment, U.S. Congress, 1976-79; mem. Sec. of State's Adv. Com. on Pvt. Internat. Law, 1979—; mem. U.S. del. UN Conf. on State Succession in Respect of Treaties, Vienna, 1978; mem. U.S. del. new internat. econ. order working group UN Commn. Internat. Trade Law, Vienna, 1981—; vis. com. Harvard Law Sch., 1996-97; mem. panel of judges World Trade Orgn., 1996-2000. Co-author: Internat. Business and Economics: Law and Policy; author: International Regulation of Multinational Corporations, 1976, Dear Mr. President: The Needed Turnaround in America's International Economic Affairs, 1984; editor: A Lawyer's Guide to International Business Transactions, 1977-87; contbr. numerous articles on internat. trade and law to profl. jours., books revs. on law and bus. to profl. jours. Coord. Anne Arundel County (Md.) Dem. Nat. Com., 1972-79; sec. Chesapeake Found., 1972-73; nat. chmn. Law Profs. for Bush and Quayle, 1988, 92, for Dole and Kemp, 1996; v.p., bd. govs. UNIDROIT Found., Rome, 1997—. Fulbright fellow, 1967, Eisenhower Exch. fellow, 1976. Mem. ABA (chmn. sect. internat. law 1978-79, ho of dels. 1982-84, mem. adv. bd. Ctrl. European and Eurasian Law Initiative), Am. Law Inst., Internat. Law Assn., Shaybani Soc. of Internat. Law (v.p.), Cosmos Club, Met. Club, Coun. Postgraduate Sch. Internat. Bus. and European Law, European Ctr. Peace and Devel. Home: 2800 35th St NW Washington DC 20007-1411 Office: Georgetown U Law Ctr 600 New Jersey Ave NW Washington DC 20001-2022

WALLACE, DOROTHY ALENE, special education administrator; b. Wright County, Mo., Sept. 11, 1942; d. Stephen Foster and Lois Alene (Breman) Dudley; widowed; children: Michael Dean Huckaby, David Lee. BS in Edn., Drury Coll., 1975, MS in Edn., 1978; Specialist in Ednl. Adminstrn., Southwest Mo. State U., 1988. Cert. tchr. and adminstr., Mo. Tchr. 3rd grade Mansfield (Mo.) R-IV Schs., 1975-78, tchr. 1st grade, 1978-85, tchr. learning disabled, 1985-89, adminstr. spl. edn., 1989-92, adminstr. spl. svcs., 1992—. Active sch. coms. on curriculum and nutrition Mansfield R-IV Schs., mem. sch./cmty. adv. coun., 1992—. Mem. Am. Salers Assn., Mo. State Tchrs. Assn., Mo. Coun. Adminstrs. of Spl. Edn., Coun. for Exceptional Children, Coun. Adminstrs. of Spl. Edn., Local Adminstrs. of Spl. Edn., Cmty. Tchrs. Assn. Avocations: raising beef cattle, writing, collecting antiques. Home: 3489 Jerico Rd Seymour MO 65746-9784

WALLACE, GERI LYNN, special education educator, landscape architect; b. Mt. Vernon, Ohio, Aug. 27, 1951; d. Richard William and Patricia Ann (Bunn) W. BS in Edn., Ashland (Ohio) Coll., 1973. Cert. tchr. health and phys. edn. Facility locator, foreman, budget analyst United Telephone Co., Mansfield, Ohio; tchr. Mt. Vernon Developmental Ctr. Named Boss of Yr., Jaycees, 1978. Mem. NEA, Devel. Edn. Assn. Address: 109 Park Rd Mount Vernon OH 43050-3825

WALLACE, HAROLD LEW, historian, educator; b. Montgomery, Ind., Nov. 9, 1932; s. Lewis Alfred and Winifred Maria (Summers) W.; m. Janice June Inman, June 22, 1957; children: Stefanie Ann, Stacy Elizabeth, Jason Lew. AB, Ind. U., 1961, MA (Univ. grantee), 1964, PhD, 1970. Tchr. history and English Mooresville (Ind.) High Sch., 1961-63; teaching asst. Ind. U., 1963-64, univ. fellow, 1964-65; asst. prof., then assoc. prof. history Murray (Ky.) State U., 1965-71; prof. history, head social sci. div. No. Ky. U., Highland Heights, Ky., 1971—, dir. oral history program, 1980—. Mem. continuing seminar community edn. Ball State U. and Mott Found., 1973—; mem. adv. bd. Ky. Oral History Commn., 1981—; vis. prof. Ky. Inst. for European Studies, Bregenz, Austria, summer 1987, Andhra U., Visakhapatnam, India, spring 1989. Author: Coal in Kentucky, 1975; Contbr. articles to profl. jours.; Editorial bd.: U. Ky. Press, 1971— ; cons., reviewer: Oceana Press, Inc, 1973— . Mem. advisory com. pub. documents, State of Ky.; Bd. dirs. Coll. Programs for No. Ky. Sr. Citizens; faculty regent No. Ky. Bd. Regents, 1985-91, pres. Ky. Conf. State AAUP, 1991—. Served with USNR, 1952-56. Recipient Svc. award State of Ind., 1957, Univ. Teaching award Andhra Univ., India, 1992; Eli Lilly fellow, 1962, 63, Smithsonian fellow, 1982; Harry S. Truman Rsch. scholar, 1965, 71; Murray State U. grantee, 1967, 71, No. Ky. State U. grantee, 1973, 76, 78, 90, Ky. Humanities Coun. grantee, 1988, 90, Ky. Oral History Commn. grantee, 1988; Fulbright grant lectr. Andhra U., India, 1992; Art Coll. Gold medal Andhra Univ., India, 1992. Mem. AAUP (pres. Ky. chpt. 1991—, Disting. Svc. award 1992), Am., So. hist. assns., Orgn. Am. Historians, Polit. Sci. Acad., AAUP, Center Study Democratic Instrn., Mensa, Intertel, Sierra Club, Alpha Epsilon Delta, Phi Delta Kappa, Phi Alpha Theta. Home: 1433 Watertree Rd Terre Haute IN 47803-7701 Office: Dept of Ed No Ky State U Highland Heights KY 41076

WALLACE, HELEN MARGARET, physician, educator; b. Hoosick Falls, NY, Feb. 18, 1913; d. Jonas and Ray (Schweizer) W. AB, Wellesley Coll., 1933; MD, Columbia U., 1937; MPH cum laude, Harvard U., 1943. Diplomate Am. Bd. Pediat., Am. Bd. Preventive Medicine. Intern Bellevue Hosp., NYC, 1938-40; child hygiene physician Conn. Health Dept., 1941-42; successively jr. health officer, health officer, chief maternity and newborn div., dir. bur. for handicapped children NYC Health Dept., 1943-55; prof., dir. dept. pub. health NY Med. Coll., 1955-56; prof. maternal and child health U. Minn. Sch. Pub. Health, 1956-59; chief profl. tng. US Children's Bur., 1959-60, chief child health studies, 1961-62; prof. maternal and child health U. Calif. Sch. Pub. Health, Berkeley, Calif., 1962-80, 99; prof., head divsn. maternal and child health Sch. Pub. Health San Diego State U., Calif., 1980—; Univ. Rsch. lectr. San Diego State U., Calif., 1985—. Cons. WHO numerous locations, including Uganda, The Philippines, Turkey, India, Geneva, Iran, Burma, Sri Lanka, East Africa, Australia, Indonesia, China, Taiwan, 1961—, traveling fellow, 1989—; cons. Hahnemann U., Phila., 1993, Ford Found., Colombia, 1971; UN cons. to Health Bur., Beijing, China, 1987; fellow Aiiku Inst. on Maternal and Child Health, Tokyo, and NIH Inst. Child Health and Human Devel., 1994; dir. Family Planning Project, Zimbabwe, 1984-87; vis. prof. U. Calif., Berkeley, 1999, 00, prof. emeritus, 2000—; mem. adv. com., faculty APHA Com. on Continuing Edn. Author, editor: 20 textbooks; editor (sr.): Health and Social Reform for Families for the 21st Century, 2d edit., 2003, Health and Welfare for Families in the 21st Century, 2003 (award Am. Coll. Nursing, Am. Jour. Nursing); contbr. 335 articles to profl. jours. Mem. coun. on Disabled Children to Media, 1991; dir. San Diego County Infant Mortality Study, 1989—, San Diego Study of Prenatal Care, 1991. Recipient Alumnae Achievement award Wellesley Coll., 1982, U. Minn. award, 1985; Ford Found. study grantee, 1986, 87, 88; fellow World Rehab. Fund, India, 1991-92, Fulbright Found., 1992—, NIH Inst. Child Health and Human Devel., 1994, Aiiku Inst. of Maternal-Child Health, Tokyo, 1994. Fellow: APHA (officer sect., chmn. com. on internat. maternal and child health, mem. faculty and adv. com. maternal and child health program 2000, Martha May Eliot award 1978, award in Internat. Maternal and Child Health 2001), Am. Acad. Pediatrics (Job Smith award 1980); mem.: AMA, Am. Sch. Preventive Medicine, Ambulatory Pediatric Assn., Am. Acad. Cerebral Palsy, Assn. Tchrs. Maternal and Child Health. Home: 850 State St San Diego CA 92101-6046

WALLACE, HELEN MARIE, secondary school educator, coach, dean; b. Chgo., Mar. 4, 1939; d. James and Birdie (Burdett) W. BS in Health and Phys. Edn., George Williams Coll., 1963, MS in Counseling Psychology, MS in Adminstrn., George Williams Coll., 1973. Cert. tchr. and adminstr., Ill. Girls and boys track, volleyball, and swimming coach Chgo. Pub. H.S.; adminstrv. asst. Chgo. Commn. on Urban Opportunity, summers 1965-68; phys. instr. Chgo. Park Dist., 1958-64; phys. edn. tchr. Chgo. Pub. Sch. Sys., 1963—, athletic dir. Harrison H.S., 1967-87, phys. edn. tchr. Lincoln Park H.S., 1987—, mem. citywide objectives for phys. edn. com., 1993-94, mem. health edn. curriculum com., 1992-94, 96-97, mem. co-chair girls track com., 1983—; phys. edn. tchr., dept. chair Lincoln Park H.S., dean students, 1997—. Mem. state track com. Ill. H.S.; co-author health edn. curriculum Chgo. Pub. H.S.'s; cons. for devel. of health and phys. edn. programs, adminstrv. guidelines, inter-intra-mural sport programs. Jr. ch. organist, celestial choir dir., organist First Bapt. Congl. Ch.; dir. and orgnaist for women's chorus Original Providence Bapt. Ch.; soprano soloist numerous functions. Mem. AAHPERD, Am. Choral Dirs. Assn., Gospel Music Workshop Am. Office: Lincoln Park HS 2001 N Orchard St Chicago IL 60614-4404

WALLACE, JACK HAROLD, employee development specialist, educator; b. Pleasant Ridge, Mich., Dec. 3, 1950; s. Jack Alfred and Mary Hilda (Hemming) W.; m. Laura Jeannine Placer, May 20, 1978. AA, Oakland Community Coll., 1972; BA, Oakland U., 1974; postgrad., Cen. Mich. U., 1984; MeD, Wayne State U., 1986, postgrad., 1988—. Cert. secondary tchr., Mich. Supply systems analyst TACOM, Warren, Mich., 1979-84; employee devel. specialist Army Tank Automotive Command, Tng. and Dev. Div., Warren, 1985—; site coord. TA COM long distance learning program Nat. Tech. U., Warren, 1993—; v.p. acad. affairs Virtual U., Bloomfield Hills, Mich., 1994—. Instr. Ferndale (Mich.) Bd. of Edn., 1976-86; instr., cons. Jordan Coll., Detroit, 1986—, Detroit Coll. Bus., Dearborn, Mich., 1986—; trainer, instr. govt. agys. Co-author: (book) Balancing the Scales of Justice, 1986, (cable TV prodn.) A Course in Law and Application in Everyday Living, 1989. Mem. Am. Soc. for Tng. and Devel., Assn. for Ednl. Comm. and Tech., Fed. Mgrs. Assn., Mich. Soc. Instructional Tech., Phi Delta Kappa. Lutheran. Avocations: reading, camping, fishing, public speaking, travel. Home: 3005 Kenmore Rd Berkley MI 48072-1684 Office: TACOM AMSTA-RM-PRT Warren MI 48397-5000

WALLACE, MARILYN JEAN, academic director; b. Oak Park, Ill., Feb. 11, 1950; d. Jay Emmons and Libbie (Novak) Phillips; m. David Stuart Wallace, Sept. 11, 1971; children: David, Douglas. BA, Principia Coll., 1972. Cert. music and edn. elem. and secondary grade levels. Music tchr. Granneman Elem., Hazelwood, Mo., 1972-73, Chicago Jr. Sch., Elgin, Ill., 1973-74, Sch. Dist. 30, Northbrook, Ill., 1974-77; 2nd grade tchr. Sch. Dist. 27, Northbrook, 1978-79; 5th grade tchr. Sch. Dist. 30, Northbrook, 1979-83, 2nd grade tchr., 1984-86; middle sch. social studies tchr. Creative Children's Acad., Mt. Prospect, Ill., 1991-92, acad. dean, 1992-93, acad. dir. Palatine, Ill., 1993—. Mem. adv. bd. Joyful Parenting, Oconomowoc, Wis., 1994—. Understanding Our Gifted, Boulder, Colo., 1994—, Nat. Louis U., Evanston, Ill., 1995—; presenter in field. Named Educator of Yr., Phi Delta Kappa, Evanston, 1993. Mem. Nat. Assn. for Gifted Children, Ill. Assn. for Gifted Children. Avocations: quilting, golfing, cooking. Home: 604 N Benton St Palatine IL 60067-3530 Office: Creative Childrens Acad 500 N Benton St Palatine IL 60067-3564

WALLACE, MARY MONAHAN, elementary and secondary schools educator; b. Teaneck, NJ, Nov. 22, 1943; d. Thomas Gabriel and Louise Grace (Monaco) Monahan; m. James Anthony Wallace, Nov. 22, 1978; (dec. May, 1992); 1 child, Meg. BS, Fordham U., 1967; MA, 1971; postgrad. in Supervision, Montclair U., 1978; postgrad. in Edn., various colls. Cert. tchr. language arts, supr., N.Y. 1st and 4th grades tchr. Holy Rosary Sch., Harlem, N.Y., 1963-65; 7th grade tchr. Immaculate Conception Sch., Bronx, N.Y., 1965-66; 8th grade tchr. St. Finbar Sch., Bklyn., 1966-68, St. Patrick Mil. Acad., Harriman, N.Y., 1968-69; English tchr. St. Stephen H.S., Bklyn., N.Y., 1969-70, Holy Rosary Acad., Union City, N.J., 1970-71, Harriman (N.Y.) Coll., 1971-72, Montclair (N.J.) Coll., 1981-82; English tchr. elem. and secondary schs. Fairlawn (N.J.) Schs., 1972—2003; clin. faculty Montclair U., 1999—2003, adj. faculty, 2003—. Advisor Fair Lawn H.S. Yearbook, 1977-80, Nat. Lang. Arts Olympiad, Fair Lawn, 1987-89; mem. Mid. Sch. Task Force Fair Lawn Schs., 1991-93, dist. wide steering com. Edn. Recognition Day, Fair Lawn, 1992-93, steering com. Fair Lawn Mid. Schs., 1994-97; exec. bd. Profl. Devel. Schs., Montclair U., 2000-03; presenter in field. Editor (newsletter) Concern, 1970-72; mem. editorial staff (newsletter) Flea Bytes, 1988-90. Participant Summer in the City U.S. Antipoverty Program, Staten Island, N.Y., 1965; pres. Bear Pond Improvement Assn., 1996—; chairperson spl. events com. marathon '99. Named Meml. Sch. Tchr. of Yr., NJ Gov.'s Recognition Program, 1993. Mem.: NEA, Nat. Mid. Sch. Assn., Fair Lawn Edn. Assn. (treas. 1990—93, pres. 1993—2003), N.J. Middle Sch. Assn., Bergen County Edn. Assn., N.J. Edn. Assn. Roman Catholic. Avocations: reading, swimming, boating, travel. Home: 20-18 Saddle River Rd Fair Lawn NJ 07410-5933 Office: Fair Lawn Edn Assn 3-13 4th St Fair Lawn NJ 07410 E-mail: fairlawn@aol.com.

WALLACE, RALPH, superintendent; b. Halifax, Nova Scotia; s. Ralph and Alberta (Warren) W.; m. Haunani Wallace, Aug. 1, 1980; children: Lianne, Travis. BEd, U. British Columbia, 1968, MEd, 1976; postgrad., U. Conn., 1986; CAGS, Boston U., 1987, EdD, 1992. Cert. supt., int. adminstr., Conn. Asst. supt. West Vancouver (B.C.) Bd. Edn., 1967-83; prin. Farmington (Conn.) Bd. Edn., 1983-85, Granby (Conn.) Bd. Edn., 1985-88, supt., 1988-92, Cheshire (Conn.) Bd. Edn., 1992-98, Ridgefield (Conn.) Bd. Edn., 1998—. Apptd. Pres. Nat. Excellence Panel. Contbr. articles to profl. jours. Dir. Gov.'s Sch., Conn. State U.; mem. Conn. Tech. Commn. Recipient Nat. Excellence award U.S. Dept. Edn.; named Conn. Supt. of Yr., 1992. Mem. ASCD, SDE (Conn. tech. com.), PDK, Am. Assn. Sch. Adminstrn., Conn. Assn. Pub. Sch. Supts. (legis), Am. Edn. Rsch. Assn., Edn. Rsch. Svc., Conn. Transp. Commn. (hon.), Conn. Tech. Commn. Home: 562 Ridgebury Rd Ridgefield CT 06877-1116 Office: Ridgefield Pub Schs 70 Prospect St Ridgefield CT 06877-4621

WALLACE, ROBERT JAMES, mathematics and science educator; b. Chgo., Sept. 1, 1942; s. James H. and Maryella (Wilder) W.; m. Amy S. Briskin, Nov. 10, 1991; children: Lisa, Brenda. BS, No. Ill. U., 1964, MA,

1970, Princeton U., PhD, 1975. Geologist CUNY, Bklyn., 1972-80; v.p. Audio Vistas, Inc., N.Y.C., 1980-85; computer cons. N.Y.C. Bd. Edn., 1984-86; computing chair St. Ann's Sch., Bklyn., 1985-93; cons. sci., math. The Harbor Acad. for Math./Sci., N.Y.C., 1985—. Cons. Packer Collegiate Inst., Bklyn., 1987-93; cons. educator Metrotech, Bklyn., 1988-90. Author: Geology Lab Manual, 1980, New York City-Wide Test Results, 1986. Adventure facilitator Harbor for Girls and Boys, N.Y.C., 1990—. Mem. AAAS, Nat. Sci. Tchrs. Assn., Sigma Xi. Avocations: tennis, bicycling, roller-skating. Office: Harbor for Girls and Boys 1 E 104th St New York NY 10029-4402 Address: 340 E 80th St Apt 1-f New York NY 10021-0928

WALLACE, WALTER L. sociologist, educator; b. Washington, Aug. 21, 1927; s. Walter L. and Rosa Belle (Boisseau) W.; children: Jeffrey Richard, Robin Claire, Jennifer Rose. BA, Columbia U., 1954; MA, Atlanta U., 1955; PhD, U. Chgo., 1963. Instr. Spelman Coll., Atlanta U., 1955-57; from lectr. to prof. sociology Northwestern U., Evanston, Ill., 1963-71; prof. sociology Princeton, 1971—. Staff sociologist Russell Sage Found., N.Y.C., 1969-77, vis. scholar, 1968; fellow Ctr. for Advanced Study in Behavioral Scis., Stanford, Calif., 1974-75. Author: Student Culture, 1966, Logic of Science in Sociology, 1971, (with James E. Conyers) Black Elected Officials, 1975, Principles of Scientific Sociology, 1983, A Weberian Theory of Human Society, 1994, The Future of Ethnicity, Race, and Nationality, 1997; editor, author: Sociological Theory, 1969; mem. social scis. adv. com. World Book, 1977-94; mem. editl. bd. Social Forces, 1984-87, Am. Sociologist, 1988-91, Sociol. Quar., 1989-92, Am. Sociol. Rev., 1997-2000, Sociol. Theory, 2000-03. Mem. exec. com. Assembly of Behavioral and Social Scis. Nat. Rsch. Coun., 1974-77. With AUS, 1950-52. Mem. Am. Sociol. Assn. (council 1971-74, theory sect. 1988—), Sociol. Rsch. Assn. Office: Princeton U Dept Sociology Princeton NJ 08544-0001

WALLACH, ALAN, art historian, educator; b. Bklyn., June 8, 1942; s. Israel and Vivian (Esner) W.; m. Phyllis Rosenzweig, Jan. 3, 1988. BA, Columbia U., 1963, MA, 1965, PhD, 1973. Assoc. prof. Kean Coll., Union, N.J., 1974-89; Ralph H. Wark prof. art and art history, prof. Am. studies Coll. William and Mary, Williamsburg, Va., 1989—. Vis. prof. UCLA, 1982-83, Stanford (Calif.) U., 1987, CUNY, 1988, U. Mich., 1989; co-curator Nat. Mus. Am. Art, Washington, 1991-94. Author: (with William Truettner) Thomas Cole: Landscape into History, 1994; Exhibiting Contradiction: Essays on the Art Museum in the United States, 1998; contbr. articles to profl. jours. Sr. Postdoctorate Rsch. award Smithsonian Inst., 1985-86. Mem. Am. Studies Assn., Coll. Art Assn. (bd. dirs. 1996-2000), Assn. Art Historians, editorial bd. Am. Quarterly. Home: 2009 Belmont Rd NW Washington DC 20009-5449 Office: Coll William and Mary Dept Art and Art History Williamsburg VA 23187-8795 E-mail: axwall@wm.edn.

WALLACH, BARBARA PRICE, classicist, educator; b. Roanoke, Va., Aug. 31, 1946; d. Benjamin Thomas and Geneva Mae (Bittinger) Price; m. Luitpold Wallach, Aug. 22, 1970 (dec. Nov. 1986). BA in Latin, Mary Washington Coll., 1968; MA in Classics, U. Ill., 1970, PhD in Classical Philology, 1974. Summer vis. lectr. U. Ill., Urbana, 1977; vis. asst. prof. U. Pitts., 1979-80; asst. prof. U. Mo., Columbia, 1980-85, assoc. prof., 1985—. Author: Lucretius and the Diatribe, 1976; contbr. articles to profl. jours. Mem. Am. Philol. Assn., Classical Assn. Middle West and South, Internat. Soc. for the History of Rhetoric, Vergilian Soc., Phi Beta Kappa. Democrat. Avocations: music, flute, reading, sports. Office: U Mo Dept Classical Studies Columbia MO 65211-0001

WALLACH-LEVY, WENDEE ESTHER, astrophotographer; b. N.Y.C., Dec. 29, 1948; d. Leonard Morris and Annette Cohen Wallach; m. David H. Levy, Mar. 23, 1997; 1 child, Nanette R. Vigil. BS in Edn., SUNY, Cortland, 1970; MA in Teaching, N.Mex. State U., 1975. Cert. tchr., N.Mex. Ret. tchr. phys. edn. Las Cruces Pub. Schs., N.Mex., 1970—96; mem. Shoemaker-Levy Observing Team, 1996—; mgr. Jarnac Obs., Vail, Ariz., 1997—; mem. Jarnac Sky Survey Team, Vail, 2001—. Intramural and athletic coord. White Sands Sch., 1970—93; instr. swimming N.Mex. State U. Weekend Coll., Las Cruces, N.Mex., 1986—96; dir., coord. learn to swim program ARC, Las Cruces, N.Mex., 1970—96; instr. phys. edn., coach volleyball and track, athletic coord. Sierra Mid. Sch., 1993—96. Co-author: Making Friends with the Stars, Cosmic Discoveries, 2001; co-host (internet radio show) LetsTalkStars.com. Instr. trainer water safety ARC, 1973-98, CPR, 1974-98; instr. trainer life guard, health and safety specialist, Doña Ana County, New Mex., 1988-96, instr. trainer std. first aid, 1991-98; chair com. health and safety svcs. Doña Ana County, Red Cross. Named Water Safety Instr. of Yr. ARC, Las Cruces, New Mex., 1986, 89, 25 Yr. Svc. award, 1992., 30 Yr. Svc. award, 1997; Asteroid 6485 named in her honor, 1997. Mem.: AAHPERD, Nat. Intramural-Recreational Sports Assn., N.Mex. Alliance Health, Phys. Edn. Recreation and Dance (spkr., aquatic chmn. 1990—92), Internat. Dark Sky Assn. (life). Democrat. Jewish. Avocations: skywatching, swimming, needlework, astro photography.

WALLEN, LINA HAMBALI, economics educator, consultant; b. Garut, West Java, Indonesia, Mar. 24, 1952; came to U.S., 1986; d. Mulyadi and Indra (Hudiyana) Hambali; m. Norman E. Wallen, Apr. 16, 1986. BA, IKIP, Bandung, Indonesia, 1975, DRA, 1984; PhD in Psychology, Columbia Pacific U., San Rafael, Calif., 1990; MA in Economics, San Francisco State U., 1993. Cert. tchr. Clk. PT Radio Frequency Communication, Bandung, 1972-74; adminstrv. mgr. CV Electronics Engring., Jakarta, Indonesia, 1974-76; exec. sec. PT Tanabe Abadi, Bandung, 1977-81; br. mgr. PT Ama Forta, Bandung, 1982-84; tchr. SMA Pembangunan, Bandung, 1976-83, Patuha Coll., Bandung, 1980-84. Faculty econ. dept. No. Ariz. U. Coll. Bus. Adminstrn., 2000—.

WALLENTINE, MARY KATHRYN, secondary educator; b. Moscow, Idaho, Dec. 27, 1943; d. Elwood Vernon and Mary Berenice (Hillard) White; m. William Edward Wallentine, Dec. 29, 1977; 1 child, Vicki. BA, Whitman Coll., 1966. Tchr. math. and art Mt. Rainier H.S., Des Moines, Wash., 1966-85; pres. Highline Edn. Assn., Seattle, 1985-89; tchr. math., dept. head Tyee H.S., SeaTac, Wash., 1988-96, ret. Tchr. leadership cadre Highline Sch. Dist., 1988-92, co-chair dist. site-based decision making com., 1989-92; tchr. leadership cadre Tyee H.S., 1995—, sr. class advisor, graduation advisor, 1994-96. Dir., editor, photographer, prodr. sr. class video Fly Me to the Moon, Tyee H.S., 1995-96. Precinct committeeperson Dem. Ctrl. Com., King County, Wash., 1980-98, state committeewoman, 1982-88, del. nat. conv., 1980—; campaign office mgr. Supt. of Pub. Instrn., 1996; mem. Bellevue Park Bd. Dirs., 1997-98; sch. grants reader Melinda and Bill Gates Found., 1999-2003. Recipient award Women's Polit. Caucus, 1997. Mem. NEA (resolutions com. 1987-92, ret. adv. coun. 2003—, nat. del. 1980—), Nat. Coun. Tchrs. Math. (spkr.), Wash. Edn. Assn. (ret., pres. 2002—, bd. dirs. 2002—). Episcopalian. Avocations: gardening, politics, visual arts, community service. Home: 860 100th Ave NE Apt 34 Bellevue WA 98004-4132

WALLER, GARY FREDRIC, English language educator, administrator, poet; b. Auckland, N.Z., Jan. 3, 1944; came to U.S., 1983; s. Fred and Joan Elsie (Smythe) W.; m. Jennifer Robyn Denham, July 2, 1966 (div. 1980); children: Michael, Andrew; m. Kathleen Ann McCormick, Nov. 12, 1988; one child, Philip. BA, U. Auckland, 1965, MA, 1966; PhD, Cambridge U., Eng., 1970. Donaldson Bye fellow Magdalene Coll., Cambridge, Eng., 1967-69; assoc. prof. English U. Auckland, New Zealand, 1969-72, Dalhousie U., N.S., Can., 1972-78; head, prof. English Wilfrid Laurier U., Waterloo, Can., 1978-83; head, prof. lit. and cultural studies Carnegie Mellon U., Pitts., 1983-92; dean arts and scis., prof. lit. and cultural studies U. Hartford, West Hartford, Conn., 1992-95; provost, v.p. acad. affairs, prof. lit. and cultural studies Purchase (N.Y.) Coll., SUNY, 1995—. Author: The Strong Necessity of Time, 1976, The Triumph of Death, 1977, Pamphilia to Amphilanthus, 1977, Dreaming America, 1979, Mary Sidney Countess of Pembroke, 1979, Sir Philip Sidney and the Interpretation of Renaissance Culture, 1984, Sixteenth Century Poetry, 1986, 2d edit., 1993, Reading Texts, 1986, Lexington Introduction to Literature, 1987, Shakespeare's Comedies, 1991, Reading Mary Wroth, 1991, The Sidney Family Romance, 1993, Edmund Spenser: A Literary Life, 1994, Lady Mary Sidney's Antonie and a Discourse of Life and Death, 1996; (poems) Other Flights, Always, 1991, Impossible Futures Indelible Pasts, 1983 Office: Purchase Coll Acad Affairs Purchase NY 10577

WALLER, GARY WILTON, administration educator, minister; b. Ft. Worth, July 16, 1948; s. Robert Preston and Lillian Lee (Taylor) W.; m. Cindy Ann Dollar, Jan. 3, 1975; children: Stephanie, RyAnn. BS in Phys. Edn., Baylor U., 1970; MRE, Southwestern Bapt. Theol. Sem., Ft. Worth, 1972, PhD, 1979, U. North Tex., 1992. Ordained to ministry, Bapt. Ch., 1979. Min. music and youth North Cleburne Bapt. Ch., Cleburne, Tex., 1970-72; min. edn. Trinity Bapt. Ch., Ft. Worth, 1972-74, Gambrell Street Bapt. Ch., Ft. Worth, 1978-82; min. edn. and evangelism North Ft. Worth Bapt. Ch., 1974-78, 1st Bapt. Ch., Waco, Tex., 1982-84; prof. adminstrn. Southwestern Bapt. Theol. Sem., 1984—, dean distance learning. Em. Com. To Nominate Coordinating Bds., Dallas, 1983-84; trustee Latham Springs Encampment, Aquilla, Tex., 1971-72, 76-78. Trustee Castleberry Ind. Sch. Dist., Ft. Worth, 1977-79; pres. bd. Aerials Gymnastics, Arlington, Tex., 1991-94. Fellow Scarborough Inst.; mem. So. Bapt. Religious Educators (v.p. 1995), Tarrant Bapt. Religious Educators (pres. 1981), Bapt. Religious Educators S.W., Am. Mgmt. Assn., Castleberry Alumni Assn. (treas. 1978-80, Outstanding Ex award 1978), Woodhaven Country Club. Avocation: golf. Office: Southwestern Bapt Theol Sem PO Box 22487 Fort Worth TX 76122-0001

WALLER, GEORGE MACGREGOR, historian, educator; b. Detroit, June 7, 1919; s. George and Marguerite (Rowl) W.; m. Martha Huntington Stifler, Oct. 16, 1943; children: Susan, Marguerite, Elizabeth, Donald, Richard. Grad., Deerfield Acad., 1937; AB, Amherst Coll., 1941; MA, Columbia U., 1947, PhD, 1953. Comml. rep. Detroit Edison Co., 1941-42; lectr. Hunter Coll., 1946-47; instr. Amherst Coll., 1948-52; chief Am. history rsch. ctr. Wis. Hist. Soc., 1952-54; prof., head dept. history and polit. sci. Butler U., Indpls., 1954-84, McGregor prof. history, 1987-89, McGregor prof. history emeritus, 1989—. Fulbright sr. scholar U. Southampton, Eng., 1961-62; vis. prof. Ind. U., 1967-69 Author: Samuel Vetch. Colonial Enterpriser, 1960, The American Revolution in the West, 1976; editor: Puritanism in Early America, 1950, rev., 1973, Pearl Harbor, Roosevelt and the Coming War, 1953, 65, 3d edit., 1976; contbr. to: Ency. So. History, World Book Ency., Dictionary of Can. Biography, Vol. I., Ency. of Indpls. Mem. Ind. Am. Revolution Bicentennial Commn., 1971-82. Lt. comdr. USNR, 1943-46. Recipient Holcomb award, 1960, Daus. of Founders and Patriots of Am. award, 1977, Disting. Hoosier award, 1989, Sagamore of the Wabash award, 1990. Mem. Ind. Acad. Social Scis. (pres. 1983), Ind. Mus. Soc. (past pres.), Internat. Platform Assn., Butler Alumni Assn. (Butler medal 1998), Phi Beta Kappa (past pres. Ind. chpt.), Phi Kappa Phi, Phi Alpha Theta. Home: 740 Broad Ave S Naples FL 34102-7330

WALLER, MARY BELLIS, psychotherapist, education educator, consultant; b. Milw., May 18, 1940; d. Ernest Anthony and Hazel Mary (Addie) Bellis; m. Michael I. Waller, May 9, 1987 (dec. Nov. 1996); children: Eric B. Griswold, Andrew D. Griswold, Megan E. Griswold Simone BS, U. Wis., Milw., 1969, MS, 1971, PhD, 1992. Coord. Wis. Coalition for Ednl. Reform, Milw., 1971-74; instr. U. Wis., Milw., 1974-77; exec. dir. Worker Rights Inst., Milw., 1977-87; adj. prof. Nat. Coll. Edn., Evanston, Ill., 1981-96; preceptor, clin. program coord. U. Wis.-Parkside, Kenosha, 1987-96; Wis. lead cons. Emprise Designs, 1993-97; psychotherapist, dir. outreach programs Achievement Assocs., Ltd., 1998—; clin. assoc. prof. U. Wis., Milw., 2002—. Cons. on drug-affected children; ctr. scientist Ctr. for Addiction and Behavioral Health Rsch., 1996—; pres. Program Devel. and Evaluation, 1993—, Priority Group, Inc., 1998—. Author: Crack-Affected Children: A Teacher's Guide, 1993, Lady of the Manor: Medieval Cooking with Herbs, 1994; author numerous articles on drug-affected children. Mem. ASCD, NAEYC, Am. Ednl. Rsch. Assn., Assn. Tchr. Educators, Phi Delta Kappa (Disting. Svc. award 1992). Home: 8316 N Regent Rd Milwaukee WI 53217-2736 E-mail: mwaller@execpc.com.

WALLER, MITZI DUNCAN, special education educator; b. Nathalie, Va., Dec. 22, 1955; d. Richard Edward Sr. and Barbara Gayle (Brown) Duncan; m. Ronnie Lee Waller, Mar. 3, 1979; children: Blair Marie, Blake Edward. BS in Therapeutic Recreation, Longwood Coll., 1979, MS in Edn., 1994. Edn. students with learning disabilities Halifax (Va.) County/South Boston City Pub. Schs., 1991—. Chmn. sch. renewal com. Volens Elem., Nathalie, Va., 1994—. Sunday sch. pianist Mulberry Bapt. Ch., Nathalie, 1980-94, Sunday sch. tchr., 1980-95; pres. North Halifax Ladies' Aux., Nathalie, 1982-84; parent Lucky Leaf 4-H Club, Nathalie, 1990—. Mem. NEA, Va. Edn. Assn. Baptist. Avocations: youth sports, reading, swimming. Home: 3098 Golden Leaf Rd Nathalie VA 24577-3480 Office: Volens Elem Sch RR 3 Box 157 Nathalie VA 24577-9514

WALLER, NEOLA SHULTZ, secondary school educator; b. Canadian County, Okla., Feb. 14, 1929; d. Lewis Ray and Alma Marie (Liebscher) Shultz; m. William Waller, May 28, 1949; children: Mary Ann, Jeffrey Scott. BA, Okla. State U., 1949; M in Tchg. of Sci., Coll. William and Mary, 1972. Secondary math. tchr. Virginia Beach (Va.) City Pub. Schs., 1963—93. Mem. Virginia Beach Arts and Humanities Commn., 1978—79; del. joint conf. U.S./Russia on edn., 1994; mem. Va. Women's Leadership Project; chmn. bd. Baylake United Meth. Ch., Virginia Beach, 1982—83; co-chair Va. Ann. Conf. United Meth. Ch. Commn. on Status and Rose of Women, 2001—. Named Secondary Math. Tchr. of Yr. for Va., Va. Coun. Tchrs. of Math., 1985. Mem.: AAUW (Va. treas. 1995—97, Va. membership v.p. 1997—98, Va. pres. 1998—2002, Ednl. Found. 2003—), Delta Kappa Gamma. Avocations: travel, reading, hammered dulcimer. Home: 3100 Shore Dr PH 52 Virginia Beach VA 23451-1199

WALLER, WILMA RUTH, retired secondary school educator and librarian; b. Jacksonville, Tex., Nov. 15, 1921; d. William Wesley and Myrtle (Nesbitt) W. BA with honors, Tex. Woman's U., 1954, MA with honors, 1963, MLS with honors, 1976. Tchr. English Dell (Ark.) High Sch., 1953-54, Jefferson (Tex.) Ind. Schs., 1954-56, Tyler (Tex.) Ind. Schs., 1956-68; librarian Wise County Schs., Decatur, Tex., 1969-71, Thomas K. Gorman High Sch., Tyler, 1971-74, Sweetwater (Tex.) Ind. Sch. Dist., 1974-86; ret. Lectr., book reviewer for various clubs. Active in past as vol. for ARC, U. Tex. Health Ctr. Ford Found. fellow, 1959; recipient Delta Kappa Gamma Achievement award, 1992. Mem. UDC, Smith County Ret. Sch. Pers., Bible Study Group, Delta Kappa Gamma. Republican. Baptist. Avocations: reading, gourmet cooking, piano, writing letters. Home: 1117 N Azalea Dr Tyler TX 75701-5206

WALLIN, LELAND DEAN, artist, educator; b. Sioux Falls, SD, Oct. 14, 1942; s. Clarence Forrest and Leona Mae (McInnis) W.; m. Meredith Maria Hawkins, Mar. 26, 1977; 1 child, Jessica Hawkins. Student, Columbus Coll. Art and Design, 1961-62; BFA in Painting, Kans. City Art Inst., Mo., 1965; MFA in Painting, U. Cin. with Cin. Art Acad., 1967. Prof. drawing, painting, sculpture St. Cloud State U., Minn., 1967-86; prof. Queens Coll., CUNY, Flushing, NY, 1983-84; prof., coord. MFA painting Marywood U., Scranton, Pa., 1985-90; prof. painting and drawing East Carolina U., Greenville, NC, 1992—; advisor Painting Guild, 1993—94. Lectr. Carnegie-Mellon U., Pitts., 1988; juror Belin Arts Grant Com., Waverly, Pa., 1989; curator Philip Pearlstein Retrospective Exhibit, Scranton, 1988; vis. prof. painting East Carolina U., Greenville, 1992-93; judge/juror No. Nat. Art Competition, 1993. One-man shows include include Mpls. Coll. Art and Design, 1978, Harold Reed Gallery, 1983, Gallery Henoch, NYC, NY, 1991, exhibited in group shows at include The Bklyn. Mus., 1983, Greenville County Mus. of Art, S.C., 1983, The Mus. of Modern Art, Fla., 1993, Huntsville Mus. Art, 1994, San Bernardino County Mus. Internat., Calif., 1995, Contemporary Realism,'96, Internat., '98, Internat., Phila, 1998, Fine Arts Ctr., Sacramento, Calif., 1999, Internat. Ctr. for Arts, Loredo, Tex., 2000, Downey (Calif.) Mus. Art, 1998, Palm Springs Desert Mus., 1999, Bellevue Art Mus., Wash., 2001, Morris Mus. of Art, Ga., 2001, Huntsville Mus. Art, Ala., 2002, Miss. Mus. Art, 2002, Represented in permanent collections represented in various collections; contbr. articles to profl. jour.; author: (book) Rescuing Bermear/ Am. Arts Quar. Fall, 2002. Named Outstanding Tchr., East Carolina U., 1994, 95; recipient numerous rsch. awards East Carolina U., 1994—. Mem. Coll. Art Assn. Am., Pa. Soc. Watercolor Painters. Home: 218 York Rd Greenville NC 27858-5601

WALLIS, RICHARD FISHER, physicist, educator; b. Washington, May 14, 1924; s. William F. and Alberta (Sigelen) W.; m. Mary Camilla Williams, Aug. 20, 1955; children: Maria Fisher, Sylvia Camilla. BS, George Washington U., 1945, MS, 1948; PhD, Cath. U. Am., 1952. Postdoctoral fellow (U. Md.), College Park, 1951-53; chemist Applied Physics Lab. Johns Hopkins U., Silver Spring, Md., 1953-56; physicist Naval Rsch. Lab., Washington, 1956-66, 67-69, head semiconductors br., 1958-66, 67-69; prof. physics U. Calif., Irvine, 1966-67, 69—; prof. emeritus, 1993—; chmn. dept. physics U. Calif., Irvine, 1972-75, 80-83. Vis. prof. U. Paris, 1975-76, 79, 85. Author: (with Maradudin and Dobrzynski) Handbook of Surfaces and Interfaces, 1980, (with Balkanski) Many-Body Aspects of Solid State Spectroscopy, 1986, (with Balkanski) Semiconductor Physics and Applications, 2000; editor: Lattice Dynamics, 1965, Localized Excitations in Solids, 1968 (with Stegeman) Electromagnetic Surface Excitations, 1986, (with Birman and Sebenne) Elementary Excitations in Solids, 1992; contbr. articles to profl. jours. Served with U.S. Army, 1945-46. Recipient Pure Sci. award Naval Rsch. Lab., 1964, Disting. Alumni Achievement award George Washington U., 1991. Fellow Am. Phys. Soc., AAAS; mem. Philos. Soc. Washington, Phi Beta Kappa, Sigma Xi Home: 2635 Alta Vista Dr Newport Beach CA 92660-4102 Office: U Calif Dept Physics Irvine CA 92697-0001

WALLIS, SANDRA RHODES, educator; b. Bel Air, Md., Nov. 16, 1945; d. Lawrence Edgar and Alverta (Kohler) Rhodes; m. W. Robert Wallis, June 25, 1977; children by previous marriage: John Robert Christopher, David Matthew Christopher. BA in Secondary Edn., U. Md., 1967; MEd in Reading, Towson U., 1974; EdD in Literacy, U. Del., 2000. Cert. tchr., Md. Tchr. Harford County Pub. Schs., Bel Air, 1968-89, reading specialist, 1972-89, supr. reading K-12, 1989-92, supr. English, lang. arts and reading, 1992-98; retired, 1998; coord. grad. reading program Goucher Coll., Balt., 1998—. Tchr. cons. Md. Writing Project, Towson, 1988—. Bd. dirs., past pres. Sexual Assault Spouse Abuse Resource Ctr.; mem. Commn. Role of the Reading Specialist. Mem. NCTE, ASCD, Harford County Reading Coun. (pres. 1986-87), State of Md. Internat. Reading Assn. (chair newspaper in edn. com. 1987-90), Alpha Delta Kappa (pres. Chi chpt. 1987-90). Democrat. Methodist. Home: 115 W Ring Factory Rd Bel Air MD 21014 Office: Goucher Coll Grad Programs Edn 1021 Dulaney Valley Rd Baltimore MD 21204-2753

WALLNER, LUDWIG JOHN, principal; b. NYC, Sept. 14, 1941; s. Ludwig and Antoinette (Maier) W.; m. Carolyn Elizabeth Holzer, Dec. 19, 1964; children: Heidi Elizabeth, Kurt Andrew. AAS, Orange County Community Coll., Middletown, N.Y., 1961; BS, SUNY, Oswego, 1964, MS, 1967; cert. advanced study, SUNY, Cortland, 1977; EdD, Highland U., 1982. Ordained deacon Episcopal Ch., 2003. Tchr. North Syracuse Ctrl. Schs., Clay, N.Y., 1964-66, sch. counselor, 1966-70, head sch. counselor, 1970-73, middle sch. asst. prin., 1973-80, house prin., 1980-86; middle sch. prin. Schalmont Ctrl. Schs., Schenectady, 1986-89, high sch. prin., 1989-95, mid. sch. prin., 1995—99; ret., 1999. Trainer Nat. Crisis Prevention Inst., Inc., Brookfield, Wis., 1994-95. Author, editor: (video) Testing Activity, 1969. Dist. chmn. Boy Scouts Am., Schenectady, 1989; bd. dirs. Hist. Soc. Saratoga Springs, Episcopal Counseling Svcs., Albany; trainer Albany Episcopal Diocese Godly Boundaries program. Recipient St. George award Episcopal Ch. (nat.), Syracuse, N.Y., 1989. Mem. Sch. Adminstrs. Assn. N.Y., Schalmont Prins. Assn. (pres. 1989-96), North Syracuse Prins. Assn. (pres. 1978), N.Am. Assn. Deacons, Epsilon Pi Tau, Inc., Phi Delta Kappa. Republican. Episcopalian. Avocations: traveling, cross-country skiing, cycling, walking, woodworking. Home: 12 Killarney Ct Saratoga Springs NY 12866-7502

WALLS, HERBERT LEROY, school system administrator; b. Springfield, Ohio, July 12, 1944; s. James Edward and Hattie Beatrice (Jackson) W.; m. Vonzile Green, Feb. 4, 1967 (div. 1975); children: Herbert Le Roy Jr., Jomica Yvette. BA in English, Calif. State U., L.A., 1972; MA in Spl. Edn., Calif. State U., Dominguez Hills, 1982; MEd, U. LaVerne, 1992, EdD, 1998; HHD (hon.), Mt. Zion Bible Sem., 1991. Cert. English tchr., spl. edn. tchr., adminstr., Calif. Tchr. Golden Day Schs., L.A., 1971-72; English tchr. M.L. King Jr. Middle Sch., Boston, 1972-74; spl. edn. tchr. Arnold RE-ED West, Carmichael, Calif., 1974-75; adminstr., tchr. Golden Day/Univ. Alternative Sch., L.A., 1975-79; dir. spl. edn. Dorothy Brown Sch., L.A., 1979-84; prin., tchr. Westside Acad., L.A., 1984-86; tchr. spl. edn. Sacramento City (Calif.) Unified Sch. Dist., 1987-93, prin., 1993—; dean Christ Temple Bible Inst., Sacramento, 1991-93. Ednl. cons. Little Citizen Schs., L.A., 1994. Contbr. poetry to anthologies. Sgt. USMC, 1962-66, Vietnam. Mem. ASCD, Calif. State U. Alumni Assn. (L.A.), Alumni U. La Verne Assn., Mt. Zion Sem. Alumni Fellowship, Phi Delta Kappa. Mem. Apostolic Ch. Avocations: watercolor impressionist painting, piano, drama, singing gospel and classical music. Home: 2600 Cadjew Ave Sacramento CA 95832-1424

WALLS-CULOTTA, SANDRA L. educational administrator; b. Milford, Del., Dec. 5, 1953; d. Thomas S. and Verna L. (Lodge) W.; 1 child, Charles H. McKinney III; m. Charles L. Culotta, July 6, 1994. BS, U. Del., 1975; MEd, Salisbury State U., 1978. Cert. prin. spl. edn., elem. and secondary adminstr., Del. Tchr. spl. edn. Indian River Sch. Dist., Frankford, Del., 1975-79, spl. edn. bldg. coord., 1979-85; tchr. spl. edn. Cape Henlopen Sch. Dist., Lewes, Del., 1985-86; program cooord. Sussex Vocat. Tech. Sch. Dist., Georgetown, Del., 1986-92; asst. prin. Sussex Tech. High Sch., Georgetown, 1992—2000; prin. Sussex Tech. H.S., Georgetown, 2000—. Adj. prof. Del. State Coll., Georgetown, 1989-90, 2000-01, Wilmington Coll., Georgetown, 2003—; expert witness Pub. Defender's Office, Worcester, Snow Hill, Md., 1989; trainer Del. Learning Resource Ctr., Georgetown, 1986-88; presenter in field. Com. chair Dem. Polit. Party, Milford, 1975-78; mem. Gov.'s Coun. for Exceptional Citizens, Dover, Del., 1980-82; coach Rookie League, T-Ball League, Ocean City, Md., 1989-92. Spl. Edn. Tng. fellow Dept. Public Inst., 1977-78; named Del. Prin. of Yr. Secondary Schs., 2003. Mem. ASCD, Nat. Assn. Sec. Sch. Prins., Nat. Coun. for Children with Behavioral Disorders, Nat. Coun. for Children with Learning Disabilities, Coun. for Exceptional Children (state pres. 1980-81, 86-87), Lower Del. Sch. Prin. Assn. (pres. 1990-91), Del. Assn. Secondary Sch. Prin. (pres.-elect 2000-03, pres. 2003—), Phi Delta Kappa (dist. rep. 1990-97). Republican. Methodist. Avocations: skiing, needlepoint, swimming, hiking, reading. Home: 6 E Clarke Ave Milford DE 19963-1803

WALMSLEY, JUDITH ABRAMS, chemistry educator; b. Oak Park, Ill., Feb. 6, 1936; d. Kenneth Frederick and Edna Martha (Grau) Abrams; m. Frank Walmsley, Aug. 29, 1959; children: Katherine Ellen, Susan Jennifer. BA in Chemistry, Fla. State U., 1958; PhD in Chemistry, U.N.C., 1962. Rsch. scientist Owens-Ill., Inc., Toledo, 1963-66; rsch. assoc., instr. Mich. State U., East Lansing, 1979-80; sr. rsch. assoc. U. Toledo, 1974-87; asst. prof. U. Tex., San Antonio, 1987-93, assoc. prof., 1993—2000, prof., 2000—, chair dept., 2001—. Instr. U. Toledo, 1968-69, 75-77, 83-87. Patentee in field; author lab. manuals, 1985; contbr. articles to profl. jours. Recipient rsch. grants Rsch. Corp., U. Tex., 1988-90, NIH, 1990—, DeArce Biomed. Rsch., U. Toledo, 1984-87. Mem. Am. Chem. Soc., AAAS, Sigma

Xi, Phi Beta Kappa, Phi Kappa Phi, Delta Gamma. Presbyterian. Avocations: reading, sewing, swimming. Office: Dept Chemistry U Tex San Antonio San Antonio TX 78249-0698

WALSH, DIANA CHAPMAN, academic administrator, sociologist, educator; b. Phila., July 30, 1944; d. Robert Francis and Gwen (Jenkins) Chapman; m. Christopher Thomas Walsh, June 18, 1966; 1 child, Allison Chapman. BA, Wellesley Coll., 1966; MS, Boston U. Sch. of Pub. Comm., 1971; PhD, Boston U., 1983; LHD (hon.), Boston U, 1994, Amer. Coll. of Greece, Athens, 1995, U. Mass., Amherst, 1999, Northeastern U., 2003. Dir. info., edn. Planned Parenthood League, Newton, Mass., 1971—74; sr. program assoc. Dept Pub. Health, Boston, 1974—76; assoc. dir. Boston U. Health Policy Inst., 1985—90; prof. Sch. Pub. Health, Sch. Medicine, Boston U., 1987—90, adj. prof. pub. health, 1990—; chair Harvard Sch. Pub. Health, 1990—93, adj. prof., 1993—; pres. Wellesley Coll., 1993—. Author: (book) Corporate Physicians, 1987; editor: Women, Work and Health: Challenges to Corporate Policy, 1980, (book series) Industry and Health Care, 1977—80; co-author: Payer, Provider, Consumer, 1977; contbr. articles to profl. jours. Bd. dirs. Planned Parenthood League of Mass., 1974—79, 1981—85, bd. overseers, 1993—94; trustee Occupl. Physicians Scholarship Fund, 1987—94, WGBH Ednl. Found., 1993—2000. Recipient Book of the Yr. award, Am. Jour. Nursing, 1980; fellow, Kellogg Nat. fellow, 1987—90. Mem.: AHA, AAAS, Consortium on Financing Higher Edn., State Street Corp., Mass. Pub. Health Assn., Soc. for the Study of Social Problems, Am. Sociol. Assn. Avocations: gender and health, social policy, writing, skiing. Office: Wellesley Coll Office of the Pres 106 Central St Wellesley MA 02481-8268

WALSH, JAMES ANTHONY (TONY WALSH), theater and film educator; b. Bklyn., Aug. 21, 1947; s. Henry Michael and Clara (Nappi) Walsh. BA in Theater, Hofstra U., 1968; MA in Theater, Adelphi U., 1976. Tchr., dir. theater N.C. Sch. of Arts, Winston-Salem, 1976-81; artistic dir. Cross and Sword/State Play of Fla., St. Augustine, 1982-91; dean Fla. Sch. of Arts, Palatka, 1982-91; dir. Inst. of Entertainment Technologies Valencia C.C., Orlando, Fla., 1992-93, dir. Ctr. Profl. Devel., 1993-96; producing dir. TV and video prodn. Valencia Coll., Orlando, 1996-2001; mng. dir. The Performing and Visual Arts Ctr. St. Johns River C.C., Orange Park, Fla., 01—, exec. dir. The Thrasher-Horn Ctr. for Arts, 2003—. Freelance theater dir., acting coach, N.Y.C., 1973-76; cons. Network of Performing and Visual Arts Schs., Washington, 1980—, Inst. Outdoor Drama, Chapel Hill, N.C., 1989—, Univ. Film and Video Assn., Sarasota, Fla., 1992, Internat. Film Workshops, Rockport, Maine, 1992, Dir. Guild Am. Educators Workshop, L.A., 1993, Dir.'s Workshop, 1996, Acad. TV Arts and Scis. Educators Seminar, L.A., 1995; writer, dir. LifeMap, PBS Teleconf., 2000. Writer PBS documentary World of Family, NCCJ, 1995; exptl. theater playwright; lyricist (off-Broadway mus.) Sugar Hill, 1990. Bd. dirs. Enzian Film Theatre, Concert on the Green, Maitland Art Ctr.; mem. adv. coun. Fla. Film Festival. NEH grantee, 1978; recipient playwriting fellowships Atlantic Ctr. for Arts, 1983, Fla. Divsn. Cultural Affairs, 1983; named Winner Fla. Playwrite Competition, 1994, Winner Best Video, Fla. Assn. C.C., 1996. Mem. Assn. Theater in Higher Edn., Fla. Motion Picture and TV Assn. (bd. dirs., v.p.), Ctrl. Fla. Film Commn. (bd. dirs.), Fla. Inst. for Film Edn. (bd. dirs.) Actors Equity Assn., Dramatists Guild N.Y.C., Players Club (N.Y.C.). Home: 2375 Coleen Lane Green Cove Springs FL 32043 Office: St Johns River CC 283 College Dr Orange Park FL 32065 E-mail: thrasherhorne@aol.com.

WALSH, JANICE MAUREEN, counselor, educator; b. Monroe, Ga., June 17, 1948; d. Herschel Thomas and Joan (Williford) Scott; m. Dennis Warner Anderson, June 24, 1967 (div. Sept. 1988); children: Jeffrey, Timothy; m. Francis Raymond Walsh, July 6, 1993 (dec. Sept. 1998). AA, Windward C.C., 1988; BA, U. Hawaii, 1990; MBA, Chaminade U., Honolulu, 1991, advanced profl. cert., 1992. Cert. clin. hypnotherapist Hawaii, 1998. Instr. Windward C.C., Kaneohe, Hawaii, 1991-92; prof. Chaminade U., Honolulu, 1993; instr., counselor Kapiolani C.C., Honolulu, 1993-99, asst. prof., 1999—. Cons. Changing Me, Kailua, Hawaii, 1993-99. Mem. disaster action team Hawaii Red Cross. Mem. ACA, Hawaii Counseling Assn. (treas., pres., past pres. 1990-97), Nat. Career Devel. Assn., Guild of Hypnotists, Hawaii Career Devel. Assn. (treas. 1995-97), Soroptomist Internat. of Windward Oahu. Avocations: bridge, movies, crossword puzzles. Office: Kapiolani C C 4303 Diamond Head Rd Honolulu HI 96816-4421

WALSH, JOANNE ELIZABETH, retired elementary school educator, librarian; b. Chgo., Nov. 25, 1942; d. Joseph Frank and Elizabeth Margaret (Gretz) Fiali; m. John Kerwin Walsh, July 17, 1976; 1 child, Kevin Joseph. BA in English, Mundelein Coll., Chgo., 1965; MEd Ednl. Adminstrn. and Supervision, Loyola U., Chgo., 1969. Tchr. Chgo. Pub. Schs., 1965-83, prin., 1983-89; tchr. libr. Burbank, Ill., 1990—93; tchr. art Tate Sch. of Discovery, Knoxville, Tenn., 1994-95; ret., 1995. Vol. Palos Cmty. Hosp., Palos Park, Ill., 1990, Palos Heights Libr., 1993; Rainbow facilitator, 1992-93; active St. John Neumann Cath. Ch., Knoxville Symphony League; decorating com. City of Farragut. Recipent Tchr. of Yr. award McCord Sch., 1992-93. Mem.: Fox Den Woman's Club, Knoxville Newcomers Club (pres. 2002—03), Knoxville Welcome Wagon Club (pres. 1999—2000). Avocations: reading, gardening, crafts, painting, golf. Home: 609 Augusta National Way Knoxville TN 37922-2536 E-mail: NDISGR8@aol.com.

WALSH, NICOLAS EUGENE, rehabilitation medicine physician, educator; b. Mpls., July 1, 1947; s. Leonard Cyril and June Alice Walsh; m. Wendy Sarah Allnutt, June 1, 1973; children: Meghan, Rorey, Katlin, Alaine. BS, USAF Acad., 1969; MS, Marquette U., 1974; MD, U. Colo., 1979. Asst. prof. naval sci. Marquette U., Milw., 1972—74; from asst. prof. to assoc. prof. rehab. medicine U. Tex. Health Sci. Ctr., San Antonio, 1982—89, prof., chmn. rehab. medicine, 1989—, exec. assoc. dean Sch. Medicine, 1999—2000, disting. prof., 2001—. Dir. Am. Bd. Phys. Medicine and Rehab., Rochester, Minn., 1994—, sec., 1996—98, chmn., 1998—; pres., CEO Univ. Physician Group, 1998—2001. Author book chpts.; editor: Rehabilitation of Chronic Pain, 1991; editor-in-chief Archives of Phys. Medicine and Rehab., Chgo., 1994—2000. Named Health Care Profl. of Yr., Gov.'s Com. for Disabled Persons, 1989; recipient Excellence in Rsch. award, Am. Jour. Phys. Medicine and Rehab., 1991. Fellow: Am. Acad. Phys. Medicine and Rehab. (Richard and Hinda Rosenthal Found. award 1991), Am. Bd. Pain Medicine (v.p. 1993—94, sec. 1994—96); mem.: Phys. Medicine and Rehab. Edn. and Rsch. Found. (pres. 1993—2000, Excellence in Rsch. award 1991), Assn. Acad. Physiatrists (v.p. 1993—95, pres. 1996—98). Office: U Tex Health Sci Ctr Mail Code 7872 7703 Floyd Curl Dr San Antonio TX 78229-3900 E-mail: walshn@uthscsa.edu.

WALSH, WILLIAM JOHN, educational administrator; b. Natrona Heights, Pa., Mar. 29, 1941; s. William Henry and Helen Constance W.; BA in Sociology, Duquesne U., 1969; MEd in Ednl. Adminstrn., Pa. State U., 1971; JD, LaSalle U., 1993; m. Carol Jean Miller, Sept. 3, 1966; children: Keirsten, Shannon. Classification analyst Pa. State U., University Park, 1969-73; asst. pers. dir. W.Va. U., Morgantown, 1973-78; exec. asst. to pres., 1977; dir. pers. adminstrn., dir. purchasing audit W.Va. Bd. of Regents, Charleston, 1978-86; dir. salary adminstrn. and benefits Pa. State U., 1986-92; dir. employee benefits and retirement U. Miami, 1992-96; exec. dir. benefits adminstrn. U. Miami, Fla., 1996—; cons. in field. Served with USMC, 1962-66; Vietnam. Mem. Coll. and Univ. Personnel Assn., South Fla. Health Coalition, Coral Gables C. of C., Med. Found. Svcs., Inc. Republican. Roman Catholic. Home: 613 Lake Blvd Weston FL 33326-3534

WALSHE, AUBREY PETER, political science educator; b. Johannesburg, Jan. 12, 1934; s. Aubrey John and Joan Kathleen (Evans) W.; m. Catherine Ann Pettifer, Jan. 28, 1957; children: Sally, Jane, Dominic, Emma. BA, Wadham Coll., Oxford, Eng., 1956, MA, 1959; PhD, St. Antony's Coll., Oxford, 1968. Vis. asst. prof. U. Notre Dame, Ind., 1962-63, asst. prof. dept. govt. and internat. studies, 1967-71, dir. African studies, 1971-77, assoc. prof., 1971-77, prof., 1977—. Sr. assoc. fellow St. Antony's Coll., Oxford, 1972-73; dir. ann. Missionary Inst. on Sub-Saharan Africa, U.Notre Dame, 1969—; lectr. and cons. in field; found. mem. So. African Rsch. Archival Project;l mem. N.Am. Support Com., Ecumenical Dialogue of Third World Theologians. Contbr. articles to profl. jours.; author: The Rise of African Nationalism in South Africa, 1971, 2d edit. 1988, Black Nationalism in South Africa: A Short History, 1975, Church Versus State in South Africa, 1983, Prophetic Christianity and the Liberation Management in South Africa, 1997; contbr. revs. to numerous jours.; occasional reader: U. Calif. Press, U. Notre Dame Press, Rev. of Politics, Social Scis. and Humanities Rsch. Coun. of Can., Ottawa, Ind. U. African Studies Pubs. Com., Cath. Inst. for Internat. Rels., London, U. Queensland, Australia. Mem. edn. com. cath. Inst. for Internat. Rels., London; adv. bd. Storypoint Ctr., Presbyn. Ch. U.S.A., N.Y.C.; cons. Nat. Coun. of Chs. of Christ, Convocation of the Kairos Document: Challenge to the Ch. in South Africa. Walsh-Price fellow Ctr. for Mission Studies, Maryknoll, N.Y., 1980-81, Helen Kellogg Inst. for Internat. Studies fellow, 1983, Inst. for Internat. Peace Studies fellow, 1987; MacArthur Found. grantee, 1989-90. Ecumenical Christian. Home: 1037 N Niles Ave South Bend IN 46617-1249 Office: Univ Notre Dame Dept Govt Notre Dame IN 46556

WALT, MARTIN, physicist, consulting educator; b. West Plains, Mo., June 1, 1926; s. Martin and Dorothy (Mantz) W.; m. Mary Estelle Thompson, Aug. 16, 1950; children: Susan Mary, Stephen Martin, Anne Elizabeth, Patricia Ruth. BS, Calif. Inst. Tech., 1950; MS, U. Wis., 1951, PhD, 1953. Staff mem. Los Alamos Sci. Lab., 1953-56; research scientist, mgr. physics Lockheed Missiles and Space Co., Palo Alto (Calif.) Rsch. Lab., 1956-71, dir. phys. scis., 1971-86, dir. research, 1986-93; cons. prof. Stanford U., 1986—. Mem. adv. com. NRC, NASA, Dept. Def., U. Calif. Lawrence Berkeley Lab. Author 2 books; contbr. articles to sci. jours. Served with USNR, 1944-46. Wis. Research Found. fellow, 1950-51; AEC fellow, 1951-53 Fellow Am. Geophys. Union, Am. Phys. Soc.; mem. Am. Inst. Physics (bd. govs.), Fremont Hills Country Club. Home: 12650 Viscaino Ct Los Altos Hills CA 94022-2517 Office: Stanford U Starlab Packard 352 Stanford CA 94305

WALTER, INGO, economics educator; b. Kiel, Fed. Republic of Germany, Apr. 11, 1940; s. Hellmuth and Ingeborg (Moeller) W.; m. Jutta Ragnhild Dobernecker, June 28, 1963; children: Carsten Erik, Inga Maria. AB summa cum laude, Lehigh U., 1962, MS, 1963; PhD, NYU, 1966. Asst. prof. econs. U. Mo., St. Louis, 1965-67, assoc. prof., chmn. dept., 1967-70; prof. econs. and fin. Stern Sch. Bus. Adminstrn. NYU, N.Y.C., 1970—, assoc. dean academic affairs, 1970-79, chmn. internat. bus. and fin. depts., 1980-85, Dean Abraham L. Gitlow chair, 1987-90; Charles Simon chair, dir. NYU Ctr., 1990—2003; dir. Stern Global Bus. Inst., N.Y.C., 2003—, NYU Global Bus. Inst., 2003—. Prof. internat. mgmt. (joint appointment) INSEAD, Fontainebleau, France, 1985—; cons. in field. Author. editor 28 books including Secret Money, 1985, 2d edit., 1990, Global Banking, 3d edit., 2003, Universal Banking in the United States, 1994, Street Smarts, 1997. High Finance in the Euro-Zone, 2000, Mergers and Acquisitions in Financial Services, 2003; contbr. articles to profl. jours. Recipient Bernhard Harms medal, 1992; Ford Found. fellow, 1974-76, Rockefeller Found. fellow, 1977-78. Mem. Am. Econ. Assn., Am. Fin. Assn., Acad. Internat. Bus., Royal Econ. Soc., So. Econ. Assn., Phi Beta Kappa, Beta Gamma Sigma, Omicron Delta Epsilon. Home: 77 Club Rd Montclair NJ 07043-2528 Office: NYU Stern Sch Bus 44 W 4th St New York NY 10012-1106 E-mail: iwalter@stern.nyu.edu.

WALTERS, CATHRYNE BRUNSON, primary school educator; b. Bladenboro, N.C., Oct. 9, 1927; m. Dempsey Aug. 12, 1947; children: Dempsey A., Keith R. BS, N.C. Agrl. Tech. State U., 1950; student, Pembroke State U., East Carolina U. Tchr. Johnson County Sch. System, Wrightsville, Ga., 1951-53, Bladen County Sch. System, Elizabethtown, N.C., 1951-52, 55-92. V.p., trustee Lumber River Baptist Housing Corp., Lumberton, N.C., 1975-89; exec. bd. Women's Baptist State Conv., Raleigh, N.C., 1965—. Trustee Lumber River Baptist Assn. Named Tchr. of Yr. Booker T. Washington Sch., Clarkton, N.C., 1984, 87; Bladen County Tchr. of Yr., 1984; Social Studies Tchr. of Yr. Booker T. Washington Sch., Clarkton, N.C., 1986. Mem. Bladen County Tchrs. Assn. (pres. 1984-85), Bellamy Scholarship Bd., N.C. Math Conf. Democrat. Baptist. Avocations: reading, public speaking, creative writing, walking. Home: PO Box 593 Bladenboro NC 28320-0593

WALTERS, D. ERIC, biochemistry educator; b. Circleville, Ohio, Jan. 20, 1951; s. David E. and Sarah G. (Riley) W.; m. Gale Climenson, 1994; children: Abigail Lee, Matthew Steven. BS in Pharmacy, U. Wis., 1974; PhD in Medicinal Chemistry, U. Kans., 1978. Postdoctoral researcher Ind. U., Bloomington, 1978-79; rsch. scientist Kraft Foods, Glenview, Ill., 1979-82, Searle Pharm. Co., Skokie, Ill., 1982-85; group leader NutraSweet Co., Mount Prospect, Ill., 1985-91; assoc. prof. Chgo. Med. Sch., North Chicago, Ill., 1991—2002; prof. Finch U. Health Sci./Chgo. Med. Sch., North Chicago, Ill. Adj. asst. prof. U. Ill., Chgo., 1987-91; cons. pharm., food, software cos.; mem. spl. study sects. NSF, Washington, 1983-84; mem. spl. study sects. NIH, Washington, 2001, 2002. Author: Opiates, 1986, Scientists Must Speak, 2002; editor: Sweeteners: Discovery, Molecular Design, Chemoreception, 1991; referee Jour. Medicinal Chemistry, Chem. Senses; contbr. articles to profl. jours. Mem. Am. Chem. Soc. (Agr. and Food Chemistry Divsn. Platinum award 1994), Bread for the World, Woodstock Inst. for Sci. and Humanitites. Lutheran. Achievements include 2 patents on new sweeteners, other patents pending; research on computational biochemistry and drug design, expert witness U.S. Internat. Trade Commn. Office: Chgo Med Sch Dept Biochem and Molec Biol 3333 Green Bay Rd North Chicago IL 60064-3037

WALTERS, DONALD LEE, education educator; b. Roachdale, Ind., Feb. 13, 1937; s. Lee and Beryl (Douglas) Walters; m. Nina Walters, June 10, 1972 (dec. Nov. 2002); 1 child, Mark R. BS, Ind. U., 1959, MS, 1960; EdD, U. Miami, 1966. Tchr. math. Kokomo (Ind.)-Ctr. Twp. Schs., 1961-63; asst. to bus. mgr. Dade County Sch. Dist., Miami, Fla., 1964-65; from prof. edn. to ret. Temple U., Phila., 1966—2002, ret., 2002, prof. emeritus, 2002—. Cons. sch. fiscal adminstrn.; spkr. in field. Author: (book) Financial Analysis for Academic Units, 1981; author: (with James J. Jones) Human Resource Management in Education, 1994; contbr. articles to profl. jours. Docent Coastal Discovery Mus., Hilton Head Island, SC, 2003—, Hilton Head, SC; cert. lay spkr. United Meth. Ch. Capt. USAR, 1959—66. Mem.: NEA, Assn. Sch. Bus. Ofcls. Internat., Am. Fedn. Tchrs., Phi Delta Kappa, Phi Kappa Phi, Phi Eta Sigma. E-mail: dwalters@temple.edu.

WALTERS, JAMES CARTER, geology educator, consultant; b. Zeeland, Mich., June 27, 1948; s. Jerome Clarwin and Dorothy Fay (Bowens) W.; m. Bonnie J. Kuhlman, June 11, 1971; children: Jennifer, Kyle. BA in Geology, Grand Valley State Coll., 1970; MPhil. Geology, Rutgers U., 1973, PhD in Geology, 1975. Teaching fellow Fairleigh Dickinson U., Madison, N.J., 1974-75; asst. prof. geology U. No. Iowa, Cedar Falls, 1975-82, assoc. prof., 1982-89, prof., 1989—, dept. head, 1995—, interim dir. environ. programs, 2003—. Vis. prof. Middlebury (Vt.) Coll., summer 1980, U. Vt., Burlington, summer 1981, disting. vis. prof., summer 1982; cons. Black Hawk County, Iowa Conservation Bd., Waterloo, 1980-82, No. Tech. Svcs., 1983, Cold Regions Rsch. Engring. Lab. U.S. Army, Hanover, N.H., 1989-2003; mem. Iowa Statemap Geologic Mapping Adv. Panel, 2000—, Iowa Sci. Found., 2001-. Contbr. articles to profl. jours. Recipient Dean's award Coll. Natural Scis., U. No. Iowa, 1991, 95 ; Nat. Park Svc. rsch. grantee, 1977-81. Fellow Geol. Soc. Am., Iowa Acad. Sci. (chair geology sect. 1983); mem. Geol. Soc. Iowa (pres. 1980, 89), Nat. Assn. Geology Tchrs., Am. Quaternary Assn., Sigma Xi (sec. 1985-95, rsch. grantee 1974), Sigma Gamma Epsilon (v.p. 1978-95, pres. 1995-2000). Avocations: travel, camping, photography. Office: U No Iowa Dept Earth Sci Cedar Falls IA 50614-0335

WALTERS, JANE, state agency administrator; MusB, BA in Music History, Rhodes Coll.; MA in Counseling, U. Memphis; PhD in Sch. Adminstrn., Duke U. Tchr., counselor Messick H.S., Memphis, asst. prin.; asst. dir. computer svcs. Memphis City Schs.; prin. Craigmont Jr. H.S., 1974-79, Craigmont Jr. and Sr. H.S., 1979-95; 21st commr. edn. State Dept. Edn., Nashville, 1995—99; exec. dir. Ptnrs. in Pub. Edn., 1999—; prin. Grizzlies Acad., Memphis, 2003—. Adv. com. edn. depts. Rhodes Coll, Christian Brothers Com., Tenn. Arts Acad.; cons. College Bd. advanced placement program. Grant reader NEA; mem. Goals for Memphis Edn. Com.; bd. dirs. World Affairs Coun, Nat. Coun. Christians and Jews, Memphis Coun. Internat. Visitors, Memphis Youth Symphony, Am. Cancer Soc., Memphis chpt. Office: 204 North Second St Memphis TN 38103*

WALTERS, LINDA JANE, marine biologist, educator, researcher; b. Easton, Pa., Aug. 2, 1961; d. Lee Rudyard and Evelyn (Hood) W.; m. Paul Eric Sacks, Aug. 2, 1992; children: Joshua. BS, Bates Coll., 1983; MS, U. S.C., 1986, PhD, 1991. Project leader Operation Raleigh, Chile, Australia, N.Z., Alaska, 1985-87; rschr. U. Hawaii-Manoa, Honolulu, 1992—94, asst. prof., 1997—2003, assoc. prof., 2003—; coord. UCF/SeaWorld Whale Watch Program, 1998—. Dir. U. Ctrl. Fla., Fellers House Field Sta., 1997—. Contbr. articles to profl. jours. Recipient Lerner-Gray award Am. Mus. Natural History, 1986; Fulbright Indo-Am. fellow, 1993; NOAA grantee, 2000—. Mem. AAUW (America fellowship 1990-91), Assn. for Women in Sci. (mentor 1992—), Ecol. Soc. Am., Soc. Comparative and Integrative Biology (sec. ecology and evolution divsn. 1999-2001), Sigma Xi (pres. chpt., outstanding grad. award 1992). Home: 556 Whipporwill Ln Oviedo FL 32765 Office: Dept Biology U Ctrl Fla Orlando FL 32816

WALTERS, SHERWOOD GEORGE, management consultant, educator; b. Detroit, May 9, 1926; s. George Henry and Helen (Parker) Walters; m. Alexandra Sielcken, Sept. 4, 1952; children: Margaret Taylor Clifford, Karen Chapin, George Alexander, Virginia Sherwood McFee. BA cum laude, W. Maryland Coll., 1949; MS, Columbia U., 1950; MBA with distinction, Columbia U., Grad. Sch. Bus., 1953; PhD hons. scholar, NYU, 1960. Assoc. prof. econ. sociology Coll. Bus. Econ., Lehigh U., Bethlehem, Pa., 1950-60; exec. v.p., dir. ctrs., retail planning mgr. Mobil Oil, N.Y.C., 1960-65; exec. officer, mktg. dir. Gen. Tire & Rubber Internat. Plastics Co., Chem. Plastics Divsn., Akron, Ohio, 1965-70; prof. Rutgers U., Newark, 1970-93, prof. emeritus mgmt. studies, 1993—, founding dir. interfunctional mgmt. program, 1970-88, founding dir. PhD mgmt. program. Cons. in field; dir. various internat. programs. Co-author: Marketing Management Viewpoints, 2d edit., 1970, Mandatory Housing Finance Programs, 1975, Managing the Industry University Cooperative Research Centers: A Guide for Directors and Other Stakeholders, 1998. Adv. nat. rep. congl. com. on tax reform, 2001; chmn. N.J. Gov. Pub. Utility Commn. Task Force, 1973—75, U./Indsl. Partnerships, John Von Neumann Ctr., Princeton, NJ, 1986; hon. chmn. bus. adv. coun. Nat. Rep. Congl. Com., 2003; elder, trustee Topsail Presbyn. Ch. 1st lt. Inf./Quatermaster Corps U.S. Army, 1944—47. Recipient Republican Presdl. Legion of Merit. Fellow: Am. Acad. Polit. Sci.; mem.: Newcomen Soc. Avocation: deep sea fishing. Home: 110 Topsail Watch Ln Hampstead NC 28443-2728 E-mail: s.george.walters@worldnet.att.net.

WALTERS-PARKER, KIMBERLY KAY, secondary school educator; b. Mt. Sterling, Ky., Apr. 9, 1961; d. Robert Wendell and Lagene Kay (Stull) Walters; m. Steve Robert Parker, July 3, 1992; 1 child, Blake. BA, Georgetown Coll., 1983; MA, Morehead State U., 1985; Rank I Cert., U. Ky., 1990. Cert. secondary English educator, reading specialist, Ky. Instr. Eastern Ky. U., Richmond, 1985-87; reading specialist Bryan Sta. High Sch. Fayette County Pub. Schs., Lexington, Ky., 1987—, dir. writing ctr., 1990—. Co-owner Walters/Parker Learning Ctr., Inc., 1993-96; cons. tech. writing and rsch. skills Ky. Sci. and Tech. Coun., 1993. Recipient Merit of Excellence award County of Fayette; grantee Ky. Dept. Edn., 1991-92, 93, Lexington Edn. Assistance Found., 1992, 96. Mem. ASCD, Nat. Coun. Tchrs. English, Internat. Reading Assn., Ky. Coun. Tchrs. English. Avocations: PhD coursework in ednl. psychology. Home: 4201 Ridgewater Dr Lexington KY 40515-6009

WALTHER, JOSEPH EDWARD, health facility administrator, retired physician; b. Indpls., Nov. 24, 1912; s. Joseph Edward and Winona (McCampbell) W.; m. Mary Margaret Ruddell, July 11, 1945 (dec. July 1983); children: Mary Ann Margolis, Karl, Joanne Landman, Suzanne Conran, Diane Paczesny, Kurt. BS, MD, Ind. U., 1936; postgrad., U. Chgo., Harvard U., U. Minn., 1945-47; DSc (hon.), Ind. U., 1997, Purdue U., 1998. Diplomate Nat. Bd. Med. Examiners, Am. Bd. Internal Medicine, Am. Bd. Gastroenterology. Intern Meth. Hosp. and St. Vincent Hosp. of Indpls., 1936-37; physician, surgeon U.S. Engrs./Pan Am. Airways, Midway Island, 1937-38; chief resident, med. dir. Wilcox Meml. Hosp., Lihue, Kauai, 1938-39; internist, gastroenterologist Meml. Clinic Indpls., 1947-83, med. dir., pres., chief exec. officer, 1947—; founder, pres. Doctors' Offices Inc., Indpls., 1947—; founder, pres., chief exec. officer Winona Meml. Found. and Hosp. (now Walther Cancer Inst.), Indpls., 1956—. Clinical asst. prof. medicine Ind. U. Sch. Medicine, Indpls., 1948-93, clin. asst. prof. emeritus, 1993—. Author: (with others) Current Therapy, 1965; mem. edit. rsch. bd. Postgrad. Medicine, 1982-83; contbr. articles to profl. jours. Bd. dirs. March of Dimes, Marion County div., 1962-66, Am. Cancer Soc., Ind. div., 1983-92. Col. USAAF, 1941-47, PTO. Decorated Bronze Star, Silver Star, Air medal; named to Pres.'s Cir., Ind. U., 1999; recipient Disting. Alumni Svc. award, 2001, Sing the Heroes award, Ind. U. Sch. Medicine, 2001, Healthcare Heroes Award for Corp. Achievement in healthcare, 2002, Living Legend award, Ind. Hist. Soc., 2003. Mem.: AMA (del. 1970—76), Hoosier Hundred, Marion County Med. Assn., Ind. Med. Assn., Soc. Cons. to Armed Forces, Am. Coll. Gastroenterology (pres. 1970—71, master and charter, Weiss award 1988), Ind. U. Alumni Assn. (life), 702 Club, Indpls. Athletic Club, Waikoloa Golf and Country Club (Hawaii), Highland Golf and Country Club (hon.). Republican. Home: 3266 N Meridian St Ste 104 Indianapolis IN 46208-5846 Office: Walther Cancer Inst 3202 N Meridian St Indianapolis IN 46208-4646

WALTHER, RICHARD ERNEST, psychology educator, library administrator; b. Des Moines, Nov. 12, 1921; s. Rudolph Herman and Ruth Viola (Leekley) W.; m. Viola Eugenia Godwin, May 4, 1951; children: Mark Edward, Diane Elaine. Student, U. Ill., 1941-42; BA, Tex. Christian U., 1949-50, MA, 1950-52; EdD, North Tex. State U., Denton, 1954-62. Cert. Lifetime Teaching Credentials, Tex. Supt. Dallas Juvenile Home, 1951-61; v.p. rsch and devel. U.S. Industries, Ednl., N.Y.C., 1961-69; pres. Walther & Assocs., Silver Springs, Md., 1969-72; dir. of libr. Ambassador U., Pasadena, Calif., 1972-90, dir., instl. rsch. Big Sandy, Tex., 1990-92, assoc. dir. Coll. Libr., prof. psychology, 1992-96; prof. emeritus, 1996—. V.p. rsch. Humane Soc. of the U.S., Washington, 1968-70; tng. cons. Bell Telephone Labs., Piscataway, N.J., 1968-72. Author: Handling Behavior Problems, 1959. Mem. APA, Am. Ednl. Rsch. Assn. Avocations: photography, writing, research. Home: PO Box 211332 Bedford TX 76095-8332 Office: 2428 Spring Valley Dr Bedford TX 76021-4352 E-mail: richrew@earthlink.net.

WALTON, CLIFFORD WAYNE, chemical engineer, researcher; b. Phila., May 14, 1954; s. John Robert and Elizabeth Baird (Hamilton) W. BSChemE, Drexel U., 1976; MSChemE, Tex. A&M U., 1977, PhD, 1987. Registered profl. engr., Nebr.; cert. electroplater-finisher. Instr. U. Coll. div. U. Md., Stuttgart, Germany, 1978-79, Tex. A&M U., College Station,

1982-84; rsch. engr. Dow Chem. Co., Freeport, Tex., 1985; asst. prof. U. Nebr., Lincoln, Nebr., 1987-91, assoc. prof., 1991-92; cons. Walton & Assocs., Lincoln, 1987-94; rsch. assoc. FMC Corp., Princeton, N.J., 1994-97, project leader, sr. rsch. assoc., 1997-00, project leader, assoc. fellow, 2000—. Cons. Lincoln Plating Co., 1987-94, Mitsui Engring. and Shipbuilding Co., Ltd., Tokyo, 1989-93, Nat. Ctr. for Mfrs. Scis., Ann Arbor, 1990-94, J.P. Industries, Ann Arbor, 1990-94. Editl. bd. Plating and Surface Finishing, 1989-95; internat. editl. bd. Jour. of Cleaner Prodn., 1990—; contbr. articles to profl. jours. Treas. Nebr. Wrestling Booster Club, Lincoln, 1990-92. 1st lt. U.S. Army, 1977-80. Named Outstanding Young Man in Am., U.S. Jaycees, 1982; recipient Ralph R. Teetor award Soc. Automotive Engrs., 1990. Mem. AIChE (sec.-treas. Nebr. br. 1989-91), ASTM (tech. com. 1989-96), Am. Electroplaters and Surface Finishers Soc. (br. pres. 1988-91, publs. bd. 1989-95, scholarship com. 1989-92, chair scholarship com. 1992-94, 95-96), Electrochem. Soc. Inc. (sec. IEEE divsn. 1996-98, symposium organizer 1989, 90, 92, 96, 97, 99—, procs. vol. editor 1990, 97, 99, vice chair IEEE divsn. 1998-00, chair IEEE divsn. 2000-02, contbg. mem. com. 1999—). Avocations: physical fitness, amateur wrestling, boxing, church choir, church youth groups. Office: FMC Corp Chem Rsch & Devel Ctr PO Box 8 Princeton NJ 08543-0008 E-mail: clifford_walton@fmc.com.

WALTON, (DELVY) CRAIG, philosopher, educator; b. L.A., Dec. 6, 1934; s. Delvy Thomas and Florence (Higgins) W.; m. Nancy Young, June 6, 1965 (div. May 1977); children: Richard, Kerry; m. Vera Allerton, Aug. 23, 1980; children: Matthew, Ruth, Peter, Benjamin. BA, Pomona Coll., 1961; PhD, Claremont Grad. Sch., 1965. Asst. prof. U. So. Calif., L.A., 1964-68, No. Ill. U., DeKalb, 1968-71, assoc. prof., 1971-72, U. Nev., Las Vegas, 1972-76, prof., 1976—, chmn. dept. philosophy, 1986-89, dir. Inst. for Ethics and Policy Studies, 1986—. Vis. prof. Friedrich Schiller Univ., Jena, Germany, 2001; presenter workshops in field. Author: De la recherche du Bien, 1972, Philosophy & the Civilizing Arts, 1975, Hobbes's Science of Natural Justice, 1987; translator: (intro.) Treatise on Ethics (Malebranche), 1992; bd. dirs. Jour. History of Philosophy, 1978—2004; contbr. articles to profl. jours. V.p. Nev. Faculty Alliance, 1984-86, pres. 95-97; mem. Clark County Sch. Dist. Task Force on Ethics in schs., 1987, 96-97. 1st lt. USAF, 1956-59. Recipient NDEA Title IV fellowship Claremont Grad. Sch., 1961-64, rsch. sabbaticals U. Nev., 1978, 85, 92, 99; Fulbright fellow Friedrich Schiller Univ., 2001; named Barrick Disting. scholar U. Nev., 1988. Mem. AAUP (pres. Nev. chpt. 1983-84), Internat. Hume Soc. (exec. com. 1979-81), Am. Philos. Assn. (excellence and innovation in philosophy programs award 2000), Soc. for Study History of Philosophy (founder and mem. exec. com. 1974-91), Internat. Hobbes Soc., Phi Beta Kappa. Democrat. Avocations: backpacking, hiking, snow-shoeing, salad-making, dog tng. Home: 6140 Eisner Dr Las Vegas NV 89131-2303 Office: U Nev Inst Ethics Policy Studies 4505 S Maryland Pkwy Las Vegas NV 89154-5049 Fax: (702) 645-3157. E-mail: cwalton@unlv.edu.

WALTON, PAULA ANDERSON, language arts educator; b. Greenville, Ala., May 6, 1937; d. Paul and Lois Alene Anderson; divorced; 1 child, Jennifer. BS, Auburn U., 1958. Tchr. Newport Richey (Fla.) Sch., 1958-59, Apopka (Fla.) Sch., 1960-61, Wellington (Mo.) High Sch., 1961-62, St. Joan of Arc, La Place, La., 1970—2001. Avocations: calligraphy, reading, travel, teaching. Office: St Joan of Arc 412 Fir St La Place LA 70068-4399 Home: 7203-A Old Sauk Rd Madison WI 53717

WALTON, WILLIAM ROBERT, academic administrator; b. Macon, Ga., Aug. 28, 1949; s. Swift Jessie and LouVenia Mattie (Helms) W.; m. Cynthia Bonell Pollock, Dec. 14, 1969; children: David Anthony, Kelly Melissa. Student, Marsh-Draughon Bus. Coll., 1968; BBA, Ga. State U., 1972, M Pub. Adminstrn., 1977. Acct. K.L. Kemp, Atlanta, 1968-72, Berman Mills & Co., Atlanta, 1972; internal auditor U. Ga. System, Atlanta, 1972-74, asst. dir. budgets, 1974-78; dir. bus. and fin. Ft. Valley (Ga.) State Coll., 1978-82; v.p. bus. affairs Roanoke Coll., Salem, Va., 1982-92; adminstr. Joseph W. Jones Ecol. Rsch. Ctr., Newton, Ga., 1992—. Treas. bd. trustees Roanoke Coll, Salem, 1983-92; trustee June Cheelsman Unitrust, Salem, 1984-92, Lois C. Fisher Unitrust, Salem, 1984-92, Harold W. Harris Unitrust, Salem, 1983-92, James W. Sieg Annuity Trust, Salem, 1984-92, T.B. & R.E. Meador Annuity Trust, Salem, 1985-92, Pendleton Hogan Unitrust, Salem, 1989-92, Francis T. West Annuity Trust, Salem, 1988-92. Pres. West Salem PTA, 1985-87; bd. dirs. Am. Lung Assn. Va., 1991-93; bd. dirs. (pres. bd. dirs. 1998—), pres. Albany Area Primary Health Care, 1993—; commr. Keep Albany-Dougherty Beautiful Commn., 1993—, vestryman St. Patrick's Episcopal Ch.; mem. Workforce Investment Bd., 2000—; mem. coun. Baker County Scho., 2001—. Mem. Nat. Assn. Coll. and Univ. Bus. Officers, Nat. Coun. Rsch. Adminstrs., Luth. Coll. Bus. Officers, Coll. and Univ. Pers. Assn., Assn. Phys. Plant Adminstrs., Salem-Roanoke County C. of C., Rotary Internat. (bd. dirs. Salem 1985-89, pres. 1987-88), South Ga. C. of C. (bd. dirs.), Baker County Collaborative (bd. dirs.), Albany C. of C., Rotary. Home: 2718 Somerset Dr Albany GA 31721-8100 Office: Joseph W Jones Ecol Rsch Ce RR 2 Box 2324 Newton GA 39870-9651 E-mail: wwalton@jonesctr.org.

WALTZ, JON RICHARD, lawyer, educator, author; b. Napoleon, Ohio, Oct. 11, 1929; s. Richard R. and Lenore (Tharp) W. BA with honors in Polit. Sci, Coll. Wooster, 1951; JD, Yale U., 1954. Bar: Ohio 1954, Ill. 1965. Assoc. Squire, Sanders & Dempsey, Cleve., 1954-64; chief prosecutor City of Willowick (Ohio), 1958-64; assoc. prof. law Northwestern U. Sch. Law, Chgo., 1964-65, prof. law, 1965-98, Edna B. and Ednyfed H. Williams prof. law emeritus; instr. med. jurisprudence Northwestern Med. Sch., 1969-74. Book critic Washington Post, Chgo. Tribune, others; Disting. vis. prof. law Ill. Inst. Tech.-Chgo.-Kent Coll. Law, 1974; lectr. Author: The Federal Rules of Evidence—An Analysis, 1973, Criminal Evidence, 1975, Chinese lang. edits., 1994, 2000, Evidence: A Summary Analysis, 1976, Introduction to Criminal Evidence, 1991, Chinese lang. edit., 1993; co-author: The Trial of Jack Ruby, 1965, Cases and Materials on Evidence, 1968, Principles of Evidence and Proof, 1968, Medical Jurisprudence, 1971, Cases and Materials on Law and Medicine, 1980, Evidence: Making the Record, 1981, Criminal Prosecution in the People's Republic of China and the United States of America: A Comparative Study, 1995; note and comment editor Yale Law Jour., 1953-54; mem. editorial adv. bd. Harcourt Brace Law Group,. 1978—; contbr. numerous articles to profl. jours. Mem. Ill. adv. com. U.S. Commn. on Civil Rights, 1971-74; mem. Ill. Criminal Justice System Policy and Planning Com., 1973-74, Ill. Jud. Inquiry Bd., 1980-88; mem. com. med. edn. AMA, 1982-83; mem. Gov.'s Task Force on Med. Malpractice, 1985; Capt. AUS, 1955-58. Decorated Commendation medal; recipient Disting. Svc. award Soc. Midland Authors, 1972, Disting. Alumni award Coll. Wooster, 1987. Mem. Assn. Am. Law Schs., Order of Coif, Phi Alpha Delta, Pi Sigma Alpha. Presbyterian. Home: 4005 Lakeridge Dr Holland MI 49424-2263

WALZER, JUDITH BORODOVKO, academic administrator, educator; b. N.Y.C., May 27, 1935; d. Isidore and Ida (Gins) Borodovko; m. Michael L. Walzer, June 17, 1956; children— Sarah, Rebecca BA, Brandeis U., 1958, MA, 1960, PhD, 1967. Dir. office women's edn. Radcliffe Coll., Cambridge, Mass., 1974-77, assoc. dean., 1976-77; Allston Burr sr. tutor, asst. dean for co-edn. Harvard Coll., Cambridge, Mass., 1977-80; asst. to the pres. Princeton U., N.J., 1980-85; provost New Sch. U., N.Y.C., 1985-98, prof. lit., 1998—. Mem. adv. com. Overseas Sch., Hebrew U. in Jerusalem, 1989—. Democrat. Jewish. Office: New Sch U 65 W 11th St New York NY 10011 E-mail: walzer@newschool.edu.

WAN, FREDERIC YUI-MING, mathematician, educator; b. Shanghai, Jan. 7, 1936; arrived in U.S., 1947; s. Wai-Nam and Olga Pearl (Jung) W.; m. Julia Y.S. Chang, Sept. 10, 1960. SB, MIT, 1959, SM, 1963, PhD, 1965. Mem. staff MIT Lincoln Lab., Lexington, 1959-65; instr. math. MIT, Cambridge, 1965-67, asst. prof., 1967-69, assoc. prof., 1969-74; prof. math., dir. Inst. Applied Math. and Stats. U. B.C., Vancouver, 1974-83; prof. applied math. and math. U. Wash., Seattle, 1983-95, chmn. Dept. Applied Math., 1984-88, assoc. dean scis. coll. arts and scis., 1988-92; prof. math., prof. mech. and aero. engring. U. Calif., Irvine, 1995—, vice chancellor rsch., dean grad. studies, 1995-2000, faculty athletics rep., 2000—. Program dir. Divsn. Math. Sci. NSF, 1986-87, divsn. dir., 1993-94; cons. indsl. firms and govt. agys.; mem. MIT Ednl. Coun. for B.C. Area of Can., 1974-83. Assoc. editor Jour. Applied Mechancs, 1991-95, Can. Applied Math. Quar., Studies in Applied Math., Jour. Dyn. Discrete, Continuous and Impulsive Sys., 1994-97, Natural Resource Modeling 1985-88, Internat. Jour. Solids & Structures; contbr. articles to profl. jours. Sloan Found. award, 1973, Killam sr. fellow, 1979. Fellow AAAS, ASME, trustee, NSF Inst. Pure & Applied Mathematics, UCLA (chmn. 1999-2001, past chmn. 2001-03) fgn. mem. Russian Acad. Natural Scis., mem. Am. Acad. Mechanics (sec. fellows 1984-90, pres.-elect 1992-93, pres. 1993-94), Soc. Indsl. and Applied Math., Can. Applied Math. Soc. (coun. 1980-83, pres. 1983-85, Arthur Beaumont Disting. Svc. award 1991), Am. Math. Soc., Math. Assn. Am., Sigma Xi. Home: 22 Urey Ct Irvine CA 92612-4077 Office: U Calif Irvine Dept Math Rm 267 MST Bldg Irvine CA 92697-3175

WAND, PATRICIA ANN, librarian; b. Portland, Oreg., Mar. 28, 1942; d. Ignatius Bernard and Alice Ruth (Suhr) W.; m. Francis Dean Silvernail, Dec. 20, 1966 (div. Jan. 19, 1986); children: Marjorie Lynn Silvernail, Kirk Dean Silvernail. BA, Seattle U., 1963; MAT, Antioch Grad. Sch., 1967; AMLS, U. Mich., 1972. Vol. Peace Corps, Colombia, S.Am., 1963-65; secondary tchr. Langley Jr. High Sch., Washington, 1965-66; asst. libr. Wittenberg U. Libr., Springfield, Ohio, 1967-69; secondary tchr. Caro (Mich.) High Sch., 1969-70; assoc. libr. Coll. of S.I. (N.Y.) Libr., 1972-77; head, access svcs. Columbia U. Librs., N.Y.C., 1977-82; asst. univ. libr. U. Oreg., Eugene, 1982-89; univ. libr. The Am. U., Washington, 1989—. Cons. Bloomsburg (Pa.) U. Libr., 1990, Banco Ctrl., Ecuador, 1998, Am. U. Sharjah, UAE, 1999; bd. dirs. CAPCON, ERIC Clearinghouse on Higher Edn. Adminstrn. Contbr. articles to profl. jours. Pres. West Cascade Returned Peace Corps Vols., Eugene, 1985-88; v.p. Friends of Colombia, Washington, 1990—; speaker on Peace Corps, 1965—, libr. and info. svcs., 1979—. Honors Program scholarship Seattle U., 1960-62, Peace Corps scholarship Antioch U., 1965-66; recipient Beyond War award, 1987, Fulbright Sr. Lectr. award Fulbright, 1989, Disting. Alumnus award Sch. of Info. and Libr. Studies, U. Mich., 1992. Mem. ALA (chmn. com. on legislation 1997-98), Assn. Coll. and Rsch. Librs. (chair budget and fin. bd. dirs. 1987-89, chair WHCLIS task force 1989-92, chair govt. rels. com. 1993-94, chair internat. rels. com. 1996-98), On-line Computer Librs. Ctr. (adv. com. on coll. and univ. librs. 1991-96), D.C. Libr. Assn. (bd. dirs. 1993-98, pres. 1996-97). Home: 4854 Bayard Blvd Bethesda MD 20816-1785 Office: Am Univ Libr 4400 Massachusetts Ave NW Washington DC 20016-8046

WANG, JAMES CHUO, biochemistry and molecular biology educator; b. Kiangsu, China, Nov. 18, 1936; came to U.S., 1960; s. Chin and H.-L. (Shih) W.; m. Sophia Shu-lan Hwang, Dec. 23, 1961; children: Janice S., Jessica A. BS, Nat. Taiwan U., 1959; MA, U. S.D., 1961; PhD, U. Mo. Coll. Arts and Sci., 1964. Asst. instr. Nat. Taiwan U., Taipei, 1959-60; rsch. fellow in chemistry Calif. Inst. Tech., Pasadena, 1964-66; asst. prof. chemistry U. Calif. at Berkeley, 1966-69, assoc. prof., 1969-74, prof., 1974-77; prof. biochemistry and molecular biology Harvard U., Cambridge, Mass., 1977-88, Mallinckrodt prof. biochemistry and molecular biology, 1988—; Chiron lectr. U. Calif., Berkeley, 1994. Chancellor's Disting. lectr. U. Calif., Berkeley, 1984; mem. molecular biology study sect. NIH, 1988-91, chair, 1990-91; disting. faculty lectr. U. Tex., M.D. Anderson Cancer Ctr., 1989. Mem. editl. bd. Quar. Rev. Biophysics, 1988-94. Guggenheim fellow Guggenheim Found., 1986-87; recipient Disting. Alumnus award U. Mo. Coll. Arts and Scis., 1991. Fellow Am. Acad. Arts and Scis.; mem. NAS (molecular biology award 1983), Third World Acad. Scis., Academia Sinica (Taipei). Office: Harvard University Dept Molecular/Cellular Biology 7 Divinity Ave Cambridge MA 02138-2019

WANG, JENNIE, literature educator; b. Shanghai, Mar. 19, 1952; came to U.S., 1979; BA in English and Am. Lit., San Francisco State U., 1983; MA in English and Am. Lit., Stanford U., 1984; PhD in English and Am. Lit., SUNY, Buffalo, 1992. Instr. Shanghai Jiao-Tong U., 1977-79; preceptor Expository Writing Program, Harvard U., Cambridge, Mass., 1992-93; asst. prof. English, 1993—97; assoc. prof. English U. No. Iowa, Cedar Falls, 1998—. Vis. scholar dept. English, U. Calif., Berkeley, 2000-01, 2003-. Author: Novelistic Love in the Platonic Tradition: Fielding, Faulkner and the Postmodernists, 1997, ; Chinese translator: Smiles on Washington Square: A Love Story of Sorts (Raymond Federman), 1999; contbr. articles on postmodern fiction, Joyce, Faulkner, Kingston and others to profl. jours. Office: U No Iowa Dept English Cedar Falls IA 50614-0502 Home: 355 Parkview Terr E 2 Vallejo CA 94589

WANG, LEON RU-LIANG, civil engineer, educator; b. Canton, China, June 15, 1932; came to US, 1959; s. Huai-Kao and Yuen-Chin (Ho) W.; m. Joyce Chieh-Chun Tien, July 22, 1961; children: Frank Yu-Heng, Mark Yu-Da, Cindy Chi-Wen. BSC.E., Cheng-Kung U., Tainan, Republic of China, 1957; MSC.E., U. Ill., 1961; ScD, MIT, 1965. Asst. prof. civil engring. Rensselaer Poly. Inst., Troy, NY, 1965-69, assoc. prof. civil engring., 1969-80; prof. civil engring. U. Okla., Norman, 1980-84, Old Dominion U., Norfolk, Va., 1984-95, chair civil engring. dept., 1984-90, prof. emeritus civil engring. dept., 1995—. Adj. prof. civil and structural engring. dept. Hong Kong U. Sci. and Tech., 1993-95; tech. cons. Watervliet (NY) Arsenal, 1966-80. Editor: Rsch. for Multiple Hazard Mitigations, 1983, Seismic Evaluation of Lifeline Systems-Case Studies, 1986. Founding mem. Chinese Cmty. Ctr., Albany, 1973. Recipient rsch. awards NSF, 1976—. Fellow ASCE (br. pres. 1987-88), Hong Kong Inst. of Engr.; mem. Earthquake Engr. Rsch. Inst., Am. Soc. Engring. Edn., Chinese-Am. Assn. Nat. Hazard Mitigation Rsch. (founding mem.).

WANG, LIHONG, biomedical engineering educator; b. Guangshui, Hubei, China, Mar. 8, 1964; came to U.S., 1988; s. Jiajun Wang and Huiqing Xiao; m. Liqiong Zheng, July 1, 1988; children, Victor Young, Julia. BS in Optical Engring., Huazhong U. Sci. and Tech., Wuhan, Hubei, China, 1984, MS in Optical Engring., 1987; PhD in Elec. Engring., Rice U., 1992. Tchr. Huazhong U. Nat. Lab. Laser Tech., 1987-88; MD Anderson Cancer Ctr.; rschr. U. Tex., Houston, 1991-93, asst. prof. biomed. engring., 1993-96, adj. asst. prof. biomed. engring., 1996—99; asst. prof. biomed. engring. Tex. A&M U., College Station, 1996—, assoc. prof., 1999—2002, prof., 2002—. Assoc. editor: Annals of Biomed. Engring., Jour. Biomed. Optics, and Applied Optics; contbr. articles to profl. jours. Recipient FIRST award NIH, 1995-2000, Outstanding Young Scientist award Johnson and Johnson Inc., 1996, Career award NSF, 1998—. Fellow Am. Inst. Med. Biol. Engring.; mem. AAAS, IEEE, Am. Phys. Soc., Optical Soc. Am., Soc. Photo-Optical Instrumentation Engrr. Achievements include patent for oblique-incidence reflectometry for measuring optical properties of turbid media; co-invention of ultrasound-modulated optical tomography and sonoluminescent tomography. Office: Tex A&M Univ College Station TX 77843-3120

WANG, PAUL WEILY, materials science and physics educator; b. Kao-Hsiung, Taiwan, Republic of China, Nov. 4, 1951; came to U.S., 1979; s. Yao Wen Wang and Yue Hua Lo; m. Diana Chung-Chung Chow, June 9, 1979; children: Agnes J., Carol H., Alfred Z. PhD, SUNY, Albany, 1986. Rsch. asst. prof. Vanderbilt U., Nashville, 1986-90; asst. prof. U. Tex., El Paso, 1990-96, assoc. prof., 1996—. Hon. prof. Dalian Inst. Light Industry, 1995—; cons. EOTec Inc., 1987-88, Midtex Comm. Instruments Inc., 1996—. Contbr. articles to Jour. Applied Physics, Nuclear Instru. and Math., Springer Series in Surface Scis., Applied Surface Sci., Applied Optics, Jour. of Am. Ceramic Soc., Jour. Materials Sci., Jour. Luminescence, Jour. Non-cyrs. Solids, Lasers, Surface and Interface Analysis, Thin Solid Films, Jour. Materials Chemistry and Physics. Fellow Inst. for Study of Defects in Solids; mem. Am. Ceramic Soc., Am. Phys. Soc., Materials Rsch. Soc., Am. Vacuum Soc. Achievements include iron in silicon gettered by thermally grown silicon dioxide thin film, dopants effects on the structure of fluoride glasses, surface modification of heavy metal doped glasses under x-ray and electron irradiations, luminescence centers in silica stimulated by particle bombardments, defects introducted by gamma-ray radiation enhance the luminescence in silica, development of defects creation mechanism in silica by 5 and 50 eV photons, investigation of silver diffuses and precipitates thermally on the surface in ion exchange sodium calcium silicate glass, investigate the radiation effects on lead silicate glasses, electron beam processing on trimethylsilane covered Si(100) surface, aluminum nitride/aluminum oxide composite films grown by plasma, conduct and manage numerous research projects in materials research. Office: U Tex Dept Physics And Materials R El Paso TX 79968-0001 Home: 1718 W Teton Dr Peoria IL 61614-2638

WANG, PING, biomedical investigator; b. Qingzhou, China, Feb. 5, 1959; arrived in U.S., 1987, naturalized, 1998; s. Tangbang Wang and Xiuzheng Quan; m. Mian Zhou, May 14, 1986; children: Stephanie M., Christie M. MD, Changwei Med. Coll., Weifong, China, 1982; MS, 3d Med. U., Chongqing, China, 1985; MA, Brown U., 1998. Rsch. assoc. U. Wash., Seattle, 1987-88, Mich. State U., East Lansing, 1988-92, asst. prof. surgery, 1992-96, Brown U. Sch. Medicine, Providence, 1996-97, assoc. prof. surgery, 1997-2000; prof. depts. surgery, pathology, physiology and biophysics U. Ala. Sch. Medicine, Birmingham, 2000—02, assoc. dir. Ctr. for Surg. Rsch., 2000—02, sr. scientist Ctr. for Metabolic Bone Disease, 2001—02, sr. scientist Clin. Nutrition Rsch. Ctr., 2001—02; chief divsn. surg. rsch. North Shore-Long Island Jewish Med. Ctr., Manhasset, NY, 2002—; investigator Ctr. for Immunology and Inflammation North Shore-Long Island Jewish Rsch. Inst., Manhasset, 2002—; prof. dept. surgery NYU Sch. Medicine, 2002—. Recipient NIH individual rsch. project awards, 1998—, ind. scientist award NIH, 1996-2001, 1st ind. rsch. support and transition award NIH, 1995-2001, grant-in-Aid award Am. Heart Assn., Dallas, 1994-98. Mem. AAAS, Am. Physiol. Soc., Shock Soc., Surg. Infection Soc., Assn. for Acad. Surgery, Soc. Critical Care Medicine, Am. Heart Assn. (cardiopulmonary and critical care coun.), N.Y. Acad. Scis. Office: North Shore-LI Jewish Rsch Inst Dept of Surg 350 Community Dr Rm 448 Manhasset NY 11030 E-mail: pwang@nshs.edu.

WANG, SHIEN TSUN, civil engineering educator; BS in Civil. Engring., Nat. Taiwan U., 1960; MS, Mich. State U., 1964; PhD, Cornell U., 1969. Teaching asst. Nat. Taiwan U., Taipei, 1961-62; rsch. asst. Mich. State U., East Lansing, 1962-64, Cornell U., Ithaca, N.Y., 1964-68, instr., rsch. assoc., 1968-69; asst. prof. civil engring. U. Ky., Lexington, 1969-75, assoc. prof., 1975-83, prof., 1983—, dir. grad. studies, 1980—84, 1988—99. Cons. to various orgns. Mem. editorial bd. Internat. Jour. Thin-Walled Structires; conbt. more than 60 articles to profl. jours. Recipient Outstanding Achievement in Engring. Edn. award Lincoln Welding Found., Cleve., 1985; named Outstanding Civil Engring. Prof., U. Ky., 1985. Mem. ASCE (chmn. and mem. tech. coms. and subcoms.), Am. Soc. Engring. Edn., Am. Acad. Mechanics, Internat. Structural Stability Rsch. Coun., Cornell Soc. Engrs., Sigma Xi, Tau Beta Pi, Chi Epsilon. Republican. Avocations: fishing, sports (basketball, tennis, soccer), travel. Office: U Ky Dept Civil Engring 373 Oliver Raymond Bldg Lexington KY 40506-0001

WANG, X. T. (XIAOTIAN WANG), psychologist, educator; b. Beijing, Oct. 10, 1957; arrived in U.S., 1987; s. Zhong Wang, Nancy Zilin Tian; m. Ying Shi, May 19, 1957; 1 child, Geng. M in Patho-physiology, Jinan U., China, 1985; MA in Physiol. Psychology, Beijing Med. U., 1991; PhD, N.Mex. State U., 1993. Lectr. Jinan U. Med. Sch., Guangzhou, China, 1986—87; grad. ass. N.Mex. State U., 1987—93; asst. prof. U. SD, Vermillion, 1993—98, assoc. prof., 1998—2003, prof., 2003—. Vis. scientist Max Planck Inst., Berlin, 1998—99; vis. prof. Hong Kong U. Sci. and Tech. Sch. Bus. and Mgmt., Hong Kong, 2000—01. Mem. editl. bd.: Jour. Behavioral Decision Making, 2002—, guest editor: Jour. Bioeconomics, 2001—02; contbr. chapters to books, articles to profl. jours. Grantee, NSF, 1999—2003, James McDonnell Found., 2000; scholar Nat. Grad. scholar, Dept. Edn. China, 1982. Mem.: Human Behavior and Evolution Soc. (Young Investigator award 1992), Soc. for Judgement and Decision Making, Psychonomic Soc., Acad. Mgmt., Behavioral and Brain Scis. (assoc.). Home: 849 Valley View Dr Vermillion SD 57069 Office: Univ SD 414 East Clark St Vermillion SD 57069 Home Fax: 605-677-6604; Office Fax: 605-677-6604. Personal E-mail: xtwang@usd.edu. Business E-Mail: xtwang@usd.edu.

WANK, GERALD SIDNEY, periodontist, educator; b. Bklyn., Jan. 20, 1925; s. Joseph and Sadie (Ikowitz) W.; m. Gloria Baum, June 4, 1949; children: David, Stephen, Daniel. BA, NYU, 1945, DDS, 1949; cert. in orthodontia, Columbia U., 1951, cert. in periodontia, 1956. Intern Bellevue Hosp., 1949-50; pvt. practice N.Y.C., Great Neck, N.Y., 1949—; instr. dept. periodontia, oral medicine NYU Dental Sch., 1956-63, asst. clin. prof. dept. periodontia, 1963-67, asst. prof. periodontia, oral medicine, former postgrad. dir. periodontal-prosthesis dept. fixed partial prosthesis, 1970—, clin. assoc. prof. periodontia and oral medicine, 1970-77, clin. prof., 1977—, postgrad. dir. periodontia, 1968-71, Disting. prof. periodontics, 2002; lectr. periodontology Harvard U. Sch. Dental Medicine, 1971—74; vis. lectr. N.Y.C. C.C. Sch. Dental Hygiene, 1960-65, Albert Einstein Coll. Medicine, 1967-96; sr. asst. attending staff North Shore U. Hosp., 1974-77, sr. asst. attending divsn. surgery, 1977—. Cons. orthodontic panel N.Y. State, N.Y.C. depts. health, 1953-80; cons. periodontal prosthesis, Goldwater Meml. Hosp., N.Y.C.; former postgrad. instr. 1st Dist. Dental Soc. Postgrad. Sch., dist. claims com.; lectr. in field; mem. com. admissions N.Y. U. Coll. Dentistry, 1975-86, chmn. fund raising, 1976-77; cons. N.Y. VA Hosp., 1996—. Contbr. to: Practice of Periodontia, 1960, Dental Clinics of North America, 1972, 81, Manual of Clinical Periodontics, 1973; contbr. articles to profl. jours. Capt. USAF, 1953-55. Recipient Alumni Meritorious Service award NYU, 1981, Coll. Dentistry Alumni Achievement award NYU, 1983, Disting. Prof. Periodontics award NYU Coll. Dentistry, 2002. Fellow Acad. Gen. Dentistry, N.Y. Acad. Dentistry (life), Internat. Coll. Dentists (life), Am. Coll. Dentistry (life), Am. Acad. Oral Medicine (pres. N.Y. sect. 1971-72), Am. Pub. Health Assn.; mem. N.Y. Coll. Dentists (dir.), ADA, Dental Soc. N.Y.C. (dir. 1st dist., chmn. ethics com. 1985-86), Fedn. Dentaire Internat., Am. Assn. Dental Schs., N.Y. State Pub. Health Assn., AAUP, Pan Am. Med. Assn. (life), AAAS, ADA, Am. Acad. Periodontology, Sci. Rsch. Soc. Am., Northeastern Soc. Periodontia (life), Am. Acad. Dental Medicine, Acad. Gen. Dentistry, Internat. Acad. Orthodontia, Am. Assn. Endodontists (life), Am. Acad. Periodontia (life), Am. Acad. Oral Medicine (life), NYU Coll. Dentistry Alumni Assn. (dir., sec. 1973-74, v.p. 1974-75, pres. 1976-77), Am. Assn. Endodontists, NYU Coll. Dentistry Dental Assocs. (charter), Acad. Oral Rehab. (hon.), First Dist. Dental Soc. (program chmn. 1984, chmn. continuing edn. 1983, sec., 1985, v.p. Eastern Dental Soc. br. 1986, pres.-elect 1987, pres. br. 1988, bd. dirs. 1989—, Meritorious Svc. award 1997), Am. Acad. Osseointegration (life), NYU Gallatin Assocs., Alumni Fedn. NYU (dir. 1976-81), N.Y. County Dental Soc. (Dist. Claims Com.), Soc. of the Torch, Masons, Century Club, NYU Club, Fresh Meadow Country Club, Omicron Kappa Upsilon (life), Alpha Omega. Jewish. Home and Office: 40 Bayview Ave Great Neck NY 11021-2819 Office: 30 E 40th St New York NY 10016-1201

WANKAT, PHILLIP CHARLES, chemical engineering educator; b. Oak Park, Ill., July 11, 1944; s. Charles and Grace Leona (Pryor) W.; m. Dorothy Nel Richardson, Dec. 13, 1980; children: Charles, Jennifer. BS in Chem. Engring., Purdue U., 1966, MS in Edn., 1982; PhD, Princeton U., 1970. From asst. prof. to C.L. Lovell disting. prof. chem. engring Purdue U., West Lafayette, Ind., 1970—, head freshman engring., 1987-95, interim dir.

continuing engring. edn., 1996, head interdisciplinary engring., 2000—. Cons. pharm. firm, 1985-94. Author: Large Scale Ads and Chromatog, 1986, Equil Staged Separations, 1988, Rate Controlled Separations, 1990, Teaching Engineering, 1993, The Effective, Efficient Professor, 2002; patentee in field. With AUS, 1962-64. Recipient award in Separations Sci. and Tech., Am. Chem. Soc., 1994. Mem. AIChE, Am. Soc. Engring. Edn. (Union Carbide Lectr. award 1997), Am. Chem. Soc. Avocations: fishing, canoeing, camping. Office: Purdue U Dept Interdisciplinary Engring West Lafayette IN 47907-1292 E-mail: wankat@ecn.purdue.edu.

WANNAMAKER, MARY RUTH, music educator; b. Ft. Collins, Colo., July 29, 1922; d. Jerry Albert and Daisy B. (Burington) Lyman; m. William H. Anderson, June 14, 1944 (dec. 1944); m. John S. Wannamaker, Sept. 7, 1946; children: Lois Wannamaker, Daisy Wannamaker Van Valkenburg. MusB, Colo. State U., 1944; M in Musicology, U. Minn., 1949, M in Ednl. Psychology, 1969. Piano tchr. U. Minn., Mpls., 1945-46; piano tchr. Drake U., Des Moines, 1945-47; prof. piano Kletzing Coll., University Park, Iowa, 1948-49; ednl. cons. Des Moines, 1975-85. Pvt. piano tchr. Des Moines, 1950—. Composer Easter ch. svc., 1965. Vol. Iowa State Hist. Libr., Des Moines, 1990—; pres. Delta Omicron Alumnae, Des Moines, 1946-50, Profl. Women's League, Des Moines, 1974-75, Iowa Pers. & Guidance Assn., Des Moines, 1978-79; violist Des Moines Symphony Orch., 1946-65; mem. Altrusa, 1970-75. Mem. Music Techs. Nat. Assn., PEO, Phi Kappa Phi (scholarship 1944). Avocations: reading, travel, concerts. Home: 200 Buffalo Hills Ln E # 107 Brainerd MN 56401-4555

WAN-TATAH, VICTOR FON, theology educator; b. Kumbo, Bui, Cameroon, Nov. 28, 1949; came to U.S., 1977; s. Samuel and Miriam (Ngaibe) Tatah; m. Margaret Kernyui Wirsiy, Sept. 15, 1973; children: Nathan, Wuyuni, Simuben. MTS, Harvard U., 1979, ThD, 1984. Assoc. prof. Youngstown (Ohio) State U., 1987-92, 1992—. Founder, coord. Concerned Citizens for Safer Youngstown, 1991. Mem. Phi Kappa Phi. Presbyterian. Avocations: jogging, table tennis, gardening. Office: Youngstown State U Dept Philosophy 410 Wick Ave Dept Youngstown OH 44555-0002

WAPNER, MYRNA, retired principal; b. Bklyn., Sept. 17, 1936; d. Nathan and Sylvia (Bromstein) Honig; divorced. BA, Bklyn. Coll., 1958, MA, 1962; postgrad., NYU, 1980. Tchr. Pub. Sch. 7, Bklyn., 1958-66, Pub. Sch. 58, Bklyn., 1966-67; asst. prin. Pub. Sch. 272, Bklyn., 1967-71, Pub. Sch. 233, Bklyn., 1971-84; prin. Pub. Sch. 135, Bklyn., 1984-98; ret. N.Y.C. Bd. Edn., 1998. Adj. lectr. Baruch Coll. Sch. Pub. Affairs, 1997—, Touro Coll., 2000—. Recipient Reliance award for excellence in edn. Elem. Sch. Prin. of Yr., Borough of Bklyn., 1991, Nat. Recognition award for outstanding sch. chpt. I math. program, 1993; named Outstanding Prin. N.Y.C., 1991. Mem. ASCD, Am. Fedn. Suprs., N.Y.C. Adminstrv. Women in Edn., N.Y. City Prin.'s Assn., Coun. Supr. Assns. (mem. dist. coun. CSA sec., mem. exec. bd. 1971-95). Avocations: reading, sewing, painting, theatre, opera. Home: 142 Amherst St Brooklyn NY 11235-4115

WARBERG, WILLETTA, concert pianist, writer, piano educator; b. Twin Falls, Idaho, June 2, 1932; d. George William Warberg and Ethel Margaret (Sargent) Warberg-Chandler; m. David Jacob Bar-Illan, Sept. 3, 1954 (div.); children: Daniela, Jeremy Oscar. Student, Colo. Women's Coll., 1950-51, Aspen Music Camp, 1951; studied with, Rudolph Firkusny, 1951-53; BS, Mannes Coll. Music, N.Y.C., 1954. Assoc. food editor Look mag., N.Y.C., 1956-61; food editor Status mag., N.Y.C., 1961-62, Ladie's Home Jour., N.Y.C., 1964-66; photog. stylist Gourmet mag., N.Y.C., 1961-64, freelance writer, photog. stylist, 1965-75; pres., owner Willettta Enterprises, advt. agy., Twin Falls, 1976-84; food columinst, music and arts critic Times News, 1978-87; duo-piano ptnr. with Robert Starer, N.Y.C., Woodstock, 1991—2000; pvt. piano tchr., Saugerties, N.Y., 1991—. Made feasibility study of restaurant situation in Israel, U.S. Dept. State ICA Point 4 Program, Washington and Israel, 1960; artist-in-residence Holy Cross Concert Series, Kingston, N.Y., 1994—. Concert pianist, Idaho, Oreg., Utah, Wash., Colo., N.Y.C., N.Y. State, 1940—; author: Cooking from Scratch, 1976, Space Age Cookery, 1977; syndicated food columnist Willetta Says, 1978-87; contbr. food and sci. articles to Cosmopolitan, Modern Maturity, Esquire, Sun Valley, Sci. Diegest, also other mags. Bd. dirs. N.W. Opera Assn., 1984-87; pres. bd. dirs. Woodstock Lyric Theatre, 1994—; v.p. bd. dirs. Woodstock Chamber Orch., 1993—; chmn. Friends of the Maverick Concerts Inc., Woodstock, N.Y., 1999—. Winner Rocky Mountain talent search contest Salt Lake Tribune and Salt Lake Telegram, 1949. Mem. Nat. Fedn. Music Clubs, Music Tchrs. Nat. Assn. (cert.), Kingston Music Soc.. Avocations: designing and sewing clothes, painting still lifes, swimming, developing recipes, writing science fiction book.

WARBURTON, RALPH JOSEPH, architectural engineer, educator; b. Kansas City, Mo., Sept. 5, 1935; s. Ralph Gray and Emma Frieda (Niemann) W.; m. Carol Ruth Hychka, June 14, 1958; children: John Geoffrey, Joy Frances W. Tracey. BArch, MIT, 1958; MArch, Yale U., 1959, M.C.P., 1960. Registered architect, Colo., Conn., Fla., Ill., La., Md., NJ, NY, Va., DC; registered profl. engr., Conn., Fla., NJ, NY; registered cmty. planner, Mich., NJ; lic. interior designer, Fla. With various archtl. planning and engring. firms, Kans. City, Mo., 1952-55, Boston, 1956-58, NYC, 1959-62, Chgo., 1962-64; chief planning Skidmore, Owings & Merrill, Chgo., 1964-66; spl. asst. for urban design HUD, Washington, 1966-72, cons., 1972-77; prof. architecture, archtl. engring. and planning U. Miami, Coral Gables, Fla., 1972-2000, chmn. dept. architecture, archtl. engring. and planning, 1972-75, assoc. dean engring. and environ. design, 1973-74, dir. grad. urban and regional planning program, 1973-75, 81, 87-93, prof. emeritus, 2000—. Advisor govt. Iran, 1970, govt. France, 1973, govt. Ecuador, 1974, govt. Saudi Arabia, 1985; cons. in field, 1972—, lectr., critic design juror in field, 1965—; mem./chmn. Coral Gables Bd. Archs., 1980-82. Assoc. author: Man-Made America: Chaos or Control, 1963; editor: New Concepts in Urban Transportation, 1968, Housing Systems Proposals for Operation Breakthrough, 1970, Focus on Furniture, 1971, National Community Art Competition, 1971, Defining Critical Environmental Areas, 1974; contbg. editor: Progressive Architecture, 1974-84; editl. adv. bd.: Jour. Am. Planning Assn., 1983-88, Planning for Higher Edn., 1986-94, Urban Design and Preservation Quar., 1987-94; contbr. over 130 articles to profl. jour.; mem. adv. panel Industrialization Forum Quar., 1969-79, archtl. portfolio jury Am. Sch. and Univ., 1993. Mem. Met. Housing and Planning Coun., Chgo., 1965-67; mem. exec. com. Yale U. Arts Assn., 1965-70; pres. Yale U. Planning Alumni Assn., 1983-89—; mem. ednl. adv. com. Fla. Bd. Architecture, 1975; mem. grievance com. The Fla. Bar, 1996-99; mem code commn.'s Nat. Fire Protection Assn., 1998-. Recipient W.E. Parsons medal Yale U., 1960; recipient Spl. Achievement award HUD, 1972, commendation Fla. Bd. Architecture, 1974, Fla. Trust Historic Preservation award, 1983, Group Achievement award NASA, 1976; Skidmore, Owings & Merrill traveling fellow MIT, 1958; vis. fellow Inst. Architecture and Urban Studies, NYC, 1972-74; NSF grantee, 1980-82. Fellow AIA (nat. housing com. 1968-72, nat. regional devel. and natural resources com. 1974-75, nat. sys. devel. com. 1972-73, nat. urban design com. 1968-73, bd. dirs. Fla. S. chpt. 1974-75, Edn. Leadership award Miami chpt. 2000, Test of Time Design award Fla. Assn. 2002), ASCE, Fla. Engring. Soc. (bd. dir. 1984-85, Miami chpt. bd. dir. 1982-83, 84-85), Nat. Acad. Forensic Engrs. NSPE; mem. Am. Inst. Cert. Planners (exec. com. dept. environ. planning 1973-74), Am. Soc. Engring. Edn. (chmn. archtl. engring. divsn. 1975-76), Dade Heritage Trust (Cmty. Svc. award 2002), Nat. Sculpture Soc. (allied profl.), Nat. Soc. Arch. Engrs. (founding), Nat. Trust Hist. Preservation (principles and guidelines com. 1967), Am. Soc. Landscape Architects (hon., chmn. design awards jury 1971, 72), Am. Planning Assn. (Fla. chpt. award excellence 1983), Am. Soc. Interior Designers (hon.), Omicron Delta Kappa, Sigma Xi, Tau Beta Pi. Home: 6600 SW 54th Ln South Miami FL 33155-6413 Office: 420 S Dixie Hwy Coral Gables FL 33146-2222 E-mail: ProfRJWarc@aol.com.

WARCH, RICHARD, academic administrator; b. Hackensack, N.J., Aug. 4, 1939; s. George William and Helen Anna (Hansen) W.; m. Margot Lynn Moses, Sept. 8, 1962; children: Stephen Knud, David Preston, Karin Joy. BA, Williams Coll., 1961; B.D., Yale Div. Sch., 1964; PhD, Yale U., 1969; postgrad., U. Edinburgh, 1962-63; H.H.D., Ripon Coll., 1980. Asst. prof. history and Am. studies Yale U., 1968-73, asso. prof., 1973-77; asso. dean Yale Coll.; dir. summer plans Yale U., 1976-77; asso. dir. Nat. Humanities Inst., New Haven, 1975-76; v.p. acad. affairs Lawrence U., Appleton, Wis., 1977-79, pres., 1979—. Cons. Nat. Humanities Faculty; ordained to ministry United Presbyn. Ch. in U.S.A., 1968; dir. Bank One of Appleton. Author: School of the Prophets, Yale College, 1701-1740, 1973; editor: John Brown, 1973. Rockefeller Bros. Theol. fellow, 1961-62 Mem. Am. Studies Assn., Soc. for Values in Higher Edn., Winnebago Presbytery. Clubs: Rotary. Home: 229 North Park Ave Appleton WI 54911 Office: Lawrence U PO Box 599 Appleton WI 54912-0599

WARD, ADRIENNE BAPTISTE BROWN, elementary school educator, writer; b. Yonkers, N.Y., Jan. 31, 1940; d. James Richard and Beatrice Elizabeth (Berbert) Baptiste; m. Ronald Michael Brown, Dec. 2, 1962 (dec. May 1989); m. Peter L. Ward, July 2, 1996. BA, CUNY, 1962; MEd, Mass. State Coll., 1964; postgrad., Plymouth (N.H.) State Coll., 1965—. Draftsman Planning Svcs. Group, Cambridge, Mass., 1962-65; tchr. 4th grade Dearborn Sch., Roxbury, Mass., 1965-66, Canaan (N.H.) Elem. Sch., 1966-67; tchr. 6th grade Thetford (Vt.) Elem. Sch., 1967-70; tchr. 4th grade Claremont (N.H.) Sch. Dist., 1971-80; tchr. sci. Orford (N.H.) Mid. Sch., 1980-82; tech. software writer Wang Labs., Lowell, Mass., 1983-84, Computac, Inc., Hanover, N.H., 1984-89; tchr. 5th and 6th grades West Fairlee (Vt.) Sch., 1989—93. Drug and alcohol counselor, coord. West Fairlee, 1989-92. Lobbyist Planned Parenthood Vt., West Lebanon, 1988-89. Mem. Geriatric Adventure Soc. (pres. 1990-91), Northern Vt. Canoe Cruisers, Appalachian Mountain Club, Mensa. Republican. Avocations: canoeing, cross country skiing, mountain climbing, backpacking, seismology. Home: PO Box 3184 Jackson WY 83001-3184

WARD, ALICE FAYE, elementary education educator; b. Swartz, La. BS, Grambling (La.) U., 1973; postgrad., N.E. U., 1976-79. Tchr. Robinson Elem. Sch., Monroe, 1971-73, Poinciana Elem. Sch., Boynton Beach, Fla., 1973-76, Melaleuca Elem. Sch., West Palm Beach, Fla., tchr., dir. after sch. program. Dir. Just Say No Club, 1994-95, K-Kid Club, 1994-95, After Sch. Program, 1994. Named Tchr. of Week Palm Beach Post Newspaper, 1994. Mem. NEA, CTA. Democrat. Baptist. Avocations: reading, bowling, traveling, dancing, helping under privileged children. Office: Melaleuca Elem Sch 5759 W Gun Club Rd West Palm Beach FL 33415-2505

WARD, CHARLES CECIL, educational administrator; b. Ft. Dix, N.J., Mar. 23, 1962; s. Charles Cecil and Shirley Kathleen (Fairchild) W.; m. Hsuying Chiou, June 20, 1994; 1 child, Jacob Lawrence. BA in Econs., U. Alaska, 1988; MEd in Ednl. Adminstrn., U. Tex. at Austin, 1992. Cert. tchr. (Type A), adminstr. (Type B), Alaska. Tchr. Lower Kuskokwim Sch. Dist., Nightmute, Alaska, 1988-91; area prin. Yukon Flats Sch. Dist., Fort Yukon, Alaska, 1992-93; site adminstr. S.W. Region Schs., Manokotak, Alaska, 1993—. Mem. ASCD, Nat. Rural Edn. Assn., Alaska Assn Secondary Sch. Prins., Kappa Delta Pi, Phi Delta Kappa, Phi Kappa Phi, Omicron Delta Epsilon. Home: PO Box 94 Manokotak AK 99628-0094 Office: Manokotak Sch PO Box 130 Manokotak AK 99628-0130

WARD, CLARE CLEERE, special education educator; b. Hastings, Nebr., Sept. 30, 1944; d. Samuel Richard and Mayme Lorene (Mitchell) Cleere; m. Joe F. Lassiter Jr., Junr 6, 1966 (div. July 1982); children: Christine Clare, Joe F. III; m. William G. Ward Jr., Sept. 21, 1986. BA, Huntingdon Coll., 1966; MEd in Spl. Edn., Auburn U., 1972, postgrad., 1986-87, 93—. Tchr. Am. history Berry H.S., Birmingham, Ala., 1966-68; substitute tchr. Ft. Benning (Ga.) Schs., 1968-69; tchr. socially maladjusted, learning disabilities Davis occupl. tng. unit Children's Ctr., Montgomery, Ala., 1969-73; staff mem. psychol. testing Greenville (S.C.) County Sch. Dist., 1973-74; co-developer learning disabled programs Greenville Pub. Schs., 1973-75; tchr. learning disabilities resource Dannelly Elem. Sch., Montgomery, 1986-93; adminstrv. asst. Camp Ikhananchi for Students with Learning Disabilities and Attention Deficit Disorders, Montgomery, 1987-90; asst. dir. Peggy Derminey's iep, Montgomery, 1987-92. Active Greenville County Crime Commn., 1977-81, chmn., 1980-81; bd. dirs. S.E. Ctr. for Attention Deficit Hyperactive Disorder/Learning Disabilities, 1997. Named Most Outstanding Tchr. Ala. Learning Disabilities Assn., 1988. Mem. Learning Disabiliites Assn., Children & Adults with Attention Deficit Disorder, Coun. Exceptional Children, Soroptomists. Home: 2404 College St Montgomery AL 36106-2123 Office: The Southeast Ctr 2167 Normandie Dr Montgomery AL 36111-2728 E-mail: sec2167@aol.com.

WARD, DAVID, academic administrator, educator; b. Manchester, Eng., July 8, 1938; arrived in U.S., 1960; s. Horace and Alice (Harwood) Ward; m. Judith B. Freifeld, June 11, 1964; children: Michael J.H., Peter F.B. BA, U. Leeds, Eng., 1959, MA, 1961; MS, U. Wis., 1961, PhD, 1963; LittD, U. Leeds, 1992. Lectr. Carleton U., Ottawa, 1963—64; asst. prof. Univ. B.C., Vancouver, 1964—66, U. Wis., Madison, 1966—67, assoc. prof., 1967—70, prof., 1970—, chmn. geography dept., 1974—77, assoc. dean Grad. Sch., 1980—88, provost and vice chancellor acad. affairs, Andrew Clark prof. geography, 1989—, chancellor, 1994—2000; pres. Am. Coun. on Edn., Washington, 2000—. Mem. exec. com. Argonne Nat. Lab., Ill., 1990—93; dir.-at-large Social Sci. Rsch. Coun., 1991—93; mem. Kellogg Commn. on Future of Land Grant Univs.; chair Internet 2, Consortium Advances Network Devel. Author: Cities and Immigrants, 1970, Geographic Perspectives on Americas Past, 1978, Poverty Ethnicity and the American City, 1989, Landscape of Modernity, 1992; contbr. articles to profl. jours. Fellow Guggenheim fellow, 1970, Einstein fellow, Hebrew U., 1980, Fulbright fellow, Australian Nat. U., 1979. Fellow: Am. Acad. Arts and Scis.; mem.: Assn. Am. Geographers (pres. 1989). Office: One Dupont Circle NW Washington DC 20036-1193 E-mail: president@ace.nche.edu.

WARD, FREDERICK CHAMPION, retired education educator; b. New Brunswick, N.J., Dec. 29, 1910; s. Clarence and Helen (Eshbaugh) W.; m. Rachel Duira Baldinger, June 13, 1936; children: Geoffrey, Andrew, Helen. BA, Oberlin (Ohio) Coll., 1932, MA, 1934; PhD, Yale U., 1937. From asst. prof. to assoc. prof. Denison U., Granville, Ohio, 1938-45, U. Chgo., 1945-58, assoc. dean coll., 1946-47, dean, 1947-54, William Rainey Harper prof. humanities, 1955-56; ednl. cons. Govt. India Ford Found., N.Y.C., 1954-58, dir. Mid. East and Africa, 1958-63, dep. v.p. internat. programs, 1963-66, v.p. edn. and rsch., 1966-71, sr. advisor edn. internat. divsn., 1971-76; ret. Mem. UNESCO's Internat. Commn. on Devel. Edn.; cons. World Bank and various founds. Editor: The Idea and Practice of General Education, Education and Development Reconsidered, 1974; contbr.: The Knowledge Most Worth Having, 1964, General Education in the Social Sciences, 1992, Humanistic Education and Western Civilisation, 1964. Mem., v.p. Greenwich (Conn.) Bd. Edn., 1974-82; trustee Oberlin Coll., 1970—; chmn. bd. dirs. Ctr. for Effective Philanthropy, Cambridge, Mass., 1986-87; chancellor New Sch. Social Rsch., N.Y.C.; chmn. White House Task Force on Edn. Gifted Persons, 1968. Democrat. Avocations: tennis, trail-blazing, volunteering, writing casuals. Home: 88 Notch Hill Rd Apt 336 North Branford CT 06471-1864

WARD, HARRY PFEFFER, physician, retired university chancellor; b. Pueblo, Colo., June 6, 1933; s. Lester L. and Alysmai (Pfeffer) W.; m. Betty Jo Stewart, Aug. 20, 1955; children— Stewart, Leslie, Elizabeth, Mary Alice, Amy. AB, Princeton U., 1955; MD, U. Colo., 1959; MS, U. Minn., 1963. Intern Bellevue Hosp., N.Y.C., 1959; resident Mayo Clinic, Rochester, Minn., 1960-63; practice medicine specializing in hematology; chief medicine Denver VA hosp., 1968-72; dean, asso. v.p. U. Colo. Sch. Medicine, 1972-78, prof. medicine, 1972; chancellor U. Ark. Med. Sci., Little Rock, 1979-2000, chancellor emeritus, 2000—. Clin. investigator VA, 1964-67 Chmn. Assn. Acad. Health Ctr., 1993-94. Mem. ACP, AMA, Am. Fedn. Clin. Research, Central Soc. Clin. Investigation, Am. Soc. Hematology, Internat. Soc. Hematology, Western Soc. Clin. Research. Home: 369 Valley Club Cir Little Rock AR 72212-2900 Office: U Ark Med Scis 4301 W Markham St Little Rock AR 72205-7101 E-mail: hpward1@msn.com.

WARD, IVA NELL BELL, special education educator; b. Grapeland, Tex., Aug. 29, 1949; d. Frenchie and Eunice (Smith) Bell; m. Edward K. Ward Jr., Sept. 1969 (div. 1972); children: Eric Kendrick, Edward Kelly III. BS, Tex. So. U., 1978; M in Edn. Mid-Mgmt., P.V. A&M U., 1998. Cert. tchr., Tex. Tchr. spl. edn. Houston Ind. Sch. Dist., 1978-85, reading specialist, program coord., 1990—. Mem. steering com. Mayor's Hearing on Children and Youth, 1990, steering com. for restructuring Houston Ind. Sch. Dist., 1991, shared decision making com. for Sch. Campus. Active City of Houston Task Force for Infant Mortality Rate, 1993; coord. 21st Century Cmty. Learning Ctr. Mem. NAACP, Nat. Women of Achievement (youth advisor, spelling bee coord., VI coord., Golden Apple award 1992), Assn. Tex. Profl. Tchrs., Houston Fedn. Tchrs. (svc. and recruitment com. 1985-86), Internat. Platform Assn., Houston Area Alliance of Black Sch. Educators, Africa Am. Reclaiming Our Cmty., Iota Phi Lambda (S.E. area coord., VIP). Home: 1700 Seaspray Ct Apt 2158 Houston TX 77008-3145

WARD, JAMES KENNETH, primary school educator; b. Lebanon, Ky., Apr. 30, 1959; s. James Charlie and Barbara Ellen (Hall) W. BA, Centre Coll., 1981; MRE, Cin. Bible, 1988; MEd, Xavier U., 1991. Tchr. The June Buchanan Sch., Pippa Passes, Ky., 1985-88, Lexington (Ky.) Christian Acad., 1988-89; tchr. U.S. history and reading Boyle County Bd. Edn., Middle Danville, Ky., 1990—. Mem. ASCD, Phi Delta Kappa, Lions Internat. Republican. Home: 1698 Mackville Rd Springfield KY 40069-9700

WARD, JAY ALAN, language professional, educator; b. Shelbyville, Ind., May 13, 1943; s. Ferald Leroy and Mary Alice (Dearinger) W.; m. Kathleen Anne Frosch, May 6, 1966. BA, Butler U., 1965; MA, Ind. Ctrl. U., 1970; PhD, Ball State U., 1977. Cert. secondary edn. educator, English, Ind. Tchr. English Warren Ctrl. H.S., Indpls., 1966-75; doctoral fellow Ball State U., Muncie, Ind., 1975-76, instr., 1976-78; asst., assoc. full prof. Thiel Coll., Greenville, Pa., 1978—. Act 101 adv. bd. Thiel Coll., Greenville, 1985—; cons. Nat. Collegiate Honors Coun., 1988—; Commonwealth spkr. Pa. Humanities Couns., 1996-98, 2002—. Author: The Critical Reputation of Byron's Don Juan in Britain, 1979; contbr. articles to Ind. English Jour., Resources in Edn. and other profl. jours. Mem. ACLU, Pa., 1980—; discussion leader Sharon (Pa.) Lifelong Learning Coun., 1992—; chair bd. dirs. Literacy Coun. of Mercer County, Inc., 2000—, Mercer Co. Family Svcs. Coord. Coun., 2002—. Recipient scholarship Lilly Endowment, 1961-65, Luth. Dept. Higher Edn. sabbatical grant, 1985, Thiel Coll. Prof. of Yr. award, 1999-2000. Mem. MLA, Coll. English Assn., Nat. Coun. Tchrs. English, Conf. on Coll. Composition and Comm., The Byron Soc., North Am. Soc. for Study of Romanticism, Am. Coun. on Romanticism, Nat. Collegiate Honors Coun., Mid-East Honors Assn. (past. pres. 1985—), Am. Forensic Assn., Nat. Forensic Assn. Avocations: European travel, attending plays and concerts, reading. Home: 305 Independence Ct Sharon PA 16146-3411 Office: Thiel Coll 75 College Ave Greenville PA 16125-2186 E-mail: jward@thiel.edu.

WARD, JO ALICE, computer consultant, educator; b. Ft. Worth, Aug. 14, 1939; d. Boyd Wheeler and Frances Elizabeth (Wheeler) Patton; m. John Oliver Ward, Mar. 19, 1960 (div. Feb. 1976); children: Russell Scott, Pamela Joan Ward Watson. BA in Math., North Tex. State U., 1961, MA in Math., 1965, postgrad., 1969-72. Instr. math. North Tex. State U., Denton, 1965-67, grad. asst., 1968-72; instr. math. Tarrant County Jr. Coll., Ft. Worth, 1967-68; math. tchr. Aldine Ind. Schs., Houston, 1973-76; math. instr. U. Houston Downtown, 1974-80; sys. analyst Conoco Inc, Houston, 1981-93; computer cons. Quality First Computer Svcs., Houston, 1994—. Vol. facilitator for family violence program Houston Area Women's Ctr., 1993-94; adminstrv. vol. Citizens for Animal Protection, 1993—; vol. Bering Comty. Svc. Found., 1995—, bd. trustees, 1997—. Recipient Outstanding Adminstrv. Vol. award Citizens for Animal Protection, 1995, Vol. of Yr. award Bering Cmty. Svcs. Found., 1997, Lay Cert. of Appreciation, Bering Meml. United Meth. Ch., 1998. Home and Office: 3333 Cummins St Apt 605 Houston TX 77027-5816

WARD, JOHN ROBERT, physician, educator; b. Salt Lake City, Nov. 23, 1923; s. John I. and Clara (Elzi) W.; m. Norma Harris, Nov. 5, 1948; children: John Harris, Pamela Lyn, Robert Scott, James Alan. BS, U. Utah, 1944, MD, 1946; MPH, U. Calif., Berkeley, 1967; Masters, Am. Coll. of Rheumatology, 1990. Diplomate Am. Bd. Internal Medicine. Intern Salt Lake County Gen. Hosp., 1947-48, asst. resident, 1949-50, resident physician internal medicine, 1950-51, asst. physician, 1957-58, assoc. physician, 1958-69; clin. fellow medicine Harvard U., Boston, 1955-57; instr. medicine U. Utah Med. Sch., Salt Lake City, 1954-58, asst. prof., 1958-63, assoc. prof., 1963, prof., 1966-93, chmn. dept. preventive medicine, 1966-70, emeritus prof. internal medicine, 1993—, chief div. rheumatology, 1957-88; prof. internal medicine emeritus U. Utah. Med. Sch., Salt Lake City, 1994—; attending physician internal medicine Salt Lake City VA Hosp., 1957-70. Nora Eccles Harrison prof. medicine U. Utah Sch. of Medcine, Salt Lake City. Served as capt. M.C. AUS, 1951-53. Master Am. Coll. Rheumatology; fellow ACP; mem. Am. Coll. Rheumatology (Disting. rheumatologist award 1994), Utah State Med. Assn. (hon. pres. 1994-95), U. Utah Sch. Medicine Alumni Assn. (Disting. Alumnus 1996). Home: 1249 E 3770 S Salt Lake City UT 84106-2446 Office: U Utah Health Scis Ctr 50 N Medical Dr Salt Lake City UT 84132-0001

WARD, JUDITH ANN KITCHENS, elementary education educator; b. Atlanta, Sept. 1, 1949; d. Leonard Oscar Jr. and Edna Viola (Kirkpatrick) Kitchens; m. Ronald Lee Ward, June 19, 1976 (div. Aug. 1990); children: Brandon Lee, Courtney Elyse. AS, Kennesaw (Ga.) State Coll., 1969; BS in Early Childhood Edn., West Ga. Coll., 1971, MEd, 1975, postgrad., 1992. Cert. tchr., Ga. Classroom tchr. 2d grade Mableton (Ga.) Elem. Sch., 1971-73; classroom tchr. Pod B (2d and 3d grades) Birney Elem. Sch., Marietta, Ga., 1973-74; grad. asst. West Ga. Coll., Carrollton, 1974-75; classroom tchr. 1st grade Temple (Ga.) Primary Sch., 1975-76; classroom tchr. 2d and 3d grades Mableton Elem. Sch., 1976-77, classroom tchr. 1st grade, 1977-78, Skyview Elem. Sch., Mableton, 1979-80; classroom tchr. 3rd grade Harmony-Leland Elem. Sch., Mableton, 1982-86, classroom tchr. kindergarten, 1986-87, classroom tchr. 3rd grade, 1987-90; learner support strategist Milford Elem. Sch., Marietta, Ga., 1990—. Presenter in field. Charter mem., sec. Austell-Mableton Community Action Team for Drug-Free Schs. and Communities, 1990—. Named Super Tchr., Turner Broadcasting System, Atlanta, 1989-90, Outstanding Educator, Ga. State Dept. Edn., Ga. Bus. Forum, 1991. Mem. NEA, Ga. Assn. Educators, Cobb County Assn. Educators, PTA (life mem., pres. Harmony-Leland Elem. 1989-90), Delta Kappa Gamma (sec. 1989-92, v.p. chpt. 1992—), Phi Delta Kappa, Alpha Delta Kappa. Avocations: community involvement, piano and music, sewing. Home: 520 Benson Hurst Dr Mableton GA 30126-1408 Office: Cobb County Bd Edn Pub Schs PO Box 1088 Marietta GA 30061-1088

WARD, KATHERINE MARIE, retired school system administrator; b. Raton, N.Mex., Oct. 31, 1936; d. Robert Lee and Lucille (Gasperetti) Davis; m. Leonard Carlin Ward, Aug. 30, 1953; children: Kathy Ann, Ronnie, Tonia, Jess. BS, Ea. N.Mex. U., 1972, MEd, 1977; edn. specialist, U. N.Mex., 1981. Data reduction tech. phys. sci. lab. N.Mex. State U., Las Cruces, 1955-61; 3d and 4th grade tchr. Clayton Pub. Schs., Amistad, N.Mex., 1972-74; 4th grade tchr. Grants/Cibola County (N.Mex.) Schs., 1974-76, Title I reading tchr., 1976-77, Title I coord., 1977-82, Chpt. I coord., 1982-89, coord. Chpt. I and drug free schs. and cmtys., 1989-90, coord. Chpt. I, drug free, DARE and Title II, 1990-92, coord. Chpt. I, Title I, drug free and Title II, 1992-96, fed. program coord., 1996-98; ret., 1999. Leader Girl Scouts U.S., Las Cruces, 1966-67, 4-H, Grants, 1977-80; mem., sec. Fighting Back Robert Wood Johnson Found. Prevent Drug and Alcohol Use Grants, 1991-96. Recipient Adminstrn. award N.Mex. Study and Rsch. Coun., 1986, Chpt. I Exemplary award U.S. Dept. Edn., 1988, Merit award DARE program Grants Police Dept., 1991. Mem. Internat. Reading Assn., Malpais Internat. Reading Assn. (pres. 1977-79, Literacy award 1979), N.Mex. Internat. Reading Assn. (Land of Enchantment Book award com. 1983-86). Avocations: grandchildren, travel, writing children's literature, recreational reading. Home: PO Box 11161 Albuquerque NM 87192-0161

WARD, LILLIAN HAZEL, music educator; b. Hastings, Colo., Sept. 19, 1920; d. Frank Joseph and Jane (Shields) Baker; m. Peter Joseph Ward, Sept. 12, 1942; children: Mary Jane Eickhoff, Michael George. Student, Western State Coll., 1938-42. Piano tchr., San Francisco, 1951-54, Los Altos, Calif., 1955—. Author: (composition for piano) Girl Scout Song Book, 1957. Leader brownies Girl Scouts USA, San Francisco, 1952-54, Los Altos, Calif., 1955-59; guardian coun. Jobs Daus., Los Altos, 1959-68; tchr., dir. United Meth. Ch., Los Altos, 1955-73. Mem. Nat. Music Tchrs. Assn., Calif. Assn. Profl. Music Tchrs. Avocations: gardening, reading, working with the blind, spending time with grandchildren, watercolor and oil painting. Home: 246 Alicia Way Los Altos CA 94022-2346

WARD, MARCIA BALMUT, secondary education educator; b. Springfield, Ohio, Aug. 5, 1946; d. Henry and Margery Louise (Zerkle) B.; m. Gregory Dow Ward, July 26, 1969; children: Katherine, Vincent, Anthony. BS in Edn., Wittenberg U., 1968; postgrad., U. Dayton, 1991—95, Wright State U., 1996; MA, Antioch U.; grad., Kushi Inst.in Macrobiotics. Tchr. Georgesville Sch. Emotionally Disturbed, Columbus, Ohio, 1968-69, Miami East Jr. High Sch., Conover, Ohio, 1969-74, Graham High Sch., St. Paris, Ohio, 1974-76; tchr. gifted edn. and gifted enrichment Graham Schs., St. Paris, 1980—84, substance abuse coord., coord. title one programs, 1990-99; tchr. human anatomy and physiology Graham H.S., St. Paris, 1999—; chair math. and sci. dept. Graham Schs., St. Paris, 1984—92. Nat. pres. Internat. Sch.-to-Sch. Experience, Urbana, Ohio, 1982—87, internat. bd., 1977—87; U.S. del. Children's Internat. Summer Village, Hexham, England, 1971; dir. Graham Digital Acad, Ohio; adv. Manatee Snorkel study Crystal Diving, Fla.; student in secondary edn. and complimentary nutrition IMA program at Antioch McGregor. Author: Do's and Dont's in CISV, 1982. Pres. St. Paris Antique Study Club, 1980; bd. dirs., grant and pub. rels. chair St. Paris Pub. Libr., 1992; chmn. Champaign County Heart Drive, Urbana, 1981; county chmn. Bicentennial Bell com.; tchr. jr. ch. 1st Christian Ch., Urbana, 1983-92; Sunday sch. tchr., jr. choir leader Westville United Meth.; chair St. Paris Pub. Libr. Levy Com. and Expansion Program, pres. Friends of St. Paris Pub. Libr.; advisor Champaign County Teen Age Sexuality and Pregnancy Prevention Advisor, Teens Opposed to Premarital Sex; del. World PRIDE Conv. and N.W. Tobacco Coalition, Nat. Sch. Bd. Conv., San Francisco; mem. bd. edn. Springfield Christian Sch. Grantee KTH Edn., 1981; Martha Holden Jennings Scholar, 1995—96, 1997—98, Cargill scholarship Mayo Clinic rsch. Mem. 4-H Clubs Am. (leader). Avocations: travel, nature study, gardening, cooking. Home: 156 Eris Rd Urbana OH 43078-8622 Office: Graham HS 7800 W Rte 36 Saint Paris OH 43072-9703

WARD, MARTHA GAIL JOINER, adult education educator; d. Wofford Johnston and Tommie Lee Joiner; m. James Edward Ward; 1 child, Jonathan Calder. Student, Brunswick (Ga.) Jr. Coll., 1971; BFA in Art Edn., Valdosta State Coll., 1974; MEd in Early Childhood Edn., Ga. So. Coll., 1985, postgrad., 1987. Reading instr. Madison County (Fla.) Sch. Bd., 1974-76; tchr. David Emanuel Acad., Stillmore, Ga., 1976-78, Candler County Bd. Edn., Metter, Ga., 1979-87; learning svcs. coord. The Job Network Ctr., Ga. So. U., Statesboro, 1987-90; adult edn. instr. Swainsboro Tech. Inst., 1990—. Reviewer series of math books: Math Matters for Adults, 1992. Recipient Most Innovative Program of the Yr. award State of Ga.'s Job Tng. Partnership Act 8% Grant, 1989. Mem. Ga. Adult Literacy Assn., Profl. Assn. Ga. Educators (state student group liaison, Candler County chpt. pres. 1986), Ga. Adult Edn. Assn., Inc., Kappa Delta Pi (chpt. pres. 1989-90), Delta Kappa Gamma Soc. Internat. (Beta Beta chpt.). Avocations: pottery, painting, camping, fishing, scuba diving. Home: RR 2 Box 110 Metter GA 30439-9548 Office: Swainsboro Tech Inst 346 Kite Rd Swainsboro GA 30401-5700

WARD, MARVIN TED, school system administrator; b. Lebanon, Ind., Feb. 4, 1950; s. Ted Frank and Reva Joan Ward; m. Hellen Louise Ward, Sept. 1, 1973; children: Brian, Erin, Andrew, Rachel. BA, U. Evansville, 1972, MA, 1974. Cert. tchr., Ind. Paraprofl. instr. physics U. Evansville, 1972-74; math. and computer tchr. Franklin (Ind.) Cmty. Schs., 1974-81, bus. mgr., 1981-85, Brownsburg (Ind.) Cmty. Schs., 1985—. Mem. Ind. Assn. Sch. Bus. Ofcls. (dir. 1984-87; chmn. rsch. com. bus. ops., profl. devel. com. registered profl., treas. 2000-01, v.p. 2001-02, pres.-elect 2002-03, pres. 2003—, named Official of Yr., 2003), Kiwanis (dir. 1988—), Greater Brownsburg C. of C. (dir., 1988-91, pres., 1991). Avocations: fishing, gardening, woodworking. Home: 8845 N County Rd 425 E Brownsburg IN 46112 Office: Brownsburg Cmty Sch Corp 444 E Tilden Dr Brownsburg IN 46112-1497

WARD, MELVIN A. nursing educator; b. Tonkawa, Okla., June 4, 1940; s. Franklin Daniel and Lottie Mae (Abel) W.; m. Sharon Lynn Ward, July 3, 1969; children: Alyssa Elizabeth, Robert Benjamin. BA, Okla. State U., 1962; MS, U. hawaii, 1964, PhD, 1969. Postdoctoral fellow U. Hawaii, Honolulu, 1969-70, Purdue U., 1970-71; teaching asst. biochemistry U. Hawaii, 1962-64; prof. biology Hawaii Loa Coll., Kaneohe, 1971-92, Hawaii Pacific U., Hawaii Loa Campus, 1992—99; dir. health sci. prog. Hawaii Loa Coll., 1976-92. Advisor pre-med. program Hawaii Pacific U., 1994-99, acad. coord. pre-med. studies, 1997-99. Contbr. articles to profl. jours. NDEA fellow, 1964-67. Mem. Nat. Assn. Advisors Health Professions, Sigma Xi. Home: 448 Noe Creek Rd Mountain Home AR 72654-0273 Address: Hawaii Pacific U 45-045 Kamehameha Hwy Kaneohe HI 96744-5297 E-mail: melward@wholedamarea.com.

WARD, MICHAEL E. superintendent of public instruction; m. Hope Morgan; children: Jason, Brooke. BEd, MEd, PhD in Edn., N.C. State U.; DHL (hon.), Catawba Coll. From tchr. to prin. Granville County Schs., NC, supt.; exec. dir. N.C. Standards Bd. for PUb. Sch. Adminstrs.; supt. pub. instrn. State of N.C., 1996—. Co-chair More at Four Task Force, Education First Task Force; adj. prof. ednl. leadership N.C. State U.; adj. prof. E.Carolina State U. Named Prin. of Yr, Granville County, 1988, Supt. of Yr., N.C.; recipient Presdl. Medallion award, Campbell U., Disting. Alumnus award, N.C. State U. Mem.: Coun. of Chief State Sch. Officers (pres. 2002—). Meth. Office: NC Dept Pub Instruction 301 N Wilmington St Raleigh NC 27601-2825

WARD, OLLIE TUCKER, counselor, educator; b. St. Louis, June 14, 1930; d. George Thomas and Luevenia (Casey) Stewart; m. George O. Tucker, Dec. 25, 1950 (div. Apr. 1969); children: George Stewart, Jeffrey Terrance; m. John Henry Ward, 1974 (dec. Sept. 1995). Student, Stowe Tchrs. Coll., 1946-50; MA, Washington U., St. Louis, 1958; postgrad., Webster U., 1972, U. Mo., 1973. From reading instr. to mid. sch. counselor St. Louis Pub. Schs., 1950-90; substitute tchr. Maplewood-Richmond Heights, 1990-97. Adj. faculty Harris Stowe State Coll., St. Louis, 1974, 84, 90; field rep. Tucker Bus. Coll., St. Louis, 1950-66, Tucker Bus. Coll. Alumni Assn., 1987—. Trustee, usher Missionary. Recipient Disting. Svc. award Iota Phi Lambda, 1988, award Nat. Bd. for Cert. Counselors, Disting. Alumae award HSSC, 1996. Mem. NAACP (double life, 1st v.p. St. Louis County br. 1988-89), CORE (So. Christian Leadership award St. Louis br. 1986), St. Louis Pers. and Guidance Assn. (pres.-elect 1984), St. Louis Sch. Counselors Assn. (pres. 1987-88, Svc. award 1990), Coalition 100 Black Women (charter mem., ad hoc chmn. 1984-85), Am. Cancer Assn. Abarasque (pres. 1977-78), Jack and Jill Am. (1st v.p., pres.-elect, assoc. 1968-91), Nat. Coun. of Negro Women (assoc.), Nat. Cert. Coun., Optimist Club (v.p. Mid County), Alpha Kappa Alpha, Iota Phi Lambda. Democrat. Methodist AME Zion. Home: 1513 Bredell Ave Richmond Heights MO 63117-2110

WARD, PAMELA MELCZER, elementary school educator; b. Phoenix, Dec. 22, 1950; d. Edward T. and Shirley (Mayer) Melczer; m. Kevin Floyd Ward, Mar. 8, 1975; children: Hilary Brook, Whitney Melczer. BS in Sociology, Ariz. State U., 1972; MEd in Reading Emphasis, Idaho State U., 1988. Cert. tchr. elem. edn., adminstrn. Title I tchr. Emerson/St. Anthony Sch., Pocatello, Idaho, 1976-78, Whittier Elem. Sch., Pocatello, 1979-81, Jefferson Elem. Sch., Pocatello, 1981-82; Chpt. I tchr. Chubbuck (Idaho) Elem. Sch., 1984-90, tchr. 2d grade, 1990—; summer sch. prin. Sch. Dist. 25, 1997—. Instr. Idaho State U., Pocatello, 1992, 96, 99, Bur. Ednl. Rsch. and Svcs., 1992—. Neighborhood canvasser March of Dimes, Pocatello; vol. Idaho State U. Natural History Mus., 1978—80; religious sch. chair Temple Emanuel, Pocatello, 1990—93; mem. vis. authors com. Idaho State U., 1988—90; organizer, presenter workshops, confs., Idaho, 1983—. Named Tchr. of the Yr., Sch. Dist. 25, Pocatello, 1988-89, Chubbuck Elem. Sch., 1988-89. Mem.: LWV, NEA, S.E. Idaho Reading Coun. (pres. 1987—88, Celebrate Literacy award 1980), Internat. Reading Assn. (Idaho coun., state coord. 2002—, pres. 1992—93, parents/reading chair 1985—87), Pocatello Edn. Assn., Idaho Edn. Assn., Alpha Delta Kappa. Democrat. Jewish. Avocations: reading, golfing, gardening, skiing. Home: 12805 W Reservation Rd Pocatello ID 83202-5103 Office: Chubbuck Elementary Sch 600 Chastain Dr Chubbuck ID 83202-2559

WARD, PATRICIA SCOTT, secondary special education educator; b. Atlanta, Feb. 2, 1937; d. Daniel M. and Susie (Ramsey) Scott; m. Albert Ray Ward, Jan. 6, 1956; children: Albert Ray Jr., Felicia Gail. BA, Spelman Coll., Atlanta, 1963; MA, Atlanta U., 1974, EdS, 1979; cert. in computer literacy, Dartmouth Coll., 1986. Cert. learning disabilities, computer literacy, info. processing, ga. Tchr. handicapped Atlanta Pub. Schs. Adj. prof. Atlanta U. Computer literacy fellow, 1986; computer grantee, 1988. Mem. ASCD, Nat. Coun. Tchrs. Math., ASPEW.

WARD, RICHARD HURLEY, dean, writer; b. N.Y.C., Sept. 2, 1939; s. Hurley and Anna C. (Mittasch) W.; children from a previous marriage: Jeanne M., Jonathan B.; m. Michelle Pierczynski, June 15, 1987; 1 child: Michelle Sophia. BS, John Jay Coll., CUNY, 1968; M in Criminology, U. Calif., Berkeley, 1969, D in Criminology, 1971. Detective N.Y.C. Police Dept., 1962-70; coord. student activities John Jay Coll., N.Y.C., 1970-71, dean students, 1971-75, v.p., 1975-77, vice chancelor, 1977-93; assoc. chancellor and prof. internat. criminology U. Ill., Chgo., 1993-98; exec. dir. Office Internat. Criminal Justice, 1985-99; exec. v.p. MBF Edn. Group, Malaysia, 1996-97; dean Coll. Criminal Justice, Sam Houston State U., Huntsville, Tex., 1999—. Vis. prof. Zagazig U., Egypt, Egyptian Police Acad., 1986, East China Inst. Politics and Law, Shanghai, 1990-91; lectr., various confs. in China, Egypt, Russia, Italy, Eng., Peru, Germany, Saudi Arabia, Finland, Taiwan, Vietnam and U.S., 1983—. Author: (with others) Police Robbery Control Manual, 1975; Introduction to Criminal Investigation, 1975, An Anti-Corruption Manual for Administrators in Law Enforcement; (with Robert McCormack) Quest for Quality, 1984; gen. editor Foundations of Criminal Justice, 46 vols., 1972-75; editor: (with Austin Fowler) Police and Law Enforcement, Vol. I, 1972; Police and Law Enforcement, Vol. II, 1975; (with Harold Smith) International Terrorism: The Domestic Response, 1982, International Terrorism: Operational Issues, 1988; co-author: (with James Osterburg) Criminal Investigation: A Method for Reconstructing the Past, 1992, 3d edit., 1999. Mem. Mayor of Chgo.'s Blue Ribbon Pannel on Police Promotion; varsity baseball coach U. Ill., Chgo., 1980-82, John Jay Coll. Criminal Justice, N.U.C., 1971-72; chief investigator Mayor's Commn. Police Integrity, 1998. Cpl. USMC, 1957-61. Recipient Leonard Reisman award John Jay Coll. Criminal Justice, 1968, Alumni Achievement award, 1978, Richard McGee award U. Calif., Berkeley Sch. Criminology, 1971, Friendship medal Peoples Republic of China, 1994, Hans Mattick award Ill. Acad. Criminology, 1999; Justice Dept. fellow U. Calif., Berkeley, 1971. Mem. ASPA, Acad. Criminal Justice Scis. (pres. 1977-78, Founder's award 1985), Internat. Assn. Chiefs of Police (chmn. edn. and tng. sect. 1974-75), Sigma Delta Chi. Office: Sam Houston State U Coll Criminal Justice Huntsville TX 77341 E-mail: on2ward@aol.com.

WARD, SANDRA JUNE, physicist, researcher, educator; b. Tadley, Hampshire, Eng., Apr. 3, 1962; d. John Leslie and Sheila Rosina (Fowles) W. BS in Physics, Royal Holloway Coll./U. London, 1983; PhD, U. London, 1986. Postdoctoral rsch. assoc., dept. physics York U., Toronto, 1986-88, U. Tenn., Knoxville, 1988-91; asst. prof. dept. physics U. North Tex., Denton, 1991-97, assoc. prof., 1997—. Contbr. articles to profl. jours. Recipient Valerie Myserscough prize U.London, 1984, 85; grantee NSF, 1992-95, U. North Tex., 1991—. Mem. Am. Phys. Soc., Inst. of Physics (assoc.), Royal Inst. of Gt. Britain, Sigma Xi. Christian. Achievements include research on the physics of electronic and atomic collisions.

WARD, SHARON DEE, secondary school educator; b. Tulsa, Okla., Sept. 15, 1958; d. Earl Edmond and Wilma Rose (Hurst) Walker; m. Ricky Lee Yates, Dec. 24, 1977 (div. Apr. 1986); children: Pamela, Lisa; m. William Eugene Ward, Apr. 8, 1988; children: Christian, William. AA, Rogers State Coll., 1987; BS cum laude, U. of the Ozarks, 1989; tchr. cert., Coll. of the Ozarks, 1992. Cert. tchr. Ark. Bus. mgr. Dr. Phillips D.D.S., Owasso, Okla., 1982-85, Dr. Franklin D.D.S., Owasso, 1986; office asst. U. Ozarks, Clarksville, Ark., 1987-89; bus. mgr. M&R Container, Berryville, Ark., 1990; office bus. mgr. Carroll County News, Berryville, 1990; v.p. of fin. The Cookie Bouquet, Inc., Dallas, 1991; vocat. bus. educator Eureka Springs (Ark.) H.S., 1992—. Mem. Eureka Springs Day Care, 1994-95; sponsor, leader First Eureka Springs Jr. Bank, Eureka Springs, 1993—; cons. Ark. Vocat. Bd., Little Rock, 1994—. Mem. cookie coun. Girl Scouts Am. Mem. Ark. Vocat. Assn., Bus. Edn. Assn., Ark. Edn. Assn. (sec. 1995—), Am. Vocat. Assn., Future Bus. Leaders of Am. Democrat. Methodist. Avocations: sewing, photography, computers, raising children. Home: 20673 Tosta Verde Gentry AR 72734-8719

WARD, WILLIAM ALLEN, principal, district curriculum coordinator; b. Chgo., Feb. 5, 1947; s. Alex and Louise (Frederick) W.; m. Linda Carole Hansen, Nov. 23, 1968; children: Kristin, William Jr. BA, DePaul U., 1968; MA, St. Xavier Coll., Chgo., 1972; Cert. Advanced Study, No. Ill. U., 1976. Tchr. Ctr. Sch. Dist. 66, Downers Grove, Ill., 1968-75, prin. elem., 1975-77; prin. Lakeview Jr. High Sch., Downers Grove, Ill., 1977—; dist. curriculum coord., 1987—; expulsion officer Sch. Dist. 99, Downers Grove, Ill., 1990—; instr. Ill. Adminstrs. Acad., 1990—. Mem. Darien (Ill.) Area In-Touch Team, 1988—. Mem. ASCD, Ill. Prin. Assn., Nat. Mid. Sch. Assn., DuPage County Jr. High Prins. Assn. Republican. Avocations: music, computers. Office: Lakeview Jr High Sch 701 Plainfield Rd Downers Grove IL 60516-4999

WARD DIDIO, PATTY, special education educator, educational diagnostician; b. McCamey, Tex., Dec. 10, 1934; d. Frank and Bertha Ellen (Hancock) McIlhaney; m. Arthur Ward Sr., Oct. 31, 1958 (div. May 1985); children: Candice Lewis, Arthur Jr., Karen Guile; m. Ugo J. DiDio, June 26, 1989. BS, U. Tex., El Paso, 1974, MEd, 1979; PhD, U. So. Miss., 1988. Cert. supt., elem. adminstr., elem. supr., spl. subject supr., psychometrist, Miss.; cert. mid mgmt. adminstr., profl. supr., profl. ednl. diagnostician, profl. counselor, profl. spl. edn. counselor, tchr., Tex. Tchr. El Paso (Tex.) Ind. Sch. Dist., 1974-79, ednl. diagnostician, 1979-86, asst. prin., 1990-91; coord. assessment Ysleta Ind. Sch. Dist., El Paso, 1991-94; ednl. diagnostician Clint (Tex.) Ind. Sch. Dist., 1991—. Part time instr. U. Tex., El Paso, 1990-93. Contbr. chpts. to book. Mem. Tex. Ednl. Diagnosticians Assn. Republican. Baptist. Avocations: reading, music, writing poetry, travel, painting. Home: PO Box 372384 El Paso TX 79937-2384

WARDEN, KAREN BARBARA, special education educator; b. Camden, N.J., Jan. 19, 1949; d. Russell James Jr. and Harriet May (Tupper) W. BS, Vanderbilt U., 1971; student, NJ Tchr.-Artist Inst. 1979,1990-94. 2000-03, Peters Valley Ednl. Ctr. 1994, 1998-2001, Elkins/Davis Coll. Augusta Heritage Seminar 1994-96, 2001, W. Va., Cedar Lake Ctr., W.Va., 1998—2002. Cert. elem. edn., spl. edn., and art edn. tchr., N.J. Tchr. of handicapped Camden County Tng. Ctr., Cherry Hill, N.J., 1979-98, sch. art coord., 1992—, spl. edn. art tchr., 1998—. Tchr., facilitator cmty. awareness program, vol. cmty. tng. program Camden County Libr., Voorhees, N.J., 1987—, Cherry Hill, N.J., 1991—; tchr., facilitator integration of spl. students Magnolia (N.J.) Pub. Schs., 1990-92. Mem. Coun. Exceptional Children, N.J. Art Educators Assn., Third Star Fiber Arts Guild (sec.), Garden Patch Quilters (photographer). Avocations: weaving, spinning, quilting, painting, gardening. Home: 216 Atlantic Ave SW Magnolia NJ 08049-1716 E-mail: cathallowstudio@aol.com.

WARDER, RICHARD CURREY, JR., dean, mechanical aerospace engineering educator; b. Nitro, W.Va., Sept. 30, 1936; s. Richard Currey and Edith Irene (Moser) W.; m. Carolyn Strickler, Mar. 7, 1964 (div. Dec. 1978); children: Jennifer, Jeffrey W.; m. Marjorie Dianne Forney, Jan. 10, 1981. BS, S.D. Sch. Mines, 1958; MS, Northwestern U., 1959, PhD, 1963. Registered profl. engr., Mo., Tenn. Asst. prof. Northwestern U., Evanston, Ill., 1963-65; mgr. energy processes research Litton Industries, Beverly Hills, Calif., 1965-68; assoc. prof. mech. and aerospace engring. U. Mo., Columbia, 1968-72, prof., 1972-94, James C. Dowell prof., 1989-94, chmn. mech. aerospace engring., 1988-94; dean U. Memphis Herff Coll. Engring., 1994—. Program mgr., head resources sect. NSF, Washington, 1974-76; mem. Engring. Accreditation Commn., 2003—; cons. to industry U.S. govt. Bd. dirs. Columbia Montessori Soc., 1971-73; bd. dirs. Columbia Soccer Club, 1976-80, pres., 1978-80; referee Maj. Indoor Soccer League, 1979-83. Fellow: ASME, AIAA (assoc.); mem.: AAAS, Am. Assn. Aerosol Rsch., Am. Soc. Engring. Edn., Am. Phys. Soc. Methodist.

WARD-STEINMAN, DAVID, composer, music educator, pianist; b. Alexandria, La., Nov. 6, 1936; s. Irving Steinman and Daisy Leila (Ward) W.-S.; m. Susan Diana Lucas, Dec. 28, 1956 (div. 1993); children: Jenna, Matthew; m. Patrice Dawn Madura, May 28, 2001. MusB cum laude, Fla. State U., 1957; MusM, U. Ill., 1958, DMA, 1961; studies with Nadia Boulanger, Paris, 1958-59; postdoctoral vis. fellow, Princeton U., 1970. Grad. instr. U. Ill., 1957-58; mem. faculty San Diego State U., 1961—, prof. music, 1968—, dir. comprehensive musicianship program, 1972—, composer in residence, 1961—, univ. research lectr., 1986-87. Faculty Eastman Sch. Music Workshop, 1969, Coll. Music Soc. Nat. Inst. for Music in Gen. Studies, U. Colo., 1983-84, Calif. State Summer Sch. for the Arts, Loyola Marymount U., 1988; Ford Found. composer in residence Tampa Bay (Fla.) Area, 1970-72, Brevard Music Ctr., N.C., 1986; acad. cons. U. North Sumatra (Indonesia), 1982; concert and lecture tour U.S. Info. Agy., Indonesia, 1982; master tchr. in residence Atlantic Ctr. for the Arts, New Smyrna Beach, Fla., 1996; vis. artist in residence Victorian Ctr. for the Arts, Melbourne, Australia, 1997, faculty Coll. Mus. Soc. Nat. Insts., San Diego, 1999, 2001, 2003, Ind., 2003. Composer: Symphony, 1959, Prelude & Toccata for orch., 1962, Concerto No. 2 for chamber orch., 1962, ballet Western Orpheus, 1964, Cello Concerto, 1966, These Three ballet, 1966, The Tale of Issoumbochi chamber opera, 1968, Rituals for Dancers and Musicians, 1971, Antares, 1971, Arcturus, 1972, The Tracker, 1976, Brancusi's Brass Beds, 1977; oratorio Song of Moses, 1964; Jazz Tangents, 1967, Childs Play, 1968; 3-act opera Tamar, 1977; Golden Apples, 1981; choral suite Of Wind and Water, 1982; Christmas cantata And In These Times, 1982; Moiré for piano and chamber ensemble, 1983, And Waken Green, song cycle on poems by Douglas Worth, 1983, Olympics Overture for orchestra, 1984, Children's Corner Revisited, song cycle, 1984, Summer Suite for oboe and piano, 1984, Quintessence for double quintet and percussion, 1985, Chroma concerto for multiple keyboards, percussion and chamber orch., 1985, Winging It for chamber orchestra, 1986, Elegy for Astronauts for orchestra, 1986, What's Left for piano, 1987, Gemini for 2 guitars, 1988, Intersections II: Borobudur, Under Capricorn, 1989, Voices from the Gallery, 1990, Cinnabar for viola and piano, 1991, Seasons Fantastic for chorus and harp, 1992, Cinnabar Concerto for Viola and Chamber Orchestra, 1993, Night Winds Quintet # 2 for woodwinds, 1993, Double Concerto for Two Violins and Orchestra, 1995, Prisms and Reflections (3rd Piano Sonata), 1996, Millennium Fanfare for symph. orch., 2000, Millennium Dances for symph. orch., 2001, FIESTA! for symphony orch., 2002, FLIGHT! for 2 Pianos, 2002; recs. include Fragments from Sappho, 1969; Duo for cello and piano, 1974, Childs Play for bassoon and piano, 1974, The Tracker, 1989, Brancusi's Brass Beds, 1984, concert suite from Western Orpheus, 1987, Sonata for Piano Fortified, 1987, Moiré, 1987, 3 Songs for Clarinet and Piano, 1987, Concerto #2 for Chamber Orchestra, 1990, Prisms and Reflections, 1999, Cinnabar, 1999, Sonata for Piano Fortified, 1999, Night Winds, 1999, Borobudur, 1999, Cello Concerto, 2000, Cinnabar Concerto, 2000, Chroma Concerto, 2000, Millennium Dances, 2001, I Am the Wind for voice and chamber ensemble, 2002; commd. by Chgo. Symphony, Joffrey Ballet, San Diego Ballet, San Diego Symphony, numerous others; author: (with Susan L. Ward-Steinman) Comparative Anthology of Musical Forms, 2 vols, 1976, Toward a Comparative Structural Theory of the Arts, 1989. Recipient Joseph H. Bearns prize in Music Columbia U., 1961, SAI Am. Music award, 1962, Dohnanyi award Fla. State U., 1965, ann. BMI awards, 1970—, Broadcast Music prize, 1954, 55, 60, 61; named Outstanding Prof., Calif. State Univs. and Colls., 1968, Outstanding Alumnus of Yr., Fla. State U., 1976; Fulbright sr. scholar La Trobe U. and Victorian Coll. Arts, Victorian Arts Ctr., Melbourne, Australia, 1989-90. Mem. Coll. Music Soc. (nat. bd. for composition 1991-93), Broadcast Music, Inc., Soc. of Composers, Inc., Nat. Assn. of Composers U.S.A., Golden State Flying Club. Presbyterian. Office: San Diego State U Dept Music San Diego CA 92182 E-mail: dwardste@mail.sdsu.edu.

WARE, BENNIE, university administrator; b. Ponca City, Okla., Sept. 21, 1946; s. Clyde Elmer and Lois Aliene (Smith) W.; m. Sheridan Lee Welch, May 28, 1967 (div. 1976); 1 child, Winston Arthur; m. Claudia Borman, Dec. 21, 1979 (div. 1998); children: Jeffrey Bright, Amelia Marie; m. Eleanor Gallagher, Mar. 7, 1998. BS in Chemistry, Okla. State U., 1968; PhD in Biophys. Chemistry, U. Ill., 1972. Asst. prof. chemistry Harvard U., Cambridge, Mass., 1972-75, assoc. prof., 1975-79; prof., chmn. dept. chemistry Syracuse U., 1979-84, Kenan prof. sci., 1984-91, v.p. rsch., 1989-92, v.p. rsch., computing, 1992—. Contbr. articles to profl. jours. Grantee NSF, 1972, 74, 77, 80, 83, 86, 89, NIH, 1972, 74, 76, 77, 79, 81, 84, 86; Alfred P. Sloan fellow, 1976-80. Fellow AAAS; mem. Phi Beta Kappa, Phi Kappa Phi. Achievements include invention of electrophoretic light scattering; first to combine laser light scattering and fluorescence photobleaching recovery to distinguish mutual and tracer diffusion; first to apply laser Doppler velocimetry to protoplasmic streaming. Home: 333 Berkeley Dr Syracuse NY 13210-3041 Office: Syracuse Univ 3-014D Ctr Sci And Tech Syracuse NY 13244-0001 E-mail: brware@syr.edu.

WARE, DOLLIE, retired nursing educator; b. Bklyn., Apr. 1, 1947; d. Solomon Henry and Lucille (Reel) Antley; m. Jim Ware, Dec. 27, 1969; children: Athena, Christopher, Monica, Jeremy. Nursing diploma, Kings County Hosp. Sch Nursing, Bklyn., 1967; BA in Health Care Psychology, Graceland Coll., Lamoni, Iowa, 1991. RN; cert. psychiat. and mental health nurse, chem. dependency nurse, addiction specialist, BCLS instr., cert. instr. Nat. Crisis Prevention Inst. Staff nurse Kings County Hosp., Bklyn.,

1967-68; asst. clin. instr. Kings County Hosp. Sch. Nursing, Bklyn., 1968-73; inservice instr. Kings County Hosp. Ctr., Bklyn., 1975-89, supr., instr. continuing edn. psychiatry-addiction, 1989—97; ret., 1997. Mem. Drug and Alcohol Nurses Assn., Nat. Consortium Chem. Dependency Nurses, Am. Psychiat. Nurses Assn., Regional Emergency Med. Svcs. Coun. N.Y.C. Inc. Avocations: reading, continuing education, walking, computer.

WARE, PEARL CUNNINGHAM, health educator; b. Greensboro, N.C., Aug. 18, 1939; d. Cyprian Reginald and Ida (Williams) Cunningham. BA summa cum laude, N.C. Agrl. and Tech. Coll., 1959; MA, Columbia U., 1962. Cert. English and spl. edn. tchr., N.Y. Tchr. Raleigh (N.C.) Pub. Schs., 1959-61; office worker Tchrs.' Coll., Columbia U., N.Y.C., 1961-62; hosp. tchr. N.Y.C. Pub. Schs., 1962—2003, ret., 2003. Candidate for N.Y. State Assembly, N.Y. State Right-to-Life Party, 1980, 82, candidate for N.Y. State Senate, 1984. Recipient plaque Boy Scouts Am., Bklyn., 1984, Honor cert. N.Y. Alliance Pub. Schs., 1987. Mem. Nat. Honor Soc. Secondary Schs., Alpha Kappa Mu, Sigma Rho Sigma, Kappa Delta Pi, Nat. Sorority Phi Delta Kappa (chpt. rec. sec. 1955-1999); health com. chairperson, 2000-. Avocations: piano, reading, swimming, hiking. Home: 91 E 91st St Brooklyn NY 11212-1501 E-mail: PEARLWARE8@aol.com.

WARE, WILLIAM BRETTEL, education educator; b. Glen Ridge, N.J., June 17, 1942; s. Howard Brettel and Helen Burd (Dickson) W.; m. Andrea Lou Gartley, June 24, 1967 (div. May 1989); children: Emily Dickson, Matthew Brettel, Erin Johanna Ware; m. Barbara Ann McClave Reynolds, Dec. 26, 1991; adopted children: Dianne Catherine, Kristin Elise. AB, Dartmouth Coll., 1964; MA in Tchg., Northwestern U., 1965, PhD, 1968. Classroom tchr. Chgo. Pub. Schs., 1964-65; asst. prof. U. Fla., Gainesville, 1968-73, assoc. prof., 1973-76, prof., 1976-78, U. N.C., Chapel Hill, 1978—. Contbr. chpts. to books and articles to profl. jours. Mgr. youth soccer team Ctrl. Carolina Youth Soccer Assn., Chapel Hill, 1980-86. Recipient J. Minor Gwynn professorship Sch. Edn., U. N.C., 1994-95, Chancellor's Award for Disting. Tchg., 1995. Mem. Am. Ednl. Rsch. Assn., Nat. Coun. on Measurement in Edn., N.C. Assn. for Rsch. in Edn. (bd. dirs., pres. 1996-97, treas. 1998—). Home: 907 Bayberry Dr Chapel Hill NC 27517-8378 Office: Sch Edn Univ North Carolina Cb # 3500 Chapel Hill NC 27599-3500

WARE, WILLIAM LEVI, physical education educator, researcher; b. Greenwood, Miss., May 15, 1934; s. Leslie and Catherine (Bowden) W.; m. Lottie Herger, Apr. 26, 1958; children: Felicia Rogene, Trevor Lesleo, Melvinia Simone. BS, Mississippi Valley State U., 1957; MA, Calif. State U., L.A., 1969; PhD, U. So. Calif., 1978. Tchr., coach Greenwood Pub. Schs., 1957-63, Bellflower (Calif.) Unified Sch. Dist., 1963-72; teaching asst. U. So. Calif., L.A., 1972-73; asst. prof. Calif. State U., Northridge, 1973-79; assoc. prof. Miss. State U., Starkville, 1979-90; prof. phys. edn., chmn. dept. Mississippi Valley State U., Itta Bena, 1990—, asst. to pres., 1995-98, cmty. outreach specialist, exec. dir. svc. learning, 1998—. Presenter in field; chmn. Delta Algebra Project Planning & Coordinating Group, 1991-93. Advisor Affirmative Action Adv. Coun., Whittier, Calif., 1977-78; bd. dirs. United Way, Starkville, 1983-86. Recipient Outstanding Svc. award Kiwanis Internat., 1985, Outstanding Educator award Greenwood Cultural Club, 1986, Presdl. citation Nat. Assn. for Equal Opportunity in Higher Edn., 1989; Inducted into Southwestern Athletic Conf. Hall of Fame, 1993; Faculty fellow Found. for Mid-South, 1994. Mem. Phi Delta Kappa (svc. award 1989), Greenwood/Leflore C. of C. (chmn. Leadership Tomorrow 1992-93). Avocations: racquetball, jogging. Office: Miss Valley State U PO Box 620 Itta Bena MS 38941-0620

WARG, PAULINE, artist, educator; b. Detroit, Mich., Oct. 15, 1951; d. Clifford Rudolf and Marguerite Evelyn (Kaiser) W.; m. Gary Dean Snider, Apr. 14, 1990. Student, Bowling Green State U., 1969-72, diploma, 1972-75; BA summa cum laude, U. So. Maine, 1999. Cert. Spl. Needs Vocat. Instr. Maine. Owner, pres. Warg Designs Inc., Scarborough, Maine, 1975—; instr. The Jewelry Inst., Providence, R.I., 1983-87; resident instr. Lexington Arts & Crafts Ctr., Lexington, Mass., 1987; asst. mgr. cons. J.S. Ritter Jewelers Tool & Supply Co., Portland, Maine, 1991-92; instr. Maine Coll. of Art, Portland, 1992—; owner, dir. metalsmithing program Future Builders, Inc., Scarborough, Maine, 1992-2001. Lectr. Paul Revere House Mus., Boston, 1981, juror League of N.H. Craftsmen, Concord, N.H., 1985-87, stds. com. juror League of N.H. Craftsman, Concord, 1985-87, exhbn. juror Boston Mus. Sch., Boston, 1992. Contbr. articles to profl. jours. Founding mem. Portsmouth Artisans, Portsmouth, N.H., 1975-77, founding owners, treas. Sail Loft Cmty. Arts Program, Portsmouth, 1977-79. Recipient Svc. award, Maine Coll. Art, Portland, 1997, 10 Yr. Svc. award, 2001. Mem. Soc. Am. Silversmiths (artisan mem. 1992—), Maine Crafts Assn., League of NH Craftsmen (state juried artisan). Democratic. Avocations: bicycling, canoeing, photography, gardening, travel. Office: Warg Designs Inc Pine Point Business Park 15 Holly St Ste 210 Scarborough ME 04074-8867 E-mail: wargine@sacoriver.net.

WARING, WALTER WEYLER, English language educator; b. Sterling, Kans., May 13, 1917; s. Walter Wray and Bonnie Laura (Weyler) W.; m. Mary Esther Griffith, Feb. 8, 1946; children: Mary Laura, Helen Ruth, Elizabeth Anne, Claire Joyce. BA, Kans. Wesleyan U., 1939; MA, U. Colo., 1946; PhD, Cornell U., 1949. Tchr., English and chemistry Belleville (Kan.) High Sch., 1939-41; instr. U. Colo., Boulder, 1941-42, 46-47; mem. faculty Kalamazoo Coll., 1949—, prof. English, 1955-85, prof. emeritus, 1985—, chmn. dept., 1953-78, dir. humanities, 1978-83. Ednl. TV lectr.; vis. prof. Kenyon Coll., 1984-86, 90-91. Painter watercolors.; author: Thomas Carlyle, 1978, also articles. Served to 1st lt. AUS, World War II, PTO. Decorated Legion of Merit. Mem. Phi Beta Kappa. Home: 8794 Keller Rd Delton MI 49046-8728

WARM, JOEL SEYMOUR, psychology educator; b. Bklyn., Sept. 28, 1933; s. Abraham and Stella (Kaplan) W.; m. Frances Goldberg, July 31, 1966; children: Eric Jay, Ellen Sue. BS, CCNY, 1956, MS, 1958; PhD, U. Ala., 1966. Rsch. assoc. US Army Med. Rsch. Lab., Ft. Knox, Ky., 1958-60; rsch. intern VA, Tuscaloosa, Ala., 1960-63; instr. U. Bridgeport, Conn., 1963-64; adj. asst. prof. U. Louisville, 1964-67; asst. prof. U. Cin., 1967-72, assoc. prof., 1972-75, prof. psychology, 1975—, dir. grad. studies, 1999—. Chair Fellows of the Grad. Sch., 1996-98, US Army multi-univ. rsch. initiative, 2002, med. rsch. devel. commd., 2003. Co-author: Psychology of Perception, 1979, Ergonomics and Human Factors, 1987; editor: Sustained Attention in Human Performance, 1984; co-editor: Viewing Psychology as A Whole: The Integrative Science of William N. Dember, 1998; mem. editl. bd. Human Factors, 1989—, Theorteical Issues in Ergonomics Sci., 2002--, Jour. Gen. Psychology, 1992-98, Internat. Rev. Rsch. in Mental Retardation, 1992-98. Fellow Grad. Sch. U. Cin., 1986, chair, 1996-97; Knothole mgr. Finneytown (Ohio) Athletic Assn., 1980. Lt. (j.g.) USNR, 1963-70. Recipient Excellence in Doctoral Mentoring award U. Cin., 1991; named Disting. Scientist Engr. and Sci. Cin., 1992; fellow Grad. Sch., U. Cin., 1984—, sr. postdoctoral fellow NRC, Cin., 1986, Disting. Summer Faculty fellow Naval Air Warfare Ctr., Warminster, Pa., 1992, grantee Fragrance Rsch. Fund, NYC, 1987-89, NASA, 1992, Naval Air Warfare Ctr., 1995, Procter and Gamble Corp., 1995-97, Mead Johnson Nutritionals, 1999, US Army Multiple U. Rsch. Initiative, 2002, US Army Med. R&D Command, 2003—. Fellow AAAS, APA, Am. Psychol. Soc., Human Factors Soc. (pres. Tri-State chpt. 1988); mem. Psychonomic Soc., So. Soc. Philosophy and Psychology (pres. 1991-92), Sigma Xi (treas. U. Cin. chpt. 1988-91, pres.-elect 1991, pres. U. Cin. chpt. 1992). Jewish. Office: U Cin Dept Psychology Cincinnati OH 45221-0001 E-mail: joel.warm@uc.edu.

WARME, JOHN EDWARD, geology educator; b. Los Angeles, Jan. 16, 1937; s. Clarence Herbert and Edna (Peterson) W.; m. Martha Fowler, 1959 (div. 1963); children: Susan Lynn, Jane Kathleen Warme Bell. BA, Augustana Coll., 1959; PhD, UCLA, 1966. Lectr. Calif. Luth. Coll., Thousand Oaks, 1961-62, instr., 1962-63; Fulbright fellow in geology U. Edinburgh, Scotland, 1966-67; prof. geology and oceanography Rice U., Houston, 1967-79; prof. geology Colo. Sch. Mines, 1979—2002, prof. emeritus, 2002—. Co-editor: The Deep Sea Drilling Project: A Decade of Progress; contbr. sci. articles to geol. jours. Named Ewing Prof. Oceanography Rice U., 1976-79; NSF Research grantee, 1969—. Fellow AAAS, Geol. Soc. Am.; mem. Soc. Econ. Paleontologists and Mineralogists (hon., pres. 1983-84), Am. Assn. Petroleum Geologists (field seminar leader in Calif., Grand Canyon, Morocco, disting. lectr. 2000-01), Internat. Assn. Sedimentologists, Soc. Econ. Paleontologists and Mineralogists Found. (pres., co-founder 1983—, bd. dirs. 1984-86). Achievements include research in stratigraphy of deepwatersandstonesof California of jurassic high atlas, Morocco, paleozoic of Algerian Sahara, devonian comet impact Breccia of Nevada. Home: 30968 Isenberg Ln Evergreen CO 80439-7129 Office: Colo Sch Mines Dept Geology & Geol Engring Golden CO 80401

WARNER, DAVID COOK, public affairs educator; b. Boston, Apr. 22, 1940; s. Roger Lewis and Dorothy Flora (Cook) W.; m. Phyllis Gail Erman, July 9, 1967; children: Ann Fitch, Michael Beers. BA, Princeton U., 1963; MPA, Syracuse U., 1965, PhD in Econs., 1969. Rsch. assoc. Ctr. Urban Studies Wayne State U., Detroit, 1969, asst. prof. econs., 1969-71; dep. dir. program analysis and budget N.Y.C. Health and Hosp. Corp., 1971-72; postdoctoral fellow Yale U., New Haven, 1972-73, lectr., 1973-75; assoc. prof. L.B.J. Sch. Pub. Affairs U. Tex., Austin, 1975-81, prof. pub. affairs, 1981—, Wilbur Cohen prof. pub. affairs, 1989—. Vis. prof. pub. health, 1983—; bd. dirs. Brackenridge Hosp., Austin, 1976—83; mem. Tex. Diabetes Coun., 1983—88, chmn., 1985—88; mem. adv. bd. Hogg Found. for Mental Health, 1990—93; vice chair quality methods tech. adv. com. Health Care Info. Coun., 1999—. Author: Health of Mexican Americans in South Texas, 1979, Developing Programs to Prevent and Control Diabetes, 1982, Maternal and Child Health on the U.S.-Mexico Border, 1987, Health Care Across the Border, 1993, NAFTA and Trade in Health Services, 1997, Cost of Diabetes in Texas in 1992, 1996, Getting What You Paid For: Extending Medicare Coverage to Retirees in Mexico, 1999; co-author: Cost of Cancer in Texas, 2001, Investing in Texas: Financing Health Coverage Expansions, 2003; editor: Toward New Human Rights, 1977, Public Affairs Comment, 1978-90; mem. editl. bd. Jour. Health, Politics, Policy and Law, 1975-93; contbr. articles to profl. jours. Mem. U.S.-Mex. Border Health Assn. (chmn. rsch., edn., tng. com. 1982-84), Am. Pub. Health Assn., Tex. Philosophical Soc. Democrat. Congregationalist. Home: 5701 Trailridge Dr Austin TX 78731-4226 Office: U Tex LBJ Sch Pub Affairs Austin TX 78713 E-mail: david.warner@mail.utexas.edu.

WARNER, ELIZABETH ROSE, librarian, educator; b. Phila., Pa., Dec. 10, 1952; d. Charles Hoffman and Elizabeth Mathilda Warner; m. Michael Joseph Dunn, Oct. 12, 1979; children: Brian Joseph Charles Warner Dunn, Colin Joseph Patrick Warner Dunn. BA, Holy Family Coll., 1974; MLS, Villanova U., 1977. Med. librarian JFK Meml. Hosp., Stratford, N.J., 1975-77; lib. coord. N.J. Sch. Osteopathic Medicine, Stratford, 1976-77; extension librarian Coll. Physicians Phila., 1977-79, reader's svcs. asst., 1975-77; med. librarian Crozer-Chester (Pa.) Med. Ctr., 1979-86; reference librarian Scott Meml. Lib. Thomas Jefferson U., Phila., 1986-90, edn. svcs. librarian, instr. info. skills workshops Scott Meml. Lib., 1991—. Vol. librarian Mummers Mus., Phila., 1976; cons., presenter in field. Contbr. numerous articles to profl. jours. Mem. Am. Lib. Assn., Med. Lib. Assn. (chair legis. com. Phila. Regional chpt. 1980-81, pres. elect, program chair, 1981-82, pres. 1982-83, mem. com. 1981-83, rep. chpt. coun. 1985-87, nominating com. 1987-88, 94-95, Achievement award 1994, edn. com. nursing and allied health resources sect. 1988-89, sec., treas. 1991-93, nominating com. 1988-89, 93-94, editor newsletter, 1992—, course designer 1993—, instr. 1993—, com. chair pub. svcs. sect., 1985-87, jury chair Ida and George prize 1992-94, Disting. mem. Acad. Health Info. Profls. 1990—), Grtr. Phila. Health Care Congress, Phila. Area Reference Librarians Info. Exchange (Bibliotecaire Sans Sobriete cert. 1993), Kappa Gamma Pi, Phi Kappa Phi. Democrat. Roman Catholic. Home: 421 E Melrose Ave Westmont NJ 08108-2510 Office: Thomas Jefferson U Scott Meml Lib 1020 Walnut St Philadelphia PA 19107-5567

WARNER, FRANK WILSON, III, mathematics educator; b. Pittsfield, Mass., Mar. 2, 1938; s. Frank Wilson Jr. and Charlotte (Walton) W.; m. Ada Woodward, June 6, 1958; children: Bruce Woodward, Clifford Powell. BS, Pa. State U., 1959; PhD, MIT, 1963. Instr. MIT, Cambridge, 1963-64; acting asst. prof. U. Calif., Berkeley, 1964-65, asst. prof., 1965-68; assoc. prof. U. Pa., Phila., 1968-73, prof. math., 1973-2000, assoc. dean Sch. Arts and Scis., 1992-95, dep. dean Sch. Arts and Scis., 1995-97, prof. emeritus, 2000—. Author: Foundations of Differentiable Manifolds and Lie Groups, 1971; contbr. articles to scholarly jours. Fellow Guggenheim Found., 1976. Fellow AAAS; mem. Am. Math. Soc., Math. Assn. Am., Sigma Xi. Achievements include research on the conjugate locus of a Riemannian manifold, on existence and conformal deformation of metrics with prescribed gaussian and scalar curvatures, on great circle fibrations of spheres. Office: U Pa 209 S 33d St Philadelphia PA 19104-6395

WARNER, JEAN ROCKWELL, education educator; b. Towanda, Pa., Nov. 9, 1938; d. Henry Tracy and Genevieve Ann (Bryant) Rockwell. AA, Rider U., 1959, BS, 1962, MA, 1964; PhD, NYU, 1970. Instr., dir. student activities evening sch. Rider U., Lawrenceville, N.J., 1962-70, asst. dean evening sch., 1975-76, assoc. prof. undergrad. edn., 1976—; instr. bus. edn. NYU, N.Y.C., 1970-71; asst. prof. bus. edn. Hunter Coll., N.Y.C., 1971-75. Advisor Collegiate Secs. Internat., 1976-90; coord. Ptnrs. in Learning, 1988-94; undergrad. coord. NCATE, 2003—. Author: Informatio Processing For Colleges, 1986, RMT Information Processing Simulation, 1992; contbr. articles to profl. jours. Named Outstanding Young Women of Am., 1968. Mem. N.J. Bus. Educators Assn., Nat. Bus. Educators Assn., Delta Pi Epsilon. Republican. Presbyterian. Avocations: skiing, gardening. Office: Rider U 2083 Lawrenceville Rd Lawrenceville NJ 08648-3099

WARNER, JUDITH (ANNE) HUSS, elementary school educator; b. Plainfield, N.J., June 15, 1936; d. Charles and Martha McMullen (Miller) Huss; m. Howard R. Warner, June 14, 1958; children: Barbara, Robert. BS in Elem. Edn., Russell Sage Coll., 1959. Elem. tchr. Pitts. Bd. Edn., 1959-60; home tchr. Napa (Calif.) Sch. Bd., 1974-77; substitute tchr. Allegheny Intermediate Unit, Pitts., 1977—94. Leader Girl Scouts U.S.A., Pitts., 1966-70; vol. Children's Hosp., Pitts., 1967-74, Jefferson Hosp., Pitts., 1977-88; pres., trustee Whitehall Libr., Pitts., 1984-92; pres., bd. dirs. Friends of Whitehall Libr., Pitts., 1969-94. Mem. AAUW, DAR. Republican. Methodist. Avocations: sailing, skiing, swimming, hiking, travel. Home: 4985 Wheaton Dr Pittsburgh PA 15236-2064

WARNER, MAUREEN JOAN, secondary education educator, English; b. Cleve., Nov. 10, 1943; d. Gilbert Frances and Helen (O'Donnell) Morrissey; children: Norman Jr., Susan. BA, Cleve. State U., 1965; MS in Edn., Nova U., 1986; EdD, U. Ctrl. Fla., 1992. Cert. secondary educator in English and gifted edn., adminstr., Fla.; nat. bd. cert. tchr., 2002. Instr. English Glenville H.S., Cleve., 1965-67; in-sch. suspension dir. Hudson (Ohio) H.S., 1978-82; instr. English Oviedo (Fla.) H.S., 1982-97; adj. prof. Nova U., Orlando, Fla., 1993—; instr. S.A.T. prep Orlando, Fla., 1993—; chair English Winter Springs (Fla.) H.S., 1997—. Secondary rep. tchr. edn. U. Ctrl. Fla., Orlando, 1991-94, gifted steering com., 1992-93; fellow NEH, Orlando, 1994; adj. instr. U. Ctrl. Fla., Seminole C.C., 1993-03. Author: (computer program) Parallel Writing Skills, 1986, (book) Florida's Writing Program, 1992; contbr. articles to profl. jours. Mem. ASCD (presenter San Francisco 1995), Fla. Coun. Tchrs. English (presenter Orlando 1993), Nat. Coun. Tchrs. English (presenter Seattle 1991, 97), Kappa Delta Phi (presenter Orlando 1994). Home: 1247 Stone Harbour Rd Winter Springs FL 32708-4523 Office: Winter Springs HS 130 Tuskawilla Rd Winter Springs FL 32708-2831

WARNER, NEARI FRANCOIS, university president; b. New Orleans, July 20, 1945; d. Cornelius and Enell (Brimmer) Francois; m. Jimmie Duel Warner Sr., June 6, 1970 (div. Sept. 1983); 1 child, Jimmie Duel Jr. BS, Grambling (La.) State U., 1967; MA, Atlanta U., 1968; PhD, La. State U., 1992. Dir. Upward Bound So. U., New Orleans, 1976-89, dean jr. divsn., 1989-94; asst. v.p. acad. affairs Grambling State U., 1994-96, v.p. student affairs, 1996-97, v.p. devel., 1997-99, acting v.p. acad. affairs, 1999, provost, v.p. acad. affairs, 1999—. Sec. Conf. La. Colls./Univs., 1999—; mem. State Funding Task Force, State of La., 1998-99; bd. dirs. La. Endowment for Humanities, 1998—; pres. La. Assn. Student Asst. Program, 1986-88. Preface writer: Interdisciplinary Approach, 1998. Mem. adv. bd. Pupil Progression Commn., New Orleans, 1989-93; mem. task force Gov.'s Tech. Prep., Baton Rouge, 1991-93, Mayor's Task Force for Edn., New Orleans, 1992, Monroe (La.) City Sch., 1995. Named Role model YWCA, New Orleans, 1992, Disting. Alumnae Nat. Assn. Equal Opportunity, Washington, 1996. Mem. AAUW, NAACP, The Links, Inc. (treas. 1999—, Unsung Hero 1993), Alpha Kappa Alpha, Kappa Delta Pi, Pi Gamma Mu Democrat. Baptist. Avocations: reading, bowling. Home: PO Box 989 Grambling LA 71245-0989 Office: Grambling State U PO Box 1170 Grambling LA 71245-1170 E-mail: nfwarner@martin.gram.edu.

WARNER, ROBERT MARK, university dean, archivist, historian; b. Montrose, Colo., June 28, 1927; s. Mark Thomas and Bertha Margaret (Rich) W.; m. Eleanor Jane Bullock, Aug. 21, 1954; children: Mark Steven, Jennifer Jane. Student, U. Denver, 1945; BA, Muskingum Coll., 1949, LL.D. (hon.), 1981; MA, U. Mich., 1953, PhD, 1958; H.H.D. (hon.), Westminster (Pa.) Coll., 1981; L.H.D. (hon.), DePaul U., 1983. Tchr. high sch., Montrose, Colo., 1949-50; lectr. dept. history U. Mich., 1958-66, assoc. prof., 1966-71, prof., 1971-97, prof. emeritus, 1997—, prof. Sch. Info., 1974-97, emeritus, 1997—, dean Sch. Info. and Library Studies, 1985-92, univ. historian, 1992—, interim dir. Univ. Libraries, 1988-90; asst. in rsch. Bentley Hist. Libr., 1953-57, asst. curator, 1957-61, asst. dir., 1961-66, dir., 1966-80; archivist of U.S., 1980-85. Mem. exec. com. Bentley Hist. Libr., 1988—; bd. visitors Sch. Libr. Sci., Case Western Res. U., 1976-80, chmn., 1980-84, Maxwell Sch. Govt., Syracuse U., 1982-87; chmn. Gerald R. Ford Presdl. Libr. Bldg. Com., 1977-79; bd. dirs., sec. Gerald R. Ford Found., 1987—; trustee Woodrow Wilson Internat. Ctr. for Scholars, 1980-85, chmn. fellowship com., 1983-85; chmn. Nat. Hist. Publs. and Records Commn., 1980-85; mem. exec. com. Internat. Coun. on Archives, 1984-88; pres. 2d European Conf. on Archives, 1989; comptroller gen. U.S. Rsch. and Edn. Adv. Com., 1988-2000; rsch. adv. com. Online Computer Libr. Ctr., 1990-93; bd. govs. Clements Libr., 1988-90, 93—, Clark Hist. Libr. Ctrl. Mich. U., 1987—; vis. prof. UCLA, 1993. Author: Chase S. Osborn, 1860-1949, 1960, Profile of a Profession, 1964, (with R. Bordin) The Modern Manuscript Library, 1966, (with C.W. Vanderhill) A Michigan Reader: 1865 to the Present, 1974, (with F. Blouin) Sources for the Study of Migration and Ethnicity, 1979, Diary of a Dream: A History of the National Archives Independence Movement, 1980-1985, 1995. Served with U.S. Army, 1950-52. Recipient Disting. Svc. award Muskingum Coll., 1990, Disting. Svc. award Nat. Hist. Pub. and Records Commn., 1992. Fellow Soc. Am. Archivists; mem. Am. Hist. Assn. (council 1981-85), Orgn. Am. Historians, ALA (council 1986-91), Assn. for Library and Info. Sci. Edn., Presbyn. Hist. Soc. (bd. dirs. 1987-91), Am. Assn. State and Local History, Hist. Soc. Mich. (trustee 1960-66, v.p. 1972-73, pres. 1973-74), Soc. Am. Archivists (mem. council 1967-71, sec., exec. dir. 1971-73, v.p. 1974-75, pres. 1976-77), Am. Antiquarian Soc., Phi Alpha Theta, Beta Phi Mu. Clubs: U. Mich. Research. Lodges: Rotary. Presbyterian. Home: 1821 Coronada St Ann Arbor MI 48103-5066 Office: U Mich Sch Info 550 E University Ave Ann Arbor MI 48109-1092 E-mail: archlib@umich.edu.

WARNER, ROLLIN MILES, JR., economics educator, real estate broker; b. Evanston, Ill., Dec. 25, 1930; s. Rollin Miles Warner Sr. and Julia Herndon (Polk) Clarkson. BA, Yale U., 1953; cert. in law, Harvard U., 1956; MBA, Stanford U., 1960; cert. in edn. adminstrn., U. San Francisco, 1974. Lic. real estate broker Calif. Asst. to v.p. fin. Stanford U., 1960-63; instr. history Town Sch., San Francisco, 1963-70, instr. econs. and history, dean, 1975—; prin. Mt. Tamalpais, Ross, Calif., 1972-74; dir. devel. Katharine Branson Sch., Ross, 1974-75, instr. econs., history, math. and outdoor edn. Author: America, 1986, Europe, 1986, Africa, Asia, Russia, 1986, Greece, Rome, 1981, Free Enterprise at Work, 1986. From scoutmaster to summer camp commr. Boy Scouts Am., San Francisco, 1956—. Served to lt. USNR, 1953—55, Korea, Pacific, Vietnam. Recipient Silver Beaver award Boy Scouts Am., 1986, Town Sch. medal Town Sch. for Boys Alumni Coun., 1995. Mem.: Marines Meml. Assn., San Francisco Yacht Club (Belvedere, Calif.), Grolier Club NY. Office: Town Sch 2750 Jackson St San Francisco CA 94115-1195 E-mail: warnerrollinm1960@alumni-gsb.stanford.edu.

WARNER, SYLVIA CLAAR, elementary school educator; b. Johnstown, Pa., Aug. 27, 1940; d. Jesse Emmert and Gladys Winifred (Albright) Claar; m. Lee Howland Warner, June 13, 1964 (div. Oct. 1981); children: Jill, Gregory Lee. BA, Juniata Coll., 1962. Cert. tchr., Fla. Tchr. Logan Area Schs., Altoona, Pa., 1962-64, Monona Grove (Wis.) Schs., 1964-65, Sun Prairie (Wis.) Schs., 1965-68, Leon County Schs., Tallahassee, Fla., 1981—. Grade-level chair, mem. sch. improvement team Astoria Park Sch., Tallahassee, 1989-95. Mem. Leon County Reading Coun. (v.p.-elect 1996, pres. 1997, treas. 1998, corr. sec. 1999), Internat. Reading Assn. (del. 1997, 98), Fla. Reading Assn. (dist. dir. 2000-01, treas. 2001—), Alpha Delta Kappa (treas. 1992-94, sgt.-at-arms 1994-96). Home: 2410 Willamette Rd Tallahassee FL 32303-3849 Office: Astoria Park Elem Sch 2465 Atlas Rd Tallahassee FL 32303-3703

WARNER, WALTER JOHN, educational administrator; b. Littleton, N.H., Mar. 2, 1955; s. Walter J. and June (Dickerman) W.; m. Laurie B. Dunlap, Aug. 24, 1988; children: Murray, Katie, Kristie, Karey. BA, Plymouth State Coll., 1980; MALS, Wesleyan U., Middletown, Conn., 1988. Tchr. chemistry New Hampton (N.H.) Sch., 1980-82, The Gunnery, Washington, Conn., 1982-94; chair sci. dept. The Seven Hills Sch., Cin., 1994-99; coord. curriculum and tech. Wyoming Sem., Kingston, Pa., 1999—2003; sch. adminstr. The Episcopal H.S. of Baton Rouge, La., 2003—. Assoc. dir. Taft Ednl. Ctr., Watertown, Conn., 1998—. Mem. ASCD, NCTM, NSTE. Office: The Episcopal HS of La Woodland Ridge Blvd Baton Rouge LA E-mail: warnerw@ehsbr.org.

WARNER, WAYNE HENRY, elementary and secondary educator; b. Phila., Oct. 11, 1941; s. Marion V. (Kreener) Warner; m. Mary JoAnn Halpert, Aug. 26, 1961; children: Stephen, Virginia, Matthew. BS in Elem. Edn., East Stroudsburg (Pa.) U., 1963; MEd, Temple U., 1969; postgrad., Trenton State Coll., Pa. State U. Cert. elem. tchr., phys. edn. tchr., ednl. media specialist. Elem. tchr., phys. edn. tchr. Bristol (Pa.) Twp. Schs., 1965-67; dir. media, tchr., head coach cross-country, gymnastics, track George Sch., Newtown, Pa., 1969-70; tchr. Centennial Schs., Warminster, Pa., 1963-65, 67-68, 1970-71, Oxford Hills Schs., South Paris, Maine, 1971-74; regional mgr. Iams Co., Dania, Fla., 1974-86; asst. media dir., coach football and gymnastics, tchr. video prodn. Northfield (Mass.) Mount Hermon Sch., 1986-89; tchr., football coach Rogersville (Tenn.) City Sch., 1989-90; dir. phys. edn./athletics, head coach cross-country, baseball and track Brandon Hall Sch., Atlanta, 1990-95; athletic dir., head coach track and football St. Andrew's (Tenn.) Sewanee Sch., 1995—. Juror Nat. Film

Festival, N.Y.C., 1988. Mem. NEA, Assn. Ednl. Rsch. and Tech., AAHPERD. Avocations: running, bicycling, camping, traveling, beekeeping. Office: St Andrew's Sewanee Sch 290 Quintard Rd NW Saint Andrews TN 37372-4000

WARNICK, JORDAN EDWARD, pharmacologist, educator; b. Boston, Mar. 21, 1942; s. Samuel William and Ruth Barbara (Hite) W.; m. Hazel Augusta Cohen, Aug. 16, 1970; 1 child, Meredith Nicole. BS in Pharmacy, Mass. Coll. Pharmacy, 1963; PhD in Pharmacology, Purdue U., 1968. Registered pharmacist, Mass. Grad. teaching asst. Purdue U., West Lafayette, Ind., 1963-65, grad. rsch. asst., 1965-68; post-doctoral fellow SUNY, Buffalo, 1968-70, NIH spl. awardee, 1970-71, asst. prof. Sch. of Pharmacy, 1971-74; asst. prof. U. Md. Sch. Medicine, Balt., 1974-80, assoc. prof., 1980-94, prof., 1994—, dir. short term rsch. tng. programs, 1983-94, dir. rsch. programs Office Student Rsch. Dir. office of student rsch. U. Md. Sch. Medicine, Balt., 1983—, dir. pathophysiology and therapeutics, 1995—, asst. dean student edn. and rsch., 1998—. Contbr. numerous articles, abstracts to profl. jours., chpts. to books. Chmn. Balt.-Rotterdam Sister City Com., 1991-97, vice-chair, 1997—. Grantee Nat. Sci. Found., 1987-92, Am. Heart Assn., 1989-96, NIH, 1985-95, 1996—. Mem. Am. Soc. for Pharmacology and Exptl. Therapeutics, Soc. for Neurosci., Academic Assn. Minority Physicians. Avocations: doll houses, electronics, computers, stamps, amateur acting. Office: U Md Sch Medicine Office Student Rsch 660 W Redwood St Baltimore MD 21201-1509

WARNKE, ROGER ALLEN, pathology educator; b. Peoria, Ill., Feb. 22, 1945; s. Delmar Carl and Ruth Armanelle (Peard) W.; m. Joan Marie Gebhart, Nov. 18, 1972; children: Kirsten Marie, Lisa Marie. BS, U. Ill., 1967; MD, Washington U., St. Louis, 1971. Diplomate Am. Bd. Pathology. Intern in pathology Stanford (Calif.) U. Med. Sch., 1971-72, resident in pathology, 1972-73, postdoctoral fellow in pathology, 1973-75, postdoctoral fellow in immunology, 1975-76, asst. prof. pathology, 1976-82, assoc. prof., 1983-90; prof., 1991—. Cons. Becton Dickinson Monoclonal Ctr., Mountain View, Calif., 1982-88, IDEC, Mountain View, 1985-90, Coulter Pharm., Inc., 1997-98; sci. advisor Ventana Med. Systems, Inc., Tucson, 1986-94. Contbr. over 300 articles to profl. jours., chpts. to books. Recipient Benjamin Castleman award Mass. Gen. Hosp., 1981; Agnes Axtel Moule faculty scholar Stanford U., 1979-82; Rsch. grantee Nat. Cancer Inst. and NIH, 1978—. Mem. So. Bay Pathology Soc., Calif. Soc. Pathologists, U.S. Can. Acad. Path., Am. Soc. Investigative Pathology, Soc. for Hematopathology, European Assn. for Haematopathology, Coll. Am. Pathologists. Home: 845 Tolman Dr Stanford CA 94305-1025 Office: Stanford U Dept Pathology Stanford CA 94305

WARREN, BARBARA DENISE, special education educator; d. Willie D. and Earnestine Loretta Davis; m. Charles Eric Warren, Sept. 7, 1976; children: Tasha Shalace, TuJuana, Charles Jr. Cert. in practical nursing, Albany Vocat. Tech. Sch., 1983; BS, Albany State U., 1998; MEd, Clark-Atlanta U., 2002, EdS, 2003. LPN, Ga. Para profl. Dougherty County Sch., Albany, Ga., 1992—97; tchr. Dekalb County Sch., Atlanta, 1997—. Mentor tchr. Dekalb County Schs., Atlanta, 2000. Mem.: Coun. Exceptional Children, Ga. Assn. Educators (bldg. rep. 2000—). Avocations: reading, gardening, music, cooking. Home: 345 Lori Ln Riverdale GA 30296 Office: Paul D West Mid Sch 2376 Headland Dr East Point GA 30344

WARREN, CLAY, communication educator; b. Lexington Park, Md., Aug. 11, 1946; s. Cassius Clay and Dorothy Dean Warren; m. Gitte Bonde Kolind, May 1, 1985; children: Laura Kolind, Daniel Clay Kolind. BS, U.S. Naval Acad., 1968; MA, U. Colo., 1973, PhD, 1976. Instr. U. Colo., Boulder, 1973-76; asst. prof. semester-at-sea program Inst. Shipbd. Edn., Laguna Hills, Calif., 1977; vis. asst. prof. U. Coll. Cape Breton, Sydney, N.S., Can., 1978, assoc. prof., 1984-90; asst. prof. Shepherd Coll., Shepherdstown, W.Va., 1978-79, U. Hawaii at Manoa, Honolulu, 1979-82; sr. lectr. Internat. People's Coll., Elsinore, Denmark, 1982-84; assoc. prof. George Washington U., Washington, 1990-91, Chauncey M. Depew prof., 1991—. Assoc. cons. M J Solutions, Westport, Conn., 1986—; dir. comm. program George Washington U., Washington, 1990-2002, Warren Consulting, Washington, 1990—. Author: Coming Around, 1986; editor: Inner Visions, Outer Voices, 1988, Democracy Is Born in Conversations, 1998; contbr. articles to scholarly jours. Mem. site team Mil. Installation Vol. Edn. Rev. Project Office of Asst. Sec. of Def., 1992—; nat. coord. CREDIT, Am. Coun. Edn., 1996—. Lt. USN, 1968-71. Latin Am. Teaching fellow Tufts U., 1977, Tompkins Inst. Rsch. fellow, 1987-89; Rudolf Dreikurs Meml. scholar Internat. Com. for Adlerian Summer Schs. and Inst., 1988; named Princeton Seminarian Acad. Consciousness Studies, Princeton U., 1994. Mem. AAUP (v.p. George Washington U. chpt. 1994-98), Nat. Comm. Assn., N.Am. Soc. Adlerian Psychology, Folk Edn. Assn. Am. (exec. coun. 1992-96). Avocations: certified scuba diver, sport parachutist, pvt. pilot, pianist, creative writer. Office: George Washington U 2130 H St NW Ste 707 Washington DC 20052-0001

WARREN, DAVID LILES, educational association executive; b. Goldsboro, N.C., Sept. 15, 1943; s. James Hubert and Katherine (Liles) W.; m. Ellen Elizabeth LeGendre, Mar. 1, 1969; children— Jamison, Mackenzie, Katrin BA in English, Wash. State U., 1965; M. Urban Studies, M.Div., Yale U., 1970; PhD, U. Mich., 1976; LittD, Elmhurst Coll., 1994, Moravian Coll., 1994; LLD, Rider U., 1996, Mt. Union Coll., 1997, Centre Coll., 1997, Mercer U., 1998, Franklin and Marshall Coll, 1999; Doctor of Public Service, Rocky Mountain Coll., 1999; LLD, Ky. Wesleyan Coll., 2000; LHD, U. of New Haven, 2001; LittD, Middlebury Coll., 2001. Gen. sec. Dwight Hall, Yale U., New Haven, 1969-76, bd. dirs., 1976—; assoc. dir. community relations Yale U., New Haven, 1976-78; sr. v.p., provost Antioch U., N.Y.C. and Yellow Springs, Ohio, 1978-82; chief adminstrv. officer City of New Haven, 1982-84; pres. Ohio Wesleyan U., Delaware, 1984-93, Nat. Assn. Indep. Colls. and Univs., Washington, 1993—; with Franklin and Marshall Coll., 1999. Cons. to hosps., sch. systems, colls., univs.; bd. dirs. Delaware County Bank; chmn. NCAA Pres. Commn., Div. III, 1990-92. Contbr. chpts. to books, articles to Yale Alumni Mag. Mem. NEw Haven Bd. Alderman, 1973-75; vice chmn. New Haven Commn. on Poverty, 1981-82; pres. North Coast Athletic Conf., 1988-90; justice of peace New Haven Dem. Party, 1974-76; state chmn. People to People, 1987; chmn. Gov.'s Task Force on Dep. Registrar, 1987; chmn. Ohio Five Coll. Commn., 1985-95, Campus Compact Nat. Exec. Com., 1987-88; bd. dirs. U.S. Health Corp., Coun. Ethics and Econs.; exec. com. Great Lakes Colls. Assn., Ctrl. Ohio Symphony Orch.; chmn. Ohio Ethics commn. Fulbright scholar Wash. State U., 1965-66; Rockefeller fellow Yale U., 1966; disting. Centennial Alumnus Wash. State U. Mem. Am. Assn. Higher Edn., Assn. Ind. Colls. Univs. (sec. 1987-88), Phi Beta Kappa Clubs: University (Columbus, Ohio); Graduate (New Haven). Democrat. Methodist. Avocations: jogging; writing; tennis. Office: Nat Assn Ind Colls & Univs 1025 Connecticut Ave NW Ste 700 Washington DC 20036-5409

WARREN, ELIZABETH CURRAN, retired political science educator; b. St. Louis, Mo., Aug. 23, 1927; d. Maurice Donovan and Florence Schulte Curran; m. Geoffrey Spencer Warren, June 26, 1949; children: Kathryn Lloyd, Patricia, Michele, Deborah Perry. BA, Bryn Mawr Coll., 1949; MA, U. Kans., 1965; PhD, U. Nebr., 1970. Adj. prof. polit. sci. Loyola U. Chgo., 1977—80, asst. prof. polit. sci., 1980—87, ret., 1987. Cons. Dept. Housing, City of Chgo., 1981; cons. on subsidized housing City of Crystal Lake, Ill., 1982. Author: Legacy of Judicial Policy-Making, 1988, God, Caesar and the Freedom of Religion, 2003; co-author: Impact of Subsidized Housing on Property Values, 1983. Village pres. Village of Glencoe, Ill., 1985—93, trustee, 1974—83; organizer, sec.-treas. Sr. Housing Aid, Glencoe, 1982—2001; mem. Glencoe Garden Club, 1989—, pres., 1997—99. Mem.: Skokie Country Club. Avocations: gardening, skiing, music, swimming, writing. Home: 900 Valley Rd Glencoe IL 60022

WARREN, EMILY P. retired secondary and adult school educator; b. Dayton, Ky., Oct. 6, 1928; d. Morris C. and Kathleen (B.) Parker; m. Richard E. Warren (dec.); children: Richard Warren Jr., George Michael. BS in Home Econs., U. Ky., 1950; MS in Edn., Barry U., 1968; postgrad., Fla. State U. Cert. tchr., Fla. Tchr. home econs., Vevay, Ind., 1950-52, H.S., Ludlow, Ky., 1952—53, Cin., 1953—54; part-time adult home econs. tchr. Sch. Practical Nursing Mt. Sinai Hosp., Miami Beach, Fla., 1955-57; elem. tchr. Dade County, Fla., 1957-59; tchr. home econs., 1960-66; coord. vocat. home econs. Dade County Pub. Schs., 1966-91. Group leader home econs. tchrs., Russia, 1993, China, 1994, Russia/Hungary, 1995; cons. in field. Named Fla. Tchr. of Yr., 1965. Mem. Am. Assn. Family and Consumer Scis., Am. Vocat. Assn., Dade County Adminstrs. Assn., Dade County Home and Family Edn. Assn., Fla. Adult Edn. Assn., Fla. Assn. for Supervision and Curriculum Devel., Fla. Assn. Family and Consumer Scis., Nat. Assn. Local Suprs. Home Econs. Econs. Assn. (pres.), Internat. Furnishings and Design Assn. (Fla. chpt. v.p. and treas.), Ret. Educators Assn. (pres. Dade County 1994-98, Delta Kappa Gamma (past pres., v.p., treas.) Home: 165 NE 162nd St Miami FL 33162-4226

WARREN, ERNESTINE HILL, elementary education educator, mayor; b. Rosebud, Tex., Dec. 17, 1927; d. Mose and Malinda (Johnson) Hill; m. Floyd Issac Warren, Apr. 12, 1962; children: Deborah Elaine, Kathy Yvonne. BS, Tex. Coll., 1951; postgrad., Baylor U., 1960, U. Tex., 1961; MEd, Prairie View A&M, 1965. Tchr. Falls County, Marlin, Tex., 1947, Rosebud (Tex.) ISD, 1950-62, Rosebud-Lott ISD, 1962—; mayor City of Rosebud, 1995—. Pres. Falls County Lake Tex. State Red Cross Assn., Rosebud, 1986-93; city counsel, Rosebud, 1985-87; pres. Cemetery Assn., Rosebud, 1986-94. Mem. Tex. Tchrs. Assn. (pres. Falls County chpt.), Nat. Coun. Tchrs. English, Delta Sigma Theta (pres. 1985). Home: 805 N 8th St Rosebud TX 76570 Office: Rosebud Lott IDS Judge Hailey Dr Rosebud TX 76556

WARREN, JERRY LEE, conductor, educator; b. Montgomery, Ala., Jan. 12, 1935; s. H.L. and Lula B. (Dowdy) W.; m. Dorothy Glen Floyd, Aug. 17, 1955; children: Dorothy Lee, Laura Ellen, John Floyd. B.M., Samford U., 1955; M.C.M., Sch. Ch. Music, So. Bapt. Theol. Sem., 1959, D.M.A., 1967. Minister music First Bapt. Ch., Cartersville, Ga., 1956-57, Auburn, Ala., 1959-63; asst. prof. music Shorter Coll., Rome, Ga., 1966-69; chmn. dept. music Belmont U., Nashville, 1969-83, dean Sch. Music, 1983-91, acting v.p. acad. affairs, 1991-92, provost, 1992—; choral performer Broadman Singers Rec. Group, Nashville, 1972-80; clinician sch. and ch. choral groups. Tenor soloist 1st Presbyn. Ch., Nashville, 1970-75, 77-79; founder, music dir. Bella Voci, 1997—. Mem. Am. Choral Dirs. Assn. (state pres. 1979-81, editor so. div. newsletter 1987-93, editorial bd. Choral Jour. 1987-94, program chair nat. conv. 1989, so. divsn. conv. 1994, pres. so. divsn. 2003—), Music Educators Nat. Conf., Tenn. Music Educators Assn. (state bd. 1976-88), Mid. Tenn. Vocal Assn. (coll. rep. 1976-88), Coll. Music Soc., Nat. Assn. Tchrs. Singing (local pres. 1974-76), Pi Kappa Lambda. Republican. Baptist. Avocations: golf, reading. Home: 5413 Barton Vale Dr Nashville TN 37211-8402 Office: Belmont U 1900 Belmont Blvd Nashville TN 37212-3757 Personal E-mail: Jerry.Warren@comcast.net. Business E-Mail: Warrenj@mail.belmont.edu.

WARREN, JOHN WILLIAM, professional society administrator; b. Clarksville, Ark., June 27, 1927; s. Frederick H. and Fannie Emily (Casey) W.; m. Marguerette Christine Cohoon, Oct. 9, 1948 (dec. Dec. 1987); children: Catherine Gail, Carolyn Anne, Eve Colette; m. Anna Jane Taylor, Feb. 10, 1990. BA, Abilene Christian U., 1949; MA, U. Ark., 1951; PhD, U. Tenn., 1961. Instr. U. Tenn., Knoxville, 1954—61; assoc. prof. David Lipscomb Coll., Nashville, 1961—62; prof., chmn. English Tenn. Tech. U., Cookeville, 1962—88; assoc. exec. dir. Phi Kappa Phi, Baton Rouge, 1988—92, exec. dir., 1992—99, exec. dir. emeritus, 1999—; v.p. Assn. Coll. Honor Socs., 1999—2001, pres., 2001—03. Author Ofcl. Lit. Map of Tenn., 1976; author: Tennessee Belles-Lettres-Guide to Tennessee Literature, 1976. Mem. Rotary (Cookeville pres. 1972-73), Phi Kappa Phi (Tenn. Tech. U. chpt. pres. 1980, SE region v.p. 1982-88, nat. bd. dirs. 1982-88). Republican. Mem. Ch. of Christ. Avocations: gardening, travel. E-mail: pkpjwarren@aol.com.

WARREN, RICHARD M. experimental psychologist, educator; b. N.Y.C., Apr. 8, 1925; s. Morris and Rae (Greenberg) W.; m. Roslyn Pauker, Mar. 31, 1950. BS in Chemistry, CCNY, 1946; PhD in Organic Chemistry, NYU, 1951. Flavor chemist Gen. Foods Co., Hoboken, N.J., 1951-53; rsch. assoc. psychology Brown U., Providence, 1954-56; Carnegie sr. rsch. fellow NYU Coll. Medicine, 1956-57, Cambridge (Eng.) U., 1957-58, rsch. psychologist applied psychology rsch. unit, 1958-59; rsch. psychologist NIMH, Bethesda, Md., 1959-61; chmn. psychology Shimer Coll., Mt. Carroll, Ill., 1961-64; assoc. prof. psychology U. Wis., Milw., 1964-66, prof., 1966-73, rsch. prof., 1973-75, disting. prof., 1975-95, adj. disting. prof., 1995—. Vis. scientist Inst. Exptl. Psychology, Oxford (Eng.) U., 1969-70, 77-78. Author: (with Roslyn Warren) Helmholtz on Perception: Its Physiology and Development, 1968, Auditory Perception: A New Analysis and Synthesis, 1999; contbr. articles to profl. jours. Fellow APA, Am. Psychol. Soc., Acoustical Soc. Am.; mem. AAAS, Am. Chem. Soc., Am. Speech and Hearing Assn., Sigma Xi. Office: U Wis Dept Psychology Milwaukee WI 53201

WARREN, RITA ROBINS, early childhood educator; b. N.Y.C., Jan. 22, 1924; d. Joseph and Anna (Levine) Robins; m. Lionel Gustave Warren, Dec. 21, 1952; children: David Harris, Matthew Marc, Steven Lewis. BA, Hunter Coll., 1945; postgrad., Towson State U., 1953-54. Cert. tchr. Md. Art dept. coord. Silberstein-Goldsmith Advt. Agy., N.Y.C., 1945-52; early childhood educator Balt. Pub. Sch., 1953-56; early childhood guidance cons. Houston Pub. Schs., 1957-60; early childhood ednl. cons. for English lang. studies Caracas (Venezuela) Pvt. Schs., 1960-63; early childhood educator New Orleans Pub. Schs., 1963-65, Jewish Cmty. Ctr. Pre-Sch., New Orleans, 1965-71; early childhood educator, dir., owner Threshold Sch., New Orleans, 1971-94. Publicity chair La. Assn. for the Edn. of Young Children, New Orleans, 1985-87, membership chair, 1988-90. Vol. interviewer New Orleans Legal Assistance Corp., 1990-95; literacy cons. Hancock County Pub. Libr., Bay St. Louis, Miss., 1995-98; vol. Hancock County Med. Ctr., 1997-2000; bd. dirs. Bay St. Louis Art Ctr., 1998-99, Walter Anderson Mus. Art. Mem. New Orleans Mus. Art. Avocations: writing travel descriptions for videos for presentations to groups, writing stories for young children in local schools and libraries. Home: PO Box 2245 Bay Saint Louis MS 39521-2245 E-mail: lgwrrw@aol.com.

WARREN, RUSSELL GLEN, academic administrator; b. Balt., Apr. 29, 1942; s. Clarence N. and Kathryn (Butler) W. BBA, U. Richmond, 1964; PhD, Tulane U., 1968. Asst. prof., then assoc. prof. U. Richmond (Va.), 1971-74, dean of Richmond Coll., 1974-76, asst. to univ. v.p., then. asst. to univ. pres., 1976-78; v.p. for acad. affairs U. Montevallo, Ala., 1978-84, James Madison U., Harrisonburg, Va., 1984-90, v.p. acad. affairs, 1986-87; acting pres. N.E. Mo. State U., Kirksville, 1990-95; Disting. prof. econs. and mgmt. Hardin-Simmons U., Abilene, Tex., 1995-97, dir. Ctr. for Rsch. on Teaching and Learning, 1995-97; exec. v.p., provost Mercer U., Macon, Ga., 1997—2002; sr. fellow Nat Assn. Ind. Colls. and Univs., Kiawah Island, SC, 2001—. Author: Antitrust in Theory and Practice, 1976, Carpe Diem, 1995. Bd. Dirs. Va. Rural Devel. Corp., Richmond, 1988-90. Capt. U.S. Army, 1969-71. Named One of Outstanding Young Men of Va., Va. Jaycees, 1976. Mem.: Am. Coun. on Edn. (coun. of fellows), Am. Assn. Colls. and Univs. (bd. dirs. 1994—95). Methodist. Avocations: golf, collecting cars. Home and Office: 175 Marsh Island Dr Kiawah Island SC 29455

WARREN, STEPHEN THEODORE, human geneticist, educator; b. Grosse Point, Mich., Nov. 30, 1953; s. Theodore Stephen and Frances (Fedo) W.; m. Karen Lee Pierce, Aug. 27, 1978; 1 child, Thomas. BS, Mich. State U., 1976, PhD, 1981. Diplomate Am. Bd. Med. Genetics. Grad. asst. Mich. State Univ., East Lansing, 1976-81; rsch. assoc. Univ. Ill., Chgo., 1981-83, instr., 1983-85; asst. prof. Emory U. Sch. of Medicine, Atlanta, 1985-91, assoc. prof., 1991-93, W.P. Timmie prof. human genetics, 1993—, chmn. dept. human genetics, 2001—; investigator Howard Hughes Med. Inst., 1992—2002. Vis. scientist European Molecular Biol. Lab., Heidelberg, Germany, 1984.; cons. Ctrs. for Disease Control, Atlanta, 1988-89, NIH, Bethesda, Md., 1989—; collaborator Ctr. D'Etude du Polymorphysme Humain, Paris, 1989—. Editor-in-chief Am. Jour. Human Genetics, 2000—; mem. editl. bd. Human Molecular Genetics, Am. Jour. Human Genetics, Cytogenetics, Cell Genetics, Mammalian Genome, others; contbr. chpts. to books and more than 200 articles to profl. jorus. Recipient Sigma Xi prize Mich. State Sigma Xi, East Lansing, 1981, NIH fellowship NIH, Bethesda, 1982, Basil O'Connor award March of Dimes, N.Y.C., 1986, Albert E. Levy award Emory Univ., Atlanta, 1987, William Rosen Rsch. award Nat. Fragile X Found., 1996. Mem. Am. Soc. Human Genetics (nominating com. 1991, awards con. 1992—, bd. dirs. 1997—, William Allan award 1999), Am. Soc. Biochemistry and Molecular Biology, Am. Soc. Microbiology, Genetics Soc. Am. Achievements include research on molecular genetic studies of the fragile X syndrome and other human genetic diseases. Home: 2305 Kimbrough Ct Atlanta GA 30350-5635 Office: Emory Univ Sch Medicine 301 Whitehead Bldg 615 Michael St Atlanta GA 30322-4218

WARRNER, ROBERT ANDREW, social studies educator; b. Spring Valley, Ill., Nov. 28, 1947; s. Robert John and Elizabeth Ann (Salisbury) W.; m. Janet McKee, June 27, 1970; children: James A., Robert D., Stephen S., Thomas J., Elizabeth L. BS, Ball State U., 1969, MA, 1972. Cert. social studies tchr. Social studies tchr. Muncie (Ind.) Schs., 1969-71, 73—; social studies instr. Ball State U., Muncie, 1971-72. Dept. chmn. Northside HS, Muncie; chmn. textbook adoption com. Muncie Schs., 1985; founding sponsor Muncie Ctrl. Jr. Historians, 1992—. Sponsor Nat. Honor Soc., 1998—. Named Tchr. of Yr. Jaycees Delaware County, 1985. Mem. NEA, Ind. State Tchrs. Assn., Muncie Tchrs. Assn. Democrat. Mem. Soc. Of Friends. Avocations: road racing, book collecting. Home: 505 N Bittersweet Ln Muncie IN 47304-3736 Office: Muncie Ctrl HS Muncie IN 47305

WARWICK, SHARON BRENDA, elementary art educator; b. El Paso, Tex., Dec. 18, 1946; d. George Clark and Charlene (Walker) W.; m. Alfonso Cortes, Sept. 14, 1978 (div. 1980); 1 child, Clark Lewis Cortes. BA, U. Tex., 1971; MEd, Tex. Woman's U., 1981, MFA, 1984. Cert. tchr. elem., art, secondary English., Tex. Art specialist Roger Williams Middle Sch., Providence, 1971-76; prof. English Instituto Allende, San Miguel de Allende, Mexico, 1977; tchr. English Krum (Tex.) High Sch., 1980-86; art specialist Borman Elem. Sch., Denton, Tex., 1986-92, Lakewood Elem. Sch., Euless, Tex., 1992-93, Shady Brook Elem. Sch., Bedford, Tex., 1993—; adj. instr. Cooke County Coll., Gainesville, Tex., 1984-85, Tex. Woman's U., Denton, 1985-86, U. North Tex., Denton, 1986-87; tchr. Cen. Jr. H.S., 1994-95; vis. asst. prof. art edn. dept. visual arts Tex. Woman's U., 1995—. V.p. It Works Inc. Pub. Co., Denton, 1979-80; assoc. rep. Tex. State Tchrs. Assn., Denton, 1989-91; guest educator Meadows Mus. Art, So. Meth. U., Dallas, 1994-96; part-time faculty Tarrant County Jr. Coll., 1995—; presenter in field. Solo exhbns. include Tex. Woman's U., Denton, 1984, Bath House Cultural Ctr., Dallas, 1989, Studio W Gallery, El Paso, Tex., 1991, Chilton Hall U. N. Tex., Denton, 1991, African Meth. Episcopal Ch., Denton, 1992, Ctr. for Visual Arts, Denton, 1996, 97; group shows include Saguarro Gallery, Denton, 1987, Lamar State U., 1989, Waterworks Gallery, 1989, Trammell Crow Ctr., Dallas, 1992, Trading Sisters Gallery, South Padre, 1993, Ctr. for Visual Arts, Denton, 1996, 97, others; solo slide/lectr. Dallas Mus. Art; contbg. author: Art Works, 1987, Spectra, 1988, Milagros, 1994, Portfolios, 1996. Hospitality chair Delta Kappa Gamma, Denton, 1992; exhbn. com. chair Greater Denton Arts Coun., 1987-97; del. Tex. Dem. Conv., Dallas, Houston, 1985-86. Recipient Yellow Rose of Tex., Gov. Ann Richards, 1991, PTA Tchr. of Yr., Shady Brook PTA, 1993-94, Founders award Denton Area Art Edn. Assn., 1996, various art awards, 1988—. Mem. Nat. Art Edn. Assn. (Nat. Mid. Divsn. Art Educator of Yr. award 1997), Am. Craft Assn., Tex. Art Edn. Assn. (elem. div. chair 1989-91, newsletter editor, bus. mgr., regional dir. visual arts scholastic event 1995—, Tex. Outstanding Art Educator - Mid. Divsn. 1996), Dallas Mus. Art, Modern Art Mus. Ft. Worth, Kimbell Mus. Art, North Tex. Inst. for Educators in the Visual Arts (leadership group, 1992), League United Latin Am. Citizens. Democrat. Unitarian Universalist. Avocations: potter, sculptor, painter. Home: 1003 Aileen St Denton TX 76201-2527 Office: Cen Jr H S 3191 W Pipeline Rd Euless TX 76040-6235

WASFIE, TARIK JAWAD, surgeon, educator; b. Baghdad, Iraq, July 1, 1946; m. Barina Y. Wasfie, Mar. 11, 1975; children: Giselle, Nissan. BS, Central U., Iraq, 1964; MD, Baghdad Med. Sch., 1970. Cert. gen. surgeon. Surg. rsch. assoc. Sinai Hosp. of Detroit/Wayne State U., 1981-85; clin. fellow Coll. Phys. & Surg., Columbia U., N.Y.C., 1985-91, postdoctoral rsch. scientist, 1987-91; attending surgeon Mich. State U./McLaren Hosp., Flint, 1991—. Contbr. articles to profl. jours. NIH grantee, 1984. Fellow ACS, Internat. Coll. Surgeons; mem. AMA, Mich. State Med. Soc., Flint Acad. Surgeons, Am. Soc. Artificial Internal Organs, Internat. Soc. Artificial Organs, Soc. Am. Gast. Endoscopic Surgeons. Achievements include production of antiidiotypic antibodies and their role in transplant immunology; development of percutenous access device. Home: 1125 Kings Carriage Rd Grand Blanc MI 48439-8715

WASHBURN, HARRIET CAROLINE, secondary education educator; b. Hallock, Minn., Mar. 15, 1920; d. John W. and Anna Melinda (Younggren) Swanson; m. Edward James Washburn, Jan. 22, 1971 (dec. 1993); children: Jacqueline Ann Batt, stepchild, Margaret; m. Ohls Batt. BA cum laude, Macalester Coll., 1941; MA in Pupil Personnel Svcs., San Jose State U., 1969. Tchr. Latin, English, phys. edn. Renville (Minn.) Pub. Sch., 1941-43; tchr. phys. edn. St. Cloud (Minn.) Jr. H. S., 1943-44, Fremont (Calif.) Unified Sch. Dist., 1958-69; recreation specialist City Recreation Dept., Lincoln, Nebr., 1946-50; dir. youth activities Trinity Meth. Ch., Lincoln, 1950-53; counselor Milpitas (Calif.) Unified Sch. Dist., 1969-75, head counselor, 1975-80; cons., trainer, speaker Stockton, Calif., 1980—; coord. bank acct. Bank of Stockton, 1989—99. Presenter Internat. Tng., Anaheim, 1978—; cons. personal, profl. devel. Personal Dynamics, Inc., Mpls., 1980-87; spkr., presenter in field. Moderator Presbyn. Women of the Stockton Presbytery PC, 2002—04. With USN, 1944—46. Recipient Sch. Counselor Svc. award Calif. Sch. Counselor Assn., Milpitas, 1980. Mem. AAUW, Lodi Investment Club, Alliance for the Mentally Ill of S.J. County, Internat. Tng. in Comm. (life), Rep. Women's Club. Presbyterian. Avocations: bridge, bible study, reading, writing.

WASHBURN, RICHARD WILBUR, secondary education educator; b. Freeport, Ill., Jan. 26, 1947; s. Wilbur William and Natalie Elaine (Staas) W.; m. Ana Iris Degado Perez, Mar. 16, 1974; children: Juan Reyes, Janette Ivonne Reyes. BS in Maths., U. Ill., 1969, MS in Maths., 1970. Cert. secondary tchr., P.R. Teaching asst. U. Ill., Champaign-Urbana, 1969-70; tchr. maths. Antilles Consolidated schs., Ceiba, P.R., 1972—. With U.S. Army, 1970-72. Mem. Math. Assn. Am., Nat. Coun. Tchrs. math., Antilles Consol. Edn. Assn. (pres. 1982-83, treas. 1993-94, 97—), Asociación Puertoriqueña de Maestros de Matemáticas, Phi Beta Kappa, Phi Kappa Phi. Avocations: wood-working, organist, electronics, computers, gardening. Home: HC 1 Box 4472 Naguabo PR 00718-9717 Office: Antilles Consolidated Schs Box 3200 Ceiba PR 00735

WASHBURN, SUSAN LYNN, educational consultant; b. Rahway, NJ, Apr. 13, 1951; d. Frank Edgar and Marie Josephine (Greene) W. BA in English, Franklin & Marshall Coll., 1973; MS in Indsl. Mgmt. Mktg., Clarkson U., 1980. Asst. dir. devel. Franklin & Marshall Coll., Lancaster, Pa., 1973-74; dir. corp. and found. rels. St. Lawrence U., Canton, N.Y., 1974-77; v.p. Centenary Coll., Hackettstown, N.J., 1977-79; dir. devel. The

Evergreen State Coll., Olympia, Wash., 1979-82, dir. coll. rels., devel., 1982-86, v.p. devel. and adminstrn., 1986—88; v.p. univ. rels. St. Lawrence U., Canton, N.Y., 1988-96; ptnr. Washburn and McGoldrick, Inc., Latham, N.Y., 1995—. Chmn., bd. trustees Coun. Advancement Support Edn., Washington, 1985-92; trustee Franklin & Marshall Coll., 1995—. Named Coun. Advancement Support Edn. Profl. Yr., 1995. Office: Washburn and McGoldrick Inc 8 Century Hill Dr Ste 1 Latham NY 12110-2116

WASHICK, RITA LUCIAN, special education educator; b. Hazleton, Pa., May 13, 1949; d. Tristram Frank Lucian and Cecilia (Meloni) DeFluri; m. Robert L. Washick, Sept. 6, 1977; children: Lindsay, Jessica. BS in Spl. Edn., Bloomsburg State U., 1975, MEd in Behavior Therapy, 1980. Cert. spl. edn., behavior therapist, Pa. Spl. educator White Haven (Pa.) State Sch. & Hosp., 1968-75; spl. edn. tchr. Carbon-Lehigh Intermediate Unit # 21, Schnecksville, Pa., 1977-92; spl. edn. elem. tchr. Nesquehoning (Pa.) Spl. Edn. Ctr., 1977-80; spl. edn. GED tchr. Hickory Run Youth Forestry Camp, White Haven, Pa., 1980-89; spl. edn. elem. resource Panther Valley Elem., Nesquehoning, 1989-92; spl. edn. secondary tchr. Jim Thorpe (Pa.) Vocat. Sch., 1992—; home sch. evaluator, 1995. Judge, vol. Sorrento Gardens Drug & Alcohol, Hazleton, Pa., 1990-92. Pres. Lake Harmony (Pa.) Ladies Aux. Fire Co., 1985; sec. Conyngham (Pa.) Park and Recreation Bd., 1992. Mem. Coun. Exceptional Children, Pa. Home Schoolers Assn. Democrat. Avocations: coordinating summer park program, cooking, sewing, stained glass, tutoring. Home: PO Box 253 360 Main St Conyngham PA 18219 Office: Carbon Lehigh Intermediate Unit # 21 200 Orchard Rd Schnecksville PA 18219 also: Carbon County Area Vo-Tech Sch 150 West 15th St Jim Thorpe PA 18229

WASHINGTON, ADRIENNE MARIE, elementary school educator; b. Chgo., June 26, 1950; d. Henry and Emily Marguerite (Sims) Robertson; m. Gregory Blake, Mar. 26, 1967 (div.); children: Emily M., Gregory D.; m. Donald Booker Washington, Apr. 18, 1990. BA, U. Mich., 1976, MA, 1977; Specialist in Arts, Ea. Mich. U., 1991. Cert. tchr., Mich. Head tchr. Second Bapt. Day Care, Ann Arbor, Mich., 1977; tchr. Willow Run Pub. Schs., Ypsilanti, 1977—. Workshop presenter Nat. Black Child Devel. Inst., detroit, 1984; pub. rels./crisis chair WREA; founder What Black History Means to Me essay contest. Youth leader NAACP, Ypsilanti, 1980's; campaign asst. Dem. orgn., Ypsilanti, 1988, 91; canvasser Mar. Dimes; corr. sec. Brown Chapel A.M.E. Ch., tchr. Bible sch., co-chair sesquecentinnel anniversary. Hon. Citizen City of Nashville, 1992, State of Tenn., 1992. Mem. Nat. Assn. Black Bus. and Profl. Women's Clubs (pres. 1984-86, Spl. Appreciation award 1997), Tenn. Black Caucus of State Legislators (hon. mem.), Elks (pres. PSP Club of Mich. 1988-95, fin. sec. Anna G. Parker Temple No. 1283). Avocations: travel, reading, sewing. Home: 10268 Bemis Rd Willis MI 48191-9742

WASHINGTON, DELPHINE CYNTHIA, special education educator, artist; b. Logansport, La., June 24, 1945; d. Roy Thomas Washington and Cuevator Francez (Singleton) Washington-Taylor; m. Howard Littlejohn, Mar., 1969 (div. Sept., 1980); 1 child, Mona Lisa Francez Washington. BEd in Art Edn. and Mentally Retarded, Grambling State U., 1974, postgrad. in Edn., 1989; MEd in Elem. Edn., Prairie View A&M U., 1981. Spl. edn. tchr. Walnut Hill Jr. High Sch., Shreveport, La., 1979-80, Second Ward High SCh., Glaster, La., 1981-82; spl. edn. and art tchr. North DeSoto High Sch., Stonewall, La., 1982—. Art tchr. summer program, Shreeveport Regional Arts Coun., 1992. Exhibited in group show at African Am. Art Exh., Ebony Expressions Art Gallery, Shreveport, La. (1st place water color painting "The Old Black Church"), 1993. Recipient Art Trophy, Spl. Edn. Supr., Mansfield La. Art Show, 1982, Key to City, Mayor Baton Rouge, La., 1992, Cert. of Appreciations, White House Art Exhibit,President Bush, 1992, Appreciation cert. Supr. Spl. Edn., 1992. Mem. NAUW, PTA (cert. appreciation 1990), Coun. Exceptional Children. Avocations: oil painting, drawing, water color, ceramics, music.

WASHINGTON, JOSEPHINE HARRIET, biologist, endocrinologist, educator; b. Demopolis, Ala., Dec. 14, 1958; d. Joseph C. and Edna (Burns) W. BS in Chemistry, Judson Coll., 1980; MS in Biology, Ala. A&M U., 1985; MEd in Biology Edn., Ala. State U., 1992; postgrad., Howard U., 1992—. Grad. rsch. asst. Ala. A&M U., Normal, 1982-85; histopathology technician VA, Biloxi, Miss., 1985-86; instr. in biology Stillman Coll., Tuscaloosa, Ala., 1986-95, asst. prof. biology, 1995—. Health career advisor Stillman Coll., 1986-95, sec. math. and sci. divsn., 1988-89, sec. profl. ethics and conduct com., 1989-90, mem. com. acad. advising, 1993-95. Grantee Dept. Edn., 1993-95, NASA, 1995. Mem. AAUW, Nat. Assn. Biology Sci. Tchrs., Alpha Zeta. Democrat. Methodist. Avocations: piano, reading.

WASHINGTON, PATRICIA LANE, retired school counselor; b. Junction City, Kans., June 23, 1943; d. LeRoy and Rose Mary (Strong) Lane; children: Janet Rosemarie, Kelly Edward. BS in Elem. Edn., Lincoln U., 1965; postgrad., U. Kans., 1968, 69, 70; specialist in counseling, U. Mo., Kansas City, 1972, postgrad., 1990-93; MS in Learning Disabilities, Ctrl. Mo. State U., 1975; postgrad., Met. C.C., Kansas City, Mo., 1979, Nat. Coll., Kansas City, 1983, Ottawa U., 1984, Avilla Coll., 1993. Cert. elem. and secondary tchr., tchr. of bevavioral disordered, learning disabled, psychol. examiner, counselor, Mo. 1st grade tchr. Kansas City Sch. Dist., 1965-68, head start instr., 1966-69, sr. instr., 1968-75, K-6 grade resource tchr., 1975-77, ednl. resource tchr. with gifted and talented students, 1979, ednl. resource tchr. early identification screening program, 1980, mem. screening team, 1980-81; sr. H.S. learning disabilities instr. Kansas City Bd. Edn., 1981, mem. spl. edn. placement team., 1981-84, sch. psychol. examiner, 1984-88, placement advisor, psychol. examiner, 1988-89, learning disabilities high sch. instr., 1989-90, elem. guidance counselor, 1990-91, mid. sch. guidance counselor, 1991-92, high sch. guidance counselor, 1992-93, chpt. I counselor grades K-5, 1993-94, mid. sch. counselor, 1994-95; ret., 1995; exec. dir., owner Upper Pathways - The Wave of the Future, Kansas City, 1996—. Dir., counselor Jackson County Ct., summer 1971; instr. Pioneer C.C., 1970-80, 80-81, 82; coord., instr. Second Bapt. Ch. Adminstr., 1983; coord. Youth As Resources Hickman Mills Sch. Dist.; spkr. in field; mentor tchr. Kansas City Sch. Dist. Pres. Host-Hostess ministry 2d Missionary Bapt. Ch. Mem. Am. Legion, Optimist Club. Democrat. Baptist. Avocations: reading, speaking, bowling, dance, travel. Home and Office: 10107 Central # 310 Kansas City MO 64114-4683

WASHINGTON, REBECCA NAN, educational association administrator; b. Amherst, Tex., Jan. 21, 1950; d. James Earl and Betty (Hinson) Parish; m. Randy Paul Washington, June 12, 1970; children: Christopher Paul, Stacy Bea. BS in Edn., Tex. Tech. U., 1973; MEd, S.W. Tex. State U., 1994. Cert. ednl. adminstr., Tex. Tchr. Round Rock (Tex.) H.S., 1976-78; dir. Hyde Park Weekday Childcare, Austin, Tex., 1979-83, Stepping Stones Presch., Georgetown, Tex., 1985-89; tchr. Georgetown Jr. H.S., 1989-94; asst. prin. Purl Elem. Sch., Georgetown, 1994-96; prin. Williams Elem., Georgetown, 1996-99, Cooper Elem. Sch., Georgetown, 1999—2001; coord. Educator Cert. Program Region 13 Edn. Svc. Ctr., Austin, Tex., 2001—. Trainor Dimensions of Learning, CHAMPS classroom discipline model, Founds. schoolwide discipline model; tchrs. leading tchrs. cohort, Regional 13 Ednl. Svc. Ctr. Adv. bd. Bapt. Gen. Conv. of Tex. Weekday Early Edn. Divsn., Dallas, 1987-89. Named Outstanding Tchr., Am. Ent. Forum, Houston, 1991. Mem. ASCD, Tex. Hist. Assn. (Commendation 1993), Tex. Elem. Prins. and Suprs. Assn., Tex. Coun. for the Social Studies, Tex. Social Studies Suprs. Assn., Phi Delta Kappa. Avocations: music, reading, sports. Office: Region 13 Education Svc Center 5701 Springdale Rd Austin TX 78723

WASHNOK, MARGUERITE BARONDEAU, nursing educator; b. Aberdeen, S.D., Aug. 15, 1954; d. Lewis Albert and Clara Janet (Deis) Barondeau; married, June 12, 1976; children: Rebecca Lynn, James Dale. B of Arts Nursing, Jamestown Coll., 1976; MSN, Tex. Woman's U., 1984; D in Nursing, Western Reserve U., 1998. Cert. clin. nurse specialist in cmty. health. Dormatory nurse S.D. Devel. Ctr., Redfield, 1977-79; nursing instr. Presentation Coll., Aberdeen, S.D., 1979-86, 90—; charge nurse pediatrics Dakota Midland Hosp., Aberdeen, 1989-91; staff nurse pediatrics St. Luke's Hosp., Aberdeen, summers 1985-86; home health nurse St. Luke's Midland Hosp., Aberdeen, 1986-89; cmty. health nurse S.D. Dept. Health, Aberdeen, 1989-90; nurse rehab. cons. Midwest Inc., Aberdeen, 1992—; assoc. prof. Presentation Coll., 1999—. Nursing instr. S.D. State U., Aberdeen, 1986-89; co-chair Immunization Coalition Aberdeen Area, 1993—; assoc. prof. nursing Presentation Coll.; presenter in field. Author video: You Can Save Your Child's Life, 1983; co-writer children's coloring book. Parent coach Odyssey of Mind, 1991-; CCD coord. St. John Bapt. Ch., Groton, S.D., 1991-; group leader Ice Carnival, Groton, 1989-; mem. edn. com. parish coun. St. John's Cath. Ch., 1992-; contact person Kids Art Day Groton, 1992-; mem. Risk Mgmt. PC, Aberdeen, 1991—; mem. ch. bd. SEAS Cath. Ch. Bush grantee in charge acad. advising. Mem. ANA, Nat. Network for Immunization Nurses and Assocs., Am. Registry of Outstanding Profls., S.D. Nursing Assn. (mem. Aberdeen area bylaws com. 1991-, cmty. health divsn. dist. 13, 1991-, pres. 1979, 90, Dist. Nurse of Yr. 1993), Jaycees (Outstanding Jaycee Groton chpt. 1991, Outstanding Jaycee Project award 1991, 93). Democrat. Roman Catholic. Avocations: working with 4h, sewing, biking, swimming, arts and crafts. Home: 406 E 7th Ave Groton SD 57445-2129 Office: Presentation Coll 1500 N Main St Aberdeen SD 57401-1299 E-mail: washnok@nvc.net.

WASINGER, MICHAELITA JEAN, principal, educator; b. Hays, Kans., July 10, 1945; d. Mike and Georgine (Windholz) W. BS, Fort Hays U., 1971, MS, 1973. Tchr. Sacred Heart Sch., Plainville, Kans., 1968-71; tchr., head tchr. Alamota Grade Sch. Unified Sch. Dist. 482, Dighton, Kans., 1972-80; tchr. Dighton Grade Sch. Unified Sch. Dist. 482, 1980-82; tchr., prin. St. Leo (Kans.) Sch., 1982-84; tchr. Blessed Sacrament Sch., Wichita, Kans., 1984-93; tchr., prin. St. Joseph Sch., Conway Springs, Kans., 1993—2001; prin. Holy Spirit Cath. Sch., Goddard, Kans., 2001—. Math. curriculum com. Cath. Diocese of Wichita, 1987—. Author: (multi-media kit) TLC About the Ageing, 1976. Mem. Kans. Assn. of Tchrs. of Math., Nat. Coun. of Tchrs. of Math. Republican. Roman Catholic. Avocations: woodworking, photography, camping. Address: PO Box 225 Goddard KS 67052-0225 Office: Holy Spirit Cath Sch 18218 W Hwy 54 Goddard KS 67052-8000 E-mail: mwasinger@holyspiritwichita.com.

WASIUK, KATHLEEN PAGE, secondary education educator; b. Princeton, N.J., Feb. 22, 1947; d. Warren Kempton amd Martha Jane (Lutz) Page; m. Joseph Steven Wasiuk, July 29, 1967; 1 child, Virginia Hope. BFA, U. Ariz., 1970; MA in Liberal Studies, Dartmouth Coll., 1988. Tchr. Tilton (N.H.) Sch., 1975-87, Northfield (Mass.) Mt. Hermon Sch., 1988—2003, chmn. history dept., 1990-94, dir. acad. resources, 1995-99, asst. to head, 1999—. Bd. dirs. Gould Farm. Named Outstanding Young Career Woman, Bus. and Profl. Women's Club N.H., 1974. Mem. Elephant Rock Assn. (pres.). Congregationalist.

WASKOW, JOYCE ANN, school administrator; b. Meriden, Iowa, Aug. 15, 1941; d. Clarence Emory and Lucille Dorothy (Horstman) Smith; m. James R. Waskow, July 6, 1963; children: Susan, Brent. BS, Iowa State U., 1963; MA, U. Mo., St. Louis, 1992. Cert. edn. specialist, Mo. Home econs./sci. tchr. Collins (Iowa) H.S., 1963-64; home economist Met. Sewer Dist., Omaha, 1964-65; home econs. tchr. Westbrook Jr. H.S., Omaha, 1965-67; home economist The Merchandising Group, N.Y.C., 1970-76; home econs. tchr. Pattonville H.S., St. Louis, 1976-79, Maplewood-Richmond Hts. H.S., St. Louis, 1979-80, Webster Groves H.S., St. Louis, 1980-93; dir. Tchr.'s Acad. Network for Ednl. Devel., St. Louis, 1989-92; asst. prin. Lafayette H.S., St. Louis, 1993—, ret., 2003. Spkr./workshop leader Network for Edn. Devel., 1987—. SASSP Assistant Principal of Year, 1998; recipient Eddy award Mo. Pub. Sch. Edn., 1999. Mem. ASCD, Nat. Assn. Secondary Sch. Prins., Am. Home Econs. Assn. (nominating com.), Suburban Home Econs. Assn. (pres. 1986-87), Nat. Assn. Vocat. Home Econs. Tchrs. (Disting. Svc. award 1989), Mo. Home Econs. Tchrs. Assn. (Tchr. of the Yr. 1987, nominating com. 1987-88), Mo. Assn. Secondary Sch. Prins. (sec.-treas. 1997—, asst. prin. of yr. 1999, pres. 2000-01), St. Louis Area Secondary Sch. Prin. Assn. (Mo. asst. prin. of yr. 1999, v.p.). Avocations: reading, whitewater rafting, hiking, antiquing, orienteering.

WASS, HANNELORE LINA, educational psychology educator; b. Heidelberg, Germany, Sept. 12, 1926; came to U.S., 1957, naturalized, 1963; d. Hermann and Mina (Lasch) Kraft; m. Irvin R. Wass, Nov. 24, 1959 (dec.); 1 child, Brian C.; m. Harry H. Sisler, Apr. 13, 1978. BA, Tchrs. Coll., Heidelberg, 1951; MA, U. Mich., 1960, PhD, 1968. Tchr. W. Ger. Univ. Lab. Schs., 1958-60; mem. faculty U. Mich., Ann Arbor, 1958-60, U. Chgo. Lab. Sch., 1960-61, U. Mich., 1963-64, Eastern Mich. U., 1965-69; prof. ednl. psychology U. Fla., Gainesville, 1969-92, prof. emeritus, 1992—, faculty assoc. Ctr. for Gerontol. Studies. Cons., lectr. in thanatology. Author: The Professional Education of Teachers, 1974, Dying-Facing the Facts, 1979, 2d edit., 1988, 3d edit., 1995, Death Education: An Annotated Resource Guide, 1980, vol. 2, 1985, Helping Children Cope With Death, 1982, 2d edit., 1984, Childhood and Death, 1984; founding editor (jour.) Death Studies, 1977-92; cons. editor: Ednl. Gerontology, 1977-92, (book series) Death Education, Aging and Health Care, 1980-96; contbr. approximately 200 articles to profl. jours. and chpts. in books. Mem. Am. Psychol. Assn., Gerontol. Soc., Internat. Work Group Dying, Death and Bereavement (bd. dirs.), Assn. Death Edn. and Counseling. Home: 6014 NW 54th Way Gainesville FL 32653-3265 Office: U Fla 346 Norman Hall Gainesville FL 32611-2053 E-mail: wass@nersp.nerdc.ufl.edu .

WASSELL, STEPHEN ROBERT, mathematics educator, researcher; b. Santa Monica, Calif., Jan. 17, 1963; s. Desmond Anthony and Catherine Ann (Stephens) W. BS in Arch., U. Va., Charlottesville, 1984, PhD in Math., 1990, M in Computer Sci., 1999. Programmer, analyst UNISYS, McLean, Va., 1984-85, graphics artist, 1986; tutor summer transition program U. Va., Charlottesville, 1987-88, tchg. asst., 1986-90; asst. prof. math. Sweet Briar (Va.) Coll., 1990-96, assoc. prof. math., 1996—2002, prof. math., 2002—, dept. chmn., 1996—97, 1999—2002. Prof. of record Ctr. for the Liberal Arts, U. Va., 1991; vis. asst. prof. math., U. Va., Charlottesville, 1992, vis. assoc. prof. computer sci., 1998-99; doctoral cons., Charlottesville, 1989-90. Author: (with Kim Williams) On Ratio and Proportion, 2002; author: Nexus 2: Architecture and Mathematics, 1998, Nexus 3: Architecture and Mathematics, 2000; editor: The Golden Section, 2003; contbr. chpt. to book. Recipient Grad. assistantship award U. Va., 1986-90; Gordon T. Whyburn fellow, 1985-86. Mem. AAUP (Sweet Briar chpt. sec.-treas. 1993-99), Am. Math. Soc., Math. Assn. Am., Am. Solar Energy Soc., Sigma Nu (Beta chpt. treas. 1985-86). Achievements include patents for solar powered lawnmover, for solar shed, for ear muffs. Home: 4500 Monacan Trail Rd North Garden VA 22959-2215 Office: Sweet Briar Coll Dept Math Scis Sweet Briar VA 24595 E-mail: wassell@sbc.edu.

WASSENBERG, EVELYN M. medical and surgical nurse, nursing educator; b. Oct. 8, 1933; d. Patrick A. and Mary A. (Kieffer) L'Ecuyer; m. Maurice P. Wassenberg, Oct. 29, 1955; children: Sherry Ann Gaines, Laura Marie O'Neil. Diploma in nursing, Marymount Sch. Nursing, Salina, Kans., 1955; BS in Nursing, Marymount Coll. of Salina, 1982; MN, Wichita State U., 1987. Cert. nurse specialist. Dir. nursing svc. Community Meml. Hosp. Inc., Marysville, Kans., 1962-79; house supr. Luth. Hosp., Beatrice, Nebr., 1980-82; primary nurse Beatrice Cmty. Hosp., 1983; instr. Ft. Scott (Kans.) C.C., 1983-2001; nurse Girard (Kans.) Hosp., 2001; ICU nurse Nevada (Mo.) Regional Health Ctr., 2001—. Mem. Mary Queen of Angels Cath. Ch. Named Nurse of Yr. Bourbon County Kans., 1992. Mem. Am. Nursing Assn., Kans. State Nursing Assn., Sigma Theta Tau. Address: 216 S Crawford St Fort Scott KS 66701-3231 Office: Nevada Regional Med Ctr 800 S Ash St Nevada MO 64772

WASSERMAN, BURTON, artist, educator; b. Bklyn., Mar. 10, 1929; s. Louis and Matilda (Kravitz) W.; m. Sarah Frances Masher, Nov. 2, 1950; 1 child, Marc. BA, Bklyn. Coll., 1950; MA, Columbia U., 1954, EdD, 1958. Art tchr. various pub. schs., L.I., N.Y., 1954-59; prof. art Rowan U., Glassboro, N.J., 1960—. Prin. art exhibition critic Art Matters, Phila., 1981—. Author: Exploring the Visual Arts, Modern Painting: The Movements, The Artists, Their Work, Bridges of Vision: The Art of Prints and the Craft of Printmaking; (with Sarita Rainey) Basic Silkscreen Printmaking, Crayon Resist Techniques; exhibited in various group shows; represented in permanent collections Phila. Mus. Art, N.J. State Mus., Stedelijk Mus., Amsterdam, Macedonian Ctr. for Contemporary Art, Thessaloniki Greece, numerous colls., cos., and pvt. collections. With U.S. Army, 1951-53. Recipient 1st prize Huntington Twp. Art League, 1956, L.I. Art Tchrs. Ann. Exhbn., 1957, 3d prize Hofstra U. Ann. Art Exhbn. L.I. Artists, 1956, 57, Brickhouse purchase prize Norfolk (Va.) Mus. Art and Scis., 1965; Kelsey Purchase prize N.J. State Mus., 1966, Ryan purchase prize, 1967; purchase prize USIA, 1970, hon. citation and Liberty Bell award City of Phila., 1992; grantee State of N.J., Rowan Coll. N.J., 1977, 78, 80, 83, 84, 86, 92. Mem. Phila. Art Alliance (bd. dirs. 1978-83); Artists Equity (past nat. pres. 1971-73). Avocations: reading, travel. Home: 204 Dubois Rd Glassboro NJ 08028-1225 Office: Wesby Art Ctr Rowan Univ Glassboro NJ 08028

WASSERMAN, EUGENE M. pediatrician, educator; b. Bklyn., Mar. 2, 1931; s. Jacob and Lena (Kartel) W.; m. Nancy C. Ziluck, Sept. 1, 1959; children: Brett D., A. Michael, Julie B. BA, Columbia U., 1952; MD, Chgo. med. Sch., 1956. Rotating intern Kings County Hosp. Med. Ctr., Bklyn., 1956-57; resident in pediat. Mt. Sinai Hosp., N.Y.C., 1957-59; practice medicine specializing in pediat. United Hosp., Port Chester, N.Y., 1961—, chmn. pediat., 1975-80; clin. asst. prof. pediat. N.Y. Med. Coll., Valhalla, 1997—. Voluntary staff Greenwich (Conn.) Hosp., 2000—. Chmn. drs.' com. Village of Mamaroneck, N.Y., 1975-85. Capt. M.C. U.S. Army, 1959-61. Fellow Am. Acad. Pediats.; mem. Med. Soc. N.Y. Jewish. Avocation: cabinet making. Office: 1600 Harrison Ave PO Box 186 Mamaroneck NY 10543-0186

WASSERMAN, PAUL, library and information science educator; b. Newark, Jan. 8, 1924; s. Joseph and Sadie (Ringelescu) W.; m. Krystyna Ostrowska, 1973; children: Jacqueline R., Steven R. BBA, Coll. City N.Y., 1948; MS in L.S., Columbia, 1949, MS, 1950; PhD, U. Mich., 1960; postgrad., Western Res. U., 1963-64. Advt. mgr. Zuckerberg Co., N.Y.C., 1946-48; asst. to bus. libr. Bklyn. Pub. Library, 1949-51, chief sci. and industry div., 1951-53; librarian, asst. prof. Grad. Sch. Bus. and Pub. Adminstrn., Cornell U., 1953-56, libr., assoc. prof., 1956-62, librarian, prof., 1962-65; dean U. Md. Coll. Library and Info. Scis., 1965-70, prof., 1970-97, prof. emeritus, 1997—. Vis. prof. U. Mich., summers 1960, 63, 64, Asian Inst. Tech., U. Hawaii, U. Hong Kong, summer 1988, Chulalongkorn U., Bangkok, 1990, U. Wash., summer 1991, U. Wis., summer 1991, U. Wis., summer 1992, C.W. Post Coll., L.I. U., 1993, Inst. Sci. and Tech. China, Beijing, 1996; Isabel Nichol lectr. Denver U. Libr. Sch., 1968; market rsch. cons. Laux Advt., Inc., 1955-59, Gale Rsch. Co., Detroit, 1959-60, 63-64; rsch. planning cons. Ind. U. Sch. Bus., 1961-62; cons. to USPHS as mem. manpower tng. rev. com. Nat. Libr. Medicine, 1966-69, Ohio Bd. Regents, 1969, Omngraphics Inc., 1988-91, VITA, summer 1987; dir. Documentation Abstracts, Inc., 1970-73, v.p., 1971-73; Fulbright prof. Warsaw U., 1993-94; rsch. project dir. Kellogg Study, 1996-98. Author: Information for Adminstrators, 1956, (with Fred Silander) Decision Making, 1958, Measurement and Evaluation of Organization Performance, 1959, Sources of Commodity Prices, 1960, 2d edit., 1974, Sources for Hospital Administrators, 1961, Decision Making: An Annotated Bibliography, supplement, 1958-63, 1964, Librarian and the Machine, 1965; Book rev. editor: Adminstrv. Sci. Quar, 1956-61; editor: Service to Business, 1952-53, Directory of University Research Bureaus and Institutes, 1960, Health Organizations of the U.S. and Canada, 1961, and 2d to 4th edit., 1977, Statistics Sources, 1962 and 4th to 8th edits., 1984, (with Bundy) Reader in Library Adminstration, 1968, Reader in Research Methods in Librarianship, 1969; mng. editor: Mgmt. Information Guide Series, 1963-83, Consultants and Consulting Organizations, 1966, 4th edit., 1979, 5th edit., 1982, Who's Who in Consulting, 1968, 2d edit., 1974, Awards, Honors and Prizes: A Sourcebook and Directory, 1969, 2d edit., 1972, 4th edit. Vol. 1, 1978, International and Foreign Awards, 1975, New Consultants, 1973-74, 76-77, 78-79, Readers in Librarianship and Information Science, 1968-78, Ency. Bus. Information Sources, 1971, 3d edit., 1976, 4th edit., 1980, 5th edit., 1983, Library and Information Services Today, 1971-75, Consumer Sourcebook, 1974, 2d edit., 1978, 3d edit., 1980, 4th edit., 1983; series editor: Contributions in Librarianship and Information Science, 1969-99; coordinating mgmt. editor: Information Guide Library, 1971-83, The New Librarianship-A Challenge for Change, 1972; mng. editor: Museum Media, 1973, Library Bibliographies and Indexes, 1975, Ethnic Groups in the United States, 1976, 2d edit., 1982, Training and Development Organizations, 1978, 2d edit., 1983, Speakers and Lecturers: How to Find Them, 1979, 2d edit., 1982, Learning Independently, 1979, 2d edit., 1983, Recreation and Outdoor Life Directory, 1979, Law and Legal Information Directory, 1980, 2d edit., 1982, Ency. Health Info. Sources, 1986, Ency. Sr. Citizen Info. Sources, 1987, Ency. Pub. Affairs Info. Sources, 1987, Ency. Legal Info. Sources, 1987; mem. editorial bd. Social Scis. Citation Index, Inst. Scientific Info., 1972-95, Jour. Library Adminstrn., 1979-89, Social Sci. Info. Studies, 1979—, 1991 Education for Info.: The Internat. Rev. of Education and Tng. in Library and Info. Sci., 1983-88, The Best of Times: A Personal and Occupational Odyssey, 2000, New York from A to Z, 2002, Washington DC from A to Z, 2003. Active U.S. Com. on Edn. and Tng. for Internat. Fedn. for Info. and Documentation, 1993-94. Served with U.S. Army, 1943-46. Decorated Purple Heart, Bronze Star; recipient ALA Ref. Svcs. Divsn./Gale Rsch. Bus. Libr. award, 1997; Fulbright scholar, Sri Lanka, 1986-87. Mem. AAUP, ALA, Am. Soc. Info. Sci., Spl. Librs. Assn. (editor, chmn. publ. project., Disting. Mem. award bus. divsn. 1996—). Home: 4940 Sentinel Dr Apt 203 Bethesda MD 20816-3552 Office: U Md Coll Info Studies College Park MD 20742-0001 E-mail: pw11@umail.umd.edu.

WASSERMAN, STANLEY, statistician, educator; b. Louisville, Aug. 29, 1951; s. Irvin Levitch and Jeanne (Plattus) W.; m. Sarah Wilson, Feb. 3, 1974; children: Andrew Joseph, Eliot Miles. BS in Econs., U. Pa., 1973; PhD in Stats., Harvard U., 1977. Asst. prof. U. Minn., Mpls., 1977-82; assoc. prof. U. Ill., Urbana, 1982-88, prof. psychology, stats., sociology, 1988—; prof. Beckman Inst., 1993—. Vis. rschr. Columbia Univ., N.Y.C., 1978; cons., expert witness EEOC, Cleve., 1979-81; cons. V.A. Med. Ctr., Mpls., 1980-82, AT&T Communications, Basking Ridge, N.J., 1988-90. Author: Social Network Analysis, 1994; assoc. editor: Sociological Methodology, 1978-81, Jour. Am. Statis. Assn., 1987—, Psychometrika, 1988-, Am. Statistician, 1993-96, Structural Analysis, 1997-2000; guest editor: Sociol. Methods and Rsch., 1992; book review editor: Chance, 1993—; consulting editor Am. Jour. Sociology, 2000—. Treas. Montessori Sch. of Champaign-Urbana, Savoy, Ill., 1990-92, bd. dirs. WEFT-FM, 2001-03. Grantee NSF, Washington, 1979-81, 84-89, 93-2003. NIH, 1995-98, 2000-, ONR, 2002--; postdoctoral fellow Social Sci. Rsch. Coun., N.Y.C., 1978. Fellow AAAS, Am. Statis. Assn.; mem. Psychometric Soc., Royal Statis. Soc., Classification Soc. N.Am. (sec., treas. 1993-95, bd. dirs. 1996-98. 99-2000, pres. 2002-03), Internat. Network for Social Network Analysis (bd. dirs. 1997--). Achievements include reseach in applied statistics, categorical data analysis, social network analysis. Home: 2066 County Road 125 E Mahomet IL 61853-8907 Office: U Ill 603 E Daniel St Champaign IL 61820-6232 E-mail: stanwass@uiuc.edu.

WASSON, ELLIS ARCHER, history educator; b. Rye, NY, Dec. 31, 1947; s. Samuel Carson and Elizabeth (Ellis) W. BA, MA, Johns Hopkins U., 1972; PhD, Cambridge (Eng.) U., 1976. Dean of faculty The Rivers Sch., Weston, Mass., 1976-86; headmaster sr. sch. Shady Side Acad., Pitts., 1986-91; chmn. history dept. Tower Hill Sch., Wilmington, Del., 1991—. Test devel. com. Coll. Bd., N.Y.C., 1985-87, cons., 1981—; adj. prof. history U. Del., 2001— Author: Whig Renaissance, 1987, AP European History, 1995, Born to Rule: British Political Elites, 2000; contbr. articles to profl. jours., chpts. to books. Treas. New Eng. History Tchrs. Assn., Boston, 1978-79; chmn. history com. Ind. Sch. Assn. Mass., Boston, 1981-83, chmn. acad. deans, 1982-86; mem. alumni admissions com. Johns Hopkins U., Pitts. and Wilmington, 1987-2000; corporator The Rivers Sch., 1986-91; convenor Am. Friends of Cambridge U., Pitts., 1986-91. Gilman fellow Johns Hopkins U., 1972, NEH fellow, 1984, rsch. fellow English Speaking Union, 1994, 2000. Fellow Royal Hist. Soc.; mem. Inst. for Hist. Rsch. (U. London), Am. Hist. Assn. (Bernadotte Schmidt fellow 1993), Athenaeum of Phila., N. Am. Conf. on Brit. Studies. Avocation: travel. Office: Tower Hill Sch 2813 W 17th St Wilmington DE 19806-1198

WASSON-SHAW, CAROL R. music teacher; b. Dayton, Ohio, Feb. 8, 1951; d. Audley Jackson and Barbara (Hickam) Wasson; m. Stephen D. Shaw, Feb. 21, 1981 (div. Apr. 1998); children: Tiffany Elise, Tia Nicole. BMusic in Piano Performance, Wright State U., Fairborn, Ohio, 1978. Pvt. tchr. piano, 1965—; pvt. tchr. violin and viola, 1980—; owner, mentor to music tchrs. Shaw's Music Ctr., Centerville, Ohio, 1993—. Lectr., tcht. piano to preschoolers. Chmn. jr. philharm. Dayton Philharm. Women's Assn., 1979-80; chmn. fundraiser South Dayton Montessori, Kettering, Ohio, 1987-88. Mem. Nat. Guild Piano Tchrs. (chmn. Dayton-Wasson Audition Ctr. 1998—), Music Tchrs. Nat. Assn., Dayton Music Club (chmn. judges Dist. IIIB Jr. Festival 1994—, co-chmn. 1999-2002, chmn. 2001—), Mu Phi Epsilon, Centerville Noon Optimists. Office: Shaw's Music Ctr 35 Marco Ln Centerville OH 45458-3818

WATANABE, MARK DAVID, pharmacist, educator; b. Santa Monica, Calif., Dec. 7, 1955; s. Jack Shigeru and Rose Nobuko (Iida) W. BA in Chemistry, U. Calif., Irvine, 1977, BS in Biol. Sci., 1978; PharmD, U. Calif., San Francisco, 1982, PhD in Pharm. Chemistry, 1990. Lic. pharmacist Calif., Oreg. Pharmacy intern various locations, San Francisco, 1979-82; pharmacist Kaiser Permanente, San Francisco, 1981-87; clin. scis. rsch. fellow in psychiat. pharmacy U. Tex., Austin, 1987-89; clin. asst. prof. pharmacy practice U. Ill., Chgo., 1989-98. Rsch. asst. U. Calif., San Francisco, 1980-87; clin. pharmacy cons. Ill. Dept. Mental Health & Devel. Disabilities, 1994-98; med. sci. mgr. Bristol-Myers Squibb, 1998-99; clin. pharmacy specialist, Alameda Co., Calif., 1999—; asst. cli. prof. clin. pharmacy, U. Calif., San Francisco, 1999—. Regents scholar U. Calif., San Francisco, 1979-82; recipient Excellence in Teaching award Long Found., San Francisco, 1984. Mem.: Am. Pharm. Assn., Am. Soc. Health-Sys. Pharmacists, Am. Coll. Clin. Pharmacy, Mensa, Rho Chi. Unitarian Universalist. Avocations: individual and fitness sports, reading, travel, music. Home: PO Box 193162 San Francisco CA 94119-3162 Office: Alameda County BHCS 2000 Embarcadero Ste 400 Oakland CA 94606-5300

WATANABE, RUTH TAIKO, music historian, library science educator; b. Los Angeles, May 12, 1916; d. Kohei and Iwa (Watanabe) W. B.Mus., U. So. Calif., 1937, AB, 1939, A.M., 1941, M.Mus., 1942; postgrad., Eastman Sch. Music, Rochester, N.Y., 1942-46, Columbia U., 1947; PhD, U. Rochester, 1952. Dir. Sibley Music Library Eastman Sch. of Music, Rochester, N.Y., 1947-84, prof. music bibliography, 1978-85, historian, archivist, 1984—. Adj. prof. Sch. Library Sci. State U. Coll. at Geneseo, 1975-83; coordinator adult edn. program Rochester Civic Music Assn., 1963-75; mem. adv. com. Hochstein Music Sch.; lectr. on music, book reviewer, 1966—; program annotater Rochester Philharmonic Orch., 1959—. Author: Introduction to Music Research, 1967, Madrigali-II Verso, 1978; editor: Scribners New Music Library, Vols. 2, 5, 8, 1973, Treasury of Four Hand Piano Music, 1979; contbr. articles to profl. jours., contbr. symphony orchs. of U.S., 1986, internat. music jours.; modern music librarianship, 1989; contbr. to Festschrift for Carleton Sprague Smith, 1989, De Mósica Hispana et aliis, 1990. Mem. overseers vis. com. Baxter Sch. Library Sci., Case Western Res. U., 1979-85, Alderman Book Com., 1986-89. Mem. ALA, AAUW (Pa.-Del. fellowship. 1949-50, 1st v.p. Rochester 1964-65, mem. N.Y. state bd. 1965-66, mem. nat. com. on soc.'s reflection on arts 1967-69, nat. com. Am. fellowships awards 1969-74, br. pres. 1969-71, hon. co-chair Capital Fund Drive, 1986-88, Woman of Yr. award 1990), Internat. Assn. Music Librs. (2d v.p. commn. on conservatory libraries, commn. research librs.), Am. Musicol. Soc., Music Libr. Assn. (v.p. 1968-70, citation 1986, mem. editl. bd. 1967-95, pres. 1979-81), Music Libr. Assn./Internat. Assn. Music Librs. (joint com., 1986-87), Civic Music Assn. Rochester, Riemenscheider Bach Inst. (hon.), Hanson Inst. Am. Music (bd. mem. 1981—), Univ. Club, Century Club, Phi Beta Kappa (pres. Iota chpt. of N.Y. 1969-71), Phi Kappa Phi, Mu Phi Epsilon (gen. chmn. nat. conv. 1956, nat. librarian 1958-60, recipient citation 1977, Ora Ashley Lambke award 1989), Pi Kappa Lambda (sec. 1978—, treas. 1980—), Delta Phi Alpha, Epsilon Phi, Delta Kappa Gamma (parliamentarian 1986-88). Home: 26 Gibbs St Rochester NY 14604-2505 Office: Eastman Sch Music 26 Gibbs St Rochester NY 14604-2505

WATERER, BONNIE CLAUSING, retired secondary school educator; b. Toledo, Sept. 25, 1940; d. Kermit Henry and Helen Ethel (Waggoner) Clausing; m. Louis P. Waterer, June 17, 1961; children: Ryan, Reid. BS in Home Econs. Edn., Ohio State U., 1962; MA in Home Econs. Edn., San Jose State U., 1966. Cert. family and consumer scis. Tchr. James Lick H.S., San Jose, 1963-67, 1973-76; adult edn. instr. Met. Adult Edn. Program, San Jose, 1968-75; home econs. instr. Independence H.S., San Jose, 1976-99, home econs. dept. chair, 1976-80; home econs. coord. East Side Union H.S. Dist., San Jose, 1980-99, coord. coll. and career resource ctrs., 1995-99. Child care occupations instr. Ctrl. County Occupl. Ctr., San Jose, 1989-99; child devel. instr. Evergreen Valley Coll., San Jose, 1995 Bd. dirs. NAMI Yavapai County, Ariz., 2001—; docent Highlands Ctr. for Natural History, 2000-. Mem.: AAUW, Home Econs. Tchrs. Assn. Calif. (pres. 1989—91, Outstanding Tchr. award 1987), Calif. Assn. Family and Consumer Sci. (Tchr. of Yr. award 1994), Am. Assn. Family and Consumer Sci., Phi Upsilon Omicron, Delta Kappa Gamma, Omicron Nu. Democrat. Methodist. Avocations: travel, computing, cooking, sewing. Home: 1052 Vantage Pt Cir Prescott AZ 86301 E-mail: bh2oer@aol.com.

WATERMAN, DANIEL, mathematician, educator; b. Bklyn., Oct. 24, 1927; s. Samuel and Anna (Robson) W.; m. Mudite Upesleja, Nov. 4, 1960; children: Erica, Susan, Scott. BA, Bklyn. Coll., 1947; MA, Johns Hopkins U., 1948; PhD, U. Chgo., 1954. Research assoc. Cowles Commn. Research in Econs., Chgo., 1951-52; instr. Purdue U., West Lafayette, Ind., 1953-55, asst. prof., 1955-59, U. Wis.-Milw., 1959-61; prof. Wayne State U., Detroit, 1961-69, Syracuse (N.Y.) U., 1969-96, prof. emeritus, 1996—, chmn. math dept., 1988-94. Cons. Martin-Marietta, Denver, 1960-61; rschr. in real and Fourier analysis, vis. prof. Fla. Atlantic U., 1997—. Author: Homeomorphisms in Analysis, 1997; editor: Classical Real Analysis, 1985: contbr. articles to profl. jours. Fulbright fellow U. Vienna, 1952-53 Mem. Math. Assn. Am., Am. Math. Soc. (coun. mem.-at-large 1975-78), JMAA (assoc. editor 1997—), Radovi Matematicki (editl. advisor 1986—), Sigma Xi. Home: 7739 Majestic Palm Dr Boynton Beach FL 33437-5413

WATERMAN, DIANNE CORRINE, artist, educator, writer, ministry leader; b. Bklyn., Feb. 9, 1949; d. Beverly D. and Bernice Iona (Dowling) Waterman; children: Christopher, Tutankhamon, Joy, Derrick, Idiah, Kia. BA, Hunter Coll., 1984; postgrad., L.I. U., 1984-86; grad., N.Y.C. Cmty. Police Acad., 2000. Cert. leisure profl., N.Y. Art instr./adminstr. Afro-Am. Experience, Hempstead, N.Y., 1968-73; art specialist/adminstr. MLK Youth Ctr., Westbury, N.Y., 1968-71; substance abuse counselor 5 Town Cmty. Ctr., Lawrence, N.Y., 1969-71; adminstr., counselor UJAMAA Acad., Hempstead, 1971-75; adminstr. asst. Inservice Learning Program Hunter Coll., 1981-84; unit mgr., youth divsn. counselor N.Y. State Divsn. for Youth, Bklyn., 1986-89; dean of women Claflin Coll., Orangeburg, S.C., 1989-90; dir. recreation and art therapy Dept. Homeless Svcs., N.Y.C., 1984-95; adj. prof. Touro Coll., Bklyn., 1995—; corrections officer Haynesville (Va.) Correctional Ctr., 1998-99; program dir. Hempstead Cmty. Action Program, 1999—; spiritual leader Loving Spirit Ministries Internat., 1999—, Women 2 Women, 2000—; asst. mgr. GAP, Inc., 2001—; project dir. Ednl. Alliance, 2001—02. Founder Renaissance Woman Cons. Internat., N.Y.C., 1984—, Artist in Focus, N.Y.C., 1991-94; pres., founder Better Living Gen. Svc., N.Y.C., 1988—; designer Ethnic Wear, Empress Fashions, N.Y.C., 1993—; project dir. Ednl. Alliance, 2001-03, Lillian Wald Cmty. Ctr. Mem. PTA (pres. Bklyn. 1985), Citizens Com. N.Y.C., 1986, Dynamics of Leadership, Bklyn., 1995; project dir. ednl. alliance Families First, 2000; mgmt. asst. Banana Republic, 2000. Recipient Outstanding Cooperation award Dept. Homeless Svcs., 1994, Outstanding Svc. award N.Y.C. Tech. Coll., 1987, Cert. of Appreciation Edwin Gould Svcs. for Children, 1984. Mem. Dress for Success Profl. Women's Group, Lioness Club, Zeta Iota Phi (sec. 1968—). Mem. Working Families Party. Avocations: art, writing, dancing, jogging, public advocacy. Home and Office: PO Box 466 Westbury NY 11590-0151

WATERMAN, MICHAEL SPENCER, mathematics educator, biology educator; b. Coquille, Oreg., 1942; s. Ray S. and Bessie E. Waterman; m. Vicki Lynn Buss, 1962 (div. 1977); 1 child, Tracey Lynn BS, Oreg. State U., 1964, MS, 1966; MA, Mich. State U., 1968, PhD, 1969. Assoc. prof. Idaho State U., Pocatello, 1969-75; mem. staff Los Alamos Nat. Lab., 1975-82, cons., 1982—; prof. math. and biology U. So. Calif., L.A., 1982—, U. So. Calif. Assocs. Endowed Chair, 1991—. Vis. prof. math. U. Hawaii, Honolulu, 1979-80; vis. prof. structural biology U. Calif.-San Francisco, 1982; vis. prof. Mt. Sinai Med. Sch., N.Y.C., 1988; 150th anniversary vis. prof. Chalmers U., 2000; Aisenstadt chair U. Montreal, 2001. Author: Introduction to Computational Biology, 1995; editor: Mathematical Methods for DNA Sequences, Calculating the Secrets of Life, 1995, Genetic Mapping and DNA Sequencing, 1996, Mathematical Support for Molecular Biology, 1999; Annals of Combinatorics, Methodology and Computing in Applied Probability, Genomics, Computational Methods in Science and Technology, Acta Biochimica et Biophysica Sinca; editor-in-chief: Jour. Computational Biology; contbr. numerous articles on math. stats., biology to profl. jours. Recipient Internat. award, Gardner Found., 2002; fellow, Guggenheim Found., 1995; grantee, NSF, 1971, 1972, 1975, 1988—, Los Alamos Nat. Lab., 1976, 1981, Sys. Devel. Found., 1982—87, NIH, 1986—99, Sloan Found., 1990—91. Fellow AAAS, Am. Acad. Arts and Scis., Celera Genomics, Inst. Math. Stats.; mem. NAS, Am. Statis. Assn., Soc. Math. Biology, Soc. Indsl. and Applied Math. Office: U So Calif Dept Biol Sci Los Angeles CA 90089-1340

WATERS, DONALD EUGENE, academic administrator; b. Muncie, Ind., Mar. 28, 1941; s. William James and Mary Harriet (Peare) W.; m. Kathryn Elaine Small, Aug. 17, 1963; children: Jill Maras, Janet Schulenburg. BS in Social Studies and English, Ball State U., 1963, MS in Guidance, 1964; EdD in Adminstrn. and Higher Edn., U. Mo., 1973. Dir. residence hall Ball State U., Muncie, 1964-66; asst. dean of students U. No. Iowa, Cedar Falls, 1966-70; with U. Mo., Columbia, 1970-73; dir. community edn. Muscatine (Iowa) Community Coll., 1973-75, dean arts and scis., 1975-77; asst. to pres. Elgin (Ill.) Community Coll., 1977-88, v.p. corp. devel., 1988-96; counselor W. Aurora H.S., 2002; ret., 2002. Councilman City of Elgin, 1980-87; mem. policy steering com. Nat. League of Cities, Washington, 1986-87; v.p., bd. dirs. United Way of Elgin, 1986-94, chair, bd. dirs. Golden Corridor Steering Com., Ill., 1986-90. Mem. Nat. Coun. Resource Devel. (pres. 1993, treas., bd. dirs. 1986-90, Lifetime Svc. award 1994), Ill. Resource Devel. Commn. (pres. 1986-87), Kiwanis (dist. pres. 1983-84). Methodist. Avocations: reading, model trains, exercise, boating. E-mail: trinkadonwaters@msn.com.

WATERS, WILLIAM CARTER, III, retired internist, educator; b. Atlanta, Dec. 12, 1929; s. William Carter and Nannie Ellen (Starr) W.; m. Sarah Ann Bankston; children: William Carter IV, Sarah Walker Waters McEntire. AB, Emory U., 1950, MD, 1958. Diplomate in internal medicine and nephrology Am. Bd. Internal Medicine. Resident in internal medicine Grady Meml. Hosp./Emory U., Atlanta, 1958-60, 61-62; fellow in nephrology New Eng. Med. Ctr., 1960-61; practice medicine specializing in internal medicine and nephrology, Atlanta, 1962—2002; from instr. to assoc. prof. Emory U. Sch. Medicine, 1962-70, clin. assoc. prof., 1970-85, clin. prof., 1985—. Chief staff internal medicine Piedmont Hosp., Atlanta, chmn. bd., 1991-94; 1st chmn. bd Promina Health Sys., Atlanta, 1994-96. Contbr. articles to med. jours. Chmn. Piedmont Hosp. Found., 2002—. Served with USAF, 1951—52. Fellow ACP (master: gov. for Ga.); mem. AMA, Med. Assn. Ga., Med. Assn. Met. Atlanta, Am. Soc. Nephrology, S.E. Clin. Club, Atlanta Country Club, Piedmont Driving Club, Big Canoe Club. Methodist. E-mail: drwaters@mindspring.com.

WATERS, WILLIAM ERNEST, microelectronics executive; b. Toronto, Aug. 18, 1928; s. Charles Lacy and Margaret Waters; m. Evelyn Elizabeth Phillips, Jan. 18, 1952; children: Kenneth Geoffrey, Brian Gregory, Kimberly William. BASc, U. Toronto, 1950. Gen. mgr. Hoskins Alloys of Can. Ltd., Toronto, 1953-59; pres. Waters Metal Products Ltd., Toronto, 1960—, Waters Metal Products, Inc., Buffalo, 1960-69, Watmet Inc., Niagara Falls, N.Y., 1968—, Microtectonics, Inc., Buffalo, 1968-71. Served with RCAF, 1946-52. Mem. Engring. Inst. Can., Ont. Assn. Profl. Engrs., Can. Soc. for Elec. Engring., Internat. Soc. Hybrid Microelectronics, Mfrs. Agts. Nat. Assn. (dir. 1973-77), Niagara Falls Golf and Country Club, Port Colborne Club, Rotary, Beta Theta Pi. Home: 554 Mountain View Dr Lewiston NY 14092

WATERS, ZENOBIA PETTUS, retired finance educator; b. Little Rock, Mar. 4, 1927; d. Henry Augustus and Lillie Liddell (Edwards) Pettus; m. Willie Waters, Jr., Jan. 29, 1949 (div. Feb. 1955); children: Pamela E. Reed, Zenobia W. Carter. BA cum laude, Philander Smith Coll., Little Rock, 1964; MEd, U. Wash., 1968. Cert. tchr. Ark., 1966. Office mgr. United Friends of Am., Little Rock, 1946—52; sec. State Dept. Edn., Little Rock, 1958—64; lectr. bus. Philander Smith Coll., Little Rock, 1965—67, asst. prof. bus., 1968—88, assoc. prof. bus. adminstrn., 1988—92, bd. dirs., faculty rep., 1976—80; asst. prof. bus. Ark. Bapt. Coll., Little Rock, 1970—84. Asst. bus. mgr. Philander Smith Coll., Little Rock, 1970—74, dir. summer sessions, 1970—81. Mem. adv. bd.: Two Centuries of Methodism in Arkansas, 2000; contbr. articles to profl. jours. Dean West Gulf Regional Sch., 1975—77; vol. Dem. Party, Little Rock, 1986—92; contact person U.S. Presdl. Campaign, Little Rock, 1992; cert. lay spkr. United Meth. Ch., 1979—; pres. so. ctrl. juris United Meth. Women, 1984—88; bd. dirs. Gen. Bd. of Global Ministries, N.Y.C., 1984—88, Aldersgate Camp, Little Rock, 1976—79, St. Paul Sch. Theology, Kansas City, Mo., 1984—88, Mount Sequoyah, Fayetteville, Ark., 1984—88. Recipient Edn. Found. award, AAUW, 1983, Svc. award, Gen. Bd. Global Ministries/Women's Divsn., 1988; fellow, Nissan, 1989; grantee Ford Found. grantee, 1967. Mem.: AAUW, Nat. Trust for Historic Preservation, United Meth. Women (pres., recognition pins 1963—2001), Phi Delta Phi, Iota Phi Lambda. Avocations: reading, walking, writing. Home: 1701 Westpark Dr Apt 219 Little Rock AR 72204

WATKINS, DENNIS H. special education educator; b. Bridgeport, Conn., Aug. 29, 1943; s. Charles Francis and Mae (Sorrentino) W.; m. Joan Marie Rahrig, Oct. 20, 1972; children: Kristen, Stephen, David. BA, Fairfield U., 1965, Cert. Advanced Study, 1971, Adminstrn. Supr. Cert., 1973; MPA, U. R.I., 1967. Cert. spl. edn. tchr., K-12, adminstr. K-8. Adminstrv. intern City of Bridgeport Comptrollers Office, 1966; spl. edn. tchr. Kolburne Sch., Norwalk, Conn., 1967-68, Helen Keller Mid. Sch., Easton, Conn., 1968—; real estate broker Dollar Dry Dock Real Estate, Stratford, Conn., 1971-96, DeWolfe Real Estate, 1997—2002, Coldwell Banker Real Estate, 2003—. Summer sch. tchr. Redding (Conn.) Elem. Sch., 1994-2002; cmty. coord. student exch. program Internat. Edn. Forum, Stratford, 1989-90; pvt. tutor. Aldermanic cand., Rep. Action League, Bridgeport, 1970; del. state conv. Rep. Party, Bridgeport, 1971. Mem. NEA, Conn. Edn. Assn., Easton Edn. Assn. (treas. 1970-75, 85-88, v.p. 1977, pres. 1978, negotiation chmn. 1979, membership chmn. 1978-91, mem. negotiation team 1970—, sec. 1998—), Coun. Exceptional Children, others. Roman Catholic. Avocations: fishing, tennis, collecting sports memorabilia, golf. Home: 381 Bridgeview Pl Stratford CT 06614-3658 Office: Helen Keller Mid Sch 360 Sport Hill Rd Easton CT 06612-1714 E-mail: mrfoxwoods@aol.com.

WATKINS, DON ORRA, public affairs educator; b. Wauseon, Ohio, Mar. 5, 1927; s. Orra Lynn and Florence Margaret (Bruner) W.; m. Barbara Jean Shelt Watkins, June 24, 1950; children: Beth, Kurt, Thomas, Christopher. BA, Denison U., 1951; MA, Yale U., 1954, PhD, 1957. Dir. Inst. of Ethics and Politics, Wesleyan U., Middletown, Conn., 1955-56; tchr., chair social studies dept. Warrensville Heights (Ohio) Schs., 1956-60; from instr. to full prof. Bklyn. Coll., CUNY, N.Y.C., 1960-70; asst. dean Bklyn. Coll. CUNY, N.Y.C., 1965-70; dean adminstrn. and fin. Medgar Evers Coll., CUNY, N.Y.C., 1970-78; v.p. for acad. affairs, dep. to pres. Hostos C.C./CUNY, N.Y.C., 1978-81; univ. dean CUNY, N.Y.C., 1981-84; prof. Bernard Baruch Coll./CUNY, N.Y.C., 1984-95, prof., ombudsman, dir. grad. programs in ednl. adminstrn. and higher edn., 1986-95, prof. emeritus, 1995—, univ. affirmative action com., 1984—. V.p. U.S.-China Edn. Found., N.Y.C., 1984—; treas., co-coord. Sino-Am. Confs. on Edn., N.Y.C. and Shanxi Province, China, 1988—; faculty assoc. Modern East Asia Seminar: China, Columbia U., 1991—; bd. dirs. Nat. Project 30 Alliance, 1991-96; rschr. and cons. on human rels., racial discrimination and higher edn. U.S., China, India, Israel. Contbr. articles to profl. jours. Mem. bd. edn. Levittown (N.Y.) Bd. Edn., 1971-77, v.p., pres., 1975, 76, 77; bd. trustees Friends World Coll., Lloyd Harbor, N.Y., 1980-89. Cpl. U.S. Army, 1945-46. Recipient Tchg. assistantship Yale U., 1953-56, Presdl. Excellence award for Disting. Svc., CUNY, 1995; Rsch. fellow Denison U. Rsch. Found., Ohio, 1951-56, Danforth fellow Danforth Found., 1966-78; Fulbright Sr. scholar Fulbright Awards, Washington, 1984. Mem. Phi Beta Kappa. Avocations: China ednl. devel. in China, reading, traveling. Home: 20 Weaver Ln Levittown NY 11756-3422 Office: US China Edn Found 361 W 36th St Apt 3A New York NY 10011

WATKINS, HORTENSE CATHERINE, middle school educator; b. St. Louis, Nov. 29, 1924; d. Isaiah S. and Katie M. (Phelps) W. BA, Harris-Stowe State Coll., St. Louis, 1946; MEd, U. Ill., 1953; postgrad. U. Chgo., InterAm. U., Saltillo, Coahuila, Mex.; postgrad., U. Seville, Spain, Webster U., St. Louis. Cert. life tchr., reading specialist, Mo. Coord. urban rural programs Carver-Dunbar Schs., St. Louis, 1975-76; adminstrv. asst. Shaw Visual Performing Arts Sch., St. Louis, 1978-82; team IV leader Woerner IGE, St. Louis, 1982-87; tchr., head lang. arts dept. Nottingham Mid. Sch., St. Louis, 1987-92. Tutor fgn.-speaking religious, presenter, lectr. numerous workshops; curriculum advisor St. Louis Pub. Schs. Active numerous comty. orgns.; bd. dirs. St. Louis Cathedral Sch., St. Louis Metro Singers, Concert Series of St. Louis Cathedral, Quartet Seraphin; bd. dirs. Cath. Family Counseling. Mem. ASCD, Nat. Coun. Tchrs. English, Mo. State Tchrs. Assn., Greater St. Louis Coun. Social Studies, Delta Sigma Theta (Golden life), Delta Kappa Gamma. Home: 5070A Enright Ave Saint Louis MO 63108-1008

WATKINS, JOAN FRANCES, retired elementary school educator; b. Linwood, N.J., Mar. 8, 1940; d. Francis Joseph and Alberta Catherine (Seabold) W. BS, St. Bonaventure U., 1967. Cert. elem. tchr., N.J. Tchr. various parochial schs., 1961-71, Atlantic City (N.J.) Pub. Schs., 1971—2003; ret., 2003. Mem. Atlantic City Edn. Assn., N.J. Edn. Assn. Roman Catholic. Avocation: working with children. Home: PO Box 714 Northfield NJ 08225-0714

WATKINS, LINDA THERESA, educational researcher; b. York, Pa., Sept. 29, 1947; d. Nathan Franklin and Madelyn Marie (Mandl) W.; m. Hugh Jerald Silverman, June 22, 1968 (div. Apr. 1983); children: Claire Christine (Silverman) Goberman, Hugh Christopher Silverman; m. Patrick Grim. BA, Muhlenberg Coll., 1968; MA, San Jose (Calif.) State Coll., 1970; PhD, Stanford (Calif.) U., 1977; cert., Hofstra U., 1991. Rsch. asst. prof. L.I. Rsch. Inst., Stony Brook, N.Y., 1977-79; asst. prof. NYU, 1979-85; rsch. assoc. dept. psychiatry SUNY, Stony Brook, 1985-87; dir. of rsch., planning and grants mgmt. Bd. Coop. Ednl. Svcs. Eastern Suffolk, Patchogue, N.Y., 1987—. Adj. lectr. SUNY Sch. Soc. Welfare, 1994; cons. Dowling Coll., Oakdale, N.Y., 1991, Tele-Niger Evaluation Project, Paris, 1972; survey cons. Redbook Mag., N.Y., 1987; interviewer Am. Inst. for Rsch., Kensington, Md., 1973. Contbr. articles to profl. jours. Rsch. grant Ronald McDonald Children's Charities, 1988, Am. Broadcasting Co., 1978, Dissertation rsch. grant Nat. Assn. of Broadcasters, 1974; NDEA fellowship, 1972. Mem. ASCD, APA, Soc. for Rsch. in Child Devel., Am. Ednl. Rsch. Assn. Avocation: house restoration. Home: 99 Sweezey St Patchogue NY 11772-4160 Office: Bd Coop Ednl Svcs Suffolk 1 15 Andrea Rd Holbrook NY 11741 E-mail: twatkins@esboces.org.

WATKINS, SHERRY LYNNE, elementary school educator; b. Bloomington, Ind., Oct. 13, 1944; d. Quentin Odell and Velma Ruth W. BSEd, Ind. U., 1966, MSEd, 1968. Tchr. 4th grade North Grove Elem. Sch., Ctr. Grove Sch. Dist., Greenwood, Ind., 1966-68; tchr. 4th and 6th grades John Strange Sch., Met. Dist. of Wash. Twp., Indpls., 1968-91; tchr. 4th grade Allisonville Sch. Met. Sch. Dist. of Wash. Twp., Indpls., 1991—. Bd. dirs. ISTA Ins. Trust and Fin. Svcs. Mem. People for Ethical Treatment of Animals. Mem.: AAUW, ACLU, NEA (nat. del. 1978—), World Confedn. Orgn. of Tchg. Profls. (del. Costa Rica 1990), Washington Twp. Edn. Assn. (pres. 1986—89), Ind. Tchrs. Assn. (state del. 1966—), Alpha Omicron Pi, Delta Kappa Gamma (chpt. pres. 1992—94, chmn. coordinating coun. Indpls. area 1994—96, state legislature chair 1997—99, state profl. affairs chair 2001—03). Avocations: traveling, cultural activities. Office: Allisonville Sch 4920 E 79th St Indianapolis IN 46250-1615

WATKINS, SYDNEY LYNN, sales executive; b. Hartford, Conn., Sept. 12, 1964; s. Robert Lee and Joan (Hardy) W. BS, Howard U., 1986, MS, 1989. Cert. U.S. Olympic Acad., Sport Adminstrn. Facility Mgmt. Inst. Water safety instr. Howard U. Satellite Youth Program, Washington, 1986, D.C. Dept. Recreation, Washington, 1986-87, phys. therapeutic recreation specialist, 1987-88; account rep. AT&T, Silver Spring, Md., 1988-90; program assoc. Amateur Athletic Found., L.A., 1991-95; program mgr. L.A. Team Mentoring, 1995-96; ind. cons., 1996—; pharm. sales cons. Wyeth-Ayerst Labs., 1997-99; dist. sales mgr. Takeda Pharms. Am., 1999—. Spl. asst. to pres. Dr. LeRoy T. Walker Found., Durham, N.C., 1993. African Am. Summit fellow NAACP, L.A., 1994; Patricia Roberts Harris grantee Howard U., 1989. Mem. AAHPERD, Alpha Kappa Alpha. Home: 3675 River Summit Trail Duluth GA 30097 E-mail: Rokwest@aol.com.

WATKINS, TED ROSS, social work educator; b. Terrell, Tex., Dec. 2, 1938; s. Daniel Webster and Iva Lucy (Lowrie) W.; m. Betty Diane Dobbs, May 30, 1959; children: Evan Scott, Brett Dobbs, James David. BA in Psychology, U. North Tex., 1961; MSW, La. State U., 1963; D of Social Work, U. Pa., 1976. Staff social worker Mercer County Mental Health Ctr., Sharon, Pa., 1963-65; chief social worker, assoc. exec. Talbot Hall Treatment Ctr., Jonestown, Pa., 1965-70; chief social worker Harrisburg (Pa.) Mental Health Ctr., 1970-71; asst. prof. social work U. Tex., Arlington, 1971-76; dir. counseling svcs. Family Svcs., Inc., Ft. Worth, 1976-79; assoc. prof. social work U. Tex., 1979-85, dir. criminal justice, 1985-87, chair dept. sociology, 1987-91, assoc. prof., grad. advisor social work, 1991-99; assoc. prof., dir. Bachelor of Social Work program S.W. Tex. State U., San Marcos, 1999—2002, prof., 2002—. Cons. in field. Author (with James Callicutt): Mental Health Policy and Practice Today, 1997; author: (with A. Lewellen and M. Barrett) Dual Diagnosis: An Integrated Approach to Treatment, 2001. Tex. del. to Pres.'s Commn. in Mental Health, Austin, 1978. Recipient Golladay Teaching award Coll. Liberal Arts, Arlington, 1990; named Outstanding Profl. Human Svcs., 1972. Mem. NASW (state bd. dirs. 1976-78, 80-82, unit chair, vol. lobbyist 1982), Acad. Cert. Social Workers (lic. master social worker, advanced clin. practitioner), World Assn. for Psychosocial Rehab., Alliance for the Mentally Ill, Nat. Assn. for Rural Mental Health, Nat. Social Sci. Assn. Democrat. Methodist. Avocations: music, painting, camping. Office: SW Tex State U Dept Social Work 601 University Dr San Marcos TX 78666-4685 E-mail: tw11@swt.edu.

WATKINS, THOMAS D. superintendent of public instruction; children: Daniel, Katherine. BS in Criminal Justice, Mich. State U., 1976; M in social work adminstrn., Wayne State U., 1979. Staff mem. Youth Living Services, 1976—80; acting exec. dir. Wayne Mental Health Ctr., Detroit, 1980—81; staff Plante and Moran, 1981—82; dep. campaign mgr. Blanchard for Gov. Com., Detroit, 1982—83; dep. chief of staff Gov. Blanchard, 1982—83; dep. dir. adminstrn. Mich. Dept. Mental Health, 1983—84; chief dep. dir. dept of mental health State of Michigan, Lansing, 1984—86; dir. mental health dept. State of Mich., Lansing, 1987—91; spl. asst. to the pres. for pub. sch. initiatives Wayne State U., Detroit; pres., CEO Econ. Coun. Palm Beach County, Fla.; exec. dir. Edn. Ptnrship. Palm Beach County, Palm Beach, Fla., 1996—99; supt. pub. instrn. Mich. Dept. Edn., Lansing, 2001—. Mailing: Mich Dept Edn 608 W Allegan St 4th Fl Lansing MI 48909

WATKISS, REGINA (REGINA MONKS), secondary school educator; b. Worcester, Mass., Apr. 21, 1952; d. Albin and Victoria (Babicz) Linga; m. G. Philip Watkiss. BA, Assumption Coll., 1974; MA, Western Md. Coll., 1980; postgrad., U. Ala.; MS, Western Md. Coll., 1992. Cert. sci. tchr., Ga., Colo. Sci. tchr. Randolph Sch., Huntsville, Ala.; sci. coord. Divine Redeemer Sch., Colorado Springs, Colo.; sci. curriculum cons. U.S. Space Found., Colorado Springs; head dept. sci. Heritage Sch., Newnan, Ga. Workshop presenter, curriculum author in field. Recipient Dreyfus Master Tchr. award in chemistry, 1986, Colo. Sci. Tchr. of Yr. award, Seismic Sleuths award State of Ga.; Woodrow Wilson fellow, 1986; State of Ala. grantee. Mem. Nat. Sci. Tchrs. Assn., Ala. Sci. Tchrs. Assn., Am. Chem. Soc. (Operation Chemistry award). Home: 285 Springwater Chase Newnan GA 30265-2298

WATLEY, MARTHA JONES, health and social services association executive; b. Jacksonville, Fla., July 18, 1936; d. Louis Kato and Annie Mae (Hartley) Jones; m. George Benjamin Watley, July 13, 1957 (dec. Aug. 1983); children: Cynthia, Harry II, Phyllis, Kevin, George IV, Baron, Sandee, Stacey. ADN, Cameron U., 1968; BA, U. Okla., 1975, MEd, 1976. RN; lic. profl. counselor; cert. drug and alcohol counselor; cert. chemo-therapist; cert. grant writer and fundraiser; cert. family life educator. Emergency supr. Comanch County Meml. Hosp., Lawton, Okla., 1963-69; Family Life Edn. Assocs. and Family Life Ctrs., program developer; nursing instr. Great Plains Area Sch., Lawton, 1969-72; nurse counselor Reynolds Army Hosp., Ft. Sill, Okla., 1972-73; nurse-therapist, supr. VA Med. Ctr., Oklahoma City, 1973-77; staff psychologist Tri City Youth and Family Svc., Choctaw, Okla.; exec. dir. Arcadia Youth Family Multipurpose Assn., Arcadia, Okla., 1978-79; chief exec. officer Arcadia Youth & Family Life Ednl. Assn., 1979—, Family Life Edn. Assocs., Oklahoma City, 1979—, program developer, 1981-86, Family Life Ctrs., Irving, Tex., 1981-86; chief exec. officer Family Life Assocs. and Family Life Ctrs., Irving, Tex., 1986—. Staff psychologist, trainer Harbingers Women Alcohol Treatment, Oklahoma City, 1977-79; cons. spl. survey projects Tri City Youth & Family, Choctaw, 1978-79; cons. spl. project aging Am. Pers. and Guidance, Midwest City, Okla., 1981; counsellor/trainer Counsellor Tng. Inst., 1999-2001. Author: Family Life Education; Family Life Centers and Life Centers, 1979. Instr. ARC, Oklahoma City, 1975—; trainer of trainers Nat. Inst. Drug Abuse, Oklahoma City, 1978; trainer Gordon's Effectiveness P.E.T. Y.E.T. T.E.T., Tex, Oklahoma City, 1976, Evangelism Explosion Internat., Dallas, 1981. Named one of Top 20 Adminstrs. in Mental Health, NIMH, 1986. Mem. AACD (Nat. Disting. Svc. Registry), ASCD, NAFE, AARP, Nat. Assn. Froensic Counselors. Democrat. Baptist. Avocations: singing, sewing, bible instruction and history. Office: Family Life Ctrs Life Ctrs PO Box 165065 Irving TX 75016-5065

WATNE, DONALD ARTHUR, accountant, educator, retired; b. Gt. Falls, Mont., Jan. 18, 1939; BA with high honors, U. Mont., 1960, MA, 1961; PhD, U. Calif., Berkeley, 1977. CPA, Oreg. Acct. Piquet & Minihan, Eugene, Oreg., 1961-65; mgr. capital investment analysis Weyerhaeuser Co., Tacoma, 1965-68; mktg. rep. IBM Corp., Portland, Oreg., 1968-70; dir. EDP Ctr. in Concejo Mcpl., Barquisimeto, Venezuela, 1971-72; prof. acctg. Portland State U., 1976-2001, prof. emeritus, 2001—. Vis. prof. Xiamen (Fujian, People's Rep. China), 1985-86, U. Otago, Dunedin, New Zealand, 1985-86, U. Newcastle, Australia, 1985-86; cons. in field; acctg. qualifications com. Oregon State Bd. Acctg., 1989-98, CPE com., 1998-2001. Author: (with Peter B.B. Turney) Auditing EDP Systems, 2d edit. 1990; contbr. chpts. to books, articles to profl. jours. Del. to Soviet Union citizen amb. program People to People Internat., 1990; active Tng. the Trainers Program, Vilnius, Lithuania, 1993; trustee, treas. First Unitarian Ch. of Portland, 2002-; mem. bd. stewards First Unitarian Ch. of Portland Found., 2002-. Mem.: AICPA, Oreg. Soc. CPAs, Mensa, Mazamas Mountain Climbing Club. Home: 2826 NE 26th Ave Portland OR 97212-3503 Personal E-mail: dawatne@msn.com.

WATNICK, ROCHELLE, principal; b. N.Y.C., June 3, 1948; d. Alexander and Tillie (Ziskin) Ockun; m. Philip Barry Watnick, Mar. 28, 1970; 1 child, Erica Joy. BA in Elem. Edn., Bklyn. Coll., 1970, MS in Urban Edn., 1972, MS in Reading, 1976; cert. advanced study in edn. adminstrn., Hofstra U., 1982. Cert. prin., N.Y.; cert. tchr., N.Y. Tchr. grades 1, 4 and English as a second lang. P.S. 113, N.Y.C. Bd. Edn., 1970; tchr. grade 6 P.S. 86, N.Y.C. Bd. Edn., 1977; tchr. grades 4-6 P.S. 183, N.Y.C. Bd. Edn., 1978, Astor tchr. of the gifted, 1981; curriculum leader CIMS Edn. Adminstr., N.Y.C., 1983; reading tchr. P.S. 197, N.Y.C. Bd. Edn., 1985; dir. lang. arts, reading Dist. 27, N.Y.C. Bd. Edn., 1988; asst. prin. P.S. 42, N.Y.C. Bd. Edn., 1990; schoolwide projects coord. Dist. 27, N.Y.C. Bd. Edn., 1990; asst. prin. P.S. 155, N.Y.C. Bd. Edn., 1991, P.S. 146, N.Y.C. Bd. Edn., 1992—; prin. P.S. 47, Broad Channel, NY, 1995—96, P.S. 97, Woodhaven, NY, 1997—98, P.S. 146, Howard Beach, NY, 2001. Tchr. Vacation Day Camp, Dist. 19, N.Y.C. Bd. of Edn., 1968-73; adminstrv. intern Dist. 27 Office of Reimbursable Funds, 1981; tchr. in charge of Vacation Day Camp 60, 1982; curriculum leader CIMS Edn. Adminstr., N.Y.C., 1983; site supr. Summer Primary Program, Dist 27, 1986, 91; instr. whole lang. in-svc. course N.Y.C. Staff Devel. Tng. Program, 1988; instr. children's lit. in-svc. course N.Y.C. Staff Devel. Tng. Program, 1989; instr. Balanced Literacy in-svc. course N.Y.C. Staff Devel. Tng., Fall 2001. Author: Gates to Learning Communication Arts: Enrichment Program for Promotional Center, 1982, (with others) Integrating Learning and Testing: Handbooks for Teachers of Grades Three and Six, 1984; editor, author Lang. Arts Newsletter, 1988, Dist. 27 Monthly Newsletter, 1990, Dist. 27 Parent Orientation Handbook, 1990; contbr. articles to profl. jours. Vol. Hewlett-Woodmere Pub. Sch. PTA, 1979-82; fundraiser, organizing chairperson P.S. 155Q/146Q, 1992; career trainer Bus. Kids T-shirts, P.S. 183Q, 1982; mem. supr. adv. coun. Educators for Gateway, N.Y. City Bd. Edn. Mem. ASCD, Nat. Coun. Tchrs. Math., Queensboro Reading Coun. (exec. bd. dirs., pres.), Phi Delta Kappa. Avocations: reading, crafts. Office: PS 146 98-01 159th Ave Howard Beach NY 11414-3543

WATROUS, ROBERT THOMAS, academic director; b. Cleve., Apr. 20, 1952; s. Frank Thomas and Marie Anne (Kmeicik) W.; m. Robin Joyce Braun, Mar. 14, 1981 (div. 1993); 1 child, Michael Francis; m. Susan J. Rupp, Mar. 8, 2003. BS, U. Dayton, 1974, MS, 1977. Dir. student ctr. for off campus cmty. rels. U. Dayton, Ohio, 1974-76, resident dir., 1976-78; dir. of housing St. Bonaventure U., Olean, N.Y., 1978-81; asst. dean of student life/housing Kutztown U. of Pa., 1981-86, dir. commuter and jud. affairs, 1986—. Faculty senate Kutztown (Pa.) U., 1986-89, 92-95; mem. Pa. Task Force on Intergroup Behavior in Higher Edn., 1991-94; trainer Pa. Interagy. Task Force on Civil Tension, Harrisburg, Pa., 1989—; exec. coun. Adult Learners Consortium, Bloomsburg, Pa., 1990-91; mem. Lehigh Valley Svc. Learning Consortium, 1994—. Bd. mgr. Tri Valley YMCA, Fleetwood, Pa., 1983-94; adv. bd. Crossroads, Kutztown, 1989-94; bd. dirs. Jr. Achievement of Berks County, Reading, Pa., 1990, Reading, Pa., 1990, Reading and Berks Coun. YMCA, 1992-96; mem. Leadership Berks, Reading, 1990; bd. dirs. Leadership Berks, 1995—, sec. 1998-99, pres., 2000—; co-founder Leading Sch. Bds., 1994—; mem. YMCA cultural diversity and internat. awareness com., 1994—; mem. Berks County Conflict Resolution Task Force, 1996—; v.p. Fleetwood Activities Booster Club, 1998—, pres., 1999-2001. Mem. Nat. Assn. Student Pers. Adminstrs. (profl. affiliate), Hawk Mt. Coun. Boy Scouts Am. (sustaining mem.), Berks County C. of C. (sch. bd. governance com. 1993—2000), Fleetwood Youth Soccer Club (v.p., pres. 1999), Fleetwood Youth Basketball Assn. (coach 1995-96). Avocations: golf, sports, gardening. Office: Kutztown Univ PO Box 37 Kutztown PA 19530-0037

WATSON, ADA, secondary education educator; b. Memphis, Oct. 21, 1951; d. Leroy and Helen Marie (Sparks) Preyer; m. William Elton Watson, June 2, 1973; children: William Elton Jr., Moneka Nésha. BS in Edn., Memphis State U., 1974, care-guidance of children endorsement, 1976; MS in Human Resource Devel., U. Tenn., 1995. Parenting educator Sea Isle Adult Vocat.-Tech. Ctr., Memphis, 1975-76; tchr. child care Sheffield Vocat.-Tech. Ctr., Memphis, 1976-88; tchr. home econs. and teen parenting edn. Booker T. Washington H.S., Memphis, 1989—. Author teen parenting videos; co-author child care curriculum. Mem. adv. bd. Golden Leaf Day Care Ctr., Memphis, 1979-81; chmn. March of Dimes, Sheffield Vocat.-Tech. Ctr., 1985-86; craft coord. Vacation Bible Sch., Greater Imani Bapt. Ch., Memphis, 1991; Sunday sch. tchr. St. Matthew Bapt. Ch., Millington, Tenn., 1992—, dir. Vacation Bible Sch., 1992-98, youth dir., 1995—. Recipient svc. award Future Homemakers Am., 1986-89. Mem. NEA, ASCD, Am. Vocat. Assn., Tenn. Edn. Assn., Memphis Edn. Assn. (faculty rep. 1978-86, bargaining com. 1981, ins. chmn. 1983, svc. awards 1981, 83, assembly rep. 1998—), Nat. Assn. Vocat. Home Econs. Tchrs. (local arrangements com., membership com., svc. award 1993), Tenn. Vocat. Assn. (v.p. home econs., svc. award 1994, pres.-elect 1997-98, pres. 1998—), Tenn. Assn. Vocat. Family and Consumer Sci. Tchrs. (bd. dirs., v.p., pres.-elect, pres. 1995, svc. award 1985, 90, 91, 92-94), Tenn. Assn. Tchrs. of Family and Consumer Sci. (chair awards com., past pres. 1996). Democrat. Avocations: sewing and crafts, singing, working with youth groups. Home: 2614 Monette Ave Memphis TN 38127-6835 Office: Booker T Washington HS 715 S Lauderdale St Memphis TN 38126-3910

WATSON, DONALD RALPH, architect, artist, educator, author; b. Providence, Sept. 27, 1937; s. Ralph Giles W. and Ethel (Fletcher) Pastene; m. Marja Palmqvist, Sept. 8, 1966 (div. Jan. 1984); children: Petrik, Elise; m. Judith Criste, Jan. 3, 1986 (dec. Oct. 8, 2000). AB, Yale U., 1959, BArch, 1962, MEd, 1969. Lic. architect Nat. Council Archtl. Registration Bds. Architect Peace Corps, Tunisia, 1962-64; archtl. cons. Govt. of Tunisia, 1964-65; pvt. practice, Trumbull, Conn., 1969—; dean Sch. Architecture, Rensselaer Poly. Inst., Troy, N.Y., 1990-95, prof., 1990—2001. Frederick C. Baker vis. prof. U. Oreg., 1995; chmn. environ. design program, Yale U., 1979-90; vis. prof. Yale U., 1995-2000. Author: Designing and Building a Solar House, 1977, Energy Conservation Through Building Design, 1979, Climatic Design, 1983, Energy Design Handbook, 1993; editor-in-chief Time Saver Standards: Architectural Design Data, 1997, Time-Saver Standards: Urban Design, 2003. Bd. dirs. Save the Children Fedn., 1979-82. Recipient Honor Design award Conn. Soc. Architects, 1974, Honor Design award region AIA, 1978, 84, 1st award Owens Corning Energy Conservation Bldg. Design Program, 1983, Excellence in housing award Energy Efficient Bldg. Assn., 1988, Lifetime Achievement award Passive and Low Energy Architecture, 1990, Best in Show Watercolors, Soc. Creative Artists, 1999, Green Bldg. Design award NESEA, 2002, Disting. Prof. award ACSA, 2002; Assn. of Collegiate Schs. of Archtecture/Am. Metals Climax rsch. fellow, 1967-69; rsch. fellow Rockefeller Found., 1978. Fellow: AIA. Home and Office: 54 Larkspur Dr Trumbull CT 06611-4652 E-mail: lakesidedj@aol.com.

WATSON, DUANE FREDERICK, religious studies educator; b. Watertown, N.Y., May 15, 1956; s. Frederick Halsted and Beverley Alice (Taylor) W.; m. JoAnn Christine Ford, June 2, 1984; 1 child, Christina Lucille. BA, Houghton (N.Y.) Coll., 1978; MDiv, Princeton Theol. Sem., 1981; PhD, Duke U., 1986. Ordained to ministry Meth. U., 1980. Asst. prof. biblical studies Ashland (Ohio) Theol. Sem., 1984-86; pastor Northwestern (N.Y.) United Meth. Ch., 1987-89; asst. prof. N.T. studies Malone Coll., Canton, Ohio, 1989-92, assoc. prof., 1992-96, prof., 1996—, chair dept. religion and philosophy, 1993-99. Owner, operator internet stoneware auction svc. Doc's Crocks. Author: Invention, Arrangement and Style, 1988, Persuasive Artistry, 1991, Rhetorical Criticism of The Bible, 1994, Commentary on Jude and 2 Peter for the New Interpreter's Bible, 1998, Intertexture of Apocalyptic Discourse in the New Testament, 2002, History of Biblical Interpretation, 2003; contbr. articles to profl. jours. and edited volumes; mem. editl. bd. Procs., Ea. Gt. Lakes and Midwest Bibl. Socs., 1993-95; co-editor: Currents in Research: Biblical Studies, 1997-2000, Rhetoric in Religious Antiquity, 1997—. Recipient Excellence in Bibl. studies award Am. Bible Soc., Houghton Coll., 1978. Mem. Studiorum Novi Testamenti Societas, Soc. Bibl. Lit. (steering com. rhetoric sect. 1990-96, program unit chair rhetoric and N.T. sect. 1997-2002), Cath. Bibl. Assn., Ea. Great Lakes Bibl. Soc. Republican. Avocations: writing, weight lifting. Office: Malone Coll 515 25th St NW Canton OH 44709-3823

WATSON, JAMES STANLEY, secondary education educator; b. Glen Ridge, N.J., Feb. 2, 1948; s. James G. and Bernice T. (Frail) W. BS in Natural Sci. Edn., U. Tenn., 1971; MA in Environ. Edn., Glassboro State Coll., 1978; postgrad., U. Tenn., 1984, 89, Coll. Atlantic, U. Maine, 1986. Cert. secondary sci. curriculum, Tenn. Tchr. geology, chemistry, biology and applied sci., asst. coach wrestling Red Bank High Sch., Chattanooga, 1972-76; tchr. earth sci. 8th grade Red Bank Jr. High Sch., Chattanooga, 1976-78; tchr. gen. sci. and ecology, coach wrestling Ooltewah High Sch., Chattanooga, 1978-81; tchr. biology, earth sci., chemistry, gen. sci., geology and physical sci., coach boys and girls soccer, asst. coach wrestling Red Bank High Sch., 1981-92; tchr. honors biology, asst. coach boys and girls soccer Soddy-Daisy High Sch., Chattanooga, 1992—; textbook reviewer for scis. Tenn. Dept. Edn., 1996—, Praxis reviewer for earth sci., 1996. Writer, tchr. new geology course Red Bank High Sch., 1973, new ecology course Ooltewah High Sch., 1979; writer energy conservation plan Hamilton County Sch. Dist., 1978, gen. sci. curriculum guide, 1979; planner, contributing writer tchr. workshop field activity design and procedures Chattanooga Nature Ctr., Keystone (Colo.) Sci. Sch., 1985, tchr. workshop volcanoes Mt. St. Helens Nat. Monument, Washington, 1986, tchr. workshop marine mammals in Gulf of Maine, 1989; writer solar energy sect. Tenn. Valley Authority Energy Source Book for Tchrs., 1985; participant Tenn. Valley Authority Water Quality Monitoring Network, 1986; presenter environ. edn. conf. N.Am. Assn., Eugene, Oreg., 1986; mem. task force on earth sci. curriculum Tenn. Dept. Edn., 1988; mem. adoption com. sci. textbooks Hamilton County Sch. Dist., 1990; textbook reader, evaluator geology, gen. sci. and phys. sci. Tenn. Dept. Edn., 1990; asst. to instr. dept. geoscis. U. Tenn., 1990, 91; presenter workshops Ctr. Excellence for Sci. and Math. Edn. Tenn. Dept. Edn., 1991. Sponsor winner Chattanooga Sci. Fair, 1973, runner-up, 1974; mem. dual team championships wrestling rules com. Tenn. Secondary Sch. Athletic Assn., 1987, speaker bureau Tenn. River Aquarium, 1990, 91, ednl. adv. com. Spangler Farm Environ. Edn. Ctr., 1991, adv. coun. Chattanooga YMCA Earth Sci. Corps, 1992; horticulture vol. Tenn. River Aquarium, 1992. Grantee Lyndhurst Found., 1982, 84, 86, Pub. Edn. Found., 1990, 94, Pub. Edn. Found., 1994, GeoTrek, 1996; recipient Soccer Coach of Yr. award News Free Press, 1985, 89, Mini-grant Chattanooga Jr. League, 1985, 87. Mem. NEA, Am. Littoral Soc., Nat. Assn. Geology Tchrs. (Outstanding Earth Sci. Tchr. award 1992, 96), Nat. Marine Edn. Assn., Ga. Assn. Marine Edn., Tenn. Edn. Assn., Hamilton County Edn. Assn. (Outstanding Svc. award 1980, trustee Hamilton County Sch. Dist. Sick Leave Bank 1982—), Tenn. Conservation League, Chattanooga Nature Ctr., Internat. Oceanographic Found., Nature Conservancy, Tenn. Earth Sci. Tchrs. Assn. (pres. 1995-97). Baptist. Avocations: hiking, mineral rock collecting, water sports, biking, yard work. Office: Soddy-Daisy High Sch 618 Sequoyah Access Rd Soddy Daisy TN 37379-4054

WATSON, JOYCE LESLIE, elementary educator; b. Riverside, N.J., May 31, 1950; d. Robert Eugene and Doris Virginia (Robinson) Stockton; 1 child, Michelle Leslie. BS, Trenton State Coll., 1972, MEd, 1978. Cert. elem. tchr., N.J., Pa. Tchr. elem. Willingboro (N.J.) Sch. Dist., 1972-81, Pennsbury Sch. Dist., Fallsington, Pa., 1987—, tchr. gifted/talented, advanced math. tchr., 1987-88, 92—, elem. demonstration tchr., 1995—97, 1998—2000, 2001—03. Coach Odyssey of the Mind, Pennwood Mid. Sch., Yardley, Pa., 1993—94; participant 8th Ann. Capital Area Space Orientation Program, Washington, 1996, NASA Educators Workshop, Kennedy Space Center, Fla., 2000, Pa. Gov.'s Inst. on Math, College Park, 2000, Share-a-thon at Nat. Congress on Aviation and Space Edn., 2002. Mem.: CAP, NEA, AIAA, Exptl. Aircraft Assn., Nat. Coun. Tchrs. Math., Women in Aviation Internat., Nat. Aero. Assn., Airplane Owners and Pilots Assn., Pa. State Edn. Assn., Pa. Assn. for Gifted Edn., League of Women Voters (Bucks County), Phi Delta Kappa. Home: 2293 Seabird Dr Bristol PA 19007 Office: Makefield Elem Sch Makefield Rd Yardley PA 19067

WATSON, KAY, educational consultant; b. Rotan, Tex., Feb. 5, 1942; d. C.M. and Marie (Reeder) W. BA, Baylor U., 1964; MA, Colo. State Coll., 1968; MEd, Sul Ross State U., Alpine, Tex., 1982; EdD, Tex. Tech. U., 1988. Tchr. grade 6 Dallas Ind. Sch. Dist., Dallas, 1964-67, counselor J.L. Long Jr. H.S., 1968-70, tchr. grade 7, 1970-72; tchr. grade 5 Weatherford (Tex.) Ind. Sch. Dist., 1972-73; spl. edn. counselor Parker County Coop., Weatherford, 1973-74, Monahans-Wickett-Pyote Ind. Sch. Dist., 1974-78; dir. spl. edn. Monahans (Tex.)-Wickett-Pyote Ind. Sch. Dist., 1978-85; supr. pre-sch. ctr. Ector County Ind. Sch. Dist., Odessa, Tex., 1985-86, prin. elem. Magnet Sch. at Travis, 1986-89, prin. LBJ Elem. Sch., 1989-90, assoc. dir. elem. edn., 1990-92, assoc. exec. dir., clusters I and II, 1992; asst. supt. Calhoun County Ind. Sch. Dist., Port Lavaca, Tex., 1992-96; vis. asst. prof. U. Tex. of the Permian Basin, Odessa, 1996-99; edn. cons., 1999—. Bd. dirs. West Tex. Educators Conf., 1997-2000. Bd. dirs. Am. Cancer Soc., Odessa, 1991-92; bd. mgrs. Ward Meml. Hosp., 1997-99, vice-chmn., 1998-99; mem. Odessa Symphony Guild, 1990-92, Port Lavaca Crisis Hotline Vol.; bd. dirs. United Way of Calhoun County, 1996; vol. Port Lavaca Crisis Hotline, 1995-96. Mem. Tex. Assn. Secondary Sch. Adminstrs., Tex. Assn. Profl. Educators, Delta Kappa Gamma Soc. Internat. Baptist. Home and Office: 1204 S Eric St Monahans TX 79756-5719 E-mail: kwatson@nwol.net.

WATSON, LINDA BARBARA, special education educator; b. Phila., Sept. 27, 1951; d. Lazarus Fuller and Louise (Blackman) Conner; m. James D. Watson, Aug. 1, 1987; children: Asher, Antonio; children from previous marriage: Dana, Janine. BA, Antioch U., 1980, MEd, 1982; postgrad., U. Del., 1992-94. Cert. spl. edn. and elem. edn. tchr., Pa. Tchr. Phila. Pub. Schs. With Delaware Valley Child Care, 1984—; pres. L.& L. Day Care Ctr. Inc., 19890—. Dep. commr. for voter registration, City of Phila., 1992—. Mem. Nat. Coalition Black Women (v.p. 1992—), Coun. Exceptional Children, Delta Sigma Theta. Democrat. Baptist. Avocations: swimming, roller skating. Home: 8041 Lindbergh Blvd Philadelphia PA 19153-1109

WATSON, MARILYN KAYE, elementary education educator; b. Liberty, Ky., Nov. 30, 1950; d. Lewis Joshua and Lois Sue (Ross) W. BA, Ea. Ky. U., 1974, postgrad., 1977, 81. Tchr. Casey County Bd. of Edn., Liberty, 1977—. Mem. NEA, Ky. Edn. Assn., Order of Eastern Star (sec. Casey chpt. 1979-85, grand Esther 1981-82, worthy matron 1989-90). Republican. Methodist. Avocations: reading, basketball, needlepoint, hiking, traveling.

WATSON, MARY ALICE, academic administrator; b. Dublin, Ga., Apr. 10, 1943; d. Jonnie Cecil and Annie Hudson (Temples) Raffield; m. Ray James Watson, Sept. 1, 1963; children: Ray Jeffry, John Adam (dec.), Sally Ann Watson-Hall. BS in Bus. Edn., Ga. Coll., 1973, MEd in Bus. Edn., 1976; Ednl. Specialist in Vocat. Edn., U. Ga., 1982; EdD, Nova Southeastern U., 1995. Cert. postsecondary edn. adminstr., secondary tchr. and adminstr. Tchr. bus. edn. Treutlen County High Sch., Soperton, Ga., 1973-74, East Laurens High Sch., Dublin, 1974-77; coord. program edn. and career exploration East Laurens Elem. Sch., Dublin, 1977-80; dep. prin. East Laurens Comprehensive High Sch., Dublin, 1980-83; v.p. instrnl. svcs. Heart of Ga. Tech. Inst., Dublin, 1983—. Mem. on-site evaluation team SACS-COEI, Houston, 1989, Paducah, Ky., 1990, Ochsner Allied Health Programs, Oschner Found. Hosp., New Orleans, 1993; presenter practicum Nova U. Summer Inst., 1989; George T. Baker Aviation Sch., Miami, 1993; Ft. Sam Houston Med. Programs, San Antonio, 1993; East Ctrl. Consortium VPISC chair, 1994-96; pres. Instrnl. Svcs. Coun., 1996—; Pinellas Tech. Edn. Ctr., Clearwater, Fla., 1996; participant various seminars and workshops. Vol. Cancer Crusade, 1983—. Mem. Nat. Coun. Community Svcs. and Continuing Edn., Am. Tech. Edn. Assn., Internat. Tech. Edn. Assn., Nat. Coun. Instrnl. Adminstrs., Nat. Coun. Local Adminstrs. Vocat. Edn., Am. Vocat. Assn., Women Bus., Ga. Vocat. Assn., Ga. Assn. Local Adminstrs. Vocat. Edn., Dublin-Laurens County C. of C., Dodge County C. of C., Order Blarney Stones, Pi Omega Pi, Iota Lambda Sigma (v.p. 1994—). Baptist. Avocations: golf, walking, gardening, reading, sewing. Office: Heart of Ga Tech Inst 560 Pinehill Rd Dublin GA 31021-1599

WATSON, MARY JO, special education educator; b. Candandaigua, N.Y., May 7, 1947; d. Joseph William and Mary (Treble) W. BS, Pembroke State U., 1970; postgrad., U. N.C., 1970, East Carolina U., 1977; MS, SUNY, Geneseo, 1983. Cert. tchr. phys. edn., N.C., tchr. phys. edn. and spl. edn., N.Y. Tchr. 3rd grade Scurlock Elem. Sch., Raeford, N.C., 1970-71; tchr. phys. edn., tennis coach, creative dance instr. E.E. Smith Sr. High Sch., Fayetteville, N.C., 1971-73; tchr. social studies and art for gifted students Reilly Rd. Elem. Sch., Fayetteville, 1973-74, specialist elem. phys. edn. resource, 1974-78; devel. specialist Craig Devel. Ctr., Sonyea, N.Y., summer 1981; tchr. spl. edn. Naples (N.Y.) Ctrl. Sch., 1984—. Mem. com. special edn. membership, Naples (N.Y.) Ctrl. Sch., special olympic com.-Cumberland County, Reilly Rd. Elem. Sch., Fayetteville, Curriculum Com. E.E. Smith Sr. High Sch., Fayetteville. Author, publisher (jour.) Teaching Exceptional Children, 1982, Learning Disabilities Advocacy Newsletter, The Advocator, 1993. Fellow ASCD, Coun. for Exceptional Children (presenter nat. conf. 1980, 81, Conn. and N.Y. state conf. 1981), N.Y. State United Tchrs., Naples Tchrs. Assn. Home: PO Box 277 Honeoye NY 14471-0277 Office: Naples Ctrl Sch 136 N Main St Naples NY 14512-9292

WATSON, REBECCA M. elementary school educator; b. Miami, Okla., July 13, 1958; d. Charles C. and Lena Mae (Jackman) W. BS, Okla. State U., 1981; MA, Northeastern Okla. State U., 1981, MA, 1987; adminstrv. cert., Nova U., 1990. Cert. elem. tchr., Okla., Nev.; K-12 reading tchr., Nev. Elem. tchr. Afton (Okla.) Pub. Sch., 1981-84, Chandler (Okla.) Pub. Sch., 1984-85, Cushing (Okla.) Pub. Sch., 1985-86, Clark County Sch. Dist., Las

Vegas, Nev., 1986—, asst. prin., 1993—. Adminstrv. asst. prin., Clark County Sch. Dist., Nev.; mem. curriculum commn., multicultiral task force Clark County Sch. Dist., Nev.; asst. site adminstr. Nova Univ., Fla.; workshop presenter. Named Outstanding Classroom Tchr.; grantee NEH. Mem. NEA, Nev. Edn. Assn., Internat. reading Assn., Clark County Tchrs. Assn., native Am. Educators Clark County Sch. Dist. (sec.), Native Ams. for Edn. (tchr. rep.), Phi Delta Kappa, Nat. Geography Assn. Home: 3758 Norton Dr Las Vegas NV 89129-5521 Office: 2801 Fort Sumter Dr North Las Vegas NV 89030-5201

WATSON, RICHARD ALLAN, philosophy educator, writer; b. New Market, Iowa, Feb. 23, 1931; s. Roscoe Richard and Daisy Belle (Penwell) W.; m. Patty Jo Andersen, July 30, 1955; 1 child, Anna Melissa BA, U. Iowa, 1953, MA, 1957, PhD in Philosophy, 1961; MS in Geology, U. Minn., 1959. Instr. philosophy U. Mich., Ann Arbor, 1961-64; asst. prof. Washington U., St. Louis, 1964-67, assoc. prof., 1967-74, prof., 1974—. Pres. Cave Research Found., Mammoth Cave, Ky., 1965-67; trustee Nat. Parks and Conservation Assn., Washington, 1969-81 Author: The Downfall of Cartesianism, 1966, Under Plowman's Floor, 1978, The Runner, 1981, The Philosopher's Diet, 1985, The Breakdown of Cartesian Metaphysics, 1987, The Philosopher's Joke, 1990, Writing Philosophy, 1992, Niagara, 1993, Caving, 1994, The Philosopher's Demise, 1995, Representational Ideas, from Plato to Patricia Churchland, 1995, Good Teaching, 1997, Cogito Ergo Sum: The Life of René Descartes, 2002;(with others) Man and Nature, 1969, The Longest Cave, 1976; editor: Classics in Speleology, 1968-73, Speleologia, 1974-79, Cave Books, 1980-2002, Jour. History of Philosophy, 1983, Jour. History of Philosophy Monograph Series, 1985-95, Jour. History of Philosophy Book Series, 2001. Served to 1st lt. USAF, 1953-55 NEH grantee, 1975; fellow Ctr. Advanced Study in Behavioral Scis., Stanford, Calif., 1967-68, 81-82, 91-92, Am. Coun. Learned Socs., 1967-68, Princeton Ctr. Internat. Studies, 1975-76, Camargo Found., 1995, Bogliasco Found., 1998. Mem. Nat. Speleological Soc. (hon. life), Am. Philos. Assn., Cave Research Found; fellow AAAS. Office: Washington U Dept Philosophy Saint Louis MO 63130-4899

WATSON, STEVEN ELLIS, school district administrator; b. Columbus, Ind., Feb. 14, 1945; s. Emerson Ellis and Emma Lee (Freeman) W.; m. Janice Faye Grau, Aug. 1, 1970; children: Daniel, David. BS in Sociology, Polit. Sci., Ball State U., 1969, MA in Sociology, 1974, EdD in Ednl. Adminstrn., 1979. Tchr. social studies Frankton (Ind.) High Sch., 1969-70; dir. alternative edn. Muncie (Ind.) Community Schs., 1971-77; asst. prin. high sch. Hammond (Ind.) City Schs., 1978-82; dir. adult and extended svcs. At-Risk Program, Hammond (Ind.) City Schs., 1982—. Mem., com. chair Gov.'s Adult Literacy Coalition, Indpls., 1983-87; bd. dirs. Calumet Area Literacy Coun., Hammond, 1988-92; cons. U.S. Dept. Edn., Ind. Div. Adult Edn., other ednl. orgns.; presenter workshops. Bd. dirs., v.p. Muncie Big Bros./Big Sisters, 1972-78, Northwest Ind. Big Bros./Big Sisters, 1981-85, Hammond YMCA, 1988—; bd. dirs. Northwest Ind. Boys and Girls Clubs, 1986-91; v.p. Hammond Lions Clubv, 1983—. Recipient award for outstanding adult and literacy program U.S. Dept. Edn., 1990; cited in Congl. Record, 1991; featured in spl. report NBC Nightly News, 1988, Parade mag., 1989; recipient program excellence award Erie (Pa.) C. of C., 1989. Mem. ASCD, Am. Assn. Adult and Continuing Edn., Ind. Assn. Adult and Continuing Edn. (bd. dirs., v.p. 1988-89, pres. 1989-91), Am. Contract Bridge League, Phi Delta Kappa. Avocations: duplicate bridge, coaching youth sports, baseball, basketball, movies. Home: 9408 Chestnut Ln Munster IN 46321-3802 Office: 5727 Sohl Ave Hammond IN 46320-2356

WATSON, WILLIAM DOWNING, JR., economist, educator; b. Durango, Colo., Aug. 9, 1938; s. William Downing and Carrie Elizabeth (Bailey) Blanchard; m. Dolores Marie Boisclair, Sept. 7, 1968; children: Kelli, Adam, Seth. BA in Math., No. Colo. U., 1964; MA in Econs., Syracuse U., 1965; PhD in Econs., U. Minn., 1970. Asst. prof. Wash. State U., Pullman, 1971-72; economist EPA-Washington, 1972-73; sr. fellow Resources for the Future, Washington, 1973-78. Adj. prof. Va. Poly. Inst. and State U., Falls Ch., 1981—; economist U.S. Geol. Survey, Reston, Va., 1978—; staff economist dirs. office U.S. Geol. Survey, Reston, 1984-88; sr. economist Ministry of Fin. and Nat. Economy Kingdom of Saudi Arabia, 1989-91; economist Office of Energy and Marine Geology U.S. Geol. Survey, Reston, 1991-95; assoc. prof. Ga. Inst. Tech., Atlanta, 1995—. Author: To Choose a Future, 1980; contbr. articles to profl. jours. With U.S. Army, 1956-59. Mem. Am. Econs. Assn., Internat. Assn. Energy Economists, Assn. Environ. and Resource Economists. Avocations: tennis, hiking, skiing. Home: 1927 Upper Lake Dr Reston VA 20191-3619 E-mail: william.watson@pubpolicy.gatech.edu.

WATSON-BOONE, REBECCA A. library and information studies researcher, educator; b. Springfield, Ohio, Mar. 7, 1946; d. Roger S. and Elizabeth Boone; m. Dennis David Ash, 1967 (div. 1975); m. Frederick Kellogg, 1979 (div. 1988); m. Peter G. Watson-Boone, May 26, 1989. Student, Earlham Coll., 1964-67; BA, Case Western Res. U., 1968; MLS, U. N.C., 1971; PhD, U. Wis., 1995. Asst. reference libr. Princeton (N.J) U., 1970-76; head cen. reference dept. U. Ariz., Tucson, 1976-83, assoc. dean Coll. Arts and Scis., 1984-89. Loaned exec. Ariz. Bd. Regents, 1988-89; pres. Ctr. for Study of Info. Profls., 1995—2002. Author: Constancy and Change in the Worklife of Research University Librarians, 1998; contbr. articles to profl. jours. Mem. ALA (div. pres. 1985-86, councilor 1988-92), Assn. for Libr. and Info. Sci. Edn., NAFE. Mem. Soc. Of Friends. Office: 7728 County Rd Y Oconto WI 54153 E-mail: csip@execpc.com.

WATT, DWIGHT, JR., (ARTHUR DWIGHT WATT JR.), computer programming and microcomputer specialist; b. Washington, Jan. 25, 1955; s. Arthur Dwight and Myrtle Lorraine (Putnam) W.; m. Shari Elizabeth Gambrell, July 30, 1988. BA, Winthrop U., 1977, MBA, 1979; EdD, U. Ga., 1989. Cert. computer and internet profl. Inst. Cert. Computer Profls., Microsoft; cert. home fire arms safety, NRA; cert. A+ personal computer technician, CompTIA; cert. sys. engr., sys. adminstr., office user specialist instr.; i-net plus cert. Comptia; Network + cert.; cert. network adminstr. and acad. instr., Cisco; Server + cert. CompTIA. Data processing instr. York Tech. Coll., Rock Hill, S.C., 1977-78; computer ctr. asst. Winthrop U., Rock Hill, 1976-79; data processing instr. Brunswick (Ga.) Coll., 1979-80; system operator, asst. programmer Sea Island (Ga.) Co., The Cloister, 1981; pvt. practice data processing cons. Swainsboro, Ga., 1981—; computer programming/microcomputer specialist instr. Swainsboro Tech. Inst., 1981-96; sr. programmer/analyst Policy Mgmt. Sys. Corp., Columbia, S.C., 1996-97; microcomputer specialist instr. Athens Tech. Coll.-Elbert County Campus, Elberton, Ga., 1997-2001; chair IT dept. Heart of Ga. Tech. Coll., Dublin, 2001—; CIO Ga. Healthcare Sys., Atlanta, 2001. Cons., spkr. in field; chmn. exec. bd. computer curricula Ga. Dept. Tech. and Adult Edn., 1990-92, 2002-, exec. bd. computer curricula, 1994-96, vice chair, 2000-02; chmn. East Ctrl. Ga. Consortium for Computer Occupations, 1990-96; co-facilitator CIS curriculum rev. and update Ga. Tech. Colls., 2001. Author: District Revenue Potential and Teachers Salaries in Georgia, 1989, Structured COBOL for Technical Students, 1998; co-author: District Property Wealth and Teachers Salaries in Georgia, 1990, Factors Influencing Teachers Salaries: An Examination of Alternative Models, 1991, Local Wealth and Teachers Salaries in Pennsylvania, 1992, School District Wealth and Teachers' Salaries in South Carolina, 1993, Test Yourself A+ Certification Practice Exams, 1998. Chmn. Emanuel County chpt. ARC, Swainsboro, 1989-90, 92-93, bd. dirs., 1989-96; pres. United Meth. Men. Swainsboro, 1984-86; trustee Greater Swainsboro Tech. Inst. Found., Inc., 1995-96. Recipient Nat. Tech. Tchr. of Yr. finalist award Am. Tech. Edn. Assn., 1994; Olympic Cmty. Hero Torchbearer, 1996. Mem. Inst. Cert. Computing Profls., Ga. Bus. Edn. Assn. (dir. dist. 1 1986, 96, dist. sec.-treas. 1993-95, dist. 1 dir.-elect 1995-96, Dist. 1 Postsecondary Tchr. of Yr. 1985, State Postsecondary Tchr. of Yr. 1995), Profl. Assn. Ga. Educators, Swainsboro Jaycees (Outstanding Young Citizen 1985, treas. 1984-89, pres. 1987-88, pres. S.E. Ga. Jaycee Fair 1995, treas. S.E. Ga. Jaycee Fair 1993-94), Ga. Jaycees (v.p. area C. mem. 1988-89, chaplain 1989-90, dir. region 6 1990-91, chmn. state shooting edn. 1991-92, chair Internat. BB Gun Match Championship 1999, co-chair match 2000, treas. match 2002), U.S. Jr. C. of C. (nat. rep. shooting edn. program 1992-95, Shooting Edn. State Program Mgr. of Yr. 1992), Kiwanis. Methodist. Home: PO Box 1637 206 Hereford Rd Swainsboro GA 30401 Office: 560 Pinehill Rd Dublin GA 31021-1253 E-mail: dwight-watt@att.net.

WATT, GLENN A. secondary school educator; b. Chgo., Feb. 9, 1952; s. Andrew Robert and Evelyn Astrid (Nelson) W. BS, Western Ill. U., 1973. Cert. secondary tchr., Ill. Quality control engr. Lasker Boiler and Engring. Corp., Chgo., 1973-76; CETA tchr. North Palos Community Sch. Dist., Palos Hills, Ill., 1976-77; substitute tchr., coach Reavis High Sch., Burbank, Ill., 1977-79, Oak Lawn (Ill.) Community High Sch., 1979-81; tchr. Independence Jr. High Sch., Palos Heights, Ill., 1981-82; tchr., coach Bradley (Ill.)-Bourbonnais High Sch., 1982-83, Grayslake (Ill.) Community High Sch., 1984—. Speaker in field. Co-author: Grayslake, A Historical Portrait; contbr. Excursions in Geometry, NSF grant, 1989. Mem. Warren-Newport Libr., Summer Leadership Acad., Ill. State U., Normal. Mem. NEA, Ill. Edn. Assn. (regional sec. 1991-92, Emerging Leaders award 1987, Bldg. Strong Locals award 1989, Beginning Bargaining Sch. award 1990, Pres. Tng. award 1992, Comm. award 1991), Grayslake Hist. Soc. (bd. dirs. 1991-93), Grayslake Edn. Assn. (pres. 1992-93, alt. rep. regional coun. 1988-89, 91-92, IEA elected position mem. 1995—), Ill. Labor History Soc., Pullman Soc., Nat. Coun. for Social Studies, Nat. Geog. Soc., Ill. Coun. for the Social Studies. Avocations: softball, golf, bowling. Office: Grayslake Community High 400 N Lake St Grayslake IL 60030-1430

WATT, WILLIS MARTIN, academic administrator, communications, adult education, leadership educator; b. Ottawa, Kans., Dec. 20, 1950; s. Gerald Omri and Shirley Arlene (Tush) W.; m. Katherine Ann Young, Feb. 14, 1970; 1 child, Derek Lee. BS in Christian Edn., Manhattan Christian Coll., 1976; BS in Secondary Edn.-Speech/Drama, Kans. State U., 1976, MA in Speech/Drama, 1978, PhD in Curriculum/Instrn./Speech, 1980; postdoctoral, Flint Hills Leadership Program, 1999; continuing edn. unit tng., Franklin/Covey, 2000, continuing edn. unit tng., 2002. Ordained to ministry Christian Ch., 1976; cert. leadership tng., 2002. Pastor Colony (Kans.) Christian Ch., 1969-71, Barnes (Kans.) Christian Ch., 1974-75, 1975-76; assoc. pastor Burlington (Kans.) Christian Ch., summers 1970-71; pastor Ogden (Kans.) Union Ch., 1979-80; elder, evangelist Hays (Kans.) Christian Ch., 1984-97; grad. tchg. asst. dept. speech, theatre and dance Kans. State U., Manhattan, 1976-78, instr., 1978-80; teaching intern speech/drama Manhattan (Kans.) Christian Coll., 1979; asst. prof. dept. speech comm. Iowa State U., Ames, 1980-84; dir. forensics dept. comm. Ft. Hays (Kans.) State U., 1984-91, chair, 1991-97; v.p. acad. affairs Manhattan (Kans.) Christian Coll., 1997-2000, dept. head adult edn., 1999-2000. Interim min. South Hutchinson (Kans.) Christian Ch., 1999-2000; adj. assoc. prof. dept. speech comm., theater and dance Kans. State U., 1999-2000; divsn. dir. profl. studies Meth. Coll., 2003—; divsn. dir. profl. studies and edn., dir. orgnl. comm. and leadership, prof. speech Meth. Coll., Fayetteville, N.C., 2000—; dir. Talking Tiger Rsch. Inst., Hays, 1985-91; mem. Comm. Tng. Consulting Svcs., Fayetteville, N.C., 1986—; exec. dir. Chi Rho Players Religious Drama Troupe, Ames, Iowa, 1981-84; adjudicator Am. Coll. Theatre Festival, Region V, 1982-2000; mem. adv. coun. for acad. affairs Ctr. for Policy in Higher Edn., 1999; artistic dir. Kyriou Drama Troupe, Manhattan, 1998-2000. Author: Fundamentals of Speech, 1988, Theory and Application for Effective Bus. and Profl. Presentations, 1994, Fundamentals of Oral Communication: Theory and Practice, 1995, Fundamentals of Oral Communication, 1997, Speech Communication: Theories & Practices, 2001; editor Kans. Speech Jour., 1994-2000; assoc. editor Nat. Forensic Jour., 1987-97; rev. editor The Forensic, 1989-95, Jour. Leadership Edn., 2003—; mem. editl. adv. bd. Privacy on Campus, 1999. Edn. divsn. leader United Way of Ellis County, Hays, 1989, mem. allocations com. Riley County (Kans.) United Way, 1999-2002; Ft. Hays State U. comm. leader, 1992; baseball coach Little League, Ames, Iowa and Hays, 1982-86; bd. dirs. ACTORS Cmty. Theatre, Ames, 1982-84; elder Fayetteville (N.C.) Christian Ch., 2002—. With U.S. Army, 1971-74. Recipient Bronze award Ellis County United Way, 1996, Outstanding Coll. Tchr. award Kans. Speech Comm. Assn., 1996, Editor's Choice award for poem Ode to Lost Love and Friends, Silver and Bronze awards for Poet of Merit Internat. Soc. Poets, 2002; inductee Mid-Am. Edn. Hall of Fame, J. Paul Jewell Ctr., Kansas City, 1998. Mem. Theta Alpha Phi (hon. drama), Pi Kappa Delta (gov. plains province 1986-88, 90-91, Exemplary Svc. award 1987, 91, Svc. award 1993, Order of Highest Distinction 1995), Pi Delta Kappa, Alpha Psi Omega. Avocations: racketball, chess, reading, writing, travel. Home: 5624 Watersplash Ln Fayetteville NC 28311-0221 Office: Meth Coll 5400 Ramsey St Fayetteville NC 28311 E-mail: wmwatt@methodist.edu.

WATTERS, EDMOND CLAIR, ophthalmologist, educator; b. Natrona Heights, Pa., Dec. 25, 1942; s. John Lomnet and Maribelle (Good) Watters; m. Comly Colwell Watters, Dec. 27, 1966; children: Christine, Jennifer, Edmond. BS Coll. William and Mary, 64; MD, George Washington U., 1968. Diplomate Am. Bd. Ophthalmology. Intern Mercy Hosp., Pitts., 1968—69; resident in ophthalmology U. Pitts., 1971—74; ophthalmologist E.H. Konnerdoll, Tarntum, Pa., 1974—77; ophthalmologist, pres. Western Pa. Surg. Eye Assn., Pitts., 1977—97, Western Pa. Surg. Eye Assn./UPMC, Pitts., 1997—. Chief ophthalmology sect. U. Pitts. Med. Ctr., St. Margaret's, 1989—, pres. med. staff, 2000—; bd. dirs. St. Margaret Found., Pitts., 1990—; assoc. clin. prof. ophthalmology U. Pitts. Elder Fox Chapel (Pa.) Presbyn. Ch., Fox Chapel, 1996—99. Capt. U.S. Army, 1969—71. Decorated Bronze Star (3). Fellow: ACS; mem.: AMA, Pa. Med. Soc., Allegheny County Med. Soc., Am. Soc. Cataract and Refractive Surgeons, Pitts. Ophthalmology Soc., Pa. Acad. Ophthalmology. Republican. Presbyterian. Avocations: golf, fishing, hunting, gardening, sailing. Home: 300 Windmere Dr Pittsburgh PA 15238

WATTLEWORTH, ROBERTA ANN, physician, medical educator; b. Sioux City, Iowa, Dec. 26, 1955; d. Roland Joseph and Elizabeth Ann (Ahart) Eickholt; m. John Wade Wattleworth, Nov. 7, 1984; children: Adam, Ashley. BS, Morningside Coll., Sioux City, 1978; D of Osteopathy, Coll. Osteo. Medicine/Surgery, Des Moines, 1981; M.Healthcare Administrn., U. Osteo. Med. & Health Scis., Des Moines, 1999. Intern Richmond Heights (Ohio) Gen. Hosp., 1981-82, resident in anesthesiology, 1982-84; anesthesiologist Doctor's Gen. Hosp., Plantation, Fla., 1984-85; resident in family practice J.F. Kennedy Hosp., Stratford, N.J., 1985-87; educator family practice U. Osteo. Medicine and Health Scis., Des Moines, 1987-89; family practitioner McFarland Clinic, P.C., Jewell, Iowa, 1989-94; lectr. family practice Osteopath. Med. Ctr., Des Moines U., 1999—. Med. dir. nursing home Bethany Manor, Story City, Iowa, 1990-99, Jewell Vol. Fire and Rescue Squad, 1990-99. Bd. dirs. Heartland Sr. Svcs., 1995—99, Iowa Rural Health Assn. Named Nat. Outstanding Osteo. Educator of Yr., Nat. Student Osteo. Med. Assn., 2001—02. Fellow Am. Coll. of Osteo. Family Physicians; mem. Am. Osteo. Assn., Am. Med. Dirs. Assn. (sec.-treas. Iowa chpt. 1997-99), Am. Geriatric Assn., Am. Coll. Osteo. Family Physicians (pres. Iowa chpt. 1995-96), Iowa Osteo. Med. Assn. (trustee 1995-99, v.p. 1999—, pres.-elect, 2000-01, pres. 2001-2002). Lutheran. Avocations: gardening, cooking, painting. Office: 3200 Grand Ave Des Moines IA 50312-4104 E-mail: Roberta.Wattleworth@dmu.edu.

WATTO, DENNIS PAUL, school system administrator, researcher, writer; b. Upland, Pa., Oct. 31, 1945; s. Paul and Helen (Kashlak) W.; m. Andrea Franzosa; children: Julie, Joseph. BS, Millersville U., 1971; MEd, East Stroudsburg U., 1977, Pa. State U., 1981, DEd, 1987. Tchr. North Schuylkill (Pa.) Sch. Dist., 1971-77; adminstr. Tamaqua (Pa.) Area Sch. Dist., 1978-88, Downingtown (Pa.) Area Sch. Dist., 1988—. V.p. Schuylkill County Inter-Scholastic Athletic Assn., Pottsville, Pa., 1978-79, 85-87, pres., 1979-85; instr. Pa. State U., 1988. Active mem. Downingtown-Uwchlan Recreation Bd.; coach Valley West Baseball Assn.; active Am. Heart Assn., Jr. Miss Pageant. With Pa. N.G., 1966-72. Mem. ASCD, Am. Ednl. Rsch. Assn., Nat. Assn. Secondary Sch. Prins., Pa. Assn. Secondary Sch. Prins., Phi Delta Kappa. Avocations: reading, music, golf, fishing, tennis. Home: 304 Millwood Ln Coatesville PA 19320-2054 Office: Downingtown Area Sch Dist Wallace Ave Downingtown PA 19335

WATTS, HAROLD WESLEY, economist, educator; b. Salem, Oreg., Sept. 30, 1932; s. Elton and Claire W.; m. Doris A. Roth, Sept. 28, 1951 (div. 1973); children— Michael Lee, Suzanne, Jane Marie, Kristin BA, U. Oreg., 1954; MA, Yale U., 1956, PhD, 1957. From instr. to assoc. prof. Yale U., New Haven, 1957-63; from assoc. prof. to prof. econs. U. Wis., Madison, 1963-76, dir. Inst. Research on Poverty, 1966-71; prof. econs. and pub. policy Columbia U., N.Y.C., 1976-98, prof. econs. and pub. policy emeritus, 1998—, dir. Pub. Policy Rsch. Ctr., 1988-93; sr. fellow Mathematica Policy Research Princeton, N.J., 1979-92; sr. rsch. assoc. Urban Inst., 1994-95. Recipient Paul Lazarsfeld award, 1980; Guggenheim fellow, 1975 Fellow Assn. Pub. Policy Analysis and Mgmt., Econometric Soc.; mem. Am. Econ. Assn., L.I. Wine Coun. (pres. 2000-02). Democrat. Home: 144 Bay Ave Greenport NY 11944-1404 Office: Ternhaven Cellars PO Box 758 Greenport NY 11944 E-mail: harold@ternhaven.com.

WATTS, JACKIE SUE, elementary education educator; b. Springfield, Mo., Mar. 12, 1959; d. William Russell and Phyllis June (Lowrey) Green; m. William Kent Watts, Mar. 22, 1981; children: Melinda Beth, Jennifer Lynn. BA, Coll. of the Ozarks, 1982. Cert. elem. edn. Tchr. lang. arts Dixon (Mo.) Mid. Sch., 1981-83; tchr. chpt. 1 math. Richards R-5, West Plains, Mo., 1983-84; primary tchr. West Plains R-7 Schs., 1984-87, Springfield R-12 Schs., 1987-95, tchr. kindergarten, 1995-98; tchr. kindergarten and primary Nixa R-2 Schs., 1998—. Tech. coord. Wanda Gray Elem., Springfield, 1992-96, lang. arts curriculum devel. com., 1996-98, math curriculum devel. com., 2001—. Children's tchr. South Gate Bapt. Ch., Springfield, 1993-96, 2001—02; girl scout leader GSA, 1996-97. Named Tchr. of Month, Springfield R-12 Schs., 1994. Mem. Internat. Reading Assn., Mo. State Tchrs. Assn., Nixa Tchr. Assn. Avocations: reading, camping, flower gardening, spending time with family. Office: John Thomas Elem Sch 312 N Market St Nixa MO 65714 E-mail: jwatts@mail.nixa.k12.mo.us.

WATTS, JOHN RANSFORD, university administrator; b. Boston, Feb. 9, 1930; s. Henry Fowler Ransford and Mary Marion (Macdonald) Watts; m. Joyce Lannom, Dec. 20, 1975; 1 child, David Allister. AB, Boston Coll., 1950, MEd, 1965; MFA, Yale U., 1953; PhD, Union Grad. Sch., 1978. Prof., ast. dean Boston U., 1958-74; prof., dean fine arts Calif. State U., Long Beach, 1974-79; dean and artistic dir. The Theatre Sch./Goodman Sch. Drama, DePaul U., Chgo., 1979-99, prof. and dean emeritus, 1999—. Mng. dir. DePaul U. Merle Reskin Theatre, 1988-99; gen. mgr. Boston Arts Festivals, 1955-64; adminstr. Arts Programs at Tanglewood, 1966-69; producing dir. Theatre Co. of Boston, 1973-75. Chmn. Mass. Coun. on Arts and Humanities, 1968-72; bd. dirs., v.p. Long Beach Pub. Cofp. for the Arts, 1975-79; mem. theatre panel Ill. Arts Coun., 1981-90. With U.S. Army, 1953-55. Recipient Lifetime Achievement award Joseph Jefferson Com., Chgo., 2000. Mem. Mass. Ednl. Comms. Commn., Am. Theatre Asasn., Nat. Coun. on Arts in Edn., Met. Cultural Alliance, U.S. Inst. Theatre Tech., League Chgo. Theatres, Chgo. Internat. Theatre Festival, St. Botolph Club (Boston), Univ. Club (Chgo.), Phi Beta Kappa, Phi Kappa Phi.

WATTS, JUDITH-ANN WHITE, secondary school educator; b. Moline, Ill., Nov. 11, 1955; d. Harry Cameron and Jennie Elizabeth (Brockevelt) White; 1 child, Cameron Paul. BSEd, Ill. State U., 1976; MSEd, Western Ill. U., 1987; postgrad., George Mason U., 1992-96, U. So. Calif., 1996-97. English tchr. United Twp. High Sch., East Moline, Ill., 1976-77, English tchr., curriculum designer/asst. theatre dir., 1978-84; county coord. Simon for Senate Campaign, Rock Island, Ill., 1984; legis. asst. U.S. Sen. Paul Simon, Washington, 1985-89; program devel. specialist NEA, Washington, 1989-90; dir. constituent rels. Nat. Coun. Accreditation Tchr. Edn., Washington, 1990-92; exec. assoc. policy devel. Nat. Bd. Profl. Teaching Standards, Washington, 1992-93; spl. asst. to pres. Va. State U., Petersburg, 1993-96; exec. asst. ofc. of the dean U. So. Calif. Sch. of Edn., L.A., 1996-97; tchr. English, theatre, speech, choral music Hillview H.S., Tustin, Calif., 1998—. V.p. bd. dirs. Rappahannock Mediation Ctr., Fredericksburg, Va., mediator, 1989-96, trainer, 1991-96. Mem. Fredericksburg Singers, 1990-96, Fredericksburg Community Chorus, 1990-96; precinct capt. Spotsylvania County (Va.) Dem. Com., 1989-96; campaign worker various polit. campaigns, Va., Ill., Calif., 1972—; exec. com. of vestry St. George's Ch., Fredericksburg, mem. ch. choir, 1990-96; family program coord. St. Paul's Episcopal Ch., Tustin, Calif., 1998-2000. Mem. NEA, ASCD, Am. Ednl. Rsch. Assn., Am. Assn. Sch. Adminstrs., Nat. Assn. Sec. Sch. Prins., Ill. Edn. Assn. (regional vice chair 1982-84, regional pub. rels. chair 1982-84), Va. Edn. Assn., Va. Meditation Network, Calif. Tchrs. Assn. Episcopalian. Avocations: sewing, singing, crafts, community theater, exercise/fitness. Home: 1131 Triumphal Way Santa Ana CA 92705-2925 E-mail: jwatts@tustin.k12.ca.us., judywatts55@hotmail.com.

WATTS, LOU ELLEN, elementary education educator; b. Conway, S.C., Sept. 23, 1940; d. Bernie Louis and Dallie Ellen (Lemons) Overhultz; m. Ervin William Watts, Feb. 3, 1963; children: William Ashley. B Music Edn., La. State U., 1962; postgrad. U. Ga., 1965; MEd, U. Ariz., 1987. Cert. elem. tchr., music tchr., Ind., Ga., La., Ariz. Music tchr. Westchester Twp. Sch., Chesterton, Ind., 1963-64; music cons. Clayton County Sch., Jonesboro, Ga., 1964-66; elem. and chorus tchr. Tucson Unified Sch. Dist., 1979—, intermediate head div. tchr., music cons., 1983-84, chorus dir., 1979-84, tchr. music and performing arts, mid. sch., 1987—; tchr., cons. archaeology, 1983—. Author (tchr./student manuals): Archaeology is More Than a Dig; contbr. articles to profl. jours. Pres., fine arts chmn., cons. Sahuaro Jr. Women's Club, Tucson, 1970-74; state consumer chmn., music award chmn. Ariz. Fedn. of Women's Club, 1970-72; mem. Tucson Panhellenic Council, 1971-72; project chmn. Southwest Children's Exploratory Ctr., Tucson; mem. music rsch. project com. Tucson Symphony Orch., U. Ariz. Tucson Enrichment Fund grantee, 1983, 90, Substance Abuse Program for Mid. Sch. Edn. grantee, 1990, Middle Sch. rsch. grantee Tucson Symphony Orchestra Univ. of Ariz. and Tucson Unified Sch. Dist., 1993, 97-98; named Clubwoman of the Year Ariz. Fedn. Jr. Women's Club, 1972. Mem. NEA, Nat. Audubon Soc., Nat. Sci. Tchr. Assn., Music Educators Nat. Conf., Ariz. Edn. Assn., Ariz. Sci. Tchr.'s Assn. (Search for Excellence in Sci. award 1985), Tucson Edn. Assn., DAR, So. Ariz. Arabian Horse Assn., Delta Kappa Gamma, Sigma Alpha Iota. Home and Office: 8740 E Summer Trl Tucson AZ 85749-9663

WATTS, MICHAEL J. geographer, educator; b. Eng., U.S. BS in Geography with first class honors, U. London, 1972; MA in Geography, U. Mich., 1974, PhD in Geography, 1979. Lectr. dept. geography U. Mich., Ann Arbor, 1975—76; postgrad. rsch. fellow dept. geography U. Ibadan, Nigeria, 1977—78; asst. prof. dept. geography U. Calif., Berkeley, 1979—85, assoc. prof., 1985—88, prof., 1988—, Chancellor's prof., 1997—2000, Class of 1963 prof. geography, 2000—, chmn. NDEA Berkeley-Stanford African Studies Ctr., 1980—, faculty assoc. Energy and Resources Group, 1983—, faculty assoc. Peace and Conflict Studies, 1984—, chmn. devel. studies major, 1986—, faculty assoc. MA Program in Internat. Studies, 1993—. Rsch. assoc. Internat. Disaster Inst., London, 1978; rsch. assoc. Ctr. for Rsch. on Econ. Devel. U. Mich., 1983—84; rsch. assoc. dept. anthropology Mus. Natural History, The Smithsonian Instn., Washington, 1990; rsch. assoc. Devel. Policy and Practice Open U., England, 1995—; vis. prof. in residence dept. geography Pa. State U., University Park, 1987; vis. prof. Inst. Developing Countries and dept. geography U. Warsaw, 1988; vis. rsch. prof. dept. geography W.Va. U.,

Morgantown, 1988; vis. lectr. Grad. Inst. Planning U. Taipei, Taiwan, 1991; vis. lectr. dept. geography U. Hawaii, Honolulu, 1992; vis. prof. in residence city and regional planning Cornell U., Ithaca, NY, 1992; vis. rsch. fellow Sch. Econs. U. Delhi, India, 1992; disting. vis. lectr. dept. geography U. Coll., London, 1994; disting. vis. prof. dept. geography U. Bergen, Norway, 1994; sr. scholar in residence Townsend Humanities Ctr. U. Calif., Berkeley, 1994—95; vis. scholar in residence dept. geography U. Copenhagen, 1995; vis. scholar in residence dept. comm. U. Bologna, Italy, 1999; mem. internat. adv. bd. South Asia Inst. U. Heidelberg, Germany, 1999—; cons. in field. Editor-in-chief, mem. editl. bd.: Critical Studies in Human Geography, 1995—; editor: African Econ. History, 1989—; mem. editl. bd.: African Studies Rev., 1982—89, Devel. Studies Rev., 1987—, Capitalism, Nature, Socialism, 1988—, ICARIA/Ecologia Politica, 1989—, Econ. Geography, 1991—94, Encyclopedia of Sub-Saharan Africa, 1991—96, Soc. and Space, 1992—, Annals of the Assn. Am. Geographers, 1993—2000, Jour. Tropical Rsch., 1993—, Rev. Internat. Polit. Economy, 1994—, Environ. History, 1994—, Oxford Geog. and Environ. Studies, 1996—, Jour. Peasant Studies, 1996—2000, Soc. for Comparative Internat. Devel., 1999—, Progress in Development Studies, 1999—, Jour. Agrarian Change, 2000—, Jour. Tech. Mgmt. and Sustainable Devel., 2001—, Routledge Series in Econ. Geography, 2002—. Recipient Disting. Tchr. award, Nat. Coun. for Geog. Edn., 1984; fellow, John Simon Guggenheim Meml. Found., 2003; grantee, Horace H. Rackham Grad. Sch., U. Mich., 1976—77, NSF, 1976—77, 1983—85, 1987—88, 1989—90, 1990—91, 1990—91, 1990—91, 1993—94, 1994—95, 1995—96, 1995—96, 1995—96, 1997—98, 1998—99, 1999—2000, 2003—, Wenner Gren Found. for Anthropol. Rsch., Inc., 1977, Social Sci. Rsch. Coun./Am. Coun. Learned Socs., 1980—81, 1992—93, U. Calif., Berkeley, 1980, 1986, 1986—87, 1991—92, Rockefeller Found., 1988—90, 1995—97, 1999—2003, MacArthur Found., 1990—93, 1997—2000, 1999—2000, 2000—03, Laird, Norton Found., 1992—93, U. Calif., 1994—96, 1995—96, 1998—99, Social Sci. Rsch. Coun., 1997, U. Calif., San Diego, 1997—98, 2000—01, Berkeley-France Fund, 1997—98, Ford Found., 1998—2000, 1999—2002, Wageningen U., 2001—, Frank Guggenheim Found., 2002—03, Nat. Geog. Soc., 2003—; Doctoral Dissertation fellow, Resources for the Future, Inc., 1976—77, Fgn. Area fellow, Social Sci. Rsch. Coun. and the Am. Coun. Learned Socs., 1976—78, predoctoral fellow, Horace H. Rackham Grad. Sch., U. Mich., 1978—79. Mem.: Assn. Concerned African Scholars, Soc. for Internat. Devel., Internat. African Inst., Assn. Am. Geographers, Assn. Am. Anthropologists, Assn. African Studies, Inst. for Food and Devel. Policy (hon.). Office: Dept Geography Univ Calif Berkeley CA 94720-4740*

WATTS, WILLIE CEPHUS, JR., elementary school principal; b. Akron, Ohio, July 27, 1951; s. Willie Cephus and Edna Louise (Williams) W.; m. Mozella Marie Cottingham, Dec. 19, 1981. BA in Edn., U. Akron, 1973, MA in Edn., 1981; PhD, Pacific Western U., 1983; JD, LaSalle U., 1992. Cert. tchr., adminstr., Ohio. Tchr., coach Mansfield (Ohio) City Schs., 1973, Akron Pub. Schs., 1974-88; adminstr., elem. sch. prin. Maple Heights (Ohio) City Schs., 1988—. Cons. Watts Cons. Svcs., Akron, 1989—. Mem. Akron Youth Commn., 1991—, Human and Community Rels. Commn., Akron, 1991—. Recipient Golden Spruce award Cuyahoga County Planning Com., Cleve., 1993. Fellow Harvard's Prin.'s Ctr.; mem. ASCD, NAACP, Am. Assn. Sch. Adminstrs., Buckeye Assn. Sch. Adminstrs., Ohio Assn. Elem. Sch. Adminstrs., Nat. Assn. Elem. Sch. Adminstrs., Rotary (pres. Maple Heights unit 1991—), Phi Delta Kappa. Democrat. Baptist. Avocations: music, reading, writing, golf, classic automobiles. Home: 964 Kingsbridge Ct Akron OH 44313-8010 Office: Maple Heights City Schs 19800 Stafford Ave Maple Heights OH 44137-1829

WATTS-WILSON, DENISE, secondary school educator; b. Bklyn., Aug. 20, 1954; d. James and Hattie (Jowers) Watts; m. Jimmy Lee Wilson, July 30, 1983; 1 child, Gregory Alexander. BA, CUNY, 1976; MA in Christian Edn., So. Bapt. Sem., Louisville, 1978, MDiv, RE, 1982. Dir. edn. and youth Bethany Bapt. Ch., Bklyn., 1978-80; substitute tchr. Jefferson County Bd. Edn., Louisville, 1980-83; min. edn. and youth South Park Bapt. Ch., Houston, 1983-84, Greenspoint Bapt. Ch., Houston, 1986-88; tchr. Barrick Elem. Sch., Houston Ind. Sch. Dist., 1985-88; tchr. history Wells Mid. Sch., Spring Ind. Sch. Dist., Houston, 1988-93; asst. pastor and minister of edn. St. Stephen Bapt. Ch., Louisville, 1993-95; tchr. U.S. history Bruce Middle Sch. Jefferson County Schs., 1995-96, tchr. computer tech. Bruce Mid. Sch., 1996-97; proprietor Gifts from Home, Louisville, 1995-99; program coord. Rites of Passage Acad., Jefferson County Schs., 1997-98; computer tech. tchr. Farnsley Mid. Sch., Jefferson County Schs., Louisville, 1998-2000, Kammerer Mid. Sch., Jefferson County Schs., Louisville, 2000—03; exploring tech./word processing tchr. Shawnee H.S., Jefferson County Schs., Louisville, 2003—; pres. Deliverance Enterprises Internat., 1999—. Youth dir. Zion Bapt. Ch., Louisville, 1982-83. Author: Devotions for Christian Staff, 1982. Founding pastor Lighthouse Christian Fellowship, LaGrange, Ky., 1997—. Benjamin Mays fellow Fund for Theol. Edn., 1981. Mem. N.G. Assn. U.S.A., N.G. Assn. Tex. (life). Republican. Avocations: walking, jogging, singing, crocheting, swimming. Office: 4018 W Market St Louisville KY 40212 E-mail: deeww@quixnet.net.

WAUGH, WILLIAM HOWARD, biomedical educator; b. N.Y.C., May 13, 1925; s. Richey Laughlin and Lyda Pearl (Leamer) W.; m. Eileen Loretta Garrigan, Oct. 4, 1952; children: Mark Howard, Kathleen Cary, William Peter. Student, Boston U., 1943, W.Va. U., 1944; MD, Tufts U., 1948, postgrad., 1949-50. Cardiovascular rsch. trainee Med. Coll. Ga., Augusta, 1954-55, asst. rsch. prof. physiology, 1955-60, assoc. medicine, 1957-60; assoc. prof. medicine U. Ky., Lexington, 1960-69; Ky. Heart Assn. Chair in cardiovascular rsch. Ky. Heart Assn., Lexington, 1963-71; prof. medicine U. Ky., Lexington, 1969-71; prof. medicine and physiology East Carolina U., Greenville, 1971—2001, rsch. prof. physiology, 2001—, prof. emeritus, 2001—. Head renal sect. U. Ky. Coll., Lexington, 1960-68; chmn. dept. clin. scis. East Carolina U., Greenville, 1971-75, chmn. policy and rev. com. on human rsch., 1972-90. Contbr. articles to profl. jours. With AUS, 1943-46; capt. USAF, 1952-54. Fellow ACP; mem. AAAS, Am. Physiology Soc., Am. Heart Assn., Am. Soc. Nephrology, Microcirculatory Soc. Republican. Achievements include basic advances in excitation contraction coupling in vasc. smooth muscle; basic advances in autoregulation of renal blood flow and urine flow; adj. therapy in acute lung edema; noncovalent antisickling agents and amino acid nutrient in sickle cell hemoglobinopathy; oral citrulline as dietary supplement in man. Home: 119 Oxford Rd Greenville NC 27858-4954 Office: E Carolina U Sch Medicine Dept Physiology Greenville NC 27858

WAUGH, WILLIAM LEE, JR., political science educator; b. Warrior, Ala., Apr. 16, 1948; s. William Lee and Frances Ruth (Hill) W.; m. Deborah McCorkle, Sept. 11, 1974. AB, u. North Ala., 1973; MA, Auburn U., 1976; PhD, U. Miss., 1980. Instr. polit. sci. Miss. State U., Starkville, 1979; asst. prof. Kans. State U., Manhattan, 1980-84; from assoc. prof. to prof. Ga. State U., Atlanta, 1985—. Author: International Terrorism, 1982, Terrorism and Emergency Management, 1990, Living with Hazards, Dealing with Disasters, 2000; co-author: State and Local Tax Policies, 1995; co-editor: Cities and Disaster, 1990, Handbook of Emergency Management, 1990, Disaster Management in the U.S. and Canada, 1996; editor-in-chief Jour. Emergency Mgmt., 2003—. With U.S. Army, 1970-71, Korea. Mem. ASPA (sect. chair 2002-03), Am. Polit. Sci. Assn., Internat. Polit. Sci. Assn., Internat. Rsch. Com. on Disasters, So. Polit. Sci. Assn., Policy Studies Orgn., Amnesty Internat., Internat. Assn. Emergency Managers. Office: Dept Pub Adminstrn & Urban Studies Andrew Young Sch Policy Studies Ga State U Atlanta GA 30303 E-mail: wwaugh@gsu.edu.

WAVLE, ELIZABETH MARGARET, college official; b. Homer, N.Y., Jan. 18, 1957; d. John Andrew Jr. and Louise Hayford (Estey) W. BMus, SUNY, Potsdam, 1979; AM in Libr. Sci., U. Mich., 1980; MS in Edn., Elmira Coll., 1990. Sr. libr. asst. U. Mich., Ann Arbor, 1979-80; pub. svcs. libr. Elmira (N.Y.) Coll., 1980-84, instr. music, 1981-97, head tech. svcs., 1984-97, coord. women's studies, 1992, 96-97; assoc. dir. collection svcs. Ithaca (N.Y.) Coll., 1998—. Mem. South Ctrl. Rsch. Libr. Coun. Interlibr. Loan Adv. Com., Ithaca, N.Y., 1991-93; mem. regional automation com. South Ctrl. Rsch. Libr. Coun., Ithaca, 1994-95, resource sharing com., 1996-97, mem. pers. com., 2000—, trustee, 2003—. Contbr. revs., essays to profl. publs. Mem. steering com. Unitarian Universalist Fellowship of Ithaca. Democrat. Avocations: music, reading, antiques. Home: 30 Washington St Trumansburg NY 14886-1008 Office: 1201 Gannett Ctr Ithaca Coll Ithaca NY 14850 E-mail: ewavle@ithaca.edu.

WAXMAN, PEARL LATTERMAN, early childhood education educator; b. Montclair, N.J., June 7, 1936; d. Louis and Fannie (Schaeffer) Latterman; m. Ronald Waxman, June 19, 1955; children: David, Roberta, Benjamin. AA, Dutchess Community Coll., 1969; BA, Vassar Coll., 1972; MS, Yeshiva U., 1976. Cert. tchr. N.Y. Head tchr. Community United Meth. Ch. Nursey Sch., Poughkeepsie, N.Y., 1972-77; lectr. VandenBerg Learning Ctr., SUNY, New Paltz, 1977-78; dir. Task Force on Child Protection, Inc., Poughkeepsie, 1978-79; trainer Dutchess County Child Devel. Com., and Office Human Resourcs, Poughkeepsie, 1980; head tchr. NOVA Child Devel. Ctrs., Inc., Arlington, Va., 1980-81; dir., head tchr. DC Jewish Community Ctr. Day Care Ctr., Washington, 1982-86; dir. World Bank Children's Ctr., Washington, 1986-90; early childhood cons. U.S. Dept. Energy, Washington, 1990-91; adj. faculty early childhood edn. program No. Va. Community Coll., Alexandria, 1981-94; adj. faculty Sch. Edn. and Human Svcs. Marymount U., Arlington, 1991—. Active No. Va. Early Childhood Adv. Com., Alexandria, 1981-94; workshop leader Montgomery County Child Care Assn., Kensington, Md., 1989—, Confs. Early Childhood Programs Businesses Orgn.; project coord. Model Comprehensive Ctr.-Based Early Childhood Tech. Assistance Project, Va. Coun. Child Day Care and Early Childhood Programs, Reston, 1992—; adj. prof. edn. dept. George Mason U., Fairfax, Va., 1993—. Mem. Va. Assn. for Early Childhood Edn. (pres. 1993—), Nat. Assn. for the Edn. Young Children (commr., mentor, validator), Acad. Early Childhood Programs, Nat. Assn. for the Edn. Young Children (reviewer), Dirs. Exch. Met. Washington. Avocations: swimming, reading, hiking, music, handicrafts. Home: 2369 Paddock Ln Reston VA 20191-2607

WAXMAN, STEPHEN GEORGE, neurologist, neuroscientist; b. Newark, Aug. 17, 1945; s. Morris and Beatrice (Levitch) Waxman; m. Merle Applebaum, June 25, 1968; children: Matthew, David. AB, Harvard U., 1967, PhD, 1970, MD, 1972; MA (hon.), Yale U., 1986. Rsch. fellow in neurosci. Albert Einstein Coll. Medicine, Bronx, NY, 1970—72; clin. fellow Boston City Hosp., 1972—75; asst. prof. neurology Med. Sch. Harvard U., Boston, 1975—77, assoc. prof., 1977—78; prof. Stanford (Calif.) U., 1978—86; vice chmn. dept. neurology Stanford U., 1981—86, chmn. neuroscis. program, 1982—86; chief neurology unit Palo Alto (Calif.) VA Hosp., 1978—86; chmn. dept. neurology Yale U., New Haven, 1986—, prof. neurology, neurobiology and pharmacology, 1986; chief neurology Yale-New Haven Hosp., 1986—. Vis. asst. prof. biology MIT, Cambridge, 1975—77, vis. assoc. prof., 1977—78; vis. prof. U. Coll. London, 1998—, Inst. Neurology, Queen Square, England, 1998—; vice chmn. dept. neurology Stanford, 1981—86, chmn. neuroscis. program, 1982—86; mem. adv. bd. Regeneration Programs VA, Washington, 1982—86; mem. sci. adv. com. Nat. Spinal Cord Injury Assn., 1982—87, Paralyzed Vets. Am., 1981—91; dir. Ctr. Rsch. Neurol. Disease VA Med. Ctr., West Haven, Conn., 1986—; mem. corp. Marine Biol. Labs., Woods Hole, Mass., 1988; mem. sci. adv. coun. Am. Paralysis Assn., 1988—92; mem. bd. sci. counselors NINDB, 1990—92; mem. bd. neurosci. and behavior Inst. Medicine, 1990; Geschwind vis. prof. Harvard U., 1996; dir. PVA/EPVA Neurosci. Rsch. Ctr. VA Hosp., West Haven, 1986—; numerous vis. lectureships. Author: Spinal Cord Compression, 1990, Correlative Neuroanatomy, 1995, 2000, The Axon, 1995, Diseases of the Spinal Cord, 2000, Form and Function in the Brain and Spinal Cord, 2001; editor: Physiology and Pathobiology of Axons, 1978; editor-in-chief: The Neuroscientist, assoc. editor: Muscle and Nerve, Jour. Neurol. Scis., mem. editl. bd.: Ann. Neurology, Brain Rsch., Internat. Rev. Neurobiology, Jour. Neurol. Rehab., Devel. Neurosci., Jour. Neurotrauma, Neurobiology of Disease, Cerebrovascular Disease, Synapse, Restorative Neurology and Neurosci. Named Nat. Multiple Sclerosis Soc. established investigator, 1987; recipient Trygve Tuve Meml. award, NIH, 1973, Rsch. Career Devel. award, 1975, Disting. Alumnus award, Albert Einstein Coll. Medicine, 1990; fellow rsch. fellow, Univ. Coll., London, 1969. Fellow: NAS, Am. Acad. Neurology (Wartenberg award 1999, Dystal prize 2003), Am. Heart Assn. (stroke coun.), Royal Soc. Medicine (Gt. Britain), Inst. Medicine; mem.: Am. Univ. Profs. Neurology, Assn. Rsch. in Nervous and Mental Diseases (trustee, pres. 1992), World Fedn. Neurology, Am. Neurol. Assn. (councillor 1980), Soc. Neurosci., Internat. Brain Rsch. Orgn. (U.S. nat. com.), Dana Alliance for Brain Initiatives, Am. Soc. Cell Biology. Office: Yale U Sch Medicine 33 Cedar St New Haven CT 06519-2314 E-mail: stephen.waxman@yale.edu.

WAYMIRE, JOHN THOMAS, principal; b. Rensselaer, Ind., June 10, 1949; s. John Frederick and Elizabeth Ann (Pettet) W.; m. Kristi Antoinette Cerny, Oct. 4, 1975; children: John Johanson, Thomas Joseph. BS, St. Joseph's Coll., 1971; MS, Ind. U., Gary, 1976; postgrad., U. Iowa, 1978-82. Cert. tchr., adminstr., Ind., Iowa, S.D. Tchr. Kankakee Valley Schs., DeMotte, Ind., 1971-73, South Ctrl. Schs., Union Mills, Ind., 1973-78; grad. asst. U. Iowa, Iowa City, 1978-79; tchr. sci. Lincoln Community Schs., Mechanicsville, Ind., 1979-80; test editorial asst. Riverside Pub. Co., Iowa City, 1980-82; prin. elem. edn. Sully Buttes Schs., Onida, S.D., 1982-86; asst. prin. Tippecanoe Valley Schs., Mentone, Ind., 1986-90; prin. Pioneer Regional Schs., Royal Center, Ind., 1990-94, Granville Wells Sch., Jamestown, Ind., 1994—. Mem. ASCD, NAESP, S.D. Assn. Elem. Sch. Prins. (dist. rep. 1985), Ind. Assn. Sch. Prins. (charter 1992), Ind. Prin.'s Leadership Acad. (grad., exec. bd. mem. 1999—), Royal Center Lions (pres. 1992-94), Jamestown Cmty. Lions Club (pres. 1998-99), Phi Delta Kappa (pres. 1989-90). Avocations: reading, model ship building, gardening, horseback riding. Home: 425 E 500 S Lebanon IN 46052-9765 Office: 5046 S State Road 75 Jamestown IN 46147-9294

WAYNE, ROBERT JONATHAN, lawyer, educator; b. Fresno, Calif., Apr. 4, 1951; s. William W. and Blanche Wayne; m. Dorothy A. Madden, Oct. 23, 1981; children: Daniel, Julia. BS, U. Oreg., 1971; JD, UCLA, 1974. Bar: Calif. 1974, Wash. 1975, U.S. Dist. Ct. (we. dist.) Wash. 1975, U.S. Ct. Appeals (9th and D.C. cirs.) 1975, U.S. Supreme Ct. 1979. Law clk. U.S. Ct. Appeals (D.C. cir.), 1974-75; assoc. Perkins, Coie, Stone, Olsen & Williams, Seattle, 1975-76; dep. prosecutor King County Prosecutor's Office, Seattle, 1976-78; pvt. practice, Seattle, 1978—. Instr. trial advocacy U. Wash., Seattle, 1977—; instr. trial advocacy Nat. Inst. Trial Advocacy, Seattle, 1980—, asst. team leader, 1990, team leader, 1991-2003, team leader nat. session, 1993, program dir. N.W. region, 1998—; lectr. implementing technology in trials; mem. faculty tchr. tng. program Harvard U., U. Colo. Mem. ATLA, NACDL (life, chmn. lawyers assistance strike force 1993-94), Wash. State Trial Lawyers Assn. (chmn. tort sect. 1983-85), Wash. State Bar Assn. (chmn. criminal law sect. 1982-83, 86-87, exec. com. 1980-88), King County Bar Assn. (jud. screening com. 1988-91), Wash. Assn. Criminal Def. Lawyers (founder, bd. govs. 1986-89, 99-2001, chmn. lawyers assistance strike force 1986-90, 91-93, chmn. ann. meeting 1989-90, 2001), Order of Coif, Order of Barristers. Avocation: flying. Office: 2110 N Pacific St Ste 100 Seattle WA 98103-9181 E-mail: bwayne@trialsnw.com.

WEAN, KARLA DENISE, secondary school educator; BS in Biology and Gen. Sci., Wheeling (W.Va.) Jesuit Coll., 1978, BA in Art, 1981; MA in Art Edn., Fla. State U., 1990; grad. Arts Mgm. Sch., N.C. State U., 1980. Cert. tchr. Nat. Bd. Tchrs., 2000. Tchr. art, chmn. dept. Mt. de Chantal Acad., Wheeling, 1978-81; tchr. fine arts Montverde (Fla.) Acad., 1981-83; instr. art Lake Sumter C.C., Leesburg, Fla., 1981-82; art and sci. tchr. Santa Fe Cath. High Sch., Lakeland, Fla., 1983-85; art tchr. Kathleen (Fla.) Jr. High/Mid. Sch., 1985-95; instr. Polk Mus. Art, Lakeland, Fla., 1989—91; musician, composer Nav Videos, Lakeland, 1990-91; tchr. art Bartow (Fla.) H.S., 1995-97, Auburndale (Fla.) H.S., 1997—. Bd. dirs. Arts on the Park, Lakeland, 1989-95, performer original music in concert entitled Seasons of Time, 1993; children's choir dir. St. John Neuman's Ch., Mulberry, Fla., 1991-95, St. Matthews, Winter Haven, Fla., 1995-96; singer, violinist, guitarist, flutist Ch. of the Resurrection, Lakeland, 1989-90, St. John Neuman's Ch. Folk Choir, 1991—; mem. Up With People, internat. song and dance group, 1978; musician, cantor, violinist, flutist, guitarist St. Anthony's Ch., Lakeland, Fla., 2003—. Composer, performer videos Look and Draw, Faces and Figures; one woman show includes Wheeling Jesuit Coll.; exhibited in group shows at Lakeland Electric, 1990, Bartow Bloomin' Arts, 1990, Lakeland Art Guild Show, 1991 (Best in Show award 2001), Strawberry Festival, 1999, 2002 (1st pl. award 1999, 3d pl. award 1999). Goodwill amb. State of W.Va., 1978; vol. sheltered workshop of handicapped, 1984-85; sec.-treas. Coastal State Rabbit Club, 1996-97, bd. dirs., 1997-98. Recipient Disting. Leadership award in teaching, 1985, Jim Harbin Fame video award State of Fla., Tallahassee, 1991, Excellence in Edn. Bahai award Bahai Assn., Lakeland, 1991, Merit award Arts on the Park Mixed Media Show, 1995, awards in various art shows. Mem. Nat. Art Edn. Assn., Fla. Art Edn. Assn.

WEATHERBEE, ELLEN GENE ELLIOTT, botanist, educator; b. Lansing, Mich., Sept. 16, 1939; d. Eugene Bradley and Wilma Alcott (Gardner) Elliott; m. Lee Weatherbee, Aug. 18, 1958 (dec. 1996); children: Anne Susan, Brent Robert, Julie Patricia. BA in Edn., U. Mich., 1960, postgrad., 1972-77; MA in English Lit., Eastern Mich. U., 1962. Cert. tchr. Tchr. adult edn. Schoolcraft Coll., Livonia, Mich., 1983-85; tchr. adult edn. lifelong learning program U. Mich./Wayne State U., Ann Arbor and Detroit, 1973-84; tchr. adult edn. Leelanau Schs./Sleeping Bear Nat. Lakeshore, 1982-86; tchr., nature trip leader adult edn. program Matthaei Bot. Gardens, U. Mich., Ann Arbor, 1984—, dir., founder adult edn. program, 1984—; cons. botanist U. Mich., Ann Arbor, 1977—. Cons. on plant and mushroom identification Mich. Hosps. Poison Control Ctr., 1978—; founder, dir. Weatherbee's Bot. Trips, 1990—; field worker for wetlands and threatened and endangered species Mich. Dept. Natural Resources and Army Corp of Engrs.; bot. cons. for wetlands permits, 1991—; botany instr. for in-svc. tng. Mich. Dept. Environ. Quality Wetland Regulators; botany trainer Mich. Dept. Environ. Quality Corps Engrs., USDA Soil Scientists in Wetland Tng., 1999. Co-author: Edible Wild Plants, A Guide to Collecting and Cooking, 1982; mem. editorial bd. Mich. Botanist, 1978—; contbr. articles to profl. jours. Constable Dem. party,Ann Arbor Twp., Mich. Mem. Austrian Mountain Climbing Soc., British Canoe Union, Fedn. Ont. Naturalists, Great Lakes Sea Kayaking Club, Mich. Acad. Sci., Mich. Bot. Club, Nature Conservancy, N.Am. Mycological Assn., Pipsissewa Chamber Music Soc. Avocations: new plants, backpacking, sea kayaking, playing cello, swimming. Home: 11405 Patterson Lake Dr Pinckney MI 48169-9747 Office: U Mich Matthaei Bot Gardens 1800 N Dixboro Rd Ann Arbor MI 48105-9741 E-mail: eew@umich.edu.

WEATHERHOLTZ, DONNA BAKER, education educator; b. Savannah, Ga., Dec. 6, 1950; m. Ruben Earnest Weatherholtz III, Dec. 19, 1970; children: Kathern Kinnett, James Earnest. BS in Elem. Edn., Coll. Charleston, S.C., 1980; MEd in Adminstrn. and Supervision, U. Va., 1988; postgrad., Ohio State U., 1993—. Cert. elem. tchr. and prin., supt., Va. Tchr. Charleston County Pub. Schs., 1980-83; adminstr. law libr. U.S. Senate Jud. Com., Washington, 1983-84; spl. asst. Office Intergovtl. & Interagy. Affairs U.S. Dept. of Edn., Washington, 1984-86; asst. prin. Shenandoah County Pub. Schs., Woodstock, Va., 1986-89; grad. teaching asst. Ohio State U., Columbus, 1993-98; pres. Donna Weatherholtz & Assocs., Ednl. Cons., 1996—. Bd. govs. S.C. Med. Malpractice Patient Compensation Fund, Columbia, S.C., 1976-83; edn. adv. bd. Shenandoah County Sch. Bd, 1990-92. Mem. nat. exec. com. S.C. Young Reps., Columbia, 1976. Named Outstanding Young Women of Am., 1976, Earl W. Anderson Leadership award, 1994, Campbell Meml. Scholarship Fund in Edn. Adminstrn., 1995, John A. Ramseyer Meml. fellowship, 1995. Mem. Am. Assn. Sch. Adminstrs., Nat. Assn. Elem. Sch. Prins., Nat. Assn. Gifted Children, Am. Ednl. Rsch. Assn., Assn. Faculty and Profl. Women, Univ. Coun. for Ednl. Adminstrn., Phi Delta Kappa. Office: 8302 Five Gates Rd Annandale VA 22003-4617

WEATHERMON, SIDNEY EARL, elementary school educator; b. Abilene, Tex., Jan. 20, 1937; s. Sidney Elliot Weathermon and Evelyn Marie (Landreth) Parker. BA, U. Colo., 1962, MA, 1968, EdD, 1976. Cert. K-12 reading tchr., elem. edn. tchr., K-12 reading specialist. Tchr. Jefferson County (Colo.) Pub. Schs., 1963-66; grades 5-6 tchr. Boulder (Colo.) Valley Pub. Schs., 1962-63, reading tchr., 1968-71, consortium dir. right-to-read project Louisville Mid. Sch., 1974-75, comm. skills program coord. Vocat.-Tech. H.S., 1976, K-12 dist. reading specialist, 1971-85, chpt. 1 tchr. grades 1-6, 1985-89, chpt. 1 kindergarten project coord., 1985-89, grade 1 tchr., 1989-95. Instr. U. Colo., Boulder, 1971-72, U. No. Colo., Greeley, 1977; adj. faculty Regis U., Denver, 1972-95, dept. edn. instr., 1982. Contbr. articles to profl. jours. Recipient Celebrate Literacy award, Boulder Coun. Internat. Reading Assn., 1986, IBM Corp. Tchr. of Yr. award, 1989, Colo./Nat. Educator, Milkin Family Found., 1990; NDEA fellow, 1966-68. Mem. NEA, Internat. Reading Assn., Colo. Edn. Assn., Boulder Valley Edn. Assn. (chair tchr. adv coun., assoc. rep., tchrs. rights and activities commn., negotiations team, profl. leave com.), Phi Delta Kappa (certs. of recognition 1987, 90), Kappa Delta Pi. Democrat. Avocation: southwest indian art. Home: 449 S Shore Dr Osprey FL 34229-9657 Office: 449 S Shore Dr Osprey FL 34229-9657 E-mail: drsidw@comcast.net.

WEATHERS, GERALD LEE, secondary school educator, educator; b. Shelby, N.C., Oct. 3, 1946; s. Samuel Monroe and Helen (Lee) W. BS, Appalachian State U., 1969; MA, MEd, U. N.C., Charlotte, 1976. Cert. math. educator, curriculum and instrn. educator, mentor. Tchr. math. Burns Sr. High Sch., Lawndale, N.C., 1969-76, Burns Jr. High Sch., Lawndale, 1976-78, Crest Sr. High Sch., Shelby, N.C., 1978—. Mem. NEA, Nat. Coun. Tchrs. Math., N.C. Coun. Tchrs. Math., N.C. Assn. Educators, Shelby Lions Club. Methodist. Avocations: golf, tennis, bowling, softball, walking. Home: 326 Woodside Dr Shelby NC 28150-5110 Office: Crest Sr High Sch 800 Old Boiling Springs Rd Shelby NC 28152-0519

WEAVER, CHARLES LYNDELL, JR., institutional and manufacturing facilities administrator, management and marketing systems consultant; b. Canonsburg, Pa., July 5, 1945; s. Charles Lyndell and Georgia Lavelle (Gardner) W.; m. Ruth Marguerite Uxa, Feb. 27, 1982; children: Charles Lyndell III, John Francis. BArch, Pa. State U., 1969; cert. in assoc. studies, U. Florence, Italy, 1968. Registered architect, Pa., Md., Mo., Va., Mass., Ky., Ga.; cert. Nat. Coun. Arch. Registration Bd.; cert. designee, Design Build Inst. Am., 2002. With Celento & Edson, Canonsburg, part-time 1966-71; project architect Meyers & D'Aleo, Balt., 1971-76, corp. dir., v.p., 1974-76; ptnr. Borrow Assocs.-Developers, Balt., 1976-79, Crowley/Weaver Constrn. Mgmt., Balt., 1976-79; pvt. practice arch. Balt., 1976-79; cons., project mgr. U. Md., College Park, 1979-80; corp. cons. architect Bank Bldg. & Equipment Corp., Am., St. Louis, 1980-83; dir. archtl. and engring. svcs. Ladue Bldg. and Engring. Inc., St. Louis, 1983-84; v.p., sec. Graphic Products Corp.; pres. CWCM Inc. Internat., 1987-2000. Dir. K-12 Edn. Market Ctr. and sr. program mgr., Sverdrup Corp., 1989-95; prin. Benham Internat. Eurasia, 1995, v.p., dir. mktg. and bus. devel. The Benham Group, St. Louis, 1995-96; v.p. Chiodini Assocs., 1997-98; asst. lectr. Washington U., 1997-2000, 2001-; cons. Stifel Cap. Start Up Venture Capital Fund; ops. mgr., generations cons. Stifel Capco

Venture Capital, 1998; dir. mktg. sys. The Maiman Co., 1998-99; dir. edn. program mgmt. The Integral Group, Atlanta, 1999-2001; vis. Alpha Rho Chi lectr. Pa. State U., 1983; vis. lectr. Washington U. Lindenwood Coll., 1987, Wentworth Inst., Boston, Am. Assn. Cost Engrs., So. Fla., 1994, with U. Houston, 2002; mem. panel Assn. Univ. Architects Conv., 1983; v.p. program mgmt. and ednl. facilities Kennedy Assoc. Inc.; participant K-12 Nat. Summit, San Diego, 2002; spkr. in field. Contbr. Planning Guide for Maintaining Facilities, U.S. Dept. Edn. Project bus. cons. Jr. Achievement, 1982-85, 2001-; mem. cluster com., advisor Explorer Program, 1982-85; mem. Design Build Inst. Am., 1998—, splty. contractor task force chmn., 2000-2002; presenter So. Ill. Econ. Devel. Conf., 1998. Recipient 5 brochure and graphic awards Nat. Assn. Indsl. Artists, 1973; 1st award Profl. Builder/Am. Plywood Assn., 1974; Honor award, 2 articles Balt. chpt. AIA, 1974; Better Homes and Gardens award Sensible Growth, Nat. Assn. Home Builders, 1975; winner Ridgely's Delight Competition, Balt., 1976. Mem. ASCD, BBC Credit Union (bd. dirs. 1983-85), AACE (conv. spkr. So. Fla. sect. 1994), Vitruvius Alumni Assn., Pa. State Alumni Assn., BOCA, NFPA, AIA, Constrn. Specifications Inst., Am. Assn. Sch. Adminstrs. (nat. coun., panel moderator 1994), Coun. Ednl. Facilities Planners, Assn. Sch. Bus. Ofcls. (Mehlville Mo. schs. program mgmt. 1992-94, Chelsea, Mass. 1993-95, Orange County, Fla. 1994-95, Macon, Ga. 1999-2000, Atlantic City, N.J. 2000-2001), Tex. Women's U., Dallas, 2002, Tex. So. U., Houston, 2002,South St. Louis,Ill. Mixed Fin. Housing Devel. Program, 2003, Alpha Rho Chi (nat. treas. 1980-82, dir. nat. found. treas. 1989-97), Optimists Internat. Office: 1318 Shenandoah Ave Saint Louis MO 63104-4123

WEAVER, CRYSTAL DAWN, interior design educator; b. Baltimore, Ohio, Feb. 9, 1957; d. Richard Laurence and Dawn Lamont (Brehm) W. BS, Morehead State U., 1979; MS, U. Tenn., 1980, PhD, 1984. Asst. prof. Ball State U., Muncie, Ind., 1983-86; assoc. prof. Mankato (Minn.) State U., 1986-89; assoc. prof. interior design Western Carolina U., Cullowhee, N.C., 1989-91; prof. interior design The Savannah Coll. Art and Design, 1992—, chair interior design dept., 1997—2001, dean Sch. Bldg. Arts, 2000—. Owner The Interiors Group, Sylva, N.C., 1989-92, Mankato, Minn., 1988-89; mem. Nat. Coun. Preservation Edn., Interior Design Educators Coun.; bd. dirs. Preservation Action Bd., U.S. Green Bldg. Coun. Curriculum/Accreditation Subcom.; lectr. in field. Mem. AIA (assoc.), ICOMOS, Internat. Interior Design Assn., Internat. Downtown Assn., Assn. Collegiate Schs. of Architecture, Assn. Preservation Tech. Internat., Am. Soc. Interior Designers-Allied, Nat. Trust for Historic Preservation, Preservation Action, Interior Design Educators Coun. Avocation: travel. Office: Savannah Coll Art and Design PO Box 3146 Savannah GA 31402-3146

WEAVER, DAVID, geography educator; Prof., chmn. geography U. Ala., Tuscaloosa, Ala., 1977—. Recipient Disting. Tchr. Coll/Univ. award Nat. Coun. for Geog. Edn., 1992. Office: Univ Alabama 202 Farrah Hall PO Box 870322 Tuscaloosa AL 35487-0001

WEAVER, ERIC JAMES, educational administrator; b. Purley, Surrey, Eng., May 14, 1938; came to U.S., 1947, naturalized, 1963; s. Edward Arthur and Amelia Cecily (Ealden) W.; m. Joyce Lynn McKean, Aug. 19, 1973; children: Stephanie Lynn, Heather Elizabeth, Jonathan Eric, Christopher James. AB, Princeton U., 1958; STB, Gen. Theol. Sem., 1961; MDiv, 1972; MS, CCNY, 1968; profl. diploma, Hofstra U., 1973; EdD, 1980. Rsch. assoc. Meadow Brook Nat. Bank, West Hempstead, N.Y., 1957-61; dir. Christian edn. and youth work Ch. Holy Cross, Bklyn., 1958-61; vicar Ch. Messiah, Ctrl. Islip, N.Y., 1961-63, St. Michael and All Angel's Ch., Gordon Heights, N.Y., 1961-63; tchr. spl. edn. Nassau County Vocat. Edn. and Extension Bd., N.Y., 1963-67; supr. ctrl. adminstrn. Nassau Bd. Coop. Ednl. Svcs., 1967-70; asst. prin. Rosemary Kennedy Sch. for Trainable Mentally Retarded, Wantagh, N.Y., 1970-73; dir. spl. edn. Middle County Schs., Suffolk County, N.Y., 1973-81, dir. spl. ednl. svcs., 1981—98. Vice chmn. Project EQUALS, 1983-86; ednl. cons., instr. Spl. Edn. Tng. Resource Ctr., 1986-98; impartial hearing officer State of N.Y., 1982-97; chmn. com. spl. edn. Middle County Schs., 1973-98, com. preschool spl. edn., 1990-98; mem. Spl. Edn. Adminstrv. Leadership Tng. Acad., 1989—; adj. asst. prof. spl. edn. C.W. Post Coll., 1979-80; ednl. cons., 1998—. Author monographs: The Sources of the First Gospel, 1958, Rudolf Bultman and Entmythologisierung, 1961, Ocular, Manual and Podiatric Dominance in a Severely Retarded Older Adolescent Population, 1968, Efforts of Special Education Administrators to Meet the Needs of Special Education Teachers by Inservice Training, 1980. Capt. Aux Police, County of Suffolk, N.Y., 1962-69; bd. dirs. Traffic Safety Bd., County of Nassau, N.Y., 1969-71, RobinPark Civic Assn.,Huntington, N.Y., 1963-66; trustee Police Hall of FAme; hon. mem. steering com. ann. art auction Lake Grove (N.Y.) Sch., 1985-90; asst. to rector Grace Ch., Huntingtyon Sta., N.Y., 1963-66, Trinity Episc. Ch., Northport, N.Y., 1966—. Fellow Am. Assn. Mental Deficiency; mem. Interagy. Coun. on Recreation for Handicapped (dir. 1970-73), Coun. Exceptional Children (pres. 1973-74), Coun. Adminstrs. Spl. Edn. (treas. 1985—), Internat. Assn. Sci. Study Mental Deficiency, Long Island Assn. Spl. Edn. Adminstrn. (sec. 1975-76, v.p. 1976-77, pres. 1977-78, exec. com. 1978—), Assn. to Help Retarded Children, Am. Ednl. Rsch. Assn., am. assn. sch. Adminstrs, Sch. Adminstrs. Assn. N.Y. State, Phi Delta Kappa. Republican. Episcopalian. Home: 8 Oceanside Ct Northport NY 11768-1301 Office: 130 Main St Northport NY 11768-1723 E-mail: eweaver@optonline.net.

WEAVER, JACQUELYN KUNKEL IVEY, artist, educator; b. Richmond, Ky., Mar. 14, 1931; d. Marion David and Margaret Tabitha (Brandenburg) Kunkel; m. George Thomas IveySr., 1951 (dec. 1989); children: George Thomas Ivey Jr., David Richard Ivey; m. Harrell Fuller Weaver, 1991. BFA, Wesleyan Coll., 1987. Owner J. K. Ivey Art, Macon, Ga., 1974-91, J.K. Ivey Bookkeeping and Tax Svc., Macon, Ga., 1976-84, Ivey-Weaver Art Studio, Macon, 1991—. Tchr. drawing, painting and sculpture, 1991—. Exhibitions include Mid. Ga. Art Assn. Gallery, Macon, 1980—, Mus. Arts and Scis., 1987, 1991, 1994, 1996, 1998, 2002, Attaway Cottage, 1990—, AAPL Salmugundi Club, N.Y.C., 1992, Frames and Art Gallery, Macon, 1995—, CLWAC Nat. Arts Club, NYC, 1995, Stofko-Dixon Fine Arts, Bolingbroke, Ga., 1996—2001, Hilton Head Island (SC) Art League, Self Family Art Ctr., 1997, 2001, Christopher Gallery, Cohasset, Mass., 1997—98, Parthenon Centennial Park, Nashville, 1998, Lowndes/Valdosta Cult. Arts Ctr., Valdosta, Ga., 1992, 1994, 1998, Brazier Art Gallery, Richmond, Va., 2002, Gallery 51, Forsyth, Ga., 2003. Bd. dirs., treas. Mid. Ga. Art Assn., Macon, 1981-84, 92, publicity chmn., 1988-89, chmn. nominating com., 1997, mem. fin. com., 1998-99, audit com., 1998. Mem.: Hilton Head Island Art League, Oil Painters of Am., Portrait Painters Am., Inc., Mid. Ga. Art Assn., Catherine Lorillard Wolf Art Club, Mus. Arts and Scis., Wesleyan Coll. Alumnae Assn., Nat. Mus. Women in Arts (charter). Presbyterian. Avocations: ballroom dancing, reading, walking, music. Office: Ivey-Weaver Art Studio 6183 Hwy 87 Macon GA 31210 Fax: 478-744-0983. E-mail: jweave550@bellsouth.net.

WEAVER, JANE MARIE, parochial school educator; b. Bklyn., Sept. 22, 1950; d. Martin Xavier and Agnes Regina (Heavey) Rochford; m. Gary Michael Weaver, May 2, 1981; children: Kathryn Marie, Frances Adele. BS in Edn., CUNY, 1972. Supr. automation processing GE, N.Y.C., 1972-75; cons. various cos., N.Y.C., 1975-77; analyst Shearman & Sterling, N.Y.C., 1977-81; internal cons. Barclays Bank, N.Y.C., 1981-83; sr. systems analyst Credit Suisse, N.Y.C., 1983-84; tchr. computer literacy Our Lady of Grace Sch., Bklyn., 1989—. Mem. computer standardization courses com. Diocese of Bklyn. Avocations: reading, sewing, writing, tutoring. Office: Our Lady of Grace Sch 385 Avenue W Brooklyn NY 11223-5399

WEAVER, LYNN EDWARD, academic administrator, consultant, editor; b. St. Louis, Jan. 12, 1930; s. Lienous E. and Estelle F. (Laspe) W.; m. JoAnn D., 1951 (div. 1981); children: Terry Sollenberger, Gwen, Bart, Stephen, Wes; m. Anita G. Gomez, Oct. 27, 1983. BSEE, U. Mo., 1951; MSEE, So. Meth. U., 1955; PhD, Purdue U., 1958. Devel. engr. McDonnell Aircraft, St. Louis, 1952-53; aerophysics engr. Convair Corp., Ft. Worth, 1953-55; instr. elec. engring. Purdue U., Lafayette, Ind., 1955-58; assoc. prof., then prof., dept. head U. Ariz., Tucson, 1959-69; assoc. dean coll. engring. U. Okla., Norman, 1969-70; exec. asst. to pres. Argonne Univs., Chgo., 1970-72; dir. sch. nuclear engring. and health physics Ga. Inst. Tech., 1972-82; dean engring., disting. prof. Auburn (Ala.) U., 1982-87; pres. Fla. Inst. Tech., Melbourne, 1987—2002, pres. emeritus, prof. elec. engring., 2002—. Cons. Ga. Power; bd. dirs. Oak Ridge Associated Univs., 1984-87, DBA Systems, Inc., Melbourne, Fla.; chmn. pub. affairs coun. Am. Assn. Engring. Soc., Washington, 1984-87; bd. advisors Ctr. for Sci., Tech. & Media, Washington; chmn. Ind. Colls. and Univs. of Fla., 1998. Author: (textbook) Reactor Dynamics & Control, State Space Techniques, 1968; exec. editor Annals of Nuclear Energy; contbr. numerous articles to tech. jours. U.S. rep. World Fedn., Engring. Orgn. Energy Com., 1981-86. Served to lt. USAF, 1951-53. Recipient Mo. Honors award for disting. svc. in engring., 1996. Fellow Am. Nuclear Soc.; mem. IEEE (sr.), Am. Soc. Engring. Edn., Sigma Xi. Clubs: Eau Gallie Yacht. Republican. Roman Catholic. Avocations: tennis, jogging. Office: Fla Inst Tech 150 W University Blvd Melbourne FL 32901-6975

WEAVER, MARIE ANTOINETTE, artist, educator; b. Wilmington, Del., Feb. 16, 1952; d. Luther Conwell and Mary Antoinette (Maucher) W.; m. Larry Leroy Sampson, Dec. 13, 1978 (div. Aug. 1983); 1 child, Ian Ezekiel; m. Stephen Craig Harvey, Jan. 3, 1987. BA, U. Vt., 1976; MFA, Syracuse U., 1989. Printmaker's asst. Tontine Press/Sabra Field, East Barnard, Vt., 1976-77; chief graphic arts U. Ala., Birmingham, 1982-85, prof. graphic design, 1990—2002; instr. U. Montevallo (Ala.), 1985-86; prin., owner Emspace Studio, Atlanta, 2003—. Owner Weaver Design, Birmingham, 1985—2002; ptnr. Weaver Miller Martin, Inc., Birmingham, 1986-88; ptnr. Emspace Studio, Atlanta, 2003— . Group exhbns., Ala., 1992-2001; design work published in books. Recipient Tchg. Excellence award U. Ala. Birmingham. Mem. Am. Inst. Graphic Arts (v.p. Birmingham 1987-89, pres. 1989-90, treas. 1994-99), Coll. Art Assn; mem. Guild of Bookworkers. Avocations: gardening, film/video, travel, hiking.

WEAVER, REG, National Education Association president; b. Danville, Ill. BS, Ill. State U.; MS, Roosevelt U., Chgo. Local Nat. Edn. Assoc. (NEA) pres., Harvey, Ill., 1967—71; pres. Ill Edn. Assoc., 1981—87; mem. NEA exec. com., 1989—95; vice-pres. NEA, 1996—2002, pres. Mem. exec. bd. Nat. Coun. for Accreditation of Tchr. Edn.; chair IEA Political Action Com. for Edn. (IPACE); appointed to Ill. Commn. for Improvement of Elementary and Secondary Edn., Ill. Project for Sch. Reform Adv. Coun., Ill. Literacy Coun., Task Force on At-Risk Youth; mem. Ill. State Bd. of Edn. Blue Ribbon Comm. on Improvement of Tchg. as a Profession. Named One of the Outstanding Men of America; recipient Ebony Mag. Influential Black Educators award, Ill. Edn. Assoc. Human Relations award. Mem.: Nat. Parent Tchr. Assn. (hon.). Office: NEA 1201 16th St NW Washington DC 20036

WEAVER-STROH, JOANNE MATEER, education educator, consultant; b. May 21, 1930; d. Kenneth Hall and Jean (Weakley) Mateer; children: Karen, Mark, Laurie. BS in Edn., U. Pa., 1952, elem. and secondary prin. cert., 1979; MS in Psychology Reading, Temple U., 1968. Tchr. Paoli (Pa.) Sch., 1952-53, Somerville Sch., Ridgewood, N.J., 1953-55, Bryn Mawr (Pa.) Sch., 1955-57, Erdenheim Sch., Springfield, Pa., 1957-58; reading specialist Abington (Pa.) Sch. Dist., 1966-67, curriculum specialist, 1967-73, coord. human rels. programs, 1973-80; prin. Rydal Elem. Sch., Abington, 1980-88, Willow Hill Elem. Sch., 1988-96; ret., 1996. Cons., tchr. Marywood Coll., Scranton, Pa., 1972—; coord. drug and alcohol abuse program Abington Sch. Dist., 1989-96; cons. Conflict Resolution, 1996—. Chmn. Abington Human Rels. Adv. Coun., 1973-88; chmn. Cmty. Rels. Com. Abington Twp., 1978—; mem. Ea. Montgomery County Human Rels. Adv. Coun., 1981-83; chmn. No Place for Hate project Abington Twp., 2003-; mediator Abington Twp.; leader Stephen Ministry program Abington Presbyn. Ch. Named Citizen of the Week Times Chronicle Newspaper, 1976; recipient award Four Chaplains Temple U., 1979, Disting. Citizens award Roslyn Jr. C. of C., 1981, Citizens for Progress Humanitarian award, 1982, Cmty. award Abington YMCA, 1987, Dr. Martin Luther King Jr. award Abington Twp., 1989, East Montgomery County/Pa. State Human Rels. Interfaith award, 2000, Citizens That Care award, Abington Cmty. Taskforce award, 2003. Mem. ASCD, NASEP, Internat. Coop. Learning Assn., Pa. Assn. Elem. Prins., Phi Delta Kappa, Delta Kappa Gamma. Republican. Home: 109 Durham Ct Maple Glen PA 19002-2854 E-mail: rwstroh@att.net.

WEBB, BEVERLY A. elementary and secondary education educator; b. Tulsa; d. Acie and Etta Lee (Clark) W. AAS in Music, Tomlinson Coll., 1981; BS in Edn., U. Tulsa, 1983; MS in Reading, Northeastern State U., 1989. Cert. reading specialist. Tchr. social studies Broken Arrow Pub. Schs., 1990—2003.

WEBB, CHARLES HAIZLIP, JR., retired university dean; b. Dallas, Feb. 14, 1933; s. Charles Haizlip and Marion (Gilker) W.; m. Kenda McGibbon, June 21, 1958; children: Mark, Kent, Malcolm, Charles Haizlip III. AB, MMus, So. Meth. U., 1955; DMus, Ind. U., 1964; DMus (hon.), Anderson. Coll., 1979. Asst. to dean Sch. Music, So. Meth. U., 1957-58; mem. faculty Sch. Music, Ind. U., 1960-97, dean, 1973-97. Mem. Nat. Rec. Preservation Found., 2002—. Dir. Indpls. Symphony Choir, 1967-81; guest condr. chorus and orch. festivals throughout U.S.; duo-pianist with Wallace Hornibrook in U.S. and Australian tour, 1973; organist First Meth. Ch., Bloomington, 1961—, mem. hymnal revision com. Meth. Ch.; mem. jury Chopin competition; mem. jury internat. piano competitions in Munich, Budapest, South Africa, Paris, Chile, Warsaw, Bolzano, London, Cologne, Japan, Israel; mem. adv. bd. Classical Insites. Chmn. adv. bd. Internat. Music Festivals, Inc.; mem. Ind. Arts Commn., 1975-83, U.S.-USSR Commn. on Music Performance Edn., Am. Coun. Learned Socs./USSR Ministry of Culture; mem. adv. panel The Music Found.; mem. recommendation bd. Avery Fisher Prize Program; bd. dirs. Busoni Found.; mem. bd. advisors Van Cliburn Internat. Piano Competition; mem. nat. adv. bd. Am. Guild Organists; trustee Indpls. Symphony Orch.; mem. Nat. Recording Preservation Found., apptd. by Libr. Congress, 2002. With U.S. Army, 1955-57. Decorated D.S.M.; recipient Disting. Alumni award So. Meth. U., 1980, Sagamore of Wabash Gov. award, 1987, 89, 97, Thomas Hart Benton medal Ind. U., 1987, Disting. Alumni award Highland Park High Sch., Dallas, 1989, Ind. Gov. award for arts, 1989, Rocking Chair award, Ind. U., 1997, Sterling Patron award Mu Phi Epsilon Internat., 1989, Ind. Gen. Assembly House Resolution # 39 for meritorious svc., 1997, Pres.'s award Ind. U., 2000; subject of tribute in U.S. Congl. Record, 1997; Rockefeller scholar Bellagio Study Ctr., 1997; named Disting. Prof. (hon.) Ind. U., 1997, Paul Harris fellow, Rotary Internat., 1997. Mem. Ind. Acad., Century Assn. of N.Y., Pi Kappa Lambda, Phi Mu Alpha, Phi Delta Theta. Home: 648 S Woodcrest Dr Bloomington IN 47401-5417

WEBB, DONNA LOUISE, academic director, educator; b. Yakima, Wash., Aug. 12, 1929; d. Manuel Lawrence and Rena May (Sewell) Matson; (div.); children: Marlene Park, Ed Webb III. AA in Vocat. Edn., Portland (Oreg.) Community Coll., 1976; BA in Psychology, Warner Pacific Coll., 1980; MEd in Career and Vocat. Edn., Oreg. State U., Corvallis, 1980, EdD in Career and Vocat. Edn., 1983. Dir. placement Andrews U., Mich., 1969-74; dir. career edn. and coop. work experience Portland, 1976-78; coord. youth program Fed. Experiment/Chronically Unemployed Youth, Vancouver, Wash., 1979; dir. career counseling Clark Coll., Vancouver, 1979; tchr. coop. edn. project Multnomah County ESD, Portland, 1981; pvt. practice counselor Portland, 1982-84; dir. career devel. & coop. edn. Walla Walla (Wash.) Coll., 1984-87; assoc. dir. Ctr. for Lifelong Learning Loma Linda (Calif.) U., 1987-91; corp. trainer Pacific Inst., Seattle, 1991-94, account mgr. consulting and rsch., 1994—. Home decorator Frederick & Nelson; payroll and computerized bookkeeper Hilo Care Ctr.; with pers. office Flour-Utah Mining; employment counselor Snelling & Snelling Employment Agy.; tchr. bus. edn. Portland Adventist Acad. Contbr. articles to profl. jours. Mem. ASTD, Assn. Per. Adminstr. (columnist San Bernardino Sun newspaper), Coun. for Adult and Exptl. Learning, Calif. Assn. for Counseling and Devel., Coop. Edn. Assn., Nat. Commn. for Coop. Edn., Phi Delta Kappa. Office: 4501 W Powell Blvd Apt 72 Gresham OR 97030-5070

WEBB, FRANCES MOORE, writer, educator; b. Summit, NJ, Nov. 5, 1929; d. Jared Blanchard and Mildred (Downs) M.; m. William David Webb; children: Andra Minío, Deena Moss, Aerie Anderson, Tara Duey. BA, Columbia U., 1952, MFA, 1973. Cons. Horabin, Polaski & Assocs., Phila., 1969-70; rschr. Assn. for Rschr. Behavior, Phila., 1971-74; coll. asst. dept. acad. skills Hunter Coll., N.Y.C., 1974-75; English lectr. CUNY Hostos C.C., 1975—91, cons. Writing Across the Cirruculum, 1991—95. Cons. for profl. writers and playwrights, 1980—; resident Millay Colony for Arts, 1985. Co-author (textbook): Worksheet, A Business-based ESL Grammar and Writing Guide, 1987; author (poetry): Punto 7, 1997; contbr. short stories to popular mags.;, author numerous poems. Recipient award Pa. Coun. on Arts, 1986. Home: 406 Crescent Rd Wyncote PA 19095-1700

WEBB, GEORGE ERNEST, science historian, educator; b. Salem, Ohio, June 17, 1952; s. James Cecil and Edna Jeanette (Santee) W. BA, U. Ariz., 1973, MA, 1974, PhD, 1978. Asst. prof. Tenn. Tech. U., Cookeville, 1978-83, assoc. prof., 1983-88, prof., 1988—. Author: (book) Tree Rings and Telescopes, 1983, Evolution Controversy in America, 1994, Science in the American Southwest, 2002; contbr. articles to profl. jour. Fellow: Tenn. Acad. Sci.; mem.: Am. Assn. Advanced Sci., Western His. Assn., History of Sci. Soc. Office: Tenn Technol Univ Dept History Cookeville TN 38505-0001

WEBB, IGOR MICHAEL, academic administrator; b. Malacky, Czechoslovakia, Nov. 8, 1941; came to U.S., 1952; s. Michael and Josephine (Nash) W.; m. Catherine Lamb (div. 1989); 1 child, Kelly Webb-Lamb; m. Marianne F. Walters, 1990; children: Rebecca Alice, Sarah Elizabeth, Benjamin Oliver, Hannah Olivia. BA, Tufts U., 1963; MA, Stanford U., 1966, PhD, 1971. Asst. prof. English Loyola U. Montreal, Can., 1968-70, U. Mass., Boston, 1971-77, assoc. prof., 1977-78; chair div. humanities Richmond Coll., London, 1979-86; spl. asst. to pres. Adelphi U., Garden City, N.Y., 1986-87, acting provost, 1987-89, provost, 1989-97, sr. v.p., 1992-97, prof. English, 1997—, acting pres., 1997. Author: From Custom to Capital, 1981, Against Capitulation, 1984. Trustee North Shore Bd. Edn., 2003—. Creative Writing fellow Nat. Endowment for Arts, 1978. Mem. Phi Beta Kappa. Office: Adelphi U Garden City NY 11530 E-mail: webb@adelphi.edu.

WEBB, LYNDAL MILLER, principal; b. Deerfield, Fla., Feb. 14, 1933; d. Bowling Dickinson Miller and Cerece Monique (Walker) Miller-Mahoney; m. Thomas Lavelle Webb, Feb. 11, 1951; children: Fredonia W. Ray, Nancy W. Nevil, Gay W. Davis, Susan W. Elsinger. BS in Edn., Valdosta State Coll., 1965, EdM in Elem. Edn., 1968, EdM in Adminstrn. and Supervision, 1971, ednl. specialist, 1982. Cert. adminstrn. and supervision in edn. Resource tchr., classroom tchr. Pine Grove Lowndes County, Valdosta, Ga., 1965-71; asst. prin. Pine Grove Primary, Valdosta, 1971-80, Pine Grove Elem., Valdosta, 1980-83; prin. Hahira Elem. Sch., Valdosta, 1984—. Bd. dirs. Locoga Credit Union, Valdosta, 1979-93; dir. vacation bible sch. Bemiss United Meth. Ch., Valdosta, 1990-94. Mem. AAUW (v.p. 1986-88), NEA, Ga. Assn. Educators, Lowndes Assn. Educators (pres.), Ga. ASCD (bd. dirs. 1992—), Internat. Reading Assn., Partnership 2000 (bd. dirs. 1994—), Phi Delta Kappa (pres.), Delta Kappa Gamma (pres. Sigma chpt. 1989-91, v.p. 1999—). Republican. Methodist. Avocations: cooking, reading, walking, grandmothering. Office: Hahira Elem Sch 350 Claudia Dr Hahira GA 31632-1568

WEBB, MARY ANN, principal; b. Wynne, Ark., Oct. 28, 1954; d. James Russell and Mary Leona (Simmons) Cartillar; m. Rex Ronald Webb, Feb. 11, 1995; 1 child, Terri Ann. M in Reading, Ark. State U., Jonesboro, 1977, BSE in Early Childhood, Elem. Edn., 1988, D in Edn. Leadership, 1998. Prin. Newark (Ark.) Pub. Schs., 1982—. Adj. prof. U. Ark., Batesville, 1998-99. Mem. Delta Kappa Gamma. Avocations: reading, playing piano, swimming, walking. Home: 2570 Walnut Grove Rd Newark AR 72562-9518 Office: Newark Pub Schs 3549 Cord Rd Newark AR 72562-9680 E-mail: awebb@nps.k12.ar.us.

WEBB, MARY CHRISTINE, reading recovery educator, in-class reading specialist; b. Ames, Iowa, Jan. 3, 1947; d. Howard Darrell and Lorena Faye (North) Webb; m. Harlen DuWayne Groe, Dec. 29, 1989 (div. Oct. 1997). BS in Elem. Edn., Iowa State U., 1969, MS in Emotional Disabilities, 1980, MEd in Learning Disabilities, 1986. Cert. tchr. K-9, learning disabilities, behavioral disabilities, multicategorical, Iowa; cert. in reading endorsement, Iowa, 2001. 1st grade tchr. Holy Spirit Sch., Carroll, Iowa, 1970; severe behavior disabilities tchr. Area Edn. Agy 7, Waterloo, Iowa, 1979-85; tchg. and rsch. assistantship Iowa State U., Ames, 1985-86; multicategorical 3-8 self contained with integration tchr. Madrid Elem. and Jr. H.S., 1986-87; behavior disability self contained with integration tchr. Des Moines Pub. Schs., 1987-88, resource rm. tchr., 1988-95, multicategorical self contained with integration tchr., 1995-99, reading recovery tchr., behavior interventionist, 1999-2000, reading recovery tchr., title reading tchr., 2000—02, reading recovery tchr., reading specialist, 2002—. Mem. People to People Spl. Edn. Del. to Mainland China, 1993. Mem.: NEA, ASCD, Iowa State Edn. Assn., Des Moines Edn. Assn. Office: King Acad Math and Sci 1849 Forest Ave Des Moines IA 50314-1336

WEBB, MYRTLE BAILEY, elementary school educator; b. Balt., Jan. 3, 1943; d. Henry Sailie and Myrtle (Dalton) Bailey; m. Harold Webb, Oct. 6, 1990; 1 child, Michele Elaine Cockrell Rochon. BS with honors, Morgan State U., 1965; MEd, Johns Hopkins U., 1970, cert. advanced studies, 1976; EdD, Temple U., 1982. Elem. sch. tchr. Balt. City Pub. Schs., 1965-67; day care tchr. Balt. Dept. Social Svcs., 1967-69; elem. sch. tchr. Balt. City Pub. Schs., 1969-77, reading specialist, 1977-95; title I facilitator/parent educator, 1995—. Mem. NAACP, Women Power, Nat. Assn. Black Sch. Educators, State of Md. Internat. Reading Assn. (bd. dirs.), Balt. City Coun. Internat. Reading Assn. (pres. elect 1992) Democrat. Roman Catholic. Avocations: reading, writing, walking. Office: Balt City Pub Schs 101 S Ellwood Ave Baltimore MD 21224-2244

WEBB, O(RVILLE) LYNN, physician, pharmacologist, educator; b. Tulsa, Aug. 29, 1931; s. Rufus Aclen and Berla Ophelia (Caudle) W.; m. Joan Liebenheim, June 1, 1954 (div. Jan. 1980); children: Kathryn, Gilbert, Benjamin; m. Jeanne P. Heath, aug. 24, 1991. BS, Okla. State U., 1953; MS, U. Okla., 1961; PhD in Pharmacology, U. Mo., 1966, MD, 1968. Diplomate Nat. Bd. Med. Examiners, Am. Bd. Family Practice; cert. medical examiner, 1999. Rsch. assoc. in pharmacology U. Okla., 1959-61; rsch. fellow NIH, 1962-66; instr. pharmacology U. Mo., Columbia, 1966-68, asst. prof., 1968-69; intern U. Mo. Med. Ctr., 1968-69; family practice New Castle, Ind., 1969-89; med. dir. VA Clinic, Lawton, Okla., 1989-94, Comanche County Hosp., 1994-98; pvt. practice medicine, 1998—; owner Comanche County Med. Clinic, Lawton, Okla., 1998—2002, Okla. Med. Clinic, Lawton, 1999—. Clin. assoc. prof. family medicine U. Okla. Coll. Medicine, 1989—; adj. assoc. prof. pharmacology U. Okla. Coll. Medicine, 1989—; mem. U. Okla. Medicine Admissions Bd., 1995-98; mem. staff Henry County Meml. Hosp., New Castle, 1969-89; guest prof. pharmacy and pharmacology Butler U. Coll. Pharmacy, Indpls., 1970-75; owner, dir. Carthage Clinic, 1975-89; clin. assoc. prof. family medicine Ind. U. Coll.

Medicine, 1986-89; county physician, jail med. dir. Henry County, Ind., 1976-89. Author: (with Blissitt and Stanaszek, Lea and Febiger) Clinical Pharmacy Practice, 1972; contbr. numerous articles to profl. jours. Bd. dirs. Lawton Philharm., 1990-95. Recipient Cert. of merit in Pharmacol. and Clin. Med. Rsch., 1970, Med. Student Rsch. Essay award Am. Acad. Neurology, 1968. Fellow Am. Acad. Family Physicians, Am. Coll. Physician Execs.; mem. AMA (ann. award recognition 1975—), AAAS, Ind. State Med. Assn., Am. Coll. Sports Medicine, Am. Coll. Occupl. and Environ. Medicine, N.Y. Acad. Scis., Am. Soc. Contemporary Medicine and Surgery, Okla. State Med. Assn., Festival Chamber Music Soc. (bd. dirs. Indpls. 1981-87), Nat. Fraternity Eagle Scouts, Mensa, Columbia Club, Skyline Club, Country Club, Kiwanis, Elks, Sigma Xi, Phi Sigma. Home: 30 Quail Creek Dr Lawton OK 73501-9026

WEBB, RUTH CAMERON, retired educator; b. Honolulu, June 1, 1923; d. William Henry and Ruth Gray (Cameron) W. AB in Psychology, Drew U., 1948; postgrad. in logopedics, U. Wichita, 1950-52; DHL, Drew U., 1972; MA, Syracuse U., 1949; PhD, U. Ill., 1963. Nursery sch. cons., Swarthmore, Pa., 1953-55; psychol. asst. Assn. Retarded Children (Pa.) Del. County, 1954-55; counseling practicum Cahnute Air Base, Rantoul, Ill., 1961-62; counseling psychologist Rehab. Inst. Jewish Vocat. Svc., Milw., 1963-66; psychologist Hamburg (Pa.) State Hosp. and Sch., 1966-67, Glenwood (Iowa) State Hosp. and Sch., 1963-84, dir. dept. devel. therapy, 1967-72, cons. devel. therapy, 1978-84, psychologist dept. spl. edn., 1984, ret., 1984. Psychol. cons. Swarthmore (Pa.) Presbyn. Nursery Sch., 1954. Author: Journey into Personhood, 1994, How AB's See Gimps, 2002; contbr. articles to profl. jours., chpts. to book. Recipient Handicapped Iowan of Yr. award Gov.'s Com. Employment Handicapped, 1971, Alumni Achievement award Drew U., 1972, Svc. award United Ch. Bd. Homeland Ministries, 1987, Ruth Suckow award Libr. Congress, 1995, Disting. Alumni award U. Ill., 1998, Harold Scharper Achievement award 2000. Mem. APA, Internat. Soc. Poets (Hall of Fame 1996), Iowa Psychol. Assn., Sigma Phi, Pi Gamma Mu. Lumbda Delta Theta, Kappa Delta Pi, Phi Beta Kappa. Home: 619 Park St Apt B104 Grinnell IA 50112-2269

WEBB, THOMPSON, geological sciences educator, researcher; b. LA, Jan. 13, 1944; s. Thompson and Diana (Stimson) W.; m. Joan Moscovitch Webb, Aug. 10, 1969; children: Rosanna, Sarah. BS with honors, Swarthmore Coll., 1966; PhD, U. Wis., 1971. Rsch. assoc. U. Mich., Ann Arbor, 1970-72; asst. prof. geol. sci. Brown U., Providence, 1972-75, assoc. prof., 1975-84, prof., 1984—. Vis. prof. U. Wis., Madison, 1976; chmn. paleoclimate adv. panel NOAA, 1994; chmn. terrestrial earth sys. history com. NSF, 1996, chmn. steering com. earth systems history program, 1997-2000. Author: (book chpt.) Late Quat. Environments of the US, vol. 2, 1983; editor: Vegetation History, 1988; contbr. articles to profl. jours. Interviewer Swarthmore Coll., Providence, 1972—, pres. 35th ReunionClass of 1966; sec. Seekonk Land Trust, 1995—. NSF fellow, 1970; vis. fellow Clare Hall, U. Cambridge, Eng., 1977; CIRES fellow U. Colo., Boulder, 1988; Bullard fellow Harvard U., 1995, Sr. fellow Wayland Coll. Fellow AAAS; mem. Ecol. Soc. Am. Office: Brown U Dept Geol Sci 324 Brook St Providence RI 02912-9019

WEBB-KERSHAW, MARIANNE ELIZABETH, elementary education educator; b. Wilmington, Del., July 17, 1957; d. Nelson Ernest and Joan Mary (Rodden) W.; m. William Michael Kershaw, Jr. Degree in child and family svc., Mansfield U., 1981, cert. elem. edn., 1982; MS in Edn., Temple U., 1992. Cert. tchr., reading specialist, Pa. Program dir. Camp Neumann, Jamison, Pa., 1979-80; residential counselor 801 House, Dover, Del., 1982-83; tchr. Corpus Christi Elem. Sch., Wilmington, 1982-85; residential counselor Siena Hall/Seton Villa, Wilmington, 1985-86; tchr. Pennsbury Sch. Dist., Fallsington, Pa., 1986—. Vol. ARC, Bucks County, Pa., 1988-92, chair disaster action team, 1992-93. Recipient Vol. Recognition award ARC, 1990, Disaster Action Team award, 1991, 92, 93. Mem. NEA, Pa. State Ednl. Assn., Pennsbury Edn. Assn. (sec. bd. dirs.). Roman Catholic. Avocations: reading, traveling, cooking. Home: 438 Lakeside Dr Levittown PA 19054-3928 Office: Pennsbury Sch Dist Village Park Sch Unity Dr Fairless Hills PA 19030-2597

WEBER, ALICE ROSE, math educator, retired; b. Danbury, Iowa, Oct. 29, 1936; d. John J. and Anna (Kleine) W. BS, DePaul U., 1967; MA, U. No. Iowa, 1972. Cert. tchr., Iowa. Tchr. St. Patrick's Sch., Clinton, Iowa, 1957-58, St. Gerald's Sch., Oak Lawn, Ill., 1958-61, Our Lady of Lourdes, Lourdes, Iowa, 1961-68, Immaculate Conception, Elma, 1968-69, Danbury (Iowa) Cath. Sch., 1969-70, Maquoketa (Iowa) Cmty. Sch. Dist., 1970—96, ret., 1996. ABC math. cons. Maquoketa Community Sch. Dist., 1981-86. Named Tchr. of Yr. Iowa Coun. Tchrs. Math., 1987, Maquoketa Edn. Assn., 1987. Home: 616 S 5th St Maquoketa IA 52060-3423

WEBER, ARNOLD ROBERT, academic administrator; b. N.Y.C., Sept. 20, 1929; s. Jack and Lena (Smith) W.; m. Edna M. Files, Feb. 7, 1954; children: David, Paul, Robert. BA, U. Ill., 1951; MA, PhD in Econs., MIT, 1958. Instr., then asst. prof. econs. MIT, 1955-58; faculty U. Chgo. Grad. Sch. Bus., 1958-69, prof. indsl. relations, 1963-69; asst. sec. for manpower Dept. Labor, 1969-70; exec. dir. Cost of Living Council; also spl. asst. to Pres. Nixon, 1971; Gladys C. and Isidore Brown prof. urban and labor econs. U. Chgo., 1971-73; former provost Carnegie-Mellon U.; dean Carnegie-Mellon U. (Grad. Sch. Indsl. Adminstrn.), prof. labor econs. and pub. policy, 1973-80; pres. U. Colo., Boulder, 1980-85, Northwestern U., Evanston, Ill., 1985-95, chancellor, 1995-98, pres. emeritus, 1998—. Cons. union, mgmt. and govt. agys., 1960—; cons. Dept. Labor, 1965; mem. Pres.'s Adv. Com. Labor Mgmt. Policy, 1964, Orgn. Econ. Coop. and Devel., 1987; vice chmn. Sec. Labor Task Force Improving Employment Svcs., 1965; chmn. rsch. adv. com. U.S. Employment Svc., 1966; assoc. dir. OMB Exec. Office of Pres., 1970—71; chmn. Presdl. R.R. Emergency Bd., 1982; trustee Com. for Econ. Devel., Nat. Multiple Sclerosis Soc.; bd. dirs. Diamond Tech. Partners Inc.; asst. sec. manpower U.S. Dept. Labor, 1969—70. Contbr. articles to profl. jours. Laureate, Lincoln Acad. Ill.; Ford Found. Faculty Rsch. fellow, 1964-65. Mem. Am. Acad. Arts and Scis., Indsl. Rels. Rsch. Assn., Nat. Acad. Pub. Adminstrn., Comml. Club Chgo. (pres., civic com. 1995-2000), Econ. Club Chgo. (pres. 1995-97), Phi Beta Kappa. Jewish. Office: Northwestern U Office of Pres Emeritus 555 Clark St 209 Evanston IL 60208-0805 E-mail: arnold-weber@nwu.edu

WEBER, DARLENE MARIE, health educator; b. Tarentum, Pa., Nov. 17, 1939; d. Thomas J. and Agnes M. (Reiger) Hohman; m. David F. Weber, Aug. 17, 1963; children: JuliLynne, Mark David. BS, SUNY, Cortland, 1961; MS, Ind. U., 1963, D of Health and Safety, 1964. Cert. vision/hearing specialist, Ill., sanitation cert., Ill. Instr. SUNY, Buffalo, 1961-62; grad. asst. Ind. U., Bloomington, 1962-63, vis. lectr., 1963-64; tchr. Martinsville (Ind.) H.S., 1964-65; area dir. Ind. Heart Assn., Indpls., 1965-66; assoc. prof. Ill. State U., Bloomington, 1967-89; health coord. Heartland Head Start, Bloomington, 1989-98; cons. health, mental health and nutrition QNET, Ohio State U., Columbus, 1989—2003. Peer reviewer region V Head Start, Chgo., 1985—; USDA cons. Ill. Dept. Edn., Springfield, 1994-96, Early Head Start, Washington, 1998—. Title I grantee HHS, Fed. Govt., 1980-82. Mem. Ill. Pub. Health Assn. Avocations: sewing, bicycling, traveling. Home: 2115 E Taylor St Bloomington IL 61701-5725 E-mail: dmweber@yahoo.com.

WEBER, DENNIS PAUL, social studies educator; b. Longview, Wash., Jan. 21, 1952; s. John L. and Emelia E. (Klein) W.; m. Kristine A. McElroy-Weber, March 26, 1977; children: Kathryn, Sarah, Juliana. BA in Polit. Sci., U. Wash., 1974; MEd, U. Portland, 1995. Cert. tchr., Wash. Social studies tchr. R.A. Long H.S., Longview, Wash., 1975-78, social studies tchr. and dept. chmn., 1985—2000; alternative edn. tchr. Natural H.S., Longview, Wash., 1978-84, sr. class adv., 2000—. Mayor City of Longview, 1984-91; mem. Rotary Internat. Group Study Exchange, Surrey, Eng., 1984. Violinist S.W. Wash. Symphony Orch., 1968-70, 74—, bd. dirs.; violinist U. Wash. Symphony Orch., 1970-73; mem. planning commn. Cowlitz County, Kelso, Wash., 1978-84, chmn. 1982-84; coun. mem. Longview City Coun., 1980-91, 2002—; mayor pro tempore 1982-84; bd. dirs. Cmty. Urban Bus. Sys. Bd., Kelso, 1984-89, chmn., 1988; bd. dirs. S.W. Wash. Air Pollution Control Authority, Vancouver, 1984-90, chmn. air pollution control authority, 1988-90; bd. dirs. Cowlitz Transit Authority, 1990-91; chair Cowlitz County Bd. Freeholders, 1997-98; mem. Cowlitz County Boundary Review Bd., 1995-2001, chair, 2001; mem. governing bd. St. John's Med. Ctr., Longview, 1991-2003; bd. dirs. Longview Cmty. Ch., 1992-96, pres., 1994-95; mem. adv. com. Cowlitz County Pub. Health, 2002—; mem. policy bd. Cowlitz County Comm. Ctr., 2002—. Recipient Outstanding Young Men in Am. award N.J. C. of C., 1978, Citizenship award Ctr for Civic Edn., 2001; named Am. Govt. and Politics fellow Taft Inst. for Teaching, 1988, 91, Sr. fellow James Madison Found., 1993. Mem. NEA (nat. del. 1980-82), LWV (sec. Cowlitz County chpt. 1993-94), Wash. Edn. Assn. (state del. 1979, Leadership in Restructuring award 1997), Longview Edn. Assn. (bd. dirs.), Wash. State Coun. for Social Studies, A Presdl. Classroom for Young Ams. Alumni Assn. (life), U. Wash. Alumni Assn. (life), Ripon Soc., Nation Conservancy. Lodges: Rotary (Paul Harris fellow 1987). Republican. Office: PO Box 1042 Longview WA 98632-7623

WEBER, ELLEN SCHMOYER, pediatric speech pathologist; b. Allentown, Pa., Oct. 6, 1952; BS in Speech Pathology, Kutztown State Coll., 1975; MS in Speech Pathology, U. So. Fla., 1982, MEd in Ednl. Leadership, 1991. Cert. tchr., ednl. adminstr., Fla. Speech therapist Schuylkill County Ind. Sch. Dist., Pottsville, Pa., 1975-76, Pinellas County Sch. Dist., Largo, Fla., 1979-95; pvt. therapist Pinellas County, Fla., 1982—87, 1994—2002; owner, dir. Children's Speech and Lang. Svcs.; speech therapist Cobb County Sch. Dist., Ga., 2002—. Staffing team coord. Pinellas County Sch. Dist., Largo, Fla., 1986-91, 93-94, mem. sch. adv. coun., 1990-93, union rep., 1989-92. Computer grantee Pinellas County Sch. Dist., 1986-87, travel grantee, 1991-92. Mem. Am. Speech-Lang.-Hearing Assn., Fla. Speech-Lang.-Hearing Assn. Avocations: travel, skiing, cycling, hiking, computer.

WEBER, JOHN PITMAN, artist, educator; b. Washington, Dec. 6, 1942; s. Palmer and Lillian (Dropkin) Weber; m. Marguerite Munch, 1966 (div. 1969); 1 child, Pascal Richard; m. Elsa Koenig, Jan. 23, 1971; children: Daniel Abraham, Alexander Samuel, Benjamin John. BA, Harvard U., 1964; MFA, Sch. Art Inst., Chgo., 1968. Art prof. Elmhurst (Ill.) Coll., 1968—. Founder Chgo. Pub. Art Group, 1970—; artist-in-residence Artists and Cmtys., 2000, State of Iowa, Spencer, Gathering Mosiac Plz. Co-author: (book) Toward a People's Art, 1977, 2d edit., 1998, Urban World, Chgo., 1997, Remembered Gates New Song, Chgo., 1999. Fellow, Govt. of France, Paris, 1964—65; Fulbright Travel fellow, 1964—66. Mem.: Coll. Art Assn., Cmty. Built Assn. Office: Elmhurst Coll 190 Prospect Ave Elmhurst IL 60126-3271 E-mail: johnw@elmhurst.edu.

WEBER, LYNN, sociology educator; BA in Sociology, Memphis State U., 1971, MA in Sociology, 1973; PhD in Sociology, U. Ill., Urbana, 1976. Asst. prof. Dept. Sociology and Social Work Memphis State U., 1976-81, assoc. prof. Dept. Sociology and Social Work, 1981-86, assoc. dir., co-founder Ctr. Rsch. on Women, 1982-88, prof. Dept. Sociology and Social Work, 1986—96; dir. Ctr. Rsch. on Women U. Memphis, 1988—96; dir. Women's Studies Program U. S.C., 1996—. Faculty devel. assignment Memphis State U., 1987-88; vis. scholar Dept. Health Edn. Temple U., 1987; faculty devel. assignment U. Memphis, 1994-95; disting. vis. prof. gender studies Dept. Sociology and Criminal Justice U. Del., 1994; mem. program com. Assn. for General and Liberal Studies, Memphis, 1993, Soc. for Applied Anthropology, 1992; coord. faculty rsch. seminar on race, class and gender MSU, 1988-90; cons. various founds. and orgns. Co-author: The American Perception of Class, 1987, Women of Color and Southern Women: A Bibliography of Social Research, 1988, 89, 91, 92, (on-line bibliographic database) Research Clearinghouse on Women of Color and Southern Women; adv. editor: The Sociological Quarterly, 1980-85, Gender & Society, 1991-94; reviewer: various scientific publs. including Social Science Quarterly, Am. Sociological Review, Social Problems, Signs: A Jour. of Women in Culture and Society, others; contbr. articles to profl. jours. Recipient numerous grants and fellowships including, NSF, 1988-91, 1995—, NIH, 1989-93, others. Mem. Am. Sociological Assn. (coun. sect. on racial and ethnic minorities 1987-90, dissertation award com. sect. on sex and gender 1990-92, chair 1992, com. on coms. 1991-93, Disting. Contbns. to Tchg. award 1993, Jessie Bernard award 1993), So. Sociological Soc. (program com. 1995), Sociologists for Women in Soc., Society for the Study of Social Problems, Alpha Kappa Delta. Home: 200 Windsor Point Rd Columbia SC 29223-1823 Office: Univ SC Womens Studies WOST Office 201 flinn Hall 1324 Pendleton St Columbia SC 29208*

WEBER, LYNNE SUZANNE, elementary education educator; b. Ottawa, Ill., July 15, 1951; d. John Joseph and Edith (Read) Corcoran; m. Kenneth Jordan, June 30, 1973 (div. 1981); 1 child, Christine Marie; m. Alan dean Weber, Dec. 20, 1986. BS in Edn., Ill. State U., 1973; MS in Tchg. Leadership, St. Xavier's U., Chgo., 1998. Tchr. lang. arts Alamogordo (N.Mex.) pub. schs., 1973-74; tchr. Streator (Ill.) Dist. 145, 1974-77, Princeton (Ill.) Elem. Sch. Dist. 115, 1980—. Mem. AAUW (pres., treas.), Bureau County Reading Coun., Optimist (treas.), Delta Kappa Gamma (v.p.). Roman Catholic. Home: 22725 2000 N Ave Princeton IL 61356-9622

WEBER, MARY LINDA, preschool educator; b. Hermon, N.Y., May 21, 1947; d. Stanley Albert and Shirley Lucille (Holland) Morrill; m. John Weber, July 23, 1966 (div. Nov. 1980); children: James, Mark. AAS, Agrl. and Tech. Coll., Canton, N.Y., 1971; BA, SUNY, Potsdam, 1973; MA, U. South Fla., 1981. Cert. pre-sch., elem. and reading K-12 tchr., N.Y., Fla. Tchr. elem. Hermon-DeKalb Ctrl. Sch., DeKalb Junction, N.Y., 1974-76, Westside Elem. Sch., Spring Hill, Fla., 1976-77; tchr. kindergarten Spring Hill Elem. Sch., 1977-89; tchr. pre-kindergarten Deltona Elem. Sch., Spring Hill, 1989-99, tchr. kindergarten, 1999—. Author mini-grant Home-Sch. Partnerships, 1990, Multi-Cultural Ctr., 1992, Family Info. Ctr., 1993, Parent Partners in Literacy, 1996, Pillars of Character, 1999. Mem. NEA (Young Children sect.), Assn. Childhood Edn. Internat., Internat. Reading Assn., So. Early Childhood Assn., Fla. Reading Assn., Hernando County Reading Coun. Avocations: reading, cross-stitch, bicycling, scrapbooks. Home: 4132 Redwing Dr Spring Hill FL 34606-2425 Office: Deltona Elem Sch 2055 Deltona Blvd Spring Hill FL 34606-3216

WEBER, STEPHEN LEWIS, university president; b. Boston, Mar. 17, 1942; s. Lewis F. and Catherine (Warns) W.; m. Susan M. Keim, June 27, 1965; children: Richard, Matthew. BA, Bowling Green State U., 1964; postgrad., U. Colo., 1964-66; PhD, U. Notre Dame, 1969; EdD (hon.), Capital Normal U., China, 1993. Asst. prof. philosophy U. Maine, Orono, 1969-75, assoc. prof., 1975-79, asst. to pres., 1976-79; dean arts and scis. Fairfield (Conn.) U., 1979-84; v.p. acad. affairs St. Cloud (Minn.) State U., 1984-88; pres. SUNY Oswego, 1988-95; interim provost SUNY Albany, 1995-96; pres. San Diego State U., 1996—. Participant Harvard Inst. Ednl. Mgmt., Cambridge, Mass., 1985. Contbr. numerous articles on philosophy and acad. adminstrn. to profl. jours. Mentor Am. Coun. Edn. Fellowship Program, Am. Coun. on Edn., Commn. on Internat. Edn. and Commn. on Govtl. Rels.; bd. govs. The Peres Ctr. for Peace, San Diego Found.; bd. dirs. San Diego Regional Econ. Devel. Corp.; mem. internat. adv. bd. Found. for the Children of the Californias. Named Outstanding Humanities Tchr., U. Maine, 1975; Rsch. fellow U. Notre Dame, 1968-69. Mem. Am. Philos. Assn., Am. Assn. Higher Edn. Democrat. Avocations: art, woodworking, swimming, boating. Office: San Diego State Univ Office Pres 5500 Campanile Dr San Diego CA 92182-8000 E-mail: presidents.office@sdsu.edu.

WEBER, WILFORD ALEXANDER, education educator; b. Allentown, Pa., Apr. 29, 1939; s. Alexander F. and Kathryn A. (Campbell) W.; children from previous marriage: Kendra L., Brad A.; m. Cheryl Angelo. BA, Muhlenberg Coll., 1963; EdD, Temple U., 1967. Tchr., counselor New Life Boys Ranch, Harleysville, Pa., 1963-65; rsch. asst. Temple U., Phila., 1965-67; asst. prof. Syracuse (N.Y.) U., 1967-71; prof. U. Houston, 1971—, chair dept. curriculum & instrn. Author approximately 165 books, monographs, papers and articles. Grantee, Syracuse U., U. Houston. Mem. Am. Ednl. Rsch. Assn., Assn. Tchr. Educators. Avocation: sports. Home: 2015 Swift Blvd Houston TX 77030-1213

WEBSTER, EDWARD GLEN, principal, school system administrator; b. Chester, Pa., Sept. 13, 1946; s. Joseph Armiger and Lois Dean (Wise) W.; m. Janice Kay Bigelow, Apr. 10, 1982; 1 child, Caitlin Bigelow. AB in English Lit., Niagara U., 1972; MA in English Lit., Gannon U., 1977; MAEd in Elem. and Secondary Adminstrn., George Wash. U., 1986; EdD in Curriculum and Instrn., W.Va. U., 1989. Cert. adminstrn., Md., Maine, Va., S.C., N.C., W.Va. English tchr. Lake Forest H.S., Felton, Del., 1972-75; grad. asst. in English Gannon U., Erie, Pa., 1975-77; English tchr. Ryken H.S., Leonardtown, Md., 1979-81; grad. asst. in secondary edn. W.Va. U., Morgantown, 1981-83; chmn. English Dept. Cumberland (Va.) County H.S., 1983-84; English tchr. Leonardtown (Md.) H.S., 1984-86; prin. Forest Hills Mid. Sch., Jackman, Maine, 1986-87; asst. prin., athletic dir. Livermore Falls (Maine) H.S., 1987-88, prin., 1988-93, Easton (Md.) H.S., 1993-95, Tucker County H.S. & Career Ctr., Hambleton, W.Va., 1995—. Contbr. articles to profl. jours. Mem. fin. com. Eaton United Meth. Ch., Livermore Falls, 1991-93. Sgt. U.S. Army, 1965-68. Recipient honorarium Allyn & Bacon, Inc., 1992, Cert. of Appreciation New Eng. Assn. Schs. and Colls., 1991. Mem. ASCD, Am. Assn. Sch. Adminstrs., Am. Ednl. Rsch. Assn., Md. Secondary Sch. Prins. Assn., Nat. Assn. Secondary Sch. Prins., W.Va. Assn. Secondary Sch. Prins., Kappa Delta Pi, Phi Delta Kappa (Cert. of Recognition 1983, 10-Yr. Membership award 1991), Rotary. Republican. Avocations: computers, jogging, reading. Home: 108 Foxhound Rd Simpsonville SC 29680-6711

WEBSTER, JOHN GOODWIN, biomedical engineering educator, researcher; b. Plainfield, N.J., May 27, 1932; s. Franklin Folger and Emily Sykes (Boody) W.; m. Nancy Egan, Dec. 27, 1954; children: Paul, Robin, Mark, Lark BEE, Cornell U., 1953; MSEE, U. Rochester, 1965, PhD, 1967. Engr. North American Aviation, Downey, Calif., 1954-55; engr. Boeing Airplane Co., Seattle, 1955-59, Radiation Inc., Melbourne, Fla., 1959-61; staff engr. Mitre Corp., Bedford, Mass., 1961-62, IBM Corp., Kingston, N.Y., 1962-63; asst. prof. elec. engring. U. Wis., Madison, 1967-70, assoc. prof. elec. engring., 1970-73, prof. elec. and computer engring., 1973-99, prof. biomed. engring., 1999—. Author: (with others) Medicine and Clinical Engineering, 1977, Sensors and Signal Conditioning, 1991, 2d edit., 2001, Analog Signal Processing, 1999; editor: Medical Instrumentation: Application and Design, 3d edit., 1998, Clinical Engineering: Principles and Practices, 1979, Design of Microcomputer-Based Medical Instrumentation, 1981, Therapeutic Medical Devices: Application and Design, 1982; Electronic Devices for Rehabilitation, 1985; Interfacing Sensors to the IBM-PC, 1988, Encyclopedia of Medical Devices and Instrumentation, 1988, Tactile Sensors for Robotics and Medicine, 1988, Electrical Impedance Tomography, 1990, Teaching Design in Electrical Engineering, 1990, Prevention of Pressure Sores, 1991, Design of Cardiac Pacemakers, 1995, Design of Pulse Oximeters, 1997, The Measurement Instrumentation, and Sensors Handbook, 1999, Encyclopedia of Electrical and Electronics Engineering, 1999, Mechanical Variables Measurement, 2000, Minimally Invasive Medical Technology, 2001, Electrical Measurement, Signal Processing and Displays, 2004, Bionstrumentation, 2004. Recipient Rsch. Career Devel. award NIH, 1971-76; NIH fellow, 1963-67; recipient Western Electric Fund award Am. Soc. Engring. Edn., 1978, Best Reference Work award, 1999, Theo C. Pilkington Outstanding Educator award, 1994. Fellow IEEE (3d Millenium medal 2000, IEEE-EMBS Career achievement award 2001), Am. Inst. Med. and Biol. Engring., Inst. Physics, Instrument Soc. Am. (Donald P. Eckman Edn. award 1974), Assn. for Advancement Med. Instrumentation (Found. Laufman-Greatbatch prize 1996). Office: Univ Wis Dept Biomed Engring 1550 Engineering Dr Madison WI 53706-1609 E-mail: webster@engr.wisc.edu.

WEBSTER, LINDA JEAN, communications educator, media consultant; b. LA, July 16, 1948; d. Stanley Stewart and Irene M. (Sabo) W. BS, So. Conn. State U., New Haven, 1981, MA, 1983; PhD, La. State U., Baton Rouge, 1987; BA, St. Gregory U., 2002. CEO CBE Enterprises, Inc., Baton Rouge, 1984-89; rsch. fellow La. State U., Baton Rouge, 1983-87; instr. speech Southeastern La. U., Hammond, 1984-89, Hancock Coll., Santa Maria, Calif., 1989; curator of edn. Lompoc (Calif.) Mus., 1989; asst. prof. speech U. Ark., Monticello, 1990-95, assoc. prof. speech, dir. honors program, 1995-2000, prof. speech and journalism, 2000—, chmn. faculty senate, 2003—. Faculty advisor student newspaper The Weevil and student yearbook The Boll Weevil, U. Ark., Monticello, yearbook dir. journalism program; exec. dir. Drew County Hist. Mus., Monticello, 1992-95; media dir. Oasis Resources-Homeless Shelter, Warren, Ark., 1991-99, chair bd. dirs., 1998-99; bur. chief Pine Bluff (Ark.) Comml., 1992-94; media consulting WZXS-FM, Holly Ridge, NC, 1995-97; apptd. State Ark. Mus. Svcs. Rev. Panel, 1997-98, re-apptd., 1999-2000, elected chair panel, 1999; chair Drew County Salvation Army, 1999-2000; faculty exec. MBA program U. Chgo., 2001-, chair faculty assembly, 2003—. Editor Jour. Comm. Studies, 1997-2000, on-line version, 2001—; assoc. editor; asst. Popular Measurement, 1998—; S.E. regional corr. Ark. Cath., 1999-2000, columnist, 2003—; contbr. chpts. to books and articles to profl. jours. Vol. Boys/Girls Club, Monticello, 1992—93, Therapy Animal; campaign dir. Gloria Wright Election, Monticello, 1995, dir. re-election campaign, 2000; campaign media dir. Ken Harper Election-Dist. 82, 1996; sec. Drew County Rep. Conv., 1998—2000; vice chair St. Mark Parish Coun., 2001—02; chair Migrant Worker Ministry to S.E. Ark.; diocesan coms. on adult faith formation Catechist Tng. Faculty; faculty Diocesan Theology Program. Recipient Noel Ross Strader award Coll. Media Advisors, Inc., 1991, Coll. Tchr. of the Yr. award Ark. State Commn. Assn., 1993, Alpha Chi Tchr. of Yr. award, 1999, Faculty Excellence Gold award, 1999; Master fellow Ark. Distance Learning Acad., 2000-01. Mem. AAUW, AAUP, Assn. for Edn. in Journalism and Mass Comm., Nat. Women's Studies Assn., Am. Soc. for History of Rhetoric, Ark. Press Women (state pres. 1993-95, Communicator of Achievement award 1991), Ark. State Comm. Assn. (1st v.p.-elect 1997-98, 1st v.p. 1998-99, pres. 1999-2000, Stds. Bearer 1997—), So. State Comm. Assn. (chair honors session 1995, constitutio com. 1997-2000), Internat. Comm. Assn., Oral History Assn., Speech Comm. Assn. (commn. chair 1993-96), Nat. Comm. Assn. (sec. sr. coll. and univ. sect. 1997-99), Edn. Comm. Assn. (campus Cath. minister 1999—), Assn. Edn. Journalism and Mass Comm. Roman Catholic. Avocations: historic preservation, gardening. Office: U Ark-Arts & Humanities Monticello AR 71656 E-mail: webster@uamont.edu.

WEBSTER, MICHAEL LEE, academic administrator; b. Fulton, N.Y., Sept. 2, 1949; s. Fred Smith and Ida Josephine (Stewart) W.; m. Donna Eileen Turk, Aug. 16, 1969; children: Andrew Michael, Bethany Sarah. BS, Clarkson U., 1971; MDiv, Trinity Evangelical Div. Sch., 1974, DMin, 1981; student, Skyline Coll., San Bruno, Calif., 1981. Ordained to ministry Koinonia Ch., Elim Fellowship, 1975. Grad. asst. Trinity Evangelical Divinity Sch., Deerfield, Ill., 1971-74; pastor Koinonia Ch., Potsdam, N.Y., 1974-78; faculty Melodyland Sch. Theology, Anaheim, Calif., 1978; pastor Coastside Christian Ctr., Pacifica, Calif., 1979-82; instr. Elim Bible Inst., Lima, N.Y., 1982-84, acad. dean, 1984-88, pres., 1988-94, pres. emeritus, 1994—; dir. Believer's Chapel Bible Inst., Cicero, N.Y., 1997—. Bd. adminstrn. Elim Fellowship, Lima, 1984-92; assoc. staff Mobilized to Serve, Lima, 1982-92; mem. NAE Commn. on Higher Edn., Network Christian Ministries; v.p. Crossroads Coun.; speaker in field. Bd. dirs. Ctr.

for Theol. Studies, Newport Beach, Calif., 1978-81. Mem. Eta Kappa Nu, Tau Beta Pi. Republican. Avocations: amateur radio, music, electronics, chess, fishing. Office: Believers Chapel 7912 Thompson Rd Cicero NY 13039-9376 Home: M5 Cobblestone Dr Cicero NY 13039

WEBSTER, MURRAY ALEXANDER, JR., sociologist, educator; b. Manila, Philippines, Dec. 10, 1941; s. M.A. and Patricia (Morse) W. AB, Stanford U., 1963, MA, 1966, PhD, 1968. Asst. prof. social rels. Johns Hopkins U., Balt., 1968-74, assoc. prof., 1974-76; prof. sociology, adj. prof. psychology U. S.C., Columbia, 1976-86; vis. prof. sociology Stanford U., 1981-82, 85, 88-89; sr. lectr. San Jose State U., 1987-89; dir. sociology program NSF, 1989-91,99-2000; prof. sociology U. N.C., Charlotte, 1993—. Author (with Barbara Sobieszek): Soruces of Self-Evaluation, 1974; author: Actions and Actors, 1975; author: (with Martha Foschi) Status Generalization: New Theory and Research, 1988; mem. editl. bd. Am. Jour. Sociology, 1976—79, Social Psychology Quar., 1977—80, 1993—, Social Sci. Rsch., 1975—. Recipient First Citizens Bank Scholars award, 2003; NIH fellow, 1966-68; grantee NSF, Nat. Inst. Edn. Mem.: N.Y. Acad. Scis., So. Sociol. Soc., Am. Sociol. Assn. Office: Univ NC Dept Sociology Charlotte NC 28223 E-mail: mawebste@email.uncc.edu.

WEBSTER, RAYMOND EARL, psychology educator, director, psychotherapist; b. Providence, Dec. 3, 1948; s. Earl Harold and Madeline (D'Antuono) W.; m. Angela Grenier, Jan. 31, 1984; children: Matthew Raymond, Patrick Gregory, Timothy Andrew. BA, R.I. Coll., 1971, MA, 1973; MS, Purdue U., 1976; PhD, U. Conn., 1978. Diplomate Am. Bd. Forensic Med., Am. Bd. Forensic Examiners; lic. psychologist, NC; cert. child forensic examiner NC. Dir. pupil svc. and spl. edn. Northeastern Area Regional Edn. Svc., Wauregan, Conn., 1978-79; dir. alternative voc. sch. Capital Region Edn. Coun., West Hartford, Conn., 1979-83; dir. sch. psychology program East Carolina U., Greenville, NC, 1983—99, prof. of psychology, 1988—. Rsch. assoc. ednl. psychology U. Conn., Storrs, 1976-78; cons. Bolton (Conn.) Pub. Sch., 1976-78, Columbia (Conn.) Pub. Sch., 1976-78, NC Dept. Instrn., Raleigh, 1983-93; textbook cons. Allyn & Bacon Pub. Co.; spkr. at profl. meetings. Guest reviewer Jour. Applied Behavior Analysis, 1975, Clin. Psychology Pub. Co., 1992, Psychol. Reports, 1993—, Perceptual and Motor Skills, 1993—; mem. editl. bd. Psychology in Sch., 1987—, The Forensic Examiner, 2000—; assoc. editor The NC Psychologist, 2000—; contbr. numerous articles to profl. jour., chpt. to books. Trustee NC Ctr. for Advancement of Tchg., Cullowhee, 1990-93. Sgt. US Army Spl. Forces N.G., 1969-75. Recipient spl. distinction award Conn. Assn. Sch. Psychologists, 1983;mem., Omicron Delta Kappa Honor Leadership Society East Carolina Univ. Mem. APA, Am. Coll. Forensic Examiners (cert. Forensic Examiner), Nat. Assn. Sch. Psychologists (cert., alt. del. 1985-86, spl. distinction in profl. devel. 1982, 83), Sigma Xi, Omicron Delta Kappa Honor Leadership Soc., Ea. Carolina Univ. Chpt. Methodist. Avocations: running, karate (3d degree black belt in goju shorin), bicycling, flower gardening. Home: 200 Williams St Greenville NC 27858-8712 Office: East Carolina U Rawl Bldg Greenville NC 27834-4353 E-mail: raymondwebsterr@earthlink.net.

WEBSTER, ROBERT LEE, accounting educator, researcher; b. Little Rock, Oct. 4, 1946; s. Daniel and Mildred LaNette (Patishall) W.; m. Mary Katherine Fiske, Aug. 26, 1967; children: Elizabeth Ashley, Jessica Lee. BA, Ouachita Bapt. U., 1968; MBA, Syracuse U., 1975; MS, L.I. U., 1986; DBA, La. Tech. U., 1993. Cert. govt. fin. mgr. Commd. 2d lt. U.S. Army, 1968, advanced through grades to lt. col., 1985; dep. contr. U.S. Army Electronics R&D Command, Adelphi, Md., 1975-80; chief of ops., comms. security NATO, Mons, Belgium, 1980-83; asst. prof. acctg. and fin. U.S. Mil. Acad., West Point, N.Y., 1983-86; prof. mil. sci. Henderson State U., Arkadelphia, Ark., 1986-88; ret. U.S. Army, 1988; asst. prof. acctg. Henderson State U., 1988-91, chair dept. acctg., econs. and bus. edn., 1991-93; chair dept. acctg. Ouachita Bapt. U., Arkadelphia, 1993—, George Young chair bus., 1995—. Bd. dirs. Hospitality Care Ctr., Arkadelphia, 1992-93; speaker in field. Editor Jour. Bus. & Behavioral Scis., 1995; author articles. Army scholar Syracuse U., 1974-75; Exch. Educator to Republic of Kazakhstan, 1994-95; recipient Dean's award for acad. achievement L.I. U., 1986. Mem. Nat. Social Sci. Assn. (bd. govs. 1992—, Outstanding Conf. Paper award 1992), Am. Acctg. Assn., Assn. of Govt. Accts., Beta Gamma Sigma, Sigma Beta Delta. Avocations: coin collecting, exercising. Home: 205 Forrest Park Dr Arkadelphia AR 71923-2811 Office: Ouachita Bapt U PO Box 3689 Arkadelphia AR 71998 E-mail: websterb@obu.edu.

WECK, MARY KATHERINE, special education educator; b. Portsmouth, Va., Feb. 3, 1962; d. Harry Eugene Dunn Sr. and Mary Ellen Dempsey; children: Donald Richard, Lindsey MaryAnn. A in Applied Bus., Lima Tech. Coll., 1992; BS in Criminal Justice, Defiance Coll., 1996; tchg. cert. spl. edn., Norfolk State U., 1999. Spl. edn. tchg. cert. Va. Legal sec. Myers & Myers Law Office, Celina, Ohio, 1992—93; investigator Child Protective Svcs., Van Wert, Ohio, 1995—96; tchr. asst. Virginia Beach (Va.) City Pub. Schs., 1997—99, spl. edn. tchr., 1999—2002. Tchr. Prins. Adv. Com., Virginia Beach, 2000—02. Voter registrar Van Wert County, 1992. Recipient Am. Scholar Collegiate award, 1995. Presbyterian. Avocations: ballroom dancing, beaches, books. Office: VBCA 273 N Witchduck Rd Virginia Beach VA 23462

WEDE, RICHARD J. school superintendent; b. Cherokee, Iowa, Nov. 11, 1949; s. Robert C. and Beatrice I. (Albers) W.; m. Carol E. Teeter, Dec. 22, 1969; 1 child, Robert D.R. BA, U. No. Iowa, 1971; MS, Iowa State U., 1979; EdS, N.W. Mo. State U., 1985; EdD, Drake U., 1996. Drivers' edn. tchr. N.W. Webster Community Sch. Dist., Barnum, Iowa, 1971, Everly (Iowa) Community Sch. Dist., 1974-75; jr. high math tchr. Blessed Sacrament Sch., Waterloo, Iowa, 1973-75; high sch. math tchr. Council Bluffs (Iowa) Community Sch. Dist., 1975-80; assoc. mid. sch. prin. Lewis Cen. Community Sch. Dist., Council Bluffs, 1980-83; sec. prin. Bedford (Iowa) Community Sch. Dist., 1983-86; supt. schs. Everly Community Sch. Dist., 1986-89, Everly & Clay Cen. Community Sch. Dists., 1989-91, Prairie Community Sch. Dist., Gowrie, Iowa, 1991-93, Cedar Valley Community Sch. Dist., 1991-93, Praire Valley Community Sch. Dist., Gowrie, Iowa, 1993-94; supt. Dunkerton (Iowa) Cmty. Sch. Dist., 1994—2001, South Winneshiek Cmty. Sch. Dist., Calmar, Iowa, 2001—. Bd. dirs. Iowa Girls H.S. Athletic Union, 2002—. Bd. dirs. Regional Transit Authority, Spencer, Iowa, 1990-91. Mem. Am. Assn. Sch. Adminstrs., Sch. Adminstrs. Iowa, Am. Legion, Westend Optimists of Council Bluffs, Dunkerton Area C. of C., Phi Delta Kappa. Roman Catholic. Office: South Winneshiek Cmty Sch Dist PO Box 430 Calmar IA 52132-0430 Home: PO Box 237 Calmar IA 52132-0237

WEDEL-COWGILL, MILLIE REDMOND, secondary school educator, performing arts educator; b. Harrisburg, Pa., Aug. 18, 1939; d. Clair L. and Florence (Heiges) Aungst; m. T.S. Redmond, 1956 (div. 1967); children: T.S. Redmond II; m. Frederick L. Wedel, Jr., 1974 (div. 1986); m. Paul R. Cowgill, May 19, 2001. BA, Alaska Meth. U., 1966; MEd, U. Alaska, Anchorage, 1972; postgrad. in comm., Stanford U., 1975-76. Lic. third class broadcasting, FCC. Profl. actress Charming Models & Models Guild of Phila., 1954-61; asst. dir. devel. in charge pub. rels. Alaska Meth. U., Anchorage, 1966, part-time lectr., 1966, 73; comm. tchr. Anchorage Sch. Dist., 1967-96; owner Wedel Prodns., Anchorage, 1976-86; cons. comms., media and edn., owner Cowgill Cons., 2003—. Pub. rels. staff Alaska Purchase Centennial Exhibit, U.S. Dept. Commerce, 1967; writer gubernatorial campaign, 1971; instr. Chapman Coll., 1990-93; adj. instr. U. Alaska, Anchorage, 1972, 77-79, 89-2001; cons. Cook Inlet Native Assn., 1978, No. Inst., 1979; judge Ark. Press Women's Writing Contest, 1990-91; sec. exec. bd. Alaska Dept. Edn. Profl. Tchg. Practices Commn., 1993-94. Bd. dirs. Sta. KAKM, Alaska Pub. TV, membership chmn., 1978-80, nat. lay rep. to Pub. Broadcasting Svc. and Nat. Assn. Pub. TV Stas., 1979; bd. dirs. Ednl. Telecom. Consortium for Alaska, 1979, Mid-Hillside Cmty. Coun., Municipality of Anchorage, 1979-80, 83-88, Hillside East Cmty. Coun., 1984-88, pres., 1984-85; rsch. writer, legal asst. Vinson & Elkins, Houston, 1981; v.p., bd. dirs. Inlet View ASD Cmty. Sch., 1994-95, pres., 1995-97; mem. Valley Forge Freedoms Found., Murdoch Scholarships, Valley Forge; bd. dirs. Rev. Richard Gay Trust, Alaska and Pa., 1992—; active Anchorage Opera Guild, Anchorage Concert Assn. Recipient awards for newspapers, lit. mags.; award Nat. Scholastic Press Assn., 1981, 82, 83, 84; Alaska Coun. Econs., 1982, Merits award Alaska Dept. Edn., 1982-93, Legis. commendation State of Alaska, Nat. Blue Ribbon Outstanding Sch. award, 1993. Mem. NEA (AEA bldg. rep., state del. 70s, 80s, 94-95), Assn. Pub. Broadcasting (charter mem., nat. lay del. 1980), Indsl. TV Assn. (San Francisco and Houston 1975-81), Alaska Press Club (chmn. high sch. journalism workshops, 1968-69, 73, awards for sch. newspapers 1972, 74, 77), Alaska Fedn. Press Women (dir. 1978-86, 94-95, pres. 1995-96, h.s. journalism competition youth projects dir., award for brochures 1978, chair youth writing contest 1994-95), Internat. Platform Assn., World Affairs Coun., Chugach Electric (chair 1990, nomination com. for bd. dirs. 1988-90), Stanford U. Alumni Club (Alaska pres. 1982-84, 90-92, 99-2000, v.p. 1998-99), Petroleum Club Anchorage, Naples Downtown Rotary, Imperial Golf Course Country Club, Club at Pelican Bay, Naples (Fla.) Philharm. League, Naples Players Theatre Guild, Pelican Bay Women's League, Delta Kappa Gamma. Presbyterian. Office: PO Box 111489 Anchorage AK 99511-1489 also: PO Box 770662 Naples FL 34107-0662

WEDEMEYER, SALLY EILEEN, special education educator; b. Arverne, N.Y., Mar. 10, 1960; d. Albert J. and Ethel I. (Graf) W. BS in Edn., Keene (N.H.) State Coll., 1982, MEd, 1988. Cert. experienced tchr., N.H. Remedial tchr. Tobey Sch., Concord, N.H., 1982-87; resource tchr. Belmont (N.H.) Elem. Sch., 1988—. Head coach Belmont Spl. Olympics Team, 1991—; participant Project Star Tree, Belmont, 1992—. Named Tchr. of Yr., Belmont Elem. Sch., 1993. Mem. NEA, Coun. for Exceptional Children (emotionally handicapped com. Shaker Regional sch. dist., workshop co-presenter Internat. Conf. Learning Disabilites, Austin, Tex. 1990). Avocations: reading, travel. Home: 897 Farrington Corner Rd Hopkinton NH 03229-2022 Office: Belmont Elem Sch 89 Gilmanton Rd E Belmont NH 03220-4813

WEE, CHRISTINE DIJOS, elementary school educator; b. Honolulu, Jan. 8, 1968; d. Cosme Wayne and Victoria Amparo Dijos; m. Phillip Ying Kin Wee, July 15, 2000; 1 child, Deanna Rae Patacsil. BEd, U. Hawaii, Manoa, 1991. Cert. tchr. Hawaii, prof. diploma in elem. edn. Univ. Hawaii, 1992. Kindergarten tchr. Island Paradise Sch., Honolulu, 1992—93, Pauoa Elem. Sch., Honolulu, 1993—94, choral dir., 1997—2002, 6th grade tchr., 1994—2002; spl. edn. summer sch. aide Wailupe Valley Elem. Sch., Honolulu; Challenger Ctr.-trained educator, NASA program Barber's Point Elem. Sch., Kapolei, Hawaii, 1996—2002. Regional conf. del. Sch.-to-Work, Honolulu, 1998; cadre mem. Roosevelt Complex Writing Inst., Honolulu, 1999; mem. music action rsch. team Hawaii State Dept. Edn., 1999—2001. Mem. coun. Sch. Cmty.-Based Mgmt. Coun., Pauoa Elem. Sch., 2001—03; vol., chmn. Honolulu Dist. Choral Festival, 1994—2002; bd. dirs. Pauoa Elem. Sch. PTA, 1996—97. Mem.: Hawaii Music Educators Assn. (3d v.p. 2000—02, chmn. 2001—02), Hawaii state tchr. assoc. (student svc. coord. 2002—03, union rep. 1995—96, 2000—01). Avocations: walking, collecting keychains and unicorns/Pegasuses, singing. Home: 823 9th Ave Honolulu HI 96816 Office: Pauoa Elem Sch 2301 Pauoa Rd Honolulu HI 96813 E-mail: christine_wee@notes.k12.hi.us.

WEED, ROGER OREN, rehabilitation services professional, educator; b. Bend, Oreg, Feb. 2, 1944; s. Chester Elbert and Ruth Marie (Urie) W.; m. Paula J. Keller BS in Sociology, U. Oreg., 1967, MS in Rehab. Counseling, 1969; PhD in Rehab. Counseling, U. Ga., 1986. Cert. rehab. counselor; cert. disability mgmt. specialist; lic. profl. counselor; cert. case mgr., cert. life care planner. Vocat. rehab. counselor State of Alaska, Anchorage, 1969-71; instr. U. Alaska, Anchorage, 1970-76; counselor Langdon Psychiat. Clinic, Anchorage, 1971-74; from asst. dir. to exec. dir. Hope Cottages, Anchorage, 1974-79; owner Profl. Resources Group, Anchorage, 1978-80; mng. ptnr. Collins, Weed & Assocs., 1980-84; assoc. dir. Ctr. for Rehab. Tech. Ga. Tech. U., Atlanta, 1986-87; catastrophic injury rehab. Weed & Assocs., Atlanta, 1984—; from asst. prof. to prof. Ga. State U., Atlanta, 1987—. Adj. faculty Ga. Inst. Tech.; courtesy faculty U. Fla., 1996—. Co-author: Vocational Expert Handbook, 1986, Transferable Work Skills, 1988, Life Care Planning: Spinal Cord Injured, 1989, 2d edit. 1994, Life Care Planning: Head Injured, 1994, Life Care Planning for the Amputee, 1992, Rehab Cons. Handbook, 1994, rev. edit., 2001; editor: Life Care Planning and Case Mgmt. Handbook, 1999; assoc. editor Jour. Lifecare Planning, 2002—; mem. editl. bd. Jour. of Pvt. Sector Rehab., 1986—, Vanguard Series in Rehab., Athens, 1988—, Jour. Forensic Vocational Analysis; contbr. articles to profl. jour. Recipient Gov.'s award Gov.'s Com. on Employment, Alaska, 1982, Goldpan Svc. award Gov.'s Com. on Employment, Alaska, 1978, Profl. Svc. award Am. Rehab. Counselors Assn., 1993. Fellow Nat. Rehab. Assn. (chmn. legis. com., bd. dir. met. Atlanta chpt. 1987-89, pres. Pacific region 1983-85, Pres.'s award Pacific region 1986), Internat. Assn. Rehab. Profls. (chmn. resh. and tng. com. 1988-93, pres. 1994-95, Educator of Yr. 1991, 97), Internat. Acad. Life Care Planning, Nat. Brain Injury Assn., Pvt. Rehab. Suppliers Ga., Rehab. Engring. Soc. N.Am., Anchorage Amateur Radio Club. Republican. Methodist. Avocations: sailing, skiing, bicycling, flying, computers. Office: Ga State U Coll of Edn Dept Counseling/Psychol Svc 9th Fl Atlanta GA 30303

WEEDEN, DEBBIE SUE, early childhood education educator; b. Tenn., Nov. 7, 1952; d. Edward Jr. and Ann Arrants; m. Gordon H. Weeden, May 5, 1979; children: Lance Edward, Lindsey Brooke. BS in Early Child Edn. magna cum laude, Va. Intermont U., 1975; MA in Reading Rsch., East Tenn. State U., 1979. Cert. K-8 reading tchr., Tenn. Kindergarten tchr. Weaver Sch., Bristol, Tenn., 1975—. V.p. Weaver Sch. PTA; tchr. rep. Weaver Sch. Mem. Career Ladder Tchrs., Alpha Delta Kappa (historian). Methodist. Avocations: crafts, volleyball. Home: 328 Orchard Ln Bluff City TN 37618-1160 Office: Weaver Sch Rte 1 Bristol TN 37620

WEED-WOLNICK, PATRICIA HURLEY, secondary education educator; b. Washington, July 11, 1956; d. Hampton Francis and Cecilia Kathleen (Hurley) Weed; m. Guy Robert Wolnick, July 12, 1986; 1 child, Sean Robert Wolnick. BA, U. Calif., Davis, 1980; MA, Calif. State U., San Francisco, 1988; postgrad., Oxford (Eng.) U., 1990; EdD, U. San Francisco, 1997; postgrad., Oxford (Eng.)' U., 1990. Cert. lang. devel. specialist, community coll. tchr., Calif. Instr. Britannia Sch., Barcelona, Spain, 1981-83, Instituto Cultural del C.I.C., Barcelona, 1983-84, Jefferson Union Adult Dist., Daly City, Calif., 1987-89; mentor tchr., ESL grades 9-12 San Francisco Unified Sch. Dist., 1984-97. Cons. Commun. Svcs., Versoix, Switzerland, 1988—, Colegio Bandeirantes, Sao Paulo, Brazil, 1991; tchr. cons. Bay Area Writing Project, Berkeley, Calif., 1989—; mem. adv. coun. Ctr. for Advancement and Renewal of Educators, San Francisco, 1991-92; instr. Foothill Coll., Los Altos, Calif., 1990-97, U. Calif. Extension, Santa Cruz, 1992-97; co-dir. Project Think/Writer, San Francisco 1988—; adult edn. tchr. Internat. Bus. Profls. Co-author curriculum guide and curriculum framework; editor: (original student writing) Facts and Fables, 1990. Mem. Leadership San Francisco of C. of C., 1991-92. Recipient Excellence in Teaching English award English Speaking Union, 1990, Dir.'s award Foghorn Press, 1990, German, Am., Israel tchr. Exchange award, 1993-94; San Francisco Edn. Fund grantee, 1989-91. Mem. TESOL, ASCD, ASTM, Ctr. for Ethics and Social Policy, Bay Area Orgn. and Devel. Democrat. Roman Catholic. Avocations: reading, running, theatre, sewing, weaving. Home: 3670 Mill Creek Rd Fremont CA 94539-5407 Office: San Francisco Unified Dist 135 Van Ness Ave San Francisco CA 94102-5207

WEEKS, ARTHUR ANDREW, lawyer, law educator; b. Hanceville, Ala., Dec. 2, 1914; s. A.A. and Anna S. (Seibert) W.; m. Carol P. Weeks; children: John David, Carol Christine, Nancy Anna. AB, Samford U., 1936; LL.B., JD, U. Ala., 1939; LL.M., Duke U., 1950; LL.D. (hon.), Widener U., 1980. Bar: Ala. 1939, Tenn. 1948. Sole practice, Birmingham, Ala., 1939-41, 1946-47, 1954-61; dean, prof. law Cumberland U. Sch. Law, 1947-54; dean, prof. Samford U., 1961-72, prof. law, 1972-74, Cumberland Sch. Law, Samford U., 1984—, Del. Sch. Law of Widener U., Wilmington, 1974-82, dean, 1974-80, interim dean, 1982-83, dean emeritus, prof., 1983—. Served to capt. AUS, 1941-46. Mem. ABA, Tenn. Bar Assn., Ala. Bar Assn., Birmingham Bar Assn., Del. Bar Assn. (assoc.), Phi Alpha Delta, Phi Kappa Phi, Delta Theta Phi Home: 1105 Water Edge Ct Birmingham AL 35244-1437

WEEKS, CATHERINE CLAIRE, elementary education educator; b. Indpls., June 12, 1928; d. Raymond Kinnear and Clara Louise (Koelliker) Van Deman; m. Robert Neal Weeks, Aug. 8, 1948 (dec. May, 1987); 1 child, Eric Neal. Student, Arthur Jordan Conservatory Music, Indpls., 1945-48; MusB magna cum laude, Washburn U., 1954; postgrad., Ind. State U., 1965, 66. Cert. tchr., Ind. Tchr. kindergarten East Indianola Sch., Topeka, 1954-59; tchr. kinderarten Newport (Ind.) Elem. Sch., 1964-66, tchr. kindergarten, music, 1967—. Active Terre Haute (Ind.) Concert Band, 1992, Montgomery County Concert Band, 1991—. Mac Vicar scholar Washburn Univ., Topeka, 1953-54; named Class Act Tchr. Sta WTWO-TV, Terre Haute, Ind., 1992. Mem. NEA, Am. Orff-Schulwerk Assn. (Ind. chpt.), Internat. Reading Assn., Music Educators Nat. Conf., Ind. Assn. Edn. Young Children, Ind. Elem. Music Educators Assn., North Vermillion Classroom Tchrs. Assn., Indpls. Matinee Musicale, ParkeCounty Mental Health Assn. (sec. 1986-89), Vigo County Mental Health Assn., Delta Kappa Gamma (Alpha Alpha chpt. chmn. music 1976-84, 86-90, 92—), Sigma Alpha Iota. Avocation: playing clarinet. Home: RR 4 Box 294 Rockville IN 47872-9271 Office: Newport Elem Sch PO Box 6 Newport IN 47966-0006

WEEKS, CLIFFORD MYERS, musician, educational administrator; b. N.Y.C., Apr. 15, 1938; s. Vernal C. and Adeline (Campbell) W.; m. Ethel Lynn Fleming, Oct. 26, 1963 (dec. 1982); children: Clifford M. Jr., Michele Lynn. Diploma in Arranging and Composition, Berklee Coll. Music, 1962; MusB magna cum laude, Boston Conservatory Music, 1963, MusM, 1975; cert. in edn. adminstrn., Boston State Coll., 1977. Cert. secondary sch. adminstr. and tchr. music, Mass. Tchr. music Boston Pub. Schs., 1964-74, condr. All-City Stage Band, 1972-79, adminstrv. asst. to asst. supt., 1974-75, coordinator instrumental music, 1975-79, asst. prin., 1979, adminstrv. asst. to asst. supt., 1979-96, acting community supt., 1983, cluster coord., 1996-2001, exec. asst. to chief of staff, 2001—. Arranger, composer, trombonist, 1963—; condr. Boston Coll. Jazz and Stage Band, Chestnut Hill, Mass., 1976-78. Composer Tryptych for tuba and piano, 1971, (oratorio) The King-Life and Teachings of Dr. Martin Luther King Jr., 1976; composer, arranger various jazz compositions, 1975. Mem. Medford (Mass.) Jaycees, 1975-76; adv. bd. Roxbury (Mass.) Boys and Girls Club, 1970—, Berklee Coll. Music, Boston, 1972. Recipient Mayor's Parkman Club award, 1999, Suskind Young at Art award Wang Ctr. Boston Theatres, 2001. Mem. Boston Assn. Sch. Adminstrs. and Suprs. (adminstrs. union 1997—), Boston Tchrs. Union, Black Educators Alliance Mass. (treas. 1972-76, award 1976), ASCAP, Adminstrv. Assts. Assn. (chmn. local chpt. 1982—), Assn. for Supervision and Curriculum Devel., Omega Psi Phi. Methodist. Office: Boston Pub Schs Office Supt 26 Court St Boston MA 02108

WEEKS, GERALD, psychology educator; b. Morehead City, NC, Nov. 20, 1948; s. Marion G. and Ada (Willis) W.; m. Kathleen Glass, Sept. 2, 1972. BA in Philosophy and Psychology, East Carolina U., 1971, MA in Gen. Psychology, 1973; PhD in Clin. Psychology, Ga. State U., 1979. Diplomate Am. Bd. Profl. Psychology (pres. 1987-88, bd. dirs. 1982-87), Am. Bd. Family Psychology, Am. Bd. Sexology; cert. marital and family therapist; lic. practicing psychologist, N.C., Pa.; registered Health Care Providers in Psychology. Intern in family therapy Harlem Valley Psychiatric Ctr., Wingdale, N.Y., 1978-79; assoc. prof. psychology U. N.C., Wilmington, 1979-85; dir. tng. Penn Coun. for Relationships, 1985—; clin. asst. prof. psychology Sch. Medicine U. Pa., Phila., 1985-87, clin. assoc. prof., 1988-98; chair, prof. dept. counseling U. Nev.-Las Vegas, 1999—. Pvt. practice Carolina Ob-gyn Ctr., Wilmington, 1980-85. Author: Promoting Change Through Paradoxical Therapy, 1985, Treating Couples: The Intersystem Model of the Marriage Council of Philadelphia, 1989, Promoting Change through Paradoxical Therapy, 1991, (with L. L'Abate) Paradoxical Psychotherapy: Theory and Practice with Individuals, Couples, and Families, 1982, (with R. Sauber, L. L'Abate) Family Therapy: Basic Concepts and Terms, 1985, (with L. Hof) Integrating Sex and Marital Therapy: A Clinicians Guide, 1987, (with S. Treat) Couples in Treatment, 1992, rev. edit., 2001, Integrative Solutions: Treating Common Problems in Couple's Therapy, 1995, (with L. Hof) Erectile Dysfunction, 2000; (with N. Gambescia) Focused Genograms: Intergenerational Assessment of Individuals, Couples and Families, 1999, (with Gambiscia) Hypoactive Sexual Desire, 2002; (with Setton and Robbins) Handbook of Family Therapy, 2003; contbr. articles to profl. jours. Fellow Am. Assn. Marital and Family Therapy (clin. mem., nat. adv. bd., approved supr.); mem. APA, Acad. Family Psychology, Interpersonal and Social Skills Assn. (founding mem.), Acad. Psychologists in Marital, Sex, and Family Therapy. Office: U Nev Dept Counseling PO Box 453045 4505 S Maryland Pkwy Las Vegas NV 89154-3045

WEEKS, MARIE COOK, health and physical education educator; b. High Point, N.C., Jan. 21, 1949; d. Paul Hue Cook and Beulah Edna (Smith) Townsend; m. Lewis Tirey Weeks, June 5, 1970; children: Gina, Corby. BS in Edn., Western Carolina U., 1971. Tchr. grades 6,7,8, math. science, health, physical edn. Ramseur (N.C.) Elem. Sch., 1971-91; tchr. grades 6,7,8, health and physical edn. Archdale-Trinity Middle Sch., Trinity, N.C., 1991—; coach girls softball and volleyball Randolph County Schs., Asheboro, N.C., 1971—. Mentor tchr. Randolph County Schs., Asheboro, 1989—; student tchr. supr. Archdale Trinity Middle Sch. 1993—, head of health and phys. edn. dept., 1993—. Coach girls' softball Hillsville (N.C.) Civitan's Youth Softball League, 1984—. Named Ramseur Sch. Tchr. of Yr., Ramseur Faculty, 1983, 89, Outstanding Young Educator Asheboro/Randolph County, Asheboro Jaycees, 1989. Mem. NEA, N.C. AAHPERD, Nat. Fedn. Coaches, N.C. Assn. Educators. Baptist. Avocations: arts and crafts, softball, family. Home: 3725 Lynn Oaks Dr Trinity NC 27370-9445 Office: Archdale-Trinity Mid Sch 5105 Archdale Rd Trinity NC 27370-9457

WEERTMAN, JOHANNES, materials science educator; b. Fairfield, Ala., May 11, 1925; s. Roelof and Christina (van Vlaardingen) W.; m. Julia Ann Randall, Feb. 10, 1950; children: Julia Ann, Bruce Randall. Student, Pa. State Coll., 1943-44; BS, Carnegie Inst. Tech. (now Carnegie Mellon U.), 1948, DSc, 1951; postgrad., Ecole Normale Superieure, Paris, 1951-52. Solid State physicist U.S. Naval Rsch. Lab., Washington, 1952-58, cons., 1960-67; sci. liaison officer U.S. Office Naval Rsch., Am. Embassy, London, 1958-59; faculty Northwestern U., Evanston, Ill., 1959—, prof. materials sci. dept., 1961-68, chmn. dept., 1964-68, prof. geol. scis. dept., 1963—, Walter P. Murphy prof. materials sci. and engring. emeritus, 1999—. Vis. prof. geophysics Calif. Inst. Tech., 1964, Scott Polar Rsch. Inst., Cambridge (Eng.) U., 1970-71, Swiss Fed. Inst. Reactor Rsch., 1986; cons. Cold Regions Rsch. and Engring. Lab., U.S. Army, 1960-75, Oak Ridge (Tenn.) Nat. Lab., 1963-67, Los Alamos (N.Mex.) Sci. Lab., 1967—; co-editor materials sci. books MacMillan Co., 1962-76. Author: Dislocation Based Fracture Mechanics, 1996, (with Julia Weertman) Elementary Dislocation Theory, 1964, 2d edit., 1992; mem. editorial bd. Metal. Trans., 1967-75, Jour. Glaciology, 1972—; assoc. editor Jour. Geophys. Rsch., 1973-75, 2000-01; contbr. articles to profl. jours. With USMC, 1943-46.

Honored with naming of Weertman Island in Antarctica.; Fulbright fellow, 1951-52; recipient Acta Metallurgica gold medal, 1980; Guggenheim fellow, 1970-71 Fellow Am. Acad. Arts and Scis., Am. Soc. Metals, Am. Phys. Soc., Geol. Soc. Am., Am. Geophys. Union (Horton award 1972, AIME Mathewson Gold medal 1977); mem. AAAS, NAE, Am. Inst. Physics, Internat. Glaciol. Soc. (Seligman Crystal award 1983), Arctic Inst., Am. Quaternary Assn., Explorers Club, Fulbright Assn., Sigma Xi, Tau Beta Pi, Phi Kappa Phi, Alpha Sigma Mu, Pi Mu Epsilon. Home: 834 Lincoln St Evanston IL 60201-2405 Office: Northwestern U Materials Sci Dept Evanston IL 60208-0001 E-mail: j-weertman2@nwu.edu.

WEERTMAN, JULIA RANDALL, materials science and engineering educator; b. Muskegon, Mich., Feb. 10, 1926; BS in Physics, Carnegie-Mellon U., 1946, MS in Physics, 1947, DSc in Physics, 1951. Physicist U.S. Naval Rsch. Lab., Washington, 1952-58; vis. asst. prof. dept. materials sci. and engring. Northwestern U., Evanston, Ill., 1972-73, asst. prof., 1973-78, from asst. prof. to assoc. prof., 1973-82, prof., 1982-99, Walter P. Murphy prof., 1989, chmn. dept., 1987-92, asst. to dean grad. studies and rsch. Tech. Inst., 1973-76, Walter P. Murphy prof. emeritus, 1999—. Mem. various NRC coms. and panels. Co-author: Elementary Dislocation Theory, 1964, 1992, also pub. in French, Japanese and Polish; contbr. numerous articles to profl. jours. Mem. Evanston Environ. Control Bd., 1972-79. Recipient Creativity award NSF, 1981, 86; Guggenheim Found. fellow, 1986-87. Fellow Am. Soc. Metals Internat., Minerals, Metals and Materials Soc. (leadership award 1997); mem. NAE, Am. Acad. Arts and Scis., Am. Phys. Soc., Materials Rsch. Soc. (Von Hipple award 2003), Soc. Women Engrs. (disting. engring. educator award 1989, achievement award 1991). Home: 834 Lincoln St Evanston IL 60201-2405 Office: Northwestern U Dept Material Sci & Engring 2220 Campus Dr Evanston IL 60208-0876 E-mail: jrweertman@northwestern.edu.

WEERTS, RICHARD KENNETH, music educator; b. Peoria, Ill., Oct. 7, 1928; s. Gerhard Nicholas and Ellen Marie (Lindeburg) W. BS, U. Ill., 1951; MA, Columbia U., 1956, EdD, 1960; MA, N.E. Mo. State U., 1973. Tchr. Lyndhurst (N.J.) Pub. Schs., 1956-57; dir. instrumental music Scotch Plains (N.J.) Pub. Schs., 1957-61; prof. music Truman State U., Kirksville, 1961—, chair dept. music, 1994—. Author: Handbook for Woodwinds, 1965, Developing Individual Skills for the High School Band, 1969, How to Develop and Maintain a Successful Woodwind Section, 1972, Original Manuscript Music, 1973, Handbook of Rehearsal Techniques for Band, 1976; numerous papers and monographs; nat. bd. editors The Quarterly, jour. of Ctr. for Rsch. in Music Learning and Teaching, 1989. Dir. music First United Meth. Ch., Kirksville, 1970—. Served with U.S. Army, 1951-55. Mem. Coun. for Rsch. in Music Edn., Nat. Assn. Coll. Wind and Percussion Instrs. (nat. exec. sec./treas. 1971—, editor jour. 1968—), Music Educators Nat. Conf., Phi Delta Kappa. Office: NACWPI Truman State U Divsn Fine Arts Kirksville MO 63501

WEGENAST, JUDY H. elementary school educator, consultant; b. Grafton, N.D., Aug. 4, 1944; d. Donald M. and Donna (Ramsey) Matter; m. Jerry G. Wegenast, May 28, 1966; children: Kim. L. Albrecht, Elisa D. Wegenast. EdB, Valley City State U., 1966; MS, N.D. State U., 1982. Tchr. St. John's, Wahpeton, N.D., 1967; remedial reading Wahpeton (N.D.) Indian Sch., 1968; tchr. West Fargo (N.D.) Pub. Sch., 1968-70, Fargo (N.D.) Pub. Schs., 1970-91, peer coach, 1991—. Instr. N.D. State U. Fargo, Grand Forks, N.D., 1986—; cons. SW Enterprises, fargo, N.D., 1985—. Bd. dirs. Yunder Farm Childrens Mus., Fargo, N.D., 1992—. Named Tchr. of Month, Fargo (N.D.) C. of C., 1989, Tchr. of Yr., IBM/Tech. and Learning, Fargo, N.D., 1992, Fargo Tchr. of Yr., 1992, N.D. Tchr. of Yr., 1992. Mem. Valley Reading Assn., N.D. Edn. Assn., Fargo Edn. Assn. NEA, ASCD, Alpha Delta Kappa. Avocations: painting, gardening, golf, reading, wood working. Office: Centennial Elem 4201 25th St S Fargo ND 58104-6800

WEGNER, JUDITH WELCH, law educator, former dean; b. Hartford, Conn., Feb. 14, 1950; d. John Raymond and Ruth (Thulen) Welch; m. Warren W. Wegner, Oct. 13, 1972. BA with honors, U. Wis., 1972; JD, UCLA, 1976. Bar: Calif. 1976, D.C. 1977, N.C. 1988, U.S. Supreme Ct. 1980, U.S. Ct. Appeals. Law clk. to Judge Warren Ferguson, U.S. Dist. Ct. for So. Dist. Calif., L.A., 1976-77; atty. Office Legal Counsel and Land & Natural Resources Divsn. U.S. Dept. Justice, Washington, 1977-79; spl. asst. to sec. U.S. Dept. Edn., Washington, 1979-80; vis. assoc. prof. U. Iowa Coll. Law, Iowa City, 1981; asst. prof. U. N.C. Sch. Law, Chapel Hill, 1981-84, assoc. prof., 1984-88, prof., 1988—, assoc. dean, 1986-88, dean, 1989-99; sr. scholar Carnegie Found. for Advancement of Tchg., 1999—; chmn. UNC Faculty, 2003—06. Spkr. in field. Chief comment editor UCLA Law Rev., 1975-76; contbr. articles to legal publs. Mem. ABA (chmn. planning com. African Law Sch. Initiative 1994, co-chmn. planning com. 1994 mid-yr. deans meeting sect. on legal edn. and admission to bar), N.C. Assn. Women Attys. (Gweneth Davis award 1989), N.C. State Bar Assn., Assn. Am. Law Schs. (mem. exec. com. sect. on law & edn. 1985-88, mem. exec. com. sect. on local govt. law 1989-92, mem. accreditation com. 1986-88, chmn. 1989-91, program chmn. 1992 ann. meeting, program chmn. 1994 ann. meeting, mem. exec. com. 1992-96, pres. 1995), Soc. Am. Law Tchrs., Nat. League Cities (coun.-mentor program 1989-91), Women's Internat. Forum, Order of Coif (nat. exec. com. 1989-91), Phi Beta Kappa. Democrat. Office: U NC Sch Law Van Hecke Wettach Hall Campus Box 3380 Chapel Hill NC 27599-3380 E-mail: judith_wegner@unc.edu.

WEGNER, KENNETH WALTER, psychology educator; b. Newton, Kans., Mar. 13, 1932; s. A. and Erna A. (Leus) W.; m. Ruth E. Brynildsen, Aug. 24, 1963; children: K. Erik, Steven S. BS in Lang. Arts, U. Kans., 1953, MEd in Counseling, 1955, EdD in Counseling Psychology, 1961. Lic. psychologist, Mass., R.I. Rehab. counselor, office mgr. Kans. divsn. Vocat. Rehab., 1958-60; counseling ctr. dir. U. Oreg., 1961-66; prof. Boston Coll., Chestnut Hill, 1966-97. Author: Guidance: Theory and Practice, 1964, (with others) Test Critiques, Vols. VI-X, 1988-94; contbr. articles to profl. jours. 1st lt. USAF, 1955-57. Mem. ACA (senator 1980-82), Am. Psychol. Assn., Nat. Career Devel. Assn. (exec. bd. 1985-88), Assn. for Counseling Edn. and Supr. (exec. bd.), Nat. Rehab. Assn. Home: 27 Dartmouth Ave Needham MA 02494-1924

WEHINGER, PETER AUGUSTUS, astronomer, educator; b. Goshen, N.Y., Feb. 18, 1938; s. George Edward and Elizabeth Marie (Goode) W.; m. Susan Wyckoff, July 29, 1967. BS in Physics, Union Coll., Schenectady, N.Y., 1960; MA in Astronomy, Ind. U., 1962; PhD, Case Western Reserve U., 1966. NASA predoctoral fellow Case Western Reserve U., Cleve., 1963-65; instr. U. Mich., Ann Arbor, 1965-67, asst. prof., 1967-70; assoc. prof. U. Kans., Lawrence, 1970-72; vis. assoc. prof. Tel Aviv U., Ramat-Aviv, Israel, 1972-75; prin. rsch. fellow Royal Greenwich Observatory, Herstmonceux, Sussex, Eng., 1975-78; vis. sr. scientist Max Planck Inst. for Astronomy, Heidelberg, Germany, 1978-80; vis. prof. Ariz. State U., Tempe, 1981-84, rsch. prof., 1984—. Project mgr. 1.3 meter telescope dept. astronomy U. Mich., 1966-70; tech. cons. Boller & Chivens divsn. Perkin Elmer Corp., South Pasadena, Calif., 1974-75, Photek Ltd., St. Leonard's-on-the-Sea, Sussex, Eng., 1992-94, Torus Precision Optics, Iowa City, 1997-99; mem. Ariz. Astronomy Bd., 1999-; vis. prof. Astronomy Ctr. U. Sussex, Brighton, Eng., 1975-78, sr. rsch. fellow dept. astronomy Ohio State U., Columbus, 1978-79; vis. prof. physics-astronomy dept. No. Ariz. U., Flagstaff, 1981-82; discipline specialist in spectroscopy Internat. Halley Watch, NASA/JPL, 1982-89; vis. rsch. fellow Mt. Stromlo Observatory and Siding Spring, Australian Nat. U., Canberra, 1986—; assoc. dir. Ariz./NASA Space Grant Consortium, Ariz. State U., 1990-94; adj. staff astronomer Steward Observatory U. Ariz., 1991-97, staff astronomer, devel. officer Dir.'s Office, 1997—; mem. Ariz. Sci. Ctr. Adv. Bd., 1995-97; vis. prof. physics and astronomy Mesa C.C., 1996-98; faculty assoc. plant biology Ariz. State U., 1997-2000. Contbr. 110 articles to profl. jours.; editor: (conf. proceedings) Observations of Recent Comets, 1990; editor electronic newsletter On Periodic Comets, 1985-90, electronic bull. bd. Halley Hotline; co-editor (CDROM Archives) Spectroscopic Observations of Comets, 1990. Grantee NASA, 1982-90, 98-99, 1983-93, 1989-94, 1995-99, GTE-Sprint, 1985-87, NSF, 1985-87, 1994-97, Ariz. Pub. Svc. Corp., 1998-2001, CEMEX Corp., 2000. Fellow Royal Astron. Soc.; mem. Am. Astron. Soc. (divsn. planetry scis.), Astron. Soc. of the Pacific, Internat. Astron. Union, Sigma Xi. Achievements include measurement of carbon isotope abundances in comets; titanium isotope abundances in red giant stars, identification of H2O+ in comets; digital imaging and spectroscopy of quasar host galaxies detected at their cosmological distances; spectroscopy of sodium torus associated with Jupiter and Io. Home: 2135 E Loma Vista Dr Tempe AZ 85282-2927 Office: U Ariz Dir Office Steward Obs 933 N Cherry Ave Tucson AZ 85721-0065 E-mail: pwehinger@as.arizona.edu.

WEHLING, ROBERT LOUIS, retired household products company executive; b. Chgo., Nov. 27, 1938; s. Ralph Joseph and Rita Helen (Casey) W.; m. Carolyn Thierry Harmon, July 5, 1958; children: Susan, Mary, Jennifer, Linda, Karen, Sandra. BA magna cum laude, Denison U., 1960; LHD (hon.), U. Cin., 1998. Brand asst. Procter & Gamble Co., Cin., 1960, 63-64, asst. brand mgr., 1964-66, brand mgr., 1966-70, assoc. advt. mgr., 1970-74, advt. mgr. bar soap and household cleaning products div., 1974-77, div. mgr. gen. advt., 1977-84, assoc. gen. advt. mgr., 1984-87, gen. mktg. svcs. mgr., 1987-88, v.p. mktg. svcs., 1988-90, v.p. pub. affairs, 1990-94, sr. v.p. advt., market rsch. and pub. affairs, 1994-99, sr. v.p. advt., market rsch. and govt. rels., 1994-99, global mktg., market rsch., consumer and market knowledge and govt. rels. officer, 1999—2001. Sr. advisor James B. Hunt, Jr. Inst.; mem. edn. task force Bus. Roundtable, 1990—; mem. Advt. Coun. Bd. (vice chmn. 1994-96, chmn. 1997-98, hon. chair 1998-99); bd. dirs. Nat. Bd. Profl. Tchg. Stds. Pres. March of Dimes, Cin., 1981-84; mem. allocations com. Fine Arts Fund, Cin., 1987—; bd. dirs. Just Say No Internat., 1991-93; co-founder with USA Today, Coalition on Edn. Initiatives, 1991—; mem. Mayor's Commn. on Children, 1992—; vice chmn. Downtown Cin., Inc.; exec. com. Cin. Youth Collaborative; trustee United Way Cin., Ohio Schs. Devel. Corp.; bd. dirs. Edn. Excellence Partnership; participant Gov.'s Edn. Mgmt. Coun.; mem. Hamilton county Family and Children First Coun., 1993-94, Greater Cin. C. of C. (trustee 1994-97, chmn. Blue Chip campaign 1994-97, chmn. 1998); numerous other civic activities. Named Citizen of Yr., City of Wyoming, 1986, One of 200 Greater Cincinnatians, Cin. Bicentennial Commn., 1988; recipient award Nat. Coun. Negro Women, 1989, Field of Svc. Organization award United Way, 1991, Chairman's award Marketing Assn. of Am., 1991, Madison Square Boys and Girls Club award, 1991, Disting. Svc. award Ohio Assn. Colls. for Tchr. Edn., 1993, award Coun. for Acad. Excellence, 1994, U.S. Dept. Edn., 1994, The Seasongood Govt. award 1994, Nat. Vol. of Yr. Elaine Whitelaw award March of Dimes, 1994, Ohio Gov.'s award, 1995, Beech Acres Children's Advocate award, 1995, Nat. Govs.' Assn. Disting. Svc. award, 1995, Community Hero Torchbearer for the 1996 Olympic Torch Relay, 1996; Bob Wehling Vol. of Yr. award named in his honor March of Dimes Southwestern Ohio chpt., 1993, numerous others. Mem. Assn. Nat. Advertisers (Robert V. Goldstein award for Disting. Svc. 1993), Advt. Coun. (campaign dir. 1988—), Greater Cin. C. of C. (trustee, exec. com.), Queen City Club, Commonwealth Club, Phi Beta Kappa. Republican. Methodist. Avocations: running, reading, education, children's issues.*

WEHRWEIN-HUNT, JERI LYNN, elementary education educator; b. New Richmond, Wis., Aug. 13, 1952; d. Harlan Fredric and Olive Angeline (Steies) Wehrwein; 1 child, Katie Lynn. BS in Elem. Edn., BS in Spl. Edn., St. Cloud State U., 1973; MEd, U. Minn., 1990. cert. elem. and spl. edn. tchr., Minn. Coord. social studies curriculum Minneapolis Pub. Schs., 1977-78, tchr., 1973—2001, asst. spl. edn. camp program coord., 1982, coord. and tchr. gifted program, 1984-86; title I and family involvement coord., 2001—. Recipient recognition for outstanding environmental activities in the classroom, Minn. Atty. Gen., 1994. Mem. Am. Fedn. Tchrs., Minn. Fedn. Tchrs. Roman Catholic. Avocations: interior decorating, singing, theater. Office: Jenny Lind Elem Sch 5025 Bryant Ave N Minneapolis MN 55430-3500 E-mail: hjh55126@aol.com.

WEI, BENJAMIN MIN, engineering educator; b. Hebei, China, Aug. 11, 1930; s. Fu Shun and Yuan Qing (Zhang) W.; m. Diana Yun Dee; 1 child: Victor Mark. BSME, Chung Cheng Inst. Tech., 1953; MSME, Concordia U., 1970; PhD, Pa. State U., 1981. Mech. engr. Ordnance Corps Arsenal, Taipei, Taiwan, 1953-59; tchr. Wenshan High Sch., Taipei, 1960-61; teaching asst. New Brunswick (Can.) U., 1962-64; supr. Domtar Constrn. Materials Co., Can., 1964-66; computer programmer McGill U., Can., 1966-67, Montreal (Can.) U., 1967-68; tchr. Pierrefond Comprehensive High sch., Que., 1970-73; prof. Norfolk (Va.) State U., 1974—. Hon. prof., cons. Taiyuan U. Polytech. Contbr. articles to profl. jours. Mem. Statistical Quality Control of China. Home: 1152 Janaf Pl Norfolk VA 23502-2631

WEI, JAMES, chemical engineering educator, academic dean; b. Macao, China, Aug. 14, 1930; came to U.S., 1949, naturalized, 1960; s. Hsiang-chen and Nuen (Kwok) W.; m. Virginia Hong, Nov. 4, 1956; children: Alexander, Christina, Natasha, Randolph (dec.). BS in Chem. Engring, Ga. Inst. Tech., 1952; MS, MIT, 1954, ScD, 1955; grad., Advanced Mgmt. Program Harvard, 1969. From rsch. engr. to rsch. assoc. Mobil Oil, Paulsboro, NJ, 1956-62, sr. scientist Princeton, NJ, 1963-68, mgr. corp. planning N.Y.C., 1969-70; Allan P. Colburn prof. U. Del., Newark, 1971-77; Sherman Fairchild distinguished scholar Calif. Inst. Tech., 1977; Warren K. Lewis prof. MIT, Cambridge, 1977-91, head dept. chem. engring., 1977-88; Pomeroy and Betty Smith prof. chem. engring. Princeton (N.J.) U., 1991—, dean Sch. Engring. and Applied Sci., 1991—2002. Vis. prof. Princeton, 1962-63, Calif. Inst. Tech., 1965; cons. Mobil Oil Corp.; cons. com. on motor vehicle emissions Nat. Acad. Sci., 1972-74, 79-80; mem. sci. adv. bd. EPA, 1976-79; mem. Presdl. Pvt. Sector Survey Task Force on Dept. Energy, 1982-83 Bd. editors Chem. Tech, 1971-80, Chem. Engring. Communications, 1972—; cons. editor chem. engring. series, McGraw-Hill, 1964—; editor-in-chief: Advances in Chemical Engineering, 1980; Contbr. papers, monographs to profl. lit., The Structure of Chemical Processing Industries, 1979. Trustee Am. U. Beirut, 1998—, Smith Coll., 1999—. Recipient Am. Acad. Achievement Golden Plate award, 1966 [e]m. AIChE (dir. 1970-72, Inst. lectr. 1968, Profl. Progress award 1970, Walker award 1980, Lewis award 1985, v.p. 1987, pres. 1988, Founders award 1990), Am. Chem. Soc. (award in petroleum chemistry 1966), Nat. Acad. Engring. (nominating com. 1981, 96, peer com. 1980-82, membership com. 1983-85, Draper award com. 1995-97, chair chem. engring. sect. 1998-99), AAAS, Am. Acad. Arts and Scis., Academica Sinica of Taiwan, Sigma Xi. Home: 571 Lake Dr Princeton NJ 08540 Office: Princeton U Engring Quadrangle Princeton NJ 08544-5263 E-mail: jameswei@princeton.edu.

WEI, TAM DANG, mental health specialist, educator; b. Nghe An, Vietnam, Jan. 2, 1926; came to U.S., 1955; d. Huong Dang Van and Hien Hoang Thi; m. Lun Shin Wei, Aug. 18, 1955; children: Michael, Max, Manuel, Aline. BA in Philosophy, U. Hanoi, Vietnam, 1949; licentiate in edn. and psychology, U. Geneva, 1955; MEd in Ednl. Psychology, U. Ill., 1958, PhD in Ednl. Psychology, 1966. Cert. sch. psychologist, administrator, bilingual tchr. French and Vietnamese, Ill. Tche. elem. and h.s. Thanh Quan and Dong Khanh Schs., Vietnam, 1948-52; instr. ednl. psychology U. Ill., Urbana, 1962-67, asst. prof., 1967-69; sch. psychologist Ford-Iroquois Counties Spl. Edn. Coop., Ford County, Ill., 1970-81; dir. bilingual edn. program Champaign (Ill.) Sch. Dist. 4, 1982-85; mental health specialist East Ctrl. Ill. Refugee Mut. Assistance Ctr., Urbana, 1986—. Cons. psychology and mental health various schs., 1975—; mem. adv. bd. Ill. Coun. Multi-Cultural Edn., Springfield, 1977-79, Ill. Adv. Home Econ. Extension, Urbana, 1978-79, Opportunity Industrialization Ctr., Champaign, 1979-81, East Ctrl. Ill. Refugee Assistance Ctr., 1981-86. Author: Piaget's Concept of Classification, 1971, Handbook for Teachers of Refugee Students, 1977, Bilingual Exceptional Child, 1984, Vietnamese Refugee Students, 1980-84. Mem. Internat. Coun. Psychologists, Ill. Sch. Psychologists, Ill. Registry Psychologists with Spl. Skills, Nat. Assn. Vietnamese, Laotian and Cambodian Educators, Bilingual Educators. Avocations: reading, walking, bicycling, music, family activities. Office: East Ctrl Ill Ref Asst Ctr 302 S Birch St Urbana IL 61801-3201

WEICKSEL, CHARLENE MARIE, principal; b. York, Pa., June 16, 1945; d. Edward A. and Mary Elizabeth (Hoffman) Debes; m. Stephen A. Weicksel, Aug. 27, 1967; children: Ann, Andrew. B Music Edn., Westminster Choir Coll., 1967; MEd, Trenton State Coll., 1986. Cert. tchr., prin., supr., N.J. Tchr. Hillsborough Twp. Bd. Edn., Neshanic, N.J., 1967-87, curriculum supr. fine and performing arts, 1987-93; prin. Triangle Rd. Elem. Sch., Hillsborough, N.J., 1993—. Bd. dirs. Lenape Swim Club, Skillman, N.J., 1990-93, Raritan Valley Chorus, Belle Mead, N.J., 1991-92. Mem. NEA, Nat. Art Educators Assn., Nat. Assn. Elem. Sch. Prins., Art Educators N.J., N.J. Edn. Assn., Jazz Educators, N.J. Prins. and Suprs. Assn. Democrat. Presbyterian. Avocations: cross-stitch, crochet, knitting, writing, travel. Home: 302 Sunset Rd Skillman NJ 08558-1628 Office: 555 Amwell Rd Hillsborough NJ 08844-3409

WEIDEMANN, CELIA JEAN, social scientist, international business and financial development consultant; b. Denver, Dec. 6, 1942; d. John Clement and Hazel (Van Tuyl) Kirlin; m. Wesley Clark Weidemann, July 1, 1972; 1 child, Stephanie Jean. BS, Iowa State U., 1964; MS, U. Wis., Madison, 1970, PhD, 1973; postgrad., U. So. Calif., 1983. Advisor UN FAO, Ibadan, Nigeria, 1973-77; ind. rschr. Asia and Near East, 1977-78; program coord., asst. prof., rsch. assoc. U. Wis., Madison, 1979-81; chief inst. and human resources US AID, Washington, 1982-85; team leader, cons. Sumatra, Indonesia, 1984; dir. fed. econ. program Midwest Rsch. Inst., Washington, 1985-86; pres., founder, pres. emeritus Weidemann Assoc., Arlington, Va., 1986-2000; pres. Weidemann Found., 2000—. Cons. U.S. Congress, Aspen Inst., Ford Found., World Bank, Egypt, Nigeria, Gambia, Pakistan, Indonesia, AID, Thailand, Jamaica, Panama, Philippines, Sierra Leone, Kenya, Jordon, Poland, India, Egypt, Russia, Finnish Internat. Devel. Agy., Namibia, pvt. client Estonia, Lativa, Russia, Japan, Internat. Ctr. Rsch. on Women, Zaire, UN FAO, Ghana, Internat. Statis. Inst., The Netherlands, Global Exch., 1986-87, Asian Devel. Bank, Mongolia, Nepal, Vietnam, Bangladesh, Indonesia, Philippines; mem. bd. visitors Sch. Human Ecology, U. Wis., 2002—; peer reviewer NRC. Author: Planning Home Economics Curriculum for Social and Econ. Develop., Agrl. Ext. for Women Farmers in Africa, 1990, Fin. Services for Women, 1992, Egyptian Women and Micro.: The Invisible Entrepreneurs, 1992, Small Enterprise Develop. in Poland: Does Gender Matter?, 1994, Micro. and Gender in India, 1995, Supporting Women's Livelihoods: Microfin. That Works for the Majority, 2002; contbr. chpts. to books, articles to profl. jours. Am. Home Econ. Assn. fellow, 1969-73; grantee Ford Found., 1987-89. Mem. Nat. Acad. Sci., Soc. Internat. Devel., Am. Sociol. Assn., Assn. for Women in Devel. (pres. 1989, founder, bd. dir.), Coalition for Women's Econ. Devel. and Global Equality (co-chair), Internat. Devel. Conf. (bd. dirs., exec. com.), Internat. Platform Assn., Pi Lambda Theta, Omicron Nu. Avocations: mountain trekking, piano/pipe organ, canoeing, photography, poetry. Office: Weidemann Assocs Inc 933 N Kenmore St Ste 405 Arlington VA 22201-2236 E-mail: jweidemann@aol.com.

WEIDEMANN, JULIA CLARK, retired principal, educator; b. Batavia, N.Y., May 21, 1937; d. Edward Thomas and Grace Eloise (Kenna) Clark; m. Rudolph John Weidemann, July 9, 1960 (dec.); 1 child, Michael John (dec.). BA in English, Daemen Coll., 1958; MS in Edn., SUNY, Buffalo, 1961, MEd in Reading Edn., 1973, postgrad, 1985-86. Cert. sch. adminstr., supr. Tchr Buffalo Pub. Schs., 1958-61, 66-67; remedial reading tchr. West Seneca (N.Y.) Cen. Sch. Dist., 1972-79, coord. chpt. I reading program, 1974-79, reading coord., 1980-87; prin. Parkdale Elem. Sch. East Aurora (N.Y.) Union Free Sch., 1987—. Adj. prof. edn. Canisius Coll., Medaille Coll., Daemen Coll.; tchr. cons. Scott Foresman Lang. Arts Textbooks; sch. support team mem. N.Y. State Edn. Dept.; chmn. elem. com. staff devel. West Seneca Ctrl. Sch., 1985-87; mem. adv. coun. Medaille Coll.; chmn. various confs.; lectr. in field. Author numerous poems; invited poet Women's Impact Gallery, Buffalo, N.Y., 1996, 97. Mem. West Seneca Dist. Computer Adv. Com., 1980-87, East Aurora Hist. Soc., 1990—; mem. cmty. adv. coun. SUNY, Buffalo, 1994—, Women's Health Initiative, 1994-96; mem. Women's Action Coalition of Buffalo, 1994; pres. Roycroft Wordsmiths; mem. steering com. Kids Voting N.Y., 1996-99. Scholar Rosary Hill Coll., 1954, N.Y. State Regents, 1954; recipient Reading award Niagara Frontier Reading Coun., 1986. Mem. AAUW (life, pres. Buffalo br. 1994-95, exec. bd. dirs., named gift ednl. found., state bd. dirs. equity in edn. com. 1995—), Assn. Compensatory Edn. (pres. 1984-85, exec. bd. Region VI 1983-87, conf. chmn. Region VI 1985-87), Internat. Reading Assn. (acting chmn. 3d ea. regional reading conf. 1980), Niagara Frontier Reading Assn. (pres. 1979-80, fin. com. chmn., bd. dirs. 1973—), Daemen Coll. Alumni Assn. (bd. govs. 1987, chmn. alumni reunion weekend, chmn. sr. reception, Disting. Alumna 1989), Assn. Supervision and Devel., Assn. Tchr. Educators, Delta Kappa Gamma (pres., Ruth Fraser scholar 1986), Beta Zeta (pres.), Phi Delta Kappa (Buffalo-South chpt. 1989). Democrat. Roman Catholic. Home: 21 Nye Hill Rd East Aurora NY 14052-2651

WEIDEN, PAUL LINCOLN, cancer researcher, oncologist, educator; b. Portland, Oreg., Aug. 21, 1941; BA, Harvard U., 1963, MD, 1967. Intern U. Hosps., Cleve., 1967-68, resident medicine, 1968-69; fellow hematology and oncology U. Wash., Seattle, 1971-73; med. dir. Nat. Marrow Donor Program Collection Ctr., 1988-2001, Dendreon Corp., Seattle, 2001—02; cons. Bartlett Regional Hosp., Juneau, Alaska, 2001—; dir. clin. oncology Sonus Pharmaceuticals, Bothell, Wash., 2002—. Chmn. stem cell transplantation com. Virginia Mason Hosp., Seattle, 1991—2001, prin. investigator cmty. clin. oncology program, 1993—2001, med. dir. cancer clin. rsch. unit, 1995—2001, chmn. rsch. adv. com., 2000—01, emeritus physician, 2001—; clin. prof. U. Wash. Med. Sch., 1991—. Fellow ACP; mem. Am. Soc. Clin. Oncology, Am. Soc. Hematology, Am. Assn. Cancer Rsch., Am. Assn. Pharm. Physicians. Office: 22026 20th Ave SE Bothell WA 98021 E-mail: plweiden@aol.com.

WEIDENBAUM, MURRAY LEW, economist, educator; b. Bronx, N.Y., Feb. 10, 1927; s. David and Rose (Warshaw) Weidenbaum; m. Phyllis Green, June 13, 1954; children: Susan, James, Laurie. BBA, CCNY, 1948; MA, Columbia U., 1949; MPA, Princeton U., 1954, PhD, 1958; LLD, Baruch Coll., 1981, U. Evansville, 1983, McKendree Coll., 1993. Fiscal economist Bur. Budget, Washington, 1949—57; corp. economist Boeing Co., Seattle, 1958—62; sr. economist Stanford Rsch. Inst., Palo Alto, Calif., 1962—63; mem. faculty Washington U., St. Louis, 1964—, prof., chmn. dept. econs., 1966—69, Mallinckrodt prof., 1971—, dir. Ctr. for Study Am. Bus., 1974—81, Washington U., St. Louis, 1982—95; chmn. Ctr. for Study Am. Bus. Washington U., St. Louis, 1995—2000; asst. sec. econ. policy Treasury Dept., 1969—71; chmn. Coun. of Econ. Advs., 1981—82; hon. chmn. Weidenbaum Ctr. on the Economy, Govt. and Pub. Policy, St. Louis, 2001—. Chmn. rsch. adv. com. St. Louis Regional Indsl. Devel. Corp., 1965—69; exec. sec. Pres.'s Com. on Econ. Impact of Def. and Disarmament, 1964; mem. U.S. Fin. Investment Adv. Panel, 1970—72; cons. various firms and instns.; chmn. U.S. Commn. to Rev. the Trade Deficit, 1999—2000. Author: Federal Budgeting, 1964, Modern Public Sector, 1969, Economics of Peacetime Defense, 1974, Economic Impact of the Vietnam War, 1967, Government-Mandated Price Increases, 1975, The Future of Business Regulation, 1980, Rendezvous With Reality: The American Economy After Reagan, 1988, Rendezvous With Reality: The American Economy After Reagan, paperback edit., 1990, Business, Government, and the Public, 1990, Small Wars, Big Defense, 1992, The Bamboo Network, 1996, Business and Government in the Global Marketplace, 2004; mem. editl. bd.: Publius, 1971—2004, Jour. Econ. Issues,

1972—75, Challenge, 1974—81, 1983—, Business and the Contemporary World, 1997—2000. With U.S. Army, 1945. Named Banbury fellow, Princeton U., 1952—54; named to Free Market Hall of Fame, 1983; recipient Alexander Hamilton medal, U.S. Dept. Treasury, 1971, Disting. Writer award, Georgetown U., award for disting. tchg., Freedoms Found., 1980, award for best book in econs., Assn. Am. Pubs., 1993. Fellow: Assn. for Pvt. Enterprise Edn. (Adam Smith award 1986), City Coll. Alumni Assn. (Townsend Harris medal 1969), Soc. Tech. Comm., Nat. Assn. Bus. Economists, Cosmos. Office: Washington Univ Weidenbaum Ctr 1 Brookings Dr Saint Louis MO 63130-4899

WEIDMAN, JOHN CARL, II, education educator, consultant; b. Ephrata, Pa., Oct. 3, 1945; s. John Carl and Mary Elizabeth (Grube) W.; m. Carla Sue Fassnacht, Aug. 20, 1967; children: Jonathan Scott, Rebecca Mary. AB in Sociology cum laude, Princeton U., 1967; AM, U. Chgo., 1968, PhD, 1974. Acting asst. prof. edn. U. Minn., Mpls., 1970-74, asst. prof. edn., sociology and Am. studies, 1974-77; sr. rsch. assoc. Bur. Social Sci. Rsch., Inc., Washington, 1977-78; assoc. prof. edn. and sociology U. Pitts., 1979-86, prof. edn. and sociology, 1986—, chmn. dept. adminstrv. and policy studies, 1986-93. Cons. Nat. Ctr. Adminstrv. Justice, Youthwork, Inc., Upper Midwest Tri-Racial Gen. Assistance Ctr., Acad. for Ednl. Devel., Asian Devel. Bank, Indonesia, Laos, Kyrgyz Republic, Uzbekistan, German Acad. Exch. Svc., Mongolia, Sema-Belgium, Uzbekistan; UNESCO chair higher edn. rsch. Maseno U. Coll., Kenya, 1993. Author: rsch. monographs; mem. editl. bd. Rev. of Higher Edn., 1984-88, Am. Ednl. Rsch. Jour., 1991-92, 96-98; co-author: Research on Higher Education in Developing Countries: Suggested Agendas and Research Strategies, 1991, Implementing a Faculty Assessment System: A Case Study of the University of Pittsburgh-USA, 1994, Higher Education Costs and Tuition, 1996, Higher Education in Korea: Tradition and Adaptation, 2000, Socialization of Graduate and Professional Students: A Perilous Passage?, 2001, Finance Higher Education, 2001; cons. editor Jour. Higher Edn., 1989—; contbr. chpts. to books, articles to profl. jours. Bd. dirs. Sch. Vol. Assn. Pitts., 1982-90, pres., 1984-87. Grantee U.S. Office Edn., 1971-73, Spencer Found., 1973-76, Nat. Inst. Edn., 1976-79, NEH, 1985-86, Asian Devel. Bank, Laos, 1995-96, Mongolia, 1997-2000, Indonesia, 2001, Krygyz Republic, 2003; Fulbright scholar U. Augsburg, Germany, 1986-87. Mem. Am. Ednl. Rsch. Assn. (sec. postsecondary divsn. 1987-89), Am. Sociol. Assn., Assn. Study of Higher Edn., Comparative and Internat. Edn. Soc., Phi Delta Kappa. Office: U Pitts 5S38 Posvar Hall 230 S Bouquet St Pittsburgh PA 15260

WEIGAND, JAN CHRISTINE, elementary education educator, computer specialist; b. Kirksville, Mo., July 22, 1952; d. Charles Leo and Helen Frances (Myers) Jeffries; m. Douglas Walter Weigand, July 29, 1978; 1 child, Jeffrey Douglas. BS in Edn., Valparaiso (Ind.) U., 1974; MEd in Tech. in Edn., Nat.-Louis U., Wheaton, Ill., 1999; MA in Edn. Tchg. and Leadership, St. Xavier U., Chgo., 2001. Tchr. 2d grade Harrison St. Sch., Geneva, Ill., 1974-77, tchr. 1st grade, 1977—, computer coord., 1987—. Mem. NEA, Ill. Edn. Assn., Internat. Reading Assn., No. Ill. Reading Coun., Geneva Edn. Assn. Methodist. Avocations: genealogy, crafts. Office: Harrison St Sch 201 Harrison St Geneva IL 60134

WEIGEL, PAUL HENRY, biochemistry educator, researcher, consultant; b. N.Y.C., Aug. 11, 1946; s. Helmut and Jeanne Weigel; m. Nancy Shulman, June 15, 1968 (div. Dec. 1987); 1 child, Dana J.; m. Janet Oka, May 17, 1992. BA in Chemistry, Cornell U., 1968; MS in Biochemistry, Johns Hopkins U., Balt., 1969, PhD in Biochemistry, 1975. NIH postdoctoral fellow Johns Hopkins U., Balt., 1975-78; asst. prof. U. Tex. Med. Br., Galveston, Tex., 1978-82, assoc. prof., 1982—94, prof. biochemistry and cell biology, 1987-94, vice chmn. dept. human biol. chemistry and genetics, 1990-93, acting chmn. dept. human biology, chemistry and genetics, 1992-93; prof., chmn. dept. biochemistry and molecular biology U. Okla. Health Scis. Ctr., Okalahoma City, 1994—; co-founder Hyalose LLC, 2000—. Mem. NIH Pathobiochemistry Study Sect., Washington, 1985-87; cons. Teltech, Mpls., 1985—, Hyalose LLC 2000—. Contbr. articles to profl. jours.; patentee in field. Treas. Bayou Chateau Neighborhood Assn., Dickinson, Tex., 1981-83, v.p., 1983-84, pres., 1984-86. With U.S. Army, 1969-71. Grantee NIH, 1979—, Office Naval Rsch., 1983-87, Tex. Biotech., 1989-94, Okla. Ctr. Advancement Sci. and Tech., 2000-03; recipient Disting. Tchr. award U. Tex. Med. Br., 1989, Disting. Rsch. award, 1989. Mem. Am. Chem. Soc., Am. Soc. Cell Biology, Am. Soc. Biochemistry and Molecular Biology (mem. pub. affairs adv. com., 2000-03), Assn. Med. and Grad. Depts. Biochemistry (web master, bd. dirs., 2002—). Democrat. Lutheran. Avocations: raquetball, basketball card collecting, poetry, camping. Home: 817 Hollowdale Edmond OK 73003-3022 Office: U Okla Health Scis Ctr Dept Biochem & Mol Biology Bmsb Rm 860 Oklahoma City OK 73190-0001 E-mail: paul-weigel@ouhsc.edu.

WEIGLE, MICHAELINE JOANNE, school system administrator; b. Schlupfing, Germany, Jan. 14, 1946; d. Michael and Kataryna (Zadora) Gratkowski; m. John Francis Weigle, Aug. 14, 1971; children: Matthew, Michael, Mark, Adrienne. BA English, Mercy Coll., Detroit, 1969. Tchr. English Immaculate Conception Ukrainian Cath. High Sch., Warren, Mich., 1984-94, prin., 1994-98; asst. prin. Mass. Ednl. Adminstrn., Wayne State U., Warren, 1998—99, prin., 1999—. Home: 4234 Parent Ave Warren MI 48092-5519 E-mail: mjweigleichs@yahoo.com.

WEIGLEY, RUSSELL FRANK, history educator; b. Reading, Pa., July 2, 1930; s. Frank Francis and Meta Beulah (Rohrbach) W.; m. Emma Eleanor Seifrit, July 27, 1963; children: Jared Francis Guldin, Catherine Emma Rohrbach. BA, Albright Coll., 1952; MA, U. Pa., 1953, PhD, 1956; HLD (hon.), Albright Coll., 1978. Instr. history U. Pa., Phila., 1956-58; asst. prof. Drexel Inst. Tech., Phila., 1958-60, assoc. prof., 1960-62, Temple U., Phila., 1962-64, prof. history, 1964-85, Disting. Univ. prof., 1985-98, prof. emeritus, 1998—. Vis. prof. Dartmouth Coll., Hanover, N.H., 1967-68; U.S. Army vis. prof. mil. history rsch. U.S. Army War Coll., U.S. Army Mil. History Rsch. Collection, Carlisle Barracks, Pa., 1973-74; pres. Am. Mil. Inst., Washington, 1975-76. Author: Quartermaster General of the Union Army: A Biography of M.C. Meigs, 1959, Towards an American Army: Military Thought from Washington to Marshall, 1962, History of the United States Army, 1967, 84, The Partisan War: The South Carolina Campaign of 1780-82, 1970, The American Way of War, 1973, Eisenhower's Lieutenants, 1981 (Atheneum of Phila. Spl. award for Nonfiction by a Phila. Author, 1983), The Age of Battles: The Quest for Decisive Warfare from Breitenfeld to Waterloo, 1991, A Great Civil War: A Military and Political History, 1862-1865, 2000 (Lincoln prize 2001); editor: The American Military: Readings in the History of the Military in American Society, 1969, New Dimensions in Military History, 1976, Philadelphia: A 300-Year History, 1982. Mem. hist. adv. commn. Dept. of Army, Washington, 1976-79, 88—92, 2003—, Pa. Hist. Records Adv. Com., Harrisburg, 1977-79; bd. dirs. Masonic Libr., Mus. of Pa., The Grand Lodge of Masons of Pa., Phila., 1990-95, 97—. Penrose Fund grantee Am. Philos. Soc., 1958; fellow John Simon Guggenheim Meml. Found., 1969-70; recipient Samuel Eliot Morison prize Am. Mil. Inst., 1989, Lincoln prize, 2001. Mem. Hist. Soc. Pa. (vice chmn. 1989-93, councilor 1983-89, 92-98, emeritus 1998—), Pa. Hist. Assn. (pres. 1975-78, v.p. 1967-75, coun. 1967—, editor jour. 1962-67), Am. Hist. Assn., Orgn. Am. Historians, Soc. Mil. Hist. (Disting. Book award 1992), So. Hist. Assn., Soc. Am. Historians Inc., Interuniv. Seminar on Armed Forces and Soc., Am. Philos. Soc., Masons (33d degree, Scottish rite supreme coun. no. Masonic jurisdiction 1999). Democrat. Unitarian Universalist. Home: 327 S Smedley St Philadelphia PA 19103-6717 Office: Temple U Dept History Philadelphia PA 19122 E-mail: rweigley@unix.temple.edu.

WEIGNER, BRENT JAMES, secondary education educator; b. Pratt, Kans., Aug. 19, 1949; s. Doyle Dean and Elizabeth (Hanger) W.; m. Sue Ellen Weber Hume, Mar. 30, 1985; children: Russell John Hume, Scott William Hume. BA, U. No. Colo., 1972; MEd, U. Wyo., 1977, PhD, 1984. Cert. Nat. Bd. for Profl. Tchg. Stds. Counselor, coach Olympia Sport Village, Upson, Wis., 1968; dir. youth sports F.E. Warren AFB, Cheyenne, 1973—74; instr. geography Laramie County Comm. Coll., Cheyenne, 1974-75; tchr. social sci. McCormick Jr. HS, Cheyenne, 1975—, Laramie County Sch. Dist. 1, Cheyenne, 1975—; head social studies dept. McCormick Jr. HS, 1987-99, 2001—02; curriculum adv. coun. chmn. Laramie County Sch. Dist. No. 1, 1988-89. Lectr. ednl. methods U. Wyo., 1989, clin. faculty, 1992-94; nat. chmn. Jr. Olympic cross-country com. AAU, Indpls., 1980-81; pres. Wyo. Athletic Congress, 1981-87; tchr. cons. Nat. Geog. Soc. Geography Inst., 1991, North Pole Marathon cons. Global Expdns.; South Pole marathon cons. and guide Adventure Network Internat., 2002-03; alt. cert. assessor Wyo. State Dept. Edn., 2002—; cons. Adventure Network Internat., 1999-2002; presenter, cons. in field. Fgn. exch. student U. Munich, 1971-72; head coach Cheyenne Track Club, 1976—, pres., 1980; race dir. Wyo. Marathon, 1978—; deacon 1st Christian Ch., Cheyenne, 1987-90, elder, 1991-93; rep. candidate gen. election Wyo. Legis., 1991; bd. dirs. United Med. Ctr. of Wyo. Found., 1995—, Cheyenne Boys and Girls Club, 1999—; keynote spkr., Okla. Marathon, 2002. Named Wyoming State bd. edn. Disting. Educator, Wyo. U.S. West Outstanding Tchr., 1989, Wyo. Coun. for the Social Studies K-8 Tchr. of Yr., 1994-95, Jr. High Coach of Yr., Wyo. Coaches Assn., 1996, Vol. of Yr., office Youth Alternatives, 2000; fellow Taft Found., 1976, Earthwatch-Hearst fellow, Punta Allen, Mex., summer 1987, Christa McAuliffe fellow, 1991-92, Wyo. Christa Mcauliffe Fellowship Selection Com., 1994, 95, 01; Fulbright grantee, Israel, summer 1984; Fulbright scholar Ghana and Senegal, 1990; People-to-People Internat. Ambassador to Vietnam, 1993; recipient Masons of Wyo. Disting. Tchr. award 1994. Mem. NEA, Nat. Network for Ednl. Renewal, Nat. Coun. Social Studies, Nat. Coun. Geog. Edn., Dominican Rep. Nat. Coun. for Geog. Edn. (Cram scholarship 1992), Wyo. Geog. Alliance (steering com., Amazon Workshop Fellowship 1998), Cheyenne Tchrs. Edn. Assn. (govtl. rels. com., instrn. and profl. devel. com.), U. No. Colo. Alumni Assn., Cheyenne C. of C., Wyo. Heritage Soc., Wyo. Edn. Assn. (World Book Ency. classroom rsch. project cons. 1976—, accountability task force 1989-90), Fulbright Alumni Assn. (life), U. Wyo. Alumni Assn. (life), Cheyenne Sunrise, Lions (bd. dirs. Cheyenne 1987, pres. 1995-96, 1st v.p. 1993-94, Melvin Jones Fellowship, 1995), Phi Delta Kappa (life, bd. dirs. Cheyenne 1989—, v.p., edn. award for rsch. 1990, pres. 1992-93, ednl. found. rep. 1993-94, area 4-D coord. 1994-95, Gerald Read Internat. Seminar scholar 1994; mem. outstanding doctoral dissertation com. 1994, 96), Phi Delta Kappa (Ed. award 2000). Achievements include first to run ultramarathon races on all seven continents, 1999; South Pole Ultramarathon champion, 2003; sr. men's nat. snowshoe champion, 2003. Home: 402 W 31st St Cheyenne WY 82001-2527 Office: McCormick Jr HS 6000 Education Dr Cheyenne WY 82009-3991 E-mail: RunWyo@msn.com.

WEIL, IRWIN, Slavic languages and literature educator; b. Cin., Apr. 16, 1928; s. Sidney and Florence (Levy) W.; m. Vivian Weil, Dec. 27, 1950; children: Martin, Alice, Daniel. AB, U. Chgo., 1948, MA, 1951; PhD, Harvard U., 1960. Sr. social sci. research analyst Library of Congress, 1951-54; teaching fellow Harvard U., 1956-58; mem. faculty Brandeis U., 1958-65; mem. faculty dept. Slavic langs. and lit. Northwestern U., Evanston, Ill., 1966—, chmn. dept., 1976-82. Vis. prof. U. Moscow, Soviet Acad. Scis.; set up series of internat. symposia between Am. scholars and USSR Acad. Scis.; founder 1st Soviet-Am. TV Student Competition in Lit., 1988-89. Author books and articles pub. in field, pub. in U.S.A. and Russia. Recipient Pushkin Internat. gold medal for outstanding teaching and research, 1984, Outstanding Teaching award Northwestern U. Alumni Assn., 1987, Tempo All-Professor Team, Humanities, Chicago Tribune, 1993; Ford Found. fellow, 1954-55. Mem. Am. Assn. Tchrs. Slavic and East European Langs. (exec. sec. 1962-68, Excellence in Teaching award 1993), Am. Coun. Tchrs. Russian (v.p. 1975-79, pres. 1980-84), Internat. Assn. Profs. Russian (founding U.S. mem.). Jewish. Achievements incude establishing TV competition on American and Russian literature between American and Russian high schoolers. Office: Northwestern U Slavic Dept Evanston IL 60208-0001

WEIL, MICHELLE COHEN, special education educator; b. N.Y.C. d. Theodore Samuel and Frances (Sadofsky) Cohen; m. Warren Jay Weil, June 14, 1959; children: Ami Lisa, Wendy Marcella, Frederic Seth. BA, U. R.I., 1959; MA in Spl. Edn., Coll. New Rochelle, 1980; 6th yr. cert., NYU, 1984. 2nd grade tchr. P.S. 165 Manhattan (N.Y.), 1959-61; tchr. learning disabled P.S. 65 Bronx (N.Y.), 1972-80; tchr. moms spl. edn. P.S. 89 Bronx, 1980-85; reading coord., tchr. emotional handicapped P.S. 17X at 92X Bronx, 1985-90; reading coord., tchr. emotionally handicapped P.S. 188X at 92X, Bronx, 1990—. Mentor, 1986—; cons. N.Y.C. Bd. Edn., Manhattan, 1989-90; del. NYSUT, 1990-93; tchr. English Poland, 1993; tchr. hosp. schs., N.Y.C.. Mem. United Fedn. Tchrs. (chpt. chair 1988, 1999-2003), Coun. for Exceptional Children, Pi Lambda Theta, Epsilon Pi Tau, Phi Delta. Avocations: sailing, archeology, travel, furniture refinishing. Home: 37 Lynwood Rd Scarsdale NY 10583-2701

WEIMAN, HEIDI, early childhood education educator; b. Chgo., July 5, 1952; d. Edwin and Sandra (Cordell) W. AA, Kendall Coll., 1972; BA summa cum laude, Northeastern Ill. U., 1992, MA in Spl. Edn., 1995; postgrad., Loyola U., 1996—. Early interventionist Home Infant Stimulation Program, Chgo., 1976-78; tchr. aid, arts and crafts tchr. Ill. Deaf-Blind Svc. Ctr. and Sch., Chgo., 1978-80; head tchr. Lad and Lassie Pre-Sch., Evanston, Ill., 1981; child care worker Jewish Children's Bur., Chgo., 1981; tchr. pre-sch. Sunshine Pre-Sch., Chgo., 1982-83; tchr. kindergarten and primary sch. aged, program coord., spl. educator, interventionist Sunshine Sch., Chgo., 1982-93; dir. George's Sunshine Preschool & Kindergarten, Chgo., 1993-95. Free lance tutor, Chgo., 1969--; adv. bd. Cook County Child Care Resource and Referral N. Satellit Dist., Chgo., 1991—; dir., head tchr., early internventionist state prekindergarten at-risk program Albany Park Comty. Ctr., Chgo., 1995; instr., acad. advisor early childhood edn. program Northeastern Ill. U., 1996; instr. child devel. program Truman Coll., City Colls. Chgo., 1997—; edn. cons., tchr. trainer, 1990—. Author, illustrator: Mother Goose Yesterday and Today; author, lyricist children's rhymes and lyrics; inventor: interactive learning materials and board games; choreographer adaptations of ethnic dances for young children; designer multicultural curriculum and costumes, 1990-95, Sunshine Sch., editor newsletter, 1991-95. Vol. tchr.'s asst. Head Start P. Sheridan Sch., Chgo., 1968; tutor Avalon Park Tutoring Project, Chgo., 1968-69; food distributor Operation Breadbasket, Chgo., 1969-72; counselor Urban Gateways, Wilmette, Winnetka, Ill., 1969; child care worker Kibbutz Palmachim and Kibbutz Sarid, Rishon Le Zion and Afula, Israel, 1973-74; vol. hotline Parental Stress Svcs./Child Abuse Prevention Svcs., Chgo., 1993-94; child life worker Children's Meml. Med. Ctr., Chgo., 1995. Recipient Excellence in Child Care award Pre-Sch. Owners Ill. Assn., 1991, Disting. Accomplishment in Scientific Literacy Workshops, Chgo. Techr.'s Ctr., 1992, Outstanding Attendance and Contribution in Adminstrv. Tng. Jane Addams Hull House Acad. Achievement award Univ. Without Walls, 1992. Mem. Nat. Ill. and Chgo. Assns. for the Edn. Young Children, Assn. for Childhood Edn. Internat. (Hall of Excellence citation 1993), Assn. for Supervision and Curriculum Devel., Ill. Sch. Age Child Care Network, Ill. Assn. Infant Mental Health, World Assn. Infant Mental Health, Coun. Exceptional Children (divsn. early childhood). Avocations: writing poetry, interior decorating, intercultural studies and dancing, tennis. Office: City Coll Chgo Truman Coll Dept Social Scis 1145 W Wilson Ave Chicago IL 60640-6063

WEINBERG, HELEN ARNSTEIN, American art and literature educator; b. Orange, N.J., June 17, 1927; d. Morris Jerome and Jeannette (Tepperman) Arnstein; m. Kenneth Gene Weinberg, Sept. 12, 1949; children: Janet Sue Weinberg Strassner, Hugh Benjamin, John Arnstein. BA in English Lit., Wellesley Coll., 1949; MA in English Lit., Western Res. U., 1953, PhD in English Lit., 1966. Teaching fellow Ohio State U., Columbus, 1949-51, Western Res. U., Cleve., 1953-57; instr. to prof. Cleve. (Ohio) Inst. Art, 1958—. Standing officer Coll. English Assn. Ohio, 1987-90; vis. tchr. NYU, 1985, Sch. Visual Art's, 1981; lecture tours Israel, 1968, 70, 71. Author: The New Novel in America: The Kafkan Mode in Contemporary Fiction, 1970. Recipient fellowship in art history NEH, Columbia U., N.Y.C., 1977-78; Recipient Am. Culture grantee NEH/Vassar Coll., 1993. Mem. AAUP, Modern Lang. Assn., Coll. Art Assn. Democrat. Jewish. Home: 3015 Huntington Rd Shaker Heights OH 44120-2407 Office: Cleve Inst Art 11141 East Blvd Cleveland OH 44106-1710

WEINBERG, LOUISE, law educator, author; b. N.Y.C. m. Steven Weinberg; 1 child, Elizabeth. AB summa cum laude, Cornell U.; JD, Harvard U., 1969, LLM, 1974. Bar: Mass. Sr. law clk. Hon. Chas. E. Wyzanski, Jr., Boston, 1971-72; assoc. in law Bingham, Dana & Gould, Boston, 1969-72; teaching fellow Harvard Law Sch., Boston, 1972-74; lectr. law Brandeis U., Waltham, Mass., 1974; assoc. prof. law Suffolk U., Boston, 1974-76, prof., 1977-80; vis. assoc. prof. law Stanford U., Palo Alto, Calif., 1976-77; vis. prof. law U. Tex., Austin, 1979; prof. law Sch. Law, U. Tex., Austin, 1980-84, Thompson prof. law, 1984-90, Andrews and Kurth prof. law, 1990-92; Fulbright and Jaworski regents rsch. prof. U. Tex., Austin, 1991-92, Angus G. Wynne, Sr. prof. civil jurisprudence, 1992-97, Fondren chair faculty excellence, 1995—, Eugene R. Smith Centennial rsch. prof. law, 1993-97, holder William B. Bates chair adminstrn. justice, 1997—. Vis. scholar Hebrew U., Jerusalem, 1989; Forum fellow World Econ. Forum, Davos, Switzerland, 1995—; pub. spkr., lectr. in field. Author: Federal Courts: Judicial Federalism and Judicial Power, 1994, and ann. supplements; co-author: Conflict of Laws, 1990, 2d edit., 2002; contbr. chpts. to books, articles to profl. jours. Bd. dirs. Ballet Austin, 1986-88, Austin Coun. on Fgn. Affairs, 1985—. Recipient Disting. Educator award Tex. Exes Assn., 1996. Mem.: Am. Constn. Soc., Maritime Law Assn., Tex. Asian C. of C., Assn. Am. Law Schs. (chmn. com. on conflict laws 1991—93, exec. com. sect. on fed. cts. 2001—02, program chair 2002—03, chair 2003—, treas. sect. on admiralty 2003—), The Philos. Soc. Tex., Am. Law Inst. (consultative com. complex litigation 1989—93, consultative com. enterprise liability 1990—95, adv. group fed. judicial code revision project 1996—2001), Scribes, Phi Kappa Phi, Phi Beta Kappa. Office: U Tex Sch Law 727 Dean Keeton St Austin TX 78705-3224 E-mail: lweinberg@mail.law.utexas.edu.

WEINBERG, RUTHMARIE LOUISE, special education educator, researcher; b. Woodbury, N.J., Feb. 9, 1953; d. Louis Albert Schopfer, Sr. and Ruth Marie (Bilse) Schopfer; m. Robert Weinberg, June 26, 1982. AS Human Svcs., Camden County Coll., 1973; BA Tchr. of the Handicapped, Glassboro State Coll., 1975; MA Sch. Adminstrn., Rowan U., 1998. Cert. tchr. of the handicapped 1975, supr. 1998, prin./supr. 1998. Supr. of cottage life, tchr. and supr. of mentally retarded Am. Inst. Mental Studies, Vineland, NJ, 1975—79; spl. edn. tchr. Haddon Heights (N.J.) H.S., 1979—. Girl Scout leader for clients Am. Inst. Mental Studies, Vineland, NJ, 1975—79, supr. summer recreation program, 1975—79. Recipient Gov.'s award for excellence in tchg., Gov. Florio and Commr. John Ellis, N.J., 1991. Mem.: Haddon Heights Ednl. Assn., N.J. Ednl. Assn., Nat. Ednl. Assn. Avocations: music, dancing, sports, nature walks, exploring new horizons. Home: 422 Austin Ave Barrington NJ 08007 Office: Haddon Heights Jr & Sr HS 301 2nd Ave Haddon Heights NJ 08035-1407

WEINBERG, SYLVAN LEE, cardiologist, educator, author, editor; b. Nashville, June 14, 1923; s. Abraham J. and Beatrice (Kottler) W.; m. Joan Hutzler, Jan. 29, 1956; children: Andrew Lee, Leslie. BS, Northwestern U., 1945, MD, 1948. From intern to resident, fellow Michael Reese Hosp., Chgo., 1947-51; attending physician Good Samaritan Hosp., Dayton, Ohio, 1953-99, chief of cardiology, 1966-99, founding dir. coronary care unit, 1967-99; clin. prof. medicine Wright State U., Dayton, 1975—; dir. med. edn. Dayton Heart Hosp., 2000—. Former panelist Med. Affairs, nat. TV; pres. Weinberg Marcus Cardiomed. Group, Inc., 1970-99; pres. Arts & Comms. Internat., Inc., 1995—. Author: An Epitaph for Merlin and Perhaps for Medicine, 1983, The Golden Age of Medical Science and the Dark Age of Health Care Delivery, 2000; founding editor Dayton Medicine, 1980—, Heart & Lung, 1972-87, The American Heart Hosp. Jour., 2002—; contbr. articles to profl. jours. Capt. U.S. Army, 1951-53, Korea. Recipient Army Commendation medal, Richard A. DeWall MD award for excellence in cardiology, Am. Heart Assn., 2001, Outstanding Pub. Svc. award, Ohio State Senate, 1980. Fellow ACP (Ohio Laureate award 1997), Am. Coll. Cardiology (editor in chief jour. ACCEL 1985-2000, pres. 1993-94), Am. Coll. Chest Physicians (pres. 1984); mem. Montgomery County Med. Soc. (pres. 1980). Avocations: writing, travel, golf. Home: 4555 Southern Blvd Dayton OH 45429-1118 Office: Dayton Heart Hosp 707 S Edwin Moses Blvd Dayton OH 45408 E-mail: slwjal@aol.com.

WEINBLATT, CHARLES SAMUEL, university administrator, employment consultant; b. Toledo, Dec. 23, 1952; s. Morris and Clara (Volk) W.; m. Frances Barbara Auslander, Aug. 12, 1973; children: Brian J., Lauren M. BA, U. Toledo, 1974. Cert. edn. and tng. counselor, Ohio. Psychiat. counselor St. Vincent Hosp., Toledo, 1974-77; vocat., rehab. counselor Goodwill Industries, Toledo, 1977-85; employment cons., pvt. practice Toledo, 1985—; tng. counselor UAW Chrysler, Perrysburg, Ohio, 1987; dir. divsn. orgn. devel. and leadership U. Toledo, 1988—. Employment svcs. cons. Employers' Assn. Toledo, 1985-90; outplacement cons. Toledo Pub. Schs., 1986; spkr. in field of labor and mgmt. rels., employee involvement. Author: Job Seeking Skills for Students, 1987. Mem. Toledo Vision Com., 1989-90. Recipient Quality Improvement award Chrysler, 1987, cert. Am. Inst. Banking, 1989. Mem. ASTD, Ohio Continuing Higher Edn. Assn., Toledo Area Human Resource Assoc., World Future Soc. Jewish. Avocations: music, sports, gardening. Home: 5118 Brenden Way Sylvania OH 43560-2223 Office: U Toledo Seagate Campus 401 Jefferson Ave Toledo OH 43604-1063 E-mail: cweinbl@utnet.utoledo.edu.

WEINER, JEROME HARRIS, mechanical engineering educator; b. N.Y.C., Apr. 5, 1923; s. Barnet and Dora (Muchar) W.; m. Florence Mensch, June 24, 1950; children: Jonathan David, Eric Daniel. B. Mech. Engring., Cooper Union U., 1943; A.M., Columbia U., 1946, PhD, 1952. Mem. faculty Columbia U., N.Y.C., 1952-68, prof. mech. engring., 1960-68, acting chmn. dept., 1961-62; L. Herbert Ballou Univ. prof. Brown U., Providence, 1968-93; L. Herbert Ballou Univ. prof. emeritus, 1993—. Author: (with B.A. Boley) Theory of Thermal Stresses, 1960, Statistical Mechanics of Elasticity, 1983. Fulbright research scholar Rome, Italy, 1958-59, Haifa, Israel, 1965- 66; Guggenheim fellow, 1965-66 Mem. Am. Phys. Soc., Am. Math. Soc., ASME Home: 24 Taber Ave Providence RI 02906-4113 Office: Brown U 79 Waterman St Providence RI 02912-9079

WEINER, KATHY CAROLE, secondary educator; b. Ardmore, Okla., Sept. 24, 1952; d. Walter Norman Cross and Carole Pearl (Cottle) Gossett; children: Nicholas, Patrick. BS in Edn., Okla. State U., 1974; MEd, Cen. State U., 1976. Tchr. Putnam City Schs., Oklahoma City, 1975-90, Durant (Okla.) Schs., 1990—. Mem. NEA, ASCD, Okla. Edn. Assn., Durant Edn. Assn., Nat. Coun. Tchrs. English, Delta Kappa Gamma. Home: 902 Crooked Oak Dr Durant OK 74701-2218 Office: Durant High Sch 802 W Walnut St Durant OK 74701-3233

WEINER, LYNN YVETTE, history educator; b. Detroit, Mich., Feb. 8, 1951; d. Charles Mendel and Audrey (Allen) W.; m. Thomas Glenn Moher, May 5, 1974; children: Andrew Allen, Jeffrey Stephen. AB, U. Mich., 1972; MA, Boston U., 1975, PhD, 1981. Rsch. assoc. Jane Addams papers project U. Ill., Chgo., 1983-84; vis. asst. prof. Northwestern U., Evanston, Ill., 1990-91; instr., lectr. history Roosevelt U., Chgo., 1985-90, assoc. prof., 1991-97, assoc. dean Arts and Scis., 1993—2001, prof., 1997—, dean Arts and Scis., 2001—, interim provist and exec. v.p., 2003—. Exec. dir.

Coordinating Com. on Women in Hist. Profession/Conf. Group on Women's History, 1989-91. Author: From Working Girl to Working Mother: The Female Labor Force in the U.S., 1820-1980, 1985 (nominated for Pulitzer prize 1985); also articles and book revs. Fellow NEH, 1988. Mem. Am. Hist. Assn., Orgn. Am. Historians (Binkley-Stephenson prize 1995), Am. Studies Assn., Chgo. Area Women's History Assn., LWV, NOW. Democrat. Jewish. Home: 527 Clinton Ave Oak Park IL 60304-1110 Office: Roosevelt U History Dept 430 S Michigan Ave Chicago IL 60605-1394

WEINER, MYRON FREDERICK, psychiatrist, educator, clinical investigator; b. Atlantic City, June 4, 1934; s. Jack and Eva (Friedman) W.; m. Jeanette Harmon; children: Daniel, Gary, Darrel, Holli. MD, Tulane U., 1957. Diplomate Am. Bd. Psychiatry, qualifications in geriatric psychiatry. Intern Parkland Hosp., Dallas, 1957-58, resident, 1960-63; fellow in geriatrics and adult devel. Mt. Sinai Med. Ctr., N.Y.C., 1984-85; clin. instr. to assoc. prof. U. Tex. Southwestern Med. Ctr., Dallas, 1963-77, prof. psychiatry, 1980—; head geriatric psychiatry U. Tex Southwestern Med. Ctr., Dallas, 1985-99; assoc. prof. neurology U. Tex. Southwestern Med. Ctr., Dallas, 1997, head clin. core Alzheimer Disease Ctr., 1988—, vice-chair clin. svcs. psychiatry, 1993—. Aradine S. Ard chair in brain rsch. U. Tex. Southwestern Med. Ctr., 1993, Dorothy L. and John P. Harbin chair in Alzheimer's Disease rsch., 1997. Author: Techniques of Group Psychotherapy, 1984, Practical Psychotherapy, 1986; editor: The Dementias: Diagnosis and Management, 1991, 3d edit., 2003; co-author: The Psychotherapist Patient Privilege, 1987. Mem. Tex. Alzheimer's Coun., 1991-98. Capt. USAF, 1958-60. Mem. AMA, Am. Psychiatric Assn., Am. Assn. Geriatric Psychiatry, Tex. Soc. Psychiatric Physicians (pres. 1985-86). Office: U Tex Southwestern Med Ctr 5323 Harry Hines Blvd Dallas TX 75390-9070 E-mail: myron.weiner@utsouthwestern.edu.

WEINER, RICHARD LENARD, hospital administrator, educator, pediatrician; b. N.Y.C., May 23, 1951; s. Irving and Martha E. (Pell) W. BA in Biology cum laude, NYU, 1972; MD, Albert Einstein Coll. Medicine, 1975. Diplomate Am. Bd. Pediat. Resident in pediats. Bronx Mcpl. Hosp. Ctr./Albert Einstein Coll. Medicine, 1975-78; instr. in pediat. Albert Einstein Coll. of Medicine, Bronx, N.Y., 1978-80, asst. prof. pediat., 1980-95, assoc. prof. pediat., 1995—; pediatrician New Rochelle (N.Y.) Hosp. Med. Ctr., 1978-80; asst. dir. pediat. Hosp. of Albert Einstein Coll. of Medicine, Bronx, 1980-86; assoc. dir. pediat. Einstein-Weiler Hosp. MMC, Bronx, 1986-97; dir. pediat. evaluation unit Einstein-Weiler Hosp., Bronx, 1990-94; dir. divsn. faculty practice Albert Einstein Coll. Medicine/Montefiore Med. Ctr., 1993-99; dir. pediatrics Montefiore Med. Group, 1999—. Coord. pediatric med. edn. New Rochelle Hosp., 1978-80; chmn. pvt. practice governance coun. dept. pediatrics Albert Einstein Coll. of Medicine, 1988-91, 97-99; pres. Temple Beth Abraham Tarrytown, N.Y., 1995-96. Mem. editl. bd. Primary Care/Emergency Decisions, 1984-88; contbr. articles to Jour. Pediat., Pediat., Pediat. Infectious Diseases, Emergency Decisions. Recipient Physician's Recognition award AMA, 1982, 86; named one of Best Doctors in N.Y., N.Y. Mag., 1998-2002. Mem. Am. Acad. Pediats., Am. Physicians Fellowship for Medicine in Israel, Ambulatory Pediat. Assn., N.Y. Acad. Scis., N.Y. Pediat. Soc., Pediat. Alumni Assn. (coord. 1980-2000), Phi Beta Kappa, Beta Lambda Sigma. Jewish. Office: 1500 Astor Ave Bronx NY 10469-5900 Fax: 718-881-7752.

WEINER, WENDY L. elementary education educator, writer; b. Milw., Jan. 2, 1961; d. Kenneth J. and Jessie M. Weiner. AA, U. Wis. Washington County, West Bend, 1981; BS, U. Wis., 1983, MS, 1987, U. Wis., Milw., 1993; prin. lic., Marian Coll., 1992. Cert. nat. cert. early childhood edn. NBPT, tchr. Wis. Tchr. Milw. Pub. Schs. Contbr. articles to profl. jours. Mem. Milw. Pub. Mus. Tchr. Adv. Coun., TV and Tech. Com., Vision in Tech. Com., Learning Mag.'s Student Best Adv. Coun.; vol. Milw. Pub. Mus., 1987-88, Channel 10/36 Spl. Event and Tours, 1986, Milw. County Zoo, 1985, Ozaukee Art Show, Milw. Area Tech. Coll. Recipient Presdl. Award in Sci. Teaching Excellence, 1994, AT&T Recognition in Sci. Teaching Excellence, 1993, Grad. Last Decade award U. Wis. Milw. Alumni Assn., 1993, Warner Cable-Teaching Creativity with Cable award, 1993, Excellence in Sci. Teaching award. Wis. Elem. Sci. Tchrs. Assn., 1993, Nat. Urban Tech. in Edn. award Coun. Great City Schs., 1992-93, Sen. Herb Kohl Tchr. Achievement award, 1992, Ameritech-Wis. Bell Gold Tchr. Recognition award, 1991, 92, Presdl. award for elem. sci. tchg. excellence, 1992; grantee Greater Mil. Edn. Trust, 1989, 90, 92, Wis. Space Grant Consortium/NASA, 1993, NSF, 1993. Mem. PTA, Wis. Aerospace Edn. Assn. (instr. mag. adviser 1996-2000, Sam's Club Tchr. of Yr. 2002), YMCA-Young Astronauts, Nat. Arbor Day Assn., Nat. Sci. Tchrs. Assn., Wis. Elem. Tchrs. Assn., Milw. Kindergarten Assn., Wis. Secondary Sci. Assn., Wis. Assn. Sch. Adminstrs., Milw. Reading Assn., Midwest Devel. Corp., Assn. Presdl. Awardees in Sci., Soc. for Elem. Presdl. Awardees, Coun. Elem. Sci. Internat., Civil Air Patrol (sr. officer). Avocations: crafts, walking. Office: Parkview Sch 4966 N 91st St Milwaukee WI 53225-4127

WEINER-HEUSCHKEL, SYDELL, theater educator; b. N.Y.C., Feb. 18, 1947; d. Milton A. and Janet (Kay) Horowitz; children: Jason, Emily; m. Rex Heuschkel, Sept. 3, 1992. BA, SUNY, Binghamton, 1968; MA, Calif. State U., L.A., 1974; postgrad., Yale U., 1968-70; PhD, NYU, 1986; MS, Calif. State U., Dominguez Hills, 1996. Lic. marriage and family therapist. Prof. theater arts, chmn. dept., dir. honors program Calif. State U. Dominguez Hills, Carson, 1984—. Guest lectr. Calif. Inst. Arts, 1988. Appeared in play Vikings, Grove Shakespeare Festival, 1988; dir. Plaza Suite, Brea (Calif.) Civic Theatre, 1982, Gypsy, Carson Civic Light Opera, 1990, Same Time Next Year, Muckehthaler, 1987, Slow Dance on the Killing Ground, Alternative Repertory Theatre, 1989; co-author: School and Community Theater Problems: A Handbook for Survival, 1978, (software) Public Speaking, 1991; contbr. Am. Jour. Psychotherapy, 1997, Jour. Clin. Psychology, 1998. Yale U. fellow, 1969; recipient Lyle Gibson Disting. Tchr. award, 1989. Mem. Screen Actors Guild, Am. Fedn. TV and Radio Artists, Calif. State U. Women's Coun. (treas. 1989-91), Phi Kappa Phi. E-mail: sweiner@csudh.edu.

WEINGOLD, ALLAN BYRNE, obstetrician, gynecologist, educator; b. N.Y.C., Sept. 2, 1930; s. Irving and Evelyne (Gold) W.; m. Marjorie Nassau, Dec. 21, 1952; children: Beth, Roberta, Matthew, Daniel BA, Oberlin Coll., 1951; MD, N.Y. Med. Coll., 1955; DSc, George Washington, 1997. Diplomate Am. Bd. Ob-Gyn. Instr. N.Y. Med.Coll., N.Y.C., 1960-63, asst. prof., 1963-67, assoc. prof., 1967-70, prof., 1970-73; prof., chmn. dept. ob-gyn George Washington U., Washington, 1973-92, v.p. med. affairs and exec. dean, 1992-96, pres. health plan, 1992-2000, mem. partnership bd., 1997-99. Cons. NIH, Bethesda, Md., 1974-97, Walter Reed Army Med. Ctr., Washington, 1974-97. Author: Principles and Practices of Clinical Gynecology, 1988; editor: Monitoring the Fetal Environment, 1969, Surgical Complications of Pregnancy, 1984. Bd. dirs. Mayor's Adv. Bd. Maternal Health, Washington, 1981-87; mem. host com. John Glenn Campaign Com., Washington, 1983-85. Maj. U.S. Army, 1957-66. Recipient Alumni award N.Y. Med. Coll., 1974 Fellow Am. Coll. Obstetricians and Gynecologists (program chmn. 1975-77), Am. Gyn.-Ob. Soc. (coun. 1988-90); mem. Assn. Profs. Ob-Gyn. (sec. 1981-84, pres. 1985-86), Soc. Perinatal Rsch., Alpha Omega Alpha. Republican. Office: George Washington U 2300 I St NW Washington DC 20037-2336

WEINKAUF, DAVID, film, animation, and photography educator; BS in TV/Radio, Ithaca Coll., 1963; MS in Film, Boston, 1965. Prodr., dir., announcer, dir. traffic WHCU-AM-FM, Ithaca, N.Y., 1960-63; grad. asst. Boston U., 1963-65; engr. WBZ-TV, Boston, 1964-65; instr. speech U. S.D., Vermillion, 1965-66; prodr./dir. radio and TV prodns. KUSD-FM TV, Vermillion, 1965-66; engr. WOR-TV, N.Y.C., summers 1966-68; asst. prof. film, animation, photography Edinboro U., Pa., 1966—. Juror Radio Fellowship awards Pa. Radio Theater/Pa. Coun. Arts, 1991, Bucks County Film Festival, 1990, Emerging Artists Series, Pitts. Filmmakers, 1989, Ann Arbor Touring Film Festival, Allegheny Coll., Meadville, Pa., 1976; vis. filmmaker Pitts. Filmmakers, 1988, Capital Children's Mus., Washington, 1987, Arts guild, Old Forge, N.Y., 1987, 72, capital U., Columbus, Ohio, 1972; curator Chuck Jones Animation Art Exhbn., Bruce Gallery, Edinboro U., 1985. Contbr. articles to profl. jours.; dir., cinematographer Fresh Seeds in the Big Apple, 1974; cinematographer Mohawk Nation, 1976; filmography includes: As Long As It Holds Out, 1964, Impressions, 1965, Face to Face: A Hundred Years Hence, 1968, Franklin: Autobiography and Beyond, 1968, To Lead Useful Lives, 1969, Band Camp, 1970, Up Front with Stephen Crane, 1970, To the Outsetting Bard, 1971, Cry for Convenience, 1971, To challenge That Which They Question, 1972, Pedagogy and Politics: Notes From a Survivor, 1972, A Space to be Me, 1973, Edinboro: A Student Notebook, 1978, Toward the Least Restrictive Environment, 1979, An Art Department Film, 1980, Chuck Jones - A Life of Animation, 1986, 90; prodr./dir. Voices from the Past series, KUSD-AM-FM, Vermillion, 1965; film designer, dir. Rashomon, 1968; prodr., dir. Edinboro: Contemporary Profiles, 1969-72, A Bag of Tricks, 1989, Three Excerpts radio series, 1986-90; prodr., dir., co-editor: The Pulse, 1990, My Father's Ways, 1993; BETA tester Video Toaster Flyer, NewTek, Inc., 1994—, Digital Equipment Corp., 1996—; media arts panelist Pa. Coun. on Arts, 1986-90, 93—; editl. bd. Film Criticism mag., 1976-80. Bd. dirs. Pa. Alliance for Arts in Edn., 1978-82; lectr. area schs., service clubs; mem. cmty. adv. bd. WQLN, 1991-96; parade marshall Conneautville Homecoming, 1990; mem. Spring Twp. Planning Commn., 1986-88; programmer film festival Best theater, Edinboro, 1966-70, others. Grantee U.S. EPA, 1970, Pa. Dept. Edn., 1978, Pa. Coun. on the Arts, 1986, 87, 88, 89, 90, 91, 92, 93, 94, 95, 96, Senate Faculty rsch. grantee, 1992, 93. Mem. Soc. Animation Studies (founding), Am. Fedn. Film Socs., Am. Fedn. Tchrs., Univ. Film Assn., Pa. Film/Video Coun., Nat. Assn. Ednl. Broadcasters, Assn. Pa. State Coll. and Univ. Faculties, Internat. Brotherhood of Elec. Workers, Internat. Alliance of Theatrical Stage Employees and Moving Picture Operators. Home: PO Box 145 Edinboro PA 16412-0145

WEINMAN, DAVID PETER, elementary education educator; b. Allentown, Pa., May 25, 1957; s. Leonard Edward and Esther (German) W.; m. Teresa Modafferi, Aug. 7, 1982; children: Christopher, Joseph. AA, Lehigh County C.C., Schnecksville, Pa., 1977; BS in Elem. Edn., Kutztown State Coll., 1979; MEd, reading specialist, East Stroudsburg U., 1983; prin. cert., Pa. State U., 1986. Fourth grade tchr. Pleasant Valley Sch. Dist., Brodheadsville, Pa., 1979-82; reading specialist grades K-4 Chestnuthill Elem.-Pleasant Valley Sch. Dist., Brodheadsville, 1982-89; reading specialist grades 3-5 J.C. Mills Elem.-Pleasant Valley Sch. Dist., Brodheadsville, 1989-93, instrnl. support tchr., 1993—. Scoutmaster Troop 98 Boy Scouts Am., Brodheadsville, 1983—. Mem. Internat. Reading Assn., Keystone State Reading Assn., Colonial Assn. Reading Educators (v.p. 1984-86, 92-94, pres., 1986-87, 94-95), Phi Delta Kappa. Democrat. Roman Catholic. Avocations: photography, camping, traveling. Office: Pleasant Valley Sch Dist Pleasant Valley Elem Sch Brodheadsville PA 18322

WEINMAN, STEVEN ALAN, emergency nurse, researcher, writer, educator, consultant; b. St. Louis, July 17, 1962; s. Stanley I. Weinman and Diana Raye (Kessler) Schrader; m. Carol Angela Daiber, July 27, 1986; children: Erin Elizabeth, Sarah Katherine. Diploma in Nursing, Jewish Hosp. of St. Louis, 1986; BSN, Webster U., Kansas City, 1996; postgrad., Webster U., 2001—. RN, Mo., NY, NJ; cert. emergency nurse. Emergency nurse Jewish Hosp. of St. Louis, 1986-87, Truman Med. Ctr.-West, Kans. City, Mo., 1987-93, clin. nurse mgr., 1987-93; clin. educator, 1993-95; emergency nurse St. Luke's Northland Hosp., Kans. City, Mo., 1996-97; prin. ptnr. Emergency Care Cons. Greater NY, Somerville, NJ, 1996—; instr. dept. emergency medicine NY Hosp.-Cornell Med. Ctr., NYC, 1997-2001; sr. dir. Med. Ed. and Custom Publ., Excepta Med. Elsevier, Hillsborough, NJ, 2001. Clin. rsch. assoc. Clin. Multiphase Rsch., Wilton, Conn., 1991—93, nurse rschr., 1991—2000; rsch. coord. dept. emergency medicine Truman Med. Ctr., Kansas City, 1991—96; mem. editl. adv. bd. Roadrunner Press/ENA, 1999—2001; per diem instr. in emergency and trauma care N.Y. Presbyn. Hosp.-Cornell Med. Ctr., N.Y.C., 2001—. Editor textbooks and monographs; mem. editl. bd. Clin. CORNERSTONE, Excerpta Medica, Inc.; contbg. author books and book chpt; contbr. articles to profl. jour. Mem. adv. bd. Kansas City chpt. ARC, 1991-94; chief nurse first aid Kans. City Spiritfest, 1989-95. Recipient Spl. Recognition award Emergency Nursing Found. Mem.: AONE, NJSNA, Nat. Assn. EMS Educators, Global Alliance for Med. Edn., Alliance for Continuing Med. Edn., Soc. Trauma Nurses, Am. Trauma Soc., Emergency Nurses Assn. (treas. Greater Kansas City chpt. 1989—91, pres. 1994, state coun. exec. com. 1993—95, sec. 1991, state del. 1991—95, Recognition award 1991, 1993, 1994, 2000, 2001, Edn. award 1993, Educator of Yr. 1994, 1996, Disting. Svc. award 2000). Avocations: photography, writing, computers/electronics, traveling. Home: 29 W Spring St Somerville NJ 08876-1627 Office: 105 Raider Blvd Ste 101 Hillsborough NJ 08844

WEINRICH, BRIAN ERWIN, mathematician, computer scientist; b. Passaic, N.J., Jan. 8, 1952; s. Erwin H. and Ann E. (Gall) Weinrich. BS, Pa. State U., 1974, MA, 1978; MS, Shippensburg (Pa.) U., 1983; postgrad. in computer engring., U. Fla., 2002—. Mathematician U.S. Dept. Agr., Agrl. Rsch. Svc., University Park, Pa., 1974-80; instr. math and computer sci. Shippensburg U., 1980-84; assoc. prof. maths. and computer sci. California U. of Pa., 1984-97, assoc. prof. emeritus of mathematics and computer scis., 1997—. Cons. in field; mem. Wall St. Jour. Panel, 1990—; devel. articulation agreements in Malaysia California U. of Pa., 1992—2001; vis. sr. lectr. in computer sci. Inti Coll., Subang Jaya, Malaysia, 1993—2001; cons. in math., sys. and database programming, 1981—2002. Author (with A. S. Rogowski): (book) Water Movement and Quality on Strip-Mined Lands: A Compilation of Computer Programs, 1984; author: (with others) Surface Mining, 1990; contbr. articles to profl. jours. Mem. mission bd. Calvary Bapt. Ch., State College, Pa., 1975—80; visitation team Prince St. United Brethren Ch., Shippensburg, 1982—84; Bible study leader, asst. Sunday sch. tchr. Libr. Bapt. Ch., 1986—92. Fellow, U. Fla., 2002—; grantee, U.S. Dept. Age, 1982—89. Mem.: Assn. Computing Machinery, Math. Assn. Am., Am. Biog. Inst. (bd. advisors 1989—), Computer Soc. of IEEE. Republican. Home: 1001 SW 16th Ave Apt 67 Gainesville FL 32601 Office: U Fla Dept Computer and Info Sci and Engring PO Box 116120 Gainesville FL 32611

WEINRICH, GLORIA JOAN CASTORIA, retired elementary education educator; b. Bklyn., Dec. 12, 1930; d. Louis and Elsie (Doddato) Castoria; m. Robert L. Weinrich, Aug. 16, 1952 (dec. 1993); 1 child, Russell Louis. BA, Hofstra U., 1952, MS, 1962. Cert. tchr., N.Y. Tchr. Oceanside (N.Y.) Bd. Edn., 1952-53, Troy (N.Y.) Bd. Edn., 1953-56, Carle Place (N.Y.) Bd. Edn., 1956-60, 69-93; ret., 1993. Lectr. to schs. and adult groups. Mem. nominating com. Western Garden City Property Owners, 1995, mem. bird sanctuary com., 1995-97; mem. dist. adv. com. to edn. Garden City Schs., 1996—. Mem. AAUW (exec. bd. Garden City chpt. 1997-98), N.Y. State Ret. Tchrs. Assn. (co-chairperson polit. action 1993-97), Carle Pl. Ret. Tchrs. Assn. (pres. 1993-95, v.p. 1997—), Alpha Upsilon, Delta Kappa Gamma (pres. 1992-96, v.p. 1997-98), Women's Club Garden City (exec. bd. 1998—). Roman Catholic. Avocations: travel, lit. groups, opera, piano, bridge. Home: 1 Hawthorne Rd Garden City NY 11530-1017

WEINRICH, MARCEL, physics educator; b. Jerdzejow, Kielce, Poland, July 23, 1927; came to U.S., 1942; s. Golda R. Weinrich; m. Eleanor A. Tulman, Aug. 30, 1958 (div. Jan. 1965); 1 child, Mason. BS magna cum laude, Bethany Coll., 1946; MS, W. Va. U., 1949; PhD, Columbia U., 1958. Instr. W.Va. U., Morgantown, 1946-49; tech. asst. Columbia U., N.Y.C., 1949-50, rsch. assoc., 1951-57; physicist GE Rsch. Lab., Schenectady, N.Y., 1957-69; prof. physics Jersey City State Coll., 1969—, chmn. dept. physics, 1969-73. Dir. Citizen's League, Schenectady, 1965-69; v.p. Schenectady Ednl. Rsch. Coun., 1965-69; mem. Human Rights Commn., Schenectady, 1967-69. Fellow AAAS; mem. Am. Physics Soc., Am. Assn. Physics Tchrs. (pres. N.J. chpt. 1970-72), N.Y. Acad. Scis. Achievements include original co-discovery of parity non conservation, determination of mu meson magnetic moment; research in controlled fusion for 12 years studying magnetic mirrors and a theta pinch. Home: 6 Broadman Pky Jersey City NJ 07305-1519

WEINSIER, PHILIP DAVID, electronics educator; b. Orlando, Fla., May 16, 1953; s. Stanley Cecil and Ruth (Potsdamer) W. BS, Berry Coll., 1978; MEd, Clemson U., 1979, EdD, 1990. Instr. West Orange High Sch., Orlando, Fla., 1980-84; grad. teaching asst. Clemson (S.C.) U., 1985-89; lectr. Appalachian State U., Boone, N.C., 1990-91; asst. prof. No. Mich. U., Marquette, 1991-95; regional tng. dir. Centerpoint Techs. Inc., Orlando, Fla., 1995—. Adj. prof. electronics U. Ctrl. Fla., 1995—; cons. Superior-Newco, Marquete, 1991, OHAB & Co., CPA, Orlando, 1995. Co-author: The Computer and Information Technology Attitude Inventory, 1988. Program dir. Fgn. Exchange Program, Orange County, Fla., 1982-84. Fulbright scholar, 1987-88; grantee Clemson U., 1989, German Sci. Found., 1989, No. Mich. U., 1992, 93. Mem. Internat. Fulbright Orgn. (life), European Assn. Rsch. on Learning and Instrn., Internat. Tech. Edn. Assn. (chmn. internat. rels. com. 1993-96, coun. tech. tchr. edn. rsch. com. 1995—), Nat. Assn. Indsl. Tech. (cert.), Nat. Assn. Indsl. and Tech. Tchr. Educators, Orange County Indsl. Arts Assn. (v.p. 1982-83, pres. 1983-84), Orange County Adult Comty. Edn. Assn. (bd. dirs. 1983-84), Epsilon Pi Tau. Avocations: international travel, foreign languages, tennis, scuba diving.

WEINSTEIN, ALVIN SEYMOUR, lawyer, educator mechanical engineer; b. Lynn, Mass., June 12, 1928; s. Samuel Jacob and Miriam (Levine) W.; m. Helené Zamcheck (div. 1982); children: Ruth Caryn, Sandra Beth, Marc Steven; m. Anne Sophie Richmond, Nov. 26, 1988. BS in Mech. Engring., U. Mich., 1951; MS in Mech. Engring., Carnegie Inst. Tech., Pitts., 1953; PhD in Mech. Engring., Carnegie-Mellon U., Pitts., 1955; JD, Franklin Pierce Law Ctr., Concord, N.H., 1983. Bar: Pa. 1983, U.S. Dist. Ct. (we. dist.) Pa. 1983, U.S. Ct. Appeals (3d cir.) 1983, U.S. Supreme Ct. 1988. Asst. prof. mech. engring. Carnegie-Mellon U., Pitts., 1955-61, assoc. prof. mech. engring., 1961-65, prof. mech. engring. and pub. policy, 1965-85, prof. emeritus, 1985—; legal and tech. cons. Weinstein Assocs., Brunswick, Maine, 1990-99, Weinstein Assocs. Internat., Delray Beach, Fla., 1999—. Adj. prof. law Franklin Pierce Law Ctr., 1986-90. Author: An Introduction to the Art of Engineering, 1976, Products Liability and the Reasonably Safe Product, 1978; contbr. articles to profl. jours. Bd. dirs. Concord (N.H.) Community Concerts Assn., 1988-90; sec. Charter Commn., Town of Phippsburg, Maine, 1993—; pres. Popham Beach Assn., Phippsburg, Maine, 1995-98, bd. dirs., 1998—. Sgt. U.S. Army, 1946-47. Mem. ASTM, ASME (recipient Melville medal 1972, chmn. design, engring. and law com.), Soc. of Automotive Engrs., Am. Boat and Yacht Coun. (bd. dirs.). Avocations: bicycling, hiking, downhill and cross country skiing. Office: Weinstein Assocs Internat 200 Macfarlane Dr Ph 6 Delray Beach FL 33483-6822 E-mail: anneal2@juno.com., walaw@ime.net.

WEINSTEIN, EILEEN ANN, elementary education educator; b. Phila., Sept. 11, 1947; d. Bernard and Eleanor (Cohen) Cobert; m. Philip Weinstein, Aug. 16, 1970; children: Lawrence, Steven. BS in Edn. with honors, Temple U., 1969, MEd with honors, 1972. Cert. elem. tchr., psychology of reading, Pa. 1st grade tchr. Phila. Sch. Dist., 1969-70, Neshaminy Sch. Dist., Langhorne, Pa., 1970-74, tchr. reading and 3d grade, 1985—; kindergarten tchr. Jewish Cmty. Ctr., Phila., 1981-85. Mem. instrnl. support team Neshaminy Sch. Dist., 1987—, mem. student assistance team, 1992—. Active Dem. Nat. Com., 1992—. Recipient Teaching award Children with ADD, 1994-95. Mem. Internat. Reading Assn., Neshaminy Fedn. Tchrs. (union rep. 1986—), Women's Am. ORT (officer, bd. mem. 1973—), Hadassah (officer and bd. mem. 1969—). Jewish. Avocations: reading, travel, music, impressionist art. Home: 83 Cypress Cir Richboro PA 18954-1653 Office: Neshaminy Sch Dist Oliver Heckman Sch Cherry St Langhorne PA 19047

WEINSTEIN, I. BERNARD, oncologist, geneticist, research administrator; b. Madison, Wis., Sept. 9, 1930; married, 1952; 3 children. BS, U. Wis., 1952, MD, 1955, DSc (hon.), 1992. Nat. Cancer Inst. spl. rsch. fellow bacteriology/immunology Harvard Med. Sch./MIT, Boston, 1959-61; career scientist Health Rsch. Coun., City of N.Y., 1961-72; assoc. vis. physician Francis Delafield Hosp., 1961-66; from asst. attending physician to assoc. attending physician Presbyn. Hosp., 1967-81, attending physician, 1981—; from asst. to assoc. prof. medicine Columbia U. Coll. Phys. and Surg., N.Y.C., 1978-90; prof. medicine Columbia U., N.Y.C., 1973—, prof. pub. health, 1978—, prof. genetics and devel., 1990—, Frode Jensen prof. medicine, 1990—, dir. comprehensive cancer ctr., 1985-96. Advisor Lung Cancer Segment, Carcinogenesis Program, Nat. Cancer Inst., 1971-74, Chem. and Molecular Biol. Segment, 1973-76; mem. interdisciplinary comm. program Smithsonian Inst., 1971-74, Pharmacology B Study ect., NIH, 1971-75, numerous sci. and adv. coms. Nat. Cancer Inst., Am. Cancer Soc., 1976-88; advisor Roswell Park Meml. Inst., Buffalo, Brookhaven Nat. Lab., Divsn. Cancer Cause and Prevention, Nat. Cancer Inst., Coun. on Analysis and Projects, Am. Cancer Soc., Internat. Agy. for Rsch. on Cancer, WHO, Lyon, France; Nakasone vis. prof., Tokyo, 1987; GM Cancer Rsch. Found. vis. prof. Internat. Agy. Rsch. Cancer, Lyon, 1988; mem. adv. coun. Nat. Inst. Environ. Health Scis., 1995—; chmn. Bristol-Myers Squibb Cancer Awards, 1993-96. Assoc. editor Cancer Rsch., 1973-76, 86-95, Jour. Environ. Pathology and Toxicology, 1977-84, Jour. Cellular Physiology, 1982-89, Oncogene, 1989-99, Clin. Cancer Rsch., 1998—. Named Louise Weissberger lectr., U. Rochester, 1981, Mary Ann Swetland lectr., Case Western Res. U., 1983, Daniel Laszlo Meml. lectr., Montefiore Med. Ctr., 1983, Samuel Kuna Disting. lectr., Rutgers U., 1985, Ester Langer lectr., U. Chgo., 1989, Harris Meml. lectr., MIT, 1989, Rufus Cole lectr., 1997, travel fellow, European Molecular Biology Orgn., 1970—71; recipient Meltzer medal, 1964, Clowes award, Am. Assn. Cancer Rsch., 1987, Silvio O. Conte award, Environ. Health Inst., 1990, Nakahara award, 1996, Anthony Dipple Carcinogenesis award, 2000, Disting. Achievement award, Am. Soc. Preventive Oncology, 2001, Am. Assn. Cancer Rsch./Am. Cancer Soc. award, 2001. Mem.: AAAS (coun. del. 1985—88), N.Y. Acad. Sci., Am. Soc. Clin. Investigation, Internat. Soc. Quantum Biology, Am. Soc. Microbiology, Am. Assn. Physicians, Am. Acad. Arts and Scis., Inst. Medicine/Nat. Acad. Sci., Am. Assn. Cancer Rsch. (pres. 1990—91). Achievements include research in cellular and molecular aspects of carcinogenesis, environmental carcinogenesis, molecular epidemiology, cancer prevention. Office: Cancer Ctr Columbia Univ 701 W 168th St New York NY 10032-2704 E-mail: ibw1@columbia.edu.

WEINSTEIN, LEONARD HARLAN, institute program director, educator; b. Springfield, Mass., Apr. 11, 1926; s. Barney Willard Weinstein and Ida Pauline (Feinberg) Weinstein Clark; m. Sylvia Jane Sherman, Oct. 15, 1950; children: Beth Rachel, David Harold (dec.). BS, Pa. State U., 1949; MS, U. Mass., 1950; PhD, Rutgers U., 1953. Postdoctoral fellow Rutgers U., New Brunswick, N.J., 1953-55; plant physiologist Boyce Thompson Inst., Yonkers, N.Y., 1955-63, program dir. Ithaca, N.Y., 1963-91, bd. dirs., 1976-96; dir. ecosystem rsch. ctr. Cornell U., Ithaca, 1988-90, William Boyce Thompson scientist emeritus, 1993—, adj. prof. dept. natural resources, 1979—96. Mem. rsch. adv. com. Oak Ridge Nat. Lab., 1985-87. Author 2 books; contbr. over 175 articles to profl. jours., chpts. to books. Mem. sci. adv. bd. EPA, Washington, 1988-91; mem. com. natural resources NASULGC, 1986-89. Grantee NIH, NSF, HEW, Am. Cancer Soc., NASA, EPA, DOE, USDA. Mem. Am. Soc. Plant Physiologists, Sigma Xi, Pi Alpha Xi, Gamma Sigma Delta. Home: 608 Cayuga Heights Rd Ithaca NY 14850-1424 Office: Cornell U 125 Boyce Thompson Inst Tower Rd Ithaca NY 14853

WEINSTEIN, RHONDA KRUGER, elementary mathematics educator, administrator; b. Boston, May 18, 1948; d. David Solomon and Henrietta Reina (Slocum) Kruger; m. Milton Charles Weinstein, June 14, 1970; children: Jeffrey William, Daniel Jay. AB, Mt. Holyoke Coll., 1970; MA, Suffolk U., 1973. Cert. supr./dir.; math. 7-12; elem. K-8; elem. prin.; supt., Mass. Tchr. grade 3 Brookline (Mass.) Pub. Schs., 1974-78, math. resource tchr. K-6, 1980-81, math. resource tchr. K-8, 1981-82, elem. curriculum coord. for math., 1982—; program evaluator Newton (Mass.) Pub. Schs., 1992-93. Part-time instr. Suffolk U., Boston, 1976, 79; mem. math. adv. bd. Ency. Britannica, Chgo., 1993-95; cons. Mass. sch. sys. including Northborough/ Southborough, 1987-88, Sudbury, 1987, North Andover, 1993; spkr. profl. meetings Assn. Tchrs. Math. in New Eng., 1990, 94, 95, ASCD, Boston, 1988. Co-author: Calculator Activities, 1987; reviewer 2 books Arithmetic Teacher, 1991. Alumnae fund vol. Mt. Holyoke Coll., South Hadley, Mass., 1985-90; vol. Am. Heart Assn., Brookline, 1982-93; mem. PTO, Baker Sch., Brookline, 1983-95. Sarah Williston scholar Mt. Holyoke Coll., 1967; grantee Brookline Found., 1994, Tchrs. and Adminstrs. Tng. Fund, 1992, 96. Mem. Nat. Coun. Tchrs. Math. (nat. conv. com. chair 1995, speaker profl. meeting 1993), Nat. Coun. Suprs. of Math. (spkr. profl. meeting 2000), Assn. Tchrs. of Math. in Mass., Boston Area Math. Specialists, Phi Beta Kappa. Avocations: cross-country skiing, gourmet cooking, walking, swimming, playing piano. Home: 50 Princeton Rd Chestnut Hill MA 02467-3061 Office: Brookline Pub Schs 88 Harvard St Brookline MA 02445-7949

WEINSTEIN, ROY, physics educator, researcher; b. N.Y.C., Apr. 21, 1927; s. Harry and Lillian (Ehrenberg) W.; m. Janet E. Spiller, Mar. 26, 1954 (dec. 1995); children: Lee Davis, Sara Lynn; m. Gail A. Birdsell, July 26, 1996. BS, MIT, 1951, PhD, 1954; ScD (hon.), Lycoming Coll., 1981. Rsch. asst. Mass. Inst. Tech., 1951-54, asst. prof., 1956-59, Brandeis U., Waltham, Mass., 1954-56; assoc. prof. Northeastern U., Boston, 1960-63, prof. physics, 1963-82, exec. officer, chmn. grad. div. of physics dept., 1967-69, chmn. physics dept., 1974-81; spokesman MAC Detector Stanford U., 1981-82; dean Coll. Natural Scis. and Math. U. Houston, 1982-88; prof. physics, 1982—; dir. Inst. Beam Particle Dynamics U. Houston, 1985-95; assoc. dir., spokesman Tex. Ctr. for Superconductivity, 1987-89. Vis. scholar and physicist Stanford (Calif.) U., 1966-67, 81-82; bd. dirs. Perception Tech., Inc., Winchester, Mass., Omniwave Inc., Gloucester, Mass., Wincom Inc., Woburn, Mass.; cons. Visidyne Inc., Burlington, Mass., Houston Area Rsch. Ctr., Stanford U., Hodotector Inc., Houston, Park Square Engrng., Marietta, Ga., Harvard U., Cambridge, Mass., Cambridge Electron Accelerator, mem. adv. com., 1967-69; adv. com. and portfolio evaluation com. Houston Venture Ptnrs., 1990-99; chmn. bd. dirs. Xytron Corp., 1986-91; dir., mem. exec. com. Houston Area Rsch. Ctr., 1984-87; chmn. organizing com. Internat. Conf. on Meson Spectroscopy, 1974, chmn. program com., 1977, mem. organizing com., 1980; chmn. mgmt. group Tex. Accelerator Ctr., Woodlands, 1985-90; chmn. Tex. High Energy Physicists, 1989-91; keynote spkr. MIT Alumni series, 1988; permanent mem. exec. com. Large Vol. Detector (Underground Neutrino Telescope, Italy), 1988—; organizer session High Temperature Superconducting Magnets 3d and 4th World Congress on Superconductivity, Munich, 1993, Orlando, 1994. Author: Atomic Physics, 1964, Nuclear Physics, 1964, Interactions of Radiation and Matter, 1964; editor: Nuclear Reactor Theory, 1964, Nuclear Materials, 1964; editor procs.: 5th Internat. Conf. on Mesons, 1977; contbr. over 200 articles to profl. jours. Active Lexington (Mass.) Town Meeting, 1973-84; vice chmn. Lexington Coun. on Aging, 1977-83. With USNR, 1945-46. Recipient Founders award World Congress Superconductivity, 1988, Materials/Devices award Internat. Superconductivity Technology Ctr., Japan, and Materials Rsch. Soc., U.S., 1995, High Current award, 1997, Excellence award for great achievements in the field of bulk superconducting materials Internat. Program Com. Processing and Applications of Large Superconducting Rare Earth Grains Worshop, 1999, NSF Rsch. awards, 1961-96, Tex. Rsch. award, 1986-87, 90—, U.S. Dept. Energy award 1974, 77, 87-97, NASA award, 1990-98, ARO award, 1994—, Elec. Power Rsch. Inst. award, 1990-95, Welch Found. award, 1997—, Nat. Cancer Inst. award, 2000—; NSF fellow Bohr Inst., Copenhagen, 1959-60, Stanford U. 1969-70, Guggenheim fellow Harvard U., 1970-71. Fellow Am. Phys. Soc. (organizer session SSC and High Energy Physics 1984); mem. Am. Assn. Physics Tchrs., Masons, Sigma Xi, Phi Kappa Phi (chpt. pres. 1977-79, Nat. Triennial Disting. Scholar prize 1980-83), Pi Lambda Phi (pres. Theta chpt. 1949-50). Unitarian Universalist. Achievements include measurement of fine structure of positronium; first measurement of rho meson coupling to gamma rays, of phi meson decay to two muons; early observation of break down in SU3 symmetry; demonstration of electron-muon universality, discovery of non-applicability of Lorentz contraction to length measured by a single observer; disproof of splitting of A2 meson; independent discovery of upsilon meson (bottom quark); achievement of highest magnetic field for any permanent magnet, in $YBa_2Cu_3O_7$, 10.1 Tesla; achievement of highest current density in textured superconductor, 0.3 megA/cm2. Home: 4368 Fiesta Ln Houston TX 77004-6603 Office: U Houston IBPD 632 SR1 Houston TX 77204-5005

WEINSTEIN, SIDNEY, neuropsychologist; b. Apr. 27, 1922; s. Celia (Schneider) W.; children: Curt, Karen, Laura; m. Margaret Carla Diamond, July 28, 1968; children: Ethan, Ari. BS, CCNY, 1949; MA in Exptl. Psychology, NYU, 1950, PhD in Physiol. Psychology, 1952. Lic. psychologist, N.Y., Conn. Dir. neuropsychol. lab., rsch. assoc. prof. Albert Einstein Coll. Medicine, N.Y.C., 1958-66, rsch. asst. prof. dept. neurology, 1958-60, rsch. assoc. prof. dept. neurology, 1960-66; rsch. assoc. neuropsychology Bronx Mcpl. Hosp. Ctr., 1958-66; pres. NeuroCommunication Rsch. Labs., Inc., Danbury, Conn., 1974-77, CEO, 1977—. Vis. assoc. prof. NYU, 1958-64, adj. clin. prof. dept. neurology, 1975—; vis. assoc. prof. Yeshiva U., 1960-67; adj. prof. CUNY, 1966—; lectr. Mt. Sinai Sch. Medicine, 1966—; prof. dept. pediat. N.Y. Med. Coll., N.Y.C., 1967-80, prof., dir. neuropsychol. lab. N.Y. Med. Coll.-Flower and Fifth Ave. Hosps., 1967-73. Author: (with others) Somatosensory Changes After Penetrating Brain Wounds in Man, 1960; The Neuropsychology of Alcohol Ingestion, 1970; editor-in-chief Internat. Jour. Neuroscience; editor Neuroscience Monographs; contbr. articles to profl. jours. Bd. dirs. Neuropsychol. Rsch. Found., Danbury, 1974—. Decorated knight of honor and merit Imperial Order St. John Jerusalem Ecumenical. Mem. AAAS, APA (pres. divsn. physiol. and comparative psychology 1963), Internat. Coun. Psychologists; mem. AAUP, Eastern Psychol. Assn., Soc. Cosmetic Chemists, Am. Acad. Neurology, Psychonomic Soc., Acad. Aphasia (bd. govs. 1966-70), Internat. Neuropsychol. Soc. (bd. govs. 1980-82), Soc. Rsch. Child Devel., Assn. Am. Med. Colls., European Brain and Behavior Soc. (charter), Soc. Neuroscience (charter), Soc. Psychophysiol. Rsch., Internat. Soc. Bioengineering and Skin, Dermal Clin. Evaluation Soc. (charter), Conn. Pyschol. Assn., N.Y. Acad. Scis., N.Y. State Psychol. Assn. (mem. divsn. exec. com. 1965-68), N.Y. Brain Function Group (charter, scribe 1964), Sigma Xi, Psi Chi. Address: 2300 Cherry Laurel Ln Chapel Hill NC 27516-8306

WEINTRAUB, RUSSELL JAY, lawyer, educator; b. N.Y.C., Dec. 20, 1929; s. Harry and Alice (Lieberman) W.; m. Zelda Kresshover, Sept. 6, 1953; children— Sharon Hope, Harry David, Steven Ross. BA, NYU, 1950; JD, Harvard U., 1953. Bar: N.Y. 1955, Iowa 1961, Tex. 1980. Tchg. fellow Harvard U. Law Sch., 1955-57; asst. prof. law U. Iowa, 1957-61, prof., 1961-65, U. Tex., 1965—, Marrs McLean prof. law, 1970-80, Bryant Smith chmn., 1980-82, John B. Connally chmn., 1982-98, Powell chmn., 1998—. Vis. prof. law U. Mich., 1965, UCLA, 1967, U. Calif., Berkeley, 1973-74, Bklyn. Law Sch., 1990, 95, Inst. Internat. Comparative Law, Paris, 1975, Florence, Italy, 1997, Barcelona, 1999, 2002, London, 2000, U. Houston, 1979-80, Inst. Internat. and Comparative Law, Oxford, Eng., 1982-83, 86-87, 92, 2003, Dublin, Ireland, 1991, La. State U., Aix-en-Provence, France, 1993, Tulane U., Spetses, Greece, 1998, Australian Nat. U., 2001; Ronald Graveson Meml. lectr. King's Coll., London, 2000; lectr. Hague Acad. Internat. Law, 1984; cons. U.S. Dept. State, 1995—; cons. in field. Author: International Litigation and Arbitration, 1994, 4th revised edit., 2003, ann. supplement; (with Eugene Scoles) Cases and Materials on the Conflict of Laws, 1967, 2d rev. edit., 1972, supplement, 1978, Commentary on the Conflict of Laws, 1971, 4th rev. edit., 2000, ann. supplement; (with Hamilton and Rau) Cases and Materials on Contracts, 1984, 2d rev. edit., 1992; (with Hay and Borchers) Cases and Materials on the Conflict of Laws, 12th rev. edit., 2004, annual supplement; contbr. articles to profl. jours. Trustee U. Iowa Sch. Religion, 1960-65. With U.S. Army, 1953-55. Recipient Disting. Prof. award U. Tex. Sch. Law, 1977, Teaching Excellence award, 1979, cert. of meritorious service Am. Bar Assn., 1977, cert. of meritorious service Tex. Bar Assn., 1978, Best Tchr. award U. Houston, 1980, Carl Fulda award scholarship in internat. law, 1993. Mem. Am. Law Inst., Am. Bar Found. (life), Tex. Bar Found. (life), Scribes. Jewish. Office: U Tex Sch Law 727 E Dean Keeton Austin TX 78705-3224 E-mail: rweintraub@mail.law.utexas.edu.

WEINTRAUB, STANLEY, arts and humanities educator, writer; b. Phila., Apr. 17, 1929; s. Ben and Ray (Segal) W.; m. Rodelle Horwitz, June 6, 1954; children: Mark, David, Erica. BS, West Chester (Pa.) State Coll., 1949; MA, Temple U., 1951; PhD, Pa. State U., 1956. Instr. Pa. State U., University Park, 1953-59, asst. prof., 1959-62, asso. prof., 1962-65, prof. English, 1965-70, research prof., 1970-86, Evan Pugh prof. Arts and Humanities, 1986-99, Evan Pugh prof. Emeritus, 2000—; dir. Inst. for Arts and Humanistic Studies, 1970-90. Vis. prof. U. Calif. at Los Angeles, 1963, U. Hawaii, 1973, U. Malaya, 1977, Nat. U. Singapore, 1982 Author: Private Shaw and Public Shaw, 1963, The War in the Wards, 1964, Reggie, 1965, The Art of William Golding, 1965, Beardlsey, 1967, The Last Great Cause, The Intellectuals and the Spanish Civil War, 1968, Evolution of a Revolt: Early Postwar Writings of T.E. Lawrence, 1968, The Literary Criticism of Oscar Wilde, 1968, Journey to Heartbreak, 1971, Whistler: A Biography, 1974, Lawrence of Arabia: the Literary Impulse, 1975, Four Rossettis, A Victorian Biography, 1977, Aubrey Beardsley: Imp of the Perverse, 1976, The London Yankees: Portraits of American Writers and Artists in England, 1894-1914, 1979, The Unexpected Shaw. Biographical Approaches to G.B. Shaw and His Work, 1982, A Stillness Heard Round the World: The End of the Great War, 1985, Victoria. An Intimate Biography, 1987, Long Day's Journey into War: December 7, 1941, 1991, Bernard Shaw: A Guide to Research, 1992, Disraeli: A Biography, 1993, The Last Great Victory-The End of World War II, July/August 1945, 1995, Shaw's People. Victoria to Churchill, 1996, Uncrowned King: The Life of Prince Albert, 1997, MacArthur's War: Korea and the Undoing of an American Hero, 2000, The Importance of Being Edward. King in Waiting, 1841-1901, 2000, Silent Night. The Remarkable 1914 Christmas Truce, 2001, Charlotte and Lionel: A Rothschild Love Story, 2003, General Washington's Christmas Farewell: A Mount Vernon Homecoming, 1783, 2003; editor: An Unfinished Novel by Bernard Shaw, 1958, C.P. Snow: A Spectrum, 1963, The Yellow Book: Quintessence of the Nineties, 1964, The Savoy: Nineties Experiment, 1966, The Court Theatre, 1966, Biography and Truth, 1967, Evolution of a Revolt: Early Postwar Writings of T.E. Lawrence, 1968, The Literary Criticism of Oscar Wilde, 1968, Shaw: An Autobiography 1856-1898, 1969, Shaw: An Autobiography, The Playwright Years, 1898-1950, 1970, Bernard Shaw's Nondramatic Literary Criticism, 1972, Directions in Literary Criticism, 1973, Saint Joan Fifty Years After: 1923/24-1973/74, 1973, The Portable Bernard Shaw, 1977, (with Anne Wright) Heartbreak House. A Facsimile of the Revised Typescript, 1979, (with Richard Aldington) The Portable Oscar Wilde, 1981, Modern British Dramatists, 1900-1945, 1982, The Playwright and the Pirate. Bernard Shaw and Frank Harris: A Correspondence, 1982, British Dramatists Since World War II, 1983, Bernard Shaw, the Diaries, 1885-1897, 1986, Bernard Shaw on the London Art Scene, 1885-1950, 1989, (with Rodelle Weintraub) Dear Young Friend. The Letters of American Presidents to Children, 2000, also editor Comparative Literature Studies, 1987-92, Shaw, The Ann. of Bernard Shaw Studies, 1956-89. Pres. Jewish Community Council of Bellefonte (Pa.) State Coll., 1966-67. Served to 1st lt. AUS, 1951-53, Korea. Decorated Bronze Star medal.; Guggenheim fellow, 1968-69; recipient Disting. Humanist award Pa. Humanities Council, 1985 Mem. The Authors' Guild, PEN. Home: 4 Winterfield Ct Newark DE 19711 E-mail: sqw4@psu.edu.

WEIR, DARLENE, principal; b. Mt. Carmel, Ill., Jan. 18, 1953; d. Benton Douglas and Norma Jean (McClane) Rayborn; m. Patrick Lee Weir, Jan. 6, 1973; children: Trinity Janeen, Destiny Ellen. AS, Wabash Valley Coll., 1973; BA, Oakland City Coll., 1988; MA in Adminstrn., Oakland City U., 2000. Cert. elem. and secondary edn., Ill. Spl. reading and math. tchr. chpt. I Bellmont (Ill.) Sch. Dist. 348, 1989-90; 2d grade tchr. South Elem. Dist. 348, Mt. Carmel, 1990—; tchr. 4th grade Bellmont Sch., 2001—02; prin. Mt. Carmel (Ill.) Mid. sch., 2002—. Mem. curriculum adv. bd. Nat. Curriculum Com., 1990-2003; mem. sci. assessment com. South Dist. 348, 1993-95; mem. Welborn full svc. schs. com. 2002-, mem. CARES com. 2000-, literacy fair co-chmn. 1996-, dist. adminstr. team mem. 2001-, parent adv. bd. mem., 2002-, others; adj. instr. Oakland City U., 2000-02, Wabash Valley Coll., 2003—; presenter workshops in field. City commr. Town Bd., Keensburg, Ill., 1979-81; explorer scout leader Boy Scouts Am., Mt. Carmel, 1979-80; first aid instr. ARC, Mt. Carmel, 1980—; aux. pres. Little League, Mt. Carmel, 1988-90; pres. Families Against Drugs, Mt. Carmel, 1988-92. Republican. Avocations: reading, travel. Office: Mt Carmel Middle Sch 1520 Poplar St Mount Carmel IL 62863

WEIR, EDWARD KENNETH, cardiologist, educator; b. Belfast, No. Ireland, Jan. 7, 1943; came to U.S. 1973; s. Thomas Kenneth and Violet Hilda (ffrench) W.; m. Elizabeth Vincent Pearman, May 29, 1971; children: Fergus G., Conor K. BA, U. Oxford, U.K., 1964; MA, BM, BCh, U. Oxford, Eng., 1967, DM, 1976. Diplomate Am. Bd. Internal Medicine. Intern Churchill Hosp., Oxford, Eng., 1968, Radcliffe Infirmary, Oxford, 1968, resident, 1970-71, Hammersmith Hosp., London, 1969, Groot Schuur Hosp., Cape Town, South Africa, 1969-70, registrar in cardiology, 1971-73; postdoctoral rsch. fellow U. Colo., Denver, 1973-75; cons. pediatric cardiologist U. Cape Town Med. Sch., 1975-76; cons. cardiologist U. Natal Med. Sch., Durban, South Africa, 1976-77; assoc. prof. medicine U. Minn., Mpls., 1978-85, prof. medicine, 1985—, prof. physiology, 1999—. Staff physician VAMC, Mpls., 1978—, chief of cardiology, 2000—; dir. Grover Confs. on Pulmonary Circulation, 1984-2000. Co-editor: Pulmonary Hypertension, 1984, The Pulmonary Circulation in Health and Disease, 1987, Pulmonary Vascular Physiology and Pathophysiology, 1989, The Diagnosis and Treatment of Pulmonary Hypertension, 1992, Ion Flux in Pulmonary Vascular Control, 1993, The Pulmonary Circulation and Gas Exchange, 1994, Nitric Oxide and Radicals in the Pulmonary Vasculature, 1996, Pulmonary Edema, 1998, Oxygen Regulation of Ion Channels and Gene Expression, 1998, The Fetal and Neonatal Pulmonary Circulations, 2000, Interactions of Blood and the Pulmonary Circulation, 2002. Fulbright scholar, 1973-75; Sr. Internat. Fogarty fellow, 1993. Fellow Am. Coll. Cardiology, Royal Coll. Physicians London; mem. Am. Heart Assn. (Minn. affiliate bd. dirs. 1989-93, Nat. Cardiopulmonary Coun. (exec. com. 1992-2003), Pulmonary Circulation Found. (treas. 1985-2001). Office: VA Med Ctr 1 Veterans Dr # 111C Minneapolis MN 55417-2300

WEIR, MORTON WEBSTER, retired academic administrator, educator; b. Canton, Ill., July 18, 1934; s. James and Frances Mary (Johnson) W.; m. Cecelia Ann Rumler, June 23, 1956; children: Deborah, Kevin, Mark. AB, Knox Coll., 1955; MA, U. Tex., 1958, PhD, 1959. Rsch. assoc., asst. prof. child devel. U. Minn., Mpls., 1959; asst. prof. child devel. U. Ill., Urbana, 1960-64, assoc. prof., 1964-68, prof., 1968-93, prof. emeritus, 1993—, head dept. psychology, 1969-71, vice chancellor acad. affairs, 1971-79, v.p. acad. affairs, 1982-88, chancellor, 1988-93, chancellor emeritus, 1993—, sr. found. rep., 1993-99; dir. Boys Town Center Study Youth Development, 1979-80. Contbr. numerous articles to profl. jours. Trustee Knox Coll., 1984—, chmn., 1995—99; trustee Menninger Found., 1993—. With AUS, 1960. NSF Predoctoral fellow, 1957-59 Fellow AAAS; mem. Soc. Rsch. in Child Devel. (chmn. bd. publs. 1971, chmn. fin. com. 1993-95), Sigma Xi, Phi Beta Kappa, Phi Kappa Phi.

WEIR, RICHARD DALE, elementary education educator; b. Diamond Springs, Calif., Oct. 2, 1940; s. Martin Gaines and Phyllis Lorene (Sargent) W.; m. Carol Jean Baker, Dec. 25, 1976; children:; David Richard, Barbara Anne, Susan Michelle, Roger Allen. BS in Elem. Edn., Oklahoma City U., 1976, MEd, 1988; BS in Mgmt. Info. Sys., Coleman Coll., LaMesa, Calif., 1987. Cert. tchr. K-8, Okla. Joined USCG, 1961, advanced through grades to chief warrant officer, 1976, adminstrv. officer, 1976-82, ret., 1982; platform instr. IBM Corp., Oklahoma City, 1985-86; mid. sch. tchr. Archdiocese Oklahoma City, 1987-88; adj. prof. Oklahoma City U., 1988-91; elem. tchr. Oklahoma City Pub. Schs., 1988—, adminstrv. intern, 1997-98; math. supr. Okla. State Dept. Edn., 1998-99; math. coord. Putnam City Pub. Schs., Warr Acres, Okla., 1999—. Cons. in tng. math.-sci. tchrs.; trainer for Activities Integrating Math./Scis. Nat. Leadership Network. Recipient Presdl. award for excellence in sci. and math. teaching NSF, Washington, 1993, Okla. Outstanding Tchr. award Math. Assn. Am., Washington, 1996. Mem. ASCD, Nat. Sci. Tchrs. Assn., Nat. Coun. Tchrs. Math., Coun. Presdl. Awardees Math., Okla. Coun. Tchrs. Math. (advisor Metro Oklahoma City), Soc. Elem. Presdl. Awardees. Republican. Methodist. Avocation: golf. Home: 9109 NW 99th Pl Yukon OK 73099-8313 Office: Putnam City Pub Schs 5401 NW 40th St Warr Acres OK 73122-3302

WEISENBURGER, THEODORE MAURICE, retired judge, poet, educator, writer; b. Tuttle, N.D., May 12, 1930; s. John and Emily (Rosenau) W.; children: Sam, Jennifer, Emily, Todd, Daniel, Dwight, Holly, Michael, Paul, Peter; m. Maylyne Chu, Sept. 19, 1985; 1 child, Irene. BA, U. N.D., 1952, LLB, 1956, JD, 1969; BFT, Am. Grad Sch. Internat. Mgmt., Phoenix, 1957. Bar: N.D. 1963, U.S. Dist. Ct. N.D. 1963. County judge, tchr. Bensen County, Minnewaukan, N.D., 1968-75, Walsh County, Grafton, N.D., 1975-87; trial judge Devils Lake Sioux, Ft. Totten, N.D., 1968-84, Turtle Mountain Chippewa, Belcourt, N.D., 1974-87; U.S. magistrate U.S. Dist. Ct., Minnewaukan, 1972-75; Justice of the Peace pro tem Maricopa County, Ariz., 1988-92; instr. Rio Salado C.C., 1992—. Tchr. in Ethiopia, 1958-59. Author: Poetry and Other Poems, 1991. 1st lt. U.S. Army, 1952-54. Recipient Humanitarian award U.S. Cath. Conf., 1978, 82, Right to Know award Sigma Delta Chi, 1980, Spirit of Am. award U.S. Conf. Bishops, 1982. Home: 4353 E Libby St Phoenix AZ 85032-1732 E-mail: tweisenburger@cox.net.

WEISMANN, DONALD LEROY, art educator, artist, filmmaker, writer; b. Milw., Oct. 12, 1914; s. Friedrich Othello and Stela Priscilla (Custer) W.; m. M. Virginia Stant; children: Anne Wilder, Christopher Thomas. BS, U. Wis., Milw., 1935; PhM, U. Wis., Madison, 1940; PhD, Ohio State U., 1950. Asst. prof. art Ill. State U., Normal, 1940-42, 47-48, Wayne U., Detroit, 1949-51; prof., head dept. art U. Ky., Lexington, 1951-54; prof., chmn. dept. art U. Tex., Austin, 1954-58, Univ. prof. arts, 1959-81, prof. emeritus, 1981—. Cons. Ford Found., N.Y.C., 1958, 66, U.S. Nat. Com. UNESCO, 1953, Rockefeller Found., 1956, Nat. Council Arts., 1966-72; spl. cons. USIS, Forence, Italy, 1961-62 Author: Language and Visual Form, 1968, Visual Arts as Human Experience, 1970, Duncan Phyfe & Drum, 1984, Follow the Bus with the Greek License Plates, 1981, Frank Reaugh, Painter to the Longhorns, 1985, The Stuff of Stories, 1999, Artifacts, Fictions and Memory, 2001, An American Fugue, 2002; contbr. articles, poems, stories and revs. to profl. jours.; painter, collagist one-man shows, Cushman Gallery, Houston, Nye Gallery, Dallas, Petite Gallery, N.Y.C., Art Mus. U. N. Mex., group shows, Bocur Gallery, N.Y.C., Chgo. Art Inst., Dallas Mus. Fine Arts, Rockefeller Ctr., N.Y.C., Vanucci Gallery, Pistoia, Italy, Villa Monte Carlo Chapala, Jalisco, Mexico; film-maker numerous productions. Served to lt. (j.g.) USN, 1942-45, PTO. Recipient Letter of Commendation Pres. U.S., 1972; honoree for book Some Folks Went West, 12th Ann. Writers Conf., Austin, 1960; grantee U. Tex. Rsch. Inst., Italy, Eng., 1961-62, 71, Pub. Broadcast Corp., 1970, 72; named fine arts scholar Harvard U., 1941 Mem. Nat. Humanities Faculty Home: 4513 Edgemont Dr Austin TX 78731-5223 Office: Am Studies U Tex Austin TX 78712

WEISS, ANN, educational association director, filmmaker, editor, writer, photographer; b. Modena, Italy, July 17, 1949; came to U.S., 1951, naturalized, 1959; d. Leo and Athalie Weiss; children: Julia Emily, Rebecca Lauren. BA magna cum laude in English Lit. and Edn., U. Rochester, 1971; MA in Info. Sci. summa cum laude, Drexel U., 1973; MA in Comm., U. Pa., 1994, postgrad. in Edn., Culture and Soc., 1994—. Editor, chief cons. monographs, articles, freelance photographer, 1974—; cataloguer Drexel U., Phila., 1971-73; libr. Akiba Lower Sch., Merion, Pa., 1973; head children's dept. Tredyffrin Pub. Libr., Strafford, Pa., 1973-79, co-head reference dept., 1979-87. Photojournalist in Ea. Europe, mainly Poland, Ukraine and Czechoslovakia, 1987—; mem. editl. bd. Studies of Shoah, 1991—; primary investigator Holocaust rsch. team U. Pa., Transcending Trauma: Psychological Mechanism of Survival, 1989—; exec. dir. Eyes From the Ashes, 1988—, curator, 1995—; facilitator/organizer Intercultural Dialogue and Understanding, 1990—. Author: The Last Album: Eyes From the Ashes of Auschwitz, 1998; dir., exec. producer (video documentary and archive creation) oral history project Inst. Pa. Hosp. U. Pa., (video documentary) The Institute: An Intimate History, 1992; dir., producer, writer, narrator, photographer (video documentary) Eyes From The Ashes, Archival Photographs from Auschwitz, 1989-90; dir., producer, writer, narrator, photographer; author, lyricist (with Thaddeus Lorentz/musical), Zosia: An Immigrant's Story; chief editorial cons. Puppetry and the Art of Story Creation, 1981, Puppetry in Early Childhood Education, 1982, Puppetry, Language and the Special Child: Discovering Alternative Language, 1984, Humanizing the Enemy...and Ourselves, 1986, Imagination, 1987; one-person photog. shows in U.S., Europe, Israel; traveling photog. exhbn. featuring archival photos from Auschwitz-Birkenau; represented in permanent collections including Martyr's Meml. Mus./Yad Vashem, Simon Wiesenthal Ctr./Mus. Tolerance. Active So. Poverty Law Ctr., Common Cause, promoting dialogue and understanding between Jews and Arabs, Jews and Poles; active Coun. for Soviet Jews, Internat. Network Children Holocaust Survivors; photographer Bob Edgar's Campaign U.S. Senate, 1985-86, David Landau's Congl. Campaign, 1986; mem. 2d generation adv. coun. U.S. Holocaust Meml. Mus., 1995—. Mem. ACLU, NOW, SANE, Free Wallenberg Alliance, Physicians for Social Responsibility, Amnesty Internat., New Israel Fund, Sierra Club, Shefa Fund. Office: PO Box 1136 Bryn Mawr PA 19010-7136

WEISS, BARRY RONALD, education administrator; b. Superior, Wis., May 12, 1946; s. Harold Nathan and Frances Ann (Fergal) W.; m. Barbara McDaniel, Aug. 15, 1988; children: Angela Jeanette, Shauna Mikail, Ben Nathan. BS in Math. Edn., SUNY, New Paltz, 1969, MA in Math., 1975; postgrad., NYU, 1992—. Cert. tchr. N.Y., edn. adminstrn. N.Y. Tchr. elem. speech therapy Fed. Head Start Program, Middletown, N.Y., 1968-69; tchr. high sch. math. Newburgh (N.Y.) Enlarged City Sch. Dist., 1969-82, dir. edn. tech., 1982—. Chmn. planning com. Mid-Hudson Tech. Fest, N.Y., 1986-91; mem. R&D tech. adv. coun. Mid-Hudson Regional Computer Ctr., N.Y., 1981—; presenter in restructuring learning and ednl. tech. Author of poems, short stories; contbr. articles to profl. jours. Mem. N.Y. State Computers and Tech. in Edn. Assn., Sch. Adminstrs. Assn. N.Y. State, Newburgh Suprs. and Adminstrs. Assn., Mega Soc., Triple Nine Soc., Four Sigma Soc. Avocations: reading, writing, outdoor adventures. Home: 51 Leslie Rd Newburgh NY 12550-1232

WEISS, CHARLES MANUEL, environmental biologist; b. Scranton, Pa., Dec. 7, 1918; s. Morris and Fannie (Levy) W.; m. Shirley Friedlander, June 7, 1942. BS, Rutgers U., 1939, postgrad., 1939-40, Harvard U., 1940; PhD, Johns Hopkins U., 1950. Fellow in marine microbiology, research assoc. in marine biology Woods Hole Oceanographic Instn., Mass., 1939-47; chemist, biologist Balt. Harbor Project, Johns Hopkins U. Dept. San Engring., 1947-50; basin biologist div. water pollution control USPHS, N.Y.C., 1950-52; biologist med. labs. Army Chem. Ctr., Edgewood, Md., 1952-56; prof. environ. biology U. N.C., Chapel Hill, 1956-89, prof. emeritus, 1989—, creator/sponsor C. & S. Weiss Urban Livability program, 1992—. Cons. limnology Duke Power Co., 1980-94; mem. ad hoc panel waste treatment Space Sci. Bd., Nat. Acad. Sci., 1966-68, chmn. panel mgmt. of spacecraft solid and liquid wastes, 1968-69, subcom. atmosphere and water contaminants of manned spacecraft, 1971; mem. triennial water quality standards rev. com. N.C. Dept. Natural Resources and Community Devel., 1982-83; cons. Nat. Health Service, Santiago, Chile, 1971; mem. Grad. Edn. Advancement Bd., U. N.C., Chapel Hill, 2001—. Author: Water Quality Investigations, Guatemala: Lake Atitlan 1968-70, 1971, Water Quality Investigations, Guatemala: Lake Amatitlan 1969-70, 1971, The Trophic State of North Carolina Lakes, 1976, The Water Quality of the Upper Yadkin Drainage Basin, 1981, Water Quality Study, B. Everett Jordan Lake, N.C., 1981-85, 87; editor N.C. Conf. AAUP Newsletter, 1985-91. Mem. Chapel Hill Planning Bd., 1969-76, chmn., 1970-72, 75-76; trustee Chapel Hill Preservation Soc., 1972; bd. dirs. Triangle Opera, 1986, 89, 91-2002; mem. adv. coun. Santa Fe Chamber Music Festival, 1990-91, 97-98, trustee, 1991-97, 98—; bd. dirs. The Chamber Orch. of the Triangle, 1997—. Recipient Gifford Phillips award Santa Fe Chamber Music Festival, 2000; Bigelow fellow Woods Hole Oceanographic Instn., 1970—. Fellow AAAS, APHA, N.Y. Acad. Scis.; mem. AAUP (chpt. pres. 1980-81, pres. N.C. conf. 1982-83, William S. Tacey award Assembly of State Confs. 1992), Am. Chem. Soc., Am. Geophys. Union, Am. Fisheries Soc., Am. Soc. Limnology and Oceanography, Ecol. Soc. Am., Soc. Internat. Limnologie, Water Pollution Control Fedn. (chmn. rsch. com. 1966-71), Am. Water Works Assn. (chmn. subcom. water quality sampling for quality control in reservoirs 1978-80), Am. Soc. Microbiology, Sigma Xi, Delta Omega. Home: 750 Weaver Dairy Rd # 2114 Chapel Hill NC 27514-1483

WEISS, ELINOR, elementary education educator; b. Bronx, Aug. 7, 1946; d. Alex and Molly Forman; m. Joel Howard Weiss; children: Sandra, Robin. B in Edn., SUNY, Buffalo, 1968, MEd in Reading, 1971. Tchr. Buffalo Bd. Edn., 1968—. Co-owner Adventure Unltd. Day Camp, Williamsville, N.Y., 1974-86. Com. Amherst Dem. Party; del. Citizens to Save the Librs.; chair Pfohl Bros. Landfill Cleanup Com.; candidate N.Y. State Assembly, 1992. Recipient Hannah G. Solomon woman of yr. award Nat. Coun. Jewish Women, Buffalo, 1991. Mem. NEA, Handgun Control, Inc., Environ. Advocates. Democrat. Jewish. Avocations: swimming, reading.

WEISS, FAEDRA LAZAR, researcher; b. Chgo., Mar. 17, 1955; d. Howard Bernard and Frances Joyce (Gameril) Lazar; m. Lewis Jay Weiss, June 1, 1980; children: Alexandra Michelle, Marjorie Ellen, Dena Nathalia. AB, Brown U., 1976; MA in Hebrew Lit., Hebrew Union Coll., Cin., 1980. Ordained rabbi 1981. Editl. asst. Hebrew Union Coll. Press, Cin., 1984-88, asst. to publs. com., 1988-89; clergy counselor Koala Hosp., Indpls., 1989-90; rsch. asst. Girls Incorp., Indpls., 1990-93, rsch. assoc., 1993—. Author: (with others) Cost-Effectiveness in the Non-Profit Sector, 1993, Informal Science Learning, 1994, Religious Methods and Resources in Bioethics, 1994, Prevention and Parity, 1996, Friendly PEERsuasion Against Substance Use: The Girls Incorporated Model and Evaluation, 1998. Coun., trainer, troop leader Hoosier Capitol coun. Girl Scouts U.S.A., Indpls., 1989—, bd. dirs., 1990—96, 2002—; mem. Indpls. Arts Chorale, 1989—, Cantabile!, 2002—, bd. dirs., 2003—; mem. Indpls. Bd. Rabbis, 1989—; mem. health profl. adv. com. March of Dimes, Cin., 1986—89, Indpls., 1989—91; bd. dirs. Big Bros./Big Sisters Ctrl. Ind., 2001—03. Mem. AAAS, Am. Ednl. Rsch. Assn., Ctrl. Con. Am. Rabbis. Jewish. Home: 7805 Mohawk Ln Indianapolis IN 46260-3339 Office: Girls Incorp Nat Resource Ctr 441 W Michigan St Indianapolis IN 46202-3287 E-mail: fweiss@girls-inc.org.

WEISS, GERALD FRANCIS, JR., secondary education educator, coach; b. Pottsville, Pa., Nov. 22, 1961; s. Gerald Francis Sr. and Joan (Marx) W.; m. Patricia Ann Lengel, Nov. 22, 1985; children: Matthew, Nicole, Caitlin. BS in Edn./Physics, Kutztown (Pa.) U., 1985; MS in Edn., Wilkes U., Wilkes-Barre, Pa., 1991. Cert. tchr., Pa. Tchr. sci. Tri-Valley Sch. Dist., Higgins, Pa., 1985-86; tchr. physics and chemistry St. Clair (Pa.) Sch. Dist., 1986-87; tchr. physics Hamburg (Pa.) Area Sch. Dist., 1987—. Instr. Alvernia Coll., 1997-98. Program dir. Camp Duportail, Hawk Mountain coun. Boy Scouts Am., summer 1995, I dian Run Dist. membership chair, 1995-98. Named Disting. Tchr. of Honor Students Pa. State U., 1994, Outstanding Young Ams., 1998; recipient Outstanding Educator award Phila. Coll. Textiles and Sci., 1994. Avocations: fishing, boating. Home: 439 Mohave Dr Auburn PA 17922-9512 Office: Hamburg Area Sch Dist Windsor St Hamburg PA 19526

WEISS, GERSON, physician, educator; b. N.Y.C., Aug. 1, 1939; s. Samuel and Lillian (Wolpe) W.; m. Linda Gordon, Dec. 24, 1959; children: Jonathan, David, Michele, Andrew. BA, NYU, 1960, MD, 1964. Diplomate Am. Bd. Ob-Gyn. (mem. divsn. reproductive endocrinology 1985-90, pres. bd. 1999-2002). Intern, fellow dept. medicine Johns Hopkins Sch. Medicine, 1964-65; resident ob-gyn NYU Med. Ctr., 1964-69; rsch. fellow physiology U. Pitts. Sch. Medicine, 1971-73; asst. prof. ob-gyn NYU Med. Ctr., 1971-76, asso. prof., 1976-80, prof., 1980-85; dir. div. reproductive endocrinology NYU Med. Center, 1975-85; prof. ob-gyn U. Med. and Dentistry N.J.-N.J. Med. Sch., 1986—, chmn. dept., 1986—; dir. divsn. reproductive endocrinology Hackensack (N.J.) U. Med. Ctr., 1996—2002. Rep. Am. Bd. Med. Specialists. Mem. editl. bd. Fertility and Sterility Jour., 1986-93, Gyn.-Ob. Investigation; contbr. rsch. articles reproductive endocrinology and gynecology to med. jours. Served to maj. MC U.S. Army, 1969-71. Rsch. grantee NIH, 1975—, United Cerebral Palsy Found., 1977-83, Mellon Found., 1982-85; John Polachek Found. Med. Rsch. fellow. Mem. ACOG, Am. Gyn-Ob. Soc., Am. Bd. Ob-Gyn. (bd. dirs., treas. 1997-98, pres. 1998-2002, chmn. 2002—, ob-gyn. residency rev. com. 1995-2000, coun. univ. chairs ob-gyn, pres.-elect, 1998-99, pres. 2000-02), Am. Bd. Med. Spltys. (coun. 2002—), Endocrine Soc., Soc. Gynecol. Investigation (pres.-elect 20004), N.Y. Obstet. Soc. (pres. 1990-91), N.Y. Gynecol. Soc. (pres. 1989-90), Soc. Study of Reprodn., Endocine Soc., Phi Beta Kappa, Sigma Xi, Alpha Omega Alpha. Home: 390 1st Ave Apt 11D New York NY 10010-4935 Office: UMDNJ NJ Med Sch Dept Ob-Gyn 185 S Orange Ave Newark NJ 07103-2757

WEISS, KENNETH JAY, education educator, reading specialist, administrator; b. N.Y.C., Mar. 26, 1950; s. Daniel and Ida (Berson) W.; m. Roberta Carol Ungar, June 10, 1973; children: Seth, Richard. BA, C.W. Post Coll., 1972; MBA, Long Island U., 1982; EdM, Rutgers U., 1989, EdD, 1993. Cert. tchr. reading specialist, adminstr., N.J. Assoc. prof. edn. Nazareth Coll., Rochester, 1993—. Mem. Nat. Coun. Tchrs. English, Internat. Reading Assn., Nat. Reading Conf., Nat. Conf. Rsch. in Lit. and Lang. Arts, Kappa Delta Pi.

WEISS, MARY ALICE, insurance economics educator; b. Cleve., June 12, 1957; d. Richard Alfred and Julianna (Scerbik) Weiss; m. J. David Cummins. BSBA, Quincy Coll., 1979; MS in Ins. Econs., U. Pa., 1982, PhD in Ins. Econs., 1984. Lectr. La Salle Coll., Phila., 1983; asst. prof. U. S.C., Columbia, 1984, Rider Coll., Lawrenceville, NJ, 1984-86, Temple U., Phila., 1986—98, prof., 1998—. Cons. IBM, N.Y.C., 1985—87; spkr. nat. and internat. ins. confs. Assoc. editor: Jour. Risk and Ins., 1985—; co-editor: Risk Mgmt. and Ins. Rev., 1999—; contbr. articles to profl. jours. Active Clean Water Action, Phila., 1986—; PhD mentor Phila., 1987—. Fellow, Huebner Found., 1979—82; presdl. scholar, Quincy Coll., 1975—79. Mem.: Risk Theory Soc., Am. Risk and Ins. Assn. (coms., nat. conf. spkr., bd. dirs., Robert I. Mehr Rsch. award 2003). Democrat. Avocation: antiques. Home: 625 New Gulph Rd Bryn Mawr PA 19010-3650 Office: Temple U Ritter Hall Annex Rm 473 Philadelphia PA 19122

WEISS, RITA SANDRA, transportation executive, educator; b. Phila., May 24, 1935; d. Jack J. and Cecelia (Alper) Brown; m. Irvin J. Weiss, Oct. 29, 1955; children: Brett David, Judith Weiss Bohn. BS in Edn., Temple U., 1955; MA in Edn., U. Md., 1976. Cert. elem. tchr., Md. Tchr. Solis-Cohen Elem. Sch., Phila., 1955-59, Geneva Nursery Sch., Rockville, Md., 1966-71; dir. Har Shalom Nursery Sch., Potomac, Md., 1971-78; ednl. cons. Am. Automobile Assn., Falls Church, Va., 1978-88; program analyst Nat. Hwy. Traffic Safety Adminstrn. U.S. Dept. Transp., Washington, 1988-93, divsn. chief Nat. Hwy. Traffic Safety Adminstrn. State and Cmty. Svcs., 1993-97; tchr. presch. Washington Hebrew Early Childhood Ctr, Potomac, Md., 1997—. Author numerous traffic safety publs. Dept. Transp. fellow, 1993-94; recipient Disting. Svc. to Safety award Nat. Safety Coun., 1994. Mem. NHTSA Profl. Women's Assn. (rec. sec., area rep.), Nat. Safety Coun. (bd. dirs., chmn. edn. resources div., chmn. community agys. sect.), Md. Community Assn. for Edn. Young Children (pres., newsletter editor, historian), Childhood Edn. Internat. (assoc.), U. Md. Alumni Assn., Women's Transp. Seminar. Avocations: needlework, reading, hiking, theater. Address: 803 Gaither Rd Rockville MD 20850

WEISS, SHIRLEY F. urban and regional planner, economist, educator; b. N.Y.C., Feb. 26, 1921; d. Max and Vera (Hendel) Friedlander; m. Charles M. Weiss, June 7, 1942. BA, Douglass Coll., Rutgers U., 1942; postgrad., Johns Hopkins U., 1949-50; M in Regional Planning, U. N.C., 1958; PhD, Duke U., 1973. Assoc. research dir. Ctr. for Urban and Regional Studies U. N.C., Chapel Hill, 1957-91, lectr. in planning, 1958-62, assoc. prof., 1962-73, prof., 1973-91, prof. emerita, 1991—; joint creator-sponsor Charles and Shirley Weiss Urban Livability Program, U. N.C., Chapel Hill, 1992—; research assoc. Inst. for Research in Social Sci., U. N.C., 1957-73; research prof. U. N.C., Chapel Hill, 1973-91, acting dir. women's studies program Coll. Arts and Scis., 1985, faculty marshal, 1988-91. Mem. grad. edn. advancement bd. U.N.C., Chapel Hill, 2001—, tech. com. Water Resources Rsch. Inst., 1976-79; mem. adv. com. on housing for 1980 census Dept. Commerce, 1976-81; cons. Urban Inst., Washington, 1977-80; mem. rev. panel Exptl. Housing Allowance Program, HUD, 1977-80; mem. adv. bd. on built environ. Nat. Acad. Scis.-NRC, 1981-83, mem. program coordinating com. fed. constrn. coun. of adv. bd. on built environ., 1982-83; mem. Planning Accreditation Bd., Site Visitation Pool, Am. Inst. Cert. Planners and Assn. Collegiate Schs. Planning, 1985—; mem. discipline screening com. Fulbright Scholar awards in Architecture and City Planning, Coun. for Internat. Exchange of Scholars, 1985-88; mem. N.Mex. adv. bd. The Enterprise Found., Santa Fe, 1997-2002; mem. governing bd. Acad. Freedom Fund, AAUP, 1997-2000. Author: The Central Business District in Transition: Methodological Approaches to CBD Analysis and Forecasting Future Space Requirements, 1957, New Town Development in the United States: Experiment in Private Entrepreneurship, 1973; co-author: A Probabilistic Model for Residential Growth, 1964, Residential Developer Decisions: A Focused View of the Urban Growth Process, 1966, New Communities U.S.A., 1976; co-author, co-editor: New Community Development: Planning Process, Implementation and Emerging Social Concerns, vols. 1, 2, 1971, City Centers in Transition, 1976, New Communities Research Series, 1976-77; mem. editl. bd.: Jour. Am. Inst. Planners, 1963-68, Rev. of Regional Studies, 1969-74, 82-92, Internat. Regional Sci. Rev., 1975-81. Trustee Friends of Libr., U. N.C., Chapel Hill, 1988-94, Santa Fe Chamber Music Festival, adv. coun., 1990-91, 97-98, trustee, 1991-97, 98—; bd. dirs. Triangle Opera, 1986-89, 91-2002, Chamber Orch. of the Triangle, 1997—. Recipient Cornelia Phillips Spencer Bell award in recognition of contbns. to life and success of U. N.C. at Chapel Hill, 1996, Disting. Alumni award in recognition of outstanding contbns. in field of city and regional planning Alumni Assn. Dept. City and Regional Planning, U. N.C., Chapel Hill, 1996, Mary Turner Lane award Assn. Women Faculty, 1994, (with Charles M. Weiss) Gifford Phillips award Santa Fe Chamber Music Festival, 2000, Disting. Alumni and Alumnus award U. N.C., Chapel, 2003; Adelaide M. Zagoren fellow Douglass Coll., Rutgers U., 1994. Emeritus fellow Urban Land Inst. (sr. fellow, exec. group, cmty. devel. coun. 1978—); mem. Am. Inst. Planners (sec., treas. southeast chpt. 1957-59, v.p. 1960-61), Am. Inst. Cert. Planners, Am. Planning Assn., Am. Econ. Assn., So. Regional Sci. Assn. (pres. 1977-78), Regional Sci. Assn. (councillor 1971-74, v.p. 1976-77), Nat. Assn. Housing and Redevelopment Ofcls., Interamerican Planning Soc., Internat. Fedn. Housing and Planning, Town and Country Planning Assn., Internat. Urban Devel. Assn., Econ. History Assn., Am. Real Estate and Urban Econs. Assn. (regional membership chmn. 1976-82, 84-85, dir. 1977-80), AAUP (chpt. pres. 1976-77, pres. N.C. Conf. 1978-79, mem. nat. coun. 1983-86, William S. Tacey award Assembly of State Confs.), Douglass Soc., Order of Valkyries, Phi Beta Kappa. Home: 750 Weaver Dairy Rd # 2114 Chapel Hill NC 27514-1483

WEISS, STEPHEN FREDRICK, computer science educator; b. Berkeley, Calif., Mar. 6, 1944; s. Irving F. and Eleanor G. Weiss; m. Iris R. Weiss, Aug. 11, 1968; children: Jeremy, Daniel. BS in Math., Carnegie Inst. Tech., 1966; MS in Computer Sci., Cornell U., 1969, PhD in Computer Sci., 1970. Prof., chmn. computer sci. U. N.C., Chapel Hill, 1970—. Home: 306 Highview Dr Chapel Hill NC 27517-7913 Office: U NC Computer Sci Dept Cb 3175 Sitterson Hl Chapel Hill NC 27599-3175

WEISS, SUSAN ELLEN, adult nurse practitioner, educator; b. Youngstown, Ohio, Oct. 25, 1951; d. Robert Cochran and Clara Olive (Cyphert) Stetson; m. Paul Wm. Weiss, Dec. 27, 1975; children: David, Rebecca, Noah. AAS, Youngstown State U., 1971, BSN, 1975; cert. adult nurse practitioner, SUNY, 1981. Cert. adult nurse practitioner, SUNY, legal nurse cons. Nurse practitioner St. Joseph Riverside Hosp., Warren, Ohio; emergency room nurse St. Elizabeth Hosp., Youngstown; ICU-CCU nurse Youngstown Osteo. Hosp.; dir. advanced nursing edn. NP Sch. Based Clinic, 1994. Mem.: AACN, Am. Acad. Nurse Practitioners, Cardiovascular Nursing Assn., Oncology Nursing Soc., Nat. League Nursing, Am. Coll. Cert. Legal Nurse Cons., Am. Coll. Nurse Practitioners. Home: 6131 Saint Andrews Dr Canfield OH 44406-9023 E-mail: weissan@aol.com.

WEISSKOPF, THOMAS EMIL, economics educator; b. Rochester, N.Y., Apr. 13, 1940; s. Victor Frederick and Ellen (Tuede) W.; m. Frederique Apffel, Mar. 23, 1963 (div. June 1969); 1 child, Marc; m. Susan Contratto, Jan. 17, 1970; children: Nicholas, Jonah. BA, Harvard U., 1961; PhD, MIT, 1966. Asst. prof. econs. dept. Harvard U., Cambridge, Mass., 1968-72; prof. econs. dept. U. Mich., Ann Arbor, 1972—. Dir. residential coll. U. Mich., 1996—. Author: Beyond the Waste Land, 1983, After the Waste Land, 1991; editor: Microeconomics in Context, 2002, The Capitalist System, 1972, 1978, 1986; author: Economics and Social Justice, 1998. Office: Univ Mich Ann Arbor MI 48109

WEISSMAN, ANN PALEY, art educator, artist, consultant; b. N.Y.C., Aug. 20, 1931; d. Bernard and Sylvia Paley; m. Arthur Weissman, Jan. 27, 1951; children: Nili, Kenneth, Margot. BA in Psychology and Sociology, Hunter Coll., 1952; student, fine and applied art, Broome C.C., 1983—. Social worker Learning Ctr., Binghamton, NY, 1968—70; dir. Hope Lodge (Am. Cancer Soc.), 1970—73; consumer advisor, cons. Cuisinarts, Greenwich, Conn., 1970—85; designer, owner Arbor Art, Binghamton, 1998—; tchr., cons. Discovery Ctr., Binghamton, 2000—. Archtl. guide Preservation Assn. S Tier, Binghamton, NY, 1981—; fin. advisor, tchr. Broome C.C. and Office for Aging, Binghamton, 1989—; fin. advisor Discovery Ctr., Binghamton, 1985—. 1850 Christmas, 2001; inventor flower collars and tree masks. Bd. mem. Commn. of Arch. and Urban Design, Binghamton, NY, 1998—; v.p. bd. Preservation Assn. of Binghamton, 1991—; docent So. Tier Roberson Meml. Mus., Binghamton, 1962—69; cons. Binghamton Planning Commn., 2000—. Mem.: Madrigal Choir of Binghamton (mem. bd. pub. rels. 1985—). Avocations: gardening, ceramics, music, cooking, decorating. Home: 5 Vincent St Binghamton NY 13905

WEISSMAN, MICHAEL HERBERT, pediatrician, educator; b. Bklyn., Jan. 15, 1942; s. George and Sipora (Silvera) W.; m. Marianne Wastcoat, July 30, 1967; children: Robert, Alexander, Samuel, Sarah, Rachel. BME, Cooper Union U., 1963; MS, PhD, Northwestern U., 1965; MD, Washington U., St. Louis, 1976. Diplomate Am. Bd. Pediat. Intern Bronx Mcpl. Hosp. Ctr., 1976-77, resident, 1977-79, chief resident, 1979-80; asst. prof. engring. Carnegie-Mellon U., Pitts., 1967-71, assoc. prof., 1971-73; practice medicine specializing in pediatrics Mount Kisco, N.Y., 1980—. Mem. staff No. Westchester Hosp. Ctr., Mount Kisco, chief pediats., 1993-98; trustee Hosp. Albert Einstein Coll. Medicine, 2002—; ptnr. Mt. Kisco Med. Group, PC, 1981-89, shareholder, 1989—; clin. asst. prof. NY Med. Coll., 1991—. Contbr. articles to profl. jours. Office: Mt Kisco Med Group 110 S Bedford Rd Mount Kisco NY 10549-3446

WEISS-SWEDE, FRANCES ROBERTA See ZAMIR, FRANCES

WEISTUCH, LUCILLE, special education educator; b. N.Y.C., July 5, 1949; d. Irving and Charlotte (Nadelman) W.; m. Alan Saffner, Aug. 21, 1977; children: Jesse, Amy. BS in Edn., CCNY, 1971, MS in Edn., 1975; PhD, Yeshiva U., 1982. Cert. spl. educator, N.J., N.Y. Tchr. Shield Inst., Bronx, N.Y., 1971-79; predoctoral fellow Ednl. Texting Svc., Princeton, N.J., 1979-82; coord. Project Child-Mercer County Spl. Svc., Trenton, N.J., 1982-83; researcher U. Med. and Dentistry of N.J., New Brunswick, N.J., 1983-89; faculty Montclair State Coll., Upper Montclair, N.J., 1989—. Dir. Lang. Project UMDNJ, New Brunswick, 1983-88; cons. Middletown Pre-sch., 1988, Essex County Consortium, Newark, 1989—. Author: Language Interaction Intervention, 1991; contbr. articles to profl. jours. Den leader Boy Scouts of Am., Middlesex County, N.J., 1990-92, brownie leader, Raritan Chpt., 1992—. Recipient H.C.E.E.P grant, 1983, State Mini-grant, N.J. State Dept. Edn., 1987. Mem. Coun. for Exceptional Children (program chair 1990—, newsletter chair 1992-93, recording sec. 1992-93). Democrat. Jewish. Avocations: kids activities, plays, movies. Home: 7 Marvin Rd Monmouth Junction NJ 08852-2929

WEITZ, JEANNE STEWART, artist, educator; b. Warren, Ohio, Apr. 30, 1920; d. William McKinley and Ruth (Stewart) Kohlmorgan; m. Loyal Wilbur Weitz, Aug. 1, 1940 (dec. 1986); children: Gail, Judith, John, Marc. BS in Art and English, Youngstown U., 1944; MEd in Art, U. Tex., El Paso, 1964; postgrad., Tex. Tech U., 1976. Indsl. engr. Republic Iron & Steel, Youngstown, Ohio, 1942-43; art tchr. pub. schs., Bessemer, Pa., 1943-44, El Paso (Tex.) Independent Sch. Dist., 1944-50, 54-78, art. cons., 1978-87; art tchr. Hermosa Beach (Calif.) Independent Sch. Dist., 1950-53, El Paso Mus. Art, 1960-65; lectr. in art U. Tex., El Paso, 1963-66; instr. El Paso Community Coll., 1970-78; free-lance artist, lectr. El Paso, 1987-91; supr. student tchr. U. Tex., El Paso, 1989-91; mgr. Sunland Art Gallery, 1994-95. Represented in group exhibitions at Sun CarnivalExhbn., 1961, El Paso Mus. Art, 1962; author highsch. curriculum guide; exhibited at LVAA Shows, 1990 (5 First Places), Westside Art Guild, 1992, LVAA, 1992 (1st in Watercolor). Coordinator art edn. El Paso Civic Planning Coun., 1985-86; chmn. art edn., art resources dept. City of El Paso, 1982-83. Recipient Purchase award El Paso Art Assn. Spring Show, 1995, 1st pl. award KCOS (PBS), 1996, 1st pl. award Westside Art Guild, 1996, 2d pl. El Paso Art Assoc., 1998, 1st pl. award West Side Art Guild, 1998, 99, H.M. El Paso Pastel Soc. Show, 1998. Mem.: Pastel Soc. N.Mex. (v.p. 2001, pres. 2003), Rio Grande Art Assn., N.Mex. Watercolor Soc., Pastel Soc. El Paso (v.p. 1999—2000), Rio Bravo Watercolorists (sec. 1998), Nat. Soc. Am. Pen Women, Westside Art Guild (pres. 1993—95), Nat. Art Edn. Assn. (sec. 1988—93, two 1st place award LVAA shows 1989), Lower Valley Art Assn. (Hon. Mention award 1988), El Paso Mus. Art Guild, Nat. Soc. Arts and Letters (sec. El Paso chpt. 1988—), Tex. Art Edn. Assn. (local orgn. 1981, conf. planner, Hon. Mention award 1972). Republican. Presbyterian. Avocations: printmaking, travel. Home: 22 Canon Escondito Sandia Park NM 87047 E-mail: jweitz@prodigy.net.

WEITZEL, MARILYN LEE, nursing educator; b. Akron, Ohio, Mar. 6, 1946; d. William and Susie Lee (York) Hupp; m. Daniel A. Weitzel, May 24, 1986; children: Laura Demastus, Edgar Demastus, Brock Demastus. Diploma, Idabelle Firestone Sch., 1967; BS, St. Joseph's Coll., North Windham, Maine, 1988; MSN, U. Akron (Ohio), 1993; PhD, U. South Ala., 2003. Cert. tchr. Staff nurse Akron City Hosp., 1967-69, Children's Hosp. Med. Ctr., Akron, 1969-80, instr., Akron Sch. Practical Nursing, 1980-94; asst. prof. nursing Cleve. State U., 1994—. Vol. N.E. Ohio Task Force on AIDS. Mem. Nat. Assn. Women's Health, Obstet. and Neonatal Nursing, Ohio Assn. Practical Nurse Educators, Ohio League for Nursing, Nursing Edn. Mobility Action Group N.E. Ohio (task force), Ala. League Nursing, Sigma Theta Tau. Anglican.

WEITZMANN, WILLIAM HENRY, education educator, photographer; b. Phila., Apr. 8, 1943; s. Henry P. and Anna H. Weitzmann; m. Susan L. Bower, June 25, 1966; children: Todd W., Amy L. BA in Indsl. Arts Edn., Pa. State U., 1966; MA in Indsl. Tech., Trenton State Coll., 1972. Cert. tchr. tech. edn. and indsl. arts. Tchr. indsl. arts East Stroudsburg (Pa.) Sch. Dist., 1966-68; curriculum coord., tchr. Stroudsburg (Pa.) Area Sch. Dist., 1968—; owner W.H. Weitzmann Photographer, Stroudsburg, 1976—. Adj. prof. East Stroudsburg (Pa.) U., 1982, 98—; bd. dirs. North Eastern Pa. Sch. Employees Fed. Credit Union, Stroudsburg. Photographs appeared in one-man show East Stroudsburg (Pa.) U., 1982. Scoutmaster Boy Scouts Am., Stroudsburg, 1973-93. Recipient award of merit Boy Scouts Am.-Pocono Dist., 1985, Silver Beaver award Boy Scouts Am.-Minsi Trails Coun., 1988, citation Pa. Ho. of Reps., 1990, 93, commendation The Gov.'s Office, 1993, commendation The Senate Pa., 1993, commendation Monroe County Commrs., 1993, Founders award North Ea. Pa. Fed. Credit Union, 1998; ITEC Microcomputer Competitive grantee Pa. Higher Edn. Assistance Agy., Stroudsburg, 1987. Mem. NEA, Pa. State Edn. Assn., Tech. Edn. Assn. Pa. (v.p. 1993-98, pres.-elect 1999, dep. pres. 2000, pres. 2001, past pres., 2002, conf. workshop chmn. 1996-98, Outstanding V.p. Svc. award 1996, Pres.' citation 2001). Avocation: classical automobile restoration. Home: 523 Queen St Stroudsburg PA 18360-2215 Office: Stroudsburg Area Sch Dist 1100 W Main St Stroudsburg PA 18360-1332 E-mail: bill.weitzmann@teap-online.org.

WEIXLMANN, JOSEPH NORMAN, JR., English educator, provost; b. Buffalo, N.Y., Dec. 16, 1946; s. Joseph Norman and Mary C. (Degenhart) W.; m. Sharron Pollack, Mar. 14, 1982; children: Seth Jacob, Adira Jenna, Benjamin Ari. AB, Canisius Coll., 1968; MA, Kans. State U., 1970, PhD, 1973. Instr. U. Okla., Norman, 1973-74; asst. prof. Tex. Tech U., Lubbock, 1974-76; from asst. prof. to prof. Ind. State U., Terre Haute, 1976—2001, assoc. dean, 1987-92, acting dean, 1992-94, dean, 1994—2001; prof. St. Louis U., 2001—, dean, 2001—02, provost, 2002—. Author: John Barth, 1976, American Short-Fiction Criticism, 1982; co-editor: Black American Prose Theory, 1984, Belief vs. Theory in Black American Literary Criticism, 1986, Black Feminist Criticism, 1988, Studies in Black Am. Lit. Ann., 1984-88; editor African Am. Rev. jour., 1976—; contbg. editor High Plains Lit. Rev., 1987-2002; adv. editor Langston Hughes Rev., 1982—. Fellow NDEA, 1970-72, NEH, 1980; Nat. Endowment for Arts grantee, 1988-95. Mem. MLA (exec. com. divsn. Black Am. Lit. and Culture 1985—), Coll. Lang. Assn., Langston Hughes Soc., Zora Neale Hurston Soc., Coun. Lit. Mags. and Presses (grantee 1977-96, Editor's grantee 1986), Coun. Editors Learned Jours. Office: Saint Louis U DuBourg Hall #106 Saint Louis MO 63103 Home: 6344 Wydown Blvd Saint Louis MO 63105-2213

WELBURN, BRENDA LILIENTHAL, professional society administrator; Grad., Howard U.; postgrad., U. Pa. Social worker, Phila.; rsch. analyst U.S. Ho. Reps. Select Com. on Assassinations; legis. asst. to Senator Paul Tsongas Mass.; dir. govtl. affairs Nat. Assn. State Bds. Edn., Alexandria, Va., 1984—88, dep. exec. dir., 1988—93, exec. dir., 1993—. Presenter in field. Author: The American Tapestry: Educating a Nation; contbr. articles to profl. jours. Office: Nat Assn State Bds Edn 277 S Washington St Alexandria VA 22314*

WELCH, BRENDA ROXSON, elementary education educator; b. Poplarville, Miss., Aug. 21, 1954; d. Perry George and Vivian Ernestine (Hodge) Stapleton; m. Jewel Edward Welch Jr., Dec. 6, 1972; children: Jewel Edward III, Tena Caroline, Jacob Samuel. BS, La. State U., 1984, Masters, 1993. Tchr. 2d grade Zachary (La.) Elem. Sch., 1984-85; tchr. 3rd grade Baker Heights Elem. Sch., Baker, La., 1985—. Adv. coun. La. Energy and Environ. Resource and Info. Ctr., Baton Rouge, 1990—; tech. advisor City Park/University Lakes Commn., Baton Rouge, 1992—; facilitator project WILD; supervising tchr. for student tchrs. math., sci., social studies La. State U.; mem. Libr. Power Writing team, Sci. Curriculum Tng. team; founder ednl facility Discovery Outpost. Author: Discovery Outpost: Activities in Hands-on Math and Science; contbg. author: Program for Leadership in Earth Science Activity Guide, Hands-on Science, 1991. Co-founder Operation R.E.D. (Recycling for Edn. against Drugs) East Baton Rouge Parish, La., 1990—; coord. East Baton Rouge Parish Earth Day, Baton Rouge, 1992, 93, East Baton Rouge Children's Coalition; speaker Save the Rainforest Internat.; active Friends of the Environment, La. Wildlife Fedn. Recipient ScienceGrasp award UpJohn Pharm., 1991, Primary Leadership award in Sci. and Math., Lawrence Hall of Sci. U. Calif., 1991; Excellence in Teaching grantee Jr. League, 1991, Dow grantee, 1992, Acad. Distinction Fund grantee 1992, 93. Mem. Nat. Sci. Tchrs. Assn. (presenter nat. and regional confs., awards and recognition selection subcom.), Nat. Coun. Tchrs. Math., Internat. Reading Assn. (presenter regional convs.), Coun. for Elem. Sci. Internat. (coord. regional Nat. Sci. Tchrs. Assn. sessions), La. Sci. Tchrs. Assn. (presenter conf., Elem. Sci. Educator of Yr. 1992), New Orleans Coun. Tchrs. Math., La. Reading Assn., Greater Baton Rouge Sci. Educators Assn. (pres. 1992-93), Capitol Area Reading Coun. (judge Young Authors). Home: 412 Douceur Dr Baker LA 70714-3830 Office: Baker Heights Elem Sch 4750 Harding St Baker LA 70714-3908

WELCH, RHEA JO, special education educator; b. Jacksonville, Ill., Jan. 26, 1957; d. James Daniel and Bobbye Jo (Weatherford) W.; 1 child, James Alexander. BA, William Woods U., Fulton, Mo., 1980; cert., U. Ill., Springfield, 1981; postgrad., MacMurray Coll., 1985, 86, 88, So. Ill. U., 1990, 91. Cert. 6-12 tchr., spl. edn., Ill. Tchr. recreational skills Ill. Sch. for Visually Impaired, Jacksonville, 1984; cross categorical tchr. Sangamon Area Spl. Edn. Dist., Springfield, 1988-89; tchr.'s aid Four Rivers Spl. Edn. Dist., Jacksonville, 1981, substitute tchr. spl. edn., 1982-86, tchr. learning disabilities, 1987, tchr. students with severe behavioral disorders, 1989—. Mem. human rights com. Jacksonville Devel. Ctr., 1992—; pub. speaker; project dir. for community svc. programs Garrison Sch., Ill. Adv. Coun. on Voluntary Action-Serve Ill.; originator Class Time Community Svc. Volunteerism Four Rivers Spl. Edn. Dist.; coord. Spl. Olympics Ivan K. Garrison Sch., 1992-93; speaker Ill. Coun. Children With Behavior Disorders, 1997. Vol. ARC, instr. HIV-AIDS, CPR, First Aid. Named Staff Mem. of Month, Ivan K. Garrison Alternative Sch., 1992, 2001; recipient 2 Disting. Svc. citations, 1992; grantee, Kraft Food Co., 1991—92. Mem. Coun. for Exceptional Children, Nat. Soc. for Experiential Edn. Episcopalian. Office: Four Rivers Spl Edn Dist 936 W Michigan Ave Jacksonville IL 62650-3113

WELCH, ROBERT DINWIDDIE, retired school administrator; b. Chgo., July 19, 1925; s. Ira Hubert Reginald and Ella Sarah (Dinwiddie) W.; m. June 18, 1955; children: Robert Dean, Richard Allen. BA summa cum laude, Dartmouth Coll., Hanover, N.H., 1948; MA in English Lit., U. Chgo., 1952; postgrad., New Sch. Social Rsch., N.Y.C., 1948-52, Wayne State U., Detroit, 1952-60. Lic. tchr., adminstr., Mich. Instr. St. Paul's Sch., Garden City, N.Y., 1948-52; instr. English/social studies Pierce Jr. H.S., Grosse Pointe, Mich., 1952-59; instr. English Grosse Pointe H.S. South, 1959-62, libr. coord., 1962-64, asst. prin. curriculum, 1964-68, Grosse Point H.S. North, 1968-75; dir. curriculum Grosse Point Pub. Schs., 1975-92; ret.; part-time master tchr. English Harvard U., Cambridge, Mass., summers 1958-66; part-time English instr., supr. Wayne County C.C., Detroit, 1970-80. Evaluator, writer North Ctrl. Assn., Detroit area, 1975-85; dir. Dept. Secondary Curriculum, Grosse Pointe Pub. Schs., 1980-92. Book reviewer Libr. Jour., 1972-83; author (curriculum books) in reading, composition, literature, grammar, 1965. Adv. bd. Grosse Point Found. Acad. Enrichment, 1983-90; chmn. social responsibilities com. Grosse Pointe Unitarian Ch., 1965, mem. bldg. com., 1960; chmn. of recorders ct. study Detroit Riots Com., 1966; advisor, spkr. Native Am. Program, East Detroit, 1978-83. Lt. (j.g.) USNR, 1942-46. Mem. Detroit Inst. Arts, Nat. Coun. Tchrs. English, U.S. Naval Res. Assn., Greenfield Village/Henry Ford Mus., Phi Beta Kappa, Phi Delta Kappa. Democrat. Home: 23313 Greencrest St Saint Clair Shores MI 48080-2564

WELCH-HILL, CONSTANCE MARCELLA, speech and language therapist, consultant; b. Wichita, Kans., Nov. 28, 1958; d. Winfred Du Bois and Graydie Marie (Bennett) Welch; m. Steven Joseph Hill, Aug. 11, 1984; 1 child, Matthew Christopher; stepson from previous marriage: Steven Marcus Hill. BS, Fontbonne Coll., 1981. Cert. speech correction K-12, Mo. Speech and lang. therapist Ware County Bd. Edn., Waycross, Ga., 1981; speech and lang. asst. Chgo. Bd. Edn., 1981-83; speech therapist in behavior mgmt. Judevine Ctr. for Autism, St. Louis, 1985—; speech and lang. therapist Franklin County Coop., St. Clair, Mo., 1989—, cons., 1992—; speech and lang. therapist R-II Sch., New Haven, Mo., 1989—. Cons. New Haven Sch. Dist., 1994—. Campaign worker Horace White for Alderman, Chgo., summer 1982. Mem. Mo. Tchrs. Accreditation Orgn. Democrat. Roman Catholic. Avocations: reading, crafts. Home: 704 Brownbert Ct Saint Louis MO 63119-1302

WELDEN, ALICIA GALAZ-VIVAR, foreign language educator; b. Valparaiso, Chile, Dec. 4, 1937; came to U.S., 1976; d. Pedro and Juanita (Vivar) Galaz; m. Oliver Welden, May 2, 1973; children: Arnold, Jacqueline, Cinthya, Jonathan. Grad., U. Chile, Santiago, 1955; PhD, U. Ala., Tuscaloosa, 1980. Prof. U. Chile, 1966-76; lectr. Appalachian State U., N.C., 1982-89; assoc. prof. U. Tenn., Martin, 1989—. Dept. chair U. Chile, Antofagasta, 1966-68; founder, editor Tebaida Lit. Rev., Chile, 1968-70. Author: Antologia de Gongora, 1962, Jaula Gruesa, 1972, Oficio de Mudanza, 1987, Alta Marea, 1989, Senas Distantes, 1990. Regional pres. Pablo Neruda's Presidential Candidacy, Chile, 1969-70. Mem. MLA, Am. Coun. Tchrs. Fgn. Langs., Tenn. Philol. Assn., Soc. Chilean Writers, Ctr. Poetical Hispanic Studies, Phi Kappa Phi. Roman Catholic. Office: Univ Tenn Modern Fgn Langs Martin TN 38238-0001

WELDON, WILLIAM FORREST, electrical and mechanical engineer, educator; b. San Marcos, Tex., Jan. 12, 1945; s. Forrest Jackson and Rubie Mae (Wilson) W.; m. Morey Sheppard McGonigle, July 28, 1968; children: William, Embree, Seth Forrest. BS in Engring. Sci., Trinity U., San Antonio, 1967; MSME, U. Tex., 1970. Registered profl. engr., Tex. Engr. Cameron Iron Works, Houston, 1967-68; project engr. Glastron Boat Co., Austin, Tex., 1970-72; chief engr. Nalle Plastics Co., Austin, 1972-73; rsch. engr. U. Tex., Austin, 1973-77, tech. dir. Ctr. Electromechanics, 1977-85, dir. Ctr. Electromechanics, 1985-93, prof., 1985-2000, Josey Centennial prof. in energy resources, 1992-2000, Josey Centennial prof. emeritus, 2000—. Mem. permanent com. Symposium on Electromagnetic Launch Tech., 1978-97, vice chmn., 1995-98, naval rsch. adv. com., 1992-97, 2001-; cons. numerous cos. and govts., 1973—; chief scientist Office Naval Rsch.-Europe, 1998-99; tech. dir. Office Naval Rsch. Internat. Field Office, 1998-99. Contbr. over 285 articles to profl. publs. Bd. dirs. Water Control & Improvement Dist. No. 10, Travis County, Tex., 1984-97. Recipient Peter Mark medal Electromagnetic Launch Symposium, 1986, IR 100 award Indsl. Rsch. mag., 1983, Navy Superior Pub. Svc. award, 1998, 99. Fellow ASME; mem. IEEE (sr.), NSPE. Achievements include 36 patents for rotating electrical machines, pulsed power, and electromagnetic propulsion.

WELKER, WILLIAM ANDREW, reading specialist; b. Shamokin, Pa., Apr. 26, 1947; s. William Howard and Dorothy Irene (Bertolette) W.; m. Margaret Jean Bainbridge, Mar. 1, 1969; children: William, Richard, Tiffany, Daniel. BS, U. Pitts., 1969, MEd, 1970; EdD, W.Va. U., 1989. Cert. tchr. health, phys. edn. K-12, Pa., W.Va., reading specialist K-12, Pa., W.Va., secondary prin. 5-12, W.Va., elem. prin. K-5, Pa., lang. arts 7-9, W.Va. Tchr. health phys. edn. Philip Murray Elem. Sch., Pitts., 1969-70, Swissvale (Pa.) Elem. Sch., 1970; tchr. 6th grade Edgington Lane Elem. Sch., Wheeling, W.Va., 1970-72; tchr. reading and English Ctrl. Cath. H.S., Wheeling, 1972-76; tchr. reading Warwood Mid. Sch., Wheeling, 1976—; adj. asst. prof. W.Va. U., Morgantown, 1991—. Mem. steering com. Rschrs. In-Sch. Environ, Ohio County Schs., Wheeling, 1990-94. Contbr. articles to profl. jours. Commr. Wheeling Human Rights Commn., 1990-93. Named W.Va. Wrestling Sportswriter of Yr., 1981, 85, 89, 96, 2000, Nat. Wrestling Sportswriter of Yr., Wrestling USA Mag., 1987-1990, W.Va. Ofcl. Wrestling Man of Yr., Wrestling USA Mag., 2001, NFHS Sect. 2 Disting. Active Ofcl. of Yr., 2001, Nat. Wrestling Ofcl. of Yr., Wrestling USA Mag., 2002, OVAC Wrestling Ofcl. of Yr., 2003; mini-grantee W.Va. Edn. Fund, Charleston, 1987, 89, 90. Mem. Internat. Reading Assn. (Columnist Svc. award 1991), Wheeling Island Lions Club. Avocations: writing, sports officiating, wrestling clinician, interpreter. Home: 110 N Huron St Wheeling WV 26003-2226 Office: Warwood Mid Sch 150 Viking Dr Wheeling WV 26003-7028 E-mail: mattalkwv@hotmail.com.

WELL, IRWIN, language educator; b. Cin., Apr. 16, 1928; s. Sidney and Florence (Levy) W.; m. Vivian Max, Dec. 27, 1950; children: Martin, Alice, Daniel. BA, U. Chgo., 1948, MA, 1951; PhD, Harvard U., 1960; D (hon.), Nevsky Inst., Petersburg, Russia, 1999. Teaching fellow Harvard U., Cambridge, Mass., 1955-58; asst. prof. Brandeis U., Waltham, Mass., 1958-65; assoc. prof. Northwestern U., Evanston, Ill., 1966-70, prof. Russian, Russian Lit., 1970—. Pres., mem. bd. dirs. Am. Coun. Tchrs. of Russian., Washington, 1967—. Author numerous books in field; contbr. articles to scholarly jours. Recipient Pushkin medal Internat. Assn. of Russian Profs. Jewish. Avocations: music, singing. Office: Northwestern U Slavic Dept Evanston IL 60208-0001

WELLBORN, OLIN GUY, III, law educator, educator; b. Galveston, Tex., Oct. 21, 1947; s. Olin Guy Jr. and Betty Jean (Merriman) W.; m. Jodi Boston, July 1, 1983; children: Olivia Boston, Olin Guy IV. AB in English magna cum laude, Harvard U., 1970, JD magna cum laude, 1973. Law clk. U.S. Ct. Appeals, San Francisco, 1973-74; asst. prof. U. Tex. Sch Law, Austin, 1974-77, prof., 1977—, William C. Liedtke sr. prof., 1985—, assoc. dean acad. affairs, 1987-91. Vis. prof. Harvard Law Sch., 1978, U. Mich. Law Sch., 1987; co-reporter Tex. Rules of Evidence, 1981—84; advisor standing com. adminstrn. rules of evidence State Bar Tex., 1983—88, 1994—2001; faculty Tex. Ctr. for Judiciary, 1992—. Author (with John F. Sutton Jr.): Cases and Materials on Evidence, 6th edit., 1987; author: 7th edit., 1992, 8th edit., 1996, Teacher's Manual to Accompany Cases and Materials on Evidence, 1992, 1996; author: (with Steven Goode and M. Michael Sharlot) Guide to the Texas Rules of Evidence: Civil and Criminal, 1988; author: 3d edit., 2002, Courtroom Handbook on Texas Evidence, 1994, 10th rev. edit., 2003; author: (with Steven Goode) Courtroom Evidence Handbook, 1995; author: 6th rev. edit., 2003, Courtroom Handbook on Federal Evidence, 1995, 9th rev. edit., 2003; author: (with David W.Robertson, William Powers Jr., David A.Anderson) Cases and Materials on Torts, 2d edit., 1998; author: Teacher's Manual to Accompany Cases and Materials on Torts, 1998, Cases and Materials on the Rules of Evidence, 2000, Teacher's Manual to Accompany Cases and Materials on the Rules of Evidence, 2000; contbr. articles to profl. jours.; : 2d edit., 2003. Mem. Phi Beta Kappa. Office: U Tex Sch Law 727 E Dean Keeton Austin TX 78705-3224

WELLER, RITA BARBARA SHEPLEY, elementary education educator; b. Reading, Pa., Aug. 26, 1951; d. Albert Raymond and Rita Barbara (Olsehfski) Shepely; m. Sherwood Dale Weller, Dec. 13, 1969 (dec. July 1985; 1 child, Theresa Marie. BA in Elem. Edn., Alvernia Coll., 1990; MS in Ednl. Tech., Lehigh U., 1993. Cert. tchr., Pa. Computer tchr. Sacred Heart Sch., West Reading, Pa., 1990-96; gov. Mifflin Sch. Dist., Shillington, Pa., 1996—. Roman Catholic. Home: 410 Pineland Rd Birdsboro PA 19508-9375 Office: Mifflin Sch Dist 10 S Waverly St Shillington PA 19607-2642

WELLINGTON, HARRY HILLEL, lawyer, educator; b. New Haven, Aug. 13, 1926; s. Alex M. and Jean (Ripps) W.; m. Sheila Wacks, June 22, 1952; children: John, Thomas. AB, U. Pa., 1947; LLB, Harvard U., 1952; MA (hon.), Yale U., 1960. Bar: D.C. 1952. Law clk. to U.S. Judge Magruder, 1953-54, Supreme Ct. Justice Frankfurter, 1955-56; asst. prof. law Stanford U., 1954-56; mem. faculty Yale U., 1956—, prof. law, 1960—, Edward J. Phelps prof. law, 1967-83, dean Law Sch., 1975-85, Sterling prof. law, 1983-92, Sterling prof. emeritus law, 1992—, Harry H. Wellington prof. lectr., 1995—; pres., dean, prof. law N.Y. Law Sch., N.Y.C., 1992-2000, dean emeritus, prof., 2000—. Ford fellow London Sch. Econs., 1965; Guggenheim fellow; sr. fellow Brookings Instn., 1968-71; Rockefeller Found. fellow Bellagio Study and Conf. Ctr., 1984; faculty mem. Salzburg Seminar in Am. Studies, 1985; John M. Harlan disting. vis. prof. N.Y. Law Sch., 1985-86; review person ITT-SEC; moderator Asbestos-Wellington Group; cons. domestic and fgn. govtl. agys.; trustee N.Y. Law Sch.; bd. govs. Yale U. Press; mem. jud. panel, exec. com. Ctr. Public Resources Legal Program; Harry H. Wellington lectr., 1995—. Author: with Harold Shepherd) Contracts and Contract Remedies, 1957, Labor and the Legal Process, 1968, (with Clyde Summers) Labor Law, 1968, 2d edit., 1983, (with Ralph Winter) The Unions and the Cities, 1971, Interpreting the Constitution, 1990; contbr. articles to profl. jours. Mem. ABA, Bar Assn. Conn., Am. Law Inst., Am. Arbitration Assn., Am. Acad. Arts and Scis., Common Cause (nat governing bd.). Office: NY Law Sch 57 Worth St New York NY 10013-2959 also: Yale U Sch Law New Haven CT 06520

WELLMAN, BONNIE WADDELL, school nurse, educator, substance abuse counselor; b. Phila., May 5, 1952; d. Russell and Arlene (Spencer) Waddell; m. Ned Allen Wellman, Sept. 14, 1974 (div. 1981); 1 child, Jeffrey Allen. BSN, Ohio State U., 1974; MA in Counseling, Trenton State Coll., 1991. RN, Pa. Sch. nurse Pennsbury Sch. Dist., Fallsington, Pa., 1985—. Bd. dirs. YWCA, Newtown, Pa., 1990; mem. Pennsbury Year Round Edn. Task Force. Mem. NEA, ACA, Pa. State Edn. Assn., Pennsbury Edn. Assn., Pa. Sch. Nurse Assn., Nat. Assn. Sch. Nurses, Bucks County Sch. Nurses Assn., Chi Sigma Iota. Republican. Presbyterian. Avocations: travel, reading. Home: 131 Windham Ct Newtown PA 18940-1750 Office: Pennsbury Sch Dist Yardley Ave Fallsington PA 19058

WELLMAN, HELEN M. administrative secretary; b. Harrisburg, Pa., Feb. 17, 1931; d. James Edwin and Elsie Laura Myers; m. Harlow Auldin Wellman, Nov. 30, 1957; children: Nancy Wason, John A., Janet Morris. Grad., John Harris High Sch., Harrisburg, Pa., 1949. Sec. Pitts. Plate Glass, Harrisburg, 1950—57, investment firm, N.Y.C., 1957, U. N.H., Durham, 1985—92; ret., 1992. Mem. zoning bd., New Durham, NH, 1997—; mem. conservation com. Exeter, NH, 1968—74; chair bd. deacons Congregational Ch., Exeter, 1980—82. Republican. Avocations: photography, knitting, kayaking. Home: 211 N Shore Rd New Durham NH 03855

WELLMAN, WILLIAM WALTER, printing executive; b. Lansing, Mich., Feb. 19, 1933; s. Ulph O. and Vera May (Barns) W.; m. Joelene Stella Richards, Apr. 24, 1954; children: Jeffrey William, Sherri Ann. B of Communications, Mich. State U., 1955. With pub. relations Farm Bur. Ins., Lansing, Mich., 1955-56; brand mgr. Kimberly-Clark Corp., Neenah, Wis., 1956-59; v.p. Wellman Press, Inc., Lansing, 1960-78, pres., 1978-86; sr. mgr. John Henry Co., Lansing, 1986—; ptnr. Wellman Enterprises, Lansing, 1986—99; oper. exec., cons. Harbor House Pubs., 1999—. Pres. Mich. Advt. Roundtable, Marshall, 1964. Bd. dirs., pres., sec., editor Harborage Condominium Assn., 1995—. Mem. Nat. Assn. Photolithographers, Mich. Communicators Assn. (pres. 1963), Mid Mich. Alumni (pres. 1981), Lansing Regional C. of C. (bd. dirs. 1978-80). Clubs: Lansing Press (pres. 1969), Walnut Hills Country (East Lansing) (bd. dirs., v.p. 1972-86). Home: 1837 Foxcroft Rd East Lansing MI 48823-2123

WELLNER, JON AUGUST, statistician, educator; b. Portland, Oreg., Aug. 17, 1945; s. Charles August and Ethel Dorothy (Wolf) W.; m. Vera Dewey, Dec. 11, 1999. BS in Math., U. Idaho, 1968; PhD in Stats., U. Wash., 1975. Asst. prof. stats. U. Rochester, N.Y., 1975-78, assoc. prof., 1978-83; prof. U. Wash., 1983—. Author: Empirical Processes with Applications to Statistics, 1986, Efficient and Adaptive Estimation for Semiparametric Models, 1993, Weak Convergence and Empirical Processes, 1996; contbr. articles to profl. jours. Served to lt. U.S. Army, 1969-71, Vietnam. Fellow John Simon Guggenheim Found., 1987-88. Fellow AAAS, Inst. Math. Stats. (assoc. editor Annals of Stats. 1983-89, 92-94, editor 2001-03). Avocations: mountain climbing, skiing, photography. Home: 1947 14th Ave E Seattle WA 98112-2801 Office: U Wash Dept Stats Box 354322 Seattle WA 98195-4322

WELLNER, MARCEL NAHUM, physics educator, researcher; b. Antwerp, Belgium, Feb. 8, 1930; came to U.S., 1949; s. Jules and Lucie (Rapoport) W.; m. Magdeleine Misselyn, Apr. 7, 1961; children: Pierre, Lucie. BS, MIT, 1952; PhD, Princeton U., 1958. Instr. Brandeis U., Waltham, Mass., 1957-59; mem. Inst. Advanced Study, Princeton, N.J., 1959-60; rsch. assoc. Ind. U., Bloomington, 1960-63; vis. scientist Atomic Energy Rsch. Establishment, Harwell, Eng., 1963-64; from asst. prof. to prof. Syracuse (N.Y.) U., 1964-95, prof. emeritus, 1995—; sr. rsch. scientist SUNY, Syracuse, 1995—. Author gen. physics textbook; contbr. numerous articles on quantum field theory, fractals and excitable media to profl. jours. Mem. Am. Phys. Soc.

WELLNITZ, CRAIG OTTO, lawyer, English language educator; b. Elwood, Ind., Dec. 5, 1946; s. Frank Otto and Jeanne (Albright) W.; m. Karen Sue Thomas, Apr. 13, 1974 (div. Sept. 1987); children: Jennifer Suzanne, Anne Katherine; m. Carol L. Hinesley, Jan. 23, 1988. BA, Purdue U., 1969; MA, Ind. U., 1972; JD, Ind. U.-Indpls., 1978. Bar: Ind. 1978, U.S. Dist. Ct. (so. dist.) Ind. 1978, U.S. Supreme Ct. 1983, U.S. Ct. Appeals (7th and Fed. cirs.) 1984, U.S. Dist. Ct. (no. dist.) 1990; registered mediator, Ind. Instr. Danville Jr. Coll., Ill., 1972-74, S.W. Mo. State U., Springfield, Mo., 1974-75; ptnr. Coates, Hatfield, Calkins & Wellnitz, Indpls., 1978-98; pub. defender criminal divsn. Marion Superior Ct., Marion County, 1979-88, master commr. criminal divsn., 1988-96, registered mediator, 1998—; ptnr. Coates, Hatfield & Wellnitz, Indpls., 1999—2002; pvt. practice Indpls., 2002—. Instr. U. Indpls., 1981-82; mem. adj. faculty dept. English Butler U., Indpls., 1982—; instr. English Ind. U.-Purdue U., Indpls., 1987-90; pres. Ind. Account Mgmt., Inspls., 1985-94; v.p. Carol Craig Assocs., Indpls., 1987—; lectr. in field. Co-author: Successful Judgment Collection in Indiana, 1996, Emerging Trends in Indiana Commercial Collections, 2001; columnist A Jury of Your Peers, 1984-86. Vice committeeman Indpls. Rep. precinct, 1978; chmn. fin. com. St. Luke's United Meth. Ch., 1985-87; sponsor Christian Children's Fund, 1990—; active Am. Mus. Natural History, Indpls. Zoo, Children's Mus. Indpls., The Royal Oak Found. Postgrad. study grantee S.W. Mo. State U., Springfield, 1975. Mem.: MLA, AAUP, Broad Ripple Village Assn., Internat. Spkrs. Network., Spkrs. U.S.A., Smithsonian Assocs., Internat. Assn. Comml. Collectors, Am. Collectors Assn. Internat., Rivera Club Indpls., Columbia Club, Elks. Office: 2575 B East 55 Pl Indianapolis IN 46220 E-mail: Indplslaw@aol.com.

WELLS, CAROLYN CRESSY, social work educator; b. Boston, July 26, 1943; d. Harris Shipman Wells and Marianne Elizabeth (Monroe) Glazier; m. Dale Reed Konle, Oct. 11, 1970 (div. Sept. 3, 1982); m. Dennis Alan Loeffler, Sept. 29, 1990. BA, U. Calif., Berkeley, 1965; MSW, U. Wis., 1968, PhD, 1973. Lic. clin. social worker, marriage and family therapist. Vol. VISTA, Espanola, N.Mex., 1965-66; social worker Project Six Cen. Wis. Colony, Madison, 1968, Milw. Dept. Pub. Welfare, 1969, Shorewood (Wis.) Manor Nursing Home, 1972; sch. social worker Jefferson (Wis.) County Spl. Edn., 1977-78; from lectr. sociology and social work to prof. Marquette U., Milw., 1972—94, prof. social work, 1994—99, U. Wis., Oshkosh, Wis., 1999—; social work therapist Lighthouse Counseling Assocs., Racine, Wis., 1989-91, The Cambridge Group, 1991-92; Achievement Assocs., 1992-95. Vis. lectr. social work U. Canterbury, Christchurch, N.Z., 1983. Author: Social Work Day to Day, 1982, 3d edit., 1999, Social Work Ethics Day to Day, 1986, Stepping to the Dance, the Training of a Family Therapist, 1998; co-author: The Social Work Experience, 1991, 4th edit., 2003. Mem. Wis. Coun. on Social Work Edn., pres., 1980-82, sec., 1985-87, mem. exec. com., 1993-96. Mem. NASW, Am. Assn. Profl. Hypnotherapists, Coun. on Social Work Edn. (mem. publs. and media com. 1989-91, site visitor for accreditation 1987—), Acad. Cert. Social Workers, Assn. Baccalaureate Program Dirs. Democrat. Avocations: writing, silent sports, celtic harp. Home: 4173 Sleeping Dragon Rd West Bend WI 53095-9296 Office: U Wis Oshkosh Dept Social Work 800 Algoma Blvd Oshkosh WI 54901 E-mail: wellsc@uwash.edu.

WELLS, CHARLES ROBERT, secondary education educator; b. Chgo., Jan. 11, 1952; s. Samuel and Wanda Jean (Few) W. BA, Harris Tchrs. Coll., St. Louis, 1978; MS in Edn., Ind. U., 1992. Cert. tchr., Ind., Mo. Tchr. social studies Gary (Ind.) Cmty. Schs., 1984—. Mem. adv. com. Ind. Dept. Edn., Indpls. Mem. Ind. Social Studies Coun., Gary Reading Coun. Lutheran. Home: PO Box 6563 Gary IN 46406-0563

WELLS, CHRISTINE VALERIE, music educator; b. Flushing, N.Y., Sept. 25, 1948; d. Roland Clifford and Frances Marie (Da Ros) Stoehr; m. Jonathan Freda Wells, June 20, 1970 (dec. Nov. 1989); children: Jennifer Lee Magee, Kevin Michael, Frederick Joseph. BMus cum laude, Bucknell U., 1970; MA, U. Md., 1974. Elem. vocal music tchr. Prince George's County Pub. Schs., Upper Marlboro, Md., 1970—2003; cantor, substitute organist Holy Trinity Cath. Ch., Glen Burnie, Md., 1980-81, St. Stanislaus Kostka Ch., Balt., 1983-2000; organist Holy Rosary Ch., Balt., 2000—; vocal music tchr. Woodmont Acad., Cooksville, Md., 2003—. Choir dir. Gregorian Singers, Glen Burnie, 1981—90; music dir. numerous plays Pasadena Theatre Co., Millersville, Md., 1981—; music dir. for plays Act II Dinner Theatre, Rosedale, Md., 1994—95, Timonium (Md.) Dinner Theatre, 1994—95, Music and Drama and Goddard Space Flight Ctr., 1997—; soprano Friday Morning Music Club Chorale, Washington, 2001—. Active fundraising Leukemia Soc., Am. Heart Assn., Glen Burnie; cantor, organist, lector Good Shepherd Cath. Ch., Glen Burnie, 1982—. Mem. Nat. Mus. Women in the Arts (charter). Republican. Roman Catholic. Avocations: traveling, music and theater, baseball, swimming, reading. Home: 303 Glenwood Ave Glen Burnie MD 21061-2233 Office: Woodmont Acad 10817 Davis Ave Woodstock MD 21163-1212 E-mail: christine.wells@verizon.net.

WELLS, DAVID JOHN, program director, academic administrator, mechanical engineer; b. Ithaca, N.Y., Jan. 4, 1949; s. Arthur John and Dorothy Helen (Edwards) W.; m. Jane Baran, July 10, 1971; children: Jacob David, Abbe Grace, Anastasia Catherine. BS in Interdisciplinary Engring. and

Mgmt., Clarkson U., 1972, MSME, 1980, PhD in Engring. Sci., 1985. Lic. profl. engr., Conn., Wyo. Planning engr. Newport News (Va.) Shipbuilding, 1973-76, Stone & Webster Engring., Boston, 1976-78; instr., counselor Clarkson U., Potsdam, N.Y., 1978-81, dir., 1986—86; project mgr., mgr. Combustion Engring., Windsor, Conn., 1981-86; dir. engring. and mgmt. program, mem. adminstrv. coun. Clarkson U., Potsdam, N.Y., 1986—, mem. exec. com., 1986-98; cons. prin. Line-up directions, 1994—; assoc. prof. U. Houston, 1999—2002; dir. Divsn. of Engring. and Physics Wilkes U., Wilkes-Barre, Pa., 2002—. Cons. in field; cons. Excellence in Edn. Action Plan, Potsdam Pub. Schs. Author: Managing Your First Years in Industry, 1994; editor Engring. Mgmt. Rev., 1994; contbr. articles to profl. jours. Bd. dirs. Windsor Pub. Schs., 1985-86. Mem. ASME, IEEE (pres. editl. bd.), Engring. Mgmt. Soc. (bd. govs. 1994—). Home: 48 Terrace St Wilkes Barre PA 18702 Office: Wilkes Univ PO Box 111 Wilkes Barre PA 18766

WELLS, LIONELLE DUDLEY, psychiatrist, educator; b. Winnsboro, SC, Nov. 22, 1921; s. Lionelle Dudley and Mary Wells; m. Mildred Wohltman, June 28, 1945 (dec. 1986); children: Lucia, Lionelle, John, Diane; m. Eilene Bromfield, Sept. 23, 1989. BS, U. S.C., 1943; MD, Med. U. S.C., 1945; grad., Boston Psychoanalytic Inst., 1960. Diplomate Am. Bd. Psychiatry and Neurology; lic. physician, S.C., Mass.; cert. in psychoanalysis. Intern Met. Hosp., N.Y.C., 1945-46; psychiatry resident VA Hosp., North Little Rock, Ark., 1948-50; asst. resident in Psychiatry Graylyn, Bowman-Gray Sch. Medicine, Winston-Salem, 1950-51; instr. psychiatry U. Ark., 1949-51, Mass. Gen. Hosp./Harvard Med. Sch., Boston, 1955-69; clin. instr. psychiatry Harvard Med. Sch., Boston, 1969-78; lectr. psychiatry Boston U. Sch. Medicine, 1977-98; asst. clin. prof. psychiatry Harvard Med. Sch., 1978-93; lectr. psychiatry Tufts U. Med. Sch., Boston, 1981—2002. Cons. staff Newton-Wellesley Hosp., Newton, Mass., 1983-95, hon. staff, 1995—; assoc psychiatrist Mass. Gen. Hosp., Boston, 1975-82, psychiatrist, 1982-96, sr. psychiatrist, 1996—; courtesy staff Waltham Deaconess Hosp. and Med. Ctr., 1977-99; cons. Edith Nourse Rogers Meml. VA Med. Ctr., Bedford, Mass., 1966—; cons. in psychiatry VA Outpatient Clinic, Boston, 1959-2002, others in past; chmn. bd., chief exec. officer Bay State Health Care, 1984-91; nominating com. Am. Managed Care and Rev. Assn., 1988-89, others. Contbr. articles to profl. jours. Recipient Robert Wilson award, Med. U. S.C., 1943, 44. Fellow Am. Coll. Physician Execs., Am. Psychiat. Assn. (disting. life); mem. AMA, Am. Psychoanalytic Assn., Am. Assn. Geriatric Psychiatry, Internat. Gero-Psychiatry Assn., Mass. Psychiat. Soc., Mass. Med. Soc., Boston Psychoanalytic Soc. and Inst., Boston Soc. for Gerontologic Psychiatry (mem. chmn. and dir. 1974-76). Home and Office: 73 Rolling Ln Weston MA 02493-2474 E-mail: Lionelle@comcast.net.

WELLS, MARTHA JOHANNA, elementary education educator; b. Rock Springs, Wyo., Feb. 25, 1941; d. Harold Richard and Mae Amber Rose (Langmack) Frey; children: Timothy Duane, Amber Jo Sutter. BA, Wayne State, 1964. Cert. tchr. grades K-9. Kindergarten tchr. Cherokee (Iowa) Cmty. Schs., 1960-63, Harris-Lake Park (Iowa) Cmty. Schs., 1964-66, Norfolk (Nebr.) Cmty. Schs., 1966-68; sr. primary tchr. Emmetsburg (Iowa) Cmty. Schs., 1969-75, first grade tchr., 1975-82, kindergarten tchr., 1982-92, second grade tchr., 1992-2000. Critical reader adv. bd. Perfection Form Co., Des Moines, 1985-86; team mem. for evaluation on Paulina (Iowa) Schs.-Dept. Edn., 1985; presenter in field. Vol. helper Party for John Glenn, Marcie Frevert's Home, Emmetsburg, 1983; bd. dirs. Emmetsburg Pub. Libr. Recipient Iowa Reading Tchr. of Yr. award, 2000, cert. of recognition Iowa Ho. of Reps., 2000, Ron Ferry award, 2000, Honor award Uniserve Unit 10, 1999-2000, cert. of recognition NEA-Iowa State Edn. Assn., 2000. Mem. AAUW, PEO, Internat. Reading Assn., Iowa Reading Assn. (zone coord. 1983-93, dir. at large 1993-95, dir. membership 1995-98, hospitality chairperson regional conf. 1995—, Appreciation cert. 1983), Iowa State Edn. Assn. (team interviewer 1994), Emmetsburg Edn. Assn. (profl. rights and responsibilities com. 1992-2000), Palo Alto Clay Kossuth Reading Coun. (newspaper in edn. com. 1990-92), Meth. Women, Kiwanis. Democrat. Avocations: golf, bridge, dance, walking, reading. Home: 1603 8th St Emmetsburg IA 50536-1442 E-mail: mwells@ncn.net.

WELLS, RUSSELL FREDERICK, biology educator; b. Bklyn., Oct. 24, 1937; s. Edwin Sutton and Dorothy Elizabeth (Meilby) W.; m. Dancy Drucilla Kelsey, Dec. 17, 1960 (div. 1974); children: Dayna Beth, Leslie Blair; m. Leigh Donaldson Berry, Sept. 1, 1975 (div. 1991). AB, Lafayette Coll., Easton, Pa., 1959; MS, Springfield (Mass.) Coll., 1962; MACT, U. N.C., Chapel Hill, 1966; PhD, Purdue U., 1970. Biology tchr./coach Charlotte (N.C.) Country Day Sch., 1962-65; asst. prof. biology Montclair (N.J.) State Coll., 1966-68; asst. prof. biol. sci. Purdue U., West Lafayette, Ind., 1970-71; vis. assoc. research physiologist U. Calif., San Diego, 1978-79; adj. prof. San Diego State U., 1978-79, 93-94; vis. fellow Australian Nat. U., Canberra, 1986-87; vis. physiologist Australian Inst. Sport, Canberra, 1986-87; asst. prof. biology St. Lawrence U., Canton, N.Y., 1971-74, assoc. prof., 1974-99, prof. emeritus, 1999—, assoc. Dean, 1981-83. Moderator Canton Unitarian Universalist Ch., 1988-91, trustee, 1992; mem. edn. com. NY State Living Mus. at Thompson Park, Watertown, 2001—. Mem. Am. Coll. Sports Medicine, Am. Alliance for Health, Physical Edn., Recreation and Dance, Masons. Unitarian Universalist. Avocation: photography. Home: 344 Rice Rd De Kalb Junction NY 13630-3191 Office: St Lawrence U Dept Biology Canton NY 13617 E-mail: rfwells@stlawu.edu.

WELLS, SHARON A(NN), primary education educator; b. Johnson City, N.Y., Dec. 6, 1943; m. WIlliam John Wells, July 29, 1967; childrne: Mardu Maree, William Mykle Jocef. BS, SUNY, Oswego, 1965; spl. edn. cert., SUNY, Binghamton, 1976; MEd, McNeese U., 1971; EdD, Nova U., 1991. Cert. early and middle childhood tchr., adminstrn. and supervision, N.Y. Tchr. Union-Endicott (N.Y.) Schs., 1965-68, 72-81, prin., 1981-82, tchr., 1982—; tchr., specialist Westlake Elem. Sch., Lake Charles, La., 1969-71; edn. coord. Broome County Head Start, 2000—. Adj. prof. Broome C.C., Binghamton, 1993—; cons., Endicott, 1986—; mem. adv. bd. Day Nursery Assn., Binghamton, 1993—. Contbr. articles to profl. jours.; author: Appleseed Day Care, 1985. Coord. Cmty. Action Fund, Endicott, 1985—. Mem. Binghamton Assn. Edn. Young Children, Binghamton Reading Assn., Woman's Aux. Legion, Pre-First and Developmentally Appropriate Edn. Home: 327 Skye Island Dr Endicott NY 13760-2763 E-mail: sawrain@aol.com.

WELLS-CARR, ELIZABETH ANTOINETTE, educational leadership trainer; b. Taft, Okla., Aug. 23, 1930; d. Horace Charlie and Daisy Magnolia (Smith) Wells; m. Columbus Carr, Dec. 13, 1953; children: Lisa Michelle, Kimberly, Trudy Eleane. BA, Oklahoma U., 1951; specialist credential, Calif. State U., San Francisco, 1976, MS in Secondary Edn., Edn. Adminstrn., 1977, '78; grad. supt.'s acad., Trinity U., 1984; postgrad., U. San Francisco, 1978-83; PhD, Calif. Coast U., 1991. Tchr. Richmond (Calif.) Unified Sch. Dist., 1964-69, tchr., acting counselor, adminstrv. curriculum designer, dept. head, 1969-79; regional dir. for right-to-read program Calif. Dept. Edn., Sacramento, 1976-77; prin. and adminstrv. vice prin. Southwood Jr. High Sch., 1978-81; prin. Am. Inst. Foreign Study, 1981-85; acting prin. and admistrv. vice prin. Oroville (Calif.) High Sch.; prin. Biggs Jr., Sr. High Sch., 1985-89; programs cons. Calif. Dept. Edn., 1989-91; trainer Calif. Sch. Leadership Acad., Sacramento, 1989-91; dir. new products devel. Josten's Learning Corp., San Diego, 1991-93; cons. pvt. practice, San Diego; owner, trainer, cons. Visions of Success. Mem. Ethnic Adv. Bd. U. Chico (Calif.), 1985-88, Tchr. Prep. Adv. Bd., U. Calif., Davis, 1988-91; assoc. prof. Butte (Calif.) C.C., 1989; liaison officer Calif. Dept. Edn., 1989—. Calif. del. Nat. Dem. Conv., 1992; chmn. Third Assembly Dist. Dem. Orgn., 1992 Recipient Martin Luther King Jr. award Butte C.C. Black Student Union, 1985; named Outstanding Reading Specialist of Yr., Calif. Dept. Edn., 1957, Outstanding Adminstr. of Year, S. San Francisco, PTA Coun., 1979, Tchrs. Assn. S. San Francisco, 1980, Grand Nat. Speaker, Bus. and Profl. Women, 1983, Outstanding Speaker, 1985, Outstanding Prin., Lions Club Internat., 1986, Calif. Gold Star Adminstr., 1989; nominee for Reader's Digest Am. Heroes award, 1988, and others. Mem. Nat. Assn. Sch. Adminstrs., Nat. Assn. Black Sch. Educators, Bus. and Profl. Women, Calif. Women in Agrl., Concow Grange 735, Sacramento Alliance of Black Scholars, Host Internat., Nat. Coun. of Negro Women, Project Literacy, Pi Lambda Theta, Phi Delta Kappa, Delta Sigma Theta and others. Presbyterian. Avocations: research, story writing, reading, travel.

WELSFORD, JAMES JOSEPH, secondary school educator; b. Rockville Centre, N.Y., Aug. 22, 1950; s. John August Sr. and Lorraine Elizabeth (Campbell) W. AA, Spokane Falls C.C., 1972; BA, Gonzaga U., 1974; postgrad., Gannon U. at U. Maria Cristina, San Lorenzo Del Escoral, Spain, summer 1978-82; cert., Opportunities Acad. Mgmt. Tng., 1978-80, Wash. Inst. Ethics, 1985; postgrad., Trinity Coll., summer 1993, 96, Marymount U., 2003. Cert. tchr., Va. Cath. Ednl. Assn., cert. in advanced religion, Arlington Diocese. Asst. dir., tchr. Spokane (Wash.) O.I.C., 1974-81; tchr. Bishop Denis J. O'Connell H.S., Arlington, Va., 1981—. Adv. bd. St. Patrick's Grade Sch., Spokane, 1978-81. Mem. Nat. Cath. Edn. Assn., Nat. Right To Life, Cath. Campaign for Am. (charter), Assn. of Miraculous Medal (Papal Blessing 1988), KC (3d degree), Legion of Mary (praesidium pres.). Roman Catholic. Avocations: chess, religious retreats, extensive travel, pilgrimages to religious shrines, writing letters and stories. Home: 2842 Cherry St Falls Church VA 22042-2249 Office: Bishop Denis J O'Connel HS 6600 Little Falls Rd Arlington VA 22213-1211 E-mail: jwelsfor@yahoo.com.

WELSH, ANDREW, English educator; b. Pitts., Nov. 20, 1937; s. Andrew Aloysius and Mercedes Angela (Donahoe) W.; m. Susan Elizabeth Booker, Oct. 2, 1971; children: Miranda Eileen, Clare Cathleen. BS in Physics, U. Pitts., 1959, MA in English Lit., 1962, PhD in English Lit., 1970. Asst. prof. English Rutgers U., New Brunswick, N.J., 1971-77, assoc. prof. English and comparative lit., 1977—. Author: Roots of Lyric, 1978 (James Russell Lowell prize 1978, Melville Cane award 1978-79); contbr. articles to profl. jours. Mem. MLA, AAUP, Internat. Soc. Anglo-Saxonists, Internat. Arthurian Soc., Celtic Studies Assn. N.Am. Office: Rutgers U English Dept 510 George St New Brunswick NJ 08901-1167

WELSH, DORIS MCNEIL, early childhood education specialist; b. Kansas City, Mo. d. Zelbert Melbourne and Anna May (Main) McNeil; children: J. Randall, Valerie M. BA, U. Calif., Berkeley, 1950, MA, 1952; postgrad., U. San Francisco, 1980-82. Cert. tchr., counselor, supr., Calif. Asst. dir. Bing Sch., Stanford, Calif., 1966-76; family devel. specialist Children's Hosp., Stanford, 1976-78; rsch. cons. Stanford U. Med. Ctr., 1970-87; dir. One Fifty Parker Sch., San Francisco, 1978-99; assoc. Lawrence Hall of Sci., U. Calif., Berkeley, 1996—. Citizen amb. del. edn. and childcare People to People Internat., St. Petersburg, Russia, Vilnius, Lithuania, Budapest, Hungary, 1993; pres. bd. dirs. Support for Parents of Spl. Children, San Francisco, 1986-87; bd. dirs. Family Svc. Assn. Mid-Peninsula, Palo Alto, Calif., 1970-80; leader Summer Camp for Pre-Schoolers, East Palo Alto, 1970-73; leader parenthood discussion groups U. Chgo., 1963-64; lectr. in field; cons., 1999—. Vol. Irving Mental Hosp., Chgo., 1963. Mem. Nat. Assn. Edn. Young Children, Assn. Childhood Edn. Internat., World Affairs Coun., Audubon Soc., Sierra Club. Avocations: natural sciences, hiking, horseback riding, gardening. Office: 26630 Ascension Dr Los Altos CA 94022-2001 E-mail: Kharis6@cs.com.

WELSH, DOROTHY DELL, columnist, writer; b. Pryor, Okla., Feb. 13, 1935; d. Roland Fields and Martha Gladys (Sheppard) Butler; m. James Robert Welsh, June 26, 1965; children: Pamela Jeanne (dec.), James Michael, Julie Marie. BA, U. Okla., 1957, MA, 1964; postgrad., U. Tex., Austin, 1983-84, U. Tex., San Antonio, 1984. Newspaper reporter Pryor Jeffersonian, Okla., 1955; tchr. English and journalism Classen H.S., Oklahoma City, 1957-61, Henderson Jr. H.S., Nev., 1961-62; dir. publs. Amarillo (Tex.) H.S., 1962-64; tchr. English Palmdale H.S., Calif., 1964-65; tchr. English and journalism Desert H.S., Edwards, Calif., 1965-66; lectr. English San Antonio Coll., 1979-88; tchg. assoc. U. Tex., San Antonio, 1986-91; reporter Swimming World mag., Sedona, Ariz., 1980—2000; freelance writer, 1992—. Lectr. journalism John Brown U., 1992. Author: Fact, Fiction and Poetic License, To Seattle for a Bone Marrow Transplant, The Butlers of Oklahoma; editor The Cresent News, 1974-80, 83-86, The Swimmer's Ear, 1983-84, Off the Blocks, 1985-86; contbr. articles to profl. jours. Bd. dirs., publicity chmn. South Tex. Swimming Assn., Austin, 1982-84; info. com. Tex. Swimming Assn., Dallas, 1983-84; v.p. Mayes County Geneal. Soc. Recipient Proficiency citation superior work journalism U. Interscholastic League, Austin, 1964, Svc. award San Antonio Aquatic Club, 1983, Outstanding Svc. award U.S. Swimming/Phillips 66, 1989, Pres.'s award Okla. Press Assn., 2003. Mem. MLA, DAR, Soc. Profl. Journalists, Journalism Edn. Assn., Okla. Anthrop. Soc., U. Okla. Assn., Mayes County Hist. Soc., Rogers County Hist. Soc., First Families Okla., Okla. Hist. Soc., Elks, Gamma Phi Beta (internat. officer 1992-94, Svc. award 1977, Internat. Merit Roll 1986, San Antonio pres. 1972-73, 87-88, v.p. 1973-74) Baptist.

WELSH, JUDITH SCHENCK, communications educator; b. Patchogue, L.I., N.Y., Feb. 5, 1939; d. Frank W. and Muriel (Whitman) Schenck; m. Robert C. Welsh, Sept. 16, 1961; children: Derek Francis, Christopher Lord (dec.). BEd, U. Miami (Fla.), 1961, MA in English, 1968. Co-organizer Cataract Surg. Congress med. meetings, 1963-76; grad. asst. instr. Dale Carnegie Courses Internat., 1967; adminstr. Office Admissions, Bauder Fashio Coll., Miami, 1976-77, instr. comms., 1977—, also pub. coll. monthly paper. Freelance writer regional and nat. publs.; guest spkr. Optifair Internat., N.Y.C., 1980, Fla. Freelance Writers Assn. ann. conf., Ft. Lauderdale, 1991, Suncoast Writers' Conf., Tampa, Fla., 2000, Book Island Festival, Fernandina, Fla., 2000; guest spkr., mem. seminar faculty Optifair West, Anaheim, Calif., 1980, Optifair Midwest, St. Louis, 1980, Face to Face, Kansas City, Mo., 1981; conf. dir. So. Fla. Writers Conf., Nat. Writers Assn./U. Miami, 1997—98, 1999—2000; guest spkr. So. Fla. Writers Conf., Fla., 2002—03. Co-editor: The New Report on Cataract Surgery, 1969, Second Report on Cataract Surgery, 1974; editor: Surgidev's Cataract Surgery N.O.W., 1982—; contbr. Miami Today, 1985, Ft. Lauderdale Sun/Sentinel, 1986, Prime Times, Club Life, Gainesville Sun, The Oklahoman, South Fla. mag., Miami Herald; staff writer (internet cos.): AOS, Press-Release-Writing.Com; author: (book) How to Write Powerful Press Releases, 2003. Mem. NAFE, Fla. Freelance Writers Assn., Nat. Writers Club (award), Nat. Writers Assn. (conf. dir. 1997-2000), Coral Reef Yacht Club, Riviera Country Club, Rotary Internat. (Paul Harris award), Delta Gamma. Congregationalist. Home and Office: 1600 Onaway Dr Miami FL 33133-2516

WELSH, MICHAEL JOHN, cell biologist, researcher, science educator; b. Houston, Oct. 9, 1947; s. Tom Christopher and Clara Marie Welsh; m. Teresa Lynn Winnitoy, Sept. 23, 1978 (div. 1996); children: Daniel Alexander, Catherine Samantha Leigh. BSc, Tex A&M U., 1970; PhD, U. Western Ont., London, Can., 1977. Instr. Baylor Coll. Medicine, Houston, 1979; asst. prof. Med. Sch. U. Mich., Ann Arbor, 1979-85, assoc. prof. Med. Sch., 1985-90, prof. Med. Sch., 1990—. Rsch. scientist reproductive scis. program U. Mich., 1983-98; prof. Mich. Cancer Ctr., 1987—, prof. dept. anesthesiology, 1988—, assoc. chair dept. anatomy and cell biology, 1994—99, acting chair dept. cell and developmental biology, 1999-2000, interim chair dept. cell and developmental biology, 2000-02. Editor-in-chief: Cell Biology and Toxicology, 2002—; contbr. articles to profl. jours. Baylor Coll. Medicine fellow, 1976; NIH fellow, 1977-79, NIH grantee, 1981—. Mem. AAAS, Am. Soc. for Cell Biology, Soc. for Study of Reprodn. (publs. com. 1990-91), Soc. Toxicology, Am. Assn. Anatomists, Soc. Developmental Biology. Achievements include first to isolate Sertoli cells in pure form for cell culture, first to observe calmodulin as a component of the mitotic spindle structure of dividing cells; discovered hsp 22. Office: U Mich Med Sch Dept Cell and Developmental Biology Ann Arbor MI 48109-0616 Home: 3569 Preserve Dr Dexter MI 48130-8402

WELSH, SHARON A. elementary and secondary school educator; b. Grand Forks, N.D., Jan. 1, 1949; d. Thomas and Alice (Kliner) Norton; m. Leonard W. Welsh, Sept. 20, 1980; children: Jennifer, John. BS, BA, Moorhead U., 1972; MA, Northwestern U., 1973, PhD, 1976; cert. in adminstrn., U. North Tex., 1985. Asst. prof., dir. edn. Marymount Coll., Salina, Kans., 1972-74; testing specialist Edn. Svc. Ctr., Richardson, Tex., 1977-85; tchr. Allen (Tex.) Ind. Sch. Dist., 1985-87; instr. computer edn. Collin County Community Coll., 1986-89; tchr. Plano (Tex.) Ind. Sch. Dist., 1987-92; staff devel. coord., 1992-98; asst. prin., 1998—. Presenter confs. Mem. ASCD, Nat. Staff Devel. Coun., Am. Ednl. Rsch. Assn., Phi Delta Kappa. Home: 1428 Debon Dr Plano TX 75075-2238

WELSTAD, KIRK, small business owner; b. Minot, N.D. m. Kim Welstad; children: Tyler, Dustin, Trey, Lindsey. Owner Connole and Somerville Heating and Air Conditioning, 1994—2003, Command Staffing and Labor, 2003—. Mem. N.D. Edn. Stds. and Practices Bd., 2001—, chmn., 2002—; mem. Minot Bd. Pub. Sch., 1993—. Mem.: N.D. Sch. Bd. Assn. (N.W. regional dir. 2002). Address: 1104 15th Ave SE Minot ND 58701 Business E-Mail: kwelstad@nglobe.com.

WELTY, GAIL ANN HARPER, physical education educator; b. Allentown, Pa., Feb. 19, 1956; d. James Adam and Doris (Bachman) Harper; 1 child, Peter Frederick. BS in Health, Phys. Edn., Lock Haven State Coll., 1978; MS in Edn., Syracuse U., 1980. Cert. tchr., Pa., Md. Asst. athletic trainer Syracuse (N.Y.) U., 1978-80; elem. tchr., then secondary tchr. Allentown Sch. Dist., 1980-83, head athletic trainer, coach, 1980-83; tchr. elem. sch. Howard County Pub. Schs., Ellicott City, Md., 1984—, coach, 1986. Coop. tchr. for student tchrs., Howard County Schs., 1989—; presenter at profl. confs. Mem. AAHPERD, Md. Assn. Health, Phys. Edn., Recreation and Dance. Avocations: swimming, gardening, crafts. Office: Atholton Elem Sch 6700 Seneca Dr Columbia MD 21046-1130

WELTY, JOHN DONALD, academic administrator; b. Amboy, Ill., Aug. 24, 1944; s. John Donald and Doris (Donnelly) W.; m. Sharon Welty; children: Anne, Elisabeth, Bryan, Darren, Heather. BS, Western Ill. U., 1965; MA, Mich. State U., 1967; Ed.D., Ind. U., 1974. Asst. v.p. for student affairs SW State U., Marshall, Minn., 1973-74; dir. residences SUNY-Albany, 1974-77, assoc. dean for student affairs, 1977-80; v.p. for student and univ. affairs Indiana U. of Pa., 1980-84, pres., 1984-91, Calif. State U., Fresno, 1991—. Lectr. in field; chair Am. Humanics. Contbr. articles to profl. jours. Recipient Chancellor's award SUNY, 1977, Chief Exec. Leadership award Coun. for Advancement and Support of Edn., 1999, John Templeton Found. award for leadership in student character devel., 1999. Mem. Fresno Bus. Coun., Fresno Econ. Devel. Commn., Sunnyside Country Club. Lodges: Rotary. Roman Catholic. Office: Calif State U 5241 S Maple Ave Fresno CA 93725-9739 E-mail: johnw@csufresno.edu.

WELU, SUZANNE MARIE, special education administrator; b. Salt Lake City, Aug. 8, 1956; d. Edward A. and Elizabeth J. (McGinn) W. BS, So. Ill. U., 1979; MEd, Nat. Coll. Edn., 1988; cert. advanced study, Nat.-Louis U., 1991. Learning disabilities resource tchr. Elgin (Ill.) Sch. Dist. U-46, 1979-91, spl. edn. adminstr., 1991—. Opening ceremonies chair Exceptional Children's Olympics, Elgin, 1979—; bd. mem. Drug Free Sch. and Community Adv. Bd., Elgin, 1988—, Ptnrs. in Edn., Elgin, 1991—. Pres. Tri-Village United Way, 1985—; vol. annual cemetary walk Elgin Hist. Soc. Recipient grant for drug prevention activities Forest Found., 1989. Mem. ASCD, Coun. for Exceptional Children, Ill. Chpt. Coun. for Exceptional Children, United Assn. for Children with Learning Disabilities, Ill. Chpt. United Assn. for Children with Learning Disabilities, Assn. Elgin Schs. Adminstrs. Home: 2176 Rob Roy Ct Hanover Park IL 60133-2959 Office: Elgin Sch Dist 355 E Chicago St Elgin IL 60120-6543

WENDEL, JOAN AUDREY, music educator; b. N.Y.C., Dec. 1, 1931; d. Adam and Edna Sophia Wohlfart; m. Ralph Aurel Wendel, July 21, 1962 (dec. May 1998); 1 child, Tracy Lynn. BA summa cum laude, Dowling Coll., 1969; MA, Adelphi U., 1971. Cert. elem. tchr., N.Y. Sec. A.C. Edwards Inc., Sayville, N.Y., 1950-53; office mgr. John V. Potter Ins., East Islip, N.Y., 1953-59, Pilger Agy., Patchogue, N.Y., 1959-66; tchr. Connetquot CSD of Islip, Bohemia, N.Y., 1969-91; pvt. music tchr. Bohemia, 1979—; music dir. Christ Luth. Ch., Cape Coral, Fla., 1996—, Sounds of Fla., Cape Coral, 1999—2003. Mem. Music Tchrs. Nat. Assn., Music Educators Nat. Conf., Assn. Luth. Ch. Musicians, Ft. Myers Music Tchrs. Assn. (v.p. 1999), Order Eastern Star (worthy matron 1964, assoc. grand marshal 1973, grand musician 1987). Republican. Lutheran. Avocations: walking, golf, music, reading. Home: 2218 SE 10th Ter Cape Coral FL 33990-6217 Office: Christ Luth Ch 2911 Del Prado Blvd S Cape Coral FL 33904-7297

WENDEL, JOSEPH ARTHUR, retired secondary education educator; b. Somerville, N.J., Mar. 19, 1926; s. Peter Fred and Lillian Stewart Wendel. BA, Kenyon Coll., 1950; MA in English, U. Iowa, 1967. Tchr. Malcolm Gordon Sch., Garrison, N.Y., 1952-54, St. Bernard's Sch., Gladstone, N.J., 1954-56, Princess Elizabeth Sch., St. John, N.B., Can., 1957-60, Fay Sch., Southborough, Mass., 1960-63; tchr., adminstr. Kingsbrook Acad., Mendham, N.J., 1972-74; asst. headmaster, tchr. St. Paul's Sch., Garden City, N.Y., 1974-83; tchr. Arlington Christian Sch., Fairburn, Ga., 1985-95. Tchr., area rep. U.S. Peace Corps, Asella, Ethiopia, 1963-65; tchr., asst. prof. Haile Selassie I. U., Addis Ababa, Ethiopia, 1967-71; tchr. Tex. Mil. Inst., San Antonio, 1983-84; instr. English Davis & Elkins Coll., Elkins, W.Va., 1984-85. Tutor Literacy Vols. Ea. Panhandle, Martinsburg, W.Va., 1995—; vol. Berkeley County Schs., Martinsburg, 1995—. Quartermaster 3/C USN, 1944-46, PTO. Home: 814 W Burke St Martinsburg WV 25401-2302

WENDELN, DARLENE DORIS, English language educator; b. Indpls., July 18, 1956; d. Robert Edward and Doris Mae (Brabender) W. BS, U. Indpls., 1978; MS, Ind. U., 1986. Lic. tchr., Ind. Secondary English tchr., coach Centerville (Ind.)-Abington Sch. Corp., 1978—. Coach girls' tennis regional and sectional championships. Mem. NEA, Nat. Coun. Tchrs. English, Ind. H.S. Tennis Coaches Assn., U.S. Tennis Assn. Lutheran. Avocations: bicycling, tennis, golf, reading. Office: Centerville High Sch Willow Grove Rd Centerville IN 47330

WENDORF, RICHARD HAROLD, library director, scholar; b. Cedar Rapids, Iowa, Mar. 17, 1948; s. Harold Albert and Jeanne Ellen (Hamblin) W.; m. Barbara Hilderman, 1970 (div. 1983); m. Diana Thanet French, 1984 (div. 1995); children: Reed Thanet Wendorf-French, Carolyn Thanet Wendorf-French; m. Elizabeth Morse, 1997. BA, Williams Coll., 1970; PhB, U. Oxford, Eng., 1972; MA, Princeton U., 1974, PhD, 1976. From asst. prof. English to assoc. prof. English Northwestern U., Evanston, Ill., 1976-86, assoc. dean, 1984-88, prof. English and art history, 1986-89; libr. dir. Houghton Libr., Harvard U., Cambridge, Mass., 1989-97; Stanford Calderwood dir. and libr. Boston Athenaeum, 1997—. Sr. lectr. fine arts Harvard U., 1990-97, acting libr. Fine Arts Libr., 1991-92; lectr. Phi Beta Kappa Assocs., 1992-96; dir. NEH summer seminars for coll. tchrs. Northwestern U., 1987, Harvard U., 1990, 92, 96, Boston Athenaeum, 2002; Robert Sterling Clark vis. prof. art history Williams Coll., 1993. Author: William Collins and Eighteenth-Century English Poetry 1981, The Elements of Life: Biography and Portrait Painting in Stuart and Georgian England, 1990, paperback edit., 1991, Sir Joshua Reynolds: The Painter in

Society, 1996; editor: Articulate Images: The Sister Arts from Hogarth to Tennyson, 1983, Rare Book and Manuscript Libraries in the Twenty-First Century, 1993, (with Charles Ryskamp) The Works of William Collins, 1979; contbr. essays in field; mem. editl. bd. Studies in 18th Century Culture, 1985-89, Word and Image, 1992-2000, Yale edit. Writings of Samuel Johnson, Old-Time New Eng., 1996-99. Trustee Mus. Fine Arts, Boston. Rsch. grantee Folger Shakespeare Libr., Washington, 1976, Am. Philos. Soc., Phila., 1977, 82, Henry E. Huntington Libr., 1979, 2003, Yale Ctr. for Brit. Art, 1983, Brit. Acad., 2003; jr. rsch. fellow Am. Coun. Learned Socs., 1978-79; summer stipend NEH, 1979; sr. rsch. fellow Am. Coun. Learned Socs., 1981-82; NEH rsch. fellow Newberry Libr., Chgo., 1988-89; fellow John Simon Guggenheim Meml. Found., 1989-90. Mem.: The Johnsonians (chmn. 1994—95, 1997—98), Nat. Com. on Stds. in Arts, Colonial Soc. Mass., Soc. Brit. Art Historians, Coll. Art Assn., Am. Soc. 18th Century Studies (pres. Midwest regional soc. 1986, Annibel Jenkins Biography prize 1998), Am. Antiquarian Soc., Keats-Shelley Assn. Am. (bd. dirs. 1993—98), Signet Soc. (assoc.), Union Club Boston, Cambridge Sci. Club, Saturday Club, Grolier Club, Phi Beta Kappa (exec. bd. Chgo. 1984—87, nominating com. 1998—2002). Office: Boston Athenaeum 10 1/2 Beacon St Boston MA 02108-3777

WENDT, CHARLES WILLIAM, soil physicist, educator; b. Plainview, Tex., July 12, 1931; s. Charles Gottlieb and Winnie Mae (Bean) W.; m. Clara Anne Diller, Oct. 15, 1955; children: Charles Diller, John William, Elaine Anne, Cynthia Lynne. BS in Agronomy, Tex. A&M U., 1951, PhD in Soil Physics, 1966; MS in Agronomy, Tex. Tech U., 1957. Research asst. Tex. Tech Coll., 1953-55, instr. agronomy, 1957-61, asst. prof., 1961-63; research asst. soil physics Tex. A&M U., 1963-65, research assoc., 1965-66; asst. prof. Tex. A&M U. (Agrl. Research and Extension Center), Lubbock, 1966-69, assoc. prof., 1969-74, prof., 1974-91, prof. emeritus, 1991—. Cons. cotton prodn. Ministry of Agr. Sudan, summer 1960; cons. Irrigation Assn., 1977-81, Office of Tech. and Assessment, 1982, S.E. Consortium for Internat. Devel., 1989, Rhone Poulenc Agrl. Co., 1992-93; prin. backstop scientist U.S. AID West African Rsch. Program on Soil-Plant0Water Mgmt., 1982-91; chmn. agrl. sect. Southwestern and Rocky Mountain divsn. AAAS, 1982-83. Contbr. articles to profl. jours., chpt. to book. Del. Lubbock County Rep. Conv., 1978; elder Westminster Presbyn. Ch.; Tex. rep. to Great Plains Coun. 1 com. on evapotranspiration; bd. dirs. Presbyn. Ctr., Inc., 1999—, Land Use and Development, Boys and Girls Club of Lubbock, 2002—; bd. dirs. divsn. land use and devel. The South Plains Food Bank, 1999—, Presbyn. Women's Clinic, 1999—. 1st lt. U.S. Army, 1951-53. Named Outstanding Researcher High Plains Research Found., 1982; recipient Superior Achievement award for rsch., soil and crop scis. dept. Tex. A&M Univ., 1987, Vice Chancellors award in excellence as mem. TROPSOILS Rsch. team Tex. A&M U., 1996; grantee industry and water dists. Dept. Interior, U.S. AID, EPA. Mem. Soil Sci. Soc. Am., Am. Soc. Agronomy, Optimist Club (1st v.p., bd. dirs. 2001—). Home: 4518 22nd St Lubbock TX 79407-2515 Office: Texas Agrl Expt Station RR 3 Lubbock TX 79403-9803 E-mail: absendt@aol.com., absendt@cox.net.

WENDT, HANS W. life scientist; b. Berlin, July 25, 1923; s. Hans O. and Alice (Creutzburg) W.; m. Martha A. Linger, Dec. 23, 1956 (div.); children: Alexander, Christopher, Sandra; m. Judith A. Hammer, June 25, 1988. MSc, U. Hamburg, Germany, 1949; PhD in Psychopharmacology, U. Marburg, Germany, 1953. Diplomate in psychology. Rsch. asst. U. Marburg, 1949-53; rsch. assoc. Wesleyan U. and Office Naval Rsch., Middletown, Conn., 1952-53; asst. prof., field dir. internat. project U. Mainz, Germany, 1955-59; engrng. psychologist to prin. human factors scientist Link Aviation, Apollo Simulator Systems, Binghamton, N.Y., 1959-61; assoc. to prof. psychology Valparaiso (Ind.) U., 1961-68; prof. psychology Macalester Coll., St. Paul, 1968-93; sr. rsch. fellow Chronobiology Labs. U. Minn., 1980—; prin. investigator A.v. Humboldt Geomedicine Collaboration (astrobiology), 1994—. Cons. and reviewer, 1961—; hon. prof. sci. U. Marburg, Germany, 1971—; vis. prof. U. Victoria, B.C., Can., U. Marburg, U. Bochum, U. Bielefeld, U. Goettingen, all Germany, 1966-89. Contbr. articles to profl. jours., chpts. to books. Recipient Disting. Sr. Scientist award, Alexander von Humboldt Found., 1976. Home: 2180 Lower Saint Dennis Rd Saint Paul MN 55116-2831

WENDT, LINDA M. educational association administrator; b. Garmisch Partenkirchen, Germany; m. Martin J. Wendt (dec.); 1 child, Angelica. BS, Western Mich. U., 1967. Cert. fund raising exec., Va. Tchr. Mich. (Tex.) Pub. Schs., 1968-80; small bus. owner Battle Creek, Mich., 1980-85; supr. Allied Stores, Battle Creek, Mich., 1985-86; pres. Jr. Achievement, Battle Creek, Mich., 1986—. Steering com. Ctr. for Workforce Excellence, Battle Creek, 1991—; edn. subcom. Econ. Devel. Forum, Battle Creek, 1991—; v.p. Volunteerism in Action, Battle Creek, 1988-91; chair Oper. GRAD Oversight, Battle Creek, 1995—. Com. chair Cereal Fest, Battle Creek, 1986-91; campaign divsn. chair United Arts Coun., Battle Creek, 1990; campaign vol. United Way, Battle Creek, 1986—; bd. dirs. Thornapple Arts Coun.; nat. leadership coun. Jr. Achievement; bd. dirs. Rotary Dist. Found., 2000—, Battle Creek Rotary Club Found., 1998—; trustee Miller Coll., 2003; regional v.p. Jr. Achievement, Inc., 2000—; sch. bd. Endeavor Charter Acad. Fellow, U.S.-China Ednl. Inst., 1995. Mem. AAUW, Rotary (com chair 1993—, bd. dirs.), Battle Creek C. of C. Avocations: tennis, boating. Office: Jr Achievement Inc 4941 Walnut Ridge Battle Creek MI 49017

WENDT, MARILYNN SUZANN, elementary school educator, principal; b. Bay City, Mich., Oct. 6, 1939; d. Clarence Henry and Margaret Viola (Rugenstein) W. AA, Bay City Jr. Coll., 1959; BA, Ctrl. Mich. U., 1962, MA, 1964; EdD, Wayne State U., 1971. Cert. elem. adminstr., Mich. Tchr., teaching prin. Baxman Sch., Bay City, 1959-62; tchr., guidance counselor, dir. elem. edn. Essexville (Mich.)-Hampton Schs., 1962-66; tchr., dir. elem. edn., dir. curriculum rsch. Bloomfield Hills (Mich.) Schs., 1966-78; elem. prin., staff development trainer, learning improvement ctr. supr. Waterford (Mich.) Schs., 1978—. Consortium facilitator Mich. Dept. Edn. Exptl. & Demonstration Ctr., Lansing, 1975-76; part time faculty mem. Wayne State U., Detroit, 1972-78. Co-author: Rational Basis for Planning School Accountability, 1976; contbr. articles to profl. jours. Trustee, v.p. Waterford Twp. Libr., 1990-95; trustee St. Mark's Bd. Edn., West Bloomfield, Mich., 1991-95. Recipient Outstanding Educator award U.S. Office of Edn.-Harold Howe II, 1968, Disting. Svc. award Bloomfield Hills Schs., 1980. Mem. ASCD, Nat. Coun. Tchrs. English, Internat. Reading Assn., Mich. Reading Assn. (Celebrate Literacy award 1989, Adminstr. of Yr. 1991), Mich. ASCD (editor newsletter, conf. planner), Oakland County Reading Assn., Oakland County State & Fed. Program Specialists, Delta Kappa Gamma (v.p. 1990-93, Woman of Distinction 1982). Avocations: reading, swimming.

WENDZEL, ROBERT LEROY, political science educator; b. May 28, 1938; married; 3 children. BA in Polit. Sci. magna cum laude, Kalamazoo Coll., 1960; PhD in Polit. Sci., U. Fla., 1965. Assoc. prof. polit. sci. U. Maine, Orono, 1977-81, 82-83; prof. internat. affairs U.S. Air War Coll., Maxwell AFB, Ala., 1981-82, prof. internat. politics, 1986-87, ednl. advisor to the Commandant, 1987-2000, prof. internat. security studies, 2002—; asst. dean arts & scis., prof. polit. sci., coord. internat. affairs program U. Maine, 1984-86; Paschal P. Vacca prof. liberal arts U. Montevallo, Ala., 2000—01; Merrill prof. polit. sci. Utah State U., Logan, 2001. Internat. affairs com., U. Maine, 1970-86, budget adv. com., 1983-86, coord. internat. affairs program, 1984-86. Author: International Relations: A Policymaker Focus, Thai edit., 1989, Relacoes Internacionais, 1985, International Politics: Policymakers and Policymaking, 1981, International Relations: A Policymaker Focus, 1977, 2d edit., 1980; co-author: America's Foreign Policy in a Changing World, 1994, Defending America's Security, 1988, 2d edit., 1990, To Preserve the Republic: The Foreign Policy of the United States, 1985, Games Nations Play, 9th edit., 1996; contbr. articles to profl. jours. Mem. Phi Beta Kappa. Home: 160 Old Field Dr Montgomery AL 36117-3938 E-mail: blw052838@aol.com.

WENG, JOHN JUYANG, computer science educator, researcher; b. Shanghai, Apr. 15, 1957; came to U.S., 1983; m. Min Guo, 1985; children: Colin S., Rodney D. BS in Computer Sci., Fudan U., Shanghai, 1982; MS in Computer Sci., U. Ill., 1985, PhD in Computer Sci., 1989. Rsch. asst. U. Ill., Urbana, 1984-88; rschr. Computer Rsch. Inst. Montreal, Can., 1989-90; vis. asst. prof. U. Ill., 1990-92; asst. prof. Mich. State U., East Lansing, 1992-98, assoc. prof., 1998—. Author: (chpt.) Early Visual Learning, 1996; co-author: (chpt.) Handbook of Pattern Recognition and Computer Vision, 1993, Motion and Structures from Image Sequences, 1993, Visual Navigation, 1997. Mem. IEEE (Computer Soc., assoc. editor IEEE Transactions on Image Processing 1994-97; assoc. editor Transactions on Pattern Analysis and Machine Intelligence 2000—), Am. Soc. Engrng. Edn., Sigma Xi, Phi Beta Delta. Achievements include contributions to understanding and computation of estimation of motion and structure from image sequences; co-inventor of Cresceptron, an experimental system for recognizing and segmenting objects from natural images; director of SHOSLIF project for a general framework for visual learning by computers; an originator of the developmental approach to artificial intelligence; dir. SAIL and DAV developmental robot projects. Office: Mich State Univ 3115 Engring Bldg East Lansing MI 48824

WENG, ROBERT ALLEN, adult education educator; b. Orange, Calif., Oct. 2, 1946; s. Norman A. and Yvonne (Mason) W.; m. Judith Lynn Farago, Jan. 25, 1969; children: Catherine, Steven, Patricia. BS in Edn., S.E. Mo. State U., 1968; MA, U. Mo., St. Louis, 1975. Tchr. U. City of Pub. Schs., University City, Mo., 1972-73; adult edn. tchr. U. Mo. Extension, St. Louis, 1973-75; master tchr./adminstrv. asst. St. Louis Pub. Schs. AEL, 1975-2000, supr., 2000—. Sec. St. John (Mo.) Park Bd., 1978-80; deacon, elder, trustee First Presbyn. Ch., Ferguson, Mo., 1983—; bd. dirs. Commn. on Adult Basic Edn., 1999—, sec. 2003—. Lt. USN, 1969-72. Mem. Mo. Assn. for Adult Continuing and Comty. Edn. (pres., sec. 1976—, Disting. Svc. award 1995), Missouri Valley Adult Edn. Assn. (bd. dirs. 1985-95, Outstanding Educator award 2000, Founders award 2002), Am. Assn. for Adult Continuing Edn., Mo. Adult Edn. and Lit. Adminstrs. Assn. (pres. 2002—). Avocations: golf, trivia, computers. Home: 18 E Drake Ave Saint Louis MO 63119-5226 Office: St Louis Pub Schs AEL 5078 Kensington Ave Saint Louis MO 63108-1010 E-mail: Robert.WEng@slps.org.

WENGER, BRUCE EDWARD, art educator, educator; b. Grand Rapids, Mich., Mar. 10, 1948; s. Gerald and Beatrice June (Bremer) W.; m. Grace Ann Glick, Dec. 30, 1982 (div. Jan. 1995); 1 child, Jesse. BS in Art, Western Mich. U., 1970; MFA, Ohio U., 1973. Prints specialist Ohio U., Athens, 1971-72; lectr. drawing Ea. Mich. U., Ypsilanti, 1974; asst. prof. art Houghton (N.Y.) Coll., 1978-86, head dept., 1982-86; asst. prof. Rochester (N.Y.) Inst. Tech. Coll. Imaging Arts and Sci., 1986—. Co-author: Design Dynamics: Integrating Design and Technology, 2003; exhibited in group shows Melville C. Brown Gallery, Laramie, Wyo., Stamford (Conn.) Art Assn., NYU, Art West Gallery, Jackson, Wyo., Memphis State U., Chattahoochee Valley Art Assn., La Grange, Ga., Viridian Gallery, N.Y.C., Schoharie County Arts Coun., Cobleskill, N.Y., Minot (N.Dak.) State Coll., 100% Real Art Gallery, Spokane, Wash., U. Ill., Chgo., U. Maine, Presque Isle, Pyramid Arts Ctr., Rochester, Day Spring Art Fair, Toronto, Ont., Can., Huntington (W.Va.) Galleries, also others. Recipient hon. mention Melville C. Brown Gallery, Schoharie County Arts Coun., Three Rivers Arts Festival, Pitts., purchase award Drawing and Print Exhbn., Ft. Hays, Kans., Ann. Maine Maritime Flatwork Exhbn., Mich. Biennial Painters and Printmakers, Grand Rapids. Office: Rochester Inst Tech Coll Imaging Arts and Sci One Lomb Memorial Dr Rochester NY 14623 E-mail: bewfaa@rit.edu.

WENGER, JOHN CHILDS, retired mathematics educator, labor union administrator; b. NYC, Jan. 13, 1941; s. Samuel and Frieda (Smigrod) W.; m. Sally Caplan, June 16, 1963; children: Susan, Karen. BS, U. Mich., 1963; MS, U. Chgo., 1966; PhD, Ill. Inst. Tech., 1979. Computer programmer Western Electric, Chgo., 1966-68; from instr. to prof. City Colls. Chgo., 1968—2002; grievance chmn. Cook County Coll. Tchr. Union, Chgo., 1986—2002; ret., 2002. Jewish. Avocation: tennis.

WENGER, LOWELL EDWARD, history educator; b. Bluffton, Ohio, Jan. 10, 1949; BA, Bowling Green State U., 1971; MA, U. Cin., 1973, postgrad., 1975-80. Instr. history U. Cin., 1975-80; tchr. history, scheduler Seven Hills Upper Sch., Cin., 1980—. Contbr. articles to profl. jours. 1st lt. U.S. Army, 1973-75, lt. col. Res., 1975-99. Recipient Gen. John J. Pershing award U.S. Army, 1989; named Coach of Yr. for girls' tennis Miami Valley Conf., 1985, 86, for boys' tennis, 1988, 92. Mem. Orgn. Am. Historians, Soc. for Historians, Am. Fgn. Rels., Soc. for Mil. History, Nat. Coun. for History Edn., Phi Alpha Theta, Omicron Delta Kappa, Phi Kappa Phi, Delta Phi Alpha. Republican. Roman Catholic. Avocations: tennis, chess, bridge, philately, travel. Home: 8136 Eastdale Dr Cincinnati OH 45255-4547 Office: Seven Hills Upper Sch 5400 Red Bank Rd Cincinnati OH 45227-1198

WENGER, SIDNEY U. psychiatrist, educator; b. Reading, Pa., Nov. 19, 1913; s. Morris and Tillie (Ullman) W.; m. June F. Klinghoffer, June 24, 1947; 1 child, Robert K. BS, Albright Coll., 1935; MD, Hahnemann Med. Coll., 1939; postgrad. psychoanalysis, Inst. Of Phila. Assn., 1951-56. Diplomate Am. Bd. Psychiatry; cert. psychoanalyst. Intern Mt. Sinai Hosp., Phila., 1939-41; Resident psychiatry Phila. Psychiat. Ctr., 1941-42, 46-47; clin. prof. psychiatry Med. Coll. Pa., Phila., 1967—; pvt. practice psychiatry and psychoanalysis Phila.; pvt. practice, 1947—. Faculty (inactive) Inst. Phila. Assn. Psychoanalysis, 1956—, Med. Coll. of Pa., Phila., 1967—; sr. attending (emeritus) Phila. Psychiat. Ctr., 1947—; cons. Jefferson Park Hosp., Phila., 1980—. Major AUS, 1942-46, NATOUSA. Recipient 50-Yr. Svc. awards Phila. County Med. Soc, 1989, Albert Einstein Med. Ctr., Phila., 1989. Mem. Phila. County Med. Soc., Pa. State Med. Soc., Phila. Assn. for Psychoanalysis, Phila. Psychoanalytic Soc., Am. Psychoanalytic Assn. (cert. in psychoanalysis), Internat. Psychoanalytic Assn., Am. Psychiat. Assn., Phila Psychiat. Soc., Pa. Psychiat. Soc. Avocations: boating, fishing. Office: D129 Presidential Apt Philadelphia PA 19131

WENGLER, MARGUERITE MARIE, educational therapist; b. Kokomo, Ind., Nov. 18, 1943; d. Eugene Ferdinand and Flavia Marie (Marullo) Scalzo; m. James Burton Wengler, Oct. 4,1969; children: James Eugene, Dale Douglas, Lauren Christine. BS in Edn., Hofstra U., 1964; MA in Moderate Spl. Needs Edn., Assumption Coll., 1991. Cert. elem. tchr. N.Y., Mass., spl. needs tchr. Mass. Spl. needs dir. Montessori Primary and Upper Schs., Lexington, Mass.; spl. edn. tchr. Lincoln-Sudbury Pub. Schs., Sudbury, Mass., 1987-88; from assoc. lectr. to sr. lectr. Program Advanced Lng. Curry Coll., Milton, Mass., 1993—, outreach dir., 1997-98. Dir. Learning Success Helpline, Acton, Mass., 1984—; profl. devel. provider towards tchr. cert. Dept. of Edn. state of Mass. Author: 60 Minutes to Much Higher Grades, coll. edit., 1995, 60 Minutes to Much Higher Grades, H.S. edit., 1997; contbg. author A Closer Look, 1995; mng. editor Shared Visions of Teaching and Learning, 1997-2001. Del. People to People/Citizen Amb., China, 1994; dir., founder A Friend in Need, Acton, Mass., 1990-96, bd. dirs. Recipient Grant to Friend in Need United Way, 1991-94, Cmty. Chest, 1993; grantee State of Mass., 1989-91. Mem. AAUP, Learning Disabilities Network. Office: Program Advancement Lng Curry Coll Blue Hill Ave Milton MA 02186-2302

WENIGER-PHELPS, NANCY ANN, media specialist, photographer; b. Kingman, Kans., Sept. 4, 1948; d. Watson and Reva Jo (Schlup) W. BA in Phys. Edn., Ottawa (Kans.) U., 1970; MA in LS, U. Denver, 1980. Cert. K-12 media specialist, secondary phys. edn. tchr., Ariz. Phys. edn. tchr. Grand Junction (Colo.) Sch. Dist., 1970-73; dist. mgr. World Book Ency., 1973-74; personal sec. Younger Bail Bond Svc., Grand Junction, 1974-76; media specialist K-12, phys. edn. tchr. Kingman (Kans.) Unified Sch. Dist., 1976-78, Ovid (Colo.) Sch. Dist., 1980-82, Sargeant Sch. Dist., Monte Vista, Colo., 1982-84, Antonito Sch. Dist., Ovid, Colo., 1984-85; photographer's asst. Bill Westenberg Photography, Alamosa, Colo., 1985-86; sch. media specialist Window Rick (Ariz.) Unified Sch. Dist., 1986-96. Profl. photographer; trainer adult and student storytellers; head dist. lib. computer program. Author: Photographic Uses in the Library; exhibited in group shows Gallup (N.Mex.) Gallery, 1989, Window Rock Elem. Sch., 1989, Sunflower Shop, Wichita, Kans. 1989-90, 96-98, also Alamosa, Colo., 1985-87, 1st Nat. Bank, Kingman (Kans.), Fernley (Nev.) Phys. Therapy, 1993, Greatest Little Art Show in Reno, Nev., 2003, Moms Arts and Crafts Show, Reno, Nev., 2003; photo consignment Trout Creek Nursery, Trucker, Calif., 2003. Mem. Washoe County Friends of Libr., Reno, Nev., vol. book sorter, vol. book sale. Mem. AAHPERD, ALA, Am. Fedn. Tchrs., Internat. Platform Assn., Ariz. Fedn. Tchrs., Window Rock Fedn. Tchrs., Ariz. Edn. Media Assn., Assoc. Photographers Internat. Ariz. Edn. Assn., Alpha Delta Kappa. Home: 3305 Farm District Rd Fernley NV 89408-8608

WENSINGER, ARTHUR STEVENS, language and literature educator, writer; b. Grosse Pointe, Mich., Mar. 9, 1926; s. Carl Franklin and Suzanne (Stevens) W. Grad., Phillips Acad. Andover, 1944; BA, Dartmouth Coll., 1948; MA, U. Mich., 1951; postgrad., U. Munich, 1948, 50-51, U. Innsbruck, 1953-54; PhD, U. Mich., 1958. Instr., asst. prof., assoc. prof. Wesleyan U., Middletown, Conn., 1955-68, prof. German and humanities, 1968-93, Marcus Taft prof. German and humanities, 1977-93, prof. emeritus, 1994—, chmn. dept. German lang. and lit., 1971-93, also sr. tutor Coll. Letters; pres. Friends of Davison Art Ctr. Mem. selection com. German Acad. Exch. Svc., 1980-92. Author: Hogarth on High Life, 1970, Plays by Arthur Schnitzler, 1982-1983, 1995; translator, editor (with W. Gropius): The Theater of the Bauhaus, 1961, rev. edit., 1996, translator, editor: The Letters and Journals of Paula Modersohn-Becker, 1983, 2d edit., 1990, Querelle: The Film Book, 1983, Franz Kafka: Pictures of a Life, 1984; translator: Marlene Dietrich: Portraits, 1984, Shabbat (Peter Stefan Jungk), 1985, Hanna Schygulla and R.W. Fassbinder, 1986, Kaethe Kollwitz: The Work in Color, 1988, Niklas Frank, In the Shadow of the Reich, 1991, (plays) Arthur Schnitzler; co-translator: Kafka: The Sons, 1989, Günter Grass, Two States-One Nation?, 1990; editor: Stone Island (Peter S. Boynton), 1973; co-editor: Hesse's Siddhartha, 1962; continuing editor: Correspondence of Norman Douglas, 1868-1952, exhbn. and symposium catalog articles on: Norman Douglas, continuing translator: plays of Schnitzler, contbr.: Columbia U. Database CD-ROM for quotations, aphorisms, 1995—; contbr. articles to profl. jours. Wesleyan Ctr. for Humanities fellow, 1974, Reynolds fellow, 1950-51, Fulbright fellow, 1954-55, Danforth fellow, 1959, Ford Found. fellow, 1970-71; Inter Nations grantee, 1978, 82, NEH rsch. grantee, 1993. Mem. MLA, Am. Assn. Tchrs. German, Heinrich von Kleist Gesellschaft, Internat. Brecht Soc., Kafka Soc. Am., Auden Soc., Soc. Preservation New Eng. Antiquities, Conn. Acad. Arts and Scis., Yale Libr. Assocs., Haddam, Conn. Land Trust, Phi Beta Kappa, Phi Kappa Phi, Delta Tau Delta. Home: Candlewood Farm 95 Jacoby Rd Higganum CT 06441-4225 Office: Wesleyan U Fisk Hall Middletown CT 06459-6082 E-mail: awensinger@wesleyan.edu.

WENTSLER, GERTRUDE JOSEPHINE, secondary school educator; b. Campbell, Ohio, July 16, 1943; d. John Tofil and Irene S. (Glass) Wallace; m. Lawrence L. Murray, Dec. 29, 1967 (div. 1978); 1 child, Carolyn Murray Joyce; m. Wm. Scott Wentsler, Mar. 4, 1989. BA, Miami U., Oxford, Ohio, 1964; MEd, Xavier U., Cin., 1967. Cert. secondary tchr., Ohio. Tchr. history Cin. Pub. Schs., 1964-71, Northwest Sch. Dist., Cin., 1974—. Dist. dir. College Hill Forum, Cin., 1972, mem. edn. com., 1970-73. Jennings scholar, 1986-87; recipient Journalism awards, 1987-89, Outstanding Tchr. award U. Chgo., 1989, Tchr. award Friends of Wm. Howard Taft Birthplace, 1992. Mem. NOW, N.W. Tchrs. Assn. (bldg. rep. 1975-77), Nat. Coun. Social Studies, Cin. Fedn. Tchrs. (membership chair 1968, bldg. rep. 1966-69). Avocations: needlework, reading, travel. Home: 2075 Connecticut Ave Cincinnati OH 45224-2368

WENTWORTH, BETTE WILSON, artist, educator; b. Paducah, Tex., Aug. 14, 1938; d. Herbert Woodrow and Mertice (Foster) Wilson; m. Nicholas Noyes Wentworth, Apr. 25, 1964; children: Mark Benning, Alan Hunter. BA, U. Tex., 1961; postgrad., Sch. Social Work Smith Coll., 1961-62, Glassell Sch. of Art, Houston, 1976-80. Social caseworker De Pelchin Faith Home, Houston, 1962-66; artist Houston, 1968-97, Austin, 1997-99; art tchr. continuing edn. Spring Br. Independent Sch. Dist., Houston, 1980-91. Juror Tenneco Internat. Children's Exhibit, 1983, Scholastic Art awards Houston Independent Sch. Dist., 1984. Exhibited in solo show at North Fourth Cafe, Albuquerque, 1997, group shows at The Art League of Houston, 1982 (2d place), 83, Watercolor Art Soc., Houston, 1983, 84, 85, 87 (1st place), 88, Jewish Cmty. Ctr. 1983, Galveston Art League, 1983, Town and Country Gallery, 1987, Aries Gallery, 1989, Aquamedia, Wash., 1988, Waterloo Watercolor Group Spring Show, 1997. Pres. Bunkerhill West Civic Club, 1988; vol. Trinity Hosp. Aux., 1999; pres. Brenham Fine Arts League, 2001—03; bd. dirs. Altharetta Yeargin Art Mus., Seton Hosp. Vol. Aux., vol. Mem. Watercolor Art Soc. Houston (chmn. 13th nat. exhibition), The Art League Houston, Waterloo Watercolor Group. Episcopalian. Avocations: walking, reading, mysteries. Home and Office: 491 Oak Forest Rd Bellville TX 77418-9617

WENTWORTH, JACK ROBERTS, business educator, consultant; b. Elgin, Ill., June 11, 1928; s. William Franklin and Elizabeth (Roberts) W.; m. Rosemary Ann Pawlak, May 30, 1956; children: William, Barbara Student, Carleton Coll., 1946-48; BS, Ind. U., 1950, MBA, 1954, DBA, 1959. Coord. displays Cadillac divsn., Gen. Motors Corp., Detroit, 1954-56; asst. prof. bus., assoc. dir. research Sch. of Bus. Ind. U., Bloomington, 1957-60, assoc. prof., dir. rsch., 1960-70, prof., 1970-93, chmn. MBA program, 1970-76, chmn. dept., faculty rep. NCAA, 1978-85, dean Sch. of Bus., 1984-93, Arthur M. Weimer prof., 1993-97, Arthur M. Weimer prof. emeritus, 1997—. Mktg. cons., Bloomington, 1960—; bd. dirs. Kimball Internat., Jasper, Ind. Editor: (monograph) Marketing Horizons, 1965; exec. editor Bus. Horizons, 1960-70 Served to 1st lt. USAF, 1950-53 Recipient Teaching award MBA Assn., 1973, 78, 81, 84, 85, Svc. award Assn. for Bus. and Econ. Rsch., 1983; Disting. Alumni Svc. award Ind. U., 1999. Mem. Am. Mktg. Assn. (v.p. 1971-73), Grad. Mgmt. Admissions Coun. (chmn. bd. trustees 1977-78), Univ. Club, Masons, Beta Gamma Sigma (pres. Alpha of Ind. chpt. 1971-72, bd. govs. 1986-98, nat. pres. 1994-96). Republican. Methodist. Avocations: athletic events; travel; bicycling; model railroading; magic. Office: Indiana Univ Sch Bus Bloomington IN 47405

WENTWORTH, LAVERNE WELLBORN, university program coordinator; b. Bryan, Tex., July 26, 1929; d. Charles Floyd and Ethel Berneice (Swanzy) Wellborn; m. Thomas Richard Wentworth (wid. 1986); children: Jason Charles, Rance Richard, Paige Lynn Wentworth Honkerkamp. BA, Baylor U., 1949, MA in Am. Civilization, 1954; postgrad., State Tchrs. Coll. N.J., Southwestern State Tchrs., Coll., San Marcus, Tex., U. Ky. Pub. sch. tchr. Tex. and N.J.; comm. edn. instr. Georgetown (Ky.) Coll., 1988—90; elderhostel program coord. U. Ky., Lexington, 1992—; Boyce Sch. instr. So. Bapt. Theol. Seminary, Lexington, 1990; pers. dept. Cardinel Hill Rehab. Hosp., Lexington, 1987-93. Tchg. cons. U.S. Steel Co., Trenton, N.J., 1957; cons., instr. Interdenominational Young People Confs., Pocono Plateau, Pa., 1958-87; field supr. U.S. Dept. Commerce, Bur. of Census, Washington, 1970-88. Author: (books) Manifest Destiny in Walt Whitman's Prose, 1954, Tryst, 1959. Pres. Princeton Theol. Seminary Wives, 1956-57,

Rotary Anne, W.Va., 1982-83; mem. Scott County Women's Club, Georgetown, 1987-93. Recipient Ship of State award W.Va. State Sec., 1983. Mem. AAUW (pres. 1987—), Scott County Hist. Assn., Georgetown Coll. Women's Assn. (life), Faith Bapt. Ch. of Georgetown. Baptist.

WENTZ, CATHERINE JANE, elementary education educator; b. Boise, Idaho, Aug. 11, 1948; d. Frank Paul and Litha Zella (Langer) W. BA, Boise State U., 1970, MA, 1975. Tchr. 2d grade Longfellow Sch., Boise, 1970-72, Taft Elem. Sch., Boise, 1972-84; tchr. 1st grade Cole Elem. Sch., Boise, 1984-87, Garfield Elem. Sch., Boise, 1987-92, Horizon Elem. Sch., Boise, 1992—. Instr. Spalding Edn. Internat., Boise, Idaho, 1980—. Active Horizon PTO. Mem. NEA, Internat. Dyslexia Assn., Idaho Coun. Internat. Reading Assn., Boise Edn. Assn., Idaho Edn. Assn., Internat. Dyselexia Assn., Alpha Delta Kappa. Avocations: singing, dancing, acting, piano, tennis. Home: 2063 E Lochmeadow Ct Meridian ID 83642-5789 Office: Horizon Elem Sch 730 N Mitchell St Boise ID 83704-9783

WERDEN, DAVID RAY, music educator; b. Davenport, Iowa, Apr. 21, 1947; s. Lawrence Otis and Dorothy Lucille W.; m. Joyce Carol Schuessler, Aug. 31, 1968 (div. Sept. 1979); 1 child, Carolyn Joyce; m. Denise Marie Werner, Feb. 2, 1980; children: Jennifer Judith, Alan David. MusB, U. Iowa, 1970; MusM, U. Conn., 1993. Clinician music edn. Boosey & Hawkes, Libertyville, Ill., 1979-89; pvt. music instr. Gales Ferry, Conn., 1980—; instr. U. Conn., Storrs, 1989-96; clinician music edn. Custom Music Co., Ferndale, Mich., 1989—, Sterling Mus. Instruments, Eng., 1989—; staff, musician USCG Acad. Band, New London, Conn., 1970-96, computer sys. coord., 1986-96; soloist, clinician Euphonium, Minnetonka, Minn., 1996—; tuba player Sheldon Theater Brass Band, Red Wing, Minn., 1996—; web devel. coord. Integrated Network Techs., Burnsville, Minn., 1996—2001; sr. web author Endurant Bus. Solutions, Eden Prairie, Minn., 2001—03; webmaster Internat. Tuba-Euphonium Assn., 2003—; web cons. Midwest Med. Ins. Co., Plymouth, Minn., 2003—. Author: The Blaikley Compensating System, 1980, Euphonium Music Guide, 1990, Scoring for Euphonium, Euphonium Compensating System Interactive, 2002; editor: The Brass Musician, 1986, Euphonium Excerpts, 1992; contbr. articles to profl. jours.; composer arrangements for solo brass and chamber ensembles. Sr. chief USCG, 1970-96. Named Euphonium Player of Yr. Sounding Brass Mag., Eng., 1980. Mem. Internat. Trombone Assn., Tubists Universal Brotherhood Assn. (euphonium coord. 1982-84, bd. dirs. 1987-89, hon. bd. advisors 1989—), Pi Kappa Lambda. Avocations: computer programming, music arranging, web page design. Home: 15800 Lake Street Ext Minnetonka MN 55345-1921 Office: The MMIC Group Tech Solutions 2800 Campus Dr Ste 150 Plymouth MN 55441-2606

WERKING, RICHARD HUME, librarian, historian, academic administrator; b. Charleston, S.C., Sept. 29, 1943; s. F. Woody and Mary S. (Prissinger) W. BA, U. Evansville, 1966; MA in Am. History, U. Wis., 1967, PhD in Am. History, 1973; MA in Librarianship, U. Chgo., 1975. Instr. history Northland Coll., Ashland, Wis., 1967-68; pers. staffing specialist U.S. Civil Svc. Commn., Indpls., 1968-69; reference libr. Lawrence U., Appleton, Wis., 1975-77; head reference dept., asst./acting libr. dir. U. Miss., Oxford, 1977-81, asst. prof. history, 1977-81; assoc. libr. dir., asst. prof. history Trinity U., San Antonio, Tex., 1981-83, libr. dir., assoc. prof. history, 1983-91; libr. dir., assoc. dean, prof. history U.S. Naval Acad., Annapolis, Md., 1991—. Author: The Master Architects: Building the U.S. Foreign Service, 1977; contbr. articles to profl. jours., chpts. to books, also papers, monographs and revs. With Ind. Nat. Guard, 1961—65, with U.S. Army, 1962. Sparks fellow Phi Kappa Phi, 1966, postdoctoral fellow Coun. on Libr. Resources, 1974. Mem. ALA (chmn. coll. librs. sect. 1987-88), Orgn. Am. Historians. Office: US Naval Acad Nimitz Libr 589 Mcnair Rd Annapolis MD 21402-1323 E-mail: rwerking@usna.edu.

WERLE, ROBERT GEARY, academic administrator; b. Washington, Mar. 28, 1944; s. Francis Bernard and Evelyn Mae (Case) W. BA, Christian Bros. Coll., 1970; MEd, U. Toronto, Ont., Can., 1976. Cert. Ednl. Adminstr. Tchr. La Salle H.S., Cin., 1970-73; tchr., adminstr. Roncalli H.S., Omaha, 1973-77; asst. prin. O'Hara H.S., Kansas City, Mo., 1977-79; dir. Stritch Retreat Ctr., Memphis, 1979-82; vocation dir. La Salle Inst., St. Louis, 1982-84; admissions counselor Christian Bros. U., Memphis, 1984-85, dir. campus ministry, 1985-86, dir. campus activities, 1986-91, assoc. dir. Stritch Conf. Ctr., 1991-94; archives and exhbn. cons., 1995—. Archivist Christian Bros. U., C.B. Midwest Dist.; curator of art Christian Bros.; archival cons. Mem. Soc. Am. Archivists, Religious Archives Assn., De La Salle Regional Archivist Assn. (founder, chair USA-Toronto region 1989—), Art Today (sec. 1997-98, treas. 1998-2000, membership chair 2000-01, archives cons. 1995—), Memphis/Shelby Urban Art Commn., Pi Kappa Phi (adv. 1986-89, 94-96, Founder's Svc. award 1989, Alumni award 1995), Memphis in May Archives Com. (Founders award 1994), Records Mgr. Assn. Democrat. Roman Catholic. Avocations: reading, graphic design, writing. Office: Christian Bros Univ O Donnell Archives 2455 Avery Ave Memphis TN 38112-4824 E-mail: rwerle@cbu.edu.

WERLICH, DAVID PATRICK, history educator; b. Mpls., Nov. 2, 1941; s. Eugene Gordon and Mary Ellen (Doran) W.; m. Sandra Cecilia Januszewski, Dec. 28, 1960; children: David A., Thomas G., Susan E. BA, U. Minn., 1963, MA, 1967, PhD, 1968. Lectr. history U. Minn., Mpls., 1966-67; asst. prof. history So. Ill. U., Carbondale, 1968-78, assoc. prof., 1978-84, prof., 1984—2003, chmn. dept. history, 1988—2000; vis. prof., 2003—. Author: Peru: A Short History, 1978, Research Tools for Latin American Historians, 1980, Admiral of the Amazon, 1990. Recipient Delta award Friends of Morris Libr., So. Ill. U., 1991. Mem. Conf. of L.Am. History, Midwest Assn. for L.Am. Studies. Office: Southern Illinois Univ Dept of History Carbondale IL 62901-4519

WERMUTH, MARY LOUELLA, secondary school educator; b. Oakland County, Mich., May 2, 1943; d. Burt and Ila A. (Cole) W.; m. David J. Kohne, Dec. 28, 1975; 1 child, John B. BA, Oakland U., 1965, MA, 1969, 81. Tchr. Rochester Cmty. Schs., Rochester Hills, Mich., 1965-96; instr., counselor Internat. Acad., Bloomfield Hills, Mich., 1996—. Farmer, 1964—; presenter in field; bd. dirs. Mich. Future Problem Solving; exchange tchr. New South Wales, Australia, 1996; ptnr. Old Indian Enterprises, 1982—; faculty Internat. Acad., dean humanities, 1996-2000; mem. adv. coun. Honors Coll., Oakland U., 2002—; ednl. travel cons. Author: Images of Michigan, 1981, Michigan Centennial Farm History, 1986. Pres. Horizons Residential Ctrs., Inc., New Baltimore, Mich., 1984—; artistic dir. Phoenix Theater Co., 1997—2001, prodr.; ptnr. Rediscovery Ctr., Holly, Mich., 2000—; bd. dirs. Honors Coll. Oakland U., 2002—; bd. dirs. Amerris Ind. Schs., 2000—. Recipient Disting. Alumni award Oakland U., 1976. Mem. NEA, Rochestern Edn. Assn., Mich. Edn. Assn., Mich. Coun. Tchrs. English (coms. 1985, 87), Oakland U. Alumni Assn. (pres. 1971-73), Mich. Centennial Farm Assn. (bd. dirs. 1979—), Mich. Assn. Gifted Edn. (v.p. 1991-93), Oakland County Tchrs. English (coms. 1985-93, editor profl. writing ad copy). Office: Internat Acad 1020 E Square Lake Rd Bloomfield Hills MI 48304-1957

WERNER, ELIZABETH HELEN, librarian, language educator; d. Fielding and Lucy Elizabeth McDearmon; m. Michael Andrew Werner, Aug. 21, 1976. BA, Mills Coll., 1966; MA, Ind. U., 1968; MLS, U. Md., 1973. Instr. Spanish McDaniel Coll., Westminster, Md., 1968—72; libr., assoc. prof. Clearwater (Fla.) Christian Coll., 1975—; chmn. Sunline Libr. Users Group Tampa Bay Libr. Consortium, 2003—. Sec. Sunline Libr. users group Tampa Bay Libr. Consortium, Tampa, Fla., 1993—94, 1998—2000, 2002—03, chmn., 2003—. Contbr. book revs. to profl. jours. Com. mem. Upper Pinellas County Post Office Customers' Adv. Coun., Clearwater, 1992—2000. Mem.: Am. Assn. Tchrs. Spanish and Portuguese, Fla. Assn. Christian Librs. (sec. 1987—90, 1995—98, 2000—, pres. 1991—94), Assn. Christian Librs. (Christian libr. consortium team coord. 1998—), Fla. Libr. Assn., Friends of Clearwater Libr. Avocations: reading, choir, travel, language study, genealogy. Office: Clearwater Christian Coll 1625 Union St Clearwater FL 33755

WERNER, GERHARD, pharmacologist, psychoanalyst, educator; b. Vienna, Sept. 28, 1921; came to U.S., 1957, naturalized, 1965; s. Rudolf and Elizabeth (Lukas) W.; m. Marion E. Hollander, July 25, 1958; children—Philip Ralph, Karen Nicole. MD, U. Vienna, 1945. With dept. pharmacology U. Vienna, 1945-50; prof. pharmacology, head dept. U. Calcutta (India) Sch. Tropical Medicine, 1952-54, U. Sao Paulo (Brazil) Med. Sch. of Ribeirao Preto, 1955-57; assoc. prof. Cornell U. Med. Sch., 1957-61; assoc. prof. pharmacology and physiology Johns Hopkins U. Med. Sch., 1963-65; v.p. prof. affairs Univ. Health Ctr., Pitts., 1975-78; prof. pharmacology, head dept. U. Pitts. Med. Sch., 1965-75, dean, 1975-78, prof. psychiatry, 1978-89, F.S. Cheever Disting. prof., emeritus prof., 1990; pres. Med. Comp, Inc., 1990—; assoc., chief of staff Dept. Vets. Affairs Med. Ctr. Highland Drive, Pitts., 1991; cons. Ctr. for Emergent Technology, Motorola, Inc., 1995—98; adj. prof. Dept. Biomedical Enging., Univ. Texas, Austin, 1999—. Cons. psychobiology program NSF, 1970-75, mem. adv. panel regulatory biology div. biology and med. sci., 1969-70, mem. primate ctr. rev. com., 1973-79; mem. chem. biol. info. panel NIH, 1967-70, mem. study sect. pharmacology and exptl. therapeutics, 1964-68; mem. study sect. Pitts. Psychoanalytic Inst., 1973-79; external examiner for Ph.D (med. scis.) U. Calcutta, 1953—; mem. adv. bd. Indian Coun. Med. Rsch., 1952-54. Mem. editorial bd. Jour. Neurophysiology, 1970-78, Internat. Jour. Neuropharmacology, Jour. Clin. Pharmacology; asso. editor Pharmacol. Revs, 1969-70; contbr. articles to profl. jours. Recipient Humboldt prize, 1984 Fellow N.Y. Acad. Sci.; mem. Soc. Neuroscis., AAAS, Harvey Soc., Am. Soc. Pharmacology and Exptl. Therapeutics, Am. Physiol. Soc., Soc. Gen. Systems Research, Internat. Union for Psychobiology, Soc. for Artificial Intelligence, Assn. for Computing Machinery, Internat. Brain Research Orgn., Am. Psychoanalytic Assn., Indian Soc. Biochemistry and Physiology, German Pharmacol. Soc., Sigma Xi. Home: 4723 Cat Mountain Dr Austin TX 78731-3507

WERNER, PATRICE (PATRICIA ANN WERNER), college president; b. Jersey City, May 31, 1937; d. Louis and Ella Blanche (Smith) W. BA in French, Caldwell Coll., 1966; MA in French, McGill U., 1970; PhD in French, NYU, 1976; postgrad. Inst. Ednl. Mgmt., Harvard U., 1991. Joined Dominican Sisters of Caldwell, 1954. Sch. tchr. Archdiocesan Sch. Systems, N.J., Ala., 1954-62; tchr. French, Latin Jersey City, Caldwell, NJ, 1962-72; instr. French Caldwell (NJ) Coll., 1973-76, dir. continuing edn., 1976-79, chair dept. fgn. langs., assoc. prof. French, 1979-85, acad. dean, prof. French, 1985-94, pres., 1994—. Trustee Caldwell Coll.; mem. corp., trustee Providence Coll.; coll. bd. Dominican Higher Edn. Coun. Vice chair exec. com. Ind. Coll. Fund N.J., bd. trustees; bd. dirs. Neylan Commn. Mem. NAICU (bd. dirs.), Am. Assn. Higher Edn., Assn. Ind. Colls. and Univs. N.J. (vice chmn. bd. dirs.), N.J. Presidents Coun. (exec. bd., treas.), Coun. of Ind. Colls., N.J. Assn. Colls. and Univs., Am. Coun. on Edn., Assn. Am. Colls. and Univs., Assn. Cath. Colls. and Univs., Assn. Governing Bds. of Colls. and Univs., N.J.'s Long Range Plan for Higher Edn. Steering Com. Avocations: tennis, reading, avid sports fan, travel. Office: Caldwell Coll 9 Ryerson Ave Caldwell NJ 07006-6195

WERNICK, RICHARD FRANK, composer, conductor; b. Boston, Jan. 16, 1934; s. Louis and Irene (Prince) W.; m. Beatrice Messina, July 15, 1956; children: Lewis, Adam, Peter (dec.). BA, Brandeis U., 1955; MA, Mills Coll., 1957. Instr. music U. Buffalo, 1964-65; asst. prof. music, dir. univ. symphony U. Chgo., 1965-68; conductor Pa. Contemporary Players, 1968-93; prof. music U. Pa., 1968-96, prof. emeritus, 1996—. Co-founder Community Youth Orch. of Delaware County; cons. Contemporary Music, The Phil. Orch., 1983-89, spl. cons. to the music dir., 1989-93; bd. dirs. Theodore Presser Co. Music dir. Royal Winnipeg Ballet Can., 1957-58; composer: Haiku of Basho, 1967, A Prayer for Jerusalem, 1971 (Naumburg award 1975), Moonsongs from the Japanese, 1972, Kaddish Requiem, 1973, String Quartet 2, 1973, Songs of Remembrance, 1974, Visions of Terror and Wonder, 1976 (Pulitzer prize 1977), Contemplations of the Tenth Muse, Book I, 1976, Book II, 1978, Introits and Canons, 1977, A Poison Tree, 1979, Concerto for Cello and Ten Players, 1980, In Praise of Zephyrus, 1981, Piano Sonata: Reflections of a Dark Light, 1982, Sonata for cello and piano: Portraits of Antiquity, 1982, The Oracle of Shimon bar Yochai, 1983, Concerto for Violin and Orch., 1983-84 (Friedheim 1st prize 1986); Oracle II for soprano, oboe and piano, 1985, Concerto for Viola and Orch., 1985-86, Musica Ptolemeica brass quintet, 1987, Symphony #1, 1988, String Quartet #3, 1988, Concerto for Piano and Orch. (Friedheim award 1992), 1989-90, Fragments of Prophecy, 1990, String Quartet #4, 1991 (Friedheim 1st prize 1991), Concerto for Saxophone Quartet and Orch., 1991, Cello Concerto #2, 1992, Symphony #2, 1993, ...and a time for peace, 1994, String Quartet #5, 1995, Cassation Music Tom Jefferson Knew, 1995, trio for violin, cello, piano, 1996, Da'ase for solo guitar, 1996, Fagotton Memories for solo bassoon, 1997, Sonata for violin and piano, 1997, Duettino for violin and oboe, 1997, String Quartet 6, 1998, Musica da Camerata, 1999, Telino's Acrobats, 1999, Piano Sonata # 2, 2000, The Name of the Game, 2000, Duo for cello and piano, 2001, Quintet for Horn & String Quartet, 2002, Suite for Unaccompanied Cello, 2003, Sextet (Flumen Lapidosum) 2003. Recipient music award Nat. Inst. Arts and Letters, 1976, Nat. Endowment Arts grantee, 1975, 79, 82; Fellow Ford Found., 1962-64, Guggenheim Found., 1976. Mem. ASCAP. Democrat. E-mail: rfwernick@aol.com.

WERT, BARBARA J. YINGLING, special education consultant; b. Hanover, Pa., May 18, 1953; d. Richard Bruce and Jacqueline Louise (Myers) Yingling; m. Barry Thomas Wert, Aug. 23, 1975; children: Jennifer Allison, Jason Frederick. BS in Elem. Edn., Kutztown (Pa.) U., 1975; MS in Spl. Edn., Bloomsburg (Pa.) U., 1990; PhD, Pa. State U., 2002. Cert. in elem. edn., spl. edn., Pa.; cert. early childhood, Pa. Dir. children's program Coun. for United Ch. Ministries of Reading, Reading, Pa., 1975-76; instr. Berks County Vo-Tech., Oley Valley, Pa., 1976-77; asst. tchr. Ostrander Elem. Sch., Wallkill, N.Y., 1982-85; spl. needs surp., instrnl. support tchr., cons. Danville (Pa.) Child Devel. Ctr., 1986—; dir. Little Learners Pre-Sch., Northumberland, Pa., 1991-94, ednl. cons., 1991—. Pvt. cons. Families with Spl. Needs, Northumberland, 1991—; adj. prof. spl. edn., Bloomsburg U., 1995, 97, 98, 99, 00. Recipient Parent Profl. Partnership award 1993. Mem. ASCD, Coun. for Exceptional Children (exec. bd. dirs. divsn. early childhood 1991—, sec. 1991-93, newsletter editor, v.p. 1993-94, pres. 1995-96), Nat. Assn. for Edn. Young Children (v.p. Pa. divsn. for early childhood 1993—, tchr. edn. divsn., coun. for behavior disorders divsn., learning disabilities divsn.), Local Autism Support and Advocacy Group. Avocations: photography, needlework, hiking, reading. Home: RR 1 Box 372-n Northumberland PA 17857-9717

WERTLIEB, DONALD LAWRENCE, psychologist, educator; b. Washington, Feb. 22, 1952; s. Norman N. and Helen (Rubin) W.; m. Lorre Beth Polinger, Aug. 12, 1973; children: Joshua Michael, Mollie Rebecca, Miriam Tamar. BS in Psychology summa cum laude, Tufts U., 1974, MA in Child Study, 1975; MA in Psychology, Boston U., PhD in Clin. and Cmty. Psychology, 1979. Instr. psychology Harvard U. Med. Sch., Boston, 1978-81; also staff psychologist Judge Baker Guidance Ctr., Boston, 1978-81; asst. prof. Eliot-Pearson dept. child study Tufts U., Medford, Mass., 1981-86, assoc. prof., 1986-89, chmn., 1989-96, prof., 1997—, chmn. dept. edn. interim, 1990-91, dir. Ctr. for Children, 1999—2002; vis. scholar Ctr. for Internat. Innovation, Leadership and Edn., Wheelock Coll., 2002—03. Sr. rsch. assoc. Harvard U. Community Health Plan, Boston, 1981-87; mem. faculty Inst. for Health Rsch., Harvard Sch. Pub. Health, 1983-87; lectr. dept. social medicine and health policy, Harvard Med. Sch., 1984-89; cons. mental health svcs. Mem. editl. bd. Profl. Psychology, 1981—, Jour. Clin. Child Psychology, 1981—2001, Jour. Pediat. Psychology, 1986—. Carmichael prize scholar, 1973; NIMH tng. fellow, 1974-76; NIMH rsch. grantee, 1977-81, 83-86, Office Spl. Edn. tng. grantee, 1981-83, NIH Biomed. Rsch. grantee, 1982; W.T. Grant Found. grantee, 1982-86; lic. psychologist, Mass. Fellow Am. Orthopscyhiat. Assn., Am. Psychol. Soc. (charter); mem. APA, Assn. Advancement Psychology, New Eng. Psychol. Assn., Mass. Psychol. Assn., Boston Inst. Devel. Infants and Parents, Soc. Psychol. Study of Social Issues, Soc. Rsch. in Child Devel., Soc. Pediatric Psychology (pres. 1996-99), Phi Beta Kappa, Psi Chi.

WERTZ, JOHN ALAN, retired secondary school educator; b. Mpls., May 28, 1945; s. John Edward and Florence (Carlson) W.; m. Margaret M. Schlangen, 1993. BS, Hamline U., 1967; MS, St. Cloud State Coll., 1973; postgrad., George Washington U., 1985. Tchr. social sci. St. Cloud Cmty. Schs., St. Cloud, Minn., 1967—2002; ret., 2002. Trainer and field rep. New Games Found., San Francisco, 1980-83; tchr.-coach Apollo H.S. Mock Trial team, 1987-2000. Mem. com. social action Minn. Synod, Luth. Ch. Am., 1971-74; chair social action com. Salem Luth. Ch. Coun., St. Cloud, 1974-76; mem. affirmative action com. St. Cloud Cmty. Schs., 1975-78, co-chair student assistance com., 1982-83, mem. site coun. Apollo H.S., 1994-96, co-chair site coun. Apollo H.S., 1995-96; chair St. Cloud Human Rights Commn., 1979-83; adv. Ctrl. Minn. Sexual Assault Ctr., 1981-83; bd. dirs. St. Cloud Area Tenants' Assn., 1975-77, St. Cloud Area Spl. Olympics, 1982-83, United Way St. Cloud Area, 1996-2001, Minn. Edn. Assn., 1996-99; bd. dirs. Great River Roundtable, 1997-2003, sec., 1997-98; mem. Edn. Minn. Transition Bd., 1998-99, Edn. Minn. Governing Bd., 1999-2002; mem. St. Cloud Area Disabilities Coun., 1995—, pres., 2002—; bd. dirs. St. Cloud Area Family YMCA, 2001-03, bd. sec., 2002-03, pres., 2003—; candidate for Minn. State Legislature, 2000, 02; counselor Sr. Corps of Ret. Execs., 2002—, chpt. chmn. 2003—. Recipient Merit award St. Cloud Area Coun. for Handicapped, 1976; grad. St. Cloud Area Leadership Program, 1995. Mem. NEA, Edn. Minn., St. Cloud Edn. Assn. (chair govtl. rels. coun. 1978-83, 88-96), Am. Hist. Soc. Germans from Russia, St. Cloud Area C. of C. (edn. divsn. 1992-97, vice-chmn. PreK-12 com. 1993-94, chair edn. recognition com. 1994-96, Thayer Youth Leadership steering com. 1995-97). Avocations: theatre arts, travel. Home: 816 Rilla Rd Saint Cloud MN 56303-1037

WESCOTT, VIRGINIA D'ARCY, special education educator; b. Camden, N.J., Apr. 11, 1953; d. Lawrence Jerry Jr. and Elizabeth Ann (Fitzgerald) W. AA, Burlington County Coll., 1975; postgrad., Stockton State Coll., Trenton State Coll.; BA, Glassboro State Coll., 1995. Cert. substitute tchr. Tchr. substitute Burlington County Sch. Sys., Westhampton, N.J., 1989—. Mem. Coun. Exceptional Children (polit. action judge 1994, network rep. 1995, pres. student assn. 1993-94). Avocations: walking, bicycle riding, sewing, gardening. Home: 215 Mannion Ave Moorestown NJ 08057-2335

WESEMAN, VICKI LYNNE, elementary school educator; b. Hastings, Nebr., Oct. 29, 1954; d. Virgil John and Vera Lillie (Berg) Kennedy; m. Creighton Lee Weseman, May 28, 1988 (div. Oct. 1999); 1 child, Jason K. BS, U. Nebr., 1977, MA, 1988. Cert. elem. tchr. Nebr., profl. tchr. Nebr. Elem. tchr. Hanover Elem. Sch., Glenvil, Nebr., 1977—2003, Lincoln Elem. Sch., Grand Isle., Nebr., 2003—. Pres. Adams County Edn. Assn., Hastings, Nebr., 1996—97; team leader stds. Adams County Schs., Hastings, 2000—01. Oregon Trail rodeo pageant coord. Adams County Agrl. Soc., Hastings, 1992—. Named Miss Rodeo, Nebr., 1977, Com. Person of Yr., Oregon Trail Rodeo, Hastings, 1999. Mem.: Nebr. Edn. Assn. (mem. selection com. 2000), Women's Profl. Rodeo Assn. Democrat. Lutheran. Avocation: barrel racing in rodeo. Home: 835 Briggs Ave Hastings NE 68901 Office: Lincoln Elem 805 Beal St Grand Island NE 68801

WESSE, DAVID JOSEPH, higher education administrator, consultant; b. Chgo., May 5, 1951; s. Herman Theodore and Lorraine Joan (Holland) W.; m. Deborah Lynn Smith, Oct. 11, 1975; children: Jason David, Eric Joseph. AA, South Suburban Coll., 1971; postgrad., Purdue U., 1971-72; BEd, Ill. State U., 1973; MS, Loyola U., Chgo., 1983. Adminstr. Reuben H. Donnelley Corp., Chgo., 1974-76; adminstrv. mgr. Loyola U., Chgo., 1976-79, Joint Commn. on Accreditation of Healthcare Orgns., Oakbrook Terrace, Ill., 1979-81; adminstrv. dir., asst. sec. Northwestern U., Evanston, Ill., 1981-97; higher edn. cons. KPMG Peat Marwick, LLP, Chgo., 1997-2000; exec. dir. U. Houston, 2000; prin. Joslyn Assocs., Alexandria, La., 2000—; asst. v.p. U. North Fla., 2000—03; vice chancellor fin. and adminstrv. svcs. La. State U., Alexandria, 2003—. Seminar leader Nat. Assn. Coll. Aux. Svcs., 1998. Contbr. numerous articles to profl. publs. Pres., bd. dirs. Riverdale (Ill.) Libr. Dist., 1975, Riverdale Youth Commn., 1975; bd. dirs. Better Bus. Bur. Chgo. and No. Ill., 1991-97, Adminstrv. Mgmt. Soc. Found., 1998—. Recipient Svc. Recognition award Riverdale Libr. Dist., 1975, Excellence in Journalism award Nat. Assn. Coll. Aux. Svcs., 1989. Mem. Adminstrv. Mgmt. Soc. (bd. dirs. Chgo. chpt. 1983-88, pres. 1986-87, bd. regents 1986-88), Acad. Adminstrv. Mgmt. (bd. regents 1992-94), Profl. Office Mgmt. Assn. Chgo. (bd. dirs. 1992-93, sec. 1993-95, pres. 1995), Nat. Mgmt. Assn. (chpt. pres. 1995), Nat. Assn. Coll. and Univ. Bus. Officers (com. mem. 1986-87, 89-90, cost reduction awards 1986-88, 90, 92), Midwest Higher Edn. Commn. (com. mem. 1996-97), Assn. Coll. Adminstrn. Profls. (seminar leader 1995, 98, 99), Chgo. Area Bus. and Support Svc. Adminstrs. (founder 1988), Big Ten Bus. and Support Svc. Adminstrs. (founder 1992), Pvt. Univ. Bus. and Support Svc. Adminstrs. (founder 1996), U. North Fla. Adminstrv. and Profl. Assn. (pres. 2002-03), Phi Theta Kappa, Lambda Epsilon. Lutheran. Office: 8216 Tom Bowman Dr N Alexandria LA 71302 E-mail: dwesse@lsua.edu.

WESSENDORF KNAU, SUANA LE, special education educator; b. Storm Lake, Iowa, Nov. 3, 1953; d. Billie and Grace Arlene (Piercy) Wessendorf; m. Gregory Charles Knau, July 27, 1991. BS in Edn., U. S.D., 1975; MEd, U. Ariz., 1980, postgrad., 1983-87, Iowa State U., 1990—. Cert. tchr., Iowa, Ariz. Spl. edn. tchr. Cherokee (Iowa) Sch. Dist., 1975-77, Ctrs. of Youth Devel. and Achievement, Tucson, 1978-79, Amphitheater Sch. Dist., Tucson, 1979-80, Tucson Unified Sch. Dist., 1980-89, Ames (Iowa) Sch. Dist., 1989-97; cons. for behavior disorders, Iowa Dept. Edn. Bur. of Children, Family and Cmty. Svc., 1998—; dir. mktg. Mktg. Concepts, Tucson, 1977-78. Master trainer Tucson Unified Sch. Dist., 1987-90; dir. Tucson Very Spl. Arts Festival, 1980-85; crisis interventionist, mem. Models of Teaching Cadre, Ames Sch. Dist., spl. edn. large vertical chair; mem. spl. edn. adv. bd. State of Iowa, 1993—; mem. Iowa Behavioral Initiative Steering Com., 1995—, State Discipline Work Group, 1997—, Success 4 Core Com., Specialized Svcs. Group, design com. 1998—; chair State of Iowa Spl. Edn. Adv. Panel, 1996-97; cons. for behavior disorders Iowa Dept. Edn., 1998—. Chair Tucson Commn. of Arts and Culture, 1980-84; mem. Christian Edn. Bd. Congl. Ch., Ames, 1993—, chair, 1994-96; mem. Tucson/Pima Arts Coun., 1984-89; mem. Beloit Adv. Com., 1999—; chair Success 4-Specialized Svcs. Group, 1998—; mem. Healthy Iowans 2010; mem. Clin. and Cmty. Adv. Coun., 1998—; mem. Iowa Mental Health Planning Coun., 1998—; mem. Iowa Plan Adv. Coun., 1998—. Recipient Recognition for Women Who Care award Gov. of Ariz., 1985, Cert. of Appreciation, Pima County Juvenile Ct., 1986. Mem. Coun. for Exceptional Children (1st v.p. 1991-92, pres.-elect 1992-93, pres. 1993-94, pres. 1994-95), Iowa Coun. for Exceptional Children (pres. 1991—, coord. political action network 1993—, Outstanding Spl. Educator award 1994, Winterstein award 1998), Iowa Coun. for Children with Behavioral Disorders (pres. 1991-92), Political Action Network, Alpha Delta Kappa (pres. 1994-96). Congregationalist. Avocations: reading, walking, collecting panda materials. Home: 914 S Dakota Ave Ames IA 50014-7920 Office: Iowa Dept Edn Bur Children Family and Cmty Svcs E14th And Grand Des Moines IA 50319-0001 E-mail: suanawessk@aol.com.

WEST, BRIAN CLAIRE, management consultant, educator; b. Balt., Oct. 3, 1956; s. Ralph Claire and Janice Marie West; m. Shirl Elaine Jones. B of Acctg. and Fin., Towson State U., 1978; M of Adminstrv. Sci., Johns Hopkins U., 1992. Acct., contr. Stephenson Aviation, Inc., Middle River, Md., 1978—80; IT project leader, mgr. Westinghouse Electirc Corp., Balt., 1980—90; mgmt. cons. Balt., 1990—93; mgr. fin. bus. analysis Merry - Go - Round Corp., Balt., 1994; sr. bus. analyst Becton Dickinson Corp., Hunt Valley, Md., 1995—97; mgmt. cons. Balt., 1997—99; dean, prof. Strayer U., Balt., 1999—. Mem.: White Marsh C. of C. Avocations: hiking, horseback riding, exercising, reading science fiction, computer technology. Home: 56 Independence Dr New Freedom PA 17349

WEST, CAROL CATHERINE, law educator; b. Phila., May 23, 1944; d. Scott G. and Helen (Young) West. BA, Miss. U. for Women, 1966; MLS, U. So. Miss., 1984; JD, U. Miss., 1970. Pub. svcs. law libr. U. Va., Charlottesville, 1966-67; catalog law libr. U. Miss., Oxford, 1967-70; legis. reference libr. Miss. Legislature, Jackson, 1970-75; law libr. Miss. Coll., Jackson, 1975-94, prof. law, 1975—. Del. White House Conf. Libr. and Info. Svcs., 1991; cons. to Parliament of Armenia, 1995, Parliament of Tanzania, 1997; mem. bd. commrs. Miss. Libr. Commn., 1993—98; mem., sec. Miss. Task Force on Gender Fairness in the Cts. Mem.: ABA, Miss. Women's Polit. Network (bd. dirs. 1998—2000), Miss. Libr. Assn., Miss. Women Lawyers Assn. (bd. dirs. 1991—93), Hinds County Bar, Miss. Bar Assn. (Susie Blue Buchanan award 2001). Methodist. Office: Miss Coll Law Sch 151 E Griffith St Jackson MS 39201-1302

WEST, CARROLL VAN, historian, educator, consultant; b. Murfreesboro, Tenn., Jan. 29, 1955; s. W. C. and Sara Pauline (Van Hooser) W.; m. Mary Sara Hoffschwelle, Nov. 29, 1980; children: Owen William, Sara Elizabeth. BA, Mid. Tenn. State U., 1977; MA, U. Tenn., 1978; PhD, Coll. of William and Mary, 1982. Interpreter Colonial Williamsburg (Va.) Fedn., 1978-81; rsch. asst. Coll. of William and Mary, Williamsburg, 1979-80, vis. asst. prof., 1980-81; hist. cons. Helena, Mont., 1981-85; assoc. prof., dir. Ctr. for Hist. Preservation, MTSU, Murfreesboro, 1985—. Assoc. fellow Coun. Gt. Plains Studies U. Nebr. Author: Travelers Companion to Montant History, 1986, Tennessee Agriculture: Century Farms, 1987, Images of Billings: A History, 1990, Capitalism on the Frontier, 1993, Tennessee's Historic Landscapes, 1995, Tennessee History, 1998, Tennessee Encyclopedia, 1998, New Deal Landscape of Tennessee, 2001, Trial and Triumph, 2002; sr. editor Tennessee Hist. Soc., 1993—. H. Hon. Smith fellow U. Tenn., 1977-78; Hill Libr. grantee James Hill Libr., 1987, 94, travel to collections grantee NEH, 1987-88. Mem. Orgn. Am. Historians, Western History Assn., Soc. for Historians of Early Republic, Nat. Trust for Hist. Preservation, Am. Assn. State and Local History (rsch. grantee 1983-84), Tenn. Hist. Soc., Vernacular Architecture Forum. Democrat. Baptist. Avocations: travel, photography. Home: 125 N Highland Ave Murfreesboro TN 37130-3824 Office: MTSU Ctr Hist Preservation PO Box 80 Murfreesboro TN 37133-0080 E-mail: cwest@mtsu.edu.

WEST, D(RUEY) TOM, JR., school administrator; b. Macon, Ga., Dec. 8, 1948; s. D.T. and Dovie Mae (Daniel) W.; m. Mary Nancy Swiney, Aug. 5, 1978; children: Dronda Sue, Leanna Marie, Ansley Hamlin, Jamie Hamlin. BA in Edn., Ga. Coll., 1971; MEd, U. Ga., 1976. Cert. sch. adminstr., Ga. Tchr. Boddie Jr. High Sch., Milledgeville, Ga., 1976-81, asst. prin., 1981-86, Baldwin High Sch., Milledgeville, 1983-91; elem. sch. prin. Southside Sch., Milledgeville, 1983-91; pers. dir. Baldwin County Schs., Milledgeville, 1991—. Dist. legis. rep. Ga. Assn. Elem. Sch. Prins., Milledgeville, 1989-91; adv. bd. Ga. Coll. Career Ctr., Milledgeville, 1989-90; prin. Nat. Sch. Excellence, 1986. Mem. ASCD, Nat. Assn. Elem. Sch. Prins., Ga. Assn. Elem. Prins., Profl. Assn. Ga. Educators, Ga. Assn. Ednl. Leaders, Milledgeville Allied Arts Assn., Ga. Sch. Pers. Assn., Phi Delta Kappa. Avocation: restoring antique jukeboxes. Home: 129 Snyder Rd NE Milledgeville GA 31061-8015 Office: PO Box 1188 Milledgeville GA 31059-1188

WEST, EULA KIRKPATRICK, retired elementary education educator; b. Fox, Okla., Oct. 16, 1930; d. William B. and Eva (Williams) Kirkpatrick; m. Billy G. West, June 6, 1948 (dec. Apr. 1977); children: William G., Carol Ann West Rushing. Student, Hills Bus. Coll., 1950; BS, U. Southern Miss., 1972. Sec. Social Security Adminstrn., Amarillo, Tex., 1952-61; tchr. Harrison County, Gulfport, Miss., 1968-70, Biloxi (Miss.) Pub. Sch., 1971-96, ret., 1996. Sunday sch. tchr., 1953—. Mem. Miss. Profl. Educators, Eastern Star, Delta Kappa Gamma (sec., treas. pres., fin. com., Women of Distinction 1993). Baptist. Home: 11471 Pine Dr Gulfport MS 39503-3997

WEST, GAIL MARCIA WEISS, special education educator; b. Queens, N.Y., Sept. 22, 1955; d. Martin Albert and Syra (Hamburg) Weiss; m. Gregg David West, Aug. 17, 1978; children: Rachel Leah, Dana Lindsay, Sasha Lynne. BS in Elem. Edn., . Wis., 1977; MS in Spl. Edn., Pepperdine U., 1980. Cert. tchr., spl. edn. tchr., Calif., Md. Asst. dir. Human Rels. Dept., Madison, Wis., 1977; tchr. La Tijera Elem. Sch., Inglewood, Calif., 1978-82; tchr. spl. edn. 153d St Sch., Gardena, Calif., 1980; tchr., tutor Specific Diagnostics, Rockville, Md., 1983-88, coord. svcs. and programs, 1985-87, ednl. diagnostician, 1987-88; ednl. cons., advocate A Helping Hand, Brookeville, Md., 1988—. Speaker at parent orgn. meetings; tutor children with learning difficulties, 1980—. Contbr. articles to profl. jours. Exec. bd. Greenwood Elem. Sch. PTA, 1988—, pres., 1991-93; exec. bd. Hadassah, 1989-91; Sherwood Cluster coord. County Level of PTA's. Mem. Wash Ind. Svcs. Ednl. Resources, Children with Attention Deficit Disorders, Parents of Gifted/Learning Disabled Children, Phi Kappa Phi. Democrat. Jewish. Avocations: aerobics, arts and crafts, reading. Home and Office: A Helping Hand 7 Saint George Ct Brookeville MD 20833-3267

WEST, KATHLEEN SHEA, special education educator, reading specialist; b. Boston, Aug. 24, 1946; d. Everett W. and Catherine (Lally) Shea; m. William S. West, Sept. 4, 1966; children: Carl, Adam. BS, SUNY, Albany, 1983; MS, Russell Sage Coll., 1989, postgrad., 1989-90. Cert. permanent K-6, spl. edn., reading tchr., N.Y. Substitute tchr. pub. schs., N.Y., 1980-84; tchr. spl. edn. Glens Falls (N.Y.) City Sch. Dist., 1984—. Speaker spl. edn. dept. Russell Sage Coll., Troy, N.Y., 1989-92. Vol. United Cerebral Palsy, Queensbury, N.Y., 1982-84; tutor Literacy Vols. Am., Glens Falls, 1992. Roman Catholic. Avocations: writing, sketching, reading, travel.

WEST, LINDA LEA, administrator; b. Sparta, Wis., Oct. 5, 1943; d. Larry C. and Florance M. (Haskell) Lomax; m. Thomas C. West, Aug. 29, 1964; children: Timothy C., Daniel H., Deborah R. AB magna cum laude, Occidential Coll., 1965; MLS, UCLA, 1966. Cert. profl. adminstrv. svcs.; cert. tchr. Calif. Libr. young adult L.A. Pub. Libr., 1966-67; libr. edn., psychology Humbolt State Coll. Libr., Arcata, Calif., 1967-68; reference libr. Monterey (Calif.) Bay Area Coop. Libr., 1969-70; instr. Hacienda La Puente & El Monte (Calif.) Adult Edn., 1976-78; instr., curriculum writer Indochinese RAP, Hacienda La Puente (Calif.) Sch. Dist., 1978-81, coord. refugee project, 1981-88; instr. adult edn. UCLA Extension, 1988—; resource tchr. Baldwin Park (Calif.) Adult Sch., 1988-90; archives mgr. Outreach & Tech. Assistance Network Hacienda La Puente Sch. Dist., 1990-94; asst. dir. Outreach and Tech. Asst. Network, Sacramento County Office of Edn., Sacramento, 1994—. Cons. in field. Comtbr. articles to profl. jours. Jr. troop leader Girl Scouts Am., West Covina, Calif., 1985-88. Mem. ALA, AAUW, Am. Assn. Adult Continuing Edn., Am. Vocat. Assn., Calif. Tchrs. English to Speakers Other Langs. (asst. adult level chmn. 1985-86, adult level chmn. 1986-87), Calif. Coun. Adult Edn., Calif. Libr. Assn., Tchrs. English to Speakers Other Langs., Phi Beta Kappa, Beta Phi Mu, Phi Alpha Theta. Democrat. Episcopalian. Avocations: tennis, tropical fish, choral singing. Home: 308 Oak Canyon Way Folsom CA 95630-1854 Office: Sacramento County Office Edn 9738 Lincoln Village Dr Sacramento CA 95827-3302

WEST, MARGARET LYNNE, computer science and mathematics educator; b. Biloxi, Miss., Sept. 13, 1950; d. George Theodore and Margaret Adriana (Leslie) Perkins; m. Adam J. Ortiz, July 4, 1973 (div. Jan. 1989); stepchildren: Margo, Mark, Daniel; m. William G. West, Dec. 23, 1989. BS, U. So. Miss., 1976, MEd, 1979, PhD, 2001; postgrad., U. Calif., Santa Barbara, 1988-90. Math. tchr. Harrison County Schs., Gulfport, Miss., 1976-79, Ocean Springs (Miss.) High Sch., 1979-81; math. tchr., dept. chair Mercy Cross High Sch., Biloxi, 1981-86; computer sci. tchr., dept. chair Biloxi Pub. Schs., 1986-92; computer sci./math. instr. Miss. Gulf Coast C.C.-Jefferson Davis Campus, Gulfport, 1992—. Adj. faculty Embry-Riddle Aero. U., Keesler AFB, Miss., 1981-86, U. So. Miss.-Gulf Park Campus, Long Beach, 1986-96; instr. Ctr. for Academically Talented and Gifted Youth, Johns Hopkins U., Redlands, Calif., 1990-91. Co-author (course curriculum) State Computer Lit. Course, 1991-92. Sunday Sch. tchr. Bapt. Ch., Biloxi, 1980—, ch. treas., pianist, 1992—; local/ch. choirs Community Chorus/Bapt. Ch., Biloxi, 1975—; mem. PTA. Recipient NSF fellowship, 1988-90, Summer Indsl. fellowship for tchrs. Naval Oceanographic Command, Miss. Gulf Coast Econ. Devel. Coun., and Johnson Controls World Svcs., Inc., 1992; nat. semi-finalist Tandy Corp.-Outstanding Tchr., 1990; named Star Tchr., State of Miss., 1986. Mem. Nat. Coun. Tchrs. Math., Miss. Coun. Tchrs. Math., Miss. Ednl. Computing Assn., Phi Delta Kappa, Delta Kappa Gamma. Republican. Avocations: piano, needlecrafts, swimming, reading, voice (singing). Home: 3122 Wayne Dr Biloxi MS 39532-8553 Office: Miss Gulf Coast CC 2226 Switzer Rd Gulfport MS 39507-3824 E-mail: margaret.west@mgccc.edu.

WEST, MARJORIE EDITH, former elementary education educator; b. Lawrence, Kans., Aug. 18, 1940; d. Merwin Hales and Helen Aletha (Fellows) Wilson Polzin; m. Hammond Dean Watkins, Feb. 17, 1968 (div. 1971); 1 child, Michele Dawn; m. Merlin Avery West, Apr. 2, 1975 (div. 1984). BA in Elem. Edn., U. No. Colo., 1962, MA in Reading, 1970; postgrad., La. State U., 1981-82, U. New Orleans, 1981-82. Cert. tchr., Colo. Tchr. Sch. Dist. 11, Colorado Springs, Colo., 1962-64, Nat. Def. Overseas Teaching Program, Wiesbaden, Fed. Republic Germany, 1964-65, Alaska On-Base Schs., Fairbanks, 1965-66, Great Bend (Kans.) Sch. Dist., 1966-67, Killeen (Tex.) Sch. Dist., 1967-68, Jefferson County Schs., Lakewood, Colo., 1969-99; ret., 1999. Trustee Nat. Tchr. Hall of Fame, 2002—. Recipient Alumni Trail Blazer award U. No. Colo., 1988; named Colo. Tchr. of Yr., 1994, finalist Nat. Tchr. of Yr., 1994; named to Nat. Tchrs.' Hall of Fame, 1995. Mem. NAFE, AAUW, NEA, PTA (by-laws com. 1989-90, hon. life mem.), Colo. Edn. Assn. (del. to assembly 1985-90), Jefferson County Edn. Assn. (spl. svcs. com. 1989-90), Internat. Reading Assn., Phi Delta Kappa, Pi Lambda Theta, Epsilon Sigma Alpha (edn. chair 1989-90, chair ways and means com. 1990-91, publicity chair 1991-93). Democrat. Avocations: football, travel, golf, reading. Home: 10810 W Exposition Ave Lakewood CO 80226-3818

WEST, MARSHA, elementary school educator; b. DeQueen, Ark., Sept. 1, 1950; d. Marshall T. and Mildred L. (Davis) Gore; m. Larry T. West, May 19, 1972; 1 child, Zachary west. BS in Edn., So. State Coll., Magnolia, Ark., 1971; MEd, U. Ark., 1975; postgrad., Henderson State Coll., Arkadelphia, Ark., Purdue U.; specialist's degree, U. Ga., 1991. Cert. elem. and spl. edn. tchr., media specialist Ga. Spl. edn. resource tchr. Gatesville (Tex.) Ind. Sch. Dist.; tchr. early childhood spl. edn. Bryan (Tex.) Ind. Sch. Dist.; elem. tchr. Tippecanoe Sch. Corp., Lafayette, Ind., Clarke County Sch. Dist., Athens, Ga., media specialist. Mem.: NEA, ALA, Clarke County Assn. Educators, Ga. Libr. Media Assn. (dit. V chair, pres.), Ga. Assn. Instrnl. Tech., Ga. Assn. Educators, Am. Assn. Sch. Librs., Kappa Delta Pi. Office: David C Barrow Elem Sch 100 Pinecrest Dr Athens GA 30605-1459

WEST, MILDRED MARIE, elementary education art educator; b. Mill Creek, Okla., July 7, 1934; d. Minor Hubert and Audrey Eunice (Baker) Hughes; m. Joe Dean West, Dec. 18, 1954; children: Michael, Jared, Adam; stepchildren: Sue, Carla. BS in Home Econs., East Ctrl. U., Ada, Okla., 1982. Cert. K-12 art edn., Okla., 6-12 home econs., Okla. Presenter in field of art edn. Columnist Ada Evening News, 1987-92; paintings exhibited Legis. Art Show, Oklahoma City, 1984-92. Mem. women's com. Farm Bur., 2002—; chmn. Farm Bur. Womens Commn.; past pres. Ada Artists, Allied Arts. Mem. AAUW (past pres.), Ada Artists Assn. (art show chmn.), Allied Arts Tanti Study Club (past pres.), Magic Brush Art Guild, Holdenville Soc. Painters and Sculptors, Beta Sigma Phi. Democrat. Member Church of Christ. Avocations: walking, aerobics, gourmet cooking, travel. Home: RR 7 Box 482 Ada OK 74820-9145 Studio: 709 E Main St Ada OK 74820-5613

WEST, NANCY LEE, music educator, performance artist, entertainer; b. Evansville, Ind., Dec. 5, 1929; d. Harold Addison and Helen Beatrice (Roland) Hill; m. Owen L. West, Aug. 2, 1952; children: Gail Ann, Janet Lee, Robert Owen. BFA, Wesleyan U., Ill., 1952. Pvt. practice, Gibson City, Ill., 1952-57, Urbana, Ill., 1957-59, Buckhannon, W.Va., 1959-68, Eureka, Ill., 1968—; music tchr. Elliott (Ill.) Elem. Sch., 1953-54; piano soloist various events. hotels, restaurants in W.Va. and Ill., 1953—; dance orch. leader various parties, clubs, benefits, Ill., 1985—; piano accompanist various musical prodns., performances in W.Va. and Ill., 1953—. Cello player Symphony Orch., Bloomington, Ill., 1950-52. Mem. adv. bd. Ctrl. Ill. Youth Symphony, Peoria, 1969-78; mem. women's bd. Eureka Coll. Recipient Purchase award Walnut Grove Fine Arts Assn., Eureka, 1978, Best of Show award, Clarksburg, W.Va., 1966, One Person Show award Volkwein Music, Pitts., 1967; winner Grand prize Salem Coll., W.Va., 1965. Mem. Am, Coll. Musicians, Music Tchrs. Nat. Assn., Am. Fedn. Musicians, AAUW, Peoria Area Music Tchrs. Assn. Mem. Christian Ch. Avocations: sewing, crafts, reading, dancing. Home and Office: 810 N Main St Eureka IL 61530-9412

WESTALL, SANDRA THORNTON, special education educator; b. Rochester, N.Y., Jan. 31, 1940; d. William Heldrith and Janice (King) Thonrton; m. Thomas Keith Westall, Jan. 10, 1965 (div. 1980); children: William Thornton, Robert Theodore. AS in Bus., So. Va. Coll. Women, 1962; BA in Early Childhood Edn., Mars Hill Coll., 1982; MA in Spl. Edn., Appalachian State U., 1989; MA in Behavioral Emotional Edn., Western Carolina U., 1990. Cert. tchr. spl. edn., learning disabilities, emotional handicapped, N.C., Fla. Tchr.'s asst. spl. edn. Mitchell County Sch., Spruce Pine, N.C., 1964-70; tchr. Pine Ridge Sch. for Learning Disabilities, Williston, Vt., summer 1985, 88, Summit Acad. for Learning Disabled Students, Waynesville, N.C., 1986-88; resource tchr. Ire B. Jones Elem. Sch. and Asheville Jr. High Sch., N.C., 1988-89; tchr. Irene Worthem Sch. for Severe/Profound Mentally Retarded, Asheville, 1989-90; resource tchr. G. Holmes Braddock High Sch., Miami, Fla., 1990-91, Kelsey L. Pharr Elem. Sch., Miami, 1991-94; tchr. severely emotionally disturbed Lakewood Elem. Sch., St. Petersburg, Fla., 1994—; night tchr. Nova U., Ft. Lauderdale, Fla., 1992—, Fla. Meml. Coll., Miami, 1992—; tchr. learning disabilities St. Leo (Fla.) Coll., 1995. Tutor, counselor Black Mountain (N.C.) Correctional Ctr. for Women, 1988-90; trainer behavior disorders No. Colo. U., Breckenridge, 1989, Willie M. Workshop, Asheville, 1989; condr. workshops on left and right brain teaching, 1980-87; speaker on learning disabled adults Harvard U., 1989; tchr. day camps for handicapped students, 1983, 84; advocate for learning disabled students and adults; del. Citizen Amb. Program field of learning disabilities, Diagnostic Ctr., various schs., Vilnius, Siauliai Pedagogical Inst., Dept. Spl. Pedagogics, Lithuania, Inst. Defectology, Russian Acad. Pedagogical, Moscow, City Coun., Inst. Econ. Problem Studies, St. Petersburg, Russia, 1993. Vol. Dade County Helpline and Dade County Schs. (in aid of Hurricane Andrew victims), swimming courses for ARC, 1980—; bd. dirs. N.C. Advocacy Ctr. for Children's Edn. and Parent Tng., 1986-90. Grantee Creative Learning for Behavior Handicapped Students, 1989; honoree ARC, 1980. Mem. Am. Coun. on Rural Spl. Edn., Assn. for Children and Adults with Learning Disabilities, The Orton Dyslexia Soc., Coun. for Exceptional Children, Coun. for Behavior Emotionally Handicapped Children. Episcopalian. Avocations: teaching, swimming, drawing, attending flea markets. Home: 751 Pinellas Bayway S Apt 205 Tierra Verde FL 33715-1946 Office: Lakewood Elem Sch 2154 27th Ave N Saint Petersburg FL 33713-4060

WESTBROOK, JAMES EDWIN, lawyer, educator; b. Camden, Ark., Sept. 7, 1934; s. Loy Edwin and Helen Lucille (Bethea) W.; m. Elizabeth Kay Farris, Dec. 23, 1956; children: William Michael, Robert Bruce, Matthew David. BA with high honors, Hendrix Coll., 1956; JD with distinction, Duke U., 1959; LLM, Georgetown U., 1965. Bar: Ark. 1959, Okla. 1977, Mo. 1982. Assoc. Mehaffy, Smith & Williams, Little Rock, 1959-62; asst. counsel, subcom. of U.S. Senate Jud. Com., Washington, 1963; legis. asst. U.S. Senate, Washington, 1963-65; asst. prof. law U. Mo., Columbia, 1965-68, asst. dean, 1966-68, assoc. prof., 1968-70, prof., 1970-76, 80—, James S. Rollins prof. law, 1974-76, 80—, Earl F. Nelson prof. law, 1982-99, emeritus prof., 1999—, interim dean, 1981-82; dean U. Okla. Coll. Law, Norman, 1976-80. George Allen vis. prof. law, U. Richmond, 1987; vis. prof. law Duke U., 1988, Washington U., St. Louis, 1996, 2001; reporter Mid-Am. Assembly on Role of State in Urban Crisis, 1970; dir. Summer Internship Program in Local Govt., 1968; cons. various Mo. cities on drafting home-rule charters; mem. Gov.'s Adv. Coun. on Local Govt. Law, 1967-68, Fed. Practice Com. U.S. Dist. Ct. (we. dist.) Mo., 1986-90; chmn. Columbia Charter Revision Commn., 1973-74; mem. spl. com. labor relations Mo. Dept. Labor and Indsl. Rels., 1975; mem., chmn. subcom. on domestic violence Task Force on Gender and Justice, Mo. Jud. Conf., 1990-93; mem. com. to rev. govtl. structure of Boone County, Mo., 1991. Author: (with L. Riskin) Dispute Resolution and Lawyers, 1987, supplement, 1993, 2d edit., 1997, abridged edit. of 2d edit., 1998; contbr. articles to profl. jours. Chair search com. for chancellor U. Mo., Columbia, 1992, chair search com. for provost, 1998. Mem. ABA, Nat. Acad. Arbitrators, Assn. Am. Law Schs. (chmn. local govt. law round table coun. 1972), Ctrl. States Law Sch. Assn. (pres. 1982-83), Mo. Bar Assn. (vice chmn. labor law com. 1986-87, chmn. 1987-88, Spurgeon Smithton award 1995), Order of Coif, Blue Key, Alpha Chi. Roman Catholic. Home: 3609 S Woods Edge Rd Columbia MO 65203-6606 Office: U Mo Sch Law Columbia MO 65211-0001

WESTBROOK, JAY LAWRENCE, law educator; b. Morristown, N.J., Dec. 11, 1943; s. Joel W. and Elaine Frances (Summers) W.; m. Pauline June Travis, Feb. 15, 1969; 1 child, Joel Mastin. BA in Polit. Sci./Philosophy, U. Tex., 1965, JD, 1968. Bar: Tex. 1968, D.C. 1969, U.S. Ct. Appeals (D.C. cir.) 1969, U.S. Supreme Ct. 1976, U.S. Ct. Appeals (4th cir.) 1978, U.S. Ct. Appeals (2d cir.) 1979. Assoc. Surrey & Morse (name now Jones, Day, Reavis, Pogue), Washington, 1969-74; ptnr. Surrey & Morse (name now Jones, Day, Reavis, Pogue, Surrey & Morse), Washington, 1974-80; mem. law faculty U. Tex., Austin, 1980—, Benno C. Schmidt Chair Bus. Law, 1991—. Vis. prof. U. London, 1990, Harvard Law Sch., 1991-92; advisor Tex. Internat. Law Jour., 1985-91; reporter Am. Law Inst. Transnat. Insolvency Project, 1994-2000; co-leader U.S. delegation to UN Commn. on Internat. Trade Law Working Group on Model Law Internation Insolvency, 1995-97, 99; sr. advisor Nat. Bankruptcy Rev. Com., 1997; mem. State Dept. Adv. Com. on Pvt. Internat. Law, 1997-2000; vis. scholar Humboldt U., Berlin, 2002. Co-author: As We Forgive Our Debtors: Bankruptcy and Consumer Credit in America, 1989 (Silver Gavel award ABA 1989), The Law of Debtors and Creditors: Text, Cases and Problems, 4th edit., 2001, Teacher's Manual, The Law of Debtors and Creditors, 4th edit., 2001, The Fragile Middle Class, 2000, Americans in Debt, 2001 (Ann. Writing award Am. Coll. Consumer Fin. Svcws. Lawyers); contbr. articles to profl. jours. Grantee U. Tex. Law Sch. Found., 1982, U. Rsch. Inst., 1982-83, NSF, 1983-86, Policy Rsch. Inst., Lyndon Johnson Sch. Pub. Affairs, 1984, Tex. Bar Found., 1985, Nat. Inst. Child Health and Human Devel., 1986, Nat. Conf. Bankruptcy Judges, 1991, 93. Mem. ABA (bus. bankruptcy com., vice chair internat. bankruptcy subcom. 1999—, Meyer rsch. grant 1986), Am. Law Inst., Am. Coll. Bankruptcy, Nat. Bankruptcy Conf., State Bar Tex. (governing coun. internat. sect. 1987-89), Internat. Bar Assn., Internat. Bankruptcy Com. (com. J), Internat. Acad. Comml. and Consumer Law, Order of Coif. Office: U Tex Sch Law 727 E Dean Keeton St Austin TX 78705-3224

WESTBROOK, JUANITA JANE, school administrator; b. Clarksville, Tex., July 15, 1947; d. James L. and S. Juanita (Dawson) Jamison; children: Jennifer L. Westbrook Cooper, Jayme Lee Westbrook. BS in Bus. Adminstrn./Edn., East Tex. State U., 1968; MS in Adult/Continuing Edn./Pers. Mgmt., U. North Tex., 1986. Cert. in mid-mgmt. adminstrn., supt. Tchr. Carroll Ind. Sch. Dist., Southlake, Tex., 1968-69; exec. sec. Tex. Instruments, Dallas, 1969-70; part-time instr. San Jacinto Coll., Pasadena, Tex., 1975-77, North Tex. State U., Denton, 1977-78; adminstrv. asst./sec. Halliburton Svcs., Duncan, Okla., 1978-80; part-time instr. Weatherford (Tex.) Coll., 1980-81; cmty. edn. coord., high sch. tchr. Weatherford Ind. Sch. Dist., 1981-82, cmty. svcs. dir., 1986—; cmty. edn. dir. Springtown (Tex.) Ind. Sch. Dist., 1982-86. Cons. Tri-County Tech. Consortium, Hubbard, Tex., 1994—; cons./grant writer Parker County Counseling Coop, Poolville, Tex., 1992-93; presenter/lectr. in field. Editor: Texas Star newspaper, 1990-92, Texas Community Educator's Practitioners Manual, 1993. Bd. dirs. Palo Pinto Cmty. Svcs., Mineral Wells, Tex., 1994—, United Way, Springtown Friends of Libr., Tex. Bus. and Edn. Coalition; grant rev. com. North Ctrl. Tex. COG, Arlington, 1994—; bd. dirs. Parker County Com. on Aging, Weatherford, 1990-93; exec. dir. Parker County Adult Literacy Coun., Weatherford, 1987—; exec. bd. Practical Parent Edn., Parker County Parenting Coalition. Named First Lady of Springtown, City of Springtown, 1984. Mem. ASCD, Tex. Cmty. Edn. Assn. (sec., pres. 1988-93, Bright Idea award 1983), Tex. Sch. Pub. Rels. Assn. (Star awards 1989-94), Tex. Assn. Sch. Adminstrs., Tex. Assn. for Alternative Edn., Assn. Tex. Profl. Educators, Nat. Assn. Ptnrs. in Edn., Nat. Cmty. Edn. Assn. (Region IV conf. program chair 1991-92, nat. conf. program co-chair 1990), Nat. Coun. State Cmty. Edn. Assns. (liaison 1991-92), Nat. Dropout Prevention Network, Nat. Sch. Pub. Rels. Assn., Tex. Assn. for Continuing Adult Edn., Tex. Assn. Supervision and Curriculum Devel., Tex. Coun. of Adult Edn. Coop Dirs., Tex. Assn. for Sch.-Age Childcare, Weatherford C. of C. Avocations: reading, crafts, sewing, gardening. Office: Weatherford Ind Sch Dist PO Box 439 Weatherford TX 76086-0439

WESTBROOK, REBECCA VOLLMER, secondary school educator; b. Hagerstown, Md., Jan. 12, 1943; d. Harry Frederick and Margaret Caldwell (Jack) Vollmer; m. John William Westbrook Jr., Apr. 4, 1972; children: Margaret Rebecca, John Williiam III. BA in French and Spanish cum laude, Thiel Coll., 1964; MAT in French and Spanish, Emory U., 1965; cert. in French studies, Inst. Am. U., Aiv-en-Provence, France, 1963. Cert. tchr. Ga., 1966, Fla., 1985. Tchr. French and Spanish Henry Grady H.S., Atlanta, 1966—70, Northside H.S., Atlanta, 1970—76, Forest H.S., Ocala, Fla., 1985—; instr. French and Spanish Jefferson C.C., Louisville, 1980—82. Cons. Itinerant Tutors, Louisville, 1983—84. Active Girl Scouts Am.; mem. Ocala Women's Club, 1989—92. Mem.: NEA, Alpha Delta Kappa, Phi Sigma Iota. Avocations: travel, antiques, reading. Home: 2630 SE 14th St Ocala FL 34471 Office: Forest HS 1614 Fort King St Ocala FL 34471

WESTERBERG, ARTHUR WILLIAM, chemical engineering educator; b. St. Paul, Oct. 9, 1938; s. Kenneth Waldorf and Marjorie Claire (Darling) W.; m. Barbara Ann Dyson, July 14, 1963; children: Kenneth (dec.), Karl. BS, U. Minn., 1960; MS, Princeton U., 1961; PhD, Imperial Coll., London, 1964. Pres. Farm Engrng. Sales Inc., Savage, Minn., 1964-65; sr. analyst Control Data Corp., San Diego, 1965-67; asst. prof., assoc. prof., prof. U. Fla., Gainesville, Fla., 1967-76; prof. chem. engrng. Carnegie-Mellon U., Pitts., 1976—, chmn. dept., 1980-83, Swearingen prof., 1982—, dir. Design Research Ctr., 1978-80, Univ. prof., 1992—; dir. Engrng. Design Rsch. Ctr., 1986-89. Co-author: Process Flowsheeting, 1979, Systematic Methods of Chemical Process Design, 1997. Recipient Murphree award Am. Chem. Soc., 1997, Steven J. Fenves Sys. Engrng. award Carnegie Mellon, 1998,

Engring. Disting. Prof. award, 2002, Robert E. Doherty Edn. award, 2003. Fellow AIChE (lectr. 1989, Computers and Sys. Tech. divsn. award 1983, Walker award 1987, McAfee award 1990, Founders Outstanding Contbns. Chem. Engring. award 1995); mem. NAE, Am. Soc. Engring. Edn. (chem. engring. divsn. lectr. 1981, GE Sr. Rsch. award 1999, CACHE Excellence in Chem. Engring. Edn. award 2003). Home: 5564 Beacon St Pittsburgh PA 15217-1972 Office: Chem Engring Dept Carnegie Mellon U Pittsburgh PA 15213 E-mail: a.westerberg@cmu.edu.

WESTERBERG, MARY L. retired secondary school educator; b. Ironwood, Mich., Nov. 17, 1942; d. Rudolph Henry and Gertrude Ethel (Saari) W. BA, Mich. State U., 1964, MA in Teaching, 1969; postgrad., U. Minn., Duluth, U. N.H. Cert. life English, history and French tchr., Minn. Tchr. Alpena (Mich.) High Sch.; tchr. English and French, Anoka (Minn.) Sr. High Sch., also chmn. Bldg. Leadership Team; ret. Organizer, co-developer workshops for parents; mem. com. on religion in pub. schs. Bd. dirs., rec. sec., program com. Finn Fest '02 Minn. Alumni disting. scholar. Mem. NEA (del. rep. assembly), Nat. Coun. Tchrs. English, Mich. Coun. Tchrs. English (legis. liaison com., censorship com., resolutions chmn., rep. to Minn. Coalition against Censorship), Minn. Edn. Assn. (IPD state coun., exec. bd., chmn. profl. growth, conf. presenter, Univ. IPD award), AHEA (v.p., chmn. settlement task force, chmn. IPD), Midwestern River Project (cons., tchr., curriculum developer), Delta Kappa Gamma (local pres., v.p.).

WESTERDAHL, JOHN BRIAN, nutritionist, health educator; b. Tucson, Dec. 3, 1954; s. Jay E. and Margaret (Meyer) W.; m. Doris Mui Lian Tan, Nov. 18, 1989; 1 child, Jasmine Leilani. AA, Orange Coast Coll., 1977; BS, Pacific Union Coll., 1979; MPH, Loma Linda U., 1981; PhD, Pacific Western U., 2001. Registered dietitian, master herbalist; cert. nutrition specialist; bd. cert. anti-aging health practitioner. From nutritionist, health educator to dir. Castle Med. Ctr., Kailua, Hawaii, 1981—89, dir. wellness and lifestyle medicine and nutritional svc., 1998—; dir. nutrition and health rsch. Health Sci., Santa Barbara, Calif., 1989-90; sr. nutritionist, project mgr. Shaklee Corp., San Francisco, 1990-96; dir. nutrition Dr. McDougall's Right Foods, Inc., South San Francisco, 1996—98; mem. faculty staff, dir. continuing edn. Am. Acad. Nutrition, 1996—; staff nutritionist Millennium Restaurant, San Francisco, 1995—. Radio talk show host Nutrition and You KGU Radio, Honolulu, 1983—89, KWAI Radio, Honolulu, 1999—; nutrition com. mem. Hawaii div. Am. Heart Assn., Honolulu, 1984—87; mem. nutrition study group Gov.s Conf. Health Promotion and Disease Prevention, Hawaii, 1985. Author: Medicinal Herbs: A Vital Reference Guide, 1998, The Millennium Cookbook: Extraordinary Vegetarian Cuisine, 1998; editor: Nourish Mag., 1995-96; nutrition editor: Veggie Life Mag., 1995—. Mem.: Seventh-day Adventist Dietetic Assn., Hawaii Dietetic Assn., Hawaii Nutrition Coun. (v.p. 1983-86, pres.-elect 1988-89, pres. 1989), Inst. Food Technologists, Am. Soc. Pharmacognosy, Am. Coll. Nutrition, Am. Dietetic Assn. (Hawaii coord. vegetarian nutrition dietetic practice group), Am. Acad. Anti-Aging Medicine, Am. Coll. Sports Medicine, AAAS. Republican. Seventh-Day Adventist. Avocations: swimming, scuba diving. Office: Castle Med Ctr Wellness & Lifestyle Med Ctr 642 Ulukahiki St Ste 105 Kailua HI 96734

WESTERFIELD, HOLT BRADFORD, political scientist, educator; b. Rome, Mar. 7, 1928; s. Ray Bert and Mary Beatrice (Putney) W.; m. Carolyn Elizabeth Hess, Dec. 17, 1960; children: Pamela Bradford, Leland Avery. Grad., Choate Sch., 1944; BA, Yale U., 1947; MA, Harvard U., 1951, PhD, 1952. Instr. govt. Harvard U., 1952-56; asst. prof. polit. sci. U. Chgo., 1956-57; mem. faculty Yale U., 1957—, prof. polit. sci., 1965-2000, chmn. dept., 1970-72, Damon Wells prof. internat. studies, 1985-2000; prof. emeritus, 2000—; rsch. assoc. Washington Center Fgn. Policy Research, Johns Hopkins Sch. Advanced Internat. Studies, 1965-66. Vis. prof. Wesleyan U., Middletown, Conn., 1967, 71; bd. visitors U.S. Joint Mil. Intelligence Coll., Washington, 1998—. Author: Foreign Policy and Party Politics: Pearl Harbor to Korea, 1955, The Instruments of America's Foreign Policy, 1963; editor: Inside CIA's Private World: Declassified Articles from the Agency's Internal Journal, 1955-92, 1995. Sheldon traveling fellow Harvard, 1951-52; Henry L. Stimson fellow Yale, 1962, 73; sr. Fulbright-Hays scholar, 1973; hon. vis. fellow Australian Nat. U., 1973. Mem. Am. Polit. Sci. Assn. (Congl. fellow 1953-54), Internat. Polit. Sci. Assn., Internat. Studies Assn. Home: 115 Rogers Rd Hamden CT 06517-3541 Office: Yale Univ Dept Polit Sci PO Box 208301 New Haven CT 06520-8301

WESTERMANN-CICIO, MARY LOUISE, academic administrator, library studies educator; b. N.Y.C., Mar. 11, 1953; d. A. Louis and Anne U. (Skelly) Morse; m. Edward L. Cicio, June 20, 1998. BS in Biology, L.I. U., 1975, MS in Libr. Sci., 1976, MPA in Health Care Adminstrn., 1986; MA in History, SUNY, Stony Brook, 1992, PhD, 2001. Con. med. libr. Nassau-Suffolk Health Systems Agy., Melville, N.Y., 1976-77; dir. John N. Shell Libr. Nassau Acad. Medicine, Garden City, NY, 1977—88; instr. L.I. U., Greenvale, N.Y., 1977-88, adj. prof., 1983-88; asst. prof. Palmer Grad. Libr. Sch., 1988-95, asst. dean, 1995—. Trustee L.I. Libr. Resources Coun., 1986-91; mem. adv. bd. Sr. Connections Program, Adelphi U., 1987-92; bd. dirs. Nassau County coun. Girl Scouts, 2002—. Recipient E. Hugh Behymer award L.I. U., 1976, Disting. Alumni award Palmer Sch. L.I. U., 1993, Jackson Turner Maid award SUNY at Stony Brook, 1993. Mem. ALA, Med. Libr. Assn. (sec. med. socs. sect. 1981-82, instr. continuing edn. 1982, chmn. med. soc. sect. 1986-87; cert. health scis. librianship, Murry E. Gottlieb award 1998), Acad. Health Info. Professions, Spl. Librs. Assn. (sec. L.I. chpt. 1978-80, bd. dirs. 1982-84, pres. elect 1988, pres. 1989-90), Cath. Libr. Assn. (instr. workshop, Libr. of Yr. award 1992), Suffolk-Nassau on-Line Retrievers (chmn. 1981), Med. and Sci. Librs. of L.I. (pres. 1980-81), Nassau County Libr. Assn. (chmn. health svcs. com. 1978-81, 83-93, bd. dirs. 1990-92), Beta Beta Beta, Beta Phi Mu (bd. dirs. Beta Mu chpt. 1987-89, Golden Anniversary award 1999), Pi Alpha Alpha. Office: LI Univ CW Post Campus Palmer Sch Libr and Info Scis Greenvale NY 11548 E-mail: westerma@liu.edu.

WESTFALL, DAVID, lawyer, educator; b. Columbia, Mo., Apr. 16, 1927; s. Wilhelmus David A. and Ruth (Rollins) W.; children: Elizabeth Stewart, William Beatty, Thomas Curwen, Katharine Putnam. AB, U. Mo., 1947; LLB magna cum laude, Harvard U., 1950. Bar: Ill. 1950, Mass. 1956. Assoc. Bell, Boyd, Marshall & Lloyd, Chgo., 1950-55; asst. prof. law Harvard Law Sch., 1955-58, prof., 1958—, John L. Gray prof., 1983—, Carl F. Schipper Jr. prof., 1996—. Author: Estate Planning Cases and Text, 1985, Every Woman's Guide to Financial Planning, 1984, Family Law, 1993; co-author: Estate Planning Law and Taxation, 4th edit., 2001; co-editor: Readings in Federal Taxation, 1983. Served as 1st lt. JAGC, AUS, 1951-53. Fellow Am. Coll. Trust and Estate Counsel (acad.); mem. ABA, Mass. Bar Assn., Am. Law Inst., Phi Beta Kappa, Phi Delta Theta. Office: 1525 Massachusetts Ave Cambridge MA 02138-2903

WESTFIELD, FRED M. economics educator; b. Essen, Germany, Nov. 7, 1926; came to U.S., 1940; s. Dietrich and Grete (Stern) W.; m. Joyce A. Horwitz Nochlin, Nov. 15, 1968; stepchildren: Steven Nochlin, Keith Nochlin. BA magna cum laude, Vanderbilt U., 1950; PhD in Indsl. Econs., MIT, 1957. Teaching asst., instr. MIT, Cambridge, 1952-53; lectr. Northwestern U., Evanston, Ill., 1953-57, asst. prof., 1957-60, assoc. prof., 1960-65; prof. econs. Vanderbilt U., Nashville, 1965-98, mem. faculty coun. Coll. Arts and Sci., 1974-76, mem. faculty senate, 1979-82, 94-95, dir. undergrad. studies dept. econs. and bus. adminstrn., 1984-87, mem. grad. faculty coun., 1991, prof. econs. emeritus, 1998—. Vis. prof. U. Colo., summers 1973-74; condr. seminars, lectr., participant univs. and rsch. orgns.; Fulbright sr. lectr. U. Nac. del Sur, Argentina, 1986; cons. Coun. Econ. Advisers, Exec. Office Pres., 1968, World Bank and Water and Power Devel. Authority, Pakistan, 1970-72, World Bank and East African Power and Light Co., Kenya, 1975, NSF, 1975, FTC, 1976-78, World Bank, UN Devel. Program and Econ. Planning Bd. South Korea, 1975-76; expert witness Tenn. Pub. Svc. Commn., 1980-89, Consumer Advocate Tenn. Atty. Gen., 1994; also others. Mem. editl. bd. Utilities Policy, 1990—2002, mem. bd. editors So. Econ. Jour., 1973—75, editl. referee Am. Econ. Rev., Jour. Polit. Economy, Econometrica, So. Econ. Jour., Econ. Inquiry; contbr. articles and book revs. to profl. jours. With U.S. Army, 1945-46. Fellow Gen. Edn. Bd., MIT, Ford Found., 1958-59. Mem. Am. Econ. Assn., Econometric Soc. (program com. 1967, chmn. conf. sessions), So. Econ. Assn. (v.p. 1976-77, chmn. conf. sessions), Phi Beta Kappa. Home: 1097 Lynnwood Blvd Nashville TN 37215-4540

WEST-HILL, GWENDOLYN, poet, educator, artist, evangelist; b. Indpls., July 30, 1951; d. Wendell Waldon West and Joyce West-Young; m. David Lee Spencer, March 12, 1972 (div. Mar. 1982); children: Hasan Abdul Spencer, Laila Marscia Spencer; m. David Lee Hill, July 25, 1985 (dec. July 1995). BA in Elem. Edn., Ind. U., 1973; Degree in Bus. Adminstrn., Butler U., 1983; degree in Comml. Art, Chas Wharton Sch. Art, 1984; student, Ga. Med. Inst., 1992, Wendell Parker's Poet Laureate Schl. Poetry, 2000—03. Prin., CEO T-Shirt Haven, Atlanta, 1990—. Exec. dir. Peace Records, Inc., Decatur, Ga., 2003. Author: Poems for the Family, 1990, Prism of Thoughts, 1998, Giving It Back To You, 2000, My Brother Phillip West, 2002; contbr. poems to newspapers, mags., and anthologies (FamousPets.Com award). Missionary House of Refuge Prayer, Coll. Park, Ga., 1993—; evangelist Dekalb United Pentecostal Ch., Stone Mountain, Ga., 2003—, The Potter's House, T.D. Jakes Ministries, Dallas, 1999. Recipient Eubie Blake award Ind. Black Expo, Indpls., 1985, award Peace Records, Inc. of Atlanta, DLM Gospel Prodn. and Promotions, Inc., 2003, Famous Poets award 2003. Fellow Delta Sigma Theta (Gamma Nu chpt.). Avocations: singing, drawing, writing, travel, teaching, speaking. Home: 4251 Parkview Ct Stone Mountain GA 30083-1294 Office: House of Refuge Prayer Mission College Park GA 30337-6243 E-mail: gospelqueen20022002@yahoo.com.

WESTIN, ALAN FURMAN, political science educator; b. N.Y.C, Nov. 11, 1929; s. Irving and Etta (Furman) W.; m. Beatrice Patricia Shapoff, June 20, 1954; children: David, Debra, Jeremy. BA, U. Fla., 1948; LLB, Harvard U., 1951, PhD, 1965. Bar: D.C. 1951. Sr. fellow Yale U. Law Sch., New Haven, 1956-57, vis. prof. polit. sci., 1960-61; asst. prof. govt. Cornell U., Ithaca, N.Y., 1957-59; assoc. prof. pub. law and govt. Columbia U., N.Y.C., 1959-66, prof., 1966-96, prof. emeritus, 1997—; dir. Ctr. Rsch. and Edn. in Am. Liberties, 1965-71; founder, pres. Ednl. Fund Individual Rights, N.Y.C., 1978-86; pres. Changing Workplaces, Englewood, N.J., 1982-87; program assoc. Harvard U., 1968-72; cons. IBM, 1973-75, U.S. Office Tech. Assessment, 1973—; pres. Ctr. Social and Legal Rsch., 1987—. Ref. Point Found., 1987-98; ptnr. Privacy Cons. Group, Washington, 1993—; chmn., CEO Toolkit Software, 1996—; CEO, Privacy Knowledge, 2001—03; dir. Privacy Exchange.org, 1998—, Japan-U.S. Privacy and Data Protection Program, 1999—; CEO Lifetime Privacy Mgr., 2003—. Cons. on privacy to Equifax, Citicorp, IBM, Am. Express, U.S. Social Security Adminstrn., Chrysler, Health Data Exch., N.Y. State Identification and Intelligence Sys., Bell Atlantic, Glaxo Wellcome, Eli Lilly; cons. on employee rights Fed. Express, Aetna Life and Casualty, Citicorp, IBM, 1980-86; acad. advisor nat. pub. surveys on privacy Louis Harris and Assocs., 1979, 90, 91, 92, 93, 94, 95, 96, 97, 98, 99, 2000; nat. pub. surveys on cons. privacy, Can., 1992, 94, U.K., Germany, 1999; dir. privacy and human genome project U.S. Dept. Energy, 1992-95; chmn. emm. adv. panels U.S. Office Tech. Assessment, 1975-92; chmn. Res. Coun. Healthy Cos., 1991-95; spkr. nat. bus., profl., govt. confs., 1960—; pres. Privacy & Am. Bus. Inst., 1993—. Author: The Anatomy of a Constitutional Law Case, 1958, reprinted, 1990 (put in Notable Trials Libr. 1995), Privacy and Freedom, 1967 (George Polk award, Sidney Hillman award, Melcher award, Van Am. Soc. award 1967), (with Barry Mahoney) The Trial of Martin Luther King, 1975, (with Michael A. Baker) Databanks in a Free Society, 1972; editor: Whistle Blowing! Loyalty and Dissent in the Corporation, 1980, Information Technology in a Democracy, 1971 (with Alfred Feliu) Resolving Employment Disputes Without Litigation, 1988, (with John D. Aram) Managerial Delemmas: Cases in Social, Legal, and Technological Change, 1988; editor-in-chief: The Civil Liberties Rev., 1973-79; polit. sci. editor: Casebook Series, 1960-66; contbr. numerous chpts. to books, articles to legal and popular publs.; mem. editl. bd. Employee Rights and Responsibilities Jour., Information Age, Jour. Computing and Society, Transnational Data Report: writer-narrator: CBS-TV Series, The Road to the White House, 1964; cons. spl. programs: ABC-TV; advisor Off Limits: Your Health, Your Job, Your Privacy, PBS Network, 1994; pub. editor-in-chief Privacy and American Business, 1993—. Mem. Nat. Wiretapping Commn., 1973-76; vice-chmn. N.J. Commn. Individual Liberty, 1977-81; sr. cons. U.S. Privacy Protection Study Commn., 1975-77. Recipient Mark Van Doren award Columbia U., 1972; recipient Disting. Alumnus award Delta Sigma Rho-Tau-Kappa Alpha, 1965; grantee Rockefeller Found., 1983, Russell Saga Found., 1969-71, 81-82 Mem. Nat. Acad. Scis. (computer sci. and engring. bd. 1969-72), Am. Polit. Sci. Assn., Assn. Computing Machinery (chmn. task force privacy 1972-73) Home: 1100 Trafalgar St Teaneck NJ 07666-1928 also: Ctr Social Legal Rsch 2 University Plaza Dr Ste 414 Hackensack NJ 07601-6209

WESTMORELAND, BARBARA FENN, neurologist, electroencephalographer, educator; b. 1940; BS in Chemistry, Mary Washington Coll., 1961; MD, U. Va., 1965. Diplomate Am. Bd. Psychiatry and Neurology and certification of added qualification in clin. neurophysiology (vice chair). Intern Vanderbilt Hosp., Nashville, 1965-66; resident in neurology U. Va. Hosp., Charlottesville, 1966-70; fellow in electroencephalography Mayo Clinic, Rochester, Minn., 1970-71, assoc. cons. neurology, 1971-73; asst. prof. neurology Mayo Med. Sch., Rochester, 1973-78, assoc. prof., 1978-85, prof., 1985—. Co-author: Medical Neurosciences, 1978, rev. edit., 1986, first author 3d edit., 1994. Mem.: Mayo History Medicine Soc. (pres. 1990—91), Am. Acad. Neurology (chair elect of sec. clin. neurophysiology 1998—2000, vice chair exam com. cert. clin. neurophysiology Am. Bd. Psych. & Neu 1998—, chair sect. clin. neurophysiology 2000—02, A.B. Baker award for lifetime achievement in edn. 2002), Ctrl. Assn. Electroencephalographers (sec.-treas. 1976—78, pres. 1979—80, chair neurology resident in-svc. tng. exam 1994—99), Am. EEG Soc. (sec. 1985—87, pres. 1991—92), Am. Epilepsy Soc. (treas. 1978—80, pres. 1987—88), Sigma Xi (pres. chpt. 1987—88).

WESTOFF, CHARLES FRANCIS, demographer, educator; b. N.Y.C., July 23, 1927; s. Frank Barnett and Evelyn (Bales) Westoff; m. Joan P. Uszynski, Sept. 11, 1948 (div. Jan. 1969); children: David, Carol; m. Leslie Aldridge, Aug. 1969 (div. Feb. 1993); m. Jane De Lung, May 1997. AB, Syracuse U., 1949, MA, 1950; PhD, U. Pa., 1953. Instr. sociology U. Pa., 1950—52; research assoc. Milbank Meml. Fund, N.Y.C., 1952—55; research assoc. Office Population Research Princeton U., 1955—62, Maurice P. During '22 prof. demographic studies and sociology, 1962—99, sr. rsch. demographer, 1999—, chmn. dept. sociology, 1965—70, assoc. dir. Office Population Research, 1962—75, dir., 1975—92; assoc. prof. sociology N.Y.U., also chmn. dept. sociology Washington Sq. Coll., 1959—62; vis. sr. fellow East-West Population Inst., Honolulu, 1979—81; Disting. vis. prof. Am. U., Cairo, 1979; mem. vis. com. Harvard-M.I.T. Joint Center for Urban Studies, 1980—83. Exec. dir. Commn. Population Growth and Am. Future, 1970—72; mem. adv. com. on population stats. U.S. Bur. Census, 1973—79; chmn. Nat. Com. for Rsch. on 1980 Census, 1981—88; bd. dirs. Alan Guttmacher Inst., 1977—88, 1989—97; sr. tech. advisor Demographic Health Surveys, 1984—; bd. dirs. Population Resource Ctr., 1985—, Population Ref. Bur., 1988—94, Population Commns. Internat., 1992—98; com. on population NAS, 1983—88. Co-author: Family Growth in Metropolitan America, 1961, The Third Child, 1963, College Women and Fertility Values, 1967, The Later Years of Childbearing, 1970, From Now to Zero, 1971, Reproduction in the United States, 1965, 1971, Toward the End of Growth: Population in America, 1973, The Contraceptive Revolution, 1976, Demographic Dynamics in America, 1977, Age at Marriage, Age at First Birth and Fertility in Africa, 1992, Unmet Need: 1990-1994, 1995, Childbearing Attitudes and Intentions, 1995, Mass Media and Reproductive Behavior in Africa, 1997, Replacement of Abortion by Contraception in Three Central Asian Republics, 1998; contbr. articles on demography and sociology to profl. jours.; co-author: Unmet Need at the End of the Century, 2002. Recipient Irene Taueber award for Outstanding Rsch. Contbns., 1995. Fellow: Am. Acad. Arts and Scis.; mem.: Internat. Union Sci. Study Population, Population Assn. Am. (bd. dirs. 1960—62, 1968—70, 1st v.p. 1972—73, pres. 1974—75), Planned Parenthood Fedn. Am. (dir. 1978—81), Inst. Medicine-NAS. Home: 1 Highland Rd Princeton NJ 08540 Office: Princeton U Wallace Hall Princeton NJ 08544

WESTON, FRANCINE EVANS, secondary education educator; b. Mt. Vernon, N.Y., Oct. 8, 1946; d. John Joseph and Frances (Fantino) Pisaniello. BA, Hunter Coll., 1968; MA, Lehman Coll., 1973; cert., Am. Acad. Dramatic Arts, N.Y.C., 1976; PhD, NYU, 1991. Cert. elem., secondary tchr., N.Y. Tchr. Yonkers (N.Y.) Bd. Edn., 1968—; aquatic dir. Woodlane Day Camp, Irvington-on-Hudson, N.Y., 1967-70, Yonkers Jewish Community Ctr., 1971-75. Creative drama tchr. John Burroughs Jr. H.S., Yonkers, 1971-77; stage lighting designer Iona Summer Theatre Festival, New Rochelle, N.Y., 1980-81, Yonkers Male Glee Club, 1981-89, Roosevelt H.S., 1980-97; freelance, 1998—; rsch. specialist Scholarship Locating Svc., 1992-94, Yonkers Civil Def. Police Aux., 1994—; master electrician NYU Summer Mus. Theatre, 1979-80; appointed program developer for Cadet Acad. of Police & Fire Scis., Pub. Safety Magnet, Roosevelt H.S., 2001. Actress in numerous comty. theater plays including A Touch of the Poet, 1979; dir. stage prodns. including I Remember Mama, 1973, The Man Who Came to Dinner, 1975; author: A Descriptive Comparison of Computerized Stage Lighting Memory Systems With Non-Computerized Systems, 1991, (short stories) A Hat for Louise, 1984, Old Memories: Beautiful and Otherwise, 1984; lit. editor: (story and poetry collection) Beautifully Old, 1984; editor: Command Post Dispatch quar., 1997—. Mem. Yonkers Civil Def. Police Aux., 1994—, adminstrv. asst. to commanding officer, 1996—, lt., capt. adminstrn., 2002—; steering com. chairperson Roosevelt H.S.-Middle States Assn. of Schs. and Colls. Self-Evaluation, 1985—88. Named Tchr. of Excellence, N.Y. State English Coun., 1990, 95, 2000; recipient Monetary award for Teaching Excellence, Carter-Wallace Products, 1992; named to Arrid Tchrs. Honor Roll, 1992. Republican. Roman Catholic. Avocations: swimming, animal related activities, anything theatrical. Office: Roosevelt High Sch Tuckahoe Rd Yonkers NY 10710

WESTON, JOHN FREDERICK, business educator, consultant; b. Ft. Wayne, Ind., Feb. 6, 1916; s. David Thomas and Bertha (Schwartz) W.; children: Kenneth F., Byron L., Ellen J. BA, U. Chgo., 1937, MBA, 1943, PhD, 1948. Instr. U. Chgo. Sch. Bus., 1940-42, asst. prof., 1947-48; prof. The Anderson Sch. UCLA, 1949—, Cordner prof. The Anderson Sch., 1981-94, prof. emeritus recalled The Anderson Sch., 1986—, dir. rsch. program in competition and bus. policy, 1969—, dir. Ctr. for Managerial Econs. and Pub. Policy, 1983-86. Econ. cons. to pres. Am. Bankers Assn., 1945-46; disting. lecture series U. Okla., 1967, U. Utah, 1972, Miss. State U., 1972, Miami State U., 1975. Author: Scope and Methodology of Finance, 1966, International Managerial Finance, 1972, Impact of Large Firms on U.S. Economy, 1973, Financial Theory and Corporate Policy, 1979, 2d edit., 1983, 3d edit., 1988, Mergers, Restructuring and Corporate Control, 1990, Takeovers, Restructuring and Corporate Governance, 3d edit., 2000, Managerial Finance, 9th edit, 1992; assoc. editor: Jour. of Finance, 1948-55; mem. editorial bd., 1957-59; editorial bd. Bus. Econs., Jour. Fin. Rsch., Managerial and Decision Econs.; manuscript referee Am. Econ. Rev., Rev. of Econs. and Statistics, Engring. Economist, Bus. Econs., Fin. Mgmt. Bd. dirs. Bunker Hill Fund. Served with Ordnance Dept. AUS, 1943-45. Recipient Abramson Scroll award Bus. Econs., 1989-94; McKinsey Found. grantee, 1965-68; GE grantee, 1967; Ford Found. Faculty Rsch. fellow, 1961-62. Fellow Nat. Assn. Bus. Economists; mem. Am. Finance Assn. (pres. 1966, adv. bd. 1967-71), Am. Econ. Assn., Western Econ. Assn. (pres. 1962), Econometric Soc., Am. Statis. Assn., Royal Econ. Soc., Fin. Analysts Soc., Fin. Mgmt. Assn. (pres. 1979-80) Home: 258 Tavistock Ave Los Angeles CA 90049-3229 Office: UCLA 258 Tavistock Ave Los Angeles CA 90049-3229

WESTON, KATH, anthropology educator; b. Ill., Nov. 2, 1958; AB, U. Chgo., 1978, AM, 1981, Stanford U., 1984, PhD, 1988. Assoc. prof. anthropology Ariz. State U. West, Phoenix, 1990-99; rsch. assoc. in sociology Brandeis U., Waltham, Mass., 2000; dir. studies in womens studies Harvard U., Cambridge, 2001—. Spkr. in field. Author: Families We Choose: Lesbians, Gays, Kinship, 1991, 2d edit., 1997 (Ruth Benedict prize), Render Me, Gender Me, 1996 (Ruth Benedict prize), Long Slow Burn: Sexuality and Social Science, 1998, Gender in Real Time: Power and Transience in a Visual Age, 2002; co-editor: The Lesbian Issue: Essays from SIGNS, 1985; contbr. articles to profl. jours. Fellow NSF, 1980-83, 85-87, AAUW, 1985-86, Rockefeller Found., U. Minn. Ctr. for Advanced Feminist Studies, 1989-90, Am. Coun. Learned Socs., 1996, Bunting Inst., Radcliffe Coll., 1996-97. Mem. Nat. Writers Union. Office: Harvard Univ Womens Studies Cambridge MA 02138

WESTPHAL, JAMES ADOLPH, planetary science educator; b. Dubuque, Iowa, June 13, 1930; s. Henry Ludwig and Nancy Kathryn (Wise) W.; m. Lois Jean, Apr. 17, 1956 (div. 1966); 1 child, Andrew Johnathan; m. Barbara Jean Webster, Nov. 2, 1967. BS, U. Tulsa, 1954. Team leader Sinclair Rsch. Labs., Tulsa, 1955-61; sr. engr. Calif. Inst. Tech., Pasadena, 1961-66, sr. rsch. fellow, 1966-71, assoc. prof., 1971-76, prof., 1976-98, prof. emeritus, 1998—; dir. Palomar Obs., Pasadena, 1994-97. Prin. investigator Hubble space telescope NASA, Calif. Inst. Tech., Pasadena, 1977—. Fellow MacArthur Found., 1991; recipient Space Science award Am. Inst. Aeronautics and Astronautics, 1995. Mem. Am. Astron. Soc. Office: Calif Inst Tech Ms 150 21 Pasadena CA 91125-0001 E-mail: jaw@caltech.edu.

WESTPHAL, KLAUS WILHELM, university museum director; b. Berlin, Mar. 20, 1939; came to U.S., 1969; s. Wilhelm Heinrich and Irmgard (Henze) W.; m. Margaret Elisabeth Dorothea Wagner, May 16, 1969; children: Barbara, Marianne, Christine. BS in Geology, Eberhard-Karls Universität, Tübingen, Germany, 1960, MS, 1964, PhD in Paleontology, 1969. Dir. geology mus. U. Wis. Madison, 1969—. Bd. dirs. natural history coun. U. Wis. Madison, 1973—, Friends of Geology Mus., Inc., 1977—; nat. speaker on paleontology Outreach, 1977—; instr. paleontology U. Wis., 1977—; leader expeditions fossil vertebrates including dinosaurs, 1977—. Participant various tchr.-tng. projects Wis. Pub. Schs. Lutheran. Home: 3709 High Rd Middleton WI 53562-1003 Office: U Wis Geology Mus 1215 W Dayton St Madison WI 53706-1600 E-mail: westphal@geology.wisc.edu.

WESTWOOD, GERALDINE E. elementary school educator; b. Buffalo, N.Y., Feb. 13, 1951; d. Robert David and Esther Norma (Fies) W. AA, Villa Maria Coll., 1971; BS, D'Youville Coll., 1973; MEd, Va. Commonwealth U., 1982; postgrad., Nova Southeastern U., 1993. Cert. tchr. K-7, elem. prin., Va. Trmedial math tchr., grades 2-4 Charles City (Va.) Pub. Schs.; kindergarten tchr. King William County (Va.) Pub. Schs., Spotsylvania (Va.) County Pub. Schs., elem. tchr. grade 3. Active Rappahannok Reading Coun. Mem. Order Eastern Star (past matron), Phi Delta Kappa (past pres. No. Va. chpt.). Home: PO Box 2607 Spotsylvania VA 22553-6815 E-mail: gwestwood@erols.com.

WETHERWAX, GEORGIA LEE (PEG WETHERWAX), elementary education educator; b. St. Louis, Oct. 7, 1931; d. Kenneth Alden and Frances Marie (Cuming) Smith; m. Alfred R. Wetherwax, Oct. 7, 1950;

children: C. Todd, Steven, Karen, Kent. BA in Elem. Edn., Calif. State U., L.A., 1955, MA in Elem. Adminstrn., 1966. Tchr. Burbank (Calif.) Unified Schs., 1955-56; tchr., vice prin. L.A. Unified Sch. Dist., 1957-68, master tchr., profl. expert, 1983-86, bi-lingual tchr., 1987-91; tchr., vice prin. Mammoth Unified Sch. Dist., Mammoth Lakes, Calif., 1969-79; asst. supt., prin. K-8, tchr. Middletown (Calif.) Unified Sch. Dist., 1979-83, ret., 1991; curriculum devel. specialist Calibre Industries, L.A., 1986-87. CEO Creative Curriculums, Thousand Oaks, Calif., 1989—. Author: Careful Mathematics Lesson Plans, 1986. Faculty Women's scholar L.A. City Coll., William Snyder scholar Calif. State U. L.A.; grantee L.A. Ednl. Partnership. Mem. Pi Lambda Theta, Delta Kappa Gamma. Avocations: quilting, photography, gardening, hiking. Home and Office: 1979 Shady Brook Dr Thousand Oaks CA 91362-1337

WETHINGTON, CHARLES T., JR., academic administrator; AB, Ea. Ky. U., 1956; postgrad., Syracuse U., 1958-59; MA, U. Ky., 1962, PhD, 1965. Instr. ednl. psychology U. Ky., Lexington, 1965-66; dir. Maysville (Ky.) C.C., 1967-71; asst. v.p. c.c. system U. Ky., Lexington, 1971-81, v.p. c.c. system, 1981-82, chancellor c.c. system, 1982-88, chancellor c.c. system and univ. rels., 1988-89, interim pres., 1989-90, pres., 1990—2001, pres. emeritus, 2001—. Chmn. legis. com. State Dirs. Community and Jr. Colls., 1983-85, chmn. nat. coun., 1985-86; commn. on colls. So. Assn. Schs. and Colls., 1978-84, vice chmn. exec. commn., 1984, trustee, 1986-89; mem. So. Regional Edn. Bd., 1988-2000, mem. exec. com., 1989-93, vice-chmn., 1991-93; pres. Southeastern Conf., 1993-95, chair exec. com. NCAA, 1999-2001. Bd. dirs. Bluegrass State Skills Corp., 1984-91, vice-chmn. bd. dirs., 1986-87; bd. visitors C.C. Air Force, 1986-90; jud. nominating commn. 22nd Jud. Dist., Fayette County, Ky., 1988-91, So. Growth Policies Bd., 1990-2000; bd. dirs. NCAA Found., 1999—; active Bus.-Higher Edn. Forum, 1999-2001. With security svc. USAF, 1957-61. Home: 2926 Four Pines Dr Lexington KY 40502 Office: U Ky 5-52 Wm T Young Libr Lexington KY 40506-0456 E-mail: cwething@email.uky.edu.

WETHINGTON, NORBERT ANTHONY, medieval scholar; b. Dayton, Ohio, Sept. 14, 1943; s. Norbert and Sophie Lillian W.; m. Martha M. Vannice, Aug. 13, 1966. BA, U. Dayton, 1965; MA, John Carroll U., 1967; postgrad., Baldwin Wallace Coll., 1968—70; PhD, U. Toledo (Ohio), 1997. Grad. asst., tchg. assoc. John Carroll U., Cleve., 1965—67; English tchr. Padua Franciscan High Sch., Parma, Ohio, 1967—70; instr., chmn. dept. tech. writing and speech N. Ctrl. Tech. Coll., Mansfield, Ohio, 1978—80, dir. pub. and cmty. svc. technologies, 1980—94; dir. humanities Terra State C.C., 1994—96, assoc. dean of instr., 1996—97; affiliate scholar Oberlin Coll., 1998—. Cons. in field. Contbr. articles. V.p. Sandusky County Bd. Health, 1979—80. Mem.: Nat. Coun. Tchrs. English, Ohio Vocat. Assn. (pres. tech. edn. divsn. 1985—86, Disting. Svc. award 1987), Am. Vocat. Assn., Nat. Coalition Ind. Scholars, MLA. Democrat. Roman Catholic. Mailing: PO Box 842 Fremont OH 43420-0842

WETMORE, RENÉE MARGARET, physical education educator; b. Grand Rapids, Mich., Feb. 25, 1966; d. Ronald Dale and Sue Beverly (Robson) W. BS in Health and Phys. Edn., Ga. Coll., 1988. Tchr. phys. edn. Bibb County Bd. Edn., Macon, Ga., 1988—, fitness cons. Wellness Ctr., 1990—. Vol. CPR instr. Am. Heart Assn. Mem. AAHPERD, Am. Running and Fitness Assn., Ga. Assn. Health, Phys. Edn., Recreation and Dance (Tchr. of Yr. award 1993). Methodist. Avocations: sailing, bicycling, tennis, back-packing, computers. Home: 124 Knights Brg Warner Robins GA 31093-8547 Office: Bruce Elem Sch 3660 Houston Ave Macon GA 31206-2497

WETSCH, PEGGY A. information systems specialist, publisher, educator, nurse; b. San Diego; d. Harvey William Henry and Helen Catherine (Thorpe) Brink; m. Gearald M. Wetsch, June 26, 1971; children: Brian Gearald, Lynette Kirstiann Nicole. Diploma, Calif. Hosp. Sch. Nursing, 1971; BSN cum laude, Pepperdine U., 1980; MS in Nursing, Calif. State U., L.A., 1985. Cert. in nursing adminstrn., human resource devel. Clin. nurse Orange County Med. Ctr./U. Calif. Irvine Med. Ctr., Orange, Calif., 1971-75; pediatric head nurse U. Calif. Irvine Med. Ctr., 1975-79; clin. nurse educator Palm Harbor Gen./Med. Ctr. Garden Grove, Calif., 1980-81; dir. ednl. svcs. Med. Ctr. of Garden Grove, 1981-85; dir. edn. Mission Hosp. Regional Med. Ctr., Mission Viejo, Calif., 1986-92; coord. computer and learning resources L.A. Med. Ctr. Sch. Nursing, 1992-95; assoc. part time faculty Saddleback Coll., 1990-94; cons. ptnr. nur.SYS-Edn. systems Cons., 1995—; sys. adminstr. Info. Resources Group, Pasadena, Calif., 1995-97, chief info. officer, 1997-98, pres., pub. L.A., 1998—. Lectr. statewide nursing program Calif. State U., Dominguez Hills, 1986-92; ednl. cons. Author: (with others) Nursing Diagnosis: Guidelines to Planning Care, 1993, 2d edit., 1994, 4th edit., 1999; contbr. articles to profl. jours. Treas. Orange County Nursing Edn. Coun., 1986-87, 88-90, pres., 1987-88. Mem. ANA, NLN, Am. Nursing Informatics Assn. (pres. 1997-98, elections com. So. Calif. chpt. 1994, coord. continuing edn., conf. planning com., webmaster 1998—), N.Am. Nursing Diagnosis Assn. (secondary reviewer Diagnostic Rev. 1989-90, expert adv. panel 1990-92, mem. diagnosis rev. com. 1992-96, chair diagnostic rev. com. 1996-98, program com. 1998—), Soc. Calif. Nursing Diagnosis Assn. (membership chmn. 1984-92, pres. 1992-94), Nat. Am. Mgmt. Assn. (charter L.A. County, U. So. Calif. Med. Ctr. chpt.), Spina Bifida Assn. Am., Phi Kappa Phi, Sigma Theta Tau (pres. Iota Eta chpt. 1990-92). Office: Ste 105 2621 Green River Rd PO Box 405 Corona CA 92882-7433

WETTSTEIN, ROBERT MARK, psychiatrist, educator; b. NYC, June 4, 1950; s. Sidney and Bonnie W.; m. Stacey Sayer; children: Zachary Sayer, Emma Rachel. BA in Natural Scis., Johns Hopkins, 1972; MD, UCLA, 1976. Adj. attending dept. psychiatry Rush-Presbyn.-St. Luke's Med. Ctr., Chgo., 1981-83; research coord. Rush-Presbyn.-Consultation Liaison Svc., Chgo., 1981-84; lectr. in psychiatry dept. psychiatry Loyola U. Stritch Sch. Medicine, Maywood, Ill., 1981-84; staff psychiatrist Isaac Ray Ctr.-Rush-Presbyn. St. Luke's Med. Ctr., Chgo., 1981-84; lectr. in psychiatry dept. psychiatry Pritzker Sch. Medicine, Chgo., 1982-84; asst. attending dept. psychiatry Rush-Presbyn.-St. Luke's Med. Ctr., Chgo., 1983-84; asst. prof. dept. psychiatry Rush Med. Coll., Chgo., 1983-84; asst. prof. psychiatry U. Pitts., 1984-96, clin. assoc. prof. psychiatry, 1997—2000, clin. prof. psychiatry, 2000—. Cons. psychiatrist Ill. Dept. Mental Health, Chgo., 1981-84; cons. Mon-Yough Corrections Program, Pitts., 1987—; co-dir. law and psychiatry program Western Psychiat. Inst. and Clinic, Pitts., 1986-96. Editor Behavioral Scis. and the Law, 1987-96; contbr. articles to profl. jours. Recipient Retirement Research Found. award, 1987-88. Mem. Am. Psychiat. Assn., Am. Acad. Psychiatry and the Law (editor newsletter, pres.-elect 2002-03), Am. Soc. Law and Medicine. Office: Ste B103 401 Shady Ave Apt B103 Pittsburgh PA 15206-4458

WETZBARGER, DONNA KAY, secondary education educator; b. Madison, S.D. d. D.H. and E.M. (Gray) Krug; m. Dale G. Wetzbarger; children: Taylor, Erin. BA, Ottawa (Kans.) U., 1973; MA, U. No. Colo., 1979. Cert. secondary edn. tchr., Colo. Tchr., Ft. Morgan, Colo., 1973-84; instr. Midland (Tex.) Coll., 1984-86; tchr. Sheridan Coll., Gillette, Wyo., 1986-87, Niwot (Colo.) H.S., 1987—. Reading specialist Improvement Plus, Longmont, Colo., 1990—. Incentive grantee St. Vrain, 1996; Sch. to Career grantee, 1997-98. Mem. NEA, Colo. Edn. Assn., Nat. Coun. Tchrs. of English. Office: Skyline High Sch 8989 Niwot Rd Longmont CO 80501 Home: 1609 Linden St Longmont CO 80501-2451 E-mail: jake2343@cris.com.

WETZEL, FRANKLIN TODD, spinal surgeon, educator, researcher; b. Wilmington, Del., Mar. 7, 1955; s. Franklin Huff and Jean Hartman (Clouser) W.; m. Patricia Ann Cassanos, May 23, 1981 (div. June 1993); m. Cathleen Ann Myers, Nov. 21, 1993 (div. May, 2002); 1 child, Colin Todd. AB, Harvard Coll., 1977; MD, U. Pa., 1981. Diplomate Am. Bd. Orthop. Surgery. Resident Yale U., New Haven, 1981-86, instr. Med. Sch., 1986-87; fellow S. Henry LaRocca, MD, New Orleans, 1987-88; asst. prof. Pa. State U., Hershey, 1988-91, assoc. prof., 1991-93, U. Chgo., 1993—, dir. Spine Ctr., 1993—, vice chair dept. surgery; chief sect. orthopedic surgery L.A. Weiss Hosp., Chgo., 1998—, chair divsn. of surgery, 2000—. Reviewer Clin. Orthops., Phila., 1993—. Assoc. editor Spine, 1990—; contbr. articles to profl. jours. Physician Armenian Gen. Benevolent, Hershey, 1988; mem. alumni coun. Wilmington Friends Sch., 1991—. Fellow Am. Acad. Orthop. Surgery; mem. Cervical Spine Rsch. Soc., N.Am. Spine Soc., Am. Neuromodulation Soc. (bd. dirs. 1994—), Acad. Orthop. Soc., Am. Pain Soc., Harvard Club (interviewer 1995—), Sigma Xi. Presbyterian. Avocations: vertebrate paleontology, vintage cars, military history, baseball, tennis, squash. Office: U Chgo Spine Ctr 4646 N Marine Dr Chicago IL 60640-5759 E-mail: twetzel@mcis.bsd.uchicago.edu.

WETZEL, JODI (JOY LYNN WETZEL), history and women's studies educator; b. Salt Lake City, Apr. 5, 1943; d. Richard Coulam and Margaret Elaine (Openshaw) Wood; m. David Nevin Wetzel, June 12, 1967; children: Meredith (dec.), Richard Rawlins. BA in English, U. Utah, 1965, MA in English, 1967; PhD in Am. Studies, U. Minn., 1977. Instr. Am. studies and family social sci. U. Minn., 1973-77, asst. prof. Am. studies and women's studies, 1977-79, asst. to dir. Minn. Women's Ctr., 1973-75, asst. dir., 1975-79; dir. Women's Resource Ctrs. U. Denver, 1980-84, mem. adj. faculty history, 1981-84, dir. Am. studies program, dir. Women's Inst., 1983-84; dir. Women in Curriculum U. Maine, 1985-86, mem. coop. faculty sociology, social work and human devel., 1986; dir. Inst. Women's Studies and Svcs. Met. State Coll. Denver, 1986—, assoc. prof. history, 1986-89, prof. history, 1990—. Speaker, presenter, cons. in field; vis. prof. Am. studies U. Colo., 1985; mem. judges panel nominations rev. Nat. Women's Hall of Fame, Seneca Falls, N.Y., 2002. Co-author: Women's Studies: Thinking Women, 1993; co-editor: Readings Toward Composition, 2d edit., 1969; contbr. articles to profl. publs. Del. at-large Nat. Women's Meeting, Houston, 1977; bd. dirs. Rocky Mountain Women's Inst., 1981-84; treas. Colo. Women's Agenda, 1987-91; mem. judges panel, nominations reviewer Nat. Women's Hall of Fame, Seneca Falls, N.Y., 2002. U. Utah Dept. English fellow, 1967; U. Minn. fellow, 1978-79; grantee NEH, 1973, NSF, 1981-83, Carnegie Corp., 1988; named to Outstanding Young Women of Am., 1979. Mem. Am. Hist. Assn., Nat. Assn. Women in Edn. (Hilda A. Davis Ednl. Leadership award 1996, Sr. Scholar 1996), Am. Assn. for Higher Edn., Am. Studies Assn., Nat. Women's Studies Assn., Golden Key Nat. Honor Soc. (hon.), Alpha Lambda Delta, Phi Kappa Phi. Office: Met State Coll Den Campus Box 36 PO Box 173362 Denver CO 80217-3362

WETZEL, JOE STEVEN, principal; b. Sherman, Tex., Aug. 7, 1948; s. Oscar Lee and Mary Elizabeth (Hash) W.; m. Patricia Fay Quattlebaum, Apr. 18, 1970; children: Jennifer Lea, Joseph Patrick. AS, Grayson County Jr. Coll., 1968; BS, East Tex. State U., 1970, MS, 1972. Tchr. Garland (Tex.) Ind. Sch. Dist., 1972-89, asst. prin., 1989—. Mem. Citizen Police Acad., membership com., 1994, v.p., 1993-94; mem. Southeastern Devel. Lab., Austin, Tex., 1993—. Mem. ASCD, Tex. Assn. Secondary Sch. Prins., Masons, Phi Delta Kappa. Democrat. Presbyterian. Avocations: golf, reading, target shooting. Home: 514 Colonial Dr Garland TX 75043-2305 Office: South Garland High Sch 600 Colonel Dr Garland TX 75043-2399

WETZEL, RICHARD DENNIS, physical education educator, administrator; b. Dayton, Ohio, July 28, 1952; m. Charlott G. Wetzel, Aug. 29, 1981; children: Nicole, Brandon. AA in Liberal Arts, Sinclair C.C., 1974; BS in Phys. Edn., U. Tenn., Knoxville, 1976; MS in Phys. Edn., U. Dayton, 1981. Cert. phys. edn. tchr., Ohio; cert. emergency med. technician; instr. first aid, CPR, BLS. Dir. Beavercreek (Ohio) Dance and Gymnastics, Inc., 1976-78; mgr. Dayton Racquetball Clubs, 1978-79; mem. faculty phys. edn., supr. phys. activity ctr. Sinclair C.C., Dayton, 1970—. Mem. AAHPERD, Ohio Alliance Health, Phys. Edn., Recreation and Dance, Am. Coll. Sports Medicine, Assn. Fitness in Bus. Avocations: jogging, triathlon. Office: Sinclair CC 444 W 3rd St Dayton OH 45402-1421 Home: 4132 Amy Brooke Cir Bellbrook OH 45305-1143

WETZEL, ROBERT GEORGE, botany educator; b. Ann Arbor, Mich., Aug. 16, 1936; s. Wilhelm and Eugenia (Wagner) W.; m. Carol Ann Andree, Aug. 9, 1959; children: Paul Robert, Pamela Jeanette, Timothy Mark, Kristina Marie. BS, U. Mich., 1958, MS, 1959; PhD, U. Calif. at Davis, 1962; PhD (hon.), U. Uppsala, Sweden, 1984. Rsch. assoc. Ind. U., Bloomington, 1962-65; asst. prof. botany Mich. State U., East Lansing, 1965-68, assoc. prof., 1968-71, prof., 1971-86, U. Mich., Ann Arbor, 1986-90; Bishop prof. biology U. Ala., Tuscaloosa, 1990—2001; prof. environ. scis. U. N.C., Chapel Hill, 2001—03, W. Kenan Disting. prof., 2003—. Cons. Internat. Biol. Program, London, 1967-75; chmn. Internat. Seagrass Commn., 1974-75; founding mem. Internat. Lake Environment Com., 1986—. Author: Limnology, 1975, 3d rev. edit., 2001, Limnological Analyses, 1979, 3d rev. edit., 2000, To Quench Our Thirst: Present and Future Freshwater Resources of the United States, 1983, Freshwater Ecosystems: Revitalizing Educational Programs in Limnology, 1996; editor: Periphyton of Freshwater Ecosystems, 1983, Wetlands and Ecotones, 1993, Recent Studies on Ecology and Management of Wetlands, 1994, Wetland Ecology, 1995, Lake Okeechobee: A Synthesis, 1995, Limnology of Developing Countries, vol. 1 1995, Limnology of Developing Countries, Vol. 2, 1999, Vol. 3, 2001, Watershed Management for Potable Water Supply, 2000, Confronting Climate Change in the Gulf Coast Region, 2001, The Missouri River Ecosystem, 2002; contbr. numerous articles on ecology and freshwater biology sys. to profl. jours.; mem. editl. bd. Aquatic Botany, 1975—, Jour. Tropical Freshwater Ecology, 1987—, Internat. Jour. Salt Lake Resources, 1991—, Biogeochemistry, 1993—, Lakes and Reservoirs, 1995—, Aquatic Ecology, 1996—, Boreal Environment Rsch., 1996—, Jour. Limnology, 1999—; N.Am. editor Archiv für Hydrobiologie, 1989—. Served with USNR, 1954—62. Recipient First T. Erlander Nat. professorship Swedish Nat. Research Council and U. Uppsala, 1982-83, award of Distinction U. Calif. at Davis, 1989; AEC grantee, 1965-75; NSF grantee, 1962— ; ERDA grantee, 1975-77; Dept. Energy grantee, 1978— Fellow AAAS; mem. Royal Danish Acaad. Scis. (elected fgn. mem. 1986), Am. Acad. Arts and Scis. (elected 1993), Am. Inst. Biol. Scis., Am. Soc. Limnology and Oceanography (edtl. bd. 1971-74, v.p. 1979-80, pres. 1980-81, G.E. Hutchinson medal 1992), Aquatic Plant Mgmt. Soc., Ecol. Soc. Am., Internat. Assn. Ecology, Freshwater Biol. Assn. U.K., Internat. Assn. Theoretical and Applied Limnology (gen. sec. treas. 1968—, editor-in-chief 2001, Baldi Meml. award 1989, Naumann-Thienemann medal 1992), Internat. Phycological Soc., Mich. Acad. Scis., N.Am. Benthological Soc., Phycological Soc. Am., Internat. Assn. Great Lakes Rsch., Internat. Consortium Salt Lake Rsch. (editl. bd. 1991—), Japanese Soc. Limnology (editl. bd. 2001—), Mich. Bot. Soc., Internat. Assn. Aquatic Vascular Plant Biologists (founder, pres. 1979-91), Water Assn. Finland (editl. bd. 1990—), Asociacion Argentina de Limnologia (hon.), Brazilian Soc. Limnology, Finnish Limnological Soc. (editl. bd. 1989—), Internat. Lake Environ. Comm. Found. (exec. bd. 1986—), Netherlands Soc. Aquatic Ecology (editl. bd. 1996—), Soc. Wetland Scientists (Lifetime Achievement award 2000), Sigma Xi, Phi Sigma. Home: 102 Songbird Ln Chapel Hill NC 27514-2650 Office: U North Carolina Dept Environ Scis-Engring Chapel Hill NC 27599-7431

WETZEL-TOMALKA, MARY MARGERITHE, retired secondary educator; b. Evanston, Ill., June 26, 1928; d. John Nicholas and Mary Elizabeth (Peckels) Maichen; m. Clarence Norman Wetzel, Aug. 25, 1951 (dec. 1993); children: Steven F., Andrew J., Bryan F., Michele M.; m. Charles Patrick Tomalka, July 23, 1994. PhB in Edn., Siena Heights Coll., 1950; MS in Edn., Ind. U., 1975. English tchr. Jr. H.S. South Bend-Fort Wayne Diocese, 1970-86. Author, pub.: Candlewick the Jewel of Imperial, 1980, 2d rev. 1995, Price Guide to Candlewick the Jewel of Imperial, 1991, Price Guide 2, 1993, Personal Inventory and Record Book, 1997, Price Guide '99, 1999, Price Guide 2002; contbr.(newsletter) Spyglass, 1980—. Recipient Offcl. Proclamation County of St. Joseph Commrs., 1985. Mem. Nat. Imperial Glass Collectors Soc. (spkr., presenter), Michiana Assn. of Candlewick Collectors (pres. 1980—). Avocations: antiques, cards, travel, cruises. Home: 1679 Colonnades Cir N Lakeland FL 33811-1522 E-mail: cndlwckmom@aol.com.

WEYAND, EDWINA WICKER, elementary school educator; b. Dublin, Ga., Jan. 20, 1964; d. Edgar Pete and Bettye Laverne (Holt) Wicker. BS in Edn., Valdosta State Coll., 1986; MEd in Ednl. Leadership, U. West Ga., 1996. Cert. tchr., Ga., La. Fitness instr. Gulfport (Miss.) YMCA, 1986-87, England AFB, Alexandria, La., 1987; recreation therapist Pinecrest State Sch., Alexandria, 1987-88; dir. youth programs, camp dir. YMCA Cen. La., Alexandria, 1988-89; camp dir. Girl Scout Camp Martha Johnston, Lizella, Ga., 1990; tchr. phys. edn. Griffin (Ga.)/Spalding County Sch. System, 1990-93; tchr. phys. edn., coach Henry County Sch. System, 1993-94; elem. phys. edn. tchr. Clayton County Sch. System, Ellenwood, Ga., 1994—. Coach cycling, event coord. Spl. Olympics, Griffin, 1990-93; vol. Dept. Family and Children's Svcs., 1994. Seven-time state cycling champion U.S. Cycling Fedn., La. and Ga., 1989-92, Olympic trials competitor, 1992; named Amateur Cyclist of Yr. Atlanta Health and Fitness mag., 1991. Mem. Profl. Assn. Ga. Educators, Ga. Assn. Health, Phys. Edn., Recreation and Dance, Spalding Sprockets Bicycle Club, Outdoor Spltys., Inc. Bicycle Racing Tean, So. Bicycle League (safety and edn. dir.), Outward Bound Alumni Assn. Methodist. Avocations: bicycle racing, camping, reading, hiking, weight-training. Home: 1308 Sablewood Dr Apopka FL 32712-2951 Office: East Clayton Elem Sch 2750 Ellenwood Rd Ellenwood GA 30294-3521

WEYANDT, LINDA JANE, physician, educator, anesthesiologist; b. Altoona, Pa., Nov. 5, 1948; d. Charles Leroy and Edna Pearl (Schaefer) W. RN, Phila. Gen. Hosp. Sch. Nursing, 1970; BA, Stephens Coll., 1978; MD, UNAM-Noreste, Mex., 1983; postgrad., North-Ctrl. U., Ariz., 1995—. Cert. trauma resolutionist Am. Inst. Med. and Psychotherapeutic Hypnosis; cert. hypnotherapist Am. Bd. Hypnotherapy. Pvt. practice anesthesia J.L. Med. Svcs., McAllen, Tex., 1986-92; staff anesthestist MD Anderson Hosp., Houston, 1992, VA Hosp., Houston, 1994-99; dir., owner Hypnosis and Pain Mgmt. Svcs. of Tex., Houston, 1993—; sr. disabilty analyst, diplomate Am. Bd. Disability Analysts. Dir. Associated Hypnotherapy and Pain Mgmt., Houston, 1991; clin. instr. dept. anesthesia Baylor Coll. Medicine, Houston. Contbr. articles to profl. jours. Fellow Am. Bd. Med. Psychotherapists & Psychodiagnosticians (diplomate); mem. AMA (Internat. Med. Grad.), Am. Med. Student Assn., Am. Acad. Pain Mgmt. (diplomate), Am. Assn. Behavior Therapists, Biofeedback Soc. Tex., Am. Soc. Clin. Hypnosis, Am. Psychotherapy and Med. Hypnosis Assn. (Advance Med. Hypnosis award 1994), Internat. Soc. Hypnosis Assn., (Australia), Am. Soc. Clin. Hypnosis, Houston Soc. Clin. Hypnosis, Alumna Assn. Stephens Coll., Alumna Assn. Phila. Gen. Hosp., NOW; student mem. APA. Avocations: ballooning, fishing, clown collecting. Home: Ste 113 7009 Almeda Rd Houston TX 77054 E-mail: drljw@earthlink.net.

WEYLAND, DEBORAH ANN, learning disabilities teacher consultant; b. Fayetteville, N.C., Aug. 19, 1959; d. William Frederick Louis and Carol Joyce (Varhall) W. BA, Fairleigh Dickinson U., 1981; MA, Montclair (N.J.) State U., 1994. Cert. tchr. nursery sch., K-8, tchr. of handicapped; cert. learning disabilities tchr. cons. Permanent substitute tchr. Franklin Jr. H.S., Nutley, N.J., 1981-82, asst. tchr. SCE program, 1982-83; tchr. grade 2 and kindergarten Saint Peter's Sch., Belleville, N.J., 1983-85; tchr. grade 5 and kindergarten Belleville Pub. Schs., 1985-91, tchr. pre-sch. handicapped program, 1991-95. Learning cons. Belleville Pub. Schs., 1994—; adv. bd. Belleville Alliance for Substance Edn., 1993—, exec. bd. 1994—; cons. Assn. of Learning, State of N.J., 1994—; cons. in field. Mem. Spl. Edn. Parent and Profls. Orgn., Belleville Edn. Assn., Women's Club Belleville, Phi Zeta Kappa, Phi Omega Epsilon. Avocations: arts and crafts, reading, walking. Office: Belleville Pub Schs 100 Passaic Ave Belleville NJ 07109-1807

WEYMOUTH, LISA ANN, microbiologist, educator; b. Washington, Jan. 11, 1946; d. Colin Crowell and Nellie Weymouth; divorced; 1 child, Kelani Katherine Larsen. BA in Zoology, Swarthmore Coll., 1967; PhD in Physiology, U. Pa., 1977. Cert. Am. Bd. Med. Microbiology. Postdoctoral assoc., fellow MIT, Cambridge, Mass., 1977-83; postdoctoral scholar dept. lab. medicine U. Calif., San Francisco, 1984-85; sr. rsch. assoc. dept. medicine New Eng. Deaconess Hosp., Boston, 1985-87; fellow dept. pathology Hartford (Conn.) Hosp., 1987-89; asst. prof. microbiology and immunology U. Rochester (N.Y.) Sch. Medicine and Dentistry, 1989-93, asst. dir. clin. microbiology lab., 1989-93; asst. prof. clin. pathology Med. Coll. Va./Va. Commonwealth U., Richmond, 1993—, assoc. dir. clin. microbiology lab., 1993-95, dir. clin. microbiology lab., 1995—. Mem. bd. exam. com. Am. Bd. Med. Microbiology, Washington, 1994—; co-dir. Am. Acad. Microbiology Accredited Postdoctoral Tng. Program in Med. and Pub. Health Microbiology at Med. Coll. Va./VCU, Richmond, 1993-95, dir., 1995-97; co-dir. Am. Acad. Microbiology Accredited Postdoctoral Tng. Program in Med. and Pub. Health Microbiology at U. Rochester Sch. Medicine, 1989-93. Author: (book chpt.) Genetic Engineering in Mammalian Cells, 1986, Cellular and Molecular Pathogenesis, 1996; editl. bd. Jour. Clin. Microbiology, 1996-98; contbr. sci. articles to profl. jours. Predoctoral fellow U.S. Pub. Health Svc., 1970-75, postdoctoral fellow Helen Hay Whitney Found., 1977-80. Mem. Am. Soc. Microbiology (mem., councilor Va. br. 1996-98, alt. councilor Va. br. 1994-96, mem. cen. N.Y. br., v.p.-elect cen. N.Y. br. 1993, councilor cen. N.Y. br. 1991-93), Am. Soc. Virology, Pan Am. Soc. for Clin. Virology, South Eastern Assn. for Clin. Microbiology. Avocations: sailing, navigation. Office: Med Coll Va Dept Pathology Box 980210 403 N 13th St Dept Richmond VA 23298-5030

WHALEN, LORETTA THERESA, religious educational administrator; b. Bklyn., May 21, 1940; d. William Michael and Loretta Margaret (Malone) Whalen; children: Ann Lindsay, Margaret Force. RN, St. Vincent's Hosp., N.Y.C., 1960; BSN, U. Pa., 1965; MA in Edn., Fordham U., 1971; cert. in sociology religion, Louvain U., Belgium, 1974; PhD in Global Edn., The Union Grad. Sch., 1994. Staff nurse Holy Family Hosp., Atlanta, 1967-69; Latin Am. communication dir. Med. Mission Sisters, Maracaibo, Venezuela, 1969-71; intensive care nurse St. Vincent's Hosp., N.Y.C., 1971-72; mem. ministry team Med. Mission Sisters, various locations, 1972-74, dir. communications Phila., 1974-77; asst. to exec. Interreligious Peace Colloquium, Washington, 1977; freelance writing, photography Ch. World Svc., N.Y.C., 1978-79; dir. Office Global Edn. Nat. Council Chs., N.Y.C., 1980-99. Co-author: Make a World of Difference: Creative Activities for Global Learning, 1990, Tales of the Heart: Affective Approaches to Global Education, 1991; mem. editorial bd., rev. editor Connections Mag., 1984-87; contbr. articles to profl. jours. Mem. Peace and Justice Commn., Archdiocese of Balt., 1985-89. Mem. Amnesty Internat., Bread for the World, NOW, World Wildlife Fund, Greenpeace, Sigma Theta Tau. Democrat. Roman Catholic. Avocations: photography, writing, racquetball, interior design, travel.

WHALEN, NORMA JEAN, special education educator; b. Albuquerque, N. Mex., Nov. 26, 1936; d. Ervin O'dell and Louise (Harcrow) Betts; m. Thomas Leo Whalen; children: Timothy, Patrick, Anna, Emily Wells, Kevin. BEd, Carson-Newman Coll., Jefferson City, Tenn., 1959. Cert. Tchr Secondary Edn. Fla., 1959, Tchr. - History Fla., 1959. Sec. sch. tchr. La Puente Jr. HS, La Puente, Calif., 1959—62; tchr. Umatilla (Fla.) Elem. Sch., 1969—70; substitute tchr. Lake County Schs., Leesburg, 1969—70, 1975—79; tchr., evening class Lee Adult H.S., Leesburg, Fla., 1979—80; elem. sch. tchr. St. Paul's Cath. Ch., Leesburg, Fla., 1980—81; spl. edn. tchr. Lee Opportunity Ctr. Lifestream Behavioral Ctr., Leeburg, Fla.,

1990—2003. Cons. curriculum devel. St. Paul's Cath. Ch., Leesburg, 1986—89, tchr. 1st communion and confession classes, 1986—2003. Dir. learning resource ctr. St. Paul Cath. Ch., Leesbug, 1986—89; Bd. dirs. Melon Patch Theater, Leesburg, Fla., 1976—81. Recipient Best Supporting actress award, Melon Patch Theater, 1979, Disting. Svc. award, 1980, Svc. award, Lake County Bd. Edn., 1999, Nat. Assn. Mentally Ill Parents Org., 2000. Mem.: NEA, Leesburg Edn. Assn. Roman Catholic. Avocations: crocheting, reading, swimming, cooking, travel. Home: 2904 Pecan Avenue Leesburg FL 34748 Office: Lee EdnOpportunity Ctr 207 Lee St Leesburg FL 34748-4914

WHALEN, PAUL LEWELLIN, lawyer, educator, mediator; b. Lexington, Ky. s. Elza Boz and Barbara Jean (Lewellin) W.; m. Teena Gail Tanner, Jan. 26, 1985; children: Ashley, Lars, Lucy. BA, U. Ky.; JD, Northern Ky. U.; cert., Bonn U., Fed. Republic Germany, 1981; student, U.S. Army J.A.G. Sch., 1988; diploma, USAF Squadron Officers Sch., 1998. Bar: W.Va. 1984, U.S. Ct. Appeals (6th cir.) 1984, Ky. 1985, U.S. Ct. Appeals (4th cir.) 1985, Ohio 1993. Assoc. Geary Walker, Parkersburg, W.Va., 1984-85; prin. Paul L. Whalen, Ft. Thomas, Ky., 1985—; prof. Def. Acquisition U., WP AFB; prof. pub. contract law Air Force Inst. Tech., 1999-2000; atty. Dept. of Air Force, Office of Chief Trial Atty. Contract Law Ctr., Wright Patterson AFB, 1988—89; hearing officer, prosecutor Ky. Dept. Ednl. Profl. Stds. Bd., 1995—97; mem. arbitration panel No. Ky., 1997—, Montgomery County, Ohio, 1998—; hearing officer Ky. Dept. Edn. IDEA, 1999—2000; impartial due process hearing officer Ohio Dept. Edn., Ohio, 2002—. Mem. Leadership No. Ky., Ft. Thomas Bd. Edn., 1987—99, chmn., 1990—94; mem. Ky. Bd. Edn., 2000—, Ky. Commn. on Human Svcs.; pres. ch. coun. Highland United Meth. Ch., 2000; mem. Campbell County Foster Care Rev. Bd., Newport, Ky., 1986; bd. dirs. Ky. Coun. Child Abuse, Inc. Com. for Kids; dir. Ky. Sch. Bd. Assn., 1993—98; mem. Air Force Bicycle Team Ride Across Iowa, 1997—2003, 2003. Recipient Commendation No. Ky. Legal Aid, 1986-2002. Fellow Commonwealth Inst. Leadership; mem. Fed. Bar Assn., No. Ky. Bar Assn., So. Assn. Schs. (mem. com.), Optimist Club, Kiwanis Club, Phi Alpha Delta. Democrat. Methodist. Avocations: freelance writing, stamp collecting, politics, amateur radio, bicycling. Home: 113 Ridgeway Ave Fort Thomas KY 41075-1333 Office: PO Box 22 Fort Thomas KY 41075 E-mail: plewellinwhalen@aol.com.

WHALEY, CAROLYN LOUISE, education educator; b. Jackson, Tenn., Apr. 4, 1952; d. James M. and Allie L. (Williams) Brown; m. Roy Lynn Whaley, Aug. 13, 1978. BA, Union U., 1974; M of Music, Southwestern Bapt. Sem., Ft. Worth, 1976, MA, 1979; EdD, Tex. Woman's U., 1996. Cert. elem. tchr., early childhood, music, spl. edn. Kindergarten tchr. Bosqueville Ind. Sch. Dist., Waco, Tex., 1987-94, multi-age primary tchr., 1994-95, tchr. music, 1995-96; pre-kindergarten tchr. Waco Ind. Sch. Dist., 1996-97; mem. faculty dept. edn. Union U., Jackson, Tenn., 1997—. Guest columnist Waco Tribune Herald, 1994-97. Vol. Prison Fellowship, Waco, 1988-94, Habitat for Humanity, Waco, 1990-94. Mem. Assn. for Childhood Edn. Internat., Nat. Assn. for Edn. of Young Children, Moo Duk Kwan Fedn. (Tae Kwon Do), Internat. Reading Assn. Home: 188 Bascom Rd Jackson TN 38305-8828 Office: Union U 1050 Union University Dr Jackson TN 38305-3697

WHALEY, LUCILLE FILLMORE, nursing consultant, educator; b. Garfield, Utah, May 17, 1923; d. Marvin W. and Isabella V. (Bennett) Fillmore; m. Bert A. Whaley, Apr. 5, 1943; children: Kathleen, Maureen. Diploma, St. Marks Hosp. Sch. Nursing, Salt Lake City, 1944; BS, San Jose State Coll., 1962; MS, U. Calif., San Francisco, 1963; EdD, U. So. Calif., 1986. Prof. emeritus nursing San Jose (Calif.) State U., 1963-83; cons. pvt. practice, Sunnyvale, Calif., 1974—. Mem. adv. bd. Assessment Techs. Inc., 1998—. Sr. author: Nursing Care of Infants and Children, 1979, 4th edit. 1991, Essentials of Pediatric Nursing, 1981, 3d edit. 1989; author: Understanding Inherited Disorders, 1974; contbr. articles to profl. jours., books. Mem. ANA, Calif. Nurses Assn., Sigma Theta Tau. Home: 1652 Lachine Dr Sunnyvale CA 94087-4207

WHALEY, ROSS SAMUEL, environmentalist, educator; b. Detroit, Nov. 7, 1937; s. Lyle John and Margaret Nielson (Semple) W.; m. Beverly Mae Heemstra, June 14, 1958; children— Heather Jean, Susan Lesli, Lindsay John. BS, U. Mich., 1959, PhD, 1969; MS, Colo. State U., 1961. Asst. prof., assoc. prof., prof. Utah State U., Logan, 1965—70, dept. head, 1967—70; assoc. dean Colo. State U., Ft. Collins, 1970—73; dept. head U. Mass., Amherst, 1973—76, dean, 1976—78; dir. econ. research USDA Forest Service, Washington, 1978—84; pres. SUNY Coll. Environ. Scis. and Forestry, Syracuse, 1984—2000, prof., 2000—. Cons. UN FAO, Rome, 1983-84, UN, Budapest, Hungary, 1974, U.S. Peace Corps., South Am., 1972, Geddes, Brecher, Qualls & Cunningham, Denver, 1971-72 Contbr. articles to profl. jours. Bd. dirs. Glynwood Ctr., Natural History Mus. of the Adirondacks, Adirondack Nature Conservancy. Fellow Soc. Am. Foresters (pres. 1991), Adirondack No. Country Assn., Nat. Audubon Soc. NY. Mem. Christian Ref. Ch. Avocations: reading, swimming, hiking, fly fishing, cross country skiing. Office: SUNY/ESF 326 Marshall Hall 1 Forestry Dr Syracuse NY 13210

WHAM, DAVID BUFFINGTON, secondary school educator; b. Evanston, Ill., May 25, 1937; s. Benjamin and Virginia (Buffington) W.; m. Joan Field Wilber, Mar. 9, 1968 (div. May, 1972); children: Benjamin, Rachel. AB cum laude, Harvard U., 1959; MA, So. Ill. U., Carbondale, 1967. Instr. U. Wyo., Powell, 1963-65, So. Ill. U., Carbondale, 1965-67; legis. asst. U.S. Congress, Washington, 1969-78; freelance writer Chgo., 1980-89; tchr. Chgo. Pub. Schs., 1994—. Speechwriter Adlai Stevenson for Gov. campaign, 1986, Dawn Netsch for Gov. campaign, 1994. Author: My Farewell to Bohemia, 1968, The Comic Genuflection, 1984, A Wave of Bright Boys, 1994. With U.S. Army, 1959-62. Recipient fiction award Columbia Pacific U., 1994. Mem. Harvard Club Chgo. (interviewer 1984—), Spee Club Harvard, Hasty Pudding Club Harvard. Democrat. Episcopalian. Home: 860 Hinman Ave # 724 Evanston IL 60202 Office: 125 S Clark St Chicago IL 60603-5200

WHARTON, KAY KAROLE, retired special education educator; b. Butler, Pa., Nov. 19, 1943; d. Clarence Henry Jr. and Alberta Elizabeth (Yost) Gilkey; m. David Burton Wharton, Nov. 28, 1975 (dec. May 1987). BS in Edn., Geneva Coll., 1965. Cert. spl. edn. tchr., Md. Tchr. 2d grade Butler Area Sch., 1965-71; resource tchr. Queen Anne County Bd. of Edn., Centreville, Md., 1971—2002, ret., 2002. Facilitator sch. improvement team Centreville Mid. Sch., 1992-95. Music dir. Diocese of Easton (Md.) Mid. Convocation Episcopal Cursillo, Old St. Paul's, Kent, 1989-91, St. Paul's, Hillsboro, 1993—; Sunday sch. supt. primary dept. St. Mark's Luth. Ch., 1966-71, St. Paul's Episcopal Ch., 1985-87; program dir. Queen Anne's County chpt. Am. Cancer Soc., Centreville, 1981-85; mem. PTA; Episcopal lay min. Meridian Nursing Home, 1978—2002. Mem. NEA, Queen Anne County Edn. Assn., Md. State Tchrs. Assn., Coun. for Exceptional Children, Internat. Reading Assn., Upper Shore Reading Assn. (sec. 1985-91, 93—99), Learning Disabled Am., Guardians Learning Disabled (sec. 1991-92), Smithsonian Assocs., Order Ea. Star (worthy matron Centreville 1977, sec. 1982-93), Nat. Geographic Soc., Town and Country Women's Club (pres. 1977, 79), Delta Kappa Gamma (Nu chpt. pres. 1992-98, rsch. com. chairperson Alpha Beta State 1993-95, membership chairperson 1995-97, music chmn., 1999-2002). Republican. Avocations: piano, embroidery, handicrafts. Home: PO Box 237 Centreville MD 21617-0237 Office: 714 Bonniebrook Rd Butler PA 16002

WHARTON, NOËLLE PARRIS, language educator, director; b. Boston, May 31, 1960; d. Noel Fitzorman Parris, Cynthia Johnson Parris; m. Winston O. Wharton, Mar. 1, 1987; children: Ky Rachel Machree, Jonathan Daniel. BA in Spanish, Swarthmore Coll., 1982; M in Translation-Interpretation, Monterey Inst. Internat. Studies, 1984. Prof. Spanish Trident Tech. Coll., Charleston, SC, 1991—, internat. edn. dir., 1995—. Pres. exec. coun. S.C. Internat. Edn. Consortium, Charleston, 2001—; pres. Trident Tek Talkers Toastmasters Internat., Charleston, 2001—; project dir. Mentoring Project Minority Males, 2002—. Fellow Fulbright Group Project Abroad, Cameroon, Fulbright Assn., 1998, Fulbright Internat. Edn. Adminstr., 1998, Fulbright Tchr. Exch., Argentina, Fulbright Assn., Dept. of State, 2000. Mem.: S.C. Tech. Edn. Assn., S.C. World Trade Ctr., Nat. Assn. Fgn. Student Advisors. Avocations: swimming, reading, travel, entertaining, writing. Office: Trident Tech Coll 7000 Rivers Ave Charleston SC 29423 Office Fax: 843-574-6540. Personal E-mail: zpwharton@yahoo.com. Business E-Mail: noelle.wharton@tridenttech.org.

WHARTON, WILLIAM RAYMOND, physicist educator; b. Knoxville, Tenn., Mar. 30, 1943; s. Joseph Bradford and Sarah (Pollard) W.; m. Gwendolyn Beryl Shumway, Sept. 2, 1967; children: Kenneth Bradford, Paul David, Ruth Michelle. BS in Physics, Stanford U., 1965; PhD of Exptl. Nuclear Physics, U. Wash., 1972. Rsch. assoc. Argonne (Ill.) Nat. Lab., 1972-74, Rutgers U., New Brunswick, N.J., 1974-75; asst. prof., assoc. prof. physics Carnegie Mellon U., Pitts., 1975-84; assoc. prof., prof. physics Wheaton (Ill.) Coll., 1984—, chair dept. physics, 1991—. Vis. prof. physics N.C. State U., Raleigh, 1990-91. Author: Lab Manual for Computer Physics, 1991; co-author: Elementary Physics Laboratory Manual, 1987; contbr. articles to profl. jours. Pres. J.B. Wharton Found., Bellevue, Wash., 1986-94. Mem. AAAS, Am. Phys. Soc., Am. Sci. Affiliation, Am. Assn. Physics Tchrs., Gt. Lakes Pew Sci. Cluster (coun. 1987-97). Evangelical. Avocations: astronomy, tennis, swimming. Home: 633 W Hawthorne Blvd Wheaton IL 60187-3427 Office: Physics Dept Wheaton College Wheaton IL 60187

WHATCOTT, MARSHA RASMUSSEN, elementary education educator; b. Fillmore, Utah, Mar. 29, 1941; d. William Hans and Evangelyn (Robison) Rasmussen; m. Robert LaGrand Whatcott, Sept. 14, 1961; children: Sherry, Cindy, Jay Robert, Justin William. Assoc., So. Utah State U., 1962; BS, Brigham Young U., 1968. Cert. tchr. early childhood, Utah. Tchr. 1st grade Provost Elem. Sch., Provo, Utah, 1968-84, kindergarten tchr., 1984-91, tchr. 3d grade, 1991—2001. Music specialist Provost Elem., 1984-87, 91-92, 93-94, art specialist, 1984-85, math. specialist, 1988-89, sci. specialist, 1994-95, 96, 97, 98-99, 99-2000; phys. edn. specialist, 1998-99, 99-2000, phys. edn. health-Olympic specialist, 2000-01; del. Utah Edn. Assn., 1989-90; bldg. rep. Provo Edn. Assn., 1993-94, 94-95; choir dir., music arranger 3d grade choir Provo City Winter Festival, Lights on Ceremony, 1995-2000; assessment and placement specialist, 2000-01. Mem. polit. action com. Provo Sch. Dist., 1982, 90, mem. profl. devel. com. Bonniville Uniserve (Provo, Alpine and Nebo Sch. Dist.), 1994-95; choir dir., music arranger 3d grade choir City Winter Festival, 1995-2000; vol. Opening and Closing Ceremonies, 2002 Olympic Games, Salt Lake City, 2001-2002, Olympic Anniversary Celebration, 2003; vice chmn. Pleasant Grove City Arts Coun., 2003-. Recipient Millard County Utah PTA scholarship, 1959-62, Golden Apple award Provo City PTA, 1984, Recognition Disting. Svc. in Edn. award Utah State Legis., 1992; named Outstanding Educator in Utah Legis. Dist. # 64, 1992, Utah State Senate Edn. Spl. award, 2001. Mem. Utah Edn. Assn. (del. 1989-90), Provo Edn. Assn. (bldg. rep. 1993-94, 94-95), Bonneville Uniserve (profl. devel. com.), vice chmn. Pleasant Grove City Arts Council, 2003-. Mem. Lds Ch. Avocations: music, gardening, art, drama, crafts. Office: Provost Elem Sch 629 S 1000 E Provo UT 84606-5204

WHATLEY, LISA, vocational school administrator; b. Rio de Janeiro, Nov. 4, 1938; came to U.S. 1965; d. Adhemar and Elzira (Ramos) Goulart; m. Lester Feldshon, Sept. 10, 1967 (div. 1974); 1 child, Lee Adhemar; m. William James Whatley, Apr. 5, 1975. Deg. in Psychology, U. Fed. de Rio de Janeiro, 1964; MEd in Vocat. Edn., Colo. State U., 1989, PhD in Sch. Adminstrn., 1991. Pres., CEO W.J. Whatley, Inc., Denver, 1979-81; owner L&W Car Wash, Denver, 1981-82; founder, pres. South American Traders, Inc., Denver, 1982-86; instr. sml. bus. mgmt. Emily Griffith Opportunity Sch., Denver, 1983-85, GED chief adminstr., 1985-86, counselor, mgr. spl. needs, 1986-91, asst. prin., instrn., 1991—. Lectr. in field; conductor seminars in field. Colo. del. White House Conf. on Sml. Bus., 1980. Mem. ASCD, Colo. Vocat. Assn., Delta Kappa Gamma, Phi Delta Kappa, Denver Transp. Club. Avocations: writing, opera, fishing. Home: Apt 4D 1901 E 13th Ave Denver CO 80206-2059

WHAYNE, THOMAS FRENCH, JR., cardiologist, educator; b. Ft. Leavenworth, Kans., Aug. 25, 1937; s. Thomas French and Mary Lutenia (Porter) W.; m. Eugenia McDonald Ingram, June 22, 1963; children: Thomas French III, James Givens, Katherine Ingram. AB in Chemistry, U. Pa., 1959, MD, 1963; PhD in Biochemistry, U. Calif., San Francisco, 1970. Intern in medicine The N.Y. Hosp., 1963-64, resident in medicine, 1964-66; fellow in cardiovascular disease Cardiovascular Rsch. Inst., San Francisco, 1966-69, U. Toronto, Ontario, Can., 1969-70; asst. prof. medicine Ohio State U., Columbus, 1970-72; assoc. prof. medicine U. Okla., Oklahoma City, 1972-77; clin. prof. medicine U. Ky., Lexington, 1977-98, prof. medicine cardiovascular medicine, 1998—. Assoc. mem. Okla. Med. Rsch. Found., 1972-77; staff cardiologist Lexington Clinic, 1977-98. Named man of yr, Okla. Heart Assn., 1975-76. Fellow ACP, Am. Coll. Cardiology, Am. Heart Assn., Coll. Physicians of Phila. Presbyterian. Avocations: spanish, golf, scuba diving, communications. Office: Divsn Cardiovascular Medicine L-543 Kentucky Clinic Lexington KY 40536-0284 E-mail: twhayn0@uky.edu.

WHEALEY, LOIS DEIMEL, humanities scholar; b. N.Y.C., June 20, 1932; d. Edgar Bertram Deimel and Lois Elizabeth (Hatch) Washburn; m. Robert Howard Whealey, July 2, 1954; children: Richard William, David John, Alice Ann. BA in History, Stanford U., 1951; MA in Edn., U. Mich., 1955; MA in Polit. Sci., Ohio U., 1975. Tchr. 5th grade Swayne Sch., Owyhee, Nev., 1952-53; tchr. 7th grade Ft. Knox (Ky.) Dependent's Sch., 1955-56; tchr. adult basic edn. USAF, Oxford, 1956-57; tchr. 6th grade Amerman Sch., Northville, Mich., 1957-58; tchr. 8th grade English, social studies Slauson Jr. High Sch., Ann Arbor, Mich., 1958-59; adminstrv. asst. humanities conf. Ohio U., Athens, 1974-76, 83. Part-time instr. Ohio U., Athens, 1966-68, 75, VISTA with Rural Action, 1996-98. Contbr. articles to profl. jours. Mem. Athens County Regional Planning Commn., 1974—78, treas., 1976—78; mem. Ohio coord. com. Internat. Women's Yr., 1977; v.p. Black Diamond Girl Scout Coun., 1980—86; chair New Day for Equal Rights Amendment, 1982; mem. Athens City Bd. Edn., 1984—90, v.p., 1984, pres., 1985; mem. Tri-County Vocat. Sch. Bd., Nelsonville, Ohio, 1984—90, v.p., 1988—89; mem. adv. com. Ohio River Valley Water Sanitation Commn., 1986—95; Ohio outreach liaison Nat. Town Meeting for Sustainable Am., 1999; bd. dirs. Ohio Environ. Coun., 1984—90, sec., 1986—90; bd. dirs. Ohio Alliance for Environ., 1994—98, v.p., 1998; bd. dirs. Organize Ohio, 1999—, bd. pres., 2001—; bd. dirs. Ohio Women, Inc., 1995—, sec., 1997—; bd. dirs. Unitarian Universalist Svc. Com., 2001—03, Ohio Meadville Dist. Unitarian-Universalist Assn., 1975—81; co-chair nat. vol. network Unitarian Universalist Svc. Com., 2003—. Recipient Unsung Unitarian Universalist award Ohio-Meadville Dist. Unitarian Universalist Assn., 1984, Thanks badge Black Diamond Girl Scout Coun., 1986, How-to award Ednl. Press Assn. Am., 1990, Donna Chen Women's Equity award Ohio U., 1994, Cmty. Svc. award Athens County Cmty. Svcs. Coun., 1998, award for an individual contbn. over a lifetime Ohio Alliance for Environment, 2002; named Woman of Achievement, Black Diamond Girl Scout Coun., 1987, Peacemaker Appalachian Peace and Justice Network, 1998, Outstanding Feminist, Athens Herstory Celebration, 2002. Mem. AAUW (pres. Athens br. 1969-70, 89-90, 93-2001, AAUW/Ohio bd. 1995—), LWV (pres. 1975-77), Phi Lambda Theta (life). Democrat. Avocations: classical music, genealogy. Home: 14 Oak St Athens OH 45701-2605

WHEATLEY, SHARMAN B. art educator, artist; b. N.Y.C., Nov. 21, 1951; d. Norman Alexander and Marjorie Grace (Biggs) Johnson; m. Simon J. Wheatley, June 21, 1975; children: Gregory Drew, Justin West. BA in Art Edn., Wagner Coll., 1973; MA in Art Edn., Coll. of New Rochelle, 1979. Cert. art educator, N.Y.; provisional cert. art educator, Conn. Art educator for multi-handicapped students Bd. Coop. Edn. Svcs., New City, N.Y., 1973-75; art educator Ardsley Pub. Schs., N.Y., 1975-76; art and humanities educator The Ursuline Sch., New Rochelle, N.Y., 1976-83; owner, dir. of tour co. Big Apple Enrichment Tours, Larchmont, N.Y., 1981-83; libr. publicist Monroe Pub. Libr., Conn., 1987-88; newspaper editor Trumbull Times, Conn., 1988; art educator Trumbull Pub. Schs., Conn., 1989-91; theatrical prodr. Little Theatre Prodns., Wilton, Conn., 1993-96; art educator Wilton Pub. Schs., Conn., 1991—. Summer crafts supr. Ardsley Pub. Schs., N.Y., 1971-79. Artist, illustrator cover design for Street Bagel mag., 1982; exhibited in group shows at Larchmont Libr., 1982, Union Trust Bank, Darien, Conn., 1983; cover illustrator Litton Pubs., N.Y.C., 1980. 1st v.p., treas., corr. sec. mem. parents coun. Monroe PTO, Conn., 1985—. Recipient 2d prize Darien Arts Coun., 1983, Adams Interior Design Ctr. award Darien Arts Coun., 1983. Mem. NEA, Conn. Edn. Assn., Met. Mus. Art, N.Y. Mus. Modern Art. Avocations: writing, dancing, sculpting, drawing, reading. Home: 44 Oakwood Dr Monroe CT 06468-2134

WHEELAN, BELLE S. state agency administrator; 1 child, Reginald. BA in Psychology and Sociology, Trinity U.; MA in Devel./Ednl. Psychology, La. State U.; D in Ednl. Adminstrn., U. Tex., 1984. Asst. prof. psychology San Antonio Coll., dir. devel. edn., dir. acad. support svcs.; dean student svcs. Thomas Nelson C.C., Hampton, Va., 1987—89; provost Tidewater C.C., Portsmouth, Va., 1989—92; pres. Ctrl. Va. C.C., 1992, No. Va. C.C., 1998—2001; sec. of edn. State of Va., Richmond, 2002—. Mem. Jobs for Va. Grads. Bd., Am. Coll. Testing Bd., Nat. Commn. on NAEP 12th Grade Assessment and Reporting, 2003—. Recipient Outstanding Alumnus award, Trinity U., 2002, Strong Men and Women award, 2003. Mem.: Nat. Coun. on Black Am. Affairs (mem. pres. roundtable). Office: Sec of Edn Ninth St Office Bldg 5th Fl 202 N 9th St Richmond VA 23219 also: PO Box 1475 Richmond VA 23218

WHEELER, BARBARA MONICA, lawyer; b. Chgo., Mar. 20, 1947; d. John Benjamin and Elizabeth (Keife) Wheeler. BA, St. Dominic Coll., 1969; cert. Lewis U. Sch. Paraprofl. Studies, 1976; JD, DePaul U., 1980. Bar: Ill. 1980. Gen. supt. Md. Manor Devel. Co., Chgo., 1970-74; v.p. Omega Constrn. Co., Chgo., 1974-78; asst. state's atty. Cook County, Ill. Mem. Bd. Edn., Community High Sch. Dist. 99, DuPage County, 1974-76, pres., 1976—; mem. Ill. Assn. Sch. Bds., dir.-at-large Tri County div., 1976-77, dir. DuPage div., 1977-78, state dir., 1982-85, v.p., 1985-87, mem. exec. com., 1984-87; bd. dirs. Sch. Mgmt. Found. Ill., 1983; mem. task force on purposes of edn. in eighties Nat. Sch. Bds. Assn. Mem. ABA, Ill. Bar Assn., Chgo. Bar Assn., Am. Mgmt. Assn., Phi Alpha Delta. Roman Catholic. Office: Nat Bd Professional Teaching Standards 1525 Wilson Blvd Ste 500 Arlington VA 22209-3276

WHEELER, DIANA JEAN MILLER, secondary education educator; b. Long Beach, Calif., May 12, 1945; d. Edward Joseph and Myrtle (Burchett) Miller. AA, Long Beach City Coll., 1965; BA, U. Calif., Long Beach, 1968; MA, credential in adminstr., Pepperdine U., 1983. Tchr. Long Beach Unified Sch. Dist., 1968—, acting co-adminstr., 1987—; dept. head Stephens Mid. Sch., Long Beach, 1975-85, faculty pres., 1984-89, faculty v.p., sch. site coun., new tchr. assoc. mentor, 1992—. Speaker Regional Mid. Sch. Conf., Palm Springs, Calif., 1992, Nat. Mid. Sch. Conf., Long Beach, Calif., 1990, Louisville, 1991. Mem. ASCD, NEA, Nat. Coun. for Self-Esteem, Nat. Mid. Sch. Assn., Calif. Tchrs. Assn., Tchrs. Assn. Long Beach (Golden Apple award 1987). Avocations: keeping in shape, fishing, bike riding. Office: 1830 W Columbia St Long Beach CA 90810-2913

WHEELER, JAMES DONLAN, chemistry educator; b. St. Louis, July 19, 1923; s. John Ingraham and Nan (Donlan) W. MS, St. Louis U., 1952, PhL, 1948, STL, 1956; PhD, U. Mo., 1965. Chemistry instr. St. Louis U. High Sch., 1950-51; prof. chemistry Rockhurst U., Kans. City, Mo., 1956—. Author: Chemistry Problem Solving, 1979. Mem. Am. Chem. Soc. (chmn. local sect. 1968), AAAS, Nat. Sci. Tchrs. Assn., Soc. for Coll. Sci. Tchrs., Rho Chi. Roman Catholic. Avocations: exercise physiology, weight-lifting. Home: 5138 Tracy Ave Kansas City MO 64110-2516 Office: Rockhurst U 1100 Rockhurst Rd Kansas City MO 64110-2508

WHEELER, JOHN ARCHIBALD, physicist; b. Jacksonville, Fla., July 9, 1911; s. Joseph Lewis and Mabel (Archibald) Wheeler; m. Janette Hegner, June 10, 1935; children: Isabel Letitia Wheeler Ufford, James English, Alison Christie Wheeler Lahnston. PhD, Johns Hopkins U., 1933; ScD (hon.), Western Res. U., 1958, U. N.C., 1959, U. Pa., 1968, Middlebury Coll., 1969, Rutgers U., 1969, Yeshiva U., 1973, Yale U., 1974; PhD (hon.), U. Uppsala, 1975; ScD (hon.), U. Md., 1977, Gustavus Adolphus U., 1981, Cath. U. Am., 1982, U. Newcastle-upon-Tyne, 1983, Princeton U., 1986, U. Conn., 1989, U. Maine, 1992, Tufts U., 1992; LLD (hon.), Johns Hopkins U., 1977; LittD (hon.), Drexel U., 1987. NRC fellow, N.Y., Copenhagen, 1933—35; from asst. prof. to assoc. prof. physics U. N.C., 1935—38; asst. prof. physics Princeton U., 1938—42, assoc. prof., 1945—47, prof., 1947—76, Joseph Henry prof. physics, 1966—76, Joseph Henry prof. physics emeritus, 1976—; prof. physics and dir. Ctr. for Theoretical Physics, U. Tex., Austin, 1976—86; Ashbel Smith prof. U. Tex., Austin, 1979—86, Blumberg prof., 1981—86, Smith and Blumberg prof. emeritus, 1986—. Cons. and physicist on atomic energy projects Princeton U., 1939—42, U. Chgo., 1942, E.I. duPont de Nemours & C, Wilmington, Del., Richland, Wash., 1943—45, Los Alamos, 1950—53; dir. Project Matterhorn (H-bomb) Princeton U., 1951—53; Guggenheim fellow, Paris and Copenhagen, 1949—50; summer lectr. U. Mich., U. Chgo., Columbia U; Lorentz prof. U. Leiden, 1956; Fulbright prof. Kyoto U., 1962; vis. fellow Clare Coll., Cambridge U., 1964; Ritchie lectr. Edinburgh, 1958; vis. prof. U. Calif.-Berkeley, 1960; Battelle prof. U. Wash., 1975; I.I. Rabi vis. prof. Columbia U., 1983; sci. advisor U.S. Senate del. to 3d ann. conf. NATO Parliamentarians, Paris, 1957; mem. adv. com. Oak Ridge Nat. Lab., 1957—65, U. Calif., Los Alamos and Livermore, 1972—77; v.p. Internat. Union Physics, 1951—54; chmn. joint com. on history of theoretical physics in 20th century Am. Phys. Soc. and Am. Philos. Soc., 1960—72; sci. adv. bd. USAF, 1961—62; chmn. Dept. Def. Advanced Rsch. Projects Agy. Project 137 (now Project Jason), 1958; mem. U.S. Gen. Adv. Com. Arms Control and Disarmament, 1969—72, 1974—77. Author: Geometrodynamics, 1962; author: (with others) Gravitation Theory and Gravitational Collapse, 1965; author: Spacetime Physics, 1966; author: (with E. Taylor) Spacetime Physics, 2d edit., 1992; author: (in German) Einstein's Vision, 1968; author: (with C.W. Misner and K.S. Thorne) Gravitation, 1973; author: (with M. Rees and R. Ruffini) Black Holes, Gravitation Waves and Cosmology, 1974; author: Frontiers of Time, 1979, A Journey into Gravity and Spacetime, 1990, At Home in the Universe, 1994; author: (with I. Ciufolini) Gravitation and Inertia, 1995; author: also translations, 1991—92; author: (with Kenneth Ford) Geons, Black Holes and Quantum Foam: A Life in Physics, 1998; editor (with W. Zurek): Quantum Theory and Measurement, 1983; contbr. 375 articles to profl. jours. Trustee Battelle Meml. Inst., 1959—89, S.W. Rsch. Inst., San Antonio, 1977—92, Unitarian Ch., 1965. Recipient A. Cressy Morrison prize for work on nuc. physics, N.Y. Acad. Scis., 1947, Albert Einstein prize, Strauss Found., 1965, Enrico Fermi award, AEC, 1968, Franklin medal, Franklin Inst., 1969, Nat. medal of Sci., 1971, Herzfeld award, 1975, Outstanding Grad. Tchg. award, U. Tex., 1981, Niels Bohr Internat. Gold medal, 1982, Oersted medal, Am. Assn. Physics Tchrs., 1983, J. Robert Oppenheimer Meml. prize, 1984, Matteucci medal, Nat. Acad. Sci. Rome, Soc. of the Forty, 1994, Wolf Found. prize in Physics, Jerusalem, 1997. Fellow: AAAS (dir. 1965—68), Am. Phys. Soc. (pres. 1966, Einstein prize 2003); mem.: NAS, Royal Danish Acad. Scis., Royal Soc. (London), Accademia Nazionale dei Lincei,

Internat. Union Physics (v.p. 1951—54), L'Academie Internationale de Philosophie des Sciences (v.p. 1987—90), Tex. Philos. Soc., Royal Acad. Sci. (Uppsala, Sweden), Philos. Soc. of Tex., Am. Philos. Soc. (councillor 1963—66, v.p. 1971—73, councillor 1976—79, Franklin medal 1989), Am. Acad. Arts and Scis., Internat. Astron. Union, Am. Math. Soc., Princeton Club (N.Y.C.), Century Assn. (N.Y.C.), Sigma Xi, Phi Beta Kappa. Unitarian Universalist. Office: Princeton U Dept Physics Princeton NJ 08544-0001 E-mail: jawheeler@pupgg.princeton.edu.

WHEELER, MARY ANNE THERESA, administrator, educator; b. Columbus, Ohio, Jan. 21, 1952; d. George Austin and Helen Beatrice (Selzer) W.; m. Ray Walter Wood, Mar. 5, 1988. BS, Miami U., 1974; MEd, U. Ill., 1978; PhD, U. Wis., 1985. Regular and spl. edn. tchr. Dayton (Ohio) Pub. Schs., 1974-76; spl. edn. tchr. Chgo. Assn. for Retarded Citizens, 1976-77, Ctrl. Wis. Ctr. Developmentally Disabled, Madison, 1978-80; teaching asst. Dept. of Studies in Behavioral Disabilities Univ. Wis., Madison, 1980-84, clinical supr., 1980-84, lectr., 1985; asst. prof. dept. edn. Boise (Idaho) State Univ., 1985-86; academic tutor Engelmann-Becker Corp., Eugene, Oreg., 1986-87; rsch. assoc. Univ. Oreg., Eugene, 1986-87, program supr., 1986-87; adminstr. spl. programs & svcs. Oak Park (Ill.) & River Forest High Sch. Dists., Oak Park, 1988-90; asst. supr. Sch. Dist. Beloit Turner, Beloit, Wis., 1990—. Cons. Ventures in Better Schooling 5: A High Sch. Improvement Conf., 1992; cons., activity leader Goodwill Rec. Resource Ctr., 1980-85; program specialist Madison Met. Sch. Dist., 1983-84; presenter in field. Editorial bd. Nat. Soc. Performance and Instruction, 1979; contbr. articles to profl. jours. Mem. ASCD, AAUW, Am. Assn. Sch. Adminstrs., Assn. Direct Instruction, Coun. Exceptional Children, Nat. Staff Devel. Coun., Whitewater Talented and Gifted Network, Wis. Assn. Supervision and Curriculum Devel., Wis. Staff Devel. Coun., Nat. Assn. Gifted Children, Pi Lambda Theta. Avocations: reading, walking, swimming, antique auction, cross stitch. Office: Sch Dist Beloit Turner 1231 Inman Pky Beloit WI 53511-1723

WHEELER, OTIS V., JR., public school principal; b. Silex, Mo., Oct. 1, 1925; s. Otis V. and Pearla F. (Howell) W.; m. Virginia Rogers, June 7, 1947; children: Jan Leigh, Mark Patrick. BBA, U. Mo., 1948, MEd, 1965, EdD, 1971. USN, 1948-52, bus. mgr., 1952-61; sci. tchr. Columbia (Mo.) Pub. Schs., 1961-63, principal, 1963-91; supt. Boone County Sch. Dist., Mo., 1971. Instr. U. Mo., Columbia, 1970-72, asst. prof. 1972-75, 78-79; cons. Midwest Ctr for Equal Ednl. Opportunities, 1972-75. Served to lt. USNR, 1943-85, World War II, Korea. Named to, Columbia Pub. Schs. Found. Hall of Leaders, 2000. Mem. Nat. Assn. Elem. Sch. Prins. (U.S. Dept. Edn., Nat. Disting. Prin. award 1985, Excellence in Edn. award 1986), Mo. Assn. Elem. Sch. Prins. (Disting. Service award 1984, editor jours. 1967-88), Mo. State Tchrs. Assn., Retired Officers Assn., U. Mo. Columbia Coll. Edn. Alumni (Citation of Merit award 1987), Nat. Soc. of the SAR, Phi Delta Kappa, Phi Delta Theta, Golden Legion. Clubs: Lake Ozark Yachting Assn. (Mo.). Methodist. Avocations: boating, dancing, travel, scuba diving. Home: 916 W Ash St Columbia MO 65203-2636 Office: Ridgeway IGE Sch 107 E Sexton Rd Columbia MO 65203-4082

WHEELER, RICHARD HERBERT, III, oncologist, educator; b. Medford, Mass., Jan. 4, 1944; s. Richard Herbert Jr. and Virginia Catherine (Loerald) W.; m. Carole Ann Wible, Feb. 12, 1966; children: Richard Lawrence, Brett Allen, Ryan James. MD, U. Mich., 1969. Asst. prof. U. Mich., Ann Arbor, 1975-82, assoc. prof. 5, 1982-83, U. Ala., Birmingham, 1983-86, prof., 1986-95. Dep. dir. Comprehensive Cancer Ctr. U. Ala., 1983-95; cons. Mayo Clinic Scottsdale; prof. Mayo Grad. Sch. of Medicine, 1996-99, prof. U. Utah Sch. of Medicine, 1999—. Contbr. articles and abstracts to profl. jours. and chpts. to books. Mem. Am. Soc. Clin. Oncology, Am. Assn. Cancer Rsch., Soc. for Biol. Therapy, AAAS. Achievements include research in developmental therapeutics, combined modality therapy. Office: Huntsman Cancer Inst 2000 Cir of Hope Salt Lake City UT 84112

WHEELER, RURIC E. mathematics educator; b. Clarkson, Ky., Nov. 30, 1923; s. Mark H. and Mary (Sullivan) Wheeler; m. Joyce Ray, May 31, 1946; children: Eddy Ray, Paul Warren. AB, We. Ky. U., 1947; MS, U. Ky., 1948, PhD, 1952. Instr. math. U. Ky., Lexington, 1948—52; asst. prof. stats. Fla. State U., 1952—53; assoc. prof. math. Samford U., 1953—55, prof., head math. dept., 1955—65, chmn. natural scis. divsn., 1965—67, asst. to dean, 1967—68; dean Howard Coll. Arts and Scis., 1968—70, v.p. acad. affairs, 1970—87, univ. prof., 1987—94, rsch. prof., 1994—. Cons. in field; dir. NSF Inst., 1961, Ala. Vis. Scientist Program, 1962—67. Author: Modern Math., 1966, 2002, Fundamental Concepts of Math, 1968, 1976, Modern Math for Business, 1969, 1986, A Programmed Study of Number Systems, 1972, Finite Mathematics, 1974, 1985, Intuitive Geometry, 1975, Mathematics, an Everyday Language, 1979, Student Activities Manual, Elementary Mathematics, 1984, Finite Mathematics (A Problem Solving Approach), 1991, Mathematicas un Lenguaje Cotidiano, 1982, Activities Manual for Elementary School Teachers, 1988, Introduccion a los Conjuntos Numericos, 1976, Modern Mathematics for Elementary School Teachers, 1994, College Mathematics (a Graphing Calculator Approach), 1996, Brief Calculus (a Graphing Calculator Approach), 1996, Chinese Translation of Brief Calculus, 1997, (novels) All Because of Polly, 2002. Mem. Birmingham Manpower Area Planning Coun., 1972—75; trustee Gorgas Found., 1968—94, chmn., 1988—92; mem. Jefferson County Ednl. Consortium, 1981—93, pres., 1986—90; mem. Commn. to Upgrade Jefferson County Schs., 1982—86; deacon Bapt. Ch. Lt. USAAF, 1943—46. Mem.: Conf. Acad. Deans So. States (pres. 1985—86), So. Conf. Deans Faculties and Acad. V.P. (pres. 1982), Am. Conf. Acad. Deans, Am. Assn. Univ. Adminstrs. (exec. com. Ala. sect. 1972—74, v.p. 1974—76, pres. 1976—77), Assn. Ala. Coll. Adminstrs. (exec. com. 1976—80, pres. 1978—79), Am. Assn. Higher Edn., Ala. Acad. Sci. (pres. 1967—69), Assn. So. Bapt. Colls. and Schs. (sec. 1973, v.p. 1974, pres. 1975, deans sect.), Assn. Math. Tchrs. Ala. (pres. 1963), Nat. Coun. Tchrs. Math., Am. Math. Assn. (chmn. SE sect. 1966—67, vis. lecture program 1989—93), Am. Math. Soc., Am. Edn. Assn., Rotary. Home: 1347 Badham Dr Birmingham AL 35216-2939

WHEELER, SUSIE WEEMS, retired educator; b. Cassville, Ga., Feb. 24, 1917; d. Percy Weems and Cora (Smith) Weems-Canty; m. Dan W. Wheeler Sr., June 7, 1941; 1 child, Dan Jr. BS, Fort Valley (Ga.) State U., 1945; MEd, Atlanta U., 1947, EdD, 1978; postgrad., U. Ky., 1959-60; EdS, U. Ga., 1977. Tchr. Bartow County Schs., Cartersville (Ga.) City Schs., 1938-44, Jeanes supr., 1946-58; supr., curriculum dir. Paulding Sch. Sys.-Stephens Sch., Calhoun City, 1958-64; summer sch. tchr. Atlanta U., 1961-63; curriculum dir. Bartow County Schs., 1963-79; ret., 1979. Pres., co-owner Wheeler-Morris Svc. Ctr., 1990—; mem. Ga. Commn. on Student Fin., 1985-95. Coord. Noble Hill-Wheeler Meml. Ctr. Project, 1983—. Recipient Oscar W. Canty Cmty. Svc. award, 1991, Woman in History award Fedn. Bus. and Profl. Women, 1995, New Frontiers Cmty. Svc. award, 1997, Outstanding Achievement for Preserving Georgia Hist., 2000; recognized for dedicated svc. on behalf of Bartow County Citizens Comm. Clarence Brown, 2003; named one of Women of Excellence, Star of the Past Bartow Women at Work, 2003. Mem. AAUW (v.p. membership 1989-91, Ga. Achievement award 1993, Edn. Found. award Cartersville-Bartow br.), Ga. Assn. Curriculum and Supervision (pres.-elect 1973-74, pres. 1974-75, Johnnye V. Cox award 1975), Delta Sigma Theta (pres. Rome alumnae chpt. 1978-80, mem. nat. bd. 1984, planning com. 1988—, Dynamic Delta award 1967, 78, Grand Chpt. cert. recognition 2002, recognition 50 plus years, Delta Sigma Theta Sorority, Inc., 2002), Ga. Jeanes Assn. (pres. 1968-70). Home: 105 Fite St Cartersville GA 30120-3410

WHEELER, TIMOTHY ARNEAL, assistant superintendent; b. Carrollton, Ga., Aug. 26, 1943; s. Ronnie Arneal and Lizzie Lillian (Huckeba) W.; m. Frances Ethelyn Massey, Dec. 20,. 1970; children: Martha Marie, Ethelyn Anne, Wesley Arneal. AB, W. Ga. Coll., 1966; MS, Ga. So. Coll., 1970; EdS, U. Ga., 1979. Cert. tchr., adminstr., Ga. Band dir., fine arts coord. Douglas County Sch. System, Douglasville, Ga., 1966-76; music dir. Jefferson City (Ga.) Schs., 1976-77; elem. prin. Jackson County Schs., Jefferson, Ga., 1977-79, high sch. prin., 1979-80, supt., 1980-88, Carroll County Sch. System, Carrollton, Ga., 1988-90; band dir. Stephens County Sch. System, Toccoa, Ga., 1990-91; asst. supt. Elbert County Sch. System, Elberton, Ga., 1991—. Music dir. Midway United Meth. Ch., Douglasville, Ga., 1966-76, '90, Jefferson 1st United Meth. Ch., 1976-88, '92—; cons. So. Assn. Colls. and Schs., 1990—; adj. prof. W. Ga. Coll., 1989—; judge at many parades and band festivals. Presenter Pub. Broadcasting System, Curriculum Issues in Ga., 1986. Vice chmn. Carroll County Bd. Health, Carrollton, 1990; mem. Jackson County Bd. Health, Jackson County Child Abuse Task Force, adv. coun. Sch. Edn. W. Ga. Coll., Carrollton, 1988-90, Emmanuel Coll., Franklin Springs, Ga., 1992—. Named Man of Yr. Douglas County C. of C., 1969, Hon. Chpt. Mem., FHA Jackson County Comprehensive High Sch., 1980, FFA, 1981, Outstanding Educator, Ga. Art Edn. Assn., 1983; recipient Leadership award, Phi Delta Kappa, 1990, Carroll County Ednl. Found., 1990; bands he directed were honored many times including invitation to play at Presidential inauguration, 1972. Mem. ASCD, Ga. Assn. Supervision and Curriculum Devel., Ga. Sch. Bds. Assn., Ga. Assn. Sch. Supts. (bd. dirs. 1985-87, pres. 9th dist. assn. 1985-86), Ga. Assn. Ednl. Leaders, Elbert County C. of C., Phi Delta Kappa. Methodist. Home: 2274 Old Kings Bridge Rd Nicholson GA 30565-2912 Office: Elbert County Bd Edn 50 Laurel Dr Elberton GA 30635-1842

WHEELOCK, KEITH WARD, retired consulting company executive, educator; b. Phila., Oct. 17, 1933; s. Ward and Margot Trevor (Williams) W.; m. Susan Bowen Kimball, June 15, 1956 (div. Nov. 1975); children: Helen Fraser, James Voorhees; m. Bente Lorentzen Ott, July 1978 (div. June 1988); m. Georgia Whidden, May 17, 1997. BA, Yale U., 1955; MA, U. Pa., 1957; MS, MIT, 1972. Fgn. svc. officer Dept. State, Washington, 1960-69; dir. programs and policy divsn. N.Y.C. Housing and Devel. Adminstrn., 1970-71; devel. officer Moody's Investors Svc., Inc., N.Y.C., 1972-74, v.p. internat. ops., 1974-75, exec. v.p., 1975-76; pres. The Fantus Co., Millburn, N.J., 1976-83; mem. Sr. Dun & Bradstreet Mgmt. Group, 1979-83; prin. Wheelock Cons., 1983-88; project dir. Mng. Growth in N.J., 1986-90; assoc. prof. Raritan Valley C.C., 1992—. Rsch. asst. Fgn. Policy Rsch. Inst., U. Pa. Author: Nasser's New Egypt, A Critical Analysis, 1960, New Jersey Growth Management, 1989. Mem. Montgomery (N.J.) Twp. Com., 1986-88; pres. adv. coun. Eisenhower Exch. Fellowship. Sloan fellow MIT, 1972. Home: 325 Mountain View Rd Skillman NJ 08558-2412 E-mail: kwheelock@rcn.com.

WHELAN, JOHN JOSEPH, education educator; b. Cleve., May 2, 1942; s. Thomas Patrick and Margaret Mary (Geddes) W; children: Sean Joseph, Thomas Gordon. BA, John Carroll U., 1965; MS, Case Western Res. U., 1970. Cert. K-8 tchr., elem. prin., Ohio. Tchr. 7th, 8th and 12th grades St. Francis Sch., Cleve., 1965-67; tchr. 6th grade Prospect Elem. Sch., East Cleveland, Ohio, 1967-69; prin. Chambers Elem. Sch., East Cleveland, 1969-90; fellow in urban edn., asst. prof. edn. John Carroll U., University Heights, Ohio, 1991—. Instr. John Carroll U., 1987, 88; apptd. peer reviewer and adv. Office Ednl. Rsch. and Improvement, 1988; panelist Chpt. 1 Nat. Program Unusually Successful Programs the Serve Disadvantaged Youth, 1988; mem. review panel Am. Educators since a Nation at Risk, 1988; mem. Whitman Award panel 1989-90, urban concersn com. Ohio Assn. Elem. Sch. Adminstrs., 1990; adv. bd. John Carroll Profl. Devel. Ctr. for Adminstrs. and Tchrs., 1990, Greater Clevel. Mental Devel. Ctr., 1991; ednl. cons. Scholarship-in-Escrow, Cleve., 1990-91; mem. parental involvement task force Cleve. Summit on Edn., 1990; spk, numerous confs. and events including Goshen (Ind.) H.S., IRA Plains Conf., S.D., Ontario Sch. Dist., Oreg. NAESD, San Francisco, Minn. Sch. Bds. Assn., 1990, Parent Tng. Inst., 1990, Pa. Sch. Bds. Assn., 1990, Met. Sch. Dist., 1990, Warrick County Sch. Corp., 1991, Minn. Elem. Prin. Assn., 1991, Ill. Renewal Inst., Saratoga Springs, N.Y., 1991, Ednl. Commn. States Nat. Forum, Denver, 1991, U. Calif., Santa Cruz., 1991, Big Springs Sch. Dist., Pa., 1991, Nat. Assn. Elem. Sch. Prins., 1992, Nat. Prins. Meeting, San Diego, 1994, Archdiocese of Denver, N.D. Reading Assn., Reading Assn. of Ireland,Dublin, Bottineau Pub. Schs. in N.D., Baldwin Coll., Cleve., NAESP, Orlando, San Diego; sr. cons. Natl. Sch. Conf. Inst./Learning 24/7, Phoenix, 2003. Bd. trustees John Carroll U.; life mem. Ohio PTA. Named Nat. Disting. Prin. Ohio, U.S. Dept. Edn., 1988-89; recipient Educator's award United Black Fund, Cleve., 1987, Ednl. Excellence award Urban League Greater Cleve., 1987, Recognition award Rotary Club Cleve., 1987. Mem. NAESP (Nat. Disting. Prin. award 1988), ASCD, Nat. Assn. for Schs. Excellence, John Carroll U. Alumni Assn. (pres. Cleve. 1992, recipient Alumni medal 1986), Phi Delta Kappa (v.p. 1986-87). Roman Catholic. Avocations: skiing, golf, jogging. Home: 344 E 276th St Euclid OH 44132-1304 Office: John Carroll U Dept Edn 20700 N Park Blvd Dept Edn University Heights OH 44118-4581

WHELAN, JOHN WILLIAM, law educator; b. Cleve., Apr. 23, 1922; s. Walter Edmund and Stacia Miriam Whelan; m. Maryrose Shields, May 29, 1947; children: Moira Ann Whelan Dykstra, Thomas M. AB, John Carroll U., 1943; JD, Georgetown U., 1948. Assoc. prof. law Columbus U., Washington, 1948-50; asst. prof. U. Va., Charlottesville, 1955-56; assoc. prof. U. Wis., Madison, 1956-59; prof. Georgetown U., Washington, 1959-67, U. Calif., Davis, 1967-75, Hastings Coll. Law U. Calif., San Francisco, 1975-91, prof. emeritus, 1991—. Mem. atomic energy com. Bd. Contract Appeals, 1965—73; cons. to atty. gen. Trust Ter. Pacific Island, 1976—78, adminstrn. law judge constrn. contracts, 1984—86; hearing examiner Medi-Cal Fiscal Intermediary Contract, 1979—82; vis. prof. Nihon U. Coll. Law, Tokyo, 1989; cons. to govt. contracts to Govt. of Poland, 92. Author (with R. S. Pasley): (book) Federal Government Contracts, 1975; author: (with K. H. York) Insurance, 1983, 2d edit., 1988, Federal Government Contracts, 1985, 2d edit., 2002; author: (with James F. Nagle) Supplement, 1989; author: Understanding Government Contracts, 1994; author: (with K. H. York, Leo Martinez) Insurance, 4th edit., 2001; editor: Yearbook of Procurement Articles, 1965—90; mem. editl. bd. Pub. Procurement Law Rev., 1991—; contbr. articles to profl. jours. With U.S. Army, 1943—45, served with JAG U.S. Army, 1950—55. Decorated Bronze Star; Ford Found. grantee, 1958—59, 1963—64, 1970. Mem.: ABA, Fed. Cir. Bar Assn., Bds. Contract Appeals Bar Assn., Nat. Contract Mgmt. Assn., DC Bar Assn., Fed. Bar Assn. Home: 306 Bristol Pl Mill Valley CA 94941-4005 Office: U Calif Hastings Coll Law 200 Mcallister St San Francisco CA 94102-4707

WHELTLE, MARGARET MAIE, secondary school educator; b. Balt., Oct. 19, 1934; d. Albert F. and Ruth (Morse) Wheltle. BA, Mt. St. Agnes Coll., 1956; JD, U. Md., 1959; postgrad., Loyola Evening Coll. Balt., 1960—61, Cath. U. Am., 1967—69; STM, St. Mary's Sem. and U. Balt., 1972. Bar: Md. 1959, U.S. Supreme Ct. 1969. Assoc. Harley Wheltle Victor & Rosser, Balt., 1959—64; asst. to pres., dir. devel., TV prodn. coord. Mt. St. Agnes Coll., Balt., 1964—67; coord. religious edn. St. Agnes Roman Cath. Congregation, Inc., Balt., 1971—74; lectr. theology Mount de Sales Acad., Balt., 1978—85, chair religion dept., 1979—85, trustee, 1979—82. Instr., dir. theology dept. Harmony Hill H.S., Watertown, SD, 1969—70; lectr. St. Martin's Home for Aged, 1975; cons. Connor Travel Agy., Inc., 1986—88; mem. spkrs. bur. Howard County Right to Life, Birthright of Md., Archdiocese of Balt. Pres. nat. alumnae Mt. St. Agnes Coll., 1961—65, mem. pres.'s coun., 1961—67; pres. Corban Corp., 1986—89; vice-chair Birthright of Md., 1975—76; co-founder, bd. chair St. Martin's Home for Aged Ladies Aux., 1973—76, bd. dirs.; adv. St. Martin's Home for Aged, 1977—80, Little Sisters of Poor, 1977—80, mem. Jeanne Jergun Assn., 2003—; mem. pub. rels. com. Archdiocese of Balt., 1975—76; Marion Burk Knott edl. cons.; v.p. parish coun. St. Mark Roman Cath. Ch., Catonsville, Md., 1986—87, pres. parish coun., 1987—88; mem. west county regional coun. Archdiocese of Balt., 1986—90; liaison Bd. Christian Formation, 1987—90; mem. sch. bd., chairperson devel. com. Resurrection-St. Paul Sch., 2001—; sodality prefect St. William of York, Balt., 1965—67, mem. parish planning team for total Christian edn., 1971, mem. total parish edn. com., 1975—76, instr. adult edn., 1976, mem. nat. catechism directory com., 1977. Recipient Cert. of Appreciation, Archdiocese Balt., 1981, Mount de Sales Acad., 1982. Mem.: Am. Soc. Law and Medicine, Internat. Platform Assn., Internat. Fedn. Cath. Alumnae (chpt. vice gov. 1964—66), Hastings Ctr. (assoc.). Home and Office: 2823 Country Ln Ellicott City MD 21042-2566

WHELTON, BARTLETT DAVID, chemical and biochemical educator; b. San Francisco, Calif., Dec. 2, 1941; BS, U. San Francisco, 1963; PhD, U. Wash., 1969. Fellow sch. pharmacy U. Alberta, Edmonton, Can., 1969-71; asst. prof. U. Pacific, Stockton, Calif., 1971-74; prof. chemistry/biochemistry Ea. Wash. U., Cheney, Wash., 1974—. Office: Ea Wash U Chemistry/Biochemistry Sci #226 526 5th St Cheney WA 99004-2440

WHICHELLO, CAROL, political scientist, educator, writer; b. Newton, N.J., Mar. 29, 1945; d. Arthur Frederick Whichello and M. W. Niper. BA, Salem Internat. U., 1967; MEd, Coll. N.J., 1978. Cert. tchr. N.J., Fla. Tchr. Freehold Twp. (N.J.) Bd. Edn., 1967—97; adj. prof. polit. sci. Indian River C.C., 1998—; sub. tchr. Martin County Sch. Bd., Fla., 2001—. Past exed. bd. dirs., legis. chairperson Freehold Twp. Edn. Assn. Mem. Stuart (Fla.) Heritage Mus., 1998—, bd. mem., 2002—. Recipient N.J. Mid. Sch.Tchr. of Yr. in Social Studies, N.J. Social Studies Tchrs., 1989. Democrat. Baptist. Avocations: writing, editing historical works. Home: 1668 SW Crossing Cir Palm City FL 34990-2460

WHIDDEN, NANCY PRINCE, principal; b. Florence, S.C., Sept. 27, 1951; d. John Bert Jr. and Marie (Gaskins) Prince; m. Johnny Lee Whidden, Sr., June 30, 1973; children: Johnny Lee, Jr., Julie Lenore. BSEd in Elem. Edn. magna cum laude, U. Ga., 1973; MEd in Adminstrn. and Supervision, Valdosta State U., 1994, EdS in Ednl. Leadership, 1996. Cert. elem. edn. educator, adminstrn. and supr. Tchr. second grade Nashville (Ga.) Elem. Sch., 1973-75; tchr. third grade Fitzgerald (Ga.) Elem., 1988-90, Ben Hill Elem., Fitzgerald, 1990-94, asst. prin., 1994-97, Ben Hill Primary Sch., Fitzgerald, 1998-2000, prin., 2000—. Mem. parent adv. com. Fitzgerald Jr. High, 1986-88, community pride com., 1985-88; prin.'s adv. com. Ben Hill Elem., 1990-92; cons. Ga. State Univ. Assessment Project, 1992-93. Bd. dirs. Am. Cancer Soc. of Ben Hill County, Fitzgerald, 1982-85, Ben Hill County Arts Coun., 1983-85; den mother Boy Scouts of Am., 1983-85. Named Ben Hill County Tchr. of Yr., 1994-95. Mem. Nat. Assn. Educators, Ben Hill County Assn. of Educators, Kiwanis Club Internat. (bd. dirs.), Delta Kappa Gamma. Baptist. Avocations: reading, walking.

WHIGHAM, MARK ANTHONY, computer scientist; b. Mobile, Ala., Jan. 14, 1959; s. Tommie Lee Sr. and Callie Mae (Molette) W. BS in Computer Sci., Ala. A&M U., 1983, MS in Computer Sci., 1990; postgrad., Ala. A&M Univ., 1995—. Computer programmer U.S. Army Corps of Engrs., Huntsville, Ala., 1985-88; programmer analyst, coord. acad. computing Ala. A&M U., Normal, Ala., 1988-89, programmer analyst II, DEC systems coord., instr. part-time computer sci. dept., 1989-91; systems engr. Advanced Bus. Cons. Inc.-La. div. Dow Chem. Co., 1991-93; owner Whigham's Computer Cons., 1990—; sys. engr. DOW Chem. Co.-USA La. Divsn., Plaquemine, La., 1991-93; instr. computer info. system Calhoun C.C., Decatur, Ala., 1993-97; network specialist/cons. Ala. A&M U., Normal, 1994—; computer info. sys. instr. Calhoun C.C., Decatur, Ala., 1994—; mgmt. info. sys. dir., CIO J.F. Drake Tech. Coll., Huntsville, Ala., 1997-98; software engr. Colsa Corp., Huntsville, Ala., 1998—99; dir. info. tech. Lane Coll., 1999—2000; instr. computer sci. Lawson State CC, 2000—. Instr. computer sci. dept. Ala. A&M U., 1989-91; network specialist, cons. Ala. A&M U., Normal, 1994—. Active Huntsville Interdenominational Ministerial Fellowship, Huntsville, 1984. Mem. Nat. Assn. Sys. Programmers, Ala. Coun. for Computer Edn., Assn. for Computing Machinery, Huntsville Jaycees, Nat. Soc. Black Engrs., Assn. Info. Tech. Profls., So. Poetry Assn., Nat. Arts Soc., Internat. Black Writers and Artists Assn., Optimists, U.S. Chess Fedn. (cert. chess coach), Future Bus. Leaders of Am.-Phi Beta Lambda, Sigma Tau Epsilon, Alpha Phi Omega. Baptist. Avocations: chess, skating, reading, playing piano. Office: Lawson State CC 3060 Wilson Rd Birmingham AL 35209-1542 Home: Apt 202 917 Valley Ridge Dr Birmingham AL 35209-1542 Office Fax: 205-929-6362. Business E-Mail: mwhigham@cougar.ls.cc.al.

WHINNA, GEORGE WALTMAN ROPER, III, secondary education educator; b. Chgo., Oct. 22, 1941; s. George Waltman Roper Jr. and Roseanna (Kepner) W. AA, Wilson Jr. Coll., Chgo., 1961; BA in History, Wartburg Coll., 1963. Cert. secondary tchr., Ill. Tchr. Roosevelt Jr. H.S., Rockford, Ill., 1963-69, West Sr. H.S., Rockford, 1969-89, Auburn Sr. H.S., Rockford, 1989—; ret., 1999. Co-chmn. Bicentennial Sch.'s Com., Rockford, 1975-76. Recipient Am. History award DAR, 1980, Rotary award Rockford Rotary, 1989; named Top Twenty Tchrs. of Distinction Golden Apple Awards program, 1998. Republican. Lutheran. Avocations: collecting books, art, glass, travel, computers. Home: 4152 Riverwood Dr Loves Park IL 61111-7669

WHIPPLE, ANDREW POWELL, biology educator; b. Columbus, Ohio, Feb. 12, 1949; s. Quentin Powell and Joan Pierce (Armstrong) W.; m. You-Ying Wang, June 23, 1973; children: Joan Chuan-Lee, Kyle Wang, Elizabeth Chuan-Fei, Daniel Wang. BS in Microbiology, Ohio State U., Columbus, 1971; MS in Biology, SUNY, Albany, 1974, PhD in Cell Biology, 1979. Rsch. asst. SUNY, Albany, 1975-78, univ. fellow, instr. biology, 1979; postdoctoral rsch. fellow Dana Farber Cancer Inst. Harvard Med. Sch., Boston, 1979-81; prof. biology Montreat (N.C.)-Anderson Coll., 1981-84, Taylor U., Upland, Ind., 1984—. Vis. prof. Biology Dept. Tunghai U., Taichung, Taiwan, 1992-93; cons. James River Corp., Neenah, Wis., 1985, Agro-K, Mpls., 1986-88; summer faculty rsch. fellow USAF, Wright-Patterson AFB, Ohio, 1987-88. Contbr. articles to profl. jours. Mem. Am. Soc. Cell Biology, Am. Sci. Affiliation, Soc. Chinese Bioscientists in Am. Republican. Presbyterian. Achievements include patent (with other) for Method for Treating Waste Fluid with Bacteria; adaptation of human lymphoblastoid cells to serum-free culture; description of response of transformed cells to growth factor stimulation as compared to their normal, non-transformed counterparts. Home: PO Box 448 Upland IN 46989-0448 Office: Taylor U Biology Dept Upland IN 46989

WHIPPLE, BEVERLY, nursing educator, researcher; b. Jersey City, June 30, 1941; d. Howard and Beatrice (Bodei) Hoehne; m. James Whipple, Sept. 15, 1962; children: Allen James, Susan Jane. BS, Wagner Coll., S.I., N.Y., 1962; MEd, Rutgers U., 1967, PhD, 1986, MSN, 1987. RN, N.J., N.Y.; diplomate Am. Bd. Sexologists; cert. sex. educator, counselor and rschr., sexologist, AASECT. Instr. Helene Field Sch. of Nursing, Camden, N.J., 1970-75; assoc. prof. nursing Gloucester County Coll., Sewell, N.J., 1975-87; prof. emerita Rutgers U., Newark, 1987—. Researcher in field. Co-author: G Spot, 1982, Safe Encounters, 1989, Outwitting Osteoporosis, 2003; contbr. numerous articles to profl. jours. Recipient Hugo Beigel award for Rsch. Excellence, Excellence in Rsch. award N.J. State Nurses Assn., Disting. Scientific Achievement award, Soc. Scientific Study of Sexuality. Fellow Am. Acad. Nursing, Soc. for Sci. Study Sexuality; mem. ANA, Am. Pain Soc., Am. Assn. Sex Educators, Counselor and Therapists, Soc. for Sex Therapy and Rsch., Sexuality Info. and Edn. Coun. U.S., Internat. Acad. Sex Rsch., Soc. for the Sci. Study of Sexuality (pres. 2002-03), Am. Assn. of Sex Educators, Counselors and Therapists (past pres., Profl. Standard of Excellence award), World Assn. Sexology (v.p. 2001—). Home: 31 N Lakeside Dr W Medford NJ 08055-9205

WHISONANT, ROBERT CLYDE, geology educator, scientist; b. Columbia, S.C., Apr. 20, 1941; s. Clyde Webb and Mary Perrylee (Lanford) W.; m. Brenda Dale Lark, June 7, 1963; children: Dell Raye, Robert Dowling. BS in Geology, Clemson U., 1963; MS, Fla. State U., 1965, PhD in Geology, 1967. Petroleum geologist Humble Oil & Refining Co., Houston, Kingsville, Tex., 1967-71, cons., 1972; mem. faculty Radford (Va.) U., 1971—, prof. geology, 1981—, chmn. dept. geology, 1981-96. Cons. Nat. Geographics, 1981; commr., Va. Oil and Gas Conservation Commn., 1982— . Contbr. articles to profl. jours. NASA grantee, 1963-66, Petroleum Rsch. Fund grantee, 1983-85, Jeffress Meml. Trust grantee, 1983-85, 86-87; recipient Neil A. Miner award, Nat. Assn. Geol. Tchrs., 1993. Fellow Geol. Soc. Am. (Penrose Rsch. grantee 1972); mem. Am. Assn. Petroleum Geologists, Soc. Econ. Paleontologists Mineralogists, Va. Acad. Sci., Lions. Methodist. Home: 29 Round Hill Dr Radford VA 24141-3611 Office: Radford Univ Geology Dept Radford VA 24142

WHITAKER, GILBERT RILEY, JR., academic administrator, business economist; b. Oklahoma City, Oct. 8, 1931; s. Gilbert Riley and Melodese (Kilpatrick) W.; m. Ruth Pauline Tonn, Dec. 18, 1953; children: Kathleen, David Edward, Thomas Gilbert. BA, Rice U., 1953; postgrad., So. Methodist U., 1956-57; MS in Econs., U. Wis., Madison, 1958, PhD in Econs. (Ford Found. dissertation fellow), 1961. Instr., Sch. of Bus. Northwestern U., 1960-61, asst. prof. bus. econs., Sch. of Bus., 1961-64, asso. prof., Sch. of Bus., 1964-66, research assoc. Transp. Center, Sch. of Bus., 1962-66; asso. prof. Washington U., St. Louis, 1966-67, prof., 1967-76, adj. prof. econs., 1968-76, asso. dean Sch. Bus. Adminstrn., 1969-76; dean, prof. bus. econs. M.J. Neeley Sch. Bus., Tex. Christian U., 1976-79; dean U. Mich., 1979-90; prof. Sch. Bus. Adminstrn. U. Mich., 1979-97; provost, v.p. acad. affairs U. Mich., Ann Arbor, 1990-93, provost, exec. v.p. acad. affairs, 1993-95; sr. advisor Andrew W. Mellon Found., 1996—; dean Jesse Jones Graduate Sch. of Mgmt./Rice U., Houston, 1997—. Dir. Am. Assembly of Collegiate Schs. of Bus., 1984-91, v.p., pres.-elect, 1988-89, pres., 1989-90, dir. Washington campus, 1980-89, chmn., 1985-88; bd. dirs. Lincoln Nat. Corp., 1986-2002; Johnson Controls, Inc., 1985-2001; Structural Dynamics Rsch. Corp., 1986-2001; sr. economist banking and currency com. U.S. Ho. of Reps., 1964; mem. Grad. Mgmt. Admissions Coun., 1972-75, chmn., 1974-75; bd. dirs. Washtenaw County United Way, 1990-96. Author: (with Marshall Colberg and Dascomb Forbush) books including Business Economics, 6th edit., 1981, (with Roger Chisholm) Forecasting Methods, 1971. Bd. trustees, sec.-treas. JSTOR, 1995-2002. With USN, 1953-56. Mem. Am. Econ. Assn., Ft. Worth Boat Club. Home: 6425 Mercer St Houston TX 77005-3733 Office: Rice University Jesse Jones Grad Sch of Mgmt PO Box 2932 Houston TX 77005-2932 E-mail: grwhit@rice.edu.

WHITAKER, JOHN KING, economics educator; b. Burnley, Lancashire, Eng., Jan. 30, 1933; came to U.S., 1967; s. Ben and Mary Whitaker; m. Sally Bell Cross, Aug. 24, 1957; children: Ann Elizabeth, Jane Claire, David John. BA in Econs, U. Manchester, 1956; A.M., Johns Hopkins U., 1957; PhD, Cambridge U., 1962. Lectr. U. Bristol, Eng., 1960-66; prof., 1966-69; vis. prof. U. Va., Charlottesville, 1967-68, prof. econs., 1969-86, chmn. dept. econs., 1979-82, Paul Goodloe McIntire prof. of econs., 1986-92, Georgia Bankard prof. of econs., 1992—2003, Georgia Bankard prof. of econs. emeritus, 2003—. Author: The Early Economic Writings of Alfred Marshall, 1867-1890, 2 vols., 1975, The Correspondence of Alfred Marshall, Economist, 3 vols., 1996. Mem. Am. Econ. Assn., Royal Econ. Soc., History of Econs. Soc. Home: 1615 Yorktown Dr Charlottesville VA 22901-3046 Office: U Va Dept Econs Rouss Hall Charlottesville VA 22903

WHITAKER, KATHLEEN K. gifted education facilitator; b. Kansas City, Mo., Mar. 26, 1940; d. Richard Ingram and Rosemary (Frost) Kidd; m. William P. Whitaker, Feb. 24, 1962 (div. 1971); children: Lorie Beth, Minda Corinne. BA, U. Mo., 1962; MS, Kans. U., 1982. Cert. learning disabilities, gifted edn. and social studies tchr.; cert. psychol. examiner. Tchr. learning disabilities Wyandotte County Spl. Edn. Coop., Kansas City, Kans., 1980-84; learning specialist diagnostic team Children's Rehab. Unit Kans. U. Med. Ctr., 1984-85; tchr. learning disabilities Turner Sch. Dist., Kansas City, Kans., 1985-89, tchr. gifted edn., 1988-89, 94—; facilitator underachieving gifted edn. Shawnee Mission (Kans.) Schs., 1989—; tchr. of gifted, 1994—. Presenter, staff mem. Rimm Underachievement Inst., 1992; presenter, developer larning materials in field; tchr., designer materials for parenting classes. Chmn. worship com. Shawnee Mission Unitarian Soc., 1991, trustee, 1992-93; adv. bd. Saramis Teddy Bear Comfort. Mem. Assn. for Edn. Gifted Underachieving Students, Kans. Assn. for Gifted, Talented and Creative, Phi Delta Kappa. Avocations: bicycling, bridge. Home: 4406 W 70th Ter Shawnee Mission KS 66208-2562 Office: Old Mission Multi-Use Ctr 4901 Reinhardt Dr Shawnee Mission KS 66205-1507

WHITAKER, LINDA M. principal; b. Blue Island, Ill., Apr. 2, 1950; d. William Martin and Evelyn Cecilia (Klucznik) Locke; m. David George Whitaker, June 10, 1972. BS in Edn. magna cum laude, No. Ill. U., 1972, MS in Edn., 1975, C.A.S., 1985. Cert. adminstrv. type 75, secondary type 9, elem. type 3. Tchr. High Sch. Dist. 218, Oak Lawn, Ill.; dean Hazelgreen Sch., Sch. Dist. 126, Alsip, Ill.; elem. sch. prin., dist. curriculum coord. Worth (Ill.) Sch. Dist. 127. Contbr. articles to profl. jours. Recipient Govs. Master Tchr. award, 1984, PTA State Life Membership award, 1988. Mem. ASCD, Ill. ASCD, Nat. Asns. Elem. Sch. Prins., Ill. Prins. Assn., Nat. Coun. for Social Studies, Mortar Board, Delta Kappa Gamma (chpt. 1st v.p.), Kappa Delta Pi, Phi Alpha Theta.

WHITAKER, THOMAS RUSSELL, English literature educator; b. Marquette, Mich., Aug. 7, 1925; s. Joe Russell and Sarah Genevieve (Houk) W.; m. Dorothy Vera Barnes, June 17, 1950 (dec. Dec. 1995); children: Thomas O'Hara, Sarah Mae, Mary Beth, Gwendolyn Anne; m. Joan Bower Horwitt, Oct. 4, 1997 (div. Sept. 2002); m. Lillian Ann Traub, Jul. 26, 2003. BA summa cum laude, Oberlin Coll., 1949; MA, Yale U., 1950, PhD, 1953. Instr. English Oberlin (Ohio) Coll., 1952-55, asst. prof., 1955-59, assoc. prof., 1959-63, prof., 1963-64; tchr. lit. Goddard Coll., Plainfield, Vt., 1964-66; prof. English U. Iowa, Iowa City, 1966-75, Yale U., New Haven, Conn., 1975-95, prof. theater studies, 1986-95, chmn. dept. English, 1979-85, Frederick W. Hilles prof. English, 1989-95; Frederick W. Hilles prof. emeritus English, 1995—. Author: Swan and Shadow: Yeats's Dialogue with History, 1964, 2d edit. with new preface, 1989, William Carlos Williams, 1968, rev. edit., 1989, Fields of Play in Modern Drama, 1977, Tom Stoppard, 1983, augmented edit., 1984, Mirrors of Our Playing: Paradigms and Presences in Modern Drama, 1999; editor: Twentieth Century Interpretations of the Playboy of the Western World, 1969, Teaching in New Haven: The Common Challenge, 1991; editor Iowa Rev., 1974-77; chmn. editorial bd. On Common Ground, 1993—; author, narrator video script: Excellence in Teaching: Agenda for Partnership, 1997; writer, advisor Yale-New Haven Tchrs. Inst. Nat. Demonstration Project, 1998-02, Yale Nat. Initiative, 2002—. Served with C.E. U.S. Army, 1944-46. Recipient Harbison award for gifted teaching Danforth Found., 1972; Am. Council Learned Socs. fellow, 1969-70; NEH-Huntington fellow, 1981 Mem. MLA. Home: 38 Wilford Rd Branford CT 06405-5321

WHITAKER, VICTORIA MANUELA KATZ, publisher, public relations executive, educator, consultant; b. N.Y.C., Mar. 12, 1941; d. Isaac William and Sylvia (Katz) Penner; m. Ronald Mark Katz, Sept. 8, 1974 (dec. Dec. 1996); m. Roger B. Whitaker, Nov. 11, 2000. BA in Journalism, Hofstra Coll., 1962. Sr. editor real estate, fin. Long Island (N.Y.) Comml. Review, 1962-72; freelance writer, publicist N.Y., 1972-74; managing editor North Shore News Group, Smithtown, N.Y., 1974-88; dir. u. news svcs. SUNY, Stony Brook, 1988-99; v.p., dir. midwest ops. Cordes Public Relations, N.Y., 1999—. Dir. Long Island Bus. Inc., Ronkonkoma, N.Y., 1965-98; adj. journalism prof. C.W. Post, Greenvale, N.Y., 1986-88, Hofstra Coll., Hempstead, N.Y., 1987. Author: (study) Smithtown Minorities, 1983. Trustee Harbor County Day Sch., St. James, N.Y., 1977-93, mktg. and pub. rels. com. mem. United Way, L.I., 1988-98; program com. mem. Mus. at Stony Brook, 1990-93; mem. Investigative Reporters & Editors; bd. dirs. Springfield Area Arts Coun. Recipient Media award for govtl. reporting Press Club L.I., 1987, 88. Mem. AAUW (past v.p.), Pub. Rels. Soc. Am. (chair steering com. L.I. chpt. 1996-97), Soc. Profl. Journalists (nat. bd. dirs., co-chair chpt. health and welfare com., regional dir. 1994-98, 2000—), Press Club L.I. Chpt. Soc. Profl. Journalists (pres. 1974, treas. 1985-93, 98-99, Deadline Club bd. 1994, program co-chair 1993, v.p. 1995-99), Headline Club (Chgo.), Am. Women in Journalism (v.p., sec. Springfield chpt.). Home: 2944 S Douglas Ave Springfield IL 62704-4912 E-mail: vkatz@racoon.com.

WHITAKER, VIVA JEANE, language therapist dyslexia, reading specialist; b. Sasakwa, Okla., Feb. 15, 1935; d. Claude Dewey and Lena Mae (Hodge) Gaines; m. Leo Whitaker, Aug. 10, 1955 (dec. Mar., 1970); children: David Leo, Linda Jeane, Sharon Diane. BS in Elem. Edn., history 1-8, Sul Ross State U., 1973, MA in Edn. Reading Specialist, 1984; Alpha Phonics Cert. Dyslexia, Scottish Rite Learning Ctr., Lubbock, Tex., 1992. Cert. tchr. elem., reading specialist, lang. therapist. 2nd grade tchr., 2nd and 3d music tchr., music dir. Buena Vista Ind. Sch. Dist., Imperial, Tex., 1974-85, reading specialist, 1985-88; tchr. basic skills 6th grade Crane (Tex.) Ind. Sch. Dist., 1988-91, alphabetic phonics tchr, dist. dir., lang. therapist, 1991—. Recipient scholarship Scottish Rite Masons, Crane, Tex., 1991, 92, leadership award, 1993. Mem. Tex. State Tchrs. Assn. (past pres.), Crane Classroom Tchrs. Assn. (past pres., v.p.), Alpha Phonics Parents Support Group (advisor), United Meth. Women (pres., v.p. 1st Meth. Ch., Crane). Democrat. Avocations: family, reading, piano, cooking, church.

WHITAKER, VON BEST, nursing educator; b. New Bern, N.C. BS, Columbia Union Coll., 1972; MS, U. Md., 1974; MA, U. N.C., 1980, PhD, 1983. Lectr. U. N.C., Chapel Hill, 1981-82; asst. prof. U. Mo., Columbia, Mo., 1982-85; asst. prof. grad. sch. Boston Coll., Newton, Mass., 1985-86; asst. prof. U. Tex. Health Sci. Ctr., San Antonio, 1986-94; assoc. prof. Ga. So. U., Statesboro, 1994—. Contbr. articles to profl. jours., chpts. to textbooks; presenter in field. Mem.: ANA, Aigma Theta Tau. Home: 5308 Bayberry Ln Greensboro NC 27455-1139

WHITAKER, WILMA NEUMAN, retired mathematics instructor; b. Chgo., Aug. 18, 1937; d. August P. and Wilma M. (Kaiser) Neuman; m. G.D. Whitaker, Mar. 28, 1970; children: Brett Allan Karlsen, Karen J. Whitaker Laflin, Mark D. Whitaker, David R. Whitaker. BA in Math., DePauw U., 1959; MEd in Math., Francis Marion Coll., 1988. Cert. secondary tchr., Ill., Mich., S.C.; cert. realtor Mich. High sch. math tchr. Dist. 209, Hillside, Ill., 1959-61, Dist. 214, Mt. Prospect, Ill., 1961-65; apprentice pharmacist Karlsen Pharmacy, Mt. Prospect, 1961-67; realtor Durbin Co., Clarkston, Mich., 1977-81; sub. tchr. Clarkston (Mich.) Cmty. Schs., 1979-80; math instr. Florence (S.C.)-Darlington Tech. Coll., 1981-85, math dept. head, 1985-87, dean arts and scis., 1987-95, instr. math., 1995-99, ret., 1999. Stephen min. St. Lukes Luth. Ch., Florence, 1991—, coun., 1989-92, tchr., 1981-98; founder, organizer Spring Cmty. Walk Along Rotary Beauty Trail, Florence, 1988, 89, 91. Named Faculty Mem. of Yr., Florence-Darlington Tech. Coll., 1987, Adminstr. of Yr., 1992, Exec. of Yr., Florence chpt. Profl. Secs. Internat., 1993. Mem. Optimist Club of Florence (v.p. 1991-92, pres. 1992-93), Optimist Internat. (lt. gov. Zone 6 S.C. 1993-94, 95-96, gov.-elect S.C. dist. 1994-95, gov. 1995-96, lt. gov. Zone 8 1996-97), Theta Sigma Phi, Delta Zeta. Avocations: antiques, bible study, travel, needlework.

WHITCOMB, MARY ELIZABETH, special education educator; b. New York, N.Y., Aug. 12, 1939; d. Alexander E. Napier, Elizabeth Virginia Atkinson; m. Michael Edward Whitcomb, Aug. 19, 1961 (div. Oct. 1, 1985); children: Linda, Kim Paskel, Michael, David, Gregory. BS in Edn., Ohio State U., 1961, MA in Edn., 1980—80. Tchr. spl. edn. Westerville North H.S., Westerville, Ohio, 1985—. Upper Arlington H.S., Upper Arlington, Ohio, 1981—85; tchr. Cin. City Schs., Cin., 1961—65. Faculty chairperson Multi-Cultural Fair Westerville North H.S., Westerville, 1995—96, chairperson North Ctrl. Evaluation Team, 1990—91; advisor Students Against Destructive Decisions, Westerville, 1985—91; del. Working Toward Peace Ohio Commn. on Dispute Resolution, Columbus, Ohio, 1995—96. Rep. Kinder Key Heart Dr. Children's Hosp. Bd., Columbus, 1980—81, chairperson Kinder Key Heart Dr. Upper Arlington, 1980—81; advisor Intern's and Resident's Wives Ohio State U. Med. Sch., Columbus, 1980—82; vol. Riverside Hosp., Columbus, 1983—85; vol. James Cancer Hosp. and Rsch. Ctr. Ohio State U., Columbus, 1998—; vol. Forums Landmark Edn., Columbus, 1991—; leader Boy/Girl Scouts of Am., Upper Arlington, 1979—80; chairperson fundraising PTO, Gaithersburg, Md., 1976—77. Grantee Conflict Mgmt. Grant, Ohio Commn. on Dispute Resolution and Conflict Mgmt./Ohio Dept. Edn., 1995 and 1996. Mem.: Westerville Edn. Assn., Ohio Edn. Assn., NEA. Mem. Brethren Ch. Avocations: travel, reading. Office: Westerville North High School 950 County Line Rd Westerville OH 43081 Personal E-mail: marynw39@aol.com. Business E-Mail: whitcomm@westerville.k12.oh.us.

WHITE, ALVIN MURRAY, mathematics educator, consultant; b. N.Y.C., N.Y., June 21, 1925; s. Max and Beatrice White; m. Myra Goldstein, Dec. 4, 1946; children: Louis, Michael. BA, Columbia U., 1949; MA, UCLA, 1951; PhD, Stanford U., 1961. Acting instr. Stanford (Calif.) U., 1950-54; asst. prof. U. Santa Clara, Calif., 1954-61; postdoctoral fellow U. Wis., Madison, 1961-62; prof. Harvey Mudd Coll., Claremont, Calif., 1962—. Vis. scholar MIT, 1975; initiator-facilitator humanistic math. network of over 2000 mathematicians worldwide; cons. coop. learning tutorial program Claremont Unified Sch. Dist. Editor: Interdisciplinary Teaching, 1981; pub., editor: Humanistic Mathematics Network Jour., Essays on Humanistic Math., Math. Assn. Am., 1993; contbr. articles to profl. jours. Served with USN, 1943-46, PTO. Grantee Fund for Improvement of Post-secondary Edn., Exxon Found. Mem. Am. Math. Soc., Math. Assn. Am., Nat. Coun. Tchrs. Math., Profl. Organizational Developers Network, Fedn. Am. Scientists, AAUP, Sigma Xi. Office: Harvey Mudd Coll 301 E 12th St Claremont CA 91711-5901

WHITE, ANNETTE JONES, retired early childhood educator, administrator; b. Albany, Ga., Aug. 29, 1939; d. Paul Lawrence and Delores Christine (Berry) Jones; m. Frank Irvin White, Nov. 13, 1964; children: Melanie Francine, Sharmian Lynell. BA, Spelman Coll., 1964; MEd, Va. State U., 1980. Tchr. Flint Ave Child Devel. Ctr., Albany, 1966-67; tchr., supr. Flintside Child Devel. Ctr., Albany, 1967-68; tchr., dir. Albany Ga. Community Sch., 1968-69; tchr. Martin Luther King Community Ctr., Atlanta, 1975-77, The Appleton Sch., Atlanta, 1977-78; sec., proofreader The Atlanta Daily World, 1978-80; tchr. kindergarten Spelman Coll., Atlanta, 1981-88, dir. nursery and kindergarten, lectr. in edn., 1988-97, asst. dir. Marian Wright Edelman Ctr., 1997-98. Cons., presenter child devel. assoc. program Morris Brown Coll., Atlanta, 1991; presenter Ga. Assn. of Young Children, 1992, ann. child care conf. Waycross (Ga.) Coll., 1993. Contbr. articles to profl. jours. including Am. Visions, Sage, So. Exposure, S.W. Georgian, Atlanta Tribune, Atlanta Daily World, Double Stitch, Choosing to Learn/An Alternative GED Curriculum Guide, 1996. Mem. Peace Action, Washington, 1990—, Children's Def. Action Coun., Washington, 1990—, Native Am. Rights Fund, Nat. Mus. Native Ams., Albany Civil Rights Mus. Mem. Nat. Coun. Negro Women, Sierra Club. Avocations: cane weaving, crocheting, cooking, drawing, reading, Alpha Kappa Alpha Sorority.

WHITE, B. JOSEPH, former dean, business educator; BS, Georgetown U., 1969; MBA, Harvard U., 1971; PhD, U. Mich., 1975. Dean bus. adminstrn. U. Mich., Ann Arbor, 1991—2001, interim pres., 2001—, Wilbur K. Pierpont Collegiate prof. leadership in mgmt. edn. and prof. bus. adminstrn. Bus. Sch., 2002—. Mng. dir. Fred Alger Mgmt., Inc., N.Y.C. Office: U Mich Bus Sch 701 Tappan St Ann Arbor MI 48109-6354 Business E-Mail: bjwhite@umich.edu..*

WHITE, BARBARA CLOUD, principal, educator; b. Chester, Pa., Oct. 18, 1952; d. Della Yarnell Cloud; m. Thomas Francis White, June 22, 1991. BA in Elem. and Spl. Edn., West Chester State U., 1974, MS in Reading, 1978; supervisory cert. spl. edn., Pa. State U., King of Prussia, 1985; elem. prin. cert., Pa. State U., Malvern, 1990; EdD, Widener U., 2003. Cert. tchr., Pa. Substitute tchr. Del. County (Pa.) Sch. Dist., 1974-75; elem. tchr. Ridley Sch. Dist., Folsom, Pa., 1975-77, learning support tchr., 1977-92, supr. spl. edn., 1992-94; prin. Lakeview Elem. Sch., Ridley, 1994—. Recipient Educator Yr. award Assn. Retarded Citizens, 1993. Mem. ASCD, Nat. Assn. Elem. Sch. Prins., U.S. Tennis Assn., Kappa Alpha Phi. Avocations: tennis, golf, reading, arts. Home: 800 Avondale Rd Apt 5D Wallingford PA 19086-6667 Office: Ridley Sch Dist 1001 Morton Ave Folsom PA 19033-2997

WHITE, BEVERLY HAWKINS, counseling administrator; b. Gholsonville, Va., Nov. 19, 1956; d. Henry Clarence and Elmer (Jones) Hawkins; m. John Raymond White, Sept. 14, 1991. BS, Va. State U., 1979, MS, 1982. Cert. tchr., Va. Tchr. Mecklenburg County Pub. Schs., South Hill, Va., 1982-85, Brunswick County Pub. Schs., Lawrenceville, Va., 1979-80, 85-88, counselor, 1989—99, ednl. diagnostician, 1999—. Treas. So. Christian Leadership Conf., Emporia, Va., 1991—; active NAACP, Emporia, 1991—. Mem.: NEA, Brunswick Edn. Assn., Va. Edn. Assn. Democrat. Baptist. Avocations: traveling, shopping, cooking, aerobics. Office: Brunswick County Pub Schs PO Box 309 Lawrenceville VA 23868-0309

WHITE, BONNIE YVONNE, management consultant, retired educator; b. Long Beach, Calif., Sept. 4, 1940; d. William Albert and Helen Iris (Harbaugh) W. BS, Brigham Young U., 1962, MS, 1965, EdD in Ednl. Adminstrn., 1976; postgrad., Harvard U., 1987. Tchr. Wilson High Sch., Long Beach, Calif., 1962-63; grad. asst. Brigham Young U., Provo, Utah, 1963-65; instr., dir. West Valley Coll., Saratoga, Calif., 1965-76; instr., evening adminstr. Mission Coll., Santa Clara, Calif., 1976-80; dean gen. edn. Mendocino Coll., Ukiah, Calif., 1980-85; dean instrn. Porterville (Calif.) Coll., 1985-89, dean adminstrv. svc., 1989-93. Rsch. assoc. SAGE Rsch. Internat., Orem, Utah, 1975-99. Mem. AAUW, Faculty Assn. Calif., Cmty. Colls., Calif., Coun. Fine Arts Deans, Assn. Calif. C.C. Adminstrs., Assn. Calif. C.C. Adminstrs. Liberal Arts, Zonta (intern), Soroptimists (intern). Republican. Mem. Lds Ch.

WHITE, CHRISTINE, physical education educator; b. Taunton, Mass., Apr. 1, 1905; d. Peregrine Hastings and Sara (Lawrence) W. Cert., Boston Sch. Phys. Edn.; BS, Boston U., 1935, MEd, 1939. Instr. Winthrop Coll., Rock Hill, S.C., 1927-29; instr., asst. prof. The Woman's Coll. U. N.C., Greensboro, N.C., 1929-41; assoc. prof., head dept. physical edn. Meredith Coll., Raleigh, N.C., 1941-43; assoc. prof., prof. chair dept. physical edn. Wheaton Coll., Norton, Mass., 1943-70, prof. emerita, 1970—. Co-editor Taunton Architecture: A Reflection of the City's History, 1981, 89. Chmn. Hist. Dist. Study Com., 1975-78, Recreation Commn., 1972-81; mem. Hist. Dist. Commn., 1979—, sec., 1979-86, acting chair, 1992-94; mem. Park and Recreation Commn., 1982—; bd. dirs. Star Theatre for the Arts, Inc., 1993—. Fellow AAHPERD; mem. AAUP (pres. Wheaton Coll. chpt. 1960-61), AAUW, LWV, Nat. Assn. Phys. Edn. in Higher Edn., Pi Lambda Theta. Avocations: travelling, historic preservation, theatre, music. Home: PO Box 1005 Berlin MA 01503-2005

WHITE, DAVID OLDS, researcher, former educator; b. Fenton, Mich., Dec. 18, 1921; s. Harold Bancroft and Doris Caroline (Olds) W.; m. Janice Ethel Russell, Sept. 17, 1923; children: John Russell, David Olds Jr., Benjamin Hill BA, Amherst Coll., 1943; MS, U. Mass., 1950; PhD, U. Oreg., 1970. Tchr. human physiology Defiance (Ohio) Coll., summer 1950; sci. tchr. Roosevelt Jr. High Sch., Eugene, Oreg., 1951-52; prin. Glide (Oreg.) High Sch., 1952-56; tchr. Munich Am. Elem. Sch., 1957-69; prin. Wurzburg (Fed. Republic Germany) Am. High Sch., 1959-60, Wertheim (Fed. Republic Germany) Am. Elem. Sch., 1960-61; tchr. Dash Point Elem. Sch., Tacoma, 1961-63, Eugene (Oreg.) Pub. Schs., 1963-81. Internat. rschr. in field. Contbr. articles to profl. publs.; patentee electronic model airplane. Staff sgt. U.S. Army, 1942-45, PTO. Fulbright grantee, 1956-57, 72-73. Mem. NEA, Fulbright Alumni Assn., Phi Delta Kappa. Home: 4544 Fox Hollow Rd Eugene OR 97405-3904

WHITE, DORIS GNAUCK, science educator, biochemical and biophysics researcher; b. Milw., Dec. 24, 1926; d. Paul Benjamin and Johanna (Syring) Gnauck; m. Donald Lawrence White Sr., Oct. 9, 1954 (div. Jan. 1986); children: Stanley, Dean, Victor, Donald Lawrence Jr. BS with honors, U. Wis., 1947, MS, 1949, PhD, 1956. Cert. tchr., Wis. Tchr. agr., chemistry, biology, gen. sci., math. U.S. Army Disciplinary Barracks, Milw., 1946-50; chairperson dept. sci. Waunakee (Wis.) High Sch., 1950-51; 4-H leader extension div. USDA, Wis., 1950-56; tchr. prof. U. Wis. Lab. High Sch., Madison, 1951-56; grad. teaching asst. health, rural, adult edn. U. Wis., Madison, 1951-56; prof. sci. edn., curriculum and instrn. William Paterson U., Wayne, N.J., from 1957; sci. teaching specialist Frankford (N.J.) Twp. Schs., 1962. Steering com. N.J. Sci. Conv., 1977—; coll. liaison, N.J. Acad. Sci. liaison N.J. Sci. Suprs., 1979—; sr. faculty and grand marshal William Paterson U., 1992—; NSF Statewide Systemic Initiatives for N.J., 1992—, Eisenhower Profl. Devel. program Belleville (N.J.) Pub. Schs., 1992-94, Vernon (N.J.) Pub. Schs., Elmwood Park (N.J.) Pub. Schs.; participant N.J. Sci. and Math. Coalition NSF grant, 1993—; judge Seiko Youth Challenge, 1994, Hudson Co. Sci. Fair, 1994-96; R&D judge 100 top internat. inventions, 1994; mentor for handicapped scientists AAAS, 1995—; active N.J. Sci. Core Curriculum Stds., Trenton, 1997, N.J. Agrl. Edn. Core Curriculum Stds., Trenton, 1998. Mem. nat. sci. tchrs. manuscript rev. panel Jour. Coll. Sci. Teaching, 1991-94. Active 4-H Club Leadership, Morristown, N.J., 1968— (N.J. 4-H Club Alumni award 1991), Geraldine Rockefeller Dodge Found. Animal Shelter, Madison, N.J., 1968—, St. Hubert's Giralda; vol. for poor and homeless of Paterson, N.J., 1971—; lic. blood tester for salmonella/fowl typhoid USDA, 1987—; mem. panel on curriculum improvement N.J. Commr. Edn., 1990-91, program com. N.J. Sci. Conv., 1978—, sex equality com. N.J. Dept. Edn., 1987, Sci. Core Proficiencies Panel, 1994-97, N.J. Sci. Coalition, 1989—; judge presdl. candidates for N.J. schs. N.J. Dept. Edn., Trenton, 1985-88; judge sci. fairs Carteret, N.J., 1991, 92, N.J. Sci. Olympiad, 1993, 95—, SEER Morristown, 1986-92, Haledon, N.J., 1957-60, Atlantic County 4-H, N.J., 1995-96, Hudson County Sci. Fair, N.J., 1994-96, numerous other local, county and state fairs; trustee N.J. Sci. Suprs. Assn. Named Outstanding Woman of Hunterdon County, N.J., 2000; recipient Silver medals, Nat. Garden Inst., 1947, 1948, Liberty Hyde Bailey Hort. medal, Cornell U., Ithaca, N.Y., 1947, Gen. Douglas McArthur Hort. medal, Nat. Garden Inst., 1947, Educator award, Am. Cancer Soc., N.J., 1967, Meth. Layleader award, 1995; grantee Dyes Rsch. grant, William Paterson U. Alumni Found., 1989—90, NSF. Fellow: N.J. Sci. Tchrs. Assn. (exec. bd. from 1978, indsl. liaison com. 1990—92, Citation Scroll award 2001); mem.: Franklin-Ogdensburg Mineral. Soc., N.J. Marine Edn. Assn., Outstanding N.J. Earth Sci. Tchrs. Assn., N.J. Sci. Tchrs. Assn., Coun. Elem. Sci. N.J., N.J. Sci. Suprs. Assn. (exec. bd. from 1979, pres. 1981), N.J. Sci. Edn. Leadership Assn., Am. Poultry Assn. (life; lic. judge from 1948), N.J. Earth Sci. Edn. Assn., N.J. Acad. Sci. (chair sci. edn. divsn. 1990—95, liaison to sci. tchrs. from 1992, judge from 1990), Nat. Sci. Leadership Assn., Nat. Sci. Suprs. Assn. (Outstanding Sci. Supr. award 1986, Pres.'s award 1992), Nat. Sci. Tchrs. Assn., Am. Chem. Soc. (Poster Contest judge from 1948), Liberty Sci. Mus. (charter), Sterling Hill Mining Mus., Am. Mus. Natural History. Republican. Methodist. Achievements include research in chromosome mapping of domestic fowl; development of 2 new varieties of winter squash which are now commercial varieties; development of penguin-like ducks, research in poultry genetics, genetics of Cucurbitaceae, ultrasound treatment of seeds concerning effects on seed germination and plant growth; using helium-neon lasers for holographic interferometry to measure plant growth occurring in seconds measured in wavelengths of light, growth regulators on flowers for parthenogenesis and for polyploidy; development of new variety of cat, herpes virus research with fowl, experiments with leaf berms for highway sound barriers; recycling waste tires stuffed with grass clippings for highway median strips covered with leaf compost; investigation of turkey head ornament colors as indicators of contentment or stress, turkey head color ornament color changes during courtship and copulation, catatonic effects in domestic fowl; design of portable methane generator, design of wave action and tidal pumps to transport glacial melt; suggested uses for incinerator ash, pollution caused by fireworks, Bernoulli's theorem as applied to bird flight, plausibility of human virgin births by cloning; improved cellular phone communication, global warming, greenhouse effect, effect of ocean floor heat vents as cause of El Nino. Home: Wake Forest, NC. Died Nov. 19, 2001.

WHITE, EDITH ROBERTA SHOEMAKE, elementary school educator; b. Hattiesburg, Miss., Feb. 24, 1948; d. Robert Ellis and Helen C.M. (Hinton) Shoemake; m. Robert Q. White, May 31, 1992 (dec. Sept. 2000). Student, Perkinston (Miss.) Jr. Coll., 1968; BS, U. So. Miss., 1970, MA, 1985. Cert. elem. tchr., Miss. Tchr. Ouachita Parish Schs., Monroe, La., Meridian (Miss.) City Schs., Lauderale County Schs., Meridian, Perry County Schs., New Augusta, Miss.; mid. sch. tchr. Hancock County Schs., Bay St. Louis, Miss., Pass Christian (Miss.) Pub. Schs. Dist. Mem. NEA, Miss. Assn. Educators. Methodist. Home: 124 Clower Ave Long Beach MS 39560-3302

WHITE, FLORENCE MAY, learning disabilities specialist; b. Ottawa, Kans., Sept. 1, 1936; d. O.C. Robert and Effie Lynne (Walker) Arnold; m. Donald L. White, June 1, 1958 (dec. Jan. 1996); children: Tab Vincent, Jacque Sue, Michelle May. BA, Ottawa U., 1958; MS, Kans. U., 1974; postgrad., Kans. U. Med. Ctr., 1975-76. Cert. reading specialist, learning disabilities specialist; cert. elem. and mid. sch. edn.: lang. arts, social studies, elem. curriculum. Classroom tchr. 2d grade Wellsville (Kans.) Elem., 1958-59; learning disabilities tchr. Olatha (Kans.) Spl. Edn. Coop., 1971-74; learning disabilities specialist, tchr. 7-9 Ottawa Mid. Sch., 1974-77; learning disabilities specialist, tchr. Paola Spl. Edn. Coop., Richmond, Kans., 1980-95; tchr. learning disabilities classes elem. level Ctrl. Heights Elem. Sch., Richmond, Kans., 2001—02. Pub. rep., speaker on learning disabilities to civic groups and local orgns., 1972-75. Den mother Boy Scouts Am. and Brownies, Ottawa, 1968-70; chair state GOP women's polit. activities Rep. State Party, Topeka, 1964-67; chair scholarship contest DAR, Ottawa dist., 1984-96; Sunday sch. tchr. Meth. Ch., Ottawa; crafts tchr. local 4-H, Ottawa; mem. Central Heights PTA (projects com. 1980-95); mem. Ottawa Arts Coun. State of Kans. scholar State Spl. Edn. Dept., 1976. Mem. Internat. Reading Assn., Kans. Reading Assn., Franklin County Reading Coun. (exec. bd. 1993-94, v.p., pres.-elect 1989-91, pres. 1991-92), PEO, Alpha Delta Kappa (projects com. 1988—, environment com., hospitality com.). Roman Catholic. Avocations: oil painting, reading, travel, music, flower arranging.

WHITE, FRANCES LAVONNE, academic administrator; b. Houston, Oct. 15, 1947; d. John Wesley Jr. and Irma Johnetta (Porter) Williams; m. Harley Sr. White, Dec. 22, 1971; 1 child, Ivan Whitney. AA in Edn., Merritt Coll., 1968; BS in Psychology, Calif. State U., Hayward, 1970, MS in Counseling and Psychology, 1972; PhD in Edn., U. Calif., Berkeley, 1990. Instr. psychology Peralta Colls., Oakland, Calif., 1980—90, dir. staff devel., 1990—91; dean social scis., arts, phys. edn. Laney Coll., Oakland, 1991—94, Evergreen Valley Coll., San Jose, Calif., 1994—96; interim chancellor San Jose/Evergreen Colls., 1996; exec. vice chancellor City Coll., San Francisco, 1996—99; pres. Skyline Coll., San Bruno, Calif., 1999—. Mem. Oakland Citizen's Adv. Bd., 1986—88; pres., bd. dirs. Adminstrs. Calif. C.C. Assn., Sacramento, 1994—2000; chmn. bd. dirs. Families on Track, South San Francisco, Calif., 1999—; mem. leadership com. United Way, San Mateo County, Calif., 2000—01; mem. cmty. adv. bd. Seton Med. Ctr., Daly City, Calif., 1999—; bd. dirs. C.C. League Calif., Sacramento, 1999—2000. Named Educator of Yr., Iota Phi Lambda, 2001; recipient Tom Lakin Leadership award, Calif. C.C. Africa American Trustees, 1997. Mem.: AAUW, San Bruno Rotary (bd. dirs. 1999—, Mem. of Yr. 2001). Avocations: reading, bicycling, singing, walking, meditation. Office: Skyline Coll 3300 College Ave San Bruno CA 94066

WHITE, GEORGE EDWARD, law educator, lawyer; b. Northampton, Mass., Mar. 19, 1941; s. George LeRoy and Frances Dorothy (McCafferty) W.; m. Susan Valre Davis, Dec. 31, 1966; children: Alexandra V., Elisabeth McC. BA, Amherst Coll., 1963; MA, Yale U., 1964, PhD, 1967; JD, Harvard U., 1970. Bar: D.C. 1970, Va. 1975, U.S. Supreme Ct. 1973. Vis. scholar Am. Bar Found., 1970-71; law clk. to Chief Justice Warren U.S. Supreme Ct., 1971-72; asst. prof. law U. Va., 1972-74, assoc. prof., 1974-77, prof., 1977-86, John B. Minor prof. law and history, 1987—2003, disting. univ. prof., John B. Minor prof. law and history, 1992—2003, David and Mary Harrison disting. prof. law, 2003—. Vis. prof. Marshall-Wythe Law Sch. spring 1988, N.Y. Law Sch., fall 1988. Author books, including: The American Judicial Tradition, 1976, 2d edit., 1988, Tort Law in America: An Intellectual History (gavel award ABA 1981), 1980, ed edit., 2003, Earl Warren: A Public Life (gavel award ABA 1983), 1982, The Marshall Court and Cultural Change, 1988, 2d edit., 1991 (James Willard Hurst prize 1990), Justice Oliver Wendell Holmes: Law and the Inner Self, 1993 (gavel award ABA 1994, Scribes award, 1994, Littleton-Griswold prize 1994, Triennial Order of the Coif award 1996), Intervention and Detachment: Essays in Legal History and Jurisprudence, 1994; Creating the National Pastime: Baseball Transforms Itself, 1903-1953, 1996, The Constitution and The New Deal, 2000; editor Studies in Legal History, 1980-86, Delegate in Law, Oxford U. Press, 1986-97. Mem. AAAS, Am. Law Inst., Am. Soc. Legal History (bd. dirs. 1978-81), Soc. Am. Historians. Office: Law Sch U Va Charlottesville VA 22903-1789 E-mail: gew@virginia.edu.

WHITE, GLADYS HOPE FRANKLIN, reading specialist; b. Elizabeth City, N.C., Mar. 22; d. Elbert and Pearl (Smithwick) Franklin; m. Frank Hollowell White, Apr. 12, 1941; children: Johnese Armelda, Sharon Faye. BS, Hampton Inst. U., 1939; MA, Columbia U., 1949; EdD, U. Sarasota, 1978. Elem. tchr. and music Brawley H.S., Scotland Neck, N.C., 1939-41; elem. critic tchr. Elizabeth City Pub. Schs., elem. tchr., music tchr. P.W. Moore H.S.; coll. edn. reading specialist Tex. Coll., Tyler; Jeanes supr. Currituck/Camden Pub. Schs., elem. supr., Wake County Pub. Schs., Raleigh, N.C.; assoc. prof. edn. and reading N.C. Agrl. and Tech. U., Greensboro, N.C., 1962-82; founder, dir. project CARE Episcopal Ch. of the Redeemer, Greensboro, 1983—. Dir. tchr. tng. inst. Nat. Def. Edn. Inst., Greensboro, 1965-68; tech. asst. reading lang. U.S. Right to Read Program, U.S. Edn. Dept., Wilmington, Del.; cons., workshop founder. Project Care exec. bd. Episcopal Ch. of Redeemer, Greensboro, N.C., 1982—; mem. Pres. Clinton's Exec. Coun. com., 1996-98; mem. Dem. Congrl. Campaign com., Washington, 1998; mem. Friends Chavis Learning Libr., Greensboro, 1982—. Mem. Internat. Reading Assn. (life, chair paraprofls., reading com.), Nat. Assn. of Bus. Profl. Womens Clubs (corr. sec., chair archives, chair scholarship com. 1960-92), Hampton U. Alumni Assn. (pres. emeritus 1990—, Greensboro chpt. past pres., Trendsetter award 1995), Lady Sertoma (life), Delta Sigma Theta (Delta Diamond award 1988, Leadership award 1991), Kappa Delta Phi. Democrat. Episcopalian. Avocations: tutoring, mentoring, sewing, crafts, reading. Home: 1206 E Side Dr Greensboro NC 27406-2149 Office: Episcopal Ch of the Redeeemer 901 E Friendly Ave Greensboro NC 27401-3103

WHITE, GLORIA WATERS, retired university administrator; b. May 16, 1934; d. James Thomas and Thelma Celestine (Brown) W.; m. W. Glenn White, Jan. 1, 1955; 1 child, Terry Anita White Glover. BA, Harris Tchrs. Coll., 1956; MA, Washington U., St. Louis, 1963; LLM, Washington U., 1980; cert. in orgnl. devel., Harvard U., 1999. Accredited exec. in pers., sr. profl. in human resources; cert. life counselor, life tchr. Tchr. St. Louis Bd. Edn., 1956-63, counselor, 1963-67; dir. office spl. projects Washington U., 1967-76, asst. to assoc. vice chancellor pers. and affirmative action, 1975-88, vice chancellor for pers., affirmative action officer, 1988-91, vice chancellor human resources, 1991-97, vice chancellor emerita, 1997—. Author: Profiles of Success in the Human Resource Management Profession, 1991. Bd. dirs. Am. Assn. Affirmative Action, 1974-77; instl. chair Arts and Edn. Fund, 1975-88; mem. Ea. Dist. Mo. Desegregation and Adv. Com., 1981-82; bd. trustees Blue Cross/Blue Shield of Mo., 1984-96, chmn., 1994-96, bd. dirs. right choice alliance, 1995—; bd. dirs. The Caring Found., 1989-98, vice chmn., 1993-96, chmn., 1996-98; adv. bd. Tchrs. Ins. Annuity Assn., 1988-91; bd. dirs. bi state chpt. officer ARC, 1989—, chmn., 1994-96, mem. north cen. regional com., 1996—, chmn. north cen. region, 1997-00; bd. dirs. Cath. Charities, 1993-94, YWCA Met. St. Louis, 1993-94, Goodwill Industries of Mo., 1994-00; active Sheldon Arts Found., 1984—, chmn. ann. fund, 1995, chmn., 1998—; chmn. Woodie award St. Louis Black Repertory Co., 1996—; bd. dirs. United Way Greater St. Louis, 1997—, exec. com., 1998—; bd. overseers Cen. Inst. for the Deaf, 1997—; bd. dirs. Girls Inc., 1997—, Repertory Theatre, 1997—, Opera Theatre of St. Louis, 1999—, Women of Achievement, 1996-99; bd. trustees Art Mus., 1999—. Recipient citations Urban League, Pres.'s award Harris State Coll., 1987, Dollars and Sense award, 1992, Clara Barton Vol. Svc. award ARC, 1993, Women of Achievement award, 1995, Martin Luther King Disting. Svc. State award, 1996, Homecoming award Habitat for Humanity, 1996, Salute to Excellence award Lifetime Achievement award, 1998, SHERO award Coalition of 100 Black Women, 1999, Founders award Fontbonne Coll., 1999, St. Louis Variety Woman of Yr. award, 2000. Mem. Coll. and Univ. Pers. Assn. (bd. dirs. 1981-88, pres. 1986-87, 87-88, v.p., Creativity award 1981, Disting. Svc. award 1988, Kathryn G. Hansen Publs. award 1989), Am. Soc. Pers. Adminstrn., Pers. Accreditation Inst. (bd. dirs.), St. Louis Symphony Soc. (exec. com., chmn. outreach com.), Delta Sigma Theta (v.p. St. Louis Alumnae chpt. 1989-91, nat. social action commr. 1988-92, pres. St. Louis Alumnae chpt. 1991-93, chmn. exec. bd., chmn. Blitz Build habitat for humanity 1994, chmn. 42d conv. 1994, dir. leadership acad. 1994-96, regional leadership team 1999—), Links, Inc. (Archway chpt. 1996—, exec. com., v.p., chmn. edn. com., chmn. membership com.). Roman Catholic. Home: 545 Delprice Ct Saint Louis MO 63124-1912 Office: Washington Univ 1 Brookings Dr PO Box 1184 Saint Louis MO 63188-1184

WHITE, HELEN FRANCES PEARSON, language educator, real estate broker; b. Bucoda, Mo., Sept. 26, 1925; d. William Sidney and Ella Myrtle Isaccs) Pearson; m. Jewel Porter White, June 21, 1942; children: Sydney LaVergne, Betty Ann, John Patrick. BA, Ark. State U., 1955; postgrad., U. Toulouse, 1965, U. Okla., 1962-64, U. Mex., 1966, Tex. A&M U., 1969; credited study tour on Creole Lang., Tex. A&M, 1969. Life time teaching lic. Mo., Tex., lic. real estate broker, lic. 1st class radio engr., FCC. High sch. English tchr., Manila, Ark., 1955-57; high sch. English, French tchr. New Madrid, Mo., 1958-63; Spanish, French tchr. Hardin Jefferson High Sch., Sour Lake, Tex., 1964-71; cons., instr. Radio Stas. KKAS & KWDX, Silsbee, Tex., 1969—; broker Accent Corner Real Estate, Silsbee, 1981—. Tour dir. Robbins Ednl. Tours, Marquand, Mo., 1957-64, Whites' Tours, Silsbee, 1968—; host family, S.E. Tex. area rep. Youth for Understanding, 1968-75; workshop participant, job tng. instr., Programs for Human Svcs., 1981-84; pvt. lang. tutor, Portageville, Mo., Silsbee. Preservationist Hist. Landmark, 1991 (Tex. Hist. Commn. award for Old Silsbee Ice House); mem. Concept of Care, Kountze, Tex., 1985-88, Hardin County Tourist Bur.; charter commr. S.E. Tex. Women's Commn., 1985-88; coun. mem. County Assn. for Retarded Persons, Silsbee, 1986-89; pres. Silsbee Libr. Adv. Bd., 1986; founder, pres. Hardin County Arts and Ednl. Found., 1987—; mem. First Meth. Ch. Grantee Tex. A&M U., 1969. Mem. AAUW (life, pres. Hardin County br. 1983-86), Hardin County Geneal. Soc., Alpha Delta Kappa. Avocations: philatelist, numismatist, writing, art appreciation. Home: 1900 J P White Dr Silsbee TX 77656-7512 Office: Accent Corner Real Estate Highway 327 W Silsbee TX 77656

WHITE, JAMES BOYD, law educator; b. Boston, July 28, 1938; s. Benjamin Vroom and Charlotte Green (Conover) W.; m. Mary Louise Fitch, Jan. 1, 1978; children: Emma Lillian, Henry Alfred; children by previous marriage: Catherine Conover, John Southworth. AB, Amherst Coll., 1960; AM, Harvard U., 1961, LLB, 1964. Assoc. Foley, Hoag & Eliot, Boston, 1964-67; asst. prof. law U. Colo., 1967-69, assoc. prof., 1969-73, prof., 1973-75; prof. law U. Chgo., 1975-83; Hart Wright prof. law and English U. Mich., Ann Arbor, 1983—. Vis. assoc. prof. Stanford U., 1972 Author: The Legal Imagination, 1973, (with Scarboro) Constitutional Criminal Procedure, 1976, When Words Lose Their Meaning, 1981, Heracles' Bow, 1985, Justice as Translation, 1990, "This Book of Starres", 1994, Acts of Hope, 1994, From Expectation to Experience, 1999, The Edge of Meaning, 2001. Sinclair Kennedy Traveling fellow, 1964-65; Nat. Endowment for Humanities fellow, 1979-80, 92; Guggenheim fellow, 1993; vis. scholar Phi Beta Kappa, 1997-98. Mem. AAAS, Am. Law Inst. Office: U Mich Law Sch 625 S State St Ann Arbor MI 48109-1215

WHITE, JANE, special education educator; b. Metuchen, N.J., Mar. 13, 1961; d. Leo A. and Marilyn C. (Sbarro) McClusky; m. William H. White. BS in Spl. Edn., Millersville (Pa.) U., 1983; MA, Montclair State U., 1988. Tchr. spl. edn. Hanover (N.J.) Park High Sch. Office: Hanover Park HS 65 Mt Pleasant Ave East Hanover NJ 07936

WHITE, JANET KELLY, english educator, secondary school educator; b. Phila., Sept. 5, 1967; d. Robert Noon and Sofia Rose (De Lucia) Kelly; m. Richard White, June 21, 1992. BS in Edn., U. Tex., 1989. Tchr. of English, reading Fort Worth Ind. Sch. Dist., 1989-91; tchr. of English Trinity Valley Sch., Ft. Worth, 1991—. Mem. Ft. Worth Dog Tng. Club. Roman Catholic. Avocations: English horseback riding, dog obedience tng., reading. Home: 10532 Del Mar Ct Benbrook TX 76126-4506 Office: Trinity Valley Sch 7500 Dutch Branch Rd Fort Worth TX 76132-4110

WHITE, JOHN AUSTIN, JR., engineering educator, university chancellor; b. Portland, Ark., Dec. 5, 1939; s. John Austin and Ella Mae (McDermott) W.; m. Mary Elizabeth Quarles, Apr. 13, 1963; children: Kimberly Elizabeth White Brakmann, John Austin III. BS in Indsl. Engring., U. Ark., 1962; MS in Indsl. Engring., Va. Poly. Inst., 1966; PhD, Ohio State U., 1969; PhD (hon.), Cath. U. of Leuven, Belgium, 1985, George Washington U., 1991. Registered profl. engr., Va. Indsl. engr. Tenn. Eastman Co., Kingsport, 1961-63, Ethyl Corp., Baton Rouge, 1965; instr. Va. Poly. Inst. and State U., Blacksburg, 1963-66, asst. prof., 1970-72, assoc. prof., 1972-75; tchg. assoc. Ohio State U., Columbus, 1966-70; assoc. prof. Ga. Inst. Tech., Atlanta, 1975-77, prof., 1977-84, Regents' prof., 1984-97, Gwaltney prof., 1988-97, dean engring., 1991-97; disting. prof. indsl. engring., chancellor U. Ark., Fayetteville, 1997—. Asst. dir. engring. NSF, 1988-90, acting dir., 1990-91; founder, chmn. SysteCon Inc., Duluth, Ga., 1977-84; exec. cons. Coopers & Lybrand, N.Y.C., 1984-93; mem. mfg. studies bd. NRC, Washington, 1986-88; bd. dirs. Russell Corp., Eastman Chem. Co., Motorola Corp., Logility Inc., J.B. Hunt Transport, Inc.; pres. Nat. Consortium for Grad. Degrees for Minorities in Engring. and Sci., Inc., 1993-95; bd. dirs. Nat. Collegiate Athletic Assn.; mem. exec. com. NCAA, 2003—; apptd. U.S. del. to the Internat. Steering Com. of the Intelligent Mfg. System, 1995-97; mem. Nat. Sci. Bd., 1994—; pres. S.E. Conf., 2002—; v.p. Malcolm Baldrige Nat Quality Award Found., 2002-03. Co-author: Facility Layout and Location: An Analytical Approach, 1974 (Book of Yr. award Inst. Indsl. Engrs. 1974), 2d edit., 1991, Analysis of Queueing Systems, 1975, Principles of Engineering Economic Analysis, 4th edit., 1998, Capital Investment Decision Analysis for Management and Engineering, 1980, 3d edit., 2003, Facilities Planning, 1984 (Book of Yr. award Inst. Indsl. Engrs. 1984), 2d edit., 1996; editor: Production Handbook, 1987; co-editor: Progress in Materials Handling and Logistics, Vol. 1, 1989; also numerous articles to profl. jours., chpts. to books and handbooks in field, conf. procs. Recipient Outstanding Tchr. award Ga. Inst. Tech., 1982, Disting. Alumnus award Ohio State U. Coll. Engring., 1984, Disting. Indsl. Engring. alumnus award Va. Polytech. Inst. and State U., 1993, Reed-Apple award Material Handling Edn. Found., 1985, Disting. Svc. award NSF, 1991, Rodney D. Chipp Meml. award Soc. Women Engrs., 1994. Fellow Am. Inst. Indsl. Engrs. (pres. 1983-84, facilities planning and design award 1980, outstanding indsl. engr. award region III 1974, region IV 1984, Albert G. Holzman disting. educator award 1988, outstanding pub. award 1988, David F. Baker disting. rsch. award 1990, Frank and Lillian Gilbreth award 1994), Am. Assn. Engring. Socs. (bd. govs., chmn. 1986, Kenneth Andrew Roe award 1989); mem. Nat. Acad. Engring., Ark. Acad. Indsl. Engring., Am. Soc. Engring. Edn. (Donald E. Marlowe award 1994), Internat. Material Mgmt. Soc. (material mgr. of yr. 1989), Soc. Mfg. Engrs. (mfg. educator award 1990), Nat. Soc. Profl. Engrs. Inst. for Ops. Rsch. and the Mgmt. Scis. (hon.), Golden Key, Sigma Xi, Alpha Pi Mu, Omicron Delta Kappa, Phi Kappa Phi, Tau Beta Pi, Omega Rho. Baptist. Avocations: reading, golf, writing. Office: Chancellor U Ark Office of the Chancellor 425 Administration Bldg Fayetteville AR 72701

WHITE, JUNE MILLER, mathematics educator, educational consultant; b. E. Bernstadt, Ky., June 13, 1938; d. James Fulton and Ida Mae (Hansel) Miller; m. Richard Allen White, Aug. 27, 1960; children: Jennifer Lynn, Richard Allen Jr. BS with high honors, Denison U., 1960; MA, U. Rochester, 1969; PhD, Bryn Mawr Coll., 1980. Engring. asst. AT&T, Kansas City, Mo., 1960-61; math. tchr. William Chrisman H.S., Independence Pub. Schs., Independence, Mo., 1961-62, Brighton (N.Y.) H.S., 1962-69, Conestoga H.S., Tredyffrin-Easttown Pub. Schs., Berwyn, Pa., 1970-72; chair math. dept. Hill Top Prep. Sch., Rosemont, Pa., 1972-76, curriculum coord., 1976-81; instr. math. St. Petersburg Jr. Coll., Clearwater, Fla., 1982-84, dir. math. program, 1984—2002, prof. math. edn., 2002—. Presenter at various confs. Author: A Collection of Mathematics Applications for College Students, 1989; editor SPECTRUM, 1983-95; contbr. articles to profl. jours. Elder Northwood Presbyn. Ch., Clearwater, 1986-90; chmn. blood drive ARC, King of Prussia, Pa., 1973-74; chmn. citizens adv. com. Upper Merion Pub. Schs., King of Prussia, 1975-76. Mem. Am. Math. Assn. of Two Yr. Colls., Math. Assn. Am. (v.p. Fla. and Caribbean sect. 1988-91, sec. 1994-99, pres.-elect 1999, pres. 2000), Nat. Coun. Tchrs. Math., Fla. Assn. Cmty. Colls., Rsch. Coun. for Diagnostic and Prescriptive Math., Pinellas County Assn. for Children and Adults with Learning Disabilities (bd. dirs. 1987-88), Phi Beta Kappa. Avocations: camping, sailing, travel. Home: 4951 Bacopa Ln S Unit 103 Saint Petersburg FL 33715-2617 E-mail: whitejune@spjc.edu.

WHITE, LEON SAMUEL, college administrator; b. West Palm Beach, Fla., Mar. 31, 1946; s. Edward Julius and Carmeta Francis (Ferguson) W.; m. Anne Fryer, Sept. 29, 1969; children: Nigel, Kanika Pele. BS, Tuskegee Inst., 1969, MEd, 1973; PhD, Ohio State U., 1976; cert. in journalism, Columbia U., 1970. Rsch. assoc. Ohio State U., Columbus, 1974—76; coord. counseling St. Augustine's Coll., Raleigh, NC, 1976—77, dean of students, 1977—81, Savannah (Ga.) State Coll., 1981—84; vice chancellor student affairs Elizabeth City (N.C.) State U., 1984—96; ednl. cons. Thomas White, PA Consultants, West Palm Beach, 1996-97, Hertford, NC, 1996—97; v.p. student affairs Cheyney U. of Pa., 1997-2000; counselor Elizabeth City (N.C.) Middle Sch., 2000—01, RCCDC YouthBuild Program, Elizabeth City, 2001—. Contbr. articles to profl. jours. Psychol. cons. Franklin County Drug Treatment Program, Columbus, Ohio, 1975-76; mentor Boys Club of Raleigh, 1978-81; vol. counselor Tidelands Cmty. Mental Health, Savannah, 1982-84. Tuskegee Inst. scholar, 1963, grad. internship, 1971. Mem. So. Assn. Coll. Student Pers., Nat. Assn. Pers. Workers, Am. Assn. Counseling and Devel., Phi Delta Kappa. Democrat. Methodist. Avocations: writing, gardening, swimming, tennis, running. Home: PO Box 2502 Elizabeth City NC 27906-2502 Office: RCCDC YouthBuild 303 W Ehringhaus St Elizabeth City NC 27909 E-mail: dr_leonswhitee@hotmail.com.

WHITE, LESLIE MILES, parochial school educator; BS in Gen. Studies, So. Oreg. Coll., 1965; MS in Edn., Portland State U., 1971; EdD, Pacific Western U., 1988; postgrad. in Ednl. Policy and Mgmt., U. Oreg. Cert. standard adminstr., K-12, elem./secondary tchr., Oreg., elem./secondary tchr., Wash. Tchr. Saint Cecilia Sch., Beaverton, Oreg., 1966-75; prin. St. Anthony Sch., Tigard, Oreg., 1975-78; chmn. social sci. dept. St. Mary of Valley High Sch., Beaverton, 1978-87, dean of acad., 1987-89; chmn. computer sci. dept. Valley Cath. High Sch., Beaverton, 1989-98; prin. Valley Catholic Middle Sch., Beaverton, 1997-98, St. Therese Sch., Portland, Oreg., 1998—. Contbg. author: Archdiocese School Policy Handbook, others. Fax: 503-281-2817.

WHITE, LINDA JACKSON, remedial reading educator; b. Orlando, Fla., Apr. 25, 1953; d. Charlie and Elnora (Slade) Jackson; m. Ernest Carlos White, Oct. 12, 1979; children: Diane, Ernest Jr., Jason. BS, Bethune-Cookman Coll., 1975. Cert. tchr., Fla. Substitute tchr. Orange County Schs., Orlando, 1975, tchr., 1975—. Verbal skills instr. Naval. Tng. Ctr., Orlando. Mem. Orange County Adult and Community Edn. Assn. (bd. dirs. 1991—), Orange County Tchrs. Assn., Adult and Community Edn. Assn. (Tchr. of Yr. 1993-94), Fla. Literacy Coalition, Zeta Phi Beta. Democrat. Baptist. Avocations: singing, reading, sewing, danc. Office: Winter Park Adult Vocat Ctr 901 W Webster Ave Winter Park FL 32789-3049

WHITE, LYNDA GAYLE, reading specialist, educational diagnostician; b. Gatesville, Tex., Mar. 11, 1943; d. Dee and Myrtle (Dunlap) White; divorced; children: Melanie Gayle, William Matthew. BS, U. Tex., 1964; MA, U. North Tex., 1979, PhD, 1983, postgrad., 1993, 94, Tex. Womans U., 1983. Cert. elem. tchr., spl. edn. tchr., supervision, spl. edn. supr., learning disabilities tchr., orthpedically handicapped tchr., reading specialist, Tex., adminstrs., ednl. diagnostician. Tchr. 2d and 4th grades, spl. edn. tchr. Irving (Tex.) Ind. Sch. Dist., 1964-79, tchr., 1982-83; 4th grade tchr. Northwest Ind. Sch. Dist., Justin, Tex., 1980-81; asst. prin. Grapevine-Colleyville Ind. Sch. Dist., Tex., 1983-87; tchr. reading improvement Carrollton (Tex.)-Farmers Branch Ind. Sch. Dist., 1988-89; cons. lang. arts Edn. Svc. Ctr. Region 10, Richardson, Tex., 1989-91; pvt. practice diagnostic reading and ednl. diagnostician Trophy Club, Tex., 1991—. Reading clinician N.Tex. State U., Denton, 1980; instr. spl. edn. U. Tex., Dallas, 1983, U Tex., Arlington, 1988; vis. prof. Tex. Women's U., Denton, 1983, 84, 87-88; h.s. resource tchr., 1997-98; diagnostician, Hillsboro, Tex., 1999; tchr. homebound handicapped, Hillsboro, 1999-2000, Irving (Tex.) Ind. Sch. Dist., 2000—; adj. developmental writing tchr. North Lake Coll., Irving, 2001—; adj. prof. reading Technique Tarrant County Coll., Tex. Author: Matt's Cats; contbr. Reading Rsch. Revisited, also revs. to Case Mgmt. Monthly Confs., Scottish Rite Hosp. and profl. jours. Facilitator Helping One Student To Succeed Reading Program, Copperas Cove, Tex. Mem. ASCD, Internat. Reading Assn. (North Tex. coun.), Learning Disabilities of Tex., Orton Disability Soc., Coun. for Exceptional Children, Phi Delta Kappa. Home: 6313 Circle Trl Fort Worth TX 76135-2412 also: 855 E Ash #613 Euless TX 76039 E-mail: lyndawhite@irvingi.s.d.tenet.edu.

WHITE, MARJORIE MARY, retired elementary school educator; b. LaCrosse, Wis., May 10, 1944; d. Knute Emil and Florence Catherine (Frederich) Johnson; m. David James White, July 6, 1985; stepchildren: Christopher Howard, Wendy Marie White Ehnert. BSE, Winona State U., 1966, MSEd, 1971. Cert. elem. tchr., Minn. Tchr. Lacrosse Cath. Schs., Wis., 1966-68, Winona County Schs., Dakota, Minn., 1968-72, Ind. Sch.

Dist., Winona, Minn., 1972—2001. Mem. NEA, AAUW (treas. 1990-92, membership co-chair 2001-03, mem.-at-large 2003—), Minn. Edn. Assn., Winona Edn. Assn. (faculty rep. 1970-96, membership chmn. 1986-96), Phi Delta Kappa (newsletter editor 1988-89, 94-98, del. 1985-91, 94-96, v.p. membership 1989-91, Svc. Key award 1991), Delta Kappa Gamma (sec. 2002--). Democrat. Roman Catholic. Avocations: needlework, hiking, gardening, reading, travel. Home: 705 W Wabasha St Winona MN 55987-2764

WHITE, MARY GEORGE, business, economics educator; b. N.Y.C. m. Charles E. White, Jr., June 20; children: Ann Marie, Cheryl, Ashley. AB in Econs., William and Mary Coll., 1963; BS in Bus. Edn., Norfolk State U., 1988; postgrad., Old Dominion U., 1990—94. Cert. bus. edn., Va. Revenue office Internal Revenue Office, Norfolk, Va., 1963—69; office adminstr. White Engring. Group, Virginia Beach, Va., 1987-91; tchr. bus. Norfolk Pub. Schs., 1988—95; tchr. I.C. Norcom H.S., Portsmouth, Va., 1995—. Mem. Am. Vocat. Assn., Nat. Ednl. Tng. Assn. Greek Orthodox. Avocations: boating, swimming, painting, camping. Home: 612 Mossycup Dr Virginia Beach VA 23462-5724 Office: Portsmouth Pub Sch IC Noncum HS 1801 London Blvd Portsmouth VA 23704

WHITE, NANCY G. journalism educator; b. N.Y.C., Oct. 21, 1923; d. John C. and Mamie (Comparetto) Giunta; m. Paul Michael White, June 16, 1946; children: Paul Michael Jr., Nancy Melissa. BA, U. Tampa, 1944; MEd, U. Fla., 1954; Advanced Masters Degree, Fla. State U., 1956. Tchr. journalism, dir. student publs. Hillsborough High Sch., Tampa, Fla., 1952-55; tchr. journalism, newspaper advisor Chamberlain High Sch., Tampa, Fla., 1956-68; tchr. journalism, head English dept., newspaper advisor Plant High Sch., Tampa, Fla., 1968-69; prof. journalism, dir. student publs. Hillsborough C.C., Tampa, Fla., 1969—. Chair profl. devel. Coll. Media Advisors, Inc., 1993-95, chair awards com., 1990-93, pub. rels. chair, 1988-90; mem. U. West Fla. Adv. Coun., Pensacola, 1984—; mem. State Dept. Edn. Common Course Numbering System Com., 1974—. Contbr. articles to profl. jours.; reporter Tallahassee Dem., 1955-57. Newsletter editor Ybor City Mus. Soc., Tampa, 1990-95; pres., newsletter editor Suncoast Aux. U.S. Submarine Vets. WWII, Tampa, 1986-92; mem., newsletter editor Tampa Women's Club, 1973—. Named to Acad. Hall of Fame, Fla. C.C. Activities Assn., 1995, Hall of Fame, Fla. C.C. Press Assn., 1991, Coll. Media Advisers Hall of Fame, 2001; recipient Columbia U. Gold Key, Columbia Scholastic Press Assn., 1971, Disting. Svc. award, Kappa Tau Alpha, 1984, Gold medallion, Fla. Scholastic Press Assn., 1989, Disting. Newspaper Adviser award, Coll. Media Advisers, 1983, Disting. Mag. Adviser award, 1988. Mem. Nat. C.C. Journalism Assn. (pres. 1992-94, named to Hall of Fame 1997), Fla. C.C. Press Assn. (pres. 1971-73, Hall of Fame 1997), Pan Am. Univ. Women (pres.-elect 1996, pres. 1997-97), Fla. Scholastic Press Assn. (pres. 1954-57), Alpha Delta Kappa (pres. 1976-78), Phi Kappa Phi, Kappa Delta Pi, Sigma Delta Chi, Alpha Psi Omega. Democrat. Methodist. Avocations: sailing, travel, reading. Home: 5105 W Homer Ave Tampa FL 33629-7522 Office: Hillsborough C C 2001 N 14th St Tampa FL 33605-3662

WHITE, RAYE MITCHELL, educational administrator; b. Gilmer, Tex., Jan. 21, 1944; d. R.E. and Addie Belle (Collum) Mullican; children: Victoria, William Brett. BS, East Tex. State U., 1966, MS, 1973; EdD, U. Ga., 1984. Cert. tchr., supr., Tex. Tchr. Arabian Oil Co., Ras Tanura, Saudi Arabia, 1978-84; cons. Region VII Edn. Svc. Ctr., Kilgore, Tex., 1985; curriculum dir. Gilmer Ind. Sch. Dist., 1985-87, 92-96; tchr., coord. at-risk mentoring program L.V. Stockard Middle Sch., Dallas, 1987-89; curriculum dir. Chapel Hill Ind. Sch. Dist., Tyler, Tex., 1989-92; part-time prof. U. Tex., Tyler, 1991-93; owner Internat. Golf, Longview and Tyler, Tex., 1996—. Mem. editorial bd. The Reading Tchr., 1987-90. Mem. ASCD, Internat. Reading Assn., Nat. Coun. Tchrs. English, Phi Delta Kappa, Kappa Delta Pi, Delta Kappa Gamma. Home: 1796 Fm 852 Gilmer TX 75644-5094 Office: Internat Golf 2608 Gilmer Rd # 3 Longview TX 75604-1820

WHITE, RAYMOND PETRIE, JR., dentist, educator; b. N.Y.C., Feb. 13, 1937; s. Raymond Petrie and Mabel Sarah (Shutze) White; m. Betty Pritchett, Dec. 27, 1961; children: Karen Elizabeth, Michael Wood. Student, Washington and Lee U., 1955—58; D.D.S., Med. Coll. Va., 1962, PhD, 1967. Diplomate Am. Bd. Oral and Maxillofacian Surgery. Postdoctoral fellow anatomy Med. Coll. Va., Richmond, 1962—67, resident in oral surgery, 1964—67; asst. prof. U. Ky., Lexington, 1967—70, asso. prof., 1970—71, chmn. dept. oral surgery, 1969—71; prof., asst. dean adminstrn. Va. Commonwealth U., Richmond, 1971—74; prof. Sch. Dentistry U. N.C., Chapel Hill, 1974—, Dalton L. McMichael disting. prof., 1993—; dean Sch. Dentistry, U. N.C., Chapel Hill, 1974—81, assoc. dean Sch. Medicine, 1981—92. Mem. staff U. N.C. Hosps., mem. exec. com., 1974—98, sec., 1977—78, assoc. chief staff, 1981—92; mem. adv. panel on dentistry U.S. Pharmacopeial Conv., 1985—; sr. program cons. The Robert Wood Johnson Found., 1982—90. Author (with E.R. Costich): Fundamentals of Oral Surgery, 1971; author: (with Bell and Proffit) Surgical Correction of Dentofacial Deformities, 1980; author: (with W.R. Proffit) Surgical Orthodontic Treatment, 1990; author: (with M.R. Tucker, B.C. Terry, J.E. Van Sickels) Rigid Fixations for Maxillofacial Surgery, 1991; co-editor: Internat. Jour. Adult Orthodontics and Orthodontic Surgery, 1985—2002; asst. editor: Jour. Oral and Maxillofacial Surgery, 1993—; author (with W.R. Profit, R.P. Jr., and D. Sarver): Contemporary Treatment of Dentofacial Deformity, 2002; contbr. sci. articles to profl. jours. Bd. dirs. Am. Fund for Dental Health, 1978—86, v.p., 1982—85. Recipient Disting. Svc. award, Am. Fund Dental Health, 1987, Dental Found. N.C., 1981, John C. Brauer award for acad. distinction, U. N.C. Alumni Assn., 2000, Daniel M. Laskin award, 2002, Rsch. Excellence award, Oral and Maxillofacial Surgery Found., 2003. Mem.: AAAS, ADA, N.C. Assn. Oral and Maxillofacial Surgeons, Am. Assn. Oral and Maxillofacial Surgeons (gen. chmn. sci. sessions com. 1974—76, chmn. strategic planning com. 1990—96, Outstanding Svc. award as committeeman 1976, William Gies award 2000, Disting. Svc. award 2003), Chalmers J. Lyons Acad. Oral Surgery, Inst. Medicine of NAS, Internat. Assn. Dental Rsch. (pres. Ky. sect. 1970), N.C. Dental Soc., Sigma Xi, Omicron Kappa Upsilon, Sigma Zeta, Alpha Sigma Chi, Delta Tau Delta, Psi Omega. Roman Catholic. Home: 1506 Velma Rd Chapel Hill NC 27514-7601 Office: U NC Sch Dentistry Dept Oral/Maxillofacial Surgery Chapel Hill NC 27599-7450

WHITE, RICHARD HUGH, dean student affairs; b. Brigham City, Utah, Dec. 3, 1933; s. Leroy Davis and Maude (Clark) White; m. Donna Mae Wood, Nov. 9, 1952 (dec. Dec. 1972); children: Richard, Marcus; m. Mary Jane Griffin, Mar. 8, 1985; children: Rhonda, Konrad. AS in Edn., Weber State Coll., 1952; BS in Edn., Utah State U., 1956, MS in Edn., 1962; D in Ednl. Adminstrn., U. Utah, 1968. Adminstrv. asst. dept. ednl. adminstrn. U. Utah, Salt Lake City, 1964-65; prin. Granite Sch. Dist., Salt Lake City, 1965-68; asst. supt. schs. Okemos (Mich.) Pub. Schs., 1968-70, Salt Lake City (Utah) Schs., 1970-72; dir. secondary edn. Am. Sch. Found., Mexico City, 1974-76; supt. schs. Pinehill (N.Mex.) Schs., 1976-80; state asst. supt. Wyo. State Dept. Edn., Cheyenne, 1985-88; state deputy supt. Nev. Stae Dept. Edn., Carson City, 1988-89; dir. tchr. edn. Sierra Nev. Coll. Lake Tahoe, Incline Village, Nev., 1989-91, dean student affairs, 1991—. Pres., cons. Educators Resource, Salt Lake City, 1972-74; pres., ptnr. Ednl. Mgmt. Systems, Tucson, 1980-83; fiscal analyst edn. Okla. State Senate, Oklahoma City, 1983-85. Active Rotarian, Murry, Utah, 1968, Lions Club, Price, Utah, 1987; instn. coord. United Fund, Salt Lake City, 1972, Carson City, 1990. Mem. AACD, Am. Assn. Sch. Adminstrs., Calif. Credential Analysts. Mem. Lds Ch. Avocations: computers, golf, writing, geneology. Office: Sierra Nev Coll PO Box 4269 800 College Dr Incline Village NV 89451-9114

WHITE, RICHARD MANNING, electrical engineering educator; b. Denver, Apr. 25, 1930; s. Rolland Manning and Freeda Blanche (Behny) W.; m. Chissie Lee Chamberlain, Feb. 1, 1964 (div. 1975); children: Rolland Kenneth, William Brendan. AB, Harvard U., 1951, AM, 1952, PhD in Applied Physics, 1956. Rsch. assoc. Harvard U., Cambridge, Mass., 1956; mem. tech. staff GE Microwave Lab., Palo Alto, Calif., 1956-63; prof. elec. engring. U. Calif., Berkeley, 1963—, Chancellor's prof., 1996-99. Chmn. Grad. Group on Sci. and Math. Edn., U. Calif. at Berkeley, 1981-85; co-dir. Berkeley Sensor and Actuator Ctr., 1986—, Co-author: Solar Cells: From Basics to Advanced Systems, Microsensors, 1991, Electrical Engineering Uncovered, 1997, Acoustic Wave Sensors, 1997; editor ElectroTechnology Rev.; patentee in field. Guggenheim fellow, 1968. Fellow AAAS, IEEE (Cledo Brunetto award 1986, Achievement award 1988, Disting. lectr. 1989, Cady award 2000); mem. Nat. Acad. Engring., Acoustical Soc. Am., Am. Phys. Soc., Phi Beta Kappa, Sigma Xi. Avocations: photography, hiking, skiing, running, music. Office: U Calif Sensor & Actuator Ctr EECS Dept Ctr Berkeley CA 94720-1774

WHITE, RICHARD NORMAN, civil and environmental engineering educator; b. Chetek, Wis., Dec. 21, 1933; s. Normal Lester and Lorna Elwilda (robinson) W.; m. Margaret Claire Howell, Dec. 28, 1957; children: Barbara Ann, David Charles. BSCE, U. Wis.-Madison, 1956, MS, 1957, PhD, 1961. Registered profl. engr., N.Y. Asst. prof. Cornell U., 1961—65, assoc. prof. civil and environ. engring., 1965-72, prof. structural engring., 1972—, dir. Sch. Civil and Environ. engring., 1978-84, assoc. dean for undergrad. programs, 1987-89, James A. Friend Family prof., 1988—98, prof. emeritus, 1999—; staff assoc. Gulf Gen. Atomic, San Diego, 1967-68. Vis. prof. U. Calif.-Berkeley, 1974-75, U. P.R., Mayaguez, 1982; cons. Def. Nuclear Agy., Washington, 1983-84, Sandia Nat. Lab., Albuquerque, 1981—, Stone & Webster Engring., 1983-87, SRI Internat., Palo Alto, Calif., 1979-83, Bakhtar Assoc., 1988—, Kamtech, 1994-95, numerous others. Author: Structural Engineering, vols. I and II, 1976, vol. III, 1974; Structural Modeling and Experimental Techniques, 1982, Building Structural Design Handbook, 1987; contbr. numerous articles to tech. jours. Served with AUS, 1957. Hon. mem. ASCE (Collingwood prize 1967), Am. Concrete Inst. (Kelly award 1992, Wason medal 1993, Structural Rsch. award 1994, pres. 1997); mem. NAE, Precast/Prestressed Concrete Inst., Sigma Xi, Tau Beta Pi, Chi Epsilon. Republican. Presbyterian. Office: Hollister Hall Cornell U Ithaca NY 14853 E-mail: rnw3@cornell.edu.

WHITE, ROBERT LEE, electrical engineer, educator; b. Plainfield, N.J., Feb. 14, 1927; s. Claude and Ruby Hemsworth Emerson (Levick) W.; m. Phyllis Lillian Arlt, June 14, 1952; children: Lauren A., Kimberly A., Christopher L., Matthew P. BA in Physics, Columbia U., 1949, MA, 1951, PhD, 1954. Assoc. head atomic physics dept. Hughes Rsch. Labs., Malibu, Calif., 1954-61; head magnetics dept. Gen. Tel. and Electronics Rsch. Lab., Palo Alto, Calif., 1961-63; prof. elec. engring., materials sci. and engring. Stanford U., Palo Alto, 1963, chmn. elec. engring. dept., 1981-86, William E. Ayer prof. elec. engring., 1985-88; exec. dir. The Exploratorium, San Francisco, 1987-89; dir. Inst. for Electronics in Medicine, 1973-87, Stanford Ctr. for Rsch. on Info. Storage Materials, 1991—2003. Initial ltd. ptnr. Mayfield Fund, Mayfield II and Alpha II Fund, Rainbow Co-Investment Ptnrs., Halo Ptnrs.; vis. prof. Tokyo U., 1975, Nat. U. Singapore, 2002; cons. in field. Author: (with K.A. Wickersheim) Magnetism and Magnetic Materials, 1965, Basic Quantum Mechanics, 1967; Contbr. numerous articles to profl. jours. With USN, 1945-46. Fellow Guggenheim Oxford U., 1969-70, Canton Hosp., Swiss Fed. Inst. Tech., Zurich, 1977-78, Christensen fellow Oxford U., 1986, IEEE Magnetics Soc. Disting. lectr., 1998; Sony sabbatical chair, 1994; vis. prof. Nat. Univ. Singapore, 2003. Fellow Am. Phys. Soc., IEEE; mem. Sigma Xi, Phi Beta Kappa. Home: 450 El Escarpado Stanford CA 94305-8431 Office: Stanford U Dept Material Sci Engr Stanford CA 94305 E-mail: white@ee.stanford.edu.

WHITE, RONALD JOSEPH, life and biomedical scientist, physiology educator; b. Opelousas, La., Dec. 4, 1940; s. John Wesley and Alma Louise (LaSalle) White; m. Margaret Helen Launey, June 8, 1963; children: Joseph LaSalle, Angela Alma, Margaret Leslie. BS in Chemistry, U. S.W. La., 1963; PhD in Phys. Chemistry, U. Wis., 1968. NSF postdoctoral fellow in theoretical chemistry U. Oxford, Eng., 1967-68; rsch. assoc. Bell Tel. Labs., Murray Hill, N.J., 1968-70; from asst. prof. to assoc. prof. math. U. S.W. La., Lafayette, 1970—76, prof. math., dir. Univ. Honors Program, 1976—80; rsch. assoc. dept. physiology and biophysics U. Miss. Med. Ctr., Jackson, 1973-75; sr. scientist GE Co./Mgmt. and Tech. Svcs. Co., Washington and Houston, 1980-85; chief scientist Life/Biomed. Scis. and Applications Divsn. NASA Life/Biomed. Scis. and Applications Divsn. NASA Hdqs., Washington, 1985—96; rsch. prof. physiology Uniformed Svcs. U. Health Scis., Bethesda, Md., 1985—96; prof. dept. otorhinolaryngology Baylor Coll. Medicine, Houston, 1996—2003; assoc. dir. Nat. Space Biomed. Rsch. Inst., 1997—2003; sr. fellow Univs. Space Rsch. Assn., Houston, 2003—. Editor (assoc. life scis.): Simulation, 1974—75; editor: (spl.) Medicine and Sci. in Sports and Exercise, 1996; contbr. numerous chpts. to books, papers to profl. jours. Vice pres. Assn. Gifted and Talented Students, La, 1977-80; pres. La. Collegiate Honors Coun., 1978-79. Recipient NASA traineeship, 1963-66, Woodrow Wilson fellowship (hon.), 1963, Am. Inst. Chemists award, 1963, Dist. Prof. award, 1978, Med. Info. Processing Best Paper award 15th ann. Hawaii Internat. Conf. on Systems Scis., 1982, Hon. Mem. award Soc. NASA Flight Surgeons, 1992, Exceptional Achievement medal NASA, 1992, IAA Luigi Mapolitano Lit. award, 1996. Mem.: Internat. Acad. Astronautics (bd. trustees 1997—, chair life scis. 2001—, commr. space life scis. 2001—, Napolitano Lit. award 1996), Am. Soc. for Gravitational and Space Biology (charter mem.), Am. Phys. Soc., Aerospace Med. Assn., Sigma Xi (rsch. award 1976), Phi Kappa Phi. Home: 1303 Primrose Ln Seabrook TX 77586-4718 Office: USRA Divsn of Space Life Sciences 3600 Bay Area Blvd Houston TX 77058

WHITE, ROSCOE BERYL, research physicist, educator; b. Freeport, Ill., Dec. 20, 1937; s. Beryl Roscoe and Merlyn (Worth) W.; m. Laura Sanguinet, July 11, 1966; 1 child, Veronica Maria. BS, U. Minn., 1959; PhD, Princeton U., 1963. Rsch. asst. Princeton (N.J.) U., 1962, instr., 1962-63, full prof., 1984—; rsch. assoc. U. Minn., 1963; exch. scientist U.S. Acad. Scis., Lebedev Inst., Moscow, 1963-64; vis. scientist Internat. Ctr. Theoretical Physics, Trieste, Italy, 1964-66; asst. prof. UCLA, 1966-72; mem. Inst. Advanced Study, Princeton, 1972-74; physicist Princeton Plasma Physics Lab., 1974—, prin. rsch. physicist, 1980—, head theory divsn., 1986-93. Vis. lectr. New Delhi U., Udaipur, 1966; vis. scientist U. Chile, Santiago, 1969; cons. Trecani Encyclopedia, Italy, 1992-93. Author: Theory of Tokanak Plasmas North Holland, 1989, 2d edit., 2002. Avocations: windsurfing, Karate, music, chess. Office: Princeton Plasma Physic Lab Princeton Univ Princeton NJ 08543

WHITE, SALLIE SNOW WILBER, retired elementary educator; b. Providence, Mar. 26, 1917; d. Bayard Frances and Mildred May (Armour) Snow; m. William J. Wilber, July 15, 1939 (dec. Dec. 1978); children: Drew B., William J., Harold B., Sallie B.; m. Jesse Freeman White, June 23, 1979 (dec. 1991). Grad. Sargent Coll., Boston U., 1938. Tchr. swimming and archery Sargent Summer Camp, Peterboro, N.H., 1937-38, counselor, 1939; tchr. sci. and math. Torsfield (Mass.) Elem. Sch., 1956-77, advisor to student tchrs., 1960-77; homemaker Naples, Fla., 1977—. Republican. Baptist. Avocations: gardening, knitting, painting, needlepoint, fishing. Home: 37 E Pelican St Naples FL 34113-4019

WHITE, SIDNEY HOWARD, English educator; b. Bangor, Maine, Aug. 29, 1923; s. Benjamin and Sadie (Sedoff) W.; m. Phyllis Evelyn Siegel, June 4, 1950 (div. Apr. 1982); children: Michael, Benjamin, Susan, Deborah; m. Pauline Elaine Allen, Oct. 22, 1982. BS, Loyola U., 1950; MA, U. So. Calif., 1951, PhD, 1962. Assoc. prof. English Marymount Coll., L.A., 1953-66; prof. English UCLA, 1962-66, U. R.I., Kingston, 1966-93. Vis. prof. English U. Victoria, B.C., 1965. Author: Critical Study of The Scarlet Letter, 1967, Critical Study of The Great Gatsby, 1968, Arthur Miller, 1970, Sidney Howard, 1977, Alan Ayckbourn, 1984; editor, reviewer books; advisor Norton Anthology of American Literature, 3d edit.; contbr. articles to profl. jours. Fundraiser March of Dimes, L.A., 1951-61. With U.S. Army, 1942-46, USAF, 1950. Decorated Okinawa Battle Star PTO. Mem. MLA. Republican. Avocations: music, gardening, tennis. Home: 34 Terrace Dr East Greenwich RI 02818-2527

WHITE, THOMAS DAVID, II, academic administrator; b. Pittsburg, Kans., Sept. 19, 1946; s. Thomas David and Audrey Marie (Parrish) White; m. Jacquelyn Lee Trone; children from previous marriage: Thomas David III(dec.), Phillip Edward. AA, Valley Forge Mil. Coll., 1967; BA, North Ga. Coll., 1969; postgrad., Pa. State U., 1978-82. Cert. adminstr., vol. svcs. Assn. Vol. Adminstrs. Dist. scout exec. Boy Scouts Am., Phila., 1969-72; vol. resource coord. Norristown (Pa.) State Hosp., 1972-74; assoc. dir. vol. resources Pennhurst Ctr., Spring City, Pa., 1974-79; dir. vol. resources Embreeville State Hosp., Coatesville, Pa., 1979-81; dir. alumni affairs and constituent rels. Valley Forge Mil. Acad., Wayne, Pa., 1981-85; assoc. univ. dir. alumni rels. Rutgers U., Newark, 1985-90; exec. dir. alumni rels. George Washington U., Washington, 1990-93; exec. dir. Nat. Assn. for Artisans and Craftsmen, Audubon, Pa., 1993-97; dean continuing edn. Montgomery County C.C., West Campus, 1997-2001; dir. alumni rels. Albright Coll., 2001—. Adj. faculty Pa. State U., 1975—76; sr. cons., co-founder Cons. Cmty., Phila., 1976—82; founder, pres. AADM Assocs., Wayne, Pa., 1983—90; prin. ptnr. Colonial Yard, 1984—. Contbr. articles to profl. publs.; author: profl. manuals; designer 18th and 19th century garden design, Early Am. Homes Mag., 1997. Sec. Roboda Cmty. Assn., Royersford, Pa., 1981—83; mem. Lower Providence Twp. Planning Commn., 1998—2002; chmn. Lower Providence Twp. Traffic Impact Com., 1999—2001; exec. com., v.p. Cornerstone of the Arts, Inc., Pottstown, Pa., 1997—99; bd. dirs. Women's Ctr. Montgomery County, 1998—2001. Mem.: Assn. Voluntary Action Scholars, Nat. Assn. Ind. Schs., Assn. Vol. Adminstrn., Coun. Advancement and Support Edn., VFMA Soc. Golden Sword (knight), Valley Forge Mil. Acad. Alumni Assn. (bd. dirs. exec. com. 1982—90), Rajah Shrine (Reading, Pa.), Rutgers Club (trustee 1985—90), Shriners, Scottish Rtie, Stichter Lodge, Masons. Republican. Avocations: American antiques, woodcarving, 19th Century landscaping, folk art, antique weapons. Home: 500 S Park Ave Audubon PA 19403-1921 Office: Albright Coll Alumni Rels PO Box 15234 Reading PA 19612-5234 E-mail: twhite@alb.edu.

WHITE, WENDEL ALBERICK, art educator, artist, photographer; b. Newark, Sept. 2, 1956; s. Howard Alberick and Symera (Hoggard) W.; m. Carmela Colon, May 23, 1981; 1 child, Amanda Rachel. BFA, Sch. Visual Arts, N.Y.C., 1980; MFA, U. Tex., 1982. Teaching asst. U. Tex., Austin, 1980-82; instr. photography Bellevue Hosp. High Sch., N.Y.C., 1983-84; photog. archivist Essence Mag., N.Y.C., 1986; workshop instr. Internat. Ctr. for Photography, N.Y.C., 1984-86; asst. prof. art Stockton State Coll., Pomona, N.J., 986—. Adj. instr. art Sch. Visual Arts, 1985-88, Cooper Union Sch. Art, N.Y.C., 1989-90; bd. dirs. Kodak Ednl. Adv. Coun., Rochester, N.Y., 1991—. Works include photog. images Indsl. Landscapes, 1988, Afro-Am. Communities in So. N.J., 1992; contbr. editor ICP Ency. of Photography, 1984; author exhbn. catalog. Bd. dirs. Atlantic City Hist. Mus., 1989—. U. Tex. fellow, Austin, 1990-81. Mem. Soc. Photog. Educators (multicultural caucus 1991—, advocacy com. 1991—), Photog. Resource Ctr., Lightwork. Democrat. Office: Stockton State Coll Div Arts And Humanitie Pomona NJ 08240

WHITEAKER, RUTH CATHERINE, retired secondary education educator, counselor; b. Monte Vista, Colo., Mar. 3, 1907; d. Samuel sigel and Vina Catherine (Becraft) Heilman; m. George Henry Whiteaker, June 23, 1946. BA, U. Denver, 1930, MA, 1954; student, Columbia U., Ohio State, and others, 1933-66. cert. tchr. Tchr./drama coach Brighton (Colo.) High Sch., 1930-36; tchr. Meeker Jr. High Sch., Greeley, Colo., 1936-42, South High Sch., Denver, 1942-52, couselor, 1952-61; tchr. Thomas Jefferson High Sch., Denver, 1961-66. Organizer first career day Greeley High Sch., 1939, Future Tchrs. Am. in Colo. High Schs. Colo. Edn. Assn., 1949-55; co-organizer Wyo. Future Tchrs. Am. Wyo. Edn. Assn., 1951; com. mem. Nat. Future Tchrs. Am. Adv. Bd., 1954. Author: (English speech units) Colo. English Guide, 1939, Denver K-12 Program, 1951; editor: (guidebook) South High Syllabus, 1952-60. Chmn. 50th reunion U. Denver Class 1930, 1980. Recipient Outstanding Contbn. to Edn. in Colo., 1954, plaque Colo. Future Tchrs. Am., 1955, Student Nat. Edn. Assn., Colo., 1955, Dedication of South H.S. Yearbook, 1958; Lifetime's Dedication to Edn. Colo. medal South Denver H.S., 1998; Heroine of S.P. Meek's Rusty, 1938; named Citizen of Week, Greeley Kiwanis Club, 1939; grantee U.S. Dept. Edn. and Mexican Ministry Edn., 1945. Mem. Bus. and Profl. Women's Club (pres. 1933, 38), Colo. Bus. and Profl. Women's Club (pres. 1945), Columbia U. Women's Club Colo. (pres. 1975-77), Rep. Ladies Roundtable, Colo. Symphony Guild, PEO Sisterhood, Meth. Women's Assn., Terr. Daus., Columbia U. Alumni Club, Alpha Gamma Delta (regional sec.-treas. 1934-36, pres. 1936-40), Delta Kappa Gamma (v.p. Colo. chpt. 1959, Cert. of Appreciation 2001). Methodist. Avocations: reading, travel, politics, lectures, theater. Home: 3455 S Corona St Apt 342 Englewood CO 80110-2871

WHITED, LINDA LEE, secondary school English language educator; b. Akron, Ohio, May 24, 1947; d. Robert Lee and Gloria Ann (Honeywill) Davis; m. Eugene Hearsel Whited, Mar. 4, 1972; children: Wendy Edna, Jefferson Eugene. BS in Secondary Edn., U. Akron, 1987, MS in Elem. Adminstrn., 1995. Sec. Goodyear Tire and Rubber Co., Akron, 1966-71, B.F. Goodrich Co., Akron, 1972-75; substitute tchr. area schs., Akron, 1987; intensive bus. tchr. Springfield H.S., Akron, 1987-92, English lang. tchr., 1992—. Cheerleading advisor Springfield H.S., 1987-95, faculty mgr., 1991-95, mem. levy com., 1991-94, mem. Spartan Booster Club, 1992-95. Active local Parent, Tchr., Student Assn., 1981—, 2nd v.p., 1981-83, 93—. Mem. NEA, Ohio Edn. Assn., Springfield Local Assn. Classroom Tchrs., Nat. Coun. Tchrs. English, Kappa Delta Pi (Mabel Riedinger scholar 1983-84), Pi Lambda Theta. Avocations: reading, travel, volleyball, swimming. Home: 2079 Waterbury Dr Uniontown OH 44685-9770

WHITEHEAD, DAVID LYNN, school counselor; b. Crockett, Tex., Mar. 24, 1950; s. Clifton Baine and Corene (Stowe) W.; m. Joyce Stalmach, June 23, 1973; children: Christopher, Kimberly, Allison. BA with honor, Sam Houston State U., Huntsville, Tex., 1972, MA, 1975. Cert. tchr., speech pathologist, learning disabilities, mental retardation, ednl. diagnostician, counseling, Tex. Speech pathologist Texas City Ind. Sch. Dist., 1972-73, Brenham (Tex.) Ind. Sch. Dist., 1973-75, ednl. diagnostician, 1975-86, Austin County Edn. Coop., Sealy, Tex., 1986-88; sch. counselor Sealy (Tex.) Ind. Sch. Dist., 1988-92; counselor Alton Elem. Sch., Brenham, Tex., 1992—. Ednl. cons., Austin County, Tex., 1987-88; reviewer spl. edn. program College Station (Tex.) Ind. Sch. Dist., 1983; feature artist Gov.'s Mansion, State of Tex., Austin, 1985. Pres. Whitehead Cemetery Assn., Grapeland, Tex., 1986-90. Mem. AACD, Tex. Assn. for Counseling and Devel., Ft. Bend County Counseling Assn., Region VI Educational Diagnosticians (pres. Bluebonnet chpt. 1977-78), Nat. Egg Art Guild (SW regional bd. dirs. 1986), Tex. Guild Egg Shell Artists (state pres. 1984-85). Mem. Brethren Ch. Avocations: gardening, reading, refinishing furniture.

WHITEHEAD, JOHN WAYNE, law educator, organization administrator, author; b. Pulaski, Tenn., July 14, 1946; s. John M. and Alatha (Wiser) W.; m. Virginia Carolyn Nichols, Aug. 26, 1967; children: Jayson Reau, Jonathan Mathew, Elisabeth Anne, Joel Christofer, Joshua Benjamen. BA, U. Ark., 1969, JD, 1974. Bar: Ark. 1974, U.S. Dist. Ct. (ea. and we. dists.) Ark. 1974, U.S. Supreme Ct. 1977, U.S. Ct. Appeals (9th cir.) 1980, Va. 1981, U.S. Ct. Appeals (7th cir.) 1981, U.S. Ct. Appeals (4th and 5th cirs.). Spl. counsel Christian Legal Soc., Oak Park, Ill., 1977-78; assoc. Gibbs & Craze, Cleve., 1978-79; sole practice law Manassas, Va., 1979-82; pres. The Rutherford Inst., Charlottesville, Va., 1982—, also bd. dirs. Frequent lectr.

colls., law schs.; past adj. prof. O.W. Coburn Sch. Law. Author: Schools on Fire, 1980, The New Tyranny, 1982, The Second American Revolution, 1982, The Stealing of America, 1983, The Freedom of Religious Expression in Public High Schools, 1983, The End of Man, 1986, An American Dream, 1987, The Rights of Religious Persons in Public Education, 1991, Home Education: Rights and Reasons, 1993, Religious Apartheid, 1994, Slaying Dragons, 1999, Grasping For the Wind, 2001, others; writer, dir.: (video series) Grasping for the Wind (Silver World medal N.Y. Film Festival), 1998-99; contbr. articles to profl. jours., chpts. to books. 1st lt. U.S. Army, 1969-71. Named Christian Leader of Yr. Christian World Affairs Conf., Washington, 1986; recipient Bus. and Profl. award Religious Heritage Am., 1990, Hungarian Freedom medal, Budapest, 1991. Mem. ABA, Ark. Bar Assn., Va. Bar Assn. Office: The Rutherford Inst PO Box 7482 Charlottesville VA 22906-7482

WHITEHEAD, WENDY LEE, special education educator; b. Wabash, Ind., Mar. 1, 1955; d. John Francis and Virginia Mae (Ritzi) W. BS, Ball State U., 1977, MS, 1981; cert. in visually impaired edn., Ind. U., Ft. Wayne, 1987. Cert. spl. edn. tchr., Ind. Tchr. of primary severe disabilities Sharp Creek Elem. Sch., Met. Sch. Dist., Wabash, Ind., 1977—. Active locla sch. dist. Assistive Tech. Team. Mem. Coun. for Exceptional Children (human rights com.). Republican. Roman Catholic. Avocations: reading, bowling, cross-stitch. Office: Sharp Creek Elem Sch 264 W 200 N Wabash IN 46992-9136

WHITEHEAD, ZELMA KAY, special education educator; b. Tupelo, Miss., Sept. 20, 1946; d. Henry Neal and Zelma Lee (Rye) W. BS in Spl. Edn., Miss. State Coll. for Women, Columbus, 1968; MEd in Spl. Edn., Miss. State U., Starkville, 1971, Edn. Specialist, 1975; postgrad., U. Miss., Oxford, 1978, 85, Miss. Coll., 1990-92. Cert. tchr. spl. edn., elem. edn., adult basic edn., spl. subject supervision, ednl. adminstrn., elem. principal, secondary principal, elem. supr. Tchr. spl. edn. Nettleton (Miss.) Elem. Sch., 1968-71; site monitor Appalachian Edn. Satellite Program Itawamba Jr. Coll., Tupelo, Miss., 1977-79, instr. spl. edn. Spl. Vocat. Edn. Ctr., 1971-85, supr. Spl. Vocat. Edn. Ctr., 1984-85, instr. adult basic edn., 1979-85; tchr. spl. prevocat. edn. Shannon (Miss.) High Sch., 1985; edn. specialist Miss. State Dept. Edn., Jackson, 1986, edn. specialist sr., 1986-90; acad. tchr. III Miss. State Hosp., Whitfield, 1990-93, coord. patient edn. and skill tng., 1993-95; adminstr. Lakeside Sch., 1995-2000, Millcreek of Pontotoc Sch., Inc., 2000—. Mem. Coun. Exceptional Children. Methodist. Avocations: softball, running, sailing. Home: 177 Little Cir Belden MS 38826-9368

WHITEHOUSE, CHARLES BARTON, avionics educator; b. Boston, Sept. 7, 1933; s. John Clifford and Pauline Barbara (Larkin) W.; m. Diana Bernier, June 9, 1962; 1 child, Clifford Bernard. BS, Ctrl. Conn. State Coll., 1957; MS, U. No. Colo., 1974, DEd, 1977. Cert. profl. tchr., Colo.; cert. flight instr., aircraft and instrument, advanced ground instr., Colo. Electrician Killywatt Elec. Co., Newington, Conn., 1951-56, Guerrard Elec. Co., New Britain, Conn., 1956-57; technician electric curriculum Opportunity Sch., Denver, 1958-60, elec. instr., 1960-68, avionics, comm. instr., 1968-92; ret. Founder, owner, seminar leader, mfr. InterTech Aviation Svcs., Littleton, Colo., 1980—; radio engr. Pacific Nomad, 1989; adj. prof. avionics, prof. aviation history aerospace dept. Met. State Coll. of Denver, 1990—. Author: FCC Exam Guide, 1991, Avionics for Aviators, 1994; contbr. manuals, study guides on avionics. Named Laureate, Colo. Hall of Fame, 2003. Mem. Colo. Aviation Hist. Soc., Air Power West, Am. Field Svc. Com., Sister Cities Internat., Wings Over the Rockies Aviation & Space Mus. (curator avionics exhibit), Colo. Pilots Assn., Assn. for Avionics Edn. (charter), Denver Radio League, Exptl. Aircraft Assn., Aircraft Owners and Pilot's Assn., Antique Wireless Assn., Silver Wings Aviation Frat., Radio Club Am. Republican. Unitarian Universalist. Home: 3 Sunset Ln Greenwood Village Littleton CO 80121 Office: InterTech Aviation Svcs 3 Sunset Ln Littleton CO 80121-1251

WHITEHURST, GROVER JAY, federal official, psychologist and educator; b. Washington, N.C., Sept. 28, 1944; s. Grover J. and Dixie (Daniel) W.; m. Janet E. Fischel, June 7, 1981; children: Owen E., Adam E. BA, East Carolina U., Greenville, 1966; MA, U. Ill., 1968, PhD, 1970. Lic. psychologist, N.Y. Asst. prof. SUNY, Stony Brook, 1970—74, assoc. prof., 1975—79, prof. psychology, 1981—2002, chair dept. psychology, 1998—2002; sr. lectr. U. N.S.W., Sydney, Australia, 1974—75; acad. v.p. Merrill-Palmer Inst., Detroit, 1979—81; dir. Inst. of Edu. Sciences, 2002—. Author: Child Behavior, 1977; editor Developmental Rev., 1981-2000; contbr. over 100 articles to profl. jours. Grantee NIH, 1985, Smith Richardson Found., 1990, Pew Charitable Trusts, 1992, U.S. Adminstrn. Children and Families, 1996, 2000. Fellow APA, Am. Assn. Profl. and Applied Psychology; Nat. Rsch. Coun. (commn. early childhood); Head Start, Nat. Adv. Bd. on Rsch. Avocation: sailing. Mailing: Dir Inst Educ Sciences US Dept Edu 555 New Jersey Ave NW Washington DC 20208-5500*

WHITELAW, JACQUELINE SUSAN, special education educator; b. Mt. Pleasant, Pa., Aug. 22, 1952; d. John Oliver and Cora Catherine (Daniels) Reed; m. Matthew Murray Whitelaw, Aug. 26, 1978; children: Kelly Moreen, Jonathan Murray. BS in Spl. Edn. and Elem. Edn., No. Ill. U., 1974, cert. in mentally impaired, visually impaired, social and emotionally disturbed, learning disabilities, 1987, cert. social/emotionally disturbed, 1994; MS in Elem. Edn., Purdue U., 1980. Cert. elem. edn. grades K-9, spl. edn. grades K-12, visually impaired. Tchr. N.W. Ind. Spl. Edn. Coop., Highland, 1974-75, South Met. Assn. for Low Incidence Handicaps, Flossmoor, Ill., 1975-95. Cons. social/emotionally disturbed program Dist. 125, Alsip, Ill., 1994—. Developer/coord. (disability awareness program) Take A Look At Being Differently-Abled, 1986—. Tchr. Christ. Luth. Ch., Hammond, 1980—, ch. choir mem., 1984—, Sunday sch. supt., 1986-92, 94—; den mother, cub master pack 280 Boy Scouts Am., Hammond, 1992—. Mem. Gavit H.S. Band Boosters (hospitality chmn. 1991—), Jefferson Elem. PTA, Gavit Jr./Sr. H.S. PTA. Democrat. Avocations: camping, crafts, sign language, bicycling, cooking. Home: 7027 Baring Ave Hammond IN 46324-2203 Office: SMA Hamlin Upper Grade Ctr Dist 125 1215 N Hamlin Ave Chicago IL 60651-2243

WHITESIDES, GEORGE MCCLELLAND, chemistry educator; b. Louisville, Ky., Aug. 3, 1939; m. Barbara Breasted; children: George Thomas, Benjamin Haile. AB, Harvard U., 1960; PhD, Calif. Inst. Tech., 1964; D Honoris Causa (hon.), U. Twente, The Netherlands, 2001. Asst. prof. dept. chemistry MIT, Cambridge, 1963—69, assoc. prof., 1969—71, prof., 1971—75, Arthur C. Cope prof., 1975—80, Haslam and Dewey prof., 1980—82; prof. dept. chemistry Harvard U., Cambridge, 1982—86, Mallinckrodt prof., 1986—. Recipient Pure Chemistry award, Am. Chem. Soc., 1975, Harrison Howe award, Rochester sect., 1979, Arthur C. Cope award, 1995, James Flack Norris award, 1994, Remsen award, 1983, Arthur C. Cope Scholar award, 1989, Disting. Alumni award, Calif. Inst. Tech., 1980, Def. Advanced Rsch. Projects Agy. award, 1996, Madison Marshall award, Am. Chem. Soc., 1996, Nat. Medal of Sci., 1998, von Hippel award, Material Rsch. Soc., 2000, World Tech. award for materials, World Tech. Network, 2001, Rschr. of Yr. award, Small Times Mag., 2002, Pitts. Analytical Chemistry award, Soc. Analytical Chemists of Pitts., 2003; fellow Alfred P. Sloan fellow, 1968. Fellow: AAAS; mem.: NAS, Am. Philos. Soc., Am. Acad. Arts and Scis. Office: Harvard U Dept of Chemistry 12 Oxford St Cambridge MA 02138-2902 E-mail: gwhitesides@gmwgroup.harvard.edu.

WHITE-WARE, GRACE ELIZABETH, elementary school educator, secondary school educator; b. St. Louis, Oct. 5, 1921; d. James Eathel, Sr. and Madree (Penn) White; divorced; 1 son, James Otis Ware II (Oloye Kunle Adeyemon). BA in Edn., H.B. Stowe Tchrs. Coll., 1943. Mgr. advt. Superior Press, St. Louis, 1935-39; tri-owner, v.p. Carolina Oil Co., St. Louis, 1938-42; with pub. relations Triangle Press, St. Louis, 1939-47, sales promotion, 1939-47; account supr. overtime payroll Bell Tel. Labs., Inc., N.Y.C., 1943-46; tchr. Dunbar Elem. Sch., St. Louis, 1946-47, Garfield Elem. Sch., Chgo., 1948-49, Betsy Ross Elem. Sch., Chgo., 1950-51, Lincoln Sch., Richmond, Mo., 1951, Dunbar Sch., Kinlock, Mo., 1952, Gladstone Elem. Sch., Cleve., 1954-61, Quincy Elem. Sch., Cleve., 1961-78, W.H. Brett Elem. Sch., Euclid Park, Cleve., 1979-82; head tchr. Head Start program, 1965; adult edn. tchr. Cleve. Bd. Edn., 1965-82; program dir. Tutoring and Nutrition Project, Delta Sigma Theta, 1982-87; tchr. TV Tonight Sch., lessons for adults, Cleve., 1972; tri-owner, v.p., social editor Style mag., St. Louis, 1947-49; owner/mgr. Wentworth Record Distbrs., Chgo., 1947-51; supr. accounts receivable div. Spiegel, Inc., Chgo., 1947-52; radio panelist Calling All Americans, Cleve., 1957-58; sec. bd. dirs. Hough Pub. Co., also Hough Area Devel. Corp., Cleve., 1968-69. Mem. child devel. parent bd. Greater Cleve. Neighborhood Centers Assn.; mem. fund raising com. Food First Program, co-chmn. woman's aux. Black Econ. Union, Cleve.; vice chmn. Cleve. com. Youth for Understanding Teenage Program; mem. Cleve. Council Human Relations; mem. Cleve. chpt. CORE; charter mem., fin. sec. Tots and Teens, Inc.; treas. Jr. Women's Civic League; mem. Cleve. bd. Afro-Am. Cultural and Hist. Soc.; women's aux. bd. Talbert Clinic and Day Care Center, Cleve.; adv. bd. Langston Hughes Library; mem. Forest City Hosp. Aux. Bd., also Women's Aux. Com. Forest City Hosp.; scholarship com. Women's Allied Arts Assn. Greater Cleve., 1972-74; mem. spl. com. Lake Erie council Girl Scouts U.S.A., 1982-84; co-coordinator Cuyahoga County Child Watch Project, 1982-83. Named Most Outstanding Vol. of Year, N.Y. Fedn. Settlements, 1944, Leading Tchr. of Community, Cleve. Call and Post, weekly newspaper, 1958; recipient Martha Holden Jennings scholar award Martha Holden Jennings Found., Cleve., 1966-67, Spl. Outstanding Tchrs. award, 1973; Outstanding Service award Black Econ. Union, 1970; Cert. of Appreciation, City of Cleve., 1973; Ednl. Service to Community award Urban League, 1986 Mem. Ohio, Cleve. edn. assns., Nat. Assn. Public Sch. Adult Edn., Nat. Assn. Minority Polit. women (treas. 1985-87), NAACP, Phillis Wheatley Assn., Moreland Community Assn., Nat. Council Negro Women, Top Ladies of Distinction (pres. Cleve. 1980-82), Nat. Assn. Univ. Women, Phi Delta Kappa (1st v.p. Cleve. 1971-73, Outstanding Achievement award 1975), Delta Sigma Theta (pres. Cleve. 1969-73), Delta Kappa Gamma, Eta Phi Beta (chpt. treas. 1975-77, regional treas. 1980-84, nat. treas. 1984-88). Democrat. Clubs: Novelette Bridge (pres. Cleve. 1973-77), Arewa Du-Du Bridge (treas. 1980-91), Hooked on Bridge (pres. 1994-97). Lodge: Kiwanis Internat. Home: 3591 E 154th St # Up Cleveland OH 44120-4913

WHITE-WINTERS, JILL MARY, nursing educator; b. Milw., June 30, 1955; d. John Paul Gabor and Ann Lorraine (Ladish) Gordy; m. Jack Mark Winters; children: Jeffrey, Eric, David, Michael. BSN, U. Wis., Milw., 1978; MS in Nursing, Marquette U., 1991; PhD, U. Wis., 1996. Nurse various hosps., Milw., 1978-84, St. Mary's Hosp., Milw., 1984-85, Peck Foods Corp., Milw., 1985-88; prof. U. Wis., Milw., 1996—2001, Marquette U., Milw., 2001—. Contbr. chpts. to books, articles to profl. jours. Grantee, Nat. Inst. Nursing Rsch., Wis. Women's Health Found., Nat. Inst. Disability and Rehab. Rsch. Mem. AACCN (grantee 1997), ANA, Midwest Nursing Rsch. Soc., Sigma Theta Tau (v.p. local chpt. 1997-99). Roman Catholic. Avocation: golf. Home: 10320 N Provence Ct Mequon WI 53092-5228 Office: Marquette U Coll Nursing PO Box 1881 Milwaukee WI 53201-1881

WHITFIELD, TAMMY J. elementary school educator, director; b. June 2, 1963; BA, Grove City Coll., 1988; MS, Robert Morris Coll., 1996; EdD, Duquesne U., 2000. Cert. prin. K-12, Pa. Tchr. Chartiers Valley Sch. Dist., Bridgeville, Pa., 1988—2000, prin. spl. programs, 2000—. Address: 67 Cowan Rd Carnegie PA 15106-1409

WHITING, LUCILLE DRAKE, retired elementary school educator, consultant; b. San Diego, Dec. 17, 1929; d. Robert Emmett and Helen Anglim; m. C. George Hewitt (div.); m. V. Edward Drake (div.); m. Erle Francis Whiting, Mar. 27, 1982; 1 child, Cecilie Anne. BA, U. Calif.-Santa Barbara, 1951; MEd, LaVerne (Calif.) U., 1975. Cert. Miller-Unruh reading specialist, spl. edn. specialist, elem. sch. tchr., adult edn. tchr., Calif. Owner, dir. Little Buckaroo Nursery Sch., Santa Barbara, Calif., 1956-65; tchr. various sch. dists. Calif., 1951-72; Title I resource tchr. Oxnard (Calif.) Sch. Dist., 1972-73, reading specialist, 1973-86; extension instr. Calif. Luth. Coll., Thousand Oaks, 1978-84, U. Calif.-Santa Barbara, 1976-82; ind. ednl. cons. Ventura, Calif., 1976-86, Cromberg, Calif., 1986—. Ind. ednl. cons. Active Plumas County Arts Commn., Quincy, Calif., 1987—, bd. dirs., 1989-90; life mem. Plumas County Mus.; bd. dirs. Quincy br. Friends of Plumas County Libr., 1990-1992, life mem.; bd. dirs. Plumas County Literacy Program, 1992-1996, founding com., v.p. 1994-1995, tutor 1992-98, advisor 1992—; vol. Cromberg Cmty. Com., 1987—; mem. Plumas County Rep. Women's Club; pres. joint com. on learning disabilities Santa Barbara and Ventura Counties, 1978-81. Mem. AAUW, Calif. Reading Assn. (ex-officio 1978-81, exemplary svc. award 1982, founding com. chair disabled reader spl. interest grou 1980), Ventura County Reading Assn. (pres. 1979-80), Reading Specialists of Calif., Orton Dyslexia Soc. (mem.-at-large Tri Counties exec. bd. 1982-85), Calif. Assn. Neurology Handicapped Children (v.p. Ventura County chpt. 1976-78), Tri-Counties Assn. Nursery Edn. (pres. 1960, adv. bd. 1961), Calif. Assn. Nursery Edn. (bd. dirs. Santa Barbara chpt. 1960-1962), Ventura County Panhellenic Assn. (v.p. 1970-72), Ben Franklin Stamp Collecting Club (leader 1989-92), Chi Omega, Phi Delta Kappa, Delta Phi Epsilon (pres. Santa Barbara chpt. 1964). Republican. Avocations: photography, travel, walking, hiking, wildflower preservation.

WHITING, MARTHA COUNTEE, retired secondary education educator; b. Marshall, Tex., Mar. 24, 1912; d. Thomas and Nannie Selena (Yates) Countee; m. Samuel Whiting, June 8, 1937; children: Jacqueline Bostic, Sammie Ellis, Nan Broussard, Tommye Casey, Martha Goddard. BA in Sci., Bishop Coll., 1934; M of Secondary Edn., Tex. So. U., 1959, postgraduate, 1962; postgrad., U. Colo., 1963. Tchr., sci., math. Houston Ind. Sch. Dist., 1942-73; researcher, local history Houston, 1973—. Lectr. in field. Mem. exec. com. (life mem.) Houston YWCA, 1977; advisor Preservation 4th Ward, Houston, 1991—; trustee Antioch Missionary Bapt. Ch., Houston, 1977; instrumental in getting the Antioch Missionary Bapt. Ch. in Christ Inc. on the Nat. Register of Hist. Places, 1976; presented Queen Elizabeth II with miniature history of Antioch Missionary Bapt. Ch. in Christ, 1991; author nomination form for Tex. hist. marker Antioch Missionary Bapt. Ch. in Christ, 1994; presenter to Harris County Heritage Soc. of Jack Yates House, the only house built by a former slave to be maintain ed by a U.S. city, and chmn. Pathfinder presentation of achievements of 64 Negro pioneers in Harris County, 1966-1986. Named Woman Courage, Houston Radcliffe Club, 1985, Black Womens Hall Fame Mus. Africal Am. Life, Dallas, 1986; recipient Friend of the Soc. award Harris County Heritage Soc., 1994. Mem. Tex. Ret. Tchrs. Assn., Houston Mus. Fine Arts, Harris County Heritage Soc. (exec. com. 1984), Bluebonnet Garden Club (pres. 1968), Jack & Jill Am. (pres. Houston chpt. 1955-57), Smithsonian, Nationwide Trust for Historic Preservation. Avocations: writing, gardening, travel, sewing, singing. Home: 3446 Southmore Blvd Houston TX 77004-6349

WHITING, WALLACE BURTON, II, chemical engineer, educator; b. Hartford, Conn., Sept. 6, 1952; s. Harold Alan and Lillian Anne (Jones) W.; m. Patricia Rose Headington Moore, June 17, 1978; children: Sharon E. Moore, Cynthia L. Moore Restivo. BS, Rensselaer Polytechnic Inst., 1974; MSChemE, Polytechnic Inst. N.Y., 1976; PhD, U. Calif., Berkeley, 1982. Registered profl. engr., Calif., W.Va., Nev. Asst. mech. engr. Pratt & Whitney Aircraft Co., East Hartford, Conn., 1973; chem. process engr. Dorr-Oliver Inc., Stamford, Conn., 1974-76; rsch. assoc. Lawrence Berkeley Lab., Berkeley, Calif., 1976-82; prof. W.Va. U., Morgantown, 1982-96. Program dir. NSF, 1991, 94; vis. prof. UCLA, 1992; prof., chair U. Nev., Reno, 1996—. Co-author: Analysis, Synthesis and Design of Chemical Processes, 1997, 2s edit., 2002; editor Fluid Phase Equilibria Jour.; contbr. articles to profl. jours. Grantee NSF, U.S. Dept. Energy. Mem. AIChE (nat. program chair for edn. 1988—), Am. Soc. Engring. Edn. (bd. dirs. nat. projects 1990—, chair programming chem. engring. and edn. divsn. 1986-90, Dow Outstanding Faculty award 1986, Centennial Svc. award 1993), Am. Chem. Soc., Internat. Gesellschaft Fuer Ingenieurpaedagogik, Assn. Environ. Engring. Profs., Sigma Xi, Tau Beta Pi. Achievements include development of a new approach to mixing rules for equations of state for asymmetric mixtures, and a new approach to quantifying uncertainties in process design caused by thermodynamic uncertainties. Office: U Nev Engring Mailstop 170 Reno NV 89557-0001

WHITING-DOBSON, LISA LORRAINE, video production educator, producer, director; b. Lansing, Mich., July 22, 1959; d. Lowell Stanton and Ruth Lorraine (Gregory) Whiting. BS in Psychology, Mich. State U., 1981, BA in Telecomm. cum laude, 1984, MA in Telecomm., 1988; AA in Dance magna cum laude, Lansing C.C., 1984. Video prodr., dir. Coll. of Comm. Arts, instr. dept. telecomm. Mich. State U., East Lansing, Mich., 1987—; prodr., dir. Cath. Diocese Lansing, 1984—; instr. media tech. Lansing C.C., 1999—. Dance instr. Synergy, 2002. Mem. Jr. League of Lansing. Office: Mich State U Dept Telecom 409 Communication Arts Bldg East Lansing MI 48824-1212 E-mail: whiting3@msu.edu.

WHITLOCK, BETTY, secondary education educator; b. Somerset, Ky., Mar. 17, 1942; d. Rual Robert and Hazel Ellen (Biers) Wilson; m. L. Craig Whitlock, June 12, 1962 (dec. 2002); children: Michael Craig, Jeffrey Robert, Katherine Elizabeth. BA, Georgetown Coll., 1964; MA, Miss. Coll., 1980, EdS, 1982; postgrad., U. So. Miss., 1986. Nat. bd. cert. tchr. Adolescence and Young Adulthood/English Lang. Arts. Tchr. kindegarten First Bapt. Ch. Kindergarten, Clinton, Miss., 1970-72, Northside Bapt. Ch. Kindegarten, Clinton, Miss., 1972-73; tchr. high sch. Miss. Bapt. High Sch., Jackson, 1973-75, Clinton High Sch., 1975—. Bd. dirs. Miss. Youth Congress, 1985—; chmn. com. Literary Map of Miss., 1985—; cons. Miss. High Sch. Activities Assn., 1991—. Co-author: Mississippi Writers: An Anthology, 1987, Mississippi Writers: Reflections on Childhood and Youth, 1988, (textbook) Dramatic Interpretation, 1994. Tchr. Sunday sch. First Bapt. Ch., Clinton, 1969—. Mem. Nat. Coun. Tchrs. English, Nat. Forensic League, Miss. Coun. Tchrs. English (chmn. maps 1975—, Outstanding Tchr. award 1992), Miss. Speech Communication Assn. (dir. congress 1973—), Miss. Profl. Educators, Miss. Forensic League (chmn. 1988-99), Jackson Cath. Forensic League (moderator 1991-93), Miss. Coll. Faculty Wives, Phi Delta Kappa. Republican. Baptist. Avocation: writing. Home: 100 Hannah Dr Clinton MS 39056-5107 Office: Clinton High Sch 401 Arrow Dr Clinton MS 39056-3108

WHITLOCK, VERONICA P. interior designer, educator; b. N.Y.C., Sept. 29, 1961; d. Emmet and Gloria Welch Whitlock; children: Alexander M. Laughlin, III, Julia W. Laughlin. BA in Studio Art and Art History cum laude, Duke U., 1983; BFA in Interior Design with distinction, N.Y. Sch. Interior Design, 1989. Cert. Nat. Coun. Interior Design Qualification, lic. interior designer Conn., cert. N.Y. Adminstrv. asst. William Doyle Galleries, N.Y.C., 1984—86; assoc. Timmins-Munn, Inc., N.Y.C., 1987—98; interior designer V.W. Interiors, Greenwich, Conn., 1994—; tchr. N.Y. Sch. Interior Design, N.Y.C., 2001—. Vol. Jr. League, Greenwich, 1999—. Mem.: Interior Designers for Licensing N.Y. (bd. mem. 0001), Am. Soc. Interior Designers (profl.), Decorators Club. Home and Office: 25 Halsey Dr Old Greenwich CT 06870

WHITLOW, DONNA MAE, daycare and primary school administrator; b. Buffalo, S.D., May 23, 1933; d. Carl Axel and Esther Johanna (Wickman) Magnuson; married, June 13, 1953; children: Debra Diane Reasy, Cathleen Denise Corallo, Lisa Mae. Diploma, Eugene Bible Coll., 1956; BA in Religious Edn., Internat. Seminary, 1985, MA, 1986. Corp. sec. various orgns., 1953-56; asst. registrar, prof. child edn. Calif. Open Bible Inst., Pasadena, 1956-57; dir. religious edn. and music, sec. to gen. bd. Jamaica Open Bible Inst., 1958-59; dir. religious edn. and music, sec. to gen. bd.. prof. on staff, bus. mgr. Trinidad Open Bible Inst., 1960-65; asst. to full-charge bookkeeper Jennings Strouss Law Firm, 1966-68; dir. religious edn. and music, mem. gen. bd., assoc. pastor Biltmore Bible Christian Ctr., Phoenix, Ariz., 1967—; founder, dir. Biltmore Bible Day Care & Kindergarten, Phoenix, 1977—. Founder bible schs. in South Africa, Argentina, Ctrl. Am., Europe, Caribbean, Singapore, and on every continent. Author: How To Start a Daycare in the Local Church, 1986. Republican. Avocations: water and snow skiing, flying, international travel. Home: 2144 E Lamar Rd Phoenix AZ 85016-1147 Office: Biltmore Bible Christian Ctr 3330 E Camelback Rd Phoenix AZ 85018-2310

WHITMAN, MARINA VON NEUMANN, economist, educator; b. N.Y.C., Mar. 6, 1935; d. John and Mariette (Kovesi) von Neumann; m. Robert Freeman Whitman, June 23, 1956; children: Malcolm Russell, Laura Mariette. BA summa cum laude, Radcliffe Coll., 1956; MA, Columbia U., 1959, PhD, 1962; LHD (hon.), Russell Sage Coll., 1972; LLD (hon.), Cedar Crest Coll., 1973, Hobart and William Smith Coll., 1973; LHD (hon.), U. Mass., 1975, N.Y. Poly. Inst., 1975; LLD (hon.) Coe Coll., 1975, Marietta Coll., 1976. Mem. faculty U. Pitts., 1962-79, prof. econs., 1971-73, disting. pub. svc. prof. econs., 1973-79; v.p., chief economist Gen. Motors Corp., N.Y.C., 1979-85, group v.p. pub. affairs, 1985-92; disting. vis. prof. bus. adminstrn., pub. policy U. Mich., Ann Arbor, 1992-94, prof. bus. adminstrn., pub. policy, 1994—. Bd. dirs. JP Morgan Chase Corp., Alcoa, Procter & Gamble Co., Unocal; mem. Trilateral Commn., 1973-84, 88-95; mem. Pres. Adv. Com. on Trade Policy and Negotiations, 1987-93; mem. tech. assessment adv. coun. U.S. Congress Office of Tech. Assessment, 1990-95; mem. Consultative Group on Internat. Econs. and Monetary Affairs, 1979—; mem. U.S. Price Commn., 1971-72, Coun. Econ. Advisers, Exec. Office of Pres., 1972-73. Author: Government Risk-Sharing in Foreign Investment, 1965, International and Interregional Payments Adjustment, 1967, Economic Goals and Policy Instruments, 1970, Reflections of Interdependence: Issues for Economic Theory and U.S. Policy, 1979, New World, New Rules: The Changing Role of the American Corporation, 1999; bd. editors: Am. Econ. Rev., 1974-77; mem. editl. bd. Fgn. Policy; contbr. articles to profl. jours. Trustee Nat. Bur. Econ. Rsch., 1993—, Princeton U., 1980-90, Inst. Advanced Study, 1999—; bd. dirs. Inst. for Internat. Econs., 1986—, Salzburg Seminar, 1994—, Eurasia Found., 1992-95; bd. overseers Harvard U., 1972-78, mem. vis. com. Kennedy Sch., 1992-98. Fellow Earhart Found., 1959-60, AAUW, 1960-61, NSF, 1968-70, Social Security Rsch. Coun.; recipient Columbia medal for excellence, 1973, George Washington award Am. Hungarian Found., 1975. Mem. Am. Econ. Assn. (exec. com. 1977-80), Am. Acad. Arts and Scis., Coun. Fgn. Rels. (dir. 1977-87), Phi Beta Kappa. Office: U Mich Gerald Ford Sch Pub Policy 411 Lorch Hall Ann Arbor MI 48109-1220 E-mail: marinaw@umich.edu.

WHITMAN, ROBERT VAN DUYNE, civil engineer, educator; b. Pitts., Feb. 2, 1928; s. Edwin A. and Elsie (Van Duyne) W.; m. Elizabeth Cushman, June 19, 1954; children: Jill Martyne Whitman Marsee, Martha Allerton (dec.), Gweneth Giles Whitman Kaebnick. BS, Swarthmore Coll., 1948, DSc (hon.), 1990; SM, MIT, 1949, ScD, 1951. Faculty MIT, 1953—, prof. civil engring., 1963-93, head structural engring., 1970-74, head soil mechanics divsn., 1970-72; prof. emeritus, 1993—. Vis. scholar U. Cambridge, Eng., 1976-77; cons. to govt. and industry, 1953—; mem. adv. com. for nat. earthquake hazard reduction program Fed. Emergency Mgmt. Agy., 1991-94, mem. commn. engring. and tech. systems NRC, 1992-97. Author: (with T. W. Lambe) Soil Mechanics. Mem. Town Meeting Lexington, Mass., 1962-76, 85—, mem. permanent bldg. com., 1968-75, mem. bd. appeals, 1979-81, 84-2000. Lt. (j.g.) USNR, 1954-56. Recipient U.S. Scientist award Humboldt Found., 1984-90; Norwegian Geotech. Inst. Rsch. fellow, 1984. Mem. NAE, ASCE (Rsch. award 1962, Terzaghi

Lecture 1981, Terzaghi award 1987, C. Martin Duke Lifeline Earthquake Engring. award 1992, James Croes medal 1994), Boston Soc. Civil Engrs. (Structural Sect. prize 1963, Desmond Fitzgerald medal 1973, Ralph W. Horne Fund award 1977), Internat. Soc. Soil Mechanics and Found. Engrs., Mex. Soc. Soil Mechanics (hon., Nabor Carrillo lectr. 2000), Earthquake Engring. Rsch. Inst. (dir. 1978-81, 84-88, v.p. 1979-81, pres. 1985-87, Disting. lectr. 1994, hon. 1997—). Achievements include research in in soil mechanics, soil dynamics, earthquake engring. and earthquake loss estimation. Home: 5 Hancock Ave Lexington MA 02420-3412 Office: MIT Dept Civil & Environ Engring Cambridge MA 02139

WHITMORE-DALTON, SANDRA ELAINE, special education educator; b. Gadsden, Ala., Dec. 12, 1950; BS, Jacksonville State Coll., 1979; MS, North Ga. Coll., 1982; Edn. Specialist, West Ga. Coll., 1984; EdD, U. Ga., 1992. Lic. adminstrn. and supervision, Ga., spl. edn. tchr., Ala., Ga. Spl. edn. tchr. Murray County Schs., Chatsworth, Ga., 1979-89, due process coord., 1989-91; dir. spl. svcs. Columbia County Schs., Appling, Ga., 1991—. Com. mem. Interagy. Community Coun., Augusta, Ga., 1991—. With U.S. Army, 1973-76. Mem. AAUW, Profl. Assn. Educators, Coun. Exceptional Children, Kappa Delta Pi, Kappa Delta Epsilon. Avocation: music. Office: Columbia County Spl Svcs 112 Ford Ave Grovetown GA 30813-2603

WHITNEY, CYNTHIA JEANNE, elementary school educator; b. Grand Rapids, Mich., Aug. 17, 1954; d. John Peter and Margaret A. (Petzold) Houk; m. John C. Whitney, Jr., June 4, 1977; children: Jack, Tom. BA, U. Wis.-Green Bay, 1976; MA, U. Wis.-Whitewater, 1989. Cert. elem. educator, instrumental music instr. Band dir. Palmyra (Wis.)-Eagle Pub. Schs., 1977-87; tchr. third grade Eagle (Wis.) Elem. Sch., 1987—. Mem. Internat. Reading Assn., Wis. State Reading Assn. (chair com.), South Kettle Moraine Reading Coun. (sec.). Home: 1517 Jamesway St Fort Atkinson WI 53538-2808 Office: Eagle Elem Sch 801 E Main St Eagle WI 53119

WHITNEY, GLAYDE DENNIS, psychologist, educator, geneticist; b. Sidney, Mont., Apr. 25, 1939; s. Russell Taylor and Althea May (Zuber) W.; m. Yvonne Marie Miels, June 20, 1965 (div. 1990); children: Scott, Timothy. BA cum laude, U. Minn., 1961, PhD, 1966. Postdoctoral fellow Inst. Behavior Genetics U. (Boulder) Colo., Boulder, 1969-70; asst. prof. psychology Fla. State U., Tallahassee, 1970-73, assoc. prof., 1973-78, prof., 1978—. Cons. NIH and NSF, Washington, 1976—; adv. group mem. Colo. Alcohol Rsch. Ctr., Boulder, 1986—. Assoc. editor Jour. Behavior Genetics, 1981-84; mem. editl. bd. Behavior Genetics, 1985-99; mem. editl. com. The Mankind Quarterly, 1997-99; contbg. editor American Renaissance, 1998—; contbr. over 200 articles to profl. jours. Capt. USAF, 1966-69. Recipient Claude Pepper award Nat. Inst. Deafness and Comm. Disorders, 1990, Mannheimer award for career contbns. to chem. senses, 1994; grantee NIH and NSF, 1970-98, Pioneer Fund, 1998—; fellow NIMH, 1963. Mem. AAAS, Nat. Assn. Scholars, Assn. Chemoreception Scis., Behavior Genetics Assn. (treas. 1978-81, pres. 1995), NRA, Phi Beta Kappa. Republican. Roman Catholic. Office: Fla State U Psychology Dept Tallahassee FL 32306-1270 E-mail: Whitney@Darwin.psy.fsu.edu.

WHITNEY, PAUL FRANCIS, gifted and talented education educator; b. N.Y.C., Sept. 28, 1947; s. William and Paula Ellen (Mehling) W.; m. Kathleen Travers, June 24, 1972. BA in History and Polit. Sci., Iona Coll., 1969, Profl. Diploma in Sch. Dist. Adminstrn., 1995; MA in Social Studies Tchg., CUNY, 1975, MS in Edn., 1981. Cert. social studies and English tchr., N.Y.; cert. sch. adminstrn. and supervision, sch. dist. adminstrn., N.Y. Guidance counselor, tchr.-mentor, dean, tchr. E.W. Stitt Jr. H.S., N.Y.C., 1970-86; coord., creator Alpha program Inwood Intermediate Sch., N.Y.C., 1994—. Mem. Dist. 6 N.Y.C. Mentor Adv. Selection Com., 1988-94. Mem. Am. Fedn. Tchrs., United Fedn. Tchrs. (chpt. chairperson 1975-78), N.Y. State United Tchrs., Nat. Coun. Tchrs. English, Phi Delta Kappa. Democrat. Roman Catholic. Avocations: reading, traveling, golfing, fishing. Home: 204 Brittany Ct Valley Cottage NY 10989-2602 Office: Inwood IS 650 Academy St New York NY 10034-5004

WHITNEY, RODGER FRANKLIN, university executive; b. Dallas, Feb. 2, 1948; s. Roger Albert and Genevieve Mae (Mohr) W. Cert. higher studies, U. Lausanne, Switzerland, 1970; BA, So. Meth. U., 1971, M Liberal Arts, 1973; EdD, Harvard U., 1978. Dir. upperclass residences So. Meth. U., Dallas, 1971-73, mem. faculty, 1973-75; dir. Mohr Edn. Found., Dallas, 1975-77; dir. North Park East, Raymond D. Nasher Co., Dallas, 1977-79; dir. Stanford Housing Ctr., asst. dean student affairs Stanford (Calif.) U., 1979-91, exec. dir. housing, 1991—. Dir. Camp Grady Spruce, YMCA, Dallas, 1971-76, bd. dirs., 1976-80. Bd. dirs. Kentfield Commons, Redwood City, Calif., 1989-91. Mem. APPA, Assn. Coll. and Univ. Housing Officers, Harvard Club San Francisco, Phi Beta Kappa. Avocations: swimming, travel, history, reading, music. Home: 861 Whitehall Ln Redwood City CA 94061-3685 Office: Stanford U Housing 565 Cowell Ln Stanford CA 94305-8512

WHITSELL, DORIS BENNER, retired educator; b. Poplar Grove, Ill., Mar. 17, 1923; d. Ralph Erwin and Sarah McKay (Mulligan) Wheeler; m. Robert M. Benner, Dec. 1945 (div. 1955); 1 child, Geoffrey Mark Benner (dec.); m. Eugene B. Whitsell, Feb. 1969 (dec. 1972). BS, No. Ill. U., 1944, MS in Secondary Edn., 1967; postgrad., Rockford Coll., 1964. Tchr. English and home econs. Lee (Ill.) High Sch., 1944-45; tchr. English Ashton (Ill.) Cmty. H.S., 1945-46; tchr. Morris Kennedy Sch., Rockford, Ill., 1952-55, William Nashold Sch., Rockford, 1955-56; tchr. English, drama Jefferson Jr. H.S., Rockford, 1956-69; tchr. English Richwoods H.S., Peoria, Ill., 1969-71; tchr. Calvin Coolidge Sch., Peoria, 1972-81. Mem. textbook selection com. Dist. 150, Peoria, 1973-75, curriculum planning com., 1974-75, tutor for homebound, 1982-83, cons. competency test seminar; cons. textbook divsn. Harcourt, Brace, Jovanovich, 1981-83; evaluator North Ctrl. Accreditation Team, Jefferson H.S., Rockford, 1980. Counselor Operation Sr. Security, Peoria, 1986-89; treas. Rockford Women's Club Fortnighty Dept., 1961-62; past deaconess 1st Federated Ch., Peoria; pres. Willow Heights Homeowner's Assn., Peoria, 1979-81; bldg. rep. Rockford Edn. Assn., 1954-56, 3d v.p., 1968-70; vol. Rockford Midway Village and Mus. Ctr., 1992, 95-96, 98, 99; bd. dirs. Forest Vale Estate Condominiums, Meadows Assn., Rockford, 1994-96, treas., 1995-97. Named for Significant Svc. to the Community, Ret. Sr. Vol. Program, Peoria, 1986. Mem.: AAUW (program v.p. 1988—89), Peoria Area Ret. Tchrs. Assn. (2d v.p. 1987—88, chmn. state bldg. fund. com. 1987—88, pres. 1989—90), Nat. Ret. Tchrs. Assn. (life), Ill. Ret. Tchrs. Assn. (life; sec. 1982—90, bd. dirs. Found. Inc. 1985—93, moderator conv. panel 1990), No. Ill. U. Alumni Assn., Delta Kappa Gamma (chmn. ins. com. Beta Gamma chpt. 1956—60, v.p. 1962—64, pres. 1964—66, mem. program com. Lambda state chpt. 1978—80, chmn. personal growth and svc. com. Nu chpt. 1988—90, mem. profl. affairs com. 1992—94, Winnebago County ret. tchrs. unit 1992—2003, mem. lit. com. 1996—98, mem. nominations com. 1999—2000, membership com. 2001—03). Avocations: reading, traveling, interior decorating, theatre. Home: 1283 Aarons Ct Rockford IL 61108-1536

WHITT, DIXIE DAILEY, microbiology educator; b. Longmont, Colo., Mar. 9, 1939; d. Herman Eden and Helen Lurissia (Stanton) Dailey; m. Gregory Sidney Whitt, Aug. 25, 1963. BS, Colo. State U., 1961, PhD, 1965. Postdoctoral trainee Yale U., New Haven, Conn., 1965-68, rsch. biologist, lectr., 1968-69; rsch. assoc. U. Ill., Urbana, 1969-87; lectr. basic scis. U. Ill. Coll. Medicine, Urbana, 1987-98, instr., 1998—. Co-author: (lab. manual) Properties of Bacterial Pathogens, 1990, (textbook) Bacterial Pathogenesis: A Molecular Approach, 1st edit., 1994, 2d edit., 2002, Microbiology: Diversity, Disease, and the Environment, 2001; contbr. articles to profl. jours. NDEA Title IV fellow, 1961-64, NIH fellow, 1964-65. Fellow Am. Acad. Microbiology; mem. AAAS, Am. Soc. Microbiology (chair membership com. 1995—), Internat. Assn. Med. Sci. Educators. Home: 1510 Trails Dr Urbana IL 61802-7052 Office: U Ill Dept Microbiology 601 S Goodwin Ave Urbana IL 61801-3709

WHITT, MARCUS CALVIN, marketing and public relations executive; b. Paintsville, Ky., Feb. 5, 1960; s. Calvin Leo and Dora Sue (Spears) W.; m. Jennifer Marie McGuire, Jan. 4, 1986; children: Emily Marie, Elizabeth Anne, Jacob Robert. BA, Eastern Ky. U., 1982, MA, 1985. Intern, dir. student rels. dept. music Eastern Ky. U., Richmond, 1982-85; assoc. for ch. rels. Cumberland Coll., Williamsburg, Ky., 1985-87; dir. communications Conv. & Visitors Bur., Louisville, 1987; staff corr. The Western Recorder, Louisville, 1987—; dir. pub. rels. Georgetown (Ky.) Coll., 1988-92; dir. pub. rels. and mktg. Campbellsville (Ky.) U., 1992-95, asst. to pres., 1995-97, v.p. advancement, 1997-2001, v.p. comms. and mktg., 2001—03, acting dir. Am. Civil War Inst., 2003—; assoc. v.p. for pub. rels. and mktg. Eastern Ky. U., Richmond, 2003—. Bd. dirs. Coun. for Advancement and Support of Edn., Ky., 1990-96, pres.-elect, 1992, pres., 1993, 94, program co-chair, 1989-91, chair III pub. and promotion, 1994, mem. program com., 1997-98, co-chair sr. profl. track, 2003; mem. program com. Bapt. Pub. Rels. Assn., Louisville, 1987; program com. co-chair CASE III Conf., 1998, bd. dirs., 1999-2001; lectr. higher edn. instrl. advancement. Contbr. articles to profl. jours. Co-founder Assn. Communicators in Baptist Edn., pres., 2002-03; chair Ky. Heartland Civil War Trails Commn., 1997—; bd. dirs. Taylor County Tourism Commn., 1995-97, Campbellsville/Taylor County Adult Edn. Commn., 2001—, Taylor County Mid. Sch. Site Base Decision Making Coun., 2002-03; comm. chair Taylor County United; mem. tourism and econ. devel. adv. coun. U.S. 2d Congl. Dist. Ky., 2003—. Recipient Gold award for Instnl. Rels., Mktg. Higher Edn., 1991, Silver medal Coun. for Advancement and Support of Edn., 1991, award of excellence, 1992, 94, 95, Spl. Merit award, 1991, 94, 95, 2001, Grand award, 1991, 94, 2000, 02, 03, Silver medal, 1991, 92, Gold medal Image Improvement Mktg. Higher Edn., 1991, Gold award Outdoor Transit Billboard, Admissions Advt. awards, 1990, 91, Merit award in TV advt. Mem. Campbellsville/Taylor County C. of C. (bd. dirs. 1995-99, pres.-elect 1996-97, pres. 1997-98, program chair 1997-2001), Leadership Scott County (publicity 1990-92), Scott County Adult Lit., Scott County Cmty. Showcase (publicity chair 1989-92), Ky. Bapt. Communicators Forum (co-founder 1991), Mil. Order of the Stars and Bars (Ky. comdr. 1987). Republican. Baptist. Avocations: music, southern and kentucky history, baseball, public speaking. Home: 601 Augusta Dr Richmond KY 40475 Office: Eastern Ky U Div PR and Mktg Coates Adminstrn Bldg CPO 7A 521 Lancaster Ave Richmond KY 40475 E-mail: Marc.Whitt@eku.edu.

WHITT, MARY F. reading educator, consultant; b. Montgomery, Ala. d. Clarence D. Whitt Sr. and Georgia Arms. BS, Ala. State U., 1958; MEd, U. Ariz., 1971; EdD, U. Ala., 1980; postgrad., various colls. ongoing. Camp counselor N.Y.C. Mission Soc., Port Jervis, summer 1956; recreation counselor Dayton (Ohio) Parks and Recreation Dept., summer 1963; adminstrv. asst. Wiley Coll./NDEA Inst., Marshall, Tex., summer 1965; tchr. Montgomery (Ala.) County Schs., 1958-62; coordinator sci. and math. Dayton (Ohio) pub. schs., 1962-67; reading and spl. edn. tchr. Vacaville (Calif.) Unified Sch. Dist., 1967-70; coord. reading Dallas Pub. Schs., 1971-72; prof. reading Ala. State U., Montgomery, 1972-98; ret. prof. edn. Contbr. articles to profl. jurs. U.S. Office Edn. fellow, 1970, 76, 77, NSF fellow, 1961, 62, 64, 66. Mem. Internat. Reading Assn., Capstone Coll. of Edn. Soc., AAUW, Phi Delta Kappa, Kappa Delta Pi. Home: 717 Genetta Ct Montgomery AL 36104-5701

WHITTAKER, DOUGLAS KIRKLAND, school system administrator; b. Westfield, N.J., July 14, 1949; s. Alfred Albert and Marion I. (Crocket) W.; m. Susan Kay Helsing, Aug. 9, 1969; children: Jessica Erin, Angela Gaye. BS, Taylor U., 1971; MA, Ball State U., 1975; EdD, Nova U., 1981. Cert. elem. educator, elem. and middle adminstrn. Tchr. Marion (Ind.) Community Schs., 1971-73, Lee County Schs., Ft. Myers, Fla., 1973-80, asst. prin., 1980-81, elem. prin., 1981-86, middle sch. prin., 1986-90, elem. prin., 1990-92, dir. curriculum svcs., 1993-95, exec. dir. curriculum and sch. improvement, 1995—2002, asst. supt. for tchg. and learning, 2002—03; dir. elem. learning Charlotte County Schs., Port Charlotte, Fla., 2003—. Adj. prof. Nova U., Ft. Lauderdale, Fla., 1983—, Barry U., Miami; trainer in field. Contbr. articles to profl. jours. Mem. ASCD, NEA, Phi Delta Kappa. Republican. Avocations: golf, travel, reading, singing, flying. Home: 9218 Palm Island Cir Fort Myers FL 33903-7120 Office: Charlotte County Pub Schs 1445 Edn Way Port Charlotte FL 33948 E-mail: d.whittaker@worldnet.att.net., doug_whittaker@ccps.k12ofl.us.

WHITTAKER, MARGARET MICHAEL, biology educator; b. Upper Darby, Pa., Aug. 27, 1940; d. Ellsworth Lorenzo and Jane Frances (Faissler) Michael; m. Richard Pawling Whittaker, June 27, 1964; children: Laura Whittaker Calizzi, Susan Whittaker Glynn, Scott, Keith. BA, U. Del., 1962; MS, U. Pa., 1964. Asst. instr. biology U. Pa., Phila., 1962-64; instr. Rosemont (Pa.) Coll., 1964-69; instr. microbiology Pa. State-Bryn Mawr Hosp., 1967-68; instr. C.C. of Phila., 1968-70; asst. biology instr. Rutgers U., Camden, N.J., 1970-71; instr. Canal Zone Coll., Balboa, Panama, 1972-74; lectr. Cabrini Coll., Radnor, Pa., 1975-83, Ursinus Coll., Collegeville, Pa., 1983-92, Pa. State U., Reading, 1993—2001; ret., 2001. Leader Girl Scouts U.S., Pottsgrove, Pa.; active tutorial program YWCA Adult Literacy Ctr., Pottstown, Pa.; bd. dirs. Schuylkill Valley br. ARC, Norristown, Pa. Mem. Montgomery County Med. Soc. Alliance (pres. 1994-96), Mortar Bd., Sigma Xi, Phi Beta Kappa, Phi Kappa Phi. Republican. Presbyterian. Home: 1300 Beaumont Ln Pottstown PA 19464-2565

WHITTEMORE, RONALD PAUL, hospital administrator, retired army officer, nursing educator; b. Saco, Maine, Aug. 10, 1946; s. Ronald B. and Pauline L. (Larson) W.; m. Judy D. McDonald, Feb. 17, 1967; 1 child, Leicia Michelle. BGS, U. S.C., 1974, MEd, 1977; BSN, Med. Coll. Ga., 1975. Enlisted U.S. Army, 1968, advanced through ranks to maj., 1985, ret., 1991; adult/oncology nurse practitioner Martin Army Cmty. Hosp.; asst. head nurse SICU, infection control practitioner Moncrief Army Cmty. Hosp.; infection control practitioner U.S. Army Hosp., Seoul, Republic of Korea; chief nurse 2nd Combat Support Hosp., Ft. Benning, Ga.; cmty. health nurse Brooke Army Med. Ctr., Ft. Sam Houston, Tex.; comty. health nurse Giessen (Germany) Mil. Cmty.; clin. instr. Eisenhower Army Med. Ctr., Ft. Gordon, Ga.; chief nursing adminstrn. E/N Frankfurt (Germany) Army Med. Ctr.; adminstr., dir. quality improvement Gracewood (Ga.) State Sch. and Hosp., 1995-97. Instr. Augusta (Ga.) Tech. Inst.; nurse epidemiologist Med. Coll. Ga., Augusta. Mem. ANA, Ga. ANA (3rd Dist. honoree, pres. 1983-85), Assn. Practitioners in Infection Control, Am. Holistic Nurses Assn., Nat. Assn. Health Care Quality Profls., Assn. for Profls. in Infection Control and Epidemiology, Sigma Theta Tau. Home: 352 Stagecoach Way Martinez GA 30907 Office: Med Coll Ga Office Nurse Rschr Augusta GA 30901-3196

WHITTEN, DAVID GEORGE, chemistry educator; b. Washington, Jan. 25, 1938; s. David Guy and Miriam Deland (Price) W.; m. Jo Wright, July 9, 1960; children: Jenifer Marie, Guy David. AB, Johns Hopkins U., 1959; MA, John Hopkins U., 1961, PhD, 1963. Asst. prof. chemistry U. N.C., Chapel Hill, 1966-70, assoc. prof., 1970-73, prof., 1973-80, M.A. Smith prof., 1980-83; C.E. Kenneth Mees prof. U. Rochester, N.Y., 1983-97, chair dept. chemistry, 1988-91, 95-97, dir. Ctr. for Photoinduced Charge Transfer, 1989-95; mem. tech. staff Los Alamos Nat. Lab., 1997-2000; co-founder, chief tech. officer QTL Biosystems, LLC, 2000—; prof. chemistry and biochemistry Ariz. State U., 2000—. Mem. adv. com. for chemistry NSF; cons. Eastman Kodak Co.; Rochester, N.Y. Editor-in-chief, Langmuir, 1998—. Alfred P. Sloan fellow, 1970; John van Geuns fellow, 1973; recipient special U.S. scientist award Alexander von Humboldt Found., 1975; Japan Soc. for Promotion of Sci. fellow, 1982 Mem. AAAS, Am. Chem. Soc. (award in colloid and surface chemistry 1992), Internat. Union of Pure and Applied Chemistry (commn. on photochemistry), Interam. Photochem. Soc. (award 1998). Democrat. Home: 5435 La Colonia Dr NW Albuquerque NM 87120 Office: QTL Biosys LLC 2778 Agua Fria St Bldg C Santa Fe NM 87507 E-mail: whitten@qltbio.com.

WHITTEN, DAVID OWEN, economics educator; b. Beaver Falls, Pa., Nov. 30, 1940; s. Paul Harry and Bula (Owens) Ehrenbergh. BS, Coll. Charleston, 1962; MA, U. S.C., 1963; PhD, Tulane U., 1970. Instr. econs. and fin. U. New Orleans, 1965-68; asst. prof. econs. Auburn U., Ala., 1968-74, assoc. prof., 1974-82, prof., 1982—; cons. U.S. Army C.E., New Orleans, summers 1964, 65. Author: Andrew Durnford: A Black Sugar Planter in Antebellum Louisiana, 1981 (La. honor award 1982), Emergence of Giant Enterprise, 1983, A History of Economics and Business at Auburn University, 1992; co-author: Democracy in Desperation: The Depression of 1893, 1998 (Choice Outstanding Acad. Title 2000); editor: (with Bessie E. Whitten) Manufacturing: A Historiographical and Bibliographical Guide Vol. 1 Handbook of American Business History, 1990, Two-Hundred Years of Eli Whitney's Cotton Gin, 1994, Andrew Durnford: A Black Sugar Planter in the Antebellum South, 1995, Extractives, Manufacturing and Services, 1992, Infrastructure and Services, 2000; editor, Contbns. in Econ. and EEcon. History, 1980-2002, Wall St. Rev. of Books, 1981-89, Bus. Libr. Rev., 1990-2002; contbr. articles to profl. jours. Served with USMCR, 1957-63. Tulane Edn. Found. fellow, 1964, 65. Mem. Am. Econ. Assn. Agrl. History Soc., Econ. History Assn., So. Econs. Assn., Bus. History Conf., Econ. and Bus. Hist. Soc. (v.p. 1988-91, pres. 1991-92, CEO 2000-01), Rexford G. Tugwell Internat. Inst. for Great Depression Era Studies (v.p., treas., dir. 1992—). Home: 102 Kimberly Dr Auburn AL 36832-6712 Office: Auburn U Dept Econs Bus Bldg 209 Auburn AL 36849 E-mail: DWhitten@Business.Auburn.edu.

WHITTEN, JOSEPH LEE, retired school librarian, elementary educator; b. Bryant, Ala., July 19, 1938; s. Jesse Nathan and Laura Lorene (Hawkins) W.; m. Gail Elaine McGeoch, May 21, 1971; 1 child, Miriam Elizabeth. BA, Bob Jones U., Greenville, S.C., 1960; M in Edn., U. Montevallo, Ala., 1977. Cert. tchr., Ala. English tchr. St. Clair Co. H.S., Odenville, Ala., 1961-70, Perry Christian Sch., Marion, Ala., 1970-71, Panama City Christian Sch., Fla., 1971-73; tchr., counselor St. Clair County H.S., Odenville, 1974-94; tchr., libr. Odenville Elem. Sch., 1994-2000. Contbr. articles to profl. jours. Bd. dirs. Ashville Mus. and Archives, 1995—, St. Clair Historical Commn., 1994-99, Cahaba Trace Commn., Montevallo, Ala., 1993-99, Nat. Endowment for Arts Continental Harmony Project: I Am A Song. Mem. NEA, Ala. Ednl. Assn., Ala. State Poetry Soc. (bd. dirs. 1998—, 2d v.p. 2000-2002, treas. 2001--, Ala. Poet of Yr. 2002), Ala. Writers Conclave. Republican. Baptist. Avocations: antiques, books, local history, writing. Home: PO Box 125 Odenville AL 35120-0125 Office: Odenville Elem Sch 400 Alabama St Odenville AL 35120-3047 E-mail: whitten93@alltel.net.

WHITTEN, LAURA A. secondary school educator; b. Lakewood, N.J., Sept. 23, 1964; AA in Gen. Studies, Southwestern Coll., Chula Vista, Calif., 1985; BA in Drama, San Diego State U., 1988; MS in Ednl. Tech., Nat. U., San Diego, 1997. English lang. tchr. Orange Glen H.S., Escondido, Calif., 1989-93; English lang. and drama tchr. Valley H.S., Escondido, Calif., 1993-98, Valley Center (Calif.) H.S., 1998—. Test preparation instr. Britannica Learning Ctr., Bonita, Calif., 1989-94, Hit Any Key Computer Learning Ctr., San Diego, 1996—. Scholarship coord. Dollars for Scholars San Diego County Office Edn., 1998. Recipient Excellence in Lang. Arts Instrn. award Old Globe Theatre, 1992, 93. Mem. NCTE, Calif. Assn. Tchrs. English, We. Assn. Schs. and Colls. (vis. com. mem. 1998), Kappa Delta Pi. Avocations: reading, baseball, computers, shopping. Home: 1230 Sybil Ct Escondido CA 92026-2129 Office: Valley Center HS Cole Grade Rd Valley Center CA 92082 E-mail: laurart@home.com.

WHITTINGTON, FREDERICK BROWN, JR., business administration educator; b. Sept. 22, 1934; m. Marjorie Ann Babington; children: Frederick Brown III, Marjorie Ellen, Lisa Anne. SB, MIT, 1958; MBA, Tulane U., 1965; PhD, La. State U., 1969. Staff economist Miss. Rsch. Commn., Jackson, 1961-64; sr. assoc. econ. rsch. Gulf South Rsch. Inst., Baton Rouge, 1966-69; asst. prof. bus. adminstrn. Emory U., Atlanta, 1969-73, assoc. prof., 1973-79, prof., 1979-96, prof. emeritus, 1997—, dir. customer bus. devel. track, 1991-94. Bd. dirs. Gwinnett Industries, Inc.; mem. forecasting panel Fed. Res. Bank Atlanta; vis. prof. Johannes Kepler U., Linz, Austria, 1983, 84, 89, 95-2003; guest lectr. Austrian Univs., Linz, Vienna, Innsbruck and Klagenfurt; presenter workshops; cons. in field. Contbr. articles and reports to profl. jours. Mktg. plan, mgmt. audit State of Miss., Park Commn.; past chmn., bd. deacons Decatur Presbyn. Ch.; mem. adv. bd. DeKalb/Rockdale Svc. Ctr., ARC. Capt. USNR, ret., 1994. Recipient Badge of Hon., Austrian Mktg. Rsch. Soc., 1996, recipient Trauner prize for ednl. innovation Upper Austrian Econ. Chamber, 1997; Sears Roebuck Found. fellow, 1965-66. Mem. Am. Mktg. Assn., Nat. Assn. Purchasing Mgmt., So. Mktg. Assn., Coun. for Logistics Mgmt., Warehousing Edn. and Rsch. Coun., Omicron Delta Kappa, Beta Gamma Sigma, Delta Tau Delta. Office: Emory U Goizueta Bus Sch Atlanta GA 30322-0001 E-mail: brown_whittington@bus.emory.edu.

WHITTINGTON, OPAL HAYES, nursing educator; b. Wynona, Okla., May 30, 1935; d. Bernie Buford and Dora Bell (Dildine) Hayes; m. William Andrew Whittington, Jan. 7, 1955; children: Joe William, Cheryl, Melanie. ASN, Miss. Gulf Coast Jr. Coll., Gulfport, 1967; BSN, Fla. So. Coll., 1985; MA in Edn., U. So. Fla., 1990. RN, Fla. Clin. nurse med./surg. Gulfport (Miss.) Meml. Hosp.; clin. nurse/surg. recovery Lakeland Reg. Med. Ctr., Fla.; dir. and instr. practical nursing, chmn. health occupations Bd. of Edn. Polk County, Bartow, Fla., 1972-97; ret. CPR instr. Am. Heart Assn.; first aid/CPR instr. ARC. Mem. Am. Nurses Assn., Fla. Nurses Assn., Am. Vocat. Assn., Fla. Vocat. Assn., Polk County Vocat. Assn., NEA, Polk Edn. Assn.

WHITTINGTON, RONALD FREDERICK, academic administrator; b. Marion, Md., July 26, 1949; s. Frederick Hubbard and Naomi (Archie) W.; m. Marilyn Elaine Portlock, June 3, 1972; 1 child, Colby. BSEd, U. Del., 1971; MBA, Cen. Mich. U., 1983. Tchr. Newark Sch. Dist., 1971-73; asst. headmaster St. Croix (V.I.) Country Day Sch., 1973-75, Goud Hope Sch., St. Croix, 1975-78; asst. dir. admissions U. Del., Newark, 1978-86, asst. dean Coll. of Bus., 1986-88, asst. to pres., 1988—. Exec. coun. Del Marva Boy Scout Coun., Wilmington, Del., 1990; exec. bd. Del. ACLU, Wilmington, 1990; com. mem. United Way of Del., Wilmington, 1986. Mem. Am. Coun. on Edn., Alpha Phi Alpha. Office: U Del 104 Hullihen Ct Newark DE 19711-3649

WHITTINGTON-BROWN, VANESSA ELIZABETH, educator; b. Boston, Apr. 15, 1960; d. Samuel Wall and Ernestine (Brazand Hundley) W; m. July, 1992. BS, Bridgewater State U., 1978; postgrad., Cambridge Coll., 1992—. Elem. tchr. Boston (Mass.) Pub. Schs., 1983—, Fauline A. Shaw, Dorchester, Mass., 1987-92; tchr. The Josiah Quincy Sch., Boston, 1992—. Adult edn. sec. Boston Pub. Schs., 1982, 83, mem. graphic learning com., 1983, impact II tchr. adaptor; musician cable TV program Gospel Expressions Prodns.; tutor Metco (after sch. program); mem. Primary Summer Source Inst., 1991; local pres. Sunshine Band, 1986, state pres., 1989-92. Mem. local Sunshine Band, 1985, state pres., 1989—; composer: Lord I'm Coming Home, 1986. Mem. Children's Mus. and the Mus. Sci., Women's Heritage Trail, 3 Regent St. Young Adult Choir, Women's Choir, Boston Writing Project, Professional Dev. Program; co-dir. Specially Trained Youth Leadership in Excellence (STYLE), 1997; church musician Church of God in Christ Church, 1976-92. With USAR, 1979-91. Mem. Assn. Supervision and Curriculum Devel., Greater Boston Reading Coun., Boston Tchrs. Union, Black Educators Alliance of Mass., Nat. Coun. Tchrs. English, Women's Heritage Trail, African Meeting House. Democrat. Avocations: music, bowling, racquetball, basketball.

WHITTINGTON-COUSE, MARYELLEN FRANCES, education administrator, organizational specialist, consultant; b. Waverly, N.Y., June 16, 1957; d. Philip John and Sheila (Dewey) Whittington; m. Daniel Couse, May 18, 1985; children: Kristen, Benjamin, Connor. BA, SUNY, Empire, 1983; M of Internat. Adminstrn., Sch. for Internat. Tng., Brattleboro, Vt., 1992. Adj. faculty Rockland C.C., 1983-85; cons. UN Non-Govtl. Liaison Svc., N.Y.C., 1987; adminstrv. asst. Manitoga Nature Ctr., Garrison, N.Y., 1987-88; coord. Intensive Tchr. Inst. Manhattanville and Coll. of New Rochelle Satellites, New Paltz, N.Y., 1990-92; dir. Bilingual ESL Tech. Assistance Ctr. N.Y. State Edn. Dept., New Paltz, 1988-2000. Orgnl. devel. cons., personal coach, 2000—; assoc. prof. SUNY, New Paltz, 1994—; diversity specialist Cornell U., 2001—; co-chair PROSPAN; mem. Parent Edn. Adv. Coun., Ulster County, 1988—. Editor: (curriculum) Teacher's Guide and Content Activities for Limited English Proficient Students, 1992; co-author video script for N.Y. State Edn. Dept., 1992. Mem. Nat. Assn Bilingual Edn., N.Y. TESOL, TESOL Internat., N.Y. State Assn. Bilingual Edn. (conf. chair 1996), Nat. Assn. Multicultural Edn. Avocations: hiking, reading, gardening. Home and Office: 19 Quaker St Tillson NY 12486 E-mail: mwhit68421@aol.com.

WHYBARK, DAVID CLAY, business educator, researcher; b. Tacoma, Wash., Sept. 18, 1935; s. Clay Alfred and Irene (Stanton) W.; m. Neva Jo Richardson, July 6, 1957; children: Michael David, Suzanne Marie (dec.). BS, U. Washington, 1957; MBA, Cornell U., 1960; PhD, Stanford U., 1967. Rsch. assoc. Stanford (Calif.) U., 1962-67; asst. prof. Ariz. State U., Tempe, 1965-66; assoc. prof. Purdue U., West Lafayette, Ind., 1967-76; prof. Ind. U., Bloomington, 1976-90; Macon G. Patton disting. prof. U. N.C., Chapel Hill, 1990—. Vis. prof. Shanghai Inst. Mech. Engring., 1986-87, Chinese U. of the Hong Kong, 1996, Victoria U., New Zealand, 1996, Canterbury U., New Zealand, 1996; adj. prof. Inst. for Mgmt. Devel., Lausanne, Switzerland, 1981-82, 85-90; dir., founder Global Mfg. Rsch. Group, 1990—; cons. in field. Author: Master Production Scheduling: Theory and Practice, 1979, Manufacturing Planning Control Systems, 1984, 5th edit., 2004, International Operations Management, 1989, Integrated Production and Inventory Management, 1993, Why ERP?, 2000; editor: Internat. Jour. Prodn. Econs., 1991-95, Global Manufacturing Practices, 1993. Recipient Lilly Alumni MBA Teaching Excellence award, 1990, Disting. Rsch. award Kenan-Flagler Sch., 1998. Fellow Decision Scis. Inst. (past pres., disting. svc. award 1984), Pan Pacific Bus. Assn. (mem. coun.), Ops. Mgmt. Assn. (pres. 1992-93); mem. Am. Prodn. Inventory Control Soc., Internat. Soc. Inventory Rsch. (mem. coun., pres. 2000-02). Avocations: travel, winemaking. Office: U NC Kenan-Flagler Sch Chapel Hill NC 27599-3490 E-mail: clay_whybark@unc.edu.

WHYTE, MARTIN KING, sociology and Chinese studies educator; b. Oklahoma City, Nov. 4, 1942; s. William Foote and Kathleen (King) W.; m. Veronica Mueller, Nov. 5, 1966 (div. 1990); children: Adam, Tracy; m. Alice Hogan, Sept. 14, 1991; 1 child, Julia. AB, Cornell U., 1964; MA, Harvard U., 1966, PhD, 1971. From asst. prof. to prof. dept. sociology U. Mich., Ann Arbor, 1969-95, assoc. chmn. dept. sociology, 1972-73, 79-81; dir. Univs. Service Ctr., Hong Kong, 1973-74; program dir.Sociology Program NSF, Washington, 1993-94; prof. dept. sociology George Washington U., Washington, 1995-2000, Harvard U., 2000—. Vis. prof. George Washington U., 1994-95; mem. joint com. on Chinese studies Am. Coun. of Learned Socs., 1978-81, 84-87; dir. Ctr. for Rsch. on Social Orgn., 1984-87, 90-92. Author: Small Groups and Political Rituals in China, 1974, The Status of Women in Preindustrial Societies, 1978; (with others) Village and Family in Contemporary China, 1978, Urban Life in Contemporary China, 1984, Dating, Mating and Marriage, 1990, Marriage in America, 2000. Mem. Am. Sociol. Assn., Assn. Asian Studies, Population Assn. Am., Phi Beta Kappa Democrat. Avocation: cycling. Home: 10015 Brunswick Ave Silver Spring MD 20910-1020 Office: Dept Sociology Harvard U 480 William James Hall Cambridge MA 02138 E-mail: mwhyte@wjh.harvard.edu.

WHYTE, NANCY MARIE, performing arts educator; b. Myrtlepoint, Oreg., Mar. 12, 1948; d. Lawrence Edward and Carol Elizabeth (Johnson) Guderian; m. Anthony John Whyte, Aug. 7, 1967 (div. Sept. 1968); 1 child, Charles Lawrence; m. Douglas Brian Graff, June 27, 1971 (div. Oct. 1974); m. Lawrence Hanson, Mar. 12, 1976 (div. Aug. 1984); m. Joseph Paul Deacon, Aug. 10, 1985; 1 child, Nina Alexandra. Student, U. Wash., 1969-72, Am. Sch. Dance, 1972; BA, Evergreen State Coll., 1987. Owner, dir. Nancy Whyte Sch. Ballet, Bellingham, Wash., 1969—; artistic dir. Garden Street Dance Players, Bellingham, 1969-72, MT Baker Ballet, Bellingham, 1975—, Alpha nd Omega Worship Dancers, 2003—; co-dir. Exptl. Performance Workshop, Bellingham, 1975-77; instr. creative dance St. Paul's Primary Sch., Bellingham, 1993-97; facilitator dance workshop Allied Arts/Whatcom Co., Bellingham, 1995—. Guest lectr. Western Wash. U., Bellingham, 1976—83, Bellingham, 1996—; guest faculty Dance Theatre N.W., Tacoma, 1995—; liturgical dance cons. Assumption Cath. Sch., 2001—; artistic dir. Alpha and Omega Worship Dancers, 2003—. Author: Memoirs of a Child of Theatre Street, 1993; soloist Raduga Folk Ballet/N.Y. Character Ballet, N.Y.C., 1978-79; choreographer numerous ballets, 1972—. Mem. Nat. Dance Assn., Dancers Over 40, Sacred Dance Guild, Vancouver Ballet Soc. Democrat. Avocations: voice, writing. Office: MT Baker Ballet 1412 Cornwall Ave PO Box 2393 Bellingham WA 98227-2393

WIATR, JEANNE MALECKI, education educator; b. Chgo., July 20, 1952; d. Aloysius John and Eugenia (Szumik) Malecki; m. Christopher Wiatr, Oct. 20, 1978; children: Kelli, C.J., Kaycee, Kirby, Nicholas. BA, Roosevelt U., 1974, MA, 1976; postgrad., No. Ill. U., 1990-95, U. Pitts., 1998. Cert. tchr., Ill. Head tchr. Chgo. Assn. for Retarded Citizens, 1974—78; children's program coord. Parklawn Sch., Oak Lawn, 1979—85; children's reference libr. Woodridge Libr., Woodridge, 1986—87; instr. Coll. of DuPage, Glen Ellyn, 1987—95, instr. kids on campus, 1989—95; art instr. Wesley Acad., 1996—97; supplemental instrn. specialist U. Pitts., 1997—2001, U. Memphis, 2001; student acad. support Rhodes Coll., 2001. Homebound tutor Dist. 203, Naperville, Ill., 1988-94; tutor, cons. Ednl. Svcs. of Glen Ellyn, 1992-95; program specialist Monyough Cmty. Svcs., 1996; storyteller, lectr. Dist. 203/204 and pvt. groups, DuPage County, Ill. and McMurray, Pa.; coord. supplemental instrn. program U. Pitts., 2001—. Master catechist St. Raphael REACH Program, Naperville, 1987-95; catechist St. Benedict The Abbot, McMurray. Roman Catholic. Avocations: cartooning and drawing, travel, golf. Home: 2910 Oakleigh Ln Germantown TN 38138-7646 E-mail: jeannewiatr@yahoo.com.

WIATT, CAROL STULTZ, elementary education educator; b. Roanoke, Va., July 9, 1946; d. Hubert Grant and Irene Ella (Barbour) Stultz (dec.); m. Alexander Lloyd Wiatt, June 14, 1969 (div.); children: Alexander Todd II, Christopher Campbell. BS in Elem. Edn., Radford U., 1968; cert., Coll. of William and Mary, 1991. Cert. elem. and mid. sch. prin., geography and elem. grades tchr. Tchr. 4th grade Roanoke County Pub. Schs. Sys., 1968-70; tchr. 6th grade Richmond (Va.) Pub. Schs. Sys., 1970-73; tchr. 5th and 6th grades Newport News (Va.) Pub. Schs. Sys., 1974-91, staff devel. specialist, 1991-93, tchr. 5th grade, 1993-99, McIntosh Elem. Sch., 1993-99; tchr. 7th grade reading, language Staunton River Mid. Sch., Moneta, Va., 1999—; tchr. 7th grade Bedford County Pub. Sch., 1999. Adj. faculty, master tchr. Hampton (Va.) U., 1988—; adj. faculty Christopher Newport U., Newport News, 1988-93, prof., 1993-94; adj. faculty U. Va., 1999—; computer specialist Newport News Pub. Schs. Sys., 1987-91; prin. Hidewood Elem. Sch., summer 1994, Newport News Pub. Sch. Enrichment Summer Sch., 1996-98; adv. com. on tech. NNPS, 1997-98; summer sch. prin. SRMS, 2003. Author: DESIGNS, 1986; contbr. articles to profl. jours. and newspapers. Active Friends of Mariners' Mus., Newport News, 1987-99; chmn. cultural arts com. Newport News Coun. PTA, 1980-83, 1st v.p., 1981-83, treas., 1983-85; mem. hospitality com. Hidenwood Sch. PTA, 1985-86, chmn. membership com., 1986-88; bd. dirs. Hidenwood Recreational Assn., Newport News, 1988-92. Recipient Hon. Mention, Tchr. of Yr. awards The Consortium for Interactive Instrn., 1987, 90; fellow Old Dominion U. Coll. Edn.; named Elem. Tchr. of Yr. Daily Press and Cannon, 1991, Tchr. of Yr., NNPS, 1991, Va. Tech. Tchr. of Yr., 1998, BCPS Rotary Tchr., 2003. Mem. ASCD, NEA, ICCE, AAUW, Va. Assn. Curriculum and Devel., Va. Edn. Assn., Va. Edn. Math. Assn., Va. Tech. Edn. Assn., Va. Geography Soc., Va. State Reading Assn. (chmn. tech. and reading com. 1997-98), Newport News Edn. Assn., Peninsula Coun. Math. of Va. (v.p. 1987-88), Newport News Reading Coun, Kappa Delta Pi. Republican. Baptist. Home: 312 Ashley Ct Vinton VA 24179-1800 Office: Staunton River Mid Sch 1293 Golden Eagle Dr Moneta VA 24121-9616

WICAL, BARBARA LOU, elementary school educator; b. Kenton, Ohio, Aug. 27, 1949; d. William Harmon and Dorothy Margaret (Seiler) Woodard; m. Eldon Craig Wical, July 12, 1980; stepchildren: Shelden Wical, Kyle Wical. BS in Edn., Ohio No. U., 1971; MS in Ednl. Adminstrn., U. Dayton, 1981. Elem. tchr. Jackson Ctr. (Ohio) Local Sch., 1971—. Named Outstanding Educator, Bus. Adv. Coun. of Sidney/Shelby County, Ohio, 1993-94; The Martha Holden Jennings Found. scholar, 1986-87. Mem. Jackson Ctr. Jr. Am. Club (sec. 1987-88, pres. 1991-93, treas. 1993-94), Delta Kappa Gamma (ways and means chair 1986-90). Lutheran. Avocations: sewing, gardening, reading, crafts, watching sports. Home: 202 S Fork Jackson Center OH 45334 Office: Jackson Center Local School 204 S Linden Jackson Center OH 45334

WICE, PAUL CLINTON, news director, educator; b. West Branch, Mich., Sept. 30, 1944; s. Clinton Harold and Viola Ruth (Potratz) W.; m. Dolores Ann Janovec, Sept. 30, 1967. BA, Kearney State Coll., 1966; MA, U. Nebr., Kearney, 1989. News anchor Sta. KHGI-TV, Kearney, Nebr., 1965-66; news editor Sta. KWBE Radio, Beatrice, Nebr., 1966-67; city editor Kearney Hub, 1968-69; news dir. Sta. KGFW-AM, Kearney, 1967-68, 69—. Adj. faculty speech communication U. Nebr., Kearney, 1981—. Bd. dirs. Kearney Literacy Coun., Kearney Cmty. Concert Assn., The SAFE Ctr. Inc.; former bd. dirs. Luth. Family Svcs. of Nebr. Mem. Soc. Profl. Jours. Home: Box 1754 2 Sycamore Pl Kearney NE 68847-8311 Office: Sta KGFW-AM PO Box 666 Kearney NE 68848-0666 E-mail: paul@kgfw.com.

WICHMAN, EDNA CAROL, media specialist, librarian; b. Dodge City, Kans., Jan. 11, 1945; d. Robert Lyle and Mabel Josephine (Woodka) Smith; m. Kenneth C. Wichman, Sept. 2, 1967; children: Lorie Jean, Curtis Clouse. BSEd, Emporia State U., 1967, MEd, 1971. Kindergarten, elem. libr. Sinai/Timmons Elem. Sch., Bonner Springs, Kans., 1967-69; with Head Start, Bonner Springs, summer 1968; tchr. 3d grade Osage City (Kans.) Elem., 1970-71, Black Lane Elem., Fairborn, Ohio, 1971-77; media specialist Cen. Jr. High Sch., Fairborn, 1977-81, Fairborn High Sch., 1981-96, Northridge Local Schs., Montgomery County, 1996-00, ret., 2000; devel. libr. Am. Rsch. Ctr. in Egypt, Cairo, 2003—. Presenter Edn. Day Western Ohio, Fairborn, 1988-90, Tech. Fair Miami U., Middletown, 1990, Ohio Dept. Edn., Columbus, 1990, OELMA conf., 1998; prof. Sch. Edn., Wright State U.; faculty edn. leadership dept. U. Dayton Edn.; librn. Am. Rsch. Ctr. Egypt, 2001. Mem. bd. elections Greene County, Xenia, Ohio; treas. Greene County Dem. Party, 1982-88, chair, 1988-90; mem. Friends of Fairborn Libr.; chairperson Greene County Mental Health Drug and Alcohol Bd., 1994-95, Ea. Miami Valley ADMH Bd., 1995-96, bd. dirs., 1995—; mem. Bath Twp. Zoning Bd., 1998—. Named Keeper of Flame Sec. State of Ohio, Dayton, 1990, Media Specialist of Yr. Ohio Sch. Libr., 1991; named to Greene County Women's Hall of Fame, Fairborn, 1990. Mem. AAUW (pres. 1984-88, Woman of Yr. Fairborn br. 1992, v.p. membership Fairborn br.), NEA (chair congl. contact team 1980-90), ALA, Am. Assn. Sch. Librs., Ohio Edn. Assn. (EPAC chair 1975-89), Fairborn Edn. Assn. (pres. 1975-76, Tchr. Salute 1977), Southwestern Ohio Young Adult Material Rev. Group (pres. 1985-87), Ohio Ednl. Libr./Media Assn. (legis. chair state bd.), Assn. Coll. and Rsch. Librs., Egyptian Libr. ASsn., Internat. Libr. Com., Phi Delta Kappa. Democrat. Lutheran. Avocations: reading, politics, gardening. Home: 1335 Yellow Springs Fairfield Rd Fairborn OH 45324 Office: Am Rsch Ctr in Egypt Garden City 2 Midan Simon Bolivar Cairo Egypt E-mail: cwichman@aol.com.

WICKER, NANCY LYNN, art history educator; b. Shelbyville, Ind. m. Matthew Leigh Murray, May 17, 1991. BA in Art History and Art Studio, Ea. Ill. U., 1975; MA in Art History, U. Minn., 1979, PhD in Ancient Studies, 1990. Adj. instr.. Minn. State U., Mankato, 1986, asst. prof., 1990-95, assoc. prof., 1995-2000, prof., 2000—02, dir. Scandinavian Studies Program, 2000—02; adminstr. asst. U. Minn., Mpls., 1986-90; prof., chair art dept. U. Miss., University, Miss., 2003—. Editor: Beyond Gender Theory, 1999, Gender and the Archaeology of Death, 2001; contbr. articles to profl. jours. Birka Internat. scholar, 1992; Am.-Scandinavian Found. fellow, 1982, NEH fellow, 2001-02; grantee Am. Coun. Learned Socs., 1990, Am. Numismatic Soc., 1994, Norwegian Ministry Fgn. Affairs, 1996, Norwegian Info. Svc., 1996, Am. Scandinavian Found., 1996, Berit Wallenberg Found., 1997, Am. Philos. Soc., 1997, Internat. Rsch. and Exchs. Bd., 1997, NEH, 2000-2001, Kress Found. grant, 2003. Mem. European Assn. Archaeologists, Soc. Am. Archaeology, Archaeol. Inst. Am., Medieval Acad. Am., Internat. Ctr. Medieval Art (bd. dirs.), Coll. Art Assn., Soc. Advancement Scandinavian Study (bd. dirs.), Soc. Medieval Feminist Scholarship, Soc. Medieval Archaeology, Soc. Historians Scandanavia (bd. dir.). Office: Univ Mississippi Art Dept PO Box 1848 University MS 38677 Fax: 662-915-5013.

WICKERT, MAX ALBRECHT, English educator, poet; b. Augsburg, Germany, May 26, 1938; came to the U.S., 1952; s. Stephan Philip and Thilde Kellner Wickert; div.; 1 child, Morgan Elaine. BA, St. Bonaventure U., 1958; MA, Yale U., 1959, PhD, 1965. Instr. Nazareth Coll. Rochester, N.Y., 1962-63, asst. prof., 1964-66, SUNY, Buffalo, 1966-71, assoc. prof., 1972—. Dir. Outriders Poetry Program, Buffalo, 1971-81; dir. summer poetry festival Artpark, Lewiston, N.Y., 1978. Author: All The Weight of The Still Midnight, 1972, Pat Sonnets, 2000; author of poetry and short stories. Recipient New Poets prize Chowan Coll., 1980, Burchfield Poetry prize Burchfield Ctr., Buffalo, 1983; Woodrow Wilson fellow Woodrow Wilson Found., 1967-68, NEH summer fellow, 1986. Mem. MLA, Dante Soc. Am., Amnesty Internat. Office: Univ Buffalo Dept English 306 Clemens Amherst NY 14260-0001 Home: 314 Highland Ave Buffalo NY 14222 E-mail: wickert@acsu.buffalo.edu.

WICKHAM, KATHLEEN WOODRUFF, education educator; b. Wilson Boro, Pa., May 31, 1949; d. Ralph E. and Ann Mary (Korp) Woodruff; m. Peter Kuntz Wickham Jr., Sept. 30, 1978; children: Matthew Peter, Timothy Kuntz. BA, Glassboro State Coll., 1971; MA, Memphis State U., 1987; EdD, U. Memphis, 1999. Reporter The Daily Advance, Dover, N.J., 1971-75, The Press, Atlantic City, N.J., 1975-77, The Star-Ledger, Newark, 1977-81; instr. U. Memphis, 1983—99; asst. prof. U. Miss., 1999—; reporter Jannett News Svc., 1999. Presenter in field. Author Math. Tools for Journalists, 2002; contbr. articles to newspapers, mags. and jours.; acad. editor Perspectives: Online Journalism, 1998. Fellow, Am. Soc. Newspaper Editors, 1999. Mem. Nat. Headliner Club, Autism Soc. Am. (Memphis chpt. pres. 1988-89, conf. co-chair 1989, 92, 95, Tenn. state soc. pres. 1989-90), Soc. Profl. Journalists (v.p. local chpt., pres. 1999-2000—), Investigative Reporters and Editors, Kappa Tau Alpha. Avocations: reading, computer technology. Office: U Miss Farley Hall Oxford MS 38677

WICKHAM, M(ARVIN) GARY, optometry educator; b. Ft. Morgan, Colo., Dec. 23, 1942; m. Irene Mary Wilhelm, Mar. 20, 1965. BS, Colo. State U., 1964, MS, 1967; PhD, Wash. State U., 1972. Rsch. physiologist VA, Gainesville, Fla., 1971-74; asst. prof. U. Fla., Gainesville, 1972-74; rsch. physiologist VA, San Diego, 1974-79; asst. rsch. biologist morphology of the eye U. Calif., San Diego, 1974-79; from assoc. prof. histology, ocular anatomy and physiology to prof. Northeastern State U., Tahlequah, Okla., 1979—97, prof. optometry, 1997—. Ad hoc reviewer vision scis. study sects. divsn. rsch. grants NIH, 1990—97. Contbr. articles to profl. jours. Recipient Glaucoma Studies grant VA, 1975, Core Em Facility grant, 1977-79, Focal Argon Laser Lesions grant, 1979; Morphology of Mammal Eyes grant NIH, 1980, Computer-Based Image Analysis grantee Nat. Eye Inst., 1990. Mem. AAAS, Soc. Integrative Comparative Biology, Am. Inst. Biol. Scis., Assn. for Rsch. in Vision and Ophthalmology. Achievements include co-development of first argon laser treatment for glaucoma; first co-documentation of movement of silicone away from clinically implanted breast prosthesis devices using EDXA; co-application of vitreous carbon as a knife-making material; confirmation of generality of occurrence of encapsulated receptors inside cetacean eyes. Office: Northeastern State U Coll Optometry Tahlequah OK 74464

WICKIZER, CINDY LOUISE, retired elementary school educator; b. Pitts., Dec. 12, 1946; d. Charles and Gloria Geraldine (Cassidy) Zimmerman Sr.; m. Leon Leonard Wickizer, Mar. 20, 1971 (div. Oct. 2003); 1 child, Charlyn Michelle. BS, Oreg. State U., 1968. Tchr. Enumclaw (Wash.) Sch. Dist., 1968-99, ret., 1999. Mem. Wash. State Ret. Tchrs. Assn., Am. Rabbit Breeders Assn. (judge, chmn. scholarship found. 1986-87, pres. 1988-94, 96-98, dist. dir. 1994-96, 2003—, Disting. Svc. award 1987, Hall of Fame 1998), Wash. State Rabbit Breeders Assn. (life, Pres.'s award 1983, 94, sec., dir., v.p. 1995-97), Vancouver Island Rabbit Breeders Assn., Wash. State Rabbit and Cavy Shows Inc. (sec. 1994—), Evergreen Rabbit Assn. (sec., v.p., pres.), Alpha Gamma Delta. Home: 20825 Star Rte 410 E PMB 196 Sumner WA 98390 E-mail: CindyWick@aol.com.

WICKWIRE, PATRICIA JOANNE NELLOR, psychologist, educator; d. William McKinley and Clara Rose (Pautsch) Nellor; m. Robert James Wickwire, Sept. 7, 1957; 1 child, William James. BA cum laude, U. No. Iowa, 1951; MA, U. Iowa, 1959; PhD, U. Tex., Austin, 1971; postgrad., U. So. Calif., 1951-66, UCLA, 1951-66, Calif. State U., Long Beach, 1951-66. Lic. ednl. psychologist, marriage, family and child counselor, Calif. Tchr. Ricketts Ind. Schs., Iowa, 1946-48; tchr., counselor Waverly-Shell Rock Ind. Schs., Iowa, 1951-55; reading cons., head dormitory counselor U. Iowa, Iowa City, 1955-57; tchr., sch. psychologist, adminstr. S. Bay Union H.S. Dist., Redondo Beach, Calif., 1962-82, dir. student svcs. and spl. edn. Cons. mgmt. and edn.; pres. Nellor Wickwire Group, 1981—; mem. exec. bd. Calif. Interagy. Mental Health Coun., 1968-72, Beach Cities Symphony Assn., 1970-82; chmn. Friends of Dominguez Hills, Calif., 1981-85. Contbr. articles in field to profl. jours. Pres. Calif. Women's Caucus, 1993-95. Mem. APA, AAUW (exec. bd., chpt. pres. 1962-72), Nat. Career Devel. Assn. (media chair 1992-98), Am. Assn. Career Edn. (pres. 1991—), L.A. County Dirs. Pupil Svcs. (chmn. 1974-79), L.A. County Pers. and Guidance Assn. (pres. 1977-78), Assn. Calif. Sch. Adminstrs. (dir. 1977-81), L.A. County SW Bd. Dist. Adminstrs. for Spl. Edn. (chmn. 1976-81), Calif. Assn. Sch. Psychologists (bd. dirs. 1981-83), Am. Assn. Sch. Adminstrs., Calif. Assn. for Measurement and Evaluation in Guidance (dir. 1981, pres. 1984-85, 98-2000), ACA (chmn. Coun. Newsletter Editors 1989-91, mem. com. on women 1989-92, mem. com. on rsch. and knowledge 1994—, chmn. 1995—, mem. and chmn. bylaws com. 1998-2001, rep. to joint com. on testing practices 2001—), Assn. Measurement and Eval. in Guidance (Western regional editor 1985-87, conv. chair 1986, editor 1987-90, exec. bd. dirs. 1987-91), Calif. Assn. Counseling and Devel. (exec. bd. 1984—, pres. 1988-89, jour. editor 1990—), Nat. Assn. for Ind.-Edn. Coop. (bd. dirs. 2002—), Internat. Career Assn. Network (chair 1985—), Pi Lambda Theta, Alpha Phi Gamma, Psi Chi, Kappa Delta Pi, Sigma Alpha Iota. Office: The Nellor Wickwire Group 2900 Amby Pl Hermosa Beach CA 90254-2216

WIDERA, GEORG ERNST OTTO, mechanical engineering educator, consultant; b. Dortmund, Germany, Feb. 16, 1938; arrived in U.S., 1950; s. Otto and Gertrude (Yzermann) Widera; m. Kristel Kornas, June 21, 1974; children: Erika, Nicholas. BS, U. Wis., 1960, MS, 1962, PhD, 1965. Asst. prof. then prof. dept. materials engring. U. Ill., Chgo., 1965-82, prof. mech. engring., 1982-91, head dept., 1983-91, acting head indsl. sys. engring. dept., 1985-86, dir off-campus engring. programs, 1987-88; from prof., chmn. mech. and indsl. engring. dept. to dir. Marquette U., Milw., 1991—2002, dir. Ctr. Joining and Mfg. Assembly, 2002—, dir. Discovery Learning Ctr., sr. assoc. dean Coll. Engring., 2001—, acting dean Coll. Engring., 2003. Gastdozent U. Stuttgart, Germany, 1968; vis. prof. U. Wis.-Milw., 1973—74, Marquette U., Milw., 1978—79; cons. Ladish Co., Cudahy, Wis., 1967—76, Howmedica, Inc., Chgo., 1972—75, Sargent & Lundy, 1970—88, Nat. Bur. Stds., 1980, bd. dirs.; cons. Engrs. and Scientists Milw., 1996—98; vis. scientist Argonne Nat. Lab., Ill., 1968. Editor: Procs. Innovations in Structural Engring., 1974, Pressure Vessel Design, 1982; assoc. editor: Pressure Vessel Tech., 1977—81, 2003—, Applied Mechanics Revs., 1987—94, Mfg. Rev., 1991—95, mem. editl. adv. bd.: Acta Mechanica Sinica, 1990—, mem. editl. bd.: Pressure Vessels and Piping Design Technology, 1982, tech. editor: Jour. Pressure Vessel Tech., 1982—93; co-editor: SME Handbook of Metalforming, 1985, 1994, Design and Analysis of Plates and Shells, 1986. Fellow Std. Oil Co. Calif., 1961—63, NASA, 1966, von Humboldt, Fed. Republic Germany, 1968—69. Fellow: WRC (chmn. subcom. design procedures for shell intersections 1983—87, chmn. com. reinforced openings and external loads 1987—91, vice chmn. com. polymer pressure components 1991—99, chmn. com. shells and ligaments 1994—97, pressure vessel rsch. coun.), ASCE (sec.-treas. structural divsn. Ill. sect. 1972—73, chmn. divsn. 1976—77, chmn. peer rev. com., tech. coun. rsch. 1984, coun. structural plastics), ASME (chmn. machine design div. Chgo. sect. 1967—68, exec. com. Chgo. sect. 1970—73, editor newsletter Chgo. sect. 1971—73, chmn. jr. awards com. applied mechanics divsn. 1973—76, chmn. design and analysis com. pressure vessel and piping divsn. 1980—83, chmn. pressure vessel rsch. com. 1982—87, bd. editors 1983—93, mem. exec. com. and program chmn. pressure vessel and piping divsn. 1985—89, vice-chmn., sec. pressure vessel and piping divsn. 1989—90, mem. bd. pressure tech. codes and stds. 1989—94, chmn. 1990—91, mem. materials and structures group 1990—91, historian, senate pressure vessel and piping divsn. 1992—93, honors and awards chmn. Milw. sect. 1992—95, mem. coun. engring. 1992—96, v.p. materials and structures group 1993—96, mem. tech. execs. com. 1993—96, soc. rep. Fedn. Materials Soc. 1994—95, Pressure Vessel and Piping award and medal 1995), Wis. Mfg. Curriculum Com. (vice-chmn. exec. com. 1998—2002), 2d China Nat. Stds. Com. Pressure Vessels (hon. cons. 1989—94), Internat. Coun. Pressure Vessel Tech. (chmn. Am. regional com. 1988—, internat. chmn. 1992—96), Am. Soc. Engring. Edn., Soc. Mfg. Engrs. (sr.), French Pressure Vessel Assn.; mem.: Wis. Assn. Rsch. Mgrs. (pres.-elect 2003). Achievements include research in in mechanics of composite materials, plate and shell structures, stress analysis (including FEM), pressure vessels, mechanics of deformation processing. Office: Marquette U Coll Engring PO Box 1881 Milwaukee WI 53201-1881 E-mail: geo.widera@marquette.edu.

WIDGERY, JEANNE-ANNA (JAN WIDGERY), retired educator; b. Upland, Pa., May 18, 1920; d. Eugene Edmond and Carol Cooke (Meeser) Ayres; m. Rolande Carpenter Widgery ; children: Carolyn Gail, Catherine Darcy, Claudia Joan. BA, Chatham Coll., Pitts., 1941; AM, Radcliffe Coll., 1946. Instr. Chatham Coll., Pitts., 1946-50; dir. of drama Ellis Sch., Pitts., 1956-60; chmn. english dept. Winchester-Thurston Sch., Pitts., 1960-75; lectr. U. Houston, 1976-77; tchr. Duchesne Acad., Houston, 1977-85; ret., 1985. Mem. adv. bd. Internat. Poetry Forum, Pitts., 1970-74; dir. creative writing workshops Carnegie Libr., Pitts., 1970-72; staff mem. Southwest Writers Conf., Houston, 1976. Author: (under pen name Jan Widgery) The Adversary, 1966, Trumpet at the Gates, 1970, Before the Burning Bush, 2002; also book revs. Vol. Family Outreach Ctr., Houston, 1989—; Bible moderator Meml. Dr. Presbyn. Ch., Houston, 1988-90. Mem. AAUW (program v.p. 1980-81), Houston Harpsichord Soc. (pres. 1981-82, treas. 1988), Mystery Writers Am., Poets and Writers Assn. Avocations: hiking, painting.

WIDGOFF, MILDRED, physicist, educator; b. Buffalo, Aug. 24, 1924; d. Leo Widgoff and Rebecca Shulimson; children— Eve Widgoff Shapiro, Jonathan Bernard Widgoff Shapiro. BA, U. Buffalo, 1944; PhD, Cornell U., 1952. Rsch. assoc. Brookhaven Nat. Lab., Yaphank, N.Y., 1952-54; rsch. fellow Harvard U., Cambridge, Mass., 1955-58; asst. prof. rsch. Brown U., Providence, 1959-66, assoc. prof. rsch., 1966-74, prof. physics, 1974-95; prof. rsch., 1995—. Fellow Am. Phys. Soc.; mem. Sigma Xi, Phi Beta Kappa, Phi Kappa Phi. Office: Brown U Dept Physics PO Box 1843 Providence RI 02912-1843

WIDMAN, ELIZABETH ANN, home economics educator; b. Pukwana, S.D., Apr. 12, 1937; d. Emmett John and DeLonde (Svoboda) Healy; m. Paul Joseph Widman, July 30, 1959; children: Cynthia, Susan, Shelly, Richard, Mark. BS in Home Econs. Edn., S.D. State U., 1959. Ext. home economist Kingsbury County, Desmet, S.D., summer 1957-58; home econs. educator Gen. Beadle Campus High Sch., Madison, S.D., 1959-60; kindergarten tchr. Henry (S.D.) Grade Sch., 1962-64; home econs. tchr. Custer (S.D.) High Sch., 1964-66, Mitchell (S.D.) High Sch., 1966-67, Mitchell Middle Sch. and High Sch., 1976—2001; retired, 2001. Lectr. Weight Watchers, Mitchell, Plankinton and Kimball, S.D., 1991-93; mem. adv. bd. S.D. State U. Coll. Home Econs., 1982-85. Mem. precinct com. Davison County Dem. Com., Mitchell, 1992; leader 4-H, 1969-81; mem. alumni coun. S.D. State U., 1974-84. Named Outstanding 4-H Alumni, S.D. 4-H Leaders, 1979, Outstanding Tchr., Mitchell Schs., 1981, Master Advisor, Future Homemakers Am., 1988, Advisor Mentor, 1992. Mem. Nat. Family andConsumer Sci. Assn. (legis. chmn. 1992, 96), S.D. Vocat. Home Econs. Tchrs. (pres. 1988, Outstanding Educator award 1990, Arch of Fame award 1991, 98, Carl Perkins Humanitarian award 1993, Outstanding Svc. to Vocat. Edn. award 1996, Vocat. Tchr. of Yr., 1990), Am. Home Econs. Assn., S.D. Home Econs. Assn., Am. Vocat. Assn., S.D. Vocat. Assn. (pres.-elect 1993-94, pres. 1994-95, past pres. 1995-96, state awards chmn. 1996-98, Outstanding Svc. award 1996), S.D. State U. Alumni Assn. (pres. 1983-84, Outstanding Alumni Leadership award 1984, Disting. Alumnus Svc. to Alumni award 1993). Roman Catholic. Avocations: sewing, reading, family.

WIDNALL, SHEILA EVANS, aeronautical educator, former secretary of the airforce, former university official; b. Tacoma, July 13, 1938; d. Rolland John and Genievieve Alice (Krause) Evans; m. William Soule Widnall, June 11, 1960; children: William, Ann. BS in Aero. and Astronautics, MIT, 1960, MS in Aero. and Astronautics, 1961, DSc, 1964; PhD (hon.), New Eng. Coll., 1975, Lawrence U., 1987, Cedar Crest Coll., 1988, Smith Coll., 1990, Mt. Holyoke Coll., 1991, Ill. Inst. Tech., 1991, Columbia U., 1994, Simmons Coll., 1994, Suffolk U., 1994, Princeton U., 1994. Asst. prof. aeros. and astronautics MIT, Cambridge, 1964-70, assoc. prof., 1970-74, prof., 1974-93, head divsn. fluid mechanics, 1975-79; dir. Fluid Dynamics Rsch. Lab., MIT, Cambridge, 1979-90; chmn. faculty MIT, Cambridge, 1979-80, chair com. on acad. responsibility, 1991-92, assoc. provost, 1992-93; sec. USAF, 1993-97; Inst. prof. MIT, Cambridge, 1997—. Trustee Sloan Found., 1998—; bd. dirs. Gen. Corp., Chemfab Inc., Bennington, Vt., Aerospace Corp., L.A., Draper Labs., Cambridge, Gencorp; past trustee Carnegie Corp., 1984-92, Charles Stark Draper Lab. Inc.; mem. Carnegie Commn. Sci., Tech. and Govt. Contbr. articles to profl. jours.; patentee in field; assoc. editor AIAA Jour. Aircraft, 1972-75, Physics of Fluids, 1981-88, Jour. Applied Mechanics, 1983-87; mem. editorial bd. Sci., 1984-86. Bd. visitors USAF Acad., Colorado Springs, Colo., 1978-84, bd. chair, 1980-82; trustee Boston Mus. Sci., 1989-93. Recipient Washburn award Boston Mus. Sci., 1987. Fellow AAAS (bd. dirs. 1982-89, pres. 1987-88, chmn. 1988-89), AIAA (bd. dirs. 1975-77, Lawrence Sperry award 1972, Durand Lectureship for Pub. Svc. award 1996, pres. 2000-01), Am. Phys. Soc. (exec. com. 1979-82); mem. ASME (Applied Mechs. award 1995, Pres. award 1999), NAE (coun. 1992-93, v.p. 1998—), NAS (panel on sci. responsibility), Am. Acad. Arts and Scis., Soc. Women Engrs. (Outstanding Achievement award 1975), Internat. Acad. Astronautics, Seattle Mountaineers. Office: MIT Bldg 33-411 77 Massachussetts Ave Cambridge MA 02139

WIDNER, NELLE OUSLEY, retired elementary education educator; b. Loyston, Tenn., May 20, 1924; d. Jacob Milas and Myrtle (Longmire) Ousley; m. John DeLozier Widner; children: Stephen John, Beth Widner Jackson, David Earl. BA, Maryville (Tenn.) Coll., 1946; postgrad., U. Tenn. Cert. profl. educator. 1st grade tchr. Alcoa (Tenn.) City Schs., 1946-50, 74-87, tchr. remedial reading, 1966-74. Mem. AAUW, Alpha Delta Kappa (publicity chmn. 1982-84, chaplain 1984-86, sec. 1994-96), Order Ea. Star (worthy matron local chpt. 1941), Chilhowee Club, Epsilon Sigma Omicron (chmn. 1991-92), Passion Play Guild. Democrat. Methodist. Avocations: reading, sports. Home: 1629 Peppertree Dr Alcoa TN 37701-1794

WIDNER, WILLIAM RICHARD, biology educator, gardener; b. Baxter County, Ark., Apr. 24, 1920; s. Walter Elum and Rena Mae (Long) W.; m. Edna Holcombe Sorelle, Aug. 17, 1962 (div. Feb. 1985); m. Dorothy Anne de Geurin, March 9, 1985. BA, Eastern N.Mex. U., 1942; MS, U. N.Mex., 1948, PhD, 1952. Rsch. asst. biomed. rsch. AEC, Los Almos, N.Mex., 1948-50; teaching asst. U. N.Mex., Albuquerque, 1950-52; indsl. hygienist AEC, Albuquerque, 1952-55; high sch. tchr. Albuquerque Indian Sch., 1955-56; chmn. biology Howard Payne Coll., Brownwood, Tex., 1956-59; biology prof. Baylor U., Waco, Tex., 1959-89, emeritus prof., 1989—. Capt. USN, 1972, USNR, 1946-80. Mem. KYCH, Masons (master 1985-86, high priest 1989, dist. dep. grand master dist. 20 1992, order of Silver Trowel 1989, royal order Jesters 1993). Republican. Southern Baptist. Avocations: gardening, hunting, photography. Home and Office: 2532 Eldridge Ln Waco TX 76710-1015

WIEBERS, DAWN RAE, secondary education educator; b. Viborg, SD, Apr. 10, 1963; d. Dean A. and Carolina R. (Meyer) W. BS in Edn., Dakota State U., 1986. Cert. tchr., Kans. Tchr. Healy (Kans.) H.S., 1987-90, Peabody (Kans.) H.S., 1990-92, Otis (Kans.)-Bison H.S., 1992—2001, Rossville (Kans.) H.S., 2001—. Ind. devel. plan chair Otis, 1993-2001; quality performance accreditation chair Unified Sch. Dist. 403, Otis, 1993—. Mem. Otis-Bison Tchr. Assn. (sec.-treas. 1993-2001), Kaw Valley Edn. Assn. (pres.). Avocations: stamp collecting, sports, gardening and lawn care, woodworking, mechanics. Home: Box 71 Rossville KS 66533

WIECHERT, ALLEN LEROY, educational planning consultant, architect; b. Independence, Kans., Oct. 25, 1938; s. Norman Henry and Serena Johanna (Steinke) W.; m. Sandra Swanson, Aug. 19, 1961; children: Kristin Nan, Brendan Swanson, Megan Ann. BArch, Kans. State U., 1962. Lic. arch., Kans.; cert. Nat. Coun. Archtl. Registration Bds. Arch. in tng. McVey, Peddie, Schmidt & Allen, Wichita, Kans., 1962-63; arch. Kivett & Myers, Kansas City, Mo., 1963-68; asst. to vice chancellor plant planning and devel. U. Kans., Lawrence, 1968-74, assoc. dir. facilities planning, 1974-78, univ. dir. facilities planning, 1978-92, univ. arch., 1993-95; campus planner Gould Evans Assocs., Lawrence, 1995-96; code enforcement officer City of Prairie Village, Kans., 1997-2001; ret.; project mgr. subs. corp. Kans. Bd. Regents, 2003—. Project mgr. Subsidiary Corp. Kans. Bd. of Regents, 2003—; mem. long range phys. planning com. Kans. Bd. Regents, 1971-95; designer, archtl. programmer ednl. facilities; bd. dirs. Kans. U. Fed. Credit Union, 1972-81, pres. bd., 1974. Editor, contbr.: Physical Development Planning Work Book, 1973. Chmn. horizons com. Lawrence Bicentennial Commn.; designer Kaw River Trail, 1976; mem. Action 80 Com., 1980-81, Lawrence-Douglas County Horizon 2020 Task Group, 1993-95; mem. standing com. Kans. Episcopal Diocese, 1976-80, pres. com., 1981, mem. diocesan coun., 1982-84, chmn. coll. work com., 1982-84, commn. on ch. arch. and allied arts, 1986-99, long range planning com., 1988; sr. warden Trinity Episc. Ch., Lawrence, 1978-80, 2001-02, mem. vestry, 1997-99; trustee Kans. Sch. Religion, 1973-80, 82-95, v.p., 1984-85, pres., 1986-92, trustee friends of the dept. of religious studies, 1995—; mem. adv. bd. Salvation Army, 1990—; bd. dirs. Trinity Group Care Home, 1973-79; advancement chmn. troop com. Boy Scouts Am., 1981-87, dist. com. Pelathe dist., 1984—, vice chmn., 1984, chmn., 1985-87; exec. bd. Heart of Am. Coun., 1985-87. 1st lt. Kans. Air N.G., 1961-67. Recipient Dist. Award of Merit, Boy Scouts Am., 1988, Silver Beaver award, 1991, Follow Me Boys award, 2002. Mem. AIA, Assn. Univ. Archs. (sec.-treas. 1986-87, v.p. 1987-88, pres. 1988-89), Nat. Hist. Trust, Kans. U. Endowment Assn. (sec. 1981-85, founder, exec. bd. Hist. Mt. Oread Fund divsn.), Nat. Cathedral Assn. (regional co-chairperson 1993—). Home: 813 Highland Dr Lawrence KS 66044-2431

WIEDMAN, TIMOTHY GERARD, management educator; b. Detroit; s. Charles Albert and Doris Gertude Wiedman. BA, Oakland U., 1976; MS, Ctrl. Mich. U., 1978; cert. profl. fin. planning, Old Dominion U., 1995. Gen. mgr. Burger Chef Sys., Inc., Detroit, 1969-75; area mgr. Fotomat Corp., Cleve., Columbus, Ohio, 1978-85; instr. bus. mgmt. Ctrl. Ohio Tech. Coll., Newark, 1986-88, Ohio U., Lancaster, 1988-92; asst. prof. Thomas Nelson C. C., Hampton, Va., 1992-95; assoc. prof. Thomas Nelson C.C., Hampton, Va., 1995—, bus. program head, 1997—. Workshop leader Va. Quality Inst., Hampton, 1994—; quality trainer Quality Union of Bus., Industry and Cmty. Program, Lancaster, 1991-92; invited spkr. Svc. Corps. Ret. Execs., Newark, 1988, USCGR Tng. Ctr., Yorktown, Va., 1994, USMCR, Hampton, 1994, So. Assn. Coll. and Univ. Bus. Officers, Memphis, 1996. Contbg. author: Great Ideas for Teaching Marketing, 1992, Great Ideas for Teaching Introduction to Business, 1994; contbr. articles to profl. jours.; author: (newsletter) The Quality Management Forum, 1993, 98. Judge regional competition Future Bus. Leaders Am., Hampton, 1993—; judge team excellence competition Ohio Mfrs. Assn., Lancaster, 1991; county rep. UNICEF, Fairfield County, Ohio, 1988-91. Mem. AAUP (chpt. treas. 1998-2000), Am. Soc. for Quality (invited speaker 1993, cert. quality mgr. 1997, recert. 2000, 2003), Nat. Assn. Profl. Fin. Planners, Va. Educator's Quality Network. Avocations: photography, travel, skiing, swimming, sailing. Office: 99 Thomas Nelson Dr Hampton VA 23666-1433 E-mail: wiedmant@tncc.vccs.edu.

WIEGAND, JULIE WILDS, secondary school educator; b. Galesburg, Ill., Apr. 14, 1954; d. John Wilson and Helen Arletta (Mitchell) Wilds; m. Michael Anthony Wiegand, Nov. 10, 1984; children: Joseph Michael, Margaret Eshe. BS, Ill. State U., 1975. Substitute tchr. Normal/Bloomington (Ill.) Schs., 1975-77; tchr. Immaculate Conception, Monmouth, Ill., 1977-79, CUSD #205, Galesburg, Ill., 1979—. Pres., sec., treas., parliamentarian Galesburg Jr. Woman's Club, 1980—; treas., sec. Ill. Fedn. of Women's Clubs, 1989-92. Mem. Galesburg Edn. Assn. (treas. 1981-85), Phi Delta Kappa (annual fund, rsch. rep. 1989-91). Democrat. Lutheran. Avocations: church outreach work, christian education, reading, traveling. Home: 1173 N Academy St Galesburg IL 61401-2646 Office: Gale Sch 1131 W Dayton St Galesburg IL 61401-1507

WIENER, DAVID L. secondary education educator; b. Utica, N.Y., Oct. 23, 1954; s. David L. Sr. and Phyllis (Jarmula) W.; m. Linda J. Ciccarelli, Sept. 22, 1979. AS, Mohawk Valley Community Coll., Utica, 1974; BS, Syracuse U., 1976; MS, U. Rochester, 1987. Photometrics lab. technician Elec. Testing Labs., Cortland, N.Y., 1977-78; digital/analog process control engr. Honeywell Inc., Amherst, N.Y., 1978-85; tchr. math. Penfield (N.Y.) High Sch., 1985, tchr. physics, 1986—. Reviewer N.Y. State Edn. Dept., albany, 1990; advisor Alfred U. Coll. Ceramic Engring. Young Scholars' Program, Penfield H.S. Chess Club; tchr. NSF Ctr., U. Rochester, summer 1993. Counselor Camp Good Days and Spl. Times, Rochester, 1985-92; instr. swimming and lifesaving ARC, Rochester, 1979-89; advisor Penfield H.S. Solar Car. Fellow U. Rochester, 1985, 86, 87, fellow N.Y. State, 1985, 86, 87; ESEA-Title II Dwight D. Eisenhower Math./Sci. Edn. grantee, 1991, Toyota/NSTA Tapestry grantee, 1992; named Outstanding Tchr. Monroe County VFW, 1991; recipient Excellence in Tchg. award U. Rochester, 1990. Mem. Am. Assn. Physics Tchrs., Jr. Engring. Tech. Soc. (advisor), Penfield High Sch. Juggling Club (advisor, founder), Rochester Juggling Club (v.p.), Internat. Star Class Yacht Racing Assn., Seneca Yacht Club, Kappa Delta Pi. Avocations: sailing, skiing, scuba diving, juggling, biking. Home: 28 Old Winding Ln Fairport NY 14450-1108

WIENER, JON, history educator; b. St. Paul, Minn., May 16, 1944; s. Daniel N. and Gladys (Aronsohn) Spratt. BA, Princeton U., 1966; PhD, Harvard U., 1971. Acting asst. prof. UCLA, 1973-74; asst. prof. history U. Calif.-Irvine, 1974-83, prof., 1984—. Vis. prof. U. Calif.-Santa Cruz, 1973; plaintiff Freedom of Info. Lawsuit against FBI for John Lennon Files, 1983—. Author: Social Origins of the New South, 1979; Come Together: John Lennon in His Time, 1984, Professors, Politics, and Pop, 1991, Gimme Some Truth: The John Lennon FBI File, 2000; contbg. editor The Nation mag.; contbr. articles to profl. jours. including The New Republic and New York Times Book Rev. Rockefeller Found. fellow, 1979, Am. Coun. Learned Socs.- Ford Found. fellow, 1985. Mem. Am. Hist. Assn., Nat. Book Critics Circle, Orgn. Am. Historians, Nat. Writers' Union, Liberty Hill Found. (bd. dirs.). E-mail: wiener@uci.edu.

WIENER, MARTIN JOEL, historian, educator; b. Bklyn., June 1, 1941; s. Harold H. and Eva (Richter) W.; m. Carol Ann Zisowitz, Sept. 22, 1964 (div. 1977); children: Wendy, Julie; m. Meredith Anne Skura, May 17, 1981; children: Rebecca, Vivian. BA, Brandeis U., 1962; MA, Harvard U., 1963, PhD in History, 1967. Asst. prof. Rice U., 1967-72, assoc. prof., 1972-80, prof. history, 1980-82, Mary Gibbs Jones prof., 1982—; chair dept. history, 1990-94. Author: Between Two Worlds: The Political Thought of Graham Wallas, 1971, English Culture and the Decline of the Industrial Spirit, 1850-1980, 1981 (Schuyler prize Am. Hist. Assn. 1981), Reconstructing the Criminal, 1990. Research fellow NEH, 1973, 86, Am. Council Learned Socs., 1982; Woodrow Wilson Scholar, 1997-98, NSF grantee, 1997-98. Fellow Royal Hist. Soc.; mem. Am. Soc. Legal History, Coun. for European Studies (steering com. 1985-90), Conf. on Brit. Studies (v.p. 1999-2001, pres. 2001—, coun. 1992-96), Social History Soc. (U.K.), Am. Hist. Assn. (coun. 1987-90). Jewish. Home: 3007 Rice Blvd Houston TX 77005-3049 Office: Rice U Dept of History 6100 Main St Dept Of Houston TX 77005-1892 E-mail: wiener@rice.edu.

WIERNICKI, LOUISE MARIE, special education educator; b. Little Falls, N.Y., Aug. 28; d. Joseph Paul and Ruth E. (Babcock) Pietrandrea; m. Kenneth Wiernicki; children: Ronald J., Anna Louise. BS, SUNY, Oswego, 1970; MS, SUNY, Cortland, 1975; postgrad., Syracuse U., 1975. Tchr. history Whitesboro (N.Y.) Ctrl. Sch., 1970-71; tchr. learning disabled Herkimer County B.O.C.E.S., Herkimer, N.Y., 1971-88; tchr. intermediate resource Frankfort-Sychule Schs., Frankfort, N.Y., 1988-89; tchr. intermediate learning disabled Little Falls (N.Y.) Ctrl. Sch., 1991—. Leader Girl Scouts U.S., Herkimer, cub scouts Boy Scouts Am., Herkimer; treas. Babe Ruth/Am. League Baseball, Herkimer. Democrat. Roman Catholic. Avocations: reading, sports, travel. Home: 204 Willis Ave Herkimer NY 13350-1026

WIERNIK, PETER HARRIS, oncologist, educator; b. Crocket, Tex., June 16, 1939; s. Harris and Molly (Emmerman) W.; m. Roberta Joan Fuller, Sept. 6, 1961; children: Julie Anne, Lisa Britt, Peter Harrison. BA with distinction, U. Va., 1961, MD, 1965; Dr. h.c., U. of Republic, Montevideo, Uruguay, 1982. Diplomate Am. Bd. Internal Medicine, Am. Bd. Med. Oncology (mem. writing com. 1981-87). Intern Cleve. Met. Gen. Hosp., 1965-66, resident, 1969-70, Osler Svc. Johns Hopkins Hosp., Balt., 1970-71; sr. asst. surgeon USPHS, 1966, advanced through grades to med. dir., 1976; sr. staff assoc. Balt. Cancer Rsch. Ctr., 1966-71, chief sect. med. oncology, 1971-76, chief clin. oncology br., 1976-82, dir., 1976-82; assoc. dir. div. cancer treatment Nat. Cancer Inst., 1976-82; assoc. dir. Albert Einstein Cancer Ctr., Bronx, 1982-98, prof. medicine, 1983-98, prof. radiation oncology, 1996-98, head divsn. med. oncology. Asst. prof. medicine U. Md. Sch. Medicine, Balt., 1971-74, assoc. prof., 1974-76, prof., 1976-82; prof. medicine and radiation oncology N.Y. Med. Coll., 1998—; cons. hematology and med. oncology Union Meml. Hosp., Greater Balt. Med. Ctr., Franklin Sq. Hosp.; bd. dirs. Balt. City unit Am. Cancer Soc., 1971-78; chmn. patient care com., 1972-75, mem. profl. edn. and grants com., N.Y.C. divsn., 1983-90, mem. nat. clin. fellowship com., 1984-96; mem. med. adv. com. Nat. Leukemia Assn., 1976-88, chmn. med. adv. com., 1989—; chmn. adult leukemia com. Cancer and Leukemia Group B, 1976-83; prin. investigator Ea. Coop. Oncology Group, 1982-94, 96—; chmn. gynecol. oncology com., 1986-88, chmn. leukemia com., 1988-94; sci. cons. Vt. Regional Cancer Ctr., 1987—; dir. OLM Comprehensive Cancer Ctr., N.Y. Med. Coll., 1998—. Editor: Controversies in Oncology, 1982, Supportive Care of the Cancer Patient, 1983, Neoplastic Diseases of the Blood, 1985, 4th edit., 2003, Adult Leukemias, 2001; editor: (assoc.) Medical Oncology and Tumor Pharmacotherapy, 1987—91; editor: (sr.), 1991—; editor: (assoc.) (jour.) Am. Jour. Therapeutics, 1994—; co-editor: Year Book of Hematology, 1986—98, Handbook of Hematologic and Oncologic Emergencies, 1988—98, Bone Marrow Transplantation (textbook), 1995, (jour.) Am. Jour. Med. Scis., 1976—81; editor (N. Am.): Jour. Cancer Rsch. and Clin. Oncology, 1986—89; mem. editl. bd. Cancer Treatment Reports, 1972—76, Leukemia Rsch., 1977—86, 1991—, Leukemia, 1986—2003, Cancer Clin. Trials, 1977—, Jour. Therapeutic Rsch., 1994—, Hosp. Practice, 1979—, Jour. Clin. Oncology, 1989—91, PDQ Nat. Cancer Inst., 1987—94, Cancer Investigation, 1998—; editor (sect. antineoplastic drugs): (jour.) Jour. Clin. Pharmacology, 1985—; contbr. articles to profl. jours., chapters to books. Recipient Z Soc. award U. Va., 1961, Byrd S. Leavell Hematology award U. Va. Sch. Medicine, 1965, Gold medal 1st Polish Congress of Oncology, 2002. Fellow AAAS, ACP, Am. Coll. Clin. Pharmacology (awards com. 1999—), Internat. Soc. Hematology, Royal Soc. Medicine (London), N.Y. Acad. Medicine; mem. Am. Soc. Clin. Investigation (instl. rep. 1997—), Am. Soc. Clin. Oncology (chmn. edn. and tng. com. 1976-79, 84, subcom. on clin. investigation 1980-82, program com. 1990, pub. issues com., 1990-95, com. on rsch. awards 1996-2000, com. on health svcs. rsch. 2000-2003), Am. Assn. Cancer Rsch. (clin. cancer rsch. com. 2002—), Am. Soc. Hematology, Am. Fedn. Clin. Rsch., Am. Acad. Clin. Toxicology, Internat. Soc. Exptl. Hematology, N.Y. Acad. Sci., Am. Soc. Hosp. Pharmacy, Am. Soc. Clin. Pharmacology and Therapeutics, Am. Radium Soc. (program com. 1987-93, exec. com. 1988-95, publ. com. 1988-92, sec. 1990-91, pres.-elect, 1992-93; pres. 1993-94, Janeway medalist, 1996), Polish Oncology Soc. (hon., finalist Gold medal), Harvey Soc., Uruguayan Hematology Soc. (hon.), Acad. Medicine Uruguay (corr.), European Assn. Cancer Rsch., European Soc. for Hematology, Phi Beta Kappa (assoc.), Sigma Xi, Alpha Omega Alpha, Phi Sigma (award 1961). Office: Comprehensive Cancer Ctr Our Lady Mercy Med Ctr 600 E 233rd St Bronx NY 10466-2604 E-mail: wiernik@jimmy.harvard.edu.

WIERWILLE, MARSHA LOUISE, elementary education educator; b. Springfield, Ohio, Mar. 19, 1951; d. Eugene Junior and Donna Catherine (Bodine) Randall; m. Bob Edward Wierwille, June 14, 1975; children: Benjamin Joseph Reuben, Jeremiah James Eugene, Samuel John Philip, Adam Joel David. BS, Ohio State U., 1973; MEd, Wright State U., 1976; postgrad., U. Dayton, Ohio, 1982, 84, 87, Coll. of Mt. St. Joseph, summer 1985, 86. Cert. elem. edn. tchr., curriculum supr., Ohio. Tchr. 1st grade New Bremen (Ohio) Sch., 1973-76, tchr. 2d grade, 1976—. Mem. NEA, Ohio Edn. Assn., Western Ohio Edn. Assn., New Bremen Tchrs. Assn. (pres. 1976-77), Ohio Coun. Tchrs. Lang. Arts, Delta Kappa Gamma. Avocations: reading, walking, biking, family, travel. Office: New Bremen Sch 202 S Walnut St New Bremen OH 45869-1297

WIESCHAUS, ERIC F. molecular biologist, educator; b. June 8, 1947; BS, U. Notre Dame, 1969; PhD in Biology, Yale U., 1974. Rsch. fellow Zool. Inst., U. Zurich, Switzerland, 1975-78; group leader European Molecular Biol. Lab., Germany, 1978-81; from asst. prof. to assoc. prof. Princeton (N.J.) U., 1981-87, prof. molecular biology, 1987—. Fellow Lab. de Genetique Moleculaire, France, 1976; vis. rschr. Ctr. Pathobiology, U. Calif., Irvine, 1977; mem. sci. adv. coun. Damon Runyon-Walter Winchell Cancer Fund, 1987-92. Contbr. articles to profl. jours. Recipient Nobel Prize in Medicine, 1995. Fellow Am. Acad. Arts and Scis.; mem. NAS. Office: Princeton U MOF 435 Dept Molecular Biology Washington Rd Princeton NJ 08544-0001*

WIESE, DOROTHY JEAN, business educator; b. Chgo., Sept. 20, 1940; d. Charles Ennis Chapman and Evelyn Catherine Flizikowski; m. Wallace Jon Wiese, Oct. 10, 1959; children: Elizabeth Jean Wiese Christensen, Jonathan Charles. BS in Edn., No. Ill. U., 1970, MS in Edn., 1976, EdD, 1994. Tchr. bus. Hampshire (Ill.) High Sch., 1970-78; prof. bus. Elgin (Ill.) C.C., 1978—. Cons. Gould, Inc., Rolling Meadows, Ill., 1984; instr. vocat. practicum McDonald's Hamburger U., Ofcl. Airline Guides, Oak Brook, Ill., 1986; spkr. SIEC, Sweden and Austria, 1987-88, Czech Republic, 1995, North Ctrl. Bus. Edn. Assn./Wis. Bus. Edn. Assn. Conv., 1992, Chgo. Area Bus. Edn. Assn., 1992, AAUW, Batavia and Geneva, 1993, Elgin, 1996; 1995 Internat. Bus. Inst. for Cmty. Coll. faculty Mich. State U., 1995. Presented paper 34th annual Adult Edn. Rsch. Conf., Pa. State U., 1993. Mem., sec. N.W. Kane County (Ill.) Airport Authority, 1987-94; bd. dirs. St. Joseph Hosp. Found., 1995—, mem. adv. bd. Cancer Wellness and Resource Ctr., 1995—; host family Am. Intercultural Student Exch., 1989-90; presenter women's seminar Trinity Luth. Ch., Roselle, Ill., 1992; mem. Leadership Ill., 1996. Mem. AAUW, Am. Women of Internat. Understanding (bd. dirs.), Nat. Bus. Edn. Assn. (internat. task force), Internat. Soc. Bus. Edn. (North Ctrl. Bus. Edn. Assn. rep. 1989-90, rep.-elect 1996), Societe Internat. pour l'Enseignment Commercial, Ill. Bus. Edn. Assn., Ill. Vocat. Assn., Women in Mgmt. (spkr., co-chair membership No. Fox Valley chpt. 1996-97), Delta Pi Epsilon (past historian Alpha Phi chpt.), Kappa Delta Pi. Lutheran. Office: Elgin CC 1700 Spartan Dr Elgin IL 60123-7189

WIESE, VICKI See GURHOLT-WIESE, VICTORIA JEAN

WIESEL, TORSTEN NILS, neurobiologist, educator; b. Upsala, Sweden, June 3, 1924; arrived in U.S., 1955; s. Fritz Samuel and Anna-Lisa Elisabet (Bentzer) Wiesel; 1 child, Sara Elisabet. MD, Karolinska Inst., Stockholm, 1954; D Medicine (hon.), Karolinska Inst, Stockholm, 1989; AM (hon.), Harvard U., 1967; D Medicine (hon.), Linköping U., 1982; ScD (hon.), NYU, 1987, U. Bergen, 1987. Instr. physiology Karolinska Inst., 1954—55; asst. dept. child psychiatry Karolinska Hosp., 1954—55; fellow in ophthalmology Johns Hopkins U., 1955—58, asst. prof. ophthalmic physiology, 1958—59; assoc. in neurophysiology and neuropharmacology Harvard U. Med. Sch., Boston, 1959—60, asst. prof. neurophysiology and neuropharmacology, 1960—64, asst. prof. neurophysiology, dept. psychiatry, 1964—67, prof. physiology, 1967—68, prof. neurobiology, 1968—74, Robert Winthrop prof. neurobiology, 1974—83, chmn. dept. neurobiology, 1973—82; Vincent and Brooke Astor prof. neurobiology, head lab. Rockefeller U., N.Y.C., 1982—98, pres., 1991—98, pres. emeritus, 1998—, dir. Leon Levy and Shelby White Ctr. for Mind, Brain & Behavior, 1998—; sec. gen. Human Frontier Sci. Program, 2000—. Ferrier lectr. Royal Soc. London, 1972, NIH lectr., 75; Grass lectr. Soc. Neurosci., 1976; lectr. Coll. de France, 1977; Hitchcock prof. U. Calif.-Berkeley, 1980; Sharpey-Schafer lectr. Phys. Soc. London; George Cotzias lectr. Am. Acad. Neurology, 1983; chmn. bd. govs. NY Acad Scis., 2001—. Contbr. numerous articles to profl. jours. Recipient Jules Stein award, Trustees for Prevention of Blindness, 1971, Lewis S. Rosenstiel prize, Brandeis U., 1972, Friedenwald award,

Assn. Rsch. in Vision and Ophthalmology, 1975, Karl Spencer Lashley prize, Am. Philos. Soc., 1977, Louisa Gross Horwitz prize, Columbia U., 1978, Dickson prize, U. Pitts., 1979, Nobel prize in physiology and medicine, 1981, W.H. Helmerich III award, 1989. Mem.: AAAS, Royal Swedish Acad. Scis. (fgn.), Royal Soc. (fgn.), Soc. Neurosci. (pres. 1978—79), Swedish Physiol. Soc., Nat. Acad. Arts and Scis., Am. Acad. Arts and Scis., Am. Philos. Soc., Am. Physiol. Soc., Physiol. Soc. (Eng.) (hon.). Office: Rockefeller U 1230 York Ave New York NY 10021-6399 E-mail: wiesel@mail.rockefeller.edu.*

WIESENBERG, JACQUELINE LEONARDI, lecturer; b. West Haven, Conn., May 04; d. Curzio and Filomena Olga (Turrinziani) Leonardi; m. Russel John Wiesenberg, Nov. 23; children: James Wynne, Deborann Donna. BA, SUNY, Buffalo, 1970; postgrad., 1970-73, 80—. Interviewer, examiner U.S. Dept. Labor, New Haven, 1948-52; sec. W.I. Clark Co., Hamden, Conn., 1952-55; acct. VA Hosp., West Haven, 1956-60; acct.-commissary USAF Missle Site, Niagara Falls, N.Y., 1961-62; tchr. Buffalo City Schs., 1970-73, 79; acct. Erie County Social Svcs., Buffalo, 1971-73; lectr., 1973—. Contbr. articles to CAP, USAF mag. Capt., Nat. Found. March of Dimes, 1969—, com. mem. telethon, 1983-86; vol. VA, 1973—; den mother Boy Scouts Am., 1961-68; chmn. Meals on Wheels, Town of Amherst, 1975-76; leader, travel chmn. Girl Scouts U.S., 1968-77; mem. Nat. Congress Parents and Tchrs., 1957—; heart fund vol. Heart Assn., 1960-86; rep. Am. Diabetes Assn., 1994—, vol. diabetes collection, 1994-95; mem. Humane Soc. U.S., ASPCA, N.Y. Srs. Coalition. Mem. AAUW, NAFE, Internat. Platform Assn., Nat. Pks. and Conservation Assn., Am. Astrol. Assn., Nat. Arbor Day Found., Western N.Y. Conf. Aging, Nat. Geog. Soc., Wilderness Soc., Nat. Wildlife Fedn., Nat. Trust for Hist. Preservation, Nature Conservancy, Ctr. for Marine Conservation, Internat. Funds Animal Welfare, North Shore Animal League, The Nature Conservancy, The Libr. Congress, U. Buffalo Found., Pvt. Land Conservancy-Nat. Park Trust, U. Buffalo Alumni Assn., Epsilon Delta Chi, Alpha Iota. Home: 14 Norman Pl Amherst NY 14226-4233

WIGFIELD, RITA L. elementary education educator; b. Mpls., Dec. 14, 1945; d. Willard Ernest and Bernice Eleanor (Peterson) Ahlquist; m. Vernon Carter Wigfield, Oct. 9, 1982. BS, U. Minn., 1967; grad., St. Thomas Coll.; postgrad., Hamlin U. Cert. elem. educator, Minn. Tchr. Alice Smith Sch., Hopkins, Minn., 1967-80, Meadowbrook Sch., Hopkins, 1980-86, Gatewood Sch., Hopkins, 1986—. Owner Swede Country, Minnetonka, Minn., 1983—; elem. team leader Prin.'s Adv. Bd.; chmn. bldg. tech. com. Hopkins Sch. Dist., past supr. bldg. sch. patrol; coop. tchrs. Gustavus Adolphus Coll.; cons. and presenter in field. Author: We Love Literature, 1991 (Grand Prize Scholastic Inc., 1991). Mem. Wooddale Choir Evang. Christian Ch., decorating com., Mission commn., organizer fellowship dinners; mem. Loaves and Fishes, Minn. Landscape Arboretum. Recipient Hon. Mention Learning Mag., 1990, Nat. Coun Econ. edn./Internat. Paper Col. Found., 1992, 2d pl. Minn. Coun. Econ. Edn., 1992, Ashland Oil award, 1994; named Minn. Tchr. of Yr., 1992. Mem. ASCD, Nat. Assn. Miniature Enthusiasts, Am. Quilting Soc., Internat. Reading Assn., Minn. Edn. Assn., Hopins Edn. Assn. (bldg. rep., treas.), Delta Kappa Gamma (pres. Beta Beta chpt.), Kappa Delta Pi. Avocations: miniatures, quilting, flowers, cross-stitch, antiques. Home: 4719 Diane Dr Hopkins MN 55343-8785 Office: Gatewood Elem Sch 14900 Gatewood Dr Minnetonka MN 55345-6731

WIGG, BRUCE JAY, social studies educator; b. Harlan, Iowa, Dec. 15, 1954; s. Barthel John and Doraine Jane (Thomsen) W.; m. Karen Jo Bortscheller, July 24, 1982; children: Aaron, Brian, Catherine, Dana. BA, Buena Vista Coll., 1977. Cert. tchr., Iowa. Social studies tchr., tennis coach, student coun. advisor Union Cmty. Schs., La Porte City, Iowa, 1977—. Mem. tchrs.' coun. Rep. Party, Des Moines, 1988-90; mem. bd. edn. Sacred Heart Cath. Ch.; former mem. La Porte City Cable Commn., 1997-98; mem. City Recreation Commn. Taft fellow U. Iowa, 1980. Mem. Union Edn. Assn. (v.p., chair govt. affairs, negotiations com., pres.), N.E. Iowa Edn. Unit (govt. affairs com.). Avocation: tennis leagues. Home: 218 Valley Dr La Porte City IA 50651-1131 Office: Union Community Schs 200 Adams St La Porte City IA 50651-1143

WIGGINS, CHARLES, secondary education educator; b. Boston, July 8, 1938; s. John and Jeanne Lee (Sargeant) W.; children: Sam, Christy. AB, Colby Coll., 1962; AM, Columbia U., 1967. Cert. tchr., Conn. Tchr. social studies Wilton (Conn.) High Sch., 1967-70, Brien McMahon High Sch., Norwalk, Conn., 1970—. Contbr. articles to profl. jours. Co-chair, co-founder Edn. 2000; mem. Sec. of State's Citizenship Task Force, 1992-93. Cpl. U.S. Army, 1963-65. NDEA grantee, U. Bridgeport, 1968, Fulbright scholar U. Ghana, 1969; named Outstanding Educator, Cornell U., 1992. Mem. Am. Fedn. Tchrs. (steward 1986-93), Conn. Coun. Social Studies (bd. dirs. 1986-89, editor Yankee Forum 1985-91). Democrat. Avocations: carpentry, travel. Office: Brien McMahon High Sch Highland St Norwalk CT 06854

WIGGINS, IDA SILVER, elementary school educator; b. Bklyn., Apr. 23; d. Joseph C. and Alice V. (Carter) Silver; m. G. Franklin Wiggins, Dec. 27, 1955; children: Bryan Franklin, Sharon-Amy. BS, NYU, 1955, MA, 1966; D Christian Letters (hon.), Shaw Divinity Sch., Raleigh, N.C., 1988. Cert. tchr., N.Y. Tchr. Durham (N.C.) County Pub. Sch., 1955-56, Johnston County Pub. Sch., Clayton, N.C., 1956-60; ednl. cons. Child Care Ctr., N.Y., 1960-61; tchr. Lakeland Cen. Schs., Shrub Oak, N.Y., 1961-91, Hudson Valley Christian Acad., Mahopac Falls, N.Y., 1991—. Tchr. adv. panel Silver Burdett Pub. Co., Morristown, N.J., 1987-88; mem. lang. arts task force, elem. math com., social studies curriculum com. Lakeland Cen Schs., 1989—; bd. dirs. Tutorial Program, Peekskill, 1986—. Writer: (choral reading) Martin Luther King, Jr., 1970. Life mem. Peekskill Hosp. Aux., 1980; former bd. mem. Peekskill YWCA, 1982, Peekskill Mus., 1988; life mem. NAACP, Peekskill, 1989; trustee Shaw U., Raleigh, N.C.; former bd. dirs. Hudson Valley Hosp. Found. Mem. AAUW, Am. Fedn. Tchrs., N.Y. State United Tchrs., Lakeland Fedn. Tchrs., Nat. Black Child Devel. Inst., Nat. Coun. Negro Women, Blacks in Govt. (life W. Point chpt.), The Links, Inc., Delta Kappa Gamma, Alpha Kappa Alpha. Baptist. Home: 1282 Maple Ave Peekskill NY 10566-4853

WIGGINS, MARY ANN WISE, small business owner, educator; b. Coushatta, La., Dec. 25, 1940; d. George Wilkinson and Maitland (Allums) Wise; m. Gerald D. Paul (div. Nov. 1977); children: John Barron, James Gordon, Brenda Michelle; m. Billy J. Wiggins, Oct. 3, 1981; children: Marshall Wade, Brian David, William Joshua, George Justin; stepchildren: Joseph James, Winona Gail. BA, Northwestern State U., Natchitoches, La., 1964, postgrad., 1994, Weatherford Coll., 1967, North Tex. State U., 1968. Lic. ins. agt., real estate agt., La., pvt. pilot. Tchr. U.S. Army Schs., Nuremberg, Germany, 1964—66, Mineral Wells Ind. Sch. Dist., 1967—70; bookkeeper Wise Dept. Store, Coushatta, La., 1966—67; amb. of good will Vietnam, 1971; owner, mgr. Mary Ann's Furniture & Hardware, Coushatta, 1977—97; tchr. Springville Mid. Sch., 1994—96, Red River Parish Alternative Sch., 1996—98, tchr. Ware Youth Ctr., 1998—. Com. mem. Instrn. and Profl. Devel. Com. La. Assn. Educators, 1998-2000, vice chmn. 1999-2002; v.p. La. Juvenile Detention Tchrs. Assn., 1999—; tchr. leader La. Tech., 2002-03. Chmn. Am. Cancer Soc., Conway, Ark., 1972, Red River Parish United Way, Coushatta, 1985; treas., bd. dirs. Hall Summit United Meth. Ch.; pres. Red River Parish Assn. Educators Polit. Action Com. Recipient German-Am. hospitality award Orgn. German-Am. Women, Nuremberg, 1965. Mem. NEA, La. Assn. Educators (chmn. legis. com.), Red River Assn. Educators (v.p. 1994, pres. 1998-2001), U.S. C. of C., Coushatta-Red River C. of C. (charter), Pi Kappa Sigma, Sigma Kappa. Democrat. Methodist. Avocations: gardening/landscaping, swimming, horseback riding, computers, week-enders with family. Home: 2217 E Carrol St Coushatta LA 71019-8567

WIGGINS, ROGER C. internist, educator, researcher; b. Tetbury, Eng., May 26, 1945; BA, Cambridge U., Eng., 1968; BChir, Middlesex Hosp. Med. Sch., London, 1971, MB, MA, 1972. House physician dept. medicine The Middlesex Hosp., London, 1971-72; house surgeon Ipswich (Eng.) and East Suffolk Hosps., 1972; sr. house officer Hammersmith Hosp., The Middlesex Hosp., Brompton Hosp., London, 1972-74; rsch. registrar The Middlesex Hosp. Med. Sch., London, 1975-76; postdoctoral fellow Scripps Clinic and Rsch. Found., La Jolla, Calif., 1976-78, rsch. assoc., 1978-79, asst. mem. 1, 1979-81; asst. prof. U. Mich., Ann Arbor, 1981-84, assoc. prof., 1984-90, prof., 1990—, chief nephrology, 1988—, dir. O'Brien Renal Ctr., 1988—, dir. NIH Nephrology Tng. Program, 1988-96. Lectr., speaker in field. Author chpts. to books; assoc. editor: Jour. Am. Soc. Nephrology, Clin. Sci.; contbr. articles to profl. jours. First Broderip scholar, 1971, Harold Boldero scholar, 1971, James McIntosh scholar, 1971, The Berkeley fellow Gonville and Caius Coll., 1976; recipient Leopold Hudson prize, 1971, The William Henry Rean prize, 1971, Disting. Rsch. Jerome W. Conn award, 1984. Fellow Royal Coll. Physicians (U.K.); mem. Am. Assn. Pathologists, Am. Assn. Immunologists, Am. Soc. Nephrology, Fedn. Clin. Rsch., Am. Soc. Clin. Investigation, Ctrl. Soc. Am. Fedn. Clin. Rsch., Assn. Am. Physicians. Office: U Mich Nephrology Div 3914 Taubman Ctr Ann Arbor MI 48109

WIGHT, DARLENE, retired speech educator, emerita educator; b. Andover, Kans., Jan. 5, 1926; d. Everett John and Claudia (Jennings) Van Biber; m. Lester Delin, Jan. 21, 1950; children: Lester Delin II, Claudia Leigh. AA, Graceland Coll., 1945; BA, U. Kans., 1948, MA, 1952. Permanent profl. cert., Iowa; life tchr.'s cert., Mo. Instr. U. Kans., Lawrence, 1949-50; instr. overseas program U. Md., Munich, 1954; speech pathologist Independence (Mo.) Pub. Sch. Dist., 1958-61; assoc. prof. Graceland Coll., Lamoni, Iowa, 1961-87, prof. emeritus. Cons. Quad-County Sch. Dist., Leon, Iowa, 1966-67, Mt. Ayr (Iowa) Cmty. Sch. Dist., 1967-70; cons. Head Start program SCIAP, Leon, 1972-75, MATURA, Bedford, Iowa, 1973-75. Co-author: Speech Communication Handbook, 1979. Mem. Common Cause, Friends of Art, Nelson-Atkins Mus. Art, Habitat for Humanity, Nat. Mus. Women in Arts, Am. Craft Coun. Recipient Award of Merit U. Kans., 1982, Award of Distinction U. Kans., 1947-48. Mem. AAUW, Am. Speech, Lang. and Hearing Assn. (speech pathology clin. competency), Coun. Exceptional Children, Archaeol. Inst. Am. Democrat. Mem. Community Of Christ Ch. Avocations: weaving/fibers, traveling, gardening, cooking. Office: Graceland U Speech Dept Lamoni IA 50140 E-mail: darlenewight@yahoo.com.

WIGHT, JAMES K. civil engineer, research scientist, educator; b. Lansing, Mich., Feb. 27, 1947; s. Claude O. and Zella T. (Mills) W.; m. Linda K. Magley, June 10, 1969; children: Danielle, Evan, Blair. BSCE, Mich. State U., 1969, MSCE, 1970; PhD, U. Ill., 1973. Asst. prof. U. Mich., Ann Arbor, 1973-78, assoc. prof., 1978-86, prof., 1986—, dir. Structural Engrng. Lab., 1987—. Editor: Earthquake Effects on Reinforced Concrete Structures, 1985—. Fellow Am. Concrete Inst. (chair concrete bldg. code com., Delmar Bloem award 1991, Joe Kelly award 1999, Boise award 2002); mem. Kiwanis. Avocations: soccer coach, golf. Home: 616 Wembley Ct Ann Arbor MI 48103-6137 Office: U Mich Dept Civil and Environ Engrng 2340 G G Brown Bldg Ann Arbor MI 48109-2125

WIGHTMAN, ARTHUR STRONG, physicist, educator; b. Rochester, N.Y., Mar. 30, 1922; s. Eugene Pinckney and Edith Victoria (Stephenson) W.; m. Anna-Greta Larsson, Apr. 28, 1945 (dec. Feb. 11, 1976); 1 child, Robin Letitia (dec. Mar. 2, 2001); m. Ludmilla Popova, Jan. 14, 1977. BA, Yale U., 1942; PhD, Princeton U., 1949; DSc, Swiss Fed. Inst. Tech., Zurich, 1969, Göttingen U., 1987. Instr. physics Yale, 1943-44; from instr. to asso. prof. physics Princeton, 1949-60, prof. math. physics, 1960-92; prof. emeritus, 1992—; Thomas D. Jones prof. math. physics Princeton, 1971-92. Vis. prof. Sorbonne, 1957, École Polytechnique, 1977-78. Served to lt. (j.g.) USNR, 1944-46. NRC postdoctoral fellow Inst. Teoretisk Fysik, Copenhagen, Denmark, 1951-52; NSF sr. postdoctoral fellow, 1956-57; recipient Dannie Heineman prize math. physics, 1969, Poincaré prize Internat. Assn. Math. Physics, 1997. Fellow NAS, Am. Acad. Arts and Scis., Royal Acad. Arts, Am. Phys. Soc.; mem. AAAS, Am. Math. Soc. Office: Princeton U 350 Jadwin Hl Princeton NJ 08544-0001

WIGHTMAN, LUDMILLA G. POPOVA, language educator, foreign educator, translator; b. Sofia, Bulgaria, Sept. 29, 1933; came to U.S., 1977; d. Genko Mateev and Liliana (Kusseva) Popov; m. Ivan Todorov Todorov, Aug. 13, 1957 (div. 1976); 1 child, Todor; m. Arthur Strong Wightman, Jan. 14, 1977. MS, U. Sofia, 1956. Cons. Nat. Libr., Sofia, 1956-58; rsch. assoc. Joint Inst. for Nuclear Rsch., Moscow, 1958-65; lectr. Russian Rutgers U., New Brunswick, N.J., 1969-70; editor Bulgarian Ency., Sofia, 1973-77; tchr. lang. Princeton (N.J.) Lang. Group, 1977—2001. Libr. Firestone Libr., Princeton U., 1983-87. Translator: Introduction to Axiomatic Field Theory, 1975, New Eng. Rev., Bread Loaf Quar., 1987, Mr. Cogito, 1989, N.Y. Rev. Books, 1990, Poetry East, 1990-91, Literary Rev., 1992, US1 Worksheets, 1992-2000, Visions International, 1993-2000, Partisan Rev., 1996, Shifting Borders: East European Poetries of the Eighties, 1993, Internat. Quarterly, 1999, Cry of a Former Dog, 2000, Forbidden Sea, 2000, Frost Flowers, 2001, Scars, 2002, Capriccio for a Goya, 2003. Avocations: bird watching, music, photography, travel. Home and Office: 16 Balsam Ln Princeton NJ 08540-5327

WIGNARAJAH, KANAPATHIPILLAI, plant physiologist, researcher, educator; b. Batticaloa, Sri Lanka, Dec. 26, 1944; came to U.S., 1988; s. Sinnathnamby and Nagaratnam (Nallathamby) K.; m. Asha Vasanti Ramcharan, Aug. 2, 1984; children: Avisha Nia, Amira Tari. BS in Botany, U. Ceylon, Colombo, Sri Lanka, 1969; PhD in Plant Physiology, U. Liverpool, Eng., 1974. Asst. lectr. in botany U. Ceylon, Sri Lanka, 1969-71; rsch. assoc. agronomy dept. U. Western Australia, 1974-75; lectr. U. Malawi, Africa, 1975-76, U. West Indies, Trinidad, 1976-84; sr. lectr. U. Guyana, S. Am., 1985-86; rsch assoc. U. Wales, Bangor, United Kingdom, 1986-87; rsch. assoc. Ctr. Nat. de la Rsch. Sci., Montpellier, France, 1987-88, U. Okla., Norman, 1988-89, U. Calif., Santa Cruz, 1989-90; sr. scientist Lockheed Martin Engrng. & Sci., Moffett Field, Calif., 1990—. Cons. Nat. Inst. for Sci. and Tech., Georgetwon, Guyana, 1985-86; Inter-Am. Inst. for Coop. in Agrl., 1985-86; reviewer for Tropical Agrl., 1980-86, Oecologia Plantarium, 1986-87, Environ. and Exptl. Botany, 1990—, Grant Proposals to NASA, 1991—. Contbr. articles to profl. jours. Sec. Ceylon Nat. Hist. Soc., Sri Lanka, 1969-71. Wheat Bd. Rsch. grant, Australian Res. Bank, Nedlands, 1974, Swedish Guest scholar The Swedish Inst., Stockholm, 1980, King Gustav Lectr. medal U. Stockholm, 1980, Yamani Found. U. fellow U. Wales, 1986, European Econ. Commn., Centre Nat. de la Rsch. Sci. fellow, Montpellier, France, 1987. Fellow Indian Chem. Soc.; mem. Scandinavian Soc. Plant Physiologists, Phytochem. Soc. Europe. Hindu. Achievements include major findings on adaptation of plants to environmental stresses, such as salinity, waterlogging and anaerobiosis. Office: Lockheed-Martin Engrng & Sci NASA Ames Rsch Ctr Moffett Field CA 94035

WIGSTON, DAVID LAWRENCE, biologist, dean; b. London, Dec. 12, 1943; came to U.S., 1993; s. Frederic Roland Wigston and Joan Mavin; m. Patricia Anne Werner, May 25, 1991; 1 child, Alexa Joan Dobinson. BSc with 1st class honors, U. Exeter, Eng., 1965; PhD in Forest Ecology, U. Exeter, 1972. Lectr. in biology Exeter Coll., 1967-69; sr. lectr. biology Coventry (Eng.) U., 1970-74; reader environ. sci. Plymouth (Eng.) U., 1974-82; prof., chair dept. forestry Papua New Guinea U. Tech., Lae, 1982-86; prof. environ. sci. No. Territory U., Darwin, Australia, 1986-93, dean faculty of sci., 1986-92; rsch. prof. U. Fla., Gainesville, 1993-96; rsch. assoc. dean U. Mich., Flint, 1996—. Vis. fellow St. Cross Coll. Oxford (Eng.) U., 1980; cons. Swedish Biomass Energy Program, 1981-82; chief wildlife scientist No. Territory (Australia) Govt., 1992-93. Narrator (symphonic works) Peter & The Wolf, Jungle Book, Hassan, 1961—. Cons. Internat. Convention Biodiversity, Australia, 1992-93; pres., bd. dirs. Gainesville Symphony Orch., 1994-96. Fellow Australian Inst. Biology (sec. No. Territory br. 1987-93); mem. Ecol. Soc. Am., Soc. Human Ecology, Soc. Econ. Botany. Avocations: music, theater, art, literature. Office: U Mich 303 Kearsley St Flint MI 48502

WIK, JEAN MARIE (JEAN MARIE BECK), librarian, media specialist; b. Aitkin, Minn., Feb. 10, 1938; d. Herman Otto Beck and Ferdina Mathilda (Petersen) Kalt; m. Richard Lyle Wik, Aug. 17, 1958; children: Steven L., Lori Jo. BS, No. State U., Aberdeen S.D., 1963; MA, U. Minn., 1972; cert. in media arts, Mankato State U., 1974. Elem. tchr. Howard Hedger Sch., Aberdeen, S.D., 1958-62; tchr. spl. edn. Westwood Sch., Bloomington, Minn., 1963-64; elem. tchr. Washburn Sch., 1964-71; media generalist elem. elem. and secondary schs., 1972-85; media generalist Kennedy High Sch., Bloomington, 1985-96; fashion coord. Weekender Casual Wear, 1993—2001. Dir. Annehurst Curriculum Classifications System project Bloomington Schs., 1976-85, dist. media leadership position, 1990-92. Chmn. Christian Women's Club, 1972-74, area rep., 1981-85. Mem. NEA, Minn. Edn. Assn., Minn. Ednl. Media Assn. Avocations: songwriting, singing, public speaking for christian groups.

WILBER, BARBARA ANN, computer science and business education educator; b. West Allis, Wis., May 9, 1951; d. Edgar Joseph and Ethel Frieda (Ellie) Smith; m. Terry B. Wilber, Sept. 27, 1949; children: Tracy Lea, Tara Ann. BS, U. Wis., Stevens Point, 1973. Cert. bus. edn., vocat. edn., computer sci. Bus. edn., computer sci. and coop. tchr. Eisenhower HS, New Berlin Pub. Sch., Wis., 1973—. Adj. instr. Lakeland Coll.; mem. tech. com. New Berlin Sch., 1981—, sch. effective tng. com., 1993—, student mgmt. com., 1993—, critical issues rep., 1994, sch. to work transition com., 1993. Mem. Future Bus. Leaders Am. (advisor 1976). Avocations: snorkeling, ocean, kayaking. Office: Eisenhower HS 4333 S Sunnyslope Rd New Berlin WI 53151-6844

WILBER, CLARE MARIE, musician, educator; b. Denver, Mar. 21, 1928; d. Thomas A. and Kathleen M. (Brennan) O'Keefe; m. Charles Grady Wilber, June 14, 1952 (dec. 1998); children: Maureen, Charles, Michael, Thomas (dec.), Kathleen, Aileen, John Joseph. AB, Loretto Heights Coll., 1948; MS, Fordham U., 1950; MM, Colo. State U., 1972. Instr. biology and music various colls. and univs., 1951-83; mgr. Ft. Collins (Colo.) Symphony, 1969-81, exec. dir., 1981-85, exec. dir. emerita, 1985—; pvt. music instr. Ft. Collins, 1973—95. Trustee Ft. Collins Symphony, 1986-95, mem. young artist competition com., 1985—. Composer Fantasie Romantique, 1972, Mass in D, 1980, Seascapes for Suzanne, 1988, Panoramas for Polly, 1990, Journeys for Jennifer, 1994, Augustine's Lament, 1996, Collage for Cynthia, 1997, Daydreams for Drew, 2001. Mem. adv. coun. Ft. Collins H.S., 1972—74; mem. adv. bd. Children's Sch. of Sci., Woods Hole, Mass., 1965—95. Recipient AT&T Crystal Clef award, 1982, Clare Wilber award named in her honor, Ft, Collins Symphony, 1992. Mem. Ft. Collins Music Tchrs. Assn. (treas. 1984-90), Colo. State Music Tchrs. Assn., Music Tchrs. Nat. Assn. (cert. music tchr. 1978—), Marine Biol. Lab. Assocs., Cosmos Club (assoc.), Sigma Xi (assoc.), Delta Omicron (local chpt. pres. 1970-72, sec. 1988—, Spl. Svc. award 1974, Star of Delta Omicron award 1995). Republican. Roman Catholic. Home and Office: 900 Edwards St Fort Collins CO 80524-3824

WILBUR, ANDREW CLAYTON, radiologist, educator; b. Phila., May 30, 1952; s. Richard Sloan and Betty Lou (Fannin) W.; m. Debra Jean Jones, June 29, 1996; children: Curtis Richard. Clayton Samuel. AB in Human Biology, Stanford U., 1974; MD, George Washington U., 1978. Diplomate Am. Bd. Radiology. Extern in diagnostic radiology Palo Alto (Calif.) Med. Found., 1978-79; resident in diagnostic radiology U. Ill. Hosp., Chgo., 1979-83, fellow in body imaging, 1983-84; asst. prof. radiology U. Ill. Coll. Medicine, Chgo., 1984-90, assoc. prof., 1990—, dir. body imaging dept. radiology, 1988—, dir. radiology residency program, 1989—. Contbr. articles to profl. jours. Mem. Radiol. Soc. N.Am., Am. Coll. Radiology, Am. Roentgen Ray Soc., Chgo. Radiol. Soc. (trustee 1996-2000). Office: Univ of Illinois Hosp M/C 931 1740 W Taylor St Chicago IL 60612-7232

WILBUR, BARBARA MARIE, elementary education educator; b. Homer City, Pa., Dec. 1, 1945; d. Nicholas and Ann (Bender) Hrebik; m. Samuel Scime, Nov. 21, 1970 (div. Jan. 1974); m. Frederick Layton Wilbur, June 21, 1986 (dec. June 1989). BS in Elem. Edn., SUNY, Buffalo, 1967, EdM in Guidance Counseling, 1971; postgrad., Harvard U., 1969; grad., John Robert Powers Modeling Sch., Buffalo, 1974. Cert. permanent elem. sch. tchr., N.Y. Elem. tchr. Buffalo Pub. Schs., 1967-70, 94—, Diocese of Ft. Lauderdale, Fla., 1971-72, Diocese of Buffalo, 1973-94. Mem. Internat. Platform Assn., State U. Buffalo Alumni Assn., State U. Coll. Buffalo Alumni Assn. (Outstanding Svc. award 1982), Buffalo State Coll. Alumni Assn. (bd. dirs. 1980-87, active various coms.). Republican. Roman Catholic. Avocations: modeling, volleyball, ice skating, tennis. Home: 20 Schimwood Ct Amherst NY 14068 Office: Buffalo Pub Schs Sch # 40 89 Clare St Buffalo NY 14206-2020

WILBUR, FRANKLIN PIERCE, education educator; b. Middleboro, Mass., Nov. 2, 1947; s. Franklin Pierce and Lillian Taylor (Arthur) W.; m. Cheryl Lynn Boyer; children: Jeffrey Taylor, Timothy Blake. BS in Elem. Edn., Bridgewater (Mass.) State Coll, 1969; MS in Instructional Tech., Syracuse U., 1970, PhD, 1976. Assoc. instrn. tech. Ctr. Instructional Devel., Syracuse U., 1972-78, dir. Project Advance, 1978—, assoc. prof. Sch. Edn., 1976—, assoc. v.p. undergrad. studies, 1990; exec. dir. Ctr. Support Tchg. and Learning Syracuse U., 1997—. Rsch. fellow Am. Assn. Higher Edn.; cons. in field. Author: Linking America's Schools and Colleges, 1994, 2d edit., 1995; contbr. papers, revs., reports in field. Mem. Am. Assn. Higher Edn., European Coun. Insternat. Schs., Internat. Learning Coop, Am. Ednl. Rsch. Assn., Am. Coun. Edn., Assn. Ednl. Comm. and Tech., Profl. and Orgnl. Network in Higher Edn., Phi Delta Kappa. Office: 400 Ostrom Ave Syracuse NY 13210-3250

WILCE, JOAN HUBBELL, elementary education educator; b. Gainesville, Fla., Feb. 20, 1931; d. Theodore Huntington and Grace (Griffin) Hubbell; m. Robert Thayer Wilce, Aug. 11, 1956 (div. 1984); children: Alexander Griffin, Andrew Thayer. BA in Zoology, U. Mich., 1954, MA in Botany, 1955, PhD in Botany, 1963; elem. edn. cert., U. Millersville, 1988. Cert. N.Y.C. Bd. Edn. Common Brs. Vis. lectr., lab. instr. dept. botany U. Mass., Amherst, 1964-67; prin. rsch. investigator NSF, Amherst, 1968-71; rsch. coord. ecol. studies at Pilgrim I Nuc. & Power Sta., Amherst, 1976-79; tchr. grades 5 and 6 The Common Sch., Amherst, 1980-82; elem. classroom tchr. N.Y.C. Bd. Edn., 1988-91, The Children's Storefront, N.Y.C., 1991-99; pre-sch./k-1 sci. tchr. The Ricardo O'Gorman Garden, N.Y.C., 1999—. Rsch. grantee NSF, 1968. Avocations: history of ancient latin american cultures, birding, gardening, traveling, camping.

WILCKE, MARILYN ANN (MIDGE WILCKE), university administrator; b. Boston, Mar. 13, 1953; d. Fred Harvey and Ann Rita (Thompson) W.; m. Robert Wilson Pollard, Apr. 2, 1983; 1 child, Ezra Lee. AB, Boston Coll., 1974; EdM, Boston U., 1979. Sec. New Eng. Merchants Nat. Bank, Boston, 1974-77; project asst. Boston U., 1977-79, asst. dir. Instrnl. Media Ctr., 1979-82; dir. univ. media svcs. Suffolk U., Boston, 1982—. Prodr. multi-image Suffolk University: A Part of Boston, 1985 (NE-AMI gold award 1985); editor Suffolk Mag., 1996 (NE-CASE gold award 1996); exec. prodr. video The Gift of Opportunity, 1996 (CASE-NE gold medal 1997), David J. Sargent Hall: A New Beginning, 1999 (CASE-NE gold medal 2000). Mem. parish com. First Parish in Brookline, Mass. Mem. Soc.

Coll. and Univ. Planners, Assn. Ednl. Comm. and Tech., Coun. Advancement and Support Edn. Democrat. Unitarian-Universalist. Home: 243 Beverly Rd Chestnut Hill MA 02467-3158 Office: Suffolk U 8 Ashburton Pl Boston MA 02108-2770

WILCOX, CHARLENE DELORIS, elementary school educator; b. Muncie, Ind., Jan. 8, 1932; d. Otto Orlando and Leona Irene (Forrest) Long;m. Arnold Henry Wilcox, Apr.17, 1955; children: George H., Roberta Lynn Cooley, Arnold Long. BS in Edn., Ohio State U., 1954; student, Mexico City Coll., 1952. Tchr. 3d grade Jackson (Mich.) Pub. Schs., 1954-56; tchr. grades 2 and 3 Wyandotte (Mich.) Pub. Schs., 1956-60; tchr. grade 4 Consolidated Schs. of Salem, N.H., 1961-62; tchr. grades 1, 2 and 4 Jackson (Mich.) Pub. Schs., 1963-86; ret. Mem. United Meth. Ch., mem. edn. com., 2001—. Mem.: NEA, AAUW (membership v.p. 1990—92, social chmn. 1992—93, program v.p. 2001—), Ch. Women United, Mich. Assn. Ext. Homemakers, Assn. of Childhood Edn. (corr. sec. 1954—56), Jackson Edn. Assn., Mich. Edn. Assn., Am. Assn. Ret. Persons, Red Hat Soc., United Meth. Women (pres. 1992—94, rec. sec. 2001, v.p. 2003—, rec. sec. 2003—, membership v.p. 2003—), Peace Coun. (sec. 1991—92), Job's Daus., Women's Club of Jackson (v.p., corr. sec. 2001—), Delta Kappa Gamma Soc. (internat. Beta Beta chpt. membership v.p. 2002—), Alpha Gamma Delta (pres. 1953—54). Methodist. Avocations: travel, reading, sewing, swimming, quilting, crafts. Address: 3144 Cypress Ct Jackson MI 49201-8690

WILCOX, CHARLES JULIAN, geneticist, educator; b. Harrisburg, Pa., Mar. 28, 1930; s. Charles John and Gertrude May (Hill) W.; m. Eileen Louise Armstrong, Aug. 27, 1955; children: Marsha Lou, Douglas Edward. BS, U. Vt., 1950; MS, Rutgers U., 1955, PhD, 1959. Registered animal scientist. Dairy farm owner, operator, Charlotte, Vt., 1955-56; prof. U. Fla., Gainesville, 1959-95; prof. emeritus, 1995—. Cons. in internat. animal agrl. Gt. Britain, France, Sudan, Pakistan, Can., Mex., El Salvador, Ecuador, Brazil, Bolivia, Peru, Colombia, Venezuela, Dominican Republic, Saudi Arabia, Sweden, Norway. Mem. editl. bd.: Genetics and Molecular Biology, 1979—; editor: Large Dairy Herd Management, 1978, 1993; author (with others): Animal Agriculture, 1973, Animal Agriculture, 2d edit., 1980, Improvement of Milk Production in Tropics, 1990. 1st Lt. U.S. Army, 1951—53, Korea. Decorated Combat Infantry Badge; recipient award of merit jr. faculty, Gamma Sigma Delta, 1968, award of merit sr. faculty, 1984, Disting. Svc. award, Fla. Purebred Dairy Cattle Assn., 1986, Internat. award for Disting. Svc. for Agr., Gamma Sigma Delta, 1987, Sr. Rsch. Scientist award, Sigma Xi, 1994. Mem.: Fla. Hostein Assn. (pres. 1979), Am. Registry Profls. Animal Sci. (examining bd. 1987—95), Am. Soc. Animal Sci., Am. Dairy Sci. Assn. (mem. editl. bd. 1999—), Fla. Guernsey Cattle Club. (pres. 1974—76), Fla. Jersey Cattle Club (bd. dir.). Republican. Avocations: spectator sports, baseball, football, basketball, tennis. Office: Univ Fla Animal Sci Dept Gainesville FL 32611-0920 E-mail: cjwgenetic@aol.com.

WILCOX, DAVID ERIC, electrical engineer, educational consultant; b. Cortland, N.Y., Sept. 4, 1939; s. James A. and Lucille (Fiske) C.; m. Phyllipa Ann Wilcox, Jan. 23, 1977; children: Terri L., Cinda A., Jana L. 0postgrad., Syracuse U., 1965; BSEE, U. Buffalo, 1961; 0postgrad., Marist Coll., Rutgers U.; MS, U. Bridgeport, 1977. Registered profl. engr., N.Y. Rsch. engrng. mgr. input/output devices Rome (N.Y.) Air Devel. Ctr., 1966-70; dir. sales Mercom Inc., Winsooki, Vt., 1970-73, dir., 1972—73; pres. Wilcox Tng. Sys., Newburgh, NY, 1973—2003; pres., CEO Global Skills Exch., 2003—. Exec. dep. dir., Nat. Skill Stds. Bd., 1998-2003, bd. dirs., 2003--; prin. Exec. Effectiveness, Inc., NYC; instr. Dale Carnegie courses. Author: Information System Sciences, 1965; contbr. articles to profl. jours.; patentee in field. Pres. N.Y. State Jaycees, 1972-73, chmn., 1973-74; dir. U.S. Jaycees, 1970-71; bd. dirs., v.p. N.Y. State Spl. Olympics, 1972-73; bd. dirs., treas. Family Counseling Svc., Inc.; mem. Orange County Pvt. Industry Coun., N.Y. State Excelsior Examiner, 1995. Lt. USAF, 1961-65. Mem. IEEE, Soc. Info. Display, N.Y. State Soc. Profl. Engrs., Internat. Transactional Analysis Assn., Internat. Platform Assn., Am. Soc. Quality Control. Methodist. Home: 528 Tobacco Quay Alexandria VA 22314 also: 30 W 60th St New York NY 10023-7902 Address: 528 Tobacco Quay Alexandria VA 22314-2042

WILCOX, PAUL HORNE, academic administrator, researcher; b. N.Y.C., Oct. 2, 1950; s. Richard Leon and Madge Muncie (Horne) W.; m. Elizabeth Winston Wyman, Aug. 24, 1985. BA, Bennington (Vt.) Coll., 1979. Coord. Aspen (Colo.) Inst. for Humanistic Studies, 1979-81; pres. Aspen Internat. Assocs., 1981-84; mgr. Nordstrom Inc., L.A., 1984-86; pres. human engrng. The Pacific Inst., Seattle, 1986-87; dir. ops. Tellsyn Group, L.A., 1987-88; chmn. Inst. for Mgmt. Studies, Seattle, 1988—. Mem. grad. rev. bd. Antioch U., Seattle, 1990—; book reviewer Synapsia The Brit. Brain Jour., Marlow, Buckinghamshire, Eng., 1990—; advisor N.W. Ethics Inst., Seattle, 1990—; founding educator Gstaad Colloquium The Lastis Found., Gstaad, Switzerland, 1988; mem. adv. bd. Lumatron Corp., 1992—. Fundraiser United Way, L.A., 1986; trustee United Ch. of Christ, Seattle, 1989—, chmn. bd. trustees, 1991—; bd. dirs. Aspen Pub. Radio Sta. NPR, 1982; vol. Wash. Lit., 1990—; bd. dirs. Wash. State Lit. Hotline, 1992—; active World Affairs Coun., 1993—; chair Statewide Lit. Outreach, 1993. Rsch. fellow U. Pa., 1991. Mem. Brain Club (bd. dirs. Marlow-Buckinghamshire chpts. 1990—), Beaver Bay Club, Hillsboro Club. Avocations: skiing, hiking, music. Office: Inst for Mgmt Studies 200 1st Ave W Ste 410 Seattle WA 98119-4219

WILCOX, RAND ROGER, psychology educator; b. Niagara Falls, N.Y., July 6, 1946; s. Howard Clinton and Phyllis Hope (Stevens) W.; m. Karen Lesley Thompson, Apr. 25, 1986; children: Quinn Alexander, Bryce Colin. BA, U. Calif., Santa Barbara, 1968, MA in Math., PhD in Ednl. Psychology, U. Calif., Santa Barbara, 1976. Sr. rsch. assoc. UCLA, 1976-81; prof. psychology U. So. Calif., L.A., 1981—. Author: New Statistical Procedures for Social Sciences, 1987, Statistics for Social Sciences, 1996, Robust Estimation and Hypothesis Testing, 1997, Fundamentals of Modern Statistical Methods, 2001, Applying Contemporary Statistical Techniques, 2003; assoc. editor Psychometrika, Computational Stats. and Data Analysis.: mem. editorial bd. 3 jours; also numerous articles . Recipient T.L. Saaty award Am. Jour. Math. & Mgmt. Scis., 1984. Fellow Am. Psychol. Soc., Royal Statis. Soc.; mem. Psychometric Soc., Am. Statis. Assn., Inst. Math. Stats., Am. Ednl. Rsch. Assn. Achievements include research on improved methods for comparing groups and measuring achievement; resistant measures of correlation and regression; substantial gains in power when testing hypotheses. Office: U So Calif Dept Psychology Los Angeles CA 90089-0001

WILCOX, SCOTT BARNES, museum curator, educator; b. Easton, Pa., Oct. 15, 1952; s. James Grant and Betty Marie (Barnes) W.; m. Carolyn Nancy Gray, Jan. 19, 1974; 1 child, Emma Elizabeth. BA, Coll. William and Mary, 1974; MLitt, Edinburgh U., Scotland, 1976; PhD, Yale U., 1984. Asst. curator prints and drawings Yale Ctr Brit. Art, New Haven, 1982-91, assoc. curator, 1991—98, curator, 1998—; lectr. history of art Yale U., New Haven, 1984—. Author: British Watercolors: Drawings of the 18th and 19th Centuries from the Yale Center for British Art, 1985, Edward Lear and the Art of Travel, 2000; co-author: Masters of the Sea, 1987, Victorian Landscape Watercolors, 1992, The Line of Beauty, 2001. Mem. Print Coun. Am., Coll. Art Assn., Historians of Brit. Art. Home: 53 Thomson Rd West Hartford CT 06107-2535 Office: Yale Ctr Brit Art 1080 Chapel St New Haven CT 06510-2302

WILD, VICTOR ALLYN, lawyer, educator; b. Logansport, Ind., May 7, 1946; s. Clifford Otto and Mary E. (Helvey) W.; 1 child, Rachel. BS in Pub. Adminstrn., U.Ariz., 1968, JD, 1974. Bar: Ariz. 1975, U.S. Dist. Ct. Ariz. 1975, Mass. 1984, U.S. Dist. Ct. Mass. 1984, U.S. Ct. Appeals (1st cir.) 1985, U.S. Ct. Appeals (9th cir.). Chief escrow officer Lawyers Title Co., Denver, 1971-72, escrow officer Tucson, 1970-71; law clk. Pima County Atty., Tucson, 1973-75, dep. county atty., 1975-81, chief criminal dep., 1981-84; asst. U.S. Atty. Dist. of Mass., Boston, 1984—. Chief gen. crimes unit U.S. Atty.'s Office, Boston, 1986-89; seminar instr. Mass. Continuing Legal Edn., Internat. Assn. Law Enforcement Investment Analysts, Dept. of Justice Office Internat. Affairs, Dept. of Labor, FBI, U.S. Postal Svc., Internat. Assn. Fin. Crims Investigators, Secret Svc., State Bar Ariz., Tucson and Phoenix, 1981-84; instr. U. Ariz., Tucson, 1981-84, Pima C.C., Tucson, 1981-84. Mem. editl. bd. Episcopal Times, Diocese of Mass., 1988—. Mem. vestry St. Michael's Episc. Ch., Marblehead, Mass., 1986-90, lay Eucharistic min., 1988—, parish warden, 1992-96; mem. Boston Ctr. for Internat. Visitors, 1989—; bd. dirs. Crime Resistors, Inc., Tucson, 1983, CODAC, Tucson, 1983, 88-Crime, Inc., Tucson, 1983, Marblehead Seaport Trust, 1987-89, Old ahd Historic Oversight Com., 1999-2000; chmn. Marblehead Capital Planning Commn., 1989—; bd. dirs. Marblehead Citizen Scholarship Found., 1997—, Marblehead Sch. Master Plan. Com., 2000—; mem. PhD rev. com. Law Policy and Soc. Northeastern U., 1991-92; bd. dirs. Davenport House Child Enrichment Ctr., Marblehead, 1986-89. With USAF, 1968-70. Recipient Commendation awards Dept. Labor, Dept. State, USCG, USIA, U.S. Postal Svc., Dept. Treasury, EOUSA Rev., Software Pub. Assn., Mass. Ins. Fraud Bur.; named Prosecutor of Yr., Office Insp. Gen., U.S. Dept. Labor, 1986, DOJ Spec. Achievement Award, 1993, 95, 96. Master Boston Inn of Ct.; mem. Ariz. Bar Assn., Mass. Bar Assn., Tau Kappa Epsilon, Delta Sigma Pi, Phi Kappa Delta. Office: US Attys Office Ste 9200 US Courthouse One Courthouse Way Boston MA 02210

WILDE, JOHN, artist, educator; b. Milw., Dec. 12, 1919; s. Emil F. and Mathilda (Lotz) W.; m. Helen Ashman, July 1943 (dec. Dec. 1966); children: Jonathan, Phoebe; m. Shirley Miller, 1969. BS, U. Wis., 1942, MS, 1948. Mem. faculty U. Wis., 1948—, prof. art, 1960—, chmn. dept. art, 1960-62, Alfred Sessler Distinguished prof. art, 1969-82, prof. emeritus, 1982—. Elected mem. Nat. Acad. Design, 1994. Works exhibited Met. Mus. Art, Mus. Modern Art, Whitney Mus. Am. Art, Corcoran Mus. Art, Mpls. Art Mus., San Francisco Mus. Art, Whitney Mus. Am. Art, 1978-80, Nat. Portrait Gallery, Smithsonian Instn., 1980, Nat. Gallery, Washington, 1988; drawing retrospective Elvehjem Mus. Art, U. Wis., 1984-85; 3-man retrospective (with Curry and Bohrod), Milw. Art Mus., 1982, 55 Yr. Retrospective Eluehjem Mus. of Art, U. Wis., Madison drawings and paintings, 1999-2000, others; represented in permanent collections, Pa. Acad. Art, Detroit Inst. Fine Art, Worcester Art Mus., Wadsworth Atheneum, Whitney Mus. Am. Art, Carnegie Inst., Nat. Collection Art, Smithsonian Instn., Yale U. Art Gallery, Butler Inst. Am. Art, Art Inst. Chgo., Sheldon Meml. Art Gallery, U. Nebr., Zimmerli Mus. Art, Rutgers U., N. Brunswick, N.J., Mus. Contemporary Art, Chgo., others, also extensive exhbns. abroad; subject of book WildeWorld, The Art of John Wilde, 1999. Recipient numerous awards for painting and drawing in regional and nat. exhbns. including, Childe Hassam purchase award Am. Acad. and Inst. Arts and Letters, 1968, 81, 87, Richard Florsheim Art Purchase award, 1994, Henry LeGrand Cannon prize Nat. Acad. Design, 2001; E.D. Found. grantee, 1995.

WILDE, MARY, secondary education educator; BS, Concordia Tchrs. Coll.; MS, U. Mo.; specialist degree, West Ga. Coll. Elem. tchr.; mid. sch. tchr. Booth Mid. Sch., Peachtree City, Ga., 1983—. Coach team Sci. Olympiad. Named Outstanding Earth Sci. Tchr., 1992. Mem. Ga. Sci. Tchrs. Assn. (pres.-elect). Office: Booth Mid Sch 250 Peachtree PkySouth Peachtree City GA 30269-1740

WILDENTHAL, C(LAUD) KERN, physician, educator; b. San Marcos, Tex., July 1, 1941; s. Bryan and Doris (Kellam) W.; m. Margaret Dehlinger, Oct. 15, 1964; children: Pamela, Catharine. BA, Sul Ross Coll., 1960; MD, U. Tex. Southwestern Med. Ctr., Dallas, 1964; PhD, U. Cambridge, Eng., 1970. Intern Bellevue Hosp., N.Y.C., 1964-65; resident in medicine, fellow cardiology Parkland Hosp., Dallas, 1965-67; research fellow Nat. Heart Inst., Bethesda, Md., 1967-68; vis. research fellow Strangeways Research Lab., Cambridge, 1968-70; asst. prof. to prof. internal medicine and physiology U. Tex. Southwestern Med. Ctr., Dallas, 1970-76, prof., dean grad. sch., 1976-80, prof., dean Southwestern Med. Sch., 1980-86, prof., pres., 1986—. Hon. fellow Hughes Hall, U. Cambridge, 1994—. Author: Regulation of Cardiac Metabolism, 1976, Degradative Processes in Heart and Skeletal Muscle, 1980; contbr. articles to profl. jours. Bd. dirs. Dallas Ctr. Performing Arts, Dallas Symphony, Dallas Opera, Dallas Mus. Art, S.W. Mus. Sci. and Tech., Dallas Citizen's Coun., Am. Friends Cambridge U., Greater Dallas C. of C. Recipient rsch. career devel. award NIH, 1972; spl. rsch. fellow USPHS, 1968-70; Guggenheim fellow, 1975-76. Mem. AMA, Inst. Medicine/NAS, Am. Soc. Clin. Investigation, Am. Coll. Cardiology, Royal Soc. Medicine Gt. Britain, Am. Physiol. Soc., Internat. Soc. Heart Rsch. (past pres. Am. sect.), Am. Fedn. Clin. Rsch., Assn. Am. Med Colls., Assn. Am. Physicians, Am. Heart Assn. (past chmn. sci. policy com.), Assn. Acad. Health Ctrs. (past chmn. sci. policy com.), British N.Am. Com., Greater Dallas C. of C. (bd. dirs.). Home: 4001 Hanover Ave Dallas TX 75225-7010 Office: U Tex Southwestern Med Ctr 5323 Harry Hines Blvd Dallas TX 75390-7208

WILDER, DOROTHY ANN, secondary school educator; b. Summerton, S.C., Sept. 11, 1950; d. Pinckney and Louise Elizabeth (Adger) W. BS in Bus. Adminstrn., Voorhees Coll., Denmark, S.C., 1972; MEd in Edn./Bus. Edn., S.C. State Coll., 1979; postgrad., U. S.C., Sumter and Columbia, 1973—. Adult edn. instr. Scott's Br. High Sch., Clarendon #1, Summerton, S.C., 1974-75; bus. edn. instr. Sumter (S.C.) High Sch. #17, 1973—. Com. mem. Sch. Referendum Com., Clarendon Sch. Dist. #1, Summerton, 1991—; student adviser Sumter High chpt. Future Bus. Leaders Am., 1977—. Mem. ASCD, NEA, Nat. Bus. Edn. Assn., S.C. Bus. Edn. Assn., S.C. Edn. Assn., Order Eastern Star, Zeta Phi Beta (chpt. phylacter 1991—). Baptist. Avocations: creative writing, public speaking, travel. Office: Sumter High Sch 2580 Mccrays Mill Rd Sumter SC 29154-6098

WILDER, FLOYDENE, primary school educator; b. Ogallala, Nebr., Nov. 21, 1952; d. Floyd and Anna (Smith) Barker; m. Dennis Wilder, Aug. 4, 1979; 1 child, Mysti. BS in Edn., U. Nebr., 1975; postgrad., Kearney State Coll., 1989. Cert. elem. tchr., Nebr. Resource tchr., speech aid ESU #12, Alliance, Nebr.; tchr. Dist. #8, Alliance, Dist. #40, Alliance; kindergarten tchr., media specialist K-6, primary tchr. Hyannis (Nebr.) Elem.; tchr. Willow Valley Sch. Mem., pres. Village Players, Inc.; active Swede Valley Lutheran Ch. Mem. NEA, Nebr. State Edn. Assn., Grant County Edn. Assn., Nat. Assn. Edn. Young Children, Nebr. Assn. Cmty. Theatres, Pi Lambda Theta. Home: PO Box 282 Hyannis NE 69350-0282

WILDER, PELHAM, JR., chemist, pharmacologist, educator, academic administrator; b. Americus, Ga., July 20, 1920; s. Pelham and Hattie (Wilder) W.; m. Alma Sterly Lebey, Mar. 20, 1945 (dec. May 1998); children: Alma Ann, Pelham III, Sterly Lebey. AB, Emory U., 1942, MA, 1943, Harvard U., 1947, PhD, 1950. Teaching fellow Harvard U., 1943-44, 46-49; instr. chemistry Duke U., 1949-52, asst. prof., 1952-58, assoc. prof., 1958-62, prof., 1962-67, prof. chemistry and pharmacology, 1967-87, Univ. Disting. Svc. prof. chemistry and pharmacology, 1987-90, Univ. Disting. Svc. prof. emeritus, 1990—, univ. marshal, chief of protocol, 1977—2000. Cons. NSF, Washington, 1960-68; Research Triangle Inst., Durham, 1965—, E.I. duPont deNemours & Co., 1966-69; Mem. advanced placement com. Coll. Entrance Exam. Bd., N.Y., 1967-75, chmn. chemistry com., 1969-75, cons., 1975— ; mem. exec. com. Gov. N.C. Sci. Advisory Com., 1962-64 Author: (with W.C. Vosburgh) Laboratory Manual of Fundamentals of Analytical Chemistry, 1956, Laboratory Manual of Physical Chemistry of Aqueous Solutions, 1967; Contbr. articles to profl. jours. Bd. dirs. Durham Acad., chmn., 1970-72; chmn. Exptl. Study of Religion and Soc., Raleigh, N.C., 1966-69. Served with USNR, 1944-46. Recipient 1st annual Alumni Distinguished Undergrad. Teaching award Duke, 1971, Disting. Pub. Svc. award USN, 1989. Mem. Am. Chem. Soc. (chmn. N.C. sect. 1956, com. on profl. tng.), Assn. Naval ROTC Colls. and Univs. (pres. 1982-88), Chem. Soc. London, Phi Beta Kappa (chpt. pres. 1974-75), Sigma Xi, Omicron Delta Kappa. Democrat. Presbyn. (ruling elder; exec. com. Ednl. Instns. Synod of N.C. 1966-72). Lodge: Rotary Club: Univ. (Durham, N.C.). Home: 2514 Wrightwood Ave Durham NC 27705-5830 Office: Duke U Dept Chemistry PO Box 90357 Durham NC 27708-0357

WILDERMUTH, ANITA JEAN, elementary school art educator; b. La Crosse, Wis., July 20, 1939; d. Arthur and Aleda Marie (Thompson) Thurin; m. Robert Berl Wildermuth, Aug. 15, 1970. BA, Luther Coll., 1961; MA in Tchg., Rockford Coll., 1977. Cert. tchr., Wis. Art tchr. Dodgeville (Wis.) Pub. Schs., 1961-62, Viroqua (Wis.) Pub. Schs., 1962-66, Beloit (Wis.) Sch. Dist., 1966-98. Supr. art Sch. Dist. Beloit, 1968-98; owner Thurin Apts., Viroqua, Wis.; sec.-treas. Wildermuth Farms, Inc. EMT Turtle Fire Dept., Beloit, 1980—; mem. U. Wis. Ext. Homemakers, So. Wis. Interest Macintosh Computer Soc. Mem. Wis. Art Educators Assn., Nat. Art Educators Assn. (amb. to China for art edn. 1988), Nat. Farmers Orgn., Art League of Beloit, Nat. Assn. Photoshop Profls., Beloit Area Ret. Educators Assn. Avocations: art, computer graphics, painting, crafts, golf. Home: 10001 S Clinton Corners Rd Clinton WI 53525-8308 E-mail: wilderm@jvlnet.com.

WILEY, ALBERT LEE, JR., physician, engineer, educator; b. Forest City, N.C., June 9, 1936; s. Albert Lee and Mary Louise (Davis) W.; m. Janet Lee Pratt, June 18, 1960; children: Allison Lee, Susan Caroline, Mary Catherine, Heather Elizabeth. B in Nuclear Engring., N.C. State U., 1958, postgrad., 1958-59; MD, U. Rochester, 1963; PhD, U. Wis., 1972. Diplomate Am. Bd. Nuclear Medicine, Am. Bd. Radiology, Am. Bd. Med. Physics, Am. Bd. Sci. in Nuclear Medicine. Nuclear engr. Lockheed Corp., Marietta, Ga., 1958; intern in surgery-medicine U. Va. Med. Sch., Charlottesville, 1963-64; resident in radiation therapy Sanford U., Palo Alto, Calif., 1964-65; resident, postdoctoral trainee U. Wis. Hosp., Madison, 1965-68; med. dir. USN Radiol. Def. Lab., San Francisco, 1968-69; nuclear safety instr. Navy Nuclear Weapons Training Ctr. North Is. Air Sta., Calif., 1968-70; staff physician Balboa Hosp., USN, San Diego, 1969-70; asst. prof. radiotherapy M.D. Anderson Hosp. U. Tex., Houston, 1972-73; assoc. dir., clin. dir. radiation oncology U. Wis., Madison, prof. radiology, human oncology, med. physics, nuclear safety ctr., 1970-88; vis. prof. U. Helsinki Hosp., Finland, 1979, The Norwegian Radium Hosp., Montebello, Norway, 1979; adj. prof. physics, chmn./prof. radiation, oncology, interim dir. cancer ctr. East Carolina U. Med. Sch., Greenville, N.C., 1988-93; clin. prof. Cancer Ctr. East Carolina U., Greenville, 2001—; prof. emeritus human oncology and radiology U. Wis., Madison, 2000—; cons. radiation medicine Watson Clinic, Lakeland, Fla., 1994—; affiliate physician U. So. Fla. Moffit Cancer Ctr., Tampa, 2000—; sr. physician Dept. Energy, Nat. Nuclear Security Agy., Oak Ridge (Tenn.) Associated Univs., 2002—. Navy rep. to meetings on radiation accidents Internat. Atomic Energy Agy., U.S. Embassy, Vienna, Austria, 1969; nuclear safety instr. Nuclear Tng. Ctr.; sr. med. officer USN Radiol. Def. Lab. Radiation Accident Team, 1968-70; cons. Los Alamos Meson Therapy Project, 1971-73, U.S. NRC, adv. com. on Nuclear Reactor Safeguards, 1981-82, Nat. Cancer Inst., VA, 1989-2000, Dept. Vet. Affairs, Dept. Homeland Security, 2002—; completed bus. adminstrv. program in med. mgmt. U. N.C.-Chapel Hill, Sch. of Bus., 1999; advisor, cons. numerous univs., govt. agys. and biotech. corps.; gov. apptd. mem. Wis. State Radioactive Waste Bd., Wis. Gov.'s Coun. on Biotech., Gov.'s Com. on UN. Author more than 150 articles and abstracts on med. physics, med. and environ. health physics, neutron radiobiology, nuclear medicine, radiation biology and treatment of pancreatic, prostate, and head/neck cancer; assoc. editor Jour. Med. Physics. Rep. candidate for U.S. Congress for 2d Wis. dist., 1982, 84; rep. primary candidate for gov., State of Wis., 1986; mem. Greenville Mayor's Drug Task Force, 1989-93; bd. dirs. Greenville Salvation Army, 1989-94; Rep. primary candidate N.C. 1st Dist. U.S. Congress, 2000; Dem. primary candidate U.S. Senate, 2002; Dem. primary candidate for U.S. Senate from N.C., 2002. Lt. comdr. USNR, 1959—89, ret. USNR, 1989. Oak Ridge Inst. Nuclear Studies fellow N.C. State U., 1958-59; Phillips Acad. Andover scholar, 1953. Fellow: N.C. Inst. Polit. Leadership, Am. Coll. Nuclear Medicine, Am. Coll. Radiology, Am. Coll. Preventive Medicine; mem.: AMA, AAUP, Fla. Vols. in Medicine, N.C. Med. Soc., Am. Acad. Health Physics, Am. Bd. Sci. Nuc. Medicine (sec.-treas.), Am. Coll. Occupl.-Environ. Medicine, N.C. Assn. Physics Tchrs., Am. Soc. Therapeutic Radiation Oncologists, Am. Assn. Physicists in Medicine, Am. Nuc. Soc., Am. Legion, U.S. Navy Inst., Am. Cancer Soc. (N.C. bd.dirs. 1989—93, pres. Polk County, Fla. 1995), VFW, Vietnam Vets. Am., Scottish Rite, Masons, N.C. Rotary, IEEE (sr.), Tau Beta Pi, Phi Eta Sigma, Sigma Phi Epsilon, Phi Kappa Phi, Sigma Xi. Avocations: fishing, politics, painting, languages, hiking. Home: PO Box 588 Salter Path Rd Salter Path NC 28575-0588 E-mail: aljanwiley@aol.com.

WILEY, DON CRAIG, biochemistry and biophysics educator; b. Akron, Ohio, Oct. 21, 1944; s. William Childs and Phyllis Rita (Norton) W.; m. Katrin Valgeirsdottir; children: William Valgeir, Lara; children from previous marriage: Kristen D., Craig S. BS in Physics and Chemistry, Tufts U., 1966; PhD in Biophysics, Harvard U., 1971; PhD (hon.), U. Leiden, The Netherlands, 1995; Doctorate (hon.), U. Leiden, Netherlands, 1995. Asst. prof. dept. biochemistry and molecular biology Harvard U., Cambridge, Mass., 1971-75, assoc. prof., 1975-79, prof. biochemistry and biophysics, from 1979, chmn. dept. molecular and cellular biology, 1992-95, investigator Howard Hughes Med. Inst., from 1987. Mem. biophys. chemistry study sect. NIH, 1981-85; Shipley Symposium lectr. Harvard Med. Sch., 1985, Peter A. Leermakers Symposium lectr. Wesleyan U., 1986, K.F. Meyer lectr. U. Calif., San Francisco, 1986, John T. Edsall lectr. Harvard U., 1987, Washburn lectr. Boston Mus. Sci., 1987, Harvey lectr. N.Y. Acad. Sci., 1988, XVI Linus Pauling lectr. Stanford U., 1989; rsch. assoc. in medicine Children's Hosp., Boston, 1990—. Contbr. numerous articles to profl. jours. Recipient Ledlie prize Harvard U., 1982, Louisa Gross Horwitz prize Columbia U., 1990, William B. Coley award Cancer Rsch. Inst., 1992, V.D. Mattia award, 1992, Passano Found. Laureate award, 1993, Emil von Behring prize, 1993, Gairdner Found. Internat. award, 1994, Lasker award, 1995, Rose Payne Disting. Scientist award, 1996, Japan prize, 1999; European Molecular Biology fellow, 1976. Fellow NAS (lectr. 1988); mem. AAAS, Am. Acad. Arts and Scis., Am. Chem. Soc. (Nichol's Disting. Symposium lectr. N.E. sect. 1988), Am. Crystallographic Assn., Am. Soc. Microbiology, Am. Soc. for Chemistry and Molecular Biology, Am. Soc. for Virology, Biophys. Soc. (Nat. lectr. 1989), Protein Soc., Am. Phil. Soc. Achievements include research on amino acid sequences of haemagglutinins of influenza viruses of the H3 subtype isolated from horses, studies of infuenza haemagglutinin mediated membrane fusion. Died Nov. 16, 2001.

WILEY, JOHN D. academic administrator; BS in Physics, Ind. U., 1964; MS in Physics, U. Wis., Madison, 1965, PhD in Physics, 1968. Tech. staff Bell Telephone Labs., Murray Hill, NJ, 1968—74; Alexander von Humboldt rsch. and tng. fellow Max Planck Inst., Stuttgart, Germany, 1974—75; mem. elec. and computer engring. faculty U. Wis., Madison, 1975—, co-founder Ctr. for X-Ray Lithography and Engring. Rsch. Ctr. for Plasma-Aided Mfg., chair Materials Sci. program, 1982—86, assoc. dean for rsch., Coll. Engring., 1986—89, dean, Grad. Sch., and sr. rsch. officer, 1989—94, provost and vice chancellor for acad. affairs, 1994—2000, chancellor, 2001—. Office: U Wis 161 Bascom Hall 500 Lincoln Dr Madison WI 53706

WILEY, MILLICENT YODER, realtor, pianist, accompanist, retired secondary school educator; b. Mercedes, Tex., June 7, 1923; d. Frank and Grace Yoder; m. William Gregory Wiley, Mar. 25, 1946; children: Sandra

Kay Wiley, Patti Gayle Wiley Stickle. BS, Tex. State Coll. Women, 1949; postgrad., U. Houston, 1950-53. Choral dir., music tchr. schs. in Tex. and La., 1945-60; music tchr. Kingsville (Tex.) Ind. Sch. Dist., 1960-80, choral dir., 1960—80, trustee, 1981-87, v.p., 1986-87; choral dir. H.M. King H.S., 1964-80, ret., 1980. Choral adjudication, Tex., 1960—; clinician for area choirs, 1965—86; area admissions advisor, adminstr. Pacific Am. Inst., 1976—80; state dir. South Tex. for Am. Internat. Edn. and Tng., 1980—83; Tex. rep. Internat. Travel Study, Inc., 1983—90; adminstr. Travel Selections, 1990—96, 2000; pianist Tex. State Fedn. Women's Clubs, 1994—96. Ch. organist various Meth. Ch., Tex. and La., 1935-65; bd. dirs. Kingsville chpt. Am. Heart Assn., 1973-78, Cmty. Concerts Assn., 1994-96, Helen Kleberg Cmty. Ctr., 1994-96, Kingsville Action Com.; adjudicator Tex. Choral Contests, 1960-96; mem. Tex. All-State Alumni Bd., 1995, 2000; active Mayor's City Com., Mayor's Future Com., 1993-96, Rep. Task Force. Recipient various certs. appreciation. Mem.: NEA, Tex. Assn. Sch. Bds. (trustee 1981—87, Kingsville ISD v.p. 1986—87), Kingsville Ret. Tchrs., Tri-City Ret. Tchrs., Fgn. Study League (counselor 1970—72, adminstr. 1973—76, advisor, prin.), Nat. Bd. Realtors, Multiple Listing Svc. Kingsville, Tex. Assn. Realtors, Kingsville Bd. Realtors (bd. dirs. 1994—95), Tex. Music Adjudicators Assn., Tex. State Tchrs. Assn., Tex. Choral Dirs. Assn. (accompanist for vocal scloists 1938—80, state clinic condr. 1977, instrumental soloists), Tex. Music Educators Assn. (clinician 1973, bd. dirs. 1973—74), Music Educators Nat. Conf., Am. Choral Dirs. Assn., Am. Sch. Bd. Assn. (trustee 1981—87), 36th Infantry Divsn. Assn. (soloist for men's meetings and ceremonies 1980—, 1st v.p. nat. ladies aux. 1989—90, pres. 1990—91, 2nd v.p. 1999—2003, pres. nat. 2003—, nat. bd. dirs. 2003—), Kingsville C. of C. Navy League (bd. dirs. 1997—, nat. dir. 1998—2002, nat. dir. emeritus 2003—), Future Homemakers (hon.), Gen. Women's Club Kingsville (parliamentarian 1992—94, pres. 1994—96), Duplicate Bridge Club, NAS Bridge Club, Kingsville Country Club, Monday Bridge Club, Exxon Bridge Club, Kiwanis (pianist Kingsville Club 1985—98), Rotary (pianist 1966—, first woman mem. 1987, chmn. membership devel. com. 1987—, fellowship chair 1997—98, mem. scholarship com. and social com. 2000—, fellowship chair 2001—03, past social chmn., program chmn. and membership chmn.), Exxon Annuitant Club (bd. dirs. 1992—94), Women's Club Kingsville (chmn. "As You Like It" dept. 1990, 1st vice chmn. 1992—94, gen. club parlimentarian 1992—94, pres. 1994—96), Music Club Kingsville (pres. 1982—84, 3d v.p. 1988—89, 1st v.p. 1989—91). Methodist. Home: 229 Helen Marie Ln Kingsville TX 78363-7305 Fax: 361-592-9300. E-mail: millie@gcol.net.

WILEY, SHIRLEY ANN, elementary education educator, musician; b. High Point, N.C.; d. Gus and Nannie L. W. BS, Winston-Salem State Coll., 1960; MS, N.C. Central U., 1966; postgrad. Harvard U., summer 1967, U. Bridgeport, 1975-86. Tchr. elem. sch. High Point City Schs., N.C., 1960-70, Bridgeport City Schs., Conn., 1970—, tchr. fgn. students, Bridgeport Bd. Edn., summer 1982, City of Bridgeport, summer 1983; music specialist Action for Bridgeport Community Devel., Bridgeport, summer 1974-78, asst. camp dir. Hall Neighborhood House, summer 1978-79, Title XX program Sacred Heart Univ., Bridgeport, summer 1979-80; dir. youth choir Stratford Baptist Ch., 1974-79. Pres. YWCA (bus. and profl. club), High Point, 1967-68. Mem. NEA, Conn. Edn. Assn., Bridgeport Edn. Assn., N.C. Tchrs. Assn. (v.p. 1964-65), Alpha Kappa Alpha. Democrat. Baptist. Avocations: piano, organ. Home: 830 Wood Ave Bridgeport CT 06604-2136 also: Darmouth Ave High Point NC 27260

WILHELM, GRETCHEN, retired secondary school educator, volunteer; b. Ames, Iowa, Sept. 30, 1938; d. Harley Almey Wilhelm and Orpha Elizabeth Lutton. BS in Math., Iowa State U., 1960; MS in Math., Oreg. State U., 1969. Permanent profl. endorsement for math. grades 7-12 and gen. sci. Iowa, life endorsement math. grades 7-12 and all scis. grades 7-12 Minn. Math. tchr. Shenandoah (Iowa) H.S., 1960—63, Robbinsdale (Minn.) Sr. H.S., 1963—68; jr. mathematician on faculty Inst. Atomic Rsch. Iowa State U., Ames (Iowa) Lab. U.S. Atomic Energy Commn., 1969; math. tchr. Robbinsdale Cooper Sr. High, New Hope, Minn., 1969—94, math. dept. chmn., 1974—76; ret., 1994. Dist. math. curriculum devel. com. Robbinsdale Sch. Dist., New Hope, 1984—89. Election judge, New Hope, 1994, 1996, 1998, 2000; charter mem. Plymouth (Minn.) Creek Christian Ch., 1978, bd. mem., 1978—79, 1982—84, 1989—91, 1997—2001. Recipient NSF Math. Inst. stipend, Oreg. State U., Corvallis, 1962, 1963, 1964, 1965. Mem.: AAUW (life; Mpls. br. bd. dirs., edn. rep. 1997—98), NEA (life), Minn. Geneal. Soc., Iowa Geneal. Soc., Women Descs. Ancient and Hon. Arty. Co., US Daus. War of 1812, Thomas Stanton Soc., Thomas Minor Soc., New Eng. Women Descs., Dau. Am. Colonists, Colonial Dames the XVII Century, Colonial Dames Am., Nat. Soc. DAR (life; chpt. 2nd vice regent 1987—88, chpt. registrar 1988—94, State constn. week chmn. 1991—95, chpt. 1st vice regent 1994—96, state registrar 1995—97, state officers club v.p., chaplain 1995—97, chpt. chaplain 1996—98, state DAR good citizen chmn. 1997—99, chpt. regent 1998—2000, state regent 2001—03, charter mem. State Regents Club 2001—, Nat. Officers Club 2001—, nat. bd. mgmt. 2001—03, hon. state regent 2003—). Republican. Mem. Christian Ch. (Disciples Of Christ). Avocation: geneaology. Home: 3925 Winnetka Ave N Minneapolis MN 55427

WILHELM, SISTER PHYLLIS, religious studies educator, director; b. Toledo, Aug. 3, 1941; d. Edward John and Ellen Catherine (Sorg) Wilhelm. BA, St. Francis Coll., 1964; MEd in Instrn., U. Wis., Superior, 1994. Joined Sisters St. Francis of Mary Immaculate, 1959; cert. tchr. Wis., elem. tchr. spl. edn. Ill. Tchr. primary St. Rita of Casica Sch., Aurora, Ill., 1963-65, St. Joseph Sch., Manhattan, Ill., 1965-74, Holy Family-St. Francis Sch., Bayfield, Wis., 1974-77, tchr., 1979-99, prin., 1979-99, peace edn. instr. K-6, 1989-99, pastoral assoc., 1999—, dir. religious edn., 2000—. Tchr. spl. edn. Guardian Angel Sch., Joliet, 1977—79. Recipient Outstanding Prin. award, Wis. Assn. Non-Pub. Schs., 1999, Sister Catherine McNamee award for leadership in promoting cultural and econ. diversity, 1999. Mem.: Superior Diocesan Prin. Assn. (treas. 1981—83, 1996—99, Educator of the Yr. award 1991), Phi Delta Kappa. Avocations: crafts, gardening, cooking. Home: PO Box 1290 232 N 1st St Bayfield WI 54814-9724 E-mail: spw803@ncis.net.

WILHELMI, MARY CHARLOTTE, education educator, college official; b. Williamsburg, Iowa, Oct. 2, 1928; d. Charles E. and Loretto (Judge) Harris; m. Sylvester Lee Wilhelmi, May 26, 1951; children: Theresa Ann, Sylvia Marie, Thomas Lee, Kathryn Lyn, Nancy Louise. BS, Iowa State U., 1950; MA in Edn., Va. Poly. Inst. and State U., 1973, cert. advanced grad. studies, 1978. Edn. coord. Nova Ctr. U. Va., Falls Church, 1969-73; asst. adminstr. Consortium for Continuing Higher Edn. George Mason U., Fairfax, Va., 1973-78, adminstr., asst. prof., 1978-83; dir. coll. mktg., pub. affairs, assoc. prof. No. Va. C.C., Annandale, 1983—. Bd. dirs. No. Va. C.C. Ednl. Found., Inc., No. Va. C.C. Real Estate Found.; v.p. audience devel. Fairfax (Va.) Symphony, 1995—; chmn. Health Systems Agy. No. Va., Fairfax; mem. George Mason U. Inst. for Ednl. Transformation. Mem. Editl. bd. Va. Forum, 1990-93; contbr. articles to profl. jours. Bd. dirs. Fairfax County chpt. ARC, 1981-86, Va. Inst. Polit. Leadership, 1995—, Fairfax Com. of 100, 1986-88, 90—, Arts Coun. Fairfax County, 1989—, Fairfax Spotlight on the Arts, Inc., 2002—; bd. dirs. Hospice No. Va., 1983-88, devel. bd., 1997-2000; steering com. Hurrah for Hospice Gala, 1999, Nat. Capital Region Hospices Gala, 2002, 2003, No. Va. Mental Health Inst., Fairfax County, 1978-81, Fairfax Profl. Women's Network, 1981; vice chair Va. Commonwealth U. Ctr. on Aging, Richmond, 1978—; supt.'s adv. coun. Fairfax County Pub. Schs., 1974-86, No. Va. Press Club, 1978—; mktg. chair, exec. com. Internat. Childrens Festival, 1997—; pres. Fairfax Ext. Leadership Coun., 1995; mem. Leadership Fairfax Class of 1992, Commonwealth Va. Combined campaign, State Adv. Coun., 1999-2003. Named Woman of Distinction, Soroptomists, Fairfax, 1988, Bus. Woman of Yr., Falls Church Bus. and Profl. Women's Group, 1993; fellow Va. Inst. Polit. Leadership, 1995. Mem. State Coun. Higher Edn. Va. (pub. affairs adv. com. 1985—), Greater Washington Bd. Trade, Fairfax County C. of C. (legis. affairs com. 1984—, millenium steering com. 1999) Va. Women Lobbyists, 1991—, No. Va. Bus. Roundtable, Internat. Platform Assn., Phi Delta Kappa (20-Yr. Continuous Svc. award 2001), Kappa Delta Alumni No. Va., Psi Chi, Phi Kappa Phi. Roman Catholic. Avocations: piano, organ, reading, hiking. Home: 4902 Ravensworth Rd Annandale VA 22003-5552 Office: NVCC 4001 Wakefield Chapel Rd Annandale VA 22003-3796 E-mail: mcwilhelmi@nvcc.edu.

WILHOIT, CAROL DIANE, retired special education educator; b. Rockford, Ill., June 2, 1950; d. Iris May (Zeigler) Cleeton; m. Jerry Dean Wilhoit, Aug. 15, 1971; children: David, Heather, Hilary, Erin. BSE, N.E. Mo. State U., 1972; MS in Edn., 1991. Cert. spl. edn. tchr., Mo. Tchr. emotionally handicapped Clarence Cannon Elem., Elsberry, Mo., 1972-73; EMH tchr. Bowling Green (Mo.) Elem., 1973-77, Clopton High Sch., Clarksville, Mo., 1979-82; tchr. learning disabilities Eugene Field Elem., Hannibal, Mo., 1982—2002; ret., 2002. Active Accelerated Sch., chair curriculum cadre, intervention cadre, steering com., 1992-93, mem. parent involvement com., 1994; del. Northeast Dist. Tchrs. Assn. Assembly, 1994. Mem. state due process subcom., 1994; PL-94-142 adv. com., 1992—. Mem. Coun. Exceptional Children (pres. 1986-88, bd. dirs. Mo. chpt. 1986, 1988-91, organizer local chpt. 1988, awards chmn., chair profl. devel. subcom., chair registration com. 1991-92, chair membership com. Mark Twain chpt. 1991—, spring conf. session leader, del. to internat. coun. assembly 1992-93, spring conf. chair 1994, del. to internat. conf. 1995), Mo. State Tchrs. Assn. (del. to state assembly 1989-90, superintendent's com. 1989-91, dist. prof. devel. com. 1990—, mentor tchr. 1990-92, state spl. edn. monitoring com. 1991-92), Hannibal Cmty. Tchrs. Assn. (bldg. rep. exec. com. 1987—, v.p. 1988, pres. 1989), Learning Disabilities Assn. Avocations: reading, crafts, sewing.

WILHOIT, GENE, school system administrator; m. Rebecca Campbell Wilhoit; children: Christopher, Kara, Jason. Bachelor's in History and Econ., Georgetown Coll.; Master's in Tchg., Polit. Sci., and Econ., Ind. U.; postgrad., W.Va. Coll. Grad. Studies. Program dir. Ind. Dept. Pub. Instrn.; exec. dir. Nat. Assn. State Bds. Edn.; chair edn. commn. State Adv. Commn., 1989—91; spl. asst. U.S. Dept. Edn.; chief state sch. officer Ark. Dept. Edn.; dep. commr. bur. learning support svcs. Ky. Dept. Edn., commr. edn., 2000—. Office: Ark Dept Edn Capitol Mall Bldg 4 Little Rock AR 72201-1049*

WILK, BARBARA, artist, educator; b. N.Y.C., Mar. 27, 1923; d. Irvin and Edith (Mittelman) Balensweig; m. Max Zalk Wilk, Oct. 28, 1949; children: David, Richard, Frances. BA, Smith Coll., Northampton, Mass., 1944; MS, U. Bridgeport, Conn., 19758. Women's editor UP Radio, N.Y.C., 1944-48; instr. Housatonic C.C., Bridgeport, 1975-78, Norwalk (Conn.) C.C., 1978-81, Fairfield (Conn.) U., 1980; art cons. Tchrs. Ctr., Fairfield, 1980-83; master tchg. artist Conn. Commn. on Arts, Hartford, 1995—. Adminstr. CETA Arts Program, Westport, 1979-81; pres. Westport-Weston Arts Coun., 1977-80. Filmmaker 5 animated films shown on pub. TV (Cine Gold Eagle award, 1st prize Filmex); exhbns. in groups shows include Crafts of the Ams., Washington, 1975, Conn. Women Artists, New Haven, 1975-78, Elements Gallery, Greenwich, N.Y.C., 1979-80, Smithsonian Traveling Crafts Show, 1975-77, U. Rochester, N.Y., 1981, Art of the N.E., Silvermine, Conn., 1989-95, Stamford (Conn.) Mus., 1988-92, Conn. allery, 1989-90, Women in the Visual Arts, New Haven, Conn., 1990-95, Ariel Gallery, N.Y.C., 1990, Discovery Mus., Bridgeport, Conn., 1991, Rachel Adler Gallery, N.Y.C., 1996-97, Seven Arts Festival, Pitts., 1999, Greer Gallery, Northport, N.Y., 1999—, Phoenix Gallery, N.Y., 1999, Paintings Direct.com, 1999—; one-woman shows include U. Conn., Storrs, 1988, Conn. Commn. on the Arts, Hartford, 1987, Silo Gallery, Milford, Conn., 1987, Satmford Mus., 1995, Discovery Mus., Bridgeport, Conn., 1995, Silvermine Guild of Artists, 1978, 87, 91, 94, 97, City Spirit Artists, New Haven, Conn., 1997, Westport (Conn.) Art Ctr., 1996, 99, Jean Cocteau Gallery, Santa Fe, 2000. Bd. mem. Westport-Weston Arts Ctr., 1984-87, Silvermine Guild Arts Ctr., 1979-82, Cultural Survival, Cambridge, 1998—; observer UN, N.Y.C., 1998—; mem. adv. bd. Helen Keller, N.Y.C., 1999—; dir. Eyes on the Future, 1996; organizer 1st Grandmother's Circle Gathering, Westport, Conn., 2002. Recipient Guggenheim Found. fellowship, N.Y.C., 1995, Presdl. Vol. Action award U.S. Pres., 1993; named one of Outstanding Women in Ct., 2003. Mem. Soc. Am. Graphic Artists (award 1999), Silvermine Guild Arts Ctr., Soc. Layerists, Artists Equity, Women's Caucus for Arts. Democrat. Avocations: tennis, aerobics. Home: 29 Surf Rd Westport CT 06880-6734 E-mail: bwilk@attglobal.net.

WILKE, CONSTANCE REGINA, elementary education educator; b. Camden, N.J., Mar. 20, 1944; d. Matthew Stanley Sr. and Regina Rita (Przeradzki) Wojtkowiak; m. Alvin Frank Wilke Jr., Apr. 20, 1968; children: Joseph Alvin, Suzanne Renee. BA in Elem. Edn., Glassboro State U., 1967, MA in Reading and Supervision, 1979. Cert. tchr. and reading speicalist, N.J. Tchr. 5th grade Bellmawr (N.J.) Bd. Edn., 1967-70; tchr. 2d grade Ethel M. Burke Sch., Bellmawr, N.J., 1970-97; tchr. 5th grade Bell Oaks Sch., Bellmawr, 1997—. Author: Wojtkowiak Family History, 1992. Vol. Gloucester (N.J.) City Libr., 1972-75, Vet.'s Standdown, Meals on Wheels, Cathedral Soup Kitchen; contact reassurance vol. Am. Heart Assn. Walk; sec. E.M. Burke Sch. PTA, Bellmawr, 1973-78, publicity person, 1980-85, pres., 1982-85, author and editor publicity book, 1980-83, rec. sec., 1995-97; advisor Cmty. Edn. Bd., Gloucester City, 1973-74; eucharistic minster St. Mary's Ch., Gloucester City, 1990—, 150 yr. Jubilee com., renew com., lector, parish coun.; dir., founder of Internat. Day at E.M. Burke Sch., dir. and founder Vet.'s Day Program, MS Read-a-thon, Jump Rope for Heart, Book It programs, Reading is the Ticket program. Named Citizen of Yr., Polish-Am. Congress, 1983, N.J. VFW Citizenship Tchr. of Yr., 2002. Mem. NEA, N.J. Epilepsy Found., N.J. Edn. Assn., West Jersey Reading Assn., Bellmawr Edn. Assn. (faculty rep.), Asthma Assn. Roman Catholic. Achievements include being instrumental in having Veteran Memorial built honoring Bellmawr veterans. Office: Bell Oaks Sch 256 Anderson Ave Bellmawr NJ 08031-1199

WILKE, DUANE ANDREW, special education educator; b. Chgo., July 2, 1948; s. Joseph V. and Helena (Komulainen) W.; m. Sue Rowley, Oct. 9, 1970; children: Mya, Kira, Noah. BS, Ill. State U., Normal, 1970; MS in Edn., No. Ill. U., 1978. Cert. tchr., Ill. Tchr. Glencoe (Ill.) Pub. Schs., 1970-71; English tchr. middle sch. U.S. Peace Corps, Daegu, S. Korea, 1971-73, tchr. tng. coord, 1973-74; diagnostician, tchr. Singer Mental Health Ctr., Rockford, Ill., 1974-78; spl. edn. cons., diagnostician Rockford Pub. Schs., 1978-90; edn. instrn. specialist EduQuest/IBM, Rockford, 1992-93; Title 1 coord. Rockford Pub. Schs., 1993—. Adj. instr. No. Ill. U., De Kalb, 1980-90; evaluator North Cen. Evaluation Team, Ottawa, Ill., 1989; instr. coord. St. Xavier U., Internat. Renewal Inst., Chgo., Rockford, 1990-94; featured spkr. 1991 conv. Coun. for Exceptional Children. Co-author: (asessment instrument) Task Asessment for Prescriptive Teaching, 1979. V.p. bd. Kantorei Boys Choir, 1996-97, pres. bd., 1998-2000; pres. bd. trustees Unitarian Ch., Rockford, 1991-93. Recipient ASCD Ill. Profl. Devel. award 1996; named Svc. Personnel of Yr., Those Who Excel, Rockford, Ill., 1987. Avocation: singing. Home: 1419 Post Ave Rockford IL 61103-6222 E-mail: wilked@rps205.com.

WILKENING, LAUREL LYNN, academic administrator, planetary scientist; b. Richland, Wash., Nov. 23, 1944; d. Marvin Hubert and Ruby Alma Wilkening; m. Godfrey Theodore Sill, May 18, 1974 BA, Reed Coll., Portland, Oreg., 1966; PhD, U. Calif., San Diego, 1970; DSc (hon.), U. Ariz., 1996. From asst. prof. to assoc. prof. U. Ariz., Tucson, 1973—80, dir. Lunar and Planetary Lab., head planetary scis., 1981—83, vice provost, prof. planetary scis., 1983—85, v.p. rsch., dean Grad. Coll., 1985—88; divsn. scientist NASA Hdqrs., Washington, 1980; prof. geol scis., adj. prof. astronomy, provost U. Washington, Seattle, 1988—93; prof. earth system sci., chancellor U. Calif., Irvine, 1993—98. Dir. Rsch. Corp., 1991-2003, Seagate Tech., Inc., 1993-2000, Empire Ranch Found., 1998-2003; vice chmn. Nat. Commn. on Space, Washington, 1984-86, Adv. Com. on the Future of U.S. Space Program, 1990-91; chair Space Policy Adv. Bd., Nat. Space Coun., 1991-92; co-chmn. primitive bodies mission study team NASA/European Space Agy., 1984-85; chmn. com. rendezvous sci. working group NASA, 1983-85; mem. panel on internat. cooperation and competition in space Congl. Office Tech. Assessment, 1982-83; trustee NASULGC, 1994-97, UCAR, 1988-89, 97-98, Reed Coll., 1992-2002. Editor: Comets, 1982. U. Calif. Regents fellow, 1966-67; NASA trainee, 1967-70. Fellow Meteoritical Soc. (councilor 1976-80), Am. Assn. Advanced Sci.; mem. Am. Astron. Soc. (chmn. div. planetary scis. 1984-85), Am. Geophys. Union, AAAS, Planetary Soc. (dir. 1994-2000, v.p. 1997-2000), Phi Beta Kappa. Democrat. Avocations: gardening, camping, swimming.

WILKERSON, PATRICIA HELEN, director child development center; b. Victoria, Tex., Aug. 2, 1936; d. Milo Andrew and Gertrude H. (Nichols) Beeman; children: Cheryl Lynn, Susan Leigh, Debra Ann, Jon Craig. Student, U. Corpus Christi, 1954-56, Del Mar Coll., 1970-71-86-88. Tax clk. Nueces County Tax Assessor, Corpus Christi, Tex., 1956—57; corr. sec. Boy Scouts of Am. Gulf Coast Coun., Corpus Christi, 1957—58; elem. dir, nursery sch. coord. First Bapt. Ch., Corpus Christi, 1972—73, pre-K tchr., sec., 1975—85; dir. child devel. ctr. 2d Bapt. Ch., Corpus Christi, 1985—99, Northway Bapt. Ch., Dallas, 1999—. ASSIST pre-sch. leader Corpus Christi Bapt. Assn., 1967-99; conf. leader, cons. Bapt. Gen. Conv., Dallas, 1967—; mem. early childhood adv. bd., Del Mar Coll., Corpus Christi, 1981-86; mem. adv. com. Tex. Bapt. Weekday Assn., Dallas, 1995-98, Gulf Coast Tng. coalition. Writer Presch. Sunday Sch. Curriculum, 1992-99, Southern Bapt. Conv. Sunday sch. tchr., various Tex. Bapt. Chs., 1959—; presch. divsn. dir. Second Bapt. Ch., Corpus Christi, 1986-98, dir. child devel. ctr., 1985-99; dir. Child Devel. Ctr., Northway Bapt. Ch., Dallas, 1999-2003; conf. leader Dallas Bapt. Assn., 2000-02, Northway (Tex.) child devel. ctr., 1999-2003. Mem. Bay Area Assn. Edn. Young Children (sec. 1981-82, co-chair conf. 1991, Week of the Young Child chair 1995-96). Avocations: reading, sewing, cats, nature study. Home: 3841 N Belt Line Rd Apt 1305 Irving TX 75038-5774 Office: Northway Bapt ChCtr 3877 Walnut Hill Ln Dallas TX 75229

WILKERSON, RITA LYNN, special education educator, consultant; b. Crescent, Okla., Apr. 22; BA, Cen. State U., Edmond, Okla., 1963; MEd, Cen. State U., 1969; postgrad., U. Okla., 1975, Kans. State U. Elem. tchr. music Hillsdale (Okla.) Pub. Sch., 1963-64; jr. high sch. music and spl. edn. Okarche (Okla.) Pub. Sch., 1965-71; cons. Title III Project, Woodward, Okla., 1971-72; dir. Regional Edn. Svc. Ctr., Guymon, Okla., 1972-81; dir., psychologist Project W.O.R.K., Guymon, 1981-90; tchr. behavioral disorders Unified Sch. Dist. 480, Liberal, Kans., 1990—; sch. psychologist Hardesty (Okla.) Schs., 1994. Cons. Optima (Okla.) Pub. Schs., 1990, Felt (Okla.) Pub. Schs., 1990, Texhoma (Okla.) Schs., 1994, Balko (Okla.) Pub. Schs., 1996; spl. edn. cons. Optima Pub. Schs., 1992—, Goodwell (Okla.) Pub. Schs., 1992—; diagnostician Tyrone, Okla. Pub. Schs., 1992-95; home svcs. provider Dept. Human Svcs., Guymon, 1990; active Kans. Dept. Social and Rehab. Svcs., 1993—; adj. tchr. Seward County C.C., 1994—. Grantee Cen. State U., 1968-69, Oklahoma City Dept. Edn., 1988-89. Mem. ASCD, NAFE, NEA (liberal Kans. chpt.), AAUW, Coun. Exceptional Children, Okla. Assn. Retarded Citizens, Okla. Assn. for Children with Learning Disabilities, Phi Delta Kappa. Republican. Avocation: crafts. Home: 616 N Crumley St Guymon OK 73942-4341 Office: Unified Sch Dist 480 7th And Western Liberal KS 67901

WILKES, SHAR (JOAN CHARLENE WILKES), elementary education educator; d. Marcus and Hattie (Ehrich) Wexman; 1 child, McKinnon. Student, U. Okla., 1973, U. Wyo., 1975—. Rsch. dirs., exhibit designer Nicolaysen Art Mus.-Children's Ctr., Casper, Wyo., 1984-85; tchr. Natrona County Sch. Dist. 1, Casper, Wyo., 1974—2002, spelling bee coord.; reading specialist Southridge Elem. Sch., 1995—2002; coord. Natrona Co. Prevention Coalition, 2002—. Enrichment coord. Paradise Valley Elem. Sch., 1993-94; co-coord. Children's Health Fair/Body Works Healthfair, Ptnrs. in Edn., Paradise Valley Elem. Sch./Wyo. Med. Ctr. and Blue Envelope, 1994; developer Fossil Trunk, Tate Museum Ednl. Program, 1999—; co-founder, dir. Ink Link, Sunday page Casper Star Tribune; spkr. Schs. to Careers Confs., S.D., Wyo. Author: Fantastic Phonics Food Factory, children's edit., 2000, parent/teacher edit., 2000. Dem. candidate Wyo. State Legis., 1986, 88; edn. chair United Way, Casper, 1988; chairperson Very Spl. Arts Festival, 1988, March of Dimes, 1989; grants person Casper Symphony, 1990; NCSD coord. Bear Trap Meadow Blue Grass Festival, 1995—; mem. Wyoming Alliance for The Arts. Recipient 3d Pl. Newspaper Across Am., 2000. Mem. NEA, Nat. Coun. Edn. Assn., Internat. Reading Assn. (lectr. Colo. coun. 2000—), Wyo. Edn. Assn., Soroptimist (charter), Phi Delta Kappa (exec. bd. 1988-98), Delta Kappa Gamma. Home: 4353 Coffman Ct Casper WY 82604-5145 Office: Mercer House 425 Cy Ave Casper WY 82601

WILKIE, DONALD WALTER, biologist, aquarium museum director; b. Vancouver, B.C., Can., June 20, 1931; s. Otway James Henry and Jessie Margaret (McLeod) W.; m. Patricia Ann Archer, May 18, 1980; children: Linda, Douglas, Susanne. BA, U. B.C., 1960, M.Sc., 1966. Curator Vancouver Pub. Aquarium, 1961-63, Phila. Aquarama, 1963-65; exec. dir. aquarium-mus. Scripps Instn. Oceanography, La Jolla, Calif., 1965-93, exec. dir. emeritus, 1993—. Cons. aquarium design, rschg. exhibit content; sci. writer and editor naturalist-marine edn. programs. coach, Scholastic Clay Targets Prog. Author books on aquaria and marine ednl. materials; contbr. numerous articles to profl. jours. Bd. mem. San Diego Shotgun Sports Assn.; pres. UCSD Retirement Assn. 1999-02. Mem. Am. Soc. Ichthyologists and Herpetologists, San Diego Zoöl. Soc., Home: 4548 Cather Ave San Diego CA 92122-2632 Office: U Calif San Diego Scripps Instn Oceanography Libr 9500 Gilman Dr La Jolla CA 92093-0219 E-mail: dwilkie@ucsd.edu., donaqua27@aol.com.

WILKIE, JACQUELINE SARAH, history educator; b. Albany, N.Y., Nov. 28, 1956; d. Lyle Howard Sr. and Patricia Maria (McDermott) W. 1 child, Miles Patrick. BA cum laude, Coll. St. Rose, Albany, N.Y., 1978; MA in Am. History, Northeastern U., Boston, 1979; DA, Carnegie-Mellon U., 1982. Teaching and rsch. asst. dept. history Northeastern U., Boston, 1978-79; curriculum designer project on social history Carnegie-Mellon U., Pitts., 1979-81, exec. asst., 1981-82, instr. dept. history, 1981, adj. asst. prof., 1982-83; asst. prof. history Ctrl. Mich. U., 1983-87, Luther Coll., Decorah, Iowa, 1987-92, assoc. prof. history, women's studies coord., 1993-97, Joyce Found. scholar-in-residence, 1991. Asst. dir. Pitts. Area Nat. History Day Contest, Carnegie-Mellon U., 1982-83; vis. scholar Inter-Univ. Consortium for Polit. and Social Rsch. summer program in quantitative methods of social rsch. U. Mich., summer 1985; coord. Mayo Found. Oral History Nursing Project, 1991-95. Author: The History of Health and Medicine, 1982; co-author: (with Peter N. Stearns) Work and Leisure in History, 1982; contbr. articles to profl. jours. Vol. Decorah Svcs. for Abused Women, 1987-98. History fellow Northeastern U., 1979. Mem. AAUP (state exec. bd. 1992-97, 2003—, sec. Iowa conf. 1995-98), AAUW, Orgn. Am. Historians, Iowa Hist. Soc., Nat. Women's Studies Assn., Am. Assn. History of Medicine. Democrat. Roman Catholic. Achievements include research on women and health, history of U.S. medicine, women in medicine and nursing history. Home: 308 Day St Decorah IA 52101-2217 Office: Luther Coll History Dept Decorah IA 52101-1045

WILKINS, CAROLYN NOREEN, early childhood educator; b. Fall River, Mass., Apr. 29, 1967; d. Thomas K. Porter Jr. and Barbara A. Wood; m. James A. Wilkins III, Feb. 22, 1992; 1 child, Zachary. BS in Edn., Lesley U., 1989. Cert. in elem. edn., Fla.; nat. bd. cert. tchr. 4-6th grade tchr. Paul

Coffee Sch., Westport, Mass., 1989-90; prekindergarten tchr. Tender Loving Child Care Ctr., New Bedford, Mass., 1990-92, My Sch. Learning Ctr., Stuart, Fla., 1992-94, St. Michael's Ind. Sch., Stuart, 1994-95; tchr. White City Elem. Sch., Ft. Pierce, Fla., 1995—. Pvt. tutor, Westport, Stuart, 1989-95. Grantee Fla. Coun. Ind. Schs., 1995-96, Fla. Power & Light Co., St. Lucie Edn. Found., 2000. Democrat. Roman Catholic. Avocation: reading. Office: 905 W 2nd St Fort Pierce FL 34982-7237

WILKINSON, ANNE WELCH, special education educator; b. Proctor, Vt., May 4, 1951; d. Richard Thomas and Margaret Mary (Rice) Welch; m. Ablert Grabowski, Aug. 11, 1973 (div. may 1986); 1 child, Jill Anne; m. Kirk Wilkinson, Aug. 24, 1991. BS, Coll. of St. Joseph, Rutland, Vt., 1973; MEd, Notre Dame Coll., Manchester, N.H., 1992. Learning disabilities specialist Nottingham (N.H.) Elem. Sch., 1973-79, Northwood (N.H.) Elem. Sch., 1973-85, Conant Elem. Sch., Concord, N.H., 1985—, Boston U. Ctr. for Assessment and of Learning, 1992-93. Exec. bd. dirs. Conant Sch. PTO, 1990-92. Mem. ASCD, Internat. Reading Assn., N.H. Soc. for Tech. in Edn., Assn. Learning Disabilities. Avocations: gardening, winter sports, reading. Home: 32 Lake St Concord NH 03301-3214 Office: Conant Elem Sch South St Concord NH 03301

WILKINSON, BEN, chancellor, evangelist, ministry organizer, writer; b. Gloster, Miss., July 6, 1932; s. Thomas Lamar and Evie (Quackenbush) W.; m. Mary Pittman; children: Evangeline Patricia Wilkinson Light, William Dwight, Manford Leighton, Glen Calvin. BA in Pub. Speaking, U. So. Miss., 1954; MDiv, Columbia Theol. Sem., Decatur, Ga., 1957, postgrad., 1964-65; DD, Whitefield Theol. Sem., 1992. Pastor Trinity Presbyn. Ch., Huntsville, Ala., 1955-62, Ga. Ave Presbyn. Ch., Atlanta, 1962-66, evangelist, 1966—, exec. dir., 1973-95. Founder, dir. Synod of the City-PEF Planting Bibl. Chs. in the Inner City, 1993—; with Presbyn. Evangelistic fellowship, Decatur, Ga.; bd. dirs. Atlanta Sch. Bibl. Studies, Westminster Bibl. Missions, World Harvest Missions, Lords Day Alliance; founder, dean, pres. Atlanta Sch. Bibl. Studies, 1971-85, chancelor, prof., 1986—. Editor: Come...Follow, 1973-95. Recipient John Calvin Internat. award The Christian Observer, 1995; Ben Wilkinson Sch. of Missions at Atlanta Sch. Bibl. Studies named in his honor, 1997. Avocations: sports, writing, reading, family life. Home: 214 Inman Dr Decatur GA 30030-3833 Office: Presbyn Evangelistic Fellowship Synod of the City 214 Inman Dr Decatur GA 30030-3833

WILKINSON, FRANCES CATHERINE, librarian, educator; b. Lake Charles, La., July 20, 1955; d. Derrell Fred and Catherine Frances (O'Toole) W.; div.; 1 child, Katrina Frances. BA in Communication with distinction, U. N.Mex., 1982, MPA, 1987; MLS, U. Ariz., 1990. Mktg. rsch. auditor Mktg. Rsch. N.Mex., Albuquerque, 1973-78; freelance photographer, 1974-75; from libr. supr. gen. libr. to assoc. dean libr. svcs. U. N.Mex., Albuquerque, 1978—2001, interim dean libr. svcs., 2001—02, assoc. dean, 2002—. Cons., trainer ergonomics univs. and govt. agys. across U.S., 1986—; bd. dirs. Friends of U. N.Mex. Librs., Aubuquerque, 1991-94; mediator Mediation Alliance, 1991-94, U. N.Mex. Faculty Dispute Resolution, 1999—; mediation coach U. N.Mex., 1999-2000. Author, editor books; editor jour. columns; contbr. articles to profl. jours. Counselor, advocate Albuquerque Rape Crisis Ctr., 1981-84. Mem.: ALA, N.Mex. Assn. Rsch. Librs., N.Mex. Preservation Alliance (vice chair 1995—96), N.Mex. Libr. Assn., N.Am. Serials Interest Group (mem. exec. bd. 1997—2001), Pi Alpha Alpha, Phi Kappa Phi (chpt. treas. 1991—92, chpt. pres. 1992—94). Home: PO Box 8102 Albuquerque NM 87198-8102 Office: U N Mex Gen Libr MSC 05 3020 1 University of New Mex Albuquerque NM 87131-0001 E-mail: fwilkins@unm.edu.

WILKINSON, JANET WORMAN, advertising and marketing consultant, reading tutor and specialist; b. Mpls., July 18, 1944; d. James Russell and Virginia Hale (Murty) Worman; m. Benjamin Delos Wilkinson, Jan. 7, 1967; children: David Delos, Steven Edward, John Douglas. BA, Wells Coll., 1966. With Met. Life Ins. Co., N.Y.C., 1966-67; elem. tchr. pub. schs. Parkersburg, W.Va. and Orange, Tex., 1968-69; on-air prin. WTAV-TV, Parkersburg, 1969-70; corp. communications educator Delmarva Power Co., Wilmington, Del., 1979-83; market mgr. W.L. Gore & Assocs., Inc., Elkton, Md., 1983-85; acvt. coord., promotion mgr. Views Mag., Chadds Ford, Pa., 1985-86; cons. mktg. communications, 1986—. Reading instr. Project ASSIST Inst., 1994; mem. Bus.-Industry Ednl. Consortium, Wilmington, 1981—83; chmn. steering com. NE Utilities Educators, 1981—83; tutor Dyslexic Children and Adults; reading specialist instructing tchrs. in alt. methods of tchg. reading, writing and spelling, 1991—; instr. Orton-Gillingham methodologies, 1992—; adj. prof. Del. Tech. and C.C. Contbg. editor Lattice News, 1984-85; editor Retailer newsletter, 1984-85. Chmn. publicity Wilmington Flower Market, 1984-85, Wells Coll. Capital Campaign Fund, Wilmington, 1983-84, Wilmington Christmas Shop, 1973-81; loaned exec. United Way, Wilmington, 1985; bd. dirs. Girls Clubs Del., 1983-84; founder, developer Help Stop the Hurt Child abuse awareness program, 1983; dir. Christian edn. Trinity Ch., Wilmington, 1982-88. Republican. Episcopalian. Avocations: sketching, watercolor, writing. Home and Office: 43 Hill Rd Wilmington DE 19806 E-mail: janplan@delanet.com.

WILKINSON, LOUISE CHERRY, psychology educator, dean; b. Phila., May 15, 1948; BA magna cum laude with honors, Oberlin Coll., 1970; EdM, EdD, Harvard U., 1974. Prof., chmn. dept. ednl. psychology U. Wis., Madison, 1976-85; prof., exec. officer Grad. Sch. Ph.D. Program CUNY, N.Y.C., 1984-86; disting. prof., dean Grad. Sch. Edn. Rutgers U., 1986—2003; dean Syracuse (NY) U., 2003—. Chairperson ednl. strategic planning Rutgers U.; mem. nat. rev. bd. Nat. Inst. Edn., 1977, 85, 87; cons. Nat. Ctr. for Bilingual Rsch., 1982, 84, U.S. Dept. Edn., 1995-96; adv. bd. Nat. Reading Rsch. Ctr., 1992-98. Co-author: Communicating for Learning, 1991; editor: Communicating in Classroom, 1982, Social Context of Instruction, 1984, Gender Influences in the Classroom, 2002; co-editor: Literacy and Language Learning, 2002; mem. editl. bds.: ; contbr. articles to profl. jours. Fellow: APA, Am. Assn. for Applied and Preventive Psychology, Am. Psychol. Soc.; mem.: NJ Coun. Acad. Policy Advisors, Am. Ednl. Rsch. Assn. (v.p. 1990—92, program chair 1997).

WILKISON, DENNIS LYLE, elementary education eductor; b. Kennett, Mo., Nov. 27, 1959; s. Kermit Lyle and Mona Lee (Kilbreth) W. BA in Ch. Ministries, Okla. Bapt. U., Shawnee, 1983, BSE, 1985; MA in Edn., Lindenwood Coll., St. Charles, Mo., 1991. Cert. in elem. edn., middle sch. lang. arts and social studies, reading, Mo. Reading tchr. 5th and 6th grades Ctrl. Elem. Sch., Moore (Okla.) Pub. Schs., 1985-87; tchr. 5th grade Mt. Hope Elem. Sch., Ft. Zumwalt Sch. Dist., O'Fallon, Mo., 1987-92; tchr. 7th grade lang. arts and social studies South Middle Sch. Ft. Zumwalt Sch. Dist., 1992-93, tchr. 6th grade reading South Middle Sch., 1993—. Music dir. Calvary Bapt. Ch., O'Fallon, 1991—. Mem. ASCD, NEA, Internat. Reading Assn., Mo. Edn. Assn., Ft. Zumwalt Edn. Assn. Baptist. Avocations: computers, music, drama, bicycling, racquetball. Home: 1202 Cypress Dr O Fallon MO 63366-1635 Office: South Middle Sch 300 Knaust Rd Saint Peters MO 63376-1716

WILKS, DUFFY JEAN, counselor, educator; b. Spur, Tex., Feb. 15, 1936; d. Rube Lee Jay and Elizabeth Audeen (Simmons) Austin; children: Vicki Ratheal, Juli Ratheal, Randy Ratheal, Rodney Ratheal; m. W.B. Wilks, Oct. 22, 1986. BA in Psychology, Tex. Tech. U., 1981, MEd in Psychology, 1984, EdD in Ednl. Psychology, 1995. Cert. substance abuse counsleor; lic. profl. counselor, Tex.; lic. marriage and family therapist, Tex. Editor writer Floydada (Tex.) newspaper, 1972-80; probation officer Adult/Juvenile Probation, Lubbock, Tex., 1982-86; pvt. practice Horseshoe Bay, Tex., 1986—. Prof. Western Tex. Coll., Snyder. Mem. ACA (mem. editl. bd. ACA Jour. 1998—), Tex. Assn. Counseling and Devel. (editorial bd. jour. 1989-91, author revs., editor Disting. Svc. award 1991), Tex. Counseling Assn. (exec. editor Tex. Counseling Assn. Jour. 1998-2000), Tex. C.C. Tchrs. Assn., Internat. Assn. for Addictions and Offender Counselors. Avocations: playing piano, writing, researching.

WILKS, JACQUELIN HOLSOMBACK, campus ministries director; b. Jan. 18, 1950; d. Jack and Ida Mae (Bass) Holsomback; m. Thomas M. Wilks, Jan. 28, 1972; children: David, Bryan. BS, La. Coll., 1972; MAT., Okla. City U., 1982; postgrad., So. Bapt. Theol. Sem., Louisville, 1974; S.E., Mo. State U., 1977; counseling cert., Cen. State Univ., 1983; PhD, Capella U., 2003. Lic. realtor Mo. Sec. to adminstr. Allen Parish Hosp., Kinder, La., 1968-69; tchr. horseback riding, swimming Triple D Guest Ranche, Warren, Tex., 1969; singer, speaker Found. Singers, 1970-71; tchr. English Pine Bluff (Ark.) H.S., 1972-74; tchr. kindergarten Doyle Elem. Sch., East Prairie (Mo.) R-2, 1974-75; tchr. 1st grade Bertrand (Mo). Elem. Sch., 1975-76; tchr. 6th grade sci. A.D. Simpson Sch., Charleston, Mo., 1976-78; dir. admissions and fin. adminstr. Control Data Inst., Control Data Corp., St. Louis, 1980-81; dir. Bapt. collegiate ministry Okla. Bapt. U., Shawnee, 2002—. Bd. dirs. Computer Commn. Svcs. Inc., 1986—, dir. tutorial svcs., instr. tutorial methods Okla. Bapt. U., 1981-83, instr. horsemanship St. Gregory's Jr. Coll., 1981; counselor Gordon Cooper Area Vocat. Tech. Sch., 1982-83, Shawnee Jr. H.S. Okla.), 1983-85, Grove Sch., Shawnee, 1989—; dir. Resource Ctr., instr. English St. Gregory's Coll., Shawnee, Okla., 1985-89; counselor Spanish tchr. North Rock Creek Sch., Shawnee; translator med. grp. missions Dominican Rep. and Guatemala, 1995, 96, Cosecha 2000, Argentina, 1998, El Salvador, 1998, 99, Ecuador, 2000; bd. dirs. Computer Commn. Svcs. Inc., Tulsa; tutor for children under jurisdiction Juvenile Ct., Jefferson County, Ark., 1972-73; leader group counseling/therapy sessions, 1972; dir. devel. Nat. Insts. Devel. Delays, 2000. Choreographer First Bapt. Ch. Youth Choir, Pine Bluff; v.p. St. Gregory's Coll. Therapeutic Horsemanship Program, 1981-82; Rep. election judge. Recipient Kathryn Carpenter award La. Bapt. Conv., 1971, real Scope award Realty World, St. Louis, 1980, NEH grantee, 1993—. Mem. Univ. Alliance Okla. Bapt. U. Baptist. Home: 18 Woodcrest Shawnee OK 74804-9048 Office: Oklla Bapt U 500 W University Shawnee OK 74804 E-mail: jackie.wilks@okbu.edu.

WILL, ANNE MARILYN, elementary education educator; b. Maryville, Mo., Mar. 9, 1940; d. Paul Gordon and Louise Madeline (Burke) Seymour; (div.); children: Eric Scott, LeAnne Elizabeth. BS in Elem. Edn., N.W. Mo. State U., 1962; Masters in Edn., Mo. U., 1983. Tchr. 5th and 6th grades, Des Moines, 1962-64; tchr. 4th grade Salem (Mo.) R-80, 1964-83, tchr. math. chpt. I, 1983—99; ret., 1999. Methodist. Avocations: reading, family activities. Home: HC 82 Box 98 Salem MO 65560-8608

WILLARD, ANN ELAM, retired special education educator; b. Luling, Tex., Mar. 23, 1932; d. George Henry and Leah (Wright) Elam; widowed; children: Sharon Darlene Denison, Rita Ann Bush, Sindy Rene Burroughs. BS, Sul Ross U., 1952; MS, U. Ala., 1971, EdS, 1975. Tchr., third grade Fort Stockton (Tex.) Pub. Schs., 1953-54; tchr., elem. music San Angelo (Tex.) Pub. Schs., 1954-55; tchr., spl. EMR class Caddo Pub. Schs., Shreveport, La., 1966-67; tchr., fourth grade Albamarl County Schs., Charlottesville, Va., 1967-69; tchr. spl. EMR class Tuscaloosa County Schs., Brookwood, Ala., 1969-70, Cresmont Elem. Sch., Northport, Ala., 1970-82; tchr. TMR/OHI Class Tuscaloosa County Schs., Northport, Ala., 1982-89; tchr. EMR class Matthews Elem. Sch., Northport, Ala., 1989-1996; ret., 1996. Tchr. adult edn. Tuscaloosa County Schs., 1974-80. Active Internat. Parents Without Ptnrs., 1980; tchr. Body Recall, First Bapt. Ch., 2003. Named Elem. Tchr. of Yr., Tuscaloosa County Schs., 1978-79, Single Parent of Yr., Parents Without Ptnrs., Tuscaloosa, 1978. Mem. AAUW (newsletter editor 1978-80), Coun. Exceptional Children (award 1981, sec. 1981, past pres. mentally retarded), Tuscaloosa County Tchrs. Assn., Toastmasters (Toastmaster of Yr. 1986, gov. of dist. #48 1995), Delta Kappa Gamma (sec. 1990-91, pres. 1992-94), Kappa Delta Pi. Baptist. Avocations: travel, reading. Home: 1737 Ridgemont Dr Tuscaloosa AL 35404-4892

WILLARD, RALPH LAWRENCE, surgery educator, physician, former college president; b. Manchester, Iowa, Apr. 6, 1922; s. Hosea B. and Ruth A. (Hazelrigg) W.; m. Norma L. Hattel, Nov. 12, 1943 (div. 1968); children: Laurie, Jane, Ann, H. Thomas; m. Margaret Dyer Dennis, Sept. 26, 1969. Student, Cornell Coll., 1940-42, Coe Coll., 1945; D.O., Kirksville Coll. Osteo. Medicine, 1949; EdD (hon.), U. North Tex., 1985; ScD (hon.), W.Va. Sch. Osteo. Medicine, 1993. Intern Kirksville Osteo. Hosp., 1949-50, resident in surgery, 1954-57; chmn. dept. surgery Davenport Osteo. Hosp., 1957-68; dean, prof. surgery Kirksville Coll. Osteo. Medicine, 1969-73; asso. dean acad. affairs, prof. surgery Mich. State U. Coll. Osteo. Medicine, 1974-75; dean Tex. Coll. Osteopathic Medicine, 1975-76, pres., 1981-85, prof. surgery, 1985-87; v.p. med. affairs North Tex. State U., Denton, 1976-81; assoc. dean W.Va. Sch. Osteo. Medicine, Lewisburg, 1988-91. Mem. Nat. Adv. Council Edn. for Health Professions, 1971-73, Iowa Gov.'s Council Hosps. and Health Related Facilities, 1965-68; chmn. council deans Am. Assn. Colls. Osteo. Medicine, 1970-73, pres., 1979-80 Served with USAAF, 1942-45; Served with USAF, 1952-53; col. USAFR, ret. Decorated D.F.C., Air medal with 4 oak leaf clusters, Meritorious Svc. medal, Legion of Merit; recipient Robert A. Kistner Educator award Am. Assn. Colls. Osteo. Medicine, 1989; named Disting. scholar Acad. Osteo. Medicine Nat. Acads. Practice, 2000. Fellow Am. Coll. Physician Execs., Am. Coll. Osteo. Surgeons; mem. Am. Osteo. Assn. (Disting. Svc. cert. 1992), Tex. Osteo. Assn., W.Va. Soc. Osteo. Medicine, Am. Acad. Osteopathy, Acad. Osteo. Dirs. Med. Edn., Quiet Birdmen, Davis-Monthan Officers Club, Masons, Shriners, Ft. Worth Rotary (Paul Harris fellow), Internat. Comanche Soc., Order of Daedalians. Democrat. Episcopalian. Address: PO Box 79267 Fort Worth TX 76179-0267 E-mail: willardrl@aol.com.

WILLE, ROSANNE LOUISE, higher education administrator; b. Hackensack, N.J., Aug. 4, 1941; d. Albert Wille and Rose Marie (Rock) Eberhardt; m. George B. Jacobs, Mar. 12, 1980; children: Leigh, Steven, Alexander, Jeffrey. M Pub. Adminstrn., Rutgers U., 1986; PhD, N.Y.U., 1980. Dept. chair Rutgers U., Newark, N.J., 1978-84, Lehman Coll., Bronx, NY, 1984-87, dean, 1987-92, provost, sr. v.p., 1992—2002; cons. for higher edn., 2002—. Contbr. articles to profl. jours. Bd. dirs. Family Support Svcs., Bronx, N.Y., 1994—, bd. dirs. South Bronx Overall Economic Devel., Inc., Bronx, 1991—. Recipient Vision award Family Support Svcs., Bronx, 1996, Thousand Points of Light award Pres. George Bush, Washington, 1991. Mem. N.Y. Acad. Scis., N.Y. Acad. Medicine, Am. Assn. Higher Edn. Avocations: aviation, golf. E-mail: rlwille@earthlink.net.

WILLI, STEVEN MATTHEW, physician, educator, researcher; b. Amityville, N.Y., Apr. 3, 1959; s. John Edward and Doris Mae (Smith) Willi; children: Matthew, Thomas; m. Maria Szpiech, July 27, 2002. BA cum laude, Johns Hopkins U., 1981, MD, 1985. Diplomate in pediatrics and pediatric endocrinology Am. Bd. Pediatrics. Resident in pediat. Children's Hosp. of Phila., 1985—88; fellow in pediatric endocrinology Children's Hosp. Phila., 1988—91; instr. pediat. U. Pa., Phila., 1991—92; asst. prof. pediat. Med. U. S.C., Charleston, 1992—98, assoc. prof., 1998—. Contbr. chpts. to books, articles to profl. jours. Med. dir. Camp Adam Fisher for Children with Diabetes, Summerton, S.C., 1995—; bd. dirs. Juvenile Diabetes Found., 1995-99. Recipient Nat. Rsch. Svc. award NIH, 1990, Clin. Assoc. Physician award NIH, 1996; Healfman scholar, 1985. Fellow Am. Acad. Pediatrics; mem. Endocrine Soc., Lawson Wilkins Pediatric Endocrine Soc., Am. Diabetes Assn. (profl. sect., mem. youth svcs. com. 1993—), So. Med. Assn., Charleston County Med. Soc. Avocations: tennis, bicycling, photography, golf. Office: Med U SC Dept Pediatrics 171 Ashley Ave Charleston SC 29425-0001 E-mail: willis@musc.edu.

WILLIAMS, ALFRED BLYTHE, management consultant, educator; b. Oakland City, Ind., Sept. 17, 1940; s. Ross Merl and Jesse Adell (Helsley) W. BS cum laude, Oakland City U., 1963; MS, Ind. U., 1964; PhD, Ga. State U., 1974. Tchr. Arlington H.S., Indpls., 1964-65, Oakland City (Ind.) U., 1965-69; editor Southwestern Pub. Co., Cin., 1969-72, cons., 1981-93; adj. prof. Ga. State U., Atlanta, 1972-74; prof. mgmt. and bus. comm. U. La., Lafayette, 1975—2002, chmn. dept., 1986-96, prof. emeritus, 2002—; ret., 2002. Cons. John Wiley Pub. Co., N.Y., 1988-89, Irwin Pub., 1989. Author study guides; editor Info. Systems Bus. Comm. Jour., 1983, 93. Patron Lafayette Cmty. Concerts, 1984—; contbr. La. and Nat. Rep. parties, Baton Rouge, Washington, 1983—. Mem. AAUP, Assn. Bus. Communicators (bd. dirs. 1986-90, Francis W. Weeks Merit award 1984), La. Assn. Higher Edn., Sierra Club, Kiwanis, Phi Delta Kappa, Phi Kappa Phi, Delta Pi Epsilon, Beta Gamma Sigma. Methodist.

WILLIAMS, ANDREW D. secondary school educator; BS in History, St. John's U., 1960, MS, 1972; EdS, Stetson U., 1984. Cert. tchr. secondary social studies and English, N.Y., N.J.; cert. prin., supr., N.J.; cert. tchr. secondary social studies and English, adminstr., supr., cert. ofcl. observer performance learning measurement system, Fla. Social studies tchr. N.Y.C. Bd. Edn., Bklyn., 1960-64, North Babylon Sr. High Sch., Babylon, N.Y., 1964-66, Glen Cove (N.Y.) High Sch., 1970-71; social studies and English tchr. Island Trees Pub. Schs., Levittown, N.Y., 1971-73; lang. arts and History tchr. Glen Ridge (N.J.) Pub. Schs., 1973-76; humanities and English tchr. Volusia County Pub. Schs., Fla., 1977-80; history and sociology tchr. Berkely Inst., Bklyn., 1980-81; lang. arts and Am. history tchr. Seminole County Pub. Schs., Fla., 1981—, social studies dept. chmn., 1993—. Part-time instr. Daytona Beach (Fla.) C.C., 1978—. Recipient Outstanding Social Studies Tchr. of Yr. award Fla. Coun. Social Studies, 1985, 94, Outstanding Tchr. Am. History 1985, 94, Outstanding H.S. Social Studies Tchr. award, 1994; named Outstanding Am. History Tchr. of Yr., DAR, 1985. Mem. Phi Delta Kappa. Office: Seminole High Sch 2701 Ridgewood Ave Sanford FL 32773-4999 Address: 42 Montauk Blvd # A Oakdale NY 11769-1320

WILLIAMS, ANNEMARIE HAUBER, secondary education educator; b. Schorndorf, Baden Württenburg, Germany, Mar. 6, 1946; came to U.S., 1951; d. William Carl and Hertha (Franze) Hauber; m. William C. Young, Nov. 23, 1972 (div.); 1 child, Niccole Anne Young; m. Evan J. Williams, Aug. 1, 1982. BA, U. S.C., 1968; postgrad., U. London Sch. Econs., 1969; MA, SUNY, New Paltz, 1974. Cert. social studies educator. Tchr. history Monticello (N.Y.) High Sch., 1968-70; tchr. history, coach male varsity and jr. varsity tennis, varsity basketball cheerleaders Yorktown (N.Y.) High Sch., 1970-71; tchr. history Hendrick Hudson High Sch., Montrose, N.Y., 1971—, coach male varsity tennis, 1971-73. Textbook rater in field. Mem. Dems. for Am., U. S.C., 1965-68. Recipient Outstanding Tchr. award U. Chgo., 1988, Inspirational Tchr. award Tufts U., 1996; Study grant U. Hawaii, 1969. Mem. ASCD, N.Y. State Coun. for Social Studies, Nat. Coun. for Social Studies. Republican. Lutheran. Avocations: tennis, gardening, reading, swimming, art collecting. Home: Box 365 336 Rock Hill Dr Rock Hill NY 12775-5019 E-mail: AWilliamsAP@hvc.rr.com.

WILLIAMS, BERTHA ELIZABETH GRIFFIN, elementary education educator; b. Maxton, N.C., Nov. 27, 1942; d. John Wright and Mary Azerlee Williams. BA in Bibl. Lit., Northeastern Bible Coll., Essex Fells, N.J., 1984; postgrad., New Brunswick Theol. Sem., 1985. Cert. elem. tchr., N.J.; ordained elder A.M.E. Ch., 1983. Accounts receivable, collections, billings clk., bookkeeper Newark Beth Israel Med. Ctr., 1964-74; outpatient and impatient billing clk., receptionist Overlook Hosp., Summit, N.J., 1975-86; elem. tchr. Newark Bd. Edn., 1985—. Asst. tchr. Headstart program Broadway Jr. High Sch., Newark, summer 1967-68; staff chaplain Hagedon Ctr. for Geriatrics, Glen Gardner, N.J., 1984—; pastor Mt. Pisgah A.M.E. Ch., Washington, N.J., 1990-93, Mt. Zion A.M.E. Ch., Princeton, N.J., 1993—; former assoc. min. St. James A.M.E., Ch., Newark; dir. Newark Dist. Bd. Christian Edn.; evangelist Newark Dist.; mem. Newark and No. N.J. Com. Churchmen; chmn. edn. com. St. James Credit Union; chmn. local bd. Christian edn. Mem. Newark Dist. Mins. Alliance (sec.), Zeta Phi Beta. Democrat. Office: Mt Zion AME Ch RFD # 4 Old Rd Princeton NJ 08540

WILLIAMS, BEVERLY BEATRICE, retired elementary education educator; b. El Nido, Calif., Mar. 30, 1932; d. James and Beatrice Idaho (Haskins) Buchholz; m. Harvey Donald Williams, Dec. 5, 1953; children: Eileen Celeste, Corinne Beth, Kevin Keoki. BS, U. Calif., 1953. Cert. elem. tchr., Calif., Hawaii. Tchr. TIVY Union Elem. Sch., Sanger, Calif., 1959-61, Armona (Calif.) Union Elem. Sch., 1963-64, Trust Ter. of The Pacific, Tinian and Saipan, 1964-66, Hawaii Dept. of Edn., Wailuku, Paia and Kula, 1966-90; retired, 1990; mem. staff H&R Block, Wailuku, Hawaii, 1988-90, Truckee, Calif., 1991-94. Grade level chmn. Iao Sch., 1970-71, 73-74, 78-79, 85-87, co-chmn. Accreditation Team, 1988; chmn. Lang. Arts dept., 1980-81. Precinct vice chmn. Dem. Party, Kahului, Hawaii, 1986-88; state del. Dem. party conv., Kahului, 1982, 84, 86; mem. PTA, PTSA, Wailuku, 1977-78, 85-90. Mem. HAwaii State Tchrs. Assn. (faculty rep. 1987-88), Nev. Fedn. Bus. and Profl. Women (state pres. HAwaii Fedn. 1985-86, Bus. Woman of Yr. HAwaii Fedn. 1988), Univ. Calif. Berkeley Alumni Assn., Christian Sci. Soc. (bd. dirs. 1990-95). Democrat. Mem. Christian Sci. Ch. Avocations: travel, reading. Home: 12075 Bavarian Way Truckee CA 96161-6120

WILLIAMS, BOBBRETTA M. educational company executive; b. Des Moines, Dec. 11, 1948; d. Robert and Margaret (Preston) Elliston; m. Cecil H. Brewton, Jr.; 1 child, Ayana Michelle. BSE, N.E. Mo. State, 1971; MSE, Drake U., 1975, EdS, 1978, EdD, 1981; BA, Upper Iowa U., 1991. Cert. adminstr., supr., tchr. Tchr. Des Moines (Iowa) Pub. Schs., 1971—90; pres. ABC Diversified, ednl. communications tng. and consultation, Des Moines, 1990—93; coord. Hiatt Jr. High Sch., Des Moines; cons. Voluntary Transfer, Des Moines; elem. prin. Longfellow Sch., Des Moines; dir. Children and Families of Iowa, 1993—2000; cons. Exec. Resources Assistance, 2000—01; dir. The Outreach Project, 2001—.

WILLIAMS, CAROL JORGENSEN, social work educator; b. New Brunswick, NJ, Aug. 12, 1944; d. Einar Arthur and Mildred Estelle (Clayton) Jorgensen; m. Oneal Alexander Williams, July 4, 1980. BA, Douglass Coll., 1966; MS in Computer Sci., Stevens Inst. Tech., 1986; MSW, Rutgers U., 1971, PhD in Social Policy, 1981. Child welfare worker Bur. Children's Svcs., Jersey City, 1966-67, Outagamie County Dept. Social Svcs., Appleton, Wis., 1967-69; supr. WIN N.J. Divsn. Youth and Family Svcs., New Brunswick, 1969-70; coord. Outreach Plainfield (N.J.) Pub. Libr., 1972-76; rsch. project dir. County and Mcpl. Govt. Study Commn., N.J. State Legislature, 1976-79; prof. social work Kean U., Union, 1979—, assessment liaison social work program, 1987-2000, dir. MSW program, 1995-2000. Chmn. faculty senate gen. edn. com. Kean U., N.J., 1990-94, chmn. faculty senate ad hoc com. for 5-yr. review of gen. edn. program, 1991-93, retention and tenure com. Sch. of Liberal Arts, 1988-94, vice chmn., 1992-94; cons. N.J. div. Youth and Family Svcs., 1979-93, Assn. for Children N.J., 1985-88; cons., evaluator Thomas A. Edison Coll., 1977—, N.J. Dept. Human Svcs., 2003; cons. advanced generalist practice La. State U. Grad. Sch. Social Work, 2002. Adv. coun. Outdoor World, 2000-03. Named Grad. Tchr. of Yr., Kean U. social work grad. students, 2001. Mem.: NASW (chpt. com. on nominating and leadership identification 1990—92, co-chmn. 1991—92), NOW, Nat. Network Social Work Mgrs., Kean U. Fedn. Tchrs., Assn. Baccalaureate Program Dirs. (com. on info tech. and distance edn. 1995—, assoc. editor of BPQ Update 2000—, mem. editl. bd. Jour. Baccalaureate Social Work), Coun. on Social Work Edn. (dir. APM Med. Tech. Ctr. 1999—2002, chair subcom. on abstract rev. 2000—02, chair electronic poster session 2002—, bd. dirs. 2003—, commn. on confs. and faculty devel. 2000—02), Outdoor

World (adv. coun. 2000—02), Good Sam Club. Democrat. Home: 32 Halstead Rd New Brunswick NJ 08901-1619 Office: Kean U Social Work Program Morris Ave Union NJ 07083-7117 E-mail: caroljwilliams@worldnet.att.net.

WILLIAMS, CAROL KUNZ, elementary education educator; b. Pitts., Sept. 21, 1954; d. John Frederick and Joan Crawford (Parker) Kunz; m. Terry Allen Williams, Aug. 7, 1982; children: Amy Elizabeth, Katherine Joan. BSEd, Ind. U. Pa., 1976; MA, W.Va. U., 1980. Remedial reading tchr. Roane County Bd. of Edn., Spencer, W.Va., 1976-77, classroom tchr., 1977—. Asst. leader Girl Scouts U.S., Spencer, 1989—; mem. PTA; pres. SPC Faculty Senate, 1993-94; facilitator W.Va. Ctr. for Profl. Devel., 1995-97, 2002-03. Mem. W.Va. Profl. Educators, Delta Kappa Gamma (treas. 1988-94, recording sec. 1994-96, 2d v.p. 1996-98, 1st v.p. 1998-2000, pres. 2000-02). Avocations: crafts, counted cross-stitch, cooking, sewing. Home: 128 Locust Ave Spencer WV 25276-1324 Office: Spencer Elem Sch PO Box 400 Spencer WV 25276-0400

WILLIAMS, CAROL MARIE, secondary school educator; b. Kansas City, Kans., June 10, 1939; d. Leonard Cropley and Minnie Marie (Wass) Nicholson; m. Howard Dean Williams, Dec. 29, 1961; children: Jeffrey Allen, Gregory Scott AA, Kansas City (Mo.) Jr. Coll., 1959; BS in Edn., Ctrl. Mo. State U., 1962. English tchr. Raytown (Mo.) H.S., 1961-62; English tchr., coord. dist. lang. arts Ruskin H.S., Kansas City, Mo., 1964-66; English tchr. Hickman Mills H.S., Kansas City, 1969-70; tchr. English, debate, history, leadership comms., student govt. Andover (Kans.) H.S., 1982-95, dist. lang. arts coord., dept. chair, 1982-95; English tchr. Olathe South (Kans.) H.S., 1996—. Coord., debate and forensics coach Andover Sch. Dist., 1982-85, chair North Ctrl. Accreditation, 1983-84, supt., prin. adv. couns., 1983-95, dist. curriculum coun., 1983-95; coord. AP Lang. Exam. Prep. Workshop; new thcr. mentor. Publicity editor The Lamp mag., 1969 (Nat. Recognition award 1969); contbg. editor Topeka mag., 1977-79; co-editor Andover Rsch. jour., 1993. Recipient Outstanding Tchr. and Mentor Recognition award U. Kans., Outstanding H.S. Edn. Recognition award Kans. Newman Coll. Mem. NEA, Kans. Olathe-NEA, Nat. Coun. Tchrs. of English, Kans. Assn. Tchrs. of English. Republican. Episcopalian. Avocations: reading, music, tennis, travel, writing. Home: 1204 W 63d St Kansas City MO 64113 Office: Olathe South HS 1640 E 151st St Olathe KS 66062-2851

WILLIAMS, CAROLYN, secondary school educator; Resource specialist, tchr. spl. needs students Bernardo Heights Middle Sch., San Diego. Past bd. mem. Internat. Dyslexia Soc. Mem.: Nat. Bd. for Profl. Tchg. Stds. (bd. mem.). Office: Bernardo Heights Middle Sch 12990 Paseo Lucido San Diego CA 92128*

WILLIAMS, CAROLYN WOODWORTH, retired elementary education educator, consultant; b. Binghamton, NY, Aug. 29, 1937; d. Charles Byron Woodworth and Dorothy Louise (Wheeler) Krum; m. James C. Williams, Mar. 29, 1958; children: Christopher, Lizette Macaluso, Matthew (dec.). BS in Elem. Edn., SUNY, Cortland, 1958; postgrad., SUNY, Geneseo, 1973-74, U. Vt., 1988; MS in Edn., SUNY, Brockport, 1989. Cert. tchr. K-6, N.Y. Elem. tchr. grade 6 Whitney Point (N.Y.) Ctrl. Sch., 1959-69, Palmyra (N.Y.)-Macedon Ctrl. Sch., 1969-71, elem. tchr. grade 4, 1971-79, 84-95, elem. tchr. grade 1, 1979-84, ret., 1995. Author, editor booklets. Active Women's Rep. Club, Binghamton, N.Y., 1959-67. Recipient Bring Local History Live into Classroom award Griffiss-McLouth Fund, 1993. Mem. ASCD, AAUW, N.Y. State United Tchrs., N.Y. State Hist. Soc., Wayne County Hist. Soc. (bicentennial history fair coord. 1989), Ea. Star (sister). Methodist. Avocations: children's welfare, literacy, women's issues, history, technology. Home: 104 Florence Dr Shohola PA 18458-3511

WILLIAMS, CHARLES MURRAY, retired computer information systems educator, consultant; b. Ft. Bliss, Tex., Dec. 26, 1931; s. Robert Parvin and Barbara (Murray) W.; m. Stanley Bright, Dec. 31, 1956; children: Margaret Allen Williams Becker, Robert Parvin, Mary Linton Williams Bondurant. BS, Va. Mil. Inst., 1953; MS, Stanford U., 1964; PhD, U. Tex., 1967. Physicist USAF, Kirtland AFB, N.Mex., 1956-58; staff mem. Sandia Labs., Albuquerque, 1958-62; programmer analyst Control Data Corp., Palo Alto, Calif., 1962-63; mathematician Panoramic Rsch., Inc., Palo Alto, 1963-64; mem. tech. staff Thomas Bede Found., Los Altos, Calif., 1964-65; rsch. scientist assoc. U. Tex., Austin, 1965-67; asst. prof. Computer Sci. Pa. State U., State College, 1967-72, Va. Poly. Inst. and State U., Blacksburg, 1972-75; assoc. prof. Computer Info. Systems Ga. State U., Atlanta, 1975-83, prof. Computer Info. Systems, 1983—99, prof. emeritus, 2000—. Cons. Visicon Inc., State Coll., 1970-72, Broomall (Pa.) Industries Inc., 1973-79, Bausch & Lomb Inc., Rochester, N.Y. 1981, Bell South Media Techs. Inc., Atlanta, 1987-90; mem. tech. staff Bell Labs., Whippany, N.J., 1979; textbook reviewer various publs. including Harper & Row, Prentice Hall, Simon & Schuster, 1976—. Contbr. articles to profl. computer graphics and image processing publs. Bd. dirs. Ga. Striders, 1993—; numerous presentations Fitness and the Fountain of Youth Seminar, 27 municipalities in 6 states, 1992—. Grantee Xerox Corp., 1985, Ga. Rsch. Alliance Telemedicine Project, 1993; recipient Silver medals in 1500-meter and 3000 meter runs 60-64 age divsn. Athletic Congress (now U.S.A. Track & Field) Nat. Masters Indoor Track and Field Championships, 1992, Gold medals in 5000-meter and 10,000-meter runs, Bronze medal in 1500-meter run, 1992, Gold medals in 1500-meter and 3000-meter runs U.S.A. Track & Field Indoor Championships, 1993, Gold medals in 5000-meter and 10,000 meter runs, Bronze medal in 1500-meter run U.S. Track and Field Outdoor Championships, 1993, Bronze medal in 5000-meter run and 10,000-meter runs U.S.A. Track & Field Outdoor Championships, 1994, Gold medal in 3000-meter run U.S.A. Track & Field Indoor Championships, 1994, Silver medal in 10,000-meter run, Bronze medal in 5,000-meter run U.S. Track and Field Outdoor Championships, 1998, Gold medal 10,000 meter run, Silver medal in 1500 meter and 5000 meter runs, U.S.A. Track & Field Outdoor Championships, 2002, Silver medals in Mile and 3000 meter runs U.S.A. Track & Field Indoor Championships, 2002, Third Place George Sheehan Meml. Mile 70+ Pontiac Fifth Ave. Mile, 2002, Bronze medals in mile and 3000 meter runs USA Track and Field Indoor Championships, 2003; ranked 3d nationally in road racing Running Times, 1992; ranked 5th, (2nd honorable mention) 1993. Mem. Nat. Computer Graphics Assn. (hon., Ga. bd. dirs. 1979-85, bd. dirs. Ga. chpt. 1985-89, sec. 1988-89), Computer Graphics Pioneers, Nat. Platform Assn., Upsilon Pi Epsilon, Omicron Delta Kappa. Republican. Episcopalian. Avocation: competitive road running (recipient numerous gold and silver medals). Home: 316 Argonne Dr NW Atlanta GA 30305-2814 E-mail: cwilliams@gsu.edu.

WILLIAMS, CHERYL A. secondary education educator; b. Neosho, Mo., July 7, 1957; d. Travestine Williams. BS in Math., Tex A&M U., 1978, postgrad., 1978-79, Rose State Coll., 1980-81, Sheppard Tech. Tng. Ctr., 1980-81; MS in Math., U. Tex., 1997. Computer scientist Tinker AFB, Oklahoma City, 1980-81, Defense Comm. Agy., Washington, 1986; tchr. Parent Child Inc., San Antonio, 1989; asst. sec. Antioch Bapt. Ch., San Antonio, 1989-92; substitute tchr. San Antonio Ind. Sch. Dist., 1990-93; instrnl. asst. Northside Ind. Sch. Dist., San Antonio, 1995-96, asst. tchr., 1994-95, North East Ind. Sch. Dist., San Antonio, 1996—2001; rep. West Telemarketing, 1998-99; math. tutor Alamo C.C. Dist., 1998—99, instr. math., 1998—, St. Philips Coll., 1998—; math. tutor Trave and G.G.'s Tutorial Svc., 1999—; instr. math. Guardian Angel Performing Arts Acad., 2002—. Asst. mgr. Fashion Pl., San Antonio, 1994—95; tax preparer H&R Block, 1994—95; distbr. Avon, 1999—2001; indep. beauty cons. Mary Kay Cosmetics, 1999—; scorer Harcourt Brace Corp., 2001, Randstad, 2001; rep. Express Svcs., 2001; cons. Prepaid Legal Svcs., Inc., 2003. Counselor YMCA, San Antonio, 1989-91; active Girl Scouts U.S., 1964-86; mem. choir, asst. sec. area ch., 1972, tutor, 1970—, tchr. Sunday Sch., 1973-86, asst. sec. Sunday Sch., 1973-86, 88—, asst. ch. sec., 1988-91; mem. Dorcas Circle, Lupus Found. Am., Biomed. Rsch. U. Tex., 1995—; mem. Epilepsy Found. Am., Tex. Head Injury Assn., Nat. Head Injury Assn., Smithsonian Instn. Mem. NEA, Tex. Edn. Assn., Mu. Alpha Theta. Avocations: jigsaw puzzles, bowling.

WILLIAMS, CLARENCE LEON, management, sociology and public policy company executive, educator; b. Longview, Tex., Aug. 9, 1937; s. Ruby Marlene (McLemore) W.; m. Kathleen Susan Robbins, June 7, 1975; children: Clarence Leon 2d, Thomas Chatterton. BA, Prairie View A&M U., 1959; MA in Sociology, Calif. State U., 1973; postgrad., U. Oreg., 1973-75. Exec. dir. Galveston County (Tex.) Community Action Coun., 1966-68, San Diego County (Calif.) Econ. Opportunity Commn., 1969-70; from assoc. dep. dir. program and contract dept. to dir. budgeting, planning, rsch. and evaluation dept. Econ. and Youth Opportunities Agy., Inc., L.A., 1970-71; dir. Rocky Mtn. Forum Internat. Issues, Denver, 1976-77; cons., adminstr. Regional Ctr. for Health Planning and Rsch. Svcs., Inc., Phila., 1977-78; with Albany (N.Y.) Interracial Coun., Inc., 1978-80; pres. Williams Academic and Pub. Policy Svcs., Fanwood, N.J., 1981—. Vis. asst. prof., assoc. prof. Grad. Sch. Internat. Studies, U. Denver, 1976-77; asst. prof., dir. Black Edn. Program Ea. Wash. State Coll., 1975-76; policy analyst, speaker, guest panelist various colls., univs., instns. nationally and internationally including U. Iowa, U. Krakow (Poland), U. Lodz (Poland), Warsaw (Poland) U., U. Erlangen (Fed. Republic Germany), Polish Inst. Sociology, Bergen County (N.J.) Ethical Culture Soc., 1965-92; policy analyst, mgmt. cons. Nat. Rural Ctr., Washington, 1976-79, Computerland and Computer Showcase Inc., N.J., 1987-88. Policy analyst, adv. mem. numerous task forces, govtl. confs. including Kettering Found. programs and confs. on econ. devel. in Asia, Africa, Latin Am., on trans-national dialog in Senegal, Mali, West Africa, 1976-80, Nat. Alliance of Businessmen, 1973-75, White House Conf. on Aging, 1967, White House Conf. on Hunger, Nutrition, Health and Poverty, 1969, Pres.' Adv. Coun. on Reorganization of OEO, 1971; regional race rels./intergroup rels. officer Home and Housing Fin. Agy., Washington, 1964-66; mem. Citizen Amb. Program, Russia and Ea. Europe, 1992. With USAF, 1961-64. Recipient Das Family Acad. Rsch. award, 1992; rsch. grantee Woodrow Wilson Nat. Found.; fellow Ford Found., Martin Luther King, Jr., Woodrow Wilson Found., U. Oreg., 1973-75; named U.S. Rep. to U.N. Human Rights 30th Anniversary Commemorative Programs, Europe, 1979-80. Mem. Alpha Kappa Delta, Phi Kappa Phi. Home and Office: 222 N Martine Ave Fanwood NJ 07023-1337

WILLIAMS, COLIN DALE, principal; b. Keokuk, Iowa, Feb. 9, 1948; s. Roger and June Williams; m. Nancy Sue Jacobsen; 1 child, Christopher Jacob. BSE, Kans. State Tchrs. Coll., 1970; MA, Northeast Mo. State U., 1979; postgrad., U. Iowa, 1982, 86. Tchr., coach Quincy (Ill.) Sr. High Sch., 1970-73, 79-80, Jefferson High Sch., Cedar Rapids, Iowa, 1973-77, Unity High Sch., Mendon, Ill., 1977-79; prin. Bennett (Iowa) Jr.-Sr. High Sch., 1980-81, Harding Middle Sch., Cedar Rapids, 1986-89; assoc. prin. McKinley Jr. High Sch., Cedar Rapids, 1981-83, Kennedy High Sch., Cedar Rapids, 1983-86; dir. staff devel. Cedar Rapids Community Schs., 1989—2002; prin. Franklin Middle Sch., 2002—. Cons. in communication skills, performance, leadership to corp. sector; presenter at profl. confs. Author: (mgmt. manual) Mastering the Change Process, 1990, (character edn. manual) Eleven Habits of Greatness, 1999. Vol. coach basketball, Cedar Rapids, 1989-90. Mem. Iowa Sch. Prins. (pres. 1988-89), Greater Cedar Rapids Jr. Golf Assn. (exec. dir. 1989—). Episcopalian. Avocations: golf, sports, travel, reading. Office: Cedar Rapids Cmty Schs 300 20th St NE Cedar Rapids IA 52402

WILLIAMS, DAVID A. lawyer, educator; b. Rochester, N.Y., July 1, 1942; s. Charles E. and Lorraine C. (Fitzgerald) W.; m. Margaret E. Ryan, May 30, 1970. BA, Williams Coll., 1964; postgrad., U. Mich., 1965; JD, U. Pa., 1968. Bar: N.Y. 1968, Vt. 1972, U.S. Dist. Ct. Vt. 1972, U.S. Ct. (we. dist.) 1990. Assoc. Law Offices of Fred G. Blum, Rochester, 1968-72; ptnr. Wolchik & Williams, Morrisville, Vt., 1972-80; sole practice Morrisville, 1980-89; ptnr. Williams and Green, P.C., Morrisville, Vt., 1989—. Adj. prof. Rochester Inst. Tech., 1969-72, Community Coll. Vt., Johnson, 1972-80, Johnson State Coll., 1973—. Author: Guide to Service of Civil Process by Vt. Sheriffs, 1980. Justice of Peace Town of Johnson, 1976-92, moderator, 1992; pres. Village of Johnson, 1978—; bd. dirs. Johnson Town Sch. Dist., 1992—. Mem. Vt. Bar Assn., Lamoille County Bar Assn. (pres. 1986-92), Sigma Phi Ednl. Found (bd. dir. 1986—). Office: P O Box 800 Morrisville VT 05661-0800

WILLIAMS, DENISE, secondary education educator; b. St. Louis, Nov. 25, 1950; d. Archie and Ivory (Payne) W. BS in Edn., Eastern Ill. U., 1971; MS in Edn., So. Ill. U., 1979. Cert. secondary edn. tchr., Ill.; cert. counselor, Ill. Substitute tchr. Madison/Venice (Ill.) Pub. Schs., 1972-74; tchr., program and curriculum developer Madison County (Ill.) CETA Program, 1974-76; tchr. life sci. Centralia (Ill.) City Schs. #135, 1976—. Sponsor, coach Cheerleaders, Centralia, 1977—, Sci. Fair, Centralia, 1977—, Just Say No Campaign, Centralia, 1977—; cons. excellence in edn. task force Ill. Edn. Assn., Springfield, 1986. Mem. NAACP, Madison, 1991—, Quad City Coun. of Ch. Women, Granite City, Ill., 1991—; mem. pianist Mt. Nebo Missionary Bapt. Ch., Madison, 1960-98; clk. Woodriver Bapt. Dist. Assn., 1973-98; active Second Bapt. Ch., Centralia, 1999—. Named one of Outstanding Tchr.'s, Masons Lodge # 86, 1989. Mem. NEA, AAUW, Nat. Sci. Tchrs. Assn., Ill. Sci. Tchrs. Assn., Centralia Edn. Assn., Ill. Edn. Assn., Ill. State Tchrs. Certification Bd., Ea. Ill. U. Alumni Assn., So. Ill. U. Alumni Assn., St. Louis Zoo Friends, St. Louis Sci. Ctr., Phi Delta Kappa, Delta Kappa Gamma. Democrat. Avocations: travel, cooking, reading, family. Home: 527 Meadowbrook Ln Centralia IL 62801-4418

WILLIAMS, DONALD HOWARD, chemist, educator, chemist, consultant; b. Ellwood City, Pa., Mar. 9, 1938; s. Howard John and Dorothy Olive (Devitt) W.; m. Susan Jane Bell, June 11, 1990; children: David Devitt, Brian Andrew. BS, Muskingum Coll., 1960; PhD, Ohio State U., 1964. Asst. prof. chemistry U. Ky., Lexington, 1964-69; assoc. prof. Hope Coll., Holland, Mich., 1969-73, prof., 1973—2003, chmn. dept. chemistry, 1979—82, dir. Inst. Environ. Quality; expert cons. U.S. Dept. of Energy, Washington, 1988-89, intermittent cons., 1989—2000. Chmn. dept. chemistry Hope Coll., 1979-82, dir. Inst. for Environ. Quality; chmn. bd. govs. Mich. Low-Level Radioactive Waste Authority, 1995-2001. Contbr. articles to profl. jours; patentor combined energy systems. Sec. Ottawa County (Mich.) Environ. Health Bd. of Appeals, 1978-89, 90-2003; mem. adv. com. minority outreach com. Mich. Dept. Edn., 1990-2000. Joyce Found. grantee, 1983-2000, GTE Lectureship Found. grantee, 1988-89. Mem. AAAS, Am. Chem. Soc., Am. Nuclear Soc., Nat. Sci. Tchrs. Assn., Rotary, Sigma Xi, Sigma Pi Sigma. Presbyterian. Achievements include patents for in combined energy systems. Avocations: photography, public speaking. Home: 4727 Heritage Meadow Dr Holland MI 49423-6951 Office: Hope Coll Dept of Chemistry Holland MI 49422-9000

WILLIAMS, DOROTHY PUTNEY, middle school educator; b. Richmond, Va., Sept. 18, 1952; d. Meriwether Vaughan and Dorothy Louise (Martin) Putney; m. Gary Davis Williams, July 24, 1982; children: Gary Davis, Michael Dale, Mark Vaughan. BA, Averett Coll., 1974. Cert. tchr., Va. Tchr. New Kent County Pub. Schs., Quinton, Va., 1974-79, Salem Ch. (Va.) Elem. Sch., Chesterfield County Schs., 1979-90, Cloverhilll Elem. Sch., Midlothian, Va., 1990-94; tchr. fgn. langs., English, social scis., history Swift Creek Middle Sch., Chesterfield County Schs., Midlothian, Va., 1994—. Mem. Fgn. Lang. Curriculum Coun., Chesterfield, 1992; delegation leader Pres. Ambs. Team-World Travel, People to People; tchr. humanities, multicultural lit. Mary Baldwin Coll. Author: A Holistic Appraoch to Foreign Languages and Cultures in the Elementary School Classroom, 1992; author fgn. langs. global awareness program, 1990; author curriculum on ancient Egypt taught at Ctr. for Gifted Edn., Coll. William and Mary. Named Tchr. of Yr., 1990-91; recipient award for Tchr. Excellence, 1992. Mem. Nat. Coun. Tchrs. of English, Internat. Reading Assn., Va. State Reading Assn., Richmond Area Reading Coun., Alpha Delta Kappa, Phi Delta Kappa (educator of the year award 1993). Baptist. Avocations: writing children's literature, world travel, anthropology, archeology, foreign languages. Home: 5118 Rock Harbour Rd Midlothian VA 23112-6211 Office: Swift Creek Middle Sch 3700 Old Hundred Rd Midlothian VA 23112-4744

WILLIAMS, DOROTHY RHONDA, gifted education consultant, educator; b. Grants, N.M., Aug. 20, 1957; d. Howard Lemuel and Betty Virginia (Bragg) Williams; m. John T. McGill, May 31, 1985. BS in Secondry Edn., U. Ark., 1979, MEd in Gifted Edn., 1985; postgrad studies in Anthropology, U. Ill., 1984-86. Cert. tchr., Class 1, Mont. High sch. math. tchr. Heber Springs (Ark.) Pub. Schs., 1979-80; math. theory instr. Ark. Gov. Sch. for Gifted, 1980; rsch. asst. U. Ark., Fayetteville, 1981-84, U. Ill., Champaign-Urbana, 1984-86; tchr. reading and English Browning (Mont.) Pub. Schs., 1986-87, tchr. 8th grade reading, 1987-91, tchr. critical thinking, 1991-92, bilingual gifted and talented specialist, 1992-95; instr. Gifted Inst. Carroll Coll., Helena, Mont., 1991—; instr. Satori Camp Ea. Washington U., Cheney, Wash., 1993—; instr. stress mgmt. for tchrs., 1995—. Presenter at peer ednl. confs., 1987—; project success enrichment trainer, 1994—, ednl. cons. 1993—; mem. curriculum writing project Mont. Office Pub. Instrn./law-related edn.; peer mediation and conflict mgmt. trainer Nat. Conf. on Peacemaking and Conflict Resolution, 1995—; conflict resolution coord. Browning Dist., 1995—; instr. conflict mgmt. cons. peer mediation programs, 1995—. Edge scholar Office of Pub. Instrn. Mont., 1990-92; Taft fellow, 1993. Mem. Assn. Gifted and Talented Edn. (planning com., presenter), Nat. Conf. on Gifted and Talented Edn. for Native People (presenter 1993, 94, 95), Glacier Reading Coun. (presenter), Mont. Reading Coun. (presenter), Internat. Reading Assn. Avocations: backpacking, hiking, reading, cooking, cultural activities. Home: PO Box 246 East Glacier Park MT 59434-0246 Office: Browning Pub Schs PO Box 610 Browning MT 59417-0610

WILLIAMS, DOYLE Z. university dean, educator; b. Shreveport, La., Dec. 18, 1939; s. Nuell O. and Lurline (Isbell) W.; m. Maynette Derr, Aug. 20, 1967; children: Zane Derr, Elizabeth Marie. BS, Northwestern State U., 1960; MS in Acctg., La. State U., 1962, PhD, 1965. CPA, Tex. Mgr. spl. edn. projects AICPA, N.Y.C., 1967-69; assoc. prof. Tex. Tech. U., Lubbock, 1969-71, prof. acctg., 1972-73, prof. area acctg., coord., 1973-78; prof. acctg. U. So. Calif., L.A., 1978-93, dean Sch. Acctg., 1979-87, interim dean Sch. Bus., 1986-88; dean Walton Coll. Bus. Adminstrn. U. Ark., Fayetteville, 1993—. Vis. prof. U. Hawaii, Honolulu, 1971-72. Author over 40 jour. articles and books. Chmn. Acctg. Edn. Change Commn., 1989-93. Named Mem. of Yr. N.Y. chpt. Nat. Assn. Accts., 1967, Outstanding Acctg. Educator Beta Alpha Psi, 1982; recipient Disting. Faculty award Calif. CPA Found., 1983, Nat. Leadership award Acad. Bus. Adminstrs., 1995, Lifetime Achievement award Ark. Soc. CPAs. Mem.: AICPA (coun. 1983—91, v.p. 1987—88, bd. dirs. 1987—91, Outstanding Educator award 1990, Gold medal 2002), Assn. to Advance Coll. Schs. Bus. Internat. (chair acctg. accreditation com. 1995—97, bus. accreditation com. 1995—97, chair acctg. accreditation com. 1999—2000, bd. dirs. 1999—, vice chair 2003—, 2003—), S.W. Bus. Dean's Assn. (pres. 1998—99), Adminstrs. Acctg. Programs (pres. 1977—78), Fedn. Schs. Accountancy (pres. 1982, Faculty Merit award 1993), Am. Acctg. Assn. (dir. edn. 1973—75, pres. 1984—85, Outstanding Educator award 1996). Home: 2447 E Boston Mountain Vw Fayetteville AR 72701-2802 Office: U Ark Sam M Walton Coll Bus Fayetteville AR 72701

WILLIAMS, EDWARD EARL, JR., entrepreneur, educator; b. Houston, Aug. 21, 1945; s. Edward Earl and Doris Jewel (Jones) W.; m. Susan M. Warren, June 28, 1983; children: Laura Michelle, David Brian. BS, U. Pa., 1966; PhD, U. Tex., 1968. Asst. prof. econs. Rutgers U., New Brunswick, N.J., 1968-70; assoc. prof. fin. McGill U., Montreal, Que., 1970-73; v.p. Svc. Corp. Internat., Houston, 1973-77; prof. adminstrv. sci. Rice U., Houston, 1978-82, Henry Gardiner Symonds prof., 1982—, prof. stats., 1995—. Chmn. bd. dirs. Edward E. Williams & Co., Houston, 1976-92; chmn. bd., pres. Tex. Capital Investment Co., 1979-95; chmn. bd. First Tex. Venture Capital Corp., 1983-92; mng. dir. First Tex. Venture Capital, LLC, 1992-2000, Svc. Corp. Internat, EQUUS II, Inc.; adv. dir. Frost Nat. Bank. Author: Prospects for the Savings and Loan Industry, 1968, An Integrated Analysis for Managerial Finance, 1970, Investment Analysis, 1974, Business Planning for the Entrepreneur, 1983, The Economics of Production and Productivity: A Modeling Approach, 1996, Entrepreneurship and Productivity, 1998, The N.Y. Times Pocket MBA Series: Business Planning, 1999, Models for Investors in Real World Markets, 2003; contbr. articles to profl. jours. Benjamin Franklin scholar, Jesse Jones scholar U. Pa., 1966; fellow Tex. Savs. and Loan League, fellow NDEA U. Tex., 1968. Mem. Am. Statis. Assn., Coll. Innovation and Entrepreneurship, Fin. Mgmt. Assn., So. Pacific Hist. and Tech. Soc., Santa Fe Rlwy. Hist. and Modeling Soc., Soc. on Econs. and Mgmt. in China, Raveneaux Country Club, Jewish Comm. North, Beta Gamma Sigma, Alpha Kappa Psi. Republican. Home: 7602 Wilton Park Dr Spring TX 77379-4672 Office: Rice U Jesse H Jones Grad Sch Mgmt Houston TX 77251 E-mail: jmkeynes@rice.edu.

WILLIAMS, ELAINE ENGSTER, primary education educator; b. New Orleans, Sept. 22, 1952; d. John Matthew and Louise (Aven) Engster; m. Charles Cullom Williams, Dec. 28, 1974; children: Erin, Amy, Brittany. BSE, U. Ark., 1974; MSE, Ark. State U., 1978. Cert. early childhood edn., Ark. Kindergarten tchr. Luxora (Ark.) Elem., 1974-76, Osceola (Ark.) Elem., 1976-79, Wilson (Ark.) Elem., 1979—. Chmn. parent/community involvement com. Wilson (Ark.) Elem., 1991-93; mem. pers. policies com. So. Mississippi County Sch. Dist., Wilson, 1992-93. Conferternity of Christian Doctrine tchr. St. Matthew's Cath. Ch., Osceola. Mem. Nat. Edn. Assn., Ark. Edn. Assn., Delta Kappa Gamma (pres. Alpha Zeta chpt. 1990-92), Kappa Delta Pi. Avocations: reading, activities with children.

WILLIAMS, ETHEL COGER, elementary education educator; b. Reeseville, S.C., Dec. 6, 1935; d. Johnny and Amanda (Toomer) Coger; m. Hoover Williams, Oct. 25, 1958; children: Terrence Donell, Damin Keith. BS, Claflin Coll., 1958; MA, NYU, 1973. Tchr. Bay Ridge Day Care Ctr., Bklyn., 1963-67, Pub. Sch. 106K, Bklyn., 1967—. Mem. Zeta Phi Beta. Office: Pub Sch 106K 1314 Putnam Ave Brooklyn NY 11221-5002

WILLIAMS, FORMAN ARTHUR, engineering science educator, combustion theorist; b. New Brunswick, N.J., Jan. 12, 1934; s. Forman J. and Alice (Pooley) W.; m. Elsie Vivian Kara, June 15, 1955 (div. 1978); children: F. Gary, Glen A., Nancy L., Susan D., Michael S., Michelle K.; m. Elizabeth Acevedo, Aug. 19, 1978. BSE, Princeton U., 1955; PhD, Calif. Inst. Tech., 1958; Doctorate (hon.), Poly. U. Madrid, 2002. Asst. prof. Harvard U., Cambridge, Mass., 1958-64; prof. U. Calif.-San Diego, 1964-81; Robert H. Goddard prof. Princeton U., N.J., 1981-88; prof. dept. mech. and aerospace engring. U. Calif., San Diego, 1988—, presidential chair in Energy and Combustion Rsch, 1994—. Adj. prof. Yale U., New Haven, 1997—. Author: Combustion Theory, 1965, 2d edit., 1985; contbr. articles to profl. jours. Fellow NSF, 1962; fellow Guggenheim Found., 1970; recipient U.S. Sr. Scientist award Alexander von Humboldt Found., 1982, Silver medal Combustion Inst., 1978, Bernard Lewis Gold medal Combustion Inst., 1990, Pendray Aerospace Literature award Am. Inst. of Aeronautics and Astronautics, 1993; named Pioneer Rschr. of the 20th Century, Japan Soc. Mech. Engrs., 1995. Fellow AIAA, Am. Phys. Soc.; mem. Combustion Inst., Soc. for Indsl. and Applied Math., Nat. Acad. Engring., Nat. Acad. Engring Mex. (fgn. corr. mem.), Sigma Xi. Home: 8258 Caminito Maritimo La Jolla CA 92037-2204 Office: U Calif San Diego Ctr Energy Rsch 9500 Gilman Dr La Jolla CA 92093-5004 E-mail: faw@ucsd.edu.

WILLIAMS, FRANCES ELIZABETH, retired secondary education educator; b. Eccles, West Virginia, May 30, 1948; d. Decolious R. and Wilhelmina (Bell) W. BA, U. DC, 1973; M, Trinity Coll., 1975, post grad., 1976-85. Keypunch operator to computer operator GSA, Washington, 1966-72; computer tape div. HHS, Washington, 1972-73; tchr. social studies H. D. Woodson Sr. High Sch., Washington, 1973—2003; ret., 2003. Mem.: U.S. Capitol Hist. Soc. Democrat. Baptist. Avocations: travel, reading, coin collecting. Home: 221 Crowne View Dr Winston Salem NC 27106

WILLIAMS, GALE CADY, secondary education educator; b. Newark, Ohio, Jan. 9, 1950; d. Paul Clifford and Betty Cady; m. Joseph Alan Williams, Jr., July 19, 1992; children: Nicholas Paul, Brian Gabriel, Rachel Elizabeth. BS, Ohio State U., 1973. Ohio secondary edn. grades 7-12 comprehensive English cert. English instr. Licking County Joint Vocat. Sch., Newark, 1973-77; ind. craftswoman Newark, 1985-90; reporter The Advocate, Newark, 1990-93; educator Newark Sr. H.S., Newark, Ohio, 1993—2000; editl. asst. Bus. First Newspaper, Columbus, Ohio, 2000—; freelance journalist Newark, 2000—. Adviser, editor Newark H.S. The Paper, 1993—2000; judge annual publs. competion Ohio Sch. Bds. Assn., 1997; spkr. in field. Edn. reporter The Adv., 1991-93, writer weekly column on edn., 1992-93; feature writer The Legend Mag., 1993-94; coord. newspaper in edn. The Newark Advocate, 1990-92. Pres. City of Newark Litter Prevention Adv. Bd., 1990—; mem. City of Newark Historic Hudson Lighting Assessment Bd., 1995; active Second Presbyn. Ch. Recipient First Pl. Cmty. Svc. award, The Associated Press, 1993. Mem. NOW, Nat. Coun. Tchrs. English, Nat. Dem. Party, Newark Tchrs. Assn. Avocations: writing, music and concerts, reading periodicals, antique shopping, family activities. Office: Newark Sr HS 314 Granville St Newark OH 43055-4483

WILLIAMS, GARY MURRAY, medical researcher, pathology educator; b. Regina, Sask., Can., May 7, 1940; s. Murray Austin and Selma Ruby (Domstad) W.; m. Julia Christine Lundberg; children: Walter, Jeffrey, Ingrid. BA, Washington and Jefferson Coll., 1963; MD, U. Pitts, 1967. Diplomate Am. Bd. Pathology, Am. Bd. Toxicology. Assoc. prof. pathology Temple U., Phila., 1971-75; mem. Fels Rsch. Inst., Phila., 1971-75; rsch. prof. N.Y. Med. Coll., Valhalla, 1975-98, prof. pathology, environ. pathology and toxicology, dir., 1999—. Mem. toxicology study sect. NIH, Bethesda, Md., 1985-87, metabolic pathol. study sect., 2003; working group Internat. Agy. Rsch. on Cancer, Lyon, France, 1976, 80, 82-83, 85-87, 89, 91, 96-99; subcom. on upper reference levels of nutrients NRC, 1999-2003; advisor joint expert com. on food additives WHO, 2001-03. Founding editor: Cell Biology and Toxicology, 1984—; mem. editl. bd. Archives of Toxicology, 1988—, European Jour. Cancer Prevention, 1991—, Drug and Chem. Toxicology, 1994—, Toxicologic Pathology, 2003—; contbr. over 470 articles to profl. jours.; editor or co-editor 8 books. Lt. comdr. USPHS, 1969-71. Recipient Sheard-Sanford award Am. Soc. Clin. Pathologists U. Pitts., 1967. Fellow Internat. Acad. Toxicol. Pathology (accreditation com.), Royal Coll. Pathologists; mem. Am. Assn. Cancer Rsch., Soc. Toxicology (Mid-Atlantic chpt., amb. in toxicology 2001, Arthur J. Lehman award 1982, Lectr. award 1996, Advancement Animal Welfare award 2002), Soc. Toxicol. Pathology, Phi Beta Kappa, Alpha Omega Alpha. Home: 8 Elm Rd Scarsdale NY 10583-1410 Office: Dept Pathology NY Med Coll Valhalla NY 10595-1549 E-mail: gary_williams@nymc.edu.

WILLIAMS, GEORGE WALTON, English educator; b. Charleston, S.C., Oct. 10, 1922; s. Ellison Adger and Elizabeth Simonton (Dillingham) W.; m. Harriet Porcher Simons, Nov. 28, 1953; children: George Walton Jr., Ellison Adger II, Harriet Porcher Stoney. BA, Yale U., 1947; MA, U. Va., 1949, PhD, 1957. Asst. cashier Carolina Savs. Bank, Charleston, 1949-54; asst. prof. English, Duke U., 1957-63, asso. prof., 1963-67, prof., 1967, chmn. dept. English, 1982-86, prof. emeritus, 1993—. Dir. summer inst. Commn. on English, Coll. Entrance Exam. Bd., 1962; pres. Durham Savoyards, Ltd., 1966-68, 81-82; sr. fellow Coop. Program in Humanities, Duke-U. N.C., 1969; Historiographer, Diocese of S.C., 1960-78; vis. prof. U.S. Mil. Acad., 1982-83 Author: St. Michael's, Charleston, 1751-1951, 1951, rev. edit., 2001, Image and Symbol in the Sacred Poetry of Richard Crashaw, 1963, The Craft of Printing and the Publication of Shakespeare's Plays, 1985, 4 children's books; editor: Romeo and Juliet, 1964, Complete Poetry of Richard Crashaw, 1970, Jacob Eckhard's Choirmaster's Book, 1971, Shakespeare's Speech-Headings, 1997; contbg. editor Dramatic Works of Beaumont and Fletcher, 1966-96; assoc. gen. editor Arden Shakespeare, 1996—. Served with inf. U.S. Army, 1943-45, ETO. Decorated Combat Inf. badge; recipient Outstanding Civilian Service medal Dept. Army, 1983; Guggenheim Found. fellow, 1977-78; Huntington Library fellow, 1981 Mem. MLA (com. on new variorum 1980-92, chmn. Shakespeare divsn. 1990), South Atlantic MLA (pres. 1980-81, J.H. Fisher award 2001), Southeastern Renaissance Conf. (editor 1960-70, 91-95, pres. 1973, hon. life 2002), Bibliog. Soc., Royal Soc. Arts London, S.C. Hist. Soc., Carolina Yacht Club (Charleston), St. Cecilia Soc. (Charleston), Elizabethan Club Yale U., Phi Beta Kappa, Phi Kappa Phi. Home: 1 Tradd St Charleston SC 29401 Office: Duke U Dept English PO Box 90015 Durham NC 27708-0015

WILLIAMS, GLADYS TUCKER, elementary school principal; d. Lee William and Cora Lena (Barksdale) Tucker; m. John Thomas Williams; children: Jon Trevor, Jamia Tiffani. BS, D.C. Tchrs. Coll., 1971; MA, George Washington U., 1981, EdD, 2003. From speech/lang. pathologist to prin. Prince Georges County Schs., Upper Marlboro, Md., 1971—. Mem. Nat. Assn. Elem. Prins. & Adminstrs., Assn. Sch.-Based Adminstrs. & Supervisors, Md. State Tchrs. Assn., Alpha Delta Kappa, Delta Kappa Gamma (v.p. 1994-95). Office: Lewisdale Elem 2400 Banning Pl Hyattsville MD 20783-2799

WILLIAMS, GLORIA LOUISE, gifted and talented education educator; b. Greenville, S.C., Sept. 29, 1949; d. Harding and Gladys Louise (Burgess) Hendricks; children: Lisa, Philip. BA, Spelman Coll., 1971; MusB, Mich. State U., 1973; MS in Edn., Ind. U., 1979. Cert. elem. tchr., Ind. Dir. christian edn. Second Christian Ch., Indpls., 1975-77; staff devel. intern Indpls. Pub. Schs., 1977-78; tchr. elem. and mid. sch. Lawrence Twp. Schs., Indpls., 1980—. Head human rels. com. Lawrence Twp. Sch., 1982-83. Part-time dir. children's ministry Light of the World Christian Ch., Indpls., 1984-89; writer Christian Bd. of Publ., St. Louis, 1998-99; grad. Tchr. Leadership Acad., 1998. Recipient Gloria and James Williams Day award Light of the World Christian Ch., 1989. Mem. Jack and Jill of Am., NAACP, Alpha Kappa Alpha. Avocations: piano, reading, singing. Office: MSD Lawrence Twp Sch 7601 E 56th St Indianapolis IN 46226-1310

WILLIAMS, GLORIA M. assistant principal; m. Rudolph E. Williams; children: Anthony E., Sharon Williams Worrell. BS in Edn. cum laude, Baruch Coll., 1983, MS in Edn. Supervision/Adminstrn., 1988, MS in Edn. Bus. Edn., 1990. Tchr. bus. edn. Midwood High Sch., Bklyn., 1983-90, coord. bus. edn., 1988-90, asst. prin. bus./tech. edn., 1990—. Mem. Bus. Edn. Assn., N.Y. Alliance Black Sch. Educators, Nat. Bus. Educators Assn., Nat. Assn. sec. Sch. Prins., Bus. Tchrs. Assn. of N.Y. State, Delta Pi Epsilon. Avocation: writing. Office: Midwood High Sch 2839 Bedford Ave Brooklyn NY 11210-2151

WILLIAMS, GREGORY HOWARD, dean, law educator; b. Muncie, Ind., Nov. 12, 1943; s. James Anthony Williams; m. Sara Catherine Whitney, Aug. 29, 1969; children: Natalia Dora, Zachary Benjamin, Anthony Bladimir, Carlos Gregory. BA, Ball State U., 1966; MA, U. Md., 1969; PhD, George Washington U., 1982, MPH, 1977, JD, 1971; LLD, Calif. Western Sch. Law, 1997; DHD, Ball State U., 1999, Coll. Wooster, 2000. Bar: Va. 1971, D.C. 1972, Ohio 1998. Dep. sheriff Delaware County, Muncie, Ind., 1963-66; tchr. Falls Ch. Public Sch., Va., 1966-70; legis. asst. U.S. Senate, Washington, 1971-73; dir. exptl. programs George Washington U., 1973-77; prof. law U. Iowa Coll. Law, Iowa City, 1977-93; assoc. v.p. Acad. Affairs U. Iowa, 1991-93; dean, prof. law Ohio State U., Columbus, 1993—. Author: Law and Politics of Police Discretion, 1984, Iowa Guide to Search and Seizure, 1986, Life on the Color Line: The True Story of a White Boy Who Discovered He Was Black, 1995. Mem. Iowa Adv. Commn. to U.S. Commn. on Civil Rights, Washington, 1978-86; chmn., mem. Iowa Law Enforcement Acad., Camp Dodge, 1979-85 Recipient Cert. of Appreciation Black Law Students Assn., 1984, GW Edn. Opportunity Program, 1977, Disting. Alumnus award George Washington U., Nat. Law Ctr., 1994, L.A. Times Book prize Current Interest Category, 1995, Disting. Alumnus award Ball State U., 1996. Mem. Assn. Am. Law Schs. (pres. exec. com. 1999). Office: Ohio State U Coll of Law 55 W 12th Ave Columbus OH 43210-1338

WILLIAMS, GWENDOLYN (ETTA) SMITH, reading specialist; b. Johnstown, Pa., Feb. 11, 1947; d. Troy and Susie Mae (Blackshire) Smith; m. Gary Lee Williams, Aug. 28, 1971; children: Marshae Blackshire, Maurice Troy. BS, Hampton U., 1969; MA, U. D.C., 1973; EdD, U. Md., 1990. Cert. elem. tchr., reading specialist, adminstr., Md. Reading specialist Prince George's County Bd. Edn., Upper Marlboro, Md., adminstr. Participant confs. in field. Adminstrv. chair Ager Rd. United Meth. Ch., Hyattsville, Md., 1989-92, lay leader, 1992; chairperson Abundant Life Ch. God in Christ, 1996—. Mem. NEA, ASCD, Md. State Tchr.'s Edn. Assn., Internat. Reading Assn. (Prince George's coun. v.p. 1988-89, pres.-elect 1989-90, pres. 1990-91, chair State of Md. intellectual freedom com. conf. 1991-93, Honor award 1990-91), Alpha Kappa Alpha (v.p. literacy com. 1991-92). Democrat. Avocations: reading novels, travel, collecting low cholesterol recipes. Home: 2540 Wayne Pl Cheverly MD 20785-3042 Office: Prince George's County Bd Edn 14201 School Ln Upper Marlboro MD 20772-2866

WILLIAMS, H. LEON, SR., school system administrator, minister; b. Walls, Miss., Apr. 3, 1945; Student, Princeton Theol. Sem.; BS in Bus. Adminstrn., Cheyney U.; student, State Tech. Inst., N.W. Miss. Jr. Coll., Southaven; MA in Christian Counseling; postgrad., LaSalle U. Asst. fin. mgr., Memphis; dir. evangelism Holly Springs, Miss., Phila., Memphis; min. Greenwood Christian Meth. Episcopal Ch., Memphis. Mem. bd. sch. dirs. Chester Upland Sch. Dist., Chester, Pa., 1987-91. Recipient cert. Nat. Christian Counselors Assn., cert. of recognition Chester Upland Sch. Dist., cert. of appreciation City of Memphis. Mem. Nat. Sch. Bd. Assn. Methodist. Home: 6431 Goodman Rd Walls MS 38680-9397

WILLIAMS, HARRIET CLARKE, retired academic administrator; b. Bklyn., Sept. 5, 1922; d. Herbert Edward and Emma Clarke (Gibbs) W. AA, Bklyn. Coll., 1958; student, Art Career Sch., N.Y.C., 1960; cert., Hunter Coll., 1965, CPU Inst. Data Processing, 1967; student, Chineses Cultural Ctr., N.Y.C., 1973; hon. certs., St. Labre Sch./St. Joseph's, Ind. Sch., Mont., 1990. Adminstr. Baruch Coll., N.Y.C., 1959-85. Mktg. researcher 1st Presbyn. Arts and Crafts Shop, Jamaica, N.Y., 1986-96; tutor in art St. John's U., Jamaica, 1986-96; founder, curator Internat. Art Gallery, Queens, N.Y., 1991—. Exhibited in group shows at Union Carbide Art Exhibit, N.Y.C., 1975, Queens Day Exhbn., N.Y.C., 1980, 1st Presbyn. Arts and Crafts Shop, N.Y.C., 1986, others; contbr. articles to profl. publs. Vol. reading tchr. Mabel Dean Vocat. High Sch., N.Y.C., 1965-67; mem. polit. action com. dist. council 37, N.Y.C., 1973-77; mem. negotiating team adminstrv. contracts, N.Y.C., 1975-78; mem. Com. To Save CCNY, 1976-77, Statue Liberty Ellis Island Found., Woodrow Wilson Internat. Ctr. Scholars, Wilson Ctr. Assocs., Washington, St. Labre Indian Sch., Ashland, Mont. Appreciation award Dist. Coun. 37, 1979; recipient Plaque Appreciation Svcs., Baruch Coll., Key award St. Joseph's Indian Sch., 1990, Key award in Edn. and Art, 1990, others. Mem. NAFE, AAUW, Women in Mil. Svc., Assn. Am. Indian Affairs, Nat. Mus. of Am. Indian, Artist Equity Assn. N.Y., Am. Indian Edn. Found., Lakota Devel. Coun., Am. Film Inst., Bklyn. Coll. Alumni, Nat. Geographic Soc., Nat. Mus. Woman in the Arts, Statue of Liberty Ellis Island Found., Inc., Alliance of Queens Artists, U.S. Naval Inst., El Museo Del Barrio, Am. Mus. Natural History, Internat. Ctr. for Scholars-Wilson Ctr. Assocs., Arrow Club-St. Labre Indian Sch., Mus. of Television and Radio, Women in Mil. Meml. Found., Nat. Mus. of Am. Indian, U.S. Holocaust Mus., Navy Meml. (adv. coun.), U.S. Golf Assn. Roman Catholic. Avocations: aerobics, vol. work, world travel, music. Office: Baruch Coll 17 Lexington Ave New York NY 10010-5518

WILLIAMS, HARRIETTE FLOWERS, retired school system administrator, educational consultant; b. L.A., July 18, 1930; d. Orlando and Virginia (Carter) Flowers; m. Irvin F. Williams, Apr. 9, 1960; children: Lorin Finley, Lori Virginia. BS, UCLA, 1952, EdD (HEW fellow), 1973; MA, Calif. State U., L.A., 1956. Tchr. L.A. Unified Sch. Dist., 1952-59, counselor, 1954-59, psychometrist, 1958-62, faculty chmn., 1956-57, student activities coord., 1955-59, leader insts. and workshops, 1952-76, dir. counseling, 1960-65, supr. Title I programs Elem. Secondary Edn. Act, 1965-68, asst. prin., 1968-76, prin., 1976-82, dir. instrn. sr. high sch. divsn., 1982-85, adminstr. ops., 1985-92; field svc. rep. Assn. Calif. Sch. Adminstrs., Culver City, 1992-2000. Asst. dir. HEW project for high sch. adminstrn. UCLA, 1971-72; adj. prof. in Masters in Sch. Adminstrn. program Pepperdine U., L.A., 1974-78, U. LaVerne, 1999—; ednl. cons. Teach for Am., 1991-94; L.A. County commr. Children and Family Commn., 1996-, vice chmn., 2001-. Recipient Sojourner Truth award Nat. Assn. Negro Bus. and Profl. Women's Clubs, L.A., 1968, Life Membership Svc. award L.A. PTA, 1972, 75, L.A. Mayor's Golden Apple award for ednl. excellence. Mem. Assn. of Adminstrs. of L.A. (pres. region 16), Assn. Calif. Sch. Adminstrs. (state chmn. urban affairs com. 1985-88, region pres. 1989-90), Nat. Assn. Secondary Sch. Prins., Sr. H.S. Asst. Prins. Assn. L.A. (bd. dirs. 1974-76, sponsor 1985-91), Sr. H.S. Prins. Orgn., Nat. Coun. Negro Women (life), Lullaby Guild Children's Home Soc. L.A. (pres. 1987-89), UCLA Gold Shield (vol. 1980—, 1st v.p. 1994-96, pres. 1998-2000), NAACP, Urban League, Inglewood-Pacific chpt. Links Inc. (sec. 1984-86, treas. 1987-89, fin. sec. 2002—), Jack and Jill of Am. (pres. L.A. chpt. 1980-82), UCLA Alumni Assn. (bd. dirs. 1979-83, 2000-03, v.p. 1992-94, donor rels. chmn. 1999—, chair support and honorary com. 2000-03, Excellence in the Cmty. award 1996), Wilfandel (pres. 1994-97, treas. 2000-03), Minerva Found. (CEO 2002—), Delta Sigma Theta (pres. L.A. chpt. 1964-66, regional dir. 1968-72, nat. committeewoman 1966-94), Pi Lambda Theta, Kappa Delta Pi, Delta Kappa Gamma (treas. 1991-94). Baptist.

WILLIAMS, IDA JONES, consumer and home economics educator, writer; b. Coatesville, Pa., Dec. 1, 1911; d. William Oscar and Ida Ella (Ruth) Jones; m. Charles Nathaniel Williams, Mar. 17, 1940 (dec. July 1971). BS, Hampton Inst., 1935; MA, U. Conn., 1965. Cert. high sch. tchr., English, sci., home econs., Va., Pa. Sci. and home econs. tchr. Richmond County H.S., Ivondale, Va., 1935-36; English and home econs. tchr. Northampton County H.S., Chesapeake, Va., 1936-40, consumer and home econs. tchr. Machipongo, Va., 1940—70, Northampton Jr. H.S., Machipongo, 1970—76. Author: Starting Anew After Seventy, 1980 (plaque 1980), News and Views of Northampton County High Principals and Alumni, 1981, Great Grandmother, Leah's Legacy-Remember You're Free, 2000; co-author: The History of Virginia State Federation of Colored Women's Clubs, Inc., 1996; editor: Fifty Year Book 1935-1985 - Hampton Institute Class, 1985, Favorite Recipes of Ruth Family & Friends, 1986. V.p. Ea. Lit. Coun., Melfa, Va., 1987-89; mem. Ea. Shore Coll. Found., Inc., Melfa, 1988-2000; mem. Gov.'s Adv. Bd. on Aging, Richmond, Va., 1992-94; instr. Ladies Community Bible Class, 1976-80 (Plaque 1980); sec., treas., v.p. Hospice Support of Ea. Shore, 1980-94; mem. Northampton/Accomack Adv. Coun., 1992-94; marshall 28th anniv. commencement Ea. Shore C.C., 1996; bd. dirs. Ea. Shore C.C. Found., 1998-2000. Named Home Econs. Tchr. of Yr., Am. Home Econs. Assn. and Family Cir., 1975, Woman of Yr., Prog. Women of E.S., 1997, Ida J. Williams scholarship fund named in her honor, Keller Ch. Christ, 1999; recipient Nat. Sojourner Truth Meritorious Svc. award, Negro Bus. and Profl. Women's Clubs, Gavel Ea. Shore Ret. Tchrs. Assn., 1994, Jefferson award, Am. Inst. Pub. Svc., Wavy-TV-Bell Atlantic and Mattress Discounters, 1991, Gov.'s award for vol. excellence, 1994, Contribution to Edn. award, Ea. Shore Coll. Found., 1997, Leadership award, 2001, trophy for outstanding and dedicated svc., 2001, plaque, Southeastern Assn. Colored Women's Clubs, Inc., 2001, award for dedicated svc., Nat. Assn. Colored Women's Club, Inc., 1998, E.S. C.C. Found., Inc. Svc. award, 2000, Exemplary Svc. award, Nat. Assn. Colored Women's Club, 2001, Black Achievement award, Ebenezer A.M.E. Ch., 2003, Achievement award, Chester County Hist. Soc. of Pa., 2003, Ednl. Achievement award for commitment to edn., Northampton County H.S. Alumni Assn., 2003. Mem. AARP (Citation award 1996, Mem. of Yr. 1997, v.p. Northampton chpt. 1998-2000), Progressive Women of Ea. Shore (pres. 1985-93, Gold Necklace 1993, Woman of Yr. 1997), C. of C., Univ. Women (v.p. Portsmouth br. 1985-87), Ea. Shore Ret. Tchrs. (pres. 1977-84), Dist. L Ret. Tchrs. (pres. 1989-91, chmn. legis. com. 1998, 99, 2001, Dedicated and Outstanding Svc. award 2003), Va. State Fedn. Colored Women's Club (pres. 1990-94, editor history com. 1994-96), Am. Assn. Ret. Persons (Va. state legis. com. 1995-2001). Mem. Ch. of Christ. Avocations: crafts, travel, writing, lecturing. Home and Office: PO Box 236 14213 Lankford Hwy Eastville VA 23347-0236

WILLIAMS, IVORY LEE, special education educator; b. White Castle, La., Nov. 8, 1953; d. Johnny and Gussie Mae (Morris) W. BA in Elem. Edn., So. U., Baton Rouge, 1975, M of Elem. Edn., 1978; postgrad. thirty plus, So. U. & Southeastern U., Baton Rouge, Hammond, La., 1990. Spl. edn. tchr. Dorseyville Elem. Sch., White Castle, La., 1975—. Leader Dorseyville 4H Club, White Castle, mem. 4H Adv. Bd., Plaquemine, La., 1981—; mem. Very Spl. Arts Com., Plaquemine, 1991; sec. Greater Progressive Bapt. Ch. Named Outstanding 4H Leader Iberville Parish 4H Club, 1991. Mem. La. Assn. Eductors (Emerging Leader 1992), Iberville Parish Assn. Educators. Democrat. Avocations: reading, sewing. Home: 57505 Hebert St White Castle LA 70788-3124 Office: Dorseyville Elem Sch PO Box 370 White Castle LA 70788-0370

WILLIAMS, JAMES FRANKLIN, II, university dean, librarian; b. Montgomery, Ala., Jan. 22, 1944; s. James Franklin and Anne (Wester) W.; m. Madeline McClellan, Jan. 1966 (div. May 1988); 1 child, Madeline Marie; m. Nancy Allen, Aug. 1989; 1 child, Audrey Grace. BA, Morehouse Coll., 1966; MLS, Atlanta U., 1967. Reference libr. Wayne State U. Sci. Libr., Detroit, 1968-69; document delivery libr. Wayne State U. Med. Libr., Detroit, 1969-70, head of reference, 1971-72, dir. med. libr. and regional med. libr. network, 1972-81, regional dir., 1975-82; assoc. dir. of librs. Wayne State U., 1981-88; dean librs. U. Colo., Boulder, 1988—. Bd. regents Nat. Libr. Medicine, Bethesda, Md., 1978-81; bd. dirs. Denver Art Mus., 1997—, pres. 1999—; bd. dirs. Ctr. Rsch. Librs., 1998—; pres. Big Twelve Plus Libr. Consortium, 2000; bd. dirs. Coun. on Librs. and Info. Resources. Mem. editl. bd. Portal: Libraries and the Academy; contbr. articles to profl. jours., chpts. to books; book editor and author. Bd. dirs. Educom, 1997-98, Boulder Cmty. Hosp., 2000—. Subject of feature interview in centennial issue Am. Librs. jour., 1976. Mem. ALA (Visionary Leader award 1988, Melvil Dewey medal 2002), Portal (editl. bd.), Assn. Rsch. Librs. (bd. dirs. 1994-96, 2000-03), Boulder C. of C. (bd. dirs.). Avocations: cycling, travel, fishing. Office: U Colo Office Dean Librs PO Box 184 Boulder CO 80309-0184

WILLIAMS, JAMES HENRY, JR., mechanical engineer, educator, consultant; b. Newport News, Va., Apr. 4, 1941; s. James H. Williams and Margaret L. (Holt) Mitchell; children: James Henry III, Mariella Louisa. Student, Newport News Apprentice Sch., 1965; BS, MIT, 1967, MS, 1968; PhD, Cambridge U., 1970. Sr. design engr. Newport News (Va.) Shipyard, 1960-70; asst. prof. mech. engring. MIT, 1970-74, assoc. prof., 1974-81, prof., 1981—2000, duPont prof., 1973, Edgarton prof., 1974-76, prof. writing and humanistic studies, 2000—. Cons. engring. to numerous cos. Contbr. articles on stress analysis, materials and nondestructive testing to profl. jours. Named Prof. of Tchg. Excellence, Sch. Engring., 1991, C.F. Hopewell faculty fellow, 1993; recipient Charles F. Bailey Bronze medal, 1961, Silver medal, 1962, Gold medal, 1963, Baker award, 1976. Mem. ASME, Am. Soc. Nondestructive Testing, Nat. Tech. Assn. Office: MIT Room 3-360 77 Massachusetts Ave Rm 3-360 Cambridge MA 02139-4307

WILLIAMS, JANE MARIE, special education educator; b. Hagerstown, Md., May 23, 1949; d. George Ernest and Marie Gertrude (Magaha) Lambillotte. BA, Wittenberg U., 1971; MA, U. Iowa, 1973; PhD, U. Md., 1984. Tchr. learning disabilities Danville (Ky.) Bd. Edn., 1973-74; diagnostic and prescriptive tchr. Chelsea (Mass.) Sch. Com., 1974-76; coord. learning disabilities program Hudson (N.H.) Sch. Dist., 1976-78; coord. work study Charles County Bd. Edn., La Plata, Md., 1978; coord. learning ctr. program Montgomery County Pub. Schs., Rockville, Md., 1978-79, tchr. spl. edn., 1979-81, 82-84, resource tchr. in spl. edn., 1984-92; edn. specialist, expert Office of Spl. Edn. Programs U.S. Dept. Edn., 1992-97; Ariz. State U. West, Phoenix, 1997-2000; assoc. dir. Ariz. K-12 Ctr., No. Ariz. U., Phoenix, 2000-01; asst. prof. U. Nev., Las Vegas, 2001—. Cons. So. N.H. Profl. Psychiat. Assn., Nashua, 1976-77, Lake Region Spl. Edn. Dist., Devil's Lake, N.D., 1990; asst. professorial lectr. George Washington U., Washington, spring 1989; presenter Internat. Spl. Edn. Congress, Cardiff, Wales, 1990. Author instrnl. materials. Ednl. cons., expert witness to atty., Rockville, 1988; reader small grant awards Found. for Exceptional Children, Reston, Va., 1985-91. Recipient Outstanding Spl. Educator award Montgomery Coun. Coun. PTA's, 1989. Mem. Coun. for Exceptional Children (sec. Md. fedn. 1982-91, gov. 1991-92, v.p. Montgomery County 1986-87, sec. 1986-87), Coun. for Learning Disabilities (sec. 1991-92), Learning Disabilities Assn. Am., Montgomery County Edn. Assn. (Broome award 1985). Avocations: running, swimming, reading. Home: 8243 Coyado St Las Vegas NV 89123-4320 Office: U Nev Las Vegas Dept Spl Edn Box 453014 4505 Maryland Pkwy Las Vegas NV 89154-3014 E-mail: janew@unlv.edu.

WILLIAMS, JOCELYN JONES, reading educator; b. Greenville, N.C., Sept. 24, 1948; d. William Edward and Elinor Suejette (Albritton) Jones; m. Robert Alexander Simpkins Jr., Sept. 7, 1969 (div. May 1972); m. Oscar James Williams Jr., July 12, 1985 (div. Mar. 1989). BS, Bennett Coll., 1970; MEd, N.C. Cen. U., 1988; MS, N.C. Agrl. & Tech. State U., 1992. Kindergarten/1st grade tchr. Greenville City Schs., 1970-74; elem./reading tchr. Orange County Schs., Hillsborough, N.C., 1974-97; Reading Recovery tchr. leader Durham (N.C.) Pub. Schs., 1997—. Mem. N.C. Reading Recovery Adv. Bd., 1994—, Reading Recovery Coun. N.Am., 1994—. Mem. NEA, ASCD, Internat. Reading Assn., Nat. Assn. Edn. Young Children, N.C. Assn. Educators, Phi Delta Kappa, Alpha Kappa Alpha, Progressive Sertoma Club. Democrat. Baptist. Avocations: reading, singing, sewing, cooking. Home: 47 Celtic Dr Durham NC 27703-2833

WILLIAMS, JOHN ALAN, secondary school educator, coach; b. Watertown, N.Y., May 30, 1949; s. John F. and Doris (Fuess) W.; m. Ana Maria Delima Moniz, Feb. 22, 1977; children: Timothy John, Katherine Evelyn. BS in Oceanography, U.S. Naval Acad., 1971; MS in Sci. Edn., Syracuse U., 1978; postgrad., SUNY, Oswego, 1989-90. Sci. tchr., coach Liverpool (N.Y.) High Sch., 1977-80, sci. tchr., coach, dir. sci. and tech. fair, 1981—, advisor, coach Olympiad Team, 1987-98; application engr. Hoffman Air & Filtration, Syracuse, N.Y., 1980-81. Coach wrestling team Liverpool High Sch., 1982—, Liverpool Optimist Wrestling Club, 1999—; coach local Pee Wee wrestling team, 1982-96; bd. dirs. sci. fair com. Syracuse Discovery Ctr., 1986-97. Lt. USN, 1971-76, Vietnam. Named Ctrl. N.Y. Sci. Tchr. of Yr. Syracuse Discovery Ctr., 1986-87, Onondaga High Sch. League-North Wrestling Coach of Yr., 1984-85, 88-89, 92-93, 97-98, 2000-01. Mem. Nat. Earth Sci. Tchrs. Assn., United Liverpool Faculty Assn., N.Y. State Sci.

Tchrs. Assn. (10 Yr. award 1990), Assn. Sci. Tech. Ctrs. (Honor Roll Tchrs. 1987), Syracuse Tech. Club (Outstanding Tchr. award 1990), NFL (Tchr. of Yr. 1990), Sigma Xi (Outstanding Sci. Tchr. award 1989). Home: 4320 Luna Crse Liverpool NY 13090-2050 Office: Liverpool High Sch 4338 Wetzel Rd Liverpool NY 13090-2098 E-mail: rocksminsandmore@aol.com.

WILLIAMS, JOHN ANDREW, physiology educator, consultant; b. Des Moines, Aug. 3, 1941; s. Harold Southall and Marjorie (Larsen) W.; m. Christa A. Smith, Dec. 26, 1965; children: Rachel Jo, Matthew Dallas. BA, Cen. Wash. State Coll., 1963; MD, PhD, U. Wash., Seattle, 1968. Staff fellow NIH, Bethesda, Md., 1969-71; research fellow U. Cambridge, Eng., 1971-72; from asst. to prof. physiology U. Calif., San Francisco, 1973-87; prof. physiology, chair dept. physiology, prof. internal medicine U. Mich., Ann Arbor, 1987—. Mem. gen. medicine study sect. NIH, Bethesda, 1985-88, NIDDK, DDK-C study sect., 1991-95. Contbr. numerous articles to profl. jours.; editor Am. Jour. Physiology: Gastrointestinal Physiology, 1985-91; assoc. editor Jour. Clin. Investigation, 1997-2001. Trustee Friends Sch. in Detroit, 1992—2000. NIH grantee, 1973—. Mem. Am. Physiol. Soc. (Hoffman LaRoche prize 1985, mem. coun. 1996-99, pres. 2003-04), Am. Soc. Cell Biology, Am. Soc. Clin. Investigation, Am. Gastroenterology Assn., Am. Pancreatic Assn. (pres. 1985-86). Democrat. Home: 1115 Woodlawn Ave Ann Arbor MI 48104-3956 Office: Dept Molecular & Intergrative Physiology Univ of Mich Med Sch Ann Arbor MI 48109 E-mail: jawillms@umich.edu.

WILLIAMS, JOHN LEICESTER, biomechanical engineering educator; b. Germiston, Transvaal, Republic of South Africa, July 22, 1952; came to U.S., 1971; s. Leicester Garnet and Drusilla Wallace (Pringle) W.; m. Lillian Yuriko Kubota, June 25, 1976; 1 child, Ian Nobuo. BS in Biology, U. Hawaii, 1975; MS, Northwestern U., 1979, PhD in Theoretical/Applied Mechanics, 1981. Asst. prof. mech. engring. Northeastern U., Boston, 1981-85, Syracuse (N.Y.) U., 1985-88, dir. univ. computer aided design and engring., 1986-88; asst. prof. orthopaedic surgery and bioengring. U. Pa., Phila., 1988-95; assoc. prof. orthopaedic surgery U. Mo., Kansas City, 1995—, assoc. prof. oral biology, 1999—. Referee Jour. Biomech. Engring., Jour. Biomechanics, Applied Mechanics Revs., J. Orthop. Rsch., Clin. Orthop. Rel. Res. Author: (with others) The Hip and Its Disorders, 1991; contbr. articles to profl.jours. Named Nat. Rsch. Svc. Tng. fellow NIH, 1976-80, grantee, 1984-86, NSF, 1985-86, Orthopaedic Rsch. and Edn. Found. Mem. ASME, Am. Soc. Biomechanics, Orthopaedic Rsch. Soc. Achievements include research in computer modeling of the spine for crash mechanics research, anisotropic mechanical and structural properties of bone and growth plate, ultrasonic characterization of bone tissue and composites and strain transduction by cells. Office: Dept Orthopaedic Surgery Truman Med Ctr 2301 Holmes St Kansas City MO 64108-2640

WILLIAMS, JOHN MICHAEL, physical therapist, sports medicine educator; b. Columbus, Ohio, Oct. 19, 1951; s. James Hutchison and Helen Lucille (Knight) W.; m. Karen Sue Eaglen, June 23, 1973; children: Michelle Rene, Elizabeth Ann. BS in Phys. Therapy, Ohio State U., 1975, MS in Allied Medicine, 1983. Lic. phys. therapist, Ohio. Asst. dir. phys. therapy Licking Meml. Hosp., Newark, Ohio, 1975-80; pvt. practice Westerville, Ohio, 1977-80; asst. dir. rehab. St. Anthony Hosp., Columbus, 1980-88; from chief phys. therapist to dir. phys. and sports medicine St. Ann's Hosp., Westerville, 1988-95; mgr. Nova Care Rehab., 1995-97. Clin. instr. Ohio State U., Columbus, 1984-97, faculty instr., 1997—; adj. faculty sports medicine Otterbein Coll., Westerville, 1989-96; cons. Licking County Arthritis Found., Newark, 1978-80; phys. therapy adv. bd. Ctrl. Ohio Tech. Coll., Newark, 1978-2001; bd. dirs. SAHCU Credit Union, Westerville; asst. prof. phys. and occupl. therapy programs U. Findlay, Ohio, 1996-2000. Author monograph. Med. team capt. Columbus Marathon, 1989—, U.S. Men's Olympic Marathon Trials, Columbus, 1992, U.S. Men's Nat. Marathon Championships, 1991, 92; mem. State of Ohio Post Critical Trauma Care Commn. 2002—. Lt. col. USAR, 1969—; exec. and spl. ops. officer 914th Combat Support Hosp., 2000—. Decorated Army Commendation medal with 3 oak leaf clusters, Meritorious Svc. medal; recipient Mayor's award for vol. svc. City of Columbus, 1993. Mem.: Am. Phys. Therapy Assn. (rep. to state assembly 1987—, state of Ohio faculty liason to state bd. dirs. 2000—02), Am. Acad. Med. Adminstrs. Episcopalian. Avocations: volleyball, golf, sailing. Home: 132 Ormsbee Ave Westerville OH 43081-1151

WILLIAMS, JOHN RALPH, school superintendent; b. Scranton, Pa., Oct. 15, 1945; s. Al and Elizabeth (Wallace) W.; m. Rita Marie Cusick, June 21, 1969; 1 child, John Jr. BS, U. Scranton, 1967; Elem. Cert., Marywood Coll., 1971; MS, U. Scranton, 1973; EdD, Lehigh U., 1985. Tchr. English Scranton Sch. Dist., 1967-68, elem. tchr., 1968-74, middle sch. asst. prin., 1974-78, elem. prin., 1978-85, dir. elem. edn., 1985-89, asst. supt., 1989-93; supt. schs., 1993—. Bd. trustees Keystone Jr. Coll., LaPlume, Pa., 1991—; pres.,PA League of Urban Sch., bd. dirs. Scranton Counseling Ctr., 1990—, Leadership Lackawanna, 1988—; mem. Mayor's Task Force on Young Children, Scranton, 1991—; pres. St. Patrick's Day Parade Assn., 1992; adv. bd. Big Bros./Big Sisters, 1985—; sec./treas., Urban Superintendant Assoc. of Am., bd. dirs. N.E. Pa. Ctr. for Ind. Living, 1990—. Recipient Matthew Gaffney award for disting. scholarship Lehigh U., 1985, Earl F. Ransom award Operation Overcome of Lackawanna County, 1990. Mem. ASCD, Pa. Sch. Bds. Assn., Am. Assn. Sch. Adminstrs., Phi Delta Kappa (past pres.). Democrat. Roman Catholic. Avocations: running, golf, tennis. Home: 1725 Penn Ave Scranton PA 18509-1927 Office: Scranton City Sch Dist 425 N Washington Ave Scranton PA 18503-1305 E-mail: williamj@ns.neiu.k12.pa.us.

WILLIAMS, J(OHN) RODMAN, theologian, educator, clergyman; b. Clyde, N.C., Aug. 21, 1918; s. John Rodman and Odessa Lee (Medford) W.; m. Johanna SerVaas, Aug. 6, 1949; children: John, Lucinda Lee, David Bert. AB, Davidson Coll., 1939; BD, Union Theol. Sem., 1943, ThM, 1944; PhD, Columbia U., 1954. Ordained to ministry Presbyn. Ch., 1943. Chaplain USNR, 1944—46; chaplain, assoc. prof. philosophy Beloit Coll., 1949—52; pastor First Presbyn. Ch., Rockford, Ill., 1952—59; prof. systematic theology and philosophy of religion Austin Presbyn. Theol. Sem., 1959—72; prof. Christian doctrine, pres. Melodyland Sch. Theology, Anaheim, Calif., 1972—82; prof. Christian theology Regent U., Virginia Beach, Va., 1982—. Author: Contemporary Existentialism and Christian Faith, 1965, The Era of the Spirit, 1971, The Pentecostal Reality, 1972, Ten Teachings, 1974, The Gift of the Holy Spirit Today, 1980, Renewal Theology, Vol. 1, God, the World, and Redemption, Vol. 2, 1988, Salvation, the Holy Spirit and Christian Living, Vol. 3, 1990, The Church, the Kingdom, and Last Things, 1992, Renewal Theology, 3 vols. in one, 1996. Home: 608 Fleet Dr Virginia Beach VA 23454-7344 E-mail: rodmwil@regent.edu.

WILLIAMS, JOHN TROY, librarian, educator; b. Oak Park, Ill., Mar. 11, 1924; s. Michael Daniel and Donna Marie (Schaffer) Williams. BA, Ctrl. Mich. U., 1949; MA in Libr. Sci., U. Mich., 1954; PhD, Mich. State U., 1973. Reference libr. U. Mich., Ann Arbor, 1955—59; instr. Bowling Green (Ohio) State U., 1959—60; reference libr. Mich. State U., East Lansing, 1960—62; 1st asst. reference dept. Flint (Mich.) Pub. Libr., 1962—65; head reference svcs. Purdue U., West Lafayette, Ind., 1965—72; head pub. svcs. No. Ill. U., DeKalb, 1972—75; asst. dean, asst. univ. libr. Wright State U., Dayton, Ohio, 1975—80; vis. scholar U. Mich., Ann Arbor, 1980—; cons. in field. Contbr. articles to profl. jours. Served U.S. Army, 1943—46. Mich. State fellow, 1963—64, HEW fellow, 1971—72. Mem.: AAUP, ALA, Coun. Fgn. Rels., Am. Sociol. Assn., Am. Soc. Info. Scis., Spl. Librs. Assn.

WILLIAMS, JUANITA LUNDY, elementary education educator; b. Phila., Apr. 29, 1939; d. James Earl and Ethel Lou (Clayton) Lundy; m. Frank Lee Lundy Williams, May 14, 1973 (div. Aug. 1989); 1 child, Christian Lundy. BS cum laude, Cheyney U., 1961, MEd in Elem. Edn., 1984. Tchr. Martha Washington Elem. Sch., Phila., 1962—, reading specialist, 1990-91; supr. pre-student tchr. Cheyney State U., 1975; grad. asst. Cheyney (Pa.) U., 1982. Writing cons. Phila. writing project U. Pa., Phila., 1988—. Tchr. Vacation Bible Sch., 1975-93; 1st v.p. Nat. Edn. Corp., 1985; participant Jr. Achievement Bus. Project, 1990, 93, Analysis of Am. Hist. textbooks for Middle Schs. in Phila. Compulsary Plus; rsch. participant establishing nat. criteria for cert. in lang. arts. for 7th & 8th grade tchrs., U. Pitts., 1992-93. Area fellow Paths/Prism, 1984. Mem. Nat. Assn. Univ. Women, Phila. Fedn. Tchrs. (bldg. rep. 1989-91), Alpha Phi Sigma. Democrat. Mem. African Methodist Episcopal Ch. Avocations: piano, reading, writing essays. Home: 8027 Mars Pl Philadelphia PA 19153-1111 Office: Martha Washington Elem Sch 44th And Aspen St Philadelphia PA 19104

WILLIAMS, JULIA REBECCA KEYS, secondary school educator; b. Bristol, Va., July 13, 1922; d. Walter King and Eleanor Fell (Fickle) K.; m. Charles Edwin, Feb. 19, 1944; children: James Edwin, Eleanor Lynn. BA, Queens Coll., Charlotte, 1943; MA, Appalachian State U., Boone, N.C., 1969; EdS, Nova U., 1989. Fla. Tchr. Cert. in Bible, History, English. Tchr. Watauga County Sch. Bd., Blowing Rock, N.C., 1943-44; bank teller, mgr. The Northwestern Bank, Boone, Blowing Rock, N.C., 1944-51; owner, mgr. Yonahlossee Motel, Blowing Rock, N.C., 1952-65; tchr. Sarasota County Sch. Bd., Fla., 1965-89. English Dept. Chmn. McIntosh Jr. High Sarasota Fla. 1976-82; English Curriculum Coordinator McIntosh Middle Sch. 1982-87. Author Poems 1986 (Golden Poet award), Interdisciplinary Units for Middle Sch., Ch. History Bee Ridge Presbyn. Ch. (elder 1981). Mem. Elder Bee Ridge Presbyn. Ch., 1990—92, 1998—2001; mem. DAR. Mem. Sarasota English and Reading Coun. (pres. 1974-75), Nat. and Fla. Coun. of English Tchrs., Presbyn. Womens Club (Life Mem. award), DAR, Delta Kappa Gamma Soc. (pres. Beta Upsilon chpt. 1990-92), Alpha Delta Kappa (pres. 1972-74). Democrat. Presbyterian. Avocations: travel, sewing, reading, movies. Home: 4509 Beacon Dr Sarasota FL 34232-5215

WILLIAMS, KARMEN PETERSEN, secondary school educator; b. Kansas City, Mo., Sept. 19, 1942; d. Hans Jorgen and Rosella Petersen; m. James Emmett Williams, Aug. 28, 1965; children: Jan Elizabeth Williams Parks, James Jorgen. BA in English, Okla. Bapt. U., 1964; MS in Edn., Ouachita Bapt. U., 1983. Cert. secondary tchr., reading specialist, K-12, Ark. Instr. English/reading Fern Creek H.S., Louisville, 1966-69; dir. kindergarten 1st Bapt. Ch., Texarkana, Ark., 1970-73; staff devel. specialist Divsn. Children & Family Svc., Pine Bluff, Ark., 1974-85; instr. English, speech, drama White Hall (Ark.) High Sch., 1985—, chairperson English dept., 1989—. Vol. Casa Women's Shelter, Pine Bluff, 1992—. Mem. MLA, Nat. Fedn. Interscholastic Speech & Debate Assn., Nat. Coun. Tchrs. English. Southern Baptist. Avocations: calligraphy, cake decorating, pastel artist, speech consultant, tutor. Home: 517 E 7th St Little Rock AR 72202-2514

WILLIAMS, KATHRYN SANDERS, elementary education administrator; b. Lexington, Ky., May 18, 1961; d. Gerald Louis and Donna Lee (Freeman) Sanders; m. R. Duane Williams, Jr., May 21, 1983; children: Bryan, Brad. BS in Elem. Edn., U. Louisville, 1983, M in Elem. Curriculum, 1990, rank I in ednl. adminstrn., 1995. Tchr. elem. sch. Indpls. Pub. Schs., 1984-85; tchr. mid. sch. Jefferson County Pub. Schs., Louisville, 1985-96; asst. prin. Mt. Washington (Ky.) Elem. Sch., 1996—. Vol. Talent Ctr. grantee, Louisville, 1990. Mem. ASCD, Ky. Assn. for Supervision and Curriculum Devel., Ky. Assn. Sch. Adminstrs., Nat. Assn. for Yr.-Round Edn., Ky. Assn. of Elem. Sch. Prins., Bullitt County Assn. of Sch. Adminstrs. Democrat. Roman Catholic. Avocations: reading, skating, sporting events. Home: 4319 Saratoga Hill Rd Jeffersontown KY 40299-8306 Office: Mt Washington Elem Sch 9234 Highway 44 E Mount Washington KY 40047-7309

WILLIAMS, LARRY BILL, academic administrator; b. Cushing, Okla., June 9, 1945; s. Louis Albert and Morene Ruth (Cox) W.; m. Pam Bryan, May 1, 1993; children: Natalie Michelle, Nicole Diane, Louis Bradley, Sharla Dianne Bryan, Vanessa Joy Bryan. BS, Ctrl. State U., Edmond, Okla., 1967, MBA, 1972; PhD, U. Okla., 1985; grad. Inst. Ednl. Mgmt. program, Harvard U., 1996. Office mgr. Okla. State U., Stillwater, 1967-69; from asst. comptr. to dir. univ. pers. svcs. Ctrl. State U., 1969-80, from asst. v.p. adminstrn. to v.p. adminstrn., 1980-87; interim pres. Southeastern Okla. State U., Durant, 1987, pres., 1987-97, Northeastern State U., Tahlequah, Okla., 1997—. Managerial cons. various municipalities; mktg. cons. State of Okla.; arbitrator Met. Fraternal Order of Police; bd. dirs. Okla. Small Bus. Devel. Ctr., Okla. Acad. State Goals, chmn. S.E. region, 1995. Bd. dirs. Bryan County Econ. Devel. Corp., 1989—, Bryan County United Way, 1988-94; mem. adv. bd. Med. Ctr. Southeastern Okla., 1987-92; bd. dirs. Bryan County Ret. Sr. Vol. Program, 1990-92, Leadership Okla. Class IV, 1991, mem. adv. bd., 1991-95; mem. exec. bd. Boy Scouts Am., 1991; com. mem. Okla. Ctr. for Advancement Sci. and Tech. Long Range Planning Task Force, Most Eminent Scholars and Rsch. Equipment, 1990-91; mem. higher edn. alumni coun. Okla. State Regent for Higher Edn. Tuition Com., mem. budget com., mem. outreach com., mem. quality initiative com., mem. capital com., chmn. legis. affairs com., chmn. acad. affairs com.; mem. adv. coun. Ea. Okla. Schs., 1987—; trustee Southeastern Found., 1990—; past pres. Kickingbird Golf Course Mgmt., Edmond; bd. dirs. Edmond C. of C., 1984; mem. Okla. State Regents for Higher Edn. Coun. of Pres., 1987—, chair, 1994; Chocktaw Nation of Okla. JTPA Adv. Coun., 1987—; mem. Okla. Regional Pres.' Coun., 1987—, chair, 1994; vice chmn. Diamond Jubilee Commn., Edmond; mem. found. bd. trustees Ctrl. State U., Edmond; mem. adv. com. Durant Airport. With USNG, 1962-70. Named One of Outstanding Young Men of Am., Edmond Jaycees, 1971, 74, 79; recipient Presdl. Leadership award Nat. U.S. Jaycee Pres., 1971, Presdl. Leadership, Achievement and Honor awards Nat. Jaycees, 1972, Nat. Presdl. award of Honor Nat. Coll. and Univ. Pers. Assn., 1973, Disting. Svc. award City of Edmond, 1974, Dwight F. Whelan Meml. award for Outstanding Leadership, Edmond, 1972, Disting. Former Student award U. Ctrl. Okla., 1996; named to Cushing Alumni Hall of Fame, 1988, recipient Nat. Order Omega (charter hon. mem), 1991. Mem. Okla. Assn. Coll. and Univ. Pers. Adminstrs. (founder, bd. dirs., chmn.), Nat. Coll. and Univ. Pers. Assn., Nat. Coll. and Univ. Bus. Officers Assn., Okla. Assn. Affirmative Action (co-founder, pres., bd. dirs.), Okla. City Pers. Assn., Am. Assn. State Colls. and Univs., Okla. Assn. Coll. and Univ. Bus. Officers (bd. dirs., pres.), Acad. Cert. Adminstrv. Mgrs., Okla. Small Bus. Devel. Ctr. (bd. dirs. 1987—), Industry Ednl. Coun. McCurtain County, Okla. Acad. for State Goals (bd. dirs. 1992—, vice chair S.E. region 1995), Okla. Advs. for Arts and Humanities (mem. steering com. 1995), Durant C. of C. (past pres., bd. dirs.), Okla. State C. of C. (bd. dirs. 1991—), Blue Key, Rotary. Lodges: Rotary (sec. Edmond club 1986-87). Democrat. Presbyterian. Avocation: golf. Office: Northeastern State Univ Office of the Pres Tahlequah OK 74464

WILLIAMS, LENA HARDING, educational administrator; b. Portsmouth, Va., June 12, 1947; d. Arthur McKinley and Mildred (Smith) Harding; m. Leroy Stephen Williams, July 8, 1966; children: Michael LaMar, Darryl LaVon, Stephen LaSean. AB in English Edn. and Speech, Norfolk State U., 1969; postgrad., U. Va., 1972-73, Norfolk State U., 1987, Old Dominion U., 1973-88, MS in Ednl. Administrn., 1993. Cert. 7-12 English and speech tchr., mid. sch. and h.s. prin., postgrad. cert., Va.; cert. Nat. Bd. for Profl. Tchg. Stds. Tchr. English S.H. Clarke Sch. Portsmouth Schs., 1969-70, tchr. English W.E. Waters Sch., 1970-71, tchr. English Churchland Mid. Sch., 1971-74, chmn. English dept., 1974-86, 88-99, cons. coll. bd. English vertical teaming, 1997, adminstrv. intern in curriculum and instrn., 1999; asst. prin. Hunt-Mapp Mid. Sch., Portsmouth, 1999—. Fieldtester Va. Standards of Learning Lang. Arts; tchr./trainer Portsmouth Schs., 1986-88, lead mentor tchr., 1990—, cons. coll. bd.; presenter SAT prep. workshop, New-Tchr. Insvc., Writing Across the Curriculum, Reading to Learn, Technology in the Classroom. Active Hodges Manor Civic League, Portsmouth, 1985—, PTA; dir. Christian edn., summer camp youth adv., coord. vol. tutorial svc., mem. sr. choir, usher, coord. youth activities, mem. ch. coun., bd. dirs. kindergarten, Edna Hyke Corbett Achievement Award Found.; coord. Multiple Sclerosis Read-a-Thon, Back to Sch. Seminar; community campaign vol. Mother's March, Am. Cancer Soc., Muscular Dystrophy, Am. Heart Assn.; co-sponsor Cavalier Manor Deep Doubles Tennis Tournament. Named State Tchr. of Yr., State Bd. Edn., Richmond, Va., 1992, Outstanding Young Educator, Portsmouth Jaycees, 1978, Va. Secondary Reading Tchr. of Yr., Secondary Reading Coun. Va., 1999; recipient 25 svc. and honor awards from local orgns. Fellow Hampton Rds. Inst. for Advanced Study of Tchg.; mem. ASCD, NEA, NAACP, Va. Edn. Assn., Nat. State Tchrs. of Yr. Assn., Nat. Coun. Tchrs. of English, Internat. Reading Assn., Va. State Secondary Reading Assn., Va. Congress English Teachers, Va. Assn. Tchrs. of English (Foster B. Gresham award 1994), Portsmouth Edn. Assn., Portsmouth Reading Coun., Tidewater Assn. Tchrs. English, Delta Sigma Theta. Democrat. Avocations: singing, speaking, reading, collecting dolls. Home: 801 Nottingham Rd Portsmouth VA 23701-2118 Office: Hunt-Mapp Middle Sch 3701 Willett Dr Portsmouth VA 23707-1295 E-mail: LLWMS2@aol.com.

WILLIAMS, LISA ROCHELLE, logistics and transportation educator; b. Toledo, Feb. 11, 1964; d. Lionel and Mary Moore; divorced; 1 child, Matthew Malik. BS, Wright State U., 1985, MBA, 1988; MA, PhD, Ohio State U., 1992. Prof. Ctrl. State U., Wilberforce, Ohio, 1988-89, Pa. State U., University Park, 1992—; prof., Oren Harris chair in logistics U. Ark. Cons. CLSA, University Park, 1992—; owner, operator Collage, State College, Pa., 1994-96. Author: Evolution, Status and Future of the Corporate Transportation function, 1991; contbr. articles to profl. jours. Mem. Coun. of Logistics Mgmt. (chmn. com. 1997—), Am. Soc. Logistics and Transp., World Conf. on Transport Rsch. (chmn. track com. 1997-98), Alpha Kappa Alpha.

WILLIAMS, LOVIE JEAN, elementary education educator; b. Kinston, N.C., Aug. 28; d. Robert Lee and Effie Mae (Hardy) W. BS, Mill. Coll. Edn., N.Y.C., 1973; MA, Columbia U., 1979, postgrad. Cert. tchr., N.Y. Instr. math. Coll. of New Rochelle, Bronx, N.Y.; tchr., asst. prin., prin. Christ Crusader Acad., N.Y.C.; elem. tchr. math. and sci. N.Y.C. Bd. Edn., Bklyn. Recipient Excellence in Teaching award, Rookie Tchr. award N.Y.C. Bd. Edn. Mem. ASCD, Elem. Sch. Sci. Assn., Math. Edn. through Mid. Grades, Delta Sigma Theta. Office: John Peter Zenger Elem Sch 502 Morris Ave Bronx NY 10451-5549

WILLIAMS, LUVENIA, academic administrator; b. Chgo. children: Dana, Andese White. BA, Roosevelt U., 1970; MA, Chgo. State U., 1980, EdD in Ednl. Leadership, 1999. English coord. Chgo. Bd. Edn.; adminstr. Chgo. (Ill.) Pub. Schs. Home: PO Box 1773 Calumet City IL 60409-7773

WILLIAMS, MARGARET LU WERTHA HIETT, nurse; b. Midland, Tex., Aug. 30, 1938; d. Cotter Craven and Mollie Jo (Tarter) Hiett; m. James Troy Lary, Nov. 16, 1960 (div. Jan. 1963); 1 child, James Cotter; m. Tuck Williams, Aug. 11, 1985. BS, Tex. Woman's U., 1960; MA, Tchrs. Coll., N.Y.C., 1964, EdM, 1974, postgrad., 1981, U. Tex., 1991-92, U. Wis.; cert. completion, U. Wis., Scotland. Cert. clin. nurse specialist, advanced practice nurse, psychiat./mental health nurse, nursing profl. devel., TNCC, PALS, ACLS, ENPC, neonatal resuscitation course. Nurse Midland Meml. Hosp., 1960-63; instr. Odessa (Tex.) Coll., 1963-67; dir. ADNP Laredo (Tex.) Jr. Coll., 1967-70; asst. prof. Pan Am. U., Edinburgh, Tex., 1970-72; rsch. asst. Tchrs. Coll., 1973-74; nursing practitioner St. Luke's Hosp., N.Y.C., 1975-79; sgt. Burns Security, Midland, 1979-81; with Area Builders, Odessa, 1981-83; field supr. We Care Home Health Agy., Midland, 1983-87; clin. educator, supr. Glenwood, A Psychiat. Hosp., Midland, 1987-92; dir. nursing Charter Healthcare Systems, Corpus Christi, Tex., 1992-93; nurse III Brown Sch., San Marcos, Tex., 1993-97; owner MTW Nursing Consultation, Whitney, Tex., 1996—, Margaret Hiett Williams RN, CNS, Whitney, Tex., 1996—; clin. devel. specialist Heritage Health Svcs., L.C., 1997—99; nurse emergency dept. Hill Regional Hosp., Hillsboro, Tex., 1999—. Co-owner, operator MTW Med. Legal Cons.; adj. prof. Pace U., 1974-75, S.W. Tex. State U., 1995; NCLEX reviewer, 1999; content expert ANCC, 2000—; reviewer in field. Mem. Gov. Richards' Exec. Leadership Coun., 1991—95, re-election steering com., 1994. Named to, Ladies 1st of Midland, 1974, Tex. Woman's U. Great 100 Nurses; recipient Isabelle Hampton-Robb award, Nat. League for Nursing, 1976, Achievement award, Cmty. Leaders of Am., 1989. Mem. NAFE, ANA, Tex. Nurses Assn. (pres. dist. 21 1962-65, dist. 32 1970-72), Am. Psychiat. Nurses Assn., Emergency Nurses Assn., Parkland Meml. Hosp. Nurses Alumnae Assn., Tex. Women's U. Alumnae Assn., Midland H.S. Alumni, Bus. and Profl. Women's Club, Mensa, Lockhart Breakfast Lions Club. Democrat. Avocations: songwriting, public speaking, singing, writing. Office: PO Box 2509 Whitney TX 76692-5509 Fax: 254-694-6335. E-mail: mhiettwilliams@hotmail.com.

WILLIAMS, MARSHA RHEA, computer scientist, educator, researcher, consultant; b. Memphis, Aug. 4, 1948; d. James Edward and Velma Lee (Jenkins) W. Cert., Schiller Coll., West Berlin, Germany, 1968; BS in Physics, Beloit Coll., 1969; MS in Physics, U. Mich., 1971; MS in Sys. and Info. Sci., Vanderbilt U., 1976, PhD in Computer Sci., 1982. Cert. data processor. Engring. coop. student Lockheed Missiles & Space Co., Sunnyvale, Calif., 1967-68; asst. transmission engr. Ind. Bell Tel. Co., Indpls., 1971-72; sys. analyst, instr. physics Memphis State U., 1972-74; computer-assisted instrn. project programmer Fisk U., 1974-76; mem. tech. staff Hughes Rsch. Labs., Malibu, Calif., 1976-78; assoc. sys. engr. IBM, Nashville, 1978-80; rsch. and tchg. asst. Vanderbilt U., Nashville, 1980-82, spl. asst. to dean Grad. Sch., spring 1981, minority engr. advisor, 1975-76; cons. computer-assisted instrn. project Meharry Med. Coll., Nashville, summer 1982; assoc. prof. computer sci. Tenn. State U., Nashville, 1982-83, 84-90, full tenured prof., 1990—, univ. marshal, 1992-97. Assoc. prof. U. Miss., Oxford, 1983-84, faculty senator; assoc. program dir. Applications of Advanced Techs. Sci. and Engring. Edn., NSF, 1987-88, apptd. USRA Sci. and Engring. Edn. Coun., Advanced Design Program, 1992-94; cons. on minority scientists and engrs. Univ. Space Rsch. Assn., Washington, 1988; vis. scientist CSNET-Minority Instn. Networking Project Bolt, Beranek & Newman, Cambridge, Mass., 1989; mem. tech. staff Bell Comm. Rsch., Red Bank, N.J., 1990; prin. investigator NSF Computer Sci., Engring. & Math. Scholarships Project, 2002-03; presenter papers profl. meetings. Editor-in-chief newspaper Pilgrim Emanuel Bapt. Ch., 1975-76. Advisr Chi Rho Youth Fellowship, Temple Bapt. Ch., 1975-81, adv. com. Golden Outreach Sr. Citizens Fellowship, 1979-80, 86-87, 89-93, Women's Day spkr., 1979-81, Ebenezer Missionary Bapt. Ch., 1993; adviser Nat. Soc. Black Engring. Students, 1983-84; founder, coord. Tenn. State U. Assn. for Excellence in Computer Sci., Math. and Physics (AE-COMP), 1986-87, coord. Tech. Opportunities Fair, 1986, 87; dir. Tenn. State U. Minorities in Sci., Engring. and Tech. Rsch. Project-MISET, 1989—; child sponsor World Vision, 1981—; mem., newsletter staff Lake Providence Missionary Bapt. Ch. Recipient Disting. Instr. award, 1984, Disting. Svc. citation Beloit Coll. Alumni Assn., 1994; grantee Digital Equipment Corp., 1989-92; rsch. grantee Tenn. State U., 1993, 94, NSF, 2002-03. Mem. AAUP, NAACP (nat. judge ACT-SO sci. olympics 1992), Assn. Computing Machinery, Assn. Info. Tech. Profls. (formerly Data Processing Mgmt. Assn.) (edn. chmn., bd. dirs. 1986), Tenn. Acad. Sci., Am. Assn. of Univ. Profs., Phi Kappa Phi. Achievements include research in developing a formally complete model information/support system (database, network and human-computer interfacing), for minority scientists, especially African American science students, and for providing/locating technical resources for developing countries. Home: PO Box 281946 Nashville TN 37228 Office: PO Box 136 Nashville TN 37203-3401

WILLIAMS, MARTHA ETHELYN, information science educator; b. Chgo., Sept. 21, 1934; d. Harold Milton and Alice Rosemond (Fox) W. BA, Barat Coll., 1955; MA, Loyola U., 1957. With IIT Rsch. Inst., Chgo., 1957-72, mgr. info. scis., 1962-72, mgr. computer search ctr., 1968-72; adj. assoc. prof. sci. info. Ill. Inst. Tech., Chgo., 1965-73, lectr. chemistry dept., 1968-70; rsch. prof. info. sci., coordinated sci. lab. Coll. Engring. U. Ill., Urbana, also dir. info. retrieval rsch. lab., 1972—, prof. info. sci. grad. sch. of libr. info. sci., 1974—, affiliate, computer sci. dept., 1979—. Chair large data base conf. Nat. Acad. Sci./NRC, 1974, mem. ad hoc panel on info. storage and retrieval, 1977, numerical data adv. bd., 1979-82, computer sci. and tech. bd., nat. rsch. network rev. com., 1987-88, chair utility subcom., 1987-88, subcom. promoting access to sci. and tech. data for pub. interest; task force on sci. info. activities NSF, 1977; U.S. rep. review com. for project on broad system of ordering, UNESCO, Hague, Netherlands, 1974; vice-chair Gordon Rshc. Conf. on Sci. Info. Problems in Rsch., 1978, chair, 1980; mem. panel on intellectual property rights in age of electronics and info. U.S. Congress, Office of Tech. Assessment; program chmn. Nat. Online Meeting, 1980-2001; founder, pres. Info. Market Indicators, Inc., 1982-; cons. in field; invited lectr. Commn. European Communities, Industrial R&D adv. com., Brussels, 1992. Editor-in-chief: Computer-Readable Databases Directory and Data Sourcebook, 1976—89, founding editor:, 1989—; editor: Ann. Rev. Info. Sci. and Tech., 1976—2001, Online Rev., 1979—92, Online and CD-ROM Rev., 1993—2000; mem. editl. adv. bd.: Database, 1978—88, mem. editl. bd.: Info. Processing and Mgmt., 1982—89, The Reference Libr., founding editor: Online Info. Rev., 2000—; contbr. articles to profl. jours. Trustee Engirng. Info., Inc., 1974-87, bd. dirs., 1976-91, chmn. bd. dirs., 1982-91, v.p., 1978-79, pres., 1980-81; regent Nat. Libr. Medicine, 1978-82, chmn. bd. regents, 1981; mem. task force on sci. info. activities NSF, 1977-78; mem. nat. adv. com. ACCESS ERIC, 1989-91. Recipient best paper of year award H. W. Wilson Co., 1975; Travel grantee NSF, Luxembourg, 1972, Honolulu, 1973, Tokyo, 1973, Mexico City, 1975, Scotland, 1976 Fellow: AAAS (mem. nominating com. 1983, 1985), Nat. Fedn. Abstracting and Info. Svcs. (hon.), Inst. Info. Scis. (hon.); mem.: NAS (mem. joint com. with NRC on chem. info. 1971—73), Internat. Fedn. for Documentation (U.S. nat. com.), Assn. Sci. Info. Dissemination Ctrs. (v.p. 1971—73, pres. 1975—77), Assn. Computing Machinery (pub. bd. 1972—76), Am. Soc. Info. Sci. (councilor 1971—72, mem. publs. com. 1974—, pres. 1987—88, councilor 1987—89, contbg. editor bull. column 1974—78, Award of Merit 1984, Pioneer Info. Sci. award 1987, Watson Davis award 1995), Am. Chem. Soc. Home: 2134 Sandra Ln Monticello IL 61856-8036 Office: U Ill 1308 W Main St Urbana IL 61801-2307 E-mail: m-will13@uiuc.edu.

WILLIAMS, MARY ELIZABETH, elementary school educator; b. Gary, Ind., Nov. 14, 1943; d. Morris O. and Mary C. (Hall) Douglas; m. Timothy Williams Jr., July 30, 1966; children: Donna M., Brian T., Derrick A. BS, Purdue U., 1965; MS, Ind. U., Gary, 1973, reading endorsement, 1990, lic. adminstr., 1994. Tchr. Hammond (Ind.) Schs., 1965-66, Gary Cmty. Sch., 1966—. Author: Building Public Confidence Through Communication, 1983. Deaconess, Sunday sch. tchr. St. John Bapt. Ch., Gary, 1967—; founder, coord. Boys and Girls Club, 1994-97. Recipient Outstanding Svc. award Kappa Delta Pi, 1991, Svc. award Nobel Sch. PTA, 1993, Adult Vol. Literacy award Gary Pub. Libr., 1991, Women of Distinction award YWCA, 1995. Mem. Am. Fedn. Tchrs., Gary Reading Coun. (sec. 1993, v.p. 1994—, pres. 1995), Ind. State Reading Assn. (mem. family involvement in reading com. 1993-97), N.W. Ind. Alliance Black Sch. Educators, Alpha Kappa Alpha (sec. 1987-90), Afrocentric Curriculum Cadre, Phi Delta Kappa (v.p. Krinon Club 1991). Democrat. Avocations: reading, sewing, cooking, photography, gardening. Home: 8535 Lakewood Ave Gary IN 46403-2250

WILLIAMS, MARY HELEN, elementary education educator; b. Lebanon, Tenn., Nov. 15, 1932; d. Magellan and Willie Neal (Douglass) White; m. Robert Lee Williams, May 16, 1954; children: Desireé Starr Williams Ehimen, Angela Deanetta. BA, Tenn. State U., 1954, MA, 1972, postgrad., 1973-75; grad., Inst. of Children's Lit., 1998. Tchr. Shelby County Sch., Memphis, 1954-55, Nashville Christian Inst., 1958-63, Metro Nashville Schs., 1964-93. Freelance writer, poet. Author: Spellbound, 2002. Recipient Editors Choice award Nat. Libr. Poetry, 1998, Five Yr. Pencil Ptnr. award 1999. Mem. NEA, Tenn. Edn. Assn., Metro Nashville Edn. Assn., Internat. Soc. Poets, Soc. Children's Book Writers, Theta Alpha Psi, Alpha Delta Omega chpt. of Alpha Kappa Alpha (leadership award, Name that Soror award), Phi Delta Kappa (family of educators award 1989, career ladder three assn. Tchr of Yr. award, 1987, Achievement award), Tenn. State Alumni Assn. Democrat. Mem. Ch. of Christ. Avocations: reading, acting, dancing, writing, storytelling. Home: 4373 Enchanted Cir Nashville TN 37218-1822

WILLIAMS, MARY IRENE, business education educator; b. Hugo, Okla., June 30, 1944; d. Primer and Hylar B. (Tarkington) Jackson; m. Lee A. Williams (div. June 1981); 1 child, Monica Ariane. BS in Bus. Edn., Langston U., 1967; MS in Bus., Emporia (Kans.) State U., 1973; EdS, U. Nev., Las Vegas, 1977; D of Bus. Adminstrn. in Internat. Bus., Alliant U., 1992. Instr. Spokane (Wash.) C.C., 1967-70; tchr. bus. Topeka Pub. Schs., 1970-73; prof. C.C. So. Nev., Las Vegas, 1973—, assoc. dean of bus., 1978—92, dean acad. support svcs., 1993—95; prof. bus. adminstrn., asst. to assoc. v.p., asst. coord. bus. Langston U., Tulsa, 1995—97, prof. bus. mgmt. Las Vegas, 1997—; prof. bus./mgmt. C.C. So. Nev., 1997—. Adj. prof. So. Nazarene U., 1996-97; adj. prof. Tulsa Jr. Coll., 1997; owner Williams Mgmt. Tng. and Cons. Co., Las Vegas, 1998—. Author: A Journey Upward, 2003. Named Educator of Yr. Nucleus Plaza Assn., 1985, New Visions, Inc., 1986. Mem. AAUW, Nat. Bus. Edn. Assn., Alpha Kappa Alpha Sorority Avocations: exercising, studying languages, reading. Office: CCSN 6375 W Charleston Blvd W2C Las Vegas NV 89146-1164

WILLIAMS, MAXINE ELEANOR, retired elementary school educator; b. Birmingham, Ala., Nov. 8, 1940; d. Ocie and Annie Bell (McCants) Easter; m. Ardre Dell Williams, Aug. 3, 1968 (div. 1988); children: Andrea Babett, Roxanne Denise, John Ashley. BS, Tuskegee Inst., 1963; MA, Mich. State U., 1970. Elem. tchr. Chester A. Moore Elem. Sch., Ft. Pierce, Fla., 1963-64, R.J. Wallis Elem. Sch., Kincheloe AFB, Mich., 1964-66, Alexander Elem. Sch., Grand Rapids, 1966-67, Brown St. Elem. Sch., Milw., 1967-68, Jefferson T.P.L.L., 1968-78; team leader Twenty First St. Sch., 1978-80; reading tchr. Bryant & Parkview Sch., 1980-81; reading resource tchr. Morse Mid. Sch., 1981-93, Parkman Mid. Sch., 1993—94, ret., 1994. Census ctr. vol. Morse Mid. Sch., 1990. Democrat. Avocation: bible study. Home: 3736 N Humboldt Blvd Apt 4 Milwaukee WI 53212-1766

WILLIAMS, MICHAEL K. agricultural production educator; b. Buffalo, Sept. 11, 1947; s. Walter K. and Della M. (Murphy) W.; m. Donna F. Wissel, Sept. 5, 1969; children: Nathan S., Mandi A. BA, Hastings Coll., 1970. Tchr. Fremont (Nebr.) Pub. Schs., 1972-79; owner Ardeles Greenhouses, Fremont, 1979-86, ECO-Soils Sys. Inc., Lincoln, Nebr., 1986-88; owner, pres. PMC Inc., Fremont, 1989—; state officer Nebr. RC&D, 2001—03; mayor. Mem. devel. and funding staff Camp Calvin Crest, Saunders County, 1983-85; dir. West African Corn Growers Project, USDA, Nebr. and Iowa, 1988-89; mem. North Bend City Couhn., 2000-02, mayor, 2002—; bd. dirs. Nebr. L.E.A.D. Alumni, 2003—. 1st lt. Nebr. N.G., 1969-75. Mem. Nat. Alliance Ind. Crop Cons., Nebr. Ind. Crop Cons. Assn. (bd. dirs. 1992-94, chair polit. com. 1994—), Nebr. Corn Growers Assn., Nebr. Soybean Assn., Loess Hill Resource Conservation Devel. Avocations: travel, reading. Home: 130 E 10th St North Bend NE 68649-4538

WILLIAMS, MINNIE CALDWELL, retired educator; b. Chapel Hill, N.C., Feb. 25, 1917; d. Bruce and Minnie (Stroud) Caldwell; m. Peter Currington Williams Sr., July 25, 1938; children— Peter Jr., Bruce, James, Jacqueline, Charles. B.S. in English, N.C. Central U., 1938, M.A. in Elem. Edn., 1942; postgrad. U. Ill., 1962, U. South Fla., 1965, Fla. State U., 1967. Cert. elem. tchr., N.C.; cert. spl. edn., Fla. Tchr. Weldon pub. schs., N.C., 1940-60, Pinellas County Sch., St. Petersburg, Fla., 1961-80, reading specialist, 1961-80, spl. edn. tchr., 1961-80. Exec. Democratic committeeman, Pinellas County, Fla., 1983-85, local campaign and poll worker; co-chairperson United Way Com; bd. mem. St. Petersburg YWCA. Recipient Ret. Tchrs. award Dixie Hollins High Sch., 1984; Ret. Tchrs. award NAACP, 1980; Panhellenic Service award Greek Orgn., 1980. Mem. Nat. Assn. Ret. Tchrs., Am. Bus. Women Assn., Profl. Bus. Women, Garden Club of St. Petersburg, Delta Sigma Theta (NAACP rep.), Kappa Delta Pi. Baptist. Avocations: Travel; reading; gardening; arts; bowling. Home: 1726 28th Ave S Saint Petersburg FL 33712-3830

WILLIAMS, NATHANIEL, JR., elementary education educator; b. Jacksonville, Fla., June 7, 1940; s. Nathaniel Sr. and Alice Elizabeth (Dusom) W.; m. Carol Ann Odom, Sept. 6, 1969; children: Monica C., Nathaniel Joshua. BS in Chemistry and Math., Bethune-Cookman Coll., Daytona Beach, Fla., 1965; M in Teaching Elem., U. Pitts., 1973. Chemist Pitts. Plate Glass Coating and Resin, Springdale, Pa., 1966-67; ins. agt. Can. Life Assurance Co., Pitts., 1967-70; tutorial tchr. Model Cities Program, Pitts., 1968-69; employment adminstr. South Oakland Citizen Coun., Pitts., 1969-70; substitute tchr. Bd. Edn., Pitts., 1970-72; elem. tchr. Penn Hills (Pa.) Sch. Dist., 1973—. Dir. edn. Pitts. Challenge, Wilkinsburg, Pa., 1974-79; bd. dirs. East End Family Ctr., Pitts., 1982-84; elem. evaluator Pa. Dept. Edn., Harrisburg, 1992—. Editor newsletter Ethnic Minority News, 1989—; coord. sci. program Invent Am., 1993. Ch. trustee, deacon Lincoln Ave. Ch. of God, Pitts., 1980-90, 94, mem. scholarship com., 1990-94. Recipient 1st place Mural award WQED/MacDonald, Pitts., 1992, plaque Ethnic Minority Caucus, Gettysburg, Pa., 1993. Mem. NEA, Pa. State Edn. Assn. (Western region com. chair 1988-94, bd. dirs. 1989-91), Penn Hills Edn. Assn. (com. chair 1983-94). Democrat. Avocations: reading, science projects, plays. Home: 218 Hawkins Ave Braddock PA 15104-2117 Office: Dible Elem Sch 1079 Jefferson Rd Pittsburgh PA 15235-4723

WILLIAMS, NELLIE JAMES BATT, secondary education educator; b. Nashville; d. Ivan C. and Lottie B. (Phillips) James; A.B., Stowe Coll., 1942; MS, U. Ill., 1945; postgrad. Ill. Inst. Tech., 1959, 64, Oberlin Coll., 1965, St. Louis U., 1962, 63, 67, 68, Rockhurst Coll., 1972, Webster Coll., 1984, 85, U. Mass, 1990; m. Napoleon Williams, July 21, 1973 (dec. 1989); 1 child by previous marriage, Charles W. Batt, Jr. Tchr. Sumner High Sch., St. Louis, 1949-54, Handly High Sch., 1954-63; tchr., head mathematics dept. Northwest High Sch., St. Louis, 1963-76; instr., dept. head, Acad. Math. and Sci., St. Louis, 1976-92; instr., head dept. Harris Teacher Coll., Forest Park C.C. Active NAACP, YWCA. NSF grantee, 1959, 62-65, 67, 72. Mem. Math. Club Greater St. Louis, Top Ladies of Distinction, Math. Assn. Am., Assn. Women in Math., Delta Sigma Theta (edn. com.). Methodist. Home: 7584 Amherst Ave Saint Louis MO 63130-2803

WILLIAMS, PAMELA R. elementary school administrator; b. Tacoma, Feb. 9, 1950; d. Richard Bartle and Elaine Staab; m. Raymond L. Williams, 1972. BA in Edn. with distinction, Wash. State U., 1972; MA in Adminstrn., Washington U., St. Louis, 1983. Cert. tchr., Mo., Colo., Calif., adminstr., Colo., Calif. Tchr. Countryside Elem., DeSoto, Kans., 1972-77, U. Chgo. Lab Sch., 1977-78, Francis Parker Sch., Chgo., 1978-80; mid. sch. tchr., coord. English, Mary Inst., St. Louis, 1980-88; elem. bilingual tchr. Boulder (Colo.) Valley Schs., 1988-91, asst. prin, 1991-96, prin., 1996-97, Riverside (Calif.) Unified Pub. Schs., 1997—. Mem. ASCD, Am. Assn. Sch. Adminstrs. (women's caucus), Nat. Assn. Elem. Sch. Prins., Assn. Calif. Sch. Adminstrs., Riverside Assn. Sch. Mgrs., CORO Women in Leadership Alumnae Assn., Phi Delta Kappa. Office: Liberty Elem Sch 9631 Hayes St Riverside CA 92503-3660

WILLIAMS, PATRICIA MARIE, middle school educator, art educator; b. Oak Park, Ill., Jan. 24, 1957; d. Norbert and Carol Estelle (Reum) Brown; m. Howard Glenn Hansen, June 3, 1989. BA in Elem. Edn., Coll. Saint Francis, Joliet, Ill., 1979; M in Natural Scis., Rensselaer Poly. Inst., 2001. Group home counselor St. Joseph's Indian Sch., Chamberlain, S.D., 1980-82; art tchr., 1982-85; 1st grade tchr. Resurrection Elem. Sch., Chgo., 1985-87; asst. sr. recreation supr. Park Dist. of Oak Park, Oak Park, Ill., 1987-90; 6th grade tchr. J.C. Orozco Cmty. Acad., Chgo., 1990-91; 2nd grade tchr. George Leland Sch., Chgo., 1991-94, art and libr. tchr., 1994-96; math tchr. Emerson Mid. Sch., Oak Park, Ill., 1996—; career modular tech. instr. Gwendolyn Brooks Mid. Sch. (formerly Emerson Mid. Sch.), Oak Park, Ill., 2002—. Arts and crafts instr. Playground and Recreation Commn., 1985-87, Park Dist. of Oak Park, 1982-87, River Forest (Ill.) Cmty. Ctr., 1986-87; math. tutor, proctor Triton Coll., River Grove, Ill., 1985-87; pottery instr. Park Dist. of Oak Park, 1991-97, Art Works, Oak Park, 1991-94. Vol. Mus. Sci. and Industry, Chgo., 1991-95, Six County Sr. Olympics, 1994-95, Chgo. Theater, 1993; presenter Young Artists Workshop, Oak Park Sch. Sys., 1994-96. Small grantee, 1991-95, Impact II Tchr. Mentor, 1993, Chgo. Found. for Edn. Mem.: Ill. Computing Educators. Avocations: gardening, creative visual arts, theater, reading, learning. Home: 625 Thomas Ave Forest Park IL 60130-1965 Office: Gwendolyn Brooks Mid Sch 325 S Kenilworth Oak Park IL 60302 E-mail: pwilliams@op97.org.

WILLIAMS, PAUL ALLAN, JR., psychiatric social worker, educator; b. New Orleans, Apr. 12, 1953; s. Paul Allan Williams and Joan Marie (Cangelosi) Wiliams; m. Maxine Lee Cook, Aug. 28, 1999; m. Janice Marie Simonelli, Oct. 29, 1977 (div. July 9, 1991); children: Tisiphonie, Alexandria. MSW, Ind. U., Indpls., 1985; BS, St. Joseph's College, Rensselaer, Ind., 1976; postgrad., Miss. State U., 1976—78; dipl. in clin. social work, 1996. Lic. clin. social worker, cert. nat. cert. gambling counselor II Nat. Coun. Problem Gambling, 2000, clin. alcohol, tobacco & other drug social worker Nat. Assn. Social Workers, 2001, alcohol and drug counselor II Ind. Counselors Assn. on Alcohol and Drug Abuse, internat. cert. alcohol and drug counselor Internat. Cert. and Reciprocity Consortium/Alcohol and Other Drug Abuse, clin. supr. Internat. Cert. and Reciprocity Consortium/Alcohol and Other Drug Abuse; LCSW diplomate NASW, 1996, lic. narriage & family therapist Nat. Assn. Social Workers. Evening-weekend counselor Fairbanks Hosp., Inc., Indpls., 1985—87; addiction program coord.-therapist Cummins Mental Health Ctr., Avon, Ind., 1987—93; pvt. practice Am. Stress & Counseling Ctr., Greenwood, Ind., 1991—92; addiction counselor Koala Hosp. & Counseling Ctrs., Indpls., 1993—94; clinical social worker The Ctr. for Mental Health, Anderson, Ind., 1994—2000; contractual therapist Family Counseling Ctr. Avon, 1992—99; pvt. practice New Choices Kokomo, Ind., 1993; psychiat. social worker Anderson Ctr. St. John's, 2000—. Facilitator sibling group Family Growth Ctr./Midtown Mental Health Ctr., Indpls., 1985—86; pvt. practice Am. Stress and Counseling Ctr., Greenwood, Ind., 1991—92; adj. faculty field lectr. Ind. U. Sch. Social Work, Indpls., 1991—2003, adj. faculty lectr., 1992—95; pvt. practice New Choices Kokomo, Ind., 1993; part -time instr. psychology Ivy Tech State Coll., Indpls., 1999—2000. Mem.: Ind. Counselors Assn. for Alcohol and Drug Abuse (case presentation evaluator 1992—2001, cert. bd. dirs. 1994—2000, 2002—03, chmn. cert. bd. 2003—04). Roman Catholic. Avocations: fly fishing, photography. Office: Anderson Center St John's 2210 Jackson St Anderson IN 46016 Home Fax: 765-778-1847. Personal E-mail: pawmsjr@netusa1.net.

WILLIAMS, PAULA MARIE SHUTER, elementary education educator; b. Portsmouth, Ohio, June 10, 1953; d. Paul Henry and Mary Elizabeth (Carr) Shuter; m. Paul Eugene Williams, Apr. 28, 1979. BS in Edn., Ohio U., 1976; M in Elem. Edn., U. Dayton, 1990. Cert. tchr. elem. edn., Ohio. Subs. tchr. Scioto County Local Schs., Portsmouth, Ohio, 1977, Portsmouth City Schs., 1977; tchr. 3rd grade Minford (Ohio) Local Schs., 1977-91, tchr. 2d grade, 1991—. Rep. career edn. Scioto County Career Edn. Dept., Lucasville, Ohio, 1986—; textbook adoption com. Scioto County Bd. Edn., Portsmouth, 1986; computer software selection com. Minford Local, 1989-90; sec. faculty coun. Minford Primary Faculty Coun., 1992-93. Mem. Alpha Delta Kappa (chaplain 1992-93). Avocations: shopping, singing. Home: 12397 State Route 139 Minford OH 45653-8717 Office: Minford Local Schs Falcon Rd Minford OH 45653

WILLIAMS, PAULINE ELIZABETH, special education educator; b. Spanish Town, Jamaica, Nov. 11, 1949; came to U.S., 1972; d. Limwell and Julia Ann (Thomas) Cranston; m. Boswell Frank Williams, May 18, 1975; children: Boswell Frank Jr., Latesha, Conrad. Student, Church Tchrs. Coll., Mandeville, Jamaica, 1969; BS in Edn., Northeastern U., 1975; MA in Pre-Sch. Handicapped, Chgo. State U., 1983; postgrad., U. Fla., 1990. Cert. English for speaker of other lang. tchr., Fla. Tchr. McAuley's Primary Sch., Jamaica, 1970-72; tchr. spl. edn. Chgo. Bd. Edn., 1975-85; varying exceptional tchr. College Park Elem. Sch., Ocala, Fla., 1985-86, Wyomina Park Elem. Sch., Ocala, 1986-87, Fessenden Elem. Sch., Ocala, 1987—. Dir. Vacation Bible Sch., Silver Springs Shores 7th-day Adventist Ch., Ocala, 1986-94. Tchr. mini-grantee Marion County Pub. Schs. Found., 1990-91. Mem. NEA, Marion Edn. Assn. (bldg. rep.), Fla. Teaching Profession. Avocations: swimming, choir, arts and crafts. Office: Fessenden Elem Sch 4200 NW 90th Ave Ocala FL 34482-1925

WILLIAMS, RANDY G. community relations executive, communication professional; b. Independence, MO, Mar. 15, 1956; s. Harold L. Williams, A. Joan Williams; m. Penny S. Robinson; children: Bradley, Kristen. Bachelor of Science, Mass Communication and Public Relations, Central Missouri State University, Warrensburg, MO, 1974—78; Certificate in Corporate Community Relations, Boston College, Boston, MA, 2000—01. Cmty. rels. dir. American Century Investments, Kansas City, Mo., 1997—2003; comm. specialist Twentieth Century Mutual Funds (now American Century), Kansas City, Mo., 1995—97; sr. media specialist AlliedSignal Inc., Kansas City, Mo., 1988—95; sr. program planner Bendix Corporation, Kansas City, Mo., 1978—88. Chapter President International Association of Business Communicators, Kansas City, MO, 1993—94. Prodr.: (Education curriculum) Tips for Kids, 2000 (IABC Gold Quill Award for Outstanding Community Relations Program, 2000). Charter bd. dirs. Mo. Jump$tart Coalition, 2003; Vice President - Public Relations Jim Eisenreich Foundation for Children with Tourette Syndrome, Kansas City, 1996—2003; mem. bd. dirs. Coterie Theater, Kansas City, 1999—2003; Kansas City Tomorrow Leadership Program Civic Council of Kansas City, Kansas City, MO, 2001—02; Nominating Committee Board Girl Scouts of Mid America, Kansas City, MO, 1999—2001; Scoutmaster Boy Scout Troop 603, Blue Springs, MO, 1997—2000. Mem.: Boston College Center for Corporate Citizenship, International Association of Business Communicators (Chapter President - Kansas City Chapter 1993—94). Methodist. Avocation: Water sports, Camping, SCUBA Diving, Community Service. Office: Am Century Cos 4500 Main St Kansas City MO 64111 Business E-Mail: rgw@americancentury.com.

WILLIAMS, RENEE LYNN, secondary mathematics educator; b. Milw., Dec. 21, 1962; d. Robert William and Myrna Rae (Wolfe) Grove; divorced; 1 child, Lyndee Rae Williams. BA in Math. Edn., Olivet Nazarene U., 1986; MS in Secondary Edn., Purdue U., 1996. Cert. secondary math. educator, Ill. Tchr. math. Bradley-Bourbonnais Cmty. H.S., Bradley, Ill., 1986—; instr. math. Olivet Nazarene U., Kankakee, Ill., 1989; instr. probability and stats. Kankakee (Ill.) C.C., 1990. Math. team head coach Mathletes-Bradley-Bourbonnais Cmty. H.S., 1990—, asst. coach, 1986-90, mem. curriculum and assessment coms., 2000—; tutor in field. Vol. tchr./leader Nazarene Ch., 1986—. Mem. NEA, Nat. Coun. Tchrs. Math., Ill. Coun. Tchrs. Math., Kappa Delta Pi, Phi Eta Sigma. Avocations: poetry, golf, word games, computers. Home: 7222 Alexander Ave Hammond IN 46323-2111 Office: Bradley Bourbonnais Sch 700 W North St Bradley IL 60915-1013

WILLIAMS, RITA CARROLL, language educator, poet; b. Norfolk, Va., Jan. 11, 1962; d. William Henry Carroll Jr. and Joyce Riddick Carroll; m. Stafford Clayton Williams Jr., Dec. 2, 1985; 1 child, Thaddeus Clayton. BA in English, BS in Geology, Elizabeth City State U., 1985. Author: (poetry) Daily Inspirations: Daily Living With God, 2002. Recipient Outstanding Achievement in Poetry award, Famous Poets Soc., 1999, Editor's Choice award, Internat. Libr. Poetry, 1999, 2003. Mem.: NEA, Internat. Soc. Poets, N.C. Assn. Educators. Avocations: writing poetry, stamp collecting, coin collecting, sports card collecting. Home: 1468 Lambs Grove Rd Elizabeth City NC 27909-7502

WILLIAMS, ROBERT CHADWELL, history educator; b. Boston, Oct. 14, 1938; s. Charles Reagan and Dorothy (Chadwell) W.; m. Ann Bennett Kingman, Aug. 27, 1960; children: Peter, Margaret, Katharine. BA, Wesleyan U., 1960; A.M., Harvard U., 1962, PhD, 1966. Asst. prof. history Williams Coll., Williamstown, Mass., 1965-70; prof. history Washington U., St. Louis, 1970-86; dean of faculty, prof. history Davidson Coll., N.C., 1986-98, Vail prof. history, 2000—03. Pres. Central Slavic Conf., 1971-72; v.p. History Assocs. Inc., Gaithersburg, Md., 1980— ; sr. research assoc. St. Antony's Coll., Oxford, 1985. Author: Culture in Exile, 1972, Artists in Revolution, 1976, Russian Art and American Money, 1980 (Pulitzer nominee), The Other Bolsheviks, 1986, Klaus Fuchs, Atom Spy, 1987, Russia Imagined, 1997, Ruling Russian Eurasia, 2000; co-author: Crisis Contained, 1982; mem. editorial bd.: Slavic Rev., 1979-82. Trustee Wesleyan U., 1996-99. Fellow Kennan Inst., 1976-77; fellow Am. Council Learned Socs., 1973-74, W. Wilson Found., 1960-61 Mem. Am. Assn. for Advancement of Slavic Studies, Phi Beta Kappa, Sigma Xi Presbyterian. Office: Davidson Coll Davidson NC 28036 E-mail: bowilliams@davidson.edu.

WILLIAMS, ROBERT JOSEPH, museum director, educator; b. Bennington, Vt., June 21, 1944; s. Joseph and Ruthe Allison (Moody) W. BS in Edn., U. Vt., 1970; MA in Interdisciplinary Social Sci., San Francisco State U., 1981. Tchr. adult edn. Mt. Anthony Union H.S., Bennington, Vt., 1972-74; columnist Bennington Banner, 1972-77; tchr. San Francisco State U., 1976-79; founder, dir. NORRAD Drug Rehab. Ctr., San Francisco, 1986-88; mus. curator Shaftsbury (Vt.) Historical Soc., 1989—. Founder, dir. Bennington Tutorial Ctr., 1971-74. Author: Toward Humanness in Education, 1981, Chalice of Leaves: Selected Essays and Poems, 1988, Modern Salvation: Guidelines from Cosmology, 1994, Gravity from Superstring Displacement, 1999; author: (with others) Intimacy, 1985. Recipient Edmunds Essay medal Vt. Historical Soc., Montpelier, 1961, award of the League of Vt. Writers, 1972, Golden Poet award World of Poetry, Sacramento, Calif., 1990. Democrat. Avocation: cosmology. Home: 102 Putnam St Bennington VT 05201-2348 Office: Shaftsbury Hist Soc PO Box 401 Shaftsbury VT 05262-0401

WILLIAMS, ROGER, academic administrator; Dir. Art Acad. Cin., 1977-94; dean Sch. Visual Arts, Savannah, Ga., 1994-96; acad. dean Ctr. for Creative Studies, Detroit, 1996—. Office: Ctr for Creative Studies 201 E Kirby St Detroit MI 48202-4048

WILLIAMS, RUTH ELIZABETH (BETTY WILLIAMS), retired secondary school educator; b. Newport News, Va., July 31, 1938; d. Lloyd Haynes and Erma Ruth (Goodrich) W. BA, Mary Washington Coll., 1960; cert. d'etudes, Converse Coll., 1961, Lycée Balzac, Tours, France, 1962. Cert. tchr., Va. French tchr. York High Sch., York County Pub. Schs., Yorktown, Va., 1960-65; French resource tchr. Newport News Pub. Schs., 1966-74, tchr. French and photography, 1974-81, tchr. French, Spanish,

German and Latin, 1981-91, ret., 1991; founder, CEO Cresset Elder Care. Pres. Cresset Publs., Williamsburg, Va., 1977—; lectr. Sch. Edn., Coll. Williamand Mary, Williamsburg, 1962-65; French tchr., coord. fgn. langs. York County Pub. Schs., 1962-65; workshop leader dept. pub. instrn. State of Del., Dover, 1965; cons. Health de Rochemont Co., Boston, 1962-71; chmn. faculty senate Dozier Intermediate Sch., Newport News, 1977-79. Driver Meals on Wheels, Williamsburg, 1989-90; contbr. Va. Spl. Olympics, Richmond, 1987—; charter mem. Capitol Soc. Colonial Williamsburg Found., Inc., 1994; mem. Colonial Williamsburg Assembly, Colonial Williamsburg Found., Inc., Chesapeake Bay Found., 1996—, W.A.R. Goodwin Soc., 1996—, Assn. Preservation Va. Antiquities, 1998—, Williamsburg Hist. Records Soc., 1998—, Mortar Bd. Nat. Found., 1998—, Williamsburg Land Conservancy; mem. Altar Guild, Bruton Parish Ch., Williamsburg, 1960—. Grantee Nat. Def. Edn. Act, 1961, 1962. Mem. AAAU, Fgn. Lang. Assn. Va., AARP (ret. tchrs. divsn.), Heritage Soc., Mary Washington Coll. Alumni Assn., Va. Hist. Soc., Am. Assn. Tchrs. French, Mortar Bd., Women in the Arts, Mary Washington Coll. Alumni Assn. (class agt. 1995—), Alpha Phi Sigma, Phi Sigma Iota. Episcopalian. Avocations: photography, coin and stamp collecting, walking, sailing, archaeology and virginia history. Home and Office: Apt D310 3800 Treyburn Dr Williamsburg VA 23185-6422

WILLIAMS, SABRINA ROSE HANCOCK, middle school education educator; b. Columbia, S.C., June 9, 1960; d. James Oscar and Hazel Frances (Phillips) Hancock; m. Keith Douglass Williams, Dec. 15, 1984; 1 child, Kathryn Elizabeth. Bachelors, U. S.C., 1983. Cert. tchr., S.C.; nat. cert. English and lang. arts. Tchr. Richland County Sch. Dist. 1, Columbia, 1984-94; chmn. lang. arts dept. Hand Mid. Sch., Columbia, 1989-93; tchr. Lexington (S.C.) Sch. Dist. 1, 1994—. Dir. Hand Found., 1992-93, dist. curriculum com., 1995—; tchr. cons. Midlands Writing Project, presenter, 1993; presenter dist. insvc., 1992; evaluator APT. Creator Cards of Life. Mem. NEA, Nat. Coun. Tchrs. English, Tchrs. Applying Whole Lang., S.C. Mid. Sch. Assn., Columbia Area Reading Coun., Dead Tchrs. Soc. Episcopalian. Avocations: music, crafts, reading, sewing, cooking. Office: White Knoll Mid Sch 116 White Knoll Way West Columbia SC 29170-3419

WILLIAMS, SANDRA CASTALDO, elementary school educator; b. Rahway, N.J., Sept. 19, 1941; d. Neil and Loretta Margaret (Gleason) Castaldo; m. Arthur Williams III, 1962; children: Arthur IV, Melinda S., Thomas N. Student, Syracuse U., 1959-61; AB, Kean Coll., 1969, MA magna cum laude, 1978. Cert. tchr. K-8, early childhood, N.J. Preschool tchr. St. Andrew's Nursery & Kindergarten, New Providence, N.J., 1973-82; kindergartern tchr. Walnut Ave. Sch. Cranford (N.J.) Sch. Dist., 1978-79; adjunct prof. Farleigh Dickinson Coll., Rutherford, Teaneck, N.J., 1983-86; tchr. 4th grade The Peck Sch., Morristown, N.J., 1986-89; dir. Summit Child Care Ctr., 1990-91; tchr. 1st grade Oak Knoll Sch. of Holy Child Jesus, Summit, N.J., 1992—, tchr. Confraternity of Christian Doctrine, 1995—. Bd. dirs. Summit Child Care Ctr., 1970-71, cons., 1991; cert. instr. Jacki Soresen Aerobic Dancing, Inc., Summit, 1990, Westfield, 1992-95. Co-chair United Way, Summit, 1991; Eucharistic min. St. Teresa's Ch., Summit, 1994—. Mem. ASCD, Internat. Reading Assn., Phi Kappa Phi, Alpha Sigma Lambda, Kappa Kappa Gamma. Republican. Roman Catholic. Avocations: needle work, gardening, church, physical fitness. Home: 8 Sunset Dr Summit NJ 07901-2323 Office: Oak Knoll Sch Holy Child Jesus 44 Blackburn Rd Summit NJ 07901-2499

WILLIAMS, SHARRON ELAINE, gifted education specialist, legal consultant; b. Cin., July 6, 1951; d. Robert and Mary (Smith) Sawyer; 1 child, Wesley. BS, Kent State U., 1973; MS, Cleve. State U., 1988; JD, U. Akron, 1979. Tchr. Akron (Ohio) Pub. Schs., 1973-79; bus. law instr. Lorain (Ohio) Cmty. Coll., 1980; law clk. Roberty Sawyer, Cleve., 1981; gifted edn. tchr. Cleveland Heights (Ohio) Schs., 1983-88; resource tchr. Coventry Sch., Cleve., 1989-90; gifted edn. specialist Shaker Heights (Ohio) Schs., 1991—. Workshop coord. Cleve. Alliance of Educators, 1994; Gestalt trainer Cleveland Heights Schs., 1990; instr. Gov.'s Summer Inst., Cleve., 1989; presenter in field. Contbg. author: Windows of Opportunity, 1994 (Nat. Coun. Tchrs. Math. award 1994). Recipient grant Marth Holden Jennings Found., 1979, grant Shaker Heights Schs., 1994. Mem. Nat. Coun. Tchrs. Math., Nat. Alliance of Black Educators, Heights Alliance of Black Educators, Delta Sigma Theta, Phi Delta Kappa (svc. coord. 1991—), Phi Alpha Delta. Avocations: foreign travel, decorating. Office: Shaker Heights City Schs 17917 Lomond Blvd Shaker Heights OH 44122

WILLIAMS, SHIRLEY J. daycare provider, educator, writer; b. Kansas City, Kans., Feb. 18, 1931; d. Anna Mae Oostebroek; d. James Ralph and Florence (Snodgrass) Akers; m. Raymond Gale Williams, Feb. 17, 1949 (dec. 2000); children: David Ray, James Ronald, Vickie Sue, Richard Gene, Randy Wayne. Tchr., owner Su-Z-Lu Ceramics, Kansas City, 1957—70; sch. bus. driver Argentine Transit Lines, Kansas City, 1959-69; ceramic tchr., owner Su-Z-Lu Ceramics, Tonganoxie, Kans., 1972-78; tchr. Ft. Leavenworth Army Post, Leavenworth, Kans., 1979-85; pres. Wagonettes Extension Homemakers Club, Forsyth, Mo., 1987-88; ceramic tchr. Crystal's Creations and Ceramic Shop, Drexel, Mo., 1995-96; owner Classic Ceramics Studio, Drexel, Mo., 1996-2001. Day-care provider for the elderly, 1990-93; founder, head Drexel Ceramic Show, 1996-2001. Weekly columnist Wyandotte West and Piper newspapers; contbr. articles to Popular Ceramics Trade Mag. Den mother Boy Scouts Am., Kansas City and Tonganoxie, 1955-66, instr., 1961; driver ARC, Kansas City, 1958-63, canteen chmn., campfire leader, 1961-64; contbr. Taney County Rep. newspaper, Forsyth, 1986-87, bd. dirs., 1987-91; mem. Univ.-Extension Coun. bd., 1988-91; vol., supt. ceramic divsn. Leavenworth County Fair, 1974-84; vol. tchr. Kester Found., 1956-57; program chmn. Sr. Citizen's Group of Drexel, Mo., 1996-97; pres. Drexel (Mo.) Sr. Citizens Assn., 1998-2000. Recipient 4-H Gold Clover, Taney County 4-H, 1987. Democrat. Avocations: photography, miniatures, crafts, short stories, ceramics. Home: 7461 Edgehill Ave Kansas City KS 66111

WILLIAMS, SONIA KAY, retired secondary school educator; b. Duluth, Minn., Jan. 13, 1939; d. Allen Parke and Ruth Adelaide (Mitchell) Swayne; m. William Fedrick Williams, Mar. 26, 1960; children: Keith Douglass, Jennifer Gay. BMus, U. Tenn., Chattanooga, 1960; M in Secondary Tchg. of English, Statesboro U., 1975; edn. specialist, Valdosta State U., 1988. Tchr. North Chattanooga Jr. H.S., 1960-61; music tchr. Savannah (Ga.) Country Day Sch., 1968-72; English tchr. Appling County Jr. H.S., Baxley, Ga., 1972-74, Appling County Comprehensive H.S., Baxley, 1974—2001; ret., 2001. Accompanist Appling Applause, Baxley, 1978-92; drama tchr. Appling County H.S., 1990-92. Prodr. videotape Sonia's Signya's, 1991. Bd. dirs., Sunday sch. tchr. First United Meth. Ch., Baxley, 1980-94; pres. Friends of Libr., Baxley, 1990-92; charter mem. Appling Hist. Soc., Baxley, 1980—, bd. dirs., 1992-94; mem. Appling Heritage Com., Baxley, 1992-94; vol. ARC, Am. Cancer Soc., So. Care Hosp. Named Star Tchr., Appling County C. of C., 1984. Mem. Nat. Coun. Tchrs. English, Appling County Assn. (pres. 1972-94), Ga. Assn. Educators (instrnl. and profl. devel. com. 1992-97, Dist. Tchr. of Yr. 1997-98), Delta Kappa Gamma (pres. 1997-99). Avocations: reading, writing, swimming, tennis, drama. Home: 177 Torrance Rd Baxley GA 31513-6726

WILLIAMS, SUSAN DIANE, language educator; b. Amsterdam, N.Y., Apr. 19, 1952; d. James Bernard and Edith Marie Martin. BA, Skidmore Coll, 1974; MS in Edn., Coll. St. Rose, Albany, N.Y., 1980; Diplôme Approfondi Langue Française, U. Franche Comte, Besancon, France, 1996; Diplôme Supérieur Etudes Françaises, CLA, U.Franche-Comté, 1996. Cert. foreign lang. tchr. N.Y., spl. edn. tchr. N.Y., elem. tchr. N.Y. French tchr. Greater Johnstown (N.Y.) Sch. Dist., 1977, North Colonie Ctrl. Shaker Sr. H.S., Newtonville, NY, 1978—79; spl. edn. lang. workshop specialist Greater Johnstown (N.Y.) Sch. Dist., 1979—81; spl. edn. tchr. Saratoga Springs (N.Y.) City Sch., 1981—87, French tchr., 1987—; Fulbright exch. tchr. Lycée François Rabelais, Dugny, France, 1994. Group leader student fgn. exchg. Rotary Exchg., Saratoga Springs, 1994—2001; Fulbright exchange tchr., Dugny, France, 1994. Ednl. advisor Congl. Youth Leadership Coun., Washington, 1999—; dist. committeeman Rep. Party, Saratoga Springs, 1979—90. Mem.: N.Y. State Assn. Fgn. Lang. Tchrs., Am. Assn. Tchrs. French (sec.-treas. 1998—). Avocations: travel, equestrian sports. Office: Saratoga Springs HS 186 West Ave Saratoga Springs NY 12866

WILLIAMS, SYLVESTER EMANUAL, III, secondary school educator, consultant; b. Chgo., Feb. 4, 1937; s. Sylvester Emanual and Carita (Brown) W.; children: Sylvia, Sylvester, Sydnee, Steven. BS, No. Ill. U., 1958; MA, Chgo. State U., 1968; PhD, U. S.C., 1992. Cert. tchr., S.C., N.C., Ill. From asst. to supt. Washington D.C. Pub. Schs., 1968-69; tchr. Chgo. Pub. Schs., 1958-68; program officer Dept. Edn., Washington, 1971-86; prof. Lander U., Greenwood, S.C., 1986-89, U. S.C., Akin, 1990-91; tchr., coach Charlotte (N.C.) Mecklenburg Pub. Schs., 1992-93; edn. devel. cons. South Shore Cmty. Ch., Chgo.; rsch. assoc. Houston Ctr., Clemson U., 1999-2000; devel. cons. Rose Garden Cmty. Svcs., Chgo., 1999-2000; cons. DHHS, 1994-2000; demographic rschr., 1992—. Bd. dirs. John de Home Sch., McCormick, S.C. Mem. Phi Delta Kappa. Republican. Baptist. Avocation: motion picture production. Home: 205 Briggs Ave Greenwood SC 29649-1603 E-mail: drsewiii@greenwood.net.

WILLIAMS, TED VAUGHNELL, physical education educator; b. Bronx, N.Y., Apr. 1, 1952; s. Joseph Alexander and Annie (Canady) W. BS, Springfield Coll., 1977. Cert. tchr., N.Y. Substitute tchr. Valhalla (N.Y.) High Sch., 1977; tchr. aide for handicapped children, tchr. spl. edn. Rye Lake Campus, Valhalla, 1978; supr. recreation activities Springfield (Mass.) Girl's Club Family Ctr., 1979; assoc. dir. boy's and men's phys. edn. dept. Trenton YMCA, 1979—; house supr. Cardinal McCloskey's Group Home, Tappan, N.Y., 1980-81; phys. edn. tchr. Our Lady of Refuge Sch., Bronx, N.Y., 1982-83; tchr. phys. edn. various Cath. elem. schs. Yonkers, N.Y., 1983—. With ops. dept. Hudson Valley Nat. Bank, 1990-92. Active Walk Am. for Healthier Babies, March of Dimes, 1990-93. Recipient Ed Steitz award Basketball Hall of Fame, 1975, Capitol award Nat. Leadership Coun., 1991; named to Wall of Tolerance, Civil Rights Meml. Ctr., Montgomery, Ala. Mem. ASCD, AAHPERD, Am. Assn. Leisure and Recreation, Hudson Valley Leisure Svcs. Assn. Democrat. Baptist. Home: 49 Bradford Ave White Plains NY 10603-2143

WILLIAMS, THEODORE JOSEPH, engineering educator; b. Black Lick, Pa., Sept. 2, 1923; s. Theodore Finley and Mary Ellen (Shields) W.; m. Isabel Annette McAnulty, July 18, 1946; children: Theodore Joseph, Mary Margaret, Charles Augustus, Elizabeth Ann. BSCh.E., Pa. State U., 1949, MSCh.E., 1950, PhD, 1955; MS in Elec. Engring., Ohio State U., 1956. Research fellow Pa. State U., University Park, 1947-51; asst. prof. Air Force Inst. Tech., 1953-56; technologist Monsanto Co., 1956-57, sr. engring. supr., 1957-65; prof. engring. Purdue U., Lafayette, Ind., 1965-94, prof. emeritus, 1995—, dir. control and info. systems lab., 1965-66; dir. Purdue Lab. Applied Indsl. Control, 1966-94, dir. emeritus, 1995—; cons., 1964—. Vis. prof. Washington U., St. Louis, 1962-65. Author: Systems Engineering for the Process Industries, 1961, Automatic Control of Chemical and Petroleum Processes, 1961, Progress in Direct Digital Control, 1969, Interfaces with the Process Control Computer, 1971, Modeling and Control of Kraft Production Systems, 1975, Modelling, Estimation and Control of the Soaking Pit, 1983, The Use of Digital Computers in Process Control, 1983, Analysis and Design of Hierarchical Control Systems - With Special Reference to Steel Plant Operations, 1985, A Reference Model for Computer Integrated Manufacturing (CIM) - A Description from the Viewpoint of Industrial Automation, 1989, The Purdue Enterprise Reference Architecture, 1992; editor: Computer Applications in Shipping and Shipbuilding, 6 vols., 1973-79, Proceedings Advanced Control Confs., 19 vols., 1974-93, Architectures for Enterprise Integration, 1996. Served to 1st lt. USAAF, 1942-45; to capt. USAF, 1951-56. Decorated Air medal with 2 oak leaf clusters. Fellow AAAS, AIChE, Instrument Soc. Am. (hon. mem., pres. 1968-69, Albert F. Sperry gold medal 1990, Lifetime Achievement award 1995), Am. Inst. Chemists, Inst. Measurement and Control (London, Sr. Harold Hartley silver medal 1975), Indsl. Computing Soc.; mem. IEEE (sr.), Internat. Fedn. for Info. Processing (Silver Core award 1978), Soc. for Computer Simulation (hon.), Am. Chem. Soc., Am. Automatic Control Coun. (pres. 1965-67), Am. Fedn. Info. Processing Socs. (pres. 1976-78), Sigma Xi, Tau Beta Pi, Phi Kappa Phi, Phi Lambda Upsilon. Home: 208 Chippewa St West Lafayette IN 47906-2123 Office: Purdue U Potter Rsch Ctr Inst Interdisciplinary Engring Studies West Lafayette IN 47907-1293 E-mail: tjwil@ecn.purdue.edu.

WILLIAMS, THOMAS RHYS, anthropologist, educator; b. Martins Ferry, Ohio, June 13, 1928; m. Margaret Martin, July 12, 1952; children: Rhys M., Ian T., Tom R. BA, Miami U., Oxford, Ohio, 1951; MA, U. Ariz., 1956; PhD, Syracuse U., 1956. Asst. prof., asso. prof. anthropology Calif. State U., Sacramento, 1956-65; vis. asso. prof. anthropology U. Calif. Berkeley, 1962; vis. prof. anthropology Stanford U., 1976; prof. anthropology Ohio State U., Columbus, 1965-78, chmn. dept, 1967-71, mem. grad. council, 1969-72, mem. univ. athletic council, 1968-74, chmn. univ. athletic council, 1973-74, exec. com. Coll. Social and Behavior Scis., 1967-71; dean Grad. Sch. George Mason U., Fairfax, Va., 1978-81, prof. anthropology, 1981—, dir. Ctr. for Rsch. and Advanced Studies, 1978-81, fed. liaison officer, 1978-81, chmn. faculty adv. bd. grad. degree program in conflict resolution, 1980-86. Author: The Dusun: A North Borneo Society, 1965, Field Methods in the Study of Culture, 1967, A Borneo Childhood: Enculturation in Dusun Society, 1969, Introduction to Socialization: Human Culture Transmitted, 1972, Socialization, 1983, Cultural Anthropology, 1990; editor, contbg. author: Psychological Anthropology, 1975, Socialization and Communication in Primary Groups, 1975; contbr. articles to profl. jours. Mem. United Democrats for Humphrey, 1968, Citizens for Humphrey, 1968. Served with USN, 1946-48. Research grantee NSF, 1958, 62, Am. Council Learned Socs.-Social Sci. Research Council, 1959, 63; Ford Found. S.E. Asia, 1974, 76; recipient Disting. Faculty award Calif. State U., Sacramento, 1961, George Mason U., 1983; Disting. Teaching awards Ohio State U., 1968, 76 Fellow Am. Anthrop. Assn., Royal Anthrop. Inst. Gt. Britain; assoc. mem. Current Anthropology; mem. AAAS, Sigma Xi. Office: George Mason U Robinson Hall B-315 4400 University Dr Fairfax VA 22030-4444

WILLIAMS, TRUDY ANNE, English language educator, college administrator; b. Winnipeg, Man., Can., Mar. 4, 1946; d. Herbert Francis and Melita French (Russell) Sly; m. Harry G. Williams, June 17, 1980; 1 child, David Langdon Jr. BA, U. Southwestern La., 1969, MA, 1970. Teaching asst. U. Southwestern La., Lafayette, 1968-72; instr. Gaston Coll., Dallas, N.C., 1980-83; asst. prof. English, St. Petersburg (Fla.) Jr. Coll., 1983—, also acting program dir., comm., program dir. acad. svcs. Adj. prof., cons. St. James Sch. Theology, Tarpon Springs, Fla., 1992—. Founding mem. Episcopal Synod of Am.; dir. Christian edn. St. Anne of Grace Episcopal Ch., Seminole, Fla. Mem. MLA, Nat. Coun. Tchrs. English, Southeastern Conf. on English in 2-Yr. Colls., Fla. Assn. Community Colls., Fla. Devel. Edn. Assn., Fla. Coll. English Assn., Pinellas County Tchrs. of English, South Atlantic Modern Lang. Assn., Fla. Coun. Instructional Affairs. Home: 8021 Bayhaven Dr Largo FL 33776-3320

WILLIAMS, VERNON J., JR., historian, educator, writer; b. Marshall, Tex., Apr. 25, 1948; s. Vernon J. Sr. and Vella D. (Roland) W.; children: Vella L., Alexander M. BA in History, U. Tex., 1969; AM in Am. Civilization, Brown U., 1973, PhD in Am. Civilization, 1977. Instr. U. R.I., Kingstown, 1978; lectr. Clark U., Worcester, Mass., 1978-79; editor Edit, Inc., Chgo., 1979-80; assoc. history dept. Northwestern U., Evanston, Ill., 1979-84; lectr. Elmhurst Coll., Chgo., 1981-82; asst. prof. U. Iowa, Iowa City, 1985, R.I. Coll., Providence, 1985-90; lectr. Boston U., 1989-90; assoc. prof. Purdue U., West Lafayette, Ind., 1990-97, prof., 1997—. Rsch. assoc. William Monroe Trotter Inst., Boston, 1987, Boston U., 1989; archives cons. Boston Anthenaeum, 1989; cons. Henry Rasof Lit. Agy., Boston, 1989-90; participant, NEH summer seminar for coll. tchrs., 1989. Author: From a Caste to a Minority, 1989, Race and Class in American Race Relations Theory, 1989, Rethinking Race, 1996; editor New England Jour. Black Studies, 1990-92; mem. editl. bd. Western Jour. Black Studies, 1998—, Jour. African Am. Studies, 2003—; contbg. editor, Transforming Anthropology, 2002—; mem. publ. commn. Nat. Coun. Black Studies, 1997-99. ACLS grantee, 1990; Clio grantee Ind. Hist. Soc., 1994, travel grantee AAAS anthropology sect., 1998. Mem. Orgn. Am. Historians, So. Hist. Assn., Afro-Am. Hist. Assn., Am. Anthrop. Assn., Assn. Black Anthropologists, Am. Sociol. Assn. Avocation: jazz collector. Office: Purdue Univ Dept History Lafayette IN 47907

WILLIAMS, VICKIE GLYN, elementary and special education educator, administrator; b. Dallas, June 2, 1954; d. Kenneth Earl and Gloria Ethelyn (McDonald) Parker; m. Jerry Roger Williams, July 22, 1978. BA, U. Tex., San Antonio, 1985. Cert. tchr. spl. edn., Tex. Sec. Great Am. Reserve Ins. Co., Dallas, 1972-76; adminstrv. asst. Vanguard Travel, Dallas, 1976-79; sec., treas. Am. Internat. Rent-A-Car Corp., Dallas, 1979-85; adminstr., tchr. Vestal Elem. Sch., San Antonio, 1985-94; tchr. Canyon Middle Sch., New Braunfels, Tex., 1994—. Recipient Trinity Excellence in Teaching award Luby's Corp., 1991, Presidential Excellence in Sci. award 1992. Mem. Nat. Sci. Tchr. Assn., Young Astronaut Coun., Tex. Coun. Elem. Sci. Tchrs., Assn. Tex. Profl. Educators (campus rep.). Republican. Baptist. Avocations: aerobics, volleyball, tennis, river activities, raising cocker spaniels. Office: Canyon Middle Sch FM 1101 New Braunfels TX 78130

WILLIAMS, VIDA VERONICA, guidance counselor; b. Charleston, S.C., May 4, 1956; d. Timothy and Dotlee (Pendarvis) W. BA, Fisk U., 1978; MS in Edn., Queens Coll., 1986, postgrad., 1994-95, profl. diploma in adminstrn./supervision, 2001. Cert. sch. counselor, spl. edn. tchr., N.Y. Job counselor Trident Work Experience, Charleston, 1980; spl. edn. tchr. Jr. High Sch. 158, Bayside, N.Y., 1983-86, Pub. Sch. 214, Bklyn., 1986-90; guidance counselor I.S. 171, 364, Pub. Sch. 214, Bklyn., 1990-95, I.S. 302, Bklyn., 1995—; dir. Springfield Garden Meth. After Sch. Tutorial Program, Jamaica, N.Y. Co-dir. I.S. 302 Gospel Chorus, 1994-95; counselor Dist. 19 Bereavement, Bklyn., 1991-95; bd. dirs. Alpha Kappa Alpha Day Care Ctr., St. Albans, N.Y., 1992-94; dir. Springfield Gardens Meml. Ch. After-Sch. Tutorial Program, 1997-98. Vol. Voter Registration, Jamaica, 1992, Increase the Peace Corps, N.Y.C., 1992, Feeding of 5,000, Jamaica, 1993, Victim Svcs., Bklyn., 1994-95; chair activities Harlem Dowling Foster Care, Jamaica, N.Y., 1995; active Allen A.M.E. Ch. Gospel Choir, 1994-95, Voices of Victory, 1994-95. Named one of Outstanding Young Women Am., 1980. Mem. Alpha Kappa Alpha. Avocations: reading, singing, sewing, arts and crafts. Home: 11240 205th St Jamaica NY 11412-2214 Office: Gifted and Talented Acad IS 59 132-55 Ridgedale St Springfield Gardens NY 11413 E-mail: wvida@aol.com.

WILLIAMS, VIVIAN LEWIE, retired counseling administrator; b. Columbia, SC, Jan. 23, 1923; d. Lemuel Arthur Sr. and Ophelia V. (McDaniel) Lewie; m. Charles Warren Williams, Apr. 4, 1947 (div. 1967); children: Pamela Ann Williams-Coote, Charles Warren Jr. (dec.). BA, Allen U., 1942; MA in Psychology, U. Mich., 1946, postgrad., 1946, 48; MS, U. So. Calif., 1971, postgrad., 1971-72. Cert. marriage and family therapist, Calif.; cert. Calif. C.C. counselor. Asst. prof. psychology Tenn. State Agrl. and Indsl. U., Nashville, 1946-47; asst. prof. edn. Winston-Salem (N.C.) State U., 1947-50; asst. prof. edn., dir. tchr. edn. Allen U., Columbia, SC, 1951-53; specialist reading, coord. lang. arts Charlotte (N.C.) Mecklenburg Schs., 1963-67, cons. comprehensive sch. improvement project, 1967-69; asst. prof. edn., psychology Johnson C. Smith U., Charlotte, 1967-69; counselor, team leader Centennial, U. So. Calif. Tchr. Corps, L.A., 1970-73; counselor Compton (Calif.) C.C., 1973—2003, adv. fgn. student, 1975-85; ret., 2003. Co-developer Hyde Park Estates and The Moors, Charlotte, N.C., 1960-63. Pres. bd. dirs. Charlotte Day Nursery, 1956-59; bd. dirs. Taylor St. USO, Columbia, S.C., 1951-53; sec. southwest region Nat. Alliance Family Life, 1973-74; sec. bd. dirs. NCCJ, Charlotte, 1959-62. Recipient Faculty Audit Program award Ford/Carnegie Found., Harvard U., Cambridge, Mass., 1968, Pub. Svc. Achievement award WSOC Broadcasting Co.; fellow U. Mich., 1946. Mem. NAACP (life, Golden Heritage mem. 1992), AAUW (life), NEA (life), Am. Fedn. Tchrs., Faculty Assn. Calif. C.C., Nat. Acad. Counselors and Family Therapists (life, clin. mem., pres. S.W. region 1989), C.C. Counselors Assn., The Links, Inc. (Harbor area chpt. historian 1985-87, chaplain 1990-94, 96-98), Jack and Jill Am. (charter mem., organizer Charlotte chpt., pres. 1954-56), Women on Target, Calif. Tchrs. Assn., Delta Sigma Theta, Alpha Gamma Sigma (Golden Apple award 1981). Democrat. Methodist. Avocations: sewing, crafts, photography. Home: 6621 Caro St Paramount CA 90723-4755

WILLIAMS, WILLIAM EARLE, artist, educator, curator; b. Vicksburg, Miss., Apr. 19, 1950; s. Willie and Estella (Steele) W.; m. Mary Katherine Meermans, Aug. 19, 1978; children: Emily Katherine, Daniel Earle. BA, Hamilton Coll., Clinton, N.Y., 1973; MFA, Yale U., 1978. Prof. art Haverford (Pa.) Coll. Author: Party Pictures, 1985; author, editor: Photographers of Sculpture, 1988; editor: Japanese Wood Block Prints, 1987, Gettysburg: Journey in Time, 1997; one-man shows include Cleve. Mus. of Art, 1990, South East Mus., 2001, Bryn Mawr Coll., 2002, exhibited in group shows at Allentown Mus. Art, 1995, Pa. Acad. Fine Arts, 1984, Bardini Mus., Florence, Italy, 1990, Phila. Mus. Art, 2000, Represented in permanent collections, Met. Mus. Art, others. Fellow in photography, Pa. Coun. on the Arts, 1986, 1997, 2002, Pew fellow, 1997, Guggenheim fellow, 2003. Mem.: Soc. Photog. Edn. (bd. dirs. 1996—2003, vice chair 2000, treas. 2001), Phila. Athenaeum, Franklin Inn Club. Avocations: running, bicycling, walking. Home: 753 College Ave Haverford PA 19041-1301 Office: Haverford Coll 370 Lancaster Ave Haverford PA 19041-1336

WILLIAMS, WILLIAM MAGAVERN, headmaster; b. Niles, Mich., Dec. 22, 1931; s. Errol Edwin and Mary Elizabeth (Magavern) W.; m. Linda Carol Grush, June 15, 1958; children: Diana, William Jr., Sarah. BA, Williams Coll., 1953, LHD (hon.), 1984; postgrad. in Philosophy, Columbia U., 1954-58, MA in Ednl. Psychology, 1966. Tchr. elem. English, history, phys. edn. McTernan Sch., Waterbury, Conn., 1953-54; head guidance, boarding, and humanities depts., instr. English, coach varsity wrestling Riverdale Country Sch., Bronx, N.Y., 1955-66; headmaster Doane Acad., Burlington, N.J., 1966-70, Poly. Prep. Country Day Sch., Bklyn., 1970-00, headmaster emeritus, 2000—. Trustee Bklyn Inst. Arts and Scis., 1972-79, Bklyn. Ctrl. YMCA, 1974-78, Profl. Children's Sch., 1976-79, Bklyn. Children's Mus., 1979-82, Plymouth Ch. Pilgrims, 1979-86, N.Y. State Assn. Ind. Schs., 1980-86; chmn. bd. dirs. Stafford (Vt.) Sch., 2002-03. Mem. Headmasters' Assn., Country Day Sch. Headmasters' Assn. (v.p. 1998-99, pres. 1999-2000), Cum Laude Soc. (regent dist. III 1971-87, dep. pres. gen. 1981-87, pres. gen. 1987-96, regent-at-large 1996—), Guild Ind. Schs. N.Y. (pres. 1986-88). Avocations: sailing, skiing, chess, travel, civil war history. Home: PO Box 26 232 Justin Morrill Mem Hwy Strafford VT 05072-9730

WILLIAMS-MONEGAIN, LOUISE JOEL, retired science educator, ethnographer; b. Chgo., June 13, 1941; d. Sylvester Emanuel Jr. and Carita Bell (Brown) Williams; m. Martin Monegain, Aug. 19, 1961; children: Michael Martin, Martin Marion II. BS, Shaw U., 1975; JD, Antioch Sch. of Law, Washington, 1979; cert. adminstrn., Roosevelt U., 1988; PhD, U. Ill., 1994. Tchr. Chgo. Archdiocese, 1968-73; assoc. dir. pub. affairs Warren Regional Planning Commn., Soul City, N.C., 1973-74; comm. specialist Coun. of the Great City Schs., Washington, 1974-76; lawyer Equal Employment Opportunity Commn., Washington, 1979-80; tchr. Olive

Harvey City Coll., Chgo., 1981-83; mgr. Joy Travel Agt., Chgo., 1981-83; owner, pres. MJS Your Travel Agt., Chgo., 1983-86; sci. tchr. Chgo. Pub. Schs., 1986-91; program leader, evaluator Argonne (Ill.) Nat. Lab., 1991-97; ethnographer Sch. Edn. and Sch. Policy Northwestern U., Evanston, Ill., 1997-98; pres. Monegain & Assocs. Program leader, evaluation rep. Nat. Cancer Program, Accra and Kamasi, Ghana, West Africa, 1995. Vol. Art Inst., Chgo., 1994; green team adv. bd. Lincoln Park Zool. Soc., Chgo., 1992—. Scholarship State of Ill., 1987. Mem. ASCD, Am. Edn. Rsch. Assn., Nat. Sci. Tchrs. Assn., Assn. for Coll. and Univ. Women, Phi Delta Kappa. Avocations: attending opera, dance performances, plays, galleries, swimming, traveling.

WILLIAMSON, CHRISTINE WILDER, preschool specialist, educational consultant, small business owner; b. Sylvester, Ga., Jan. 1, 1929; d. Thomas Herman and Irene (Beverly) Wilder; m. James Bryant Williamson, Aug. 10, 1947; children: James Robert, Joseph Nathan, Janet Marie. BS, Tift Coll., Forsyth, Ga., 1972; MEd, Mercer U., 1973; D Ministry, Luther Rice Sem., Jacksonville, Fla., 1983. Tchr. Houston County Bd. Edn., Warner Robins, Ga., 1947-50, Kathleen Pape Kindergarten, Macon, Ga., 1963-66, Vineville Bapt. Kindergarten, Macon, 1966-71; elem. dir. Vineville Bapt. Ch., 1971-80; presch. specialist, cons. Ga. Bapt. and So. Bapt. Conv., 1970—. Instr. Macon Tech. Inst., 1980-85; owner, founder Splendid Difference Ent., 1990—. Author: I Can Do It Myself, 1983, Creative Art Activities for Children, 1991. Fund raiser Ga. Cancer Assn., Macon, 1970-88; dir. Mission Friends, Macon Bapt. Women's Missionary Union, 1989—; dir. Royal Ambassadors. Mem. Nat. Assn. Edn. Young Children, So. Assn. Children under Six, Ga. Assn. Young Children, Ga. Presch. Assn. (pres. 1984-86, chaplain 1990—), Bibb County Presch. Assn. (pres. 1975-77, chaplain, treas. 1988—), MADD. Democrat. Avocations: walking, aerobics, watching sports events, travel, reading. Home and Office: 577 Old Lundy Rd Macon GA 31210-4305

WILLIAMSON, DEBRA FAYE, performing arts educator; b. Longview, Wash., Apr. 15, 1953; d. Harvey Homer and LoEtta (Crumb) Yaden; m. Bruce Laird Williamson, June 10, 1977; children: Amber Marie, John Lee, David Andrew. BA, St. Martin's Coll., 1975. Dance tchr. Tugaw Sch. Dance, Longview, 1971-73; tchr. secondary edn. Kelso (Wash.) Sch. Dist., 1975—; tchr. Huntington Jr. High. Owner, tchr. Performing Arts Acad., Longview, 1980—; nat. judge, master tchr. Spotlight Dance Events. Choreographer The Student Prince, 1971, 1776, 1976. Named Top Choreographer Dupree Enterprises, 1995-2002. Mem. Dance Masters Am. (bd. dirs. 1983-89, sec.-treas. 1983-88). Republican. Methodist. Avocations: reading, travel, gardening. Office: Performing Arts Acad 1215 1/2 Commerce Ave Longview WA 98632-3026

WILLIAMSON, DOROTHY JUNE, art consultant, artist, educator, writer; b. Mpls., June 13, 1929; d. Louis William and Hazel Irene (Johnson) W. BA, Asbury Coll., 1951; MA, U. Minn., 1963, postgrad., 1969-71. Cert. edn. Art tchr. Hopkins Pub. Schs., Minn., 1952-53; art cons. Owatonna Pub. Schs., Minn., 1953-54; art tchr. Richfield Pub. Schs., Mpls., 1954-86; art educator, fine arts educator, lectr. Augsburg Coll., Mpls., 1970-91; art cons. Mpls., 1990—. Mem. com. art edn. Mpls. Soc. Fine Art, 1956; grants reader, evaluator U.S. Office of Edn., Washington, 1969—70; sole art del. U.S. Office of Edn.-Ednl. Profl. Devel. Program, Washington, 1971; participant, seminar leader discipline based art edn. Getty Found., Phoenix, 1985; sole art del.-global edn. Minn. State Dept. Edn., St. Paul, 1990—91; spkr. many confs. in field; judge art shows; participant Owatonna Art Project. Contbg. author: Discover Art Series, 1986—; exhibitor Minn. State Arts Exhibit; also in pvt. collections. Bd. mem. Women's Aux. Minn. Hist. Soc., 1988—94, chair pub. rels., 1994—96; mem. sch. arts bd., 1976—80; outreach bd. Colonial Ch. of Edina, 1992—95, mem. mission bd., 1996—99, sr. min., 1994—96, mem. search com. Mem.: Internat. Soc. Edn. Art, U.S. Soc. Art, Art Edn. Minn. (pres. 1966—69), Nat. Art Edn. Assn. (regional v.p. 1969—71, chair summer confs., del. rep. mem. search com., exec. sec. 1971—72, chmn. nat. membership 1976—78), Christians in Visual Arts (founding mem.). Congregationalist. Avocations: photography, swimming, travel, printmaking, ceramics. Home: 4053 21st Ave S Minneapolis MN 55407-3071

WILLIAMSON, JEAN ELIZABETH, office manager; b. Norfolk, Va., Nov. 12, 1933; d. Benjamin Davis and Hattie Agnes (Thomas) Hood; m. Tony Randolph Baum, Nov. 9, 1951 (dec. June 1963); children: Deborah Jean Baum Jankiewicz, Steven Randolph Baum, Jacqueline Kay Baum Gearles, Lynn Hood Baum, Deanna Leigh Baum King; m. Lenworth Earl Williamson, Jan. 27, 1973. Banking cert., Am. Banking Inst., 1951; student, Old Dominion Univ., 1963-64, Tidewater Coll., 1975-80. Proof and transit operator Va. Nat. Bank, Norfolk, 1950-51; bookkeeper machines Norfolk Savings & Loan, Norfolk, 1951; parts dept. Kline Chevrolet, Norfolk, 1963-65; sec., office mgr. Norfolk Pub. Schs., Norfolk, 1965-95. Quilter speaker, Lake Waccamaw and Whiteville, N.C., 1995—; spl. projects speaker, 1995—. Contbr. articles to profl. jours.; quilter on various quilts. Chmn. Lake Waccamaw Presby. Flower Communcator, 1997—; mem. Lake Waccamaw Presby. Ch. Choir, 1995—; girl scouts mem. Norfolk, 1949; mem. bible chaplain Order of Eastern Star, 1963-78; asst. chmn. Tidewater Quilters Guild, 1985-86; speaker on quilts to cmty. Mem. Lake Waccamaw Depot Mus (bd. dirs.), N.C. Quilters Guild, Lake Waccamaw Book Club, SouthEastern Genelogical Soc., Lake Waccamaw Womans Club (fine arts chmn. 1996), Lake Waccamaw Extension Dept. Homemakers, Southeastern Oratorio Soc. Avocations: music, painting, quilting, genealogist, gardening. Office: Norfolk Pub Schs 1384 Kempsville Rd Norfolk VA 23502-2206

WILLIAMSON, JOHN HENRY, III, school administrator; b. San Mateo, Calif., Feb. 20, 1960; s. Ronald Clay and Kathryn (Kennedy) W.; m. Trisha Glenell Hair, Aug. 11, 1990; 1 child, Matthew. BA, St. Mary's Coll. of Calif., 1982; MA, Monterey Inst. Internat. Studies, 1984. Cert. tchr. Calif. Tchr. Ojai (Calif.) Valley Sch., 1985-92; acad. dean Ojai Valley Sch., 1987-89, asst. headmaster, 1989-90, dean of faculty, 1990-92, dir. summer sch. and camp, 1988-92, assoc. dir. admissions, 1992-96, dir. of admission, 1997—. Mem. Western Boarding Schs. Assn. (steering com. 1992-95). Avocations: reading, running, camping. Home: 381 Baker Ave Ventura CA 93004-1558

WILLIAMSON, JUDY DARLENE GREENLEE, secondary school educator, librarian; b. Gallipolis, Ohio, Nov. 10, 1948; d. Byron Jr. and Margaret Mae Greenlee; m. Lannes Clay Williamson, Aug. 29, 1984. AB, Glenville State Coll., 1970; MA, Marshall U., 1973, postgrad., 1994. Librarian, tchr. Mason County Bd. Edn., Point Pleasant, W.Va., 1970—; acting dir. Mason County Pub. Library, Point Pleasant, 1986-87. Cons. Found. for Library Research, Point Pleasant, 1983—; adj. faculty Marshall U., Mid Ohio Valley Ctr. C.C., 1996-2000. Created the Automated Library System computer software; contbr. articles to profl. jours. Treas. Point Pleasant Emergency Med. Svcs., 1976-82; mem. chpt. 2 com. Mason County Bd. Edn., 1983—, mem. computer com., 1984—; mem. bicentennial steering com. City of Point Pleasant, 1987; chmn. Mason County Tech. com., 1993-2002, Point Pleasant H.S. Tech., 1993-2002. Grantee W.Va. Dept. Edn., 1981, 82, 97. Mem. W.Va. Libr. Assn., W.Va. Edn. Assn., Mason County Reading Coun., W.Va. Ednl. Media Assn., Alpha Delta Kappa, Delta Kappa Gamma. Republican. Methodist. Avocations: flowers, reading, travel. Home: 2764 Us Route 35 Southside WV 25187-9730 Office: Point Pleasant HS RR 1 Box 4 Point Pleasant WV 25550-9702 E-mail: jwilliam@access.K12.wv.us.

WILLIAMSON, NORMA BETH, adult education educator; b. Hamilton, Tex., Nov. 2, 1939; d. Joseph Lawrence and Gladys (Wilkins) Drake; m. Stuart Williamson, Mar. 14, 1981. BA, Baylor U., 1962; MA, Tex. A&M U., 1969; postgrad., Tex. Tech. U., 1976-80, CIDOC, Cuernavaca, Mex., 1973, 75. Instr. English, Tex. Southmost Coll., Brownsville, 1969-81; sr. English tchr. The Woodlands McCulloch H.S., 1981-83; lectr. in English Sam Houston State U., 1983-85; coll. prep. tchr. Tex. Dept. Corrections, 1985-95; ret., 1995. Lectr. Spanish Sam Houston State U.; faculty advisor Circle K, Sam Houston State. Vol., reading mentor Houston Elem. Sch.; pres. S.W. Dist. Unitarian Universalist Assn., 1982-86; treas. Huntsville Cmty. Theatre. Mem. AAUW (pres. Huntsville br. 1995-96), Huntsville Kiwanis (pres. 1999-2000), Walker County Geneal. Soc. (editor newsletter), Delta Kappa Gamma, Alpha Mu (pres. 1980-81), Upsilon (pres. 1994-96). Home: 794A Round Prairie Rd Bedias TX 77831-3238 E-mail: betwil@aol.com., fol.nbw@shsu.edu.

WILLIAMSON, OLIVER EATON, economics and law educator; b. Superior, Wisconsin, Sept. 27, 1932; s. Scott Gilbert and Lucille S. (Dunn) W.; m. Dolores Jean (Celeni), Sept. 28, 1957; children: Scott, Tamara, Karen, Oliver, Dean. BS, Mass. Inst. Tech., 1955; MBA, Stanford U., 1960; PhD, Carnegie Mellon U., 1963, Norwegian Sch. Econ. and Bus. Adminstrn., 1986; PhD in Econ. sci. (hon.), Hochschule St. Gallen, Switzerland, 1987, Groningen U., 1989, Turku Sch. Econ. and Bus. Admin, St. Petersburg, Russia, 1996, HEC, Paris, 1997, Copenhagen Bus. Sch., 2000, U. Chile, 2000. Project. engr. U.S. Govt., 1955-58; asst. prof. econ. U. Calif., Berkeley, Calif., 1963-65; assoc. prof. Pa. State U., Phila., 1965-68, prof., 1968-83, Charles and William L. Day prof. econ. and social sci., 1977-83; Gordon B. Tweedy prof. econ. law and orgn. Yale U., 1983-88; Transam. prof. of bus., econ. and law U. Calif., Berkeley, Calif., 1988-94, Edgar F. Kaiser prof. bus. adminstrn., prof. econ. and law, 1994—. Spl. econ. asst. to asst. atty. gen. for antitrust Dept. Justice, 1966—67; dir. Ctr. for Study of Orgnl. Innovation, U. Pa., 1976—83; cons. in field. Author: The Economics of Discretionary Behavior, 1964; Corp. Control and Bus. Behavior, 1970; Markets and Hierarchies, 1975; The Econ. Instn. of Capitalism, 1985; Econ. Orgn., 1986, Antitrust Economics, 1987; The Mechanisms of Governance, 1996; assoc. editor, Bell. Jour. Econ., 1973-74; editor, 1975-82; co-editor Jour. Law, Econ. and Orgn., 1983—2003. Fellow Ctr. for Advanced Study in Behavioral Sci., 1977-78; Guggenheim fellow, 1977-78; Fulbright scholar, 1999; Am. Acad. Arts and Sci. fellow, 1983; recipient Alexander Henderson Award Carnegie-Mellon U., 1962, Alexander von Humboldt Rsch. prize, 1987, Irwin Award Acad. of Mgmt., 1988, John von Newmann prize, 1999. Fellow Econometric Soc.; Am. Acad. Polit. and Social Sci.; mem. NAS, 1995; Internat. Soc. for New Instnl. Econ. (pres. 1999-2001); Am. Econ. Assn. (v.p. 2000-01); Am. Law and Econ. Assn. (pres. 1997-98); Western Econ. Assn. (pres. 1999-2000). Office: Univ Calif Dept Econ Berkeley CA 94720-0001

WILLIAMSON, RICHARD ANTHONY, music educator, conductor; b. Anderson, S.C., Apr. 2, 1962; MusB, Furman U., 1983; MusM, MA, Eastman Sch. Music, 1986; D in Music Arts, U. Ill., 1993. Cert. permanent tchr., N.Y.; cert. profl. tchr., S.C.; cert. tchr., Ga. Secondary tchr. music Rome (N.Y.) City Schs., 1986-89; choir dir. 1st Bapt. Ch., Champaign, Ill., 1989-93; K-8 tchr. music Chestfield County Schs., Chesterfield, S.C., 1993-94; tchr. music Warner Robins (Ga.) H.S., 1994-96; asst. prof. music Anderson (S.C.) Coll., 1996—2002, assoc. prof. music, 2002—. Dir. music Rome Choral Soc., 1987-89; instr. music Danville (Ill.) Area C.C., 1991-93; guest condr., composer, lectr., 1988—; presenter in field. Composer: Christmas Scenes for Strolling Strings (commd. Bartlesville Wesleyan Coll. 1989); also numerous songs. Presser scholar Furman U., 1982; grad. fellow Eastman Sch. Music, 1983-86; Univ. fellow U. Ill., 1989-90. Mem. Music Educators Nat. Conf., S.C. Music Educators Assn., Coll. Music Soc., Am. Choral Dirs. Assn., Soc. for Music Theory, Phi Beta Kappa, Pi Kappa Lambda, Kappa Delta Pi, Phi Kappa Phi. Baptist. Avocations: cooking, travel, gardening. Office: Anderson Coll Box 1131 316 Boulevard Anderson SC 29621 E-mail: rwilliamson@ac.edu.

WILLIAMSON, ROBERT THOMAS, JR., educational administrator; b. Detroit, Nov. 6, 1946; s. Robert Thomas and Sarah Jane (Simmons) Williamson; m. Jean Thompson Simmonds, Aug. 23, 1969; children: Robert Thomas III, Josephine Simmonds, Katherine Grace, Rebecca Jean. BA, Coll. Wooster, 1968; JD, U. Balt., 1975. Officer USN, 1968-70; coord. new products legal dept. McCormick & Co., Inc., Hunt Valley, Md., 1970-76; dir. econ. devel./tech. asst. ctr. SUNY, Plattsburgh, 1976-82; v.p. external rels. Clarkson U., Potsdam, N.Y., 1982-87, exec. v.p., 1987-97; pres. Westminster Coll., New Wilmington, Pa., 1997—. Bd. dirs. Jamison Hosp., New Castle, Pa.; mem. jud. commn. Pa. Bar Assn., 2000—. Avocations: golf, tennis, outdoor activities.

WILLIAMSON, SAMUEL RUTHVEN, JR., historian, emeritus university president; b. Bogalusa, La., Nov. 10, 1935; s. Samuel Ruthven and Frances Mitchell (Page) Williamson; m. Joan Chaffe Andress, Dec. 30, 1961; children: George Samuel, Treeby Andress, Thaddeus Miller. BA, Tulane U., 1958; AM, Harvard U., 1960, PhD, 1966, grad. advanced mgmt. program, 1986; degree (hon.), Furman U., Va. Theol. Sem., Centre Coll. Asst. prof. U.S. Mil. Acad., 1963—66; from instr. history to asst. dean Harvard U., 1966—69, asst. to dean of Harvard Coll., 1969—70; rsch. assoc. Inst. Politics, faculty assoc. Ctr. for Internat. Affairs, 1971—72; mem. faculty J.F. Kennedy Sch. Govt., 1971—72; from assoc. prof. history to provost U. N.C., Chapel Hill, 1972—84, provost univ., 1984—88; pres., vice chancellor U. of South, Sewanee, Tenn., 1988—2000, vice chancellor emeritus, prof. history, 2000—. Robert M. Ayres Jr. disting. univ. prof., 2001—. Cons. historian's office Office of Sec. Def., 1974—76; vis. fellow Churchill Coll., 1976—77; mem. vis. com. Harvard Coll., 1986—92; dir. Rsch. Triangle Inst., 1984—88; trustee N.C. Sch. Sci. and Coll., 1976—77, Day Found., 1990—93; mem. bd. visitors Air U., 1994—2002. Author: The Politics of Grand Strategy: Britain and France Prepare for War 1904-1914, 1969, 1990; co-author: The Origins of U.S. Nuclear Strategy, 1945-53, 1993, Soldiers, Statesmen and the Coming of the Great War, 2003, July 1914: Soldiers, Statesmen, and the Coming of the Great War, 2003; editor: The Origins of a Tragedy, July 1914, 1981, War and Soc. Newsletter, 1973—88; co-editor: Essays on World War I: Origins and Prisoners of War, 1983, Austria-Hungary and the Origins of the First World War, 1991. Mem. cen. com. Morehead Found., 1978—93; vice chmn. bd. visitors Air U., 1996—98, chmn. bd. visitors, 1998—2000. Capt. U.S. Army, 1963—66. Fellow Woodrow Wilson fellow, 1958—63, Danforth fellow, 1958—63, NEH, 1976—77, Nat. Humanities Ctr., 1983; grantee, Ford Found., 1976; scholar Fulbright scholar, U. Edinburgh, 1958—59, Woodrow Wilson Ctr. scholar, Washington, 2002. Mem.: Nat. Assn. Colls. and Univs. (vice chmn., chmn. bd. dirs. 1993—95), Internat. Inst. Strategic Studies, Am. Hist. Assn. (George Louis Beer prize 1970). Democrat. Episcopalian. Home: PO Box 837 Sewanee TN 37375-0837 Office: U of South duPont Libr Sewanee TN 37383-1000 E-mail: swilliam@sewanee.edu.

WILLIAMSON, THOMAS ARNOLD, publishing company executive; b. Sagamore, Pa., Oct. 4, 1939; s. Thomas and Mabel (Kennedy) W.; m. Kathryn Steiner White, Mar. 1, 1980; 1 child, Thomas J. Grad., Phillips Exeter Acad., 1957; AB, Harvard U., 1961. From sales person to sr. v.p. Harcourt Brace & Co., N.Y.C., 1962—88, sr. v.p., 1988—95; pres. The Psychol. Corp., San Antonio, 1982-88; v.p. Holt Rinehart & Winston, Harcourt Brace, 1989-95, pres. Sch. Pubs., 1989-93, pres. Ednl. Devel. Group, 1993-94; pres. The Learning Initiative, Austin, Tex., 1994—, T. Williamson Assocs., Inc., Austin, Tex., 1995—, Focused Learning, Ltd., Austin, Tex., 1998—. Bd. dirs. The Austin Project. Co-chmn. vis. com. to psychology dept. U. Tex., Austin, 1986-89, 95-98; vol., chair chpt. 249, SCORE. Mem.: The Hills Country Club, Town and Gown Club, Harvard Club N.Y.C. Home: 5 Cheverly Ct Austin TX 78738-1511 Office: T Williamson Assoc Inc PO Box 340097 Austin TX 78734-0097

WILLIAMSON, VIKKI LYN, university official, financial executive; b. Huntington, W.Va., June 30, 1956; d. Ernest E. and Wanda C. (Cole) W. BA in Secondary Edn., English, Temple U., 1978; postgrad. in Acctg. and Fin., U. Cin., 1984-86; MA in Mgmt., Antioch U., 2002. CPA, Ohio; cert. tchr., Tenn., Ohio. Tchr. Springfield Christian Acad., Tenn., 1978-79; acctg. asst. Children's Hosp. Med. Ctr., Cin., 1979-84; asst. dir. fin. svcs. U. Cin. Med. Ctr., 1984-85, dir. fin. svcs., 1985-88, dir. fin. and adminstrn., 1988-91, dep. dir., CFO, 1991-2000; chief fin. adminstrv. officer Antioch U McGregor, Yellow Springs, Ohio, 2000—02; dir. budget and fin. planning Ctrl. State U., 2002—. Bd. dirs. Contemporary Dance Theatre, 1987-90. Bd. dirs. Habitat for Humanity-Hamilton, 1991-94, v.p., 1991, pres., 1992; v.p. PTA, 1997-98, pres., 1989-99, treas. 1999-2001; treas., bd. dirs. Tawawa Cmty. Devel. Found., 2002—. Mem. AICPA, Healthcare Fin. Mgmt. Assn., Am. Assn. Blood Banks, Ohio Assn. Blood Banks (fin. com. 1986-90, treas. 1991-97), Am.'s Blood Ctrs. (fin. com. 1991-2000, alt. trustee 1991-2000), Assn. Women Adminstrs. (fin. com. 1987-90), Assn. Mid-Level Adminstrs. (bd. dirs. 1987-90), Alpha Epsilon Theta, Beta Gamma Sigma, Delta Mu Delta. Office: Central State Univ PO Box 1004 Wilberforce OH 45384 E-mail: vwilliamson@csu.ces.edu.

WILLIAMS-PEREZ, KENDRA BETH, nursing educator; b. Fort Dodge, Iowa, June 11, 1963; d. Roger H. and Shirley K. (Holtz) W.; m. Hector Perez, June 27, 1992 (dec.); children: Sophia Marie, Alexandra Kae. BSN, Coe Coll., 1986; MSN, U. Tex. Health Sci. Ctr., San Antonio, 1991; postgrad., U. No. Iowa, 1999—. Staff nurse, asst. head nurse U.S. Army-Ft. Sam Houston, San Antonio, 1986-90; staff nurse Humana Hosp. Village Oaks, San Antonio, 1990-91; nursing instr. Stephen F. Austin State U., Nacogdoches, Tex., 1991-93; asst. prof. Allen Coll., Waterloo, Iowa, 1993—2001, assoc. prof., 2001—. Capt. U.S. Army, 1986-90. Decorated Commendation medal U.S. Army, 1986. Mem. PEO, ANA, Iowa Nurses Assn., Sigma Theta Tau (Iota Rho chpt.), Phi Delta Kappa. Democrat. Methodist. Avocations: reading, walking, bicycling. Office: Allen Coll Waterloo IA 50703

WILLIAMS-WENNELL, KATHI, human resources consultant; b. Danville, Pa., Sept. 22, 1955; d. Raymond Gerald and Julia Dolores (Higgins) Williams; m. Mark Kevin Wennell, Apr. 3, 1982; children: Ryan Christopher, Lauren Ashley. BA, Immaculata Coll., 1977; MEd, Pa. State U., State College, 1978. Cert. rehabilitation counselor, Pa.; cert. profl. human resources. From project dir. to coord. devel. activities Community Interactions, Blue Bell, Pa., 1978-83; from mgmt. trainee to coord. coll. recruiting and rels. Meridian Bancorp, Inc., Reading, Pa., 1983-86, mgmt. recruiter, 1986-88, compensation analyst, 1989-93, recruiter, spl. projects, 1993-96; cons. Chet Mosteller & Assocs., Reading, Pa., 1996—. Cons. Norristown (Pa.) Life Ctr., 1981; instr. Immaculata (Pa.) Coll., 1981-83, Alvernia Coll., Reading, 1988-89. Meridian campaign coord. United Way Berks County, Reading, 1985. Named Recruiter of Yr. LaSalle U., Phila., 1986; recipient Excellence in Programming award Nat. Assn. Bank Women, Pa., 1986. Mem. Soc. Human Resources Mgmt. Republican. Roman Catholic. Avocations: walking, golf, tennis, piano, reading. Home: 69 S Hampton Dr Wyomissing PA 19610-3108

WILLIG, ROBERT DANIEL, economics educator; b. Bklyn., Jan. 16, 1947; s. Jack David and Meg W.; m. Virginia Mason, July 8, 1973; children: Jared Mason, Scott Mason, Brent Mason, Alexandra Mason. BA, Harvard U., 1967; MS in Ops. Rsch., Stanford U., 1968, PhD in Econs, 1973. Lectr. Stanford U., Palo Alto, Calif., 1971-73; tech. staff Bell Labs., Holmdel, NJ, 1973-77, supr. dept. econs. rsch., 1977-78; prof. econs. and pub. affairs Princeton U., 1978—; task force on future of postal svc. Aspen Inst., 1978-80; dep. asst. atty. gen. U.S. Dept. Justice, Washington, 1989-91. Cons. in field; rsch. fellow U. Warwick, Eng., 1977; organizing com. Telecom Policy Rsch. Conf., 1977-78; rsch. adv. bd. Am. Enterprise Inst., 1980-88; mem. N.J. Gov.'s Task Force on Market-Based Pricing of Electricity, 1987; bd. dirs. Consultants in Industry Econs., Inc., Competition Policy Assocs., Inc.; mem. Def. Sci. Bd. Task Force on Antitrust for the Def. Industry, 1993-94, Transp. Rsch. Bd. Task Force, 1995-96; advisor Inter-Am. Devel. Bank, 1997—. Author: Welfare Analysis of Policies Affecting Prices and Products, 1973, Contestable Markets and the Theory of Industry Structure, 1982; editor: Handbook of Industrial Organization, 1986, Can Privatization Deliver: Infrastructure for Latin America, 1999, Second Generation Reforms in Infrastructure Services, 2002; contbr. articles to profl. jours.; mem. editl. bd. MIT Press Series on Govt. Regulation, 1978—, Am. Econ. Rev., 1980-83, Jour. Indsl. Econs., 1985-89, Utility Policy, 1989-2001. Adv. bd. B'nai B'rith Hillel Found., Princeton U., 1978-89. Grantee, NSF, 1979—85. Fellow Econometric Soc. (program com. 1978-81); mem. Am. Econ. Assn. (nominating com. 1980-81). Office: Princeton Univ Economics Dept Princeton NJ 08540

WILLINGHAM, JOYCE JARRETT, elementary education educator, gifted education educator; b. Pine Bluff, Ark., May 12, 1951; d. Johnnie and Hazel (Hill) Jarrett; m. Lee Odis Willingham, Dec. 29, 1973; children: LaDonna Marie, Lee Jarrett. BS, Ark. M&N Coll., 1973; MEd, U. Ark., Fayetteville, 1979; postgrad., U. Ark., Little Rock, 1989, 92. Cert. in elem. edn., elem. gifted and talented edn., cert. elem. prin., Ark. Early childhood tchr. Dumas (Ark.) Sch. Dist., 1973-82; elem. tchr. Little Rock Sch. Dist., 1982-87, gifted specialist, 1987—. Adj. instr. U. Ark.-Little Rock Coop. Tchrs. Adv. Bd., 1987-90; gifted revision and multi-ethnic com. mem. Little Rock Sch. Dist., 1992—. Block coord. Muscular Dystrophy Assn., Little Rock, 1989; sickle cell coord., Little Rock, 1991; Just Say No coord. Pecan Lake, Little Rock, 1991—; Richard Anderson's ATA Taekwood Hospitality vol. coord., 1993; com. mem. home study guide for parents Little Rock Sch. Dist., 1993; vol. art tchr. Eigth Ave Bapt. Ch. Bible Sch., 1993. Rockefeller Found. grantee, 1987, 90. Mem. Natl. Edn. Assn., Ark. Edn. Assn., Ark. Gifted and Talented Edn. Assn., Little Rock Classroom Tchr.'s Assn., Epsilon Zeta Pi Beta. Baptist. Home: 5601 Pecan Lake Rd Little Rock AR 72204-8593

WILLINGHAM, THORNTON, physical education specialist; b. Macon, Ga., Feb. 2, 1952; d. Thomas Slade and Jean Thornton (Saunders) W. BS, Ga. State U., 1981, MEd, 1988. Cert. tchr., Ga. Tchr. Fulton County Schs., Atlanta, 1982—. Named Fulton County Elem. Phys. Edn. Tchr. of the Yr., Phys. Edn. Elem. Specialists, 1990. Home: 20 Anastasia Dr Mableton GA 30126-1461 Office: Fulton County Schs 9425 Barnwell Rd Alpharetta GA 30022-6147

WILLIS, ARNOLD JAY, urologic surgeon, educator; b. Phila., Feb. 12, 1949; s. Alexander and Rosaline May (Dortort) W.; m. Lilian Marie Mortensen, Aug. 29, 1981; children: Adam Mark, Simon Matt, Andreas Morton. BA, Franklin & Marshall U., 1970; MD, Thomas Jefferson Med. Ctr., 1974. Intern George Washington U. Hosp., Washington, 1974-75, resident in surgery, 1975-77, resident in urology, 1977-80; instr. in urology George Washington U. Med. Ctr., Washington, 1980-82, asst. clin. prof., 1982-88, assoc. clin. prof., 1988—. Founder, dir. Met. Ambulatory Urologic Inst.; mem. Del Marva Found. Med. care, Washington, 1985-90; mem. profl. adv. bd. Nat. Kidney Found., Washington, 1988-92; cons. Caremark Internat., Washington, 1990-93, Managed Care Options, Bethesda, Md., 1993-95; med. dir., founder Met. Ambulatory Urologic Inst., Mid Atlantic Prostate Inst., Mid Atlantic Cryotherapies, LLC; med. dir., founder Continence Treatment Ctr. of Md.; urologic cons. Johnson & Johnson; expert on transgluteal brachytherapy for prostate cancer; med. dir., founder Met. Brachytherapy Assocs.; keynote spkr. 12th Copenhagen Urologic Symposium on Brachytherapy. Mem. editl. bd. Health Educator, 1995-96; contbr. articles to sci. jours.; inventor ultrasound guide. Founder profl. sports league/major league roller hockey; owner world champion Washington Power profl. hockey team. Clin. Oncology Tng. grantee NIH, 1974; named Tchr. of Yr., Georgetown Family Practice Residency, 1991. Fellow Internat. Coll. Surgeons (v.p. U.S. sect. 1986—, Washington regent); mem. Am. Urologic Assn., Am. Assn. Clin. Urologists, Washington Urol. Assn. (Resident's prize 1980). Jewish. Avocations: tennis, squash, skiing, fishing, sailing. Home: 2011 Whiteoaks Dr Alexandria VA 22306-2432 Office: 650 Pennsylvania Ave SE Ste 450 Washington DC 20003-4339

WILLIS, CRAIG DEAN, academic administrator; b. Cambridge, Ohio, Mar. 21, 1935; s. John Russell and Glenna (Stevens) W.; m. Marilyn Elaine Foster, June 9, 1956; Mark Craig, Bruce Dean, Todd Laine, Garth John. BA, Ohio Wesleyan U, 1957; MA, Ohio State U., 1960, PhD, 1969. Registrar Ohio Wesleyan U., 1964-69; dir. admissions Wright State U., 1970-72, dean, 1971-77; v.p. acad. affairs Concord Coll., 1977-82; pres. Lock Haven U. Pa., 1982—. Chmn. internat. affairs com. Am. Assn. State Colls. and Univs.; A.C.E. pres.'s commn. on internat. edn.; vice chmn. Clinton region Mellon Bank Ctr., 1987, chmn., 88, also bd. dirs.; bd. dirs. Lock Haven U.; cons. Ellis Assocs., Princeton, W.Va., 1980—82. Chmn. bd. Kirkmont Preschool, Beavercreek, Ohio, 1974-77, Beavercreek Library, 1976-77, Regional Edn. Service Agy., Beckley, W.Va., 1978-82; mem. N.E.-Midwest leadership Coun., 1989—. Recipient Disting. Alumnus award dept. edn. Ohio Wesleyan U., 1991; scholar Sohio Oil, 1953, Govt. of France, Paris, 1964, Shell Oil Co, 1967. Mem. Commn. State Coll. and Univ. Pres., Assn. State Colls. annd Univs., Clinton County C. of C. (pres.), Rotary (v.p., pres. elect, Citizen of Yr. award Lock Haven 1989), Ohio Wesleyan U. Alumni Assn. (Disting. Sesquicentennial Alumnus of the Edn. 1992), Phi Kappa Phi, Kappa Kappa Psi, Phi Delta Kappa, Kappa Delta Pi. Presbyterian. Office: Lock Haven U North Fairview St Lock Haven PA 17745

WILLIS, DOLLIE P. adult education educator; b. West Union, Ohio, Nov. 13, 1957; d. Arbra Edgar and Mallie Mae (Erwin) Plymail; m. Orland Willis, Aug. 14, 1983; children: Emerson, Thomas. Student, So. State Coll., Fincastle, Ohio, 1977; BS in Edn., Morehead (Ky.) State U., 1979; MEd, Coll. Mt. St. Joseph, Ohio, 1991. Cert. tchr. vocat. home econs., reading, reading supr. Substitute tchr. Ohio Valley Local Schs., West Union, 1983—, Highland County Schs., Hillsboro, Ohio, 1983—; pvt. tutor/owner Eclectic Reading Svc., Hillsboro, 1989—; tchr. jr. high sci. Lynchburg-Clay (Ohio) Schs., 1990-91, alternative classroom tchr., 1993—. Instr., Orton-Gillian tutor Jobs for Ohio Grads. Den mother, leader Boy Scouts Am.; career specialist Folsom (Ohio) United Meth. Ch., 1983—. Mem.: Internat. Reading Assn., Ohio Reading Assn., Eagle Aux., Family Readiness Ohio Army Nat. Guard, Internat. Dyslexia Assn. Republican. Avocations: ceramics, horses, gardening, needlepoint. Home: 7360 Oakridge Rd Hillsboro OH 45133-9682

WILLIS, DOUGLAS MACARTHUR, secondary education educator, consultant; b. Ironton, Ohio, Oct. 11, 1945; s. Brady C. and Mary T. (Dodson) W.; m. Karen K. Cory, June 8, 1969; children:: Andrew M., Matthew D. BS in Indsl. Arts, Morehead (Ky.) State U., 1968; MS in Indsl. Edn., Ctrl. Mo. State U., 1973. Cert. permanent K-12 tchr., Ohio. Tchr. indsl. arts Dawson-Bryant H.S., Coal Grove, Ohio, 1968-71, Little Miami H.S., Morrow, Ohio, 1971-72; grad. asst. Ctrl. Mo. State U., Warrensburg, 1972-73; tchr. indsl. arts Ankeney Jr. H.S., Beavercreek, Ohio, 1973-75, tchr. unified arts, 1975-80, tchr. tech., dept. chmn., 1980-2000; ret., 2000. Mem. Greene County Tech. Edn. Curriculum Com., Xenia, Ohio, 1980-00, Beavercreek Tech. Study Com., 1992-00; western rep. State Stds. Task Force, Columbus, Ohio, 1991-00. Mem. Xenia Twp. Vol. Fire Dept., 1974-89, pres., 1980-82. Recipient cert. of accomplishment Ohio Ho. of Reps., 1995. Mem. Internat. Tech. Edn. Assn., Ohio Tech. Edn. Assn., Western Ohio Tech. Edn. Assn., Ohio Tech. Edn. Leadership Coun. (pres. 1993-94). Avocation: custom woodworking. Home: 985 Jane Ave Xenia OH 45385-1517

WILLIS, ELEANOR LAWSON, university official; b. Nashville, Sept. 15, 1936; d. Harry Alfred Jr. and Helen Russell (Howse) Lawson; m. Alvis Rux Rochelle, Aug. 25, 1956 (div. Mar. 1961); m. William Reese Willis Jr., Mar. 7, 1964 (div. June 1994); children: Alfred Russell Willis, William Reese III, Brent Lawson. BA cum laude, Vanderbilt U., 1957. Host children's syndicated TV show Sta. WSIX-TV, Nashville, 1961-64; tchr. head start program Metro Pub. Sch., Nashville, 1965-67; co-investigator cognitive edn. curriculum project Peabody Coll., Nashville, 1979-81; dir., founder Heads Up Child Devel. Ctr., Inc., Nashville, 1973-87; dir. Tenn. Vols. for Gore for Pres. Campaign, Nashville, 1987-88; dir. devel. Vanderbilt Inst. Pub. Policy Studies, Vanderbilt U., Nashville, 1988—. Bd. dirs. Vanderbilt Child Devel. Ctr. Author: (with others) I Really Like Myself, 1973, I Wonder Where I Came From, 1973. Pres. Nashville Bar Aux., 1967-68, Nashville Symphony Guild, 1984-85, W.O. Smith Nashville Community Music Sch., 1987-03; founder, bd. dirs. Rochelle Ctr., Nashville, 1968-03; vice-chmn. Century III Com., Nashville, 1978-80; Homecoming 1986 Steering Com., Nashville, 1985-86; mem. Cheekwood Fine Arts Ctr., Nashville City Ballet, Nashville Symphony Assn., Dem. Women of Davidson County; appointed Metro Arts Commn., 1992, Metro Ednl. Access Corp.; exec. dir. Friends of Warner Park, 1994; leadership coun. John F. Kennedy Ctr., 1995—; founder Nashville Tree Found.; bd. dirs. Cumberland Region Tomorrow, 2001. Recipient Leadership Nashville award, 1982; Seven Leading Ladies award Nashville Mag., 1984; Eleanor Willis Day proclaimed by City of Nashville, 1987; named to Acad. for Women of Achievement, 2003. Mem. Exchange Club of Nashville, Vanderbilt Alumni Assn. Presbyterian. Avocations: reading, camping, running. Office: 50 Vaughn Rd Nashville TN 37221-3706

WILLIS, ISAAC, dermatologist, educator; b. Albany, Ga., July 13, 1940; s. R.L. and Susie M. (Miller) W.; m. Alliene Horne, June 12, 1965; children: Isaac Horne, Alliric Isaac. BS, Morehouse Coll., 1961, DSc (hon.), 1989; MD, Howard U., 1965. Diplomate Am. Bd. Dermatology. Intern Phila. Gen. Hosp., 1965-66; fellow Howard U., Washington, 1966-67; resident, fellow U. Pa., Phila., 1967-69, assoc. in dermatology, 1969-70; mem. staff Phila. Gen. Hosp., 1969-70; instr. dept. dermatology U. Pa., Phila., 1970-72; mem. staff Moffit Hosp. U. Calif., San Francisco, 1970-72; asst. prof. Johns Hopkins U., Johns Hopkins Hosp., Balt., 1972-73; mem. staff Johns Hopkins Hosp., Balt. City Hosp., Good Samaritan Hosp., Balt., 1972-73; asst. prof. Emory U., Atlanta, 1973-77; mem. staff Crawford W. Long Meml. Hosp., Atlanta, 1974—, West Paces Ferry Hosp., Atlanta, 1974-2000; assoc. prof. Emory U., Atlanta, 1977-82; prof. Morehouse Sch. Medicine, Atlanta, 1982—, chief dermatology, 1991—; mem. staff Piedmont Hosp., Atlanta, 2000—. Dep. commdr. of 3297th USA Hosp. (1000B), 1990-; mem. gen. medicine group IA study sect., NIH, 1985-; mem. grants review panel EPA, 1986—; adv. bd. Arthritis and Musculoskeletal and Skin Diseases, 1991-, U. Pa. Sch. Medicine, 1995-, adv. bd. U. of Calif. Sch. of Engring. LaJolla, 2000-, Emory U., 1994-; chmn. inst. review bd., mem. pharmacy and therapeutic com.; bd. dirs. Comml. Bank Gwinnett, Comml. Bank of Ga., Heritage Bank, Landmark Bank Fla., Learning Framework, West Paces Med. Ctr., Lupus Specialists, Inc., InterVu, Inc., Lupus Erythematosus Found., Jacquelyn McClure Lupus Erythematosus Clinic, Skin Cancer Found., World Network Solutions; bd. dirs., chmn. audit com. Comml. Bank of Ga., 2000-, Landmark Bank of Fla., 1999-; mem. med. staff Piedmont Hosp., 2000-; adv. bd. Enable, Inc.; mem. adv. coun. U. Calif. Jacobs Sch. Engring., San Diego, 2001-; cons. in field. Author: Textbook of Dermatology, 1971; contbr. articles to profl. jours. Trustee Friendship Bapt. Ch., Atlanta, 1980-82; mem. gov.'s commn. on effectiveness and economy in govt. State of Ga. Human Resources Task Force, 1991—, Ga. State Bd. of worker's Compensation Med. subcom., 1997—; mem. nat. alumni coun. U. Pa., 1995—; mem. coun. of advisors U. Calif. San Diego Jacobs Sch. Engring., 2001--. Col. USAR, 1983-95. Named Internat. Scientist of Yr. Internat. Biog. Inst. of Cambridge, Eng., 2002; EPA grantee, 1980—. Fellow Am. Acad. Dermatology, Am. Dermtol. Assn., Am. Soc. Laser Medicine and Surgery, Inc.; mem. AAAS, AMA, Nat. Cancer Inst., Soc. Investigative Dermatology, Nat. Med. Assn., Internat. Soc. Tropical Dermatology, Pan Am. Med. Assn., Am. Fedn. Clin. Rsch., Am. Soc. Photobiology, U. Pa. Nat. Alumni Adv. Coun., State of Ga. Dermatology Found., Frontiers Internat., Sportsman Internat., Phi Beta Kappa, Omicron Delta Kappa. Achievements include a patent for the development of a shaving composition and method for preventing Pseudofollientitis Barbae, 1999; subspecialties in the areas of dermatology and cancer research (medicine), Internat. Sci. of the Yr.,(IBC), 2002. Home: 1141 Regency Rd NW Atlanta GA 30327-2719 Office: NW Med Ctr 3280 Howell Mill Rd NW Ste 342 Atlanta GA 30327-4109 E-mail: iwmd@bellsouth.net.

WILLIS, JERRY WELDON, computer systems educator, writer; b. Tuscumbia, Ala., Jan. 27, 1943; s. Elbert Cartr and Lavice Mae (McAlpin) W.; m. Dee Anna Smith, Mar. 28, 1987 (div. 1997); 1 child, Amy Elizabeth. BA, Union U., 1966; MA, PhD, U. Ala., 1970. Asst prof. U. Guelph, Ong., Can., 1972-74, U. Westrn Ont., London, 1974-76, U. B.C., Vancouver, 1976-78; prof. edn. Tex. Tech. U., Lubbock, 1978-87; dean Edn. and Home Econs. Miss. U. for Women, 1987-88; prof., program coord. Instrnl. Tech.-Ednl. Computing, E. Carolina U. Sch. Edn., 1988-91; prof., dir. ctr. for info. tech. and tchr. edn. Coll. of Edn., U. Houston, 1991-98; prof. curriculum and tech. Iowa State U., 1998—, dir., Ctr. for Tech., Learning and Tchg., 1999—. Pres. Willis Pub. Group; adv. Pres's. Panel on Tech. in Edn., 1995. Author: Peanut Butter and Jelly Guide to Computers, 1978 (Outstandig Computer Book, Am. Libr. Jour.); Nailing Jelly to a Tree, 1981, Computers for Everybody, 1981 (Outstanding Computer Book, Am. Libr. Jour.), Computers for People, 1982, Computers, Teaching and Learning, 1983, The Essential Commodore 128 User's Guide, 1986, The Essential Atari ST User's Guide, 1986, Super Calc 3: Learning, Mastering and Using, 1986, Using Super Calc 4, 1987, Desktop Publishing with your IBM PC and Compatible, 1987, Educational Computing: An Introduction, 1986, 96, Computer Simulations: A Guide to Educational Applications, 1986, Teaching with Artificial Reality, 1990, Works Tutorial and Applications, 1990, Computers, Reading and Language Arts, 1996; assoc. editor: Computers in the Schools; contbg. editor Educational Technology; also 34 other books and transls. in 9 langs.; contbr. chpt. to book. Mem. Internat. Soc. for Tech. in Edn., Assn. for Computing Machinery, Assn. for Tchr. Educators, Soc. for Info. Tech. and Tchr. Edn. (founder, pres. 1991-95, jour. co-editor 1991—, Outstanding Contbns. award 1996). Home: 619 Onyx St Ames IA 50010-8405 Office: Iowa State U CTLT Coll of Edn Ames IA 50010

WILLIS, RALPH HOUSTON, mathematics educator; b. McMinnville, Tenn., Dec. 26, 1942; s. Carl Houston and Carrie Lee (Hill) W.; m. Gayle Catherine Celestin, June 29, 1973 (div. Apr. 1985); m. Velma Inez Church, Aug. 10, 1985; 1 stepchild, Bobbie Lynn White Buckner. BS in Math., Mid. Tenn. State U., 1964, MA in Math., 1966. Cert. secondary edn. Instr. depts. math. & computer sci. Western Carolina U., Cullowhee, N.C., 1968-73, asst. prof., 1973-83, assoc. prof., 1983—. Co-founder N.C. State Math. Contest & Contest Network, 1977-78, state maths. contest com., 1977-78, western regional rep. exec. steering com., 1978—, recording sec., 1978—; co-founder N.C. Math. League, 1981-82, mem. problem writing com., 1981-84. Editor: (newsletters) Abelian Grapevine-Secondary Math. 1970-88, The Child of Mathematics-Elementary-Middle Grade Math., 1972-78; mem. editl. bd. The Centroid, 1995-00; contbr. articles to profl. jours. Founder, dir., coord. High Sch. Math. Contest, Western Carolina U., 1970—, solicitor-coord. Math. Contest Scholarship Program, 1971-82, founder, coord. math dept. student awards program, 1970—, initiator-coord. math. dept.'s Vis. Speaker Program, 1974-77; founder, faculty sponsor N.C. Coun. Tchrs. Math. Student Affiliate, Cullowhee, 1988—; coord. state road paving project Univ. Heights Cmty. Devel. Orgn., 1974-76, chmn., founder cmty. watch., 1978-79, coord. public water sys. upgrade project, 1980-84; founder, coord., bd. dirs., trustee Hunerwadle Cmty. Cemetery Assn., Beersheba, Tenn., 1983—; co-founder N.C. State Math. Contest and Contest Network, 1977-78. Recipient Paul A. Reid Disting. Svc. award Western Carolina U., 1991, hon. mention N.C. Gov.'s Award for Excellence, 1991, Innovator award N.C. Coun. Tchrs. in Math., 1994, Exemplary Site award State Math. Contest Com., 1990, W.W. Rankin Meml. award for Excellence in Math. Edn., 2001, First Career Svc. award Coll. Arts and Scis., Western Carolina U., 2003. Mem. Nat. Coun. Tchrs. Math., N.C. Coun. Tchrs. Math. (historian 1993-98, Innovator award 1994. editl. bd. Centroid 1995-2000, W.W. Rankin award 2001), Phi Kappa Phi, Kappa Mu Epsilon. Avocations: genealogy, gardening, military history, model building, die cast model collector. Office: Western Carolina U Math Dept Stillwell Bldg Cullowhee NC 28723

WILLMERT, LOIS ANN, elementary education educator; b. Frost, Minn., Dec. 7, 1951; d. Ronald Floyd and Gladys Rebecca (Alfson) W. BS, Mankato State Coll., 1973; postgrad., Hamline U., 1979, Mankato State U., 1980-85. Cert. tchr., Minn. Receptionist, bookkeeper Dr. Lewis Hanson, MD, Frost, 1965-73; tchr. Frost Pub. Sch., 1973-74, Winnebago (Minn.) Community Sch., 1974—. Cons., speaker South Ctrl. Ednl. Coop. Svc. Unit, Mankato, 1990-91, New Ulm (Minn.) Cath. Schs., 1991, Challenge 2000 - Outcome Based Edn., St. Cloud, Minn., 1992; creator Winnebago Gifted Edn. Program, 1982-85. Dir. Winnebago Area Mus. Players, 1980—. Mem. NEA, Minn. Edn. Assn., S.W. Minn. Reading Coun. (exec. bd. dirs. 1980-81, Cert.), Winnebago C. of C. (exec. bd. dirs. 1990-93). Lutheran. Avocations: musical theater, reading, walking, piano. Home: 105 1st Ave SE Winnebago MN 56098-1086 Office: Winnebago Elem Sch 132 1st Ave SE Winnebago MN 56098-1052

WILLON, MYCHAEL COLE, school system administrator, educator; b. Cambridge, Md., Apr. 1, 1955; s. Wallace Edwin and Iris Mary (Slacum). BS, U. Md., 1973-77, MEd, 1984; PhD, LaSalle U., 1992. Notary pub., Kans. Tchr. Charles Co. Bd. of Edn., Pomfret, Md., 1977-78, Howard Co. Bd. of Edn., Columbia, Md., 1978-85, gifted and talented resource tchr., 1985-86; asst. prin. Frederick County Bd. Edn., Md., 1986-88, gifted and talented coord., 1987; prin. McCollom Elem. Sch., Wichita, Kans., 1988-89, coord. spl. projects in curriculum, 1989-90, coord. elem. social studies, 1990-91, dir. elem. programs, 1991-93, asst. to supt., 1993-95; dir. Horace Mann/Irving/Park Complex, 1995—. Recipient MATE Cooperating Teacher of the Year. Md. Assoc. of Teacher Education, 1984, Excellence in Teaching award Howard County C. of C., Columbia, Md. 1984. Mem. Wichita Reading Assn., Am. Numismatic Soc., U. Md. Alumni Assn., Assn. Tchr. Educators. Republican. Avocations: traveling, running. Home: 8 Laurel Ter Cherry Hill NJ 08002-1939 Office: Unified Sch Dist # 259 HIP Complex 1243 N Market St Wichita KS 67214-2834

WILLOUGHBY, JULIA ANN, secondary school educator; b. Lander, Wyo., Mar. 3, 1958; d. William Emory and Martha Jeanette (Woods) Willoughby; m. Douglas Richard Gilmer, Jan. 29, 1979 (div.); children: Gregory Scott, Lillian Jeanette. BA in Math. with high honors, U. Wyo., 1979, BS in Math. Edn., 1982, MS in Natural Sci., 1985. Cert. secondary math., physics, gen. and earth sci. tchr., Wyo. Sci. rsch. aide U. Wyo., Laramie, 1980-81, math. tutor, 1982-83, grad. teaching asst., 1984-85; computer operator and programmer IN-SITU, Inc., Laramie, 1982-83; tchr. math. Albany County Sch. Dist. 1, Laramie, 1983-84; tutor, Laramie, 1985-86; tchr. math. and sci. Scottsbluff (Nebr.) Sch. Dist. 32, 1986-88; mem. adj. faculty math. dept. Laramie County Community Coll., Cheyenne, Wyo., 1988-89; substitute tchr. Fremont County Sch. Dist. 1, Lander, 1990-91; tchr. sci. Fremont County Sch. Dist. 14, Ethete, Wyo., 1991-92; tchr. math and sci. Fremont County Sch. Dist. 1, Lander, 1992—. Tchr.-presenter Nebr. Assn. Tchrs. Math., 1987; adj. math instr. Ctrl. Wyo. Coll., 1992—. Vol. young parents program Panhandle Community Svcs., Gering, Nebr., 1987-88; vol.; Sunday sch. tchr. United Meth. Ch., Lander, 1990-91. Mem. Wyo. Sci. Tchrs. Assn., Phi Beta Kappa, Phi Kappa Phi. Republican. Avocations: downhill and cross-country skiing, sketching, reading, hiking, family activities. Home: 1826 Hillcrest Dr Lander WY 82520-9775

WILLOUGHBY, SARAH-MARGARET C. chemist, educator, chemical engineer, consultant; b. Bowling Green, KY, Oct. 15, 1917; d. Austin Burrell Claypool and Minerva Dallas Renfrow-Claypool; m. John Richard Evans, II, Aug. 30, 1938 (dec. Dec. 1942); 1 child, Richard Claypool Evans; m. Olief Glenn Willoughby, June 18, 1948 (dec.); children: Sarah, Stephen(dec.). BS, Western Ky. U., 1938; PhD, Purdue U., 1950. Registered profl. engr., Ind., Tex. Chemist Devoe-Reynolds, Inc., Louisville, 1941—42; jr. engr. chem. lab. div. Curtiss-Wright Corp., Louisville, 1942—44; tech. asst. Purdue U., West Lafayette, Ind., 1944—46, fellow, 1946—50; rsch. chemist, coatings divsn. Monsanto Chem. Co., Boston, 1950—52; assoc. prof. of chemistry U. Tex., Arlington, 1954—84, co-dir. Ctr. for Microcrystalline Polymer Rsch. Studies, 1978—82, prof. emeritus chemistry, 1984. Cons. Albert H. Halff Assocs., Dallas, 1980—86. Nominee Dallas-Ft. Worth Trailblazer award, 1996; named to Hall of Disting. Alumni, Western Ky. U., 1994; recipient Outstanding Chem. Engr. award, Purdue U., 1996. Fellow: Am. Inst. Chemists; mem.: N.Y. Acad. Sci., Soc. Women Engrs. (sr.), Am. Chem. Soc. (emeritus mem.), Nat. Soc. Daughters of Founders and Patriots (v.p. N.E. Tex. chpt. 1997—), Friends of St. George, Plantagenet Soc., Colonial Dames Am., Nat. Soc. Colonial Dames of XVII Century (chpt. regent 1980—82), Nat. Soc. DAR (chpt. regent 1967—69, nat. bicentennial com. mem. 1975—76), Nat. Soc. Children of Am. Revolution (Tex. sr. state pres. 1968—70), Nat. Soc. Magna Carta Dames (Tex. state pres. 1986—88), Colonial Order of the Crown, Soc. Descendants of Knights of the Most Noble Order of the Garter, Sovereign Colonial Soc. Ams. of Royal Descent, Order Ky. Cols., Sigma Xi (emeritus mem.), Alpha Chi Omega (Lambda Epsilon chapt.). Home: 1630 Pecan Park Dr Arlington TX 76012

WILLS, GARRY, journalist, educator; b. Atlanta, May 22, 1934; s. John and Mayno (Collins) Wills; m. Natalie Cavallo, May 30, 1959; children: John, Garry, Lydia. BA, St. Louis U., 1957; MA, Xavier U., Cin., 1958, Yale U., 1959, PhD, 1961; LittD (hon.), Coll. Holy Cross, 1982, Columbia Coll., 1982, Beloit Coll., 1988, Xavier U., 1993, St. Xavier U., 1993, Union Coll., 1993, Macalester Coll., 1995, Bates Coll., 1995, St. Ambrose, 1997, George Washington U., 1999, Spring Hill Coll., 2000, Siena Heights U., 2001, Gettysburg Coll., 2002, Am. Univ., 2003. Fellow Ctr. Hellenic Studies, 1961—62; assoc. prof. classics Johns Hopkins U., 1962—67, adj. prof., 1968-80; Henry R. Luce prof. Am. culture and public policy Northwestern U., 1980—88, adj. prof., 1988—. Author: (book) Chesterton, 1961, Politics and Catholic Freedom, 1964, Roman Culture, 1966, Jack Ruby, 1967, Second Civil War, 1968, Nixon Agonistes, 1970, Bare Ruined Choirs, 1972, Inventing America, 1978, At Button's, 1979, Confessions of a Conservative, 1979, Explaining America, 1980, The Kennedy Imprisonment, 1982, Lead Time, 1983, Cincinnatus, 1984, Reagan's America, 1987, Under God, 1990, Lincoln at Gettysburg, 1992 (Pulitzer Prize for gen. non-fiction, 1993), Certain Trumpets: The Call of Leaders, 1994, Witches and Jesuits: Shakespeare's Macbeth, 1994, John Wayne's America, 1997, St. Augustine, 1999, A Necessary Evil, 1999, Papal Sin, 2000, Venice, Lion City, 2001, St. Augustine's Childhood, 2001, James Madison, 2002, Why Am I a Catholic, 2002, St. Augustine's Memory, 2002, Mr. Jefferson's University, 2002, St. Augustine's Sin, 2003, Negro President, 2003. Recipient Merle Curti award, Orgn. Am. Historians, Nat. Book Critics Cir. award (2), Wilbur Cross medal, Yale U., Peabody award, NEH Presdl. medal, 1998, John Hope Franklin award. Mem.: AAAL, Am. Philos. Soc., Am. Antiquarian Soc., Am. Acad. Arts and Scis., Mass. Hist. Soc. Roman Catholic. Office: Northwestern U Dept History Evanston IL 60201

WILLS, J. ROBERT, academic administrator, drama educator, writer; b. Akron, Ohio, May 5, 1940; s. J. Robert and Helen Elizabeth (Lapham) W.; m. Barbara T. Salisbury, Aug. 4, 1984 (dec. 1998); m. Jeanne Hokin, June 2002. BA, Coll. of Wooster, 1962; MA, U. Ill., 1963; PhD, Case-Western Res. U., 1971; cert. in arts adminstrn, Harvard U., 1976. Instr. to asst. prof., dir. theatre Wittenberg U., Springfield, Ohio, 1963-72; assoc. prof., dir. grad. studies, chmn. dept. theatre U. Ky., Lexington, 1972-77, prof. theatre, dean Coll. Fine Arts, 1977-81; prof. drama, dean Coll. Fine Arts U. Tex., Austin, 1981-89, Effie Marie Cain Regents chair in Fine Arts, 1986-89; provost, prof. theatre Pacific Luth. U., Tacoma, Wash., 1989-94; prof. theatre, dean coll. fine arts Ariz. State U., Tempe, 1994—. Cons. colls., univs., arts orgns., govt. agencies Author: The Director in a Changing Theatre, 1976, Directing in the Theatre: A Casebook, 1980, rev. edit., 1994; dir. 92 plays; contbr. articles to profl. jours. Bd. dirs. various art orgns., Ky., Tex., Wash., Ariz. Recipient grants public and pvt. agencies. Mem. Nat. Assn. State Univs. and Land-Grant Colls.(chmn. commn. on arts 1981-83), Coun. Fine Arts Deans (exec. com. 1984-89, sec./treas. 1986-89), Univ. and Coll. Theatre Assn. (pres. 1981-82), Assn. for Communication Adminstrn. (pres. 1986-87), Ky. Theatre Assn. (pres. 1976). Office: Ariz State U PO Box 872102 Tempe AZ 85287-2102 E-mail: bob.wills@asu.edu.

WILLS, KATHERINE V. TSIOPOS, English language educator; b. St. Louis, Sept. 30, 1957; d. Vasilios and Kalliope (Stratos) Tsiopos. BA, Washington U., 1979; MA, Ind. U., 1990. Rsch. dir. U. Chgo. Gynecology, 1980-82, Northwestern U., Chgo., 1982-86; pres. Port of Nashville (Ind.) Inc., retailer of nautical items and antiques, 1986—. Vis. lectr. English dept. Ind. U. Purdue U., Indpls., 1991—; vol. Women's Writers' Conf. Contbr. articles and poetry to jours. Recipient essay award Scholastic Mag., Inc., 1973, award for acad. excellence and community svc. Am. Hellenic Progessvie and Ednl. Assn., A poetry award Wednesday Club of St. Louis, Mo., 1977, Roger Conant Hatch hon. mention for writing, Washington U., 1977. Greek Orthodox. Home: 7772 Bellsville Pike Nashville IN 47448-8995

WILLS, LOIS ELAINE, religious education educator; b. Dayton, Ohio, Feb. 26, 1939; d. Harold Otto and Marjorie Elizabeth (Schmidt) Wallen; m. David P. Wills, Sept. 26, 1960 (dec.); children: Marianne, Melody, Michele. Degree, Coll. of Mount St. Joseph, Cin. Cert. catechist. Educator, substitute various schs., 1985-90; gallery dir. Studio San Giuseppe, Cin., 1987-90; curator Murdock Art and Antiques, Cin., 1990-92; mgr. Cin. Antique Mall, 1992-93; dir. religious edn. St. John the Bapt., Dover, Ind., 1993-96, Blessed Sacrament, Ft. Mitchell, Ky., 1996—. Group exhibits include Clermont County Libr., Batavia, Ohio, 1990, Murdock Gallery, Cin., 1990, Studio San Giusseppe, Mount St. Joseph Coll., Cin., 1990, Milford Libr., Cin., 1991, Cathedral Fresh Art Exhibit, Covington, Ky., 1998 (1st pl.); represented in pvt. collections. Mem. Youth Encouragement Svcs., Aurora, Ind., 1985—; active Dearborn Highland Arts Coun., Lawrenceburg, Ind., 1990-95; mem. Rev. Club, Lawrenceburg, 1985—; dir. religious edn. Blessed Sacrament Parish, Ft. Mitchell, Ky., 1996—. Mem. Greendale Garden Club. Avocations: art, reading, traveling, gardening, swimming. Home: 1286 Indian Woods Trl Lawrenceburg IN 47025-8678 Office: 2407 Dixie Hwy Fort Mitchell KY 41017-2936

WILLSON, CHARLES EMERY, school system administrator; b. Bunkerhill, Kans., Jan. 16, 1936; s. Emery J. and Clara Louise (Marsh) W.; m. Margaret Sue Caldwell, Sept. 23, 1960; children: Nanci Sue, Wade Hunter, Amy Louise. BS in Edn., Emporia State U., 1960; MS in Edn., Ft. Hays State U., 1965; postgrad., Kans. U., Iowa State U. Cert. tchr., adminstr., Kans. Classroom tchr., coach Unified Sch. Dist. 208, WaKeeney, Kans., 1960-63; classroom tchr. USD 489, Hays, Kans., 1963-64; classroom tchr., coach R-1 Jefferson County Schs., Lakewood, Colo., 1964-67, bldg. adminstr., 1967-74, Unified Sch. Dist. 407, Russell, Kans., 1974-78, adminstr., 1985-87; banking, ins. exec. Home State Bank, Russell, 1978-85; asst. supt. Unified Sch. Dist. 234, Ft. Scott, Kans., 1987-91; supt. schs. Unified Sch. Dist. 449, Easton, Kans., 1991—. Tchr./trainer Tchr. Effectiveness and Student Achievement, Ft. Scott, 1988—; presenter, coord. Outcomes Based Edn./Effective Schs., Kans., 1987—. Cast mem. Russell Arts Coun., 1981; mem. sch. bd. Unified Sch. Dist. 407, 1980; chmn. bd. trustees Trinity United Meth. Ch., Russell, 1976-86; mgr., coach Am. Legion Baseball, Russell, 1985-86; mem. Leadership Ft. Scott, 1988. Mem. ASCD, Am. Assn. Sch. Adminstrs., United Sch. Adminstrs. Kans., Kans. Assn. Sch. Adminstrs., Kans. Assn. Supervision and Curriculum Devel., Kans. State Bd. Edn. (coun. supts. 1993-95), Greater Kansas City Assn. Supervision and Curriculum Devel., Kansas City Learning Exch., Masons, Phi Delta Kappa (coord. 1988). Avocations: golf, hunting, classical music. Home: 22715 W 49th Ter Shawnee Mission KS 66226-3848 Office: Unified Sch Dist 449 32502 Easton Rd Easton KS 66020-7260

WILMERDING, JOHN, art history educator, museum curator; b. Boston, Apr. 28, 1938; s. John Currie and Lila Vanderbilt (Webb) W. AB, Harvard U., 1960, AM, 1961, PhD, 1965. Asst. prof. art Dartmouth Coll., 1965-68, asso. prof., 1968-73, Leon E. Williams prof., 1973-77, chmn. dept. art, 1968-72, chmn. humanities divsn., 1971-72; sr. curator Am. art Nat. Gallery of Art, 1977-83, dep. dir., 1983-88; Sarofim prof. Am. art Princeton (N.J.) U., 1988—, chmn. dept. art and archeology, 1992-99. Vis. lectr. history of art Yale U., 1972; vis. prof. fine arts Harvard U., 1976; vis. prof. art U. Md., 1979; vis. prof. art history U. Del., 1982; hon. curator painting Peabody Mus., Salem, Mass.; vis. curator Met. Mus., 1988—. Author: Fitz Hugh Lane, American Marine Painter, 1964, A History of American Marine Painting, 1968, Pittura Americana dell' Ottocento, 1969, Robert Salmon, Painter of Ship and Shore, 1971, Fitz Hugh Lane, 1971, Winslow Homer, 1972, Audubon, Homer, Whistler and 19th Century America, 1972, The Genius of American Painting, 1973, American Art, 1976, American Light, The Luminist Movement, 1980, American Masterpieces from the National Gallery of Art, 1980, An American Perspective, 1981, Important Information Inside, 1982, Andrew Wyeth, The Helga Pictures, 1987, American Marine Paintings, 2d edit., 1987, Paintings by Fitz Hugh Lane, 1988; American Views: Essays on American Art, 1991, The Artist's Mount Desert: American Painters on the Maine Coast, 1994, Compass and Clock: Defining Moments in American Culture, 1999. Trustee Coll. of the Atlantic, Bar Harbor, Maine, Guggenheim Mus., N.Y.C., N.E. Harbor Libr., Maine, Wendell Gilley Mus., S.W. Harbor, Maine, Wyeth Endowment for Am. Art, Wilmington, Del.; trustee emeritus Shelburne Mus., Vt.; mem. trustees' coun. Nat. Gallery Art, Washington. Guggenheim fellow, 1973-74. Fellow Phila. Atheneum (hon.); Mem. Coll. Art Assn., Am. Studies Assn. Office: Princeton U Dept Art and Archaeology 105 Mccormick Hl Princeton NJ 08544-1018

WILMETH, DON BURTON, theatre arts educator, theatre historian, administrator, editor; b. Houston, Dec. 15, 1939; s. Perry Davis and Pauline W.; m. Judy Eslie Hansgen, June 10, 1963; 1 child, Michael Tyler. BA, Abilene Christian U., 1961; MA, U. Ark., 1962; PhD, U. Ill., 1964; MA ad Eundem (hon.), Brown U., 1970. Tchg. asst. U. ARk., Fayetteville, 1961-62; U. Ill., Urbana, 1962-64; asst. prof., head drama dept. Eastern N.Mex. U., Portales, 1964-67; from asst. to prof. theatre arts, dept. chmn. Brown U., Providence, 1967—. Curator (hon.) H. Adrain Smith Collection of Conjuring Books and Magicana, 1988—; Asa Messer chair H. Adrain Smith Collecitons of Conjuring Books and Magicana, 1998—2003; cons. Internat. Exch. Scholars (Fulbright), Washington, 1982—84, Am. Memory Libr. Congress, 1992—95, Am. Theatre Series Sta. WNET-TV, N.Y.C., Shaw Theatre Festival, Ont., 1993—; juror George Freedley Theater Book Award com., 1971—93, 1994—, Barnard Hewitt Book award com., 1985—89; mem. com. hist. figures Theatre Hall of Fame, 1993—; D.R. and Eva Mitchell vis. disting. prof. Trinity U., San Antonio, 1995; faculty Trintiy Repertory Theatre/Brown U. Consortium, 2001—. Dir.: numerous theatrical prodns. including (Brown U. Prodns.) Carousel (Rodgers and Hammerstein), 1968, The Devils, 1969, The Night of the Iguana (Tennessee Williams), 1970, Much Ado About Nothing (Shakespeare), Too True to Be Good, 1972, Dial "M" for Murder, 1972, The Beggar's Opera (John Gray), 1973, Company (Stephen Sondheim), 1974, Look Homeward, Angel, 1975, Secret Service, 1976, Romeo and Juliet (Shakespeare), 1977, The Hostage (Brendan Behan), 1978, The Seagull (Chekhov), 1979, The Importance of Being Ernest (Oscar Wilde), 1980, The Playboy of the Western World (J.M. Synge), 1982, The Rivals (Sheridan), 1983, Our Town (Thornton Wilder), 1985, Philadelphia Story, 1987, Mrs. Warren's Profession (Shaw), 1989, The Duchess of Malfi (John Webster), 1992, The Illusion, 1994, Sweeney Todd, 1998, Candide, 2002, also numerous prodns. at other venues; actor: Twelfth Night (Colo. Shakespeare Festival), 1960, The Tempest (Champlain Shakespeare Festival), 1962, The Passion of Dracula, 1979, The Runner Stumbles, 1984, Follies, 1991; author: The American Stage to World War I, 1978, American and English Popular Entertainment, 1980, George Frederick Cooke, 1980, The Language of American Popular Entertainment, 1981, Variety Entertainment and Outdoor Amusements, 1982; co-author: Theater in the United States: A Documentary History, Vol. I, 1750-1915, 1996; co-editor: Plays by Augustin Daly, 1984, Plays by William Hooker Gillette, 1983, Mud Show, American Tent Circus Life, 1988, Cambridge Guide to American Theatre, 1993, sole edit., 1996; editor: (book series) Cambridge Studies Am. Theatre and Drama, 1992—; coeditor: Cambridge History of Am. Theatre, 3 vols., 1998—2001 (Freedley and Barnard Hewitt awards, 1999), Cambridge Guide to World Theatre, 1988, Cambridge Guide to Theatre, 1995, Staging the Nation, 1998; cons., interviewer (documentaries) (PBS) Houdini, 2000; contbr. articles, chapters to books; contbr. book revs., World Book Ency., Dictionary Am. Biography, Ency. N.Y.C., other ref. material, adv. editor 7 jours. Bd. dirs. Am. Inst. Am. Theatre Studies, Bloomington, Ind., 1981—84; corp. mem. Providence Pub. Libr., 1983—; bd. mgrs. Players of Providence, 1966—80; mem. adv. bd. East Lynne Theatre Co., Secaucus, NJ, 1981—, Langston Hughes Cultural Arts Ctr., Providence, 1982—92, Actors Theatre of Louisville, 1987—; grants panelist R.I. State Coun. Arts, Providence, 1981—. Recipient New Eng. Theatre award for theatre contbn. on nat. level, 1998, award, U. Ark., 1998, Anthony Denning award, Eng., 2001, Career Achievement award in Academic Theatre, Assn. Theatre in Higher Edn., 2001, Sustained Excellence in Editing award, 2003; John Simon Guggenheim fellow, 1982. Mem.: Nat. Theatre Conf., Coll. Fellows Am. Theatre (bd. dirs. 1995—96, dean 1996—98), Soc. Advancement Edn. (bd. trustees 1977—91, N.Y.C.), Am. Soc. Theatre Rsch. (exec. com. 1976—78, 1980—83, 1985—88, pres. 1991—94, sec. 1995—2002, Disting. Scholarship award 2001), Am. Theatre and Drama Soc. (mem. exec. bd. 1995—99, Betty Jean Jones award 1999), Internat. Fed. Theatre Rsch. (exec. bd. 1995—97), Theatre Libr. Assn. (v.p. 1981—84). Avocations: reading, collecting theatre books and memorabilia, bookbinding. Home: 525 Hope St Providence RI 02906-1630 Office: Brown U Dept Theatre Speech and Dance PO Box 1897 Providence RI 02912-1897 E-mail: Don_Wilmeth@brown.edu.

WILSEY, PHILIP ARTHUR, computer science educator; b. Kewanee, Ill., Sept. 24, 1958; s. George A. and Mary Lee (Smith) W.; m. Marilyn L. Hargis, Jan. 2, 1982; children: Patrick A., Zackary E., Alexis L. BS in Math., Ill. State U., 1981; MS in Computer Sci., U. La., Lafayette, 1985, PhD in Computer Sci., 1987. Computer programmer Union Ins. Group, Bloomington, Ill., 1980-81, Bob White Computing & Software, Bloomington, 1981-82; rsch. asst. U. La., Lafayette, 1983-87; asst. prof. U. Cin., 1987-2000; ptnr. Bubu Soft, LLC, 1998—2003; pres. Clifton Labs., Inc., 1997—; assoc. prof. U. Cin., 2000—03, prof., 2003—; ptnr. Palm Properties, LLC, 2003—. Cons. MTL, Dayton, 1992-99; mem. editorial bd. VLSI Design, 1993—2002. Assoc. editor: Potentials Mag., 1992-98, 2003—, editor-in-chief, 1999—2003; contbr. articles to profl. jours. Mem. IEEE (sr.), Assn. Computing Machinery. Home: 3678 Fawnrun Dr Cincinnati OH 45241-3834 Office: Exptl Computing Lab Design Lab Dept ECECS PO Box 210030 Cincinnati OH 45221-0030 E-mail: philip.wilsey@ieee.org.

WILSON, ANGELA SABURN, nursing educator; b. Norfolk, Va., May 24, 1961; d. Richard Ruben and Rosa Faye (Mobley) Saburn; m. Robert Walker Wilson, Mar. 4, 1989. Diploma, Norfolk Gen. Hosp. Sch. Nsg., 1987; BSN, Old Dominion U., 1989, MSN, 1993; PhD in Nursing, U. Va., 2001. RN, Va.; cert. pediatric nurse. Staff nurse Children's Hosp. of King's Daus., Norfolk, 1987-90, staff devel. coord., 1990-94, nurse educator, 1994-95; nursing instr. DePaul Hosp., Norfolk, 1995-96, Christopher Newport U., 1996—2001, asst. prof., dept. chair, 2001—03; assoc. prof., dept. chair U. of Va., Coll. at Wise, 2003—. Mem.: Va. Nurses Assn., Phi Kappa Phi, Alpha Chi, Sigma Theta Tau (Region 13 coord., past pres. Epsilon Chi chpt., mem. Beta Kappa chpt.), Golden Key Honor Soc. Home: 5709 Warning St Virginia Beach VA 23464 E-mail: asw5u@uvawise.edu.

WILSON, ANNETTE SIGRID, elementary school educator; b. Harlan, IA, Jan. 30, 1953; d. Anker Christian and Ruth Edith Eastergard; m. John Roger Wilson, Dec. 21, 1974; children: Elicia Ruth, Elizabeth Annette. BS, Bob Jones U., 1975; MAE, U. No. Iowa, 2001. Educator Arlington Bapt. Sch., Baltimore, Md., 1976—78, Calvary Bapt. Sch., Normal, Ill., 1978—80, Walnut (Iowa) Pub. Sch., 1986—2000, Council Bluffs (Iowa) Cmty. Schs., 2000—03; trainer Area Edn. Agy., Council Bluffs, 1994—98. Homebound spl. edn. instr.1984, 1983—84. Recipient Optimist Award for Outstanding Tchr., 1992, 1996, Leadership award, Area XIII, 1998. Mem.: Phi Delta Kappa Internat. Home: 902 Baldwin St Harlan IA 51537

WILSON, BARBARA T. retired physical education educator; b. Pisgah, Ala., June 5, 1944; d. Jesse Leroy and Lillie Belle (Long) Tinker; m. Jimmy Dale Wilson, June 30, 1963; childern: Eric Dale, Christopher, Chadwick, Jeremy Lance. BS in Heatlh Phys. Edn., Biology, Jacksonville State U., 1967; MS in Health Phys. Edn., U. Ala., 1969, AA/EdS in Health Edn., 1980. Cert. tchr. Tchr. Calhoun County Bd. Edn., Anniston, Ala., 1967-74, Jacksonville (Ala.) State U., 1974-97; ret., 1997. Author: Aqua Robics, 1991; co-author: Curriculum Voices, 1986; editor Jacksonville State U. H.P.E.R. Alumni newsletter, 1993-95. Mem. AAHPERD, NEA, Coll. Assn. Health, Phys. Edn., Recreation and Dance (sec., treas. 1986-87, 84-85, pres.-elect 1994-95, pres. 1995-96, Coll.-Univ. Profl. of Yr. award 1998, Pathfinder award 2001), Ala. State Assn. Health, Phys. Edn., Recreation and Dance, Ala. Edn. Assn., Delta Kappa Gamma (pres. Beta Phi chpt. 1989-92, 96-98, dist. II dir. 1994-96). Avocations: walking, painting, gardening, cooking, traveling.

WILSON, BENNIE JAMES, III, business educator; b. San Antonio, Aug. 5, 1943; s. Bennie James Jr. and Claressa (Deary) W.; m. Karen Inez Wanda Paul, Aug. 8, 1981; children: Benét Jenene, Claressa Delores. BS, San Jose (Calif.) State Coll., 1965; MBA, U. Rochester, N.Y., 1969; EdD, Auburn (Ala.) U., 1979. Sr. profl. in human resources Soc. for Human Resource Mgmt.; chief adminstrv. officer credentials C.C. State of Calif. Sr. rsch. fellow Nat. Def. U., Washington, 1982-83; dep. base comdr., dir. pers. Edwards (Calif.) AFB, 1983-86; vice comdr., dir. testing U.S. Mil. Entrance Processing Command, Gt. Lakes, Ill., 1986-90; asst. chief of staff for pers. and adminstrn. U.S. Forces, Seoul, Republic of Korea, 1990-92; interim comdr., vice commandant Air Force Inst. of Tech., Dayton, Ohio, 1992-95; dir. human resource devel. San Antonio State Hosp., 1996-97; gen. mgr. Lucent Techs. Svcs. Co., Inc., 1997-98; asst. dean, sr. lectr. Coll. of Bus. U. Tex., San Antonio, 1998—. Bd. of advisors Hidea Innovative Products, LLC, San Antonio. Editor: The Guard and Reserve in the Total Force: The First Decade, 1983. Trustee City of San Antonio Housing Trust Fund, San Antonio, 1998-2002; mem. City of San Antonio Citizen Adv. Action Bd., 1998-2002, Greater San Antonio C. of C., 1998-2002; sec., bd. dirs. The Estates at Champions Run Homeowners Assn.; chmn. City of San Antonio Commn. on Literacy, 2002. Col. USAF, 1965-95. Mem. Am. Legion, Mensa, Phi Delta Kappa, Omega Psi Phi. Avocation: golf. Home: 73 Champions Run San Antonio TX 78258-7704 Office: U of Tex at San Antonio Coll of Bus 6900 N Loop 1604 W San Antonio TX 78249-1130 E-mail: bjwilson@utsa.edu.

WILSON, BEVERLY MANGHAM, secondary education educator, artist; b. Columbus, Ga., Mar. 31, 1944; d. Jesse Roger and Ethel Shealy (Webster) Mangham; divorced; children: Altaira Lea, Rion Troy. BA Art Edn., U. Southwestern La., Lafayette, 1967; MA Art Edn., La. State U., 1987. Cert. tchr., La. Art tchr. Gen. George S. Patton Sch., Chgo., 1966-67; tchr. 6th grade Loda, Ill., 1967-69; religious edn. dir. Unitarian Ch. Baton Rouge, La., 1974-82; art tchr. Catholic High Sch., Baton Rouge, 1980-87, La. State U., 1989—, U. Lab. Sch.; tchr. art internat. baccalaureate degree program La. State Lab. Sch., 2001—. With ind. study program La. State U., 1990—; faculty Southea. La. U., 1993. Exhibited in juried shows Savannah Sch. Savannah, Ga., 2002, La. State U. Union Gallery, 2000, Xian (China) Arts Coun.,1998, La. State U. Gallery, Baton Rouge, 1999, La. State U. Sch. Design Gallery, 1997, Unitarian Ch. of Baton Rouge, 1996; curator, exhibitor Artists Who Teach, La. Arts and Sci. Ctr., Baton Rouge, 1993, others; contbr. articles to profl. jours. Apptd. mem. La. State Arts Coun.; religious edn. dir. Unitarian Ch. Baton Rouge; sponsor Nat. Art Honor Soc., Student Nat. Art Edn. Assn., Univ. Lab. Sch. Art Club. Rrecipient Vol. in Pub. Schs. commendation award, 1984, 86, 87, 88, State of La. Cert. Commendation, 1983, 85, 86; fellow Kappa Kappa Gamma, 1988. Mem. Nat. Art Edn. Assn., Nat. Assn. Lab. Schs., La. Art Edn. Assn. (La. Secondary Art Educator of Yr. 1993, La. Art Educator of Yr. 1996, Disting. Svc. within the Profession award 1999), Assn. Gifted and Talented, Youth Art Coun. Am., Phi Delta Kappa, Phi Kappa Phi. Unitarian Universalist. Avocations: painting, quilting, reading. Office: U Lab Sch La State U Baton Rouge LA 70803-0001

WILSON, BLENDA JACQUELINE, foundation administrator; b. Woodbridge, N.J., Jan. 28, 1941; d. Horace and Margaret (Brogsdale) Wilson; m. Louis Fair Jr. AB, Cedar Crest Coll., 1962; AM, Seton Hall U., 1965; PhD, Boston Coll., 1979; DHL (hon.), Cedar Crest Coll., 1987, Loretto Heights Coll., 1988, Colo. Tech. Coll., 1988, U. Detroit, 1989; LLD (hon.), Rutgers U., 1989, Ea. Mich. U., 1990, Cambridge Coll., 1991, Schoolcraft Coll., 1992; DHL (hon.), Cambridge Coll., 2001, Antioch U., 1999, Salve Regina U., 2002; DPublic Svc. (hon.), U. Mass., 2002; DHL (hon.), Merrimack Coll., 2001. Tchr. Woodbridge Twp. Pub. Schs., 1962-66; exec. dir. Middlesex County Econ. Opportunity Corp., New Brunswick, N.J., 1966-69; exec. asst. to pres. Rutgers U., New Brunswick, N.J., 1969-72; sr. assoc. dean Grad. Sch. Edn. Harvard U., Cambridge, Mass., 1972-82; v.p. effective sector mgmt. Ind. Sector, Washington, 1982-84; exec. dir. Colo. Commn. Higher Edn., Denver, 1984-88; chancellor and prof. pub. adminstrn. & edn. U. Mich., Dearborn, 1988-92; pres. Calif. State U., Northridge, 1992-99, Nellie Mae Found., Braintree, Mass., 1999—. Am. del. U.S./U.K. Dialogue About Quality Judgments in Higher Edn.; adv. bd. Mich. Consolidated Gas Co., Stanford Inst. Higher Edn. Rsch., U. So. Col. Dist. 60 Nat. Alliance, Nat. Ctr. for Rsch. to Improve Postsecondary Teaching and Learning, 1988-90; bd. dirs. Alpha Capital Mgmt.; mem. higher edn. colloquium Am. Coun. Edn., vis. com. Divsn. Continuing Edn. in Faculty of Arts & Scis., Harvard Coll., Pew Forum on K-12 Edn. Reform in U.S., The Coll. Bd., Federated Dorchester Neighborhood Ho., Fed. Res. Bank of Boston. Dir. U. Detroit Jesuit High Sch., Northridge Hosp. Med. Ctr., 1993-99, Arab Cmty. Ctr. for Econ. and Social Svcs., Union Bank, J. Paul Getty Trust, James Irvine Found., 1996-99, Internat. Found. Edn. and Self-Help, Achievement Coun., L.A.; dir., vice chair Met. Affairs Corp.; exec. bd. Detroit area coun. Boy Scouts Am.; bd. dirs. Commonwealth Fund, Henry Ford Hosp.-Fairlane Ctr., Henry Ford Health System, Met. Ctr. for High Tech., United Way Southeastern Mich.; mem. Nat. Coalition 100 Black Women, Detroit, Race Rels. Coun. Met. Detroit, Women & Founds., Greater Detroit Interfaith Round Table NCCJ, Adv. Bd. Valley Cultural Ctr., Woodland Hills; trustee assoc. Boston Coll.; trustee emeritus Cambridge Coll.; trustee emeritus, bd. dirs. Found. Ctr.; trustee Henry Ford Mus. & Greenfield Village, Sammy Davis Jr. Nat. Liver Inst. Mem. AAUW, Assn. Governing Bds. (adv. coun. of pres.'s), Edn. Commn. of the States (student minority task force), Am. Assn. Higher Edn. (chair-elect), Am. Assn. State Colls. & Univs. (com. on policies & purposes, acad. leadership fellows selection com.), Assn. Black Profls. and Adminstrs., Assn. Black Women in Higher Edn., Women Execs. State Govt., Internat. Women's Forum, Mich. Women's Forum, Women's Econ. Club Detroit, Econ. Club, Rotary. Office: Nellie Mae Edn Found 1250 Hancock St 205N Quincy MA 02169-4331

WILSON, BONNIE JEAN, lawyer, educator, investor; b. Alameda County, Calif. d. August and Violet Adeline (Lockard) Ritzenthaler; m. Allan Nicholas Wilson (dec.); children: Albert Clyde, Bruce Allan. BA, cert. in elem. tchg., U. Calif., Berkeley; JD, Thomas Jefferson SOL, 1981. Bar: Calif.; cert. tchr., Calif. Elem. sch. tchr. Contra Costa and San Diego Counties; intern San Diego County Dist. Atty. Office, 1981; pvt. practice La Jolla, Calif., 1982—. Mem., adv. dir. La Jolla Presbyn. Ch., San Diego Opera Assn., San Diego Symphony Assn., Friends of the La Jolla Libr.; edn. activist, 1972-76. Mem. Calif. State Bar Assn., San Diego County Bar Assn., La Jolla Newcomer's Club (bd. dirs. 1968-69), U. Calif. Berkeley Alumni Club (bd. dirs. San Diego chpt. 1961-62), Am. Assn. Ind. Investors (bd. dirs. 1991-97), La Jolla Beach and Tennis Club. Presbyterian. Home: 2235 Bahia Dr La Jolla CA 92037-7007

WILSON, CAROLYN ROSS, retired school administrator; b. Lake Charles, La., June 25, 1941; d. Charles Wesley and Lucille Gertrude (Payne) Ross; m. James David Wilson, Apr. 10, 1971; 1 child, Charlise. BS in Music Edn. cum laude, Xavier U., 1962; MMus in Music Edn., Cath. U., Washington, 1968; postgrad., U. D.C., 1985-86, George Washington U., 1987-88, Harvard U., 1989. Tchr. Xavier U. Jr. Sch. Music, New Orleans, 1960-61, Orleans Parish Schs., New Orleans, 1962-63, D.C. Pub. Schs., Washington, 1964-87, curriculum writer, summer 1984, 85, adminstrv. intern Ea. High Sch., 1987-88, asst. prin. Cardozo High Sch., 1988-89, asst. prin. Duke Ellington Sch. of Arts, 1989-93; prin. Duke Ellington Sch. Arts, Washington, 1993-97—; proposal reader U.S. Dept. Edn., 1998, 98, 99. Curriculum writer music dept. D.C. Pub. Schs., Washington, 1984-85, dir. All City High Sch. Chorus, 1973. Composer: A Dedication to Federal City Alumnae Chapter of Delta, Sigma Theta Sorority. Inc., 1973. Lector Immaculate Conception Ch., Washington, 1986—; named D.C. Tchr. of Yr., 1987. Recipient Cert. of Merit-Outstanding Tchr. and Prin. award D.C. Govt., 1994; U.S. Dept. Edn. Effective Schs. grantee, Washington, 1992. Mem. ASCD, Instn. for Devel. Ednl. Activities (6th yr. fellow, session chair 1988, seminar leader 1991, 92, 93, 94), Delta Sigma Theta (Federal City Alumnae chpt.). Roman Catholic. Avocations: reading, travel, bowling, musical arranging, playing the piano.

WILSON, CAROLYN TAYLOR, librarian; b. Cookeville, Tenn., June 10, 1936; d. Herman Wilson and Flo (Donaldson) Taylor; m. Larry Kittrell Wilson, June 14, 1957 (dec.); children: Jennifer Wilson Rust, Elissa Anne Wilson. BA, David Lipscomb Coll., 1957; MLS, George Peabody Coll., 1976. Tchr. English Fulton County Sch. System, Atlanta, 1957-59; serials cataloger Vanderbilt U. Libr., Nashville, 1974-77; asst. libr. United Meth. Pub. House, Nashville, 1978-80; collection devel. libr. David Lipscomb U., Nashville, 1980—, acting dir. Beaman Libr., 1998, dir. Beaman Libr., 1999—. Cons. and rschr. in field; project dir. Tenn.'s Lit. Legacy for Tenn. Humanities Coun., 1994—, ALA grant, Frontier in Am. Culture, 1996-98; project dir. Tenn. Humanities Coun. grant, 1998—; rep. Tenn. Avd. Coun. Librs., Acad. Librs., 1999—. Rsch. asst. Handbook of Tennessee Labor History, 1987-89. Adv. bd. So. Festival of Books, Nashville, 1988-90, 90—, vol. coord., 1989, 90—; project dir. Women's Words (summer grant program) for Tenn. Humanities Coun., Tenn.'s Literary Legacy (summer grant program), 1994-96, Growing Up Southern (summer grant), 1996—, ALA grant The Frontier in Am. Culture, 1996—. Recipient Nat. Honor Soc. award Phi Alpha Theta, 1956, Internat. Honor Soc. award Beta Phi Mu, 1980, Frances Neel Cheney award Tenn. Libr. Assn., 1992; nominee Athena award, 1992; Growing Up Southern summer grantee, 1996—. Mem. ALA, Tenn. Hist. Soc., Tenn. Libr. Assn. (Frances Neel Cheney award 1992), Southeastern Libr. Assn. (chmn. outstanding S.E. author award com. 1991-92, chmn. So. Books competition 1992-94, sec. exec. bd. 1997—), Women's Nat. Book Assn. (pres., v.p., treas., awards chmn. 1980—), Disciples of Christ Hist. Soc. (bd. dirs. 2002—), Tenn. Writers Alliance (bd. dirs. 1995—). Democrat. Avocations: reading, cooking, jogging, sailing. Office: David Lipscomb U Beaman Libr # 310 Nashville TN 37204 E-mail: carolyn.wilson@lipscomb.edu.

WILSON, CATHERINE PHILLIPS, elementary education educator; b. Calif., July 19, 1935; d. Harry Leland and Catherine (Waterbury) Phillips; m. Henry S. Wilson Jr., Apr. 12, 1958 (dec. Jan. 1979); children: Lee, Janell, Carey, Kimberly, Blake. Student, U. of the Pacific, 1953-54; BA in Edn. and Psychology, Calif. State Coll., San Jose, 1957; postgrad., Portland State U., 1981-89, Chapman U., Danville, Calif., 1990-93. Cert. tchr., Oreg. Sales coord. The Donatello Hotel, San Francisco, 1981-82; ind. mgmt. cons. A. Cal Rossi, Inc., San Francisco, 1983-84; tchr. 5th grade Portland (Oreg.) Pub. Schs., 1985, tchr. Glencoe Sch., 1987-89; tchr. 1st grade Oakland (Calif.) Unified Dist., 1989-90; tchr. 2d grade Martin Luther King Elem. Sch. Portland Pub. Schs., 1990-93, tchr. 2d grade Lent Elem. Sch., 1993—. Author: Soaring to Success, 1986, Escape to Freedom, 1987, Journey Through the Galazies, 1988. Named Oreg. Tchr. of Yr., U.S. West, 1991, Spirit of the N.W., KATU Channel 2, Portland, 1992; recipient Tchrs. Making a Difference award Nationwide Ins., 1994, Impact II award Reading in a Castle of Dreams, 1994, KEX-Fred Meyer Tchr. award, 1994. Mem. Oreg. Edn. Assn., Kiwanis Early Risers, Kappa Alpha Theta, Alpha Delta Kappa. Republican. Roman Catholic. Avocations: reading, writing, collecting, speaking to groups. Office: Lent Elem Sch 5105 SE 97th Ave Portland OR 97266-3747

WILSON, CECILIA ANN, special education educator; b. Corning, N.Y., Feb. 8, 1959; d. Leroy Eugene and Helen Esther (Rodman) W. BA, Manhattanville Coll., Purchase, N.Y., 1981; M Spl. Edn., Mansfield (Pa.) U., 1986. Cert. tchr., tchr. asst., N.Y. Asst. tchr. mid. sch. Corning (N.Y.)-Painted Post Sch. Dist.; jr.-sr. high sch. tchr. spl. edn. Steuben-Allegany Bd. Coop. Ednl. Svcs., Bath, N.Y.; mid. sch. tchr. spl. edn. Penn Yan (N.Y.) Sch. Dist.; jr.-sr. high sch. resource room tchr., chmn. com. spl. edn. Avoca (N.Y.) Cen. Sch.; resource room tchr. Elmira (N.Y.) City Sch. Dist. Mem. com. special edn. Resource Room, Cohocton (N.Y.) Ctrl. Sch. Dist.; coord. student affairs Empire State Speech & Hearing Clinic, Inc. Sec. N.Y. State area 15 Spl. Olympics. Mem. NEA. Home: 223 Pritchard Ave Corning NY 14830-1735

WILSON, CHERYL YVONNE, elementary school educator, secondary school educator; b. Dayton, Ohio, Sept. 25, 1958; d. Samuel Wesley Wilson Sr. and Hazel Oneida Wilson; m. Henry Heard Cofield Jr., July 27, 1985. Student, Ohio State U., 1976—81; AA, Miami U., 1987. Legal sec. Raymond W. O'Neal, Sr. Atty. at Law, Middletown, Ohio, 1982—83; reorder buyer Dason's Hardware Ctr., 1984—85; Writer's Digest Novel Writing Workshop Middletown City Sch. Dist., 1986—87; deputy clk. Butler County Clk. Cts., Hamilton, 1990—91; mail room clk. Butler County Printing Co., 1992—95; mail courier, security officer Johnson Controls Svcs., Inc., 1998—2000. Pres., CEO Ohio Writer's Pub. Co., Middletown, 1987—, 1991—. Mem. U.S. Bicentennial Commn., 2003—, curator, exec. dir., 2003. Nominee 87th Spingarn medal award, NAACP, 1998, 2001, Coretta Scott King book award, 2002, Oprah Winfrey Angel Network Use Your Life award, 2003. Mem.: NAACP (life Broze Plaque award 2002), Internat. African Am. Genealogy Rsch. Pub. Assn. (curator 2003—, exec. dir. 2003—), Middleton Hist. Soc. (life). Republican. Mem. Lds Ch. Avocations: writing, reading, photography.

WILSON, CHRISTINE ANN, biologist, educator; b. Kitchener, Ont., Can., Sept. 26, 1953; came to U.S., 1979; d. Harry and Fernande Marie (Giguère) Mazurek; m. George Harlan, Apr. 26, 1974; children: James Owen, Benjamin, Nathaniel Aaron. BS with honors in Biology, U. Waterloo (Can.), 1977, MS in Biology, 1980. Adj. prof. biology Thiel Coll., Greenville, Pa., 1988-92, Pa. State U., Sharon, 1989-92; asst. prof. biology C.C. Allegheny County, Monroeville, Pa., 1992—98; assoc. prof. biology U. Md., 2000—. Cons. Internat. Field Studies, 1996-98. Co-author (lab. manual) Ecological Field Studies, 1996; contbr. articles to profl. jours. Active Cub Scouts and Boy Scouts Am., 1988—; vol. Osprey reintroduction program Moraine Preservation Soc., 1991-96. C.C. Allegheny County mini-grantee, 1994, 96. Mem. Human Anatomy and Physiology Soc. (N.E. regional conf. advisor and coord. 1996), Am. Microbiol. Soc., Bartramian Audubon Soc., Sigma Xi Sci. Rsch. Soc. Presbyterian. Achievements include work as coordinator 1996 N.E. regional human anatomy and physiology conf., Pitts.; coordinator first C.C. Allegheny County International field studies program for environmental studies in Nicaragua.

WILSON, CLARENCE SYLVESTER, JR., lawyer, educator; b. Bklyn., Oct. 22, 1945; s. Clarence Sylvester and Thelma Louise (Richards) W.; m. Helena Chapellin Iribarren, Jan. 26, 1972. BA, Williams Coll., 1967; JD, Northwestern U., 1974. Bar: Ill., 1975; U.S. Supreme Ct., 1985, U.S. Tax Ct. 1985, U.S. Ct. Appeals (7th cir.) 1985. Fgn. Svc. Res. officer U.S. Dept. of State, 1968-74; vice consul 3d sec. Am. Embassy, Caracas, Venezuela, 1969-71; adj. prof. law Kent Coll. of Law, Ill. Inst. Tech., Chgo., 1981-94; lectr. Columbia Coll., Chgo., 1996—; mem. vis. com. music dept., visual arts, U. Chgo., 1991-2003; mem. bd. govs. Sch. of Art Inst. of Chgo., 1994-2002; vice chmn. Jazz Mus. of Chgo., 1994-97; adj. prof. The John Marshall Law Sch., 1999-2000. Trustee Chgo. Symphony Orch., 1987-96, Art Inst. Chgo., 1990—; mem. adv. bd. Chgo. Dept. Cultural Affairs, 1988-97; bd. dirs. Arts Midwest, Mpls., 1985-89, Harold Washington Found., Chgo., 1989-91; mem. MERIT Music Program, 1991-96, Ill. Arts Coun., 1984-89; project mgr. Dept. Justice Task Force. The Pres.'s Pvt. Sector Survey on Cost Control in the Fed. Govt. (Grace Commn.), 1982-84. Mem. com. Ptnrs. in Excellence panel Ill. Arts Coun., 1998—2003. Mem. Lawyers for the Creative Arts (pres. 1987-88). Republican. Episcopalian. Avocations: music, art collecting. Office: 1130 S Michigan Ave #4303 Chicago IL 60605-2325 Fax: 312-583-0646. E-mail: hcwilson@ix.netcom.com.

WILSON, DARLENE ANDERSON, elementary school educator; b. L.A., 1935; d. Alfred and Alyce Anderson; m. Charles Cecil Wilson, Apr. 18, 1958; 1 child, Scott Wilson. BA, Occidental U., Eagle Rock, Calif., 1957; MA, Calif. State U., 1978. Gen. Elem., Kindergarten Primary, Adminstrv. Svcs., Calif. Kindergarten tchr. Buchanan St. Sch., Highland Park, Calif., 1957-58, Valley View Elem. Sch., Hollywood, Calif., 1959-60; 2nd and 3rd grade tchr. Fair Ave. Sch., N. Hollywood, Calif., 1960-61; kindergarten tchr. Napa St. Sch., Northridge, Calif., 1962-84. 5th grade tchr., acting prin., tng. tchr. Chatsworth Park Elem. Sch., Calif., 1984-95; grad. student advisor Milken Educator Awards, Beverly Hills, Calif., 1991. Tchr., chair Local Sch. Leadership Coun., Chatsworth, 1989-91. Recipient Hon. Svc. award Napa St. PTA, Northridge, Calif., 1983. Mem.: CRTA. Democrat. Avocations: tennis, hiking, dancing, reading, theatre. Home: 8419 Jason Ave Canoga Park CA 91304-3114 Office: Chatsworth Park Elem Sch 22005 Devonshire St Chatsworth CA 91311-2841

WILSON, DAVID GORDON, mechanical engineering educator; b. Sutton Coldfield, Warwick., Eng., Feb. 11, 1928; s. William and Florence Ida (Boulton) W.; m. Anne Ware Sears, July 18, 1963 (div. May 1988); children: John M.B., Erica Sears; m. Ellen Cecilia Warner, Dec. 30, 1988; 1 child, Susan Speck. Postgrad., MIT, Harvard U., 1955-57; BS with honors, U. Birmingham, UK, 1948; PhD, U. Nottingham, UK, 1953. Brush fellow, rsch. asst. Nottingham U., 1950-53; ship's 7th engr. officer Donaldson Line, Glasgow, UK, 1953; engr. Brush Elec. Engring. Co., Ltd., UK, 1953-55; sr. gas-turbine designer Ruston & Hornsby, Lincoln, UK, 1957-58; sr. lectr., mech. engring. U. Ibadan, Zaria, Nigeria, 1958-60; v.p., tech. dir. No. Rsch. and Engring. Corp., Cambridge, Mass., also U.K., 1960-66; assoc. prof. mech. engring. MIT, Cambridge, 1966-71, prof., 1971-94; prof. emeritus, 1994—; co-founder, chief sci. officer Wilson TurboPower, Inc., Woburn, Mass., 2001—. Vis. engr., Boeing Airplane Co., 1956-57; vis. fellow MIT and Harvard U., 1955-56; cons., lectr. in field. Author: The Design of Gas-Turbine Engines, 1991, The Design of High-Efficiency Turbomachinery and Gas Turbines, 1984, (with T.P. Korakianitis), 2d edit., 1998; co-author: (with Frank Rowland Whitt) Bicycling Science, 1974, 2d edit., 1982, 3d edit., 2004, (with Richard Wilson et al) The Health Effects of Fossil-Fuel Burning, 1981, (with Douglas Stephen Beck) Gas-Turbine Regenerators, 1996; co-editor: (with Allan V. Abbott) Human-Powered Vehicles, 1995; editor: Solid-Waste-Management Handbook, 1977, The Treatment and Management of Urban Solid Waste, 1972; editor Human Power, 1984-2002. Recipient T. Bernard Hall prize Inst. Mech. Engrs., 1954, Lord Weir 1st prize Inst. Mech. Engrs., 1955, Indsl. Rsch. IR-100 award, 1974, Reclamation Industries Internat. prize, 1974; Power-Jets-Sch. scholar, 1954; Commonwealth Fund fellow MIT and Harvard U., 1955-57. Avocations: human power, biking, hiking, tennis, music. Office: MIT/Mech Engring Rm 7-040 Cambridge MA 02139

WILSON, DAVID JAMES, chemistry researcher, educator; b. Ames, Ia., June 25, 1930; s. James Calmar and Alice Winona (Olmsted) W.; m. Martha Carolyn Mayers, Sept. 6, 1952; children: John Wesley, Charles Steven, William David, Andrew Lyman, Joyce Ballin. BS in Chemistry, Stanford U., 1952; postgrad., 1952-53, 55-57; PhD, Calif. Inst. Tech., 1958. Mem. faculty U. Rochester, N.Y., 1957-69, assoc. prof., 1963-67, prof. phys. chemistry, 1967-69; prof. Vanderbilt U., Nashville, 1969-95, prof. chemistry and environ. engring., 1977-95, prof. emeritus, 1995—, Alexander Heard disting. service prof., 1983-84; sr. rsch. assoc. Eckenfelder/Brown and Caldwell, Nashville, 1988-95, sr. rsch. fellow, 1995—. Vis. sr. lectr. chemistry U. Ife, Nigeria, 1964-65; vis. prof. U. Málaga, Spain, 1993-94; mem. Rochester Com. for Sci. Info., 1960-69, v.p., 1966-69; chmn. Nashville Com. for Sci. Info., 1971-74. Author: (book) Foam Flotation: Theory and Applications, Hazardous Waste Site Soil Remediation, Modeling of In Situ Techniques for Treatment of Contaminated Soils. Pres. Tenn. Environ. Coun., 1985-87. With AUS, 1953-55. Sp-3 U.S. Army, 1953—55, Army Chemical Center, Maryland. Recipient award Monroe County Conservation Coun., 1967, Tenn. Conservation League, 1971; Alfred P. Sloan Found. fellow, 1964-66. Mem. AAAS, Am. Chem. Soc., Tenn. Acad. Sci., Sigma Xi, Phi Beta Kappa. Avocations: ornithology, music, travel, hiking. Home: 11544 Quirk Rd Belleville MI 48111

WILSON, DAVID PAUL, computer educator, elementary education specialist; b. Pensacola, Fla., Jan. 31, 1957; s. Julian L. and Gertrude M. Wilson. AA, Pensacola Jr. Coll., 1982; BA, U. West Fla., 1984; MEd, U. Western Fla., 2001. Tchr. 4th grade Escambia County Sch. Bd., Pensacola, 1984-85, tchr. 5th grade, 1985-87, drop out prevention tchr., 1987-89, instr., 1989—. Team leader C. A. Weis Sch., Pensacola, 1989—, adminstrv. asst. summer sch. program, 1990, network adminstr., 1993—, CCTU tech. dir., 1994—. Mem. Fla. Assn. Computer Educators. Office: CA Weis Computer Sci Lab 2710 N Q St Pensacola FL 32505-5616

WILSON, DEBORAH SUE, elementary education educator; b. Ft. Riley, Kans., Feb. 16, 1966; d. George Nathaniel and Barbara Sue (Deavers) W. BA in History and Edn., Agnes Scott Coll., 1988; MEd, Ga. State U., 1993. Cert. tchr., Ga. Tchr. Atlanta Pub. Schs., 1989—. Active ch. neighborhood ctr. Peachtree Presbyn. Ch., Atlanta, 1991—. Mem. Nat. Assn. Edn. Young Children, PEO, Kappa Delta Pi. Avocations: reading, hiking, travel. Home: 4169 Spring Cove Dr Duluth GA 30097-2841 Office: Atlanta Pub Schs 1485 Woodland Atlanta GA 30316

WILSON, DEBORRAH, physical education educator; b. Tachikowa, Japan, Aug. 5, 1950; BS in Phys. Edn. and Health, U. Del., 1972; MEd, Wilmington Coll., 2000. Elem. phys. edn. tchr. Downes Elem. Sch.; instr. of programs, teen dir. YWCA, 1972—78; phys. edn. specialist Christina Sch. Dist., 1978—. Recipient Alumni award U. Del., 1993, Disting. Svc. award Maclary PTA, 1993, Del. Congress Parents and Tchrs. Inc.; named Ea. Region Elem. Sch. Phys. Edn. Tchr. of Yr., Nat. Assn. Sport and Phys. Edn., 1993, Elem. Phys. Edn. Tchr. of Yr., State of Del., 1993. Home: 731 Art Ln Newark DE 19713-1208

WILSON, DIANE BAER, health educator, dietitian, cancer prevention researcher; b. Flint, Mich., Feb. 10, 1949; d. John Henry and Phyllis Mae (Noyle) Baer; m. Stephen Russell Wilson, Oct. 2, 1971 (div. 1996); children: April Lynn, Robin Elaine. BS, U. Del., 1971; MS, La. State U., 1975; EdD in Health Edn. Adminstrn., U. S.C., 1991. Registered dietitian, S.C. Adj. instr. Fla. Internat. U., Miami, 1976-77; cons. Nutrition Cons. Svcs., Miami, 1977-79; dietitian Coral Reef Hosp., Miami, 1979-80; cons. dietitian Baker Hosp., Charleston, S.C., 1980-83; adj. asst. prof. dept. phys. edn. and health Coll. of Charleston, 1985-94; dir. MS in Health Professions Edn. Med. U. S.C., Charleston, 1994-97, assoc. prof., 1996—. Mem. exec. bd. PTA, George Fishburne Elem. Sch., 1990-93. U.S. Dept. HHS fellow, 1998. Mem. Am. Dietetic Assn. (mem. S.C. nutrition coun. exec. bd. 1993-94), S.C. Dietetic Assn. (treas. 1981-83, pres. 1984-85), Assn. Tchrs. Preventive Medicine, Otranto Civic Club Charleston, Omicron Nu, Gamma Sigma Delta, Phi Delta Kappa, Phi Upsilon Omicron. Republican. Avocations: reading, skiing. Office: Med U SC Coll Health Professions MS Program Health Prof Edn Charleston SC 29425

WILSON, DONALD WALLIN, academic administrator, communications educator; b. Poona, India, Jan. 9, 1938; s. Nathaniel Carter and Hannah Myrtle Wilson; children: Carrie, Jennifer, Gregory, Andrew. BA, So. Missionary Coll., 1959; MA, Andrews U., 1961; PhD, Mich. State U., 1966. Dean applied arts and tech. Ont. (Can.) Colls., North Bay, 1968-73; acad. dean Olivet Coll., 1973-76; pres. Castleton State Coll., 1976-79, Southampton Coll., 1979-83, prof. communications and history, 1973-83; pres., prof. Pittsburg State U. (Kans.), 1983-95; pres. Kilang Nusantara Pacific, 1995—; exec. v.p. Shepherd of the Hills Entertainment Group, Branson, Mo., 1997—. Author: The Untapped Source of Power in the Church, 1961, Long Range Planning, 1979, The Long Road From Turmoil to Self Sufficiency, 1989, The Next Twenty-Five Years: Indonesias Journey Into The Future, 1992, The Indispensable Man: Sudomo, 1992. Mem. Kans. Adv. Coun. of C.C.'s; bd. dirs. Internat. U. Thailand; pres. Internat. Univ. Found. Named Alumnus of Achievement Andrews U., 1981; recipient Outstanding Alumni award Mich. State U., 1984. Mem. Speech Communication Assn., Assn. Asian Studies, Internat. Univ. Found. (pres.), Rotary. Methodist. Office: Kilang Nusantara Pacific Office of Pres Frontenac KS 66763 Address: 503 Ohio St Pittsburg KS 66762-6429 E-mail: wdonaldwilson@aol.com.

WILSON, DONNA MAE, administrator, foreign language educator; b. Columbus, Ohio, Feb. 25, 1947; d. Everett John and Hazel Margaret (Bruck) Palmer; m. Steven L. Wilson, Nov. 16, 1968. BA, Ohio State U., 1973, MA, 1976; postgrad studies, U. Wash., Seattle Pacific U., U. Mass., 1980-93; cert., U. Salamanca, Spain, 1985. Tchg. assoc. Ohio State U., Columbus, 1974-76; lectr. U. Wash., Seattle, 1977-78; grants officer Seattle U., 1978-82; adj. prof. Shoreline Coll., Seattle, 1982-84; coord. fgn. langs., prof. Spanish Bellevue (Wash.) Coll., 1984-87; prof. Spanish Highline Coll., Des Moines, Wash., 1987-98, chair fgn. lang. dept., 1990-94, chair arts and humanities, 1994-98; assoc. dean acad. affairs Greenfield (Mass.) Coll., 1998—. Spkr. at lang. orgns., confs. regional and nat., 1985—. Editor: (book) Fronteras: En Contacto, 1992-93; (jours.) Modern Lang. Jour., 1991, 92, 94, 96, 97, Hispania, 1993, 95; text editor D. C. Heath and Co., Harcourt, Brace and Jovanovich, Houghton Mifflin, Prentice Hall; contbr. articles to profl. jours., chpt. to English of Science and Technology Learning, 2000. Mem. Mass. Bd. Higher Edn. Exit Assessment; pres. Mass. Coun. Acad. Deans, 2000-2001; assoc. deans think tank New England Resource Ctr. Higher Edn. Recipient cert. of excellence Phi Theta Kappa, 1990, Pathfinder award Phi Beta Kappa, 1995; fellowshp grant Coun. Internat. Edn. Exchange, Santiago, Chile, 1992. Mem. Nat. Coun. Instr. Adminstrns., Am. Assn. Tchrs. of Spanish (v.p. Wash.), Am. Coun. Tchrs. of Fgn. Langs. (cert. oral proficiency), Assn. Dept of Fgn. Langs. (exec. bd. 1994-97), Pacific N.W. Coun. Fgn. Langs., 1986-98, Nat. Assn. Fgn. Lang. Suprs., Sigma Delta Mu. (nat. exec. sec. 1992-98), Women in Highter Edn. Avocations: travel, assessment rsch. on 2d lang., outdoors. E-mail: donna123@educ.umass.edu.

WILSON, DORIS FANUZZI, learning disabilities consultant, educator; b. N.Y.C., Oct. 17, 1935; d. Vitoantonio and Rose (Colavito) Panzarino; children: James Douglas Fanuzzi, Robert Alan Fanuzzi; m. Richard Gerard Wilson, Aug. 21, 1977 (div. 1987). BA cum laude, Hunter Coll., 1956; MA, Montclair State U., 1978; supr. cert., Trenton State Coll., 1996. With Tri-County Ednl. Vocat. High Sch., Totowa, N.J., 1979-80; learning disabilities tchr., cons. Fairlawn (N.J.) Bd. Edn., 1980-82, Somerville (N.J.) Bd. Edn., 1982-83, Regional Child Study Team, Franklin, N.J., 1983-84; cons. curriculum and instrn. divsn. devel. disabilities N.J. Dept. Human Svcs., Trenton, 1984-91; program dir. The ARC/Mercer, 1993; learning cons. Highlands (N.J.) Bd. Edn., 1993-94, Trenton (N.J.) Bd. Edn., 1994-96, Bergen County Spl. Svcs. Sch. Dist., 1996-97, Piscataway Bd. Edn., 1998—. Apptd. by gov. audiology and speech-lang. pathology adv. com., 1993-1998. Active Nat. Women's Polit. Caucus; co-founder, exec. advisor Capital Caucus (Md., DC, Va.); former vice chmn. Rep. Task Force. Mem. Assn. Learning Cons., Pub. Rels. Soc. Am. (internat. com.), Learning Disabilities Assn., Friends of Decatur House, Capitol Hill Club. Avocations: tennis, reading, ballroom dancing, foreign travel. E-mail: dariswilson@yahoo.com.

WILSON, DOROTHY ANN, retired special education educator; b. Statesboro, Ga., Feb. 10, 1937; d. Julian and Sylvania (Collins) W.; divorced, 1972; children: William Kevin Brown, Lori Anne Brown. AS in Social Work, BS in Early Childhood Edn., Adelphi U., 1983, MS in Spl. Edn., 1985. Tchr. spl. edn. N.Y.C. Bd. Edn., 1983-92, tchr. homebound after sch. program, 1984-85, articulation coord., 1990-92, tchr. aft and crafts after sch. program, 1990-91. Recipient award for sci. teaching to spl. edn. children. N.Y.S. United Tchrs., 1992; fellow NEH, 1992. Mem. Am. Fedn. Tchrs., United Fedn. Tchrs., N.Y. State United Tchrs., Nat. Alliance Black Sch. Educators, Adelphi U. Alumni Assn. Roman Catholic. Avocations: arts and crafts, gardening, sewing and designing, interior decorating, bowling. Home: 11137 Poachers Run Chesterfield VA 23832-7925

WILSON, EDWARD OSBORNE, biologist, educator, writer; b. Birmingham, Ala., June 10, 1929; s. Edward Osborne and Inez (Freeman) W.; m. Irene Kelley, Oct. 30, 1955; 1 child, Catherine Irene. BS, U. Ala., 1949, MS, 1950, LHD (hon.), 1980; PhD, Harvard U., 1955; DPhil, Uppsala (Sweden) U.; DS (hon.), Duke U., 1978, Grinnell Coll., 1978, U. West Fla., 1979, Lawrence U., 1979, Fitchburg State Coll., 1989, Macalester Coll., 1990, U. Mass., 1990, Oxford U., 1993, Ripon Coll., 1994, U. Conn., 1995, Ohio U., 1996, Bates Coll., 1996, Coll. Wooster, 1997, U. Guelph, 1997, U. Portland, 1997; LHD (hon.), Hofstra U., 1986, Muhlenburg Coll., 1998, Yale U., 1998, Pa. State U., Bradford Coll., 1997, Conn. Coll., 2000, U. S. Ala., 2003; DHC, U. Madrid Complutense, 1995, Conn. Coll., 2000; LLD, Simon Fraser U.; DrRerNat, U. Würzburg, 2000; DS (hon.), Kenyon Coll., 2002, U. of the South, 2002, U. South Ala., 2003. Jr. fellow Soc. Fellows, Harvard U., 1953—56, mem. faculty, 1956—, Baird prof. sci., 1976—94, Pellegrino U. prof., 1994—97, univ. rsch. prof., 1997—2002, curator entomology, 1971—97, hon. curator entomology, 1997—. Mem. selection com. Guggenheim Found., 1982—89; bd. dirs. World Wildlife Fund, 1983—94, Orgn. Tropical Studies, 1984—91, N.Y. Bot. Garden, 1991—95, Am. Mus. Natural History, 1992—2002, Am. Acad. Liberal Edn., 1993—, Nature Conservancy, 1994—2002, Conservation Internat., 1997—. Author: The Insect Societies, 1971, Sociobiology: The New Synthesis, 1975, On Human Nature, 1978 (Pulitzer prize for non-fiction, 1979), Promethean Fire, 1983, Biophilia, 1984, Success and Dominance in Ecosystems, 1990, The Diversity of Life, 1992 (Nat. Wildlife Assn. award, Deutsche Umweltstiftung Book award, Sir Peter Kent Conservation prize), Naturalist, 1994 (L.A. Times Book prize sci., 1995), In Search of Nature, 1996, Consilience: The Unity of Knowledge, 1998 (Forkosch award Internat. Acad. Humanism, 2000), Biological Diversity: The Oldest Human Heritage, 1999, The Future of Life, 2002 (Natural World Book prize, U.K., 2002), Pheidole in the New World: A Dominant, Hyperdiverse Ant Genus, 2003 (Julia Ward Howe prize, 2003); author: (with R.H. MacArthur) The Theory of Island Biogeography, 1967; author: (with C.J. Lumsden) Genes, Mind and Culture, 1981; author: (with Bert Holldobler) The Ants, 1990 (Pulitzer prize for non-fiction, 1991), Journey to the Ants, 1994 (Phi Beta Kappa prize sci., 1995); others. Recipient Cleve.-AAAS rsch. prize, 1967, Nat. Medal Sci., 1976, Leidy medal, Acad. Natural Sci., Phila., 1979, Disting. Svc. award, Am. Inst. Biol. Scis., 1976, Mercer award, Ecol. Soc. Am., 1971, Archie Carr medal, U. Fla., 1978, Tyler Ecology prize, 1984, Silver medal, Nat. Zool. Park, German Ecol. Inst. prize, 1987, Weaver award scholarly letters, Ingersoll Found., 1989, Crafoord prize, Royal Swedish Acad. Scis., 1990, Prix di'Inst. de la Vie, Paris, 1990, Revelle medal, 1990, Gold medal, Worldwide Fund for Nature, 1990, Achievement award, Nat. Wildlife Fedn., 1992, Shaw medal, Mo. Bot. Garden, 1993, Internat. prize biology, Govt. of Japan, 1993, Eminent Ecologist award, 1994, Audubon award, Audubon Soc., 1995, Pub. Understanding Sci. award, AAAS, 1995, John Hay award, Orion Soc., 1995, Schubert prize, Germany, 1996, Washburn award, Mus. Sci., 1996, Hutchinson medal, Garden Club Am., 1997, Stone award, New Eng. Aquarium, 1999, Nonino prize, Letters and Sci., Italy, 2000, King Faisal Internat. prize for sci., 2000, Kistler prize, Found. for the Future, 2000, Phillips Meml. medal, World Conservation Union, 2000, Lewis Thomas prize, Rockefeller U., 2001, Nierenberg prize, Scripps Oceanographic Inst., 2001, Thoreau medal, Thoreau Soc., 2001, Lifetime Achievement award, Time, 2001, Global Environment Citizens award, Harvard U., 2001, Busk medal, Royal Geog. Soc., 2002, Presdl. medal, Republic of Italy, 2002, Silver Cross of Christopher Columbus, Dominican Republic, 2003, others; fellow Guggenheim Found., 1978. Fellow: Deutsche Akad. Naturforsch, Am. Philos. Soc. (Franklin medal 1998), Am. Acad. Arts and Scis.; mem.: NAS, Royal Soc. Sci. Uppsala (Sweden), Russian Acad. Nat. Sci., Royal Entomol. Soc. (hon. life), Finnish Acad. Sci. and Letters, Royal Soc. London, Netherlands Entomol. Soc. (hon. life), Assn. Tropical Biology (hon. life), Acad. Humanism (hon. life), Am. Humanist Assn. (Disting. Svc. award 1982, hon. life, Humanist of Yr.), Zool. Soc. London (hon. life), Entomol. Soc. Am. (Founders Meml. award 1972, L.O. Howard award 1985, hon. life), Brit. Ecol. Soc. (hon. life), Am. Genetics Assn. (hon. life). Home: Apt A-208 1010 Waltham St Lexington MA 02421 Office: Harvard U Mus Comparative Zoology Cambridge MA 02138 E-mail: ewilson@oeb.harvard.edu.

WILSON, IRA LEE, middle school educator; b. Taylor, La., Dec. 20, 1927; d. Henry and Sadie Mae (Milbon) Parker; m. Odie D. Wilson, Jr., May 11, 1946; children: Ervin Charles, Annie Jo, Carrido Michelle. BS, Grambling State U., 1954; postgrad., Pepperdine U., 1974, postgrad., 1976; MEd, La Verne Coll., 1976. Tchr. Willowbrook Sch. Dist., Los Angeles, 1955-67, Compton (Calif.) Unified Sch. Dist., 1968—. Grade level chairperson Roosevelt Middle Sch. P.T.A., Compton, 1988—; corr. sec., 1988—, sch. site leadership resource team; mem. associated student body coun. advisor Roosevelt Middle Sch., 1993-95, mem. discipline com., 1994-95. Asst. sec. Los Angeles Police Dept. Sweethearts Area Club, Los Angeles, 1988-95; mem. planning activities com. L.A. Football Classic Found., 1989; chairperson higher edn. Travelers Rest Bapt. Ch., 1992—. Recipient Perfect Attendance award Compton Unified Sch. Dist., 1987-88, S.W. Area Sweethearts for Outstanding Svcs. Los Angeles Police Dept., 1988, Disting. Svc. award Compton Edn. Assn., 1987-88, 83, Cert. of Achievement Roosevelt Jr. High Sch., 1984-85, Perfect Attendance award Roosevelt Middle Sch., 1984, Cert. of Achievement Mayo Elem. Sch., 1973-74, Roosevelt Mid. Sch., 1989, Disting. Svc. award Compton Edn. Assn., 1987-88, Key of Success award Am. Biog. Inst., Inc., 1990. Mem. NEA, Calif. Tchr. Assn., Grambling State U. Alumni Assn. (life, asst. activity chairperson 1987—), Black Women's Forum, Block Club. Democrat. Baptist. Avocations: reading, horticulture, attending sports events. Home: 828 W 126th St Los Angeles CA 90044-3818

WILSON, JAMES MILLER, IV, cardiovascular surgeon, educator; b. Atlanta, Mar. 11, 1946; s. James Miller Wilson III and Sara Sharp; m. Lisa VanLandingham; children: James Miller V, Robert Paul, Michael Simpson, Sara Ann. Student, Emory U.; MD, Duke U., 1971. Diplomate Am. Bd. Surgery, Am. Bd. Thoracic Surgery. Intern N.Y. Hosp., 1971-72; resident N.Y. Hosp.-Cornell Med. Ctr., 1972-73, U. Calif., San Francisco, 1975-80; attending staff Christ Hosp., Cin., 1980—, Bethesda Hosp., Cin., 1980—, Jewish Hosp., Cin., 1980—, Univ. Hosp., Cin., 1982—, Deaconess Hosp, Cin., 1982—; chmn. dept. cardiovasc. surgery Deaconess Hosp., Cin., 1985—; attending staff VA Med Ctr., Cin., 1983—, Children's Hosp., Cin., 1984—, Good Samaritan Hosp., Cin., 1994—; assoc. prof. clin. surgery U. Cin. Coll. Med., 1985—; dir. cardiac surgery Mercy Hosp., chmn. dept. cardiovasc. surgery, 2001. Open heart surgery adv. com., Ohio, 1995—; dir. cardia surgery Mercy Hosp., 2001; mem. Thoracic Surgery Found.; lectr. in field. Contbr. articles to profl. jours. Lt. Comdr. submarine svc. USN, 1973-75. Fellow ACS, Am. Coll. Cardiology; mem. AMA, U.S. Naval Submarine League, UDT/SEAL Assn., U.S. Submarine Vets., Inc., Am. Assn. Thoracic Surgery, Thoracic Surgery Found., Assn. Acad. Surgery, Soc. Thoracic Surgeons, Am. Heart Assn. (mem. cardiovasc. coun.), Ohio State Med. Assn., Cin. Acad. Medicine, Howard C. Nafziger Soc. Avocations: music, diving, hiking, skiing, horses. Office: 311 Straight St Cincinnati OH 45219-1018

WILSON, JANET MARIE, art educator; b. Erie, Pa., Nov. 1, 1952; d. John Howard and Agnes M. (Jackson) W. BS in Art Edn., Edinboro U., 1978. Cert. art tchr., Pa. Substitute tchr. Sch. Dist. of the City of Erie, Pa., 1979-86, substitute contract art tchr., 1987-88, art tchr. traveling to elem. grades, 1988—. Asst. dir. Dr. G. Barber Ctr., Erie, 1977, camp counselor, 1976; arts and crafts supr. City of Erie and Erie YMCA, 1973. Exhibited in group shows at Jury Show at Edinboro U., 1977, Printmaking Show, Edinboro U., 1976. Named Tchr. of Yr., McKinley Elem., 1989. Mem. NEA, Pa. Art Edn. Assn., Nat. Art Edn. Assn., Pa. State Edn. Assn., Erie Edn. Assn., Erie Art Mus. Democrat. Presbyterian. Avocations: photography, biking, golfing, reading, painting. Home: 644 W 7th St Erie PA 16502-1201 Office: Pfeiffer-Burleigh Elem Sch 235 E 11th St Erie PA 16503-1009

WILSON, JOHN I. educational association administrator, educator; b. N.C. BS in Edn., Western Carolina U., 1970; MEd, N.C.U., 1971. Spl. edn. tchr. Wake County Sch. System, 1972—92; mgr. govt. rels. N.C. Assn. Educators, 1992—95, exec. dir., 1995—2000, NEA, Washington, 2000—. Pres. Student N.C. Assn. of Educators, 1969—70, Raleigh Assn. Classroom Tchrs., NC, N. C. Classroom Tchrs. Assn., Wake County Assn. Classroom Tchrs., N.C. Assn. of Educators, 1981; mem. NEA Exec. Com., 1983—89. Co-founder Covenant for N.C. children; lobbyist NC Educators Assn. Office: NEA 1201 16th St NW Washington DC 20036

WILSON, KATHY, principal; b. East Providence, R.I., Aug. 10, 1951; d. Marion A. and Rita (Castergine) Higdon; m. Paul O. Wilson, Dec. 21, 1974; children: Casey Rose, Fletcher Todd. BS in Edn., U. Mo., 1973, MA in Edn., 1976. Cert. in tchg., Mo. Social sci. rsch. analyst Dept. Labor, Washington, 1977-80; nat. pres. Nat. Women's Polit. Caucus, Washington, 1981-85; substitute tchr. Alexandria (Va.) City Pub. Schs., 1989-91; tchr. Resurrection Children's Ctr., Alexandria, Va., 1991-93; dir. Abracadabra Child Care & Devel. Ctr., Alexandria, Va., 1993—. Model tchr. The Danny Chitwood Early Learning Ctr., Alexandria, Va., 1993, The Danny Chitwood Early Learning Inst. Family Child Care, Alexandria, 1992-93; jr. gt. books tchr. Maury & Lykes Crouch Elem. Schs., 1986-89. Contbr. articles to newspapers. Youth Soccer Coach Alexandria Soccer Assn., 1989-90; recording sec. PTA, gift wrap chmn.; chmn. All Night Grad. Party, T.C. William H.S., 1995—; mem. adv. bd. Nat. Womens Polit. Caucus; founder, bd. dirs. Nat. Rep. Coalition for Choice, Washington, 1989-91. Received award for one of Washington's Most Influential Washington Mag., 1985;

named one of Am.'s 100 Most Important Women Ladies Home Jour. editl. bd., 1983. Mem. Nat. Assn. for the Edn. of Young Children, Alexandria Child Care Dirs. Assn. (co-chmn. 1995—). Republican. Baptist. Avocations: reading, writing, soccer, politics, friends. Home: 1402 Orchard St Alexandria VA 22302-4216 Office: Abracadabra Child Care & Devel Ctr 700 Commonwealth Ave Alexandria VA 22301-2308

WILSON, KATIE JEAN, elementary education educator; b. Montgomery, Ala. d. Nathaniel and Annie (Williams) Potts; m. Norman Wilson, June 19, 1968; 1 child, Yasmin Shalon. BS, Ala. State U., 1966; postgrad, U. Wis., 1968; MA, Case Western Res. U., 1977; reading cert., John Carroll U., Cleve., 1987. Tchr. South Bend (Ind.) City Schs., 1966-68, East Cleveland (Ohio) Schs., 1968—. Fundraiser United Negro Coll. Fund, Cleve., 1992. Recipient Crystal Apple award of tchr. excellence, 1991, PTA Coun. Excellence award, 1992. Mem. NEA, NAACP, Ohio Edn. Assn., Zeta Phi Beta. Mem. Ch. of Christ. Avocations: reading, swimming, jogging. Office: Mayfair Sch 13916 Mayfair Ave East Cleveland OH 44112-3713

WILSON, KEITH B. rehabilitation educator; b. Spartanburg, S.C., Feb. 19, 1962; s. George and Helen Annette Wilson; m. Beverly Jean Gaither, June 13, 1992; 1 child, Aliya Imani. BA, Wilberforce U.; MEd, Kent State U., 1985; PhD, Ohio State U., 1997. Cert. rehab. counselor. Case mgr. Ohio Bur. Vocat. Rehab., Canton, 1985; counseling coord. Savannah (Ga.) State U., 1986—89; dir. counseling svc. Brewton-Parker Coll., Mt. Vernon, Ga., 1989—94; grad. program asst. Ohio State U., Columbus, 1994—95, tchg. asst., 1995—97; asst. prof. Pa. State U., State College, 1997—. Cons. Brewton-Parker Coll., Mt. Vernon, 1993; mem. adv. bd. Pa. Office Vocat. Rehab., Harrisburg, 1998—; cons. Indiana U. Pa., 2000. Author: (newsletter) Mosaic, 2001; co-editor: Rehab. Counseling Bull., 2002. Judge Pa. State Grad. Exhbn., State College, 2001; chairperson Multicultural Ad. Com., Harrisburg, 2002—; bd. dirs. Inst. Sci. Advancement, Harrisburg, 2001. Recipient Bobbie Atkins Rsch. award, Nat. Assn. Multicultural, 2001. Mem.: Pa. Counseling Assn. (Named Outstanding Rschr. 2000), Pa. Rehab. Assn., Phi Beta Kappa. Home: 109 Berwick Dr Boalsburg PA 16827 Office: Pa State U Counselor Edn 308 Cedar Bldg State College PA 16802-3110 Office Fax: 814-863-7750. Business E-Mail: kbw4@psu.edu.

WILSON, KENNETH GEDDES, physics research administrator; b. Waltham, Mass., June 8, 1936; s. E. Bright and Emily Fisher (Buckingham) Wilson; m. Alison Brown, 1982. AB, Harvard U., 1956, DSc (hon.), 1981; PhD, Calif. Tech. Inst., 1961, U. Chgo., 1976. From asst. prof. to prof. physics Cornell U., Ithaca, NY, 1963—88, James A. Weeks prof. in phys. sci., 1974—87; Hazel C. Youngberg Trustees Disting prof. The Ohio State U., Columbus, 1988—. Co-author: Redesigning Education, 1974. Recipient Nobel prize in Physics, 1982, Dannie Heinemann prize, 1973, Boltzmann medal, 1975, Wolf prize, 1980, A.C. Eringen medal, 1984, Franklin medal, 1982, Aneesur Rahman prize, 1993. Mem.: NAS, Am. Acad. Arts and Scis., Am. Phys. Soc., Am. Philos. Soc.

WILSON, L(ETITIA) ALEXANDRA, elementary school educator; b. Ft. Bragg, N.C., Aug. 17, 1943; d. Frank Grant and Elizbeth L. (Campbell) Schnerr; m. J.T. Lewis Wilson, June 18, 1966; children: John T.L. Jr., Mary Elizabeth. BS, Moore Coll. of Art, Phila., 1966; MEd, Millersville U., 1985. Cert. tchr., S.C. Kindergarten tchr. Private Sch., Santa Monica, Calif., 1966-68; layout artist Cooke Pub. Co., St. Davids, Pa., 1972-77; admistr. Head Start Lancaster County, Pa., 1977-84; elem. art tchr. Florence (S.C.) Sch. Dist., 1985—. Mem. curriculum writing com. Florence Sch. Dist., 1986-91, mem. grant writing com., 1990-92, mem. 1st summer inst. Winthrop Coll. DBAE curriculum devel., 1989; pvt. art tutor, Florence, 1987—; mem. S.C. Curriculum Congress. Editor (newsletter) Episcopal Diocese of S.C. Mem. Florence Fine Arts Coun., MacDowell Evening Music Club, 1986—. Grantee Pee Dee Edn. Found., Florence, 1989. Mem. NEA, S.C. Art Educators Assn. (ea. region coord., youth art month coord. 1992—), Nat. Art Educators Assn. (program standards award), S.C. Edn. Assn., Pee Dee Artisans Guild (mem. organizing bd.). Episcopalian. Address: PO Box 903 Sheridan MT 59749-0903

WILSON, LEVON EDWARD, law educator, lawyer; b. Charlotte, N.C., Apr. 2, 1954; s. James A. and Thomasina Wilson. BSBA, Western Carolina U., 1976; JD, N.C. Ctrl. U., 1979; Ed D, 2001. Bar: N.C. 1981, U.S. Dist. Ct. (mid. dist.) N.C. 1981, U.S. Tax Ct. 1981, U.S. Ct. Appeals (4th cir.) 1982, U.S. Supreme Ct. 1984; lic. real estate broker, N.C.; cert. mediator N.C. Alternative Dispute Resolution Commn., arbitrator BBB. Pvt. practice, Greensboro, N.C., 1981-85; asst. county atty. Guilford County, Greensboro, 1985-88; asst. prof. N.C. Agrl. & Tech. State U., Greensboro, 1988-91, Western Carolina U., Cullowhee, NC, 1991-96, prof., 1996—, prof., head dept. bus. adminstrn., law and mktg., 1996—2002; pres. Integrated Mgmt. Resources, Inc., 2000—. Pres. Trade Brokers Cons.; legal counsel, bd. dirs. Rhodes Assocs., Inc., Greensboro, 1982—; legal counsel Guilford County Sheriff's Dept., Greensboro, 1985-88; bd. dirs. Webster Enterprises, Inc. Contbr. articles to profl. jours. Bd. dirs. Post Advocacy Detention Program; active mem. Prison Litigation Study Task Force, Adminstrn. Justice Study Com. Recipient Svc. award Blacks in Mgmt., 1980, Excellence in Tchg. award Jay I. Kneedler Found. of Western Carolina U., 1994-95; Student in Free Enterprise fellow. Mem. ABA, N.C. Bar Assn.., Acad. Legal Studies in Bus., Southeastern Acad. Legal Studies in Bus. (former editor-in-chief Jour. of Legal Studies in Bus., mng. editor), N.C. Assn. Police Attys., N.C. Real Estate Educators Assn., So. Acad. Legal Studies in Bus., Phi Delta Phi, Beta Gamma Sigma. Democrat. Methodist. Home: PO Box 620 Cullowhee NC 28723-0620 Office: Western Carolina U Coll of Bus Cullowhee NC 28723 Personal E-mail: levonwilson@msn.com. Business E-Mail: lwilson@wcu.edu.

WILSON, LINDA B. education specialist, medical association administrator; b. Kingston, Pa., Apr. 15, 1962; MSN in Critical Care and Trauma, Thomas Jefferson U., 1985. RN, Pa., N.J.; cert. ambulatory perianesthesia nurse, post anesthesia nurse, nursing continuing and staff devel. Resident N.J./Bermuda Perianesthesia Nurses, 1994-98; dir. edn. Thomas Jefferson U. Hosp., Phila., 1998—, ASPAN, 1999—. Cert. post anesthesia nurse, ambulatory perianesthesia nurse, nursing continuing edn. and staff devel. Mem. Am. Soc. Perianesthesia Nurses (co-chair nat. conf. 1998).

WILSON, LINDA SMITH, academic administrator; b. Washington, Nov. 10, 1936; d. Fred M. and Virginia D. (Thompson) Smith; 1 child, Helen K. Whatley; m. Paul A. Wilson, Jan. 22, 1970; 1 stepchild, Beth A. BA, Tulane U., 1957, HLD (hon.), 1993; PhD, U. Wis., 1962; DLitt (hon.), U. Md., 1993. Rsch. assoc. U. Md., College Park, 1962—64, rsch. asst. prof., 1964—67; vis. asst. prof. U. Mo., St. Louis, 1967—68; asst. to vice chancellor for rsch., asst. vice chancellor for rsch., assoc. vice chancellor for rsch. Washington U., St. Louis, 1968—75; assoc. vice chancellor for rsch. U. Ill., Urbana, 1975—85; assoc. dean U. Ill. Grad. Coll., Urbana, 1978—85; v.p. for rsch. U. Mich., Ann Arbor, 1985—89; pres. Radcliffe Coll., Cambridge, Mass., 1989—99, pres. emeritus, 1999; sr. lectr. Harvard Grad. Sch. Edn., 1989—2003; bd. dirs. Myriad Genetics, Tulane U., Tulane Murphy Found. Chmn. adv. com. office sci. and engring. pers. NRC, 1990—96; dir.'s adv. coun. NSF, Washington, 1980—89, adv. com. edn. and human resources, 1990—95; mem. Nat. Commn. on Rsch., Washington, 1978—80; com. on govt.-univ. relationships NAS, 1981—83, govt.-univ.-industry rsch. roundtable, 1984—89, coord. coun. for edn., 1991—93; rsch. resources adv. coun. NIH, Bethesda, Mass., 1978—82; energy rsch. adv. bd. Dept. of Energy, 1987—90; sci., tech. and states task force Carnegie Commn. on Sci., Tech. and Govt., 1991—92; overser Mus. Sci., Boston, 1992—2001; bd. dirs. Myriad Genetics, Inc.; mem. bd. vis. U. Wis. Coll. Letters and Sci.; dean's adv. coun. Newcomb Coll.; bd. dirs. Tulane U., Tulane Murphy Found.; bd. vis. Coll. Letters and Sci. U. Wis., 1999—; mem. dean's adv. coun. Newcomb Coll., 1999—. Contbr. articles to profl. jours. Adv. bd. Nat. Coalition for Sci. and Tech., Washington, 1983—87; bd. govs. YMCA, Champaign, Ill., 1980—83; trustee Mass. Gen. Hosp., 1992—99, hon. trustee, 1999—2002; trustee Com. on Econ. Devel., 1995—; with string quartet Friends of Daponte; bd. dirs. Friends of DaPonte String Quartet. Named One of 100 Emerging Leaders, Am. Coun. Edn. and Change, 1978; recipient Centennial award, Newcomb Coll., 1986, Disting. Alumni award, U. Wis., 1997, Radcliffe medal, 1999. Fellow: AAAS (bd. dirs. 1984—88); mem.: Am. Coun. Edn. (commn. on women in higher edn. 1991—93, chair 1993), Inst. Medicine (coun. mem. 1986—89), Assn. for Biomed. Rsch. (bd. dirs. 1983—86), Nat. Coun. Univ. Rsch. Adminstrs., Soc. Rsch. Adminstrs. (Disting. Contbn. to Rsch. Adminstrn. award 1984), Am. Chem. Soc. (bd. coun. com. on chemistry and pub. affairs 1978—80), Phi Kappa Phi, Phi Delta Kappa, Alpha Lambda Delta, Sigma Xi, Phi Beta Kappa. Home: 47 Keene Neck Rd Bremen ME 04551

WILSON, LORRAINE M. medical/surgical nurse, educator; b. Mich., Nov. 18, 1931; d. Bert and Frances Fern (White) McCarty; m. Harold A. Wilson, June 9, 1953; children: David Scott, Ann Elizabeth. Diploma in nursing, Bronson Meth. Sch. Nursing, Kalamazoo, Mich., 1953; BS in Chemistry, Siena Heights Coll., 1969; MSN, U. Mich., 1972; PhD, Wayne State U., Detroit, 1985. RN Mich. Staff nurse U. Mich. Med. Ctr., Ann Arbor, 1953-54, Herrick Meml. Hosp., Tecumseh, Mich., 1954-69; asst. prof. nursing U. Mich., Ann Arbor, 1972-78, Wayne State U., Detroit, 1978-79; assoc. prof. nursing Sch. of Nursing Oakland U., Rochester, Mich., 1986-89; prof. nursing Ea. Mich. U., Ypsilanti, 1989—. Rschr. in field; bd. advisors Profl. Fitness Sys., Warren, Mich., 1986—; cons. wellness and exercise program GM CPC Hdqs., Warren, 1986; cons., faculty liaison nurse extern program in critical care, MSN program dir. Ea. Mich. U. Catherine McAuley Health Ctr., 1989—. Author (with S. Price and L. Wilson): (book) Pathophysiology, 6th edit., 2003; author: (with Sylvia Price) Pathophysiology: Clinical Concepts of Disease-Processes, 6th edit., 2003; contbr. articles to profl. jours. Vol. Cmty. Health Screening Drs., Tecumseh, 1960—70; leader Girl Scouts U.S., Tecumseh, 1960; mem. PTA; Sunday sch. tchr. Gloria Dei Luth. Ch., Tecumseh, 1960. Grantee, Mich. Heart Assn., 1984, 1988, R. C. Mahon Found., 1988. Mem.: NOW, ANA (various offices and com. chairs), Nat. League Nursing, Mich. Nurses Assn. (del.), Midwest Nursing Rsch. Soc. (v.p., sec.-treas., bd. dirs.), Sigma Theta Tau. Lutheran. Avocations: travel, theater, jogging. Home: 1010 Red Mill Dr Tecumseh MI 49286-1145 Office: Ea Mich U 53 W Michigan Ave Ypsilanti MI 48197-5436 E-mail: LWIL@LNI.net.

WILSON, LOUISE ASTELL MORSE, home economics educator; b. Corning, N.Y., Oct. 26, 1937; d. James Leland and Hazel Irene (Bratt) Morse; m. Robert Louis Wilson, Dec. 26, 1965 (dec. June 1981); 1 child, Patricia Louise. BS, SUNY, Buffalo, 1960; MS, Elmira Coll., 1971. Cert. home economist, N.Y. Tchr. Corning City Sch. Dist., 1960—. Com. mem. Corning Sch. Dist., 1991—. Mem. Internat. Fed. Home Econs. (area rep. 1991—), Am. Home Econs. Assn., Am. Vocat. Assn., N.Y. Home Econs. Assn. (treas. 1989-91), N.Y. State Home Econs. Tchrs. Assn. (area coord. 1988-89, Tchr. of Yr. 1993-94), Am. Coun. consumer Interests, Corning Tchrs. Assn. (exec. coun. 1981-91, 93—), Order Ea. Star (past matron), Corning Country Club. Republican. Methodist. Avocations: photography, sports, needlework, glassware, coins. Home: PO Box 2 Coopers Plains NY 14827-0002

WILSON, MARGARET EILEEN, retired physical education educator; b. Kansas City, Mo., Aug. 4, 1925; d. Edward Leslie and Bertha Mae (Coe) W. BS in Edn., U. Ark., 1944, MS, 1949; PhD, U. Iowa, 1960. Cert. secondary tchr., Ark. Recreation dir. Pine Bluff (Ark.) Arsenal, 1944-45; instr. Ctrl. High Sch., Muskogee, Okla., 1945-48; grad. asst. U. Ark., Fayetteville, 1948-49; instr. Fayetteville High Sch., 1949-52; from instr. to asst. prof. Ark. Poly. Coll., Russellville, 1952-57, assoc. prof., 1959-65; grad. asst. U. Iowa, Iowa City, 1957-59; prof. Tex. Tech. U., Lubbock, 1965-90, dept. chair health, phys. edn. and recreation for women, 1967-76, prof. emerita, 1990—. Mem. Tex. Tech. Faculty Senate, 1978-90, pres., 1978-79, 85-86. Active Lubbock County Dem. Com., 1993, 94, 96. Recipient AMOCO Found. Disting. Tchg. award, 1978, Disting. Faculty award in Tex. Tech. Moms and Dads Assn., 1987. Mem. AAHPERD (life), Tex. Assn. for Health, Phys. Edn., Recreation and Dance (Honor award 1979, David K. Bruce award 1992), Tex. Tech. Faculty Legal Action Assn. (pres. 1990-96), Lubbock Ret. Tchrs. Assn. (cmty. svc. chair 1994-96, co-treas. 1996-99), Double T Connection (chair membership 1991-94), Delta Gamma (house corp. treas. 1982-91, Cable award 1978), Delta Kappa Gamma (chpt. pres. 1972-74, Chpt. Achievement award 1976, state corr. sec. 1979-81, state conv. chair 1979-80, state nominations com. 1985-87, state pers. com. 1987-89, State Achievement award 1987, state necrology com. 1993-95, state fin. com. 1995-96). Presbyterian. Avocations: gardening, needlepoint, reading. Home: 5411 46th St Lubbock TX 79414-1513 Office: Tex Tech U Womens Gymnasium Lubbock TX 79409

WILSON, MARGARET MARY, special education educator; b. Chgo., Dec. 27, 1950; d. George August and Gertrude (Ras) W. BA in Learning Disabilities, Elem. Edn., Northeastern Ill. U., Chgo., 1972; M of Health Scis., Govs. State U., University Park, Ill., 1984. Cross categorical tchr. Chgo. Bd. Edn., 1975—; substance abuse counselor St. Elizabeth Hosp., Chgo., 1981-85; cmty. prof. Govs. State U., 1985—. Spl. edn. adv. com. Chgo. Bd. Edn., 1991. Mem. Coun. for Exceptional Children, Chgo. Tchrs. Union (spl. edn. com. 1989—, vice chair tchrs. task force 1992-93, 97-98, pres. 1999-00), Tchrs. With Disabilities United (pres.). Home: 3236 N Ozark Ave Chicago IL 60634-3012

WILSON, MARGARET SULLIVAN, retired executive dean, consultant; b. Norwich, Conn., Mar. 21, 1924; d. John Joseph and Margaret Ellen (Connelly) Sullivan; BS, Eastern Conn. State U., 1944; MA, U. Conn., 1949; m. William Robert Wilson, July 20, 1950 (dec.); children: Margaret Ellen, William Robert. Reading cons. Greenwich (Conn.) Pub. Schs., 1948-50; asst. prof. early childhood, chmn. dept. early childhood Eastern Conn. State U., Willimantic, 1967-77, exec. asst. to pres., 1977-78, v.p. adminstrv. affairs, 1978-80, exec. dean, 1980-89, emeritus dean, 1989—; commr. Nat. Commn. Prevention Infant Mortality, 1986-93, chair Norwich Econ. Devel. Commn., 1988-91, Southeastern Connecticut regional Planning Comm., 1999-2001(mem. 1993—); dir. Rose City Community Land Trust Housing, Com. on City Plan, 1992—; del. White House Conf. on Children, 1970, 80, White House Conf. on Travel and Tourism, 1995; corporator Chelsea Groton Savs. Bank, Norwich, Conn. Mem. Conn. Mental Health Bd., 1979-83; mem. adv. bd. Norwich Hosp.; chmn. rev. com. Conn. Health Coordinating Council; mem. Eastern Regional Mental Health Bd., 1976-83, chmn., 1979-81; mem. Norwich Bd. Edn., 1954-69, 80-83, adv. coun. head start and day care programs, 1986-91; mem. Conn. Dem. Cen. Com., 1966-82, Dem. Town Com., 1964-82, 86-90; chmn. Blue Ribbon Commn. To Establish Goals for U. Conn. Health Ctr., 1975-76; sr. warden Ch. of Resurrection, Norwich., 1988-91, Dio Com on Ministry Higher Edn. Named Citizen of Yr., C. of C., 1970; recipient Disting. Alumni award Eastern Conn. State U., 1972, Mental Health Bell award Conn. Mental Health Assn., 1972, Valiant Women award Council Ch. Women, 1976, Woman of Yr. award Bus. and Profl. Women, 1978, Jefferson award Inst. Pub. Service, 1982, pres. Norwich Mus. Trust, Inc., 1992—; mem., vice chair Southeastern Conn. Regional Planning Commn., 1993—; dir. Family Svc. Southeastern Conn., 1995—, Southeastern Conn. Enterprise Region, Norwich Comm. and Tech. Learning Ctr.; past-pres. Eastern Conn. Cmty. Found.; del. White House Conf. on Aging, 1995. Mem. Norwich Area C. of C. (dir. 1979-81), Greater Willimantic C. of C. (edn. com. 1980-88), United Ch. Women Conn. (bd. dirs.). Democrat. Home: 27 Canterbury Tpke Norwich CT 06360-1812 Office: 83 Windham St Willimantic CT 06226-2211

WILSON, MARGIE JEAN (MARJORIE WILSON), elementary school educator, writer; b. San Francisco, Nov. 2, 1950; d. Robert Barry and Priscilla Jean (Small) Clarfield; m. Michael E. Wilson, July 3, 1976; children: Christopher Michael and Robert Alexander. BA, U. Calif., Santa Barbara, CA., 1972; post grad., Calif. State U., Hayward, CA.; post grad. Contra Costa Adult Edn., U. Calif., Berkeley, Ca. Cert. elem. and middle sch. tchr., Calif. Adminstrv. asst. Spreckels Sugar, San Francisco, 1974-76; sales exec. Cromwell and Co., Nashville, 1976-77; legal sec., paralegal Latham and Watkins, L.A., 1977-79; legal sec. James C. Monroe, Santa Rosa, Calif., 1979-81; adminstrv. asst. Benefit Plan Securities, Santa Rosa, Calif., 1982-84, Bruce Kassel, MSW, Santa Rosa, Calif., 1984-85, Curriculum Assoc., Santa Rosa, Calif., 1985-86; editor Events Mag., Santa Rosa, Calif., 1987-95; contract editor and proofreader Kodansha Internat. Pubs., Tokyo, 1996—; substitute tchr. West Sonoma County Sch., Calif., 1995—; ptnr. Wordsworth, Santa Rosa, Calif., 1983—; contract editor Nolo Press, Occidental, Calif., 1998—2000. Publicity coord., dir., Jack London Found., Glen Ellen, Calif., 1990—. Author: Jack London Coloring and Activity Book, 1993, 500 Ways to Say Said, 1985, second edition, 2001. The Wit & Wisdom of Jack London, 2001, Mastering the Art of Scratchboard, 2002; editor: The Ruelle, Hardisty, Stefani, and Molinari Families, 2003, Larry's Letters, 2002, The Chronicles of an Abstract Youth, 2001, Riding the East Wind, 2000, Animal Origami, 1997, True Love Poems from the Heart, 1996, As I Recall, 1993, Beauty and the Feast, 1995, Jack London's Klondike Adventure, 2001, Ozark Hillbilly CEO, 1999; contbr. articles to various publ. Vol. USA-USSR Inst., San Francisco, 1974-76, Oak Grove & Forestville Unified Sch. Dist., Sonoma County, 1986—, Russian River Rodeo, Guerneville, 1996-2001, Hallberg Butterfly Gardens, 1999, Youth Essay Contest Chairperson, 1993; Market Day coord. U. Calif. Santa Barbara, Hot Breakfast program, Goleta, Calif., 1973, 74, Dem. party Sonoma and Santa Barbara counties, 1970—, Redwood Empire Lyric Theater, Santa Rosa, 1990-98, Save the Redwoods, 1990—, Super Playground, Sebastopol, Calif., 1992. Life mem. Calif. Scholarship Found., life mem. Delta Kappa Gamma, Internat. Assn. Machinists & Aerospace Workers, Eastern Star. Home: 2524 S Edison St Graton CA 95444-9352 Office: Wordsworth PO Box 7132 Santa Rosa CA 95407-0132 Fax: 707-829-2316. E-mail: margiewilson@getyourwordsworth.com.

WILSON, MARILYN IONE, retired educator; b. Austin, Minn., Nov. 15, 1931; d. Raymond Harold and Florence O. (Benson) Bray; m. Clinton C. Hertle, Oct. 6, 1951 (div. June 1976); children: Sherri Maloney, Lori Carlson, Barbara Beattie (dec.); m. Wendell Wilson, Sr., June 11, 1994. BS, Winona State U., 1971; MS in Elem. Edn., Mankato State U., 1978. Tchr. Mower County Rural Sch., Austin, 1950-51, 55-56; substitute tchr. Dist. 492 Pub. Schs., Austin, 1958-71, classroom tchr., 1971-92. Mem. NEA, Minn. Edn. Assn., Austin Edn. Assn. Baptist. Avocations: traveling, cooking, reading, hiking, playing with 6 grandsons. Home: 14453 Fairway Dr Eden Prairie MN 55344-1931

WILSON, MARK MOFFETT, secondary school educator; b. New Castle, Pa. s. William James and Eileen Anise (Moffett) W.; m. Mary Elizabeth Hart, May 13, 1988. BS in Secondary Edn., Clarion (Pa.) State Coll., 1975; MS in Bus. Adminstrn., Robert Morris Coll., Pitts., 1986. Cert. tchr. secondary social studies, driver/safety edn., Ohio, Pa. Social studies tchr. Berea (Ohio) City Schs., 1976-79, North Allegheny Schs., Pitts., 1979—, chair dept. social studies, 1993—. Mem. pub. libr. bd. dirs. Cranberry Cmty. Pub. Libr., Cranberry Twp., Pa., 1984-85. Mem. ASCD, Pa. Geog. Soc. (Disting. Tchr. award 1994), Nat. Coun. for Geog. Edn. (Disting. Tchr. award 1994), Pa. Geog. Alliance (mem. steering com. and tchr. cons. 1990—), Nat. Coun. for the Social Studies, Hist. Soc. of Western Pa. Home: 140 Johns School Rd Renfrew PA 16053-8614 Office: North Allegheny Schools 350 Cumberland Rd Pittsburgh PA 15237-5410

WILSON, MICHAEL JOHN, biologist, educator; b. Iowa City, June 3, 1942; s. James H. and Doris E. (Lackender) W.; m. Martha J. Swartzwelter, June 7, 1969; 1 child, Matthew. AA, Divine Word Coll., 1962; BA, St. Ambrose Coll., 1964; MS, U. Iowa, 1967, PhD, 1971. Rsch. fellow Harvard Med. Sch. Boston, 1971-73; scientist VA Med. Ctr., Mpls., 1975-82, Career Rsch. scientist, 2000—; rsch. assoc. U. Minn., Mpls., 1973-75, asst. prof., 1975—82, assoc. prof., 1982-2000, prof., 2000—. Mem. regional adv. bd. Inst. Disability Studies, 1989-93. Mem. editl. bd. Jour. of Andrology, 1998—; contbr. articles to profl. jours. Chmn. spl. edn. coun. St. Paul Pub. Schs., Minn., 1982-85; bd. dirs. United Cerebral Palsy Minn., 1985-96; mem. devel. disabilities com. Ramsey County Citizens Adv. Coun., 1997-2003; mem. assistive tech. bd. Courage Ctr., 2001—. Mem. Am. Soc. Study Cell Biology, Soc. for Study Reprodn., Am. Soc. Andrology, Internat. Soc. Proteolysis, Soc. Basic Urologic Rsch. Democrat. Roman Catholic. Home: 2053 Dayton Ave Saint Paul MN 55104-5732 E-mail: wilso042@tc.umn.edu.

WILSON, P. CRAIG, program director, marketing professional, consultant; b. Erie, Pa., Nov. 2, 1943; s. Percy Walter and Jean Marie (Orton) W.; m. Darlene Anne Ford; children: Allen, Dain. BA in Polit. Sci., Gannon U., Erie, 1965; MA in Founds. of Edn., Troy (Ala.) State U., 1971; EdS in Higher Edn. Adminstrn., George Washington U., 1978, EdD in Higher Edn. Adminstrn., 1991. Commd. USAF, 1966, advanced through grades to maj., ret., 1986; benefits mgr. Coll. William and Mary, Williamsburg, Va., 1986-87; mktg. cons., pres. Career Transition Inc., Hampton, Va., 1987—; mktg. program mgr. George Washington U., Hampton, 1987—, asst. prof. Washington, 1989—. Adj. faculty St. Leo Coll., Hampton, 1976-84, Golden Gate U., Hampton, 1976-84. Contbr. articles to profl. jours. Pres. Willow Oaks Civic Assn., Hampton, 1990, membership chmn., 1989; bd. dirs. Big Bros., Big Sisters, Hampton, 1984. Named Pers. Office of the Yr. USAF, 1979. Mem. NRA, Learning Resources Network, Assn. Continuing Higher Edn., S.E. Va. Live Steamers (pres. 1991—), Kiwanis (v.p. 1987—). Republican. Lutheran. Avocations: live steam locomotive technology, woodcraft, hunting. Office: George Washington Univ One Enterprise Pky Hampton VA 23666

WILSON, PATRICIA POTTER, library science and reading educator, educational and library consultant; b. Jennings, La., May 3, 1946; d. Ralph Harold and Wilda Ruth (Smith) Potter; m. Wendell Merlin Wilson, Aug. 24, 1968. BS, La. State U., 1967; MS, U. Houston-Clear Lake, 1979; EdD, U. Houston, 1985. Cert. tchr., learning resources specialist (libr.), Tex. Tchr. England AFB (La.) Elem. Sch., 1967-68, Edward White Elem. Sch./Clear Creek Ind. Schs., Seabrook, Tex., 1972-77; libr. C.D. Landolt Elem. Sch., Friendswood, Tex., 1979-81; instr./lectr. children's lit. U. Houston, 1983-86; with U. Houston/Clear Lake, 1984-87, asst. prof. libr. sci. and reading, 1988-94, assoc. prof. learning resources and reading edn., 1994—2001, assoc. prof. emeritus, 2001—, faculty devel. com. chair, 1995-97, mem faculty senate, 1992-93, reading search com. chair, tchg. task force, 1997-98, reading and libr. sci. program chair, 1997-98, mem. Piper award com., 1996—98, U. Faculty award com., 1997, U. learning assessment task force, 1997-98, promotion and tenure com. chair, 1999. Cons. Hermann Hosp., Baywood Hosp., 1986-87, Bedford Meadows Hosp., 1989-90, Wetcher Clinic, 1989; co-owner, v.p. Potter Farms, Inc., 1994—. Editor: A Review Sampler, 1985—86, 1989—90; author: Happenings: Developing Successful Programs for School Libraries, 1987, The Professional Collection for Elementary Educators, 1996, Premiere Events: Library Programs That Inspire Elementary Patrons, 2001, Leadership for Today's School Library, 2001, Igniting the Spark: Library Programs that Inspire High School Patrons, 2001, Center Stage: Library Programs That Inspire Middle School Patrons, 2002; contbg. editor: Tex. Libr. Jour., 1988—94; contbr. articles to profl. jours. Trustee Freeman Meml. Libr., Houston, 1982—87, v.p., 1985—86, pres., 1986—87; trustee Evelyn Meador Libr., 1993—94, adv. bd., 1994—; mem. Bay Area Houston Symphony League, Assistance League of the Bay Area, 1997—, Clear Lake Area Panhellic Assn., 2002—, Clear Lake Area Econ. Devel. Found., 2002—, Banquet Com.; founder

Friends of Neumann Libr., 1998; chmn. hospitality com. Lunar Rendevous Festival, 1998—2001; gen. chmn. Lunar Rendezvous Festival, 2002; vice chmn. Clear Lake Met. Ballet, 2003—; co-chmn. Kickoff Reception, 2003; mem. adv. bd. Bay Area Soc. Prevention Cruelty Animals, 1994—98, Bay Area Turning Point, 1998—; bd. dirs. Sta. KUHT-TV, 1984—87, Friends of Neumann Libr., 1998—99; vice chair bd. dirs. Bay Area Houston Ballet and Theatre, 2003—; dir. Learning Resources Book Rev. Ctr., 1989—90; bd. dirs. UHCL Alumni Assn., 1988—2001, v.p. adminstrn., 2000, anniversary hon. com., 1999—2000, mem. 25th anniversary com., 1999, alumni ball com., 1999; mem. Armand Bayou Nature Ctr., Houston, 1980, bd. dirs., 1989—94; vice-chmn. Clear Lake Met. Ballet., 2003—04. Named Outstanding Vol. of Yr., Houston's Nat. Philanthropy Day, 1999; named one of 10 Men and Women of Heart, Bay Area Turning Point, 2001; recipient Rsch. award, Tex. State Reading Assn., 1993, Pres. award, Tex. Coun. Tchrs. English, Disting. Tchg. award, Enron Corp., 1996, Disting. Alumni award, U. Houston-Clear Lake, 1998, Disting. Alumna award, U. Houston-Main Campus, Coll. Edn., 2002; grantee, Tex. Libr. Assn., 1993. Mem. ALA, Am. Assn. Sch. Librs., Internat. Reading Assn., Nat. Coun. Tchrs. English (Books for You rev. com. 1985-88, 97-98, Your Reading rev. com. 1993-96), Tex. Coun. Tchrs. English, Antarctican Soc., Alumni Assn. U. Houston-Clear Lake (bd. dirs. 1998-2001, v.p. adminstrn. 2000, anniversary hon. com. 1999-2000, 25th anniversary com. 1999, alumni ball com. 1999), Bay Area Houston Econ. Partnership, Bay Oaks Country Club, Clear Lake Panhellenic, Phi Delta Kappa, Phi Kappa Phi (sec. 1997-98, pres. 1998-99), Lakewood Yacht Club. Methodist.

WILSON, PAULETTE ADASSA, language educator, writer; b. St. Thomas, Jamaica, Dec. 15, 1954; came to U.S., 1986; d. Robert Ashton and Inez Celestine (Grant) W. Diploma, Shortwood Tchrs. Col., Kingston, Jamaica, 1978; BA, U. West Indies, Kingston, Jamaica, 1984; MA, Rutgers U., 1993, PhD, 1996. Tchr. St. Hugh's H.S., Kingston, Jamaica, 1977-78, Morant Bay H.S., St. Thomas, Jamaica, 1978-81, Kingston Coll., Jamaica, 1984-86; lectr. spanish & portuguese dept. Rutgers U., New Brunswick, N.J., 1991-95; visiting prof. langs. dept. Clemson U., Clemson, S.C., 1995-96, asst. prof., 1996—. Advisor Sigma Delta Pi, Clemson (S.C.) U., 1995—, African/Carribean Students Assn., Clemson U., 1995-96. Mem. MLA, Am. Assn. Tchrs. Spanish & Portuguese. Avocations: travel, basketball, gardening, writing. Office: Clemson U PO Box 341515 Clemson SC 29634-0001 Home: Apt 9C 95 Cedar Ln Florence NJ 08518-2903

WILSON, PEGGY JO, secondary education educator; b. Marysville, Kans., Oct. 8, 1950; d. Allen L. and June A. (Ritter) Holeman; m. John Frederick Wilson, May 27, 1972; children: Bradley, Craig. BA in Math. cum laude, Kans. State U., 1972, MEd, 1975. Cert. tchr., Kans. Tchr., math. Unified Sch. Dist. #501, Topeka, 1972—79, Seaman Unified Sch. Dist. #345, Topeka, 1979—80; rsch. asst. Menninger Found., Topeka, 1980—82; tchr., math. Auburn-Washburn Unified Sch. Dist. #437, Topeka, 1984—. Active Friends of Topeka Libr., Friends of Topeka Zoo, Friends of KTWU. Mem. NEA, Auburn Washburn NEA, Nat. Coun. Tchrs. of Math., Phi Kappa Phi, Phi Delta Kappa. Methodist. Avocations: reading, piano, walking. Office: Washburn Rural High Sch 5900 SW 61st St Topeka KS 66619-2008

WILSON, REBECCA ANN, English and special education educator, retired; b. Balt., Md., Feb. 21, 1945; d. Bertram Bradford and Nancy Ann Wiley; m. David Lloyd Wilson, July 29, 1967; children: Laura Beth, Amy Lynn. BA in Secondary Edn., Shepherd Coll., 1967; postgrad., W.Va. U. Cert. Spl. Edn. Tchr. W.Va., 1968. Tchr. Jefferson County Schs., Charles Town, W.Va., 1967—72, substitute tchr., 1975—79. Vol. Jefferson County Spl. Olympics, Charles Town, W.Va., 1986—97; judge Jefferson County Fair, 1968—; adv. com. Jefferson County Bd. Edn., Charles Town, W.Va., 1990; chmn. W.Va. Adv. Coun. for Edn. Exceptional Children, Charleston, 1986—92; mem. Gov. Sch. Adv. Coun., Charleston, 2001—; mem. bd. edn. Jefferson County, Charles Town, W.Va., 1994—98; mem. bd. dirs. Shepherdstown Day Care Ctr., Regional Edn. Svc. Agy. Mem.: AAUW (life), Internat. Assn. Jazz Edn., Homakers Club, Shepherdstown Women's Club (pres. 2000—), Md. 4-H All Stars (life), Order of Ea. Star. Democrat. Episcopalian. Avocations: travel, attending national conventions, reading, cooking. Home: 103 Prospect Ave PO Box 624 Shepherdstown WV 25443

WILSON, ROBERT FOSTER, cardiologist, educator; b. Oak Park, Ill., Apr. 30, 1953; s. Robert Foster and Mary Elizabeth (Clark) W.; m. Betsy V. Wilson; children: Rebecca, Adam, Jessica. BS, Pa. State U., 1973; MD, U. Iowa, 1977. Diplomate Am. Bd. Internal Medicine with subspecialty in cardiovascular diseases. Resident U. Tex., San Antonio, 1977-80; fellow in cardiovascular disease U. Iowa, Iowa City, 1982-85, asst. prof., 1985-86, U. Minn., Mpls., 1986-91, assoc. prof., 1991—, dir. cardiac catheterization lab., 1991—. Founder, chmn. bd. ACIST Med. Sys., Mpls., Mpls., 1994—. Fellow Am. Heart Assn. (coun. circulation 1991—, pres. Northland affiliate 1999-2000). Achievements include development of Doppler catheters and the ACIST angiographic injection technology; assessment of coronary physiology and innervation in humans; coronary angioplasty device development. Office: U Minn Cardiovascular Divsn 420 Delaware St SE # 508 Minneapolis MN 55455-0374 E-mail: sf2@qwest.net.

WILSON, ROBLEY CONANT, JR., English educator, editor, author; b. Brunswick, Maine, June 15, 1930; s. Robley Conant and Dorothy May (Stimpson) W.; m. Charlotte A. Lehon, Aug. 20, 1955 (div. 1991); children: Stephen, Philip; m. Susan Hubbard, June 17, 1995. BA, Bowdoin Coll., 1957, D.Litt (hon.), 1987; M.F.A., U. Iowa, 1968. Reporter Raymondville Chronicle, Tex., 1950-1951; asst. publicity dir. N.Y. State Fair Syracuse, 1956; instr. Valparaiso U., Ind., 1958-63; asst. prof. English U. No. Iowa, Cedar Falls, 1963-69, assoc. prof., 1969-75, prof., 1975-2000, prof. emeritus, 2000—, editor N.Am. Rev., 1969-2000. Author: The Pleasures of Manhood, 1977, Living Alone, 1978, Dancing for Men, 1983 (Drue Heinz Lit. prize, 1982), Kingdoms of the Ordinary (Agnes Lynch Starrett award, 1986), Terrible Kisses, 1989, A Pleasure Tree, 1990 (Soc. Midland Authors Poetry award, 1990), The Victim's Daughter, 1991, A Walk Through the Human Heart, 1996, Everything Paid For, 1999, The Book of Lost Fathers, 2001; co-editor: 100% Pure Florida Fiction, 2000. Bd. dirs. Associated Writing Programs, Norfolk, Va., 1983-86; pres. Iowa Woman Endeavors, Inc., 1986-90. With USAF, 1951-55. Guggenheim fellow, 1983-84, Nicholl Screenwriting fellow, 1996. Mem.: PEN, Authors' Guild. Home: PO Box 4009 Winter Park FL 32793-4009

WILSON, ROOSEVELT LEDELL, secondary education educator; b. Baton Rouge, La., Aug. 8, 1941; m. Barbara Batiste; 1 child, Janile. BS, So. U., 1964, MEd, 1970; MS, U. Okla., 1973; PhD, U. Iowa, 1975. Cert. tchr. math. and sci., La. Tchr. East Baton Rouge Parish Sch. Bd., 1964-75, 81—; teaching asst. U. Iowa, Iowa City, 1974; asst. prof. Jackson (Miss.) State U., 1976-81; tchr. earth and physical sci., dean of students Baton Rouge Prep. Acad., 1994—. Club sponsors, dept. chairperson McKinley Mid. Magnet, Baton Rouge, 1981—; dir. workshops E. Baton Rouge Parish Schs., 1983, 85; coord. after-sch. tutorial program Jordan United Meth. Ch., Baton Rouge, 1992—; participant adminstrv. internship program E. Baton Rouge Parish, 1993-94. Contbr. articles to profl. jours. Mem. male chorus Jordan United Meth. Ch., Baton Rouge. Fellow Nat. Fellowship Fund; grantee NSF. Mem. NEA, Nat. Sci. Tchrs. Assn., La. Assn. Educators, Phi Delta Kappa. Methodist. Avocations: golf, tennis, fishing. Home: 21253 Old Scenic Hwy Zachary LA 70791-6920 Office: Baton Rouge Prep Acad 5959 Cadillac St Baton Rouge LA 70811-5802

WILSON, ROSE EATON, elementary education educator; b. Monroe, La., July 7, 1941; d. Wyatt and Olivia (Walker) Eaton; m. Elvin Gene Wilson Sr., July 30, 1989; stepchildren: Karen Patricia, Elvin Jr. BS, Grambling Coll., 1966; MEd, Northeast La. U., 1977, postgrad., 1984. Cert. tchr., supr., La. Tchr. Monroe City Schs., 1966—, tchr. gifted program, 1980-86, assessment tchr., 1986—, liaison mem. spl. edn. adv. bd., 1988—. Mem. beautification bd. City of Monroe, 1985-87; mem. Mayor's Commn. for Women, Monroe, 1989-90; commr. Franklin Parish Voter Registration, 1992—. Mem. La. Edn. Assessment Tchrs. Assn. (region rep. 1992—), Delta Sigma Theta (v.p. 1982-83). Democrat. Baptist. Avocations: basketball, reading, cooking, shopping. Home: 1202 Gum St Apt C Winnsboro LA 71295-2855

WILSON, SAMUEL V. academic administrator; Pres. Hampden-Sydney Coll., Va., 1992—2000, chmn. in leadership, 2000—.*

WILSON, SONJA MARY, retired secondary school educator, poet; b. Lake Charles, La., Mar. 28, 1938; d. Albert Ronald and Annelia (DeVille) Molless; m. Willie McKinley Williams, Apr. 28, 1956 (div. May 1969); children: William P., Dwayne L., Rachelle A., Devon A., Lisa M., Ricardo Soto; m. Howard Brooks Wilson, Nov. 12, 1982 (div. Dec. 1999); stepchildren: Howard N. Wilson, Yvonne Wilson. AA in Social and Behavioral Scis., Mt. St. Jacinto Coll., 1992; designated subjects credential, U. Calif., San Bernardino, 1983; student, Calif. State Poly. U., 1986; M in Adminstrn., Laverne U., 1985; BS in Edn. Methodologies, So. Ill. U., 1995; postgrad., Riverside (Calif.) City Coll., 1988—89, postgrad., 1994. Prin.'s sec. Elsinore (Calif.) H.S., Elsinore Jr. H.S., 1974-83, tchr. bus. and adult vocat. edn. coord., 1979-88, class adviser, 1983-88; ret., 1988. Long-term substitute tchr. Perris H.S. Dist., 1991—94; spkr. in field. Judge Lake Elsinore Unified Sch. Dist. Bd., 1986—, clk., 1988, pres., 1988, 98, 2002; clk., Lake Elsinore Elem. Sch. Bd., 1976-88; pres., sec.-treas., v.p. Riverside County Sch. Bds. Assn., 1979-98; assoc. sponsor, advisor Black Student Union/Future Leaders of Am., 1984-90; svc. unit rep., leader Girl Scouts U.S.A., bd. dirs. San Gorgonio coun., 1995—, nominating com., 1998—; den leader Boy Scouts Am.; active Ctrl. Dem. Com., 1989-91; del. PTSA, 1991-93; mem. Econ. Devel. Com., Elsinore; vol. United Way, 2003—. Tribute in her honor Black Student Union/Future Leaders Am., 1989, Wall of Tolerance, 2003; recipient Excellence in Edn. award Hilltop Community Ctr. Club, 1989, Leadership award Black Art and Social Club, 1989, Svc. award Sojourner Truth Media Network, 1989, Proclamation award City of Elsinore, 1989, County of Riverside, 1984, Golden Leaf award PTSA; named Outstanding Poet, Nat. Libr. of Congress, 1994, 95. Mem. NAACP (life, charter mem. Lake Elsinore affiliate; treas. 1998-2000, pres. 2000-02, plaque), Calif. Sch. Bds. Assn. (legis. com. 1981-97, regional dir. 1988-92, nominations com. 1988, conf. planning com. 1989, media com., dir. at large black 1993-95, audit com. 1993, dir./del. trainer 1993, alt. del., sgt. at arms 1994-95, Fed. Rels. Network del. 1992, 95), Calif. Elected Women Ofcls. Assn., Calif. Sch. Employees Assn. (pres., treas., regional rep. asst., state negotiation com., del. to conf.), Calif. Ret. Tchrs. Assn. (resource rep. 2001—), Internat. Soc. Poets, Lake Elsinore C. of C., Calif. Coalition Black Sch. Bd. Mems. (v.p., program liaison 1989, pres. 1990), Nat. Sch. Bds. Assn. (alt. del. 1994-95), Nat. Coalition Black Sch. Bd. Mems. (dir. 1989-94, v.p. 1995-2000, sec.-treas. 1998—), Nat. Coun. Negro Women (life, charter, Willa Mae Taylor sect.), Black Art and Social Club, Lake Elsinore Black Art Culture Club (treas. 1997—, Vol. of Yr. 1999-2000, RTA com.), Hilltop Cmty. Club (plaque), Eta Phi Beta (all offices Gamma Alpha chpt., pres. 1992-94, Resurrection choir 1996—, Western region dir. 1997-2001, nat. chaplain 2002—, cmty. rev. team 2003—, plaque, Vol. of Yr. award 2000). Avocations: travel, writing poetry, gardening, childcare, dancing. Home: 30402 Jernigan St Lake Elsinore CA 92530-5045 E-mail: sonjawilson@msn.com., Sonja.Wilson@leusd.k12.ca.us.

WILSON, STANLEY CHARLES, artist, educator, curator, art gallery director, consultant; b. Los Angeles, Feb. 2, 1947; s. Ernest Charles and Eleanor (Reid) W.; m. Jacquelyn Bellard, June 3, 1978; 1 child, Jendayi Asabi. BFA, Otis Art Inst., 1969, MFA, 1971. Asst. prof. Southwestern Coll., Chula Vista, Calif., 1972-73; prof. art Calif. Poly U., Pomona, 1973—; dir. univ. gallery Calif. Poly. U., Pomona, 1988—; instr. Otis Parsons Watts Towers, Los Angeles, 1981-88; dir. univ. art gallery Calif. State Poly. U., Pomona, 1988-89, prof. emeritus, 2002—. Mem. bd. artists Brockman Gallery Prodns., L.A., 1980-85; bd. dirs. Watt Towers Art Ctr., L.A.; vis. artist dept. art U. Nev., Las Vegas, 1990; vis. prof. sculpture Otis Art Inst., L.A., 1991-92; bd. advisors The Armory Gallery, Pasadena, Calif.; apptd. Nat. Edn. Com., Princeton, N.J., 1996; chair Pasadena (Calif.) Arts Commn., 1997; co-chair sculpture panel Coll. Art Assn., L.A., 1999; Disting. artist lecture Calif. State U., Northridge, 2001; grad. reviewer Memphis Coll. of Art and Design, Memphis, 2001; co-curator exhbn. Armony Ctr. for Arts, Pasadena, 2002; mem. various awards panels; slide lectr., disting. artist series Calif. State U., Northridge, 1002; vis. artist, grad. reviewer Memphis Coll. Art and Design. One-man shows include Sol Del Rio Gallery, San Antonio, 1980, Brockman Gallery, 1982, Daniel Maher Gallery, 1983, Southwest Coll., 1984; 2 person exhbn. Calif. State U., Bakersfield, 2002; exhibited in group shows at Oranges/Sardines Gallery, 1984, Sparc Gallery, 1985, Mus. Of African Am. Art, 1985, Los Angeles Art Gallery, 1986, Muni Art Gallery Calif. State U. Dominguez Hills, Altars, Icons & Sacred Places, San Antonio Art Inst., 1992, Gallery 1078, Chico, Calif., Calif. State U., 2002; represented in permanent collections Calif. Mus. Afro-Am. History and Culture, Prairie View Coll., 1977, Tex. A&M U., 1977, Atlanta Life Ins. Co., 1984, Golden State Life Ins., 1985, Broadway Fed. Savs. & Loan Corp., Los Angeles, 1986, LACTC Metro Rail Commn.; artist in residence Studio Mus. Harlem, N.Y., Spokane (Wash.) Coll.; contbr. articles to profl. jours. Chmn. Pasadena Arts Commn. NEA fellow, 1986; Visual Arts fellow Pasadena Art Commn., 1991; advanced placement, Studio Art Devel. Com.; Brody visual art fellow, L.A., 1998; recipient Gold Crown award in visual arts Pasadane Arts Coun., 1998. Democrat. Avocations: music, landscape gardening, archtl. designs, sports. Office: Calif Poly U Dept Art 3801 W Temple Ave Pomona CA 91768-2557

WILSON, WANDA KAY, special education educator; b. Big Spring, Tex., June 21, 1941; d. Carl Abercrombie and Wanda Maxine (Smith) Coleman; m. Albert Gene Wilson, July 6, 1963 (div. 1980); 1 child, D'Carlon Wilson Mata. BS in Edn., Abilene Christian Coll., 1962; cert. in emotional disturbed, Texas Tech, 1973. Tchr. Pease Elem. Sch., Odessa, Tex., 1962-68; spl. edn. tchr. Big Spring State Hosp., 1971-84, Big Spring (Tex.) High Sch., 1984—. Mentor, Alternative Edn. Region 18-Terminal, Big Spring, 1989-93. Chair So. Assn. Com. for Spl. Edn., Big Spring, 1989-90; mem. 14th and Main Ch. of Christ. Named to Big Spring H.S. Hall of Fame, 2002. Mem. NEA, Tex. Tchrs. Assn. Avocations: sports, ceramics, school and church related activities. Office: Big Spring Ind Sch Dist 11th Pl Big Spring TX 79720

WILSON, WENDY MELGARD, kindergarten and special education educator; b. Fargo, N.D., Jan. 13, 1952; d. Howard A. Melgard and Grace B. (Alphson) Watkins; m. Henry Milton Wilson II, July 31, 1982; children: Andrew J., Aaron C. BA/BS in Edn., U. N.D., 1972-77; postgrad., Drake U., 1984-86, Simpson Coll., 1992-94, U. No. Iowa, 1998—. Secondary spl. edn. tchr. Ctrl. Decatur Community Schs., Leon, Iowa, 1978-80; work experience instr. Green Valley AEA, Creston, Iowa, 1980-82; elem. spl. edn. tchr. Stuart (Iowa) Menlo Community Schs., 1983-86, Greenfield (Iowa) Community Schs., 1986-93, kindergarten tchr., 1993-98; elem. spl. edn. tchr. Spirit Lake (Iowa) Sch. Dist., 1998-99; kindergarten tchr. Spirit Lake (Iowa) Cmty. Schs., 1999—. Pres., bd. dirs. Little Lambs Presch., Greenfield, 1991-92; sec., v.p. bd. Sunshine Daycare Ctr., Greenfield, 1987-90; co-chairperson S.W. Iowa Very Spl. Art Festival, Creston, 1981; innkeeper, co-owner Wilson Home Bed & Breakfast, 1986-95; team mem. New Iowa Schs. Devel. Corp., 1996-98; mem. Spirit Laek Sch. Dist. Bldg. and Dist. Improvement Teams, 2001--. Com. mem. Greenfield Tourism Com., 1988-94; mem. Greenfield Mother's Club, 1987-98, sec., 1991; mem. Adair County Meml. Hosp. Aux., 1987-98, Greenfield Elem. PTA, Grace Luth. Ch., Spirit Lake. Mem. NEA, PEO, Iowa State Edn. Assn., Greenfield Edn. Assn. (pres., v.p., com. ch. 1989-98), Nat. Assn. for Educating Young Children, Iowa Bed and Breakfast Innkeepers Assn. (sec. 1990-92), Spirit Lake Edn. Assn. (v.p. 1999-2000, pres. 2000-01), Greenfield C. of C., Winterset C. of C., Greenfield Bus. Women, Iowa Aviation Preservation Soc. Home: 13926 240th Ave Spirit Lake IA 51360-7048 E-mail: whaa@mchsi.com.

WILSON, WINNIE RUTH, elementary education educator, reading specialist; b. San Antonio, Nov. 8, 1927; d. T. A. and Louise (Edwards) Hamilton; m. James C. Wilson, Feb. 13, 1949; children: James C. Jr., Karen Lynn. BS in Phys. Edn., W.Va. State Coll., 1949; MEd in Learning Disabilities, U. Ill., 1970. Cert. tchr. elem. edn., Ill. Tchr. project promise program Champaign (Ill.) Sch. Dist. Unit 4, 1966-69; title 1 reading tchr. Champaing (Ill.) Sch. Dist. Unit 4, 1969-84, facilitator, 1981-83, chpt. 1 reading specialist, 1984-92, dir. compensatory edn., 1990-92. Mem. Ill. Chpt. I Dirs., 1990-92. Active PTA; vol. Salvation Army, Champaign-Urbana, Ill., 1991-92. Recipient Educator's award Regional Office Edn., 1987. Mem. NEA (life), Altrusa Internat, Inc., Delta Kappa Gamma, Phi Delta Kappa. Democrat. United Methodist. Avocations: reading, walking. Home: 2007 S Vine St Urbana IL 61801-5819

WILSON-SMITH, BARBARA ANN, reading specialist; b. Enterprise, Ala., Sept. 10, 1945; d. William Franklin and Opal Elizabeth (Jones) W. BA, Stetson U., 1970, MEd, 1979, EdS in Ednl. Leadership, 1994. Cert. early childhood, elem., reading, specific learning disabilities, emotionally handicapped tchr., ednl. leadership, Fla. Ednl. cons. Macmillan Pub. Co., N.Y.C., 1984-89; tchr. Lake County Bd. Edn., Tavares, Fla., 1970-76, Chpt. I rsch. tchr., 1976-79, primary specialist, 1979-84, Chpt. I reading program specialist, 1989-97; nat. math. cons. Macmillan Pub. Co., N.Y.C., 1989; asst. prin., 1997-98; supr. compensatory edn., 1998-2001. Mem. ASCD, Reading Suprs. Fla., Fla. Reading Assn., Internat. Reading Assn. Avocations: reading, swimming, tennis. Home: 2453 Broadvue Ave Eustis FL 32726-7626 Office: Lake County Bd Edn 201 W Burleigh Blvd Tavares FL 32778-2407

WILSON-WEBB, NANCY LOU, education administration consultant, rancher; b. Maypearl, Tex, Jan. 20, 1932; d. Madison Grady Wise and Mary Nancy Pearson-Bedford (Haney) Wilson; m. John Crawford Webb, July 29, 1972. BS magna cum laude, Abilene Christian U., Tex., 1953; EdM (hon.), Tex. Christian U., 1985. Cert. tchr., mid-mgmt., sch. adminstr., Tex. Tchr. elem. grades Ft. Worth Ind. Sch. Dist., 1953-67, adult edn. tchr., 1967-73; dir. adult edn. consortium for 38 sch. dists. Tex. Edn. Agy., 1973-2000. Pres. Nat. Commn. on Adult Basic Edn., "Most Outstanding adult ed. Admin. in US" by AAAC; 1994-95; pres. Tex. Adult Edn. Adminstrn., 1994; apptd. mem. Tex. State Literacy Coun., 1987-94, Tex. State Sch. Bd. Commn., 1994-99; exec. bd. Tex. Coun. Co-op Dir., 1989-2001, Bd. Nat. Assn. of AAACE, 1988; pres., 1994—; apptd. to Gov. Ann Richard's Task Force for Edn.; ranch owner, mgr., 1998-2003. Cons. to textbooks, 1994-98; editor textbooks, 1999. Pres. Jr. Womans Club, Ft. Worth, 1969, Fine Arts Guild, Tex. Christian U., Ft. Worth, 1970-72, Ft. Worth Womens Civic Club Coun., 1970, pres. Aquarius Women's Club; active Exec. Libr. Bd., Ft. Worth, 1990-2003, Jewel Charity Ball, 1988-2003; bd. dirs. Literacy Plus in North Tex., 1988-99, pres., 2001—; bd. dirs. Greater Ft. Worth Literacy Coun., 1976-88, 2002—, pres., 2001-03; commr. Ed-16 Task Forces Tex. Edn. Agy., 1985-94; literacy bd. dir. Friends of Libr., 1967-2002, Opera Guild Bd. Ft. Worth, 1965-85, Ft. Worth Ballet Guild, Johnson County (Tex.) Corr. Bd., 1990-2000; bd. dirs. Salvation Army, Ft. Worth, 1996-2003, Ft. Worth Libr.; active Tarrant County Bd. on Aging, 1997-98, Commn. Status of Women, Ft. Worth, 1973-99, Southside Ch. of Christ. Recipient Bevy award Jr. Womans Club, 1968, Proclamation Commr. Ct. Outstanding 43 Yr. Literacy Svc. to Tarrant County Com. Ctr., 1994, Tarrant County Woman of Yr. award, Fort Worth Star Telegram, 1995, Outstanding Leadership award Ft. Worth ISD Sch. Bd., 1985, 95, Mayor's Proclamation of Nancy Webb Week, 1996; named one of Most Outstanding Educators in U.S. Nat. Assn. Adult Edn., 1983, Most Outstanding Woman Edn., City of Ft. Worth, 1991, others; nominated to Tex. Hall of Fame for Women, 1991; named to Ft. Worth Hall of Fame, 1992; scholar Germany, 1983. Mem. NEA, DAR (Mary Isham Keith chpt. 1985-2002, Nat. Literacy award 1992, Leadership Literacy award 1985-87, 89, 94, Nat. Educators award 2003), AAUW, Am. Assn. Adult and Continuing Edn. (v.p. 1987-89, chair 1993 internat. conv. 1992, Nat. Adminstr. of Yr. in Adult Edn. 1998, Most Outstanding Adminstr. Adult Edn. in US 1999), Tex. Assn. Adult and Cont. Edn. (pres. 1985-86, Most Outstanding Adult Adminstr. in Tex. 1984), Tex. Coun. Adult Edn. Dirs. (pres. nat. com. on edn., Nat. Dept. Labor award 1992), Coun. World Affairs (bd. dir. 1980-2002), Am. Bus. Women's Assn., Ft. Worth C. of C., Lecture Found., Internat. Reading Assn. (Literacy Challenge award 1991), Ft. Worth Adminstrv. Assn., Southwest Cattle Raisers Assn., Ligon Assn., Zonta, Tanglewood Garden Club, Ft. Worth Garden Club (exec. bd. dirs. 2000-03), Woman's Club, Ft. Worth Petroleum Club, Carousel Dance Club, Met. Dinner Dance Club, Ridglea Country Club, Girls Svc. League, Aquarius (pres. 2001-02), Crescent Club (Dallas), Alpha Delta Kappa (Nat. Literacy award 1992), Greater Ft. Worth Literacy Coun. (pres. 2000-03), Phi Delta Kappa, Mary Isham Keith DAR (Nat. award 1993, Nat. Found. award 2003). Democrat. Mem. Lds Ch. Home: 3716 Fox Hollow St Fort Worth TX 76109-2616

WILSTED, JOY, elementary education educator, reading specialist, parenting consultant; b. St. Marys, Pa., Aug. 12, 1935; d. Wayne and Carrie (Neiger) Furman; m. Richard William Wilsted, Feb. 14, 1982; 2 children. BA, Fla. Atlantic U., 1970; MS in Edn., Old Dominion U., Norfolk, Va., 1975. Cert. reading specialist, elem. tchr., Mo.; cert. permanent tchr., N.Y. Tchr. creative dramatics Hillsboro Country Day Sch., Pompano Beach, Fla., 1966-68; tchr. PTA Kindergarten, Boca Raton, Fla., 1968-69; tchr. creative dramatics Wee-Wisdom Montessori Sch., Delray Beach, Fla., 1969-70; elem. tchr. Birmingham (Mich.) Pub. Schs., 1970-72; classroom and reading resource tchr. Chesapeake (Va.) Pub. Schs., 1972-79; reading coord. Harrisonville (Mo.) Pub. Schs., 1979-81; Chpt. I reading tchr., reading improvement tchr. North Kansas City Pub. Schs., Kansas City, Mo., 1981-96. Instr. continuing edn. U. Mo., Kansas City, 1980-87, Ottawa U., Overland Park, Kans., 1990—; cons. Young Authors' Conf., Oakland U., Rochester, Mich., 1971; coord. fine arts Alpha Phi Alpha Tutorial Project, Chesapeake, 1973-75; presenter Chpt. I Summer Inst., Tech. Asistance Ctr., Mo., 1984; cons. on parenting Reading Success Unltd., Gallatin, Mo., 1987—; mem. adv. bd. Parents & Children Together, Ind. U. Family Literacy Ctr., Bloomington, 1990-93; keynote speaker ann conf. Nat. Coalition of Chapter I Parents. Author: Dramatics for Self-Expression, 1967, Now Johnny CAN Learn to Read, 1987, Reading Songs and Poems of Joy, 1987, Character-Building Poems for Young People. Mem. Internat. Reading Assn. (mem. coun., pres. local coun. 1986-88, state chmn. parents and reading com. 1988-89, mem. nat. parents and reading com. 1989-92, keynote spkr. IRA Conf. Inst. 1990, local coun., Literacy award 1989). Office: Reading SUCCESS Unltd PO Box 215 Gallatin MO 64640-0215

WILTROUT, ANN ELIZABETH, foreign language educator; b. Elkhart, Ind., Aug. 3, 1939; d. F. LeRoy and Margaret Elizabeth (Williams) W. BA, Hanover Coll., 1961; MA, Ind. U., 1964, PhD, 1968. Vis. asst. prof. Ind. U., Bloomington, 1968-69; asst. prof. Miss. State U., Mississippi State, 1969-71, assoc. prof., 1971-87, prof., 1987—2002, prof. emerita fgn. lang., 2002—. NEH fellow in residence Duke U., 1977-78. Author: A Patron and a Playwright in Renaissance Spain, 1987; contbr. articles to profl. publs. Recipient Disting. Svc. cert. Inst. Internat. Edn., 1986; named Humanities Tchr. of Yr., 1998. Mem. AAUP, MLA (del. to assembly 1975-78), Assn. Internat. Hispanistas, Cervantes Soc. Am., Am. Assn. Tchrs. of Spanish and Portuguese, Assn. Hispanic Classical Theater, Soc. Scholars in Arts and Scis., Phi Kappa Phi, Sigma Delta Pi. Avocations: Shakespeare, travel, reading, roses. Office: Miss State U Dept Fgn Langs Drawer FL Mississippi State MS 39762 E-mail: wiltrout@ra.msstate.edu.

WIMMER, KATHRYN, retired elementary school educator; b. St. Louis, May 8, 1929; d. Arthur Jordan and Louise Clara Sykes; m. Harry William Wimmer, Aug. 4, 1951; children: Robert William, Richard Jordan. BS in Edn., U. Mo., 1951; postgrad., U. South Fla., 1971—72. Cert. tchr. Mo., Fla. Tchr. Affton (Mo.) Sch., 1951—52, Heege Sch., Affton, 1965—67, Gulf Gate Sch., Sarasota, Fla., 1967—72; piano tchr. Crestwood, Mo., 1963—65. Artist, musician. V.p. Southgate Cmty., Sarasota, 1989—90; pres. bd. dirs. Assoc. Women's Club, Sarasota, 1990—91, bd. dirs., 1986—93; vol. Gulf Gate Libr., Sarasota, 1993—2003. Recipient tennis trophy, Bath and Racquet Tennis Club, Sarasota, 1979, swimming trophy, Southgate Cmty. Assn., 1987, 1988. Mem.: Mysterium High IQ Soc., Delta Gamma (scholarship chmn., treas., rush chmn., social chmn.). Democrat. Presbyterian. Avocations: sewing, literature, cards, dancing, travel.

WIMMERS, INGE CROSMAN, French literature and theory educator; b. Hamm, Westphalia, Germany, Jan. 17, 1940; arrived in U.S., 1954; d. Ewald Otto and Hildegard Margarete Karalus; m. Robert True Crosman, Sept. 1967 (div. 1984); 1 child, Christopher; m. Eric Walter Wimmers, June 22, 1984. AB, Douglas Coll., 1958-62; MA, Columbia U., 1965, PhD, 1971. Instr. French and German Bradford (Mass.) Jr. Coll., 1963—64; lectr. French Bklyn. Coll., 1964—65; asst. prof. French Williams Coll., Williamstown, Mass., 1969—72; prof. French studies Brown U., Providence, 1973—, chair dept. French Studies, 1994—97. Author: Metaphoric Narration: The Structure and Function of Metaphors in A la recherche du temps perdu, 1978, Poetics of Reading: Approaches to the Novel, 1988, Proust and Emotion. The Importance of Affect in A la recherche du temps perdu, 2003; co-editor: The Reader in the Text: Essays on Audience and Interpretation, 1980, Approaches to Teaching Proust's Fiction and Criticism, 2003; asst. lit. editor: French Review, 1987-92. AAUW fellowship, 1968-69; Humboldt Rsch. fellow, 1979-80, 83. Mem. AAUW, MLA (exec. com. div. on prose fiction 1983-87), Amis de Marcel Proust, Proust Gesellschaft, Phi Beta Kappa. Avocations: music, hiking. Office: Brown U Dept French Studies PO Box 1961 Providence RI 02912-1961

WIMPEE, MARY ELIZABETH, elementary school educator; b. Karnes City, Tex., Nov. 23, 1952; d. Bernarr Floyd and Mary Jane (Putnam) Plummer; m. William Eugene Wimpee, June 7, 1975; 1 child, Matthew David. BS in Elem. Edn., Baylor U., 1974. Cert. elem. tchr., Tex. Resource tchr. 1st and 2nd grades Kenedy (Tex.) Ind. Sch. Dist., 1975-76; kindergarten tutor Stride Learning Ctr., F.E. Warren AFB, Wyo., 1976-78, infant stimulation therapy asst., 1978-80; kindergarten tchr. Stockdale (Tex.) Ind. Sch. Dist., 1980-81, Edgewood Ind. Sch. Dist., San Antonio, 1981-83, 1st grade tchr., 1983-85, 2nd grade tchr., reading lang., gifted and talented tchr., 1989-93, instrnl. specialist, gifted and talented tchr., 1993-94; 3rd grade tchr. Winston Elem. Sch., San Antonio, 1994—, 2nd grade tchr., 1996-97; 3rd grade tutor Wake County, Cary, N.C., 1985-86, 3rd grade tchr., 1986-89; 2nd grade tchr. Stafford Elem. Sch., 1998—, sci. head tchr., 2001—03. 2d grade rep. Edgewood Dist. Edn. Improvement Coun., 1998-2001. Co-author: Curriculum Writing for Kindergarten and Second Grade Gifted and Talented, 1991. Mem.: Assn. Tex. Profl. Educators, Edgewood Classrm. Tchrs. Assn. (rep. 1990—94). Baptist. Avocations: longaberger basket collecting, cross stitching, reading, collecting cook books, collecting cat meow houses. Home: 9658 Chelmsford San Antonio TX 78239-2308 E-mail: bill_mary_wimpee@hotmail.com.

WINCHELL, GEORGE WILLIAM, curriculum and technology educator; b. Coldwater, Mich., Nov. 12, 1948; s. Elwood F. and Ethel L. (DeBray) W.; m. Marcia A. Hersh, June 7, 1969 (dec.); 1 child, Paul Michael. BA, Mich. State U., 1969; diploma, Leningrad (USSR) State U., 1967; MA, Mich. State U., 1973; EdS, Cen. Mich. U., 1982. Cert. elem., secondary, Russian, lang. arts and social sci. tchr.; cert. adminstr., supt., elem. prin. Elem. tchr. Silverton (Colo.) Pub. Schs.; tech. edn. cons. Stanton, Mich.; off-campus instr. Cen. Mich. U., Mt. Pleasant; profl. devel. coord., facilitator strategic planning, dir. instrnl. tech. Montcalm Area Intermediate Sch. Dist., Stanton, 1997-99; dir. tech. edn. Cen. Montcalm Pub. Sch., Stanton, 1969—99; grants coord., v.p. Crystal Automation Sys., Inc.; master online instr. Mich. Virtual HS, 1999—, regional ambassador. Regional amb. Mich. Virtual HS. Mem. ASCD, Internat. Soc. Tech. Edn., Am. Soc. Distance Learning, Am. Soc. Quality, Mich. Assn. Computer Users in Learning, Nat. Staff Devel. Coun. Office: Crystal Automation Sys Inc 617 E Lake St Stanton MI 48888-8902

WINCOR, MICHAEL Z. psychopharmacology educator, clinician, researcher; b. Chgo., Feb. 9, 1946; s. Emanuel and Rose (Kershner) W.; m. Emily E.M. Smythe; children: Meghan Heather, Katherine Rose. SB in Zoology, U. Chgo., 1966; PharmD, U. So. Calif., 1978. Rsch. project specialist U. Chgo. Sleep Lab., 1968-75; psychiat. pharmacist Brotman Med. Ctr., Culver City, Calif., 1979-83; asst. prof. U. So. Calif., L.A., 1983-97, assoc. prof., 1997—, interim chair dept. pharmacy, 2001—02, assoc. dean external programs, 2003—. Cons. Fed. Bur. Prisons Drug Abuse Program, Terminal Island, Calif., 1978—81, Nat. Inst. Drug Abuse, Bethesda, Md., 1981, The Upjohn Co., Kalamazoo, 1982—87, 1991—92, Area XXIV Profl. Stds. Rev. Orgn., L.A., 1983, Brotman Med. Ctr., Culver City, Calif., 1983—88, SmithKline Beecham Pharms., Phila., 1990—93, Tokyo Coll. of Pharmacy, 1991, G.D. Searle & Co., Chgo., 1992—97, 1999—2001, Pfizer, NY, 1998—, Wyeth-Ayerst, Phila., 1999—2001, Novartis, East Hanover, NJ, 2002—, AstraZeneca, Wilmington, Del., 2002—. Contbr. more than 75 articles to profl. jours., chpts. to books, papers presented at nat. and internat. meetings and reviewer. Mem. adv. coun. Franklin Avenue Sch., 1986-89; bd. dirs. K.I. Children's Ctr., 1988-89; trustee Sequoyah Sch., 1992-93; mem. tech. com. Ivanhoe Sch., 1993-96; U. So. Calif. Amb., 2000—. Recipient Cert. Appreciation, Mayor of L.A., 1981, Bristol Labs Award, 1978, DuPont Pharma Innovative Pharmacy Practice award, 1995, Pharmacy Coun. Mental Health award, 1996, Outstanding Chpt. Advisor award Am. Pharm. Assn.-Acad. of Students of Pharmacy, 2003; Faculty scholar U. So. Calif. Sch. Pharmacy, 1978. Mem. Am. Coll. Clin. Pharmacy (chmn. constn. and bylaws com. 1983-84, mem. credentials com. 1991-93, 95-97, ednl. affairs com. 1994, constn. and bylaws com. 1999-00), Am. Assn. Colls. Pharmacy (focus group on liberalization profl. curriculum 1990-92, mem. pharmacy practice planning commn. 1996-97, chmn. pharmacy practice awards com. 1998-2000, mem. bylaws and policy devel. com. 2001-03, mem. computer tech. in edn. task force 2001-02, chmn. coun. of faculties strategic planning and resolutions com. 2001-03), Am. Soc. Health-Sys. Pharmacists (chmn. edn. and tng. adv. working group 1985-88, chmn. com. on academia 1996-97), Am. Pharm. Assn. (del. ann. meeting ho. of dels. 1989, 1998, Acad. Students of Pharmacy Outstanding Chpt. Advisor 2003), Sleep Rsch. Soc., Am. Acad. Sleep Medicine, Calif. Pharmacists Assn. (trustee 1997-2001, chmn. editl. rev. com. 1998-2003), U. So. Calif. Sch. Pharmacy Alumni Assn. (bd. dirs. 1979—, pres. 1998—), Rho Chi. Avocation: photography. Office: 1985 Zonal Ave Los Angeles CA 90089-9121

WINDEL, ROBERT EUGENE, school system administrator; b. New York Mills, Minn., Mar. 2, 1944; s. Adolph H. and Dora Ellen (Ramsay) W.; children from previous marriage: Jonathan, Jill; m. Patricia Dianne Tschetter, July 1, 1977; children: Pamela, Timothy, Robert J. BS, Concordia Coll., 1966; MS, Mankato State U., 1973; EdS, Tri-Coll. U., 1981; EdD, Mont. State U., 1991. Cert. adminstr., Mont., tchr. elem. edn., adminstr., Minn. Tchr. Prior Lake (Minn.) Elem. Sch., 1966-69; team leader Sweeney Elem. Sch., Shakopee, Minn., 1969-70, 71-73; tchr. sci. Grant Elem. Sch., Duluth, Minn., 1970-71; team leader, asst. prin. William Byrne Elem. Sch., Burnsville, Minn., 1973-77; elem. prin. Lake PArk (Minn.) Elem. Sch., 1977-79; asst. supt. Lake Park Pub. Schs., 1979-81; adminstrv. asst. supt. West Fargo (N.D.) Pub. Schs., 1981-86; supt. schs. Havre (Mont.) Pub. Schs., 1986—. Keynote speaker Ann. Regional Adminstrv. Conf., Saskatchewan, Can., 1987; chmn. sch. adminstrn. Cert./Aspiring Prins., Mont, 1991-93; pres. Vanguard Paradigm, Inc., 1992—, corp. pres. sch. reform initiative, 1992. Bd. dirs. No. Mont. Health Care, Inc., Havre; pres. Hi Line Sch. Adminstrn. Assn., 1989-91. Mem. Am. Assn. Sch. Adminstrs. (reader, evaluator conf. proposals 1992), Internat. Reading Assn. (presenter nat. convention 1990), Minn. Assn. Elem. Sch. Prins. (presenter confs. 1977-81), Mont. Conf. Edn. Leadership (sectional leader 1988, 89, 91, 92), Active Corp. Execs., Rotary, Havre C. of C. Avocation: hunting. Office: Havre Pub Schs 425 6th St Havre MT 59501-4032

WINDSOR, PATRICIA (KATONAH SUMMERTREE, PERRIN WINTERS), author, educator, lecturer; b. NYC, Sept. 21, 1938; d. Bernhard Edward and Antoinette (Gaus) Seelinger; m. Laurence Charles Windsor, Jr., Apr. 3, 1959 (div. 1978); children: Patience Wells, Laurence Edward; m. Stephen E. Altman, Sept. 21, 1986 (div. 1989). Student, Bennington Coll., 1956-58, Westchester Community Coll.; AA, NYU. V.p. Windsor-Morehead Assoc., NYC, 1960—63; info. mgr. Family Planning Assn., London, 1974-76; faculty mem. Inst. Children's Lit., Redding Ridge, Conn., 1976-94, 99—; editor-in-chief AT&T, Washington, 1978-80; instr. U. Md. Writers Inst., Open Univ., Washington, 1980-82; creative developer, faculty mem. Long Ridge Writer's Group, Danbury, Conn., 1988-2000; dir. Summertree Studios, Savannah, Ga., 1992—. Dir. Wordspring Lit. Cons., 1989—, Wordworks Writing Cons., 1999—; dir. Devel. Writing Workshops, Katonah, NY, 1976-78; judge Internat. Assn. Bus. Communicators, Washington, 1979, 89; lectr. LI U., Jersey City State Coll., Skidmore Coll., others, 1987—; instr. Coastal Ga. Ctr. for Continuing Edn., 1996—, Armstrong Atlantic U. Continuing Edn., 1997-2000, Anne Arundel (Md.) C.C., 2000—, workshop coord., 2000—. Author: The Summer Before, 1973 (ALA Best Book award 1973, transl. 1980 Austrian State prize 1980, also Brit., Norwegian, German edits.), Something's Waiting for You, Baker D, 1974 (starred selection Libr. Jour., Brit., Japanese edits.), Home Is Where Your Feet Are Standing, 1975, Diving for Roses, 1976 (NY Times Outstanding Book for Young Adults award, starred selection Libr. Jour.), Mad Martin, 1976, Killing Time, 1980, Demon Tree, 1983 (pen name Colin Daniel), The Sandman's Eyes, 1985 (Edgar Allan Poe Best Juvenile Mystery award Mystery Writers Am.), How a Weirdo and a Ghost Can Change Your Life, 1986, The Hero, 1988 (highest rating Voice of Youth Advocate), Just Like the Movies, 1990, The Christmas Killer, 1991 (Edgar nominee, Brit., Danish, French edits.), Two Weirdos and a Ghost, 1991, A Weird and Moogly Christmas, 1991, The Blooding, 1996 (YALSA pick for reluctant readers), The House of Death, 1996; columnist The Blood Rev., 1990-92, Savannah Parent, 1990-92; columnist Coastal Senior, 1997-99; also short stories in anthologies and mags.; actress: The Haunting of Hill House, City Lights Theatre Co., 1991. Mem. City Lights Theatre Co., Savannah, Ga., 1991. Mem. Children's Book Guild, Authors Guild, Poetry Soc. Ga., Savannah Storytellers. Avocations: skiing, painting, modern dance. Office: Born Author Dot Com PO Box 799 Severna Park MD 21146

WINEBERG, HOWARD, social studies educator, researcher; b. N.Y.C., Aug. 30, 1955; s. Moe and Ruth (Blinder) W. BA, Bowling Green (Ohio) State U., 1977, MA, 1980; PhD, Johns Hopkins U., 1985. Demographer Indian Nations Coun. of Govts., Tulsa, 1985; sr. rsch. assoc. Inst. Aging, prof. cmty. health, urban studies and planning Portland (Oreg.) State U., 1986—. Co-founder Oreg. Demographic Group, Portland, 1990; Oreg. rep. to Fed.-State Coop. Program for Population Estimates, 1986-98; mem. steering com. Fed.-State Coop. Program for Population Estimates, 1994-98. Author: Do All Trails Lead to Oregon? Population Estimates for Oregon 1980-90, 91-97, A Portrait of Older Oregonians, 1997; mem. editl. bd. Jour. Divorce and Remarriage, 1996—; contbr. articles to profl. jours. Johns Hopkins U. fellow, 1980-82; Children's Svcs. Commn., grantee, 1989. Mem. Internat. Soc. for Philos. Enquiry, Population Assn. Am., Population Reference Bur., Soc. for Study of Social Biology (v.p. 1998—), Oreg. Acad. Sci., Internat. Platform Assn. Avocations: racquetball, music. Office: Portland State U Inst on Aging 632 SW Hall St Portland OR 97201-5215

WINEGARDNER, ROSE MARY, special education educator; b. Granite City, Ill., Feb. 4, 1933; d. Arthur Udell and Margaret Helen (Brown) Barco; m. Carl Norman Winegardner, July 23, 1954; children: Laura Helen, Thelma Rose Winegardner Gordon, Jacob Harrison (dec.). BS in Edn., Mo. U., Columbia, 1954; MA in Ednl. Adminstrn., Wyo. U., 1977; edn. specialist, Nebr. U., 1988. Cert. tchr., Nebr., Iowa, Mo. Tchr. Elem. Sch. Grandview & Belton, Mo., 1957-64; tchr. mid. sch. Schleswig (Iowa) Community Schs., 1978-82; spl. edn. resource tchr. Ednl. Svc. Unit #4, Auburn, Nebr., 1982-94, Kans. U. Inst. Rsch. Learning trainer strategy implementation model, 1989—; spl. edn. resource tchr. Dawson-Verdon Consol. Schs., 1990—. Grantee Nebr. Dept. Edn., 1990-93. Mem. Internat. Reading Assn., Coun. for Exceptional Children (v.p. S.E. Nebr. chpt. 1990-92, pres. 1992-94, 94-96), DAR, Phi Delta Kappa, Zeta Tau Alpha. Lutheran. Home: 2100 23rd St Auburn NE 68305-2400

WINEMAN, ALAN STUART, mechanical engineering and applied mechanics educator; b. Wyandotte, Mich., Nov. 17, 1937; s. Meyer Michael and Sophia Ethel (Cohen) W.; m. Carol Sue Frank, Dec. 20, 1964; children— Lara, Daniel BSE., U. Mich., 1959; PhD, Brown U., 1964. Asst. prof. mech. engrng. and applied mechanics U. Mich., Ann Arbor, 1964-69, assoc. prof. mech. engrng. and applied mechanics, 1969-75, prof. mech. engrng. and applied mechanics, 1975—. Contbr. articles to profl. jour. NSF grantee Mem. ASME, Soc. Rheology, Am. Acad. Mechanics, Soc. Natural Philosophy, Soc. Engrng. Sci. Avocations: singing; appearing in amateur musical productions. Office: U Mich Dept Mech Engrng Ann Arbor MI 48109

WINER, WARD OTIS, mechanical engineer, educator; b. Grand Rapids, Mich., June 27, 1936; s. Mervin Augustus and Ina Katherine (Wood) W.; m. Mary Jo Wielinga, June 15, 1957; children: Mathew Owen, James Edward, Paul Andrew, Mary Margaret. Asso., Grand Rapids Jr. Coll., 1956; BS, U. Mich., 1958, MS, 1959, PhD, 1962; PhD (Cavendish Lab. fellow), Cambridge (Eng.) U., 1964. Asst. prof. dept. mech. engrng. U. Mich., Ann Arbor, 1963-66, assoc. prof., 1966-69; assoc. prof. mech. engrng. Ga. Inst. Tech., 1969-71, prof., 1971-84, Regents' prof., 1984—, mem. exec. bd., 1983-88, chmn., 1984-86, dir. and chmn. Sch. Mech. Engrng., 1988—, Eugene C. Gwaltney Jr. chair George W. Woodruff Sch. Mech. Engrng., 2001—. Chmn. Gordon Research Conf. on Friction, Lubrication and Wear, 1980; mem. NRC, 1980-88; chmn. Com. on Recommendations for U.S. Army Basic Sci. Research, 1985-87; mem. div. mech., structural, materials engrng. adv. bd. NSF Engrng. Directorate, 1984-89. Co-editor: Wear Control Handbook, 1980; tech. editor: Jour. Lubrication Tech., 1980-84, Jour. of Tribology, 1984-87; contbr. articles to profl. jours. Democratic precinct chmn., 1967-68; Mem. exec. bd. Horace H. Rackham Sch. Grad. Studies, U. Mich., 1968. Recipient Disting. Faculty Svc. award Coll. Engrng. U. Mich., 1967, Alumni Merit award, 1998, Cert. Recognition, NASA, 1977, Clarence E. Earle Meml. award Nat. Grease Lubricating Inst., 1979, Disting. Prof. award Ga. Inst. Tech., 1987; named Hon. Alumni, Ga. Tech., 2003. Fellow AAAS, ASME (bd. comms. 1987-91, v.p. rsch. 1989-93, Melville medal 1975, Centennial medallion 1980, Mayor D. Hersey award 1986, Charles Russ Richards Meml. award 1988), Soc. Tribologists and Lubrication Engrs. (bd. dirs. 1983-86, Internat. award 1997), Brit. Tribology Trust (gold medal 1987); mem. Am. Soc. Engrng. Educators (Benjamin Garver Lamme award 1995, Donald Marlowe award 1996), NAE, Metro Atlanta Engrng. Soc. (Engr. of Yr. 1989), Am. Acad. Mechanics, Soc. Rheology, Soc. Engrng. Sci. (dir. 1980-84), AAUP (pres. Ga. Tech. chpt. 1972-74, v.p. state conf. 1973-75), Sigma Xi (chpt. pres. 1982-83, Sustained Rsch. in Engrng. award 1975), Tau Beta Pi, Pi Tau Sigma, Phi Kappa Phi. Home: 1025 Mountain Creek Trl NW Atlanta GA 30328-3535 E-mail: ward.winer@me.gatech.edu.

WING, ADRIEN KATHERINE, law educator; b. Aug. 7, 1956; d. John Ellison and Katherine (Pruitt) Wing; children: Che-Cabral, Nolan Felipe. AB magna cum laude, Princeton U., 1978; MA, UCLA, 1979; JD, Stanford, 1982. Bar: N.Y. 1983, U.S. Dist. Ct. (so. and ea. dists.) N.Y. 1983, U.S. Ct. Appeals (5th and 9th cirs.). Assoc. Curtis, Mallet-Prevost, Colt & Mosle, N.Y.C., 1982-86, Rabinowitz, Boudin, Standard, Krinsky & Lieberman, 1986-87; assoc. prof. law U. Iowa, Iowa City, 1987-93, prof., 1993—, disting. prof. law, 2001—. Mem. alumni council Princeton U., 1983-85, 96-2000, mem. exec. com., 2002—, trustee Class of '78 Alumni Found., 1984-87, 93—, v.p. Princeton Class of 1978 Alumni, 1993-98, trustee Princeton U. 1995; mem. bd. visitors Stanford Law Sch., 1993-96; vis. prof. U. Mich., 2002. Mem. bd. editors Am. J. Comp. Law, 1993—. Mem. Iowa Commn. on African Ams. in Prisons, 1999—. Mem.: ABA (exec. com. young lawyers sect. 1985—87, law sch. site inspector 2002—), U.S. Assn. Constl. Law (bd. dir.), Am. Assn. of Law Schs. (minority sect. bd. 1996—, chair 2002), Am. Friends Svc. Com. (bd. dirs. Mid. East 1998—), Am. Soc. Internat. Law (exec. coun. 1986—89, exec. com. 1988—99, nominating com. 1991, 1993, group chair S. Africa 1993—95, membership com. 1994—95, exec. coun. 1996—99), Internat. Assn. Dem. Lawyers (UN rep. 1984—87), Nat. Conf. Black Lawyers (chmn. internat. affairs sect. 1982—95, UN rep.), Internat. Third World Legal Studies Assn. (bd. dirs. 1996—, nominating trustee Princeton com. 1997—2000), Coun. on Fgn. Rels., Iowa Peace Inst. (bd. dirs. 1993—95), Iowa City Fgn. Rels. Coun. (bd. dirs. 1989—94), Transafrica Scholars Forum Coun. (bd. dirs. 1993—95), Black Alumni of Princeton U. (bd. dirs. 1982—87). Democrat. Avocations: photography, writing, poetry. Office: U Iowa Sch Law Boyd Law Bldg Iowa City IA 52242 E-mail: adrien-wing@uiowa.edu.

WINGATE, ANN, early childhood education educator; b. Ocilla, Ga., Jan. 12, 1952; d. Amos Leonard and Winnie Lavada (Brown) W. AA, Abraham Baldwin Agrl. Coll., 1972; BS in Edn., Ga. So. U., 1974, MS in Edn., 1978; edn. specialist, Valdosta State Coll., 1989. Cert. tchr., Ga. Tchr. Atkinson County Bd. Edn./Willacoochee (Ga.) Elem. Sch., 1974—. Mem. Atkinson County Dem. Com. Mem. NEA, Ga. Edn. Assn., Atkinson County Assn. Educators (pres.-elect, then pres. 1977-82), Am. Home Econs. Assn., Phi Upsilon Omicron. Baptist. Avocations: piano, organ, reading. Home: Atlantic Ave PO Box 67 Willacoochee GA 31650-0067

WINGATE, BETTYE FAYE, librarian, educator; b. Hillsboro, Tex., Oct. 31, 1950; d. Warren Randolph and Faye (Gilmore) W. BA summa cum laude, Baylor U., 1971, MA, 1975; MLS, Tex. Womans U., 1985. Cert. prov. sec., learning resources endorsement. English tchr. Mexia HS, Tex.; reading tchr. Connally Ind. Sch. Dist., Waco, Tex.; reading tchr., libr. Grapevine-Colleyville Ind. Sch. Dist., Grapevine, Tex.; libr., ret., May 02 Crockett Mid. Sch., Irving, Tex. Mem. librs. coms., Campus Action Planning Com., 1989-93, Irving Ind. Sch. Dist. Site Based Decision-Making Com., 1992-94, mem. staff devel. coun., 1994-96, chair media fair com., 1996-2001; rev. Linworth Pub.; spkr., presenter in field. Founding sponsor Challenger Ctr., Air Force Meml. Found. Recipient Tex. Media awards, 1988, 89, 94. Mem. ALA, NEA, Am. Assn. Sch. Libr. (vol. libr. Kids Connect), Tex. State Tchr. Assn. (assn. rep.), Tex. Libr. Assn. (chmn. state media awards com. 1989-91), Tex. Assn. Edn. Tech., Tex. Computer Edn. and Tech., Assn. Ednl. Comm. and Tech., Planetary Soc., Nat. Space Soc., Nat. Parks & Conservation Assn., Baylor Alumni Assn. (life), Wilderness Soc., Sierra Club, Beta Phi Mu, Delta Kappa Gamma (scholar 1985). E-mail: bettye.winate@yahoo.com.

WINGATE, C. KEITH, law educator; b. Darlington, S.C., May 12, 1953; s. Clarence L. and Lilly W.; m. Gloria Farley; stepchildren: Brenda, Marvin, Terry and Oliver Champion. BA in Polit. Sci., U. Ill., 1974, JD cum laude, 1978. Bar: Calif., 1978. Assoc. litigation dept. Morrison & Foerster, San Francisco, 1978-80; from asst. to assoc. prof. law U. Calif.-Hastings, San Francisco, 1980-86, prof., 1986—. Dir. Coun. Legal Edn. Opportunity Region I Inst., 1989; vis. prof. law Stanford Law Sch., fall 1990, 94, spring 1998; chair Minority Law Tchrs.' Conf. Com., 1990; mem. acad. assistance work group, 1991; trustee Law Sch. Admission Coun., 1997-2001. Author: (with David I. Levine and William R. Slomanson) Cases and Materials on California Civil Procedure, 1991, (with William R. Slomanson) California Civil Procedure in a Nutshell, 1992, (with Donald L. Doernberg) Federal Courts, Federalism and Separation of Powers, 1994, 2nd edit., 2000. Bd. dirs. Cmty. Housing Devel. Corp., North Richmond, 1990-99. Recipient 10 Outstanding Persons award U. Ill. Black Alumni Assn., 1980; Harno fellow U. Ill., Coll. of Law, 1976. Mem. Assn. Am. Law Schs. (chair sect. minority groups 1990, exec. com. mem. sect. civil procedure 1991), Charles Houston Bar Assn., Phi Sigma Alpha. Office: U Calif Hastings Coll Law 200 Mcallister St San Francisco CA 94102-4707

WINGATE, THOMAS MARIE JOSEPH, assistant headmaster; b. Guildford, Surrey, England, May 23, 1959; came to the U.S., 1993; s. Peter Henry and Therese M. (Vachon) W.; m. Maria Elena Espinosa de los Reyes Bolanos, July 10, 1982; children: Elenita, Juliet, Thomas Philip. BA in English, History, Theory Art, U. Kent, Canterbury, Kent, U.K., 1981; postgrad. cert. in edn. in English, U. Leeds, U.K., 1982; MEd, Ga. State U., 1996. English tchr. St. George's Coll., Weybridge, Surrey, 1985-86, Brit. Internat. Sch., Mexico City, 1986-89, head English, 1989-91, head intermediate sch., 1991-93; lang. arts tchr. Wesleyan Sch., Atlanta, 1993-94, prin., 1994-96, asst. headmaster, 1996—. Author: The Chapel on the Heath, 1985. Vol. Saint Vincent de Paul Soc., Atlanta, 1994. Grantee Ga. State U., Atlanta, 1993-94, Wesleyan Sch. Governing Bd., Atlanta, 1994. Mem. ASCD, Kappa Delta Pi. Roman Catholic. Avocations: photography, mountain climbing, cricket, coin collecting. Office: Wesleyan Sch 5405 Spalding Dr Norcross GA 30092-2614

WINICK, HERMAN, physicist, educator; b. N.Y.C., June 27, 1932; s. Benjamin and Yetta (Matles) W.; m. Renee Feldman, May 31, 1953; children: Alan Lee, Lisa Frances, Laura Joan. AB, Columbia Coll., 1953; PhD, Columbia U., 1957. Rsch. assoc., instr. U. Rochester, N.Y., 1957-59; from staff physicist to asst. dir. Cambridge (Mass.) Electron Accelerator Harvard U., 1959-73; dep. dir. Stanford (Calif.) Synchrotron Radiation Lab. Stanford Linear Accelerator Ctr., 1973-96. Rsch. prof. applied physics Stanford U., 1983-97, prof. emeritus, 1998—; chair tech. rev. com. Synchrotron Radiation Rsch. Ctr., Taiwan, 1984-93. Mem. editl. bd. Nuclear Instruments and Methods, 1982—; co-editor: Synchrotron Radiation Research, 1980; editor: Synchrotron Radiation Sources: A Primer, 1994. Recipient Humboldt Sr. Scientist award, 1986, Energy Related Tech. award U.S. Dept. Energy, 1987, U.S. Particle Accelerator Sch. prize, 1995, Disting. Assoc. award, U.S. Dept. Energy, 2000. Fellow AAAS, Am. Phys. Soc. (chmn. com. on internat. freedom of scientist 1992). Achievements include development of first wiggler and undulator magnets for synchotron radiation research. Home: 853 Tolman Dr Stanford CA 94305-1025 Office: SSRL SLAC 2575 Sand Hill Rd Menlo Park CA 94025-7015 E-mail: winick@slac.stanford.edu.

WINKELMAN, MARY LYNN, middle school educator; b. May 22, 1950; children: Candice, Joseph. Student, U. Wis., 1968-70, BS, 1975. Cert. tchr. 1-8, Wis. 6th grade tchr. St. Williams Sch., Waukesha, Wis., 1979-90; 7th grade tchr. Waukesha Cath. Sch. Sys., St. Joseph's Middle Sch., Waukesha, 1990—. Mem. Phi Kappa Phi. Avocations: reading, softball. Office: Waukesha Cath Sch Sys St Josephs 822 N East Ave Waukesha WI 53186-4808

WINKLE, SUSAN RENEE, elementary education educator; b. Rochester, Pa., May 28, 1952; d. Allen Jordan and Patricia Ielene (Whittingham) Wachob; m. Raymond Frank Winkle, Aug. 17, 1974; children: Timothy Frank, Joseph Allen. BS in Edn., Edinboro (Pa.) State U., 1974; MS in Edn., Old Dominion U., Norfolk, Va., 1992. Cert. tchr., Pa., Va. Substitute tchr. Norfolk City Schs., 1975; children's shoes clk. Kauffmann's Store, Rochester, Pa., 1982-84; tutor Rochester, 1984; kindergarten tchr. Kindercare Day Care, Newport News, Va., 1984-86, daycare dir., 1986; transitional 1st grade tchr. Newport News Schs., 1986-93, REACH reading tchr., 1993—.

Mentor Christopher Newport U., Newport News, 1992; workshop facilitator. Contbg. author: K/T-1 Cross Reference Curriculum Guide, 1990. Active Apostles Luth. Ch., Gloucester, Va., 1987—. Primary Block grantee, 1994. Mem. ASCD, Odyssey of the Mind (judge, ofcl.), Va. Reading Coun., Newport News Reading Coun., So. Early Childhood Assn., Tidewater Assn. Early Childhood Edn. (2d v.p. 1994), Sch. Improvement Team. Avocations: gardening, reading. Home: 1787 Chiskiake St Gloucester Point VA 23062-2403 Office: Richneck Elem Sch 205 Tyner Dr Newport News VA 23608-1660

WINKLE, WILLIAM ALLAN, music educator; b. Rapid City, S.D., Oct. 10, 1940; s. Curis Powell and June Ada (Alexander) W.; m. Carola Kay Croll, June 16, 1968; children: Brenda, Rachelle. MusB, Huron U., 1962; MA, U. Vt., 1971; ArtsD, U. Northern Colo., 1976; postgrad., North Tex. State U. Dir. choral and band Arlington (S.D.) High Sch., 1962-64; band dir. DeSmet (S.D.) High Sch., 1964-67; coord. music Huron (S.D.) Pub. Schs., 1967-69; head of instrumental music Huron Coll., 1969-71; dir. bands, prof. music Chadron (Nebr.) State Coll., 1971—. Instr. tuba music camp S.D. State U., Brooking, 1969-71, Internat. Music Camp, Dunseith, Nebr., 1977—, high sch. sessions U. Vt., Burlington, 1964-71; tubist, bassoonist Huron Symphony/Huron Mcpl., 1957-69, Nebr. Panhandle Symphony & Symphonia, Chadron, 1971—; tubist Blue Jean Philharmonic, Estes Park, Colo., 1960-64, Internat. Brass Quintet, 1985—; conductor, tour dir. Am. Youth Symphony and Chorus, European Tours, 1967-78; performing artist, clinician Yamaha Music Corp. USA, 1977—. Author: List of Tuba/Euphonium Solos, 1984; co-author: Art of Tuba, 1992; contbr. articles to mags. Moderator, trustee, deacon, conf. bd. dirs. United Ch. of Christ, 1974-90. Recipient Freedom Found. award, 1972, Chadron State Coll. Rsch. Inst. 5 awards, 1974-78; Paul Harris fellow, 2002. Mem. Chadron C. of C., Nebr. State Bandmasters (dist. VI and coll. rep. 1978-84, pres. 1998—), Internat. Music Camp (bd. dirs. 1980-86, Disting. Svc. award 1987), Tubist Universal Brotherhood Assn. (internat. rep. 1971—, Nat. Sem. award 1975, 77), Music Educators Nat. Conf., Internat. Assn. Jazz Educators, Concert Bands Am., Nat. Band Assn. (chmn. Nebr. chpt. 1996—, citation of excellence 1999), Coll. Band Dirs. Nat. Assn., Nebr. Bandmasters Assn. (pres. 1999), Phi Beta Mu (pres. Alpha Theta chpt. 1999—), Kappa Kappa Psi, Kappa Delta Pi. Republican. Avocation: cycling. Home: 318 Ann St Chadron NE 69337-2412 Office: Chadron State Coll 10th Main Chadron NE 69337

WINKLER, ALLEN WARREN, lawyer, educator; b. Chgo., Dec. 11, 1954; s. Maurice A. and Florence (Klein) W.; m. Bett C. Gibson, Nov. 1, 1986. BS, No. Ill. U., 1977; JD, Tulane U., 1981. Bar: La. 1982, Ill. 1982, U.S. Dist. Ct. (ea. dist.) La. 1982, U.S. Dist. Ct. (mid. dist.) La. 1987. Atty. Tulane Law Clinic, New Orleans, 1980—81, La. Legal Clinic, New Orleans, 1982-84; pvt. practice law New Orleans, 1984-85; staff atty. Oak Tree Savs. Bank, S.S.B., New Orleans, 1985-87, sr. atty., asst. v.p., 1987-90; atty. FDIC/Resolution Trust Corp., Baton Rouge, 1991-92, sr. atty. Atlanta, 1992-95; sr. corp. counsel Fleet Fin., Inc., Atlanta, 1996-97; pres. Legal Ease Inc., Atlanta, 1996—; corp. counsel Prudential Bank, Atlanta, 1997; gen. counsel, v.p. NCS Mortgage Svcs., Norcross, Ga., 1998-2000, gen. counsel, 1999-2000; exec. v.p., COO Companion Servicing Co., LLC, 1999-2000; corp. counsel Provident Bank, Atlanta, 2000-2001; sr. atty., v.p. SunTrust Bank, Atlanta, 2001—. Mem. faculty Franklin Coll. Ct. Reporting, Metairie, La., 1981-88; cons., guest lectr. paralegal studies Tulane U., New Orleans, 1982-90; guest lectr. U. New Orleans, 1988-90. Vol. Hawkins for Judge campaign, New Orleans. Mem. La. Bar Assn., Ill. Bar Assn. Home: 4754 Forest Glen Court Marietta GA 30066 Office: SunTrust Bank 2950 SunTrust Plz 303 Peachtree St NE Atlanta GA 30308 E-mail: allen.winkler@suntrust.com.

WINKLER, HENRY RALPH, retired academic administrator, historian; b. Waterbury, Conn., Oct. 27, 1916; s. Jacob and Ethel (Rieger) W.; m. Clare Sapadin, Aug. 18, 1940; children— Allan Michael, Karen Jean; m. Beatrice Ross, Jan. 28, 1973. AB, U. Cin., 1938, MA, 1940; PhD, U. Chgo., 1947; hon. degrees, Lehigh U., 1974, Rutgers U., 1977, No. Ky. U., 1978, St. Thomas Inst., 1979, Hebrew Union Coll., 1980, Xavier U., 1981, U. Akron, 1984, U. Cin., 1987, Thomas More Coll., 1989. Instr. U. Cin., 1939-40; asst. prof. Roosevelt Coll., 1946-47; mem. faculty Rutgers U., 1947-77, prof. history, 1958-77, chmn. dept., 1960-64; dean Faculty Liberal Arts, 1967, vice provost, 1968-70, acting provost, 1970, v.p. for acad. affairs, 1970-72, sr. v.p. for acad. affairs, 1972-76, exec. v.p., 1976-77, U. Cin., 1977, pres., 1977-84, pres. emeritus, 1984—, Univ. prof. history, 1977-86, prof. emeritus, 1986—. Mng. editor Am. Hist. Rev., 1964-68; vis. prof. Bryn Mawr Coll., 1959-60, Harvard, summer 1964, Columbia, summer 1967; faculty John Hay Fellows Inst. Humanities, 1960-65; bd. overseers Hebrew Union Coll., 1984—. Author: The League of Nations Movement in Great Britain, 1914-19, 1952, Great Britain in the Twentieth Century, 1960, 2d edit., 1966; editor: (with K.M. Setton) Great Problems in European Civilization, 1954, 2d edit., 1966, Twentieth-Century Britain, 1977, Paths Not Taken: British Labour and International Policy in the Nineteen Twenties, 1994; mem. editorial bd. Historian, 1958-64, Liberal Edn., 1986—; mem. adv. bd. Partisan Rev., 1972-79; contbr. articles to jours., revs. Nat. chmn. European history advanced placement com. Coll. Entrance Exam. Bd., 1960-64; mem. Nat. Commn. on Humanities in Schs., 1967-68, Am. specialist Eastern Asia, 1968; exec. com. Conf. on Brit. Studies, 1968-75; chmn. bd. Nat. Humanities Faculty, 1970-73; chmn. adv. com. on history Coll. Entrance Exam. Bd., 1977-80; mem. council on acad. affairs, mem. bd. trustees, chmn., 1982-84; pres. Highland Park (N.J.). Bd. Edn., 1962-63; mem. exec. com. Nat. Assn. State Univs. and Land-Grant Colls., 1978-81, mem. Cin. Lit. Club, 1978—, pres., 1993—; bd. dirs. Am. Council on Edn., 1979-81; trustee Seasengood Good Govt. Found., 1979—, pres., 1991-93; trustee Thomas More Coll., 1986-93; mem. Ohio Indsl. Tech. and Enterprise Bd., 1983-89; bd. dirs. Nat. Civic League, 1986—, Planning Accreditation Bd., 1988—; mem. adv coun. U. Va.'s Coll at Wise, Ohio Humanities Coun., 1994— With USNR, 1943-46. Recipient Lifetime Achievement award N.Am. Conf. on Brit. Studies, 1995, Bishop William Hughes award for disting. svc. to Cath. higher edn. Thomas More Coll., 1997. Mem. Am. Hist. Assn., Phi Beta Kappa, Tau Kappa Alpha, Phi Alpha Theta. Clubs: Comml., Bankers, Cin., Lit. Office: U Cin 571 Langsam Library Cincinnati OH 45221-0001 E-mail: Henry.Winkler@uc.edu.

WINKLER, JOANN MARY, secondary school educator; b. Savanna, Ill., Dec. 17, 1955; d. Donald Edgar and Genevieve Eleanor (Withhart) Winkler; m. Russell Arthur Ehlers, May 25, 1990; 1 child, Genevieve Rose Winkler Ehlers. BS in Art Edn., No. Ill. U., 1979; MA in Art Edn., N.E. Mo. State U., 1984. Tchr. art, chmn. dept. art Clinton (Iowa) H.S., 1979—. Coll. for Kids instr. Area Edn. Agy. #9, Clinton, summers, 1986—, Davenport, summers, 1987—; instr. St. Ambrose U., Clinton, 1990, Mt. St. Clare Coll., Clinton, 1993-98. Costume designer Utah Mus. Theatre, "Two by Two," 1987; exhibited in group shows at Clinton Art Assn., 1990-93. Judge Art in the Park, Clinton, 1988, 93; co. mgr. Utah Mus. Theager, Ogden, 1987; founding bd. dirs. Art's Alive, Clinton, 1985-86; bd. dirs. Gateway Contemporary Ballet, Clinton, 1987-89; founding com. mem. Louis Sullivan's Van Allen Bldg. Jr. Mus., Clinton, 1991-93. Recipient Gold Key Group award Clinton Sch. Bd., 1990, Gold Key Individual award, 1989; R.I. Sch. Design scholar, 1989, Alliance for Ind. Colls. of Art scholar, summers 1988. Mem. NEA, Ill. Art Edn. Assn., Chgo. Art Inst., Clinton Art Assn., Art Educators of Iowa, Nat. Art Edn. Assn., PEO. Avocations: swimming, travel, theater. Home: 722 Melrose Ct Clinton IA 52732-5508 Office: Clinton High Sch 817 8th Ave S Clinton IA 52732-5698

WINKLER, KATHERINE MAURINE, management consultant, educator; b. Louisville, Nov. 29, 1940; d. Myrick and Maurine (Holland) W. Cert. in foreign studies, Inst. for Am. Univs., 1961; BA, Transylvania U., 1963. Market rsch. field supr. Procter & Gamble, Cin., 1963-65; Eng. tchr. Louisville Ky. Sch. System, 1967-68; mgmt. and staff positions in sales, mktg., human resources, total quality mgmt. and edn. IBM, Louisville, Lexington, Ky., Mpls., Cin., and Westchester, N.Y., 1968-93; pvt. practice N.Y.C., Richmond, Va., 1993—. Adj. prof. NYU. Author: Leadership, 1982, Across the Board, Executive Excellence, Westchester Historian, The Scarsdale Inquirer; contbr. articles to publs. Com. mem. Mpls. Cultural Affairs Com., 1970, Village of Tarrytown (N.Y.) Main St. com., 1981—82; bd. dirs., chair trustee affairs com. Westchester County Hist. Soc., Elmsford, NY, 1989—99; mem. mgmt., bus., econs. study group NYU, 1995—97; vol. cons. White Plains Hosp. Ctr., 1998—2000; bd. dirs. Fan Dist. Assn., Richmond, chair pub. rels. com., 2003—. Named Outstanding Young Woman of Am., 1972. Mem. ASTD, Human Resource Planning Soc., Ky. Col., Soc. for Human Resource Mgmt., New Directions Human Resource Consultants Roundtable, Fan Dist. Assn. (dir., chair pub. rels. com. 2003—), Fan Woman's Club (bd. dirs. 2002-). Home: 1423 Grove Ave Richmond VA 23220-4601 E-mail: kittywink@ATTGlobal.net.

WINN, FRANCIS JOHN, JR., medical educator; b. Detroit, Aug. 12, 1946; s. Francis John and Margaret (Aubuchon) Winn; m. Cathy Mannion, Aug. 24, 1974 (div. Dec. 1980); m. Gloria Elizabeth Morrow, Feb. 6, 1981; children: Francis John III, Paige Whitney. BS in Psychology, Mich. State U., 1968; MA in Physiol. Psychology, Ctrl. Mich. U., 1974; PhD in Psychology and Stats., Tex. Tech U., 1977. Commd. USPHS, 1978, advanced through grades to comdr., 1984, ret., 1997; chief mental health svcs. and Atlantic area psychiat. screening unit USCG Outpatient Clinic, Governor's Island, NY, 1978-83; staff rsch. psychologist, cons. to chief psychiatry br. USCG Tng. Ctr., Cape May, NJ, 1983-86; sr. scientist psychophysiology & biomechanics sect. Nat. Inst. Occupl. Safety and Health, Cin., 1986-91; sr. rsch. support scientist officer Nat. Inst. Drug Abuse, 1991-92, Substance Abuse and Mental Health Svc. Adminstrn., 1992-95, sr. health statistician Ctr. Substance Abuse Prevention, 1995-97; clin. asst. prof. E. Carolina U., Greenville, NC, 1997—. Cons. assoc. Duke U. Sch. Nursing, 1998—; program evaluation cons. New Bold Assocs., 1998—2001; asst. adj. prof. Med. Coll. Ga., 1995—; bd. collaborators N.C. Agro-Med. Inst., 1998—. exec. com., 2000—01; vis. asst. prof. dept. psychology U. Tex., El Paso, 1977—78; adj. assoc. prof. dept. human svcs., counseling St. John's U., Jamaica, NY, 1980—82; lectr. Stockton State Coll., Pomona, NJ, 1985—86; adj. asst. prof. U. Cin., 1989—91; mem. adv. bd. Conf. Engring. and Aging, Stein Gerontol. Inst., Drexel U., 1990—91; mem. sci. program com. 2d Internat. Conf. Aging and Work, Danish Working Environ. Fund, 1998; program chair tech. group aging Triennial Congress Internat. Ergonomics Assn., 2000; spkr. in field. Assoc. editor: Exptl. Aging Rsch.; contbr. articles to profl. jours. Mem.: DAV, Internat. Soc. Occupl. Ergonomics and Safety (mem. at large to exec. com.), Internat. Commn. Occupl. Health (mem. sci. com. aging and work 2002—), Soc. Air Force Psychologists, Gerontol. Soc. Am., Soc. Exptl. Biology and Medicine, Am. Psychol. Soc., Assn. Physician Assist Programs, Res. Officers Assn., Sigma Xi. Home: 3401 Cutler Ct Greenville NC 27834-7621 Office: E Carolina U W Rsch Campus 1157 V Site 'C' Rd Greenville NC 27834 E-mail: winnf@mail.ecu.edu.

WINN, JOHN STERLING, chemist, educator; b. Lexington, Va., Oct. 8, 1947; s. Sterling Wilbur and Nancy Margaret (Mahady) W. SB in Chemistry, SB in Physics, MIT, 1969; PhD in Chemistry, U. Calif., Berkeley, 1973; MA, Dartmouth Coll., 1992. Rsch. fellow Harvard U., Cambridge, Mass., 1973-75; prof. U. Calif., Berkeley, 1975-82; prin. investigator Lawrence Berkeley (Calif.) Lab., 1977-82; prof. Dartmouth Coll., Hanover, N.H., 1982—, chair dept. chemistry, 1994—98. Author: Physical Chemistry, 1994. Alfred P. Sloan fellow Alfred P. Sloan Found., 1978-80. Mem. Am. Chem. Soc., Am. Phys. Soc., Sigma Xi. Office: Dartmouth Coll 6128 Burke Lab Hanover NH 03755

WINSLOW, JANET LUCAS, elementary education educator; b. Scotland Neck, N.C., May 2, 1939; d. Ernest and Cora Wilma (Dixon) Lucas; m. Roy L. Winslow, Dec. 27, 1969; 1 child, Sally L. BS in Edn., Old Dominion U., 1965; student, U. Va., Norfolk State U. Cert. collegiate profl. K-7. Tchr. Norfolk (Va.) City Schs., 1965-95, ret., 1995, mem. all city teaching team, tchr. mentor adv. coun., 1970, 85, 90, 91. Great books leader, tchr. corps. program. Program dir. Girl Scout Camp Matoaka. Recipient Sch. Bell award, 1989-90, 1990-91. Mem. NEA, Va. Edn. Assn., Edn. Assn. Norfolk, PTA (life). Home: 3378 Finch Ave Norfolk VA 23518-5713

WINSLOW, NORMA MAE, elementary education educator; b. Pawling, N.Y., Oct. 18, 1942; d. Franklin Norman and Florence (Chandler) Timpson; m. Donald Arthur Winslow, Aug. 5, 1961; children: Gregory Donald (dec.), Kevin Craig. AA in Liberal Arts, Adirondack Coll., 1970; BS in Edn. summa cum laude, Castleton State U., 1973; MS in Adminstrn. and Supervision, SUNY, Plattsburg, 1990; CAS, Plattsburgh State U., 1993. Cert. elem. and secondary tchr., N.Y., SAS and SDA in Adminstrn. Tchr. Ft. Ann Ctrl. Sch., NY, 1973-77, Corinth Ctrl. Sch., 1977—, grade chair, 1984-89, dir. student svcs. adminstrn., 2002—03. Dir. music Corinth Theatre Guild, 1980—. Named Outstanding Tchr. of English, N.Y. State English Coun., 1981, One of 2000 Notable Women, 1995. Mem. Corinth Tchrs. Assn. (pres. 1980-86, 94-95), Rotary (pres. Corinth chpt. 1992, Paul Harris fellow), Delta Kappa Gamma (officer Beta Omega chpt. 1980—). Avocation: music. Home: 320 Center St Corinth NY 12822-1104 Office: Corinth Cen Sch 105 Oak St Corinth NY 12822-1203

WINSTON, DONNA CAROL, nursing educator, nurse practitioner; b. Cin., Aug. 3, 1938; BS, Tex. Christian U., 1978; BBA, U. Cin., 1960; MS, U. Ariz., 1982; PhD, Tex. Woman's U., 1988. Cert. geriatric nurse practitioner, nutritional specialist. Clin. nurse specialist Harris Hosp., Ft. Worth, 1982-84; nursing specialist U. Tex., 1985-86; dir. edn. AMI-North Tex. Med. Ctr., McKinney, 1987; asst. prof. Wayne State U., Detroit, 1988-90, Ariz. State U., Phoenix, 1990-93; geriatric NP in pvt. practice, 1993; adult NP St. Joseph's Med. Ctr., Phoenix, 1994—96. Cons. Samaritan Corp., 1993, Streich Lang Law Firm, 1995, Med. Rsch. Methodologies, 1996—. Mem. Am. Mktg. Assn., Internat. Soc. Human Ethology, Sigma Theta Tau.

WINSTON, JANE KAY, secondary education educator, artist; b. Omaha, July 5, 1947; d. Paul Henry and Jean (Irwin) Kupfer; 1 child, Daniel. BFA in Edn., U. Nebr., Lincoln, 1969; student, Midland Luth. Coll., Fremont, Nebr., 1965-67. Art tchr. Beveridge Jr. High, Omaha, 1969-73, Idaho Falls (Idaho) H.S., 1975-80, Skyline H.S., Idaho Falls, Idaho, 1987—. Mem. Idaho Falls Snowfest Com., 1991. Named Idaho Secondary Art Educator of Yr., 1996; Idaho Falls Edn. Found. grantee, 1992. Mem. Idaho Falls Art Guild, Idaho Art Edn. Assn., Nat. Art Edn. Assn., Eagle Rock Art Guild (life), Delta Kappa Gamma. Avocations: reading, playing board and card games, travel. Home: 5845 S Holmes Ave Idaho Falls ID 83404-7619 Office: Skyline High School 1767 Blue Sky Dr Idaho Falls ID 83402-4802

WINSTON, KRISHNA, foreign language professional; b. Greenfield, Mass., June 7, 1944; d. Richard and Clara (Brussel) W.; 1 child, Danielle Billingsley. BA, Smith Coll., 1965; MPhil, Yale U., 1969, PhD, 1974. Instr. Wesleyan U., Middletown, Conn., 1970-74, asst. prof., 1974-77, assoc. prof., 1977-84, prof., 1984—, acting dean, 1993-94. Coord. Mellon Mays Undergrad. Fellowship, 1993—. Author: O v. Horváth: Close Readings of Six Plays, 1975; translator: O. Schlemmer, Letters and Diaries, 1972, S. Lenz, The Heritage, 1981, G. Grass, Two States, One Nation, 1990, C. Hein, The Distant Lover, 1989, G. Mann, Reminiscences and Reflections, 1990, J. W. V. Goethe, Wilhelm Meister's Journeyman Years, 1989, C. v. Krockow, The Hour of the Women, 1991, E. Heller, With the Next Man Everything Will be Different, 1992, R. W. Fassbinder, The Anarchy of the Imagination, 1992, G. Reuth, Goebbels, 1994, E. Lappin; editor: Jewish Voices, German Words, 1994, P. Handke, Essay on the Jukebox, 1994, P. Handke, My Year in the No-Man's-Bay, 1998, G. Grass, Too Far Afield, 2000, P. Handke, On a Dark Night I Left My Silent House, 2000, G. Grass, Crabwalk, 2003. Vol. Planned Parenthood, Middletown, 1972-77; mem. Recycling Task Force, Middletown, 1986-87; chmn. Resource Recycling Adv. Coun., Middletown, 1989—; trustee Ind. Day Sch., Middlefield, Conn., 1989—. Recipient Schlegel-Tieck prize for translation, 1994, 2001, Helen and Kurt Wolff prize for transl., 2001; German Acad. Exch. Svc. fellow, Kahn fellow Smith Coll., 2000-01. Mem. MLA, ALTA, Soc. for Exile Studies, Am. Assn. Tchrs. German, PEN, Phi Beta Kappa (pres. Wesleyan chpt. 1987-90). Home: 655 Bow Ln Middletown CT 06457-4808 Office: Wesleyan Univ German Studies Dept Middletown CT 06459-0040 E-mail: kwinston@wesleyan.edu.

WINSTON, MICHAEL RUSSELL, foundation executive, historian; b. NYC, May 26, 1941; s. Charles Russell and Jocelyn Anita Prem Das Winston; m. Judith Ann Marianno, Aug. 10, 1963; children: Lisa Marie, Cynthia Eileen. BA magna cum laude, Howard U., 1962; MA, U. Calif.-Berkeley, 1964, PhD, 1974. Instr. dept. history Howard U., Washington, 1964-66, asst. dean Coll. Liberal Arts, 1968-69, asst. prof. dept. history, 1970-73, v.p. acad. affairs, 1983-90, prof. emeritus, 1990—; assoc. dir. Inst. Svc. to Edn., Washington, 1966; fellow Haus. Hof-und Staatsarchiv, Vienna, 1969; dir. Moorland Spingarn Rsch. Ctr., 1973-83; v.p., bd. dirs. Alfred Harcourt Found., Silver Spring, Md., 1992-93, pres., 1993—. Cons. Smithsonian Instn., 1979—, nat. Inst. Edn., 1978-85, NSF, 1985—. Author: (with R.W. Logan) The Negro in the United States, 1970, The Howard Univ.Dept. of History, 1913-73, 1973; editor: (with R.W. Logan) Dictionary of Am. Negro Biography, 1982, (with G.R. McNeil) Hist. Judgements Reconsidered, 1988; mem. editl. bd. Washington History, 1993-97. Mem. exec. bd. Nat. Capital Area coun. Boy Scouts Am., 1988—90; trustee spl. contbn. fund NAACP, 1980—82; trustee D.C. Pub. Defender Svc., 1985—88; bd. trustees Woodrow Wilson Nat. Fellowship Found., 1997—; bd. mgrs. Hist. Soc. Washington; bd. dirs. Harcourt Brace Jovanovich, 1980—91, D.C. Pub. Libr. Found., 1994—2002, pres., 1995—99, Nat. Coun. for History Standards; mem. bd. overseers' com. to visit dept. history Harvard U., 1996—; mem. nat. adv. com. and coun. of scholars Libr. of Congress; nat. adv. bd. Protect Historic Am.; mem. Commn. on Coll. and Univ. Nonprofl. Studies ABA; mem. Nat. Ctr. for History in the Schs. UCLA/NEH. Moten fellow U. Edinburgh, 1962, Wilson fellow U. Calif., 1962, Ford fellow, 1969-70, Woodrow Wilson Internat. Ctr. Scholars fellow, 1979-80; sr. scholar, 2001—. Mem.: Nat. Coun. for History Standards, Coun. on Foreign Relations, Atlantic Coun. of U.S., Hist. Soc. Washington, Am. Antiquarian Soc., Orgn. Am. Historians, Am. Hist. Assn., Grolier Club, Century Assn., Cosmos Club (Washington), Phi Beta Kappa (Ralph Waldo Emerson prize com. 2000). Democrat. Episcopalian. Home: 1371 Kalmia Rd NW Washington DC 20012-1444 Office: Alfred Harcourt Found 8401 Colesville Rd Silver Spring MD 20910-3352 E-mail: mwinston@erols.com.

WINSTON, ROLAND, physicist, educator; b. Moscow, USSR, Feb. 12, 1936; s. Joseph and Claudia (Goretskaya) W.; m. Patricia Louise LeGette, June 10, 1957; children: Joseph, John, Gregory. AB, Shimer Coll., 1953; BS, U. Chgo., 1956, MS, 1957, PhD, 1963. Asst. prof. physics U. Pa., 1963-64; mem. faculty U. Chgo., 1964—, prof. physics, 1975—, chmn. physics dept., 1989-95. Recipient Kraus medal Franklin Inst., 1996, First Solar Personality of the Yr. award, Bangalore, India, 1999. Fellow: Am. Solar Engery Soc., Am. Optical Soc., Am. Phys. Soc., AAAS; mem.: Internat. Solar Energy Soc. ((Abbot award 1987, Farrington Daniels award 2001)), Franklin Inst. (hon.). Achievements include patent for ideal light collector for solar concentrators. Home: 5217 S University Ave Apt C Chicago IL 60615-4439 Office: Physics Dept U Chgo 5640 S Ellis Ave Chicago IL 60637-1433 E-mail: r-winston@uchicago.edu.

WINTER, CHESTER CALDWELL, physician, surgery educator, historian, writer; b. Cazenovia, N.Y., June 2, 1922; s. Chester Caldwell and Cora Evelyn (Martin) W.; m. Mary Antonia Merullo, Oct. 22, 1983; children by previous marriage: Paul, Ann, Jane. BA, U. Iowa, 1943, MD, 1946. Diplomate: Am. Bd. Urology. Intern Meth. Hosp., Indpls., 1946-47; med. resident St. Luke's Hosp., Cedar Rapids, Iowa, 1947; resident gen. surgery VA Hosp., Los Angeles, 1952-53; resident urology VA Hosp.-UCLA Med. Ctr., 1953-57; physician Calif., 1950-51; clin. asst. surgery UCLA, 1954-57, instr. surgery and urology, 1957-58, asst. prof. surgery and urology, 1958-59, asst. prof. Step II, 1959-60; prof. surgery and urology Ohio State U., 1960-88, prof. emeritus surgery and urology, 1988—, Louis Levy prof. urology, 1980-88. Dir. urology Ohio State U. Hosp., Columbus, 1960-78; cons. urology VA, Air Force hosps., Dayton, 1960-80. Author: Radioisotope Renography, 1963, Correctable Renal Hypertension, 1964, Nursing Care of Patients with Urologic Diseases, 4th edit, 1977, Practical Urology, 1969, Vesicoureteral Reflux, 1969, A Concise History of the U.S. and the State of Ohio, 2002, A Bicentennial History of the State of Ohio, 2003; editl. cons.: Exerpta Medica: Nuclear Medicine, Jour. AMA; editl. bd.: Andrology, Jour. Urology; Contbr. articles to profl. jours. Served to capt. M.C. U.S. Army, 1943-46, 48-49. Fellow Am. Acad. Pediatricians, Am. Coll. Surgeons; mem. Am. Assn. Genitourinary Surgeons, Am. Urol. Assn., Soc. Univ. Surgeons, Soc. Pediatric Urology, Soc. Univ. Urologists, Internat. Soc. Urology, Urol. Investigators Forum, Ohio State Med. Assn., Columbus Surg. Soc., Central Ohio Urology Soc., Columbus Acad. Medicine, Ohio State U. Med. Soc. Home: 6425 Evening St Worthington OH 43085-3054 E-mail: cwinter3@ameritech.net.

WINTER, ELIZABETH H. educational administrator; b. Upper Darby, Pa., Nov. 9, 1950; d. Stanley Jackson and Thurley Lillian (Blanchard) Shurtleff; m. Gary Winter, Apr. 24, 1982; children: Elizabeth Jackson, Alexander Cameron. AA, Lasell Coll., 1970; BA, Newton Coll. of Sacred Heart, 1972; MBA, Babson Coll., 1975. Sales rep. Xerox Corp., Boston, 1975-77; admissions counselor Lasell Coll., Newton, Mass., 1977-78, dir. fin. aid, asst. dir. admissions, 1978-79, contr., 1979-80, dir. fin. affairs, 1980-83, dean of adminstrn., 1983-88, v.p. bus. and finance, 1988—. Bd. dirs. Newton Television Found., 1989—; treas. Williams Sch. PTA, Newton, 1991. Mem. Nat. Assn. Coll. and Univ. Bus. Officers, Eastern Assn. Coll. and Univ. Bus. Officers (small coll. com. 1990-92). Avocations: golf, skiing, gardening. Home: 69 Maple St Newton MA 02458-1711 Office: Lasell Coll 1844 Commonwealth Ave Auburndale MA 02466-2709

WINTERGERST, ANN CHARLOTTE, language educator; b. Memmingen, Bavaria, Germany, Mar. 11, 1950; came to U.S., 1958; d. Martin and Charlotte Frieda (Denk) W. BA summa cum laude, St. John's U., 1972; MA, Columbia U., 1978, EdM, 1981, EdD, 1989. Teaching fellow U. Pa., Phila., 1972-73; lang. arts tchr. Our Lady Miraculous Medal Sch., Ridgewood, N.Y., 1973-81; assoc. tchr. Columbia U., N.Y.C., 1978-82; asst. prof. St. John's U., Queens, N.Y., 1981-86, 92-93, dir. ESL, 1986-91, assoc. prof., 1993—. Cons. Ednl. Testing Svc., Oakland, Calif., 1989-99, Bd. Regents N.Y. State, Albany, 1992-95, St. Martin's Press, N.Y.C., 1993-95, UN, N.Y.C., 1994-95, 96-97. Author: Second-Language Classroom Interaction, 1994; co-author: Crossing Cultures in the Language Classroom, 2004; editor: Focus on Self-Study, 1995; contbr. articles to profl. jours. Mem. Dem. Nat. Com., Washington, 1990—. Recipient N.Y. State TESOL's James A. Lydon Disting. Svc. award, 1998, Recognition award Nat. Assn. Bilingual Edn. Coun. for World Langs. and Cultures, 2000. Mem. N.Y. State TESOL (officer, 1st v.p. 1994-95, pres. 1995-96, immediate past pres. 1996-97), N.Y. State Coun. Langs. (officer, pres. 1988-90), Internat. TESOL (higher edn. chair 1993-94, officer). Democrat. Roman Catholic. Avocations: soprano in diocesan choir, german folkdancer, traveling, bowling, skiing. Home: 70-15 71st Pl Glendale NY 11385-7326 Office: St Johns Univ Dept Langs and Lits Jamaica NY 11439-0001 E-mail: winterga@stjohns.edu.

WINTERHALTER, DOLORES AUGUST (DEE WINTERHALTER), art educator; b. Pitts., Mar. 22, 1928; d. Joseph Peter and Helen August; m. Paul Joseph Winterhalter, June 21, 1947 (dec.); children: Noreen, Audrey,

Mark. Student, Yokohama, Japan, 1963-64, Paris, 1968-70, La Romita Sch. Art, Terni, Italy, 2001. Cert. tchr. Japanese Flower Arranging, Kamakuri Wood Carving. Tchr. YWCA, Greenwich, Conn., 1978-84, Friends of the Arts and Scis., Sarasota, Fla., 1992—; tchr./lectr. Classes & Workshops, 2004—04. Lectr. Sarasota Art Assn, 1984—; tchr., workshop presenter, Bangkok, 1971; mem. staff Hilton Leech Art Studio and Gallery, Sarasota; events chmn. State of Fla. Watercolor Exhbn., Sarasota, 1995; cultural exch. tchr. univs., fine arts acads., China; mem., tchr. Venice Art Ctr., Sarasota, 1996—2003, Art Ctr., Sarasota, 1999—2002; Hilton Leech Tchr., Sarasota, 1996—99; mem. Women's Caucus of Arts in Am., 1996—98; selected demonstrator Fine Arts of Sarasota, 1995—98; paper cons. D'Arches Watercolor Paper Co., Paris, 1983—2000; tchr., lectr., judge Sumie Inks; demonstrator Fla. Watercolor Conv., Ocala, 2000; workshop instr. Venice (Fla.) Watercolor/Monoprint and Sumi-e, 2003; tchr. home studio. Exhbns. Xiam, China, 1994, Creators Tour of Fine Arts Soc. Sarasota, 1994-2001; numerous works in watercolor, ink, oriental brushwork; paintings in numerous corp. collections. Pres., Am. Women's Club, Genoa, Italy, 1962; participant to help raise money for scholarships Collectors and Creators Tour of Fine Arts Soc. of Sarasota, 1994. Recipient numerous awards Old Greenwich (Conn.) Art Assn., 1971-84, Sarasota, 1985, Collectors and Creators Tour award Fine Arts Soc. Sarasota, 1994, Pat Buckman award, 2000; named Artist of Yr., Fine Arts Soc. Sarasota, 1994, Venice Art Ctr., 2000. Mem. Suncoast Fla. Watercolor Soc. (life), Fla. Watercolor Soc., Long Boat Key Art Assn., Sarasota Art Assn., Sumi-e Soc. Am., Nat. League Am. PEN Women (pres. 1994-96, scholarship bd. 1996-98), Internat. Soc. Marine Printers, Venice Art Ctr., Art Sarasota, Womens Contemporary Arts Soc. (tchr.). Democrat. Roman Catholic. Avocations: wood carving, travel, bridge, creative design in crochet and fashion. Home and Office: 4027 Westbourne Cir Sarasota FL 34238-3249

WINTER-NEIGHBORS, GWEN CAROLE, art and special education educator, consultant; b. Greenville, SC, July 14, 1938; d. James Edward and Evelyn (Lee) Walters (dec. 1998); m. David M. Winter Jr., Aug., 1963 (dec. Feb. 1980); children: Robin Carole Winter, Charles G. McCuen, Dustin Winter TeBrugge; m. Thomas Frederick Neighbors, Mar. 24, 1989. BA in Edn. and Art, Furman U., 1960, MA in Psychology, 1967; cert. in guidance/pers., Clemson U., 1981; EdD in Youth and Mid. Childhood Edn., Nova Southeastern U., 1988; postgrad., U. S.C., Spartanburg, 1981-89; cert. clear specialist instrn. with honors, Calif. State U., Northridge, 1991; art edn. cert., Calif. State U., L.A., 1991; JD, Glendale U., 1999. Cert. tchr. art, elem. edn., psychology, secondary guidance, S.C. Tchr. 7th grade Greenville Jr. H.S., 1960-63; art tchr. Wade Hampton H.S., Greenville, 1963-67; prin. adult edn. Woodmont H.S., Piedmont, S.C., 1983-85, Mauldin H.S., Greenville and Mauldin, S.C., 1981; tchr. ednl. psychology edn. dept. Allen U., Columbia, S.C., 1969; activity therapist edn. dept. S.C. Dept. of Corrections, Columbia, 1973-76; art specialist gifted edn. Westcliffe Elem. Sch., Greenville, 1976-89; tchr. self-contained spl. day class Elysian Heights Elem. Sch., Echo Park and L.A., Calif., 1989-91; art tchr. medh. drawing Sch. Dist. Greenville County Blue Ridge Mid. Sch., Greer, 1991-95; tchr./asst. head edn. dept. N. Creenville Coll., 2001—02. Participant nat. conf. U.S. Dept. Edn./So. Bell, Columbia, 1989; com. mem. nat. exec. com. Nova Southeastern U., 1988—89; asst. chmn., tchr. edn. dept. North Greenville coll., 2001; adm., staff North Greenville Coll., 2001, U. S.C., Spartanburg; adj., student tchr., supr. U. SC, 2002; adv. bd. S.C. Gov. Sch. for Arts & Humanities; parent/tchr. adv. bd. Spl. Edn.; adj. prof U. SC Univ. Ctr., Greenville, 2002—03. Mozart Book, 1988; author: (drama) Let's Sing a Song About America, 1988 (1st pl. Nat. Music award, 1990); contbr. The International Library of Poetry Ode to Stardust', 2002. Life mem. Rep. Presdl. Task Force, 1970—; mem. voter registration com. Lexington County Rep. Party, 1970—80; grand jury participant 13th Jud. Ct. Sys., Greenville, 1986—88, guardian ad litem, 1988—2003; mem. arts educators adv. task force S.C. Gov. Sch. Arts and Humanities, 2002—; mem. spl. edn. parent adv. bd. representing Sue Cleveland Elem. Sch. Greenville Co. Sch. Dist., Spl. Edn. Topics and Trends, 2001—02; poll manager Greenville Co. Tchr. Incentive grantee Sch. Dist. Greenville County, 1986-88, Project Earth grantee Bell South, 1988-89, 94-95, Edn. Improvement Act/Nat. Dissimination Network grantee S.C. State Dept. Edn., 1987-88, Targett 2,000 Arts in Curricular grantee S.C. Dept. Edn., 1994-95, Alliance grantee Bus. Cmty. Greenville, 1992-95, Greer Art Rsch. grantee, 1993-94, S.C. Govs. Sch. Study grantee, 1994, Edn. Improvement Act Competitive Tchr. grantee S.C. Dept. Edn., 1994-95, Alliance Grand grant, 1995-96; recipient Am. Jurisprudence Bancroft-Whitney award Glendale U. Sch. Law, 1997, 98, Excellence Recognition in Real Property award Glendale Law Faculty, 1997, Excellence in Art of Appellate Advocacy, Glendale U. Sch. Law, 1998, Am. Jurisprudence Bancroft-Whitney award Constl. Law I, 1998. Mem.: ABA, Palmetto State Tchr. Assn., S.C. Art Edn. Assn., S.C. Arts Alliance, Nat. Mus. Women in Arts, Nat. Art Edn. Assn., Phi Delta Kappa. Baptist Avocations: computers, art, writing, music composition, law. Home: 26 Charterhouse Ave Piedmont SC 29673-9139 E-mail: neighborslaw@wmconnect.com.

WINTERS, CHARLENE ADRIENNE, nursing educator; b. Long Beach, Calif., Jan. 6, 1952; d. Albert J. and Jean Janis Worrick; m. Don Winters, Jan. 8, 1977; children: John, Scott. AS, Long Beach City Coll., 1976; BS, Calif. State U., Long Beach, 1979, MS, 1984; DNSc, Rush U., 1998. Staff nurse ICU St. Mary Med. Ctr., Long Beach, 1976-81, clin. educator, 1980-84; asst. prof. Mont. State U., Bozeman, 1984-88, 92—; nursing faculty Salish Kootenai Coll., Pablo, Mont., 1988-92. Staff nurse ICU/PAR St. Patrick Hosp., Missoula, Mont., summers, 1986-93. Mem. Am. Assn. Critical Care Nurses, Sigma Theta Tau (Recognition award, Dissertation award), Western Inst. of Nursing.

WINTERS, CYNTHIA SAINTSING, middle school education educator; b. Winston-Salem, N.C., Oct. 14, 1969; d. Estus Benniewayne and JoAnne Meredith Saintsing; m. Jeffrey Mark Winters, Jan. 1, 1994; children: John Estus, Abigail Lee. BA, U. N.C., Greensboro, 1991. Econ., govt. tchr. So. Vance H.S., Henderson, N.C., 1991-92; spl. edn. tchr. South Davidson H.S., Thomasville, N.C., 1992; 8th grade tchr. Brown Mid. Sch., Thomasville, 1992-94, 6th grade tchr., 1994—, social studies dept. chair, 1995—, 7th grade tchr., 1997-99, computer tchr., 0199—2000; 6th grade tchr. Ledford Middle Sch., 2001—. Ch. youth leader Unity United Meth. Ch., Thomasville, 1992-95. Mem. N.C. Edn. Assn., N.C. Geography Alliance, Phi Beta Kappa, Delta Kappa Gamma. Republican. Avocations: reading, travel, crafts, cooking. Home: 185 Beech Ridge Rd Thomasville NC 27360-9708

WINTERS, VIRGINIA ROSEMARY, counselor, education consultant; b. Portchester, N.Y., Feb. 22, 1954; d. Oliver William Sr. and Virginia Elizabeth (Quamily) W. BA in Edn., Marygrove Coll., 1975; MEd, Wayne State U., 1985. Cert. tchr., guidance counselor, Mich.; cert. tchr., N.J. Tchr. vocal music Martin L. King Sch., Newark, 1975-76; tchr. elem. grades Most Holy Trinity Sch., Detroit, 1976-87; tchr. 2d grade Schulze Elem. Sch., Detroit, 1978-79; tchr. elem. grades McKenny Elem. Sch., Detroit, 1979-87; tchr., guidance counselor Parker Elem. Sch./McGraw Elem. Sch., Detroit, 1987-90; guidance counselor Parker Elem. Sch., Detroit, 1987—. Presenter seminars, workshops; cons. in field. Author workbook, decision-making curriculum, 1993. Recipient Educator's award Booker T. Washington Bus. Assn., 1991; grantee various institutions. Mem. ASCD, ACA, Am. Sch. Counselors Assn., Mich. Assn. Counseling and Devel., Guidance Assn. Met. Detroit, Detroit Reading Coun. Avocations: singing opera, choir directing. Office: Parker Elem Sch 12744 Elmira St Detroit MI 48227-3732

WINTERSTEIN, JAMES FREDRICK, academic administrator; b. Copperas Cove, Tex., Apr. 8, 1943; s. Arno Fredrick Herman and Ada Amanda Johanna (Wagnr) W.; m. Diane Marie Bochmann, July 13, 1963; children: Russell, Lisa, Steven, Amy. Student, U. N.M., 1962; D of Chiropractic cum laude, Nat. Coll. Chiropractic, 1968; cert., Harvard Inst. for Ednl. Mgmt., 1988. Diplomate Am. Chiropractic Bd. Radiology; lic. chiropractic, Ill., Fla., S.D., Md. Night supr. x-ray dept. DuPage Meml. Hosp., Elmhurst, Ill., 1964-66; x-ray technologist Lombard (Ill.) Chiropractic Clinic, 1966-68, asst. dir., 1968-71; chmn. dept. diagnostic imaging Nat. Coll. Chiropractic, Lombard, Ill., 1971-73, chief of staff, 1985-86; pres. Nat. U. Health Scis., Lombard, Ill., 1986—; pvt. practice West Chicago, Ill., 1968-73, 1973-85. Faculty Nat. Lincoln Coll. Post-Profl., Grad. and Continuing Edn., 1967—; chmn. x-ray test com. Nat. Bd. Chiropractic Examiners, 1971-73; govs. adv. panel on coal worker's pneumoconiosis and chiropractic State of Pa., 1979; v.p. Am. Chiropractic Coll. Radiology, 1981-83; mem. adv. coun. on radiation protection Dept. Health and Rehabilitative Svcs. State of Fla., 1984-85; cons. to bd. examiners State of S.C., 1983-84, State of Fla., 1980-85; cons. to peer review bd. State of Fla., 1980-84; trustee Chiropractic Centennial Found., 1989-90; mem. adv. com. Aids Alternative Health Ptnrs., 1996-2000, Consortial Ctr. for Chiropractic Rsch., 1998—; bd. dirs. Fedn. Ill. Ind. Colls. and Univs., 1995—; bd. dirs. Alternative Medicine, Inc., 1999—; spkr. in field. Pub. Outreach (Nat. Univ. Health Scis. monthly); author numerous monographs on chiropractic edn. and practice; co-inventor composite shielding and mounting means for x-ray machines; contbr. articles to profl. jours. Chmn., bd. dirs. Trinity Luth. Ch., West Chgo., 1970-72, Luth. High Sch., Pinellas County, Fla., 1979-82, St. John Luth. Ch., Lombard, 1988; chmn. bd. edn. First Luth. Sch., 1975-79; chmn. First Luth. Congregation, Clearwater, Fla., 1979-82; chmn. bldg. planning com. Grace Luth. Ch. and Sch., St. Petersburg, Fla., 1984-85; bldg. planning com. ch. expansion, new elem. sch., First Luth. Sch., 1975-79; stewardship adv. coun. Fla./Ga. dist. Luth. Ch. Mo. Synod, 1983-85; trustee West Suburban Regional Acad. Consortium, 1993-99. With U.S. Army, 1961-64. Recipient Cert. Meritorious Svc. Am. Chiropractic Registry of Radiologic Technologists, Cert. Recognition for Inspiration, Guidance, and Support Delta Tau Alpha, 1989, Cert. Appreciation Chiropractic Assn. South Africa, 1988, 1st pl. Fund Raiser Ride for Kids award Pediat. Brain Tumor Found. U.S., 1997, Cert. Appreciation Ill. Chiropractic Soc., 1997, Hope and Support award Alternative Health Ptnrs., 1998, NUHS Bd. Trustees Disting. Svc. award, 2002, Chiropractor of Yr., Ill. Chiropractic Soc., 2000, Person of the Yr., Alternative Medicine, Inc., 2001. Mem. APHA, Am. Chiropractic Assn., Am. Chiropractic Coll. Radiology (pres. 1983-85, exec. com. 1985-86), Am. Chiropractic Coun. on Diagnostic Imaging, Am. Chiropractic Coun. on Diagnosis and Internal Disorders, Am. Chiropractic Coun. on Nutrition, Nat. Univ. Alumni Assn., Am. Acad. Chiropractic Physicians (sec.), Assn. Chiropractic Colls. (sec.-treas. 1986-91), Coun. Chiropractic Edn. (sec.-treas. 1988-90, v.p. 1990-92, pres. 1992-94, immediate past pres. 1994-96), Fla. Chiropractic Assn. (chmn. radiol. health com. 1977-85, Disting. Svc. award 1999). Republican. Lutheran. Avocations: reading, automobile rehabilitation, harley-davidson motorcycles, fishing.

WINTON, CALHOUN, literature educator; b. Ft. Benning, Ga., Jan. 21, 1927; s. George Peterson and Dorothy (Calhoun) W.; m. Elizabeth Jefferys Myers, June 30, 1948; children: Jefferys Hobart, William Calhoun. Student, Ga. Inst. Tech., 1944-46; BA, U. of the South, 1948; MA, Vanderbilt U., 1950, Princeton U., 1954, PhD, 1955. Instr. Dartmouth Coll., Hanover, N.H., 1954-57; asst. prof. U. Va., Charlottesville, 1957-60; asst. prof. then assoc. prof., asst. dean Grad. Sch. U. Del., 1960-67; prof. dept. English U. S.C., Columbia, 1967-75, chmn. dept., 1970-73; prof. U. Md., College Park, 1975-97, dir. Rsch. Ctr. for Humanities, 1988-90, prof. emeritus, 1997—. Del. Jt. Nat. Com. on Langs., Washington, 1986-90, 95-99. Author: (biography) Captain Steele, 1964, Sir Richard Steele, 1970; editor: Plays of Aaron Hill, 1981, John Gay and the London Theatre, 1993; author (with others) Colonial Book in the Atlantic World, 2000; contbr. entries Oxford Dictionary of National Biography. Pres. faculty guild U. Md., 1986-89; bd. dirs. Md. Fedn. Tchrs., Balt., 1986-89. Capt. USN, 1944-47, 50-52. Am. Philos. Soc. grantee, 1960; Guggenheim Found. fellow, 1965-66, Folger Shakespeare Libr. fellow, Washington, 1970, John Carter Brown Libr. fellow, Providence, 1995, 20033 Fulbright Commn. lectureship, Ankara, Turkey, 1979-80. Mem. MLA (exec. com. South Atlantic chpt. 1977-80), Am. Soc. 18th-Century Studies (founder 1970—), East Cen. Soc. 18th Century Studies (pres. 1987), Assn. Princeton Grad. Alumni (exec. bd. 1986-90), Cosmos Club Washington, Princeton Club (N.Y. and Washington), Am. Antiquarian Soc., Literary Soc. Washington. Democrat. Episcopalian. Avocations: swimming, book collecting. Home: 6700 Belcrest Rd Hyattsville MD 20782 Office: U Md Dept English College Park MD 20742-0001 E-mail: cw41@umail.umd.edu.

WIRSZUP, IZAAK, mathematician, educator; b. Wilno, Poland, Jan. 5, 1915; came to U.S., 1949, naturalized, 1955; s. Samuel and Pera (Golomb) W.; m. Pola Ofman, July 19, 1940 (dec. 1943); 1 son, Vladimir (dec. 1943); m. Pera Poswianska, Apr. 23, 1949; 1 dau., Marina (Mrs. Arnold M. Tatar). Magister of Philosophy in Math, U. Wilno, 1939; PhD in Math, U. Chgo., 1955. Lectr. math. Tech. Inst. Wilno, 1939-41; dir. Bur. d'Études et de Statistiques Spéciales, Société Centrale d'Achat-Société Anonyme des Monoprix, Paris, 1946-49; mem. faculty U. Chgo., 1949—, prof. math., 1965-85, prof. math. emeritus, 1985—, prin. investigator U. Chgo. Sch. Math. Project (sponsored by Amoco Found., also dir. resource devel. component), 1983—, dir. Internat. Math. Edn. Resource Ctr., 1988—. Dir. NSF Survey Applied Soviet Rsch. in Math. Edn., 1985-91; cons. Ford Found., Colombia, Peru, 1965-66, Sch. Math Study Group, 1960, 61, 66-68; participant, writer tchr. tng. material African Math. Program, Entebbe, Uganda, summer 1964, Mombasa, Kenya, summers 1965-66; assoc. dir. Survey Recent Ea. European Math. Lit., 1956-68, dir., 1968-84; dir. NSF program application computers to mgmt., 1976-83; cons. NSF-AID Sci. Edn. Program, India, 1969; mem. U.S. Commn. on Math. Instn., 1969-73; co-prin. investigator U. Chgo.-Polk Bros. Found. Program for the Devel. of Math. Tchrs. in Chgo. Pub. Schs., 1999—. Contbr. articles to profl. jours.; Editor Math. books, transls., adaptions from Russian.; Adviser math.: Ency. Brit., 1971—. Recipient Lewellyn John and Harriet Manchester Quantrell award U. Chgo., 1958, Univ. Alumni Svc. medal, U. Chgo., 1994; resident master Woodward Ct., U. Chgo., 1971-85; endowed Wirszup Lecture Series, U. Chgo., 1986. Mem. N.Y. Acad. Scis., Am. Math. Soc., Math. Assn. Am., AAAS, Nat. Council Tchrs. Math. (chmn. com. internat. math. edn. 1967-69, Lifetime Achievement medal for Leadership, Tchg., and Svc. in Math. Edn. 1996) Home: 5750 S Kenwood Ave Chicago IL 60637-1744 Office: U Chgo Dept Math 5734 S University Ave Chicago IL 60637-1514

WIRTZ, DOROTHY MARIE, retired language educator; b. Keokuk, Iowa, Mar. 9, 1915; d. John and Alma Adelaide (Schard) Wirtz. BA, U. Iowa, 1939; MA, U. Wis., 1940, PhD, 1944. Tchg. asst. U. Wis., 1939—44; asst. prof. French U. Minn., ., 1944—50; dir., French House U. Wis., 1945; sec. Ariz. Tax Commn., Phoenix, 1952—58; dep. state treas. of Ariz., 1956—58; prof., French Ariz. State U., 1958—73; ret., 1973. Sec. to Dem. whip Ariz. Ho. of Reps., Phoenix, 1950—52. Contbr. articles to profl. pub. and poetry magazines.; author: (poetry) Evalution, 2003. Pres. Ariz. Fgn. Lang. Soc., Phoenix, 1968. Mem.: AAUW (cultural chmn.), Phi Beta Kappa (pres., Phoenix Chap., 1974). Democrat. Mem. United Ch. Of Christ. Avocations: art, music, literature, travel. Home: 1711 W State Ave Phoenix AZ 85021

WISE, SUSAN TAMSBERG, management and communications consultant, speaker; b. Memphis, Nov. 16, 1945; d. Joseph Lane and Mable Rosa (Koth) Tamsberg; m. Roy Thomas Wise, June 29, 1968; children: Kristin Rebecca, Mary Catherine. BA in Math., Columbia (S.C.) Coll., 1967; M in Edn., Ga. State U., Atlanta, 1986. Tchr. high sch. math. various pub. schs., N.C., S.C., and Ga., 1967-73; instr. Cen. Piedmont Community Coll., Charlotte, N.C., 1979; devel. dir. Classique, Inc., Kannapolis, N.C., 1979-81; asst. v.p. First Nat. Bank of Atlanta, 1981-87; Ga. dir. The Exec. Speaker, Inc., Atlanta, 1987-90; pres. TrimTime, Inc., Atlanta, 1988—, Wise Consulting Inc., Atlanta, 1990—. Speaker Girl Scouts USA, Jr. League, numerous med. assns., Atlanta and S.E. area, 1985—; affiliate Exec. Coaching Network, Inc. Tng. cons. Jr. League of Atlanta, 1988-89; bd. dirs. Incarnation Luth. Ch., Atlanta, 1984; mem. ch. coun., bd. dirs, Luth. Ch. of the Redeemer, 1994. Mem. ASTD (v.p., bd. dirs., Leadership award 1987), Kappa Delta Pi. Republican. Avocations: international traveling, antiques, needlework.

WISE-JOHNSON, KIMBERLY ANN, middle school educator; b. Ellsworth AFB, S.D., Dec. 7, 1956; d. Bruce Franklin and Mildred Marie (Getz) Wise; m. David Denzle Johnson, Aug. 2, 1980; children: Matthew Bruce Johnson, Katherine Marie Johnson. BA, Calif. State U., Sacramento, 1980; MEd in Classroom Guidance, U. LaVerne, Calif., 1995. Cert. tchr. early adolescence, English, lang. arts. Music tchr. St. John Evangelist Sch., Carmichael, Calif., 1979-81, tchr. 1st grade, 1981-86; tchr. 7th grade lang. arts Arcade Fundamental Mid. Sch., Sacramento, 1986—, dept. chair, 1995—2001. Mem. St. John's Sch. Bd., Carmichael, 1993-95. Author poetry. Named Tchr. Yr. San Juan Unified Dist., 1990, 94, 2000, Dist. Exemplary Tchr., San Juan Unified Dist., 1991; named Outstanding CTA Educator Yr., San Juan Tchrs. Assn., 2003. Mem.: Calif. Tchrs. Assn. (Named Outstanding Educator of Yr. 2003), Nat. Coun. Tchrs. of English. Republican. Roman Catholic. Avocations: music, reading. Office: Arcade Fundamental Mid Sch 3500 Edison Ave Sacramento CA 95821-2710

WISEMAN, DENNIS GENE, academic administrator; b. Anderson, Ind., Sept. 25, 1947; s. Harold Leslie and Lillian Loetta (Woods) W.; m. Susan Jean Reidenbach, June 10, 1971; children: Matthew Benjamin, Andrew Joseph. BA, U. Indpls., 1969; MA, U. Ill., 1970, PhD, 1974; postgrad., Ind. U., 1970-71. Tchr. Indpls. Pub. Schs., 1970-71; rsch. asst. U. Ill., Urbana, 1971-74, clinician, supr., 1972-74, coord. Office for Profl. Svc., 1973-74; dir., tchr. Champaign (Ill.) pub. schs., 1972-73; asst. prof. U. S.C. Coastal Carolina Coll., Conway, 1974-77, assoc. prof., 1977-84, prof., 1982—, dean Sch. Edn., 1982-2000; assoc. provost, spl. asst. to pres. Coastal Caroline U., Conway, 2000—. Field disseminator Social Sci. Edn. Consortium, Boulder, Colo., 1979-81; reviewer Ethnic Heritage Studies Program, U.S. Office Edn., Washington, 1980-81; cons. S.C. State Dept. Edn., Columbia, 1986—; dir. Oxford program U. S.C. Coastal Carolina Coll., summer, 1990; evaluator So. Assn. Colls. and Schs., Atlanta, 1991; folio reviewer for Nat. Coun. for Social Studies, Nat. Coun. for Accreditation of Tchr. Edn., 1994-2000; field reader U.S. Dept. Edn., Higher Edn. Program, 1999-2001; spl. asst. to pres. U./Schs. Collaboration, 2001—. Co-author: Effective Teaching, 1984, 3d edit., 1999, Wondering about Thinking, 2003, The Middle Level Teachers' Handbook: Becoming a Reflective Practitioner, 1998, Best Practice in Motivation and Management in the Classroom, 2001, The Modern Middle School: Addressing Standards and Student Needs, 2003; contbr. articles to profl. jours. Mem. Horry County Human Rels. Coun., Conway, 1990-93; mem. curriculum frameworks rev. panel S.C. Dept. Edn., 1993-2000. Named Tchr. of Yr., U. S.C. Coastal Carolina Coll., 1980; S.C. Com. for the Humanities grantee, 1984, S.C. Com. on Higher Edn. grantee, 1985, 86; Japan Study Program scholar U.S. Office Edn., 1980. Mem. S.C. Assn. Colls. for Tchr. Edn. (pres. elect 1989, pres. 1989-91, treas. 1997-2001), Coun. Edn. Deans (pres. 1986-90, pres. 1996-2000), Nat. Coun. for the Social Studies, Am. Assn. Colls. for Tchr. Edn. (instl. rep. 1980-2000), Assn. Tchr. Educators, Phi Delta Kappa (pres. Coastal Carolina chpt. 1984-85). Methodist. Avocations: reading, travel, writing. Office: Coastal Carolina U PO Box 261954 Conway SC 29528-6054 E-mail: dwiseman@coastal.edu.

WISHART, LEONARD PLUMER, III, army officer; b. Newark, Sept. 24, 1934; s. Leonard Plumer and Mabel Dorothea (Womsley) W.; m. Sandra Frances De Vito, Apr. 12, 1958; children: Leonard Plumer IV, Scott Brian. Student, Va. Mil. Inst., 1952-53; BS in Engring., U.S. Mil. Acad., 1957; MS in Nuclear Physics, U. Va., 1966. Commd. 2d lt. U.S. Army, 1957, advanced through grades to lt. gen., 1988; served in Germany and Vietnam; tactical officer U.S. Mil. Acad., West Point, N.Y., 1971-73; sr. mil. asst. to Sec. of Army, 1975-76; comdr. 1st Brigade, 24th Inf. Div., Ft. Stewart, Ga., 1977-78; chief of staff 24th Inf. Div., 1979, VII Corps in Germany, 1979-81; asst. div. comdr. 1st Armored Div., 1981-83; dep. comdr. CACDA, Ft. Leavenworth, Kans., 1983-86; comdr. 1st Inf. Div., Ft. Riley, Kans., 1986-88, Combined Arms Command, Ft. Leavenworth, Kans., 1988-91; dep. comdr. TRADOC, Ft. Leavenworth, Kans., 1988-91, ret., 1991; assoc. Burdeshaw Assocs. Ltd., Bethesda, Md., 1991-92. Apptd. 1st dir. non-legis. and fin. svcs. U.S. Ho. of Reps., Washington, 1992—94, resigned., 1994; assoc. Burdeshaw Assocs., Ltd., Bethesda, Md., 1994—; mgr. ind. study Army N.G. INNOLOG, McLean, Va., 1996—98. Active in cmty. activities; pres. Army Distaff Found., Washington, 1997-99, chmn., bd. govs. 5th Cavalry Regiment Assn., 1998—. Decorated Disting. Service Medal (2), Legion of Merit (2), D.F.C., Bronze Star medal (2), Army Commendation medal, Air medals. Mem. Assn. U.S. Army, Assn. Grads. U.S. Mil. Acad., Alumni Assn. U. Va., VFW, Soc. of the First Divsn., First Cavalry Divsn. Assn. Methodist. Office: Burdeshaw Assocs Ltd 4701 Sangamore Rd Bethesda MD 20816-2508

WISHERT, JO ANN CHAPPELL, music educator, elementary and secondary education educator; b. Carroll County, Va., July 10, 1951; d. Joseph Lenox and Helen Alata (Wagoner) Chappell; m. Clarence Hinnant Wishert, Jr., June 10, 1987; 1 child, Kelly Marie. BA, Oral Roberts U., 1974; MS, Radford U., 1977; degree in advanced postgrad studies, Va. Poly. Inst. and State U., 1981; postgrad., U. S.C., Spartanburg, 1990, U. S.C., Columbia, 1995, The Citadel, 1996, Winthrop U., 1995, 96, postgrad., 2003. Cert. elem. music supr., Va., elem. and secondary music tchr., S.C., music tchr., ednl. specialist, N.C. Head start tchr. Rooftop of Va., Galax, 1975; elem. music tchr. Carroll County Pub. Schs., Hillsville, 1975-78; grad. asst., supr., course advisor Coll. Edn., Va. Poly. Inst. and State U., Blacksburg, 1975-81, pregrad. interviewer placement svcs., 1981-83; music dir. Heritage Acad., Charlotte, N.C., 1984-85, fine arts specialist, 1985-86; choral dir. Chester County Schs., Chester, 1986—2002; music tchr. Old Pointe Elem./Rock Hill Sch. Dist. #3, 2002—; chmn. fine arts Chester H.S., 1995—2002. Fine arts chairperson Chester H.S., 1995-2002, adept evaluator, 1996—, chmn., spl. areas dept. chair, 2003; guest condr. workshop Patrick County Schs., Stuart, Va., 1980; liaison for Chester County Schs. to S.C. Gov.'s Sch. for Arts, 1990-91; faculty mem., sponsor Tri-M Music Honor Soc.; guest spkr. Curriculum Leadership Arts, 2003; guest spkr Rock Hill Sch. Dist. Tchr. Forum, 2003-2004. Soloist PTL TV Network, Charlotte, 1984-85. Guest spkr. on battered women and marital abuse to chs. and workshops; entertainer; co-dir. Chester City Schs. Choral Festival; active Arts Coun. Chester County, 1988—, S.C. Arts Alliance and Arts Advocacy, Winthrop Consortium for the Arts, Rock Hill Sch. Dist. Tchr. Forum, 2003—, Inst. for Arts, Wintrhop U., 2003; sponsor Tri-M Music honor soc., 1991—2002, Beta Club. Named Tchr. of the Yr., Chester Sr. H.S., 1989, Chester County Schs., 1991, Educator of Yr., Chester County C. of C., 1992, Tchr. of the Week, The Herald, 1995, Rock Hill Sch. Dist. Educator of the Day, 2002, 2003. Mem. ASCD, AAUW (mem. bylaws com. Chester br. 1987-93, sec. 1988-89, fine arts chmn. 1995-2002), Music Educators Nat. Conf., S.C. Music Educators Assn. (del. pub. rels. network Chester County Schs. 1991), S.C. Edn. Assn., Palmetto State Tchrs. Assn., Am. Ednl. Rsch. Assn., Am. Assn. Choral Dirs., Chester County Edn. Assn., Nat. Assn. Secondary Music Edn. (team evaluator divsn. tchr. edn. cert. 1989, 91-2002), S.C. State Coun. Internat. Reading Assn., S.C. Reading Assn., State So. Assn. Schs. and Colls. (mem. evaluation team, mem. steering com.), All U.S.A. Chorus Student Group (alumni), Tri-M Music Honor Soc. (sponsor), 4-H Club (life), Phi Delta Kappa., Old Pointe Elem. (spl. areas dept. chair, 2003-2004). Republican. Baptist. Avocations: reading, cross stitch, needlepoint, music. Home: 1122 Virginia Dare Dr Rock Hill SC 29730-9669 E-mail: jwishert@rock-hill.k12.sc.us.

WISMER, PATRICIA ANN, retired secondary education educator; b. York, Pa., Mar. 23, 1936; d. John Bernhardt and Frances Elizabeth Loreen Marie (Fry) Feiser; m. Lawrence Howard Wismer, Aug. 4, 1961. BA in English, Mt. Holyoke Coll., 1958; MA in Speech/Drama, U. Wis., 1960;

postgrad., U. Oreg., 1962, Calif. State U., Chico, 1963-64, U. So. Calif., 1973-74. Tchr., co-dir. drama program William Penn Sr. High Sch., York, 1960-61; instr. English, dir. drama York Jr. Coll., 1961-62; assoc. church editor San Francisco Examiner, 1962-63; reporter, publicist News Bur. Calif. State U., Chico, 1963-64; chmn. English Dept. Chico Sr. H.S., 1966-96; mentor tchr. Chico Sr. High Sch., Chico Unified Sch. Dist., 1983-93. Judge writing awards Nat. Coun. Tchr. English, 1970—; cons. No. Calif. Writing Project, 1977—; curriculum cons., freelance writer and photographer, 1996—. Author: My Life with Vanessa: A Journal of the Plagued Years, 1998, 40 Year Photo Retrospective, 2002; newsletter editor Chico Cat Coalition, 1999—. Mem. Educators for Social Responsibility, Planetary Soc., Upper Calif. Coun. Tchrs. English (bd. dirs. 1966-85, pres. 1970-71), Calif. Assn. Tchrs. English, Nat. Coun. Tchrs. English, NEA, Calif. Tchrs. Assn., Chico Unified Tchrs. Assn. Democrat. Lutheran. Avocations: photography, play prodn., video prodn. Home: 623 Arcadian Ave Chico CA 95926-4504 Office: PO Box 1250 Cannon Beach OR 97110-1250 E-mail: pwismer@aol.com.

WISNIEWSKI, RICHARD, retired dean; Dir. Office Urban Edn. and assoc. prof. edn. sociology U. Wash.; assoc. dean Sch. Edn. U. Wis.; dean Coll. Edn. U. Okla., U. Tenn., Knoxville, 1983—97, dir. Inst. Ednl. Innovation, 1997—98, dean and prof. emeritus, 1998—. Vis. prof. Evergreen State Coll., Olympia, Wash., 1998—99. Author: Reforming a College: The University of Tennessee Story, 2000. Mem.: Tenn. Assn. Colls. Tchr. Edn. (past pres.), Nat. Coun. Accreditation Tchr. Edn. Bd. Examiners (chair exec. com.), Assn. Colls. and Schs. Edn. in State Univs. and Land Grant Colls. and Affiliated Pvt. Univs. (past pres.), Am. Assn. Colls. Tchr. Edn. (past pres.). Office: U Tenn Inst Ednl Innovation 329 Claxton Addition Knoxville TN 37996*

WISSLER, ROBERT WILLIAM, physician, cardiovascular pathologist, educator; b. Richmond, Ind., Mar. 1, 1917; s. William Oscar and Muriel (Thomas) W.; m. Elizabeth Anne Polk, Jan. 9, 1940; children: Barbara Anne Wissler-Mayers, Mary Linda Wissler Graham, David William, John Polk. AB, Earlham Coll., Richmond, 1939, DSc (hon.), 1959; MS, U. Chgo., 1943, PhD, 1946, MD with honors, 1948; MD (hon.), Heidelberg (Germany) U., 1973, U. Siena, Italy, 1982; DSc (hon.), UMDNJ, Newark, 1982, Ohio State U., 1990. From instr. to assoc. prof. U. Chgo., 1943-57, prof. McLean Inst., 1953-80, prof. dept. pathology, 1957-82, prof. in the Coll., 1965-80, chmn. dept. pathology, 1957-72, Donald N. Pritzker prof. pathology, 1972-87, Disting. Svc. prof. pathology, 1977-87, emeritus prof., 1987—. Vis. scientist Theodor Kocher Inst., U. Berne, Switzerland, 1963, Baker Inst. for Med. Rsch., Melbourne, Australia, 1985; vis. prof. pathology Nihon U. Sch. Medicine, Tokyo, 1974; mem. faculty Given Inst. Pathology, Aspen, Colo., 1964, 71-73, 78-81; dir. U. Chgo. Spl. Ctr. Rsch. Atherosclerosis, 1972-82., program dir. Pathobiol. Determinates Atherosclerosis Youth, 1985-96. Editor, co-editor monographs; contbr. chpts. to books, more than 300 articles to profl. jours. Scout leader Boy Scouts Am., Chgo., 1951-56, 61-67; trustee First Unitarian Ch., Chgo., 1960-64, chmn. bd., 1962-64; trustee Earlham Coll., 1968-71, 75-85, chmn. edn. com., 1977-85; mem. Hyde Park-Kenwood Cmty. Conf., Chgo., 1960—. Recipient award of merit Am. Heart Assn., Dallas, 1971, Disting. Achievement award Modern Medicine, 1977, Joseph B. Goldberger award AMA, 1979, Coeur d'Or award Chgo. Heart Assn., 1982, Gold Headed Cane award, Am. Assn. Pathologists, 1983, U. Chgo. Gold Key award, 1984, Career Achievement award Internat. Atherosclerosis So., 1994, Rising Sun award Emperor of Japan, 1995. Mem. Am. Soc. Exptl. Pathology (pres. 1961-62), Am. Heart Assn. (chmn. coun. on arteriosclerosis 1965-66), Assn. Pathology Chairmen (pres. 1967-68), Coll. Am. Pathologists (chmn. edn. com. 1985-95), Univ. Assocs. for Rsch. and Edn. in Pathology (bd. dirs., pres. 1969-71), Am. Assn. Pathologists and Bacteriologists, 1952-90 (pres. 1968), others. Avocations: gardening, photography, playing clarinet. Home: 5550 S South Shore Dr Apt 515 Chicago IL 60637-5053 Office: U Chgo Med Ctr MC 3083 5841 S Maryland Ave Chicago IL 60637-1463

WITHERELL, NANCY LOUISE, education educator; b. Bridgewater, Mass., Aug. 1, 1952; d. Anthony and Bertha Eunice (Smith) Kopcych; m. Peter Walker Witherell, Aug. 27, 1973; children: Paul William, Jonathan Lewis, Thomas Clayton. BA in Sociology, U. Mass., Dartmouth, 1974; EdM in Elem. Sch. Adminstrn., U. Md., 1979; EdD in Lang. Arts and Literacy, U. Mass., Lowell, 1993. Cert. tchr., Mass. Elem. tchr. Prince Georges County Pub. Sch., Hyattsville, Md., 1974-80, Norton (Mass.) Pub. Schs., 1980-81; tchrs. asst. U. Mass., Lowell, summer 1992; vis. lectr. Bridgewater (Mass.) State Coll., 1985-93, assoc. prof., 1993—, sec. media literacy task force, 1995—2000. Cons., 1993—. Co-author: Graphic Organizer and Activities to Differentiate Instruction in Reading, 2002. Great Books coord., bd. dirs. Raynham (Mass.) Vol. Edn., 1986—; chairperson, bd. edn. Pilgrim Congl. Ch., Taunton, Mass., 1987—. Mem.: ASCD, Nat. Coun. Tchrs. English, Internat. Reading Assn., Assn. Colls. U. Reading Educators (past pres.), Internat. Reading Assn. (publ. proposal reviewer), Southea. Regional Reading Coun. (past pres.), Mass. Reading Assn. (com. parent-child comm. 1993—94, tech. com. 1996—, nominating chair 2002—03, Sylvia D. Brown scholar 1993), Pi Lambda Theta (Virginia B. Biggy scholar 1992). Avocations: reading, skiing, sailing. Home: 345 Elm St Raynham MA 02767 Office: Bridgewater State Coll Hart Hall Dept Elem Edn Bridgewater MA 02324 E-mail: nwitherell@bridgew.edu.

WITHEROW, JIMMIE DAVID, secondary school educator; b. Dalton, Ga., Nov. 13, 1961; s. Jimmie W. and Jimmie Lou (Nixon) W. BA in English, Emory U., 1983; MEd in Secondary Edn., Ga. State U., 1989, PhD in Communicative Arts Edn., 1999. Cert. English tchr., Ga. Tchr. SE Whitfield High Sch., Whitfield County Bd. Edn., Dalton, 1983-92, Murray County High Sch., Chatsworth, Ga., 1992—. Contbr. article to profl. jour. Mem. NEA, Nat. Coun. Tchrs. English, Ga. Edn. Assn., Ga. Coun. Tchrs. English, Kappa Delta Pi. Home: PO Box 891 Chatsworth GA 30705-0891

WITHERS, DINAH LEA, special education educator; b. Amarillo, Tex., Mar. 14, 1953; d. John Eugene and Janelle (Williamson) W. BA in Spl. Edn., Ariz. State U., 1992. Cert. spl. edn. tchr., Ariz., Calif.; cert. child devel. credential. Kindergarten tchr., asst. dir., dir. Palo Alto Presch., Mesa, Ariz., 1978-84; tchr. Kachina County Day Sch., Phoenix, 1984-85; tchr. aide to handicapped Parkway Sch., Mesa, 1986; classroom aide to phys. handicapped Manzano H.S., Albuquerque, 1986-87; classroom aide/driver in head trauma classroom Devereaux Ctr., Scottsdale, Ariz., 1987-88; tchr. Tesseract Sch., Paradise Valley, Ariz., 1988-91; residential care technician Tempe Ctr. for Habilitation, Tempe, Ariz., 1991; residential staff, tchr. Victory House Discovery Ctr., Mesa, 1991; spl. edn. tchr. cross categorical Roosevelt Sch. Dist., Phoenix, 1992-93; spl. edn. tchr. San Leandor (Calif.) Unified Sch. Dist., 1993—. Master tchr. San Leandro Unified Sch. Dist., 1994—. Grantee Kiwanis Club, 1997, Community Edn. Fund., 1994-97, East Bay Cmty. Found., 1997-2000. Mem. Coun. for Exceptional Children, Golden Key Nat. Honor Soc., Phi Kappa Phi.

WITKIN, MILDRED HOPE FISHER, psychotherapist, educator; b. N.Y.C. d. Samuel and Sadie (Goldschmidt) Fisher; m. Jorge Radovic, Aug. 26, 1983; children: Georgia Hope, Roy Thomas, Laurie Philips, Kimberly Hope, Nicole Sue, Scott Benjamin, Joshua William, Jennifer Ivy, Jacob Glen. AB, Hunter Coll.; MA, Columbia U., 1968; PhD, NYU, 1973. Diplomate Am. Bd. Sexology, Am. Bd. Sexuality. Head counselor Camp White Lake, Camp Emanuel, Long Beach, N.J.; tchr. econs., polit. sci. Hunter Coll. H.S.; dir., group leader follow-up program Jewish Vacation Assn., N.Y.C.; investigator N.Y.C. Housing Authority; psychol. counselor Montclair State Coll., Upper Montclair, N.J., 1967-68; mem., lectr. Creative Problem-Solving Inst., U. Buffalo, 1968; psychol. counselor Fairleigh Dickinson U., Teaneck, N.J., 1968; dir. Counseling Ctr., 1969-74; pvt. practice psychotherapy N.Y.C., also Westport, Conn.; sr. faculty supr., family therapist and psychotherapist Payne Whitney Psychiat. Clinic, N.Y. Presbyn. Hosp., Cornell Med. Ctr., 1973—; clin. asst. prof. dept. psychiatry Cornell U. Med. Coll., 1974—; assoc. dir. sex therapy and edn. program N.Y. Presbyn. Hosp. and Weill Med. Coll., Cornell U., 1974—. Cons. counselor edn. tng. programs N.Y.C. Bd. Edn., 1971—75; cons. Health Info. Sys., 1972—79; supr. master's and doctoral candidates NYU, 1975—82; sr. cons. Kaplan Inst. Evaluation and Treatment of Sexual Disorders, 1981—96; chmn. sci. com. 1st Internat. Symposium Female Sexuality, Buenos Aires, 1984; pvt. practice psychotherapy and sex therapy, N.Y.C., Westport, Conn.; vis. prof. numerous colls. and univs.; lectr. internat. and nat. workshops, radio and TV. Author: (book) 45-And Single Again, 1985, Single Again, 1994; contbr. articles to profl. jours., chpts. to textbooks. Chmn. edn. legislation com. PTA, Yonkers, 1955; Scarsdale chmn. mothers com. Boy Scouts Am., 1961—64; mem. Morrow Assn. Correction N.J., 1969—91; bd. dirs. Girl Scouts Am.; publicity chmn. United Jewish Appeal, Scarsdale, 1959—65. Recipient Bronze medal for svcs., Hunter Coll., plaque, United Jewish Appeal, 1962, Founders Day award, NYU, 1973, citation, N.Y. Hosp.-Cornell U. Med. Ctr., 1990. Fellow: Am. Acad. Clin. Sexologists, Internat. Coun. Sex Edn. and Parenthood of Am. U.; mem.: LWV, ACA, AAUW, APA, Conn. Assn. Marriage and Family Therapy, Am. Assn. Sexology (diplomate), Nat. coun. Women in Medicine, Am. Women's Med. Assn., Am. Assn. Counseling and Devel., Profl. Women's Caucus, Assn. Counselor Supervision and Edn., Am. Assn. Higher Edn., Creative Edn. Found., N.J. Psychol. Assn., N.Y. Psychol. Assn., Am. Pers. and Guidance Assn., Ackerman Family Inst., N.J. Assn. Marriage and Family Counselors, Am. Assn. Marriage and Family Counselors, Eastern Assn. Sex Therapists, Soc. Sci. Study Sex Therapy and Rsch., Argentine Soc. Human Sexuality (hon.), Am. Assn. Sex Educators, Counselors and Therapists (regional bd., nat. accreditation bd., cert. internat. supr.), Nat. Assn. Women Deans and Counselors, Am. Coll. Pers. Assn. (nat. mem. commn. II 1973—76), N.Y. Acad. Sci., Women's Med. Assn. N.Y.C., Am. Coll. Sexuality (cert.), Internat. Assn. Marriage and Family Counselors, Assn. Counseling Supervision, Alpha Chi Alpha, Kappa Delta Pi, Pi Lambda Theta. Home: 9 Sturges Commons Westport CT 06880-2832 Office: NY Presbyn Hosp Cornell Med Ctr 35 Park Ave New York NY 10016-3838 Business E-Mail: mwitkin903@aol.com.

WITMER, DIANE F. communications educator; b. Pasadena, Calif., Jan. 20, 1945; d. Stanley Lamar and Mary Evelyn Witmer; 1 child, David William Penkoff. AA, Golden West Coll., Huntington Beach, Calif., 1977; BS in BA, U. LaVerne (Calif.), 1980; MS in Sys. Mgmt., U. So. Calif., L.A., 1989; MA in Communication Arts, U. So. Calif., 1993, PhD in Orgnl. Comm., 1994. Dir. pub. rels. Weight Watchers, Santa Ana, Calif., 1980-84; dir. comm. March of Dimes, Costa Mesa, Calif., 1986-90; prin. Penkoff Comm. Resources, L.A., 1990-92; instr. Calif. State U., Fullerton, 1990-94; asst. lectr. comm. arts and scis. U. So. Calif., University Park, 1991-94; asst. prof. Purdue U., West Lafayette, Ind., 1994-97; assoc. prof. Calif. State U., Fullerton, 1997—. Editor, The Paper Weight, 1981-84. Chmn. award com. March of Dimes, Costa Mesa, nat. vol., 1980—; pub. info. officer in disaster Orange County chpt. ARC, Santa Ana, Calif. Mem. Pub. Rels. Soc. Am. (accredited mem.), U. So. Calif. Alumni Assn., Pacific Chorale. Avocation: choral singing.

WITMER, ELIZABETH, education minister; b. The Netherlands; m. Cameron Witmer; children: Scott, Sarah. BEd, U. Western Ontario. Tchr. Ontario Schs.; elected min. Ontario Legis. Assembly, Toronto, 1990—, min. of labor, 1995, min. of health, 1997, min. of health and long-term care, 1999—2001, min. of environ., 2001, dep. premier and minister edn., 2002—. Named Woman of Yr., Kitchener-Waterloo, 1987; recipient Dr. Harry Paikin award of merit, Ontario Pub. Sch. Bds. Assn., 1996, Philippe Pinel award, 2001. Mem.: Registered Nurses Assn. of Ontario (hon.), Kichener=Waterloo Rotary Club (Paul Harris fellow 1997). Office: Ont Ministry of Edn Mowat Block 22d Fl 900 Bay St Toronto M7A 1L2 Canada Office Fax: 416-325-2608.

WITT, ANNE CLEINO, musician, education educator; b. Winston-Salem, N.C., May 14, 1945; d. Edward Henry and Elizabeth Anne (White) Cleino; m. Robert Ernest Witt, Nov. 23, 1977; children: Peter Ivy, Karen Ivy. BS in Music Edn., U. Ala., 1967; MMus, U. Tex., 1974, PhD in Music Edn., 1983. Choral dir. Lee H.S., Huntsville, Ala., 1967-70; profl. cellist Austin (Tex.) Symphony Orch., 1974-95; pvt. cello tchr. Austin, 1990-93; orch. dir. and string tchr. Lamar Mid. Sch. and McCallum H.S., Austin, 1974-80, 83-90; lectr. edn. U. Tex., Austin, 1990-93; dir. U. Tex. String Project, Austin, 1993-95; adjunct assoc. prof. of music. Clinician conv. sessions, insvc. tng., 1980—. Author: Recruiting for the School Orchestra, 1984, 2d edit. 1987; co-author: A Rhythm a Week, 1998; editor: Teaching Stringed Instruments, 1991, Strategies for Teaching Strings and Orchestra, 1996. Mem. Am. String Tchrs. Assn. (past pres., Citation for Exceptional Leadership and Merit 1988, 96, nat. pres. 1992-94), Tex. Orch. Dirs. Assn. (pres. 1991-92), Music Educators Nat. Conf. (life), Tex. Music Educators Assn., Suzuki Assn. of Americas. Episcopalian. Home: 2329 Table Rock Ct Arlington TX 76006-2761 Office: Univ of Texas Dept Of Music Arlington TX 76019-0001

WITT, DENISE LINDGREN, operating room nurse, educator; b. Rockville Centre, N.Y., July 4, 1959; d. Edwin J. and Alice Lindgren; m. Donald T. Witt, July 30, 1982; children: Evan, Brandon. BSN magna cum laude, Adelphi U., 1986; MA in Health Adminstrn., Hofstra U., 1995. Cert. operating room nurse, surg. technologist, CPR, AORN Nurse Edn./Clinical Nurse specialist. Prof. surg. tech. Nassau Community Coll., Garden City, NY. Mem. Assn. Oper. Rm. Nurses, Assn. Surg. Technologists, Am. Diabetes and Juvenile Diabetes, N.Y. State Assn. of Two Year Colls. Home: 22 Anchor Dr Massapequa NY 11758-7821

WITT, DENNIS RUPPERT, secondary school mathematics educator; b. Buffalo, Apr. 25, 1954; s. Carlton Albert and Elinor Marie (Ruppert) W.; m. Donna Violet Endres, July 9, 1983; 1 child Ashley Witt. BS in Math., SUNY, Fredonia, 1976; cert. in Cobol programming, Erie C.C., 1979; MS in Edn., Canisius Coll., 1981, MS in Ednl. Adminstrn., 1993. Cert. math. tchr. and sch. dist. adminstr., N.Y. Tchr. jr. high math. Frontier Ctrl. Sch., Hamburg, N.Y., 1977-90, tchr. sr. high math., 1988-2001, tchr. middle sch. math., 2001—. Cons. spl. computer projects Goldome Realty Credit Corp., Amherst, N.Y., 1985-87, Chevrolet/GMC Saginaw divsn., Buffalo, 1988, Faulring's Cabinet Making, North Collins, N.Y., 1989, Avanti Corp., 1987, Gen. Mills, 1975-77; adminstrv. asst. prin., Frontier Summer Sch., 1993-96; curriculum cons. in field. Named Girls Cross-Country Coach of Yr., Channel 7 TV, Buffalo, 1987. Mem.: Frontier Ctrl. Tchrs.' Assn. (rep. coun. 1995—, mem. exec. com. 2002—, chmn. membership com. 2002—, trustee benefit fund 2002—). Avocations: coaching, running. Office: Frontier Ctrl Sch 2751 Amsdell Rd Hamburg NY 14075-1335

WITT, ELIZABETH NOWLIN (BETH WITT), special education educator, speech-language pathologist; b. Columbus, Miss., Apr. 11, 1941; d. Mervyn Davis and Elizabeth (Moody) Smith; m. Lawrence V. Witt Jr., Feb. 10, 1963; children: Lawrence V. III, Ben, John, Catherine, Elizabeth. BS in Journalism and English, Miss. U. for Women, Columbus, 1963; MA in Spl. Edn., La. Tech. U., Ruston, 1979; postgrad., La. State U., 1990—. Cert. in English, learning disabilities, mental retardation, presch. handicapped severe/profound, also prin., ednl. cons., ednl. diagnostician, La.; lic. speech-lang. pathologist. Tchr. spl. edn. Caddo-Bossier Assn. for Retarded Citizens, Shreveport, La., 1976-79; tchr presch. handicapped Bossier Parish Schs., Bossier City, La., 1979-83; ednl. diagnostician Caddo Parish Schs., Shreveport, 1983-96. Ednl. cons. Ruston (La.) State Sch., summer 1981; instr. La. Tech. U., 1990-95; mem. author adv. bd. Comm. Skill Builders, Tucson, 1986-88; ex-officio mem. Region VII Infant Coun., Shreveport, 1990-92; bd. dirs. Childcare of N.W. La., Shreveport, 1986-90, Head Start, Shreveport, 1984-85., asst. prof. Speech-Language Pathology La. Tech. U., Ruston, 1996-97; speech pathologist C-BARC Early Intervention Program, Shreveport, 1996-97; instr. dept. comm. disorders La. State U. Med. Ctr., 1997—. Mem. editl. adv. bd. JCCD, DCCD, 1990-95; mem. editl. bd. AJSLP, 1998—; author lang. activity kits and programs and textbook chpts. Vol. edn. cons. Lighthouse Presch. Program, Vols. of Am., Shreveport, 1986—; elder First Presbyn. Ch., Bossier City, 1989-91. Mem. Am. Speech and Hearing Assn., Coun. for Exceptional Children (editor newsletter La. Fedn. 1988-90, pres. La. div. early childhood 1989-90, pres. La. div. mental retardation 1986-87, editl. rev. bd., jour. DCCD-CEC 1990-95). Avocations: reading, anthropology, archaeology, ethnography, travel. Office: Mollie E Webb Speech & Hearing Ctr 2919 Southern Ave Shreveport LA 71104-2955

WITT, JUDITH ANNE, elementary education educator; b. Danville, Ill., Mar. 8, 1949; d. Dale Norman and Ruby Lou (Stonecipher) Shideler; m. Robert Witt, Feb. 24, 1970; children: Eric, Sean, Ryan. BA, U. Ariz., 1971; MA, U.S. Internat. U., San Diego, 1990; EdS, Point Loma Nazarene Coll., 1993. Tchr. Ovid-Elsie (Mich.) Schs., 1971-73; tchr., coord. gifted and talented edn. Poway (Calif.) Unified Sch. Dist., 1987-91; tchr., dist. gifted and talented coord. Ramona (Calif.) Unified Sch. Dist., 1991-95; dist. GATE coord. Castro Valley (Calif.) Unified Sch. Dist., 1995—. Presenter local sch. and dist. insvc. days, state and nat. confs.; Calif. mentor tchr. learning styles. Active community orgns. Mem. ASCD, Calif. Assn. for Gifted, Phi Delta Kappa.

WITTE, RAYMOND HENRY, psychologist, educator; b. Dayton, Ky., Mar. 22, 1957; s. Raymond Henry and Irma Mae (Henry) W.; m. Susan Evans Weih; children: sarah, Ashleigh. BA, U. Ky., 1979, MS, 1982, PhD, 1991. Nat. cert. sch. psychologist; std. sch. psychology, Ky.; lic. sch. psychologist. Prof. Midway (Ky.) Coll., 1981-87; rsch. asst., neuropsychologist Albert Chandler Med. Ctr., Univ. Ky., Lexington, 1985-87; sch. psychologist Jessamine County Sch. System, Nicholasville, Ky., 1988-93, preschool co-dir., 1992-93; assoc. prof. Miami U., Oxford, Ohio, 1993—. Contbr. articles to profl. jours. Recipient Univ. scholarship U. Ky., Lexington, 1978. Mem. APA, Nat. Assn. Sch. Psychologists, Ohio Sch. Psychol. Assn. Avocations: horses, hiking.

WITTEN, MARK LEE, lung injury research scientist, educator; b. Amarillo, Tex., June 23, 1953; s. Gerald Lee and Polly Ann (Warren) W.; m. Christine Ann McKee, June 10, 1988; 1 child, Brandon Lee. BS in Phys. Sci., Emporia State U., 1975; PhD, Ind. U., 1983. Postdoctoral fellow U. Ariz., Tucson, 1983-88; instr. in medicine Harvard Med. Sch., Boston, Mass., 1988-90; rsch. prof. U. Ariz., Tucson, 1990—, head Airborne Particulates Rsch. Ctr., 1998—, head Lung Injury Lab., 1998. Cons. Ames Life Scis. Space Sta. program NASA; grant cons. USAF, Washington, 1991—, NSF, 1995, U.S. Army, 1995. Contbr. articles to profl. jours.; patentee in field. Grantee USAF, 1991—, Health Effects Inst., 2001, Tng. grant Dept. of Def., 1992—, NIH, 1991—, Upjohn Pharm., 1992, Dept. of Army, 1993, Eli Lilly, 2002. Mem. AIAA, Am. Physiol. Soc., N.Y. Acad. Scis., Soc. Toxicology. Methodist. Achievements include first animal model of cigarette smoke exposure to show cigarette smoke increases lung permeability, animal model of passive cigarette smoke, to demonstrate pulmonary edema in a microgravity model, studies of fluid regulation in space biology models; patents for anti-cancer and immunostimulatory properties of substance P. Office: U Ariz Dept Pediatrics Ahsc 1501 N Campbell Ave Tucson AZ 85724-0001

WITTEN, THOMAS JEFFERSON, JR., mathematics educator; b. Welch, W.Va., Feb. 10, 1942; s. Thomas Jefferson and Gladys Marium (McMeans) W.; m. Barbara Phyllis Honaker, Feb. 20, 1965; children: Thomas Jefferson III, Rebecca A. Dye, Timothy A., Stephanie L. Dye. BS in Edn., Concord Coll., Athens, W.Va., 1965; MA in Edn., W.Va. U., Morgantown, 1971. Cert. tchr., Va., W.Va. Tchr. math. McDowell County Schs., Gary (W.Va.) High Sch., 1965-71, asst. prin., 1971-73; asst. prin. inst. Tazewell County Schs., Richlands (Va.) High Sch., 1973-87; secondary supr. Jackson County Schs., Ripley, W.Va., 1987-88; asst. prof. math., tech. prep. dir. Southwest Va. C.C., Richlands, 1988—. Math. cons. S.W. Va. C.C. Computer Math. Grant Project, Richlands, 1988-90; coord. S.W. Va. Tech Prep Consortium, 1992—; co-dir. Eisenhower Math Grant, 1996-97, 2002, dir., 1998-2002. Mem. sch. bd. Tazewell (Va.) County Schs., 1990-91, 95—, chair 1996-97, vice chmn. 1999-2001, chmn., 2002-03. Recipient K-8 Tchr. Improvement grant, 1992-93. Mem. Va. C.C. Assn., Mountain Math Alliance (chmn. 1990—), PTA (life, pres. 1979-81), Richlands Rotary (pres. 1989-91, 99-2000, asst. gov. 2000-2001, dist. chmn.), Masons (jr. deacon 1966-68), Shriners. Democrat. Methodist. Avocations: painting, cross-stitch, reading, computers, old cars, writing. Home: 744 Terry Dr Richlands VA 24641-2616 Office: SW Va C C Box SVCC Richlands VA 24641 E-mail: tom.witten@sw.edu., wit10@netscope.net.

WITTLINGER, CHERYL A. elementary education educator; b. Lakewood, Ohio, Mar. 30, 1950; d. Richard Lawrence and Beverly Jane (Leighton) Riedel; children: Brian E., Jasen E, Ashley T. Student, Kent State U., 1968-70; AA, Lorain County Community Coll., Lorain, Ohio, 1977; BA in Visual Arts, Cleve. State U., 1982; postgrad., Coll. Mt. St. Joseph, Cin., 1987. Tchr. art Lorain (Ohio) City Schs., 1983—. Presenter in field; chmn. Lorain County Very Spl. Arts Festival, 1988; judge Lorain County Consortium for Gifted Edn. Fair, 1989. Endowment grantee Lorain City Schs., 1987, 88, 91, 98, 2000. Mem. AAUW, Ohio Art Edn. Assn. (conf. presenter 1986-88, 90, Outstanding Art Tchr. for Northeastern Ohio region award 1991, 2001), N.E. Ohio Art Edn. Assn. (newsletter editor), Lorain Edn. Assn., Ohio Alliance for Arts Edn. Presbyterian. Avocations: breeding cocker spaniels, painting, travel, tole painting on clothes. Home: 527 Ashley Cir Avon Lake OH 44012-2131 Office: Lorain Middle Sch 602 Washington Ave Lorain OH 44052

WITTSCHE, VALERIE JOSEPHINE, elementary education educator, special education educator; b. Yankton, S.D., Jan. 11, 1959; d. Vernon Joseph and Anita Marie (Bruening) Blaschke; m. Gregory Donald Wittsche, Aug. 6, 1983; 1 child, Jesse Donald. BA, Mt. Marty Coll., 1981; MEd in Spl. Edn., Tex. Woman's U., 1992. Cert. tchr., gifted and talented edn., Tex. Tchr. St. Mary's Sch., Osmond, Nebr., 1981-82, St. Rose of Lima, Crofton, Nebr., 1982-85, Red Oak (Tex.) Ind. Sch. Dist., 1985—. Presenter Gifted Students Inst., Dallas, 1991, Primary, Intermediate, Gifted Symposium, Mesquite, Tex., 1991-94. Mem. Tex. Assn. for the Gifted and Talented (facilitator 1992, presenter 1990-93), Tex. Coun. Exceptional Children. Avocations: reading, outdoor recreation, creative writing, public speaking. Home: 937 Highgate Dr Lewisville TX 75067-6147 Office: Red Oak Ind Sch PO Box 9000 Red Oak TX 75154-9000

WITTY, ELAINE P. former dean, education educator; m. Jack P. Witty; children: Janeen, Jack P., Jr. BS, Jackson State U., 1956; MS, Vanderbilt U., 1961, EdD, 1965; postgrad., U. Ga., 1978. Tchr. English McCullough High Sch., Monticello, Miss., 1956-58; mid. sch. tchr. Jackson (Miss.) State U. Lab. Sch., 1958-59, asst. prin., 1963-65; libr. asst. Jackson State U., 1959-60, dir. student teaching and field svcs., 1965-69; head dept. elem. edn. Norfolk (Va.) State U., 1969-79, dean sch. edn., 1979—98, assoc. v.p. acad. affairs, 1998—99, dean emeritus, 1998—. Dir. Norfolk Tchr. Corps Project, 1970-74; mem. Norfolk U. Long Range Planning Com., 1976-79, numerous univ. coms., 1969—; dir. univ. self study for accreditation Nat. Coun. Accreditation in Tchr. Edn., 1970, 80, 91, bd. appeals, 1977-80, vis. com. mem., 1977-83; dir. univ. self study for accreditation So. Assn. Colls. and Schs., 1986-88, vis. com. mem., 1976—; bd. dirs. Am. Assn. Colls. in Tchr. Edn., 1977-80, 85-88, mem. com. multicultural edn., 1980-83, nat. adv. bd. for the study of minority tchr. edn. achievement, 1990; mem. Nat. Tchr. Examinations Policy Bd., 1985-87, advanced edn. com. for GRE, 1983-88; bd. dirs. Va. ASCD, 1985-86; lectr. in field. Contbr. articles to profl. jours. including The Gifted Child Qaurterly, Jour. Tchr. Edn., Jour. Negro Edn., Assn. Tchr. Educators Jour. and Essence; dir. video tapes, 1991;

prodr. video tape, 1992. Trustee Presbyn. Sch. Christian Edn., 1974-76, Union Theol. Sem., 1979-82; mem. gen. assembly mission bd. Presbyn. Ch. (USA), 1982-87, exec. com. nat. coun. ch. and race, 1984-87; chair edn. com. Urban League of Hampton Roads, 1987-91, 93—; bd. dirs. Children's Camp Fund of Hampton Roads, 1985—, Tidewater Red Cross, 1992—; campaign mgr. Va. House of Dels., Va. State Senate, 1984-91. Recipient Lola Parker Nat. Achievement award Iota Lambda Sorority, 1989, Eula Glover Regional Achievement award Norfolk chpt. Alpha Kappa Alpha Sorority, 1991, Pemeroy award Am. Assn. Colls. and Tchr. Edn., 1994. Office: Norfolk State U 2401 Corprew Ave Norfolk VA 23504-3993*

WITTY, THOMAS EZEKIEL, III, psychologist, researcher; b. Greensboro, NC, Oct. 11, 1955; s. Thomas Ezekiel Jr. and Peggy (Coggins) Witty; m. Ginger Lynell Kissee, June 28, 1997; children: Ezekiel Thomas, Zoe Anne. BA in English, U. N.C., Greensboro, 1980; MS, Va. Commonwealth U., 1989; PhD, U. Mo., 1995. Lic. psychologist Miss. Tchr. secondary English, debate and cross-country coach Henry County Pub. Schs., Collinsville, Va., 1981-87; fin. aid. counselor asst. Va. Commonwealth U., Richmond, 1987-89; substance abuse counselor Dist. 19 Alcoholism Svcs., Petersburg, Va., 1990; grad. rsch. asst. U. Mo., Columbia, 1990-94, grad. instr., 1992-94; postdoctoral fellow Rusk Rehab. Ctr., Columbia, 1995-98; chief psychology Mo. Rehab. Ctr., Mt. Vernon, 1998-2001; psychologist North Miss. Med. Ctr., Tupelo, 2001—. Rsch. cons. Coun. on Rehab. Edn., Inc., Champaign, Ill., 1991; ad hoc reviewer Jour. Rehab. Psychology, 1995—98; internship selection com. U. Mo. Health Svcs. Consortium, Columbia, 1996—98; adj. faculty Family Medicine Residency Ctr., Tupelo, Miss., 2001—; alt. mem. instl. rev. bd. North Miss. Med. Ctr., Miss., 2002—. Contbr. articles to profl. jours. NIH postdoctoral fellow in rehab. rsch., 1995-98, Walter Scott Monroe rsch. fellow U. Mo., 1992-95; rsch. grantee U. Mo. Rsch. Bd., 1997. Mem.: Nat. Rehab. Counseling Assn., Am. Pain Soc., Miss. Psychol. Assn., APA (divsn. 17, 22, 38, 50, program rev. com. divsn. 22 1996—), Sierra Club, KC, Kappa Delta Pi. Democrat. Roman Catholic. Avocations: running, swimming, cycling, hiking, camping. Office: North Miss Med Ctr Dept Behavioral Health 830 S Gloster St Tupelo MS 38801 Fax: 662-377-7035. E-mail: twitty@nmhs.net.

WITZ, GISELA, scientist, educator; b. Breslau, Federal Republic of Germany, Mar. 16, 1939; came to U.S., 1955. d. Gerhardt Witz and Hildegard (Sufeida) Minzak. BA, NYU, 1962, MS, 1965, PhD, 1969. Assoc. rsch. scientist NYU Med. Ctr., N.Y.C., 1970-73, rsch. scientist, 1973-77, asst. prof., 1977-80, U. Medicine and Dentistry of N.J.-Robert Wood Johnson Med. Sch., Piscataway, NJ, 1980-86, 1986—93, prof., 1993—2000, prof. emeritus, 2001—. Dep. dir. Joint Grad. Program in Toxicology, Rutgers U./Univ. Medicine and Dentistry of N.J.-Robert Wood Johnson Med. Sch., 1988, assoc. dir. 1992-2000; cons. Nat. Rsch. Coun., Washington, 1982-83, 85-86. Recipient Dupont Teaching award, NYU, 1966, Univ. Scholar, Founders Day award, N.Y. U., 1969, Student Appreciation award Rutgers Assn. Toxicology Grad. Students, 1996; honoree 3d Ann. Women in Sci. Symposium, 2000. Fellow Oxygen Soc.; mem. Am. Assn. Cancer Rsch., Am. Chem. Soc., Soc. Toxicology, N.Y. Acad. Sci., Sigma Xi. Avocation: gardening. Office: U Medicine and Dentistry NJ Robert Wood Johnson Med Sch Piscataway NJ 08854 E-mail: witz@eohsi.rutgers.edu.

WOBUS, REINHARD ARTHUR, geologist, educator; b. Norfolk, Va., Jan. 11, 1941; s. Reinhard Schaffer and Oral (Phares) W.; m. Sheridan Whitcher, Mar. 18, 1967; children: Erik Reinhard, Cameron Wright. BA, Washington U., St. Louis, 1962; MA, Harvard U., 1963; PhD, Stanford U., 1966. Asst. prof. geology Williams Coll., Williamstown, Mass., 1966-72, assoc. prof., 1972-78, prof., 1978-85, Edna McConnell Clark prof. geology, 1985—, dept. chmn., 1988-96. Geologist U.S. Geol. Survey, Denver, 1967-86; vis. prof. Colo. Coll., Colorado Springs, 1976, 82-83, Colo. State U., Ft. Collins, summers 1977-84; bd. dirs. Colo. Outdoor Edn. Ct., Florissant, Williamstown Rural Lands Found.; co-founder Keck Twelve-Coll. Geol. Consortium, mem. governing bd., 1986—. Contbr. maps and articles on Precambrian geology of So. Rocky Mountains to profl. jours. Danforth fellow, 1962, Woodrow Wilson fellow, 1962, NSF fellow, 1962-66. Fellow Geol. Soc. Am.; mem. Am. Geophys. Union, Nat. Assn. Geosci. Tchrs., Coun. on Undergrad. Rsch., Colo. Sci. Soc., Mineral Soc. Am., Phi Beta Kappa, Sigma Xi. Achievements include current work: Petrology and geochronology of Precambrian igneous and metamorphic rocks and mid-Tertiary volcanic rocks, so. Rocky Mountains. Subspecialties: Petrology, Geology. Home: 20 Grandview Dr Williamstown MA 01267-2528 Office: Williams Coll Dept Geoscis Williamstown MA 01267 E-mail: rwobus@williams.edu.

WOERNER, ALFRED IRA, medical device manufacturer, educator; b. Jersey City, N.J., Sept. 21, 1935; s. Theodore and Miriam (Mann) W.; m. Margaret R. Martin, Nov. 27, 1959; children: John, Michael, Judith. DME, Stevens Inst., 1956; MS, Stevens, 1961; MBA, NYU, 1965; LLB, LaSalle U., 1963; PhD, Calif. State U., 1990; diploma for motorcycle tech., Thomson-Direct Edn. U., 2002. Gen. program mgr. Becton Dickenson & Co., Ruthuferd, N.J., 1959-63; group v.p., asst. to pres. Howmet Corp., N.Y.C., 1963-69; gen. mgr., v.p. Wide Range Industries, N.Y.C., 1969-72; pres., owner New World Market Ltd., Westwood, N.J., 1972—, Fairfield Surg. Corp., Stanford, Conn., 1972—. Cons. Woerner Assocs., Westwood; prof. Fairleigh Dickinson U., Teaneck, N.J., 1969-96. Author: Program Management, 1988. Pres. Bd. Edn., Westwood, 1978-86; adv. Stevens Inst. Tech., Hoboken, N.J., 1972-80; commodore Bay Island Marina, 2002—; musician Fla. Sun Coast Jazz Band, 2002—. Mem. AMA, ASME, Am. Acad. Cons., Am. Statistical Assn., Fla. Condo Assn. (dir. 2002—). Achievements include five patents in Medical Industry; development of new process in orthopedic surgery industry. Home: 7560 Bay Island Dr S South Pasadena FL 33707-4562 Office: Fairleigh Dickinson U 1000 River Rd Teaneck NJ 07666-1996 E-mail: mrwaiw@aol.com.

WOGAMAN, JOHN PHILIP, retired minister and educator; b. Toledo, Mar. 18, 1932; s. Donald Ford and Ella Louise (Kilbury) W.; m. Carolyn Jane Gattis, Aug. 4, 1956; children: Stephen Neil, Donald George, Paul Joseph, Jean Ann. BA, U. Pacific, 1954; STB, Boston U., 1957, PhD, 1960. Ordained to ministry United Meth. Ch., 1957. Pastor First Meth. Ch., Marlborough, Mass., 1956-58; staff asst. div. world missions United Meth. Ch., 1960-61; asst. prof., then assoc. prof. U. Pacific, 1961-66; prof. Christian social ethics Wesley Theol. Sem., Washington, 1966—2002, dean, 1972-83, prof. emeritus, 2002. Sr. pastor Foundry United Meth. Ch., Washington, 1992—2002; mem. com. religious and civil liberties Nat. Coun. Chs., 1966-2003; chairperson United Meth. Infant Formula Task Force, 1980-84, Muskie Com., 1982-91, World Meth. Coun., 1986-91, United Meth. Gen. Conf., 1988, 92, 96, 2000; pres. Interfaith Alliance, 1997-99; chmn. bd. dir. Interfaith Conf. of Met. Washington. Author: Methodism's Challenge in Race Relations, 1960, Protestant Faith and Religious Liberty, 1967; Guaranteed Annual Income: The Moral Issues, 1968, A Christian Method of Moral Judgement, 1976, Christians and the Great Economic Debate, 1977, Faith and Fragmentation, 1985, Economics and Ethics, 1986, Christian Perspectives on Politics, 1988, rev. edit., 2000, Christian Moral Judgement, 1989, Making Moral Decisions, 1990, Christian Ethics, 1993, To Serve the Present Age, 1995, Speaking the Truth in Love, 1999, From the Eye of the Storm: A Pastor to the President Speaks Out, 1999; editor: The Population Crisis and Moral Responsibility, 1973, Readings in Christian Ethics, 1996. Pres. Stockton (Calif.) Fair Housing Com., 1963-64, Suburban Md. Fair Housing, 1970; mem. Calif. Dem. Ctrl. Com., 1964-66. Lilly fellow, 1959-60; recipient rsch. award Assn. Theol. Schs., 1975. Mem.: Am. Theol. Soc. (v.p. 2003—), Soc. Christian Ethics (pres. 1976—77), Cosmos Club (Washington). Home: 4620 45th St NW Washington DC 20016-4479

WOGAN, GERALD NORMAN, toxicology educator; b. Altoona, Pa., Jan. 11, 1930; s. Thomas B. and Florence E. (Corl) W.; m. Henrietta E. Hoenicke, Aug. 24, 1957; children: Christine F., Eugene E. BS, Juniata Coll., 1951; MS, U. Ill., 1953, PhD, 1957. Asst. prof. physiology Rutgers U., New Brunswick, N.J., 1957-61; asst. prof. toxicology MIT, Cambridge, 1962-65, assoc. prof., 1965-69, prof. toxicology, 1969—, head dept. applied biol. scis., 1979-88, prof. chemistry, 1989-96, dir. divsn. toxicology, 1988-99, also prof. chemistry. Cons. to nat. and internat. govt. agys., industries. NIH grantee, 1963— Mem. editl. bd. Cancer Rsch., 1971-79, Applied Microbiology, 1971-79, Chem.-Biol. Interactions, 1975-78, Toxicology, Environ. Health, 1974-84, Jour. Nat. Cancer Inst., 1988—; contbr. articles and revs. to profl. jours. Recipient Disting. Alumni award U. Ill. Fellow Am. Acad. Microbiology; mem. AAAS, NAS, Inst. Medicine, Am. Assn. Cancer Rsch., Am. Soc. Pharmacology and Exptl. Therapeutics, Am. Soc. Microbiology, Soc. Toxicology, Am. Inst. Nutrition, Sigma Xi. Office: MIT Divsn Bioengr/Environ Health 77 Mass Ave Rm 26-009 Cambridge MA 02139-4307

WOGEN, CATHY LYNN, academic director; b. Farmington, Minn., Aug. 5, 1957; d. Normand Ernest and Betty Ann (Cline) deVaudreuil; m. David Lee Wogen, June 13, 1981; children: Carlene, Elizabeth, Glen. BS in Computer Sci., St. Cloud State U., 1980; student, Alnwick (Eng.) Tchrs. Acad., 1976-77. Cons. MCOS, St. Cloud, Minn., 1985-89; evening computer instr. St. Cloud Bus. Coll., 1983-90, evening dir., 1990-92, acad. dir., 1992—. Post/secondary rep. Bus./Edn. Partnership, St. Cloud, 1993; mem. at large Parochial Sch. Bd., 2000-2002, sec., 2002-03, chmn. diversity enhancement com., 1998-2003. Mem. St. Cloud C. of C. Democratic. Lutheran.

WOHL, DAVID, humanities educator, college dean-theatre director; b. Washington, Nov. 28, 1950; s. Joseph Gene and Carol (Weiss) W.; m. Sherry Simmers; children: Isaac, Gabriele. BA, Clark U., 1972; MA, U. Conn., 1975; PhD, Kent State U., 1988. Staff asst. Am. Theatre Assn., Washington, 1975-76; prof. W.Va. State Coll., Institute, 1976-79, chmn. dept. comm., 1979-88, dean sch. arts and humanities, 1988—; artistic dir. Charleston (W.Va.) Stage Co., 1991—2002. Gen. mgr. Porthouse Theatre, Cuyahoga Falls, Ohio, 1984-85; cons. U. South Ala., Mobile, 1988; bd. dirs., treas., pres. Southeastern Theatre Conf., 1993-98; coord. W.Va. Gt. Tchrs. Seminar. Stage dir. Kanawha Players, 1978—, Nutmeg Summer Playhouse, 1975-76, W.Va. Theatre Festival, Charleston Playhouse; prodr.: (films) Chillers, 1985, Strangest Dreams, 1990, Paradise Park, 1992 (Gold medal Houston Internat. Film Festival 1992, 1st place award Chgo. Film Festival 1992); contbr. articles to theatre jours. Bd. dirs. Kanawha Arts Alliance, Charleston, 1979-81, Kanawha Players, 1982-85; pres. W.Va. Theatre Conf., 1987-89; v.p. Arts Advocacy W.Va., 1994—. NEH Fellow, 1977, 80; Dept. Edn. teaching fellow, 1976-77. Mem. Assn. for Theatre in Higher Edn. Home: 13 Hidden Cv Cross Lanes WV 25313-1171 Office: W Va State Coll PO Box 28 Institute WV 25112-0028

WOHLERT, EARL ROSS, health care analyst; b. Phila., Oct. 19, 1963; s. Anton Emil and Dona Lee (Zimmerman) W.; children: Ryan Chandler, Maia Katharine; m. Heather Lunne Enos, Sept. 15, 2002. BA, Hawaii Loa Coll., Kaneohe, 1986; MBA, U. New Haven, 1992. Acct. Yale U. Sch. Medicine, New Haven, 1987-88, fin. analyst, 1988-90, assoc. adminstr. fin., 1990-93, assoc. adminstr. fin. svcs., 1993-95; health care analyst M.D. Health Plan, North Haven, Conn., 1995-96, dir. healthcare analysis, 1996—2000; dir. med. action planning CIGNA Healthcare, Hartford, Conn., 2000—. Mktg. and mgmt. cons. Lt. USNR, 1992. Avocations: sailing, tennis, golf, traveling. Home: 25 Farm River Rd Branford CT 06405 Office: 900 Cottage Grove Rd Hartford CT 06152

WOJAHN, DAVID, poet, literature educator; MFA, U. Ariz., 1980. Instr. U. Chgo., U. Houston, U. Ala.; prof. English, dir. Creative Writing Program Ind. U.; poet, prof. English Va. Commonwealth U., 2003; mem. MFA faculty Vt. Coll. Author: Icehouse Lights, 1982 (Yale Younger Poets award, 1981, William Carlos Williams Book award Poetry Soc. Am.), Glassworks, 1987, Mystery Train, 1990, Latin Empire, 1994, The Falling Hour, 1997, Strange Good Fortune: Essays on Contemporary Poetry, 2001; editor: The Only World, 1995, author poetry and essays. Recipient Book award, Soc. Midland Authors, George Kent Meml. prize, Poetry mag., Celia B. Wagner award, Poetry Soc. Am., three Pushcart prizes; fellow, Fine Arts Work Ctr., Provincetown, John Simon Guggenheim Meml. Found., 2003; Creative Writing fellow in poetry, Ind. and Ill. Arts Couns., Nat. Endowment for the Arts, Amy Lowell Travelling Poetry scholar. Office: Va Commonwealth Univ Dept English Hibbs Bldg 900 Park Ave PO Box 842005 Richmond VA 23284-2005*

WOJCICKI, ANDREW ADALBERT, chemist, educator; b. Warsaw, May 5, 1935; s. Franciszek Wojcicki and Janina (Kozlowa) Hoskins; m. Marba L. Hart, Dec. 21, 1968; children: Katherine, Christina. BS, Brown U., 1956; PhD, Northwestern U., 1960; postdoctoral fellow, U. Nottingham, Eng., 1960-61. Asst. prof. chemistry Ohio State U., Columbus, 1961-66, assoc. prof., 1966-69, prof., 1969-2000, prof. emeritus, 2001—, acting chmn., 1981-82, assoc. chmn., 1982-83, 84-86. Vis. prof. Academia Sinica, Taipei, Taiwan, 2002-03, Case Western Res. U., 1967, U. Bologna, Italy, 1988, Nat. Sci. Council Chemistry Rsch. Promotion Ctr., Taiwan, 1994, U. Sydney, Australia, 1998; vis. researcher U. Coll. London, 1969; sr. U.S. scientist Alexander von Humboldt Found., Mulheim/Ruhr, Germany, 1975-76; vis. scholar U. Calif.-Berkeley, 1984; assoc. dean Coll. of Math. and Phys. Scis., Ohio State U., 1996-98. Contbr. articles to profl. jours. Guggenheim fellow U. Cambridge (Eng.), 1976; recipient Disting. Teaching award Ohio State U., 1968, Humboldt Sr. award Humboldt Found., 1975, 76, Casimir Funk Natural Sci. award, Polish Inst. of Arts and Scis. in Am., 2001. Mem.: Am. Chem. Soc. (Columbus sect. award 1992), Phi Lambda Upsilon, Sigma Xi. Home: 825 Greenridge Rd Columbus OH 43235-3411 Office: Ohio State U 100 W 18th Ave Columbus OH 43210-1185

WOJCICKI, STANLEY GEORGE, physicist, educator; b. Warsaw, Mar. 30, 1937; came to U.S., 1950; s. Franciszek and Janina (Kozlow) W.; m. Esther Denise Hochman, Nov. 17, 1961; children: Susan Diane, Janet Maia, Anne Elizabeth. AB, Harvard U., 1957; PhD, U. Calif., Berkeley, 1962. Physicist Lawrence Radiation Lab., Berkeley, 1961-66; asst. prof. physics Stanford U., 1966-68, assoc. prof., 1968-74, prof., 1974—, chmn. dept., 1982-85, dep. dir. Superconducting Supercollider Central Design Group, 1984-89; chmn. Stanford Linear Accelerator Center Exptl. Program Adv. Com., 1979-81. Chmn. High Energy Physics Adv. Panel, 1990-96. Assoc. editor Phys. Rev. Letters for Exptl. High Energy Physics, 1978-80. Recipient Alexander von Humboldt Sr. Am. Scientist award, 1981; NSF fellow, 1964-65; Sloan Found. fellow, 1968-72; Guggenheim fellow, 1973-74 Fellow Am. Phys. Soc. Office: Stanford U Dept Physics Stanford CA 94305-4060

WOLDMAN, EVELYN JANDORF, computer information specialist, educator; b. Balt., Mar. 4, 1950; d. Bernard Joseph and Lottie (Kaufman) Jandorf; m. James Arthur Woldman, Aug. 26, 1979; children: Robyn Nancy(dec.), Susan Ami, Rachel Lynne. BA, Boston U., 1972, MEd, 1977; Cert. Advanced Grad. Study, Lesley U., 1986. Tchr. Holliston Pub. Sch., Mass., 1972—82; resource staff Miller Sch., 1982—83; computer coord. K-12 Holliston Sch., 1983—85; part-time faculty Lesley U., 1983—; ptnr. Ednl. Tech. Software specialist Chtp. 1 Computer Ctr., 1989—95, Framingham State Coll., 1995—96; edn. coord. Mass. Elem. Sch. Prin. Assn. Tech. Ctr., 1996—; mem. Commonwealth Inservice Inst., Mass. Dept. Edn. Contbr. articles to profl. publs.; resource author Computers and the Social Studies, 1988; co-author 6 software programs. Recipient Pathfinder award, Mass. Computer Using Educators, 2001. Mem.: ASCD, Mass. Elem. Sch. Prins. Assn. (tech. ctr. coord. 1996—, edn. coord. 1996—), Holliston Fedn. Tchrs., Internat. Coun. on Computers in Edn., Nat. Coun. Social Studies, Mass. Coun. for Social Studies (newsletter editor), Hadassah, B'nai B'rith, Pi Lambda Theta. Democrat. Jewish. Home: 18 Cudworth Ln Sudbury MA 01776-1386

WOLF, BARRY, genetics, pediatric educator; b. Chgo., June 19, 1947; s. Bert D. and Toby E. (Urkoff) W.; children: Michael Loren, Bryan Phillip. BS, U. Ill., 1969; MD, U. Ill. Coll. Medicine, 1974; PhD, U. Ill., 1974. Diplomate Am. Bd. Pediatrics, Med. and Biochem. Genetics. Intern, resident in pediatrics Childrens Meml. Hosp., Northwestern U., Chgo., 1974-76; fellow Yale U. Sch. Medicine, New Haven, Conn., 1976-78; prof. human genetics Med. Coll. Va., Richmond, 1978-2001, vice chair for rsch. dept. pediatrics, 1996-2000; dir. rsch. Conn. Children's Med. Ctr., 2001—. Assoc. chair, dir. rsch. dept. pediats. U. Conn. Sch. Medicine, 2001—. Author over 175 jour. articles and book chpts. dealing with inherited disorders of metabolism and biochem. genetics, specifically disorders of biotin metabolism. Recipient E. Mead Johnson award for pediatric rsch. Am. Acad. Pediatrics, 1988, Borden award in nutrition Am. Inst. Nutrition, 1987, Outstanding Scientist of Va. award Va. Sci. Mus., 1986, Ounce of Prevention award Action for Prevention of Va., 1985. Mem. Am. Soc. Clin. Investigation, Am. Pediat. Soc., Soc. Pediatric Rsch., Soc. for Inherited Metabolic Diseases, Am. Soc. Clin. Nutrition, Am. Inst. Nutrition, Soc. for the Study of Inborn Errors of Metabolism, Am. Soc. Human Genetics. Avocation: japanese cloisonne. Office: Conn Childrens Med Ctr 282 Washington St Hartford CT 06106 E-mail: bwolf@ccmckids.org.

WOLF, CHARLES, JR., economist, educator; b. NYC, Aug. 1, 1924; s. Charles and Rosalie W.; m. Theresa van de Wint, Mar. 1, 1947; children: Charles Theodore, Timothy van de Wint. BS, Harvard U., 1943, M.P.A., 1948, PhD in Econs., 1949. Economist, fgn. service officer U.S. Dept. State, 1945-47, 49-53; mem. faculty Cornell U., 1953-54, U. Calif., Berkeley, 1954-55; sr. economist The Rand Corp., Santa Monica, Calif., 1955-67, head econs. dept., 1967-81; dean The Rand Grad. Sch., 1970-97, sr. econ. advisor, 1981—, corp. fellow in internat. econs., 1996—; sr. fellow Hoover Inst., 1988—. Bd. dirs. Capital Income Builder Fund, Capital World Growth Fund; lectr. econs. UCLA, 1960-72; mem. adv. bd. ctr. internat. bus. and econ. rsch., UCLA Anderson Grad. Sch., 1996—. Author: The Costs and Benefits of the Soviet Empire, 1986, Markets or Governments: Choosing Between Imperfect Alternatives, 1989, 2d edit., 1993, Linking Economic Policy and Foreign Policy, 1991, Long-Term Economic and Military Trends: The United States and Asia, 1994-2015, 1995, The Economic Pivot in a Political Context, 1997; co-author: Economic Openness: Many Facets, Many Metrics, 1999, Asian Economic Trends and Their Security Implications, 2000, European Military Prospects, Economic Constraints and the Rapid Reaction Force, 2001, Straddling Economics and Politics: Cross-Cutting Issues, in Asia, the United States and the Global Economy, 2002, Fault Lines in China's Economic Terrain, 2003; mem. editl. bd.: Korean Jour. Def. Econs., 1995—, Society, 1997—; contbr. articles to profl. jours. Mem. Assn. for Public Policy Analysis and Mgmt. (pres. 1980-81), Am. Econs. Assn., Econometric Soc., Coun. on Fgn. Rels., Internat. Inst. Strategic Studies London. Clubs: Cosmos (Washington); Riviera Tennis (Los Angeles); Harvard (N.Y.). Office: The Rand Corp 1700 Main St Santa Monica CA 90407-2138 Business E-Mail: wolf@rand.org.

WOLF, CONSTANCE SLOGGATT, artist, educator; b. Merrick, N.Y., June 25, 1959; d. Arthur Hastings Sloggatt and Dorothea Mae Sloggatt-Rush; m. Charles Robert Wolf. BFA in Painting, Pratt Inst., 1982; MFA in Painting, L.I. U., 1987; studies in edn., art and computers, 1990—. Asst. painting tchr. L.I. U., Greenvale, N.Y., 1985-87; asst. to dir. Fine Arts Mus. L.I., Hempstead, N.Y., 1987-89; art instr. Huntington (N.Y.) Twp. Art League, summer 1991, 94, 95; secondary art tchr. Northport (N.Y.)-East Northport Sch. Dist., 1991—. Coord. ednl. resource Women Artists Visual Resource Collection, 1994-95, Student Portfolio on Laser Disc, 1994-95, Portfolio on CD ROM; presenter in field. One woman show Northport (N.Y.) Cmty. Gallery, 1994; two-person shows include Alfred Van Loen Gallery, Huntington, 1996; represented in numerous pvt. collections. Sponsor, co-sponsor Nat. Art Honor Soc., Northport H.S., 1992-. Recipient mini grant Western Suffolk Tchrs. Ctr., 1994-95. Mem. NOW, Nat. Art Edn. Assn., Nat. Mus. for Women in Arts, Huntington Twp. Art League (instr.), N.Y. State Art Tchrs. Assn., Girls, Inc. Office: Northport-E Northport Sch D Art Dept Laurel Hill Rd Northport NY 11768

WOLF, CYNTHIA TRIBELHORN, librarian, library educator; b. Denver, Dec. 12, 1945; adopted d. John Baltazar and Margaret (Kern) Tribelhorn (dec.); m. H.Y. Rassam, Mar. 21, 1969 (div. Jan. 1988); children: Najma Christine, Yousuf John; adopted children: Leonard Joseph Lucero, Lakota E. Rassam-Lucero, McKinley William Osborn, Kevin Trey, Jackson Andrew Lee, Rachel A.; m. Walter Larry Peck, June 21, 1965 (div. Feb. 1967). BA, Colo. State U., 1970; MLS, U. Denver, 1985. Cert. permanent profl. librarian, N.Mex. Elem. tchr. Sacred Heart Sch., Farmington, N.Mex., 1973-78; asst. prof. libr. sci. edn. U. N.Mex., Albuquerque, 1985-91, dir. libr. sci. edn. divsn., 1989-91; pres. Info. Acquisitions, Albuquerque, 1990-99; libr. dir. Southwestern Coll., Santa Fe, 1992-94; mem. youth resources Rio Grande Valley Libr. Sys., Albuquerque, 1994-95, adult reference svc., 1995-98; with Albuquerque Pub. Schs., 1998—, coach nat. sch. reform policy, 2000—; instr. U. N.Mex., 1998-99. Fine arts resource person for gifted edn. Farmington Pub. Schs., 1979-83; speaker Unofficial Mentorships and Market Rsch., 1992-98. Mem. Farmington Planning and Zoning Commn., 1980-81; bd. dirs. Farmington Mus. Assn., 1983-84; pres. Farmington Symphony League, 1978. Mem. ALA, N.Mex. Library Assn., LWV (bd. dirs. Farmington, 1972-74, 75, pres.). Avocations: mixed media graphics design, market research, creative approaches to personal journals, board game design.

WOLF, EDITH MALETZ, retired educator; b. Warsaw, Nov. 12, 1922; came to U.S., 1923; d. Michael and Sonia Chai (Ingerov) Maletz; m. Jordan Melvin Wolf, July 7, 1946; 1 child, David Richard (dec.). BS, U. Wis., 1944, MS, 1968. Cert. tchr. Wis. Tchr. Milw. Pub. Schs., 1945-85, acting vice prin., 1980-81, ret., 1985. Author: The Magic Dreydle, 1962, The New Governess, 1970, (play) The Dream. Mem. Saturday Arts, Milw., 1970-80, Wis. Painters and Sculptors, Milw., 1944—. Scholarship Dudley Krafts Watson, 1944. Mem. AAUW, Hadassah (sec. 1980-81, pres. emeritus, donor chair, program chair), Nat. Mus. Women in the Arts, Florentine Opera Club (founding mem.), U. Wisc. Alumni Assn., Cousteau Soc. Avocations: reading, writing fiction, plays, painting, gardening.

WOLF, EMIL, physics educator; b. Prague, July 30, 1922; naturalized U.S. citizen, 1967; BSc, U. Bristol, Eng., 1945, PhD, 1948; DSc, U. Edinburgh, Scotland, 1955; Dr. (hon.), U. Groningen, 1989, U. Edinburgh, 1990, Palacky U., Czechoslovakia, 1992, U. Bristol, 1997, Laval U., Que., Can., 1997, Aalborg (Denmark) U., 1999, U. d. Franche Compté, France, 1999. Rsch. asst. observatory Cambridge U., Eng., 1948-51; rsch. asst., lectr. math. and physics U. Edinburgh, 1951—53; rsch. fellow theoretical physics U. Manchester, 1954—58; vis. rsch. scientist Courant Inst. NYU, 1957; assoc. prof. optics U. Rochester, N.Y., 1959-61, prof. physics, 1961—, prof. optics, 1978—, Wilson prof. optical physics, 1987—. Guggenheim fellow, vis. prof. U. Calif., Berkeley, 1966-67; vis. prof. U. Toronto, 1974-75; disting. vis. prof. U. Ctrl. Fla., 1998, disting. provost's rsch. prof., 2002. Author: (with M. Born) Principles of Optics, 1959, 7th edit., 1999, (with L. Mandel) Optical Coherence and Quantum Optics, 1995; editor: Progress in Optics, Vol. 1-44, 1961-2003; (with L. Mandel) Selected Papers on Coherence and Fluctuations of Light, 2 vols., 1970, Selected Works of Emil Wolf with Commentary, 2001; contbr. articles to profl. jours. Recipient Marconi medal Italian Nat. Rsch. Coun., 1987, Gold medal Czechoslovak Acad. Sci., 1991, medal Union of Czechoslovak Mathematicians and Physicists, 1991, Gold medal Palacky U., Olomouc, Czechoslovakia, 1991. Fellow Optical Soc. Am. (hon., dir.-at-large 1972-74, v.p. 1976, pres. 1978, Frederic Ives medal 1977, Max Born award 1987,

Esther Hoffman Beller award 2002), Am. Phys. Soc., Brit. Inst. Physics, Am. Inst. Physics (governing bd. 1977-78), Franklin Inst. (Albert A. Michelson medal 1980), Optical Soc. India (hon.), Optical Soc. Australia (hon.). Office: U Rochester Dept Physics & Astronomy Rochester NY 14627 E-mail: ewlupus@pas.rochester.edu.

WOLF, JOAN D. education educator; b. Cannon, Del., July 9, 1934; d. Floyd Henry and Catherine (Baker) W.; m. Robert Wolf, Mar. 5, 1951 (div. 1991); children: Cynthia, Catherine, Robert. AA, Canada C.C., Redwood City, Calif., 1982; BA, San Francisco State U., 1984. Thcr. Monterey (Calif.) Salinas Schs., 1992—. Author poetry. Mem. Nat. Libr. of Poetry.

WOLF, JOAN MANGON, health occupations instructor, nursing educator; b. Dover, Ohio, June 25, 1936; d. William James and Ruth (Metcalf) M.; m. Robert Charles Wolf. Diploma in Nursing, St. Luke's Sch. Nursing, 1957; Bachelor, Kent State U., 1978; MS, U. Dayton, 1979. RN, Ohio, Fla.; cert. secondary tchr., sch. nurse, sch. guidance counselor, Ohio, Fla. Charge nurse St. Luke's Hosp., Cleve., 1957-58; staff nurse Union Hosp., Dover, Ohio, 1959-64; sch. nurse Buckeye Career Ctr., New Philadelphia, Ohio, 1980-82, health occupl. instr., 1982—98, adult edn. coord. nurse aid tng. program, 1991—98; ind. nurse provider, 1998—; sch. nurse Indian Valley Sch. Dist., 2000—. Co-author Diversified Health Occupation Lab Mmgmt Guide, 1992. Lay del. East Ohio conf. of Gnadenhutten United Meth. Ch., Lakeside, Ohio, 1991—, Order of St. Luke; vol. Am. Cancer Soc., New Philadelphia, 1960—, Am. Heart Assn., New Philadelphia, 1960—, Cmty. Bloodmobile Program, Canton, Ohio, 1980—, ARC. Recipient Rockefeller Found. grant Ohio State U., 1959; Jennings scholar, 1996-97. Mem. Buckeye Edn. Assn. (chmn., founder scholarship com. 1986), Ohio Edn. Assn., Nat. Edn. Assn., Am. Vocat. Assn., Ohio Vocat. Assn. (Disting. Svc. award 1992, Pacesetter award 1995), Alpha Tau Delta, Delta Kappa Gamma. Avocations: red cross nurse, red cross first aid and cpr instr. Office: Indian Valley Sch Dist 100 N Walnut St Gnadenhutten OH 44629

WOLF, KELLY, secondary school educator; b. Amsterdam, N.Y., Oct. 17, 1959; d. Daniel and Barbara Ann (Strazewski) Haberek; m. Sampson Little Wolf, Feb. 20, 1994. BA in English edn., Siena Coll., 1980; MS in Ednl. Psychology, Coll. St. Rose, Albany, N.Y., 1984; postgrad. holistic nutrition, Clayton Coll. Natural Health. Cert. tchr. secondary school English, N.Y.; cert. psychosynthesis practitioner. Lang. arts/writing tchr. St. Mary's Acad. of North Country, Glens Falls, N.Y., 1981-82; life skills/opportunities instr. Pvt. Industry Coun., Amsterdam, summers 1990-93; life skills instr. Tryon Resdl. Facility, Johnstown, N.Y., summer 1994; tchr. English Northville (N.Y.) Ctrl. Sch., 1983—. Counselor, holistic ednl. cons. The Wolf Within, Northville, N.Y., 1996-; mem. Site Based Mgmt. Team, North Ctrl., Northville, 1996. Author poetry. Mem. Nat. Coun. Tchrs. English, N.Y. State English Coun. (English Educator of Excellence 1997), Assn. for Advancement of Psychosynthesis. Avocations: reading, esoteric/spiritual studies. Office: 1011 Tennantville Rd Northville NY 12134-3605

WOLF, MARION ESTHER, reading educator; b. N.Y.C., Oct. 25, 1953; d. Fred and Lotte (Wilmers) W. B, Douglass Coll., New Brunswick, N.J., 1975; M, Columbia Tchrs. Coll., 1977. Cert. elem. sch. tchr., tchr. reading. Asst. tchr. Cmty. Sch., Englewood, N.J., 1976-77; reading specialist Spence Sch., N.Y.C., 1977-88; tchr. Ramapo Ridge Mid. Sch., Mahwah, N.J., 1988-93; reading tchr. Joyce Kilmer Sch., Mahwah, 1993—. Presenter readers theater workshops Spence Sch., Hewitt Sch., Assn. Tchrs. Ind. Schs. Confs., N.Y.C., 1982-88, Mahwah Schs., 1988; mem. delegation reading tchrs. Citizens Amb. Program, People-to-People, Budapest, St. Petersburg, Moscow, 1992. Trustee Temple Emeth, Teaneck, 1997—. Mem. Internat. Reading Assn., Phi Beta Kappa. Avocations: readers theater, travel. Office: Joyce Kilmer Sch 80 Ridge Rd Mahwah NJ 07430-3401

WOLF, THOMAS MARK, psychologist, educator; b. Cin., Dec. 25, 1944; s. Herbert and Ursula (Wachtel) W.; m. Valerie Barbara Winchester, Sept. 20, 1969 (dec.); 1 child, Mark Benjamin. BA, U. Cin., 1966; MA, Miami U., Oxford, Ohio, 1967; PhD, U. Waterloo, Ont., Can., 1971; fellow, St. Louis U., 1974-76. Lic. psychologist, La. From asst. to assoc. prof. SUNY, Cortland, NY, 1970-75; from assoc. to prof. La. State Health Scis. Ctr., New Orleans, 1975—. Cons. psychologist St. Bernard Group Homes, Chalmette, La., 1979-86, Cen. City Mental Health Clinic, New Orleans, 1980-89, Assoc. Cath. Charities, New Orleans, 1987-89, Child and Adolescent Mental Health Program, New Orleans, 1989-96, New Orleans Target Cities Project, 1996-99, Office Dist. Atty. New Orleans, 1999—. Contbr. chapters to books, articles to profl. jours. Mem. APA, La. Psychol. Assn., Soc. Behavioral Medicine. Democrat. Jewish. Avocations: jogging, camping, gardening. Home: 7046 Camp St New Orleans LA 70118-4808 Office: La State U Health Scis Ctr Dept Psychiatry 1542 Tulane Ave New Orleans LA 70112-2825

WOLF, WAYNE HENDRIX, electrical engineering educator; b. Washington, Aug. 12, 1958; s. Jesse David and Carolyn Josephine (Cunningham) W.; m. Nancy Jane Porter, Aug. 12, 1989. BS with distinction, Stanford U., 1980, MS, 1981, PhD, 1984. Lectr. Stanford (Calif.) U., 1984; staff mem. AT&T Bell Labs., Murray Hill, N.J., 1984-89; asst. prof. elec. engring. Princeton (N.J.) U., 1989-95, assoc. prof., 1995-98, prof., 1998—. Program chair First Internat. Workshop Hardware-Software Co-Design, 1991, gen. chair, 1993; program chair Internat. Conf. on Computer Design, 1995. Author: Modern VLSI Design, 1994, Computers as Components, 2000; co-editor: High-Level VLSI Synthesis, 1991; contbg. author: Physical Design Automation of VLSI Systems, 1989. Fellow: IEEE (editor-in-chief Transactions on VLSI Sys. 1999—2000), Assn. Computing Machinery (editor-in-chief Transactions on Embedded Computing Sys. 2001—); mem.: Am. Soc. Elec. Engrs. (Frederick E. Terman award 2003), Tau Beta Pi, Phi Beta Kappa. Avocations: bicycling, photography, films, flying. Office: Princeton U Dept Elec Engring Princeton NJ 08544-0001

WOLF, WERNER PAUL, physicist, educator; b. Vienna, Apr. 22, 1930; arrived in U.S., 1963, naturalized, 1977; s. Paul and Wilhelmina Wolf; m. Elizabeth Eliot, Sept. 23, 1954; children: Peter Paul, Mary-Anne Githa. BA, Oxford (Eng.) U., 1951, DPhil, MA, Oxford (Eng.) U., 1954; MA (hon.), Yale U., 1965. Rsch. fellow Harvard U., 1956-57; Fulbright travelling fellow, 1956-57; Imperial Chem. Industries rsch. fellow Oxford U., 1957-59, univ. demonstrator, lectr., 1959-62; lectr. New Coll., 1957-62; faculty Yale U., 1963—2001, prof. physics and applied sci., 1965-76, dir. grad. studies dept. engring. and applied sci., 1973-76, Becton prof., 1976-84, chmn. dept. engring. and applied sci., 1976-81, chmn. council engring., 1981-84, Raymond J. Wean prof. engring. and applied sci., prof. physics, 1984—2001, prof. emeritus, 2002—, dir. undergrad. studies dept. applied physics, 1987-94, dir. grad. studies coun. engring., 1989, chmn. dept. applied physics, 1990-97, chair commn. on econ. status of faculty, 1990-92, dir. ednl. affairs for engring., 1994-99. Cons. Dupont Exptl. Sta., Wilmington, Del., 1957, Hughes Aircraft, Culver City, Calif., 1957, GE Rsch. Lab., Schenectady, N.Y., 1960, Mullard Rsch. Labs., Salfords, England, 1961, IBM, Yorktown Heights, N.Y., 1962-66, Brookhaven Nat. Lab., 1966-80, GE R & D Ctr., Schenectady, 1966-93, U. Bridgeport, 1995-96, Nat. U. Singapore, 1994-96; vis. prof. Technische Hochschule, Munich, Germany, 1969; Sci. Research Council sr. vis. fellow Oxford U., 1980, 84; vis. fellow Corpus Christi Coll., 1984, 87; mem. program com. Conf. Magnetism and Magnetic Materials, 1963, 65, 86, chmn., 1968, mem. adv. com., 1964-65, 70-76, 85-88, chmn., 1972, steering com., 1970-71, conf. gen. chmn., 1971; mem. organizing, program coms. Internat. Congress on Magnetism, 1967, internat. program com., 1978-79, planning com., 1979-85; vis. physicist Brookhaven Nat. Lab., 1966, 68, vis. sr. physicist, 1970, research collaborator, 1972, 74, 75, 77, 80; mem. vis. com. dept. phys./sci. U. Del., 1980, 84, 86; mem. NATO Advanced Study Inst. Program Com., 1983, 85, internat. adv. bd. Yamada Conf. XXV on Magnetic Phase Transitions, 1990; mem. bd. visitors Fairfield U. Sch. Engring., 1996—. Editor: CASE Reports, 1988-90; contbr. papers on magnetic materials and low temperature physics. Named vis. guest fellow, Royal Soc. London, 1987; recipient sr. U.S. scientist award, Alexander von Humboldt Found, 1983, Sheffield Disting. Tchg. award, Yale U. Faculty Engring., 2000. Fellow IEEE (life), Am. Phys. Soc. (edn. com. 1977-80, program dir. Indsl. Grad. Intern Program 1978-79, chmn. fellowship com., Div. Condensed Matter Physics 1981-83); mem. Conn. Acad. Sci. and Engring., Yale Sci. and Engring. Assn. (Meritorious Svc. award 1985). Home: 37 Apple Tree Ln Woodbridge CT 06525-1258 Office: Yale U Dept Applied Physics PO Box 208284 New Haven CT 06520-8284 E-mail: werner.wolf@yale.edu.

WOLFE, CHRISTOPHER RANDALL, psychologist, researcher, educator; b. Ann Arbor, Mich., Mar. 10, 1959; s. Donald M. and Annette I (Grossman) W. BA in Philos. Analysis, Behavioral Scis., Denison U., 1981; MS in Psychology, U. Bridgeport, 1984; MS in Cognitive Psychology, U. Pitts., 1987, PhD in Cognitive Psychology, 1989. Prof. interdisciplinary studies Miami U., Oxford, Ohio, 1989—, assoc. dept. psychology, 1989—, dir. quantitative reasoning and instrnl. computing, dir. quantitative reasing and instrnl. computing, 1989—. Dir., creator websites; cons.; condr. workshops, presenter in field. Author: Learning and Teaching on the World Wide Web, 2001; contbr. articles and abstracts to profl. jours., chpts. to books; software developer Internet list owner; developer of world wide web; mem. exec. bd. Ctr. for Human Devel., Learning and Tchg. Grantee Miami U., 1990, 92, NSF, 1995, Dept. Edn., 2002, others; recipient awards for website, USA Today, 1997, Eisenhower Nat. Clearinghouse for Sci. and Math., 1997, Microsoft Internet Explorer Home Users website, 1998, Web This Week, 1999. Mem. Am. Psychol. Soc. (charter), Assn. for Integrative Studies, Psychonomic Soc. (assoc.), Soc. for Computers in Psychology (sect., treas.), Soc. for Judgment and Decision Making, Ctr. for Learning, Tech. and Assessment U. Ariz. (affiliate). Home: 333 W Sycamore St Oxford OH 45056-1134 Office: Miami U Western Coll Program Oxford OH 45056 Fax: (513) 529-5849. E-mail: WolfeCR@MUOhio.edu.

WOLFE, DEBORAH CANNON PARTRIDGE, government education consultant, educator, minister; b. Cranford, N.J. d. David Wadsworth and Gertrude (Moody) Cannon; 1 son, H. Roy Partridge. BS, N.J. City U.; MA, EdD, Tchrs. Coll., Columbia U.; postgrad., Vassar Coll., U. Pa., Union Theol. Sem., Jewish Sem. Am.; hon. doctorates, Seton Hall U., 1963, Coll. New Rochelle, 1963, Morris Brown U., 1964, Glassboro/Rowan Coll., 1965, Bloomfield Coll., 1988, Monmouth Coll., 1988, William Paterson Coll., 1988; LLD (hon.), Kean Coll., 1981; LHD (hon.), Stockton State Coll., 1982; LLD (hon.), Jersey City State Coll., 1987, Centenary Coll., William Paterson Coll., 1989, Tuskegee U., 1989, Glassboro State Coll., 1985, Tuskegee U., 1989, St. Peter's Coll., 1989, Rider Coll., 1989, Georgian Court Coll., 1990; DSc (hon.), Stevens Inst. Tech., 1991; LLD (hon.), Rutgers U., 1992, Thomas Edison Coll., 1992; DSc, U. Med. and Dentistry N.J., 1989, CUNY, 2001, LHD (hon.), 2001. Former prin., tchr. pub. schs., Cranford, also Tuskegee, Ala.; faculty Tuskegee Inst., Grambling Coll., NYU, Fordham U., U. Mich., Tex. Coll., Columbia U.; supervision and adminstrn. curriculum devel., social studies U. Ill., summers; prof. edn., affirmative action officer Queens Coll., officer; prof. edn. and children's lit. Wayne State U.; edn. chief U.S. Ho. of Reps. Com. on Edn. and Labor, 1962—. Fulbright prof. Am. lit. NYU; U.S. rep. 1st World Conf. on Women in Politics; chair non-govtl. reps. to UN (NGO/DPI exec. com.), 1983—; editl. cons. Macmillan Pub. Co.; cons. Ency. Brit.; adv. bd. Ednl. Testing Svc.; mem. State Bd. Edn., 1964-94; chairperson N.J. Bd. Higher Edn., 1967-94; mem. nat. adv. panel on vocat. edn. HEW; mem. citizen's adv. com. to Bd. Edn., Cranford; mem. Citizen's Adv. Com. on Youth Fitness, Pres.'s Adv. Com. on Youth Fitness, White House Conf. Edn., 1955, White House Conf. Aging, 1960, White House Conf. Civil Rights, 1966, White House Conf. on Children, 1970, Adv. Coun. for Innovations in Edn.; v.p. Nat. Alliance for Safer Cities; cons. Vista Corps, OEO; vis. scholar Princeton Theol. Sem., 1989—; chairperson Human Rels. Coun., N.J., 1994—; vis. prof. U. Ill., U. N.C., Wayne State U.; theologian-in-residence Duke U.; mem. trustee bd. Sci. Svc.; mem. N.J. Commn. on Holocaust Edn., 1996. Contbr. articles to ednl. publs. Bd. dirs. Cranford Welfare Assn., Cmty. Ctr., 1st Bapt. Ch., Cranford Cmty. Ctr. Migratory Laborers, Hurlock, Md.; trustee Sci. Svc., Seton Hall U., bd. regents; mem. Pub. Broadcasting Authority, N.J. Commn. on Holocaust Edn., 1996—, Tuskegee U. Alumni, 1995; mem. N.J. Conv. of Progressive Baptists, 1995, v.p., 1996—, pres., 1999-2001; parliamentarian Progressive nat. Bapt. Conv.; sec. Kappa Delta Pi Ednl. Found., nat. bd. dirs., 2001—, laureate rep.; mem. adv. com. Elizabeth and Arthur Schlesinger Libr., Radcliffe Coll., trustee Edn. Devel. Ctr., 1965—; assoc. min. 1st Bapt. Ch.; chair Human Rels. Commn., Monroe, 1995; v.p., then pres. N.J. Conv. Progressive Bapt., 1996—; parliamentarian Progressive Nat. Baptist Conv.; mem. exec. com. Nat. Coun. Agrl. Rsch., Ext. and Teaching, 1997—; mem. N.J. Holocaust Commn., 1996— Named N.J. Educator of Yr., 2003; named to, NABSE Hall of Fame; recipient Woman of Yr. award, Delta Beta Zeta, Morgan State Coll., Medal of Honor, DAR, 1990, Disting. Svc. medal, Nat. Top Ladies of Distinction, 1991, Disting. Svc. award, Nat. Assn. State Bds. Edn., 1992, 1994, Disting. Svc. to Edn. award, N.J. Commn. on Status of Women, 1993, Svc. to Children award, N.J. Assn. Sch. Psychologists, 1993, Disting. Medal award, U. Medicine and Dentistry N.J., Union Coll., citation, N.J. State Coun. on Vacat. Edn., 1994, N.J. State Bd. Edn., 1994, Svc. award for 50 Yrs., Cranford Bd. Edn., 1995, Women Who Count award, Zonta Internat., 1996, Minister's Appreciation award, Progressive Nat. Bapt. Conv., 1996, Edn. award, Tuskegee U. Alumni, 1996, Women Who Make a Difference award, Zonta Internat., 1995, Dr. George Washington Carver award, Pa. Acad. Sci., 1998, Lifetime Svc. award, William Patterson U., 1999, Triumph award, N.J. Dept. State, 2001. Mem.: NAACP (Medal of Honor 1994), AAUP, AAUW (nat. edn. chmn.), NCCJ, NEA (life), ASCD (rev. coun.), AAAS (chmn. tchr. edn. com.), LWV, N.J. Conv. of Progressive Bapts. (1st woman elected pres. 1999), Alliance Black Clergywomen (pres.), Nat. Assn. State Univs. and Colls. and Land Grant Colls. (mem. exec. bd. 1996, mem. coun. on agr. ext. and tchg.), Ch. Women United (UN rep., mem. exec. com.), Internat. Platform Assn., Am. Coun. Edn. (mem. commn. fed. rels.), Nat. Soc. Study Edn., Internat. Assn. Childhood Edn., Am. Acad. Polit. and Social Sci., Comparative Edn. Soc., Internat. Reading Assn., Fellowship So. Churchmen, Am. Tchrs. Assn., N.Y. Tchrs. Assn., Nat. Assn. Black Educators (pres.), Nat. Assn. Negro Bus. and Profl. Women (chmn. spkrs. bur., Nat. Achievement award 1958), Nat. Panhellenic Coun. (dir.), Am. Coun. Human Rights (v.p.), Coun. Nat. Orgns. Children and Youth, N.J. Commn. Holocaust Edn., N.J. Holocaust Commn., N.J. Fedn. Colored Women's Clubs, UN Assn.-USA (mem. exec. com.). Home: 4102 Monroe Village Monroe Township NJ 08831

WOLFE, EDWARD WILLIAM, II, music educator, composer; b. Albuquerque, Sept. 24, 1946; s. Edward William and Mary Ellen (Gabriele) W.; m. Nancy Jean Brown, Aug. 16, 1980. B in Music Edn., U. N.Mex., 1968, MA, 1973. Cert. tchr., N.Mex., Calif. Tchr. Grant Jr. High Sch., Albuquerque, 1970-75, Manzano High Sch., Albuquerque, 1974-75, Hoover Mid. Sch., Albuquerque, 1975-77, San Dimas (Calif.) High Sch., 1977-85; instr. music Calif. Poly. State U., Pomona, Calif., 1984; tchr. Bonita High Sch., LaVerne, Calif., 1985-89, Lone Hill Mid. Sch. and Feeders, San Dimas, Calif., 1989—2001, San Dimas High Sch., 2001—. Tchr. Hummingbird Music Camp, Jemez, N.Mex., 1970-76; cons. BUSD, San Dimas, 1980—; presenter jazz edn. SCSBOA fall conf., 1995. Author: The Language of Music, 1974, rev. 1993; composer Quartet for Horns, 1967, Oboe Sonata, 1967, Trio for Flute, Violin and Horn, 1968, Caverna, 1972, Quintet for Brass, 1993, numerous compositions and jazz arrangements, 1972—. Mem. Task Force on Mid. Sch. Reform, 1990. Recipient award Juvenile Justice Commn. City of San Dimas, 1984, 93; named to BUSD Hall of Fame, 1991. Mem. Music Educators Nat. Conf. (adjudicator 1969-77, 80—, v.p. dist. 7 1972, pres. 1975-76), Calif. Music Educators Assn. (task force on mid. sch. reform 1990, Outstanding Music Edn. cert. 1991), Nat. Assn. Jazz Educators (adjudicator 1980—, treas. N.Mex. chpt. 1972), Calif. Tchrs. Assn., So. Calif. Sch. Band and Orch. Assn., Bonita United Teaching Assn., Phi Mu Alpha. Avocation: model railroader. Home: 817 S Dumaine Ave San Dimas CA 91773-3808

WOLFE, ELIZABETH ANNE, elementary education educator; b. Washington, July 26, 1954; d. William Arthur and Eleanore Elizabeth (Smith) Walsh; m. Christopher James Wolfe, Feb. 10, 1979; children: Daniel James Wolfe, Jeffrey Taylor Wolfe. AA, St. Petersburg Jr. Coll., Clearwater, Fla., 1975; BA, U. Md., 1977. Cert. elem., early childhood tchr., Fla. Kindergarten tchr. High Point Elem. Sch., Clearwater, 1978-83; 1st grade tchr. Curlew Creek Elem. Sch., Palm Harbor, Fla., 1983-87, 3rd grade tchr. math., social sci., 1987-89, 1st grade tchr., 1989-90, 5th grade lang. tchr., 1990-92, 4th grade lang. tchr., 1992-94, 5th grade self-contained classroom tchr., 1994-2000; 4th grade self-contained classroom tchr. Belcher Elem. Sch., Clearwater, Fla., 2000—. Cub Scout den leader Boy Scouts Am., Clearwater, 1991; coach Odyssey of the Mind, Curlew Creek Elem. Sch., 1991-97. Recipient sci. fiction reading, writing grant Fla. Coun. Elem. Edn., 1992, sci. communication grant Dept. Instrnl. Tech., 1992, newspapers in edn. grant Teach for Excellence Edn. Found., 1990, mini-economy grant Teach for Excellence Edn. Found., 1988; winner Odyssey of the Mind State Championship, 1997; named Tchr. of Yr., Pinellas County Edn. Found., 1997. Mem. PTA, Pinellas Coun. Social Studies (elem. rep. 1990-92), Pinellas Classroom Tchrs. Assn., Pinellas Reading Coun. Avocations: tae kwon do (black belt), roller blading, tap dance, computering.

WOLFE, ELLEN DARLENE, school librarian, elementary school educator; b. Mattoon, Ill., Dec. 16, 1952; d. Floyd Dale and Irma Jane (Hensley) Robinson; m. Walter Ray Wolfe, Mar. 12, 1994; children: Gregory David, William Scott, Joseph Dean, Brian Matthew, Joshua Paul. BS, Ind. State U., 1987. Cert. elem. educator, Ill. Reading tchr. Marshall (Ill.) Community Dist. 2, 1987-91; law libr. Robinson (Ill.) Correctional Ctr., 1991-94; libr. Palestine (Ill.) Cmty. Unit Sch. Dist. # 3, 1994—. Libr. City of Marshall, 1986—; dir. summer camp Clark County Handicapped Assn., Marshall, 1988—; law libr. Robinson Correctional Ctr., 1991. Coord. Jr. youth group St. Mary's Cath. Ch. Mem. Correctional Edn. Assn., Home Ext. Club, Kappa Delta Pi, Phi Delta Kappa. Roman Catholic. Home: 18993 E River Rd Palestine IL 62451-2430 Office: Robinson Correctional Ctr PO Box 1000 Robinson IL 62454-0919

WOLFE, EVA AGNES, retired educator; b. Stockport, Iowa, Jan. 13, 1910; d. Marion J. and Hattie Florence (Webber) Munson; m. Donald Earl Wolfe, 1937; 1 child, Sharon Dawn. BA, Iowa Wesleyan U., 1951; student, U. Minn., 1928-89, State U. Iowa, 1928, 29, 30. Tchr. rural schs. Van Buren County, Stockport, 1929-30, grade sch. tchr. Keosauqua, Iowa, 1930-37, Pleasant Lawn Consol. Sch., Mt. Pleasant, Iowa, 1946-50; tchr. home econs., English Danville (Iowa) Consol. High Sch., 1951-60; tchr. home econs. West Burlington (Iowa) Pub. Schs., 1961-74; ret., 1974. Mem. Am. Assn. Ret. Persons. Mem. DAR, AAUW, Henry County Ret. Tchrs. (pres. 1976-78), Daus of Nile, Order of Eastern Star, White Shrine, Alpha Xi Delta. Democrat. Methodist. Avocations: music, reading, sewing, dancing, exercise. Office: c/o Harold Munson 3199 Wheat Blvd Lockridge IA 52635-8054

WOLFE, GEORGE CROPPER, retired private school educator, artist, writer; b. New Orleans, Sept. 6, 1933; s. Howard Edward and Amaryllis (Brannen) Wolfe; m. Catherine Vasterling, June 2, 1955; children: David, Michael, Philip. BFA, La. State U., 1956; MEd, U. New Orleans, 1972, MS in Urban Planning, 1975; postgrad., Tex. Tech U., Junction, 1986-93, Northwestern State U., La. Cert. tchr. art, social studies La. Elem. tchr. Live Oak Manor Sch., Waggaman, La., 1962-65; tchr. art Isidore Newman Sch., New Orleans, 1965-96; adj. prof. art Northwestern State U., Natchitoches, La., 1997-99; co-owner design studio Wolf Patrol Prodns. Author: (video) Sculpture in Motion, 2000 (Silver Telly award, 2001), 3-D Wizardry (Telly award, 1996), Papier Maché Plaster and Foam; contbr. articles to profl. jours.; one-man shows include Hanchley Gallery, Northwestern U., 1999, exhibited in group shows at New Alexandria (La.) Mus. Art, commn. sculpture, Echo Totem, Alexandria Mus. Art, 1998, Alex the Red, 1998, Hands Supporting Hands, Wesley Found., 1999, commn. life size puppets, Two by Two, Northwestern State U. Summer Theatre, 1999. With USCG, 1956—58. Mem.: La. Art Edn. Assn. (pres. 1978—79), Nat. Art Edn. Assn. (La. Art Educator of the Yr. 1990, Ret. Art Educator of the Yr. 2000—01, Victor Lowenfeld award 2002), Phi Delta Kappa (v.p., Rsch. award 1996), Kappa Delta Pi. Home: 342 Jefferson St Natchitoches LA 71457-4382

WOLFE, GERALDINE, administrator; b. Monticello, Ark., Mar. 29, 1944; d. John Wesley and Hazeline (Daniels) Fisher; 1 child, Arin. BA, Keuka Coll., 1965; MA, Mt. Holyoke Coll., 1967; MSEd, Elmira Coll., 1981; cert. ednl. adminstrn. SUNY-Brockport, 1985; PhD Cornell U., 1988. Tchr. biology and health Corning Sch. Dist., N.Y., 1967-90; asst. prof. SUNY, Plattsburgh, 1990-93; adminstr. Saranac Lake Ctrl. Sch. Dist., 1993-96; asst. supt. Schenectady City Sch. Dist., 1996-99; supt. Catskill (N.Y.) Ctrl. Sch. Dist., 1999—. Mem. Mid. States Evaluation Team, 1985; chmn. bd. trustees Friendship Bapt. Ch., Corning, 1984-90; bd. dirs. Hamilton Hill Arts Ctr., 1996-99, Oslo scholar U. Oslo, 1964, Coop. Ext., Common Ground of Catkill, Workforce Investment Act, Youth Coun., Grene County Collubirative Community Partnership for Youth; Mem. N.Y. State Profl. Health Educators Assn., Women in Ednl. Adminstrn., LWV, Sigma Xi, Sigma Lambda Sigma. Club: Cosmopolitan (officer 1979-81) (Elmira). Mem. allocations com. United Way, 1982-90; mem. edn. com. Planned Parenthood, 1984-90. Mem. NAACP, ASCD, Nat. Assn. Sec. Sch. Prins., Am. Assn. Sch. Adminstrs., Nat. Alliance Black Sch. Educators, N.Y.S. Assn. for Computers and Technologies in Edn., N.Y.S. Assn. Compensatory Educators, N.Y. State Coun. Sch. Supts., Cornell Edn. Soc., Jr. League of Elmira, Rotary Club of Catskill, Capital District Assn. of Women Adminstrs., Delta Kappa Gamma, Phi Delta Kappa. Avocations: tennis; cross countryskiing; travel; piano; reading. Home: 7 Forest Hills Dr Elmira NY 14905-1141 Office: Catskill Ctrl Sch Dist 343 W Main St Catskill NY 12414-1621

WOLFE, JOHN RAYMOND, education educator; b. Abilene, Kans., May 17, 1955; s. Raymond Edward and Frances Marie (Berry) W.; m. Nancy Lynn Isley, Aug. 25, 1979; children: Natalie, Lauren, Tyler. AA, Donnelly Coll., Kansas City, Kans., 1975; BS, Benedictine Coll., 1976; MS, Kans. State U., 1978; PhD, Bowling Green State U., 1995. Lic. tchr., Kans. Instr./coord. Happy Hearts Inc./Highland C.C., Atchison, Kans., 1977-79, adminstr., 1978-79; asst. dir. summer ESL program Acad. Mt. St. Scholastica, Atchison, 1980, dir. summer ESL program, 1981-83; dir. Ctr. for Gen. Studies Benedictine Coll., Atchison, 1980-86, dir. continuing edn., 1983-86; dir. learning resources/adj. asst. prof. edn. Wright State U., Celina, Ohio, 1986—2000; dir. academic & instructional services Wright State U. - Lake Campus. Lectr./cons. Learning Ctr., Benedictine Coll., 1979. Mem., sec. Coll. Cmty. Arts Coun., Celina, 1995—; mem. Adult Edn. Adv. Bd., St. Mary's Ohio, 1987, 88, 89; judge, moderator, rm. capt. Scholastic Bowl, Celina, 1987—; judge Kiwanis scholarship, 1991; judge Midwest Electric, St. Mary's, 1994-96. Title III grantee, 1982, Enrollment Planning Coun. grantee, others; named to Outstanding Young Men of Am., 1984. Mem. Nat. Assn. for Developmental Edn., Am. Assn. Higher Edn., Ohio Assn. for Developmental Edn., Delta Epsilon Sigma. Democrat. Roman Catholic. Avocations: travel, gardening, art. Office: 7600 State Route 703 Celina OH 45822-2952

WOLFE, LILYAN, special education clinical educator; b. N.Y.C., Mar. 17, 1937; d. Alexander and Molly (Springer) Aven; m. Richard Wolfe, June 8, 1957; children: Brian, Stacey. BBA, CUNY, 1957; postgrad., Hunter Coll., 1962-65; MA, NYU, 1982, postgrad., 1983-85. Cert. tchr., N.J., N.Y.; cert. tchr. of handicapped, N.J. Tchr. PS 101 Manhattan, N.Y.C., 1962-65, Hazlet

Twp. (N.J.) Schs., 1976-81; tchr. at risk mother-toddler program U. Medicine and Dentistry N.J., Newark, 1982-85, tchr. therapeutic nursery, 1982-84, head tchr., 1984-97; ret., 1997. Recipient cert. appreciation, Essex County Child Care Coalition, Newark, 1992. Mem. Nat. Assn. Edn. Young Children, NYU Alumni Assn., Kappa Delta Pi. Avocations: piano, gourmet cooking, travel, reading. Home: 1629 Starling Dr Sarasota FL 34231-9121

WOLFE, MARTHA, elementary education educator; b. Centralia, Ill., Apr. 16, 1944; d. Elmer A. and Dorothy L. (Stonecipher) Krietemeyer; children: Kimberly S., Debora L. BS, So. Ill. U., 1967, MS, 1973, adminstrv. cert., 1987. Cert. elem. tchr., K-12 adminstrn., Ill. Tchr. Title I reading, dir., tech. coord. Cobden Unit Sch. Dist., Ill. Presenter in field. Recipient Master Tchr. award Gov. of Ill., 1984. Mem. NEA, Internat. Reading Assn., So. Ill. Reading Assn. (pres., v.p., bd. dirs.), Delta Kappa Gamma (Lambda State scholar 1986). Home: 106 Evergreen Dr Anna IL 62906-2122

WOLFE, MINDY RENÉ, early childhood special education educator; b. Norton, Kans., Dec. 10, 1963; d. Roger L. and Celia Dee (Boxberger) W. Student, Colby C.C., 1982-83; BSBA, Ft. Hays State U., 1986, BS in Elem. Edn., 1988. Cert. tchr., Kans.; endorsement in early childhood spl. edn. Associated Colls. Cen. Kans. Tutor Ind. Teaching Svc., Norton, 1989-90; substitute tchr. Unified Sch. Dist. 211, Norton, 1989-90, Unified Sch. Dist. 295, Jennings, Kans., 1989-90, Kiddie Kampus Pre-sch., Norton, 1990; lead tchr. Jolly Junction Child Care Ctr., Lindsborg, Kans., 1990-92; policy adviser, toddler program dir. Children's Ctr., Lindsborg, 1992-93; dir. Newcomer Day Care Ctr., Marquette, Kans., 1993; asst. dir. Children's Ctr., Lindsborg, 1993-94; coord. early childhood spl. needs N.W. Kans. Ednl. Svc. Ctr., Oakley, 1994-95; head start tchr. Oakley, Kans., 1995-98, N.W. Kans. Ednl. Svc. Ctr., Oakley, 1995-98; early childhood spl. edn. tchr. Smith Center, Kans., 1998—. Mem. Kans.-NEA, Nat. Assn. Edn. Young Children, Coun. for Exceptional Children, Kans. Head Start Assn., PEO (officer), Beta Sigma Phi (pres. Kappa Xi chpt. 2000-01). Methodist. Avocations: crafts, fashion sewing, stationary bicycle, piano, church choir. Home: 115 E 3d St Smith Center KS 66967-2008

WOLFE, STEVEN ALBERT, secondary education educator; b. Des Moines, Iowa, Feb. 24, 1949; s. Edward Jr. and Necia Lee (Hill) W.; m. Nina Joyce Wagner, Apr. 25, 1973; children: Ivan Angus, Rebekah, Nina Ellen, Rainbow, Tamara, Ross, Rosemary. BS, Brigham Young U., 1974; Masters Arts Teaching, Alaska Pacific U., 1988. Cert. tchr., Idaho, Alaska. Tchr. North Gem High Sch., Bancroft, Idaho, 1974-76, Homer (Alaska) Mid. Sch., 1976-77, Homer Jr. High Sch., 1977-85, Homer High Sch., 1985—. Coach wrestling Homer High Sch., 1976-91, coach football, 1983-90. Author: Comprehensive Index to Wrestling Rules, 1991. Scoutmaster troop 365 Boy Scouts Am., Homer, 1988—; coach state championship wrestling teams Alaska Sch. Activities Assn., 1982, 85, 86. Named Nat. Coach of Yr., Franklin Inst., 1988. Mem. Alaska Wrestling Coaches Assn. (pres. 1989-91, inductee Hall of Fame 1990), Kenai Penninsula Wrestling Ofcls. Assn. (pres. 1992—). Mem. Lds Ch. Avocations: amateur wrestling (4 gold medals at AAU Grant Nats. in 1995), genealogy, landscaping. Home: 5007 Clover Ln Homer AK 99603-8116 Office: Homer High Sch 600 E Fairview Ave Homer AK 99603-7678

WOLFF, CHRISTIAN, composer, music and classics educator; b. Nice, France, Mar. 8, 1934; AB, Harvard U., 1955, MA, 1957, PhD, 1963. Instr. classics Harvard U., 1962-65, asst. prof., 1965-71; assoc. prof. classics, comparative lit. and music Dartmouth Coll., Hanover, N.H., 1971-78, prof. classics and music, 1978-80, Strauss prof. music and classics, 1980—; emeritus, 1999. Vis. composer Deutscher Akademischer Austauschdient, Berlin, 1974; vis. prof. classics Harvard U., 1980 Author: Ueber form, 1960, Orestes, In Euripides: A Collection of Critical Essays, 1968, On Political Texts and New Music, SONUS, 1980, Euripides in Ancient Writers: Greece and Rome, 1982; CUES, collected writings and interviews on music, 1998, Euripides, Hercules, Introduction and notes, 2001; contbr. articles to profl. jours.; compositions recorded on Hat Art CD, 1994, 96, Mode CD, 1995, 98, 99, 2002, 03.; numerous CD recordings, Timescraper, 1996, Content, 1998, 2003, Syr, 1999, Etcetera, 2000, Tzadik, 2001, Matchless, 2002. Loeb bequest grantee Harvard U., 1967-68; fellow Ctr. Hellenic Studies, Washington, 1970-71; recipient Music award Am. Acad. and Nat. Inst. Arts and Letters, 1974 Office: Dept of Music Dartmouth College Hanover NH 03755

WOLFF, CHRISTOPH JOHANNES, music historian, educator; b. Solingen, Germany, May 24, 1940; came to U.S., 1970; s. Hans Walter and Annemarie (Halstenbach) W.; m. Barbara Mahrenholz, Aug. 28, 1964; children: Katharina, Dorothea, Stephanie. Ed., U. Berlin, 1960-63, U. Freiburg, Germany, 1963-65; Dr. Phil., U. Erlangen, Germany, 1966; MusD, New Eng. Conservatory, 1999; LHD, Valparaiso U., 2002. Lectr. U. Erlangen, 1966-69; asst. prof. U. Toronto, Ont., Can., 1968-70; assoc. prof. musicology Columbia U., 1970-73, prof., 1973-76; prof. musicology Harvard U., 1976—, William Powell Mason prof., 1985—2002, Adams Univ. prof., 2002—, dept. chmn., 1980-88, 90-91. Vis. prof. Princeton U., 1973, 75; hon. prof. U. Freiburg, Germany, 1990—; acting dir. Harvard U. Libr., 1991—92; dir. Bach Archive, Leipzig, Germany, 2001—; dean Grad. Sch. Arts and Scis., 1992—2000. Author: Der Stile Antico in der Musik J.S. Bachs, 1968, The String Quartets of Haydn, Mozart and Beethoven, 1980, Bach Compendium, 7 vols., 1986—89, Bach: Essays on His Life and Music, 1991, Mozart's Requiem, 1994, The World of Bach Cantatas, 1997, The New Bach Reader, 1998, Johann Sebastian Bach: The Learned Musician, 2000; contbr. articles to profl. jours.; editor: Bach-Jahrbuch, 1974—, critical edits. of music by Scheidt, Buxtehude, Bach, Mozart and Hindemith. Recipient Dent medal, Royal Mus. Assn., London, 1978, Humboldt prize, Alexander von Humboldt Found., 1996. Fellow: Am. Philos. Soc., Am. Acad. Arts and Scis.; mem.: Gesellschaft fuer Musikforschung, Saxon Acad. of Scis. (Leipzig), Am. Musicol. Soc., Internat. Musicol. Soc. Home: 182 Washington St Belmont MA 02478-3560 Office: Harvard U Dept Music Cambridge MA 02138-5723

WOLFF, CYNTHIA GRIFFIN, humanities educator, author; b. St. Louis, Aug. 20, 1936; d. James Thomas and Eunice (Heyn) Griffin; m. Robert Paul Wolff, June 9, 1962 (div. 1986); children— Patrick Gideon, Tobias Barrington; m. Nicholas J. White, May 21, 1988. BA, Radcliffe Coll., 1958; PhD, Harvard U., 1965. Asst. prof. English Manhattanville Coll., Purchase, N.Y., 1968-70; asst. prof. English U. Mass., Amherst, 1971-74, assoc. prof., 1974-76, prof., 1976-80; prof. humanities MIT, Cambridge, 1980-85, Class of 1922 prof. lit. and writing, 1985—. Exec. com. for Am. lit. MLA, 1979-81; mem. selection bd. Literary Classics Am., 1981—; exec. bd. for fgn. grants Am. Council Learned Socs., 1981-84. Author: (literary criticism) Samuel Richardson, 1972, (literary biography) A Feast of Words: The Triumph of Edith Wharton, 1977, 2d edit., 1995, Emily Dickinson, 1986; bd. editors Am. Quar., 1979-84. Grantee AAUW, 1964-65, NEH, 1975-76, 1983-84, 97-98; Am. Council Learned Socs., 1984-85, Guggenheim, 1998—. Mem. Am. Studies Assn.

WOLFF, SIDNEY CARNE, astronomer, observatory administrator; b. Sioux City, Iowa, June 6, 1941; d. George Albert and Ethel (Smith) Carne; m. Richard J. Wolff, Aug. 29, 1962 BA, Carleton Coll., 1962, DSc (hon.), 1985; PhD, U. Calif., Berkeley, 1966. Postgrad. research fellow Lick Obs. Santa Cruz, Calif., 1969; asst. astronomer U. Hawaii, Honolulu, 1967-71, assoc. astronomer, 1971-76; astronomer, assoc. dir. Inst. Astronomy, Honolulu, 1976-83, acting dir., 1983-84; dir. Kitt Peak Nat. Obs., Tucson, 1984-87, Nat. Optical Astronomy Observatories, 1987-2001; dir. Gemini Project Gemini 8-Meter Telescopes Project, 1992-94; astronomer, project scientist Large Synoptic Survey Telescope, 2001—. Pres. SOAR Inc., 1999—; project scientist Large Synoptic Survey Telescope, 2002—. Author: The A-Type Stars--Problems and Perspectives, 1983, (with others) Exploration of the Universe, 1987, Realm of the Universe, 1988, Frontiers of Astronomy, 1990, Voyages Through the Universe, 1996, 2nd edit., 2003, Voyages to the Planets, 1999, 2nd edit., 2003, Voyages to the Stars and Galaxies, 1999, 2nd edit., 2003; founding editor: Astronomy Edn. Rev., 2002; contbr. articles to profl. jours. Trustee Carleton Coll., 1989—, chair acad. affairs com., 1995—. Rsch. fellow Lick Obs. Santa Cruz, Calif., 1967; recipient Nat. Meritorious Svc. award NSF, 1994. Fellow Royal Astronical Soc.; mem. Astron. Soc. Pacific (pres. 1984-86, bd. dirs. 1979-85), Am. Astron. Soc. (coun. 1983-86, pres.-elect 1991, pres. 1992-94). Office: Nat Optical Astronomy Obs PO Box 26732 950 N Cherry Ave Tucson AZ 85719-4933

WOLFGANG, JAMES STEPHEN, history educator, minister; b. Indpls., Dec. 8, 1948; s. James Harold and Alma Jean (Cowgill) W.; m. Bette Ashworth, June 5, 1969; children: Lesley Dawn, Lindsay Brooke. BA, Ind. Wesleyan U., 1970; MA, Butler U., 1975; MDiv, So. Bapt. Theol. Sem., 1978; MA, Vanderbilt U., 1990; PhD, U. Ky., 1997. Ordained min., Ch. of Christ, 1969. Minister Expwy. Ch. of Christ, Louisville, 1975-79, Danville (Ky.) Ch. of Christ, 1979-98; instr. history U. Ky., Lexington, 1994-97. Vis. prof. Internat. Christian U., Vienna, Austria, 1990; vis. instr. Redlands Coll. Brisbane, Australia, 1993; instr. history Lexington C.C., 1993—. Mem. editl. adv. bd. Louisville Courier-Jour., 1994-95; news anchor Sta. WUKY-FM, 1994—; contbr. articles to profl. jours. Recipient Grosswirth-Salny award Mensa Ednl. Rsch. Found., 1990, Lester London award, 1991. Mem. Am. Hist. Assn., Am. Soc. Ch. History, Orgn. Am. Historians, So. Hist. Assn., Mensa (Bluegrass chpt., bd. govs. 1990-94), Hospice (Heritage chpt., bd. dirs. 1993—, v.p. 1995-98, pres. 1998-99). Home: 803 Sunset Dr Danville KY 40422-1156 Office: U Ky/Lexington CC 227 Moloney Bldg Lexington KY 40506-0001

WOLFGANG, JERALD IRA, economic development educator; b. Niagara Falls, N.Y., Apr. 8, 1938; s. Louis and Rose (Jochnowitz) W.; m. Joan Barbara Winter, Aug. 18, 1968; 1 child, Lynn Jessica. BS in Edn., SUNY, Buffalo, 1962, MS in Adminstrn., 1966. Tchr. Niagara Falls Schs., 1962-68; asst. to Gov. Rockefeller Albany, N.Y., 1968-71; dep. commr. for State of N.Y. Dept. Motor Vehicles, 1971-75; with N.Y. State Senate, Buffalo, 1976; spl. asst. to minority leader N.Y. State Assembly Office of Minority Leader, Buffalo, 1977-83; dir. Western N.Y. Edn. Ctr. for Econ. Devel., Buffalo, 1983—. Bd. dirs., Southern Tier West Regional Planning and Devel.; adv. bd., State of N.Y. Small Bus. Assn., Western N.Y. Council for Edn. and Employment Equity, Western N.Y. Economic Devel. Corp., N.Y. State Economic. Devel. Corp., Western N.Y. Internat. Trade Council, Inc. Active Niagara County Am. Cancer Soc., Niagara Univ. Council, Mt. St. Mary's Hosp., Lewiston, Camp Nia-Y, Lewiston-Porter All Sports Scholarship Dinner; chmn. Niagara County Republican Com, 1978-86; sec. N.Y. Republican State Com, 1982-88; chmn. bd. dirs. A Festival of Lights, 1997-2000; sec. bd. dirs. St. Mary's Hosp., 1997-98; bd. vice chmn. St. Mary's Hosp. Found.; chmn. bd. dirs. United Way, 2000—; apptd. mem. Work Investment Bd. Niagara County, 2000. Named Rep. of Year, 1977, Man of Year, Niagara Taxpayers League, Inc., 1987, Lewiston Kiwanian of Yr., 1999; recipient Top Hat award for Outstanding Svc. to Cmty., WHLD Radio and Niagara Frontier Svcs., 1978, Disting. Achievement award, SUNY Buffalo United U. Professions, Pres.'s award for outstanding club leadership, Lewiston Kiwanis, 1979, Pathfinder award, 1999, Leader of Year award, Leadership Niagara, 2001. Mem. Am. Vocational Assn., Assn. of Vocational Edn. Administrators of N.Y. State, Greater Buffalo C. of C., Help and Instruct Residents in Edn., Nat. Assn. of Small Bus. Internat. Trade Educators., N.Y. Assn. for Continuing Community Edn., N.Y. State Council on Vocational Edn., Niagara County Labor Mgmt. Council, Niagara Frontier Industry Edn. Council, Lewiston Kiwanis, Niagara Falls County Club. Republican. Jewish. Avocations: golf, racquetball. Home: 4267 Lower River Rd Youngstown NY 14174-9753 Office: W NY Edn Ctr Econ Devel 355 Harlem Rd West Seneca NY 14224-1825 E-mail: jwolfgan@eriel.wnyric.org.

WOLFINGER, RAYMOND EDWIN, political science educator; b. San Francisco, June 29, 1931; s. Raymond Edwin and Hilda (Holm) W.; m. Barbara Kaye, Aug. 7, 1960; 1 son, Nicholas Holm. AB, U. Calif.-Berkeley, 1951; MA, U. Ill., 1955; PhD, Yale U., 1961. Asst. prof. polit. sci. Stanford (Calif.) U., Calif., 1961-66; assoc. prof. Stanford U., Calif., 1966-70, prof., 1970-71, U. Calif.-Berkeley, 1971—, Heller prof. polit. sci., 1995—. Dir. U. Calif. Data Archive and Tech. Assistance, 1980-92; chmn. bd. overseers Nat. Election Studies, Ann Arbor, Mich., 1982-86 Author: The Politics of Progress, 1974, (with others) Dynamics of American Politics, 1976, 80, (with Steven J. Rosenstone) Who Votes, 1980, (with others) The Myth of the Independent Voter, 1992; mem. editorial bd. Brit. Jour. Polit. Sci., 1980-84, Am. Polit. Sci. Rev., 1985-88. Bd. dirs. S.W. Voter Rsch. Inst., San Antonio, 1988-96, Consortium of Social Sci. Assns., 1987-93, pres. 1988-90. 1st lt. U.S. Army, 1951-53. Fellow Ctr. for Advanced Study in Behavioral Scis., 1960-61; Guggenheim fellow, 1965; Ford Found. faculty research fellow, 1970-71 Fellow Am. Acad. Arts and Scis. (chair Class III membership com. 1998-99); mem. Am. Polit. Sci. Assn. (sec. 1981-82), AAUP (council 1981-84), Western Polit. Sci. Assn. (v.p. 1988-89, pres. 1989-90). Democrat. Office: U Calif Dept Polit Sci Berkeley CA 94720-1950

WOLFMAN, BERNARD, lawyer, educator; b. Phila., Pa., July 8, 1924; s. Nathan and Elizabeth (Coff) W.; m. Zelda Bernstein, Dec. 25, 1948 (dec. Oct. 1973); children: Jonathan L., Brian S., Dina A.; m. Toni A. Grotta, June 12, 1977. AB, U. Pa., 1946, JD, 1948; LLD (hon.), Jewish Theol. Sem., 1971, Capital U., 1990. Bar: Pa. 1949, Mass. 1976. Mem. law firm Wolf, Block, Schorr & Solis-Cohen, Phila., 1948-63; prof. law U. Pa. Law Sch., 1963-76, dean, 1970-75, Kenneth W. Gemmill prof. tax law and tax policy, 1973-76, chmn. Faculty Senate, 1969-70; Fessenden prof. law Harvard U., 1976—. Vis. prof. Stanford U. Law Sch., summer 1982, NYU Law Sch., 1987-88; Irvine lectr. Cornell U. Law Sch., 1980; Halle lectr. Case Western Res. U. Law Sch., 1983; Cleve. State U. Sch. Law; Sugarman lectr., 1989; Altheimer lectr. U. Ark. Sch. Law, Little Rock, 1994; Polisher lectr. Dickinson Coll. Law, 1998; mem. editl. bds. law divsn. Aspen Law & Bus. (formerly Little Brown & Co.), Jour. Corp. Taxation; gen. counsel AAUP, 1966-68, mem. coun., 1979-82; prof.-in-residence tax divsn. Dept. Justice, 2003; cons. to ind. counsel Lawrence E. Walsh (Iran-Contra prosecution), 1987-89; mem. adv. group to commr. internal revenue, 1966-67; cons. tax policy U.S. Treasury Dept., 1963-68, 77-80; chmn. Task Force Univ. Governance, U. Pa., 1968-70; mem. steering com. IRS project Adminstrv. Conf. U.S., 1974-80; vice chmn. bd. advs. NYU-IRS Continuing Profl. Edn. Project, 1981-85; mem. legal activities policy bd. Tax Analysts, 1974—; mem. exec. com. Fed. Tax Inst. New Eng., 1976—. Author: Federal Income Taxation of Corporate Enterprise, 1971, 3d edit., 1990; (with J. Holden and D. Schenk) Ethical Problems in Federal Tax Practice, 1981, 3dedit., 1995, (with J. Holden and K. Harris) Standards of Tax Practice, 1991, 5th edit. 1999; sr. author: Dissent Without Opinion: The Behavior of Justice William O. Douglas in Federal Tax Cases, 1975; contbr. articles to profl. jours. Adv. com. Commn. Philanthropy and Pub. Needs, 1973-75; mem. Phila. regional council Pa. Gov.'s Justice Commn., 1973-75; trustee Found. Center, NYC, 1970-76, Fedn. Jewish Agys. Greater Phila., 1968-74; bd. dirs. Phila. Lawyers Com. Civil Rights Under Law, 1970-74, Phila. Defender Assn., 1955-69; mem. Nat. Lawyers Adv. Council of Earl Warren Legal Tng. Program. Served with AUS, 1943-45. Fellow Am. Bar Found., Am. Coll. Tax Counsel (regent 1st cir.); mem. ABA (past chmn. com. on taxation, coun. sect. individual rights and responsibilities 1978-82, coun. sect. taxation 1982-85), Am. Law Inst. (cons. fed. income tax project 1974—), ACLU (nat. dir. 1973-75), Order of Coif (exec. com. 1982-91, v.p. 1986-89, pres. 1989-91), Phi Beta Kappa. Home: 229 Brattle St Cambridge MA 02138-4623 Office: Harvard Law Sch Cambridge MA 02138

WOLFMAN, BRUNETTA REID, education educator; b. Clarksdale, Miss., Sept. 4, 1931; d. Willie Orlando and Belle Victoria (Allen) Reid Griffin; m. Burton Wolfman, Oct. 4, 1952; children: Andrea, Jeffrey. BA, U. Calif., Berkeley, 1957, MA, 1968, PhD, 1971; DHL (hon.), Boston U., 1983; DP (hon.), Northeastern U., 1983; DL (hon.), Regis Coll., 1984, Stonehill Coll., 1985; DHL, Suffolk U., 1985; DET (hon.), Wentworth Inst., 1987; AA (hon.), Roxbury Community Coll., 1988. Asst. dean faculty Dartmouth Coll., Hanover, N.H., 1972-74; asst. v.p. acad. affairs U. Mass., Boston, 1974-76; acad. dean Wheelock Coll., Boston, 1976-78; cons. Arthur D. Little, Cambridge, Mass., 1978; dir. policy planning Dept. Edn., Boston, 1978-82; pres. Roxbury C.C., Boston, 1983-88, ACE sr. assoc., 1988-94, NAWE sr. assoc., 1994-98; assoc. v.p. acad. affairs George Washington U., Washington, 1989-92, prof. edn., 1992-96, prof. edn. emeritus, 1996—. Accreding commission on edn. on health svcs. adminstrn. (ACEHSA); ACE-MIVER cons.; pres. bd. dirs. Literacy Vols. of Capitol Region; mem. comm. com. bd., pub. rels. com. LVA, Inc.; bd. dirs. Am. Coun. Edn., Harvard Cmty. Health Plan. Author: Roles, 1983; contbr. articles to profl. jours. Mem. bd. overseers Wellesley Coll., 1981, Boston Symphony Orch.; trustee Mus. Fine Arts, Boston; mem. Coun. on Edn. for Pub. Health; chair Provincetown bd. Coun. on Aging, 1999—; bd. dirs. Boston-Fenway Program, 1977, Freedom House, Boston, 1983, Boston Pvt. Industry Coun., 1983; bd. dirs., co-chmn. NCCJ, Boston, 1983. Named Wolfman Courtyard in their honor, Evergreen Ctr., 2000; recipient Freedom award, NAACP No.Calif., 1971, Amelia Earhart award, Women's Edn. and Indsl. Union, Boston, 1983; scholar Nat. Assn. Women in Edn. Mem. AAUW, Am. Sociol. Assn., Assn. Black Women in Higher Edn., Greater Boston C. of C. (edn. com. 1982), Sierra Club, Mass. Audubon Soc., Cosmos Club (Washington), Provincetown Art Assn. (sec. bd. trustees, mus. sch. com.), Alpha Kappa Alpha (Humanitarian award 1984), Phi Delta Kappa. Home: 657 Commercial St Provincetown MA 02657-1759 E-mail: bruburt2@comcast.net.

WOLFSON, AARON HOWARD, radiation oncologist, educator; b. Nashville, May 13, 1955; s. Sorrell Louis and Jacqueline Adele (Falis) W.; m. Adrienne Sue Mates, Dec. 16, 1979; children: Alexis Ellyn, Andrew Lane. BA, U. Fla., 1978, MD, 1982. Diplomate Am. Bd. Radiology. Intern internal medicine Jackson Meml. Hosp., Miami, Fla., 1982-83; staff physician Pub. Health Svc., Miami, 1983-85; pvt. practice Palm Beach Gardens, Fla., 1985-86; resident in radiation oncology Med. Coll. Va., Richmond, 1986-89; from instr. radiation oncology to prof. U. Miami (Fla.) Sch. Medicine, 1989—2003, prof., 2003—. Co-dir. Gynecology Site dis. group, Sylvester Cancer Ctr., 2001—. Contbr. articles to profl. jours. Bd. dirs. Children's Home Soc., Ft. Lauderdale, Fla., 1993—, Temple Beth Israel, Sunrise, Fla., 1994—; mem. spkrs. bur. U. Miami, 1993—; vol. spkr. Broward County Schs., 1990—; exec. v.p. Temple Beth Israel, 1996-98, pres., 1998-99. Sylvester Cancer Ctr. grantee, 1992. Mem. Gynecologic Oncology Group, Radiation Therapy Oncology Group, Am. Soc. Therapeutic Radiology and Oncology. Jewish. Achievements include research on malignant tumors of the female genital tract. Office: Univ of Miami 1475 NW 12th Ave # D-31 Miami FL 33136-1002 E-mail: awolfson@med.miami.edu.

WOLOSHCHUK, CANDACE DIXON, secondary school educator, artist, consultant; b. Joliet, Ill., Jan. 11, 1947; d. Harold Russell and Beatrice Diane (Johnson) Dixon; m. Christopher Ralph Jose, Mar. 1, 1969 (div. Sept. 1982); children: Amy Russell, Jennifer Seavey; m. Thomas Woloshchuk, Dec. 23, 1988; stepchildren: Michael, Debbie, Paul, John. BA in Art, Salem Coll., 1969; postgrad., Merrimac Coll., 1969; MA in Art Edn., U. Hartford, 1977; Cert. Dir. Fine Arts, Fitchburg State Coll., 1994; student, CAGS Mus., 2000. Cert. tchr., Mass., Conn. Art dir. Fred D. Wish Sch., Hartford, Conn., 1969-71; art tchr. Timothy Edwards Jr. H.S., South Windsor, Conn., 1971-72; art coord. Hebron (Conn.) Elem. Sch., Gilead Hill Sch., 1974-78; art tchr. Longmeadow (Mass.) Pub. Schs., 1978-82, Agawan (Mass.) Pub. Schs., 1982-85; visual arts coord. Wilbraham (Mass.) Mid. Sch., 1985—. Coord. medieval festival Wilbraham Mid. Sch., 1986-87, coord. Oriental festival, 1987-88; pres., owner Scholarships Unltd., Monson, Mass., 1992-94; mem. tchr.-trainer program U. Hartford, 1974-78; enrichment, art tchr. Elms Coll., 1988-93; v.p. Pioneer Valley Decorative Painters, 1996-97. One-women show Garrett Gallery, 1981; group shows include Spencer Arts Ctr., 1993, Craft Adventure Expo '93, 1993 (2nd and 3rd pl. awards), Craft Expo '92, 1992 (2nd pl. award), Wilbraham Pub. Libr., 1992, 93, 94. Chairwomen, mem. Wilbraham Arts Lottery Coun., 1987-88; program chairwoman Pioneer Valley Decorative Painters of Mass., 1996—, v.p., 1997—. Recipient Outstanding Visual and Performing Arts Edn. award, Mass. Alliance for Arts Edn., 1988, gold award Am. Sch. Food Svc. Assn., 1987. Mem. ASCD, NAFE, Nat. Art Edn. Assn., Mass. Art Edn. Assn., Mass. Tchrs. Assn., Wilbraham Tchrs. Assn., Am. Craft Coun. Republican. Avocations: sailing, painting, equestrian riding. Office: Wilbraham Mid Sch 466 Stony Hill Rd Wilbraham MA 01095-1574 E-mail: cwoloshchuk@hwrsd.org., cwoloshchuk@samnet.net.

WOLOTKIEWICZ, MARIAN M. business executive; b. Camden, N.J., Apr. 22, 1954; d. Edward J. and Rita J. Wolotkiewicz; m. Paul J. Sagan, Mar. 31, 1984 (div. Aug. 1, 1994). AB in Polit. Sci., Mount Holyoke Coll., 1976; JD, Suffolk U., 1979; MBA Clark U., 1995. Notary pub., Mass. Manuscript editor Little, Brown & Co., Boston, 1979-84; freelance editor, 1984-88; freelance writer Camp Dresser & McKee Inc., 1985-87; dir. pub. info. Regis Coll., Weston, Mass., 1988-90; assoc. dir. planned giving Clark U., Worcester, Mass., 1990-93; dir. gift planning & policy Mus. Fine Arts, Boston, 1993-94; pvt. practice cons. Boston, 1994-96; project mgr. Global Bus. Process Integration The Gillette Co., Boston, 1996-99; bus. cons., 1999—2001; adminstrv. dir. CMT Ind. Labs., Ltd., Ballston Spa, NY, 2001—; owner Photos4You.com, 1999—, AsktheDivas.com, 1999—. Various writing, editing and communications activities for Mass. Bar Assn., 1978-83, Womens Bar Assn., 1979-83; freelance editor for publishers including Little, Brown & Co., Artech Ho., Ballinger, Butterworth, 1984-88. Chmn. adv. com. Stow (Mass.) Cable TV, 1983-94; active fundraising Mass. Assn. Womens Lawyers charity auction, 1984, Mt. Holyoke Coll., 1986-96; pres. Boston Alumnae Club, Mt. Holyoke Coll., 1997-99. Mem. Phi Delta Phi.

WOLPER, ALLAN, journalist, educator; b. N.Y.C. s. Sydelle Wolper; m. Joanna Wolper; children: Jill Miller, Richard, Kim Arminen. BS, NYU, 1965. Reporter Providence Jour., 1965-67; polit. writer AP, N.Y.C., 1967-69, N.Y. Post, N.Y.C., 1970-73; writer, producer WABC Eyewitness News, N.Y.C., 1974-75; managing editor, columnist Soho Weekly News, N.Y.C., 1974-82; host, writer, producer of Right to Know Suburban Cablevision and N.J. Network, Sta. WNYC-TV, N.Y.C., Newark and Avenel, N.J., 1982-89; host, producer series on media Right to Know Right to Know syndicated pub. radio series on the media, Newark, 1989-93; assoc. prof. journalism Rutgers U., 1978-92, prof. journalism, 1995—; commentator on media urban issues WBGO-FM, 1993—. Host, prodr., writer documentary The Marielitos, 1984, Hillside: Desegregation, 1985, Impact, 1988, TV spl. The First Amendment, 1989 (Joseph Brechner First Amendment award 1995); columnist Sports Media, Washington Journalism Rev., 1980-82, media N.J. Reporter, Princeton, 1982-85; ethics columnist, contbg. editor Editor and Pub. mag., 1987—. Recipient best pub. affairs program award Internat. TV and Video Festival, 1985, Nat. Cable TV Assn., 1986, award for cable excellence, 1986, 3 Aces award Nat. Cable TV, 1985, 86, Lowell Mellett award Pa. State U., 1985, Alfred I. DuPont award Columbia U., 1985, award in broadcast journalism (1st cable prodr. to win) N.J. Press Assn., 1987, N.J. Bell Enterprise award for best radio documentary, 1992, Best Radio Commentary and Media Nat. Headliner award 1993, Hildy Johnson award North Jersey Press Club, 2000, First Place Best Personal Column, Deadline Club N.Y., 2000, Bart Richards award for media criticism, 2002, second place, tied, Best Personal Column award, Deadline Club, 2003, Paul Mongerson award of distinction for investigative reporting on news coverage Ctr. Media Pub. Affairs, 2003. Mem.: AAUP, Soc. Profl. Journalists (chmn. freedom of info. com. Deadline Club N.Y.C. br. 1980, Outstanding Broadcast Journalism award 1984, 1987, Disting. Svc. award 1989, spl. award N.J. chpt. media criticism 1991, radio documentary 1992, investigative report 1992, 1st pl. Pub. Svc. award Mag. N.J. chpt. 1994, Brechner 1st Amendment award 1996, Best Column, Deadline Club, N.Y. chpt. 2000, spl. award N.J. chpt., 1st pl. Bicentennial Broadcast Competition 1989). Office: 327 Central Park W New York NY 10025-7631 also: Rutgers U Journalism Dept Bradley Hall Newark NJ 07102 Office Fax: 973-353-5119.

WOLSEY, THOMAS DEVERE, middle school educator; b. Salt Lake City, Mar. 6, 1962; d. T. Mark and Lynn Wolsey. BS, So. Utah State Coll., 1986; MA in Ednl. Adminstrn., Calif. State U., San Bernardino, 1990. Cert. tchr., Utah; mid. sch. endorsement, reading, English tchr., adminstrv. svcs., Calif. Tchr. adult edn., tchr. English San Bernardino City Unified Sch. Dist., 1986-89; ESL tutor Alpine Sch. Dist., American Fork, Utah, 1981-84; tchr. U.S. History and English Lake Elsinore (Calif.) Unified Sch. Dist., 1989—. Adj. faculty sch. of edn. and human svcs./reading methodology Nat. Univ., 1995—. Mem. editl. adv. bd.: The Jour. of Adolscent & Adult Literacy, 1997—, The Reading Tchr., 1998. Mem. Nat. Coun. Tchrs. English, Internat. Reading Assn. (mem. pubs. com. 2001-03), Lake Elsinore Tchrs. Assn. (pres. 1996-98). Home: 31996 Corte Ruiz Temecula CA 92592-3621 Office: Elsinore Mid Sch 1203 W Graham Ave Lake Elsinore CA 92530-3318

WOLTERING, MARGARET MAE, retired secondary school educational consultant; b. Trenton, Ohio, July 24, 1913; d. David Lindy and Nellie Stevenson; m. Elmer Charles Woltering, Apr. 9, 1938 (dec. Oct. 1994); 1 child, Eugene Anthony. Student, Mercy Sch. Nursing, Hamilton, Ohio, 1931-34; BS, Miami U., 1962, MEd, 1968, postgrad., 1975. RN Ohio, cert. tchr., curriculum supr., Ohio Pub. Health. Pub. health nurse Ohio State Dept. Health, Butler County, 1936-49; supr. Swedish Hosp., Seattle, 1944-45; various h.s. teaching positions Cin., 1968-78; ednl. cons., 1981-94. Cons., Ohio, 1981—96; ednl. cons. specializing in curriculum devel., 1980—91; book reviewer Friends of Libr., 1991—93; lectr. Sr. Citizens Ctr., 1992—98; instr. Bible Study, 2000—. Author: The National Library of Poetry Anthology, 2000—03, spelling book, numerous poems. Chmn. Hosp. Svc. for Children, Hamilton, 1981—85; chmn. vol. tutorial program Hamilton H.S., 1989—93, 1994—2000. Recipient Order of St. Louis IX medallion, 2003. Mem.: AAUW, Toastmasters. Democrat. Roman Catholic. Avocations: reading, theater, art collecting, China porcelain painting.

WOLYNES, PETER GUY, chemistry researcher, educator; b. Chgo., Apr. 21, 1953; s. Peter and Evelyn Eleanor (Etter) W.; m. Jane Lee Fox, Nov. 26, 1976 (div. 1980); m. Kathleen Cull Bucher, Dec. 22, 1984; children: Margrethe Cull, Eve Cordelia, Julia Jean. AB with highest distinction, Ind. U., 1971; AM, Harvard U., 1972, PhD in Chem. Physics, 1976; DSc (hon.), Ind. U., 1988. Rsch. assoc. MIT, Cambridge, 1975-76; asst. prof., assoc. prof. Harvard U., Cambridge, 1976-80; vis. scientist Max Planck Inst. für Biophysikalische Chemie, Gottingen, Fed. Republic Germany, 1977; assoc. prof. chemistry U. Ill., Urbana, 1980-83, prof. chemistry, 1983-2000, prof. physics, 1985-2000, prof. physics and biophysics, 1989-2000, mem. Ctr. for Advanced Study, 1989-2000; William H. and Janet LyCan prof. chemistry Ctr. for Advanced Study U. Ill., Urbana, 1993-96, Robert Eiszner prof., 1996-2000; prof. chemistry and biochemistry U. Calif., San Diego, 2000—, Francis H.C. Crick prof., 2001—. Vis. prof. Inst. for Molecular Sci., Okazaki, Japan, 1982, 87; vis. scientist Inst. for Theoretical Physics, Santa Barbara, Calif., 1987, Ecole normale Supérieure, Paris, 1992; Merski lectr. U. Nebr., 1986; Denkewalter lectr. Loyola U., 1986; Hinshelwood lectr. Oxford U., 1997; Harkins lectr. U. Chgo., 1997; FMC lectr. Princeton U., 1998; Matsen lectr. U. Tex., 2002. Contbr. numerous articles to profl. jours. Sloan fellow, 1981-83, J.S. Guggenheim fellow, 1986-87; Beckman assoc. Ctr. for Advanced Study, Urbana, 1984-85; Fogarty scholar NIH, 1994-98. Fellow AAAS, Am. Phys. Soc., Am. Acad. Arts and Scis., The Biophys. Soc.; mem. NAS, Am. Chem. Soc. (Pure Chemistry award 1986, Peter Debye award 2000), N.Y. Acad. Scis., Phi Beta Kappa, Sigma Xi, Phi Lambda Upsilon (Fresenius award 1988), Sigma Pi Sigma, Alpha Chi Sigma. Home: 12737 Sandy Crest Ct San Diego CA 92130-2795 Office: U Calif San Diego Dept Chem and Biochemistry 9500 Gilman Dr MC 0371 La Jolla CA 92093-0371 E-mail: pwolynes@ucsd.edu.

WOLYNIES, EVELYN See GRADO-WOLYNIES, EVELYN

WONG, TIMOTHY C. language and literature educator; b. Hong Kong, Jan. 24, 1941; came to U.S., 1951; s. Patrick J. and Rose (Poon) W.; m. Elizabeth Ann Steffens, Dec. 18, 1970; children: Sharon Elizabeth, Rachel Margaret, Laura Katherine. BA, St. Mary's Coll., Moraga, Calif., 1963; MA, U. Hawaii, 1968; PhD, Stanford U., 1975. Vol. U.S. Peace Corps, Thailand, 1963-65; asst. prof. Ariz. State U., Tempe, 1974-79, assoc. prof., 1979-85; resident dir. Coun. on Internat. Ednl. Exchange Peking Univ., China, 1984-85; assoc. prof. Ohio State U., Columbus, 1985-95; prof. Ariz. State U., Tempe, 1995—, dir. Ctr. for Asian Studies, 1995—2002. Author: Wu Ching-tzu, 1978, Stories for Saturday: Twentieth-Century Chinese Popular Fiction, 2003. Mem. Chinese Lang. Tchrs. Assn., Assn. Asian Studies, Am. Oriental Soc. (dir.-at-large 1996-2000, v.p. western br. 2000-02, pres., 2001-03). Democrat. Roman Catholic. Office: Ariz State U Dept Langs and Lits Tempe AZ 85287-0202 E-mail: timothy.wong@asu.edu.

WONNACOTT, PAUL, economics educator; b. London, Ont., Can., Mar. 16, 1933; s. Gordon Elliott and Muriel Johnston Wonnacott; m. Donna Elizabeth Cochrane, July 2, 1960; children: David, Ann, Alan, Bruce. BA, U. Western Ont., 1955; MA, Princeton U., 1957, PhD, 1959. Instr., asst. prof. econs. Columbia U., N.Y.C., 1958-62; assoc. prof. then prof. econs. U. Md., College Pk., 1962-91, prof. emeritus, 1992. Mem. Pres.'s Coun. Econ. Advisers, 1991-93; Alan Holmes prof. econs. Middlebury Coll., 1994-2000; rsch. staff Royal Commn. Banking and Fin., Toronto, 1962; sr. staff economist Coun. Econ. Advisers, Washington, 1968-70; assoc. dir. divsn. internat. fin. Fed. Res. Bd., Washington, 1974-75; vis. scholar Office Internat. Monetary Rsch., U.S. Treasury, 1980; econ. adviser to Under Sec. of State, 1990-91. Author: The Canadian Dollar, 1960, 2d rev. edit., 1965, (with R.J. Wonnacott) Free Trade between the United States and Canada: The Potential Economic Effects, 1967, (with H.G. Johnson and H. Shibata) Harmonization of National Economic Policies under Free Trade, 1968, Macroeconomics, 1974, 3d rev. edit., 1984, (with R.J. Wonnacott) Economics, 1979, 4th rev. edit. 1990, Spanish edit., 1981, 3d rev. edit., 1987, (with Y. and C. Crusius) Portuguese edit., 1982, 2d rev. edit., 1985, (with A. Blomquist) Can. edit., 1983, 4th rev. edit., 1994, Lithuanian edit., 1998, The United States and Canada: The Quest for Free Trade, 1987; contbr. articles to profl. jours. Fellow Brooking Inst., 1957-58, Ford Found., 1963-64; vis. fellow Inst. Internat. Econs., 1986, 93-94 Avocation: skiing. Home: 10100 Bevern Ln Potomac MD 20854-2130 E-mail: paulwon@wam.umd.edu.

WONSER, MICHAEL DEAN, retired public affairs director, art history educator; b. Long Beach, Calif., Mar. 12, 1940; s. Franklin Henry and Dorothy Mae (Harris) W.; children: Therice Michele, Sherice Michele, Christopher Franklin; m. Mary L. Van Epps, Dec. 22, 1990. BS, U. Oreg., 1963, MFA, 1965; postgrad., U. Colo., 1976. Instr. Cen. Oreg. Coll., Bend, 1966-68; prof. Adams State Coll., Alamosa, Colo., 1969-91, dir. pub. affairs, 1982-90; adj. prof. art history Ctrl. Oreg. C.C., Bend. Pres. Colo. Faculty Com. Trustees, 1980-82. Mem. Chamber Edn. Com., Monte Vista, Colo., 1982-88; pres. Luth. Ch. Alamosa, 1980-85; bd. dirs. Creede Repertory Theatre, 1989-91; mem. Commerce Comm. and Resources Comm., 1995, Cmty. Improvement Commn., Sisters, Oreg., 1996-97. Mem. Higher Edn. Assn. of Rockies (pres. Colo. chpt. 1985-88), C. of C. Ambassador (treas. 1982), Alamosa, C. of C. Tourism Bd., Alamosa (chmn. 1987-89), Sisters C. of C. (v.p. 1995-97, pres. 1996-97, bd. dirs.), Rotary (pres. Alamosa County 1990-91), Lambda Chi Alpha (Hall of Fame 1993). Republican. Avocations: golf, skiing. Home: 24 NW Shasta Pl Bend OR 97701-2633 E-mail: mmwonser@bendcable.com.

WOOD, BARBARA BUTLER, secondary language arts and television production educator; b. L.A., Oct. 19, 1946; d. E. Reynolds and Frances (Swain) Butler; m. John M. Wood, Aug. 12, 1978; 1 child, Mark Douglas. BS in Edn., No. Ariz. U., 1968; MS in Cinema Edn., U. So. Calif., 1974. Lic. English tchr., Calif., secondary sch. English tchr., Ariz. Tchr. Whittier (Calif.) Union High Sch. Dist., 1968-73; mem. mgmt. staff Ramada Inns, Inc., Phoenix, 1975-79; tchr. Glendale (Ariz.) Union High Sch. Dist., 1985—; mem. part-time faculty English Glendale C.C., 1990-94; designer CD-ROM curriculum, English course developer Ednl. Mgmt. Group, Scottsdale, Ariz., 1996-97, 98-99; instr. cinematography and English U. of Advancing Computer Tech., 1997-98; online course developer, adj. faculty mem. Rio Salado C.C., 1999—. Mem. adv. bd. on at-risk edn. Glendale Union High Sch. Dist., 1989-90, editor Viewpoint newsletter, 1991-92; cons. Ariz. Bus. Leaders for Edn., Phoenix, 1989-92. Active Jr. League Phoenix, 1983-87, Phoenix Zoo Aux., 1980-91. NEH fellow, Newark, N.J., 1990; grantee Wells Fargo Found., 1999; recipient Take Charge of Edn. scholarship Target, 2000; named Intel Corp. Teach to the Future Tchr., 2000. Mem. ASCD, Nat. Coun. Tchrs. English, Ariz. Tech. Edn. Assn. Office: Moon Valley HS 3625 W Cactus Rd Phoenix AZ 85029-3122

WOOD, BARBARA LYNN, elementary education educator; b. Syracuse, NY; d. Robert Hilton and Carol (Flynn) W. BS, Springfield (Mass.) Coll., 1974; Cert. in advanced study in adminstrn., Cortland Coll., 1990; MS, Tex. Woman's U., 1991. Tchr. phys. edn. Homer (N.Y.) Cen. Sch., 1974-87, 88—. Designed, produced and impmented A Home/Sch. Based Devel. Phys. Edn. Program K-2, 1989-91. Author: School Based Home Developmental P.E. Program, 1998. Recipient coaches award Onondaga High Sch. League, 1984. Mem. AAHPER and Dance, N.Y. State Assn. Health, Phys. Edn., Recreation and Dance (conf. speaker 1990). Avocations: stained glass projects, woodworking, sailing. Home: 28 Abdallah Ave Cortland NY 13045-3303

WOOD, BERENICE HOWLAND, retired secondary school educator; b. Newport, R.I., Oct. 21, 1910; d. Horatio Gates and Margaret Lorraine (Doyle) W. AB, Vassar Coll., 1934; MA, Columbia U., 1936; postgrad., U. R.I., 1961-65. Clk. 1st Dist. Ct. R.I., Newport, 1942-50; home service dir. ARC, Newport, 1950-61; tchr. Cranston, R.I., 1961-62, Elmhurst Sch., Portsmouth, R.I., 1962-64, Newport, 1964-82. Sec. to mayor City of Newport, 1941. Pres. Coun. Social Agys., Newport, 1955—57; active Hist. Soc. Newport, Art Mus. Newport, Redwood Libr., Newport, Preservation Soc., Newport, Hill Assn., Newport. Mem. Point Assn. Newport, Nat. Trust Hist. Preservation. Roman Catholic. Avocations: maintaining and preserving antiquities, foreign travel. Home: 82 Mill St Newport RI 02840-3146

WOOD, CAROLYN JANE, educational leadership educator; b. Niles, Mich., Sept. 1, 1942; d. Jerome W. and Priscilla J. (Barbary) W. BA, Drake U., Des Moines, 1964; MA, U. Denver, 1968; PhD, Washington U., St. Louis, 1977. Cert. chr. social studies, 7-12, cert. adminstr. Social studies tchr. Howard Cmty. Schs., Niles, 1964-66; asst. residence hall dir. U. Denver, 1966-68; asst. dean of students Bowling Green (Ohio) State U., 1968-71; faculty Washington U., St. Louis, 1972-76; asst. prof. U. N.Mex., Albuquerque, 1977-81, assoc. prof., 1981-93, prof. ednl. leadership, chair dept. ednl. leadership and orgn. learning, 2003—. Part-time instr. Webster Coll., St. Louis, spring 1975, Maryville Coll., St. Louis, summer 1977; evaluator N.Mex. Fellows for the Advancement of Math. Edn., NSF, 1991-94; project dir. AWARE-NM (Assisting Women to Advance Through Resources and Encouragement), Albuquerque, 1987-92. Contbr. articles to profl. jours.; co-creator multimedia: Do Flowers Always Grow from Planted Seeds?, 1993, Does Systemic Change Teach Helplessness or Resourcefulness?, 1994, Are People Learning to be Helpless or Resourceful?, 1994. Sec. and mem. N.Mex. Corrections Commn., Santa Fe, 1983-85; chmn. bd. United Way of Greater Albuquerque, 1991. Recipient Rsch. award U. N.Mex. chpt. Phi Delta Kappa, 1979, Outstanding Tchr. of the Yr. for Grad. Instrn. award U. N.Mex., 1982, Gov.'s Award for Outstanding N.Mex. Women, 1991, Rsch. award Nat. Rural Edn. Assn., 2000; grantee U.S. Office Elem. and Secondary Edn., 2002—. Mem. ASCD, Am. Ednl. Rsch. Assn., Phi Delta Kappa. Home: 2521 Harold Pl NE Albuquerque NM 87106-2515 Office: Univ of N Mex Edn Office Bldg Albuquerque NM 87131-0001 E-mail: cwood@unm.edu.

WOOD, CLINTON WAYNE, middle school educator; b. Birmingham, Ala., Nov. 13, 1954; s. Clinton Mason and Dorothy Ann (Pullen) W. BA, U. Mobile, 1978. Cert. secondary edn. tchr., Ala. Tchr., coach Westminster Christian Sch., Gadsden, Ala., 1978-79, Simmons Mid. Sch., Hoover, Ala., 1979—. Author: Bob Finley: A Class Act; author, editor: The Marble Valley Boys, 1986; co-author: Kiss Sweet Little Lillah For Me; contbr. articles to profl. jours. Named one of Outstanding Young Men of Am., 1985. Mem. Nat. Edn. Assn., Ala. Edn. Assn., Coaches Assn. (state and nat.), SAR, SCV. Baptist. Avocations: sports, camping, reading, hiking, traveling. Home: 3400 Treeline Ct Apt 604 Hoover AL 35216-5714 Office: Simmons Mid Sch 1575 Patton Chapel Rd Birmingham AL 35226-2257

WOOD, DANIEL BRIAN, educational consultant; b. Roseburg, Oreg., Mar. 5, 1960; s. Jack Livingston and E. June (Gamble) W. BS, U. Oreg., 1982, MS, 1985, PhD, 1989. Cert. folklore and ethnic studies. Fare policy analyst Lane Transit Dist., Eugene, Oreg., 1984-85; asst. to dean for internships Univ. Oreg., Eugene, 1987-88; rsch. analyst Oreg. System Higher Edn., Eugene, 1988; pvt. practice in ednl. rsch., specializing in applications of machine sys. control theory to problems of social and ednl. measurement Eugene, 1988—. Co-designer, co-author statewide exam. and analysis of transfer student performance in Oreg. higher edn.; manuscript reviewer for refereed jours.; vis. asst. prof., rsch. assoc. U. Miss., 1992-93; active Statewide Task Force on Transfer Followup, 1987-88. Reviewer Internat. Jour. Intercultural Rels., 1995-96; contbr. articles to profl. jours. Mem. Am. Soc. Pub. Adminstrn., Oreg. Sect. Pub. Adminstrn. Edn., Pi Lambda Theta (pres.), Phi Delta Kappa. Home and Office: 122 E Howard Ave Eugene OR 97404-2617 E-mail: drdbwood@webtv.net.

WOOD, DAVID LAURENCE, artist, art educator, consultant; b. Hollywood, Calif., Sept. 1, 1944; s. E. Laurence and Natalie Georgette (Sheckles) W.; m. Terry Lynn Ezell Wood, Aug. 11, 1973 (div. Aug. 1983); children: Caynan, Jennifer; m. Pamela Forster, July 14, 2000. BA in art history, U. Calif., 1968; MA in printmaking, Calif. State U., 1976. Fine art dept. chair John Burroughs H.S., Burbank, Calif., 1992-93, art instr., 1969-94, Santa Monica (Calif.) H.S., 1994—. Chmn. Partnership com. Visual Arts, Burbank, 1988-94; lectr. I.V.A.E. J. Paul Getty Ctr., Santa Monica, 1992-93. Pres. Fine Arts Fedn. Burbank, 1993—2001; bd. dirs. Task Force for the Cultural Arts, 1991-92, Glendale Regional Arts Coun., Glendale, Calif., 1988-92, Design Review Bd., Burbank, 1969-73. Recipient Bronze award Information Film Producers of Am., Hollywood, 1980; named Outstanding Art Tchr., Creative Art Ctrs., Burbank, 1989, 90, 91, 92, 93. Mem. Am. Soc. Appraisers. Home: 3921 Davana Rd Sherman Oaks CA 91423-4633 E-mail: davidlwood@earthlink.net.

WOOD, DAVID LEE, entomologist, educator; b. Jan. 8, 1931; BS, SUNY, Syracuse, 1952; PhD, U. Calif., Berkeley, 1960. Lic. forester, Calif. Prof. entomology, emeritis dept. Environ. Sci. Policy, Mgmt. U. Calif., Berkeley, 1960—. Lectr., reviewer, cons. in field. Contbr. articles to profl. jours. Recipient Silver medal Swedish Coun. for Forestry and Agril. Rsch., 1983, Founder's award Western Forest Insect Work Conf. 1992. Fellow Entomol. Soc. Can., Entomol. Soc. Am. (Founder's award 1986); mem. AAAS, AIBS, Entomol. Soc. Am., Entomol. Soc. Can., Internat. Soc. Chem. Ecology (Silver medal 2001), Soc. Am. Foresters, Sigma Xi. Home: 26 Hardie Dr Moraga CA 94556-1134 Office: U Calif Divsn Insect Biology 201 Wellman Hall Berkeley CA 94720-3112 E-mail: bigwood@nature.berkeley.edu.

WOOD, DIANE MARY, special education educator; b. Athol, Mass., Feb. 11, 1953; d. Harold Warren and Ann Theresa (Karluk) Wood. BS, So. Conn. State U., New Haven, 1974; MS, So. Conn. State U., 1975; PhD, SUNY-Albany, 1994. Reading clinician New London (Conn.) pub. schs., 1975-77; developmental reading specialist Marlborough (N.H.) Sch. Dist. 29, 1977-78; spl. edn. tchr. Keene (N.H.) Sch. Dist., 1978-84, Ravena-Coeymans-Selkirk (N.Y.) Sch. Dist., 1984-89; teaching asst. SUNY-Albany, 1989-90; cons. tchr. Ravena-Coeymans-Selkirk Sch. Dist., 1990—. Ednl. cons. Keene Sch. Dist., 1983—84; adj. faculty SUNY, Albany, 1990—2003; lectr. Coll. of St. Rose, 1990—. Dir. YMCA Day Camp, Cheshire County, Richmond, summer 1979; driver, vol. Albany Meals on Wheels, 1989-90; bd. dirs. Monadnock Task Force on Child Abuse and Neglect, Keene, N.H., 1982-84; active Big Bros./Big Sisters, Keene, 1982-84. Mem. Coun. for Exceptional Children, Am. Ednl. Rsch. Assn., Learning Disabilities Assn. Am. Avocations: reading, skiing. Office: AW Becker Elem Sch RR 9 # W Selkirk NY 12158

WOOD, DIANE PAMELA, judge; b. Plainfield, N.J., July 4, 1950; d. Kenneth Reed and Lucille (Padmore) Wood; m. Dennis James Hutchinson, Sept. 2, 1978 (div. May 1998); children: Kathryn Hutchinson, David Hutchinson, Jane Hutchinson. BA, U. Tex., 1971, JD, 1975, Georgetown U., 2003. Bar: Tex. 1975, D.C. 1978, Ill. 1993. Law clk. U.S. Ct. Appeals (5th cir.), 1975—76, U.S. Supreme Ct., 1976—77; atty.-advisor U.S. Dept. State, Washington, 1977—78; assoc. Covington & Burling, Washington, 1978—80; asst. prof. law Georgetown U. Law Ctr., Washington, 1980—81, U. Chgo., 1981—88, prof. law, 1988—95, assoc. dean, 1989—92, Harold J. and Marion F. Green prof. internat. legal studies, 1990—95, sr. lectr. law, 1995—; spl. cons. antitrust divsn. internat. guide U.S. Dept. Justice, 1986—87, dep. asst. atty. gen. antitrust divsn., 1993—95; judge U.S. Ct. Appeals (7th cir.), 1995—. Contbr. articles to profl. jours.; bd. editors: Am. Jour. Internat. Law. Bd. dirs. Hyde Park-Kenwood Cmty. Health Ctr., 1983—85. Mem.: Am. Law Inst. (elected coun. mem. 2003), Am. Soc. Internat. Law, Phi Alpha Delta. Democrat.

WOOD, DOLORES IDEL, retired Spanish and French languages educator; b. Warren, Ohio, Feb. 22, 1938; d. Robert Childs Wellmon and Retha Idel (Westmoreland) Morris; m. Robert Dean Wood, June 6, 1959; children: Barry Lloyd, Bryan Scott. BA, So. Nazarene U., 1958; MA, U. Okla., 1965. Spanish, fgn. language in elem. schs. tchr. Dist 11 Schs., Colorado Springs, Colo., 1959-62, 65-66; assoc. prof. Spanish So. Nazarene U., Bethany, Okla., 1967—2000, modern lang. dept. chair, 1985-94; ret., 2000. Interpreter, translator, Oklahoma City; interpreter Okla. Lang. Bank, polic, chs., community agys., Oklahoma City. Recipient Teaching Excellence and Campus Leadership award Sears-Roebuck Found., 1991. Mem. Am. Coun. Teaching Fgn. Lang., Am. Assn. Tchrs. Spanish and Portuguese, N.Am. Assn. Christian Fgn. Lang. and Lit. Faculty, Okla. Fgn. Lang. Tchrs. Assn. Republican. Mem. Ch. of Nazarene. Avocations: quilting, reading, scherenschnitte. Home: 8209 NW 31st St Bethany OK 73008-4341

WOOD, EMILY CHURCHILL, educator, educational consultant; b. Summit, N.J., Apr. 11, 1925; d. Arthur Burdett and Ruth Vail (Pierson) Churchill; m. Philip Warren Wood, June 22, 1946; children: Martha, Arthur, Warren, Benjamin. BA, Smith Coll., 1946; MA in Teaching, Manhattanville Coll., 1971; postgrad., U. Tulsa, 1974-79, Langston U., 1990-92. Cert. tchr. social studies, learning disabilities, elem. edn., econs., Am. history, world history. Tchr. Miss Fines Sch., Princeton, N.J., 1946-47, Hallen Ctr. for Edn., Portchester, N.Y., 1973-74, Town and Country Sch., Tulsa, Okla., 1974-79, Tulsa Pub. Schs., 1979-97, Heritage Acad., Tulsa, 1998—; adj. instr. Tulsa C.C., Tulsa, 1998—. Ednl. cons. Tulsa, 1997—; leader colloquia Bill of Rights Arts and Humanities Coun., Tulsa, 1989; mem. literacy task force Tulsa 2000 Edn. Com., 1990-92; chmn. internat. student exch. Eisenhower Internat. Sch., Tulsa, 1992-97. Author: (with others) Visual Arts in China, 1988, Applauding Our Constitution, 1989, The Bill of Rights: Who Guarantees What, 1993; contbr. articles to profl. jours. Leader, founder Am. Field Svc., Tulsa, 1982—84; pres., v.p. Booker T. Washington H.S. PTA, Tulsa, 1985; campaign mgr. auditors race Dem. Party, Tulsa, 1988, 1992, 1994; bd. dirs. Smith Coll. Alumnae, Northampton, Mass., 1956—59, Sister Cities Internat., Tulsa, 1992—2001, nominations chair, 1999—2001; bd. dirs. Tulsa Global Alliance; trustee Okla. Found. for Excellence, 2000—. Named Tulsa Tchr. of Yr. Tulsa Classroom Tchrs. Assn., 1988, Nat. Elem. Tchr. of Yr., Nat. Bar Aux., 1992, Outstanding Elem. Social Studies Tchr., Nat. Cound. or Social Studies, 1999; recipient Elem. Medal of Excellence, Okla. Found. for Excellence, 1990, Valley Forge Tchrs. medal Freedoms Found., 1992, Paragon award Tulsa Commn. on Status of Women, 1996, Pinnacle award Mayor's Commn. on Status of Women, 1998, Liberty Bell award Tulsa Bar Assn., 1998, Global Vision award Tulsa Global Alliance, 2002. Mem. UN Assn. Ea. Okla. (pres. 2000—), Nat. Coun. Social Studies (religion program com. 1984—, bd. dirs. 1997—), DAR, Okla. Edn. Assn., Okla. Coun. Social Studies (pres. 1995, tchr. of yr. 1984), Okla. Bar Assn. (law related com. 1988—, tchr. of yr. 1990), Okla. Coun. Econ. Edn. (state and nat. awards 1981, 89, 92), Kent Place Alumnae Assn. (disting. alumna award 1992). Avocations: reading, swimming, travel, walking. Home: 3622 S Yorktown Pl Tulsa OK 74105-3452 E-mail: emily_wood46@hotmail.com

WOOD, ERIC FRANKLIN, earth and environmental sciences educator; b. Vancouver, B.C., Can., Oct. 22, 1947; s. Lorne George and Olga Eugena (Hryvnak) W.; m. Katharine Holding Schwed; children: Eric Alexander, Emily Holding. BASc with hons., U. B.C., 1970; SM, MIT, 1972, MSCE, 1973, ScD, 1974. Rsch. asst. MIT, Cambridge, 1970-73; rsch. scholar Internat. Inst. for Applied Systems Analysis, Vienna, Austria, 1974-76; prof. civil engring. Princeton (N.J.) U., 1976—. EOS sci. steering com. NASA, 1984-87, sci. adv. working group, 1992, land surface processes adv. com., 1985-90, Landsat sci. working group, 1992-93, MTPE Biennial Rev. Panel, 1997; mem. Continental Internat. Project sci. steering com. World Climate Rsch. Program, 1993-95; mem. policy adv. panel Continental Water-Energy Climate Project, NOAA, Office of Global Programs, 1996-97. Co-author: An Introduction to Groundwater Contamination from Hazardous Wastes, 1984; assoc. editor: Water Resources Research, 1977-82, Applied Math. and Computation, 1983—, Jour. of Forecasting, 1984-2000, Rev. in Geophysics, 1988-93; editor (books) Recent Developments in Real-Time Forecasting/Control of Water Resources Systems, 1980, Scale Effects in Hyrology, 1986, Land Surface-Atmospheric Interactions for Climate Models: Observations, Modeling and Analysis, 1990; contbr. numerous articles to profl. jours. Recipient Rheinstein award Princton U., 1980. Fellow Am. Geophys. Union (mem. editl. bd. Water Resources Monographs, 1980-85, exec. mem. hydrology sect. 1984-85, 88-92, 94-95, union fellows com. 1994-98, chair 1998-2000, Fall meeting com., 2001-03, Horton Medal Com. 2002-, union meeting com. 1988-90, chmn. remot sensing com., 1988-92, Horton rsch. com. 1992-95, Robert E. Horton award 1988), Am. Meteorol. Soc. (coun. 1999-2002, Atm awards 2003-, hydrology com. 1987-90, chair 1997—, Robert E. Horton Lctr., 2001); mem. INFORMS, NAS (com. on flood levee policy, water sci. technology bd. 1997-2000, bd. atmospheric sci. and climatology 1999-2002, com. on hydrologic sci. 1999—, chair 2002-), NSF (mem. com. of flood hazard mitigation 1979-80, panel on engring. and global climate change 1991). Avocations: squash, sailing, skiing. Office: Princeton U Dept Of Civil Engring Princeton NJ 08544-0001

WOOD, GLADYS BLANCHE, retired secondary education educator, journalist; b. Sanborn, N.D., Aug. 12, 1921; d. Charles Kershaw and Mina Blanche (Kee) Crowther; m. Newell Edwin Wood, June 13, 1943 (dec. 1990); children: Terry N., Lani, Brian R., Kevin C.; m. F.L. Stutzman, Nov. 30, 1991. BA in Journalism, U. Minn., 1943; MA in Mass Comm., San Jose State U., 1972. Cert. secondary tchr., Calif. Reporter St. Paul Pioneer-Dispatch, 1943-45; editor J.C. Penney Co., N.Y.C., 1945-46; tchr. English and journalism Willow Glen H.S., San Jose, Calif., 1968-87. Freelance writer, photographer, 1947—; cons. in field. Named Secondary Journalism Tchr. of Yr. Calif. Newpaper Pubs. Assn., 1977. Mem. AAUW, AMA Alliance, Inc., Soc. Profl. Journalists, Journalism Edn. Assn., Calif. Ret. Tchrs. Assn., Women in Comm., Friends of Libr., Santa Clara County Med. Assn. Alliance, Saratoga Foothill Club, Delta Kappa Gamma, Theta Sigma Phi, Alpha Omicron Pi. Republican. Methodist. Avocations: music, journalism, photography, travel. Home: 14161 Douglass Ln Saratoga CA 95070-5535

WOOD, JACALYN KAY, education educator, educational consultant; b. May 25, 1949; d. Carleston John and Grace Anna (Schumacher) W. BA, Georgetown Coll., 1971; MS, Ohio State U., 1976; PhD, Miami U., 1981. Elem. tchr. Bethel-Tate Schs., Ohio, 1971-73, Columbus Christian Sch., 1973-74, Franklin (Ohio) Schs., 1974-79; tchg. fellow Miami U., Oxford, Ohio, 1979-81; cons. intermediate grades Erie County Schs., Sandusky, Ohio, 1981-89, presenter, tchr. insvc. tng. Mem. coun. Sta. WVIZ-TV, 1981-88; assoc. prof. Ashland U., Elyria, Ohio, 1989, dir. elem. edn., 1989—; mem. Lorain County 20/20, mem. strategic planning bd., 1992—. Mem. Leadership Lorain County, 1994—; mem. exec. com. Perkins Cmty. Schs., 1981-85; bd. edn. Open Door Christian Schs., 1997—; active Love, Inc. of Lorain County, 1992—, sec., 1995—; mem. cmty. adv. bd. Sandusky Vols. Am., 1985-89, Sandusky Soc. Bank, 1987-88; vol. Firelands Cmty. Hosp., 1986-87; active Leadership Lorain County, 1994-95. Mem. AAUW, ASCD, Am. Businesswomen's Assn. (local pres. 1985), Internat. Reading Assn., Assn. Childhood Edn. (internat. publs. com. 1996), Ohio Sch. Suprs. Assn. (regional pres. 1986, state pres. 1986-87), Phi Delta Kappa (local sec. 1985, 86, v.p. 1991-93, pres. 1993—), Phi Kappa Phi, Kappa Delta Pi (local adv. 1991-93). Baptist. Home: 35873 Westminster Ave North Ridgeville OH 44039-1380 Office: Ashland U at LCCC 1005 N Abbe Rd Elyria OH 44035-1613

WOOD, JAMES ALBERT, foreign language educator; b. Enterprise, Oreg., Nov. 9, 1949; s. Ralph Albert and Charlotte Lavona (Johnson) Wood; m. Maritza Wood, Apr. 14, 1977; 1 child, Jamie Maritza. BS in Health and Phys. Edn., David Lipscomb U., Nashville, 1975; BA in Spanish, MA in Health and Phys. Edn., So. Oreg. Univ., 1979; EdD, Tex. A&M U., Kingsville, 1986; postgrad., U. Tenn., 1981-82. Cert. health and phys. edn. tchr., K-12, Spanish-ESL tchr., mid-mgmt. supr., supt., elem., bilingual all level ESL, Tex. Tchr. Spanish and ESL Galena Park Ind. Sch. Dist., Houston, 1986-88; tchr. ESL and reading Rice Consol. Ind. Sch. Dist., Altair, Tex., 1988-89; ESL tchr. K-5 Royalwood Elem.Sch., Sheldon Ind. Sch. Dist., Houston, 1989-90; vol. Peace Corps, El Salvador, 1976-77; sr. program devel. specialist bilingual programs U. Okla., Norman, 1990-92; prof. bilingual edn. Sul Ross State U. Rio Grande Coll., Uvalde, Tex., 1992—. Adj. prof. Tex. So. U., Houston, U. Houston, Clear Lake, Tex., 1988-90. Contbr. articles to profl. jours. Sgt. U.S. Army, 1970-73. Dean's grantee Tex. A&M U.-Kingsville. Mem. ASCD, TESOL, Nat. Assn. Bilingual Edn., Tex. Assn. Bilingual Edn., Tex. Tchr. Educators Assn., Non-Commd. Officers Assn. (life), Am. Legion, VFW (life). Home: PO Box 1415 Uvalde TX 78802-1415

WOOD, JOETTA KAY, special education educator; b. Kirksville, Mo., Sept. 30, 1951; d. Vernon John Wood and Hazel Ellen (Lake) Ammon. BS in Elem. Edn., N.W. Mo. State U., 1973; MS in Spl. Edn., S.W. Mo. State U., 1993. Cert. tchr., Mo. Kindergarten Livingston County Sch., Wheeling, Mo., 1973-75; 1st grade tchr. Mercer (Mo.) Sch., 1975-77, Maysville (Mo.) Sch., 1978-80; learning disabilities tchr. Lakeland Sch., Lowery City, Mo., 1980-81, Tri-County Sch., Jamesport, Mo., 1981-84, Plato (Mo.) Sch., 1984—. Adj. faculty Columbia Coll., 1995. Mem. Coun. for Exceptional Children, Mo. State Tchrs. Assn. Home: PO Box 8 Plato MO 65552-0008

WOOD, KATHERINE, physical education educator; b. Chipley, Fla., Sept. 9, 1958; d. William Lester and Pamela (deBoer) Kitching; m. Jonathan Wood, June 27, 1980; children: Caroline, Victoria. BS, Fla. State U., 1980. Phys. edn. tchr. Longwood (Fla.) Elem. Sch., 1980-82; sci. tchr. Hamilton County Middle Sch., Jasper, Fla., 1982-85, J.L. Wilkinson Middle Sch., Middleburg, Fla., 1985-86; phys. edn. tchr. Holly Hill (Fla.) Middle Sch., 1986-91, Mainland High Sch., Daytona Beach, Fla., 1991—. Co-leader Brownie troop #1171 Spruce Creek Elem. Sch., 1993—. Mem. AAHPERD, Fla. Assn. for Health, Phys. Edn., Recreation, Dance, and Phys. Edn. (co-chair program 1994—, Tchr. of Yr. 1994), NEA. Democrat. Baptist. Avocations: volleyball, light cooking, children. Office: Mainland High Sch 125 S Clyde Morris Blvd Daytona Beach FL 32114-3954

WOOD, LARRY (MARY LAIRD), journalist, author, university educator, public relations executive, environmental consultant; b. Sandpoint, Idaho; d. Edward Hayes and Alice (McNeel) Small; children: Mary, Marcia, Barry. BA summa cum laude, U. Wash., 1939, MA summa cum laude, with highest honors, 1940; postgrad., Stanford U., 1940-43, U. Calif., Berkeley, 1946-47, cert. in photography, 1971; postgrad. journalism, U. Wis., 1971-72, U. Minn., 1971-72, U. Ga., 1972-73; postgrad. in art, architecture and marine biology, U. Calif., Santa Cruz, 1974-76, Stanford Hopkins Marine Sta., 1977-80. Lifetime secondary and jr. coll. teaching cert., Wash., Calif. Feature writer and columnist Oakland Tribune and San Francisco Chronicle, Calif., 1939—; archtl. and environ. feature and travel writer and columnist San Jose (Calif.) Mercury News (Knight Ridder), 1972-90; teaching fellow Stanford U., 1940-43; dir. pub. rels. 2-counties, 56-park East Bay Regional Park Dist., No. Calif., 1948-68; pres. Larry Wood Pub. Rels., 1946—; pub. rels. dir. Calif. Children's Home Soc., 1947-58. Prof. pub. rels., mag. writing, journalism, investigative reporting San Diego State U., 1974-75; disting. vis. prof. journalism San Jose State U., 1976; assoc. prof. journalism Calif. State U., Hayward, 1978; prof. sci. and environ. journalism U. Calif. Berkeley Ext. grad. divsn., 1979—; press del. nat. convs. Am. Geophys. Union Internat. Conf., 1986—, AAAS, 1989—, Nat. Park Svc. VIP Press Tour, Yellowstone after the fire, 1989—, Nat. Assn. Sci. Writers, 1989—, George Washington U./Am. Assn. Neurol. Surgeons Sci. Writers Conf., 1990, Am. Inst. Biol. Scis. Conf., 1990, Nat. Conf. Sci. Writers, Am. Heart Assn., 1995, Internat. Cardiologists Symposium for Med./Sci. Writers, 1995, Annenberg Program Electronic Media Symposium, Washington, 1995; EPA del. to USSR and Ea. Europe; expert witness on edn., pub. rels., journalism and copyright; cons. sci. writers interne project Stanford U., 1989—; spl. media guest Sigma Xi, 1990—; mem. numerous spl. press corps; selected White House Spl. Media, 1993—; selected mem. Duke U. 14th Ann. Sci. Reporters Conf., 1995; internat. press guest Can. Consulate Gen. Dateline Can., 1995—, French Govt. Tourist Office, 1996—, Ministerio delle Risorse Agricole Alimentari e Forestali and Assocs. Conf., 1995; appeared in TV documentary Larry Wood Covers Visit of Queen Elizabeth II Contbr. over 5,500 articles to newspapers, nat. mags., nat. and internat. newspaper syndicates including L.A. Times-Mirror Syndicate, Knight-Ridder Syndicate, Washington Post, Phila. Inquirer, Chgo. Tribune, Miami Herald, Oakland Tribune, Seattle Times, San Francisco Chronicle, Parade, San Jose Mercury News (Nat. Headliner award), Christian Sci. Monitor, L.A. Times/Christian Sci. Monitor Worldwide News Syndicate, Washington Post, Phila. Inquirer, Hawaiian Airlines In Paradise and other in-flight mags., MonitoRadio, Donnelly Pubs., Sports Illus., Life, Mechanix Illus., Popular Mechanics, Parents (contbg. editor), House Beautiful, Am. Home (awards 1988-89), Archl. Digest, Better Homes and Gardens, Sunset, Architectural Digest, National Geographic World, Travel & Leisure, Chevron USA/Odyssey (Calif. Pub.'s award 1984), Xerox Edn. Publs., Europe's Linguapress, PSA Mag., Off Duty, Oceans, Sea Frontiers, AAA Westways, AAA Via, Travelin', others; home and garden columnist and editor, 5-part series Pacific Coast Ports, 5-part series Railroads of the West, series Immigration, Youth Gangs, Endangered Species, Calif. Lighthouse Chain, Lighthouses of the World, Pacific Coast Wetlands, Elkhorn Slough Nat. Estuarine Res., Ebey's Landing Nat. Hist. Island Res., Calif. Water Wars, BLM's Adopt a Horse Program, Mt. St. Helen's Eruption, Oreg's Covered Bridges, Loma Prieta Earthquake, Oakland Firestorm, Missing Children, Calif. Prison Reform, Columbia-Alaska's Receding Glacier, Calif. Underwater Parks, and many others; author: Wonderful U.S.A.: A State-by-State Guide to Its Natural Resources, 1989; co-author: McGraw-Hill English for Social Living, 1944, Fawcett Boating Books, 1956-66, Fodor's San Francisco, Fodor's California, 1982-89, Bell and Howell/Charles Merrill Focus on Life Science, Focus on Physical Science, Focus on Earth Science, 1983, 2d edit, 1987, State of California's Golden State Travel Guide, 1998; contbr. Earth Science 1987; 8 works selected for use by Europe's Woltors-Nordoff-Longman English Language Texts, U.K., Netherlands, 1988; author: (with others) anthology West Winds, 1989; reviewer Charles Merrill texts, 1983-84; book reviewer Profl. Communicator, 1987—; selected writings in permanent collections Oakland Pub. Libr., U. Wash. Main Libr.; environ. works included in Dept. Edn. State of Md. textbook; contbr., author Journalism Quar.; author script PBS/AAA America series, 1992; contbg. editor: Parents, Fashion Showcase, Spokane Mag. Nat. chmn. travel writing contest for U.S. univ. journalism students Assn. for Edn. in Journalism and Mass Communication/Soc. Am. Travel Writers, 1979-83; judge writing contest for Nat. Assn. Real Estate Editors, 1982—; cons. S. Carolina Dept. Parks, Recreation and Tourism, 1999—; press del. 1st Internat. Symposium Volcanism and Aviation Safety, 1991, Coun. for Advancement of Sci. Writing, 1977—, Rockefeller Media Seminar Feeding the World-Protecting the Earth, 1992, Global Conf. on Mercury as Pollutant, 1992, Earth Summit Global Forum, Rio de Janeiro, 1992; invited Nat. Park Svc. Nat. Conf. Sci. Writers, 1985, Postmaster Gen.'s 1992 Stamps, 1991, Internat. Geophys. Union Conf., 1982—, The Conf. Bd., 1995—, Corp. Comm. Conf., Calif. Inst. Tech.'s Media and Sci. Seminar, 1995—, Medical Writers Delegation to Russia and Estonia, 1997, N.Y. Times Opinion Rsch. Co. Corp. Image Conf., 1999, EPA and Dept. Energy Tech. Conf., 1992, Am. Soc. Photogrammetry and Remote Sensing Internat. Conv. Mapping Global Change, 1992, U.S. Conf. on Oceans, 1998, N.Y. Mus. Modern Art Matisse Retrospective Press Rev. and all media previews, 1992—, celebration 150th anniversary Oreg. Trail, 1993, Nat. Coun. Advancement Sci. Writing, 1977-2003, Sigma Xi Nat. Conf., 1988-2003, Nat. Sci. Writers Confs., 1977-2003, PRSA Travel and Tourism Conf., 1993—, Internat. Conf. Environment, 1994, 95, Quality Life Europe, Prague, 1994, Calif. Sesquicentennial, 1996, 14th Ann. Sci. Writers Conf., 1996, Picasso Retrospective, 1996, others; mem. Gov.'s Conf. Tourism N.C., 1993-2002, Calif., 1976—, Fla., 1987—, N.C. Govs. conf. on tourism and film, 2000-, U.C. Irvine Calif. Computer Sci. Symposium, 2000, Sea Grant's conf. on sci. in the news, 2000, N.Y. conf. bd. conf. on environ. journalism, 2000, on economics, 2001; press guest 14 U.S. states and 12 fgn. countries' Depts. Tourism, 1986—. Named to Broadway Hall of Fame, U. Wash., 1984; recipient Broadway Disting. Alumnus award, 1995; citations for environ. writing Nat. Park Svc., U.S. Forest Svc., Bur. Land Mgmt., Oakland Mus. Assn., Oakland C. of C., Chevron USA, USN plaque and citation, Best Mag. articles citation Calif. Pubs. Assn., 1984, U.S. Treasury award, 1946; co-recipient award for best Sunday newspaper mag. Nat. Headliners, citation for archtl. features Oakland Mus., 1983; honoree for achievements in journalism Nat. Mortar Bd., 1988, 89; named one of 10 V.I.P. press for Yellowstone Nat. Park field trip on "Let Burn" rsch., 1989, Calif.'s top 40 Contemporary Authors for writings on Calif. underwater parks, 1989, nat. honoree Social Issues Resources Series, 1987, Gov.'s Calif. Women of Achievement award, 1988-90; invited V.I.P. press, spl. press guest . Mem. AAAS, Am. Bd. Forensic Examiners, Calif. Acad. Scis., San Francisco Press Club, Nat. Press Club, Pub. Rels. Soc. Am. (charter mem. travel, tourism, environment and edn. divs.), Nat. Sch. Pub. Rels. Assn., Environ. Cons. N.Am., Am. Assn. Edn. in Journalism and Comm. (exec. bd. nat. mag. div. 1978, panel chmn. 1979, 80, author Journalism Quar. jour.), Women in Comm. (nat. bd. officer 1975-77, book reviewer Prof. Communicator), Soc. Profl. Journalists (nat. bd. for hist. sites 1980—), Nat. Press Photographers Assn. (hon. life, cons. Bay Area interne project 1989—, honoree 1995), Investigative Reporters and Editors (charter), Bay Area Advt. and Mktg. Assn., Nat. Assn. Sci. Writers, Calif. Writers Club (state bd., Berkeley bd. 1989—, honoree ann. conv. Asilomar, Calif. 1990), Am. Assn. Med. Writers, Internat. Assn. Bus. Communicators, Soc. Environ. Journalists (charter), Am. Film Inst., Am. Heritage Found. (citation 1986, 87, 88), Soc. Am. Travel Writers, Internat. Oceanographic Found., Oceanic Soc., Calif. Acad. Environ. News Writers, Seattle Advt. and Sales Club (former officer), Nature Conservancy, Smithsonian Audubon Soc., Nat. Wildlife Fedn., Nat. Parks and Conservation Assn., Calif. State Parks Found., Calif. Environ. Leadership Roundtable (trustee), Fine Arts Mus., San Francisco, Seattle Jr. Advt. Club (charter), U. Wash. Comm. Alumni (Sch. Comm. alumni, life, charter mem. ocean scis. alumni, Disting. Alumni 1987), U. Calif., Berkeley Alumni (life, v.p., scholarship chmn. 1975-81), Stanford Alumni (life), Mortar Board Alumnae Assn. (life, honoree 1988-89), Am. Mgmt. Assn., Nat. Soc. Environ. Journalists (charter), Calif. Environ. Leadership Roundtable, Phi Beta Kappa (v.p., bd. dirs. Calif. Alumni Assn., statewide chmn. scholarship awards 1975-81), Purple and Gold Soc. (planning com., charter, 1995—), Pi Lambda Theta, Theta Sigma Phi. Home: Piedmont Pines 6161 Castle Dr Oakland CA 94611-2737

WOOD, LINDA SHERRILL, secondary education educator; b. Birmingham, Ala., Aug. 16, 1947; d. Virgil Alton and Anna Ruth (Boston) W. BS, Auburn U., 1969, MEd, 1973. Tchr. math. Elberta (Ala.) Jr. High Sch., 1970-85, Foley (Ala.) High Sch., 1985—2003, counselor, 2003—. Mem. NEA, Ala. Edn. Assn., Baldwin County Edn. Assn. Office: Foley High Sch 1 Pride Pl Foley AL 36535-1100

WOOD, MAGGIE ETHEL, social studies educator; b. Saranac Lake, N.Y., Dec. 11, 1948; d. Albert Carlos and Margaret (Stewart) Skeels; m. Bennie Franklin Lewis, Jan. 24, 1968 (div. Nov. 1980); children: Jeremy S., Daniel V.; m. Bruce Alvin Wood, Aug. 14, 1982 (div. May 1988); children: Raymond A., Joshua D.; m. Larry Wayne Lane, Aug. 20, 1991. BS in Edn., SUNY, Plattsburgh, 1971; MS in Edn., U. So. Calif., 1976. Cert. tchr., N.Y., N.C. Tchr. Dept. Def. Schs., Kaiserslautern, Germany, 1973-77, Bossier Parish Schs., Benton, La., 1977-78, Webster Parish Schs., Minden, La., 1979-80, Caddo Parish Schs., Shreveport, La., 1980-84, Wayne County Pub. Schs., Goldsboro, N.C., 1985-93, Harnett County Schs., Lillington, N.C., 1993—. Lit. vol. Wayne County, Goldsboro, 1989—; ESL instr. Wayne C.C., Goldsboro, 1990-92, N.C. Coun. Social Studies. Mem. N.C. Coun. for Social Studies. James Iredell fellow Bicentennial Commn., Cullowhee, N.C., 1989. Mem. NEA, N.C. Assn. Educators, Laubach Internat., Tchr. Acad., Found. for Tchg. Econs. Avocations: sewing, reading. Home: PO Box 552 Mamers NC 27552-0552 Office: RR 5 Box 395 Lillington NC 27546-9014

WOOD, MARY MARIE, secondary education educator; b. Enon, Mo., Aug. 16, 1928; d. Ely Emerson and Maggie Mae (Campbell) W. AA, Southwest Bapt. Coll., 1951; BSBA, Cen. Mo. State U., 1955, MS in Edn., 1962. Cert. bus. educator, Mo. Tchr. bus. Cole R-1 Schs., Russellville, Mo., 1955-67; tchr. vocat. bus. edn. California (Mo.) R-1 Schs., 1967—. Recipient Most Influential Tchr. award U. Mo., 1991-92; named Calif. R-1 Outstanding Educator, 1987, 93-94. Mem. Nat. Bus. Edn. Assn., Mo. Tchrs. Assn., Mo. Bus. Edn. Assn., California Cmty. Tchrs. Assn. (past officer), Mo. Vocat. Assn., Moniteau County Hist. Soc., Daus. Am. Colonists (libr.). Home: 800 S Randolph St California MO 65018-2011 Office: California R-1 Sch 205 Owen St California MO 65018

WOOD, MILDRED HOPE, special education educator; b. Alta, Iowa, Apr. 19, 1920; d. Jesse L. and Hazel E. (David) Fisher; m. William O. Wood, June 23, 1940 (dec. 1988); children: Larry A., Donald D. BA, U. No. Iowa, 1956, MA, 1962, Edn. Specialist, 1963; EdD, Ind. U., 1970. Tchr. 1st and 2nd grades Rowley (Iowa) Consolidated Sch., 1939-40; speech therapist Black Hawk County (Iowa) Schs., 1956-60; instr. spl. edn. U. No. Iowa, Cedar Falls, 1961-65; demonstration tchr. mental retarded U. No. Iowa Lab. Sch., Cedar Falls, 1961-66; instr. ext. svc. for Headstart tchrs. Ind. U., Bloomington, 1969-70; edn. cons. and diagnostician Black Hawk & Buchanan County Schs., 1965-75; coord. learning disabilities prog. Cedar Falls (Iowa) pub. schs., 1968-72; vis. instr. learning disabilities U. No. Iowa, 1969—; child advocate Iowa Assn. for Children and Adults, 1978—. Edn. cons.; lectr. in field. Author: Communication Skills for the Mentally Retarded, 1966; co-author: Pre-Academic Learning Inventory (PAL), 1975; contbg. author: Language Arts Curriculum Guide, 1972; writer on learning disabilities Waterloo (Iowa) Courier, 1987—. Bd. dirs. Human Devel. Commn., Cedar Falls, 1975-82, Housing Community Devel. Task Force, 1975-80; mem. Black Hawk County Youth Shelter adv. bd., Waterloo, 1980-85. Named Outstanding Tchr. in Exceptional Edn., Acad. Ther. Pub., 1975, Helping Hand award, 1976, others. Mem. Learning Disability Assn., Coun. for Exceptional Children, Iowa Assn. for Children with Learning Disabilities (pres. 1979), Nat. League Am. Pen Women (pres. Iowa 1992-94), LWV, Pi Lambda Theta, Delta Kappa Gamma. Avocations: reading, bridge, travel, drama, creative writing.

WOOD, PAUL WILLIAM, language educator; b. Cin., Mar. 24, 1933; s. Walter John and Marie Sophie (Lott) W.; m. Mary Lou Donovan, Aug. 20, 1960; children: Paul Jr., Suzanne, Douglas, Rebecca. BA, Athenaeum of Ohio, Cin., 1954; MA, U. Cin., 1960; PhD, Northwestern U., 1970. Tchr. Forest Hills Sch. Dist., Cin., 1960-62; instr. Loyola U., Chgo., 1962-67; asst. prof. U. Akron, Ohio, 1967-71; prof. dept. modern lang. St. Bonaventure U., Olean, N.Y., 1971—. Participant Project Rendez-Vous, Ministry Affaires Etrangeres, Paris, 1985; mem. 2d Lang. Acquisition Coun., Buffalo, 1985-89; symposium leader Heidelberg (Germany) U., 1986; fgn. lang. program evaluator Commonwealth of Pa., Edinboro, 1987. Editor: Creating an Environment for Second Language Learning, 1987; contbr. to profl. publs. Pres. Friends of Libr., Olean, 1985-88; chmn. selection com. Big Thirty Acad. Scholarship, Olean, 1990; bd. dirs. Cattaraugus County Coun. on Alcoholism and Substance Abuse, Inc., 1993-2000. With U.S. Army, 1955-57, Korea. Named grand knight Olean Coun. 338, 1988-2000, faithfull navigator, 2000—. Mem. N.Y. State Assn. Fgn. Lang. Tchrs. (v.p. 1983-85, 93—, pres. 1985-86, Ferdinand D. Bartholo Disting. Leadership award 1985), Western N.Y. Fgn. Lang. Educators' Coun. (pres. 1978-80), Coll. Consortium Internat. Study (del. 1984-93), N.Y. State Coun. on Langs. (pres. 1986-88), Pi Delta Phi (v.p. 1991-97, pres. 1998—). Roman Catholic. Office: St Bonaventure U Box BQ Saint Bonaventure NY 14778 E-mail: pwood@sbu.edu.

WOOD, RUBY FERN, writer, retired elementary educator; b. Strauss, Kans., Aug. 17, 1922; d. John Elijah and Mildred Floy (Cole) Morrow; m. Leonard Edgar Wood, Oct. 18, 1942; children: Michael Wood, Sherry Wood Ruddell, Toni Wood Treaster. BS in Elem. Edn., Pittsburg (Kans.) State U., 1961, MS in Elem. Edn., 1965. Cert. tchr. elem. edn., secondary English, reading, lit., social studies, psychology, Kans. Tchr. grades 1-8 Cunningham Sch., Labette County, Kans., 1939-41, Centennial Sch., Montgomery County, Kans., 1941-42, Overfield Sch., Montgomery County, 1942-43, Foster Sch., Montgomery County, 1946-47, Racob-Wetzel Sch., Montgomery County, 1955-58; elem. tchr. Cherryvale (Kans.) Unified Sch. Dist. 447, 1961-87. Pres. Cherryvale Tchrs. Assn., 1971-72; mem. selection panel Master Tchrs. Kans., Emporia, 1983-85. Author: (biography) Pop and Bud, 1981, (hist. fiction) The Benders-Keepers of the Devil's Inn, 1992; editor: 10-Year History of the SWC Region of AAUW, 1986, (anthology) Memories of a Country School, 1989; editor, contbg. author: Southeast Kansas: Land of Discovery, 1993. Coord. Heritage 200 Day, Cherryvale, 1976; guest White House briefing, Washington, 1984; coord. spl. exhibits Cherryvale Mus., 1980—. Recipient 1st prize Tulsa Professionalism in Writing Conf., 1991. Mem. AAUW (Kans. pres. 1983-85), Kans. Authors Club (pres. 3d dist. 1989-93, state pres. 1995-97, 1st prize Eisenhower theme 1990), Kans. Coun. Women, Internat. Platform Spkrs. Assn., Phi Theta Kappa, Delta Kappa Gamma. Democrat. Methodist. Avocations: writing, research, church work, travel. Home: RR 2 Box 114 Cherryvale KS 67335-9726

WOOD, SAMUEL EUGENE, college administrator, psychology educator; b. Brotherton, Tenn., Aug. 16, 1934; s. Samuel Ernest and Daisy J. (Jernigan) W.; m. Helen J. Walker, June 2, 1956; children: Liane Wood Kelly, Susan Wood Benson, Alan Richard; m. Ellen Rosenthal Green, Sept. 8, 1977; stepchildren: Bart M. Green, Julie Alice Green. BS in English and Music, Tenn. Tech. U., 1961; M in Edn. Adminstrn., U. Fla., 1967, D in Edn., 1969. Asst. prof. edn. W.Va. U., 1968-70, U. Mo., St. Louis, 1970-75, mem. doctoral faculty, 1973-75; dir. rsch. Ednl. Devel. Ctr., Belleville, Ill., 1976-81; prof. psychology Meramec Coll., St. Louis, 1981-94; pres. Higher Edn. Ctr., St. Louis, 1985—; prof. psychology Lindenwood Coll., 1995—. Exec. dir. Edn. Opportunity Ctrs., St. Louis, 1985—, Project Talent Search, St. Louis, 1991—; bd. commrs. Pub. TV Com., St. Louis, 1985—; planning com. St. Louis Schs., 1985-90; adminstr. German-Am. student exch. program Internat. Bus. Students, 1985—; sponsor Higher Edn. Ctr. Internat. Edn. Coun., 1985—; co-founder, pres. Higher Edn. Cen. Cable TV Channel, Sta. HEC-TV, St. Louis, 1986; v.p. St. Louis County Cable TV Commn., 1991—. Musician, composer with USN Band, 1956-59; composer A Nautical Musical Comedy, A Child's Garden of Verses in Song, 1979; numerous poems set to music; co-author: (with Ellen Green Wood) (textbook) The World of Psychology, 1993, 4th edit., 2002, Can. edit., 1996, The Essential World of Psychology, 2000; contbr. articles to ednl. and sci. jours. Served with USN, 1955-59. US Office Edn. grantee 1976-81, 85—. Mem. Internat. Edn. Consortium (bd. dirs. 1985-91), Phi Kappa Phi. Democrat. Baptist. Avocations: writing, reading, music composition and performance. Home: 853 Longacre Dr Apt B Saint Louis MO 63132-4736 Office: Apt B 853 Longacre Dr Saint Louis MO 63132-4736

WOOD, SHELTON EUGENE, education educator, consultant, minister; b. Douglas, Ga, May 20, 1938; s. Shelton and Mae Lillie (Pheil) Wood; m. Edna Louise Wood, Aug. 25, 1961; children: Shelton John, Deirdre Louise. AA, St. John's U., 1958; BA, U. Nebr., 1959; MEd, Coll. William and Mary, 1971; PhD, Sussex U., 1973; EdD, Southeastern U., 1975; MBA, Ctrl. Mich. U., 1977; MA, U. Okla., 1980; D in Ministry, Wesleyan Bible Coll., 1999; Cert. in Internt. Rels., Fgn. Svc. Inst., 1971; Cert. in Mgmt., Indsl. Coll. Armed Forces, 1970. Area mgr. Marshall Fields Corp., Fla., 1957-58; transp. supr. Greyhound Corp., Jacksonville, Fla., 1959-62; officer US Army, 1963, advanced through grades to inf. col., 1996; with Redstone Readiness Group, 1977-80; chief studies and analysis divsn. Korean Inst. for Def. Analysis, 1981-83; faculty St. John River C.C., 1984-90; nat. and internat. bus. and mgmt. cons., 1995—; sr. pastor Fellowship Wesleyan Ch., Spring Hill, Fla., 1998—. Mem. faculty Wesleyan Bible U., 1997—, dean Grad. Sch. Author: Strategic for Implementing A Family Life Ministry Ctr., 1997; contbr. over 120 articles and reports in field of mil. tng., edn., mgmt., pastoral studies, and practical theology. Active Boy Scouts Am., 1977—90; lay leader United Meth. Ch., Falls Ch., Va., 1977—79, St. James United Meth. Ch., 1986—90; mem. dist. bd. ministerial develop. Fla. Dist. of Wesleyan Ch., 1999, chair evangelism and ch. growth com., 1999—; bd. dir. Baby Love. Decorated Bronze Star with 2 oak leaf clusters, Air medal with 3 oak leaf clusters, Purple Heart with 2 oak leaf clusters; Sussex Coll. fellow, 1969-70. Mem. NEA, Am. Soc. Trainers and Developers (pres. S.E. chpt. 1974-75), Am. Def. Preparedness Assn., Putnam County C. of C. (pres. 1990-91), Toastmasters Internat. (Disting. Toastmaster 1989), Kiwanis (pres. 1989-90), Phi Kappa Delta, Phi Delta Kappa. Address: 8485 Chatsworth St Spring Hill FL 34608

WOOD, VIVIAN POATES, mezzo soprano, educator, writer; b. Washington, Aug. 19, 1923; d. Harold Poates and Mildred Georgette (Patterson) W. Studies with Walter Anderson, Antioch Coll., 1953-55; Denise Restout, Saint-Leu-A-Forget, France and Lakeville, Conn., 1960-62, 64-70; Paul A. Pisk, Saint-Leu-La-Fôret, France and Lakeville, Conn., 1968-71; Paul Ulanowsky, N.Y.C., 1958-68; Elemer Nagy, 1965-68, Vyautas Marijosius, 1967-68; MusB, Hartt Coll. Music, 1968; postgrad. (fellow), Yale U., 1968; MusM (fellow), Washington U., St. Louis, 1971, PhD (fellow), 1973. Debut in recital series Internat. Jeunesse Musicals Arts Festival, 1953; solo fellowship Boston Symphony Orch., Berkshire Music Ctr., Tanglewood, 1964, St. Louis Symphony Orch., 1969, Washington Orch., 1949, Bach Cantata Series Berkshire Chamber Orch., 1964, Yale Symphony Orch., 1968. Appearances in U.S. and European recitals, oratorios, operas, radio and TV, 1953-68; soloist Landowska Ctr., Lakeville, 1969, Internat. Harpsichord Festival, Westminister Choir Coll., Princeton, N.J., 1973; prof. voice, head voice area Sch. of Music, U. So. Miss., Hattiesburg, 1971-2000, ret. 2000, prof. emerita, 2000—; asst. dean Coll. Fine Arts, 1974-76, acting dean, 1976-77; guest prof. Hochschüle für Musik, Munich, 1978-79; prof. Italian Internat. Studies Program, Rome, 1986; Miss. coord. Alliance for Arts Edn., Kennedy Ctr. Performing Arts, 1974—; mem. Miss. Gov.'s Adv. Panel for Gifted and Talented Children, 1974—, 1st Miss. Gov.'s Conf. on the Arts, 1974—. Author: Polenc's Songs: An Analysis of Style, 1971. Recipient Young Am. Artists Concert award N.Y.C., 1955; Wanda Landowska fellow 1961-68. Mem. Miss. Music Tchrs. Assn., Nat. Assn. Tchrs. of Singing, Music Tchrs. Nat. Assn., Am. Musicology Soc., Golden Key, Mu Phi Epsilon, Delta Kappa Gamma, Tau Beta Kappa (hon.), Pi Kappa Lambda. Democrat. Episcopalian.

WOOD, WELLINGTON GIBSON, III, biochemistry educator; b. Balt., Dec. 29, 1945; s. Wellington Gibson Jr. and Elsie Bernice (Johnson) W.; m. Beverly Jean Beaver, Feb. 8, 1969; children: Wellington Gibson IV, Katherine Brittingham. BA, Tex. Tech U., 1971, PhD, 1976. Postdoctoral fellow Syracuse (N.Y.) U., 1976-77; staff scientist Bangor (Maine) Mental Health Inst., 1978-80; evaluation coord. VA Med. Ctr., St. Louis, 1980-89, assoc. dir. for edn. and evaluation Mpls., 1989—; asst. prof. St. Louis U. Sch. Medicine, 1982-87, assoc. prof., 1987-89; assoc. prof. dept. pharmacology U. Minn. Sch. Medicine, Mpls., 1990-96, prof. dept. pharmacology, 1996—. Mem. sci. editorial bd. Alcoholism and Drug Rsch. Comm. Ctr., Austin, Tex., 1990-96; mem. biochemistry, physiology and medicine study sect. NIH-Nat. Inst. Alcohol Abuse and Alcoholism, 1992-96, bd. sci. counselors, 1997-2002; bd. dirs. Minn. Inst. for Vets. Rsch. Assoc. editor Exptl. Aging Rsch., 1977-82; contbr. numerous articles to profl. jours. Nat. Inst. on Alcohol Abuse and Alcoholism postdoctoral fellow, 1976-77; grantee Nat. Inst. on Alcohol Abuse and Alcoholism, Nat. Inst. on Aging, Dept. Vets. Affairs, NATO Dept. Def. Mem. Am. Soc. Cell Biology, Soc. Neurosci., Am. Soc. for Neurochemistry, Internat. Soc. for Neurochemistry, Am. Soc. Biochemistry and Molecular Biology. Achievements include elucidating the role of cholesterol in brain neuronal structure and function, particularly with respect to the neuronal plasma membrane; this work has focused on mechanisms that are involved in the regulation of membrane cholesterol domains and how changes in cholesterol domains may contribute to neuronal dysfunction induced by alcoholism, aging, and Alzheimer's disease. Home: 16091 Huron Path Lakeville MN 55044-8874 Office: VA Med Ctr GRECC 11G Minneapolis MN 55417 Business E-Mail: woodx002@umn.edu.

WOODALL, SUSAN KAY, language educator, librarian; b. Terre Haute, Ind., Mar. 13, 1951; d. James H. and Frances E. (Erxleben) Anderson; m. John P. Ramsey, Aug. 8, 1978 (div. May 1987); children: Jamie Sue, Jessica Leora; m. John Omar Rodriguez, Nov. 21, 1990 (div. Oct. 1996); m. Michael Taylor Woodall, May 21, 2002. Student, Cambridge (Eng.) U., spring 1972; BA in Latin, English and Psychology cum laude, Valparaiso U., 1973; MA with distinction in English, Ind. State U., 1976, MA in Libr. Sci., 1985; gifted/talented edn. endorsement, Purdue U., 1990. Lic. lifetime tchr.; cert. tchr. secondary English, Latin and psychology, Ind.; cert. in elem. and secondary gifted and talented edn., Ind.; lic. lifetime elem. and secondary libr. Tchr. English and Latin Clinton (Ind.) H.S., 1973-77, Austin (Ind.) H.S., 1977-78; tchr. Latin, English and psychology South Putnam H.S., Greencastle, Ind., 1978-85, tchr., libr. head dept., 1995—. Past drama coach, yearbook instr. South Putnam H.S., acad. team coord., 1985-97; adj. instr. libr. sci. Ind. State U., Terre Haute, summers 1986, 87; Fulbright exch. tchr. Southwood Secondary Sch., Cambridge, Ont., Can., 1994-95; adj. tchr. gifted and talented edn., libr. cons. Sacred Heart Sch., Terre Haute, 1994-95; cons. Dist. III Ind. Classical Conf., 1975-77. Contbr. articles to profl. publs. Mem. VFW aux.; past participant Habitat for Humanity. Named Creative Latin Tchr. of Yr., Ind. Classical Conf., 1976, 77; recipient Exch. cert. Fulbright Assn., Washington, 1995. Mem. NEA, Ind. Collective Svcs. Auth. (South Putnam Sch. Corp. rep. 1989—, mem. exec. com. 1989-95), Stone Hills Area Libr. Svcs. Authority (bd. dirs. Bloomington, Ind. br. 1989-95, treas., bd. dirs. 1993, 94, cons., mem. com. for cons./dir. rev. 1992, Dedicated Svc. award 1995), Acad. Coaches Assn. (Ind. br.), Ont. Libr. Assn., Ind. Coop. Libr. Svcs. Auth. Episcopalian. Avocations: writing, travel. Office: Ind South Putnam Libr Svcs 1780 E Us Highway 40 Greencastle IN 46135-8722

WOODBURY, DIXON JOHN, physiologist, educator, research scientist; b. Seattle, Dec. 31, 1956; s. John Walter and Betty (Gunderson) Woodbury; m. Susan Diana Harvey, Mar. 20, 1980; children: James Dixon, Thomas Walter, Emily Susan, Kara Leigh. BS in Physics and Chemistry magna cum laude, U. Utah, 1980; PhD in Physiology and Biophysics, U. Calif., Irvine, 1986. Postdoctoral fellow in biochemistry Brandeis U., Waltham, Mass., 1986-89; rsch. assoc. Howard Hughes Med. Inst., Waltham, 1989-90; asst. prof. Wayne State U., Detroit, 1990-97, assoc. prof., 1997-2001, Brigham Young U., Provo, Utah, 2001—03, prof., 2003—. Unit commr. Boy Scouts Am., 1984—86, 1996—98; bishopric Ch. Jesus Christ LDS, 1997—99. Fellow, U. Calif., 1980, 1981, 1985, Muscular Dystrophy Assn., 1986—88. Mem.: IEEE, Biophysical Soc., Soc. Neuroscience. Office: Brigham Young U 574 Widtsoe Bldg Provo UT 84602-5255

WOODBURY, RICHARD BENJAMIN, anthropologist, educator; b. West Lafayette, Ind., May 16, 1917; s. Charles Goodrich and Marion (Benjamin) W.; m. Nathalie Ferris Sampson, Sept. 18, 1948. Student, Oberlin Coll., 1934-36; BS in Anthropology cum laude, Harvard U., 1939, MA, 1942, PhD, 1949; postgrad., Columbia U., 1939-40. Archeol. research, Ariz., 1938, 39, 1940, 1947-49, 1953-56, Tehuacan, Mex., 1964; archaeologist United Fruit Co. Zaculeu Project, Guatemala, 1947-50; assoc. prof. anthropology U. Ky., 1950-52, Columbia U., 1952-58; rsch. assoc. prof. anthropology interdisciplinary arid lands program U. Ariz., 1959-63; curator archeology and anthropology U.S. Nat. Mus., Smithsonian Instn., Washington, 1963-69, acting. head office anthropology, 1965-66, chmn. office anthropology, 1966-67; prof., chmn. dept. anthropology U. Mass., Amherst, 1969-73, prof., 1973-81, prof. emeritus, 1981—, acting assoc. provost, dean grad. sch., 1973-74. Mem. divsn. anthropology and psychology NRC, 1954-57; bd. dirs. Archaeol. Conservancy, 1979-84, Valley Health Plan, Amherst, 1981-84, Mus. of No. Ariz., 1983-90; liason rep. for Smithsonian Instn., Com. for Recovery of Archeol. Remains, 1965-69; assoc. seminar on ecol. systems and cultural evolution Columbia U., 1964-73; mem. exec. com. bd. dirs. Human Relations Area Files, Inc., New Haven, Conn., 1968-70; cons. Conn. Hist. Commn., 1970-72. Author (with A.S. Trik) The Ruins of Zaculeu, Guatemala, 2 vols., 1953, Prehistoric Stone Implements of Northeastern Arizona, 1954, Alfred V. Kidder, 1973, Sixty Years of Southwestern Archaeology, 1993, (chpt.) (with James A. Neely) The Prehistory of the Tehuacan Valley, Vol. 4, 1972; editor: (with I.A. Sanders) Societies Around the World (2 vols.), 1953, (with others) The Excavation of Hawikuh, 1966, Am. Antiquity, 1954-58, Abstracts of New World Archaeology; editor-in-chief: Am. Anthropologist, 1975-78; mem. editorial bd.: Am. Jour. Archeology, 1957-72. Mem. sch. com., Shutesbury, Mass., 1979-82; chmn. finance com. Friends of Amherst Stray Animals (Dakin Animal Shelter), 1983-85, trustee, 1991—; sec. Shutesbury Hist. Commn., 1999—. With USAF, 1942-45. Fellow Mus. No. Ariz., 1985. Fellow AAAS (coun. rep. Am. Anthrop. Assn. 1961-63, com. on desert and arid zones rsch. Southwest and Rocky Mountains divsn. 1958-64, vice-chair 1962-64, com. arid lands 1969-74, sec. 1970-72), Am. Anthrop. Assn. (exec. bd. 1963-66, A.V. Kidder award 1989), Archeol. Inst. Am. (exec. com. 1965-67); mem. Soc. Am. Archeology (treas. 1953-54, pres. 1958-59, chmn. fin. com. 1987-89, Fiftieth Anniversary award 1985, Disting. Svc. award 1988), Ariz. Archeol. and Hist. Soc., Nature Conservancy, Archeol. Conservancy (life). Office: U Mass Dept Anthropology Machmer Hall Amherst MA 01003

WOODBURY, STEPHEN ABBOTT, economics educator; b. Beverly, Mass., Oct. 25, 1952; s. Stephen E. and Barbara (Sandberg) W.; m. Susan Pozo, May 29, 1982 (div. June 1992); 1 child, Ricardo Pozo; m. Virginia Baldwin, Dec. 7, 1996. AB, Middlebury (Vt.) Coll., 1975; MS, U. Wis., 1977, PhD, 1981. Asst. prof. of econs. Pa. State U., University Park, 1979-82, Mich. State U., East Lansing, 1982-88, assoc. prof. econs., 1988-94; prof. econs., 1994—; sr. economist W.E. Upjohn Inst., Kalamazoo, Mich., 1984—. Dep. dir. Fed. Adv. Coun. on Unemployment Compensation, Washington, 1993-94, cons., 1994-96; cons. U. Hawaii/State of Hawaii, Honolulu, 1991-96, State of Mich. Task Force, Lansing, 1989-90, U.S. Dept. Labor, Washington, 1988, 96—, European Communities Commn., Brussels, 1987-88; vis. prof. U. Stirling, Scotland, 1992; vis. scholar Fed. Res. Bd., Washington, 1992. Author: Tax Treatment of Fringe Benefits, 1991; editor: Search Theory and Unemployment, 2002, Employee Benefits and Labor Markets in the U.S. and Canada, 2000, Reform of the Unemployment Insurance System, 1998, Long-Term Unemployment and Reemployment Policies, 2000; contbr. articles to profl. jours. Recipient Rsch. grants William H. Donner Found., 1991, U.S. Dept. Health and Human Svcs., 1985, 99, U.S. Dept. Labor, 1995, 98, 2002. Filene Rsch. Inst., 1996, Ctr. Credit Union Rsch., U. Wis., 1997, AMA, 2001. Mem. Am. Econ. Assn., Am. Statis. Assn., Assn. for Evolutionary Econs., Indsl. Rels. Rsch. Assn., Midwest Econs. Assn. (1st v.p. 1993-94, pres. 1998-99), Nat. Acad. Social Ins., Soc. Labor Economists, Nat. Tax Assn. Office: Dept Econs Marshall Hall Mich State U East Lansing MI 48824 also: WE Upjohn Inst 300 S Westnedge Ave Kalamazoo MI 49007-4630

WOODE, MOSES KWAMENA ANNAN, medical and chemistry educator, scientist; b. Takoradi, Ghana, June 27, 1947; came to U.S., 1981; s. Emmanuel Kwamena and Georgina Aba (Arthur) W.; m. Eunice Adjaottor, Aug. 24, 1974; children: Linda-Marie, Timothy. BS in Chemistry and Math., U. Ghana, Legon, Accra, 1971, BS in Chemistry with honors, 1972, MS in Chemistry; PhD in Chem. Crystallography, Sch. Tech. and Medicine, London, 1978. Assoc. prof. med. edn. and chemistry U. Va., Charlottesville, 1986-93, dir. Assisting Students Achieve Med. Degrees, 1987—, asst. dean, acad. support, 1988-91, assoc. dean acad. support and strategic programs, 1992—, rsch. assoc. prof. chemistry, assoc. prof. ob-gyn., 1986-93, prof. med. edn., ob-gyn. rsch. prof. chemistry, 1993—. Contbr. articles to profl. jours. Grantee NIH, 1987—, Robert Wood Johnson Found., 1988—, U.S. Dept. HHS, 1990—. Fellow Am. Inst. Chemists; mem. APHA, ACA, Am. Crystallographic Assn., Sigma Xi. Achievements include design of academic enrichment programs at high school, college and medical school levels; contribution to understanding of structure-function relationships of biologically important molecules and liquid crystals. Office: U Va Sch Medicine PO Box 446 Charlottesville VA 22902-0446

WOODEN, REBA FAYE BOYD, guidance counselor; b. Washington, Ind., Sept. 21, 1940; d. Lester E. and Opal M. (Burch) Boyd; m. N. Nuel Wooden, Jr., Dec. 23, 1962 (div. 1993); children: Jeffrey Nuel, Cynthia Faye. BA, U. Indpls., 1962; MS, Butler U., 1968, Ind. U., 1990. Cert. tchr., counselor, Ind. Tchr. Mooresville (Ind.) High Sch., 1962-66, Perry Meridian High Sch., Indpls., 1974-92, counselor, 1992—. Part-time instr. Ind. U.-Purdue U. at Indpls., 1994-95; humanist counselor, Celebrant, 2001—. Named Outstanding High Sch. Psychology tchr. APA, 1987. Mem. NEA, AAUW (coord.), Ind. State Tchrs. Assn., Perry Edn. Assn., Am. Humanists, ACLU, ACLU Coun. for Secular Humanists, Ind. Civil Liberties Union, Freedom from Religion Found., Secular Humanists, Humanist Friendship Group Ctrl. Ind. (founder), Indpls. Hiking Club (bd. mem.). Humanist. Avocations: reading, travel, hiking. Home address. Home: 113 Severn Dr Greenwood IN 46142-1880 Office: Perry Meridian High Sch 401 W Meridian School Rd Indianapolis IN 46217-4215 E-mail: rboydw@webtv.net.

WOODFORD, MARY IMOGENE STEELE, secondary school educator; b. Balt., Jan. 7, 1919; d. Percy Howard and Mary Imogene (Waring) Steele; m. Hackley Elbridge Woodford, MD, June 7, 1940; children: Peggy, John, Joan, Barbara. BA, Howard U., 1940; MA, U. Chgo., 1960. Tchr. Benton Harbor Sch., Mich., 1960-70, Jr. and Sr. HS, Pasadena, Calif., 1971-75, LA, 1975-84. Bd. dir. Girl Scouts of US, Benton Harbor, Mich., 1947-50; mem. Ys Neighbors, YWCA, Benton Harbor, St. Joseph, Mich., 1947-70. Lotta Crabtree Estate scholar, Wayland, Boston 1936. Mem. AAUW, Tuskegee Airmen Inc. (membership chair 1995-96), The Links, Inc. (Mothr of Yr. 1994), Delta Sigma Theta. Democrat. Presbyterian. Avocations: reading, travel, crossword puzzles, sewing, swimming. Home: 16071 Avenida Lamego San Diego CA 92128-3151

WOODING, GAYLE MCAFEE, nursing educator, consultant; b. Pitts., Jan. 2, 1937; d. Ralph W. and Harriet L. (Hulbert) McA. Diploma, Shadyside Hosp., 1959; BS in Nursing, Med. Coll. Ga., 1977; MS in Nursing, U. Fla., 1987. Commd. 2d lt. U.S. Army, 1960, advanced through grades to col., 1987, resigned, 1975; nurse epidemiologist Good Samaritan Hosp., West Palm Beach, Fla., 1977; surg. supr. VA Med. Ctr., Gainesville, Fla., 1978-86; dir. nursing Bradford Hosp., Starke, 1986; educator, cons. pvt. practice, Gainesville, Fla., 1987—, Nationwide Ins., Gainesville, Fla., 1991—. Contbr. articles to profl. jours. With USAR, 1975—. Mem. Assn. of Mil. Surgeons of the U.S., Res. Officers Assn., Am. Assn. Legal Nurse Cons., Sigma Theta Tau.

WOODMAN, JEAN WILSON, educator, consultant; b. New Brunswick, N.J., June 3, 1949; d. Richard and Doris (Pappa) Wilson; m. G. Roger Woodman; 1 child, Kevin. BA in English, St. Mary-of-the-Woods Coll., Terre Haute, Ind., 1971; MA in Tchg. magna cum laude, Monmouth U., West Long Branch, N.J., 1981. Cert. tchr., N.J. Tchr., chmn. English dept. St. Peter Sch., Point Pleasant, N.J., 1973-77, 80-85, Holy Family Sch., Lakewood, N.J., 1985-89; tchr. ESL and supplemental instrn. Lakewood Prep. Sch., Howell, N.J., 1991-93; tchr. St. Gregory the Great Sch., Hamilton Square, N.J., 1993—. Ednl. cons. J.W. Woodman Assocs., Lakewood, 1982—; sr. v.p. Cynosure Cons., Inc., Lakewood, 1987—. Contbr. poems to profl. publs. Mem. ASCD, Nat. Cath. Ednl. Assn. Avocations: writing, swimming, theater, ice skating.

WOODRUFF, GENE LOWRY, nuclear engineer, university dean; b. Greenbrier, Ark., May 6, 1934; s. Clarence Oliver and Avie Erscilla (Lowry) W.; m. Marylou Munson, Jan. 29, 1961; children— Gregory John, David Reed BS with honors, U.S. Naval Acad., 1956; MS in Nuclear Engring., MIT, 1963, PhD in Nuclear Engring., 1966. Registered profl. engr., Wash. Asst. prof. nuclear engring. U. Wash., Seattle, 1965-70, assoc. prof., 1970-76, prof., 1976-93, chmn. dept., 1981-84, dir. nuclear engring. labs., 1973-76, dean Grad. Sch., 1984-93, prof. chem. engring. environ. studies, 1989-98, dean emeritus, prof. emeritus, 1998—. Vice-chair, chair-elect Grad. Record Exam., 1991-92, chair, 1992-93; cons. to govt. and industry. Contbr. numerous articles to sci. and tech. jours. Served to lt. USN, 1956-60 Mem. Nat. Soc. Profl. Engrs. (Achievement award 1977), Am. Nuclear Soc. (Achievement award 1977, chmn. honors/awards com. 1981-84, nat. program com. 1971-75, exec. com. fusion div. 1976-80, vice chmn. edn. div. 1983-84, Arthur Holly Compton award 1986), Am. Soc. Engring. Edn., Assn. Grad. Schs. (v.p./pres.-elect 1990-91, pres. 1991-92). Democrat. Home: 19081 11th Ave NW Shoreline WA 98177-2610 Office: U Wash Box 351750 Seattle WA 98195-1750 E-mail: woodruff@u.washington.edu.

WOODRUFF, KATHRYN ELAINE, English language educator; b. Ft. Stockton, Tex., Oct. 12, 1940; d. James Arthur and Catherine H. (Stevens) Borron; m. Thomas Charles Woodruff, May 18, 1969; children: Robert Borron, David Borron. BA, Our Lady of the Lake U., San Antonio, 1963; MFA, U. Alaska, 1969; PhD, U. Denver, 1987. Cert. tchr., Tex., Colo. English and journalism tchr. Owensboro (Ky.) Cath. High Sch., 1963-64, Grand Junction (Colo.) Dist. 12, 1964-66; English tchr. Monroe High Sch., Fairbanks, Alaska, 1966-67; teaching asst. U. Alaska, Fairbanks, 1967-69, instr., 1969-70, U. Colo., Boulder, 1979, Denver, 1988-89, Regis Coll., Denver, 1987-89; asst. prof. Econs. Inst., Boulder, 1989-92; assoc. prof. English Colo. Christian U., Lakewood, 1993—. Tchr. Upward Bound, Fairbanks, 1968; instr. ethnic and women writers course U. Colo., Denver, 1988-93; mem. Assoc. Writing Programs; soprano Boulder Chorale, Cantabile Singers, St. John's Cathedral Choir, Augustana Chamber Choir; mem. Women's Studies Delegation to South Africa, 1998; active in missionary work in Ecuador, 1998, European Singing Tour with Augustana Arts, 1998, 2000. Author: (poetry) Before the Burning, 1994; poetry readings in Colo., Tex. and Paris; poems publ. in Denver Quarterly, The Incliner, Southwestern Am. Lit. Friend Chautauqua Music Festival, Boulder, 1985—; dir. 12th Annual Arts Festival, Fairbanks, 1969; active Augustana Chamber Chorus, St. John's Cathedral Choir; bd. mem. Denver Bach Soc. Recipient Poet's Choice award Internat. Soc. Poetry, 1997; named one of Outstanding Young Women Am., 1966; nominated for Poet Laureate of Colo., 1996; NEH grantee, 1996. Mem. AAUW, MLA, Am. Assn. Univ. Professors, Assoc. Writing Programs, Soc. Internat. Devel. UN Assn., Nat. Women's Hall of Fame, Acad. of Am. Poets, Denver Bach Soc. (bd. dirs. 2003), Internat. Women's Writing Guild. Democrat. Mem. Christian Ch. Avocations: singing, tennis, skiing, volleyball, travel. Office: Colo Christian U 180 S Garrison St Lakewood CO 80226-1053

WOODRUFF, MARY BRENNAN, elementary education educator; d. John L. and Josephine (Martino) Brennan; m. Paul R. Woodruff; children: Christopher, Jeffery. BS, SUNY, Brockport; MS, SUNY, Buffalo, 1987. Cert. Elem. Edn. Tchr. Third grade tchr. Middleport (N.Y.) Elem., fifth grade tchr., 1979—2003, math specialist K-6, 2003—. Sch. improvement presenter, mem., dist. curriculum guide, facilitator Social Studies curriculum, Royalton-Hartland Cen. Sch., Middleport, NY, 1989—, co-author mentor program for Royalton-Hartland District, Project "Deep" Elem. Econ. faciliator Contributing author Royalton-Hartland Curriculum Guide 1989; designer of spelling program 5th grade. Campaign mgr. Rep. Legislator, Orleans County, 1979-87. NY State United Tchs. Leadership Award, 1997 Exec. coun., v.p., NY State United Tchrs., v.p. Royalton-Hartland Tchrs. Assn.Mem. ASCD, pres.Royalton-Hartland Tchrs. Assn. (grievance chmn.), Delta Xi Sorority, Assn., Delta Kappa Gamma. Avocations: political action, writing, reading.

WOODRUFF, SHIRLEY, middle school educator; b. Richmond, Calif., May 30, 1951; d. Vern LeRoy and Betty Jo (Salyer) Cole; m. Carl Woodruff, June 22, 1974; children: Dan, David, Ben, Mark, Joseph. AA, Solano C.C., Rockland, Calif., 1971; BA in Social Sci., Calif. State U., Sacramento, 1973; postgrad., Idaho State U., 1972-73; student, Contra Costa Jr. Coll., San Pablo, Calif., 1969-70; postgrad., Brigham Young U. Cert. reading specialist, secondary and elementary credentials, kindergarten endorsement, reading endorsement K-12, social studies K-12, Idaho, Calif. Tchr. grades 5 and 6, tchr. art and music Sch. Dist. 91, Idaho Falls, Idaho, 1973-74; chpt. I tchr., 1979-82; tchr. kindergarten Bonneville Joint Dist. 93, Idaho Falls; 3rd grade tchr., 1982-85; elem. tchr. Bonneville Joint Dist. 93, Idaho Falls; 9th grade reading tchr., Book Fair chmn. Sandcreek Mid. Sch., Idaho Falls, Idaho, 1992-97; tchr. reading Bonneville Joint Dist. 93, Idaho Falls, 7th grade reading, geography, and lit. tchr. study skills, 1985—, mem. dist. curriculum com. lang. arts dept., 1995-96, bldg. cons. for accelerated reader program, 1996—, chairperson lang. arts dept. for state evaluations. Past editor Hi-Hopes Idaho Coun. Internat. Reading Assn. state newsletter; past editor Edn. Coalition Newsletter Goals 2000, Idaho Falls, 1992-93; writer ch. newsletter. Libr. Sunday sch. tchr.; chmn. Multiple Sclerosis read-a-thon Iona Elem. Sch., 1980; adv. Reading Club, Sandcreek Mid. Sch., 1990-97, team leader Team of Tchrs., 1992-93, 96-98, book fair chmn., 1992-97; bldg. rep. East Idaho Reading Coun., 1992-95; mem. steering com. Edn. Coalition, Idaho Falls, 1991-93; chmn. Spelling Bee, 1988-89, 96-97. Mem. NEA, Nat. Coun. Tchrs. English, Internat. Reading Assn. (Pres.'s award Idaho coun.), East Idaho Reading Coun. (rep. 1990-97, membership chair, bldg. rep. 1994-95, past pres., past v.p.), Idaho Edn. Assn., Bonneville Edn. Assn. (bldg. rep. 1994-95). Home: 5511 Concord Cir Idaho Falls ID 83401-6328

WOODRUFF, VALERIE, secretary of education; m. Frank Woodruff; 1 child, Scott 1 stepchild, Sheri. BEd in Secondary Edn., Alderson Broaddus Coll., W. Va.; MA in guidance and counseling, U. Del.; postgrad. studies in vocat. edn. and curriculum devel., Temple U., 1999—. From tchr. to prin. New Castle County, Del., Cecil County Md.; assoc. sec. for curriculum and instructional improvement Del. Dept. Edn., Dover, Del., 1992—99, acting sec., 1999—2000, sec, 2000—. Office: Del Dept Edn Townsend Bldg #279 401 Federal St Ste 2 Dover DE 19903-1402

WOODRUFF, WANDA LEA, elementary education educator; b. Woodward, Okla., May 2, 1937; d. Milton Casper and Ruth Arlene (Bradshaw) Shuck; m. William Jennings Woodruff, Aug. 18, 1962; children: Teresa Kaye, Bruce Alan, Neal Wayne. BS, Northwestern State U., 1959; MA in Edn., Olivet Nazarene U., 1973. Cert. K-8th grade tchr. Elem. tchr. Anthony (Kans.) Pub. Schs., 1959-60, transition class tchr., 1960-61, elem. tchr., 1961-62, Versailles (Ky.) Pub. Schs., 1962-63, Bradley (Ill.) Elem. Schs., 1968-93; presch. vol. Concern Ctr., Bartlesville, Okla., 1994—. Com. chmn. Bus. and Profl. Women, Anthony, 1959-62; sec. com. PTA, Anthony, 1959-63, Bradley (Ill.) PTA, 1968-93. Recipient grant for edn. First of Am. Bank, 1991-92, 92-93. Mem.: Nazarene World Mission Soc. (local pres. 1999—2002), Bartlesville Pilot Club Internat. (edn./patriotism chairperson 1994—95, dir. 1995—96, mem. Spl. Olympics Com. 1995—98, pres.-elect 1996—97, pres. 1997—98). Avocations: jogging, reading, baking, working with children and young people. Home: 2373 Mountain Dr Bartlesville OK 74003-6952

WOODS, ALMA JEAN, elementary educator; b. Pueblo, Colo., Aug. 26, 1937; d. Melvin Leroy and Lillian Roberta (Ullrich) W. Assoc., Pueblo (Colo.) Jr. Coll., 1958; BA, Western State Coll., Gunnison, Colo., 1960; MA, U. No. Colo., Greeley, 1964. Lic. elem. educator. Elem. tchr. Sch. Dist. 60, Pueblo, 1960-93; substitute elem. tchr., 2000—. Travel-cultural spkr., educator So. Colo. Sch., Colorado Springs. Bd. dirs. YWCA, 1996—, Pueblo 2010 Recreation and Leisure Task Force, 1996-02; vol. to patients Sangre de Cristo Hospice, Pueblo, 1994—; historic docent Rosemount Mus. Mem. Pueblo Colo. Ret. Educators, Ark. Valley Audubon, Alpha Delta Kappa (chpt. pres. 1982-84). Democrat. Methodist. Avocations: walking, water aerobics, photography, stamp collecting. Home: 124 W 22nd St Pueblo CO 81003-2520

WOODS, CYNDY JONES, secondary educator, researcher; b. Phoenix, Oct. 26, 1954; d. Glenn Billy and Helen Marie (Harrison) Jones; m. Clifford R. Woods, Apr. 3, 1975; children: Sean, Kathleen, Connor. AA in English, St. John's Coll., 1974; BA in English, Ariz. State U., 1992, M in Secondary Edn., 1994. Cert. secondary and ESL tchr., c.c. instr., Ariz. Tchr. grades 6-8 John R. Davis Sch., Phoenix, 1993, Thomas J. Pappas Sch., Phoenix, 1994—98, Maya H.S., Phoenix, 1998—; adj. faculty English and lit. Glendale C.C., 1997—98; asst. prin. Maya H.S., Phoenix, 2000—03;

faculty mgr. Connected U., 2003—. Adj. faculty English and lit. Rio Salado C.C., 1995—; treas. Martin Luther Sch. Bd., Phoenix, 1985-89; presenter in field; chair TIF tech. and specialist depts. Conn. U., 2000-03. Contbr. poetry to anthologies Dance on the Horizons, 1993, The Sound of Poetry: Best Poems of 1995, Across the Universe, 1996; cmty. columnist Ariz. Republic, 2002—; contbr. articles to profl. jours. Mem. St. Francis Xavier Sch. Bd., Phoenix, 1995; v.p. City/County Child Care Bd., Phoenix, 1988-92; youth group advisor Mt. Calvary Luth. Ch., Phoenix, 1988-96; mem. SRP Ednl. Adv. Coun., 1996-98; mem. Maricopa County Juvenile Cmty. Justice Com., 1997; Fulbright master tchr., 2001. Fulbright Tchr. scholar, 1998. Mem. Ariz. Edn. Assn., Brophy Coll. Prep. Mother's Guild, Xavier Coll. Prep. Mother's Guild. Democrat. Avocations: computers, homeless issues, at-risk issues, volleyball, writing. Home: PO Box 5115 Glendale AZ 85312-5115 E-mail: cyndywrites@yahoo.com.

WOODS, DENNIS CRAIG, school superintendent; b. Akron, Ohio, Nov. 29, 1946; m. Janice Mary Matvey, Apr. 21, 1971; children: Gregory, Jeffrey, Mark. BA, Brown U., 1968; MA, U. Akron, 1974; postgrad., Ohio State U., 1990-92. Job placement specialist Summit County Bd. Edn., Akron, 1971-72; tchr. English, athletic dir. South H.S., Akron, 1972-77; unit prin. Buchtel H.S., Akron, 1977-80; asst. prin. Firestone H.S., Akron, 1980-81, prin., 1987-90, Ellet H.S., Akron, 1981-87; grad. rsch. assoc. Policy Rsch. for Ohio Based Edn., Columbus, 1990-91; asst. dir. Sch. Study Coun. of Ohio, Columbus, 1991-92; supt. Sandy Valley Local Schs., Magnolia, Ohio, 1992-96, Bay Village (Ohio) City Sch. Dist., 1996—. Instructional audit team Sch. Effectiveness Trainers, Columbus, 1992-96; presenter adminstr.'s acad. Middletown (Ohio) City Sch. Dist., 1994; presenter Ohio Acad. for Sch. Improvement, Columbus, 1993, Supts. Transition Project, The Ohio State U., 2000—, others; site visitor Blue Ribbon Schs. Program, Washington, 1991; presenter in field. Mem. Brown U. Alumni Schs. Program, 1981—; advancement chair Troop 50, Boy Scouts Am., Akron, 1986—93; Founding mem. Sandy Valley TAP Group, Magnolia, 1993—96; trustee The Bay Village Ednl. Found., 1996—, The Bay Village Found., 1997—; governance com. Ohio H.S. Athletic Assn., 2001—02; mem. com. of practitioners Ohio Dept. Edn., 2002—03; E &A coalition DeRolph Mediation Response Team; mem. Ohio Leadership for Integrating Tech., 2002—03; hon. life mem. PTA; mem. cmty. bd. Fairview Hosp., 2003—; mem. Gov.'s Blue Ribbon Task Force on Sch. Funding, 2003—; mem. cmty. bd. Fairview Hosp., 2003—; mem. Govs. Blue Ribbon Task Force Sch. Funding, 2003—; eucharistic min. St. Raphael Ch., 1994—; mem. cmty. bd. St. John West Shore Hosp., 1998—; mem. governing bd. Cuyahoga Spl. Edn. Svc. Ctr., 1999—, chmn., 2003—; bd. dirs. long range planning com. Lake Erie Ednl. Computer Assn., 1999—2003; bd. dirs. Mohican Inst., 2000—; mem. articulation and transfer adv. coun. Ohio Bd. Regents, 2001—02. Lt. (j.g.) USNR, 1968—70. Recipient Outstanding Secondary Prin. award Akron Secondary Prins. Assn., 1985, 89, Pyramid award Nat. Sch. Pub. Rels. Assn., 1997, Exemplary Svc. award Sandy Valley Bd. Edn., 1996; E.E. Lewis fellow Ohio State U., 1991, Eikenberry scholar, 1990; fellow Knowledgeworks Found., 2002-. Mem. ASCD, Horace Mann League (Amb. award 2000), Ohio Assn. Local Supts., Ohio Sch. Bds. Assn., Ohio Inst. Effective Sch. Leadership (first cohort 1995), Am. Assn. Sch. Adminstrs. (del. assembly 2000-03, presenter 2000), Mid-Am. Assn. Sch. Supts., Ohio Assn. Local Sch. Supts., Greater Cleve. Sch. Supts. Assn., Buckeye Assn. Sch. Adminstrs. (exec. and pub. rels. com. 1995, legis. com. 1996-97, chmn. state dept. com. 1998-2000, constn. and by-laws com., 2000-03, pres.-elect 2000, pres. 2001, chmn. 2003, Exemplary Leadership award 2000, Disting. Svc. award 2003, Ohio Supt. of Yr. award 2003), Sandy Valley C. of C., Midwest Suburban Supts. Assn., Bay Kiwanis Club, Touchdown Club, Phi Delta Kappa. Avocations: reading, physical fitness, ornithology. Office: Bay Village City Sch Dist 377 Dover Center Rd Bay Village OH 44140-2304 E-mail: dwoods@Leeca.org.

WOODS, GWENDOLYN ANNETTE, retired secondary education educator; b. Jacksonville, Ill., May 31, 1920; d. Robert L. and Genevieve L. (Dorsey) Brim; m. Mervin R. Woods, Aug. 20, 1943; children:Roger, Kristine Woods Camphouse, Kerry David, Loraine Woods Berquist. BA, Ill. Coll., Jacksonville, 1942. Cert. secondary tchr., Ill. Tchr. math., Latin, and phys. edn. Franklin (Ill.) High Sch., 1942-46; tchr. math., Latin, and French Perry (Ill.) High Sch., 1946-95. Leader Perry 4-H Stitchers, 1947—. Honored Citizen, Perry Pioneer Day Com., 1991. Mem. Nat. Coun. Math. Tchrs., Perry PTA (officer), Am. Legion Aux. (past officer), Perry Garden Club (officer), DAR (regent Nancy Ross chpt. 1995-99, historian 1999—), Pike-Calhoun Retired Tchrs, Abbie Hatch Chautauqua Cir. (reader, officer). Avocations: reading, sewing, gardening. Home: PO Box 65 Perry IL 62362-0065

WOODS, JEAN FRAHM, science educator; b. Boise, Idaho, Oct. 24, 1931; d. Theodore Roosevelt and Bonnie Mae (Gross) Frahm; m. Lonnie Lee Woods, June 24, 1951 (dec. May 7, 1977); children: Jeffrey Lee, Nicholaus Lon, Karl Eugene. BS in Sci. Edn., Home Econs., U. Idaho, Moscow, 1954; MS in Zoology, U. Wis., 1960. Tchr. 4th grade Rapid City (S.D.) Schs., 1954-55; tchr. 7th and 8th grades Lovelock (Nev.) Schs., 1956-57; tchr. biology, chemistry, home econs. Richfield (Idaho) H.S., 1957-59; dietitian U. Idaho, Moscow, 1961-62; tchr. sci., home econs. Eagle (Idaho) Jr. H.S., 1962-63; sci. tchr. 7th grade Meridian (Idaho) Schs., 1981-97. Tchr. of Yr. Meridian Schs., 1987. Mem. AAUW, Nat. Sci. Tchrs. Assn., Idaho Sci. Tchrs. Assn., Boise Home Economists (treas. 1968, pres. 1969), Native Daus. of Idaho, Delta Kappa Gamma (1st v.p.) 2001-03. Avocations: reading, biking, bird watching. Home: 3518 Catalina Rd Boise ID 83705-4604

WOODS, JEANNIE MARLIN, theatre educator; b. Shreveport, La., Oct. 6, 1947; d. Charles Raymond and Orlando (Crossett) Smith; m. Daniel Carl Woods, Sept. 6, 1973. BA, U. Idaho, 1970; MA, Hunter Coll., 1987; MPh, CUNY, 1988, PhD, 1989. Actress Germinal Stage, Third Eye Theatre, Denver, 1971-80; lectr. CCNY, N.Y.C., 1987, Baruch Coll., 1988; asst. prof. theatre Winthrop U., Rock Hill, SC, 1989-95, assoc. prof., 1995—2000, dir office for effective tchg., 1996—98, prof., 2000—, assoc. dean Coll. Visual & Performing Arts, 2001—; artistic dir. New Stage Ensemble Theatre, 1993—. Author: Theatre to Change Men's Souls, The Artistry of Adrian Hall, 1993, Maureen Stapleton: A Bio-Bibliography, 1992; contbg.author: Notable Women in American Theatre, 1989; co-translator: (with Chi Mei Wang) The Bride and Her Double. Fellow, CCNY, 1988—89; scholar Fulbright, Nat Inst of Arts, Taipei, Taiwan, 1998—99. Mem. Assn. for Theatre in Higher Edn., V.P. for Profl. Devel.2003-05, Fulbright Assn. Office: Winthrop Univ Coll Visual and Performing Arts Rock Hill SC 29733-0001

WOODS, JOHN JOSEPH, school system administrator; b. Syracuse, N.Y., Nov. 10, 1926; s. John Joseph and Agnes C. (Mooney) W.; m. Gertrude B. Fuchs, June 16, 1956 (div. Oct. 15, 1976); m. Ann M. Sorheide, Dec. 16, 1976; children: Gregory, Douglas, Lori, Carrie. BS, SUNY, Rochester, 1981; MS, SUNY, Brockport, 1982; Cert. of Advanced Studies, SUNY, 1982; EdD, U. Rochester, 1987; student, Harvard U., 1988-91. Cert. sch. dist. adminstr., N.Y. Dir. pers. and pub. rels. Alliance Tool Corp., Rochester, N.Y., 1956-78; pres. N.Y. State Sch. Bds. Assn., 1975-76, Woods Pers. Cons. Svcs., 1978-79; sch. supt. Rochester Tooling & Machining Inst., 1979-85; exec. dir. Monroe County Sch. Bds. Assn., Rochester, 1986—. Speaker in field; lectr. U. Rochester, Grad. Sch. of Edn. and Human Devel.; adj. prof., lectr. SUNY Coll. at Brockport; tutor SUNY Empire State Coll. of Rochester; lectr. Rochester Inst. Tech., Roberts Wesleyan Coll.; chmn. Fed. Elem. Secondary Edn. Act Title III State Adv. Coun., 1973-75. Contbr. articles to profl. jours. Trustee grad. sch. edn. U. Rochester, 1990-96. Recipient Scholar fellowship U. Rochester, Monroe County Sch. Bds. Assn. "Good Guy" award. Mem. ASCD, Monroe County Bar Assn. (sch. atty.'s com.), Kappa Delta Pi, Phi Delta Kappa. Home: 626 Rumson Rd Rochester NY 14616-1249

WOODS, LEIGH ALAN, theatre educator; b. Whittier, Calif., Mar. 3, 1948; s. Harry Braxton and Phyllis Jean (Hunnicutt) W.; m. Agústa Gunnarsdóttir, June 12, 1982; children: Livia Arndal, Bryndís Arndal. BA in English, Harvard Coll., 1970; MFA in Acting, Columbia U., 1972; PhD in Dramatic Arts, U. Calif., Berkeley, 1979. Tchr. grades 5-12 Spence Sch., N.Y.C., 1972-75; teaching asst. U. Calif., 1976-79, lectr. acting, 1979-80; asst. prof. Ind. U., Bloomington, 1980-86, assoc. prof., 1986-87, U. Mich., Ann Arbor, 1987-96, head grad. studies, acad. adviser, prof., 1996—. Author: Garrick Claims the Stage, 1984, On Playing Shakespeare, 1991, Public Selves, Political Stages, 1997; co-editor: Playing to the Camera: Film Actors Discuss Their Craft, 1998. Mem. Am. Soc. Theatre Rsch. (mem. nominating com. 1994—), Actors' Equity Assn., Phi Beta Kappa. Avocation: tennis. Home: 2411 Darrow Dr Ann Arbor MI 48104-5205 Office: U Mich Dept Theatre & Drama 2540-D Frieze Ann Arbor MI 48109-1285

WOODS, PENDLETON, college director, author; b. Ft. Smith, Ark., Dec. 18, 1923; s. John Powell and Mabel (Hon) W.; m. Lois Robin Freeman, Apr. 3, 1948; children: Margaret, Paul Pendleton, Nancy Cox. BA in Journalism, U. Ark., 1948. Editor, asst. pub. mgr. Okla. Gas & Electric Co., Oklahoma City, 1948-69; dir. Living Legends of Okla., Okla. Christian U., Oklahoma City, 1969-82; project, promotion dir. Enterprise Square and Am. Citizenship Ctr., 1982-92, dir. Nat. Edn. Program and Am. Citizenship Ctr., 1992. Arbitrator BBB; leader youth seminars in field; state pub. affairs officer Employer Support Guard and Res. Author: You and Your Company Magazine, 1950, Church of Tomorrow, 1964, Myriad of Sports, 1971, This Was Oklahoma, 1979; recorded Sounds of Scouting, 1969, Born Grown, 1974 (Western Heritage award Nat. Cowboy Hall of Fame), One of a Kind, 1977, Countdown to Statehood, 1982, The Thunderbird Tradition, 1989, A Glimpse at Oklahoma, 1990, Historic Oklahoma County, 2002; editor Libertas. Vol. reader Okla. Libr. for the Blind; past pres. Okla. Assn. Epilepsy, Keep Okla. Beautiful, Okla. City Mental Health Clin.; pub. rels. chmn. Okla. County chpt. A.R.C.; past chmn. Western Heritage award Nat. Cowboy Hall of Fame; past pres., hon. lifetime dir. Variety Health Ctr.; Am. Freedom Coun.; charter dir. Okla. Vets. Med. Rsch. Found.; cons. Exec. Svc. Corps.; ex-state comdr. Am. ex-Prisoners of War; mem. Coun. Pub. Affairs; vol. Okla. City VA Hosp.; state historian Okla. N.G.; chmn. Okla. City Independence Day Parade; exec. com. Okla. City Centennial Commn.; bd. dirs. Campfire Girls Coun., Okla. Jr. Symphony, past pres.; bd. dirs. Zoo Amphitheater of Okla. City, Will Rogers Centennial Commn., Greater Okla. City Tree Bank Found., Boy Scout Am. (life); bd. dirs., co-founder Ctrl. Pk. Neighborhood Assn.; dir. Okla. for Resource Preservation; chmn. State Directional Signage Task Force. With U.S. Army, WWII and Korean War, ret. col. Named Outstanding Young Man of Yr., Oklahoma City Jr. C. of C., 1953; recipient Silver Beaver award Boy Scouts Am., 1963, Wokan award Okla. City Coun. Camp Fire girls, 1968, Silver medal Advt. Fedn. Am., Disting. Cmty. Svc. award Neighborhood Devel. and Conservation Ctr., Gold and Silver Patrick Henry Patriotism medals Mil. Order of the World Wars, 2 Commendation awards Am. Assn. for State and Local History, 4 honor medals Freedoms Found., Jefferson Davis medal United Daus. of the Confederacy, Okla. Disting. Svc. medal (2), Outstanding Contbn. to Okla. Mus., Okla. Mus. Assn., 1987, Outstanding Contbn. to Okla. Tourism award Okla. Dept. Tourism, 1989, Cmty. Svc. award U. Ark. Alumni Assn., 1992, Citizenship and Patriot award SAR, 1992, 5 Who Care award KOCO-TV, 1993, Jefferson award Am. Inst. for Pub. Svc., 1993, Mayor's award in Beautification, 1994, George Washington award Youth Leadership Found., St. Augustine, Fla., 1993, Golden Rule award J.C. Penney Found., 1999, Lifetime Achievement award Keep Okla. Beautiful; inducted into Okla. Journalism Hall of Fame, 2001, Okla. Mil. Hall of Fame, 2002, U. Ark. Journalism Hall of Fame, 2002. Mem.: VFW, DAV, Okla. Distributive Edn., Okla. Jr. C. of C. (hon. life, past internat. dir.), Ctrl. Okla. Bus. Communicators (past pres., hon. life mem.), Advt. Fedn. Am. (past dist. dir.), Soc. Assoc. Indsl. Editors (past v.p.), Okla. Vets. Coun. (chmn.), Mil. Order World Wars (regional comdr., Okla. City comdr., Okla. State comdr., nat. staff), Okla. Travel Industries Assn., Okla. Heritage Assn., Okla. City Beautiful (publ. editor), Okla. Safety Coun. (publ. editor), Okla. County Hist. Soc. (dir., past pres.), 45th Inf. Div. Assn. (past pres.), Korean War Vets Assn., Am. Legion, Mus. Unassigned Lands (chmn.), Okla. Hist. Soc. (life; publ. editor,), Words of Jesus Found. (pres.), Okla. Zool. Soc. (past pres.), Okla. Geneal. Soc., Okla. County Sr. Nutrition Found. (sec., bd. dirs.), Freedom's Found. (v.p.), Nat. Eagle Scout Assn. (Okla. chmn.), U. Ark. Alumni Assn. (charter pres. Okla. City chpt.), Okla. Lung Assn. (pub. rels. com.), Am. Cancer Soc. (dir. Okla. County chpt.), Okla. City Hist. Preservation Commn., Am. Ex-Prisoners of War (state comdr.), Okla. City Clean and Green Coalition, Lincoln Pk. Country (pres.), Oklahoma City Advt. Club (past pres., hon. life mem.), Kappa Sigma (nat. commr. publs.), Sigma Delta Chi. Home: 541 NW 31st St Oklahoma City OK 73118-7334 E-mail: penwoods@cox.net.

WOODS, PHYLLIS MICHALIK, librarian; b. New Orleans, Sept. 12, 1937; d. Philip John and Thelma Alice (Carey) Michalik; 1 child, Tara Lynn Woods. BA, Southea. La. U., 1967. Cert. speech and English tchr., libr. sci., La. Tchr. speech, English and drama St. Charles Parish Pub. Schs., Luling, La., elem. tchr., secondary tchr. remedial reading, Chpt. I reading specialist, Wicat tchr. coord., elem. sch. libr.; media specialist Jefferson Parish Pub. Sch. System. Tchr. cons. St. Charles parish writing project La. State U. Writing Project. Author: Egbert, the Egret, Egbert's Picnic, Egbert Visits Sammy, Angel Without Wings, The Necklace and Egbert's Calf, The Hurricane, The Cleanup Day, The Rainbow, The Fair, The Tornado; songwriter; musical compositions include The Fruits of the Spirit, Father's Day Song, Mother's Day Song; contbr. articles and poems to River Parish Guide, St. Charles Herald. Sch. rep. United Fund, St. Charles Parish Reading Assn.; parish com. mem. Young Authors, Tchrs. Who Write; active 4-H leader; bd. trustees Michalik Scholarship Trust. Mem. ASCD, Internat. Platform Assn., Internat. Reading Assn., Am. Fedn. Tchrs., St. Charles Parish Reading Coun., Newspaper in Edn. (chmn., historian), La. Assn. Newspapers in Edn. (state com.), Jefferson Parish Libr. Assn., Jefferson Parish Reading Assn., Jefferson Parish Tchrs. Union.

WOODS, SHERWYN MARTIN, psychiatrist, educator; b. Des Moines, Iowa, June 25, 1932; m. Nancy Bricard. BS with high honors, U. Wis., Madison, 1954, MD with high honors, 1957. Diplomate Am. Bd. Psychiatry and Neurology. Intern Phila. Gen. Hosp., 1957-58; resident in psychiatry U. Wis., Madison, 1958-60, chief resident in psychiatry, 1960-61; instr. psychiatry U. Wis. Med. Sch., Madison, 1961; asst. prof. dept. psychiatry U. So. Calif., L.A., 1963-68, assoc. prof., 1968-74, prof., 1974—98, emeritus prof., 1998—. Sr. physician LAC-USC Med. Ctr.; asst. instr., instr., now supervising and tng. analyst So. Calif. Psychoanalytic Inst.; vis. prof. U. Wis., 1966-74, U. N.C., 1974, U. B.C., 1977, Pa. State U., 1978, Hebrew U. Med. Sch., Jerusalem, 1979, U. Tex. Med. Sch., 1979, Loma Linda U., 1982, UCLA, 1983, U. Calif.-Davis, 1983; cons. in field. Editl. bd. Contemporary Psychiatry: Jour. Critical Rev., 1981—, Jour. Psychiat. Edn., 1988, Acad. Psychiatry, 1989—; psychiatry editor Med. Grand Rounds, 1982-87; book series editor Critical Issues in Psychiatry, 1986-94; reviewer various med. jours.; contbr. articles to profl. jours. Capt. USAF, 1961—63. Grantee NIMH, 1964-66. Fellow Am. Acad. Psychoanalysis, Am. Coll. Psychiatrists, Am. Coll. Psychoanalysts, Am. Psychiat. Assn. (disting. life); mem. AMA, AAUP, Am. Assn. Dirs. Psychiat. Residency Tng., Am. Psychoanalytic Assn., Assn. Acad. Psychiatry, Assn. Advancement Psychotherapy, Group for Advancement Psychiatry, Internat. Psychoanalytic Assn., Psychiat. Alumni Continuing Edn., So. Calif. Psychiat. Assn., So. Calif. Psychoanalytic Soc., Salerni Collegium. Office: Univ So Calif Sch Medicine Los Angeles CA 90033-1011

WOODS, SUSAN LOUISE, nursing educator; b. L.A., Nov. 6, 1946; d. Charles John and Mary Jane (Roach) Blank; m. Thomas W. Glenn, June 8, 1968 (div. 1972); m. James Earl Woods, Aug. 2, 1975; children: Jaime Rose, Jennifer Mary. Diploma in Nursing, L.A. County/U. So. Calif. Med., 1967; BSN, U. Wash., 1973, MSN, 1975; PhD, Oreg. Health Scis. U., 1991. RN, Wash. Staff nurse Los Angeles County/U. So. Calif. Med. Ctr., L.A., 1967-69, Drs. Hosp., Phoenix, 1969-70, VA Hosp., Seattle, 1970-71; head nurse CCU, USPHS Hosp., Seattle, 1971-75; from instr. to assoc. prof. nursing U. Wash., Seattle, 1975-93, prof., 1993—, assoc. dean acad. programs, 1996—. Author: Cardiac Nursing, 1982 (AJN Books of Yr. award), 4th edit. 1995, Medical Surgical Nursing, 1986 (AJN Books of Yr. award), 2d edit., 1991; editor Cardiovascular Medications for Cardiac Nursing, 1990, Cardiovascular Critical Care Nursing, 1983; contbg. author in field. Recipient Nursing Edn. award U. Wash., 1975, Disting. Alumnus of Yr. award Oreg. Health Scis. U., 1996; grantee HEW, 1977-79, Dept. HHS, 1981-86. Fellow Am. Heart Assn. (coun. on cardiovascular nursing 1988, K. Lembright award 1995), Am. Nurses Assn., Am. Acad. Nursing, Commn. on Colligate Nursing Edn. (founding bd. mem.); mem. Am. Assn. Critical Care Nurses (award 1985), Am. Heart Assn. (award 1979), Sigma Theta Tau. Republican. Roman Catholic. Home: 3629 1st Ave NW Seattle WA 98107-4904 Office: U Wash PO Box 357260 Seattle WA 98195-7260

WOODS, WILLIE G. dean, English language and education educator; b. Yazoo City, Miss., 1943; d. John Wesley and Jessie Willie Mae Woods. BA, Shaw U., Raleigh, N.C., 1965; MEd, Duke U., 1968; postgrad., Pa. State U., 1970, postgrad., 1980—82, Temple U., 1972, U. N.H., 1978, NYU, 1979, Indiana U. of Pa., 1986—88. PhD, 1995. Tchr. sch. in N.C. and Md., 1965—69; mem. faculty Harrisburg Area C.C., Pa., 1969—99, assoc. prof. English and edn., 1976—82, prof., 1982—94, sr. prof., 1994—, supr. Writing Ctr., 1975—78, coord. Act 101Basic Studies Program, 1978—83, dir. Acad. Founds. program, 1983—87, asst. dean acad. affairs Acad. Found. and Basic Edn. Div., 1987—89, asst. dean acad. affairs, chmn. social sci., pub. svcs. and basic edn. div., 1989—94, dean social sci., pub. svcs. and basic edn. divsn., 1994—96, 1998—, chmn. dirs. coun., 1981—82, acting v.p. faculty and instrn., 1996—98, tchr. Cmty. Resources Inst., 1975—90; dean divsn. arts and sci. Chesapeake Coll., Md., 1999—. Moderator workshops; cons. in field. Asst. editor: Black Conf. Higher Edn. Jour., 1980. Mem. Harrisburg Mayor's Commn. Lit., 1995—, Pa. Gov.'s Interagy. Coun. Lit., 1997—; sec., exec. com. People for Progress, 1971—73; bd. mgrs., exec. com. Camp Curtin br. YMCA, 1971—79; bd. dirs. Alternative Rehab. Communities, 1978—; bd. mgrs. Youth Urban Svcs., Harrisburg Area YMCA, 1981—92; bd. dirs. Dauphin Residences, Inc., 1981—88. Recipient cert. of merit for cmty. svcs., City of Harrisburg, 1971, Youth Urban Svcs. Vol. of Yr. award, 1983, Black Student Union award, Harrisburg Area C.C., 1984; Kellogg fellow in expanding leadership diversity in cmty. coll. program, 1994—95. Mem.: AAUP, Nat. Coun. on Black Am. (instl. rep. 1983—), Am. Assn. Cmty. and Jr. Colls., Pa. Edn. Assn., Nat. Coun. Tchrs. English, Pa. Black Conf. Higher Edn. (Outstanding Svc. award 1980, Ctrl. Region award 1982), Pa. Assn. Devel. Educators (chmn. conf. 1980, sec. 1981—82, v.p. 1986—87, pres. 1987—88), Phi Kappa Phi, Alpha Kappa Mu, Alpha Kappa Alpha (Outstanding Svc. award 1983, 1997, Basileus award 1984, Ida B. Wells Excellence in Media award 1994, Ivy Honor Roll of Clips award 1994). Baptist. Home: 8708 Mulberry Dr Easton MD 21601 Office: Chesapeake Coll 1000 College Dr PO Box 8 Wye Mills MD 21679

WOODSIDE, LISA NICOLE, humanities educator; b. Portland, Oreg., Sept. 7, 1944; d. Lee and Emma (Wenstrom) W. Student, Reed Coll., 1962-65; MA, U. Chgo., 1968; PhD, Bryn Mawr Coll., 1972; cert., Harvard U. Inst. Ednl. Mgmt., 1979; MA, West Chester U., 1994. Cert. tchr. ecstatic trance postures Cuyamungue Inst., New Mex., 2003, wellness counseling, creative energy options. Mem. dean's staff Bryn Mawr Coll., 1970-72; asst. prof. Widener U., Chester, Pa., 1972-77, assoc. prof. humanities, 1978-83, asst. dean student svcs., 1972-76, assoc. dean, 1976-79, dean, 1979-83; acad. dean, prof. humanities Holy Family Coll., Phila., 1983—, v.p., dean acad. affairs, prof. humanities, 1990-98, prof. humanities, 1998—. Cons. State N.J. Edn. Dept., 1990; accreditor Commn. on Higher Edn., Middle States Assn., 1977-83, 94; reader for test of spoken English, Ednl. Testing Svc., 2002-03. Co-author: New Age Spirituality: An Assessment. City commr. for cmty. rels., Chester, 1980-83; mem. Adult Edn. Coun. Phila. Recipient Crasilneck award for best paper Am. Soc. Clin. Hypnosis; Am. Assn. Papyrology grantee Bryn Mawr Coll., also S. Maude Kaemmerling fellow. Mem.: MLA, AAUW (univ. rep. 1975—83), APA, Pa. Coll. Tchrs. Assn., Mid. States Classics Assn., Am. Philol. Assn., Audubon Soc., Psi Chi, Alpha Sigma Lambda, Phi Eta Sigma. Home: 360 Saybrook Ln # A Media PA 19086-6761 Office: Humanities Dept Holy Family Univ Torresdale Philadelphia PA 19114

WOODSON, ADRIANNE MARIE, secondary school educator and coordinator; b. Chgo., Sept. 1, 1951; d. Theodore Roosevelt and Adah Mae Hull; m. Rudolph Woodson, June 26, 1976; children: Porsha M., Patrice A., Kellen E., Karley A. BS, Lincoln U., 1973; MS, Ind. U., South Bend, 1981. Lic. sch. adminstr. Spl. edn. tchr. Gary (Ind.) Cmty. Sch. Corp., 1973-76; spl. edn. multi-category tchr. South Bend (Ind.) Cmty. Schs., 1976-77; spl. edn. resource tchr. Sch. City of Hammond, Ind., 1977-86, facilitating tchr., 1986-97, homebound instr., 1997—, spl. edn. coord., 1998—. Student tchr. supr. Purdue U. Calumet, Hammond, summers 1993—, mem. spl. edn. search com.; participant for standardizing nat. diagnostic test W.I.A.T., Westchester, Ind., 1990; presenter at state conf. Coun. for Exceptional Children, Indpls., 1987, 99; spl. edn. dir.'s program Cohort 2000, Bloomington, Ind., 1999-2000. Pres. Jack and Jill Am., Inc.; children's program dir. Delaney United Meth. Ch., pianist. Mem. Ind. Coun. Adminstrs. in Spl. Edn., Lincoln U. Alumni Assn. (sec.-treas.), Sigma Gamma Rho (com. chairperson, Membership award 2000), Delta Kappa Gamma (v.p.). Democrat. Methodist. Avocations: travel, fashion, home and interior decorating, singing, playing the piano. Office: 5727 Sohl Ave Hammond IN 46320-2356 Fax: 219-933-2498. E-mail: amwoodson@m1.hammond.k12.in.us.

WOODS-STELLMAN, DONNA SUE, education educator, reading consultant; b. Springhill, La., Jan. 15, 1954; children: Klaten A. Woods, Matthew M. Woods, Laura E. Woods, Gabriele E. Woods; m. Felix A. Stellman II, June 28, 1997; 1 stepchild, Kellie N. Stellman. BA, La. Tech U., 1975; MEd, La. State U., 1983; EdD, Okla. State U., 1992. Cert. English, social studies, gifted edn. tchr., La.; cert. English, gifted edn. and reading tchr., Okla. Tchr. English, Grawood (La.) Christian Schs., 1979-80; tchr. spl. edn. Bossier Parish Sch. Bd., Benton, La., 1981-83, curriculum developer, 1990; tchr. gifted Curtis Elem. Sch., Bossier City, La., 1983-88; tchr. lang. arts Elm Grove (La.) Jr. High Sch., 1988-90; teaching asst., univ. rep. Okla. entry yr. assistance Okla. State U., Stillwater, 1990-92, co-dir., instr. 13th ann. reading workshop, 1991, instr. Coll. Vet. Medicine, 1991, developer, dir. student tchr. seminar, 1992; asst. prof. Coll. Edn. Northwestern Okla. State U., Alva, 1992-95; dir. reading and literacy Okla. State Dept. Edn., Oklahoma City, 1995-97; asst. prof. dept. urban edn. U. Houston-Downtown, 1997—, asst. chair dept. urban edn., 2001. Adj. instr. Oklahoma City C.C., 1991-92, U. Okla., 1995-97. Tutor YWCA, Shreveport, La., 1975; supt. youth Sun. schs. 1st Presbyn. Ch., Edmond, Okla., 1991, youth choir dir., 1994-97, youth handbells dir., 1995-97; mem. Greater Houston (Tex.) Area Reading Counsel. Named Favorite Tchr. of Yr., Bossier C. of C., 1987, Outstanding Instr. FB Urban Educators, 1999; Centennial scholar Okla. State U. Coll. Edn. Alumni Assn., 1992. Mem.: Okla. Early Childhood Tchrs. Assn. (conf. presenter 1991), Greater Houston Area Reading Coun., Okla. Reading Assn. (conf. presenter 1993—97), Internat. Reading Assn. (conf. presenter 1996, 2001), Phi Delta Kappa, Kappa Delta Pi, Alpha Upsilon Alpha (faculty sponsor 1994—95). Avocations: reading, music, quilting, sailing. Home: 8326 Bo Jack Dr Houston TX 77040-1535

WOODWARD, CLINTON BENJAMIN, JR., civil engineering educator; b. El Paso, Tex., Mar. 4, 1943; s. Clinton Benjamin and Iris Elizabeth (Zant) W.; m. Willie Ann Shollenbarger, June 14, 1969 (div. June 1976); m. Deon Bennett Speir, Nov. 22, 1979; 1 child, Clinton Benjamin III. BSET, N.Mex. State U., 1976; MS, Colo. State U., 1978; MSCE, N.Mex. State U., 1984,

PhD, 1986. Registered profl. engr., N.Mex. From asst. mgr. to pres. Woodward Enterprises Co., Inc., Las Cruces, N.Mex., 1968-82; prof., program dir. structural engring. N.Mex. State U., 1987—. Contbr. articles to profl. jours. With USN, 1962-66. Mem. ASCE, Am. Soc. for Engring. Edn., Forest Products Soc., Soc. Wood Sci. and Tech., Tau Beta Phi, Chi Epsilon, Phi Kappa Phi, Sigma Xi. Avocations: camping, fly fishing.

WOODWARD, DEBBIE CAROL, special education educator; b. Lufkin, Tex., Mar. 1, 1953; d. Robert Charles and Peggy Jean Beddingfield; m. Allen Wiley, Aug. 15, 1975 (div. Aug. 1984); 1 child, Richard Charles Wiley; m. Lee George Woodward, July 24, 1998. BS, Stephen F. Austin State U., Nacogdoches, Tex., 1995. Tchr. 5th grade Lufkin Ind. Sch. Dist., Tex.; owner Wiley's Wee Wons Nursery, Bryan, Tex., Wiley's Wee Wons Day Sch. and Nursery, Lufkin; faculty Ctr. for Retarded, Houston; spl. edn. tchr. Galena Park Ind. Sch. ., Houston, Channelview Ind. Sch. Dist., Tex. Homebound spl. svcs. provider and cons. Galena Park Ind. Sch. Dist., Houston, Channelview Ind. sch. Dist.; salesperson Avon Products. Active Cystic Fybrosis Found., Susan G. Komen Breast Cancer Found., Shriners Hosps., Inc.; pvt. cons. for families and schs. of terminally children in Galena Park and Channelview. Mem.: Coun. for Exceptional Children, Order Ea. Star.

WOODWARD, ISABEL AVILA, educational writer, foreign language educator; b. Key West, Fla., Mar. 14, 1906; d. Alfredo and Isabel (Lopez) Avila; m. Clyde B. Woodward, June 6, 1944 (dec.); children: Joy Avis Ball, Greer Isabel, Woodward Sucke. Student, Fla. State Coll. for Women, 1925, AB in Edn., 1938; cert. in tchg. Spanish, U. Miami, 1961; summer study, U. Fla., Eckerd Coll.; postgrad., St. Lawrence U., U. Miami. Tchr., Key West, 1927-42; remedial reading cons., 1941-42; reading tchr., asst. reading lab. and clinic St. Lawrence U., summer 1941; Spanish translator U.S. Office of Censorship, Miami Beach, 1943; tchr. Central Beach Elem. Sch., Miami Beach, 1943-44, Silver Bluff Elem. Sch., 1943-50, Henry West Lab. Sch., Coral Gables, Fla., 1955-57, Dade Demonstration Sch., Miami, 1957-61. Author 125 sch. radio lessons for tchg. Spanish Workshop for Fla.; spkr. poetry and short story writing, 1977; guest lectr. on writing the short story Fla. Inst. Tech., Jensen Beach, 1981; guest lectr. Cicle Bay Yacht Club, Stuart, Fla., 1995. Freelance writer; contbr. to Listen Mag., Sunshine Mag., Lookout Mag., Christian Sci. Monitor, Miami Herald, Three/Four, Child Life, Wee Wisdom, Fla. Wildlife, Young World: sponsor Port St. Lucie Jr. Woman's Club, 1983. Recipient Honoris Causa award Alpha Delta Kappa, 1972-74, award Contra Costa Times, Calif., 1985, 1st prize for short story in nat. Ark. writers conf. contest, 1992; named one of 5 Outstanding Fla. Tchrs. 1972-74. Mem. Nat. League Am. Pen Women (1st v.p. Greater Miami br. 1974-76, historian 1978—, librarian 1978—, awards for writing 1973, 74, 77, 1st and 3d pl. state writing awards for adult and juvenile fiction 1983, state 1st prize short story 1985), AAUW, Alpha Delta Kappa, Psi Psi Psi. Address: 1950 SW Palm City Rd Apt 6-301 Stuart FL 34994-4310

WOODWARD, JAMES HOYT, academic administrator, engineer; b. Sanford, Fla., Nov. 24, 1939; s. James Hoyt and Edith Pearl (Breeden) W.; m. Martha Ruth Hill, Oct. 13, 1956; children: Connie, Tracey, Wade. BS in Aero. Engring. with honors, Ga. Tech. Inst., 1962, MS in Aero. Engring., 1963, PhD in Engring. Mechanics, 1967; MBA, U. Ala.-Birmingham, 1973. Asst. prof. engring. mechanics USAF Acad., Colo., 1965-67, assoc. prof., 1967-68; asst. prof. engring. mechanics N.C. State U., 1968-69; assoc. prof. engring. U. Ala., Birmingham, 1969-70, assoc. prof., 1973-77, prof. civil engring., 1977-89, asst. v.p., 1973-78, dean engring., 1978-84, acad. v.p., 1984-89; chancellor U. N.C., Charlotte, 1989—. Dir. tech. devel. Rust Engring. Co., Birmingham, 1970-73; cons. in field. Contbr. articles to profl. jours. With USAF, 1965-68. Mem. ASME, Am. Soc. Engring. Edn., Am. Mgmt. Assn., Sigma Xi. Methodist. Office: U NC Charlotte Office of Chancellor 9201 University City Blvd Charlotte NC 28223-0002

WOODWARD, KATHERINE ANNE, secondary education educator; b. Detroit, Apr. 6, 1942; d. Walter E. and Helen (Leuer) Roberts; m. Clifford Edward Woodward, July 1, 1967; children: Ted, Bob, Chris, John-Paul. BA in History, Webster U., 1964; student, St. Louis U., 1966; MA in History, Sam Houston State U., 1991. Cert. tchr., Tex., Mo. Tchr. world history Oxford (Ala.) High Sch., 1967-69; tchr. English Santa Fe Jr. High Sch., Altaloma, Tex., 1969; tchr. world history Jersey Village High Sch., Houston, 1985—. Co-founder, pres. Brazoria County Cay Care, Alvin, Tex., 1970-73; co-funder Cypress Creek Emergency Med. Svc., Houston, 1975. Named Outstanding Young Women in Am., 1976. Mem. ASCD, AAUW (pres. North Harris County 1976-77), Tex. Coun. Social Studies, Cypress-Fairbanks Coun. Social Studies (pres. 1994-95, scholarship 1990), Nat. Coun. Social Studies, Tex. Coun. for History Edn. (mem. steering com.). Avocations: travel, reading, dutch painting, music, boating. Office: Jersey Village High Sch 7600 Solomon St Houston TX 77040-2199

WOODWARD, RALPH LEE, JR., historian, educator; b. New London, Conn., Dec. 2, 1934; s. Ralph Lee and Beulah Mae (Suter) W.; m. Sue Dawn McGrady, Dec. 30, 1958; children: Mark Lee, Laura Lynn, Matthew McGrady; m. Janice Chatelain, Aug. 8, 1996. AB cum laude, Central Coll., Mo., 1955; MA, Tulane U., 1959, PhD, 1962. Asst. prof. history Wichita (Kans.) U., 1961-62, U. S.W. La., Lafayette, 1962-63; asst. prof. history U. N.C., Chapel Hill, 1963-67, asso. prof., 1967-70; prof. history Tulane U., New Orleans, 1970-99, head dept. history, 1973-75, chmn. dept. history, 1986-88; dir. Tulane Summer in C. Am., 1975-78; prof. in charge Tulane Jr. Year Abroad, Paris, 1975-76; Penrose prof. L.Am. studies Tex. Christian U., Ft. Worth, 1999—2003; ret., 2003. Fulbright lectr. U. Chile, U. Catolica de Valparaiso, Chile, 1965-66, U. del Salvador, Universidad Nacional, Buenos Aires, 1968; vis. prof. U.S. Mil. Acad., West Point, N.Y., 1989; regional liaison officer Emergency Com. to Aid Latin Am. Scholars, 1974. Author: Class Privilege and Economic Development, 1966, Robinson Crusoe's Island, 1969, Positivism in Latin America, 1850-1900, 1971, Central America: A Nation Divided, 1976, 3d edit., 1999, Tribute to Don Bernardo de Galvez, 1979, Belize, 1980, Nicaragua, 1983, 2d edit., 1994, El Salvador, 1988, Guatemala, 1992, Rafael Carrera and the Emergence of the Republic of Guatemala, 1993 (Alfred B. Thomas Book award); editor: Central America: Historical Perspectives on the Contemporary Crises, 1988, Here and There in Mexico: The Travel Writings of Mary Ashley Townsend, 2001; assoc. editor: Revista del Pensamiento Centroamericano, 1975, Research Guide to Central America and the Caribbean, 1985, Encyclopedia of Latin American History and Culture, 1996; contbg. editor: Handbook of Latin American Studies, 1987-90; series editor: World Bibliographical Series, 1987-2000; contbr. articles to profl. jours. Capt. USMC, 1955-58. Recipient Alfred B. Thomas Book award Southeastern Coun. Latin Latin Am. Studies, 1994; Henry L. and Grace Doherty Found. fellow Tulane U., 1962; named La. Humanist of Yr. La. Endowment for Humanities, 1995, Disting. Svc. award, Conf. Latin Am. History, 2002. Mem. Am. Hist. Assn. (mem. Conf. L.Am. History, pres. 1989, mem. gen. com. 1974-76, Disting. Svc. award 2002), Southeastern Conf. L.Am. Studies (program chmn. 1975, pres. 1975-76), L.Am. Studies Assn., Com. on Andean Studies (chmn. 1972-73), Geography and History Acad. Guatemala. Home: 206 Boardman Ave Bay Saint Louis MS 39520 E-mail: clioclio@bellsouth.net.

WOODWARD, ROBERT SIMPSON, IV, economics educator; b. Easton, Pa., May 7, 1943; s. Robert Simpson and Esther Evans (Thomas) W.; m. Mary P. Hutton, Feb. 15, 1969; children: Christopher Thomas, Rebecca Marie. BA, Haverford Coll., 1965; PhD, Washington U., St. Louis, 1972. Econ. policy fellow HEW, Washington, 1975-76; asst. prof. U. Western Ont., London, Can., 1972-77; asst. prof. Sch. Medicine Washington U., St. Louis, 1978-86, assoc. prof., 1986-2001; McKerley prof. health econ. U. N.H., Durham, 2001—. Pres. Writing Assessment Software, Inc., 1987-91. Contbr. articles to profl. jours. Mem. adv. coun. Mo. Kidney Program, 1980-86, vice-chmn., 1983, chmn., 1984-85; coop. mem. Haverford Coll., 1968-90. NDEA fellow, 1968-71, Kellogg Nat. fellow, 1981-84. Mem. Am. Econs. Assn., Am. Statis. Assn. Home: 131 Wednesday Hill Rd Lee NH 03824-6546 Office: U NH Dept Health Mgmt and Policy Hewitt Hall Durham NH 03824-3563 E-mail: rsw@unh.edu.

WOODWARD, THEODORE ENGLAR, medical educator, internist; b. Westminster, Md., Mar. 22, 1914; s. Lewis Klair and Phoebe Helen (Neidig) Woodward; m. Celeste Constance Lauve Woodward, June 24, 1938; children: William E., R. Craig, Celeste L. Woodward Applefeld, Lewis O.(dec.). BS, Franklin and Marshall Coll., 1934, DSc (hon.), 1954; MD, U. Md., 1938; DSc (hon.), Western Md. Coll., 1950, Hahnemann U., 1993. Diplomate Am. Bd. Internal Medicine. Asst. prof. medicine U. Md. Sch. Medicine, Balt., 1946—48, assoc. prof., also dir. sect. infectious disease, 1948—54, prof., 1954—83, prof. emeritus, 1983—, chmn. dept., 1954—81; attending physician Balt. VA Med Ctr., 1949—. With Armed Forces Epidemiol. Bd., Washington, 1952—92, mem. commns., 1952—72, pres. bd., 1976—78, Washington, 1980—92; mem. U.S./Japan Coop. Med. Sci. Program, Washington, 1965—95, emeritus, 1995—; disting. physician Cen. VA, Washington, 1981—87. Author: Chloramphemicol, 1958, 200 Years of Medicine in Baltimore, 1976, A History of the Department of Medicine, University of Maryland, 1807-1981, 1987, A History of Armed Forces Epidemiological Board, 1940-1990, 1990, Carroll County (Md.) Physicians of the 19th and Early 20th Centuries, 1990, The Armed Forces Epidemiological Board: The History of the Commissions, 1995, Make Room for Sentiment: A Physician's Story, 1998, Research on Infectious Diseases at the University of Maryland School of Medicine and Hospital. A Global Experience: 1807-2000, 2000; contbr. chpts. to textbooks. Life trustee Gilman Sch., Balt., 1955—. Lt. col. Medical Svc. Corp U.S. Army, 1941—46, ETO, PTO. Decorated Order of the Sacred Treasure Gold and Silver Star Govt. of Japan; named Student Coun. Faculty awardee of Yr., U. Md., 1966, 1972, 1974—78, 1981—93, 1985—89, 1991, 1993—96, 1998, 2000; recipient U.S.A. Typhus Commn. medal, Dept. Def., 1945, Exceptionally Disting. Svc. award, 1990, Outstanding Civilian Svc. medal with oak leaf cluster, Dept. Army, 1981, Louis Pasteur medal, Inst. Pasteur, 1961, Disting. Svc. award, AMA, 1995. Master: ACP (gov. Md. regent 1969—70, James D. Bruce Meml. award 1970, Disting. Tchr. award 1992); mem.: Inst. Medicine NAS, Infectious Disease Soc. Am. (pres. 1976—77, Finland award 1972, Bristol award, Kass award 1991), Am. Clin. and Climatol. Assn. (pres. 1969—70), Mayo Fellows Assn. (hon.), Hamilton St. Club, Elkridge Club (Towson, Md.). Republican. Avocations: photography, gardening, raising wild fowl. Home: 1 Merrymount Rd Baltimore MD 21210-1908 Office: Balt VA Med Ctr 10 N Green St Baltimore MD 21210

WOODWORTH, BETH ELAINE, business owner; b. Olean, N.Y., Feb. 22, 1951; d. Glenn Walter and Marjorie Elaine (Platt) Bernreuther; m. Donald James Woodworth; children: Mathew, Jennifer, Melissa. BA, SUNY, Albany, 1973; MS in Edn., St. Bonaventure U., 1977, MS in Edn., 1986; EdD, SUNY, Buffalo, 1996. Cert. elem. and secondary tchr., N.Y.; cert. sch. adminstr., N.Y. Tchr. English Scio (N.Y.) Ctrl. Sch., 1973-76; instructional support svcs. asst. Allegany County Bd. Coop. Ednl. Svcs., Belmont, N.Y., 1977-81; dir. Wellsville (N.Y.) Child Care Ctr., 1981; substitute tchr. various schs., N.Y., 1982; tchr. English Angelica (N.Y.) Ctrl. Sch., 1984-85; owner Woodworth Nurseries, Scio, 1982-89; sec., treas. Parallel Processing, Inc., Bergen, N.Y., 1982—; pres. Dustables, Inc., Bergen, 1995—. Mem. rsch. team SUNY, Buffalo, 1988-90, Western N.Y. Ednl. Svc. Coun., Inc., Buffalo, 1989-90; presenter in field. Contbr. articles to profl. jours. Neighborhood chmn. Seven Lakes coun. Girl Scouts U.S., Phelps, N.Y., 1977-80, 84-85, leader, 1977-80, 84-85, bd. dirs. 1978-80, 81-84, educator family life., 1982-83, mem. troop com. Genesee Valley coun., Rochester, N.Y., 1987-90, leader, 1990-99; badge counselor Iroquois Trail coun. Boy Scouts Am., Lockport, N.Y., 1987-90; mem. coop. planning team Byron-Bergen (N.Y.) Ctrl. Sch., 1994-96. Presdl. fellow, 1987-90. Mem. Phi Delta Kappa, Pi Lambda Theta. Avocations: reading, writing. Home and Office: 5866 W Sweden Rd Bergen NY 14416-9516

WOODY, JOHN FREDERICK, retired secondary education educator; b. Indpls., Apr. 27, 1941; s. Ralph Edwin and Crystal Oleta (Thomas) W.; m. Nancy Ann Henry, July 7, 1963; children: Michael, Laura. BS in Secondary Sch. Teaching, Butler U., 1963, MS in Edn., 1967, adminstrn. lic., 1979, postgrad., 1991—, UCLA, 1980-82, Ind. U., 1990, U. Amsterdam, The Netherlands, 1985, Mont. State U., 1993, Purdue U., 1994. Tchr. Pub. Sch. 90, Indpls., 1963-66, Broad Ripple High Sch., Indpls., 1966-89; tchr., head social studies dept. Arlington H.S., Indpls., 1989—2003; ret., 2003. Author: (resource kits for hist. events) Cram, Inc., 1976-81, (filmstrips) Lowe Sheldrew, 1976-81; contbr. articles to profl. jours. and sch. materials. Sponsor Rep. Nat. Com., 1982—; deacon North Star Bapt. Ch., 1983—; mem. U.S. Congress German Bundestag Select Com. Ind., 1986-93. Fulbright scholar U.S. Info. Agy., 1985. Mem. ASCD, Nat. Coun. Social Studies, Ind. Coun. Social Studies, Arlington Acad. Com. Avocations: reading, writing, swimming, lifting weights. Home: 7362 Woodside Dr Indianapolis IN 46260-3137 Office: Arlington High Sch 4825 N Arlington Ave Indianapolis IN 46226-2499

WOOLEVER, GAIL WALUK, elementary school educator, artist, secondary school educator; b. Auburn, Ind., Apr. 26, 1952; d. Edward and Dorothy Mae (Rieke) Waluk; m. Stephen J. Woolever, July 18, 1981; 1 child, Zachary. BA, Valparaiso U., 1974; MS, Ind. U., 1979. Cert. permanent tchr., Ind. Art tchr. Kankakee Valley Sch. Corp., Wheatfield, Ind., 1974—. One-woman show includes Munce Art Ctr., 1988; group show includes studio show, 1990, PAC Show, 2000; designer 8 sets of stained glass windows, 1993-95, logo design for sch., 1992; stained glass window designer and constn. with two other tchrs. for intermediate sch., 2001; owner Heart to Hand Art Studio; coord. and designer, fused glass window Wheatfield Elem. Sch., 2003, Grace Fellowship, 2003. Den leader Cub Scouts, DeMotte, Ind., 1989-94; Sunday sch. tchr. jr. high Demotte United Meth., 1993-97, jr. high youth leader, 1995-96; sec. Little League, Wheatfield, Ind., 1994-95. Eli Lilly Grant, 2000, Grace Fellowship, Sr. High S. Sch., 2003. Mem. NEA, Nat. Art Edn. Assn., Ind. State Tchrs. Assn., Prairie Arts Coun., Hobart Arts League, Delta Kappa Gamma. Avocations: artist, reading, gardening, cooking, sewing. Home: 3219 W 1700 N Wheatfield IN 46392-8935 Office: Wheatfield Elem Sch PO Box 158 Wheatfield IN 46392-0158

WOOLF, AMY KASPAR, librarian, storyteller; b. Peoria, Ill., June 7, 1954; d. Edgar Armand and Gwendolyn Eleanor (Mackenzie) Kaspar; m. William Randolph Woolf, Oct. 7, 1978; children: Katherine Michele, Sarah Elizabeth. BA magna cum laude, Bradley U., 1976; MS in LS, U. Ill., 1977. Children's libr. Wichita (Kans.) Pub. Libr., 1978—86; head libr. Botanica, The Wichita Gardens, 1987—2002; artist, storyteller Arts Ptnrs., Wichita, Kans., 2002—. Storyteller Wichita Pub. Schs., 1986-98. Chmn. Children's Libr. Assn., 1984—; mem. William Allan Colite Children's Book Award Selection Com., 1985—. Mem.: Wichita Area Libr. Assn. Avocations: quilting, gardening. Office: Arts Ptnrs 201 N Water Ste 300 Wichita KS 67202

WOOLF, WILLIAM BLAUVELT, retired association executive; b. New Rochelle, N.Y., Sept. 18, 1932; s. Douglas Gordon and Katharine Hutton (Blauvelt) W. AA, John Muir Jr. Coll., 1951; student, U. Calif. at Berkeley, 1951; BA, Pomona Coll., 1953; MA, Claremont (Calif.) Grad. Sch., 1955; PhD, U. Mich., 1960. Instr., asst. prof., asso. prof. U. Wash., Seattle, 1959-68; assoc. sec., dir. adminstrn. AAUP, Washington, 1968-79; mng. editor Math. Revs., Am. Math. Soc., Ann Arbor, Mich., 1979-90, acting exec. editor, 1984-85; assoc. exec. dir. Am. Math. Soc., Providence, 1990-96. Bd. dirs. Nat. Child Rsch. Ctr., Washington, 1975-77; trustee Friends Sch., Detroit, 1985-90, treas., 1986-90; mem. Law and Justice Coun., Jefferson County, Wash., 1998—, chmn., 2001; mem. Wash. State U. Jefferson County Adv. Team, 1999-2003, chmn., 2002-2003, Jefferson County Edn. Com., 1998-2003, chmn., 1999-2001; bd. dirs. Jefferson County Farmers Market Assn., 2002-03. Fulbright research fellow U. Helsinki, Finland, 1963-64 Fellow AAAS; mem. ACLU (life, treas. Washington 1966-68, bd. dirs. Washtenaw County and Mich. State 1989-90, bd. dirs. R.I. State 1993-95, treas. 1994-95, chmn. Jefferson County chpt. 2003—), Am. Math. Soc., Math. Assn. Am. Mem. Soc. Of Friends. Home: PO Box 225 Port Townsend WA 98368-0235

WOOLFORD, KATHLEEN MARIE, special education educator, secondary school educator; b. Racine, Wis., May 25, 1962; d. Norbert Ley and Shirley Mae Klar; m. Alan Robert Woolford, July 19, 1984; children: Adrianne Chantelle, Kassondra Lynn. BS in Vocat. Rehab. with concentration in spl. edn., U. Wis.-Stout, Menomonie, 1984; MS in Edn., U. Wis., LaCrosse, 1992. Lic. tchr. mental retardation, learning disabilities and emotional disturbance. Ride operator Marriotts Great Am., Gurnee, Ill., 1979—81; camp counselor Camp Friendship, Annandale, Minn., 1981—84; substitute tchr. Highland (Wis.) H.S., 1984; vocat. spl. edn. tchr. Lowry H.S., Winnemucca, Nev., 1984—86; spl. edn. tchr. Lancaster (Wis.) H.S., 1986—; customer svc. rep. Land's End, Inc., Dodgeville, Wis., 1992—96; admitting rep. S.W. Health Ctr., 2002—03; office mgr. Oak Pk. Dental, 2003—. Edn. rep. polit. action and grievance Lancaster Cmty. Schs., 1995—; Lancaster rep. Grand County Transition Adv. Team, Lancaster, 1998—99; mem. faculty senate Lancaster H.S., 2001. Treas. Westview Elem. PTO, Platteville, Wis., 1997—99; vol. Badger State Games; phone vol. Pregnancy Helpline; mem. Platteville Parent in Edn., 1998—; uniform coord. Platteville Power Soccer Club, 2001—; soccer coord. City of Platteville (Wis.) Pk. and Recreation, 2003; sec. St. Mary Cath. Ch. Coun. Cath. Women, Platteville, Wis., 1996—99. Mem.: Wis. Assn. Children with Behavior Disorders, Coun. for Exceptional Children. Roman Catholic. Avocations: cross stitch, reading, sports, travel. Home: 1470 Country Club Ct Platteville WI 53818 Office: Lancaster HS 806 E Elm St Lancaster WI 53813

WOOLLEY, JEAN GIBSON, instructional designer, consultant; b. L.A., Oct. 13, 1939; d. Robert Everett and Marie Laura (Butler) G.; m. William Jon Woolley, July 29, 1961; children: William Allen, Pamela Jean, Stephen Douglas, Jennifer Lynn. BA, U. Colo., 1961; MS, Ind. U., 1966. Cert. supr./coord., curriculum specialist, English and social studies tchr., Wis. Tchr. grade 4 Plaza Elem. Sch., Virginia Beach, Va., 1961-63, East Elem. Sch., Martinsville, Ind., 1963-64; comm./social sci. inst. educator Moraine Park Tech. Coll., Fond du Lac, Wis., 1976-81; curriculum planner Moraine Park, Fond du Lac, 1981-86, dean gen. edn./instrnl. support, 1986-97; mgr. tng. and cons. Wis. Instrnl. Design Sys., Ripon, 1997—. Gen. edn. task force Wis. tech. Coll. Sys., Madison, 1989-94, mem. bd. gen. edn. deans, 1986-97, chmn., 1996-97. Chpt. advisor Alpha Delta Pi at Ripon (Wis.) Coll., 1969-75, 89-95; Sunday sch. tchr., liturgist at local ch., Ripon, 1986—. Recipient Excellence in Vocat. Adminstrn. award Moraine Park Vocat. Assn., 1986, 94. Mem. Am. Vocat. Assn., Wis. Vocat. Assn. Methodist. Avocations: downhill skiing, biking, travel, opera. Home: 611 Hillside Ter Ripon WI 54971-1605 Office: WIDS Worldwide Instrnl Design Sys 203 Blackburn St PO Box 67 Ripon WI 54971-0067

WOOLLS, ESTHER BLANCHE, library science educator; b. Louisville, Mar. 30, 1935; d. Arthur William and Esther Lennie (Smith) Sutton; m. Donald Paul Woolls, Oct. 21, 1953 (div. Nov. 1982); 1 son, Arthur Paul AB in Fine Arts, Ind. U., 1958, MA in Libr. Sci., 1962, PhD in Libr. Sci., 1973. Elem. libr. Hammond Pub. Schs., Ind., 1958-65, libr. coord., 1965-67, Roswell Ind. Schs., N.Mex., 1967-70; prof. libr. sci. U. Pitts., 1973-97; prof., dir. Sch. Lib. and Info. Sci. San Jose (Calif.) State U., 1997—. Exec. dir. Beta Phi Mu, 1981-95. Author: The School Library Media Manager, 1995, 2d edit., 1999, So You're Going to Run a Library, 1995, Ideas for School Library Media Centers, 1996; co-author: Information Literacy, 1999; editor: Continuing Professional Education and IFLA: Past, Present, and a Vision for the Future, 1993, Delivering Lifelong Continuing Professional Education Across Space and Time, 2001. Fulbright scholar, 1995-96; recipient disting. svc. award Pa. Sch. Librs. Assn., 1993. Mem. ALA (mem. coun. 1985-89, 95—), Am. Assn. Sch. Librs. (bd. dirs. 1983-88, pres. 1993-94, disting. svc. award 1997), Pa. Learning Resources Assn. (pres. 1984-85), Internat. Assn. Sch. Librs. (pres. 1998-2001), Internat. Fedn. Libr. Assns. (mem. standing com. sch. librs. sect. 1991-99, sec. Continuing Profl. Edn. Round Table 2000—). Home: 130 E San Fernando St #403 San Jose CA 95112-3600 Office: San Jose State U Sch Lib & Info Sci 1 Washington Sq San Jose CA 95192-0029

WOOLSEY, THOMAS ALLEN, neurobiologist; b. Balt., Apr. 17, 1943; s. Clinton Nathan and Harriet (Runion) W.; m. Cynthia Tull Ward, June 8, 1969; children: Alix, Timothy. BS, U. Wis., 1965; MD, Johns Hopkins, 1969. Asst. prof. anatomy Washington U. Sch. Medicine, St. Louis, 1971-75, asst. prof. anatomy, neurobiology, 1975-77, assoc. prof. anatomy, neurobiology, 1977-80, assoc. prof. anatomy, neurobiology, physiology biophysics, 1980-83, coord. neurosci. program, 1980-84, sr. neuroscientist, 1982—, prof. neurology, neurological surgery, 1984—, dir. experimental neurology, neurological surgery, 1984—. Chmn., Washington U. Teaching Space Evaluation, 1989-90. Contbr. articles to profl. jours. First v.p. Pub. Info. Com. Acad. Sci., St. Louis, 1989—. NIH Rsch. grantee, 1970—; George H. and Ethel R. Bishop scholar, 1984—; recipient McKnight Neurosci. Devel. award, 1982-85. Mem. Am. Assn. Anatomists, Am. Acad. Neurology, St. Louis Acad. Sci., Soc. Neurosci., Johns Hopkins Med. Surgical Assn., Cajal Club. Avocations: hiking, history, woodworking. Office: Washington U Sch Medicine 660 S Euclid Ave # 8057 Saint Louis MO 63110-1010

WOOLWORTH, SUSAN VALK, primary school educator; b. Toledo, Ohio, Apr. 24, 1954; d. Robert Earl and Alice (Melick) Valk; children: Alison Valk, Andrew Baker. BA, Pine Manor Jr. Coll., Chestnut Hill, Mass., 1974; BS, Boston U., 1976. Tchr. kindergarten Lancaster (Pa.) Country Day Sch., 1986—. Bd. dirs. Fulton Opera House; past bd. dirs. Planned Parenthood, Vis. Nurse Assn., Hands-On House. Mem.: Jr. League (sustainer), Sigma Gamma. Republican. Episcopalian. Avocations: walking, gardening, tennis, decorating.

WOOTAN, GERALD DON, osteopathic physician, educator; b. Oklahoma City, Nov. 19, 1944; s. Ralph George and Corrinne (Loafman) W. BA, Ctrl. State U., Edmond, Okla., 1970, BS, 1971, MEd, 1974; MB, U. Okla., Oklahoma City, 1978; DO, Okla. State U., 1985. Dir. mfg. engring. lab. GE, Oklahoma City, 1965-70; counseling psychologist VA Hosp., Oklahoma City, 1970-76; physician asst. Thomas (Okla.) Med. Clin., 1978-81; pvt. practice, Jenks, Okla., 1986—; intern Tulsa Regional Med. Ctr., 1985-86; assoc. prof. Okla. State U. Coll. Osteo. Medicine, 1986—, with Springer Clinic, 1995-98; owner Jenks (Okla.) Health Team LLC, 1998—. Chmn. gen. practice quality assurance Tulsa Regional Med. Ctr., 1989-91; v.p. New Horizons Counseling Ctr., Clinton, Okla., 1977-81; sr. aviation med. examiner FAA, Tulsa, 1991—; pres. S.W. Diagnostics, Inc., Tulsa, 1989-91, Okla. Edn. Found. Osteo. Medicine, Tulsa, 1988-89, 96, trustee Tulsa Long Term Care Authority; med. dir. Grace Living Ctr. Contbr. articles to profl. jours.; patentee for human restraint. Advancement chmn., chmn. Eagle bd. rev. Boy Scouts Am., Tulsa, 1987-88; trustee Tulsa Long Term Care Authority, 1988-91; trustee Tulsa Community Found. for Indigent Health Care, Inc., 1988-91. With USN, 1962-64. Named Clin. Preceptor of Yr., U. Okla., 1980, Outstanding Alumni award Okla. State U. Coll. Osteo. Medicine, 1990. Mem.: Am. Coll. Osteo. Family Physicians (cert. of added qualification in geriatrics 1982, bd. cert. 1993, pres. Okla. chpt. 1993—94, qualified hyperbaric oxygen therapy 2001, med. dir. Narconon Drug Treatment Ctr.), Okla. Acad. Gen. Practitioners (pres.), Am. Coll. Gen. Practitioners, Am. Acad. Physician Assts., Tulsa Dist. Osteo. Soc. (pres. 1991—92), Okla. Osteo. Assn. (legis. bur. 1986—2001, trustee 1998—2001, membership bur. 1998—2001, bur. on membership benefits

1998—2001), Am. Osteo. Assn., Okla. State U. Coll. Osteo. Medicine Alumni Assn. (pres. 1988—89). Avocations: scuba diving, aviation medicine. Home: 4320 E 100th St Tulsa OK 74137-5305 Address: 715 W Main St Ste S Jenks OK 74037-3553 Office: Ste S 715 W Main St Jenks OK 74037-3553

WOOTEN, FRANK THOMAS, retired research facility executive; b. Fayetteville, N.C., Sept. 24, 1935; s. Frank Thomas and Katherine (McRae) Wooten; m. Linda Walker, July 14, 1962; children: Laurin Walker, Patrick Thomas, Ashley Tripp. BSEE, Duke U., 1957, PhD, 1964. Engr. Corning Glass Works, Raleigh, NC, 1964—66; from engr. to pres. Rsch. Triangle Inst., Research Triangle Park, NC, 1966—89, pres., 1989—99, ret., 1999. Bd. dirs. N.C. Biotech. Ctr., Troxler Electronics Labs., N.C. Biosci. Investment Fund. Contbr. articles on semiconductors and biomedical engring. to profl. publs.; patentee semiconductors tech. Lt. (j.g.) USN, 1957—59. Recipient Disting. Engring. Alumnus award, Duke U., 1991; fellow, Shell, 1961. Mem.: IEEE, Nat. Inst. Statis. Scis. (corp. 1990—98), Ballistic Missile Def. Orgn. (tech. application rev. panel 1990—94), Assn. for Advancement Med. Instrumentation (chmn. com. on aerospace tech. 1971—77). Baptist.

WOOTEN, ROBERT E. musician, educator; b. Chgo., Feb. 17, 1930; s. John and Flora (Waits) W.; m. Frances Louise Carter, Aug. 26, 1956; children: Robert Jr., Carol Lynne, John D. BMus, Chgo. Conservatory Music, 1956; M in Music Edn., Roosevelt U., 1968; D in Music Edn., Va. Seminary & Coll., 1983. Min. music Beth Eden Bapt. Ch., Chgo., 1941—; founder, dir. Wooten Choral Ensemble, 1949—; dir. music Greater Harvest Bapt. Ch., 1950-86. Music dept. chair Parker H.S., Chgo., 1957-62; staff asst., Chgo. Pub. Schs. 1962-75, dist. adminstr., 1976-95. Mem. Am. Choral Dirs., Music Educators Nat. Conf. Home: 9531 S Union Ave Chicago IL 60628-1031

WOOTEN-BRYANT, HELEN CATHERINE, principal; b. Houston, Feb. 24, 1940; d. Johnny Clement and Roberta (Glenn) Steward. BS in Elem. Edn., Prairie View A&M U., 1962, MEd in Adminstrn. and Supervision, 1966. Cert. elem. tchr. Tchr. Chgo. Bd. Edn., 1962-83; prin. Vanderpoel Magnet Sch. Humanities, Chgo., 1984—. Communion minister St. James Cath. Ch. Recipient Phi Delta Kappa Educator award, 1998. Mem. Nat. Women of Achievement (pres. Chgo. chpt. 1988—, Excellence award 1988), Chgo. Prin. Assn., Prairie View A&M U. Alumni Assn. (founder, pres. Chgo. chpt., 1987—), Sigma Gamma Rho (pres. 1981-83, chairwoman cen. regional nominating com. 1982-84, chairwoman polit. action com. 1985—, Karrie Regional award 1980, Outstanding Pres. award Chgo. Alumnae chpt., 1987, Fred Hampton Inst. award 1990). Republican. Roman Catholic. Avocations: golf, bridge. Office: Vanderpoel Magnet Sch Humanities 9510 S Prospect Ave Chicago IL 60643-1296

WOOTTON, JOHN FRANCIS, physiology educator; b. Penn Yan, N.Y., May 31, 1929; s. John Edenden and Margaret Eliza (Smith) W.; m. Joyce Albertine Mac Mullen, Aug. 28, 1959; children: J. Timothy, David M., Barbara H., Bruce C. BS, Cornell U., 1951, MS, 1953, PhD, 1960. Grad. rsch. asst. Cornell U., Ithaca, N.Y., 1956-60; post doctoral fellow U. Coll., London, 1960-62; from asst. prof. to assoc. prof. dept. physiology Cornell U., 1962-70, prof. dept. physiology, 1970—, assoc. dean Grad. Sch., 1980-83. Grad. faculty rep. field of physiology Cornell U., 1990-92, 93-97, chmn. dept. physiology, 1997-98, co-chmn. dept. biomed. scis., 1998-99, chmn. 1999-2000; vis. scientist MRC Molecular Biology, Cambridge, Eng., 1969-70, Nat. Inst. Med. Rsch., London, 1985-86, 92-93, 2002; temporary sr. rsch. assoc. Stanford (Calif.) U., 1977-78. Contbr. articles to profl. jours. 1st lt. USAR, 1954-56. Rsch. and Travel grantee NIH, USDA Burroughs Wellcom Fund, Med. Rsch. Coun., Cornell Biotech. Program. Mem. AAAS, Am. Soc. Biochemistry, Molecular and Cell Biology, Am. Chem. Soc., Biophys. Soc., Protein Soc., Sigma Xi (v.p., pres. Cornell chpt.). Avocations: travel, choral singing, gardening, art, fishing. Office: Cornell U Dept Biomed Scis T8-014 Vet Rsch Tower Ithaca NY 14853-5908

WORKMAN, GAYLE JEAN, physical education educator, educator; b. Mt. Vernon, Ohio, Sept. 26, 1959; d. Willard L. Workman and Joyce (Pealer) Workman-Garvic. BS in Phys. Edn., Bowling Green State U., 1982; MS in Sport Studies, Slippery Rock U., 1991; PhD, Ohio State U., 1995. presenter in field, 1992—. Elem. phys. edn. tchr., coach East Knox Sch. Dist., Howard, Ohio, 1983-89; teaching asst. Slippery Rock (Pa.) U., 1989-91; adj. prof. Butler (Pa.) C.C., 1991; prof. Kutztown (Pa.) U., 1992; teaching asst. Ohio State U., Columbus, 1992-95; asst. prof. U. Akron, Ohio, 1995—. Presenter Midwest Conv. of Adult Edn., Columbus, 1993. Mem. AAHPERD. Avocations: golf, jogging, racket sports, reading, backpacking. Home: 1543 Garfield St Hollywood FL 33020-3748

WORKMAN, KAYLEEN MARIE, special education and adult education educator; b. Paola, Kans., Aug. 25, 1947; d. Ralph I. and Pearl Marie (Shults) Platz; m. John Edward Workman, Aug. 10, 1980; children: Andrew Ray, Craig Michael. BS in Edn., Emporia State U., 1969, MS in Edn., 1983. Tchr. English/speech Lincoln (Kans.) High Sch., 1969-70, substitute tchr., 1970-71, Hudson (Wis.) Sch. Dist., 1971-72; tchrs. aide learning disabilities Park Forest South (Ill) Jr. High Sch., 1978—97; learning disabilities/English instr. George York Sch., Osawatomie, Kans., 1978-97, instr. math and sci., spl. edn., 2003—; adult edn. instr. Adult Edn. Ctr., Osawatomie State Hosp., 1997-2000; spl. edn. tchr. Ottawa (Kans.) H.S., 2000—02; math. and sci. tchr. spl. edn. George York Cmty. Sch., Osawatomie, Kans., 2003—. Supr. Loose Ends Clown Troop, 1988-91; presenter in field. Author of poems. Com. mem., sec. Cub Scouts, Osawatomie, 1987-88, com. mem. Boy Scouts Am., 1988-91, sec., 1990-91; forensics judge Osawatomie H.S. Forensics Team, 1991-92; hunter's safety instr. Osawatomie Sportsman's Club, 1982-86; mem. Osawatomie Cmty. Band, 1990-92. Mem. Osawatomie-NEA (v.p. 1982-83, 93-94, pres. 1983-84, 94-95, sec. 1986), Kans.-NEA (Sunflower uniserv adminstrv. bd. 1985, Sunflower uniserv coord. coun.), Learning Disabilities Assn., Delta Kappa Gamma. Avocations: hunting, fishing, collecting santa clauses, writing poetry, shopping.

WORRALL, CHARLES HARRISON, elementary education educator; b. Phila., Sept. 4, 1956; s. Joseph Harrison Worrall and Mae (Cadwalader) Hollenback; m. Vickianne Marie Mrugal, Sept. 5, 1981; children: Anna Cadwalader, Coeli Martin. BS in Edn., Psychology, Elmira Coll., 1979. Cert. tchr., N.Y. Tchr. mid. sch. Montgomery Mid. Sch., Wynnewood, Pa., 1982-87, assoc. dir. admissions, 1985-87, dir. summer programs, 1984-86; tchr., head dept. history, athletic dir. Gulf Stream (Fla.) Mid. Sch., 1987-93; asst. head mid. sch. Shipley Sch., Bryn Mawr, Pa., 1993-98, head of mid. sch., 1998—. Mem. Secondary Sch. Admission Testing Bd., Princeton, N.J., 1987—. Mem. ASCD, Fla. Coun. Ind. Schs. (evaluation tema 1989, citation for teaching history 1990). Avocations: reading, golf, tennis, sailing, ice hockey. Office: 814 Yarrow St Bryn Mawr PA 19010-3525 Home: # B 3408 Goshen Rd Newtown Square PA 19073-3424

WORRELL, BETTY CARTRETTE, elementary school educator; b. Whiteville, N.C., Mar. 26; d. J. D. Cartrette and Earlie Mae (Boswell) Jones; m. Charles Worrell. AA, Southeastern C.C., 1985; BA in Early Childhood Edn., U. N.C., Wilmington, 1988; M in Elem. Edn., Pembroke State U., 1991; degree in G level reading specialist, Fayetteville State U., 1998. Nat. bd. cert. in lang. arts.; trainer CRISS, 2002, Framework for Teaching Students Who Live in Poverty, 2003, NC Writing, 2003. Tchr. reading grades 4-8 Boys Home Sch., Lake Waccamaw, N.C., 1991-92; Chpt. I reading tchr. Old Dock/Guideway, Tabor City, N.C., 1992-94; lit./curriculum coord. Guideway Elem. Sch., Tabor City, 1994-95, mid. sch. lang. arts tchr., 1995—2003. Trainer N.C. Tchr. Acad., 1996—2003. Named Columbus County Tchr. of Yr., 2002. Mem. ASCD, Internat. Reading Assn., N.C. Reading Tchrs. Assn., Mid. Sch. Assn. (mem. svc. com.), Nat. English Tchrs. Assn., N.C. English Tchrs. Assn., Cape Fear Reading Assn., N.C. Writing Project, N.C. Assn. Educators, Kappa Delta Pi. E-mail: betty_worrell@yahoo.com.

WORRELL, RICHARD VERNON, orthopedic surgeon, college dean, dean; b. Bklyn., June 4, 1931; s. John Elmer and Elaine (Callender) Worrell; m. Audrey Frances Martiny, June 14, 1958; children: Philip Vernon, Amy Elizabeth. BA, NYU, 1952; MD, Meharry Med. Coll., 1958. Diplomate Am. Bd. Orthop. Surgery, Nat. Bd. Med. Examiners. Intern Meharry Med. Coll., Nashville, 1958—59; resident in gen. surgery Mercy-Douglass Hosp., Phila., 1960—61; resident in orthop. surgery State U. N.Y. Buffalo Sch. Medicine Affiliated Hosps., 1961—64; resident in orthop. pathology Temple U. Med. Ctr., Phila., 1966—67; pvt. practice orthop. surgery Phila., 1967—68; asst. prof. acting head divsn. orthop. surgery U. Conn. Sch. Medicine, 1968—70; attending orthop. surgeon E.J. Meyer Meml. Hosp., Buffalo, Millard Fillmore Hosp., Buffalo, VA Hosp., Buffalo, Buffalo State Hosp.; clin. instr. orthop. surgery SUNY, Buffalo, 1970—74; chief orthop. surgery VA Hosp., Newington, Conn., 1974—80; asst. prof. surgery (orthop.) U. Conn. Sch. Medicine, 1974—77, assoc. prof., 1977—83, asst. dean student affairs, 1980—83; prof. clin. surgery SUNY Downstate Med. Ctr., Bklyn., 1983—86; dir. orthop. surgery Brookdale Hosp. Med. Ctr., Bklyn., 1983—86; prof. orthop. U. N.Mex. Sch. Medicine, 1986—97, prof., vice chmn. dept. orthop., 1997—99, prof. emeritus, 1999—; dir. orthop. oncology U. N.Mex. Health Scis. Ctr., 1987—99; mem. med. staff U. N.Mex. Cancer Ctr., 1987—99; chief orthop. surgery VA Med. Ctr., Albuquerque, 1987—97. Cons. in orthop. surgery Newington (Conn.) Children's Hosp., 1968—70; mem. sickle cell disease adv. com. NIH, 1982—86. Bd. dirs. Big Bros. Greater Hartford. Served to capt. M.C. USAR, 1962—69. Fellow: ACS, Royal Soc. Medicine, London, Am. Acad. Orthop. Surgeons; mem.: AMA, N.Mex. Soc. Clin. Oncology, Internat. Soc. Orthop. Surgery and Traumatology, Orthop. Rsch. Soc., Internat. Fedn. Surg. Colls. (assoc.), Am. Soc. Clin. Oncology, Am. Soc. Clin. Pathologists, Am. Orthop. Assn., Alpha Omega Alpha.

WORTHAM, DEBORAH LYNNE, school principal; b. Chgo., May 13, 1949; d. Leon Cabot and Bessie (Summers) Smith; m. Chester Hopes Wortham, Jan. 29, 1972; children: Shelley Sharon, Chester Hopes III. BS, U. Wis., 1972; MS, Morgan State U., 1981; EdD, Nova Southeastern U., 1997. Tchr., reading tchr., support tchr. Balt. City Pub. Schs., 1972-87, asst. prin., 1988-90, prin. Samuel Coleridge Taylor Sch., 1990-94, dir. efficacy, 1994-97, prin. K-8, 1997—, dir. profl. devel., 2000—. Program facilitator Balt. Schs.-Johns Hopkins U., 1987-88; dean of edn. Higher Dimensions Learning Ctr., Balt., 1985—. Author: Teaching by Signs and Wonders, 1992. Recipient Mayor's Citation for Volunteerism, Balt., 1982, Am. Best Elem. Sch. for Significant Improvement award Redbook Mag., 1993, 95; cited Administrator's Class Act, Channel ll TV, Balt., 1991. Mem. ASCD, Phi Delta Kappa, Alpha Kappa Alpha. Democrat. Pentecostal. Office: Bd Edn 2500 E Northern Pkwy Baltimore MD 21214-1199

WORTHAM, MAXINE ALLINE, early childhood education executive director; b. Jackson, Tenn., June 23, 1947; d. Willie and Alline (Hayes) W. BS, Lane Coll., 1968; MS, Ill. State U., 1973, PhD, 1985. Adminstrv. endorsement and superintendency, Ill. Tchr. math. and sci. Roosevelt and Trewyn Sch., Peoria, Ill., 1968-72; tchr. spl. edn. Lincoln Elem. Sch., Peoria, 1973-76, tchr., 1976-78; dean students Manual H.S., Peoria, 1978-86; adminstrv. asst. Blaine Sumner Mid. Sch., Peoria, 1986-87; prin. Glen Oak Primary Sch., Peoria, 1987-88; dir. pers. Peoria Pub. Schs., 1988-89, exec. dir. pers., 1989-91, exec. dir. primary schs., 1991-92. Pres. bd. Ill. Assn. Sch., Coll. and Univ. Staff, 1992-93. Author: The Constitutionality of the Illinois Public Schools Finance System, 1985. Pres. bd. dirs. Tri-County Urban League, Peoria, 1983-84; fellow Edn. Policy Fellowship Program, 1985-86; mem. adv. bd. Peoria (Ill.) Pub. Libr., 1986-89, Salvation Army, Peoria, 1987-93, Ctrl. Ill. Light Co., Peoria, 1991-94; bd. mem. Peoria (Ill.) Assn. Retarded Citizen, 1994—; pres. Tri-Urban League Guild; steward Ward Chapel African Meth. Episc. Ch. Recipient Martin Luther King Jr. Leadership award Southside Pastors Assn., Peoria, 1989, Profl. award YWCA, Peoria, 1989, Ill. Those Who Excel award Ill. State Bd. Edn., 1998; named Outstanding Young Women in Am., 1983. Mem. Alpha Kappa Alpha, Delta Kappa Gamma (v.p.), Phi Delta Kappa, Rotary. Methodist. Home: 6908 N Michele Ln Peoria IL 61614-2625 Office: Peoria Pub Schs 3202 N Wisconsin Ave Peoria IL 61603-1260

WORTHEN, ELLIS CLAYTON, retired fine arts administrator, educator; b. Ferron, Utah, May 28, 1936; s. Peter Clayton and Vernell (Seeley) W.; m. Olga Mae Gilbert, Aug. 28, 1959; children: Douglas, Joseph, Steven, Roger, Brenda, Paul. AS, Coll. Ea. Utah, 1956; BA, Brigham Young U., 1958, MA, 1966, PhD, 1972. Cert. elem. and secondary music edn., adminstrv./supervisory. Music tchr. West Side Sch. Dist., Dayton, Idaho, 1960-62, Uintah H.S., Vernal, Utah, 1962-65; grad. asst. Brigham Young U., Provo, Utah, 1965-67; chmn. music dept. No. Mont. Coll., Havre, 1967-70; music tchr. Ch. Coll. Western Samoa, Apia, 1970-73, Granger H.S., West Valley City, Utah, 1974-75; fine arts adminstr. Granite Sch. Dist., Salt Lake City, 1975-97, ret., 1997. Pres. Young Audiences of Utah, Salt Lake City, 1988-92; chmn. State Music Festivals, Utah, 1987-97; adv. com. Utah Symphony, Ballet West, Utah Opera, Salt Lake City, 1975-97. Composer (piano) Minuet, 1966, (percussion ensemble) Percussionata, 1967, (orch.) Contrasts, 1967, (brass sextet) Sextet, 1967. Active LDS Ch., Utah, Idaho, Mont., Calif., Western Samoa. Sgt. U.S. Army Res., 1955-66. Recipient Minute Man award Utah Nat. Guard, Salt Lake City, 1980, Disting. Svc. award Utah H.S. Activities Assn., 1997; named Outstanding Adminstr. Granite Edn. Found., Salt Lake City, 1994. Mem. Music Educators Nat. Conf., Nat. Sch. Orch. Assn. (disting. svc. award 1990), Nat. Fedn. H.S. Activities Assn. (outstanding music educator 1992, 98), Utah Music Educators Assn. (festival chair 1975-94, spl. svc. award 1986), Utah Alliance Arts and Humanities Edn. (bd. mem.), Young Audiences Utah (bd. mem., pres. 1988-92, excellence award 1992). Avocations: books, camping, hunting, gardening. Home: 3623 Kempner Rd Salt Lake City UT 84109-3642

WORTHEN, JOHN EDWARD, retired academic administrator; b. Carbondale, Ill., July 15, 1933; s. Dewey and Annis Burr (Williams) W.; m. Sandra Damewood, Feb. 27, 1960; children: Samantha Jane, Bradley Edward. BS in Psychology (Univ. Acad. scholar), Northwestern U., 1954; MA in Student Pers. Adminstrn., Columbia U., 1955; EdD in Adminstrn. in Higher Edn. (Coll. Entrance Exam. Bd. fellow), Harvard U., 1964; PhD (hon.), Yeungnam U., Daegu, Korea, 1986; DL (hon.), Ball State U., 2001. Dean of men Am. U., 1959-61; dir. counseling and testing and asst. prof. edn., 1963-66; asst. to provost and asst. prof., 1966-68; acting provost and v.p. acad. affairs, 1968; assoc. provost for instrn., 1969; v.p. student affairs, 1970-75; v.p. student affairs and adminstrn., 1976-79; pres. Ind. U. of Pa., 1979-84, Ball State U., Muncie, Ind., 1984-2000; ret., 2000. Cons. to universities and public schs. Bd. dirs. Ball State U. Found.; mem. adv. bd. Muncie-Delawaare County Found.; mem. Cmty. Alliance to Promote Edn. Mem. Am. Assn. State Colls. and Univs. (chair, bd. dirs. 1999), Rotary Internat., Phi Delta Kappa, Kappa Delta Pi. E-mail: johneworthen@aol.com.

WORTHINGTON, DANIEL GLEN, lawyer, educator; b. Rexbury, Idaho, Aug. 15, 1957; BA magna cum laude, Brigham Young U., 1982, MEd, 1986, EdD, JD cum laude, Brigham Young U., 1989; LLM in Taxation, U. Fla., 2002. Bar: Utah 1990. Asst. to assoc. dean students Brigham Young U., 1986—88, cons., 1987—89, mgr. planned giving, tech. cons., 1989—90, adj. prof. law and edn., 1989—; asst. dean students Coll. Eastern Utah, 1985—86; assoc. dean, exec. dir. devel. Porterville Coll. Found., 1990—91; prin. Worthington & Assoc., Provo, Utah, 1991—93; mng. atty., ptnr. Walstad & Babcock, Provo; assoc. dean U. SD Sch. Law, 1994—95, exec. v.p. found., 1995—2001. Assoc. v.p. gen. counsel U. Ctrl. Fla. Found., Orlando, adj. faculty Masters of Tax Program; sr. cons. Fla. Hosp. and the U. S.D. Bus. Sch., 1997—2001; cons. Citigroup Trust Svcs., 1997—2001; sr. cons. Fla. Hosp., 1997—99, v.p. gen. counsel, 1999—2003. Editor-in-chief jour. Edn. & Law Perspectives, 1986-88, co-chair, exec. adv. bd., dir., 1988-91; mem. editl. bd. Planned Giving Design Ctr., 2002—, Endowment Devel. Svc., 1999—; contbr. articles to profl. jour. Exec. v.p. SD Planned Giving Coun., 1994-2001; nat. assembly del. Nat. Com. on Planned, 1994—; mem. Nat. Valuation Task Force, 2002—; pres. Greater Orlando Planned Giving Round Table, 1999—; v.p., gen. counsel Fla. Hosp. Found., 1999-2003. Pres. Wealth Mgmt. Group, 2003—; sr. cons., maranatha volunteers Internat.; Fla. conf. of Seventh-Day Adventists Cmty. Found. of ctrl. Fla. Boys & Girls Club of Ctrl. Fla., 2002-; bd. dir. SD Trust Co., 2002—; pres. Family Bank Design Ctr., 2002—; Editorial Bd., Planned Giving Design Ctr., 2002; Editorial Bd., Endowment Develop. Svc., 1999-; With USAFR, 1982-88. Mem. Supreme Ct. Hist. Soc., Federalist Soc., mem., Am. Judicature Soc., 1994; Nat. Soc. Fund Raising Exec., Nat. Eagle Scout Assn., Phi Kappa Phi. E-mail: dan.worthington@flhosp.org.

WORTHINGTON, PATRICIA, elementary education educator; b. Mineola, N.Y., Sept. 25, 1948; d. George Edward and Thelma (Carson) Donnelly; m. Michael Worthington, July 16, 1977. BS, Parsons Coll., Fairfield, Iowa, 1970; postgrad., Morningside Coll., Davenport, Iowa, Drake U. Cert. tchr., Iowa. Elem. tchr. Gilmore City (Iowa) Bradgate Comunity Sch., 1970—. Co-chmn. Phase III, Iowa Dept. Edn.; chairperson for Cmty. Svc. Grant, 1996, 97. Mem. success 4 com. Nat. Geog. Kids Network, mem. pioneer team for IM series. Career edn. grantee, 1977, Roy J. Carver grantee Nat. Geog. Kids Network, 1990. Mem. Iowa Edn. Assn. (past sec.-treas., pres.), Delta Kappa Gamma (v.p. Alpha Omega chpt. 2000-02, pres. 2002—). Home: 2014 W River Dr Humboldt IA 50548-2634 Office: 412 S E Ave Gilmore City IA 50541

WORTHINGTON, WARD CURTIS, JR., university dean, anatomy educator; b. Savannah, Ga., Aug. 8, 1925; s. Ward Curtis I and Pearl Mabel (Farris) W.; m. Floride Calhoun McDermid, June 21, 1947; children: Ward Curtis III, Amy Lynne Worthington Hauslohner. BS, The Citadel, 1952; MD, Med. U. S.C., 1952. Intern Boston City Hosp., 1952-53; instr. anatomy John Hopkins, 1953-56; asst. prof. anatomy U. Ill., 1956-57; asst. prof., assoc. prof. Med. U. S.C., Charleston, 1957-66; prof. anatomy Med. U. S.C., Charleston, 1966-91; prof. emeritus, 1991—. prof. history med. scis. M. U. S.C., Charleston, 1987—, asst. dean curriculum, 1966-69, chmn. dept. anatomy, 1969-77, acting v.p. acad. affairs, 1975-77, v.p. acad. affairs, 1977-82, assoc. dean acad. affairs, 1982—, dir. Waring Hist. Library, 1982—. Contbr. articles to profl. jours. Bd. dirs. Charleston Symphony Orch. Assn., 1980-84, 2d v.p., 1982. Served with USNR, 1944-46. Research grantee The Commonwealth Fund, 1957-61, NIH, 1962-73; NIH spl. fellow, 1964-65. Mem. Waring Library Soc., S.C. Acad. Sci., S.C. Med. Assn., Charleston County Med. Soc., Endocrine Soc., Am. Physiol. Soc., Am. Assn. Anatomists, Sigma Xi, Alpha Omega Alpha. Episcopalian. Lodge: Rotary (bd. dirs. 1982-83). Home: 17 Morton Ave Charleston SC 29407-7231 Office: 171 Ashley Ave Charleston SC 29425-0001

WORTHY, FRED LESTER, computer science educator; b. Greeley, Colo., Mar. 8, 1936; s. William and Gladys (Walburn) W.; m. Susan Worthy, June 4, 1963; children: Michael (dec.), Nina E. BS in Math., Colo. State Coll., 1959; MA in Physics, Colo. State U., 1965; cert. computer sci., Clemson U., 1978; student Computer Tchrs. Inst., Ctrl. State U., Edmond, Okla., 1989-90. Physics tchr. Littleton (Colo.) H.S., 1959-63, King H.S., Tampa, 1963-65; prof. physics Ga. So. Coll., Statesboro, 1965-66; rschr. USAF (NASA), Tullahoma, Tenn., 1966-68; prof. physics Bapt. Coll., Charleston, S.C., 1968-78, registrar, asst. dean, 1969-70; prof. computer sci. Charleston So. U., 1978—; bus. cons. Charleston, 1981—. Dir. Developed Creative Physics Labs. for H.S. as part of Self-Paced Physics, 1962-63, Established Hands-On Computer Curriculum, 1979-86, Hands-On Teaching Labs. for Computers Across the Curriculum, 1987-93; developer new physics labs. for coll. NSF, Bapt. Coll., Charleston, 1970-72. Author: Twenty-Five Self-Paced Computer Laboratories, 1986-93. Chmn., deacon Summerville (S.C.) Bapt. Ch., 1978-85; chmn. judge com. Miss Charleston-Miss America, Charleston, 1992—; mem. Miss S.C. Judges List, 1991—. Avocation: photography. Home: 104 Three Iron Dr Summerville SC 29483-2937

WORTMAN, RICHARD S. historian, educator; b. N.Y.C., Mar. 24, 1938; s. Joseph R. and Ruth (Nacht) W.; m. Marlene Stein, June 14, 1960; 1 child, Leonie. BA, Cornell U., 1958; MA, U. Chgo., 1960, PhD, 1964. Instr. history U. Chgo., 1963-64, asst. prof., 1964-69, asso. prof., 1969-76, prof., 1976-77; prof. history Princeton U., 1977-88, dir. Russian studies, 1982-88; prof. history Columbia U., 1988—; Bryce prof. history, 2001—. Trustee Nat. Council for Soviet and Eastern European Research, 1983-89; sr. fellow Harriman Inst., 1985-86 Author: The Crisis of Russian Populism, 1967, The Development of a Russian Legal Consciousness, 1976, (with Leopold Haimson and Ziva Gallili) The Making of Three Russian Revolutionaries: Voices from the Menshevik Past, 1987, Scenarios of Power: Myth and Ceremony in Russian Monarchy, vol. I, 1995, vol. II (George L. Mosse prize Am. Hist. Assn.), 2000. Social Sci. Rsch. Coun. grantee, 1975-76; Guggenheim fellow, 1981-82 Mem. Am. Assn. Advancement Slavic Studies (pres. Mid-Atlantic Slavic Conf. 1982-83), AAUP., Am. Hist. Assn. Home: 410 Riverside Dr Apt 91 New York NY 10025-7924 E-mail: rsw3@columbia.edu.

WORZBYT, JOHN CHARLES, counseling education educator; b. Auburn, N.Y., Sept. 9, 1943; s. John and Audrey (Loomis) W.; m. Jean Ann Vogelsperger, Mar. 26, 1967; children: Jason, Janeen. BS in Elem. Edn., SUNY, Oswego, 1965; EdM, U. Rochester, 1968, EdD in Counselor Edn., 1971. Cert. grades K-8 and common br. subjects, N.Y., cert. guidance, N.Y., nat. cert. counselor, lic. profl. counselor, 2002. Tchr. Union Springs (N.Y.) Bd. Edn., 1965-67; elem. guidance counselor West Genesee Bd. Edn., Camillas, NY, 1970-72; prof. Indiana (Pa.) Univ. of Pa., 1972—. Coord. of doctoral studies Dept. of Counselor Edn., Indiana Univ. Pa., 1986—; project coord. U.S. Dept. Edn. Rsch., Washington, 1989-91; cons. R. J. S. Films, Inc., Altoona, Pa., 1989—, T.E.A.M. Fight Against Drugs, Phila., 1990—. Author: Beating the Odds, 1991, 3R's Decision Making, 1991; co-author: Assessment and Behavior Problem Children, 1983, Elementary School Counseling, 1989, Caring Children Make Caring Choices, 1998, co-author: Support Groups for Children, 1996, Elementary School Counseling: A Commitment to Caring and Community Building, 2003. Pres. bd. YMCA, Indiana, 1991; bd. mem. Indiana (Pa.) County Child Care, 1991; chairperson Pastor Parish Rels.-Meth. Ch., Marion Center, Pa., 1991. Recipient U.S. Dept. Edn. grant Drug Free Schs. & Communities grant, 1989, Faculty Recognition Award, Outstanding Accomplishments as a Tchr., Scholar, Coll. of Edn., Ind. Univ. of Pa., 1992, Eminent Practitioner Award, Pa. Counseling Assn., 1997, Counselor Educator of the Yr. Award, Pa. Sch. Counselors Assn., 2001. Mem. AACD (Nat. Disting. Svc. registery 1989), Am. Sch. Counselors Assn. (Rsch. award 1990), Assn. for Counselor Edn. & Supervision, Nat. Bd. for Cert. Counselors, Nat. Ctr. for Self Esteem, Nat. Assn. for Humor and Creativity, Phi Delta Kappa. Avocations: hiking, swimming, traveling, profl. speaking. Home: 2672 Route 119 Home PA 15747-9438

WOSK, JULIE, humanities educator; m. Averill M. Williams. BA, Washington U., St. Louis, 1966; MAT, Harvard U., 1967; PhD, U. Wis., 1974. Prof. SUNY Maritime Coll., Bronx, 1975—. Author: Breaking Frame, 1992, Women and the Machine, 2001; contbr. articles to profl. jours. Grantee Alfred P. Sloan Found., N.Y.C., 2000. Mem. Soc. for History of Tech., Internat. Soc. for History of Tech. Office: SUNY Maritime Coll Dept Humanities 6 Pennyfield Ave Ft Schuyler Bronx NY 10465

WOSZCZYK, WIESLAW RICHARD, audio engineering educator, researcher; b. Czestochowa, Poland, Jan. 9, 1951; arrived in Can., 1974; s. Waclaw Konstanty and Krystyna Maria (Malek) W.; m. Trudy Elizabeth Erickson, Dec. 28, 1978; children: Jake, Magda. MA, State Acad. Music Warsaw, Poland, 1974; PhD, Chopin Acad., Warsaw, 1984. Rsch. asst. McGill U., Montreal, Can., 1974-75; recording engineer Basement Recording Co. Inc., N.Y.C., 1975-76; sound dir. Harry Belafonte Enterprises Inc., N.Y.C., 1977; chief engr. Big Apple Recording Studios, N.Y.C., 1976-78; asst. prof. McGill U., Montreal, 1978-84, chmn. grad. studies in sound recording, 1979—, assoc. prof., 1984-91, full prof., 1991—. Tech. dir. McGill Records, Montreal, 1987—; owner, cons. Sonologic Registered, Montreal, 1988—; chmn. internat. conf. TV Sound Today and Tomorrow, 1991; vis. prof. Bang and Olufsen A/S, Denmark, 1994, James McGill prof. in sound recording, 2000-, dir., Ctr. for Interdisciplinary Rsch. in Music Media and Tech., 2000-. Recording engr. over 50 records and films, 1975-85; prodr. over 30 compact discs, 1985—; mem. rev. bd. Jour. Audio Engring., 1992; contbr. articles to profl. jours. Recipient Grand Prix du Disque award Can. Coun. for Arts, 1978, Bd. Govs. award Audio Engring. Soc., 1991; Major Rsch. SSHRC grantee Rsch. Coun. Can., 1986, 93; Indsl. grantee Sony Classical, 1992, Bruel & Kjaer, 1991. Mem. Audio Engring. Soc. (gov., chmn. membership com. 1991—), Acoustical Soc. Am., Sigma Xi. Roman Catholic. Achievements include 3 patents on audio transducers; major rsch. on the design and application of transducers for music recording, auditory design in sound recording, multi-channel sound recording, reprodn. and audio-visual interactions. Office: McGill U Faculty Music 555 Sherbrooke St W Montreal QC Canada H3A 1E3

WOTIPKA, CHRISTINE MIN, education educator; BA in Internat. Rels. and French with highest honors, U. Minn., Twin Cities, 1993; MA in Sociology, Stanford U., 1999, PhD in Internat. Comparative Edn., 2001. Vol. U.S. Peace Corps, Thailand, 1993—95; econ. rschr., English editor 1st Econ. Rsch. Inst., 1995—96; rsch. asst. Comparative Sociology Workshop, 1996—2001; cons. MentorNet, 2001; asst. prof. edn., dir. master's program in internat. and comparative edn. Stanford (Calif.) U., 2001—. Faculty affiliate Expansion and Impact of World Human Rights Regime project, 2002—; MacArthur Consortium affiliate Ctr. for Internat. Security and Coop., 2000—; mem. adv. bd. sci. and tech. TV Digital Turbulence, 2002—. Office: Stanford U Sch Edn 485 Lasuen Mall Stanford CA 94305-3096*

WRENN, WALTER BRUCE, marketing educator, consultant; b. Mobile, Ala., Nov. 9, 1950; s. Walter P. and Winona A. (Jeffrey) W.; m. Jan F. Carmichael, June 12, 1971. BS, Auburn U., 1973; M of Mgmt., Northwestern U., 1974, PhD, 1989. Market analyst The UpJohn Co., Kalamazoo, 1974-78; asst. prof. mktg. Andrews U., Berrien Springs, Mich., 1978-89; assoc. prof. Ind. U., South Bend, 1995—2001, prof., 2002—. Cons. The UpJohn Co., Kalamazoo, 1982, N.Am. Div. SDA, Washington, 1983, Worthington (Ohio) Foods, 1985—, Adventist Health System, Austin, Tex., 1986, Leco, 1991, Bio-Met, 1991, Maple Leaf Farms, 1998. Co-author: Marketing for Congregations, 1994, The Marketing Research Guide, 1997, Marketing Planning Guide, 1997, Marketing Research: Text and Cases, 2002, Marketing Essentials, 2002, Marketing Management: Text and Cases, 2004; contbr. articles to profl. jours. Dir. University Press, Berrien Springs, 1986-89, Sta. WAUS, Berrien Springs, 1987—. Named Outstanding Young Man of Am. Jr. C. of C., 1980; univ. scholar Northwestern U., 1980-83. Mem. Am. Mktg. Assn. (Outstanding Mktg. Student 1973), Acad. Mktg. Sci., Phi Kappa Phi, Alpha Mu Alpha, Omicron Delta Epsilon, Delta Sigma Pi, Delta Mu Delta. Seventh Day Adventist. Avocation: golf. Home: 5027 E Bluffview Dr Berrien Springs MI 49103-1435 Office: Ind Univ 1700 Mishawaka Ave South Bend IN 46615-1400

WRIGHT, ANITA BETH, speech-language pathologist; b. Plainview, Tex., Apr. 18, 1953; d. Floyd B. and Billie E. (Ross) Ehresman; m. David Mel Wright, Nov. 24, 1973; children: David Jess, Kevin Scott. BS, U. Tulsa, 1980, MA, 1983. Cert. clin. competence. Speech-lang. pathologist Verdigris (Okla.) Pub. Schs., 1981-86, High Plains Regional Edn. Coop., Springer, N.Mex., 1986-95, Citizens for Developmentally Disabled, Raton, N. Mex., 1995-98, Cimmarron Mcpl. Schs., 1998—. Trainer N.Mex. State Paraprofl. Tng. Network, Springer, 1988-89; chairperson lang. curriculum guide com. Verdigris Pub. Schs., 1983-84, staff devel. com., 1983-84. Com. sec. troop # 67 Boy Scouts Am., Springer, 1993-95; chairperson Maxwell (N.Mex.) Fire Fighters' Aux., 1994. Mem. Am. Speech Lang. Hearing Assn., N.Mex. Speech Lang. Hearing Assn., Tulsa Area Speech Pathologists and Audiologists (recording sec. 1985-86), Delta Kappa Gamma (pres. Omicron chpt. 1990-92, sec. 1998). Avocations: gardening, reading. Home: 203 Parque Ave Maxwell NM 87728 Office: Cimarron Mcpl Schs PO Box 605 Cimarron NM 87714 E-mail: anita_87728@yahoo.com.

WRIGHT, BYRON T. physicist, educator; b. Waco, Tex., Oct. 19, 1917; s. Wilbur and Dora (Thompson) W.; m. Lorna Doone Bloemers, Oct. 21, 1944 (dec. 1964); children— Carol Ann, Susan Lee, Gail Elizabeth. BA, Rice U., 1938; PhD, U. Calif. at Berkeley, 1941. Physicist Naval Electronics Lab., 1941-42, Manhattan Project, 1942-46; mem. faculty UCLA, 1946—, prof. physics, 1956—, asso. dean grad. div., 1972-80. Ford Found. vis. scientist CERN, 1963-64 Fulbright research scholar, 1956-57; Guggenheim fellow, 1963-64 Fellow Am. Phys. Soc. Spl. research accelerator devel., nuclear structure physics. Home: 1225 Chickory Ln Los Angeles CA 90049-1403

WRIGHT, C. T. ENUS, former academic administrator; b. Social Circle, Ga., Oct. 4, 1942; s. George and Carrie Mae (Enus) W.; m. Mary Stephens, Aug. 9, 1974. BS, Fort Valley State U. (Ga.), Ga., 1964; MA, Atlanta U., 1967; PhD, Boston U., 1977; LHD, Mary Holmes Coll., 2000. Tchr. Ga. Pub. Schs., Social Circle, 1965-67; mem. faculty Morris Brown Coll., Atlanta, 1967-73, divsn. chmn., 1973-77; program dir., asst. provost Eastern Wash. U., Cheney, 1977-81; v.p. acad. affairs Talladega Coll. (Ala.), 1981-82; pres. Cheyney U. Pa., Cheyney, 1982-85; v.p. and provost Fla. Meml. Coll., 1985-89; pres. Internat. Found. and Coord. African-African Am. Summit, 1989-2001; pres., CEO IFESH, 2001—. Cons. and lectr. in field; bd. dirs. Internat. Found. for Edn. and Self Help, England, Leow Sullivan Trust, So. Africa, Peoples Investment Fund for Africa. Author: (booklet) The History of Black Historical Mythology, 1980; contbr. articles to profl. jours. Commnr., Wash. Pub. Broadcasting, Olympia, 1980-84; exec. com. Boy Scouts Am., Phila., 1982—; Goodwill Amb. State of Ga., 1997—. Human Rels. scholar, 1969, Nat. Tchg. fellow Boston U., 1971. Mem. Am. Assn. Colls. and Univs. (coms. 1982—), Am. Hist. Assn. (coms. 1970—), Assn. Study Afro-Am. Life & History (coms. 1965—), Nat. Assn. Equal Opportunity in Higher Edn. (coms. 1982—), NEA (coms. 1965—). Am. Baptist. Clubs: Lions (Cheyney, Wash. (v.p. 1979-81), Tuscan, Fountain Hills Times, Atlanta Constitution. Address: 17420 E Dull Knife Dr Fountain Hills AZ 85268 E-mail: wrightjack@aol.com.

WRIGHT, CECILIA POWERS, gifted and talented educator; b. Phila., Sept. 30, 1946; d. Robert Francis and Rosemary (Redditt) Powers. BS, West Chester (Pa.) U., 1968; MS, Pa. State U., 1972; MA, Gratz Coll., Melrose Park, Pa., 1996. Tchr. Haverford Twp. Sch. Dist., Havertown, Pa., 1968—73; author/editor and instr. McGraw Hill, Paoli, Pa., 1973—78; tchr. Lower Merion Sch. Dist., Wynnewood, Pa., 1987—90; tchr. of gifted West Chester Area Sch. Dist., 1990—. Instr., cons. Regional Tng. Ctr., Gratz Coll., Randolph, NJ, 1996—; seminar presenter Coll. of N.J., Trenton, 1998—2000. Author (and editor): Careers: A Multicultural View, 1977 (Excellence award, 1977). Leader Girl Scouts U.S., Havertown, 1983—87; chairperson good citizens DAR, Chester County, Pa., 1996—. Named to Leaders in Am. Elem. Edn., Haverford Twp. Sch. Dist., 1971; recipient award, Nat. Band Assn., 2000—01. Mem.: NEA, Band and Orch. Assn. (pres. 2000), Pa. State Edn. Assn. (rep. 1998—). Avocations: watercolor, travel, biking. Home: 15 E Wilmot Ave Havertown PA 19083

WRIGHT, CHARLES PENZEL, JR., English language educator; b. Pickwick Dam, Tenn., Aug. 25, 1935; s. Charles Penzel and Mary Castleman (Winter) Wright; m. Holly McIntire, Apr. 6, 1969; 1 child, Luke Savin Herrick. BA, Davidson Coll., 1957; MFA, U. Iowa, 1963; postgrad., U. Rome, 1963—64. Mem. faculty U. Calif., Irvine, Calif., 1966—83, prof. English, 1976—83; mem. faculty U. Va., Charlottesville, Va., 1983—. Vis. prof. N.Am. Lit. U., Padua, Italy, 1968—69; disting. vis. prof. U. Degli Studi, Florence, Italy, 1992. Translator: The Storm and Other Poems (Eugenio Montale), 1978, Orphic Songs (Dino Campana), 1984. With AUS, 1957—61. Recipient Pen Transl. prize, 1979, Nat Book award for Poetry, 1983, citation in poetry, Brandeis U. Creative Arts Awards, 1987, L.A. Times Book prize, 1997, award, Nat. Book Critics Circle, 1997, Pulitzer Prize, 1998, Ambassador Book award, 1998; fellow Guggeheim fellow, 1976, Ingram Merrill fellow, 1980, 1993; scholar, Fulbright Found., 1963—65. Mem.: Acad. Am. Poets (chancellor), Am. Acad. Arts and Sci., Am. Acad. Arts and Letters, Fellowship of So. Writers. Home: 940 Locust Ave Charlottesville VA 22901-4030 Office: English Dept Univ Va Charlottesville VA 22901

WRIGHT, CHATT GRANDISON, academic administrator; b. San Mateo, Calif., Sept. 17, 1941; s. Virgil Tandy and Louise (Jeschien) W.; children from previous marriage: Stephen Brook, Jon David, Shelley Adams; m. Janice Teply, Nov. 28, 1993. Student, U. Calif., Berkeley, 1960-62; BA in Polit. Sci., U. Calif., Davis, 1964; MA in Econs., U. Hawaii, 1968. Instr. econs. U. Hawaii, Honolulu, 1968-70; mgr. corp. planning Telecheck Internat., Inc., Honolulu, 1969—70; economist State of Hawaii, Honolulu, 1970—71; adminstr. manpower City & County of Honolulu, 1971-72; bus. adminstr., dean. Hawaii Pacific U., Honolulu, 1972-74, v.p., 1974-76, pres., 1976—. Mem. City and County of Honolulu Manpower Area Planning Commn., 1976—82; mem. Mayor's Salary Commn. City and County of Honolulu, 1977—80; mem. Honolulu City Ethics Commn., 1978—84, City and County of Honolulu Labor Market Adv. Coun., 1982—84; bd. dirs. Hawaii Econ. Devel. Corp., 1980—84; trustee Queen's Med. Ctr., Honolulu, 1986—92, Honolulu Armed Svcs. YMCA, 1984—86, Hawaii Maritime Ctr., 1990—92; chmn. bd. trustees Hist. Hawaii Found., 1995—96, trustee, 1990—96; mem. adv. bd. Cancer Rsch. Ctr. Hawaii, 1987; trustee St. Andrew's Priory Sch., 1994—98; bd. dirs. Hawaii Visitors Bur., 1995—97; bd. dir. Downtown Improvement Assn., 1988—96; bd. dirs. Outrigger Duke Kahanamoku Found., 1996—98, Hawaii Opera Theatre, 1997—99; bd. govs. Hawaii Coun. on Econ. Edn., 1998—; trustee Oceanic Inst., 1998—, chmn., 2003—; mem. Hawaii Execs. Coun., 1996—, chmn., 2002, Hawaii Exec. Conf., 2002; bd. govs. Hawaii Med. Libr., 1989—92; mem. adv. bd. Aloha coun. Boy Scouts Am., 1991—2002; trustee Molokai Gen. Hosp., 1991—92; mem. Pacific Asian Affairs Coun., 1998—2001; steering com. Asian Devel. Bank, 2000—. With USN, 1968—70. Recipient Pioneer award Pioneer Fed. Savs. Bank, 1982, Stephen J. Jackstadt award, 1998; named Sales Person of Yr., Sales and Mktg. Execs. of Honolulu, 1998; Paul Harris fellow Rotary, 1986. Mem.: Hawaii Assn. Ind. Colls. and Univs. (chmn. 1986), Western Coll. Assn. (exec. com. 1989—92), Hawaii Joint Coun. Econ. Edn. (bd. dirs. 1982—88), Nat. Assn. Intercollegiate Athletics (mem. 1985—98, vice chair NAIA coun. of pres. 1994), Assn. Governing Bds. Univs. and Colls., Am. Assn. Higher Edn., Soc. Sci. Assn. (mem. 1994—99), Japan-Am. Soc. Honolulu, Waialae Country Club, Plaza Club (bd. govs. 1992—97), Pacific Club (Honolulu), Outrigger Canoe Club. Republican. Episcopalian. Avocations: hunting, fishing, reading, travel. Office: Hawaii Pacific U Office of Pres 1166 Fort Street Mall Honolulu HI 96813-2708 E-mail: president@hpu.edu.

WRIGHT, CONNIE SUE, special education educator; b. Nampa, Idaho, Aug. 26, 1943; d. Ruel Andrew and Renabel Carol (Graham) Farwell; m. Roger R. Wright, July 5, 1968; 1 child, Jodi C. BA, N.W. Nazarene Coll., 1967; MA in Spl. Edn., Boise State U., 1990. Cert. elem. tchr. grades kindergarten through 8th, cert. spl. edn. tchr. grades kindergarten through 12th, Idaho. Tchr. 3rd and 4th grades Vallivue Sch. Dist. 139, Caldwell, Idaho, 1967-69; tchr. 2nd grade Nampa Sch. Dist. 131, 1969-70; tchr. 3rd grade Caldwell Sch. Dist. 132, 1970-73; tchr. spl. edn. grades kindergarten through 3rd Hubbard Elem. Sch., Kuna (Idaho) Joint Sch. Dist. 3, 1985-92; tchr. adolescents CPC Intermountain Hosp. of Boise, 1992-93; tchr. spl. edn. Pioneer Elem. Sch., Meridian, Idaho, 1993—, Spalding Elem. Sch., Meridian, Idaho, 1997—. Mem. Internat. Edn. Conf. Between Russia and U.S., 1994. Libr. Horizon's Reading Coun., 1990-91. Named Tchr. Yr. Pioneer Elem. Sch., 1994-95; recipient Cert. of Recognition, Devel. D.C. Mem. Coun. for Exceptional Children, Coun. for Learning Disabilities, Coun. Learning Disabilities, Assn. Curriculum & Supr., Delta Kappa Gamma Soc. Internat. (Omicron chpt.). Avocations: reading, doll making, computers.

WRIGHT, DAVID RAY, secondary school educator; b. Lampasas, Tex., Oct. 31, 1953; s. James Arlen and Peggy Pauline (Hail) W. BS, S.W. Tex. State U., 1976; postgrad., Baylor U., 1989-90. Cert. tchr., Tex. Tchr./coach Copperas Cove (Tex.) I.S.D., 1976—; dept. chmn. Jewell Elem. Sch., Copperas Cove, 1997-98. Supt. adv. com. Copperas Cove I.S.D., 1987-89, 96-97, profl. consultation com.. 1989-90; test devel. advisor TAAS Instr. Objectives for Wellness, Tex. Edn. Agy., Austin, 1993. Actor: (motion picture) Gilbert Grape, 1993; dancer/actor: (motion picture for TV) Another Pair of Aces, 1991, Seduction in Travis County, 1992, Big T, 1992; singer Bluegrass Gospel Band; mem. First Bapt. Players Drama group, San Saba Actors Theatre, 1999—, Vive Les Arts Theatre, Killeen, Tex., 1999—. Actor: "The Butler Did It", Viva Les Arts Theatre, Killeen, Tex., 1998, Father Son and Holy Coach, Vive Les Arts Theatre, Killeen, 2000, also Carousel, 2003, Ragtime, 2003; portrayed Jesus in The Passion Play, First Bapt. Ch., Copperas Cove, 1996-98, ch. historian. Recipient Excellence in Teaching award Killeen Daily Herald, 1987; tchr. of the Yr. award Copperas Cove Vets. of Foreign Wars, Post 8577, 1991. Mem. Nat. Dance Assn., AAHPERD, Tex. Assn. of Health, Phys. Edn., Recreation, and Dance (clinician State Convs. 1991, 93, chair Phys. Edn. Pub. Info. Com. 93-94, state dance com. 2000—), Tex. Clogging Coun. (dance awards com. 2001—), Lloyd Shaw Found., Country Song and Dance Found., Western Swing Hall of Fame. Baptist. Home: 1608 E Robertson Ave Copperas Cove TX 76522-3175 E-mail: davidw@ccisd.com.

WRIGHT, ERIN DEAN, graphic design educator; b. Denver, July 24, 1959; s. Elton Stanley and Roxene Roi (Weichel) W.; m. Lisa Dawn Womack, Nov. 25, 1983 (div. Jan. 1988); m. Elizabeth Laura Montgomery, Dec. 12, 1992. BFA, Colo. State U., 1982; MFA, U. Ariz., 1990. Tech. illustrator Woodward-Clyde Cons., Denver, 1982-88; graphic designer, illustrator Tucson, 1988-89; acting asst. prof. La. State U., Baton Rouge, 1989-90, asst. prof., 1990—. Panelist Higher Edn. Art Conf., Prescott, Ariz., 1988; co-chmn. Resources Pro Bono, Baton Rouge, 1994—; area coord., graphic designer La. State U., Baton Rouge, 1993—, curator Boelts/Carson exhbn., 1994. Artist, designer: (mag. cover) Graffiti, 1988, (trademarks) Comty. Fund for the Arts, 1993, The Epilepsy Assn., 1993, (poster) Boelts/Carson Exhbn., 1994; exhibited works at Soc. Illustration Sch. Comp., N.Y.C., 1989. Bd. dirs. The Epilepsy Assn., Baton Rouge, 1993—. Recipient Citation of Excellence, 7th Dist. Regional Addys, 1993, Addy award Advt. Fedn., 1993, 95; computer animation grantee Coun. on Rsch., La. State U., 1993. Mem. Art Dirs. and Designers Assn. New Orleans, Advt. Fedn. Greater Baton Rouge. Episcopalian. Avocations: mountain biking, backpacking, collecting comic books. Office: La State U 123 Design Ctr Baton Rouge LA 70803-0001

WRIGHT, ESTHER ESTELLE, educational consultant; b. N.Y.C., Mar. 9, 1941; d. Hyman Weiser and Sophie (Salinas) Gray; m. Edward Rosenblueth, July 11, 1964 (div. Apr. 1982); 1 child, Stephen. BA, San Francisco State U., 1962, MA, 1963. Tchr. Alhambra (Calif.) City Schs., 1964-65, Hayward (Calif.) Pub. Schs., 1965-67, San Francisco Unified Schs., 1967-76, program cons., 1976-92; tchr. trainer, lectr. San Francisco State U., 1989—99; ednl. cons. Teaching From the Heart, San Francisco, 1988—. Author: Good Morning Class-I Love You, 1988, Loving Discipline A to Z, 1994, The Heart and Wisdom of Teaching, 1997, Why I Teach, 1999. Mem. Calif. Learning Disability Assn. (v.p. 1993-94, bd. dirs. 1992-94), San Francisco Learning Disability Assn. (pres. 1989-92). Democrat. Jewish. Avocations: personal growth, philosophy, eastern religions. Office: Teaching From the Heart PO Box 460818 San Francisco CA 94146-0818 E-mail: dearesther@aol.com.

WRIGHT, ETHEL, secondary education educator; b. Apr. 5, 1947; m. James A. Wright, Sept. 26, 1969; children: Cassandra, Hannibal, Omari. BS in English, Alcorn State U., Lorman, Miss., 1970; MS in Edn., Butler U., Indpls., 1975. Tchr. Simmons H.S., Arcola, Miss., 1970-71; tchr. English Indpls. Pub. Schs., 1971—. Mem. textbook adoption com. Indpls. Pub. Schs., 1979, liaison for Tchrs. Ctr., mem. film preview com. Clk., Dem. Com., Indpls. Recipient ABCD award Indpls. Pub. Schs., 1985, 92; Gregg and Reed scholar Indpls. Pub. Schs. Mem. NEA, Indpls. Edn. Assn. Avocations: reading, gardening, sewing, growing houseplants, travel.

WRIGHT, GLADYS STONE, music educator, composer, writer; b. Wasco, Oreg., Mar. 8, 1925; d. Murvel Stuart and Daisy Violet (Warren) Stone; m. Alfred George Wright, June 28, 1953. BS, U. Oreg., 1948, MS, 1953. Dir. bands Elmira (Oreg.) U-4 High Sch., 1948-53, Otterbein (Ind.) High Sch., 1954-61, Klondike High Sch., West Lafayette, Ind., 1962-70, Harrison High Sch., West Lafayette, 1970-84. Organizer, condr. Musical Friendship Tours, Cen. Am., 1967-79; v.p., condr. U.S. Collegiate Wind Band, 1975—; bd. dirs. John Philip Sousa Found. 1984—; chmn. Sudler Cup, 1986—, Sudler Flag, 1982; pres. Internat. Music Tours, 1984—, Key to the City, Taxco, Mex., 1975. Editor: Woman Conductor, 1986—; composer: marches Big Bowl and Trumpets and Tabards, 1987; contbg. editor: Informusica (Spain). Bd. dirs. N. Am. Wildlife Park, Battleground, Ind. 1985. Recipient Medal of the order John Philip Sousa Found., 1988, Star of Order, 1991, Internat. Contbrn. to Music award Phi Beta Mu, 2000; 1st woman guest condr. U.S. Navy Band, Washington D.C., 1961, Goldman Band, N.Y.C., 1958, Kneller Hall Band, London, 1975, Tri-State Music Festival Massed Orch., Band, Choir, 1985; elected to Women Bd. Dirs. Hall of Fame of Disting. Women Condr., 1994; inductee Hall of Fame Disting. Condrs., Nat. Band Assn., 1999. Mem. Am. Bandmasters Assn. (bd. dirs. 1993, 1st woman mem.), Women Band Dirs. Nat. Assn. (founding pres. 1967, sec. 1985, recipient Silver Baton 1974, Golden Rose 1990, Hall of Fame 1995), Am. Sch. Band Dirs. Assn., Nat. Band Assn. (Citation excellence 1970), Tippecanoe Arts Fedn. (bd. dirs. 1986-90), Tippecanoe Fife and Drum Corps. (bd. dirs. 1984), Daughters of Am. Revolution, Col. Dames-Pre Quitanen Chpt., New England Women, Tau Beta Sigma (Outstanding Svc. to Music award 1970), Phi Beta Mu (1st hon. women mem. 1972), North Am. Wildlife Park (bd dirs, 1990—). Avocations: historic preservation, environ. activities.

WRIGHT, JAMES EDWARD, academic administrator, historian, educator; b. Madison, Wis., Aug. 16, 1939; s. Donald J. and Myrtle (Hendricks) Wright; m. Joan Bussan, Sept. 3, 1962 (div.); children: James J., Ann Marie, Michael J.; m. Susan DeBevoise, Aug. 18, 1984. BS, Wis. State U., 1964; MS, U. Wis., 1966, PhD, 1969; MA (hon.), Dartmouth Coll., 1980. From asst. prof. to assoc. prof. history Dartmouth Coll., Hanover, NH, 1969—80, prof. history, 1980—, assoc. dean faculty, 1981—85, dean faculty, 1989—97, acting pres., 1995, provost, 1997—98, pres., 1998—. Sr. historian U. Mid Am., Lincoln, Nebr., 1976—77; humanist-in-residence Colo. Humanities Coun., Georgetown, 1975. Author: Galena Lead District, 1966, Politics of Populism, 1974, Progressive Yankees, 1987; author: (co-editor) Great Plains Experience, 1978. Trustee Kimball Union Acad., Meriden, NH, 1990—94; dir. Sherman Fairchild Found., Greenwich, Conn., 1991—; chair Hanover Dem. Town Com., 1970—74; bd. dirs. Divsn. 1 NCAA, 2001—03. Cpl. USMC, 1957—60. Danforth fellow, 1964—69, Guggenheim fellow, 1973—74, Charles Warren fellow, Harvard U., 1980—81. Fellow: Am. Acad. Arts and Scis.; mem.: Western History Assn. (chair Caughey prize 1986—87), The Century Assn., Orgn. Am. Historians (chair film, media com. 1983—85), Phi Beta Kappa. Home: 1 Tuck Dr Hanover NH 03755-3575 Office: Dartmouth College Office of the President 207 Parkhurst Hall Hanover NH 03755 E-mail: james.wright@dartmouth.edu.

WRIGHT, JAMES THOMAS, SR., education educator; b. Montgomery County, Ark., July 17, 1925; s. Joel Schooley and Loretta Cornelia (Grant) W.; m. Pauline A. Williams, Dec. 19, 1959; 1 child, James Thomas Jr. BA in Bus. Adminstrn./Phys. Edn., Ouachita Bapt. Coll., Arkadelphia, Ark., 1950; MS in Secondary Edn., U. Ark., 1957, EdD in Elem. Edn., 1965. Secondary tchr., coach pub. schs., Ark., 1950-55; elem. tchr., prin. pub. schs., Elida and Carlsbad, N.Mex., 1955—61; grad. asst. U. Ark., Fayetteville, 1961-62; head elem. edn. dept., prof. Wayland Bapt. Coll., Plainview, Tex., 1962-64; chmn. elem. edn., dir. student teaching Sul Ross State Coll., Alpine, Tex., 1964-67; assoc. prof. edn. Ouachita Bapt. Coll., Arkadelphia, 1967-68; prof., chmn. elem., early childhood and spl. edn. Henderson State U., Arkadelphia, 1968-90, adj. faculty, 1990—. Adv. coun. Bapt. Student Union, Henderson State U., Arkadelphia, 1990—, pres., 1994—. Mem. exec. bd. Ouachita Area Coun. Boy Scouts Am., Hot Springs, Ark., 1973—; mem. bd. Ione Bynum Childcare Ctr., Arkadelphia; mem. Comprehensive Outcomes Evaluation teams schs. in S.W. Ark., 1992—; mem. Gov.'s Task Force on Early Childhood Edn. Gov. of Ark. Recipient Silver Beaver and Dist. Award of Merit Ouachita Area Coun. Boy Scouts Am., Hot Springs, Vigil Honors and Founders award Order of Arrow, Boy Scouts Am., H. award Henderson State U. Alumni Assn., Arkadelphia, 1994. Mem. Am. Assn. Ret. Persons (del. White House Conf. on Aging 1995, mem. state legis. com. 1993—), Ark. Silver Haired Legislature, Assn. Bapt. for Scouting, Phi Delta Kappa. Baptist. Home and Office: PO Box 1976 Glenwood AR 71943-1976

WRIGHT, JEAN NORMAN, elementary education educator; b. Norristown, Pa., June 20, 1931; d. John Rich and Mildred (Hitchcock) Norman; m. John A. Wright (dec. Mar. 1979); children: Lori Wright Lutter, Larry. BA cum laude, Cedar Crest Coll., Allentown, Pa., 1953. Cert. tchr., Pa. Elem. tchr. Upson Sch., Euclid, Ohio, 1953-55; tchr. art and music Schuylkill Elem. Sch., Phoenixville, Pa., 1965-70, elem. tchr., 1970—. Mem. alumni bd. dirs. Cedar Crest Coll., 1980-84; mem. Phoenixville Community Concert Bd., 1986—. Mem. NEA, Pa. Edn. Assn., Cedar Crest Coll. Alumnae Club (pres. 1962-64), Delta Kappa Gamma (pres. 1990-92). Republican. Presbyterian. Avocations: barbershop singing, tennis. Office: Schuylkill Elem Sch Whitehorse Rd Phoenixville PA 19460

WRIGHT, JEFF REGAN, civil engineering educator; b. Spokane, Wash., Nov. 25, 1950; s. Harold U. and Gail Virginia (Hodgson) W.; m. Delores Jeanne Finch, Sept. 14, 1972; children: Kelly Hodgson, Myka Kristine. BA, U. Wash., 1975, BS, 1976, MSCE, 1977; PhD, Johns Hopkins U., 1982. Asst. prof. civil engring. Purdue U., West Lafayette, Ind., 1982-86, assoc. prof., 1986-90, prof., 1990—, dir. Ind. Water Resources Rsch. Ctr., 1989—. Asst. dean engring. Purdue U., West Lafayette; v.p. OMTEK Engring., West Lafayette, 1986—. Author: Civil and Environmental Systems Engineering, 1996, Expert Systems Applications to Urban Planning, 1989; contbr. articles to profl. jours. Mem. ASCE (editor-in-chief Jour. Infrastructure Sys.), Ops. Rsch. Soc. Am., Inst. Mgmt. Scis. Office: Purdue U WRRC Sch Civil Engring West Lafayette IN 47907-1284

WRIGHT, JERRY JAYE, physical education educator; b. Richmond, Ind., July 30, 1944; s. Robert Evan and Janet W. (Jay) W.; m. Mary Lee Cathey, Dec. 27, 1980. AA, Art Acad., Cin., 1964; BA, Saginaw Valley State U., 1974; MEd, Bowling Green State U., 1976; PhD, The Ohio State U., 1980. Illustrator Advt. Svcs., Richmond, Ind., 1964-71; asst. baseball coach Bowling Green (Ohio) State U., 1974-75; asst. baseball and basketball coach Saginaw (Mich.) Valley State U., 1975-77; asst. prof. U. No. Iowa, Cedar Falls, 1980-81, U. Wis., Milw., 1981-86; head tennis coach Penn State U., Altoona, Pa., 1986-91, assoc. prof., 1986—. Chair dept. exercise and sports sci. sport historian Penn State U., Altoona, 1989—. Author: Phys. Educator Jour., 1986, Jour. of Sport History, 1988, Strategies Jour., 1991, 1992, Baseball Rsch. Jour., 1992, The National Pastime, 1993, Encyclopedia of Major League Baseball Teams, 1993, Nine: A Journal of Baseball History and Social Policy Perspectives, 1994, 95, 96, Canadian Journal of the History of Sport, 1994, International Journal of the History of Sport, 1994, Baseball's First Stars, 1996. Sport historian Blair County Hist. Soc., Altoona, 1989—. Sgt. U.S. Army, 1965-67. Mem. North Am. Soc. for Sport History, Orgn. for Am. Historians, Soc. for Am. Baseball Rsch., Am. Alliance for Phys. Edn., Phys. Edn. in Higher Edn. Avocations: coll. sport memorabilia, baseball cards, tennis, golf, sport historian rsch. Office: Pa State U 3000 Ivyside Park Altoona PA 16601-3760

WRIGHT, JOAN MCANALLY, English educator; b. Belmont, Mass., Nov. 3, 1949; d. James S. and Mary (Ivy) McAnally; m. Gary M. Wright; children: Kristi Joan, Shawn. BS, Morehead State U., 1971; MA, U. Miss., 1990. Cert. tchr., Miss. Tchr. English, creative writing Belmont (Miss.) High Sch., 1973—. Mem. Miss. Writing Thinking Inst., Starkville, 1988—; mem. writing assessment team Nat. Assessment Edn. Progress, 1992. Mem. NAFE, ASCD, Nat. Coun. Tchrs. English, Ole Miss. Writing Project. Methodist. Office: Belmont High Sch PO Box 250 Belmont MS 38827-0250

WRIGHT, JOHN C., II, physician, educator; b. Sodus, N.Y., June 16, 1927; s. John Embry and Frances Louise (Horton) W.; m. Jane A. Atwood, Oct. 27, 1956 (dec. Aug. 1990); children: Kim A., Tamilyn A. Jerilyn A., John C. III. BA, U. Buffalo, 1950; MD, N.Y. Med. Coll., 1955. Diplomate Am. Bd. Family Practice. Intern Waterbury (Conn.) Hosp., 1955-56, resident in medicine, 1956-57; pvt. practice Manchester, Conn., 1957-72; dir. Family Practice Residency Program, Middletown, Conn., 1972-75; asst. prof. dept. cmty. medicine U. Conn., 1972-75; vice chmn., assoc. prof. dept. family practice Wright State U., Dayton, Ohio, 1975-78; assoc. prof. dept. family practice U. Louisville, 1978-92, prof., 1992-95, chmn. dept. family practice, 1978-81, dir. geriatric programs, 1981-92, dir. predoctoral edn., 1978-86, chief geriatric divsn., 1990-92, acting dir. Urban Ctr. on Aging, 1985-91, prof. emeritus, 1995—. Med. dir. Hurstbourne Care Ctr. at Stony Brook, Louisville, 1991-99—, Christian Health Ctr., Louisville, 1985-92; mem. staff St. Anthony Hosp., Louisville, 1978-90, Univ. Hosp., U. Louisville, 1983—, St. Elizabeth Med. Ctr., Dayton, 1976-78, Miami Valley Hosp., Dayton, 1976-78, Good Samaritan Hosp., Dayton, 1976-78, Children's Med. Ctr., Dayton, 1976-78, Frazier Rehab. Ctr. Inc., Louisville, 1986—, Jewish Hosp., Louisville, 1989—, Audubon Hosp., Louisville, 1992—, Kosair Children's Hosp., Louisville, 1990—. Patentee adjustable ski racks, 1979; contbr. articles to profl. jours. Mem. health care and edn. com. Louisville and Jefferson County Bd. Health, 1979-81; mem. vestry St. Francis in the Fields Episc. Ch., 1983-86, mem. choir, 1978-90; founding mem., chair Lifespan: A Teaching Gerontologic Cmty., 1987-90; mem. Nat. Ski Patrol, 1981—. With USNR, 1946-47. Fellow Am. Acad. Family Physicians; mem. AMA, Am. Geriatric Soc., Soc. Tchrs. of Family Medicine, Ky. Med. Assn., Jefferson County Med. Assn., Am. Med. Dirs. Assn. (cert.), Am. Heart Assn. (mem. coun. on epidemiology sect. on hypertension). Home: 3696 Webb Rd Simpsonville KY 40067-6435 Office: MedCenter One 501 E Broadway 2d Fl Louisville KY 40202

WRIGHT, JOHN COLLINS, retired chemistry educator; b. Oak Hill, W.Va., Aug. 5, 1927; s. John C. and Irene (Collins) W.; m. Margaret Ann Cyphers, Sept. 11, 1949; children: Jeffrey Cyphers, John Timothy, Curtis Scott, Keith Alexander. BS, W.Va. Wesleyan Coll., 1948, LLD, 1974; PhD, U. Ill., 1951; DSc (hon.), U. Ala., 1979, W.Va. Inst. Tech., 1979. Research chemist Hercules, Inc., 1951-57; mem. faculty W.Va. Wesleyan Coll., 1957-64; asst. program dir. NSF, 1964-65; dean Coll. Arts and Scis., No. Ariz. U., 1966-70, W.Va. U., Morgantown, 1970-74; vice chancellor W.Va. Bd. Regents, Charleston, 1974-78; pres. U. Ala., Huntsville, 1978-88, prof. chemistry, 1988-95, prof. emeritus, 1995—; interim pres. W.Va. Coll. Grad. Studies, Institute, 1975-76. Hon. research asso. Univ. Coll., London, Eng., 1962-63; cons. NSF, 1965—, Army Sci. Bd., U.S. Army, 1979-82. Served with USNR, 1945-46. Mich. fellow Center Study Higher Edn., U. Mich., 1965-66 Mem. AAAS, NSTA. Office: 2312 Carlton Cove Blvd Huntsville AL 35802

WRIGHT, JOHN CURTIS, chemist, educator; b. Lubbock, Tex., Sept. 17, 1943; s. John Edmund and Jean Irene (Love) W.; m. Carol Louise Swanson, Aug. 17, 1968; children: Dawna Lynn, John David. BS, Union Coll., 1965; PhD, Johns Hopkins U., 1970; postgrad., Purdue U., 1972. From asst. to assoc. prof. U. Wis., Madison, 1972-80, prof., 1980—. Contbr. articles to profl. jours. Recipient William F. Meggers award Applied Spectroscopy Soc. 1981. Mem. Am. Chem. Soc. (Spectrochem. Analysis award 1991), Am. Phys. Soc. Achievements include pioneering work in site selective laser spectroscopy; discovery of multi-dimensional four wave mixing spectroscopy; development of line narrowed nonlinear electronic and vibrational spectroscopy; patent for Chemical Analysis of Ions Incorporated in Lottices using Coherent Excitation Sources. Office: Univ Wis Dept Chemistry 1101 University Ave Madison WI 53706-1322

WRIGHT, JOHN HARRISON, JR., retired headmaster; b. Humboldt, Tenn., Apr. 25, 1930; s. John Harrison and Florence (Smith) Wright; m. Winston Case, Apr. 12, 1858; children: John Harrison III, Catherine Isabel, Elizabeth Fullerton, Victoria Winston. BA, U. of the South, 1954; EdM, Harvard U., 1966. Tchr., dir. admissions Sewanee (Tenn.) Mil. Acad., 1954-59; tchr. Liceo Scientifico "A. Tassoni", Modena, Italy, 1959-61; adminstr. Maqased Coll., Beirute, Lebanon, summer 1960; dean of faculty Chatham (Va.) Hall, 1961-68; headmaster Gill & Gill/St. Bernard's, Bernardsville, N.J., 1968-80, The Masters Sch., Dobbs Ferry, N.Y., 1980-90, Bermuda H.S., 1990-95, St. Luke's Sch., Mobile, Ala., 1996-2000. Trustee Matheny Sch. for Cerebral Palsied Children, Peapack, N.J., 1970-77, St. Mary's Hall-Doan Acad., Burlington, N.J., 1976-78, Loaves and Fish Homeless Coalition, Mobile, Ala., 2000—; founding headmaster N.J. Sch. Consortium, Morristown, 1971-80. Sgt. USAF, 1950-53, commd. officer, 1954. Tchg. fellow Fulbright Commn., Modena, 1959-61; adminstrn./tchg. fellow The Smith/Mundt Commn., Beirut, 1960. Mem. The Athelston Club, Harvard Club of N.Y.C. (admissions com. 1999—), Nat. Assn. Prins. of Sch. for Girls (assoc., various offices), Headmistresses of the East (assoc.), Elem. Sch. Head Assn. (hon.). Democrat. Episcopalian. Avocations: gardening, travel. Home: 45 Buerger Rd Mobile AL 36608-1801

WRIGHT, JOHN SPENCER, school system administrator; b. Washington, May 8, 1948; s. Clarence S. and Florence (Nagel) W.; m. Debra Kim Buck, Aug. 4, 1973; 1 child, Deanna Michelle. BA in Econs., U. Va., 1969, MEd in Secondary Adminstrn., 1971, EdD in Adminstrn. and Supervision, 1976. Cert. social studies tchr., prin., supt., fin. officer, N.C.; registered sch. bus. adminstr. Tchr. govt. and social studies Lane H.S., Charlottesville, Va., 1969-72, spl. asst. to prin., 1972-74; supr. Sch. Gen. Learning Charlottesville H.S., 1974-75; exec. dir. Va. Assn. Sch. Execs., Charlottesville, 1976-78; prin. E.C. Glass H.S., Lynchburg, Va., 1978-82; dir. bus. svcs. Lynchburg Pub. Schs., 1982-86, dir. fin. and planning svcs., 1986; asst. supt. bus. and fin. svcs. Greensboro (N.C.) Pub. Schs., 1986-90, assoc. supt. human and fin. resources, 1990-93; assoc. supt. adminstrv. svcs. Guilford County (N.C.) Schs., 1993—2003, chief adminstrv. officer, 2003—. Investigating probation officer 8th Regional Juvenile and Domestic Rels. Ct., Charlottesville, 1970-71; grad. asst., teaching asst. Sch. Edn., U. Va., 1975-76; rsch. asst. Tayloe Murphy Inst., U. Va., 1975-76; asst. prof. Grad. Sch. Edn., U. Va., 1976-78; part time asst. prof. Grad. Sch. Edn., U. Va., 1978-80; adj. prof. U. Va., Sch. Continuing Edn., 1983, 86. Co-author: Charlottesville Change Project: Year End Report, 1974; editor: Developments in School Law, 1976-78; contbr. articles and reviews to profl. jours. Former bd. dirs. Triad Sickle Cell Anemia Found.; former bd. dirs. Presbyn. Home and Family Svcs., Inc.; past v.p. deductible fund Local Govt. Ins. Funds, Greensboro, Guilford, N.C., past pres. liability fund; former mem. N.C. Profl. Rev. Com., 1993-98; former mem. N.C. Profl. Practices Commn., 1996-98; mem. Com. 100, Greensboro Human Rels. Commn.; Former mem. dean's coun. U. Va. Sch. Edn. Found. Mem. Am. Assn. Sch. Adminstrs., Am. Assn. Sch. Pers. Adminstrs., Assn. Sch. Bus. Ofcls., (editl. bd. 2003—) Southeastern Assn. Sch. Bus. Ofcls., N.C. Assn. Sch. Bus. Ofcls. (past region chmn., vice-chair and mem. state exec. com.), N.C. Assn. Sch. Adminstrs. (bd. dirs. 2002—), Edn. Law Assn., Distributive Edn. Clubs Am. (hon. life), Greensboro C. of C. (govtl. affairs coun., former minority/women bus. devel. coun.), U. Va. Alumni Assn. (former class agt.), Va. Student Aid Found., Greensboro Civitans (v.p. 1993-94, bd. dirs. 1994-96), Human Resources Mgmt. Assn. Greensboro (bd. dirs. 1997-98), High Point C. of C (edn. com.), Phi Delta Kappa (Triad chpt. pres. 2003—), Kappa Delta Pi, others. Presbyterian. Home: 4610 Charlottesville Rd Greensboro NC 27410-3655 Office: Guilford County Schools PO Box 880 Greensboro NC 27402-0880

WRIGHT, JUDITH MARGARET, law librarian, educator, dean; b. Jackson, Tenn., Aug. 16, 1944; d. Joseph Clarence and Mary Catherine (Key) Wright; m. Mark A. Johnson, Apr. 17, 1976; children— Paul, Michael BS, U. Memphis, 1966; MA, U. Chgo., 1971; JD, DePaul U., 1980. Bar: Ill. 1980. Librarian Oceanway Sch., Jacksonville, Fla., 1966-67; program dir. ARC, South Vietnam, 1967-68; documents and reference librarian D'Angelo Law Library, U. Chgo., 1970-74, reference librarian, 1974-77, dir., lectr. in law, 1980-99, assoc. dean for libr. and info. svcs., lectr. in law, 1999—. Mem. adv. bd. Legal Reference Svcs. Quar., 1981—. Mem. ABA, Am. Assn. Law Libraries, Chgo. Assn. Law Libraries. Democrat. Methodist. Office: U Chgo Law Sch D'Angelo Law Libr 1121 E 60th St Chicago IL 60637-2745 Fax: 773-702-2889. E-mail: jm-wright@uchicago.edu.

WRIGHT, KATHI BROWN, elementary educator; b. Linton, Ind., Dec. 30, 1954; d. Bill D. and Kathryn L. (Wray) Brown; m.; 1 child, Hallie Swearingen. BS in Edn., Memphis State U., 1978, MEd, 1981; postgrad., Trevecca Nazarene Coll., Nashville, 1992. Tchr. Ross Elem. Sch., Memphis, 1978-90, Southwind Elem. Sch., Memphis, 1990—. Sponsor Environ. Club, 1998—. Mem. NEA, Tenn. Edn. Assn., Shelby County Edn. Assn., Tenn. PTA (hon., life). Republican. Presbyterian. Avocations: crafts, reading, decorating.

WRIGHT, KATHY DIANE, secondary school educator; b. Warner Robins, Ga., Sept. 23, 1961; d. Thomas Neal and Mary Rose Wright. BS, Fla. State U., 1983, MS, 1987. Tchr. Colquitt County Bd. Edn., Moultrie, Ga., 1983—93, Decatur County Bd. Edn., Bainbridge, Ga., 1993—94, Colquitt County H.S., Moultrie, 1994—. Mem.: Am. Choral Dirs. Assn. (Ga. pres. 2001—03), Music Educators Nat. Conf. (dist. chair 1985—90, 2002—). Home: 833 Georgia Hwy 111 Moultrie GA 31768 Office: Colquitt County High Sch 1800 Park Ave Moultrie GA 31768

WRIGHT, KATIE HARPER, educational administrator, journalist; b. Crawfordsville, Ark., Oct. 5, 1923; d. James Hale and Connie Mary (Locke) Harper; m. Marvin Wright, Mar. 21, 1952; 1 child, Virginia K. Jordan. BA, U. Ill., 1944, MEd, 1959; EdD, St. Louis U., 1979. Elem. and spl. edn. tchr. East St. Louis (Ill.) Pub. Schs., 1944-65, dir. Dist. 189 Instrnl. Materials Program, 1965-71, dir. spl. edn. Dists. 188, 189, 1971-77, asst. supt. programs, 1977-79; interim supt. East St. Louis Sch. Dist. 189, 1993-94. Adj. faculty Harris/Stowe State Coll., 1980, adj. prof. edn. emeritus; mem. staff St. Louis U., 1989—; interim supt. Dist. 189 Schs., 1994—; mem. Pres.'s Commn. on Excellence in Spl. Edn. Author: Delta Sigma Theta/East St. Louis Chapter History, 1992; contbr. articles to profl. jours.; feature writer St. Louis Argus Newspaper, 1979—. Mem. Ill. Commn. on Children, 1973-85, East St. Louis Bd. Election Comms., East St. Louis Fin. Adv. Authority, 1999—; pres. bd. dirs. St. Clair County Mental Health Ctr., 1970-72, 87—; bd. dirs. River Bluff coun. Girl Scouts USA, 1979—, nat. bd. dirs., 1981-84; bd. dirs. Jackie Joyner-Kersee Youth Ctr. Found., 1991—, United Way, 1979—, Urban League, 1979—, Provident Counseling Ctr., 1995-98; pres. bd. trustees East St. Louis Pub. Libr., 1972-77; pres., bd. dirs. St. Clair County Mental Health Ctrs., 1987; mem. adv. bd. Magna Bank; charter mem. Coalition of 100 Black Women; mem. coord. coun. ethnic affairs Synod of Mid-Am., Presbyn. Ch. U.S.A.; mem. Ill. Dept. Corrections Sch. Bd., 1995—; charter mem. Metro East Links Group, Gateway chpt. The Links, Inc.; mem. Ill. Minority/Female Bus. Coun., 1991—; mem. Pres.'s Commn. on Excellence in Spl. Edn., 2001--. Recipient of more than 150 awards including Lamp of Learning award East St. Louis Jr. Wednesday Club, 1965, Outstanding Working Woman award Downtown St. Louis, Inc., 1967, Ill. State citation for ednl. document Love is Not Enough, 1974, Delta Sigma Theta citation for document Good Works, 1979, Girl Scout Thanks badge, 1982, award Nat. Coun. Negro Women, 1983, Cmty. Svc. award Met. East Bar Assn., 1983, Journalist award Sigma Gamma Rho, Spelman Coll. Alumni award, 1990, A World of Difference award, 1990, 92, Edn. award St. Louis, YWCA, 1991, SIU-E-Kimmel award, 1991, St. Clair County Mental Health award, 1992, Gateway East Met. Ministry Dr. M.L. King award, 1993, Nat. Coun. Negro Women Black Leader of Yr., 1995, Disting. Alumni award U. Ill., 1996, Pioneer award Mosque 28B, 2000, Tri Del Globe award, 2001, Urban League Merit award, 2002, Ill. Office of Edn. award, 2002, Eugene B. Redmond Writers Club award, 2002; named Woman of Achievement, St. Louis Globe Democrat, 1974, Outstanding Adminstr. So. region III Office Edn., 1975, Woman of Yr. in Edn. St. Clair County YWCA, 1987, Nat. Top Lady of Yr., 1988, Disting. Alumnus U. Ill., 1996, Vashon H.S. Hall of Fame, 1989, Citizen Amb., 1994, Citizen Amb., 1996, Sr. Illinoisan Hall of Fame, 1997. Mem. Am. Librs. Trustees Assn. (regional v.p. 1978-79, 92, nat. sec. 1979-80), Ill. Commn. on Children, Mensa, Coun. for Exceptional Children (mem. pres.'s commn. excellence spl. edn.), Top Ladies of Distinction (pres. 1987-91, nat. editor 1991—, Journalism award 1992, Media award 1992), Delta Sigma Theta (chpt. pres. 1960-62, Letters award 2000), Kappa Delta Pi (pres. So. Ill. U. chpt. 1973-74), Phi Delta Kappa (Svc. Key award 1984, chpt. pres. 1984-85), Iota Phi Lambda, Phi Lambda Theta (chpt. pres. 1985-87), East St. Louis Women's Club (pres. 1973-75). Republican. Home: 733 N 40th St East Saint Louis IL 62205-2138

WRIGHT, LILYAN BOYD, physical education educator; b. Upland, Pa., May 11, 1920; d. Albert Verlenden and Mabel (Warburton) Boyd; m. Richard P. Wright, Oct. 23, 1942; 1 child, Nicki Wright Vanek. BS, Temple U., 1942, MEd, 1946; EdD, Rutgers U., 1972. Tchr. health and phys. edn. Woodbury (N.J.) High Sch., 1942-43, Glen-Nor High Sch., Glenolden, Pa., 1944-46, Chester (Pa.) High Sch., 1946-54; chmn. women's dept. health and phys. edn. Union (N.J.) High Sch., 1954-61; with Trenton State Coll., 1961-90, head women's program health and phys. edn., 1967-77, chmn. dept. health, phys. edn. and recreation, 1977-86, adj. faculty mem., 1990-92, prof. emeritus, 1991—. Mem. N.J. State Com. Div. Girls and Women's Sports, 1958-80; chmn. New Atlantic Field Hockey Sectional Umpiring, 1981-85; chmn. New Atlantic Field Hockey Assn., 1985-90; with recreation after sch. program Newport Counseling Ctrl., 1992-93; vol. coach field hockey Goshen-Lempster Coop. Sch., 1995—. Active Chester United Fund; water safety, first aid instr.; vestry Ch. Epiphany, Newport, N.H., 1992—, sr. warden, 1995-99; vestry St. Luke's Episcopal Ch., 1988-91, clk. of the vestry, 2000—; trustee Olive Pettis Libr., Goshen, 1992—, chair of trustees, 1998—, Goshen budget com., 1999—; dist. ednl. improvement team for Goshen-Lempster Sch. Dist., 1995—, mem. sch. bd., 2001—. Recipient U.S. Field Hockey Assn. award, 1989; ARC Scholarship in her honor N.J. Athletic Assn. Girls, 1971; named to Hall of Fame, Temple U., 1976; named Nat. Honorary and Emeritus Field Hockey Umpire. Mem. AAHPERD (chmn. Ea. Dist. Assn. Div. Girls and Women's Sports, sec. to coun. for svcs. Ea. Dist. Assn. 1979-80, chmn. 1980-81, chmn. com. on aging and adult devel. of ea. dist. 1993-97, 2001—, N.J. rep. to council for convs. 1984-85, Honor Fellow award 1986), N.J. AHPER (pres. 1974-75, past pres. 1975-76, v.p. phys. edn. div., parliamentarian 1990—, Disting. Service and Leadership award 1969, 93, Honor Fellow award 1977, Presdl. Citation award 1993, 95, 96, 97, 98, 99, Disting. Leadership award 1994), N.J. Women's Lacrosse Assn. (umpiring chmn. 1972-76), Nat. Assn. Phys. Edn. in Higher Edn., Eastern Assn. Phys. Edn. Coll. Women, North Jersey, Ctrl. Jersey bds. women's ofcls., Am., Pa. (v.p. 1953-54), Chester (pres. 1949-54) fedns. tchrs., U.S. Field Hockey Assn. (exec. com., chair honorary umpire award com. 1992), North Jersey Field Hockey Assn. (past pres.), N.H. Field Hockey Umpires' Assn., No. New Eng. Lacrosse Officials Bd., U.S. Women's Lacrosse Assn. (Honorary and Emeritus Umpiring Rating award), Kappa Delta Epsilon, Delta Psi Kappa (past pres. Phila. alumni chpt.), Kappa Delta Pi. Home: PO Box 239 Goshen NH 03752-0239

WRIGHT, MARIE ANNE, management information systems educator; b. Albany, N.Y., Oct. 21, 1953; d. Arthur Irving and Ethel (Knickerbocker) W. BS, U. Mass., Boston, 1981; MBA, Clarkson U., 1984; PhD, U. Mass., Amherst, 1989. Grad. asst. Clarkson U., Potsdam, N.Y., 1982; sys. analyst St. Lawrence U., Canton, N.Y., 1983-84; instr. Bentley Coll., Waltham, Mass., 1984-85; tchg. asst. U. Mass., 1985, rsch. asst., 1986; computer cons. Amherst (Mass.) Police Dept., 1986-88; asst. prof. Elms Coll., Chicopee, Mass., 1986-89; assoc. prof. Western Conn. State U., Danbury, Conn., 1990—2002, prof., 2002—. Cons. Ctr. for Human Devel., Springfield, Mass., 1986-87, Early Childhood Ctr., 1986-87. Contbr. articles to profl. jours. and mags. Recipient MIS award U. Mass., 1981. Mem. AAUW, IEEE, Assn. Computing Machinery, Internat. Computer Security Assn., Info. Sys. Security Assn., Am. Soc. Indsl. Security, Computer Security Inst., Assn. Info. Sys., Am. Coll. Forensic Examiners Internat., Beta Gamma Sigma. Democrat. Avocations: cross-country skiing, swimming, reading. Office: Western Conn State U MIS Dept Danbury CT 06810

WRIGHT, MARTHA HELEN, elementary education educator; b. Leesburg, Fla., Nov. 6, 1955; d. Richard and Helene (McRae) Wright; children: Robert L., Micah R. BS, Bethune-Cookman Coll., 1977. Cert. tchr., Fla. Payroll clk. Inland Container Corp., Orlando, Fla., 1978; computer operator So. Bell Telephone, Orlando, 1978-79; tchr. 4th and 5th grades Orange County Pub. Schs., Orlando, 1979-80; homeparent Health Rehab. Svcs., Orlando, 1980-81; elem. tchr. Pinar Elem. Sch., Orlando, 1981-83, Central Ave Elem. Sch., Kissimmee, Fla., 1983—. Program coord. U. Ctrl. Fla., Orlando, summer 1990; program dir. Frontline Outreach, Inc., Orlando,. summers 1984-89; youth counselor The Pvt. Industry Coun., Orlando, summers 1991-92. Author plays; poet; choreographer dance recital. Inner city tutor Frontline Outreach, summer 1987; founder Adopt-A-Grandparent, Kissimmee, 1986—; dir., creator UN Day/Cultural Awareness, 1991-92. Recipient Community Svc. award Walt Disney World, 1991, 92, Youth Group Vol. of Yr. award Beverly Enterprises, 1993, Teacherrrific award Walt Disney Co., 1996-97, other awards. Avocations: writing, playing piano, reading, choreography, modern dance, and motivational speaking. Home: PO Box 1370 Orlando FL 32802-1370

WRIGHT, MELVA POLK, school administrator; b. Salisbury, Md., July 16, 1960; d. Melville Tesco and Shirley Annabelle (Morris) Polk; m. Jeffrey Wright, July 13, 1991; 1 child, Mallory Paige. BS, Towson State U., 1982; MEd, Salisbury State U., 1990. Cert. elem. and mid. sch. tchr., adminstr., supr., Md. Math. tchr. Riverview Mid. Sch., Denton, Md., 1982-83; classroom tchr. West Salisbury Elem. Sch., 1983-90; vice prin. Westside Primary Sch., Quantico, Md., 1990-91, C. H. Chipman Elem. Sch., Salisbury, 1991—. Sec. supply Woman's Home and Overseas Missionary Soc. African Methodist Episcopal Zion Ch., Phila./Balt. Conf., 1987—. Mem. Nat. Assn. Elem. Sch. Prins., Md. Assn. Elem. Sch. Adminstrs., Wicomico County Assn. Elem. Sch. Adminstrs., Assn. Pub. Sch. Adminstrs. and Suprs. of Wicomico County. Democrat. Avocations: singing, family activities, bowling. Home: RR 2 Box 135A Delmar MD 21875-9802 Office: Charles H Chipman Elem Sch 711 Lake St Salisbury MD 21801-3514

WRIGHT, NANCY JANE, English language educator; b. Springfield, Ill., Feb. 28, 1939; d. William Joseph and Elizabeth (Walton) Lucasey; m. Arthur Lee Wright, Aug. 21, 1960; 1 child, John Arthur. BS magna cum laude, Western Ill. U., 1961; MS summa cum laude, So. Ill. U., 1963; PhD, Tex. A&M U., 1975. Tchg. asst. So. Ill. U., Carbondale, 1961-62; instr. Ferris State Coll., Big Rapids, Mich., 1962-65, Christian Coll., Columbia, Mo., 1965-70; tchg. asst. then instr. Tex. A&M U., College Station, 1971-76; instr. lit. Blinn Coll., Bryan, Tex., 1977—, chmn. divsn. humanities, 1997—. Mem. Am. Disabilities Task Force, Blinn Coll., Bryan, 1994—, mem. curriculum com., 1993-94, acad. advisor coord., 1995—; workshop leader. Co-author: How to Prepare for the Tasp, 1991, 2d edit., 1994. Vol. instr. LIFT Program, Dallas, 1970-71; dir. music, pianist/accompanist First Christian Ch., Bryan. Mem. Blinn Coll. Profl. Assn. (founding pres.), Nat. Coun. Tchrs. English, Tex. Jr. Coll. Tchrs. Assn. Republican. Mem. Christian Ch. (Disciples Of Christ). Home: 1008 Holt St College Station TX 77840-2621

WRIGHT, NORMAN ALBERT, JR., middle school educator; b. Suffern, N.Y., July 21, 1948; s. Norman A. and Eleanor (Schultz) W.; 1 child, Kami Renee. BA, Pace U., Pleasantville, N.Y., 1970; MA, William Paterson Coll., Wayne, N.J., 1974. Tchr. 6th grade Nanuet (N.Y.) Pub. Schs., 1970-77; tchr. 5th grade Alpine (N.J.) Pub. Schs., 1977-78; tchr. 6th grade Englewood Cliffs (N.J.) Pub. Schs., 1978-79; tchr. 5th grade Woodcliff Lake (N.J.) Pub. Schs., 1979-80, tchr. middle sch. math., 1980-82, tchr. middle sch. sci., 1982—. Mem. profl. devel. com. Woodcliff Lake Pub. Schs., 1988-90, co-chair, 1990-2000, mem. supts. curriculum coord. com., 1988-2000, dist. and regional sci. articulation team, 1988—, chmn. dist. sci. team, 1994-2000, mid. sch. program devel. com., 1990—; clin. faculty Montclair State U., 1998—. Judge Seiko Challenge Nat. Sci. Competition, Our Lady of Mercy Sch. Sci. Fair; mem. Woodcliff Lake PTA. Mem. NEA, ASCD, NSTA, Nat. Mid. Level Sci. Tchrs. Assn., Nat. Coun. Tchrs. Math., Nat. Coun. Tchrs. English, Am. Mus. Natural History, Nat. Geog. Soc., N.J. Edn. Assn., N.J. Sci. Tchrs. Assn. (conf. presenter) N.J. Marine Edn. Assn., N.J. Earth Sci. Tchrs. Assn., North Jersey Weather Observers, Am. Chem. Soc. (tchr. affiliate), N.J. Assn. Environ. Edn., N.J. Assn. Mid. Level Educators, Hudson Valley Orienteering, U.S. Orienteering Fedn., Woodcliff Lake Edn. Assn., N.Y. Zool. Soc., Internat. Soc. Tech. in Edn., Internat. Reading Assn., Astron. Soc. Pacific, Activities Integrating Math. and Sci. Edn. Found., N.Y. State Middle Sch. Assn., The Planetary Soc., N.Y. Acad. Scis. Avocations: walking, rowing, bicycling, photography, reading. Office: Woodcliff Sch 134 Woodcliff Ave Westwood NJ 07677-8296

WRIGHT, REBECCA DIANE, program director; b. Springfield, Ohio, Dec. 5, 1947; d. Earl William and Diane Adele (Johns) W.; m. Charles Spaeth, Nov. 15, 1974 (div. April 1977); m. George De La Pena, Nov. 2, 1984; children: Matthew, Alexander. Grad. h.s., 1966. Ballerina Joffrey Ballet, N.Y.C., 1966-75, Am. Ballet Theatre, N.Y.C., 1975-82; ballet mistress Twyla Tharp, N.Y.C., 1983; prof. Calif. State U., Long Beach, 1986—93; dir. dance program Adelphi U., Garden City, N.Y., 1997-99; dir. Wright Moves, Inc., Garden City, NY, 1998; dir. summer intensives Am. Ballet Theatre, 1997—2003; dir. dance program St. Paul's Sch., 1999—. Vis. prof. UCLA, 1993—97; mem. steering com. Fosse Scholarship Awards, 1996—98; panelist LA Arts Coun., 1998—99; site visitor NEA. Starring role: Broadway Musical Merlin, N.Y.C., 1982-83, Broadway Musical On Your Toes, L.A. and N.Y.C., 1983. Ford Found. scholar, 1964. Mem. Am. Coll. Dance Assn. (bd. dirs.). Avocations: cooking, reading, writing. E-mail: rqright@sps.edu.

WRIGHT, RICHARD OSCAR, III, pathologist, educator, clinical ethicist; b. La Junta, Colo., Aug. 9, 1944; s. Richard O. Jr. and Frances R. (Curtiss) W.; m. Bernale Trout, May 31, 1969; children: Lauren Diane, Richard O. IV. BS in Biology, Midwestern State U., 1966; MS in Biology, U. Houston, 1968; DO, U. Health Sci., 1972; MA in Bioethics, Midwestern U., 2001. Cert. anatomic pathology and lab. medicine Am. Osteo. Bd. Pathology. Sr. attending pathologist Normandy Met. Hosps., St. Louis, 1977-81, Phoenix (Ariz.) Gen. Hosps., 1981-97, dir. med. edn., 1989-92, 96—; clin. asst. prof. pathology Coll. Osteo. Medicine, Western U., Pomona, Calif., 1985—; dir. labs., chmn. dept. John C. Lincoln Hosp., Deer Valley, 1997—, dir. med. edn., dir. labs., 1997—; v.p. Osteo. Postdoctoral Tng. Inst., Kirksville, Mo., 1998—. Clin. instr. pathology Ohio U. Coll. Osteo. Medicine, Athens, 1976—77; clin. prof. pathology Kirksville Coll. Osteo. Medicine, 1985—; vis. lectr. pathology New Eng. Coll. Osteo. Medicine, Biddeford, Maine, 1989—92; clin. asst. prof. pathology Midwestern U. Ariz. Coll. Osteo. Medicine, 1997—; cons. pathologist Phoenix Indian Med. Ctr., 1992—94; adv. bd. Inter Soc. Coun. Pathology, Chgo., 1992—; sec. med. staff John C. Lincoln Hosp.-Deer Valley, 1997—99, v.p. med. staff, 2000—03; dir. John C. Lincoln Health Network Bd., 2001—. Active Ariz. Rep. Party, Phoenix, Rep. Nat. Coun., Washington; precinctman Dist. 18 Maricopa County, Ariz., 1996-98, Madison Heights Precinct, 1996-98; dir. John C. Lincoln Healthcare Network, 2001—; chmn. bd. trustees Phoenix (Ariz.) Gen. Hosp., 1994-95; ex-officio, trustee, 1995-97; dir. John C. Lincoln Health Network Guild, 1997—; dir., v.p. found. adv. coun. Lincoln Health Found.-Phoenix Gen. Hosp. Osteo. Endowment Fund. Recipient Mead-Johnson award Nat. Osteo. Assn., 1975. Fellow Am. Osteo. Coll. Pathologists (disting., pres. 1989-90, bd. govs. 1984-91), Coll. Pathologists, Coll. Am. Pathologists, Am. Soc. Clin. Pathologists; mem. Ariz. Osteo. Med. Assn. (del. dist. 2 ho. of dels. 1998), Ariz. Soc. Pathologists, Century Club Alumni Assn., AAAS, Alpha Phi Omega, Rho Sigma Chi, Psi Sigma Alpha. Presbyterian. Office: Anatomic Pathology Assoc 19829 N 27th Ave Phoenix AZ 85027-4001 E-mail: rwrigh@jcl.com.

WRIGHT, ROBERT ROSS, III, law educator; b. Ft. Worth, Nov. 20, 1931; m. Susan Webber; children: Robert Ross IV, John, David, Robin. BA cum laude, U. Ark., 1953, JD, 1956; MA (grad. fellow), Duke U., 1954; SJD (law fellow), U. Wis., 1967. Bar: Ark. 1956, U.S. Supreme Ct. 1968, Okla. 1970. Instr. polit. sci. U. Ark., 1955-56; mem. firm Forrest City, Ark., 1956-58; ptnr. Norton, Norton & Wright, Forrest City, 1959; asst. gen. counsel, asst. sec. Crossett Co., Ark.; atty. Crossett div. Ga.-Pacific Corp., 1960-63; asst. sec. Pub. Utilities Co., Crossett, Triangle Bag Co., Covington, Ky., 1960-62; faculty U. Ark. Law Sch., 1963-70; asst. prof., dir. continuing legal edn. and research, then asst. dean U. Ark., Little Rock, 1965-66, prof. law, 1967-70; prof. U. Okla., 1970-77; dean U. Okla. Coll. Law; dir. U. Okla. Law Center, 1970-76; vis. prof. U. Ark., Little Rock, 1976-77; Donaghey Disting. prof. U. Ark, 1977-99, Donaghey disting. prof. emeritus, 1999—. Vis. disting. prof. U. Cin., 1983; vis. prof. law U. Iowa, 1969-70; vis. prof. U. Ark., Little Rock, 1976-77; Ark. commr. Nat. Conf. Commrs. Uniform State Laws, 1967-70; past chmn. Com. Uniform Eminent Domain Code; past mem. Com. Uniform Probate Code, Ark. Gov.'s Ins. Study Commn.; chmn. Gov. Commn. on Uniform Probate Code; chmn. task force joint devel. Hwy. Research Bd.; vice chmn. Okla. Jud. Council, 1970-72, chmn., 1972-75; chmn. Okla. Center Criminal Justice, 1971-76 Author: Arkansas Eminent Domain Digest, 1964, Arkansas Probate Practice System, 1965, The Law of Airspace, 1968, Emerging Concepts in the Law of Airspace, 1969, Cases and Materials on Land Use, 3d edit., 1982, supplement, 1987, 5th edit., 1997, Uniform Probate Code Practice Manual, 1972, Model Airspace Code, 1973, Land Use in a Nutshell, 1978, 4th edit., 2000, The Arkansas Form Book, 1979, 2d edit., 1988, Zoning Law in Arkansas: A Comparative Analysis, 1980, Old Seeds in the New Land: A History and Reminiscences of the Bar of Arkansas, 2001; contbr. articles to profl. jours. Mem. Little Rock Planning Commn., 1978-82, chmn., 1982. Named Ark. Man of Year Kappa Sigma, 1958. Fellow: Am. Coll. Trust and Estate Counsel (acad.), Am. Law Inst.; mem.: ABA (past chmn., exec. coun. gen. practice, solo and small firm sect., former chmn. new pubs. editl. bd., sect. officers conf., ho. of dels. 1994—2000, standing com. fed. jud. improvements 1998—), Pulaski County Bar Assn., Ark. Bar Assn. (life; exec. coun. 1985—88, ho. of dels., chmn. eminent domain code com., past mem. com. new bar ctr., past chmn. preceptorship com., exec. com. young laywers sect.), Okla. Bar Assn. (past vice-chmn. legal internship com., former vice-chmn. gen. practice sect.), U. Ark. Alumni Assn., U. Wis. Alumni Assn., Duke U. Alumni Assn., Omicron Delta Kappa, Phi Alpha Delta, Phi Beta Kappa, Order of Coif. Episcopalian. Home: 249 Pleasant Valley Dr Little Rock AR 72212-3170

WRIGHT, RUTH P. primary education educator, photographer, writer; b. Ogden, Utah, Sept. 19, 1928; d. Russell Beers Petty and Josephine Volker (dec.); stepmother Lucile Owen; m. Charles David Wright, June 23, 1955 (dec. July 1978); children: David Hugh, Vivian. BS in Child Devel., Utah State U., 1950; MA in Early Childhood Edn., U. Mich., 1952; cert. elem. adminstr., Albertson Coll., 1984-85. Cert. elem. edn. Edn. dir., elem. tchr. various locations, 1950-58; rsch. assoc. Frank Porter Rsch. Ctr., Chapel Hill, N.C., 1965-68; dir., tchr. pvt. presch., Chapel Hill, 1967-72; dir. tchr. tng. State Idaho Headstart Program, Boise, 1972-73; prin. Boise Ind. Schs., 1973-75, kindergarten/1st grade tchr., 1975-93. Instr. child devel. Iowa State U., Merrill Palmer, Detroit, 1952-54; tchr. trainer Headstart, U. N.C., Chapel Hill, 1964; evaluator N.C. Day Care Ctrs., Fed. Govt., Chapel Hill, 1967; adj. faculty photography Boise State U., 1985-86; presenter in field. Pub.: book Mrs. Greiner Does Barbie and Other Adventures in Kindergarten. Bd. dirs., docent Boise Art Mus., 1992-2000; bd. dirs. Garden City (Idaho) Libr., 1992-98; originator book mobile Bells for Books, 1994-97; chair book sale Anne Frank Exhbn., Idaho Hist. Mus., 1995; organizer, bd. dirs. Log Cabin Literary Ctr., Boise, 1996; organizer kids writing camp Log Cabin Summer Camp, 1996-97. Recipient Anne Frank on Human Rights award, Idaho Voices of Faith, Boise, 1996, J.C. Penny Golden Rule award, 1996, Achievement award, Literacy High Risk Children, Assn. Idaho Cities State Assn., 1996, Women of Distinction award, Soroptomist Club, Garden City, 1997, Lifetime Achievement award, Silver Sage Girl Scout Coun., Boise, 1998, Boise Mayor's award for excellence in the arts, 2001. Mem. NEA (life), Idaho Commn. on the Arts (mem. at large 1997—), Boise Art Mus., U. Mich. Alumnae Assn. (life).

WRIGHT, STEPHANIE M.G. aerospace educator; b. Boulder, Colo., Apr. 9, 1948; d. Henry J. and Dorothy J. (Puvodnic) Gerjovich; m. Brian Harry, Aug. 23, 1975; children: Henry Gordon, Harry Charles. BA, U. Del., 1970, MEd, 1976; DEd, Temple U., 1987. Music educator Alexis I. DuPont Sch. Dist., Del., 1970-78, Red Clay Consol. Dist., Del., 1978-89; space ambassador NASA, Washington, 1985—; dir. aerospace edn. Del. Tchr. Ctr., Dover, 1989—. Pres., dir. Del. Aerospace Edn. Found./Del. Aerospace Acad., 1990—; adv. bd. Del. NASA space grant, 1990-, steering mem. Challenger Ctr., Alexandria, Va., 1988—. Contbr. articles to profl. jours. Tchr. in Space award Dept. Pub. Instruction, NASA, Del., 1985, Christa McAuliffe fellowship Dept. Edn., Women in Aerospace Edn. award, Washington, 1988, Aerospace Educator award, 1992, 5-Yr. Svc. pin Challenger Ctr. for Space Sci. Edn., Alexandria, Va., 1993, Cen. East Region Aerospace award AFA, 1995, Edn. Achievement award Aerospace States Assn., 1995, Disting. Citizen award Dover AFB, 1995, Edn. Achievement award AeroSpace States Assn., 1995, Educator Achievement award, AIAA, 2001, numerous others. Mem. Alumni Assn. U. Del. (exec. bd. mem. 1990-93, Hall of Fame 1989), Edn. Alumni Assn./U. Del. (exec. bd., pres. 1986-94), Sci. Alliance (bd. dirs. 1992-94, Sci. Recognition award 1992), Air Force Assn. (exec. bd. dir., state v.p. 1991—, Premier Salute 1993), AAUW, Phi Delta Kappa. Home: 5 Essex Dr Bear DE 19701-1602

WRIGHT, STEPHEN GAILORD, civil engineering educator, consultant; b. San Diego, Aug. 13, 1943; s. Homer Angelo and Elizabeth Videlle (Ward) W.; m. Ouida Jo Kennedy; children: Michelle, Richard. BSCE, U. Calif., Berkeley, 1966, MSCE, 1967, PhD CE, 1969. Prof. civil engring. U. Tex., Austin, 1969—. Contbr. numerous tech. papers & research reports, 1969—. Mem. ASCE. Republican. Presbyterian. Home: 3406 Shinoak Dr Austin TX 78731-5739 Office: U Tex Go Tech Engring Dept Civil Engring C1700 Austin TX 78712

WRIGHT, SYLVIA, government agency administrator; b. Balt. BA, Temple U., 1963, MA, 1965. Group leader Sch. Improvement Program Office U.S. Dept. Edn., Washington, dir. Sch. Support and Tech. Programs, 2001—. Office: US Dept Edn FB6 Rm 3E121 400 Maryland Ave SW Washington DC 20202*

WRIGHT, VICKI LYNN, gifted and talented education educator; b. Sioux Falls, S.D., Sept. 20, 1956; d. Victor Eugene and Thenetta Lou (Lancaster) Nield; m. John Albert Paul Wright, July 28, 1979. BA in Art and Spanish, Augustana Coll., Sioux Falls, 1978, MA in Gifted Edn., 1990. Tchr. art Sioux Falls Pub. Schs., 1982-87, gifted edn. tchr., 1987-92, West Des Moines (Iowa) Cmty. Schs., 1992—. Innovative Project grantee Sioux Falls Pub. Schs., 1991-92; Artists in Schs./Cmty. New Residency Program grantee Iowa Arts Coun., 1993; Iowa Arts Coun. program grantee, 1993-95. Mem. ASCD, NEA, Iowa Edn. Assn., West Des Moines Edn. Assn. (bldg. rep. 1993-94). Avocations: computers, cruising the internet, computer graphics, reading, telecomputing. Office: Crossroads Elem Sch 1050 50th St West Des Moines IA 50266-4902

WRIGHT, VIRGINIA BAXTER, retired economics educator; b. Concordia, Kans., May 21, 1939; BA magna cum laude in Polit. Sci., Kans. State U., 1961; PhD, George Washington U., 1971. Computer programmer federal systems div. IBM Corp., Bethesda, Md., 1962; rsch. asst. govtl. studies div. The Brookings Inst., Washington, 1963-66; sr. staff assoc. Nat. League of Cities/U.S. Conf. Mayors, Washington, 1971-74; rsch. dir. Commn. on Correctional Facilities & Svcs. ABA, Washington, 1974-76; sr. rsch. assoc. state and local govt. program The Urban Inst., Washington, 1976-77; vis. asst. prof. dept. econs. SUNY, Albany, 1977-78, project dir. Inst. on Man & Sci., 1978-80; exec. dir. Growth & Rsch. Orgn. for Women, Inc., Lexington, Ky., 1980-81; prof. econs. Eastern Ky. U., Richmond, 1982-99, ret. Rsch. assoc. dept. econs. George Washington U., 1971; mem. Com. on Status of Women in the Econs. Profession; sec.-treas. GROW Conf. for Women Researchers, 1989-93. Woodrow Wilson fellow, 1961, NDEA fellow, 1966-69. Mem. AAUW (internat. fellowships panel 1987-90), Am. Econ. Assn., Ky. Econ. Assn. (bd. dirs. 1989-92), Phi Kappa Phi. Home: 1004 Palmetto Dr Richmond KY 40475-8224

WRIGHTON, MARK STEPHEN, chemistry educator; b. Jacksonville, Fla., June 11, 1949; s. Robert D. and Doris (Cutler) Wrighton; children: James Joseph, Rebecca Ann. BS, Fla. State U., 1969; PhD, Calif. Inst. Tech., 1972; DSc (hon.), U. West Fla., 1983. From asst. prof. chemistry to provost MIT, Cambridge, 1972—90, provost, 1990—95; prof., chancellor Washington U., St. Louis, 1995—. Bd. dirs. A.G. Edwards, Inc., Cabot Corp., Ionics, Inc., Helix Tech. Corp., Optical Imaging Sys., Inc., Danforth Plant Sci. Ctr., Nidus Ctr. for Sci. Enterprise, Barnes Jewish Hosp., BJC HealthCare; mem. Nat. Sci. Bd.; bd. dirs. Nat. Assn. of Independent Colleges and Univs. Author: Organometallic Photochemistry, 1979. Trustee St. Louis Art Mus., Mo. Bot. Garden, St. Louis Symphony, St. Louis Sci. Ctr.; bd. dirs. United Way Greater St. Louis. Recipient Herbert Newby McCoy award, Calif. Inst. Tech., 1972, Disting. Alumni award, 1992, E.O. Lawrence award, Dept. Energy, 1983, Halpern award in photochemistry, N.Y. Acad. Scis., 1983, Fresenius award, Phi Lambda Upsilon, 1984, Dreyfus tchr.-scholar, 1975—80; fellow, Alfred P. Sloan, 1974—76, MacArthur fellow, 1983—88. Fellow: AAAS; mem.: Acad. of Sci. of St. Louis, Electrochem. Soc., Am. Chem. Soc. (award in pure chemistry 1981, award in inorganic chemistry 1988), Am. Philos. Soc., Am. Acad. Arts and Scis. Office: Washington Univ Office of Chancellor One Brookings Dr # 1192 Saint Louis MO 63130-4899

WRISLEY, ROBERT LYMAN, business educator; b. Montique, Mass., Nov. 28, 1941; s. Lyman A. Jr. and Mildred (Vachula) W.; m. Mary Ellen Davis, June 10, 1967; children: Robert Jr., Scott, Ellen. B of Edn., Mid. Tenn. State U., 1966, MEd, 1968; EdD, U. Ga., 1978. Tchr. English, sci., social studies Walker County Schs., Flintstone, Ga., 1967-68, instr., 1967-72; tchr., chmn. bus. office edn. Chickamauga (Ga.) City Schs., 1968-74; adminstrv. asst. to chmn. of div. vocat. edn. U. Ga., Athens, 1975-78; asst. prof. bus. edn. Fayetteville (N.C.) State U., 1978-85; cons. bus. edn. N.C. State Dept. Pub. Instruction, Raleigh, 1985-89; asst. prof. dept. bus., vocat. and tech. edn. East Carolina U., Greenville, N.C., 1989—. Researcher and presenter in field. Contbr. articles to profl. jours. State chpt. advisor Future Bus. Leaders of Am., 1985-89. Mem. Nat. Bus. Edn. Assn., Am. Vocat. Assn., So. Bus. Edn. Assn. (exec. bd. 1992—), N.C. Bus. Edn. Assn. (treas. 1991, chmn. ann. conf. 1991, chmn. bylaws com. 1984-85, 2d v.p. 1983-84, chmn. pub. rels. com. 1982-83, bd. dirs. 1992—), N.C. Vocat. Assn. (chmn. audit com. 1989—, chmn. nominating com. 1988-89, bd. dirs. 1982-85, pres. bud. edn. divsn. 1984-85), Delta Pi Epsilon (nat. svc. projects com. 1980-84, historian Beta Delta chpt. 1977-79), Pi Omega Pi, Phi Delta Kappa. Lutheran. Office: East Carolina U 2313 Gen Classroom Bldg Greenville NC 27858

WRITER, SHARON LISLE, secondary education educator; b. L.A., Aug. 29, 1939; d. Harlan Lawrence and Emma Mae (Cordery) Lisle; m. Robert Vincent Writer, Dec. 30, 1961; children: Martin Carl, Cynthia Louise, Brian Robert, Scott Andrew. BS, Mt. St. Marys Coll., 1961; MS in Sci. Edn., Calif. State U., Fullerton, 1989; postgrad., U. Calif., Irvine, 1987, Colo. Sch. Mines, 1994. Cert. secondary tchr., Calif. Tchr. St. Mary's Acad., L.A., 1961-62, Escambia High Sch., Pensacola, Fla., 1962-63; rsch. asst. U. So. Calif., L.A., 1964-65, U. Calif., Irvine, 1965-66; tchr. aide Cerro Villa Jr. High Sch., Villa Park, Calif., 1975-76, tchr., 1976-88, Villa Park High Sch., 1988—98, mentor tchr., 1990—97; lectr. Calif. State Univ., Long Beach, 1999—; CA Dir. of Sci. Olympiad, Southern Section, 2000—. Tchr. of yr. com. Orange (Calif.) Unified Sch. Dist., 1992, supt. adv. coun., 1990-1998, curriculum sci. com., 1991-1997. Active Villa Park Womens League, 1975—, Assistance League of Orange, 1991—; project leader, county coord. Orange County 4-H Assn., Anaheim, Calif., 1975-84; bd. sec. Orange County Sci. Fair, 1986-91, awards chmn., 1991-94, pres., 1994—; mem. judging policy adv. com. Calif. State Sci. Fair, 1996-2001. Recipient Outstanding Sci. Tchr. award Orange County Sci. Tchrs. Assn., 1993; named Tchr. of Yr. Villa Park High Sch., 1990, 94, Outstanding Coach Orange County Sci. Olympiad, 1990, 92, 94, 96, Calif. State Sci. Olympiad, 1987. Mem. NSTA (conv. hospitality com. 1989, 90, hospitality co-chair 1994 nat. conv.), Am. Chem. Soc., Calif. Sci. Tchr. Assn., Orange County Sci. Educators Assn. (Disting. Sci. Tchr. award 1993). Roman Catholic. Avocations: tennis, swimming, water skiing, needlepoint. Home: 18082 Rosanne Cir Villa Park CA 92861-6431 Office: CSULB Dept Sci Edn 1250 Bellflower Blvd Long Beach CA 90840-4501

WRUCK, ERICH-OSKAR, retired foreign language educator, administrator; b. Gross-Kroessin/Pomerania, Germany, Oct. 29, 1928; came to U.S., 1952, naturalized, 1954; s. Erich Albert and Erna (Kroening) W.; m. Esther Emmy Schmidt, Oct. 3, 1953; children: Eric Gordon, Karin Esther, Krista Elisabeth. BA magna cum laude, Rutgers U., 1959; MA, 1961, PhD, 1969. Asst. instr. Rutgers U., New Brunswick, N.J., 1959-62; asst. prof. Davidson (N.C.) Coll., 1962-69, assoc. prof., 1969-73, prof., chmn. dept. German, 1983-87; established exch. program Marburg (Germany) U., 1963; with U. Würzburg, Germany, 1985; dir. Davidson abroad program Marburg, 1966-67, 71-72; jr. yr. abroad program Würzburg, 1986-87, 89-92; ret., 1994. Cons. faculty U.S. Army Command and Gen. Staff Coll., 1974-85. 1st lt. U.S. Army, 1953-57, to col. USAR, 1988. Recipient Julius Maximilians medal U. Wuerzburg, 1987; named to Arty. OCS Hall of Fame, 1996; Henry Rutgers scholar. Mem. Goethe Assn., Freies Deutsches Hochstift, Schiller Assn., Goethe Soc. of N. Am. (charter), Soc. German Am. Studies. Lutheran. Avocations: painting, photography, soaring, skiing, running.

WRUCKE-NELSON, ANN C. elementary education educator; b. Mankato, Minn., Nov. 5, 1939; d. G.F. and Dorothy (Thomas) Wrucke; children: Chris, Dor-Ella. BS, Mankato State U., 1961; MLA, So. Meth. U., 1974; postgrad., U. Minn., 1963, Tex. Woman's U., EdD in Early Childhood Edn., 1992. Cert. elem., kindergarten, ESL, history tchr., Tex. Tchr. Rochester (Minn.) Pub. Schs., Christ the King Sch., Dallas; dir., tchr. Norway Christian Presch., Dallas; Every Student Learns Lang. program kindergarten tchr. Dallas Ind. Sch. Dist., 1971—. Tchr. summer session Tex. Woman's U., 1991; presenter in field. Producer video: A Year of Language Learning, 1990. Sunday sch. tchr. Holy Trinity Ch. Recipient Tchr. of Yr. award, 1989, Tex. TESOL scholarship, 1994; Bill Martin Literacy Conf. scholar; named ESL Tchr. of Yr., 1991. Mem. Internat. Reading Assn., Assn. for Childhood Edn. Internat., So. Assn. on Children Under Six, TESOL, Kindergarten Tchrs. Tex., Tex. TESOL, Dallas Assn. for Edn. of Young Child, Phi Delta Kappa. Office: 201 N Adams Ave Dallas TX 75208-4624

WU, GUOYAO, animal science, nutrition and physiology educator; b. China, July 28, 1962; s. Fanjiu Wu and Meixiao Huang; m. Yan Chen, Aug. 7, 1995; 1 child, Neil David. BS in Animal Sci., South China Agrl. U., 1982; MS in Animal Nutrition, Beijing Agrl. U., 1984; MS in Animal Biochemistry, U. Alta., Can., 1986, PhD in Animal Biochemistry, 1989; postgrad. in metabolism/diabetes, McGill U., Mont., Can., 1989-91; postgrad. in biochemistry, Meml. U. Nfld., Can., 1991. Grad. tchg. asst. U. Alta., 1985-88; postdoctoral rschr. Royal Victoria Hosp., McGill U., 1989-91, Meml. U. Nfld., 1991; asst. prof. dept. animal sci. and faculty nutrition Tex. A&M U., College Station, 1991-96, assoc. prof., 1996—. Reviewer Amino Acids, Am. Jour. Clin. Nutrition, Am. Jour. Physiology, Analytical Biochemistry, Biochimica et Biophysica Acta, Can. Jour. Physiology and Pharmacology, Diabetes, Diabetologia, Gastroenterology, Gene, Hormone and Metabolic Rsch., Jour. Animal Sci., Jour. Nutrition, Jour. Nutritional Biochemistry, Jour. Cellular Physiology, Metabolism,, Poultry Sci., Reproduction-Nutrition-Devel., Can. Diabetes Assn., Med. Rsch. Coun. Can., U. Toronto Banting and Best Ctr., Can.; editl. advisor Biochem. Jour., 1993—; mem. editl. bd. Jour. Nutrition, 1997—; contbr. articles to profl. jours. Grantee Tex. A&M U., 1992—, Ajinomoto Inc., Japan, 1992, USDA, 1992—, Houston Livestock Show and Rodeo, 1992-95, Am. Heart Assn., 1995—; nat. scholarship for grad. studies abroad Ministry Edn. China, 1984-86, grad. tchg. assistantship U. Alta., 1985-88, dissertation fellowship, 1989, Ctr. Rsch. Fund award, 1988, Andrew Stewart Grad. prize, 1989, U. Alberta, Can. Rsch. Inst. fellowship Royal Victoria Hosp., 1988, fellowship Can. Diabetes Assn., 1989, Med. Rsch. Coun. Can. fellow, 1989-91; established investigator Am. Heart Assn., 1998—. Mem. AAAS, Am. Diabetes Assn., Am. Heart Assn., Am. Soc. for Nutritional Scis., Am. Heart Assn., Am. Physiol. Soc., Am. Soc. Animal Sci., Biochem. Soc. U.K., Can. Soc. Nutritional Scis., Juv. Diabetes Found. Internat. (grantee 1992-94), Soc. for the Study of Reproduction. Home: 4707 Shoal Creek Dr College Station TX 77845-4410 Office: Tex A&M Univ Dept Animal Sci College Station TX 77843-0001

WU, INA ZHIQING, art educator; b. Tianjin, China; arrived in U.S., 1987. d. Wenjin Wu and June Yuru Ao. Attended, Tianjin Art Inst., 1978-80; BFA, U. Wash., 1994, MFA, 1997. Artistic designer Printers and Plastics Manufactory, Tianjin, China, 1974-78; import, export adminstr. Linda Garment Manufactory, Hong Kong, 1980-87; art instr. Seattle Ctrl. C.C., 1997—2001; art prof. Olympic Coll., Bremerton, Wash., 2001—. Exhibited in group shows, Wismer Ctr. Gallery Seattle U.; Art Ctr. Gallery Seattle Pacific U.; Univ. Gallery; Pacific Luth. U.; Wash. State Conv. Trade Ctr.; Seattle (honorable mention award), Kinsey Art Gallery, Seattle U.; Art Gallery Seattle Ctrl. C.C.; Art Gallery North Seattle C.C.; Is Is Collectibles Gallery, Seattle; Judith Schorr Gallery, Seattle; Jacob Lawrence Gallery, Seattle; Henry Art Gallery, Seattle; Van de Griff Gallery, Santa Fe; Heping Art Gallery, China; Tianjin Art Mus., China; work reviewed in books and mag. Recipient: curricular grant, Seattle Ctrl. C.C., 1998, president's fund, 1998, faculty devel. grant, 1997, Nordstrom scholarship, 1996, Gonzales scholarship. Mem.: Coll. Art Assn. Avocations: painting, art, reading, golf. Office: Olympic Coll Art Bldg Room 115 1600 Chester Ave Bremerton WA 98337-1699

WU, JUNRU, physics educator; b. Shanghai, Apr. 5, 1944; came to U.S., 1980; s. Xien Zhon and Meizhen (Li) W.; m. Yiying Lin, Jan. 28, 1976; children: Kathy H., Jane. MS in Physics, UCLA, 1981, PhD in Physics, 1985. Tchg. asst. UCLA, 1980-85, adj. asst. prof., 1985-87; asst. prof. physics U. Vt., Burlington, 1987-93, assoc. prof., 1993-96, prof., 1996—, chmn. physics dept., 1998—. Contbr. more than 80 articles to Jour. Acoustics Soc. Am., Ultrasound in Medicine and Biology. Rsch. grantee NIH, 1990—. Fellow Acoustical Soc. Am., Am. Inst. Ultrasound in Medicine (mem. bioeffect com. 1992-95, mem. tech. standards com. 1996—). Office: U Vt Dept Physics Burlington VT 05405-0001

WU, TAI TE, biological sciences and engineering educator; b. Shanghai, Aug. 2, 1935; m. Anna Fang, Apr. 16, 1966; 1 son, Richard. MB, BS, U. Hong Kong, 1956; BS in Mech. Engring, U. Ill., Urbana, 1958; SM in Applied Physics, Harvard U., 1959, PhD in Engring. (Gordon McKay fellow), 1961. Rsch. fellow in structural mechanics Harvard U., 1961-63; rsch. fellow in biol. chemistry Harvard U. (Med. Sch.), 1964, rsch. assoc., 1965-66; rsch. scientist Hydronautics, Inc., Rockville, Md., 1962; asst. prof. engring. Brown U., Providence, 1963-65; asst. prof. biomath. Grad. Sch. Med. Scis., Cornell U. Med. Coll., N.Y.C., 1967-68, assoc. prof., 1968-70; assoc. prof. physics and engring. scis. Northwestern U., Evanston, Ill., 1970-73, prof., 1973-74, prof. biochemistry and molecular biology and engring. scis., 1973-85, acting chmn. dept. engring. scis., 1974, prof. biochem., molecular biology, cell biology and biomed. engring., engring. scis., applied math., 1985-94, prof. biochemistry, molecular biology, cell biology, biomed. engring., 1994—. Author (with E.A. Kabat and others): Variable Regions of Immunoglobulin Chains, 1976, Sequences of Immunoglobulin Chains, 1979, Sequences of Proteins of Immunological Importance, 1983, Sequences of Proteins of Immunological Interest, 1987, 5th edit., 1991; editor: New Methodologies in Studies of Protein Configuration, 1985, Analytical Molecular Biology, 2001; contbr. articles to profl. jours. Recipient progress award Chinese Engrs. and Scientists Assn. So. Calif., Los Angeles, 1971; C.T. Loo Scholar, 1959-60; NIH Research Career Devel. awardee, 1974-79 Mem. Am. Soc. Biochem. and Molecular Biology, Biophys. Soc., Sigma Xi, Tau Beta Pi, Pi Mu Epsilon. Office: Northwestern U Dept Biochem Molecular and Cell Biology Evanston IL 60208-0001 E-mail: tt@immuno.bme.nwu.edu.

WU, TAI TSUN, physicist, educator; b. Shanghai, Dec. 1, 1933; came to U.S., 1950, naturalized, 1964; s. King Ching and Wei Van (Tsang) W.; m. Sau Lan Yu, June 18, 1967. BS, U. Minn., 1953; S.M., Harvard U., 1954, PhD, 1956. Jr. fellow Soc. Fellows Harvard U., 1956-59, asst. prof., 1959-63, assoc. prof., 1963-66, Gordon McKay prof. applied physics, 1966—, prof. physics, 1994—. Mem. Inst. Advanced Study, Princeton, 1958-59, 60-61, 62-63; vis. prof. Rockefeller U., 1966-67; sci. assoc. Deutsches Elektronen-Synchrotron, Hamburg, Ger., 1970-71, 82-83; Kramers prof. U. Utrecht, Netherlands, 1977-78; sci. assoc. CERN, Geneva, Switzerland, 1977-78, 86—. Author: (with Ronold W.P. King) Scattering and Diffraction of Waves, 1959, (with Barry M. McCoy) Two-Dimensional Ising Model, 1973, (with Ronold W.P. King, Glenn S. Smith and Margaret Owens) Antennas in Matter: Fundamentals, Theory and Applications, 1981, (with Hung Cheng) Expanding Protons: Scattering at High Energies, 1987, (with Raymond Gastmans) The Ubiquitous Photon: Helicity Method for QED and QCD, 1990, (with Ronold W.P. King and Margaret Owens) Lateral Electromagnetic Waves: Theory and Applications to Communications, Geophysical Exploration, and Remote Sensing, 1992. Recipient

Alexander von Humboldt award, 1985; Putnam scholar, 1953; fellow A.P. Sloan Found., 1960-66; fellow NSF, 1966-67; Guggenheim Found., 1970-71. Mem. Am. Acad. Arts and Sci., Sigma Xi, Eta Kappa Nu, Tau Beta Pi. Home: 35 Robinson St Cambridge MA 02138-1403 Office: Harvard U Physics Dept 204B Pierce Hall Cambridge MA 02138-2901

WUBAH, DANIEL ASUA, microbiologist, educator, dean; b. Accra, Ghana, Nov. 6, 1960; arrived in U.S., 1984; s. Daniel Asua and Elizabeth Bruba (Appoe) Wubah; m. Judith A. Dadson, Dec. 17, 1993; children: Vera Bruba, Abena, Araba. BSc with honors, BEd, U. Cape Coast, Ghana, 1984; MS, U. Akron, 1988; PhD, U. Ga., 1990. Cert. in hazardous waste site ops. and emergency response health and safety. Postdoctoral fellow U.S. EPA Rsch. Lab., Athens, Ga., 1991-92; asst. prof. dept. microbiology Towson (Md.) U., 1992-97, assoc. prof., 1997-2000, dept. chair, 1998-2000; assoc. dean Coll. Sci. and Math. James Madison U., 2000—, prof., 2002—, pre-med. coord., 2002—. Councillor Coun. Undergrad. Rsch. Assoc. editor: Mycologia; contbr. articles to profl. publs. Sr. warden Sherwood Episcopal Ch., Cockeysville, Md., 1998-2000; bd. govs. Nat. Aquarium Balt. Recipient Paul Acquarone award U. Akron, 1985, Palfrey award U. Ga., 1989; Faculty Rsch. grantee Towson State U., 1992, 94, 97; grantee NSF, 1993, 98—, USDA, 1994, Univ. Sys. Md., 1998-2000, NIH Bridges, 1998—, NSF Undergrad. Mentoring in Environ. Biology, 2000—. Mem. AAAS, Mycological Soc. of Am., Am. Soc. Microbiology, Med. Mycological Soc. of Am., Internat. Soc. for Human and Animal Mycology, CUR (councilor biology divsn.), Sigma Xi (pres. Towson chpt. 1996-97), Coun. on Undergrad. Rsch. (listserver adminstr.), Project Kaleidoscope F21. Episcopalian. Achievements include first description of the resting stage of anaerobic zoosporic fungi from rumen; first isolation of rumen zoosporic fungi from nature; description of a novel morphological development in rumen fungus; demonstration that hitherto fungi belonging to different species were the same. Home: 415 Confederacy Dr Penn Laird VA 22846-9625 Office: James Madison U Office Dean Coll Sci And Math Harrisonburg VA 22807-0001 E-mail: wubahda@jmu.edu.

WUBBELS, GENE GERALD, chemistry educator; b. Preston, Minn., Sept. 21, 1942; s. Victor and Genevieve M. (Sikkink) W.; m. Joyce Ruth Honebrink, Aug. 26, 1967; children: Kristen, Benjamin, John. BS, Hamline U., 1964; PhD, Northwestern U., 1968. Asst. prof. Grinnell Coll., Iowa, 1968-73; assoc. prof., 1973-79; prof. chemistry, 1979-92; Dack prof., 1986-92; provost, dean of coll., prof. chemistry Washington Coll., Chestertown, Md., 1992-95; sr. vice chancellor acad. affairs, 1995-97; prof. chemistry U. Nebr., Kearney, 1995—. Editor: Survey of Progress in Chemistry, vol. 10, 1983. Program dir. NSF, Washington, 1990-92; moderator United Ch. of Christ Congl., Grinnell, 1980-82, 83-84; bd. dirs. Edgerton Explorit Ctr., Aurora, Nebr., 1996—. Grantee NSF, 1971-95; recipient Sci. Faculty Prof. Devel. award NSF, 1981-82, Catalyst award for excellence in tchg. Chem. Mfrs. Assn., 1989. Fellow Iowa Acad. Sci.; mem. ACS (rsch. grantee 1970-86, mem. editl. adv. bd. Accounts Chme. Rsch. 1977-83, adv. bd. Petroleum Rsch. Fund 1986-89, pres. Chem. Coun. Undergrad. Rsch. 1986-87). Republican. Avocation: music. Office: U Nebr Kearney 905 W 25th St Kearney NE 68849-0002 E-mail: wubbelsg@unk.edu.

WUEBBELS, THERESA ELIZABETH, art educator; b. Breese, Ill., Nov. 8, 1950; d. Wilson Theodore and Selma Maria (Haake) W. BA, Notre Dame Coll., St. Louis, 1972; postgrad., Boston Coll., 1976-79, Pembroke State U., 1988. Teaching nun Sch. Sisters of Notre Dame, St. Louis, 1969-80; art tchr. Cathedral Sch., Belleville, Ill., 1972-76, Sacred Heart Sch., Fort Madison, Iowa, 1976-80; missionary sister Little Sisters of Jesus, 1980-87; visual art tchr. Balden County Schs., Clarkton, N.C., 1989—, magnet schs. grant coord., 1998—. Visual art tchrs. coord. Bladen County Schs., Elizabethtown, N.C., 1991—; bd. dirs. N.C. Alliance for Arts. Coord. Celebration of the Arts Festival for Bladen County, 1992—; task force mem. founding Clarkton Sch. Discovery, Clarkton, N.C., 1993-94. Named Tchr. of Yr. Clarkton Sch. of Discovery, 1992-93, 93-94, 94-95. Mem. N.C. Art Edn. Assn., Nat. Art Edn. Assn., Visual Art Guild. Roman Catholic. Avocations: fossils, shells, pottery, cats, nature. Home: 653 Poe Elkins Rd Clarkton NC 28433-7243 Office: Clarkton Sch Discovery PO Box 127 Clarkton NC 28433-0127

WUELLNER, KATHLEEN D. school counselor, former English educator; b. Indpls., Dec. 30, 1953; d. Russell E. and Mary Catherine (Fisk) Pritchard; m. Curtis C. Wuellner, June 26, 1976; children: Thomas N., Jason R. BA, Valparaiso U., 1975; MA, No. Ky. U., 1986; postgrad., Ind. U., 1976-77, Xavier U., 1996-99. Cert. tchr., Ky. Tchr. English/Latin MSD Wayne Twp. Schs., Indpls., 1975-78, Boone County Schs., Florence, Ky., 1978-79; tchr. English/journalism Kenton County Bd. Edn., Erlanger, Ky., 1988-99, guidance counselor, 1999—. Faculty rep. Dixie Hts. Site Based Coun., Ft. Mitchell, Ky., 1997-98. Mem. Dixie Hts. Athletic Boosters, Ft. Mitchell, 1993-2000. Named Champion of Learning, Kenton County Bd. Edn., 1995, 97-99; recipient Golden Apple Achiever award Ashland Oil, 1997. Mem. NEA, Ky. Edn. Assn., Ky. Counseling Assn. Am. Sch. Counselors Assn., Nat. Coun. Tchrs. English. Avocations: reading, golf, decorating, baseball.

WUENSCH, BERNHARDT JOHN, ceramic engineering educator; b. Paterson, NJ, Sept. 17, 1933; s. Bernhardt and Ruth Hannah (Slack) W.; m. Mary Jane Harriman, June 4, 1960; children: Stefan Raymond, Katrina Ruth. SB in Physics, MIT, 1955, SM in Physics, 1957, PhD in Crystallography, 1963; DEng (hon.), Hanyang U., Seoul, 2003. Rsch. fellow U. Bern, Switzerland, 1963-64; asst. prof. ceramics MIT, Cambridge, 1964-69, assoc. prof. ceramics, 1969-74, prof., 1974—, TDK chair materials sci. and engring., 1985-90, dir. Ctr. Materials Sci. and Engring., 1988-93, acting dept. head dept. materials sci. and engring., 1980. Vis. prof. Crystallographic Inst., U. Saarland, Fed. Republic Germany, 1973; physicist Max Planck Institut für Festkorperforschung, Stuttgart, Fed. Republic Germany, 1981; mem. U.S. nat. com. for crystallography NRC, NAS, 1980-82, 89-94; mem. N.E. regional com. for selection of Marshall Scholars, 1970-73, chmn., 1974-80. Co-editor: Modulated Structures, 1979, Neutron Scattering in Materials Science, 1995; adv. editor: Physics and Chemistry of Minerals, 1976—85; assoc. editor Can. Mineralogist, 1978—80; editor: Zeitschrift fuer Kristallographie, 1981—88, Jour. Ceramic Processing Rsch., 2000—. Ford Found. postdoctoral fellow, 1964-66. Fellow Am. Ceramic Soc. (Outstanding Educator award 1987), Mineral. Soc. Am.; mem. AAAS, Am. Crystallographic Assn., Mineral. Assn. Can., Materials Rsch. Soc. Episcopalian. Home: 190 Southfield Rd Concord MA 01742-3432 Office: MIT 77 Massachusetts Ave Rm 13-4037 Cambridge MA 02139-4307 E-mail: wuensch@mit.edu.

WUGHALTER, EMILY HOPE, physical education educator; b. Bklyn., Nov. 24, 1954; d. Milton and Leah (Isaacs) W. BA in Phys. Edn. and Teaching, CUNY, 1977; MS in Phys. Edn. and Motor Learning, Univ. Colo., 1978; EdD, U. Ga., 1981. Tchr. math. COMPASS House, N.Y.C.; tchr. phys. edn. St. Pius. High Sch., Bronx, Hebrew Acad. of West Queens, 1976-77; instr. Boulder City Parks and Recreation, 1977; grad. asst. Univ. Ga., 1978-81; assoc. prof. NYU, 1981-91; prof. San Jose Univ., 1991—. Measurement, design, and evaluation cons. N.Y. Alliance for the Pub. Schs.; phys. fitness evaluator N.Y.C. Affiliate Am. Heart Assn.; exercise science trainer Young Women's Christian Assn. Author: (with A.L. Rothstein) Basic Stuff Series I- Motor Learning, 1987; contbr. articles to profl. jours. Recipient Recognition award N.Y.C., 1989 and 1990, Mable Lee award, 1992; Curricular Change grantee N.Y.U., 1987, 91, Spencer Found. Young Scholars Rsch. award grantee, 1982-83, and numerous others. Mem. Am. Alliance of Health, Phys. Edn., Recreation, and Dance, Am. Coll. of Sports Medicine, Am. Edn. Rsch. Assn., Nat. Assn. for Phys. Edn. in Higher Edn., Nat. Women's Studies Assn., Western Soc. for Phys. Edn. Coll. Women, No. Am. Soc. for the Study of Psychol. of Sport and Phys. Activity, Calif. Assn. of Health, Phys. Edn. Recreation and Dance. Home: 358 Hihn St Felton CA 95018-9201 Address: San Jose Univ Dept of Human Performance 1 Washington Sq San Jose CA 95192-0001

WUKASCH, DORIS LUCILLE STORK, educator, counselor; b. Somerville, Tex., Dec. 30, 1924; d. Edwin William and Clara Rofine (Fuchs) Stork; B.A. with high honors, U. Tex., 1944, M.Ed., 1969; m. Joe Eugene Wukasch, July 7, 1945 (div. 1971); children— Linda Thiering, Susan Wukasch Richter, Jean Wukasch Mihalik, Jonathan. Chemist Tex. Dept. Health, Austin, 1944-45; microbiologist Terrell Labs., Ft. Worth, 1946-47; exec. sec. Wukasch Architects and Engrs., Austin, 1954-66; editorial asst. Steck-Vaughn Pubs., Austin, 1966; rehab. caseworker, job counselor Mary Lee Sch., Austin, 1969-70; spl. tchr. career edn. Austin Ind. Sch. 1970-85. Instr. ARC, 1972—; vol. tchr. Austin State Sch., 1958-68, Papua New Guinea, 1986. Area chmn. Am. Cancer Soc., 1970; mem. Women's Archtl. Guild, 1954-71, pres., 1964; mem. Women in the Arts, 1987—, Smithsonian Assn., 1972—, Wycliffe Assos., 1973—, Summer Inst. Linguistics, 1986, Wycliffe Bible Translators, 1986; active Stephen Minister. HEW grantee, 1968-69. Cert. rehab. counselor. Mem. Nat. Trust Historic Preservation, Austin Heritage Soc., Austin Poetry Soc., Kwill Klub, Tex. State Poetry Soc., Christian Bus. and Profl. Women's Council, AAUW, Phi Beta Kappa. Lutheran. Contbr. poems and articles to mags. and newspapers. Home: 12463 Los Indios Tr Austin TX 78729-7931

WULF, JANIE SCOTT MCILWAINE, gifted and talented education educator; b. Smithfield, Va., Mar. 30, 1934; d. Porter O'Brien and Claire (Bennett) Scott; m. Harro Biner Wulf, Sept. 22, 1962; children: Susan, Thomas, Katherine, Jane. BS, Longwood Coll., Farmville, Va., 1955; MEd in Guidance, George Mason U., Fairfax, Va., 1975; postgrad., U. Va. Cert. home econs., upper elem. tchr., guidance counselor, g/t cert., Va. Tchr. kindergarten Faith Luth. Day Sch., Arlington, Va.; tchr. home econs. Annandale H.S., Fairfax; tchr. sci. Chesterfield County Pub. Schs., Chester; tchr. English gifted and talented edn. Fairfax County Pub. Schs., Fairfax, also mid. sch. team leader, 1990-91; team leader, supervising tchr. Fairfax County Frost Sch., 1990-98; ret., 2000. Mem. Am. Fedn. Tchrs. English, Nat. Geneal. Soc., Va. Mid. Sch. Assn., Va. Assn. Tchrs., VA. Hist. Soc., Va. Geneal. Soc., Fairfax County Fedn. of Tchrs.,

WULF, WILLIAM ALLAN, computer information scientist, educator, federal agency administrator; b. Chgo., Ill., Dec. 8, 1939; s. Otto H. and Helen W. (Westermeier) Wulf; m. Anita K. Jones, July 1, 1977; children: Karin, Ellen. BS, U. Ill., 1961, MSEE, 1963; PhD in Computer Sci., U. Va., 1968. Prof. computer sci. Carnegie-Mellon Univ., Pitts., 1968—81; chmn., CEO Tartan Labs., Pitts., 1981—87; AT&T prof. computer sci. U. Va., Charlottesville, Va., 1988—; asst. dir. Nat. Sci. Found., Washington, 1988—90; pres. Nat. Acad. of Engring., Washington, 1996—. Bd. dir. Charles Strak Draper Labs., Cambridge, Mass., Nat. Action Coun. Minorities Engring., Inst. Women and Tech.. Biblioteque Alexandrina; cons. various computer mfr. Author: Fundamental Structures of Computer Science, 1981. Bd. dirs. Pitts. High Tech. Coun., 1982—88; trustee Charles Babbage Inst. Fellow: AAAS, IEEE, Assoc. Women in Sci., Assoc. Computing Machinery; mem.: Am. Acad. Arts and Sci., Nat. Acad. Engring. Avocations: woodworking, photography. Office: Nat Acad Engring 2101 Constitution Ave NW Washington DC 20418-0007

WULFF, DONALD HENRY, research center director, assistant dean; b. Billings, Mont., Aug. 5, 1944; s. Orville H. and Elsie B. (Evans) W.; children: Shaun S., Darci H. BS, Mont. State U., 1966; MA, U. Mont., 1975; PhD, U. Wash., 1985. Secondary instr. Roundup (Mont.) Sch. Dist. 55, 1965-71, Missoula (Mont.) County H.S., 1971-82; teaching asst. U. Wash., Seattle, 1982-83; from staff cons. to asst. dir. Ctr. for Instrnl. Devel. and Rsch./U. Wash., Seattle, 1983-92, assoc. dir., 1992-2000; interim dir., interim asst. dean U. Wash., Seattle, 2000—01. Co-author: Working Effectively with Graduate Student Assistants, 1996; co-editor: To Improve the Academy, vol. II, 1992, Preparing Teaching Assistants for Instructional Roles, 1992, Preparing the Professorate of Tomorrow to Teach, 1991; mem. editl. bd. Jour. Grad. Teaching Asst. Devel., 1993—. Named Outstanding Young Educator, Roundup, Mont., 1970, Missoula, 1979, one of Outstanding Educators Of Am., 1970; recipient Disting. Teaching award U. Wash. Alumni Assn., 1984. Mem. Profl. and Orgnl. Devel. Network in Higher Edn. (bd. dirs. 1989-95, exec. com. 1992-95, pres. 1993-94), Am. Assn. for Higher Edn., Speech Comm. Assn. (editl. bd. mem. 1991—), Western Speech Comm. Assn. (co-dir. basic course conf. 1984), Mont. Assn. Tchrs. English (sec.-treas., v.p. 1976-80). Avocations: sports, singing, playing piano. Office: U Wash Ctr Instrnl Devel Rsch Box 351725 396 Bagley Hall Seattle WA 98195-1725 E-mail: wulff@cidr.washignton.edu.

WULFF, VIRGINIA MCMILLAN, association executive; b. Glendale, Calif., May 27, 1958; d. Reginald Joseph and Virginia Ellen (Cavett) McMillan; m. Robert Reid Wulff, June 20, 1981; children: Kellyn Melissa, Katharine Cooper, Kyle Reid. BA in English with honors, Stanford U., 1980. Prodn. mgr. Addison Wesley/Benjamin Cummings Pub., Menlo Park, Calif., 1980-82; ways and means chair Oak Elem. PTA, Los Altos, Calif., 1988-89, pres., 1990-91, Los Altos/Mountain View PTA Coun., Los Altos, 1992-93; v.p. coms. Sixth Dist. PTA, San Jose, Calif., 1995-99, editor The Bell, 1995-99. Sec., mem. exec. bd. Peninsula Youth Theatre, Mountain View, Calif., 1994—; pres. San Juan Sensations Team, Los Altos, 1995—. Editor: The Bell, 1995-98. Oak chair Measure A Com., Los Altos, 1993, 95, 97; mem. parcel taxes bond measure coms. Los Altos Elem.; mem. Mountain View/Los Altos H.S. Dist. Bond Com., 1996, 97; lead parent rep. Castilleja Sch., 1998—; legislation chair Blach PTA, 1999—, Sixth Dist. PTA, San Jose, CA, 1995-98. Mem. AAUW. Home: 136 Waverly Pl Mountain View CA 94040-4573

WULKER, LAURENCE JOSEPH, portfolio manager, educator, financial planner; b. Cin., Apr. 6, 1945; s. Joseph Laurence and Dorothea Clare (Link) W. BS, Xavier U., Cin., 1967, MA, 1971; cert. fin. planner, Coll. Fin. Planner, 1985. Instr. Lloyd High Sch., Erlanger, Ky., 1967-68, Elder High Sch., Cin., 1968-73, Peoples High Sch., Cin., 1973-74, Regina High Sch., Cin. Tech. U., Cin., 1974-75; stockbroker Harrison-Bache, Cin., 1976-78; portfolio mgr., fin. planner, v.p. investments Paine Webber, Cin., 1978—, formed Wulker/Cummins Group, 1997; instr. U. Cin., 1981-98, Nat. Inst. Fin., South Plainfield, N.J., 1986-88; systems operator, Fin. Planning Forum Tristate Online, Cin., 1991—93. Speaker at numerous seminars 1984—; systems operator Investor Forum, Compuserve, 1985-86. Author column Japanese-Am. League Newsletter, 1985-96; contbr. articles to Cin. Enquirer, Cin. Post, Cin. Bus. Courier. Bd. dirs., v.p., pres. No. Ky. Symphony, 1993-99; treas. Friends of Findlay Market, Findlay Market Assn., 1999—; bd. dirs. Riverwinds Condo Assn., Behringer- Crawford Mus., 2003—. Fulbright scholar Dept. Health, Edn. and Welfare, 1972; named one of best 200 Stockbrokers, Country-Money mag., 1987. Mem. Fulbright Soc., Order Ky. Cols. Roman Catholic. Avocations: computers, tennis, golf, volleyball, reading. Home: Riverwinds Condos 558 Davenport Ave No 11 Cincinnati OH 45204-1362 Fax: 513-369-4020. E-mail: laurence.wulker@ubs.com.

WUNDER, HAROLDENE FOWLER, taxation educator; b. Greenville, S.C., Nov. 16, 1944; d. Harold Eugene Fowler and Sarah Ann (Chaffin) Crooks. BS, U. Md., 1971; M Acctg., U. S.C., 1975, PhD, 1978. Vis. asst. prof. U. S.C., Columbia, 1977-78; asst. prof. U. Pa., Phila., 1978-81; vis. asst. prof. U. N.C., Chapel Hill, 1981-82; asst. prof. U. Mass., Boston, 1982-86; vis. assoc. prof. Suffolk U., Boston, 1986-87; assoc. prof. U. Toledo, 1987—93; prof. Calif. State U., Sacramento, 1993—. Contbr. articles to profl. and acad. jours. Fellow George Olson fellowship, 1975. Mem.: AICPA, Nat. Tax Assn., Am. Taxation Assn., Am. Acctg. Assn., Calif. Soc. CPAs, Beta Gamma Sigma. Avocation: reading. Office: Calif State U Sch Bus Adminstrn Sacramento CA 95819-6088 E-mail: wunderh@csus.edu.

WUNDERLICH, BERNHARD, physical chemistry educator; b. Brandenburg, Germany, May 28, 1931; came to U.S., 1954, naturalized, 1960; s. Richard O. and Johanne (Wohlgefahrt) W.; m. Adelheid Felix, Dec. 28, 1953; children: Caryn Cornelia, Brent Bernhard. Student, Humboldt U., Berlin, Germany, 1949-53, Goethe U., Frankfurt, Germany, 1953-54, Hastings Coll., 1954-55; PhD, Northwestern U., 1957. Instr. chemistry Northwestern U., Evanston, Ill., 1957-58, Cornell U., Ithaca, N.Y., 1958-60, asst. prof., 1960-63; assoc. prof. phys. chemistry Rensselaer Poly. Inst., Troy, N.Y., 1963-65, prof. phys. chemistry, 1965-88, prof. emeritus, 1988—; prof. chemistry U. Tenn., Knoxville, 1988-2001, prof. emeritus, 2001—; Disting. scientist div. chemistry Oak Ridge Nat. Lab., 1988-2001. Cons. E.I. duPont de Nemours Co., 1963-88; dir. Lab. for Advanced Thermal Analysis; rsch. in solid state of linear high polymers and thermal analysis, 1980-2001. Author: Macromolecular Physics, Vol. 1, 1973, Vol. 2, 1976, Vol. 3, 1980, Thermal Analysis, 1990; author computer and audio courses on Crystals of Linear Macromolecules, and Thermal Analysis of Materials; contbr. over 500 articles to profl. jours.; mem. editl. bd. Chemistry, 1965-68, Makromolekulare Chemie, 1966-96, Jour. Thermal Analysis and Calorimetry, 1963-2001; mem. adv. bd. Jour. Polymer Sci., 1963-2001, Macromolecules, 1984-88, Polymers for Advanced Tech., Macromolecular Sci., 1988-2001, Phys. and Thermochim. Acta, 1996-2001. Recipient Humboldt award, 1987-88, award for applied chem. thermodynamics Swiss Soc. for Thermal Analysis and Calorimetry, 1993, TA Instruments award Internat. Conf. Thermal Analysis and Calorimetry, 1996. Fellow Am. Phys. Soc., N.Am., Thermal Analysis Soc. (Mettler award in thermal analysis 1971, Disting. Svc. award 2002); mem. Am. Chem. Soc. Home: 200 Baltusrol Dr Knoxville TN 37922-3707

WURSTER, DALE ERIC, pharmacy educator; b. Madison, Wis., Jan. 19, 1951; s. Dale Erwin and June M. (Peterson) W.; m. Pamela Ann Marvin, May 31, 1975; children: Elizabeth Ann, Kristin Gail, Dale Edward. BS in Chemistry, U. Wis., 1974; PhD in Phys. Pharmacy, Purdue U., 1979. Asst. prof. Sch. Pharmacy U. N.C., Chapel Hill, NC, 1979—82; asst. to assoc. prof. Coll. Pharmacy U. Iowa, Iowa City, 1982—95, prof. Coll. Pharmacy, 1996—, divsn. head pharmaceutics, 2000—01, assoc. dean Grad. Coll., 2002—. Cons. Nat. Assn. Bds. of Pharmacy, Park Ridge, Ill., 1982—; apptd. to U.S. Pharmacopeial Conv. Com. of Revision, 1995—; cons. in field. Contbr. articles to profl. jours. Fed. and indsl. grantee. Fellow Am. Assn. Pharm. Scientists; mem. Am. Chem. Soc., Am. Assn. Colls. Pharmacy, Materials Rsch. Soc., Sigma Xi. Achievements include research in tablet coatings for controlled release, surface phenomena, solution and differential scanning calorimetry, chemical kinetics; dissolution kinetics and testing, physics of tablet compression, analytical applications of Fourier transform infrared spectroscopy. Home: 3808 County Down Ln NE North Liberty IA 52317-9388 Office: Coll Pharmacy S215 Iowa City IA 52242 also: Grad Coll 205G Gilmore Hall Iowa City IA 52242 Address: Univ Iowa Grad Coll 205G Gilmore Hall Iowa City IA 52242 E-mail: dale-e-wurster@uiowa.edu.

WURSTER, DALE ERWIN, pharmacy educator, university dean emeritus; b. Sparta, Wis., Apr. 10, 1918; s. Edward Emil and Emma Sophia (Steingraeber) W.; m. June Margaret Peterson, June 16, 1944; children: Dale Eric, Susan Gay. BS, U. Wis., 1942, PhD, 1947. U. Wis. Sch. Pharmacy, Madison, 1958-71, mem. faculty, 1947-71; prof., dean N.D. State U. Coll. Pharmacy, 1971-72; prof. U. Iowa Coll. Pharmacy, Iowa City, 1972—, dean, 1972-84, dean emeritus, 1984—. George B. Kaufman Meml. lectr. Ohio State U., 1968; Hancher Finkbine Medallion prof. U. Iowa, 1984; Joseph V. Swintosky disting. lectr. U. Ky., 2000; cons. in field; phys. sci. adminstr. USN, 1960-63; sci. advisor U. Wis. Alumni Rsch. Found., 1968-72; mem. revision com. U.S. Pharmacopoeia, 1961-70; mem. pharmacy rev. com. USPHS, 1966-72; mem. tech. adv. com. contraceptive R&D program Ea. Va. Med. Sch., 1987-2002, rsch., U. Wis. Contbr. articles to profl. jours., chpts. to books; patentee in field. With USNR, 1944-46. Recipient Superior Achievement citation Navy Dept., 1964, merit citation U. Wis., 1976, Disting. Alumni award U. Wis. Sch. Pharmacy, 1984; Dale E. Wurster Chr. Pharm. Tech. at U. Iowa named in his honor. Fellow Am. Assn. Pharm. Scientists (founder, sponsor Dale E. Wurster rsch. award 1990—, Disting. Pharm. Scientist award 1991); mem. Am. Assn. Colls. Pharmacy (exec. com. 1964-66, chmn. conf. tchrs. 1960-61, vis. scientist 1963-70, Disting. Educator award 1983), Acad. Pharm. Scis. (exec. com. 1967-70, chmn. basic pharmaceutics sect. 1965-67, pres. 1975, Indsl. Pharm. Tech. award 1980), Am. Pharm. Assn. (chmn. sci. sect. 1964-65, rsch. achievement award 1965, Wis. Disting. Svc. award 1971), Iowa Pharmacists Assn. (Robert G. Gibbs award 1983), Wis. Acad. Scis., Arts and Letters, Soc. Investigative Dermatology, Rumanian Soc. Med. Sci. (hon.), Am. Found. Pharm. Edn. (bd. grants 1987-92), Sigma Xi, Kappa Psi (past officer), Rho Chi, Phi Lambda Upsilon, Phi Sigma. Home: 16 Brickwood Cir NE Iowa City IA 52240-9129

WURTMAN, RICHARD JAY, physician, educator, inventor; b. Phila., Mar. 9, 1938; s. Samuel Richard and Hilda (Schreiber) W.; m. Judith Joy Hirschhorn, Nov. 15, 1959; children: Rachael Elisabeth, David Franklin. AB, U. Pa., 1956; MD, Harvard U., 1960. Intern Mass. Gen. Hosp., 1960-61, resident, 1961-62, fellow medicine, 1965-66, clin. assoc. in medicine, 1985—; research assoc., med. research officer NIMH, 1962-67; mem. faculty MIT, Cambridge, 1967—, prof. endocrinology and metabolism, 1970-80, prof. neuroendocrine regulation, 1980-94, Cecil H. Green disting. prof., 1994—; dir. Clin. Rsch. Ctr., MIT, Cambridge, 1985—; prof. neuroscience MIT, 1984-94. Lectr. medicine Harvard Med. Sch., 1969—; prof. Harvard-MIT Divsn. Health Scis. and Tech., 1978—; Smithies lectr. Oxford U., 2002; sci. dir. Ctr. for Brain Scis. and Metabolism Charitable Trust, 1981—; invited prof. U. Geneva, 1981; Sterling vis. prof. Boston U., 1981; vis. fellow Balliol Coll., Oxford U., 1997; mem. small grants study sect. NIMH, 1967-69, preclin. psychopharmacology study sect., 1971-75; behavioral biology adv. panel NASA, 1969-72; coun. basic sci. Am. Heart Assn., 1969-74; rsch. adv. bd. Parkinson's Disease Found., 1972-80, Am. Parkinson's Disease Assn., 1978—; com. phototherapy in newborns NRC-Nat. Acad. Scis., 1972-74, com. nutrition, brain devel. and behavior, 1976, mem. space applications bd., 1976-82; mem. task force on drug devel. Muscular Dystrophy Assn., 1980-87; chmn. life scis. adv. com. NASA, 1979-82; chmn. adv. bd. Alzheimer's Disease Assn., 1981-84; assoc. neurosci. rsch. program MIT, 1974-82; chmn. life scis. adv. bd. USAF, 1985—; Bennett lectr. Am. Neurol. Assn., 1974; Flexner lectr. U. Pa., 1975; founder, chmn. sci. adv. bd. Interneuron Pharms., Inc., 1989-99; co-founder Wurtco, 1999, Back Bay Sci., 1999. Author: Catecholamines, 1966; (with others) The Pineal, 1968; editor: (with Judith Wurtman) Nutrition and the Brain, Vols. I and II, 1977, Vols. III, IV, V., 1979, Vol. VI, 1983, Vol. VII, 1986, Vol. VIII, 1990, also some 1000 other articles and books; mem. editl. bd. Endocrinology, 1967-73, Jour. Pharmacology and Exptl. Therapeutics, 1968-75, Jour. Neural Transmission, 1969-88, Neuroendocrinology, 1969-72, Metabolism, 1970-80, Circulation Research, 1972-77, Jour. Neurochemistry, 1973-82, Life Scis., 1973-81, Brain Rsch., 1977—. Mem. bd. overseers Boston Symphony Orch., 1997—; bd. dirs. Fenway Cmty. Health Ctr., Boston, 1998—, Provincetown Art Assn. and Mus., 2000—. Recipient Alvarenga prize and lectureship Phila. Coll. Physicians, 1970, CIBA-Geigy Drew award in Biomed. Rsch., 1982, Roger Williams award in Preventive Nutrition, 1987, NIMH Merit award, 1989—, Internat. Prize for Modern Nutrition, 1989, Hall of Fame Disting. Alumni award Ctrl. H.S. Phila., 1992; Disting. lectr. Purdue U., 1984; Rufus Cole lectr., Rockefeller U., 1985; Pfizer lectr. NYU Med. Sch., 1985; Grass Fedn. lectr. U. Ga., 1985, Alan Rothballer Meml. lectr., N.Y. Med. Coll., Valhalla, N.Y., 1989, Gretchen Kerr Green lectr in the neurosics., 1989; Wellcome Vis. Prof. Washington State U., Pullman, 1989; Julius Axelrod Disting. lectr. in neurosci., CUNY, 1990, Sigma Tau Found. lectr. on aging, Rome, 1990, Disting. lectr. in neurosci. La. State U., 1991, McEwen lectr. Queen's U., Ont., 1991; Plenary lectr. 3d Internat. Symposium on Microdialysis, 1993; Hans Lindner Meml. lectr. Weizmann Inst., 1993, Waldo E. Nelson Meml.

lectr. St. Christopher's Hosp., Phila., 1997, Sidney Kibrick M.D. lectr. Boston U. Med. Sch., 1998. Mem. Am. Soc. Clin. Investigation, Endocrine Soc. (Ernst Oppenheim award 1972), Am. Physiol. Soc., Am. Soc. Biol. Chemists, Am. Soc. Pharmacology and Exptl. Therapeutics (John Jacob Abel award 1968), Am. Soc. Neurochemistry, Soc. Neuroscis., Am. Soc. Clin. Nutrition, Am. Inst. Nutrition (Osborne & Mendel award 1982). Clubs: Harvard (Boston). Achievements include some 60 U.S. patents on new treatments for diseases and conditions; invention of melatonin for promoting sleep, of dexfenfluramine for treating obesity, of citicoline for treating stroke and of Prozac (Sarafem) for the treatment of premenstrual syndrome. Home: 300 Boylston St Boston MA 02116-3923 Office: Mass Inst Tech 45 Carleton St # E25-604 Cambridge MA 02142-1323 E-mail: dick@mit.edu.

WURTZ, BETTY LOU, retired educator; b. Dayton, Ohio, June 13, 1925; d. Herbert Eugene and Pauline Edith (Elwell) Cashner; m. Conrad R. Wurtz, Aug. 29, 1948; children: Patricia, Richard, Douglas, Gary, Stewart. BA, U. Iowa, 1949; MS in Tchg., Drake U., 1970. Reservation agt. Am. Airlines, Indpls., 1946-48; dir., tchr. Kinderhaus Day Care, Des Moines, 1970-72, Temple Shalom Nursery Sch., Auburn, Maine, 1973-85; supr. Maine State Foster Grandparents, Pownal, 1985-92; tutor Auburn Sch. Sys., 1992-94, ret., 1994. Chair Women's Internat. League for Peace and Freedom, Des Moines, 1968-70; workshop facilitator on conflict resolution Am. Friends Svc. Com., Portland, 1978-90; co-chair Maine Assn. for Edn. of Young Children, Portland, 1978-79, Educators for Social Responsibility, So. Maine, 1985-93; chair conflict resolution com. Peace Action Maine, Portland, 1992-94. Unitarian Universalist. Avocations: kayaking, camping, music, travel, drumming. Home: 19 Meguier Rd New Gloucester ME 04260-4403

WUTTKE, DIETER, philology and art history educator; b. Fuerstenwalde, Germany, Oct. 12, 1929; s. Walther Gustav Hugo and Charlotte (Weichert) W.; m. Helga Anna Geller, Nov 2, 1965; children: Carolin, Henrike. PhD, U. Tuebingen, Fed. Republic Germany, 1958; habilitation, U. Goettingen, Fed. Republic Germany, 1971. Tchr. Altes Gymnasium, Bremen, Fed. Republic Germany, 1957-62; postgrad. scholar, lectr. U. Bonn, Fed. Republic Germany, 1962-66; oberstudienrat i.h. U. Goettingen, 1966-71, prof., 1971-79, U. Bamberg, 1979—95, prof. emeritus, 1995—. Dir. Seminar fuer Deutsche Philologie U. Goettingen, 1972-79; holder of chair Deutsche Philologie des Mittelalters und der Fruehen Neuzeit U. Bamberg, 1979-95; vis. prof. U. Hamburg, 1975, 76. Author: Die Historia Herculis, 1964, Deutsche Germanistik und Renaissanceforschung, 1968, Von der Geschichtlichkeit der Literatur, 1984, Humanismus als integrative Kraft, 1985, Nuremberg: Focal Point of German Culture and History, 2nd edit., 1988, Sebastian-Brant-Bibliographie, 1990, Aby M. Warburgs Methode, 4th edit., 1991, Der Humanist Willibald Pirckheimer, 1994, Das Institut: Eine Einführung, 1995, Dazwischen: Kulturwissenschaft auf Warburgs Spuren, 1996, Aby M. Warburg-Bibliographie 1866-1995, 1998, Die Belle Époque und der Fragebogen, 1999, Para uma visão holística das ciências e das artes, 2002, Ueber den Zusammenhang der Wissenrchaflen und Kuenste, 2003; author, editor: Aby M. Warburg, 3d edit., 1992, Caritas Pirckheimer 1467-1532, 1982, Commedia dell'arte, 2d edit., 1983, E.R. Curtius und das Warburg Inst:, 1989, W. Pirckheimers Briefwechsel, Vol. III, 1989, Fastnachtspiele, 6th edit., 1998, E. Panofsky: Hercules am Scheidewege, 1997, E. Panofsky-Korrespondenz, vol. I (1910-1936), 2001, vol. II (1937-1949), 2003; editor: Probleme Alfgermanistischer Editionen, 1968, Das Verhältnis der Humanisten zum Buch, 1976, Gratia, 1977—, Probleme der Edition mittel- und neulateinischer Texte, 1978, Ethik im Humanismus, 1979, Saecula Spiritalia, 1979—, From Wolfram and Petrarch to Goethe and Grass: Festschrift L. Forster, 1982, Philologie als Kulturwissenschaft: Festschrift K. Stackmann, 1987, S. Brant: Das Narrenschiff, 1994, Festschrift: Poesis et Pictura, 1989, Artibus, 1994, Schimpf und Ernst, 1995. Named Knight of the Order of Merit, Fed. Republic of Germany, 2003. Fellow The Warburg Inst. U. London, Westfield Coll. U. London, Ctr. Advanced Study in Visual Arts Nat. Gallery (Washington), Volkswagenstiftung, Getty Ctr. History of Art and the Humanities, Prague Acad.; mem. Inst. Advanced Study in Princeton, N.J., Inst. Germanic Studies U. London (corr.). Lutheran. Home: Obere Seelgasse 8 D-96049 Bamberg Germany Office: Univ Bamberg D-96045 Bamberg Germany

WYATT, FOREST KENT, university president emeritus; b. Berea, Ky., May 27, 1934; s. Forest E. and Almeda (Hymer) W.; m. Janice Collins, Mar. 4, 1956; children: Tara Janice Wyatt Mounger, Elizabeth Pharr Wyatt Mitchell. BS in Edn., Delta State U., Cleveland, Miss., 1956; MEd, U. So. Miss., 1960; EdD, U. Miss., 1970; postgrad., Harvard Inst. Ednl. Mgmt., 1975. Instr., coach Univ. Mil. Sch., Mobile, Ala., 1956-60; tchr., adminstr. Bolivar County dist. schs., Cleveland, Miss., 1960-64; alumni sec. Delta State U., 1964-69, adminstrv. asst. to pres., dir. adminstrv. services, asso. prof. edn., 1969-75, pres., 1975-99, pres. emeritus, 1999—; dir. Union Planters Bank of Northwest Miss., 1995—. Dir. Grenada Bank. Contbr. articles to profl. jours. Past bd. dirs. United Givers Fund, Cleveland Beautification Commn.; past bd. dirs., past v.p. Miss. Com. for Humanities, Delta Area coun. Boy Scouts Am. Friends of State Libr. Commn.; past chmn. Indsl. Devel. Found.; past pres. Cleveland Crosstie Arts Coun.; past trustee So. Bapt. Theol. Sem.; past bd. dirs. Miss. Econ. Coun.; past pres. Gulf South Conf.; bd. dirs. Southeastern Regional Vision for Edn. With U.S. Army, 1957-58. Recipient Kossman award for Outstanding Community Svc. C. of C., 1987. Mem. Miss. Assn. Educators, Am. Coun. on Edn. (mem. com. on govtl. rels.), Am. Coun. on Tchrs. Edn., Miss. Assn. Sch. Adminstrs., Am. Assn. State Colls. and Univs. (bd. dirs., past chmn. athletic com., com. governance, com. profl. devel. task force on athletics), NCAA (coun., past chmn. student-athlete adv. com., pres's. commn., gender equity com., exec. dir. search com., past chmn. athletics cert. study com. divsn. II, chmn. divsn. II project team eligibility, amateurism project team), Miss. Assn. Colls. (past pres.), So. Assn. Colls. and Schs. (Commn. on Colls.), Inter-Alumni Coun., Cleve. C. of C. (past pres.), Cleve. Country Club (dir.), Lions, Phi Delta Kappa, Omicron Delta Kappa, Kappa Delta Pi. Address: Delta State U Cleveland MS 38733

WYATT, JOE BILLY, academic administrator; b. Tyler, Tex., July 21, 1935; s. Joe and Fay (Pinkerton) Wyatt; m. Faye Hocutt, July 21, 1956; children: Joseph, Sandra Faye. BA, U. Tex., 1956; MA, Tex. Christian U., 1960. Systems engr. Gen. Dynamics Corp., 1956—65; mgr. Digital Computer Lab., 1961—65; dir. computer ctr., assoc. prof. computer sci. U. Houston, 1965—72; dir. Office Info. Tech. Harvard U., 1972—76, sr. lectr. computer sci., 1972—82, v.p. adminstrn., 1976—82; chancellor Vanderbilt U., Nashville, 1982—2000, chancellor emeritus, 2000. Faculty Harvard U. Kennedy Sch., 1976—82; bd. dirs., chmn. com. on math/sci. Am. Coun. of Edn.; bd. dirs. El Paso Energy, Inc., Ingram Micro., Inc., Advanced Networking and Sys. Corp., Hercules Corp., Aerostructures Corp.; prin. Washington Adv. Group. Author (with others): Financial Planning Models for Colleges and Universities, 1979; editor-in-chief: Jour. Applied Mgmt. Sys., 1983; contbr. articles to profl. jours.; patentee in field. Trustee EDUCOM, Princeton, NJ, 1973—81, Harvard U. Press, 1976—83, pres., 1975—76, chmn. bd., 1976—79; trustee Leadership Nashville, 1983—93; active Coun. Competitiveness; bd. dirs. Nashville Inst. Arts, 1982—83, Ingram Industries, 1990—96; chmn. adv. com. IST, NSF, 1978—85; vice-chmn. bd. Mass. Tech. Devel. Corp., Boston, 1977—83; alumni bd. dirs. Harvard Bus. Sch., 1982—92; chmn. New Am. Schs., 2002—, Edn. Quality Inst., 2002—. Named Outstanding Tennessean, Gov. of Tenn., 1986; recipient award for exemplary leadership, CAUSE, 1982, Nat. Tree of Life award, Jewish Nat. Fund, 1988; fellow, Gallaudet Coll., 1981—83. Fellow: AAAS; mem.: IEEE, Bus. Higher Edn. Forum (exec. com. 1990—93), So. U. Rsch. Assn., Inc. (chmn. coun. pres. 1988—89), U. Rsch. Assn. (bd. trustees 1988—, chmn. 1997—), Assn. Computing Machinery (pres. Dallas and Ft. Worth chpt. 1963—65), Am. Coun. Edn. (chmn. adv. com. on tech. edn. 1980—81, bd. dirs. 1990—92), Nat. Assn. Ind. Colls. and Univs. (policy bd. 1980—82), Hosp. Corp. Am. (bd. dirs. 1984—89), Assn. Am. Univs. (chmn. exec. com. 1990—91), Govt. Univ. Industry Rsch. Roundtable (chmn. 1998—), Nashville C. of C. (bd. dirs. 1983—86, pres. 1996—97), Experimental Aircraft Assn. (pres. adv. com., found. bd. 1997—), Aircraft Owners and Pilots Assn., Harvard Club, Beta Gamma Sigma, Sigma Xi, Phi Beta Kappa (hon.). Methodist. Office: Vanderbilt U 2525 West End Ave Ste 1430 Nashville TN 37203 E-mail: joe.b.wyatt@vanderbilt.edu.

WYATT, MARCIA JEAN, fine arts educator, administrative assistant; b. Petersburg, Va., Nov. 2, 1959; d. Andrew Ezekiel and Lillian (Bonner) Wyatt; m. Nicholas Charles Cooper-Lewter, Nov. 29, 1986 (div. 1998). BS in Elem. Edn., Va. State U., Ettrick, 1984; MEd in Spl. Edn., 1993; Degree in Adminstrv. Ednl. Leadership, St. Mary's U., Mpls., 2000. Lic. minister, 1987; ordained to clergy, 1990. Tchr. Marion (Ind.) Community Schs., 1985-86, Inglewood (Calif.) Unified Schs., 1986-87; office mgr. C.R.A.V.E. Christ Counseling, Tustin, Calif., 1986—; asst. minister New Garden of Gethsemane B.C., L.A., 1987-90; assoc. minister New Hope Bapt. Ch., St. Paul, 1990—; assoc. pastor New Garden of Gethsemane B.C., L.A., 1990—; assoc. minister New Hope Bapt. Ch., 1990—, pulpit coord., 2002; pres. C.R.A.V.E. Christ Singers, L.A., 1987-90; adminstr. asst. Eldorado Bank, Orange, Calif., 1988-90; tchr. fine arts Broadway Cmty. Sch., Mpls., 1996—, Mpls. Sch. Dist., 1990—; assessment coord. Broadway Cmty. Sch., Mpls., 1999—; with Wyatt Consulting, Shoreview, Minn., 1986—; 4th grade tchr. Hall Cmty. Sch., Mpls. Founder, dir. Diversity in Motion program for A.A. students, 1992—; stage dir. Babu's Magic with dancer Chuck Davis, 1994; cons. Everyday Learning Corp., 1996—; assessment coord., curriculum writer Mpls. Pub. Schs., 1999—; 4th/5th grade curriculum instrn. assessment team lead. Nominated to Pres.'s Commn. White House Fellowships, 1993; mem. C.R.A.V.E. Christ Ministries (Relax in Christ, Affirm with Christ, Visualize Christ, Experience Christ); pulpit coord. New Hope Bapt. Ch. Imagination grantee Star Tribune, 1994, 95-96, Fulbright grantee, Namibia, 1996, African studies grantee U. Wis., 1995-96, FASSE grantee U. Minn., 1996. Mem. NAFE, Alpha Kappa Alpha. Avocations: reading, music, fish breeding. E-mail: mwyatt@mpls.k12.mn.us.

WYCKOFF, ALEXANDER, stage designer, educator; b. Leonia, N.J., Aug. 17, 1898; s. James Talmage and Wilhelmina (Ludwig) W.; 1 child, Peter Talmage. Student, Columbia Coll., 1916-17, 19, Carnegie Inst. Tech., 1920. Designer, H. Robert Law Studios, N.Y.C., 1920-21, 24-25; instr., designer drama dept. Carnegie Inst. Tech., Pitts., 1921-24; dir. Memphis Little Theatre, 1927-30; art dir. U. Mich., Ann Arbor, 1932-41, 50; supr. design Phila. Mus. Sch., 1933-43; writer, illustrator, stage designer, Leonia, N.J., 1950-69, Tustin, Calif., 1971-88; art dir. pageant Rensselaer Poly. Inst., 1924, U.S. Govt., Yorktown, Va., 1931, Joint City/Producers Corp., Alexandria, Va., 1949; art dir. Cin. Art Theatre, 1925-26. Author: (with Edward Warwick and Henry Pitz) Early American Dress, 1964; editor: Arts of Design-Dunlap, 1965; author/illustrator: 19th Century Dress, 1966-81, 1600 World Dress, 1982-83, Sketchbook of Aboriginal Dress, Western Hemisphere, Post-Glacial to 1866 A.D., 1987. Pres., bd. dirs. Leonia players Guild, N.J., 1920-53, Leonia Pub. Library, 1962-69, Wyckoff House Found. (hon.); vol. advisor Performing Arts, Tustin High Sch., Calif., 1975-88. Served with U.S. Army, 1917-18. Mem. Nat. Theatre Conf. (founding, bd. dirs.). Address: 1308 Kempton Dr Libertyville IL 60048-5216

WYLIE, ANN GILBERT, geology educator; b. Tulsa, Mar. 31, 1944; d. Charles Churchill Gilbert and Dorothy Jean McIntyre Banks; m. John Voorhees Wylie, Dec. 16, 1971; children: John Voorhees Jr., Alice Belle, Eva Ann, Annabelle Gilbert. BA, Wellesley Coll., 1966; PhD, Columbia U., 1972. Asst. prof. U. Md., College Park, Md., 1972-79, assoc. prof., 1979-92, prof., 1992—, Disting. Scholar-Tchr., 1994, assoc. provost, 2000—01, asst. pres. chief of staff, 2001—. Contbr. articles to profl. jours. Fellow Geol. Soc. Am.; mem. Mineral Soc. Can., Soc. Econ. Geologists, Geol. Soc. Washington (Bradley prize 1989). Episcopalian. Office: Office of the Pres Univ Md College Park MD 20742-0001 E-mail: awylie@umd.edu.

WYLIE, JAMES MALCOLM, educator; b. NYC, Mar. 16, 1938; s. James M. and Nancy Beatrice (Worthy) Wylie. BS, Boston U., 1960. Columnist Mexico City Times, 1964; assoc. prof. The Cooper Union Coll., N.Y.C., 1986—. Author: The Lost Rebellion, 1971, The Homestead Grays, 1977, The Sign of Dawn, 1981; participant Spoleto Festival U.S.A., 2001. Office: 51 Astor Pl New York NY 10003-7132

WYMAN, VIOLA BOUSQUET, elementary educator; b. Woonsocket, R.I., Dec. 6, 1923; d. Philias and Lela (Ladouceur) Bousquet; m. James Vernon Wyman, June 24, 1950; children: J. Vernon, Douglas Philip, Carolyn Wyman Blumenkrantz. B of Edn, R.I. Coll., 1945. Elem. tchr. Mansfield (Mass.) Sch. Dept., 1945-46, Woonsocket (R.I.) Sch. Dept., 1946-50, Needham (Mass.) Sch. Dist., 1950-52, Swansea (Mass.) Sch. Dept., 1952-53, Cumberland (R.I.) Sch. Dept., 1961-90. Mem. R.I. Supreme Ct. Disciplinary Coun., Providence, 1996—2001; jud. evaluation com. R.I. Supreme Ct., Providence, 1997—99; chmn. of bd. R.I. Supreme Ct., Providence, 2001—. Mem. NEA, AAUW. Avocations: photography, tennis, reading.

WYMER, BARBARA SUE, elementary educator; b. Wood County, Ohio, Sept. 6, 1961; d. Robert Lee and Eileen Nettie (Snyder) Gore; m. Edward A. Wymer, Nov. 19, 1976; children: Graig, Larissa, Scott. BS in Edn., Bowling Green (Ohio) State U., 1981, postgrad., 1984—. Tchr. kindergarten North Baltimore (Ohio) Pub. Schs., 1982-84, tchr. 1st grade, 1984-88, 1998—. Penta sci. grantee. Mem. Kappa Delta Pi.

WYMORE, LUANN COURTNEY, education educator; b. Kansas City, Mo., Feb. 22, 1942; d. Clifford Willis and Lola (Moore) Courtney; m. George Philip Wymore, Dec. 27, 1964; children: Courtney, Kristin, Ryan. BA, William Jewell Coll., 1964; MA, U. Mo., Kansas City, 1969; PhD, Mo. U., 1989. Cert. elem., biology, Englisy tchr., Mo. Elem. tchr. Sch. Dist. North Kansas City, Mo., 1964-69; assoc. prof. elem. edn. Mo. Valley Coll., Marshall, 1989—. Presenter in field. Contbr. articles to profl. jours. Leader Girl Scouts U.S.A., Slater, Mo., 1980's, 4-H Club, Orearville, Mo., 1980's. Mem. ASCD, PEO, Internat. Reading Assn. Democrat. Avocations: reading, piano, organ, travel. Home: 820 Rich St Slater MO 65349-1258 Office: Mo Valley Coll 500 E College St Marshall MO 65340-3109

WYNDEWICKE, KIONNE ANNETTE (ANNETTE JOHNSON MOORER), reading educator; b. Preston, Miss. d. Clifton Thomas and Missouria (Jackson) Johnson; m. Eugene C. Moorer, Sept. 23, 1961 (div.). BS, Ill. State U., 1961; postgrad., Williams Coll., 1972, Columbia Coll., 1972; MEd, Nat. Coll. Edn., 1982. Social worker Cook County Dept. Pub. Aid, 1961; tchr. reading Chgo. Bd. Edn., 1961—; asst. to news dir. Sta. WCIU-TV, 1972-74; asst. women's editor Chgo. Defender, 1970-72; social sec. Dr. William R. Clarke, 1972—. Part-time photog. model, fashion commentator, pub. relations cons., pub. spkr. Contbr. articles to local newspapers. Co-chmn. installation Profl. Womens Aux., Provident Hosp., 1961, corr. sec., 1969, publicity chmn., 1969-72, 74-77. Selected as one of 13 persons in U.S. to attend Innovative Tchr. Tng. Seminar, funded by Henry Luce Found. at Williams Coll., 1972, Woman of the Day, WAIT Radio, 1978; one of 25 Black Women of Chgo. at receive Kizzy award, 1977; recipient Outstanding Cmty. Svc. award Beatrice Caffrey Youth Svc., Inc., 1978, 83, 85. Mem. Ill. Speech and Theatre Assn., Speech Comm. Assn. Am., Ret. Tchrs. Assn. Chgo., Internat. Platform Assn., Art Inst. Chgo., YWCA. Lutheran. Home: 2901 S King Dr Apt 1514 Chicago IL 60616-3314

WYNN, GAINES CLORE, artist, educator, museum consultant; b. Lamesa, Tex., Jan. 13, 1946; d. Hugh Ebert and Ruth Lee (Hodges) Gaines; m. Albert Russell Wynn, May 2001; 1 child from previous marriage, Meredith Gaines Clore. BA in Fine Arts, Tex. Tech U., 1968; MFA, Ariz. State U., 1971, postgrad., 1972. Cert. in secondary edn., Md., D.C. Created art dept. for Urban League Sch. Washington Urban League, 1973-75; chair dept. art Calvert H.S., Prince Frederick, Md., 1975-80; owner, gallery dir. Ocean Hand Art Gallery, Ocean City, Md., 1980-82; freelance graphic designer Laurel, Md., 1982-85; h.s. programs coord. Nat. Mus. Women in the Arts, Washington, 1986-90, mus. programs cons., 1990—; chair dept. fine arts Forestville (Md.) H.S., 1990—, Flowers H.S., 2000—. Curator Expanding Visions Exhbn. WCA honorees at Nat. Mus. Women in the Arts, 1991, Corinne Mitchell: A Glimpse of Joy Exhbn. at Nat. Mus. Women in the Arts, 1992, Pulse Point exhbn. Harvard Coll., 1996; writer exhbn. catalogue Norm Parish Catalogue-Norm Parish Gallery Georgetown, Wash., 1996; curator, writer exhbn. catalog Violence Against Women: Breaking the Silence, at Greenbelt Arts Ctr., 2002; owner Gaines Clore Wynn Studio, Greenbelt Arts Ctr., 2001—; artist, art cons.; cons. to nat. adv. bd. Nat. Mus. Women in the Arts; art cons. 21st Century Learning Ctrs., Suitland, Md.; curator Seven Artists St. Marrten. Author: Gumba Ya Ya--Anthology of African American Women Artists, 1994 (exhbn. catalog), Corinne Mitchel : A Glimpse of Joy, 1992: exhibited paintings in shows at West Beth Gallery, N.Y.C., 1990, 92, Rahr-West Art Mus., Manitowoc, Wis., 1990, Appleton (Wis.) Gallery of Art, 1991, Charles Allis Art Mus., Milw., 1991, Susan Conway Gallery, Washington, 1992, Bowie (Md.) State U., 1993, Soho 20 Gallery, 1996, 97; creator, prodr. Role Model Series Nat. Mus. Women in the Arts, 1988. Founder Art Honor Soc. (now Nat. Art Honor Soc.), 1975; bd. dirs. Art for the People, 2003—; appointed mem. Md. State Arts Coun., 2002—, grants com., 2003. Mem.: DAR, Nat. Art Edn. Assn. (Presdl. award 1995), Dem. Spouse Orgn., Congl. Black Caucus Spouse Orgn., Women's Caucus for Art (membership chair 1990—, nat. bd. dirs.). Democrat. Episcopalian. Avocation: gardening.

WYNN, SHERRI LORRAINE, educational administrator; b. Indpls., July 9, 1953; d. Clay M. and Norma L. (Price) Mace; m. James Stephen Wynn, Aug. 19, 1972; children: Shea, Shawn, Shannon. BS in Edn., Ind. U., Indpls., 1975, MS in Spl. Edn., 1988; EdS in Sch. Adminstrn., Ind. U., Bloomington, 1994, EdD in Sch. Adminstrn., 1997. Cert. tchr., adminstr., Ind. Tchr. MSD Warren Twp., Indpls., 1973-78; tchr. spl. edn. Blue River Spl. Edn. Coop., Shelbyville, Ind., 1986-88; tchr. Indpls. Pub. Schs., 1988-93, dir. spl. project, 1991-93; dist. site coord. modern red schoolhouse project Hudson Inst., 1993—; coord. Modern Red Schoolhouse edn. reform project Beech Grove (Ind.) City Schs., 1993-96; prin. MSD Warren Twp., Indpls., 1996—. Assoc. faculty Ind. U., Bloomington, 1992; mem. adv. bd. Organized Assn. Southside Indpls. Schs., 1992—; univ. liaison U. Indpls., 1992—, assoc. mem. faculty, 1993; presenter in field. Author: What Parent Think About Outcome-Based Education, 1997. Bd. dirs. New Palestine (Ind.) Community Libr., 1982-84, Indian Creek Christian Ch., Indpls., 1986—. Grantee Community Leaders Allied for Superior Schs., Ameritech Super Sch., 1991—, Ind. Dept. Edn. Mem. ASCD, Coun. Exceptional Children, Kappa Delta Pi, Phi Delta Kappa, Alpha Lambda Delta. Avocations: quilting, reading, counted cross-stitch, bread making. Home: 6718 Bloomfield Dr Indianapolis IN 46259-1234

WYNNE, TERRY LYNNE, career counselor, trainer, writer; b. Ridgeland, SC, Mar. 28, 1951; d. Herbert Ray and Carolyne (Taylor) W. BA, Ga. State U., 1972, MEd, 1974, EdS, 1977. Lic. profl. counselor, Ga.; nat. cert. counselor, career counselor; master career counselor, career devel. profl.; cert. practitioner Myers-Briggs Type Indicator. Asst. Ernest L. Robinson, PhD, Atlanta, 1976-77; various SunTrust Bank, Atlanta, 1971-75, 77-84; trainer, spkr., writer Atlanta, 1980-90; product info. specialist Unisys Corp., Atlanta, 1984-87; career counselor Emory U., Atlanta, 1987-96, 97—, Charter Behavioral Health Sys., Atlanta, 1995-97; owner, sole propr. Profl. Edge, Tucker, Ga., 1990—. Ice skating instr. Omni Internat. Ice Skating, 1980-82; career counselor, tng. cons. grad. sch. USDA, Atlanta, 1996-2002. Recipient 3d pl. Maupintour Travel Photography Contest, 1991, Sullivan award Furman U., 1969; Ednl. Opportunity grantee Furman U., 1968. Mem. ACA, MENSA, Nat. Career Devel. Assn., Lic. Profl. Counselors Ga. Assn., Ga. Career Devel. Assn. Avocations: ballroom dance, writing, ice skating, travel, photography. E-mail: tlwynne@bellsouth.net.

WYRICK, DANIEL JOHN, science/health textbook editor, science specialist; b. Oakland, Calif., May 22, 1952; s. Charles Truman and Thelma Lillian (White) W.; m. Christine Evelyn Ingels, Nov. 10, 1972; children: Aimee, Emilie. BA, Pacific Union Coll., 1977, MA, 1984. Cert. tchr., Calif. Tchr. Pine Hills Jr. Acad., Auburn, Calif., 1977-81; prin., tchr. Fort Bragg (Calif.) Seventh Day Adventist Elem. Sch., 1981-85; sci. tchr. Lodi (Calif.) Adventist Elem. Sch., 1985-89; sci./health textbook editor N.Am. Div. of Seventh Day Adventist, Silver Spring, Md., 1989-95; sci. specialist Lodi Adventist Elem. Sch., 1995—. Co-author: Life series sci./health textbooks, 1993—, Every Friday, 1987. Youth leader Fairmont Seventh Day Adventist Ch., Lodi, 1986-91, ch. elder, 1988; youth leader English Oaks Seventh Day Adventist Ch., Lodi, 1991-93, ch. elder, 1991—; mem. Lodi Acad. Sch. Bd., 1992-95. Mem. Nat. Sci. Tchrs. Assn., Calif. Sci. Tchrs. Assn., Calif. Assn. Pvt. Schs. Republican. Avocations: fishing, camping, photography, outdoor education. Office: Lodi Acad 1230 S Central Ave Lodi CA 95240-5999

WYRSCH, JAMES ROBERT, lawyer, educator, writer; b. Springfield, Mo., Feb. 23, 1942; s. Louis Joseph and Jane Elizabeth (Welsh) W.; m. B. Darlene Wyrsch, Oct. 18, 1975; children: Scott, Keith, Mark, Brian, Marcia. BA, U. Notre Dame, 1963; JD, Georgetown U., 1966; LLM, U. Mo., Kansas City, 1972. Bar: Mo. 1966, U.S. Ct. Appeals (8th cir.) 1971, U.S. Ct. Appeals (10th cir.) 1974, U.S. Ct. Appeals (5th cir.) 1974, U.S. Ct. Appeals (6th cir.) 1982, U.S. Ct. Appeals (11th cir.) 1984, U.S. Ct. Appeals (7th cir.) 1986, U.S. Ct. Appeals (4th cir.) 1990, U.S. Ct. Appeals (9th cir.) 1998, U.S. Ct. Mil. Appeals 1978, U.S. Tax Ct. 1983, U.S. Supreme Ct. 1972. Assoc. Wyrsch, Hobbs & Mirakian P.C., Kansas City, 1970-71, of counsel, 1972-77, ptnr., 1978—, pres., shareholder, 1988—; adj. prof. U. Mo., 1981—. Mem. Mo. Supreme Ct. Proceducres Com., 1983—; mem. adv. coun. legal assts. program U. Mo. at Kansas City, 1985-88; mem. cir. ct. adv. com. Jackson County, Mo., 1998—; mem. jud. selection com. U.S. Magistrate we. dist., Mo., 1985; mem. fed. practice subcom. we. dist. U.S. Dist. Ct., Mo., 1985-88; mem. subcom. to draft model criminal instrns.for dist. cts. of 8th cir., 1986—; bd. dirs. Kansas City Bar Found.; Mo. membership co-chmn. U.S. Supreme Ct. Hist. Soc., 2002—. Co-author: Missouri Criminal Trial Practice, 1994; contbr. articles to profl. jours. Capt. U.S. Army, 1966—69. Recipient Joint Svcs. Commendation medal U.S. Army, 1969, U. Mo. Kansas City Svc. award Law Found., 1991-92, Lawyer of Yr. award Mo. Lawyers Weekly, 2001, Dean of Trial Bar award Kansas City Met. Bar Assn., 2002, Practitioner of the Yr. award U. Mo. Kans. City Law Sch. Alumni Assn., 2002; named Best of the Bar, Kansas City Bus. Jour., 2002. Fellow: Mo. Bar Found., Am. Coll. Trial Lawyers (access to justice com., Mo. State com. 2002—03), Am. Bar Found. (life); mem.: ATLA, ABA, Nat. Lawyers Assn. (chmn. criminal law com. 2003), Coll. Master Advs. and Barristers (sr. counsel), Mo. Assn. Criminal Def. Attys. (dir. 1978, sec. 1982), Nat. Assn. Criminal Def. Attys., Am. Bd. Trial Advs. (adv.), Kansas City Bar Assn. (chmn. anti-trust com. 1981, chmn. bus. tort, anti-trust, franchise com. 1998), Mo. Bar Assn. (vice chmn. criminal law com. 1978—79), Am. Arbitration Assn. (panel arbitrators 1976—2000), U.S. Supreme Ct. Hist. Soc., Country Club of Blue Springs, Kansas City Club, Phi Delta Phi. Democrat. Roman Catholic. Home: 1501 NE Sunny Creek Ln Blue Springs MO 64014-2044 Office: Wyrsch Hobbs & Mirakian PC 1101 Walnut St Fl 13 Kansas City MO 64106-2134

WYSCHOGROD, EDITH, philosophy educator; b. N.Y.C. d. Morris and Selma Shurer; m. Michael Wyschogrod, Mar. 6, 1955; children: Daniel, Tamar. AB, Hunter Coll., 1957; PhD, Columbia U., 1970. Prof. philosophy

Queens Coll., Flushing, N.Y., 1967-92; J. Newton Rayzor prof. philosophy and religious thought Rice U., Houston, 1992—2003, emerita, 2003—. Author: Emmanuel Levinas: The Problem of Ethical Metaphysics, 1974, 2d edit., 2000, Spirit in Ashes, 1985, Saints and Postmodernism, 1990, An Ethics of Remembering: History, Heterology and the Nameless Others; co-editor: Lacan and Theological Discourse, 1989, The Enigma of Gift and Sacrifice, 2002, The Ethical, 2003. Nat. Humanities Ctr. fellow, 1981, Woodrow Wilson Ctr. fellow, 1987-88, Guggenheim fellow, 1995-96. Fellow Am. Acad. Arts and Scis.; mem. Am. Acad. Religion (pres. 1992-93). Home: 211 W 92d St # 62 New York NY 10025 E-mail: stedith@rice.edu.

WYSZYNSKI, RICHARD CHESTER, musician, writer, conductor, educator; b. Chgo., Feb. 15, 1933; s. Ignatius John and Victoria (Gerlich) W. MusB, B of Music Edn., Northwestern U., 1955; cert. in music criticism, U. So. Calif., 1967; studies with Marcel Moyse, Brattleboro, Vt., 1961-65. Instr. flute DeLaSalle Inst., Chgo., 1952-56; chmn. music dept. Adult Edn. Ctrs., Chgo., 1957-60; prin. flutist N.C. Symphony Orch., Chapel Hill, 1960, Shreveport (La.) Symphony Orch., 1960-61, Camelot Nat. Touring Co., N.Y.C., 1964; asst. condr., flutist Man of La Mancha Nat. Touring Co., N.Y.C., 1967-70; dir., solo flutist Cardinal Woodwind Quintet, Chgo., 1970—; condr. Cardinal Chamber Orch., Chgo., 1972—; prin. flutist Jesus Christ Superstar Nat. Tour, N.Y.C., 1977; instr. Monnacep-Oakton Community Coll., Des Plaines, Ill., 1977—; co-prin. flutist Chgo. Symphonic Wind Ensemble, 1978—. Instr. music Exptl. Coll. U. So. Calif., Los Angeles, 1972, Cen. YMCA Community Coll., Chgo., 1976, Norris Ctr., Northwestern U., Evanston, Ill., 1979-81, Loyola Continuing Edn., Chgo., 1980-84; condr. Lincolnwood (Ill.) Community Mus. Theatre, 1976, Stuart Ctr., De Paul U., Chgo., 1978-80; lectr. music Newberry Library, Chgo., 1979, Chgo. Office Fine Arts, 1985-86; dir. Singleforum, Chgo., 1986—. Editor, pub. Interplay mag., 1951-54; music critic Old Town Voice, 1962-65; scriptwriter documentary films for Atwood Films, 1964-65 (N.Y. Film Festival, Cine award); producer, announcer Sta. WHPK-FM, 1973-76; featured in 1995 Reading series, by Chgo. Writers in the Emerging Artists Project, A. Montgomery Ward Found., Chgo. Dept. Cultural Affairs and Ill. Arts Coun.; dir. demonstration Cardinal Chamber Ensemble. Rockefeller Found. fellow, 1965-67, Chgo. Office Fine Arts grantee, 1985-86. Mem. Am. Fedn. Musicians. Clubs: Classical Music Rap Sessions for Singles (dir. 1984—) (Chgo.). Roman Catholic. Home and Office: 851 N Leavitt St Chicago IL 60622-7116

WYVILL, J. CRAIG, research engineer, program director; b. Washington, May 8, 1951; s. Andrew J. and Rach. C. Wyvill; m. Peggy T. Wyvill. BSME, Ga. Tech, 1973; MBA, Ga. State U., 1981. Registered profl. engr., Ga., Va. Energy sys. engr. Union Carbide Corp., Charleston, W.Va., 1973-75; project officer EPA, Washington, 1975-79; rsch. engr. Ga. Tech Rsch. Inst., Atlanta, 1979—, dir. agrl. tech. rsch. program, 1982—, dir. office food industry programs, 1994-99, chief food processing divsn., 1999—. Mem. ASME, Soc. Mfg. Engrs. (chpt. chmn. 1990, 93-94), Inst. Food Technologists, Ga. Agribus Coun. Office: Ga Tech Rsch Inst Ipst Engring Ctr Atlanta GA 30332-0823 E-mail: craig.wyvill@gtri.gatech.edu.

XIA, JIDING, chemical engineering educator; b. Jiangyin, Jiangsu, China, Mar. 23, 1921; s. Baogen Xia; m. Ming Yu, Oct. 1, 1958; children: Wei, Men. BS, Zhejiang U., Hangzhou, China, 1945, MS, 1948. Assoc. prof. Haijiang U., Fujian, China, 1949-50, Nanjing (China) Normal U., 1953-54; dir. teaching and rsch. divsn. Southeast U. (China), 1954-58; assoc. prof. and dir. teaching/rsch. divsn. Wuxi (China) U. Light Industry, 1958-85; prof. chem. engring. Wuxi U. of Light Industry, 1985-92; rsch. chemist U. Wis., Madison, 1995-96. Vis. prof. Wayne State U., Detroit, 1993-95; mem. expert group synthetic detergents and fatty acids, Ministry of Light Industry China, 1979-86; vis. prof. The VI Univ. of Paris, 1986;, evaluation com. acad. degree Authorized U., 1980-84, Jiangsu Light Industry Sr. Engrs., 1982-92; project evaluator China Nat. Natural Sci. Found. Surface Chemistry, 1985—; cons. Chemithon Co., Seattle, 1990-93, Aging Toilet Soap Factory, China, 1991—, Tianjin Rsch. Inst. Interface and Colloid Scis., 1993, Stepan Co., Chgo., 1994, Proctor & Gamble Co., Cin., 1994-95, Vista Chem. Co., Houston, 1994—;mem. adv. com. Internat. Symposium on Surfactants in Solution, 1993. Author: Synthetic Detergents, 1976, Chemistry and Technology of Surfactants and Detergents, 1997; author and editor: Protein-Based Surfactants, 2001, Gemini Surfactants-Synthesis Interface Behavior and Applications, 2003; editor: Composite Soaps, 1987; translator: Comprehensive Refining of Sunflower Seed Oil, 1956, Chemistry of Oil and Fats, 1958, Manufacture of Detergents, 1986; mem. editl. bd. Jour. Surfactant Industry, 1982-90, Jour. Petro-Finechemicals, 1982, Chinese Ency. LIght Industry, 1987-91; contbr. more than 120 articles to acad. jours. Recipient award Ministry of Petroleum Industry for EOR Project, 1992, Outstanding Contbn. to Chinese Higher Edn. award State Coun., 1992, Ministry of Light Industry for rsch. on composite soaps, 1983, Remarkable Achievement in Sci. and Tech. Invention and Innovation, UN, 1994; Excellent Advanced Sci. Rsch. fellow Wuxi, 1990, 93. Mem. China Assn. Surfactants and Detergent Industry (hon. dir. 1992, standing dir. 1983-92), Jiangsu Soc. of Daily Chem. Industry (chmn. 1978-85), Am. Chem. Soc. Home: 500 E Irving Ave Apt 620 Madison Heights MI 48071-1957 E-mail: xiajiding@aol.com.

XIAO, SHU-YUAN, medical educator; b. Wuhan, China, Feb. 1, 1963; s. Shihe Xiao and Yuxiang Lei; m. Fang Liu; children: Stephanie, Emily. MD, Hubei Med. U., Wuhan, 1987. Diplomate Am. Bd. Pathology. Mem. faculty Wuhan U. Med. Sch., 1987—88; J.E. Fogarty vis. fellow NIH, Bethesda, Md., 1988—90; NRC sr. assoc. US Army Med. Rsch. Inst. of Infectious Diseases, Frederick, Md., 1990—92; J.E. Fogarty vis. assoc. NIH, Bethesda, 1992—94; resident U. Chgo. Hosp., 1994—98, fellow in gastrointestinal and liver pathology, 1998—99; asst. prof. U. Tex. Med. Br., Galveston, 1999—2001, assoc. prof. pathology and internal medicine, 2002—. Contbr. articles to profl. jour. Mem.: U.S. and Can. Acad. of Pathology, Am. Soc. Virology, Am. Soc. Tropical Medicine and Hygiene, Am. Soc. Investigative Pathology. Office: U Tex Med Br 301 University Blvd Galveston TX 77555-0588

XIDIS, KATHLEEN O'CONNOR, history educator; b. Fort Wayne, Ind., May 17, 1939; d. John Arthur and Harriet Sloan (Stimmel) O'C.; m. Robert D. Xidis, Dec. 28, 1972; 1 child, Elizabeth Claire. BA, St. Mary's Coll., Notre Dame, Ind., 1961; MA, Ind. U., 1964, PhD, 1970. Secondary tchr. Bishop Noll H.S., Hammond, Ind., 1961-63; legis. asst. U.S. Ho. of Reps., Washington, 1965-66; faculty Johnson County C.C., Overland Park, Kans., 1970—. Reader for advanced placement tests in U.S. history Ednl. Testing Svc., Princeton, N.J., 1990, 91, 92, 95. Author: Hints and Help for History Students, 1994; co-author: Writing in History Class: A Guide for College Students, 1991. Mem. Am. Hist. Assn., Orgn. Am. Historians, Tomahawk Soc., Nat. Soc., Children of the Revolution (sr. pres. 1991—), Nat. Coun. for History Edn. (charter mem.), DAR (Quivira Crossing chpt.). Home: 10220 Long St Lenexa KS 66215-1826 Office: Johnson County CC 12345 College Blvd Overland Park KS 66210-1283

XIN, JACK, mathematician, educator; BS in Math., Peking U., 1985; MS in Math., NYU, 1988, PhD in Math., 1990. Postdoctoral fellow Math. Scis. Rsch. Inst., Berkeley, Calif., 1990—91, Inst. for Advanced Study, Princeton, NJ, 1991—92; asst. prof. math. U. Ariz., 1991—97, assoc. prof., 1997—99; prof. math. U. Tex., Austin, 1999—. Invited prof. Math. Inst. Stuttgart (Germany) U., 1998; invited prof. Multimedia Lab. Hokkaido (Japan) U., 2000; invited prof. Inst. de Henri Poincaré, Paris, 2002. Contbr. articles to profl. jours. Fellow, John Simon Guggenheim Meml. Found., 2003; grantee, NSF, 1993—96, 1996—99, Army Rsch. Office, 1999—2000, 2000—02, 2002—03, Info. Tech. Rsch., NSF, 2002—; NFR Rsch. fellow, Swedish Natural Sci. Rsch. Coun., Inst. Mittag-Leffler, Sweden, 1994. Office: Dept Math Univ Tex Austin Austin TX 78712*

YABLUN, RONN, secondary education educator, small business owner; b. Chgo., July 11, 1950; s. Sidney and Phyllis (Bender) Y.; m. Anna Yablun, Dec. 17, 1977 (div. Jan. 1987); children: Melissa, Alex, Mark, William, Brandon BS in Edn., No. Ill. U., 1972. Cert. tchr., Ill., Calif. Tchr. art Page Sch., Beverly Hills, Calif., 1977-78; tchr. math. Calif. Prep. Sch., Encino, 1978-80; dir. of instruction The Reading Game, Encino, 1980-83; tchr. math. and computers Northridge (Calif.) Jr. High Sch., 1983—, math. dept. chairperson, 1991-94; owner, dir. Mathamazement, Tarzana, Calif., 1983—. Leadership sponsor Northridge Jr. H.S., 1985-88, pentathlon coach, 1985-89, theatrical dir., 1989—, dean of students, 1995-96, gifted coord., 1997-98. Contbr. articles to jours.; author: How to Develop Your Child's Gifts and Talents in Math, Mathamazement. GTE fellow, 1989; grantee L.A. Unified Schs.; recipient Outstanding Classroom Tchr. award L.A. Unified Schs.. 1989. Mem. NEA, United Tchrs. L.A. (chpt. chmn. 1994-99), Calif. Tchrs. Assn., Phi Kappa Sigma (sec., social chmn.). Avocations: choreographer, director.

YACKEL, JAMES WILLIAM, mathematician, academic administrator; b. Sanborn, Minn., Mar. 6, 1936; s. Ewald W. and Marie E. (Heydlauff) Y.; m. Erna Beth Seecamp, Aug. 20, 1960; children: Jonathan, Juliet, Carolyn. BA, U. Minn., 1958, MA, 1960, PhD, 1964. Rsch. instr. dept. math. Dartmouth Coll., Hanover, N.H., 1964-66; asst. prof. dept. stats. Purdue U., West Lafayette, Ind., 1966-69, from assoc. prof. to prof., 1969-76, assoc. dean sci., 1976-87; vice chancellor acad. affairs Purdue U. Calumet, Hammond, Ind., 1987-90, chancellor, 1990-2001, chancellor emeritus, 2001—. Rsch. mathematician Inst. Def. Analysis, Washington, 1969. Author: Applicable Finite Mathematics, 1974; editor Statistical Decision Theory, 1971; contbr. articles to profl. jours. Fellow AAAS; mem. Am. Math. Soc., Math. Assn. Am., Inst. Math. Stats. Achievements include research on Ramsey's theorem and finite graphs. E-mail: yackelj@calumet.Purdue.edu.

YAKLIN, LORI STILLWAGON, government agency administrator; BBA, U. Mich.; M in Adminstrn., Ctrl. Mich. U. Founding exec. dir. Mich. Sch. Bd. Leaders Assn.; dir. Sch. Choice Office of the Under Sec. U.S. Dept. Edn., sr. advisor on family ednl. rights Office of Innovation and Improvement. Spkr. in field. Office: US Dept Edn FOB-6 Rm 7E306 400 Maryland Ave Washington DC 20202*

YALE, SEYMOUR HERSHEL, dental radiologist, educator, university dean, gerontologist; b. Chgo., Nov. 27, 1920; s. Henry and Dorothy (Kulwin) Y.; m. Muriel Jane Cohen, Nov. 6, 1943; children: Russell Steven, Patricia Ruth. BS, U. Ill., 1944, D.D.S., 1945, postgrad., 1947-48, Spertus Inst. Jewish Studies, 1995—. Pvt. practice of dentistry, 1945-54, 56—; asst. clin. dentistry U. Ill., 1948-49, instr. clin. dentistry, 1949-53, asst. prof. clin. dentistry, 1953-54, assoc. prof. dept. radiology Coll. Dentistry, 1956, prof., head dept. Coll. Dentistry, 1957-65, adminstrv. asst. to dean Coll. Dentistry, 1961-63, asst. dean Coll. Dentistry, 1963-64, acting dean Coll. Dentistry, 1964-65, dean, 1965-87, dean emeritus, 1987—, also mem. grad. faculty dept. radiology Coll. Medicine, prof. dentistry and health resources mgmt. Sch. Pub. Health, 1987—. Sr. dental dir. Dental Care Plus Mgmt. Corp., Chgo.; pres., dir. dental edn. Dental Care Plus Mgmt. Ednl. Svcs., Ltd.; health care facilities planner; dir. tng. Dental Technicians Sch., U.S. Naval Tng. Ctr., Bainbridge, md., 1954-56; mem. subcom. 16 Nat. Com. on Radiation Protection; mem. Radiation Protection Adv. Bd., State of Ill., 1971, City of Chgo. Health Sys. Agy.; founder Ctr. for Rsch. in Periodontal Disease and Oral Molecular Biology, 1977; organizer, chmn. Nat. Conf. on Hepatitis-B in Dentistry, 1982; organizer, dir. Univ. Taskforce Primary Health Care Project, U. Ill., Chgo.; chmn. U. Ill.-U. Stockholm-U. Gothenberg Conf. on Geriatrics, 1985; dir. planning AMVETS/UIC Tchg. Nursing Home Project, 1987-91; co-sponsor 1st Egyptian Dental Congress, 1984; adj. prof. Ctr. for Exercise Sci. and Cardiovasc. Rsch., Northeastern Ill. U., Chgo., 1991, Northwestern U. Sch. Dentistry Divsn. Behavioural Scis., Evanston, Ill., 1996—. Editor-in-chief Dental Care Plus Mgmt. Digest, 1995—. Bd. dirs., co-benefactor (with wife) World Heritage Mus., U. Ill., Urbana, 1985; mem. Hillel Bd., U. Ill.-Chgo.; life mem. (with wife) Bronze Circle of Coll. Liberal Arts, U. Ill., Urbana; mem. (with wife) Pres.' Council, U. Ill. Recipient centennial research award Chgo. Dental Soc., 1959; Distinguished Alumnus award U. Ill., 1973; Harry Sicher Meml. Lecture award Am. Coll. Stomologic Surgeons, 1983 Fellow Acad. Gen. Dentistry (hon.), Am. Coll. Dentists; mem. Ill. Dental Soc. (mem. com. on radiology), Chgo. Dental Soc., Internat. Assn. Dental Rsch., Am. Acad. Oral Roentgenology, Am. Dental Assn., Odontographic Soc. Chgo. (Award of Merit 1982), Council Dental Deans State Ill. (chmn.), N.Y. Acad. Scis., Gerontol. Soc. Am., Pierre Fauchard Acad. (Man of Yr. award Ill. sect. 1988), Am. Pub. Health Assn., Gerontol. Soc. Am., Omicron Kappa Upsilon, Sigma Xi, Alpha Omega (hon.) Achievements include established (with wife) collection of Coins of Ottoman Empire and Related Mohammedan States and supplemental antique map collection at World Heritage Mus., U of Ill.; established Muriel C. Yale Collection, antique maps of Holy Land collection at Spertus Inst. Jewish Studies. Home: 155 N Harbor Dr Chicago IL 60601-7364 Office: 30 N Michigan Ave Chicago IL 60602-3402 E-mail: ddssy@uic.edu.

YAMADA, TETSUJI, health economist, educator; M of Internat. Affairs, Columbia U., 1978; MPhil, CUNY, 1983, PhD in Econs., 1987. Instr. CUNY, NYC, 1982—86; postdoc. fellow Grad. Ctr. of CUNY, N.Y.C., 1987; asst. prof. dept. econs. Rutgers U., Camden, NJ, 1987—91; assoc. prof. Ritsumeikan U., Kyoto, 1991-92; rsch. fellow NBER, 1987-90, rsch. assoc., 1991-94; health economist Internat. Leadership Ctr. Longevity and Society, 1993-94; rsch. assoc. Ctr. Pacific Basin Fed. Res. Bank, San Francisco, 1990—; assoc. prof. Rutgers U., 1993—2003, prof., 2003—, chair dept. econs., 1996-99; exec. bd. China East Inst. Soc. Ins., China, 1998—. Rep. Japan Econ. Fedn., Ditchley, Oxford, England, 1994; vis. rsch. scholar Inst. Policy and Planning Scis., Tsukuba U., Japan, 1997—2002; temp. advisor WHO, 1999; faculty assoc. The Walter Rand Inst., 1999—; ctr. assoc. The Ctr. for Children and Childhood Studies, 2000—; cons. Japan Found., 2001; reviewer and referee profl. jours., books and rsch. grants. Contbr. articles to profl. jours. Fellow postdoctoral fellow, Grad. Ctr. CUNY, 1987; grantee Ministry of Edn., Japan, 1991, Iryo Kagaku Kenkyu Jo, Japan, 1991-92, 96-97, Pfizer Health Rsch. Found., 1992-93, 21st Century Cultural Rsch. Found., Japan, 1993, Ministry of Health and Welfare, Japan, 1993-94, Nomura Found., Japan, 1995-96, Iryo Keizai Kenkyu Kiko, Japan, 1997-98, Rutgers U. ORSP, 1992-, Ctr. for Children and Childhood Studies, 2000-2001, Ministry of Edn., Sci., Sports and Culture of Japan, 2002—; Rutgers U. Dialogues grantee, 2002—03. Mem. Am. Econ. Assn., So. Econs. Assn., Western Econ. Assn., Internat. Health Econ. Assn., Japan Econ. Sem., Omicron Delta Epsilon (award). Home: 300 East 40th St #4M New York NY 10016 Office: Dept Econs-CCAS Rutgers Univ State Univ NJ Camden NJ 08102 Fax: 212-297-0192. E-mail: ytetsuji@aol.com., tyamada@crab.rutgers.edu.

YAMAKAWA, ALLAN HITOSHI, academic administrator; b. San Francisco, Oct. 18, 1938; s. Victor Tadashi and Alice Tsugie (Sato) Y.; m. Nancy Ann Habel, Apr.17, 1977 (div. Mar 1987); children: Bryan Allan, David Scott. BS, Roosevelt U., 1962, MEd, 1970. Tech. svcs. dir. audio visual libr. Roosevelt U., Chgo., 1958-60; dean, exec. dir. Ency. Britannica Schs., Inc., Chgo., 1960-67; curriculum svcs. dir. Field Enterprises Newspaper Div., Chgo., 1967-70; edn. svcs. dir. Chgo. Tribune Co., 1970-76; tng. svcs. dir. Dialogue Systems Inc., N.Y.C., 1976-79; orgn. devel. dir. U. Ill., Chgo., 1979-99. Cons., trainer Can. Daily Newspaper Pub. Assn., Toronto, 1973-84, Am. Newspaper Pub. Found., Reston, Va., 1972-80, Gifted Students Found. Dallas, 1974-75; cons. Cedars Sinai Med. Ctr., Beverly Hills, Calif., 1983-98, W. K. Kellogg Found., 1987-2000; developer Nat. Leadership Program; faculty Internat. Ctr. for Health Leadership Devel., 1996-2000. Author: Handbooks of Teaching Methods, 1974, Communicate, 1975, Catalysts For Change, 1976, Evaluation of Senior Administrators, 1994; patentee experiential learning method. Instr. ARC, Chgo., 1954-85; bd. dirs. Edison Regional Gifted Ctr. Sch., Chgo., pres., 1989-93; dist. program chmn. Boy Scouts Am., 1985—. Recipient Founders award Boy Scouts Am., 1997. Mem. ASTD, ASCD, Soc. Programmed and Automated Learning, Toastmasters (pres. 1974-76), Order of Arrow. Avocations: photography, computer programming, electronics, pyrotechnics, film production. Office: 1524 W Pratt Blvd Unit G Chicago IL 60626-4297 E-mail: ahy26@hotmail.com.

YAMAMOTO, HIRO-AKI, toxicology and pharmacology educator; b. Shimonoseki, Japan, July 9, 1947; s. Hanzo and Haruko (Watanabe) Y.; m. Kyoko Kinoshita, Sept. 24, 1976; children: Takeomi, Mika. Grad. in pharmacy, Fukuoka (Japan) U., 1970; MS, Kyushu U., Fukuoka, 1972, PhD, 1975. Postgrad. researcher in pharmacology U. Calif., San Francisco, 1975-76, vis. scientist, 1979-80; vis. fellow NIH, Bethesda, Md., 1976-77; prof. Fukuyama (Japan) U., 1983-89; asst. prof. toxicology and pharmacology U. Tsukuba, Japan, 1977-83, assoc. prof., 1989—. Vis. prof. U. Mo., 1981-82. Author: Calcium and Biological Systems, 1985, Higienic Chemistry and Public Health, 1990; contbr. articles to sci. jours. Mem. Fukuyama Pollution Measures Com., 1984-89. Mem. N.Y. Acad. Scis., Am. Soc. Pharm. and Exptl. Therapeutics, Japan Soc. Toxicology (trustee). Avocations: tennis, baseball. Home: Otto Minami 1-chome 26 Tsuchiura 300-0845 Japan Office: U Tsukuba Inst Cmty Medicine 1-1-1 Tsukuba Tsukuba 305-8575 Japan E-mail: hiro_aki@d4.dion.ne.jp., hiroaki@md.tsukuba.ac.jp.

YAMAYEE, ZIA AHMAD, engineering educator, dean; b. Herat, Afghanistan, Feb. 2, 1948; came to U.S., 1974; s. Sayed and Merjan Ahmad. BSEE, Kabul (Afghanistan) U., 1972; MSEE, Purdue U., 1976, PhD, 1978. Registered profl. engr., Calif., Wash. Mem. faculty of engring. Kabul U., 1978; engr. Systems Control, Inc., Palo Alto, Calif., 1979-81; sr. engr. Pacific N.W. Utilities, Portland, Oreg., 1981-83; assoc. prof. elec. engring. Clarkson U., Potsdam, N.Y., 1983-85; assoc. prof. Gonzaga U., Spokane, 1985-87, dean Sch. Engring., 1988-96; prof., chair elec. engring. dept. U. New Orleans, 1987-88. Part-time rsch. engr. La. Power and Light Co., New Orleans, 1987-88; sr. cons. Engring. and Cons. Svcs., Spokane, 1989-96. Contbr. articles, reports to profl. jours. Bd. dirs. Wash. State Math., Engring. Sci. Achievement, Seattle, 1989-96; mem. Spokane Intercollegiate Rsch. and Tech. Inst. Adv. Coun., 1990-96. NSF grantee. Mem. Am. Soc. Engring. Edn., IEEE (sr.). Office: University of Portland 5000 N Willamette Blvd Portland OR 97203-5798 E-mail: yamayee@up.edu.

YAMAZAKI, MAKOTO, economics educator; b. Tokyo, Dec. 19, 1948; s. Motoi and Mutsuko (Yamamoto) Y.; m. Abigail Elizabeth Burford, Aug. 4, 1984. BA in Law, Keio U., Japan, 1971; BA in Econs. and Polit. Sci., Wittenberg U., 1972-74; MA in Internat. Rels., The Fletcher Sch. of Law and Diplomacy, 1976; PhD in Econs., Duke U., 1984. Instr. Wittenberg U., Springfield, Ohio, 1972-74, asst. to program dir., 1973-75; vis. lectr. Tufts U., Medford, Mass., 1976, teaching asst. 1977-79; teaching asst. Duke U., Durham, N.C., 1982; asst. prof. W.Va. State Coll., Institute, 1984-85; vis. asst. prof. Wittenberg U., Springfield, Ohio, 1985-87; asst. prof. Aguinas Coll., Grand Rapids, Mich., 1987—; prin. Grand Rapids Japanese Sch., 1990—; pres. Global Trade Cons., Grand Rapids, 1990-91; chmn. M&M Hilmont Internat., Inc., 1991—, Living Space Internat., Inc., 1997—; faculty advisor Internat. Honor Soc. in Econs., 1988—, Student in Free Enterprise, 2002; exec. com. U.S./Japan Grassroots Seminar, 1993—; chmn. bus. adv. coun. Nat. Rep. Congl. Com., 2002; bd. mem. U.S. Japan Econ. Bus. and Cultural Form, 2003-, Green Build Japan, 2003-; Advisor Assn. Internat. des Etudients en Scis. Economiques Commerciales in French acronym, Grand Rapids, 1990. Recipient Nat. Leadership award Nat. Rep. Congl. com., 2002, Disting. Tchr. award Aquinas Coll., 2002; named Businessman of Yr., Nat. Rep. Congl. Com., 2002; Wittenberg U. scholar, 1972; Grad. scholar Duke U., 1980; recipient rsch. grants Wittenberg U., 1986, Aquinas Coll., 1988. Mem. Am. Econ. Assn., Grand Rapids Home Builders Assn. (lifetime design com., 1999), Organic Trade Assn., U.S.A. Track and Field, Omicron Delta Epsilon. Congregationalist. Avocations: tennis, running, swimming, cooking, gardening. Home: 1131 Fernridge Ave SE Grand Rapids MI 49546-3818 Office: Aguinas Coll Econs Dept Grand Rapids MI 49506

YAMMARINO, FRANCIS JOSEPH, management educator, consultant; b. Buffalo, Dec. 25, 1954; s. Peter Anthony and Helen Ann (Giangrisostomi) Y.; m. Cathy Ann Apa, July 4, 1982; children: Kayla M., Anthony J. BS, SUNY-Buffalo, 1976, MBA, 1979, PhD, 1983. Services coordinator Buffalo Savs. Bank, 1972-76; research assoc., instr. SUNY-Buffalo, 1977-79, research fellow, 1979-81, project dir., 1980-81; asst. prof. mgmt. U. Ky., Lexington, 1982-85, SUNY-Binghamton, 1985-90, assoc. prof., 1990—95, prof. 1995-2003, disting. prof., 2003—, dir. Ctr. for Leadership Studies, 2000—; mgmt. cons. Fortune 500 cos., several orgs. and agys. Author: (with F. Dansereau and J.A. Alutto) Theory Testing in Organizational Behavior: The Varient Approach, 1984, Multiple Level Approaches to Leadership, 1998, Research in Multi-Level Issues, 2002, 6 others; sr. editor Leadership Quarterly; mem. editl. review bd. of 7 jours.; contbr. over 100 articles to profl. jours. Recipient 2 Corning Glass Rsch. and Innovation awards, numerous grants. Fellow Am. Psychol. Soc., Ctr. for Leadership Studies SUNY-Binghamton (rsch. grantee); mem. Am. Psychol. Assn., Soc. Indsl. and Organizational Psychology, Soc. for Human Resources Mgmt., N.Y. Acad. Scis., Acad. Mgmt., Internat. Assn. Applied Psychology, Beta Gamma Sigma. Democrat. Office: SUNY Binghamton Sch Mgmt PO Box 6000 Binghamton NY 13902-6000

YANCEY, ELEANOR GARRETT, retired crisis intervention clinician; b. Ga., Oct. 24, 1933; adopted d. Overton LaVerne Garrett; m. Robert Grady Yancey, Nov. 10, 1961 (div. Apr. 1968); children: Katherine La Verne, David Shawn. Student, High Mus. Art Inst., 1952-53, Ga. State U., 1953-55, 78; BA, La Grange Coll., 1957. Social worker, case worker Fulton County Dept. Family and Children's Svcs., Atlanta, 1957-61; asst. tchr. Atlanta (Ga.) Bd. Edn., 1973-85; mental health crisis intervention clinician Dekalb County Bd. Health, Decatur, 1985-95, acting dir. crisis intervention, 1988-90; ret., 1995. Performed summer stock with Rogers & Co., 1969-70; band booster pres. Henry Grady H.S., Atlanta, 1977-78, v.p. PTA, 1978-79; pres. PTA Morningside Elem. Sch., Atlanta, 1977; grand juror Dekalb County, Decatur, 1983; active Sesquicentennial Celebration of Ala. Statehood. Mem. Kappa Kappa Iota (Lambda chpt. state pres. 1987-88, Eta pres. local chpt. 1992-97, mem. chi chpt. 1999—). Democrat. Avocations: drawing, gardening, travel, music. Home: 3425 Regalwoods Dr Doraville GA 30340-4019

YANDELL, CATHY MARLEEN, foreign language educator; b. Anadarko, Okla., Dec. 27, 1949; d. Lloyd O. and Maurine (Dunn) Y.; m. Mark S. McNeil, Sept. 7, 1974; children: Elizabeth Yandell McNeil, Laura Yandell McNeil. Diplôme d'études, Inst. des Professeurs de Français à l'Etranger, Sorbonne, Paris, 1970; BA, U. N.Mex., 1971; MA, U. Calif., Berkeley, 1973, PhD, 1977. Teaching asst. U. Calif., Berkeley, 1971-75, acting instr., 1976-77; asst. prof. Carleton Coll., Northfield, Minn., 1977-83, assoc. prof., 1983-89, prof. French, 1989—. Chair commn. on the status of women Carleton Coll., Northfield, 1983-85, ednl. policy com., 1985-86, 96-97, romance langs. and lits., 1990-94, chair faculty affairs com., 2000-02, pres. of faculty, 1991-94, Bryn-Jones disting. tchg. prof. humanities, 1996-99, mentor to jr. faculty, 1996—, W.I. and Hulda F. Daniell prof. French lit. lang. and culture, 1999—; dir. Paris French Studies Program, 1998. Author: Carpe Corpus: Time and Gender in Early Modern France, 2000; co-author: Vagabondages: Initiation ã la litt. d'expression française, 1996; contbr. to Art & Argumentation: The Sixteenth Century Dialogue, 1993, French Texts/American Contexts: French Women Writers, 1994, Montaigne: A Collection of Essays, Vol. 4, Language and Meaning, 1995, Reflexivity in Women Writers of the Ancien Régime, 1998, High Anxiety,

2002, Ronsard, figure de la variété, 2002, Lectrices d'Ancien Régime, 2003; editor: Pontus de Tyard's Solitaire Second, ou prose de la musique, 1980; contbr. articles to profl. jours. Active exec. com., then mem. Amnesty Internat., Northfield, 1980—. Regents' Travelling fellow, U. Calif. at Berkeley, 1975—76, Faculty Devel. grantee, Carleton Coll., 1988, 1991, NEH Rsch. fellow., 1994—95, Mellon Faculty fellow, 2003. Mem. MLA (del. 1989-92, exec. com. French 16th century lit., 2001—, 16th century studies coun. 2001—). Democrat. Home: 514 5th St E Northfield MN 55057-2220 Office: Carleton College 1 N College St Northfield MN 55057-4044 E-mail: cyandell@carleton.edu.

YANDLE, ANNA COBB, gifted/talented education educator; b. Rock Hill, S.C., Dec. 12, 1961; d. James Neil Sr. and Susan E. (Louthian) Cobb; m. David Alan Yandle, Aug. 8, 1987. BA in Comm., Winthrop Coll., 1985, postgrad., 1985-91, U. S.C., 1985-91. Cert. elem. and drama tchr., S.C. Pers. Am. Energy Corp., Rock Hill, 1982-83; mgmt. and sales staff Stereo Village, Inc., Charlotte, N.C., 1983-86; elem. tchr. Kershaw (S.C.) Elem., 1986-87, Clover (S.C.) Sch. Dist., 1987-90, gifted/talented tchr., 1990—. Sch. rep. Supt. Adv. Coun., Clover, 1989-90, 92—; chair Kinard Elem. Sch. Improvement Coun., Clover, 1988-90. Author numerous poems; producer (video) Aliens, 1989, Expressions, 1992; contbr. articles to profl. jours. Founder, coord. Benny D. Pate Camp for Space, Sci. and Tech., Clover, 1992—; asst. tchr. Summer Voyages Starship Earth, Clover, 1990-91; founder, instr. CompuTerrific Comm. Computer Camp, Clover, 1991—; coach, asst. coach various youth sports leagues, Clover, 1981-88, 92; active PTO, 1986—, PTA, 1990—. Grantee Innovative Tchr. Clover LEAF Found., 1989-93, Target 2000 S.C. State Dept. Edn., 1989-90. Mem. NAFE, S.C. Sci. Tchrs. Assn. Avocations: multimedia computer production, outdoor sports, writing music, plays and educational material. Home: 56 Marina Rd Lake Wylie SC 29710-9219 Office: Clover School District #2 Bethel St Clover SC 29710

YANDLE, STEPHEN THOMAS, dean; b. Oakland, Calif., Mar. 7, 1947; s. Clyde Thomas and Jane Walker (Hess) Y.; m. Martha Anne Welch, June 26, 1971. BA, U. Va., 1969, JD, 1972. Bar: Va. 1972. Asst. dir. admissions U. Va. Law Sch., Charlottesville, 1972-76; from asst. to assoc. dean Northwestern U. Sch. Law, Chgo., 1976-85; assoc. dean Yale U. Law Sch., New Haven, 1985—2002; exec. dir. Housing Authority of New Haven, 2002—. Bd. dirs. The Access Group; lectr. in law Yale Law Sch., 2002—. Commr. New Haven Housing Authority, 1998-2002; trustee Nat. Assoc. for Law Placement Found. for Rsch. and Edn., 2000—. Capt. U.S. Army, 1972. Mem. Law Sch. Admission Coun. (programs, edn. and prelaw com. 1978-84), Assn. Am. Law Schs. (chmn. legal edn. and admissions sect. 1979, nominations com. 1987, chmn. adminstrn. of law schs. sect. 1991), Nat. Assn. for Law Placement (pres. 1984-85, co-chmn. Joint Nat. Assn. com. on placement 1986-88), New Haven Legal Assistance Assn. (bd. dirs., treas. 1992-98). Office: Yale Law Sch PO Box 208215 New Haven CT 06520-8215 E-mail: stephen.yandle@yale.edu.

YANG, BAIYIN, adult education educator; b. Changshu, Jiangsu, China, Mar. 17, 1962; came to U.S., 1992; s. Zongde Yang and Feng Ying Gu; m. Xiaoping Lu, Dec. 14, 1987; children: Zhuowei, Zhuoyu. BS, Nanjing U., 1982; M Continuing Edn., U. Saskatchewan, Can., 1992; PhD, U. Ga., 1996. Lectr. The Chinese Acad. Scis., Nanjing, 1982-87, coord. tng. and devel., 1987-90; computer lab. advisor U. Saskatchewan, Saskatoon, 1990-92; stat. cons. U. Ga., Athens, 1993-96; asst. prof. adult edn. Auburn (Ala.) U., 1996-98; prof. adult edn. and human resources devel. U. Idaho, 1998—. Rsch. asst. U. Ga., 1992-96, tchg. asst. summer 1992; rsch. asst. U. Saskatchewan, 1990-91. Contbr. articles to profl. jours. Mem. APA, Am. Ednl. Rsch. Assn., Am. Assn. Adult and Continuing Edn., Acad. Human Resource Devel., Kappa Delta Pi. Office: U Idaho 800 Park Blvd Ste 200 Boise ID 83712-7742

YANG, CHAO YUH, chemistry educator; b. Pingtung, Taiwan, May 8, 1939; came to U.S., 1982; s. Shang-Sheng and Kuei-Mei (Lee) Y.; m. Manlan Lou Yang; children: Tseming, Tseliang, Thomas. BS, Tamkang U., Taipei, Taiwan, 1962; MS, Georg-August U., Goettingen, Germany, 1970, PhD, 1973. Tchr. Chiatung Agr. High Sch., Pingtung, Taiwan, 1963-64; chemist Kuantu Glass Plant, Taipei, 1964-68; postdoctoral fellow dept. molecular biology Max-Planck Inst. for Exptl. Medicine, Goettingen, 1973-75, scientist dept. immunochemistry, 1975-82; asst. prof. biochemistry Baylor Coll. Medicine, Houston, 1982-89, asst. prof. dept. medicine, 1983-86, rsch. assoc. prof. dept. medicine, 1986-90, rsch. assoc. prof. dept. biochemistry, 1989-91, rsch. prof. medicine, 1990-95; rsch. prof. biochemistry, 1991-95; prof. medicine and biochemistry, 1995—. Dir. peptide core Nat. Rsch. and Demonstration Ctr. in Arteriosclerosis, Baylor Coll. Medicine, 1984-96, internal adv. com., 1986-96; organizing com. 10th Internat. Conf. on Methods in Protein Structure Analysis, Snowbird, Utah, 1994; sci. com. Internat. Conf. on Methods in Protein Sequence Analysis, Berlin, 1988, Sweden, 1990; reviewer grants Biomed. Rsch. rev. Com., Nat. Inst. on Drug Abuse, NSF, Washington; lectr. in field. Reviewer papers for Jour. Chromatography, Jour. Lipid Rsch., Jour. Protein Chemistry, Molecular and Cellular Biochemistry, Biochemistry, Arteriosclerosis; contbr. numerous articles to profl. jours. Pres. Taiwanese Am. Citizens League of Houston, 1988-90, Taiwanese Am. Assn. Houston, 1985-86. Grantee BRSG Funds, 1982-83, NIH, 1986-96, 2001—, AHA, 1985-90, 97-99, Meth. Hosp. Found., 1988-91, AHA Tex., 1997-2001, ADA, 2003—. Home: 4102 Levonshire Dr Houston TX 77025-3915 Office: Baylor Coll Medicine Dept Medicine/Atherosclerosis MSA601 6565 Fannin MS A601 Houston TX 77030-3411 E-mail: cyang@bcm.tmc.edu.

YANG, DAVID CHIE-HWA, business administration educator; b. Taiwan, Republic of China, Nov. 7, 1954; came to U.S., 1977; s. Wen-Shen and Chin-Huei (Lee) Y. BA, Nat. Taiwan U., Taipei, 1977; MBA, U. Calif., Berkeley, 1979; PhD, Columbia U., 1985. Prof., sch. accountancy U. Hawaii, Honolulu, 1985—. Rsch. assoc. Acctg. Rsch. Ctr. Grad. Sch. Bus. Columbia U., N.Y.C., 1981-84; vis. prof. Beijing (People's Republic of China) Inst. Chem. Engring. Mgmt., 1988-89; cons. to China Nat. Chem. Constrn. Corp., 1990, 91, CIEC CPAs, Shanghai Acad. Social Scis. CPAs, China; past tchr. Peking U., Nat. Taiwan U. Author: Modern Western Financial Management, 1992, The Association Between SFAS 33 Information and Bond Ratings, 1985, Accounting and Auditing in China, 1998, China's Economic Powerhouse, 2002; co-editor: FASB Statement 33 Data Bank Users Manual, 1985, FASB Statement 36 Data Bank Users Manual, 1985. Recipient Title VI Grant U.S. Dept. Edn., 1987, curriculum devel. grant Coopers S. Lybrand Found, N.Y.C., 1987, ednl. improvement fund award U. Hawaii, 1987. Mem. Inst. Mgmt. Accts., Am. Acctg. Assn., Inst. of Internal Auditors, EDP Auditors Assn., Assn. Chinese Scholars in Hawaii (pres. 2000-01), Chinese Acctg. Profs. Assn. N.Am. (pres. 1997-98), Assn. for Chinese Mgmt. Educators (v.p. 1999-2000), Inst. Mgmt. Accts., Beta Gamma Sigma, Beta Alpha Psi (Outstanding Prof. 1989, 91, 92, 96, 97, Dennis Ching 1st Interstate Bank Meml. Teaching award 1993). Office: U Hawaii Coll Bus Adminstrn 2404 Maile Way Honolulu HI 96822-2223

YANG, HENRY T. academic administrator, educator; b. Chungking, China, Nov. 29, 1940; s. Chen Pei and Wei Gen Yang; m. Dilling Tsui, Sept. 2, 1966; children: Maria, Martha. BSCE, Nat. Taiwan U., 1962; MSCE, W.Va. U., 1965; PhD, Cornell U., 1968; D honoris causa, Purdue U., 1996, Hong Kong U. Sci. and Tech., 2002. Structural engr. Gilbert Assocs., Reading, Pa., 1968—69; asst. prof. Sch. Aeros. and Astronautics, Purdue U., West Lafayette, Ind., 1969—72, assoc. prof., 1972—76, prof., 1976—94, Neil A. Armstrong Disting. prof., 1988—94, sch. head, 1979—84; dean engring. Purdue U., 1984—94; chancellor U. Calif., Santa Barbara, 1994—. Mem. sci. adv. bd. USAF, 1985—89; mem. aero. adv. com. NASA, 1985—89; mem. engring. adv. com. NSF, 1988—91; mem. mechanics bd. vis. ONR, 1990—93; mem. def. mfg. bd. DOD, 1998—99, def. sci. bd., 1989—91; mem. acad. adv. bd. NAE, 1991—94; mem. tech. adv. com. Pratt & Whitney, 1993—95; mem. Naval Rsch. Adv. Com., 1996—98. Recipient 12 Best Tchg. awards, Purdue U., 1971—94, Outstanding Engr. award, 1999. Fellow: AIAA, Am. Soc. Engring. Edn. (Centennial medal 1993, Benjamin Garver Lamme award 1998); mem.: NAE, Academia Sinica. Office: U Calif Chancellors Office Santa Barbara CA 93106

YANG, RENE IKAN, university administrator; b. Shanghai, Peoples Republic of China, Sept. 25, 1951; s. Fred Tse and Alice Hsing (Lee) Y.; m. Debbie J. Cayton, Apr. 22, 1977; children: Kanani, Kami, Keilani. BS, Brigham Young U., Laie, Hawaii, 1978; MA, Cen. Mich. U., 1980. Dir. MIS Brigham Young U. Hawaii, 1984—. Pres. Living Environment Classroom Lang. System, Honolulu, 1988-92; cons. LEC Taiwan, Beabeeca Presch., Taipei, Taiwan, 1988—; bd. dirs. The Jade Joss Inc., Arcadia, Calif., Shangai, China, Coast Chain Enterprise Inc., Walnut, Calif. Chmn. housing com. Laie Community Assn., 1985-90. Mem. Nat. Prime User Group (pres. 1987-90). Office: Brigham Young U Hawaii # 1960 Laie HI 96762

YANKEE, MARIE, publishing executive, educator; m. J.R. Yankee, June 6, 1956; children: Michael, David, Stephen, Jennifer. Diploma Montessori edn., Montessori Inst. Am., 1968; MS, Southeastern U., Greenville, S.C., 1980, PhD, 1981. Chief exec. officer The Fernhaven Studio, Los Angeles, 1966—. Montessori Ednl. Environment, Los Angeles, 1974—, Yankee Montessori Mfg., L.A., 1980-86; pres. Internat. Montessori Inst. Tchr. Ednl. Programs, Sage, Calif., 1980—; rsch. editor Edn. Systems Pub., L.A., 1982—; dir. EEI, Inc., L.A., 1987—. Cons. Calif. pub. schs., 1976; prof. Univ. Coll. Vancouver. Author: Montessori Curriculum, 1985, Reading Program, 1981, Science for Preschool, 1981, Geography for Preschool, 1982. Mem. Am. Montessori Soc., Montessori Inst. Am. Home: 38395 Trifone Rd Hemet CA 92544-9693 Office: 38395 Trifone Rd Hemet CA 92544-9693

YANKOVICH, JAMES MICHAEL, education educator; b. Richmond, Va., Mar. 15, 1935; s. Michael James and Edna Mae (Mann) Y.; m. Ann Page Richardson, Aug. 11, 1956; children: Kathy, Julie, Michael. BA, U. Richmond, 1957; M.Ed., U. Va., 1961; Ed.D., U. Mich., 1971. Tchr., Henrico County, Va., 1958-60; guidance counselor, 1960-61; prin. Glen Echo Elem. Sch., 1961-62, Varina Elem. Sch., 1962-64, Johnson Elem. Sch., Charlottesville, Va., 1964-65; asst. supt. schs. Charlottesville, 1965-66; asst. prof. U. Mich., Flint, 1968-71, assoc. prof., 1971-74, dean acad. affairs, 1971-74; dean Sch. Edn., Coll. of William and Mary, Williamsburg, Va., 1974-83, 93-95, prof. edn., 1983-92; dean Sch. Edn., 1992—. Bd. dirs. Inst. Ednl. Mgmt., Harvard U., 1973 C.S. Mott leadership fellow, 1966-67 Mem. Phi Delta Kappa. Home: 116 Yorkshire Dr Williamsburg VA 23185-3983 Office: Coll William and Mary Williamsburg VA 23187-8795

YANNAS, IOANNIS VASSILIOS, polymer scientist, educator; b. Athens, Apr. 14, 1935; s. Vassilios Pavlos and Thalia (Sarafoglou) Yannas; m. Stamatia Frondistou (div. Oct. 1984); children: Tania, Alexis. AB, Harvard U., 1957; SM, MIT, 1959; MS, Princeton U., 1965, PhD, 1966. Asst. prof. mech. engring. MIT, Cambridge, 1966-68, duPont asst. prof., 1968-69, assoc. prof., 1969-78, prof. polymer sci. and engring. dept. mech. engring., 1978—, prof. dept. materials sci. and engring., 1983—; prof. Harvard-MIT Div. Health Scis. and Tech., Cambridge, 1978—. Vis. prof. Royal Inst. Tech., Stockholm, 1974. Author: (book) Tissue and Organ Regeneration in Adults, 2001; mem. editl. bd. Jour. Biomed. Materials Rsch., 1986—, Jour. Materials Sci. Materials Medicine, 1990—, Tissue Engring., 1994—; contbr. articles to profl. jours. Recipient Founders award, Soc. Biomaterials, 1982, Clemson award, 1992, Fred O. Conley award, Soc. Plastics Engrs., 1982, award in medicine and genetics, Sci. Digest/Cutty Sark, 1982, Doolittle award, Am. Chem. Soc., 1988; fellow, Shriners Burns Inst., Mass. Gen. Hosp., 1980—81; Pub. Health Svc. fellow, Princeton U., 1963. Fellow: Biomaterials Sci. and Engring., Am. Inst. Med. and Biol. Engrs. (founding mem.), Am. Inst. Chemists; mem.: Inst. Medicine Nat. Acad Scis. Achievements include patents in field. Office: MIT Bldg 3-332 77 Mass Ave Cambridge MA 02139-4307

YANOFSKY, CHARLES, biology educator; b. N.Y.C., Apr. 17, 1925; s. Frank and Jennie (Kopatz) Y.; m. Carol Cohen, June 19, 1949, (dec. Dec. 1990); children: Stephen David, Robert Howard, Martin Fred; m. Edna Crawford, Jan. 4, 1992. BS, CCNY, 1948; MS, Yale U., 1950, PhD, 1951, DSc (hon.), 1981, U. Chgo., 1980. Rsch. asst. Yale U., 1951-54; asst. prof. microbiology Western Res. U. Med. Sch., 1954-57; mem. faculty Stanford U., 1958—2000, prof. biology, 1961—2000, Herzstein prof. biology, 1966—2000, prof. emeritus, 2000—. Career investigator Am. Heart Assn., 1969-95. Served with AUS, 1944-46. Recipient Lederle Med. Faculty award, 1957, Eli Lilly award bacteriology, 1959, U.S. Steel Co. award molecular biology, 1964, Howard Taylor Ricketts award U. Chgo., 1966, Albert and Mary Lasker award, 1971, Townsend Harris medal Coll. City N.Y., 1973, Louisa Gross Horwitz prize in biology and biochemistry Columbia U., 1976, V.D. Mattia award Roche Inst., 1982, medal Genetics Soc. Am., 1983, Internat. award Gairdner Found., 1985, named Passano Laureate, Passano Found., 1992; recipient William C. Rose award in biochemistry and molecular biology, 1997, Abbott Lifetime Achievement award Am. Soc. Microbiology, 1998. Mem. NAS (Selman A. Waksman award in microbiology 1972), Am. Acad. Arts and Scis., Genetics Soc. Am. (pres. 1969, Thomas Hunt Morgan medal 1990), Am. Soc. Biol. Chemists (pres. 1984), Royal Soc. (fgn. mem.), Japanese Biochem. Soc. (hon.) Home: 725 Mayfield Ave Stanford CA 94305-1016 Office: Stanford U Dept Of Biological Sci Stanford CA 94305

YANOWITZ, EDWARD STANLEY, allergist, educator; b. N.Y.C., July 4, 1950; s. Robert Donald and Betty (Lewis) Y.; m. Jean Wendy Temeck, Oct. 25, 1986. BA, Yale U., 1972; MD, Autonomous U. Guadalajara, 1978; student 5th pathway program, Booth Meml. Med. Ctr., 1978-79. Diplomate Am. Bd. Pediat., Am. Bd. Allergy and Immunology. Intern in pediat. The Roosevelt Hosp., N.Y.C., 1979-80; resident in pediat. St. Luke's-Roosevelt Hosp. Ctr., N.Y.C., 1980-82; fellow in allergy and immunology N.Y. Hosp./Cornell Med. Ctr., N.Y.C., 1982-84; allergy assoc. Allergy Care Assocs., N.Y.C., 1984-87; asst. prof. medicine George Washington U. Med. Ctr., Washington, 1987-97, clin. asst. prof., 1997—; allergy assoc. Asthma and Allergy Care Am. of Md., P.C., 1997—2000, pres., 2000—. Vis. clin. fellow Columbia U., 1979-82; clin. fellow divsn. allergy and immunology dept. pediat., Cornell U., 1982-84, instr. pediat., 1984-87; asst. attending physician The New York Hosp., 1984-87; cons. staff dept. pediat. St. Luke's Hosp., Newburgh, N.Y., 1984-87. Co-author: Handbook of Pulmonary Drug Therapy, 1994. Fellow Am. Acad. Pediat., Am. Acad. Allergy and Immunology; mem. Joint Coun. Allergy and Immunology, N.Y. Med. Soc. (mem. com. fgn. med. grads. 1982, mem. membership com. 1986), N.Y. Allergy Soc., Med. Soc. State of N.Y., Alumni Assn. Autonomous U. Guadalajara. Office: Allergy and Asthma Care of Md PC 8508 Cedar St Silver Spring MD 20910-4322 E-mail: eyanowitz@juno.com.

YAO, DAVID DA-WEI, engineering educator; b. Shanghai, July 14, 1950; came to U.S., 1983, naturalized, 1990; s. William Kang-Fu and Nancy Yun-Lan (Lu) Y.; m. Helen Zhi-Heng Chen, Jan. 31, 1979; children: Henry, John. MASc, U. Toronto, Ont., Can., 1981, PhD, 1983. Assoc. prof. systems engring. Harvard U., Cambridge, Mass., 1986-88; asst. prof. indsl. engring. and ops. rsch. Columbia U., N.Y.C., 1983-86, prof., 1988—, Thomas Alva Edison prof., 1992—. Acad. visitor AT&T Bell Labs., Holmdel, N.J., 1989, T.J. Watson Rsch. Ctr., IBM, Yorktown, N.Y., 1990—. Co-author: Monotone Structure in Discrete-Event Systems, 1994, Fundamentals of Queueing Networks, 2001, Dynamic Control of Quality in Production-Inventory Systems, 2002; contbr. over 150 articles to profl. jours. including Maths. Ops. Rsch., Jour. of Assn. Computing Machinery, Advances in Applied Probability. Recipient Presdl. Young Investigator award NSF, Washington, 1987-92, Guggenheim fellow John Simon Guggenheim Meml. Found., N.Y.C., 1991-92. Fellow IEEE; mem. Soc. Indsl. and Applied Math. (Outstanding Paper prize 2003), Ops. Rsch. Soc. Am. (George Nicholson prize 1983, Franz Edelman award 1999). Achievements include development of theory of algebraic structures in discrete-event systems, theory of stochastic convexity and its applications in queuing networks, stochastic network models for manufacturing systems and supply chains, methodologies in the optimization and control of stochastic discrete-event systems. Home: 1261 Underhill Ave Yorktown Heights NY 10598-5718 Office: Columbia U IEOR Dept 302 Mudd Bldg New York NY 10027-6699 E-mail: yao@ieor.columbia.edu.

YARBOROUGH, NELLIE CONSTANCE, principal, minister; b. Cedar Groove, N.C. d. Anderson and Bessie Y.. BA, Ea. Nazarene Coll., Quincy, Mass., 1978; MA, Antioch U./Cambridge (Mass.) Coll., 1979. Co-founder, exec. sec. Mt. Calvary Holy Ch., Boston, 1944—92, nat. youth pres., 1948—88, state sec. and treas., 1962—95; nat. missionary pres. Mt. Calvary Ch., Boston, 1960—90; founder, prin. Dr. Brumfield Johnson Acad., Boston, 1992—; founder, dean NCY Bible Inst., Boston, 1992—. Editor: (manual) YPHA Book, 1944; asst. editor: Jesus the Son of God, 1968, Spiritual Voice, 1948—72. Mem. adv. bd. Vision New Eng., Acton, Mass., 1998—; bd. dirs. Roxbury (Mass.) Multi-Svc. Ctr., 1970—85, Consumer's Credit, Boston, 1978—85, Project Right, Boston, 1991—, Blue Hill Task Force, Boston, 1995—. Named Pastor of the Yr., Vision New Eng., 1995, Woman of the Yr., Urban League of Ea. Mass., 1996; recipient Sojourner Truth award, Boston Profl. League, 1993. Democrat. Pentecostal. Avocations: reading, exercise, travel, motivational speaking. Home: 250 Seaver St Boston MA 02121 Office: Mt Calvary Holy Ch Am 9-19 Otisfield St Boston MA 02121 Fax: 617-427-1595.

YARBRO, BILLY RAY, elementary school educator, basketball coach; b. Linden, Tenn., Mar. 22, 1957; s. Nashel and Melvina (Vaughn) Y.; m. Diane Wynn, Feb. 2, 1982 (div. June 1990); children: Crystal, Lindsey; 1 stepchild, Lisa Wynn; m. Darlene Johnson, May 26, 1993; 1 stepchild, Crystal Brooks. BS, Freed Hardeman U., 1979; MA, Austin Peay U., 1988. Cert. tchr., Tenn. Tchr. Pope Elem. Sch., Linden, 1980-83, prin., 1983-87; asst. prin. Linden Elem. Sch., 1987-89, phys. edn. tchr., 1989-90, math. tchr., basketball coach, 1990—. Mem. Perry County Edn. Assn. (pres. 1990-92). Mem. Ch. of Christ. Avocations: playing and umpiring baseball, softball and basketball. Home: PO Box 359 Linden TN 37096-0359 Office: Linden Elem College St Linden TN 37096

YARBROUGH, JOHN WILLIAM, secondary school educator; b. Dallas, June 2, 1946; s. Lonnie Jordan and Emma Joe (Robinson) Y. BA in History, U. North Tex., 1968; M in Liberal Arts, So. Meth. U., 1987; postgrad., U. Tex., Arlington, 1986, U. Dallas, 1990. Cert. tchr., Tex. Tchr. Delay Mid. Sch., Lewisville, Tex., 1971-73; tchr., advanced placement dir. Lewisville H.S., 1973-80, Casady Sch., Oklahoma City, Okla., 1980-82, Episcipal Sch. Dallas, 1982-85; tchr. W.T. White H.S., Dallas, 1985-86; tchr., dept. chair James Madison H.S., Dallas, 1986-92; tchr. Stockard Mid. Sch., Dallas, 1992-93, Holmes Mid. Sch., Dallas, 1993—. Cons. Am. history S.W. Region of Coll. Bd., Austin, Tex., 1979-81; panelist Luther Quincentenary, U. North Tex., Denton, 1984; participant Advanced Placement Workshop, Southwestern Region Coll. Bd., 1990, 92, Inst. for Tchrs. of Talented Students, Carleton Coll., 1992, 95, Coop. Learning in the Social Studies, Nat. Coun. for the Social Studies, 1993, Architecture in the Classroom, Nat. Trust for Historic Preservation, 1994. Del. Tex. Dem. State Conv., 1972-96. Woodrow Wilson Nat. Found. fellow U. Tex., Dallas, 1995. Mem. ASCD, Nat. Coun. for the Social Studies, Am. Hist. Assn., Dallas Coun. for the Social Studies, Orgn. Am. Historians, Tex. Coun. for the Social Studies. Avocations: reading, music. Office: OW Holmes Classical Acad and Mid Sch 2001 E Kiest Blvd Dallas TX 75216-3300

YARWOOD, DEAN LESLEY, political science educator; b. Decorah, Iowa, Mar. 17, 1935; s. Harold Nicholas and Elsie Mabel (Roney) Y.; m. Elaine Delores Bender, Sept. 2, 1956; children: Lucinda, Kent, Keith, Douglas, Dennis. BA, Iowa U., 1957; MA, Cornell U., 1961; PhD, U. Ill., 1966. Tchr. social studies, acting jr. high prin. Mid-Prairie Community Sch., Wellman, Iowa, 1957-59; asst. prof. Coe Coll., Cedar Rapids, Iowa, 1963-66, U. Ky., Lexington, 1966-67, U. Mo., Columbia, 1967-70, assoc. prof., 1970-78, prof., 1978—, dir. grad. studies dept. polit. sci., 1970-72, 88, 94-97, chmn. dept. polit. sci., 1988-91, 98-99, Frederick A. Middlebush prof. polit. sci., 1992-95, prof., 1978-2000, prof. emeritus, 2000—. Editor: The National Administrative System: Selected Readings, 1971, Public Administration, Politics, and the People: Selected Readings for Managers, Employees and Citizens, 1987; author, co-author numerous articles in polit. sci. jours. Recipient Bradish Meml. scholarship, 1953-57, Iowa Merit scholarship, 1956-57, Woodrow Wilson fellowship, 1959-60, James Garner fellowship, 1961-62, Woodrow Wilson Dissertation fellowship, 1962-63. Mem. Am. Soc. Pub. Adminstrn. (chmn. sect. on pub. adminstrn. edn. 1986-87, publs. com. 1986-89, com. on orgnl. rev. and evaln. 1995-97, Ctrl. Mo. chpt. coun. 1979-80, pres. 1980-81, ex-officio mem. coun. 1981-83), Am. Polit. Sci. Assn., Mo. Polit. Sci. Assn. (v.p. 1990-91, pres. 1991-92), Mo. Inst. for Pub. Adminstrn. (coun. 1976-77, v.p. 1977-78, pres. 1978-79, Pub. Adminstr. of Yr. 1998), Phi Beta Kappa. Office: U Mo Dept Polit Sci 206 Professional Building Columbia MO 65211-6040

YATES, ALBERT CARL, academic administrator, chemistry educator; b. Memphis, Tenn., Sept. 29, 1941; s. John Frank and Sadie L. (Shell) Y.; m. Ann Young; children: Steven, Stephanie, Aerin Alessandra, Sara Elizabeth. BS, Memphis State U., 1965; PhD, Ind. U., 1968. Research assoc. U. So. Calif., Los Angeles, 1968-69; prof. chemistry Ind. U., Bloomington, 1969-74; v.p. research, grad. dean U. Cin., 1974-81; exec. v.p., provost, prof. chemistry Washington State U., Pullman, 1981-90; pres. Colo. State U., Fort Collins, 1990—; chancellor Colo. State U. System, Fort Collins, 1990—. Mem. grad. record exam. bd. Princeton (N.J.) U., 1977-81; undergrad. assessment program coun. Ednl. Testing Svc., 1977-81, NRC, 1975-82, Office Edn., HEW, 1978-80; mem. exec. coun. acad. affairs Nat. Assn. State Univs. and Land Grant Colls., 1983-87, Am. Coun. on Edn., 1983-87, nat adv. coun. gen. med. scis. NIH, 1987-90. Contbr. research articles to Jour. Chem. Physics; research articls to Phys. Rev.; research articles to Jour. Physics, Phys. Rev. Letters, Chem. Physics Letters. Served with USN, 1959-62. Recipient univ., state and nat. honors and awards Mem. AAAS, Am. Phys. Soc., Am. Chem. Soc., Sigma Xi, Phi Lambda Upsilon. Home: 1744 Hillside Dr Fort Collins CO 80524-1965

YATES, BRENDA H. CARROLL, secondary school educator; b. Carrolltown, Ga., Sept. 16, 1949; d. Buford Bledsoe and Lovie Beatrice (Thaxton) Holmes; m. Kenneth Wayne Carroll, Aug. 23, 1969 (div. Aug. 1984); children: Kenneth W. Jr., Samuel Mark; m. Gwendolyn Ray Yates, Dec. 10, 1987. BA in Secondary Edn. Social Studies, West Ga. Coll., 1970, MEd in Secondary Edn. English, 1974, EdS in Secondary Edn. English, 1988. Cert. tchr., Ga. Social studies and lang. arts tchr. Rockmart (Ga.) H.S., 1970-78; lang. arts tchr., dept. head Douglas County Comprehensive H.S., Douglasville, Ga., 1978—. Adj. instr. Mercer U., Lithia Springs, Ga., 1990—. Named Star Tchr., State of Ga., 1994. Mem. NEA, Ga. Assn. Educators. Democrat. Baptist. Avocation: reading. Home: 4978 Pebblebrook Dr Douglasville GA 30135-4520 Office: Douglas County Comp HS 8705 Campbellton St Douglasville GA 30134-2202

YATES, CHERYL ANN, home economist, educator; b. Cheyenne, Wyo., Oct. 11, 1945; d. Robert Watson and Harriette Julia (Oberg) Yates. BS, U. Wyo., 1968; MA, Ariz. State U., No. Ariz. U. Cert. home econ. tchr. Ariz. Tchr. Carson Jr. HS, Mesa, Ariz., 1968—69; tchr., chmn. home econs. dept. Powell Jr. HS, Mesa, 1970—80; tchr. Mountain View HS, Mesa, 1980—81, Dobson HS, Mesa, 1981—, dept. chair, 1981—. Contbr. articles to mags. in field. Active Friends of Channel 8. Mem.: NEA, Mesa Edn. Assn., Ariz. Edn. Assn. Republican. Office: 1502 W Guadalupe Rd Mesa AZ 85202

YATES, DONALD ALFRED, retired literature educator; b. Ayer, Mass., Apr. 11, 1930; s. Alfred Craig Yates and Bessie Mae Cambridge; m. Mary Dodd, June 24, 1951 (div. Mar. 1961); children: Brian Donald, Juliet Marie; m. Lynn P. Taylor, Mar. 31, 1962 (div. May 1975); 1 child, John Allan; m. Joanne Margaret Mueller, Mar. 21, 1977. AB in Spanish, U. Mich., 1951, MA in Spanish, 1954, PhD in Spanish, 1961. Tchg. fellow U. Mich., Ann Arbor, 1953-57; instr. Mich. State U., East Lansing, 1957-61, asst. prof. Spanish-Am. lit., 1961-64, assoc. prof., 1964-67, prof., 1967-83, prof. emeritus, 1983—. Pres. Internat. Inst. Latin-Am. Lit., Pitts., 1971-73. Author: Jorge Luis Borges: Life, Work & Criticism, 1985; editor, translator: Latin Blood: Best Crime Stories of Latin America, 1972; co-editor, translator: Labyrinths: Selected Writings of Jorge Luis Borges, 1962; co-editor: (textbook) Imaginación y Fantasía, 1960, 6th edit., 1999. With U.S. Army, 1951-53. Translation grantee NEA, 2000-01. Mem. MLA, Mystery Writers of Am., Baker St. Irregulars (The Greek Interpreter 1972), Sherlock Holmes Soc. London. Democrat. Home: 555 Canon Park Dr Saint Helena CA 94574-9726 E-mail: mrmelas72@earthlink.net.

YATES, ELSIE VICTORIA, retired secondary school educator; b. Newport, R.I., Dec. 16, 1916; d. Andrew James and Rachel Agnes (Sousa) Tabb; m. George Herman Yates, July 12, 1941 (div. Apr. 1981); children: Serena, George Jr., Michael, Elsie French, David. AB in English and History, Va. Union U., 1938; postgrad., U. R.I., 1968-73, Salve Regina U., 1968-73. Life cert. in secondary English and reading specialist, R.I. Reading specialist grades 7 and 8 title I Newport (R.I.) Sch., 1971-74, secondary English educator, 1975-87; ret., 1987. Mem. adult com. Young Life, Newport, 1981-93; active Newport (R.I.) Substance Abuse Force, 1989-93; chmn. multicultural curriculum com. New Visions for Newport (R.I.) Schs., 1991-94; mem. edn. com. Swinburne Sch., Newport, 1992-94; active Equity in Edns. Com.-Concerned Citizens Group. Recipient Outstanding Ednl. Contbn. Under Title I award U.S. Office Edn., Bur. Sch. Sys., 1976, Presdl. citation Nat. Edn. Assn. R.I., 1987, Appreciation for Svc. award Cmty. Bapt. Ch., Newport, 1988, Outstanding Svc. award in field of edn. to the youth in cmty. Queen Esther Chpt. 2, Newport, 1992. Mem. NAACP (life), R.I. Ret. Tchrs. Assn., Newport Ret. Tchrs. Assn. Baptist. Avocations: reading, handicrafts, community activities. Home: The John Clarke Retirement Center 600 Valley Road Apt 121 Middletown RI 02842

YATES, JOHN THOMAS, JR., chemistry educator, research director; b. Winchester, Va., Aug. 3, 1935; s. John Thomas and Kathryn (Barnett) Y.; m. Kerin Joyce Narbut, Oct. 18, 1958; children: Geoffrey, Nathan. BS, Juniata Coll., 1956; PhD, MIT, 1960. Asst. prof. chemistry Antioch Coll., Yellow Springs, Ohio, 1960-63; NRC fellow, rsch. chemist Nat. Bur. Standards, Washington, 1963-82; R.K. Mellon prof. chemistry U. Pitts., 1982—, dir. Surface Sci. Ctr., 1982—. Co-dir. materials rsch. ctr. U. Pitts., 1994, R.K. Mellon prof. chemistry and physics, 1994—. Author: Experimental Innovations in Surface Science, 1997; co-author: The Surface Scientist's Guide to Organometallic Chemistry, 1987; co-editor: Vibrational Spectroscopy of Molecules on Surfaces, 1987, Chemical Perspectives of Microelectronic Materials, Vol. 131; assoc. editor: Studies in Surface Science and Catalysis, 1986; series editor: Methods of Surface Characterization, 1987; bd. editors Ann. Rev. Phys. Chemistry, 1983-85, Jour. Phys. Chemistry, 1983-88, Jour. Chem. Physics, 1984-87, Jour. Catalysis, 1987-91, Chem. Revs., Langmuir, Surface Sci., Applications of Surface Sci., Accounts Chem. Rsch.; assoc. editor Langmuir, 1991-98; contbr. revs. and articles to profl. jours.; inventor desorption spectrometer, 1981. Sherman Fairchild Disting. scholar Calif. Inst. Tech., 1977-78; recipient Silver medal Dept. Commerce-Nat. Bur. Stds., 1973, Stratton award, 1981, Gold medal Dept. Commerce Nat. Bur. Stds., 1981, Pres.'s Disting. Rsch. award U. Pitts., 1989, Proctor & Gamble award, 1989, Alexander von Humboldt Sr. Rsch. award, 1994, Linnett lectr. Cambridge U., 2000, named Among 100 Most Highly Cited Chemists in World 1984--, G.N. Lewis award U. Calif.-Berkeley, 2002; fellow Sidney Sussex Coll., 2000. Fellow Am. Phys. Soc. (bd. dirs. divsn. chem. physics 1991—, chmn. divsn. chem. physics 1989), Am. Vacuum Soc. (chmn. surface sci. divsn. 1973, 92, trustee 1975, bd. dirs. 1982-85, M.W. Welch award 1994, fellow 1994); mem. NAS, Am. Chem. Soc. (chmn. divsn. colloid and surface chemistry, Langmuir lectr. 1979, Kendall award in colloid of surface chemistry 1986, Morley prize Cleve. chpt. 1990, Peter Debye lectr. Cornell U. 1993, Pitts. award 1998, A.W. Adamson award 1999), Pitts.-Cleve. Catalysis Soc. Office: U Pitts Surface Sci Ctr Dept Chemistry Pittsburgh PA 15260

YATES, MARGERY GORDON, elementary education educator; b. Walton, N.Y., July 3, 1910; d. McClellan Gordon and Marcia Beulah (Ramsdell) Gordon-Strahl; m. James McKendree Yates, Aug. 11, 1933; 1 child, Sally. BS, U. Houston, 1943, MS, 1948; MA, Stanford U., 1952. Tchr. Baldwin (N.Y.) Sch. Dist., 1928-34, Houston Sch. Dist., 1943-48; supr. primary edn. Watsonville (Calif.) Sch. Dist., 1948-53; edn. cons. San Mateo County Office Edn., Redwood City, Calif., 1953-58; supr. primary edn. Jefferson Elem. Sch. Dist., Daly City, Calif., 1958-65; tchr. Hillsborough (Calif.) Sch. Dist., 1965-75. Instr. U. Houston, 1956, San Jose State Coll., 1957. Mem. AAUW (edn. area rep. 1987-88, 89-90, 91-92, 92-93, 93-94, Fellowship award honoree 1991), Burlingame Music Club (pres. 1992-93, 93-94), Commonwealth Club Calif., Alpha Delta Kappa (corr. sec. Calif. state bd. 1981-82, Gamma Beta chpt. pres. 1971-74, treas. 1985-89, 94—). Republican. Mem. Ch. Christian Sci. Avocations: gardening, travel, music, dancing, theater.

YATES, MILDRED CAMPBELL, retired literature educator; b. Beaumont, Tex., Jan. 1, 1920; d. William Holland and Eula Mildred (Owens) Campbell; m. Reed Henry Kirkpatrick Yates, Jr., May 17, 1944; children: Reed Henry III, Mary Campbell Yates Kirkpatrick. BFA, U. Ga., 1940; MA in English, Lamar U., 1962. Cert. tchr. grades 5-12, Tex. Tchr. elem. lang. arts and music Beaumont (Tex.) Ind. Sch. Dist., 1953-67; asst. prof. elem. lang. arts edn. Lamar U., Beaumont, 1968-70; tchr. Am. lit. and world civilization French H.S., Beaumont, 1970-79. Bd. dirs. Mental Health Assn., Austin, Tex., 1972-76; commr. Beaumont Landmark Corp., 1980-84; dir. of bd. Arts Related Curriculum, Beaumont, 1982-89; docent French Hist. House, Beaumont, 1979—. Co-author: (devel. reader) Images, 1971, Keystone, 1975; co-author, co-editor: With a Dome More Vast, 1986 (Kate Warnick award 1986); author: (essay) Beaumont Women, A Memoir, 1992. Pres. Beaumont Heritage Soc., 1980-82; genealogist Tex. Gulf Hist. Soc., Beaumont, 1986—; pres., sec. Tyrrell Hist. Libr. Assn., Beaumont, 1987—; tchr. adult classes First United Meth. Ch., Beaumont, 1998—; bd. dirs. Beaumont Music Commn., 1988—, chmn. Speaker's Bur., Jefferson Theatre Restoration, 1998—. Nominee for Jefferson award Beaumont Enterprise, 1996; recipient Preservation award Main St. Project, Beaumont, 1997. Mem. Art Mus. of Tex., Pi Beta Phi (sec.). Methodist. Avocations: reading, travel, hist. preservation, volunteering.

YATES, PATRICIA ANN THOMPSON, elementary school educator; b. Louisville, Feb. 22, 1942; d. Albert Gregory and Eleanor (Bloemer) Thompson; m. Ronald Anthony Yates, Aug. 24, 1963; children: Robert Eric, Kristin Yates Sutton, Kurt Daniel. BA, Aquinas Coll., Grand Rapids, Mich., 1963; MEd, Xavier U., Cin., 1976. Cert. reading specialist (K-12), reading supr. Remedial reading tchr. Cin. Pub. Schs., 1977—; asst. coord. The Olympus Ctr., Cin., 1992—. Cons. Cin. Ctr. for Developmental Disorders, 1995—. Author: Root Word Program, 1990. Bd. dirs. Ohio Valley br. Orton Dyslexia Soc., Cin., 1989—; ednl. adv. com. edn. dept. Coll. Mount St. Joseph, Cin., 1990-94. U. Cin. grantee, 1988. Mem. Internat. Reading Assn. Avocations: reading, tennis, sewing. Office: The Olympus Ctr 2230 Park Ave Cincinnati OH 45206-2710

YATVIN, JOANNE INA, education educator; b. Newark, Apr. 17, 1931; d. John and Mary Edna (Cohen) Goldberg; m. Milton Brian Yatvin, June 8, 1952; children: Alan, Bruce, Lillian, Richard. Ba, Douglass Coll., 1952; MA, Rutgers U., 1962; PhD, U. Wis., 1974. Cert. sch. adminstr. Tchr. Hamburg Pub. Sch., NJ, 1952-53, New Brunswick Pub. Sch., NJ, 1953-55, Mayaguez Sch., PR, 1958-59, Milltown Pub. Sch., NJ, 1959-62, East Brunswick Pub. Sch., NJ, 1962-63; tchr., prin. Madison Met. Sch. Dist., Wis., 1963-88; supt. Cottrell Sch. Dist., Boring, Oreg., 1988-97, prin., 1997-2000; mem. faculty Portland State U., Oreg., 2000—. Adv. bd. mem. Big Books Mag., 1990-91; cons. various sch. dist.; apptd. to nat. reading panel Nat. Inst. of Child Health and Devel., 1998-2000. Author: Learning Language Through Communication, 1986, (monograph) A Whole Language Program for a Whole School, 1991, (monograph) Beginning a School Literacy Improvement Project: Some Words of Advice, Kdg Teachers Guide, Pegasus Reading Program, Kendall Hunt, 2000; contbr. chpts. in books and articles to profl. jour. Named Elem. Prin. of Yr., Wis. Dept. Edn., 1985, Wis. State Reading Assn., 1985; recipient Excellence in Print award, Washington Edpress, 1987, Disting. Elem. Edn. Alumni award, U. Wis., 1988, Kenneth S. Goodman In Def. of Good Tchg. award, Dept. Lang. and Learning U. Ariz., 2001. Mem.: ASCD, Oreg. Reading Assn., Nat. Coun. Tchrs. English (chair com. on ctrs. excellence 1986—89, mem. commn. on curriculum 1999—2002), Internat. Reading Assn. (pres. Portland coun. 2002—, Portland Coun. Celebrate Literacy award 2002), Phi Delta Kappa. Home: 5226 SW Northwood Ave Portland OR 97201-2832 Office: Grad Sch Edn Portland State U PO Box 751 Portland OR 97207-0751

YAU, KING-WAI, neuroscientist, educator; b. Canton, Kwangtung, China, Oct. 27, 1948; came to U.S., 1968; s. Tin-Man and Wai-Hing (Chan) Y.; m. Crystal Lin, Dec. 27, 1975; children: Emily, Jason. AB, Princeton U., 1971; PhD, Harvard U., 1975. Rsch. assoc. Stanford (Calif.) U., 1976-79, Cambridge (Eng.) U., 1979-80; from asst. prof. to prof. U. Tex. Med. Br., Galveston, 1980-86; prof. neurosci. Johns Hopkins Sch. Medicine, Balt., 1986—. Investigator Howard Hughes Med. Inst., Balt., 1986—. Recipient Rank prize in optoelectronics, London, 1980, Rsch. Career Devel. award NIH, 1981-86, Merit award, 1992-2002, Alcon Rsch. Inst. award, 1994, Magnes prize The Hebrew U., Jerusalem, 1996. Fellow Am. Acad. Arts & Scis.; mem. Soc. Neurosci., Soc. Gen. Physiologists, Assn. Rsch. Vision and Opthalmology (Friedenwald award 1993), Biophys. Soc., Physiol. Soc. (U.K.). Achievements include rsch. on mechanisms of visual and olfactory transductions. Office: Johns Hopkins U Sch Med 725 N Wolfe St Baltimore MD 21205-2105 E-mail: Kwyau@mail.jhmi.edu.

YAU, SHING-TUNG, mathematics educator; b. Swatow, China, Apr. 4, 1949; arrived in U.S., 1969; m. Yu-Yun Kuo; children: Isaac, Michael. PhD, U. Calif., Berkeley, 1971, Chinese U. Hong Kong, 1980, Harvard U., 1987. Mem. Inst. Advanced Study, Princeton, N.J., 1971-72; asst. prof. math. SUNY, Stony Brook, 1972-73; prof. math. Stanford (Calif.) U., 1974-79, Inst. Advanced Study, Princeton, 1979-84, U.Calif.-San Diego, La Jolla, 1984-87, Harvard U., Cambridge, Mass., 1987—. Vis. prof., chair math. dept. U. Tex., Austin, 1986; spl. chair Nat. Tsing Hua U., Hsinchu, Taiwan, 1991—; Wilson T.S. Wang Disting. vis. prof. Chinese U., Hong Kong, 1991—. Contbr. articles to profl. publs. Named Honorable prof., Fudan U. China, Academia Sinica China; recipient Sr. Scientist award, Humboldt Found. fellow, 1985, Crafoord prize, 1994, Veblen prize, 1981, Fields medal, 1982, Certy prize, 1980. Mem.: AAAS, NAS, Chinese Acad. Sci. (fgn. mem.), Acad. Sinica (Taiwan), Soc. Indsl. Applied Math., Am. Phys. Soc., Am. Math. Soc., Acad. Arts and Scis. Boston, N.Y. Acad. Scis. Office: Harvard U Dept Math 3d Fl Sci Ctr 1 Oxford St Cambridge MA 02138-2901

YAXLEY, JACK THOMAS, secondary education educator; b. Detroit, June 30, 1943; s. Thomas William Yaxley and Evelyn Dora (Chandler) Dahlman. AS, Broward Community Coll., 1964; BS, Fla. Atlantic U., 1965, MEd, 1966, postgrad., 1968, 70-73, Brown U., 1969, Bowdoin Coll., 1972, B.C.C. Field Sch., Mex., 1979-80, Hope Coll., 1986, English for Speakers of Other Langs. Inst., 1991-92, Broward Schs. Macintosh Computer Tng. Inst., 1992. Cert. assoc. master tchr., tchr. English for speakers of other langs. Tchr. chemistry N.E. High Sch., Ft. Lauderdale, Fla., 1966-70; tchr. honors chemistry, chemistry, advanced placement chemistry South Plantation (Fla.) High Sch., from 1971, instr. gifted and honors earth/space sci., from 1990, sci. dept. head, from 1994. Chem. analyst Alfinco/Russell-Anaconda, Oakland Park, Fla., 1968-70; part-time instr. Fla. Atlantic U., 1970-71; cons. Broward Dist. Schs., Ft. Lauderdale, 1971-87, tchr. gifted summer camp, 1983-85; lab. instr. Broward C.C., 1982-83, lectr. chemistry, 1988-90; cons. textbooks Modern Chemistry, CBS/Holt-Rinehart, 1983, Holt. Phys. Sci., 1984, Modern Phys. Sci., 1984-85, Exploring Matter and Energy: Phys. Sci., 1990; presenter, editor workshop NSF, Broward Sch., 1986; presenter Dist. VIIa Leadership Tng. Inst. Phi Delta Kappa, 1991, 93; mem. bd. advisors, bd. dirs. com. Lake Emerald Svcs. Co., Inc.; panel mem. Home Testing Inst., Port Washington, N.Y.; instr. Sch. Tech. Inservice, 1995. Columnist Reflections of Lake Emerald, 1985-88. Mem., bd. dirs. Lake Emerald Owners Assn., 1983-93, chairperson activities com., 1985-88, security com., 1985-86, 89-92, handicapped facilities com., 1992, beautification com., 1993, v.p. bd. dirs., 1989-91, pres., 1991, v.p., 1992, mem. negotiations com., 1992-93, corp. sec., 1993, mem. budget and fin. com., 1994. Named Tchr. of Yr., Fla. Engring. Soc., 1985; recipient Tchr. of 3d Acad. Quarter award Fla. Power and Light, 1989, Outstanding Tchr. award Tandy Tech. Scholars, 1991-92, 92-93; fellow NSF, 1969, 72, 86. Mem. NEA (life, Broward faculty rep. 1987—), Fla. Assn. Sci. Tchrs. (life), Fla. Teaching Profession-NEA, Fla. Atlantic U. Alumni Assn. (bd. dirs. 1966-71), Fla. Atlantic U. Coll. Edn. Alumni Assn. (founding benefactor), Planetary Soc., Phi Delta Kappa (scholarship fund raising com. auction, treas. 1990-93, bd. dirs. 1990—, Victoria C.T. Reed Adopt a Scholar program com. 1991—, v.p. for programs 1993-94, mem. scholarship ball com. 1993, mem. juvenile diabetes project com. 1994-95, rsch. rep. 1994-95, Disting. Svc. award 1987, 88, 91, 93). Republican. Roman Catholic. Avocations: cultural anthropology, ethnographic research in mex. Home: Macomb, Mich. Died Mar. 22, 2000.

YAZINSKI, JUDY, special education educator; b. Scranton, Pa., Feb. 21, 1950; d. James Patrick and Marie (Corcoran) McLane; m. Ronald F. Yazinski, Apr. 28, 1973; children: Jeremy, Tara. BS, Marywood Coll., Scranton, 1972, MS, 1979. Cert. instrnl. II, Pa. Tchr. spl. edn. Northeastern Ednl. Unit 19, Mayfield, Pa., 1972-76; enumerator, interviewer U.S. Dept. Commerce, Phila., 1978-81; tchr. spl. edn. Scranton City Sch. Dist., 1981—98; tchr. West Scranton Intermediate Sch., 1998—. Bd. dirs. North Pocono Pre Sch., Moscow, Pa. Alumni fundraiser Marywood Coll., 1973—; treas. Moscow Elem. Sch. PTA, 1979-81; coord. Scranton Spl. Olympics, 1981—; sec. North Pocono Booster Assn., Moscow, 1991-92; lector St. Catherine of Sienna PTA, 1989—; trustee libr. bd. Lackawanna County Sys., 2000—, v.p., 2002—; inservice coun. Scranton Sch. Dist., 2002—. Recipient svc. award Scranton Sch. Dist. Spl. Olympics, 1992. Democrat. Roman Catholic. Avocations: travel, sports, quilting. Home: RR 3 Box 3122 Moscow PA 18444-9415 Office: West Scranton Intermed Sch Parrott and Fellows Scranton PA 18504

YEAGER, BERNICE WHITTAKER, elementary and secondary school educator; b. Bethany, W.Va., June 26, 1915; d. Robert Helsabeck and Louise (McGraw) Whittaker; m. Roy Harold Yeager (dec. 1967). AB, Concord Coll., W.Va., 1934; MS, U. Tenn., 1937. Tchr./prin. Mercer County Schs., Princeton, W.Va., 1934-45, supr. instrn., 1945-47; asst. prof., supervising tchr. Winthrop Tng. Sch.-Winthrop Coll., Rock Hill, S.C., 1948-64; coordinator reading Lancaster (S.C.) City Schs., 1964-70, Lancaster County Schs., 1970-75; tchr. Catawba Acad., Rock Hill, S.C., 1975-82; substitute tchr. Charlotte-Mecklenburg Schs., Charlotte, N.C., 1983—. Cons. in field. Chmn. youth activities ARC, Rock Hill, 1970-75. Named Woman of the Yr., Rock Hill Bus. and Profl. Women, 1977, others. Mem. NEA, S.C. Edn. Assn., AAUW, S.C. Ret. Tchrs. Assn., Phi Kappa Phi, Delta Kappa Gamma. Lutheran. Address: 862 Mary Knoll Ct Rock Hill SC 29730-3727

YEAGER, CAROL ANNETTE, instrumental music educator; b. Seattle, Mar. 14, 1948; d. Marion Jack and Leonora Annette (Alinder) Y. AA, Bergen C.C., 1972; BA, Jersey City State Coll., 1974; MEd, U. Nev., 1982. Cert. music tchr., classroom tchr., adminstr., Nev. Instr. gen. music Brownsville (Tex.) Ind. Sch. Dist., 1974-76; instr. gen. music and band Port Isabel (Tex.) Ind. Sch. Dist., 1976-77; instr. gen. music Washoe County Sch. Dist., Reno, 1977-78; instr. instrmental music Carson City (Nev.) Sch. Dist., 1978—. Coord. Music in Our Schs., Brownsville Ind. Sch. Dist., 1976; dir. Elem. Jazz Band Carson City Sch. Dist., 1980—; coord. band festival Carson City Sch. Dist., 1993; instr. Adult Beginning Band, Carson City, 1989—. Musician Reno Mcpl. Band, 1978—, Sierra Nev. Coll. Wind Ensemble, Incline Village, Nev., 1990—; musician, asst. dir. Capital City Community Band, Carson City, 1980—. Mem. ASCD, Omsby County Edn. Assn. Avocations: woodworking, gardening. Office: Carson City Sch Dist PO Box 603 Carson City NV 89702-0603

YEAGER, LOUISE BARBARA LEHR, secondary education educator; b. New Haven, Feb. 24, 1943; d. Michael Adolf and Rosa (Gabold) Lehr; m. Charles Edward Yeager, Sept. 13, 1967; 1 child, William. BS in Math. and Physics, Cen. Conn. State U., 1965, postgrad., 1974. Tchr. math. West Haven (Conn.) High Sch., 1965—67, 1971—2002. Mem. Nat. Coun. Tchrs. Math., Assoc. Tchrs. Math. in Conn. Lutheran. Avocation: golf. Home: 30 Cedar Ln Northford CT 06472-1608 Office: West Haven H S Circle St West Haven CT 06516

YEAGER, MARGIE ANN, English language educator; b. Paducah, Ky., Oct. 27, 1953; d. Victor M. and S. Auneen (Word) Sanderson; m. Leslie C. Yeager Jr., Aug. 10, 1975; children: Andrew S., Elizabeth A. BA, Ind. State U., 1974; MS, Ind. U./Purdue U., 1980. Cert. in secondary edn. English tchr. Connersville (Ind.) H.S., 1975—, dept. chair, 1981-98. Edn., field experience adv. bd. Ind. U. East, Richmond, 1985-95; adj. prof. Ind. U. Advanced Coll. Project, 1985—. Mem. Nat. Coun. Tchrs. of English, Am. Fedn. Tchrs., Internat. Reading Assn., Ind. Libr. Fedn., Delta Kappa Gamma. Lutheran. Avocation: reading.

YEAGER, MYRON DEAN, English language educator, business writing consultant; b. Evansville, Ind., Oct. 27, 1950; s. Robert Paul and Sarah Mazol (Hunt) Y. BA, Grace Coll., 1972; MA, Purdue U., 1974, PhD, 1980. Cert. tchr., Calif. Prof. Grace Coll., Winona Lake, Ind., 1976-84, Chapman U., Orange, Calif., 1984—. Cons. numerous firms, 1980—; faculty chmn. Chapman U., Orange, 1991-92, dept. chmn., 1990-93, dean sch. comm. arts, 2001—; dept. chmn. Grace Coll., Winona Lake, 1981-84. Co-author: The Hutton Story, 1998; co-editor The Chesterfield Papers Project, 1998, Procs. of the West Coast Conf. on Corp. Commn., 1994; contbr. articles to profl. jours. and mags. Recipient UCLA Clark postdoctoral fellowship, 1982, David Ross fellowship Purdue U., 1980, Valerie Scudder award for outstanding tchg., 1992. Mem. Am. Soc. Eighteenth-Century Studies, Samuel Johnson Soc. So. Calif (sec.), Assn. Bus. Comm., Phi Beta Delta, Sigma Tau Delta. Office: Chapman Univ One University Dr Orange CA 92866-1099 E-mail: yeager@chapman.edu.

YEAGLEY, KATHLEEN LUX, community health nurse, educator; b. Columbus, Ohio, Nov. 17, 1953; d. Donald Gregory and Harriet Hope (Harmer) Lux. BS, Ohio State U., 1975, PhD, 1992; MS, U. Hawaii, 1988. Cert. health edn. specialist. Asst. charge nurse Dr.'s North Hosp., Columbus, 1975-76; team leader Ohio State U. Hosp., Columbus, 1976-77; flight nurse USAF, 1977-84; EMT instr. City Colls. Chgo., 1981-82; nursing and health svcs. chair ARC, Rhein Main, Germany, 1984-85; parent educator, clinic coord. Kapiolani Hosp., Honolulu, 1985-86; family planning nurse student and health svcs. U. Hawaii, Honolulu, 1986-87, rsch. asst., 1988; grad. tchg. assoc. Ohio State U., Columbus, 1988-92, lectr., 1992-93, asst. prof., 1993-96, 1999—; tng. and rsch. coord. Next Era Med., Columbus, 1997-98; perinatal program mgr. Columbus Health Dept., 2000—02; clin. educator Hacking Valley Cmty. Hosp., Logan, Ohio, 2003—. Mem.: AAHPERD, APHA, Ohio Assn. Health, Phys. Edn., Recreation and Dance (exec. dir. 1993—), Res. Officer's Assn., Phi Kappa Phi, Eta Sigma Gamma, Sigma Theta Tau. Republican. Roman Catholic. Office: Hacking Valley Cmty Hosp PO Box 966 601 State Rt 664 N Logan OH 43138 E-mail: hvchadm3@ohiohills.com.

YEAMANS, GEORGE THOMAS, librarian, educator; b. Nov. 7, 1929; s. James Norman and Dolphine Sophia (Manhart) Yeamans; m. Mary Ann Seng, Feb. 1, 1958; children: Debra, Susan, Julia. AB, U. Va., 1950; MLS, U. Ky., 1955; EdD, Ind. U., 1965. Asst. audio-visual dir. Ind. State U., Terre Haute, 1957—58; asst. film libr. Ball State U., Muncie, Ind., 1958—61, film libr., 1961—69, assoc. prof. libr. sci., 1969—72, prof., 1972—95, prof. emeritus, 1995—. Cons. Pendleton (Ind.) Sch. Corp., 1962, 67, Captioned Films for the Deaf Workshop, Muncie, 1963—65, Decatur (Ind.) Sch. Sys., 1978; adjudicator Ind. Media Fair, 1979—93, David Letterman Scholarship Program, 1993. Author: Projectionists' Programmed Primer, 1969, rev. edit., 1982, Mounting and Preserving Pictorial Materials, 1976, Tape Recording, 1978, Transparency Making, 1977, Photographic Principles, 1981, Computer Literacy — A Programmed Primer, 1985, Building Effective Creative Project Teams, 1996, Designing Dynamic Media Presentations, 1996; : rev. edit., 2000; ; songwriter: Branson Bound, 1996; contbr. articles to profl. jours. Campaign worker Wilson for Mayor, Muncie, 1979. With USMC, 1950—52. Recipient Citations of Achievement, Internat. Biog. Assn., Cambridge, England, 1973, Am. Biog. Assn., 1976, Mayor James P. Carey award for achievement for disting. contbns. to Ball State U. and City of Muncie, 1988; Video Info. Sys. grantee, Ball State U., 1993. Mem.: ALA, NEA (del. assembly dept. audiovisual instrn. 1967), Audio-Visual Instrn. Dirs. Ind. (exec. bd. 1962—68, pres. 1966—67), Thomas Jefferson Soc. Alumni U. Va., Ind. Pub. Libr. Assn., Ind. Acad. Libr. Assn., Ind. Corp. and Network Libr. Assn., Ind. Libr. Fedn., Assn. Ednl. Comm. and Tech., Autisim Soc. Am., Assn. Ind. Media Educators (chmn. auditing com. 1979—81), Ind. Assn. Ednl. Comms. and Tech. (dist. dir. 1972—76), Am. Assn. Sch. Librs., Phi Delta Kappa. Republican. Unitarian-Universalist. Avocations: photography, philately, numismatics, genealogy. Home: 4507 W Burton Dr Muncie IN 47304-3575

YEATMAN, HARRY CLAY, biologist, educator; b. Ashwood, Tenn., June 22, 1916; s. Trezevant Player and Mary (Wharton) Y.; m. Jean Hansford Anderson, Nov. 24, 1949; children— Henry Clay, Jean Hansford. AB, U. N.C., Chapel Hill, 1939, MA, 1942, PhD, 1953; student, Cornell U., summer 1937. Asst. prof. biology U. of South, Sewanee, Tenn., 1950-54, asso. prof., 1954-60, prof., 1960—, Kenan prof., 1980—, chmn. dept., 1972-76, elderhostel tchr., 1987-88. Vis. prof. marine biology Va. Inst. Marine Sci., Gloucester Point, summer 1967; cons. Smithsonian Instn., Sci. Applications, Inc., La Jolla, Calif., Ctrs. for Disease Control, Atlanta, WHO, Ecol. Analysts, Inc., Balt., Duke Power Co., Charlotte, N.C. Contbr. articles to profl. jours. Served with AUS, 1942-46. Gen. Edn. Bd. fellow, 1941-42; Brown Found. fellow, 1984 Fellow AAAS; mem. Soc. Systematic Biology (charter), Soc. Limnology and Oceanography (charter), Soc. Ichthyology and Herpetology, Tenn. Acad. Sci., Am. Micros. Soc., Am. Ornithologists Union, Tenn. Ornithol. Soc., Tenn. Archeol. Soc., Nat. Speleological Soc., Blue Key, Phi Beta Kappa, Sigma Xi, Omicron Delta Kappa, Sigma Nu. Republican. Episcopalian. Home: PO Box 356 Jumpoff Rd Sewanee TN 37375 Office: 735 University Ave Sewanee TN 37383-1000 Office Fax: 931-598-1145.

YEATS, SYLVIA ANITA, special education educator; b. Bay City, Tex., July 24, 1951; d. Amos Morales and Bertha (Mendeola) Garcia; m. David Arthur Yeats, Aug. 10, 1981. AA, Wharton County Jr. Coll., 1971; BA, Tex. Arts and Industries Univ., 1973; teaching cert., Southwest Tex. State U., 1980; MS, U. Houston, 1993. Cert. tchr., Tex. Tchr. Dept. Edn., Agat, Guam, 1985-86, Alvin (Tex.) Ind. Sch. Dist., 1991—. Active Nat. Geog. Soc. Mem. Coun. Exceptional Children (divsn. learning disabilities, emotionally disturbed children), Univ. Houston Clear Lake Alumni Assn. Roman Catholic. Avocations: reading, playing chess, basketball, tennis. Home: 411 Holly Fern Dr League City TX 77573-5950 Office: Alvin ISD 301 E House St Alvin TX 77511-3581

YEAZELL, RUTH BERNARD, English language educator; b. N.Y.C., Apr. 4, 1947; d. Walter and Annabelle (Reich) Bernard; m. Stephen C. Yeazell, Aug. 14, 1969 (div. 1980). BA with high honors, Swarthmore Coll., 1967; MPhil, Yale U., 1970, PhD, 1971. Asst. prof. English Boston U., 1971-74, UCLA, 1975-77, assoc. prof., 1977-80, prof., 1980-91, Yale U., 1991—, dir. grad. studies, 1993-98, Chace family prof., 1995—, chair, 2000—. Author: Language and Knowledge in the Late Novels of Henry James, 1976, Death and Letters of Alice James, 1981, Fictions of Modesty: Women and Courtship in the English Novel, 1991, Harems of the Mind: Passages of Western Art and Literature, 2000; assoc. editor Nineteenth-Century Fiction, 1977-80; editor: Sex, Politics and Science in the 19th Century Novel, 1986, Henry James: A Collection of Critical Essays, 1994. Dir. Lewis Walpole Libr., 1996—. Woodrow Wilson fellow, 1967-68, Guggenheim fellow, 1979-80, NEH fellow, 1988-89, Pres.'s rsch. fellow U. Calif., 1988-89. Mem. MLA (exec. coun. 1985-88), English Inst. (supervising com. 1983-86). Office: Yale U Dept English New Haven CT 06520-8302

YECKE, CHERI PEARSON, education agency administrator, columnist, author; b. St. Paul, Feb. 5, 1955; d. Leo Sylvester and Marceline Mae (Intihar) Pierson; m. Dennis Joseph Yecke, Dec. 22, 1973; children: Anastasia, Tiffany. BA, U. Hawaii, 1975; MST, U. Wis., River Falls, 1984; postgrad., U. Va. Apptd. mem. State Bd. Edn., 1995—98, dep. sec. edn., 1998—2001, sec. edn., 2001—02; dir. tchr. quality and pub. sch. choice US Dept. Edn., 2002—03; sr. adv. to White House on USA Freedom Corps., 2003; commr. edn. State of Minn., 2003—. Author: The War Against Excellence: The Rising Tide of Mediocrity in America's Middle Schools, 2003. Mem.: Edn. Leaders Coun. Republican. Home: 2106 Arnold Palmer Dr Blaine MN 55449

YEEND, STACEY BROWN, special education educator; b. Chattanooga, Jan. 13, 1967; d. Winfred Eugene and Gloria Ann (Meacham) B.; m. Adam D. Yeend. BS, U. South Ala., 1989; M in Mental Retardation, Auburn U. at Montgomery, 1993. Cert. spl. edn. tchr., Ala. Tchr. of severe/profound Children's Ctr. of Montgomery, Ala., 1989—2000, dept. chair, 1990-91; resource tchr. Dalraida Elem. Sch., 2000—01, Dannelly Elem. Sch., Montgomery, 2001—. 1st v.p. Children's Ctr. PTA, 1991-92, 92-93, 2d v.p., 1994-95. Mem.: NEA. Avocations: cross-stitch, reading, cooking. Home: 536 Lynnhurst Ct Montgomery AL 36117-2945 Office: Dannelly Elem Sch Carter Hill Rd Montgomery AL 36111

YEGGY-DAVIS, GERALDINE MARIE, elementary reading and special education educator, school system administrator; b. Riverside, Iowa, July 25, 1922; d. Henry Clair and Mary Maurine Yeggy; m. Henry Louis Davis, Dec. 28, 1976. BA, Marycrest Internat. U., Davenport, Iowa, 1947; MA, U. Detroit, 1970; postgrad., UCLA; Ednl. Specialist degree, Western Ill. U., 1976; PhD in Reading Edn., La Salle U., 1995. Cert. permanent tchr., ednl. adminstr., reading specialist, learning disabilities, Iowa. Primary tchr. numerous sch. systems, including, Davenport, Ottumwa, Iowa, Ft. Madison, Des Moines, Mpls., Rock Island, Ill.; reading specialist, primary tchr. Chpt. I, title I Davenport Community Schs.; tchr. spl. edn. Child Devel., Inc., Milan, Ill.; pres. Child Devel. Inc., Milan, Ill.; adminstr. C.O.P.E. Tutoring Sch. Inc., Milan, Ill., 1998-99; founder, pres., adminstr., curriculum counselor H.O.M.E. Values Schooling, Inc., Milan, 2000—. Founder, adminstr., dir. not-for-profit sch.; workshop presenter curriculum of perceptual/conceptual experiences program; adminstr. C.O.P.E. Tutorial School Inc. for primary children, intermediate, jr. h.s. and h.s. students with learning disabilities, Milan Ill., bd. dirs., pres. Contbr. numerous publs. for children. Bd. dirs. Quad-Cities Spl. Presons Encounter Christ (S.P.E.C.). Recipient Ind. U. Sch. Project award for Effective Teaching of Reading, 1983, Golden Apple award Scott County, 1991; fellow Wall St. Jour., 1964. Mem. NEA, ASCD, Ill. ASCD, Nat. Coun. Tchrs. English, Internat. Reading Assn., Ill. State Edn. Assn., Iowa Reading Assn., Miss. River Bend Reading Assn., Nat. Learning Disabilities Assn., Ill. Learning Disabilities Assn., Early Childhood Edn. Assn., Nat. Coun. Tchrs. Math. Home: 509 33rd Ave W Milan IL 61264-3753 Office: COPE Tutoring and HOME ValuesSch Inc 228 2nd Ave W Milan IL 61264-2429

YEH, HSU-CHONG, radiology educator; b. Taipei, Taiwan, Mar. 30, 1937; came to US, 1973; s. Ping-Hui and Ah-Chu (Chuang) Y.; m. Cha-Pying Yeh, Sept. 26, 1964; children: David, Benjamin. MD, Nat. Taiwan U., Taipei, 1962. Diplomate Am. Bd. Radiology. Rotating intern U. Alberta Hosp., Edmonton, Can., 1964-65; resident in diagnostic radiology Montreal Gen. Hosp., McGill U., Canada, 1969-72, fellow in diagnostic ultrasound, 1972-73; mem. active med. staff Soldier's Meml. Hosp., Campbellton, Canada, 1967-69; assoc. Mt. Sinai Sch. Medicine, NYC, 1973-75, asst. prof. radiology, 1976-78, assoc. prof., 1979-86, prof., 1986—. Cons. radiology VA Hosp., Bronx, NY, 1977-87. Author: Radiology of the Adrenals, 1982; contbg. author: Progress in Liver Disease, 1979, Frontiers in Liver Disease, 1981, Ultrasound Annual, 1982, 85, Ultrasound in Urology, 1984, Ultrasonography of the Urinary Tract, 1991, Surgical Management of Urologic Disease, 1991; contbr. articles to med. jour. 2d lt. Armored Corps, Taiwan Army, 1962-63. Fellow Soc. Radiologists in Ultrasound; mem. Am. Inst. Ultrasound in Medicine (sr.), Radiol. Soc. N.Am. (sci. exhibit award 1988-2000), Computerized Radiology Soc., Am. Roentgen Ray Soc. (sci. exhibit award 1988), NY Roentgen Ray Soc. Avocations: fine art painting, sculpture, jogging, movies. Office: Mt Sinai Med Ctr One Gustave L Levy Pl New York NY 10029-6574

YEH, PAUL PAO, electrical and electronics engineer, educator; b. Sung Yang, Chekiang, China, Mar. 25, 1927; came to U.S., 1956, naturalized, 1963; s. Tsung Shan and Shu Huan (Mao) Y.; m. Beverley Pamela Eng, May 15, 1953; children: Judith Elaine, Paul Edmond, Richard Alvin, Ronald Timothy. Student, Nat. Cen. U., Nanking, China, 1946—49; B.A.Sc., U. Toronto, Ont., Can., 1951; MSEE, U. Pa., 1960, PhD, 1966. Registered profl. engr., Ont. Design engr. Can. Gen. Electric Co., Toronto, 1951-56; asst. prof. SUNY, Binghamton, 1956-57; sr. engr. H.K. Porter, ITE & Kuhlman, Phila. and Detroit, 1957-61; assoc. prof. N.J. Inst. Tech., Newark, 1961-66; supr. rsch. and devel. N.Am. Rockwell, Anaheim, Calif., 1966-70; sr. R&D engr. Skunk Works Lockheed Calif. Co., Burbank, Calif., 1970-72, 78-89; mem. tech. staff The Aerospace Corp., El Segundo, Calif., 1972-78; sr. R&D engr. Lockheed Advanced Devel. Co., Burbank, 1978-89; chief scientist Advanced Systems Rsch., Pasadena, Calif., 1989—. With Consol. Edison Co., N.Y.C., 1963-64, Pub. Svc. Elec. and Gas Co. N.J., 1965-66, Zhejiang Sci. and Tech. Exch. Ctr. with Fgn. Countries, 1995—; sr. lectr. State U. Calif., Long Beach, 1967-73; cons. prof. Chung Shan Inst. Sci. and Tech., 1989-92; vis. prof. Tsinghua U., 1993—, South China U. Sci. and Tech., 1997--; vis. chair prof. S.E. U., 1994—, Zhejiang U., 1994—; cons. prof. Northwestern Poly. U., 1993—, Shanghai U., 1994—; hon. prof. Beijing U. Aeronautics and Astronautics, 1993—, Zhejiang U. Sci. and Tech., 1994—; chair, prof. Nanjing U. Aeronautics & Astronautics, 1999—, Wuyi U., 1999—; rschr. power sys. design and control, 1951-66; investigator R&D Stealth tech. electronic warfare, anti-jam warfare, avionics, IR/EO Tech, nuclear hardening, anti-submarine warfare. Recipient Achievement award for anti-submarine warfare/magnetic anomaly detection sys. Lockheed Corp. Mem. IEEE (sr., life), Nat. Mgmt. Assn. (life), Nat. Def. Indsl. Assn., Assn. Old Crows, Chinese Am. Engring./Sci. Assn. So. Calif. (life; pres. 1969-71), Nat. Ctrl. U. Alumni Assn. (life; pres. 1977), Beijing Assn. for Sci. and Tech. Exchs. with Fgn . Countries, (hon. dir.), Assn. Profl. Engrs. of Ont., N.Y. Acad. Scis., Air Force Assn., Zhejiang Assn. for Sci. and Tech. Exchs. with Fgn. Countries (advisor), Armed Forces Comms. and Electronics Assn., U.S. Naval Inst., Assn. U.S. Army. Republican. Presbyterian. Achievements include patent for Non-Capacitive Transmission Cable. Home: 78278 Quail Run Palm Desert CA 92211 Office: Advanced Systems Rsch Inc 33 S Catalina Ave Ste 202 Pasadena CA 91106-2426 E-mail: Drpaulpyeh@ieee.org.

YEH, RAYMOND WEI-HWA, architect, educator; b. Shanghai, Feb. 25, 1942; came to U.S., 1958, naturalized, 1976; s. Herbert Hwan-Ching and Joyce Bo-Ding (Kwan) Y.; m. Hsiao-Yen Chen, Sept. 16, 1967; children—Bryant Po Yung, Clement Chung-Yung, Emily Su-Yung. BA, U. Oreg., 1965, B.Arch., 1967; M.Arch., U. Minn., 1969. Cert. Nat. Coun. Archtl. Registration Bds.; registered architect, Tex., Okla., Calif., Hawaii. Draftsman, designer various archtl. firms, 1965-68; design architect Ellerbe Architects, St. Paul, 1968-70; v.p., dir. design Sorey, Hill, Binnicker, Oklahoma City, 1973-74; prin. architect Raymond W.H. Yeh & Assos., Norman, Okla., 1974-80; asst. prof. to prof. U. Okla., Norman, 1970-79; head dept. architecture, prof. Calif. Poly. State U., San Luis Obispo, 1979-83; dean Coll. Architecture U. Okla., Norman, 1983-92; prin. architect W.H. Raymond Yeh, Norman, 1983-93; dean sch. architecture U. Hawaii at Manoa, Honolulu, 1993—. Profl. adviser Neighborhood Conservation and Devel. Center, Oklahoma City, 1977 79 Works include: St. Thomas More U. Parish and Student Center, Norman, Summit Ridge Center Retirement Community, Harrah, Okla., (recipient Nat. Design award Guild Religious Architecture 1978). Nat. Endowment for Arts fellow, 1978-79 Fellow AIA (dir., pres. Okla. chpt. 1986, design awards, nat. com. chmn. 1989); mem. Calif. Coun. Archtl. Edn. (dir., pres. 1982-83), Okla. Found. for Architecture (founding chair bd. 1989-90), Asian Soc. Okla. (award of Excellence 1992), Asia Pacific Ctr. for Arch. (founding bd. dirs. 1996). Presbyterian. Office: U Hawaii Manoa Sch Architecture Honolulu HI 96822

YELTON, DIANNE BURGESS, secondary school educator; b. Albuquerque, Nov. 23, 1954; d. Robert Allen and Elizabeth (Donnelly) B.; m. Steven John Yelton, Aug. 13, 1988. BS in Edn., Miami U., 1977, MEd, 1983. Tchr. Defiance (Ohio) City Schs., 1977-78; jr. high devel. handicapped tchr. Princeton City Schs., Cin., 1978-79, Oak Hills Local Schs., Cin., 1979-82, tchr. primary developmentally handicapped, 1982-88; tchr. Ft. Thomas (Ky.) Ind. Schs., 1988—. Supr. student tchrs. various sch. dists., 1980—; spkr. convs. and inservice workshops, 1979—. Mem. No. Ky. Leadership Class, 2003. Recipient Outstanding Woman of No. Ky., 1998, Golden Apple Achiever award Ashland Oil, 1998, Ky. Post Golden Apple award, 1997, Tchg. Excellence award Jiffy Lube, 1997. Mem. NEA, Internat. Reading Assn., Nat. Coun. Tchrs. English, PTA. Methodist. Avocations: aerobics, spectator sports, dining out. Office: Highlands Mid Sch 2350 Memorial Pkwy Fort Thomas KY 41075-1111 E-mail: dbyelton@yahoo.com.

YELTON, ELEANOR O'DELL, retired reading specialist; b. Maryville, Tenn., Jan. 21, 1929; d. Rondie Bliss and Maxie (Williams) O'Dell; m. Doran Yelton, Aug. 26, 1951; children: Doran II, Marshall, David, Holly. BS, East Tenn. State U., 1951. Cert. tchr., Fla. Tchr. Rozelle Sch., Memphis, 1952-55; tchr. English Clay High Sch., Green Cove Springs, Fla., 1963-66, reading specialist, 1986-96, The Bolles Sch., Jacksonville, Fla., 1966-84; ret., 1995. Chair adv. coun. Clay High Sch., Green Cove Springs, 1991-92. Author: (newsletters) PERKS, 1990 (Secondary Reading Coun. Fla. award 1991), Parents' Link, 1993. Mem. Internat. Reading Assn., Fla. Reading Assn., Secondary Reading Coun. Fla., Clay County Acad. Excellence, Clay County Reading Coun. (founder Books for Babies program Humana Hosp. 1990, pres. 1990-91, Literacy award 1995). Avocations: traveling, reading, computers. Home: 3161 River Rd N Green Cove Springs FL 32043-8768

YELVERTON, DEBORAH SUE, middle school art educator; b. Wilson, N.C., Mar. 17, 1956; d. George Elliott and Hadilene (Coley) Yelverton. BS, Atlantic Christian Coll., 1978. Cert. art educator, N.C. Tchr. art Frink Jr. High Sch., LaGrange, N.C., 1978-79, Wayne County Schs., Goldsboro, N.C., 1979—. Mem. judge panel Youth Art Month Art Exhibit, Raleigh, N.C., 1983, mem. Youth Art Month Com., 1982-84; judge panelist Western N.C. Scholastic Arts Competition, Greensboro, 1990, Seymour Johnson AFB Adult Divsn. Arts/Crafts Contest, Goldsboro, 1988-94, 95; mem. Wayne County Mid. Sch. Task Force, Goldsboro, 1990-91. Group photography exhibits include Wayne County Artists that Teach, 1985, N.C. Black/White Photography Travel Exhibit, 1980. Grantee Arts in Schs. program, Cmty. Arts Coun. Wayne County, 1987-88, 89-90; recipient Zeno Spence Art Educator award, 1996; named Outstanding Young Educator Goldsboro Jaycees, 1994. Mem. Nat. Art Edn. Assn., N.C. Art Edn. Assn. Avocations: music, photography, collecting unicorns, dancing. Home: 2601 Cashwell Dr Apt H Goldsboro NC 27534-4228 Office: Ea Wayne Mid Sch 3518 Central Heights Rd Goldsboro NC 27534-8027

YENERICH, WALLACE CHRISTIAN, mathematics educator; b. Ashton, Ill., June 28, 1921; s. Wesley H. and Minnie J. (Krug) Y.; m. Twyla M. Yeoman, Oct. 7, 1944; children: Phyllis, Marlene, Paul, Camilla, Ruth. BA, North Ctrl. Coll., Naperville, Ill., 1944; MA, U. Ill., 1948; postgrad., Purdue U., 1956, DePauw U., 1958. Tchr. math., sci., and phys. edn. Plato Twp. H.S., Plato Center, Ill., 1944-47; math., sch. and phys. edn. tchr. Beason (Ill.) Cmty. H.S., 1948; math. and sci. tchr. Ashton (Ill.) H.S., 1948-55; math. tchr. Rochelle (Ill.) Twp. H.S., 1955-79, Red Bird Mission Sch., Beverly, Ky., 1979-81; ind. math. tchr. Ashton, 1981—. Treas. Ashton United. Meth. Ch., 1981—; trustee Village of Ashton, 1950-58. Mem. Nat. Tchrs. Math., Ill. Ret. Tchrs. (chmn. com. 1992—). Avocation: waterskiing. Home: PO Box 278 Ashton IL 61006-0278

YEOMAN, LYNN CHALMERS, medical educator; b. Evanston, Ill., May 17, 1943; m. Carol J. Yeoman; children: Caroline, Christopher, Sarah. BA, DePauw U., 1965; PhD, U. Ill., 1970. Instr. Baylor Coll. Medicine, Houston, 1972-73, asst. prof., 1973-76, assoc. prof., 1976-84, prof., 1984—; assoc. dir. Bristol-Baylor Lab, Houston, 1989-90; assoc. dir. anti-cancer drug discovery and cell and molecular biology Bristol-Myers Co., Wallingford, Conn., 1989-90; dir. curriculum database program Baylor Coll. Medicine, Houston, 1995—, dir. integrated problem solving program, 1997—, dir. ednl. resource ctr., 2001—. Cons. Litton Bionetics, Ft. Detrick, Md., 1977-78, Colon Cancer Working Group, Houston, 1985-86, Oncos, Ltd., Houston, 1985-87, Bristol-Myers Co., Wallingford, Conn., 1985-89, U. Tex. Med. Br., Galveston, 1998, Ubiquitex Techs. Corp., 1995-96; mem. com. revision U.S. Pharmacopeial Conv., 1985-90, 1995—, chmn. expert com. on biotech. and natural therapeutics and diagnostics, complex actives exec. com., 2000—. Editor: Methods in Cancer Research, Vols. 19 and 20, 1982; mem. editl. bd. Frontiers in Biosci., Med. Edn. Online; contbr. articles to profl. jours. Parliamentarian, Marilyn Estates Civic Assn., Houston, 1984. NCI grantee, 1987—. Mem. Am. Chem. Soc., Am. Soc. Biochem. and Molecular Biology, Group on Ednl. Affairs. Methodist. Achievements include patent for detection of antigen gp650 in sera and other specimens from cancer patients with anti-gp650 monoclonal antibody. Home: 5454 Rutherglenn Dr Houston TX 77096-4032 Office: 1 Baylor Plz Houston TX 77030-3411 Business E-Mail: lyeoman@bcm.tmc.edu.

YEOMANS, GORDON ALLAN, retired education educator; b. Cherry Valley, Ohio, Sept. 30, 1921; s. Ralph Carey Yeomans and Margaret Warner; m. Marjorie Jo Roberts, Feb. 27, 1949; 1 child, Lynne Leigh Yeomans Craver. BA, U. S.W. La., 1951; MA, La. State U., 1952, PhD, 1966. Instr. U. Miss., Oxford, 1952; assoc. prof. Samford U., Birmingham, Ala., 1952-66, U. S.W. La., Lafayette, 1966-67; prof., dept. head Miss. U. for Women, Columbus, 1967-68; prof. U. Tenn., Knoxville, 1968-87, prof. emeritus, 1987. Cons. Andersen Electric Corp., Leeds, Ala., 1958, John Williamson Co., Birmingham, 1960-61, Birmingham (Ala.) Trust Bank, 1962, Union Carbide Corp., Oak Ridge, Tenn., 1969-81, Magnavox Corp., Asheville, N.C., 1975. Author: A Handbook for Speakers, 1969; contbr. author: The Heart of the Valley, 1976, Pamphlets and The American Revolution, 1976; contbr. articles to profl. jours. Program chmn. Knoxville Religious Bicentennial, 1976; adv. coun. Knoxville Alcohol and Drug Rehab. Ctr.; mem. 1st United Meth. Ch., Knoxville, religious drama dir.. With USAAF, 1940-45. Tchr. grantee Danforth Found., 1956-57, summer 1963, Rsch. grantee U. Tenn., 1974, 75; named Speech Tchr. of Yr., State of Tenn., 1984. Mem. Speech Communication Assn., So. Speech Communication Assn., East Tenn. Hist. Soc., Knoxville Civil War Roundtable. Democrat. Avocation: antiquarian book dealer and collector. Home: 805 Noragate Rd Knoxville TN 37919-7016

YERUSHALMI, YOSEF HAYIM, historian, educator; b. NYC, May 20, 1932; s. Leon and Eva (Kaplan) Y.; m. Ophra Pearly, Jan. 4, 1959; 1 child, Ariel. BA, Yeshiva U., 1953; M in Hebrew Lit., Jewish Theol. Sem. Am., 1957; MA, Columbia U., 1961, PhD, 1966; MA (hon.), Harvard, 1970; DHL (hon.), Jewish Theol. Sem. Am., 1987; LHD (hon.), Hebrew Union Coll., 1996; PhD (hon.), U. Haifa, 1997, Ludwig Maximilians U., 1997; DHL (hon.), Spertus Inst., 2002; PhD (hon.), Ecole Pratique des Hautes Etudes Sorbonne Paris, 2003. Instr. Jewish history Rutgers U., New Brunswick, N.J., 1963-66; asst. prof. Hebrew and Jewish History Harvard U., 1966-70, prof., 1970-78, Jacob E. Safra prof. Jewish history and Sephardic civilization, 1978-80, chmn. dept. near eastern langs. and civilizations, 1978-80, Salo Wittmayer Baron Prof. of Jewish History, Culture, Soc.; dir. Ctr. for Israel and Jewish Studies Columbia U., N.Y.C., 1980—. Author: From Spanish Court to Italian Ghetto: Isaac Cardoso, A Study in Seventeenth-Century Marranism and Jewish Apologetics, 1971, Haggadah and History, 1975, The Lisbon Massacre of 1506, 1976, Zakhor: Jewish History and Jewish Memory, 1982, Freud's Moses: Judaism Terminable and Interminable, 1991, A Field in Anatot: Essays on Jewish History (in German), 1993, Servants of Kings and Not Servants of Servants: Some Aspects of the Political History of the Jews (in German), 1995, Sefardica: Essays on the History of the Jews, Marranos and New Christians of Hispano-Portuguese Origin (in French), 1998; author (in Hebrew): Spinoza on the Survival of the Jews, 1983; contbr. articles to profl. publs. on Spanish and Portuguese Jewry and history of psychoanalysis; chmn. publs. com. Jewish Publ. Soc., 1972-84; pres. Leo Baeck Inst., 1986-91. Bd. dirs. Conf. Jewish Social Studies, Psycho analytic Research and Devel. Fund, Editorial Bd., History and Memory. Recipient Newman medal CUNY, 1975, Nat. Jewish Book award, 1983, 92,Ansley award Columbia U. Press, 1968, medal of achievement in history Nat. Found. for Jewish Culture,1995; Kent fellow, 1963, travel fellow Nat. Found. for Jewish Culture, 1964, fellow NEH, 1976-77, Rockefeller fellow in humanities, 1983-84, Guggenheim fellow, 1989-90; Carl Friedrich von Siemens Stiftung fellow (Munich), 1996-97. Fellow Am. Acad. Jewish Research, Am. Acad. Arts and Scis., Academia Portuguesa da História Lisbon (hon.) Office: Columbia U 511 Fayerweather Hall 1180 Amsterdam Ave New York NY 10027-7039

YETMAN, LEITH ELEANOR, academic administrator; b. Kellits, Clarendon, Jamaica, West Indies; came to U.S., 1967; d. 2nd child of 12 children of Percival Augustus and Grace Elizabeth (Anderson) Y.; m. Noel W. Miller, Apr. 8, 1961 (div. 1977); children: Donovan, Jo-Ann, Kirk, Lori-Anne; adopted children: LaFara, Samantha, Brandon Ryan. Attended, Bethlehem Teachers Coll., St. Elizabeth, Jamaica, 1960; BSC, Baruch Coll., 1976; MA, Columbia U., 1979. Cert. tchr., N.Y.; accredited Grace Inst. Bus. Tech., Bklyn., 1998. Legal sec. various law firms, N.Y.C., 1969-76; instr. Taylor Bus. Inst., N.Y.C., 1977-79; founder, pres., dir. N.Y. Inst. English and Bus. (formerly N.Y. Inst. Bus. Tech., N.Y.C., 1981—; founder Grace Inst. Bus. Tech., Bklyn., 1996. Founder Grace Inst. Bus. Tech., Bklyn., 1996. Recipient Outstanding Achievement award Baruch Coll. Alumni Assn., 1989, Outstanding Achievement award Baruch Coll. Alumni Assn., citations Hon. Virginia Fields, Gov. N.Y. State, Hon. George E. Pataki, letters of recognition and praise Ex-First Ladies Barbara Bush, Hillary Clinton, Ex-Pres. Bill Clinton, Senator Charles Rangel, Ex-Mayor David Dinkins, others; Leith E. Yetman Day proclaimed June 1, 1994 by Manhattan Borough Pres. Office: NY Inst English and Bus 248 W 35th St New York NY 10001 E-mail: ny1eb02@aol.com.

YETT, SALLY PUGH, elementary school educator, gifted and talented educator; b. St. Louis, Feb. 15, 1935; d. John D. and Esther Ruth Pugh; m. Donald Edward Yett, June 19, 1964; children: Stephen Edward, John Harold. BFA, Washington U., St. Louis, 1956; tchg. credential, Calif. State U., L.A., 1989. Cert. gen. clear multiple subject and art supplementary Calif. Dept. Edn. Recreation therapist ARC, San Antonio, 1956-58; dir. recreation therapy dept. Jewish Hosp., St. Louis, 1958-64; tchr. art-gifted class Juan Cabrillo Elem., Malibu, Calif., 1975-78; educator pre-kindergarten Malibu Meth. Pre-Sch., 1979-81; educator grades 9-12 Santa Monica (Calif.) Sch. Dist., 1981-89; spl. edn. educator grades 1-6 art L.A. Unified Sch. Dist.-Visual and Performing Arts Magnet, 1990—; resource tchr., art edn. advisor Calif. State U., L.A., 2001—. Judge Making History, L.A., 1998—; participant UCLA Tchrs. and Scholars Symposium, 1999—2003; cons. edn. dept. Calif. State U., L.A.; state judge History Day in Calif., 2003. Exhibitions include Malibu Art Festival, 1976 (3rd place award), Malibu Art Assn. Show, 1984 (3rd place award), Roberts Art Gallery, 1989, CAEA State Conv.-Calif. State Bakersfield Exhibit, 2001; contbr. articles to profl. jours. PTA pres. Juan Cabrillo Elem., Malibu, 1976—78, Malibu Park Jr. HS; pres. Santa Monica Jr. Programs, 1979—81; 2d, 3d, and 4th v.p. Santa Monica/Malibu PTA Coun., 1982—85; pres. Malibu Art Assn., 1992—93. Nominee Tchr. of Yr., Walt Disney Co.; recipient Honoree Bravo award, L.A. Music Ctr., award, Calif. Cmty. Found., 2003; grantee, 2003—, 2003. Mem.: Internat. Studies Overseas Program, East West Players Orgn., Calif. Alliance Arts Edn., Ams. for the Arts, Smithsonian Inst., Huntington Mus., Gene Autrey Mus., Nat. Mus. Women, Mus. Natural History, Calif. Art Edn. Assn., Calif. Coun. Social Studies, Soc. Calligraphy (bd. dirs., pub. rels. 1987—91), Tchrs. and Writers Collaborative, Nat. Art Edn. Assn., Art Mus. Long Beach, Metro. Mus. Art, Shakespeare Festival/L.A., UCLA Fowler Mus. Cultural History, L.A. County Art Mus., S.W. Mus., Mus. Contemporary Art, Craft and Folk Mus., Pacific Asia Mus., Smithsonian Nat. Mus. Am. Indian, Mus. L.Am. Art, People to People Internat. (Indigenous Art del. to New Zealand, Australia 1998), UCLA Book Club, Kappa Alpha Theta. Avocations: travel, reading, calligraphy, hiking, gardening. Home: 2042 Hanscom Dr South Pasadena CA 91030-4012

YETTER, RICHARD ALAN, engineering educator; b. Trenton, N.J., May 23, 1952; s. Albert Lewis Jr. and Marcella Fern (Snook) Y. BS, Syracuse U., 1974; MS, Cornell U., 1981; MA, Princeton U., 1981, PhD, 1985. Rsch. engr. Ford Motor Co., Dearborn, Mich., 1976-79; rsch. collaborator Brookhaven Nat. Lab., Upton, N.Y., 1983-87; rsch. staff dept. mech. and aerospace engring. Princeton (N.J) U., 1985-90, rsch. scientist, 1990-96, sr. rsch. scientist, 1996—, lectr., 1990—. Cons. Cabot Corp., Ill., 1991, British Oxygen Corp., N.J., 1990-91, U.S. Army & HR Rsch., 1988-92, Rsch. Cottrell & Efthimion Enterprises, N.J., 1989-92. Dep. editor Combustion Sci. and Tech., 1996—; contbr. chpts. to books and articles to profl. jours.; patentee asymmetric whirl combustion. Exxon Edn. Found. fellow, 1980-84. Mem. SO. Automotive Engrs., Combustion Inst., Pi Tau Sigma, Tau Beta Pi. Avocations: running, tennis, sailing.

YI, JENNY KISUK, public health educator; b. Korea, Sept. 8, 1958; came to U.S., 1973; d. Moon Se and Kyong Suk (Yim) Y. BS in Biology, U. Wash., 1982; BS in Nutrition, U. Minn., 1986, MPH, 1987; PhD in Pub. Health, U. Mass., 1992. Pub. health nutritionist Minn. Health Dept., Mpls., 1986-87; sr. pub. health nutritionist Cape Cod WIC Program, Hyannis, Mass., 1987-88; acad. advisor U. Mass., Amherst, 1990-92; asst. prof. U. Houston, 1992—. Bd. dirs. Asian Am. Health Coalition, Houston; mem. adv. bd. Baylor Coll. Medicine Breast Cancer Edn. Project, Houston, 1995—. Contbr. articles to profl. jours. Recipient Cert. of Appreciation, Everywoman's Ctr., U. Mass., 1991. Fellow Okura Health Leadership

Found.; mem. APA, Nat. Women's Health Network, Asian Am. Psychol. Assn. Avocations: travel, playing piano, gardening, reading mystery novels. Office: Univ Houston 3855 Holman St Houston TX 77004-4710

YIM, SOLOMON CHIK-SING, civil engineering educator, consultant; b. Hong Kong, Sept. 11, 1952; came to U.S., 1972; s. Fuk-Ching and San-Chan (Leung) Y.; m. Lenore S. Hata, Aug. 27, 1983; children: Rachel L., Joshua A. BSCE, Rice U., 1976; MSCE, U. Calif., Berkeley, 1977, MA in Math., 1981, PhD in Civil Engring., 1983. Registered profl. engr., Oreg. Rsch. asst. U. Calif., 1976-83, vis. lectr., 1983-84, vis. assoc. prof., 1993-94; sr. rsch. engr. Exxon Prodn. Rsch. Co., Houston, 1984-87; asst. prof. civil engring. Oreg. State U., Corvallis, 1987-91, assoc. prof., 1991-97, prof., 1997—, asst. dept. head, 1998-2000, dir. Transp. Rsch. Inst., 1999—. Cons. engr., 1977—; mem. ship structures com. NRC, 1990-96; mem. grad. fellowship com. in sci. and engring. Dept. Def., 1989-99; sr. vis. scientist Norwegian Coun. for Sci. and Indsl. Rsch., Trondheim, 1994. Fellow Office Naval Rsch., 1988-91; sr. faculty rsch. fellow USN, 1993. Mem. ASCE (publ. com. 1993-96, editl. bd. 1996—), ASME (assoc. editor 2000—), Soc. Naval Architecture and Marine Engrs., Internation Soc. Offshore and Polar Engrs. (charter, conf. tech. program com. 1992-98). Achievements include research in nonlinear stochastic dynamics and reliability of ocean and structural systems, in nonlinear response of structures to earthquakes. Office: Oreg State U 202 Apperson Hall Corvallis OR 97331-8522 E-mail: solomon.yim@orst.edu.

YIN, FANG-FANG, medical physicist, educator; b. Ningbo, Zhejiang, China, Sept. 14, 1958; came to U.S., 1985; s. Shisheng Yin and Xiaoxian Ma; m. Li Sun, Feb. 14, 1986; children: Moli Yin, Lucy Yin. BS, Zhejiang U., 1982; MS, Bowling Green (Ohio) State U., 1987; PhD, U. Chgo., 1992. Cert. medical physicist Am. Bd. Radiology. Lectr. Industry U. of East China, Shanghai, 1982-85; grad. asst. Bowling Green State U., 1985-87; rsch. asst. U. Chgo., 1987-88, researcher, 1989-91; asst./med. physicist U. Rochester, N.Y., 1992-93, sr. instr./med. physicist, 1994—, asst. prof./med. physicist, 1994—. Chief Oncologic Imaging Rsch. Lab., Rochester, 1994—; divsn. head med. physics Henry Ford Health System, Dept. Radiation Oncology, Detroit, 1998—. Contbr. articles to profl. jours.; patentee for automated method and system for the detection and classification of abnormal lesions and parenchymal distortions in med. images. Recipient Overman Summer fellowship Bowling Green State U., 1986; rsch. grantee Am. Cancer Soc., 1994, The Whitaker Found., 1995-98. Mem. Am. Assn. Physicists in Medicine. Avocations: tennis, ping pong. Office: Henry Ford Health Sys Dept Radiation Oncology 2799 W Grand Blvd Detroit MI 48202-2608

YITTS, ROSE MARIE, nursery school executive; b. Bridgeport, Conn., Apr. 29, 1942; m. Richard Francis Yitts, Dec. 28, 1963; children: Anthony Michael, Jennifer Lisa, Heather Michelle. BS, So. Conn. State Coll., 1963; MS, So. Conn. State U., 1983. Tchr. Trumbull Bd. Edn., Conn., 1963-69; substitute tchr. Seymour and Oxford Bd. Edn., Conn., 1970-79; tchr. aide spl. edn. Oxford Bd. Edn., 1979-82; dir., founding ptnr., pres. and treas. Strawberry Tyme Nursery Sch. and Day Care Ctr. Ltd., Seymour, 1983—. Den leader, com. chmn. Boy Scouts Am., Seymour, 1973-77; troop leader Girl Scouts U.S., Seymour, 1978-80; chair fundraisers, coach George J. Hummel Little League, Seymour, 1982-86, 1st woman pres., 1987-88, player agt., 1990; tchr., spl. edn. curriculum developer Ch. of Good Shepherd, mem. parish coun., 1984-86; elected mem., corr. sec. Seymour Libr., bd. dirs., 1983-89; elected mem. Republican Town Com., 1996-, mem. exec. bd., 2000, GOP 5 State, 1998—2002; elected mem. Seymour Bd. Edn., 1999—. Recipient award of merit, honorable mention, Golden Poet award, World of Poetry, 1987, Editor's Choice award, Nat. Libr. Poetry, 1994, 1995, Joseph Gido award, Seymour Rep. Town. Com., 2001—. Mem. Nat. Assn. for Edn. of Young Children, Oxford Bus. Assn. (membership com. 1993-95), Seymour Hist. Soc. (life, bd. dirs. 2003—). bd. dirs. Seymour Hist. Soc., 2003-. Republican. E-mail: michmax2@aol.com.

YLINIEMI, HAZEL ALICE, educational administrator; b. Rural Becker County, Minn., Jan. 30, 1941; d. Isacki and Aili Maria (Haanpaa) Y. BS in English Edn., Moorhead State U., 1967; MS in Media Edn., Mankato State U., 1973; postgrad., Tri-Coll. U., 1973—, U. N.D., 1980—. Clk. group ins. Northwestern Nat. Life, Mpls., 1959-60; cosmetologist Looking Glass Dayton's, Mpls., 1961-63; clk. group ins. N.Am. Life & Casualty, Mpls., 1963-64; English tchr. grades 10, 12 Hibbing (Minn.) High Sch., 1967-69; English tchr. grades 10, 11 Carlton (Minn.) High Sch., 1969-71; libr. media specialist Fargo (N.D.) South High Sch., 1973-80; dir. instrnl. resources Fargo Pub. Sch. System, 1980—. Mem. program com. AECT/DSMS, 1990; reviewer video tapes; treas. 16th Plains Internat. Reading Conv., Fargo, 1988. Sch. rep. N.D. Centennial State Kick-Off Celebration, Fargo, 1989. Recipient Literacy award Valley Reading Coun., Fargo, 1989. Mem. ALA, Am. Assn. Sch. Librs. (del. affiliate assembly of AASL 1980-81, 84-90, 93, region IV coord. affiliate assembly 1988-90), Young Adult Libr. Svc. Assn. (media selection and usage com. 1989-93, selected films and videos for young adults com. 1993-95), Phi Delta Kappa, Delta Kappa Gamma (pres. Beta chpt. 1984-86). Lutheran. Avocations: walking, reading, movies. Home: 17948 County Highway 38 Frazee MN 56544-8576 Office: Fargo Pub Schs 415 4th St N Fargo ND 58102-4514

YOCUM, CHARLEEN ELAINE, educational administrator, counselor; b. Denver, June 21, 1941; d. Charles Marston and Margie Ellen (Terwilliger) Macy; m. Gilbert Lee Yocum, Mar. 22, 1964; children: David, Dean, Danelle. AB in Teaching, U. No. Colo., 1963; MEd, Colo. State U., 1984, postgrad., 1991—. Cert. tchr., job devel. specialist, Colo. Sec. various cos., Denver, 1957-63; tchr. North High Sch., Denver, 1963, Metro Youth Ctr., Denver, 1966; instr. Red Rocks C.C., Lakewood, Colo., 1971-78; tchr. Jefferson County Schs., Arvada, Colo., 1978-89, adminstr. Lakewood, 1989-93; career counselor Standley Lake High Sch., 1993—. Facilitator numerous curriculum guides, 1988—. Co-chmn. Arvada West Bus. Adv. Coun., 1980-88; mem. Exec. Bus. Coun., Golden, Colo., 1985-88; mem., co-facilitator Jeffco County Adv. Com., Golden, 1988-92; charter mem. Eldorado Homeowners Assn., 1971-75; block organizer Am. Heart Assn., Diabetes Found., 1980-88; participant Ronald MacDonald House; mem. Leaders Industry, Bus., Edn. Relating To Youth, Lakewood, 1991-92. Named Outstanding Bus. Tchr., Nat. Mgmt. Assn., Instr. of Excellence, Women's Leadership Inst., 1990; scholar Leadership Lakewood, 1991. Mem. Am. Vocat. Assn., Colo. Vocat. Assn., Jefferson County Adminstrs. Assn., Colo. Mktg. Assn., Colo. For and About Bus., Leadership Lakewood Alumnae Assn. Avocations: bridge, golf, bowling, watching football, baseball and soccer, church activities. Office: Standley Lake High Sch 9300 W 104th Ave Broomfield CO 80021-3686

YOCUM, CHARLES FREDRICK, biology educator; b. Storm Lake, Iowa, Oct. 31, 1941; s. Vincent Cary and Olive Lucille (Cammack) Y.; m. Patricia Joan Bury, Jan. 1, 1981; 1 son, Erik Charles. BS, Iowa State U., 1963; MS, Ill. Inst. Tech., 1968; PhD, Ind. U., 1971. Rsch. biochemist Ill. Inst. Tech. Rsch. Inst., Chgo., 1963-68; grad. fellow Ind. U., Bloomington, 1968-71; postdoctoral fellow Cornell U., Ithaca, N.Y., 1971-73; asst. prof. U. Mich., Ann Arbor, 1973-77, assoc. prof., 1978-82, prof. biol. scis. and chemistry, 1983—. Alfred S. Sussman collegiate prof. biology, 1998—, chmn. dept. biology, 1985-91; vis. prof. Mich. State U., East Lansing, 1980-81; cons. NSF, Washington, 1982—. Editl. bd. Plant Physiology, Photosynthesis Rsch., Biochimica et Biophysica Acta; contbr. articles to various publs. Fulbright fellow, 1996; rsch. grantee NSF, 1978—, USDA, 1978—; recipient Henry Russel award U. Mich., 1977; fellow J.S. Guggenheim Found., 2002-03. Fellow AAAS; mem. Am. Chem. Soc., Am. Soc. Plant Physiologists, Am. Soc. Biol. Chemists, Am. Soc. Photobiology. Avocations: classical music, travel. Office: Dept Biology Univ of Mich Ann Arbor MI 48109-1048 E-mail: cyocum@umich.edu.

YOCUM, HARRISON GERALD, horticulturist, botanist, educator, researcher; b. Bethlehem, Pa., Apr. 2, 1923; s. Harrison and Bertha May (Meckes) Y. BS, Pa. State U., 1955; MS, Rutgers U., 1961. Horticulture instr. U. Tenn., Martin, 1957-59; biology tchr., libr. asst. high schs., El Paso, Tex., 1959-60; rsch. asst. geochronology lab. U. Ariz., Tucson, 1960-67, rsch. asst. environ. rsch. lab., 1969-76; landscaping supt. Tucson Airport Authority, 1976-82; instr. Pima C.C., Tucson, 1976—. Contbr. articles to profl. jours. Founder Tucson Bot. Gardens, 1964. Recipient 1st Unique Gardener award Gardeners Am. Mem. Am. Hort. Soc., Nat. Trust Historic Preservation, Ariz. Preservation Found., Men's Garden Club Tucson (pres. 1991), Tucson Cactus & Succulent Soc. (pres. 1991, 92), Internat. Palm Soc. (charter), El Paso Cactus and Rock Club (life), Tucson Gem and Mineral Soc., Old Pueblo Lapidary Club, Deming Mineral Soc., Nat. Geog. Soc., Ariz.-Sonora Desert Mus., Huachuca Vigilantes, Penn State Alumni Assn. (life), Pa. Club Tucson, Fraternal Order Police Assocs., Nature Conservancy, N.Am. Hunting Club (life), Boyce-Thompson Arboretum, Shriners, Masons, Scottish Rite (life). Lutheran. Home: 1628 N Jefferson Ave Tucson AZ 85712-4204

YODER, ANNA A. elementary school educator; b. Beach City, Ohio, Sept. 5, 1934; d. Abram J. and Barbara D. (Miller) Y. BS, Ea. Mennonite Coll., 1966; MEd, Frostburg State Coll., 1974. Cert. elem. tchr., Ohio, recreational leader. Tchr. Garrett County Schs., Oakland, Md., 1966-70, prin. elem. sch., 1970-74; tchr. E. Holmes Local Schs., Berlin, Ohio, 1974-98, ret., 1998. Chairperson edn. com. German Culture Mus., Berlin, Ohio, 1987-90; cons. bilingual edn. E. Holmes Local Schs., Berlin, Ohio, 1982-98, ret., 1998. Supporting mem. German Culture Mus., Berlin, Ohio, 1983—; mem. Killbuck (Ohio) Valley mus., 1988—, Holmes County Hist. Soc., Millersburg, Ohio, 1989—; life mem. Mennonite Info. Ctr., Berlin, Ohio, 1985—; sustaining mem. The Wilderness Ctr., Wilmot, Ohio, 1974—. Jennings scholar Martha Holden Jennings Found., 1983-84; Silver Poet award World of Poetry, 1986. Mem. AAUW (v.p. Holmes County chpt. 1994, chpt. v.p. 2002-), Creative Arts Soc. (sec.-treas. 1987-89), Delta Kappa Gamma (sec. Beta Iota chpt. 1987-90, pres. 1990-92, pres. 1998-2000). Mennonite. Avocations: nature studies-birds and flowers, handcrafts. Home: 5229 State Route 39 Millersburg OH 44654-8408

YODER, ANNA MARY, reading educator; b. Iowa County, Iowa, Nov. 14, 1933; d. Kores M. and Sadie Rebecca (King) Y. BS in Elem. Edn., Ea. Mennonite U., 1959; MA in Linguistics, Hartford Sem. Found., 1968; MA in Curriculum and Instruction, U. Tenn., 1975; postgrad., U. Iowa, 1975-81. Tchr. Am. Sch., Tegulcigalpa, Honduras, 1969-70, Escuela Internat. Sch., San Pedro Sula, Honduras, 1970-75; tchr. bilingual Muscatine (Iowa) Cmty. Schs., 1977-78, tchr., supr. title I, 1978-79; tchr. Escuela Internat. Sch., 1979-80; tchr. home room Muscatine Cmty. Schs., 1980-87, reading tchr., 1987-99. Nat. dir. adult educators Alfalit Spanish Univ. of Lit., Honduras, 1963-69; Reading Recovery tchr., 1995-2000. Author/editor: Pre-Cartilla de Alfalit, 1968. Mem. Sisters Cities, Muscatine, 1994, bd. dirs., 1995-99; vol. Mid Prairie Sch. Dist., Wellman, Iowa. Mem. NEA, Internat. Reading Assn. Avocations: gardening, cats, reading, tutoring, volunteering.

YODER, EDGAR PAUL, education educator; b. Millersburg, Ohio, June 20, 1946; s. Albert Daniel Yoder and Ella Marie (Bontrager) Erb; m. Deborah Jean Barnhart, June 12, 1971; children: Scott, Suzan. BSA, Ohio State U., 1968, MS, 1972, PhD, 1976. Cert. tchr., counselor, prin., Ohio, Va. Tchr. agr. and sci. Conotton Valley Schs., Bowerston, Ohio, 1968-69, East Holmes Schs., Berlin, Ohio, 1969-72; curriculum specialist Ohio State U., Columbus, 1972-74, project dir., 1974-76; asst. prin. Montgomery County Schs., Blacksburg, Va., 1976-77; asst. prof. Va. Poly. Inst. and State U., Blacksburg, 1977-78, Pa. State U., University Park, 1978-84, assoc. prof. tchr. edn., 1984-94, prof., 1994—, interim dept. head, 1995-98. Cons. Poland Ministry Edn., Warsaw, 1994, Swaziland Ministry Agr., Mbane, 1985, 87, U. Peredenyia, Kandy, Sri Lanka, 1984. Author text: Ag Supplies and Services, 1974; (with others) Undergraduate Education in Agriculture, 1989, also chpt. to book. Chmn. community svc. Sertoma Internat., Columbus, 1975; asst. dir. Va. HSA Assn., Blacksburg, 1978; sect. chmn. Am. Heart Assn., State College, Va., 1981; pres. Ferguson Twp. PTO, State College, 1983-84; bd. dirs. RAFT Drug Rehab. Ctr., Radford, 1976-78, Nat. Future Farmers Am., Alexandria, Va., 1981-83. Recipient hon. degree, Nat. Future Farmers Am., 1983. Mem. Nat. Assn. Coll. Tchrs. Agr. (pres., teacher fellow 1987, Regional Outstanding Teaching award 1992), Am. Assn. Agr. Educators (legis. chmn. 1985), Am. Assn. Ednl. Rsch., Am. Vocat. Edn. Rsch. Assn., Assn. Internat. Agr. and Extension Edn., Phi Delta Kappa, Gamma Sigma Delta (Teaching award of Merit 1987). Avocations: collecting sports memorabilia, restoring antiques, classic cars. Office: Penn State U Rm 323 Ag Adminstrn Coll Agricultural Scis University Park PA 16802

YODER, EDWIN MILTON, JR., columnist, educator, editor, writer; b. Greensboro, N.C., July 18, 1934; s. Edwin M. and Mytrice M. (Logue) Y.; m. Mary Jane Warwick, Nov. 1, 1958; children: Anne Daphne, Edwin Warwick. BA, U. N.C., 1956; BA, MA (Rhodes scholar), Oxford (Eng.) U., 1958; D.H.L. (hon.), Grinnell Coll., 1980, Elon Coll., 1986; DLitt (hon.), U. N.C., 1993, Richmond Coll., London. Editorial writer Charlotte (N.C.) News, 1958-61; editorial writer Greensboro Daily News, 1961-64, assoc. editor, 1965-75; asst. prof. history U. N.C., Greensboro, 1964-65; editorial page editor Washington Star, 1975-81; syndicated columnist Washington Post Writers Group, 1982-97; prof. journalism and humanities Washington and Lee U., 1992—2002, prof. emeritus, 2002—. Hon. fellow Jesus Coll., Oxford, Eng., 1998—. Author: Night of the Old South Ball, 1984, The Unmaking of a Whig, 1990, Joe Alsop's Cold War, 1995, The Historical Present, 1997; contbr. articles to periodicals. Trustee Inst. for Early Am. History and Culture, Nat. Humanities Ctr., 1991-97. Recipient awards editorial writing N.C. Press Assn., 1958, 61, 66, Walker Stone award Scripps-Howard Found., 1978, Pulitzer prize editorial writing, 1979; Disting. Alumnus award U. N.C., Chapel Hill, 1980 Mem. Nat. Conf. Editorial Writers, Am. Soc. Newspaper Editors. Democrat. Episcopalian. Home: 4001 Harris Pl Alexandria VA 22304-1720 E-mail: yoderem@aol.com.

YODER, MYRON EUGENE, secondary school educator; b. Reading, Pa., Oct. 28, 1953; s. Robert W. and Carmen D. (Keinard) Y.; m. Debra Kuper, Dec. 27, 1975; children: Joshua B., Rebecca A. BE cum laude, Kutztown U., 1976; Masters Equivalency, Pa. Dept. Edn., 1979; MEd cum laude, Kutztown U., 1981. Cert. secondary social studies tchr., Pa. With maintenance ride repair Dorney Pk, Allentown, Pa., 1968-72; postal asst. Lehigh County U.S. P.O. SCF180, Allentown, 1972-73; insp. Fairtex Mills, Allentown, 1973-74; correctional officer Lehigh County Prison, Allentown, 1974-76, emergency prison counselor, 1979-84; mgr., supr. Hosp. Cen. Svcs., Allentown, 1976; curriculum coord. Allentown Sch. Dist., 1986—. Adj. prof. edn. Cedar Crest Coll., 2000-02, DeSales U., 2003—; tchr. trainer Ctr. for Civic Edn., Bicentennial Commn., Calabasas, Calif., 1987—, Temple U. LEAP, 1987-2000; sch. coord. Boy Scouts Am. Awareness Post, Allentown, 1989-2000; scholar Pa. Humanities Coun., Phila., 1991; Pa. Congl. Dist. 15 coord. for We the People Citizen and Constn. Program, 1992—; apptd. commr. Pa. Profl. Standards and Practices Commn.; mem. social studies student standards devel. team Pa. Dept. Edn., 1996; mem. assessment and student standard exercise devel. team Social Studies State Collaborative, 1996. Photographer (Kinisa Local award 1980, 83); computer programmer Class Dues Record Keeper, 1987-88 (1st dist., 2nd regional runner-up computer learning award), Study Hall Record Keeper, 1988 (1st dist., 2nd regional award); contbr. articles to profl. publs. Chmn. Borough of Emmaus Operation Homecoming, 1991; discussion leader Pa. Humanities Coun., Emmaus, 1992, Allentown, 96; com. mem. Allentown Columbus Quincentenary, 1991, Allentown Black History Month Com., 1990-91; coord. We the People program Pa. Congl. Dist. 15; bd. dirs. Jr. Achievement of Lehigh Valley, 1993, Korea/Vietnam Meml. Nat. Ednl. Ctr., 1993. Recipient Applied Econs. Tchr. Yr. award Jr. Achievement of Lehigh Valley, 1990, 93, Jr. Achievement Applied Econs. Tchr. of Yr. for Pa. award, 1991, Pa. DAR Am. History Tchr. of Yr. award, 1993, Nat. Soc. DAR Am. History medal, 1993, cooperating Tchr. award Kutztown U., 1994, SAR Silver Good Citizenship medal, 1994, Letter of Commendation Pa. Sec. Edn., 1999; selected by Jr. Achievement to travel to Soviet Union to train Soviet tchrs. in using Jr. Achievment applied econs., 1991; finalist Pa. Tchr. of Yr., 1995. Mem. NEA, Nat. Coun. Social Studies, Pa. Coun. Social Studies (Outstanding Secondary Social Studies Tchr. 1992), Pa. State Edn. Assn. (internat. rels. com. region chmn. 1987, vice chmn. state com., 1996-97, tchr. trainer student assessment tng. cadre), Lehigh Valley Coun. Social Studies, Lehigh U. Coll. Edn. Alumni Coun. (Outstanding Tchr. award 1992), Allentown Edn. Assn. (v.p. 1991-96), Kiwanis. Republican. Lutheran. Avocation: photography. E-mail: yoderm@allentownsd.org., mey11@aol.com.

YODER-WISE, PATRICIA SNYDER, education educator; b. Wadsworth, Ohio, July 2, 1941; d. Belford Grant and Leona Cora (Mohler) Snyder; m. Robert Thomas Wise, Feb. 17, 1973; children: Doreen Ellen, Deborah Ann. BSN, Ohio State U., 1963; MSN, Wayne State U., 1968; EdD, Tex. Tech. U., 1984. RN, Tex. Interim dir. nursing ctr. Tex. Tech. U. Health Sci. Ctr. Sch. Nursing, Lubbock, 1988-89, interim assoc. dean practice program, 1989-90, interim dean, prof., 1991-93, dean and prof., 1993-2000, prof., 2000—; clin. prof. U. Tex. Health Sci. Ctr., San Antonio, 1993—2000. Mem. rev. panel Nursing Outlook, 1993—; mem. adv. com. GlaxoWellcome, 1996-2000; v.p. Am. Nurses Credentialing Ctr., 2000-2003; mem. Nat. Quality Forum Provider Panel, 2001-04. Author (editor): Leading and Managing in Nursing, 1994 (Book of Yr. award, 1996, 1999, 2003); peer reviewer: Jour. Profl. Nursing, 1984—2003, mem. editl. bd.: Jour. Continuing Edn. in Nursing, 1978—; editor, 1988—. Participant Leadership Tex.-Found. for Women's Resources, 1997-98; mem. Leadership Tex., 1998-99, Leadership Am., 1999-2000. Recipient of Woman of Excellence in Medicine, YWCA, Lubbock, 1996. Fellow: Am. Acad. Nursing (chair Inst. for Nursing Leadership 1999—2002, mem. planning com. 2004); mem.: ANA (del. 1995—2000, chair constituent assembly 1998—2000, sec. 2000—02, 1st v.p. 2002—), Tex. Nurses Assn. (pres. 1995—99). Office: Texas Tech Univ HSC Sch Nursing 7309 93rd St Lubbock TX 79424-4939

YOGANATHAN, AJIT PRITHIVIRAJ, biomedical engineer, educator; b. Colombo, Sri Lanka, Dec. 6, 1951; came to U.S., 1973; s. Ponniah and Mangay (Navaratnam) Y.; m. Tripti Yoganathan. BSChemE with honors, Univ. Coll., U. London, 1973; PhDChemE, Calif. Inst. Tech., 1978. Engring. asst. Shell Oil Refinery, Stanlow, Eng., 1972; tchg. asst. Calif. Inst. Tech., 1973-74, 1976, rsch. fellow, 1977-79; asst. prof. Ga. Inst. Tech., 1979-83, assoc. prof., 1983-88, chmn. bioengring. com., 1984-88, prof. chem. engring., 1988-94, dir. Bioengring. Ctr., 1989—, prof. mech. engring., 1989-94, co-dir. Emory U.-Ga. Tech. Biomed. Tech. Ctr., 1992—, Regents prof., 1994—, assoc. chair biomed. engring., 1998—. Adj. assoc. prof. U. Ala., 1985—. Founding fellow Am. Inst. Med. & Biol. Engring., 1992; recipient Edwin Walker prize Brit. Inst. Mech. Engrs., 1988, Humboldt fellowship, 1985, Am. Heart Assn.-Ga. Affiliate Rsch. Investigatorship award, 1980-83, Calif. Inst. Tech. fellowship, 1973-77, Goldsmid Medal and prize Univ. Coll., 1972-73, Brit. Coun. scholarship, 1971-73. Mem. AIChE, ASME (Bioengring. div., H.R. Lissner award 1997), Biomed. Engring. Soc., Am. Soc. Echocardiography (dir. 1987-91). Office: Sch Biomed Engring Ga Tech/Emory Atlanta GA 30332-0535 Office Fax: 404-894-4243. E-mail: ajit.yoganathan@bme.gatech.edu.*

YOKEN, MEL B(ARTON), French language educator, writer; b. Fall River, Mass., June 25, 1939; s. Albert Benjamin and Sylvia Sarah (White) Y.; m. Cynthia Stein, June 20, 1976; children: Andrew Brett, David Ryan, Jonathan Barry. BA, U. Mass., 1960; MAT, Brown U., 1961, PhD, 1972. Instr. French U. Mass., Dartmouth, 1966-72, asst. prof., 1976-81, prof., 1981-2001, chancellor prof., 2001—. Dir. French summer study program French Inst., 1981-88; radio commentator Am. Field Svc., 1971—, pres., 1984-86, v.p., 2001—; vis. prof. Wheaton Coll., 1987, U. of Montreal, 1981-88; translator New Bedford Superior Ct., New Bedford, Mass., 1985—, Fall River Superior Ct., Fall River, Mass., 1985—; reader, cons. AP Exams in French, 1997—; mem. nominating com. Nobel Prize for lit., 1972—, Acad. Am. Poets, 1999—. Author: Claude Tillier, 1976, Speech is Plurality, 1978, Claude Tillier (1801-44): Fame and Fortune in His Novelistic Work, 1978, Entretiens Quebecois I, 1986, Entretiens Quebecois II, 1989, Letters of Robert Molloy, 1989, Festschrift in Honor of Stowell Goding, 1993, Entretiens Quebecois III, 1999; contbr. articles to profl. jours. Pres. Friends of Fall River Pub. Libr., 1972-80, pres., bd. dirs., 1972-80; pres. New Bedford Pub. Libr., 1980-82; bd. dirs. Am. Field Svc., 1980—, pres., 1984-86, v.p., 2001—; v.p. Friends of U. Mass. Libr., 1998—, pres., 1999—; dir. Boivin Ctr., 1999—. Decorated Officier dans l'Ordre des Palmes académiques, 2001—; recipient Disting. Svc. award City Fall River, 1974, 80, Excellence in Tchg. French award, 1984, 85, Gov.'s citation, 1986, Nat. Disting. Leadership award, 1990, Dist. Svc. award Mass. Foreign Lang. Assn., 1992, Medaille de Vermeil du Rayonnement de la Langue Française, L'Academie Française, 1993, Outstanding Cmty. Svc. award, 1997, Disting. Alumni award, Durfee H.S., 1998, Golden Apple award Fall River Herald News, 1998; Govt. of Que. grantee, 1981-85, 87-89, Can. Embassy grantee, 1986, 87, Southeastern Mass. U. grantee, 1985, 89, 90; Mel Yoken Day proclaimed by Mayor of New Bedford, 1990. Mem. MLA (life), Am. Assn. Tchrs. French (life), Am. Coun. Tchrs. Fgn. Langs., Middlebury Amicale (life), N.E. MLA (coord. 1987-91), New Eng. Fgn. Lang. Assn., Mass. Fgn. Lang. Assn. (bd. dirs. 1985-90, disting. svc. award 1992), N.Y. State Assn. Fgn. Lang. Tchrs., Internat. Platform Assn., Francophone Assn. (v.p. 1990-98), Assn. Literary Scholars and Critics, Fall River C. of C., Brown U. Alumni Assn. (rep.), Richelieu Internat., Universal Manuscript Soc. (v.p. 1993-95). Avocations: traveling, languages, baseball, postcards, meteorology. Home: 261 Carroll St New Bedford MA 02740-1412 Office: U Mass Dartmouth Lang Dept Old Westport Rd North Dartmouth MA 02747-2512 E-mail: myoken@umassd.edu.

YOO BOWNE, HELEN, otolaryngologist, educator; b. Seoul, Aug. 27, 1961; arrived in U.S., 1970; d. Kun Yul Yoo and Young Ja Lee; m. Wilbur Bowen Fairfax Bowne, Sept. 23, 2000. BA, NYU, 1987; MD, Albert Einstein Coll. Medicine, 1994. Diplomate Am. Bd. Otolaryngology-Head and Neck Surgery. Intern in surgery Beth Israel Med. Ctr., N.Y.C., 1994—96; resident in otolaryngology N.Y. Eye and Ear Infirmary, N.Y.C., 1996—2000; head and neck fellow Beth Israel Med. Ctr., N.Y.C., 2000—01; asst. prof., attending physician St. Vincents Hosp., N.Y.C., 2001—. Contbr. articles to profl. jours. Mem.: AMA, N.Y. Head and Neck Soc., Am. Acad. Otolaryngology. Office: St Vincents Hosp Ste 422 36 7th Ave New York NY 10011

YOPCONKA, NATALIE ANN CATHERINE, computer specialist, educator, business owner; b. Taylor, Pa., July 21, 1942; d. Michael Joseph and Natalie Ann Lucille (Panek) Y. BS with high honors, U. Md., 1965; MBA, George Washington U., 1976, MA in Edn. and Human Devel., 1988, postgrad., 1990—96. Mgmt. analyst, adminstrv. trainee, computer programmer U.S. Dept. Commerce, Maritime Adminstrn., Washington, 1965-67; computer programmer, computer specialist U.S. Dept. Labor, Washington, 1967-78; instr. computer sci. Assn. for Computing Machinery, Washington, 1978; instr. computer sci. and mgmt. tech. Montgomery Coll., Takoma Park and Rockville, Md., 1979; sr. programmer analyst Dynamic Data Processing, Inc., Silver Spring, Md., 1979; instr. Nat. Bus. Sch., Inc., Alexandria, Va., 1980; cons. McLeod Corp., Washington, 1980; lectr. computer sci., coop. coord. U. Md., College Park, 1980-81; sr. adminstrv. applications analyst programmer Data Transformation Corp., Washington, 1981; sr. sys. analyst Singer Link Simulation Sys. Divsn., Silver Spring, 1981-82; accessory designer, 1982-83; market rschr. Washington Fin. Svc., 1982-83;

lectr. computer info. and sys. sci. U. D.C., Rockville, Md., 1983; prof. computer programming and mgmt. info. sys. Benjamin Franklin U., Washington, 1983; rschr. Info. U.S.A., Potomac, Md., 1983-85; admissions rep. Brook-Wein Bus. Inst., Washington, 1985; pvt. distbr. Hyattsville, Md., 1979—86; distbr. AMWAY Corp., 1979—92. Course developer, instr. Grad. Sch. USDA, Balt., 1986-87; chmn. Cert. for Computing Profls. Exam. Review Course for Balt. Washington, D.C. corridor, 1994-95; agent Kivex, Inc., 1996-97, Information Builders, Inc., 1997-2000, 3COM Corp., 1997-99; field interviewer Nat. Drug Abuse Bur., 1989-90; pvt. distbr. Hyattsville and Columbia, Md., 1979-1992, distbr. AMWAY Corp., 1979-92; bus. owner, cons. Sys. and Edn. Enterprises, 1979—; pvt. cons. Columbia, Md., 1987—. Mem. Takoma Park Disability Com., Mayor's Com. on Energy, Housing and Planning, 1980-81; mem. Vision 2030 Balt./Howard County, 2002-2003; mem. Missionary Oblates of Immaculate Mary; mem. choir Our Lady of Sorrows Cath. Ch., 1977-82; mem. various choirs, St. John the Evangelist Cath. Ch., eucharistic min.; active Suburban Md. High Tech. Coun., 1994-95, Howard County High Tech. Coun., 1994-95, Citizens Adv. Com. to Bd. Edn., Howard County, 1991-92; computer adv. com. Bd. Edn. Howard County, 1993-95; mem. internet com. St. John the Evangelist Roman Cath. Ch., 1996-97. Mem. NAFE, IEEE (Balt. sect.), Info. Sys. Audit and Control Assn., Assn. for Computing Machinery (edn. com., instr. 1978-79, edn. com. 1980-81, profl. devel. com. 1982-83), Data Processing Mgmt. Assn. (chmn. cert. for computing profls. exam. rev. course for Balt.-Washington corridor 1994-95), Balt. Washington Info. Sys. Educators (consortium com. 1984-85, program com. for 1986 regional tng. conf. 1985-86, vendor com. 1988-89), Fed. Automatic Data Processing Users Group (various coms. 1976-1983), Am. Automobile Assn., IEEE Computer Soc. (mem. various coms), IEEE Software Stds. Assn., Armed Forces Comm. and Electronics Assn., Balt. Coun. Fgn. Affairs, Am. Assn. Ret. Persons, Nat. Assn. Ret. Fed. Employees (sec. Howard County chpt.), U. Md. Howard County Alumni Club (scholarship com. 1989), Columbia (Md.) Assn., Phi Delta Gamma (scholarship com. 1977-78, social com. 1980-81, hospitality com. 1982-83, sec. 1989-90).

YORK, DARRYL ROBERT, health and physical education educator; b. Marietta, Ga., Sept. 14, 1963; s. Robert L. and Carol (Copeland) Y.; m. Sherri Williams, June 23, 1990; children: Parker Copeland, Preston Williams. Student, West Ga. Coll., 1981-82; BS in Edn., Kennesaw State Coll., 1986; MEd, Ga. State U., 1994. Cert. tchr., Ga. Tchr. phys. edn. Dodgen Mid. Sch., Marietta, 1986-88; tchr. health and phys. edn. Simpson Mid. Sch., Marietta, 1988—. Coach Walton High Sch., Marietta, 1988-90, athletic trainer, 1988-91; presenter pre-planning workshop Simpson Mid. Sch., 1990, life skills pilot program Cobb Mega Conf., 1992. Instr. CPR ARC, Marietta, 1990—; pres. Homeowners Assn., Acworth, Ga., 1992; field svcs. supr. Ga. State Games, Atlanta, 1992; active Simpson PTA, 1988—. Mem. AAHPERD, Ga. Assn. of Health, Phys. Edn., Recreation and Dance. Avocations: computers, camping, cooking. Office: Simpson Mid Sch 3340 Trickum Rd Marietta GA 30066-4663

YOUNAN, NICOLAS HANNA, electrical engineering educator; BSEE, Miss. State U., 1982, MSEE, 1984; PhD in Elec. Engring., Ohio U., 1988. Asst. prof. Miss. State U., Starkville, 1990-93, assoc. prof., 1993—2001, prof., 2001—, grad. program dir., 1995—. Vis. asst. prof. Miss. State U., 1988-90; rsch. scientist Praxis Internat., Exton, Pa., 1989-90. Contbr. articles to profl. jours. Grantee in field. Mem. IEEE (sr., chmn. N.E. Miss. subsect. 1993-94, vice-chmn. 1992-93, sec./treas. 1991-92), N.Y. Acad. Sci., Phi Kappa Phi, Tau Beta Pi, Eta Kappa Nu. Office: Miss State U Dept Elec/Computer Engring PO Box 9571 Mississippi State MS 39762-9571

YOUNG, BETTY MAE, special education educator; b. Winona, Miss., Sept. 27, 1957; d. Robert Wall and Pearlie Mae (McCarrell) Y. BS in Edn., Jackson State U., 1978, MS in Edn., 1979. Cert. Nat. Reach Trainer. Tchr. Unified Sch. Dist. 501, Topeka, 1980—. First asst. coach volleyball Jardine Mid. Sch., Topeka, 1986—, advisor to leader base team, 1987-96, spl. svcs. rep. sch. site adv. coun., 1992—, head track coach 1990—, tng. team multicultural curriculum, 1991—, staff devel. trainer 1992—, rep. spl. edn. component outcomes based staff devel. tng. team, 1992, dept. head spl. edn. Named Disting. Mid. Sch. Tchr., Selection Com., Topeka, 1990-91; recipient Bldrs. award Topeka Pks. and Recreation, 1991. Mem. NEA (chpt. v.p. 1991-93), Topeka Alliance Black Sch. Educators (memberships chairperson 1990—, conv. chairperson 1993, Disting. Black Educator 1993, pres. elect 1994—), Kansans of Color (planning com. 1992-96). Avocations: reading, exercising, shopping, decorating, social activities. Home: PO Box 4274 Topeka KS 66604-0274 Office: Jardine Mid Sch 260 SW 23rd St Topeka KS 66611

YOUNG, BETTYE JEANNE, retired secondary education educator; b. Chgo., Nov. 2, 1929; d. Frank M. Forbish and Mary Bernice (Phillips) Lunde; m. Dale Eugene Young, July 22, 1950; 1 child, Debra Jeanne. AA, Vallejo Jr. Coll., 1964; BA in History, Dominican Coll., 1968. Tchr. North Star Elem., Anchorage, 1978, Inlet View Elem., Anchorage, 1978-82, tchr.-in-charge, 1979-82; tchr. Ctrl. Jr. High Sch., Anchorage, 1982—, chair social studies dept., 1994-95; vol. tchr. reading and math. Anacortes Elem. Sch., 1997—. Chairperson N.W. Accreditation for Ctrl. Jr. High Sch., 1983; mem. Supt.'s Apprasal Com., Anchorage, 1983-85, Anchorage Sch. Dist.'s Talent Bank, 1979-93, Social Studies Curriculum Com., 1979-95, exec. bd. State Coun. Social Studies, 1990-92; chair social study dept. Ctrl. Jr. H.S., 1994—, established youth ct. Author: Thematic Approach to U.S. History, 1989 (Merit award Alaska State Dept.), Immigration Unit for U.S. History, 1988 (Merit award Alaska State Dept.), others in field. Voter registrar, Anchorage, 1984; del. Rep. Caucus, Fairbanks, Alaska, 1984; facilitator marriage seminars, Anchorage, 1989-90; mem. Ch. choir, music dept., Anchorage, 1978-93; mem. adv. bd. Law Related Edn., Anchorage, 1993-94; bd. dirs. Alaska Jr. Coll., 1993-94; vol. reading and math. tchr. elem. schs.; vol. Anacortes Aux. Patrol Police, 1995—. Named Tchr. of Month Anchorage Sch. Dist., 1981; recipient Jr. Achievement Appreciation award, Project Bus., 1987-92, Support of Social Studies award, Alaska Dept. Edn., 1991, 92; grantee Law Related Edn. Fed. Govt., ABA, 1990-94. Mem. NEA, Anchorage Edn. Assn. (chair instrnl. profl. devel. 1984-85), Anchorage Area Social Studies Coun. (sec. 1983-84, v.p. 1988-90, pres. 1990-92), Nat. Coun. Social Studies, Alaska Coun. Social Studies (secondary tch. of the yr. 1991), Phi Delta Kappa (Cook Inlet chpt., v.p. 1990-92), Delta Kappa Gamma. Avocations: travel, camping, motorcycle riding, reading, writing. Home: 3909 W 6th St Anacortes WA 98221-1295 Office: Ctrl Jr High Sch 1405 E St Anchorage AK 99501-5098

YOUNG, CHARLES EDWARD, academic administrator; b. San Bernardino, Calif., Dec. 30, 1931; s. Clayton Charles and Eula May (Walters) Young. AA, San Bernardino Coll., 1954; AB, U. Calif., Riverside, 1955; MA, UCLA, 1957, PhD, 1960; DHL (hon.), U. Judaism, L.A., 1969; DHL (hon.), Occidental Coll., L.A., 1997. Congl. fellow, Washington, 1958—59; adminstrv. analyst Office of the Pres., U. Calif., Berkeley, 1959—60; asst. prof. polit. sci. U. Calif., Davis, 1960, UCLA, 1960—66, assoc. prof., 1966—69, prof., 1969—97, asst. to chancellor, 1960—62, asst. chancellor, 1962—63, vice chancellor, adminstrn., 1963—68, chancellor, 1968—97; pres. U. Fla., Gainesville, 1999—. Bd. dirs. Intel Corp., Acad. TV Arts and Sci. Found., L.A. Met. Project; cons. Peace Corps., 1961—62, Ford Found. on Latin Am. Activities, 1964—66. Mem. Nat. Com. on U.S.-China Rels.; adminstrv. bd. Internat. Assn. Univs; mem. Knight Found. Commn. on Intercollegiate Athletics, Calif. Coun. on Sci. and Tech., Town Hall of Calif., Carnegie Comm. Task Force on Sci. and Tech. and the States, Pacific Coun. on Internat. Policy, NCAA Pres.'s Commn., Coun. for Govt.-Univ.-Industry Rsch. Roundtable and the Nat. Rsch. Coun. Adv. Bd.-Issues in Sci. and Tech.; chancellor's assocs. UCLA; coun. trustees L.A. Ednl. Alliance for Restructuring Now; past chair. Assn. Am. Univs., Nat. Assn. State Univs. and Land-Grant Colls.; past co-chair Calif. Campus Compact; trustee UCLA Found.; bd. dirs. Found. Internat. Exchange Sci. and Cultural Info. by Telecom., L.A. Internat. Visitors Coun., Greater L.A. Energy Coalition, L.A. World Affairs Coun. With USAF, 1951—52. Named Young Man of Year, Westwood Jr. C. of C., 1962; recipient Inter-Am. U. Cooperaton award, Inter-Am. Orgn. Higher Edn., Neil H. Jacoby Internat. award, UCLA Student Ctr., 1987, Edward A. Dickson Alumnus of Yr. award, UCLA Alumni Assn., 1994, Disting. Svc. award, U. Calif. Riverside Alumni Assn., 1996, Treasure of L.A. award, L.A. Ctrl. City Assn., 1996, Albert Schweitzer Leadership award, Hugh O'Brien Youth Found., 1996; fellow, UCLA Coll. Letters and Sci., 1996. Fellow: AAAS; mem.: Nat. Collegiate Athletic Assn. Pres. Commn. Office: U Fla 226 Tigert Hall PO Box 113150 Gainesville FL 32611-3150*

YOUNG, DANIEL EDWIN, principal; b. Akron, Ohio; s. Eugene E. and Allys M. (Holmes) Y. BS in Edn., No. Ariz. U., 1969, MA in Edn., 1972; postgrad., Ariz. State U., 1993—. Cert. elem., jr. high, high sch., prin., supt., supr., spl. edn., social studies, elem. grades K-8. Tchr. Cross Categorical Spl. Edn., Flagstaff, Ariz., 1969-71, Emotionally Handicapped Jr. High, Mesa, Ariz., 1971-73; tchr., cons. spl. edn., emotionally handicapped, trainable mentally handicapped, Mesa, 1973-74; asst. prin. C. D. Poston Jr. High Sch., Mesa, 1974-78; prin. D. Mac Arthur Elem. Sch., Mesa, 1978-81, J. J. Rhodes Jr. High Sch., 1981-85, V.E. Johnson Elem. Sch., 1986-90, W.S. Porter Elem. Sch., 1991-96, Barbara Bush Elem. Sch., Mesa, 1996—. Co-faciliator conf. and workshop ASU and No. Ariz. U., 1978—; north ctrl. evaluation chair North Ctrl. Accreditation-Tucson, 1980—; on-site visitor nat. blue ribbon panelist U.S. Dept. Edn., Washington, 1984—; workshop cons. State Dept Edn.; co-facilitator to Ariz. Dept. Edn. Principal's Acad.; negotiations facilitator. Author: Guidelines to Supervising Student Teachers, 1972. Named Prin. of Leadership, Nat. Sch. Safety Ctr., 1990, Ariz. Top Ten Elem. Sch. Adminstr., 1990. Mem. Ariz. ASCD (Excellence in Supervision award 1990), Nat. Assn. Elem. Adminstrs./Prins., Mesa Assn. for Sch. Adminstrs., Phi Delta Kappa, Maricopa County Sheriff Posse (life mem.). Avocations: travel, antiques, films, theater, family. Office: B Bush Elem Sch 4924 E Ingram St Mesa AZ 85205-3315

YOUNG, DAVID WILLIAM, management educator; b. L.A., Feb. 8, 1942; s. William Albert and Hilda Mary (Cook) Y.; m. Ernestine M.L. Van Schaik, Oct. 4, 1968 (div. 1975); m. Francesca Michela Larson, Jan. 28, 1984; children: Christian William, Anthony Edwin. BA, Occidental Coll., 1963; MA, UCLA, 1966; D in Bus. Adminstrn., Harvard U., 1977. Systems engr. IBM, Glendale, Calif., 1963-64; asst. to pres. Lundberg Survey, Inc., Hollywood, Calif., 1964-66; program economist U.S. AID, El Salvador, 1966-69; cons. Thomas Goldsmith & Assoc., Cambridge, Mass., 1969-71; mng. dir. Commonwealth Mgmt. Sys., Cambridge, 1971—; assoc. prof. mgmt. Harvard U. Sch. Pub. Health, Boston, 1976-85, adj. faculty mem., 1985—; prof. mgmt. Boston U. Sch. Mgmt., 1985—, chmn. dept. acctg., 1986-91, dir. acctg. MBA program, 1989-93, dir. inst. acctg. rsch. and edn., 1989-93, dir. health care mgmt. program, 1991-94; prin. The Crimson Group, Cambridge, 1994—. Vis. prof. mgmt. control Instituto de Estudios Superiores de la Empresa, Barcelona, Spain, 1984. Author: The Managerial Process in Human Service Agencies, 1979, Financial Control in Health Care, 1984, The Hospital Power Equilibrium, 1985, Management Control in Nonprofit Organizations, 1984, 7th edit., 2003, Introduction to Financial and Management Accounting: A User Perspective, 1994, Primer on Financial Accounting, 1998, Primer on Management Accounting, 1999, Managing Integrated Delivery Systems: A Framework for Action, 1999, The Manager's Guide to Creative Cost Cutting: 181 Ways to Build the Bottom Line, 2003, Techniques of Management Accounting,: An Essential Guide for Managers and Financial Professionals 2003; contbr. articles to profl. jours. Trustee Roxbury Comprehensive Cmty. Health Ctr., 1983-86, Art Inst., Boston, 1990-96, Mass. Eye and Ear Infirmary, Boston, 1990-92, Symmes Hosp., Arlington, 1993-94, The Atrium Sch., 1995-97, Youville Hosp., 1997-2000, Coolidge Corner Theatre Found., 2000—, Spaulding Rehab. Hosp., 2001—; commr., chair Mass. Hosp. Payment Sys., 1992-95. Milton Fund fellow Harvard Med. Sch., 1984. Mem.: Am. Acctg. Assn. Democrat. Office: Boston U Sch Mgmt 595 Commonwealth Ave Boston MA 02215-1704 E-mail: dwy204@cs.com.

YOUNG, EDWIN HAROLD, chemical and metallurgical engineering educator; b. Detroit, Nov. 4, 1918; s. William George and Alice Pearl (Hicks) Y.; m. Ida Signe Soma, June 25, 1944; children: David Harold, Barbara Ellen. BS in Chem. Engring, U. Detroit, 1942; MS in Chem. Engring, U. Mich., 1949, MS in Metall. Engring, 1952. Chem. engr. Wright Air Devel. Center, Dayton, Ohio, 1942-43; instr. U. Mich., Ann Arbor, 1946-52, asst. prof., 1952-56, assoc. prof., 1956-59, prof. chem. and metall. engring., 1959-89, prof. emeritus chem. and metall. engring., 1989—. Mem. Mich. Bd. Registration for Profl. Engrs., 1963-78, chmn., 1969-70, 72-73, 75-76; mem. Mich. Bd. Registration for Architects, 1963-78 Author: (with L.E. Brownell) Process Equipment Design, 1959; contbr. articles to profl. jours. Dist. commr. Boy Scouts Am., 1961-64; mem. Wolverine coun., 1965-68. With USNR, 1943-46, to capt. Res. ret., 1978. Fellow ASME, ASHRAE, AIChE (Donald Q Kern award 1979), Am. Inst. Chemists, Engring. Soc. Detroit; mem. Am. Chem. Soc., Am. Soc. Engring. Edn., Nat. Soc. Profl. Engrs. (pres. 1968-69, award 1977), Mich. Soc. Profl. Engrs. (pres. 1962-63, Engr. of Year award 1976), Mich. Assn. of Professions (pres. 1966, Distinguished award 1970), Nat. Council Engring. Examiners, Naval Res. Assn., Res. Officers Assn., Sigma Xi, Tau Beta Pi, Phi Kappa Phi, Phi Lambda Upsilon, Alpha Chi Sigma. Republican. Baptist. Home: 609 Dartmoor Rd Ann Arbor MI 48103-4513 E-mail: ehyoung@engin.umich.edu.

YOUNG, FREDDIE GILLIAM, educational administrator; b. Miami, Fla., Nov. 1, 1939; d. Thomas and Myrtle (Gibson) Gilliam. BS, Fla. A&M U., 1961; MS, Hunter Coll., 1970; postgrad., U. Ghana, 1970; EdD, Nova U., 1990. Cert. in supervision and adminstrn., African studies, elem. and jr. coll.; cert. asst. prin. Tchr. Collier County Pub. Schs., Naples, Fla., N.Y.C. Pub. Schs., Bronx, N.Y., Dade County Pub. Schs., Miami, prin.; adj. lead prof. Nova U. Presenter Am. Assn. Ethnic Studies Conf., Fla. Atlantic U., 1991, Assn. Carribean Studies Cairo, 1993, Georgetown, Guyana, 1994, Nat. Assn. African Am. Studies, Houston, 2000, Nat. Commn. on Educating the Black Child, others. Del. 19th congl. dist. Dem. conv., 1988; mem. Am. Jewish Com., African Am. Summitt, London, South Africa, Zimbabwe, West Africa, First Emancipation Independence Day, Ghanna, West Africa, 1998. Named Most Outstanding Black Woman, S. Fla., Women's C. of C., Educator of Yr. Zeta Phi Beta; recipient 50 outstanding svc. awards Prin. Ctr. Harvard U. Sch. Edn., 1989, Metro Dade County commendation for dedicated svc., Ida B. Wells Awd., Nat. Alliance of Black Sch. Educators; finalist for Adminstr. of Yr., 1991, DCSHA. Mem. AAUW, ASCD, Am. Jewish Com., Nat. Alliance Black Educators, S. Fla. Exec. Educators, Leadership Miami, Miami Alliance Black Educators, Nat. Black Women's Polit. Caucus, Dade County Adminstrs. Assn. (chair), Fla. Reading Assn., Dade Reading Coun., Fla. A&M U. Alumni Assn. (pres. Miami-Dade chpt.), Nova U. Alumni Assn. (sec. Miami chpt.), Phi Delta Kappa. Home: 12390 SW 144th Ter Miami FL 33186-7419

YOUNG, GLENNA ASCHE, elementary education educator; b. Lodi, Ohio, Apr. 14, 1955; d. Virgil Eugene and B. Lucille (Johnson) Asche; m. William Young, Aug. 6, 1983. BS, Ohio State U., 1977, cert. learning-behavioral disorders, 1981; MS, Ashland Coll., Columbus Ohio, 1988. Cert. K-12 phys. edn. tchr., Ohio. Kindergarten and elem. phys. edn. tchr. West Jefferson (Ohio) Local Schs., 1979-82; high sch. tchr. severe behavioral handicapped Madison County Schs., London, Ohio, 1982-86; elem. tchr. learning disabled SW Licking Local Sch. Dist., Etna, Ohio, 1986-88, tchr. elem. phys. edn., 1988—. Treas. Etna Sch. PTO, 1989-91. Recipient Golden Apple award Ashland Oil Co. Mem. West Jefferson Edn. Assn. (Disting. Svc. award, President's award), SW Licking Local Edn. Assn. (bldg. rep. 1989-92, sec. 2002—). Home: 9550 Haaf Farm Dr Pickerington OH 43147-8401 E-mail: gyoung@laca.org.

YOUNG, GORDON, elementary education educator; Tchr. Grandview H.S., Aurora, Colo. Recipient Tchr. Excellence award Internat. Tech. Edn. Assn., Colo., 1992. Office: Grandview H S 20500 E Rapaho Rd Aurora CO 80016

YOUNG, HOBART PEYTON, economist, mathematician, educator; b. Evanston, Ill., Mar. 9, 1945; s. Hobart Paul and Louise (Buchwalter) Y.; m. Fernanda Toueg, Mar. 27, 1982; children: Hobart Patrick, Benjamin Morris Chandler. BA, Harvard Coll., 1966; PhD, U. Mich., 1970. Econ. Nat. Water Commn., Arlington, Va., 1971; from asst. to assoc. prof. CUNY, 1971-75; rsch. scholar, dep. chmn. systems and decision sci. Internat. Inst. for Applied Systems Analysis, Laxenburg, Austria, 1975-81; prof. pub. policy U. Md., College Park, 1981-94; prof. econ. Johns Hopkins Univ., 1994—; sr. fellow in econ. The Brookings Inst., 1998—. Adv. panel John D. and Catherine T. MacArthur Found., 1997-99; external faculty Santa Fe Inst., 2001—. Author: Fair Representation, 1982, Equity, 1994, Individual Strategy and Social Structure, 1998; editor: Cost Allocation, 1985, Fair Allocation, 1985, Negotiation Analysis, 1991, Social Dynamics, 2001; assoc. editor: Games and Economic Behavior, 1989—, Social Choice and Welfare, 1990-97. NSF grantee, 1975-86, 90-91, 96-2002, Office Naval Rsch. grantee, 1986-89, Russell Sage Found. grantee, 1989-91; Erskine fellow in Econs., 1990; recipient Lester R. Ford award Math. Assn. Am., 1976; Named Fulbright Disting. Chair in Econs., 2003-. Fellow Econometric Soc.; mem. Am. Polit. Sci. Assn., Ops. Rsch. Soc. Am., Cosmos Club, European Econ. Assn., Crane Theory Soc. (coun. mem.). Episcopalian. Avocations: choral singing, canoeing. Office: Johns Hopkins Univ Dept Econ Baltimore MD 21218 also: The Brookings Instn 1775 Massachusetts Ave NW Washington DC 20036-2103 E-mail: pyoung@jhu.edu.

YOUNG, IRMA JEAN, elementary education educator; b. Water Valley, Miss., Jan. 2, 1939; d. Fulton Wright and Nettie Jewell (Phillips) Hudson; m. Booker T. Young, Mar. 2, 1958; children: Linda Gayle, Deborah Denise. BS, Memphis State U., 1975, MEd, 1982. Elem. edn. tch. Dunbar Elem., Memphis, Tenn., 1975-80, Oakshire Elem., Memphis, 1980—. Tchr. New Hope Tutorial Ministry, Southaven, Miss., 1977—, New Hope Vacation Bible Sch., 1980—; mem. New Hope Bapt. Ch., 1964, New Hope Inspirational Choir, 1986. Mem. NEA, NAACP, Memphis Edn. Assn. (faculty rep. 1977-78), Tenn. Edn. Assn. Democrat. Office: Oakshire Elem 1765 E Holmes Rd Memphis TN 38116-9160

YOUNG, JAMES JULIUS, university administrator, retired army officer; b. Fort Ringgold, Tex., Nov. 28, 1926; s. John Cooper and Violet Thelma (Ohl) Y.; m. June Agnes Hillstead, Dec. 17, 1948; children: Robert Michael, Steven Andrew, Patrick James, Mary Frances. BS, U. Md., 1960; M.H.A., Baylor U., 1962; PhD in Hosp. and Health Adminstrn, U. Iowa, 1969. Commd. 2d lt. U.S. Army, 1947, advanced through grades to brig. gen., 1977; comdr., med. ops. officer, dir. tng. field med. units in European Command, 1949-53; comdr. Mil. Med. Leadership Sch., 1953-54; med. advisor (Nationalist Army of China), 1955-57; asst. adminstr. Fitzsimons Army Med. Center, 1957-60; med. plans and ops. officer (US Forces), Korea, 1962-63; sr. field med. instr., chief field med. service Med. Field Service Sch., 1963-66; dir. health care orgn. and mgmt. analysis Office of Surgeon Gen., 1969-71; dir. med. plans and ops. directorate Office of the Surgeon, Military Assistance Command, Vietnam, 1971-72; exec. officer, chief adminstrv. services Silas Hays Army Hosp., 1973-74; military health analyst, military health care study OMB, Exec. Office of Pres., 1974-76; dep. dir. resources mgmt. and cons. for health care adminstrn. Office of Surgeon Gen., 1976-77; chief med. svcs. corps U.S. Army, 1977-81; dir. resources mgmt. Office of Surgeon Gen., 1977-81; ret., 1981; instr. U. Iowa, 1967-69; asst. prof., preceptor Baylor U., 1973-74; vice chancellor for health affairs W.Va. Bd. Regents, Charleston, 1982-87; dean sch. of allied health scis. U. Tex. Health Sci. Ctr., San Antonio, 1987-90, interim dean Sch. Medicine, 1988-89, dean Sch. Medicine, 1989—, dean emeritus, 2000—. Cons. to Min. of Health, Republic of Vietnam, 1971-72, 1989-2000; adj. prof. Baylor U., 1977-81, George Washington U., 1975-76, W.Va. U., 1986; prof. U. Tex. health Sci. Ctr., San Antonio, 1989-2000. Contbr. articles to profl. jours. Decorated D.S.M., Legion of Merit, Meritorious Service medal, others; recipient Walter Reed medallion for service, 1981; Army Med. Dept. medallion for contbn. to health service, 1981, Order of Mil. Med. Merit, 1981, U. Tex. Health Scis. Ctr. Hon. medallion Fountains of Progress, 2000; recipient Humanism in medicine award Health Care Foun. N.J., 2000. Mem. APHA, Coun. Deans, Assn. of Am. Med. Colls., Bexar Cty. Med. Soc., Tex. Med. Assn., Assn. Mil. Surgeons (chmn. med. svc. sect. 1978), Assn. U.S. Army, Interagy. Inst. Fed. Health Execs., Phi Kappa Tau. Roman Catholic. Home: 1610 Anchor Dr San Antonio TX 78213-1943 E-mail: jyoung51@satx.rr.com.

YOUNG, JOYCE HENRY, adult education educator, consultant; b. Oak Park, Ill., July 3, 1930; d. Jesse Martin and Adelina Patti (Gillander) H.; m. James Edward Young, Apr. 26, 1958; children: Richard Allen, Patti Ann. BA, Calif. State U., Fresno, 1951; MA, Northwestern U., 1952; EdD, U. So. Calif., 1986. Tchr. Glencoe (Ill.) Pub. Schs., 1952-53, Hayward (Calif.) Schs., 1953-59, Honolulu Dept. Edn., 1969-83, Kamehameha Schs., Honolulu, 1987; instr. Hawaii Pacific Coll., Honolulu, 1987, Honolulu Community Coll., 1988, Chaminade U., Honolulu, 1990, Kansai Gaidai Hawaii Coll., 1991-93, U. Hawaii, Manoa, 1994, instr. emeritus, 1994—. Cons. Computer Lab., Honolulu, 1988. Mem. AAUW, Am. Ednl. Rsch. Assn., Educom, Delta Epsilon, Kappa Delta Pi, Pi Lambda Theta. Democrat. Presbyterian. Avocations: german shepherds, exotic birds.

YOUNG, JULIA ANNE, librarian, elementary education educator; b. El Campo, Tex., July 25, 1958; d. Harold Lane and Marcella Jeanne (Payne) Y. BA in English and French, Sam Houston State U., Huntsville, Tex., 1979; MBA, Sam Houston State U., 1982; M in Libr. and Info. Sci., U. Tex., 1986. Cert. tchr. secondary bus., elem. and secondary English 1-12, talented and gifted K-12, PK-12 learning resource ctrs., K-8 elem. gen., Tex. Cataloguer Sam Houston State U., 1976-85; mem. acquisitions and serials staff Tex. State Libr., Austin, 1985-86; cataloguer PCL Grad. Libr. U. Tex., Austin, 1985-86; libr., tchr. Dallas Ind. Sch. Dist., 1986—. Vol. voter registration, Huntsville, 1982—83; active Common Cause, Dallas, 1976, 2000; leader Girl Scouts U.S., Huntsville, 1976, Dallas, 1987—88; sec. PTA, 1998—2000; fin. com. adminstrv. bd. Highland Park United Meth. Ch., 1995—97; ch. choir Oak Lawn United Meth. Ch., 2001—02, mem. handbell choir, 2001—. Grantee, Jr. League, Dallas, 1994, 1996, 2002, 2003, Spanish Embassy, 2002, scholarship to study in Spain, Tex. Edn. Agy., 2002. Mem. AAUW, Tex. Libr. Assn., Dallas Emmaus Cmty., Dallas Assn. Sch. Librs. Democrat. Avocations: swimming, reading, walking, needlework, writing. Home: PO Box 190403 Dallas TX 75219-0403

YOUNG, KATHERINE ANN, education educator; b. Castleford, Idaho, Apr. 9, 1941; d. Ross and Norna (Scully) Stoner; m. Virgil Monroe Young, Dec. 20, 1964; 1 child, Susan Annette. BS in Elem. Edn., U. Idaho, 1965; MEd, Ea. Washington U., 1969; EdD, Utah State U., 1980. Cert. advanced elem. tchr., Idaho. Tchr. spl. edn. Coeur d'Alene (Idaho) Sch. Dist., 1965-66; tchr. elem. grades Coeur d' Aleue (Idaho) Sch. Dist., 1966-67, Boise (Idaho) Sch. Dist., 1967-88, prof. edn., 1988—2002; prof., coord. elem. edn. Boise State U., 1993—; prof. emeritus Boise (Idaho) State U., 2002—; dir. Alliance of Idaho Geographers/Nat. Geographic Soc., 1993—2002. Co-author: (resource book) The Story of Idaho Author's, 1977, The Story of Idaho Guide and Resource Book, 1993; author: The Utah Activity Book, 1980, Constructing Buildings, Bridges, and Minds, 1993; cons., contbr. (nat. edn. jour.) Learning, 1991—. Named Idaho Tchr. of Yr., State Dept. of Edn., Boise, 1983; attended luncheon at White House, Pres. Ronald Reagan, Washington, 1983; Recipient Outstanding Young Educator award Boise Jaycees, 1983; profiled in Idaho Centennial pub.,

1990; travel to Japan grantee Rocky Mountain Region Japan Project, 1990. Mem. ASCD, Nat. Coun. for Social Studies, Idaho Law Found., Alliance Idaho Geographers-Nat. Geog. Soc. (state coord.). Avocations: travel, reading.

YOUNG, LAUREN SUE JONES, education educator; b. San Diego, July 21, 1947; d. Warren Calvin and Lola Esther Jones; 1 child, Forest McRay Young. AB, Occidental Coll., 1969; MS, San Diego State U., 1971; EdM, Harvard U., 1979, EdD, 1984. Adminstrv. asst. Child Devel. Research Unit, Nairobi, Kenya, 1969-70; asst. prof. San Diego State U., 1974—78, assoc. dir. Tchr. Corps., 1971—78; co-chmn. and mem. Harvard Ednl. Review, Cambridge, Mass., 1979-81; research assoc. The Huron Inst., Cambridge, 1980-82, Atari Cambridge Research Lab., Cambridge, 1982-84; policy analyst N.Y. State Dept. Social Services, Albany, 1984-85, spl. asst. to commr., 1985-87; assoc. prof. Mich. State U., East Lansing, 1987-2001; sr. program officer, dir. The Spencer Found., Chgo., 1998—. Cons. Am. Insts. for Rsch., Cambridge, 1980, Tchr. Corps, Boston area, 1978-80, instr., Pago Pago, Am. Samoa, 1979; rsch. assoc. A Study of H.S.'s, Cambridge, 1980-82; disting. visitor John D. and Catherine T. MacArthur Found., 1995-96. Co-editor: Too Little, Too Late, 1988; mem. editorial bd. Evaluation Rev. Jour., 1984-88, Jour. Negro Edn. Team mem. Operation Crossroads Africa, Morogoro, Tanzania, 1968; mem. program adv. bd. Spencer Found., 1992. Recipient Danforth Found. fellow, St. Louis, 1978-84, tchr. scholar award, M.S.U., 1993. Mem. Am. Ednl. Research Assn. Office: The Spender Found 875 N Michigan Ave Ste 3930 Chicago IL 60611-1803

YOUNG, LAURENCE RETMAN, biomedical engineer, educator; b. N.Y.C., Dec. 19, 1935; s. Benjamin and Bess (Retman) Y.; m. Joan Marie Fisher, June 12, 1960; children— Eliot Fisher, Leslie Ann, Robert Retman. AB, Amherst Coll., 1957; SB, MIT, 1957, SM, 1959, ScD, 1962; Certificat de License (French Govt. fellow), Faculty of Sci. U. of Paris, France, 1958. Registered profl. engr., Mass. Engr. Sperry Gyroscope Co., Great Neck, N.Y., 1957; engr. NASA Instrumentation Lab., MIT, 1958-60, asst. prof. aero. and astronautics, 1962-67, assoc. prof., 1967-70, prof., 1970—, payload specialist spacelab life sci., 1991-93; Apollo Program prof., chair in astronautics MIT, Cambridge, 1995—; prof. Baylor Coll. Medicine, Houston, 1996—. Dir. Nat. Space Biomed. Rsch. Inst., 1997-01; summer lectr. U. Ala., Huntsville, 1966-68; lectr. Med. Sch. Harvard U., 1970-78; mem. tng. com. biomed. engring. NIH, 1971-73; mem. com. space medicine and biology Space Sci. Bd., NAS, 1974-77, chmn. vestibular panel summer study of life scis. in space, 1977; mem. com. engring. and clin. care NAE, 1970; mem. Air Force Sci. Adv. Bd., 1979-85; mem. Air Force Studies Bd., NRC, 1982, Aeros. and Space Engrs. Bd., 1982-87; mem. NRC Com. on Space Sta., 1987, 1991—, Com. on Human Exploration Space, 1990, Com. on Human Factors, 1990—; CHABA coun. NASA Task Force on Sci. Uses of Space Sta., 1982-85; vis. prof. Swiss Fed. Inst. Tech., Zurich, 1972-73, Conservatoire Nationale des Arts and Metiers, Paris, 1972-73, Stanford U., 1987-88; vis. scientist Kantonsspital Zurich, 1972-73; prin. investigator vestibular expts. on Spacelabs— 1, SLS-1, 2 and D-1, 1977—; cons. Applied Sci. Lab., NASA, Gulf & Western, Link div. Singer Co., Boeing, Lockheed, others; payload specialist Space Shuttle STS-58 (Spacelab SLS-2), NASA Johnson Space Ctr., 1992—. Contbg. author: chpt. on vestibular system Medical Physiology, 1974, Handbook of Physiology, 1983, Encyclopedia of Neuroscience, 1987; editorial bd. chpt. on vestibular system Internat. Jour. Man-Machine Studies, 1966-75, Neurosci., 1976-92; contbr. numerous articles to profl. jours. Recipient Pub. Svc. Group Achievement award NASA, 1984, Exceptional Civilian Svc. award USAR, 1985, Koetser Found. prize, 1998. Fellow IEEE (Franklin V. Taylor award 1963, First Ann. Space Life Sci. lectr. 1990), AIAA (Dryden lectr. 1981), Aerospace Medical Assn. (Jeffries Medical Rsch. award 1992), Aerospace Human Factor Assn. (Paul Hensen award 1995), U.S. Ski Assn. (award of merit 1976), Explorers Club; mem. NAE, Inst. Medicine, Am. Physiol. Soc. (1st lectr. in aerospace life scis. 1990), Biomed. Engring. Soc. (founding/charter mem., dir. 1972-75, pres. 1979-80, Alza lectr. 1984), Aerospace Med. Assn., ASTM (com. on snow skiing 1975—, chmn. 1988-93), Internat. Soc. Skiing Safety (bd. dirs. 1977-85), Internat. Fedn. Automatic Control (tech. com. biomed. engring. 1975-85), AIAA (working group for simulator facilities 1976-80), Nat. Acad. Engrs., Inst. Medicine, Internat. Acad. Astronautics (corr.), Barany Soc., Cosmos Club, Tau Beta Pi. Home: 217 Thorndike St Apt 108 Cambridge MA 02141-1504 Office: MIT Man-Vehicle Lab Rm 37-219 Cambridge MA 02139

YOUNG, LINDA IRENE, school district administrator; b. Fort Smith, Ark., Dec. 2, 1948; d. Charles Holt and Wanda Louise (Graves) Y.; children: Charles, Patrick. BS Edn., U. Ark., 1970, MEd, 1971. Cert. tchr., adminstr., supr., Ark. Tchr. Fayetteville (Ark.) Pub. Schs., 1970-72, Bauxite (Ark.) Pub. Schs., 1972-75, Pulaski Acad., Little Rock, 1975-76, elem. prin., 1976-78; asst. dir. summer reading program U. Ark.-Little Rock, 1985-88, instr., 1987-88; dir. restructuring/new futures liaison Little Rock Sch. Dist., 1988—. Bd. mem. Ark. Mid. Level. Assn., 1989—; fellow Ctr. for Leadership in Sch. Reform, Louisville, 1990—; mem. adv. bd. Ctr. for Mid. Level. Edn., Fayetteville, 1992—, cons., 1993; bd. mem. Ark. Mid. Level Grade Task Force, 1991—. Mem. editorial bd. MidSouth Jour. Mid. Level Edn. Mem. Ark. Arts Ctr. Alumni Orgn., Little Rock, 1985—; pres. Ark. Symphony Orch. Guild, Little Rock, 1986-87; bd. dirs. Ark. Symphony Orch. Assn., 1986-87. Recipient Juvenile Justice Recognition award Div. Children and Family Svcs., State of Ark., 1990. Mem. ASCD, Nat. Assn. Secondary Sch. Prins., Nat. Mid. Sch. Assn., Phi Delta Kappa. Democrat. Methodist. Avocations: reading, music, tennis, water sports, gardening. Home: 13820 Windsor Rd Little Rock AR 72212-3209 Office: Little Rock Sch Dist 810 W Markham St Little Rock AR 72201-1306

YOUNG, LOIS CATHERINE WILLIAMS, poet, former reading specialist; b. Wakeman, Ohio, Mar. 10, 1930; d. William McKinley and Leona Catherine (Woods) Williams; m. William Walton Young; children: Ralph, Catherine, William. BS, NYU, 1957; MS, Hofstra U., 1962, profl. diploma, 1967, EdD, 1981; M Pub. Adminstrn., Fla. Internat. U., 1988. Cert. tchr., sch. supr., N.Y., pub. mgmt., Fla. Tchr. Copiaque (N.Y.) Schs., 1957-59; research assoc. Columbia and Hofstra Univs., Hempstead, N.Y., 1964-69; tchr. Half Hollow Hills Pub. Schs., Dix Hills, N.Y., 1970-72; instr. Conn. Coll., New London, 1972-73; tchr., supr., reading coordinator Hempstead (N.Y.) Pub. Schs., 1975-85; cons. South African project AID Fla. Meml. Coll., Miami, Fla., 1987-88. Clinician Hofstra U., Hempstead, 1962-64; tchr. trainer Amityville (N.Y.) Pub. Schs., 1965, Hofstra Univ., 1982; key speaker Internat. Reading Assn., N.Y., Calif., Caribbean Islands, 1982-86. Author numerous poems. Sec. Nassau County (N.Y.) chpt. Jack and Jill of Am., 1960-62; pres. PTA, Uniondale, N.Y., 1962-68; active Boy Scouts Am., Uniondale, N.Y., 1963-65; bd. dirs. Miami chpt. UN Assn./USA, 1987-92, 1st v.p. 1989-91, Broward Fort Lauderdale chpt., 1993—; active multilateral project, 1987-90; contbr. Procs. South African Project, 1987. Recipient Lifetime Membership award PTA, 1964, rsch. grant N.Y. State Fed. Programs, 1978, Laurel Wreath award Doctoral Assn. of N.Y. Educators, 1982, Cert. of award UN Assn./USA, 1987, 88, Outstanding Achievement award Fla. Internat. U., 1988, Golden Poet award World of Poetry, 1990, 91; fellow Fla. Internat. U., 1987. Mem. Internat. Soc. Poets (life, lifetime adv. panel 1993—, award, Nat. Libr. of Poetry award 1994, 95, Poetry Today 1996), Fla. Internat. U. Alumni Assn., NYU Alumni Assn. (bd. dirs. 1983-90, 2d v.p. 1986-87), Hofstra U. Alumni Assn., Tuskegee Airmen, Inc., Weston (Fla.) Toastmasters Club (charter), Toastmasters Internat., Kappa Delta Pi, Alpha Kappa Alpha, Theta Iota Omega (global affairs com. 1984-86), Phi Delta Kappa. Avocations: creative writing, travel, tennis, radio reading for unsighted, golf. Home: 1221 Devonshire Way West Palm Beach FL 33418-6864

YOUNG, MALCOLM EUGENE, JR., social studies secondary educator; b. Sulphur Springs, Tex., Sept. 27, 1943; s. Malcolm Eugene Sr. and Cleo Lessie (Wilson) Y.; m. Frances Jeane Tatum, Aug. 27, 1966; children: Robert, Kerri, Scott. BS, Howard Payne U., 1967; MEd, North Tex. State U., 1969. Lic. tchr., Tex. Tchr., coach Travis Jr. High Sch., Irving, Tex., 1967-69, MacArthur High Sch., Irving, 1969-71, North Jr. High Sch., Richardson, Tex., 1971-72, Westwood Jr. High Sch., Richardson, 1972-75, J.J. Pearce High Sch., Richardson, 1975-78, tchr., 1978—. Tchr. participant Close Up, Washington, 1989, Law-Related Edn. Summer Inst., Austin, 1993, 96, 97; sponsor, participant Close Up-Citizen Bee regional competition, Dallas, 1990-96, 98. Taft Seminar for Tchrs. fellow, Austin, Tex., 1995. Mem. Nat. Coun. Social Studies, Assn. Tex. Profl. Educators, Tex. Coun. Social Studies, Richardson Assn. Tex. Profl. Educators. Methodist. Avocations: leather work, hunting, fishing, camping. Office: Richardson Ind Sch Dist 1600 N Coit Rd Richardson TX 75080-2805

YOUNG, MARGARET CHONG, elementary education educator; b. Honolulu, May 8, 1924; d. Henry Hon Chin and Daisy Kyau (Tong) Chong; m. Alfred Y.K. Young, Feb. 21, 1948; children: Robert S.W., Richard S.K., Linda S.K. EdB, 5th yr. cert., U. Hawaii, 1945. Cert. tchr., Hawaii. Tchr. Waipahu (Hawaii) Elem. Sch., Manoa Housing Sch., Hawaii Dept. Edn., Honolulu, Pauoa Elem. Sch., Honolulu. Author: And They Also Came, History of Chinese Christian Association, Hawaii's People From China; contbr. numerous articles to profl. jours. Ch. sch. tchr., supt. United Ch. Christ-Judd St. Grantee San Francisco State Coll. Mem. NEA, Hawaii State Tchrs. Assn., Hawaii Congress of Parents and Tchrs. (hon. life mem.), Kappa Kappa Iota (Disting. Educator award 1986-87), Delta Kappa Gamma (internat.).

YOUNG, MICHAEL KENT, dean, lawyer, educator; b. Sacramento, Nov. 4, 1949; s. Vance Lynn and Ethelyn M. (Sowards) Young; m. Suzan Kay Stewart, June 1, 1972; children: Stewart, Kathryn, Andrew. BA summa cum laude, Brigham Young U., 1973; JD magna cum laude, Harvard U., 1976. Bar: Calif. 1976, N.Y. 1985. Law clk. to Justice Benjamin Kaplan, Supreme Jud. Ct. Mass., Boston, 1976-77; assoc. prof., prof., Fuyo prof. Japanese law Columbia U., N.Y.C., 1978-98; dir. Ctr. Japanese Legal Studies Ctr. for Korean Legal Studies, N.Y.C., 1985-98; dir. Program Internat. Human Rights and Religious Liberties Columbia U., N.Y.C., 1995-98; dep. legal advisor U.S. Dept. State, Washington, 1989-91, dep. under sec. for econ. affairs, 1991-93, amb. for trade and environ. affairs, 1992-93; law clk. to Justice William H. Rehnquist U.S. Supreme Ct., Washington, 1977-78; dean, Lobingier prof. comparative law and jurisprudence George Washington U. Sch. of Law, Washington, 1998—. Chair U.S. Commn. on Internat. Religious Freedom, 2001—02, vice chair, 2002—; vis. scholar law faculty U. Tokyo, 1978—80, 1983; vis. prof. Waseda U., 1989; chmn. bd. advisors Japan Soc., 1996—98; counsel select subcom. on arms transfers to Bosnia U.S. Ho. of Reps., 1996; mem. steering com. Law Profs. for Dole, 1996; mem. com. on internat. jud. rels. U.S. Jud. Conf., 1999—; mem. Brown v. Bd. Edn. 50th Anniversary Commemoration Com.; chair NAFTA labor agreement adv. com. Dept. of Labor, 2002—; mem. trade and environ. policy adv. com. U.S. Trade Rep. Office, 2003—. Author: Fundamentals of U.S. Trade Law, 2001, Japanese Law in Context, 2001. Bd. visitors USAF Acad., 2000—02. Fellow, POSCO Rsch. Inst., 1995—98, Japan Found., 1979—80, Fulbright, 1983—84. Fellow: Am. Bar Found.; mem.: Coun. Fgn. Rels. Mem. Lds Ch. Avocation: Avocations: skiing, scuba diving, photography. Fax: 202-994-5157. E-mail: myoung@law.gwu.edu.

YOUNG, MICHAEL WARREN, geneticist, educator; b. Miami, Fla., Mar. 28, 1949; s. Lloyd George and Mildred (Tillery) Y.; m. Laurel Ann Eckhardt, Dec. 27, 1978; children: Natalie, Arissa. BA, U. Tex., 1971, PhD, 1975. NIH postdoctoral fellow Stanford (Calif.) U. Med. Sch., 1975-77; asst. prof. genetics The Rockefeller U., N.Y.C., 1978-83, assoc. prof., 1984-88, prof., 1988—, dir. Levy/White Ctr. Mind, Brain and Behavioral Studies, 2000—02; head Rockefeller unit NSF Sci. and Tech. Ctr. Biol. Timing, 1991—2001. Investigator Howard Hughes Med. Inst., N.Y.C., 1987-96; adv. panel on genetic biology NSF, Washington, 1983-87; spl. advisor Am. Cancer Soc., N.Y.C., 1985—; spl. reviewer genetics study sect. NIH, Bethesda, Md., 1990—, cell biology study sect., 1993-97. Contbr. articles to profl. jours. Meyer Found. fellow, N.Y.C., 1978-83. Fellow N.Y. Soc. Fellows; mem. AAAS, Genetics Soc. Am., Am. Soc. Microbiologists, N.Y. Acad. Scis., Harvey Soc. (treas. 2001—). Achievements include research on transposable DNA elements, molecular genetics of nerve and muscle development, biological clocks, molecular control of circadian rhythms. Home: 51 Greenwoods Rd Old Tappan NJ 07675-7018 Office: The Rockefeller Univ 1230 York Ave New York NY 10021-6399

YOUNG, NANCY HENRIETTA MOE, retired elementary education educator; b. Athens, Ohio, June 25, 1936; d. Charles N. Moe and Mary E. (Sams) Moe-Oyler; m. Henry O. Young, May 13, 1956; children: Pamela Sue Young Paustenbach, Patrick H. BA in Elem. Edn., Ohio U., 1973, degree in elem. edn., 1983. Tchr. 3rd grade Berne Union Sch., Sugar Grove, Ohio, 1968-86, tchr. 4th grade, 1987-94, head dept., 1992-94; tchr. 8th grade English and reading Berne Union Mid. Sch., Sugar Grove, Ohio, 1995-96, 6th grade English, reading and sci. tchr., 1996-98. Music tchr. Fairfield Christian Acad., Lancaster, Ohio, 1999—. Jennings scholar Capital U., 1980-81. Mem. NEA, Ohio Edn. Assn., Berne Union Edn. Assn., Delta Kappa Gamma. Republican. Mem. 1st Ch. of God. Avocations: music, reading, traveling, family. Home: 2410 Blue Valley Rd SE Lancaster OH 43130-9019

YOUNG, NANCY M. retired secondary school educator, artist; b. Pensacola, Fla., May 24, 1933; d. Mark Bodenheimer Mayer and Elsie Nobles; m. Richard S. Young, June 7, 1955 (dec. Oct. 1996); children: Deeann, Sandra, Mark. BS, Fla. State U., 1955. Tchr. pub. schs., Athens, Ala., 1955—56; artist Sunnyvale, Calif., 1961—67; tchr. pub. schs., Arlington, Va., 1968—70; piano tchr. McLean, Va., 1968—75; salesperson art and pottery McLean and Annapolis, Md., 1975—81; salesperson Dee Real Estate, Bronxville, NY, 1981—83; travel agt. Travco, McLean, 1984—87. Mem. Beautification Bd., Cape Canaveral, Fla., 1989—96, Libr. Bd., Cape Canaveral, 1984—96. Avocation: watercolor painting. Home: 673 Heatherstone Dr Merritt Island FL 32953

YOUNG, PAULA ERNESS, corporate trainer; b. Memphis, Sept. 20, 1957; d. Erneest Leroy and Carrie Louise (Watson) Y. BS, Memphis State U., 1978; MPA, Atlanta U., 1981; EdD in Ednl Adminstrn., U. Cin., 1993. Asst. dir. grants and contracts Nat. Assn. for Equal Opportunity in Higher Edn., Washington, 1981-83, clearinghouse and conf. exhibits mgr., 1981-83; dir rsch. and proposal devel. Clark Coll., Atlanta, 1984-87; asst. v.p. for devel. Johnson C. Smith U., Charlotte, N.C., 1987-88; v.p. instl. advancement Bennett Coll., Greensboro, N.C., 1988-90; spl. asst. to dean Coll. Arts and Scis., N.C. Agrl. and Tech. State U., Greensboro, 1990-98; sr. instrl. design specialist Fed. Express Corp., 1998—. Mem. Women of Color Com., 1994; mem. Greensboro Minority/Women Bus. Enterprise Adv. Bd., 1993; mem. Greensboro Human Rels. Commn., 1990; founder African Am. Atelier Art Gallery; vol. Girl Scouts U.S.A., 1985-86; active YWCA, NAACP. Woodrow Wilson fellow, 1981-83, 85-87. Mem. Nat. Assn. Negro Bus. and Profl. Women's Clubs, Nat. Soc. Fund Raising Execs., Toastmasters Internat., Alpha Kappa Alpha. Avocations: ceramic artwork, reading. Address: 7617 Windsong Dr Memphis TN 38125-6513

YOUNG, RAYMOND JAMES, retired education educator; b. Howard, Kans., Nov. 2, 1922; s. Raymond Everett and Ethel Belle Young; m. Blenda E. Thompson, Nov. 14, 1942 (dec. 1980); children: Judy Rae, Dwight Paul; m. Ruby I. Wright, Aug. 24, 1962; children: Runell A., Raven J. BS, Kans. State Tchrs. Coll., 1948, MS, 1949; EdD, U. Colo., 1950; postgrad., U. Idaho, 1986. Cert. tchr., Kans. Tchr., prin. Elk County Sch. Dist., Howard, Kans., 1941-42; asst. prof. Okla. State U., Stillwater, 1950-54; assoc. prof. U. Okla., Norman, 1954-55, U. Ill., Champaign, 1955-59; prof. U. Mich., Ann Arbor, 1959-69, Wash. State U., Pullman, 1976-89; ret., 1990; sr. cons. edn. Arthur D. Little, Inc., Cambridge, Mass., 1969-75; prin. assoc. McMannis Assocs., Inc., Washington, 1975-76. Co-author: The School and The Community, 1955, Summer Sessions in Colleges and University, 1991; contbr. over 150 articles to profl. jours. Editor, historian 602nd Tank Destroyer Battalion Assn., Inc., 1986—, pres., 2000—. Sgt. U.S. Army, 1943-45, ETO. Mem. Am. Legion (post comdr. 1997-2000, dist. comdr. 1998-99), Coun. Study Comty. Colls., VFW, DAV, NEA, Elks, Ind. Order Odd Fellows, Phi Delta Kappa. Achievements include development of citizens participatory process for starting new 2-yr. colls., and holds record for the number started in the U.S; dir. major study projects in Algeria, Greece, and Holland. Avocations: fishing, golf, hunting, boating. Home: PO Box 4573 East Lansing MI 48826-4573

YOUNG, RENEE LENOIRE JOYEUSAZ, English educator; b. Ft. Meade, Md., July 5, 1952; BA, U. Del., 1974; MA, Del. State U., 1991; EdD, Wilmington Coll., 1996. Cert. tchr., Del. Advt. rep. Del. State News, Dover, 1976-80; adj. prof. English Del. Tech. C.C., Dover, 1987-92; adj. prof. English, writing ctr. dir. Wesley Coll., Dover, 1988-91; dept. asst. Del. State U., Dover, 1991-92, instr., 1992-96, assoc. prof. English, 1996—, coord. writing ctr., 1997—. Mem. adv. bd. Alpha-Capital Sch. Dist., Dover, 1984-87; faculty senator Del. State U., 1993—; cons. MBNA, Newark, 1995. Contbr. articles to profl. jours. Judge Odyssey of the Mind State Finals, Del., 1990; presenter regional confs.; facilitator 4th Conf. on Minority Issues in Higher Edn., Del. State U., 1996. Recipient advt. award Md.-Del.-D.C. Press Assn., 1979. Mem. Nat. Writing Ctrs. Assn., Nat. Coun. Tchrs. English, Mid. Atlantic Writing Ctrs. Assn. (bd. dirs. 1991—), Delta Kappa Gamma (organizer Outreach to Student Tchr. Del. State U. 1997-2003, pres. 2003—), Phi Delta Kappa. Episcopalian. Avocation: antique collector. Home: 385 Troon Rd Dover DE 19904-2356 Office: Del State Univ DuPont Hwy Dover DE 19904

YOUNG, RICHARD ALAN, association executive; b. Oak Park, Ill., Mar. 17, 1935; m. Carol Ann Schellinger, June 28, 1958; children: Steven, Karen, Christopher. BA, U. Iowa, 1958; MS, PhD, Western State U., 2000. Chief engr. Cardox Corp., Chgo., 1958-61; asst. chief engr. Goodman Mfg. Co., Chgo., 1961-63; plant and environ. engr. Signode Corp., Glenview, Ill., 1963-68; editor Pollution Engring. Tech. Pub. Co., Barrington, Ill., 1968-81; exec. dir. Nat. Registry of Environ. Profls., 1988—; pub. Cahners Pub. Co., Des Plaines, Ill., 1990-95. Adj. prof. George Williams Coll.; mcpl. pollution control adviser and enforcement officer for 24 cities and state govts; ofcl rep. and pollution control expert U.S. Govt. at tech. transfer meetings; exec. dir. Internat. Certification Accreditation Bd., 1999—. Editor 26 books on environ. engring.; pollution engring.; series editor, Marcel Dekker Inc., N.Y.C.; contbr. articles to profl. jours.; patentee in field. Recipient Jesse H. Neal certificate for outstanding editorial writing Am. Bus. Press, Inc., 1971, Outstanding Service award Western Soc. Engrs., Charles Ellet award as Most Outstanding Engr. of Yr. 1970; Environ. Quality award EPA, 1976 Mem. Internat. Assn. for Pollution Control (dir.), Am. Soc. Bus. Press Editors (Editl. Excellence award 1980, Design Excellence award 1982), Am. Inst. Plant Engrs. (past nat. chmn. environ. quality), Internat. Congress Environ. Profls. (mng. dir.), Nat. Inst. Hazardous Materials Mgmts. (dir. 1984-88, cert. hazardous materials mgr.).

YOUNG, RICHARD ALAN, retired sports administration educator, athletic director; b. Ohio, Jan. 3, 1932; m. Alexandra (Sandy) Waddell, Mar. 20, 1954; children: Pamela, Alyson. Student, Denison U., 1950-51; B of Phys. Edn. & Recreation cum laude, Ohio State U., 1954, MA in Edn., 1959; PhD in Ednl. Adminstrn., Bowling Green State U., 1975. Adminstrv. asst. health, phys. edn., athletics Bowling Green (Ohio) State U., 1959-71, acting chmn., 1971, dir. athletics, 1971-78, Okla. State U., Stillwater, 1978-83, Wash. State U., Pullman, 1983-87; dir. athletics and campus recreation Fla. Internat. U., Miami, 1987-93; prof. sports adminstrn., dir. intercollegiate athletics Lynn U., Boca Raton, Fla., 1993—2002; interim athletic dir. Fla. Atlantic U., 2002—, ret., 2003. Instr. Bowling Green State U., 1959-64, asst. prof., 1964-71, assoc. prof., 1971-78, prof., 1978-83, head baseball coach, 1959-71, asst. football coach, head freshman football coach, 1959-68; lectr. Wash. State U., 1983-87; grad. asst. football coach Ohio State U., 1958-59; adj. prof. Fla. Internat. U., 1987-93 Bd. dirs. Boy Scouts Am., Big Bros., Rotary, C. of C.; state dir. Fellowship of Christian Athletes. Lt. USN, 1955-58, (naval aviator). Recipient Spl. Achievement award Bowling Green State U., 1974; named Big Ten Scholar-Athlete Ohio State U., 1954, All-Am. Scholar Football Team Ohio State U., 1954. Mem. U.S. Sports Acad. Adv. Bd., Nat. Collegiate Athletic Assn. (divs. I steering com. 1981-84, post-season football com. 1982-85, television com. 1983-85, postgrad. scholar com. 1985-92), Nat. Assn. Collegiate Dirs. Athletics (bd. dirs.), Trans Am. Athletic Conf. (v.p. 1991-93), New South Athletic Conf. (v.p. 1988-90, pres. 1990-92, Bowling Green State U. Hall of Fame, U.S. Sports Acad. Disting. Svc. award, 2003).

YOUNG, RICHARD ROBERT, logistics and transportation educator; b. Passaic, NJ, July 18, 1946; s. William Frederick and Helen Mae (Smith) Y.; m. Mary Frances Braccio, Nov. 27, 1971. BS in Commerce, Rider Coll., 1968; MBA, SUNY, Albany, 1971; postgrad., U. Mass., 1973-77; PhD, Pa. State U., 1993. Admitted to practice FMC. Materials handling engr. Thatcher Glass Mfg. Co., Elmira, N.Y., 1968-69; mgr. customer svc. Cooper Labs., Wayne, N.J., 1971; materials mgr. of contracts Sprague Electric Co., North Adams, Mass., 1971-75, mgr. corp. purchasing, 1975-77; mgr. purchasing adminstrn. Am. Hoechst Corp., Somerville, N.J., 1977-80, mgr. group purchasing, 1980-84; mgr. group distbn. Hoechst Celanese Corp., Somerville, 1984-89; asst. prof. bus. logistics Pa. State U., 1989—2002, assoc. prof., supply chain mgmt., 2002—, dir. logistics exec. program in Singapore, 1996-2000; acting divsn. head engring., bus. and computer sci. Pa. State U.-Berks-Lehigh Valley Coll., 2002—03. Bd. dirs. Guildcraft Inc., York, Pa., vice-chmn., 1992-94, chmn., 1995-2003; mem. adv. com. World Trade Inst., N.Y.C., 1985-98; cons. indsl. and svc. sector clients world-wide 1995—; affiliate rschr. Idaho Inst. Bus. and Environ., 1995-98; external examiner Sch. Bus., Temasek Poly., Singapore, 2002-2003; mem. Fulbright German Studies Seminar, 2003. Contbr. articles to logistics jours. Bd. dirs. No. Berkshire Child Care Commn., North Adams, Mass., 1972-76; mem. Union Twp. (N.J.) Zoning Bd., 1985-89, vice chmn., 1989; v.p. Union Twp. Rep. Club, 1983-87; alt. mem. Hunterdon County (N.J.) Rep. Com., 1987; ordained Presbyn. elder. Fellow Chartered Inst. Transport (U.K.); mem. Can. Assn. Logistics and Supply Chain Mgmt. (mem. rsch. com.), Phillipsburg R.R. Historians (co-founder), Acad. Mgmt., Decision Sci. Inst., Nat. Assn. Purchasing Mgmt. (cert.), Am. Soc. Transp. and Logistics (sustaining assoc. examiner 1989-98), Assn. for Psychol. Type, Fulbright Assn., Masons, Hamilton Club Lancaster, Delta Sigma Pi. Presbyterian. Avocations: travel, sailing, photography. Home: 222 Heatherstone Way Lancaster PA 17601-4975 Office: Pa State U 149 Franco Bldg Reading PA 19610 Personal E-mail: rry1@aol.com. Business E-Mail: rry100@psu.edu.

YOUNG, ROBERT DONALD, physicist, educator; b. Chgo., Apr. 20, 1940; s. Robert Joseph and Nellie Y.; children: Robert Gerald, Jennifer Ann Rolinski; m. BJ Marymont, Feb. 14, 1981; 1 child, Emily Sexton. BS in Physics, Ill. Inst. Tech., 1962; MS in Physics, Purdue U., 1965, PhD in Physics, 1967. Asst. prof. physics Ill. State U., Normal, 1967-73, assoc. prof., 1974-78, prof., 1979-2000, prof. emeritus, 2000—, dir. rsch. Coll. Arts and Scis., 1994-95, assoc. v.p. for rsch., dean grad. studies, 1995-97, chair dept. physics, 1997-2000. Adj. prof. physics U. Ill., Urbana, 1986—2001; adj. prof. physics and astronomy No. Ariz. U., Flagstaff, 2003—. Named Rschr. of Yr., Ill. State U., 1989. Mem.: Biophy Soc., Am. Assn. Phys. Tchg., Am. Phys. Soc. Achievements include research in physics of proteins, usage of computer techniques in physics education, individualized modular approach in physics education. Home: 838 N Lone Oak Way Flagstaff AZ 86004-5819 Office: No Ariz Univ Dept Physics & Astronomy Campus Box 6010 Flagstaff AZ 86011-6010

YOUNG, RUSSELL LESLIE, education educator; b. San Diego, June 5, 1956; s. Edward Billy and Dolly (Hom) Y.; m. Liling Chen, Jan. 10, 1984; children: Christopher, Brandon. BA in Psychology, U. Calif., San Diego, 1978; MEd, U. Hawaii, 1980; PhD in Edn., San Diego State U. and Claremont Grad. Sch., 1987. Instr. Nat. Chengchi U., Taipei, Taiwan, 1982-83, Nat. Taiwan Normal U., Taipei, 1982-83; evaluator San Diego (Calif.) State Found., 1987-90, adj. prof., lectr., 1987-90, prof., 1990—, San Diego State U. Adj. faculty Nat. U., San Diego, 1987-88; prof. Nat. Kaohsiung (Taiwan) Normal U., 1991-93; mem. Asian Pacific Edn. Coun. to San Diego (Calif.) City Schs., 1990-91. Author: Language Maintenance and Language Shift Among the Chinese on Taiwan, 1989, Dragon Song: A Fable for the New Millennium. Recipient Excellence in Children's Lit. award Taiwan Provincial Dept. Edn., 1986; grantee Pacific Cultural Found., Taiwan, 1986, Multicultural Infusion Inst., San Diego, 1991, Republic of China Nat. Sci. Coun., Taiwan, 1993. Mem. Nat. Assn. for Multicultural Edn. (recipient Children's Book award), Assn. for Asian Studies, Am. Ednl. Rsch. Assn., Yale-China Assn., Phi Beta Delta. Office: San Diego State Univ Coll of Edn San Diego CA 92182

YOUNG, SARAH MOSKOWITZ, educational and computer consultant, journalist; b. Galveston, Tex., June 10, 1947; d. Irving Leonard and Joyce (Schreiber) Moskowitz; children: Clement Clarke III, Leonard Arthur. B Tech. Edn., postgrad., Nat. U., San Diego, 1984; EdD, Calif. Coast U., San Diego, 1989, postgrad. Adult edn. and community coll. credentials, cert. vision and hearing tech., pers. cons., Calif.; cert. first aid and CPR instr. trainer. Tchr. Vista High Sch., San Diego, 1980-81; project dir. Robert Harrow Co., San Diego, 1981-82; instr. North County Coll., Eldorado Coll., San Diego County, 1982-84, Bangkok U., Kasesart U., 1985-86; assoc. dean, chmn. dept. edn. Phillips Coll., New Orleans, 1988-89; instr., radio performer Am. Lang. Tng., Jakarta, Indonesia, 1989-90; ednl. cons., journalist various mags. and newspapers, 1980—. Seminar speaker Sci. Rsch. Assocs., 1980; tng. officer Naval Sea Cadets, Monterey, Calif., 1988-89; mem. nat. curriculum com. Am. Assn. Med. Transcriptionists, 1978-88; med. instr. Kelsey-Jenney Coll., San Diego, 1990-91; founder Disabled Individuals Suggesting Computer Solutions. Mem., bd. dirs. Mira Mesa Town Coun., San Diego, 1980-84, sec., 1983-84; bd. dirs. Mira Mesa Community Coun., 1982-84; precinct chmn. San Diego Mayoral Election Com., 1982-84. Scholar Nat. U., 1984. Mem. NAFE, Leadership Edn. Awareness and Devel., San Diego Computer Soc., Mensa (chmn. mayor's adv. com. San Diego 1982-84, career day 1983), San Diego Press Club, Tetra Soc. San Diego (founder), Delta Omicron Epsilon. Avocations: artist, musician, world culturee, languages, animals. Home and Office: 10257 Trails End Cir San Diego CA 92126-3517

YOUNG, SHARON LAREE, mathematics educator; b. San Bernardino, Calif., Jan. 28, 1945; d. Richard Austin and Freida Belle (Southerland) Uzzel; m. Randall Lee Young, June 19, 1966; children: Gillian, Courtney. BA, U. Redlands, 1966; MA, Denver U., 1976; PhD, U. Colo., 1979. Cert. tchr., Calif. Social worker Los Angeles County, Glendale, Calif., 1966-67; tchr. Spottswood (N.J.) Sch. Dist., 1967-68; tchr., then program specialist North Sacramento Sch. Dist., 1968-74; lectr., tchg. asst. U. Colo., Boulder, 1977-80; author, cons. Addison-Wesley Pub. Co., Menlo Park, Calif., 1980-94; assoc. prof. Seattle Pacific U., 1995-99, 2000—. Vis. asst. prof. W.Va. U., Morgantown, 1981-82; asst. prof. La. State U., Baton Rouge, 1982-86; cons. Ednl. Cons. Assocs, Englewood, Colo., 1976-79, Good Apple, Inc., Carthage, Ill., 1980-83. Author: Harry's Math Books, Set A, 1997, Set B, 1998, Geometry Books, 2001, Numbers 1-20 Books, 2002, More Geometry Books, 2003, Spatial Concept Books, 2003, 1-20 Counting Books, 2002, Addison-Wesley Mathematics; co-author textbooks; contbr. articles to profl. publs. Mem. Nat. Assn. Suprs. Math., Nat. Coun. Tchrs. Math., Assn. Math. Tchr. Educators.

YOUNG, SONIA WINER, public relations director, educator; b. Aug. 20, 1934; d. Meyer D. and Rose (Demby) Winer; m. Melvin A. Young, Feb. 24, 1957; 1 child, Melanie Anne. BA, Sophie Newcomb Coll., 1956; M in Ednl. Psychology, U. Tenn.-Chattanooga, 1966. Cert. speech and hearing specialist Am. Speech and Hearing Assn. Speech therapist Chattanooga-Hamilton County Speech and Hearing Ctr., 1961-66, ednl. psychology, 1966-78; staff psychologist Chattanooga Testing and Counseling Svcs., 1978-80; ins. rep. Mut. Benefit Life Ins. Co., Chattanooga, 1980-84; columnist Chattanooga Times, 1982-84; comty. affairs reporter Sta. WRCB-TV, Chattanooga, 1983-84; pub. rels. and promotions dir. Purple Ladies, Inc., Chattanooga, 1984—. Cons. psychology Ga. Dept. Human Resources, also Cheerhaven Sch., Dalton, 1970-78; adj. prof. psychology U. Tenn.-Chattanooga, 1971-80, adj. prof. dept. theatre and speech, 1988—; pres. Speak Out; bd. dirs. M. Young Comm., Vol. Ctr., 1995—, Arthritis Found., 1995-98; spl. projects dir. Chattanooga State Tech. C.C., 1995—; bd. dirs. M. Young Comm.; bd. dirs. Purple Lady, Inc. Author (columnist): (jour.) Lookout Mountain Mirror, Signal Mountain Mirror; contbg. editor: Chattanooga Life and Leisure Mag. Pres. Chattanooga Opera Guild, 1973-74, Chattanooga Opera Assn., 1979-80; bd. dirs., sec. Chattanooga-Hamilton County Bicentennial Libr., 1977-79; pres. Little Theatre of Chattanooga, 1984-90, bd. dirs., 1974—; v.p. Girls Club, Chattanooga, 1979-80; bd. dirs. March of Dimes, 1988, Chattanooga Symphony Guild, Mizpah Congregation, Chattanooga Area Literacy Coun., Chattanooga Cares, 1993—, Tourist Devel. Agy., 1990—; mem. alumni coun. U. Tenn.-Chattanooga; mem. selection com. Leadership Chattanooga, 1984-86; sec. Allied Arts Greater Chattanooga, 1978-80, residential campaign chmn., 1985; bd. dirs. Chattanooga Ctr. for the Dance, Ptnrs. for Acad. Excellence, 1987—, Chattanooga Mental Health Assn., 1988, Chattanooga Symphony Opera Assn., 1999—; chmn. March of Dimes Mother's March, 1988, One of a Kind-the Arts Against AIDS-Chattanooga Cares, 1993, 94; co-chair Am. Heart Assn. Gala, 1994, chmn., 1995; chair Little Theatre Capital Campaign, 1995; chmn. Galactic Gala fundraiser Chattanooga State Coll., 1996, Chattanooga Theatre Ctr. Endowment Campaign, 1998-99, April in Paris fundraiser, Chattanooga St. Coll., 1997, Chattanooga H.S. Ctr. for the Creative Arts fundraising, 1999, chmn. Broadway Lights Broadway Nights, 1999; adv. coun. Hamilton County Magnet Schs., 1999; bd. dirs. Chattanooga Symphony Opera Assn., 1999, 2000, fundraiser Evening in Provence, 2000, 2001, fundraiser Evening in Tuscany, 2001, Evening in New Orleans, 2003; bd. dirs. Chattanooga Ballet, 2000—, Chattanooga Theatre Ctr., 2002—, AIM Ctr., 2002—, Chattanooga Cares, 2002, Chattanooga Zoo, 2002—. Recipient Disting. Citizens award City of Chattanooga, 1975, Steakley award Little Theatre Chattanooga, 1982, Pres. award, 1991, 92, Vol. of Yr., 1995, Woman of Distinction award Am. Lung Assn., 1995, Vol. of Yr. award, 1995, Penney's Golden Rule award Chattanooga Cares, 1994, Vol. of Yr., 1995, Best Actress award Chattanooga Theatre Ctr., 2000. Mem. Phi Beta Kappa (pers. Chattanooga chpt. 1978-79). Jewish. Home: 1025 River Hills Cir Chattanooga TN 37415-5611 Office: U Tenn Theatre & Speech Dept 615 Mccallie Ave Chattanooga TN 37403-2504 E-mail: purplesoni@aol.com.

YOUNG, SUSAN EILEEN, elementary education educator; b. New Haven, Aug. 8, 1956; d. James William and Rosemary Ann (Drotar) Tobin; m. Randy Harold Young, May 17, 1986; 1 child, Sarah Elizabeth. BA, Annhurst Coll., 1978; postgrad., George Mason U., 1988-91; student, Mary Washington Coll. Cert. tchr., Conn., Va. Tchr. St. Mary Sch., Branford, Conn., 1978-81, Holy Spirit Sch., Annandale, Va., 1990-92; tchr. asst. West Gate Sch., Manassas, Va., 1994-97; presch. spl. edn. paraprofl. Ferry Farm Sch., Stafford, Va., 1997-99, kindergarten paraprofl., 1999-2000, reading ctr. paraprofl., 2000—. Substitute tchr. Fairfax (Va.) Sch. System, Prince William County (Va.) County Sch. System, Diocese of Arlington Schs., 1987-90; home tutor, Dale City, Va., summer 1991. Vol. Spl. Olympics, Denver, 1983. With USN, 1983-87. Mem. Kappa Delta Pi, Phi Delta Kappa. Roman Catholic. Avocations: piano, sports, crafts, reading.

YOUNG, SUSAN JEAN, music specialist; b. Chgo., Nov. 9, 1940; d. Walter Lawrence and Grace Helen (Blue) Pennie; m. Peter R. Young Jr., June 23, 1962; children: Laura Jane, Beth Ann. B.Mus.Ed (scholar), Northwestern U., 1962; M.Mus.ED (grad.scholar), Am. Conservatory of Music, Chgo., 1974; cert. advanced study in gen. adminstrn., Nat.-Louis U., 1995. Music specialist Skokie (Ill.) Sch. Dist., 1962-63, Northbrook (Ill.) Sch. Dist. # 28, 1974—. Lectr. music edn. North Park Coll., 1995-96, Northwestern U., 1997—; pvt. piano tchr., 1963-74; pres. Stevenson High Choral Guild, 1979-81; music dir., choir dir. Wheeling Community Ch., 1981-93; choir dir. Ivanhoe United Ch. of Christ, 1995-96; dir. Y'all Come Choir, 1991—; music dir. Northbrook Children's Theatre, 1981-88, Glenview Community Theatre, Northbrook Community Theatre. Mem. ASCD, Music Educators Nat. Conf., Ill. Music Educators Assn. (chmn. Jr. High Choral Fest 1987-90, Mary E. Hoffman award for tchg. excellence 2003), Music Tchrs. Nat. Assn., Ill. Music Tchrs. Assn., Nat. Registered Music Educator, Am. Choral Dirs. Assn., Soc. Am. Musicians, Delta Kappa Gamma (pres. Beta Tau chpt. 1992-96, Ill. State music chmn. 1995-99, internat. music rep. 2002—), Mu Phi Epsilon, NICE, ISTE. Home: 3161 N Southern Hills Dr Wadsworth IL 60083-9289 Office: 1475 Maple Ave Northbrook IL 60062-5418

YOUNG, TAYLOR LYNN, education administrator; b. Evansville, Ind., Dec. 7, 1952; s. James Taylor and Luvenia (Welborn) Y.; 1 child, Virginia Melin. BS in Edn., Ea. Ill. U., 1975; MS in Edn., Ill. State U., 1980; PhD in Edn., U. Denver, 1988. Tchr. spl. edn. St. Joseph (Ill.)-Ogden High Sch. Dist. 305, 1975-80; dir. Mid-State Spl. Edn. Coop., Hillsboro, Ill., 1980-81; dir. spl. edn. Mountain Bd. Coop. Svcs., Leadville, Colo., 1981-87; sr. cons. on sch. fin., cons. on spl. edn. Colo. Dept. Edn., Denver, 1987-88; prin. Laremont Sch., Spl. Edn. Dist. Lake County, Gurnee, Ill., 1988-89; dir. edn. Colo. Christian Home, Denver, 1989-92; spl. edn. tchr. El Paso County Dist. 11, Colorado Springs, Colo., 1992-93, spl. edn. supr., 1992—2000, Title 1 literacy supr., 2000—02, dir. Title 1, 2002—. Cons. Project Choice, Ill. Bd. Edn., Springfield, 1989-90. Republican. Avocations: golf, travel. Home: 4780 Paramount Pl Colorado Springs CO 80918-9030 Office: Schl Dist 11 1115 N El Paso St Colorado Springs CO 80903-2599

YOUNG, TERESA GAIL HILGER, adult education educator; b. Modesto, Calif., Mar. 4, 1948; d. Richard George and Jessie Dennie (Dennis) Long; m. Charles Ray Young, June 22, 1974; 1 child, Gregory Paul. BS in Edn., Abilene (Tex.) Christian U., 1970; MEd in Curriculum, Tarleton State U., Stephenville, Tex., 1976; postgrad., Tex. Tech U., 1990-92. Cert. supr., mid-mgmt., supt., Tex. Tchr. sci. Tex. Youth Coun., Gatesville, 1970-73, Gatesville Ind. Sch. Dist., 1973-81; coord. Edn. and Tng. Ctr., Cen. Tex. Coll., Gatesville, 1983; tchr. Tex. Dept. of Criminal Justice-ID, 1984—2002. Conf. presenter. Trustee Jonesboro (Tex.) Ind. Sch. Dist., 1988-96. Teacher of the Year for Region II of Tex. Dept. of Criminal Justice, 1997-98. Mem. Am. Fedn. Tchrs., Assn. Tex. Profl. Educators. E-mail: tyoung@htcomp.net.

YOUNG, TOMMIE MORTON, social psychology educator, writer; b. Nashville; BA cum laude, Tenn. State U., 1951; MA, Vanderbilt U., 1955; PhD, Duke U., 1977; postgrad., U. Okla., 1967, U. Nebr., 1968. Coord. Young Adult Program Lucy Thurman br. YWCA, 1951-52; instr. edn. Tenn. State U., Nashville, 1956-59; instr. coord. media program Prairie View Coll. (Tex.), 1959-61; asst. prof. edn., assoc. prof. English, dir. IMC Ctr. U. Ark., Pine Bluff, 1965-69; asst. prof. English and edn., dir. learning lab N.C. Central U., Durham, 1969-74; prof., dir./chairperson libr. /dir. Afro-Am. Family Project, prof. philosophy sociol. found. N.C. Agrl. and Tech. State U., Greensboro, 1975—92; adj. prof. langs., lit. and philosophy, dir. schs. history project Tenn. State U., Nashville, 1994—. Dir. workshops, grants; pres., dir. Ednl. Cons. Svcs.; owner Historic Black Nashville Tours. Co-author: Afro-Am. Genealogy Sourcebook, 1987, Oral Histories of Former All-Black Public Schs., 1991, After School Program for At-Risk Youth and Their Families, 1997, Sable Scenes, 1996, Genealogist's Guide to Discovering Your African Ancestors, 1997, A Sister Speaks, 1998, Nashville, Tennessee, 2000; contbr. poem to Poetry: American Heritage; contbr. rsch. papers, articles to profl. jours. Nat. chmn. Com. to Re-Elect the Pres.; past sec. Fedn. Colored Women's Clubs; bd. dirs. Southwestern div. ARC, Nashville area, 1994—, dir. Volun-Teens; chairperson schs. div. Durham County Unit Am. Cancer Soc.; past mem. adv. bd., bd. dirs. YMCA, Atlanta; chair Guilford County Commn. on Needs of Children; bd. advisors NIH, N.C. Coun. of the Arts; mem. Guilford County Involvlement Coun.; chmn. N.C. adv. com. U.S. Civil Rights Com.; mem. exec. planning com. Greensboro; hon. staff mem. 54th Legis. Dist., Nashville, 1996; pres. Davidson County Dem. Women, 2003—. Recipient awards ARC, 1968, 73, NAACP, 1973, HEW, 1978, U.S. Commn. on Civil Rights, 1982, cert. of Accomplishement Contributing to Youth Devel. Bus. and Profl. Women, 2000; named Disting. Alumni Tenn. State U., 1994. Mem. AAUW (honor award 1983, pres. Greensboro br., chairperson internat. rels. com.), ALA (divsn. coll. and rsch. librs., past chair), NAACP (life, 1st v.p. Durahm br., exec. bd. Greensboro br. dir. parent edn./child advocacy program, Woman of Yr. 1992), NEA, Assn. Childhood Ednl. Internat., Comperative and Internat. Edn. Assn., Archives Assoc., Internat. Platform Assn., Nat. Hist. Soc., Greenboro Jr. League (community adv. bd. 1991—), African Am. Gen. Soc. Tenn. (founder 1994), Zeta Phi Beta (chairperson polit. action com. eastern region, nat. grammateus, Polit. and Civic Svc. award 1974, Outstanding Social-Polit. Svc. award 1982, Woman of Yr. 1977), Comm. on Status of Women (Woman of Achievement 1991), Phi Kappa Phi (Disting. Alumni award Tenn. State U. 1994, Disting. Alumni NAFEO award, 1995, Carl Rowan-Oprah Winfrey lectr. Tenn. State U., 1995, Excellence in Journlism award SPJ, 1995, Tenn. Outstanding Achievement award, 1997), 100 Black Women, Steering Com., Tenn. Trust for Historic Preservation, 1999 (named Woman of Distinction Top Ladies, 2001). Home: PO Box 281613 Nashville TN 37228-8506

YOUNG, VERA LEE HALL, educational administrator, association executive; b. Natchitoches, La., Jan. 9, 1944; d. Sidney and Gertrude (Bell) H.; m. Willie L. Young, Aug. 21, 1965 (div. June 1971). BS, Grambling State U., 1967; MS, Bank St. Coll., 1977; PhD with distinction, Century U., 1985. Cert. tchr., La., N.J., N.Y. Ednl. cons. family day care program N.Y.C. Community Sch. Dist. 6; ednl. dir. Leslie Freeman Daycare Ctr., Bklyn., 1973-74; tchr. West N.Y. Bd. of Edn., 1978—; exec. dir., founder Operation Super Inst., Ft. Lee, N.J., 1986—. Lectr., tchr., panelist and cons. in field; participant Statewide Child Care Adv. Coun. Conf., N.J., 1980, State Ill. Tchrs. Conf., 1987, U. S.C. Tchrs. Conf., Georgetown, 1989; discussant Speaking for Schools radio program, N.J., N.Y.; program developer N.Y. Pub. Schs., 1996; del. 24th Internat. Congree Arts and Comms., 1997; instr. Funda C.C., Soweto, South Africa, 1998. Author: A Day Care Solution in America: The Learning Center, 1985; contbr. articles to field. Recipient Internat. Order of Merit award (# 320 of 500 world-wide), Internat. Biog. Ctr., Cambridge, Eng.; named Educator or Yr., Black Achievement and Awards, 1988; Dept. Labor grantee, Jerusalem, 1982-83 Mem. NEA, Nat. Alliance Bus., N.J. Edn. Assn. (conf. participant 1987), N.J. Women Bus. Ownership Orgn., Internat. Platform Assn., Internat. Reading Assn., Minority & Women Owned Bus. N.Y., Bank St. Coll. Alumni Assn., Gambling Coll. Alumni Assn. Mem. Dutch Reform Ch. Avocations: reading, travel, sports. Office: Operation Super 229 Main St # 1834 Fort Lee NJ 07024-5709

YOUNG, VIRGIL MONROE, education educator; b. Santa Rosa, Calif., Sept. 24, 1936; s. Virgil M. and Vesta May (Huyett) Williams; stepson Louis H. Young; m. Katherine Ann Young, Dec. 20, 1964; 1 child, Susan Annette. BS, U. Idaho, 1958, EdD, 1967. Cert. advanced secondary edn. educator, sch. supt., Idaho. Tchr. Moscow (Idaho) Sch. Dist., 1959-63; adminstrv. asst. to supt. Coeur d'Alene (Idaho) Sch. Dist., 1965-67; prof. edn. Boise (Idaho) State U., 1967-96, head dept. edn., 1989-96, prof. emeritus, 1996—. Author: (elem. textbook) The Story of Idaho, 4 edits.; co-author: The Story of the Idaho Guide and Resource Book, 1993; author: (with others) Year 2000 Grolier Multimedia Encyclopedia, 2000; designer, author ednl. Internet websites, 1999—. Capt. USAR. Mem. N.W. Assn. Tchr. Educators (past pres.), Idaho Assn. Colls. Tchr. Edn. (past pres.), Phi Delta Kappa (past pres.).

YOUNG, WILLIAM BENJAMIN, retired special education educator; b. Wichita, Kans., Jan. 30, 1929; s. Ernest William and Florence Belle (McCann) Y.; m. La Vona P., Feb., 1949 (div. 1973); children: Lynda, David, Timothy; m. Patricia Sue Reber, Aug., 1974. Student, Southwestern Coll., Winfield, Kans., 1947-48; B in Gen. Edn., U. Omaha, 1961; MS in Pers. Counseling, Miami U., Oxford, Ohio, 1965; PhD in Exceptional Edn., Adminstrn. and Counseling, Ohio State U., 1972. Cert. elem. and secondary adminstr., tchr., counselor, psychologist, psychometrist, spl. edn., mental retardation, learning disabled/behavior disordered, emotionally handicapped, Ind.; cert. K-12 guidance counselor and edn. leadership, Fla.; lic sexologist, flight instr.; lic. Coast Guard capt. Enlisted USAF, 1948, commd. 2nd lt., 1955, advanced through grades to capt., 1960, ret., 1966; numerous teaching and counseling positions as civilian, 1966-91; co-owner, instr. Ft. Wayne (Ind.) Ground Schs., 1984-88; marriage and family counselor, pvt. practice, 1966-91; tchr., counselor, behavior specialist Broward County Schs., Ft. Lauderdale, Fla., 1989-99; ret., 1999. Cons., internat. presenter/lectr. learning and behavior problems. Vol. instr. AARP Safe Driving Course; vol. support group leader for dementia caregivers support. Mem. ACA, Coun. for Exceptional Children, Coun. Behavior Disorders, Fla. Counseling Assn., 32 degree Masons. Avocations: travel, golf, swimming. Home and Office: 1101 SW 70th Ter Plantation FL 33317-4135 E-mail: wby130@aol.com.

YOUNGBERG, ROBERT STANLEY, principal, consultant; b. Chgo., Apr. 21, 1932; s. Holger Raymond and Eva Boyd (Carr) Y.; m. Catherine Jane Fitzpatrick, June 19, 1954; children: Kevin, Melissa, Margo Jenkins, Brian. BS, U. Ill., 1954; MEd, Wayne State U., 1959; PhD, U. Mich., 1975. Tchr. Hanneman-Herman-Dixon, Detroit, 1956-62; counselor Barbour Jr. High/Ruddman Jr. High Sch., Detroit, 1962-67, Redford High Sch., Detroit, 1967-70; prin. mid. sch. Novi, Mich., 1970-79; prin. high sch., 1979-92; pvt. practice edn. cons. Clearwater, Fla., 1992—. Site evaluator secondary recognition program U.S. Dept. Edn., Mich. Dept. Edn., 1988-97; immigration and customs inspector U. S. Dept. Justice, 1961-64; summer camp dir. Mich. and Wis., 1965-70; cons. in field. Chmn. citizens adv. com. Sch. Facilities, Detroit, 1958-59; chmn. Citizens Adv. Com. on Mid. Schs., Novi, 1972-74, Citizens Adv. Com. on Humanities and Arts, 1975, Great Cities Sch. Improvement Project, Detroit, 1962-64, Dist. Curriculum Coun., Novi, 1972-80; bd. dirs. Youth Assistance Bd., Novi, 1975-79; site vis. North Ctrl. Assn., 1968-91; bus. cons. Mgmt. Style for Retail Merchants, Novi, 1988-91. With U.S. Army, 1954-56. Mem. Mich. Assn. Sch. Adminstrs., Mich. Assn. Secondary Sch. Prins., Nat. Assn. Secondary Sch. Prins., Nat. ASCD, Kensington Valley Activities Conf. (bd. dirs.), Phi Delta Kappa. Avocations: physical fitness, senior games, racquetball, basketball, track and field events. Office: 2427 Bond Ave Clearwater FL 33759-1204

YOUNGBLOOD, BETTY J. academic administrator; b. Detroit; m. Ralph P. Youngblood; 1 child. BS in Political Sci., Oakland U., Rochester, Mich.; MA in South Asian Studies, PhD in Political Sci., U. Minn. Formerly mem. faculty West Ga. Coll., Tex. Tech U.; various adminstrv. positions Kennesaw State Coll., Marietta, Ga.; v.p. acad. affairs MacMurray Coll., Jacksonville, Ill., Wesley Coll., Dover, Del.; vice chancelllor acad. affairs, dean faculty, prof. polit. sci. U. Wis.-Superior, 1990-91, acting chancellor, 1991-92, chancellor, 1992—96; pres. Lake Superior State U., Mich., 2002—. Cons., evaluator North Ctrl. Assn. Colls. and Schs. Contbr. articles to profl. jours. Bd. dirs. United Way, Superior. Rsch. grantee for study in N.W. India. Mem. Superior C. of C., Rotary. Office: Lake Superior State Univ 650 W Easterday Ave Sault Sainte Marie MI 49783*

YOUNGER, JUDITH TESS, lawyer, educator; b. N.Y.C., Dec. 20, 1933; d. Sidney and Kate (Greenbaum) Weintraub; m. Irving Younger, Jan. 21, 1955; children: Rebecca, Abigail M. BS, Cornell U., 1954; JD, NYU, 1958; LL.D. (hon.), Hofstra U., 1974. Bar: N.Y. 1958, U.S. Supreme Ct 1962, D.C. 1983, Minn. 1985. Law clk. to judge U.S. Dist. Ct., 1958-60; asso. firm Chadbourne, Parke, Whiteside & Wolff, N.Y.C., 1960-62; mem. firm Younger and Younger, and (successors), 1962-67; adj. asst. prof. N.Y. U. Sch. Law, 1967-69; asst. atty. gen. State of N.Y., 1969-70; assoc. prof. Hofstra U. Sch. Law, 1970-72, prof., assoc. dean, 1972-74; dean, prof. Syracuse Coll. Law, 1974-75; dep. dean, prof. law Cornell Law Sch., 1975-78, prof. law, 1975-85; vis. prof. U. Minn. Law Sch., Mpls., 1984-85, prof., 1985-91, Joseph E. Wargo Anoka County Bar Assn. prof. family law, 1991—. Of counsel Popham, Haik, Schnobrich & Kaufman, Ltd., Mpls., 1989-95; cons. NOW, 1972-74, Suffolk County for Revision of Its Real Property Tax Act, 1972-73; mem. N.Y. Gov.'s Panel To Screen Candidates of Ct. of Claims Judges, 1973-74; mem. Minn. Lawyers' Profl. Responsibility Bd., 1991-93. Contbr. articles to profl. jours. Trustee Cornell U., 1973-78 Mem.: AAUP (v.p. Cornell U. chpt. 1978—79), ABA (council legal edn. 1975—79), Minn. Bar Assn., Assn. of Bar of City of N.Y., Am. Law Inst. (adv. restatement property 1982—84). Home: 3520 W Calhoun Pkwy Minneapolis MN 55416-4657 Office: U Minn Law Sch Minneapolis MN 55455 E-mail: young001@umn.edu.

YOUNG-OSKEY, SUSAN MARIE, elementary education educator; b. Astoria, N.Y., July 30, 1964; d. Thomas Bernard and Carole Marion (Fleming) Y. AA, Suffolk Coll., 1987; BA, Dowling Coll., 1989; MA in Liberal Studies Edn., SUNY, Stony Brook, 1992. Kindergarten asst. tchr. First Steps Sch., East Setauket, N.Y., 1986-88, pre-kindergarten/toddler tchr., 1989-90; kindergarten/pre-kindergarten tchr. Our Lady of Lourdes Sch., West Islip, N.Y., 1990-94, tchr. 1st grade, 1994—. Vol. Rainbow Program Our Lady of Lourdes Parish, 1992. Mem. Reading Specialists Coun. Suffolk (reading specialist 1990-91). Republican. Home: 755 Expressway Dr N Medford NY 11763-2003

YOUNGS, DIANE CAMPFIELD, learning disabilities specialist, educator; b. Margaretville, NY, Feb. 16, 1954; d. Richard Maxwell and Charlotte June (Rickard) Campfield; m. William H. Youngs, June 30, 1984. BS in Edn., SUNY, Geneseo, 1976, MS in Edn., 1977. Professionally recognized spl. educator. Tchr. educable mentally retarded Tompkins-Seneca-Tioga Bd. Coop. Ednl. Svcs., Ithaca, NY, 1978-80; tchr. learning disabled Joint Svc. for Spl. Edn., Mishawaka, Ind., 1980-97; assoc. faculty Ind. U.-South Bend Grad. Sch. Edn., 1996-98. Vis. lectr. dept. edn. Ind. U., South Bend, 1998-2002, lectr., 2002—; mem. Task Force for Reorgn. Spl. Edn., Mishawaka, 1990-91; coord. Tiny Talkers Summer Speech/Lang. Camp, 1994—. Mem. AAUP, Coun. for Exceptional Children, Learning Disabilities Assn., Coun. for Learning Disabilities, Ind. Prof. Reading, Internat. Reading Assn., Nat. Coun. Tchrs. English, Kappa Delta Pi, Psi Iota Xi. Republican.

YOUNT, GWENDOLYN AUDREY, humanities educator; b. Indpls., July 24, 1957; d. August de Alba and Hena Yount; 1 child, Clark. AA, L.A. City Coll., 1977; BA, UCLA, 1979, MA, 1982, Candidate in Philosophy, 1987. Cert. C.C. lifetime credential Calif., bilingual cert. competence. Ednl. aide Alexander Hamilton H.S., Los Angeles, 1975—76; tchg. fellow UCLA, 1981—88; instr. L.A. Unified Sch. Dist., 1982—90; prof. Institut Franco-Americain de Mgmt., Paris, 1983—84; instr. Santa Monica (Calif.) Coll., 1987—88; lectr. U. of Calif., Riverside, 1988—91; instr. Beverly Hills (Calif.) Adult Sch., 1986—88; assoc. prof. Riverside (Calif.) C.C., 1990—. Dir. RCC Study Abroad Program in Spain, Salamanca, Spain, 1998—2002,

RCC Study Abroad Program in Costa Rica, San Jose, Costa Rica, 1993, UCLA Spanish Program in Mex., Guadalajara, Mexico, 1987. Dancer (ballet performance) Celebrate Dance, 2000; actor: (mus. theater) La Cage Aux Folles, 1998; singer: (vocal performance) Montreux Jazz Festival, 1993. Adminstr. G. Yount scholarship Riverside County Found., 1998—2003; sen. Acad. Senate, Riverside, 1997—2003; mem. Spanish lang. steering com. Riverside Pub. Libr., 1989—91; charter mem. Mus. of Tolerance, L.A., 1994—2003. Named Most Influential Instr., RCC Disabled Student Svcs., 1993, 1998, Tchr. of Distinction, LDS Ch., 1998, 2000, 2001, 2002, Tchr. of the Yr., Riverside C.C., 1999—2000, 2000—01, 2002—03; grantee Univ. grantee for grad. study, UCLA, 1979. Mem.: Philol Soc. of the Pacific Coast, Assn. for Tchrs. of Spanish, Sigma Tau Sigma, Alpha Mu Gamma (pres. 1977—78), Sigma Delta Pi (v.p. 1985—86). Liberal. Avocations: travel, reading, studying. Office: Riverside C C 4800 Magnolia Ave Riverside CA 92506 Office Fax: 909-222-8149. Business E-Mail: gwen.yount@rcc.edu..

YOURZAK, ROBERT JOSEPH, management consultant, engineer, educator; b. Mpls., Aug. 27, 1947; s. Ruth Phyllis Sorenson. BCE, U. Minn., 1969; MSCE, U. Wash., 1971, MBA, 1975. Registered profl. engr., Wash., Minn. Surveyor N.C. Hoium & Assocs., Mpls., 1965-68, Lot Surveys Co., Mpls., 1968-69; site layout engr. Sheehy Constrn. Co., St. Paul, 1968; structural engring. aide Dunham Assocs., Mpls., 1969; aircraft and aerospace structural engr., program rep. Boeing Co., Seattle, 1969-75; engr., estimator Howard S. Wright Constrn. Co., Seattle, 1976-77; dir. project devel. and adminstrn. DeLeuw Cather & Co., Seattle, 1977-78; sr. mgmt. cons. Alexander Grant & Co., Mpls., 1978-79; mgr. project sys. dept., project mgr. Henningson, Durham & Richardson, Mpls., 1979-80; dir. project mgmt., regional offices Ellerbe Assocs., Inc., Mpls., 1980-81; pres. Robert Yourzak & Assocs., Inc., Mpls., 1982—. Lectr. engring. mgmt. U. Wash., 1977-78; lectr., adj. asst. prof. dept. civil and mineral engring. and mech./indsl. engring. Ctr. for Devel. of Tech. Leadership, Inst. Tech.; mem. strategic mgmt. and orgn. dept., mgmt. scis. dept. Sch. Mgmt., U. Minn., 1979-90, 96—; bd. adv. inst. tech., 1989-93; founding mem., membership com., mem. U. of Minn. com. Minn. High Tech. Coun., 1983-95; instr. principles mgmt. dept. bus. and pub. policy Concordia U., 1997, instr. constrn. mgmt., constrn. estimating and scheduling, bldg. orgn. and tech., and project mgmt. and planning skills Inver Hills C.C., 1998—; instr. introduction to engring. and design, statics, mechanics of materials, ops. mgmt. North Hennepin C.C., 2002—; adj. instr. ops. mgmt. Hamline U., St. Paul, 2001; spkr. in field. Author: Project Management and Motivating and Managing the Project Team, 1984, (with others) Field Guide to Project Management, 1998. Chmn. regional art group experience Seattle Art Mus., 1975-78; mem. Pacific N.W. Arts Coun., 1977-78, ex-officio adviser Mus. Week, 1976; bd. dirs. Friends of the Rep. Seattle Repertory Theatre, 1973-77; mem. Symphonics Seattle Symphony Orch., 1975-78. Named Outstanding Young Man of Am., U.S. Jaycees, 1978; scholar Boeing Co., 1967-68, Sheehy Constrn. Co., summer 1967. Fellow ASCE (chmn. continuing edn. subcom. Seattle chpt. 1976-79, chmn. program com. 1978, mem. transp. and urban planning tech. group 1978, Edmund Friedman Young Engr. award 1979, chmn. continuing edn. subcom. 1979-80, chmn. energy com. Minn. chpt. 1980-81, bd. dirs. 1981-89, sec. 1981-83, v.p. profl. svcs. 1983-84, v.p. info. svcs. 1984-85, pres. 1986-87, past pres. 1987-89, spkr.), PMI Project Mgmt. Inst. (cert. project mgmt. prof., spkr., founding pres. 1985, chmn., adv. com. 1987-89, bd. dirs. 1984-86, program com. chmn. and organizing com. mem. Minn. chpt. 1984, spkr., project mgr. internat. mktg. program 1985-86, chmn. internat. mktg. standing com. 1986, long range and strategic planning com. 1988-93, chmn. 1992, v.p. pub. rels. 1987-88, ex-officio dir. 1989, 92, internat. pres. 1990, chmn. bd. 1991, ex-officio chmn. 1992, internat. bd. dirs., chmn. nominating com. 1992, PMI fellow 1995, chmn. exec. dir. selection com. 1996-97, Robert J. Yourzak Scholarship Award established Minn. chpt. 1998—), Inst. Indsl. Engrs. (pres. Twin Cities chpt. 1985-86, chmn. program com. 1983-84, bd. dirs. 1985-88, awards com., chmn. 1984-89, fellow 1999, spkr.); mem. ASTD (So. Minn. chpt.), Am. Cons. Engrs. Coun. (peer reviewer 1986-89), Am. Arbitration Assn. (mem. Mpls. panel of constrn. arbitrators), Minn. Surveyors and Engrs. Soc., Cons. Engrs. Coun. Minn. (chmn. pub. rels. com. 1983-85, vice chmn. 1988, chmn. 1989, program com. chmn. Midwest engrs. conf. and exposition 1985-90, spkr., Honor award 1992), Inst. Mgmt. Cons. (cert. mgmt. cons.), Mpls. Soc. Fine Arts, Internat. Facility Mgmt. Assn., Am. Soc. Engring. Edn., Rainer Club (co-chmn. Oktoberfest), Sierra club, Chowder Soc., Mountaineers, North Star Ski Touring, Chi Epsilon (life). Office: 7320 Gallagher Dr Ste 325 Minneapolis MN 55435-4510

YOUSEF, FATHI SSLAAMA, communication studies educator, management consultant; b. Cairo, Jan. 2, 1934; arrived in U.S., 1968, naturalized, 1973; s. Salaama and Rose (Tadros) Yousef; m. Marjan El-Faizy Lowies, June 24, 1994. BA, Ain Shams U., Cairo, 1955; MA, U. Minn., 1970, PhD, 1972. Svc. ctr. supt. Shell Oil Co., Cairo, 1955-61; indsl., mgmt. tng. instr. ARAMCO, Dhahran, Saudi Arabia, 1961-68; tchg. assoc. U. Minn., Mpls., 1968-72; comm. studies prof. emeritus Calif. State U., Long Beach, 1972—. With orgn. and indsl. engring. dept. ARAMCO, 1978—80. Co-author: An Introduction to Intercultural Communication, 1975, 1985; contbr. Grantee, NSF, 1981, 1982, 1983. Mem.: Assn. Egyptian Am. Scholars. Democrat. Office: Calif State U Dept Comm Studies Long Beach CA 90840-2407 E-mail: fyousef@csulb.edu.

YOUSHAW, DENNIS GORDON, surgeon, educator; b. Butler, Pa., July 24, 1939; s. Stephen P. and Lenore I. (List) Y.; m. Judith Ann Berkheimer, June 19, 1965; 1 child, Susan Lynn. A.B., Lycoming Coll., 1961; M.D., Hahnemann U., 1965. Diplomate Am. Bd. Surgery. Intern, Allegheny Gen. Hosp., Pitts., 1965-66; resident Henry Ford Hosp., Detroit, 1966-70; gen. surgeon Altoona Hosp., Pa., 1972—, chmn. dept., 1984-92. Past pres. chpt. Am. Cancer Soc. Served to maj. USAF, 1970-72. Mem. Am. Trauma Soc. (past chpt. pres.), AMA, Pa. Med. Assn., Blair County Med. Assn., ACS. Clubs: Spruce Creek Rod and Gun (Pa.). Avocation: fishing. Home: 603 Ridge Ave Altoona PA 16602-1333 Office: UBlais Med Ctr 501 Howard Ave Ste A204 Altoona PA 16601-4810

YOUST, DAVID BENNETT, career development educator; b. May 14, 1938; s. Howard Page and Agnes (Bennett) Y.; m. Faye Phillips; children: Stacy Sillen, Shawna Sannier, Liesl Berger, Genny Phillips, Elizabeth Curley. BS, SUNY-Albany, 1959; MS, Syracuse (N.Y.) U., 1961; PhD, Mich. State U., 1969. Cert. career counselor Nat. Bd. Counselor Cert. Tchr. sci. North Syracuse schs., 1959-61; adminstr. student pers. Mich. State U., 1961-63; counselor, prin., program dir. Rochester (N.Y.) schs., 1963-70; sr. rsch. technologist Eastman Kodak Co., Rochester, 1970-72; asst. dean Nat. Tech. Inst. for the Deaf, Rochester Inst. Tech., 1972-74; mem. faculty Empire State Coll., SUNY, Rochester, 1974-78; exec. dir. Career Devel. Coun., Corning, N.Y., 1978-84; mgr. engring. tng. Corning Inc., N.Y., 1984-90; ptnr. Phillips Tng. Sys., Inc., 1989—. Former adj. faculty Corning C.C., Elmira Coll., C.W. Post Coll.; mediator cmty. dispute resolution Bd. of Dir. Cmty. Dispute Resolution Ctr., Ithaca, NY; instr. MSF motorcycle safety; EEO mediator U.S. Postal Svc. Author guide, articles in field; former mem. editl. bd. Career Devel. Quar. Former bd. dirs. 171 Cedar Arts Ctr. Mem. ASTD, ACA, Nat. Career Devel. Assn. (Merit award 1970, 84), Am. Ednl. Rsch. Assn., Assn. Measurement and Evaluation in Guidance. Republican. E-mail: youst@empacc.net.

YOVICH, DANIEL JOHN, education educator; b. Chgo., Mar. 5, 1930; s. Milan D. and Sophie (Dorociak) Y.; m. Anita Barbara Moreland, Feb. 7, 1959; children: Daniel, Amy, David, Julie Ann. Ph.B., DePaul U., 1952; MA, Governors State U., 1975, MS, 1976. Cert. reality therapist, cert. profl. mgr., PMA instr. Formulator Nat. Lead Co., 1950-52, 56-59; researcher Montgomery Ward, Chgo., 1959-62; tech. dir. Riley Bros., Inc., Burlington, Iowa, 1962-66, Mortell Co., Kankakee, Ill., 1966-70; exec. dir. Dan Yovich Assos., 1970-79; asst. prof. Purdue U., Hammond, Ind., 1979-84, assoc. prof., 1984-90, prof., 1990-2000, prof. emeritus, 2000—. Instr. Army Security Agy. Sch., 1954—56, Napoleon Hill Acad., 1965—66, Kankakee C.C. Continuing Edn., 1976; cons. Learning House, 1964—; assoc. Hill, Zediker & Assocs. Psychologists, Kankakee, 1975—79; mem. adv. bd. Nat. Congress Inventor Orgns., 1984; vis. prof. Grand Valley State U., 2000—, Northwood U., 2001—. Author: Applied Creativity; prdr., moderator: (program) Careers Unlimited, Sta. WCIU-TV, Chgo., 1967; creator: Salute, A Patriotic Celebration, 1999-; contbr. articles to profl. jours.; patentee game Krypto, coating Sanitane. Mem. cmty. adv. coun. Governors State U., 1978; mem. Hammond (Ind.) Hist. Soc. Served to 1st lt. AUS, 1952-56. Recipient Outstanding Citizen Award News Pub. Co. Am., 1971, Outstanding Tchr. award Purdue U., 1980, 82, 83, Faculty Service award Nat. U. Continuing Edn. Assn., 1984, Disting. Service award Purdue U.-Calumet Alumni Assn., 1988, Arthur Young award Venture Mag., 1988, Entrepreneurial Edn. award Inc. Mag., 1990, Indiana Spirit of Innovation award, 1996. Mem. ASTD, World Future Soc., Nat. Mgmt. Assn., Am. Soc. Profl. Supervision (exec. sec. 1986), Inventors and Entrepreneurs Soc. Am. (founder, exec. dir. 1984, prodr. Salute Vet. Recognition Programs 1999—), Global Intuition Network, Internat. Creativity Network, Infantry Officer Cand. Sch. Alumni Assn. (life), Napoleon Hill Found., Inst. Reality Therapy, Inst. Contemporary Living, Soc. Am. Inventors (life), Am. Legion, K.C., Vets. of the Battle of the Bulge (historian), Army and Navy Club of Grand Rapids. Home: 3527 Whispering Brook Dr SE Kentwood MI 49508-3733 E-mail: danyovich@prodigy.net.

YSSELDYKE, JAMES EDWARD, psychology educator, dean; b. Grand Rapids, Mich., Jan. 1, 1944; 2 children. Student in psychology, Calvin Coll., 1962-65; BA in Psychology and Biology, Western Mich. U., 1966; MA in Sch. Psychology, U. Ill., 1968, PhD, 1971. Lic. cons. psychologist, Minn. Tchr. spl. edn. Kent County Juvenile Ct. Ctr., Grand Rapids, 1966-67; rsch. asst. U. Ill. Inst. Rsch. on Exceptional Children, 1969-70, tchg. asst. dept. ednl. psychology, 1970; sch. psychology intern Oakland County Schs., Pontiac, Mich., 1970-71; asst. prof. sch. psychology Pa. State U., 1971-75, assoc. prof., 1975, U. Minn., Mpls., 1975-79, prof., 1979-91, dir. Inst. Rsch. on Learning Disabilities, 1977-83, dir. Nat. Sch. Psychology Insvc. Tng. Network, 1977-83, dir. sch. psychology program, 1987-93, dir. Nat. Ctr. on Ednl. Outcomes, 1991-99, assoc. dean for rsch., 2000—. Emma Birkmaier endowed prof. U. Minn., 1998-2000; advisor, cons. and researcher in field. Author: (with J. Salvia) Assessment in Special and Remedial Education, 1985, 9th edit., 2003, (with B. Algozzine and M. Thurlow) Critical Issues in Special and Remedial Education, 1992, 3d edit., 2000, Strategies and Tactics for Effective Instruction, 1997, (with S.L. Christenson) Functional Assessment of Academic Behavior, 2003; editor: Exceptional Children, 1984-90; assoc. editor: The School Psychologist, 1972-75, mem. editorial bd., cons. editor numerous jours.; contbr. chpts. to books and articles to jours. Recipient Disting. Tchg. award U. Minn., 1988, Disting. Alumni award U. Ill. Coll. Edn., 1998; fellow NIMH, 1967-69; grantee in field. Fellow APA (Lightner Witmer award 1973); mem. APA, NASP, Am. Ednl. Rsch. Assn., Coun. for Exceptional Children (Rsch. award 1995), Coun. for Ednl. Diagnostic Svcs. Office: Coll of Edn and Human Devel 104 Burton Hall 178 Pillsbury Dr SE Minneapolis MN 55455-0296 E-mail: jim@umn.edu.

YU, PAULINE RUTH, former dean, educational association administrator; b. Rochester, N.Y., Mar. 5, 1949; d. Paul N. and Iling (Tang) Y.; m. Theodore D. Huters, Aug. 23, 1975, Emily Elizabeth, Matthew Charles, Alexander David. BA in History and Lit. magma cum laude, Harvard U., 1971; MA in Comparative Lit., Stamford U., 1973, PhD in Comparative Lit., 1976. Asst. prof., then assoc. prof. U. Minn., Mpls., 1976-85; assoc. prof., then prof. Columbia U., N.Y.C., 1985-89; prof., founding chair dept. East Asian langs. and lit. U. Calif., Irvine, 1989-94; dean humanities UCLA, 1994—2003, prof. East Asian langs. and culture, 1994—2003; pres. Am. Coun. Learned Socs., N.Y.C., 2003—. Author: The Poetry of Wang Wei, 1980, The Reading of Imagery in the Chinese Poetic Tradition, 1987; editor and contbg. author: Voices of the Song Lyric in China, 1994, Culture and State in Chinese History: Conventions, Accomodations, and Critiques, 1997, Ways with Words: Writing about Reading Texts from Early China, 2000; mem. editl. bd. Tang Studies, Chinese lit., 1993—. Guggenheim fellow, 1983-84, ACLS fellow, 1983-84; recipient Profl. Achievement award U. Calif. at Irvine Alumni Assn., 1993. Mem. MLA, Assn. Asian Studies (mem. China and Inner Asia coun. 1982-85), Am. Comparative Lit. Assn. (mem. SSRC joint com. on Chinese studies 1987-93, mem. SSRC joint adv. com. on internat. studies 1994—), Phi Beta Kappa. Office: Am Coun Learned Societies 633 Third Ave New York NY 10017-6795 E-mail: paulineyu@acls.org.*

YU, ROBERT KUAN-JEN, biochemistry educator; b. Chungking, China, Jan. 27, 1938; came to U.S., 1962; m. Helen Chow, July 1, 1972; children: David S., Jennifer S. BS, Tunghai U., Taiwan, 1960; PhD, U. Ill., 1967; Med.ScD. (hon.), Tokyo, 1980; MA (hon.), Yale U., 1985. Rsch. assoc., instr. Albert Einstein Coll. Medicine, Bronx, 1967-72; asst. prof. Yale U., New Haven, 1973-75, assoc. prof., 1975-82, prof., 1983-88; prof. biochemistry, chmn. dept. Med. Coll. Va. Va. Commonwealth U., Richmond, 1988-2000; dir. Inst. Mol. Med. Genetics Med. Coll., Augusta, Ga., 2000—. Mem. study sect. NIH, Washington, 1980-84, 96—; mem. Bd. Lab. Svcs., Va., 1994-98. Editor: Gangioside Structure Function and Biomedical Potential, 1984, New Trends in Ganglioside Research, 1988; contbr. over 500 articles to profl. publs. Josiah Macy scholar, 1979; grantee NIH, 1975—; recipient Va. Outstanding Scientist of Yr. award, 1995, Jacob Javits award NIH, 1984-91, Alexander von Humboldt award, 1990, GRA Eminent scholar, 2000. Mem. AAAS, Am. Soc. Cell Biology, Am. Soc. Neurochemistry (mem. coun. 1983-86, 91-95, pres. 2001-03), Internat. Soc. Neurochemistry, Soc. Neurosci., Am. Soc. Biochemistry and Molecular Biology, Am. Chem. Soc., N.Y. Acad. Sci. Home: 821 River Bluff Rd North Augusta SC 29841-6056 Office: IMMAG Med Coll Ga 1120 15th St Augusta GA 30912-0004 E-mail: ryu@mail.mcg.edu.

YUAN, JASON XIAO-JIAN, medical researcher, educator; b. Xintian, Hunan, People's Republic of China, May 9, 1963; arrived in U.S., 1988, naturalized, 1998; s. Tian-Lin Yuan and Li-Hua Chen. MD, Suzhou (China) Med. Coll., 1983; PhD in Physiology, Peking Union Med. Coll., Beijing, 1993; postgrad., U. Md., 1993. Intern Suzhou Med. Coll. Hosp., 1982-83; resident Lanzhou (China) Med. Coll. Hosp., 1983-84; mem. sci. cadre Office Sci. and Tech. Gansu Environ. Protection Bur., Lanzhou, 1984; rsch. assoc. dept. environ. medicine Gansu Inst. Environ. Scis., Lanzhou, 1984-85; postdoctoral fellow dept. physiology and medicine U. Md. Sch. Medicine, Balt., 1988-93, rsch. asst. prof. dept. physiology, 1993-96, rsch. asst. prof. divsn. pulmonary and critical care med., 1993-96, asst. prof., 1996-98, assoc. prof., 1998-99, U. Calif.-San Diego Sch. Medicine, 1999—2003, prof., 2003—. Lectr. in field; ad hoc reviewer grant applications NIH, 1995—, mem. lung biology and pathology study sect., 2002-03, mem. respiratory physiology study sect., 2003—; mem. study sect. Am. Heart Assn., 1995-97, 98—, mem. exec. com., 1999—, editor newsletter, 2001—; ad hoc reviewer rsch. grant applications Wellcome Trust (London), 1995, 98, U.S. Dept. Vets. Affairs, 1995; mem. lung biology and pathology study sect., NHLBI, 2002—.; hon. prof. The Fourth Mil. Med. U., Xian, China, 1999—, China. Acad. Med. Scis. and Peking Union Med. Coll., 2002—. Author: Olympic Complete Words, 1988; editorial asst. Gansu Assn. Environ. Scis., 1984-85; mem. editl. bd. Am. Jour. Physiology Lung Cellular and Molecular Physiology Respiratory Rsch., 2001—; contbr. articles to profl. jours. Parker B. Francis fellow, 1994-97. Mem. AAAS, Am. Heart Assn. (Md. affiliate rsch. fellow 1990-92, exec. com. 1999—, grantee 1990-92, 93-95, 96-98, Cournand and Comroe Young Investigator award 1995, Best Abstract award 1996, Established Investigator award 1998), Am. Physiol. Soc. (Giles F. Filley Meml. award 1995, Rsch. Career Enhancement award 1995, Lamport award 1998), Am. Thoracic Soc., Biophys. Soc., Chinese Assn. Physiol. Sci. (editl. asst. 1987-88), Soc. Chinese Bioscientists in Am. (Dr. C.W. Dunker award 1993). Home: 12952 Brome Way San Diego CA 92129 Office: U Calif San Diego Med Ctr Divsn Pulmonary CC Medicine 200 W Arbor Dr San Diego CA 92103-1911

YUDOF, MARK GEORGE, law educator, university system chancellor; b. Phila., Oct. 30, 1944; s. Jack and Eleanor (Parris) Y.; m. Judith Lynn Gomel, July 11, 1965; children: Seth Adam, Samara Lisa BA, U. Pa., 1965, LLB, 1968. Bar: Pa. 1970, U.S. Supreme Ct. 1974, U.S. Dist. Ct. (we. dist.) Tex. 1975, U.S. Ct. Appeals (5th cir.) 1976, Tex. 1980. Law clk. to judge U.S. Ct. Appeals (5th cir.), 1968-69; assoc. gen. counsel to ABA study FTC, 1969; rsch. assoc. Harvard Ctr. Law and Edn., 1969-70, sr. staff atty., 1970-71; lectr. Harvard Grad. Sch. Edn., 1970-71; asst. prof. law U. Tex., Austin, 1971-74, prof., 1974—97, assoc. dean, 1979-84, James A. Elkins Cent. chair in law, 1983-97, dean, 1984-94, exec. v.p., provost, 1994-97, John Jeffers rsch. chair in law, 1991-94; pres. U. Minn., 1997—2002; chancellor U. Tex. Sys., 2002—, Jamail regents chair higher edn. leadership, 2002—, Wright chair fed. courts, 2002—. Of counsel Pennzoil vs. Texaco, 1987. Author: When Government Speaks, 1983 (Scribes Book award 1983, cert. merit ABA 1983), (with others) Educational Policy and the Law, 1992, (with others) Gender Justice, 1986. Mem. Tex. Gov.'s Task Force on Sch. Fin., 1989-90, Tex. Gov.'s Select Com. on Edn., 1988; bd. dirs. Freedom to Read Found., 1989-91; mem. Austin Cable Commn., 1981-84, chmn., 1982; mem. nat. panel on sch. desegregation rsch. Ford Found., 1977-80; mem. state exec. com. Univ. Interscholastic League, 1983-86; bd. dirs. Jewish Children's Regional Svc., 1980-86; mem. Gov.'s Select Task Force on Pub. Edn., 1995; mem. Telecomms. Infrastructure Fund Bd., State of Tex., 1995-97; adv. bd. Nat. Inst. for Literacy, 2002-. Recipient Teaching Excellence award, 1975, Most Meritorious Book award Scribes, 1983, Humanitarian award Austin region NCCJ, 1988, Antidefamation League Jurisprudence award, 1991; hon. fellow Queen Mary and Westfield Coll., U. London. Fellow: Am. Acad. Arts & Sci., Am. Bar Found., Tex. Bar Found.; mem.: Edn. Testing Svc. (mem. bd. dirs. 2000—02), Am. Coun. Edn. (mem. com. on leadership and instl. effectiveness 2000), Assn. Am. Law Schs. (chmn. law and edn. sect. 1983—84, exec. com. 1988—90), Tex. Bar Found., Am. Law Inst. Avocation: collecting antique maps. Office: U Texas System 601 Colorado St Austin TX 78701-2904

YUILL, THOMAS MACKAY, academic administrator, microbiology educator; b. Berkeley, Calif., June 14, 1937; s. Joseph Stuart and Louise (Dunlop) Y.; m. Ann Warnes, Aug. 24, 1960; children: Eileen, Gwen. BS, Utah State U., 1959; MS, U. Wis., 1962, PhD, 1964. Lab. officer Walter Reed Army Inst. Rsch., Washington, 1964-66; med. biologist SEATO Med. Rsch. Lab., Bangkok, 1966-68; asst. prof. U. Wis., Madison, 1968-72, assoc. prof., 1972-76, prof., 1976—2003, dept. chmn., 1979-82, assoc. dean, 1982-93, dir. Gaylord Nelson Inst. Environ. Studies, 1993—2003, emeritus prof. and dir., 2003—. Cons. NIH, Bethesda, 1976-86; chmn. Viral Diseases Panel, U.S.-Japan Biomed. Scis. Program, 1979-86, Am. Com. Arbovirology, 1982—; bd. dirs. Cen. Tropical Agrl. Res. Teaching, Turrialba, Costa Rica, 1988-96. Contbr. chpts. to books, articles to profl. jours. Served to capt. U.S. Army, 1964-66. Recipient grants state and fed. govts., 1968—. Mem. Orgn. Tropical Studies (pres. 1979-85), Wildlife Disease Assn. (treas. 19880-85, pres. 1985-87, editl. bd. 1989-2003), Am. Soc. Tropical Medicine and Hygiene (editl. bd. 1984-96), Nat. Assn. State Univ. Land Grant Colls., EPA Task Force (co-chair 1994-2002), Sigma Xi. Avocations: flying, cross-country skiing, music. Office: U Wis Sch Vet Medicine 2015 Linden Dr W Madison WI 53706-1404 E-mail: tmyuill@facstaff.wisc.edu.

YUNDT, BETTY BRANDENBURG, elementary education educator; b. Corydon, Ind., Sept. 23, 1957; d. Melvin Marion and Lena Beatrice (Blake) Brandenburg; m. Randall Gene Yundt, Apr. 2, 1978; 1 child, Cameron Blake. BS, Ind. U. SE, New Albany, 1981, MS with highest distinction, 1989. Cert. elem. tchr. Rank I, Ind., Ky. Tchr. pre-kindergarten Keneseth Israel Sch., Louisville; tchr. Dept. Def. Dependent Sch., Goppingen, Fed. Republic Germany; curriculum coord. Iroquois and West End Child Devel. Ctr., Louisville; elem. tchr. Ft. Knox (Ky.) Sch. Dist. KERA Fellows II cohort. Named Tchr. of Yr., Ft. Knox, Ky., 2003. Mem. NEA, ASCD, Internat. Reading Assn., Ind. Coun. Tchrs. Math., Louisville Assn. for Children Under Six, Kappa Delta Pi, Phi Lambda Theta, Alpha Chi. Home: 40 Springdale Rd Guston KY 40142-7151 Business E-Mail: byundt@knox.odedodea.edu. E-mail: byundt@bbtel.com.

YUSKA, IRENE MARIE, special education educator; b. Streator, Ill., Apr. 11, 1965; m. Lee Yuska; children: Michael Fioravanti children: Robert Fioravanti III. MA, Gov.'s State U.; BS, Ea. Ill. U., 1987; MEd, St. Xavier U., 2001. Spl. edn. dir. Evergreen Park H.S., Evergreen Park, Ill., 1996—, tchr. spl. edn., 1992—96; tchrs. spl. edn. in therapeutic day sch. Krejci Acad., Naperville, Ill., 1990—92; elem. tchr. Sch. Dist. #144, Hazel Crest, Ill., 1987—90; dir. Morton West H.S., Berwyn, Ill., 2002, bldg. adminstr., asst. spl. edn., 2002—. Mem.: Coun. Exceptional Children. Avocations: reading, scrapbooks. Home: 9558 S Sacramento Evergreen Park IL 60805 Office: Evergreen Park High School 9901 S Kedzie Evergreen Park IL 60805 Office Fax: 708-424-7497. Personal E-mail: Leerene@aol.com.

YUSSOUFF, MOHAMMED, retired physicist, educator; b. Cuttack, India, Aug. 14, 1942; arrived in U.S., 1991; s. Haji and Nurunnisa Fakhruddin; m. Farhana Begum, Apr. 6, 1969; children: Ashraf, Zeenat, Mustafa. MSc, Delhi U., 1963; PhD, Indian Inst. Tech., Kanpur, 1967. Prof. physics Indian Inst. Tech., Kanpur, 1967-90; vis. prof. physics Mich. State U., East Lansing, 1991—; ret., 1999. Guest scientist Ford Rsch., Dearborn, Mich., 1991-97, GM Tech. Ctr., Warren, Mich., 1997-98, Delphi Tech. Ctr., Warren, 1999—; vis. scientist U. Köln, Germany, 1972-74, U. Western Ont., London, Can., 1990-91; Humboldt scientist Atomic Energy Agy, Jülich, Germany, 1979-81; vis. prof. U. Konstanz, Germany, 1986-89; mem. com. physics examination Pub. Svc. Commn., Delhi, India, 1976-86, rsch. grants Univ. Grants Commn., Delhi, 1985-90; dir. Internat. Sch. on Band Structure, Indian Inst. Tech., 1986; creator Slow Pace program for tchg. sci. and engring. to deficient students with poor econ. or sch. backgrounds. Editor: Electronic Band Structure and Its Applications, 1987, The Physics of Materials, 1987. Mem.: Am. Phys. Soc., Internat. Ctr. Theoretical Physics (assoc.). Moslem. Achievements include patents for monitoring the catalytic converters in cars; research in theory of freezing; kinetic model of catalysis; theory of disordered systems, chanelling, clusters, electronic structure, ionic conductors, exhaust gas sensors, superconductors, zeolites; fundamental rate constants of catalytic reactions and foundations of quantum theory. Home: 5920 Crystal Lake Dr Romulus MI 48174 E-mail: yussouf2@hotmail.com.

Z, CHRIS, internist, medical educator; b. Corning, N.Y., Sept. 10, 1960; s. Chris and Potoula Roulidis; m. Maria Eugenia Hallas, May 24, 1987. BA with distinction, U. Va., 1982, MD, 1986. Diplomate Am. Bd. Internal Medicine. Resident U. Calif., San Francisco, 1988-91; assoc. Yater Med. Group, Washington, 1991-92; asst. clin. prof. Georgetown U., Washington, 1993-95; assoc. Duke U. Affiliated Physicians, Durham, N.C., 1995-96; asst. clin. prof. dept. medicine Duke U., Durham, 1996-2000, Emory U., Atlanta, 2001—. Gen. Internal Medicine fellow Georgetown U., 1992-93. Fellow: ACP; mem.: AMA. Avocations: music, piano, flute, bonsai, golf. Office: Emory U 1525 Clifton Rd NE Atlanta GA 30322

ZABEL, BARBARA, art historian, educator; b. Boston, Jan. 28, 1947; d. Carroll and Grace (Kamerling) Z.; m. G. Thomas Couser. BA, U. Colo., 1969; MA, U. Tex., 1971; PhD, U. Va., 1978. Asst. prof. Hobart and William Smith Colls., Geneva, N.Y., 1975-76; assoc. prof. Conn. Coll., New London, 1983—96, prof., 1996—. Fellow for arts and tech. Conn. Coll., New London, 1993-98. Author: Assembling Art: The Machine and the American Avant-Garde, 2004; contbg. author: Making Mischief: Dada

Invades New York, 1996, Modernism, Gender and Culture, 1997, Women in Dada, 1998; contbr. numerous articles to profl. jours. and arts mags. Bd. dirs. Lyman Allyn Art Mus., New London, Conn., 1988-2004. Predoctoral fellow Smithsonian Instn., 1973-75; vis. scholar grantee Nat. Mus. Am. Art., 1988, sr. scholar Nat. Portrait Gallery, Smithsonian Inst., 2003. Mem. Coll. Art Assn., Assn. Historians Am. Art. Office: Conn Coll 270 Mohegan Ave New London CT 06320-4126

ZABEL, VIVIAN ELLOUISE, secondary education educator; b. Randolph AFB, Tex., July 28, 1943; d. Raymond Louis and Dolly Veneta (Lyles) Gilbert; m. Robert Lee Zabel, Feb. 18, 1962; children: René Lynne, Robert Lee Jr., Randel Louis, Regina Louise. BA in English and Speech, Panhandle State U., 1977; postgrad., U. Ctrl. Okla., 1987-92. Cert. tchr., Okla. Tchr. English, drama, speech, debate Buffalo (Okla.) H.S., 1977-79; tchr. English, drama, speech Schulter (Okla.) H.S., 1979-80; tchr. English Morris (Okla.) H.S., 1980-81; tchr. speech, drama, debate Okla. Christian Schs., Edmond, 1981-82; tchr. English, drama, debate, speech/debate coach Braman (Okla.) H.S., 1982-83; debate coach Pawhuska (Okla.) H.S., 1983-84; tchr. English, French, drama, speech and debate coach Luther (Okla.) H.S., 1984-95; tchr. debate, forensics, yearbook, newspaper, mag., creative writing, competitive speech Deer Creek H.S., Edmond, Okla., 1995—2001; ret., 2001. Dir. drama Nazarene Youth Impact Team, Collinsville, Okla., 1979-81; tchr. h.s. Sun. sch. class Edmond Ch. of Nazarene, 1991-94; mem. cmty.-sch. rels. com. Luther Pub. Schs., 1991-92, supt.'s adv. com., 1992-94. Editor: Potpourri mag., 1975—77; author (under name Vivian Gilbert Zabel): Reflected Images; author: poetry, short stories, novels. Adult supr. Texas County 4-H, Adams, Okla., 1975-77; double diamond coach NFL; adjudicator and tournament dir. qualifying OSSAA Tournaments. Recipient Disting. Svc. award NFL, 1994, Editor's Choice award for poetry, 1997, 1998, 1999, Tchr. of Excellence, 1996, Outstanding Poet award, 1997, 1998, 1999, 2001. Mem. Nat. Debate Coaches Assn., Nat. Fedn. Interscholastic Speech and Debate Assn., Okla. Speech Theatre Comms. Assn., Okla. Tchrs. English, Internat. Soc. Poets. Republican. Nazarene. Home: 2912 Rankin Ter Edmond OK 73013-5344 E-mail: vzabel@juno.com.

ZABELSKY, WILLIAM JOHN, choral and band director; b. Homestead, Pa., May 2, 1954; s. William John Sr. and Elizabeth Jean (Tisza) Z.; m. Leslie Jane Sloan, June 11, 1977; children: Jennifer Ann, Amy Elizabeth, Sarah Jane. BS in Music Edn., Duquesne U., 1976. Cert. music tchr. Substitute tchr. Pitts. Area Schs., 1976-79; gen. music tchr. Gardnerville (Nev.) Elem. Sch., 1979-85; band and choir dir. Douglas High Sch., Minden, Nev., 1985—. Rep. presdl. inaugural parade, Nev., 1989, 2001; chmn. Nev. Allstate Choir, 1997. Mem. NEA, Am. Choral Dirs. Assn., Music Educators Nat. Conf., Nat. Band Assn., Nev. Music Educators Assn. (v.p. 1989-91, pres. 1991-93, 97-99, editor Nev. Notes), Douglas County Profl. Edn. Assn. (pres. 1981-84, 85-87, 90-91, 94-96), Phi Mu Alpha. Democrat. Roman Catholic. Avocations: reading, golf, music. Office: Douglas HS PO Box 1888 Minden NV 89423-1888

ZABETAKIS, PAUL MICHAEL, nephrologist, educator; b. Washington, Pa., July 30, 1947; s. Michael G. and Rebecca A. (Banakas) Z.; m. Martha Robinson, Oct. 3, 1970; 1 child, Amy Shannon. BA, Washington & Jefferson Coll., 1969; mD, U. Tenn., 1972. Diplomate Am. Bd. Internal Medicine, Am. Bd. Nephrology. Intern in medicine U. Pitts., 1972-73, resident in medicine, 1973-75; fellow in nephrology Yale U., New Haven, 1975-77; asst. chief nephrology-hypertension Lenox Hill Hosp., N.Y.C., 1977-82, assoc. chief nephrology-hypertension, 1978-99, dir. home peritoneal dialysis, 1985-99; asst. prof. clin. medicine N.Y. Med. Coll., Valhalla, N.Y., 1980-88, assoc. prof. clin. medicine, 1988-92; clin. asst. prof. medicine Cornell U., N.Y.C., 1992-93; clin. assoc. prof. medicine NYU, N.Y.C., 1993-99; exec. v.p., COO Everest Healthcare Svc., Oak Park, Ill., 1999-2001; CEO Extracorporeal Alliance Fresenius Med. Care, N.Am., 2001—. Mem. editl. bd. Clinical Nephrology, 1979—, Clinical and Experimental Dialysis and Apheresis, 1983-86, Geriatric Nephrology and Urology, 1995—, Advances in Renal Replacement Therapy, 1999—; nephrology cons. Nicholas Inst. Sports Medicine and Athletic Trauma Lenox Hill Hosp., N.Y.C., 1978-99, rsch. physician, 1982-99; mem. hypertension svc. adv. com. ARC, N.Y.C., 1981-99; mem. exec. com. End Stage Renal Disease Network N.Y. Inc., 1986-99, treas., 1992-93, chmn. long-range planning com., 1994; bd. dirs. Physician Hosp. Orgn. Lenox Hill Hosp., chmn. bd. dirs., 1996-99, v.p. med. bd., 1997-99; vice-chmn. quality improvement, med. dir. Everest Healthcare Svcs., Chgo., 1996-99. Contbr. numerous chpts. to books; patentee in field; lectr. in field; contbr. articles to profl. jours. Fellow ACP, Am. Coll. Preventive Medicine, Am. Coll. Sports Medicine; mem. N.Y. County Med. Soc., Med. Soc. of State of N.Y., Am. Heart Assn., Westchester Heart Assn., N.Y. Soc. Nephrology, Am. Soc. Nephrology, Internat. Soc. Nephrology, N.Y. Acad. Scis., N.Y. State Fedn. Profl. Health Educators, Am. Fedn. Clin. Sch., Internat. Soc. Peritoneal Dialysis, Am. Soc. Artificial Internal Organs (program com. 1995-99), Soc. Critical Care Medicine, Am. Coll. Nutrition, Internat. Soc. for Renal Nutrition and Metabolism, Internat. Soc. Geriatric Nephrology and Urology (founding mem., sec-treas. 1994-99). Avocation: sailboat racing. E-mail: paul.zabetakis@fmc-na.com.

ZABILKA, IVAN L. secondary education educator; b. Oskaloosa, Iowa, Aug. 14, 1939; s. J. Harvey and Marion (Pooley) Z.; m. Virginia Marcus, June 9, 1962 (div. Oct. 1990); children: Eric John, Laura Lynne; m. Carol Lindsay, May 21, 1992. AB, Asbury Coll., 1961; MDiv & ThM, Asbury Theol. Sem., 1965, 68; MA, U. Ky., 1976, PhD, 1980. Cert. secondary tchr., history, math., physics. Instr., math. Asbury Coll., Wilmore, Ky., 1966-68, registrar, dir. admissions, 1968-71; registrar, asst. dean Asbury Theol. Sem., Wilmore, 1971-74; tchr., secondary sch. Jessamine County (Ky.) & Johnson County (ind.), 1977-80; asst. registrar U. Mo., Columbia, 1980-87; instr., math. Bryan Sta. Mid. Sch., Lexington, Ky., 1987—99; program cons. Ky. Dept. Edn., 1999—2002; policy analyst The Family Found. of Ky., 2002—; instr. math Lexington Christian Acad., Lexington, Ky., 2003—. Presenter in field. Author: Scientific Malpractice, 1992, The Lottery Lie, 1998; contbr. over 20 articles to profl. jours. Mem. Jessamine County Sch. Bd., 1971-74; del. Rep. State Conv., 1972. Methodist. Avocation: hiking.

ZACEK, JANE SHAPIRO, director; b. N.Y.C., Nov. 10, 1938; d. Charles and Dorothy (Gintzler) Perlberg; m. Alan Shapiro, 1961; children: Leslie, Peter; m. Joseph Frederick Zacek, 1979. BA in Polit. Sci. with honors, Cornell U., 1960; cert. Russian Inst., MA in Polit. Sci., Columbia U., 1962, PhD in Polit. Sci., 1967; diploma nat. security affairs, The Nat. War Coll., 1979. Prof. polit. sci. Manhattanville Coll., Purchase, N.Y., 1965-78; prof. nat. security affairs The Nat. War Coll., Washington, 1978-80; divsn. mgmt./confidential affairs N.Y. State Gov.'s Office of Employee Rels., Albany, N.Y., 1980-86; dir. mgmt. resource project Gov.'s Office and Rockefeller Inst., Albany, 1986-89; sr. project dir. Rockefeller Inst. Govt. SUNY, Albany, 1989-91; pvt. rsch. and orgnl. cons. Albany, 1991-93; assoc. dean and dir. grad. studies Union Coll., Schenectady, N.Y., 1993-96, dir. office of grant support, 1996—. Rsch. cons. Yankelovich, Skelly, White, N.Y.C., 1976-78; adj. prof. polit. sci. SUNY, Albany, 1983, 90-93. Author, compiler: Governing the Empire State: An Insider's Guide, 1988; editor: The Gorbachev Generation: Issues in Soviet Foreign Policy, 1988, The Gorbachev Generation: Issues in Soviet Democracy, 1989; co-editor: Communist Systems in Comparative Perspective, 1974, Change and Adaptation in Soviet and East Politics, 1976, Politics and Participation under Communist Rule, 1983, Reform and Transformation in Communist Systems, 1991, Establishing Democratic Rule: The Reemergence of Local Governments in Post-Authoritarian Systems, 1993, Legacy of the Soviet Bloc, 1997; contbr. chpts. to books and articles to profl. jours. Pres. Women's Equity Action League, N.Y., 1991—; bd. dirs., v.p. YWCA of Albany, N.Y., 1991-94; bd. dirs. Albany (N.Y.-Russia) Tula Alliance, 1994-99, ARC of Northeastern N.Y., 1994-2002. Mem. Phi Beta Kappa. Avocations: walking dog, exercise. Home: 104 Manning Blvd Albany NY 12203-1742 Office: Union Coll 807 Union St Schenectady NY 12308 E-mail: zacekj@union.edu.

ZACHARIA, MATHEW VARIKALAM, educational administrator, management consultant; b. Edathua, Kerala, India, July 9, 1947; came to U.S., 1969; s. Varikalathil Mathew and Annamma (Thomas) Z.; m. Elizabeth Rajeena Cherian, June 13, 1953; children: Manoj Mathew, Melanie Elizabeth. AAS, Manhattan Coll., Bronx, 1971, BS, 1973; MPA, L.I. U., 1990. Adminstrv. dir. Mercy Cmty. Hosp., Port Jervis, N.Y., 1977-86; mgmt. cons. Port Jervis, 1986—; instr. Orange County C.C., Middletown, N.Y., 1990-91. Pres. Crossroad Books and Gifts, Port Jervis, 1994—. Mem. sch. bd. Port Jervis City Schs., 1993—; mem. Orange County Christian Coalition, 1993—; Sun. sch. tchr. St. Thomas Marthoma Ch., Yonkers, N.Y., 1987—; organizer Kerala Samajam of Greater N.Y., Manhattan, 1969-70. Mem. Lions. Republican. Avocations: evangelism, bible reading, touring the holy land and israel. Home: PO Box 196 14 Highland Ave Sparrow Bush NY 12780-5415

ZACHARIAS, DONALD WAYNE, academic administrator; b. Salem, Ind., Sept. 28, 1935; s. William Otto and Estelle Mae (Newlon) Z.; m. Tommie Kline Dekle, Aug. 16, 1959; children: Alan, Eric, Leslie. BA, Georgetown (Ky.) Coll., 1957, LLD (hon.), 1983; MA, Ind. U., 1959, PhD, 1963. Asst. prof. communication and theatre Ind. U., 1963-69; assoc. prof. U. Tex., Austin, 1969-72, prof., 1972-79, asst. to pres., 1974-77; exec. asst. to chancellor U. Tex. System, 1978-79; pres. Western Ky. U., 1979-85, Miss. State U., Starkville, 1985-97, pres. emeritus, 1998—. Bd. dirs. First Fed. Savs. & Loan Assn., Bowling Green, Ky., Inst. for Tech. Devel., Sanderson Farms, Inc., Miss. Econ. Coun.; dir. John Grisham Libr., Starkville, 1998. Author: In Pursuit of Peace: Speeches of the Sixties, 1970. Bd. dirs. Greenview Hosp.; pres. Southeastern Conf., 1989-91. With U.S. Army, 1959-60. Named Mississippian of Yr. Data Processing Mgmt. Assn.; recipient Teaching award Ind. U. Found., 1963, Cactus Teaching award U. Tex., 1971, Justin Smith Morrill award U.S. Dept. Agriculture, 1992, Disting. Teaching award Honors Program, 2000. Mem. Inst. Tech. Devel. (bd. dirs. 1985-92), Nat. Assn. State Univs. and Land-Grant Colls. (exec. com. 1990-92), Phi Kappa Phi (pres. 1978). Democrat. Episcopalian.

ZACHARIASEN, FREDRIK, physics educator; b. Chgo., June 14, 1931; s. William Houlder and Ragni (Durban_Hansen) Z.; m. Nancy Walker, Jan. 27, 1957; children: Kerry, Judith. BS, U. Chgo., 1951; PhD, Calif. Inst. Tech., 1956. Instr. MIT, Cambridge, 1955-56; rsch. physicist U. Calif., Berkeley, 1956-57; asst. prof. physics Stanford U., Calif., 1957-60; prof. Calif. Inst. Tech., Pasadena, 1960—. Assoc. dir. Los Alamos Nat. Lab., 1982-83. Author: Structure of Nucleons, 1960, Hadron Physics, 1973, Sound Fluctuation, 1979. Sloan fellow, 1960-64, Guggenheim fellow, 1970; Green scholar Scripps Instn. Oceanography, 1997-98. Home: 2235 Villa Heights Rd Pasadena CA 91107-1103 Office: Calif Inst Tech 1201 E California Blvd Pasadena CA 91125-0001

ZACHER, VALERIE MARIE, art educator; b. Duluth, Minn. d. Patrick Moore and Mary Jane (Younge) Langston; m. William John Zacher, Aug. 30, 1941; children: Michael William, Steven Patrick. Degree, State Tchrs. Coll.; student, Duluth Art Inst.; postgrad., U. Md. Docent Basil's Art Gallery, Duluth, Minn., 1956-58; instr. Sketch Pad Studio, Duluth, 1958—, Vocat. Inst. Tech., 1962-68, Latchkey Program, St. Petersburg, Fla., 1985-90; art specialist YMCA, St. Petersburg, 1990-95; adult instr. recreation dept. Gulfport, Fla., 1994-96. Instr. adult edn. painting class Yankee Trailer Park, Largo, Fla., 1991-96. Pres. Suntan Art Ctr., St. Petersburg; steering com. Pinellas Art Coun.; active with physically and mentally challenged children Adult Edn. Program; active PTA, Duluth. Recipient Outstanding Achievement award, 1990; named Vol. of Yr., St. Mary's Hosp., 1960. Mem. AAUW, Nat. Mus. Women in Arts, Mus. Fine Art, Smithsonian Instn. Lutheran. Avocations: painting, sketching, reading, travel.

ZACHERT, VIRGINIA, psychologist, educator; b. Jacksonville, Ala., Mar. 1, 1920; d. R.E. and Cora H. (Massee) Z. Student, Norman Jr. Coll., 1937; AB, Ga. State Woman's Coll., 1940; MA, Emory U., 1947; PhD, Purdue U., 1949. Diplomate: Am. Bd. Profl. Psychologists. Statistician Davison-Paxon Co., Atlanta, 1941-44; research psychologist Mil. Contracts, Auburn Research Found., Ala. Poly. Inst.; indsl. and research psychologist Sturm & O'Brien (cons. engrs.), 1958-59; research project dir. Western Design, Biloxi, Miss., 1960-61; self-employed cons. psychologist Norman Park, Ga., 1961-71, Good Hope, Ga., 1971-99. Rsch. assoc. med. edn. Med. Coll. Ga., Augusta, 1963-65, assoc. prof., 1965-70, rsch. prof., 1970-84, rsch. prof. emeritus, 1984—, chief learning materials divsn., 1973-84, faculty senate, 1976-84, acad. coun., 1976-82, pres. acad. coun., 1983, sec., 1978; mem. Ga. Bd. Examiners Psychologists, 1974-79, v.p., 1977, pres. 1978; adv. bd. Comdr. Gen. ATC USAF, 1967-70; cons. Ga. Silver Haired Legislature, 1980-86, senator, 1987-93, pres. protem, 1987-88, pres., 1989-93, rep., spkr. protem, 1993-96, spkr., 1997-98, Nat. Silver-Haired Congress rep., 1995—, spkr. 1997-99; govs. appointee White House Conf. on Aging, 1971, 96, Ga. Coun. on Aging, 1988-96; U.S. Senate mem. Fed. Coun. on the Aging, 1990-93; senator appointee White House Conf. on Aging, 1995; Ga. Health Decision's appointee to Ga. Coalition for Health, 1996-98. Author: (with P.L. Wilds) Essentials of Gynecology-Oncology, 1967, Applications of Gynecology-Oncology, 1967. Del. White House Conf. on Aging, 1981, 95. Served as aerologist USN, 1944-46;aviation psychologist USAF, 1949-54. Recipient Jane Kennedy Excellence Aging award, 1999. Fellow AAAS, Am. Psychol. Assn.; mem. AAUP (chpt. pres. 1977-80), Sigma Xi. (chpt. pres. 1980-81) Baptist. Home: 4275 Owens Rd # 403 Evans GA 30809

ZACK, STEVEN JEFFREY, master automotive instructor; b. Middletown, Conn., Oct. 12, 1955; s. Mathias Charles and Sylvia Ann (Berkowitz) Z. AAS, Williamsport Area C.C., 1976. Cert. EPA instr. Automotive technician Bob Sharp Nissan, Danbury, Conn., 1976-79; svc. engr. Ingersoll Rand, Painted Post, N.Y., 1979-85; tech. svc. rep. Chrysler Motor Corp., Metairie, La., 1985-87; automotive instr. Hartford (Conn.) Tech. Inst., 1988-92; master automotive instr. SPX/Automotive Diagnostics, Kalamazoo, Mich., 1992-97, SPX/OTC, Owatonna, Minn., 1997—. Tng. cons. Conn. DMV, North Haven, 1994—; with Coun. of Advanced Automotive Trainers, Lisle, Ill., 1995—; master instr. EPA/Coalition Safer Cleaner Vehicles, Albany, N.Y., 1994—. Contbr. articles to trade jours. Mem. Coalition for Safer Cleaner Vehicles. Achievements include designed electric car heat exchanger motor; designed, patent Zack cycle engine; holder 10 copyrights; developed over 75 technical diagnostic and equipment training classes. Home: 280 East Main St Unit B7 Clinton CT 06413

ZAFERSON, WILLIAM S. philosophy educator, publisher; b. Kalavrita, Greece, Feb. 10, 1925; came to U.S., 1953; s. Steven A. and Katharine (Michael) Z.; m. Toni Adelgunde Humberg, Oct. 15, 1955. BA in Lit. cum laude, U. Athens, Greece, 1952; MA in Classical Lang. and Lit., U. Chgo., 1965; DPhil magna cum laude, U. Athens, 1976; postgrad., Truman Coll., 2000; Internat. Scholar in Tr origin. classical texts. Asst. prof. U. Upper Iowa, Fayette, 1966-68, Marymount Coll., Salina, Kans., 1968-70; prof. philosophy St. Mary's U., San Antonio, Tex., 1970-72. Internat. scholar translating original classical texts. Author: The Meaning of Metempsychosis, 1965, The Universe, Its Elements and Justice, 1974, A Hymn to Health, 1975, The Platonic View of Moral Law and the Influence of the Tragedians on Plato's Thoughts, 1976, The Perfect Family, 1986, The Heraclitean Logos, 1996; author, pub.: The Songs of the Muses for Gods and Men, 1999, (70 poems set to music) Hephaestus, 2000, (poem set to music) Hermes to King Odysseus, 2001, (lyrics and music) Mother Gaea's Reprobation, 2001, (lyrics and music) Pluto and Persephone (A Look into the Elusinian Mysteries Verifying Every Soul's Immortality), 2002, (poem set to music) Hymn to the Earth: Mother of All, 2002, (music) The Throne of Virtue, 2002, The Titans (War of Ideologies. Vice versus Virtue, words & music), 2003, others. A. Daniel L. Shorey fellow, U. Chgo., 1955. Mem. NRTA, AAUP, Am. Philos. Assn. (ctrl. divsn. emeritus), U. Chgo. Alumni Assn., Am. Assn. Learned Socs., Goethe-Institut Chgo., Nat. Assn. Scholars. Avocations: poetry, classical music, opera, hiking, swimming.

ZAGANO, PHYLLIS, religious studies educator; BA in English, Marymount Coll., 1969; MS in Pub. Rels., Boston U., 1970; MA in English, L.I.U., 1972; PhD in English, SUNY, Stony Brook, 1979; MA in Theology, St. John's U., Jamaica, N.Y., 1990. Program officer Nat. Humanities Ctr., N.Y.C., 1979-80; asst. prof. comms. Fordham U., Bronx, N.Y., 1980-84; rschr. Archdiocese of N.Y., 1984-86; ind. rschr. N.Y.C., 1986-88; assoc. prof. comm. Boston U., 1988—98, dir. inst. for democratic comm., 1998; spl. assoc. prof. religious studies Hofstra U., Hempstead, NY, 2003—. Author: Religion and Public Affairs, 1987, Social Impact of the Mass Media, 1991, Woman to Woman, 1993, On Prayer, 1994, Ita Ford: Missionary Martyr, 1996, Twentieth Century Apostles, 1999, Things Now and Old, 1999, Holy Saturday: An Argument for the Restoration of the Formale Diaconaizs in the Catholic Church, 2000 (Book award Catholic Press Assn. 2001, Coll. Theology Soc. 2002), DorothyDay: In My Own Words, 2003; monthly radio host Boston U. World of Ideas, 1992-97. Lector, lay minister Ch. St. Vincent Ferrer, NYC, 1980-92, Our Lady of the Miraculous Medal Ch., 1996—, Newman Ctr., Boston U., 1992-96. Comdr. USNR, 1976—. Faculty Rsch. grantee Fordham U., 1983, Rsch. grantee Nat. Inst. Peace, 1989, Rsch. grantee Wabash Ctr., 2003; Coolidge fellow Episcopal Divinity Sch., 1987; recipient citation for heroism Nassau County (N.Y.) Fire Commn., 1995. Mem. Am. Acad. Religion (co-chair Roman Cath. Studies, 1991-2001), Am. Cath. Philos. Assn., Assn. Profs. Religious Studies, Naval Res. Assn., Soc. for Study of Christian Spirituality. Roman Catholic. Office: 115 Hofstra Univ Hempstead NY 11549

ZAGARE, FRANK COSMO, political science educator; b. Bklyn., June 7, 1947; s. Domenick Joseph and Josephine Ann (Stager) Z.; m. Patricia M. Sclafani, May 26, 1974; children: Catherine, Ann, Elizabeth. BA, Fordham U., 1969; MA, NYU, 1972, PhD, 1977. Asst. prof. Boston U., 1978-87; assoc. prof. SUNY, Buffalo, 1987-91, prof., 1991—, chmn. dept. polit. sci., 1991-94, 96—. Author: Game Theory, 1984, Dynamics of Deterrence, 1987; co-author: Perfect Deterrence, 2000; contbr. articles to profl. publs. MIT/Harvard fellow 1984; grantee U.S. Inst. Peace, 1989-90, NSF, 1992-94, 96-98. Mem. Am. Polit. Sci. Assn. (coun. mem. conflict processes sect. 1986-89), Internat. Studies Assn., Midwest Polit. Sci. Assn. Home: 123 Morris Ave Buffalo NY 14214-1609 Office: SUNY Buffalo 520 Park Hall Buffalo NY 14260-4100

ZAHNER, DOROTHY SIMKIN, elementary education educator; b. Chengdu, Szechuan, China, May 01; came to US in the 1930s; d. Robert Louis and Margaret Isadore (Timberlake) Simkin; divorced; children: Mary De Avilan, Robert Louis. BA in Sociology, Whittier Coll.; MLS, U. So. Calif., L.A. Cert. tchr. Calif., Ariz. Tchr. LA and Pasadena Sch., Calif., 1969-93; dir., owner Betty Ingram Sch., North Hollywood, Calif., 1976-79; dir. Foothill Nursery Sch., La Crescenta, Calif., 1970s; tchr. L.A. Unified Sch. Dist.; guest tchr. Washington Unified Sch. Dist., Phoenix, 1994-97. Guest tchr. Osborn Sch. Dist., 1998-2000, Madison Sch. Dist., Phoenix, 1999-2001. Author: (poetry) Yucca Poetry Workshop, 1993-94, Treasured Poems of America, 1993, Silver Quill, 1996, internat. poetry publ., numerous others; poems pub. in Eng., 1998, 99, 2000, 01. Bd. dirs. Ariz. Tenants Assn., Phoenix, 1994, 95; vol. Am. Friends Svc. Com., Phila., Calif., 1985—, Common Cause, LA, 1990, Internat. Rescue Com., Dem. Candidates, LA and Phoenix. Recipient award for a poem, Ariz. State Poetry Soc., Phoenix, 1995, 2000; hon. mention for poem publ. Sandcutters, 2000. Mem.: Ariz. State Poetry Soc. (pres. 2002—03), Alameda Writers Group, Phoenix Poetry Soc. (pres. 1998, anthology editl. co. 2001, com. mem., Poet of Yr. 2000), Phoenix Writers Club (sec. 1998). Avocations: theatre, films, music, swimming, reading.

ZAHRLY, JANICE HONEA, management educator; b. Ft. Payne, Ala., Sept. 27, 1943; d. John Wiley and Lillian (McKown) Honea. BA, U. Fla., 1964; MBA, U. Ctrl. Fla., 1980; PhD, U. Fla., 1984. Tchr. Hope Mills (N.C.) H.S., 1964-65, Satellite Beach (Fla.) H.S., 1965-69; realtor-assoc. WD Webb Realty, Melbourne, Fla., 1969-70; realtor Aero Realty, Melbourne, 1970-72, Albert J. Tuttle, Realtor, Melbourne, 1972-74; mktg. mgr. Cypress Woods Devel., Orlando, Fla., 1974-76; regional campaign mgr. Pres. Ford Com., 1976; ednl. researcher Peace Corps, Korea, 1976-78; rsch. analyst, tech. writer Rsch. Sys. Inc., Orlando, 1979-80; rsch. asst., lectr. U. Fla., Gainesville, 1980-84; asst. prof. Wayne State U., Detroit, 1984-89; assoc. prof. Old Dominion U., Norfolk, Va., 1989-94, U. N.D., Grand Forks, 1994—. Mem. Melbourne Bd. Realtors, 1969-76, orientation chair, 1972, pub. rels. chair, 1973, civic affairs chair, 1973, grievance com., 1975; cons. Wayne County Retarded Persons Assn., Detroit, 1985, Gov.'s Conf. on Women Entrepreneurs, Mich., 1986, Oakland County AAUW Conf. on Women, Mich., 1987, 88, Coll. Bus. and Pub. Adminstrn. Inst. of Mgmt., Old Dominion U., Norfolk, 1990, U.S. Army Corps Engrs., Norfolk, 1990; presenter in field. Editl. rev. bd., Case Rsch. Jour., 2000—; contbr. chpts. to books, articles to profl. jours. and procs. Vol. Tidewater AIDS Crisis Task Force, Norfolk, 1990-93, bd. dirs., 1990-92, v.p., 1991, rec. sec., 1992; mem. occupational adv. com. Brevard County Mental Health Ctr., Fla., 1973-74; mem. Brevard County Libr. Bd., 1973-74; bd. dirs. Fla. Dist. 12 Mental Health Bd., 1973-74, sec. 1973-74; bd. dirs. Alachua County Crisis Ctr., Gainesville, 1982-84, chair, 1983-84; vol. Open Door, Detroit, 1986-89; bd. dirs. United Way Grand Forks area, 1996-97; pres. bd. dirs. Cherry Arms Condominium Assn., 1996-97. Recipient Best Paper award Midwest Soc. for Human Resources/Indsl. Rels., 1989, F.W. Lawrence award U. N.D., 1996; rsch. fellow Fed. Mogul Corp., 1987-88; rsch. grantee Wayne State U., 1985-89, Old Dominion U., 1990, U. N.D., 1995, 96, 98; repipient Tate award (best case) N. Am. Case Rsch. Assn. 2002. Mem. AAUW (bd. dirs. 1974-75), Acad. Mgmt., Assn. for Rsch. on Nonprofit Orgns./Vols., N.Am. Case Rsch. Assn. (nonprofit track chair 1999-2000, procs. editor 2001-2002), So. Mgmt. Assn., Hampton Rds. Gator Club (co-founder, treas. 1989-91), Alpha Omicron Pi (bd. dirs. alumnae chpt. 1969-73, v.p. 1969-73). Avocations: travel, writing fiction, photography, music. Home: 3424 Cherry St Apt A1 Grand Forks ND 58201-7692

ZAHS, DAVID KARL, secondary school educator, educational administrator; b. Mt. Clemens, Mich., June 2, 1957; s. William Karl and Shirley Ann Zahs. BEd magna cum laude, U. Toledo, 1982, postgrad. in adminstrn. Student tchr. Waterville Elem. and Monclova Elem. Schs., Ohio, 1982; substitute tchr. Anthony Wayne H.S., Whitehouse, Ohio, 1982, Bowsher H.S., Toledo, 1982-83; tchr. Toledo Pub. Schs., 1983-88; human svc. program adminstr. vocation, vols. and adult edn. Warrensville (Ohio) Devel. Ctr. MR/DD, 1988-98; substitute tchr., coach girls basketball, boys soccer Garfield Heights (Ohio) H.S., 1989—, head coach, 1989—; boys soccer coach Strongville H.S., 1997; adapted phys. edn. instr. Brunswick (Ohio) City Schs., 1999—; site mgr. summer program HELP Found., 1999—. Coach soccer and basketball Ctrl. Cath. H.S., Toledo, 1983-88; coach boys' track DeVilbiss H.S., Toledo, 1986-87 (State Champions 1987); head coach girls' soccer Brunswick H.S.; referee soccer h.s./USSF Grade 7, 1984-99; instr. Rocket Soccer Camp U. Toledo, 1985-88; asst. Maumee Valley Soccer Sch., 1982-84, head coach girls' team, 1982; dir. Bulldog Basketball Camp, 1992—. Named divsn. 1 Coach of Yr. N.E. Ohio AP, 1997. Mem. AAHPERD, Fellowship of Christian Athletes. Lutheran. Avocations: soccer, distance running. Home: 23215 Chandlers Ln Olmsted Falls OH 44138-3221 Office: Brunswick City Schs 3643 Center Rd Brunswick OH 44212-3619 E-mail: dzahs@brunswick.org.

ZAHUMENY, JANET MAE, secondary education educator; b. Rahway, N.J., Mar. 23, 1945; d. Richard Evans and Elsie Mae (Walling) Franklin; m. Edward Zahumeny, Dec. 21, 1966 (div. 1987); 1 child, Carole Ann. BA, Newark State Coll., 1967; MEd, William Paterson Coll., 1990; MA, Kean Coll., 1994. Cert. secondary tchr., N.J. Math. tchr. Hunterdon Cen. High Sch., Flemington, N.J., 1967-68; math., computer tchr. Roselle Park (N.J.) High Sch., 1968—. Instr. computers Roselle Park Adult Sch., 1987-88; instr. computer tech. William paterson Coll., 1992—, U. Calif., Berkeley, 1995—; cons. Gray's Appraisal, Cranford, N.J., 1987; textbook editor Prentice Hall, 1989; computer group asst. Bell Labs., Whippany, N.J., summers 1972-73; chmn. Dist. Computer Study Com., 1988; in-svc. tchr. tng., 1988—; 8th grade computer coord., 1988-89; mem. Mid. State Evaluation Team, 1972, 82, 85; liaison com. RPHS, 1985—, dist. tech. com., 1996—; cooperating tchr. Kean Coll., 1990—, Montclair State U.; adminstrv. asst. to v.p. Alpha Wire, summer 1991—; participant Computing Inst., 1983, Woodrow Wilson Inst., 1991, 96, NSF Inst., 1991; mem. Key Curriculum Press Profl. Devel. Team, 1993—; webmaster, Roselle Pk., N.J. Home Page, 1995—. Mem. Web Site editl. bd. William Paterson Coll. Inst. for Tech. in Math. Active Crandford PTA, Roselle Park PTSA; cons. Roselle Park Web Site. Named Outstanding Acad. Tchr., Cittone Inst., Edison, N.H., 1988, Outstanding Tchr., N.J. Gov.'s Recognition Program, 1989, Outstanding Computer/Math. Tchr. Tandy Techs., 1991; recipient Grad. Scholarship Kean Coll., Union, N.J., 1992, Computer Grant award 1993, Presdl. award for excellence in math. tchg., 1994, 95. Mem. NEA, Nat. Coun. Tchrs. Math., Assn. Math. Tchrs. N.J., N.J. Edn. Assn., Roselle Park Edn. Assn., N.J. Assn. for Ednl. Tech., WPC Inst. for Tech. in Math., Mensa, Kean Coll. Alumni Assn., William Paterson Coll. Alumni Assn., Cranford Mcpl. Alliance, Papermill Playhouse Theater Guild, Pi Lambda Theta, Kappa Delta Pi, Phi Kappa Phi. Avocations: computers, embroidering, sailing, bowling, bridge. Office: Roselle Park High Sch 185 W Webster Ave Roselle Park NJ 07204-1699

ZAIDI, EMILY LOUISE, retired elementary school educator; b. Hoquiam, Wash., Apr. 20, 1924; d. Burdick Newton and Emily Caroline (Williams) Johnston; m. M. Baqar Abbas Zaidi, June 12, 1949 (dec. Dec. 1983). BA in Edn. and Social Studies, Ea. Wash. State U., 1948; MEd, U. Wash., 1964, EdD, 1974. Tchr. 4th grade Hoquiam Schs., 1948-49; tchr. grades 5-6 Lake Washington Sch. Dist., Kirkland, Wash., 1949-51; tchr. grades 2-3 Port Angeles (Wash.) Schs., 1951-54; tchr. grade 2 Seattle Schs., 1954-55; tchr., reading specialist Northshore sch. Dist., Bothell, Wash., 1955-69, Sacramento City Schs., 1969-87; ret. Mem. Calif. State Instructional Materials Panel, Sacramento, 1975. Mem. Sacramento Opera Assn., 1986—, Sacramento Ballet Assn., 1987-2000. Fulbright Commn. Exchange Tchr., 1961-62. Mem. Reading Club. Democrat. Avocations: writing, children's literature, reading, travel. Home: 4230 N River Way Sacramento CA 95864-6055

ZAKARAUSKAS, PIERRE, physicist, educator; b. Amos, Que., Can., Dec. 25, 1958; s. Joseph and Réjeanne (Latreille) Z. BSc, U Que., 1980; PhD, U. B.C., Vancouver, 1984. Def. scientist Def. Rsch. Establishment Atlantic, Dartmouth, N.S., 1984-86, Def. Rsch. Establishment Pacific, Victoria, B.C., 1986-95. Rsch. assoc. dept. psychology U. B.C., 1988-93, asst. prof. dept. ophthalmology, 1993—; CTO Wavemakers Inc. Contbr. articles and referee to profl. jours. including Jour. Acoustical Soc. Am., IEEE Transaction on Signal Processing, Neural Network for Ocean Engring., IEEE Proceedings, Hearing Res., Phys. Rev. D. Mem. Acoustical Soc. Am., Can. Acoustical Assn. Achievements include research on ice-cracking noise in Arctic, complexity analysis of nearest-neighbor search, applying neural networks to acoustic localization, computational theories of sound localization, and classification, high-energy particle physics. Home: 655 Moberly Rd Ste 507 Vancouver BC Canada V5Z 2B4 Office: Ste 302 134 Abbott St Vancouver BC Canada V6B 2K4 E-mail: pierre@wavemakers.com.

ZALINSKY, SANDRA H. ORLOFSKY, school counselor; b. Elizabeth, N.J., July 11, 1959; d. Marion E. (Carrajat) Orlofsky; m. Thomas J. Zalinsky, Apr. 12, 1985. BA in Math. & Sci. Edn., Glassboro State Coll., 1981; MA in Adminstrn., Jersey City State Coll., 1985, MA in Counseling, 1990; EdD in Child & Youth Studies, Nova Southeastern U., 1994. Nat. cert. sch. counselor; master addictions counselor. Sr. cam counselor Brick (N.J.) Recreation Dept., 1978-81; tchr. high sch. math. and sci. Brick (N.J.) Twp. Bd. Edn., 1981-88; counselor, cons. pvt. agys., Ocean County, N.J., 1988—; counselor high sch. Brick Twp. Bd. Edn., 1988-98; dept. head guidance Brick Twp. H.S., 1995-98; counselor So. Reg. H.S., Manahawkin, N.J., 1998—. Speaker in field. Mem. ASCD (nat. cert. counselor), N.J. Counseling Assn., N.J. Sch. Counselors Assn., N.J. Edn. Assn. (sch. rep. 1981—), Ocean County Pers. and Guidance Assn. (pres. 1997—), Skippers Cove Yacht Club, Phi Delta Kappa. Avocations: sailing, scuba diving, photography, tennis, travel. Home: 20 Davey Jones Way Waretown NJ 08758-2106 Office: Southern Regional Bd of Edn 75 Cedar Bridge Rd Manahawkin NJ 08050-3056

ZAMBONE, ALANA MARIA, special education educator, consultant; b. Vineland, N.J., Sept. 17, 1952; d. L. Alan and Joyce (Bernero) Z. AB in Spl. Edn. and Elem. Edn., U. N.C., Chapel Hill, 1974; MS in Human Devel. Liaison, George Peabody Coll. Tchrs., 1978; PhD in Spl. Edn., Vanderbilt U., 1984. Cert. spl. edn., elem. edn., visual impairments, mental retardation, N.C. Tchr., counselor Orange County Assn. for Retarded Citizens, Chapel Hill, N.C., 1973-74; lead tchr. Shelbyville-Bedford (Tenn.) County Adult Svc. Ctr., 1974; program coord. Dickson (Tenn.) County Adult Svcs., 1974-75; dept. head, habilitative svcs. CloverBottom Devel. Ctr., Nashville, Tenn., 1975-76; exec. dir. Waves, Inc. Adult Svcs., Fairview, Tenn., 1976-77; from vocat. cons. to liaison, Peabody Tchrs. Coll. Vanderbilt U., 1977-80; chairperson, bd. dirs. Residential Svcs., Inc., Nashville, 1976-80; asst. prof., coord., dept. curriculum N.C. State U., Raleigh, N.C., 1981-84; coord. and asst. prof., div. spl. edn. Minot (N.D.) State U., 1984-86; coord. internat. outreach svcs. Hilton-Perkins Internat. Program Perkins Sch. for the Blind, Watertown, Mass., 1989-94; assoc. prof., dir. Inst. for Visually Impaired Pa. Coll. Optometry, Phila., 1994—. Co-founder, sr. rsch. fellow Walker-Wheelock Inst. for Equity in Edn., sr. project dir. exceptional needs assessment devel. lab. Edn. Devel. Corp., Newton, Mass., 1998—; co-coord. grad. program tchrs. of students with spl. needs, mem. grad. faculty infant toddler program evaluator Danforth cmty. devel. project Wheelock Coll., 1995-98; nat. cons. Am. Found. for the Blind, N.Y.C., 1986-89; adj. asst. prof. div. spl. edn., Columbia U., 1987—; co-dir. model infant/toddler program, sch. medicine, U. N.C., Chapel Hill, 1983-84; project dir., mem. grad. faculty severe and multiple disabilities Simmons Coll., 1990—; bd. dirs. N.D. Coun. for the Arts; adv. bd. Blind Babies Found.; mem. adv. com. Robert E. Miller, Inc., Community Residential Svcs. for Disabled Children; bd. dirs. Specialized Svcs. for Children, Inc.; sch. edn. rep. to fac. N.C. State U., sch. edn. fac. senate, among others. Grantee Busch Found., N.D. Coun. Arts, Nat. Coun. on the Arts, Dean's Grant Program, Burlington/No. Found., Kate B. Reynolds Found., Nat. Rural Spl. Edn. Consortium, U.S. Office Human Devel. Svcs., U.S. Office of Spl. Edn. Mem. Coun. for Exceptional Children (past dir. div. visual handicaps), Assn. for Retarded Citizens, Assn. for Persons with Severe Handicaps, Am. Assn. Mental Deficiency, Am. Assn. for Applied Behavior Analysis, Nat. Assn. for Parents of the Visually Impaired, Internat. Assn. for the Edn. of the Deaf-Blind, Assn. for the Edn. and Rehab. of the Blind and Visually Impaired (pre-sch. div., multihandicaps div., chairperson multiple disabilities div.), Internat. Coun. Educators of Children and Youth Who Are Blinded or Visually Impaired (co-coord. functions curriculum devel. project 1993—). Avocation: scuba diving. Office: Inst for Equity in Schs Affiliate Walker Home & Sch 1968 Central Ave Needham MA 02492-1410 also: Edn Devel Corp 35 Chapel St Newton MA 02458-1010 E-mail: zambone790@earthlink.net.

ZAMIR, FRANCES ROBERTA (FRANCES ROBERTA WEISS-SWEDE), educational compliance specialist; b. Bklyn., Nov. 6, 1944; d. Martin and Jean (Roskosky) Swede. BA in English, Calif. State U., Northridge, 1967, MA in Spl. Edn., 1975; MA in Ednl. Adminstrn., Calif. State U., L.A., 1987. Credential adminstrv. svcs., std. elem, spl. edn.-learning handicapped, Calif; cert. resource specialist. Former childrens' ctr. tchr., gen. edn. and spl. edn. tchr., resource specialist, mentor tchr., program specialist/region advisor, asst. prin., prin. L.A. Unified Sch. Dist., compliance specialist. Formerly owner, ptnr. Best Bet Ednl. Therapy/Tutoring Referral Svc.; former cons. Academics Plus Tutoring Referral Svc.; former asst. prof. resource specialist cert. program Calif. State U., Dominguez Hills; former instr. early and regular edn. credential program UCLA; former mem. Cluster 5 Instrnl. Cabinet L.A. Unified Sch. Dist., former asst. prin. steering com. Region C; former adminstr. portfolio documentation subcom. Adminstrv. Tng. Acad.; former sch. site rev. coms. Calif. State Dept. Edn., former mem. ad hoc com. on quality indicators. Former mem. spkrs. bur. Commn. on Jews with Disabilities. Mem.: NEA, Women in Ednl. Leadership, Calif. Tchrs. Assn., Calif. Assn. Resource Specialists (former state v.p. and conf. chair, state pres., bd. dirs.), Calif. Assn. Sch. Adminstrs. (former spl. edn. com. L.A. chpt.), Calif. Assn. Program Specialists (former So. Calif. regional rep.), L.A. Rep. Coun. (former elem. asst. prin. rep.), Assoc. Adminstrs., Friends of Calif. State, Phi Delta Kappa, Kappa Delta Pi. Office: L A Unified Sch Dist 450 N Grand Ave Los Angeles CA 90012-2123

ZAMORANO, WANDA JEAN, secondary education educator; b. Mertzon, Tex., Aug. 11, 1947; d. A.L. and Billie Louise (Byler) Sawyer; married; 1 child, Anna. BS, Sul Ross State Univ., 1970; MEd, Tex. Tech., 1974; EdD, Nova Southeastern U., 1994. Cert. tchr., Tex. Migrant edn. tchr. Balmorhea (Tex.) ISD, 1970-72; reading tchr. Hurst-Euless Bedford (Tex.) ISD, 1972-92; owner cons. firm WZ Enterprizes. Cons. Tex. Tech. U., 1980-81; demonstration tchr. Ednl. Svcs. Ctr., Austin, 1975; instr. Richland Coll., Dallas, 1982; mem. nat. faculty Turner Ednl. Svcs. Inc.; adj. prof. Tex. Woman's U.; presneter 67th annual So. N.Mex. Tech. Conf., 1994. Contbr. articles to profl. jours. Active Bedford Jr. High PTA. Named Tchr. of Yr., Bedford, 1984, Most Prominent Educators Tex., 1983, Cable Tchr. of Yr., 1991, Tchr. of Month, Bronco News, 1993; TCI Cable grantee, 1995. Mem. NEA, AAUW (Named USA Today faculty mem.), Hurst-Euless-Bedford Tex. State Tchrs. Assn. NEA (v.p. 1994-95, Internat. Reading Assn., Tex. State Tchr. Assn. (exec. bd.), The Governor's Club (charter), Kappa Delta Pi. Democrat. Avocations: reading, travel, card playing. Home: 531 Ranch Trl Apt 157 Irving TX 75063-7614 Office: Bedford Jr High 325 Carolyn Dr Bedford TX 76021-4195

ZANCHETTI, PAMELA JOAN, elementary education educator; b. Milw., Jan. 25, 1950; d. Joseph William and Jane Florence (Gorski) Hess; m. Mark Anthony Zanchetti, Mar. 17, 1973; children: Christina, Nicole. BS in Edn., U. Wis., Whitewater, 1972. Primary tchr. St. Roman Sch., Milw., 1972-74; elem. tchr. St. Kilian Sch., Hartford, Wis., 1974-81, 86—. Mem. English Lang. Arts Reading Com., Hartford, 1986-93, Washington County Reading Coun., West Bend, Wis., 1990-93, Washington County Young Writers, West Bend, 1991-92. Mem. ASCD, Wis. State Reading Assn., Wis. Cath. Edn. Assn. Roman Catholic. Avocations: traveling, reading, cross-country skiing, biking, camping. Home: N844 Franklin Rd Oconomowoc WI 53066-9527 Office: St Kilian Sch 245 High St Hartford WI 53027-1196

ZANDER, ARLEN RAY, retired physics educator; b. Shiner, Tex., Dec. 12, 1940; s. Elton A. and Lillie G. (Malina) Z.; m. Dorothy Marie Mayer, Feb. 1, 1964; children: Melanie, Aaron, Bryan. BS in Physics, U. Tex., 1964; PhD in Physics, Fla. State U., 1970. Asst. prof. physics East Tex. State U., Commerce, 1970-74, assoc. prof. physics, 1975-79, prof. physics, 1980-89, coord. external grants, 1974-77, asst. dean arts and sci., 1982-86, dean arts and sci., 1986-89; provost, v.p. acad. affairs U. La., Monroe, 1989-2000. Liaison superconducting super collider E. Tex. State U., Commerce, 1987-89; lectr. fgn. countries; commentator weekly radio show Sci. Update, 1981-82. Contbr. articles to profl. jours.; author weekly newspaper column Halley's Comet (Sci. Writing award Coun. for Advancement and Support of Edn. 1986), 1985-86. Campaign chmn. United Way, Commerce, 1988; bd. govs. Monroe Symphony Orch., 1991. Numerous grants various agys.; NATO fellow, 1982. Mem. Am. Assn. Physics Tchrs., West Monroe C. of C. (chmn. 1994), Lions (bd. dirs. internat. youth camp 1983-86), Sigma Xi. Avocations: jogging, reading, racquetball, classical music. Home: 100 Bluff Dr West Monroe LA 71291-9434 Office: U La-Monroe 700 University Ave Monroe LA 71209-9000 E-mail: zander@ulm.edu.

ZANGENEH, FEREYDOUN, pediatrics educator, pediatric endocrinologist; b. Tehran, Iran, July 11, 1937; came to U.S., 1962, 86; married. MD, U. Tehran, Iran, 1961. Diplomate Am. Bd. Pediatrics and Pediatric Endocrinology. Intern Washington Hosp. Ctr., 1962; resident in pediatrics U. Chgo. Hosps. & Clinics, 1963-65; fellow in pediatric endocrinology Children's Memorial Hosp., Chgo., 1965-66, U. Wash., Seattle, 1966-68; asst. prof. to prof. U. Tehran, Iran, 1968-86; assoc. prof. pediatrics Marshall U. Sch. of Medicine, Huntington, W.Va., 1986-89, W.Va. U., Charleston, 1989-95, prof. pediatrics, 1995—, dir. pediatric endocrinology, 1989—. Instr. pediatrics U. Wash., Seattle, 1967-68; dir. dept. endocrinology Children's Hosp. Med. Ctr., Tehran, Iran, 1968-86; dir. pediatric endocrinology Marshall U. Sch. Medicine, Huntington, 1986-89; mem. W.Va. Adv. Com. on Newborn Metabolic Screening, W.Va. Adv. Com. on Diabetes Mellitus. Author: (with others) Pediatric Endocrinology and Metabolism; contbr. articles and abstracts to profl. jours. Bd. dirs., rsch. com., camp com. Am. Diabetes Assn., W.Va. affiliate, Charleston, active in Huntington W.Va. affiliate, 1986-89; bd. dirs. Diabetes Camp of W.Va. Recipient Gharib Rsch. award, Iranian Pediatric Soc., Tehran, 1976. Fellow Am. Acad. Pediatrics, Am. Coll. Endocrinology; mem. Internat. Pediatric Assn. (adv. expert panel 1977-83), Union Mid. Ea. and Mediterranean Pediatric Socs. (exec. coun. 1979-85), Lawson Wilkins Pediatric Endocrine Soc., Endocrine Soc., Am. Assn. Clin. Endocrinologists, Am. diabetes Assn., Internat. Soc. Pediatric and Adolescent Diabetes. Office: WVa U Dept Pediatrics 830 Pennsylvania Ave Ste 104 Charleston WV 25302-3389

ZANNI, CHRISTINA MARIE, art educator; b. Mt. Clemens, Mich., July 3, 1951; d. Julian Victor and Marie Ann (De Grandis) Z. BS in Edn., Wayne State U., 1973, continuing cert., 1976, endorsement in Lang. Arts, 1977, MA in Edn., 1978. Cert. art tchr., secondary humanities tchr., secondary lang. arts tchr., elem. tchr., Mich. Art instr. Marlette (Mich.) Community Schs., 1973-75, Chippewa Valley Schs., Clinton Township, 1975—. Integrated arts con. Chippewa Valley Schs., Clinton Township, 1977-79, art curriculum coun., 1988—. Illustrator (cartoons-caricatures) Zany Kids, 1982; free lance illustrator, 1980—. Recipient Chippewa Valley We Make It Happen award, 1992-93; named Chippewa Valley Elem. Tchr. of Yr., 1998; Gov.'s scholar Wayne State U., 1970-73. Mem. Nat. Art Edn. Assn., Mich. Art Edn. Assn. Roman Catholic. Avocations: plays, musicals, baking, illustrating. Office: Chippewa Valley Schs 19120 Cass Ave Clinton Township MI 48038-2301

ZAPFFE, NINA BYROM, retired elementary education educator; b. Independence, Mo., Aug. 17, 1925; d. Richmond Douglas and Nina Belle (Howell) Byrom; m. Robert Glenn Fessler, June 25, 1946 (dec. June 1947); 1 child, Robert Glenn Fessler Zapffe; m. Fred Zapffe, July 1, 1952 (dec. Dec. 1999); children: Paul Douglas, Carl Raymond. BA, So. Meth. U., 1946. Fin. sec. Tyler St. Meth. Ch., Dallas, 1948-49; tchr. Dallas Ind. Sch. Dist., 1949-52, Norman (Okla.) Pub. Schs., 1966-74; cert. chief reader for GED Writing Skills Test Part II GED Testing Svc., Am. Coun. on Edn., Washington, 1990-98. Adv. com. (Acad. Resource Ctr.) Moore-Norman Tech. Ctr., 1988—. Adv. bd. Norman Salvation Army, 1978-90; organizer, historian Norman Salvation Army Womens Aux., 1983-2000; organizer, past pres. Norman Literacy Coun., 1976—; organizing com., past pres. Norman Interfaith Coun., 1974-93; organizing com., past treas. Friends of the Norman Libr., 1979—; mem. McFarlin Meml. United Meth. Ch., historian 2-in-1 Sunday Sch. class, 1990-2002, lay leader, 1980-81. Named Woman of Yr., Norman Bus. and Profl. Women, 1999; named to Literacy Hall of Fame, Pioneer Libr. Sys., Norman, 1995; recipient medal of appreciation, SAR, 2002. Mem. DAR (regent Black Beaver chpt. 1998-2000, state literacy chmn. 2000-02), Nat. Soc. Daus. 1812 (state treas. 1996-2000), Old Regime Study Club (pres. 1998-99), Coterie Club (pres. 1996, 2002), Delta Delta Delta Alumnae. Republican. Avocation: genealogy. Home: 2717 Walnut Rd Norman OK 73072-6940

ZAPHIRIOU, GEORGE ARISTOTLE, lawyer, educator; b. July 10, 1919; came to U.S., 1973, naturalized, 1977; s. Aristotle George and Callie Constantine (Economou) Z.; m. Peaches J. Griffin, June 1, 1973; children: Ari, Marie. JD, U. Athens, 1940; LLM, U. London, 1950. Bar: Supreme Ct. Greece 1946, Eng. 1956, Ill. 1975, Va. 1983. Gen. counsel Counties Ship Mgmt. and R & K Ltd., London, 1951-61; practicing barrister, lectr. City of London Poly., 1961-73; vis. prof. Ill. Inst. Tech.-Chgo. Kent Coll. Law, 1973-76; pvt. practice Northbrook, Ill., 1976-78; prof. law George Mason U. Sch. Law, 1978-94, prof. law emeritus, adj. prof., 1994—. Prof. internat. transactions George Mason U. Internat. Inst., 1992-94; mem. Odin, Feldman & Pittelman P.C., Fairfax, Va., 1994-96; mem. study group on internat. elec. commerce conv. and other pvt. internat. law convs. U.S. Dept. of State. Author: Transfer of Chattels in Private International Law, 1956, U.S. edit., 1981, European Business Law, 1970; co-author: Declining Jurisdiction in Private International Law, 1995; joint editor: Jour. Bus. Law, London, 1962-73; bd. dirs. and bd. editors Am. Jour. Comp. Law of Am. Soc. Comparative Law, 1980-94; contbr. articles to profl. jours. Mem.: ABA (sect. internat. law and practice and dispute resolution), George Mason Am. Inn of Ct. (founder, master, emeritus), Am. Arbitration Assn. (panel comml. arbitrators), Chgo. Bar Assn., Ill. Bar Assn. Home: 400 Green Pasture Dr Rockville MD 20852-4233 Fax: 301-984-1164. E-mail: gzaphiri@gmu.edu.

ZAPKE, CLIFFORD F. secondary education educator; b. N.Y.C., Dec. 28, 1946; s. Edward and Edith (Bellion) Z.; m. Sue Gebhart, Aug. 16, 1969; children: Heather, Allison. BA, U. Dubuque, 1969; MA, No. Ill. U., 1974. Cert. social studies and English tchr., adminstr., Ill. Tchr. social studies Machesney Park (Ill.) Schs., 1969—. Chief negotiator Harlem Fedn. Tchrs., Machesney Park, 1984-88; founder Ill. Future, Harlem Schs., Machesney Park, 1987-2003, gifted cons., 1984-89, VFW Dist. 6, Ill tchr. of the yr., 2003. Mem. blue print commn. Rockford (Ill.) Cmty., 1994. Recipient Holland and Knight Found. award Workshop on Holocaust, 2003; named Econs. Tchr. of Yr., Jr. Achievement, Rock River Valley, 1990. Mem. Nat. Coun. Scoial Studies, Ill. Coun. on Teaching Econs. Edn. (award for excellence in tchg. 1995, 97, 99, 2001, 02), Ill. Fedn. Tchrs., Machesney Park C. of C. (ednl. com. 1995). Avocations: investing, coaching, train collecting, antiques. Home: 3648 Doreen Dr Roscoe IL 61073-8918

ZAPPE, JOHN PAUL, city editor, educator, newspaper executive; b. N.Y.C., July 30, 1952; s. John Paul and Carolyn (Pikor) Z. JD, Syracuse (N.Y.) U., 1978. Reporter Poughkeepsie Jour., 1973-75, Nev. State Jour., Reno, 1979-80; prin. Am. Media Bold, Oakland, Calif., 1981-83; reporter Press-Telegram, Long Beach, Calif., 1983-88, city editor, 1988-97, webmaster PT Connect, 1995-97, mgr. new media, 1997-98; dir. new media Riverside (Calif.) Press-Enterprise, 1998-2000; v.p. new media L.A. Newspaper Group, Woodland Hills, Calif., 2000—03; prin. Zappe Media Svcs., 2003—; consulting gen. mgr. Mother Lode Internet, 2003—. Tchr. Syracuse U., 1976-78, Calif. State U., 1985-87, U. So. Calif., 2003—; adj. faculty U. So. Calif., 2003—; cons. Am. Media Bold, 1981-83. Chmn. Local 69 Newspaper Guild, Long Beach, 1984-87. Mem. Investigative Editors and Reporters, NAA New Media Fedn. E-mail: jzappe@charter.net.

ZARE, RICHARD NEIL, chemistry educator; b. Cleveland, Nov. 19, 1939; s. Milton and Dorothy (Amdur) Zare; m. Susan Leigh (Shively), Apr. 20, 1963; children: Bethany Jean, Bonnie Sue, Rachel Amdur. BA, Harvard U., 1961; post grad., U. Calif., Berkeley, 1961—63; PhD (hon.), Harvard U., 1964; DS (hon.), U. Ariz., 1990, Northwestern U., 1993, ETH, Zürich, 1993, Columbia U., 2000, State U. West Ga., 2001; DP (hon.), Uppsala U., Sweden, 2000; PhD U. York (hon.), 2001; PhD (hon.), Hunan U., 2002. Postdoctoral fellow Harvard U., 1964; rsch. assoc. Joint Inst. for Lab. Astrophysics, 1964—65; asst. prof., chemistry MIT, 1965—66; asst. prof., dept. physics and astrophysics U. Colo., 1966—68, assoc. prof. physics, astrophysics, chemistry, 1968—69; prof. chemistry Columbia U., 1969—77, Higgins prof. natural sci., 1975—77; prof. Stanford U., 1977—, Shell, disting. prof. chemistry, 1980—85, Marguerite Blake Wilbur prof., natural sci., 1987—, prof., physics, 1992—. Cons. Aeronomy Lab, NOAA, 1966—77; radio standards physics divsn. Nat. Bur. Std., 1968—77, Lawrence Livermore Lab., U. Calif., 1974—, SRI, Internat., 1974—, Los Alamos Sci. Lab., U. Calif., 1975—; fellow adj. Joint Inst. Lab. Astrophysics, U. Colo.; sci. adv. com. IBM, 1977—92; chmn. commn. on phys., scis., and math applications Nat. Rsch. Coun., 1992—95; chmn. bd. dir. Ann. Rev., Inc., 1995—. Contbr. articles to profl. jour.; editor: Chem. Physics Letters, 1982—85. Named Calif. Scientist of Yr., 1997; recipient Fresenius Award, Phi Lambda Upsilon, 1974, Michael Polanyi Medal, 1979, Nat. Medal Sci., 1983, Spectroscopy Soc. Pitts. Award, 1983, Michelson-Morley Award, Case Inst. Tech., Case We. Res. U., 1986, ISCO Award for significant contbn. to instrumentation for biochemical separations, 1990, Ea. Analytical Symposium Award, 1997, Exceptional Sci. Achievement Award, NASA, 1997, Space award Aviation Week and Space Tech., 1997, Disting. Svc. Award, Nat. Sci. Bd., 1998, Centennial Medal, Harvard U., The Welch Award, 1999, Faraday Medal, Royal Soc. Chemistry, 2001, Bing Fellowship Tchg. Award, 1996; fellow Non-resident fellow, Joint Inst. for Lab. Astrophysics, 1970—, Alfred P. Sloan fellow, 1967—69, Christensen fellow, St. Catherine's Coll. Oxford U., 1982, Stanford U., 1984—86. Fellow: AAAS, Inst. of Physics, Royal Soc. Chemistry (hon.), Calif. Acad. Sci. (hon.); mem.: NAS (coun. mem., Chem. Sci. Award 1991), Royal Soc. London, Chem. Soc. London, Am. Philos. Soc., Am. Chem. Soc. (Harrison Howe Award 1985, Remsen Award 1985, Kirkwood Award 1986, Willard Gibbs Medal 1990, Peter Debye Award in phys. chemistry 1991, Linus Pauling Medal 1993, Dannie-Heineman Prize 1993, The Harvey Prize 1993, Analytical Chemistry Divsn. Award in chem. instrumentation 1995, Analytical Chemistry Award 1998, G.M. Kosalapoff Award 1998, E. Bright Wilson award in spectroscopy 1999, Nobel Laureate Signature Award 2000, Charles Lathrop Parsons award 2001, Madison Marshall award 2001), Am. Phys. Soc. (Earle K. Plyler prize 1981, Irving Langmuir Prize 1985, Arthur L. Schawlow prize in laser sci. 2000), Am. Acad. Arts and Scis., Phi Beta Delta, Phi Beta Kappa. Achievements include research in laser chemistry and chem. physics. Office: Stanford U Dept Chemistry Stanford CA 94305-5080

ZARECKI, ANGELA ROSE, special education educator; b. Berlin, Wis., June 14, 1965; d. William Franklin and Doris Mae (Rollmann) Belfeuil; m. Kevin Lee Zarecki, June 13, 1992; children: Isaac Lee, Tate Elliot. BS in Edn., U. Wis., Oshkosh, 1987. Tchr. emotionally disturbed Chilton (Wis.) H.S., 1987-88; tchr. mentally retarded Chilton Elem. Sch., 1988-91; cognitive disabilities tchr. Abraham Lincoln Sch., Monroe, Wis., 1991-93; cognitive disabilities borderline tchr. Northside Sch., Monroe, 1993—98; tchr. emotionally disturbed Pardeeville, Wis., 1998—99; tchr. cognitively disabled John Muir Elem. Sch., Portage, Wis., 1999—. Tchr. young artists workshop St. Norbert Coll., DePere, Wis., summer 1987. Spl. Olympics coach CESA 7, Chilton, 1988-91, Green County Spl. Olympics, Monroe, 1991—. Fellow Coun. for Exceptional Children, Wis. Edn. Assn. Avocations: reading, crafts, family.

ZAREMBKA, PAUL, economics educator; b. St. Louis, Apr. 17, 1942; BS, Purdue U., 1964; MS, PhD, U. Wis., 1967. Asst. prof. U. Calif., Berkeley, 1967-72; vis. prof. Heidelberg (Fed. Republic Germany) U.,

1970-71, Gottingen (Fed. Republic Germany) U., 1972; assoc. prof. SUNY, Buffalo, 1973-76, prof., 1976—, dir. grad. studies dept. econs., 1995—99. Sr. rsch. officer Internat. Labor Office, Geneva, 1974-77; researcher Louis Pasteur U., Strasbourg, France, 1978-79; Fulbright-Hayes lectr. Coun. Internat. Exchange of Scholars, Poznan, Poland, 1979. Author: Toward a Theory of Economic Development, 1972; editor: Frontiers in Econometrics, 1974, Research in Political Economy, 1977—; co-editor: Essays in Modern Capital Theory, 1976; contbr. articles to profl. publs. Active Buffalo Ctr. chpt. exec. bd. United Univ. Professions, 1981—, pres., 1991-95, grievance officer acad., 1995-97; active AFL-CIO Buffalo Labor Coun., 1982-83, 96-97, Commn. on Quality Edn. in Buffalo for the 1990s, 1990-91; mem. subcom. on capital appropriations City of Buffalo, 1990-2000, citizens adv. com., 1997-2000; bd. dirs. United Parents, 1991-94; chair Labor Party, Buffalo, 1996. NSF grantee, 1969-72. Office: SUNY Dept Econs 415 Fronczak Hall Buffalo NY 14260-1520

ZARLE, THOMAS HERBERT, academic administrator; b. Akron, Ohio, Oct. 11, 1939; BS, Springfield Coll., 1963; MA, Ohio U., 1965; PhD, Mich. State U., 1970; MPH, Harvard U., 1978. V.p. instl. advancement Bentley Coll., Waltham, Mass., until 1988; pres. Aurora U., Ill., 1988—. Office: Aurora U Office of Pres 347 S Gladstone Ave Aurora IL 60506-4892

ZARR, MELVYN, lawyer, law educator; b. Worcester, Mass., Aug. 29, 1936; m. Gail Sclar, Aug. 29, 1971. AB, Clark U., 1958; LL.B., Harvard U., 1963. Bar: Mass. bar 1964, Maine bar 1973. Staff atty. NAACP Legal Def. & Edn. Fund, Inc., N.Y.C., 1963-69; co-dir. Mass. Law Reform Inst., Boston, 1970-73; prof. law U. Maine, 1973—; U.S. magistrate, Portland, Maine, 1977-82. Mem. Am. Law Inst. Home: 19 Mckinley Rd Falmouth ME 04105-1913 Office: U Maine Sch Law 246 Deering Ave Portland ME 04102-2837 Business E-Mail: mzarr@usm.maine.edu.

ZARRELLA, ARTHUR M. superintendent of schools; b. Providence, July 30, 1936; s. Joseph and Flora (Santoro) Z.; m. Ann Miletta, Aug. 19, 1960; children: Matthew, Mark, Chris, Paul. BS, U. R.I., 1960; D of Pedagogy (hon.), R.I. Coll., 1985. Cert. bus. edn., history, social studies, guidance and counseling, critic tchr., secondary sch. prin., secondary sch. asst. prin., supt. of schs. Tchr. bus. edn. Cranston H.S. West, 1961-62, Mt. Pleasant H.S., 1962-65, tchr. social studies, 1965-68; head social studies dept. Ctrl. H.S., 1968-70, head guidance dept., 1970-72, adminstr. student rels., 1972-76, prin., 1976-87, Classical H.S., 1987-88, acting asst. supt. for secondary edn., 1988-89, asst. supt. for secondary edn., 1989-90, asst. supt. secondary edn./dep., 1990—, acting supt. schs., 1991-92, supt. schs., 1992-99. Asst. coach track and field Mt. Pleasant H.S., 1961-64, head coach track and field, 1964-69; tchr. Brown U., 1970, Providence Coll., 1973-74, 74-75, 86—, advisor adminstrv. internship program, 1976-82; tchr. R.I. Coll., 1980, 82, 95—, social worker practicum supervision U. R.I., 1976-78; advisor adminstrv. internship program Harvard U., 1985-86; cons. Inst. for Ednl. Leadership, Inc., Hartford, 1985; instr. Solve Regina U., 1999—, dir. secondary edn. dept., 1999—; presenter in field, many others. Contbr. articles to profl. jours. Bd. dirs. Mt. Pleasant Little League, 1973-76, treas., 1973-75, pres., 1976; bd. dirs. West End Community Assn., 1976-89, Wiggins Village Tenants Assn., 1980—, Young Vols. of R.I., 1982-84, Urban Edn. Ctr., 1982—, R.I. Leadership Acad., 1983-85, Keep Providenc Beautiful, 1984-85, Providence Edn. Fund, 1985-88, West End Community Ctr., 1986-90, Todd Morsilli Fund, 1987—, chairperson, 1989-91; scholarship chairperson Italian Am. Sports Hall of Fame, 1988-89; others. With USNG, 1959-65. Recipient Delta Sigma Theta Sorority's Comty. Svc. award, 1986, Mayor's citation for comty. svc., 1989, R.I. Ho. of Reps. citation for comty. svc., 1989, Gov.'s citation for comty. svc., 1989, R.I. Senate citation for comty. svc., 1989, Youth Dirs. Assn. Comty. Svc. award, 1989, NAACP Edn. award, 1989, R.I. Ho. of Reps. citation for commitment to substance abuse programs, 1991, Mayor's Citizen citation, 1991, Roberto Clemente Citizen award, 1991, Excellence in Edn. award U. R.I. Alumni Assn., 1996; fellow Danforth Found., 1994—, Annemberg fellow, 1994—. Mem. Nat. Assn. Secondary Sch. Prins., R.I. Assn. Secondary Sch. Prins., R.I. Sch. Adminstrs. Assn., Barnard Club. Roman Catholic. Home: 468 Kingstown Rd Apt 7 South Kingstown RI 02879-3618

ZARTMAN, DAVID LESTER, animal sciences educator, researcher; b. Albuquerque, July 6, 1940; s. Lester Grant and Mary Elizabeth (Kitchel) Z.; m. Micheal Aline Plemmons, July 6, 1963; children: Kami Renee, Dalan Lee. BS, N.Mex. State U., 1962; MS, Ohio State U., 1966, PhD, 1968. Cert. dairy cattle specialist, Am. Registry Profl. Animal Scientists. Jr. ptnr. Marlea Guernsey Farm, Albuquerque, 1962-64; grad. rsch. assoc. Ohio State U., Columbus, 1964-68; asst. prof. dairy sci. N.Mex. State U., Las Cruces, 1968-71, assoc. prof., 1971-79, prof., 1979-84, Ohio State U., Columbus, 1984—. Chmn. dept. Ohio State U., Columbus, 1984-99; pres. Mary K. Zartman, Inc., Albuquerque, 1976-84; cons. Bio-Med. Electronics, Inc., San Diego, 1984-89, Zartemp, Inc., Northbrook, Ill., 1990, Recom Applied Solutions, 1993-2000, Am. Registry of Profl. Animal Scientists, 1996—. Contbr. articles to profl. jours.; patentee in field. Recipient State Regional Outstanding Young Farmer award Jaycees, 1963, Disting. Rsch. award N.Mex. State U. Coll. Agr. and Home Econs., 1983, Outstanding Svc. award Ohio Poultry Assn., 1999, Grazier of Yr. award Gt. Lakes Internat. Grazing Conf., 2001, hon. state degree Ohio FFA, 2000; course acclaimed by Humane Soc. of U.S.; named one of Top 100 Agr. Alumni, N.Mex. State U. Centennial, 1987; spl. postdoctoral fellow NIH, New Zealand, 1973; Fulbright-Hayes lectr., Malaysia, 1976. Fellow AAAS; mem. Am. Dairy Sci. Assn., Am. Soc. Animal Sci., Dairy Shrine Club, Ohio Farm Bur., Sigma Xi, Gamma Sigma Delta, Alpha Gamma Rho (1st Outstanding Alumnus N.Mex. chpt. 1985), Alpha Zeta, Phi Kappa Phi. Home: 7671 Deer Creek Dr Worthington OH 43085-1551 Office: Ohio State U 2027 Coffey Rd Columbus OH 43210-1043 E-mail: zartman.3@osu.edu.

ZARZOUR, ROBIN ANN, special education educator; b. Parma, Ohio, Apr. 14, 1964; d. Robert Halim and Rosalie Frances (Ezzie) Z. AAS in Early Childhood Edn., Cuyahoga C.C., 1985; BS in Spl. Edn., Cleve. State U., 1990, MA in Early Childhood Spl. Edn., 1993. Early childhood spl. edn. aide Middleburg Spl. Presch., Middleburg Heights, Ohio, 1983-86; counselor Camp Sunshine, Parma, Ohio, 1986-88; early childhood spl. religious tchr. St. Charles, Parma, Ohio, 1988-89; early childhood spl. edn. tchr. Parma City Sch. System, 1990—. Mem. Cleve. Assn. Mid. Ea. Orgn., 1992—; core mem. St. Charles Young Adult Group, 1999—. Recipient Tchr. of Yr. award Cuyahoga Spl. Edn. Svc. Ctr., 1993—. Mem. Coun. for Exception Children, Parma Edn. Assn. (union bldg. rep. 1992—). Democrat. Roman Catholic. Avocations: golf, working out, movies, music.

ZASLAVSKY, CLAUDIA, mathematics education consultant, author; b. N.Y.C., Jan. 12, 1917; d. Morris and Olga (Reisman) Cogan; m. Sam Zaslavsky, July 19, 1941; children: Thomas, Alan. BA, Hunter Coll., 1937; MA, U. Mich., 1938; postgrad., Columbia U., 1974-78. Cert. secondary math. tchr., N.Y. Cost acct. Block Drug Co., Jersey City, 1938-42; jr. engr. Remington Arms, Ilion, N.Y., 1942-43; music tchr. various music schs., N.Y.C., 1954-59; tchr. math., chair dept. New Rochelle (N.Y.) Acad., 1959-65; tchr. math. Woodlands H.S., Hartsdale, N.Y., 1965-77; adj. asst. prof. math. Coll. New Rochelle, 1979-81; math textbook cons. Macmillan/McGraw-Hill and other pub. cos., 1991-96; math. edn. cons. U. Alaska, Fairbanks, 1993—2000. Mem. task force on multiculturalism and gender Nat. Coun. Tchrs. Math., Reston, Va., 1993-94; condr. workshops and seminars on multicultural math., 1970—. Author: Africa Counts: Number and Pattern in African Culture, 1973, 99, Fear of Math, 1994, The Multicultural Math Classroom, 1996, 10 others; contbr. articles to profl. jours. and books. Trustee Davis-Putter Scholarship Fund, 1982-99; bd. dirs. Girls Inc. "Eureka" Program, N.Y., 1992-95; Educators for Social Responsibility, N.Y., 1984—; adv. bd. Educators Against Racism and Apartheid, N.Y., 1986-94. NSF grantee, 1960-70. Mem. Internat. Study Group on Ethnomath., Am. Fedn. Tchrs., Authors Guild, Nat. Coun. Tchrs. Math., Women's Internat. League for Peace and Freedom, Phi Beta Kappa. Avocations: playing violin, singing a capella, folk dancing.

ZASLAVSKY, ROBERT, secondary school educator; b. Phila., Feb. 26, 1942; s. Harry and Sally (Zwick) Z.; div.; 1 child, Cordelia Helena. AB in Philosophy, English Lit., Temple U., 1964; MA in Philosophy, New Sch. Social Rsch., 1969, PhD in Philosophy, 1978; postgrad., Cabrini Coll., 1989-91. Substitute tchr. math. and English Phila. Bd. Edn., 1964; caseworker Phila. Dept. Pub. Assistance, 1964-65, N.Y.C. Dept. Welfare, 1965-68; instr. philosophy Villanova U., 1971-73; instr. philosophy of art Immaculata Coll., 1975; libr. interlibr. loan and reference Bryn Mawr (Pa.) Coll., 1973-86; exec. producer, on-air performer, camera oper. Studio 9 Video Prodns., 1986—; adj. instr. English and religion, student tchr. adviser Cabrini Coll., 1990; instr. lit. Main Line Sch. Night, 1991-95; instr. humanities Akiba Hebrew Acad., Merion Station, Pa., 1990-96; instr. English Marine Mil. Acad., Harlingen, Tex., 1997-99; instr. Latin and English Fort Worth Ind. Sch. Dist., 1999—. Job counselor Kingston (N.Y.) Community Ctr., 1968; presenter seminars; guest lectr. Greek lit. Bryn Mawr Coll., 1976-78, Villanova U., 1978-81; assoc. Greater Phila. Philosophy Consortium, 1983-86; instr. Rittenhouse Acad., 1989, Haverford Twp. Adult Sch., 1989, Valley Forge Mil. Acad., 1989-90; instr. Elderhostel program Cabrini Coll., 1990, 91, Valley Forge Hist. Soc., 1991. Contbr. articles, revs. to lit. publs. Mem. ASCD, MLA, Nat. Coun. Tchrs. English, Core Knowledge Found., Acad. Am. Poets, Am Coun. Tchrs. Fgn. Langs., S.W. Conf. on Lang. Tchg., Tex. Fgn. Lang. Assn., Am. Classical League. Home: 6412 Wildwood Cir S Apt 815 Fort Worth TX 76132-5124 E-mail: RobertZ466@aol.com.

ZATLIN, PHYLLIS, Spanish language educator, translator; b. Green Bay, Wis., Dec. 31, 1938; d. Frank L. and Ellen Mary (Butler) Z.; m. George Boring Kelly, Aug. 20, 1962; children: William, Lee. BA, Rollins Coll., 1960; postgrad., U. Grenoble, France, 1960-61; MA, U. Fla., 1962, PhD, 1965. Cert. Spanish to English translator Am. Translators Assn. Instr. Rutgers U., New Brunswick, N.J., 1963-66, asst. prof., 1966-71, assoc. prof., 1971-79, assoc. dean, 1974-80, prof. Spanish, 1979—, chair dept. Spanish, grad. dir., 1980-87. Mem. discipline adv. com. Coun. Internat. Exch. Scholars', 1990—93; spkr. in field. Co-author: Lengua y Lectura: Un Repaso y Una Continuación, 1970; author: Elena Quiroga, 1977, Víctor Ruiz Iriarte, 1980, Jaime Salom, 1982, Cross Cultural-Approaches to Theatre: The Spanish-French Connection, 1994, The Novels and Plays of Eduardo Manet: An Adventure in Multiculturalism, 2000; editor: (Francisco Ayala) El Rapto, 1971, (Víctor Ruiz Iriarte) El Landó de Seis Caballos, 1979, (Jaime Salom) La Piel del Limón, 1980, (Antonio Gala) Noviembre y un Poco de Yerba. Petra Regalada, 1981, (Francisco Nieva) Combate de Opalos y Tasia. Sombra y Quimera de Larra. La Magosta, 1990, El teatro alternativo español, 2001; co-editor: The Contemporary Spanish Theater. A Collection of Critical Essays, 1988, Homenaje (A Tribute to Martha T. Halsey), 1995; co-editor: Entre Actos: Diálogos sobre teatro español, 1999, Un escenario propio (A Stage of Their Own), 1998; co-guest editor jour. Art Teatral. Cuadernos de Minipiezas Ilustradas, 1996; translator play edits.: (J.L. Alonso de Santos) Going Down to Marrakesh, 1992, Hostages in the Barrio, 1997, (Paloma Pedrero) Parting Gestures (The Color of August, A Night Divided, The Voucher, With Tonight in the Subway, 1999, (Jaime Salom) A Bonfire at Dawn, 1992, (Jean-Paul Daumas) The Elephant Graveyard, 1994, (Eduardo Manet) Lady Strass, 1992, 97, also performances; assoc. editor Estreno, 1992-2001, editor Estreno Plays, 1998—; mem. editl. bd. Western European Stages, Espana Contemporanea, others. State pres. Women's Equity Action League, N.J., 1971-72, nat. bd. dirs., Washington, 1973, 76-77. Fellow Fulbright Found., 1960-61, Woodrow Wilson Found., 1961-62; recipient Disting. Alumna award Rollins Coll., 1985, Profl. award Fgn. Lang. Educators of N.J., 1989, Outstanding Alumna award Romance Langs., U. Fla., 2003. Mem. AAUP (mem. nat. coun. 1987-90), MLA (mem. commn. on status of women 1978-81), Dramatists Guild, Soc. Gen. de Autores y Editores (Profl. award 1997). Democrat. Avocations: biking, jogging, travel. Home: 5 Timber Rd East Brunswick NJ 08816-2941 Office: Rutgers Univ 105 George St New Brunswick NJ 08901-1414 E-mail: pzatlin@spanport.rutgers.edu.

ZAWACKI, GAIL MARIE, religious studies educator, school principal; b. Bridgeport, Conn., Apr. 25, 1947; d. Raymond Walter and Marie Fausta (Homza) Z. B.A. in Psychology, Sacred Heart U., 1969. Tchr., Westport, Conn., 1969-74, San Marino, Calif., 1974-81; prin., San Marino, Calif., 1981-82, Montrose, Calif., 1982— . Mem. Nat. Cath. Ednl. Assn., Assn. Supervision and Curriculum Devel. Office: 2361 Del Mar Rd Montrose CA 91020-1403

ZAWADA, EDWARD THADDEUS, JR., physician, educator; b. Chgo., Oct. 3, 1947; s. Edward Thaddeus and Evelyn Mary (Kovarek) Z.; m. Nancy Ann Stephen, Mar. 26, 1977; children: Elizabeth, Nicholas, Victoria, Alexandra. BS summa cum laude, Loyola U., Chgo., 1969; MD summa cum laude, Loyola-Stritch Sch. Medicine, 1973. Diplomate Am. Bd. Internal Medicine, Am. Bd. Nephrology, Am. Bd. Nutrition, Am. Bd. Critical Care, Am. Bd. Geriatrics, Am. Bd. Clin. Pharm., Am. Bd. Forensic Examiners, Am. Bd. Forensic Medicine; specialist Hypertension, Am. Soc. Hypertension. Intern UCLA Hosp., 1973, resident, 1974-76; asst. prof. medicine UCLA, 1978-79, U. Utah, Salt Lake City, 1979-81; assoc. prof. medicine Med. Coll. Va., Richmond, 1981-83; assoc. prof. medicine, physiology & pharmacology U. S.D. Sch. Medicine, Sioux Falls, 1983-86, Freeman prof., chmn. dept. Internal Medicine, 1987—2002, prof. emeritus, 2002—, chief div. nephrology and hypertension, 1983-88, pres. univ. physician's practice plan, 1992—95; v.p. sci. affairs, dir. dialysis Avera Health Sys., 2002—. Chief renal sect. Salt Lake VA Med. Ctr., 1980-81; asst. chief med. service McGuire VA Med. Ctr., Richmond, 1981-83. Editor: Geriatric Nephrology and Urology, 1984; contbr. articles to profl. publs. Pres. Minnehaha div. Am. Heart Assn., 1984-87, pres. Dakota affiliate Am. Heart Assn., 1989-91. VA Hosp. System grantee, 1981-85, 85-88; Health and Human Svcs. grantee Pub. Health Scvs. Rsch. Adminstrn. Bureau Health Profl., 1993—. Fellow ACP, Am. Coll. Chest Physicians, Am. Coll. Nutrition, Am. Coll. Clin. Pharmacology, Internat. Coll. Angiology, Am. Coll. Angiology, Am. Coll. Clin. Pharmacology, Am. Coll. Forensic Examiners, Royal Soc. Medicine, Soc. for Vascular Medicine and Biology; mem. Internat. Soc. Nephrology, Am. Soc. Nephrology, Am. Soc. Pharmacology and Exptl. Therapeutics, Am. Physiol. Soc., Am. Inst. Nutrition, Am. Soc. Clin. Nutrition, Am. Geriatric Soc., Am. Soc. Transplant Physicians, Westward Ho Country Club. Democrat. Roman Catholic. Avocations: golf, tennis, skiing, cinema, music. Home: 2908 S Duchess Ave Sioux Falls SD 57103-4826 Office: North Ctrl Kidney Inst 911 E 20th St Ste 601 Sioux Falls SD 57105

ZAWADZKI, KATHERINE MARY, physical education educator, coach; b. Grosse Pointe, Mich., Nov. 9, 1964; d. John Thaddeus and Marilyn Theresa (Stevens) Z. BS in Biology, U. Houston-Clear Lake, 1987; MA in Exercise Physiology, U. Tex., 1991. Coord. children's summer sports sch. U. Tex., Austin, 1990—, aquatic specialist dept. kinesiology and health edn., 1991—. Personal coach, trainer, Austin, 1991—. Contbr. articles and abstract to profl. publs. Instr. Centex chpt. ARC, Austin, 1990—; vol. Planned Parenthood, Austin, 1992—. Mem. AAHPERD, Am. Coll. Sports Medicine, Tex. Alliance for Health, Phys. Edn., Recreation and Dance, Swim Instrs. Assn., Triathlon Fedn. U.S.A. Avocations: triathlons, gardening, her dog. Office: 1900 E Campus Dr Austin TX 78712-1105

ZAWICKI, JOSEPH LEO, science educator; b. Batavia, N.Y., Sept. 24, 1958; s. Leo Stanley Zawicki, Rita Zawicki; m. Ann Marie Hartley, July 27, 1984; children: Richard John, Erin Kathleen, Lee Joseph, Sean Michael. BA, Canisius Coll., 1980; MSEd, U. Rochester, 1989; PhD in Sci. Edn., SUNY, Buffalo, 2002. Cert. tchr. certificate N.Y. Lab technologist Strong Meml. Hosp., Rochester, NY, 1984—89; tchr., dept. chair Elba Ctrl. Sch., Elba, NY, 1989—2002; asst. prof. Buffalo State Coll., Buffalo, 2002—. Lectr. Buffalo State Coll., NY, 2001—02, U. Buffalo, 2002; item writer, cons. N.Y. State Edn. Dept., Albany, 1995—; physics mentor N.Y. State Mentor Network, Oneonta, 1996—; bd. dirs. N.Y. Sci. Edn. Leadership Assn. Developer Optic Bench Sci., 2001. Bd. dirs. Cornell Coop. Ext., Batavia, 1996—98; dir. religious edn. Our Lady of Fatima, Elba, 1999—. Recipient St. Joseph the Worker award, Diocese of Buffalo, 2001; grantee Environ. Empowerment, N.Y. State, 1998. Mem.: Nat. Assn. Rsch. in Sci. Tchg., N.Y. State Edn. Leadership Assn., Sci. Tchrs. Assn. N.Y., Am. Assn. Physics Tchrs., Am. Chem. Soc. Avocation: Avocations: reading, science education, youth programs. Home: PO Box 172 7 S Main St Elba NY 14058-0172 Office: Buffalo State Coll Sci 130 Dept Earth Scis and Sci Edn 1300 Elmwood Ave Buffalo NY 14222

ZAX, JEFFREY STEPHEN, economist, educator; b. Gulfport, Miss., Dec. 7, 1954; s. Melvin and Joanne Sylvia (Prives) Z.; m. Judith Eleanor Graham, July 31, 1988; children: Jacob M., Talya E. BA, Harvard U., 1976, PhD, 1984. Rsch. economist Nat. Bur. Econ. Rsch., 1983—91; asst. prof. econs. CUNY, 1984-89, assoc. prof., 1989-90, U. Colo., 1990—96, prof., 1996—. Author: Residential Location Theory and the Measurement of Segregation, 2003, The Evolution of Entrepreneurial Activity in Urban China, 1988-1995, 2000, Immigration, Race and Space, 1998, Latent Demand for Urban Housing in the People's Republic of China, 1997, When is a Move a Migration?, 1994, The Substitution Between Moves and Quits, 1991, Compensation for Commutes in Labor and Housing Markets, 1991, Race and Commutes, 1989, Reform City Councils and Municipal Employees, 1990, Election Methods, Black and Hispanic Council Membership, 1990, Initiatives and Government Expenditures, 1989, Quits and Race, 1989, Is There a Leviathan in Your Neighborhood?, 1989, Employment and Local Public Sector Unions, 1989, Fringe Benefits, Tax Exemptions and Implicit Subsidies, 1988, Wages, Nonwage Compensation and Municipal Unions, 1988, The Effects of Jurisdiction Types and Numbers on Local Public Finance, 1988; author: (with D.I. Rees) IQ, Academic Performance, Environment and Earnings, 2002; author: (with J. Lynch) The Rewards to Running: Prize Structure and Performance in Professional Road Racing, 2000; author: (with G.L. Yang) Gender-linked Income Differences in Transitional Urban China, 2000; author: (with H. Li) Economic Transition and Labor Supply in Urban China, 2000; author: (with J.F. Kain) Moving to the Suburbs: Do Relocating Companies Leave Their Black Employees Behind?, 1996; author: Commutes, Quits and Moves, 1991; author: (with M.S. Skidmore) Property Tax Rate Changes and the Rate of Development, 1994; author: (with C. Ichniowski) Right to Work Laws, Free Riders and Unionization in the Local Public Sector, 1991, Excludability and the Effects of Free Riders: Right-to-Work Laws and Local Public Sector Unionization, 1991, Bargaining Laws and Unionization in the Local Public Sector, 1990, Today's Associations, Tomorrow's Unions, 1990, The Effects of Public Sector Unions on Payroll, Employment and Municipal Budgets, 1988; author: (with R.B. Freeman and C. Ichniowski) Collective Organization in the Public Sector, 1988; contbr. articles to profl. jours. Mem. Am. Econ. Assn., Soc. Labor Economists, Chinese Economists Soc. Office: U Colo Dept Econs Boulder CO 80309-0256

ZAYAS-BAZAN, EDUARDO, foreign language educator; b. Camagüey, Cuba, Nov. 17, 1935; came to U.S., 1962, naturalized, 1969; s. Manuel Eduardo and Aida Modesta (Loret de Mola); children: Eduardo, Elena María. Dr. en Derecho, U. Nacional José Martí, 1958; MS, Kans. State Tchrs.' Coll., 1966. Social worker Cuban Refugee Asst. Program, 1962-64; Spanish tchr. Plattsmouth High Sch., 1964-65, Topeka West High Sch., 1965-66; Spanish instr. Appalachian State U., 1966-68; asst. prof. East Tenn. State U., Johnson City, 1968-73, assoc. prof., 1973-79, prof., 1979-99, chmn. fgn. lang. dept., 1973-93, prof. emeritus, 1999—. Author (with P. Ferreiro): Cómo dominar la redacción, 1989; author: (with G. Fernández de la Torriente) Cómo aumentar su vocabulario 3; author: Cómo escribir cartas eficaces, 1989; author: (with N.A. Humbach and José B. Fernández) Nuestro mundo, 1990; author: (with José Fernández) iArriba!, 1993, 1997, 2001; author: (with Carolyn M. Novak) No se equivoque con el inglés, 1993; author: El inglés que usted no sabe que sabe, Primera y Segunda Serie, 1993; author: (with Susan Bacon and Dulce García) Conexiones, 1999; author: (with Susan Bacon and Dulce García), 2002; editor (with Anthony G. Lozano): Del amor a la revolución, 1975; editor: (with L. Suárez) De aquí y de allá, 1980; editor: (with G. J. Fernández) Así somos, 1983; translator: Secret Report on Cuban Revolution, 1981. Pres. Sister Cities Internat., Johnson City, 1971-76. Recipient Disting. Faculty award E. Tenn. State U., 1978 Mem.: Cuban Cultural Heritage Assn. (bd. dirs. 2000—02, sec. 2003—), Nat. Assn. Cuban-Am. Educators (pres. 1991—93, chair bd. dirs. 1994—2002, pres. 2002—), Tenn. Fgn. Lang. Teaching Assn. (pres. 1980, Jacqueline Elliott award 1989), Am. Assn. Tchrs. Spanish and Portuguese (pres. 1985, assoc. editor Hispania 1994—98), Am. Coun. Tchrs. Fgn. Langs., Municipality of Camagüey in Exile (editor El Camagüeyano Libre 2002—, pres. 2000—02), Sigma Delta Pi (Premio Martel 1984). Home: 265 Grapetree Dr Apt 122 Key Biscayne FL 33149-2749

ZAYDON, JEMILLE ANN, English language and communications educator; b. Peckville, Pa., Feb. 21; d. Joseph and Catherine Ann (Hazzouri) Z. Student, Barry Coll. for Women; BS, Marywood U.; MS in Edn., Wilkes U.; doctoral candidate, Temple U. Tchr. St. Hugh Elem. Sch., Coconut Grove, Fla., Allapattah Elem. Sch., Miami, Columbus Elem. Sch., Westfield, N.J.; comm. instr. Keystone Job Corps, Drums, Pa.; vol. instr. Keystone Rehab. Ctr., Scranton, Pa.; curriculum cons. for mentally retarded Vienna; prof. English and reading Lackawanna Jr. Coll., Scranton, head dept. English, speech and reading, chmn. dept. arts, humanities and social studies; assoc. prof. Marywood U., Wilkes U. Adj. prof. English U. Scranton; comm. instr. Lackawanna County Vocat. Tech. Sch. Editor Lebanese Am. Jour. Supr. recreation program, Hazleton, Pa., summer; founder, adviser Keystone Kourier; sec. Fedn. Youth, William W. Scranton; coord. annual Christmas for Mentally Retarded Keystone City Residence, Scranton; supr. students Heart Fund campaign; developer program mentally retarded Allied Svcs. for Handicapped Scranton; Class rep. Marywood Univ. Fund Dr.; gen.; faculty coord. Am. Cancer Soc.; active ARC, March of Dimes, Heart Fund, Leukemia and United Fund drives, also Sickle Cell Anemia Found.; bd. dirs. Michael F. Harrity Meml. Fund.; mem. exec. bd. Northeastern Pa. Environ. Coun., also co-chmn. pub. edn. and funding. Recipient Faculty Mem. of Yr. award, Keystone Job Corps, Humantarian award, Outstanding Educators award, 1992, Educators award Dade County; named Tchr. of Yr., Tchr. We Will Never Forget, Dade County Allpattah Elem. Students, 1991, N.E. Woman by Scranton Sunday Times, 1993; Svc. scholar Barry Coll. Mem. NEA, Pa. State Edn. Assn., Beta Lambda Tau, Sigma Tau Delta, Theta Chi Beta (charter pres.), Lambda Iota Tau (life). Democrat. Roman Catholic (instr. Confraternity Christian Doctrine). Home: 608 N Main Ave Scranton PA 18504-1870

ZBAR, LLOYD IRWIN STANLEY, otolaryngologist, educator; b. Jersey City, June 2, 1939; m. Margo Wally, Mar. 25, 1965; children: Ross I.S., Brett I.W. MD, Queen's U., Kingston, Ont., Can., 1964. Cert. in otolaryngology. Intern Beth Israel/Harvard, Boston, 1964; resident in surgery French Hosp., N.Y.C., 1965-66; resident in otolaryngology Bellevue Hosp. Ctr.-NYU, N.Y.C., 1966-69, fellow in otolaryngology, 1969-70; chmn. med. edn. com. Mountainside Hosp., Montclair, N.J., 1979-89, dir. otolaryngology, 1990-97, 99—. Sec. med. bd. Mountainside Hosp., Glen Ridge, N.J., 1986-90, clin. assoc. prof. otolaryngology NYU Sch. Medicine. Contbr. rev. to New Eng. Jour. Medicine, 1988. Mem. exec. bd. Boy Scouts of Am., Essex County, N.J., 1984-95; pres. Mountainside Physicians Scholarship Loan Fund, 1972-85. Fellow ACS, Am. Acad. Otolaryngology-Head and Neck Surgery, Royal Soc. Medicine. Office: 200 Highland Ave Glen Ridge NJ 07028-1528 Fax: 973-743-3111. E-mail: liszmd@yahoo.com.

ZBIEGIEN, M. ANDREA, chaplain, religious education educator, consultant, educational administrator; b. Berea, Ohio, May 12, 1944; d. Leopold and Anna Meri (Voskovich) Z. BS in Edn., St. John Coll., 1969, MS in Edn., 1973; MDiv, Grad. Theol. Union, 1986, D of Ministry, 1988. Tchr. jr. h.s. Diocese of Cleve., 1964-76, instr. dept. religious edn., 1971-82, dir. religious edn., 1976-82; diocesan dir. religious edn. Diocese of Toledo, 1982-87; instr. Dept. Christian Formation Diocese of Savannah, Ga., 1987—2001; dir. religious edn. Diocese of Savannah, 1987—2001; bus. builder/asst. supr. Shaklee Corp., 1978—. Substitute tchr., Cleve., also Brunswick, Ga., 1976-2001; cons. Benziger Pub. co., Ohio, 1971-78, Our Sunday Visitor Pubs., 1978-90, Silver Burdett Ginn, St. Augustine Diocese, 1988—; adj. prof. St. John U., Collegeville, Minn., Grad. Theol. Union, San Anselmo, Calif., summers 1978—. Author: RCIA: Parish Team Formation, 1987, Poetic Prayers, 2003; producer, author: (videos) RCIA: Parish Team Formation, 1987; contbr. articles to profl. jours. Facilitator Bishop's Task Force Action for a Change, Cleve., 1969-72; adv., facilitator Systematic Techniques of Effective Parenting, 1982—; mem. Bishop's Commn. on Worship, Diocese of Savannah; 1999-2001; vol. Med. Assistance for World's Poor; tour host Ednl. Opportunities. Recipient scholarship KC, Cleve., 1961-69. Mem. AAUW, Nat. Assn. Pastoral Coords. and Dirs., Sisters for Christian Cmty., Ind. Order Foresters, Shaklee Bus. Builder. Avocations: fiberarts, creative writing, photography, and sketching. Home: 11557 Tyndel Creek LN Jacksonville FL 32223-8706 E-mail: azbiegi86@earthlink.net.

ZDANIS, RICHARD ALBERT, academic administrator; b. Balt., July 15, 1935; s. Albert Francis and Elsie (Kral) Z.; m. Barbara Rosenberger, June 5, 1955; children: Michael Richard, Carole Lynn. BA, Johns Hopkins U., 1957, PhD in Physics, 1960. Rsch. assoc. Princeton (N.J.) U., 1960-61, instr., 1961-62; asst. prof., then assoc. prof. Johns Hopkins U., Balt., 1962-69, prof., 1969-88, assoc. provost, 1975-79, v.p. for adminstrv. svcs., 1977-79, vice provost, 1979-88; provost Case Western Res. U., Cleve., 1988-2000, retired, 2000. Cons. Naval Ordnance Lab., 1967-68, 69-74. Bd. dirs. Great Lakes Mus., 1990—, Cleve. Edn. Found., 1990-96; mem. governing coun. Ohio LINK, 1994-2000; mem. Cleve. Initiative for Edn., 1999—. Mem.: Associated Univs. Inc. (bd. dirs.), Am. Phys. Soc.

ZEHNER, CONSTANCE WENDELL, gifted and talented, science education educator; b. Port Arthur, Tex., Oct. 22, 1953; d. Robert Edward and Catherine (Baldwin) Wendell; m. James L. Lord Jr., July 14, 1976 (div. July 1982); m. Warren Bacon, Aug. 18, 1984. BS, Corpus Christi State U., 1982, MS, 1984. Cert. tchr., Tex. Dir. Westminster Weekday Schs., Houston, 1984-85; tchr. Alief Ind. Sch. Dist., Houston, 1985-88, sci. specialist, 1989-91; tchr. Garland (Tex.) Ind. Sch. Dist., 1988-89; coord. vol. svcs. Tex. Water Commn., Houston, 1991—. Cons. Alief Ind. Sch. Dist., 1991—; mem. steering com. Brazos River Authority, Waco, Tex., 1992, Galveston Bay Nat. Estuary Program Monitoring, 1992—, Galveston Bay Found. Monitoring, 1992—; mem. employee devel. seminar com. Tex. Water Commn. Field Ops., 1992—; mem. Chem. Literacy Consortium, Houston, 1992. Author: (tng. manual) Texas Watch, 1992, (trainer's manual) Texas Watch, 1993. Counselor Harvest of Hope, Soc. St. Andrews, Houston, 1988-90, coord., 1991. Mem. Tex. Outdoor Educators Assn., Sci. Tchrs. Assn. Tex., Tex. Marine Educators Assn., Delta Kappa Gamma (v.p. 1992-94), Phi Delta Kappa. Avocations: singing, home decorating, floral arrangement, wildlife rehabilitation.

ZEHNER, JEANNE MADELYN, school system administrator; b. NYC; d. Humphrey and Sadye (Scelfo) Rella; m. Harold V. Zehner (dec.), Sept. 11, 1938; children: Harold V., Jr. (dec.), Geraldine P. McElroy. BA, Fordham U., 1971, MS, 1973; Montessori Cert., New Rochelle (N.Y.) Coll., 1976. Tchr., N.Y. Model, sect. mgr. R.H. Macy & Co., N.Y.C., 1934-40; mgr. Plymouth Shops, N.Y.C., 1940-71; tchr. Archdiocese N.Y., N.Y.C., 1971-88, Bd. Edn., N.Y.C., 1988—. Vol. Providence Rest Home for the Aged, N.Y., Our Lady of Charity, N.Y.C., 1974—. Presdl. scholar, 1969-70; named Tchr. of Yr N.Y. State, 1984. Mem. Manor Club, Rosary Altar Soc., Delta Kappa, Lambda Xi. Avocations: mentoring, antiques, travel. Home: 536 Highbrook Ave Pelham NY 10803-2252

ZEHR, AMY JO WURCH, elementary education educator; b. Webster City, Iowa, Feb. 16, 1967; d. John William and Vivian Allene (Hassebrock) W. BS, U. Iowa, 1989. Tchr. 4th grade East Union Cmty. Sch., Afton, Iowa, 1989-92; tchr. 3d grade Boone (Iowa) Cmty. Sch., 1992—. Conflict mgmt. trainer Boone Cmty. Sch. Dist., 1994—, cons., at-risk com., 1990—, mem. vol. adv. bd., 1993—. Co-author: Math Alternative Assessments, 1994, Language Arts Alternative Assignments, 1994; editor: (video) It's A Wonderful World, 1993-94. Active PTA, Boone, 1989—; tchr. Bible Sch., St. Paul's Luth. Ch., Webster City, 1985, 86; supr. Univ. Parents Care Collective, Iowa City, 1987-88. Cessna scholar, 1985; Teresa Sterns scholar, 1985. Mem. NEA, Iowa State Edn. Assn., Boone Edn. Assn. (assessment team 1994-95), Chi Omega. Avocations: reading, refinishing, water skiing, organ, dance. Home: 1703 130th St Boone IA 50036-7315 Office: Boone Schs Franklin Elem Sch 19th and Crawford Boone IA 50036

ZEIGLER, ROBERT G. physical education educator emeritus; b. Harrisburg, Pa., Oct. 4, 1931; s. Guy Wilson and Hazel (Groce) Z.; m. Lenore Virginia Duncan, Sept. 5, 1953; children: Daniel, Ronald, Kenneth, Robert. BS, West Chester State Coll., 1958; MS, Pa. State U., 1960, EdD, 1970. Tchr. S. York County Sch. Dist., Glen Rock, Pa., 1959-60; asst. prof. Bloomsburg (Pa.) State Coll., 1960-63; camp dir. Cen. Pa. Synod Luth. Ch. Am., Harrisburg, 1963-64; advisor Pa. State Dept. Edn., Harrisburg, 1964-71; prof. Towson (Md.) State U., 1971-95. Chmn. Md. Sr. Olympic Commn., Towson, 1980-2002, chmn. emeritus, 2002—. Named to Hall of Fame, Md. Commn. on Phys. Fitness, Md. Sr. Citizen Hall of Fame, 1996; recipient Honor award Pa. Assn. Health, Phys. Edn., Recreation and Dance, Silver Eagle award Pres. Coun. on Phys. Fitness and Sport, 1995. Mem. AAHPERD (Outstanding Profl. award in phys. edn. 1993), Md. Assn. Health, Phys. Edn., Recreation and Dance (exec. dir. 1987-97, Burdick award 1982, presdl. citation 1984, R. Tait McKenzie award 1992). Avocations: painting, woodworking.

ZEILINGER, ELNA RAE, elementary educator, gifted-talented education educator; b. Tempe, Ariz., Mar. 24, 1937; d. Clayborn Eddie and Ruby Elna (Laird) Simpson; m. Philip Thomas Zeilinger, June 13, 1970; children: Shari, Chris. BA in Edn., Ariz. State U., 1958, MA in Edn., 1966, EdS, 1980. Bookkeeper First Nat. Bank of Tempe, 1955-56; with registrar's office Ariz. State U., 1956-58; piano tchr., recreation dir. City of Tempe; tchr. Thew Sch., Tempe, 1958-61; elem. tchr. Mitchell Sch., Tempe, 1962-74, intern prin., 1976, personnel intern, 1977; specialist gifted edn. Tempe Elem. Schs., Tempe, 1977-86; elem. tchr. Holdeman Sch., Tempe, 1986-89; tchr. grades 1-12 and adult reading, lang. arts, English Zeilinger Tutoring Svc., 1991—. Grad. asst. ednl. adminstrn., Iota Workshop coordinator Ariz. State U., 1978; presenter Ariz. Gifted Conf., 1978-81; condr. survey of gifted programs, 1980; reporter pub. rels. Tempe Sch. Dist., 1978-80, Access com. for gifted programs, 1981-83. Author: Leadership Role of the Principal in Gifted Programs: A Handbook, 1980; Classified Personnel Handbook, 1977, also reports, monographs and paintings. Active Tempe Hist. Assn., liaison, 1975, Tempe Art League; freedom train com. Ariz. Bicentennial Commn., 1975-76; bd. dirs. Maple Property Owners Assn., 1994-2002; storyteller Tempe Hist. Mus., 1997—; dir. pagentry Daus. of the Nile, 2002-03. Named Outstanding Leader in Elem. and Secondary Schs., 1976' Ariz. Cattle Growers scholar, 1954-55; Elks scholar, 1954-55; recipient Judges award Tempe Art League, 1970, Best of Show, Scottsdale Art League, 1976. Mem.: Daus. of the Nile (dir. pageantry 2002—03). Democrat. Congregationalist.

ZEITLIN, EUGENIA PAWLIK, librarian, educator, writer; b. N.Y.C., Jan. 29; d. Charles and Pauline (Klimowski) Pawlik; m. Herbert Zakary Zeitlin, July 3, 1949; children: Mark Clyde, Joyce Therese Zeitlin Harris, Ann Victoria, Clare Katherine. BA in English, Bklyn. Coll., 1945; MA in English, NYU, N.Y.C., 1951; MALS, Rosary Coll., 1968. Teaching credential N.Y., Ariz., Calif., Ill. English tchr., Sea Cliff, L.I., NY, 1945—47; English, math. tchr. Merrick (N.Y.) Sch. Dist., 1948—49; English tchr. Wilson Sch. Dist., Phoenix, 1949—50; counselor West Phoenix (Ariz.) High Sch., 1953—56; asst. prof. English Wright Coll., Chgo., 1965—66; asst. prof. English, asst. to v.p. curriculum and instrn. Oakton C.C., Des Plaines, Ill., 1970—76; libr. Pasadena City Coll., L.A., 1979—84, L.A. Pub. Libr., 1984—. Contbr. articles to profl. jours. Named Northridge City Employee of Yr., 1986. Mem. AAUW (br. pres. Lancaster, Calif. 1959-60), Thoreau Soc. (life), Beta Phi Mu. Avocations: freelance writing and editing, book collecting. Home: 20124 Phaeton Dr Woodland Hills CA 91364-5633

ZELBY, LEON WOLF, electrical engineering educator, consulting engineer; b. Sosnowiec, Poland, Mar. 26, 1925; came to U.S., 1946, naturalized, 1951; s. Herszel and Helen (Wajnryb) Zylberberg; m. Rachel Kupfermintz, Dec. 28, 1954; children: Laurie Susan, Andrew Stephen. BSEE, Moore Sch. Elec. Engring., 1956; MS, Calif. Inst. Tech., 1957; PhD, U. Pa., 1961. Registered profl. engr., Pa., Okla. Mem. staff RCA, Hughes R & D Labs., Lincoln Lab., MIT, Sandia Corp., Argonne (Ill.) Nat. Labs., Inst. for Energy Analysis; mem. faculty U. Pa., 1959-67, assoc. prof., 1964-67; assoc. dir. plasma engring. Inst. Direct Energy Conversion, 1962-67; prof. U. Okla., Norman, 1967-95, dir. Sch. Elec. Engring., 1967-71; ret., 1995. Cons. RCA, 1961-67, Moore Sch. Elec. Engring., 1967-68, also pvt. firms. Editor Tech. and Soc. mag., 1990-93; contbr. articles on energy-associated problems and issues to profl. jours. With AUS, 1946-47. Cons. Electrodynamic Corp. fellow Calif. Inst. Tech., 1957, Mpls.-Honeywell fellow U. Pa., 1957-58, Harrison fellow, 1958. Mem. IEEE, Franklin Inst., Sigma Xi, Tau Beta Pi, Eta Kappa Nu, Pi Mu Epsilon, Sigma Tau, Phi Kappa Phi. Home: 1009 Whispering Pines Dr Norman OK 73072-6912

ZELDIS, JEROME BERNARD, medical foundation executive, educator, physician; b. Waterbury, Conn., Apr. 6, 1950; s. Milton Zeldis and Norma M. (Gratz) Berger; m. Sharon W. Stamm, May 28, 1978; children: Cara, Micah, Sydney. AB, MS, Brown U., 1972; MPhil, Yale U., 1977, MD, PhD, 1978. Diplomate Am. Bd. Internal Medicine, Am. Bd. Gastroenterology, Nat. Bd. Med. Examiners. Intern in internal medicine UCLA Med. Ctr., L.A., 1978-79, jr. asst. resident in internal medicine, 1979-80, resident in internal medicine, 1980-81; rsch. fellow med. scientist tng. program Yale U., New Haven, 1972-78; rsch. fellow in medicine Harvard Med. Sch., Boston, 1981-84; clin. and rsch. fellow in-medicine Mass. Gen. Hosp., Boston, 1981-84; from instr. medicine to asst. prof. medicine Harvard Med. Sch., 1984-88; from asst. prof. medicine to assoc. prof. medicine U. Calif., Davis, 1988-95; clin. asst. prof. medicine Cornell U. Med. Sch., 1995, clin. assoc. prof. medicine, 1996—; from asst. physician to assoc. physican Beth Israel Hosp., Boston, 1984-88; asst. attending physician N.Y. Hosp., N.Y.C., 1995-96, assoc. attending physician, 1996—; chief med. officer, v.p. med. affairs Celgene Corp., 1997—. Clin. rsch. physician Sacramento Med. Found. Ctr. for Blood Rsch., 1990—; consulting physician Spaulding Rehab. Hosp., Boston, 1982, Sacramento VA Clinic, 1993-94; clin. asst. in medicine Mass. Gen. Hosp., Boston, 1984; assoc. dir. clin. R&D, med. expert in gastroenterology Sandoz Rsch. Inst., East Hanover, N.J., 1994-95; dir. med. devel. Janssen Rsch. Inst., Titusville, N.J., 1995-97; keynote spkr. Korean Soc. for Hematology, Seoul, 1990; vis. prof. Hunan Med. U., Changsha, China, 1990, others. Mem. editl. bd.: Jour. of History of Medicine and Allied Scis., 1973-74, Yale Jour. Biology and Medicine, 1974-78, Hepatology, 1993—; assoc. editor: Hepatitis Knowledge Base, New Eng. Jour. Medicine, 1993—; contbr. numerous articles, abstracts and reports to med. jours., chpts. to books. Recipient Barry Rosen Meml. award, 1972, Fulton award, 1972, Mosby award for scholastic achievement, 1978, Am. Liver Found. Postdoctoral Tng. award, 1983, Pfizer Postdoctoral Rsch. Fellowship award, 1984-87, AGA Travel award, 1986, Hans Popper Faculty Scholar award Am. Liver Found., 1986. Fellow ACP; mem. AAAS, Am. Assn. Immunologists, Am. Gastroenterol. Assn. (trainee mem.), Am. Assn. for Study of Liver Disease, European Assn. for Study of Liver Disease (corr. mem.), Am. Soc. for Gastrointestinal Endoscopy, Am. Fedn. for Clin. Rsch., Western Soc. Clin. Investigation, Phi Beta Kappa, Sigma Xi. Achievements include patent for assay to detect presence of live virus in vitro; research in molecular biology of viral hepatitis; immunology of viral hepatitis; etiology of hepatocellular carcinoma, GI motility disorders. Office: Celgene Corp 7 Powderhorn Dr Ste 1 Warren NJ 07059-5190

ZELINSKI, JOSEPH JOHN, engineering educator, consultant; b. Glen Lyon, Pa., Dec. 30, 1922; s. John Joseph and Lottie Mary (Oshinski) Z.; m. Mildred G. Sirois, July 22, 1946; children: Douglas John, Peter David. BS, Pa. State U., 1944, PhD, 1950. Grad. fellow Pa. State U., University Park, 1946-50; project supr. applied physics lab. Johns Hopkins U., Silver Spring, Md., 1950-58; staff scientist Space Tech. Labs. (now TRW, Inc.), Redondo Beach, Calif., 1958-60; head chem. tech. div. Ops. Evaluation Group MIT, Cambridge, 1960-62; prin. rsch. scientist Avco Everett (Mass.) Rsch. Lab., 1962-64; prof. mech. engring. Northeastern U., Boston, 1964-85, prof. emeritus, 1985—; pres. World Edn. Resources, Ltd., Tampa, Fla., 1984—. Cons. Avco Everett Rsch. Lab., 1964-71, Pratt & Whitney Aircraft, East Hartford, Conn., 1966-70, Modern Electric Products and Phys. Scis. Co., Inc., Boston, 1980-82, Morrison, Mahoney and Miller, Boston, 1984; vice-chmn., chmn. exec. com. Univ. Grad. Coun., Northeastern U., Boston, 1980-84, dir. mech. engring. grad. program, 1982-85; del. 4th World Conf. Continuing Engring. Edn., Beijing China People to People, Spokane, Wash., 1989. Contbr. articles to profl. jours. Prin. Confraternity Christian Doctrine, Andover, Mass., 1961-64; pres. Andover Edn. Coun., 1962-64; vice chmn. Dem. Town Com., Boxford, Mass., 1980-84. Lt. (j.g.) USNR, 1943-46, PTO. Mem. AAAS, ASME, Am. Chem. Soc., N.Y. Acad. Scis., Combustion Inst. Democrat. Roman Catholic. Achievements include U.S. and foreign patents for coal combustion system for magnetohydrodynamic power generation, for fuel-cooled combustion systems for jet engines flying at high Mach numbers; prediction of optical observables of re-entry vehicles from analysis of decomposition mechanisms of heat-shield materials; invention of high-temperature furnace for production of crystalline graphite; development and verification of a design method for ramjet combustors.

ZELINSKY, DANIEL, mathematics educator; b. Chgo., Nov. 22, 1922; s. Isaac and Ann (Ruttenberg) Z.; m. Zelda Oser, Sept. 23, 1945; children: Mara Sachs, Paul O., David. BS, U. Chgo., 1941, MS, 1943, PhD, 1946. Rsch. mathematician applied math group Columbia U., N.Y.C., 1944-45; instr. U. Chgo., 1943-44, 46-47; Nat. Rsch. Coun. fellow Inst. Advanced Study, Princeton, N.J., 1947-49; from asst. to assoc. prof. dept. math. Northwestern U., Evanston, Ill., 1949-60, prof., 1960-93, prof. emeritus, 1993—, acting chmn. math. dept., 1959-60, chmn., 1975-78. Vis. prof. U. Calif. Berkeley, 1960, Fla. State U., Tallahassee, 1963, Hebrew U., Jerusalem, 1970-71, 85, others; vis. scholar Tata Inst., 1979; mem. various coms. Northwestern U.; lectr. in field. Author: A First Course in Linear Algebra, 1968, rev. edit., 1973; contbr. articles to profl. jours. Fulbright grantee Kyoto U., 1955-56, grantee NSF, 1958-80; Guggenheim fellow Inst. Advanced Study, 1956-57, Indo-Am. fellow, 1978-79. Fellow AAAS (mem. nominating com. sect. A 1977-80, chmn. elect sect. A 1984-85, chmn. 1985-86, retiring chmn. 1986-87), Am. Math. Soc. (mem. coun. 1961-67, editor Transactions of A.M.S. 1961-67, mem. various coms., mem. editorial bd. Notices of A.M.S. 1983-86, chmn. editorial bds. com. 1989, chmn. ad hoc com. 1991-92). Jewish. Home: 613 Hunter Rd Wilmette IL 60091-2213 Office: Northwestern U Dept Math Evanston IL 60208-0001 E-mail: d.zelinsky@comcast.net.

ZELL, BLOSSOM ANN, educator; b. McKeesport, Pa., Jan. 13, 1957; d. Aron and Janet Adele (Fenster) Zell; m. Means Johnston III, June 26, 1980 (div. Nov. 1992); children: Holden Joseph, Evan Michael. BS, U. Md., 1979; MEd, Am. U., 1981. Cert. elem. tchr., mid. sch., spl. edn. Group leader Community Psychiat. Clinic, Bethesda, Md., summers 1983-85; regular educator Montgomery County Pub. Schs., Rockville, Md., 1979-80, spl. edn. tchr. emotionally disturbed elem., 1981—96; spl. edn. tchr. learning disabilities Ctrl. York Sch. Dist., York, Pa., 1996—. Fellow Orthopsychiat. Assn.; mem. ASCD, Coun. for Exceptional Children (divsn. learning disabilities), Coun. for Children with Behavioral Disorders. Home: 12 Hunting Park Ct York PA 17402-3614 Office: Ctrl York Sch Dist 775 Marion Rd York PA 17402 E-mail: bzell@suscom.net.

ZELLER, FRANCIS JOSEPH, dean; b. Chgo., July 31, 1943; s. Charles Joseph and Erma J. (Kile) Z.; m. Frances Joan McGrath, Aug. 3, 1968; children: Patrick, Brian. BA in English, Lewis U., 1967; MA in Edn. Adminstrn., No. Ill. U., 1970, EdD in Edn. Adminstrn., 1983. Chmn. Robert Frost Jr. High Sch., Schaumburg, Ill., 1967-69; asst. bus. mgr. Park Ridge (Ill.) Elem. Sch., 1970-71; bus. mgr. Barrington (Ill.) High Sch., 1971-73; dean bus. svcs. Illinois Valley Community Coll., Oglesby, Ill., 1973-2000; v.p. Guenther Bradford & Co. Ednl. Cons., 2000—. Contbr. articles to profl. jours. Mem. adv. com. state Univ. Retirement System, Champaign, Ill., 1983-90. Named Outstanding Life Rotarian La Salle (Ill.) Rotary Club, 1976. Mem. NEA, Ill. C.C. Chief Fin. Officers (bd. dirs. 1984-87, chair 1993-95), Ill. Assn. Sch. Bus. Ofcls. (past pres., life mem. 1972—). Internat. Assn. Sch. Bus. Ofcls. (chair comm. col. com.), Ottawa C. of C., Golden Triangle Club, Art Inst. Chgo., Delta Sigma Pi. Avocations: tennis, cross-country skiing, bicycling. E-mail: Zeller@The Ramp.net. Office: Ill Valley Cmty Coll 815 N Orlando Smith St Oglesby IL 61348-9692

ZELLER, MICHAEL EDWARD, physicist, educator; b. San Francisco, Oct. 8, 1939; s. Edward Michael and Marie (Eschen) Z.; m. Linda Marie Smith, June 12, 1960; children: Jeffrey, Daniel. BS, Stanford U., 1961; MS, UCLA, 1964, PhD, 1968. Research assoc. UCLA, 1968-69; instr. physics Yale U., New Haven, 1969-70, asst. prof., 1970-76, assoc. prof., 1976-82, prof., 1982—, chmn., 1989-95, Henry Ford II prof., 1996—. Recipient DeVane medal Phi Beta Kappa, 1980 Fellow Am. Phys. Soc.; mem. N.Y. Acad. Sci., Sigma Xi, Sigma Pi Sigma Democrat. Jewish. Home: 135 Newton Rd Woodbridge CT 06525-1534 Office: Yale U Physics Dept 260 Whitney Ave New Haven CT 06511-8903

ZELLER, MICHAEL FRANK, science educator; b. Des Moines, Feb. 4, 1953; s. Richard Frank and Alice (Leslie) Z.; m. Linda Stoos, May 29, 1976; 1 child, Anne Marie. BA, Westmar Coll., 1975; MS in Edn., Iowa State U., 1992. Cert. sci. tchr., Iowa. Sci. tchr. Dumont (Iowa) Community Schs., 1976-77; tchr. sci. and phys. edn. Woodward-Granger Community Sch., Woodward, Iowa, 1977—. Apptd. Governing Bd. Iowa Coalition for Math and Sci., 1994—. Mem. AAAS, ASCD, NEA, Nat. Sci. Tchrs. Assn. (student programs com. 1994-95), Nat. Assn. Biology Tchrs., Iowa Acad. Sci. (Iowa Tchrs. sect., Excellence Sci. Tchg. award 1993), Iowa Alliance for Sci. Com., Iowa State Edn. Assn., Woodward-Granger Edn. Assn. (biotechnology edn. program adv. com.). Avocations: hunting, fishing, outdoor activities. Office: Woodward-Granger Sch 306 W 3rd St Woodward IA 50276-1000 Address: 120 1/2 S Water St Apt 3 Madrid IA 50156-1157

ZELLER, MICHAEL JAMES, psychologist, educator; b. Des Moines, Dec. 3, 1939; s. George and Lila (Fitch) Zeller. BS, Iowa State U., 1962, MS, 1967. Instr. psychology Minn. State U., Mankato, 1967-73, asst. prof., 1974-89, assoc. prof., 1990-2001, prof. emeritus, 2001—. Mem. social sci. edn. Mankato State U., 1976—; ednl. cons. Random Ho., Scott Foresman, West Pub. Co-author: (book) Unit Mastery Workbook, 1974, Test Item File to Accompany Psychology, 1974, Test Item File to Accompany Psychology, 2d edit., 1976, Unit Mastery Workbook, 2d edit., 1976, Psychology: A Personal Approach, 1982, Psychology: A Personal Approach, 2d edit., 1984, Test Field for Psychology, 3d edit., 1988, Test Item File to Accompany Introduction to Psychology, 5th edit., 1989; editor: Test Item File to Accompany INtroduction to Psychology, 6th edit., 1992; contbr. chapters to books. With USAR, 1964—70. Mem.: APA, Am. Psychol. Soc., Psi Chi (award 1988). Achievements include development of and research on educational materials; methods of instruction and career opportunities for psychology majors. Home and Office: PO Box 150 Mc Cormick SC 29835 E-mail: mil9584762@wctel.net.

ZELLIOT, ELEANOR MAE, history educator; b. Des Moines, Oct. 7, 1926; d. Ernest A. and Minnie (Hadley) Z. BA, William Penn Coll., 1948; MA, Bryn Mawr (Pa.) Coll., 1949; PhD, U. Pa., 1969. Assoc. editor The Am. Friend, Richmond, Iowa, 1950-58; tchr. Scattergood Sch., West Branch, Iowa, 1958-60; editor Pendle Hill Pubs., Wallingford, Pa., 1960-62; acting instr., asst. prof. U. Minn., Mpls., 1966-69; researcher South Asia Hist. Atlas, Mpls., 1966-69; from asst. prof. to assoc. prof. Carleton Coll., Northfield, Minn., 1969-79, prof., 1979-97, dept. chair, 1989-92, Laird Bell prof., 1993-97, prof. emerita, 1997—. Pres. Midwest Conf. on Asian Affairs, 1996-97. Author: From Untouchable to Dalit, 1992, 96, 2000; editor: Experience of Hinduism, 1988, (jour. issue) Marathi Sampler, 1982; contbr. articles to profl. jours. Mem. Dem. Farmer Labor Party, Minn., LWV. Fellowship NEH, 1987, Fulbright, 1992. Mem. Minn. Consortium for South Asia, Am. Inst. of Indian Studies (v.p. 1994-97, bd. trustees, fellowship 1985, 89), Assn. of Asian Studies (Disting. Svc. award 1999). Mem. Soc. Of Friends. Avocations: walking, cooking. Address: Carleton Coll Dept History Northfield MN 55057

ZELLNER, KENNETH KERMIT, elementary education educator; b. Allentown, Pa., Sept. 4, 1945; s. Mellis Myron and Thelma Amanda (Bortz) Z.; m. Jean Elizabeth Welsh, June 24, 1978; children: Todd Benjamin, Amanda Elizabeth. BS, Kutztown U., 1967, MEd, 1971. Cert. elementary and secondary edn., environ. edn., supervision elementary edn., Pa. Tchr. Parkland Sch. Dist., Allentown, 1967—, environ. lab. cons., 1980-97. Cooperating tchr. East Stroudsburg (Pa.) U., 1973-97, Lehigh U., Bethlehem, Pa., 1992-94, sci. camp instr. SMART Ctr., 1993-94; faculty mentor Pa. Gov.'s Sch. of Excellence for Teaching Pa. Dept. Edn., Harrisburg, 1992. Contbr. articles to profl. jours. Mem. little Lehigh watershed curriculum task force Wildlands Conservancy, Emmaus, Pa., 1984-97; mem. newspapers in edn. adv. coun. Allentown Morning Call, 1988-89. Recipient Presdl. Award for Excellence in Sci. and Math. Teaching NSF, 1992, Regional Catalyst award for Excellence in Sci. Teaching Chem. Manufacturers Assn., 1994, Nat. Educators award Milken Family Found., 1994, Congrl. Citation for Outstanding Sci. Teaching Pa. Ho. of Reps., 1994. Mem. Pa. Sci. Tchrs. Assn., Nat. Sci. Tchrs. Assn., Coun. for Elem. Sci. Internat., Assn. Presdl. Awardees in Sci. Teaching, Soc. Elem. Presdl. Awardees, Masons (worshipful master 1985). Republican. Lutheran. Avocations: woodworking, antique and classic cars, snow skiing. Home: 9022 Reservoir Rd Germansville PA 18053-2731 Office: Parkland Adminstrn Bldg 1210 Springhouse Rd Allentown PA 18104-2119

ZELMAN, SUSAN TAVE, school system administrator; DEd, U. Mich.; D in Pub. Edn. (hon.), U. Rio Grande, Ohio; D in Humanities (hon.), Youngstown U. Assoc. prof. edn. Emmanuel Coll., Boston, chair dept. edn.; assoc commr. ednl. dept. personnel Mo. Dept. Edn., Jefferson City, 1988—94; dep. commr. Mo. Dept. Elem. and Secondary Edn., Jefferson City, 1994—99; supt. pub. instrn. Ohio Dept Edn., Columbus, 1999—. Rschr. Edn. Tech. Ctr. Harvard Grad. Sch. Edn. Recipient Nat. Sci. Rsch. Opportunity award, Columbus Tchrs. Coll. Office: Ohio Dept Edn 25 S Front St Columbus OH 43215-4183

ZELNIK, REGINALD ELY, education educator, researcher; b. N.Y.C., May 8, 1936; s. Simon Bernard and Salomea (Czysz) Z.; m. Elaine Rosebery, 1956; children: Pamela, Michael David. BA, Princeton U., 1956; MA, Stanford U., 1961, PhD, 1966. Lectr. dept. history Ind. U., Bloomington, 1963-64; from acting asst. prof. to assoc. prof. dept. history U.

Calif., Berkeley, 1964-76, prof., 1976—, chmn. dept. history, 1994—97, vice chmn. for grad. affairs, 2003—. Chmn. Joint Com. on the Soviet Union and its Successor States, 1993-95. Author: Labor and Society in Tsarist Russia, 1971, Law and Disorder on the Narova River, 1995; editor, translator: A Radical Worker in Tsarist Russia: The Autobiography of Semen Kanatchikov, 1986 (Babra award 1987); editor: Workers and Intelligentsia in Late Imperial Russia, 1999; co-editor: The Free Speech Movement: Reflections on Berkeley in the 1960s, 2002; mem. editl. bd. Jour. Social History, 1968—, Kritika, 2000—; Am. Hist. Rev., Slavic Rev., Jour. Modern History; bd. dirs. NCEEER; contbr. articles to profl. jours. Bd. dirs. Mental Health Assn. Alameda County, Calif. Lt. (j.g.) USN, 1957-59. Fulbright fellow U. Vienna, 1956-57, Guggenheim fellow, 1971-72, Ctr. for Study & Behavior Scis. fellow, 1989-90; grantee NEH, Ford Found. Mem. Am. Hist. Assn., Am. Assn. for Advancement Slavic Studies. Democrat. Jewish. Avocations: reading, music, conversation, travel. Home: 1975 El Dorado Ave Berkeley CA 94707-2441 Office: Univ Calif Dept History 3229 Dwinelle Hall Berkeley CA 94720-2550 E-mail: zelnik@socrates.berkeley.edu.

ZENANKO, CARL MICHAEL, learning center educator; b. Little Rock, Ark., June 23, 1950; s. Carl and Mary Elizabeth (Womack) Z.; children: Alexander Michael, Natasha Anne. BA in Humanities, Hendrix Coll., 1976; MEd in Sci. Edn., Vanderbilt U., 1986. Cert. tchr. Tenn., Ark., Tex., Ala. Tchr. Perryville (Ark.) H.S., 1979-80, 86-89; tchr., coach Montgomery Bell Acad., Nashville, 1980-84; tchr. Plainview (Tex.) H.S., 1988-89; coord. supervision of multimedia instrnl. labs. Jacksonville (Ala.) State U., 1989—, dir. instructional svcs. unit. Chief editor Standard Tutoring Newsletter, 1992-95. Pres. Kitty Stone Elem. PTA, 1994-95. Mem. Nat. Orgn. Tutoring (organizer 1992, mem. exec. bd., editor newsletter 1996-98). Avocations: sculpture, layout computer graphics. Home: 210 Mayfield Ln NE Jacksonville AL 36265-1159

ZENG, ZHAO-BANG, geneticist, educator; b. Wuhan, China, Dec. 8, 1957; came to the U.S., 1986; s. Guangming and Yulan (Ni) Z.; m. Jia Ma, Sept. 9, 1983; 1 child, Jiemin. BS, Huazhong Agrl. U., 1981; PhD, U. Edinburgh, 1986. Asst. lectr. Huazhong Agrl. U., Wuhan, 1982-83; postdoctoral rsch. assoc. N.C. State U., Raleigh, 1986-90, vis. asst. prof., 1990-91, rsch. asst. prof., 1992-94; rsch. assoc. prof., 1994-99; rsch. prof., 1999—2001; prof., 2001—. Adj. prof. Hunzhong Agrl. U., Wuhan, China, 1995—, Zhejiang U., Hangzhou, 2000—. Assoc. editor Genetics, 1994-2002, Theoretical Population Biology, 1995-2000; contbr. articles and revs. to profl. jours. Grantee NIH, 1990—, NSF, 1993—, USDA, 1994—. Mem. Am. Soc. Genetics, Soc. for Study Evolution, Biometric Soc., Phi Kappa Phi, Sigma Xi. Avocations: computer games, jogging, classical music, reading. Home: 112 Kirkfield Dr Cary NC 27511-6815 Office: NC State U PO Box 7566 Raleigh NC 27695-7566 E-mail: zeng@stat.ncse.edu.

ZENILMAN, MICHAEL E. surgeon, educator; b. Far Rockaway, N.Y., Mar. 14, 1958; s. David and Dorothy Zenilman; married. BS with highest honors, SUNY, Stony Brook, 1980; MD summa cum laude, SUNY, Bklyn., 1984. Diplomate Am. Bd. Surgery. Resident in surgery, fellow, then chief resident Barnes Hosp.-Washington U. Sch. Medicine, St. Louis, 1984-91; asst. prof. surgery, chief geriatric surgery Johns Hopkins U. Sch. Medicine, Balt., 1991-93; assoc. prof., chief of surgery Albert Einstein Sch. Medicine, Bronx, N.Y., 1993-2000, vice chmn. dept. surgery, 1998-2000; prof., chmn. dept. surgery SUNY Downstate Med. Ctr., Bklyn., 2000—. Editor: Geriatric Surgery, 2001; contbr. articles on surgery and basic sci. to sci. jours. Fellow ACS; mem. Assn. Acad. Surgery, Soc. for Surgery Alimentary Tract, Am. Gastroent. Assn., Soc. Univ. Surgeons, Am. Physiol. Soc., Am. Pancreatic Assn., Sages, Internat. Soc. Digestive Surgery, Phi Beta Kappa, Alpha Omega Alpha. Office: SUNY Downstate Med Ctr 450 Clarkson Ave Brooklyn NY 11203

ZENTZ, MARLENE KAY, education specialist; b. Billings, Mont., July 27, 1953; d. Clifford and Sybil (Dehrer) Z.; children: Alisan Ashcraft, Holly Ashcraft. BA in French/Liberal Arts, U. Mont., 1976; MS in Spl. Edn., Mont. State U., Billings, 1978; BA in History, Mont. State U., 1994. Cert. tchr. French, spl. edn., elem. edn. and history. Itinerant resource tchr. Fergus County Rural Coop., Lewistown, Mont., 1978-79; tchr. spl. edn. Billings Pub. Schs., 1980-84, tchr. English and geography, 1987—, tech. integration specialist, 1996-98; assoc. project dir., tech. integration specialist Mont. State U., Billings. Cons. No. Lights Ednl. Consortium, Billings, 1993—; com. mem. Mont. Tchrs. Edn. Program Standards for Social Studies, Helena, Mont., 1991-93; tchr. facilitator mus. interactive exhibit No. Lights TeleGeography, 1993. Co-prodr.: (laser disc and CD) Norther Lights TeleGeography Project Overview, 1994; co-author: (rsch.) Norther Lights TeleGeography Project: An Ethnographic Case Study, 1994. Fund for Innovation in Edn. grantee U.S. Dept. Edn., 1991, 92; classroom curriculum grantee Billings Pub. Schs., 1988-90. Mem. NEA, ASCD, Nat. Indian Edn. Assn., Nat. Coun. for Social Studies, Mont. Coun. for Social Studies (v.p. 1994—), Mont. Coun. for Computers in Edn. Avocation: educational technologies. Office: Coll Edn and Human Svcs Mont State U--Billings 1500 N 30th St Billings MT 59101-0298 E-mail: mzentz@msubillings.edu.

ZEPF, THOMAS HERMAN, physics educator, researcher; b. Cin., Feb. 13, 1935; s. Paul A. and Agnes J. (Schulz) Z. BS summa cum laude, Xavier U., 1957; MS, St. Louis U., 1960, PhD, 1963. Asst. prof. physics Creighton U., Omaha, 1962-67, assoc. prof., 1967-75, prof., 1975—2002, prof. emeritus, 2002—, acting chmn. dept. physics, 1963-66, chmn., 1966-73, 81-93, coord. allied health programs, 1975-76, coord. pre-health scis. advising, 1976-81. Cons. physicist VA Hosp., Omaha, 1966-71; vis. prof. physics St. Louis U., 1973-74; program evaluator Am. Coun. on Edn., 1988—. Contbr. articles and abstracts to Surface Sci., Bull. Am. Phys. Soc., Proceedings Nebr. Acad. Sci., The Physics Tchr. jour., others. Recipient Cert. Recognition award Phi Beta Kappa U. Cin. chpt., 1953, Disting. Faculty Svc. award Creighton U., 1987, Excellence in Teaching award Creighton U., 1997. Mem. AAPT, Am. Phys. Soc., Am. Assn. Physics Tchrs. (pres. Nebr. sect. 1978), Nebr. Acad. Sci. (life, chmn. physics sect. 1985—), Internat. Brotherhood Magicians, Soc. Am. Magicians (pres. assembly #7, 1964-65), KC, Sigma Xi (Achievement award for rsch. St. Louis chpt. 1963, pres. Omaha chpt. 1993-94), Sigma Pi Sigma. Roman Catholic. Office: Creighton U Dept Physics Omaha NE 68178-0001

ZERNIAL, SUSAN CAROL, education educator, consultant, editor; b. L.A., July 2, 1948; d. Gus Edward and Gladys Elizabeth (Hale) Z. BA, Calif. State U., Long Beach, 1973; MA, Calif. State U., 1975; EdD, U. San Francisco, 1992. Cert secondary and elementary tchr.; libr. credential. Libr. Clovis (Calif.) Unified Schs., 1975-78; media specialist Anaheim (Calif.) Union High Sch. Dist., 1975; libr. Benicia (Calif.) Unified Sch. Dist., 1978-80; tchr. Atascadero (Calif.) Unified Schs., 1985-93; adj. prof. Edn. Adams State Coll., Alamosa, Colo., 1993—. Sr. acquisitions editor Librs. Unltd./Tchrs. Ideas Press, Englewood, Colo. Recipient Scholarship, Calif. Assn. Sch. Librs., 1974. Mem. ASCD, Am. Rsch. Assn., Phi Delta Kappa. Avocations: camping, hiking, reading, writing.

ZEROKA, DANIEL, chemistry educator; b. Plymouth, Pa., June 22, 1941; s. Michael and Mary (Klimchak) Z.; m. Alexandra S. Kotulak, May 27, 1967; children: Daniel Michael, Andrea Marie. BS, Wilkes Coll., 1963; PhD, U. Pa., 1966. Asst. prof., chemistry Lehigh U., Bethlehem, Pa., 1967-74, assoc. prof., chemistry, 1974-90, prof., chemistry, 1990—. Vis. rsch. scientist duPont Cen. R & D, Wilmington, Del., summer 1984; sabbatical leave Cornell U., Ithaca, N.Y., spring 1985; U.S. Army summer rsch. faculty Edgewood (Md.) Area of Aberdeen Proving Ground, summers 1989, 90, 91; sr. rsch. assoc. NRC, 1997-98. Contbr. articles to Jour. Chem. Physics, Jour. Phys. Chemistry, Langmuir, Internat. Jour. Quantum Chemistry, Jour. Am. Chem. Soc., Theochem. Named NASA Predoctoral fellow, U. Pa., 1964-66, NSF Postdoctoral fellow, Yale U., 1966-67. Mem. Am. Chem. Soc. (sec. Lehigh Valley sect. 1989-90, chmn. Lehigh Valley sect, 1993, alt. councilor 1995-2000, treas. 2000-01), Am. Phys. Soc., Sigma Xi (LU chpt. treas. 1995-97, pres. 2001). Home: 7617 Tilghman St PO Box 14 Fogelsville PA 18051-0014 Office: Lehigh U Dept Chemistry 6 E Packer Ave Bethlehem PA 18015-3172

ZERUBAVEL, EVIATAR, sociologist, educator; BA in Sociology, Anthropology and Polit. Sci., Tel-Aviv U., 1971; MA in Sociology, U. Pa., 1973, PhD, 1976. Asst. prof. psychiatry and sociology U. Pitts., 1976—80; assoc. prof. sociology Columbia U., 1980—84, Queens Coll., 1984—85; prof. sociology SUNY, Stony Brook, 1985—88, Rutgers U., 1988—, dir. sociology grad. program, 1992—2001. Author: Patterns of Time in Hospital Life: A Sociological Perspective, 1979, Hidden Rhythms: Schedules and Calendars in Social Life, 1981, The Seven-Day Circle: The History and Meaning of the Week, 1985, The Fine Line: Making Distinctions in Everyday Life, 1991, 1993, Terra Cognita: The Mental Discovery of America, 1992, Social Mindscapes: An Invitation to Cognitive Sociology, 1997, 1999, The Clockwork Muse: A Practical Guide to Writing Theses, Dissertations, and Books, 1999, Time Maps: Collective Memory and the Social Shape of the Past, 2003. Fellow, John Simon Guggenheim Meml. Found., 2003. Mem.: Am. Sociol. Assn. (chair culture sect. 2000—01). Office: Rutgers Univ Dept Sociology 54 Joyce Kilmer Ave Piscataway NJ 08854

ZEXTER, ELEANOR M. secondary education educator; b. Providence, R.I., Sept. 7, 1936; d. Morris and Anna Rae (Cantor) Marks; m. D. Ronald Zexter, Dec. 24, 1958; children: Francine Deborah, Judith Blair. BA, Brown U., 1958, MAT, 1962. Cert. tchr. R.I., Calif. Tchr. French and English Hope H.S., Providence, 1959—69, Nathan Bishop Mid. Sch., Providence, 1970—93; tchr. English and social studies Harkham Hillel Hebrew Acad., Beverly Hills, Calif., 1993—99. Mktg. dir. DRZ Sales; grant writer Nathan Bishop Mid. Sch., Providence, 1980-93, choral dir., 1985-93, founder Famous Authors, 1987-93; cons. substance abuse program, Brown U., 1987-93; ednl. cons. Vol. tutor Harkham Hillel Hebrew Acad., 1993-99, French club coord., Harkham Hillel Acad., 1993-99. Recipient Citizen Citation for outstanding efforts with Providence children, Mayor, 1990, McClorin award, 1991. Mem. Am. Assn. French Tchrs., Alliance Francaise, R.I. Assn. Foreign Language, Beverly Hills Country Club (tennis team capt.). Avocations: tennis, antique collecting, reading clubs, bridge, travel. Home: 8544 Burton Way Apt 401 Los Angeles CA 90048-3390

ZGUSTA, LADISLAV, linguist, educator; b. Libochovice, Czechoslovakia, Mar. 20, 1924; came to U.S., 1970, naturalized, 1977; s. Ladislav and Sonya (Bernasova) Z.; m. Olga Janouskova, Apr. 10, 1948; children: Monica, Richard. PhD, Caroline U., Prague, Czechoslovakia, 1949; D.Sc., Czech Acad. Scis., 1964. Asst. prof. Caroline U., Prague, Czechoslovakia, 1948-52; sr. research mem. Oriental Inst., Prague, 1952-70, head dept. lexicography, 1958-69; vis. prof. Cornell U., Ithaca, N.Y., 1970; prof. linguistics and classics U. Ill., Urbana, 1970—, dir. Ctr. Advanced Study, permanent mem. Ctr. Advanced Study. Head dept. lexicography German Acad. Scis., Berlin, 1960-70; instr. U. Brno, Czechoslovakia, 1965-69; Ford Found. instr., India, 1975, 89, Philippines, 1979; rsch. cons. Linguistics Rsch. Ctr., U. Tex., Austin, 1970-72; condr. seminar NEH, 1978; cons. NSF. Author: Personennamen griech. Stadte, 1955, Kleinasiatische Personennamen, 1964, Anatol. P.N. Sippen, 1964, Neue Beitrage, 1970, Manual of Lexicography, 1971, Chinese transl., 1984, Kleinasiatische Ortsnamen, 1984, Lexicography Today, 1988; contbr. articles to profl. publs. Guggenheim fellow, 1977, 84; Am. Council Learned Socs. grantee, 1973, 81, Deutsche Forschungsgemeinschaft grantee, 1971, 72, 73, 74, NEH grantee, 1989-91. Fellow Dictionary Soc. N.Am. (pres. 1983-85); mem. Am. Acad. Arts and Scis., Linguistic Soc. Am., Am. Names Soc. (hon.), Indogermanische Gesellschaft (exec. com. 1956-64), Austrian Acad. Scis. (corr.) Home: 912 W Illinois St Urbana IL 61801-3029 Office: 4096 FLB 707 S Mathews Ave Urbana IL 61801-3625

ZHANG, CHUN CHUCK, industrial engineer, educator; b. Beijing, Apr. 24, 1964; arrived in U.S., 1989; s. Xigen Zhang and Baorui Yan. BS, Nanjing (China) Aero. Inst., 1984; MS, SUNY, Buffalo, 1991; PhD, U. Iowa, 1993. Asst. prof. Fla. State U., Tallahassee, 1993-98, assoc. prof., 1998—. Lectr. Nanjing Aero. Inst., 1987-88; guest scientist Nat. Inst. Standards Tech., Gaithersburg, Md., 1995-96; mem. rev. bd. Natural Sci. Engring. Rsch. Coun. Can., Ottawa, 1995. Guest editor Internat. Jour. Engring. Design Automation, 1996; reviewer ASME Trans., Jour. Mfg. Sys., others; contbr. articles to profl. jours. Grantee NSF, 1995, Defense Adv. Rsch. Projects Agy., 1996. Mem.: Soc. Mfg. Engrs. Recipient Outstanding Young Mfg. Engr. award, Soc. Mfg. Engring. Office: Dept Indsl Engring Fla State U 2525 Pottsdamer St Tallahassee FL 32310-6046

ZHANG, LIANJUN, forestry educator, researcher; b. Jinan, Shandong, China, Apr. 21, 1956; arrived in US, 1985; s. Ziyuan Zhang and Yuelan Yang; m. Yufeng Yang, Mar. 7, 1981; children: Jennifer Y., Annie F. BS, Agrl. U., Shandong, 1982; MS, U. Idaho, 1987, PhD, 1990. Rsch. assoc. U. Idaho, Moscow, 1991-93; asst. prof. Ala. A&M U., Huntsville, 1993-94, SUNY, Syracuse, 1994—2000, assoc. prof., 2000—. Contbr. articles to profl. jours. including Forest Sci., Can. Jour. Forest Rsch., Annals Botany, Hortisci. Recipient Michaux Fund award Am. Philos. Soc., 1993. Mem. Internat. Chinese Statis. Assn., Soc. Am. Foresters, Am. Statis. Assn., Biometrics. Office: SUNY ESF One Forestry Dr Syracuse NY 13210

ZHANG, XIAODONG, computer scientist, educator, researcher; b. Beijing, July 16, 1958; came to the U.S., 1983; s. Min and Yishan (Jiang) Z.; m. Yan Meng, July 20, 1985; 1 child, Simon. BS, Beijing (China) Poly. U., 1982; MS, U. Colo., 1985, PhD, 1989. Rsch. asst. Beijing (China) Poly. U., 1982-83, Environ. Rsch. Lab., Boulder, Colo., 1983-85, U. Colo., Boulder, 1985-89; tech. staff Toplogix Inc., Denver, 1989; asst. prof. U. Tex., San Antonio, 1989-92, assoc. prof., 1993-97, chair computer sci., 1993, dir. high performance computing and software lab., 1993—; prof. Coll. William and Mary, Williamsburg, Va., 1997—, dir. grad. studies, 1999-2001, chair computer sci., 2003—; prog. dir. NSF, Arlington, Va., 2001—. Vis. scientist Rice U., 1990-91; guest prof. Wuhan U., China, 1995-97; guest rsch. prof. U. Sci. and Tech. of China, 1997—, guest prof. Northwestern Poly. U., China, 1998—; tech. cons. NASA ICASE, 1998—; mem. overseas expert assessor Chinese Acad. Scis., 1999—; adv. panelist NSF, 1995, 96, 97, 99, 2000; program chair 4th Internat. Workshop on Modeling, Analysis and Simulation of Computer and Telecomm. Systems; keynote spkr. 8th Internat. Conf. on Parallel and Distributed Computer Sys., 1996. Co-author: Multiprocessor Performance, 1994; editor Jour. of Parallel Computing, 1994-95; contbr. articles to profl. jours. Recipient Disting. Rsch. Achievement award U. Tex., 1993, Best Paper award 9th Internat. Conf. on Supercomputing, 1995; grantee NSF, 1990—, Southwestern Bell, 1992-97, USAF, 1993-97, AFOSR, 1995—, ONR, 1995-97, Sun Microsystems, 1998. Mem. IEEE (sr., chmn. tech. com. on supercomputing applications, disting. visitor, program coms., program com. 7th Symposium on Parallel and Distributed Processing 1995, 8th Symposium, 1996, 4th Internat. Symposium on High Performance Computer Arch. 1998, Supercomputing '99, others, mem. steering com. Supercomputing '96, '97, 98, 99, High Performance Computing Asia '97, 98, 99, 2000, internat. conf. on parallel processing 2000, editl. bd. Transactions on Parallel and Distributed Sys. IEEE Micro), Assn. Computing Machinery (nat. lectr., program coms., program com. 10th Internat. Conf. on Supercomputing), Soc. Indsl. and Applied Math. Office: Coll William and Mary Computer Sci Williamsburg VA 23187

ZHAO, JIAN HUI, electrical and computer engineering educator; b. Nanping, Fujian, China, Aug. 2, 1959; came to U.S., 1983; s. Yumao Zhao and Su Qing Chen; m. Menghan Pan, Apr. 28, 1992. BS in Physics, Amoy U., China, 1982; MS in Physics, U. Toledo, 1985; PhD in E.E., Carnegie Mellon U., 1988. Rsch. asst. Nonlinear Optics Lab. U. Toledo, Ohio, 1983-85; rsch. asst. Solid State Elec. Lab. Carnegie Mellon U., Pitts., 1985-88; asst. prof. electric and computer engring. dept. Rutgers U., New Brunswick, N.J., 1988-93, assoc. prof. electric and computer engring. dept., 1993-99, prof. dept. electric and computer engring., 1999—. Cons. Army Rsch. Lab., Ft. Monmouth, 1991—, Westinghouse, Pitts. Contbr. numerous articles to profl. jours. Henry Rutgers fellow Rutgers U., New Brunswick, N.J., 1989, 90; recipient Initiation award NSF, 1990, Best Teaching Performance award Rutgers Eta Kappa Nu, 1991. Mem. IEEE (sr.), Am. Phys. Soc., Materials Rsch. Soc., N.Y. Acad. Sci. Achievements include patents for InP/InGaAsP optoelectronic high speed thyristor, an AlGaAs/GaAs-based optothyristor for ultra-high power switching, field effect real space transfer transistor, electrical tunable superlattice detector for wavelength division demultiplexing applications. Office: Rutgers Univ Elec & Computer Engring Dept PO Box 909 Piscataway NJ 08855-0909

ZHAO, MEISHAN, chemical physics educator, researcher, writer; b. Shanxian, Shandong, People's Republic of China, Nov. 5, 1958; s. Zhong Chen Zhao and Ming Rong Zhang; m. Linlin Cai, Sept. 2, 1983; children: Fang, Yuan, Nan. MS in Physics, U. Minn., 1986, PhD in Chem. Physics, 1989. Lectr. physics S.E. U. China, Nanjing, 1982-84; teaching asst., rsch. asst. U. Minn., Mpls., 1984-89; rschr. James Franck Inst. and dept. chemistry U. Chgo., 1990—, dir. Gen. Chemistry Lab., 1999—. Contbr. articles to profl. jours. Mem. AAAS, Am. Phys. Soc. (internat. editl. bd. Internal. Physics Edn., Chinese ed., 1991-92), N.Y. Acad. Sci. Home: 1443 Keats Ave Naperville IL 60564 Office: Univ Chgo James Franck Inst 5640 S Ellis Ave Chicago IL 60637-1433 E-mail: m-zhao@uchicago.edu.

ZHDANKIN, VIKTOR VLADIMIROVICH, chemistry educator; b. Sverdlovsk, Russia, June 6, 1956; came to U.S., 1990; s. Vladimir M. and Rimma V. (Lukanina) Z.; m. Olga Y. Geraskina, Sept. 20, 1980; children: Vasili V., Vladimir V. BS, MS, Moscow State U., 1978, PhD, 1981, DSc, 1987. Rsch. fellow Moscow State U., 1982-86; vis. scientist U. Minn., Duluth, 1987-88; rsch. prof. Moscow State U., 1988-89; instr., sr. rsch. assoc. U. Utah, Salt Lake City, 1990-93; asst. prof. U. Minn., Duluth, 1993-96, assoc. prof., 1996-99, prof., 1999—. Panel mem. Internat. Sci. Found., Washington, 1993-95. Contbr. articles to profl. jours.; mem. editl. bd. Russian Jour. Organic Chemistry, 1989-93, Jour. Mendeleev Chem. Soc., 1989-95, Mendeleev Comm., 1998—. Grantee, Rsch. Corp., 1993—96, Petroleum Rsch. Fund/Am. Chem. Soc., 1994—96, NSF, 1995—, Civilian R&D Found., 2000—02, NIH, 2002—. Mem. Am. Chem. Soc., Coun. Undergrad. Rsch., Sigma Xi. Achievements include discovery of new phenomena in physical-organic chemistry; preparation of new iodine reagents; development of organic chemistry of xenon. Office: U Minn Dept Chemistry 10 University Dr Duluth MN 55812-2403 E-mail: vzhdanki@d.umn.edu.

ZHOA, YONG, academic administrator, educator; BA in English lang. edn., Sichuan Internat. Studies U., 1986; MA in edn., U. Ill., 1994, PhD in ednl. Psychology, 1996. Tchr. Aiangjiang Middle Sch., China, 1986—87; vis. scholar, adj. faculty Linfield Coll., Edn. Dept., 1992—93; grad. tchg. rsch. asst. U. Ill., Urbana-Champaign, 1993—95; coord. Williamette U., Lang. Learning Ctr., Salem, Oreg., 1995—96; instr. tech. spec. Mellon Lang. Tech. Consortium, Colgate U. and Hamilton Coll., Hamilton, NY, 1996; dir. Mich. State U., Tchg. and Tech., Coll. Edn., 1999—; asst. prof. Mich. State U., 1996—2001; assoc. prof. tech. in tchg. and learning Mich. State U., Dept. Counseling, Edn. Psychology and Spec. Edn., 2001—. Co-dir. US China Elanguage Project. Office: Mich State U Coll Edn 115D Erickson Hall East Lansing MI 48824 E-mail: zhayo@msu.edu.*

ZHOU, MING DE, aeronautical scientist, educator; b. Zhejiang, China, June 26, 1937; s. Pin Xiang and Ang Din Xia; m. Zhuang Yuhua, Aug. 12, 1936; children: Zhengyu, Yan Zhuang. BS, Beijing U. Aero. and Astron., 1962; MS, Northwestern U. Tech., 1967; PhD, Internat. Edn. Rsch. Found., 1992. Tchr. Harbin (China) U. Tech., 1962-64, 67-73; from lectr. to prof. Nanjing (China) U. Aeronautics and Astronautics, 1973-86, 86—; dean bd. postgrad. studies Nanjing (China) U. Aeros. and Astronautics, 1985-89; nationally qualified PhD advisor China, 1989—; rsch. scientist U. Ariz., Tucson, 1991-93, rsch. prof., 1993—2003, adj. prof., 2003—. Vis. scholar Cambridge (Eng.) U., 1980—82; guest scientist Inst. Exptl. Fluid Mechanics, Göttingen, Germany, 1983—84, 1985, 87; sr. vis. scientist Tech. U., Berlin, 1988, 90, 99; rsch. assoc. U. So. Calif., L.A., 1989—90; adj. prof. and sr. rsch. scientist state key lab. for studies of turbulence and complex sys. Peking Univ., China, 2001—. Author: (with others) Viscous Flows and Their Measurements, 1988, (with others) Introduction to Vorticity and Vortex Dynamics, 1992; mem. editl. com. Chinese Jour. Exptl. Mechanics, 1986-89; contbr. articles to profl. jours. including Jour. Fluid Mechanics, Physics of Fluids, Aero. Jour. U.K., Experiments in Fluids, AIAA Jour., Chinese Jour., Aeronautics. Co-recipient Nat. award Progress in Sci. and Tech. first class, Peoples Republic of China, 1985. Mem. AIAA (sr.), N.Y. Acad. Scis., Am. Phys. Soc., Chinese Soc. Aeronautics, Chinese Soc. Mechanics (mem. acad. group exptl. fluid mechanics 1986-89), Chinese Soc. Aerodynamic Rsch. (acad. group unsteady flow and vortex control 1985-89). Achievements include patent for techniques and device of artificial boundary layer transition. E-mail: zmd@u.arizona.edu.

ZHU, BO-QING, cardiovascular research specialist; b. Huhan, Hube, China, Feb. 24, 1941; arrived in U.S., 1986; s. Han-Chang and Zhi-wen (Chen) Z.; m. Jin-Zhen Qiu, Dec. 14, 1967; 1 child, Frank. MD, Shanghai (China) Med. Coll., 1963. Resident Hua Shan Hosp./Shanghai Med. U., 1963-80; attending physician Hua Shan Hosp., Shanghai, 1980-86; vis. prof. U. Calif., San Francisco, 1986-88, asst. rsch. cardiologist, 1988-90, rsch. assoc. specialist, 1990—. Contbr. articles to profl. jours. Fellow: Am. Coll. Cardiology. Office: U Calif San Francisco 505 Parnassus Ave San Francisco CA 94143-0124 E-mail: zhu@medicine.ucsf.edu.

ZHU, ZHEN, educator; b. Nantong, Jiangsu, China, July 22, 1963; came to the U.S., 1986; s. Guang Shen and Lianzhen Zhu; m. Liping Ma, July 30, 1986; 2 children, Alexander and Angela. BA, People's U., Beijing, 1985; MA, Bowling Green State U., 1987; PhD, U. Mich., 1994. Tchg. asst., instr. econs. U. Okla., Norman, 1989-94, asst. prof. internat. fin., econometrics and macroecons., 1994-2000; asst. prof. econs., bus. statistics U. Cen. Okla., Edmond, 2000—; sr. economist C.H. Guernsey & Co., Oklahoma City, 2000—. Contbr. articles to profl. jours. Mem. Am. Econ. Assn., Am. Fin. Assn. Home: 4105 Gloucester Ln Norman OK 73072-2282 Office: U Cen Okla 218 Thatcher Hall Edmond OK 73034 E-mail: zzhu@ucok.edu.

ZIAVRAS, SOTIRIOS GEORGE, computer and electrical engineer, educator; came to the U.S., 1984; s. George Spyros and Sofia George Z. Diploma in elec. engring., Nat. Tech. U., Athens, 1984; MS, Ohio U., 1985; DSc, George Washington U., 1990. Rschr. Riso (Denmark) Nat. Lab., 1983; teaching and rsch. asst. Ohio U., Athens, 1984-85; disting. grad. teaching asst. George Washington U., Washington, 1985-89, rsch. asst., 1986; from asst. prof. to assoc. prof. N.J. Inst. Tech., Newark, 1990-2001, prof., 2001—, assoc. chmn. grad. studies, 2001—. Rschr. Walter Reed Army Inst. Rsch., Silver Spring, Md., 1987-88; rsch. asst. U. Md., College Park, 1988-89; vis. prof. George Mason U., Fairfax, Va., 1990; dir. internet engring. program N.J. Inst. Tech., 2000—01; vice chmn. faculty coun., N.J. Inst. Tech., 2000-01, chmn., 2001-02. Contbr. articles to profl. jours.; assoc. editor: Pattern Recognition Jour., 1994—. Recipient Rsch. Initiation award NSF, 1991, New Millenium Computing Point Design award NSF/DARPA, 1996; grantee Dept. Energy, 2002—. Mem. IEEE (sr.), Assn. for Computing Machinery, N.Y. Acad. Scis. (adv. bd. CIS sect. 1994-97), Eta Kappa Nu. Achievements include development of class of high-performance, low-cost interconnection networks for massively parallel computers called reduced hypercubes; introduction of class of multilevel architectures for high-performance multiresolution image analysis, reconfigurable computing project for the Power Grid funded by Dept. Energy to investigate parallel processing with FPGAS. Office: NJ Inst Tech Elec Computer Engring Dept Newark NJ 07102 E-mail: ziavras@njit.edu.

ZICHEK, SHANNON ELAINE, retired secondary school educator; b. Lincoln, Nebr., May 29, 1944; d. Melvin Eddie and Dorothy Virginia (Patrick) Z. AA, York (Nebr.) Coll., 1965; BA, U. Nebr., Kearney, 1968; postgrad., U. Okla., Edmond, 1970, 71, 72, 73, 74, 75, U. Nebr., Kearney, 1980, 81, 82, 89, 92. Tchr. history and English, N.W. H.S., Grand Island, Nebr., 1948-1999, ret., 1999. Republican. Christian. Home: 2730 N North Rd Grand Island NE 68803-1143

ZICHERMAN, DAVID L. lawyer, educator, financial consultant; b. N.Y.C., Oct. 12, 1961; BA in Psychology magna cum laude, W.Va. U., 1984; JD, MPIA, U. Pitts., 1989. Bar: Del. 1990, Pa. 1990, D.C. 1990. Assoc. Richards, Layton & Finger, Wilmington, Del., 1989-92, Klehr Harrison et al, Phila., 1992-94, Kelly Grimes Pietrangelo & Vakil, P.C., Media, Pa., 1994-97. Adj. prof. Widener U. Law Ctr., Wilmington, 1993-95, fin. cons., Merrill Lynch, 1998—. Editor: State Legislation Forum newsletter, 1991-93; editor Delaware County Legal Jour., 1995-97; contbr. chpt. to book, articles to profl. jours. Bd. dirs. Nat. Tay Sachs and Allied Diseases Assn. Delaware Valley, 1998-2001; mem. tech. com. Rose Tree Media Edn. Found., 1998-2000. Avocations: sports, photography, creative writing, travel. Office: Merrill Lynch PO Box 748 Media PA 19063-0748

ZIEGELMEIER, PATRICIA KAY, music educator, executive secretary; b. Colby, Kans., July 14, 1944; d. Lon Elmer and Mary Marie (Saddler) Sowers; m. Carl Ernest Ziegelmeier, June 9, 1963; children: Matt, Steve, Lisa, Amy, Lori. BA in Music Edn., U. Wyo., 1967; MS in Ednl. Adminstrn., Ft. Hays State U., 1991. Tchr. music, sub. tchr. Golden Plains Schs., Rexford, Kans., 1969-72; pvt. piano instr. Gem, Kans., 1972-87; ch. organist Gem and Colby, Kans., 1968—; instr. music Colby C.C., 1988—. Cmty. leader 4-H, Gem, 1980-88, 99—; bd. dirs. Thomas County Ext. Coun., Colby, 1982-86, 94-95. Mem. NEA, Music Tchrs. Nat. Assn., Kans. Music Tchrs. Assn. (bd. dirs. 1981—, exec. sec. 1987—, Outstanding Tchr. award 1994), Western Plains Arts Assn. (exec. dir. 1989—), Northwest Kans. Piano Assn. (clinic chair 1973—). Methodist. Avocations: reading, music listening, playing piano, walking. Office: Kans Music Tchrs Assn 2154 County Road 27 Gem KS 67734-9008 E-mail: patz@colby.ixks.com.

ZIEGLER, CHRISTINE BERNADETTE, psychology educator, consultant; b. Syracuse, N.Y., Mar. 22, 1951; d. Salvatore and Beverlie (Hopkins) Capozzi; m. Steven Jon Ziegler, Jan. 7,1979;1 child. Justin. Bs, SUNY, Brockport, 1978; MS, Syracuse U., 1980, PhD, 1982. Adj. asst. prof. SUNY, Cortland, N.Y., 1983-86, Syracuse (N.Y.) U., 1984-86, LeMoyne Coll., Syracuse, 1986-87; rsch. cons. Syracuse (N.Y.) U., 1982-86; from assoc. prof. to prof. Kennesaw (Ga.) State U., 1987—. Dean continuing edn. East Cobb Mid. Sch.; parent facilitator Ga. Coun. Child Abuse, Atlanta, 1990—; cons. Dissertation Rsch. UGA, Atlanta; cons. aggression reduction tng. N.W. Regional Hosp., Rome, Ga.; presenter numerous profl. confs. in field. Reviewer for Teaching of Psychology Jour., Jour. Undergrad. Rsch.; contbr. articles to profl. jours. Mem. Juvenile Ct. Panel, Health Children's Initiative; mem. sch. adv. com., Marietta, Ga., 1989, mem. sch. bond com., 1989. Recipient fellowship Syracuse U., 1982. Mem. APA, AAAS, NAS, Ga. Psychol. Assn., Southeastern Psychol. Assn., Soc. Philosophy and Psychology, Soc. for Rsch. in Child Devel., Psychology Club (advisor), Blue Key (chpt. v.p.). Avocations: camping, gardening, environmental protection, conservation. Office: Kennesaw State Univ 1000 Chastain Rd NW Kennesaw GA 30144-5591

ZIEGLER, MARK DOUGLAS, secondary school educator; b. Tomah, Wis., Mar. 8, 1969; s. Keith John and Isabelle Lucille (Felber) Z. BS in Biology and Edn., U. Wis., La Crosse, 1992. Cert. tchr., Wis. Mem. curriculum devel. com. Norskedalen, Coon Valley, Wis., 1991; sci. tchr., wrestling coach Spencer (Wis.) H.S., 1992-98, softball coach, 1994-96; sci. tchr., wrestling coach Logan H.S., 1998—. Wrestling coach La Crosse Logan, 1989-92. Grantee Honeywell Corp., 1994; named Marathon County Spl. Edn., Regular Edn. Tchr. of Yr., 1998. Mem. Wis. Wrestling Coaches Assn., Western Wis. Sci. Tchrs., BioNet.

ZIEGLER, MICHAEL GREGORY, medical educator, researcher; b. Chgo., May 12, 1946; s. William John and Agnes (Finlayson) Z.; m. Carole Lowrey, Dec. 12, 1970; children: Barbara, Matthew. BS in Biology, Loyola U., Chgo., 1967; MD, U. Chgo., 1971. Diplomate Am. Bd. Internal Medicine. Intern Kans. Med. Sch., Kansas City, 1971-72, resident, 1972-73; pharmacologist NIMH, Bethesda, Md., 1975-76; asst. prof. clin. pharmacology U. Tex. Med. Br., Galveston, 1976-80; asst. prof. dept. medicine U. Calif., San Diego, 1980-86, assoc. prof. San Deigo, 1986-90, prof., 1991—, program dir. Clin. Rsch. Ctr., 1993—. Program dir. Clin. Rsch. Ctr., 1993—; cons. NASA Extended Duration Orbiter Program, Univ. Space Rsch. Assn. Author: Norepinephrine: Frontiers of Clinical Neuroscience, 1984, The Catecholamines in Psychiatric and Neurologica Disorders, 1985; mem. editorial bd. Hypertension, 1981-86, Psychosomatic Medicine, 1991—. Mem. sci. adv. bd. Khalsa Found. Lt. comdr. USPHS, 1971-73. NIH grantee, 1992—. Mem. Am. Soc. Hypertension, Am. Fedn. for Clin. Rsch., Am. Soc. Nephrology, Am. Heart Assn. (kidney coun.), Physicians for Social Responsibility, Am. Soc. Clin. Investigation. Avocation: surfing. Office: U Calif San Diego Med Ctr Mail Code 8341 200 W Arbor Dr San Diego CA 92103-9000

ZIEGLER, ROBERT OLIVER, retired music and special education educator; b. Cullman, Ala., Sept. 6, 1939; s. Mary Catherine (Taylor) McDonald; adopted Edgar and Kathryn Ziegler; m. Gladys L. Friese, May 3, 1962 (div. Jan. 1970); children: Robert, Edgar, Lesha, Kathy. BS, U. Ala., Tuscaloosa, 1961, MA, 1964, PhD, 1970. Cert. spl. edn. tchr., sch. counselor, music tchr., Ga. Band dir. Phillips Jr. H.S., Mobile, Ala., 1961-62, Wiggins (Colo.) H.S., 1962-63, Eastwood Jr. H.S., Tuscaloosa, 1963-65, McAdory H.S., McCalla, Ala., 1966-70, Calera (Ala.) H.S., 1971-72; prof. music edn. Tift Coll., Forsyth, Ga., 1972-78; jr. H.S. counselor Clayton County Schs., Jonesboro, Ga., 1978-80; elem. sch. counselor Rockdale County Schs., Conyers, Ga., 1980-82; spl. edn. tchr. Henderson Jr. H.S., Jackson, Ga., 1982-87, Clayton County Schs., Jonesboro, Ga., 1987-92, gen. music tchr., 1996-99; spl. edn. tchr. City Schs. of Decatur, Ga., 1992-96; elem. sch. music tchr. Clayton County Schs., 1996-99. Clarinetist Mobile (Ala.) Symphony Orch., 1961-62; vis. lectr. Stillman Coll., Tuscaloosa, Ala., 1970-71; prof. grad. sch. Mercer U., Macon, 1972-74; vis. lectr. in music Wesleyan Coll., Macon, Ga., 1975-76; acting head music dept. Tift Coll., Forsyth, Ga., 1976-77; curriculum cons. South Metro Psychoednl. Ctr., Atlanta City Schs., 1989. Contbr. articles to profl. publs. Minister of music, choir dir. United Meth. Ch., 1961-90, lay leader, 1989-94; mem. South Metro Concert Band, Morrow, Ga., 1978—, Tara Wind Band, Jonesboro, Ga., 1987-88. Recipient Cert. of Appreciation United Meth. Ch., 1990, Spl. Mission Recognition award United Meth. Women, 1983; U. Ala. grantee, 1960-61 Mem. Profl. Assn. Ga. Educators (bldg. rep. 1994-96), Soc. for Preservation and Encouragement of Barber Shop Quartet Singing in Am. (founding mem., co-dir. Fayetteville chpt. 1990, co-founder, 1st dir. So. Crescent Chorus 2001). Avocations: tennis, ragtime piano playing, singing gospel music. Home: 2669 Jodeco Dr Jonesboro GA 30236-5311 E-mail: bobmzieg@aol.com.

ZIGLER, EDWARD FRANK, psychologist, educator; b. Kansas City, Mo., Mar. 1, 1930; s. Louis and Gertrude (Gleitman) Z.; m. Bernice Gorelick, Aug. 28, 1955; 1 child, Scott. BA, U. Mo.-Kansas City, 1954; PhD, U. Tex., 1958; MA (hon.), Yale, 1967; DSc (hon.), Boston Coll., 1985; LHD (hon.), Bank St. Coll. Edn., 1989, U. New Haven, 1991, St. Joseph Coll., 1991; PhD (hon.), Hon. degree, CUNY, 1995; LLD (hon.), Gonzaga U., 1995; HHD, Park U., 2000; LHD, McGill U., 2001. Psychol. intern Worcester (Mass.) State Hosp., 1957-59; asst. prof. psychology U. Mo., 1958-59; mem. faculty Yale U., 1959—, prof. psychology and child study center, 1967—, Sterling prof., 1976—, dir. child devel. program, 1961-76, chmn. dept. psychology, 1973-74; head psychology sect. Yale Child Study Center, 1967—; dir. Bush Center in Child Devel. and Social Policy, 1977—. Chief Children's Bur. NEW, Washington, 1970-72; cons. in field, 1962—; mem. nat. steering com. Project Head Start, 1965-70, chmn. 15th anniversary Head Start com., 1980; mem. nat. adv. com. Nat. Lab. Early Childhood Edn., 1967-70; nat. rsch. adv. bd. Nat. Assn. Retarded Children, 1968-73; nat. rsch. coun. Project Follow-Through, 1968-70; chmn. adv. com. Vietnamese Children's Resettlement, 1975; mem. Pres.'s Com. on Mental Retardation, 1980; joint appointee Yale U. Sch. Medicine, 1982—, chmn. Yale Infant Care Leave Commn., 1983-85, Parents as Tchrs., 1986—; mem. adv. com. Head Start Quality and Expansion, 1993; mem. adv. com. on svcs. for families with infants and toddlers HHS, 1994; mem. 25th Anniversary hon. com. Children's Def. Fund, 1997; mem. program com. Head Start's 5th Nat. Rsch. Conf., 1998—; mem. nat. adv. panel hon. chair, hist. mentor Nat. Head Start Assn.: Fulfilling the Promise 2010 Project 1998-2000; mem. adv. com. Head Start Rsch. and Evaluation for Adminstrn. for Children and Families, 1999—, Nat. Partnership's Family Leave Income Initiative, 1999—. Author, co-author, editor books and monographs; contbr. articles to profl. jours. With AUS, 1951-53. Recipient Gunnar Dybwad Disting. scholar in behavioral and social sci. award Nat. Assn. Retarded Children, 1964, 69, Social Sci. Aux. award, 1962, Alumni Achievement award U. Mo., 1965, Alumnus of Yr. award, 1972, C. Anderson Aldrich award Am. Acad. Pediatrics, 1985, Nat. Achievement award Assn. for Advancement of Psychology, 1985, Dorothea Lynde Dix Humanitarian award for svc. to handicapped Elwyn Inst., 1987, Sci. Leadership award Joseph P. Kennedy Jr. Found., 1990, Mensa Edn. and Rsch. Found. award for excellence, 1990, Nat. Head Start Assn. award, 1990 Founders award, 1995, Bldg. dedication Edward Zigler Head Start Ctr., 1990, As They Grow award in edn. Parents mag., 1990, Excellence in Edn. award Pi Lambda Theta, 1991, Friend of Edn. award Conn. Edn. Assn., 1991, Loyola-Mellon Social Sci. award 1991, Pres.'s award Conn. Assn. Human Svcs., 1991, Harold W. McGraw, Jr. prize in edn., 1992, Disting. Achievement in Rsch. award Internat. Assn. Sci. Study of Mental Deficiency, 1992, Disting. Svc. award Coun. Chief State Sch. Officers, 1993, Outstanding Fed. Leadership in Support of Head Start Rsch., Adminstrn. on Children, Youth and Families, 1993, Child and Family Advocacy award Parents as Tchrs. Nat. Ctr., 1994, Nat. Distinction award U. Pa. Edn. Alumni Assn., 1994, Disting. Fellow award So. Conn. State U. chpt. Phi Delta Kappa, 1997, Lifetime Achievement award in Applied and Preventive Psychology Am Assn. Applied and Preventive Psychology, 1998, Recognition award Coun. for Early Childhood Profls., Child Devel. Assocs., 1999, Heinz award pub. policy, 1999, Nat. Head Start Assn. award appreciation, 2000, Disting. Svc. medal Tchrs. Coll. Columbia U., 2000, Disting. Alumnus U. Tex., 2000, Key to the City, Independence, Mo., 2000, Nat. Head Start Assn. award appreciation, 2000, Disting. Svc. medal Tchrs. Coll. Columbia U., 2000, Lifetime Mentoring award, ACYF, 2000, Lifetime Contbn. psychology award CT Psychol. Assn., 2000, Lifetime Commitment to comty. svc. award Ct dept. higher edn. and CT commn. on nat. and comty. svc., 2001, Florence Halpern award disting. profl. contbns. in clin. psychology APA, 2001, Bridges Over Barrtiers awrd, Family REsources Youth Svcs. Coalition Ky., 2002, others; named Hon. Commr. Internat. Yr. of Child, 1979. Fellow Am. Orthopsychiat. Assn. (Blanche F. Ittleson award 1989, pres. 1993-94), APA (pres. divsn. 7, 1974-75, G. Stanley Hall award 1979, award for disting. contbns. to psychology in pub. interest 1982, Nicholas Hobbs award 1985, award for disting. profl. contbns. to knowledge 1986, Edgar A. Doll award 1986, award for disting. contbn. to cmty. psychology and cmty. mental health 1989, pres.-elect divsn. 37 1997, pres. 1998, past pres. 1999, Bronfenbrenner Lifetime Contbn. award divsn. 7 1998, Florence Halpern award for disting. profl. contbns. in clin. psychology divsn. 12 2001); mem. Inst. Medicine of NAS, AAAS, Am. Acad. Mental Retardation (Career Rsch. award 1982), Soc. Psychol. Study Social Issues (Kurt Lewin meml. award 1995), Zero to Three (Dolley Madison award 1995), P.R. Head Start Assn. (Outstanding Leadership award 1995, True Father of Headstart recognition award 1996, award of appreciation for lifelong support and participation 1997), Am. Psychol. Found. (gold medal for life contbn. 1997, Parents Child Care award for advocacy 1998, Heinz award in pub. policy, 1999). Home: 177 Ridgewood Ave North Haven CT 06473-4442 Office: Yale U Dept Psychology PO Box 208205 2 Hillhouse Ave New Haven CT 06520-8205 E-mail: edward.zigler@yale.edu.

ZIGLER, TED ALAN, principal; b. Bryan, Ohio, Apr. 29, 1952; s. Olan A. and Patsy A. Zigler; m. Beth E. Auby, Sept. 1, 1973; children: Scott, Amy. EdB, U. Toledo, 1974, EdM, 1977; EdD, U. Cin., 1992. Tchr., coach Montpelier (Ohio) Local Schs., 1974-78; tchr., counselor, coach Bright Local Schs., Mowrystown, Ohio, 1978-79; tchr., coach Margaretta Local Schs., Castalia, Ohio, 1979-84, Northwest Local Schs., Cin., 1984-87, asst. prin. middle sch., 1987-91, asst. prin. H.S., 1991-94; prin. Harrison H.S. Southwest Local Schs., Harrison, Ohio, 1994—. Adj. faculty mem. U. Cin., Ohio, 1992—, Mt. St. Joseph, Cin.; presenter in field; mem. various confs. in field; reviewer manuscripts for Corwin Press. Mem. Am. Ednl. Rsch. Assn., Midwest Ednl. Rsch. Assn., Nat. Assn. Secondary Sch. Prins., Ohio Assn. Secondary Sch. Adminstrs., Midwest Ednl. Rsch. Assn., Univ. Coun. Ednl. Adminstrn. Avocations: open wheel racing, college basketball. Office: Wm Henry Harrison HS 960 West Rd Harrison OH 45030

ZIGNAUSKAS, DOROTHY ELIZABETH, special education educator; b. Jersey City, Dec. 8, 1949; d. Sheldon and Rose Lucy (Stabile) Horowitz; m. John A. Zignauskas, May 2, 1982; children: John Jr., Jennifer Rose. BA in Spl. Edn., Jersey City State Coll., 1971, MA in Spl. Edn., 1978. Cert. tchr. handicapped, N.J. Spl. edn. tutor Quitman Street Sch., Newark, 1972-74, tchr. handicapped, 1972-94, 18th Ave. Sch., Newark, 1994—. Active mem. Lincroft Sch. PTA, 1987—; leader Girl Scouts U.S., Lincroft, 1994; den mother Boy Scouts Am., Lincroft, 1988-94; food and clothing dr. organizer Quitman St. Sch., 1972-82. Mem. Coun. for Exceptional Children, Children with Attention Deficit Disorder, Living with Attention Deficit Disorder Evenly and Rationally. Republican. Roman Catholic. Avocations: ceramics, sewing, bowling, travel, theater. Office: Newark Bd of Edn 18th Avenue Newark NJ 07108

ZIL, J. S. psychiatrist, physiologist; b. Chgo; s. Stephen Vincent and Marillyn Charlotte (Jackson) Z.; 1 child, Charlene-Elena. BS magna cum laude, U. Redlands, 1969; MD, U. Calif., San Diego, 1973; MPH, Yale U., 1977; JD with honors, Jefferson Coll., 1985. Med. clk. Clinica de Casa de Todos, Tijuana, Mexico, 1968—70; intern, resident in psychiatry and neurology U. Ariz., 1973-75; fellow in psychiatry, advanced fellow in social, cmty. and forensic psychiatry, Yale cmty. cons. toections Conn. State Dept. Corrections, 1975-77; instr. psychiatry Yale U., 1976-77; instr. physiology U. Mass., 1976-77; unit chief Inpatient and Day Hosp., Conn. Mental Health Ctr., Yale-New Haven Hosp., 1973—77; asst. prof. psychiatry U. Calif., San Francisco, 1977-82, assoc. prof. psychiatry and internal medicine, 1982—86, vice-chmn. dept. psychiatry, 1983-86; prof. natural sci. Calif. State U., 1985-87; assoc. prof. bioengring. and internal medicine U. Calif., Berkeley, San Francisco, 1982-92, clin. faculty Davis, 1991-99, legis. liaison Ctrl. Office Berkeley, 1988—; med. dir. Sierra Vista Hosp., 2003—. Chief psychiatry and neurology VA Med. Ctr., Calif., 1977—86; prin. investigator Sleep Rsch. and Physiology Lab., 1980—86; chmn. dept. psychiatry and neurology U. Calif., San Francisco, Ctrl. San Joaquin Valley Med. Edn. Program and Affiliated Hosps. and Clinics, 1983—86; chief psychiatrist State Calif. Dept. Corrections, 1986—89, chief forensic Psychiatrist, 1986—2003; chmn. State of Calif. Inter-Agy. Tech. Adv. Com. on Mentally Ill Inmates & Parolees, 1986—92; mem. med. adv. com. Calif. State Pers. Bd., 1986—95; apptd. counciloor Calif. State Mental Health Plan, 1988—93; cons. Nat. Inst. Corrections, 1992—94; invited faculty contbr. and editor Am. Coll. Psychiatrist's Resident in Tng. Exam, 1981—86; commr. physician's adv. bd. Pres. Commn. on Bus., U.S. Ho. of Reps., 2002—; med. dir. Sierra Vista Hosp., Sacramento, 2003—. Author: The Case of the Sleepwalking Rapist, 1992, Mentally Disordered Criminal Offenders, 5 vols., 1989, 2nd edit., 1991, 3rd edit., 1996, 4th edit., 1996; co-author: The Measurement Mandate: On the Road to Performance Improvement in Health Care, 1993, Psychiatric Services in Jails and Prisons, 2nd edit., 2000, 2nd printing, 2001; assoc. editor Corrective and Social Psychiatry Jour., 1978—97, referee, 1980—, reviewer, 1981—; contbr. articles; author: Suicide Prevention handbook, 1987. Commr. Presdl. Commn. on Bus., 2002—. Nat. Merit scholar, 1965; recipient Nat. Recognition award Bank of Am., 1965, Julian Lee Roberts award U. Redlands, 1969, Kendall award Internat. Symposium in Biochemistry Rsch., 1970, Campus-Wide Profl. Achievement award U. Redlands, 1994. U. Calif., 1995-1996. Fellow Royal Soc. Health, Am. Assn. Social Psychiatry; mem. AAUP, APHA, Am. Psychiat. Assn., Am. Assn. Mental Health Profls. in Corrections (nat. pres. 2002—), Nat. Coun. on Crime and Delinquency, Calif. Scholarship Fedn. (past pres.), Delta Alpha, Alpha Epsilon Delta. Office: PO Box 160208 Sacramento CA 95816-0208 E-mail: corrmentalhealth@aol.com.

ZILBERT, ALLEN BRUCE, education educator, computer consultant; b. Bronx, N.Y., May 26, 1957; s. Murray and Perla Z.; m. Barbara Dale Palley, July 1, 1984; children: Heather Robynne, Jared Lee. BA in Econ., CUNY, 1978; MBA, St. Johns U., 1980, advanced profl. cert., 1982; MEd in Adminstrv. Computer Systems Edn., Columbia U., 1986, EdD, 1988; postgrad., Kennedy-Western U., 1995—. Instr. bus. computer info. systems & quantitative methods Hofstra U., Hempstead, N.Y., 1981-83; asst. prof. info. systems Pace U. Sch. Computer Sci. and Info. Systems, N.Y.C., 1983-89; dir. ancillary systems Advanced Med. Systems, Rockville Centre, NY, 1989-90; asst. prof. mgmt. Long Island U. Sch. Bus., Coll. Mgmt., Brookville, N.Y., 1990-94; asst. prof. mgmt. info. sys. Sy Syms Sch. Bus., David Zysman prof. of mgmt. info. sys. Yeshiva U., N.Y.C., 1994-2000; assoc. prof. math./computer sci. Molloy Coll., Rockville Centre, 2000—03, dir. computer sci. and computer info. systems programs, 2000—03; assoc. prof. computer info. sys. Briarcliffe Coll., Patchogue, NY, 2003—, chair computer info. sys. dept., 2003—. Mem. curriculum com. Pace U. Sch. Computer Sci. and Info. Sys., 1983-89; chmn. personal computer resources com. Advanced Med. Sys., 1989-90; mem. campuswide computer com. L.I. U., 1991-94, chmn., 1993-94, chmn. scholarship awards com., 1990-91; assembly collegiate schs. bus. curriculum planning com. Coll. Mgmt., 1993-94, chmn. computer needs, usage and stds. com., 1990-93, chmn. mgmt. dept. computer com., chmn. scholar awards com., 1992-93; book and software reviewer. Contbr. articles to profl. jours. Mem. IEEE, Assn. for Computer Tng. and Support, Assn. for Computing Machinery, Assn. of Info. Tech. Profls., Internat. Assn. for Computer Info. Sys., Internat. Assn. Mgmt., Info. Resources Mgmt. Assn. E-mail: azilbert@bcl.edu.

ZIMET, LLOYD, sport psychologist, health planner, educator; b. Bklyn., Oct. 5, 1951; s. Victor R. and Marcia (Sorkin) Z. BA, Whittier (Calif.) Coll., 1973; MA, U. Md., 1983, PhD, 1984; MPH, NYU, 1989. Head basketball coach Aarhus (Denmark) U., 1973—78, 1980—82, 1985—86; resident dir. U. Md., College Park, 1978—80; sports supr. Montgomery County (Md.) Dept. of Recreation, 1978, 1982—84; dir. health promotion Optimal Fitness Inc., N.Y.C., 1986—91; internat. cons. cmty. and occupational health, 1984—; dir. World of Discovery Day Camp, Bklyn., 1997—2000. Dir. edn. AIDS Ctr. of Queens (N.Y.) County, 1989-90; bd. dirs. Patricia Manning Meml. Fund childhood cancer Am. Cancer Soc., Queens, 1988-95; mem. AIDS adv. com. N.Y.C. Bd. of Edn., 1989-90; mem. adv. bd. Adolescent Health Network, Queens, 1989-90; keynote speaker NYU Health Edn. Alumni, 1990, USPHS Region II Conf., 1991. Bd. govs. U.S. Amateur Boxing Fedn., Colorado Springs, Colo., 1988-91; bd. dirs. Met. Amateur Boxing Fedn., N.Y.C., 1988-91; mem. USA Boxing Nat. Scholarship com., 1984-88. Fellow: Soc. Pub. Health Educators; mem.: AAHPERD, APA, APHA, Internat. Soc. Sport Psychology, N.Am. Soc. Psychology Sport & Phys. Activity, Assn. for Advancement of Applied Sport Psychology, Am. Alliance Health Educators.

ZIMMER, GRETA GAY, secondary school educator; b. Goldthwaite, Tex., Mar. 19, 1941; d. Edwin John and Lillian (Elkins) Drueckhammer; m. Henry Junior Stagemeyer (div.); 1 child, Thomas David Dietrich; m. David LeRoy Zimmer, July 16, 1982. BA, Tex. Luth. U., Seguin, 1963; MS, Kearney (Nebr.) State U., 1969. Tchr. Channing (Tex.) Ind. Sch. Dist., 1963-64, Arapahoe (Nebr.) Ind. Sch. Dist., 1964-65, Loomis (Nebr.) Ind. Sch. Dist., 1965-68, Galena Park Ind. Sch. Dist., Houston, 1969-71, LaPorte (Tex.) Jr. High Sch., 1972-86; tchr. English and German, LaPorte High Sch., 1986-96; ret., 1996. Trainer N.J. Writing Inst. in Tex., LaPorte, 1990-93. Author short stories and poetry. Mem. NEA, Tex. State Tchrs. Assn., LaPorte Edn. Assn. (pres. 1990-91). Lutheran. Home: PO Box 827 La Porte TX 77572-0827

ZIMMER, STUART, retired secondary school educator; b. Bklyn., Sept. 20, 1942; s. Joseph and Rose (Sachs) Z.; m. Joan Beth Heyman, June 26, 1965; children: Todd, Ronald. BA, L.I. U., 1964; MA, Bklyn. Coll., 1966. Tchr. area high sch., Bklyn., 1964-67, Canarsie H.S., Bklyn., 1967-77, August Martin H.S., Queens, N.Y., 1977-87, Jamaica (N.Y.) H.S., 1987-95. Writer curriculum N.Y.C. Bd. Edn., 1983; presenter numerous workshops and tchg. confs. Author: Government and You, 1985, Economics and You, 1987, Key to Understanding Global Studies, 1988, Key to Understanding U.S. History and Government, 1988, Comprende Tu Mundo, 1989, Los Estados Unidos, 1990, Mastering Global Studies, 1991, Mastering U.S. History and Government, 1992, Mastering Ohio's 9th Grade Citizenship Test, 1993, Mastering Ohio's 12th Grade Citizenship Test, 1994, Ohio: Its Land and Its People, 1994, Historia y Gobierno de los Estados Unidos, 1995, Principios de Economia, 1995, Ohio: Its Neighbors, Near and Far, 1995, Texas: Its Land and Its People, 1996, New York: Its Land and Its People, 1996, North Carolina: The Tar Heel State, 1997, Michigan: Its Land and Its People, 1997, The Key to Understanding Global History, 1998, Mastering the M.E.A.P. Test in Social Studies, 1998. Recipient Cert. of Recognition, N.Y.C. Deputy Police Commissioner, 1987, Spl. Achievement citation Am. Flag Inst., N.Y.C., 1987, resolution honoring his many achievements N.Y. State Legislature, Albany, 1989. Mem. Nat. Coun. Social Studies Tchrs., Assn. Tchrs. of Social Studies (assoc. editor publ. 1984-93). Avocations: reading, jogging, autograph collecting. Home: 12 Elmore Pl East Northport NY 11731-5627

ZIMMERMAN, ANITA ELOISE, elementary education educator; b. Wilkes-Barre, Pa., Apr. 27, 1954; d. Edward Martin and Ada Eloise (Jacoby) Mushal; m. Jeffrey Zimmerman, June 19, 1976. BS in Elem. Edn./Early Childhood Edn., Coll. Misericordia, 1976; M Equivalency, various univs., State of Pa., 1986. Cert. elem. edn. and early childhood edn. tchr., Pa. Tchr. third grade Hunlock Creek (Pa.) Elem. N.W. Area Sch. Dist., 1976—. Rif co-coord. Hunlock Elem. PTO, 1978—, newsletter coord., 1978—, numerous offices to pres. 1992—; tchr. mentor N.W. Area Sch. Dist., Shickshinny, Pa., 1989, coop. master tchr. student tchrs., 1989—; coach Odyssey of the Mind, 1997-98, cons., 1998-99. Pianist Roaring Brook Bapt. Ch., 1980—, asst. organist, 1980—, asst. music dir., 1980—. Recipient Encouragement of Outstanding Young Writers award Luzerne County Poetry Soc., Wilkes-Barre, 1990. Mem. N.W. Area Edn. Assn. (rep. 1986-87). Republican. Avocations: pianist, vocal soloist, organist, reading, author children's plays. Office: Hunlock Creek Elem RR 1 Hunlock Creek PA 18621-9801

ZIMMERMAN, BARRY JOSEPH, educational psychology educator, researcher; b. Sheboygan, Wis., Nov. 23, 1942; s. Victor J. and Ida M. (Dekeyser) Z.; m. Diana J. Conley, Aug. 6, 1966; children: Kristin L., Shana M. BA, U. Ariz., 1965, PhD, 1969; MA, N.Mex. State U., 1966. Asst. prof.

U. Ariz., Tucson, 1970-72, assoc. prof., 1972-74; assoc. prof. grad. sch. CUNY, 1974-78, prof. grad. sch., 1978-96, disting. prof., 1996—. Head human learning Devel. and Instrn. Area; vis. scholar Stanford (Calif.) U., 1991; co-investigator Columbia Coll. Physicians and Surgeons, N.Y.C., 1987-98. Co-author: Social Learning and Cognition, 1978, Developing Self-Regulated Learners: Beyond Achievement to Self-Efficacy, 1996; co-editor: Functions of Language and Cognition, 1979, Self-Regulated Learning and Academic Achievement, 1989, 2d edit., 2001, Self-Regulation of Learning and Performance, 1994, Developing Sel-Regulated Learners: From Teaching to Self-Reflective Practice, 1998, Educational Psychology: A Century of Contributions, 2003; mem. editl. bd. Devel. Rev., 1980—, Merrill-Palmer Quar., 1979-80, Contemporary Ednl. Psychology, 1975-90, 95—, Jour. Applied Devel. Psychology, 1983-90, Am. Ednl. Rsch. Jour., 1992-95, Jour. Ednl. Psychology, 1993—, Sch. Psychology Quarterly; editor jour. issue Self-Regulated Learning, 1990. Bd. dirs. Am. Lung Assn., 1988-90, coun. mem., 1991-93, chmn. sch. health com., 1988-92, rsch. coord. com., 1989-91. Rsch. Support grantee Nat. Inst. Heart, Lung and Blood, 1987—98, grantee Nat. Inst. Edn., 2001—. Fellow APA (divsn. 7, 15, 16, pres. divsn. 15 1996-97, coun. mem., 1999-2003, Sr. Scientist award divsn. 16 1994), Am. Psychol. Soc.; mem. AAUP, Am. Ednl. Rsch. Assn. (asst. chmn. divsn. C 1991-92, Sylvia Scribner award 1999), Am. Thoracic Soc. (chmn. behavioral sci. assembly 1991-93), Soc. for Rsch. in Child Devel., Leonia Tennis Club. Avocations: music, travel, tennis, skiing. Office: CUNY Grad Sch 365 5th Ave New York NY 10016-4309

ZIMMERMAN, HAROLD SEYMOUR, elementary school educator; b. Bklyn., June 3, 1928; BA, Bklyn. Coll., 1950; MA, So. Ill. U., Edwardsville, 1970; postgrad., various, 1950-90. 8th grade English, Social Studies, Reading tchr. Sherwood Day Sch., Chesterfield, Mo., 1956-64; 7th grade core curriculum, English, Social Studies tchr. Nipher Jr. High Sch., Kirkwood, Mo., 1964-70; 7th grade Social Studies, team teaching tchr. Brittany Woods Sch., University City, Mo., 1971-91; tchr. Russian lit. OASIS, 1995; tchr. Russian Art Oasis, 1996, 98. Adj. prof. Russian studies Lindenwood Coll., St. Charles, Mo., 1975—, Washington U., 1972-91; participant 1st U.S./Russia Joint Conf. on Edn., 1994; cons. in field. Author: Facing Issues of Family Living; contbr. articles to profl. jours. Chairperson bd. trustees Indian Meadows subdivsn., Olivette, Mo.; chairperson Youth Commn., Olivette; vol. OASIS, St. Louis Zoo; past pres., program chmn. People to People, St. Louis; pres. Ashford Condo. Corp.; mem. Fgn. Rels. Com., St. Louis. Mem. NEA, ASCD, Mo. Edn. Assn., Nat. Coun. Social Studies (spl. interest groups psychology, tchr. edn., religion in schs.), Mo. Geog. Alliance Tchr. Cons., People to People, World Coun. of Affairs, Bus. for Russia. Home: 450 E Lockwood Ave Webster Groves MO 63119-3128

ZIMMERMAN, JAY, secondary education educator; Tchr. Physics Brookfield (Wis.) Ctrl. High Sch., 1980—. Recipient Disting. Svc. Citation, 1993. Office: Brookfield Ctrl High Sch 16900 Gebhardt Rd Brookfield WI 53005-5138

ZIMMERMAN, JUDITH ROSE, elementary art educator; b. Youngstown, Ohio, Jan. 17, 1945; d. Emery and Josephine Leona (Terlecki) Ference; m. William Carl Zimmerman, Jr., Nov 27, 1965; children: Shawn, William III. BFA in Art Edn., Kent State U., 1977, MEd in Curriculum and Instruction, 1992. Cert. art tchr., Ohio. Elem. art tchr. Sandy Valley Sch. Dist., Magnolia, Ohio, 1977—. Instr. art Massillon (Ohio) Art Mus., Canton (Ohio) Mus. Art. Adv. com. Edn. Enhancement Partnership Coun., Canton, Ohio, 1992; active Little Art Gallery, 1992, Massillon Art Mus. Mem. NEA, Nat. Art Edn. Assn., Ohio Edn. Assn., Ohio Art Edn. Assn. (chair east cen. divsn. 1985-90, elem. divsn. 1989-91, Art Educator of Yr. 1983, Featured Art Tchr. of Month 1990), Ohio Alliance for Art Edn., Canton Art Inst. (state team art assessment, Art Educator of Yr. 1992), Phi Delta Kappa (newsletter editor McKinley chpt., Nat. Newsletter award 1997). Roman Catholic. Avocations: reading, tennis, music, oil painting, walking. Home: 6897 Deer Trail Ave NE Canton OH 44721-2081 Office: Sandy Valley Sch Dist RR 2 Magnolia OH 44643-9802

ZIMMERMAN, MICHAEL RAYMOND, pathology educator, anthropologist; b. Newark, Dec. 26, 1937; s. Edward Louis and Bessie (Herman) Z.; m. Barbara Elaine Hoffman, Dec. 25, 1960; children: Jill Robin, Wendy Vida. BA, Washington and Jefferson Coll., 1959; MD, NYU, 1963; PhD, U. Pa., 1976. Diplomate Am. Bd. Pathology. Intern in surgery Kings County Hosp., Bklyn., 1963-64; resident-fellow in pathology NYU- Bellevue Med. Ctr., N.Y.C., 1964-68; pathologist Lankenau Hosp., Phila., 1970-72; assoc. prof. pathology and anthropology U. Mich., Ann Arbor, 1977-80; pathologist Jeanes Hosp., Phila., 1982-85; dir. pathology and lab. svcs. Coney Island Hosp., Bklyn., 1985-87; asst. prof. pathology U. Pa., Phila., 1972-77, prof. anthropology, 1985—; assoc. prof. pathology Hahnemann U., Phila., 1980-87, prof. pathology and lab. medicine, 1987-94, chmn. exec. faculty, 1991-94; prof. pathology Mt. Sinai Sch. of Medicine, 1994-95; dir. clin. labs. Maimonides Med. Ctr., Bklyn., 1995-99. Cons. pathologist U. Scranton, Pa., 1985—; rsch. assoc. Univ. Mus., Phila., 1982—; mem. faculty paleopathology course Armed Forces Inst. Pathology, Washington, 1992. Author: Foundations of Medical Anthropology, 1980; co-author: Atlas of Human Paleopathology, 1982; co-editor, author: Dating and Age Determination of Biological Materials, 1986; mem. editl. adv. bd. Advance for Adminstrn. Labs., 1992-94; also articles in Arctic Anthropology, Annals Clin. Lab. Sci. Trustee Martin's Run Life Care Retirement Community, Broomall, Pa., 1988-94. Rackham faculty rsch. grantee U. Mich., 1978-80. Mem. Am. Soc. Clin. Pathologists, Coll. Am. Pathologists (insp. 1988—), Am. Assn. Phys. Anthropologists, Paleopathology Assn. (charter). Achievements include research in paleopathology; field work in Egypt and Alaska. Office: Dept Anthropology U Penn Mus Philadelphia PA 19104

ZIMMERMAN, MURIEL, university official; b. Boston, Nov. 22, 1938; d. Nathan and Edna (Droz) Laden; m. Everett Zimmerman, Apr. 28, 1963; children: Andrew, Daniel. BS, Temple U., 1959, PhD, 1967. Lectr. tech. communications MIT, Cambridge, 1983-85; dir. writing program U. Calif., Santa Barbara, 1985—98. Co-author: MIT Guide to Science and Engineering Writing; editor Energy Rev., 1974-82; contbr. articles to profl. jours. NDEA fellow, 1960-63. Mem. Soc. Tech. Communication, Assn. Tchrs. Tech. Writing, Profl. Communication Soc. of IEEE. Home: 1822 Prospect Ave Santa Barbara CA 93103-1950

ZIMMERMAN, SALLY GAIL, elementary education educator; b. Effingham, Ill., Feb. 22, 1965; d. Billy Dean and Donna Lorene (Nobel) Wills; m. Stephen Scott Zimmerman, July 25, 1993. BS in Elem. Edn., Eastern Ill. U., 1986, MS in Elem. Edn., 1988. Tchr. presch., dir. Rainbow Factory Day Care Ctr., St. Elmo, Ill., 1986-87; grad. asst. Eastern Ill. U., Charleston, 1987-88; tchr. remedial reading Ill. Valley Ctrl. #321, Chillicothe, 1988-91; tchr. reading Altamont (Ill.) C.U.S.D. #10, 1991-94, tchr. 1st grade, 1994—. Mem. Nat. Read Reading Coun., Internat. Reading Assn., Kappa Delta Pi, Phi Delta Kappa. Avocations: reading, piano, travel. Home: RR 2 Box 124 Vandalia IL 62471-9505 Office: Altamont Grade Sch 407 S Edwards St Altamont IL 62411-1799

ZIMMERMAN, VICTORIA ANNMARIE, elementary education educator, administrator; b. Salamanca, N.Y., Aug. 23, 1953; d. Benny John and Catherine Theresa (Oliverio) Vecchiarella; children: Alexia, Samuel. AA in Adminstrn., Ctrl. Tex. U., Killeen, 1986, BS, 1988, postgrad. Dept. asst. Ctrl. Tex. Coll., 1988, coll. instr., 1988-89, developer instrnl. materials, 1987-88; supr., tchr. Seneca Nation Johnson O'Malley Program, Salamanca, 1989—; part-time adult edn. tchr. Catt County BOCES, Olean, N.Y., 1994—. Mem. adv. bd., office adminstrn. dept. Ctrl. Tex. Coll., 1991—; mem. SHARE, Salamanca, 1991-94; dir. JOM Summer Camp, Salamanca, 1990, 91, 92. Recipient Outstanding Cmty. Svc. award Ft. Hood Youth Activities, 1986, Employee of Yr. award Seneca Nation, 1989-90. Roman Catholic. Avocations: reading, pistol target shooting, drawing, computers, tennis.

ZIMMERMANN, PAMELA SEMMENS, secondary education educator; b. Cleve., Jan. 8, 1953; d. Thomas Michael and Katherine (Tehan) Semmens; m. Ronald Howard Murrison, Feb. 28, 1992; 1 child, Geoffrey. BS, U. Ill., 1975; MS, No. Ill. U., 1981, EdD, 1997. Lic. tchr., sch. svc. pers., adminstrn., Ill. Tchr. West Chicago (Ill.) H.S., 1975-80; tchr., gifted coord. Lisle (Ill.) H.S., 1980-85; tchr. Hinsdale (Ill.) Ctrl. H.S., 1985-92; assoc. prin. Adlai Stevenson H.S., Lincolnshire, Ill., 1992—. Speaker Am. Studies Conf., 1988, 90, 92; coord., organizer Am. Studies Ann. Conf., 1991; mem. sch. improvement com. Hinsdale Ctrl. H.S. Author thematic curriculum, world cultures curriculum project. Precinct committeeman Dem. party Milton Twp., DuPage County, Ill., 1986—. Recipient Those Who Excel award of excellence Ill. State Bd. Edn., 1997; James scholar U. Ill. Mem. ASCD, Nat. Coun. Social Studies, Com. on Am. Studies Edn. (mem. steering com.), Phi Delta Kappa. Avocations: piano, travel, athletics. Home: 825 W Hawthorne Blvd Wheaton IL 60187-3476 Office: 1 Stevenson Dr Lincolnshire IL 60069-2824

ZIMMERMANN, THOMAS CALLANDER PRICE, retired historian, educator; b. Bryn Mawr, Pa., Aug. 22, 1934; s. R.Z. and Susan (Goodman) Z.; m. Margaret Upham Ferris. BA, Williams Coll., 1956, Oxford U., 1958, MA, 1964; AM, Harvard U., 1960, PhD, 1964. Asst. prof. Reed Coll., Portland, Oreg., 1964-67, assoc. prof., 1967-73, prof. history, 1973-77, chmn. dept. history, 1973-75; v.p. acad. affairs Davidson (N.C.) Coll., 1977-86, Charles A. Dana prof. History, 1986-99, Charles A. Dana prof. history emeritus, 1999-2000, ret., 2000. Mem. Oreg. Com. for Humanities NEH, 1971—77; mem. Region 14 selection com. Woodrow Wilson Nat. Fellowship Found., Princeton, NJ, 1967—70. Author: Paolo Giovio: The Historian and the Crisis of Sixteenth-Century Italy, 1995 (Helen and Howard R. Marraro Book prize Am. Hist. Assn. 1996, Presdl. Book award Am. Assn. for Italian Studies 1997); co-editor of collected works of Paolo Giovio, 1985; contbr. articles to profl. jours. Pres. Am. Alpine Club, N.Y.C., 1979-82, bd. dirs., 1975-83; bd. dirs. Charlotte Opera Assn., N.C., 1980-82, N.C. Outward Bound Sch., Morgantown, 1978-81; bd. advisors Lowell Obs., 1988-93; mem. Rome Prize Jury (Post-Classical Humanistic Studies) Am. Acad. in Rome, 1993. Danforth fellow, 1956-62, Fulbright fellow, Italy, 1962-64, Villa "I Tatti" fellow Harvard U. Ctr., 1970-71; Am. Council of Learned Socs. fellow, N.Y.C., 1975-76. Mem. Renaissance Soc. Am., Sixteenth Century Studies Conf., Soc. Italian Hist. Studies, Am. Assn. Italian Studies, Phi Beta Kappa.

ZIMMETT, MARK PAUL, lawyer, educator; b. Waukegan, Ill., July 4, 1950; s. Nelson H. Zimmett and Roslyn (Yastrow) Zimmett Grodzin; m. Joan Robin Urken, June 11, 1972; children: Nora Helene, Lili Eleanor. BA, Johns Hopkins U., 1972; JD, NYU, 1975. Bar: N.Y. 1976, U.S. Dist. Ct. (so. and ea. dists.) N.Y. 1976, U.S. Dist. Ct. (no. dist.) Calif. 1980, U.S. Ct. Appeals (2d cir.) 1980, U.S. Supreme Ct. 1981, U.S. Ct. Appeals (5th cir.) 1986, U.S. Ct. Appeals (9th cir.) 1988. Assoc. Shearman & Sterling, N.Y.C., 1975-83, ptnr., 1984-90; adj. assoc. prof. internat. law NYU, 1986-88; lectr. internat. comml. litig. and arbitration Practicing Law Inst., 2000—02. Author: Letters of Credit, New York Practice Guide Business and Commerical Law, 1990; contbr. articles to profl. jours. Mem. ABA (subcom. on letters of credit, com. on uniform comml. code sect. bus. law), N.Y. State Bar Assn., Assn. of the Bar of the City of N.Y., N.Y. County Lawyers Assn. (com. on bus. bankruptcy law), Citizens Union. Democrat. Jewish. Office: 126 E 56th St New York NY 10022-3613

ZIMPHER, NANCY LUSK, academic administrator; b. Gallipolis, Ohio, Oct. 29, 1946; d. Aven Denzle and Elsie Gordon (Hammond) L.; 1 child from a previous marriage, William Fletcher Zimpher; m. Kenneth R. Howey, May 8, 1987. BS, Ohio State U., 1968, MA, 1971, PhD, 1976. Cert. K-12 Tchr., Ohio. English tchr. Montgomery County Schs., Md., 1968, Reynoldsburg (Ohio) Schs., 1970; substitute tchr. Rolla (Mo.) City Schs., 1970-71; tchr. Phelps County Schs., Mo., 1971-72; grad. teaching assoc. Coll. Edn. Ohio State U., Columbus, 1972-73; dir. Coll. of Edn. Ohio State U., Columbus, 1973-74, grad. adminstrn. asst. to dean, 1974-76, dir. field experiences alumni rels., 1976-80, coord. undergraduate programs, 1980-84; asst. prof. Ednl. Policy and Leadership Ohio State U., 1984-86, assoc. prof., 1986-91, full prof., 1991-98, assoc. dean, 1992, dean, 1993, exec. dean, 1994; chancellor, prof. curriculum and instrn. U. Wis., Milw., 1998—2003; pres. U. Cincinnati, 2003—. Prin. investigator U.S. Office Edn. Field Devel. Grant, 1981-83, 85-88; co-principal investigator Metro. Life Found. Grant. 1989—, 1992—; cons. The Holmes Group, Lansing, Mich., 1991—. Book rev., editor: Journal of Teacher Education, 1986-89; co-author: Book Profiles of Preservice Teacher Education, 1989, RATE Profiles, 1987-92. Chair Faculty Compensation and Benefits Commn., 1989-90, Fiscal Com., 1991-92, Spousal Equivalency Com., 1990-91, Search Com., v.p. for Fin., 1992, Ohio State U; pres., chair bd. dirs. Holmes Partnership, 1997; chair edn. vision coun. United Way Franklin County, 1997; chair bd. dirs. United Way Franklin County, 1998. Fellow Com. for Instnl. Coop., Acad. Leadership Program. 1989-90; recipient Disting. Rsch. award, Disting. Teacher Educator award Assn. Tchr. Educators, 1990, Adams Professorshi Coll. Edn. Ind. State U., 1990—, Alumni Disting. Teaching award, The Ohio State U., 1992; named YWCA Woman of Achievement, 1997. Mem. AAUP, Am. Edn. Rsch. Assn., Am. Assn. Coll. Teacher Edn. Rsch. Comm., Assn. Tchr. Educators, ASCD, Phi Delta Kappa. Democrat. Episcopalian. Avocations: watercolorist, golf, sewing. Office: U Cincinnati Cincinnati OH 45221*

ZINAMAN, HELAINE MADELEINE, gifted and talented education educator; b. N.Y.C., Sept. 11, 1951; d. Harold Joseph and Charlotte (Orenstein) Z. BA, Am. U., 1973; MEd, U. Md., 1979. Spl. edn. resource tchr. John Eager Howard Elem. Sch., Capitol Heights, Md., 1973-85; coord. talented and gifted program Glenarden Woods TAG Magnet, Lanham, Md., 1985-96; coord. Owens Rd. Math., Sci. and Tech. Sch., Oxon Hill, Md., 1992-93, Walker Mill Mid. Sch., Capital Heights, Md., 1993-94. Pvt. tutor, Washington, 1982-85, 92—; talented and gifted specialist Talented and Gifted Office, Capitol Heights, 1996-2000, talented and gifted program supr., 2000—; tchr. overview course GED, Bladensburg, Md., 1983; instr. creative thinking Prince George's Community Coll., Largo, Md., 1983, 85; instr. Thinktank, U. Md., College Park, 1989—; mem. Math., Sci. and Tech. Network, 1989; writer curriculum for gifted children, 94, 95. Asst. editor Sci. Bowl, 1990-92. Judge Md. State Odyssey of the Mind Competition; talent on "Count on Us" Cable TV Math. Show. Washington Post grantee, 1989, 95; recipient Bowie Excellence in Edn. award, 1991. Mem. Nat. Assn. for Gifted Children, Assn. for Supervision and Curriculum Devel., Md. State Tchrs. Assn., Nat. Educators Assn. Democrat. Jewish. Avocations: travel, tennis, calligraphy. Home: 4222 38th St NW Washington DC 20016-2258 Office: Talented and Gifted Office 301 9201 E Hampton Dr Capitol Heights MD 20743-3812

ZINBERG, DOROTHY SHORE, science policy educator; b. Boston; m. Norman E Zinberg (dec.); children: Sarah Zinberg Mandel, Anne. BA, MA, Boston U.; PhD, Harvard U., 1966. Research chemist Lever Bros., Cambridge; sr. research assoc. Daniel Yankelovich, Inc., N.Y.C., and; Cambridge Center for Research in Behavioral Scis., 1966-68; NSF research sociologist dept. chemistry U. Coll. London, 1968-69; lectr. Harvard U., 1960—. Mem. adv. com. Office Sci. Pers. NRC, Washington, 1971—74, bd. on engrng. edn., 1991; spl. adviser Aspen Inst.; cons. MacArthur Found., 1989—93; vis. scholar NAS, China, 1987, Nat. Inst. Sci. and Tech., Tokyo, 1991; vis. lectr. Inst. for Human Scis., Vienna, 1995; mem. adv. bd. Erik Erikson Inst. for Edn. and Rsch., 1996—; vis. prof. Imperial Coll., London, 2001—. Columnist: London Times Higher Educ Supplement, 1993—2001, NY Times Syndication, 1994—96. Mem. internat. sci. exchs. NAS, 1994—96, mem comt int relations, 1977—80, mem comt int human resources; chmn adv coun int div NSF, 1978—81; mem coun Int Exchange Scholars, 1978—81; mem comt int exchange engrs NAE, 1987—88; mem adv panel Office Technology Assessment Educ and Employment Scientists and Engrs, 1986—88; trustee Simon's Rock Col, 1971—75; mem panel sci and tech policy NATO, 1995—99; bd. dirs. Fine Arts Workshop, Provincetown, Mass., 1970—86, Bill T. Jones Found for Dance Promotion, 1997—99; bd dirs Gen Scanning, Inc, 1998—99; bd dirs eng educ NRC, 1990—95. Fellow: AAAS (mem comt sci freedom and responsibility 1972—74, comt opportunities in sci 1973—76, comt sci, eng, and pub policy 1982—88, comt exchange scientists with Fed Republic Germany 1987—91, 1991); mem.: NAS (mem comt to evaluate Int Sci and Technology Ctr Moscow 1995—97), Int Sci Policy Found (mem adv bd 1988—), Coun Foreign Relations, Fedn Am Scientists (mem coun 1980—85). Home: 3 Acacia St Cambridge MA 02138-4818 Office: Harvard U 79 JF Kennedy St Cambridge MA 02138 E-mail: dorothy_zinberg@harvard.edu.

ZINK, DAVID DANIEL, retired English educator, writer; b. Kansas City, Mo. s. David Daniel and Virginia (Taylor) Z.; m. Joan Wilson (div. July 13, 1982); children: Laurie Wilson Zink, David Paul Zink; m. Joann Nelson Rocha, Oc.t. 29, 1982 (filed for dissolution of marriage Dec. 19, 1988); 1 child, Christopher Stewart. BJ, U. Tex., 1952; MA in English, U. Colo., 1957, PhD in Victorian Lit., 1962. Instr./assoc. prof. English USAF Acad., Colo. Springs, Colo., 1957-65; prof. English Lamar U., Beaumont, Tex., 1965-77. Part-time English instr., Pasadena City Coll., Pasadena, Calif., 1984-89; exec. recruiter, L.A., 1980-84. Author: (book) The Ancient Stones Speak: A Photographic and Archaeological Atlas of the Megalithic Sites of the World, 1979, Stones of Atlantis, 1990, on camera cons. Leslie Stephen, 1972; co-author: (with wife Joan) You are the Mystery, 1976; in Bolivia for NBC series In Search of..., 1976, to Cousteau Soc. at Bimini Island for PBS special Calypso's Search for Atlantis, 1976; contbr. to TV specials on Atlantis, 1993-98; co-rschr. Kirlian photography project, 1973. Mem. Internat. Explorers Soc. expdn. to Mosquito Coast, NE Honduras, 1976; led 10 underwater projects (the Poseidia expdns.) to an archaeol. site off Bimini Island, 1974-79. Capt. USAF, 1952-65, comdr. mt. top radio relay detachments, 1953-54, Korea. Explorer of Yr. Internat. Explorers Soc., 1976; appointed dir. of rsch. (hon.) Bahamas Antiquities Inst., Nassau, 1975; Poseidia project listed in Spirit of Enterprise from the Rolex Awards, 1978. Fellow Explorer's Club (N.Y.C.). Home: 4060 NW 110th Ave Ocala FL 34482

ZINN, MARY FARRIS, educator; b. Salisbury, NC, July 7, 1937; d. Melbourne R. and Elizabeth (Lingle) Farris; m. Grover A. Zinn, Jr., July 28, 1962; children: Jennifer A., G. Andrew. BS, Wake Forest U., 1959; MA, Duke U., 1962, PhD, 1965. Teaching fellow Duke U., Durham, NC, 1961-62, rsch. assoc. Med. Sch., 1964-66; rsch. and tchg. asst. U. Glasgow, Scotland, 1962-63; asst. prof. Cleve. State U., 1966-68, 75-78; tchr. chemistry, chmn. dept. sci. Lake Ridge Acad., Elyria, Ohio, 1978—2002. Lectr. Cuyahoga C.C., Cleve., 1969, 75-76, Lorain County C.C., Elyria, Ohio, 1971-72, 73-74; asst. prof. Oberlin (Ohio) Coll., 1974-75; US Dept. Energy tchr. rsch. assoc. Los Alamos (N.Mex.) Nat. Lab., 1992. Contbr. articles to sci. jour. Woodrow Wilson fellow, 1960-61; grantee Dept. Energy and NEH, summer 1979, Inst. Chem. Edn., summer 1986; Teaching Rsch. Assoc. fellow Dept. Energy, summer 1992. Mem. NSTA, Am. Chem. Soc., Phi Beta Kappa, Sigma Xi. Democrat. Episcopalian. Avocations: swimming, hiking, reading. Home: 61 Glenhurst Dr Oberlin OH 44074-1423

ZINNI, HANNAH CASE, foreign language educator; b. Cin., Oct. 10, 1944; d. John Persinger and Althea Kay Case; m. Thomas Arthur Copeland, Aug. 27, 1966 (div. Sept. 1977); m. Chester Samuel Zinni, Sept. 23, 1977; children: Chester, Peter, Meredith. BA, Oberlin Coll., 1966; MA, Northwestern U., Evanston, Ill., 1967, PhD, 1971. Prof. French Slippery Rock (Pa.) U., 1970—. Author: Art and the Artist in the Works of Samuel Beckett, 1975. Coun. mem. Pa. Humanities Coun., Phila., 1996-2002; founder, pres. French Club New Castle, Pa., 1986—. Recipient Humanities grant Pa. Humanities Coun., 1989, 92, Social Equity grant Commonwealth Pa., 1992. Mem. MLA, Samuel Beckett Found., Am. Assn. Tchrs. French, Pa. Modern Lang., Phi Beta Kappa. Avocations: choral singing, tennis, travel. Office: Slippery Rock U Dept Modern Langs/Cultures Slippery Rock PA 16057 Fax: 724-738-2263. E-mail: hannah.zinni@sru.edu.

ZINS, MARTHA LEE, elementary education educator, media specialist; b. Mankato, Minn., Dec. 14, 1945; d. Hubert Joseph and Rose Marie (Johannes) Z. BS in History, Mankato State U., 1966, BA in English, 1967; MLS, Western Mich. U., 1971; postgrad., U. Minn. Tchr. history Worthington H.S., Minn., 1966-67; sch. media generalist Hopkins West Jr. H.S., Minn., 1967-83, Curren Elem. Sch., Hopkins, Minn., 1986—2003; dir. media svcs. Hopkins Sch. Dist., Minn., 2003—. Mem. Hopkins Dist. Tech. Com., 1986—; co-chair Hopkins Elem. Sci. Com., 1991—94. Contbr. articles to profl. jours.; presenter and speaker at confs. Pres. Saddlewood Patio Homes Assn. Inc., Minnetonka, 1991-95, bd. dirs., 1987-95; mem. various Minn. Gov.'s Task Forces; del. Ngo Forum 95, Beijing; mem. WILPF's Internat. Peace Train (Helsinki to Beijing), 1995; co-chair Minn. Metro WilPF, 1998-99; mem. Metronet Adv. Com., 1994-96. Mem. NEA (bd. dirs. 1976-77, 91-97, Woman Educator of Yr. 1975), ALA, ACLU, Minn. Edn. Assn. (bd. dirs. 1975-86, 91-97, v.p. 1977-83, pres. 1983-86, Human Rels. award 1979), Minn. Civil Liberties Union (bd. dirs. 1982-95), State of Minn. Tchrs. Retirment Assn. (bd. dirs. 1989—), Minn. Ednl. Media Orgn. (co-founder, v.p. 1990), Delta Kappa Gamma (Beta Beta chpt., co-founder, chpt. treas.), Beta Phi Mu, Phi Alpha Theta. Mem. Dem. Farm Labor Party. Roman Catholic. Avocations: travel, reading, photography, volunteer work, environmental/hunger concerns. Home: 17509 Saddlewood Ln Minnetonka MN 55345-2663 Office: Curren Sch Dept Media 1600 Mainstreet Hopkins MN 55343-7409 E-mail: marti_zins@hopkins.k12.mn.us.

ZINSER, ELISABETH ANN, academic administrator; b. Meadville, Pa., Feb. 20, 1940; d. Merle and Fae Zinser. BS, Stanford U., 1964; MS, U. Calif., San Francisco, 1966, MIT, 1982; PhD, U. Calif., Berkeley, 1972. Nurse VA Hosp., Palo Alto, Calif., 1964-65, San Francisco, 1969-70; instr. Sch. Nursing U. Calif., San Francisco, 1966-69; pre-doctoral fellow Nat. Inst. Health, Edn. and Welfare, 1971-72; adminstr. Sch. Medicine U. Wash., Seattle, 1972-75, Coun. Higher Edn., State of Ky., 1975-77; prof., dean. Coll. Nursing U. N.D., Grand Forks, 1977-83; vice chancellor acad. affairs U. N.C., Greensboro, 1983-89; pres. Gallaudet U., Washington, 1988, U. Idaho, Moscow, 1989-95; chancellor U. Ky., Lexington, 1995—. Bd. dirs. Am. Coun. Edn., Washington, 1995-98; chmn. commn. on outreach and tech. transfer; bd. dirs. Nat. Assn. State Univs. and Land Grant Colls., Am. Assn. Colls. and Univs., 1999—, Ctr. Acad. Integrity, 1998—; co-chair Bd. Oceans and Atmosphere, 1998—; cons. in field. Primary author: (with others) Contemporary Issues in Higher Education, 1985, Higher Education Research, 1988; spkr. in field. Bd. dirs. Humana Hosp., Greensboro, 1986-88; v.p., bd. dirs. Ea. Music Festival, Greensboro, 1987-89; trustee N.C. Coun. Econ. Edn., 1985-89, Greensboro Day Sch., 1987-89; ann. mem. Truman Found. Panel; bd. dirs. YMCA, Lexington, 1999—. Leadership fellow Bush Found., 1981-82. Office: U Ky 111 Adminstrn Bldg Lexington KY 40506-0001

ZIPPIN, CALVIN, epidemiologist, educator; b. Albany, N.Y., July 17, 1926; s. Samuel and Jennie (Perkel) Z.; m. Patricia Jayne Schubert, Feb. 9, 1964; children: David Benjamin, Jennifer Dorothy. AB magna cum laude, SUNY, Albany, 1947; ScD, Johns Hopkins U., Balt., 1953. Rsch. asst. Sterling-Winthrop Rsch. Inst., Rensselaer, NY, 1947-50, Johns Hopkins U., Balt., 1950—53; instr. biostats. Sch. Pub. Health, U. Calif., Berkeley, 1953-55; asst. to full rsch. biostatistician Sch. Medicine U. Calif., San

Francisco, 1955-67, asst. prof. preventive medicine, 1958-60; post doctoral fellow London Sch. Hygiene and Tropical Medicine, 1964-65; prof. epidemiology U. Calif., San Francisco, 1967-91, prof. emeritus, 1991—. Vis. assoc. prof. stats. Stanford U., 1962; adv. WHO, 1969—; vis research worker Middlesex Hosp. Med. Sch., London, 1975; various coms. Am. Cancer Soc. and Nat. Cancer Inst., 1956—; faculty adviser Regional Cancer Centre, Trivandrum, India, 1983—; cons., lectr., vis. prof. in field. Co-author book, book chpts.; author or co-author papers primarily on biometry and epidemiology of cancer; editorial advisor Jour. Stats. in Medicine, Boston, 1981-86. Mem., alt. mem. Dem. Ctrl. Com., Marin County, Calif., 1987-96. Recipient Disting. Alumnus award SUNY, Albany, 1969, also awards, fellowships and grants for work in cancer biometry and epidemiology. Fellow Am. Statis. Assn., Am. Coll. Epidemiology, Royal Statis. Soc. Gt. Britain; mem. Biometric Soc. (mem. internat. coun. 1978-81, pres. Western N.Am. region 1979-80), Calif. Cancer Registrars Assn. (hon.), Internat. Assn. Cancer Registries (hon.), B'nai B'rith (pres. Golden Gate lodge 1970-71, pres. Greater San Francisco Bay area coun. 1974-75), Phi Beta Kappa, Sigma Xi, Delta Omega. Office: Univ Calif Dept Epidemiology Biostats San Francisco CA 94143-0560 E-mail: czippin@itsa.ucsf.edu.

ZIRAKZADEH, ARMANDO ARDESHIR, elementary educator; b. Tehran, Iran, Nov. 16, 1955; came to U.S., 1956; s. Aboulghassem and Refugio (Flores) Z.; m. Twila Jean Townsend, Aug. 25, 1979; children: Sabrina Renee, Donovan Aboul. BFA, Colo. State U., 1981, art teaching cert., 1989. Cert. K-12 art specialist, Colo. Owner, operator Master Screen Art, silkscreening, Ft. Collins, 1984-91; tchr. art, co-chmn. sch. improvement team Eisenhower Elem. Sch., Boulder, Colo., 1990—. Mem. art steering com., 1992; chmn. art curriculum com. Boulder Valley Sch. Dist., 1992—, author proficiency and outcomes standards. Mem. Paul Douglas Scholarship com., 1991, 92. Roman Catholic. Home: 961 Eldorado Ln Louisville CO 80027-3105

ZIRILLI, FRANCESCO, mechanical engineer, engineering educator; b. Buenos Aires, Apr. 23, 1956; s. Giuseppe and Giuseppa (Nucifora) Z.; m. Joanne A. Long, July 8, 1994; 3 stepchildren: Jim Long, Kristen Long, Lisa Long. BSME, Clarkson U., Potsdam, N.Y., 1977, MSME, 1979, PhD in Mech. Engring., 1985. Assoc. engr. GE Co., Schenectady, N.Y., 1978-80; cons. engr. Stress Tech., Inc., Rochester, N.Y., 1983-84; project mgr. Xerox Corp., Rochester, 1984—; sr. lectr. U. Rochester, 1986-96. Contbr. articles to profl. jours. Mem. ASME, TAPPI, Pi Tau Sigma. Achievements include 2 patents. Office: XEROX Corp 800 Phillips Rd # 207-1Z Webster NY 14580-9791

ZIRKIND, RALPH, physicist, educator; b. N.Y.C., Oct. 20, 1918; s. Isaac and Zicel (Lifshitz) Z.; m. Ann Goldman, Nov. 22, 1940; children: Sheila Zirkind Knopf, Elaine Zirkind Gorman, Edward I. BS, CCNY, 1940; MS, Ill. Inst. Tech., 1945; postgrad., George Washington U., 1946-47; PhD, U. Md., 1950; D.Sc., U. R.I., 1968. Physicist Navy Dept., 1945-50, chief physicist, 1951-60; physicist Oak Ridge Nat. Lab., 1950-51, Advanced Research Project Agy., Washington, 1960-63; prof. Poly. Inst. Bklyn., 1963-70, U. R.I., Kingston, 1970-72, adj. prof., 1972—; physicist Advanced Research Projects Agy., Arlington, Va., 1972-74; cons. Advanced Rsch. Projects Agy., Arlington, Va., 1974—. Lectr. U. Md., 1947-48, 48-50, George Washington U., 1952-53, U. Mich., 1964, 66, Haifa Inst. Tech., 1971; cons. ACDA, Jet Propulsion Lab., Calif. Inst. Tech.; cons. to industry, 1974—. Contbg. author: Jet Propulsion Series, 1952, FAR Infrared Properties of Materials, 1968, NAS Study Biology and Exploration of Mars, 1966; editor: Electromagnetic Sensing of Earth, 1967, Procs. SPIE-Developments in Electronic Imagining Techniques, vol. 32, 1972; mem. editl. bd. Infrared Physics, 1963—; contbr. articles profl. jours. Recipient Meritorious Civilian Svc. award Navy Dept., 1957; Meritorious Civilian Svc. award Dept. Def., 1970; Outstanding Educator of Am. medal, 1972; Maj. Contbn. award BMDO/AIAA, 1994; Spl. Lifetime Achievement Award for Pioneering Work in Sensors, SPIE, 2002. Mem. Am. Phys. Soc., N.Y. Acad. Scis., Sigma Xi, Sigma Pi Sigma (SPIE Aerosense Lifetime Achievement award 2002), Eta Kappa Nu. Home: 820 Hillsboro Dr Silver Spring MD 20902-3202 Office: 4001 Fairfax Dr Ste 700 Arlington VA 22203-1618

ZITARELLI, DAVID EARL, mathematics educator; b. Chester, Pa., Aug. 12, 1941; s. Earl John and Claire (Nungesser) Z.; m. Anita Helene Paul; children: Paul, Nicole. Student, Pa. Mil Coll., 1959-62; BA, Temple U., 1963, MA, 1965; PhD, Penn State U., 1970. Asst. prof. Temple U., Phila., 1970-76, assoc. prof., 1976—. Visiting prof. Vanderbilt U., Nashville, Tenn., 1976. Author: Ascent of Mathematics, 1984, Finite Mathematics, 1989, 3d edit., 1997, Finite Mathematics with Calculus, 1989, 2d edit., 1992, Calculus, 1989, 2d edit., 1993, Brief Calculus, 1990, 2d edit., 1993, Linear Algebra LABS with MATLAB, 1994, 3d edit., 2003, A Collaborative Approach to Mathematics, 1999. Recipient Excellence in Teaching award Temple U. Alumni Assn., 1989, Lindbach award for disting. tchg., 2001. Mem. Am. Math. Soc., Math. Assn. of Am., Canadian Soc. for History and Philosophy of Math., Brit. Soc. for the History Math., History of Sci. Soc. Avocations: running, coaching girls softball. Home: 1012 Westwood Dr Media PA 19064-3731 Office: Temple U Dept Math Philadelphia PA 19122

ZITTO, RICHARD JOSEPH, physics educator; b. Lisbon, Ohio, Sept. 1, 1945; s. Tony Joseph and Olive Lucille (Davison) Z.; m. Pamela Daryl Irons, July 22, 1967; children: Angela Marie, Elena Michelle. BS in Sci. Edn., Ohio State U., 1968, MA in Phys. Sci. Edn., 1978. Tchr. sci. Kenton (Ohio) Jr. H.S., 1968-70; tchr. physics and sci. Kenton Sr. H.S., 1970-76; tchr. physics Boardman H.S., Youngstown, Ohio, 1976-99; physics educator Youngstown State U., 1981—, coord. Physics Olympics, 1994—. Dir. Youngstown Area Physics Alliance, 1987—. Trustee Hardin Meml. Hosp., Kenton, 1971-76; bd. dirs. Blue Cross of Lima, Ohio, 1973-76, Nat. Multiple Sclerosis Soc. N.E. Ohio, 1981-91; trustee Columbiana Pub. Libr., 1990—, pres., 1993-95, 2000—. Recipient Outstanding Young Educator award Kenton Jaycees, 1972, Outstanding Sci. Tchr. Youngstown State U. Sigma Xi, 1980, Career Educator award Ohio State U. Coll. Edn., 1997; A. Jennings scholar Martha Holden Jennings Found. Fellow Ohio Acad. Sci.; mem. ASCD, Am. Assn. Physics Tchrs. (physics tchg. resource agt. 1986—, pres. Ohio sect. 1989-90, mem. physics in high schs. com. 1991-94, History and Philosophy com. 1999-2002), Ont. Assn. Physics Tchrs., Nat. Sci. Tchrs. Assn., N.E. Ohio Edn. Assn. (co-chmn. sci. workshop 1979—), Sci. Edn. Coun. Ohio, United Tchg. Profession, Lions, Rotary (sec. 1978-79), Elks. Republican. Presbyterian. Avocations: woodworking, tennis, history of science, collecting antique physics apparatus. Home: 332 W Park Ave Columbiana OH 44408-1242 Office: Physics & Astronomy Dept Youngstown State Univ Youngstown OH 44555-0001 E-mail: rjzitto@ysu.edu.

ZIZIC, THOMAS MICHAEL, physician, educator; b. Milw., Dec. 9, 1939; s. Michael Mitchell Zizic and Dorothy (Batas) Ciric; m. Karen Owens, June 15, 1962 (div. Sept. 1967); m. Martha Ann Ardos, Nov. 22, 1967; children: Lara Ann, Kristine Michelle. BS, U. Wis., 1961; MD, Johns Hopkins U., 1965. Intern Johns Hopkins Hosp., Balt., 1965-66, asst. resident, 1966-67, fellow in internal medicine, 1969-71, instr. dept. medicine, 1971-73, asst. prof. medicine, 1971-81, assoc. prof. medicine, 1981—. Pvt. practice, Balt., 1988—; co-dir. Chesapeake Osteoporosis Ctr., Balt., 1988—; dir. med. affairs Murray Electronics, 1993—; v.p. med. quality care Physicians Quality Care, 1995—; pres. U.S. Osteoporosis Network, Inc., 1996—; co-founder, dir. Creative Environ. Solutions, Inc., 1996—; cons. in field. Contbr. numerous articles and abstracts to profl. jours. V.p. Md. chpt. Arthritis Found., Balt., 1976-77; chmn. Md. Commn. on Arthritis and Related Diseases, 1986-90. Fellow Am. Coll. Rheumatology, 1986; Md. Soc. Rheumatic Diseases (pres. 1975-76), D.C. Rheumatism Assn., Balt. City Med. Soc., Johns Hopkins Hosp. Med. Soc., Arthritis Found. (fellow 1971-73, v.p. 1976-77, med. and sci. com. 1977-79, chmn. profl. edn. com. 1977-78, govtl. affairs com. 1979-83), Phi Beta Kappa, Phi Kappa Phi, Phi Eta Sigma. Avocations: skiing, tennis. Office: 5601 Loch Raven Blvd Baltimore MD 21239-2905

ZOFFER, H. JEROME, business educator, university dean; b. Pitts., July 23, 1930; s. William and Sarah Leah (Fisher) Z.; m. Maye Rattner, July 19, 1959; children: Gayle Risa, William Michael. BBA, U. Pitts., 1952, MA, 1953, PhD, 1956; CPCU, Am. Inst., Phila., 1954. Sales and mgmt. cons., 1952-60; instr. Sch. Bus. Adminstrn., U. Pitts., 1953-56; asst. prof. Sch. Bus. Adminstrn. U. Pitts., 1956-59, assoc. prof. Joseph M. Katz Grad. Sch. Bus., 1959-66, prof. Sch. Bus. Adminstrn., Grad. Sch. Bus., 1966—, chmn. dept. real estate and ins., 1958-60, dir. spl. studies, 1960-62, asst. dean for acad. affairs, 1962-65, assoc. dean for adminstrn., 1965-68, dean Grad. Sch. Bus., 1968-96. Bd. dirs. Emerald Growth Fund, Emerald Banking and Fin. Funds, Emerald Tech. Fund; Ford Found. fellow in applied math. U. Pa., Phila., 1961—62; mem. visitation com. Am. Assembly Collegiate Schs. of Bus., 1972—2000, mem. stds. com., 1974—78, mem. exec. com., 1975—87, chmn. accreditation rsch. com., 1974—84, v.p. bd. dirs., 1984—85, pres., 1985—86, chmn. Mid. State Evaluation Accrediting Teams, 1967—85. Author: The History of Automobile Liability Insurance Rating: 1900-1958, 1959; also monographs.; contbr. articles to profl. jours. Bd. dirs., v.p. Leadership Inst. for Community Devel., 1968-73, Allegheny chpt. Epilepsy Found. Am., 1971-77; bd. dirs. Pitts. Dist. Export Coun., 1974-77, Czech Mgmt. Ctr.; bd. govs. Internat. Ins. Seminars, Inc., 1968-77; pres. Temple Sinai Congregation, 1979-81; mem. festival bd. Three Rivers Art Festival, 1988-93; mem. steering com. Leadership Pitts., 1986-91; sec. Am. Jewish Com., 1993-95; bd. dirs. Student Cons. Project, U. Pitts., 1970-96, Consortium for Coop. and Competitiveness, 1986-96, Moral Force in the Workplace, 1986-96; investment com. United Jewish Fedn., 1992-95; sec.-treas. David Berg Found. Named Man of Yr. in Edn., Vectors Pitts., 1986, Disting. Alumnus, 1989, U. Pitts. Alumni Assn. Mem. Soc. Psychol. Study Social Issues, Mid. Atlantic Assn. Colls. Bus. Adminstrn. (pres. 1972-73), Am. Assn. Univ. Adminstrs. (exec. com. 1971-79, pres. 1975-77, dir. 1980-83, pres. found. 1983-95), Univ. Club (bd. dirs. 1988-94, sec. 1990-91, v.p. 1991-92, pres. 1992-93), Omicron Delta Gamma, Beta Gamma Sigma (pres. Beta chpt. 1964-68). Home: 220 N Bellefield Ave Ph 1201 Pittsburgh PA 15213-1468 Office: U Pitts Pitts Campus Katz Grad Sch Bus Pittsburgh PA 15260 E-mail: zoffer@katz.pitt.edu.

ZOIS, CONSTANTINE NICHOLAS ATHANASIOS, meteorology educator; b. Newark, Feb. 21, 1938; s. Athanasios Konstantinos and Asimina (Speros-Blekas) Z.; m. Elyse Stein, Dec. 26, 1971; children: Jennifer, Jonathan. BA, Rutgers U., 1961; MS, Fla. State U., 1965; PhD, Rutgers U., 1980. Draftsman Babcock and Wilcox Corp., Newark, 1956; designer Foster Wheeler Corp., Carteret, N.J., 1956; instr. Rutgers U., New Brunswick, N.J., 1961-62; grad. asst. Fla. State U., Tallahassee, 1962-65; rsch. meteorologist Nat. Weather Svc., Garden City, L.I., N.Y., 1965-67; prof. Kean Coll. N.J., Union, 1967—. Founder meteorology program Kean Coll., N.J.; cons. Connell, Foley and Geiser, Roseland, N.J., 1986-88; chmn. Kean Coll. All-Coll. Promotion com., 1991-93. Author, editor: Papers in Marine Science, 1971; author: Observation of the Newark N.J. Nocturnal Heat Island and Its Consideration in Terms of a Physical Model, 1980, Dynamical and Physical Oceanography, 1988, Atmospheric Dynamics: Exercises and Problems, 1988, Climatology Workbook, 1988, Weather Map Folio, 1989; contbg. author: Outcomes Assessment at Kean College of N.J., 1992, Synoptic Meterology-Exercises and Readings, Vols. 1-3, 1995. Mem. AAAS, Nat. Weather Assn., Am. Meteorol. Soc. (pres. N.J. chpt. 1980-81), N.Y. Acad. Scis. (vice chmn. atmospheric scis. sect. 1986-87, chmn. 1987-88, adv. com. atmospheric sci. sect., 1988—), N.J. Marine Scis. Consortium, Phi Beta Kappa. Republican. Greek Orthodox. Avocations: guitar, banjo, fishing, baseball, snorkeling. Home: 2798 Carol Rd Union NJ 07083-4831 Office: Kean Coll of NJ Dept Meterology Morris Ave Union NJ 07083-7117

ZOLLER, MICHAEL, otolaryngologist, head and neck surgeon, educator; b. New Orleans, July 21, 1947; s. Harry and Mildred (Daitch) Z.; m. Linda Kramer, Dec. 21, 1974; children: Rebecca, Jonathan. BS, U. New Orleans, 1971; MD, Tulane U., 1972. Resident in gen. surgery Jewish Hosp., St. Louis, Washington U. Sch. Medicine, 1972—74; resident in otolaryngology Mass. Eye and Ear Infirmary, Harvard U. Med. Sch., Boston, 1974—77; pres. Ear, Nose and Throat Assocs., Savannah, Ga., 1977—2003; chmn. Eye, Ear, Nose & Throat Dept. Candler Hosp., 1996—98. Asst. clin. prof. surgery Med. Coll. Ga., Augusta, 1982—96, assoc. clin. prof. surgery, 1996—2003; assoc. prof. surgery Mercer Med. Sch., 2000—03; dir. otology otoneurology dept. St. Joseph's Hosp., Savannah, 1994—2003. Chmn. med. divsn. United Way, Savannah, 1990, chmn. profl. divsn., 1991, 94-2001, vice chmn. campaign, 2002, bd. dirs., 2002-03, allocation panel, 1997-2002, chmn. campaign, 2003; bd. dirs. Am. Cancer Soc., Savannah, 1993-2000, pres. Chatham County unit, 1996-97, chmn. bd., 1997-98; bd. dirs. Savannah Country Day Sch., 1993-97, chmn. ann. campaign, 1995-96; bd. dirs. Candler Hosp. Found., 2001-03; pres. Savannah Jewish Fedn., 1991-93; active Savannah Jewish Fedn. Endowment Bd., 1995-99; mem. med. adv. bd. South Coll., 1996-2000; mem. parents coun. Washington U., St. Louis, 1997-2001, Tulane U., 2002-03; bd. dirs. Leadership Savannah, 1996-98. Recipient Young Leadership award Savannah Jewish Fedn., 1985, Boss of Yr. award Savannah Jaycees, 1993, Celebrate Savannah award for outstanding contbns. to Savannah, Ga. Guardian, 1996; Harvard U. Med. Sch. fellow, 1976-77. Fellow: ACS; mem.: AMA, Ga. Soc. Otolaryngology (pres. bd. trustees 1997—98, editor newsletter 1998—2001), So. Med. Assn., Med. Assn. Ga. (mem. ho. of dels. 1990—2003, bd. dirs. 1995—2003, editl. bd. 2001—03, Ga. Cup award 1993, Ayest-Wyth Cmty. Svc. award 1996, Cmty. Svc. award 2001), 1st Dist. Med. Assn. (pres. 1987—88), Ga. Med. Soc. (pres. 1992, chmn. bd. trustees 1997, John B. Rabun Cmty. Svc. award 1995, Hero's award 2001), Am. Neurotology Soc., Am. Soc. Head and Neck Surgery, Am. Acad. Otolaryngology and Head and Neck Surgery (tonsils and adenoids com. 1996—99, sleep disorders com. 1996—2002, pediatric otolaryngolgoy com. 2003—). Office: Ear Nose and Throat Assocs Savannah 5201 Frederick St Savannah GA 31405-4501 E-mail: MZ47ent@aol.com.

ZOLOTOW, ELLEN See DRAGONWAGON, CRESCENT

ZONDLER, JOYCE EVELYN, kindergarten educator; b. Jersey City, N.J., June 28, 1952; d. Vincent Roger and Marta (Gruber) Hohmann; m. Kenneth P. Zondler, June 20, 1976 (div.). BA, Jersey City State Coll., 1974, MA, 1981. Cert. elem., early childhood tchr., N.J. Kindergarten tchr. Robert Fulton Sch., North Bergen, N.J., 1974—. Mem. curriculum rev. coms. for math. and sci. North Bergen Schs., 1993—, for lang. arts, 1992-93, mem. report card rev. com. Mem. exec. bd. Fulton Sch. PTA, 1976-86, sec., 1978-80, v.p. 1980-82, treas. 1982-86. Recipient Gov.'s Recognition award, 1991, Tchr. Recognition Awd., 1999. Mem. North Bergen Edn. Assn. (sec. 1989-91, v.p. 1991-93, pres. 1993-98). Democrat. Roman Catholic. Office: Robert Fulton Sch 7407 Hudson Ave North Bergen NJ 07047-5698

ZOOK, MERLIN WAYNE, meteorologist, educator; b. Connellsville, Pa., July 2, 1937; s. Ellrose Durr and Frances Adeline (Loucks) Z.; m. Maxine Beatrice Hartzler, May 1, 1965; children: Kevin Ray, Kathleen Joy. BA, Goshen (Ind.) Coll., 1959; MS, Pa. State U., 1961. Cert. consulting meteorologist. Rsch. assoc. U. Mich., Ann Arbor, 1958; grad. asst. Pa. State U., University Park, 1960-61; audio-visual asst., staff meteorologist Mennonite Cen. Com., Akron, Pa., 1961-63; air quality program specialist Pa. Dept. Environ. Protection, Harrisburg, Pa., 1963-2000; ret., 2000. Book reviewer Sci. Edn. Dept. Boston U., 1990-92, Nat. Weather Assn., Temple Hills, Md., 1983-88, book rev. editor, 1988-92; scientist, participant AAAS-Bell Atlantic Found., Washington, 1989-90; lectr. Goshen (Ind.) Coll., Messiah Coll., Grantham, Pa. Author, contbr.: (chpt.) Behind the Dim Unknown, 1966. Guest lectr. Millersville (Pa.) State U., 1988, 90, Boy Scouts Am., Camp Hill, Pa., 1990, Pa. State U., Middletown, 1990, 91—, Cub Scouts Am., Camp Hill, 1991—. Mem. Am. Meteorol. Soc., Union of Concerned Scientists. Achievements include development of models for the daily prediction of the Air Quality Index of Pa.; collection of cloud type photographs with classifications for study of cloud characteristics/physics; research in meso-scale meteorology and localized forecasting, on the relationship between solar radiation and formation of ozone in urban areas in Pa., research and development of mathematical models for the prediction of ozone episodes in urban areas; on migratory patterns of local birds influenced by meteorological conditions. Home: 105 June Dr Camp Hill PA 17011-5069 E-mail: mwzook@itech.net.

ZOPF, EVELYN LANOEL MONTGOMERY, guidance counselor; b. Laurel, Miss., July 10, 1932; d. Arthur LaNoel and Ruby Lee (Lewis) Montgomery; m. Paul Edward Zopf Jr., Aug. 5, 1956; 1 child, Eric Paul. MusB in Edn., U. So. Miss., 1953, MA, 1954. Guidance counselor U. So. Miss., 1953-54, U. Fla., 1954-56; tchr. New Orleans City Schs., 1956-57; pub. sch. music tchr., band dir., choral dir. Putnam County Schs., Fla., 1957-59; pvt. music tchr. voice, piano, clarinet and trumpet, 1953-61; substitute tchr. Guilford County Schs., 1959-93; mem. arts series com. Guilford Coll., 1973-77; interim choir dir. New Garden Friends Meeting, 1961, chmn. music com., 1974-76; adviser to fgn. students, 1954-56, 59-62; mem. First Internat. Congress on Quaker Edn. Com., 1987-88, Guilford Coll.'s Sesquicentennial Com., 1985-87; speaker various religious and art groups. Vol. ARC, Boy Scouts Am.; mem. U. Fla. Union Bd., 1955-56; precinct del. County Dem. Conv., 1977, 79, precinct worker, 1980, campaign worker, 1980; bd. dirs. Greensboro Friends of Music, 1970-71, Greensboro chpt. N.C. Symphony Bd., 1979-93, mem. feeder bd. The Guilford Coll. Friends of the Lib. Bd., 1993-94, mem. exec. bd., 1994-95. Mem. United Soc. of Friends Women (pres. 1979-81), Internat. Fellowship Quaker Women, Guilford Coll. Community Chorus, Phi Mu. Clubs: Women's Soc. (dir. 1978-82), Guilford Coll. Arts Appreciation (v.p. 1980-81, pres. 1981-82), Guilford Gourmet. Home: 815 George White Rd Greensboro NC 27410-3317

ZOPF, PAUL EDWARD, JR., sociologist; b. Bridgeport, Conn., July 9, 1931; s. Paul Edward and Hilda Ernestine (Russell) Z.; m. Evelyn Lanoel Montgomery, Aug. 5, 1956; 1 child, Eric Paul. BS, U. Conn., 1953; MS, U. Fla., 1955, PhD, 1966. Asst. prof. sociology Guilford Coll., Greensboro, N.C., 1959-66, assoc. prof., 1966-70, prof., 1970-72, Dana prof. sociology, 1972-93; Dana prof. sociology emeritus, 1993—; chief. coll. marshal, 1997—. Cons. U.S. Dept. Agrl., local govt. agys. Author: North Carolina: A Demographic Profile, 1967, Demography: Principles and Methods, 1970, 76, Principles of Inductive Rural Sociology, 1970, Profile of Women in Greensboro: 1990, 1977, Sociocultural Systems, 1978, Cultural Accumulation in Latin America, 1980, Population: An Introduction to Social Demography, 1984, Income and Poverty Status of Women in Greensboro, 1985, America's Older Population, 1986, American Women in Poverty, 1989, Mortality Patterns and Trends in the United States, 1992; editor Guilford Coll. Self-Study Accreditation Report; contbr. articles to profl. jours. Recipient Teaching Excellence award Guilford Coll., 1978; grantee Kenan Found., 1970-79, Guilford Coll., 1979-93. Mem. Am. Sociol. Assn., Internat. Union Sci. Study Population, So. Sociol. Soc., Rural Sociol. Soc., Population Reference Bur. Mem. Soc. Of Friends. Home: 815 George White Rd Greensboro NC 27410-3317 Office: Guilford Coll Dept Sociology Greensboro NC 27410

ZORITCH, GEORGE, dance educator, choreographer; b. Moscow, June 6, 1917; came to U.S., 1935; s. Serge and Helen (Grunke) Z. Diploma, Lady Deterding's Russian Sch., Paris, 1933. Mem. Ida Rubinstein Ballet Co., Paris, 1933-34, Pavlova's Co., Eng., W.I., Australia, India, Egypt, 1934-35, Col. W. de Basil's Balle Russe de Monte-Carlo, U.S., Europe, 1935-37; soloist Denham Ballet Russe de Monte-Carlo, U.S., Can., S.Am., Europe, 1938-42; actor, dancer in plays, musicals, concert tours, Broadway and across U.S., S.Am. and Europe, 1943-50; actor 17 movies in Hollywood and Rome; premier danseur noble Grand Ballet de Marquis de Cuevas, Europe, Africa, S.Am., 1951-57, Denham Ballet Russe de Monte Carlo, U.S.A., 1957-62; founder George Zoritch Sch. Classical Ballet, West Hollywood, Calif., 1963-73; prof. fine arts, mem. dance faculty com. fine arts U. Ariz., 1973-87. Freelance engagements, 1973—; symposium panelist New Orleans Internat. Ballet Conf. for A Ballets Russes Celebration, 2000; hon. guest IX Internat. Competition of Ballet Artists, June 2001, courtesy of Bolshoi Theatre, Moscow; adjudicator ballet competitions including Arabesque Perm, Russia, 1996, 2002. Author: (memoir) Ballet Mystique, 2000; editor records: George Zoritch for Classical Ballet, 1962-65. Hon. guest Bolshoi Ballet, Moscow, Russia, 2001. Recipient Key to Jacksonville (Fla.), 1968, Bolshoi Theatre medallion of merit award IV Internat. Ballet Competition, Moscow, 1981, Ariz. Dance Treasures award Ariz. Dance Arts Alliance and Ariz. State U. Dept. Dance, 1992, Merit award Acad. Choreographic Sch. A. Vaganova, 1993, Vaslav Nijinsky medallion of merit award Consulate Gen. of Poland, 1994, Diaghilev House Silver Medallion of Merit award 6th Dance Competition of Paris, 1994, U. Ariz. Spl. Tribute, 2001, Life Time Achievement award Western Mich. U., 2002; named Amb. San Antonio World Hemisphere, 1968. Mem. Ariz. Dance Arts Alliance (hon. life), Phoenix Ballet Gild (hon.), Nat. Soc. Arts and Letters (Medallion of Merit award Valley of Sun chpt. 1990). E-mail: zoritch@dakotacom.net.

ZORN, ROBERT LYNN, education educator; b. Youngstown, Ohio, Mar. 22, 1938; s. Robert S. and Frances L. Zorn; B.S. Ed., Kent State U., 1959; M.Ed., Westminster Coll., 1964; Ph.D., U. Pitts., 1970; m. Joan M. Wilkos, Apr. 26, 1957; children: Deborah Lynn, Patricia Lynn. Tchr., West Branch (Ohio) Schs., 1961-62; elem. prin. Poland (Ohio) Schs., 1962-67, supt. schs., 1976— ; high sch. unit prin. Boardman (Ohio) Schs., 1967-70; dir. adminstrv. services Mahoning County (Ohio) Schs., 1970-73, asst. supt., 1973-76; adj. prof. edn. Westminister Coll., 1985—; chmn. Ohi Adv. Com. to State Dept. Edn.; chmn. McGuffey Hist. Soc. Nat. Educator's Hall of Fame. Chmn. Mahoning County chpt. Am. Cancer Soc.; pres. bd. trustees Poland Methodist Ch.; trustee Mahoning County chpt. Am. Heart Assn. Served to lt. USAF, 1959-61. Mem. Doctoral Assn. Educators (life), Am. Assn. Sch. Adminstrs., Ohio PTA (life; Educator of Yr. 1980-81), Phi Delta Kappa. Republican. Clubs: Fonderlac County, Rotary, Protestant Men's. Author numerous books including Speed Reading, 1989, rev. edit., 1997; contbr. articles to profl. jours. Office: 30 Riverside Dr Youngstown OH 44514-2049

ZRULL, JOEL PETER, psychiatry educator; b. Detroit, Jan. 10, 1932; s. Arthur Benjamin and Mildred (Bazy) Z.; m. Nancy Jane Eichenlaub, June 19, 1954; children: Mark Christian, Lisa Carol. BA with honors, U. Mich., 1953, MD, 1957. Diplomate Am. Bd. Psychiatry, Am. Bd. Child Psychiatry. From instr. to assoc. prof. psychiatry U. Mich. Med. Sch., Ann Arbor, 1962-73; prof., chief child psychiatry Med. Coll. Ohio, Toledo, 1973-75, prof., chmn. dept. psychiatry, 1975-97, prof. emeritus, 1997—. Cons. Monroe (mich.) County Intermediate Sch. Dist., 1961—; pres. Associated Physicians MCO, Inc., Toledo, 1983-84, 87-90; chief of staff Med. Coll. Hosps., Toledo, 1984-86; mem. com. on cert. in child psychiatry Am. Bd. Psychiatry and Neurology, 1986-91, chmn. 1990-91. Editor: Adult Psychiatry: New Directions in Therapy, 1983; contbr. articles to profl. jours. Grantee NIMH, 1974-76, Ohio Dept. Mental Health, 1978-86. Fellow Am. Psychiat. Assn. (life), Am. Acad. Child and Adolescent Psychiatry (chmn. com. tng. 1984-87, chmn. comm. memls. and awards 1992-95), Am. Coll. Psychiatrists, Am. Ortho-Psychiat. Assn.; mem. AMA, Soc. Profs. of Child and Adolescent Psychiatry (sec. treas. 1989-92, pres.-elect 1992-94, pres.

1994-96). Roman Catholic. Avocations: tennis, bridge. Home: 6133 Wyandotte Rd W Maumee OH 43537-1334 Office: Med Coll Ohio Kobacker Ctr 3130 Glendale Ave Toledo OH 43614-5811

ZUBER, NORMA KEEN, career counselor, educator; b. Iuka, Miss., Sept. 27, 1934; d. William Harrington and Mary (Hebert) Keen; m. William Frederick Zuber, Sept. 14, 1958; children: William Frederick Jr., Michael, Kimberly, Karen. BS in Nursing, U. Southwestern La., 1956; MS in Counselling, Calif. Luth. U., 1984. Nat. cert. counselor, nat. cert. career counselor; registered profl. career counselor, Calif.; master career counselor. Intensive care nurse Ochsner Found. Hosp., New Orleans, 1956-59; career devel. counselor BFC Counseling Ctr., Ventura, Calif., 1984-87; founder, prin., counselor Career & Life Planning-Norma Zuber & Assocs., Ventura, 1987—. Instr. adult continuing edn. Ventura C.C., 1987—; instr. Calif. State U., Northridge, 1988-89; instr. U. Calif. Santa Barbara, Antioch U.; mem. adv. coun. on tchr. edn. Calif. Luth. U., Thousand Oaks, 1984-87; mem. adv. bd. for development of profl. career counseling cert. program U. Calif., San Diego, 1991—; co-chair legis. com. Calif. Coalition Counselor Licensure. Co-author: The Nuts and Bolts of Career Counseling: How to Set Up and Succeed in Private Practice, 1992. Chmn. bd. dirs. women's ministries Missionary Ch., Ventura, 1987-90. Recipient profl. contbn. award H.B. McDaniel Found.-Stanford U. Sch. Edn., 1988, Govt. Rels. Com. Cert. of Appreciation, Am. Assn. for Counseling and Devel., Career Devel. Practitioner of the Year award Internat. Career Conf., 1998, Spirit of Networking award Ventura Profl. Women's Network, 2001; featured in Nat. Assn. of Women bus. Owners Bravo award, Ventura, Calif. Mem. NAFE, ACA, Nat. Career Devel. Assn. (western region trustee 1994-97, master cancer counselor 2002—), Calif. Assn. Couseling and Devel. (chmn. legis. task force 1987-89, Jim Saum govt. rels. award 1989), Internat. Platform Assn., Nat. Career Devel. Assn. (western regional trustee 1995-98), Internat. Career Conf. (Career Devel. Practitioner of Yr. 1998), Calif. Career Devel. Assn. (bd. dirs. 1985-98, membership dir. 1991-92, pres. 1992-93, Leadership and Professionaliam award 1988, 89), Calif. Career Conf. (program chair 1993), Ventura County Profl. Women's Network (dir. membership 1990-91, pres. 1998-99), Calif. Registry Profl. Counselors and Paraprofls. (bd. dirs. 1990-94, chair 1995-97), Chi Sigma Iota. Republican. Home: 927 Sentinel Cir Ventura CA 93003-1202 Office: Career and Life Planning Norma Zuber and Assocs 3585 Maple St Ste 237 Ventura CA 93003-9117

ZUBERBIER, JO ANN, elementary school educator; b. Perryville, Mo., Mar. 8, 1936; d. Henry Herman and Marcella Mae (Koeneman) Schaefer; m. Orlan Gene Zuberbier, June 11, 1960; children: Todd Alan, Gregg Milo, Dawn Cheryl Zuberbier Flatt. BA magna cum laude, U. Wis., Green Bay, 1971. Cert. life tchr., Wis. Tchr. St. John's Luth. Sch., Red Bud, Ill., 1954-55, St. Paul's Luth. Sch., Mt. Prospect, Ill., 1956-61, Kennedy Elem. Sch., Green Bay, Wis., 1971-92, Christa McAuliffe Elem. Sch., Green Bay, 1992—97; ret., 1997. Vol. tchr. St. Croix County Jail, Hudson, Wis. Mem. ASCD, NEA, Green Bay Edn. Assn., WEAC. Home: 1146 County Rd H New Richmond WI 54017-6125

ZUBOV, LYNN, special education educator, researcher; b. Bklyn., Dec. 3, 1960; d. David P. Roche III. BS in Spl. Edn., St. John's U., Jamaica, N.Y., 1983; MS in Spl. Edn., St. John's U., 1988, EdS in Supervision and Adminstrn., 1990; PhD in Spl. Edn., Vanderbilt U., Nashville, 1996. Tchr. asst. Little Village Sch., Garden City, N.Y., 1981-82; tchr. of emotionally disturbed J.H.S. 8, Jamaica, N.Y., 1983-86, Poseidon, Los Angeles, 1986-87; ednl. coord., mainstream coord. P.S. 80, Jamaica, N.Y., 1987-91; rsch. asst. Peabody Coll. Vanderbilt U., Nashville, 1991-95; asst. prof., program dir. Canisius Coll., Buffalo, 1995-99; asst. prof., program coord. Winston-Salem State U., 1999—. Spl. edn. cons. Paul J. Cooper, Bklyn., 1991; mem. project Basics I.H.S. 8, Jamaica, N.Y., 1983-86; sec. Pupil-Pers. Commn., P.S. 80, Jamaica, 1987-91. Cons., instr. How To Use The Apple Computer, How to Make Inclusion Work, Developing Positive Behavioral Support Plans Through the Use of a Functional Analysis of Behavior; co-author: Handbook for the Special Education Paraprofessional, 1990. Mem. CEC, N.Y. State Coun. for Exceptional Children (past pres.). Republican. Roman Catholic. Home: 229 Engleman Ave Burlington NC 27215-4801 Office: Winston-Salem State U 601 Martin Luther King Jr CB 19360 Winston Salem NC 27157 E-mail: zubovle@wssu.edu.

ZUCCARELLI, SHARRON ADELE, educator; b. Sacramento, Nov. 14, 1943; d. John Clark and Edith Winifred (Thompson) Ames; m. Anthony Joseph Zuccarelli, Dec. 23, 1968; children: Cara Nicole, Anthony Alexander. BS, Pacific Union Coll., 1965; MA, Loma Linda U., 1988. Cert. secondary tchr. Sec. White Meml. Med. Ctr., L.A., 1965-66; tchr. bus. San Gabriel (Calif.) Acad., 1966-67, Arcadia (Calif.) High Sch., 1968-71; instr. bus. San Bernardino (Calif.) Valley Coll., 1976-84, Crafton Hills Community Coll., Yucaipa, Calif., 1982-86; tchr. bus. Showline Unified Sch. Dist., Phelan, Calif., 1986—. Cons. vol. Loma Linda (Calif.) Elem., 1983-84; sec. Loma Linda U., 1983-85, instr. bus., 1985. Calif. Lottery Monies grantee, 1988. Mem. Calif. Bus. Edn. Assn., Nat. Bus. Edn. Assn., Sponsor Future Bus. Leaders Am. (sponsor 1986—). Adventist. Avocations: sewing, piano and organ playing, foreign languages. Home: 2173 Wild Canyon Dr Colton CA 92324-9521

ZUCHOWSKI, BEVERLY JEAN, chemistry educator; b. Toledo, Ohio, Jan. 11, 1950; d. Frank I. and Esther C. (Steinke) Patronik; m. Mark G. Zuchowski, May 21, 1971; children: Caroline H., Mark J., Gregory S., Beverly A. BS in Edn., Bowling Green State U., 1974, MAT in Chemistry, 1989. Cert. tchr. physics, chemistry and math. 7-12, Ohio. Instr. chemistry and physics Eastwood Schs., Luckey, Ohio, 1974-77, Perrysburg (Ohio) Pub. Schs., 1978-88, Owens Tech. Coll., Perrysburg, 1981-88; grad. asst. Bowling Green (Ohio) State U., 1988-89; chemistry instr. Perrysburg Pub. Schs., 1989—. Mem. Ohio Dept. Edn. Sci. Proficiency Content Com., 1995—; tchr. intern Ctr. of Sci. and Industry, Columbus, Ohio, 1987; tchr. chaperone, Young Exptl. Scientist, Columbus, 1988-92, Women in Sci., Bowling Green, 1989-95. Mem. Rossford (Ohio) Bd. Edn., 1988—, v.p., 1991-92, 2000—; mem. Penta County Vocat. Sch. Bd. Edn., 1994-95; leader Girl Scouts U.S., Rossford, 1978-95; precinct worker Wood County Bd. of Elections, 1982-87. Recipient Award of Achievement Ohio Sch. Bd. Assn., 1998, 99, 2000. Mem. NEA, Ohio Edn. Assn., Nat. Sci. Tchrs. Assn., Ohio Coun. Tchrs. Math., Ohio Acad. Sci., Sci. Edn. Coun. Ohio, Perrysburg Edn. Assn. (treas. 1981), Rossford Community Svc. League (sec. 1992), Ohio Womens Caucus, Rossford Lions Club (charter), Toledo Mothers of Twins Club. Democrat. Lutheran. Avocations: camping, gardening, water sports. E-mail: pbhs_st_bz@noeca. Home: 3 Riverside Dr Rossford OH 43460-1130 Office: Perrysburg High Sch 13385 Roachton Rd Perrysburg OH 43551-1363

ZUCKERMAN, HARRIET, sociologist, educator; b. N.Y.C., July 19, 1937; d. Harry and Anne D. (Wiener) Z; m. Robert K. Merton, 1993. AB, Vassar Coll., 1958; PhD, Columbia U., 1965. Asst. prof. sociology Columbia U., 1965-72, assoc. prof., 1972-78, prof., 1978-92; prof. emerita, 1993—; sr. rsch. scholar, 1993—; chmn. dept. Columbia U., 1978-81; v.p. Andrew W. Mellon Found., 1991-98, sr. v.p., 1998—. Vis. scholar Russell Sage Found., 1971-72, 85-87; mem. adv. bd. Social Sci. Citation Index, Inst. Sci. Information, 1972-98; dir. Annual Revs., Inc., 1974— ; trustee Am. Savs. Bank, 1978-83 Author: Scientific Elite: Nobel Laureates in the United States, 1977, rev. edit., 1996; co-editor: Toward A Metric of Science: The Advent of Science Indictors, 1978, The Outer Circle: Women in the Scientific Community, 1991; mem. editorial bd. Scientometrics, 1977—, Am. Jour. Sociology, 1972-74, 77-79, Am. Sociol. Rev, 1972-74, 87-91, Sci., 1985-86; contbr. articles to profl. jours. Bd. dirs. Social Sci. Rsch. Coun., 1974-76, AAAS, 1980-84, Women's Forum, 1989-91; trustee Ctr. for Advanced Study in Behavioral Scis., 1976-88, 89-2001, 03—; mem. ednl. adv. bd. John Simon Guggenheim Meml. Found., 1986-93, mem. com. on selection, 1989-91. Woodrow Wilson fellow, 1958-59; Center for Advanced Study in Behavioral Scis. fellow, 1973-74; Guggenheim fellow, 1980-81; Phi Beta Kappa vis. scholar, 1982-83; recipient Dean's award for Disting. Achievement Columbia U. Grad. Sch., 1998. Mem. Am. Philos. Soc. (councillor 1997-03, chmn. Class III membership com. 2002—), Am. Acad. Arts and Scis. (chmn. class III membership com. 1991-94), Soc. Social Studies Sci. (pres. 1989-91), The Century Assn., Coun. on Fgn. Rels.

ZUCKERMAN, NANCY CAROL, learning disabilities specialist, consultant; b. Jersey City, Aug. 14, 1951; d. Bernard Milton and Shirley (Stepner) Solomon; m. Marshall Howard Zuckerman, Aug. 20, 1978; 1 child, Seth Michael. BA, Rider U., 1973; MEd, William Paterson Coll., 1977. Cert. elem. tchr., spl. edn. and learning disabilities tchr., prin., N.J. Tchr. elem. edn. North Bergen (N.J.) Bd. Edn., 1973-76; tchr. state compensatory edn. Bayonne (N.J.) Bd. Edn., 1977, tchr. cons. learning disabilities, 1977—. Chairperson Child Study Team, Bayonne, 1988-99. Mem. adv. bd., sec., asst. pack leader Cub Scouts Pack 35, Bayonne, 1996-2000, com. chair Troop 35, 2002—; bd. dirs. Temple Beth Am, Bayonne, 1975-79, 97—, edn. chmn., 1975-79. Mem. CEC, Assn. Learning Consultants, Pi Lambda Theta. Jewish. Home: 21 E 35th St Bayonne NJ 07002-3924 Office: Bayonne Bd Edn Bayonne NJ 07002 E-mail: N@LDTC@aol.com.

ZUCKERMAN, STUART, psychiatrist, forensic examiner, educator; b. Syracuse, N.Y., Feb. 18, 1933; s. George and Cassie (Kolsan) Z. Student, U. Kans., 1950-51; BS, U. Ala., 1954; DO, Phila. Coll. Osteo. Medicine, 1958. Diplomate Am. Osteo. Bd. Neurology and Psychiatry, Am. Nat. Bd. Psychiatry, Am. Coll. Forensic Medicine, Bd. Forensic Medicine, Bd. Forensic Examiner; cert. correctional health profl. Rotating intern Hosps. Phila. Coll. Osteo. Medicine, 1958-59; psychiat. fellow, resident Phila. Mental Health Clinic, 1959-62, Psychoanalytic Studies Inst., Phila., 1959-62; chief resident, 1962; chief div. neuropsychiatry Grandview Hosp., Dayton, Ohio, 1962-65; asst. med. dir., chief children's and adolescent's unit N.J. State Hosp., Ancora, 1967-70; chief outpatient dept. Atlantic City, 1970-72; practice specializing in neuropsychiatry Atlantic City, 1965—; founding prof. psychiatry, chmn. dept. Ohio U. Coll. Osteo. Medicine, Athens, 1976-77, clin. prof., 1977—; mem. faculty U. Pa. Sch. Medicine, Phila. Coll. Osteo. Medicine, 1972-76, with Benjamin Franklin scholar spl. studies faculty; lectr. U. Pa., 1977-79; prof. dept. psychiatry, charter faculty Sch. Medicine, Marshall U., 1977-78, clin. prof., 1979-80, N.Y. Coll. Osteo. Medicine, 1979—; chief mental hygiene VA Hosp., Huntington, W.Va., 1978-79; liaison psychiatrist, acting chief VA Med. Center, Perry Point, Md., 1979-80; med. dir. Mental Health Clinic of Ocean County, Toms River, N.J., 1980-85, Ventnor (N.J.) Mental Health Ctr.; chief psychiatrist N.J. Dept. Corrections So. State Correctional Facility, 1985-96. Physician Atlantic City Beach Patrol, 1961-63; attending psychiatrist Atlantic City, Shore Meml., Kessler Meml., Washington Meml., Atlantic County Mental hosps., 1965-76; attending psychiatrist, asst. dir. dept. psychiatry Phila. Gen. Hosp., 1972-76; med. dir. Shawnee Mental Health Center, (Adams, Lawrence, Scioto counties), Portsmouth, Ohio, 1977-78; cons. psychiatrist Athens Mental Health and Mental Retardation Ctr., 1976-77, Scioto Meml., So. Hills, Mercy hosps., Portsmouth, 1977-78, Lansdowne Cmty. Mental Health Center, (Greenup, Carter counties), Ashland, Ky., 1977-78, Atlantic City Med. Ctr., 1984-97, Cmty. Meml. Hosp., Toms River, N.J., 1984-91, So. Ocean County Hosp., Manahawkin, N.J., 1984-91, Paul-Kimball Med Ctr., Lakewood, N.J., 1984-97, Obleness Meml. Hosp., Clin. Services of Athens, Vinton, Hocking Counties, Hudson Health Ctr., Ohio U., 1976-77; cons. Bayside State Prison, Leesburg, N.J., 1989-96, Atlantic County Justice System, Mays Landing, N.J., 1992-93, child study spl. svcs. S. Jersey sch. systems; chmn. profl. adv. com. Atlantic County Mental Health Bd., 1969-71; mem. nominating com. Mental Health Assn., Atlantic County, 1972-75; exam. psychiatrist Jersey Police and Fire depts.; mem. Atlantic County Mental Health Bd.; mem. profl. adv. com. N.J. Dept. Corrections; cons. N.J. Dept. Pub. Advocate; mem. panel med. cons. N.J. State Med. Bd., 1998—. Mem. adv. bd. Osteo. Physician, 1975-98; assoc. editor Bull. Am. Coll. Neuropsychiatrists, 1963-70, Jour. Corr. Health Editl. Bd.; contbr. articles to profl. jours. Bd. dirs. Atlantic County Family Svcs. Assn., 1968-74, Cape May County Drug Abuse Coun., 1973-76, Nat. Comm. Correctional Health Care, 1988-97; mem. Ventnor City Beautification Com., 1996—; sponsor, house physician Friends of the Pops Ocean City (N.J.) Music Pier. Fellow Am. Coll. Forensic Psychiatry, Am. Coll. Neuropsychiatrists (bd. reps.), Am. Acad. Disability Evaluating Physicians (charter), Acad. Psychosomatic Medicine, Acad. Medicine N.J., Coll. Physicians of Phila.; mem. AMA (Physicians Recognition award 1985—), AAUP, Am. Bd. Forensic Examiners (cert. 1994), Am. Coll. Forensic Medicine (bd. cert. 1996), World Psychiat. Assn., Am. Psychiat. Assn., N.J. (confidentiality, pub. psychiatry com., gen. hosp. psychiatry com., law com., mkgt. benefits com.) Psychiat. Assn., Am. Assn. Psychiatrists in Alcohol and Addictions (founder), Am., N.J. pub. health assns., Am. Osteo. Assn. (hosp. inspection team 1971-75, bd. reps.), Am. Assn. CMHC Psychiatrists, Am. Assn. Psychiatrists in Pvt. Practice, Internat. Assn. Med. Specialists, Am. Soc. Law and Medicine, Am. Acad. Clin. Psychiatrists, Corp. Advancement Psychiatry, Am. Med. Writers Assn., Nat. Council Community Mental Health Ctrs., Nat. Alliance Mentally Ill (profl. assoc. mem.), Met. Coll. Mental Health Assn., Am. Soc. Criminology., South Jersey Neuropsychiat. Soc., Psychiat. Outpatients Ctrs. Am., Am. Coll. Legal Medicine, Acad. Psychiatry and Law (pub. info. com., edn com., internat. affairs com.), Am. Acad. Forensic Scis., Am. Assn. Acad. Psychiatry, Am. Coll. Emergency Physicians (charter mem.), Am. Acad. Psychotherapists, Am. Assn. Mental Deficiency, Am. Assn. Psychiat. Services for Children, N.J. (chmn. com. on confidentiality, liaison com. health human svcs., corrections), Fla. assns. osteo. physicians and surgeons, N.J. Hosp. Assn., Am. Vocat. Assn., Am. Assn. Group Therapy, Am. Soc. Clin. Psychopharmacology, Assn. Mil. Surgeons U.S., Nat. Assn. VA Physicians, Am. Assn. Psychiat. Adminstrs., Am. Assn. Adolescent Psychiatry, World Med. Assn., Am. Assn. Mental Health Adminstrs., Am. Assn. Gen. Hosp. Psychiatrists, Human Factors Soc., Orthopsychiat. Assn., Am. Physicians Fellowship, Assn. for Research Nervous and Mental Diseases, Atlantic County Osteo. Med. Soc. (pres. 1970-72), N.J. Assn. Mil. Surgeons U.S. (v.p.), Am. Assn. Correctional Health Care, Am. Coll. Forensic Psychiatry (diplomate 1984), charter mem. Soc. of Correctional Physicians. N.J. State bd. of Med. Examiners Specialty Adv. Panel, 1998—. Home: 6700 Atlantic Ave Ventnor City NJ 08406-2618

ZUERCHER, NANCY TOZER, English language educator; b. Buffalo, May 6, 1936; d. Richard John Tozer and Flora Fordyce; children: James Frederick, William John. BA with honors, Ohio Wesleyan U., 1958; MA, U. Wyo., 1961; EdD, U. S.D., 1986. Tchr. Rocky River (Ohio) H.S., 1958-60, El Segundo (Calif.) Jr. H.S., 1961-63, Santa Monica (Calif.) H.S., 1963-65; from instr. to asst. prof. U. S.D., Vermillion, 1963-89, assoc. prof., 1989—. Mem. panel of scholars S.D. Coun. on Humanities Coun., Brookings, 1990-92, scholar, discussant, 1988—; state dir. Dakota Writing Project, 1989—. Editor: (newsletter) The Write Connections, 1990—; co-author: (book chpt.) Teachers Are Researchers, 1993; co-author: (book chpt.) Winning Ways of Coaching Writing, 2001. Treas. Vermillion Area Arts Coun., 1970-72. Recipient summer stipend NEH, 1977. Mem. Internat. Reading Assn., Nat. Coun. Tchrs. of English, S.D. Coun. Tchrs. of English (pres. 1976-78, Tchr. of Yr. 1989), Conf. on English Edn., Conf. on Coll. Composition and Comm. Avocations: running, mountain biking, photography, hiking. Home: 423 Linden Ave Vermillion SD 57069-3511 Office: U SD 414 E Clark St Vermillion SD 57069-2307

ZUHLKE, MARYBETH, curriculum consultant, educator, coordinator; b. Kenosha, Wis., Jan. 16, 1946; d. Charles Casmir and Elizabeth (Mulich) Safransky; m. Lee VanLunduyt, Aug. 24, 1968 (div. 1985); children: Kyle, Ravi; m. Tom Zuhlke, Sept. 9, 1990. Student, U. Dallas, 1965-67; BS, U. Wis., Whitewater, 1968; MS, U. Wis., Milw., 1973, postgrad., 1988-89, Marquette U., 1978-81. Cert. elem. tchr., prin., coord. instruction, Wis. Tchr. second grade Kenosha Unified Sch. Dist., 1968-70, community liaison tchr., 1974-79, dissemination specialist, 1979-82, curriculum cons., 1982—; site coord.-Kenosha, Cardinal Strich U., Milw., 2001—. Cons. Conn. Facilitator, North Haven, 1984-86, South Ocean Internat. Sch., Datong, China, 1995—; prin. McKinley Elem. Sch., Kenosha, 1988-89. Co-author: Kenosha Model Kindergarten Manual, 1985, Kenosha Model Math. Manual, 1986; editor: Kenosha Model Language Experience, 1979. Mem. Racine (Wis.) Arts Coun., 1980—. Mem. ASCD, Internat. Reading Assn., Parent Edn. and Childhood Assn. (exec. bd. 1976-83), Inst. of World Affairs, Wis. State and Fed. Specialists (newsletter editor 1986-87), Assn. Wis. Sch. Administrs., (Co-Chmn.), Exhibits Team, Imaginarium Children's Museum, Phi Delta Kappa. Avocations: reading, nature. Home: 1419 Crabapple Dr Racine WI 53405-1703 E-mail: mrszuhlke@aol.com.

ZUICK, DIANE MARTINA, elementary education educator; b. Gary, Ind., May 19, 1951; d. Arnold and Matilda (Chaimovitz) Herskovic; m. Norman Robert Zuick, Aug. 12, 1973; children: Scott, Amy. BS in Edn., Ind. U., 1972, MS in Edn., 1974. Cert. nat. bd. cert. tchr. early childhood generalist Nat. Bd. for Profl. Tchg. Stds. Tchr. 5th grade George L. Myers Sch., Portage, Ind., 1972-73, tchr. 3d grade, 1973-83, tchr. 1st grade, 1983-90, tchr. 2d grade, 1990—. Mem. prime time com. Portage Twp. Schs., 1991—, mem. reading curriculum com., 1987-88, mem. devel. com., 1983-85, mem. math. curriculum coun., 1999-2003; mem. adv. K'ton Ton Pre-Sch., Highland, Ind., 1984-86; mem., chair adv. group Ind. Profl. Stds. Bd., 1999-2001; mentor candidates Nat. Bd. Cert. Tchrs., 1999—; mem. adv. com. Beginning Tchr. Mentor Tng. Program, 2003-. Chair sch. bd. Congregation Beth Israel, Hammond, Ind., 1993-95, mem. sch. bd., 1992-95, mem. exec. bd., 1994—, bd. dirs., 1996-; mem. B'nai B'rith, Hammond, 1993—, mem. dist. bd. govs., 1995-97. Recipient Ind. Dept. Instrn. Prime Time award, 1988, 89; Portage Twp. Schs. grantee, 1993, 94. Mem. NEA, Ind. State Tchrs. Assn., Portage Assn. Tchrs., Tchrs. Applying Whole Langs., Internat. Reading Assn., Ind. U. Alumni Assn, Delta Kappa Gamma. Avocations: reading, travel, piano, nature, music. Home: 58 Cedar Ln Schererville IN 46375-1107 Office: Portage Twp Schs 6240 Us Highway 6 Portage IN 46368-5057

ZUKOWSKA, ZOFIA MARIA, cardiovascular physiologist, educator; b. Sosnowiec, Poland, July 16, 1949; came to U.S., 1980; d. Wladyslaw and Natalia (Kiewszynis) Zukowska; children: Anna Natalia, Wojtek Pawel Grojec. MD, Med. Acad., Warsaw, Poland, 1972, PhD, 1979. Med. diplomate. From resident to sr. resident dept. hypertension Med. Acad., Warsaw, 1972-74, asst. prof. dept. hypertension, 1974-80; vis. fellow NIMH/NIH, Bethesda, Md., 1980-83; vis. assoc. NINDS/NIH, Bethesda, 1983-85; asst. prof. dept. physiology Georgetown U., Washington, 1985-91, prof. dept. physiology, 1991—. Cons. Astra Zeneca, Sweden, 1997—, dept. hypertension Acad. Med., Warsaw, 1990—; Polish-Am. sci. exch./vis. prof. Nat. Heart, Lung and Blood Inst./Cardiology Program, Bethesda and Warsaw, 1990—, prin. investigator R01, Bethesda, 1996—. Author: (book chpt.) The Biology of NPY, 1992; contbr. articles to Sci., Proc. NAS, Am. Jour. Physiology, Cir. Rsch. Recipient Adele Holmes Established Investigatorship award D.C. chpt. Am. Heart Assn., 1988. Fellow Coun. for High Blood Pressure Rsch. Am. Heart Assn.; mem. Polish Acad./Hypertension Soc. (hon.), Soc. Neurosci. Achievements include discovery of high sensitivity of males to vasoconstrictor effects of neuropeptide Y (NPY) and stress-induced release of NPY; beneficial effects of NPY in treatment of shock and mitogenic and angiogenic activities of NPY. Office: Georgetown U Dept Physiology 3900 Reservoir Rd NW Dept Washington DC 20007-2188

ZULAUF, SANDER WILLIAM, educator, poet; b. Paterson, N.J., Nov. 5, 1946; s. S. William Z. and Marion Ann Zulauf; m. Christianne Beresford, June 15, 1968 (div. 1976); 1 child, Scott; m. Madeline Ruth Slocum, May 26, 1979; stepchildren: Michael, Mary Beth. BA, Gettysburg Coll., 1968; MA, Ind. U., 1973. Tchr. Martin Luther King Sch., Paterson, NJ, 1968—69, Hanover Park Regional H.S., East Hanover, NJ, 1969-71; prof. County Coll. Morris, Randolph, NJ, 1973—. Editor, pub. Ars Poetica, Lake Hopatcong, N.J., 1996-99. Author of poems, including collection Succasanna New Jersey, 1987; editor Jour. N.J. Poets, 1989—; founding editor, Index of American Periodical Verse, 1971-82. Committeeman County Com., Byram Twp., N.J., 1994—; sec. treas. Forest South Homeowners Assn., Byram Twp., 1989-94; lay eucharistic min. St. Dunstan's Episcopal Ch., Succasunna, N.J., 1974—. Recipient Allen Ginsberg award Poetry Ctr., Passaic, N.J., 1993, 2001, 2002, Excellence in Print award for Jour. of N.J. Poets Pub. Radio's Poet and the Poem, 2002, Jour. N.J. Poets; N.J. Arts Coun. grantee, 1992-93; NEH fellow, Princeton, 1987; named 1st Poet Laureate Diocese of Newark, 1999—. Mem. Acad. Am. Poets, Poetry Soc. Am., Poets House, Kenneth Burke Soc., Thoreau Soc., Associated Writing Programs, Skylands Writers & Artists Assn. (sec. treas. 1994-98, v.p. 1999-2000). Democrat. Episcopalian. Avocations: camping, boating, environmental preservation, gardening, travel. Office: County Coll Morris 214 Center Grove Rd Randolph NJ 07869-2007 E-mail: szulauf@ccm.edu.

ZUMBRUN, ALVIN JOHN THOMAS, law and criminology educator; s. Orrell Sylvester Tilton and Mary Kathryn (Sprinkle) Z.; m. Marianne Jane Nolan; children: Mary Susan, Alvin J.T. Jr., Steven M., Diane, MaryAnn, Mary Kathleen. BA, U. Md., 1952, MA, 1956; MEd in Spl. Edn., Coppin State U., 1972, MEd in Adminstrn., 1974; JD, U. Balt., 1970. Probation officer Supreme Bench of Balt., 1950-52; budget and program dir. Cmty. Chest, Balt., 1953-55; mng. dir. Criminal Justice Commn., Balt., 1956-59; exec. dir., criminologist Md. Crime Investigating Com., Balt., 1960-96; dept. chmn., prof. criminal justice Catonsville (Md.) C.C., 1968-94; dept. chmn., dir. grad. program, prof. criminal justice U. Balt., 1974-76. Adj. prof. criminal justice U. Md., Hood Coll., Coppin State U., Md. State Police Acad., Balt. County Police Acad., 1969—; mem. adv. bd. U. Balt. Criminal Justice Program, 1976-94; cons. Am. Edn. Assn., Washington, 1980-1985; mem. senate Catonsville C.C., 1970-83; mem. Nat. Disaster Med. System, 1993—; mem. acad. stds. senate com. U. Md., College Park, 1997-99. Author: Maryland Crime Report, 5 vols., 1959-94, Directory of Criminal Justice Agencies, 22 vols., 1962-94, Civil Disturbance Riots of 1968, 69, also rsch. in field. Mem. scholarship com. Md. Troopers Assn., Pikesville, 1990-93; mem. adv. bd. articulation com. U. Md., College Park, 1977-94; lay pres., mem. coun. Salem Luth. Ch., Catonsville, 1956-59, 65-68; pres. Maplewoods Home Owners Assn., 1996-97. Served to lt. (j.g.) USN. Recipient Superior Pub. Svc. award Afro Am. Newspaper, 1962, Excellence in Teaching award Md. State Bd. C.C.s, 1987, Superior Ednl. Svcs. award Balt. County Police Chief, 1994, Gov.'s citation for ednl. achievements Gov. of Md., 1994, Hon. Trooper 25 Yrs. Acad. Teaching Md. State Police, 1995. Mem. VFW (life), Am. Legion (life), Md. Acad. Criminal Justice Profs. (pres. 1971-94), Internat. Soc. Criminology, Nat. Dist. Attys. Assn., Internat. Assn. Chiefs of Police, Maplewoods Homeowners Assn. (pres. 1995-96). Avocations: walking, biking, family activities, world travel. Home and Office: 438 Maple Forest Rd Catonsville MD 21228-1783 E-mail: azumbrun@comcast.net.

ZUMPE, DORIS, ethologist, researcher, educator; b. Berlin, May 18, 1940; came to U.S., 1972; d. Herman Frank and Eva (Wagner) Z. BSc, U. London, 1961, PhD, 1970. Asst. to K.Z. Lorenz, Max-Planck-Inst. für Verhaltensphysiologie, Seewiesen, Fed. Republic Germany, 1961-64; rsch. asst. and assoc., lectr. Inst. Psychiatry, U. London, 1965-72; rsch. assoc. Emory U. Sch. Medicine, Atlanta, 1972-74, asst. prof. psychiatry (ethology), 1974-77, assoc. prof., 1977-87, prof., 1987—. Reviewer NSF, 7 sci. jours. Contbr. over 150 articles to profl. jours. NIMH grantee, 1971-2000. Mem. AAAS, Internat. Soc. Psychoneuroendocrinology, Internat. Primatological Soc., Internat. Soc. for Human Ethology, Soc. Behavioral Neuroendocrinology, Am. Soc. Primatologists, N.Y. Acad. Scis., Earl Music Am., Viola da Gamba Soc. Am. Avocation: music. Office: Emory U Sch Medicine Dept Psychiatry Atlanta GA 30322-0001

ZUMWALT, NANCY EILEEN WILLIAMS, health occupations educator; b. Ferndale, Mich., Aug. 14, 1927; d. Joseph A. and Marcella N. (Wahl) Williams; diploma Highland Park Gen. Hosp. Sch. Nursing, 1948; R.N., BA, Eastern Ill. U., 1976, MS Ed. in Community Counseling, 1980; m. Bruce G. Zumwalt, Jan. 28, 1950; children: Marcy, B. Joseph, Frank, John. Various nursing positions, 1948-71; dir. Iroquois Meml. Hosp. Home Health Agency, Watseka, Ill., 1968-71, dir. nursing Vermilion County Health Dept., Danville, Ill., 1971-74; adminstr. Iroquois County Health Dept., Watseka, 1974-77; instr. health occupations Iroquois Area Career Ctr., Watseka, 1980-90; instr. Kankakee Community Coll Sch. Nursing, 1992—; past pres. Ill. Council Home Health Svcs., Ill. Assn. Local Health Dept. Nursing Adminstrs. Mem. regional bd., sec. East Central Ill. Health Service Agy.; past pres., mem. exec. bd. Iroquois County Mental Health Center; pres. Iroquois County Heart Assn.; precinct committeeman Concord Twp. Dem. Party; mem. Iroquois County Bd., 1992—. Mem. Iroquois Meml. Hosp. Aux. Club: Am. Legion Aux. Home and Office: 3101 E 1900 N Rd Sheldon IL 60966-9341

ZUNDE, PRANAS, information science educator, researcher; b. Kaunas, Lithuania, Nov. 26, 1923; came to U.S., 1960, naturalized, 1964; s. Pranas and Elzbieta (Lisajevic) Z.; m. Alge R. Bizauskas, May 29, 1945; children: Alge R., Audronis K., Aurelia R., Aidis L., Gytis J. Dipl. Ing., Hannover Inst. Tech., 1947; MS, George Washington U., 1965; PhD, Ga. Inst. Tech., 1968. Dir. project Documentation Inc., Bethesda, Md., 1961-64, mgr. mgmt. info. system, 1964-65; sr. research scientist Ga. Inst. Tech., Atlanta, 1965-68, assoc. prof., 1968-72, prof. dept. computer sci., 1973-91, prof. emeritus, 1991—. Cons. UNESCO, Caracas, Venezuela, 1970-72, Esquela Polit. Nacional, Quito, Ecuador, 1974-75, State of Ga., Atlanta, 1976-78, Royal Sch. Librarianship, Copenhagen, 1985-87, Clemson (N.C.) U., 1987—, N.Y. State Dept. Edn., 1993; vis. prof. Simon Bolivar U., Caracas, 1976, J. Kepler U., Austria, 1981; vis. scientist Riso Nat. Lab., Roskilde, Denmark, 1983, Lithuanian Acad. Scis., Vilnius, 1988-89. Author: Agriculture in Soviet Lithuania, 1962, National Science Information Systems in Eastern Europe, 1972; editor: Procs. Info. Utilities, 1974, Procs. Fouds. of Info. and Software Sci., 1983-90; contbr. articles to tech. and sci. jours. Mem. senate Vitoldus Magnus U., Kaunas, Lithuania, 1990—. NSF grantee; Fulbright prof. NAS, 1975. Mem. Am. Soc. Info. Sci., Semiotic Soc. Am., Soc. Sigma Xi. Roman Catholic. Office: Ga Inst Tech Coll Computing North Ave Atlanta GA 30332-0001

ZUNZ, OLIVIER JEAN, history educator; b. Paris, July 19, 1946; s. Jean R. and Monique M. (Blin) Z.; m. Christine M. Crommen, July 3, 1970; children: Emmanuel, Sophie. Licence in history and geography, U. Paris X, 1968, M in History, 1969; Doctorat-ès-Lettres, U. Paris I, Panthéon-Sorbonne, 1982. Scientist Ctr. Nat. de la Recherche Scientifique, Paris, 1976-78; asst. prof. dept. history U. Va., Charlottesville, 1978-83, assoc. prof., 1983-88, prof., 1988-99, Commonwealth prof., 1999—. Vis. prof. Ecole des Hautes Etudes en Scis., Sociales, Paris, 1985—, Coll. France, 1997; dir. seminar for Coll. Tchrs. NEH, 1989, 92. Author: The Changing Face of Inequality: Urbanization, Industrial Development, and Immigrants in Detroit, 1980-1920, 1982, Making America Corporate, 1870-1920, 1990, Why the American Century?, 1998; editor, co-author: Reliving the Past: The Worlds of Social History, 1985; co-editor: (with David Ward) The Landscape of Modernity: Essays on New York City, 1900-1940, 1992, (with Leonard Schoppa and Nobuhiro Hiwatari): Social Contracts under Stress: The Middle Classes of America, Europe, and Japan at the Turn of the Century, 2002, (with Alan S. Kahan): The Tocqueville Reader: A Life in Letters and Politics, 2002; mem. editl. bd. Revs. in Am. History, 1990-98; contbr. articles, book revs. to profl. jours. Jr. fellow Mich. Soc. Fellows, 1973-76, John Simon Guggenheim Meml. Found. fellow, 1986-87; grantee U. Mich.-Ford Found. Population Devel. Fund, 1974-76, NSF, 1976-78, NEH, 1979-81, 84-87; also recipient numerous rsch. grants. Mem. Am. Hist. Assn., Orgn. Am. Historians, The Tocqueville Soc. (pres. 2001—). Home: 1368 Hilltop Rd Charlottesville VA 22903-1225 Office: U Va Corcoran Dept of History PO Box 400180 Randall Hall Charlottesville VA 22904-4180 Office Fax: 434-924-7891. E-mail: oz@virginia.edu.

ZURAV, FRANKIE STALFORD, special education educator; b. Newark, Dec. 16, 1929; d. William and Anna (Bader) Stalford; m. David B. Zurav, Mar. 18, 1951; children: Ilene Halprin, Edward H. BS, Syracuse U., 1951; MA, Newark State U., 1966. Cert. clin. competence, speech pathologist, N.J., Am. Speech-Language-Hearing Assn. Speech pathologist Cerebral Palsy Ctr., Morristown, N.J., 1965-66; specialist speech-lang. Bd. Edn., Plainfield, N.J., 1966—. Mem. Am. Speech-Lang.-Hearing Assn., N.J. Speech-Lang.-Hearing Assn. (legis. com. 1972-74), Union County Speech-Lang.-Hearing Assn. Home: 1 Archbridge Ln Springfield NJ 07081-2702

ZURAW, KATHLEEN ANN, special education and physical education educator; b. Bay City, Mich., Sept. 29, 1960; d. John Luke and Clara Josephine (Kilian) Z. AA with high honors, Delta Community Coll., 1980; BS with high honors, Mich. State U., 1984, MA, 1987. Cert. spl. edn., mentally impaired phys. edn. grade K-12, adaptive phys. edn. tchr., Mich. Summer water safety instr. Camp Midicha, Columbia, Mich., 1982, Bay Cliff Health Camp, Big Bay, Mich., 1983; summer spl. edn. tchr. Jefferson Orthopedic Sch., Honolulu, 1984, 85, 86, Ingham Intermediate Sch. Dist., Mason, Mich., 1987; spl. edn. tchr. Bay Arenac Intermediate Sch. Dist., Bay City, 1985-87, Berrien County Intermediate Sch. Dist., Berrien Springs, Mich., 1987—. Mem. citizen amb program fitness delegation People's Republic China, 1991. Area 17 coach Mich. Spl. Olympics, Berrien Springs, 1987—; mem. YMCA, St. Joseph, Mich., 1987—, Y-Ptnrs., 1989, Coun. Exceptional Children; participant Citizen Ambassador Delegation to People's Republic of China, 1991. Mem. Am. Alliance Health, Phys. Edn., Recreation and Dance, Phi Theta Kappa, Phi Kappa Phi, Phi Delta Kappa. Roman Catholic. Avocations: sports, crafts. Home: 7306 W S Saginaw Rd Bay City MI 48706

ZUSPAN, FREDERICK PAUL, obstetrician, gynecologist, educator; b. Richwood, Ohio, Jan. 20, 1922; s. Irl Goff and Kathryn (Speyer) Z.; m. Mary Jane Cox, Nov. 23, 1943; children: Mark Frederick, Kathryn Jane, Bethany Anne. BA, Ohio State U., 1947, MD, 1951. Intern Univ. Hosps., Columbus, Ohio, 1951-52, resident, 1952-54, Western Res. U., Cleve., 1954-56, Oblebay fellow, 1958-60, asst. prof., 1958-60; chmn. dept. bo-gyn. McDowell (Ky.) Meml. Hosp., 1956-58, chief clin. svcs., 1957-58; prof., chmn. dept. ob-gyn. Med. Coll. Ga., Augusta, 1960-66; Joseph Boliver DeLee prof. ob-gyn., chmn. dept. U. Chgo., 1966-75; obstetrician, gynecologist in chief Chgo. Lying-In Hosp., 1966-75; prof., chmn. dept. ob-gyn. Ohio State U., Columbus, 1975-87, R.L. Meiling prof. ob-gyn. Sch. Medicine, 1984-90, prof. emeritus, 1991—. Founding editor Lying In, Jour. Reproductive Medicine; editor-in-chief Am. Jour. Ob-Gyn. and Ob-Gyn. Reports, (with Lindheimer and Katz) Hypertension in Pregnancy, 1976, Current Developments in Perinatology, 1977, (with Quilligan) Operative Obstetrics, 1981, 89, Manual of Practical Obstetrics, 1981, 90, Clin. and Exptl. Hypertension in Pregnancy, 1979-86, (with Rayburn) Drug Therapy in Ob-Gyn., 1981, 3rd edit., 1992; editor: (with Christian) Controversies in Obstetrics and Gynecology; contbr. articles to med. jours., chpts. to books. Pres. Barren Found., 1974-76. With USNR, 1942-43; 1st lt. USMCR, 1943-45. Decorated DFC, Air medal wth 10 oak leaf clusters. Mem.: Perinatal Rsch. Soc., Soc. Perinatal Obstetrics, Am. Gynecology and Obstetrics Soc. (pres. 1986—87), Internat. Soc. Study of Hypertension in Pregnancy (pres. 1981—83), Soc. Gynecol. Investigation (Pres.'s award 2001), Am. Soc. Clin. Exptl. Hypnosis (exec. sec. 1968, v.p. 1970), Ctrl. Assn. Ob-Gyn. (cert. of merit, rsch. prize 1970), South Atlantic Assn. Ob-Gyn. (Found. prize for rsch. 1962), Assn .Profs. Gynecology and Obstetrics, Am. Coll. Ob-Gyn., Am. Acad. Reproductive Medicine (pres.), Columbus Ob-Gyn. Soc. (pres. 1984—85), Chgo. Gynecol. Soc., Am. Assn. Ob-Gyn., Soc. Gynecol. Investigation, Alpha Omega Alpha, Sigma Xi, Alpha Kappa Kappa. Home: 10520 Button Willow Dr Las Vegas NV 89134-7346 E-mail: FPZUS@aol.com.

ZUSTIAK, GARY BLAIR, youth minister, educator; b. Cottage Grove, Oreg., Mar. 7, 1952; s. George J. and Janice M. (Garrison) Z.; m. Mary S. Seablom, Nov. 27, 1970; children: Joshua B., Aaron J., Caleb C. BA, Boise Bible Coll., 1976; MA, MDiv, Lincoln Christian Sem., 1982; D of Ministry, Abilene Christina U., 1994. Ordained to ministry, Christian Ch., 1976. Youth min. First Christian Ch., Emmett, Idaho, 1973-77, Farmer City, Ill., 1977-78; min. Broadwell (Ill.) Christian Ch., 1978-82; assoc. min. First Christian Ch., Sandpoint, Idaho, 1982-86; prof. Ozark Christian Coll., Joplin, Mo., 1986-99; dir. youth ministries and resources Christ in Youth, Joplin, Mo., 1999—. Author: The Next Generation, 1996, Reasons to Believe, 1998; contbr. articles to profl. jours. Founder Parents Support Group, Sandpoint, 1985-86; mem. Insight Drug Intervention Program, Sandpoint, 1985-86; chmn. Recreation Com. for City, Sandpoint, 1985-86; vol. 4-State Community AIDS project, Joplin, 1989—. Recipient scholarships, Eastern Star, 1978-82. Republican. Avocations: chess, Tae Kwon Do, motor-cross, guitar. Office: Christ in Youth Box B Joplin MO 64802

ZUTTER-BROCK, PAMELA JEAN, secondary school educator; b. Lima, Peru, Feb. 8, 1951; d. Louis Eric and Georgia Nell (Carpenter) Zutter; m. Carrol Bruce Brock, June 11, 1978; 1 child, Eric David. BA English, McKendree Coll., 1969-73; degree in Spanish and French, So. Ill. U., Edwardsville, 1973-74. Tchr. and chair French, Spanish, English Wright City (Mo.) High Sch., 1974-83; tchr. Francis Howell H.S., St. Charles, Mo., 1983—; world lang. chair Francis Howell High Sch., St. Charles, Mo., 1987—. Sponsor Spanish Club, St. Charles; pres. Community Tchrs. Assn., Wright City, 1980-81. New mem. followup First United Meth. Ch., St. Charles, 1992, 93, 94, bd. mem., 1985-87; mem. Rennaisance, St. Charles, 1993-98, co-chair, 1998—. Mem. Am. Assn. Tchrs. Spanish and Portuguese, Fgn. Lang. Tchrs. Assn. Greater St. Louis. Methodist. Avocations: travel, reading, wood carvings. Home: 175 Quail Run Dr Defiance MO 63341-1706 E-mail: zutterbrock@aol.com.

ZUZOLO, RALPH CARMINE, biologist, educator, researcher, consultant; b. Dente Cane, Avellino, Italy, Sept. 5, 1929; came to U.S., 1930; s. Antonio and Assunta (Nardone) Z.; m. Betty Ann Fong, July 22, 1972. PhD in Cell/Cellular Physiology and Micro-Surgery, NYU, 1960. Asst. prof. CCNY of CUNY, 1965-75, assoc. prof., 1975-93, prof., 1993—, dir. masters program, dept. biology, 1993—; dep. chmn. dept. biology, 1993—; grad., undergrad. advisor, 1993—; co-dir. Robert Chambers Lab. for Cell Micro-Manipulation and microinjection CCNY, 1978—, supr. dept. biology Sch. Gen. Studies, 1968-91; adj. rsch. scientist NYU, N.Y.C., 1965-78; dir. course and standing CCNY, 1978—88. Cons. Robert Chambers Lab. CCNY, 1978—. Author: (manuals) Cellular Micromanipulation, 1992, Manual of Ruby Laser Microsurgery, 1993; co-author: Manual in Cell and Molecular Biology, 1992. Cpl. USMC, 1951-52, Korea. Recipient Rsch. fellowship U. Tex., 1966-68, grant Olympus Corp. of Am., 1981-2000. Mem. AAUP, Nat. Tissue Culture Assn., Applied Spectroscopy, N.Y. Microscopical Soc., Sigma Xi. Achievements include development of instrumentation and methods for microinjection of macromolecules into single plant and animal cells and embryos. Office: CCNY Convent Ave at 138th St New York NY 10031

ZVARA, CHRISTINE C. middle school education educator; BS in Physical Edn. and Adaptive Physical Edn., U. Wis. Mid. and secondary physical edn. specialist grades 6-12 Gibraltar Schs., Fish Creek, Wis. Coord. Dance for Heart Event; mem. swim team bd. Door County YMCA, 1991-95; vol. Sister Bay Fall Classic Run, 1988-91; mem. Sturgeon Bay Sch. Booster Club, 1992—, Sturgeon Bay Band Parents Club, 1991—, Friends of Gibraltar PTO, 1982—. Named Coord. of Yr. Wis. Northeast Dist. Jump Rope for Heart, 1993. Home: 205 S 10th Ave Sturgeon Bay WI 54235-1803 Office: Gibraltar Sch RR 1 Box 205-g Fish Creek WI 54212-9801*

ZWEIER, RICHARD JOSEPH, JR., secondary school educator, education supervisor; b. Lebanon, Pa., Jan. 5, 1951; s. Richard Joseph and Verna Ruth (Leedy) Z.; m. Deborah Ann Troxel, Aug. 11, 1973 (div. 1985); 1 child, David Richard; m. Nancy Patricia Baylock, Mar. 3, 1985. BS in Music Edn., Lebanon Valley Coll., Annville, Pa., 1972; MMus, Manhattan Sch. Music, 1980. Tchr. Franklin (N.J.) Pub. Schs., 1973-75; tchr., choral dir. Vernon (N.J.) Twp. High Sch., 1975—, music supr. 9-12, 1985-93; music supr. K-12 Vernon Twp. Pub. Schs., 1991-93; music area coord. Vernon (N.J.) Twp. High Sch., 1993—, coord. performing arts dept., 1994—. Pvt. voice instr., Vernon, 1977—; condr. N.J. All-State Chorus, Atlantic City, 1984, N.J. All-State Opera Festival Chorus, East Orange, 1989, Miss. State Music Camp Chorus, Starkville, summers 1988, 89. Artistic dir., prin. condr. Community Choral Soc., Vernon, 1989-95; conductor selection com. N.J. All-State Chorus, 1996-98. Mozart seminar fellow NEH, 1994, Humanities fellowship award Coun. for Basic Edn., 1997. Mem. NEA, Music Educators Nat. Conf. (nationally registered), N.J. Music Educators Assn. (state bd. dirs. 1980-83, 87-90, chmn. choral procedures com. 1988-90), North Jersey Sch. Music Assn., Am. Choral Dirs. Assn. Avocations: music history, reading, shortwave radio, opera, theatre. Home: 29 Woodland Dr Vernon NJ 07462-3517 Office: Vernon Twp High Sch PO Box 800 Vernon NJ 07462-0800

ZWERVER, PETER JOHN, linguistics educator; b. Grouw, Friesland, The Netherlands, Sept. 3, 1942; came to U.S., 1959; m. Margot Anne Otters, July 16, 1978. AA in Fgn. Langs., Cerritos Coll., 1963; BA in German and English, Calif. State U., Long Beach, 1963; MA in Edn., Azusa Pacific U., 1971; PhD in Edn., Pacific Western U., 1980; PhD in Linguistics, Clayton U., 1988; BS in Liberal Studies, SUNY, Albany, 1989; BA in Archtl. Arts, Clayton U., 1995; EdD (hon.), City Univ. L.A., 2003. Cert. standard elem., jr. high sch. and gen. secondary tchr., Calif.; cert. in standard supervision and adminstrv. svcs. grades kindergarten through 12, Calif. Tchr. math. and woodworking Monrovia (Calif.) Unified Sch. Dist., 1966-96; assoc. prof. applied linguistics Pacific Western U., L.A., 1984-92, prof., 1992—93; v.p. adminstrv. svcs. Am. M & N U., Metairie, La., 1993—; rep. ITT Tech. Inst., West Covina, Calif., 1997-98; prof. human svcs. City Univ. L.A., 1996—. Fellow in community arts and architecture Am. Coastline U., New Orleans, 1989; mem. acad. adv. coun. Pacific Western U., 1984—; chmn. acad. coun. Am. Coastline U., 1988—. Editor jour. Internat. Inst. for Ind. Scholarship, Pacific Western U., 1983-87; contbg. author: Poetic Voices of America, 1993; columnist Foothill Inter-City Newspapers, 1983-86. Pres. Monroe Sch. PTA, 1975, Santa Anita Family Svc., Monrovia, 1982, Arcadian Christian Sch., Arcadia, Calif., 1974. Recipient Hon. Svc. award Nat. Congress of Parents and Tchrs., 1976. Mem. Nat. Assn. Scholars, Doctorate Assn. N.Y. Educators, Phi Delta Kappa (rsch. rep. U. So. Calif. chpt. 1990-91, Rsch. award 1987, Intrnat. Svc. Key, 1993). Avocations: woodworking, attending concerts, museums, architecture, reading.

ZWICK, REBECCA, education educator; BA in Psychology and Edn., Antioch Coll., 1974; MA in Quantitative Methods, U. Calif., Berkeley, 1981; PhD in Quantitative Methods, 1983; MS in Stats., Rutgers U., 1989. NIMH postdoctoral fellow L.L. Thurstone Psychometric Lab. U. N.C., Chapel Hill, 1983—84; rsch. scientist Psychometrics Rsch. Group Ednl. Testing Svc., Princeton, NJ, 1984—89, dir. data analysis and scale devel. Nat. Assessment Ednl. Progress, 1990—91, sr. rsch. scientist Rsch. Stats. Group, 1991—95, prin. rsch. scientist Rsch. Stats. Group, 1995—96; prof. dept. edn. U. Calif., Santa Barbara, 1996—. Cons., workshop presenter on psychometrics and stats. Clin. Svcs. Rsch. Tng. Program U. Calif., San Francisco, 1986—; sr. fellow Consortium of Univs. U.S. Def. Dept., 1998—; tech. design team Nat. Assessment of Adult Literacy, 1999—; reviewer for reports or proposals Nat. Ctr. for Edn. Stats., 1998, 2001, Nat. Acad. Scis., 1999, NSF, 2000, Nat. Inst. Statis. Scis., 2002, Springer Pubs., 2002. Editor: (spl. issue) Jour. Ednl. Stats., 1992, Jour. Ednl. Measurement, 1995—98; cons. editor: Jour. Consulting and Clin. Psychology, 1985—89, Psychol. Assessment, 1988—91, reviewer: Jour. Am. Statis. Assn., Psychometrika, Psychol. Methods, Applied Psychol. Measurement, Applied Measurement in Edn., Multivariate Behavioral Rsch., Jour. Ednl. Measurement, Jour. Ednl. and Behavioral Stats., Ednl. Measurement: Issues and Practice, Can. Jour. Behavioral Scis., Jour. Math. Psychology. Fellow: APA; mem.: Psychometric Soc., Nat. Coun. on Measurement in Edn. (chair publs. com. 2001—03, faculty advisor grad. student issues com. 1999—2001), Am. Stats. Assn., Am. Ednl. Rsch. Assn. (sec.-treas. 1988—90, program chair conv. 1995, pres. ednl. statisticians spl. interest group 1995—96), Soc. for Multivariate Experimental Psychology. Office: Univ Calif Santa Barbara 2216 Phelps Hall Santa Barbara CA 93106-9490*

ZWIREN, JANET, holistic professional, educator; b. Orange, N.J., Aug. 3, 1952; d. John Paul and Martha Ann (Gallik) Bachmann; m. Steven Scott Zwiren, Sept. 25, 1971 (div. Feb. 1986); children: Paula Marie, Lisa Michelle. AA in Home Econs., Centenary Coll., Hackettstown, N.J., 1975; BA in Psychology, Coll. St. Elizabeth, Convent Station, N.J., 1987; Reiki master, Unltd. Potential, West Orange. N.J., 1994; grad., Realtors Inst., Edison, N.J., 1994. Cert. residential specialist. Title searcher Chelsea Title, New Brusnwick, N.J., 1972, Stewart Title, Morristown, N.J., 1973-75; title searcher, officer Heritage Abstract, Morristown, 1976-84; mortgage banker Fin. Investement Resources, Morristown, 1987-88, Greater Metro, Wayne, N.J., 1988; realtor residential sales Weichert Realtors, Succasunna, N.J., 1988-91, Re/Max Renown Realty, Randolph, N.J., 1991-99; Reiki Master, Shamanic practitioner Universal Life Energy Healing Ctr., Succasunna, 1994—97; dir., Shaman, Reiki master Oasis for the Soul, 1997—. Pvt. cons. Bus. Mktg. and Mgmt., Succasunna, 1995—. Leader Girl Scouts U.S.A., Succasunna, 1993, 1985, 88, Denville, N.J., 1981, 84; town coun. reporter League Women Voters, Randolph, 1975. Mem. Nat. Assn. Realtors, N.J. Assn. Realtors (Million Dollar Club bronze and silver awards 1988-98, Remax Internat. Hall of Fame, 1997), Morris County Bd. Realtors, Residential Spl. Coun., Grad. Realtors Inst., Remax Internat. 100 Club. Democrat. Avocations: sailing, reading, hiking, writing, travel. Home: 16 Meadowview Ave Succasunna NJ 07876-1737 Office: Oasis for the Soul PO Box 85 Succasunna NJ 07876-0085

ZWISLOCKI, JOZEF JOHN, neuroscience educator, researcher; b. Lwow, Poland, Mar. 19, 1922; came to U.S., 1951; s. Tadeusz and Helena (Moscicki) Z.; m. Ruth Gerber, Oct. 29, 1945 (div. May 1954); m. Sylvia Claire Goldman, July 11, 1954 (dec. July 17, 1992); m. Jadwiga M. Morrison, Dec. 2, 1993. Diploma, Fed. Tech. Inst., Zurich, Switzerland, 1944, Sc.D., 1948; D. honoris causa, U. Adam Mickiewicz, Poznán, Poland, 1991. Head electroacoustic lab. dept. otolaryngology U. Basel, Switzerland, 1945-51; research fellow psychoacoustic lab. Harvard U., Cambridge, Mass., 1951-57; dir. Bioacoustic Lab. Syracuse U., N.Y., 1958-63, founder, dir. Lab. of Sensory Communication, 1963-73, founder dir. Inst. for Sensory Research, 1973—84, prof. neurosci., 1984—88, disting. prof. neurosci., 1988—92, disting. prof. emeritus, 1992—; prof. communicative disorders dept. spl. edn. Syracuse U. Sch. Edn., 1982—92; research prof. SUNY Health Sci. Ctr., Syracuse, 1967—. Affiliate prof. bioengring. L.C. Smith Coll. Engring., Syracuse U., 1986-92; Carhart Meml. lectr. Am. Auditory Soc., 1992; mem. exec. coun. Com. Hearing, Bioacoustics and Biomechanics, NRC, Washington, 1965-68, chmn., 1967-68; mem. rev. panel on communicative scis. NIH, Bethesda, Md., 1966-70, chmn., 1969-70; mem. Communicative Disorders Program Project rev. com. NIH, Bethesda, 1971-75; chmn. Bd. Sci. Advs. Ctr. Health Scis., U. Wis., Madison, 1975-78. Inventor acoustic ear simulator, acoustic bridge, several types of ear defenders; contbr. articles to profl. jours.; author: Auditory Sound Transmission: An Autobiographical Perspective, 2002. Recipient Faculty Research award Syracuse chpt. Sigma Xi, 1973, Internat. Ctr. Ricerche e Studi Amplifon prize, 1976, Chancellor's citation, Syracuse U., 1980, Javits Neurosci. Investigator award NIH, 1984, Kwiek medal Acoustics Inst., A. Mickiewicz U., Poland, 1991, medal Acoustical Soc. Poland, 1991, Hugh Knowles prize Northwestern U., 1992. Fellow Acoustical Soc. Am. (chmn. tech. com. on psychol. and physiol. acoustics 1962, 63, exec. coun. 1982-85, recipient 1st Bekesy medal 1985, chmn. long-range planning com. 1983-86, nominating com. 1986-87, mem. com. on tutorials 1988-91, com. on meetings 1988-91, chmn. spring meeting, 1989), Am. Speech and Hearing Assn., The Polish Inst. of Arts and Scis. of Am.; mem. NAS, Polish Acad. Scis., Internat. Soc. Audiology (v.p. 1967-72), Internat. Union of Physiol. Scis. (commn. on auditory physiology 1982-89), Internat. Union Pure and Applied Physics (Commn. on Acoustics 1982-89), Collegium Oto Rhino Laryngologicum Amicitiae Sacrum, Assn. for Rsch. in Otolaryngology (award of merit 1988), Hearing Rsch. (editl. bd.). Avocations: skiing, tennis, trout fishing, inventions.

Professional Index

ADULT EDUCATION

UNITED STATES

ALABAMA

Huntsville
Hollowell, Jan Bennett *adult education educator*

Prattville
Moorer, Frances Earline Green *vocational educator*

ARIZONA

Flagstaff
Bacon, Roger Lee *English educator, consultant*

Fort Huachuca
Adams, Frank *education specialist*

Tempe
Axford, Roger William *adult education educator, consultant*

ARKANSAS

Fayetteville
Farrell, Karolyn Kay McMillan *adult education educator*

CALIFORNIA

Downey
Brooks, Lillian Drilling Ashton (Lillian Hazel Church) *adult education educator*

El Cajon
Thomas, Esther Merlene *elementary and adult education educator*

Fresno
Faderman, Lillian *adult education educator*

Long Beach
Duran, Matias Martin *adult education educator*

Mill Valley
Nelson, Anita Josette *adult education educator*

Modesto
Davis, Julie Lynda *adult and secondary education educator*

Morro Bay
Scholer, Margaret D. *adult education educator*

San Diego
Schade, Charlene Joanne *adult and early childhood education educator*

San Francisco
Zhu, Bo-qing *cardiovascular research specialist*

San Jose
Holyer, Erna Maria *adult education educator, writer, artist*

Santa Monica
Tigue, William Bernard *adult education educator*

FLORIDA

Fort Lauderdale
Guest, Suzanne Mary *adult education educator, artist*

Miami
Brown, Warren Donald *adult education educator, retired police officer*
McLaughlin, Margaret Brown *educator, writer*

Monticello
Hooks, Mary Linda *adult education educator*

Tampa
Hunt, Janice Lynn *adult education educator*

GEORGIA

Athens
Andrews, Grover Jene *adult education educator, administrator*

Savannah
Taggart, Helen M. *nurse*

Swainsboro
Ward, Martha Gail Joiner *adult education educator*

IDAHO

Boise
Yang, Baiyin *adult education educator*

ILLINOIS

Chicago
Murray, Robb *software educator, voiceover professional*

Madison
Purdes, Alice Marie *retired adult education educator*

Marseilles
Nellett, Gaile H. *university level educator*

Murphysboro
Novara Murphy, Amy *court reporter*

Peoria
Dries, Colleen Patricia *adult education educator*

INDIANA

Gary
Hall, James Rayford, III, *adult educator*

Westville
LeRoy, Elizabeth Reichelt *retired adult education educator*

KANSAS

Kansas City
Hall, Helene W. *retired adult education educator*

Olathe
Dennis, Patricia Lyon *adult education educator*

LOUISIANA

Alexandria
Hughes, Mary Alice *adult education educator*

MICHIGAN

Ann Arbor
Turner, Hazel M. *adult education educator*

Dearborn
Bergin, Barbara Dawn *adult education educator*

Detroit
Miller, Annetta *university administrator*
Rezabek, Christina JoAnn *adult education educator*

Southfield
Hartman-Abramson, Ilene *adult education educator*

Traverse City
Miller, Patricia Ann *adult education educator*

MISSOURI

Republic
Traylor, Joyce Elaine *adult education educator*

Saint Louis
Martens Balke, Patricia Frances *adult education educator*
Weng, Robert Allen *adult education educator*

MONTANA

Great Falls
Gray, Chris Hables *adult education educator, writer*

NEBRASKA

Omaha
Ng, Peter Ann-Beng *computer science educator, researcher*

NEVADA

Las Vegas
Chance, Patti Lynn *school leadership educator*

NEW HAMPSHIRE

Londonderry
Kennedy, Ellen Woodman *elementary and home economics educator*

NEW JERSEY

Roselle Park
Scarpelli, Vito *adult education educator, administrator*

Teaneck
Hart, Denise Marie *adult education educator, director*

NEW YORK

Fayetteville
Hiemstra, Roger *adult education educator, writer*

New York
King, Kathleen Palombo *adult education educator, consultant*
Newman, Phyllis *adult education educator, psychologist*

Saratoga Springs
McKnight, Joyce Sheldon *adult educator, community organizer, mediator*

Schenectady
Helmar-Salasoo, Ester Anette *literacy educator, researcher*

Yonkers
Liggio, Jean Vincenza *adult education educator, artist*

NORTH CAROLINA

Charlotte
Nassar-McMillan, Sylvia C. *adult education educator*

Durham
Glasco, JoAnn *adult education educator, consultant*

Raleigh
Martin, Donnis Lynn *adult education educator*

OHIO

Columbus
Klayman, Elliot Irwin *adult education educator*

Hillsboro
Willis, Dollie P. *adult education educator*

Medina
Pilat, Janet Louise B. Oberholtzer *adult education educator*

Oberlin
MacKay, Gladys Godfrey *adult education educator*

Waverly
Lovett, Francis William, Jr., *adult education educator*

OKLAHOMA

Enid
Taylor, Donna Lynne *adult training coordinator*

PENNSYLVANIA

Harrisburg
Boyer, Cheryl Moen *adult education educator*

State College
Aitken, Ruth Elaine Willson *educational and career/job search consultant*

SOUTH CAROLINA

Columbia
Muzekari, Thomasine Dabbs *adult education educator*

TENNESSEE

Knoxville
Brockett, Ralph Grover *adult education educator*

TEXAS

Bedias
Williamson, Norma Beth *adult education educator*

Bryan
Beal, Mary Frances *adult education educator*

Dallas
Scott, John Roland *business law educator*

El Paso
Grimes, William Gaylord *adult education educator*

Fort Worth
Wilson-Webb, Nancy Lou *education administration consultant, rancher*

Houston
Stryker, Daniel Ray *adult education educator*

San Antonio
McSorley, Rita Elizabeth *adult education educator*

UTAH

Ogden
Grant, Sandra Kay *adult education educator*

VERMONT

South Duxbury
Villemaire, Diane Davis *adult education educator*

VIRGINIA

Centreville
Madison-Colmore, Octavia Dianne *adult education educator*

Reston
Rowen, Betty J. (Rose) *adult education educator*

Richmond
Blank, Florence Weiss *literacy educator, editor*

Staunton
Hagen, Agnes Mary *adult education educator, writer*

WASHINGTON

Nine Mile Falls
Payne, Arlie Jean *parent education administrator*

Tacoma
Ingram, Artonyon S. *psychology educator*

WEST VIRGINIA

Martinsburg
Baccala, Beverly Anne *adult education educator*

WISCONSIN

Fox Point
Ellis, Nancy Kempton *adult education educator*

Hales Corners
Michalski, Wacław (Żur-Żurowski Wacł Michalski) *adult education educator*

Menomonee Falls
Nelson, Mary Ellen Genevieve *adult education educator*

Wausau
Olszewski, Sharon Ann *adult education educator*

NIGERIA

Calabar
Morah, Frank Nwokedi Igbekwe *adult education educator, researcher*

ADDRESS UNPUBLISHED

Albarracin-Nwoke, Luz G. *adult education educator*
Bayard, Susan Shapiro *adult education educator, small business owner*
Brewer, Patricia Rose *adult education educator*
Conover, Mona Lee *retired adult education educator*
Evans, Bonita Dianne *adult education educator*
Fleming, Jean Anderson *adult and community education educator*
Heap, Sylvia Stuber *educator*
Hertel, Suzanne Marie *training and development specialist*
Kozma, Helene Joyce Marie *adult educator*
Ledbury, Diana Gretchen *adult education educator*
Moistner, Mona Sue *adult education educator*
O'Brien, Kathy Mosdal *educator*

Sanders, Catharine Downer *retired adult educator, historical researcher*
Spingola, Jeannie Saundra *college, special education and adult educator, counselor*
Young, Joyce Henry *adult education educator, consultant*
Young, Teresa Gail Hilger *adult education educator*

ASSOCIATION ADMINISTRATION

UNITED STATES

ALABAMA

Birmingham
Hames, Carl Martin *educational administrator, art dealer, consultant*

Montgomery
Oswalt, (Eugene) Talmadge *educational administrator*

ALASKA

Anchorage
Jones, Mark Logan *educational association executive, educator*

Delta Junction
Mauer, Richard I. *educational association administrator*

ARIZONA

Paradise Valley
Moya, Sara Dreier *educational association administrator*

Prescott
Garvey, Daniel Edward *foundation administrator, educator, academic administrator*

Scottsdale
Milanovich, Norma JoAnne *training and development company executive*

Tucson
Drachman, Sally Spaid *educational foundation administrator*
Lovejoy, Jean Hastings *social services counselor*

ARKANSAS

Little Rock
Malone, David Roy *educational association administrator, director*

CALIFORNIA

Berkeley
Myers, Miles Alvin *educator, educational association administrator*

Citrus Heights
Leisey, Donald Eugene *educational materials company executive, educator*

Cupertino
Bradley, Richard James *educational association administrator*

Long Beach
Lee, Isaiah Chong-Pie *social worker, educator*

Los Angeles
Jaggers, Velma Mary Lee *foundation administrator, educator*
Munitz, Barry *arts and foundation administrator*

Menlo Park
Schulman, Lee S. *educational association administrator*
Smith, Marshall Savidge *foundation executive*

Mountain View
Wulff, Virginia McMillan *association executive*

Oakland
Lennon, Joanna Leslie *conservation organization executive*

Palo Alto
Robinson, Agnes Claflin *educational administrator*

Salinas
Butler, Billie Rae *educational administrator*

San Diego
Swanson, Mary Catherine *educational reform program founder*

San Francisco
Brown, Bernice Leona Baynes *foundation consultant, educator, consultant*
Carleton, Mary Ruth *development professional, consultant*
Egan, Patricia Jane *foundation executive, former university development director, writer*
Harvey, Glen H. *educational association administrator*
Mikuriya, Mary Jane *retired educational agency administrator*

Santa Barbara
Shreeve, Susanna Seelye *educational planning facilitator*

Santa Clarita
Melonakos, Christine Marie *educational administrator*

Santa Monica
Foley, Jane Deborah *foundation executive*

Whittier
Harvey, Patricia Jean *special education administrator, retired*
Meardy, William Herman *retired educational association administrator*

COLORADO

Arvada
Leafgreen, Lisa Diane *education coordinator*

Boulder
Johnstone, Sally Mac *educational association administrator, psychology educator*
Longanecker, David A. *educational association administrator*

Denver
Dion, Susan M. *education director, educator*
Fevurly, Keith Robert *educational administrator*
Fujioka, Jo Ann Ota *educational administrator, consultant*
Henry, Ernestyne Ethel Thatch *educational administrator*
Jones, Jean Correy *organization administrator*
Loeup, Kong *cultural organization administrator*
Sanders, Ted *educational association administrator*

Fort Collins
Cummings, Sharon Sue *state extension service youth specialist*

Louisville
Jonsen, Richard Wiliam *retired educational administrator*

Louviers
Murdoch, John T., II, *academic organization administrator, publishing company executive*

Westminster
Campagna, Timothy Nicholas *institute executive*

CONNECTICUT

Waterbury
Harper, Barbara Clara *counselor, educational program administrator, counselor*

DELAWARE

Newark
Gronka, M(artin) Steven *educational association executive, film and television producer*
Townsend, Brenda S. *educational association administrator*

Wilmington
Fleming, Blanche Miles *educational administrator*

DISTRICT OF COLUMBIA

Washington
Alberts, Bruce Michael *research organization executive*
Barclay, Ellen S. *not-for-profit developer*
Binkley, Marilyn Rothman *educational research administrator*
Bray, Sarah Hardesty *newspaper editor, writer*
Elliott, Thomas Michael *retired association executive, educator, consultant*
Feldman, Sandra *labor union executive*
Friedman, Miles *trade association executive, financial services company executive, university lecturer*
Gaiter, Jatrice Martel *educational administrator*
Huband, Frank Louis *educational association executive*
Ingram, Richard Thomas *educational association executive*
Kane, Cheryl Marie *education program developer*
Kolb, Charles Chester *humanities administrator*
Levine, Felice *educational association administrator*
Magrath, C. Peter *educational association executive*
Raizen, Senta Amon *educational administrator, researcher*
Rayburn, Wendell Gilbert *educational association executive*
Rich, Dorothy Kovitz *writer, educational administrator*
Robinson, Sharon Porter *professional society administrator*
Russell, William Joseph *educational association administrator*
Schneider, Carol Geary *educational association administrator*
Tse, Man-Chun Marina *educational association administrator*
Warren, David Liles *educational association executive*
Weaver, Reg *National Education Association president*
Wilson, John I. *educational association administrator, educator*

FLORIDA

Coral Springs
Orenstein, Janie Elizabeth *educational association administrator, educator*

Jacksonville
Burney, Betty Seabrook *educational administrator*

Melbourne
Dale, Cynthia Lynn Arpke *educational administrator, retired*
Sieloff, Debra Ann *educational administrator, consultant*

Orlando
Thomas, Sandra Marie *training company executive*

Saint Petersburg
Giffin, Barbara Haines *education coordinator*

Stuart
Bourque, Anita Mary *social services administrator*

West Palm Beach
Moody, Cheryl Anne *social services administrator, social worker, educator*

GEORGIA

Atlanta
Axon, Michael *education association field representative*

Bainbridge
McRae, John Henry *educational administrator*

Cordele
Wade, Benny Bernar *educational administrator*

Lagrange
Gaston, Pat Benefield *educational administrator*

Millen
Cowart, Veronica *education administrator*

Riverdale
Rhoden, Mary Norris *educational center director*

Saint Simons Island
Bell, Ronald Mack *university foundation administrator, consultant*

Waycross
Battle, Romona Anita *educational administrator, consultant*

ILLINOIS

Chicago
Donovan, Margaret *educational association administrator*
Fanton, Jonathan Foster *foundation administrator*
Lutz, Carlene *educational association administrator*
Ree, Donna *social services administrator, educator*
Richman, Harold Alan *social welfare policy educator*

Dekalb
Folgate, Cynthia A. *social services administrator*

Lansing
McKeown, Mary Elizabeth *educational administrator*

Lisle
Nykiel, Karen Ann *development administrator*

Machesney Park
Canova, John Richard *educational administrator*

Naperville
L'Allier, James Joseph *educational multimedia company executive, instructional designer*

River Grove
O'Sullivan, Gerald Joseph *association executive*

Springfield
LaVista, Daniel J. *educational association administrator*
Steiner, Janet *educational association administrator*

Vernon Hills
Michalik, John James *legal educational association executive*

Wheaton
Votaw, John Frederick *educational foundation executive, educator*

INDIANA

Indianapolis
Barcus, Robert Gene *retired educational association administrator*
Kreegar, Phillip Keith *educational administrator*
Riesz, Wanda Wallace *educational consultant*

Muncie
Durr, Melissa Ann *nonprofit executive*

West Lafayette
Baumgardt, Billy Ray *professional society administrator, agriculturist*

IOWA

Iowa City
Ferguson, Richard L. *educational administrator*

KANSAS

Atwood
Okeson, Dorothy Jeanne *educational association administrator*

Olathe
Shelton, Jody *educational association administrator*

Wichita
Lowrey, Annie Tsunee *retired cultural organization administrator*

KENTUCKY

Berea
Stephenson, Jane Ellen *educational association administrator*

Covington
Moore, Charlotte Chandler *educational association administrator*

Hardin
Morrow, Bruce William *educational administrator, business executive, consultant, author*

Lexington
DeVries, Brigid Larkin *educational association administrator*
Sexton, Robert Fenimore *educational organization executive*

Louisville
Appleberry, James Bruce *higher education consultant*

Utica
Mountjoy, Helen W. *educational association administrator*

MAINE

Falmouth
Gulliver, Jean K. *educational association administrator*

Windham
Mulvey, Mary Crowley *retired adult education director, gerontologist, senior citizen association administrator*

MARYLAND

Aberdeen Proving Ground
Tobin, Aileen Webb *educational administrator*

Baltimore
Manno, Bruno Victor *foundation administrator*

College Park
Khoury, Bernard V. *educational administrator*

Greenbelt
Miller, Alwin Vermar *educational advisor, consultant*

Lanham Seabrook
Littlefield, Roy Everett, III, *association executive, legal educator*

Owings Mills
Tapp, Mamie Pearl *educational association administration*

Rockville
Standing, Kimberly Anna *educational researcher*

Saint Michaels
Batistoni, Ronald *educational association administrator*

Silver Spring
Camphor, James Winky, Jr., *educational administrator*
Winston, Michael Russell *foundation executive, historian*

Takoma Park
Lancaster, Alden *educational and management consultant*

MASSACHUSETTS

Bedford
Kampits, Eva *accrediting association administrator, educator*

Boston
Franks, Peter John *educational administrator*

Cambridge
Brown, Lloyd David *association executive, management educator*
Hehir, Thomas F. *educational administrator*

PROFESSIONAL INDEX — ASSOCIATION ADMINISTRATION

Framingham
Harrington, Joseph Francis *educational company executive, history educator*

Orleans
Marquand, Jean MacMurtry *educational administrator*

Quincy
Wilson, Blenda Jacqueline *foundation administrator*

Sharon
Reilley, Dennen *research agency administrator, educator*

MICHIGAN

Ann Arbor
Porter, John Wilson *education executive*

Battle Creek
Richardson, William Chase *foundation executive*
Wendt, Linda M. *educational association administrator*

East Lansing
Mitstifer, Dorothy Irwin *honor society administrator*

Manistee
Behring, Daniel William *educational and business professional, consultant*

Rochester Hills
Niemann, Birgie Ann *university fundraiser*

Saint Joseph
Phenix, Gloria Gayle *educational association administrator*

Troy
Hunia, Edward Mark *foundation executive*

MINNESOTA

Minnetonka
Fogelberg, Paul Alan *continuing education company executive*

Saint Paul
Anderson, Gordon Louis *foundation administrator*
Skillingstad, Constance Yvonne *social services administrator, educator*
Stauber, Karl Neill *foundation administrator*
Swanson, Gordon Ira *former educational administrator*

MISSISSIPPI

Jackson
Marks, Michael *association administrator*

MISSOURI

Earth City
Anderhalter, Oliver Frank *educational organization executive*

Jefferson City
Kellerman, James S. *educational association administrator*

Kirksville
French, Michael Francis *non-profit education agency administrator*

Richmond Heights
Chandler, James Barton *international education consultant*

Saint Louis
Anderson, Bruce John *foundation administrator*

Stanberry
Beatty, Judy Iola Spencer *educational specialist*

NEBRASKA

Bancroft
Neihardt, Hilda *foundation administrator, writer, educator*

Hastings
Scherr, Stephen A. *educational association administrator*

Mc Cook
Koetter, Leila Lynette *children's services administrator*

NEVADA

Las Vegas
Spencer, Carol Brown *association executive*

Pahrump
Nowell, Linda Gail *organization executive*

NEW HAMPSHIRE

Hampstead
Scott, Bradwell Davidson *educational administrator, writer, consultant*

NEW JERSEY

Jersey City
Degatano, Anthony Thomas *educational association administrator*

Lyndhurst
Ridenour, James Franklin *fund raising consultant*

Mahwah
Beasley, Diana Lee *educational administrator*

Princeton
Bomba, Cheryl Lynne *educational researcher*

South Orange
Stringile, Marie Elizabeth *educational administrator*

Trenton
Dahme, Maud *educational association administrator*

West Orange
Rinsky, Judith Sue Lynn *foundation administrator, educator consultant*

NEW MEXICO

Santa Fe
Atencio, Pedro Luis *educational administrator*

NEW YORK

Albany
Bellizzi, John J. *law enforcement association administrator, educator, pharmacist*
Bradley, Joseph Anthony *education program director*
Huxley, Carole Frances Corcoran *educational administrator*

Armonk
Cannella, Nancy Anne *educational administrator*

Breesport
Peckham, Joyce Weitz *foundation administrator, former secondary education educator*

Centereach
Chassman, Karen Moss *educational administrator*

Elmhurst
Matsa, Loula Zacharoula *social services administrator, educator*

Jamaica
Keys, Martha McDougle *educational administrator*

New York
Berkovits, Annette Rochelle *educational association administrator, biologist, educator*
Brown, John S. *educational association administrator*
Grabois, Neil Robert *foundation administrator, former college president*
Gregorian, Vartan *foundation administrator*
Ilchman, Alice Stone *foundation administrator, former college president, former government official*
Iselin, John Jay *foundation president*
Kardon, Peter Franklin *foundation administrator*
Levy, Gerald Dun *nonprofit organization administrator*
Lewis, Richard A. *educational association administrator, writer*
McPherson, Mary Patterson *charitable foundation executive*
Slaughter, John Brooks *professional society administrator*

Potsdam
Stevens, Sheila Maureen *teachers union administrator*

Sparrow Bush
Zacharia, Mathew Varikalam *educational administrator, management consultant*

Syracuse
Clark, Kate Helen *educational administrator*
Rountree, Patricia Ann *youth organization administrator*

Tonawanda
Bennett, Robert M. *educational association administrator*

NORTH CAROLINA

Chapel Hill
Krasno, Richard Michael *foundation executive, educator*

Charlotte
Blaschke, Robert Carvel *education coordinator*

Clinton
Griffin, Betty Lou *not-for-profit developer, educator*

Greensboro
Simpson, Bradford Van *education association executive*

Raleigh
Parker, Charles Brand, Jr., *training company executive*

Rocky Mount
Bell, Kim A. *educational program administrator, consultant*

OHIO

Canton
McIlwain-Massey, Nadine *foundation administrator*

Cincinnati
Freter, Lisa *non-profit association administrator*

Cleveland
Calkins, Hugh *foundation executive*

OKLAHOMA

Lawton
Henry, Patricia Jean *educational association administrator, consumer products company executive*

Oklahoma City
Maton, Anthea *education consultant*
McLaughlin, Lisa Marie *educational administrator*

OREGON

Bandon
Millard, Esther Lound *foundation administrator, educator*

Portland
Hudson, Jerry E. *foundation administrator*
Thomas, Carol F. *educational association administrator*

Salem
Kirk, Jill *educational association administrator*

Sherwood
Stroemple, Ruth Mary Thomas *social welfare administrator*

PENNSYLVANIA

Bryn Mawr
Weiss, Ann *educational association director, filmmaker, editor, writer, photographer*

Chester
Ciociola, Cecilia Mary *development specialist*

Drexel Hill
Schiazza, Guido Domenic (Guy Schiazza) *educational association administrator*

Erie
De Backer, David Pierre *educational administrator*

Harrisburg
Amell, Robert Edward *educational facility administrator, business owner*

New Hope
Koljian, Hollis Ann *educational association administrator*

Newtown
De Champlain, Andre Fernand *educational researcher*

Philadelphia
Hochberg, Mark Stefan *professional society administrator, cardiac surgeon*
Scheffer, Ludo Carel Peter *educational researcher, consultant*

Pittsburgh
Grinberg, Meyer Stewart *educational institute executive*

York
Donley, Donald Charles *educational administrator*

RHODE ISLAND

Providence
DiPrete, James A. *educational association administrator*
Littky, Dennis *educational association administrator*

Woonsocket
Dubuc, Mary Ellen *educational administrator*

SOUTH CAROLINA

Beaufort
Barton, Rayburn *educational administrator*

Columbia
Sheheen, Fred Roukos *education agency administrator*

Easley
Moncrief, James Loring *educational administrator*

Florence
Alley, Mary Dean Brewer *medical foundation executive*

Spartanburg
Glassick, Charles Etzweiler *academic foundation administrator*
Owens, Hilda Faye *management and leadership development consultant, human resource trainer*

Woodruff
Childers, Bob Eugene *educational association executive*

TENNESSEE

Chattanooga
Morton, Michael Rader *career and technology education director*
Piatt, Albert Earl *educator, researcher, consultant*

Cleveland
Lockhart, Madge Clements *educational organization executive*

Memphis
Brookins, Dolores *educational consulting organization executive*

Nashville
Bransford, John D. *educational association administrator*
McCullough, Hubert L., Jr., *educational association administrator*
Rhoda, Richard G. *educational administrator*

TEXAS

Austin
Bonjean, Charles Michael *foundation executive, sociologist, educator*
Nasworthy, Carol Cantwell *education and public policy researcher*
Pettigrew, Jo Arnold *educational association administrator*
Washington, Rebecca Nan *educational association administrator*

Dickinson
Sawyer, Cheryl Lynne *foundation administrator, educator, consultant*

El Paso
Schmidt, Mary Berry *educational administrator*

Houston
Albrecht, Kay Montgomery *early childhood educator, author, child advocate*

Irving
Green, John Howard *scouting association administrator*

Levelland
Tilley, Suzanne Denise *education specialist*

Odessa
Boyd, Claude Collins *educational specialist, consultant*

San Antonio
Moder, John Joseph *non-profit administrator*
Montes, Felix Manuel *educational researcher, technological consultant*

Waco
Moran, Doris Ann *educational consultant, mathematics educator*

UTAH

Salt Lake City
Mendenhall, Robert W. *educational executive*

VERMONT

Bondville
Ambach, Gordon Mac Kay *educational association executive*

Plainfield
Mossberg, Barbara Clarke *educational writer and speaker*

VIRGINIA

Alexandria
Butler, Susan Lowell *educational association executive, writer*
Carter, Gene Raymond *professional association executive*
Turner, Mary Jane *educational administrator*
Welburn, Brenda Lilienthal *professional society administrator*

Arlington
Shannon, Thomas Alfred *retired educational association administrator emeritus*

Charlottesville
Thompson, Kenneth W(inifred) *educational association administrator, writer, editor, social sciences educator*

Fairfax
Gray, William H., III, *association executive, former congressman*

Manassas
Neal, Richard Glenn *educational management company executive*

ASSOCIATION ADMINISTRATION

Norfolk
Meslang, Susan Walker *educational administrator*

Reston
Gates, James David *retired association executive, consultant*
Madry-Taylor, Jacquelyn Yvonne *educational administrator*
Mahlmann, John James *music education association administrator*
Mogge, Harriet Morgan *educational association executive*

Richmond
Combs, Sandra Lynn *state parole board official*
Ralph, Deborah Malone *social services administrator, educator*

Sterling
Munger, Paul David *company executive, educational administrator*

Virginia Beach
Reece-Porter, Sharon Ann *international human rights educator*

Warrenton
Fox, Raymond Graham *educational technologist*

Weems
Merrick, Roswell Davenport *educational association administrator*

Williamsburg
Sass, Arthur Harold *educational executive*

Yorktown
Feldt, Glenda Diane *educational administrator*

WASHINGTON

Port Townsend
Woolf, William Blauvelt *retired association executive*

Redmond
Teeley, Kevin *educational association administrator*

Tacoma
Hinkley, Nancy Emily Engstrom *foundation administrator, educator*

WEST VIRGINIA

Charleston
Persinger, Howard Moses, Jr., *educational association administrator*

WISCONSIN

Allenton
Ellis, Maxine Ethel *social services administrator, educator*

Madison
Higby, Gregory James *historical association administrator, historian*

TERRITORIES OF THE UNITED STATES

VIRGIN ISLANDS

St Thomas
Creque, Linda Ann *non-profit educational and research executive, former education commissioner*

ADDRESS UNPUBLISHED

Adams, Jeanette Brown *educational association administrator*
Babb, Roberta Joan *educational administrator*
Bailey, Tracey L. *educational association administrator*
Boysen, Thomas Cyril *educational association administrator*
Brown, Steven E. *retired educational association administrator*
Bryant, Anne Lincoln *educational association executive*
Burt, Aurelia Thomas *educational administrator, middle school consultant*
Butcher, Harry William *educational administrator, educator, historian*
Butterfield, Karen *educational association administrator*
Dickson, Suzanne Rathbone (Sue Dickson) *educational administrator*
Dozier, Therese Knecht *educational association administrator, educator*
Edwards, Margaret Sally *retired educational administrator*
Franklin, Phyllis *retired professional society administrator*
Gadsden, Marie Davis *educational agency administrator*
Jacoby, Thomas S. *cultural organization administrator*
Johnson, Christine *educational administrator*
Kahrmann, Robert George *educational administrator*
Kussrow, Nancy Esther *educational association administrator*
McWethy, Patricia Joan *educational association administrator*

Mitchell, Carolyn Cochran *foundation administrator's executive assistant*
Morrison, Barbara Haney *educational administrator*
Morse, Jean Avnet *higher education administrator, lawyer*
Navarro, Richard *educational association administrator*
Peck, Robert David *educational foundation administrator*
Peri, Winnie Lee Branch *educational director*
Piraino, Ann Mae *seminar trainer, leader, vocational counselor*
Ponder, Henry *educational association administrator*
Pratt, Alice Reynolds *retired educational administrator*
Prescott, Barbara Lodwich *educational administrator*
Quam, Jon *educational association administrator*
Ryan, John William *association executive*
Saunders-Smith, Gail Ann *educational administrator, consultant*
Scott, Jacqueline Delmar Parker *educational association administrator, business administrator, consultant, fundraiser, educator*
Seamans, Patrick William *international education consultant, architect*
Smith, Laverne Byrd *educational association administrator*
Smith, Sheryl Velting *organization administrator*
Stern, Harrian Micha Burttschell *educational diagnostician*
Stewart, Marilyn Epstein *educational administrator, consultant*
Swain, Virginia M. *executive mentor, conflict resolution, reconciliation and peace education consultant, educator*
Temkin, Terrie Charlene *professional non-profit administrator, educator*
Warren, John William *professional society administrator*
Whalen, Loretta Theresa *religious educational administrator*
Williamson, Robert Thomas, Jr., *educational administrator*

COUNSELING/CAREER PLANNING

UNITED STATES

ALABAMA

Montgomery
Chamberlain, Kathryn Burns Browning *retired career officer*
Walker, Annette *retired counseling administrator*

ARIZONA

Phoenix
Karabatsos, Elizabeth Ann *career counseling services executive*
Meddles, Sharon Diane Gunstream *school counselor*

CALIFORNIA

Alameda
Carter, Roberta Eccleston *therapist, counselor*

Anaheim
Guajardo, Elisa *counselor, educator*

Covina
Aguilar, Gladys Maria *counselor, educator*

Hemet
Fitzsimmons, Terri Kathleen *educator, counselor*

Lodi
Reinold, Christy Diane *school counselor, consultant*

Long Beach
Culton, Paul Melvin *retired counselor, educator, interpreter*

Los Angeles
Coker, Sybil Jane Thomas *counseling administrator*
Harvey, James Gerald *educational counselor, consultant, researcher*
McGee, Lynda Plant *guidance counselor*

Orange
Gerhard, Nancy Lucile Dege *school counselor, educator*

Palos Verdes Peninsula
Miller, Francie Loraditch *counseling administrator*

Paramount
Williams, Vivian Lewie *retired counseling administrator*

Petaluma
Mulkern-Kolosey, Sandy Kathleen *college counselor, educator, realtor*

San Diego
King, Verna St. Clair *retired school counselor*

Ventura
Zuber, Norma Keen *career counselor, educator*

COLORADO

Denver
Antonoff, Steven Ross *educational consultant, author*
Augustine, Rosemary *vocational counselor, writer*

Nederland
Morrison, K. Jaydene *education counseling firm executive*

Parker
Fedak, Barbara Kingry *retired technical center administrator*

CONNECTICUT

Bridgeport
Perryman-Joines, Keith (Keith P. Joines) *school counselor*

Farmington
Dawson-Thompson, Mary Marquetta *guidance counselor*

Trumbull
Madigan, Rita Duffy *career education coordinator*

DELAWARE

New Castle
Johnson, Dorothy Sutherland *school guidance counselor*

Wilmington
Chagnon, Lucille Tessier *workforce development and literacy specialist*
Fletcher, Lawrence Francis *guidance counselor*

DISTRICT OF COLUMBIA

Washington
Hall, Samuel M., Jr., *career educator, career development consultant*

FLORIDA

Clearwater
Stilwell, Charlotte Finn *vocational counselor*

Gainesville
Slattery, William Joseph *school psychologist*

Jacksonville
Boyles, Carol Ann Patterson *career development educator*

Miami
Allen, Nancy *vocational rehabilitation counselor*
Jones-Koch, Francena *school counselor, educator*
Perez, Mary Christine *guidance counselor, small business owner*

Orlando
Kornrumph, Joan O. *counseling administrator, educator*

Palatka
Rowe, Devona Powell *guidance counselor, social worker*

Tampa
McNair, Gloridine Deloris *counseling administrator*

Winter Park
McDowell, Annie R. *retired counselor*

GEORGIA

Albany
Keith, Carolyn Austin *secondary school counselor*

Atlanta
Bailey, Joy Hafner *counselor educator*
Curry, Toni Griffin *counseling center executive, consultant*
Walker, Carolyn Smith *college services administrator, counselor*

Columbus
Abrahamson, William Gene *retired school counselor*

Conyers
Bouchillon, John Ray *education coordinator*

Dublin
Fatum, Delores Ruth *school counselor*

Smyrna
Force, Crystal Ann *school counselor*

Suwanee
Trice, Mary Sue Williams *guidance counselor*

Zebulon
Bizzell Yarbrough, Cindy Lee *school counselor*

HAWAII

Honolulu
Walsh, Janice Maureen *counselor, educator*

Waipahu
O'Brien, Nancy A. *youth counselor*

IDAHO

Mountain Home
Graves, Karen Lee *counselor*

Pocatello
Eichman, Charles Melvin *school counselor, career assessment educator*

ILLINOIS

Charleston
Eberly, Charles *counseling and student development educator*

Chicago
Roberson, Carolyn A. *elementary school counselor*

Downers Grove
Soder-Alderfer, Kay Christie *counseling administrator*

Jacksonville
Moe-Fishback, Barbara Ann *counseling administrator*

Moline
Schauenberg, Susan Kay *retired counseling administrator*

Olney
Boyer, A(deline) Nadine *guidance counselor*

South Holland
Larsen, Mary Ann Indovina *counselor, educator*

West Peoria
McBride, Sharon Louise *counselor, technical communication educator*

INDIANA

Indianapolis
Fletcher, Brady Jones *vocational education career specialist*
Metzner, Barbara Stone *university counselor*
Wooden, Reba Faye Boyd *guidance counselor*

Muncie
Holt, Gerald Wayne *retired counseling administrator*

Warren
Pattison, Deloris Jean *retired counselor, university official*

IOWA

Cedar Rapids
Hutton, Mary J. *guidance counselor*

KANSAS

Bonner Springs
Jarrett, Gracie Mae *middle school guidance counselor*

Shawnee Mission
Baughman, Pamela Ann *secondary school counselor*

Wichita
Sherwood, Joan Karolyn Sargent *retired career counselor*

KENTUCKY

Covington
Berg, Lorine McComis *retired guidance counselor*

Hodgenville
Morrison, Helena Grace *guidance counselor*

Lexington
Crouch, Dianne Kay *secondary school guidance counselor*
Lawson, Frances Gordon *child guidance specialist*

Liberty
Brady, Sherry Sluder *guidance counselor*

Paintsville
Fannin, Juanita Jude *guidance counselor*

Union
Franklin, Dorothy Ann *guidance counselor*

LOUISIANA

Abbeville
Camel, Peggy Thurston *guidance counselor*

Alexandria
Vandersypen, Rita DeBona *guidance counselor, academic administrator*

Franklin
Fairchild, Phyllis Elaine *school counselor*

MARYLAND

Bowie
Moseley, Theresa A. *guidance counselor, actress*

PROFESSIONAL INDEX

MASSACHUSETTS

Frederick
Hamilton, Rhoda Lillian Rosén *guidance counselor, language educator, consultant*

Boston
Daukantas, George Vytautas *counseling practitioner, educator*

Burlington
Dubois, Cindy A. *guidance counselor*

MICHIGAN

Detroit
Winters, Virginia Rosemary *counselor, education consultant*

Royal Oak
Pricer, Wayne Francis *counseling consultant*

MINNESOTA

Saint James
Jones, Patricia Louise *elementary counselor*

MISSISSIPPI

Cleveland
Baker-Branton, Camille *counselor, educator*

Jackson
Dansby-Giles, Gloria F. *counselor, educator*
Trigg, Glyn Ray *guidance counselor, educational administrator, customer service representative*

MISSOURI

Kansas City
Washington, Patricia Lane *retired school counselor*

Kirkwood
Foster, Diane Marie *elementary school counselor*

Richmond Heights
Ward, Ollie Tucker *counselor, educator*

Saint Louis
Flanagan, Joan Wheat (Maggie Flanagan) *educational therapist*

Versailles
Beyer, Teresa Lynn *elementary counselor*

NEBRASKA

Offutt A F B
Wade, Rebecca Haygood *education professional*

NEVADA

Reno
Mulert, Lynne Carol *school counselor*

NEW HAMPSHIRE

Plymouth
DeCotis, Ruth Janice *career planning administrator, educator*

NEW JERSEY

Jersey City
McGhee, Elaine Simmons *school director, consultant*

Manahawkin
Zalinsky, Sandra H. Orlofsky *school counselor*

Paramus
Plucinsky, Constance Marie *school counselor, supervisor*

Princeton
Pimley, Kim Jensen *financial training consultant*

Teaneck
Smith, Susan Elizabeth *guidance director*

Wharton
Sarubbi, Judith Alice Clearwater *guidance counselor*

NEW MEXICO

Albuquerque
Edwards, Louise Wiseman *career counselor, educator*

NEW YORK

Amherst
Pachan, Mary Jude Kathryn Dorothy *guidance counselor*

Bemus Point
Rollinger, Mary Elizabeth *school counselor*

Brooklyn
Curry, David *guidance staff developer*

Sarni, Carol A. *school psychologist*

Buffalo
Schobert, Melody A. *counseling educator*

Mahopac
Silbert, Linda Bress *educational counselor, therapist*

New Rochelle
Conte, Susan *secondary school counselor*

New York
Anderson, Carol Lynn *counseling, career planning administrator*
Mullin, Mary Ann *career counselor*

Oakdale
Hogeboom, Patricia Ann Schrack *high school guidance counselor*

Peconic
Aldcroft, George Edward *guidance counselor*

Springfield Gardens
Williams, Vida Veronica *guidance counselor*

NORTH CAROLINA

Greensboro
Zopf, Evelyn LaNoel Montgomery *guidance counselor*

Raleigh
Drew, Nancy McLaurin Shannon *counselor, consultant*

OHIO

Broadview Heights
Jergens, Maribeth Joie *school counselor*

Cincinnati
Ashley, Lynn *educator, consultant, administrator*

Cleveland
Sabik, Joseph Andrew *psychometrist, counselor*

Fairfield
Brown, Cheryl Ann *high school counselor*

Houston
Borchers, Kay Elizabeth *school counselor*

Hudson
Goheen, Janet Moore *counselor, sales professional*

Parma
Newman, Andrea Haas *school counselor, educator*

Toledo
Marcus, Carol A. *counseling administrator, educator*

OKLAHOMA

Claremore
Davis, Carol Anderson *school counselor*

Oklahoma City
Parker-Broiles, Diana Marie *school counselor*

OREGON

Fairview
Sizemore, Robert Dennis *school counselor, educational administrator*

Lake Oswego
Meltebeke, Renette *career counselor*

Merrill
Porter, Roberta Ann *counselor, educator, school system administrator*

PENNSYLVANIA

Belle Vernon
Kline, Bonita Ann *middle school guidance counselor, educator*

Flourtown
Moore, Sandra Kay *counselor, administrator*

Malvern
Darby, Samuel Edward *guidance counselor*

Mertztown
Allison, Robert Harry *school counselor*

Perkasie
Ferry, Joan Evans *school counselor*

Philadelphia
Styer, Antoinette Cardwell *middle school administrator*

RHODE ISLAND

Barrington
Hart, Michael Allen *educator, counselor*

Central Falls
Leclerc, Leo George *guidance counselor*

SOUTH DAKOTA

Aberdeen
Fouberg, Glenna M. *career planning administrator*

TENNESSEE

Hendersonville
Poynor, Robert Allen, Jr., *retired guidance counselor*

Knoxville
Anderson, Yasmin Lynn Mullis *educational consultant, small business owner*

Memphis
Maxwell, Sandra Elaine *guidance counselor*

TEXAS

Austin
Lewis, Nancy Louine Lambert *school counselor*

Dallas
Smith, Valerie Gay *school counselor*

Denton
Coy, Doris Rhea *counselor, educator*

Edna
Schrimsher, Joanne Johnson *professional counselor*

Frisco
Phelps, Deanne Elayne *educational counselor, consultant*

Houston
Bui, Khoi Tien *college counselor*

Lubbock
Mayekawa, Mary Margaret *education counselor*

Plainview
Norris, Kathy Horan *school counselor*

San Antonio
Barrera, Elvira Puig *counselor, therapist, educator*
DeNice, Marcella L. *counseling administrator*
Evans, Linda Marie *educational diagnostician, secondary education educator*

UTAH

Logan
Price, Susan Kay Lind *employment training organization administrator*

VIRGINIA

Lawrenceville
White, Beverly Hawkins *counseling administrator*

Newport News
Levy, Robin Carole *elementary guidance counselor*

Richmond
Batch, Mary Lou *guidance counselor, educator*

Roanoke
Street, Terri Evans *counselor, consultant*

Williamsburg
Polk-Matthews, Josephine Elsey *school psychologist*

WASHINGTON

Kent
Chandler, Karen Regina *career guidance specialist*

Seattle
Cottingham, Mary Patricia *vocational rehabilitation counselor*
Fetterly, Mary E. *counseling administrator*

WEST VIRGINIA

Charleston
Davis, Billie Johnston *school counselor*

Hinton
McBride, Karen Sue *school guidance counselor*

WISCONSIN

Bayside
Topetzes, Fay Kalafat *retired school guidance counselor*

Kenosha
Armstrong, Leona May Bottrell *retired counselor, educator*

Waukesha
Mansur, Sharif Samir *counselor, education educator*

TERRITORIES OF THE UNITED STATES

NORTHERN MARIANA ISLANDS

Saipan
King, Tanya *counseling administrator, public school educator*

ADDRESS UNPUBLISHED

Barnett, Linda Kay Smith *vocational guidance counselor*
Buckler, Marilyn Lebow *school psychologist, educational consultant*
Conover, Nancy Anderson *retired secondary school counselor*
Dickson, Max Charles *retired career counselor, coordinator*
Dillard, Teresa Mary *school counselor*
Enlow, Donna Lee *elementary school counselor*
Frey, Margo Walther *career counselor, columnist*
Goertz, Roger Lamar *retired education counselor*
Goldfarb, Helene Diane *school counselor, retired*
Huffman, Sandra Jean *academic counselor, educator*
Koch, Joanne Ellen *guidance counselor*
Lee, Barbara Catherine *career counselor*
Martir, Wilfredo R. *school counselor*
McLean-Wainwright, Pamela Lynne *educational consultant, college educator, counselor, program developer, clinical therapist*
Neighbors, Patsy Jean *school counselor*
President, Toni Elizabeth *counseling administrator, guidance counselor, former elementary educator*
Resing, Maryloretto Rachel *guidance counseling administrator, elementary school educator, pastoral counselor*
Statman, Jackie C. *career consultant*
Stuckey, Helenjean Lauterbach *counselor educator*
Thomas, Ethel Colvin Nichols (Mrs. Lewis Victor Thomas) *counselor, educator*
Thorne, Barbara Lockwood *guidance counselor, secondary education educator*
Valentine, Phyllis Louise *counseling administrator*
Whitehead, David Lynn *school counselor*
Wilks, Duffy Jean *counselor, educator*
Wuellner, Kathleen D. *school counselor, former English educator*
Wynne, Terry Lynne *career counselor, trainer, writer*

EDUCATION: OTHER

UNITED STATES

ALABAMA

Birmingham
Davis, Gwendolyn Louise *air force officer, English educator*

Equality
Jordan, Ramona Pierce *home economics educator, art education educator, elementary education educator*

Huntsville
Hawley, Harold Patrick *educational consultant*

Montgomery
Fry, Donna Marie *military officer, educator*
Riley, Robert *governor*

Normal
Lane, Rosalie Middleton *extension specialist*

ALASKA

Wasilla
Hogue, Bonnie Marie Kifer Gosciminski *child care educator, consultant*

ARIZONA

Glendale
Sweat, Lynda Sue *cooking instructor, catering company owner, deaconess*

Phoenix
Kotinas, Demetra *advocate, educator*

Sedona
Sasmor, James Cecil *publishing representative, educator*

Tucson
Powers, Stephen *educational consultant, researcher*

ARKANSAS

Little Rock
Killingsworth, Elizabeth Ann *educational consultant*

Warren
Shaw, Laurie Jo *counseling and assessment center administrator*

EDUCATION: OTHER

CALIFORNIA

Bakersfield
Thompson, Joyce Ann *education consultant*

Ben Lomond
Sikora, James Robert *educational business consultant, financial analyst*

Berkeley
Krooth, Richard *sociology and political studies educator*

Carmel
Faul, June Patricia *education specialist*

Claremont
Pedersen, Richard Foote *diplomat and academic administrator*
Rudder, Robert Sween *Spanish language educator*

Costa Mesa
Hugo, Nancy *county official, alcohol and drug addiction professional*

Culver City
Kamm, Jacqueline Ann *elementary reading specialist*

Cypress
Friess, Donna Lewis *children's rights advocate*

Davis
Redenbach, Sandra Irene *educational consultant*

Escondido
Sanders, Adrian Lionel *educational consultant*

Foster City
Berman, Daniel K(atzel) *educational consultant, university official*

Fullerton
O'Donnell, Edith J. *educational and information technology consultant, writer, musician*

Glendale
Edwards, Kathryn Inez *educational technology consultant*
Shelburne, Merry Clare *public information officer, educator*

Glendora
Schiele, Paul Ellsworth, Jr., *education business owner, writer*

Hemet
Yankee, Marie *publishing executive, educator*

Huntington Beach
Shishkoff, Muriel Mendelsohn *education writer*

La Mirada
Terry, Alice Rebecca *educational consultant*

La Quinta
DeLong, Diane Margene *educator resource specialist*

Lodi
Nusz, Phyllis Jane *not-for-profit fundraiser, consultant, educational consultant*
Wyrick, Daniel John *science/health textbook editor, science specialist*

Los Angeles
Caldwell Portenier, Patty Jean Grosskopf *advocate, educator*
Ireland, Robert Abner, Jr., *education consultant*
Shapiro, Mel *playwright, director, drama educator*

Los Gatos
Hastings, Reed *film company executive, educational association administrator*

Monterey Park
Hurwitz, Saundra Harriet (Sandi Hurwitz) *analyst, educator*

Oakland
Haiman, Franklyn Saul *author, communications educator*
Howatt, Sister Helen Clare *former human services director, former college library director*

Palmdale
Valenti, Betty Janet *resource specialist, educator*

Pasadena
Pings, Cornelius John *educational consultant, director*

Rialto
Johnson, Ruth Floyd *educational consultant*

Sacramento
Contreras, Dee (Dorothea Contreras) *municipal official, educator*

San Diego
Young, Sarah Moskowitz *educational and computer consultant, journalist*

San Francisco
Pierce, Deborah Mary *educational administrator*
Wright, Esther Estelle *educational consultant*

San Jose
Cates, Michelle Renee *air force reserve officer, consultant*
Ritzheimer, Robert Alan *educational publishing executive*

Stanford
Kennedy, Donald *editor, environmental scientist, educator*

Upland
Hung, Jenny *development specialist*

Walnut Creek
McCarthy, Helen H. *civic worker, retired educator*

COLORADO

Arvada
Bert, Carol Lois *retired educational assistant*

Denver
Billig, Shelley Hirschl *educational research and training consultant*
Driggs, Margaret *educator*

Lakewood
Heitsmith, William Richard *educational consultant*

Littleton
Bennett, Janice Lynn *publisher, educator*

Vail
McGee, Michael Jay *protective services official, educator*

CONNECTICUT

Bridgeport
Simoneau, Cynthia Lambert *newspaper editor, journalism educator*

Hartford
Cross, Vivian Alicia *university educator*

Milford
Dorneman, Penny Lee Harding *educational products developer*

Stamford
Hayashida, Ralph Francis *educational publishing company executive*

Trumbull
Lang, James Richard *education consultant*

DELAWARE

Laurel
Kile, Kenda Jones *educational consultant*

Newark
Pifer, Ellen I. *literary critic, educator*

Wilmington
Higgins, Roxanne Snelling *educational consultant*

DISTRICT OF COLUMBIA

Washington
Andrews, John Frank *editor, author, educator*
Baxter, Ruth Howell *educational administrator, psychologist*
Carney, Mark *financial executive*
Christian, Mary Jo Dinan *educational administrator, educator*
Elliott, Emerson John *education consultant, policy analyst*
Gentry, Barbara Beatrice *educational consultant*
Griffin, Paul, Jr., *navy officer, engineer, educator*
Gwaltney, Corbin *editor, publishing executive*
Hassan, Aftab Syed *education specialist, author, editor*
Johnson, Karen *legislation and congressional affairs secretary*
Mantyla, Karen *distance learning consultant*
Miller, Mary Rita *former college educator*
O'Brien, Timothy Andrew *writer, journalist, lawyer, educator*
Odom, William Eldridge *army officer, educator*
Pelavin, Sol Herbert *research company executive*
Semas, Philip Wayne *editor*
Towle, Alexis Charles (Lex Towle) *education advocate*

FLORIDA

Coral Gables
Stano, Carl Randolph (Randy Stano) *newspaper editor, art director, educator*

Fort Lauderdale
Edmund, Norman Wilson *educational researcher*

Longboat Key
Kaye Johnson, Susan *educational consultant*

Melbourne
Jeffers, Barbara Clark *learning clinic administrator*

Ormond Beach
Hodges, Elizabeth Swanson *educational consultant, tutor*

Port Charlotte
Van Patten, Muriel May *educational consultant*

Punta Gorda
Eliason, Nancy Carol *education consultant*

Saint Petersburg
Buchan, Russell Paul *publisher, gas company executive, entrepreneur*

Sarasota
Lee, Ann McKeighan *curriculum specialist*
Scheman, Blanche *reading specialist*
Stevens, Leonard Berry *educational consultant*

Spring Hill
Wood, Shelton Eugene *education educator, consultant, minister*

Sun City Center
Stanton, Vivian Brennan (Mrs. Ernest Stanton) *retired guidance counselor*

Tallahassee
Lynn, Gwendolyn Renaye *physical and health education educator*

Titusville
Barnes, Jacqueline C. Linscott *education consultant, retired educator*

GEORGIA

Athens
David, Martha Lena Huffaker *educator*

Atlanta
Allensworth, Diane DeMuth *academic association director*
Laney, James Thomas *former ambassador, educator*
Rucker, Kenneth Lamar *law enforcement officer, educator, military officer*

Barnesville
Barnard, John Phillip *technology educator*

Bowdon
Henson, Diana Jean *county official*

Columbus
Tidd, Joyce Carter *etiquette educator*

Decatur
Murphy, Shirley Hunter *reading specialist*

Fort Benning
Ramsey, Russell Wilcox *national security affairs educator*

Lagrange
Donehew, Pamela K. *reading specialist*

Midland
Hadden, Mayo Addison *chamber of commerce executive, military officer, educator*

Rocky Face
Phelps, Carolyn Sue *educational consultant*

HAWAII

Honolulu
Doi, Dorothy Mitsue Yano *educator, consultant*
Hack, Randolph C. *advocate, educator, counselor*

IDAHO

Hagerman
Skaar, Sarah Henson *editor, educator*

ILLINOIS

Bethalto
Gallinot, Ruth Maxine *educational consultant*

Bloomington
Key, Otta Bischof *retired educator*

Champaign
Espeseth, Robert D. *park and recreation planning educator*

Chicago
Ayman, Iraj *educational consultant*
Buniak, Raymond *educational professional*
Keryczynskyj, Leo Ihor *county official, educator, lawyer*
Kubistal, Patricia Bernice *educational consultant*
Monaghan, M. Patricia *education educator, writer, poet*
Scribner, Margaret Ellen *educational consultant, consultant*

Marion
Coil, Carolyn Chandler *educational consultant*

New Lenox
Marzan, Suzanne M. *foreign language educator*

Normal
Grever, Jean Kempel *business education and adminstrative services educator*

Ringwood
Tomlinson, Ferol Martin *reading and learning center media specialist*

Springfield
Maloney, Edward Dennis *state senator, assistant principal*

Urbana
Hale, Allean Lemmon *writer, educator*
Wilson, Winnie Ruth *elementary education educator, reading specialist*

Virden
Rohrer, Susan Jane *mayor*

INDIANA

Bloomington
Collyer, Esther Ritz *volunteer, educator*

Indianapolis
Eames, Sherry Diane *educational consultant*
Eikenberry, Kevin Leon *training consultant*
Vann, Lora Jane *reading educator, retired*

Muncie
Felsenstein, Frank Arjeh *educator*

IOWA

Des Moines
Blake, Darlene Evelyn *political worker, consultant, educator, author*

Elliott
Hunt, Colleen A. *educational consultant*

Fort Dodge
Hickey, Sharon Marie *councilman, elementary school educator, Mayoral aide*

Grinnell
Webb, Ruth Cameron *retired educator*

Iowa City
Gray, George Trumon *test development professional*
Paulina, Diana *alternative school educator*

Maquoketa
Weber, Alice Rose *math educator, retired*

KANSAS

Downs
La Barge, William Joseph *tutor, researcher*

Fort Leavenworth
Schneider, James Joseph *military theory educator, consultant*

Lawrence
Levine, Stuart George *editor, English literature educator, author*
Romzek, Barbara S(ue) *public administration educator*

Olathe
Goodwin, Becky K. *educational technology resource educator*

Overland Park
Schnapp, Diana Corley *speech communication educator*

KENTUCKY

Crestwood
Keith, Penny Sue *mayor, educator*

Frankfort
Henry, Stephen Lewis *lieutenant governor, orthopedic surgeon, educator*
Richards, Jody *state legislator, journalism educator, small business owner*

Hindman
Thompson, Marcia Slone *choral director, educator*

LOUISIANA

Alexandria
Miller, Stanley Odell *educational diagnostician*

Baton Rouge
Conerly, Evelyn Nettles *educational consultant*

Grambling
Porter, Wilma Jean *educational consultant*

Metairie
Smethurst, Jacqueline *educational consultant*

MAINE

Auburn
Umpierre, Luz María *women studies educator, foreign language educator*

Augusta
Desmond, Mabel Jeannette *state legislator, educator*

Brownfield
Kloskowski, Vincent John, Jr., *educational consultant, writer, educator*

Portland
Bowman, Tillian *educational consultant, writer*

Presque Isle
Davidshofer, Claire H. *college instructor*

MARYLAND

Annapolis
Holston, A. Frank *retired broadcaster, communications educator*

PROFESSIONAL INDEX — EDUCATION: OTHER

Baltimore
Babarinde-Hall, 'Bunmi *administrator educational cable station*
Bradshaw, Cynthia Helene *educational administrator*
Jones, Raymond Moylan *strategy and public policy educator*
Keller, George Charles *higher education consultant, writer*
Norris, Karen W. *grants specialist*

Bethesda
Olson, Lynn *editor*
Wishart, Leonard Plumer, III, *army officer*

Burkittsville
Aughenbaugh, Deborah Ann *mayor, retired educator*

Cumberland
Johnson, Rex Ray *automotive education educator*

Owings Mills
Berg, Barbara Kirsner *health education specialist*

Potomac
Kuykendall, Crystal Arlene *educational consultant, lawyer*

Princess Anne
Bing, Sarah Ann *educational psychologist*

Silver Spring
Carson, Steven Lee *newspaper publisher*

Union Bridge
Hannah, Judy Challenger *private education tutor*

Upper Marlboro
Reed, Jacqueline K(emp) *educational researcher*
Williams, Gwendolyn (Etta) Smith *reading specialist*

MASSACHUSETTS

Acton
Kittross, John Michael *retired communications educator*

Beverly
Murray, Mary *educational consultant*

Cambridge
Smith, David Julian *educational consultant*

Groton
Campbell, Patricia Barbara *educational research company executive, consultant*

Lincoln
Fletcher, Mary Beth *reading specialist, educator*

Lowell
Cheney, Liana DeGirolami *art history educator*

Medford
Tilger, Justine Tharp *research director*

New Bedford
Cordeiro, Elizabeth Dalein *law enforcement training educator*

Northampton
Sherr, Richard Jonathan *educator*

Williamstown
Chandler, John Wesley *educational consultant*

Worcester
Vick, Susan *playwright, educator, director, actress*

MICHIGAN

Ann Arbor
Lewis, Robert Enzer *lexicographer, educator*

Dowagiac
Ott, C(larence) H(enry) *citizen ambassador, accounting educator*

Grand Rapids
Flory, Betsy J. *educator*
Kunze, Linda Joye *educator*

Ironwood
Sobolewski, Jane Ann *business educator*

Jackson
Saunders, Doris Evans *editor, educator, business executive*

Muskegon
Roy, Paul Emile, Jr., *county official*

New Buffalo
Jessup, Sally Ann *adult educator, educational consultant*

Rochester Hills
Anderson, Susan Elaine Mosshamer *education and organization consultant, musician*

Southfield
Lee, James Edward, Jr., *educational consultant*

Ypsilanti
Corriveau, Arlene Josephine *educational specialist*
Olmsted, Patricia Palmer *educational researcher*

MINNESOTA

Blaine
Yecke, Cheri Pearson *education agency administrator, columnist, author*

Bloomington
Powell, Christa Ruth *educational training executive*

Cushing
Perfetti, Robert Nickolas *educational consultant*

Eden Prairie
Lashbrook, Velma Janet *research and development executive*

Minneapolis
Fraser, Arvonne Skelton *former United Nations ambassador*

Owatonna
Shea, Thomas Joseph *educator*

MISSISSIPPI

Jackson
Musgrove, David Ronald *governor*

Leland
Ayres, Mary Jo *professional speaker, writer, composer*

MISSOURI

Blue Springs
Hatley, Patricia Ruth *business/education partnership coordinator*

Florissant
Ordinachev, Joann Lee *special education counselor and administrator*

Joplin
LeTendre, Brenda Guenther *educational consultant*

Saint Louis
Leonard, Judith Price *educational advisor*
Meyer, Ruth Ann *retired physical education and dance educator*

MONTANA

Billings
Zentz, Marlene Kay *education specialist*

Helena
Richmond, Paul, Jr., *educational consultant*

NEBRASKA

Kearney
Wice, Paul Clinton *news director, educator*

NEVADA

Las Vegas
Carter, Connie Beverly *education consultant*
Chevers, Wilda Anita Yarde *former state official and educator*

Minden
Bednark, James David *company executive*

NEW HAMPSHIRE

Boscawen
Clarke, Claire Diggs *academic counselor*

New Durham
Wellman, Helen M. *administrative secretary*

Windham
Greenleaf, Diana Crampton *school media generalist*

NEW JERSEY

East Orange
Teller, Lorraine Helen *reading specialist and basic skills educator*

Edison
Kushinsky, Jeanne Alice *SAT tutor*

Flemington
Buckleitner, Warren William *editor, former elementary school educator*

Gladstone
Turner, Ann Coffeen *reading specialist educator*

Lodi
Looney, JoAnn Marie *learning disabilities consultant, educator*

Marlboro
Francisco, Deborah Antosh *educational administrative professional*

Middletown
Shields, Patricia Lynn *educational broker, consultant*

Monroe Township
Martin, Marie Theresa *school counselor*

Wolfe, Deborah Cannon Partridge *government education consultant, educator, minister*

Montclair
Delgado, Ramon Louis *educator, author, director, playwright, lyricist*

New Brunswick
Horowitz, Irving Louis *publisher, educator*

Newark
Hooper-Perkins, Marlene *technical editor, educator*

Oakland
Butterfield, Charles Edward, Jr., *educational consultant*

Randolph
Zulauf, Sander William *educator, poet*

Short Hills
Robbins-Wilf, Marcia *educational consultant*

Skillman
Rhett, Haskell Emery Smith *educator*

Trenton
Faulkner, Juanita Williams *educational administrator*

Union City
Sheehy, Janice Ann *education technology coordinator*

Woodstown
Tatnall, Ann Weslager *reading educator*

NEW MEXICO

Albuquerque
Harlow, Judith Leigh *educational institute executive, consultant*

Los Alamos
Engel, Emily Flachmeier *educational consultant*
Mendius, Patricia Dodd Winter *editor, educator, writer*

NEW YORK

Albany
Branigan, Helen Marie *educational consultant, administrator*

Amherst
Wiesenberg, Jacqueline Leonardi *lecturer*

Auburn
Ohl, Thomas Anthony *school counselor*

Bainbridge
Goerlich, Shirley Alice Boyce *publishing executive, educator, media consultant*

Bronx
Sedacca, Angelo Anthony *protective services official, educator*

Brooklyn
Palm, Marion *educator*

Holbrook
Watkins, Linda Theresa *educational researcher*

Hudson
Vile, Sandra Jane *leadership training educator*

Latham
McGoldrick, William Patrick *educational consultant*
Washburn, Susan Lynn *educational consultant*

Mount Kisco
Appelbaum, Judith Pilpel *editor, consultant, educator*

New York
Arndt, Cynthia *educational administrator*
Barolini, Teodolinda *literary critic*
Caperton, W. Gaston *former governor, educational association administrator*
Charendoff, Mark Stuart *educator*
Gartner, Alan P. *municipal official*
Jervis, Kathe *educational consultant, researcher*
Landau, Sarah Bradford *fine arts educator, author*
Marks, Lillian Shapiro *secretarial studies educator, author*
Mirenburg, Barry Leonard *publishing executive, educator*
Ranald, Ralph Arthur *former government official, educator*
Rosenfeld, Herb *educational consultant*
Wylie, James Malcolm *educator*

North Syracuse
Long, Stephen James *clergyman*

Port Jefferson
Strong, Robert Thomas *former mayor, middle school educator*

Poughkeepsie
Kim, David Sang Chul *publisher, evangelist, retired seminary president*

Rye
Jay, Barbara *educational consultant*

Staten Island
Berman, Barbara *educational consultant*

Syracuse
Collins, William John *educational administrator*

Valley Stream
Rodgers, John Joseph, III, *educational administration consultant, educator*

NORTH CAROLINA

Boone
Hearron, Patricia Folino *child development specialist, educator*

Chapel Hill
Klompmaker, Jay Edward *business administration educator*

Charlotte
Mercer, Evelyn Lois *retired guidance counselor*

Greenville
Reichelt, Susan Ann *educator*

Pinehurst
Roberts, Francis Joseph *retired army officer, retired educational administrator, global economic advisor*

Raleigh
Gulledge, Karen Stone *educational administrator*
Lee, Howard N. *state senator, concessions company executive*
McAllister, David Franklin *publishing executive*

Sanford
Harrington, Anthony Ross *radio announcer, educator*

Waynesville
Ingle, Marti Annette *protective services official, educator*

Wilmington
Rorison, Margaret Lippitt *reading consultant*

NORTH DAKOTA

Grand Forks
DeMers, Judy Lee *former state legislator, university dean*

Sheyenne
Tossett, Gloria Vay *educator, administrator*

OHIO

Amherst
Gerstenberger, Valerie *media coordinator*

Austintown
Gugliotti, Robert Anthony *sports publishing and media relations specialist*

Canton
Lyon, James Hugh *education specialist, legislative consultant*

Chillicothe
Basil, Brad L. *technology education educator*

Cleveland
Spicer, Michael William *university educator*

Columbus
Lowe, Clayton Kent *radio film critic, educator*
Mitchell, Carol Elaine *publishing executive, writer, educator*
Parks, Darrell Lee *vocational education contultant, administrator*
Riedinger, Edward Anthony (Ted Riedinger) *international educator, Brazilianist*

Crestline
Maddy, Janet Marie *retired physical education educator, dean*

Dayton
Crowe, Shelby *educational specialist, consultant*

Gahanna
Sherman, Ruth Todd *government advisor, counselor, consultant*

Lima
Sametz, Lynn *educator*

Painesville
Davis, Barbara Snell *college educator*

Reynoldsburg
D'Onofrio, Peter Joseph *protective services official, educator*

Zanesville
Higginbotham, Lark *family and consumer sciences educator*

OKLAHOMA

Broken Bow
Baggs, Patricia R. *county educational administrator*

Edmond
Zhu, Zhen *educator*

Norman
Jackson, David Lee *industrial education educator*

EDUCATION: OTHER

Oklahoma City
Shao, John Jianping *educator*

Tahlequah
Grant, Kay Lallier *early childhood education educator*

Tulsa
Cardwell, Sandra Gayle Bavido *university admissions professional*

OREGON

Coos Bay
Shannon, Willa L. *community college instructor, data analyst*

Eugene
Wood, Daniel Brian *educational consultant*

Portland
Pepper, Floy Childers *educational consultant*

PENNSYLVANIA

Aspers
Saltzman, Charles McKinley *educational consultant*

California
Langham, Norma E. *playwright, educator, poet, composer, inventor*

Camp Hill
Hughes, William Francis, Jr., *educational consultant*

Cheltenham
Kuziemski, Naomi Elizabeth *educational consultant, counselor*

Enola
Myers, Alfred Frantz *retired state education official, educator*

Gettysburg
Kile, Marcia Ann *education consultant*

Hatfield
Jesberg, Robert Ottis, Jr., *educational consultant, science educator*

Hellertown
Claps, Judith Barnes *educational consultant*

Holland
Hosey, Sheryl Lynn Miller *editor, educator, theater director*

Johnstown
Puto, Anne-Marie *reading specialist*

Kingston
Benovitz, Madge Klein *civic volunteer*

Langhorne
King, Ann D. *educational consultant*

Norristown
Raquet, Maureen Graham *protective services official, educator*

Philadelphia
Christman, Jolley Bruce *educational research executive, educator*

Pittsburgh
George, Charlene Colette *mathematics educator*
Pollock, Marc *media fundraising executive, consultant*

Roslyn
Roberts, Kevin Lee *township recreation administrator*

Springfield
Lynch, Maria Rosaria *mathematics educator, private tutor*

Swarthmore
Berger, Dianne Gwynne *family life educator, consultant*

Unionville
Martin, Helen Elizabeth *educational consultant*

Williamsport
Bryant, Martha Jean *reading specialist*

RHODE ISLAND

East Greenwich
Humbyrd, Shirley J. *educational consultant, counselor, therapist*

SOUTH CAROLINA

Charleston
Karesh, Janice Lehrer *special education consultant*

Columbia
Alford, Elisabeth M. *technical communication educator*
Badders, Rebecca Susanne *military officer, educator, writer*
Sinclair, Linda Drumwright *educational consultant*

Gaffney
Davis, Lynn Hambright *culinary arts educator*

Kershaw
Lucas, Dean Hadden *retired home economics educator*

Laurens
Prescott, Peggy Collins *higher education administrator*

Liberty
Mitchell, William Dewey, Jr., *educational consultant*

SOUTH DAKOTA

Pierre
Hawley, Tom *retired military officer, state agency administrator, educator*

TENNESSEE

Athens
Brown, Sandra Lee *art association administrator, watercolorist*

Brentwood
Smith, Charles Edward *education consultant*

Clarksville
Bowers, Carolyn Powers *county official, educator*

Dandridge
Shipe, Kelly Ann *music educator, director, professional harpist,*

Kingsport
Reed-Wright, Karen *school administrator*

Knoxville
Griffin, Mary Jane Ragsdale *educational consultant, writer, small business owner*

Mc Minnville
Martin, Ron *editor, superintendent of schools, consultant, minister*

Nashville
Loper, Linda Sue *special collections librarian*

Newport
Kridler, Jamie Branam *children's advocate, social psychologist*

TEXAS

Amarillo
Petty, John Ernest *education specialist, consultant*

Arlington
Reber, Barbara Lee *diagnostician, school administrator*

Austin
Ashworth, Kenneth Hayden *public affairs specialist*
Herrin, David Leslie *educator*
Johnson, Sandra Lynn Terry *education consultant*
Warner, David Cook *public affairs educator*
Williamson, Thomas Arnold *publishing company executive*

Beaumont
Rogers, Linda Gail *educator, consultant*

Blanco
Dudley, Brooke Fitzhugh *educational consultant*

Dallas
Cirilo, Amelia Medina *educational consultant, supervisor*
Gajewski, Ronald S. *consulting and training company executive*
Hansen, William *educational consultant*
Newman, Rita Gray *retired education specialist*
Shambaugh, Irvin Calvin, Jr., *aptitude test firm executive*

Denton
Noble, Diane Kay *education specialist*

Denver City
Taylor, Sharon Kay *elementary school counselor*

El Paso
Tackett, Stephen Douglas *education services specialist*

Fort Hood
Reid, Sharon Lea *educational facilitator*

Fort Worth
Marquez, Hope *school system worker, educator*

Garland
Michaels, Cindy Whitfill (Cynthia G. Michaels) *educational consultant*

Granbury
Scogin, Martha Aduddell *public information officer*

Houston
Belcher Randall, Mary Sue *remedial reading educator*
Caram, Dorothy Farrington *educational consultant*
Coleman, Mabeth Hallmark *newspaper publishing professional*
Eckhardt, Karen Boyce *educational consultant*
Lopez, Herminia G. *bilingual educator*

Oliphant, Jodie Jenkins *secondary school consultant*

Kingwood
Squire, James Robert *retired publisher, consultant*

Lancaster
Hajek, Eloise *educational consultant, educator*

Monahans
Watson, Kay *educational consultant*

Odessa
Folsom, Hyta Prine *educational grant writer, consultant*

Port Isabel
Pon-Salazar, Francisco Demetrio *diplomat, educator, deacon, counselor*

Round Rock
Ledbetter, Sharon Faye Welch *retired educational consultant*

Royse City
Antony, Rose Mary *physical education educator*

San Antonio
Garcia, Yolanda Vasquez *educational services manager, educator*
Hill, William Victor, II, *retired army officer, secondary school educator*
Messina, Paul Francis *education consultant*
Reneau, Marvin Bryan *military officer, business educator*

Sherman
Gunn, Edgar Lindsey *educational consultant*

Spring
Jackson, Guida Myrl *writer, magazine editor, book editor, publisher*

Stephenville
Seawright, Gaye Lynn *education consultant*

Taylor
Holubec, Edythe Johnson *educational consultant*

Waco
Corum, Janet Maupin *child development specialist, child care administrator*

UTAH

Bountiful
Burningham, Kim Richard *former state legislator*

Kaysville
Steele, David H. *state legislator*

VERMONT

Charlotte
Ohanian, Susan *freelance education writer*

VIRGINIA

Alexandria
Kuhn, Nancy Jane *educator*
Montgomery, Gillespie V. (Sonny Montgomery) *former congressman*
Smith, Canda Banks *educational consultant*
Stevens, Alice Marie *educational consultant*

Arlington
Stout, Mary Webb *education program specialist*

Charlottesville
Jordan, David Crichton *ambassador, educator*
Newsom, David Dunlop *foreign service officer, educator*

Fredericksburg
Boyd, Den Cook, Jr., *educational consultant*

Hillsville
Jackson, Thomas Micajah *former state legislator, lawyer*

Middleburg
Kaplan, Jean Gaither (Norma Kaplan) *reading specialist, retired educator*

Millboro
Minetree, James Lawrence, III, *retired military officer, educator*

Norfolk
Taylor Claud, Andrea *educational consultant*
Williamson, Jean Elizabeth *office manager*

Reston
Miller, John Edward *army officer, technology executive, educational administrator*

Richmond
Dilworth, Robert Lexow *career military officer, educator*
Inlow, D(avid) Ronald *university administrator, food service consultant, consumerism lecturer*
Miles, Donna Regina *educator, researcher*
Stith, Leah Drake *legislative aide, school system administrator*
Torrence, Rosetta (Phillips) *educational consultant*

Vienna
Jackson, Juanita Wallace *educational consultant*

WASHINGTON

Bainbridge Island
Lawrence, Lu *educator, photographer*

Bremerton
Milander, Henry Martin *educational consultant*

Carnation
Beshur, Jacqueline E. *special needs educator*

Seattle
Baker, Roland Jerald *educator*
Ostrom, Katherine Elma *retired educator*
Strahilevitz, Meir *inventor, researcher, psychiatry educator*

WEST VIRGINIA

Philippi
Shearer, Richard Eugene *educational consultant*

WISCONSIN

Madison
Lawton, Barbara *lieutenant governor*
Van Deburg, William Lloyd *educator*

Racine
Rodrigues-Pavao, Antonio *vocal music teacher*

Ripon
Woolley, Jean Gibson *instructional designer, consultant*

River Falls
Standiford, Sally Newman *technology educator*

Watertown
Henry, Helga Irmgard *liberal arts educator*

TERRITORIES OF THE UNITED STATES

PUERTO RICO

Bayamon
Berio, Blanca *editor*

MILITARY ADDRESSES OF THE UNITED STATES

PACIFIC

Apo
Chung, Tchang-Bok *management analyst, consultant*

CANADA

BRITISH COLUMBIA

Victoria
Bond, Shirley *legislator, educator*

NORTHWEST TERRITORIES

Yellowknife
Ootes, Jake *minister education, culture and employment*

NOVA SCOTIA

Halifax
MacIsaac, Angus *education minister*

Fredricton
Furlong, Dennis J. *education minister, physician*

Iqualuit
Kilabuk, Peter *education and human resources minister*

Québec
Reid, Pierre *education minister*

St John's
Reid, Gerry *education minister*
Thistle, Anna *youth services and post-secondary education minister*

Toronto
Witmer, Elizabeth *education minister*

Whitehorse
Edzerza, John *legislator*

Winnipeg
Lemieux, Ron *education and youth minister*
McGifford, Diana *legislator, writer, elementary school educator*

SAUDI ARABIA

Riyadh
Kawmy, Susan Yost *educational consultant*

ADDRESS UNPUBLISHED

Archuleta, Walter R. *educational consultant, language educator*
Bachtel, Ann Elizabeth *educational consultant, researcher, educator*
Bashore, Irene Saras *art association administrator*
Beck, Janice McKloskey *government affairs educator*
Berkowitz, Eric Neal *school administrator, consultant*
Brandt, Mitzi Marianne *retired educational specialist*
Brandt, Ronald Stirling *retired editor, researcher*
Buell, Jon Alfred *education and curriculum development administrator*
Charlton, Shirley Marie *educational consultant*
Clarke, Walter Sheldon *independent military consultant, educator*
Dalsimer, Anthony Stearns *retired foreign service officer, educator*
Dickinson, Gail Krepps *educator*
Duncan, Verne Allen *state legislator, dean, education educator*
Elmen, Gary Warren *educational consultant*
Emmett, Rita *professional speaker*
Ficht, Angela Kay *middle school counselor*
Fistell, Ira J. *newspaper editor, adult education educator, newswriter, radio and television personality*
Fleetwood, Mary Annis *education association executive*
Fodrea, Carolyn Wrobel *educational researcher, publisher, consultant*
Foster, Michele *educator*
Franklin, Billy Joe *international higher education specialist*
Gile, Mary Stuart *state legislator, educational executive*
Goldoff, Anna Carlson *public administration educator*
Graves, Ruth Parker *educational executive, educator*
Greer, Susan Anne *educational materials writer*
Hansen, Sally Jo *educational consultant*
Heimbold, Margaret Byrne *publisher, educator, consultant*
Henry, Gary Norman *air force officer, astronautical engineer*
Hurtig, Shane Brent *multimedia and music industry writer, educator, consultant*
Johnson, Maryann Elaine *educational administrator*
Joseph, Geri Mack (Geraldine Joseph) *former ambassador, educator, journalist*
King, Jane Cudlip Coblentz *volunteer educator*
Kinnel, Mary Lou *college recruitment executive*
Korologos, Ann McLaughlin *public policy, communications executive*
Lai, Feng-Qi *instructional designer, educator*
Langdon, Karen Sims *consultant*
Luft, Cecile E. *music educator*
Manson, Malcolm Hood *educational consultant*
Meyers, Dorothy *education consultant, writer*
Miller, Norman Charles, Jr., *editor, reporter*
Miller, Robert Michael *publishing executive*
Mitchell, Peter Kenneth, Jr., *educational consultant*
Mowrer-Reynolds, Elizabeth Louise *educational psychology educator*
O'Connell, William Raymond, Jr., *educational consultant, retired academic administrator*
Oerding, James Bryan *military educator*
Paino, Ronald Thomas *education consultant*
Paolucci, Anne Attura *playwright, poet, English and comparative literature educator, educational consultant*
Patrick, Brenda Jean *educational consultant*
Pendleton, Gail Ruth *newspaper editor, writer, educator*
Petrou, Anastasis D. *consultant, adjunct faculty*
Press, Aida Kabatznick *former editor, writer, poet*
Ramsay, Karin Kinsey *publisher, educator*
Riggs, Jacki Pieracci *educational consultant*
Rosado, Elizabeth Schaar *elementary bilingual and ESL program coordinator*
Sanders, Marlene *anchor, journalism educator*
Schatz, Lillian Lee *playwright, molecular biologist, educator*
Schieffelin, George Richard *educational consultant*
Scott, L. Carol *educational consultant*
Silvius, Donald Joe *educational consultant*
Smith, Mary Lex *victim's advocate*
Tauber, Rosalyn *educational therapist, learning consultant*
Trusdell, Mary Louise Cantrell *retired state educational administrator*
Tucker, Janet Grace *university educator, researcher*
Welsh, Dorothy Dell *columnist, writer*
Whiting, Lucille Drake *retired elementary school educator, consultant*
Widgery, Jeanne-Anna (Jan Widgery) *retired educator*
Williams, Bobbretta M. *educational company executive*
Wolf, Edith Maletz *retired educator*
Young, Richard Alan *association executive*

Zappe, John Paul *city editor, educator, newspaper executive*

GIFTED AND TALENTED/SPECIAL EDUCATION

UNITED STATES

ALABAMA

Anniston
Turner, Elnora Crankfield *special education educator and administrator*

Bessemer
Johnsey-Robertson, Anita Colleen *special education educator*

Birmingham
Bean, Sandra G. *special education educator*

Decatur
Clark, Kathleen Vernon *special education educator*

Gadsden
Massaro, Traci Lynn *special education educator*

Hueytown
Gilbert, Melba Caldwell *special education and early childhood educator*

Huntsville
Elliott, Sally Ann *special education educator*
Helton, Norma Jean *special education educator*
Krueger, Kathleen Susan *special education administrator*

Jones
Tidwell, Betty Davenport *special education educator*

Mc Calla
Godsey, Cheryl Partridge *administrator*

Montgomery
Hardin, Glenda Kendrick *retired special education educator*
Ladner, Ann-Marie Calvo *special education educator*
Mathewson, Judith Jeanne *special education educator*
Stanley, Janice Faye *special education educator*
Ward, Clare Cleere *special education educator*
Yeend, Stacey Brown *special education educator*

Newton
Brazzelle, Merry Elizabeth *special education educator*

Rainsville
Richards, Mark Anthony *special education educator*

Sylacauga
Harvard, Mary Ruth *special education educator*

Talladega
Anderson, Sharon Rice *special education educator*
Morgan-Lawler, Barbara *speech educator*

Tuscaloosa
Searcy, Jane Berry *retired educational administrator, counselor*
Willard, Ann Elam *retired special education educator*

Wetumpka
Curlee, Robert Glen, Jr., *special education educator*

ALASKA

Fairbanks
Rudig, Stephanie Scott *gifted and talented education educator*

Haines
Haas, June F. *special education educator, consultant*

Juneau
May, Scott C. *special education educator*

ARIZONA

Chinle
Quell, Margaret Anne *special education educator*

Flagstaff
Casmir, Mina G. Halliday *speech educator, consultant*

Glendale
Hays, Sandra Lynn *gifted education educator*

Oro Valley
Alvarado, Ivy Elizabeth *special education educator*
Scoville, Lynda Sue *special education educator, writer*

Peoria
Jesse, Sandra Elizabeth *special education educator*

Phoenix
Cloyd, Sandra Gomez *bilingual educator*
Culnon, Sharon Darlene *reading specialist, special education educator*
Penwell, Patricia Lee *special education educator*

Sierra Vista
Revak, JoAnn *special education educator*

Tucson
Dyer-Raffler, Joy Ann *special education diagnostician, educator*
Madden, James A. *gifted and talented educator*
Tompkins, Jeannie Kay *special education educator*

ARKANSAS

Dermott
Bynum, Judith Lane *gifted and talented education educator*

El Dorado
Daymon, Joy Jones *school psychology specialist*

Fort Smith
Pointon, Mary Lou *special education educator*

Hartford
Roller Hall, Gayle Aline *gifted and talented education educator*

Little Rock
Duncan, Adren Lee *special education educator*

North Little Rock
Dow, Teresa Elmerick *guidance and special needs professional*

Siloam Springs
Poindexter, Tonya Dawn *special education educator*

Vilonia
Lomax, Peggy Quarles *gifted and talented education educator*

Wynne
Vance, Tammy Rena *special education educator*

CALIFORNIA

Alameda
Greene, Jamie Candelaria *special education educator*
Verrill, Kathleen Wills *special education educator*

Bakersfield
Oliver, Beverly Gail *special education educator*
Steele, Julius Raynard *special education educator*

Castaic
Ashton, Tamarah M. *special education educator, consultant*

Cerritos
Taguchi, Aileen Takayo *special education educator*

Concord
Small, Leslie Jane *special education administrator*
Snyder, Lynn Nelson *special education educator*

Costa Mesa
Candelaria, Angie Mary *special education educator*

Cupertino
Machamer, Sylvia Geraldine *special education educator*

Downey
Carrico, Deborah Jean *special education teacher*
Denmon, Frances *resource specialist educator*
Ruecker, Martha Engels *retired special education educator*

Elk Grove
Landon, JoJene Babbitt *special education educator*

Eureka
Harvey, Carol Sammons *educator*

Fremont
de Roque, Barbara Penberthy *special education educator, consultant*

Glendora
Acevedo, Elizabeth Morrison *special education educator*

Hacienda Heights
Mieux, Donna Marie *special education educator*

Hayward
Laycock, Mary Chappell *gifted and talented education educator, consultant*

La Mirada
Cronk, Mildred Schiefelbein (Mili Cronk) *special education consultant*

Laguna Niguel
Teitelbaum, Marilyn Leah *special education educator*

Laguna Woods
Epley, Thelma Mae Childers *retired gifted and talented education educator*

Lancaster
Schneider, Elaine Fogel *special education educator, consultant*

Los Angeles
Simon, Sheila Sandra *special education educator, administrator*
Sohaili, Monira *special education educator, writer*

Modesto
Heiny, Robert Wayne *special education educator*
Johnson-Cole, Luella Emily *educator*

Montebello
Dible, Rose Harpe McFee *special education educator*

Monterey
Boger, Gail Lorraine Zivna *reading specialist*

Moreno Valley
Hathaway, Katherine Jane *special education educator*
Moran, Patricia Eileen *special education educator*

North Hollywood
Burman, Sheila Flexer Zola *special education educator*

Oakland
Dibble, David Van Vlack *visually impaired educator, lawyer*

Pacific Grove
Longman, Anne Strickland *special education educator, consultant*

Palm Springs
Hartman, Rosemary Jane *retired special education educator*

Pasadena
Almore-Randle, Allie Louise *special education educator*

Pomona
Callaway, Linda Marie *special education educator*

Rialto
Bauza, Christine Diane *special education educator*

Riverside
Fontana, Sandra Ellen Frankel *special education educator*
Joyce, Vicki Marie *special education educator*

Rohnert Park
Gordon, Sharon J. *special education educator*

San Bernardino
Okino, Wendy Jean *special education educator*
Plotkin, Judy Ann *special education educator*

San Diego
Hill, Gerry A. *special education educator, consultant*
Owen, Sally Ann *gifted and talented education educator*
Rief, Sandra Fáye *special education educator, consultant*

San Francisco
Lichtenwalner, Pamela Smith *special education educator, consultant*

San Jose
Lobig, Janie Howell *special education educator*
Merriam, Janet Pamela *special education educator*

San Rafael
Adcock, Muriel W. *special education educator*
Fagersten, Barbara Jeanne *special education educator*

Santa Cruz
Davis, Geraldine Sampson *special education educator*

Santa Rosa
Cheung, Judy Hardin *retired special education educator*

Selma
Rezac, Debra Dowell *bilingual educator*

Stockton
Cooper, Iva Jean *special education educator*

CALIFORNIA (cont.)

Tustin
Greene, Wendy Segal *special education educator*

Twentynine Palms
Huffman, Donald Gerald *special education educator*

COLORADO

Arvada
Reed, Joan-Marie *special education educator*

Aurora
Fuller, Elthopia Vivens *gifted and talented education educator*

Boulder
Cline, Timothy Byron *special education educator*

Colorado Springs
Young, Taylor Lynn *education administrator*

Denver
Cannon, Elizabeth Anne *special education educator*
Colasanti, Georgette Elizabeth *special education educator*

Fort Collins
Jones, Leslie Susan *special education educator*

Greeley
Green, Vickie Lee *gifted and talented educator, music educator*
Murry, Francie Roberta *special education educator*

Hudson
Starks, Elizabeth Vial *gifted/talented education educator*

CONNECTICUT

Ansonia
Goldson, Terri Drew *special education educator, consultant*

Cos Cob
Sorese, Denise Powers *reading and language arts consultant, educator*

Danbury
Heller, Maryellen *special education educator*
Tracey, Valerie Lewis *special education educator*

Easton
Watkins, Dennis H. *special education educator*

Falls Village
Gaschel-Clark, Rebecca Mona *special education educator*

Hartford
Marchand, Sheila Anne Haley *special education educator, consultant*
Perez-Silva, Glaisma *special education teacher*

Mystic
Infantino, Nancy Strong *special education educator*

Newington
Vassar, William Gerald *gifted and talented education educator*

Norwalk
Nelson, Paula Morrison Bronson *educator*
Schaefer-Wicke, Elizabeth *reading consultant, educator*

Suffield
Black, Maureen McWeeny *special education educator*
D'Aleo, Penny Frew *special education educator, consultant*

Trumbull
Smith, Gail Marie *special education educator, educational consultant*

Windsor
Mulvagh, Charlene Frances *special education educator*

Wolcott
Topazio, Lawrence Peter *special education educator*

DELAWARE

Seaford
Palmer, Danna Swain *special education educator*
Petrea, Patricia Beth *special education educator*

Wilmington
Heald, Deborah Ann *special education educator, counselor*

DISTRICT OF COLUMBIA

Washington
Long, Levitha Owens *special education educator*
McBride, David Francis *special education educator*
Valdez, Felicia M. *special education educator*

FLORIDA

Altamonte Springs
Egli, Jacqueline Rae *special education educator*

Archer
Sarver, Vernon Thomas, Jr., *gifted education educator*

Bartow
Hubkaba, Nancy Pletts *special education educator*
Mercadante, Anthony Joseph *special education educator*

Boca Raton
Marraffino, Ellen Talenfeld *retired special education educator*

Boynton Beach
Pallowick, Nancy Ann *special education educator*

Brooksville
Sarnecki, Thomas George *special education educator*

Clearwater
Jacobs, Marilyn Arlene Potoker *gifted education educator, consultant, author*

Cocoa Beach
Coppola, Phyllis Gloria Cecire *retired special education educator*

Coral Springs
Heydet, Nathalie Durbin *gifted and talented education educator*

Delray Beach
Terry, Margaret Smoot *special education educator*

Fort Lauderdale
Grish, Marilyn Kay *speech educator*
Mirabal, Angela Prince *special education educator*

Jacksonville
Carter, Paula Stanley *special education educator*
Hinely, Bethany Knoll *special education educator*
Reese, Dorothy Harmon *special education educator*
Smith, Stephen Mark *special education educator, music educator*

Jensen Beach
Kraynak, Helen *special education consultant*

Leesburg
Whalen, Norma Jean *special education educator*

Lighthouse Point
Cooper, Penny McEwen *special education professional*

Longwood
Brown, Barbara Jean *special and secondary education educator*

Manalapan
Phipard, Nancy Midwood *retired special education educator, poet*

Marco Island
Stride, June *special education educator, author*

Miami
Quigley, John Joseph *special education educator*
Rodriguez-Walling, Matilde Barcelo *special education educator*

New Smyrna Beach
Fraser, Beverly Ann *assistive technology and special education consultant, physical therapist*

Oakland Park
Krauser, Janice *special education educator*
Slater, Constance *special education educator, educator*

Ocala
Dougherty, Michael Kevin *special education educator*
Phillips, Margaret Crouse *gifted and talented educator*
Renda, Rosa A. *special education educator*
Williams, Pauline Elizabeth *special education educator*

Okeechobee
Saine, Christy Watson *special education educator*

Orlando
Birkes, Marilyn *guidance resource teacher, behavior specialist, special education educator*
Cacciatore Sinnott, Ann Frances *special education educator*
Taylor, Patricia Lee *special education educator*

Palm Coast
Myckaniuk, Maria Anna *elementary and special education educator*

Panama City
Deeds, Barbara Catherine *special education vocational educator*
Green, Catherine L. *special education educator*

Pensacola
Galloway, Sharon Lynne *special education educator*
Gregory, Flaudie Stewart *special education educator*

Plantation
Young, William Benjamin *retired special education educator*

Pompano Beach
Hellwege, Nancy Carol *special education educator*

Saint Petersburg
Westall, Sandra Thornton *special education educator*
Williams, Minnie Caldwell *retired special education educator*

Sanford
Tossi, Alice Louise *special education educator*

Sarasota
Wolfe, Lilyan *special education clinical educator*

Seffner
Straub, Susan Monica *special education educator*

Tampa
Gatewood, Linda Layne *special education educator*
Wade, Sally Moseley *special education educator*

Tavares
Wilson-Smith, Barbara Ann *reading specialist*

Winter Garden
Gillet, Pamela Kipping *special education educator*

Winter Haven
McCutchan, Judith Katherine *special education educator*

Winter Park
White, Linda Jackson *remedial reading educator*

GEORGIA

Albany
Stanley-Chavis, Sandra Ornecia *special education educator, consultant*

Atlanta
Dixon, Lori-Renee *special education diagnostician*
Ignatonis, Sandra Carole Autry *special education educator*
Parko, Edith Margaret *special education educator*

Augusta
Mitchell, Brenda Joyce *special education educator, consultant*

Carrollton
Butler, Jody Talley *gifted education educator*

Columbus
Beall, Charles Donald *former special education educator*
Duncan, Frances Murphy *retired special education educator*
Matheny, Elizabeth Ann *special education educator*

Conyers
Griffey, Karen Rose *special education educator*

Daisy
Sands, Miriam Linda *special education educator*

Douglas
Purvis, Mary Ruth Moore *special education educator*

East Point
Warren, Barbara Denise *special education educator*

Eastman
Hall, Lula *retired special education educator*

Greensboro
Brock, Lori Anne Sowar *special education educator*

Grovetown
Whitmore-Dalton, Sandra Elaine *special education educator*

Jonesboro
Fleming, Janelle Smith *gifted and talented education educator*
Ziegler, Robert Oliver *retired music and special education educator*

Lagrange
Ault, Ethyl Lorita *special education educator, consultant*

Lawrenceville
Quinn, Carolyn Anne *special education educator*

Lilburn
Allen, Judith Marchese *special education educator*

Macon
Cummings, Crystal Sneed *special education educator*

Marietta
Simmons Smith, Mona Jean (Monica Simmons) *special education educator, writer*

Savannah
Thompson, Larry James *retired gifted education educator*

Tunnel Hill
Martin, Teresa Ann Hilbert *special education educator*

West Point
Hart, Brenda Rebecca *retired gifted and talented educator*

Winder
Hutchins, Cynthia Barnes *special education educator*

HAWAII

Honolulu
Schimmelfennig, Ladona Beth *special education educator, management analysis and compliance specialist*

Kailua
Rodgers, Marilyn Carol *special education educator*

IDAHO

Boise
Ellis-Vant, Karen McGee *elementary and special education educator, consultant*
Griffin, Sylvia Gail *reading specialist*

Middleton
Brown, Ilene De Lois *special education educator*

Ola
Farr, Reeta Rae *special education administrator*

Saint Anthony
Blower, John Gregory *special education educator*

ILLINOIS

Alton
Day-LeBlanc, Maria Anne *special education educator, reading specialist*

Anna
Fahlberg, Sheree Lynn *special education educator*

Burbank
Prokes, James Otto *special education educator*

Cary
Passaglia, Candace V. *special education educator*

Catlin
Asaad, Kolleen Joyce *special education educator*

Chicago
Abularach, Gloria *special education educator*
Bernadetta, Sister Maria *special education educator*
Bohm, Susan Mary *special education educator*
Buck, Catherine Ann *special education educator*
Cooper, Wylola *retired special education educator*
Fontánez-Phelan, Sandra María *special education director, consultant*
Gantz, Suzi Grahn *special education educator*
Javaras, Barbara Kariotis *special education educator*
Jones, Trina Wood *special education educator*
Kasik, Maribeth Montgomery *special education educator, educator*
Kubon, Walter Joseph, Jr., *bilingual history educator*
Rumbler, Sandra Lynn *special education educator*
Whitelaw, Jacqueline Susan *special education educator*
Wilson, Margaret Mary *special education educator*

Chicago Heights
Nowocin, Debra Terese *gifted and talented secondary education educator*

Cicero
Strejcek, Elizabeth Geierman *reading specialist, educator*

Downers Grove
Arnold, Nancy Ann *special education educator, researcher*

Elk Grove Village
Stoffregen, Gertrude Boettcher *retired gifted education educator*

Evergreen Park
Yuska, Irene Marie *special education educator*

Grayslake
Taylor, Sharen Rae (Sharen McCall) *special education educator*

Gurnee
Hutten, Angela Clare *special education educator*
Proctor, Susan Delaney Cobbs *special education educator, consultant*

Highland
Franklin, Patricia Lynn Powell *special education educator*

Hoffman Estates
Crane, Beverley Doris *special education educator*

Ingleside
Currie, Leah Rae *special education educator, retired*

Jacksonville
Welch, Rhea Jo *special education educator*

Joliet
Caamano, Kathleen Ann Folz *gifted and talented educator*
Morris, Diane Marie *special education consultant, travel consultant*

Lake Zurich
Schwarz, Cheryl Marita *special education educator*

Livingston
Brooke, Dolores Ann *special education educator*

Marion
Patterson, Kelley René *special education educator*

Milan
Yeggy-Davis, Geraldine Marie *elementary reading and special education educator, school system administrator*

Momence
Holland, Leslie Ann *special education educator*

Naperville
Florence, Ernest Estell, Jr., *special education educator*

Normal
Myers, Marilyn Conn *elementary education educator*

Northfield
Fleischer, Cynthia Silverman *special education educator*

Oak Park
Venerable, Shirley Marie *gifted education educator*

Orland Park
Brott, Barbara Jo *gifted and talented education educator*

Paris
Essinger, Susan Jane *special education educator*

Park Forest
Skummer, Mary Anne *hearing impaired educator, coordinator*

Pecatonica
Smith, Janet Faye *special education educator*

Richmond
Pech, Rose Ann *special education educator*

Rochelle
Chrestman, Shirley J. *special education educator*

Rock Island
Adams, Stewart Lee *special education educator*
Brauch, Merry Ruth Moore *gifted education consultant*

Rockford
Anderzon, Nancy Joy *special education educator*
Boyer, Karen Jo Ann *retired secondary gifted education educator*
Wilke, Duane Andrew *special education educator*

Romeoville
Smith, Sandra Jean *special education educator*

South Holland
Schaap, Marcia *special education educator*

Springfield
Stover, Gary Lee *special education educator*

Sterling
Albrecht, Beverly Jean *special education educator*

Tinley Park
Guzak, Debra Ann *special education educator*

Villa Park
Smith, Barbara Ann *gifted education coordinator*

Washington
McKinney-Keller, Margaret Frances *retired special education educator*

White Hall
Moore, Tara Sue *special education educator*

INDIANA

Bedford
Bundy, Kelly Jane *learning disabilities educator, consultant*

Boonville
Sureck, Karen Eileen *special education educator*

Carmel
McCarthy, Patricia Sue *retired special education educator*

Cloverdale
Mann, Mary Louise *special education educator*

Crawfordsville
Spurgeon, Nannette SuAnn (Susie Spurgeon) *special education educator*

Dale
Hayes, Mary Joanne *special education educator*

Elkhart
Thompson, Nancy Jo *special education educator, elementary education educator, consultant*

Fort Wayne
Lewark, Carol Ann *special education educator*

Franklin
Farrar, Susan Lee *special education educator, consultant*

Greencastle
Houck, Carolyn Marie Kumpf *special education educator*

Hobart
Hanley, Roberta Lynn *alternative education coordinator, educator*

Indianapolis
Huizer, Eveline Marina *special education educator*
Pruett, Lindy Newton *special education educator*
Sandberg, Marilyn Lee *special education educator*
Williams, Gloria Louise *gifted and talented education educator*

Nappanee
Dodson, Robin Powell *special education educator*

New Albany
Straughn, Laura Hamilton *special education educator*

Noblesville
Calvert, David Randall *educational interpreter, consultant*

Valparaiso
Grskovic, Janice Ann *special education educator*

Vincennes
Ax, Joanne E. *special education educator*

Wabash
Whitehead, Wendy Lee *special education educator*

IOWA

Carlisle
Stump, Patricia Ann VerPloegh *educator*

Cedar Falls
McDonald, Linda Wirkler *special education educator*

Cedar Rapids
Smith, Cindy Thompson *special education educator*
Stirler, Karen Sue *special education educator, adult education educator*

Des Moines
Jeschke, Thomas *gifted education educator*
Webb, Mary Christine *reading recovery educator, in-class reading specialist*
Wessendorf Knau, Suana Le *special education educator*

Eddyville
Kelderman Van Polen, Carole Ann *special education educator*

Essex
Drahn, Priscilla Charlotte *special education educator*

Harlan
Ahrenholtz, Mary Mickelson *special education educator*

Honey Creek
Hansen, Cherry A. Fisher *special education educator*

Iowa City
Porter, Nancy Lefgren *reading recovery educator*

Sloan
Ullrich, Roxie Ann *special education educator*

West Des Moines
Wright, Vicki Lynn *gifted and talented education educator*

KANSAS

Americus
Grimsley, Bessie Belle Gates *retired special education educator*

Beloit
Niemczyk, Karen Sue *special education educator*

Colby
Squibb, Sandra Hildyard *special education educator*

Dodge City
Ekum, Kristi Ann *special education educator*

El Dorado
Good, Mary Martha *special education educator*

Goddard
Kastens, Beverly Ann *special and elementary education educator*

Halstead
McGinn, Jill Marie *special education educator, speech pathologist*

Kansas City
Cummings, Penelope Dirrig *special education educator*

Lawrence
Hilt, Betty Marie *special education educator*
Peterson, Nancy *special education educator*
Schnose, Linda Mae *special education educator*

Liberal
Wilkerson, Rita Lynn *special education educator, consultant*

Oakley
Ptacek, Elaine Valetta *special education counselor, consultant*

Pleasanton
Starr, Darlene R. *special education educator, education educator*

Russell
Anschutz, Mary Anna *special education educator*

Salina
Dubuc-Schindler, Deborah Jo *special education educator*
Hammond, Deborah E. *special education educator, consultant*
Nelson, Charlotte Coleen *special education educator*

Shawnee Mission
Whitaker, Kathleen K. *gifted education facilitator*

Topeka
Owsley, Tina Kathleen *special education educator*
Young, Betty Mae *special education educator*

Winchester
Sedlak, Jo Ann *special education educator*

KENTUCKY

Carrollton
Heilman, Mary Joanne *gifted education educator*

Coxs Creek
Davenport, William Bruce, Jr., *special education educator*

Harrodsburg
Cummins, Bonnie Norvell *gifted and talented education educator*

Lexington
Curiel, Laura Taylor *special education educator*
Spaulding, Melinda Duncan *special education educator*

Louisville
Cannon, Dannie Parker *special education educator*
Martin, Janice Lynn *special education educator*

Owensboro
Hays, Suzanne Ryan *family resource center care worker*

Somerset
Kincaid, Carolyn Wade *special education educator*

LOUISIANA

Albany
Scott, Paula Lagrue *special education educator*

Baton Rouge
Harris, Marvin DeWitt *special education educator*
Kirk, Victor Clark *special education educator*
McElroy, Patricia Ann *special education educator*

Bossier City
Russell, Shannon Ferguson Darling *special education educator*

Deridder
Hill, Christine Lucille *gifted and talented education educator*

Hammond
Cook, Myrtle *special education educator*

Houma
Bordelon, Dena Cox Yarbrough *retired special education educator, director*

Kenner
Regan, Siri Lisa Lambourne *gifted education educator*

Leesville
Lytle, Ellen Juanita Wilson *special education educator*

Marrero
Love, Gayle Magalene *special education educator*

Metairie
Andersson, Billie Venturatos *school learning specialist*
Flake, Leone Elizabeth *special education educator*

New Iberia
Ledbetter, Deidre Leday *special education educator*

New Orleans
Novakov, George John, Jr., *gifted and talented educator, consultant, administrative assistant*

Newllano
Boren, Lynda Sue *gifted education educator*

Pineville
Matthews, Betty Parker *special education educator*

Quitman
Davis, Ella Delores *special education educator, elementary school educator*

Ruston
Freasier, Aileen W. *special education educator*

Shreveport
Driscoll, Barbara Hampton *special education educator*
Knight, Diane *special education educator*
Witt, Elizabeth Nowlin (Beth Witt) *special education educator, speech-language pathologist*

White Castle
Williams, Ivory Lee *special education educator*

MAINE

Bangor
Jackson, Diane West *special education educator, consultant*

Casco
Chandler, Patricia Ann *retired special education educator*

Fort Kent
Taggette, Deborah Jean *special education educator*

Lubec
Hudson, Miles *retired special education educator*

Scarborough
Russo, Joan Mildred *special education educator*

Tenants Harbor
Holland, Robert James *special education educator*

MARYLAND

Annapolis
Stern, Margaret Bassett *retired special education educator, author*

Baltimore
Allen, Rocelia J. *retired special education educator*
Allison, Brenda Kaye *special education educator, administrator*
Esterson, Morton M. *special education educator*
Jackson, Stanley Edward *retired special education educator*
Mask-Monroe, Rose Maria *reading specialist, educator*
Rose, Sara Margaret *English as a second language educator*

Bowie
Francis, Maxine Beth *special education educator*

Boyds
Carpenter, Dorothy Schenck *special education educator*

Brookeville
West, Gail Marcia Weiss *special education educator*

Capitol Heights
Zinaman, Helaine Madeleine *gifted and talented education educator*

Crisfield
Purnell, Ronald Jerry *special education educator*

Crofton
Clark, Marcia Hileman *special education educator*

Glenwood
Rossetti, Linda Elaine *special education educator*

Laurel
Barcome, Marigail *special education educator*

Middletown
Setzer, Kathleen Russell *special education educator*

Perryville
Stokes, Melissa Anne *special education educator*

Rockville
Lockhart, Virginia King *reading specialist*
Salzman, Joanna Michele *special education educator*

Upper Marlboro
Underdue, Marilyn Rosetta *special education educator*

MASSACHUSETTS

Chelmsford
Dunn, Mary Denise *reading specialist, freelance editor*

Chicopee
Czerwiec, Irene Theresa *gifted education educator*
Fishman, Gail Barbara *special education educator*

Dighton
Buote, Rosemarie Boschen *retired special education educator*

Hyde Park
Harris, Emily Louise *special education educator*

Jamaica Plain
Tirella, Theresa Mary *special education educator*

Lakeville
Barry, Marilyn White *retired special education educator, dean*

Lexington
France-Litchfield, Ruth A. *reading and early literacy specialist*

Longmeadow
Katz, Barbara S. *special education educator*

Mansfield
Ratcliffe, Barbara Jean *special education educator*

Marblehead
Tamaren, Michele Carol *special education educator*

Methuen
Conran, Lisa Ann *special education educator*

Milton
Wengler, Marguerite Marie *educational therapist*

Needham
Zambone, Alana Maria *special education educator, consultant*

New Bedford
Nunes, Pricilla O. *special education educator, artist*

Oakham
Poirier, Helen Virginia Leonard *elementary education educator*

Peabody
Stahl, William Martin *professional training director*

Petersham
Kenney, Joseph Edmund *special education educator*

Revere
DeLuca, Rose Marie *special education educator*
Ferrante, Olivia Ann *retired educator, consultant*

South Yarmouth
Thompson, Cheryl Ann *special education educator*

Spencer
Anderson, Valerie Lee *reading educator*

Springfield
Conway, Mary Patricia *speech educator*

Wales
Letendre, Jacquelyn Lee *special education consultant*

MICHIGAN

Bay City
Zuraw, Kathleen Ann *special education and physical education educator*

Bloomfield Hills
Hitchcock, Lillian Dorothy Staw *speech and English educator, actress, artist*

Brighton
Baranski, Lois Mae *special education educator*

Cadillac
McKay, Laurie Marie *special education educator*

Caro
Edwards, Mary Ann *special education educator*

Chesterfield
Broad, Cynthia Ann Morgan *special education educator, consultant*

Clinton Township
Darby, Lewis Randal *special education educator*
Fontanive, Lynn Marie *special education administrator*

Detroit
Corbitt, Eumiller Mattie *elementary and secondary education educator, special education educator*
Rutledge, Barbara Jean *special education educator*

Dexter
Beaulieu, Carol Marie *special education educator*

Farwell
Schepperley, Karen L. *special education educator*

Flint
Czekai, Lynnette Marie *special education educator*
Reska-Hadden, Marcia Ann *special education educator*

Garden City
Polin, Colleen Marie *special education educator*

Grand Blanc
Bogan Allen, Joyce *special education educator, consultant*

Grand Rapids
Kammeraad, Stephanie D. *special education educator*

Holland
Schieringa, Paul Kenneth *special education educator, entertainer*

Kalamazoo
Green, Cynthia Diane *special education educator*

Lake Orion
Brewer, Judith Anne *special education educator, consultant*

Midland
McDaniels, Peggy Ellen *special education educator, consultant*

Muskegon
Hadiaris, Marie Ellen *special education educator*

Olivet
Fuller, Judith Kay Altenhein *special education educator*

Pinckney
Duquet, Suzanne Frances *special education educator*

Saint Clair Shores
Black, Patricia Anne *special education educator*

Sterling Heights
Nanasi, Madonna *reading educator*

Sturgis
Thieme, Georgia Lee *special education educator*

Traverse City
Stepnitz, Susan Stephanie *special education educator*

Trenton
Beebe, Grace Ann *retired special education educator*
Vos, Gail Ann *talented and gifted educator*

Ypsilanti
Fleming, Thomas A. *former special education educator*

MINNESOTA

Bertha
Peterson, Myra M. *special education educator*

Cloquet
Ellison, David Charles *special education educator*

Minneapolis
Rogers, Karen Beckstead *gifted studies educator, researcher, consultant*

Minnetonka
Danahy, Marcia Karen *gifted education resource educator*

Moorhead
Holtz, Jane Kay *special education educator*

Remer
McNulty-Majors, Susan Rose *special education administrator*

Saint Cloud
Bates, Margaret Helena *special education educator*

MISSISSIPPI

Belden
Whitehead, Zelma Kay *special education educator*

Biloxi
Simpson, Elizabeth Ann *reading and language arts educator*

Columbia
Stepney, Joyce Harriett *special education educator*

Hattiesburg
Slade, Barbie Evette Delk *special education educator*

Jackson
Chambers-Mangum, Fransenna Ethel *special education educator*
Everly, Jane *gifted education educator*

Senatobia
Freeman, Mary Coleman *special education educator*

Shelby
Campany, Sarah Wilson *special education educator*

Vicksburg
Keulegan, Emma Pauline *special education educator*

Waveland
Pearce, Belinda Allen *elementary reading recovery educator*

MISSOURI

Arnold
Dismang, Debra Carole *special education educator*

Ballwin
Guinther, Christine Louise *special education educator*

Belton
Ludwick, Kathleen *special education educator*

Butler
Cochran, Beth *gifted and talented educator*

Camdenton
Vandergriff, Susan Ellen *special education educator*

Chesterfield
Shepperd, Susan Abbott *special education educator*

Chula
Murphy, Jenny Lewis *special education educator*

Cleveland
Long, Linda Sue *special education educator*

Fair Grove
Pickering, Becky Ruth Thompson *special education educator*

Florissant
Gallen, Maryanne B. *special education educator*
James, Dorothy Louise King *special education educator*

Fulton
Ebersole, Judy Ann *special education educator*

Imperial
Usher, Mary Margaret *special education educator*

Independence
Muñoz, Margaret Ellen *reading specialist*
Stoner, Connie Kay *special education educator*

Jefferson City
Gonder, Sharon *special education educator*

Kansas City
Sturges, Gloria June *learning disabilities educator*

Lees Summit
Griffith-Thompson, Sara Lynn *resource reading educator*

Lexington
Terrill, Julia Ann *elementary education educator*

Linn
Gove, Peter Charles *special education educator*

Maryville
Belcher, Rebecca Newcom *special education educator*

Plato
Wood, Joetta Kay *special education educator*

Raytown
Coppenbarger, Cecelia Marie *special education educator*

Saint Charles
Mager, Margaret Julia Eckstein *special education educator*
Newcomb, Carolyn Jeanne *special education educator*

Saint Joseph
Correu, Sandra Kay *special education educator*

Saint Louis
Bubash, Patricia Jane *special education educator*
Dulatt, Lorraine Edwina Simon *special education educator, reading specialist*
Hilyard, Veronica Marie *education administrator*
Mitchell, Louise Tyndall *special education educator*
Scheffing, Dianne Elizabeth *special education educator*
Thomas, Pamela Adrienne *special education educator*

Savannah
Walker, Frances Morine *retired special education educator*

Sedalia
Hazen, Elizabeth Frances *retired special education educator*

Smithville
Parker, Brenda Jean *secondary education educator*

West Plains
Gunter, DeVona Elizabeth (Betty Gunter) *retired special education educator*

Willow Springs
Evins, Marylou *retired special education educator*

MONTANA

Bigfork
Keller, Barbara Lynn *special education educator, reading teacher*

Browning
Williams, Dorothy Rhonda *gifted education consultant, educator*

Miles City
Emilsson, Elizabeth Maykuth *special education educator*

NEBRASKA

Auburn
Winegardner, Rose Mary *special education educator*

Columbus
Rieck, Janet Rae *special education educator*

Holdrege
Amen, Betty Jean *special education educator*

Omaha
Hill, John Wallace *special education educator*
Rosse, Therese Marie *reading and special education educator, curriculum, school improvement and instruction consultant*

Peru
Nichols, Virgil *special education educator*

Valley
Lerew, Everett Duane *special education administrator, poet, writer*

NEVADA

Boulder City
Calvo, Rhonda Lynne *special education educator*

Henderson
Thomas, James Patrick *special education educator*

Las Vegas
Obenhaus, Kathy Ann *special education educator*
Williams, Jane Marie *special education educator*

Reno
Myers, Geraldine Ruth *special education educator, consultant*

Sparks
Manley, Molly Elizabeth *special education educator, elementary school educator*

NEW HAMPSHIRE

Belmont
Wedemeyer, Sally Eileen *special education educator*

Berlin
Fowler, Katrina Joan *special education educator*

Concord
Wilkinson, Anne Welch *special education educator*

Hudson
Marshall, Annette *special education educator*

Lebanon
Tinker, Averill Faith *special education educator*

Littleton
McGruder-Houlihan, Ruby Lee *special education educator*

Merrimack
Delano, Marilyn Ann *special education educator*

Swanzey
Snyder, Deborah Jean *special education educator*

Wilton
Packer, Lee Ann *special education educator*

NEW JERSEY

Absecon
Douglas, Margaret Ann *special education educator*

Atlantic Highlands
Fink, Dolores Hesse *special education educator*

Avalon
Barker, Ralph Merton, Jr., *special education and gifted education educator*

Basking Ridge
Besch, Lorraine W. *special education educator*

Bayonne
Zuckerman, Nancy Carol *learning disabilities specialist, consultant*

Belleville
Weyland, Deborah Ann *learning disabilities teacher consultant*

Cape May Court House
Sadler, Charlotte Brooks *special education educator*

Cherry Hill
Brenner, Lynnette Mary *reading specialist, educator*
Bryan, Richard Arthur *retired special education educator*

Chester
Gray, Pamela *special education educator*

Clifton
Hochman, Naomi Lipson *special education educator, consultant*

East Brunswick
Candelmo, Lee France *special education educator*
Chinni, Anthony Patrick *special education and industrial education educator*

East Hanover
White, Jane *special education educator*

Edison
Dunn, Deborah Dechellis *special education educator*

Elmer
Slavoff, Harriet Emonds *learning disabilities teacher, consultant*

Elmwood Park
Jollin, Paula *special education educator*

Flemington
Blades, Jane M. *special education educator*
Coleman, Paul John *special education educator*
Foti, Margaret Mai *education consultant*

Haddon Heights
Weinberg, Ruthmarie Louise *special education educator, researcher*

Haddonfield
Kinee-Krohn, Patricia *special education educator*

Hammonton
Berenato, Patrice Simon *special education educator*

Kinnelon
Petrozzino, Jane A. *learning consultant*

Little Falls
Regan-Geraci, Theresa Elizabeth *learning disability educator, consultant*

Magnolia
Warden, Karen Barbara *special education educator*

Mahwah
Wolf, Marion Esther *reading educator*

Maplewood
Leuchs, John James, Jr., *elementary gifted education educator*

Medford
Della Croce, Nora Lee *special education educator*

Mendham
Nassoura, Nancy Kathryn *special education educator*

Monmouth Junction
Weistuch, Lucille *special education educator*

Moorestown
Wescott, Virginia D'Arcy *special education educator*

Morganville
Karp, Stefanie *special education educator*

Newark
Zignauskas, Dorothy Elizabeth *special education educator*

Nutley
Bukovec, Joseph Aloysius *special education educator*

Oceanport
Meibauer, Amery Filippone *special education educator*

Old Bridge
Dittus, Carolyn Helen *special education educator, consultant, realtor*

Oradell
DiGiovachino, John *special education educator*

Parsippany
Panian, Barbara Anne Marie *special education educator*

Paterson
Filippelli, Alice Marie *special education educator*

Perth Amboy
Santiago, Theresa Marie *special education educator*

Phillipsburg
Farley, Cynthia Crocket *special education educator, consultant*

Piscataway
Coppola, Sarah Jane *special education educator*

Plainfield
Montford, Claudian Hammond *retired gifted and talented education educator*

Plainsboro
Cevera, Eileen Levy *special education educator*

Princeton
Fenske, Edward Charles *special education educator, consultant*

Roseland
Bolger, Mary Phyllis Judge *special education educator*

Roselle
Di Marco, Barbaranne Yanus *special education educator*
Smith-Gomes, Kathleen Marie *special education educator*

South Orange
Gruenwald, Renee *special education educator*

Springfield
Zurav, Frankie Stalford *special education educator*

Summit
Starks, Florence Elizabeth *retired special education educator*

Toms River
Cebula, Mary Ann Antionette *special education educator, speech correctionist*

Trenton
Duda, Patricia Mary *gifted education educator, owner cosmetics company*

Union City
Bull, Inez Stewart *special education, gifted music educator, coloratura soprano, pianist, editor, author, curator*

Vineland
Hesser, Lorraine M *special education educator*
Vivarelli, Daniel George, Sr., *special education and learning disabilities educator, consultant*

Waldwick
Greenberg, Rita Moffett *special education educator, consultant*

West Long Branch
Harriott, Wendy A. *special education educator*

West New York
Rosenberg, Raymond David *special education educator, consultant*

West Orange
Pollara, Joanne *learning disabilities educator consultant*

Westwood
Cullen, Ruth Enck *reading specialist, elementary education educator*

NEW MEXICO

Albuquerque
Mullen, Nancy Lee *reading specialist, educator, travel consultant*

Carlsbad
Pinching, Deborah Anne Odell *special education educator*

Farmington
Charley, Marilyn Rose *special education educator*

Las Vegas
Simpson, Dorothy Audrey *retired speech educator*

Los Lunas
Denzler, Mary Joanne *special education, early childhood educator*

Mesilla Park
Shutt, Frances Barton *special education educator*

NEW YORK

Albany
Turner, Faith Mosseau *special education educator*

Amenia
Lopardo, Susan Joan *special education educator*

Baldwinsville
Kline, Carole June *special education educator*

Barker
Godshall, Barbara Marie *educational administrator*

Bay Shore
Pinsker, Tillene Giller *retired special education administrator*

Brewster
Evans, Kathleen Tara *special education administrator*

Bronx
Alicea, Yvette *special education educator*
Foster, Marcia Veronica *gifted and talented education educator*
Giaccio, Maria *special education educator, administrator*
Sarojini, Guruguntla Venkatraman *special education educator*

Brooklyn
Brown, Kevin L. *special education administrator*
Duato, Arlene Chana Leah *special education educator, consultant*
Heger, Claudine Lynn *special education educator*

Buffalo
Perrin, Janice Helen Davis *special education educator*

Chazy
Ratner, Gayle *special education educator*

Clarence
Trinkus, Laima Mary *special education educator*

Clay
Mathews, Barbara Bailey *special education educator*

Clifton Park
Preston, Carol Ann *special education educator*

Corning
Wilson, Cecilia Ann *special education educator*

Deposit
Hanstine, Barbara Ann *reading specialist*

Fairport
Halpern, David Rodion *special education administrator*

Fallsburg
Sperber, Marilyn Janice *special education educator*

Flushing
Carlton, Doreen Charlotte *special education supervisor and administrator*

Gainesville
MacWilliams, Debra Lynne *language arts consultant*

Glen Cove
Chun, Arlene Donnelly *special education educator*

Glen Head
Swift, Ronni *special education educator*

Guilderland
Escobar, Deborah Ann *gifted and talented education educator*

Hauppauge
Oschmann, Joan Edythe *gifted and elementary education educator*

Herkimer
Wiernicki, Louise Marie *special education educator*

Howard Beach
Livingston, Barbara *special education educator*

Irvington
Harris, Maria Loscutoff *special education educator, consultant*

Island Park
Feir-Stillitano, Elisabeth *gifted/talented education educator*

Levittown
Gould, Helen Jane *special education educator*

Lindenhurst
Deeds, Zoe Ann *special education educator, department chairman*

Malone
McClain, Angela Mary *special education educator*

Malverne
Alesse, Judith *special education educator*

Medford
Haig, Monica Elaine Nachajski *special education educator*

Naples
Watson, Mary Jo *special education educator*

New Paltz
Emanuel-Smith, Robin Lesley *special education educator*

New Rochelle
Shrage, Laurette *special education educator*

New York
Lang, Mary Ann *special education educator, administrator*
Lanquetot, E. Roxanne *retired special education educator*
Maesaka, Martha H. *special education educator*
Pulanco, Tonya Beth *special education educator*
Whitney, Paul Francis *gifted and talented education educator*

North Rose
Anderson, Nancy Marie Greenwood *special education educator*

North Salem
Adams, Patricia Murphy *special education educator*

Olcott
Sansone, Rosemary Margaret *retired gifted and talented education educator*

Orchard Park
Galluzzo, Charles Anthony *special education educator*

Owego
Coppens, Laura Kathryn *special education educator*

Rego Park
Marchese, Melissa J. *special education educator, director*

Rochester
Everett, Claudia Kellam *retired special education educator*
Newell, William James *sign language educator*

Rockaway Park
Goldsmith, Cathy Ellen *retired special education educator*

Saratoga Springs
Piccirillo, Lou Anne *special education educator*
Riley, Dawn C. *educational philosopher, researcher*

Saugerties
Falzano, Colleen *special education educator*

Scarsdale
Weil, Michelle Cohen *special education educator*

Selkirk
Wood, Diane Mary *special education educator*

Sherrill
Cramer, Carolyn Marie *special education educator*

Sparkill
Nelson, Marguerite Hansen *special education educator*

Springwater
Palmer-Sacchitella, Kelley Anne *special education educator*

Staten Island
Reing, Alvin Barry *special education educator, psychologist*

Tuckahoe
Doyle, Joellen Mary *special education educator*

Valatie
Deily, Ann Beth *special education educator, consultant*

West Hempstead
Conway-Gervais, Kathleen Marie *reading specialist, educational consultant*

White Plains
Szolnoki, John Frank *special education educator, administrator*

Williamsville
Hamp-Lane, Sandra N. *special education educator*

Yonkers
Atkins, Leola Mae *special education educator*
Hoar, Mary Margrette *gifted education educator*

NORTH CAROLINA

Ash
Minton, Denise Dawson *special education educator*

Cary
Krotee, Leslie Latshaw *special education educator*

Deep Gap
Tompkins, James Richard *special education educator*

Fayetteville
Hagans, Valerie Mae Gee *special education educator*

Gibsonville
Crawford, Kathrine Nelson *special education educator*

Greenville
Kirby, Jamie McGuire *gifted and talented educator*

Hamlet
Walker, Wanda Gail *special education educator*

Hampstead
Leaven, Glorious Sharpless *special education educator, reading specialist*

Kernersville
Hosier, Linda Grube *educator*
Litton, Daphne Napier Rudhman *special education educator*

Micro
Loose, Vicky Dianne *special education educator*

Raleigh
Davis, Susan Wells *special education educator*
Lawson, Elizabeth Louise *special education educator*
Page, Anne Ruth *gifted education educator, education specialist*
Sardi, Elaine Marie *special education educator*
Syster, Cheryl Lu *special education administrator*

Sparta
Adams, Marion Ruth Allison *special education educator*

Terrell
Maltby, Sue Ellen *special education educator*

Waynesville
Carpenter, Margaret Mary *state legislator, information technology manager*

Wilkesboro
Dale, Brenda Stephens *gifted and talented educator*

Williamston
Hoggard, Minnie Coltrain *gifted education educator, consultant*

Wilson
Jones, Llewellyn Williams *special education educator*

Winston Salem
Crowder, Lena Belle *retired special education educator*
Marshall, Walter *special education educator*
Roth, Marjory Joan Jarboe *special education educator*
Volz, Annabelle Wekar *learning disabilities educator, consultant*
Zubov, Lynn *special education educator, researcher*

NORTH DAKOTA

Bismarck
Jarrett, Twila Marie *special education educator*

Grand Forks
Ashe, Kathy Rae *special education educator*
Lindquist, Mary Louise *special education educator*

Minot
Bullen, Theresa Ann *special education coordinator*

OHIO

Akron
Buzzelli, Charlotte Grace *special education educator*

Alliance
Dunagan, Gwendolyn Ann *special education educator*

Avon
Smolen, Cheryl Hosaka *special education educator*

Batavia
Nichols, Marci Lynne *gifted education coordinator, educator, consultant*

Bedford
Hodge-Clotman, Alma R. *special education educator, consultant*

Bucyrus
Foley, Tracy Yevonne Lichtenfels *special education educator*

Cadiz
Puskarich, Lynn M(ary) *special education educator*

Canton
Rustifo, Phyllis Marie Wehr *special education educator*

Centerville
Geier, Sharon Lee *special education educator*

Chillicothe
New, Eloise Ophelia *special education educator*

Cincinnati
Cyr, Kathleen Kirley *special education educator*
Hoffman, Donna Coy *learning disabilities educator*
Murphy, Patricia Hurlburt *special education educator*
Sheffield, Elizabeth Baker *special education educator, lecturer, consultant*

Cleveland
Callesen-Gyorgak, Jan Elaine *special education educator*
Cohen, Suzette Francine *reading specialist*
Hanlon, Mary Jo *special education educator, early intervention specialist*
Madden, Antoinette Liadis *special education educator*
Quigney, Theresa Ann *special education educator*

Columbus
Gampp, Teresa Lee Lavender *special education educator*
Hayes, Karla Rene *special education educator*

Dayton
Allen, Rose Letitia *special education educator*

Dover
Tremba, Leatrice Joy *special education educator*

Dublin
Conrad, Marian Sue (Susan Conrad) *special education educator*

Elyria
Skillicorn, Judy Pettibone *gifted and talented education coordinator*

Fairfield
Hanby, Donna M. Weiss *gifted/talented education educator*
Lapp, Susan Bolster *learning disability educator*

Fremont
Richter, Virginia Ann *special education educator*

Groveport
Keck, Vicki Lynn *special education educator*

Hudson
Eidson, Colleen (Kelly) Frances *elementary counselor*

Lancaster
Gault, Teressa Elaine *special education educator*

Lewis Center
Strip, Carol Ann *gifted education specialist, educator*

London
Crouch, Mercedes Cain *special education educator*

Madison
Tinck, Elizabeth Ann *special education educator*

Medina
Carrick, Cynthia Anne *special education educator, educational administrator*

Mount Vernon
Wallace, Geri Lynn *special education educator, landscape architect*

New Bremen
Poppe, Beverly Reed *special education educator*

Newark
Paul, Rochelle Carole *special education educator*

Niles
Linden, Carol Marie *special education educator*

Northfield
Heath, Linda A. *gifted and talented educator*

Oxford
Davis, Sherie Kay *special education educator*
Schirmer, Barbara Rose *special education educator*

Parma
Pisarchick, Sally *special education educator*

Proctorville
Coleman, Debra Kay *special education educator*

Rio Grande
Lepley, Charmaine Gunnoe *special education educator*
Shibley, Ralph Edwin, Jr., *special education and career-technical education*

Shaker Heights
Lichtman, Lillian Margaret Yaeger *special education educator*
Williams, Sharron Elaine *gifted education specialist, legal consultant*

Sunbury
Hoke, Eugena Louise *special education educator*

Toledo
Goldstein, Margaret Franks *special education educator*
Knuth, Marya Danielle *special education educator*

Trotwood
Kiefer, Jacqueline Lorraine *special education educator, consultant*

University Heights
Starcher-Dell'Aquila, Judy Lynn *special education educator*

Waldo
Hollaway, Lisa Jean *secondary education educator*

Warren
McFarland, Leslie King *special education educator*

Washington Court House
Fichthorn, Fonda Gay *gifted and talented educator, retired principal*

West Carrollton
Ernst, Kelli Anne *special education educator*

Westerville
Whitcomb, Mary Elizabeth *special education educator*

Wheelersburg
Keller, Julie Elizabeth *elementary and learning disabilities educator*

OKLAHOMA

Kansas
Pemberton, Merri Beth Morris *special education educator*

Miami
Vanpool, Cynthia Paula *special education educator, special services consultant*

Muskogee
Meyer, Billie Jean *special education educator*

Norman
Curtis, Janet Lynn *elementary education educator*

Oklahoma City
Admire, Sherilynn *special education educator*
Dooley-Hanson, Barbara Ann *special education educator*
Johnson, Lonnie *special education educator*
Kraker, Deborah Schovanec *special education educator*
Lackey, Joyce *special education educator*
Runion, Katherine Goetz *special education educator*

Owasso
Roberts, Linda Taylor *reading specialist*

Prague
Stefansen, Peggy Ann *special education educator*

Tulsa
Barnes, Cynthia Lou *retired gifted and talented educator*
Wood, Emily Churchill *educator, educational consultant*

OREGON

Portland
Latini, Nancy Jane *special education administrator*

Roseburg
Bowser, M. Gayl *special education coordinator*

Salem
Hill, JoAnne Miller *special education educator, consultant*

PENNSYLVANIA

Ardmore
Dagna, Jeanne Marie *special education educator*

Aston
Carroll, Claire Barry *special education educator*

Blain
Sassaman, Paula *reading specialist*

Butler
Wharton, Kay Karole *retired special education educator*

Coatesville
Campenni, Carol M. *special education educator*
Smith, Patricia Anne *special education educator*

Conshohocken
Holleran, Priscilla Hook *special education educator*

Doylestown
Murray, Karen Lee *special education educator*

Du Bois
Spafford, Michelle *special education educator*

Easton
Bolash, Susan Roberts *special education and corrections education program director*
Snyder, Nancy Susan *reading specialist*

Elliottsburg
Carter, Amy Harpster *special education educator*

Enola
Harman, Lisa Elaine *special education educator*

Erie
Barber, Michele A. *special education educator*
Drexler, Nora Lee *retired gifted and talented educator, writer, illustrator*

Franklin
Moore, Mary Julia *special education educator*

Greensburg
Brady, Elisa Genevieve *special education educator*

Harrisburg
Walker, Paulette Patricia *special education educator*

Havertown
Wright, Cecilia Powers *gifted and talented educator*

Hollsopple
Saylor, Rosellen Beth *special education educator*

Honey Brook
Johnson, Marjorie R. *special education educator*

Jermyn
Crotti, Rose Marie *special education educator*

Lafayette Hill
Delacato, Janice Elaine *learning consultant, educator*

Levittown
Quay, Sharon Rose *special education educator*

Lewistown
Grego, Lauren Harris *reading specialist*

Mc Donald
Maurer, Karen Ann *special education educator*

Mechanicsburg
Hoffman, Diane Mae *special education educator*

Media
Comeforo, Jean Elizabeth *hearing impaired educator*

Millerton
Kipferl, Christiana A. *special education educator*

Monessen
Tarquinio, Antoinette Camille *special education educator*

Nanticoke
Dalmas-Brown, Carmella Jean *special education educator*

Newtown
Sandler, Julia Ann *special education educator*

Northumberland
Wert, Barbara J. Yingling *special education consultant*

Oreland
Wagman, Michael Mark *gifted and talented educator*

Penn Run
Scanlon, Patrick Lee *special education educator*

Perkasie
Rivera, Jane Markey *special education educator*

Philadelphia
Felts, George William, Sr., *special education educator*
Guyer, Hedy-Ann Klein *special education educator*
Schipani, Sister Kathleen Monica *special education educator*
Watson, Linda Barbara *special education educator*

Pittsburgh
Bradick, Angella Velvet *special education educator*
Hendricks, Laura Venturino *special education educator*
Stella, Janet Louise *special education educator, researcher*

Quarryville
Schreiner, Helen Ann *special education educator*

Schnecksville
Washick, Rita Lucian *special education educator*

Scranton
Staff, Mary Clare *special education educator*
Yazinski, Judy *special education educator*

Sharon
Milo, Elizabeth *special education educator*

Tobyhanna
Custis, Diane Camille *special education educator*

Verona
Bruno, Louis Vincent *special education educator*

Wallingford
Purcell, Mary Hamilton *speech educator*

Waynesboro
Drooger, Jacquelyn Marie *special education educator*

West Aliquippa
Peya, Prudence Malava *retired elementary education educator*

West Chester
Keiser, Mary Ann Myers *special education educator*

West Mifflin
Edwards, Keith David *special education educator*

West Newton
Sleith, Barbara Ann Balko *special education educator*

Willow Grove
Burtt, Anne Dampman *special education educator*

Yardley
Watson, Joyce Leslie *elementary educator*

York
Zell, Blossom Ann *educator*

RHODE ISLAND

Cranston
McAulay, Dianne Lucy *gifted education educator*

Cumberland
LaFlamme-Zurowski, Virginia M. *secondary school special education educator*

Kingston
Smith, Sareba G. *special education educator*

Narragansett
Pierson, Douglas H. *special education educator*

Wood River Junction
Carlson-Pickering, Jane *gifted education educator*

SOUTH CAROLINA

Aiken
Sheppard, Deborah Cody *hearing handicapped educator, clinician*

Charleston
Suggars, Candice Louise *special education educator*

Clover
Yandle, Anna Cobb *gifted/talented education educator*

Columbia
LeClair, Betty Jo Cogdill *special education and early childhood educator*

Florence
Lott, Melinda Jo *special education and secondary education educator*
Rutherford, Vicky Lynn *special education educator*

Gilbert
McGill, Cathy Broome *gifted and talented education educator*

Greenville
Jordan, Betty Sue *retired special education educator*
Sutton, Joe Perry *special education educator*

Hartsville
Covington, Lynn Norris *special education educator*

Ladson
Cannon, Major Tom *special education educator*

Myrtle Beach
Treese, Lisa Maureen *deaf educator*

Piedmont
Winter-Neighbors, Gwen Carole *art and special education educator, consultant*

Spartanburg
McPherson, Frances Anne *university special education educator*

Sumter
Bach, Linda Wallinga *special education educator*

SOUTH DAKOTA

Aberdeen
Mundschenk, Jane Marie *special education educator*

Box Elder
Schmidt, Laura Lee *elementary and middle school gifted and talented educator, special education educator*

Freeman
Mutchelknaus, Audrey J. *special education educator*

Lemmon
Grey Eagle, Sandra Lee *special education educator*

Sioux Falls
Casey, Beverly Jane *special education educator*
Davis, Ann Katherine *special education educator*

TENNESSEE

Bolivar
Buchanan, Bennie Lee Gregory *special education educator*

Collierville
Gagne, Ann Marie *special education educator*

Gainesboro
Walker, Leann Fox *special education educator*

Henderson
England, Richard C., Jr., *special education educator*

Knoxville
Bodenheimer, Sally Nelson *reading educator, retired*
Royse, Sue Marion *special education educator*

Maryville
Jacobus, Sara Wilson *special education educator*

Memphis
McGlown, Brenda Pryor *special education educator*

Midway
Pruitt, Melinda Douthat *elementary school special education educator*

Oak Ridge
Evans, Carole Clinton *special education educator*

Pleasant Hill
Hull, Charles William *retired special education educator*

Sewanee
Lorenz, Anne Partee *special education educator, consultant*

Strawberry Plains
Blanchard, Pamela Snyder *special education educator*

Townsend
Tomlinson, Linda Sue *special education educator*

TEXAS

Alamo
Forina, Maria Elena *gifted education educator*

Alice
Thomas, Katherine Carol *special education educator*

Alvin
Yeats, Sylvia Anita *special education educator*

Amarillo
Sutterfield, Deborah Kay *special education educator*

Austin
Luedecke, Sharon Annette *special education educator, speech therapist*
Mauzy, (Martha) Anne *retired deaf educator, audiologist*
Wukasch, Doris Lucille Stork *special education educator, consultant*

Big Spring
Wilson, Wanda Kay *special education educator*

Channelview
Ursprung, Deborah Lynn *special education educator, counselor*

Conroe
Marsh, Sue Ann *special education educator*

Dallas
Grotjan, Elizabeth Gayle *special education educator*
Jaffe-Blackney, Sandra Michelle *special education educator*
Wilkerson, Patricia Helen *director child development center*

Denton
Bullock, Lyndal Marvin *special education educator*
Miller, April D. *special education educator*
Pettigrew, Johnnie Delonia *educational diagnostician*

El Paso
Jesinsky, Susan Gail *special education educator*
Ward DiDio, Patty *special education educator, educational diagnostician*

Elgin
Shelby, Nina Claire *special education educator*

Forney
Ellis, Donna Litton *special education educator*

Fort Worth
Killingsworth, Maxine Armatha *special education educator*
Sullivan, Lynn Davis *special education educator*
White, Lynda Gayle *reading specialist, educational diagnostician*

Grapevine
Bloyd, Ruthanne *gifted and talented mathematics educator*

Hillsboro
Divin, Nancy Gail *gifted and talented student educator*

Houston
Anderson, Claire W. *computer gifted and talented educator*
Berry, James Declois *special education and history educator*
Boggs, Barbara Jean *special education educator*
Hammack, Gladys Lorene Mann *reading specialist, educator*
Kinnaird, Susan Marie *special education educator*
Mansell, Joyce Marilyn *special education educator*
Ross, Melanie Ann *education specialist*
Sayer, Coletta Keenan *gifted education educator*
Sykes, Ruth L. *special education educator*
Ward, Iva Nell Bell *special education educator*

Hurst
Dodd, Sylvia Bliss *special education educator*

Katy
Gibert, Charlene West *gifted education educator*

Killeen
Harvey, Hilda Ruth *special education educator*

Lancaster
Schlachter, Deborah Bristow *special education educator, consultant*
Sykes, Mary Lou Strain *retired reading educator*

Laredo
Reuthinger, Georgeanne *special education educator*

Lubbock
Nes, Sandra Lee *learning disabilities educator*

Mabank
Smith, Patricia Jean *gifted and talented education educator*

Mesquite
Holt, Mildred Frances *special education educator*
Palmer, Jeannette Ursula *counselor, educator*

Odessa
Bridges, Judy Cantrell *gifted and talented education educator*

Omaha
Moos, Verna Vivian *special education educator*

Plano
Chomistek, Catherine *special education educator*
Fleming, Christina Samusson *special education educator*

Quitman
Blackwell, Carol Diane *special education educator*

Rio Grande City
González, Olga Estela *special education educator*

Rockwall
Mierow, Sharon Ann *special education educator*

San Angelo
Harrison, Arthurlyn Carol *special education educator*
McLaren, Karlene Marie *special education educator*

San Antonio
Jackman, Harry Emekona, III, *special education educator*
Kucinkas, Katherine Ann Mansur *special education consultant, writer*
Robertson, Samuel Luther, Jr., *special education educator, therapist, researcher*
Senecal, Connie Montoya *special education educator*
Slay-Barber, Doris A. *educational administrator*
Stephens, Sunny Courington *special education educator*

San Marcos
Carman, Mary Ann *retired special education educator*

Sonora
Solis, Lori *special education educator*

Sulphur Springs
Clayton, Pamela Sanders *special education educator*

Sweetwater
Cogburn, Alton O. *special education administrator*

Texarkana
McHenry, Louisa Beth *special education educator*

Universal City
Trevor, Leslie Jean *special education educator*

Waco
Girouard, Tandy Denise *special education educator, psychology educator*

UTAH

Delta
Nielson, Barbara Broadhead *special education administrator*

Ferron
Becket, Johanna Nina *special education educator*

Logan
Hunsaker, Scott Leslie *gifted and talented education educator*

Salt Lake City
Baxter, Sharon A. *special education educator*
Henderson, Sharlene Ottesen *special education educator*
Huefner, Dixie Snow *special education educator*
Kerikas, Sharon Marel *special education educator*
Magleby, Florence Deming *special education educator*
Schowe, Sheral Lee Speaks *special education educator*

VERMONT

Brattleboro
Steffens, Annie Laurie *sign language educator, interpreter*

Poultney
Cooper, Charleen Frances *special and elementary education educator*

Richmond
O'Connell-Pope, Mary Anne Prudence *diagnostic special education*

VIRGINIA

Alexandria
Edgell, Karin Jane *reading specialist, special education educator*

Amherst
Herbert, Amanda Kathryn *special education educator*

Annandale
Del Conte, L. Catherine *special education educator*
Heyer, Laura Miriam *special education educator*

Arlington
Mattson, Beverly Louise *special education educator*

Blacksburg
Candelas, Teresa Bush *special education educator*

Boyd Tavern
Darden, Donna Bernice *special education educator*

Catharpin
Rankin, Betty Hill *retired special education educator*

Charlottesville
Walker, Sharon Louise *gifted education educator*

Chesapeake
Gomer, Edith Anne *special education educator*
King, Ingrid Payton *special education educator*

Chesterfield
Perdue, Julie Diane *special education educator*
Wilson, Dorothy Ann *retired special education educator*

Colonial Heights
Jamison, Mary Ruffin *special education educator*

Farmville
Dotson, Vicky Lynn *special education educator*

Fredericksburg
Hedke, Richard Alvin *retired gifted education educator*

Gretna
Sorrell, Rebecca Sue *special education educator*

Hamilton
Pegues, Kathleen Garcia *gifted and talented educator*

Hampton
Silva, Monica *gifted education educator*

Lexington
Ryan, Halford Ross *speech educator*

Marshall
Savignac, Amy Lynn Norris *special education educator*

Melfa
Harmon, Patricia Marie *special education educator*

Midlothian
Alligood, Mary Sale *special education educator*

Nathalie
Waller, Mitzi Duncan *special education educator*

Newport News
Meade, Angela Kaye *special education educator*
Tracy, Tracy Faircloth *special education educator*

Norfolk
Golembiewski, Gae S. *gifted education educator*

Reston
Hill, Carol Card *special education educator, coordinator*

Richmond
Sasser, Ellis A. *gifted and talented education educator*
Usry, Jana Privette *special education educator*

Roanoke
Rowe, Vickie Caldwell *reading resource educator*

Round Hill
Bergeman, Clarissa Hellman *special education educator, retired*

Saxe
Andrews, Marie Staylor *special education educator*

Springfield
Bayer, Karen Elaine *special education educator*
Leavitt, Mary Janice Deimel *special education educator, civic worker*

Staunton
Fauber, Anita P. *special education educator*

Suffolk
Matson, Virginia Mae Freeberg (Mrs. Edward J. Matson) *retired special education educator, author*

Surry
Sprouse, Earlene Pentecost *special education educator*

Virginia Beach
Franz, Carol Anne *special education educator*
Weck, Mary Katherine *special education educator*

Williamsburg
Chandler, Kimberley Lynn *educational administrator*

Winchester
Martin, Pamela Aileen *special education educator*

Woodbridge
Breene, Norma Wylie *special education educator*

WASHINGTON

Bellevue
Bergstrom, Marianne Elisabeth *program coordinator, special education educator*

Benton City
Kromminga, An-Marie *special education educator*

Bothell
Fortier, Sharon Murphy *special education educator*

Bremerton
Fischer, Mary E. *special education educator*

Naches
Glover, Marie Elizabeth *special education educator, speech language pathologist*

Olympia
Humphrey, Camilla Marie *retired special education educator*

Poulsbo
Pack, Nancy J. *special education educator, speech therapist*

Seattle
Hampton, Shelley Lynn *hearing impaired educator*
Wagness, Lorraine Melva *gifted education educator*

Wapato
Parish, Synthia Lee *special education educator*

Woodinville
Bentz, Penny Lennea *special education educator*

WEST VIRGINIA

Charleston
Roberts, Linda Sue McCallister *gifted and talented education educator*

Glen Jean
Beverly, Laura Elizabeth *special education educator*

Martinsburg
Bovey, Lisa Dawn *special education educator*

Moorefield
Hill, Nancy Elizabeth Wilson *special education educator, journalist*

Paw Paw
Palmer, Robert Jeffrey *special education educator*

Ridgeley
Unger, Roberta Marie *special education educator*

Shepherdstown
Wilson, Rebecca Ann *English and special education educator, retired*

Wellsburg
Miller, Linda Kay *reading specialist*

WISCONSIN

Brookfield
Kemp, Patricia Mary *reading educator*

Cedarburg
Steffens, Donna Irene *gifted and talented education coordinator*

Cleveland
Gurholt-Wiese, Victoria Jean (Vicki Wiese) *special needs educator*

Eagle River
Nieuwendorp, Judy Lynell *special education educator*

Greenwood
Kern-Ystad, Carol Rae *special education educator*

La Crosse
Davis, Laurie Lee *special education educator*

Lancaster
Woolford, Kathleen Marie *special education educator, secondary school educator*

Madison
Becker, Katharine Elizabeth *special education educator*

Manitowoc
Nelson, Robert Louis *special education educator, consultant*

Medford
Novinska, Deirdre Ann *special education educator*

Milwaukee
Doehr-Hodkiewicz, Denise Louise *special education educator*

Oak Creek
Thomae, Mary Joan Pangborn *special education educator*

Rice Lake
Sanborn, Marie Louise *special education educator*

Thiensville
Schlei, Robin *gifted and talented education coordinator*

Whitewater
Busse, Eileen Elaine *special education educator*

WYOMING

Cheyenne
Robertson, Susan Joyce Coe *special education educator*

Cody
Christman, Donald Ray *special education educator*

Edgerton
Malson, Verna Lee *special education educator*

Glenrock
Marr, Jo Ann *special education educator*

TERRITORIES OF THE UNITED STATES

NORTHERN MARIANA ISLANDS

Saipan
Kaufer, Connie Tenorio *retired reading specialist*

THAILAND

Bangkok
Kruck, Donna Jean *special education educator, consultant*

ADDRESS UNPUBLISHED

Alberg, Joni Yale *special education educator, jewelry designer*
Alligood, Elizabeth Ann Hiers *retired special education educator*
Alstat, George Roger *special education educator*
Armstrong, Karen Lee *special education educator*
Arnold, Leslie Ann *special education educator*
Arnold, P. A. *special education educator*
Barber, Muriel P. *retired special education educator*
Barefoot, Constance Maureen *special education educator*
Beach, Nancy Ann Helen *special education educator, educator*
Beatty, Marilyn Barton *special education educator*
Beaudin, Kimberly Ann *special education educator*
Bellflower, Deborah K. *gifted and talented education educator, special education educator*
Beyer, La Vonne Ann *special education educator*
Blach, Amanda Carolyn W. *special education educator*
Black, Cheryl Ann *special education educator*
Black, Rebecca Leree *special education educator*
Black, Rhonda Stout *special education educator*
Boise, Audrey Lorraine *retired special education educator*
Bragg, Vicki Stewart *special education educator*
Brostrom, Theresa Anne *home educator*
Brown, Deborah Joyce *special education educator*
Brown, Shari K. *special education educator*
Bryant, Janice Ann *special education department administrator*
Buck, Lori Ann *special education educator*
Calandra, Linda Claudia *special education educator*
Calfapietra, Elizabeth Anne *special education educator*
Chernesky, Barbara Jean *special education educator*
Chester, Margaret Jane *special education educator*
Childers, Susan Lynn Bohn *special education educator, administrator, human resources and transition specialist, consultant*
Cicero, Dianne *special education educator*
Clement, Betty Waidlich *literacy educator, consultant*
Clough, Lauren C. *retired special education educator*
Cummings, Carole Edwards *retired special education educator*
Davis, Janet Holmes *special education educator*
Davis, Karen Ann (Karen Ann Falconer) *special education educator*
Dirst, Stephanie Lemke *special education administrator*
Dodds, Linda Carol *special education educator*
Dudycha, Anne Elizabeth *retired special education educator*
Duncan, Sylvia Lorena *gifted education educator*
Dwinell, Ann Jones *retired special education educator*
Eacho, Esther MacLively *special education educator*
Eaton, Emma Parker *special education educator*
Essenberg, Louise Marie *special education, physical education educator*
Evert, Jill Lorene *elementary special education educator*
Finley, Gerry *special education educator, primary school educator*
Firestone, Sheila Meyerowitz *retired gifted and talented education educator*
Fletcher, Patrice Tomasky *special education educator*
Foltiny, Stephen Vincent *special education educator*
Fountain, Cornelia Wilkes *special education educator*
Franklin, Inga Sivills Knupp *special education educator*
Gates, Donna Marie *special education educator*
Gavin, Joan Elaine *special education educator*
Gifford, Mary Ann *retired special education educator*
Gilmore, Norma J. *special education educator*
Glime, Ann Elizabeth *special education educator*
Goché, Joyce Priscilla Hughey *special education and gifted education educator*
Gore, Carolyn Williams Gardner *special education educator, reading specialist*
Hammer, Joyce Mae *gifted and talented education educator*
Harader, Dana L. *behavior consultant*
Harville, Martha Louise *special education educator*
Hattaway, Linda *special education educator*
Hausler, Sara Fincham *learning disabilities specialist, educator*
Hawkins, Christine Marguerite *special education educator*
Hayden, Colleen *advanced placement secondary school educator*
Hermance, Betty Jean *special education educator*
Herrmann, Janice Rae *remedial educator*
Hines, Voncile *special education educator*
Hobart, Margery Anne *retired special education educator*
Hood, Luann Sandra *special education educator*
Huff, Janet House *special education educator*
Huntington, Irene Elizabeth *special education educator*
Iannella, Penny Marie *learning disabilities educator, consultant*
Jensen, Anna Bernice *retired special education educator and nurse*
Johnson, Delores *special education educator*
Johnson, Judith Ann *special education educator*
Jones, Susan McGowan *gifted and talented educator*
Kampe, Carolyn Jean *elementary art and special education educator*
Kellar, Marie Terese *special education educator*
Keller, Jami Ann *special education educator*
Kessler, Joan Miriam *retired special education educator, learning consultant*
Kilbourne, Diane Custeau *special education educator*
Kleeman, Nancy Gray Ervin *retired special education educator*
Klein, Mary Ann *special education educator*
Knabenshue, Catherine Sue *special education educator*
Lahann, Jeanne Marie *special education educator*
Laird, Roberta Jane *reading specialist*
Lanyon, Susan Wenner *special education educator*
Levering, Emma Gertrude *special education educator*
Lewis, Kathleen F. *special education educator*
Loyd, Judy *special education educator*
Lynch, Linda Lou *reading and language arts specialist, educator*
Mallett, Deborah Glenn *gifted talented education educator, coordinator*
Marcus, H. Louise *special education educator, writer*
Marshall, Maryann Radke *special education consultant*
Martin, Marta *learning disability specialist, educator*
Mascia-Strickler, Martha *special education educator*
Mayer, Wendy Wiviott *special education educator*
McElyea, Barbara Jeanette *special education educator*
McIntosh, Joyce Eubanks *special education educator, educator*
Melman, Cynthia Sue *special education educator*
Mencey, Helen Veronica Louise *special education educator*
Menhennett, Victoria Ann *special education educator*
Meyer, Kathleen Marie *gifted education educator, writer*
Meyer, Pauline Marie *retired special education educator*
Monroe, Sidni McCluer *special education educator*
Mullen, Terri Ann *retired special education educator*
Naglieri, Eileen Sheridan *special education educator*
Newman, Barbara Mae *retired special education educator*
Newton, Charles Kennedy *special education educator, educator*
Noyes, Dirk Arnold *special education educator, education educator*
Olson, Cheryl Ann *reading educator*
Oskin, JoEllen Ross *special education educator, school librarian*
Osnes, Pamela Grace *behavior analyst*
Owens, Cheryl Michelle *behavior specialist*
Papineau, Patricia Agnes *special education educator*
Patron, Nicholas Victor *special education educator*
Peavy, Sally Hudgins *special education educator, diagnostician, school psychologist*
Pitale-Sampson, Maria *special education educator*
Pizzuro, Salvatore Nicholas *special education educator*
Puder, Janice *special education educator*
Regn Fraher, Bonnie *special education educator*
Reynolds, Geneva B. *special education educator*
Reynolds, Lynne Warren *special education educator, speech pathologist*
Rhodes, Rhoda Ellen *gifted education educator*
Rice, Gary Russell *special education educator*
Rice, Patricia Oppenheim Levin *special education educator, consultant*
Roberts, Antonette *retired special education educator*
Rohrer, Jane Carolyn *retired gifted education specialist, academic administrator, poet, consultant*
Rollo, Mary-Jo Vivian *special education educator*
Samples, Rita Karmelin *special education educator*
Sand, Phyllis Sue Newnam (Phyllis Sue Newnam) *retired special education educator*
Sandwell, Kristin Ann *special education educator*
Scala, Marilyn Campbell *literacy and inclusion consultant, writer*
Scandary, E. Jane *special education educator, consultant*
Scheer, Terri Lynn *special education educator*
Shaw, Valeen Jones *special education educator, elementary school educator*
Shellman-Lucas, Elizabeth C. *special education educator, researcher*
Shernoff, Elise Rubin *special education educator*
Shields, Rana Colleen *special education educator*
Siegel, Carol J. *special education educator*
Siper, Cynthia Dawn *special education educator*
Solper, Sherrie Ann *learning disabilities educator*
Speer, Max Michael *special education educator*
Squires, Connie Jo *special education educator*
Starr, Joyce Ives *special education educator*
Stephen-Cossie, Elizabeth Ann *retired special education educator*
Stewart, Lucille Marie *retired special education coordinator*
Stuck, Wanda Marie *special education educator*
Stucky, Nancy L. *special education educator*
Sundstrom, Aileen Lois *speech educator*
Sutton, Julia Zeigler *retired special education educator*
Tanner, Merrilee *special education educator*
Tasker, Greta Sue *English as second language educator*
Thomas, Beverly Irene *special education educator, educational diagnostician, substance abuse counselor*
Tiemann, Barbara Jean *special education educator*
Toomey, Paula Kathleen *special education educator, educational technologist, consultant*
Troxclair, Debra Ann *gifted education educator*
Volkering, Mary Joe *special education educator*
Volpe, Eileen Rae *retired special education educator*
Ward, Patricia Scott *secondary special education educator*
Washington, Delphine Cynthia *special education educator, artist*
West, Kathleen Shea *special education educator, reading specialist*
Whitaker, Viva Jeane *language therapist dyslexia, reading specialist*
White, Florence May *learning disabilities specialist*
Wilhoit, Carol Diane *retired special education educator*
Wilson, Doris Fanuzzi *learning disabilities consultant, educator*
Withers, Dinah Lea *special education educator*
Wood, Mildred Hope *special education educator*
Woodward, Debbie Carol *special education educator*
Workman, Kayleen Marie *special education and adult education educator*
Wright, Connie Sue *special education educator*
Wulf, Janie Scott McIlwaine *gifted and talented education educator*
Yoder, Anna Mary *reading educator*
Youngs, Diane Campfield *learning disabilities specialist, educator*
Zarecki, Angela Rose *special education educator*
Zarzour, Robin Ann *special education educator*
Zehner, Constance Wendell *gifted and talented, science education educator*

GOVERNMENT ADMINISTRATION

UNITED STATES

ALASKA

Juneau
Sampson, Roger *education commissioner*

PROFESSIONAL INDEX

ARIZONA

Scottsdale
Mathes, Mary Louise *state official, retired educator*

CALIFORNIA

Davis
Eastin, Delaine Andree *federal agency administrator*

Sacramento
Burns, John Francis *state official, educator*
Mazzoni, Kerry *state agency administrator*

Stanford
Shultz, George Pratt *former government executive, economics educator*

CONNECTICUT

Putnam
LeClair, Peter R. *state agency supervisor, mental retardation services professional*

DELAWARE

Dover
Woodruff, Valerie *secretary of education*

DISTRICT OF COLUMBIA

Washington
Andersen, Margo K. *federal agency administrator*
Andrade, Jeffrey R. *government educational secretary*
Bailey, John P. *director educational technology*
Banfield, Marian D. *federal agency administrator*
Brown, Dale Susan *government administrator, educational program director, writer*
Bryant, Wilbert *government counselor*
Chittum, Loretta Petty *federal agency administrator*
Conaty, Joseph C. *federal agency administrator*
Corwin, Thomas Michael *federal agency administrator*
Danielson, John M. *federal official*
de Kanter, Adriana Alison *federal agency administrator*
Dorfman, Cynthia Hearn *government agency administrator*
Ferrier, Maria Hernandez *federal official, educator*
Fiegel, John *federal agency administrator*
Fleischer, Rebecca *federal agency administrator*
Francis, Shari *federal agency administrator*
Garcia, Francisco *federal agency administrator*
Garnette, Cheryl Petty *government agency administrator*
Ginsburg, Alan L. *federal agency administrator*
Gore, Patricia W. *federal agency administrator*
Guard, Patricia J. *federal agency administrator*
Harvey, Edith M. *federal agency administrator*
Hickok, Eugene W. *federal agency administrator*
Higgins, John P., Jr., *inspector general U.S. Department of Education*
Horn, Sharon K. *government agency administrator*
Hunt, Earl Stephen *federal agency administrator*
Jackson, Jacquelyn C. *federal agency administrator*
Jones, Brian W. *federal official*
Jones, Linda W. *federal agency administrator*
Keegan, Lisa Graham *state agency administrator*
Klenk, Jack *federal agency administrator*
Leidinger, William John *federal official*
Lim, Jeanette J. *federal agency administrator*
Lord, Jerome Edmund *education administrator, writer*
Luigart, Craig *federal official*
Magaziner, Ira *government agency administrator*
Marburger, Darla A. *federal agency administrator*
Martin, Jack *federal agency administrator*
Modzeleski, William *government agency administrator*
Moniz, Ernest Jeffrey *government official, former physics educator*
Myers, Raymond A. *government education administrator*
Paige, Roderick R. *secretary of education*
Pastorek, Paul G. *federal agency administrator*
Patrick, Susan D. *government agency administrator*
Rees, Nina Shokraii *federal official, writer*
Reynolds, Gerald A.(Jerry) *assistant secretary of education for civil rights, lawyer*
Rich, Laurie M. *federal official, educator*
Rooker, LeRoy S. *federal agency administrator*
Schagh, Catherine *federal agency administrator*
Sclafani, Susan K. *federal official*
Shaw, Theresa (Terri) S. *federal official*
Simmons, Enid Brown *retired state agency administrator*
Simon, Doug *government educational administrator*
Spearman, Leonard H. O., Sr., *federal official*
Stroup, Sally *federal agency administrator*
Thompson, Tommy George *secretary of health and human services, former governor*
Vasques, Victoria L. *federal agency administrator*
Wright, Sylvia *government agency administrator*
Yaklin, Lori Stillwagon *government agency administrator*

FLORIDA

Boca Raton
Brogan, Frank T. *former lieutenant governor*

Pensacola
Droegemueller, Lee *state education official*

Tallahassee
Braswell, Jackie Boyd *state agency administrator*
Thomas, James Bert, Jr., *government official*

GEORGIA

Atlanta
Cox, Kathy *education commissioner*

HAWAII

Honolulu
Aizawa, Herman *state agency administrator*

ILLINOIS

Champaign
Semonin, Richard Gerard *retired state official*

INDIANA

Indianapolis
Hill, Patricia Jo *workforce development specialist*

KANSAS

Topeka
Tompkins, John Andy *commissioner of education*

LOUISIANA

Baton Rouge
Franklin, Bobby Jo *state education agency administrator*

MAINE

Augusta
Gendron, Susan Ann *commissioner, educator*

Kennebunk
Martin, Leo G. *educational consultant*

MASSACHUSETTS

Boston
Peyser, James *state agency administrator*

Brant Rock
Petrilli, Michael J. *federal agency administrator*

Cambridge
Mankiw, Nicholas Gregory *federal agency administrator, economics educator*
Summers, Lawrence *former government official, academic administrator*

Malden
Driscoll, David P. *commissioner, educator*

MICHIGAN

Lansing
Watkins, Thomas D. *superintendent of public instruction*

West Bloomfield
Ho, Leo Chi Chien *Chinese government official*

MISSISSIPPI

Jackson
Johnson, Henry L. *superintendent of education*

MISSOURI

Columbia
McClain, Charles James *educator*

Jefferson City
King, D. Kent *education commissioner*
Peeno, Larry Noyle *state agency administrator, consultant*

Saint Louis
King, Joseph, Jr. *government administrator, educator, consultant*

MONTANA

Helena
McCulloch, Linda *state official*

NEBRASKA

Lincoln
Bonaiuto, John A. *state education official*

NEW HAMPSHIRE

Concord
Donohue, Nicholas C. *education commissioner*

NEW JERSEY

Trenton
Librera, William *education commissioner*

NEW MEXICO

Santa Fe
Davis, Michael J. *public instruction superintendent*

NEW YORK

Clifton Park
Nolan, Donald James *retired state educational commisioner*

Hadley
Gray-Aldrich, Gretchen Elise *retired state agency administrator, nursing educator*

NORTH CAROLINA

Raleigh
Ward, Michael E. *superintendent of public instruction*

OKLAHOMA

Ada
Stewart, Steven Elton *state agency administrator*

Yukon
Thompson Pybas, Joyce Elizabeth *retired state education official*

PENNSYLVANIA

West Chester
Dinniman, Andrew Eric *county commissioner, history educator, academic program director, international studies educator*

SOUTH CAROLINA

Clemson
Nielsen, Barbara Stock *state educational administrator*

Columbia
Tenenbaum, Inez Moore *superintendent of education*

Lexington
Resch, Mary Louise *town agency administrator*

SOUTH DAKOTA

Pierre
Melmer, Rick *state agency administrator*

TENNESSEE

Memphis
Walters, Jane *state agency administrator*

Nashville
Seivers, Lana C. *commissioner of education*
Thomas, Hazel Beatrice *state official*

TEXAS

Austin
Alanis, Felipe *education commissioner*
Butler, Douglas M *state agency administrator, educator*
Forgione, Pascal D., Jr., *state superintendent*
Joplin, Claudia Phillips *state education administrator*

UTAH

Ogden
Hardy, Duane Horace *retired federal agency administrator, educator*

VIRGINIA

Annandale
Dugan, John Vincent, Jr., *legislative affairs specialist, researcher*

Arlington
Umminger, Bruce Lynn *government official, scientist, educator*

Richmond
DeMary, Jo Lynne *state official, elementary school educator*
Heiss, Frederick William *public administrator and policy researcher, political scientist, educator*
Wheelan, Belle S. *state agency administrator*

WASHINGTON

Springfield
Jones, Bonnie Damschroder *government agency administrator*

Williamsburg
Drum, Joan Marie McFarland *federal agency administrator, educator*

WASHINGTON

Olympia
Markham, J. David *educator, writer, historical consultant*

WEST VIRGINIA

Charleston
Hechler, Ken *former state official, former congressman, political science educator, writer*

WISCONSIN

Madison
Deer, Ada E. *former federal agency official, social worker, educator*

WYOMING

Cheyenne
Blankenship, Trent *state official, educator*
Catchpole, Judy *state official*
Simons, Lynn Osborn *state agency administrator*

TERRITORIES OF THE UNITED STATES

NORTHERN MARIANA ISLANDS

Saipan
Sablan, Rita Aldan *state agency administrator*

VIRGIN ISLANDS

St Thomas
Michael, Noreen *commissioner, educator*

CANADA

PRINCE EDWARD ISLAND

Charlottetown
Gillan, Chester *education commissioner*

Toronto
Cunningham, Dianne *minister of intergovernmental affairs*

MEXICO

Mexico City
Tamez Guerra, Reyes S. *secretary of public education for Mexico*

ADDRESS UNPUBLISHED

Arveson, Raymond Gerhard *retired state official*
Billings, Judith A. *state education official*
Bishop, C. Diane *state agency administrator, educator*
Guay, Gordon Hay *federal agency administrator, marketing educator, consultant*
Henderson, Geraldine Thomas *retired social security official, educator*
Heyman, Ira Michael *federal agency administrator, museum executive, law educator*
Holloway, Shirley J. *state agency administrator*
Johnstone, Stowell *former state agency administrator*
Morgan, Alan Douglas *state education official*
Randall, William Theodore *state official*
Skarr, Michael W. *state agency administrator*
Sorter, Bruce Wilbur *federal program administrator, educator, consultant*
Surbeck-Harris, Joyce Annette *special education administrator*

HIGHER EDUCATION ADMINISTRATION

UNITED STATES

ALABAMA

Anniston
Cain, William Vernon *academic administrator*

Auburn
Gropper, Daniel Michael *college assistant dean, business educator*
Voitle, Robert Allen *college dean, physiologist*

Birmingham
Corts, Thomas Edward *university president*

Deal, William Brown *physician, educator, author, medical school dean*
Reynolds, W(ynetka) Ann *academic administrator, educator*

Enterprise
Heck, Charles Ralph *university dean*

Florence
Barfield, Kenny Dale *religious school administrator*
Howard, G. Daniel *university administrator*
Potts, Robert Leslie *academic administrator*

Hanceville
Galin, Jerry Dean *college dean*

Huntsville
Franz, Frank Andrew *university president, physics educator*

Jacksonville
Dunaway, William Preston *retired educator*

Jasper
Rowland, David Jack *academic administrator*

Livingston
Green, Asa Norman *university president*

Mobile
Curry, Catharine Terrill *health care and marketing executive*
Kreisberg, Robert A. *dean, medical educator*

Montgomery
Ducharme, Adele *educational administrator*
Ritvo, Roger Alan *vice chancellor, health management-policy educator*

Opp
Patterson, Polly Jones *academic director, marriage and family therapist*

Rainsville
Reece, Marilyn King *college dean*

Tuscaloosa
Dolly, John Patrick *educational psychologist, educator*
Thomas, Joab Langston *retired university president, biology educator*

Tuscumbia
Hutchens, Eugene Garlington *college administrator*

Tuskegee
Green, Elbert P. *retired university official*

ALASKA

Eagle River
Standley, Mark *school program administrator, consultant*

Fairbanks
Abels, Michael Alan *university administrator*
Alexander, Vera *dean, marine science educator*

Homer
Swartz, Carol I. *academic administrator*

ARIZONA

Flagstaff
Abata, Duane *dean*

Fountain Hills
Wright, C. T. Enus *former academic administrator*

Glendale
Stauffer, Thomas Michael *former university president*

Phoenix
Coor, Lattie Finch *university president*
Forster, Bruce Alexander *dean*
Schou, Gayle Evelyn *academic administrator*
Taylor, Mark Alan *academic administrator*

Scottsdale
Mayer, Robert Anthony *retired college president*
Stone, Alan Jay *retired college administrator*

Sun Lakes
Smith, Eleanor Jane *university chancellor, retired, consultant*

Tempe
Peck, Ernest James, Jr., *academic administrator*
Wills, J. Robert *academic administrator, drama educator, writer*

Tucson
Di Pasquale, Pasquale, Jr., *education consultant*
Garner, Girolama Thomasina *retired educational administrator, educator*
Humphrey, John Julius *university program director, historian, writer*
Likins, Peter William *university administrator*
Miles, Suzanne Laura *dean*
Sevigny, Maurice *dean*

ARKANSAS

Arkadelphia
Dunn, Charles DeWitt *academic administrator*
Elrod, Ben Moody *academic administrator*
Futrell, Alvin *director*

Camden
Owen, Larry Gene *academic administrator, educator, electronic and computer integrated manufacturing consultant*

Fayetteville
Ferritor, Daniel E. *chancellor emeritus*
Williams, Doyle Z. *university dean, educator*

Little Rock
Fribourgh, James Henry *university administrator*
Keaton, William Thomas *academic administrator, pastor*

Magnolia
Gamble, Steven G. *academic administrator*

CALIFORNIA

Aptos
Hirsch, Bette G(ross) *college administrator, foreign language educator*

Arcata
McCrone, Alistair William *retired academic administrator*
Slinker, John Michael *academic director*

Azusa
Gray, Paul Wesley *university dean*

Bakersfield
Arciniega, Tomas Abel *university president*
Black, Lori Annette *academic administrator*
Thomas, Tom Eldon *corrections educator*

Berkeley
Berdahl, Robert Max *academic administrator, historian, educator*
Kerr, Clark *academic administrator emeritus*
Lederer, C. Michael *energy researcher, academic administrator*
Miles, Raymond Edward *former university dean, organizational behavior and industrial relations educator*
Ralston, Lenore Dale *academic policy and program analyst*
Semoff, Deirdre Paula *special education administrator, academic director*

Beverly Hills
Grant, Michael Ernest *educational administrator, institutional management educator*

Calexico
Aguilar, Isabel (Chavela) *counselor, university official*

Camarillo
Rush, Richard R. *academic administrator*

Campo
Jermini, Ellen *educational administrator, philosopher*

Carson
Mori, Allen Anthony *academic administrator, consultant*

Chico
Esteban, Manuel Antonio *academic administrator, language educator*

Claremont
Bekavac, Nancy Yavor *academic administrator, lawyer*
Douglass, Enid Hart *educational program director*
Gann, Pamela Brooks *academic administrator*
Maguire, John David *academic administrator, educator, writer*
Riggs, Henry Earle *academic administrator, engineering educator*
Stanley, Peter William *former academic administrator*
Strauss, Jon Calvert *academic administrator*

Davis
Kearney, Patricia Ann *university administrator*
Kraft, Rosemarie *dean, educator*
Vanderhoef, Larry Neil *academic administrator*

El Centro
Fragale, Richard P. *academic administrator*

El Dorado Hills
Bartlett, Robert Watkins *educator, consultant, metallurgist*

Encino
Bach, Cynthia *educational program director, writer*

Fallbrook
Evans, Anthony Howard *university president*

Fountain Valley
Purdy, Leslie *community college president*

Fresno
Welty, John Donald *academic administrator*

Fullerton
Beers, Susan Alice *dean*

Glendale
Hurley, Patricia Ann *college official*

Hayward
Rees, Norma S. *academic administrator*

Hemet
Shea, Robert Stanton *retired academic administrator*

Indian Wells
Trotter, F(rederick) Thomas *retired academic administrator*

Irvine
Cicerone, Ralph John *academic administrator, geophysicist*
Peltason, Jack Walter *foundation executive, educator*

Kentfield
McCarthy, Marie Geraldine *program director, coordinator, educator*

La Jolla
Frieman, Edward Allan *academic administrator, educator*
Trybus, Raymond J. *higher education executive, psychologist*

La Verne
Morgan, Stephen Charles *academic administrator*

Laguna Beach
Martinez, Vera *academic administrator*

Livermore
Roshong, Dee Ann Daniels *dean, educator*

Long Beach
Reed, Charles Bass *chief academic administrator*
Thompson, William Ancker *intramural-recreational sports director, educator*

Los Altos
Fong, Bernadine Chuck *academic administrator*

Los Angeles
Armstrong, Lloyd, Jr., *university official, physics educator*
Bice, Scott Haas *dean, lawyer, educator*
Carnesale, Albert *academic administrator*
Dewey, Donald Odell *dean, academic administrator*
Lim, Larry Kay *university official*
Mitchell, Theodore Reed *academic administrator*
Moore, Donald Walter *academic administrator, school librarian*
Rosser, James Milton *academic administrator*
Ryan, Stephen Joseph, Jr., *ophthalmology educator, university dean*
Sample, Steven Browning *university executive*
Taylor, Leigh Herbert *college dean*
Venis, Linda Diane *academic administrator, educator*
Wagner, William Gerard *university dean, physicist, consultant, information scientist, investment manager*

Malibu
Benton, Andrew Keith *university administrator, lawyer*

Mission Viejo
Hodge, Kathleen O'Connell *academic administrator*

Northridge
Syms, Helen Maksym *educational administrator*

Oakland
Atkinson, Richard Chatham *university president*
Chook, Edward Kongyen *academic administrator, medical educator*
Diaz, Sharon *education administrator*
Dynes, Robert C. *academic administrator*
Heydman, Abby Maria *academic executive*
Holmgren, Janet L *college president*

Oceanside
Beaulieu, Rodney Joseph *academic administrator, education educator*
Pena, Maria Geges *academic services administrator*

Orange
Schrodi, Tom *instructional services director*

Orinda
Glasser, Charles Edward *university president emeritus*

Oxnard
Auston, David Henry *former academic administrator, electrical engineer, educator*

Pasadena
Baltimore, David *academic administrator, microbiologist, educator*
Everhart, Thomas Eugene *retired university president, engineering educator*

Pleasanton
Lucas, Linda Lucille *dean*

Pomona
Ambrose, William Wright, Jr., *dean, educator, academic administrator*

Redlands
Appleton, James Robert *university president, educator*

Rohnert Park
Arminana, Ruben *academic administrator, educator*

Sacramento
Gerth, Donald Rogers *university president*
Stegenga, (Preston Jay *international education consultant*
West, Linda Lea *administrator*

San Bernardino
Butler, Arthur Maurice *university administrator*

San Bruno
White, Frances LaVonne *academic administrator*

San Diego
Lauer, Jeanette Carol *college dean, history educator, writer*
Lazarus, Francis Martin *academic administrator*
Lyons, Mary E. *academic administrator*
Meno, Lionel R. *academic administrator*
Weber, Stephen Lewis *university president*

San Francisco
Albino, Judith Elaine Newsom *university president*
Cannon, Tyrone *dean*
Corrigan, Robert Anthony *academic administrator*
Hudson, Suncerray Ann *analyst, research grants manager*
Kane, Mary Kay *dean, law educator*
Runyon, Steven Crowell *university administrator, communications educator*
Stephens, Elisa *college president*

San Luis Obispo
Bailey, Philip Sigmon, Jr., *university official and dean, chemistry educator*
Baker, Warren J(oseph) *university president*

San Marino
Mothershead, J. Leland, III, *dean*

San Rafael
Fink, Joseph Richard *academic administrator*

Santa Ana
Hernandez, Edward, Jr., *community college administrator*
Moghadam, Amir *consultant, educational administrator*

Santa Barbara
Allaway, William Harris *retired university official*
Yang, Henry T. *academic administrator, educator*
Zimmerman, Muriel *university official*

Santa Clarita
Lavine, Steven David *academic administrator*

Santa Monica
Robertson, Piedad F. *college president*

Signal Hill
Vandamert, William Eugene *retired academic administrator*

Stanford
Casper, Gerhard *law educator, former academic administrator*
Hennessy, John L. *academic administrator*
Palm, Charles Gilman *university official*
Raisian, John *academic administrator, economist*
Spence, A(ndrew) Michael *dean, finance educator*
Whitney, Rodger Franklin *university executive*

Sun Valley
Mayhue, Richard Lee *provost, dean, pastor, writer*

Valley Springs
Perry, Richard Lee *retired academic administrator, physics educator*

Ventura
Lawson, William Harold *college dean, labor economist*

Walnut Creek
Lilly, Luella Jean *academic administrator*

Weimar
Kerschner, Lee R(onald) *academic administrator, political science educator*

COLORADO

Aurora
Beckman, L. David *university chancellor*

Boulder
Vigil, Daniel Agustin *academic administrator*
Williams, James Franklin, II, *university dean, librarian*

Colorado Springs
Adams, Bernard Schroder *retired college president*
Celeste, Richard F. *academic administrator, former ambassador, former governor*
Spears, Suzanna D. *educational administrator*

Denver
Burrows, Bertha Jean *retired academic administrator*
Ellis, Sylvia D. Hall *development and library education consultant*
Fulkerson, William Measey, Jr., *college president*
Halgren, Lee A. *academic administrator*
Horton, Frank Elba *university official, geography educator*
Mornes, Amber J. Bishop *consultant, computer software trainer, analyst*
Poynter, James Morrison *travel educator, travel company executive*
Ritchie, Daniel Lee *academic administrator*

Durango
Barter, Mary F. *academic administrator*

Fort Collins
Baldwin, Lionel Vernon *retired university president*

Jaros, Dean *university official*
Maher, Thomas George *academic administrator, producer, media educator*
Yates, Albert Carl *academic administrator, chemistry educator*

Glenwood Springs
Mayer, Dennis Marlyn *academic administrator, consultant*

Golden
Bickart, Theodore Albert *university president emeritus*

Greeley
Afoaku, Oyibo Helisita *academic administrator*
Bond, Richard Randolph *foundation administrator, legislator*

Littleton
Greenberg, Elinor Miller *university official, consultant*
Marion, John Martin *academic administrator*

CONNECTICUT

Cos Cob
McElwaine, Theresa Weedy *academic administrator, artist*

Danbury
Roach, James Richard *university president*
Stewart, Albert Clifton *college dean, marketing educator*

Enfield
Reuter, Joan Copson *retired program director*

Fairfield
Cernera, Anthony Joseph *academic administrator*
Kelley, Aloysius Paul *university administrator, priest*

Farmington
Paplauskas, Leonard Paul *academic administrator, health science educator*

Greens Farms
Johnson, Jamieson Dregallo *women's athletics director*

Hartford
Frost, James Arthur *former university president*
Reynolds, Scott Walton *academic administrator*

Middletown
Bennet, Douglas Joseph, Jr., *university president*

New Britain
Boyea, Ruthe W. *retired educator*

New Haven
Gaudiani, Claire Lynn *retired academic administrator*
Haines, Jacqueline Irene *institute director*
Kronman, Anthony Townsend *law educator, dean*
Lamar, Howard Roberts *educational administrator, historian*
Levin, Richard Charles *academic administrator, economist*
Rosner, Diane A. *academic administrator*
Yandle, Stephen Thomas *dean*

New London
Fainstein, Norman *college president*

Norfolk
O'Malley, John Patrick *retired dean*
Potter, Elizabeth Stone *academic administrator*

North Haven
Sommers, Alexis Nigel *academic administrator, engineering educator, manufacturer*

Waterbury
Brown, Lillian Hill *retired academic administrator*
Sanders, Richard L. *academic administrator*

West Hartford
Malone, Thomas Francis *academic administrator, meteorologist*
Tonkin, Humphrey Richard *academic administrator, educator*

Willimantic
Carter, David George, Sr., *university administrator*
Enggas, Grace Falcetta *university administrator*
Eshoo, Barbara Anne Rudolph *academic official*
Wilson, Margaret Sullivan *retired executive dean, consultant*

Wilton
Reilly, Kathleen C. *director, retired secondary school educator*

DELAWARE

Dover
Sessoms, Allen Lee *academic administrator, former diplomat, physicist*
Sorenson, Liane Beth McDowell *women's affairs director, state legislator*

New Castle
Doberstein, Audrey K. *college president*

Newark
Carter, Mae Riedy *retired academic official, consultant*
Roselle, David Paul *university president, mathematics educator*
Schiavelli, Melvyn David *academic administrator, science educator, researcher*
Whittington, Ronald Frederick *academic administrator*

DISTRICT OF COLUMBIA

Washington
Alatis, James Efstathios *university dean emeritus*
Anroman, Gilda Marie *college program director, lecturer, educator*
Boggs, George Robert *academic administrator*
Bradshaw, Rebecca Parks *academic administrator*
Burris, James Frederick *federal research administrator, educator*
Caputo, Anne Spencer *knowledge and learning programs director*
Cortright, Jane Brigid Moynahan *educational administrator*
Cronin, Richard James *university official, educator*
DeGioia, John J. *university president*
Duffey, Joseph Daniel *academic administrator*
Easterling, Christine Davis *educational administrator*
Friedenthal, Jack H. *former dean*
Harding, Ilo-Mai *program director*
Howard, Kenneth Lee *university official, consultant*
Ingold, Catherine White *academic administrator*
Jordan, Irving King *university president*
Karelis, Charles Howard (Buddy Karelis) *former academic administrator, humanities educator*
Lovett, Clara Maria *university administrator, historian*
Mohrman, Kathryn J *academic administrator*
Nwagbaraocha, Joel Onukwugha *academic administrator, educator*
O'Donovan, Leo Jeremiah *former academic administrator, priest, theologian*
Ranck, Edna Runnels *academic administrator, researcher*
Riccards, Michael Patrick *academic administrator*
Starr, Stephen Frederick *academic administrator, historian*
Swygert, Haywood Patrick *university president, law educator*
Trachtenberg, Stephen Joel *university president*
Van Ummersen, Claire A(nn) *academic administrator, biologist, educator*
Ward, David *academic administrator, educator*

FLORIDA

Boca Raton
Jurewicz, John Thomas *university dean, engineer*

Bokeelia
Adams, Alfred Hugh *retired college president*

Bonita Springs
Becker, Richard Charles *retired college president*
McManigal, Shirley Ann *university educator, dean emerita*

Brandon
Blomgren, David Kenneth *dean, pastor*

Clearwater
Edmonds, Maria Nieves *college administrator*

Cocoa
Gamble, Thomas Ellsworth *academic administrator*

Coral Gables
Lewis, Elisah Blessing *university official*
Shalala, Donna E. *university administrator, former federal official, political scientist, educator*

Daytona Beach
Ebbs, George Heberling, Jr., *university executive*

Deland
Lee, Howard Douglas *academic administrator*

Destin
Asher, Betty Turner *academic administrator*

Fort Lauderdale
Preziosi, Robert Charles *dean, business educator*

Gainesville
Chambers, Robert Hunter, III, *college president, American studies educator, consultant*
Neims, Allen Howard *university dean, medical scientist*
Phillips, Winfred Marshall *dean, biomedical research executive, mechanical engineer, educator*
Stroh, Robert Carl, Sr., *university official*
Young, Charles Edward *academic administrator*

Holmes Beach
Dunne, James Robert *academic administrator, management consultant, business educator*

Jacksonville
Jenkins, Jimmy Raymond *university president*

Kennedy Space Center
Feldman, Stephen *academic administrator*

Melbourne
Catanese, Anthony James *academic administrator*
Weaver, Lynn Edward *academic administrator, consultant, editor*

Merritt Island
McClanahan, Leland *university director*
Thompson, Hugh Lee *academic administrator*

Miami
Foote, Edward Thaddeus, II, *university president, lawyer*
Magnusen, Olga Cristina *career planning and placement director*
Maidique, Modesto Alex *academic administrator*
Temares, M. Lewis *university dean, academic administrator*

Miami Beach
Gitlow, Abraham Leo *retired dean*

Newberry
Thornton, J. Ronald *technology consultant*

North Fort Myers
Philippi, Dieter Rudolph *retired academic administrator*

Ocala
Kinney, Thomas John *academic administrator*

Orlando
Ady, Laurence Irvin *academic administrator*
Clinton, Stephen Michael *academic administrator*
Holland, Kathie Kunkel *university official, educator*

Oviedo
MacKenzie, Charles Sherrard *academic administrator*

Palm Beach Gardens
Turner, V(eras) Dean *dean*

Ponte Vedra Beach
Hartzell, Karl Drew *retired university dean, historian*
Patterson, Oscar, III, *university program administrator*

Saint Augustine
Proctor, William Lee *college chancellor*

Saint Petersburg
Armacost, Peter Hayden *academic administrator*
Estenes, Joseph John, Jr., *academic administrator*
Kuttler, Carl Martin, Jr., *academic administrator*
Nussbaum, Leo Lester *retired college president, consultant*

Sarasota
Atwell, Robert Herron *higher education executive*
Christ-Janer, Arland Frederick *college president*
Reagan, Larry Gay *college vice president*

South Miami
Price, Anna Maria *university administrator*

Tallahassee
Foss, Donald John *university dean, research psychologist*
Humphries, Frederick S. *university president*
Sliger, Bernard Francis *academic administrator, economist, educator*
Spiegel, Samuel Albert *program director*
Tull, Trent Ashley *college administrator*

Tampa
Troxell, Raymond Robert, Jr., *college administrator*

Venice
Thomas, David Ansell *retired university dean*

Weston
Walsh, William John *educational administrator*

GEORGIA

Americus
Batson, Stephen Wesley *university administrator, consultant*

Athens
Adams, Michael Fred *university president, political communications specialist*
Castenell, Louis Anthony *academic administrator*
Crowther, Ann Rollins *academic administrator, political science educator*

Atlanta
Bickerton, Jane Elizabeth *university research coordinator*
Bright, David Forbes *academic administrator, classics and comparative literature educator*
Clough, Gerald Wayne *academic administrator*
Farokhi, Helen Elizabeth (Beth) *university official*
Henry, Ronald James Whyte *university official*
Hogan, John Donald *retired college dean, finance educator*
Keiller, James Bruce *college dean, clergyman*
Meredith, Thomas C. *academic administrator*
Meyer, Ellen L. *academic administrator*
Patton, Carl Vernon *academic administrator, educator*
Schuppert, Roger Allen *retired university official*

Augusta
Puryear, Joan Copeland *academic administrator*
Tedesco, Francis Joseph *university administrator*

Carrollton
Brewer, A. Bruce *university administrator*

Clarkesville
Melichar, Barbara Ehrlich *educational administrator*

Cochran
Halaska, Thomas Edward *academic administrator, director, engineer*

Decatur
Wilkinson, Ben *chancellor, evangelist, ministry organizer, writer*

Dublin
Watson, Mary Alice *academic administrator*

Gainesville
Burd, John Stephen *academic administrator, music educator*

Lawrenceville
English, John Rife *educational administrator*

Marietta
Rossbacher, Lisa Ann *university president, geology educator, writer*

Milledgeville
Bader, Carol Hopper *dean*
Deal, Therry Nash *college dean*

Newton
Walton, William Robert *academic administrator*

Savannah
Hayes, Willis Boyd *academic program director*
Rowan, Richard G. *academic administrator*

Toccoa Falls
Alford, Paul Legare *college and religious foundation administrator*

Valdosta
Bailey, Hugh Coleman *university president*
Kellner, Robert Dean *college official*
Krotseng, Marsha Van Dyke *higher education administrator*

Vidalia
Parker, Lisa E. *developmental studies educator*

HAWAII

Hilo
Best, Mary Lani *university program coordinator*

Honolulu
Dobelle, Evan Samuel *academic administrator*
Gee, Chuck Yim *dean*
Keith, Kent Marsteller *academic administrator, educator, writer, lawyer*
Wright, Chatt Grandison *academic administrator*

Laie
Yang, Rene Ikan *university administrator*

IDAHO

Boise
Maloof, Giles Wilson *academic administrator, educator, author*
Ruch, Charles P. *academic administrator*

Caldwell
Hendren, Robert Lee, Jr., *academic administrator*

Moscow
Sebald, Jama Lynn *academic administrator*

Pocatello
Jolly, Michael John *college administrator*
Lawson, Jonathan Nevin *academic administrator*

Sandpoint
Rigas, Anthony Leon *university department director*

ILLINOIS

Aurora
Zarle, Thomas Herbert *academic administrator*

Blue Island
Troy, Cherryl April *secondary education educator*

Calumet City
Williams, Luvenia *academic administrator*

Carbondale
Covington, Patricia Ann *university administrator*

Champaign
Blanchard, Rosemary Ann *university program administrator, consultant, educator*
Cantor, Nancy *academic administrator*

Charleston
Thornburgh, Daniel Eston *retired university administrator, journalism educator*

Chicago
Burton, Erlie P. *academic administrator*
Champagne, Ronald Oscar *academic administrator, mathematics educator*
Craine, Thomas Knowlton *non-profit administrator*
Cross, Dolores Evelyn *former university administrator, educator*
Driskell, Claude Evans *college director, educator, dentist*
Gómez, Fabiola *university official*
Gross, Theodore Lawrence *university administrator, author*
Hamada, Robert S(eiji) *educator, economist, entrepreneur*

Harris, Charles Upchurch *seminary president, clergyman*
Hayes, Alice Bourke *academic administrator, biologist, educator*
Helms, Byron Eldon *academic administrator*
Henikoff, Leo M., Jr., *academic administrator, medical educator*
Khan, M. Wasi *academic administrator*
McPherson, Michael Steven *former academic administrator, economist*
O'Neill, Walter John Hugh *university director, consultant*
Pellegrino, James William *college dean, psychology educator*
Randel, Don Michael *academic administrator, musicologist*
Richardson, John Thomas *academic administrator, clergyman*
Sulkin, Howard Allen *college president*
Yamakawa, Allan Hitoshi *academic administrator*

Dekalb
Coakley, Michael James *university administrator*

Downers Grove
Fjortoft, Nancy Fay *univeristy administrator, educator*

East Dubuque
Kussmaul, Donald *academic administrator*

Eureka
Hearne, George Archer *academic administrator*

Evanston
Boye, Roger Carl *journalism educator, writer*
Christian, Richard Carlton *university dean, former advertising agency executive*
Weber, Arnold Robert *academic administrator*

Galesburg
Sunderland, Jacklyn Giles *former alumni affairs director*

Glen Carbon
Lazerson, Earl Edwin *academic administrator emeritus*

Gurnee
Jennings, Gary Harold *college administrator*

Hinsdale
Taylor, Ronald Lee *academic administrator*

Lake Forest
Ferrari, Michael Richard, Jr., *university administrator*

Libertyville
Bermingham, John Scott *business executive, educator*

Naperville
Heuer, Michael Alexander *dean, endodontist educator*

Northbrook
Beljan, John Richard *university administrator, medical educator*

Oglesby
Zeller, Francis Joseph *dean*

Peoria
Bunch, Dale *academic administrator*

Rock Island
Bahls, Steven Carl *academic administrator, educator*
Horstmann, James Douglas *college official*

Urbana
Glick, Karen Lynne *college administrator*
Stukel, James Joseph *academic administrator, mechanical engineering educator*

Wheaton
Sweetser, Ruth Emilie Ziemann *academic administrator*

Wheeling
Kieffer, Connie Welch *academic administrator*

Wilmette
Smutny, Joan Franklin *academic director, educator*

INDIANA

Anderson
Edwards, James Lee *university president*

Bloomington
Collins, Dorothy Craig *retired educational administrator*
Dunning, Jeremy David *industrial research director, educator, dean*
Herbert, Adam William, Jr., *academic administrator, educator*
Palmer, Judith Grace *university administrator*
Webb, Charles Haizlip, Jr., *retired university dean*

Carmel
Rand, Leon *academic administrator*

Crawfordsville
Ford, Andrew Thomas *academic administrator*

Fort Wayne
Balthaser, Linda Irene *retired academic administrator*
Dahl, John Clarence, Jr., *academic administrator*

Greencastle
Bottoms, Robert Garvin *academic administrator*

Huntington
Lahr, Beth M. *college administrator*

Indianapolis
Bepko, Gerald Lewis *university administrator, law educator, lecturer, consultant, lawyer*
Boyd, Rozelle *retired university administrator, educator*
Brand, Myles *academic administrator*
Brenner, Mark Lee *academic administrator, physiologist, educator*
Clark, Charles M., Jr., *medical school administrator*
D'Amico, Carol *educational administrator*
Huffman-Hine, Ruth Carson *adult education administrator, educator*
Paradysz, Marsha L. *academic administrator*
Stookey, George Kenneth *retired director, retired dental educator*

Kokomo
Person, Ruth Janssen *academic administrator*

Muncie
Amman, E(lizabeth) Jean *university official*
Brownell, Blaine Allison *university administrator, history educator*

New Harmony
Rice, David Lee *university president emeritus*

North Manchester
Switzer, Jo Young *academic administrator, dean*

Notre Dame
Hatch, Nathan Orr *university administrator*
Malloy, Edward Aloysius *academic administrator*
O'Meara, Onorato Timothy *academic administrator, mathematician*

South Bend
Rodgers, Grace Anne *university official*

Terre Haute
Dando, William Arthur *academic administrator, geography and geology educator*
Moore, John William *former university president*

Upland
Kesler, Jay Lewis *academic administrator*

Valparaiso
Harre, Alan Frederick *academic administrator*

West Lafayette
Beering, Steven Claus *academic administrator, medical educator*
Carney, Thomas Quentin *academic administrator, educator, pilot*
Frick, Gene Armin *university administrator*
Jischke, Martin C. *academic administrator*
Moyars-Johnson, Mary Annis *university official*
Singleton, Gregory Ray *dean*

Westville
Alspaugh, Dale William *university administrator, aeronautics and astronautics educator*

IOWA

Des Moines
Maxwell, David E. *academic executive, educator*

Dubuque
Garfield, Phyllis H. *international program administrator, educational consultant*
Kerrigan, John E. *academic administrator*

Epworth
Anich, Kenneth James *priest, college administrator*

Grinnell
Osgood, Russell King *academic administrator*

Iowa City
Boyd, Willard Lee *academic administrator, educator, museum administrator, lawyer*
Brennan, Robert Lawrence *educational director, psychometrician*
Feldt, Leonard Samuel *university educator and administrator*
Hines, N. William *dean, law educator, administrator*
Roe, Gerald Bruce *director, writer*
Vaughan, Emmett John *academic dean, insurance educator*

Pacific Junction
Krogstad, Jack Lynn *associate dean, accounting educator*

KANSAS

Baldwin City
Lambert, Daniel Michael *academic administrator*

El Dorado
Edwards, James Lynn *college dean*

Emporia
Schallenkamp, Kay *academic administrator*

Frontenac
Wilson, Donald Wallin *academic administrator, communications educator*

Hays
Hammond, Edward H. *university president*

Lawrence
Locke, Carl Edwin, Jr., *academic administrator, engineering educator*
Wiechert, Allen LeRoy *educational planning consultant, architect*

Liberal
Rodenberg, Anita Jo *academic administrator*

Manhattan
May, Cheryl Elaine *university official*
Muir, William Lloyd, III, *academic administrator*

Pittsburg
Smoot, Joseph Grady *university administrator*
Sullivan, F(rank) Victor *university administrator, retired educator*

Salina
Talley, Melvin Gary *academic administrator*

Topeka
McFarland, William Joseph (Joe McFarland) *academic administrator*

Wichita
Kindrick, Robert LeRoy *academic administrator, dean, English educator*

KENTUCKY

Bowling Green
Beck, Ronald Dudley *university administrator*

Danville
Roush, John A *academic administrator*

Lexington
Peck, Claudia Jones *associate dean*
Southgate, Paul Gregory *information administrator*
Taylor, Paul Franklin *college dean*
Thelin, John Robert *academic administrator, education educator, historian*
Wethington, Charles T., Jr., *academic administrator*
Zinser, Elisabeth Ann *academic administrator*

Louisville
Kmetz, Donald R. *retired academic administrator*
Swain, Donald Christie *retired university president, history educator*

LOUISIANA

Alexandria
Wesse, David Joseph *higher education administrator, consultant*

Baton Rouge
Hamilton, John Maxwell *university dean, writer*
Smith, Michael *college president*

Grambling
Warner, Neari Francois *university president*

Lake Charles
Hebert, Robert D. *academic administrator*

New Orleans
Cowen, Scott S. *academic administrator*
Crisp, John N. *engineering educator, former dean*
Kelly, Eamon Michael *university president emeritus*
Sherman, Edward Francis *dean, law educator*

MAINE

Augusta
Huffman, Durward Roy *college system official, electrical engineer*

Bar Harbor
Krevans, Julius Richard *university administrator, physician*

Bremen
Wilson, Linda Smith *academic administrator*

Fairfield
Douglas, Jeanne Masson *academic administrator, education educator*

Fort Kent
Cost, Richard Willard *university administrator, educator*

Lewiston
Hansen, Elaine T. *academic administrator*

Oakland
Asmussen, J. Donna *retired educational administrator, researcher, artist*

Orono
Rauch, Charles Frederick, Jr., *retired university official and business educator*

Portland
Gilmore, Roger *college consultant*
Pattenaude, Richard Louis *university administrator*

Waterville
Adams, WilliaM D. *academic administrator*
Cook, Susan Farwell *associate director planned giving*

MARYLAND

Annapolis
Keller, Michael Jay *research director*
Nuesse, Celestine Joseph *retired university official*

Baltimore
Behm, Mark Edward *university administrator, consultant*
Brody, William Ralph *academic administrator, radiologist, educator*
Ellis, Brother Patrick (H. J. Ellis) *academic administrator*
Fletcher, Sherryl Ann *higher education administrator*
Gifford, Donald George *legal educator*
Hrabowski, Freeman Alphonsa, III, *university president*
Lazarus, Fred, IV, *college president*
McPartland, James Michael *university official*
Poehler, Theodore Otto *university provost, engineer, researcher*
Resides, Diane Louise *academic administrator*
Richardson, Earl Stanford *university president*
Ross, Richard Starr *medical school dean emeritus, cardiologist*
Trabilsy, David Mitchell *academic administrator*

Bethesda
August, Diane L. *independent education consultant, policy and reading researcher*
Pruitt, France Juliard *international educational consultant*

Bowie
McManus, Mary Hairston *academic administrator*

Chevy Chase
Curris, Constantine William *university president*
Ostar, Allan William *academic administrator, higher education consultant*

College Park
De Salvo, Lorraine Constance *academic administrator*
Prentice, Ann Ethelynd *university dean*
Stumpff, Robert Thomas *academic administrator*
Szymanski, Edna Mora *dean*
Toll, John Sampson *university president, physics educator*

Hagerstown
Spruill, Howard Vernon *former academic administrator, minister*

Kennedyville
Schiff, Gary Stuart *academic administrator, educator, consultant*

Millington
Blackston, Barbara Jean *dean*

Princess Anne
Hytche, William Percy *university president*
Merwin, Debra Lee *university counseling director*

Saint Michaels
Feisel, Lyle Dean *retired dean, electrical engineer, educator*

Salisbury
Bello, Zakri Yau *academic administrator*
Randrup, Joy Davidson *college administrator*

Silver Spring
Boykin, Nancy Merritt *academic administrator*
Coles, Anna Louise Bailey *retired university official, nurse*
Pearman, Reginald James *educational administrator*
Schick, Irvin Henry *academic administrator, educator*

Stevenson
Hyman, Mary Bloom *science education programs coordinator*
Manning, Kevin James *academic administrator*

Swanton
Cummins, Delmer Duane *academic administrator, historian*

Towson
Boucher, Laurence James *educator, chemist*

Westminster
Rosenthal, Michael Ross *academic administrator, consultant*

Wye Mills
Woods, Willie G. *dean, English language and education educator*

MASSACHUSETTS

Amherst
MacKnight, Carol Bernier *educational administrator*
Marx, Anthony W. *academic administrator*
Prince, Gregory Smith, Jr., *academic administrator*

Auburndale
Winter, Elizabeth H. *educational administrator*

Boston
Berk, Lee Eliot *academic administrator*
Caldwell, Ann Wickins *academic administrator*
Cass, Ronald Andrew *dean*
Chobanian, Aram *medical school dean, cardiologist*
Dujon, Diane Marie *director, activist*

Freeland, Richard Middleton *academic administrator, historian*
Maganzini, Brother John Bernard *academic administrator*
Penney, Sherry Hood *university president, educator*
Rittner, Stephen Lee *academic administrator*
Ronayne, Michael Richard, Jr., *academic dean*
Shattuck, Lawrence William *admissions director*
Silber, John Robert *university chancellor, philosophy and law educator*
Wilcke, Marilyn Ann (Midge Wilcke) *university administrator*

Cambridge
Baumgartner, Mary Anne Sgarlat *academic administrator, entrepreneur*
Fox, John Bayley, Jr., *university dean*
Gray, Paul Edward *academic official*
Khoury, Philip S. *academic administrator*
Rowe, Mary P. *organizational ombudsman, management educator*
Schmalensee, Richard Lee *dean, economist, former government official, educator*
Seaman, Jeffrey Richard *academic administrator*
Vest, Charles Marstiller *academic administrator*

Chestnut Hill
Altbach, Philip *director, educator*
Leahy, William P. *academic administrator, historian, educator*
Smyer, Michael Anthony *dean, educator, gerontologist*

Concord
Brown, Linda Weaver *academic administrator*

Great Barrington
Rodgers, Bernard Francis, Jr., *academic administrator, dean*

Haverhill
Kelley, David Brian *community college dean, educator, consultant*

Holland
McGrory, Mary Kathleen *retired college president*

Lexington
Kilson, Marion *college dean*

Medford
Bacow, Lawrence Seldon *academic administrator, environmental educator*
Gittleman, Sol *university official, humanities educator*
Swap, Walter Charles *academic dean, psychology educator*

North Andover
Gannon, Patricia J. *academic administrator*

North Falmouth
Green, Linda C. *education specialist administrator, researcher*

Northampton
Christ, Carol Tecla *academic administrator*

Plymouth
Paul, Carol Ann *retired academic administrator, biology educator*

Shrewsbury
Onorato, Nicholas Louis *retired program director, economist*

South Hadley
Creighton, Joanne Vanish *academic administrator*

Springfield
Caprio, Anthony S. *academic administrator*
Courniotes, Harry James *academic administrator*
Scibelli, Andrew M. *academic administrator*

Sudbury
Campbell, Elaine Josephine *retired educational director, writer, critic, educator*

Swansea
Curry, Thomas John *academic administrator*

Waltham
Reinharz, Jehuda *academic administrator, history educator*

Wellesley
Auerbach, Jerold S. *university educator*
Tucker, John Avery *retired academic administrator, electrical engineer*
Walsh, Diana Chapman *academic administrator, sociologist, educator*

Williamstown
Schapiro, Morton Owen *university administrator*

Worcester
Berth, Donald Frank *university official, consultant*
Lazare, Aaron *dean, psychiatrist*
McFarland, Michael C. *academic administrator*
Orwig, Timothy Thomas *academic administrator, writer*
Traina, Richard Paul *academic administrator*

MICHIGAN

Adrian
Caine, Stanley Paul *college administrator*

Ann Arbor
Cole, David Edward *university administrator*
Copeland, Carolyn Abigail *retired university dean*
Duderstadt, James Johnson *academic administrator, engineering educator*
Paul, Ara Garo *university dean*
Sullivan, Thomas Patrick *academic administrator*
Warner, Robert Mark *university dean, archivist, historian*
White, B. Joseph *former dean, business educator*

Battle Creek
Bishop, Joyce Ann *director*
Mawdsley, Jack Kinrade *retired education program administrator*

Benton Harbor
Smith, Cathy *academic administrator*

Berrien Springs
Lesher, William Richard *retired academic administrator*

Big Rapids
Ryan, Ray Darl, Jr., *academic administrator*

Detroit
Alford, Sandra Elaine *university official*
Barrett, Nancy Smith *university administrator*
Semanik, Anthony James *instructional technology supervisor*
Williams, Roger *academic administrator*

East Lansing
Honhart, Frederick Lewis, III, *academic director*
McPherson, Melville Peter *academic administrator, former government official*
Zhoa, Yong *academic administrator, educator*

Grand Rapids
Calkins, Richard W. *former college president*
Lubbers, Arend Donselaar *retired academic administrator*

Holland
Nyenhuis, Jacob Eugene *college official*

Houghton
Tompkins, Curtis Johnston *academic administrator*

Kalamazoo
Haenicke, Diether Hans *academic administrator emeritus, educator*

Lansing
Butcher, Amanda Kay *retired university administrator*
Straus, Kathleen Nagler *education administrator, consultant*

Midland
Chen, Catherine Wang *provost*

Mount Pleasant
Carlson, Charles Evans *university official*

Olivet
Mahmoudi, Hoda *academic administrator, sociology educator*

Pontiac
Decker, Peter William *academic administrator*

Riverview
Thompson, LaVerne Elizabeth Thomas *college official*

Sault Sainte Marie
Youngblood, Betty J. *academic administrator*

University Center
Gilbertson, Eric Raymond *academic administrator, lawyer*

MINNESOTA

Bemidji
Norris, Gerald Lee *dean*

Burnsville
Freeburg, Richard L. *primary education educator*

Hopkins
Ramberg, Patricia Lynn *college president*

Marshall
Danahar, David C. *academic administrator, historian, educator*

Minneapolis
Johnson, David Chester *university chancellor, sociology educator*
Jorgensen, Daniel Fred *academic executive*
Schuh, G(eorge) Edward *university dean, agricultural economist*

Moorhead
Dille, Roland Paul *college president*

Northfield
Oden, Robert A., Jr., *academic administrator*

Saint Paul
Brushaber, George Karl *academic administrator, minister*
McCormick, James Harold *academic administrator*

Winona
Krueger, Darrell William *academic administrator*

MISSISSIPPI

Cleveland
McArthur, W(illiam) Frank, Jr., *academic administrator*
Wyatt, Forest Kent *university president emeritus*

Hattiesburg
Henry, Myron *academic administrator*

Jackson
Harmon, George Marion *academic administrator*
Johnson, Curtis *alumni affairs administrator, enrollment management administrator*
Lindsay, Susan Ruchti *school director*

Mississippi State
Hewitt, Patricia Bradley *academic administrator*
Rent, Clyda Stokes *academic administrator*

University
Sam, Joseph *retired university dean*

MISSOURI

Columbia
Fluharty, Charles William *policy institute director, consultant, policy researcher*

Hallsville
Christy, Shelia *university official, information specialist*

Kansas City
Barry, Louise McCants *retired college official*
Oliver, Bernard *academic dean*
Sizemore, William Christian *retired academic administrator, county official*

Kimberling City
Stovall, Richard L. *retired academic administrator*

Kirksville
Dixon, Barbara Bruinekool *provost*

Lees Summit
Smith, Dwyane *university administrator*

Maryville
Hubbard, Dean Leon *university president*

Saint Louis
Briggs, Cynthia Anne *educational administrator, clinical psychologist*
Byrnes, Christopher Ian *academic dean, researcher*
Danforth, William Henry *retired academic administrator, physician*
Dodge, Paul Cecil *academic administrator*
Kennelly, Sister Karen Margaret *retired academic administrator, church administrator, nun*
Koff, Robert Hess *academic administrator*
Lovin, Keith Harold *academic administrator, philosophy educator*
Pflueger, M(elba) Lee Counts *academic administrator*
Reed, Sheila Kaye *academic administrator*
Seligman, Joel *dean*
White, Gloria Waters *retired university administrator*
Wood, Samuel Eugene *college administrator, psychology educator*

Springfield
Good, Stephen Hanscom *academic administrator*
Gordon, Marshall *former university president*
Hawkins, Ralph G(erald) *university media administrator, educator*
Quiroga, Ninoska *university official*
Smith, Judith Ann *academic administrator*

Trenton
Hannaford, Karla *college official*

Troy
Lawrence, John R. *academic administrator*

Unity Village
Boehm, Toni Georgene *seminary dean, nurse, minister*

MONTANA

Dillon
Jimeno, Cheri Annette *dean*

Havre
Lanier, William Joseph *college program director*

Helena
Morton, Claudette *education administrator*
O'Reilly, Frances Louise *academic administrator*

NEBRASKA

Blair
Christopherson, Myrvin Frederick *college president*

Lincoln
Grew, Priscilla Croswell *university official, geology educator*
Hermance, Lyle Herbert *retired college official*
Omtvedt, Irvin Thomas *academic administrator, educator*
Schkade, Anthony Roland *academic administrator*
Smith, Lewis *academic administrator, educator*

Omaha
Bruckner, Martha *academic administrator*
Moskus, Jerry Ray *academic administrator, educator*
Schlegel, John P. *academic administrator*

NEVADA

Carson City
Wadman, William Wood, III, *educational director, technical research executive, consulting company executive*

Incline Village
White, Richard Hugh *dean student affairs*

Las Vegas
Hall, Gene E. *dean*
Harter, Carol Clancey *university president, English language educator*
Rice, Stephen Landon *university official*

Reno
Crowley, Joseph Neil *university president, political science educator*
Lilley, John Mark *academic administrator, dean*

NEW HAMPSHIRE

Chester
Hoar, John Bernard *dean*

Durham
Eggers, Walter Frederick *academic administrator*
Farrell, William Joseph *university chancellor*

Hanover
Freedman, James Oliver *former university president, lawyer*
Wright, James Edward *academic administrator, historian, educator*

Keene
Donnelly, Joan Mary *college program director*

Manchester
Sullivan, Robert Martin *educational fundraiser*

Rindge
Palmer, Bruce Harrison *academic administrator*

NEW JERSEY

Caldwell
Ott, Walter Richard *academic administrator*
Werner, Patrice (Patricia Ann Werner) *college president*

Camden
Lawrence, Francis Leo *former university president, language educator*
Leontiades, Milton *dean*

Cherry Hill
Kapel, David Edward *retired academic administrator, education educator*

Elizabeth
Rocha, Pedro, Jr., *academic administrator, educator*

Fort Lee
Young, Vera Lee Hall *educational administrator, association executive*

Glassboro
Gephardt, Donald Louis *university official*
James, Herman Delano *former college administrator*
Libro, Antoinette Christine *university dean*

Hackettstown
Quade, Robert Thomas *business educator*

Lawrenceville
Rozanski, Mordechai *academic administrator*

Lodi
Pivinski, Sister Mary Lorene *academic administrator*

Madison
Kean, Thomas H. *academic administrator, former governor*
Mertz, Francis James *university president*

Matawan
Liggett, Twila Marie Christensen *academic administrator, public television executive*

New Brunswick
Chasek, Arlene Shatsky *academic director*
Henry, Paula Louise (Paula Louise Henry Coover) *academic administrator*
McCormick, Richard Levis *academic administrator*
Paz, Harold Louis *dean, medical educator, internist*
Sapirman, Nadine Kadell *university official*

Newark
Bergen, Stanley Silvers, Jr., *retired university president, physician*
Fenster, Saul K. *university president emeritus*
Gibson, David M. *dean*

North Arlington
Batshaw, Marilyn Seidner *education administrator*

Piscataway
Dill, Ellis Harold *university dean*
Lee, Barbara Anne *educator, lawyer*

Pomona
Colijn, Geert Jan *academic administrator, political scientist*
Comfort, Priscilla Maria *retired college official, human resources professional*

Princeton
Dobin, Hank (Howard) *academic administrator, English language and literature educator*
Malkiel, Nancy Weiss *dean, historian, educator*
Ramana, M. V. *director*
Shapiro, Harold Tafler *former academic administrator, economist*
Tilghman, Shirley Marie *academic administrator, biology educator*

South Amboy
Moskal, Anthony John *former dean, professor, management and education consultant*

Stratford
Schurig Rollins, Sandra L. *academic administrator*

Trenton
Pruitt, George Albert *college president*

West Long Branch
Gaffney, Paul Golden, II, *academic administrator, military officer*

NEW MEXICO

Albuquerque
Caldera, Louis Edward *academic administrator, former federal official*
Garcia, F. Chris *academic administrator, political science educator, public opinion researcher*
Lattman, Laurence Harold *retired academic administrator*
Trojahn, Lynn *academic administrator*

Hobbs
Stanley, Sheryl Lynn *college administrator*

Portales
Byrnes, Lawrence William *dean*
Dixon, Steven Michael *university administrator*

Santa Fe
Harcourt, Robert Neff *educational administrator, journalist, genealogist*

NEW YORK

Albany
Lipetz, Ben-Ami *dean, information science educator*
Long, David Russell *academic program director*
Thornton, Maurice *retired academic administrator*

Alfred
Coll, Edward Girard, Jr., *university president*
Hunter, John Orr *college president*

Annandale On Hudson
Botstein, Leon *academic administrator, conductor, historian*

Aurora
Leybold-Taylor, Karla Jolene *college official*

Bellport
Schultheis, Edwin Milford *dean, business educator*

Binghamton
DeFleur, Lois B. *university president, sociology educator*
Meador, John Milward, Jr., *university dean*

Brentwood
Manning, Randolph H. *academic administrator*

Briarcliff Manor
Coppola, Jean Frances *university program administrator*

Brockport
Campbell, Jill Frost *university official*
Stier, William Frederick, Jr., *academic administrator, educator*

Bronx
Damico, Debra Lynn *college official, English and French educator*
Fernandez, Ricardo R. *university administrator*
Purpura, Dominick P. *dean, neuroscientist*
Samuels, Angella V. *academic administrator*
Scanlan, Thomas Joseph *college president, educator*

Bronxville
Myers, Michele Tolela *academic administrator*

Brooklyn
Lacey, John Derek *university administrator, admissions counselor*
Madama, Patrick Stephen *academic official*
May, David A. *retired dean*

Buffalo
Durand, Henry J., Jr., *academic administrator*
Greiner, William Robert *university administrator, educator, lawyer*
Gress, Edward J(ules) *educator, consultant*
Herdlein, Richard Joseph, III, *college official and dean, educator*
Thurston, John Thomas *university advancement official*

Catskill
Wolfe, Geraldine *administrator*

Cazenovia
Durgin, Patricia Harte *college administrator, chemistry educator, counselor*

Cicero
Webster, Michael Lee *academic administrator*

Clinton
Havens, Pamela Ann *college official*

Commack
Cohen, Judith W. *retired academic administrator*

Crown Point
Dajany, Innam *academic administrator*

Dix Hills
Gee, David E. *academic administrator*

East Hampton
Goldstein, Judith Shelley *reading and learning specialist*
Schetlin, Eleanor M. *retired university official*

Falconer
Benke, Paul Arthur *academic administrator*

Farmingdale
Cipriani, Frank Anthony *former college president*

Fayetteville
Mirucki, Maureen Ann *retired academic administrator*

Garden City
Fanelli, Sean A. *college president*
Scott, Robert Allyn *academic administrator*
Shuart, James Martin *retired academic administrator*
Webb, Igor Michael *academic administrator*

Geneseo
Mooney, Michael C. *athletic administrator, soccer coach*

Grafton
McGowan, Sister Mary Kenan *retired alumni affairs director*

Greenvale
Shenker, Joseph *academic administrator*
Steinberg, David Joel *academic administrator, historian, educator*
Westermann-Cicio, Mary Louise *academic administrator, library studies educator*

Hamilton
Chopp, Rebecca S. *university president*

Hempstead
Berliner, Herman Albert *university provost and officer, economics educator*
Salten, David George

Huntington Station
Kelly, Michael Joseph *academic administrator, consultant*

Ithaca
Lehman, Jeffrey Sean *academic administrator, educator*
Nesheim, Malden C. *academic administrator, nutrition educator*
Wavle, Elizabeth Margaret *college official*
Weinstein, Leonard Harlan *institute program director, educator*

Jackson Heights
Gall, Lenore Rosalie *educational administrator*

Jamaica
Harrington, Donald James *university president*
McGuire, Patrick Pearse *academic administrator*
McKenzie, André *academic administrator, educator*
Mullen, Frank Albert *former university official, clergyman*

Long Island City
Lieberman, Janet Elaine *academic administrator*

Melville
Atkins, William Allen *academic administrator*

Merrick
Garfinkel, Lawrence Saul *academic administrator, educator, television producer*

Morrisville
Cleland, Gladys Lee *university administrator, adult education educator*

New Paltz
Poskanzer, Steven Gary *university administrator, lawyer*

New Rochelle
Sweeny, Stephen Jude *academic administrator*

New York
Amster, Jeanne E. *school director*
Bollinger, Lee Carroll *academic administrator, law educator*
Boylan, Elizabeth Shippee *academic administrator, biology educator*
Brademas, John *retired university president, former congressman*
Budig, Gene Arthur *former chancellor, professional sports executive*
Claster, Jill Nadell *university administrator, history educator*
Cochran, Raymond Martin *university auditor*
Conyard, Shirley Jean *college dean*
Ewers, Patricia O'Donnell *university administrator*
Feldberg, Meyer *university dean*
Gerety, Tom *academic administrator, lawyer, educator, philosopher*
Gottschalk, Alfred *retired college chancellor, museum executive*
Grossman, Allen, III, *educational administrator*
Haffner, Alden Norman *university official*
Hartstein, Sam *public relations professional*
Hood, Donald Charles *university administrator, psychology educator*
Horowitz, Frances Degen *academic administrator, psychology educator*
Jelinek, Vera *university director*
Jeynes, Mary Kay *college dean*
Joel, Richard Marc *academic administrator, law educator, dean*
Lamm, Norman *academic administrator, rabbi*
Lattin, Vernon Eugene *academic administrator*
Laurenson, David James *academic director*
Leebron, David Wayne *dean, law educator*
Levine, Naomi Bronheim *academic administrator*
Lynch, Gerald Weldon *academic administrator, psychologist*
Marcus, Steven *dean, English educator*
Marcuse, Adrian Gregory *academic administrator*
Mills, Barry *academic administrator, lawyer*
Morreale, Joseph Constantino *higher education administrator, public administration educator, economic and financial consultant*
Oliva, Lawrence Jay *former academic administrator, history educator*
Pawliczko, George Ihor *academic administrator*
Polisi, Joseph W(illiam) *academic administrator*
Rhodes, David J. *academic administrator*
Rosensaft, Jean Bloch *university administrator*
Rudenstine, Neil Leon *former academic administrator, educator*
Rupp, George Erik *not-for-profit administrator*
Scaffidi, Judith Ann *academic administrator*
Sexton, John Edward *academic administrator, law educator*
Shapiro, Judith R. *academic administrator, anthropology educator*
Shields, James Joseph *education administrator, educator, author*
Socol, Sheldon Eleazer *university official*
Somville, Marilyn F. *retired dean*
Walzer, Judith Borodovko *academic administrator, educator*
Williams, Harriet Clarke *retired academic administrator*
Yetman, Leith Eleanor *academic administrator*
Yu, Pauline Ruth *former dean, educational association administrator*

Old Westbury
Dibble, Richard Edward *academic administrator*
Saueracker, Edward *academic administrator*

Oneonta
Markuson, Cira Profit *college administrator*

Oyster Bay
Hoxie, Ralph Gordon *educational administrator, author*

Painted Post
Trombley, Donald B. *academic administrator*

Potsdam
Ratliff, Gerald Lee *academic administrator*

Poughkeepsie
Conklin, D(onald) David *academic administrator*
Cox, Gerard Anthony *academic director*
Fergusson, Frances Daly *college president, educator*
Pollak, Joel Michael *director*

Remsenburg
Hirsch, Ann Ullman *retired academic administrator*

Rexford
Schmitt, Roland Walter *retired academic administrator*

Riverhead
Connors, William Francis, Jr., *dean*

Rochester
Cohen, Jules *physician, educator, former academic dean*
Jackson, Thomas Humphrey *academic administrator, lawyer*
McKenzie, Stanley Don *academic administrator, English educator*

Saratoga Springs
Glotzbach, Philip A. *academic administrator*

Schenectady
Hull, Roger Harold *academic administrator*
Zacek, Jane Shapiro *director*

Staten Island
Springer, Marlene *university administrator, educator*

Stony Brook
Kenny, Shirley Strum *academic administrator*

Syracuse
Coliz, James Russell *university administrator, telecommunications consultant*
Fairbanks, Mary Joanne *educational administrator*
Miles, Kenneth Ontario *academic program director*
Rubin, David M. *dean, educator*
Ware, Bennie *university administrator*

Tarrytown
Berg, Sister Marie Majella *retired academic administrator*

Troy
Judd, Gary *university administrator*

Valhalla
Hankin, Joseph Nathan *college president*

NORTH CAROLINA

Banner Elk
Thomas, John Edwin *retired academic administrator*

Bolivia
Hewett, Joyce Parker *educational administrator*

Boone
Durham, Harvey Ralph *academic administrator*

Chapel Hill
Carroll, Roy *retired academic administrator*
Magill, Samuel Hays *academic administrator, higher education consultant*
Moeser, James Charles *university chancellor, musician*
Murphy, James Lee *college dean, economics educator*
Roper, William Lee *dean, physician*
Sanders, John Lassiter *retired academic administrator*

Charlotte
Calhoun, Mary Lynne *dean*
Hardin, Elizabeth Ann *academic administrator*
Mosier, Stephen Russell *college program director, physicist*
Tyson, Cynthia Haldenby *academic administrator*
Woodward, James Hoyt *academic administrator, engineer*

Conover
Sims, Janette Elizabeth Lowman *educational director*

Cullowhee
Coulter, Myron Lee *retired academic administrator*
Reed, Alfred Douglas *retired academic administrator*

Davidson
Vagt, Robert F. *academic administrator*

Durham
Keller, Thomas Franklin *business administration educator*
Keohane, Nannerl Overholser *university president, political scientist*
Kuniholm, Bruce Robellet *university administrator*
Schmalbeck, Richard Louis *university dean, lawyer*
Stanley, Carol Jones *academic administrator, educator*

Elizabeth City
Burnim, Mickey L. *academic administrator*
White, Leon Samuel *college administrator*

Fayetteville
Friedman, Deborah Leslie White *educational administrator*
Watt, Willis Martin *academic administrator, communications, adult education, leadership educator*

Fletcher
Jahnke, Jessica Jo *university administrator, dean*

Greensboro
Alston, Charlotte LeNora *college administrator*
Averett-Short, Geneva Evelyn *college administrator*
Barnett, Dorothy Prince *retired university dean*
Buford Speight, Velma Ruth *retired alumni affairs director*
Fort, Edward Bernard *university chancellor*
McNemar, Donald William *academic administrator*
Moran, William Edward *academic administrator*

Greenville
Eakin, Richard Ronald *academic educator, mathematics educator*
Leggett, Nancy Porter *university administrator*
Muse, William Van *academic administrator*

High Point
Martinson, Jacob Christian, Jr., *academic administrator*

Kinston
Matthis, Eva Mildred Boney *retired academic administrator*
Scott, Stephen Carlos *academic administrator*

Lake Junaluska
Stanton, Donald Sheldon *academic administrator*

Laurinburg
Deegan, John, Jr., *academic administrator, researcher*

Morganton
Knox, George Charles *college dean*

New Bern
Hemphill, Jean Hargett *college dean*

Pembroke
Meadors, Allen Coats *health administrator, educator*

Raleigh
Robinson, Prezell Russell *academic administrator*

Salisbury
Heymann, Hans Paulsen *community college administrator*

Summerfield
Appenzeller, Herb Thomas *retired education administrator, coach*

Wilmington
DePaolo, Rosemary *dean, academic administrator*
Leutze, James Richard *academic administrator, television producer and host*

Winston Salem
Ewing, Alexander Cochran *retired chancellor*
Hall, Dorothy Louise Parzyk *academic administrator*
Hearn, Thomas K., Jr., *university president*
Hobgood, E(arl) Wade *college chancellor*
Suttles, Donald Roland *retired academic administrator, business educator*
Thrift, Julianne Still *academic administrator*

NORTH DAKOTA

Dickinson
Conn, Philip Wesley *academic administrator*

Grand Forks
Page, Sally Jacquelyn *university official*

Minot
Shaar, H. Erik *academic administrator*

OHIO

Ada
Baker, Kendall L. *academic administrator*
Freed, DeBow *academic administrator*

Akron
Dietz, Margaret Jane *retired public information director*

Ashland
Drushal, Mary Ellen *educator, former university provost*

Athens
Bruning, James Leon *academic administrator, educator*
Moreno, Rosa-Maria *modern languages educator*

Berea
Hairston, Jay Timothy *college administrator*

Canton
Niece, Richard Dean *academic administrator*

Cincinnati
Berry, Michael Cody *educational administrator*
Boothe, Leon Estel *academic administrator emeritus, consultant*
Callan, Terrance Dennis, Jr., *dean, religious studies educator*
Dykes, Bill G. *principal, administrator*
Jackson, Cynthia Lynn *academic dean*
Nester, William Raymond, Jr., *retired academic administrator and educator*
Smith, Gregory Allgire *college administrator*
Winkler, Henry Ralph *retired academic administrator, historian*
Zimpher, Nancy Lusk *academic administrator*

Cleveland
Ainsworth, Joan Horsburgh *university development director*
Cavanagh, Peter Robert *academic administrator, department chairman, science educator, researcher*
Cerone, David *academic administrator*
Hundert, Edward M. *academic administrator*
Jones, Rosemary *college official*

Columbus
Alutto, Joseph Anthony *university dean, management educator*
Baughman, George Washington, III, *retired university official, financial consultant*
Dietrich, Carol Elizabeth *educator, former dean*
Fields, Henry William *college dean*
Heinlen, Daniel Lee *alumni organization administrator*
Miller, Wayne Clayton *student services administrator, notary public*
Otte, Paul John *academic administrator, consultant, trainer*
Perrone, Ruth Ellyn *university administrator*
Williams, Gregory Howard *dean, law educator*

Delta
Miller, Beverly White *former college president, educational consultant, consultant*

Elyria
Bowen, Thomas Lee *academic administrator*
Ugwu, David Egbo *academic director, consulting company executive*

Findlay
Martin, Richard Howard *academic program director*

Gambier
Nugent, S. Georgia *academic administrator*

Highland Hills
Sender, Maryann *director*

Kent
Cartwright, Carol Ann *university president*
Gaston, Paul Lee *academic administrator, language educator*

Stevens, George Edward *dean, academic administrator*

Lima
Meek, Violet Imhof *retired dean*

Mansfield
Riedl, John Orth *university dean*

Oberlin
Dye, Nancy Schrom *academic administrator, historian, educator*

Oxford
Shriver, Phillip Raymond *academic administrator*

Sidney
Seitz, James Eugene *retired college president, freelance writer*

Springfield
Kinnison, William Andrew *retired university president*

Toledo
Jacobs, Ruth Ann *program director*
Weinblatt, Charles Samuel *university administrator, employment consultant*

Uniontown
Pettigrew, Frank Edwin, Jr., *assistant dean, physical education educator*

Westerville
Diersing, Carolyn Virginia *educational administrator*

Wilberforce
Henderson, John L. *academic administrator*
Svager, Thyrsa Anne Frazier *university administrator, retired educator*
Walker-Taylor, Yvonne *retired college president*
Williamson, Vikki Lyn *university official, financial executive*

Youngstown
Atwater, Tony *provost, dean, educator*
Becker, Karen Ann *university program administrator*
Cochran, Leslie Herschel *university administrator*
Loch, John Robert *university administrator*

OKLAHOMA

Altus
Brown, Roger Dale *academic administrator*

Bethany
Crabtree, John Michael *college administrator, consultant*

Disney
Hamilton, Carl Hulet *retired academic administrator*

Enid
Jones, Kathryn Anne *academic administrator*

Norman
Van Horn, Richard Linley *academic administrator*

Oklahoma City
Alexander, Patrick Byron *university administrator*
Sibley, William Arthur *academic administrator, physics educator, consultant*
Woods, Pendleton *college director, author*

Ponca City
Rice, Sue Ann *dean, industrial and organizational psychologist*

Pryor
Titsworth, Tobie Richard, III, *academic administrator*

Shawnee
Wilks, Jacquelin Holsomback *campus ministries director*

Stillwater
Halligan, James Edmund *university administrator, chemical engineer*

Tahlequah
Howard, James Kenton *academic administrator, journalist*
Williams, Larry Bill *academic administrator*

Tulsa
Donaldson, Robert Herschel *university administrator, educator*
Roger, Jerry Lee *academic administrator*
Trennepohl, Gary Lee *university administrator, finance educator*

Union City
Strange, Frances Rathbun *financial aid administrator, therapist*

Woodward
Fisher, Deena Kaye *social studies education administrator*

OREGON

Albany
Smart, Ann Catherine *dean*

Corvallis
Byrne, John Vincent *higher education consultant*

Healey, Deborah Lynn *education administrator*
Parker, Donald Fred *college dean, human resources management educator*
Risser, Paul Gillan *academic administrator, botanist*
Verts, Lita Jeanne *university administrator*

Eugene
Foley, Charles Bradford *university dean, music educator*
Heiss, James Edward *university administrator, accountant*
McMillan, Adell *retired educational administrator*
Pickett, Stephen Wesley *academic administrator, consultant*

Gresham
Webb, Donna Louise *academic director, educator*

Joseph
Gilbert, David Erwin *retired academic administrator, physicist*

Mcminnville
Howland, Peter McKinnon *academic administrator*

Oceanside
Wadlow, Joan Krueger *academic administrator*

Portland
Cox, Joseph William *former academic administrator, education educator*
Diver, Colin S. *academic administrator, educator*
Fawcett, Lee C. *retired dean*
Lawson, Lolita Agnes *academic administrator*
Martin, Ernest Lee *academic administrator, historian, theologian, writer*
Tufts, Robert B. *academic administrator*

Roseburg
Johnson, Doris Ann *educational administrator*

Salem
Haring-Smith, Tori *academic administrator*
Pelton, M Lee *academic administrator*

PENNSYLVANIA

Allentown
Procopio, Marylouise Elizabeth *college program director*

Annville
Pollick, G. David *academic administrator, philosopher*

Bethlehem
Farrington, Gregory C. *university administrator*

Blue Bell
Brendlinger, LeRoy R. *academic administrator*
Rizzo, Gary Edward *academic administrator*

Bryn Mawr
Smith, Nona Coates *academic administrator*
Vickers, Nancy J. *academic administrator*

Carlisle
Durden, William G. *academic administrator*

Center Valley
Gambet, Daniel G(eorge) *college president, clergyman*

Chester
Bruce, Robert James *retired academic administrator*
Buck, Lawrence Paul *academic administrator, educator*

Coatesville
Strauser, Simeon John *academic administrator*

Devon
Garbarino, Robert Paul *retired administrative dean, lawyer*

Du Bois
Schoch, Jacqueline Louise *retired academic administrator*

Easton
Rothkopf, Arthur J. *college president*

Erie
Daly, Mary *college administrator*
Dever, Merrill Thomas *academic administrator, retired police chief*

Gettysburg
Haaland, Gordon Arthur *psychologist, university president*

Gibsonia
Korchnak, Lawrence C. *educational administrator, consultant, writer*

Harrisburg
Hample, Judy G. *academic administrator*

Haverford
Tritton, Thomas Richard *academic administrator, biologist, educator*

Hazleton
Stevens, Linda Tollestrup *academic director*

Indiana
Pettit, Lawrence Kay *university president*

Kutztown
McFarland, David E. *university official*

La Plume
Boehm, Edward Gordon, Jr., *college administrator, educator*

Lancaster
Drum, Alice *academic administrator, educator*
Fry, John Anderson *university president*
Kneedler, Richard (Alvin Kneedler) *former academic administrator*

Langhorne
Babb, Wylie Sherrill *college president*

Latrobe
Mans, Thomas Charles *academic administrator*

Lincoln University
Nelson, Ivory Vance *academic administrator*

Lock Haven
Willis, Craig Dean *academic administrator*

Macungie
Rubin, Arthur Herman *retired university official, consultant*

Martinsburg
Neff, Robert Wilbur *academic administrator, educator, minister*

Moon Township
Tannehill, Darcy Anita Bartins *academic administrator*

Nanticoke
Donohue, Patricia Carol *academic administrator*

New Castle
Halm, Nancye Studd *retired private school administrator*

Orefield
Shappell, Vaughn Scott *education director, educator*

Philadelphia
Aversa, Dolores Sejda *educational administrator*
Bates, James Earl *academic administrator*
Caplan, Arthur *university program director, educator*
Cohen, David Walter *academic administrator, periodontist, educator*
Dunn, Mary Maples *former university dean*
Lentz, Bernard Frederic *university administrator*
Ludwig, Kurt James *residence director*
Nahary, Levia L. *campus programming director*
Presseisen, Barbara Zemboch *retired educational director, researcher*
Quillen, Mary Ann *university administrator, consultant*
Reichenbach, M. J. Gertrude *retired university program director, consultant*
Ricks, Thomas Miller *Middle East historian, university administrator*
Rodin, Judith Seitz *academic administrator, psychology educator*
Romer, Daniel *university official, psychologist, educator*
Rubenstein, Arthur Harold *medical school official, physician*
Rudczynski, Andrew B. *academic administrator, medical researcher*
Sheehan, Donald Thomas *retired academic administrator*
Sibolski, Elizabeth Hawley *higher education administrator*
Tawyea, Edward Wayne *university administrator, librarian*

Pittsburgh
Binstock, Linda Grossmann *educational administrator*
Cohon, Jared L. *academic administrator*
Gilbert, Shandel Sue *academic educational director, reading educator*
Howse, W. Frances *academic administrator*
McHoes, Ann McIver *academic administrator, computer systems consultant*
Summers, Tony Edward *academic administrator*

Reading
White, Thomas David, II, *academic administrator*

Scranton
Passon, Richard Henry *English language educator, former administrator*

Slippery Rock
Smith, Grant Warren, II, *university administrator, physical sciences educator*
Smith, Robert Mason *academic administrator*

Springboro
Lillie, Marshall Sherwood *college safety and security director, educator*

Swarthmore
Bloom, Alfred Howard *academic administrator, educator*

University Park
Shearer, Rick Leland *university official*
Spanier, Graham Basil *university president*
Tippeconnic, John W., III, *director, educator*

Upper Darby
Hudiak, David Michael *academic administrator*

Villanova
Dobbin, Edmund J. *university administrator*
Fitzpatrick, M. Louise *dean, nursing educator*

Washington
Mitchell, Brian Christopher *college president*

Wernersville
Panuska, Joseph Allan *academic administrator*

West Chester
Adler, Madeleine Wing *academic administrator*

West Mifflin
Archey, Mary Frances Elaine (Onofaro) *academic administrator, educator*
Gerity, Patrick Emmett *university executive director*

Wilkes Barre
Skvarla, Lucyann M. *college official*
Wells, David John *program director, academic administrator, mechanical engineer*

RHODE ISLAND

Kingston
Carothers, Robert Lee *academic administrator*
Springston, James Raymond *college administrator, educator*

Providence
Blumstein, Sheila Ellen *former academic administrator, linguistics educator*
Cooper, Caroline Ann *hospitality faculty dean*
Gaebe, Morris J. *academic administrator*
Greer, David S. *university dean, physician, educator*
Mandle, Earl Roger *design school president, former museum executive*
Simmons, Ruth J. *academic administrator*

Smithfield
Lema, Jo-Anne S. *academic administrator*

SOUTH CAROLINA

Aiken
Alexander, Robert Earl *university chancellor, educator*

Anderson
Martin, Terrell Owen *retired university administrator*

Central
Bell, Gloria Jean *academic administrator, literature educator, dean*

Charleston
Curtis, Marcia *university dean*
Hunter, Jairy C., Jr., *academic administrator*
Worthington, Ward Curtis, Jr., *university dean, anatomy educator*

Columbia
Kendrick, Richard Lofton *university administrator, consultant*
McCulloch, Anne Merline Jacobs *college dean*
Palms, John Michael *academic administrator, physicist*
Plyler, Chris Parnell *university administrator, dean*
Ruff, Dan George *academic administrator*

Conway
Wiseman, Dennis Gene *academic administrator*

Gaffney
Griffin, Walter Roland *college president, historian, educator*

Greenville
Brown, Wilbur C. *college director*
Payne, George Frederick *academic administrator*

Greenwood
Koenig, Daniel Dean *college dean*
Morgan, John Augustine *university executive, consultant*

Kiawah Island
Warren, Russell Glen *academic administrator*

Laurens
Dixon, Albert King, II, *retired university administrator*

Lexington
Gatch, Charles Edward, Jr., *academic administrator*

Mount Pleasant
Gilbert, James Eastham *academic administrator*

Prosperity
Hause, Edith Collins *college administrator*

Spartanburg
Fields, George D., Jr., *former college president*

SOUTH DAKOTA

Aberdeen
Ruud, Jay Wesley *dean*

Brookings
Miller, Peggy Gordon Elliott *university president*

Madison
Tunheim, Jerald Arden *academic administrator, physics educator*

TENNESSEE

Chapel Hill
Christman, Luther Parmalee *retired dean, consultant*

Chattanooga
Bartoo, Eugene Chester *academic administrator, educator*
Obear, Frederick Woods *academic administrator*
Stacy, Bill Wayne *academic administrator*

Cookeville
Peters, Ralph Martin *academic administrator*
Volpe, Angelo Anthony *former university president, chemistry educator*

Henderson
Gardner, Elmer Claude *academic administrator*

Jackson
Agee, Bob R. *academic administrator, educator, minister*
Barefoot, Hyran Euvene *academic administrator, educator, minister*

Jefferson City
Butler, Vickie Burkhart *college official*

Johnson City
Bishop, Wilsie Sue *dean, nursing educator*

Knoxville
South, Stephen A. *academic administrator*
Wisniewski, Richard *retired dean*

Memphis
Daughdrill, James Harold, Jr., *academic administrator*
Dunathan, Harmon Craig *college dean*
Hardy, Joy Miller *academic administrator, consultant*
Nesin, Jeffrey David *academic administrator*
Troutt, William Earl *academic administrator*
Werle, Robert Geary *academic administrator*

Murfreesboro
Kimbrell, Edward Michael *university administrator, journalism educator, talk show host*

Nashville
Clinton, Barbara Marie *university health services director, social worker*
Gee, Elwood Gordon *academic administrator*
Hazelip, Herbert Harold *academic administrator*
Manning, Charles W. *university chancellor*
Porter, Andrew Calvin *academic administrator, psychologist, educator*
Ramer, Hal Reed *academic administrator*
Willis, Eleanor Lawson *university official*
Wyatt, Joe Billy *academic administrator*

Oak Ridge
O'Neil, Charlotte Cooper *environmental education administrator*
Sternfels, Ronald Julian *academic program administrator*

Sewanee
Bonner, Thomas Perry *academic administrator*
Croom, Frederick Hailey *academic administrator, mathematician, educator*
Cunningham, Joel Luther *university president, vice-chancellor*
Patterson, William Brown *dean, history educator*

TEXAS

Abilene
Kim, Thomas Kunhyuk *college administrator*

Alpine
Morgan, Raymond Victor, Jr., *university administrator, mathematics educator*

Amarillo
Green, Karen Ann *college administrator*

Austin
Brewer, Thomas Bowman *retired university president*
Cunningham, William Hughes *former academic administrator, marketing educator*
Fair, Harry David *academic administrator, physicist*
Faulkner, Larry Ray *university official, chemistry educator*
Kelley, Henry Paul *university administrator, psychology educator*
Livingston, William Samuel *university administrator, political scientist*
Ryan, Randa Catherine *university administrator, business owner*
Shilling, Roy Bryant, Jr., *academic administrator*

Beaumont
Brentlinger, William Brock *college dean*

Belton
Ham, Clarence Edward *university administrator*

Brownsville
Garcia, Juliet Villarreal *university administrator*

Buchanan Dam
Miloy, Leatha Faye *university program director*

Canyon
Long, Russell Charles *academic administrator*

College Station
Bowen, Ray Morris *academic administrator, engineering educator*
Sayavedra, Leo *academic administrator*
Vandiver, Frank Everson *institute administrator, former university president, author, educator*

Commerce
Morris, Jerry Dean *retired academic administrator*

Corpus Christi
Furgason, Robert Roy *university president, engineering educator*
Harper, Sandra Stecher *university administrator*

Dallas
Attanasio, John Baptist *dean, law educator*
Cook, Gary Raymond *university president, clergyman*
Friedheim, Jan V. *education administrator*
Hester, Linda Hunt *retired dean, counseling administrator*
Turner, Robert Gerald *university president*

Denton
Baier, John Leonard *university educator*
Hurley, Alfred Francis *historian, academic administrator emeritus, retired air force officer*

Edinburg
Esparza, Thomas, Sr., *academic athletics administrator*

El Paso
Erskine, William Crawford *academic administrator, accountant, health facility administrator*
Natalicio, Diana Siedhoff *academic administrator*
Provenghi, Lesa Christine *educational administrator*

Fort Worth
Bickerstaff, Mina March Clark *university administrator*
Boschini, Victor John, Jr., *academic administrator*
Helton, Lucille Henry Hanrattie *academic administrator*
Tucker, William Edward *academic administrator, minister*

Galveston
Goodwin, Sharon Ann *academic administrator*

Hillsboro
Auvenshine, William Robert *college president*

Houston
Burgos-Sasscer, Ruth *chancellor emeritus*
Carroll, Michael M. *academic dean, mechanical engineering educator*
Geisinger, Kurt Francis *university administrator, psychometrician*
Gillis, Malcolm (Stephen Gillis) *academic administrator, economics educator*
Kellar, William Henry *university official, history educator*
Pickering, James Henry, III, *academic administrator, educator*
Smith, Arthur Kittredge, Jr., *academic administrator, political science educator*
Tucker, Aubrey Stephen *composer, music industry consultant*
Tyson, Carla Lea *director*
Whitaker, Gilbert Riley, Jr., *academic administrator, business economist*

Huntsville
Hopper, Margaret Sue *academic administrator, educational diagnostician, consultant*
Ward, Richard Hurley *dean, writer*

Kingsville
Ibanez, Manuel Luis *university official, biological sciences educator*

Laredo
Black, Clifford Merwyn *academic administrator, sociologist, educator*

Longview
Austin, Alvin O. *academic administrator*

Los Fresnos
Martin, José Ginoris *education administrator*

Lubbock
Schmidly, David J. *university president, biology educator*

Odessa
Grubbs, Donald Ray *educational director, educator, welder*

Pasadena
Blue, Monte Lynn *college president*

Plainview
Davis, Wallace Edmond, Jr., *former university administrator, educator*

San Antonio
Calgaard, Ronald Keith *university president*
Henderson, Dwight Franklin *dean, educator*
Romo, Ricardo *academic administrator, history educator*
Young, James Julius *university administrator, retired army officer*

San Marcos
Supple, Jerome H. *academic administrator*

Tyler
Sharpe, Aubrey Dean *college administrator*

Waco
Reynolds, Herbert Hal *academic administrator*
Selke-Kern, Barbara Ellen *university official, writer*

Wichita Falls
Leavell, Landrum Pinson, II, *seminary administrator, clergyman, educator*
Rodriguez, Louis Joseph *academic administrator, economist, educator*

Wimberley
Jennett, Joseph Charles *retired academic administrator, engineering educator*

UTAH

Logan
Ahlstrom, Callis Blythe *university official*
Emert, George Henry *former academic administrator, biochemist*
Gay, Charles W., Jr., *academic administrator*

Provo
Samuelson, Cecil O. *academic administrator*

Salt Lake City
Bassis, Michael Steven *academic administrator*
Drew, Clifford James *university administrator, special education and educational psychology educator*
Morris, Sylvia Marie *university official*

Sandy
Sabey, J(ohn) Wayne *academic administrator, consultant*

VERMONT

Middlebury
McCardell, John Malcolm, Jr., *academic administrator*
Rader, Rhoda Caswell *academic program director*

Winooski
Fellows, Diana Potenzano *educational administrator*

VIRGINIA

Alexandria
Jenkins, John Smith *retired academic dean, lawyer*
Pastin, Mark Joseph *association executive*
Smith, Harold Allen *education administrator, researcher, educator*

Annandale
Ernst, Richard James *former academic administrator*

Arlington
Aguerrebere, Joseph A. *academic administrator*
John, Martha Tyler *dean, education educator*
Ramaley, Judith Aitken *former university president, endocrinologist*
Violand-Sanchez, Emma Natividad *school administrator, educator*

Blacksburg
Brown, Gregory Neil *university administrator, forest physiology educator*
Torgersen, Paul Ernest *academic administrator, educator*

Charlottesville
Casteen, John Thomas, III, *university president*
O'Neil, Robert Marchant *university administrator, law educator*
Scott, Robert Edwin *dean, law educator*

Chatham
Ripley, John Walter *academic administrator*

Dulles
Hegarty, George John *university rector, English educator*

Fairfax
Kettlewell, Gail Biery *academic administrator*
Merten, Alan Gilbert *academic administrator*
Powell, Karan Hinman *academic administrator*

Falls Church
Copes, Marvin Lee *college president*

Hampton
Wilson, P. Craig *program director, marketing professional, consultant*

Harrisonburg
Carrier, Ronald Edwin *academic administrator, director*
Lemish, Donald Lee *university athletics director*

Lexington
Burish, Thomas Gerard *academic administrator*
McCloud, Anece Faison *academic administrator*

Lynchburg
Husted, Stewart Winthrop *dean, marketing educator, consultant*

Middleburg
Larmore, Catherine Christine *university official*

Norfolk
Koch, James Verch *academic administrator, economist*
Myers, Donald Allen *university dean*
Ridley, Dennis Raymond *university director*
Witty, Elaine P. *former dean, education educator*

Radford
Carter, Fletcher Fairwick *university administrator, education educator*
Liss, Ivan Barry *dean, computer science educator*

Richmond
Boudinot, Frank Douglas *dean*
Drain, Cecil B. *university dean, nurse anesthetist educator, retired army officer*

Fishback, Patricia Davis *academic administrator, educator*
Heilman, E. Bruce *academic administrator*
Trani, Eugene Paul *university president, educator*

Virginia Beach
Jones, Felicia M. *director*
Selig, William George *university official*

Williamsburg
Cross, Dennis Wayne *academic administrator*
Reveley, Walter Taylor, III, *dean*

Wise
Lemons, L. Jay *academic administrator*

WASHINGTON

Bellingham
Masland, Lynne S. *university official*
Morse, Karen Williams *academic administrator*

Kenmore
Jennerich, Edward John *university official and dean*

Olympia
Averill, Ronald Henry *dean*
Ponder, William Stanley *university administrator*

Seattle
Banks, James Albert *educational research director, educator*
Carlson, Dale Arvid *university dean*
Gerberding, William Passavant *retired university president*
Ginorio, Angela Beatriz *university research administrator, educator*
Huntsman, Lee *university provost, academic administrator*
Kelley, Lucille Marie Kindely *dean, psychosocial nurse*
McMahon, John Joseph *college official*
Plotnick, Robert David *educator, economic consultant*
Stringer, William Jeremy *university official*
Tschernisch, Sergei P. *academic administrator*
Wilcox, Paul Horne *academic administrator, researcher*
Wulff, Donald Henry *research center director, assistant dean*

Spokane
Coughlin, Bernard John *university chancellor*

Tacoma
King, Gundar Julian *retired university dean*

Toppenish
Ross, Kathleen Anne *college president*

Walla Walla
Cronin, Thomas Edward *academic administrator*

WEST VIRGINIA

Beckley
Thompson, Novella Woodrum *college administrator, psychotherapist*

Huntington
Baker, Winston Alexander, Sr., *academic administrator*
Gould, Alan Brant *academic administrator*

Martinsburg
Ohl, Ronald Edward *academic administrator*

Morgantown
Brooks, Dana D. *dean*
Bucklew, Neil S. *educator, past university president*
Hardesty, David Carter, Jr., *university president*

Saint Albans
Smith, Robert Carlisle *department administrator, welding educator*

WISCONSIN

Appleton
Tincher, Barbara Jean *university official*
Warch, Richard *academic administrator*

Baraboo
Umhoefer, Aural M. *retired dean, educational consultant*

Beloit
Burris, John Edward *academic administrator, biologist, educator*
Wheeler, Mary Anne Theresa *administrator, educator*

Hudson
Dahle, Johannes Upton *retired academic administrator*

Janesville
Taylor, Timothy Leon *college dean*

Madison
Cantu, Kathleen Marie *academic administrator*
Kreuter, Gretchen V. *academic administrator*
Lyall, Katharine C(ulbert) *academic administrator, economics educator*
Simone, Beverly Sue *academic administrator*
Wiley, John D. *academic administrator*
Yuill, Thomas MacKay *academic administrator, microbiology educator*

Menomonie
Shaw, Dennis Lee *academic administrator*

Mequon
Ellis, William Grenville *academic administrator, management consultant*

Milwaukee
Aman, Mohammed Mohammed *dean, library and information science educator*
Coffman, Terrence J. *academic administrator*
Iaquinta, Leonard Phillip *university official*
Read, Sister Joel *academic administrator*
Sankovitz, James Leo *retired development director, lobbyist*

Oconto
Watson-Boone, Rebecca A. *library and information studies researcher, educator*

Platteville
Lindahl, Thomas Jefferson *retired university dean*

Rhinelander
Hansen, Paula J. *academic administrator*

River Falls
Thibodeau, Gary A. *academic administrator*

Solon Springs
Kleven, Bruce Alan *academic administrator*

Whitewater
Greenhill, H. Gaylon *retired academic administrator*

TERRITORIES OF THE UNITED STATES

AMERICAN SAMOA

Pago Pago
Ili, Esther Kaili *educational administrator*

GUAM

Hagatna
Hall, Charles Worth Leo *college administrator*

Mangilao
Iyechad, Theodore Melengoes *youth program director*

PUERTO RICO

Guayama
Febres-Santiago, Samuel F. *retired academic administrator*

San German
Mojica, Agnes *academic administrator*

CANADA

ALBERTA

Edmonton
Schwabe, Marcus Christopher *medical foundation executive*

MANITOBA

Winnipeg
Stalker, Jacqueline D'Aoust *academic administrator, educator*

NOVA SCOTIA

Wolfville
Ogilvie, Kelvin Kenneth *university president, chemistry educator*

ONTARIO

Belleville
Buckley, Edward Joseph *retired academic dean*

Ottawa
Brombal, Douglas Nereo *retired university official, consultant*
Philogene, Bernard J. R. *academic administrator, science educator*

Thunder Bay
Gilbert, Frederick Franklin *academic administrator, natural resource sciences educator*

Toronto
Ebedes, Allan Norman *academic administrator*

QUEBEC

Montreal
Lajeunesse, Marcel *university administrator, educator*

Toronto
Bereiter, Carl *academic administrator, educator*

GUATEMALA

Guatemala City
Harris, Randy Jay *university official, finance executive*

JAPAN

Amagasaki
Oikawa, Hiroshi *college president, materials science educator*

ADDRESS UNPUBLISHED

Aaslestad, Halvor Gunerius *college dean, retired*
Aiken, Michael Thomas *former academic administrator*
Allen, Charles Eugene *university administrator, agriculturist, educator*
Armacost, Mary-Linda Sorber Merriam *former academic administrator, consultant*
Armstrong, Warren Bruce *former university president, historian, educator*
Aug, Alberta J. *educational administrator*
Baker, Robert M. L., Jr., *academic administrator*
Balis, Jennifer Lynn *academic administrator, computer technology educator*
Barnard, Ann Watson *retired academic administrator, educator, writer*
Baron, James Neal *organizational behavior and human resources educator, researcher*
Bassist, Donald Herbert *retired academic administrator*
Begin, Jacqueline Sue *environmental education specialist*
Bernstein, I. Melvin *university official and dean, materials scientist*
Blackledge, David William *retired academic administrator*
Blagg, James Douglas, Jr., *university administrator*
Blood, Peggy A. *academic administrator*
Bolek, Catherine *university research director*
Boyle, Betsy H. *educational administrator*
Brenner, Theodor Eduard *academic foundation administration*
Burke, Joseph C. *former university official*
Burrell, E. William *retired university adminstrator, educator*
Casler, Frederick Clair, Sr., *academic administrator, law enforcement educator*
Chace, William Murdough *former university administrator*
Chaim, Robert Alex *dean, educator*
Chandler, Alice *higher education consultant, university president*
Cheek, Barbara Lee *college reading program director, educator*
Clawson, Roxann Eloise *college administrator, computer company executive*
Cochrane, Walter E. *academic administrator, music educator, conductor*
Coleman, Mary Sue *academic administrator*
Compton, Norma Haynes *retired university dean, artist*
Conway, Edward Gerald, Jr., *university educational technology administrator*
Costilow, Susan Lynn *education and conference coordinator*
Cummins, Patricia Willett *academic administrator*
Darke, Charles Bruce *academic administrator, dentist*
Davis, Joseph Lloyd *educational administrator, consultant*
Debs, Barbara Knowles *former college president, consultant*
Diamond, Robert Mach *higher education administrator*
DiBiaggio, John A. *university president*
Dorsey, Rhoda Mary *retired academic administrator*
Duff, John Bernard *college president, former city official*
Edelman, Norman Herman *medical educator, university dean and official*
Elliott, Cindy Sue *academic administrator*
Erfani, Shervin *academic administrator, engineering educator*
Essig, Kathleen Susan *university official, management consultant*
Evans, James Handel *university administrator, architect, educator*
Falk, Marshall Allen *retired university dean, physician*
Farris, Vera King *former college president*
Feldstein, Joshua *educational administrator*
Felicetti, Daniel A. *academic administrator, educator*
Fenton, Marjorie *university official, consultant*
Foldesi, Robert Stephen *education administrator, management educator*
Ford, Loretta C. *lecturer, consultant, retired university dean, nurse*
Foster, Martha Tyahla *educational administrator*
Fountain, Andre Ferchaud *academic program director*
Franklin, Mary Ann Wheeler *educator, higher education and management consultant*
Fritschler, A. Lee *retired college president, public policy educator*
Frost, Everett Lloyd *anthropologist, academic administrator*
Gabel, Katherine *retired academic administrator*
Galloway, Pamela Eilene *university official emeritus*
Gilmore, Connie Sue *director*
Glaze, Lynn Ferguson *development consultant*
Glennen, Robert Eugene, Jr., *retired university president*
Goerke, Glenn Allen *university administrator*
Golden, Beth *Special Olympics administrator*
Gordis, David Moses *academic administrator, rabbi*
Gray, Richard Moss *retired college president*
Grebstein, Sheldon Norman *university administrator*
Green, Nancy Loughridge *newspaper executive*
Guskin, Alan E. *university president*
Guzman, Ana Margarita *university administrator*
Haak, Harold Howard *university president*
Hall, James William *university chancellor*
Harris, Dolores M. *retired academic administrator*
Hart, James Warren *retired academic administrator, retired football player*
Hasselmo, Nils *academic administrator, linguistics educator*
Hazel, Mary Belle *university administrator*
Hersh, Richard H. *academic administrator*
Hill, Emita Brady *academic administrator, consultant*
Hill, Virgil Lusk, Jr., *academic administrator, naval officer*
Hoffman, Neil James *academic administrator*
Hughes, Eugene Morgan *university president*
Hunt-Clerici, Carol Elizabeth *retired academic administrator, counselor*
Jackson, Lambert Blunt *academic administrator*
Jackson, Miles Merrill *retired university dean*
Jaji, Lazarus Musekiwa *educational administrator, leadership educator, consultant, researcher*
Janeway, Richard *university official*
Jervis, Jane Lise *college official, science historian*
Johnson, Duane P. *retired academic administrator, consultant*
Johnson, Sylvia Sue *university administrator, educator*
Johnstone, D. Bruce *university administrator*
Jones, Joel Mackey *academic administrator*
Kappner, Augusta Souza *academic administrator*
King, John Ethelbert, Jr., *academic administrator*
King, Maxwell Clark *former academic administrator*
Koleson, Donald Ralph *retired college dean, educator*
Kormondy, Edward John *retired academic administrator, retired science educator*
Kraemer, Linda Gayle *associate dean*
Kubiak, John Michael *academic administrator*
Kuykendall, John Wells *academic administrator, educator*
Lantz, Joanne Baldwin *academic administrator emeritus*
Lawrence, Sally Clark *academic administrator*
Link, David Thomas *dean, lawyer*
Loser, Joseph Carlton, Jr., *dean, retired judge*
Luedeke, J. Barton *academic administrator*
Lusztig, Peter Alfred *university dean, educator*
Lynn, Naomi B. *academic administrator*
MacGregor, Bonnie Lynn *school administrator*
Machen, Ethel Louise Lynch *retired academic administrator*
Malcolm, Richard Ward *academic administrator, consultant*
Mañas, Rita *educational administrator*
Massey, Thomas Benjamin *retired academic administrator, educator*
Matsuda, Fujio *retired university president*
Maybury, Greg J. *academic administrator*
McCoy, Eileen Carey *academic dean*
McDyer, Susan Spear *academic administrator*
McGee, Harold Johnston *former academic administrator*
McPeak, Allan *career services director, educator, lawyer, consultant*
Mehne, Paul Randolph *associate dean, medical educator*
Melady, Thomas Patrick *academic administrator, ambassador, author, public policy expert, educator*
Meskill, Victor P. *academic administrator, educator*
Miller, Arjay *retired university dean*
Mollo, Joseph Anthony *university administrator*
Monteith, Larry King *chancellor emeritus*
Morgan, Ruth Prouse *academic administrator, educator*
Mossman, Kenneth Leslie *academic administrator, health physicist, radiobiologist*
Myers, Harold Mathews *academic administrator*
Narduzzi, James Louis *college dean, consultant*
Neff, Diane Irene *university administrator*
O'Hare, Joseph Aloysius *academic administrator, priest*
Oliveira, Mary Joyce *university official*
O'Malley, Thomas Patrick *academic administrator*
O'Neil, William Francis *academic administrator*
Orr, Kenneth Bradley *academic administrator*
Pacheco, Manuel Trinidad *retired academic administrator*
Park, John Thornton *academic administrator*
Parker, Paulette Ann *academic administrator*
Parko, Joseph Edward, Jr., *emeritus educator*
Patterson, Howard Yates *academic athletics administrator*
Paxton, Juanita Willene *retired university official*
Pearson, Susan Winifred *dean, consultant*
Pettigrew, L. Eudora *retired academic administrator*
Pierce, Susan Resneck *academic administrator, English language educator*
Pouncey, Peter Richard *academic administrator, classics educator*
Price, Barbara Gillette *college administrator, artist*
Prieto, Claudio R. *academic administrator, lawyer*
Prins, Robert Jack *retired academic administrator*
Pruitt, Anne Loring *academic administrator, education educator*
Puryear, James Burton *college administrator*
Rada, Ruth Byers *college dean, author*
Raleigh, Cheryl Elaine *academic director, educator*
Ramirez, Maria C(oncepción) *retired educational administrator*

Rehnke, Mary Ann *academic administrator*
Riddle, James Douglass *retired academic administrator*
Rinsland, Roland DeLano *retired university official*
Robertson, Wyndham Gay *university official, journalist*
Rocheleau, James Romig *retired university president*
Rochelle, Lugenia *academic administrator*
Rohan, Virginia Bartholome *college development director*
Rohwer, William D., Jr., *university dean*
Rowell, Barbara Caballero *retired academic administrator*
Ryder, Georgia Atkins *university dean, educator*
Schure, Alexander *university chancellor*
Schwartz, Eleanor Brantley *academic administrator*
Seidner, Stanley S. *academic administrator, educator*
Shannon-Hallam, Isabelle Louise *education director*
Shaw, Helen Lester Anderson *retired dean, nutrition educator, researcher*
Shearer, Charles Livingston *academic administrator*
Shelton, Leslie Habecker *adult literacy and learning specialist*
Sherratt, Gerald Robert *retired academic administrator*
Shields, Cynthia Rose *college administrator*
Shipley, Melody Lea *director, mathematician, educator*
Sicuro, Natale Anthony *academic and financial administrator, consultant*
Slorp, John S. *retired academic administrator*
Smith, Clodus Ray *academic administrator*
Smith, Hoke LaFollette *university president*
Smith, Samuel Howard *academic administrator, plant pathologist*
Solmssen, Peter *retired academic administrator*
Sonnenschein, Hugo Freund *academic administrator, economics educator*
Spielmann, Diane Ruth *research center public services director*
Stauff, William James *college official*
Stein, Dale Franklin *retired university president*
Stewart, Joan Hinde *academic administrator*
Taylor, Mary Lee *retired college administrator*
Tobias, Judy *university development executive*
Troupe, Marilyn Kay *educational administrator*
Uehling, Barbara Staner *educational administrator*
Vinson, James Spangler *academic administrator*
Volpe, Edmond L(oris) *college president*
Wagner, Robert Todd *university president, sociology educator*
Warder, Richard Currey, Jr., *dean, mechanical aerospace engineering educator*
Waters, Donald Eugene *academic administrator*
Watts, John Ransford *university administrator*
Weir, Morton Webster *retired academic administrator, educator*
Wentworth, LaVerne Wellborn *university program coordinator*
Wilkening, Laurel Lynn *academic administrator, planetary scientist*
Wille, Rosanne Louise *higher education administrator*
Wilson, Samuel V. *academic administrator*
Winterstein, James Fredrick *academic administrator*
Wogen, Cathy Lynn *academic director*
Worthen, John Edward *retired academic administrator*
Wright, Rebecca Diane *program director*
Young, Michael Kent *dean, lawyer, educator*
Young, Richard Alan *retired sports administration educator, athletic director*
Zacharias, Donald Wayne *academic administrator*
Zdanis, Richard Albert *academic administrator*

HIGHER EDUCATION: ARCHITECTURE AND DESIGN

UNITED STATES

CALIFORNIA

Irvine
Kraemer, Kenneth Leo *architect, educator, urban planner*

La Jolla
Brandt, Maryclare *interior designer, educator*

Orange
Shirvani, Hamid *architect, educator, author, administrator, philosopher*

Pauma Valley
Rutz, Miriam Easton *landscape architecture educator*

COLORADO

Denver
Prosser, John Martin *architect, educator, urban design consultant*

Fort Garland
Boyer, Lester Leroy, Jr., *architecture educator, consultant*

CONNECTICUT

Fairfield
Ingis, Gail *interior designer, educator, writer, photographer, artist*

Old Greenwich
Whitlock, Veronica P. *interior designer, educator*

Trumbull
Watson, Donald Ralph *architect, artist, educator, author*

DISTRICT OF COLUMBIA

Washington
Freschi, Bruno Basilio *architect, educator*
Miller, Iris Ann *landscape architect, urban designer, educator*
Prigmore, Kathryn Bradford Tyler *architecture educator, architect*

FLORIDA

Gainesville
Schueller, Wolfgang Augustus *architectural educator, writer*

Tallahassee
Pugh, Thomas Doering *architecture educator, educator*

GEORGIA

Atlanta
Fash, William Leonard *retired architecture educator, college dean*
Nwagbara, Chibu Isaac *industrial designer, consultant*

Savannah
Weaver, Crystal Dawn *interior design educator*

HAWAII

Honolulu
Yeh, Raymond Wei-Hwa *architect, educator*

ILLINOIS

Champaign
Anthony, Kathryn Harriet *architecture educator*
Baker, Jack Sherman *architect, designer, educator*
Selby, Robert Irwin *architect, educator*

INDIANA

Notre Dame
Stroik, Duncan Gregory *architect, architectural design educator*

KANSAS

Manhattan
Chang, Amos Ih-Tiao *retired architecture educator*

LOUISIANA

Lafayette
Cazayoux, Edward Jon *architect, educator*

New Orleans
Klingman, John Philip *architect, educator*
Latorre, Robert George *naval architecture and engineering educator*

MARYLAND

Garrett Park
Stites, M(ary) Elizabeth *architecture educator*

MASSACHUSETTS

Cambridge
Anderson, Stanford Owen *architect, architectural historian, educator*
Porter, William Lyman *architect, educator*
Szabo, Albert *architect, educator*

Newton
Lewis-Kausel, Cecilia *interior design educator*

Woods Hole
Newman, John Nicholas *naval architect educator*

MICHIGAN

Ann Arbor
Beckley, Robert Mark *architect, educator*
Marans, Robert Warren *architect, planner*

MISSOURI

Columbia
Tofle, Ruth Brent *design educator, researcher, educator*

Springfield
Liu, Yuan Hsiung *drafting and design educator*

NEVADA

Las Vegas
Serfas, Richard Thomas *architecture educator, urban planner, county official*

NEW JERSEY

Newark
Goldman, Glenn *architecture educator, architect*

Princeton
Graves, Michael *architect, educator*

NEW YORK

Jamaica
Gati, William Eugene *architect, designer and planner*

New York
Body-Lawson, Victor F. *architect, educator*
Ranalli, George Joseph *architect, educator*
Robinson, James LeRoy *architect, educator, developer*

Syracuse
Smardon, Richard Clay *landscape architecture and environmental studies educator*

Utica
Labuz, Ronald Matthew *design educator*

NORTH CAROLINA

Chapel Hill
Stipe, Robert Edwin *design educator*

OKLAHOMA

Norman
Sipes, James Lamoyne *landscape architect, educator*

OREGON

Eugene
Matthews, Kevin Michael *architecture educator, researcher*

PENNSYLVANIA

Erwinna
Auerbach, Kathryn Ann *architecture and preservation educator, consultant*

Philadelphia
Malkawi, Ali Mahmoud *architecture educator, researcher*
Mertins, Detleff *architect, educator, architect, department chairman*

Pittsburgh
Becherer, Richard John *architecture educator*

RHODE ISLAND

Wakefield
Phipps, Lynne Bryan *interior architect, educator, minister*

TEXAS

Austin
Garstka, John Edward *interior design educator*

College Station
Greer, John Only *architect, educator*

Houston
Ivanov, Lyuben Dimitrov *naval architecture researcher, educator*

UTAH

Salt Lake City
Miller, William Charles *architect, educator*

VIRGINIA

Blacksburg
Bliznakov, Milka Tcherneva *architect, educator*
Crawford, Peggy Smith *design educator*
Rodriguez-Camilloni, Humberto Leonardo *architect, historian, educator*

WASHINGTON

Pullman
Carper, Kenneth Lynn *architect, educator*

Seattle
Bosworth, Thomas Lawrence *architect, architecture educator*
Jacobson, Phillip Lee *architect, educator*
Johnston, Norman John *retired architecture educator*
Lovett, Wendell Harper *architect, educator*
Moudon, Anne Vernez *urban design educator*
Sutton, Sharon Egretta *architect, educator, artist, musician*

Shelton
McClelland, Craig Alexander *architect, educator, business owner*

ADDRESS UNPUBLISHED

Anderson, Ruth Lucille *interior designer, educator, artist, librarian, archivist*
Loss, John C. *architect, retired educator*
Ramirez, Martin Ruben *architect, engineer, educator, cognitive scientist, consultant*
Rogers, Kate Ellen *interior design educator*
Schuth, Mary McDougle *interior designer, educator*
Thiel, Philip *design educator*

HIGHER EDUCATION: EDUCATION

UNITED STATES

ALABAMA

Auburn
Vazsonyi, Alexander Thomas *education educator*

Birmingham
Clarke, Juanita M. Waiters *education educator*
Lee, James Michael *religious education educator, publisher*

Decatur
Kuby, Patricia Ann Williams *early childhood education educator*

Eufaula
Vandenberg, Donald *retired education educator, philosopher*

Fairhope
Gwin, John Michael *retired education educator, consultant*

Jacksonville
McCrary, Judy Hale *education educator*

Mobile
Byrd, Mary Jane *education educator*
Dansak, Daniel Albert *medical educator, consultant*

Troy
Marsicano, Hazel Elliott *education educator*

ALASKA

Kotzebue
O'Brien, Annmarie *education educator*

ARIZONA

Chandler
Stewart, Nancy Sue Spurlock *education educator*

Green Valley
Berwald, Helen Dorothy *education educator*

Phoenix
McGrath, Jane Lee *education educator, writer*

Prescott
Halvorson, Mary Ellen *education educator, writer*

Sun Lakes
Johnson, Marian Ilene *education educator*

Tempe
Guzzetti, Barbara Jean *education educator*
Haggerson, Nelson Lionel, Jr., *education educator*

Tucson
Porreca, Betty Lou *education educator*

ARKANSAS

Fayetteville
Henry, Ann Rainwater *retired education educator*
Schoppmeyer, Martin William *education educator*
Van Patten, James Jeffers *education educator*

Glenwood
Wright, James Thomas, Sr., *education educator*

Jonesboro
Blake, Sally Steinsiek *education educator, researcher*

Rogers
Searles, Anna Mae Howard *educator, civic worker*

Russellville
Morris, Lois Lawson *education educator*

PROFESSIONAL INDEX — HIGHER EDUCATION: EDUCATION

State University
McClain, Veda *education educator, department chairman*

CALIFORNIA

Altadena
Prober, Alexandra Jaworski *education educator*

Aptos
Bohn, Ralph Carl *educational consultant, retired educator*

Berkeley
Freedman, Sarah Warshauer *education educator*
Kay, Herma Hill *education educator*
Linn, Marcia Cyrog *education educator*
Zelnik, Reginald Ely *education educator, researcher*

Claremont
Monte, William David *education educator, educator*

Colton
Dybowski, Douglas Eugene *education educator, economist*

Encino
Green, Kenneth Charles *education educator, researcher*

Folsom
Jantzen, J(ohn) Marc *retired education educator*

Fresno
Veaco, Lelia *retired education educator*

Fullerton
Donoghue, Mildred Ransdorf *education educator*

Irvine
Chen, Chuansheng *education educator*

La Jolla
Lowe, Lisa *education educator, department chairman*

Laguna Beach
Fry, Edward Bernard *education educator, retired*

Long Beach
Armstrong, Joanna *education educator*
Hellmer, Lynne Beberman *education educator*
Knudson, Ruth Esther *education educator*
Mandarino, Candida Ann *education educator, consultant*

Los Angeles
Agnew, John A. *education educator*
Astin, Alexander William *education educator*
Cohen, Arthur M. *education educator*
Gilbert, Richard Keith *education educator, researcher*
Simun, Patricia Bates *education educator, consultant*

Menlo Park
Chapin, June Roediger *education educator*

Monterey
Di Girolamo, Rosina Elizabeth *education educator*
Gamiere, Constance Anne *education educator, counselor*

Palm Desert
Haugh, Joyce Eileen Gallagher *education educator, volunteer*
Sexson, Stephen Bruce *education writer, educator*

Petaluma
O'Hare, Sandra Fernandez *education educator*

Pinole
Grogan, Stanley Joseph *educational and security consultant*

Riverside
Dutton, Jo Sargent *education educator, researcher, consultant*
Fischer, John Martin *education educator, researcher*
Savage, Marsha Kay *education educator*

San Bernardino
Norton, Ruth Ann *education educator*

San Diego
Mayer, George Roy *education educator*
Young, Russell Leslie *education educator*

San Francisco
Ada, Alma Flor *education educator, writer*
Clifford, Geraldine Joncich (Mrs. William F. Clifford) *education educator*

Santa Barbara
Boyan, Norman J. *retired education educator*
Tettegah, Sharon Yvonne *education educator*
Zwick, Rebecca *education educator*

Santa Clara
Ling, Nam *educator*

Santee
Morris, Henry Madison, Jr., *education educator*

Sonoma
Hobart, Billie *education educator, consultant*

Stanford
Ball, Arnetha *education educator*
Barron, Brigid *education educator*

Boaler, Jo *education educator*
Bridges, Edwin Maxwell *education educator*
Cohen, Elizabeth G. *education and sociology educator, researcher*
Cuban, Larry *education educator, researcher*
Darling-Hammond, Linda *education educator*
Eisner, Elliot W. *education educator*
Grossman, Pamela Lynn *education educator*
Kirst, Michael Weile *education educator, researcher*
Loeb, Susanna *education educator*
Lotan, Rachel *education educator*
Pea, Roy *education educator*
Perry, William James *education educator, former federal official*
Shavelson, Richard *education educator*
Stipek, Deborah *education educator, dean*
Strober, Myra Hoffenberg *education educator, consultant*
Wotipka, Christine Min *education educator*

Upland
Doyle, Michael James *education educator, organist*

Victorville
Ceseña, Carmen *education educator, education administrator*

COLORADO

Boulder
Borko, Hilda *education educator*

Colorado Springs
Englebretson, Rosann Camille *education educator, writer*

Denver
Biram, Geraldine Louise *elementary education educator*
Davis, W. Alan *education educator*
Ellis, Voleen *education educator, researcher*
Peebles, Lucretia Neal Drane *policy and administration educator*

Estes Park
Guest, Linda Sand *education educator*

Greeley
King, Richard Auld *education educator*

Pueblo
Lightell, Kenneth Ray *education educator*

CONNECTICUT

Bridgeport
Lange, Linda Diane *education educator, researcher*

Danbury
Caruso, John, Jr., *education and educational psychology educator*

Hartford
Lavoie, Norma Yolanda Berberian *education educator*

New Haven
Green, Donald Philip *education educator*
Miller, Christopher L *education educator*
Sachdev, Subir *education educator*
Skelly, David K *education educator*

North Branford
Ward, Frederick Champion *retired education educator*

North Haven
Fuggi, Gretchen Miller *education educator*
Montagna, Bernice Donna *education educator*

Preston
Makara, Carol Pattie *education educator, consultant*

Storrs Mansfield
Lee, Tsoung-Chao *education educator*

West Hartford
Echols, Ivor Tatum *retired educator, assistant dean*

Willimantic
Stoloff, David L. *education educator, academic administrator, web site designer*

DISTRICT OF COLUMBIA

Washington
Fisher, Miles Mark, IV, *education and religion educator, minister*
Halbrook, Arthur Marshall *educational educator, assessment specialist*
Jackson, Barbara Talbert *education educator*
Savukinas, Robert Steven *education educator, director*
Timpane, Philip Michael *education educator, policy analyst*

FLORIDA

Boca Raton
Connor, Frances Partridge *retired education educator*

Bradenton
Driscoll, Constance Fitzgerald *education educator, writer, consultant*

Coral Gables
Sternberg, Leonel da Silveira Lobo *education educator*

Coral Springs
Delaney, Eleanor Cecilia Coughlin *education educator, consultant*

Daytona Beach
Green, Betty Nielsen *education educator, consultant*

Fort Lauderdale
McCan, James Lawton *education educator*
McMahon-Dumas, Carmen Elethea *education educator*

Fort Myers
Canham, Pruella Cromartie Niver *retired educator*

Jacksonville
Cook, Mary Shepard *education educator*
Main, Edna Dewey (June Main) *education educator*

Melbourne
Cahill, Gerard Albin *university educator*

Miami
Brotherson, Mary Lou Nelson *education educator*
Dottin, Erskine S. *education educator*
Leathers, Katherine Anne *education educator*
Stolzenberg, Lisa Ann *education educator*

Naples
Loft, Bernard Irwin *education educator, consultant*

Orlando
DuVall, Rick *education educator*

Port Saint Lucie
Centerbar, Alberta Elaine *education educator, research specialist*
Guglielmino, Lucy Margaret Madsen *education educator, researcher, consultant*

Sarasota
Gourley, Mary E. *education educator*

Tallahassee
Crider, Irene Perritt *education educator, small business owner, consultant*
Lick, Dale Wesley *educational leadership educator*
Mills, Belen Collantes *early childhood education educator*

Tampa
Anderson, Robert Henry *education educator, writer*
Fries, Mary Kim *AIDS education educator, educational consultant*
Kaywell, Joan *education educator*

Venice
Myers, Virginia Lou *education educator*

West Melbourne
Robsman, Mary Louise *education educator*

West Palm Beach
Bechtol, Dennis L. *education educator, sport and business management consultant*

GEORGIA

Ailey
Claxton, Melba Sammons *education educator*

Athens
Smagorinsky, Peter *education educator*

Atlanta
Lee, Hamilton H. *education educator*
Nweke, Winifred Chinwendu *education educator*
Rogers, Brenda Gayle *educational administrator, educator, consultant*

Augusta
Hunter, William Andrew *education educator*

Carrollton
Mizell, Jill Angelique *education educator, consultant*
Morgan, Harry New *education educator*
Van Brackle, Anita Short *early childhood education educator*

Cleveland
Raznoff, Beverly Shultz *education educator*

Macon
Hunnicutt, Victoria Anne Wilson *education educator*
Popper, Virginia Sowell *education educator*

Milledgeville
Manley, Jo Ann Seagraves *education educator, consultant*

Rome
Barnes, Wendell Wright, Jr., *education educator*

Statesboro
Strauser, Beverly Ann *education educator*

Sylvania
Smith, Benjamin Alexander, II, *education educator, geography educator*

Valdosta
Cripe, Juliann Woods *education educator*

Peace, Barbara Lou Jean *education educator*

HAWAII

Honolulu
Bogart, Louise Berry *education educator*
Burniske, Richard William, Jr., *education educator*

Laie
James, Mark Olov *education educator*

Pearl City
Uyeno, Lani Akemi *education educator*

IDAHO

Boise
Beach, John Douglas *education educator*
Palmer, Rosemary Gudmundson *education educator*

Kimberly
Coonts, Janet Rodman *education educator*

Pocatello
Pemberton, Cynthia Lee A. *educational leadership educator*

ILLINOIS

Carbondale
Snyder, Carolyn Ann *education educator, librarian*

Champaign
Farmer, James Alexander, Jr., *retired education educator*
Ikenberry, Stanley Oliver *education educator, former university president*
Keen, Maria Elizabeth *retired educator*
Spodek, Bernard *early childhood educator*

Charleston
Buckellew, William Franklin *retired education educator*

Chicago
Adelman, Pamela Bernice Kozoll *education educator*
Beck, John Matthew *education educator*
Bordage, Georges *physician, medical education educator*
Bryk, Anthony S. *education educator*
Cyganowski, Carol Klimick *educator, writer*
Johnson, Barbara Elaine Spears *retired education educator*
Landerholm, Elizabeth Jane *early childhood education educator*
Litvin, Faydor Leiba *education educator, researcher*
McCoy, John Elbert *education educator*
Mindes, Gayle Dean *education educator*
Panko, Jessie Symington *education educator*
Rosenbluth, Marion *educator, consultant, psychotherapist*
Schubert, William Henry *curriculum studies educator*
Schwarzkopf, Gloria A. *education educator, psychotherapist*
Young, Lauren Sue Jones *education educator*

Dekalb
Morrison, Harriet Barbara *retired education educator*
Simmons, Deborah Anne *environmental educator*

Elmhurst
Hillman, Carole Dorothy *education educator*

Evanston
Lewis, Dan Albert *education educator*

Hazel Crest
Freed, Melvyn Norris *retired higher education administrator and educator, writer*

Normal
Hickrod, George Alan Karnes Wallis *educational administration educator*

Peoria
McMullen, David Wayne *education educator*

Springfield
Craig, John Charles *educational researcher, consultant*

Sugar Grove
Burch, Susan Ann *human resource developer, educator*

Urbana
Davidson, Fred *education educator*

INDIANA

Bloomington
Mehlinger, Howard Dean *education educator*
Smith, Carl Bernard *education educator*

Indianapolis
Mendenhall, Gordon Lee *education educator*
Speth, Gerald Lennus *education and business consultant*

Lafayette
Vaughn, Vicki Lynn *education educator*

Marion
Dixon, Ruth Ann Storey *education educator*

Muncie
Marchant, Gregory John *education educator*

New Albany
Riehl, Jane Ellen *education educator*

Notre Dame
Johnstone, Joyce Visintine *education educator*

Plymouth
Cardinal-Cox, Shirley Mae *education educator*

Terre Haute
Jerry, Robert Howard *retired education educator*
Van Til, William *education educator, writer*

Upland
Kitterman, Joan Frances *education educator*

Valparaiso
Maletta, Diane Stanley *education educator*

West Lafayette
Moskowitz, Herbert *management educator*

IOWA

Ames
Herwig, Joan Emily *developmental education educator, researcher*
Manatt, Richard *retired education educator*

Cascade
Peryon, Charleen D. *education educator, consultant*

Cedar Falls
Herring, Mary Corwin *education technology educator*

Cedar Rapids
Rosberg, Merilee Ann *education educator*

Davenport
Hudson, Celeste Nutting *education educator, reading clinic administrator, consultant*

Des Moines
Beisser, Sally Rapp *education educator*

Garner
Mestad, Gary Allen *education educator*

Iowa City
Duffy, William Edward, Jr., *retired education educator*

Keokuk
Mills, Sylvia Janet *secondary education educator*

Morning Sun
Byers, Elizabeth *education educator*

KANSAS

Kansas City
Bach, Michele *education educator*

Lawrence
Greenberg, Marc Leland *education educator*

North Newton
Ediger, Marlow *education educator*

Topeka
Diffley, Judy High *educator*
Smith, Loran Bradford *education educator*

Wichita
Penn, Patricia Whitley *education educator*

KENTUCKY

Cold Spring
Malayery, Nasrin *educator, consultant*

Georgetown
Powell, Rebecca Gaeth *education educator*

Lexington
Guskey, Thomas Robert *education educator*
Logan, Joyce Polley *education educator*

Louisville
Highland, Martha (Martie) *retired education educator, consultant*

Ludlow
Stull, Thomas James *education educator, coach*

Masonic Home
Schweichler, Mary Ellen *childhood education educator, consultant*

Owensboro
Glenn, Cornelia Jarmon *education educator*

Paducah
Hoffman, Rey *education educator, writer*

LOUISIANA

Baton Rouge
Litton, Nancy Joan *education educator*
Maxcy, Spencer John *education educator*

Hammond
Nauman, Ann Keith *education educator, department chairman*

Monroe
Hardin, Dawn Thomley *education leadership educator*

New Orleans
Levitt, Gregory Alan *education educator*
Longstreet, Wilma S. *curriculum and instruction educator*

MAINE

Ashland
Millett, Michael Fredric *education educator*

Machias
Rosen, David Matthew *education educator*

Orono
Butterfield, Stephen Alan *education educator*

MARYLAND

Baltimore
Lectka, Thomas *education educator*

Bel Air
Miller, Dorothy Eloise *education educator*

Bethesda
Jameson, Sanford Chandler *education educator*

Cambridge
Beath, Paula Marie Ruark *education educator, consultant*

Cockeysville
Cuninggim, Whitty Daniel *education educator*

Columbia
King, Ora Sterling *education educator, consultant*

Frostburg
Root, Edward Lakin *education educator, university administrator*

Salisbury
Verbeke, Karen Ann *education educator*

Towson
Hildebrand, Joan Martin *education educator*

MASSACHUSETTS

Amherst
Page, Max *education educator*

Ayer
Sizer, Theodore R. *education educator*

Boston
Backus, Ann Swift Newell *education educator, consultant*
Coleman, K(atherine) Ann *behavioral psychology educator*

Bridgewater
Nelson, Marian Emma *education educator*
Witherell, Nancy Louise *education educator*

Cambridge
Cazden, Courtney B(orden) *education educator*
Elmore, Richard F. *education educator*
Fischer, Kurt Walter *education educator*
Graham, Patricia Albjerg *education educator*
Harris, Joseph C. *education educator*
Lagemann, Ellen Condliffe *history and education educator*

Leominster
Suskind, Diana Lee *education educator*

Lowell
LeBaron, John Francis *education educator*

Marstons Mills
Martin, David Standish *education educator*

Medford
Reid, Peter Laurence Donald *education educator*

Provincetown
Wolfman, Brunetta Reid *education educator*

South Attleboro
Hanson, Barbara Jean *education educator*

Worcester
Donnelly, Carol Burns *education educator*
Johnson, Nancy Ann *education educator*

MICHIGAN

Ann Arbor
Ball, Deborah Loewenberg *education educator*
Cohen, David K. *education educator*
Merte, Herman, Jr., *education educator, mechanical engineer*

Detroit
Abel, Ernest Lawrence *education educator*
Hagman, Harlan Lawrence *education educator*
Kelly, James Arthur, Jr., *educator*
Rogers, Richard Lee *education educator*
Walker, Michael Leon *education educator*

East Lansing
Brophy, Jere Edward *education educator, researcher*
Hickey, Howard Wesley *retired education educator*
Young, Raymond James *retired education educator*

Grand Rapids
Bosma, Bette DeBruyn *education educator*
Margesson, Maxine Edge *educator*

Kalamazoo
Brashear, Robert Marion *retired education educator, consultant*
Burns, James W. *education educator*
Fager, Jennifer Jeanne *education educator*
Stufflebeam, Daniel LeRoy *education educator*

Kentwood
Yovich, Daniel John *education educator*

Lansing
Piveronus, Peter John, Jr., *education educator*

Macomb
Farmakis, George Leonard *education educator*

Rochester
Packard, Sandra Podolin *education educator, consultant*

Saint Clair Shores
McDonald, Patricia Leslie *education educator*

Traverse City
Petersen, Evelyn Ann *education consultant*

Ypsilanti
Gwaltney, Thomas Marion *education educator, writer*

MINNESOTA

Cambridge
Kittock, Claudia Jean *education educator*

Grand Marais
Kreitlow, Burton William *retired adult education educator*

Northfield
Kohl, Herbert Ralph *education educator*

Rochester
Sherman, Thomas Francis *education educator*

Winona
Nasstrom, Roy Richard *retired education educator, consultant*

MISSISSIPPI

Alcorn State
Felder-Wright, Pamela Theresa *education educator*

Columbus
Daffron, Martha *retired education educator*

Courtland
Lindgren, Carl Edwin *educational consultant, antiquarian, historian*

Hattiesburg
Culberson, James O. *retired rehabilitation educator*

Jackson
McLeod, Stephen Glenn *education educator, language educator*

Leakesville
Dobbins, Dolores Pauline *education educator, counselor*

Mississippi State
Gillaspie, Lynn Clara *education educator, educator*

Oxford
Wickham, Kathleen Woodruff *education educator*

Ridgeland
Lovette, Lillie Faye *education educator*

MISSOURI

Boonville
Cline, Dorothy May Stammerjohn (Mrs. Edward Wilburn Cline) *education educator, consultant*

Cape Girardeau
McMahan, Gale Ann Scivally *education educator*

Columbia
Hatley, Richard V(on) *education educator*

Marshall
Wymore, Luann Courtney *education educator*

Saint Louis
Gooch, Audrey Smith *retired education educator*
Miller, Jo Ann *education educator, college official*
Turner, Gwendolyn Yvonne *education educator*

MONTANA

Missoula
Rowland, Paul McDonald *education educator*

NEBRASKA

Lincoln
Heusel, Gary Lee *educator*
McGowan, Thomas *education educator, dean*

Omaha
Ho, David Kim Hong *education educator*

NEVADA

Las Vegas
Kassouf, Esther Kay *education educator*

NEW HAMPSHIRE

Concord
Twomey, Elizabeth Ann Molloy *education educator*

Durham
DeMitchell, Todd Allan *education educator*
Hart, Ann Weaver *educational administration educator*

Keene
Hickey, Delina Rose *retired education educator*

Manchester
Stefanik, Jean Marianne *retired education educator, naturalist*

Nashua
Mitsakos, Charles Leonidas *education educator, consultant*

New London
Taylor, Deborah Ann *education educator*

NEW JERSEY

Cherry Hill
Rovner, Leonard Irving *education educator*

Lawrenceville
Tharney, Leonard John *education educator, consultant*
Warner, Jean Rockwell *education educator*

New Brunswick
Durnin, Richard Gerry *education educator*
Garner, Charles William *educational administration educator, consultant*
Strickland, Dorothy *education educator*
Tanner, Daniel *curriculum theory educator*

Nutley
Pugliese, Joanne Gallagher *education educator*

Princeton
Howarth, William (Louis Howarth) *education educator, writer*

Warren
Hennings, Dorothy Grant (Mrs. George Hennings) *education educator*

Wayne
Goetz, William Walter *education and history educator*

West Long Branch
Bass, Mary Lee *education educator, administrator*

NEW MEXICO

Albuquerque
Drummond, Harold Dean *retired education educator*
Wood, Carolyn Jane *educational leadership educator*

Las Cruces
Heger, Herbert Krueger *education educator*

Raton
Robinson, Janie Monette *education educator*

Santa Fe
Sandoval, Isabelle Medina *education educator*

NEW YORK

Attica
Taylor, Karen Marie *education educator*

Binghamton
Coffey, Margaret Tobin *education educator, county official*
Okpewho, Isidore O *education educator*

Bronx
Rothstein, Anne Louise *education educator, college official*

Canandaigua
Malinowski, Patricia A. *community college educator*

Coxsackie
Santora, Olga Marie *retired education educator*

Delmar
Houghton, Raymond Carl, Jr., *education educator*

Dix Hills
Braun, Ludwig *educational technology consultant*

HIGHER EDUCATION: EDUCATION

East Amherst
Raven, Ronald Jacob *education educator, researcher, consultant*

Elmhurst
Lester, Lance Gary *education educator, researcher*

Elmira
Pratt, Linda *reading educator*

Grand Island
Muck, Ruth Evelyn Slacer (Mrs. Gordon E. Muck) *education educator*

Great Neck
Fried, Belle Warshavsky *education educator*

Hempstead
Gold, Ruth Forman *education educator*

Howard Beach
Iorio, John Emil *retired education educator*

Huntington Station
Devlin, Jean Theresa *educator, storyteller*

Ithaca
Green, Edward Thomas, Jr., *education educator*
Harris-Warrick, Ronald Morgan *education educator*
Steinberg, Michael P *education educator*

Jamaica
Cline, Janice Claire *education educator*
Faust, Naomi Flowe *education educator, poet*

Lockport
March, Cathleen Case *education educator*

Manlius
Booth, Patricia Vogt (Trish Booth) *education consultant*

Mastic Beach
Pagano, Alicia I. *education educator*

New Paltz
Edwards, Peter *education educator, writer*

New Rochelle
Gallagher, John Francis *education educator*

New York
Kopp, Wendy *teaching program administrator*
Monson, Robert Joseph *education educator*
Reutter, Eberhard Edmund, Jr., *education and law educator*
Rust, Frances O'Connell *education educator, department chairman*
Seidenberg, Rita Nagler *education educator*
Sobol, Thomas *education educator*
Townsend-Butterworth, Diana Barnard *educational consultant, author*
Vázquez, José Antonio *education educator*

Niagara University
Foote, Chandra Jeanet *education educator, writer, elementary school educator*

Nyack
Phillips, Kevin G. *education educator*

Oneonta
MacCreery, Neal Joseph *education educator*

Orangeburg
Hsu, Donald Kung-Hsing *education educator, management consultant*

Potsdam
Ha, Andrew Kwangho *education educator*

Poughkeepsie
Brakas, Nora Jachym *education educator*

Purchase
Caporino, Grace Connolly *education educator, consultant*

Rego Park
Tsui, Soo Hing *educational research consultant*

Sands Point
Cullinan, Bernice E(llinger) *education educator*

Southampton
Ferrara-Sherry, Donna Layne *education educator*

Syracuse
Burstyn, Joan Netta *education educator*
Schmidt, Patricia Ruggiano *education educator*
Wilbur, Franklin Pierce *education educator*

Utica
Boyle, William Leo, Jr., *educational consultant, retired college president*

White Plains
Robinson, Joan *education educator*

NORTH CAROLINA

Boone
Morris, Robert Darrell *reading education educator*

Chapel Hill
Salgado, Maria Antonia *education educator*
Ware, William Brettel *education educator*

Durham
Lindsey, Lydia *education educator, researcher*

Greenville
Hudgins, Herbert Cornelius, Jr., *education educator, department chairman*
Stuart, Andrew Michael *education educator*

Hickory
Painter, Lorene Huffman *retired education educator, psychologist*

Indian Trail
Hinson, Robert Wayne *education educator*

Kinston
Richardson, Vanessa *education educator*

Pembroke
Preston, Debra Sue *counselor, educator*

Raleigh
Baker, Stanley Beckwith *education educator*
Burris, Craven Allen *retired college administrator, educator*
Penick, John E. *education educator*

Winston Salem
Harris, Frederick Holladay deBrosche *business educator*

NORTH DAKOTA

Grand Forks
Olson, Myrna Raye *education educator*

OHIO

Ashland
McKinley, Norma Elizabeth *education educator*

Canton
Friesen, Bruce K. *education educator*

Celina
Wolfe, John Raymond *education educator*

Chillicothe
Leedy, Emily L. Foster (Mrs. William N. Leedy) *retired education educator, consultant*

Cincinnati
Mallory Harrison, George William *education educator, consultant*

Cleveland
Samson, Gordon Edgar *educator, consultant*

Columbia Station
Goll, Paulette Susan *education educator*

Columbus
Culbertson, Jack Arthur *education educator*

Dayton
Gies, Frederick John *education educator*

East Sparta
Cook, Martha Jane *educator, counselor*

Elyria
Wood, Jacalyn Kay *education educator, educational consultant*

Kent
DeBerry, Patricia Yvonne *education educator*

Kingston
Mathew, Martha Sue Cryder *retired education educator*

Kingsville
Poluga, Judith *education educator*

Marietta
Montgomery, Jerry Lynn *retired education educator*

Mechanicsburg
Maynard, Joan *education educator*

Medina
Hunter, Brinca Jo *education specialist*

Oxford
Thompson, Bertha Boya *retired education educator, antique dealer and appraiser*

Sylvania
Sampson, Earldine Robison *education educator*

Toledo
Romanoff, Marjorie Reinwald *retired education educator*

University Heights
Whelan, John Joseph *education educator*

Youngstown
Zorn, Robert Lynn *education educator*

OKLAHOMA

Edmond
Harryman, Rhonda L. *education educator*

Lawton
Cates, Dennis Lynn *education educator*
Smiley, Frederick Melvin *education educator, consultant*

Norman
Schindler, Barbara Francois *education educator*

Oklahoma City
Abram, Darlene Ruth Sheppard *education educator, consultant*
Childs, Gayle B(ernard) *retired education educator*

Tulsa
Barker, Colin George *education educator*
Robards, Shirley Jean Needs *education educator*

OREGON

Beaverton
Nikolich-Zugich, Janko *biomedical scientist, educator*

Corvallis
Lumpkin, Margaret Catherine *retired education educator*

Eugene
Matthews, Esther Elizabeth *education educator, consultant*

Portland
Hanna, Sami A. *education educator*
Leupp, Edythe Peterson *retired education educator*
Yatvin, Joanne Ina *education educator*

Yachats
Robeck, Mildred Coen *education educator, writer*

PENNSYLVANIA

Aliquippa
Drobac, Nikola (Nick Drobac) *education educator, consultant*

Bala Cynwyd
Oswald, James Marlin *education educator*

Chester
Rozycki, Edward George *education educator*

Clarion
Dingle, Patricia A. *education educator, artist*

Coraopolis
Southworth, Horton Coe *educational educator, education scholar*

Erie
Anderson, Cathie Kellogg *education educator*
Eberlin, Richard D. *education educator*

Gladwyne
Castetter, William Benjamin *retired education educator, educational director*

Indiana
Thibadeau, Eugene Francis *education educator, consultant*

Johnstown
Kushner, Boris Abraham *education educator*

Kutztown
Sunderland, Ray Thoburn *education educator, administrator*
Sychterz, Teresa A. *education educator*

Maple Glen
Weaver-Stroh, Joanne Mateer *education educator, consultant*

Media
Strunk, Betsy Ann Whitenight *education educator*

Philadelphia
Slaughter-Defoe, Diana Tresa *education educator*

Pittsburgh
Spinella, Dennis Michael *education educator*
Weidman, John Carl, II, *education educator, consultant*

Robesonia
Evaul, Charleen McClain *education educator*

Spring City
Middleton, Dawn E. *education educator*

State College
McKeel, Lillian Phillips *retired education educator*

Stroudsburg
Weitzmann, William Henry *education educator, photographer*

University Park
Fuhrman, Susan H *education educator*
Nicely, Robert Francis, Jr., *education educator, administrator*
Nolan, James Francis, Jr., *education educator*
Yoder, Edgar Paul *education educator*

Villanova
Heitzmann, Wm. Ray *education educator, coach*

SOUTH CAROLINA

Aiken
Gregg, Paula Ann *education educator*

Charleston
Smith, J. Roy *education educator*
Voorneveld, Richard Burke *education educator, college official*

Columbia
Sears, James Thomas *educator, researcher*

Greenville
Hill, Grace Lucile Garrison *education educator, consultant*

Hartsville
Rubinstein, Joseph Harris *education educator*

Spartanburg
Mahaffey, James Perry *education educator, consultant*

SOUTH DAKOTA

Aberdeen
Tebben, Sharon Lee *education educator*

TENNESSEE

Franklin
Guthrie, Glenda Evans *academic counselor, development specialist*

Germantown
Burnett, Suzanne Katherine *education educator*
Wiatr, Jeanne Malecki *education educator*

Jackson
Whaley, Carolyn Louise *education educator*

Knoxville
Yeomans, Gordon Allan *retired education educator*

Mc Minnville
Brock, Angela Eulene Douglass *education educator*

Memphis
Hill, Martha Nell *education educator*
Meredith, Cathy *education educator*
Pezeshki, S. Reza *education educator*

Nashville
Bloome, David Michael *education educator*
Farran, Dale Clark *education educator*
Madden, Paul Herman *education educator*
Quick, Beth Nason *education educator*
Reschly, Daniel J. *education educator, psychologist, educator*

Telford
Mashburn, Donald Eugene *education educator*

Tullahoma
Collins, S(arah) Ruth Knight *education educator*

TEXAS

Abilene
Harper, Dorothy Glen *education educator*

Austin
De Hart, Flora Ballowe *education educator*
Hunter, Brother Eagan (Donald J. Hunter) *retired education educator*
Justiz, Manuel Jon *education educator, researcher*

Carrollton
Last, Susan Walker *training developer*

College Station
Linn, Brian M *education educator*
Oxley, Mary Boone *early childhood education educator*
Sadoski, Mark Christian *education educator*

Commerce
Vornberg, James Alvin *education educator*

Conroe
Corley, Donna Jean *education educator, language arts educator*

Crosby
Shanklin, Annie Thomas *retired education educator*

Denton
Crocker, Betty Charlotte *education educator*
Greenlaw, Marilyn Jean *education educator, consultant, writer*

Fort Sam Houston
Robinson, Naomi Jean *educational training systems educator*

Fort Worth
Mays, Glenda Sue *retired education educator*

Georgetown
Davis, O. L., Jr., *education educator, researcher*

Houston
Beckingham, Kathleen Mary *education educator, researcher*
DiRosa, Linda Mary *education specialist, diagnostic company executive*
Ferguson, Jennifer Lee Berry *education educator*
Poats, Lillian Brown *education educator*
Wagner, Paul Anthony, Jr., *education educator*
Weber, Wilford Alexander *education educator*
Woods-Stellman, Donna Sue *education educator, reading consultant*

Laredo
Desiderio, Mike Francis *education educator*

HIGHER EDUCATION: EDUCATION

Longview
Fouse, Anna Beth *education educator*

Lubbock
Askins, Billy Earl *education educator, consultant*
Murray, John Patrick *education educator*
Yoder-Wise, Patricia Snyder *education educator*

Marfa
Hill, Celia Ann *retired education educator*

Marshall
Dahl, Shirley Ann Wise *education educator*

Mesquite
Vaughan, Joseph Lee, Jr., *education educator, consultant*

Moody
McNiel, Norbert Arthur *retired educator*

Pasadena
Herrera, Mary Cardenas *education educator, music minister*

Rancho Viejo
Garza, Roberto Jesus *retired education educator*

Richardson
Bray, Carolyn Scott *education educator*

San Angelo
Davison, Elizabeth Jane Linton *education educator*

San Antonio
Horowitz, Rosalind *education educator, researcher*

San Marcos
Fite, Kathleen Elizabeth *education educator*
Moore, Betty Jean *retired education educator*

Tye
Hill, Emma Lee *education educator*

Tyler
Marsh, Owen Robert *education educator, researcher*

Victoria
Hutto, Nora Marguerite Nelson *education educator*

Waco
Rogers, Douglas W. *education educator*
Stauber, Donna Beth *education educator*

UTAH

Provo
Allred, Ruel Acord *education educator*
Tunnell, Michael O'Grady *education educator*

Salt Lake City
Bennion, John Warren *urban education educator*

VERMONT

Burlington
Son, Mun Shig *education educator*

East Corinth
Freeman, Carole Cook *education educator*

VIRGINIA

Alexandria
Mallette, Lila Gene Mohler (Gurudev Sri Rasalilananda) *education educator, writer, editor*

Annandale
Weatherholtz, Donna Baker *education educator*
Wilhelmi, Mary Charlotte *education educator, college official*

Arlington
Freitag, Patricia Koenig *education educator*

Charlottesville
Miller, Margaret Alison *education educator*
Taylor, Alton Lee *education educator*

Lynchburg
Schewel, Rosel Hoffberger *education educator*

Manassas
Archer, Chalmers, Jr., *retired education educator*

Newport News
Eastman, John Robert *education educator*

Norfolk
Bucher, Katherine Toth *education educator, librarian*
Mallory, Sara Brockwell *education educator*
Ritz, John Michael *education educator*

Orange
Duncan, Douglas Allen *education educator*

Radford
Hanna, Mary Ann *education educator*

Rapidan
Powers, Evelyn Mae *education educator*

Reston
Waxman, Pearl Latterman *early childhood education educator*

Richmond
Maitre, Joan *education educator*
Smith, Charles H. *education educator*

Williamsburg
Carson, Barbara Gilbert *education educator, consultant*
Van Tassel-Baska, Joyce Lenore *education educator*
Yankovich, James Michael *education educator*

WASHINGTON

Anacortes
Felger, Ralph William *education educator, retired military officer*

Bellevue
Clark, Richard Walter *education consultant*

Bothell
Banks, Cherry Ann McGee *education educator*

Camas
Howe, Robert Wilson *education educator*

Seattle
Abbott, Robert Dean *education scientist*
Goodlad, John Inkster *education educator, writer*
Grembowski, David Emil *educator, researcher*

WISCONSIN

Barron
Johnson, Eleanor Mae *education educator*

Greenfield
Carlin, Carol Ruth *education educator*

Madison
Berggren-Moilanen, Bonnie Lee *education educator*
Odden, Allan Robert *education educator*

Milwaukee
Rheams, Annie Elizabeth *education educator*

WYOMING

Jackson
Massy, William Francis *education educator, consultant*

Laramie
Chatton, Barbara Ann *education educator*

TERRITORIES OF THE UNITED STATES

PUERTO RICO

Ponce
Chamorro Meléndez, Digna *education educator*

Rio Piedras
López de Mendez, Annette Giselda *education educator*
Medina-Diaz, Maria del Rosario *education educator*

VIRGIN ISLANDS

St Thomas
Shuck, Annette Ulsh *education educator*

CANADA

BRITISH COLUMBIA

Langley
Van Brummelen, Harro Walter *education educator*

Vancouver
Haycock, Kenneth Roy *education educator, consultant, administrator*

ONTARIO

Toronto
Blomberg, Douglas Gordon *education educator*

DENMARK

Odense
Laursen, Finn *education educator*

ESTONIA

Tallinn
Lippmaa, Endel *education educator, science educator*

ADDRESS UNPUBLISHED

Baney, Lori A. *education educator*
Barcus, Nancy B. *education educator, writer*
Becker, Dorothy Loretta *education educator, librarian*
Becker, Robert Dean *retired education educator, retired academic administrator*
Bridger, Teresa Lynne *education educator*
Brimijoin, Kay Rothgeb *education educator*
Brown, Abbie Howard *education educator, researcher*
Brownfield, Sally Ann *education educator*
Burow, Sharon Ruth *education educator*
Butler, Orton Carmichael *earth science educator, climatologist*
Cannon, Lena Ferrara Lee *retired education educator*
Carlin, Betty *education educator*
Colage, Beatrice Elvira *education educator*
Collinson, Vivienne Ruth *education educator, researcher, consultant*
Cooper, James Michael *education educator*
Cross, Kathryn Patricia *education educator*
Dias, Mari Nardolillo *education educator, consultant*
Doby, Janice Kay *education educator, science educator*
Ebert, Robert Peter *education educator*
Edwards, June Caroline *retired education educator*
Elliott, Willie Lawrence *education educator, department chairman*
Endicott, Jennifer Jane Reynolds *education educator*
Facciano, Pauline Rose *education educator*
Filchock, Ethel *education educator*
Fitzpatrick, Ruth Ann *education educator*
Frey, Katie Manciet *education educator*
Gardner, David Chambers *adult education educator, psychologist, business executive, author*
Garner, Doris Traganza *education educator, director*
Gass, Saul Irving *retired education educator*
Gehring, Donald D. *education educator*
Gibson, Orpha Ray *retired education educator*
Gittman, Elizabeth *education educator*
Gladstone, Carol Lynn *education educator*
Gordon, Margaret Louise *former education educator*
Grabill, James R., Jr., *education educator, editor, writer*
Hancock, Charles R. *education educator*
Haneke, Dianne Myers *retired education educator*
Hastings-Bishop, Susan Jane *education educator*
Haugland, Susan Warrell *education educator, consultant*
Heestand, Diane Elissa *education educator, medical educator*
Henderson, William Eugene *education educator*
Huffman, Janice Kay *middle school educator, curriculum coordinator*
Jefferis, Bernice K. *education educator*
Johnson, Olin Chester *education educator*
Kelley, Patricia Colleen *education educator, researcher*
Keyes, Joan Ross Rafter *education educator, author*
Kirkpatrick, Dorothy Louise *retired education educator, program coordinator*
Klucking, Gail Marie *education educator*
Kravetz, Nathan *education educator, writer*
Larson, Robert William *education educator, consultant*
Lester, Robin Dale *education educator, writer, former headmaster*
Lewicke, Catherine Pearl *retired education educator*
Lewis, Philip *educational and technical consultant*
Lindsay, Beverly
Lindsey, Ruth *retired education educator*
Little, Claire Long *education educator, humanities educator*
Macko, Stephen Alexander *education educator*
Martin, David Jerner *education educator*
Martin, John Swanson *retired education educator*
Mattice, Howard LeRoy *retired education educator*
McGregor, F. Daniel *education educator*
McLoone, Eugene P. *education educator*
Morgan, Mary Lou *retired education educator, civic worker*
Munuz, Florence Batt *education educator*
Murphy, Jeanette Carol *education educator*
Nelson, Murry Robert *education educator*
Noddings, Nel *education educator, writer*
Parker, Marilyn *elementary school and education educator, assistant principal, school/special education counselor, entrepreneur*
Parks, Julia Etta *retired education educator*
Patterson, Mildred Lucas *retired teaching specialist*
Peabody, Merle Andrew *education educator*
Perry, Raymond Carver *education educator*
Posch, Margaret A. *education educator, researcher*
Pyle, Wilma J. *retired education educator*
Roberts, Patricia Lee *education educator*
Rudden, Jane Frances *education educator*
Russell, Louise *education educator, folklorist*
Schaffer, Eugene Carl *education educator*
Schuster, Sylvia M. *education educator*
Scordias, Margaret Ann *education educator*
Sherman, Richard H. *education educator*
Sizemore, Barbara Ann *Black studies educator*
Southworth, Jamie MacIntyre *retired education educator*
Stark, Joan Scism *education educator*
Stoecklin, Sister Carol Ann *education educator*
Stoker, Howard W. *former education educator, educational administrator, consultant*
Stomfay-Stitz, Aline Maria *education educator*
Tanner, Laurel Nan *education educator*
Tapp, Anne Renee Goss *education educator*
Thompson, Raymond Eugene, Jr., *education educator*
Tonjes, Marian Jeannette Benton *education educator*
Turnbull, Vernona Harmsen *retired residence counselor, education educator*
Walters, Donald Lee *education educator*
Weiss, Kenneth Jay *education educator, reading specialist, administrator*
Wolf, Joan D. *education educator*
Young, Katherine Ann *education educator*
Young, Virgil Monroe *education educator*
Zernial, Susan Carol *education educator, consultant, editor*
Zilbert, Allen Bruce *education educator, computer consultant*

HIGHER EDUCATION: ENGINEERING

UNITED STATES

ALABAMA

Auburn
Blakney, William Gilbert Grover *engineer, educator*
Cicci, David Allen *aerospace engineer, educator*
Foster, Winfred Ashley, Jr., *aerospace engineering educator*
Picha, Kenneth George *mechanical engineering educator*
Rainer, Rex Kelly *civil engineer, educator*

Huntsville
Balint, David Lee *engineering company executive*
Vaughan, Otha H., Jr., *retired aerospace engineer*

Tuscaloosa
Barfield, Robert F. *retired mechanical engineer, educator, dean*
Moynihan, Gary Peter *industrial engineering educator*
Park, Duk-Won *mining/civil engineer, educator*
Pitt, Robert Ervin *environmental engineer, educator*
Turner, Daniel Shelton *civil engineering educator*

ARIZONA

Chandler
Fordemwalt, James Newton *microelectronics engineering educator, consultant*

Flagstaff
Scott, David Robin *electrical engineering educator*
Vadasz, Peter *engineering educator, consultant*

Prescott
Bieniawski, Zdzislaw Tadeusz Richard *engineering educator emeritus, writer, consultant*
Kahne, Stephen James *systems engineer, educator, academic administrator, engineering executive*

Tempe
Laananen, David Horton *mechanical engineer, educator*
Robertson, Samuel Harry, III, *transportation safety research engineer, educator*
Schroder, Dieter Karl *electrical engineering educator*
Si, Jennie *engineering educator*

Tucson
Bahill, A. Terry *systems engineering educator*
Jones, Roger Clyde *retired electrical engineering educator*
Ogilvie, T(homas) Francis *engineer, educator*
Slack, Donald Carl *agricultural engineer, educator*

ARKANSAS

Fayetteville
White, John Austin, Jr., *engineering educator, university chancellor*

CALIFORNIA

Arcata
Chaney, Ronald Claire *environmental engineering educator, consultant*

Belmont
Hollis, Mary Frances *aerospace educator*

Berkeley
Berger, Stanley Allan *mechanical and biomechanical engineering educator*
Birdsall, Charles Kennedy *electrical engineer*
Cairns, Elton James *chemical engineering educator*
Carey, Van Patrick *mechanical engineering educator, researcher*
Chopra, Anil Kumar *civil engineering educator*
Dornfeld, David Alan *engineering educator*
Evans, James William *metallurgical engineer*
Hodges, David Albert *electrical engineering educator*
Hu, Chenming *electrical engineering educator*
Kastenberg, William Edward *engineering educator, science educator*

Koshland, Catherine Preston *mechanical engineer, educator*
Kuh, Ernest Shiu-Jen *electrical engineering educator*
Leitmann, George *mechanical engineer, educator*
Ma, Fai *mechanical engineering educator*
Monismith, Carl Leroy *civil engineering educator*
Muller, Richard Stephen *electrical engineer, educator*
Pister, Karl Stark *engineering educator*
Polak, Elijah *engineering educator, computer scientist*
Prausnitz, John Michael *chemical engineer, educator*
Skabardonis, Alexander *civil engineering educator*
Tien, Chang-Lin
Tomizuka, Masayoshi *mechanical engineering educator, researcher*
White, Richard Manning *electrical engineering educator*

Canyon Country
Hawkins, Dale Cicero *aviator, educator, engineer*

Claremont
Dym, Clive Lionel *engineering educator*
Molinder, John Irving *engineering educator, consultant*
Monson, James Edward *electrical engineer, educator*
Tanenbaum, Basil Samuel *engineering educator*

Clovis
Brahma, Chandra Sekhar *civil engineering educator*

Cool
Trybul, Theodore Nicholas *engineering educator*

Cupertino
Franson, C(arl) Irvin *aerospace material and process engineer, educator*

Davis
Gardner, William Allen *electrical engineering educator*
Hakimi, S. Louis *electrical and computer engineering educator*

Fairfield
Mayers, Jean *aerospace engineering educator*

Fullerton
Tehrani, Fleur Taher *electrical engineer, educator, researcher*

Irvine
Chelapati, Chunduri Venkata *civil engineering educator*
Orme, Melissa Emily *mechanical engineering educator*

La Jolla
Chang, William Shen Chie *electrical engineering educator*
Coler, Myron A(braham) *chemical engineer, educator*
Karin, Sidney *computer science and engineering educator*
Williams, Forman Arthur *engineering science educator, combustion theorist*

La Mirada
Kong, Xiangli (Charlie Kong) *mechanical and control engineer, educator*

Lincoln
Chiang, George Djia-Chee *retired engineer, educator*

Long Beach
Dillon, Michael Earl *engineering executive, mechanical engineer, educator*
Kumar, Rajendra *electrical engineering educator*

Los Angeles
Alwan, Abeer *electrical engineering educator*
Chobotov, Vladimir Alexander *aerospace engineer, educator*
Friedlander, Sheldon Kay *chemical engineering educator*
Kim, Jeongbin John *mechanical engineering educator*
Maxworthy, Tony *mechanical and aerospace engineering educator*
McKellop, Harry Alden *biomechanical engineering educator*
Mehrabian, Robert *aerospace engineer, academic administrator*
Rauch, Lawrence Lee *aerospace and electrical engineer, educator*
Saravanja-Fabris, Neda *mechanical engineering educator*
Udwadia, Firdaus Erach *engineering educator, consultant*
Vasileiadis, Savvas *chemical engineer, environmental engineer, materials engineer, educator*

Marina Del Rey
Philpott, Lindsey *civil engineer, researcher, educator*

Menlo Park
Shah, Haresh Chandulal *civil engineering educator*

Monterey
Newberry, Conrad Floyde *aerospace engineering educator*
Platzer, Max F. *aeronautics and astronautics educator*

Morro Bay
Wagner, Peter Ewing *physics and electrical engineering educator*

Northridge
Rengarajan, Sembiam Rajagopal *electrical engineering educator, researcher, consultant*

Oakland
King, Cary Judson, III, *chemical engineer, educator, university official*

Palo Alto
Quate, Calvin Forrest *engineering educator*

Palos Verdes Peninsula
Seide, Paul *civil engineering educator*

Pasadena
Flagan, Richard Charles *chemical engineering educator*
Gavalas, George R. *chemical engineering educator*
Hornung, Hans Georg *aeronautical engineering educator, science facility administrator*
Jennings, Paul Christian *civil engineering educator, academic administrator*
Yeh, Paul Pao *electrical and electronics engineer, educator*

Pomona
Bernick, Robert Lloyd *engineering educator*

San Diego
Anderson, Paul Maurice *electrical engineering educator, researcher, consultant*
Auld, Robert Henry, Jr., *biomedical engineer, educator, consultant, author*
Butler, Geoffrey Scott *systems engineer, educator, consultant*
Plotkin, Allen *aerospace engineer, educator*

San Francisco
Keller, Edward Lowell *electrical engineer, educator*
Svensson, Bengt Anders *engineering educator*

San Jose
Haque, Mohammed Shahidul *electrical engineer, educator*
Jacobson, Albert Herman, Jr., *industrial and systems engineer, educator*

San Luis Obispo
Cummings, Russell Mark *aerospace engineer, educator*
Moazzami, Sara *civil engineering educator*

Santa Barbara
Bruch, John Clarence, Jr., *engineer, educator*
McMeeking, Robert Maxwell *mechanical engineer, educator*

Santa Clara
Chen, Wai-Kai *electrical engineering and computer science educator, consultant*

Stanford
Aziz, Khalid *petroleum engineering educator*
Boudart, Michel *chemical engineer, chemist, educator, consultant*
Cox, Donald Clyde *electrical engineering educator*
Franklin, Gene Farthing *engineering educator, consultant*
Gibbons, James Franklin *electrical engineering educator*
Goodman, Joseph Wilfred *electrical engineering educator*
Gray, Robert M(olten) *electrical engineering educator*
Harris, Stephen Ernest *electrical engineering and applied physics educator*
Kailath, Thomas *electrical engineer, educator*
Kane, Thomas Reif *engineering educator*
Kruger, Paul *nuclear civil engineering educator*
Levitt, Raymond Elliot *civil engineering educator*
Macovski, Albert *electrical engineer, educator*
Marhic, Michel Edmond *engineering educator, entrepreneur, consultant*
McCarty, Perry Lee *civil and environmental engineering educator*
Pease, Roger Fabian Wedgwood *electrical engineering educator*
Reynolds, William Craig *mechanical engineer, educator*
Roth, Bernard *mechanical engineering educator, researcher*
White, Robert Lee *electrical engineer, educator*

Walnut Creek
Hanson, Robert Duane *civil engineering educator*

COLORADO

Bayfield
Haug, Edward Joseph, Jr., *retired mechanical engineering educator, simulation research engineer*

Boulder
Cathey, Wade Thomas *retired electrical engineering educator*
Corotis, Ross Barry *civil engineering educator, academic administrator*
Sture, Stein *civil engineering educator*
Timmerhaus, Klaus Dieter *chemical engineering educator*
Waite, William McCastline *electrical engineer educator, consultant*

Centennial
Ballard, Jack Stokes *engineering educator*

Denver
Alaghband, Gita *computer engineer, educator*

Fort Collins
Kaufman, Harold Richard *mechanical engineer and physics educator*
Richardson, Everett Vern *hydraulic engineer, educator, administrator, consultant*

Grand Junction
Rybak, James Patrick *engineering educator*
Tavossi, Hasson M. *physics and engineering educator, consultant*

Littleton
Whitehouse, Charles Barton *avionics educator*

Westminster
Dalesio, Wesley Charles *former aerospace educator*

CONNECTICUT

Branford
Ma, Tso-Ping *electrical engineering educator, researcher, consultant*

Mystic
Lincoln, Walter Butler, Jr., *marine engineer, educator*

New Britain
Czajkowski, Eva Anna *aerospace engineer, educator*

New Haven
Haller, Gary Lee *chemical engineering educator*
Horváth, Csaba *chemical engineering educator, researcher*

Orange
Lobay, Ivan *mechanical engineering educator*

DELAWARE

Bear
Wright, Stephanie M.G. *aerospace educator*

Newark
Allen, Herbert Ellis *environmental chemistry educator*
Brockenbrough, Thomas William *civil engineer, educator*
Christy, Charles Wesley, III, *industrial engineering educator*
Kaler, Eric William *chemical engineer, educator*
Lomax, Kenneth Mitchell *agricultural engineering educator*
Sandler, Stanley Irving *chemical engineering educator*
Vinson, Jack Roger *mechanical engineer, educator*

Wilmington
Valentini, Jose Esteban *chemical engineering director, scientist, educator*

DISTRICT OF COLUMBIA

Washington
Arkilic, Galip Mehmet *mechanical engineer, educator*
Chen, Ho-Hong H. H. *industrial engineering executive, educator*
Khozeimeh, Issa *electrical engineer, educator*
Pickholtz, Raymond Lee *electrical engineering educator, consultant*
Thigpen, Lewis *engineering educator*

FLORIDA

Boca Raton
Furht, Borivoje *computer engineer, educator, researcher*
Han, Chingping Jim *industrial engineer, educator*
Pajunen, Grazyna Anna *electrical engineer, educator*
Su, Tsung-Chow Joe *engineering educator*

Clearwater
Fehr, Ralph Edward, III, *electrical engineer, educator*

Coral Gables
Modestino, James William *electrical engineering educator*
Warburton, Ralph Joseph *architectural engineer, educator*

Fort Myers
Sechrist, Chalmers Franklin, Jr., *electrical engineering educator*

Gainesville
Orazem, Mark Edward *chemical engineering educator*
Schmertmann, John Henry *civil engineer, educator, consultant*
Sherif, S. A. *mechanical engineering educator*
Shyy, Wei *aerospace and mechanical engineering researcher, educator*
Tia, Mang *civil engineering educator*
Verink, Ellis Daniel, Jr., *metallurgical engineering educator, consultant*

Jacksonville
Joyce, Edward Rowen *retired chemical engineer, educator*

Miami
Chaves, Juan Carlos *mechanical engineering educator, consultant, researcher*

Daumas Ladouce, Pablo *engineer, educator, consultant*

Orlando
Biegel, John Edward *retired industrial engineering educator*

Saint Cloud
Everett, Woodrow Wilson *electrical engineer, educator*

Sarasota
Deutsch, Sid *bioengineer, educator*

Sun City Center
Edwards, Paul Beverly *retired science and engineering educator*

Tallahassee
Arce, Pedro Edgardo *chemical engineering educator*
Chen, Ching Jen *mechanical engineering educator, research scientist*
Zhang, Chun Chuck *industrial engineer, educator*

Tampa
Givens, Paul Edward *industrial engineer, educator*
Wade, Thomas Edward *electrical engineering educator, university research administrator*

GEORGIA

Athens
Tollner, Ernest William *agricultural engineering educator, agricultural radiology consultant*

Atlanta
Armanios, Erian Abdelmessih *aerospace engineer, educator*
Ellingwood, Bruce Russell *structural engineering researcher, educator*
Hess, Dennis William *chemical engineering educator*
Lohmann, Jack R. *engineering educator*
McDowell, David Lynn *mechanical engineering educator*
Parsonson, Peter Sterling *civil engineer, educator, consultant*
Pence, Ira Wilson, Jr., *material handling research executive, engineer*
Porter, Alan Leslie *industrial and systems engineering educator*
Simitses, George John *retired engineering educator, consultant*
Stacey, Weston Monroe, Jr., *nuclear engineer, educator, physicist*
Tedder, Daniel William *chemical engineering educator*
Teja, Amyn Sadrudin *chemical engineering educator, consultant*
Thuesen, Gerald Jorgen *industrial engineer, educator*
Wadsworth, Harrison Morton, Jr., *industrial engineering educator, consultant*
Winer, Ward Otis *mechanical engineer, educator*
Wyvill, J. Craig *research engineer, program director*
Yoganathan, Ajit Prithiviraj *biomedical engineer, educator*

Marietta
Ranu, Harcharan Singh *biomedical scientist, administrator, orthopaedic biomechanics educator*

Savannah
Hsu, Ming-Yu *engineering educator*

IDAHO

Boise
Affleck, Stephen Bruce *chemical and civil engineer, educator*
Pline, James Leonard *civil engineer, educator*

Moscow
Johnson, Brian Keith *electrical engineering educator*

Pocatello
Bennion, John Stradling *engineering educator, consultant*

ILLINOIS

Argonne
Miller, Shelby Alexander *chemical engineer, educator*

Champaign
Sohn, Chang Wook *energy systems researcher, educator*

Chicago
Aggarwal, Suresh Kumar *mechanical and aerospace engineering educator*
Arastoopour, Hamid *chemical engineering educator*
Banerjee, Prashant *industrial engineering educator*
Dix, Rollin C(umming) *mechanical engineering educator, consultant*
Kennedy, Lawrence Allan *mechanical engineering educator*
Murad, Sohail *engineer educator*
Russo, Gilberto *engineering educator*

Edwardsville
Gu, Keqin *mechanical engineering educator*

Evanston
Achenbach, Jan Drewes *engineering educator, scientist*
Backman, Vadim *biomedical engineer, educator*
Bankoff, Seymour George *chemical engineer, educator*
Belytschko, Ted *civil and mechanical engineering educator*
Brazelton, William Thomas *chemical engineering educator*
Carr, Stephen Howard *materials engineer, educator*
Cheng, Herbert Su-Yuen *mechanical engineering educator*
Chung, Yip-Wah *engineering educator*
Daniel, Isaac Mordochai *mechanical engineering educator*
Daskin, Mark Stephen *civil engineering educator*
Goldstick, Thomas Karl *biomedical engineering educator*
Haddad, Abraham Herzl *electrical engineering educator, researcher*
Krizek, Raymond John *civil engineering educator, consultant*
Kung, Harold Hing-Chuen *engineering educator*
Liu, Wing Kam *mechanical engineering educator*
Ottino, Julio Mario *chemical engineering educator, scientist*
Plonus, Martin Algirdas *electrical engineering educator*
Rubenstein, Albert Harold *industrial engineering and management sciences educator*
Taflove, Allen *electrical engineer, educator, researcher, consultant*
Tankin, Richard Samuel *fluid dynamics engineer, educator*

Normal
Devinatz, Victor Gary *industrial relations educator*

Peoria
Kroll, Dennis Edwards *industrial engineering educator*
Polanin, W. Richard *engineering educator*

Schaumburg
Kornowski, Robert Richard *engineer, science educator*

Urbana
Axford, Roy Arthur *nuclear engineering educator*
Benekohal, Rahim Farahnak *civil engineering educator, researcher, consultant*
Chato, John Clark *mechanical and bioengineering educator*
Coleman, Paul Dare *electrical engineering educator*
Jacobson, Sheldon Howard *engineering educator*
Maxwell, William Hall Christie *civil engineering educator*
Miley, George Hunter *nuclear and electrical engineering educator*
Prussing, John Edward *aerospace engineer, educator, researcher*
Sentman, Lee H. *aerospace engineer, educator*

INDIANA

Angola
Lin, Ping-Wha *engineering educator, consultant*

Evansville
Bennett, Paul Edmond *engineering educator*

Fort Wayne
Hwang, Santai *electrical engineering educator*

Hammond
Neff, Gregory Pall *mechanical engineer, educator*

Indianapolis
Fer, Ahmet F. *electrical engineer, educator*

Kokomo
Miller, Robert Frank *retired electronics engineer, educator*

Lafayette
Bernhard, Robert James *mechanical engineer, educator*
Caldwell, Barrett Scott *industrial engineering educator*
Fox, Robert William *mechanical engineering educator*
Ransom, Victor Harvey *engineering educator*

Muncie
Seymour, Richard Deming *technology educator*

Notre Dame
Incropera, Frank Paul *mechanical engineering educator*
Jerger, Edward William *mechanical engineer, university dean*
Schmitz, Roger Anthony *chemical engineer, educator, academic administrator*

Terre Haute
Malooley, David Joseph *electronics and computer technology educator*

West Lafayette
Barany, James Walter *industrial engineering educator*
Cohen, Raymond *mechanical engineer, educator*
Drnevich, Vincent Paul *civil engineering educator*
Grace, Richard Edward *engineering educator*
Greenkorn, Robert Albert *chemical engineering educator*
Neudeck, Gerold Walter *electrical engineering educator*
Pierret, Robert F. *electrical engineering educator*
Taylor, Raymond Ellory *engineering executive*
Tomovic, Mileta Milos *mechanical engineer, educator*
Wankat, Phillip Charles *chemical engineering educator*
Williams, Theodore Joseph *engineering educator*
Wright, Jeff Regan *civil engineering educator*

IOWA

Ames
McGee, Thomas Donald *materials engineer, educator*
Tannehill, John C. *aerospace engineer, educator*

Cedar Falls
Rao, Posinasetti Nageswara *manufacturing engineering educator*

Iowa City
Andersland, Mark Steven *electrical and computer engineering educator*
Kusiak, Andrew *manufacturing engineer, educator*

Oakdale
Huq, Mansur U. Kennedy *chemical engineer, materials scientist, educator, entrepreneur*

KANSAS

Lawrence
Darwin, David *civil engineering educator, researcher, consultant*
Green, Don Wesley *chemical and petroleum engineering educator*
Moore, Richard Kerr *electrical engineering educator*
Vossoughi, Shapour *chemical and petroleum engineering educator*

Manhattan
Erickson, Larry Eugene *chemical engineering educator*
Steichen, James Matthew *agricultural engineer, educator*

Salina
Delker, David Glen *electronic engineering technology educator, consultant*

Wichita
Paarmann, Larry Dean *electrical engineering educator*

KENTUCKY

Lexington
Radun, Arthur Vorwerk *electrical engineering educator*
Wang, Shien Tsun *civil engineering educator*

Louisville
Cornelius, Wayne Anderson *electrical and computer engineering consultant*
Hanley, Thomas Richard *engineering educator*
Taylor, G. Don *industrial engineering educator*

Winchester
Studebaker, John Milton *utilities engineer, consultant, educator*

LOUISIANA

Baton Rouge
Chen, Peter Pin-Shan *electrical engineering, computer science and internet/web educator, data processing executive*
Pike, Ralph Webster *chemical engineer, educator, university administrator*
Reible, Danny David *environmental chemical engineer, educator*
Valsaraj, Kalliat Thazhathuveetil *chemical engineering educator*

Dubach
Straughan, William Thomas *engineering educator*

Grambling
Harrison, Edward Matthew *retired industrial educator*

Natchitoches
Christensen, Raymond Lyle *electrical engineer, educator*

New Orleans
Lintinger, Gregory John *electrical engineer, educator*

Ruston
Sterling, Raymond Leslie *civil engineering educator, researcher, consultant*

MAINE

Auburn
Bastow, Richard Frederick *civil engineer, educator, surveyor*

Eastport
Kennedy, Robert Spayde *electrical engineering educator*

Waterville
Laurence, Robert Lionel *chemical engineering educator*

MARYLAND

Baltimore
Ball, William Parks *environmental engineer and educator*
Carmi, Shlomo *mechanical engineering educator, scientist*
Fisher, Jack Carrington *environmental engineering educator*
Jelinek, Frederick *electrical engineer, educator*
Meneveau, Charles Vivant *mechanical engineering and applied sciences educator, researcher*
Sharpe, William Norman, Jr., *mechanical engineer, educator*
Sincero, Arcadio Pacquiao *engineering educator*

Bethesda
Di Marzo, Marino *engineering researcher, educator*
Nimeroff, Phyllis Ruth *electronic engineer, visual artist*

College Park
Newcomb, Robert Wayne *electrical engineer educator*

Frederick
Bryan, John Leland *retired engineering educator*

Hyattsville
Berger, Bruce Sutton *mechanical engineering educator*
Kirk, James Allen *mechanical engineering educator*

MASSACHUSETTS

Amherst
Schaubert, Daniel Harold *electrical engineering educator*

Belmont
Merrill, Edward Wilson *chemical engineering educator*

Boston
Baillieul, John Brouard *aerospace engineering and applied mathematics educator*
Buchanan, Walter Woolwine *electrical engineer, educator, academic administrator*
Grenzebach, William Southwood *nuclear engineer, consultant, historian*
Rappaport, Carey Milford *electrical engineering educator*
Saleh, Bahaa E. A. *electrical engineering educator*
Schubert, E. Fred *electrical engineer, educator*
Teich, Malvin Carl *electrical engineering educator*

Cambridge
Ben-Akiva, Moshe Emanuel *civil engineering educator*
Brenner, Howard *chemical engineering educator*
Brockett, Roger Ware *engineering and computer science educator*
Brown, Robert Arthur *chemical engineering educator*
Chen, Sow-Hsin *nuclear engineering educator, researcher*
Corbato, Fernando Jose *electrical engineer and computer science educator*
Covert, Eugene Edzards *aerospace engineer, physics educator*
Cummings-Saxton, James *chemical engineer, consultant, educator*
de Neufville, Richard Lawrence *engineering educator*
Dewey, Clarence Forbes, Jr., *engineering educator*
Eagleson, Peter Sturges *civil engineer, environmental engineer, educator*
Gallager, Robert Gray *electrical engineering educator*
Glicksman, Leon Robert *mechanical engineering educator*
Greitzer, Edward Marc *aeronautical engineering educator, consultant*
Griffith, Peter *mechanical engineering educator, researcher*
Gyftopoulos, Elias Panayiotis *mechanical and nuclear engineering educator*
Heywood, John Benjamin *mechanical engineering educator*
Howard, Jack Benny *chemical engineer, educator, researcher*
Kamm, Roger Dale *biomedical engineer, educator*
Kazimi, Mujid Suliman *nuclear engineer, educator*
Kong, Jin Au *electrical engineering educator*
Ladd, Charles Cushing, III, *civil engineer, educator*
Latanision, Ronald Michael *materials science and engineering educator, consultant*
Mann, Robert Wellesley *biomedical engineer, educator*
Markey, Winston Roscoe *aeronautical engineering educator*
McGarry, Frederick Jerome *civil engineering educator*
Milgram, Jerome H. *marine and ocean engineer, educator*
Remington, Paul James *mechanical engineer, educator*
Rogers, Peter Phillips *environmental engineering educator, city planner*
Russell, Kenneth Calvin *metallurgical engineer, educator*
Saltzer, Jerome Howard *computer science educator*
Siebert, William McConway *electrical engineering educator*
Smith, Kenneth Alan *chemical engineer, educator*
Sonin, Ain A. *mechanical engineering educator, consultant*
Triantafyllou, Michael Stefanos *ocean engineering educator*
Trilling, Leon *aeronautical engineering educator*
Troxel, Donald Eugene *electrical engineering educator*
Tuller, Harry Louis *materials science and engineering educator*
Vander Velde, Wallace Earl *aeronautical and astronautical educator*
Vunjak-Novakovic, Gordana *chemical engineer, educator*
Whitman, Robert Van Duyne *civil engineer, educator*
Williams, James Henry, Jr., *mechanical engineer, educator, consultant*
Wilson, David Gordon *mechanical engineering educator*
Wuensch, Bernhardt John *ceramic engineering educator*
Yannas, Ioannis Vassilios *polymer scientist, educator*
Young, Laurence Retman *biomedical engineer, educator*

Lexington
Morrow, Walter Edwin, Jr., *electrical engineer, university laboratory administrator*

Lincoln
Kerrebrock, Jack Leo *aeronautics and astronautics engineering educator*

Lowell
Paikowsky, Samuel G. *civil engineering educator*

Medford
Astill, Kenneth Norman *mechanical engineering educator*
Howell, Alvin Harold *engineer, company executive, educator*

North Dartmouth
Cory, Lester Warren *electrical engineering educator*

Pittsfield
Shammas, Nazih Kheirallah *environmental engineering educator, consultant*

South Hadley
Randall, Hermine Maria *retired power plant engineer*

Springfield
Masi, James Vincent *electrical engineering educator*

Swampscott
Kaufman, William Morris *engineer consultant*

Worcester
Norton, Robert Leo, Sr., *mechanical engineer, educator, researcher*
Parrish, Edward Alton, Jr., *electrical and computer engineering educator, academic administrator*
Rencis, Joseph John *engineering educator, mechanical and civil engineer*

MICHIGAN

Ann Arbor
Assanis, Dennis N. (Dionissios Assanis) *mechanical engineering educator*
Director, Stephen William *electrical and computer engineering educator, academic administrator*
England, Anthony Wayne *electrical engineering and computer science educator, astronaut, geophysicist*
Felbeck, David Kniseley *mechanical engineering educator*
Gibala, Ronald *metallurgical engineering educator*
Green, Paul Allan *scientist, engineer, educator*
Haddad, George Ilyas *engineering educator, research scientist*
Hryciw, Roman D. *civil engineering educator*
Kammash, Terry *nuclear engineering educator*
Kearfott, Kimberlee Jane *nuclear engineer, health physicist, educator*
Leith, Emmett Norman *electrical engineer, educator*
Liu, Vi-Cheng *aerospace engineering educator*
Lyons, Harvey Isaac *mechanical engineering educator*
Martin, William Russell *nuclear engineering educator*
Mazumder, Jyotirmoy *mechanical and materials engineering educator*
O'Brien, William Joseph *materials engineer, educator, consultant*
Powell, Kenneth Grant *aerospace engineering educator*
Root, William Lucas *electrical engineering educator*
Schwank, Johannes Walter *chemical engineering educator*
Ulaby, Fawwaz Tayssir *electrical engineering and computer science educator, research center administrator*
Wight, James K. *civil engineer, research scientist, educator*
Wineman, Alan Stuart *mechanical engineering and applied mechanics educator*
Young, Edwin Harold *chemical and metallurgical engineering educator*

HIGHER EDUCATION: ENGINEERING

Dearborn
Kendall, Laurel Ann *geotechnical engineer*
Little, Robert Eugene *mechanical engineering educator, materials behavior researcher, consultant*

Detroit
Rathod, Mulchand *mechanical engineering educator*

East Lansing
Asmussen, Jes, Jr., *electrical engineer, educator, consultant*
Goodman, Erik David *engineering educator*
Radcliffe, Clark Jeffrey *mechanical engineering educator*
von Bernuth, Robert Dean *agricultural engineering educator, consultant*

Houghton
Lumsdaine, Edward *mechanical engineering educator*
Pandit, Sudhakar Madhavrao *engineering educator*
Pelc, Karol Ignacy *engineering and technology management educator, researcher*

Iron Mountain
Jamar, John Woodbridge *technology education educator, consultant*

Kalamazoo
Engelmann, Paul Victor *plastics engineering educator*

Madison Heights
Xia, Jiding *chemical engineering educator*

Marquette
Curtis, Mark Allen *engineering educator, author, consultant*

MINNESOTA

Minneapolis
Anderson, John Edward *mechanical engineering educator*
Davis, Howard Ted *engineering educator*
Finkelstein, Stanley Michael *engineering educator, research biomedical engineer*
Goldstein, Richard Jay *mechanical engineer, educator*
Hepworth, Malcolm Thomas *civil engineer, educator*
Keller, Kenneth Harrison *engineering educator, science policy analyst*
Kvalseth, Tarald Oddvar *mechanical engineer, educator*
Parhi, Keshab Kumar *electrical and computer engineering educator*
Shulman, Yechiel *engineering educator*

Saint Paul
Maze, Thomas H. *engineering educator*

MISSISSIPPI

Mississippi State
Truax, Dennis Dale *civil engineer, educator, consultant*
Younan, Nicolas Hanna *electrical engineering educator*

Starkville
Jacob, Paul Bernard, Jr., *electrical engineering educator*

University
Smith, Charles Edward *electrical engineering educator*
Uddin, Waheed *civil engineer, educator*

MISSOURI

Ballwin
Arantes, José Carlos *industrial engineer, educator*

Kansas City
Lowe, Forrest Gilbert *mechanical engineering educator*
Williams, John Leicester *biomechanical engineering educator*

Rolla
Adams, Craig David *environmental engineering educator*
Belarbi, Abdeldjelil *civil engineering educator, researcher*
Finaish, Fathi Ali *aeronautical engineering educator*
Grayson, Robert Larry *mining engineering educator, mining executive*
Numbere, Daopu Thompson *petroleum engineer, educator*
Sarangapani, Jagannathan *embedded systems and networking educator, researcher*
Sauer, Harry John, Jr., *mechanical engineering educator, university administrator*

Saint Louis
Birman, Victor Mark *mechanical and aerospace engineering educator, academic administrator*
Craig, Jerry Walker *engineering graphics educator*
Mathieu, Richard Graber *business educator*
Shrauner, Barbara Wayne Abraham *electrical engineer, educator*
Szabo, Barna Aladar *mechanical engineering educator, mining engineer*

MONTANA

Bozeman
Stanislao, Joseph *consulting engineer, educator*

NEBRASKA

Lincoln
Lou, David Yeong-Suei *mechanical engineering educator*
Rajurkar, Kamlakar Purushottam *mechanical engineering educator*

NEVADA

Reno
Batchman, Theodore Earl *electrical engineering educator, researcher*
Bautista, Renato Go *chemical engineer, educator*
Danko, George *engineering educator*
Whiting, Wallace Burton, II, *chemical engineer, educator*

NEW HAMPSHIRE

Hanover
Graves, Robert John *industrial engineering educator*
Hutchinson, Charles Edgar *engineering educator*
Long, Carl Ferdinand *engineering educator*
Queneau, Paul Etienne *metallurgical engineer, educator*

New Castle
Klotz, Louis Herman *structural engineer, educator, consultant*

NEW JERSEY

Atco
Beard, Richard Burnham *engineering educator emeritus, researcher*

Cherry Hill
Melick, George Fleury *mechanical engineer, educator*

Englewood
Deresiewicz, Herbert *mechanical engineering educator*

Glassboro
Slater, C. Stewart *chemical engineering educator*

Hopewell
VanMarcke, Erik Hector *civil engineer, educator*

Little Ferry
Shuch, H. Paul *radio astronomer*

Newark
Bar-Ness, Yeheskel *electrical engineer, educator*
Carpinelli, John Dominick *computer engineering educator*
Meyer, Andrew U(lrich) *electrical engineer, educator, consultant*
Spillers, William Russell *civil engineering educator*
Ziavras, Sotirios George *computer and electrical engineer, educator*

Piscataway
Benaroya, Haym *aerospace engineer, educator, researcher*
Boucher, Thomas Owen *engineering educator, researcher*
Flanagan, James Loton *electrical engineer, researcher, engineering educator*
Guo, Qizhong *engineering educator, researcher, consultant*
Mammone, Richard James *engineering educator*
Zhao, Jian Hui *electrical and computer engineering educator*

Plainsboro
Sorensen, Henrik Vittrup *electrical engineering educator*

Princeton
Curtiss, Howard Crosby, Jr., *mechanical engineer, educator*
Dickinson, Bradley William *electrical engineering educator*
Glassman, Irvin *mechanical and aeronautical engineering educator, consultant*
Liu, Bede *electrical engineering educator*
Miles, Richard Bryant *mechanical and aerospace engineering educator*
Poor, Harold Vincent *electrical engineering educator*
Prud'homme, Robert Krafft *chemical engineering educator*
Salkind, Alvin J. *electrochemical engineer, biomedical engineer, educator, dean*
Stengel, Robert Frank *engineering and applied science educator*
Verdu, Sergio *engineering educator*
Walton, Clifford Wayne *chemical engineer, researcher*
Wei, James *chemical engineering educator, academic dean*
Wolf, Wayne Hendrix *electrical engineering educator*

Springfield
Goldstein, Irving Robert *mechanical and industrial engineer, educator, consultant*

Teaneck
Pfeffer, Robert *chemical engineer, academic administrator, educator*

NEW MEXICO

Albuquerque
Dorato, Peter *electrical and computer engineering educator*
Hall, Jerome William *research engineering educator*

Las Cruces
Colbaugh, Richard Donald *mechanical engineer, educator, researcher*
Genin, Joseph *engineering educator, researcher*

Los Alamos
Nunz, Gregory Joseph *aerospace engineer, program manager, educator, entrepreneur*

NEW YORK

Alfred
Pian, Carlson Chao-Ping *mechanical engineering educator, researcher*

Baldwin
Brown, Pamela Ann *chemical engineering educator*

Bergen
McCarty, Richard Joseph *consulting engineer*

Bethpage
Conti, James Joseph *chemical engineer, educator*

Brooklyn
Beaufait, Frederick W(illiam) *civil engineering educator*
Ortiz, Mary Theresa *biomedical engineer, educator*
Shaw, Leonard Glazer *electrical engineering educator, consultant*

Buffalo
Chang, Ching Ming (Carl Chang) *engineering executive, mechanical engineer, educator*
Felske, James David *mechanical engineering educator*
Landi, Dale Michael *industrial engineer, academic administrator*
Reinhorn, Andrei M. *civil structural engineering educator, consultant*

Endicott
Schwartz, Richard Frederick *electrical engineering educator*

Franklin Square
Cantilli, Edmund Joseph *safety engineering educator, translator, writer, consultant*

Ithaca
Fuchs, W. Kent *engineering educator*
George, Albert Richard *mechanical and aerospace engineering educator*
Lynn, Walter Royal *civil engineering educator, university administrator*
Maxwell, William Laughlin *retired industrial engineering educator*
Stedinger, Jery Russell *civil and environmental engineer, researcher*
White, Richard Norman *civil and environmental engineering educator*

Jamaica
Vasilopoulos, Athanasios V. *engineering educator*

Katonah
Bashkow, Theodore Robert *electrical engineering consultant, former educator*

Melville
Bilenas, Jonas *mechanical engineer, educator*

New Rochelle
Schwarz, Ralph Jacques *retired engineering educator*

New York
Ahmad, Jameel *civil engineer, researcher, educator*
Asadorian, Diana C. *electrical engineer, educator*
Denn, Morton Mace *chemical engineering educator*
Diament, Paul *electrical engineering educator, consultant*
Harris, Colin Cyril *mineral engineer, educator*
Klein, Morton *industrial engineer, educator*
Lai, W(ei) Michael *mechanical engineer, educator*
Manassah, Jamal Tewfek *electrical engineer, educator, management consultant*
Mow, Van C. *engineering educator, researcher*
Paaswell, Robert Emil *civil engineer, educator*
Schwartz, Mischa *electrical engineering educator*
Smaili, Ahmad *mechanical engineering educator*
Yao, David Da-Wei *engineering educator*

Potsdam
Carroll, James Joseph *electrical and computer engineering educator*
Chin, Der-Tau *chemical engineering educator*
Pillay, Pragasen *engineering educator*

Rochester
Freckleton, Jon Edward *engineering educator, consultant, retired military officer*
Haines, Charles Wills *mathematics and mechanical engineering educator*
Niznik, Carol Ann *electrical engineer, educator, consultant*

Rome
Suter, Bruce Wilsey *electrical engineering educator, researcher*

Schenectady
Bucinell, Ronald Blaise *mechanical engineer, educator*

Staten Island
Rajakaruna, Lalith Asoka *civil engineer, land surveyor*

Stony Brook
Chiang, Fu-Pen *mechanical engineering educator, researcher*

Syracuse
Engbretson, Gustav Alan *bioengineering educator, neuroscientist*

Tappan
Cardenas, Raul Rodolfo, Jr., *engineering executive, educator*

Troy
Belfort, Georges *chemical engineering educator, consultant*
Block, Robert Charles *nuclear engineering and engineering physics educator*
Feeser, Larry James *civil engineering educator, researcher*
Fish, Jacob *civil engineer, educator*
Gerhardt, Lester A. *engineering educator, dean*
Glicksman, Martin Eden *materials engineering educator*
Gutmann, Ronald J. *electrical engineering educator*
McDonald, John Francis Patrick *electrical engineering educator*
Sanderson, Arthur Clark *engineering educator*
Shephard, Mark Scott *civil and mechanical engineering educator*
Stoloff, Norman Stanley *materials engineering educator, researcher*

Upton
Qian, Shinan *optical engineer, researcher, educator*

Wallkill
Rosenthal, Lee *electrical engineer, educator*

Webster
Zirilli, Francesco *mechanical engineer, engineering educator*

Wellsville
Tezak, Edward George *mechanics educator*

NORTH CAROLINA

Charlotte
Keanini, Russell Guy *mechanical engineering educator, researcher*

Columbus
Brooks, Jerry Claude *safety engineer, educator*

Durham
Board, John Arnold, Jr., *electrical engineer educator, computer engineer*
Casey, H(orace) Craig, Jr., *electrical engineering educator*
Strohbehn, John Walter *engineering science educator*
Utku, Senol *civil engineer, computer science educator*

Greensboro
Adewuyi, Yusuf Gbadebo *chemical engineering educator, researcher, consultant*
Cazel, Hugh Allen *industrial engineer, educator*
Shen, Ji Yao *mechanical engineering educator*
Shivakumar, Kunigal Nanjundaiah *aerospace engineer, educator*

New Bern
Moeller, Dade William *environmental engineer, educator*

Pilot Mountain
Rumer, Ralph Raymond, Jr., *civil engineer, educator*

Raleigh
Bourham, Mohamed Abdelhay *nuclear and electrical engineering educator*
Havner, Kerry Shuford *civil engineering and solid mechanics educator*
Meier, Wilbur Leroy, Jr., *industrial engineer, educator, former university chancellor*
Sneed, Ronald Ernest *engineering educator emeritus*

Swannanoa
Stuck, Roger Dean *electrical engineering educator*

NORTH DAKOTA

Fargo
Li, Kam Wu *mechanical engineer, educator*
Rogers, David Anthony *electrical engineer, educator, researcher*
Varma, Amiy *civil engineer, educator*

OHIO

Akron
Haritos, George Konstantinos *engineer, educator, military officer*
Isayev, Avraam Isayevich *polymer engineer, educator*
Sancaktar, Erol *engineering educator*

Athens
Chen, Hollis Ching *electrical engineering, computer science educator*
Rabelo, Luis Carlos *engineering educator, consultant*

Cincinnati
Buchanan, Relva Chester *engineering educator*
Fried, Joel Robert *chemical engineering educator*
Greenberg, David Bernard *chemical engineering educator*

Cleveland
Merat, Francis Lawrence *engineering educator*
Rudy, Yoram *biomedical engineer, biophysicist, educator*
Saada, Adel Selim *civil engineer, educator*
Savinell, Robert Francis *engineering educator*

Columbus
Altan, Taylan *engineering educator, mechanical engineer, consultant*
Bailey, Cecil Dewitt *aerospace engineer, educator*
Bodonyi, Richard James *engineering educator, researcher*
Cruz, Jose Bejar, Jr., *engineering educator*
Fentiman, Audeen Walters *nuclear engineer, educator*
Fenton, Robert Earl *electrical engineering educator*
Houser, Donald Russell *mechanical engineering educator, consultant*
Ozkan, Umit Sivrioglu *chemical engineering educator*
Peters, Leon, Jr., *electrical engineering educator, research administrator*
Rizzoni, Giorgio *engineering educator*
Sebo, Stephen Andrew *electrical engineer, educator, researcher, consultant*
Singh, Rajendra *mechanical engineering educator*
Smith, Philip John *industrial and systems engineering educator*

Dayton
Jain, Surinder Mohan *electronics engineering educator*

Lima
Oruma, Francis Obatare *mechanical engineering educator, consultant*

Tipp City
Demers, Gerald Zoel *engineering educator*

Toledo
Oh, Keytack Henry *industrial engineering educator*
Randolph, Brian Walter *civil engineer, educator*

Wadsworth
Atwood, Glenn Arthur *engineer, educator*

Wright Pat
King, Paul Irvin *aerospace engineering educator*

Wright Patterson AFB
Mitchell, Philip Michael *aerospace engineer, consultant, educator*

Wright Patterson Afb
Mall, Shankar *engineering mechanics educator, researcher*

Youngstown
Kim, Hyun Wang *mechanical engineering educator*

OKLAHOMA

Norman
Abousleiman, Younane Nassib *civil engineer, researcher, educator*
Altan, M(ustafa) Cengiz *mechanical engineering educator*
Bert, Charles Wesley *mechanical and aerospace engineer, educator*
Cronenwett, William Treadwell *electrical engineering educator, consultant*
Mallinson, Richard Gregory *chemical engineering educator*
McCann, Patrick John *electrical engineering educator, researcher*
O'Rear, Edgar Allen, III, *chemical engineering educator*
Shah, Subhash Nandlal *petroleum engineering educator*
Trafalis, Theodoros Vassilios *industrial engineering educator*
Zelby, Leon Wolf *electrical engineering educator, consulting engineer*

Stillwater
Foutch, Gary Lynn *chemical engineering educator, entrepreneur*

OREGON

Beaverton
Edlich, Richard French *biomedical engineering educator*

Corvallis
Yim, Solomon Chik-Sing *civil engineering educator, consultant*

Hillsboro
Rotithor, Hemant Govind *electrical engineer, educator*

Klamath Falls
Lomas, Charles Gardner *engineering educator, retired, psychotherapist*

Portland
Chrzanowska-Jeske, Malgorzata Ewa *electrical engineering educator, consultant*
Kocaoglu, Dundar F. *engineering management educator, industrial and civil engineer*
Li, Fu *electrical engineering educator, editor*
Perkowski, Marek Andrzej *electrical engineering educator*
Pham, Kinh Dinh *electrical engineer, educator, administrator*
Savery, C(lyde) William *mechanical engineering educator*
Yamayee, Zia Ahmad *engineering educator, dean*

Salem
Dixon, Robert Gene *retired manufacturing engineering educator, retired mechanical engineering company executive*

PENNSYLVANIA

Allentown
Hansel, James Gordon *engineer, educator*
Lesak, David Michael *safety engineer, educator, consultant*

Beaver
Vogeley, Clyde Eicher, Jr., *engineering educator, artist, consultant*

Beaver Falls
Shaw, David William *engineering educator*

Bethlehem
Neti, Sudhakar *mechanical engineering educator*
Roberts, Richard *mechanical engineering educator*

Coopersburg
Siess, Alfred Albert, Jr., *engineering executive, management consultant*

Danville
Cheung, Joseph Yat-Sing *biomedical scientist, nephrologist*

Gibsonia
Shoub, Earle Phelps *engineer, industrial hygienist, educator*

Indiana
Soule, Robert D. *safety and health educator, administrator*

Lancaster
Adams, Joseph Brian *operations research engineer, mathematics and computer science educator*

Philadelphia
Bau, Haim Henrich *mechanical engineering educator*
Engheta, Nader *electrical engineering educator, researcher*
Haas, Charles Nathan *environmental engineering educator*
Humphreys, Donald Wayne *environmental engineering educator*
Ku, Yu H. *electrical engineer, educator*
Soslowsky, Louis Jeffrey *bioengineering educator, researcher*
Van der Spiegel, Jan *engineering educator*

Pittsburgh
Akay, Adnan *mechanical engineer, educator*
Casasent, David Paul *electrical engineering educator, data processing executive*
Charap, Stanley Harvey *electrical engineering educator*
Li, Ching-Chung *electrical engineering and computer science educator*
Maly, Wojciech P. *engineering educator, researcher*
Meiksin, Zvi H. *electrical engineering educator*
Reznik, Alan A. *petroleum engineering educator*
Russell, Alan James *chemical engineering and biotechnology educator*
Sun, Haiyin *optical engineer, educator*
Westerberg, Arthur William *chemical engineering educator*

Spring House
Jayjock, Michael Anthony *environmental engineer, educator*

State College
Barton, Russell Richard *business and engineering educator, academic administrator*
Benson, Richard Carter *mechanical engineering educator*

Swarthmore
Krendel, Ezra Simon *systems and human factors engineering consultant*

University Park
Grimes, Craig Alan *electrical engineering educator*
Helfferich, Friedrich G. *chemical engineer, educator*
Jenkins, William Kenneth *electrical engineering educator*
Knott, Kenneth *engineering educator, consultant, expert witness*
Maughmer, Mark David *aerospace engineering educator*
Ramani, Raja Venkat *mining engineering educator*
Reed, Joseph Raymond *civil engineering educator, academic administrator*
Thompson, William, Jr., *engineering educator*
Ventsel, Eduard Sergeevich *engineering mechanics educator*

Villanova
McLaughlin, Philip VanDoren, Jr., *mechanical engineering educator, researcher, consultant*

Wilkes Barre
Arora, Vijay Kumar *electrical engineering educator, researcher*

RHODE ISLAND

Kingston
Lee, Kang-Won Wayne *engineer, educator*

Portsmouth
Durgin, Scott Benjamin *radio frequency engineer, physics educator, engineering executive*

Providence
Hazeltine, Barrett *electrical engineer, educator*
Preparata, Franco Paolo *computer science and engineering educator*
Richman, Marc Herbert *forensic engineer, educator*
Suuberg, Eric Michael *chemical engineering educator*
Symonds, Paul Southworth *mechanical engineering educator, researcher*
Weiner, Jerome Harris *mechanical engineering educator*

SOUTH CAROLINA

Clemson
Kimbler, Delbert Lee, Jr., *industrial engineering educator*

Mauldin
Harris, Daniel Frederick *biomechanical analyst, educator*

Orangeburg
Isa, Saliman Alhaji *electrical engineering educator*

SOUTH DAKOTA

Brookings
Hamidzadeh, Hamid Reza *mechanical engineer, educator, consultant*

Rapid City
Gowen, Richard Joseph *electrical engineering educator, academic administrator*
Ramakrishnan, Venkataswamy *civil engineer, educator*

TENNESSEE

Cookeville
Chowdhuri, Pritindra *electrical engineer, educator*
Darvennes, Corinne Marcelle *mechanical engineering educator, researcher*
Sissom, Leighton Esten *engineering educator, dean, consultant*

Knoxville
Brown, Donald Vaughn *technical educator, engineering consultant*
El-Ghazaly, Samir *electrical engineering educator*
Hungerford, John Charles *mechanical engineer, educator*
Uhrig, Robert Eugene *nuclear engineer, educator*

Memphis
Hochstein, John Isaac *mechanical engineering educator*
Maksi, Gregory Earl *engineering educator*

Nashville
Galloway, Kenneth Franklin *engineering educator*

Old Hickory
Thomas, Jonathan Wayne *engineering educator*

TEXAS

Austin
Aggarwal, Jagdishkumar Keshoram *electrical and computer engineering educator, research administrator*
Armstrong, Neal Earl *civil engineering educator*
Baker, Lee Edward *biomedical engineering educator*
Carey, Graham Francis *engineering educator*
Dougal, Arwin Adelbert *electrical engineer, educator*
Fair, James Rutherford, Jr., *chemical engineering educator, consultant*
Fowler, David Wayne *architectural engineering educator*
Fowler, Wallace T. *engineering educator*
Frank, Karl Heinz *civil engineer, educator*
Himmelblau, David Mautner *chemical engineer*
Hixson, Elmer L. *retired engineering educator*
Hughes, Thomas J.R. *mechanical engineering educator, consultant*
Hull, David George *aerospace engineering educator, researcher*
Koen, Billy Vaughn *mechanical engineering educator*
Koepsel, Wellington Wesley *electrical engineering educator*
Liljestrand, Howard Michael *environmental engineering educator*
Mc Ketta, John J., Jr., *chemical engineering educator*
Nichols, Steven Parks *mechanical engineer, lawyer, educator*
Paul, Donald Ross *chemical engineer, educator*
Peppas, Nikolaos Athanassiou *chemical and biomedical engineering educator, consultant*
Reese, Lymon Clifton *civil engineering educator*
Richards-Kortum, Rebecca Rae *biomedical engineering educator*
Schmidt, Philip S. *mechanical engineering educator*
Streetman, Ben Garland *electrical engineering educator*
Swartzlander, Earl Eugene, Jr., *engineering educator, former electronics company executive*
Tucker, Richard Lee *civil engineer, educator*
Wright, Stephen Gailord *civil engineering educator, consultant*

College Station
Hall, Kenneth Richard *chemical engineering educator, consultant*
Holste, James Clifton *chemical engineering educator*
Holtzapple, Mark Thomas *biochemical engineer, educator*
Kihm, Kenneth David (Ken Kihm) *mechanical engineering educator*
Lu, Mi *computer engineer, educator*
Lytton, Robert Leonard *civil engineer, educator*
Neff, Ray Quinn *electric power educator, consultant*
Parlos, Alexander George *systems and control engineering educator*
Patton, Alton DeWitt *electrical engineering consultant*
Toliyat, Hamid Abolhasani *electrical engineer, educator*
Wang, Lihong *biomedical engineering educator*

Corpus Christi
Umfleet, Lloyd Truman *electrical engineering technology educator*

Dallas
Kalyanaram, Gurumurthy *engineering educator, consultant*

Houston
Akers, William Walter *chemical engineering educator*
Cheatham, John Bane, Jr., *retired mechanical engineering educator*
David, Yadin B. *biomedical engineer, health care technology consultant*
Grigoriadis, Karolos Michail *mechanical engineering educator*
Hirasaki, George Jiro *chemical engineer, educator*
Kobayashi, Riki *chemical engineer, educator*
Lienhard, John Henry, IV, *mechanical engineer, educator*
McIntire, Larry Vern *biomedical engineering educator*
Mo, Yi-Lung *structural engineering educator*
Ostrofsky, Benjamin *business and engineering management educator, industrial engineer*

Lubbock
Giesselmann, Michael Guenter *electrical engineer, educator, researcher*

Prairie View
Akujuobi, Cajetan Maduabuchukwu *systems engineer, electrical engineering educator, researcher*

San Antonio
Redfield, Carol Ann Luckhardt *engineering educator*
Shadaram, Mehdi *electrical engineering educator*

Sugar Land
Finch, Robert David *mechanical engineer, educator, consultant*

The Woodlands
Reddy, Gopal Baireddy *engineering educator*

Waco
Farison, James Blair *electrical biomedical engineer, educator*
Solomon, Charles Francis *electronics educator*

UTAH

Kaysville
Rushforth, Craig K. *retired electrical engineering educator, researcher*

Salt Lake City
Kopecek, Jindrich *biomedical scientist, biomaterials and pharmaceutics educator*
Sohn, Hong Yong *chemical engineer, educator, metallurgical engineer, educator*
Stringfellow, Gerald B. *engineering educator*

VIRGINIA

Alexandria
Poehlein, Gary Wayne *retired chemical engineering educator*
Rassai, Rassa *electrical engineering educator*
Wilcox, David Eric *electrical engineer, educational consultant*

Arlington
Bordogna, Joseph *engineer, educator*

Blacksburg
Batra, Romesh Chander *engineering mechanics educator, researcher*

Brown, Gary Sandy *electrical engineering educator*
Gray, Festus Gail *electrical engineer, educator, researcher*
Inman, Daniel John *mechanical engineer, educator*
Mitchell, James Kenneth *civil engineer, educator*
O'Brien, Walter Fenton *mechanical engineering educator*
Perumpral, John Verghese *agricultural engineer, administrator, educator*
Safaai-Jazi, Ahmad *electrical engineering educator, researcher*
Simpson, Roger Lyndon *aerospace and ocean engineering educator, researcher*

Burke
Lynch, Charles Theodore, Sr., *materials science engineering researcher, consultant, educator*

Charlottesville
Fink, Lester Harold *engineering company executive, educator*
Gelmont, Boris L. *engineering research educator*
Haimes, Yacov Yosseph *systems and civil engineering educator, consultant*
Hudson, John Lester *chemical engineering educator*
Theodoridis, George Constantin *biomedical engineering educator, researcher*
Townsend, Miles Averill *aerospace and mechanical engineering educator*

Falls Church
Spivak, Steven Mark *textile and standards engineer, educator*

Great Falls
Skeen, David Ray *systems engineer, consultant, engineering executive, educator*

Norfolk
Wei, Benjamin Min *engineering educator*

Richmond
Bandyopadhyay, Supriyo *electrical engineer, educator, researcher*

WASHINGTON

Federal Way
Studebaker, Irving Glen *mining engineering consultant*

Mill Creek
Sengupta, Mritunjoy *mining engineer, educator*

Pullman
Funk, William Henry *retired environmental engineering educator*

Seattle
Bowen, Jewell Ray *chemical engineering educator*
Clark, Robert Newhall *electrical and aeronautical engineering educator*
Davis, Earl James *chemical engineering educator*
Ishimaru, Akira *electrical engineering educator*
Kalonji, Gretchen *engineering educator*
Lewis, Mark Richard *aerospace engineer, educator*
McCormick, Norman Joseph *mechanical engineer, nuclear engineer, educator*
Mc Feron, Dean Earl *mechanical engineer, educator*
Ratner, Buddy Dennis *bioengineer, educator*
Roeder, Charles William *structural engineering educator*
Spindel, Robert Charles *electrical engineering educator*
Woodruff, Gene Lowry *nuclear engineer, university dean*

WEST VIRGINIA

Fairmont
Brizendine, Anthony Lewis *civil engineering educator*

Morgantown
Dadyburjor, Dady B. *chemical engineering educator, researcher*
Gray, Donald Dwight *civil engineering educator*

WISCONSIN

Brookfield
Curfman, Floyd Edwin *engineering educator, retired*

Madison
Boyle, William Charles *civil engineering educator*
Carbon, Max William *nuclear engineering educator*
Chang, Y. Austin *materials engineer, educator*
Converse, James Clarence *agricultural engineering educator*
DeVries, Marvin Frank *mechanical engineering educator*
Loper, Carl Richard, Jr., *metallurgical engineer, educator*
Lumelsky, Vladimir Jacob *engineering educator*
Malkus, David Starr *retired mechanics educator, applied mathematician*
Shohet, Juda Leon *electrical and computer engineering educator, researcher, high technology company executive*
Skiles, James Jean *electrical and computer engineering educator*
Webster, John Goodwin *biomedical engineering educator, researcher*

Milwaukee
Landis, Fred *mechanical engineering educator*
Widera, Georg Ernst Otto *mechanical engineering educator, consultant*

TERRITORIES OF THE UNITED STATES

PUERTO RICO

Gurabo
Kuruganty, Sastry Pratap *electrical engineering educator*

Mayaguez
Suarez, Luis Edgardo *civil engineering educator*

CANADA

BRITISH COLUMBIA

Coquitlam
Fei, Lin *engineering educator, engineering executive*

Vancouver
Grace, John Ross *chemical engineering educator*

Victoria
Antoniou, Andreas *electrical engineering educator*

ONTARIO

Hamilton
Bandler, John William *electrical engineering educator, consultant*

Oshawa
Esmailzadeh, Ebrahim *mechanical engineering educator, consultant*

Windsor
Hackam, Reuben *electrical engineering educator*

QUEBEC

Montreal
Haccoun, David *electrical engineering educator*
Selvadurai, Antony Patrick Sinnappa *civil engineering educator, applied mathematician, consultant*

Sainte-Foy
LeDuy, Anh *engineering educator*

MEXICO

Mexico City
Favela-Lozoya, Fernando *engineering educator*

CHINA

Beijing
Shu, Wenlong *environmental engineer, educator*

GREECE

Athens
Halkias, Christos Constantine *electronics educator*

ISRAEL

Ramat-Aviv
Seifert, Avi *aerodynamic engineering educator and researcher*

JAPAN

Nara
Hayashi, Tadao *engineering educator*

ADDRESS UNPUBLISHED

Andrea, Mario Iacobucci *engineer, scientist, gemologist, appraiser*
Baddour, Raymond Frederick *chemical engineer, educator, entrepreneur*
Bamberger, Joseph Alexander *mechanical engineer, educator*
Becerra-Fernandez, Irma *electrical engineer, researcher, educator*
Beebe, Larry Eugene *quality engineering educator, management consultant*
Berger, Frederick Jerome *electrical engineer, educator*
Bergfield, Gene Raymond *engineering educator*
Bers, Abraham *electrical engineering and physics educator*
Bertin, John Joseph *aeronautical engineer, educator, researcher*
Bloch, Erich *retired electrical engineer, former science foundation administrator*
Bowen, Douglas Glenn *electrical engineer, consultant*
Bradshaw, Peter *engineering educator*
Carlson, Robert Codner *industrial engineering educator*
Cha, Soyoung Stephen *mechanical engineer, educator*
Chapanis, Alphonse *human factors engineer, ergonomist*
Day, Donald Lee *retired engineering educator, researcher*
Donohue, Marc David *chemical engineering educator*
Fish, Andrew Joseph, Jr., *electrical engineering educator, researcher*
Gussow, Milton *electrical engineer, educator*
Hanson, John M. *civil engineering and construction educator*
Herakovich, Carl Thomas *civil engineering, applied mechanics educator*
Hoeppner, David William *mechanical engineering educator*
Hogan, Neville John *mechanical engineering educator, consultant*
Hutchinson, John Woodside *mechanical engineer, educator*
James, Charles Franklin, Jr., *engineering educator, educator*
Jolles, Mitchell Ira *engineering consultant*
Juricic, Davor *mechanical engineering educator*
Kirk, Robley Gordon *mechanical engineering educator*
Kiser, Kenneth M(aynard) *chemical engineering educator*
Kolbe, Ronald Lynn *research engineer*
Kruger, Charles Herman, Jr., *mechanical engineering educator*
Leburton, Jean-Pierre *electrical engineering educator*
Liang, Junxiang *retired aeronautics and astronautics engineer, educator*
Liu, Y. A. *engineering educator*
Luenberger, David Gilbert *electrical engineering educator*
Lui, Eric Mun *civil engineering educator, practitioner*
Madix, Robert James *chemical engineer, educator*
McDermott, Kevin J. *engineering educator, consultant*
Meldrum, Deirdre Ruth *electrical engineering educator*
Meyer, John Edward *nuclear engineering educator*
Morgan, James John *environmental engineering educator*
Mortimer, Richard Walter *mechanical engineer, educator*
Munger, Paul R. *civil engineering educator*
Nguyen, Charles Cuong *engineering educator, researcher, dean*
Salamon, Miklos Dezso Gyorgy *mining engineer, educator*
Salkind, Michael Jay *technology administrator*
Sandry, Karla Kay Foreman *industrial engineering educator*
Schmidt, Robert *retired mechanics and civil engineering educator*
Schultz, Albert Barry *engineering educator*
Sheridan, Thomas Brown *mechanical engineering and applied psychology educator, researcher, consultant*
Skelland, Anthony Harold Peter *chemical engineering educator*
Somasundaran, Ponisseril *surface and colloid engineer, applied science educator*
Soukup, Rodney Joseph *electrical engineer, educator*
Sreenivasan, Katepalli Raju *mechanical engineering educator*
Stallings, Viola Patricia Elizabeth *systems engineer, educational systems specialist, retired information technology manager*
Swift, Jill Anne *industrial engineer, educator*
Uygur, Mustafa Eti *materials and mechanical engineering educator*
Wang, Leon Ru-Liang *civil engineer, educator*
Weinsier, Philip David *electronics educator*
Weldon, William Forrest *electrical and mechanical engineer, educator*
Woodward, Clinton Benjamin, Jr., *civil engineering educator*
Yetter, Richard Alan *engineering educator*
Zelinski, Joseph John *engineering educator, consultant*

HIGHER EDUCATION: FINANCE AND BUSINESS

UNITED STATES

ALABAMA

Birmingham
Lockamy, Archie, III, *operations management educator*

Deatsville
Owen, Larry Lesli *management educator, retired military officer, small business owner*

Dothan
Cross, Steven Jasper *finance educator*

Florence
Brown, Sarah Ruth *accountant, educator*
Richardson, Ruth Delene *retired business educator*

Huntsville
Stewart, Verlindsey Laquetta *accounting educator*

Montrose
Haynie, Betty Jo Gillmore *personal property appraiser, antiques dealer*

Pelham
Bell, Nancy Sutton *finance educator*

Tuscaloosa
Gup, Benton Eugene *banking educator*

ALASKA

Anchorage
Behrend, Donald Fraser *environmental educator, university administrator*

Homer
Gillon, Stephen John *business educator, consultant*

ARIZONA

Flagstaff
Giovale, Virginia Gore *health products executive, volunteer*

Kingman
Baker, Richard Earl *business management educator*

Phoenix
Currie, Constance Mershon *investment services professional*
Denning, Michael Marion *marketing professional, educator*
Hutchinson, Ann *management consultant*
Proffitt, Dennis Lewis *finance educator*

Tempe
Meehan, Robert Henry *human resources executive, electronics company executive, business educator*
Roy, Asim *business educator*
Sackton, Frank Joseph *public affairs educator*

Tucson
Nixon, Robert Obey, Sr., *business educator*
Seay, Suzanne *financial planner, educator*
Taylor, William Malcolm *environmentalist, educator, executive recruiter*

ARKANSAS

Arkadelphia
Webster, Robert Lee *accounting educator, researcher*

Conway
Horton, Joseph Julian, Jr., *economics and finance educator*
Moore, Herff Leo, Jr., *management educator*

Fayetteville
Combs, Linda Jones *management company executive, researcher*
Cook, Doris Marie *accountant, educator*
Orr, Betsy *business education educator*

Hot Springs National Park
Aqeel, Sulaiman Rafeeq Saadiq (Lawrence Emerold Bonner) *small business owner, minister, elementary school educator*

Jonesboro
Sullivan, Virginia L. *public affairs educator, consultant*

Little Rock
Flournoy, Jacob Wesley *internal audit director*
Waters, Zenobia Pettus *retired finance educator*

Monticello
Webster, Linda Jean *communications educator, media consultant*

State University
Ruby, Ralph, Jr., *vocational business educator*

CALIFORNIA

Altadena
Eisen, Glenn Philip *management consultant, teacher*

Anaheim
Torbat, Akbar Esfahani *investment advisor, economics educator, researcher*

Atherton
Goodman, Sam Richard *electronics company executive*

Bakersfield
Bacon, Leonard Anthony *accounting educator*
Lowenstein, Henry *business educator, dean*

Berkeley
Bucklin, Louis Pierre *business educator, consultant*

Carmel
Allan, Robert Moffat, Jr., *corporate executive, educator*
Creighton, John Wallis, Jr., *novelist, publisher, former management educator, consultant*

Claremont
Lipman-Blumen, Jean *public policy and organizational behavior educator*
Moriarty, J. Joseph *management and technology consultant*

Clovis
Kellam, Becky *business educator, consultant*

Concord
Miller, John Nelson *banker, educator*

Corona Del Mar
O'Brien, John William, Jr., *investment management company executive, finance educator*

Costa Mesa
Metzger, Vernon Arthur *management educator, consultant*

Culver City
Buskirk, Bruce David *marketing educator*

Davis
Naik, Prasad Anand *marketing educator*

Downieville
Forbes, Cynthia Ann *small business owner, marketing educator*

Escondido
Strong, James Thompson *management, security, human resources consultant*

Glendora
Richey, Everett Eldon *religious studies educator*

Hayward
Doctors, Samuel Isaac *management educator, researcher director*
Kam, Vernon Tam Siu *accounting educator*

Huntington Beach
Dang, James Bac *business planner, educator*

La Jolla
Freedman, David Noel *religious studies educator*

Lancaster
Houck, John Dudley *investment adviser, educator*

Long Beach
Lowentrout, Peter Murray *religious studies educator*

Los Angeles
Allen, Suzanne *financial planning executive, insurance agent, writer*
Allison, Laird Burl *business educator*
Drummond, Marshall Edward *business educator, university administrator*
Jensen, David Gram *marketing professional, consultant, sales trainer*
Krieger, Martin H. *planning and design educator*
Lin, Thomas Wen-shyoung *accounting educator, researcher, consultant*
Nadler, Gerald *management consultant, educator*
Roussey, Robert Stanley *accountant, educator*
Stewart, David Wayne *marketing educator, psychologist, consultant*
Walendowski, George Jerry *accounting and business educator*
Weston, John Frederick *business educator, consultant*

Lynwood
Dove, Donald Augustine *city planner, educator*

Malibu
Baskin, Otis Wayne *business educator*

Mountain View
Harrison, Wendy Jane Merrill *insurance company executive*

Newport Coast
Mc Guire, Joseph William *business educator*

Northridge
Orenstein, Michael (Ian Orenstein) *philatelic dealer, columnist*

Oakland
Michael, Gary G. *retired retail supermarket and drug chain executive, university administrator*
Randisi, Elaine Marie *accountant, educator, writer*

Oceanside
Asato, Susan Pearce *business executive, educator*
Hough, J. Marie *realtor*

Palo Alto
Stephens, Bess *computer company executive*

Palos Verdes Peninsula
Manning, Christopher Ashley *finance educator, consultant*

Pleasant Hill
Seefer, Carolyn Marie *business educator, curriculum developer*

Poway
Mueller, Gerhard G(ottlob) *retired financial accounting standard setter, retired educator*

Redding
Streiff, Arlyne Bastunas *business educator, educator*

Redlands
Barnes, A. Keith *management educator*
Pick, James Block *business educator, demographer*

Redondo Beach
Matthews, Steven Richard *culinary instructor, chef, consultant*

Sacramento
Boekhoudt-Cannon, Gloria Lydia *business education educator*
Wunder, Haroldene Fowler *taxation educator*

San Clemente
Petruzzi, Christopher Robert *business educator, consultant*

San Diego
Edwards-Tate, Laurie Ellen *human services administrator, educator*
Evans, John Joseph *management consultant, executive, educator, writer*
Gee, Roger Allan *accounting educator, writer*
Gengor, Virginia Anderson *financial planning executive, educator*

San Francisco
August-deWilde, Katherine *banker*
Chen, Roger (Rongxin Chen) *management educator*
O'Neill, Michael *management educator*
Tyau, Gaylore Choy Yen *business educator*

San Jose
Morrison, William Fosdick *business educator, retired electrical company executive*
Smith, David Eugene *business administration educator*

San Luis Obispo
Thatcher, Janet Solverson *financial advisor, writer*

San Mateo
Helfert, Erich Anton *management consultant, writer, educator*
Hopkins, Cecilia Ann *business educator*

Santa Clara
Martin, Norman Francis *public relations executive*

Santa Monica
Moore, Timothy Joel *health and fitness consultant*

Santee
Schenk, Susan Kirkpatrick *nurse educator, consultant, business owner*

Saratoga
Rollo, F. David *hospital management company executive, health care educator*

Sherman Oaks
Koonce, John Peter *investment company executive, educator*

Stanford
Holloway, Charles Arthur *public and private management educator*
Martin, Joanne *educator*
McDonald, John Gregory *financial investment educator*
Miller, William Frederick *research company executive, educator, business consultant*
Pfeffer, Jeffrey *business educator*
Porterfield, James Temple Starke *business administration educator*
Saloner, Garth *management educator*

Stockton
Hackley, Carol Ann *public relations director, educator, consultant*
Hoberg, Michael Dean *management analyst, educator*
Plovnick, Mark Stephen *business educator*
Post, Gerald V. *business educator*

Tehachapi
Smith-Thompson, Patricia Ann *public relations consultant, educator*

Victorville
Caldwell, Patricia Frances *financial consultant, lecturer*

Woodside
Concannon, George Robert *business educator*

COLORADO

Aspen
Bradford, Diane Goldsmith *multimedia marketing and product consultant*

Boulder
Melicher, Ronald William *finance educator*
Stanton, William John, Jr., *marketing educator, author*

Broomfield
Lybarger, John Steven *human resources development consultant, trainer*

Colorado Springs
Ansorge, Iona Marie *musician, educator*
Marsh, Peter Jerome *credit union officer, former educator*
Stienmier, Saundra Kay Young *aviation educator*

Denver
Cheris, Elaine Gayle Ingram *business owner*
Lutsky, Sheldon Jay *financial and marketing consultant, writer*

Evergreen
Saxton, Mary Jane *management educator*

Golden
Van Dusen, Donna Bayne *communications consultant, educator, researcher*

Granby
Hamilton, Penny Rafferty *research executive, writer, educator*

Grand Junction
Freeman, Neil *accounting and computer consulting firm executive*
Mallory, Elgin Albert *business educator, management consultant, small business owner, school system administrator*

Greeley
Clinebell, Sharon Kay *management educator*

Lakewood
Porter, Lael Frances *retired communication consultant, educator*

Littleton
Moore, Dan Sterling *insurance executive, sales trainer*

Wheat Ridge
Leino, Deanna Rose *business educator*

CONNECTICUT

Avon
Kling, Phradie (Phradie Kling Gold) *small business owner, educator*

Clinton
Zack, Steven Jeffrey *master automotive instructor*

Danbury
Goldstein, Joel *finance and statistics educator, researcher*
Proctor, Richard Jerome, Jr., *business educator, accountant, expert witness*

East Hartford
Druckman, Margaret Smith *consultant, retail executive, administrator*

Farmington
Muse, James Michael *bank executive, finance educator*

Hamden
He, Xiaohong *finance educator*

Hartford
Generas, George Paul, Jr., *finance educator, lawyer*
Olson, Peter Wesley *international business educator*

Milford
Penkala, Antoinette Marie *mortgage company executive*

New Britain
Darius, Franklin Alexander, Jr., (Chip Darius) *safety consultant, educator*
Detmar-Pines, Gina Louise *business strategy and policy educator*

New Haven
Abdelsayed, Wafeek Hakim *accounting educator*
Buck, Donald Tirrell *retired finance educator*
Jacob, Deirdre Ann Bradbury *manufacturing executive, business educator, consultant*
Meeks, Wayne A. *religious studies educator*

Old Lyme
Fairfield-Sonn, James Willed *management educator and consultant*

Portland
Chapman, Allen Floyd *management educator, college dean*

Prospect
Powell, Raymond William *financial planner, school administrator*

Stamford
O'Connor, Frank M. *business educator, sales professional*

West Haven
Mendez, Angela M. *small business owner*

DELAWARE

Newark
Byrne, John Michael *energy and environmental policy educator, researcher*

Wilmington
Landgraf, Kurt M. *chemicals executive*
Wilkinson, Janet Worman *advertising and marketing consultant, reading tutor and specialist*

DISTRICT OF COLUMBIA

Washington
Cafritz, Peggy Cooper *communications executive*
Darman, Richard *investor, educator*
Dessaso, Deborah Ann *freelance writer, online communications specialist, consultant*
Droms, William George *finance educator, investment advisor*
Fischetti, Michael Joseph *accounting educator*
Heumann, Judith *bank executive*
Kaludis, George *management consultant, book company executive, educator*
MacLaury, Bruce King *financial institution executive*
Mc Nallen, James Berl *marketing executive*
Roomkin, Myron J. *management educator, arbitrator, consultant*
Wade, Robert Hirsch Beard *international consultant, former government and educational association official*
Walker, David A(lan) *finance educator, educator*

FLORIDA

Apopka
Rufenacht, Roger Allen *accounting educator*

Boca Raton
Demes, Dennis Thomas *religious studies educator*
Jessup, Joe Lee *business educator, management consultant*
Konrad, Agnes Crossman *retired real estate agent, retired educator*
Levin, Marlene *human resources executive, educator*

Cocoa
Vilardebo, Angie Marie *management consultant, parochial school educator*

Coral Gables
Fitzgerald, John Thomas, Jr., *religious studies educator*

Crystal River
Lewis, Christina Lynn *human services administrator*

Deland
Tedros, Theodore Zaki *real estate broker, appraiser, educator*

Fort Lauderdale
Abraham, Rebecca Jacob *finance educator*
Beatty, Robert Clinton *religious studies educator*
Castro, Stephanie L. *business management educator*
Vasquez, William Leroy *business educator, consultant*

Fort Myers
Massa, Conrad Harry *religious studies educator*

Grand Island
Johnson, Tesla Francis *data processing executive, educator*

Jacksonville
Bodkin, Ruby Pate *corporate executive, real estate broker, educator*
Tomlinson, William Holmes *management educator, retired army officer*

Lady Lake
Tolleson, Nanette Brittain *realtor, educator*

Lake Park
Portera, Alan A. *religious studies educator, director*

Miami
George, Stephen Carl *reinsurance executive, educator, medical and life consultant, expert witness, expert witness*
Pomeranz, Felix *accounting educator*

Naples
LaRusso, Anthony Carl *company executive, educator*

Orlando
Armacost, Robert Leo *management educator, former coast guard officer*

Palm Bay
Jurgevich, Nancy J. *retail executive, educator*

Palm Coast
Owens, Garland Chester *accounting educator*

Palmetto
Roehl, Nancy Leary *marketing professional, educator*

Pensacola
Carper, William Barclay *management educator*

Safety Harbor
Fay, Carolyn M. *education marketing business owner*

Saint Petersburg
Barney, Linda Susan *manufacturing specialist*

Stuart
Donohue, Edith M. *human resources specialist, educator*

Tallahassee
Handy, F. Philip *investment company executive, educational association administrator*

Tampa
Cannella, Deborah Fabbri *accountant*
Ortinau, David Joseph *marketing specialist, educator*

Winter Park
Matulich, Serge *accounting educator, author*
Starr, Martin Kenneth *management educator*

GEORGIA

Athens
Aronson, Jay Ellis *management information systems educator, consultant*
Bamber, Linda Smith *accounting educator*

PROFESSIONAL INDEX — HIGHER EDUCATION: FINANCE AND BUSINESS

Hofer, Charles Warren *strategic management, entrepreneurship educator, consultant*
Smith, Richard Alton *mechanical contracting company executive*

Atlanta
Beres, Mary Elizabeth *management educator, organizational consultant*
Malhotra, Naresh Kumar *management educator*
Sheth, Jagdish Nanchand *business administration educator*
Whittington, Frederick Brown, Jr., *business administration educator*

Columbus
Huff, Lula Lunsford *controller, accounting educator*
Ingersoll, Margaret Lee *personnel professional*

Dalton
Evans, Thomas Passmore *business and product licensing consultant*

Decatur
Becker, Robert Stephen *digital multimedia producer*

Duluth
Watkins, Sydney Lynn *sales executive*

Folkston
Crumbley, Esther Helen Kendrick *retired real estate agent, retired secondary school educator, former councilwoman*

Lagrange
Hawkins, Frances Pam *finance educator*

Macon
Denham, Elaine Birdsong *business educator*

Milledgeville
Engerrand, Doris Dieskow *business educator*

Morrow
Terrell, Natalie Dorethea *contractor*

Statesboro
Murkison, Eugene Cox *business educator*

HAWAII

Honolulu
Kam, Thomas Kwock Yung *accountant educator*
Kwok, Reginald Yin-Wang *urban planning and development educator, architect*
Misawa, Mitsuru *finance educator*
Ng, Wing Chiu *accountant, educator, application developer, lawyer, educator, advocate*
Seiler, Michael Joseph *finance educator, researcher*
Yang, David Chie-Hwa *business administration educator*

Laie
Bradshaw, James R. *business educator*

IDAHO

Boise
Ilett, Frank, Jr., *trucking company executive, educator*
Luthy, John Frederick *management consultant*
Steinfort, James Richard *financial consultant*

ILLINOIS

Antioch
Dahl, Laurel Jean *human services administrator*

Carbondale
Jugenheimer, Donald Wayne *advertising and communications educator, university administrator*
Mathur, Ike *finance educator*

Charleston
Garrett, Norman Anthony *business education educator*

Chicago
Bolnick, Howard Jeffrey *insurance company executive, educator, investor*
Dowling, Doris Anderson *business owner, educator, consultant*
Fregetto, Eugene Fletcher *marketing educator*
McGrath, Mary Ann Pauline *consumer researcher, marketing educator*
Nadas, Julius Zoltan *data processing educator*
Shannon, Donald Sutherlin *accounting educator*

Downers Grove
Clement, Paul Platts, Jr., *performance technologist, educator*

Edwardsville
Giamartino, Gary Attilio *university administrator, management educator*

Elgin
Wiese, Dorothy Jean *business educator*

Evanston
Caywood, Clarke Lawrence *marketing educator, public relations executive*
Dranove, David *business educator, consultant, economist*
Neuschel, Robert Percy *management consultant, educator*

Freeport
Ryan, Bonnie Mae *business office technology educator*

Loves Park
Sylvester, Nancy Katherine *management consultant*

Northbrook
Afterman, Allan B. *accountant, educator, researcher, consultant*

Oakbrook Terrace
Keller, Dennis James *management educator*

River Forest
Batlivala, Robert Bomi D. *oil company executive, economics educator*

Rockford
Albert, Janyce Louise *human resources specialist, retired business educator, banker, consultant, human resources specialist*

Springfield
Whitaker, Victoria Manuela Katz *publisher, public relations executive, educator, consultant*

Urbana
Lakner, Hilda Buckley *consumer behavior educator*

Vernon Hills
Powers, Anthony Richard, Jr., *educational sales professional*

INDIANA

Bloomington
DeHayes, Daniel Wesley *management executive, educator*
Perkins, William Clyde *business educator*
Ravellette, Barbara Lynn *account executive*
Wentworth, Jack Roberts *business educator, consultant*

Carmel
Fadely, James Philip *public relations executive, educator, writer*
Kellison, Donna Louise George *accountant, educator*

Franklin
Link, E. G. (Jay Link) *corporate executive, family wealth counselor*

Huntington
Paff, John William *public relations executive*

Indianapolis
Larsen, Glen Albert, Jr., *finance educator*
Smith, Andrew MacLellan *business administration educator*

Jeffersonville
McMichael, Jeane Casey *real estate company executive, educator*

Lafayette
Lazarus, Bruce I. *restaurant and hotel management educator*

Muncie
Kuratko, Donald F. *entrepreneur, educator, consultant*

Notre Dame
Reilly, Frank Kelly *business educator*
Shannon, William Norman, III, *marketing and international business educator, food service executive*
Vecchio, Robert Peter *business management educator*

South Bend
McDonnell, G. Darlene *retired business educator*
Metzger, Carolyn Dibble *accountant, educator*
Wrenn, Walter Bruce *marketing educator, consultant*

Vincennes
Cutshall, Rex Ralph *operations manager, educator, administrator*

West Lafayette
Feinberg, Richard Alan *consumer science educator, consultant*
Lewellen, Wilbur Garrett *management educator, consultant*
Plante, Robert Donald *management educator, university dean*

IOWA

Ames
Hunger, J(ohn) David *business educator*

Cedar Falls
Schrage, Christine Rosetta *swine production executive, educator*

Davenport
Asadi, Anita Murlene *business educator*
Sievert, Mary Elizabeth *small business owner, retired secondary school educator*

Des Moines
Smith, Diana Marie *business educator*
Snell, Michelle Louise *underwriter*

Iowa City
Clark, Dianne Elizabeth *religious studies and reading educator*

Waverly
Koob, Kathryn Loraine *religious studies educator*

KANSAS

Emporia
Berghaus, Nona Rose *business education educator*

Overland Park
Parker, Cheryl Jean *small business owner*

Pittsburg
Darling, John Rothburn, Jr., *business educator*

Stilwell
Roeseler, Wolfgang Guenther Joachim *city planner*

Wichita
Jabara, Francis Dwight *merchant banker, educator, entrepreneur*

KENTUCKY

Bowling Green
Ahmed, S. Basheer *research company executive, educator*

Fort Thomas
Hill, Esther Dianne *business education educator*

Louisville
Gott, Marjorie Eda Crosby *conservationist, former educator*
McKinney, Owen Michael *retired security executive, consultant*
Min, Hokey *business educator*

Owensboro
Glenn, James H., Jr., *business educator*

Richmond
Whitt, Marcus Calvin *marketing and public relations executive*

LOUISIANA

Baton Rouge
Simmons, Dolores Brown *finance officer, accountant*

Coushatta
Wiggins, Mary Ann Wise *small business owner, educator*

Crowley
Martin, Edythe Louviere *business educator*

Grambling
Fields, Hall Ratcliff *finance educator*

Lake Charles
Heiserman, Russell Lee *electronics educator*

New Orleans
Cook, Victor Joseph, Jr., *marketing educator, consultant*
Smith, John Webster *retired energy industry executive, consultant*

Pineville
Beall, Grace Carter *business educator*

Ruston
Posey, Clyde Lee *business administration and accounting educator*

Thibodaux
Fairchild, Joseph Virgil, Jr., *accounting educator*

MAINE

Andover
Kaltsos, Angelo John *electronics executive, educator, photographer*

Bar Harbor
Cohen, William John *city and regional planner, educator, photographer*

Castine
Potoker, Elaine Sharon *international trade services company executive, business educator*

MARYLAND

Baltimore
Dodge, Calvert Renaul *education and training executive, author, educator*
Laric, Michael Victor *management and marketing administrator*

Chevy Chase
Blaunstein, Phyllis Reid *communications and marketing executive*

College Park
Gordon, Lawrence Allan *accounting educator*
Lamone, Rudolph Philip *business educator*

Columbia
Kurlander, Neale *accounting and law educator, lawyer*

Crofton
Gongwer, Carolyn Jane *human factors engineer*

Frostburg
Groer, Connie Jean *accounting educator*

Gaithersburg
Brown, Dorothea Williams *technology consulting company executive*

Hagerstown
Seibert, Barbara Ann Welch *business educator*

Potomac
Higgins, Nancy Branscome *management and counseling educator*

Riva
Barto, Bradley Edward *small business owner, educator*

Rockville
Lee, James Jieh *environmental educator, computer specialist*
Proffitt, John Richard *business executive, educator*
Weiss, Rita Sandra *transportation executive, educator*

Salisbury
Ezell-Grim, Annette Schram *business management educator, academic administrator*

Silver Spring
Cathey, Mary Ellen Jackson *religious studies educator*
Shih-Carducci, Joan Chia-mo *cooking educator, biochemist, medical technologist, author, writer*

Takoma Park
Urciolo, John Raphael, II, *real estate developer, real estate and finance educator*

MASSACHUSETTS

Amherst
Roberts, Chris *strategy and finance educator, researcher*

Boston
Aber, John William *finance educator*
Boyd, David Preston *business educator*
Buchin, Stanley Ira *management consultant, finance educator*
Bunker, Beryl H. *retired insurance executive, community volunteer*
Harris, Virginia Sydness *religious studies educator*
Hudson, Bradford Taylor *management educator*
McFarlan, Franklin Warren *business administration educator*
Reiling, Henry Bernard *business educator*
Rosen, David Michael *public relations administrator, public affairs consultant*
Sloane, Carl Stuart *educator and management consultant*
Young, David William *management educator*

Cambridge
Hax, Arnoldo Cubillos *management educator, industrial engineer*
Little, John Dutton Conant *management scientist, educator*
Magnanti, Thomas L. *management educator, engineering educator*
Susskind, Lawrence Elliott *urban and environmental planner, educator, public dispute mediator*
Widnall, Sheila Evans *aeronautical educator, former secretary of the airforce, former university official*

Chestnut Hill
Bartunek, Jean Marie *management educator*

Hanson
Norris, John Anthony *health products executive, lawyer, educator*

Lexington
Frieden, Bernard Joel *urban studies educator*
Klein, Lawrence Allen *accounting educator*

Norwood
Carpenter, Pamela Prisco *bank officer, foreign language educator*

Ocean Bluff
Kelley, Albert Joseph *global management strategy consultant*

Quincy
Britt, Margaret Mary *finance educator*

South Orleans
Hale, Margaret Smith *insurance company executive, educator*

Springfield
Vincensi, Avis A. *sales executive, medical educator*

Sudbury
Buono, Anthony Francis *business educator*

Taunton
McMullen, John Henry, Jr., *manufacturing company executive, educator*

Waltham
Buchholz, William James *communications executive, educator*
Curnan, Susan P. *social policy and management educator*

MICHIGAN

Ann Arbor
Huntington, Curtis Edward *actuary*
Seyhun, Hasan Nejat *finance educator, department chairman*

Big Rapids
Hardy, Victoria Elizabeth *management educator*

Center Line
Rose, Mary Philomena *business educator*

Dearborn
Ghoul, Wafica Ali *finance educator*
Lee, Hei Wai *finance educator, researcher*

Detroit
Cavanagh, Gerald Francis *business educator*
Kahalas, Harvey *business educator*

East Lansing
Melnyk, Steven Alexander *business management educator*
Schmidgall, Raymond Stanley *accounting and finance educator*

Grand Rapids
Beals, Paul Archer *religious studies educator*
Kumar, Ashok *operations management educator*

Keego Harbor
Gee, Sharon Lynn *funeral director, educator*

Marquette
Camerius, James Walter *marketing educator, corporate researcher*

Olivet
Kiebala, Susan Marie *accounting and management educator*

Orchard Lake
Ingram, Robert John *business education educator*

Pontiac
Popadak, Geraldine L. *organizational development consultant, educator*

Saginaw
Scharffe, William Granville *academic administrator, educator*

Tecumseh
Taylor, Robert Lee *financial services and sales executive, information systems account executive, educator*

Three Rivers
Truesdell, Timothy L. *private investor*

University Center
Hall, David McKenzie *business and management educator*

Warren
Wallace, Jack Harold *employee development specialist, educator*

MINNESOTA

Apple Valley
Kettle, Sally Anne *consulting company executive, educator*

Bloomington
McGlone, Mary Ellen *marketing and fashion consultant, writer*

Duluth
Feroz, Ehsan Habib *accounting educator, researcher, writer*
Nelson, Dennis Lee *finance educator*

Mankato
Janavaras, Basil John *business educator, consultant*

Minneapolis
Kroll, Paul Benedict *insurance consultant*
Mohanty, Sunil K. *finance educator, researcher*
Schwartz, Howard Wyn *business/marketing educator, consultant*
Yourzak, Robert Joseph *management consultant, engineer, educator*

Minnetonka
Gillies, Donald Richard *marketing and advertising consultant, educator*

Oakdale
Be Vier, William A. *religious studies educator*

Saint Cloud
Reha, Rose Krivisky *retired business educator*

Saint Paul
Dresbach, David Philip *financial consultant, educator*

MISSISSIPPI

Hattiesburg
Doty, Duane Harold *business educator*
Duhon, David Lester *business educator, management consultant*

Jackson
Skelton, Gordon William *data processing executive, educator*

Mississippi State
Chrisman, James Joseph *management educator*
Vance, David A. *information systems educator*

Ocean Springs
Bates, Mable Johnson *retired business technology educator*

Tupelo
Nash, Henry Warren *marketing educator*

Vicksburg
Lee, Thomas Lindsey, Jr., *business educator*

MISSOURI

Columbia
Geiger, Mark Watson *management educator*
Grundler, Mary Jane Lang *business education educator*
Nikolai, Loren Alfred *accounting educator, writer*

Kansas City
De Lurgio, Stephen Anthony *management educator*
Pruitt, Stephen Wallace *finance educator*
Shaw, Richard David *marketing and management educator*

Saint Louis
Brockhaus, Robert Herold, Sr., *business educator, consultant*
Carlson, Arthur Eugene *accounting educator*
Poole, William *bank executive*
Ricks, David Artel *business educator, editor*
Supanvanij, Janikan *finance educator*
Weaver, Charles Lyndell, Jr., *institutional and manufacturing facilities administrator, management and marketing systems consultant*

Warrensburg
Schwepker, Charles Henry, Jr., *marketing educator*

NEBRASKA

Lincoln
Digman, Lester Aloysius *management educator*

North Bend
Williams, Michael K. *agricultural production educator*

Omaha
Brailey, Susan Louise *quality analyst, educator*
Roskens, Ronald William *international business consultant*

NEVADA

Las Vegas
Bovee, Courtland Lowell *business educator*
Leong, G. Keong *operations management educator*
Nold, Aurora Ramirez *business and economics educator*
Opfer, Neil David *construction educator, consultant*
Sevalstad, Suzanne Ada *accounting educator*
Williams, Mary Irene *business education educator*

Reno
Munro, Roderick Anthony *business improvement coach*
Neidert, Kalo Edward *accountant, educator*

NEW HAMPSHIRE

Dover
Elder, Jennifer Howard *accounting educator*

Hanover
Anthony, Robert Newton *management educator emeritus*

Manchester
Bramante, Fredrick J., Jr., *retail executive*
Levins, John Raymond *investment advisor, management educator, educator*
Poloian, Lynda Gamans *retailing educator*

NEW JERSEY

Avon By The Sea
Bruno, Grace Angelia *accountant, retired educator*

Berkeley Heights
Gottheimer, George Malcolm, Jr., *insurance executive, educator*

Cherry Hill
Bennett, Mary Ellen *tax consultant, accounting consultant, business consultant*

Fair Lawn
Kourkoumelis, Nick *financial analyst, consultant, finance educator*

Fanwood
Williams, Clarence Leon *management, sociology and public policy company executive, educator*

Florham Park
Ohn, Jonathan K. *business educator*

Jackson
Hunter, Lynn *sales executive, writer, elementary school educator*

Jamesburg
Barcus, Gilbert Martin *medical products executive, business educator*

Kinnelon
Richardson, Irene M. *management consultant*

Morristown
Mooney, Patricia Anne *sales executive, educator*

Newark
Contractor, Farok *business and management educator*
Norwood, Carolyn Virginia *business educator*

Point Pleasant
Albano, Pasquale Charles *management educator, management and organization development consultant*

Princeton
Lincoln, Anna *company executive, foreign languages educator*
Stackhouse, Max Lynn *Christian ethics educator*

Skillman
Tenenbaum, Bernard Hirsh *entrepreneur, educator*
Wheelock, Keith Ward *retired consulting company executive, educator*

Somers Point
McCullough, Eileen (Eileen McCullough LePage, Elli McCullough) *financial consultant, writer, editor, educator*

Teaneck
Connola, Donald Pascal, Jr., *management consultant*
Woerner, Alfred Ira *medical device manufacturer, educator*

Warren
Blass, Walter Paul *consultant, management*
DiPietro, Ralph Anthony *marketing and management consultant, educator*

NEW MEXICO

Albuquerque
D'Anza, Lawrence Martin *management consultant*
Frazier, James R. *management educator*

Los Alamos
Sankaran, Harikumar *finance educator*

Santa Fe
Jurkat, Martin Peter *mathematician, statistician, management educator*

NEW YORK

Amherst
Jen, Frank Chifeng *finance and management educator*

Averill Park
Traver, Robert William, Sr., *management consultant, author, lecturer, engineer*

Bergen
Woodworth, Beth Elaine *business owner*

Bethpage
Marrone, Daniel Scott *business, production and quality management educator*

Binghamton
Taylor, Kenneth Douglas *stockbroker, finance and computer consultant, educator*
Yammarino, Francis Joseph *management educator, consultant*

Brooklyn
Abrams, Roni *business education educator, communications consultant, trainer*
Frisch, Ivan Thomas *computer and communications company executive*
Galatianos, Gus A. *computer executive, information systems consultant, real estate developer, educator*
Roche, John Edward *educator, human resources consultant*
Stiner, Frederic Matthew, Jr., *accounting educator, consultant, writer*

Buffalo
Bennett, Shirley Ann *maintenance executive, business technologist educator*
Eagan, John Gayle *business educator*
Shick, Richard Arlon *finance educator*

Cazenovia
Adamo, Joseph Francis *management educator*

Greenlawn
Brassell, Robert James, Jr., *small business owner*

Hempstead
Comer, Debra Ruth *management educator*
Evans, Joel Raymond *marketing educator*
Lee, Keun Sok *business educator, consultant*
Zagano, Phyllis *religious studies educator*

Huntington
Ruppert, Mary Frances *management consultant, school counselor*

Ithaca
Elliott, John *accountant, educator, dean*
Kelly, Eileen Patricia *management educator*
Kimes, Sheryl Elaine *business educator*
Lesser, William Henri *marketing educator*

Jamaica
Angerville, Edwin Duvanel *accountant, educator*
Konecsni, John-Emery *marketing company executive, philosophy educator, university official*

Lyons
Lyons, Patrick Joseph *management educator*
Ruggieri, Catherine Josephine *management educator*

Lewiston
Waters, William Ernest *microelectronics executive*

Merrick
Beckman, Judith Kalb *financial counselor and planner, educator, writer*

Morrisville
Coppola, Joseph Angelo *computer professional, educator*

New Hyde Park
DeLuca, James Patrick *graphic arts and advertising educator, consultant*

New York
Altfest, Karen Caplan *diversified financial services company executive, director*
Assael, Henry *marketing educator*
Becker, Susan Kaplan *management and marketing communication consultant, educator*
Berkowitz, Alice Orlander *management consultant, hearing and speech educator*
Cavanagh, Richard Edward *research association executive*
Craig, Charles Samuel *marketing educator*
Creamer, German Gonzalo *bank executive, educator*
Das, T. K. *management educator, consultant*
Fischer, Stanley *bank executive, economist, educator*
Hollis, Loucille *risk control administrator, educator*
Johnson, Thomas Stephen *banker*
Kaufman, Henry *financial services executive*
Kover, Arthur Jay *marketing educator, consultant*
Mintz, Norman Nelson *investment banker, educator*
Putney, Mary Lynn *bank administrator, educator*
Savas, Emanuel S. *public management and public policy educator*
Sharp, J(ames) Franklin *finance educator, portfolio manager*

Nyack
Stratis, George *finance educator*

Old Westbury
Barbera, Anthony Thomas *accountant, educator*

Orchard Park
Keenan, John Paul *leadership and management educator, consultant, psychologist*
Oliver, Dominick Michael *business educator*

Pleasantville
Cozzolino, John Michael, Jr., *management educator*
Reps, David Nathan *finance educator*

Poughkeepsie
Gagne, Margaret Lee *accounting educator*

Pound Ridge
Darcy, Keith Thomas *finance company executive, educator*

Rye
Finnerty, John Dudley *financial consultant*

Saint Bonaventure
Pandit, Vinay Yeshwant *business educator*

Stony Brook
Koppelman, Lee Edward *regional planner, educator*

Sunnyside
Privo, Alexander *finance educator, department chairman*

Syracuse
Marcoccia, Louis Gary *accountant, university administrator*
Whaley, Ross Samuel *environmentalist, educator*

Troy
Phan, Phillip Hin Choi *business educator, consultant*

Valhalla
Christesen, John Denis *business educator*

Westbury
Silverman, Judith *human resource educational services director, author, consultant*

NORTH CAROLINA

Chapel Hill
Lynch, Luann Johnson *business educator*
Rondinelli, Dennis A(ugust) *business administration educator, researcher*
Roth, Aleda Vender *business educator*
Weiss, Shirley F. *urban and regional planner, economist, educator*
Whybark, David Clay *business educator, researcher*

Charlotte
Spangler, Clemmie Dixon, Jr., *construction company executive*

Durham
Bettman, James Ross *management educator*
Oakley, Wanda Faye *management consultant, educator*

Greensboro
Kondeas, Alexander G. *finance educator*

Lenard, Mary Jane *accounting and information systems educator*
Lloyd, Lila G. *business educator*

Greenville
Wrisley, Robert Lyman *business educator*

Hampstead
Walters, Sherwood George *management consultant, educator*

Hertford
McClung, Kenneth Austin, Jr., *training executive, performance consultant*

Hillsborough
Eustice, Russell Clifford *consulting company executive, academic director*

Morganton
Hartley, Helen Rosanna *business educator*

Pembroke
Bukowy, Stephen Joseph *accounting educator*

Raleigh
Godfrey, Albert Blanton *former research and management consulting company executive, writer, educator*

NORTH DAKOTA

Grand Forks
Zahrly, Janice Honea *management educator*

Minot
Welstad, Kirk *small business owner*

OHIO

Ada
Cooper, Ken Errol *retired management educator*

Akron
Arnett, James Edward *retired insurance company executive, retired secondary school*
Kim, Il-Woon *accounting educator*

Athens
Miller, Peggy McLaren *retired management educator*

Bellefontaine
Hagerdon, Kathy Ann (Kay Hagerdon) *electric power industry executive, educator*

Canton
Thomas, Suzanne Ward *public relations executive, communications educator, radio personality*
Watson, Duane Frederick *religious studies educator*

Chagrin Falls
Stevenson, Thomas Herbert *management consultant, writer, executive coach*

Cincinnati
Anderson, Jerry William, Jr., *technical and business consulting executive, educator*
Hawkins, Lawrence Charles *management consultant, educator*
Hoermann, Edward Richard *urban planning educator*
Wulker, Laurence Joseph *portfolio manager, educator, financial planner*

Cleveland
Anders, Claudia Dee *occupational therapist*
Eagan, Susan Lajoie *finance educator, consultant*
Key, Helen Elaine *accountant, educator, consulting company executive*
Noetzel, Arthur Jerome *business administration educator, management consultant*
Poza, Ernesto *business consultant, educator*
Sudow, Thomas Nisan *marketing services company executive, broadcaster, chamber of commerce executive*

Columbus
Collier, David Alan *management educator*
Hanna, Sherman Davie *financial planning educator*
Schlesinger, Leonard Arthur *retail executive*

Dayton
Anderson, Ruth Yarnnelle *real estate professional, educator*
Cox, Myron Keith *business educator*

Dublin
Heneman, Robert Lloyd *management educator*

Grove City
Purdy, Dennis Gene *insurance company executive, education consultant*

Highland Hills
Haldar, Frances Louise *business educator, accountant, treasurer*

Hillsboro
Roark, Peggy Jean *business educator, academic specialist, consultant*

Marysville
Agin, Dennis Michael *aircraft manufacturer, orthodontist educator*

Painesville
Luhta, Caroline Naumann *airport manager, flight educator*

Pickerington
Callander, Kay Eileen Paisley *business owner, retired education educator, writer*

Reynoldsburg
Gunnels, Lee O. *retired finance and management educator, manufacturing/research company director, inventor*

Springboro
Walden, James William *accountant, educator*

Springfield
Rowland-Raybold, Roberta *insurance agent, music educator*

Toledo
Cole, Jeffrey Clark *public relations professional*
Lazur, James Joseph *accounting educator*
Vonderembse, Mark Anthony *management educator*

Westerville
Arch, Gail Thelma *international business educator*

OKLAHOMA

Lawton
Davis, Ellen Marie *business educator*

Miami
Taylor, Vesta Fisk *real estate broker, educator*

Oklahoma City
Atlee, Debbie Gayle *sales consultant, medical educator*
Rex, John Williams *assurance company executive*

Tulsa
Gaddis, Richard William *management educator*
Imhoff, Pamela M. *marketing educator*

OREGON

Ashland
Farrimond, George Francis, Jr., *management educator*

Bend
Wonser, Michael Dean *retired public affairs director, art history educator*

Eugene
Lindholm, Richard Theodore *economics and finance educator*

Portland
Lavigne, Peter Marshall *environmentalist, lawyer, educator*
Munroe, Donna Scott *marketing executive, healthcare and management consultant, educator*
Watne, Donald Arthur *accountant, educator, retired*

PENNSYLVANIA

Allentown
Coyle, Charles A. *marketing educator*

Bethlehem
Barsness, Richard Webster *management educator, administrator*
Gupta, Parveen P. *accounting educator, consultant, researcher*

Blue Bell
Hirsch, Robert W. *sales executive, consultant*

Chester
DiAngelo, Joseph Anthony, Jr., *finance educator, dean*

Dunmore
Pencek, Carolyn Carlson *treasurer, educator*

Enola
Baumann, Matthew Louis *business education educator, elementary school educator*

Indiana
McPherson, Donald Scott *employment relations educator, arbitrator/mediator*
Stevenson, Charles Beman *business educator*

Johnstown
Smiach, Deborah *accountant, educator, consultant*

Kutztown
Ogden, James Russell *marketing educator, consultant, lecturer, writer*

Lancaster
Taylor, Ann *human resources specialist, educator*

Latrobe
Fazzi, Charles *accounting educator*

Lebanon
Deysher, Paul Evans *training consultant*

Loretto
Benham, Philip Owen, Jr., *business marketing educator, consultant*

Monaca
Nutter, James Randall *management educator*

New Freedom
West, Brian Claire *management consultant, educator*

Newry
LaBorde, Terrence Lee *audit consultant, negotiator*

Newtown
Fiore, James Louis, Jr., *public accountant, educator, professional speaker, trainer consultant*

Philadelphia
Andrisani, Paul J. *business educator, management consultant*
Blume, Marshall Edward *finance educator*
Choi, Jongmoo Jay *finance educator, educator*
Gerrity, Thomas P. *management educator*
Goldsmith, Nancy Carrol *business and health services management educator*
Keim, Donald Bruce *finance educator*
Mazzarella, James Kevin *business administration educator*
Oliva, Terence Anthony *marketing educator*
Rowan, Richard Lamar *business management educator*
Santomero, Anthony M. *bank executive, public policymaker*
Shils, Edward B. *management educator, lawyer, arbitrator and mediator*
Useem, Michael *management consultant educator*

Pittsburgh
Bonner, Shirley Harrold *business communications educator*
Cornuejols, Gerard Pierre *operations research educator*
Means, Dwight Bardeen, Jr., *financial consultant, educator*
Miles, Leon F. (Lee Miles) *marketing educator*
Zoffer, H. Jerome *business educator, university dean*

Radnor
Marland, Alkis Joseph *rental company executive, computer scientist, educator, financial planner*

Reading
Young, Richard Robert *logistics and transportation educator*

Reedsville
Farrell, Rodney Alan *management consultant*

Saint Davids
Rogers, James Gardiner *accountant, educator*

Schuylkill Haven
Bonawitz, Mary Feeney *accountant, educator*

Shippensburg
Stone, Susan Ridgaway *marketing educator*

Shiremanstown
Nesbit, William Terry *small business owner, consultant*

University Park
Muscarella, Christopher James *finance educator*

Villanova
Cox-Klaczak, Karen Michelle *marketing educator, computer company official*

Wynnewood
Frankl, Razelle *management educator*

Wyomissing
Williams-Wennell, Kathi *human resources consultant*

RHODE ISLAND

Providence
Allio, Robert John *management consultant, educator*
Satterthwaite, Franklin Bache, Jr., *management educator, executive coach, author*

Wakefield
Doody, Agnes G. *communications educator, management and communication consultant*

SOUTH CAROLINA

Anderson
Caperton, Richard Walton *photographer, automobile repair company executive, educator, consultant*

Clemson
Petzel, Florence Eloise *textiles educator*
Sheriff, Jimmy Don *accounting educator, academic dean, administrator*

Columbia
Luoma, Gary A. *accounting educator*
Pritchett, Samuel Travis *finance and insurance educator, researcher, consultant*

Graniteville
Learnard, James Michael *middle school educator, former finance company executive, special education educator*

Rock Hill
Click, John William *communication educator*
Cornick, Michael F(rederick) *accounting educator*

Spartanburg
Pate, John Gillis, Jr., *financial consultant, accounting educator*

Summerville
Sexton, Donald Lee *retired business administration educator*

Sumter
van Bulck, Margaret West *financial planner, educator*

SOUTH DAKOTA

Mina
Beck, John Herman *retired business education educator*

Mitchell
Luckett, Jerry Lynne *business administration educator*

TENNESSEE

Atoka
Haas, Robert Donnell *flight instructor, airline transport pilot, lawyer, retail executive, retail executive*

Brighton
Iles, Roger Dean *business educator*

Chattanooga
Vance, Phoebe Avalon *educator*
Young, Sonia Winer *public relations director, educator*

Gatlinburg
Flanagan, Judy *special events professional, entertainment and marketing specialist, professional public speaker*

Jackson
Holt, Michael Kenneth *management and finance educator, consultant, city councilman*

Johnson City
Bayes, Paul Eugene *accounting educator*
Morgan, Robert George *accounting educator, researcher*

Knoxville
Mynatt, Marvin Dennis *utilities company training executive*

Martin
Haddad, Mahmoud Mustafa *management educator*

Memphis
Young, Paula Erness *corporate trainer*

Murfreesboro
Lee, John Thomas *finance educator, financial planner*

Nashville
Deel, Rebecca Lynne *business educator*
Richmond, Samuel Bernard *management educator*

TEXAS

Aledo
Barton, Charles David *religious studies educator, writer, historian, researcher*

Allen
Garner, Julie Lowrey *occupational therapist*

Amarillo
Strickland, Anita Maurine *retired business educator, librarian*

Archer City
Long, Ashley Diane *finance educator, technology educator*

Argyle
Pettit, John Douglas, Jr., *management educator*

Arlington
Swanson, Peggy Eubanks *finance educator*

Austin
Anderson, Urton Liggett *accounting educator*
Daly, John Augustine *communications management researcher and educator*
Larson, Kermit Dean *accounting educator*
Lenoir, Gloria Cisneros *consultant, educator*
McCullough, Benjamin Franklin *transportation researcher, educator*
McElroy, Maurine Davenport *financier, educator*
Parrino, Robert *finance educator*
Sturdevant, Wayne Alan *executive management consultant*

Cleburne
Marak, Randy Barton *computer educator*

College Station
Cocanougher, Arthur Benton *business administration educator*

Commerce
Carraher, Shawn Michael *management educator*

Corpus Christi
Stanford, Jane Herring *management consultant and educator, author*

Dallas
Martinez, Guillermo Bill *administrator*

Miller, Geraldine (Tincy) *real estate company executive, educational association administrator*
Peavy, John Wesley, III, *investment advisor, educator, investment advisor, educator, consultant, financial consultant*
Smiles, Ronald *management educator*

Denton
Prybutok, Victor Ronald *business educator*
Taylor, Sherrill Ruth *management educator*

Dripping Springs
Guess, Aundrea Kay *accounting educator*

Fort Worth
Pappas-Speairs, Nina *financial planner, educator*
Waller, Gary Wilton *administration educator, minister*

Frisco
Kern, Ronald Paul *computer company executive, academic dean, curriculum consultant*

Garland
Hurst, Linda Whittington *small business owner, educational administrator*
Leigh-Manuell, Robert Allen *training executive, educator*

Houston
Chatterjee, Amitava *finance educator, consultant*
Crystal, Jonathan Andrew *executive recruiter*
Margotta, Maurice Howard, Jr., *management consultant*
McComas, Marcella Laigne *marketing educator*
Wagner, Charlene Brook *publishing consultant*
Williams, Edward Earl, Jr., *entrepreneur, educator*

Huntsville
Sower, Victor Edmund *management educator*
Stowe, Charles Robinson Beecher *management consultant, educator, lawyer*

Lubbock
Lawson, Melanie Kay *management administrator, early childhood consultant*
Sears, Robert Stephen *finance educator, university dean*

Richardson
Merville, Lawrence Joseph *finance educator*

San Antonio
Allison, Genevieve J. *business educator*
Cottingham, Stephen Kent *real estate development executive, researcher, minister, educator*
Sun, Minghe *business educator*
Wilson, Bennie James, III, *business educator*

San Marcos
Taylor, Ruth Arleen Lesher *marketing educator*

Santa Fe
Lambert, Willie Lee Bell *mobile equipment company owner, educator*

Stephenville
Collier, Boyd Dean *finance educator, management consultant*

Tyler
Tarry, (Jimmie) Patricia *real estate broker, retired elementary education educator*

Waco
Flanders, Henry Jackson, Jr., *religious studies educator*

UTAH

Logan
Arbuthnot, Jeanette Jaussaud *apparel executive, design educator, researcher*
Brackner, James Walter *retired finance educator*

Orem
Snow, Marlon O. *trucking executive, state agency administrator*

Provo
Newitt, Jay *construction management educator*

Salt Lake City
Sullivan, Claire Ferguson *retired marketing educator*

VERMONT

Burlington
Mead, Philip Bartlett *healthcare administrator, obstetrician, educator*

Ludlow
Mueller, Diane *hotel executive*

Middlebury
Benoit, Philip Grosvenor *communications executive, educator, writer*

Shelburne
Giles, Scott Andrew *finance company executive*

VIRGINIA

Abingdon
Ramos-Cano, Hazel Balatero *caterer, chef, innkeeper, restauranteur, entrepreneur*

Alexandria
Smith, Robert Luther *management educator*

Arlington
Hengels, Charles Francis *management consultant, business educator*
Missal, Joseph Bannan *mathematics and business educator*

Ashland
Bowles, Betty Jones *business education educator*

Blacksburg
Kincade, Doris Helsing *apparel marketing educator*
Patterson, Douglas MacLennan *finance educator*

Charlottesville
DeMong, Richard Francis *finance and investments educator*
Scott, Charlotte H. *business educator*
Verstegen, Deborah A. *policy and finance educator*

Chesterfield
Harris, Valerie Coleman *office assistant*

Crozet
Rosenblum, John William *finance educator*

Emory
Kellogg, Frederic Richard *religious studies educator*

Farmville
Bacon, Frank William *finance educator, consultant*

Fort Belvoir
Gould, Jay William, III, *management development educator, lecturer, author, international consultant*

Gretna
Miller, Bernice Dearing *funeral director, member school board*

Hampton
Wiedman, Timothy Gerard *management educator*

Hopewell
Eastman, Tamara Jane *private investigator, educator*

Lynchburg
Gilmore, Philip Nathanael *finance educator, accountant*

Manassas
Foley, Michael Patrick *marketing professional educator*

Mc Lean
Lane-Maher, Maureen Dorothea *marketing educator, consultant*

Norfolk
Dungan, William Joseph, Jr., *insurance broker, economics educator*
Haug, James Charles *business and management educator*
McKee, Timothy Carlton *taxation educator*
Pharr, Naomi H. Morton *business educator*

Reston
Foster, William Anthony *management consultant, educator*
Fox, Edward A. *business executive*

Richmond
Harris, Ruth Hortense Coles *retired accounting educator*
Winkler, Katherine Maurine *management consultant, educator*

Williamsburg
Pearson, Roy Laing *business administration educator*

Winchester
Sample, Travis Lamar *business educator*

Woodbridge
Rose, Marianne Hunt *business educator*

WASHINGTON

Edmonds
Bell, Nancy Lee Hoyt *real estate investor, middle school educator, volunteer*

Everett
Vujovic, Mary Jane *education and employment training planner*

Gig Harbor
Cuzzetto, Charles Edward *accountant, financial analyst, educator*

Malaga
Nanto, Roxanna Lynn *marketing professional, management consultant*

Mount Vernon
Gaston, Margaret Anne *retired business educator*

Pullman
Nofsinger, John *finance educator, consultant*

Seattle
Gist, Marilyn Elaine *organizational behavior and human resource management educator*
Sundem, Gary Lewis *accounting educator*

Shoreline
Hutton, Winfield Travis *management consultant, educator*

Spokane
Fowler, Walton Berry *franchise developer, educator*
Teets, Walter Ralph *accounting educator*

WEST VIRGINIA

Elkins
Payne, Gloria Marquette *business educator*

Inwood
Cloyd, Helen Mary *accountant, educator*

Martinsburg
Ayers, Anne Louise *small business owner, consultant, counselor*

Parkersburg
Everson, Nina Marie Brode *small business owner, preschool educator*

Triadelphia
McCullough, John Phillip *management consultant, educator*

WISCONSIN

Bayfield
Wilhelm, Sister Phyllis *religious studies educator, director*

Janesville
Butters, John Patrick *travel company executive, educator*

Madison
Aldag, Ramon John *management and organization educator*
Haynes, Marilyn Mae *accountant, educator*

Middleton
Cotherman, Audrey Mathews *management and policy consultant, administrator*

New Berlin
Wilber, Barbara Ann *computer science and business education educator*

West Bend
VanBrunt-Kramer, Karen *business administration educator*

Whitewater
Long, Ellen Joyce *accounting/business educator*

WYOMING

Green River
Thoman, Mary E. *business and marketing educator, rancher*

Laramie
Spiegelberg, Emma Jo *business education educator, academic administrator*

CANADA

ALBERTA

Calgary
Schulz, Robert Adolph *management educator, management consultant*

BRITISH COLUMBIA

Burnaby
Tung, Rosalie Lam *business educator, consultant*

ONTARIO

Ottawa
Goodine, Isaac Thomas *development executive, educator*

Toronto
Carrothers, Gerald Arthur Patrick *environmental and city planning educator*
Hore, John Edward *commodity futures educator*

Windsor
Faria, Anthony John *marketing educator, consultant, researcher*

QUEBEC

Montreal
Gabbour, Iskandar *city and regional planning educator*

HONG KONG

Shatin
Tang, Yingchan Edwin *marketing educator*

HUNGARY

Budapest
Rice, Kenneth Lloyd *environmental services executive, educator*

SINGAPORE

Singapore
Frank, Ronald Edward *marketing educator*

ADDRESS UNPUBLISHED

Alexakos, Frances Marie *counselor, business owner, psychology educator, researcher, producer, editor*
Amadio, Bari Ann *metal fabrication executive, former nurse*
Amatangelo, Nicholas S. *retired financial printing and document management services executive*
Ashcraft, Charles Olin *business educator*
Banis, Robert Joseph *pharmaceutical company executive, educator, publisher*
Baxter, Barbara Morgan *Internet service provider executive, educator*
Benenson, Claire Berger *investment and financial planning educator*
Benjoseph, Dan C. *travel company executive, educator*
Bertucelli, Robert Edward *accountant, educator*
Blomberg, Susan Ruth *training executive*
Bryan, Mary Jo W. *realtor, artist, art educator*
Carter, Richard Duane *business educator*
Chapman, Geneva Joyce *entrepreneur, educator, writer*
Chia, Felipe Humberto *management marketing educator, author, consultant*
Chinula, Donald McLean *religious studies educator*
Cittone, Henry Aron *hotel and restaurant management educator*
Coates, Shirley Jean *finance educator, secondary school educator*
Conti, Indalicio Palomar *accountancy educator*
Cooper, Jon Charles *environmentalist, educator, lawyer*
Cunningham, Nancy Schieffelin *business educator*
Dasso, Jerome Joseph *real estate educator*
Dendrinos, Dimitrios Spyros *urban planning educator*
Denning, Karen Craft *finance educator*
Dietz, Janis Camille *business educator*
Duncan, Robert Bannerman *strategy and organizations educator*
Edleson, Michael Edward *economist, finance educator, consultant, writer*
Elliott, Marion Louise Dick *arts education and management consultant*
Farrigan, Julia Ann *retired small business owner, educator*
Forester, Jean Martha Brouillette *innkeeper, retired librarian, educator*
Goehring, Maude Cope *retired business educator*
Gray, Margaret Ann *management educator, consultant*
Hand, Herbert Hensley *finance educator, writer, entrepreneur*
Hochschild, Carroll Shepherd *computer company and medical equipment executive, educator*
Hodgen, Maurice Denzil *management consultant, retired education educator*
Humphrey, Doris Davenport *publishing company executive, consultant, educator*
Ihlanfeldt, William *investment company executive, consultant*
Jackson, Vivian Michele *church administrator, consultant*
Jerrytone, Samuel Joseph *financial broker*
Kaplan, Erica Lynn *typing and word processing service company executive, pianist, educator*
Kilmann, Ralph Herman *business educator*
King, Algin Braddy *retired marketing educator*
Kirk, Donald James *accountant, consultant*
Lee, Nancy T. *human services administrator, educator*
Letcher, Naomi Jewell *quality engineer, educator, counselor*
Magoon, Donald W. *retired business educator*
Maltin, Freda *retired university administrator*
Mason, George Henry *business educator*
Meek, Forrest Burns *retired trading company executive*
Melroy, Jane Ruth *business educator*
Mikiska, Jenifer Ann *public relations executive*
Miller, Carl Chet *business educator*
Mobley, William Hodges *management educator, researcher, author, executive*
Morita, Toshiyasu *technology professional*
Munlu, Kamil Cemal *finance educator*
Needles, Belverd Earl, Jr., *accountant, educator*
Neelankavil, James Paul *marketing educator, consultant, researcher*
Orem, Cassandra Elizabeth (Sandra Orem) *small business owner, educator, holistic health consultant and practitioner*
Paonessa, M. Suzanne *budget analyst*
Patillo, Sylvia Jane *human resources executive, educator*
Pierce, Lisa Margaret *telecommunications executive, product and market development manager, lecturer*
Richards, Carmeleete A. *computer training executive, network administrator, consultant*
Richardson, Thomas Andrew *business executive, educator*
Robertson, Jack Clark *accounting educator*
Rogan, Robert William *management educator, consultant, osteopath, psychiatrist*
Royston, Lloyd Leonard *educational marketing consultant*
Ryan, Leo Vincent *business educator*
Sagafi-Nejad, Tagi *business educator*
Sandage-Mussey, Elizabeth Anthea *retired market research executive*
Sanquist, Nancy Johnson *facitliy management executive*
Schmoldt, Peggy Sue *cosmetology educator*
Shelan, Debbie Levin *travel agency administrator, school system administrator*

Shore, Harvey Harris *business educator*
Shultis, Robert Lynn *finance educator, cost systems consultant, retired professional association executive*
Solberg, Ronald Louis *investment adviser*
Sorgi, Deborah B(ernadette) *educational software company executive*
Sorstokke, Ellen Kathleen *marketing executive, educator*
Sowa, Frank Xavier *entrepreneur, futurist, educator, speaker*
Srinivasan, Venkataraman *marketing and management educator*
Strength, Janis Grace *management executive, educator*
Strong, John Scott *finance educator*
Substad Lokensgard, Kathryn Ann *small business owner, career consultant*
Sullivan, Sarah Louise *management and technology consultant*
Sunderman, Deborah Ann *apparel executive, fashion and business educator*
Swanson, Lauren A. *consultant, entrepreneur, educator, researcher*
Thomas, Rhonda Robbins *marketing educator, consultant*
Trent, Robert Harold *retired business educator*
Tyler, Richard James *personal and professional development educator*
Ulosevich, Steven Nils *social scientist, management consultant, educator, trainer*
Velazquez, Joseph *management and mathematics educator*
Vu, Joseph Duong *financial educator*
Wald, Mary S. *retired risk management and personal finance educator*
Wehling, Robert Louis *retired household products company executive*
White, Bonnie Yvonne *management consultant, retired educator*
Williams, Alfred Blythe *management consultant, educator*
Williams, Lisa Rochelle *logistics and transportation educator*
Wise, Susan Tamsberg *management and communications consultant, speaker*
Wolotkiewicz, Marian M. *business executive*
Youst, David Bennett *career development educator*

HIGHER EDUCATION: HEALTHCARE

UNITED STATES

ALABAMA

Auburn
McEldowney, Rene *healthcare educator, consultant*
Parsons, Daniel Lankester *pharmaceutics educator*

Birmingham
Caulfield, James Benjamin *pathologist, educator*
DiMicco, Wendy Ann *nurse educator*
Falls, Jacqueline O'Barr *psychotherapist, educator*
Frenette, Luc *anesthesiologist, educator*
King, Charles Mark *dentist, educator*
Meezan, Elias *pharmacologist, educator*
Oakes, Walter Jerry *pediatric neurosurgeon*
Omura, George Adolf *medical oncologist*
Perry, Helen *medical/surgical nurse, secondary school educator*
Pittman, Constance Shen *physician, educator*
Pittman, James Allen, Jr., *physician, educator*
Siegal, Gene Philip *pathology educator*
Thorson-Houck, Janice Hargreaves *speech, language pathologist*
Tilden, Samuel Joseph *pediatrician, educator*

Florence
Foote, Dorothy Gargis *nursing educator*

Huntsville
Burg, Fredric David *physician, university dean*
Noble, Ronald Mark *sports medicine facility administrator*
Steinbuchel, Carla Faye *pediatrics nurse, nursing educator*

Mobile
Barik, Sailen *biomedical scientist, educator*
Brady, Sylvia Eltz *medical/surgical and pediatric nurse, educator*
Esham, Richard Henry *internist, educator, geriatrician, educator*
Guarino, Anthony Michael *pharmacologist, educator, consultant, counselor*
Itaya, Stephen Kenji *neuroanatomist, educator*
Littleton, Jesse Talbot, III, *radiology educator*
Stevens, Gail Lavine *community health nurse, educator*

Orange Beach
Conrad, Marcel Edward *hematologist, educator*

Tuscaloosa
Orcutt, Ben Avis *retired social work educator*
Sinclair, Robert Ewald *physician, educator*

Tuskegee Institute
Cooley, Fannie Richardson *counselor, educator*

Valley
Striblin, Lori Ann *critical care nurse, Medicare coordinator, nursing educator*

ALASKA

Valdez
Devens, John Searle *natural resources administrator*

ARIZONA

Flagstaff
Braunstein, Ethan Malcolm *skeletal radiologist, paleopathologist, educator*

Glendale
Chavez, Mary Lynn *pharmacy educator*

Mesa
Hagen, Nicholas Steward *medical educator, consultant*

Payson
Lasys, Joan *medical nurse, writer, educator, publisher*

Phoenix
Anderson, Christina Susanne *speech and language therapist*
Holloway, George Allen, Jr., *physician, educator*
Mc Mahon, Margaret Garvey *nursing educator*
Mitchell, Wayne Lee *health care administrator*
Murcko, Anita Cecilia *medical consultant, educator*
Steward, Lester Howard *psychiatrist, academic administrator, educator*
Wright, Richard Oscar, III, *pathologist, educator, clinical ethicist*

Sonoita
Scott, William Coryell *medical executive*

Sun City West
Roush, Dorothy Evelyn *medical laboratory educator, consultant*

Tucson
Graham, Anna Regina *pathologist, educator*
Harris, David Thomas *immunology educator*
Hughes, John Harold *surgeon, educator*
Witten, Mark Lee *lung injury research scientist, educator*

ARKANSAS

Eureka Springs
McCullough, V. Beth *pharmacist, educator*

Fayetteville
Cook, Daniel Walter *rehabilitation education educator*

Hot Springs National Park
McDaniel, Ola Jo Peterson *retired social worker, educator*

Little Rock
Bissada, Nabil Kaddis *urologist, educator, researcher, author*
Cave, Mac Donald *anatomy educator*
Mrak, Robert Emil *neuropathologist, educator, electron microscopist*
Sotomora-von Ahn, Ricardo Federico *pediatrician, educator*
Ward, Harry Pfeffer *physician, retired university chancellor*

Mountain Home
Ward, Melvin A. *nursing educator*

Sherwood
Eddy, Nancy C. *counselor*

State University
Rutherford, Mary Jean *laboratory administrator, science educator*

CALIFORNIA

Agoura Hills
Merchant, Roland Samuel, Sr., *hospital administrator, educator*

Alhambra
Kilburn, Kaye Hatch *medical educator*
Mabee, John Richard *physician assistant, educator*

Alta Loma
Fenison, Eddie *health science educator*

Altadena
Branin, Joan Julia *health services management educator*

Arcadia
Anderson, Holly Geis *women's health facility administrator, commentator, educator*
Gamboa, George Charles *retired oral surgeon, educator*

Berkeley
Diamond, Marian Cleeves *anatomy educator*
Duhl, Leonard *psychiatrist, educator*
Harris, Michael Gene *optometrist, educator, lawyer*
Little, Angela Capobianco *nutritional science educator*
Tempelis, Constantine Harry *immunologist, educator*

Beverly Hills
Allen, Howard Norman *cardiologist, educator*
Catz, Boris *endocrinologist, educator*

Campbell
Tran, Nam Van *health education specialist*

Carson
Carroll, Marilyn Jeanne *medical technologist, educator*
Kearns, Ellen Hope *health sciences educator*

Claremont
Johnson, Jerome Linné *cardiologist, educator*
Ross, Mary Caslin *medical researcher*

Clovis
Benefiel, Diane Marie *home health nurse supervisor*

Corte Madera
Epstein, William Louis *dermatologist, educator*

Culver City
Hadley, Robert Gordon *rehabilitation counselor educator, consultant*

Davis
Cardiff, Robert Darrell *pathology educator*
Kay, Douglas Harold *optometrist, educator*
Ruebner, Boris Henry *pathologist, educator*
Schenker, Marc Benet *preventive medicine educator*

Duarte
Li, Jian Jian *medical educator*

Fresno
Khouzam, Hani Raoul *psychiatrist, physician, educator*
Leigh, Hoyle *psychiatrist, educator, writer*

Fullerton
Griffin, Kirsten Bertelsen *nursing educator*

Gardena
Duenes Brown, Elena Marie *speech/language pathologist*

Hayward
Bachicha, Joseph Alfred *physician, educator*
Hosang, Robert Anthony *obstetrician-gynecologist, educator*

Huntington Beach
Pacino, Frank George *physician, educator*

Irvine
Quilligan, Edward James *obstetrician, gynecologist, educator*

La Jolla
Covell, Ruth Marie *medical educator, medical school administrator*
Covington, Stephanie Stewart *psychotherapist, writer, educator*
Dalessio, Donald John *internist, neurologist, educator*
Jorgensen, Judith Ann *psychiatrist, educator*
Katzman, Robert *medical educator, neurologist*
Marshall, Sharon Bowers *nursing educator, director clinical trials*

La Verne
McDonough-Treichler, Judith Dianne *medical educator, consultant*

Laguna Woods
Ross, Mathew *medical educator*

Lemoore
Davis, Cynthia Almarinez *nursing educator*

Loma Linda
Behrens, Berel Lyn *physician, academic and healthcare administrator*
Bull, Brian Stanley *pathology educator, medical consultant, business executive*
Green, Lora Murray *immunologist, researcher, educator*

Lompoc
Wagner, Geraldine Marie *nursing educator, consultant*

Long Beach
Aguilar, Félix *public health physician, educator*
Elftman, Susan Nancy *physician assistant, childbirth-lactation educator, research director*
Friis, Robert Harold *epidemiologist, health science educator*
Hall, Phyllis Charlene *therapist, counselor*
Mills, Don Harper *pathology and psychiatry educator, lawyer*
Pineda, Anselmo *neurosurgery educator*
Talmadge, Mary Christine *nursing educator*

Los Angeles
Archie, Carol Louise *obstetrician and gynecologist, educator*
Askanas-Engel, Valerie *neurologist, educator, researcher*
Baron, Melvin Farrell *pharmacy educator*
Bernstein, Sol *cardiologist, educator*
Brautbar, Nachman *physician, educator*
Chuksorji, Jean Caulfield *nursing educator*
Cowan, Marie Jeanette *nurse, pathology and cardiology educator*
Datar, Ram Hemant *pathologist, educator*
De Cherney, Alan Hersh *obstetrics and gynecology educator*
Fonkalsrud, Eric Walter *pediatric surgeon, educator*
Giannotta, Steven Louis *neurosurgery educator*
Giesser, Barbara Susan *neurologist, educator*
Goldstein, Charles Meyer *dental educator*
Gorney, Roderic *psychiatry educator*
Gray, Gregory Edward *physician, administrator, educator*
Hahn, Bevra Hannahs *medical educator*
Hallegua, David Samuel *internist, rheumatologist, educator*
Lewis, Mary Ann *nursing educator*
Liu, Ming Wei *cardiologist, educator*
Lubman, Richard Levi *physician, educator, research scientist*
Maloney, Robert Keller *ophthalmologist, medical educator*
McCaffery, Margo *pain consultant, lecturer, author*
Noble, Ernest Pascal *pharmacologist, biochemist, educator*
Parham, Linda Diane *occupational therapist, researcher, educator*
Parker, Robert George *radiation oncology educator, academic administrator*
Raghavan, Derek *oncologist, medical researcher and educator*
Scheibel, Arnold Bernard *psychiatrist, educator, research director*
Siegel, Stuart Elliott *physician, pediatrics educator, cancer researcher*
Straatsma, Bradley Ralph *ophthalmologist, educator*
Wincor, Michael Z. *psychopharmacology educator, clinician, researcher*
Woods, Sherwyn Martin *psychiatrist, educator*

Martinez
McKnight, Lenore Ravin *child psychiatrist, educator*

Menlo Park
Marton, Laurence Jay *researcher, educator, clinical pathologist*

Modesto
Suntra, Charles Ratapol *surgeon, educator*

Newport Beach
Connolly, John Earle *surgeon, educator*

Norwalk
Bao, Joseph Yue-Se *orthopedist, microsurgeon, educator*

Oak Park
Caldwell, Stratton Franklin *kinesiology educator*

Oakland
Killebrew, Ellen Jane (Mrs. Edward S. Graves) *cardiologist, educator*
King, Janet Carlson *nutrition educator, researcher*
Watanabe, Mark David *pharmacist, educator*

Orange
Chang, Jae Chan *hematologist, oncologist, educator*
Jolley, Weldon Bosen *surgery educator, research executive*
Schneider, Max Alexander *physician, educator*

Palm Springs
Boyajian, Timothy Edward *public health officer, educator, consultant*

Palmdale
Kinzell, La Moyne B. *school health services administrator, educator*

Palo Alto
Bagshaw, Malcolm A. *radiation oncologist, educator*
Benitz, William Edwin *medical educator*
Holman, Halsted Reid *medical educator, physician*
Keeffe, Emmet Britton *medical educator*
Litt, Iris Figarsky *pediatrics educator*
Salvatierra, Oscar, Jr., *transplant surgeon, urologist, educator*
Silverman, Norman Henry *cardiologist, educator*

Palos Verdes Estates
Nelson, Ronald John *retired cardiothoracic surgeon, educator*

Palos Verdes Peninsula
Thomas, Claudewell Sidney *psychiatry educator*

Pasadena
Cole, Roberta Carley *retired nursing educator*
Holmes, Louis Ira *physician assistant, educator, photojournalist*
Short, Elizabeth M. *physician, educator, federal agency administrator*

Rancho Mirage
Ausman, James I. *neurosurgeon, educator*

Redondo Beach
Cardin, Suzette *nursing educator*

Richmond
Hancock, Nannette Beatrice Finley *mental health educator, consultant*

Riverside
Chang, Sylvia Tan *health facility administrator, educator*
Radtke, Karen Dorothy *school nurse*
Shoji, Hiromu *orthopedic surgeon, educator*

Rolling Hills Estates
Bellis, Carroll Joseph *surgeon, educator*

Sacramento
Bogren, Hugo Gunnar *radiology educator*
Ellis, William Gene *neuropathologist*
Farrell, Francine Annette *psychotherapist, educator, author*
Merwin, Edwin Preston *healthcare educator, consultant*
Zil, J. S. *psychiatrist, physiologist*

San Diego
Abrams, Reid Allen *surgeon, educator*

Benirschke, Kurt *pathologist, educator*
Cosman, Bard Clifford *surgeon, educator*
Goltz, Robert William *physician, educator*
Jamieson, Stuart William *surgeon, educator*
Neuman, Tom S. *emergency medical physician, educator*
Parthemore, Jacqueline Gail *internist, educator, hospital administrator*
Ross, John, Jr., *cardiologist, educator*
Scherger, Joseph Edward *family physician, educator*
Stewart, Jean Catherine *critical care and neuroscience emergency trauma nurse, educator*
Teguh, Collin *physician, educator*
Wallace, Helen Margaret *physician, educator*
Yuan, Jason Xiao-Jian *medical researcher, educator*
Ziegler, Michael Gregory *medical educator, researcher*

San Dimas
Flores, Frank Cortez *public health researcher, educator, administrator*

San Francisco
Aird, Robert Burns *neurologist, educator*
Arsham, Gary *medical educator*
Chater, Shirley Sears *health educator*
Cummerton, Joan Marie *social work educator*
Hess, Patricia Alice *nursing educator, geriatrics nurse consultant*
Hoffman, Julien Ivor Ellis *pediatric cardiologist, educator*
Khosla, Ved Mitter *oral and maxillofacial surgeon, educator*
Kline, Howard Jay *cardiologist, educator*
Lee, Philip Randolph Randolph *medical educator*
Lull, Robert John *nuclear medicine physician, educator*
Lustig, Robert Howard *pediatrician, educator*
Miller, Walter Luther *pediatrician, educator*
Patti, Marco Giuseppe *surgeon, educator*
Phillips, Theodore Locke *radiation oncologist, educator*
Robinson, Effie *social worker, educator*
Rosenthal, Eleanor *psycho-physical therapist, educator*
Schachter, Julius *epidemiology educator*
Schmid, Rudi (Rudolf Schmid) *internist, educator, academic administrator*
Schmidt, Robert Milton *physician, scientist, educator, administrator*
Stannard, Daphne Evon *nursing educator*
Zippin, Calvin *epidemiologist, educator*

San Jose
Demers, Mary Adelaide *psychotherapist, educator*
Lippe, Philipp Maria *physician, surgeon, neurosurgeon, educator, administrator*

San Mateo
Bocobo, Christian Reyes *rehabilitation medicine educator*
Richens, Muriel Whittaker *marriage and family therapist, educator*

Santa Ana
Chenhalls, Anne Marie *nurse, educator*
Rockoff, Sheila G. *nursing and health facility administrator, nursing and health occupations educator*

Santa Barbara
Gutmann, Barbara Lang *nurse, educator, administrator, consultant*
Steckel, Richard J. *radiologist, academic administrator*

Santa Cruz
Kline, Sybil Rose *researcher*

Santa Maria
Phillips, Dorothy Lowe *nursing educator*

Santa Monica
Lymberis, Maria T. *psychiatrist, psychiatric educator*

Sausalito
Groah, Linda Kay *nursing administrator, educator*
Seymour, Richard Burt *health educator*

South Lake Tahoe
Bruce, Veronica Helene *nursing educator*

Stanford
Basch, Paul Frederick *international health educator, parasitologist*
Carstensen, Laura Lee *gerontology educator*
Farquhar, John William *physician, educator*
Greco, Ralph Steven *surgeon, researcher, medical educator*
Mansour, Tag Eldin *pharmacologist, educator*
Marmor, Michael Franklin *ophthalmologist, educator*
McDevitt, Hugh O'Neill *immunologist, educator*
Paffenbarger, Ralph Seal, Jr., *epidemiologist, educator*
Payne, Anita Hart *reproductive endocrinologist, researcher*
Tessier-Lavigne, Marc Trevor *neurobiologist, researcher*
Warnke, Roger Allen *pathology educator*

Suisun City
Atiba, Joshua Olajide O. *internist, pharmacologist, oncologist, educator, philanthropist*

Sun City
Olim, August Souza *counselor*

Sunnyvale
Whaley, Lucille Fillmore *nursing consultant, educator*

Temecula
Keenan, Retha Ellen Vornholt *retired nursing educator*

Thousand Oaks
Baynes, Roy Dennis *hematologist, educator*
Farshidi, Ardeshir B. *cardiologist, educator*
Friedman, H. Harold *cardiologist, internist*

Torrance
Brass, Eric Paul *internal medicine and pharmacology educator*
Hansen, James Edward *medical educator, researcher*
McIntyre, Hugh Baxter *neurology educator*
Swerdloff, Ronald S. *medical educator, researcher*

Vacaville
Feldman, Stephen Michael *retired periodontist, dental educator*

Ventura
Bircher, Andrea Ursula *psychiatric nurse practitioner*

Westminster
Nguyen, Lan Thi Hoang *physician, educator*

Yucaipa
Holbrook, James Robert *medical technology educator, consultant*

COLORADO

Basalt
Jaffrey, Ira *oncologist, educator*

Boulder
Braddock, David Lawrence *health science educator*
Dalton, Alice L. Gorgen *nursing educator, consultant*

Castle Rock
Thornbury, John Rousseau *radiologist, physician*

Colorado Springs
Anderson, Paul Nathaniel *oncologist, educator*

Denver
Beresford, Thomas Patrick *psychiatry educator, alcoholism researcher*
Brand, Ely *gynecologic surgeon, cancer surgeon, educator*
Bristow, Michael *cardiologist, researcher, medical educator*
Campbell, David Neil *physician, educator*
Cohn, Aaron I. *anesthesiologist, educator*
Kraizer, Sherryll A. *child safety and interpersonal violence prevention educator*
Lee, Lela A. *dermatology educator, researcher*
Lillehei, Kevin Owen *neurosurgeon, educator*
Lyons, Cherie Ann *researcher, writer*
Nett, Louise Mary *nursing educator, consultant*
Plummer, Ora Beatrice *nursing educator, trainer*
Thomas, Enolia *nutritionist, educator*

Fort Collins
Schatz, Mona Claire Struhsaker *social worker, educator, consultant, researcher*

Glenwood Springs
Candlin, Frances Ann *psychotherapist, social worker, educator*

Grand Junction
Dillin, Jake Thomas, Jr., *healthcare facility executive*

Greeley
Gritts, Gerald Lee *home health nurse, AIDS care nurse, AIDS educator*

Guffey
McCaslin, Kathleen Denise *child abuse educator*

CONNECTICUT

Branford
Feinstein, Alvan Richard *physician, educator, epidemiologist, educator*

Bridgeport
McAuliffe, Catherine A. *counselor, psychology educator, psychotherapist*

Darien
Newman, Fredric Alan *plastic surgeon, educator*

Derby
Jekel, James Franklin *physician, public health educator*

Farmington
Bonkovsky, Herbert Lloyd *gastroenterologist, educator*
Damato, Kathryn Leathem *dental hygienist, educator*
McCawley, Austin *psychiatrist, educator*
O'Rourke, James *ophthalmologist, pathologist, educator*

Glastonbury
Pearson, Karen Leiter *speech and language pathologist*

Hamden
Cole-Schiraldi, Marilyn Bush *occupational therapy educator*

Hartford
Gordan, Dennis Stuart *physiatrist, educator*
Jung, Betty Chin *epidemiologist, research analyst, educator, medical/surgical nurse*
Klimek, Joseph John *physician, educator*
Wohlert, Earl Ross *health care analyst*

Manchester
Milewski, Stanislaw Antoni *ophthalmologist, educator*

New Haven
Aghajanian, George Kevork *medical educator*
Bolognia, Jean Lynn *academic dermatologist*
Comer, James Pierpont *psychiatrist, educator*
Cooper, Jack Ross *pharmacology educator, researcher*
De Rose, Sandra Michele *psychotherapist, educator, supervisor, administrator*
Dolan, Thomas Francis, Jr., *pediatrician, educator*
Genel, Myron *pediatrician, educator*
Goodrich, Isaac *neurosurgeon, educator*
Heninger, George Robert *psychiatry educator, researcher*
Jones, Ervin *physician, educator*
Krauss, Judith Belliveau *nursing educator*
Lentz, Thomas Lawrence *biomedical educator, dean, researcher*
Musto, David Franklin *physician, educator, historian, consultant*
Nwangwu, John Tochukwu *epidemiologist, public health educator*
Patwa, Huned S. *neurology educator*
Prusoff, William Herman *biochemical pharmacologist, educator*
Ritchie, J. Murdoch *pharmacologist, educator*
Shulman, Gerald I. *physician, scientist, educator*
Spiro, Howard Marget *physician, educator*
Tamborlane, William V., Jr., *physician, biomedical researcher, pediatrics educator*
Waxman, Stephen George *neurologist, neuroscientist*

North Branford
Gordon, Martin Eli *physician, educator*

North Haven
Phillips, Elizabeth Vellom *social worker, educator*

Norwalk
Boles, Lenore Utal *nurse psychotherapist, educator*
Needham, Charles William *neurosurgeon, educator*

Simsbury
Voroscak, Robert Anthony *rehabilitation specialist, educator*

Stamford
Gefter, William Irvin *physician, educator*
Goodhue, Peter Ames *obstetrician and gynecologist, educator*

Storrs Mansfield
Organek, Nancy Strickland *nursing educator*
Packard, Sheila Anne *nursing educator, researcher*

Stratford
Russell, Cynthia Pincus *social worker, educator*

Trumbull
Vaidya, Kirit Rameshchandra *anesthesiologist, educator*

Waterbury
Dudrick, Stanley John *surgeon, scientist, educator*

Watertown
Sherwood, James Alan *physician, scientist, educator*

Westport
Dakofsky, LaDonna Jung *radiation oncologist, educator*

DELAWARE

Dover
Millon-Wisneski, Sharon Marie *critical care nurse, educator*

Newark
Dadmarz, Kewmars Ebrahim *physician, educator*
Lieberman, Joseph Aloysius, III, *physician, educator*

Wilmington
Gonzalez, Ricardo *surgeon, educator*
Inselman, Laura Sue *pediatrician, educator*

DISTRICT OF COLUMBIA

Washington
Baer, Alfred *physician, educator*
Burris, Boyd Lee *psychiatrist, psychoanalyst, physician, educator*
Corless, Dorothy Alice *nurse educator*
Curfman, David Ralph *neurosurgeon, educator, civic leader, musician*
Curry, Sadye Beatryce *gastroenterologist, educator*
Dennis, Gary C. *neurosurgeon, educator*
Epps, Roselyn Elizabeth Payne *pediatrician, educator*
Geelhoed, Glenn William *surgeon, educator, writer*
Gray, Bradford Hitch *health policy researcher*
Harland, Barbara Ferguson *nutritionist, educator*
Hussain, Syed Taseer *biomedical educator, researcher*
Korn, David *educator, pathologist*
Little, John William *plastic surgeon, educator*
Lombardo, Fredric Alan *pharmacist, educator*
Mann, Oscar *retired physician, internist, educator*
Njie, Veronica P.S. *nurse educator, clinical nurse*
Oskoui, R. *cardiologist, educator*
Paup, Donald C. *psychology educator*
Peña, Maria Teresa *surgeon, educator, otolaryngologist*
Schuelein, Marianne Ida *neurologist, educator*
Sivasubramanian, Kolinjavadi Nagarajan *neonatologist, educator*
Spagnolo, Samuel Vincent *internist, pulmonary specialist, educator*
Stephan, Dietrich A. *pediatrician, educator, geneticist*
Theiss, Patricia Kelley *public health researcher, educator*
Weingold, Allan Byrne *obstetrician, gynecologist, educator*
Willis, Arnold Jay *urologic surgeon, educator*
Zukowska, Zofia Maria *cardiovascular physiologist, educator*

FLORIDA

Amelia Island
Schiebler, Gerold Ludwig *pediatrician, educator*

Boca Raton
Monaghan, W(illiam) Patrick *immunohematologist, retired naval officer, health educator, consultant*

Bokeelia
Grottanelli, Pamala N. *nursing administrator, educator*

Bonita Springs
Dougherty, James *orthopedic surgeon, educator, author*

Boynton Beach
Leapman, Phyllis Lenore *retired nursing educator*

Brandon
Applegate, Minerva Irons *nursing educator, nurse*

Clearwater
Fromhagen, Carl, Jr., *obstetrician, gynecologist*

Coral Springs
Carrington, J.P. (Jossif Peter Bartolotti) *nutritionist, psychoanalyst, research scientist, educator*

Defuniak Springs
Bonner, Kathryn Esther *nursing administrator, nursing educator*

Deltona
Bondinell, Stephanie *counselor, academic administrator*

Dunedin
Barlis, Bettye Montgomery *medical center administrator, elementary educator*

Fort Lauderdale
Flemenbaum, Abraham *psychiatrist, educator*
Price, Judith *nursing educator*
Siegel, Wilma Bulkin *oncologist, educator, artist*

Fort Myers
Harr, Alma Elizabeth Tagliabue *nursing educator*

Fort Pierce
Clunn, Patricia Ann *nursing educator, writer*

Gainesville
Aranda, Juan M., Jr., *cardiologist, medical educator*
Mahla, Michael E. *anesthesiologist, educator*
Malasanos, Lois Julanne Fosse *nursing educator*
McMahon, Pamela Sue *dietitian, educator*
Rhoton, Albert Loren, Jr., *neurological surgery educator*
Rubin, Melvin Lynne *ophthalmologist, educator*

Jacksonville
Bosworth, William Posey *physician, physical education educator*
Cherry, Barbara Waterman *speech and language pathologist, physical therapist*
Huddleston, John Franklin *obstetrics and gynecology educator*
Peters, Thomas Guy *surgeon, educator*
Raynor, Eileen Margolies *otolaryngologist, educator*

Lakeland
Spraley, Judith Ann *nursing educator, administrator*

Marco Island
Sundberg, Ruth Dorothy *physician, educator*

Margate
Ory, Steven Jay *physician, educator*

Melbourne
Magee, Thomas Henry *medical doctor, medical educator*

Miami
Alvarez, Ofelia Amparo *medical educator*
Andreas, Cynthia Barbara *art therapist*
Blechman, Wilbur Jordan *medical educator*
Conde, Cesar Augusto *cardiologist, educator*
Duchowny, Michael S. *physician, educator*

Freshwater, Michael Felix *plastic surgeon, educator*
Ganz, William Israel *radiology educator, medical director, researcher*
Himburg, Susan Phillips *dietitian, educator*
Martínez, Luís Osvaldo *radiologist, educator*
Parchment, Yvonne *nursing educator*
Poblete, Rita Maria Bautista *physician, educator*
Regan, Marie Christine *nursing educator*
Ricordi, Camillo *surgeon, transplant and diabetes researcher*
Saland, Deborah *psychotherapist, educator*
Salerno, Tomas Antonio *cardiothoracic surgeon, educator*
Temple, Jack Donald, Jr., *physician, medical educator*
Wolfson, Aaron Howard *radiation oncologist, educator*

Middleburg
Brown, Linda Lockett *nutrition management executive, nutrition consultant*

Mount Dora
Crone, Eugene N. *addictions counselor, retired educator*
Shyers, Larry Edward *mental health counselor, educator*

Naples
Cinotti, Alfonse Anthony *ophthalmologist, educator*

Orlando
Sharp, Christina Krieger *nursing educator, researcher*

Palm Beach
Seggev, Meir *radiologist, educator*

Pineland
Donlon, Josephine A. *diagnostic and evaluation counseling therapist, educator*

Port Saint Lucie
Hogan, Roxanne Arnold *nursing consultant, risk management consultant, educator*

Saint Petersburg
Linhart, Joseph Wayland *retired cardiologist, educational administrator*

Sanford
Balk, Mary Dale *drug prevention specialist, elementary school educator*

Sarasota
Iverson, Robert Louis, Jr., *internist, physician*
Sturtevant, Ruthann Patterson *anatomy educator*

South Miami
Bauman, Sandra Spiegel *nurse practitioner, mental health counselor*

Tallahassee
Coble, Daniel Bruce *nursing administrator*

Tampa
Courey, Michael Herbert *health physicist*
Frias, Jaime Luis *pediatrician, educator*
Hubbell, David Smith *surgeon, educator*
Jacobson, Howard Newman *obstetrics and gynecology educator, researcher*
Liller, Karen DeSafey *public health educator*
Lopez, Guillermo *obstetrician-gynecologist, educator*
Muroff, Lawrence Ross *nuclear medicine physician, educator*
Murtagh, Frederick Reed *neuroradiologist, educator*
Perez-Valdes, Yvonne Ann *nurse, educator*
Pollara, Bernard *immunologist, educator, pediatrician*
Rhodin, Johannes Arne Gösta *medical educator*
Slonim, Charles Bard *ophthalmic plastic surgeon, educator*
Sullebarger, John Thompson *internist, cardiologist, educator*

Tavares
Osborne, Glenna Jean *social and health services administrator*

Vero Beach
Cobb, Ronald David *pharmacist, educator*

West Palm Beach
Atkinson, Regina Elizabeth *medical social worker*

Winter Park
Douglas, Kathleen Mary Harrigan *retired psychotherapist, educator*

GEORGIA

Albany
Gates, Roberta Pecoraro *nursing educator*

Alpharetta
Harris, James Herman *pathologist, neuropathologist, consultant, educator*

Atlanta
Barnett, Crawford Fannin, Jr., *internist, educator, cardiologist, travel medicine specialist*
Correa-Villaseñor, Adolfo *epidemiologist, physician*
Dutt, Kamla *medical educator*
Harbin, Thomas Shelor, Jr., *ophthalmologist, educator*
Horowitz, Ira R. *gynecologic oncologist, educator*
Hug, Carl Casimir, Jr., *anesthesiology and pharmacology, educator*
Khuri, Fadlo Raja *oncologist, educator*
Letton, Alva Hamblin *surgeon, educator*
Sherbinski, Linda Anne *nurse anesthetist, nursing educator*
Tissue, Mike *medical educator, respiratory therapist*
Weed, Roger Oren *rehabilitation services professional, educator*
Willis, Isaac *dermatologist, educator*
Z, Chris *internist, medical educator*
Zumpe, Doris *ethologist, researcher, educator*

Augusta
Chandler, Arthur Bleakley *pathologist, educator*
Feldman, Elaine Bossak *medical nutritionist, educator*
Gambrell, Richard Donald, Jr., *endocrinologist, educator*
Lee, Gregory Price *neuropsychology educator*
Puchtler, Holde *histochemist, pathologist, educator*
Whittemore, Ronald Paul *hospital administrator, retired army officer, nursing educator*

Brunswick
Perniciaro, Charles Vincent *dermatologist, educator, entrepreneur*

Clarkston
Thatcher, Sharon Louise *medical educator*

Doraville
Yancey, Eleanor Garrett *retired crisis intervention clinician*

Fort Valley
Swartwout, Joseph Rodolph *obstetrics and gynecology educator, administrator*

Jonesboro
Dame, Laureen Eva *nursing administrator, educator*

Kennesaw
Barnett, Benjamin Lewis, Jr., *retired physician, educator*

Lagrange
Rhodes, Eddie, Jr., *medical technologist, phlebotomy technician, educator*

Lyons
Frey, Bob Henry *psychotherapist, sociologist, educator, poet, canon lawyer*

Macon
Keating, Thomas Patrick *health care administrator, educator*
Mathis, David Edwin *internist, educator*
Robinson, Joe Sam *neurosurgeon, educator*

Marietta
Holtz, Noel *neurologist, educator*

Martinez
Colborn, Gene Louis *anatomy educator, researcher*
Nesbitt, Robert Edward Lee, Jr., *physician, educator, scientific researcher, writer, poet*

Quitman
McElroy, Annie Laurie *nursing educator, administrator*

Rome
Papp, Leann Ilse Kline *respiratory therapy educator*

Savannah
Barnette, Candice Lewis *speech/language pathologist*
Hoskins, William John *obstetrician, gynecologist, educator*
Zoller, Michael *otolaryngologist, head and neck surgeon, educator*

Statesboro
Bartels, Jean Ellen *nursing educator*

Valdosta
Backes, Lora Stephens *speech/language pathologist*

Warner Robins
Beck, Rhonda Joann *paramedic, educator, writer*

HAWAII

Honolulu
Ardolf, Deborah Ann *speech language pathologist*
Fischer, Joel *social work educator*
Kane, Thomas Jay, III, *orthopaedic surgeon, educator*
Katz, Alan Roy *public health educator*
Lum, Jean Loui Jin *nursing educator*
Roberson, Kelley Cleve *health care administrator*
Sugiki, Shigemi *ophthalmologist, educator*
Terminella, Luigi *critical care physician, educator*

Kailua
Westerdahl, John Brian *nutritionist, health educator*

Kamuela
Morgan, Andrew Lane *urologist, educator*

Kaneohe
Lange-Otsuka, Patricia Ann *nursing educator*

Lihue
Culliney, John James *radiologist, educator*

Waianae
Miguel, Linda J. *critical care nurse, nursing educator*

IDAHO

Pocatello
Heberlein, Alice LaTourrette *healthcare educator, physical education educator, coach*

ILLINOIS

Aurora
Buffum, William Erwin *social worker, educator*

Berwyn
Galinsky, Dennis Lee *radiation oncologist, educator*
Hudik, Martin Francis *hospital administrator, educator, consultant, writer*

Bloomington
Weber, Darlene Marie *health educator*

Carbondale
Sarvela, Paul D. *health facility administrator, educator*

Charleston
Drake, Anne Kelly *social worker, educator*

Chicago
Abramowicz, Jacques Sylvain *obstetrician, perinatologist, educator*
Albazzaz, Faiq Jaber *physician, researcher, educator*
Boggs, Joseph Dodridge *pediatric pathologist, educator*
Boshes, Louis D. *physician, scientist, educator, historian, author*
Chan, Lawrence Siu-Yung *dermatologist, educator*
Cohen, Louis *medical educator, cardiologist, inventor*
Datta, Syamal Kumar *medical scientist, educator, researcher*
Dayal, Vijay Shanker *medical educator, physician*
Fitch, Frank Wesley *pathologist educator, immunologist, educator, administrator*
Frohman, Lawrence Asher *endocrinology educator, scientist*
Gewertz, Bruce Labe *surgeon, educator*
Ginsberg, Norman Arthur *physician, educator*
Hahn, Yoon Sun *pediatric neurosurgeon, educator*
Hanlon, C. Rollins *physician, educator*
Hellman, Samuel *radiologist, physician, educator*
Jones, Richard Jeffery *internist, educator*
Kraft, Sumner Charles *physician, educator*
Leventhal, Bennett Lee *psychiatry and pediatrics educator, administrator*
Logemann, Jerilyn Ann *speech pathologist, educator*
Malkinson, Frederick David *dermatologist, educator*
Moon, Catherine Hyland *art therapist, art therapy educator*
Nemickas, Rimgaudas *cardiologist, educator*
Nyhus, Lloyd Milton *surgeon, educator*
Osiyoye, Adekunle *obstetrician, attorney medical and legal consultant, gynecologist, educator*
Palmer, Martha H. *counseling educator, executive*
Peruzzi, William Theodore *anesthesiologist, intensivist, educator*
Plate, Janet Margaret Dieterle *immunology educator, scientist*
Reder, Anthony Thomas *neurologist, educator*
Rhone, Douglas Pierce *pathologist, educator*
Sabbagha, Rudy E. *obstetrician, gynecologist, educator*
Schade, Stanley Greinert, Jr., *hematologist, educator*
Schilsky, Richard Lewis *oncologist, researcher*
Sewitch, Deborah E. *health science association administrator, educator, sleep researcher*
Short, Marion Priscilla *neurogenetics educator*
Siegler, Mark *internist, educator*
Smith, Earl Charles *nephrologist, educator*
Swerdlow, Martin Abraham *physician, pathologist, educator*
Thomas, Leona Marlene *health information educator*
Tomar, Russell Herman *pathologist, educator, researcher*
Vigen, Kathryn L. Voss *nursing administrator, educator*
Wetzel, Franklin Todd *spinal surgeon, educator, researcher*
Wilbur, Andrew Clayton *radiologist, educator*
Wissler, Robert William *physician, cardiovascular pathologist, educator*
Yale, Seymour Hershel *dental radiologist, educator, university dean, gerontologist*

Danville
Prabhudesai, Mukund M. *pathology educator, laboratory director, researcher, administrator*

Darien
Gardner, Howard Garry *pediatrician, educator*

Dekalb
Bukonda, Ngoyi K. Zacharie *health care management educator*
Flanagan, Joan Marie *nursing educator, dean*

Des Plaines
D'Anca, John Arthur *psychotherapist, educator*

East Saint Louis
Martin, Betty J. *speech, language pathologist*

Elmwood Park
Oryshkevich, Roman Sviatoslav *retired physician, physiatrist, dentist, educator*

Glen Ellyn
Tomkins, Joanne Kark *health physicist, educator*

Glencoe
Grabow, Beverly *learning disability therapist*

Glenview
Coulson, Elizabeth Anne *physical therapy educator, state representative*

Grayslake
Devney, Anne Marie *nursing educator*

Gurnee
Enz, Diane S. *rehabilitation services professional, therapist, educator*

Harrisburg
Endsley, Jane Ruth *nursing educator*

Hines
Folk, Frank Anton *surgeon, educator*

Hinsdale
Beatty, Robert Alfred (R. Alfred) *surgeon, educator*
Brueschke, Erich Edward *physician, researcher, educator*
Finley, Robert Coe, III, *interventional cardiologist, consultant, educator*

Homewood
Schumacher, Gebhard Friederich Bernhard *obstetrician-gynecologist*

Joliet
Lynch, Priscilla A. *nursing educator, therapist*

Kampsville
Schumann, Alice Melcher *medical technologist, educator, sheep farmer*

Lake Forest
Pawl, Ronald Phillip *neurosurgery educator*
Somberg, John Charin *medicine and pharmacology educator*

Lisle
Renegar, Delilah A. *chiropractor, educator*

Macomb
Morton, Patsy Lou *social worker*

Matteson
Rodos, Joseph Jerry *osteopathic physician, educator*

Maywood
Joehl, Raymond Joseph *surgeon, educator*

Naperville
Schwab, Paul Josiah *psychiatrist, educator*
Tang, Debby Tseng *counselor*

North Chicago
Barsano, Charles Paul *medical educator, dean*
Gall, Eric Papineau *physician, educator*
Kim, Yoon Berm *immunologist, educator*
Nair, Velayudhan *pharmacologist, medical educator*
Rudy, David Robert *physician, educator*
Sierles, Frederick Stephen *psychiatrist, educator*

Oak Brook
Schultz, Karen Rose *clinical social worker, author, publisher, speaker*

Oak Park
Matsuda, Takayoshi *surgeon, educator, biomedical researcher*
Rossof, Arthur Harold *internal medicine educator*

Peoria
Brewer, Cheryl Ann *obstetrician and gynecologist, educator*

Plainfield
Cook, Bruce Lawrence *research analyst*

River Grove
Hillert, Gloria Bonnin *anatomist, educator*
Hill-Hulslander, Jacquelyne L. *nursing educator and consultant*

Rockford
Rifkin, Gary D. *physician, educator*

Sheldon
Zumwalt, Nancy Eileen Williams *health occupations educator*

Springfield
Campbell, Kathleen Charlotte Murphey *audiology educator, administrator, researcher*

Streamwood
Samuelson, Rita Michelle *speech language pathologist*

Tinley Park
Daniels, Kurt R. *speech and language pathologist*

University Park
Leftwich, Robert Eugene *oncological and adult nursing educator*
Samson, Linda Forrest *nursing educator and administrator*

Urbana
Kocheril, Abraham George *physician, educator*

Tripp, April *special education services professional*

Wheaton
Blair, Rosemary Kasul *social work educator*

INDIANA

Anderson
Williams, Paul Allan, Jr., *psychiatric social worker, educator*

Beverly Shores
Barowsky, Harris White *physician, educator*

Bloomington
Torabi, Mohammad R. *healthcare educator*

Coalmont
Salesman, Janet Fay *speech language pathologist*

Corydon
Kelty, Paul David *physician, educator*

Fort Wayne
Flynn, Pauline T. *speech pathologist, educator*
Harwood, Virginia Ann *retired nursing educator*
Richardson, Joseph Hill *physician, medical educator*

Goshen
Deuschle, Constance Joan *counselor, educational consultant*

Hammond
Smokvina, Gloria Jacqueline *nursing educator*

Indianapolis
Atkins, Clayton H. *family physician, epidemiologist, educator*
Bowman, Elizabeth Sue *psychiatrist, educator, editor*
Brady, Mary Sue *nutrition and dietetics educator*
Broxmeyer, Hal Edward *medical educator*
Christen, Arden Gale *dental educator, researcher, consultant*
Chuang, Tsu-Yi *dermatologist, epidemiologist, educator*
Dere, Willard Honglen *internist, educator*
Hill, Beverly Ellen *health sciences educator*
Kesler, Kenneth Allen *thoracic surgeon, educator*
Molitoris, Bruce Albert *nephrologist, educator*
Moore, Regina Denise *healthcare facility educator, therapist*
Orazi, Attilio *anatomic pathologist, researcher, educator*
Tisdale, James Edward *pharmacy educator, pharmacotherapy researcher*
Van Scoder, Linda I. *medical educator, department chairman*
Walther, Joseph Edward *health facility administrator, retired physician*
Weiss, Faedra Lazar *researcher*

Linton
Schnabel, Diane Susan *speech pathologist, educator*

Marion
Lau, Patrick Hing-Leung *radiologist, educator*

Michigan City
Moldenhauer, Nancy A. *social worker, educator*

Munster
Singh, Manmohan *orthopedic surgeon, educator*

Nappanee
Borger, Michael Hinton Ivers *osteopathic physician, educator*

South Bend
Ivory, Goldie Lee *retired social worker, educator*

Terre Haute
Sawyer, Thomas Harrison *health, physical education and recreation director*

West Lafayette
Rutledge, Charles Ozwin *pharmacologist, educator*
Tacker, Willis Arnold, Jr., *medical educator, researcher*

Westville
Topp, Janice *mental health and clinical nurse specialist, educator*

IOWA

Cedar Falls
Downs, William Robert *social worker, educator*

Cedar Rapids
Brooks, Debra L. *healthcare executive, neuromuscular therapist*
Stephens, Ralph Renne *massage therapy educator*

Des Moines
Moos, Pamela Sue *family development specialist*
Wattleworth, Roberta Ann *physician, medical educator*

Iowa City
Abboud, Francois Mitry *physician, educator*
Bar, Robert S. *endocrinologist, educator*
Baumert, Paul Willard, Jr., *physician, educator*
Berg, Mary Jaylene *pharmacy educator, researcher*
Butler, John Edward *biomedical sciences educator, consultant*
Callaghan, John Joseph *orthopaedist, surgeon, educator*
Clifton, James Albert *physician, educator*
Damasio, Antonio R. *physician, neurologist*
Fellows, Robert Ellis *medical educator, medical scientist*
Hammond, Harold Logan *oral and maxillofacial pathologist, educator*
Kirchhoff, Louis Vaughn *biomedical researcher, educator, internist*
Lainson, Phillip Argles *dental educator*
Rankin, Margaret Ann *retired nursing educator*
Richerson, Hal Bates *physician, internist, allergist, immunologist, educator*
Wurster, Dale Eric *pharmacy educator*
Wurster, Dale Erwin *pharmacy educator, university dean emeritus*

Waterloo
Williams-Perez, Kendra Beth *nursing educator*

West Des Moines
Herwig, Steven Roger *osteopathic physician, otolaryngologist, educator*

KANSAS

Goodland
Paxton, Lisa Ann *speech language pathologist*

Kansas City
Godwin, Harold Norman *pharmacist, educator*
Lee, Kyo Rak *radiology educator*
Mathews, Paul Joseph *health educator*
Mathewson, Hugh Spalding *anesthesiologist, educator*
Ternus, Jean Ann *nursing educator*

Newton
Dyck, George *psychiatry educator*

Oakley
Hubert, Shelby Ann *speech/language pathologist*

Olathe
Jones, Robert Lyle *emergency medical services leader, financial planner, educator*
Moore, William Paul *educational psychologist, researcher*

Overland Park
Dockhorn, Robert John *physician, educator*

Topeka
Varner, Charleen LaVerne McClanahan (Mrs. Robert B. Varner) *nutritionist, educator, administrator, dietitian*

Wichita
Huntley, Diane E. *dental hygiene educator*
Park, Chan Hyung *cell biologist, physician*
Rider, Sherri Eileen *critical care nurse, educator*

KENTUCKY

Brandenburg
Bowen, Patricia Lederer *dental educator*

Danville
Nickens, Harry Carl *medical association administrator*

Elizabethtown
Rahman, Rafiq Ur *oncologist, educator*

Lexington
Gilliam, M(elvin) Randolph *retired urologist, educator*
Glenn, James Francis *urologist, educator*
Hagen, Michael Dale *family physician educator*
Kraman, Steve Seth *physician, educator*
Scott, Samuel Russell *internal medicine educator*
Whayne, Thomas French, Jr., *cardiologist, educator*

Louisville
Bloemer, Gary Fred *orthopedic surgeon, educator*
Callen, Jeffrey Phillip *dermatologist, educator*
Cook, Christine L. *endocrinologist, gynecologist, educator*
Elin, Ronald John *pathologist, educator*
Hines-Martin, Vicki Patricia *nursing educator, researcher*
Rao, Ch. V. *endocrinologist, educator*
Syed, Ibrahim Bijli *medical educator and physicist, author, philosopher, theologist, public speaker, writer*
Wright, John C., II, *physician, educator*

Madisonville
Ellis, Wayne Enoch *nursing educator, retired air force officer*

Richmond
Brown, Julie Baldwin *nursing educator*

Russellville
Harper, Shirley Fay *nutritionist, educator, consultant, lecturer*

LOUISIANA

Baton Rouge
Cormier-Thomas, Mary Irma *speech and language pathologist*
Kidd, James Marion, III, *allergist, immunologist, naturalist, educator*

Benton
Dunnihoo, Dale Russell *physician, medical educator*

Gretna
Cochiara, Suzette Belsom *speech pathologist, administrator*

Hammond
Hejtmancik, Milton Rudolph *medical educator*

Lafayette
Boudreaux, Gloria Marie *nursing educator*
Cade, Toni Marie *medical educator*

Leesville
Gutman, Lucy Toni *school social worker, educator, counselor*

Mandeville
Pittman, Jacquelyn *retired mental health nurse, nursing educator*

Metairie
Lake, Wesley Wayne, Jr., *internist, allergist, educator*
Massare, John Steve *medical association administrator, educator*
Spruiell, Vann *psychoanalyst, educator, editor, researcher*

Monroe
Ifediora, Okechukwu Chigozie *nephrologist, educator*

New Orleans
Abdelghani, Assaf A. *medical educator*
Corrigan, James John, Jr., *pediatrician, dean*
Davis, Verda Merlyn *nursing educator, educator*
Dildy, Gary Andrew, III, *maternal fetal medicine physician, educator*
Edmonds, Velma McInnis *nursing educator*
Gatipon, Betty Becker *medical educator, consultant*
Gould, Harry J., III, *neurology educator*
Hyman, Albert Lewis *cardiologist, educator*
Lewy, John Edwin *pediatric nephrologist*
Martin, Louis Frank *surgery and healthcare outcomes analyst*
Newman, Patricia Anne *nurse anesthesia educator*
Nichols, Ronald Lee *surgeon, educator*
Olubadewo, Joseph Olanrewaju *pharmacologist, educator*
Pankey, George Atkinson *internist, educator, researcher*
Remley, Theodore Phant, Jr., *counseling educator, lawyer*
Schabelman, Sergio Eduardo *cardiologist, educator*

Pineville
McAllister, Ann Marie *social worker, educator*

Shreveport
Albores-Saavedra, Jorge *pathologist, educator*
Conrad, Steven Allen *critical care and emergency physician, biomedical engineer, educator*
Fort, Arthur Tomlinson, III, *physician, educator*
George, Ronald Baylis *physician, educator*
Griffith, Robert Charles *allergist, educator, planter*
Misra, Raghunath Prasad *physician, educator*
Mukherjee, Debi Prasad *medical educator*
Preston, Loyce Elaine *retired social work educator*
Sayles, Sandra *nursing educator*

West Monroe
Ott, Paula Nisbet *nursing and emergency medical technician educator*

MAINE

Canton
Parsons, Lorraine Leighton *nurse, child care professional*

Orono
Marston-Scott, Mary Vesta *nurse, educator*

Starks
Medeiros, M. Joyce *community health educator*

MARYLAND

Arnold
Gagné, Doreen Frances *nursing educator*

Baltimore
Bergey, Gregory Kent *neurology educator, neuroscientist*
Bottomley, Paul Arthur *radiology educator*
Boyer-Shick, Kathy Marie *special education and mental health consultant*
Brieger, Gert Henry *medical historian, educator*
Carrier, France *medical educator*
Dang, Chi Van *hematology and oncology educator*
Fedder, Donald Owen *pharmacist, educator*
Ferencz, Charlotte *pediatrician, epidemiology and preventive medicine educator*
Gimenez, Luis Fernando *physician, educator*
Hungerford, David Samuel *orthopedic surgeon, educator*
Imboden, John Baskerville *psychiatry educator*
Johns, Richard James *physician, educator*
Korniewicz, Denise M. *nursing educator*
Lee, Carlton K. K. *clinical pharmacist, consultant, educator*
Maultsby, Marilyn D. *health science association administrator*
McKhann, Guy Mead *physician, educator*
Myslinski, Norbert Raymond *medical educator*
Silverstein, Arthur Matthew *ophthalmic immunologist, educator, historian*
Udvarhelyi, George Bela *neurosurgery educator emeritus, cultural affairs administrator*
Walker, Wilbur Gordon *physician, educator*
Warnick, Jordan Edward *pharmacologist, educator*
Woodward, Theodore Englar *medical educator, internist*
Zizic, Thomas Michael *physician, educator*

Bethesda
Coleman, C. Norman *radiation and medical oncologist, researcher, educator*
Feller, William Frank *surgery educator*
Govern, Frank Stanley *health facility administrator, consultant, healthcare educator, writer*
Hoyer, Mary Louise *social worker, educator*
Hutton, John Evans, Jr., *surgery educator, retired military officer*
Jones, Dionne Juanita *health science association administrator, educator*
Miller, Nancy Ellen *health facility administrator, educator*
Ommaya, Ayub Khan *neurosurgeon, educator*
Pacher, Pál *pharmacologist, educator, researcher*
Silverman, Charlotte *epidemiologist, educator*

Brandywine
Galvin, Noreen Ann *nurse, educator*

Capitol Heights
Cox, Pierre Napoleon *health education consultant*

Chevy Chase
Hersh, Stephen Peter *psychiatrist, psycho-oncologist, educator*

Cockeysville Hunt Valley
Dans, Peter Emanuel *medical educator*

Columbia
Chaiklin, Harris *retired social work educator*

Fort Washington
Isom, Virginia Annette Veazey *retired nursing educator*

Gaithersburg
Stanford, Jennifer Laura *nurse educator*

Hagerstown
Harrison, Lois Smith *hospital executive, educator*

Kensington
Mirkin, Gabe Baron *allergist, pediatrician, medical writer, educator, radio personality, talk show host*

Lutherville Timonium
Dembo, Donald Howard *cardiologist, medical administrator, educator*

Olney
Michael, Jerrold Mark *public health specialist, former university dean, educator*

Potomac
Grimley, Judith Lee *speech and language pathologist*

Rockville
Gulya, Aina Julianna *neurotologist, surgeon, educator*
Shuren, Jeffrey Eliot *behavioral neurologist, lawyer*
Smith, Shelagh Alison *public health educator*

Salisbury
Rankin, Elizabeth Anne DeSalvo *nurse, psychotherapist, educator, consultant*

Severna Park
Simonds, Valerie Deverse *prehospital educator*

Silver Spring
Eliot, John *psychologist, educator*
Kaiser, Hans Elmar *pathology educator, researcher*
Nevans, Laurel S. *rehabilitation counselor*
Yanowitz, Edward Stanley *allergist, educator*

Takoma Park
Stephenson, Patricia Ann *public health researcher, educator*

Timonium
Forrester, Alfred Whitfield *psychiatrist, educator*

Towson
Thompson, John Tilynn *ophthalmologist, educator*

MASSACHUSETTS

Acton
Buck-Moore, Joanne Rose *nursing administrator, educator*

Auburndale
Kibrick, Anne *retired nursing educator and university dean*

Bedford
Letts, Lindsay Gordon *pharmacologist, educator*

Boston
Adelstein, S(tanley) James *physician, educator*
Aisenberg, Alan C. *physician, educator, researcher*
Alpert, Joel Jacobs *medical educator, pediatrician*
Arky, Ronald Alfred *medical educator*
Austen, K(arl) Frank *internist, educator*

Bacigalupe, Gonzalo Manuel *family therapist, educator*
Bebo, Joseph Anthony *counselor, educator*
Calkins, David Ross *physician, medical educator*
Caplan, Louis Robert *neurology educator*
Carey, Martin Conrad *gastroenterologist, molecular biophysicist, educator, medical geneticist*
Coffman, Jay Denton *physician, educator*
Cohen, Brian Jeffrey *internist, nephrologist, educator*
DeJong, H. William *health educator*
Epler, Gary Robert *physician, author, educator*
Erban, John Kalil *medicine educator, cancer specialist, researcher*
Estes, Nathan Anthony Mark, III, *cardiologist, medical educator*
Federman, Daniel David *medical educator, educational administrator, endocrinologist*
Friedman, Lawrence Samuel *gastroenterologist, educator*
Goldstein, Jill M. *psychiatric epidemiologist, clinical neuroscientist, psychiatry educator*
Goumnerova, Liliana Christova *physician, neurosurgeon, educator*
Grove, Geoffrey Eric *emergency medical technician, educator*
Hedley-Whyte, John *anesthesiologist, educator*
Huvos, Andrew *internist, cardiologist, educator*
Klein, Jerome Osias *pediatrician, educator*
Lavine, Leroy Stanley *orthopedist, surgeon, consultant*
Levinsky, Norman George *physician, educator*
McNeil, Barbara Joyce *radiologist, educator*
Merk, Frederick Bannister *biomedical educator, medical researcher*
Moneta, Giovanni Battista *research educator*
Morgan, James Philip *pharmacologist, cardiologist, educator*
Pallotta, Johanna Antonia (Johanna Stephen) *physician, educator, researcher*
Quickel, Kenneth Elwood, Jr., *physician, medical center executive*
Ransil, Bernard J(erome) *research physician, methodologist, consultant, educator*
Rohrer, Richard Jeffrey *surgeon, educator*
Ryan, Kenneth John *physician, educator*
Sachs, David Howard *surgery and immunology educator, researcher*
Sadeghi-Nejad, Abdollah *pediatrician, educator*
Schildkraut, Joseph Jacob *psychiatrist, educator*
Shields, Lawrence Thornton *orthopaedic surgeon, educator*
Spellman, Mitchell Wright *surgeon, academic administrator*
Taveras, Juan Manuel *physician, educator*
Theoharides, Theoharis Constantin *pharmacologist, physician, educator*
Vandam, Leroy David *anesthesiologist, educator*

Brighton
Smith, Edward Herbert *radiologist, educator*

Brookline
Koretsky, Sidney *internist, educator, paper historian*

Cambridge
Brusch, John Lynch *physician, educator, hospital administrator*
Clifton, Anne Rutenber *psychotherapist, educator*
Coles, Robert *child psychiatrist, educator, author*
Friedman, Jeffrey Robert *psychiatrist, educator*
London, Irving Myer *physician, educator*
Wurtman, Richard Jay *physician, educator, inventor*

Charlestown
Murphy-Lind, Karen Marie *health educator, dermatology nurse*

Chestnut Hill
Dahlben, Salin Abraham *neuropsychiatrist*
Thier, Samuel Osiah *physician, educator*

Dartmouth
Leclair, Susan Jean *hematologist, clinical laboratory scientist, educator*

Fitchburg
Scannell, Ann Elizabeth *nurse, educator*

Framingham
Austin, Sandra Ikenberry *nurse educator, consultant*

Jamaica Plain
Pierce, Chester Middlebrook *retired psychiatrist, educator*

Lenox
Pirani, Conrad Levi *pathologist, educator*

Lexington
Paul, Norman Leo *psychiatrist, educator*

Lowell
Cocanour, Barbara Ann *anatomy educator*
Richards, Constance Ellen *nursing school administrator, consultant*

Marion
McPartland, Patricia Ann *health educator and administrator*

Newton
Benedict, Mary-Anne *nursing educator, consultant*
Solomon, Mildred Zeldes *educational psychologist, health services researcher, medical ethics educator*

Newton Center
Veeder, Nancy Walker *social work educator*

Newton Centre
Kaneko, Sylvia Yelton *clinical social worker, educator*

Quincy
Luo, Hong Yuan *biomedical scientist, educator*

Springfield
Friedmann, Paul *surgeon, educator*
McGee, William Tobin *intensive care physician*
Saia, Diane Plevock DiPiero *nutritionist, educator, legal administrator*
Sloan, David James *sonographer*

Taunton
Anderson, Peter D. *pharmacist, forensic scientist*

Waltham
Brink, Stuart Jay *pediatric endocrinologist, educator*

Wellesley
Pierce, Donald Shelton *retired orthopedic surgeon, educator*
Sexton, John Joseph *oral and maxillofacial surgeon, educator*

West Hatfield
Bandman, Elsie Lucier *mental health nurse, ethicist*

West Roxbury
Cohen, Carolyn Alta *health educator*

West Springfield
Moore, Janet Ruth *nurse, educator*

Weston
Wells, Lionelle Dudley *psychiatrist, educator*

Williamstown
Conklin, Susan Joan *psychotherapist, educator, corporate staff developer, TV talk show host*

Worcester
Bernhard, Jeffrey David *dermatologist, editor, educator*
Cashman, Suzanne Boyer *health services administrator, educator*
Lanza, Robert Paul *medical scientist*
Tonkonogy, Joseph Moses *physician, neuropsychiatrist, researcher*

MICHIGAN

Alma
Caputo, Janette Susan *clinical neuropsychologist, educator*

Ann Arbor
Ash, Major McKinley, Jr., *dentist, educator*
Bloom, David Alan *pediatric urology educator*
Brooks, Sharon Lynn *dentist, educator*
Burke, Robert Harry *surgeon, educator*
Cerny, Joseph Charles *urologist, educator*
Clark, Noreen Morrison *behavioral science educator, researcher*
Craig, Robert George *dental science educator*
Davis, Wayne Kay *medical educator*
Doyle, Constance Talcott Johnston *physician, educator, medical association administrator*
Ferrara, James Lawrence Michael *medical educator, physician, scientist*
Gross, Milton David *internist, educator, nuclear medicine physician*
Hoff, Julian Theodore *physician, educator*
Humes, H(arvey) David *nephrologist, educator*
James, Sherman Athonia *social epidemiologist, educator*
Ketefian, Shaké *nursing educator*
Konnak, John William *surgery educator*
Kuhl, David Edmund *physician, nuclear medicine educator*
Lichter, Paul Richard *ophthalmology educator*
Miller, Josef M. *otolaryngologist, educator*
Pitt, Bertram *cardiologist, educator, consultant*
Simms, Lillian Miller *nursing educator*
Simpson, Robert Urquhart *medical educator, researcher*
Smith, Donald Cameron *physician, educator*
Tandon, Rajiv *psychiatrist, educator*
Wiggins, Roger C. *internist, educator, researcher*

Benton Harbor
Alsbro, Donald Edgar *health educator*

Berrien Springs
Merling, Stephanie Caroline *speech and language pathologist*

Big Rapids
Cron, Michael Thomas *pediatric optometry educator*

Bloomfield Hills
Klosinski, Deanna Dupree *medical educator, consultant*
Rosenzweig, Norman *psychiatry educator administrator*

Chelsea
Apgar, Barbara Sue *physician, educator*

Clinton Township
Ho, Robert En Ming *neurosurgeon, educator*

Dearborn
Sears, Richard Bruce *speech and language pathologist*
Suchy, Susanne N. *nursing educator*

Detroit
Balon, Richard *psychiatrist, educator*
Ginsburg, Kenneth Alan *obstetrician-gynecologist, educator*
Jacox, Ada Kathryn *nurse, educator*
Kithier, Karel *pathologist, educator*
Lupulescu, Aurel Peter *medical educator, researcher, physician*
Masse', Donald Duane *obstetrician, gynecologist, educator*
Moghissi, Kamran S. *obstetrician, retired gynecologist*
Phillips, Eduardo *surgeon, educator*
Redman, Barbara Klug *nursing educator*
Sima, Anders Adolph Fredrik *neuropathologist, neurosciences researcher, educator*
Sokol, Robert James *obstetrician, gynecologist, educator*
Tse, Harley Y. *immunologist, educator*

East Lansing
Beckmeyer, Henry Ernest *anesthesiologist, medical educator, pain management specialist*
Schemmel, Rachel Anne *food science and human nutrition educator, researcher*
Waite, Donald Eugene *medical educator, consultant*

Farmington
Gordon, Craig Jeffrey *oncologist, educator*

Flint
Cawood, Thomas Fred *retired music therapist*

Grand Blanc
Wasfie, Tarik Jawad *surgeon, educator*

Hastings
Adrounie, V. Harry *public health administrator, scientist, educator, environmentalist*

Lansing
Sauer, Harold John *physician, educator*

Mount Pleasant
Parkhurst, Connie Lou *audiologist*

Negaunee
Matero, Janet Louise *counselor, educator*

Paw Paw
DuCharme, Donald Walter *pharmacologist, educator*

Petoskey
Beierwaltes, William Henry *physician, educator*

Royal Oak
Keye, William Richard, Jr., *physician, educator*
Lechner, Jon Robert *nursing administrator, educator*
McCarroll, Kathleen Ann *radiologist, educator*

Southfield
Hammel, Ernest Martin *medical educator, academic administrator*
Perez-Cruet, Mick Jorge *neurological surgeon, educator*

Sterling Heights
Genovich-Richards, Joann *health care services consultant, educator*

University Center
Shannon, Marcia Rucker *mental health nurse, educator*

West Bloomfield
Sarwer-Foner, Gerald Jacob *physician, educator*
Seidman, Michael David *surgeon, educator*

Ypsilanti
Krajewski-Jaime, Elvia Rosa *social worker*
Wilson, Lorraine M. *medical/surgical nurse, educator*

MINNESOTA

Detroit Lakes
Eginton, Charles Theodore *surgeon, educator*

Duluth
Sebastian, James Albert *obstetrician, gynecologist, educator*

Excelsior
Anderson, William Robert *pathologist, educator*

Mankato
Huot, Rachel Irene *biomedical educator, research scientist, physician*

Minneapolis
Dahl, Gerald LuVern *psychotherapist, educator*
Doubek, Fayola Marie *nurse, educator*
Gerdner, Linda Ann *nursing researcher, educator*
Kennedy, B(yrl) J(ames) *medicine and oncology educator*
Kralewski, John Edward *health service research educator*
Luepker, Russell Vincent *epidemiology educator*
Odegaard, Daniel Owen *dentist, educator*
Schultz, Alvin Leroy *retired internist, endocrinologist, retired university health science facility administrator*
Staba, Emil John *pharmacognosy and medicinal chemistry educator*
Thompson, Theodore Robert *pediatric educator*
Verby, John Edward, Jr., *physician, educator*
Weir, Edward Kenneth *cardiologist, educator*
Wilson, Robert Foster *cardiologist, educator*

Palisade
Kilde, Sandra Jean *nurse anesthetist, educator, consultant*

Rochester
Beahrs, Oliver Howard *surgeon, educator*
Butt, Hugh Roland *gastroenterologist, educator*
Kummeth, Patricia Joan *nursing educator*
Lanier, William Lovel, Jr., *anesthesiologist, educator*
McKean, David Jesse *medical science researcher*
Rogers, Roy Steele, III, *dermatology educator, dean*
Sands, Amy Catherine *nursing administrator, educator*
Scott, John Paul *medical educator*
Suelto, Consuelo Quilao *retired nursing educator*

Saint Paul
Joyce, Michael Daniel *personal resource management therapist and consultant, neurolearning therapist*
Michael, Alfred Frederick, Jr., *physician, medical educator*
Sher, Phyllis Kammerman *pediatric neurology educator*

MISSISSIPPI

Brookhaven
Mitchell, Penny *school counselor*

Gautier
Egerton, Charles Pickford *anatomy and physiology educator*

Gulfport
Stafford, Betty Trammell *psychiatric nursing educator*

Jackson
Cruse, Julius Major, Jr., *pathologist, educator*
Freeland, Alan Edward *orthopedic surgery educator, physician*
Kermode, John Cotterill *pharmacology educator, researcher*
Tchounwou, Paul Bernard *environmental health specialist, toxicologist, educator*

Ocean Springs
Parker, Rebecca Mary *special education facility administrator, educator*

MISSOURI

Branson
Coscia, Robert Lingua *surgeon, educator*

Columbia
Allen, William Cecil *physician, educator*
Barrett, James Thomas *immunologist, educator*
Boedeker, Ben Harold *anesthesiologist, educator*
Cowden, John Williams *eye physician, educator*
Eggers, George William Nordholtz, Jr., *anesthesiologist, educator*
Silver, Donald *surgeon, educator*

Crystal City
Lourwood, David Lee, Jr., *pharmacotherapist, educator*

Holts Summit
Melton, June Marie *nursing educator*

Independence
Sturges, Sidney James *pharmacist, educator, investment and development company executive*

Kansas City
Heymach, George John, III, *physician, educator, health facility administrator, consultant*
Jonas, Harry S. *medical education consultant*
Smith, Roger Perry *obstetrics and gynecology educator*
Thompson, Catherine Rush *physical therapist, educator*

Mexico
Rice, Marvin Elwood *dentist*

Nevada
Wassenberg, Evelyn M. *medical and surgical nurse, nursing educator*

Raytown
Shymanski, Catherine Mary *health facility administrator*

Rogersville
Utley, Rose *nursing educator and researcher*

Saint Charles
Panagos, Rebecca Jean Huffman *university educator, researcher, consultant*

Saint Louis
Anderhub, Beth Marie *medical educator*
Cryer, Philip Eugene *medical educator, scientist, endocrinologist*
Dodson, W(illiam) Edwin *child neurology educator*
Evens, Ronald Gene *radiologist, medical center administrator*
Galofre, Alberto *medical educator*
Geltman, Edward Mark *cardiologist, educator*
Griffing, George Thomas *medical educator, endocrinologist*
Kipnis, David Morris *physician, educator*
McCown, Linda Jean *medical technology educator*
Molloff, Florence Jeanine *speech and language therapist*
Morgan, Stephan Shane *ophthalmologist, educator*
Myerson, Robert J. *radiation oncologist, educator*
North, Carol Sue *psychiatrist, educator*
Peck, William Arno *physician, educator, university official and dean*
Singh, Inderjit *nephrologist, internist, medical educator*

Stencer, Mark Joseph *healthcare administrator, consultant*
Welch-Hill, Constance Marcella *speech and language therapist, consultant*

Smithville
Vitek, Victoria Lynn *speech-language pathologist*

Warrensburg
Engle, Mary Elizabeth *dietitian, educator*

MONTANA

Billings
England, John David *neurologist, educator*

Hamilton
Soden, Ruth M. *geriatrics nurse, educator*

Missoula
Stevenson, Marolane *counselor*

NEBRASKA

Fremont
Hawks, Jane Esther Hokanson *nursing educator*

Gering
Judy, Janice M. *nurse, educator*

Lincoln
Koszewski, Bohdan Julius *retired internist, medical educator*

Omaha
Baldwin, Jeffrey Nathan *pharmacy educator*
Casey, Murray Joseph *physician, educator*
Dash, Alekha K. *pharmaceutical scientist, educator*
Huurman, Walter William *pediatric orthopaedic surgeon, educator*
Korbitz, Bernard Carl *retired oncologist, hematologist, educator, consultant*
Mardis, Hal Kennedy *urological surgeon, educator, researcher*
Ramaprasad, Subbaraya *medical educator*
Recker, Robert R. *medical educator, internist*
Swanson, Darlene Marie Carlson *speech therapist, educator, speaker, writer*

NEVADA

Hawthorne
Sortland, Trudith Ann *speech and language therapist, educator*

Las Vegas
Bingham, James Frederick *healthcare educator*
Kowalski, Susan Dolores *critical care nurse, educator*
Ramsey, Nancy Lockwood *nursing educator*
Records, Raymond Edwin *ophthalmologist, medical educator*
Zuspan, Frederick Paul *obstetrician, gynecologist, educator*

Reno
Graham, Denis David *marriage and family therapist, educational consultant*
Kurtz, Kenneth John *physician, educator*
Mathews, Cheri Rene *speech pathologist*

Sparks
Allen, Judith Martha *nursing administrator, educator, career officer*

NEW HAMPSHIRE

Lebanon
Boardman, Maureen Bell *community health nurse, educator*
Cohen, Jeffrey Allen *neurologist, educator*
Dixon-Vestal, Ruth Elaine *nurse, educator*
Racusin, Robert Jerrold *psychiatry educator*

Manchester
Merideth, Susan Carol *healthcare educator*

Portsmouth
Michelsen, W(olfgang) Jost *neurosurgeon, educator, retired*

NEW JERSEY

Bridgewater
Hirsch, Paul J. *orthopedist, surgeon, medical executive, educator, editor*

Browns Mills
Henderson, Kathleen Denise Ross *medical/surgical nurse, nursing educator*

Camden
Ances, I. G(eorge) *obstetrician, gynecologist, educator*

Cape May Point
Lee, Betty Jane *nursing educator*

Cherry Hill
Brachfeld, Jonas *cardiologist, educator*
Grado-Wolynies, Evelyn (Evelyn Wolynies) *clinical nurse specialist, educator*
Olearchyk, Andrew *cardiothoracic surgeon, educator*
Swibinski, Edward Thomas *physician, educator*

Dover
Chung, Tae-Soo *physiatrist, educator*

Edison
Angelakos, Evangelos Theodorou *physician, physiologist, pharmacologist, educator*

Fair Lawn
Dadurian, Medina Diana *pediatric dentist, educator*

Franklin Park
Perry, Arthur William *plastic surgeon, educator*

Glen Ridge
Zbar, Lloyd Irwin Stanley *otolaryngologist, educator*

Hamilton
Reid-Merritt, Patricia Ann *social worker, educator, author, performing artist*

Hillsborough
Weinman, Steven Alan *emergency nurse, researcher, writer, educator, consultant*

Hillsdale
Rosenstein, Beverly Bella *speech and language pathologist*

Kirkwood Voorhees
Barone, Donald Anthony *neurologist, educator*

Linwood
Cohen, Diana Louise *psychology, educator, psychotherapist, consultant*

Livingston
Rickert, Robert Richard *pathologist, educator*
Rokosz, Gregory Joseph *emergency medicine physician, lawyer, educator*

Long Branch
Daniels, Richard Alan *retired internist, educator*

Lumberton
Losse, Catherine Ann *pediatric nurse, critical care nurse, educator, clinical nurse specialist, family nurse practitioner*

Marlton
Kahn, Sigmund Benham *retired internist and dean*
Letizia, Dorothy *nursing educator*

Medford
Whipple, Beverly *nursing educator, researcher*

Montville
Keefe, Deborah Lynn *cardiologist, educator*

Mountainside
James, Barbara Frances *school nurse, special education educator*

New Brunswick
Brilliant, Eleanor Luria *social work educator*
Chandler, James John *surgeon, educator*
Knuppel, Robert Alan *obstetrics-gynecology educator, healthcare consultant*
Laraya-Cuasay, Lourdes Redublo *pediatric pulmonologist, educator*
Nosko, Michael Gerrik *neurosurgeon, educator*
Sherman, Richard Arthur *nephrologist, educator*
Trelstad, Robert Laurence *pathology educator, cell biologist*

Newark
Fu, Shoucheng Joseph *biomedicine educator*
Haycock, Christine Elizabeth *retired medical educator, health educator*
Healy-Sova, Phyllis M. Cordasco *school social worker*
Kantor, Mel Lewis *dental educator, researcher*
Lee, Young Bin *psychiatry educator, neurologist*
Leevy, Carroll Moton *medical educator, hepatology researcher*
Leung, Christopher Chung Kit *anatomy educator*
Shane, Paul Gauguin *social worker, educator, sociologist*
Weiss, Gerson *physician, educator*

Ocean Grove
Davis, John Mihran *surgeon, educator*

Old Bridge
Romeo, Christina Ioannides *speech language pathologist*

Park Ridge
Ablin, Richard Joel *immunologist, educator*

Paterson
DeBari, Vincent Anthony *medical researcher, educator*

Perth Amboy
Buckelew, Carolyn Rose Pierce *nursing educator*

Phillipsburg
Drago, Joseph Rosario *urologist, educator*

Pomona
Bukowski, Elaine Louise *physical therapist, educator*

Red Bank
Brown, Valerie Anne *psychiatric social worker, educator*
Gutentag, Patricia Richmand *social worker, family counselor, occupational therapist*
Murray, Abby Darlington Boyd *psychiatric clinical specialist, educator*

Scotch Plains
Touretzky, Muriel Walter *nursing educator*

Sewell
Libby, Joseph Anthony *physician, educator*

Skillman
Schirber, Annamarie Riddering *speech and language pathologist, educator*

South Orange
Breines, Estelle Borgman *occupational therapy educator*
Hansell, Phyllis Shanley *nursing educator, administrator, researcher, consultant*

Sparta
Alberto, Pamela Louise *oral and maxillofacial surgeon, educator*

Succasunna
Pool, Nancy Ellen *school social worker*
Zwiren, Janet *holistic professional, educator*

Teaneck
Scotti, Dennis Joseph *educator, researcher, consultant*

Toms River
Hines, Patricia *social worker, educator*

Turnersville
Cammarota, Marie Elizabeth *nursing educator*

Union
Williams, Carol Jorgensen *social work educator*

Ventnor City
Zuckerman, Stuart *psychiatrist, forensic examiner, educator*

Warren
Laskin, Oscar Larry *clinical pharmacology educator, virologist*
Zeldis, Jerome Bernard *medical foundation executive, educator, physician*

Wayne
Oriji, Gibson K. *medical educator, medical researcher*

West New York
Kelly, Lucie Stirm Young *nursing educator*

West Orange
Brodkin, Roger Harrison *dermatologist, educator*
Ghali, Anwar Youssef *psychiatrist, educator*
Hill, George James *physician, educator*
Stock, Jeffrey Allen *urologist, educator*

Westfield
Lisman, Elias *pediatric dentist, educator*

Woodbridge
Estok, Rosemarie DeNorscio *educational administrator*

Woodbury
Stambaugh, John Edgar *oncologist, hematologist, pharmacologist, educator*

NEW MEXICO

Alamogordo
Snowberger, Jane Ardeth *geriatrics nurse, educator, consultant*

Albuquerque
Addis, Marguerite Christjohn (Chris Addis) *physical therapist*
Bennett, Max Dial *internal medicine educator*
Lee, Roland Robert *radiologist, educator*
Mapel, Douglas Wayne *epidemiologist, educator, health facility administrator*
Omer, George Elbert, Jr., *orthopaedic surgeon, educator*
Rayburn, William Frazier *obstetrician, gynecologist, educator*
Stevenson, James Richard *radiologist, lawyer*

Cimarron
Wright, Anita Beth *speech-language pathologist*

Gallup
Crouch, Altha Marie *health educator, consultant*

Las Cruces
Mata, Josefina *health education coordinator, educator*

Roswell
Johnston, Mary Ellen *retired nursing educator*

NEW YORK

Albany
Ambros, Robert Andrew *pathologist, educator, writer*
Curry, Robert Richard *health facility administrator*
DeNuzzo, Rinaldo Vincent *pharmacy educator*
Henrikson, Ray Charles *retired anatomy educator*
Mayer, Dan Michael *emergency medicine educator*
Veille, Jean-Claude *maternal-fetal medicine physician, educator*

Alfred
Prigmore, Charles Samuel *social work educator*

Amagansett
Fleetwood, M. Freile *psychiatrist, educator*

Armonk
Mellors, Robert Charles *physician, scientist, educator*

Bay Shore
Altchek, Edward M. *neurosurgeon, educator*

Bayside
Du Mont, Allen André *pyschotherapist, educator*

Bronx
Kanofsky, Jacob Daniel *psychiatrist, educator*
Moshe, Solomon L. *neurology and pediatrics educator*
Nanna, Michele *cardiologist, educator*
Opler, Lewis Alan *psychiatrist, educator, researcher*
Rubinstein, Arye *pediatrician, microbiologist, educator, immunologist, educator*
Weiner, Richard Lenard *hospital administrator, educator, pediatrician*
Wiernik, Peter Harris *oncologist, educator*

Brooklyn
Adasko, Mary Hardy *speech pathologist*
Bendo, Audrée Argiro *anesthesiologist, educator*
DeHovitz, Jack Alan *physician, educator, health facility administrator*
Donovan, Rita R. *nurse anesthetist, trauma and critical care nurse, educator*
El Kodsi, Baroukh *gastroenterologist, educator*
Feit, Alan *cardiologist, internist, medical educator*
Gaglioti, Linda Crista *nurse midwife, educator*
Gotta, Alexander Walter *anesthesiologist, educator*
Greenberg, Deborah *speech and language pathologist*
Harris-Olayinka, Verda (Lorraine Harris-Olayinka) *health agency administrator, cultural consultant*
Marsala-Cervasio, Kathleen Ann *medical/surgical nurse, administrator*
Mittman, Neal *nephrologist, medical educator*
Norstrand, Iris Fletcher *psychiatrist, neurologist, educator*
Radice, Beatrice Rosemarie *family nurse practitioner*
Reddy, Chatla V. Ramana *internist, cardiologist, educator*
Shulman, Abraham *otolaryngology educator, hospital administrator*
Spiegel, Allen D. *medical educator, consultant*
Ware, Pearl Cunningham *health educator*
Zenilman, Michael E. *surgeon, educator*

Buffalo
Bankert, Richard Burton *immunologist, educator*
Blane, Howard Thomas *research institute administrator*
Brody, Harold *neuroanatomist, gerontologist*
Enhorning, Goran *obstetrician, gynecologist, educator*
Fischman, Stuart Lee *oral medicine educator, dentist*
Halbreich, Uriel Morav *psychiatrist, educator*
Krackow, Kenneth Alan *orthopaedic surgeon, educator, inventor*
Kurlan, Marvin Zeft *surgeon, educator*
Milgrom, Felix *immunologist, educator*
Naughton, John Patrick *cardiologist, educator*
Schentag, Jerome John *pharmacy educator*
Vladutiu, Adrian O. *physician, educator*

Canaan
Coon, Thomas Gary *alcohol and substance abuse counselor*

Chaumont
Schell, Jacquelyn Ann *speech pathology/audiology services professional*

Cheektowaga
Richmond, Allen Martin *speech pathologist, educator*

Chestnut Ridge
Day, Stacey Biswas *medical educator*

Cobleskill
Colony, Pamela Cameron *medical researcher, educator*

East Hampton
Paton, David *ophthalmologist, educator*

East Meadow
Feinfeld, Donald Allen *nephrologist, educator*

Elmhurst
Masci, Joseph Richard *medical educator, physician*

Elmira
Bellohusen, Ronald Michael *orthodontist, educator*

Fayetteville
Pirodsky, Donald Max *psychiatrist, educator*

Flushing
Dubov, Spencer Floyd *podiatrist, educator*

Forest Hills
Gold, Roslyn *social worker, educator*

Garden City
Nicklin, George Leslie, Jr., *psychoanalyst, educator, physician, author*

Glen Cove
Mallow, Alissa Jane *social worker, educator*

Great Neck
Dines, David Michael *surgeon, educator*
Gross, Lillian *psychiatrist, educator*
Mayer, Susan Lee *nurse, educator*
Shons, Alan Rance *plastic surgeon, surgical oncologist, educator*

Great River
Hayman, Martin Arthur *psychiatrist, educator*

Huntington
Joseph, Richard Saul *cardiologist, educator*
Salcedo-Dovi, Hector Eduardo *anatomist, educator, surgeon*

Hurley
Petruski, Jennifer Andrea *speech and language pathologist*

Ithaca
Habicht, Jean Pierre *healthcare educator, nutritionist*
Pagliarulo, Michael Anthony *physical therapy educator*

Jackson Heights
Chang, Lydia Liang-Hwa *social worker, educator*

Jamaica
Cohen, Wayne Roy *obstetrician-gynecologist, educator*

Malone
Oakes, Anita Gwynne *physical therapist, educator*

Malverne
Ryan, Suzanne Irene *nursing educator*

Mamaroneck
Wasserman, Eugene M. *pediatrician, educator*

Manhasset
Boal, Bernard Harvey *cardiologist, educator, author*
Feinberg, Arthur Warren *medical educator*
Wang, Ping *biomedical investigator*

Maryland
Rogers, Evelyn M. *retired speech and language pathologist*

Massapequa
Witt, Denise Lindgren *operating room nurse, educator*

Melville
Copperman, Stuart Morton *pediatrician, educator*

Mount Kisco
Weissman, Michael Herbert *pediatrician, educator*

New Hartford
Eidelhoch, Lester Philip *physician, educator, surgeon*

New Hyde Park
Rai, Kanti Roop *hematologist, oncologist, medical educator*

New York
Abramson, Sara Jane *radiologist, educator*
Armenakas, Noel Anthony *medical educator*
Aviv, Jonathan Enoch *otolaryngologist, educator*
Baden, Michael M. *pathologist, educator*
Ballard, Bruce Laine *psychiatrist*
Bansinath, Mylarrao *pharmacologist, educator*
Barnhill, John Warren *psychiatrist, educator*
Barnum, Barbara Stevens *writer, retired nursing educator*
Beerman, Joseph *health educator*
Ben-Zvi, Jeffrey Stuart *gastroenterologist, internist*
Berk, Paul David *physician, scientist, educator*
Braff, Robert Alan *cardiologist, educator*
Braun, Norma Mai Tsen Wang *physician, educator*
Brook, Judith Suzanne *psychiatry and psychology researcher and educator*
Burkhardt, Ann *occupational therapist, clinical educator*
Cammisa, Frank P., Jr., *surgeon, educator*
Cancro, Robert *psychiatrist, educator*
Caruana, Joan *educator, psychotherapist, nurse*
Cosgriff, Stuart Worcester *internist, consultant, medical educator*
Costa, Rosann *research associate*
Cutler, Mary Jane Venger *nursing administrator, educator*
Cuttner, Janet *hematologist, educator*
DeAngelis, Lisa Marie *neurologist, educator*
Du Mont, Nicolas *psychiatrist, educator*
Erlenmeyer-Kimling, L. *psychiatrist, researcher*
Fahn, Stanley *neurologist, educator*
Freiman, Alvin Henry *cardiologist, educator*
Frommer, Herbert Henry *educator*
Froum, Stuart Jay *periodontist, educator*
Gerber, Linda Maxine *epidemiology educator*
Gliklich, Jerry *physician, educator*
Godman, Gabriel Charles *pathology educator*
Golde, David William *physician, educator*
Goldsmith, Michael Allen *oncologist, educator*
Goldsmith, Stanley Joseph *nuclear medicine physician, educator*
Goldstein, Marc *microsurgeon, urology and reproductive medicine educator, administrator*
Gotto, Antonio Marion, Jr., *internist, educator*
Grant, Alfred David *orthopaedic surgeon, educator*
Green, Wayne Hugo *psychiatrist, psychoanalyst*
Greenberg, Henry Morton *physician, educator*
Harris, Matthew Nathan *surgeon, educator*
Jacobs, Joseph Barry *otolaryngologist, educator*
Jacobs, Thomas Price *internal medicine educator*
Jonas, Saran *neurologist, educator*
Kahn, Norman *pharmacology and dentistry educator*
Kalayjian, Anie *psychotherapist, nurse, educator, consultant*
King, Thomas Creighton *thoracic surgeon, educator*
Kron, Leo *psychiatrist, educator*
Kyman, Wendy *sex therapist, health educator*

Lane, Joseph M. *orthopedic surgeon, educator, oncologist*
Lawson, William *otolaryngologist, educator*
Lombardi, Linda Catherine *health facility administrator, educator*
Loo, Marcus Hsieu-Hong *urologist, physician, educator*
Lopez, Ralph Ivan *pediatrics educator*
Macken, Daniel Loos *physician, educator*
MacKinnon, Roger Alan *psychiatrist, educator*
Mandracchia, Violet Ann Palermo *psychotherapist, educator*
Manly, Carol Ann *speech pathologist*
Marks, Arthur *prosthodontist, educator*
Marks, Paul Alan *oncologist, cell biologist, educator*
Matera, Cristina *obstetrician-gynecologist, educator*
Matorin, Susan *social work administrator, educator*
Michels, Robert *psychiatrist, educator*
Mishne, Judith Marks *social work educator, psychotherapist*
Moss, Melvin Lionel *anatomist, educator*
Naidich, Thomas Paul *neuroradiologist, educator*
Noback, Charles Robert *anatomist, educator*
Omura, Yoshiaki *physician, educator*
Ordorica, Steven Anthony *obstetrician, gynecologist, educator*
Ossenberg, Hella Svetlana *psychoanalyst*
Pardes, Herbert *psychiatrist, educator*
Phoon, Colin Kit-Lun *pediatric cardiologist, medical educator*
Raab, Edward Leon *ophthalmologist, educator, lawyer*
Richard, Elaine *educational therapist*
Rosenberg, Victor I. *plastic surgeon, educator*
Rumore, Martha Mary *pharmacist, educator*
Sager, Clifford J. *psychiatrist, educator*
Salzer, Jacqueline Ann *anesthesiologist, educator*
Sanchez, Miguel Ramon *dermatologist, educator*
Sarno, Martha Taylor *speech and language pathologist, educator*
Scarola, John Michael *dentist, educator*
Schaffler, Mitchell Barry *research scientist, anatomist, educator*
Seiler, Jerome Saul *obstetrician, gynecologist, educator*
Shortliffe, Edward Hance *internist, medical educator, computer scientist*
Simon, Jane *psychiatrist, educator*
Spiegel, Herbert *psychiatrist, educator*
Sternberg, Stephen Stanley *pathologist, educator*
Sun, Tung-Tien *medical science educator*
Tortolani, Anthony John *surgeon, educator*
Turino, Gerard Michael *physician, medical scientist, educator*
Wank, Gerald Sidney *periodontist, educator*
Weinstein, I. Bernard *oncologist, geneticist, research administrator*
Witkin, Mildred Hope Fisher *psychotherapist, educator*
Yeh, Hsu-Chong *radiology educator*
Yoo Bowne, Helen *otolaryngologist, educator*

Old Westbury
Chaudhry, Humayun Javaid *physician, medical educator, flight surgeon, writer*

Orangeburg
Nixon, Ralph Angus *psychiatrist, educator, research neuroscientist*
Pratt, Christina Carver *social work and women's studies educator*

Plainview
Kelemen, John *neurologist, educator*
Krauss, Leo *urologist, educator*

Plattsburgh
Bedworth, David Albert *health educator*

Rochester
Agrawal, Govind Prasad *optics educator*
Akiyama, Toshio *cardiologist, educator, researcher*
Burton, Richard Irving *orthopedist, educator*
Marriott, Marcia Ann *health facility administrator, finance educator*
Moore, Duncan Thomas *optics educator*
Papadakos, Peter John *critical care physician, educator*
Peters, Cathy J. *nurse practitioner, education consultant*
Schmidt, John Gerhard *neurologist, educator, researcher*
Shields, Cleveland George *family therapist, researcher, educator*
Sparks, Charles Edward *pathologist, educator*

Sands Point
Lear, Erwin *anesthesiologist, educator*

Scarsdale
Liston, Mary Frances *retired nursing educator*

Schenectady
Fulco, John Dominick *diagnostic radiologist*
O'Baire, Marika *community health nurse, writer*

Seneca Falls
Norman, Mary Marshall *educator, counselor, therapist*

Speculator
Mulleedy, Joyce Elaine *nursing service administrator, educator*

Staten Island
Bloomfield, Dennis *physician, educator, dean*
Villanueva, E. Gary *internist, educator*

Stony Brook
Badalamente, Marie Ann *orthopedist, educator*
Edmunds, Leland Nicholas *biology educator*
Jasiewicz, Ronald Clarence *anesthesiologist, educator*

Kuchner, Eugene Frederick *neurosurgeon, educator, neuroscientist*
Liang, Jerome Zhengrong *radiology educator*
Ricotta, John Joseph *vascular surgeon, educator*

Syracuse
Alao, Adekola Olatunji *psychiatrist, educator*
Dewan, Mantosh Jaimani *psychiatrist, educator*
Farah, Fuad Salim *dermatologist, educator*
Gerle, Richard Darlington *radiologist, educator*
Streeten, Barbara Wiard *ophthalmologist, medical educator*

Tarrytown
Andreen, Aviva Louise *dentist, researcher, academic administrator, educator*

Troy
Medicus, Hildegard Julie *retired dentist, orthodontist, educator*

Tuxedo Park
Regan, Ellen Frances (Mrs. Walston Shepard Brown) *ophthalmologist, educator*

Valhalla
Couldwell, William Tupper *neurosurgeon, educator*
Kline, Susan Anderson *medical school official and dean, internist*
Marks, Stephen J. *neurologist, educator*
McGoldrick, Kathryn Elizabeth *anesthesiologist, educator, writer*
Moussouttas, Michael M. *medical educator*
Williams, Gary Murray *medical researcher, pathology educator*

White Plains
Blass, John Paul *medical educator, physician*
Hariton, Jo Rosenberg *psychotherapist, educator*
Pfeffer, Cynthia Roberta *psychiatrist, educator*

Whitestone
Dressler, Brenda Joyce *health educator, consultant, book and film reviewer*
Helmreich, Helaine Gewirtz *speech pathology professional*

NORTH CAROLINA

Asheville
Ellis, Virginia Lynn *gerontology services educator*

Chapel Hill
Berkey, Douglas Bryan *dental educator, researcher, gerontologist, clinician*
Bondurant, Stuart *physician, educational administrator*
Burnham, Steven James *physician, educator*
Coles, William Henry *ophthalmologist, educator*
Collier, Albert M. *pediatric educator, child development center director*
Droegemueller, William *gynecologist, obstetrician, medical educator*
Drossman, Douglas Arnold *medical investigator, educator, gastroenterologist*
Graham, John Borden *pathologist, writer, educator*
Hawkins, David Rollo, Sr., *psychiatrist, educator*
Hershey, H(oward) Garland, Jr., *orthodontist, university administrator*
Houpt, Jeffrey Lyle *dean, psychiatrist, educator*
Lee, Joseph King Tak *radiologist, medical educator*
Pagano, Joseph Stephen *physician, researcher, educator*
Prentice, William Edward *athletic trainer, physical therapist, educator*
Usher, Charles Lindsey *social work educator, public policy analyst*
White, Raymond Petrie, Jr., *dentist, educator*

Charlotte
Carper, Barbara Anne *nursing educator*
Chapel, Sally Jo *behavioral scientist, nurse, educator, minister*
Morris, Tama Lynn *nursing educator*

Durham
Anderson, William Banks, Jr., *ophthalmology educator*
Bashore, Thomas Michael *cardiologist, educator*
Bennett, Peter Brian *researcher, hyperbaric medicine*
Branch, Laurence George *health policy researcher, educator, gerontologist*
Brodie, Harlow Keith Hammond *psychiatrist, educator, past university president*
Buckley, Rebecca Hatcher *physician, educator*
Christmas, William Anthony *internist, educator*
Cohen, Harvey Jay *physician, educator*
Durack, David Tulloch *physician, educator*
Falletta, John Matthew *pediatrician, educator*
Gebhardt, Richard George *therapist, educator*
Hammond, Charles Bessellieu *obstetrician, gynecologist, educator*
Klitzman, Bruce *physiologist, plastic surgery educator, researcher*
Newborg, Barbara Carol *retired medical educator*
Soper, John Tunnicliff *obstetrician-gynecologist, educator*
Stiles, Gary Lester *cardiologist, molecular pharmacologist, educator*

Elizabeth City
Griffin, Gladys Bogues *critical care nurse, educator*

Greensboro
Bland, Annie Ruth (Ann Bland) *nursing educator*
Price Lea, Patricia Jean *nurse educator*
Whitaker, Von Best *nursing educator*

Greenville
Hoffman, Donald Richard *pathologist, educator*
Lee, Kenneth Stuart *neurosurgeon, educator*
Monroe, Edwin Wall *physician, former university dean*
Waugh, William Howard *biomedical educator*
Winn, Francis John, Jr., *medical educator*

Hampstead
Solomon, Robert Douglas *pathology educator*

Hillsborough
Wallace, Andrew Grover *physician, educator, medical school dean*

Pembroke
Marson, Stephen Mark *social work educator*

Raleigh
Berry, Joni Ingram *hospice pharmacist, educator*
Garrett, Leland Earl *nephrologist, educator*
Hammon, Kathleen Campbell *health science association administrator, educator*
Parks, Suzanne Lowry *psychiatric nurse, educator*

Roxboro
Broyles, Bonita Eileen *nursing educator*

Salter Path
Wiley, Albert Lee, Jr., *physician, engineer, educator*

Sherrills Ford
Stynes, Barbara Bilello *integrative health professional, educator*

Siler City
Allred, Rachel Hall *retired nurse, educator*

Southern Pines
Penick, George Dial *pathologist*

Winston Salem
Eldridge, J. Charles *endocrinologist, researcher, medical educator, medical educator*
Toole, James Francis *medical educator*

NORTH DAKOTA

Belfield
Oe, Emily Norene *counselor, play therapist*

Center
Kautzman, Jean L. Pfliger *nurse educator*

Fargo
Scott, David Michael *pharmacy educator*

Minot
Mohler, Marie Elaine *nurse educator*

OHIO

Akron
Evans, Douglas McCullough *surgeon, educator*
Litman, George Irving *physician, educator*

Ashtabula
Freitas, Frances Anne *nursing educator, consultant*

Athens
Chila, Anthony George *osteopathic educator*

Bidwell
Matura, Raymond Carl *gerontologist, sociologist, educator*

Boardman
Giannini, A. James *psychiatrist, educator, researcher, author*

Bowling Green
Scherer, Ronald Callaway *voice scientist, educator*

Canfield
Weiss, Susan Ellen *adult nurse practitioner, educator*

Canton
Starchman, Dale Edward *medical educator*

Cincinnati
Azizkhan, Richard George *pediatric surgeon, educator*
Cudkowicz, Leon *medical educator*
Repaske, David Roy *pediatric endocrinologist, educator*
Rothenberg, Marc Elliot *pediatrics educator*
Scott, Ralph C. *physician, educator*
Sherman, Kenneth Eliot *medicine educator, researcher*
Stinson, Mary Florence *retired nursing educator*
Wilson, James Miller, IV, *cardiovascular surgeon, educator*

Clayton
Childers, Frances Carole *nursing director, educator, emergency nurse*

Cleveland
Agich, George John *medical educator, educator*
Bambakidis, Peter *neurologist, educator*
Bowerfind, Edgar Sihler, Jr., *physician, medical administrator*
Chao, Jason *family physician, educator*
Chukwumerije, Nkemdirim *medical educator*
Cowan, Dale Harvey *internist, lawyer*
Daniel, Thomas Mallon *medical educator, researcher*
Hokenstad, Merl Clifford, Jr., *social work educator*

Kumar, Mary Louise *physician, educator*
Macklis, Roger Milton *physician, educator, researcher*
Narsavage, Georgia Roberts *nursing educator, researcher, dean, associate dean*
Neuger, Sanford *orthodontics educator*
Newman, Lynda Nittskoff *medical/surgical nurse, nurse educator*
Spirnak, John Patrick *urologist, educator*
Stern, Robert C. *physician, educator*
Strome, Marshall *otolaryngologist, educator*

Columbus
Abrahms, Shawna K. *special education services professional*
Agarwal, Anil Kumar *nephrologist, educator*
Balcerzak, Stanley Paul *physician, educator*
Boué, Daniel Robert *pediatric pathologist, neuropathologist, educator*
Carr, Michele Paige *dental hygienist, educator*
Furste, Wesley Leonard, II, *surgeon, educator*
Hicks, William James *internist, oncologist, educator*
Jacko, Jean Anne *nurse, educator*
Jolly, Daniel Ehs *dental educator*
Senhauser, Donald A(lbert) *pathologist, educator*
Toomey, Beverly Guella *social work educator*
Tzagournis, Manuel *physician, educator, university administrator*
Vermilyea, Stanley George *prosthodontist, educator*

Copley
Smith, Joan H. *retired women's health nurse, educator*

Dayton
Hawley, H(arrison) Bradford *physician, educator*
Ruegsegger, Donald Ray, Jr., *radiological physicist, educator*
Weinberg, Sylvan Lee *cardiologist, educator, author, editor*

Fairfield
Goodman, Myrna Marcia *school nurse*

Gahanna
Kaye, Gail Leslie *healthcare consultant, educator*

Gnadenhutten
Wolf, Joan Mangon *health occupations instructor, nursing educator*

Groveport
Hall, Dorothy Marie Reynolds *dental educator*

Independence
Van Kirk, Robert John *nursing case manager, educator*

Kenton
Mackey, Ruth Elizabeth (Betty Mackey) *nutrition and food educator, real estate broker*

Lakewood
Kane, Karen Ann *speech language pathologist*

Lancaster
Snider, Gordon B. *retired medical educator*

Logan
Yeagley, Kathleen Lux *community health nurse, educator*

Massillon
Vaughn, Lisa Dawn *physician, educator*

New Carlisle
Peters, Elizabeth Ann Hampton *retired nursing educator*

Oberlin
Lapham, Lowell Winship *physician educator, researcher*

Richmond Heights
Bowman, James Arthur, Jr., *obstetrician-gynecologist, educator*

Saint Clairsville
Sidon, Claudia Marie *psychiatric and mental health nursing educator*

Springfield
Kurian, Pius *nephrologist, educator*

Strongsville
Nelson, Jill Elaine *nurse attorney, health care consultant, health facility administrator, instructor, researcher*

Toledo
Danso, Daniel Y. *physician, educator*
Early, Johnnie L., II, *pharmacy educator*
Kurczynski, Thaddeus Walter *neurologist, geneticist, educator*
Lessick, Mira Lee *nursing educator*
Lynn, Christopher Kenneth *internist, educator*
Martin, John Thomas *physician, author, educator*
Zrull, Joel Peter *psychiatry educator*

Warren
VanAuker, Lana *recreational therapist, educator*

Westerville
Williams, John Michael *physical therapist, sports medicine educator*

Worthington
Winter, Chester Caldwell *physician, surgery educator, historian, writer*

Youngstown
Valenta, Janet Anne *substance abuse professional*

Zanesville
Ray, John Walker *otolaryngologist, educator, broadcast commentator*

OKLAHOMA

Ada
Davenport, Ann Adele Mayfield *retired home care agency administrator*

Broken Arrow
Muller, Patricia Ann *nursing administrator, educator*

Claremore
McCall, Charles Barnard *health facility administrator, educator*
McClain, Marilyn Russell *counselor*

Edmond
Roy, Johnny Bernard *urologist, educator*

Jenks
Wootan, Gerald Don *osteopathic physician, educator*

Lawton
Lewis, Gary Alan *radiologic technologist, educator*
Webb, O(rville) Lynn *physician, pharmacologist, educator*

Norman
Jones, Linda Karen *speech, language pathologist*
Lowell, Jeanne *nursing educator, psychiatric-mental health nurse*

Oklahoma City
Andrews, M. Dewayne *dean, internist, educator*
Brooks, Clifton Rowland, Sr., *pediatrician, educator, enviromental medicine*
Halverstadt, Donald Bruce *urologist, educator*
McEwen, Irene Ruble *physical therapy educator*
Perez-Cruet, Jorge *physician, psychopharmacologist, psychophysiologist, psychiatrist, educator, addictionologist, geropsychiatrist*
Shillingburg, Herbert Thompson, Jr., *dental educator*
Thadani, Udho *physician, cardiologist*

Sapulpa
Fletcher, Shirley Faye *counselor*

Tahlequah
Wickham, M(arvin) Gary *optometry educator*

Tulsa
Allen, Thomas Wesley *medical educator, dean*
Cherry, Andrew Lawrence, Jr., *social work educator, researcher*
Friedman, Mark Joel *cardiologist, educator*
Hannah, Barbara Ann *nurse, educator*
Kalbfleisch, John McDowell *cardiologist, educator*
Lewis, Corinne Hemeter *psychotherapist, educator*
Nebergall, Robert William *orthopedic surgeon, educator*
Nettles, John Barnwell *obstetrics and gynecology educator*

Vinita
Neer, Charles Sumner, II, *orthopedic surgeon, educator*

OREGON

Ashland
Masters, Robert Edward Lee *psychotherapist, neural researcher, human potential educator, philosopher*

Bend
Sabatella, Elizabeth Maria *clinical therapist, educator, mental health facility administrator*

Central Point
Brown, Christopher Patrick *health care administrator, educator*

Coos Bay
Ballinger, Kathryn Annette (Phelps) *mental health counseling executive, consultant*

Corvallis
Engle, Molly *program evaluator, preventive medicine researcher, medical educator*
Hafner-Eaton, Chris *health services researcher, medical educator, policy analyst*

Cove
Kerper, Meike *family violence, sex abuse and addiction educator, consultant*

Forest Grove
Gryde, Carol Joan *occupational therapy educator, administrator*

Milwaukie
Sklovsky, Robert Joel *naturopathic physician, pharmacist, educator*

Portland
Baker, Timothy Alan *healthcare administrator, educator, consultant*
Jacob, Stanley Wallace *surgeon, educator*
Kohler, Peter Ogden *physician, educator, university president*
Korb, Christine Ann *music therapist, researcher, educator*
Morton, William Edwards *environmental epidemiology educator, occupational medicine specialist*
Riddle, Matthew C(asey) *physician, educator*
Saslow, George *psychiatrist, educator*
Vines, Diane Welch *psychotherapist, educator*

PENNSYLVANIA

Acme
Babcock, Marguerite Lockwood *addictions treatment therapist, educator, writer*

Allentown
Adamshick, Pamela Zenz *nursing educator*
Berman, Muriel Mallin *optometrist, humanities lecturer*

Altoona
Youshaw, Dennis Gordon *surgeon, educator*

Annville
Scott, Ronald William *educator, physical therapist, lawyer, writer*

Bellefonte
Kelley, Earl W., Jr., *managed care administrator*

Boyertown
Dickey, Susan B. *nursing educator*

Bryn Mawr
Price, Trevor Robert Pryce *psychiatrist, educator*

Camp Hill
Pendrak, Robert Francis *internist, insurance company executive*

Clearfield
Boykiw, Norma Severne *nutritionist, educator, retired nutritionist*

Easton
Grunberg, Robert Leon Willy *nephrologist, educator*

Erie
Michaelides, Doros Nikita *internist, medical educator*

Factoryville
Simmons, Ruth Doris *retired women's health nurse, educator*

Fallsington
Wellman, Bonnie Waddell *school nurse, educator, substance abuse counselor*

Forty Fort
Buczynski, Mary Frances *speech therapist*

Hanover
Davis, Ruth Carol *pharmacy educator*

Harrisburg
Chernicoff, David Paul *osteopathic physician, educator*

Haverford
Aronson, Carl Edward *pharmacology and toxicology educator*

Home
Worzbyt, John Charles *counseling education educator*

Indiana
Nelson, Linda Shearer *child development and family relations educator*

Johnstown
Schultz, Carolyn Joyce *nursing educator*

Kennett Square
Mather, Elizabeth G. Tiffany *occupational therapist, educator*

Lancaster
Brod, Roy David *ophthalmologist, educator*
Falk, Robert Barclay, Jr., *anesthesiologist, educator*

Loretto
Sackin, Claire *retired social work educator*

Malvern
Stuckey, Susan Jane *perioperative nurse, consultant*

Merion Station
Lewis, Paul Le Roy *pathology educator*

Myerstown
Corby, Joy E(lizabeth) *psychotherapist, educator, marriage and family therapist*

Narberth
Comer, Nathan Lawrence *psychiatrist, educator*
Strom, Brian Leslie *internist, educator*

New Tripoli
Hess, Darla Bakersmith *cardiologist, educator*

Newtown Square
Sacks, Susan Bendersky *mental health clinical specialist, educator*

Norristown
Steinberg, Arthur Irwin *periodontist, educator*
Tornetta, Frank Joseph *anesthesiologist, educator, consultant*

Oakmont
Balog, Theresa Gallagher *nursing educator*

Philadelphia
Aiken, Linda Harman *nurse, sociologist, educator*
Austrian, Robert *physician, educator, department chairman*
Bagley, Demetrius H. *urologist, educator, researcher*
Barchi, Robert Lawrence *clinical neurologist, neuroscientist, educator*
Barker, Clyde Frederick *surgeon, educator*
Beck, Sharon Ellen *nursing educator, nursing administrator*
Butler, Marie Gladys *nursing educator*
Chu, Mon-Li Hsiung *dermatology educator*
Cooper, Edward Sawyer *cardiologist, internist, educator*
Dalinka, Murray Kenneth *radiologist, educator*
Dasgupta, Indranil *physician, educator*
Doty, Richard L. *medical researcher*
García, Celso-Ramón *obstetrician, gynecologist, educator*
Gault, Janice Ann *ophthalmologist, educator*
Gerner, Edward William *medical educator*
Glick, John H. *oncologist, medical educator*
Jensh, Ronald Paul *anatomist, educator*
Johnson, Mark Paul *obstetrics and gynecology educator, geneticist*
Kaji, Hideko *pharmacology educator*
Kaye, Robert *pediatrics educator*
Kefalides, Nicholas Alexander *physician, educator*
Kelley, William Nimmons *physician, educator, science administrator, dean*
Kotler, Ronald Lee *physician, educator*
Manson, Lionel Arnold *immunology educator, researcher*
Marino, Ignazio Roberto *transplant surgeon, educator, researcher*
Miyamoto, Curtis Trent *medical educator*
Myers, Allen Richard *rheumatologist*
Pappas, Charles Nicholas, III, *dentist, educator*
Piccolo, Joseph Anthony *hospital administrator*
Pyeritz, Reed Edwin *medical geneticist, educator, research director*
Reinhardt, Eleanor Hollister *nursing educator*
Rollins, Diann E. *nurse, primary school educator*
Rubin, Stephen Curtis *gynecologic oncologist, educator*
Rustgi, Anil K (umar) *gastroenterologist, educator*
Salganicoff, Leon *pharmacology educator*
Savage, Michael Paul *medicine educator, interventional cardiologist*
Schwartz, Gordon Francis *surgeon, educator*
Segal, Bernard Louis *physician, educator*
Smith, David Stuart *anesthesiology educator, physician*
Solomon, Phyllis Linda *social work educator, researcher*
Steinberg, Janet DeBerry *optometrist, educator, researcher*
Strauss, Jerome Frank, III, *physician, educator*
Stunkard, Albert James *psychiatrist, educator*
Vanarsdall, Robert Lee, Jr., *orthodontist, educator*
Walinsky, Paul *cardiology educator*
Wenger, Sidney U. *psychiatrist, educator*
Zimmerman, Michael Raymond *pathology educator, anthropologist*

Phoenixville
Seiderman, Arthur Stanley *optometrist, consultant, author*

Pittsburgh
Bruno, Audrei Ann *nurse educator, administrator*
Cockerham, Kimberly Peele *ophthalmologist, educator*
Constantino-Bana, Rose Eva *nursing educator, researcher, lawyer*
Gallagher, Patricia Hirsch *nurse, educator*
Gorr, Elaine Gray *therapist, elementary education educator*
Grufferman, Seymour *medical educator, researcher*
Levenson, David Jeffrey *nephrologist, educator*
Mitchell, Ann Margaret *nursing educator, psychiatric nurse practitioner*
Perel, James Maurice *pharmacology and psychiatry educator, researcher*
Pistella, Christine Ley *public health educator*
Pollock, Bruce Godfrey *psychiatrist, educator*
Price, Fredric Victor *physician, educator, medical researcher*
Scott, C. Paul *psychiatrist, educator*
Stanger, Robert Henry *psychiatrist, educator*
Suzuki, Jon Byron *medical educator, periodontist, microbiologist*
Tobon, Hector *gynecologic pathologist, educator*
Vogel, Victor Gerald *medical educator, researcher*
Watters, Edmond Clair *ophthalmologist, educator*
Wettstein, Robert Mark *psychiatrist, educator*

Radnor
Giordano, Antonio *medical educator*

Rydal
Kolodner, Ellen Jayne Lichtenstein *occupational therapy manager and educator*

State College
Wilson, Keith B. *rehabilitation educator*

University Park
Rolls, Barbara Jean *nutritionist, educator, director*

Wynnewood
Alter, Milton *neurologist, educator*
Frankl, William Stewart *cardiologist, educator*
Marks, Gerald *surgeon, educator*

Yardley
Somma, Beverly Kathleen *medical and marriage educator*

Youngwood
Gediminskas, Rebecca Ann *critical care nurse, nurse educator*

RHODE ISLAND

North Providence
Stankiewicz, Andrzej Jerzy *physician, biochemistry educator*

Pawtucket
Crowley, James Patrick *hematologist, medical educator, immunologist*
Poses, Roy Maurice *physician, educator*

Providence
Biron, Christine Anne *medical science educator, researcher*
Crisafulli, Frederick Salvatore *internist, educator*
Kane, Steven Michael *psychotherapist, educator*
Metrey, George David *social work educator, academic administrator*
Shetty, Taranath *neurologist, educator*
Vezeridis, Michael Panagiotis *surgeon, educator*

SOUTH CAROLINA

Aiken
Bransome, Edwin Dagobert, Jr., *internal medicine educator*
Voss, Terence J. *human factors scientist, educator*

Anderson
Pruitt, Rosanne Harkey *nursing educator, human services researcher*

Charleston
Beale, Mark Douglas *psychiatrist, educator*
Dorman, B(ruce) Hugh *anesthesiologist, educator*
Lavelle, Mary Lee Demetre *psychiatric nursing educator*
Lutz, Myron Howard *obstetrician, gynecologist, surgeon, educator*
Oldham, John Michael *physician, psychiatrist, educator*
Osguthorpe, John David *otolaryngologist, educator*
Othersen, Henry Biemann, Jr., *pediatric surgeon, physician, educator*
Reves, Joseph Gerald *dean, anesthesiology educator*
Simson, Jo Anne *retired anatomy and cell biology educator, biologist, educator*
Stine, Gordan Bernard *dentist, educator*
Willi, Steven Matthew *physician, educator, researcher*
Wilson, Diane Baer *health educator, dietitian, cancer prevention researcher*

Columbia
Ballington, Don Avell *medical educator*
Brannon, William Lester, Jr., *neurologist, educator*
Donald, Alexander Grant *psychiatrist, educator*
Flanagan, Clyde Harvey, Jr., *psychiatrist, psychoanalyst, educator*
Fowler, Linda McKeever *hospital administrator, management educator*
Hwang, Te-Long *neurologist, educator*
Kowalski, Timothy Joseph *child and adolescent psychiatrist, educator*
Lin, Tu *endocrinologist, educator, researcher, academic administrator*

Conway
Nale, Julia Ann *nursing educator*

Easley
Howe, Linda Arlene *nursing educator, writer*

Edisto Island
Cooper, William Allen, Jr., *audiologist, educator*

Greenville
Bonner, Jack Wilbur, III, *psychiatrist, educator, administrator*
Davis, Maureen Flynn *nursing educator, administrator*

Hilton Head Island
Kearney-Nunnery, Rose *nursing administrator, educator, consultant*

Lake City
Mims, Albert Durant *physician, educator*

Myrtle Beach
Killian, Greg *mental health services professional*

Pendleton
Fehler, Polly Diane *neonatal nurse, educator*

Spartanburg
Carson, Beth H. *nursing educator*
Chauhan, Suneet Bhushan *medical educator*

SOUTH DAKOTA

Aberdeen
Washnok, Marguerite Barondeau *nursing educator*

Brookings
Singh, Yadhu Nand *pharmacology educator, researcher*

Rapid City
Foland, Kay Lynn *nurse therapist, nursing educator*

Sioux Falls
Tilstra, Sally Ann *computer information systems educator, clinical laboratory scientist*
Zawada, Edward Thaddeus, Jr., *physician, educator*

TENNESSEE

Alcoa
Lucas, Melinda Ann *pediatrician, educator*

Bristol
Moore, Marilyn Patricia *community counselor*

Chattanooga
Holmes, Everlena McDonald *health science administrator, consultant, retired dean*

Cookeville
Musacchio, Marilyn Jean *nurse midwife, educator, administrator*

Johnson City
Raidl, Martha Anne *nutrition and dietetics educator, dietitian*

Knoxville
Filston, Howard Church *pediatric surgeon, educator*
Lee, Jan Louise *nursing educator*
McGuire, Sandra Lynn *nursing educator*

Memphis
Cannito, Michael Phillip *speech language pathologist, educator*
Cowan, George Sheppard Marshall, Jr., *surgeon, educator, research administrator*
Dagogo-Jack, Samuel E. *medical educator, physician scientist, endocrinologist*
Fields, W(ade) Thomas *dental educator*
Heimberg, Murray *pharmacologist, biochemist, physician, educator*
Huget, Eugene Floyd *dental educator, researcher*
Mirvis, David Marc *health administrator, cardiologist, educator*
Pui, Ching-Hon *hematologist, oncologist, educator*
Tutko, Robert Joseph *law enforcement officer, radiology administrator*
Van Arsdale, Stephanie Kay Lorenz *cardiovascular clinical specialist, nursing educator, researcher*

Milligan College
Fabick, Mary Marie *medical and surgical and emergency nurse, educator*

Nashville
Bates, George William *obstetrician, gynecologist, educator, medical products executive*
Brown, Wendy Weinstock *nephrologist, educator*
Byrne, Daniel William *biostatistician, educator*
Jones, Evelyn Gloria *medical technologist, educator*
Parker, John Randolph *pathologist, educator*
Riley, Harris DeWitt, Jr., *pediatrician, medical educator*
Ross, Joseph Comer *physician, educator, academic administrator*
Thornton, Spencer P. *ophthalmologist, educator*

New Tazewell
Money, Max Lee *family nurse practitioner*

TEXAS

Abilene
Godsey, Martha Sue *speech-language pathologist*
Morrison, Shirley Marie *nursing educator*

Amarillo
Bohachef, Janet Mae *medical educator*

Arlington
Adams, Phyllis Curl *nursing educator*
Rugari, Susan Marie *medical/surgical nurse, nursing educator*

Austin
Austin, John Riley *surgeon, educator*
Dlabal, Paul William *cardiologist, educator*
Hayes, Patricia Ann *health facility administrator*
Johnson, Mildred Snowden *retired nursing educator*
Martin, Frederick Noel *audiology educator*
Richardson, Betty Kehl *nursing educator, administrator, counselor, researcher*
Werner, Gerhard *pharmacologist, psychoanalyst, educator*

Beaumont
Phan, Tâm Thanh *medical educator, psychotherapist, consultant, researcher*
Tucker, Gary Wilson *nursing educator*

Bryan
Dirks, Kenneth Ray *pathologist, medical educator, army officer*

Castroville
Strickland, Sandra Jean Heinrich *nursing educator*

College Station
Potter, Charlotte Ann *health education educator, physical education educator*

Corpus Christi
Gaylor, James Leroy *biomedical research educator*
Kirksey, Kenn M. *nursing educator*
Lim, Alexander Rufasta *neurologist, clinical investigator, clinical neurophysiologist, educator, writer*
Stetina, Pamela Eleanor *nursing educator*

Dallas
Anderson-Cermin, Cheryl Kay *orthodontics, educator*
Bashour, Fouad Anis *cardiology educator*
Bick, Rodger Lee *hematologist, oncologist, researcher, educator*
Byrd, Ellen Stoesser *school nurse administrator*
Dietschy, John Maurice *gastroenterologist, educator*
Eden, Becky DeSpain *dental educator*
Emmett, Michael *physician, educator*
Friedberg, Errol Clive *pathology educator, researcher*
Fyfe, Alistair Ian *cardiologist, scientist, educator*
Harrington, John Norris *ophthalmic plastic and reconstructive surgeon, educator*
Homan, Richard Warren *neurologist, academic administrator, medical educator*
Hurd, Eric Ray *rheumatologist, internist, educator*
Johnson, Robert Lee, Jr., *physician, educator, researcher*
Maddrey, Willis Crocker *medical educator, internist, academic administrator, consultant, researcher*
McGregor, Scott Duncan *optometrist, educator*
Nieswiadomy, Rose Marie *nursing educator, researcher*
Parkey, Robert Wayne *radiology and nuclear medicine educator, research radiologist*
Race, George Justice *pathology educator*
Rohrich, Rodney James *plastic surgeon, educator*
Romero, Jorge Antonio *neurologist, educator*
Simon, Theodore Ronald *physician, medical educator*
Southern, Paul Morris, Jr., *internist, educator, microbiologist*
Stone, Marvin Jules *physician, educator*
Weiner, Myron Frederick *psychiatrist, educator, clinical investigator*
Wildenthal, C(laud) Kern *physician, educator*

Denton
Cissell, William Bernard *health studies educator*

Edinburg
Nieto, Beatriz Chavez *nursing educator*

El Paso
Mitchell, Paula Rae *nursing educator, college dean*
Tomita, Tatsuo *pathologist, educator, diabetes researcher*

Fort Sam Houston
Gordon, Ella Dean *health and nurse educator, women's health and orthopedic nurse*

Fort Worth
Bowling, John Robert *osteopathic physician, educator, academic administrator*
Brooks, Lloyd William, Jr., *osteopath, interventional cardiologist, educator*
Curry, Linda Carolyn *nursing educator*
McNairn, Peggi Jean *speech pathologist, educator*
Siede, Wolfram *research scientist*
Strength, Danna Elliott *retired nursing educator*
Willard, Ralph Lawrence *surgery educator, physician, former college president*

Galveston
Dawson, Earl Bliss *obstetrics and gynecology educator*
Dinh, Tung Van *obstetrician, gynecologist, pathologist, educator*
Heggers, John Paul *surgery, immunology, microbiology educator*
James, Thomas Naum *cardiologist, educator*
Kvale, Janice Keller *nurse-midwifery educator*
Lefeber, Edward James, Sr., *medical educator, physician*
McKendall, Robert Roland *neurologist, virologist, educator*
Xiao, Shu-Yuan *medical educator*

Garland
Varnon, Suzanne *speech language pathologist*

Georgetown
Sawyer, William Dale *physician, educator, university dean, foundation administrator*

Houston
Alford, Bobby Ray *physician, educator, university official*
Bahl, Saroj Mehta *nutritionist, educator*
Barcenas, Camilo Gustavo *physician*
Barrett, Bernard Morris, Jr., *plastic and reconstructive surgeon*
Bast, Robert Clinton, Jr., *medical researcher, medical educator*
Bedikian, Agop Y. *internist, oncologist, educator*
Bevers, Therese Bartholomew *physician, medical educator*
Bodey, Gerald Paul *medical educator, physician*
Borromeo, Annabelle R *critical care nurse, educator, consultant*
Caggins, Ruth Porter *nursing educator*
Casscells, Samuel Ward, III, *cardiologist, educator*
Conrad, Charles A. *neurologist, neuro-oncologist*
Corriere, Joseph N., Jr., *urologist, educator*
Davis-Lewis, Bettye *nursing educator*
DeBakey, Michael Ellis *cardiovascular surgeon, educator, scientist*
Dominguez, Patricia Brown *nursing educator*
Dunbar, Burdett Sheridan *anesthesiologist, pediatrician, educator*
Duvic, Madeleine *dermatologist, educator, scientist*
Engelhardt, Hugo Tristram, Jr., *physician, educator*
Entman, Mark Lawrence *cardiologist, biomedical scientist, educator*
Ertan, Atilla *medical educator, physician, researcher, health facility administrator*
Gibson, Kathleen Rita *anatomy and anthropology educator*
Glassman, Armand Barry *physician, pathologist, scientist, educator, administrator*
Gleason, Wallace Anselm, Jr., *medical educator and researcher*
Goldman, Stanford Milton *medical educator*
Hall, Robert Joseph *physician, medical educator*
Hrna, Daniel Joseph *pharmacist, lawyer*
Hsu, Katharine Han Kuang *pediatrics educator*
Ingersoll, Maryann E. Patterson *health educator, holistic nurse*
Jankovic, Joseph *neurologist, educator, scientist*
Jenkins, Daniel Edwards, Jr., *retired physician, educator*
Jordan, Paul Howard, Jr., *surgeon, educator*
Kaplan, Alan Leslie *gynecology educator, oncologist*
Kavanagh, John Joseph *medical educator*
Kelly, Dorothy Helen *pediatrician, educator*
Lavis, Victor Ralph *internist, educator*
Layne, Charles Shannon *medical educator*
Low, Morton David *physician, educator, policy consultant*
Lynch, Edward Conover *hematologist, educator*
Marshall, Gailen Daugherty, Jr., *physician, scientist, educator*
McKechnie, John Charles *gastroenterologist, educator*
Raijman, Isaac *gastroenterologist, endoscopist, educator*
Rapini, Ronald Peter *dermatology educator*
Ross, Patti Jayne *obstetrics and gynecology educator*
Rudolph, Andrew Henry *dermatologist, educator*
Schachtel, Barbara Harriet Levin *epidemiologist, educator*
Schoolar, Joseph Clayton *psychiatrist, pharmacologist, educator*
Vassilopoulou-Sellin, Rena *clinician investigator*
Weyandt, Linda Jane *physician, educator, anesthesiologist*
Yeoman, Lynn Chalmers *medical educator*
Yi, Jenny Kisuk *public health educator*

Irving
Watley, Martha Jones *health and social services association executive*

Keene
Adams, Lavonne Marilyn Beck *critical care nurse, nursing educator*

Keller
Hewlett, Sandra Marie *clinical consultant*

Killeen
Perry, John Wesley, Sr., *psychotherapist*

Lubbock
Beck, George Preston *anesthesiologist, educator*
Kurtzman, Neil A. *medical educator*
Partlow, Shara Sue *nursing educator*

Lufkin
Dean, Odell Joseph, Jr., *urologist, educator*

Magnolia
Girard, Louis Joseph *ophthalmologist, educator*

Midland
Sullivan, Patricia G. *maternal, child and women's health nursing educator*

Missouri City
Chang, Jeffrey Chai *dentist, educator, researcher*

Pampa
Lane, Jerry Ross *alcohol and drug abuse service counselor*

Pasadena
Mullins, Jack Allen *cardiologist, educator*
Stahl, Charlyn Beth *medical educator*

Rockport
Acker, Virginia Margaret *nursing educator*

San Antonio
Hall, Brad Bailey *orthopaedic surgeon, health care administrator*
Hawken, Patty Lynn *retired nursing educator, dean of faculty*
Langland, Olaf Elmer *retired dental educator*
Munoz, Ricardo, Jr., *obstetrician-gynecologist, educator*
Neel, Spurgeon Hart, Jr., *physician, retired army officer*
Nguyen, Vung Duy *radiologist, educator*
O'Rourke, Robert A. *cardiologist, educator*
Piest, Kenneth Lee *ophthalmic plastic surgeon, educator*
Pigno, Mark Anthony *prosthodontist, educator, researcher*
Rebolledo, Jose Rafael *pediatrician, educator*
Reuter, Stewart Ralston *retired radiologist, lawyer, educator*
Riddle, Katharine Parker *nutrition educator*
Schneider, Frank David *family physician*
Swansburg, Russell Chester *medical administrator educator*
Townsend, Frank Marion *pathology educator*
Walsh, Nicolas Eugene *rehabilitation medicine physician, educator*

San Marcos
Mooney, Robert Thurston *health care educator*
Watkins, Ted Ross *social work educator*

Seabrook
Patten, Bernard Michael *neurologist, writer, educator*

Sherman
Sikes, Connie Sue Bond *nursing educator*

Temple
Dyck, Walter Peter *gastroenterologist, educator, university official*
Holleman, Vernon Daughty *physician, internist*

Tow
Shepherd, Elizabeth Poole *health science facility administrator*

Whitney
Williams, Margaret Lu Wertha Hiett *nurse*

Willis
Rappaport, Martin Paul *internist, nephrologist, educator*

UTAH

Orem
Sauter, Gail Louise *speech pathologist*

Park City
Carmichael, Paul Louis *ophthalmic surgeon*

Salt Lake City
Bauer, A(ugust) Robert, Jr., *surgeon, medical educator*
Burke, John Patrick *internist, educator*
Kanner, Richard Elliot *physician, educator*
Middleton, Anthony Wayne, Jr., *urologist, educator*
Moser, Royce, Jr., *physician, medical educator*
Murtaugh, Maureen Ann *nutrition educator*
Nelson, Russell Marion *surgeon, educator*
Parkin, James Lamar *otolaryngologist, educator*
Vanderhooft, Jan Eric *orthopedic surgeon, educator*
Ward, John Robert *physician, educator*
Wheeler, Richard Herbert, III, *oncologist, educator*

Smithfield
Burris, Ann *nursing educator*

VERMONT

Burlington
Prelock, Patricia A. *speech pathologist*

Dorset
Bamford, Joseph Charles, Jr., *gynecologist, obstetrician, educator, medical missionary, writer*

Lyndon Center
Boykin, Catherine Marie *health care administrator, educator*

Norwich
Mills, Letha Elaine *physician, educator*

Randolph
Sax, Daniel Saul *neurologist, educator*

VIRGINIA

Alexandria
Buhain, Wilfrido Javier *medical educator*
Mullen, Charles Frederick *health educator*

Annandale
Greenspan, Valeda Clareen *nursing educator*

Arlington
Sanchez, Janice Patterson *psychotherapist, educator*

Blacksburg
Baudoin, Antonius B. A. M. *plant pathologist, educator*

Charlottesville
Carey, Robert Munson *medical educator, physician*
Chevalier, Robert Louis *pediatric nephrologist, educator, researcher*
Dalton, Claudette Ellis Harloe *anesthesiologist, educator, university official*
Gross, Charles Wayne *physician, educator*
Hostler, Sharon Lee *pediatrics educator, rehabilitation center executive*
Pate, Robert Hewitt, Jr., *counselor educator*
Woode, Moses Kwamena Annan *medical and chemistry educator, scientist*

Colonial Heights
Crowder, Dorothy Sholes *nursing educator*

Fairfax
Knee, Ruth Irelan (Mrs. Junior K. Knee) *social worker, health care consultant*
Robertson, Patricia Aileen *adult and geriatric nurse practitioner*

Fredericksburg
Nelson Sargeant, Susan Marie *speech pathology/audiology services professional*

Keswick
Johansen, Eivind Herbert *special education services executive, former army officer*

Lexington
DeSilvey, Dennis Lee *cardiologist, educator, university administrator*

Mc Lean
Cuffe, Robin Jean *nursing educator*
Obrien, Barbara Ann *speech and language pathologist*

Monterey
Tabatznik, Bernard *retired physician, educator*

Nassawadox
Fisher, Ramona Faye *hospital child care center administrator*

Norfolk
Davis, Russell Haden *consultant*
Evett, Russell Dougherty *internist, educator*
Oelberg, David George *neonatologist, educator, researcher*

North Garden
Moses, Hamilton, III, *medical educator, hospital executive, management consultant*

Radford
Carter, Kimberly Ferren *nursing educator*
Scartelli, Joseph Paul *music therapy educator, dean*
Southern, Ann Gayle *nurse, educator*

Reston
Schwartz, David Taylor *urologist, educator*

Richmond
Bentley, Kia Jean *social worker, educator*
Gandy, Gerald Larmon *rehabilitation counseling educator, psychologist, writer*
Hardy, Richard Earl *rehabilitation counseling educator*
Kaplowitz, Lisa Glauser *physician, educator*
Laskin, Daniel M. *oral and maxillofacial surgeon, educator*
Neal, Marcus Pinson, Jr., *radiologist, medical educator*
Seeds, John William *obstetrician-gynecologist, educator*
Sirica, Alphonse Eugene *pathology educator*
Small, Ralph Edward *pharmacy educator, consultant*
Thompson, William Taliaferro, Jr., *internist, educator*

Roanoke
Dagenhart, Betty Jane Mahaffey *nursing educator, administrator*

Salem
Chakravorty, Ranes Chandra *surgeon, educator*

Sterling
Block, Robert Michael *endodontist, educator, researcher*

Suffolk
Carroll, George Joseph *pathologist, educator*

Virginia Beach
Lawrence, Joyce Wagner *health facility administrator, educator*
Wilson, Angela Saburn *nursing educator*

Williamsburg
Maloney, Milford Charles *retired internal medicine educator*

Winchester
Billeter, Marianne *pharmacy educator*

WASHINGTON

Bellevue
Bender, Maurice *health science administrator, consultant*

Bothell
Weiden, Paul Lincoln *cancer researcher, oncologist, educator*

Coupeville
Mayhew, Eric George *medical researcher, educator*

Federal Way
Mail, Patricia Davison *public health specialist*

Issaquah
Duncan, Elizabeth Charlotte *retired marriage and family therapist, educational therapist, educator*

Marysville
Steele, Sandra Elaine Noel *nursing educator*

Pullman
Chermak, Gail Donna *audiologist, speech and hearing sciences educator*

Seattle
Aldea, Gabriel S. *cardiothoracic surgeon, educator*
Benson, Karen A. *nursing educator*
Cardenas, Diana Delia *physician, educator*
Day, Robert Winsor *preventive medicine physician, researcher*
Dear, Ronald Bruce *social work educator*
Dorpat, Theodore Lorenz *psychoanalyst*
Freeman, Melvin Irwin *ophthalmic surgeon, educator, municipal official*
Hackman, Robert Cordell *pathology educator, researcher*
Halar, Eugen Marian *physiatrist, educator*
Henshaw, Christine Marie *nursing educator*
Herring, Susan Weller *dental educator, oral anatomist*
Hickok, Lee Richard *obstetrician, gynecologist, educator*
Karl, Helen Weist *pediatric anesthesia and pain management educator, researcher*
Kolbeson, Marilyn Hopf *holistic practitioner, educator, artist, advertising executive*
Kozarek, Richard Anthony *gastroenterologist, educator*

Krohn, Kenneth Albert *radiology educator*
Martin, George M. *pathologist, gerontologist, educator*
Neff, John Michael *health facility administrator, educator, dean*
Nicholls, Stephen Charles *surgeon, educator*
Pagon, Roberta Anderson *pediatrics educator*
Petersdorf, Robert George *physician, medical educator, academic administrator*
Plorde, James Joseph *physician, educator*
Reichenbach, Dennis Dale *physician, pathology educator*
Swanson, August George *physician, retired association executive*
Thompson, Arlene Rita *nursing educator*
Woods, Susan Louise *nursing educator*

Seaview
McNeil, Helen Jo Connolly *nursing educator, public health administrator*

Shoreline
Merendino, K. Alvin *surgical educator*

Spokane
Cope, Kathleen Adelaide *critical care and parish nurse, educator*
Robinson, Herbert Henry, III, *educator, psychotherapist*
Shogan, Maureen Gordon *clinical nurse specialist, nursing consultant*
Valdez, Maria del Rosario *perinatal nurse, educator*

Tacoma
Fought, Sharon Gavin *nursing educator*
Maloney, Patsy Loretta *nursing educator*

WEST VIRGINIA

Charleston
Ukoha, Ozuru Ochu *surgeon, educator*
Zangeneh, Fereydoun *pediatrics educator, pediatric endocrinologist*

Gap Mills
Henry, Cynthia Ann *retired gerontology nurse, educator*

Huntington
Brown, Bruce Joseph *medical technology educator*
Cocke, William Marvin, Jr., *plastic surgeon, educator*

Lewisburg
Mazzio-Moore, Joan L. *radiology educator, physician*

Morgantown
Hill, Ronald Charles *surgeon, educator*
Leslie, Nan S. *nursing educator, womens' health nurse*
Li, Qingdi Quentin *physician, research scientist, medical educator*
Ponte, Charles Dennis *pharmacist, educator*
Sikora, Rosanna Dawn *emergency physician, educator*

WISCONSIN

Brookfield
Scheving, Lawrence Einar *anatomy educator, scientist*

Jackson
Hoffmann, Marlene Ethel *rehabilitation administrator*

Madison
Brooks, Benjamin Rix *neurologist, educator*
Leavitt, Lewis A. *pediatrician, medical educator*
Owen, Bernice Doyle *nursing educator*
Pitot, Henry Clement, III, *pathologist, educator*

Mequon
Mandel, Trudy Ann *medical/surgical nurse, theology studies educator*

Milwaukee
Effros, Richard Matthew *medical educator, physician*
Feinsilver, Donald Lee *psychiatry educator*
Morris, George L. *neurologist, educator*
Rodgers, Beth L. *nursing educator, researcher*
Terry, Leon Cass *neurologist, educator*
Wagner, Marvin *general and vascular surgeon, educator*
Waller, Mary Bellis *psychotherapist, education educator, consultant*
White-Winters, Jill Mary *nursing educator*

Nekoosa
Hamin, Amy Lynn *speech and language pathologist*

Oak Creek
Kim, Zaezeung *allergist, immunologist, educator*

Oconomowoc
Schacht, Ruth Elaine *nursing educator*

Oshkosh
Cooper, Janelle Lunette *neurologist, educator*
Wells, Carolyn Cressy *social work educator*

Verona
Stein, Michael Alan *cardiologist, medical educator*

WYOMING

Casper
Boyer, Patricia Ann *social worker, educator*

Ethete
Tepper, Marcy Elizabeth *drug education director*

TERRITORIES OF THE UNITED STATES

PUERTO RICO

Aguada
Vélez-Juarbe, Luis Antonio *industrial pharmacy educator*

Mayaguez
Sahai, Hardeo *medical statistics educator*

San Juan
Ghaly, Evone Shehata *pharmaceutics and industrial pharmacy educator*

CANADA

ALBERTA

Edmonton
Kumar, Shrawan *university educator physical therapy, ergonomics consultant*
Oberg, Lyle *physician, academic administrator*

BRITISH COLUMBIA

West Vancouver
Knauff, Hans Georg *physician, educator*

MANITOBA

Winnipeg
Persaud, Trivedi Vidhya Nandan *anatomy educator, researcher, consultant*

ONTARIO

Burlington
MacLeod, Stuart Maxwell *health science administrator, educator, pharmacologist, physician*

London
Dunn, Wesley John *dental educator*

Markham
Calkin, Joy Durfée *healthcare executive, consultant, educator*

Toronto
Eisenberg, Howard Edward *physician, psychotherapist, consultant, educator, writer*
Hindmarsh, Kenneth Wayne *pharmacy dean, educator*
Page, Linda Jewel *professional coaching and mental health care educator*
San, Nguyen Duy *psychiatrist, educator*

Windsor
Ferguson, John Duncan *medical research educator*

QUEBEC

Montpellier
Poirier, Louis Joseph *neurology educator*

Montreal
Clermont, Yves Wilfrid *anatomy educator, researcher*
Goltzman, David *endocrinologist, educator, researcher*

BELGIUM

Brussels
Rombouts, Jean Jacques *orthopaedic surgery educator, dean*

BULGARIA

Varna
Belcheva, Anna Beronova *pharmacology educator*

CHINA

Guangzhou
Li, Jing Rong *neurosurgeon, educator, consultant*

FRANCE

Saint Priest en Jarez
Gilloz, André-Pierre *urologist, educator*

GERMANY

Mannheim
Gattaz, Wagner Farid *psychiatry educator*

ISRAEL

Givatayim
Kornel, Ludwig *medical educator, physician, scientist*

ITALY

Firenze
Buffoni, Franca *pharmacology educator*

Perugia
Corea, Luigi *cardiologist, educator*

JAPAN

Aichi
Toyama, Hiroshi *radiologist, educator*

NETHERLANDS

Amsterdam
Prahl-Andersen, Birte *orthodontics educator*

NIGERIA

Enugu
Ozumba, Benjamin Chukwuma *obstetrician, gynecologist*

Ibadan
Grillo, Isaac Adetayo *surgery educator, consultant*

REPUBLIC OF KOREA

Gwangju
Hwang, Hyeon-Shik *orthodontist, educator, dean*

ADDRESS UNPUBLISHED

Abbott, Regina A. *neurodiagnostic technologist, consultant, business owner*
Abdullaev, Yalchin *neuroscientist, physician, educator*
Adekson, Mary Olufunmilayo *therapist, counselor educator*
Adisman, I. Kenneth *prosthodontist, educator*
Ambrosi, Sandra Elizabeth *retired nurse, educator*
Applebaum, Edward Leon *otolaryngologist, educator*
Armstrong, Edward Bradford, Jr., *oral and maxillofacial surgeon, educator*
Barker, Virginia Lee *nursing educator*
Bass, Lynda D. *retired medical/surgical nurse, retired nursing educator*
Beattie, Edward James *surgeon, educator*
Becker, Bruce Carl, II, *physician, educator, health facility administrator*
Begley, Nan Elizabeth *psychotherapist, psychology educator*
Benz, Edward John, Jr., *physician, educator*
Berger, Miriam Roskin *creative arts therapy director, educator, therapist*
Berlin, Fred Saul *psychiatrist, educator*
Biegel, David Eli *social worker, educator*
Blau, Helen Margaret *molecular pharmacology educator*
Bloom, Eugene Charles *gastroenterologist, educator*
Braun, Mary Lucile Dekle (Lucy Braun) *therapist, consultant, counselor, educator*
Brem, Andrew Samuel *pediatric nephrologist, educator*
Brown, Warnella Charlie *speech and language pathologist*
Bryant, Gail Annette Grippen *nurse, educator*
Bullough, Vern LeRoy *sexologist, historian, nursing educator, researcher*
Burakoff, Steven James *immunologist, educator*
Cabanas, Elizabeth Ann *nutritionist, educator*
Canarina, Opal Jean *nurse, administrator, educator, consultant, lecturer*
Carson, Mary Silvano *career counselor, educator*
Carson, Regina E. *healthcare administrator, geriatric specialist, pharmacist, educator*
Carter, Frances Monet *nursing educator*
Casamento, Maria M. *speech pathology/audiology services professional, special education educator*
Cash, Deanna Gail *retired nursing educator*
Cason, Nica Virginia *nursing educator*
Castro, Maria Graciela *medical educator, geneticist, researcher*
Charalambous, Susan F. *nursing educator, consultant*
Cheah, Keong-Chye *psychiatrist, educator*
Chin, Hong Woo *oncologist, educator, researcher*
Chin, Jennifer Young *public health educator*
Chorpenning, Frank Winslow *immunology educator, researcher*
Chung, Ed B(aik) *pathologist, educator*
Claudio, Manuel P.A. *medical educator, health facility administrator*
Clemendor, Anthony Arnold *obstetrician, gynecologist, educator*
Clyde, Wallace Alexander, Jr., *pediatrics and microbiology educator*
Conley, Susan Bernice *medical school faculty pediatrician*
Cooper, Eugene Bruce *speech, language pathologist, educator*
Cooper, Signe Skott *retired nurse educator*
Cory, Miriam Elaine *speech and language pathologist, retired*
Dalessandri, Kathie Marie *surgeon, educator*
Davis, Ada Romaine *nursing educator*
Davis, Erlynne P. *social work educator*
Dawson, Karen Oltmanns *nursing educator*
Degann, Sona Irene *obstetrician, gynecologist, educator*
Diana, Joanne Mercedes *retired medical/surgical nurse, nursing educator*
Diorio, Eileen Patricia *retired medical technologist, philosophy educator*
Duarte, Cristobal G. *nephrologist, educator*
Duffy, Brian Francis *immunologist, educator*
Dziewanowska, Zofia Elizabeth *neuropsychiatrist, pharmaceutical executive, researcher, educator*
Edelstein, Rosemarie (Rosemarie Hublou) *medical/surgical nurse, educator, medical and legal consultant*
Edwards, Larry David *internist, educator*
Elgart, Mervyn L. *dermatologist, educator*
English, Jujuan Bondman *women's health nurse, educator*
Fein, Adrienne Myra *nursing administrator*
Felgar, Raymond E(ugene) *pathologist, medical educator*
Ferstenfeld, Julian Erwin *internist, educator*
Fine, David Jeffrey *hospital executive, educator, consultant, lecturer*
Fischer, Linda Marie *nursing educator*
Fischman, Gary Joseph *podiatrist, educator*
Fletcher, J. S. *health educator*
Fomon, Samuel Joseph *physician, educator*
Franco, Kenneth Lawrence *surgery educator*
Gable, Karen Elaine *health science educator*
Gabriel, Judith A. *bodywork therapist, educator, writer*
Garza, Cutberto *nutrition educator*
Gilchrist, Gerald Seymour *pediatric hematologist, oncologist, educator*
Giles, Melva Theresa *nursing educator*
Gillett, Patricia *family and acute care nurse practitioner, clinical nurse*
Gilmore, Linda Louise Traywick *nursing educator, educator*
Glass, Dorothea Daniels *physiatrist, educator*
Gonzales, Richard Robert *counselor*
Gordon, Audrey Kramen *healthcare educator*
Gordon, Susan Marquis *researcher*
Graven, Stanley Norman *pediatrician, educator*
Greenfield, Linda Sue *nursing educator*
Griffith, B(ezaleel) Herold *physician, educator, plastic surgeon*
Gupta, Narendra Kumar *physician, educator*
Hall, Mina Elaine *geriatrics nurse*
Handford, H. Allen *retired psychiatrist, educator*
Hansen, Meredith Jane *physician assistant educator*
Hansen-Kyle, Linda L *managed health care nurse, nursing educator*
Harrigan, Rosanne Carol *medical educator*
Hart-Kepler, Virginia Lynn *nurse, educator*
Hartmann, Ruth Annemarie *health care education specialist*
Hayes, Judith *psychotherapist, educator*
Heffelmire, Virginia Ann *school nurse*
Heifner, Carol Joan *social work educator*
Heiner, Douglas Cragun *pediatrician, educator, immunologist, allergist*
Herman, Martin Neal *neurologist, educator*
Hirose, Teruo Terry *surgeon, educator*
Hoeffer, Beverly *nursing educator, researcher*
Hoffman, Jerry Irwin *retired dental educator*
Hooper, Billy Ernest *retired medical association administrator*
Howe, John Prentice, III, *health science center executive, physician*
Howell, Mary Ellen Helms *nursing educator, neonatal nurse*
Huggins, Charles Edward *obstetrician, gynecologist, educator*
Hutcheon, Duncan Elliot *physician, educator*
Illanes, Alejandro Mora *physician, educator, researcher*
Jackson, Jo Anne *speech pathologist*
Jacobs, Arthur Dietrich *educator, researcher, health services executive*
Jacobsen, Egill Lars *dentist, educator*
Jarczynski, Elaine Childs *nurse educator*
Jefferies, William McKendree *internist, educator*
Jenkins, Peggy Jean *nurse educator*
Jensen, Robert Travis *physician, educator, researcher*
Johnson, Barbara Ann *health services educator*
Johnson, John Patrick *neurosurgeon, educator*
Journeay, Glen Eugene *physician, educator*
Kalipolites, June Eleanor Turner *rehabilitation professional*
Kapitan, Mary L. *retired nursing administrator, educator*
Karst, Nancy Joan Shobe *dental hygiene educator*
Kenyon, Elinor Ann *retired social worker*
Kilpatrick, Georgia Lee *nurse educator*
King, Hueston Clark *retired otolaryngologist, educator*
King, Imogene M. *retired nursing educator*
Kirby, Deborah Louanna *nursing administrator*
Knopf, Tana Darlene *counselor, music educator*
Koerber, Marilynn Eleanor *gerontology nursing educator, consultant, nurse*
Kowlessar, Muriel *retired pediatric educator*
Kreutzer, Rita Kay *speech and language pathologist*
Kundel, Harold Louis *radiologist, educator*
Lai, Eric Pong Shing *family physician, educator*
Landgarten, Helen Barbara *art psychotherapist, educator*
Latimer, Margaret Petta *retired nutrition and dietetics educator*
Lauterbach, Edward Charles *psychiatric educator*
LeBlanc, Jeanette Amy *psychotherapist, educator, writer, consultant*
Leonetti, Evangeline Phillips *retired nursing educator*
LeWitt, Michael Herman *physician, educator*
Lim, Shun Ping *cardiologist, educator*
Long-Middleton, Ellen *family nurse practitioner, educator, researcher*
Luddy, Paula Scott *nursing educator*
Luke, Robert George *nephrologist, medical educator*
Makins, James Edward *retired dentist, dental educator, educational administrator*
Mandell, Barbara Deborah *clinical social worker, educator*
Mansergh, Gordon Dwight *health maintenance and prevention researcher*
Markowitz, Phyllis Frances *retired mental health services administrator, psychologist*
Martof, Mary Taylor *retired nursing educator*
Masten, W. Yondell *nursing educator*
Mathews, William Edward *neurological surgeon, educator*
Mattson, Richard Henry *neurologist, educator*
Mayer, Patricia Lynn Sorci *mental health nurse, educator*
McCausland, Catherine Laird *nursing educator*
McDunn, Kathleen Evelyn *nurse, nursing educator*
McGee, Sue *pediatrics nurse, educator, administrator*
McKenna, Richard Henry *consultant*
Meeks, Linda Mae *women's health nurse, educator*
Mendel, Lisa Lucks *audiologist, educator*
Mendez, C. Beatriz *obstetrician, gynecologist, educator, gynecologist, consultant*
Mich, Connie Rita *mental health nurse, educator*
Middleton, Charlene *retired medical and surgical nurse, educator*
Miller, Lillie M. *nursing educator*
Miller-Young, Corriene Calhoun *nursing educator*
Montgomery, John Richard *pediatrician, educator*
Moos, Daniel James *retired surgeon, educator*
Mountain, Clifton Fletcher *surgeon, educator*
Mueller, Charles Barber *surgeon, educator*
Murphy, Margaret A. *nursing educator, adult nurse practitioner*
Napodano, Rudolph Joseph *internist, medical educator*
Nardozzi, Peter Michael *pharmacist, clinical educator, lecturer, entrepreneur*
Nealis, James Garry Thomas, III, *pediatric neurologist, educator, author*
Neiberger, Richard Eugene *pediatrician, nephrologist, educator*
Nelson, William Rankin *surgeon, educator*
Nichols, Carol Jean *nurse educator*
Nicholson, June C. Daniels *retired speech pathologist*
Nora, James Jackson *physician, writer, educator*
Norris, Charley William *retired otolaryngologist, educator*
Nowak, Felicia Veronika *endocrinologist, molecular biologist, educator*
O'Brien, MaryAnn Antoinette *retired nursing educator*
Odell, William Douglas *endocrinologist, educator*
Ongkingco, Florence Kagahastian *health facility educator*
Ortel, Thomas Lee *oncologist, hematologist, educator*
Park, Jon Keith *dentist, educator*
Parker, Carol Tommie *psychotherapist, educator*
Patterson, James Willis *pathology and dermatology educator*
Peeler, Richard Nevin *internist, educator*
Perinelli, Marguerite Rose *women's health nurse, educator*
Pesch, LeRoy Allen *physician, educator, health and hospital consultant, business executive*
Peterson, Veronica Marie (Ronnie Peterson) *clinical nurse manager*
Pinedo, Myrna Elaine *psychotherapist, educator*
Poppers, Paul Jules *anesthesiologist, educator*
Poston, Iona *nursing educator*
Quaife, Marjorie Clift *retired nursing educator*
Reyes, Edward *pharmacology educator*
Reynolds, Kasandra Massingill *nursing educator*
Richburg, W. Edward *nurse educator*
Rindone, Joseph Patrick *clinical pharmacist, educator*
Ritter, Frederick Edmond *plastic surgeon, educator*
Robbins, Dick Lamson *internist, educator*
Rofman, Ethan Samuel *psychiatrist, educator*
Roman, Stanford Augustus, Jr., *medical educator, dean*
Rothman, Juliet Cassuto *social work educator, writer*
Rubin, Phyllis Getz *health association executive*
Rudan, Vincent Thaddeus *nursing educator, administrator*
Ruskaup, Calvin *therapist, history professor*
Sacha, Robert Frank *osteopathic physician*
Salazar, Omar Mauricio *radiation oncologist, educator*
Salerno, Sister Maria *nursing educator, adult and gerontological nurse*
Sandt, John Joseph *psychiatrist, educator*
Scarlett, Novlin Rose *public health nurse, educator*
Schatz, Pauline *dietitian*
Schneider, Thomas Aquinas *surgeon, educator, retired surgeon*
Schooley, Robert T. *medical educator*
Schwartz, David Alan *infectious diseases and placental and obstetrical pathologist, educator, epidemiologist*
Scott, Amy Annette Holloway *nursing educator*
Servage, Bonnie Lee *nursing educator, administrator*
Shapiro, Marcia Haskel *speech and language pathologist*
Shemansky, Cindy Ann *nursing educator*
Shih, Chiaho *biomedical researcher, educator*
Smith, Thomas Hunter *ophthalmologist, ophthalmic plastic and orbital surgeon*
Sobol, Bruce J. *internist, educator, researcher*
Soffer, Rosemary S. *community health nurse, consultant, educator*
Stewart, Barbara Lynne *geriatrics nursing educator*
Stiles, Anne Scott *nursing educator*
Stockwell, Vivian Ann *nursing educator*
Stonnington, Henry Herbert *physician, medical executive, educator*
Sullivan, Colleen Anne *physician, educator*
Swenson, James Reed *physician, educator*
Taleff, Michael James *chemical dependency educator, consultant*
Taylor, Lesli Ann *pediatric surgery educator*
Tchakarova, Bogdana *retired radiologist, educator*
Timmreck, Thomas C. *health sciences and health administration educator*
Towne, Kathleen Dugan *counselor, educator*
Turndorf, Herman *anesthesiologist, educator*
Tuttle, Laura Shive *healthcare educator, administrator*
Uzsoy, Patricia J. *nursing educator and administrator*
Vogel, H. Victoria *psychotherapist, trauma, post-traumatic stress disorder and addiction recovery counselor and educator, author*
Volkman, Alvin *physician, research scientist, educator, retired*
von Schwarz, Carolyn M. Geiger *psychotherapist, educator*
Walker, Michael James *surgeon, educator*
Ware, Dollie *retired nursing educator*
Waters, William Carter, III, *retired internist, educator*
Weber, Ellen Schmoyer *pediatric speech pathologist*
Weitzel, Marilyn Lee *nursing educator*
Westmoreland, Barbara Fenn *neurologist, electroencephalographer, educator*
Whittington, Opal Hayes *nursing educator*
Wilson, Linda B. *education specialist, medical association administrator*
Winston, Donna Carol *nursing educator, nurse practitioner*
Winters, Charlene Adrienne *nursing educator*
Wooding, Gayle McAfee *nursing educator, consultant*
Worrell, Richard Vernon *orthopedic surgeon, college dean, dean*
Zabetakis, Paul Michael *nephrologist, educator*

HIGHER EDUCATION: HUMANITIES

UNITED STATES

ALABAMA

Birmingham
Allen, Lee Norcross *historian, educator*
Hull, William Edward *theology educator*
Long, Sheri Spaine *foreign language educator*
Morrison, Gregg Scott *theology educator, college administrator*
Morton, Marilyn Miller *retired genealogy and history educator, lecturer, researcher, travel executive, director*

Decatur
Simmons, Robert Burns *history and political science educator*

Gadsden
Holley, Charlotte Buggs *English language educator*

Greensboro
Massey, James Earl *clergyman, educator*

Huntsville
Hughes, Kaylene *historian, educator*
Marks, Marsha Kass *history educator*

Jacksonville
Spector, Daniel Earl *historian, educator*
Zenanko, Carl Michael *learning center educator*

Mobile
Donalson, Malcolm Drew *classics educator*
Hamner, Eugenie Lambert *English educator*

Montgomery
Bailey, Randall Charles *religious studies educator, consultant*
Gribben, Alan *English language educator, research consultant*
Richburg, Terri Scroggins *English educator*
Robinson, Ella Scales *language educator*
Whitt, Mary F. *reading educator, consultant*

Troy
McPherson, Milton Monroe *history educator*

ALASKA

Anchorage
Crawford, Ronald Merritt *history and geography educator*
Haley, Michael Cabot *English educator, researcher*
Namias, June *historian, educator, writer*

ARIZONA

Apache Junction
Ransom, Evelyn Naill *language educator, linguist*

Duncan
Ouzts, Eugene Thomas *minister, secondary education educator*

Flagstaff
Brown, Burton Ross *humanities educator, university administrator*
Marcus, Karen Melissa *foreign language educator*

Glendale
Galletti, Marie Ann *English language and linguistics educator*
Tuman, Walter Vladimir *Russian language educator, researcher*

Kingman
Jones, Barbara Christine *linguist, creative arts designer, educator*

Mesa
Fierro, Marcella *language educator*

Phoenix
Campbell, Maynard Thomas *English language educator*
Drnjevic, Jonathan Mark *language educator*
Kohi, Susan *bilingual educator, translator*
Wirtz, Dorothy Marie *retired language educator*

Prescott
Trejos, Charlotte Marie *humanities educator, consultant*

Tempe
Green, Monica H. *history educator*
Honegger, Gitta *language educator*
Ruiz, Vicki Lynn *history educator*
Wong, Timothy C. *language and literature educator*

Tucson
Gaines, Kendra Holly *English language educator, editorial and writing consultant*
Hammond, Michael *linguistics educator*
Mattoon, Sara Halsey (Sally Mattoon) *consultant, director*
Milton, Corinne Holm *art history educator*
Neff-Encinas, Julie Gay *bilingual education specialist, consultant*
Rabuck, Donna Fontanarose *English writing educator*
Schulz, Renate Adele *German studies and second language acquisition educator*

ARKANSAS

Arkadelphia
Hicks, Billy Ferrell *minister, educator*

Conway
Kearns, Terrance Brophy *English language educator*

Eureka Springs
Dragonwagon, Crescent (Ellen Zolotow) *writer, educator*

Fayetteville
Levine, Daniel Blank *classical studies educator*

Little Rock
Quick, Edward Raymond *museum director, educator, curator*

State University
Schichler, Robert Lawrence *English language educator*

CALIFORNIA

Alpine
Butler, Evelyn Anne *writer, educator, editor*

Arcadia
Sloane, Beverly LeBov *writer, consultant*

Azusa
Shoemaker, Melvin Hugh *religious educator*

Bakersfield
Gunderson, Sarah Chloe (Chloe Sarah Burns) *historian, educator*

Berkeley
Altieri, Charles Francis *English language educator*
Chihara, Charles Seiyo *philosophy educator*
Di Carlo, Armando *Italian language educator*
Gallagher, M. Catherine *English literature educator*
Herr, Richard *history educator*
Hull, Glynda *language educator*
Long, Anthony Arthur *classics educator*
Nagler, Michael Nicholas *peace and conflict studies educator*
Tracy, Robert (Robert Edward Tracy) *English language educator, poetry translator*
Wakeman, Frederic Evans, Jr., *historian, educator*

Camarillo
Christopher, Renny Teresa *liberal studies educator*
Derr, Jeannie Combs *bilingual educator, anthropology educator*

Cambria
Salaverria, Helena Clara *retired language educator*

Carmichael
Donaldson, Robert Charles *history educator*
Ertel, Grace Roscoe *freelance non-fiction writer, educator*

Chula Vista
Nelson, Carl Alfred *international business educator*

Citrus Heights
Knight, Arthur Winfield *English educator*

Claremont
Atlas, Jay David *philosopher, consultant, linguist*
Davis, Nathaniel *humanities educator*
Dolence, Michael G. *writer, consultant, educator*
Elsbree, Langdon *English language educator*
Lofgren, Charles Augustin *legal and constitutional historian, history educator*
Moss, Myra Ellen (Myra Moss Rolle) *philosophy educator*
Pinney, Thomas Clive *retired English language educator*
Post, Gaines, Jr., *retired history educator, dean, administrator*
Sontag, Frederick Earl *philosophy educator*

Cupertino
Russi, John Joseph *priest, educational administrator*

Daly City
Gao, Luji *foreign language educator, columnist*

Dublin
Ingram, Judith Elizabeth *writer, counselor, educator*

El Cajon
Dana-Davidson, Laoma Cook *English language educator*

Fresno
Bundy-DeSoto, Teresa Mari *language educator, vocalist*
Garrison-Finderup, Ivadelle Dalton *writer, educator*
Patterson, Carolyn F. *retired English educator*

Fullerton
Carrithers, Joseph Edward *English composition and literature educator*

Glendale
de Grassi, Leonard *art historian, educator*

Grass Valley
Hotchkiss, Bill *author, educator*

Healdsburg
Myers, Robert Eugene *writer, educator*

Imperial
Montenegro, Jean Baker *English language educator*

Irvine
Lehnert, Herbert Hermann *foreign language educator*

Kensington
Nathan, Leonard Edward *writer*

La Jolla
Miyoshi, Masao *literature educator, writer*

Laguna Niguel
Teitelbaum, Harry *English educator*

Livermore
Hiskes, Dolores G. *language educator*

Long Beach
Beebe, Sandra E. *retired English language educator, artist, writer*
Locklin, Gerald Ivan *language educator, poet, writer*
Nguyen, Huong Tran *English language professional, federal agency official*
Snider, Clifton Mark *English educator, writer, poet*
Tang, Paul Chi Lung *philosophy educator*
Yousef, Fathi Sslaama *communication studies educator, management consultant*

Los Angeles
Allen, Michael John Bridgman *English educator*
Amneus, D. A. *English language educator*
Burns, Robert Ignatius *historian, educator, clergyman*
Caram, Eve La Salle *English educator, writer*
Cortinez, Veronica *literature educator*
Dumitrescu, Domnita *Spanish language educator, researcher*
Hawley, Cherie *reading and language arts educator*
Hsu, Kylie *language educator, researcher, linguist*
Hundley, Norris Cecil, Jr., *history educator*
Lehan, Richard D'Aubin *English language educator, writer*
Nakanishi, Don Toshiaki *Asian American studies educator, writer*
Shideler, Ross Patrick *foreign language and comparative literature educator, writer, translator, poet*
Smith, Bruce R. *English language educator*
Tangherlini, Timothy R. *literature educator*
Thomas, Shirley *author, educator, business executive*

Marina
Boldyrev, Peter Matveevich *Russian language and culture educator, writer*

Merced
Elliott, Gordon Jefferson *retired English language educator*

Mission Viejo
Bander, Carol Jean *German and English language educator*

Monterey
Peet, Phyllis Irene *women's studies educator*

Moorpark
Hall, Elton Arthur *philosophy educator*

Moraga
Lashof, Carol Suzanne *literature educator*

Northridge
Soffer, Reba N. *history educator*

Oakland
Patten, Bebe Harrison *minister, chancellor*

Oceano
Scott, Donald Michael *writer, educator*

Ontario
Cook, Stanley Joseph *retired language educator*

Orange
Stevens, Cherita Wyman *writer, educator*
Yeager, Myron Dean *English language educator, business writing consultant*

Oxnard
Hill, Alice Lorraine *history, genealogy and social researcher, educator*

Palo Alto
Knoles, George Harmon *history educator*
Tsumura, Yumiko *Japanese language and culture educator, consultant*
Walker, Carolyn Peyton *English language educator*

Pleasant Hill
Ashby, Denise Stewart *speech educator, communication consultant*

Pomona
Cranston, John Welch *historian, educator*
Montgomery, Elizabeth Anne *English language educator*

Portola Valley
Carnochan, Walter Bliss *retired humanities educator*

Rancho Dominguez
Corominas, Juan M. *language educator, priest*

Rancho Palos Verdes
Thomas, Pearl Elizabeth *English educator*

Redondo Beach
Battles, Roxy Edith *novelist, consultant, educator*

Riverside
Andersen, Frances Elizabeth Gold *religious leadership educator*
Cortés, Carlos Eliseo *historian, educator*
Huang, Kai-Loo *religion educator emeritus*
Yount, Gwendolyn Audrey *humanities educator*

Sacramento
Gerringer, Elizabeth (The Marchioness de Roe Devon) *writer, lawyer*
Madden, David William *English language educator*
Meindl, Robert James *English language educator*
Reed, Nancy Boyd *English language and elementary education educator*

Saint Helena
Yates, Donald Alfred *retired literature educator*

Salinas
Smith, Jerilynn Suzanne *educational coordinator*

San Bernardino
Hansen, Anne Katherine *poet, retired elementary education educator*

San Carlos
Palmer, Patricia Ann Texter *English language educator*

San Diego
Amstadt, Nancy Hollis *retired language educator*
Cayleff, Susan Evelyn *women's studies educator, department chairman*
Darby, Joanne Tyndale (Jaye Darby) *arts and humanities educator*
Dunlop, Marianne *retired English as second language educator*
Thurber, Barton Dennison *English literature educator, writer*

San Francisco
Alayeto, Ofelia Luisa *writer, researcher, educator*
Batchelor, Karen Lee *English language educator*
Costa-Zalessow, Natalia *foreign language educator*
DuBose, Francis Marquis *clergyman*
Felstiner, Mary Lowenthal *history educator*
Gamson, Joshua Paul *sociology educator*
Mann, Charles Frederick *language educator, translator, author*
Sanazaro, Leonard Rocco *language educator, writer*
Satin, Joseph *language professional, university administrator*

San Jose
Chae, Yoon Kwon *minister, educator*
Kerkoc, Ruth Ann *Spanish educator*
Pickering, Mary Barbara *history educator, writer*

San Juan Capistrano
Carlson, Lawrence Arvid *retired English language educator, real estate agent*

San Marcos
Rolle-Rissetto, Silvia *foreign languages educator, writer, artist*
Tanner, John Douglas, Jr., *history educator, writer*

San Mateo
Petit, Susan Yount *French and English language educator*

Santa Ana
Mallory, Lee Wesley, III, *English and French language educator, poet*

Santa Barbara
Abbott, H(orace) Porter *English language educator*
Avalle-Arce, Juan Bautista *Spanish language educator*
Bazerman, Charles *English language educator, writing researcher*
Brownlee, Wilson Elliot, Jr., *history educator*
Collins, Robert Oakley *history educator*
Dunn, Francis Michael *classicist, educator*
Gordon, Helen Heightsman *English language educator, writer, publisher*
Kelm, Bonnie G. *art museum director, educator*
Kuczynski, John-Michael Maxime *humanities educator, writer*
Mahlendorf, Ursula Renate *literature educator*
Rose, Mark Allen *humanities educator, educator*

Santa Clara
Kain, Philip Joseph *philosophy educator*

Santa Cruz
Lieberman, Fredric *ethnomusicologist, educator, composer*
Lynch, John Patrick *classics educator, university official*

Saratoga
deBarling, Ana Maria *language educator*

Solana Beach
Gilliam, Vincent Carver *religion educator, minister, writer*

Stanford
Baker, Keith Michael *history educator*
Fredrickson, George Marsh *history educator*
Gardner, John William *writer, educator*
Hilton, Ronald *international studies educator*
Kennedy, David Michael *historian, educator*
Martin, Richard Peter *classics educator, consultant*
Offen, Karen Marie *historian, educator*
Perloff, Marjorie Gabrielle *English and comparative literature educator*
Predmore, Michael Pennock *Spanish language and literature educator*
Stansky, Peter David Lyman *historian*

Temple City
Perkins, Floyd Jerry *retired theology educator*

Torrance
Anderson, Marilyn Wheeler *English language educator*

Tulare
Gorelick, Ellen Catherine *museum director, curator, artist, educator, civic volunteer*

Turlock
Blodgett, Harriet *English educator*

Vallejo
Landauer, Elvie Ann Whitney *humanities educator, writer*

Venice
Murez, Melanie Goodman *linguist, language services company owner, former educator*

Wilmington
Brown, Nancy Ellen *language educator, writer*
Smith, June Burlingame *English educator*

COLORADO

Boulder
Barchilon, Jacques *foreign language educator, researcher, writer*
Colwell, James Lee *humanities educator*
Engel, Barbara Alpern *history educator*
Gonzalez-del-Valle, Luis Tomas *Spanish language educator*
Moore, George Barnard *poet, educator*
Preston, Michael James *English and folklore educator, consultant*

Colorado Springs
Anderson, Katheryn Lucille *language arts educator and author*
Austerman, Donna Lynne *Spanish language educator*

Denver
Fasel, Ida *English language educator, writer*
Klein, William Wade *religious educator*
Nemiro, Beverly Mirium Anderson *author, educator*
Osborn, Susan Chaney *educator, writer*
Wetzel, Jodi (Joy Lynn Wetzel) *history and women's studies educator*

Durango
Smith, Duane Allan *history educator, researcher*

Englewood
Bardsley, Kay *historian, archivist, dance professional*

Erie
Dilly, Marian Jeanette *humanities educator*

Fort Collins
Rolston, Holmes, III, *theologian, educator, philosopher*
Tremblay, William Andrew *English language educator, writer*

Lakewood
Hickman, Ruth Virginia *Bible educator*
Joy, Carla Marie *history educator*
Kleinfeld, Elizabeth Anne *English literature educator*
Woodruff, Kathryn Elaine *English language educator*

Littleton
Champney, Linda Lucas *reading educator*
Elrick, Billy Lee *English language educator*

Parker
Sieveke-Pearson, Starla Jean *language educator*

Pueblo
Farwell, Hermon Waldo, Jr., *parliamentarian, educator, former speech communication educator*

CONNECTICUT

Ansonia
Mendyk, Sandra L. *English educator*

Branford
Whitaker, Thomas Russell *English literature educator*

Danbury
Edelstein, David Simeon *historian, educator*

East Hampton
Tucceri, Clive Knowles *science writer and educator, consultant*

Fairfield
Lachowicz, Franciszek *foreign language educator*
Michael, Mary Amelia Furtado *freelance writer, retired educator*

Hamden
Dittes, James Edward *psychology of religion educator*
Magnarelli, Sharon Dishaw *Spanish language educator*
McClellan, Edwin *Japanese literature educator*
Pelikan, Jaroslav Jan *history educator*

Hartford
Clark, Patricia Ruth *foreign language educator*
Cohn, Jan Kadetsky *American literature and American studies educator*
Decker, Robert Owen *history educator, clergyman*
Ogden, Hugh *English literature educator, poet*

Killingworth
Sampson, Edward Coolidge *humanities educator*

Middletown
Gillmor, Charles Stewart *history and science educator, researcher*
Heimann-Hast, Sybil Dorothea *language arts and literature educator*
Meyer, Priscilla Ann *Russian language and literature educator*
Pomper, Philip *history educator*
Reed, Joseph Wayne *American studies educator, artist*
Schwarcz, Vera *history educator, poet*
Slotkin, Richard Sidney *American studies educator, writer*
Stowe, William Whitfield *English language educator*
Turco, Alfred, Jr., *English language educator*
Wensinger, Arthur Stevens *language and literature educator, writer*
Winston, Krishna *foreign language professional*

Naugatuck
Scheithe, Jeanne Marie *language educator*

New Britain
Emeagwali, Gloria Thomas *humanities educator*

New Haven
Alexandrov, Vladimir Eugene *Russian literature educator*
Alwood, Edward McQueen *writer, journalist, media specialist*
Borroff, Marie *English language educator*
Brooks, Peter (Preston) *French and comparative literature educator, department chair, writer*
Dupré, Louis *retired philosopher, educator*
Fink, Hilary Lynn *Slavic languages educator*
Gilbert, Creighton Eddy *art historian*
Gilman, Todd Seacrist *librarian, scholar, educator, musician*
Glier, Ingeborg Johanna *German language and literature educator*
Greene, Thomas McLernon *language professional, educator*
Harries, Karsten *philosophy educator, researcher*
Hartman, Geoffrey H. *language professional, educator*
Hayden, Dolores *author, architect, educator*
Hickey, Leo J(oseph) *museum curator, educator*
Hollander, John *humanities educator, poet*
Holquist, James Michael *Russian and comparative literature educator*
Insler, Stanley *philologist, educator*
Kennedy, Paul Michael *history educator*
Mazzotta, Giuseppe Francesco *Italian language and literature educator*
Palisca, Claude Victor *musicologist, educator*
Peterson, Linda H. *English language and literature educator*
Pollitt, Jerome Jordan *art history educator*
Prown, Jules David *art historian educator*
Rawson, Claude Julien *English educator*
Sammons, Jeffrey Leonard *foreign language educator*
Sanneh, Lamin *religion educator*
Schenker, Alexander Marian *Slavic linguistics educator*
Underdown, David Edward *historian, educator*
Valesio, Paolo *Italian language and literature educator, writer*
van Altena, Alicia Mora *language educator*
Wilcox, Scott Barnes *museum curator, educator*
Yeazell, Ruth Bernard *English language educator*

New London
Zabel, Barbara *art historian, educator*

North Branford
Thacher, Barbara Auchincloss *history educator*

Southbury
Normann, Margaret Ella *deacon, educator*

Southport
Ei, Susan M(ichelle) *English language educator*

Storrs Mansfield
Coons, Ronald Edward *historian, educator*

Waterbury
Donahue, Linda Wheeler *retired English educator, writer*
Meyer, Judith Chandler Pugh *history educator*

West Hartford
Collins, Alma Jones *English educator, writer*
Edwards, Sarah Alexander *minister, educator*

Westport
Amodio, Barbara Ann *philosophy educator, educational administrator*

Windsor
Auten, Arthur Herbert *history educator*

Woodbridge
Ecklund, Constance Cryer *French language educator*
Kleiner, Diana Elizabeth Edelman *art history educator, administrator*

DELAWARE

Dover
Young, Renee Lenoire Joyeusaz *English educator*

Newark
Andrews, Deborah Crehan *English studies educator*
Day, Robert Androus *English language educator, former library director, editor, publisher*
Lathrop, Thomas Albert *language educator, educator*
Steiner, Roger Jacob *linguistics educator, writer, researcher*
Weintraub, Stanley *arts and humanities educator, writer*

Wilmington
Frederick, Albert Bruce *historian, educator*

DISTRICT OF COLUMBIA

Washington
Bennett, Betty T. *English literature educator, university dean, writer*
Birnbaum, Norman *author, humanities educator*
Carter, Yvonne Johnson *writer, editor, English educator*
Caws, Peter James *philosopher, educator*
Davidson, Dan Eugene *Russian language and area scholar, academic administrator*
Farr, Judith Banzer *writer, literature educator*
Felton, Zora Belle *emerita museum educator*
Fisher, Elizabeth Ann *classics educator*
Jensen, Joseph (Norman) *priest, educator*
Keenan, Edward Louis *history educator*
Kennedy, Dane Keith *history educator*
King, Thomas M. *theology educator, priest*
Langan, John Patrick *philosophy educator*
Levy, David Corcos *museum director*
Miller, Jeanne-Marie Anderson (Mrs. Nathan J. Miller) *English language educator, academic administrator*
Mujica, Barbara Louise *language educator, writer*
Poos, Lawrence Raymond *history educator*
Robb, James Willis *Romance languages educator*
Rojer, Olga Elaine *German studies educator, translator*
Rosenblatt, Jason Philip *English language educator*
Ross, Robinette Davis *publisher*
Salamon, Linda Bradley *English literature educator*
Severino, Roberto *foreign language educator, academic administration executive*
Simko, Jan *English, foreign language and literature educator*
Veatch, Robert Marlin *philosophy educator, medical ethics researcher*
Voll, John Obert *history educator*
Wogaman, John Philip *retired minister and educator*

FLORIDA

Boca Raton
Adriazola, Ana *Spanish and Latin American culture educator*
Collins, Robert Arnold *English language educator*
Eisenberg, Robin Ledgin *religious education administrator*

Brooksville
Henton, M. Lois Smith *English language arts educator*

Cape Coral
Martin, Thomas Sherwood *history and political science educator*

Coral Gables
Lemos, Ramon Marcelino *philosophy educator*

Davie
Speiller-Morris, Joyce *English educator*

Daytona Beach
Bronson, Oswald Perry, Sr., *religious organization administrator, clergyman*

Delray Beach
Stone, Elizabeth Walker *English educator*

Fort Lauderdale
Van Alstyne, Judith Sturges *retired language educator*

Fort Myers
Schultz, Samuel Jacob *clergyman, educator*

Fort Pierce
Bynum, Henri Sue *education and French educator*

Gainesville
Brown, William Samuel, Jr., *communication sciences and disorders educator*
Emch-Dériaz, Antoinette Suzanne *historian, educator*

Gulfport
Davis, Ann Caldwell *history educator*

Homestead
Reeder, Cecelia Painter *English educator*

Jacksonville
Afflick, Clive Henry *minister, guidance counselor*
Gentry, Robert Bryan *humanities educator, writer*
Lloyd, Jacqueline *English language educator*
Stanton, Robert John, Jr., *English language educator*
Zbiegien, M. Andrea *chaplain, religious education educator, consultant, educational administrator*

Key Biscayne
Zayas-Bazan, Eduardo *foreign language educator*

Labelle
Payne, Alma Jeanette *English language educator, author*

Lakeland
Piatt, Richard C., II, *senior pastor, educator*

Largo
Williams, Trudy Anne *English language educator, college administrator*

Leesburg
Fletcher, Mary H. *English language educator*

Madison
McCauley, Barbara Lynne *language educator*

Melbourne
Jones, Elaine Hancock *humanities educator*

Miami
Hargitai, Peter J. *English language educator*
Johnson-Cousin, Danielle *French literature and cultural studies educator*
Jones y Diez Arguelles, Gastón Roberto *language educator, educator*
Neu, Charles Eric *historian, educator*
Newson, Adele Sheron *English educator*

Mulberry
Bowman, Hazel Lois *retired English language educator*

Naples
Griffin, Linda Louise *English language and speech educator*
Siddall, Patricia Ann *retired English language educator*
Waller, George Macgregor *historian, educator*

New Port Richey
McCabe, Sharon *humanities educator, art educator*
Morgan, Lona Scaggs *speech professional educator*

North Port
Seiler, Charlotte Woody *retired educator*

Ocala
Zink, David Daniel *retired English educator, writer*

Oldsmar
Craft Davis, Audrey Ellen *writer, educator*

Orlando
Raffa, Jean Benedict *author, educator*

Palm Beach
Artinian, Artine *French literature scholar, collector*

Pensacola
Arnold, Barry Raynor *philosophy educator, medical ethicist, clergyman, counselor*
Maddock, Lawrence Hill *retired language educator*

Plantation
Belmonté, Kathryn (KiKi Belmonté) *writer, small business owner*

Pompano Beach
Kaskinen, Barbara Kay *author, composer, songwriter, musician, music educator*

Saint Petersburg
Sherburne, Donald Wynne *philosopher, educator*

Stuart
Woodward, Isabel Avila *educational writer, foreign language educator*

Tallahassee
Burroway, Janet G. *English language educator, novelist*
Dorn, Charles Meeker *art education educator*
Kirby, David *literature educator*
Laird, Doris Anne Marley *humanities educator, musician*
Palladino-Craig, Allys *museum director*

Tampa
Mitchell, Mozella Gordon *English language educator, minister*
Perry, James Frederic *philosophy educator, writer*

Tequesta
Ragno, Nancy Nickell *educational writer*

Valrico
Peeler, Scott Loomis, Jr., *foreign language educator*

West Palm Beach
Nolan, Richard Thomas *clergyman, educator*
Young, Lois Catherine Williams *poet, former reading specialist*

Winter Garden
Earls, Irene Anne *art history educator*

Winter Haven
Kerner, Howard Alex *English and communications educator, writer, literary manager*

Winter Park
Wilson, Robley Conant, Jr., *English educator, editor, author*

GEORGIA

Americus
Isaacs, Harold *history educator*

Athens
McGregor, James Harvey Spence *comparative literature educator*
Miller, Ronald Baxter *English language educator, writer*
Moore, Margaret Bear *American literature educator*
Moore, Rayburn Sabatzky *American literature educator*
Spears, Louise Elizabeth *minister, secondary school educator*

Atlanta
Blumenthal, Anna Catherine *English educator*
Burns, Thomas Samuel *history educator*
Manley, Frank *retired English language educator, writer*
Schaumann, Caroline *language educator*
Trethewey, Natasha *poet, literature educator*

Augusta
Dyer, James Harold, Jr., *language educator, educator*

Bellville
Porter, James Logan *humanities educator*

Brunswick
Choate, Jean Marie *history educator*

College Park
Payne, Harry Charles *historian, educator*
West-Hill, Gwendolyn *poet, educator, artist, evangelist*

Dalton
Mathews, Marsha Anderson *English educator, poet, minister*

Decatur
Dillingham, William Byron *literature educator, author*
Morris, Robert Renly *minister, clinical pastoral education supervisor*
Pepperdene, Margaret Williams *English educator*

Dublin
Claxton, Harriett Maroy Jones *retired language educator*

Dunwoody
Duvall, Marjorie L. *English and foreign language educator*

Macon
Huffman, Joan Brewer *history educator*

Marietta
Rainey, Kenneth Tyler *English language educator*

Robins A F B
Head, William Pace *historian, educator*

Valdosta
Adler, Brian Ungar *English language educator, program director*

HAWAII

Hilo
Kinney, Jeanne Kawelolani *English studies educator, writer*

Honolulu
Hoffmann, Kathryn Ann *humanities educator*
Pagotto, Louise *English language educator*
Peterson, Barbara Ann Bennett *history educator, television personality*

Kaneohe
Nagtalon-Miller, Helen Rosete *humanities educator*

Makawao
Moore, Rosemary Kuulei *art gallery administrator*

Waianae
Perkins, Lily Leialoha *humanities educator, writer*

IDAHO

Boise
Nguyen, King Xuan *language educator*
Steiner, Stanley F. *literature educator*

Moscow
Greever, Janet Groff *history educator*

Pocatello
Smith, Evelyn Elaine *language educator*

ILLINOIS

Benton
Andros, Hazel Laverne (Brissette Andros) *speech professional, educator*

Bridgeport
McMillen, Julie Lynn *English, speech educator*

Carbondale
Hickman, Larry Allen *philosophy educator*
Spees, Emil Ray *philosophy educator*

Chicago
Aronson, Howard Isaac *linguist, educator*
Barbour, Claude Marie *minister, educator*
Baumhart, Raymond Charles *Roman Catholic church administrator*
Bevington, David Martin *English literature educator*
Biggs, Robert Dale *Near Eastern studies educator*
Booth, Wayne Clayson *English literature and rhetoric educator, author*
Brinkman, John Anthony *historian, educator*
Chambers, Richard Leon *retired Turkish language and civilization educator*
Davidson, Arnold I. *philosophy educator*
Doherty, Sister Barbara *religious institution administrator*
Frantzen, Allen John *English language educator*
Golden, Lily Oliver *humanities educator*
Gray, Hanna Holborn *history educator*
Harris, Mildred Clopton *clergy member, educator*
Haugeland, John *philosophy educator*
Headrick, Daniel Richard *history and social sciences educator*
Hellie, Richard *Russian history educator, researcher*
Hurley, William James, Jr., *English language educator*
Ingham, Norman William *Russian literature educator, genealogist*
James, Marie Moody *clergywoman, musician, vocal music educator*
Johnson, Raymonda Theodora Greene *humanities educator*
McGinn, Bernard John *religious educator*
Melnick, Jane Fisher *journalism, creative writing and literature educator*
Miller, Angela Perez *bilingual and special education educator*
Mueller, Rose Anna Maria *humanities educator*
Nakamura, Kimiko *language educator*
Odishoo, Sarah A. *English language educator*
Rodriguez, David Gonzalez, Jr., *priest, art and religion educator*
Rodriguez-Florido, Jorge Julio *language educator, mathematics educator*
Romano-Magner, Patricia R. *English studies educator, researcher*
Shanahan, Timothy Edward *urban education educator, researcher*
Sherwin, Byron Lee *religion educator, college official*
Stratman, Deborah *filmmaker, film and video educator*
Van Patten, Bill *foreign language educator*
Weiner, Lynn Yvette *history educator*

Dekalb
Michael, Colette Verger *language educator, writer*
Townsend, Lucy Forsyth *historian, educator*

Des Plaines
Krupa, John Henry *English language educator*

Edwardsville
Cataldi, Suzanne Laba *philosophy educator*
Swalley, Gary William *history educator*

Elgin
Duffy, John Lewis *retired Latin, English and reading educator*
Parks, Patrick *English language educator, humanities educator*

Evanston
Lems, Kristin *English language educator, songwriter*
May, Norma Butler *reading educator*
McCurry, Stephanie *historian, educator*
Romanowski, Sylvie *French literature educator*
Van Zanten, David Theodore *humanities educator*
Weil, Irwin *Slavic languages and literature educator*
Well, Irwin *language educator*

Glen Ellyn
Georgalas, Robert Nicholas *English language educator*

Highland Park
Greenblatt, Miriam *writer, editor, educator*

Itasca
Bradshaw, Linda Jean *English language educator*

Lake Forest
Hahn, Cynthia Therese *foreign language educator*
Taylor, Barbara Ann Olin *writer, educational consultant*

Libertyville
Schroeder, W(illiam) Widick *religion educator*

Lincoln
Sackett, Glenn Charles *theology studies educator*

Lisle
Fortier, Mardelle LaDonna *English educator*

Macomb
Leonard, Virginia Waugh *history educator, writer, researcher*

Moline
Johnson, Mary Lou *lay worker, educator*

Mount Carmel
Owens, Patricia Ann *history educator*

Mount Vernon
Hall, Sharon Gay *retired language educator, artist*

Normal
Shields, John Charles *American studies and African American studies and literature educator*

Northbrook
Ehrmann, Susanna *foreign language educator, writer, photographer*
Stamper, James M. *retired English language educator*
Young, Susan Jean *music specialist*

Oak Lawn
Laird, Jean Elouise Rydeski (Mrs. Jack E. Laird) *author, adult education educator*

Ottawa
Ballowe, James *English educator, author*

Palatine
Hull, Elizabeth Anne *retired English language educator*
Keres, Karen Lynne *English language educator*

Palos Heights
Higgins, Francis Edward *history educator*

Palos Hills
Phillips, Keith *Spanish language educator*

River Forest
O'Meara, Thomas Franklin *priest, educator*

Riverside
Marty, Martin Emil *religion educator, editor*

Rockford
Hoshaw, Lloyd *retired historian, educator*
Provo, Wade Arden *foreign language educator*

Tuscola
Cisna, Susan Jo *language arts educator*

Urbana
Baron, Dennis E. *English language educator*
Carringer, Robert *English language and film educator*
McKay, John Patrick *history educator*
Mortimer, Armine Kotin *literature educator*
Sousa, Ronald Wayne *foreign language educator*
Spence, Mary Lee *historian, educator*
Steinberg, Mark David *history educator*
Stillinger, Jack Clifford *English educator*
Sullivan, Zohreh T. *English educator*
Talbot, Emile Joseph *French language educator*
Zgusta, Ladislav *linguist, educator*

Wilmette
McClure, Julie Anne *literature educator*
Stockman, Robert Harold *religious organization administrator, educator*

INDIANA

Bloomington
Choksy, Jamsheed Kairshasp *historian, religious scholar, language professional, humanities educator*
Gealt, Adelheid Maria *museum director*
Gros Louis, Kenneth Richard Russell *humanities educator*
Hanson, Karen *philosopher, educator*
Lebano, Edoardo Antonio *foreign language educator*
Nordloh, David Joseph *English language educator*
Pfingston, Roger Carl *writer photographer, retired educator*
Stoeltje, Beverly June *liberal studies educator*

Centerville
Wendeln, Darlene Doris *English language educator*

Chesterton
Hayduk, John Matthew *English and journalism educator*

Crawfordsville
Barnes, James John *history educator*

Evansville
Bigham, Darrel E. *history educator*
Grabill, Virginia Lowell *retired English educator*

Fort Wayne
Crismore, Avon Germaine *English language educator, researcher*

Franklin
Cain, Clifford Chalmers *chaplain, educator*

Greencastle
Woodall, Susan Kay *language educator, librarian*

Howe
Bowerman, Ann Louise *writer, genealogist, educator*

Indianapolis
Geib, George Winthrop *history educator*
Nnaemeka, Obioma Grace *French language and women's studies educator, consultant, researcher*
Plater, William Marmaduke *English language educator, academic administrator*

Lafayette
Williams, Vernon J., Jr., *historian, educator, writer*

Mount Vernon
Sorenson, Sharon Orilla *language arts author and consultant*

Muncie
King, Adele Cockshoot *French language educator*

Nashville
Wills, Katherine V. Tsiopos *English language educator*

North Manchester
Naragon, Steven Scott *philosophy educator*

Notre Dame
Delaney, Cornelius Francis *philosophy educator*
De Santis, Vincent Paul *historian, educator*
Doody, Margaret Anne *English language educator*
Dougherty, James Patrick *English language educator*
Jemielity, Thomas John *language educator*
Lanzinger, Klaus *language educator*
MacIntyre, Alasdair *philosophy educator*
Matthias, John Edward *English literature educator*
McInerny, Ralph Matthew *philosophy educator, writer*
McMullin, Ernan Vincent *philosophy educator*
Rosenberg, Charles Michael *art historian, educator*
Sayre, Kenneth Malcolm *philosophy educator*

Rensselaer
Garrity, Robert John *philosophy and English language educator*

Richmond
Hamm, Thomas Douglas *archivist, history educator*
Siatra, Eleni *English educator*
Turk, Eleanor Louise *history educator*

Salem
Morris, Marjorie Lynne *language arts educator*

Terre Haute
Brennan, Matthew Cannon *English literature educator, poet*
Clouse, Robert Gordon *history educator, minister*

Valparaiso
Peters, Judith Griessel *foreign language educator*

West Lafayette
Broden, Thomas Francis, III, *French language educator*
Garfinkel, Alan *language educator*

IOWA

Ames
Dial, Eleanore Maxwell *foreign language educator*

Avoca
Hardisty, William Lee *English language educator*

Buffalo Center
Coxson, Betty Jane *retired secondary school and humanities educator*

Burlington
Freeland, Deborah Jane *English educator*

Cedar Falls
Clohesy, William Warren *philosopher, educator*
Schnucker, Robert Victor *history and religion educator*
Wang, Jennie *literature educator*

Cedar Rapids
Berry, Jay Robert, Jr., *English educator*

Cleghorn
Anderson, Marilyn Ruth *retired multi-media specialist*

Davenport
Kruse, Marylin Lynn *retired foreign language educator*
Orozco, LuzMaría *language educator, educator*
Stauff, Jon William *history educator*

Decorah
Wilkie, Jacqueline Sarah *history educator*

Dubuque
Bloesch, Donald George *theologian, writer, educator*
Burkhart, John Ernest *theology studies educator*

Grinnell
Kintner, Philip L. *history educator*
Michaels, Jennifer Tonks *foreign language educator*

Iowa City
Aikin, Judith Popovich *languages educator, academic administrator*
DiPardo, Anne *English language and education educator*
Folsom, Lowell Edwin *language educator*
Gelfand, Lawrence Emerson *historian, educator*
Hawley, Ellis Wayne *historian, educator*
Kerber, Linda Kaufman *historian, educator*
Percas de Ponseti, Helena *foreign language and literature educator*
Solbrig, Ingeborg Hildegard *German literature educator, writer*

Lamoni
Wight, Darlene *retired speech educator, emerita educator*

Pella
Den Adel, Raymond Lee *classics educator*

Sioux City
Nichols, Roger Sabin *genealogist, retired school counselor*

University Park
Murphree, Jon Tal *clergyman, philosophy and theology educator, academic administrator*

Waverly
Blair, Rebecca Sue *English educator, lay minister*
Lindell, Terrence Jon *history educator*

KANSAS

Atchison
Homan, Thomasita *English language and literature educator*

Chanute
Dillard, Dean Innes *English language educator, academic administrator*

Cherryvale
Wood, Ruby Fern *writer, retired elementary educator*

Great Bend
Gunn, Mary Elizabeth *retired English language educator*

Hays
Smith, Wilda Maxine *history educator*

Kansas City
Haen, Joanne Lee *English educator*

Lawrence
Boyd, Beverly *English literature educator*
Cateforis, David Christos *art history educator*
Debicki, Andrew Peter *foreign language educator*
Eldredge, Charles Child, III, *art history educator*
Gunn, James E. *English language educator*
Low-Weso, Denise Lea *writing educator*
Parker, Stephen Jan *Slavic language and literature educator*
Seaver, James Everett *historian, educator*

PROFESSIONAL INDEX — HIGHER EDUCATION: HUMANITIES

Manhattan
Higham, Robin *historian, editor, publisher*
Suleiman, Michael Wadie *humanities educator*
Walker Schlageck, Kathrine L. *museum educational administrator, educator*

Ottawa
Tyler, Priscilla *retired English language and education educator*

Overland Park
Xidis, Kathleen O'Connor *history educator*

Pittsburg
Beer, Pamela Jill Porr *writer, retired vocational school educator*

KENTUCKY

Ashland
St. Clair, Philip Roland *humanities educator, poet*

Bowling Green
Minton, John Dean *historian, educator*

Campbellsville
Benningfield, Troy Lee *language arts educator*

Danville
Newhall, David Sowle *history educator*

Elizabethtown
Cantrell, Douglas Eugene *history educator, author*

Falmouth
Conrad, Kerry S. *language educator*

Fort Mitchell
Wills, Lois Elaine *religious education educator*

Highland Heights
Wallace, Harold Lew *historian, educator*

Lexington
Allaire, Gloria Kaun *Italian language educator*
Hargreaves, Mary-Wilma Massey *retired history educator*
Wolfgang, James Stephen *history educator, minister*

Louisville
Ford, Gordon Buell, Jr., *literature educator, writer*
Garcia-Varela, Jesus *language educator, literature educator*
Kearney, Anna Rose *history educator*
Nuessel, Frank Henry *linguistics educator*
St. Clair, Robert Neal *English language and linguistics educator*
Schultze, Sydney Patterson *language educator*

Williamsburg
Fish, Thomas Edward *English language and literature educator*
Sharp, Jolly Kay *English language educator*

LOUISIANA

Baton Rouge
Olney, James *English language educator*
Ricapito, Joseph Virgil (Giuseppe Ricapito) *Spanish, Italian and comparative literature educator*
Sasek, Gloria Burns *English language and literature educator*

Hammond
Thorburn, James Alexander *retired humanities educator*

La Place
Walton, Paula Anderson *language arts educator*

Lafayette
Poe, (Lydia) Virginia *reading educator*

Lake Charles
Goodaker, Dianne McCrystal *language educator*

Metairie
Baisier, Maria Davis *English language educator, theater director*

New Orleans
Bischof, Günter Josef *history educator*
Brumfield, William Craft *Slavic studies educator*
Carter, James Clarence *pastor, educator*
Gelderman, Carol *English educator, writer*
Paolini, Gilberto *literature and science educator*
Pizer, Donald *author, educator*
Pollock, Linda Anne *history educator*
Reck, Andrew Joseph *retired philosopher, educator*
Sturges, Robert Stuart *English language educator*
Thompson, Annie Laura (Anne) *foreign language educator*

Pineville
Tapley, Philip Allen *language educator, literature educator*

Ruston
Halliburton, Lloyd *Romance philology educator*

MAINE

Brunswick
Levine, Daniel *historian, educator*

Hancock
Kimball, Anne Spofford *French language educator*

Kennebunk
Escalet, Frank Diaz *art gallery owner, artist, educator*

Scarborough
Campbell, Edward Fay, Jr., *religion educator*

Waterville
Roisman, Hanna Maslovski *classics educator*

MARYLAND

Baltimore
Baldwin, John Wesley *history educator*
Cacossa, Anthony Alexander *Romance languages educator*
Chapelle, Suzanne Ellery Greene *history educator*
Child-Olmsted, Gisèle Alexandra *language educator*
Del Rosso, Jeana Marie *literature educator*
Irwin, John Thomas *humanities educator, educator*
Kessler, Herbert Leon *art historian, educator, university administrator*
Knight, Franklin W. *history educator*
Lidtke, Vernon LeRoy *history educator*
Natividad, Evangelia de Hitta *Spanish educator, court interpreter, translator*
Nichols, Stephen George *Romance languages educator*
Paulson, Ronald Howard *English and humanities educator*
Pritchett, Robert Marvin, Jr., *religious organization administrator*
Ranum, Orest Allen *historian, educator*
Russell-Wood, Anthony John R. *history educator*
Skinner, Daniel Thomas *language educator*
Terborg-Penn, Rosalyn Marian *historian, educator*
Thompson-Cager-Strand, Chezia *literature educator, writer, performance artist*

Bethesda
Briend-Walker, Monique Marie *French and Spanish language educator*
Lurensky, Eleanor Goldman *humanities educator*
Raffini, Renee Kathleen *foreign language professional, educator*

Bowie
Sterling, Richard Leroy *English and foreign language educator*

Chevy Chase
Cline, Ruth Eleanor Harwood *translator*

College Park
Berlin, Ira *historian, educator*
Brush, Stephen George *historian, educator*
De Lorenzo, William E. *foreign language educator*
Lichtenberg, Judith A. *philosophy educator*
Olson, Keith Waldemar *history educator*
Pasch, Alan *philosopher, educator*
Winton, Calhoun *literature educator*

Ellicott City
Veasel, Walter *minister, educator*

Emmitsburg
Stay, Byron Lee *rhetoric educator, college administrator*

Hyattsville
Rodgers, Mary Columbro *literature educator, writer, academic administrator*

Kingsville
Clark, Wilma Jean Marshall *English language educator*

Pocomoke City
Kerbin, Diane Leithiser *history educator*

Rockville
Goldenberg, Myrna Gallant *English language/literature and Holocaust educator*

Salisbury
Cubbage, Elinor Phillips *English language educator*

Severna Park
Windsor, Patricia (Katonah Summertree, Perrin Winters) *author, educator, lecturer*

Silver Spring
Edwards, Kamala Doris *humanities educator*
Papas, Irene Kalandros *English language educator, poet, writer*

Upper Marlboro
Carroll, Cyril James *speech communication and theatre educator*

Westminster
Scott, Susan Clare *art history educator, editor*

MASSACHUSETTS

Amesbury
Bahre, Jeannette *English language and literature educator, education educator, librarian, educational consultant and tutor*
Labaree, Benjamin Woods *history educator*

Amherst
Beekman, Eric M. *language educator*

Gibson, Walker *retired English language educator, poet, writer*
Kinney, Arthur Frederick *literary history educator, writer, editor*
Rosbottom, Ronald Carlisle *French, arts and humanities educator*
Stavans, Ilan *Latin American studies educator, writer*

Belchertown
Kitchell, Kenneth Francis, Jr., *classical studies educator*

Belmont
Dohanian, Diran Kavork *art historian, educator*

Boston
Glick, Thomas F. *history educator*
Knott, Bill *poet, literature educator*
Scanlon, Dorothy Therese *history educator*
Terrill, Ross Gladwin *writer, educator*
Tobin, Daniel Eugene *poet, English language educator*

Bridgewater
Farrar, Ruth Doris *reading and literacy educator*

Byfield
Kozol, Jonathan *writer*

Cambridge
Asani, Ali S. *foreign language and religious studies educator*
Badian, Ernst *history educator*
Bailyn, Bernard *historian, educator*
Buell, Lawrence Ingalls *English language educator*
Chomsky, (Avram) Noam (Avram Chomsky) *linguistics and philosophy educator*
Cohn, Marjorie Benedict *curator, art historian, educator*
Conley, Tom Clark *literature educator*
Craig, Albert Morton *Asian studies educator*
Cuno, James *art museum director*
Damrosch, Leo *English educator*
Engell, James Theodore *English educator*
Fisher, Philip J. *English language and literature educator*
Flier, Michael Stephen *Slavic languages educator*
Ford, Patrick Kildea *Celtic studies educator*
Gaskell, Ivan George Alexander De Wend *art museum curator*
Goldfarb, Warren (David Goldfarb) *philosophy educator*
Graham, William Albert *religion educator, history educator*
Guthke, Karl Siegfried *foreign language educator*
Halle, Morris *linguist, educator*
Hanan, Patrick Dewes *foreign language professional, educator*
Heaney, Seamus Justin *poet, educator*
Henrichs, Albert Maximinus *classicist, educator*
Hutchison, William Robert *history educator*
Iriye, Akira *historian, educator*
Jones, Christopher Prestige *classicist, historian*
Kennedy, Roger George *museum director, park service executive*
Laiou, Angeliki Evangelos *history educator*
Maier, Charles Steven *history educator*
Maier, Pauline *history educator*
Mazlish, Bruce *historian, educator*
McCormick, Michael *history educator*
McDonald, Christie Anne *Romance languages and literature educator, writer*
Mowry, Robert Dean *art museum curator, educator*
O'Neil, Wayne *linguist, educator*
Ozment, Steven *historian, educator*
Parsons, Charles Dacre *philosophy educator*
Pipes, Richard *historian, educator*
Rosenberg, Charles Ernest *historian, educator*
Rotberg, Robert Irwin *historian, political economist, educator, editor*
Sevcenko, Ihor *history and literature educator*
Shinagel, Michael *English literature educator*
Singer, Irving *philosophy educator*
Sollors, Werner *English language, literature and American studies educator*
Thernstrom, Stephan *historian, educator*
Vendler, Helen Hennessy *literature educator, poetry critic*
Wolff, Christoph Johannes *music historian, educator*

Chestnut Hill
Barth, John Robert *English educator, priest*
Hachey, Thomas Eugene *British and Irish history educator, consultant*
Valette, Rebecca Marianne *Romance languages educator*

Dalton
Fumento, Rocco *retired English and film educator*

Fairhaven
Lopes, Myra Amelia *writer*

Fall River
Powers, Alan William *literature educator*

Framingham
Casper, Leonard Ralph *American literature educator*

Gardner
Cosentino, Patricia Byrne *English educator, poet*

Leverett
Margolis, Nadia *foreign language educator, medievalist, translator*

Lincoln
Donald, David Herbert *author, history educator*

Ludlow
Tetherly, Jonathan Collieson *chaplain, educator*

Medford
Bedau, Hugo Adam *philosophy educator*
Fyler, John Morgan *English language educator*
Gardner, Geoffrey *writer, English language educator*
Laurent, Pierre-Henri *history educator*
Marcopoulos, George John *history educator*
O'Leary, David Michael *priest, educator*

Natick
Ma, Jing-Heng Sheng *East Asian languages educator*

Newburyport
Lyons, Thomas Tolman *history educator*

Newton
Scheffler, Israel *philosopher, educator*
Tannenwald, Leslie Keiter *rabbi, justice of peace, educational administrator, chaplain*

North Dartmouth
Sitarz, Paula Gaj *writer*
Yoken, Mel B(arton) *French language educator, writer*

Plymouth
Mulligan, Louise Eleanore *retired English literature educator*

Revere
Herron, Carolivia *novelist, English educator*
Rega, Frances Louise *English educator*

Rutland
Cormick, Albina *foreign language educator*

Salem
Gozemba, Patrica Andrea *women's studies and English language educator, writer*

Sherborn
Cushing, Steven *linguist, educator, writer, researcher, consultant*

South Hadley
Farnham, Anthony Edward *English language educator*
Johnson, Richard August *English language educator*
Mazzocco, Angelo *language educator, cultural historian, linguist*

Springfield
Bonemery, Anne M. *language educator*
Porter, Burton Frederick *philosophy educator, writer, dean*
Varnum, Robin Ranelle *English language professional, educator*

Stoughton
Hall, Roger Lee *musicologist, educator, composer*

Swampscott
Truog, Dean-Daniel Wesley *educator, consultant*

Waltham
Delaney, Mary Anne *retired theology studies educator*
Hale, Jane Alison *French and comparative literature educator*
Reisman, Bernard *theology educator*

Watertown
Feld, Marjorie Nan *history educator*
Regan, Thomas Joseph *priest, educator*
Rivers, Wilga Marie *foreign language educator*

Wellesley
Jacoff, Rachel *Italian language and literature educator*
Lefkowitz, Mary Rosenthal *Greek literature educator*
Martin, Tony *humanities educator*
Mistacco, Vicki E. *foreign language educator*
Piper, Adrian Margaret Smith *philosopher, artist, educator*
Putnam, Ruth Anna *philosopher, educator*

Wenham
Flint-Ferguson, Janis Deane *English language and literature educator*

West Stockbridge
Stokes, Allison *pastor, researcher, religion educator*

Weston
Jarzavek, John Brian *English and art history educator*
Vetterling, Mary-Anne *Spanish language and literature educator*

Williamstown
Bell-Villada, Gene H. *literature educator, writer*
Eusden, John Dykstra *theology educator, minister*
Fuqua, Charles John *retired classics educator*
Graver, Lawrence Stanley *English language professional*
Graver, Suzanne Levy *English literature educator*
Norton, Glyn Peter *French literature educator*
Oakley, Francis Christopher *history educator, former college president*
Pistorius, George *language educator, educator*
Raab, Lawrence Edward *English educator*

Worcester
Kom, Ambroise *literature educator*
Manfra, Jo Ann *history educator, lawyer*
Scanlon, Peter Joseph *priest*
Vaughan, Alden True *history educator*

HIGHER EDUCATION: HUMANITIES

Wrentham
Ferreira, Joseph John, Jr., *history educator, theatre/drama educator*

MICHIGAN

Adrian
Peeradina, Saleem *English educator, poet*

Albion
Baumgartner, Ingeborg *foreign language educator*

Allendale
Cata, Isabelle Marie Gros *foreign language educator*

Ann Arbor
Bailey, Richard Weld *English language educator*
Blouin, Francis Xavier, Jr., *history educator*
Bornstein, George Jay *literary educator*
Cambers, Philip William *pastor, music minister, music educator*
Cart, Pauline Harmon *minister, educator*
Izzo, Herbert John *language and linguistics educator, researcher*
McCarus, Ernest Nasseph *retired language educator*
Munro, Donald Jacques *philosopher, educator*
Nelson, Roy Jay *retired French educator*
Perkins, Bradford *history educator*
Pernick, Martin Steven *history educator*
Scodel, Ruth *humanities educator*
Trautmann, Thomas Roger *history and anthropology educator*

Battle Creek
Cline, Charles William *poet, pianist, rhetoric and literature educator*

Big Rapids
Mehler, Barry Alan *humanities educator, journalist, consultant*

Birmingham
Reeves, Kathleen Walker *English and French language educator*

Bloomfield Hills
Gossett, Kathryn Myers *language professional, educator*

Davison
McCann, Martha Sue Powers *reading and language arts educator*

Dearborn
Hess, Margaret Johnston *religious writer, educator*
Little, Daniel Eastman *philosopher educator, university program director*

Delton
Waring, Walter Weyler *English language educator*

Detroit
Haase, Donald Paul *German language, literature and culture educator*
Walker-Shivers, Dauphine *humanities educator*

East Lansing
Anderson, David Daniel *retired humanities educator, writer, editor*
Bresnahan, Roger Jiang *humanities educator, researcher*
Dewhurst, Charles Kurt *museum director, cultural administrator, curator, folklorist, English language educator*

Eastpointe
Humita, Tiberius Ted *languages educator*

Flushing
Lemke, Laura Ann *language educator, principal*

Grand Rapids
Diephouse, David James *humanities educator, historian*
Henry, Karen Lee *writer, lecturer*

Harper Woods
Havrilcsak, Gregory Michael *history educator*

Holland
Pannapacker, William Albert, III, *humanities educator*

Jackson
Feldmann, Judith Gail *language professional, educator*

Kalamazoo
Julien, Catherine *history educator*
Raaberg, Gloria Gwen *literature educator*
Ruoff, Cynthia Osowiec *foreign language educator*

Livonia
Holtzman, Roberta Lee *French and Spanish language educator*

Mount Pleasant
Steffel, Susan Elizabeth *English language and literature educator*

New Era
Minty, Judith Makinen *poet, literature and creative writing educator*

Olivet
Walker, Donald Edwin *history educator*

Saginaw
Houshiar, Bobbie Kay *language arts educator*

Sterling Heights
Ice, Orva Lee, Jr., *history educator, retired*

Temperance
DeBoer, Annabel *English language educator*

Ypsilanti
Cere, Ronald Carl *languages educator, consultant, researcher*
Duley, Margot Iris *historian, educator*

MINNESOTA

Coon Rapids
Carlson, Linda Marie *language arts educator, consultant*

Cottonwood
Curtler, Hugh Mercer, Jr., *philosophy educator*

Duluth
Tezla, Albert *English educator*

Grand Rapids
Merrill, Arthur Lewis *retired theology educator*

Inver Grove Heights
Koenig, Robert August *clergyman, educator*

Minneapolis
Battle, Willa Lee Grant *clergywoman, educational administrator*
Cohen, Andrew David *language educator, applied linguist*
Evans, Sara Margaret *history educator*
Farah, Caesar Elie *Middle Eastern and Islamic studies educator*
Fergus, Patricia Marguerita *English language educator emeritus, writer, editor*
Garner, Shirley Nelson *English language educator*
Hauch, Valerie Catherine *historian, educator*
Jewell, H. Richard *English language educator*
Ross, Donald, Jr., *English language educator, university administrator*

Moorhead
Coomber, James Elwood *English language educator*

Northfield
Iseminger, Gary Hudson *philosophy educator*
McKinsey, Elizabeth *humanities educator, consultant*
Paas, John Roger *language educator*
Sipfle, David Arthur *retired philosophy educator*
Soule, George Alan *literature educator, writer*
Swanson, Stephen Olney *minister, retired English educator*
Yandell, Cathy Marleen *foreign language educator*
Zelliot, Eleanor Mae *history educator*

Ortonville
Schrom, Elizabeth Ann *writer, educator*

Preston
Schommer, Trudy Marie *pastoral minister, religion education*

Saint Cloud
Braun, Janice Larson *language arts educator*
Specht-Jarvis, Roland Hubert *fine arts and humanities educator, dean*
Van Buren, Phyllis Eileen *Spanish and German language educator*

Saint Paul
Davis, Joy Lee *English language educator*
Klejment, Anne *historian, educator*
Monson, Dianne Lynn *literacy educator*

Waseca
Strand, Melvin LeRoy *English educator*

MISSISSIPPI

Bay Saint Louis
Woodward, Ralph Lee, Jr., *historian, educator*

Gulfport
Swetman, Glenn Robert *English language educator, poet*

Hattiesburg
Harvey, Tamara Maureen *English literature and women's studies educator*

Jackson
Curtis, Verna Polk *reading educator*
Palmer, Dora Deen Pope *English and French language educator*

Magnolia
Coney, Elaine Marie *English and foreign languages educator*

Mississippi State
Wiltrout, Ann Elizabeth *foreign language educator*

Pascagoula
Irving, Thomas Ballantine *retired Spanish language educator, consultant*

Senatobia
Banham, Sandra Rodgers *language educator*
Bunce, Robert Winford *literature educator*

University
Brinkmeyer, Robert Herman, Jr., *American literature and Southern studies educator*
Hall, J(ames) R(obert) *English educator*
Murchison, Margaret Lynne *educator*

Wicker, Nancy Lynn *art history educator*

MISSOURI

Boonville
McVicker, Mary Ellen Harshbarger *museum director, art history educator*

Branson
Ford, Jean Elizabeth *former English language educator*

Columbia
Anderson, Donald Kennedy, Jr., *English educator*
Schwartz, Richard Brenton *English language educator, dean, writer*
Vallentyne, Peter Lloyd *philosophy educator*
Wallach, Barbara Price *classicist, educator*

Florissant
Ashhurst, Anna Wayne *foreign language educator*

Joplin
Butler, Paul Thurman *retired religious studies educator*
Zustiak, Gary Blair *youth minister, educator*

Kansas City
Hebenstreit, Jean Estill Stark *religion educator, practitioner*

Kirksville
Iles, Lawrence Irvine *liberal arts educator, historian*
Siewert, Gregg Hunter *language professional, educator*

Laddonia
Scheffler, Lewis Francis *pastor, educator, research scientist*

Lees Summit
Himes, Brian David *reading educator*

Maryville
Heusel, Barbara Stevens *English scholar and educator*

Saint Louis
Arneill, B. Porter *arts program educator*
Bagley, Mary Carol *literature educator, writer, announcer*
Boyd, Robert Cotton *English language educator*
Brown, Virginia Suggs *writer, language arts educator, consultant*
Corbett, Suzanne Elaine *food writer, marketing executive, food historian*
Montesi, Albert Joseph *retired English educator*
Perry, Elisabeth Israels *historian, educator, administrator*
Robbert, Louise Buenger *retired historian*
Sand, Gregory William *history educator, researcher*
Watson, Richard Allan *philosophy educator, writer*
Weixlmann, Joseph Norman, Jr., *English educator, provost*

Springfield
Burgess, Ruth Lenora Vassar *speech and language educator*

Warrensburg
Robbins, Dorothy Ann *foreign language educator*

West Plains
Smith, Allison London *English language educator, real estate developer*

MONTANA

Big Arm
Dale, David Wilson *English educator, poet*

Big Timber
Agnew, Kathleen Dianne Crosbie *language educator*

Missoula
Chin, Beverly Ann *literature educator*
Talbot, Susan Anderson *French language educator*

NEBRASKA

Hastings
McEwen, Larry Burdette *retired English and theater arts educator, author*

Lincoln
Levin, Carole *history educator*

Murray
Tiedemann, Ruth Elizabeth Fulton (Sunnye Tiedemann) *writer, educator*

Omaha
Okhamafe, Imafedia *English literature and philosophy educator*
Tate, Michael Lynn *history educator*
Vierk, Janice Marie *English educator*

Trenton
Goodenberger, Mary Ellen *English educator*

NEVADA

Las Vegas
Gafford, Mary May *humanities educator*

Walton, (Delvy) Craig *philosopher, educator*

North Las Vegas
Green, Michael Scott *history educator, columnist*
Logsdon, Richard M. *English language educator, magazine editor*
Miller, Eleanor *English language and literature educator*
Schmitt, Paul John *history and geography educator*

NEW HAMPSHIRE

Derry
Holmes, Richard Dale *history consultant*

Durham
Linden, Blanche Marie Gemrose *history educator*

Hanover
Bien, Peter Adolph *English language educator, author*
Daniell, Jere Rogers, II, *retired history educator, consultant, public lecturer*
Garthwaite, Gene Ralph *historian, educator*
Gert, Bernard *philosopher, educator*
Heffernan, James Anthony Walsh *language and literature educator*
Kritzman, Lawrence David *humanities educator*
Mansell, Darrel Lee, Jr., *English educator*
Scher, Steven Paul *literature educator, educator*
Scherr, Barry Paul *foreign language educator*
Shewmaker, Kenneth Earl *history educator*

Jaffrey
Van Ness, Patricia Wood *religious studies educator, consultant, author*

Keene
Long, Mark Christopher *English educator*

Mount Sunapee
Marashio, Paul William *humanities educator*

Orford
Beale, Georgia Robison *historian, educator*

Swanzey
Nichols, Diane Linda Clark *French language educator*

NEW JERSEY

Asbury Park
Schwerin, Alan Kenneth *philosophy educator*

Belleville
Lewandoski, Suzanne Taylor *English educator*

Brielle
McIntyre, Elizabeth Jones *multi-media specialist, educator*

Burlington
Holmes-Baxter, Maureen Olivia *language arts educator*

Caldwell
Campbell, Sister Maura *religious studies and philosophy educator*

Cherry Hill
Bryan, Henry Collier *clergyman, retired secondary school educator*

Clifton
Ressetar, Nancy *foreign language educator*
Stalbaum, Bernardine Ann *English language educator*

Dayton
Adickes, Sandra Elaine *English language educator, writer*

Glassboro
Ashton, Dianne Cheryl *American studies educator*

Hackensack
Fatemi, Saeid *language educator, writer, researcher*

Hainesport
McKay, Dianne Adele Mills *humanities educator, educator*

Hightstown
Davis, Jacquetta Anderson *English language educator*

Holmdel
Buyanovsky, Sophia *linguist, educator*

Jersey City
D'Ambra, Eve *art historian*
Lane, Ted *literacy education educator*

Lincroft
Jones, Floresta D. *English educator*

Livingston
Saffer, Amy Beth *foreign language educator*

Madison
Edwards, Lillie Johnson *history educator*
Perriman, Wendy Karen *poet, educator*

Mahwah
Padovano, Anthony Thomas *theologian, educator*

Manasquan
Hope, Jaime Lynn *foreign language educator*

Metuchen
Breen, Vincent De Paul *bishop*

Morristown
Sandonato, Ernest R. *English language educator*

New Brunswick
Chambers, John Whiteclay, II, *history educator*
Hartman, Mary S. *historian, educator*
Levine, George Lewis *English language educator, literature critic*
Mora, Gabriela *language educator, researcher*
Speer, Mary Blakely *French language educator*
Tripolitis, Antonia *religion, classics and comparative literature educator*
Welsh, Andrew *English educator*
Zatlin, Phyllis *Spanish language educator, translator*

Newark
Hadas, Rachel *poet, educator*
Schweizer, Karl Wolfgang *historian, educator, author*
Sher, Richard B. *historian, educator*

Paramus
Brandes, Margot *humanities educator, artist*

Princeton
Aarsleff, Hans *linguistics educator*
Bermann, Sandra Lekas *English language educator*
Brombert, Victor Henri *literature educator, author*
Brown, Leon Carl *history educator*
Cooper, John Madison *philosophy educator*
Darnton, Robert Choate *history educator*
Ermolaev, Herman Sergei *Slavic languages educator*
Harman, Gilbert Helms *philosophy educator*
Hollander, Robert B., Jr., *Romance languages educator*
Itzkowitz, Norman *history educator*
Jenson, Pauline Alvino *retired speech and hearing educator*
Kay, James Franklin *religion educator*
Kelly, Sean Dorrance *philosophy educator*
Mc Pherson, James Munro *history educator*
Metzger, Bruce Manning *clergyman, educator*
Ober, Josiah *history educator*
Painter, Nell Irvin *historian, author*
Peterson, Willard James *Chinese history educator*
Rigolot, François *French literature educator, literary critic*
Rodgers, Daniel Tracy *history educator*
Townsend, Charles Edward *Slavic languages educator*
Wightman, Ludmilla G. Popova *language educator, foreign educator, translator*

Ridgewood
Molnar, Thomas *philosophy and religion educator, writer*

River Edge
Haynes, Barbara Judith *language educator*

Rumson
Rosoff, Barbara Lee *religious education administrator*

Secaucus
Walka, Anne Lauraine *English language educator*

Somerset
Fama, Katherine *English and journalism educator, multicultural literature consultant*

Somerville
D'Alessio, Jacqueline Ann *English educator*

Teaneck
Czin, Felicia Tedeschi *Italian language and literature educator, small business owner*
Dowd, Janice Lee *foreign language educator*
Walensky, Dorothy Charlotte *foreign language educator*

Toms River
Bosley, Karen Lee *English and journalism educator*

Wayne
Rogoff, Paula Drimmer *English and foreign language educator*

NEW MEXICO

Albuquerque
Valdez, Dianna Marie *language educator, consultant*

Carlsbad
Sandford, Mary Ann *Spanish language educator*

Gallup
Martinez, Marcella *language educator*

Portales
Overton, Edwin Dean *campus minister, educator*

Santa Fe
Gaustad, Edwin Scott *historian, educator*
Vivelo, Jacqueline Jean *author, English language educator*

NEW YORK

Amherst
Kurtz, Paul *philosopher, educator, writer, publisher*
Wickert, Max Albrecht *English educator, poet*

Ballston Spa
Barba, Harry *author, educator, publisher*

Bronx
Asare, Karen Michelle Gilliam *reading, math and English language educator*
Cammarata, Joan Frances *Spanish language and literature educator*
Hallett, Charles Arthur, Jr., *English and humanities educator*
Hilfstein, Erna *science historian, educator*
Himmelberg, Robert Franklin *historian, educator*
Kirmse, Sister Anne-Marie Rose *nun, educator, researcher*
Maddox, Utricia Antoinette *English educator, communications educator*
Ruffing, Janet Kathryn *spirituality educator*
Spatt, Hartley Steven *humanities educator, educator*
Ultan, Lloyd *historian, educator*
Wosk, Julie *humanities educator*

Bronxville
Pollin, Burton Ralph *English educator*
Swann, Lois Lorraine *writer, editor, educator*

Brooklyn
Bonaffini, Luigi *language and literature educator, translator*
Everdell, William Romeyn *humanities educator, educator*
Gisolfi, Diana (Diana Gisolfi Pechukas) *art history educator*
Harkavy, Roberta Susan *retired humanities educator*
Jaffe, Louise *English language educator, creative writer*
King, Margaret Leah *history educator*
Mulvihill, Maureen Esther *writer, educator, scholar*

Buffalo
Gracia, Jorge Jesus Emiliano *philosopher, educator*
Hare, Peter Hewitt *philosophy educator*
Levine, George Richard *English language educator*
Merini, Rafika *foreign language, cultures and literatures educator*
Nelson, Herbert James *philosophy educator*
Payne, Frances Anne *literature educator, researcher*
Peradotto, John Joseph *classics educator, editor*
Siedlecki, Peter Anthony *English language and literature educator*

Castleton On Hudson
VanVliet, Mary Lynne *English language educator, photography assistant*

Cedarhurst
Solymosy, Hattie May *writer, publisher, storyteller, educator*

Chatham
Sninchak, Faye Rita *humanities educator*

Churchville
Clarke, Stephan Paul *retired language educator, retired writer*

Delmar
Schwarz, Louise A. *band director*

Dobbs Ferry
Sax, Boria *intellectual history studies educator, writer*

Elmira
Pucci, Anthony J. *English language educator*

Fairport
Graham, Susette Ryan *retired English educator*

Fayetteville
Olson, Ann Martin *language education specialist*

Flushing
Lonigan, Paul Raymond *language professional, educator*
Raines, Judi Belle *language educator, historian*
Ranald, Margaret Loftus *English literature educator, author*

Forest Hills
Kra, Pauline Skornicki *French language educator*

Fredonia
Smith, Claire Laremont *language educator*
Strada, Christina Bryson *retired humanities educator, librarian*

Garden City
Diamandopoulos, Peter *former philosopher, educator*

Grand Island
Kutlina, Mary Louise *language educator*

Great Neck
Rapoport, Florence Rosenberg *English language educator*

Guilderland
Ryan, Nancy Marie *Spanish-English educator*

Guilderland Center
Bloom, Michelle *foreign language educator*

Hamilton
Busch, Briton Cooper *historian, educator*
Staley, Lynn *English educator*

Hastings On Hudson
Barolini, Helen *writer, translator, educator*
Del Duca, Rita *language educator*

Schieber, Phyllis *writer, learning disabilities specialist*

Hempstead
McPhee, Martha *literature educator*
Tucker, Joseph *clergyman, former dean*

Herkimer
Martin, Lorraine B. *humanities educator*

Hurley
Davila, Elisa *language educator, literature educator*

Indian Lake
Schoenberg, Margaret Main *former English language educator*

Ithaca
Colby-Hall, Alice Mary *Romance studies educator*
Kammen, Carol Koyen *historian, educator*
Kronik, John William *Romance studies educator*
McCoy, Maureen *novelist, writing educator*
Norton, Mary Beth *history educator, writer*

Jamaica
Harmond, Richard Peter *historian, educator*
Wintergerst, Ann Charlotte *language educator*

Kings Point
Brickman, Jane Pacht *history educator*

Massapequa
Vaccaro, Nicholas Carmine *English language and media educator*

New Paltz
Brown, Peter David Gilson *German language educator*
Hathaway, Richard Dean *retired language educator*
Hauptman, Laurence Marc *history educator*
Urbanski, Henry *foreign language educator*

New Rochelle
Confalone, Patricia Cullen *language arts and reading specialist*

New York
Alazraki, Jaime *Romance languages educator*
Arac, Jonathan *English language educator*
Ashbery, John Lawrence *language educator, poet, playwright, art critic*
Ashdown, Marie Matranga (Mrs. Cecil Spanton Ashdown Jr.) *writer, educator, lecturer, cultural organization administrator*
Bagnall, Roger Shaler *history educator*
Belknap, Robert Lamont *Russian and comparative literature educator*
Berghahn, Volker Rolf *history educator*
Birstein, Ann *writer, educator*
Block, Ned *philosopher, educator*
Bogen, Nancy *writer, English educator*
Cahn, Steven Mark *philosopher, educator*
Caws, Mary Ann *French language and comparative literature educator, critic*
Colon, Elsie Flores *American and English literature educator*
Compagnon, Antoine Marcel *French language educator*
Costello, John Robert *linguistics educator*
Danto, Arthur Coleman *author, philosopher, art critic*
Deak, Istvan *historian, educator*
Dore, Anita Wilkes *English language educator*
Driver, Martha Westcott *English language educator, writer, researcher*
Foner, Eric *historian, educator*
Freedberg, David Adrian *art educator, historian*
Friedman, Herbert A. *rabbi, educator, fund raising executive*
Gay, Peter *history educator, author*
Ginter, Valerian Alexius *urban historian, educator*
Gluck, Carol *history educator*
Gutfreund, Owen David *historian, educator*
Howard, Jean Elizabeth *English educator*
Javitch, Daniel Gilbert *comparatist, educator*
Johnson, Samuel Frederick *English and literature educator emeritus*
Kafka, Barbara Poses *writer*
Kaiser, Walter *English language educator*
Kalmus, Ellin *art historian, educator*
Karsen, Sonja Petra *retired American-Hispanic literature educator*
Klass, Sheila Solomon *English language educator, writer*
Koch, Kenneth *poet, playwright*
Kroeber, Karl *English language educator*
Levi, Isaac *philosophy educator*
Lewyn, Ann Salfeld *retired English as a second language educator*
London, Herbert Ira *humanities educator, institute executive*
Lorch, Maristella De Panizza *medieval and Renaissance scholar, writer*
Lunardini, Christine Anne *writer, historian, school administrator*
Luten, Karen A. *English language educator*
Malefakis, Edward E. *history educator*
Malin, Irving *English literature educator, literary critic*
Malone, Joseph Lawrence *linguistics educator*
May, Gita *language educator, literature educator*
Maysilles, Elizabeth *speech communication professional, educator*
Mazzucelli, Colette Grace Celia *author, multimedia educator*
McCullough, David *writer, educator*
Meisel, Martin *English and comparative literature educator*
Meléndez, Zulma Cecilia *bilingual/bicultural education evaluator*
Mendelson, Edward James *English literature educator*

Middlebrook, Diane Wood *English language educator, writer*
Milford, Nancy Winston *writer, English educator*
Miller, Peter N. *historian, educator*
Moberg, Verne *Swedish language educator, translator*
O'Donnell, Mark Patrick *writer, drama educator*
Olson, Roberta Jeanne Marie *art historian, author, educator, curator*
Paxton, Robert Owen *historian, educator*
Plottel, Jeanine Parisier *foreign language educator*
Ponsot, Marie *poet*
Pool, Mary Jane *writer, lecturer*
Root, William Pitt *poet, educator*
Rosenberg, John David *English educator, literary critic*
Rothberger, Sue Ellen *language educator*
Rothenberg, Jerome *author, visual arts and literary educator*
Rothman, David J. *history and medical educator*
Rowen, Ruth Halle *musicologist, educator*
Salemi, Joseph Salvatore *classics and humanities educator, poet, writer*
Schaffner, Cynthia Van Allen *writer, curator, lecturer*
Schorsch, Ismar *clergyman, Jewish history educator*
Steinberg, Leo *art historian, educator*
Stempleski, Susan *English language professional, writer*
Stephens, Gary Ralph *American literature and journalism educator*
Stern, Fritz Richard *historian, educator*
Stimpson, Catharine Roslyn *English language educator, writer*
Swann, Brian *writer, humanities educator*
Taran, Leonardo *classicist, educator*
Umeh, Marie Arlene *English language educator*
Walkowitz, Daniel Jay *historian, filmmaker, educator*
Wallace, Barbara Faith *linguistics educator*
Wortman, Richard S. *historian, educator*
Wyschogrod, Edith *philosophy educator*
Yerushalmi, Yosef Hayim *historian, educator*

Newburgh
Adams, Barbara *English language educator, poet, writer*

Niagara Falls
Gromosiak, Paul *historian, consultant, writer, science and math educator*

North Tonawanda
Bilotta, James Dominic *history educator*
Powers, Bruce Raymond *writer, English language educator, consultant*

Oneonta
Malhotra, Ashok Kumar *philosophy educator*
Shrader, Douglas Wall, Jr., *philosophy educator*
Travisano, Thomas Joseph *English language educator*

Orchard Park
Perry, Marion J.H. *English educator*

Oyster Bay
Gable, John Allen *historian, association executive, educator*
Garone, Frank *English language educator*

Pittsford
French, Henry Pierson, Jr., *historian, educator*

Pleasantville
Martini, Joseph T(homas) *language educator, music educator, data processing executive*

Potsdam
Cross, John William *foreign language educator*
Regan, Marie Carbone *retired language educator*

Poughkeepsie
Brakas, Jurgis (George) Hoegh *philosopher, educator*
Sharp, Ronald Alan *English literature educator, dean, author*

Purchase
Clark, Mary Twibill *philosopher, educator*
Lucas, Billy Joe *philosophy educator*
Waller, Gary Fredric *English language educator, administrator, poet*

Queens Village
Acuña-Reyes, Rita *foreign language educator*

Rochester
Ganley, Beatrice *English educator, writer*
Hollis, Susan Tower *history educator*
Joyce, John Joseph *English language educator*
Kneeland, Timothy William *historian, researcher*
Ousley, Laurie M. *English educator*
Watanabe, Ruth Taiko *music historian, library science educator*

Rockville Centre
Smalbach, Barbara Schiller *foreign language educator*

Sagaponack
Appleman, Philip *poet, writer, educator*

Saint Bonaventure
Wood, Paul William *language educator*

Sanborn
Michalak, Janet Carol *reading education educator*

Saratoga Springs
Rogoff, Jay *poet, educator*
Williams, Susan Diane *language educator*

Sayville
Lippman, Sharon Rochelle *art historian, art therapist, filmmaker*

Scarsdale
Graff, Henry Franklin *historian, educator*

Schenectady
Baker, Robert Bernard *philosophy educator*

Sound Beach
Everett, Graham *English language educator, poet, publisher*

Staten Island
Bernhardt, William Wolf *English language educator*
Lombardi, Giancarlo *Italian language educator*
Popp, Lilian Mustaki *writer, educator*

Stony Brook
Bethin, Christina Y. *linguist, language educator*
Harris, Alice Carmichael *linguist, educator*
Levin, Richard Louis *English language educator*

Syracuse
Alston, William Payne *philosophy educator*
Waddy, Patricia A. *architectural history educator*
Walker, Amy Melissa *English as second language educator*

Troy
Phelan, Thomas *clergyman, academic administrator, educator*

Vestal
Quataert, Donald *history educator*

Wappingers Falls
Pastrana, Ronald Ray *Christian ministry counselor, Biblical theology educator, former school system administrator*

White Plains
Benjamin, Barbara Bloch *writer, editor*

Yonkers
Agli, Stephen Michael *English language educator, literature educator*
Viola, Mary Jo *art history educator*

NORTH CAROLINA

Cary
Mata, Elizabeth Adams *English language educator, land investor*
Slaatté, Howard Alexander *minister, philosophy educator*

Chapel Hill
Davis, Sarah Irwin *retired English language educator*
Ludington, Townsend *English and American studies educator*
Semonche, John Erwin *history educator, lawyer, consultant*
Stanberry, D(osi) Elaine *English literature educator, writer*
Strauss, Albrecht Benno *English educator, editor*

Charlotte
Grigg, Eddie Garman *minister, educator*
Hill, Ruth Foell *language consultant*
Preyer, Norris Watson *history educator*

Cullowhee
Blethen, Harold Tyler, III, *history educator*
Farwell, Harold Frederick, Jr., *English language educator*

Davidson
Goldstein, Irwin Stuart *philosophy educator*
Williams, Robert Chadwell *history educator*

Durham
Crenshaw, James L(ee) *theology educator*
Davis, Calvin De Armond *historian, educator*
Jonassaint, Jean *French and Francophone literatures educator*
Meyers, Eric Mark *religion educator*
Thomas, Jean-Jacques Robert *Romance languages educator*
Williams, George Walton *English educator*
Williams, Jocelyn Jones *reading educator*

Elizabeth City
Williams, Rita Carroll *language educator, poet*

Fayetteville
Conley, Raymond Leslie *English language educator*
McMillan, Bettie Barney *English language educator*

Franklin
Johnson, Herbert Alan *history and law educator, lawyer, chaplain*

Greensboro
Gaines, Sarah Fore *retired foreign language educator*
Penninger, Frieda Elaine *retired English language educator*

Hillsborough
Idol, John Lane, Jr., *English language educator, writer, editor*

Laurinburg
Bayes, Ronald Homer *English language educator, author*

Raleigh
de Cuba, Marjorie Herrmann *retired bilingual educator*

Ryan, Bryan *college administrator, language educator, writer, editor*
Slatta, Richard Wayne *historian, educator, writer*

Wilmington
Graham, Otis Livingston, Jr., *history educator*

Woodland
Burgwyn, Anna Poole *English language educator*

NORTH DAKOTA

Grand Forks
Caldwell, Mary Ellen *English language educator*

Mayville
Brunsdale, Mitzi Louisa, (Mallarian) *English language educator, book critic*

Wahpeton
Reubish, Gary Richard *English language educator*

OHIO

Akron
Burton, June Rosalie Kehr *history educator*
Clinefelter, Ruth Elizabeth Wright *historian, educator*

Athens
Jellison, Katherine Kay *historian, educator*
Perdreau, Cornelia Ruth Whitener (Connie Perdreau) *English as a second language educator, international exchange specialist*
Ping, Charles Jackson *philosophy educator, retired university president*
Whealey, Lois Deimel *humanities scholar*

Brecksville
Pappas, Effie Vamis *English and business educator, writer, poet, artist*

Canton
Dickens, Sheila Jeanne *family preservation educator*

Chagrin Falls
Rawski, Conrad H(enry) *humanities educator, medievalist*

Cincinnati
Alexander, John Kurt *history educator*
Anderson, Joan Balyeat *religion educator, minister*
Ciani, Alfred Joseph *language professional, associate dean*
Neman, Beth S. *English educator*
Rosen, Roberta *philosophy educator*
Schrier, Arnold *historian, educator*

Cleveland
Anderson, David Gaskill, Jr., *Spanish language educator*
Benseler, David Price *foreign language educator*
Harrison, Dennis I. *archivist*
Juhlin, Doris Arlene *French language educator*
Khabeer, Beryl Jean *poet, playwright, educator*
Robinson, Alice Helene *English language educator, administrative assistant*
Salem, Dorothy Carlson *social science and history educator*
Spencer, James Calvin, Sr., *humanities educator*
Taylor, Margaret Wischmeyer *retired language educator*
Weinberg, Helen Arnstein *American art and literature educator*

Columbus
Battersby, James Lyons, Jr., *English language educator*
Beja, Morris *English literature educator*
Findley, Carter Vaughn *historian, educator*
Jarvis, Gilbert Andrew *humanities educator, writer*
Jebsen, Harry Alfred Arthur, Jr., *history educator*
Nakayama, Mineharu *Japanese language professional, educator*
Stephan, Alexander Friedrich *German language and literature educator*

Cuyahoga Falls
Walker, Suzannah Wolf *language educator*

Dayton
Alexander, Roberta Sue *history educator*
Romaguera, Enrique *foreign language educator, corporate interpreter*
Triulzi, Daniel Albert *classical and modern languages educator, priest*

Delaware
Lewes, Ulle Erika *English educator*

Dublin
Davis, Harrison Ransom Samuel, Jr., *English language educator*

Fairborn
Shevin, David A. *English literature educator*

Findlay
Fry, Charles George *theologian, educator*

Fremont
Wethington, Norbert Anthony *medieval scholar*

Granville
Baishanski, Jacqueline Marie *foreign language educator*
Lisska, Anthony Joseph *humanities educator, philosopher*
Santoni, Ronald Ernest *philosophy educator*

Hamilton
Inness, Sherrie Anne *English language educator*

Huron
Ruble, Ronald Merlin *humanities and theater communications educator*

Kent
Apseloff, Marilyn Fain *English educator*
Georgopoulos, Nenos Aristides *philosophy educator*
Harkness, Bruce *English language educator*
Hassler, Donald Mackey, II, *English language educator, writer*
Marovitz, Sanford E. *English language and literature educator*
Remley, R. Dirk *English educator, consultant*

Loveland
Grimmet, Alex J. *clergyman, school administrator, elementary and secondary education educator*

Macedonia
Schmidt, Nancy Charlene Linder *English and journalism educator*

Mansfield
Joyce, Steven James *German and comparative studies educator*

Marietta
Neu, Irene Dorothy *historian, educator*

Mc Arthur
Shuter, David Henry *foreign language educator*

North Canton
Heaphy, Leslie Anne *history educator*

Oberlin
Care, Norman Sydney *philosophy educator*
Collins, Martha *English language educator, writer*
Ganzel, Dewey Alvin *English language educator*
Soucy, Robert Joseph *history educator*

Portsmouth
Payne, Joyce Taylor Gillenwater *art specialist, art museum consultant, educator*

Saint Clairsville
Fisher, Sandra Irene *English educator*

Salem
Booth, Stephane Elise *history and women's studies educator, assistant dean*

Solon
Gallo, Donald Robert *retired English educator*

University Heights
Goral, Judith Ann *educator*

West Farmington
Smith, Agnes Monroe *history educator*

Yellow Springs
Fogarty, Robert Stephen *historian, educator, editor*

Youngstown
Sullivan, Dolores P. *writer, former educator*
Wan-Tatah, Victor Fon *theology educator*

OKLAHOMA

Bethany
Wood, Dolores Idel *retired Spanish and French languages educator*

Durant
Baskin, Vlasta Jana Marie *language educator, educator*

Edmond
Ackerman, Judy Kay *English educator*

Norman
Fears, Jesse Rufus *historian, educator, academic dean*
Hobbs, Catherine Lynn *English language and literature educator*
Leitch, Vincent Barry *literary and cultural studies educator*
Taylor, Kenneth Lapham *history and science educator*

Oklahoma City
Hall, James Granville, Jr., *history educator*
Hampton, Carol McDonald *priest, educator, historian*
Holt, Karen Anita Young *English educator*
Meeks, Patricia Lowe *language educator*
Prichard, Barbara Ann *English educator*

Stillwater
Fischer, LeRoy Henry *historian, educator*

Tulsa
Chew, Pamela Christine *language educator*

Weatherford
Craig, Viki Pettijohn *English and Spanish languages educator*

OREGON

Central Point
Curler, (Mary) Bernice (Mrs. Albert Elmer Curler) *writer, educator*

Eugene
Birn, Raymond Francis *historian, educator*

Lansdowne, Karen Myrtle *retired English language and literature educator*
White, David Olds *researcher, former educator*

Netarts
Hartman-Irwin, Mary Frances *retired language professional*

Newberg
Tsohantaridis, Timotheos *minister, religion educator*

North Bend
Shepard, Robert Carlton *English language educator*

Portland
Englert, Walter George *classics and humanities educator*
Karant-Nunn, Susan Catherine *history educator*
Knapp, Robert Stanley *English language educator*
Schmidt, Stanley Eugene *retired speech educator*
Steinman, Lisa Malinowski *English literature educator, writer*

Turner
Ratzlaff, Ruben Menno *religion educator, minister*

PENNSYLVANIA

Allentown
Huang, Guiyou *English studies educator, writer*

Ardmore
Gutwirth, Marcel Marc *French literature educator*

Aston
Bahl, Janice Miriam *director religious education*
Valdata, Patricia *English language educator, aviation writer*

Bala Cynwyd
Murphey, Murray Griffin *history educator*

Beaver Falls
Lambert, Lynda Jeanne *humanities and arts educator, artist*

Bethlehem
Orsi, Martha D. *literature educator, language educator*
Steffen, Lloyd Howard *minister, religion educator*

Blue Bell
Roden, Carol Looney *retired language educator*

Bryn Mawr
Dudden, Arthur Power *historian, educator*
Hamilton, Richard *Greek language educator*
King, Willard Fahrenkamp (Mrs. Edmund Ludwig King) *Spanish language educator*
Lane, Barbara Miller (Barbara Miller-Lane) *humanities educator*
Levine, Steven Z *humanities educator, department chairman*
Trout, Charles Hathaway *historian, educator*

California
Schwerdt, Lisa Mary *English language educator*

Chadds Ford
Curtis, James Malcolm *language educator*

Clinton
Talbot, Mary Lee *minister*

Edinboro
Kinch, Janet Carolyn Brozic *English and German language and literature educator, academic administrator*

Elizabethtown
Kraybill, Donald Brubaker *humanities educator, writer*

Erie
Allshouse, Robert Harold *history educator*
Nies, Katherine Ann *English teacher*

Glenside
Pelham, Fran O'Byrne *writer, teacher*

Greenville
Ward, Jay Alan *language professional, educator*

Harrisburg
Borie, Renee Debra *English language educator*
Boswell, James Aurthur, Jr., *English language educator*
Gibson, Shere Capparella *foreign language educator*
Khanzhina, Helen P. *English educator, translator*

Haverford
Kee, Howard Clark *religion educator*
Spielman, John Philip, Jr., *historian, educator*

Hermitage
Durek, Dorothy Mary *retired English language educator*

Indiana
Roumm, Phyllis Evelyn Gensbigler *retired literature educator, writer*

Kittanning
Smits, Ronald Francis *English educator, poet*

Kutztown
Cortés-Hwang, Adriana *Spanish language educator*

Meyer, Susan Moon *speech language pathologist, educator*

Lafayette Hill
Green, Rose Basile (Mrs. Raymond S. Green) *poet, author, educator*

Lewisburg
Edgerton, Mills Fox, Jr., *retired foreign language educator*
Payne, Michael David *English language educator*

Merion Station
Littell, Franklin Hamlin *theologian, educator*
Littell, Marcia Sachs *Holocaust and genocide studies educator*

Millersville
Craven, Roberta Jill *literature and film educator*
Miller, Steven Max *humanities educator*

Mont Alto
Russo, Peggy Anne *English language educator*

New Freedom
Sedlak, Valerie Frances *retired English language educator, retired academic administrator*

New Wilmington
Perkins, James Ashbrook *English language educator*

Philadelphia
Beeman, Richard Roy *historian, educator*
Daemmrich, Horst Sigmund *German language and literature educator*
de Francesco, John Kenneth *foreign language educator*
Dyson, Robert Harris *museum director emeritus, archaeologist, educator*
Feldscher, Sharla *writer, public relations executive*
Fusco, Richard *English literature educator*
Fussell, Paul *author, English literature educator*
Gross Alvarez, Cynthia Marie *bilingual education coordinator*
Hoenigswald, Henry Max *linguist, educator*
Lowry, Ralph James, Sr., *retired history educator*
Means, John Barkley *foreign language educator, association executive*
Paglia, Camille *writer, humanities educator*
Regan, Robert Charles *English language educator*
Tobia, Susan J. *reading educator*
Tripole, Martin R. *religion educator, priest*
Waks, Leonard Joseph *philosophy and education educator*
Weigley, Russell Frank *history educator*
Woodside, Lisa Nicole *humanities educator*

Phoenixville
Clark, Kathleen Mulhern *foreign language and literature educator*

Pittsburgh
Chase, William John *history educator*
Drescher, Seymour *history educator, writer*
Gale, Robert Lee *retired American literature educator and critic*
Goldstein, Donald Maurice *historian, educator*
Hsu, Cho-yun *history educator*
Jaffe, Gwen Daner *museum educator*
Klancher, Jon Paul *English language educator*
McCormick, David James *English language educator*
Paulston, Christina Bratt *linguistics educator*
Petesch, Natalie L. Maines *English language educator, author*
Rosen, Robert Stephen *humanities, theatre arts, TV and English educator*
Seligson, Mitchell A. *Latin American studies educator*

Reading
Robinson, Donald Lee *clergyman, educator*

Scranton
De Celles, Charles Edouard *theologian, educator*
Gougeon, Len Girard *literature educator*
Hoffman, Barbara Ann *English language educator*
Zaydon, Jemille Ann *English language and communications educator*

Shippensburg
Long, Kim Martin *language and literature educator*

Slippery Rock
Cobb, Larry Russell *ethics educator*
Zinni, Hannah Case *foreign language educator*

State College
Schmalstieg, William Riegel *retired Slavic languages educator*
Strasser, Gerhard Friedrich *German language and comparative literature educator*

Sunbury
Ely, Donald J(ean) *clergyman, secondary school educator*

Swarthmore
Bannister, Robert Corwin, Jr., *historian, educator*
Frost, Jerry William *religion and history educator, library administrator*
Lacey, Hugh Matthew *philosophy educator*
Swearer, Donald Keeney *Asian religions educator, writer*

Titusville
Mulcahy, Richard Patrick *history educator, consultant*

University Park
Brault, Gerard Joseph *French language educator*
Halsey, Martha Taliaferro *Spanish language educator*
Lacy, Norris J. *literature educator*

Villanova
Bergquist, James Manning *history educator*
DeLaura, David Joseph *English language educator*
Hunt, John Mortimer, Jr., *classical studies educator*
McDiarmid, Lucy *English educator, author*
Radan, George Tivadar *art history and archaeology educator*
Sullivan, Mark White *art history educator*

West Chester
Gougher, Ronald Lee *foreign language educator and administrator*

Williamsport
Feinstein, Sascha *English language educator*

Wyncote
Webb, Frances Moore *writer, educator*

York
Sarfo, Kwasi *history and political science educator*

RHODE ISLAND

East Greenwich
White, Sidney Howard *English educator*

Providence
Ackerman, Felicia *philosophy educator, writer*
Anderson, James Arthur *humanities educator, academic director*
Bensmaia, Reda *French studies educator, researcher*
Blasing, Mutlu Konuk *English language educator*
Boegehold, Alan Lindley *classics educator*
Donovan, Bruce Elliot *classics educator, university dean*
Gill, Mary Louise Glanville *educator of classics and philosophy*
Gleason, Abbott *history educator*
Harshman, Thomas Ringwood *writer*
Kim, Jaegwon *philosophy educator*
Konstan, David *classics and comparative literature educator, researcher*
Monteiro, George *English educator, writer*
Putnam, Michael Courtney Jenkins *classics educator*
Ribbans, Geoffrey Wilfrid *Spanish educator*
Saint-Amand, Pierre Nemours *humanities educator*
Schmitt, Richard *philosopher, educator*
Sosa, Ernest *philosopher, educator*
Wimmers, Inge Crosman *French literature and theory educator*

SOUTH CAROLINA

Anderson
Mims, Frances Larkin Flynn *retired English language educator*

Beaufort
Shaw, Nancy Rivard *museum curator, art historian, consultant*
Villena-Alvarez, Juanita I. *language educator, consultant*

Chapin
Branham, Mack Carison, Jr., *retired theological seminary educator, minister*

Charleston
Wharton, Noëlle Parris *language educator, director*

Clemson
Nicholas, David *history educator*
Wilson, Paulette Adassa *language educator, writer*

Columbia
Fried, Morris Louis *retired humanities educator*
Synnott, Marcia Graham *history educator*
Vazsonyi, Nicholas *foreign languages educator*

Denmark
Lebby, Gloria C. *history educator*

Greenville
Henderson, Alan Scott *humanities educator*

Greenwood
Figueira, Robert Charles *history educator*

Hilton Head Island
Knox, John, Jr., *philosopher, educator*

North Myrtle Beach
Damerst, William *English and humanities educator*

Orangeburg
Johnson, Alex Claudius *English language educator*

Pawleys Island
Ford, Anna Maria *language educator*

Rock Hill
Land, Betty Lou Jackson *reading educator, writer*

Spartanburg
Epps, Edwin Carlyle *English language educator*

Shand, Rosa *English educator*

Taylors
Vaughn, John Carroll *minister, educator*

SOUTH DAKOTA

Aberdeen
Iwerks, Carol Joy *minister*

Brookings
Evans, David Allan *English educator*

Huron
Rich, Gretchen Garnet *English educator*

Sioux Falls
Carlson Aronson, Marilyn A. *English language and education educator*
Olson, Gary Duane *history educator*

Vermillion
Zuercher, Nancy Tozer *English language educator*

TENNESSEE

Athens
Armstrong, Thomas Field *history educator, college administrator*

Bethel Springs
Mehr, Vern Conrad *minister, educator*

Big Sandy
Chastain, Kenneth Duane *retired foreign language educator*

Cookeville
Campana, Phillip Joseph *German language educator*
Webb, George Ernest *science historian, educator*

Gallatin
Flynn, John David *writer, educator*
Osaitile, Andy Eldo *English language and literature educator*

Jackson
Agee, Nelle Hulme *retired art history educator*
Fant, Gene Clinton, Jr., *English language educator*
Glosson, Julie Ann McDade *language educator*

Jefferson City
Millsaps, Ellen McNutt *English language educator*

Kingsport
Egan, Martha Avaleen *history educator, archivist, consultant*

Knoxville
Cutler, Everette Wayne *history educator*

Martin
Welden, Alicia Galaz-Vivar *foreign language educator*

Maryville
Brigance, Albert Henry *educational writer, publisher*

Memphis
Jolly, William Thomas *foreign language educator*
Jones, Marguerite Jackson *English language educator*
Michta, Andrew Alexander *educator, researcher*
Vest, James Murray *foreign language and literature educator*
Vinson, Mark Alan *English language and literature educator*

Murfreesboro
Rupprecht, Nancy Ellen *historian, educator*
West, Carroll Van *historian, educator, consultant*

Nashville
Cook, Ann Jennalie *English language educator*
Dickerson, Dennis Clark *history educator*
Graham, Hugh Davis *history educator*
Hassel, Rudolph Christopher *English educator*
Jarman, Mark Foster *English language educator*
Lachs, John *philosopher, educator*
McGinnis, Harrill Coleman *humanities educator*
Risko, Victoria J. *language educator*
Sullivan, Walter Laurence *writer, educator*

Sewanee
Williamson, Samuel Ruthven, Jr., *historian, emeritus university president*

TEXAS

Abilene
Smith, Ronald Aubrey *theology educator*

Amarillo
Lindsay, Robby Lane *English educator*

Arlington
Kubecka, Ronna Denise *English language and art educator, psychotherapist*

Austin
Alofsin, Anthony *art historian, writer, educator*
Arens, Katherine Marie *language educator, educator*
Braybrooke, David *philosopher, educator*
Dulles, John Watson Foster *history educator*
Farrell, Edmund James *retired English language educator, writer*

Gustafsson, Lars Erik Einar *writer, educator*
Justus, Carol Faith *linguistics educator*
Minault, Gail *history educator*
Neeld, Elizabeth Harper *author, retreat and workshop leader, consultant*
Staley, Thomas Fabian *language professional, academic administrator*
Tyler, Ronnie Curtis *historian*

Bertram
Albert, Susan Wittig *writer, English educator*

Canyon
Hanson, Trudy L. *speech professional, educator*
Roper, Beryl Cain *writer, publisher, retired library director*

College Station
Berger, Harris Merle *ethnomusicologist, educator*
Dunsford, Deborah Williams *English language, journalism educator*
Ezell, Margaret J. *language educator*
Harner, James Lowell *English language educator*
Kallendorf, Craig William *English, speech and classical languages educator*
Martin, Carol Jacquelyn *literature educator, artist*
Van Domelen, John Emory *retired English studies educator, gemstone dealer*
Wright, Nancy Jane *English language educator*

Commerce
Grimshaw, James Albert, Jr., *English language educator*

Corpus Christi
McCoy, Dorothy Eloise *writer, educator*
Snouffer, Nancy Kendall *English and reading educator*

Dallas
Chawner, Lucia Martha *English educator*
Davis, Daisy Sidney *history educator*
Davis, Elise Miller (Mrs. Leo M. Davis) *writer, educator*
Gross, Harriet P. Marcus *religious studies and writing educator*
Ndimba, Cornelius Ghane *language educator*
París, Kevin *English educator*

Edinburg
Barrera, Eduardo *Spanish language and literature educator*

El Paso
Clement-Fouts, Shirley George *educational services executive*
Lujan, Rosa Emma *bilingual specialist, trainer, consultant, assistant principal, assistant principal*
Ucles, Maureen Ellen *bilingual educator*

Fort Worth
Garrett, James Leo, Jr., *theology educator*
Robin, Clara Nell (Claire Robin) *English language educator*
Toulouse, Mark Gene *religion educator*
White, Janet Kelly *english educator, secondary school educator*

Georgetown
Rippy, Frances Marguerite Mayhew *English language educator*

Harlingen
Roberts-Parast, Ann Talbot *English and foreign language educator*

Houston
Arnold, James Phillip *religious studies educator, history educator*
Belk, Joan Pardue *English educator*
Castañeda, James Agustín *language educator, golf coach*
Chance, Jane *English literature educator*
de Kanter, Ellen Ann *English and foreign language educator*
Drew, Katherine Fischer *history educator*
Edwards, Susan Freda *history educator*
Grandy, Richard E. *philosophy educator*
Haskell, Thomas Langdon *history educator*
Hyman, Harold M. *history educator, consultant*
Martin, James Kirby *historian, educator*
McEvoy-Jamil, Patricia Ann *English language educator*
Mc Fadden, Joseph Michael *history educator*
McPhail, JoAnn Winstead *writer, publisher, art dealer*
Meeks, Herbert Lessig, III, *pastor, former school system administrator*
Pasternak, Joanna Murray *humanities educator*
Pryor, William Daniel Lee *humanities educator*
Smith, Richard Joseph *history educator*
Temkin, Larry Scott *philosopher, educator*
Thompson, Ewa M. *foreign language educator*
Vallbona, Rima-Gretel Rothe *foreign language educator, writer*
Wiener, Martin Joel *historian, educator*

Kerrville
Lich, Glen Ernst *writer, consultant, business executive*

Kingsville
Hunter, Leslie Gene *history educator*

Longview
Carl, Harold Francis *theology educator*

Lubbock
Angstadt, Frances Virginia *language arts and theatre arts educator*
Hurst, Mary Jane *English language educator*

Mesquite
Davis, Vivian *English language educator*

HIGHER EDUCATION: HUMANITIES

Mineral Wells
McKimmey, Martha Anne *writer*

Montgomery
Kelsey, Clyde Eastman, Jr., *philosophy and psychology educator*

Odessa
Forsyth, Beverly K. *language educator, writer*

Plano
France-Deal, Judith Jean *language educator*
Miller, Ken Leroy *religious studies educator, consultant, writer*

Ranger
Jones, Roger Walton *English language educator, writer*

Round Rock
Lee, Susan Joye *minister, educator*

San Antonio
Gonzalez Pino, Barbara *foreign languages educator*
Lonchar, Patricia Paulette *English educator*
Myers, Ellen Howell *historian, educator*
Passty, Jeanette Nyda *English language educator, writer*
Rogers, Frances Evelyn *author, retired educator and librarian*
Teran, Sister Mary Inez *retired nun, educator*
Walker, William Oliver, Jr., *retired theology studies educator, dean*

San Marcos
Beebe, Steven Arnold *communication educator, author*
Beebe, Susan Jane *English language educator*

Silsbee
White, Helen Frances Pearson *language educator, real estate broker*

Spring
Hunt, T(homas) W(ebb) *retired religion educator*

Stephenville
Huggins, Mary Louise White *English educator, small business owner*

Uvalde
Wood, James Albert *foreign language educator*

Waco
Lewis, Martha Nell *Christian educator, minister, expressive arts therapist*
McManness, Linda Marie *language educator*

West
Atlas, Diane Allen *Spanish language educator*

Wichita Falls
Bourland, D(elphus) David, Jr., *linguist, educator*

UTAH

Logan
Bame, James Edwin *English educator*

Ogden
Harrington, Mary Evelina Paulson (Polly Harrington) *religious journalist, writer, educator*
Larsen, Lila Duncan *curator, educator*
LeTourneau, Mark Stephen *English language educator, researcher*

Provo
Alexander, Thomas Glen *history educator*
Cracroft, Richard Holton *English literature educator*
Hall, John Franklin *classicist, educator*
Skinner, Andrew Charles *history educator, religious writer*

Salt Lake City
Lima, Marilynne *foreign language educator, consultant*
Olsen, Glenn Warren *historian, educator*

Springville
Paulsen, Linda Grayson *contract consultant, artist, poet*

VERMONT

Bennington
Bernard, April *poet, literature educator*

Burlington
Flores, Yolanda *literature educator*
Scrase, David Anthony *German language educator*

Middlebury
Cohen, Robert *language educator, writer*

Norwich
Carlson, Elizabeth Borden *historian, educator*

Plainfield
Hamlin, Wilfrid Gardiner *retired literature and philosophy educator*

Shaftsbury
Williams, Robert Joseph *museum director, educator*

Wilmington
Reeve, Franklin D. *writer, literature educator*

VIRGINIA

Alexandria
Brignoni, Gladys *foreign language educator*
DeZarn, Guy David *English language educator*

Annandale
Hutcheon, Wallace Schoonmaker *history educator*

Arlington
Irizarry, Estelle Diane *foreign language educator, writer, editor*
Porterfield, Daniel Ryan *English educator*
Solimando, Dominic Anthony, Jr., *writer, consultant, pharmacist, educator*

Ashland
Inge, Milton Thomas *American literature and culture educator, author*

Blacksburg
Baumgartner, Frederic Joseph *history educator*
Ochsenwald, William Leo *history educator, consultant*
Ulloa, Justo Celso *Spanish educator*

Bridgewater
Piepke, Susan L. *foreign language educator, researcher, writer*

Charlottesville
Arnold, Albert James *foreign language educator*
Battestin, Martin Carey *retired English language educator*
Casey, John Dudley *writer, English language educator*
Chase, Karen Susan *English literature educator*
Cherno, Melvin *humanities educator*
Colker, Marvin Leonard *classics educator*
Davidson, Hugh MacCullough *French language and literature educator*
Dove, Rita Frances *poet, English language educator*
Garrett, George Palmer, Jr., *creative writing and English language educator, writer*
Hirsch, Eric Donald, Jr., *English language educator, educational reformer*
Humphreys, Paul William *philosophy educator, consultant*
Kellogg, Robert Leland *English language educator*
Kett, Joseph Francis *historian, educator*
Lane, Ann Judith *history and women's studies educator*
Lyons, John David *French, Italian and comparative literature educator*
McGann, Jerome John *English language educator*
McGrady, Donald Lee *retired Spanish language educator*
Megill, Allan D. *historian*
Midelfort, Hans Christian Erik *history educator*
Nohrnberg, James Carson *English language educator*
Perkowski, Jan Louis *language and literature educator*
Rubin, David Lee *humanities educator, publisher*
Schuker, Stephen Alan *historian, educator*
Schutte, Anne Jacobson *historian, educator*
Shaw, Donald Leslie *Spanish language educator*
Spearing, Anthony Colin *English literature educator*
Stocker, Arthur Frederick *classics educator*
Wagoner, Jennings Lee, Jr., *history educator*
Wright, Charles Penzel, Jr., *English language educator*
Zunz, Olivier Jean *history educator*

Fairfax
Elstun, Esther Nies *foreign language educator*
Stearns, Peter Nathaniel *history educator*

Fort Lee
Sterling, Keir Brooks *historian, educator*

Great Falls
Castro-Klaren, Sara *Latin American literature educator*
Kagan, Constance Henderson *philosopher, educator, consultant*

Hampden Sydney
Bagby, George Franklin, Jr., *English language educator*
Jagasich, Paul Anthony *language educator, translator*

Hampton
Long, Thomas Lawrence *English educator*

Harrisonburg
Alotta, Robert Ignatius *historian, educator, writer*

Hmpden Sydney
Arieti, James Alexander *classics educator, writer*

Kingstowne
Hixson, Stanley G. *speech, language and computer technology educator*

Lexington
Ray, George Washington, III, *English language educator*
Sessions, William Lad *philosophy educator, administrator*
Simpson, Pamela Hemenway *art historian, educator*
Stuart, Dabney *poet, author, English language educator*

Lynchburg
Bell, Carolyn Wilkerson *English educator*

Mc Lean
García-Godoy, Cristián *historian, educator*

Newport News
Thomas, Dorothy Worthy *English educator*

Norfolk
Bazin, Nancy Topping *retired English language educator*
McCoy, Elizabeth Mills *French educator*
Perry, Ruth Anna *English language educator*

North
Fang, Joong *philosopher, mathematician, educator*

Petersburg
Garrott, Carl Lee *foreign language educator*

Portsmouth
Jackson, Cheryl K. *English educator*
Mapp, Alf Johnson, Jr., *writer, historian*

Purcellville
Laughlin, Faith Ann *language educator*

Richmond
Gordon, John L., Jr., *historian, educator*
Hall, James H(errick), Jr., *philosophy educator, writer*
Hart, Philip Ray *religion educator, minister*
Rilling, John Robert *history educator*
Terry, Robert Meredith *foreign language educator*
Wojahn, David *poet, literature educator*

Roanoke
Miller, Sally Liples *English language teacher*

Salem
Gathercole, Patricia May *modern foreign languages educator*

Spotsylvania
Kozloski, Lillian Terese D. *museum educator, consultant, lecturer*

Springfield
Murri, Luella Davis *personnel and language professional*

Surry
Wachsmann, Elizabeth Rideout *reading specialist*

Sweet Briar
Horwege, Ronald Eugene *foreign language educator*

Virginia Beach
Dickerson, Nancy Knewstep *language educator*
Williams, J(ohn) Rodman *theologian, educator, clergyman*

Williamsburg
Chappell, Miles Linwood, Jr., *art history educator*
Crapol, Edward P. *history educator*
Dowling, John Clarkson *language educator*
Esler, Anthony James *historian, novelist, researcher*
Harris, James Franklin *philosophy educator*
McLane, Henry Earl, Jr., *philosophy educator*
Nettels, Elsa *English language educator*
Sherman, Richard Beatty *history educator*
Wallach, Alan *art historian, educator*

WASHINGTON

Auburn
Sims, Marcie Lynne *English language educator, writer*

Bellingham
Highland, Frederick *writer, humanities educator*

Lacey
Edwards, Margaret H. *English as second language instructor*

Port Angeles
Kinney, Beverly Jean *English language educator*

Port Townsend
Kahn, Sy Myron *humanities educator, poet*

Pullman
Bennett, Edward Moore *historian, educator*

Seattle
Burrows, Elizabeth MacDonald *religious organization executive, educator*
Gross, Catherine Mary (Kate Gross) *writer, educator*
Keyt, David *philosophy and classics educator*
Mini, Anne Alexandra Apostolides *writer, educator*
Rullkoetter, Jill E. *museum education administrator*
Snow-Smith, Joanne Inloes *art history educator*

Spokane
Swinton, Janet Ruth (Peterson) *English language educator*

Tacoma
Curley, Michael Joseph *English language educator*
Pan, Rosalie Jia-Ling *English language educator*
Thomas, Ronald Robert *English literature educator, writer*

Walla Walla
Carlsen, James Caldwell *musicologist, educator*
Krieger, William Carl *English language educator*

Yakima
Meshke, George Lewis *drama and humanities educator*

WEST VIRGINIA

Charles Town
Na, Tsung Shun (Terry Na) *Chinese studies educator, writer*

Charleston
Leasor, Jane *religion and philosophy educator, musician*

Institute
Wohl, David *humanities educator, college dean-theatre director*

Morgantown
Bruner, Jeffrey Benham *foreign language educator*
Singer, Armand Edwards *foreign language educator*

New Milton
Radcliff, Melinda Sue *language arts teacher*

WISCONSIN

Appleton
Doeringer, Franklin M. *historian, educator*
Herscher, Susan Kay *English language educator*

Chippewa Falls
Schmider, Mary Ellen Heian *American studies educator, academic administrator*

Delafield
Gulgowski, Paul William *German language, social science, and history educator*

Horicon
Bohn, Monica J. *multi-media specialist, educator*

Madison
Brandt, Deborah *English educator*
Brembeck, Winston Lamont *retired speech communication educator*
Fox, Michael Vass *Hebrew educator*
Hamalainen, Pekka Kalevi *historian, educator*
Hutchison, Jane Campbell *art history educator, researcher*
O'Brien, James Aloysius *foreign language educator*
Shaw, Joseph Thomas *Slavic languages educator*
Spear, Thomas Turner *history educator*
Vogt, Sharon Madonna *writer, educator*
Westphal, Klaus Wilhelm *university museum director*

Manitowoc
Tadych, Renita *English eduator*

Milwaukee
Backes, Nancy Constance *English educator*
Dziewanowski, Marian Kamil *history educator*
Hribal, C. J. *language educator*
Kainz, Howard Paul *philosophy educator*
Preston, Patricia Ann *language educator, researcher*
Swanson, Roy Arthur *classicist, educator*
Wagner, Diane M(argaret) *theology educator, chaplain*

Oshkosh
Burr, John Roy *philosophy educator*

Superior
Sutter, Barton E. *literature educator, writer*

WYOMING

Casper
Gunderson, Mary Alice *writer, educator*

Laramie
Boresi, Arthur Peter *writer, educator*
Nye, Eric William *English language and literature educator*

Sheridan
Aguirre-Batty, Mercedes *Spanish and English language and literature educator*

TERRITORIES OF THE UNITED STATES

PUERTO RICO

Rio Piedras
Plata, Miriam Ruth *English language and ESL educator*

San Juan
Ramos Moreau, Iris Violeta *English educator*

CANADA

ALBERTA

Edmonton
McMaster, Juliet Sylvia *English language educator*

Edmonton
Raaflaub, Vernon Arthur *religion educator*

BRITISH COLUMBIA

Clayburn
Van Kleek, Laurence McKee (Laurie Van Kleek) *minister, librarian, educator*

Prince George
Keyes, Gordon Lincoln *history educator*

ONTARIO

Richmond Hill
Kuby, Lolette *English educator, writer*

Toronto
Grisé, Catherine *French educator*
McWilliam, Joanne Elizabeth *retired religion educator*

PRINCE EDWARD ISLAND

Montague
Cregier, Don Mesick *historian, educator, researcher, consultant*

QUEBEC

Montreal
Hamel, Reginald *history educator*

CHINA

Hong Kong
Chiang, Samuel Edward *theological educator, humanities educator*

DENMARK

Odense
Mey, Jacob Louis *linguistics educator*

ENGLAND

Cambridge
Harrison, Jonathan *philosophy educator*

GERMANY

Bamberg
Wuttke, Dieter *philology and art history educator*

ITALY

Bari
Laneve, Cosimo Raffaele *humanities educator*

NETHERLANDS

Groningen
Holz, Hans Heinz *philosophy educator*

REPUBLIC OF KOREA

Seoul
Newman, Jeanne Johnson *sociolinguistic educator, researcher*

ADDRESS UNPUBLISHED

Abernethy, Sharron Gray *language educator*
Andrade, Carolyn L. *foreign language educator*
Ansbro, John Joseph *philosopher, educator*
Aptekar, Sheldon I. *speech, theatre, and performing art educator*
Archibold, Mildred Haynes *bilingual education educator*
Armstrong, (Arthur) James (Arthur Armstrong) *minister, educator, consultant, writer*
Azodo, Ada Uzoamaka *French language, African women's studies educator, writer*
Bangs, Susan Elizabeth *bilingual educator*
Barker, Verlyn Lloyd *retired minister, educator*
Becker, Lawrence Carlyle *philosopher, educator, writer*
Beisch, June *freelance/self-employed writer, literature educator, poet*
Ben-Ghiat, Ruth *historian, educator*
Berndt, Jane Ann *writer, poet, researcher, educator*
Bernstein, Vivian D. *special education author, educational consultant*
Black, David *writer, educator, producer*
Blackbourn, David Gordon *history educator*
Blum, Lawrence Alan *moral philosophy educator*
Bonner, Thomas, Jr., *English language educator*
Boyd-Brown, Lena Ernestine *history educator, education consultant*
Brewer, Wanda Eastwood *retired educator in English, art museum docent*
Bronars, Joseph Charles, Jr., *philosophy educator*
Brown, Clarence Fleetwood *comparative literature educator*
Bullard, Pamela *writer, educational consultant*
Burrill, Kathleen R. F. (Kathleen R. F. Griffin-Burrill) *Turkologist, educator*
Busch, Frederick Matthew *writer, literature educator*
Caldwell, Howard Bryant *English language educator*
Calleo, David Patrick *history, political, economy and international relations educator*
Carls, Alice Catherine *history educator*
Carroll, Rosemary Frances *historian, educator, lawyer*
Cartwright, Talula Elizabeth *writing and leadership educator, consultant*
Caswell, Frances Pratt *retired English language educator*
Cecil, Elizabeth Jean *writer*
Chaffee, Steven *communication educator*
Chalfant-Allen, Linda Kay *retired Spanish language educator*
Chandra, Pramod *art history educator*
Chess, Sonia Mary *retired language educator*
Clark, Eve Vivienne *linguistics educator*
Clogan, Paul Maurice *English language and literature educator*
Collins, Jean Katherine *English educator*
Cornbleet, Aileen Gail Hirsch *English language and social studies educator*
Cuppo Csaki, Luciana *foreign language educator, writer*
Davidson, Mark *writer, educator*
Defever, Susanna Ethel *English language educator*
DeSando, John Anthony *retired humanities educator*
Dias, Kathleen R. *foreign language educator*
Doyle, Robert Charles *historian, educator*
Duffy, Patricia Lynne *English language educator*
Dyson, Anne Haas *English language educator*
Eby, Carl Peter *English educator*
Eby, Cecil DeGrotte *English language educator, writer*
Egelston, Roberta Riethmiller *writer*
Esterhammer, Angela *literary theorist, educator*
Farmer, Ann Dahlstrom *English language educator*
Feal, Gisele Catherine *foreign language educator*
Fisher, Anita Jeanne (Kit Fisher) *language educator*
Fleischauer, John Frederick *retired English language educator, administrator*
Fleming, Donald Harnish *historian, educator*
Foote, Stephanie *English educator*
Foster, Dorothy Jean Peck *language educator*
Garza, Deborah Jane *bilingual education educator*
Gasteyer, Carlin Evans *museum administrator, museum studies educator*
Geiselhart, Lorene Annetta *English language educator*
Gerlach, Jeanne Elaine *English language educator*
Gerrard, Ruth Ann *retired English educator*
Gish, Robert Franklin *English language educator, writer*
Glaysher, Frederick *English language educator*
Goldfarb, Ruth *poet, educator*
Goldstein, Phyllis Ann *art historian, educator*
Gonzalez-Vales, Luis Ernesto *historian, educational administrator*
Gradie, Charlotte May *history educator*
Grant, Leonard Tydings *clergyman*
Gray, Clarence Jones *foreign language educator, dean emeritus*
Greenberg, Nathan Abraham *retired classics educator*
Greene, Elinore Aschah *speech and drama professional, writer*
Gregory, Myra May *religious organization administrator, educator*
Greve, Sally Doane *English educator*
Gumpel, Liselotte *retired language educator*
Gutke, Jeffrey Alan *Spanish language educator*
Haber, Lynn Becker *English language educator*
Hall, Marie-Joyee Faith *Spanish and English language educator*
Hamrock, Margaret Mary *retired educator, writer*
Hartman, Marilyn D. *English and art educator*
Haviland, Kay Lynn (Kade Haviland) *English literature educator*
Havran, Martin Joseph *historian, educator, author*
Haworth, Dale Keith *art history educator, gallery director*
Hermand, Jost *German language educator*
Hernandez, Ramon Robert *retired clergyman and librarian*
Hewes, Dorothy Walker *history educator*
Hoart, Gladys Gallagher *English language educator*
Hoffman, Daniel (Gerard) *literature educator, poet*
Holloway, Kimberley Michele *freelance/self-employed writer, communications executive, language educator*
Houston, Gloria *author, educator, consultant*
Hsu, Patrick Kuo-Heng *retired languages educator, librarian*
Hughes, Edward Thomas *retired English educator, consultant*
Hund, Barbara Maurer *English educator and speech broadcasting educator*
Irwin, Anna Mae *English language educator*
Jay, Karla *English language educator, women's studies educator*
Jentsch, Lynda Jeanne *language educator*
Johnsen, Barbara Parrish *writer, educator*
Johnson, Clifton Herman *historian, archivist, former research center director*
Jolley, Betty Cornette *history educator*
Jones, Charlott Ann *museum director, art educator, retired*
Jones, Suejette Albritton *basic skills educator*
Kane, Loana *foreign language educator*
Kaplan, Harold *humanities educator, author*
Kaspar, Victoria Ann *school administrator*
Kaufman, Janice Horner *foreign language educator, women's and gender studies educator*
Keeter, Lynn Carpenter *English educator*
Kimbrell, Grady Ned *writer, educator, retired school system administrator*
Kohler, Sheila M. *humanities educator, writer*
Kolb, Harold Hutchinson, Jr., *English language educator*
Lee, Corinne Adams *retired English teacher*
Lehman, Barbara Albu *foreign language educator, translator*
Lewy, Phyllis *English educator*
Lindboe, Berit Roberg *language educator, literature educator*
Loughran, James Newman *philosophy educator, college administrator*
Lucente, Gregory L. *humanities educator*
MacDonald, Robert Alan *language educator, educator*
Maehl, William Harvey *historian, educator*
Mali, Paul *publisher, retired management educator*
Manrique, Jaime *writer, educator*
Martinez, William, Jr., *Spanish language educator, multicultural issues consultant*
Mattar, Philip *writer*
McEwen, Inger Theorin *retired secondary education educator, consultant*
McGann, Lisa B. Napoli *language educator*
McGrady, Stephanie Jill *speech communications educator*
Meister, Elyse S. *reading specialist*
Melzer, Barbara Evelyn *minister*
Mender, Mona Siegler *writer, music educator*
Miscella, Maria Diana *humanities educator*
Molloy, Sylvia *Latin American literature educator, writer*
Moore, Nancy Newell *English language educator*
Morales, Marcia Paulette Merry *language educator, archaeologist*
Moront-Figuero, Patricia *language educator*
Morrison, Sarah Lyddon *author*
Morse-McNeely, Patricia *poet, writer, retired middle school educator*
Murphy, Robert James *language educator, consultant*
Newbery, Ilse Sofie Magdalene *German language educator*
Nugent, Walter Terry King *historian*
O'Connor, Patrick Joseph *writer, musician, university educator*
Osterholm, J(ohn) Roger *humanities educator*
Palmer, Marilyn Joan *English composition educator*
Palter, Robert Monroe *humanities educator*
Paxton, Laura Belle-Kent *English language educator, management professional*
Pemberton, Janett E. Matthew *language educator*
Perdigó, Luisa Marina *foreign language and literature educator*
Perlingieri, Ilya Sandra *art history scholar, writer*
Ping-Robbins, Nancy Regan *musicologist, educator*
Poole, Rosemary Jean *art history educator*
Porter, Marsha Kay *language professional and educator*
Quint Sehat, Arlene *art history educator, curator, museum administrator*
Ragans, Rosalind Dorothy *textbook author, retired art educator*
Ransom, Nancy Alderman *sociology and women's studies educator, university administrator*
Rebay, Luciano *Italian literature educator, literary critic*
Reciniello, Karen Mary *language educator*
Reed, Thomas Lee, II, *minister, social worker, educator*
Reeves, Barbara *writer, educator*
Rektorik-Sprinkle, Patricia Jean *classics consultant, retired Latin language educator*
Riasanovsky, Nicholas Valentine *retired historian, educator*
Richards, David Gleyre *German language educator*
Rickard, Ruth David *retired history and political science educator*
Ridill, Winifred Marie Meyers *retired English educator*
Ruoff, A. LaVonne Brown *English language educator*
Sabat-Rivers, Georgina *Latin American literature educator*
Sandford, Virginia Adele *motivational speaker, writer*
Sandy, Stephen *writer, educator*
Sawai, Dahleen Emi *language educator*
Schmidt, Lawrence Kennedy *philosophy educator*
Schmiel, David Gerhard *clergyman, religious education administrator*
Schmitz, Dennis Mathew *English language educator*
Sessions, Bettye Jean *humanities educator*
Shattuck, Roger Whitney *author, educator*
Sheffey, Ruthe Garnet *English and humanities educator, speaker*
Sherman, Susan Jean *writer, educator, editor*
Shillingsburg, Miriam Jones *English educator, academic administrator*
Sices, David *language educator, translator*
Smith, Brenda Joyce *author, editor, social studies educator*
Snyder, Susan Brooke *retired English literature educator*
Stanley, Myrtle Brooks *minister, educational and religious consultant*
Stavropoulos, Yvette *editor, writer, educator*
Steinhauser, Janice Maureen *arts administrator, educator, artist*
Stone, Marilyn *foreign language educator, consultant*
Strong, Carol Joan *speech professional, researcher*
Strong, Virginia Wilkerson *freelance writer, former educator*
Swinyard, Sharon Joan *language professional, educator, administrator*
Takacs, Kristy B. *educator*
Tayler, Irene *English literature educator*
Tedesco, Paul Herbert *humanities educator*
Thackray, Arnold Wilfrid *historian, foundation executive*
Thomson, Virginia Winbourn *humanities educator, writer*
Tobias, Sheila *writer, educator*
Tong, Rosemarie *medical humanities and philosophy educator, consultant and researcher*
Vestal, Thelma Shaw *history educator*
Von Gonten, Kevin Paul *priest, liturgist, theologian*
Wiener, Jon *history educator*
Wilson, Donna Mae *administrator, foreign language educator*
Wolff, Cynthia Griffin *humanities educator, author*
Woodman, Jean Wilson *educator, consultant*
Wruck, Erich-Oskar *retired foreign language educator, administrator*
Wyatt, Marcia Jean *fine arts educator, administrative assistant*
Yates, Mildred Campbell *retired literature educator*
Yeager, Margie Ann *English language educator*
Zaferson, William S. *philosophy educator, publisher*
Zimmermann, Thomas Callander Price *retired historian, educator*
Zwerver, Peter John *linguistics educator*

HIGHER EDUCATION: LAW

UNITED STATES

ALABAMA

Birmingham
Weeks, Arthur Andrew *lawyer, law educator*

ARIZONA

Phoenix
Koester, Berthold Karl *lawyer, law educator, retired honorary German consul*
Sutton, Samuel J. *lawyer, educator, engineer*
Swartz, Melvin Jay *lawyer, writer*
Weisenburger, Theodore Maurice *retired judge, poet, educator, writer*

Tempe
Furnish, Dale Beck *lawyer, educator*

Tucson
Falbaum, Bertram Seymour *law educator, investigator*
Fortman, Marvin *law educator, consultant*

Yuma
Hossler, David Joseph *lawyer, law educator*

ARKANSAS

Little Rock
Murphey, Arthur Gage, Jr., *law educator*
Wright, Robert Ross, III, *law educator*

CALIFORNIA

Berkeley
Choper, Jesse Herbert *law educator, university dean*
McNulty, John Kent *lawyer, educator*
Mishkin, Paul J. *lawyer, educator*
Moran, Rachel *lawyer, educator*
Post, Robert Charles *law educator*
Scheiber, Harry N. *law educator*

California City
Friedl, Rick *lawyer, former academic administrator*

Chico
Ragland, Carroll Ann *law educator, judicial officer*

Chino
Van Wagner, Ellen *lawyer, law educator*

Claremont
Ferguson, Cleve Robert *lawyer, educator*

Corona
Everett Nollkamper, Pamela Irene *legal management company executive, educator*

Davis
Johnson, Kevin Raymond *law educator*

Encino
Greer, Cynthia Faye *mediator, law educator, consultant*

Fullerton
Frizell, Samuel *law educator*

La Jolla
Wilson, Bonnie Jean *lawyer, educator, investor*

Larkspur
Ratner, David Louis *retired law educator*

Los Angeles
Abrams, Norman *law educator, university administrator*
Carrey, Neil *lawyer, educator*
Dudziak, Mary Louise *law educator, lecturer*
Follick, Edwin Duane *law educator, dean, chiropractor*

HIGHER EDUCATION: LAW

Green, Kenneth Norton *law educator*
Gross, Ariela Julie *law educator*
Parks, George Brooks *land development consultant, university dean*
Reinstein, Todd Russell *lawyer, educator*
Rosett, Arthur Irwin *lawyer, educator*
Seto, Theodore Paul *lawyer, educator*
Spitzer, Matthew Laurence *law educator, dean*

Menlo Park
Ehrlich, Thomas *law educator*

Newport Beach
Mandel, Maurice, II, *lawyer, educator, mediator*

North Fork
Flanagan, James Henry, Jr., *lawyer, writer, business educator*

Orinda
Hetland, John Robert *lawyer, educator*

Oroville
Chapman, Joyce Eileen *court reporting educator, administrator*

Pomona
Palmer, Robert Alan *lawyer, educator*

Richmond
Kirk-Duggan, Michael Allan *retired law, economics and computer sciences educator*

Ridgecrest
Long, Andre Edwin *law educator, lawyer*

Sacramento
Goodart, Nan L. *lawyer, educator*
Hartman, Patricia Jeanne *lawyer, educator*
Malloy, Michael Patrick *law educator, consultant*

San Diego
Begovich, Michael *public defender, law educator*
Fauchier, Dan R(ay) *mediator, arbitrator, educator, construction management consultant*
Slomanson, William Reed *law educator, legal writer*

San Francisco
Allen, Paul Alfred *lawyer, educator*
Folberg, Harold Jay *lawyer, mediator, educator, university dean*
Hilton, Stanley Goumas *lawyer, educator, writer*
Jung, David Joseph *law educator*
Knapp, Charles Lincoln *law educator*
Lynch, Timothy Jeremiah-Mahoney *lawyer, educator, theologian, realtor, writer*
Marcus, Richard Leon *lawyer, educator*
Park, Roger Cook *law educator*
Rossmann, Antonio *lawyer, educator*
Whelan, John William *law educator*
Wingate, C. Keith *law educator*

Santa Ana
Harley, Robison Dooling, Jr., *lawyer, educator*

Stanford
Franklin, Marc Adam *law educator*
Friedman, Lawrence M. *law educator*
Goldstein, Paul *lawyer, educator*
Mann, J. Keith *retired law educator, arbitrator*
Rhode, Deborah Lynn *law educator*
Scott, Kenneth Eugene *lawyer, educator*

Walnut
McKee, Catherine Lynch *law educator, lawyer*

Woodland Hills
Barrett, Robert Matthew *law educator, lawyer*
Johnson-Champ, Debra Sue *lawyer, educator, writer, artist*

COLORADO

Boulder
Corbridge, James Noel, Jr., *law educator, educator*
DuVivier, Katharine Keyes *lawyer, educator*
Purvis, John Anderson *lawyer, educator*

Commerce City
Trujillo, Lorenzo A. *lawyer, educator*

Denver
Dauer, Edward Arnold *law educator*
Olsen, M. Kent *lawyer, educator*

Lakewood
Isely, Henry Philip *association executive, integrative engineer, writer, educator*

Loveland
DiFalco, John Patrick *lawyer, arbitrator*

CONNECTICUT

Derby
McEvoy, Sharlene Ann *law educator*

Hartford
Appel, Robert Eugene *lawyer, educator*
Blumberg, Phillip Irvin *law educator*
Pepe, Louis Robert *lawyer, educator*
Schroth, Peter W(illiam) *lawyer, management and law educator*

New Canaan
Hatch, Roberta Anne *lawyer, educator*

New Haven
Ackerman, Bruce Arnold *law educator, lawyer*
Burt, Robert Amsterdam *lawyer, educator*
Calabresi, Guido *judge, law educator*
Clark, Elias *law educator*
Duke, Steven Barry *law educator*
Gewirtz, Paul D. *lawyer, legal educator*
Goldstein, Abraham Samuel *lawyer, educator*
Langbein, John Harriss *lawyer, educator*
Priest, George L. *law educator*
Rose-Ackerman, Susan *law and political economy educator*
Simon, John Gerald *law educator*

Stamford
Margolis, Emanuel *lawyer, educator*

Storrs Mansfield
Tucker, Edwin Wallace *law educator*

Torrington
Lippincott, Walter Edward *law educator*

DELAWARE

Newark
Elson, Charles Myer *law educator*

DISTRICT OF COLUMBIA

Washington
Aaronson, David Ernest *law educator, lawyer*
Bloch, Susan Low *law educator*
Blumenfeld, Jeffrey *lawyer, educator*
Caplin, Mortimer Maxwell *lawyer, educator*
Carter, Barry Edward *lawyer, educator, administrator*
Chused, Richard Harris *law educator*
Dam, Kenneth W. *lawyer, law educator, federal agency administrator*
Donegan, Charles Edward *lawyer, educator*
Elliott, Edwin Donald, Jr., *law educator, federal administrator, environmental lawyer*
Ginsburg, Martin David *lawyer, educator*
Goldblatt, Steven Harris *law educator*
Gutman, Harry Largman *lawyer, educator*
Guttman, Egon *law educator*
Haythe, Winston McDonald *lawyer, educator, consultant, real estate investor*
Horlick, Gary Norman *lawyer, legal educator*
Isbell, David Bradford *lawyer, educator*
Jackson, John Howard *lawyer, educator*
Jamar, Steven Dwight *law educator*
Jones, Kelsey A. *law educator, law administrator*
Kovacic-Fleischer, Candace Saari *law educator*
Miller, John T., Jr., *lawyer, educator*
Mwenda, Kenneth Kaoma *legal consultant, advisor, educator*
Page, Joseph Anthony *law educator*
Rice, Paul Jackson *lawyer, educator*
Rohner, Ralph John *lawyer, educator, university dean*
Ross, Douglas *lawyer*
Shakow, David Joseph *lawyer, former educator*
Starrs, James Edward *law and forensics educator, consultant*
Stewart, David Pentland *lawyer, educator*
Tatel, David Stephen *federal judge*
Tigar, Michael Edward *law educator*
Tushnet, Mark Victor *law educator*
Wallace, Don, Jr., *law educator*

FLORIDA

Clearwater
Bairstow, Frances Kanevsky *arbitrator, mediator, educator*

Coral Gables
Rosenn, Keith Samuel *lawyer, educator*
Swan, Alan Charles *law educator*

Daytona Beach
Barker, Robert Osborne (Bob Barker) *educator, mediator*

Delray Beach
Weinstein, Alvin Seymour *lawyer, educator mechanical engineer*

Edgewater
Dunagan, Walter Benton *lawyer, educator*

Fort Lauderdale
Jarvis, Robert Mark *law educator*
Mintz, Joel Alan *law educator*

Gainesville
Israel, Jerold Harvey *law educator*

Hollywood
Tannen, Ricki Lewis *lawyer, depth psychologist, educator*

Jacksonville
Beytagh, Francis Xavier, Jr., *law educator*

Melbourne
Dixon, Richard Dean *lawyer, educator*

Merritt Island
Sharett, Alan Richard *lawyer, environmental and disability litigator, mediator and arbitrator, law educator*

Miami
Jackson-Holmes, Flora Marie *lawyer, educator*
Leslie, Richard McLaughlin *lawyer, educator*
Stansell, Leland Edwin, Jr., *lawyer, mediator, educator*

North Miami
Dellagloria, John Castle *city attorney, educator*

Palm Beach
Hastings, Lawrence Vaeth *lawyer, physician, educator*

Palm Beach Gardens
Kahn, David Miller *lawyer, educator*

Polk City
Closen, Michael Lee *retired law educator*

Saint Petersburg
Carrere, Charles Scott *law educator, judge*
Jacob, Bruce Robert *law educator*

Sarasota
Clarke, Garvey Elliott *lawyer*

Tallahassee
Schroeder, Edwin Maher *law educator*

Tampa
Baynes, Thomas Edward, Jr., *judge, lawyer, educator*

GEORGIA

Athens
Davis, Claude-Leonard *lawyer, university official*
Ellington, Charles Ronald *lawyer, educator*
Huszagh, Fredrick Wickett *lawyer, educator, information management company executive*
Shedd, Peter Jay *law educator*

Atlanta
Dobbs, C. Edward *lawyer, educator*
Fernandez, Henry A. *lawyer, consultant*
Knowles, Marjorie Fine *lawyer, educator, dean*
Landau, Michael B. *law educator, musician, writer*
Marvin, Charles Arthur *law educator*
Podgor, Ellen Sue *law educator*
Winkler, Allen Warren *lawyer, educator*

Valdosta
Sinnott, John Patrick *lawyer, educator*

HAWAII

Honolulu
Bloede, Victor Carl *lawyer, academic executive*
Bourgoin, David L. *lawyer, real estate broker, trade broker, educator, video/television producer*

Kula
Richardson, Robert Allen *retired lawyer, educator*

Lihue
Budd, Nancy J. *lawyer, school system administrator*

ILLINOIS

Champaign
Kindt, John Warren *lawyer, educator, consultant*
Stone, Victor J. *law educator*

Chicago
Allen, Ronald Jay *law educator*
Alschuler, Albert W. *law educator*
Appel, Nina Schick *law educator, dean*
Baird, Douglas Gordon *law educator, dean*
Crane, Charlotte *law educator*
D'Amato, Anthony *law educator*
Felsenthal, Steven Altus *lawyer, educator*
Heinz, John Peter *lawyer, educator*
Helmholz, R(ichard) H(enry) *law educator*
Hilliard, David Craig *lawyer, educator*
Landes, William M. *law educator*
Landsberg, Jill Warren *lawyer, educator, arbitrator*
Meltzer, Bernard David *law educator*
Meltzer, Robert Craig *lawyer, educator*
Minow, Newton Norman *lawyer, educator*
Murdock, Charles William *lawyer, educator*
Neumeier, Matthew Michael *lawyer, educator*
Presser, Stephen Bruce *lawyer, educator*
Robbins, Ellen Sue *lawyer, educator*
Shapo, Marshall Schambelan *lawyer, educator*
Steinman, Joan Ellen *law educator*
Stone, Geoffrey Richard *law educator, lawyer*
Wilson, Clarence Sylvester, Jr., *lawyer, educator*

Evanston
Morrison, John Horton *lawyer*

Highland Park
Ruder, David Sturtevant *lawyer, educator, government official*

Joliet
Hablutzel, Nancy Zimmerman *lawyer, educator*

Marion
Dibble, Elizabeth Jeane *lawyer, educator*

Naperville
Larson, Mark Edward, Jr., *lawyer, educator, financial advisor*

River Forest
Marcello, Frank F. *lawyer, educator, writer*

Springfield
Darby, Karen Sue *legal education administrator*
Kerr, Gary Enrico *lawyer, educator*

Western Springs
Mudd, Anne Chestney *mediator, law educator, real estate broker*

INDIANA

Bloomington
O'Leary, Rosemary *law educator*

Shreve, Gene Russell *law educator*

Danville
Baldwin, Jeffrey Kenton *lawyer, educator*

Indianapolis
Funk, David Albert *retired law educator*
Wellnitz, Craig Otto *lawyer, English language educator*

Lagrange
Brown, George E. *judge, educator*

Notre Dame
Gunn, Alan *law educator*
Robinson, John Hayes *law educator*

West Lafayette
Scaletta, Phillip Jasper *lawyer, educator*

IOWA

Burlington
Hoth, Steven Sergey *lawyer, educator*

Des Moines
Duckworth, Marvin E. *lawyer, educator*
Edwards, John Duncan *law educator, librarian*

Iowa City
Bonfield, Arthur Earl *lawyer, educator*
Gittler, Josephine *law educator*
Stensvaag, John-Mark *legal educator, lawyer*
Tomkovicz, James Joseph *law educator*
Wing, Adrien Katherine *law educator*

KANSAS

Lawrence
Casad, Robert Clair *legal educator*
Turnbull, H. Rutherford, III, *law educator, lawyer*

Topeka
Dimmitt, Lawrence Andrew *retired lawyer, law educator*

Wichita
Fisher, Randall Eugene *lawyer, educator*

KENTUCKY

Fort Thomas
Whalen, Paul Lewellin *lawyer, educator, mediator*

Louisville
Palmer, Larry Isaac *lawyer, educator*

Prospect
Mayfield, William Stephen *law educator*

LOUISIANA

Baton Rouge
Hawkland, William Dennis *law educator*
Schroeder, Leila Obier *retired law educator*

New Orleans
Crusto, Mitchell Ferdinand *lawyer, educator, consultant*
Lorio, Kathryn Venturatos *lawyer, law educator*
Osakwe, Christopher *lawyer, educator*
Palmer, Vernon Valentine *law educator*
Riess, George Febiger *lawyer, educator*

MAINE

Portland
Zarr, Melvyn *lawyer, law educator*

MARYLAND

Baltimore
Schochor, Jonathan *lawyer, educator*

Catonsville
Zumbrun, Alvin John Thomas *law and criminology educator*

Gaithersburg
McDowell, Donna Schultz *lawyer, educator*

Owings Mills
Granat, Richard Stuart *lawyer, educator*

Park Hall
Lacer, Alfred Antonio *lawyer, educator*

Riverdale
Meyers, William Vincent *lawyer*

Rockville
De Jong, David Samuel *lawyer, educator*
Zaphiriou, George Aristotle *lawyer, educator*

Silver Spring
McDermitt, Edward Vincent *lawyer, educator, writer*

MASSACHUSETTS

Boston
Abrams, Roger Ian *law educator, arbitrator*
Auerbach, Joseph *lawyer, educator, retired*
Carter, T(homas) Barton *law educator*
Fischer, Thomas Covell *law educator, consultant, writer, lawyer*

Freehling, Daniel Joseph *law educator, law library director*
Hrones, Stephen Baylis *lawyer, educator*
Park, William Wynnewood *law educator*
Wild, Victor Allyn *lawyer, educator*

Cambridge
Andrews, William Dorey *law educator, lawyer*
Bartholet, Elizabeth *law educator*
Bok, Derek *law educator, former university president*
Dershowitz, Alan Morton *lawyer, educator*
Fisher, Roger Dummer *lawyer, educator, negotiation expert*
Frug, Gerald E. *law educator*
Haar, Charles Monroe *lawyer, educator*
Kagan, Elena *law educator*
Kaplow, Louis *law educator*
Kaufman, Andrew Lee *law educator*
Miller, Arthur Raphael *law educator*
Sander, Frank Ernest Arnold *law educator*
Schauer, Frederick Franklin *law educator*
Steiner, Henry Jacob *law and human rights educator*
von Mehren, Arthur Taylor *lawyer, educator*
Westfall, David *lawyer, educator*
Wolfman, Bernard *lawyer, educator*

Medford
Salacuse, Jeswald William *lawyer, educator*

Newton
Coquillette, Daniel Robert *lawyer, educator*
Huber, Richard Gregory *lawyer, educator*

Waltham
Dickie, Robert Benjamin *lawyer, consultant, educator*

Watertown
Singsen, Antone G., III, *lawyer, educator*

Westfield
Ettman, Philip *business law educator*

MICHIGAN

Ann Arbor
Allen, Layman Edward *law educator, research scientist*
Anderson, Austin Gothard *lawyer, consultant, academic administrator*
Browder, Olin Lorraine *legal educator*
Cooper, Edward Hayes *lawyer, educator*
Kamisar, Yale *lawyer, educator*
Krier, James Edward *law educator, writer*
Lempert, Richard Owen *lawyer, educator*
MacKinnon, Catharine Alice *lawyer, law educator, legal scholar, writer*
St. Antoine, Theodore Joseph *retired law educator, arbitrator*
Schneider, Carl Edward *law educator*
Waggoner, Lawrence William *law educator*
White, James Boyd *law educator*

Bloomfield Hills
Solomon, Mark Raymond *lawyer, educator*

Dearborn
Kahn, Mark Leo *arbitrator, educator*

Detroit
Mengel, Christopher Emile *lawyer, educator*
Volz, William Harry *law educator, administrator*

East Lansing
Bassett, Debra Lyn *lawyer, educator*

Grosse Pointe Park
Centner, Charles William *lawyer, educator*

Holland
Waltz, Jon Richard *lawyer, educator, author*

Lansing
Brennan, Thomas Emmett *lawyer*
Fox, Mark Richard *lawyer, educator, political consultant*
Mead, Irene Marie *lawyer, engineer, educator*

Northville
Hariri, V. M. *arbitrator, mediator, lawyer, educator*

Southfield
Hotelling, Harold *law and economics educator*
Shpiece, Michael Ronald *lawyer, educator*

MINNESOTA

Minneapolis
Clary, Bradley G. *lawyer, educator*
Frase, Richard Stockwell *law educator*
Karan, Bradlee *lawyer, educator*
Kilbourn, William Douglas, Jr., *law educator*
Kirtley, Jane Elizabeth *law educator*
Lazar, Raymond Michael *lawyer, educator*
Morrison, Fred LaMont *law educator*
Nord, Beryl Annette *judge, educator*
Radmer, Michael John *lawyer, educator*
Tanick, Marshall Howard *lawyer, law educator*
Younger, Judith Tess *lawyer, educator*

Rochester
Larson, Bruce Robert *lawyer, educator*

Saint Joseph
Olheiser, Mary David *lawyer, educator*

Saint Paul
Daly, Joseph Leo *law educator*
Failinger, Marie Anita *law educator, editor*
Haynsworth, Harry Jay, IV, *lawyer, educator*

MISSISSIPPI

Greenwood
Deaton, Charles Milton *lawyer*

Jackson
West, Carol Catherine *law educator*

MISSOURI

Columbia
Moore, Mitchell Jay *lawyer, law educator*
Westbrook, James Edwin *lawyer, educator*

Independence
Cady, Elwyn Loomis, Jr., *medico legal consultant, educator*

Kansas City
Wyrsch, James Robert *lawyer, educator, writer*

Saint Louis
Ellis, Dorsey Daniel, Jr., *lawyer, educator*
Evans, Lawrence E. *lawyer, educator*
Luberda, George Joseph *lawyer, educator*
Ringkamp, Stephen H. *lawyer, educator*

MONTANA

Whitehall
Bernard, Donald Ray *law educator, international business counselor*

NEBRASKA

Lincoln
Ogle, Robbin Sue *criminal justice educator*

Omaha
Forbes, Franklin Sim *lawyer, educator*

NEVADA

Las Vegas
Goodwin, John Robert *lawyer, law educator, author*
O'Connell, John F. *lawyer, retired law educator*

NEW HAMPSHIRE

Exeter
DeMitchell, Terri Ann *law educator*
Vogelman, Lawrence Allen *law educator, lawyer*

Hanover
Prager, Susan Westerberg *law educator, provost*

Hollis
Lumbard, Eliot Howland *lawyer, educator*

NEW JERSEY

Edison
Fink, Edward Murray *lawyer, educator*
Goldfarb, Ronald C. *lawyer, educator*

Flemington
Nielsen, Lynn Carol *educational consultant*

Greenwich
Lane, Mark *lawyer, educator, writer*

Hackensack
Cipollone, Anthony Dominic *judge, educator*
Curtis, Robert Kern *lawyer, physics educator*

Mc Afee
Fogel, Richard *lawyer, educator*

Princeton
Katz, Stanley Nider *law history educator*

Rahway
Reldan, Robert Ronald *law educator, psychological consultant, poet*

Ridgewood
Harris, Micalyn Shafer *lawyer, educator, arbitrator, mediator*

Saddle Brook
Knopf, Barry Abraham *lawyer, educator*

NEW MEXICO

Los Lunas
Pope, John William *judge, law educator*

Santa Fe
Noland, Charles Donald *lawyer, educator*

NEW YORK

Albany
Barsamian, J(ohn) Albert *lawyer, judge, educator, criminologist, arbitrator*
Hanna, John, Jr., *lawyer, educator, arbitrator, mediator*

Ballston Spa
Alman, Emily Arnow *lawyer, sociologist, educator*

Bronx
Cornfield, Melvin *lawyer, university institute director*

Brooklyn
Barabash, Claire *lawyer, special education administrator, psychologist*
Schussler, Theodore *lawyer, physician, educator, consultant*

Dobbs Ferry
Juettner, Diana D'Amico *lawyer, educator*

East Meadow
Hyman, Montague Allan *lawyer, educator*

Fresh Meadows
Greenberg, Robert Jay *law educator*

Hawthorne
Jacobs, Jeffrey Lee *lawyer, education network company executive*

Huntington
Glickstein, Howard Alan *law educator*
Grant, J. Kirkland *law educator, lawyer*
Liput, Andrew Lawrence *lawyer, educator*

Ithaca
Alexander, Gregory Stewart *law educator, educator*
Barcelo, John James, III, *law educator*
Clermont, Kevin Michael *law educator*
Cramton, Roger Conant *law educator, lawyer*
Eisenberg, Theodore *law educator*
Roberts, E. F. *lawyer, educator*
Rossi, Faust F. *lawyer, educator*
Simson, Gary Joseph *law educator*
Summers, Robert Samuel *lawyer, author, educator*

New York
Amsterdam, Anthony Guy *law educator*
Arlen, Jennifer Hall *law educator*
Bear, Larry Alan *lawyer, educator*
Bell, Derrick Albert *law educator, author, lecturer*
Black, Barbara Aronstein *legal history educator*
Bruner, Jerome S. *law educator*
Chase, Oscar G(ottfried) *law educator, consultant, author*
Chiang, Yung Frank *law educator*
Dorsen, Norman *lawyer, educator*
Edgar, Harold Simmons Hull *legal educator*
Estreicher, Samuel *lawyer, educator*
Eustice, James Samuel *legal educator, lawyer*
Farber, Donald Clifford *lawyer, educator*
Farnsworth, E(dward) Allan *lawyer, educator*
Feerick, John David *law educator*
First, Harry *law educator*
Gordon, Jeffrey Neil *law educator*
Grad, Frank Paul *law educator, lawyer*
Grant, Paula DiMeo *lawyer, nursing educator, mediator*
Greenawalt, Robert Kent *lawyer, law educator*
Greenberg, Jack *lawyer, law educator*
Greenberger, Howard Leroy *lawyer, educator*
Guggenheim, Martin Franklin *law educator, lawyer*
Hansmann, Henry Baethke *law educator*
Hill, Alfred *lawyer, educator*
Iannuzzi, John Nicholas *lawyer, author, educator*
Kaden, Lewis B. *law educator, lawyer*
Kandel, William Lloyd *lawyer, mediator, arbitrator, educator, writer*
King, Lawrence Philip *lawyer, educator*
Klapper, Molly *lawyer, educator*
Levitan, David M(aurice) *lawyer, educator*
Liebman, Lance Malcolm *law educator, lawyer*
Lowenfeld, Andreas Frank *law educator, arbitrator*
Marcus, Maria Lenhoff *lawyer, law educator*
Maxfield, Guy Budd *lawyer, educator*
Merrill, Thomas Wendell *lawyer, educator*
Mundheim, Robert Harry *law educator*
Naftalis, Gary Philip *lawyer, educator*
Redlich, Norman *lawyer, educator*
Reid, John Phillip *law educator*
Russo, Thomas Anthony *lawyer*
Sandler, Ross *law educator*
Schmertz, Eric Joseph *lawyer, educator*
Schwartz, William *lawyer, educator*
Schwind, Michael Angelo *law educator*
Seidel, Selvyn *lawyer, educator*
Siegel, Stanley *lawyer, educator*
Smit, Hans *law educator, academic administrator, lawyer*
Sovern, Michael Ira *law educator*
Stewart, Richard Burleson *law educator*
Strauss, Peter L(ester) *law educator*
Wellington, Harry Hillel *lawyer, educator*
Zimmett, Mark Paul *lawyer, educator*

Syracuse
Ackerman, Kenneth Edward *lawyer, educator*
Engel, Richard Lee *lawyer, educator*

West Point
Olejniczak, Julian Michael *lawyer, publications executive*

White Plains
Carlisle, Jay Charles, II, *lawyer, educator*
Robinson, Nicholas Adams *lawyer, educator*
Sloan, F(rank) Blaine *law educator*

NORTH CAROLINA

Chapel Hill
Brower, David John *lawyer, urban planner, educator*
Hardin, Paul, III, *law educator*
Wegner, Judith Welch *law educator, former dean*

Charlotte
Durham, J(oseph) Porter, Jr., *lawyer, educator*

Cullowhee
Wilson, LeVon Edward *law educator, lawyer*

Durham
Carrington, Paul DeWitt *lawyer, educator*
Christie, George Custis *lawyer, educator, author*
Cox, James D. *law educator*
Demott, Deborah Ann *lawyer, educator*
Horowitz, Donald Leonard *lawyer, educator, researcher, political scientist, arbitrator*

Fayetteville
Mitchell, Ronnie Monroe *lawyer, educator*

Greensboro
Swan, George Steven *law educator*

Kure Beach
O'Keefe, Raymond Peter *lawyer, educator*

Raleigh
Hall, John Thomas *lawyer, educator*

Winston Salem
Foy, Herbert Miles, III, *lawyer, educator*
Walker, George Kontz *law educator*

OHIO

Ada
Streib, Victor Lee *dean*

Beachwood
Lewis, Cherie Sue *lawyer, English language and journalism educator*

Cincinnati
Christenson, Gordon A. *law educator*
Dornette, W(illiam) Stuart *lawyer, educator*
Meyers, Karen Diane *lawyer, educator, corporate officer*

Cleveland
Mehlman, Maxwell Jonathan *law educator*
Spero, Keith Erwin *lawyer, educator*

Columbus
Blackburn, John D(avid) *legal educator, lawyer*
Frasier, Ralph Kennedy *lawyer, banker*
Hill, Kathleen Blickenstaff *lawyer, mental health nurse, nursing educator*

Mount Vernon
Rose, Kim Matthew *lawyer, educator*

OKLAHOMA

Oklahoma City
Epperson, Kraettli Quynton *lawyer, educator*
Kline, David Adam *lawyer, educator, writer*
Necco, Alexander David *lawyer, educator*
Simpson, Michael Wayne *lawyer, educator*
Steinhorn, Irwin Harry *lawyer, educator, corporate executive*

Tahlequah
Moore, Jerry Scott *lawyer, law educator*

Tulsa
Belsky, Martin Henry *law educator, lawyer*

OREGON

Portland
Schuster, Philip Frederick, II, *lawyer, writer, law educator*
Sokol, Larry Nides *lawyer, educator*

Salem
Nafziger, James Albert Richmond *lawyer, educator*

PENNSYLVANIA

Bala Cynwyd
Kane-Vanni, Patricia Ruth *lawyer, paleontology educator*

Chambersburg
Cleaver, David Charles *lawyer, educator*

Erie
Nichols, Caleb Leroy *lawyer, educator, employment consultant*

Harrisburg
Diehm, James Warren *lawyer, educator*
Sheldon, J. Michael *lawyer, educator*
Van Zile, Philip Taylor, III, *lawyer, educator*

Kennett Square
Conard, Alfred Fletcher *legal educator*

Media
Zicherman, David L. *lawyer, educator, financial consultant*

Philadelphia
Adamany, David Walter *law and political science educator*
Aronstein, Martin Joseph *law educator, lawyer*
Bernard, John Marley *lawyer, educator*
Burbank, Stephen Bradner *law educator*
Chang, Howard Fenghau *law educator, economist*
Keene, John Clark *lawyer, educator*
Klasko, Herbert Ronald *lawyer, law educator, writer*
Klein, Howard Bruce *lawyer, law educator*
Levin, A. Leo *law educator, retired government official*
Mannino, Edward Francis *lawyer, educator*
Pollak, Louis Heilprin *judge, educator*
Pollard, Dennis Bernard *lawyer, educator*

HIGHER EDUCATION: LAW

Reitz, Curtis Randall *lawyer, educator*
Strazzella, James Anthony *law educator, lawyer*
Summers, Clyde Wilson *law educator*

Pittsburgh
Burkoff, John Michael *law educator, lawyer*
Flechtner, Harry Marshal *law educator*
Hellman, Arthur David *law educator, consultant*
Lally-Green, Maureen Ellen *superior court judge, law educator*
Litman, Roslyn Margolis *lawyer, educator*
Murray, John Edward, Jr., *lawyer, educator, university president*
Nordenberg, Mark Alan *law educator, academic administrator*
Rosen, Richard David *lawyer*
Sell, William Edward *law educator*

Villanova
Frankino, Steven P. *lawyer, law educator*

York
Hoffmeyer, William Frederick *lawyer, educator*

RHODE ISLAND

Bristol
Bogus, Carl Thomas *law educator*

SOUTH CAROLINA

Columbia
McCullough, Ralph Clayton, II, *lawyer, educator*
Rouse, LeGrand Ariail, II, *retired lawyer, educator*

Georgetown
Terhune, Jane Howell *legal assistant, educator*

Greenville
Riley, Richard Wilson *lawyer, former federal official*

TENNESSEE

Knoxville
Phillips, Jerry Juan *law educator*

Memphis
Patton, Charles Henry *lawyer, educator*

Nashville
Blumstein, James Franklin *law educator, lawyer, consultant*
Bostick, Charles Dent *retired lawyer, educator*
Charney, Jonathan Isa *law educator, lawyer*
Ely, James Wallace, Jr., *law educator*
Harris, James Harold, III, *lawyer, educator*
Tuke, Robert Dudley *lawyer, educator*

TEXAS

Austin
Bobbitt, Philip Chase *writer, educator, public official*
Churgin, Michael Jay *law educator*
Gibson, William Willard, Jr., *law educator*
Hager, Julie-Ann *lawyer, educator*
Hamilton, Dagmar Strandberg *lawyer, educator*
Hamilton, Robert Woodruff *law educator*
Jentz, Gaylord Adair *law educator*
Laycock, Harold Douglas *law educator, writer*
Mullenix, Linda Susan *lawyer, educator*
Sherman, Max Ray *lawyer, academic executive, former state senator*
Sturley, Michael F. *law educator*
Sullivan, Teresa Ann *law and sociology educator, academic administrator*
Weinberg, Louise *law educator, author*
Weintraub, Russell Jay *lawyer, educator*
Wellborn, Olin Guy, III, *law educator, educator*
Westbrook, Jay Lawrence *law educator*
Yudof, Mark George *law educator, university system chancellor*

Beaumont
Cavaliere, Frank Joseph *lawyer, educator*

Dallas
Burns, Sandra *lawyer, educator*
Busbee, Kline Daniel, Jr., *law educator, lawyer*
Elkins-Elliott, Kay *law educator*
Garner, Bryan Andrew *law educator, consultant, writer*
Johnson, James Joseph Scofield *lawyer, judge, educator, author*

Fort Worth
Reade, Kathleen Margaret *paralegal, author, educator*

Houston
Engerrand, Kenneth G. *lawyer, law educator*
Foster, Charles Crawford *lawyer, educator*
Goldman, Nathan Carliner *lawyer, educator*
Graving, Richard John *law educator*
Gutheinz, Joseph Richard, Jr., *lawyer, former politician, investigative consultant, retired army officer and NASA official, educator, author*
Lopez, David Tiburcio *lawyer, educator, arbitrator, mediator*
Moroney, Linda L.S. (Muffie) *lawyer, educator*
Moya, Olga Lydia *law educator*

Kerrville
Cole, Barbara Ann *lawyer, educator*

Lubbock
Skillern, Frank Fletcher *law educator*

Plano
Hemingway, Richard William *law educator*

San Antonio
Castleberry, James Newton, Jr., *retired law educator, dean*
Reams, Bernard Dinsmore, Jr., *lawyer, educator*
Ross, James Ulric *lawyer, accountant, educator*
Schlueter, David Arnold *law educator*

Tyler
Patterson, Donald Ross *lawyer, educator*

UTAH

Salt Lake City
Shea, Patrick A. *lawyer, educator*

VERMONT

Morrisville
Williams, David A. *lawyer, educator*

Rutland
Faignant, John Paul *lawyer, educator*

VIRGINIA

Arlington
Anthony, Robert Armstrong *lawyer, educator*
Mossinghoff, Gerald Joseph *lawyer*
Wheeler, Barbara Monica

Blacksburg
Jensen, Walter Edward *lawyer, educator*

Charlottesville
Bonnie, Richard Jeffrey *law educator, lawyer*
Henderson, Stanley Dale *lawyer, educator*
Kitch, Edmund Wells *lawyer, educator, private investor*
Martin, David Alan *law educator*
Meador, Daniel John *law educator*
Menefee, Samuel Pyeatt *lawyer, anthropologist*
Monahan, John T. *law educator, psychologist*
O'Brien, David Michael *law educator*
Wadlington, Walter James *law educator*
White, George Edward *law educator, lawyer*
Whitehead, John Wayne *law educator, organization administrator, author*

Mc Lean
Redmond, Robert *lawyer, educator*
Susko, Carol Lynne *lawyer, accountant*

Norfolk
Johnson, Thomas G., Jr., *lawyer*

Richmond
McFarlane, Walter Alexander *lawyer, educator*

Williamsburg
Marcus, Paul *law educator*
Sullivan, Timothy Jackson *law educator, academic administrator*

WASHINGTON

Seattle
Bailey, William Scherer *lawyer, educator*
Price, John Richard *lawyer, law educator*
Starr, Isidore *law educator*
Wayne, Robert Jonathan *lawyer, educator*

WEST VIRGINIA

Charleston
Brewer, Lewis Gordon *judge, lawyer, educator*

WISCONSIN

Madison
Michaelis, Karen Lauree *law educator*

Milwaukee
Kircher, John Joseph *law educator*

Ripon
Prissel, Barbara Ann *paralegal, law educator*

WYOMING

Laramie
Fulton, Jo Ann *lawyer*

TERRITORIES OF THE UNITED STATES

PUERTO RICO

San Juan
Ramos-Gonzalez, Carlos Eduardo *law educator, university dean*

CANADA

Whale Cove
Rodnunsky, Sidney *lawyer, educator*

GUATEMALA

Guatemala City
Mayora-Alvarado, Eduardo Rene *lawyer, law educator*

ADDRESS UNPUBLISHED

Amar, Akhil Reed *law educator*
Anderson, John Bayard *lawyer, educator, former congressman*
Bakken, Gordon Morris *law educator*
Berry, Robert Worth *lawyer, retired law educator, retired military officer*
Brewer, Edward Cage, III, *law educator*
Califano, Joseph Anthony, Jr., *lawyer, public health policy educator, writer*
Clark, Robert Charles *law educator*
Crawford, Muriel Laura *lawyer, author, educator*
Cronen, Michael James *lawyer, educator*
Damaska, Mirjan Radovan *law educator*
Davis, Frederick Benjamin *retired law educator*
Dickerson, Claire Moore *lawyer, educator*
Dowben, Carla Lurie *lawyer, educator*
Dunfee, Thomas Wylie *law educator*
Dutile, Fernand Neville *law educator*
Fink, Norman Stiles *lawyer, educational administrator, fundraising consultant*
Fiss, Owen M. *law educator, educator*
Fox, Eleanor Mae Cohen *lawyer, educator, writer*
Freedman, Monroe Henry *lawyer, educator, columnist*
Fried, Charles *law educator*
Greenberg, Ronald David *lawyer, law educator*
Heppe, Karol Virginia *lawyer, educator*
Hermann, Donald Harold James *lawyer, educator*
Holtzschue, Karl Bressem *lawyer, author, educator*
Johnson, James Terence *lawyer, educator, minister*
Jones, William Rex *law educator*
Lang, Michael Benjamin *law educator*
Lathrope, Daniel John *law educator*
Latovick, Paula R(ae) *lawyer, educator*
Lipsman, Richard Marc *lawyer, educator*
Long, Charles Thomas *lawyer, history educator*
Martin, Connie Ruth *retired lawyer*
Missan, Richard Sherman *lawyer, educator*
Mlyniec, Wallace John *law educator, lawyer, consultant*
O'Dell, Joan Elizabeth *lawyer, mediator, business executive, educator*
Paulus, Norma Jean Petersen *lawyer*
Phillips, Florence Tsu *lawyer, choreographer, dance educator*
Pooley, Beverley John *law educator, librarian*
Roe, Mark J. *law educator*
Sax, Joseph Lawrence *lawyer, educator*
Schlueter, Linda Lee *law educator*
Schmidt, Kathleen Marie *lawyer*
Schmoll, Harry F., Jr., *lawyer, educator*
Schuck, Peter Horner *lawyer, educator*
Seaver, Robert Leslie *retired law educator*
Siegan, Bernard Herbert *lawyer, educator*
Smith, Ronald Ehlbert *lawyer, educator, pastor, public speaker, writer, motivator, real estate developer*
Termini, Roseann Bridget *law educator*
Wood, Diane Pamela *judge*
Worthington, Daniel Glen *lawyer, educator*

HIGHER EDUCATION: LIFE SCIENCES

UNITED STATES

ALABAMA

Auburn University
Bakhtiyarov, Sayavur Ispandiyaroglu *rheologist, educator, researcher*

Dauphin Island
Cowan, James Howard, Jr., *fishery scientist, biological oceanographer*

Huntsville
Gillani, Noor Velshi *atmospheric scientist, researcher, educator*

Mobile
French, Elizabeth Irene *biology educator, violinist*
Taylor, Aubrey Elmo *physiologist, educator*

Normal
Coleman, Tommy Lee *soil science educator, researcher, laboratory director*
Mays, David Arthur *agronomy educator*
Sabota, Catherine Marie *horticulturist, educator*

ARIZONA

Flagstaff
Price, Peter Wilfrid *ecology educator, researcher*
van Riper, Charles, III, *biology educator*

Glendale
Collins, Richard Francis *microbiologist, educator*

Phoenix
Davey, Eleanor Ellen *science educator*
Leary, Rosemary Frech *science educator*
Revie, Jean E. *science educator*

Prescott
Sloan, Marjorie Hawkins *science educator, retired advertising executive*

Taylor
Kerr, Barbara Prosser *research scientist, educator*

Tempe
Pinkava, Donald John *botany educator, researcher*

Tucson
Gerba, Charles Peter *microbiologist, educator*
Yocum, Harrison Gerald *horticulturist, botanist, educator, researcher*

ARKANSAS

Fayetteville
Riggs, Robert Dale *plant pathology and nematology educator, researcher*

CALIFORNIA

Alameda
Luther, John Stafford *biology educator, consultant*

Berkeley
Barrett, Reginald Haughton *biology educator, wildlife management educator*
Chandler, David *scientist, educator*
Getz, Wayne Marcus *biomathematician, researcher, educator*
Levine, Michael Steven *science educator*
Lichtenberg, Allan Joseph *science educator*
Perloff, Jeffrey Mark *agricultural and resource economics educator*
Schachman, Howard Kapnek *molecular biologist, educator*
Spear, Robert Clinton *environmental health educator, consultant*
Taylor, John W. *mycologist, educator*
Wake, David Burton *biology educator*
Wood, David Lee *entomologist, educator*

Beverly Hills
Smith, Marilyn Noeltner *retired science educator*

Campbell
Pak, Nomyon *biologist, educator*

Carmel
Epel, David *biologist, educator*

Davis
Hess, Charles Edward *environmental horticulture educator*
Horwitz, Barbara Ann *physiologist, educator, consultant*
Kester, Dale Emmert *pomologist, educator*
Qualset, Calvin O. *plant genetics and agronomy educator*

Fairfield
Redfield, David Allen *chemistry educator*

Gardena
Hu, Steve Seng-Chiu *scientific research company executive, academic administrator*

Hercules
Hardy, Joel Allen *microbiologist, educator*

Hermosa Beach
Chi, Lois Wong *emeritus biology educator, research scientist*

Irvine
Demetrescu, Mihai Constantin *research scientist, educator, computer company executive*
Silverman, Paul Hyman *science administrator, former university official*

La Jolla
Helinski, Donald Raymond *biologist, educator*
Johnson, Paul Christian *physiologist, educator*
Wilkie, Donald Walter *biologist, aquarium museum director*

La Verne
Neher, Robert Trostle *biology educator*

Loma Linda
Aloia, Roland Craig *scientist, administrator, educator*

Long Beach
Toma, Ramses Barsoum *food science and nutrition educator*

Los Altos
Nye, Reba Rhodes *science and home economics educator*

Los Angeles
Buth, Donald George *biology educator*
Davies, Kelvin James Anthony *research scientist, educator, consultant, author*
Grinnell, Alan Dale *neurobiologist, educator, researcher*
Gunsalus, Robert Philip *microbiologist, educator, molecular geneticist*
Haglund, Thomas Roy *research biologist, consultant, educator*
Lu, John Kuew-Hsiung *physiology educator, endocrinologist*
Melnick, Michael *geneticist, educator*
Shen-Miller, Jane *research biologist*
Sullivan, Cornelius Wayne *marine biology educator, university research foundation administrator, government agency administrator*

Malibu
Hunt, Valerie Virginia *electrophysiologist, educator*

Merced
Olsen, David Magnor *chemistry and astronomy educator*

Moffett Field
Friedmann, Roseli Ocampo *microbiologist, educator*
Wignarajah, Kanapathipillai *plant physiologist, researcher, educator*

Oceanside
Paxton, Mary Jean Wallace *science educator*

Palo Alto
Briggs, Winslow Russell *plant biologist, educator*

Pasadena
Davidson, Eric Harris *molecular and developmental biologist, educator*
Konishi, Masakazu *neurobiologist, educator*
Lewis, Edward B. *biology educator*
Meyerowitz, Elliot Martin *biologist, educator*
Revel, Jean-Paul *biology educator*

Pomona
Saccoman, Stefanie Ann *science educator*

Riverside
Erwin, Donald Carroll *plant pathology educator*

San Diego
Hogan, Sheila Maureen *biology educator, nurse*
Savage, Jay Mathers *biology educator*

San Francisco
Borchardt, Kenneth Andrew *microbiology consultant, educator*
Levinson, Warren Edward *physician, microbiologist, educator*
Márquez-Magaña, Leticia Maria *biology educator*
Randall, Janet Ann *biology educator, desert biologist*

San Marcos
Sheath, Robert Gordon *botanist, educator*

Santa Barbara
Badash, Lawrence *science history educator*

Santa Cruz
Griggs, Gary Bruce *science administrator, oceanographer, geologist, educator*

Santa Monica
Honour, Lynda Charmaine *research scientist, educator, psychotherapist*

Stanford
Campbell, Allan McCulloch *bacteriology educator*
Cohen, Stanley Norman *geneticist, educator*
Djerassi, Carl *writer, retired chemistry educator*
Ehrlich, Paul Ralph *biology educator*
Falkow, Stanley *microbiologist, educator*
Hanawalt, Philip Courtland *biology educator, researcher*
Matin, A. *microbiology educator, consultant*
Shapiro, Lucille *molecular biology educator*
Shooter, Eric Manvers *neurobiology educator, consultant*
Yanofsky, Charles *biology educator*

Thousand Oaks
Rosenberg, Fred Allan *microbiology educator*

Walnut
Shannon, Cynthia Jean *biology educator*

Winters
Low, Donald Gottlob *retired veterinary medicine educator*

COLORADO

Arvada
Reynolds-Sakowski, Dana Renee *science educator*

Boulder
Staehelin, Lucas Andrew *cell biology educator*

Broomfield
DuPee, Pamela Annette *fisheries biologist, educator, consultant*

Brush
Gabriel, Donald Eugene *science educator*

Colorado Springs
Heim, Werner G(eorge) *biology educator*

Denver
Heifets, Leonid *microbiologist, educator*

Fort Collins
Hendrix, John Edwin *biology educator*
Hughes, Harrison G. *horticulture educator*
Phemister, Robert David *veterinary medical educator*

Golden
Bergeron, Sheila Diane *retired science educator, educational consultant*

CONNECTICUT

Darien
Burchenal, Joan Riley *science educator*

Fairfield
Braun, Phyllis Cellini *biology educator*

Hartford
Wolf, Barry *genetics, pediatric educator*

Milford
Turko, Alexander Anthony *biology educator, hypnotherapist*

New Haven
Altman, Sidney *biology educator*
Aronson, Peter Samuel *medical scientist, physiology educator*
Brudvig, Gary W. *chemistry educator*
Brunson, Kenneth Wayne *cancer biologist*
Cohen, Lawrence Baruch *neurobiologist, educator*
Giebisch, Gerhard Hans *physiology educator*
Hoffman, Joseph Frederick *physiology educator*
Stolwijk, Jan Adrianus Jozef *physiologist, biophysicist*
Tanaka, Kay *genetics educator*
Wagner, Günter Paul *biologist educator*

Storrs Mansfield
Salamone, John Dominic *neuroscientist, educator*

West Simsbury
Morest, Donald Kent *neuroscientist, educator*

DELAWARE

Dover
Peiffer, Randel Aaron *agricultural sciences educator, researcher*

Newark
Campbell, Linzy Leon *molecular biology researcher, educator*

DISTRICT OF COLUMBIA

Washington
Apple, Martin Allen *science executive, scientist, educator*
Case, Larry D. *agricultural education specialist*
Coleman, Bernell *physiologist, educator*
De Fabo, Edward Charles *photobiology and photoimmunology, research scientist, educator*
Holmes, George Edward *molecular biologist, educator*
James, Charles Clinton *science education educator, consultant*
Kapetanakos, Christos Anastasios *science administrator, physics educator*
Kramer, Jay Harlan *physiologist, researcher, educator*
Soloway, Rose Ann Gould *clinical toxicologist*
Tingus, Steven James *physiologist researcher, educator*

FLORIDA

Coral Gables
Schaiberger, George Elmer *microbiologist educator*

Fort Lauderdale
Silfen, Roberta Dawn *wildlife hospital administrator*

Gainesville
Cantliffe, Daniel James *horticulture educator*
Dilcher, David Leonard *paleobotany educator, research scholar*
Hochmuth, George J. *horticultural educator*
Jaeger, Marc Julius *physiology educator, researcher*
Jones, David Alwyn *geneticist, botany educator*
Jones, Richard Lamar *entomology educator*
Quesenberry, Kenneth Hays *agronomy educator*
Seale, James Lawrence, Jr., *agricultural economics educator, international trade researcher*
Shanmugam, Keelnatham T. *microbiology educator*
Teixeira, Arthur Alves *food engineer, educator, consultant*
Wilcox, Charles Julian *geneticist, educator*

Jacksonville
Tardona, Daniel Richard *cognitive ethologist, writer, park ranger, educator*

Largo
Beck, Donald James *veterinarian, educator*

Margate
Franks, Allen P. *research institute executive, educator*

Orlando
Walters, Linda Jane *marine biologist, educator, researcher*

Oviedo
Koevenig, James Louis *biology educator, artist*

Punta Gorda
O'Neal, Lyman Henry *biology educator*

Sarasota
Sanderson, Kenneth Chapman *horticulture educator, consultant, researcher*

Tallahassee
Hunter, Pamela Ann *veterinarian, educator*
Onokpise, Oghenekome Ukrakpo *agronomist, educator, forest geneticist, agroforester*

Tampa
Hickman, Hugh V. *science educator, researcher*
Keith, Mary Agnes *food scientist, educator*

West Palm Beach
Miao, Shili *plant biology and wetland ecology researcher*

GEORGIA

Athens
Atwater, Mary Monroe *science educator*
Brackett, Benjamin Gaylord *physiology and pharmacology educator*
Karnok, Keith J. *agronomist, educator*
Shotts, Emmett Booker, Jr., *microbiology educator, researcher*

Atlanta
Black, Carolyn Morris *microbiologist, educator, science administrator*
Carey, Gerald John, Jr., *retired research institute director emeritus, former air force officer*
Carmichael, Willie Franklin, Jr., *science educator*
Circeo, Louis Joseph, Jr., *research scientist, civil engineer*
Clifton, David Samuel , Jr., *research executive, economist*
Matthews, Hewitt William *science educator*
Schwartz, Miriam Catherine *biology educator*
Warren, Stephen Theodore *human geneticist, educator*

Augusta
Hayes, John Thompson *biology educator, educational administrator*
Kutlar, Ferdane *genetics educator, researcher*
Yu, Robert Kuan-jen *biochemistry educator*

Columbus
Riggsby, Ernest Duward *science educator, educational development executive*

Griffin
Doyle, Michael Patrick *microbiologist, educator, director*

Macon
Carson, Juanita Elaine *biologist, educator*

HAWAII

Honolulu
Brewbaker, James Lynn *crop science and genetics educator*
Sherman, Martin *entomologist, educator*
Silva, James Anthony *soil scientist, educator*
Smith, Dean Orren *physiology educator*

Tamc
Uyehara, Catherine Fay Takako (Catherine Yamauchi) *physiologist, educator, pharmacologist*

IDAHO

Boise
Woods, Jean Frahm *science educator*

ILLINOIS

Argonne
Schriesheim, Alan *research administrator*

Champaign
Stout, Glenn Emanuel *retired science administrator*

Chicago
Baumgartner, Donald Lawrence *entomologist, educator*
Castignetti, Domenic *microbiologist, biology educator*
Cherif, Abour Hachmi *biology and science educator*
Desjardins, Claude *physiologist, dean*
Drantz, Veronica Ellen *science educator and consultant*
Houk, James Charles *physiology, educator*
New, John Gerard *neuroscientist, educator*
Peeples, Mark Edward *virology researcher, educator*
Racker, Darlene Katie *cardiovascular anatomist and electrophysiologist*
Rymer, William Zev *research scientist, administrator*
Schreckenberger, Paul Charles *clinical microbiologist, educator*
Straus, Lorna Puttkammer *biology educator*
Tarnow, Fredric Herman *science educator*

Danville
Konsis, Kenneth Frank *forester, educator*

Dekalb
King, Kenneth Paul *science educator*
Meganathan, Rangaswamy *microbiologist, educator*

Edwardsville
Brugam, Richard Blair *biology educator*

Evanston
Wu, Tai Te *biological sciences and engineering educator*

Lombard
Velardo, Joseph Thomas *molecular biology and endocrinology educator*

Normal
Anderson, Roger Clark *biology educator*
Brown, Lauren Evans *zoologist, researcher, educator*

North Chicago
Albach, Richard Allen *microbiology educator*
Chang, Kwang Poo *microbiology educator*

River Grove
Gardner, Sandi B. *biology educator*

Urbana
Anastasio, Thomas Joseph *neuroscientist, educator, researcher*
Cheryan, Munir *agricultural studies educator, biochemical engineering educator*
Crang, Richard Francis Earl *plant and cell biologist, research center administrator*
Dziuk, Philip John *animal scientist educator*
Feng, Albert *science educator, researcher*
Greenough, William Tallant *psychobiologist, educator*
Hoeft, Robert Gene *agriculture educator*
Holt, Donald A. *agronomist, consultant, retired academic administrator*
Rebeiz, Constantin A. *plant physiology educator, laboratory director*
Robinson, Gene Ezia *biologist, educator*
Waldbauer, Gilbert Peter *entomologist, educator*
Whitt, Dixie Dailey *microbiology educator*

INDIANA

Bloomington
Hammel, Harold Theodore *physiology and biophysics educator, researcher*
Heiser, Charles Bixler, Jr., *botany educator*
Rebec, George Vincent *neuroscience researcher, educator, administrator*

Goshen
Jacobs, Merle Emmor *zoology educator, researcher*

Indianapolis
Christian, Joe Clark *medical genetics researcher, educator*
Cliff, Johnnie Marie *mathematics and chemistry educator*
Lahiri, Debomoy Kumar *molecular neurobiologist, educator*

Lafayette
Guo, Peixuan *molecular virology educator*

Muncie
Hendrix, Jon Richard *biology educator*

New Albany
Baker, Claude Douglas *biology educator, researcher, environmental activist*

Notre Dame
Jensen, Richard Jorg *biology educator*
Lafield, Karen Woodrow *science educator, demographer*
Lamberti, Gary Anthony *biology educator*

Richmond
Foos, K. Michael *biology educator*

Upland
Whipple, Andrew Powell *biology educator*

West Lafayette
Carlson, Gary Patrick *toxicologist, educator*
Hunt, Michael O'Leary *wood science and engineering educator*
Johannsen, Chris Jakob *agronomist, educator, administrator*
Nelson, Philip Edwin *food scientist, educator*
Nyquist, Wyman Ellsworth *biometry educator*
Scott, Terry Alan *science education educator*

IOWA

Ames
Moore, Kenneth James *agronomy educator, scientist*
Mullen, Russell Edward *agricultural studies educator*
Pearce, Robert Brent *agricultural studies educator*
Rothschild, Max Frederick *animal science educator*

Des Moines
Finnerty, Edward Patrick *neuroscience educator, clinical chemist*

Estherville
Klepper, Robert Rush *science educator*

Iowa City
Bettis, Elmer Arthur, III, *physical science educator*
Chapleau, Mark William *physiologist, educator*
Lim, Ramon (Khe-Siong Lim) *neuroscience educator, researcher*

Larchwood
Onet, Virginia C(onstantinescu) *research scientist, educator, writer*

Woodward
Zeller, Michael Frank *science educator*

KANSAS

Emporia
Sundberg, Marshall David *biology educator*

Hays
Talbott, Nancy Costigan *science educator*

Kansas City
Samson, Frederick Eugene, Jr., *neuroscientist, educator*

Lawrence
Bovee, Eugene Cleveland *protozoologist, emeritus educator*
Michener, Charles Duncan *entomologist, educator, researcher*

Manhattan
Erickson, Howard Hugh *veterinarian, physiology educator*
Fick, Walter Henry *range research scientist, educator*
Ham, George Eldon *retired soil microbiologist, educator*
McKee, Richard Miles *animal studies educator*

KENTUCKY

Berea
Barnes, Richard Nearn *biology educator emeritus*

Hazard
Globig, Sabine A. *biology educator*

Lexington
Barnhart, Charles Elmer *animal sciences educator*
Palmer, Brent David *environmental physiology educator, biologist*

Owensboro
Oetinger, David Frederick *biology educator*

LOUISIANA

Baton Rouge
Chapman, Russell Leonard *botany educator*
Hansel, William *biology educator*
Liuzzo, Joseph Anthony *food science educator*
Murai, Norimoto *plant molecular biologist, educator*

Metairie
Curry, Mary Grace *environmental executive*

New Orleans
Andersson, Hans Christoph *human geneticist, educator*

MAINE

Brunswick
Sherman, Thomas Fairchild *biology educator*

Lee
Avery, Pasco Bruce *secondary science educator*

Orono
Bushway, Rodney John *food science educator*

Presque Isle
Lord, Richard Newell, Jr., *science educator*

Rockland
Desaulniers, Paul Roger *physics, marine science, and aquaculture educator, consultant*

MARYLAND

Baltimore
Goldberg, Alan Marvin *toxicologist, educator*
Grollman, Sigmund Sidney *physiology educator*
Massof, Robert William *neuroscientist, educator*
Privalov, Peter L. *biology and biophysics educator*
Roberts, Randolph Wilson *health and science educator*
Seydoux, Geraldine *molecular biologist*
Suskind, Sigmund Richard *microbiology educator*
Trpis, Milan *vector biologist, scientist, educator*
Yau, King-Wai *neuroscientist, educator*

Bethesda
Bunger, Rolf *physiology educator*
Chan, Wai-Yee *geneticist, educator*
Petralia, Ronald Sebastian *entomologist, neurobiologist*
Rubin, Gerald Mayer *molecular biologist, biochemistry educator*
Ryan, Kevin William *virologist, researcher, science educator, clinical research administrator*

Claiborne
Moorhead, Paul Sidney *geneticist*

College Park
Mather, Ian Heywood *cell biologist, educator*

Greenbelt
Thomas, Lindsey Kay, Jr., *research ecology biologist, educator, consultant*

Millersville
Sipple, William Stanton *ecologist, educator*

Towson
Shah, Shirish Kalyanbhai *computer science, chemistry and environmental science educator*

Wye Mills
Lednum, Florence Nash *biological sciences educator*

MASSACHUSETTS

Amherst
Francis, Frederick John *food science educator*
Schumann, Gail L. *plant pathologist, educator*

Bedford
Patton, Cindy Anne *biology educator*

Boston
Broitman, Selwyn Arthur *microbiologist, educator*
El-Baz, Farouk *science administrator, educator*
Lehman, William Jeffrey *physiology educator*

Brookline
Rosner, Anthony Leopold *research director, biochemist*

Cambridge
Ashton, Peter Shaw *tropical forest science educator*
Berg, Howard C. *biology educator*
Branton, Daniel *biology educator*
Dowling, John Elliott *biology educator*
Fox, Maurice Sanford *molecular biologist, educator*
Gilbert, Walter *molecular biologist, educator*
Hastings, John Woodland *biologist, educator*
Hynes, Richard Olding *biology researcher, educator*
Knoll, Andrew Herbert T. *biology educator*
Levins, Richard *biologist, educator*
Pardue, Mary-Lou *biology educator*
Pfister, Donald Henry *biology educator*
Sharp, Phillip Allen *biologist, educator*
Wilson, Edward Osborne *biologist, educator, writer*
Wogan, Gerald Norman *toxicology educator*

Fitchburg
Boisvert, Dorothy Lozowski *science educator*

Ipswich
Appa, Anna Aniko *biology educator, Latin educator, writer, poet, editor*

Lowell
Eby, G. Nelson *geoscience educator*

Methuen
Bonanno, A. Richard *weed management scientist, educator*

Woods Hole
Ebert, James David *research biologist, educator*

Worcester
Dobson, James Gordon, Jr., *cardiovascular physiologist, scientist, educator*
Leonard, Thomas J. *biologist, department chairman*

MICHIGAN

Adrian
Husband, Robert Wayne *biology educator*

Albion
Stowell, Ewell Addison *botany educator, forestry consultant*

Ann Arbor
Gelehrter, Thomas David *medical and genetics educator, physician*
Kleinsmith, Lewis Joel *cell biologist, educator*
Richardson, Rudy James *toxicology and neurosciences educator*
Sloat, Barbara Furin *cell biologist, educator*
Weatherbee, Ellen Gene Elliott *botanist, educator*
Welsh, Michael John *cell biologist, researcher, science educator*
Williams, John Andrew *physiology educator, consultant*
Yocum, Charles Fredrick *biology educator*

Detroit
Bhalla, Deepak Kumar *cell biologist, toxicologist, educator*
DeRoo, Sally Ann *biology, geology and environmental science educator*
Grossman, Lawrence I. *molecular biology educator*
Phillis, John Whitfield *physiologist, educator*
Subramanian, Marappa Gounder *reproductive physiologist, educator*

East Lansing
Patterson, Maria Jevitz *microbiology-pediatric infectious disease educator*

Flint
Wigston, David Lawrence *biologist, dean*

Highland Park
Crittenden, Mary Lynne *science educator*

Kalamazoo
Gómez Lance, Betty Rita *sciences and foreign language educator, writer*

Mount Pleasant
Novitski, Charles Edward *biology educator*

Troy
Tai, Wei-Hua *mechanics scientist, educator*

MINNESOTA

Duluth
Heller, Lois Jane *physiologist, educator, researcher*

Mapleton
John, Hugo Herman *natural resources educator*

Minneapolis
Lee, Hon Cheung *physiology educator*
Low, Walter Cheney *neuroscience and physiology educator*
Scott, Rebecca Andrews *retired biology educator*

Rochester
Roberts, Glenn Dale *microbiologist, educator*

Saint Paul
Barnwell, Franklin Hershel *zoology educator*
Cheng, H(wei) H(sien) *soil scientist, agronomic and environmental science educator*
D'Cruz, Osmond Jerome *research scientist, educator*
Fan, David P. *scientist biologist, educator*
Hueg, William Frederick *agronomy educator, dairy owner*
Kommedahl, Thor *plant pathology educator*
Leonard, Kurt John *plant pathologist, retired university program director*
Marini, John Joseph *medical scientist, physician*
McKinnell, Robert Gilmore *retired zoology, genetics and cell biology educator*
Newman, Raymond Melvin *biologist, educator*
Phillips, Ronald Lewis *plant geneticist, educator*
Pomeroy, Benjamin Sherwood *veterinary medicine educator*
Wendt, Hans W. *life scientist*
Wilson, Michael John *biologist, educator*

MISSISSIPPI

Lorman
Ezekwe, Michael Obi *animal science educator*

Macon
Hatcher, Lucille Robinson *science educator*

MISSOURI

Columbia
Blevins, Dale Glenn *agronomy educator*
David, John Dewood *biology educator*
Morehouse, Lawrence Glen *veterinarian, educator*

Kansas City
Hagsten, Ib *animal scientist, livestock consultant*

Saint Louis
Bourne, Carol Elizabeth Mulligan *biology educator, phycologist*
Curtiss, Roy, III, *biology educator*
Dutcher, Susan K. *geneticist, educator*
Woolsey, Thomas Allen *neurobiologist*

Springfield
Falls, Harold Brown, Jr., *biomedical sciences educator, physiologist*
Myers, Richard Lee *microbiology and immunology educator*
Scheusner, Dale Lee *microbiologist, educator*

Windyville
Condron, Barbara O'Guinn *metaphysics educator, school administrator, publisher*

NEBRASKA

Lincoln
Barrett, Leverne A. *agricultural studies educator*
Genoways, Hugh Howard *systematic biologist, educator*
Massengale, Martin Andrew *agronomist, university president*

Omaha
Badeer, Henry Sarkis *physiology educator*
Nipper, Henry Carmack *toxicology educator*

NEVADA

Las Vegas
Golding, Lawrence Arthur *physiology educator*
Himes, John G. *biologist, educator*

NEW HAMPSHIRE

Lebanon
Ou, Lo-Chang *physiology educator*

NEW JERSEY

Beach Haven
McLellan, Laura John *biology educator*

Carlstadt
Siri, Walter Alan *retired science educator*

Jersey City
Singer, Howard Jack *biology educator*

Kinnelon
Richardson, Joseph Blancet *retired science educator, educational consultant*

Madison
Demain, Arnold Lester *microbiologist, educator*

New Brunswick
Day, Peter Rodney *geneticist, educator*
Ehrenfeld, David William *biology educator, writer*

Newark
Lachance, Paul Albert *food science educator, clergyman*
Solberg, Myron *food scientist, educator*

Gagna, Claude Eugene *molecular biologist, biochemist, anatomist*
Geskin, Ernest S(amuel) *science administrator, consultant*
Jonakait, Gene Miller *developmental neurobiologist, neuroimmunologist, educator*
Ledeen, Robert Wagner *neurochemist, educator*

Piscataway
Essien, Francine B. *geneticist, educator*
Liu, Alice Y. C. *biology educator*
Stevenson, Nancy Roberta *physiologist, educator*
Stollar, Victor *microbiology educator*
Tischfield, Jay Arnold *genetics educator*

Princeton
Ballou, Janice Donelon *research director*
Gould, James L. *biology educator*
Grant, Peter Raymond *biologist, researcher, educator*
Rubenstein, Daniel Ian *biology educator*
Steinberg, Malcolm Saul *biologist, educator*
Wieschaus, Eric F. *molecular biologist, educator*

Wayne
White, Doris Gnauck *science educator, biochemical and biophysics researcher*

NEW MEXICO

Albuquerque
O'Neil, Daniel Joseph *scientist/engineer, research executive, educator*
Roberts, Scott Owen *exercise physiologist, educator*

Carlsbad
Nance, Raymond G. *science educator*

Santa Fe
Myers, Charlotte Will *biology educator*

NEW YORK

Albany
Trimble, Robert Bogue *research biologist*

Alfred
Buckwalter, John David *biologist educator*

Annandale On Hudson
Ferguson, John Barclay *biology educator*

Batavia
Marcus, Bernard Andrew *biology educator*

Bronx
Espinoza, Fernando *science education educator*
Lisowy, Donald C. *conservation and science educator*

Brooklyn
Altura, Bella T. *physiologist, educator*
Altura, Burton Myron *physiologist, educator*
Levin, Norman Lewis *biology educator*

Buffalo
Isseroff, Hadar *molecular parasitologist*
Zawicki, Joseph Leo *science educator*

Canton
Wells, Russell Frederick *biology educator*

Cobleskill
Ingels, Jack Edward *horticulture educator*

Cooperstown
Harman, Willard Nelson *malacologist, educator*

Cortland
Mason, Elliott Bernard *biologist, educator*

East Patchogue
Metz, Donald Joseph *retired science educator*

Flushing
Aaronson, Sheldon *microbiology educator*
Ben-Harari, Ruben Robert *research scientist, medical writer, medical communications consultant*
Calhoon, Robert Ellsworth *biology educator*

Fredonia
Tomlinson, Bruce Lloyd *biology educator, researcher*

Garden City
Podwall, Kathryn Stanley *biology educator*

Hempstead
Blumenthal, Ralph Herbert *natural science educator*

Ithaca
Ballantyne, Joseph M. *science educator, program administrator, researcher*
Crepet, William Louis *botanist, educator*
Earle, Elizabeth Deutsch *biology educator*
Gillett, James Warren *ecotoxicology educator*
Hairston, Nelson George, Jr., *ecologist, educator*
Hudler, George *plant pathologist, educator*
Viands, Donald Rex *plant breeder, educator*
Walcott, Charles *neurobiology and behavior educator*
Wootton, John Francis *physiology educator*

Manorville
Esp, Barbara Ann Lorraine *educational researcher, educator*

New Paltz
Meng, Heinz Karl *biology educator*

New York
Babich, Harvey Jerome *biology educator*
Calame, Kathryn Lee *microbiologist, educator*
Clarke, Marjorie Jane *environmental educator, consultant, author, researcher*
Cohen, David Harris *neurobiology educator, university official*
Garvey, Michael Steven *veterinarian, educator*
Lederberg, Joshua *geneticist, educator*
Lutton, John Dudley *medical educator, cell biology/hematology-immunology educator*
Morse, Stephen Scott *virologist, immunologist, epidemiologist*
Rabino, Isaac *biology and health science educator, researcher*
Ribary, Urs *neuroscientist, researcher, educator*
Scott, Walter Neil *physiology educator*
Shelanski, Michael L. *cell biologist, educator*
Telang, Nitin T. *cancer biologist, educator*
Tierno, Philip Mario, Jr., *microbiologist, educator, researcher*
Wiesel, Torsten Nils *neurobiologist, educator*
Young, Michael Warren *geneticist, educator*
Zuzolo, Ralph Carmine *biologist, educator, researcher, consultant*

Rochester
Frisina, Robert Dana *sensory neuroscientist, educator*
McCormack, Grace *retired microbiology educator*
Rustchenko, Elena *geneticist, educator*
Schanfield, Moses Samuel *geneticist, educator*

Setauket
Misener, Alan Francis *science educator*

Syracuse
Ames, Ira H. *cell biologist, educator*
Zhang, Lianjun *forestry educator, researcher*

Troy
Berg, Daniel *science and technology educator*

NORTH CAROLINA

Chapel Hill
Huang, Eng-Shang *virology educator, biomedical engineer*
Peet, Robert Krug *ecology educator*
Weiss, Charles Manuel *environmental biologist*
Wetzel, Robert George *botany educator*

Charlotte
Pharr, Jacqueline Anita *biology educator*

Elizabeth City
Blackmon, Ronald H. *biologist, science educator*

Greensboro
Van Pelt, Arnold Francis, Jr., *biologist, researcher*

Greenville
Fulghum, Robert Schmidt *microbiologist, educator*

Morrisville
Andersen, Melvin Ernest *toxicologist, educator*

Raleigh
Davey, Charles Bingham *soil science educator*
Dunphy, Edward James *crop science extension specialist*
Hassan, Hosni Moustafa *microbiologist, biochemist, toxicologist and food scientist, educator*
Havlin, John Leroy *soil scientist, educator*
Hawkins, Eleanor Carroll *veterinary educator*
Noga, Edward Joseph *aquatic animal veterinary medicine educator*
Peacock, Charles H. *agricultural studies educator*
Pharr, David Mason *horticulture educator*
Sanders, Douglas Charles *horticulturist, researcher, educator*
Zeng, Zhao-Bang *geneticist, educator*

Southern Shores
Aukland, Elva Dayton *retired biologist, educator*

Wilmington
Roer, Robert David *physiologist, educator*

Winston Salem
Gmeiner, William Henry *science educator*
Laxminarayana, Dama *geneticist, researcher, educator*

NORTH DAKOTA

Bisbee
Keller, Michelle R. *science educator, secondary education educator*

Fargo
Grier, James William *zoology educator*

Minot
Royer, Ronald Alan *entomologist, educator*

Tioga
Nelson, Marlow Gene *agricultural studies educator*

OHIO

Ashland
Rueger, Daniel Scott *horticulture educator*

Chillicothe
Curtis, Timothy Jack *science educator*

Cincinnati
Cameron, Guy N. *biologist, educator*
Sperelakis, Nicholas, Sr., *physiology and biophysics educator, researcher*

Columbus
Cohen, Robert Alan *agricultural administrator, educator*
Jensen, William August *plant biology educator*
Kapral, Frank Albert *medical microbiology and immunology educator*
Kolodziej, Bruno John *retired biology educator*
Ockerman, Herbert W. *agricultural studies educator*
Selamet, Ahmet *science educator*
Snyder, Susan Leach *science educator, writer*
Stansbery, David Honor *ecologist, malacologist*
Tuovinen, Olli Heikki *microbiology educator*
Zartman, David Lester *animal sciences educator, researcher*

Dublin
Baughman, Paul Earl *agriculture educator*

Elmore
Rosato, Laura Marie *toxicologist, educator*

Granville
Haubrich, Robert Rice *biology educator*

Newark
Greenstein, Julius Sydney *zoology educator*

Oxford
Miller, Harvey Alfred *botanist, educator*

Springfield
Hobbs, Horton Holcombe, III, *biology educator*

Wooster
Grewal, Parwinder S. *biologist, educator*
Nault, Lowell Raymond *entomology educator*

Youngstown
Sturm, Nicholas *biological sciences educator, author*

OKLAHOMA

Ada
Thompson, Rahmona Ann *plant taxonomist*

Edmond
Caire, William *biologist, educator*
Radke, William John *biology educator*

Norman
Brown, Harley Procter, Jr., *zoology educator, entomology researcher*
Sonleitner, Frank Joseph *zoology educator*

Oklahoma City
Barber, Susan Carrol *biology educator*

Stillwater
Campbell, John Roy *animal science educator, academic administrator*
Langwig, John Edward *retired wood science educator*

Tahlequah
Clifford, Craig William *physiologist, educator*

Tulsa
Korstad, John Edward *biology educator*

OREGON

Ashland
Christianson, Roger Gordon *biology educator*

Corvallis
Castle, Emery Neal *agricultural and resource economist, educator*

PENNSYLVANIA

Aston
Given, Mac F. *biologist, educator*

Bloomsburg
Klinger, Thomas Scott *biology educator*

Bradford
Fedak, John G. *biology education educator*

Bryn Mawr
Hung, Paul Porwen *biotechnologist, educator, consultant*

Elizabethtown
Pepper, Rollin Elmer *microbiology educator, consultant*

Haverford
Schwabe, Calvin Walter *veterinarian, medical historian, medical educator*

Hershey
Demers, Laurence Maurice *science educator, biochemist, consultant, editor*

Indiana
Lord, Thomas Reeves *biology educator*

Kennett Square
Benson, Charles Everett *microbiology educator*

Lewisburg
Sojka, Gary Allan *biologist, educator, university official*

Mifflintown
Varner, Vance Sieber *science educator*

Philadelphia
Dornburg, Ralph Christoph *biology educator*
Kaji, Akira *microbiology scientist, educator*
Lynch, Peter Robin *physiology educator*
Patterson, Donald Floyd *human, medical and veterinary genetics educator*

Pittsburgh
Davis, Eleanor Lauria *biology educator, volunteer, lecturer*
Kiger, Robert William *botanist, science historian, educator*
Kuster, Janice Elizabeth *biology educator, researcher*
Li, Mengfeng *molecular biologist, virologist, educator*
Murphy, Robert Francis *biology educator and researcher*
Nettrour, Lila Groff *biology educator*
Tung, Frank Yao-Tsung *microbiologist educator*

Pottstown
Whittaker, Margaret Michael *biology educator*

Schuylkill Haven
Sarno, Patricia Ann *biology educator*

Scranton
Clymer, Jay Phaon, III, *science educator*

Slippery Rock
Kefeli, Valentin Ilich *biologist, botanist, educator, researcher*

State College
Cowen, Barrett Stickney *microbiology educator*
Hettche, L. Raymond *research director*
Rubba, Peter Anthony, Jr., *science educator*

Swarthmore
Gilbert, Scott Frederick *biologist, educator, author*

University Park
Buskirk, Elsworth Robert *physiologist, educator*
Hagen, Daniel Russell *physiologist, educator*
Hamilton, George Wesley *agronomist, educator*
Hood, Lamartine Frain *agriculture educator, former dean*
Kim, Ke Chung *entomology, systematics, and biodiversity educator, researcher*
Kuhns, Larry J. *horticulturist, educator*
Macdonald, Digby Donald *scientist, science administrator*
Stinson, Richard Floyd *retired horticulturist, educator*
Traverse, Alfred *palynology educator, clergyman*

Wilkes Barre
Hayes, Wilbur Frank *retired biology educator*

RHODE ISLAND

Cranston
Vavala, Domenic Anthony *medical scientist, retired military officer*

Providence
Freiberger, Christine Holmberg *biologist*
Gerbi, Susan Alexandra *biology educator*
Schmitt, Johanna Marie *plant population biologist, educator*

SOUTH CAROLINA

Anderson
Rhoe, Wilhelmina Robinson *retired science educator*

Clemson
Birrenkott, Glenn P., Jr., *poultry science educator*
Caldwell, Judith *horticultural educator*
Jones, Ulysses Simpson, Jr., *agronomy and soils educator, consultant*

Greenville
Cureton, Claudette Hazel Chapman *biology educator*
Gray, W(illiam) Michael *biology educator*

Prosperity
Long, William McMurray *physiology educator*

Rock Hill
Mitchell, Paula Levin *biology educator, editor*

SOUTH DAKOTA

Brookings
Malo, Douglas Dwane *soil scientist, educator*
Parsons, John Gordon *dairy chemistry educator*

TENNESSEE

Cookeville
Boswell, Fred C. *retired soil science educator, researcher*

Johnson City
Miyamoto, Michael Dwight *neuroscience educator, researcher*

Knoxville
Chen, James Pai-fun *biology educator, researcher*

Memphis
Blatteis, Clark Martin *physiology educator, researcher*
Chung, King-Thom *microbiology, educator*
Van Middlesworth, Lester *physiology, biophysics and medicine educator*

Sewanee
Yeatman, Harry Clay *biologist, educator*

Smithville
Vaughn, Eulalia Cobb *retired science educator, mathematician*

TEXAS

Austin
Biesele, John Julius *biologist, educator*
Bronson, Franklin H. *zoology educator*
Fryxell, Greta Albrecht *marine botany educator, oceanographer*
Lariviere, Janis Worcester *biology educator*
Turner, Billie Lee *botanist, educator*

Cedar Park
Albin, Leslie Owens *biology educator*

College Station
Armstrong, Robert Beall *physiologist, educator*
Beaver, Bonnie Veryle *veterinarian, educator*
Brown, Robert Dale *wildlife science educator, department head*
Hesby, John Howard *agricultural educator*
Storey, J. Benton *horticulturalist, educator*
Stranges, Anthony Nicholas *science history educator*
Wu, Guoyao *animal science, nutrition and physiology educator*

Corpus Christi
Schake, Lowell Martin *animal science educator*

Dallas
Baker Dailey, Alice Ann *exercise physiologist, exercise educator*
Bates, Barry Leon *biology educator*
Hewlett, Gloria Louise *rancher, retired educator, civic volunteer*
Norgard, Michael Vincent *microbiology educator, researcher*
Sinton, Christopher Michael *neurophysiologist, educator*

El Paso
Conway, John Bell *biologist, educator*
Johnson, Jerry Douglas *biology educator*

Fort Worth
Holcomb, Anna Louise *physical science educator*
Jensen, Harlan Ellsworth *veterinarian, educator*

Galveston
Albrecht, Thomas Blair *microbiology educator, researcher, consultant*
Baskaran, Mahalingam *marine science educator*
Budelmann, Bernd Ulrich *zoologist, educator*
Fleischmann, William Robert, Jr., *microbiologist, educator*
Santschi, Peter Hans *marine sciences educator*
Smith, Eric Morgan *virology educator*
Thompson, Edward Ivins Bradbridge *biological chemistry and genetics educator, molecular endocrinologist, department chairman*

Graham
James, Tanys Gene *biology educator, consultant*

Hempstead
Propst, Catherine Lamb *biotechnology company executive*

Houston
DeBakey, Selma *science communications educator, writer, editor, lecturer*
Hung, Mien-Chie *cancer biologist*
Schultz, Stanley George *physiologist, educator*
Seaton, Alberta Jones *biologist, educator, consultant*
White, Ronald Joseph *life and biomedical scientist, physiology educator*

Kingsville
Brennan, Leonard Alfred *research scientist, administrator*

Lubbock
Wendt, Charles William *soil physicist, educator*

San Antonio
Blystone, Robert Vernon *cell biologist, educator*
Poarch, Mary Hope Edmondson *science educator*

Sherman
Redshaw, Peggy Ann *molecular biologist, educator*

Waco
Jackson, Janis Lynn *biology educator*
Widner, William Richard *biology educator, gardener*

UTAH

Logan
Rashid, Kamal A. *university administrator, research educator*

HIGHER EDUCATION: LIFE SCIENCES

Orem
Crookston, R. Kent *agronomy educator*

Provo
Crandall, Keith Alan *science educator*
Tolman, Richard Robins *zoology educator*
Woodbury, Dixon John *physiologist, educator, research scientist*

Salt Lake City
King, R. Peter *science educator, academic center director*

VERMONT

Burlington
Etherton, Bud *botanist, educator, researcher*

Hinesburg
Fay, Glenn Mills, Jr., *science educator*

VIRGINIA

Big Stone Gap
Ogbonnaya, Chuks Alfred *entomologist, agronomist, environmentalist*

Blacksburg
Fell, Richard D. *entomology educator*
McKenna, James Richard *agronomy educator*

Charlottesville
Brunjes, Peter Crawford *neurobiology educator*

Fairfax
Geller, Harold Arthur *earth and space sciences executive, educator*
Soyfer, Valery Nikolayevich *geneticist, biophysicist*

Falls Church
Shah, Syed-Waqar *science educator*

Harrisonburg
Wubah, Daniel Asua *microbiologist, educator, dean*

Manassas
Isbister, Jenefir Diane Wilkinson *microbiologist, researcher, educator, consultant*

Martinsville
Hardy, Margaret Antoinette Kumko *science educator*

Mc Lean
Talbot, Lee Merriam *ecologist, educator, foundation administrator*

Richmond
Ching, Melvin Chung-Hing *retired physiologist, anatomy educator, researcher*
Formica, Joseph Victor *retired microbiology educator*
Gregory, Jean Winfrey *ecologist, educator*
Weymouth, Lisa Ann *microbiologist, educator*

Virginia Beach
Simmons, Marsha Thrift *science and reading educator, musician*

WASHINGTON

Kirkland
Pigott, George Morris *food engineering educator, consulting engineer*

Seattle
Boersma, P. Dee *marine biologist, educator*
Edwards, John Stuart *zoology educator, researcher*
Ho, Rodney Jin Yong *educator, medical researcher*
Hood, Leroy Edward *molecular biologist, educator*
Karr, James Richard *ecologist, educator, research director*
Kohn, Alan J. *zoology educator*
Kruckeberg, Arthur Rice *botanist, educator*
Orians, Gordon Howell *biology educator*
Riddiford, Lynn Moorhead *zoologist, educator*
Tukey, Harold Bradford, Jr., *horticulture educator*

Silverdale
Tozer, William Evans *entomologist, educator*

Wenatchee
Schrader, Lawrence Edwin *plant physiologist, educator*

WEST VIRGINIA

Morgantown
Gladfelter, Wilbert Eugene *physiology educator*
Ong, Tong-man *microbiologist, educator*

WISCONSIN

Brookfield
Sevilla-Gardinier, Josefina Zialcita *biology educator, musician*

Cottage Grove
Lund, Daryl Bert *food science educator*

Madison
Becker, Wayne Marvin *biologist, educator, retired biologist*

Dolan, Terrence Raymond *neurophysiology educator*
Ensign, Jerald C. *bacteriology educator*
Iltis, Hugh Hellmut *plant taxonomist-evolutionist, educator*
Jeanne, Robert Lawrence *entomologist, educator*
Marth, Elmer Herman *bacteriologist, educator*
Olson, Norman Fredrick *food science educator*
Rueckert, Roland Rudyard *retired virologist, educator*
Schatz, Paul Frederick *laboratory director*
Tibbitts, Theodore William *horticulturist, researcher*

Sheboygan
Marr, Kathleen Mary *biologist, educator*

WYOMING

Laramie
Laycock, William Anthony *range management educator*

TERRITORIES OF THE UNITED STATES

PUERTO RICO

San Juan
Orkand, Richard Kenneth *neurobiologist, researcher, educator*

VIRGIN ISLANDS

Christiansted
Odell, Daniel H. *science educator, scuba instructor*

CANADA

BRITISH COLUMBIA

Vancouver
Schluter, Dolph A. *biologist, educator*

Victoria
Finlay, Audrey Joy *environmental educator, consultant, naturalist*

ONTARIO

Downsview
Forer, Arthur H. *biology educator, researcher, editor*

London
Brooks, Vernon Bernard *neuroscientist, author*
Locke, Michael *zoology educator*

Ottawa
Bousfield, Edward Lloyd *biologist, educator*
Sells, Bruce Howard *biomedical sciences educator*

Toronto
Mustard, James Fraser *research institute executive*

PRINCE EDWARD ISLAND

Valleyfield
Cregier, Sharon Ellis *ethologist, information skills educator*

QUEBEC

Montreal
Krnjevic, Kresimir Ivan *neurophysiologist*

SASKATCHEWAN

Saskatoon
Khachatourians, George (Gharadaghi) *microbiologist, educator*

BELGIUM

Liege
Verstegen, John P.L. *theriogenologist, educator*

CHINA

Guangzhou
Jian, Haoran *microbiology educator*

CZECH REPUBLIC

Plzeň
Kunes, Josef *science educator, consultant*

FRANCE

Dijon
Bézard, Jean Alphonse *science educator*

Saint Etienne
Vergnaud, Jean-Maurice *science educator, researcher*

HONG KONG

Kowloon
Kung, Shain-dow *molecular biologist, academic administrator*

ITALY

Messina
Gimbo, Angelo *veterinary pathology educator, researcher*

JAPAN

Kohoku-ku
Matsuoka, Yoshiyuki *science educator, researcher*

Tsukuba
Yamamoto, Hiro-Aki *toxicology and pharmacology educator*

NIGERIA

Calabar
Ebenso, Eno Effiong *chemistry educator*

POLAND

Olsztyn
Groth, Izydor Pawel *agricultural studies educator*

REPUBLIC OF KOREA

Pohang
Kwak, Jin-Hwan *molecular biologist, educator*

Seoul
Chun, Jang Ho *science educator, researcher*

Taejon
Kim, Dojin *science educator*

ADDRESS UNPUBLISHED

Allen, Densil E., Jr., *retired agricultural studies educator*
Andrews, Richard Vincent *physiologist, educator*
Atkin, J Myron *science educator*
Baldwin, C. Andrew, Jr., *retired science educator*
Bernard, Richard Lawson *retired geneticist, educator*
Birchem, Regina *cell biologist, environment consultant, educator, writer*
Black, Kathie M. *science educator*
Borgman, Lois Marie *biology educator, college science administrator*
Brock, Lucy Ray Brannen *science educator*
Burdett, Barbra Elaine *biology educator*
Burkes, Lionel Seaton *science educator, writer, researcher*
Buss, Leo William *biologist, educator*
Carlquist, Sherwin *biology and botany educator*
Cheng, Zhen-Qiang *research scientist*
Cockerham, Lorris G. *radiation toxicologist*
Collins, Angelo *science educator*
Coyle, Marie Bridget *retired microbiology educator, laboratory director*
Cronholm, Lois S. *center administrator*
Cross, Harold Zane *agronomist, educator*
Crowell, Kenneth Leland *biology educator*
Dole, Jim Walter *biology educator*
Edwards, Julie Ann *science researcher*
Fan, Hung Y. *virology educator, consultant*
Feir, Dorothy Jean *entomologist, physiologist, educator*
Foglesong, Paul David *molecular biology and microbiology educator*
Garruto, Ralph Michael *research anthropologist, educator, biologist, neuroscientist*
Giordano, James Joseph *neuroscientist, pathologist, pain specialist*
Hall, Geraldine Cristofaro *biology educator*
Hauke, Richard Louis *retired science educator*
Hebert, Mary Schroller Kordisch (Mrs. Douglas Hebert) *retired zoology educator, genetic consultant*
Helgeson, John Paul *plant physiologist, researcher*
Hildebrand, Verna Lee *human ecology educator*
Holliday, Charles Walter, Jr., *physiology and biology educator*
Hunt, Ronald Duncan *veterinarian, educator, pathologist*
Iacono, James Michael *research center administrator, nutrition educator*
Ingram, Gloria Batie *science educator*
Isacson, Ole *neuroscientist, educator*
Jacobs, Hyde Spencer *soil chemistry educator*
James, Susanne Marie *biology educator*
Jane, Jay-lin *food science educator*
Katz, Anne Harris *biologist, educator, writer, aviator*
Kollar, Edward James *retired biology educator*
Langer, Glenn Arthur *cellular physiologist, educator*
Leath, Kenneth Thomas *research plant pathologist, educator, agricultural consultant*
Leventhal, Ruth *retired parasitology educator, university official*
Maroni, Donna Farolino *biologist, researcher*
McCann, Peter Paul *biology researcher, educator*
Metzler, Ruth Horton *genealogical educator*
Miller, Patrick William *research administrator, educator*
Murarka, Shyam Prasad *science and engineering educator, administrator*
Nutter, June Ann Knight *exercise physiologist, educator*
Peaslee, Margaret Mae Hermanek *zoology educator*
Perkes, Victor Aston *science education educator*
Poccia, Dominic Louis *biology educator*
Prazak, Bessmarie Lillian *science educator*
Rogers, Jack David *plant pathologist, educator*
Rothman, Frank George *biology educator, biochemical genetics researcher*
Shahied, Ishak I. *science educator*
Simon, Melvin I. *molecular biologist, educator*
Spiess, Eliot Bruce *biologist, educator*
Stefano, George B. *neurobiologist, researcher*
Taylor, Roy Lewis *botanist, educator*
Thomas, Teresa Ann *microbiologist, educator*
Topolski, Catherine *science educator*
Troll, Ralph *biology educator*
Washington, Josephine Harriet *biologist, endocrinologist, educator*
Wilson, Christine Ann *biologist, educator*
Wooten, Frank Thomas *retired research facility executive*
Zwislocki, Jozef John *neuroscience educator, researcher*

HIGHER EDUCATION: MATHEMATICS AND COMPUTERS

UNITED STATES

ALABAMA

Auburn
Govil, Narendra Kumar *mathematics educator*

Birmingham
Kinzey, Ouida Blackerby *retired mathematics educator, photographer, photojournalist*
Peeples, William Dewey, Jr., *mathematics educator*
Wheeler, Ruric E. *mathematics educator*
Whigham, Mark Anthony *computer scientist*

Florence
Foote, Avon Edward *web developer/producer, communications educator*

Pelham
Przybyzewski, Leslie Camille *mathematics educator*

Tuscaloosa
Rice, Margaret Lucille *computer technology educator*

ALASKA

Anchorage
Mann, Lester Perry *mathematics educator*

ARIZONA

Chandler
Rudibaugh, Melinda Campbell *mathematics educator*

Tempe
Bristol, Stanley David *mathematician, educator*
Downs, Floyd L. *mathematics educator*

Tucson
Lomen, David Orlando *mathematician, educator*

ARKANSAS

Conway
McDermott, Cecil Wade *mathematics educator, educational program director*

Fort Smith
Smith-Leins, Terri L. *mathematics educator*

Monticello
Annulis, John Thomas *mathematics educator*

Pangburn
Perry, Pamela Jo *mathematician, educator*

Texarkana
Spears, Melinda Katharyne *mathematics educator*

CALIFORNIA

Berkeley
Bickel, Peter John *statistician, educator*
Freedman, David Amiel *statistics educator, consultant*
Frenkel, Edward Vladimir *mathematician, educator*
Hyman, Edward Jay *forensic psychologist, cognitive and information scientist, consultant, educator, television news commentator*

Kahan, William M. *mathematics educator, consultant*
Moore, Calvin C. *mathematics educator, administrator*
Osserman, Robert *mathematician, educator, writer*
Schoenfeld, Alan Henry *mathematics and education educator*
Séquin, Carlo H. *computer science educator*
Smith, Alan Jay *computer science educator, consultant*

Carmel
Banathy, Bela Henrich *systems science educator, author, researcher*

Carson
Kowalski, Kazimierz *computer science educator, researcher*

Claremont
Coleman, Courtney Stafford *mathematician, educator*
White, Alvin Murray *mathematics educator, consultant*

Corona
Wetsch, Peggy A. *information systems specialist, publisher, educator, nurse*

Costa Mesa
Arismendi-Pardi, Eduardo J. *mathematics educator*
Demille, Dianne Lynne *mathematics educator, administrator*
Savage, Sandra Hope Skeen *mathematics educator, curriculum writer*

Danville
Lowery, Lawrence Frank *mathematic science and computer educator*

Davis
Mulase, Motohico *mathematics educator*

El Cerrito
Stenmark, Jean Kerr *mathematics educator*

Fairfield
Martin, Gary William *computer and information science educator*

Foster City
Scheer, Janet Kathy *mathematics educator*

Fremont
Stannard, William A. *mathematics educator*

Hayward
Prada, Gloria Ines *mathematics and Spanish language educator*

Irvine
Schechter, Martin *mathematics educator*
Wan, Frederic Yui-Ming *mathematician, educator*

La Jolla
Buss, Samuel Rudolph Rudolph *mathematics educator, researcher*

Long Beach
Colman, Ronald William *computer science educator*

Los Angeles
Chacko, George Kuttickal *systems science educator, consultant*
Rector, Robert Wayman *mathematics and engineering educator, former association executive*
Waterman, Michael Spencer *mathematics educator, biology educator*

Newport Beach
Cook, Marcy Lynn *mathematics educator, consultant*

Oakland
Lubliner, Irving *mathematics educator, consultant*

Oxnard
Neilson, Jane Scott *mathematics educator*

Palo Alto
Amin, Massoud *executive, systems science and mathematics educator*

Pasadena
Franklin, Joel Nicholas *mathematician, educator*

Riverside
Bhanu, Bir *computer information scientist, educator, director university program*

Rohnert Park
Ledin, George, Jr., *computer science educator*

Rolling Hills Estates
Clewis, Charlotte Wright Staub *mathematics educator*

Rosemead
Hattar, Michael Mizyed *mathematics educator*

San Bruno
Olson, Julie Ann *systems consultant, educator*

San Diego
Rubin, Stuart Harvey *computer science educator, researcher*

San Francisco
Cruse, Allan Baird *mathematician, computer scientist, educator*

San Luis Obispo
Hsu, John Yu-Sheng *computer scientist, educator*

San Marino
Lashley, Virginia Stephenson Hughes *retired computer science educator*

Santa Clara
Halmos, Paul Richard *mathematician, educator*

Stanford
Karlin, Samuel *mathematics educator, researcher*
Keller, Joseph Bishop *mathematician, educator*
McCarthy, John *computer scientist, educator*
Ornstein, Donald Samuel *mathematician, educator*
Schoen, Richard Melvin *mathematics educator, researcher*
Ullman, Jeffrey David *computer scientist, educator*

Stockton
Hitt, Alan Berkley *computer programmer, systems analyst, educator*

Tarzana
Bakenhus, August Anthony *mathematics educator, computer specialist*

Wilmington
Bornino-Glusac, Anna Maria *mathematics educator*

COLORADO

Colorado Springs
Soifer, Alexander *mathematics educator*

Denver
Mendez, Celestino Galo *mathematics educator*

Longmont
Venrick, Kristie Lund *mathematics educator*

CONNECTICUT

Danbury
Scalzo, Robert Edward *middle school mathematics educator*
Wright, Marie Anne *management information systems educator*

Enfield
Oliver, Bruce Lawrence *information systems specialist, educator*

Fairfield
Eigel, Edwin George, Jr., *mathematics educator, retired university president*

Farmington
Nash, Judith Kluck *mathematics educator*

Middletown
Hager, Anthony Wood *mathematics educator*
Linton, Fred Ernest Julius *mathematics educator*
Reid, James Dolan *mathematics educator, researcher*

New Haven
Howe, Roger Evans *mathematician, educator*
Margulis, Gregory A. *mathematics educator, researcher*
Massey, William S. *mathematician, educator*

Norwalk
DiCostanzo, Pamela S. *science and mathematics educator*

West Haven
Fischer, Alice Edna Waltz *computer science educator*

DELAWARE

Newark
Chester, Daniel Leon *computer scientist, educator, consultant*
Cook-Ioannidis, Leslie Pamela *mathematician, educator*

DISTRICT OF COLUMBIA

Washington
Kotz, Samuel *statistician, educator, translator, editor*
McCue, Edmund Bradley *mathematics educator*
Nolan, John Patrick *mathematician, educator*
Rao, Mamidanna Seshagiri *biostatistics educator, consultant, researcher*
Sandefur, James Tandy *mathematics educator*
Singpurwalla, Nozer Darabsha *statistician, engineer, educator*
Wulf, William Allan *computer information scientist, educator, federal agency administrator*

FLORIDA

Boynton Beach
Waterman, Daniel *mathematician, educator*

Cocoa Beach
Gillette, Halbert George *mathematics educator*

Coral Gables
Howard, Bernard Eufinger *mathematics and computer science educator*

Coral Springs
Hawn, Micaela (Micki Hawn) *mathematics educator*

Delray Beach
Hegstrom, William Jean *mathematics educator*

Fort Lauderdale
Kontos, George *computer science educator*
Littman, Marlyn Kemper *information scientist, educator*

Gainesville
Bednarek, Alexander Robert *mathematician, educator*
Keesling, James Edgar *mathematics educator*
Noffsinger, William Blake *computer science educator, academic administrator*
Weinrich, Brian Erwin *mathematician, computer scientist*

Jacksonville
Robinson, Christine Marie *mathematics educator*

Melbourne
Lakshmikantham, Vangipuram *mathematics educator*

Miami
Marinas, Carol Ann *mathematics educator*

Montverde
Carlo-Melendez, Arnaldo *mathematics educator*

North Miami Beach
Su, Hui Fang Huang *mathematician, educator*

Orange Park
Howard, Aughtum Smith *retired mathematics educator*

Pensacola
Wilson, David Paul *computer educator, elementary education specialist*

Punta Gorda
Smith, Charles Edwin *computer science educator*

Saint Petersburg
White, June Miller *mathematics educator, educational consultant*

Tallahassee
Mason, Robert McSpadden *technology management educator, consultant*
Nichols, Eugene Douglas *mathematics educator*
Traphan, Bernard Richard *computer scientist, educator*

Tamarac
Marged, Judith Michele *information technology educator*

Tampa
Couturier, Gordon Wayne *computer information systems educator, consultant*
Thompson, Denisse R. *mathematics educator*

West Palm Beach
Still, Mary Jane (M. J. Still) *mathematics educator*

Winter Park
Johnson, Constance Ann Trillich *web site designer*

GEORGIA

Athens
Lynch, James Walter *mathematician, educator*
Neter, John *statistician, educator*

Atlanta
Foley, James David *computer science educator, consultant*
King, K(imberly) N(elson) *computer science educator*
Pan, Yi *computer science educator*
Williams, Charles Murray *retired computer information systems educator, consultant*
Zunde, Pranas *information science educator, researcher*

Brunswick
Mihal, Sandra Powell *systems analyst*

Decatur
Pierre, Charles Bernard *mathematician, statistician, educator*

Dublin
Watt, Dwight, Jr., (Arthur Dwight Watt Jr.) *computer programming and microcomputer specialist*

Gainesville
Reed, Gina Fulton *mathematics educator*

Macon
Bass, Gloria Bailey *mathematician, educator*

Marietta
Rutherfoord, Rebecca Hudson *computer science educator*

Norcross
Bennett, Catherine June *information technology executive, educator, consultant*

HAWAII

Hilo
Gersting, Judith Lee *computer scientist, educator, computer scientist, researcher*

Honolulu
Reed, Nancy Ellen *computer science educator*

Kihei
Herrera, Robert Bennett *retired mathematics educator*

Pearl City
Takemoto, Cory Noboru *mathematics educator*

ILLINOIS

Ashton
Yenerich, Wallace Christian *mathematics educator*

Canton
Godt, Earl Wayne, II, *technology education educator*

Champaign
Philipp, Walter Viktor *mathematician, educator*
Wasserman, Stanley *statistician, educator*

Chicago
Bona, Jerry Lloyd *mathematician, educator*
Deliford, Mylah Eagan *mathematics educator*
Ong, Michael King *mathematician, educator, banker*
Sloan, Robert Hal *computer science educator*
Wirszup, Izaak *mathematician, educator*

Chicago Heights
Galloway, Sister Mary Blaise *mathematics educator*

Dekalb
Sons, Linda Ruth *mathematician, educator*

Des Plaines
Drezdzon, William Lawrence *retired mathematics educator*

Edwardsville
Ehlmann, Bryon Kurt *computer science educator*

Elmhurst
MacInnes, Sally Ackerman *computer education educator*

Evanston
Bellow, Alexandra *mathematician, educator*
Chen, Gui-Qiang *mathematician, educator, researcher*
Davis, Stephen Howard *applied mathematics educator*
Gasper, George, Jr., *mathematics educator*
Gomez, Louis M. *computer scientist, educator*
Kalai, Ehud *decision sciences educator, researcher in economics and decision sciences*
Matkowsky, Bernard Judah *applied mathematician, educator*
Zelinsky, Daniel *mathematics educator*

Harrisburg
Mummert, Jack R. *mathematics educator*

Henry
Bonacorsi, Larry Joseph *mathematics educator*

Highland
Probst, Carol Jean *mathematics educator*

Hinsdale
Bazik, Edna Frances *mathematics educator*

Lisle
Townsley, Lisa Gail *mathematics educator*

Morton
Grisham, George Robert *mathematics educator*

Normal
Jones, Graham Alfred *mathematics educator*

O Fallon
Bjerkaas, Carlton Lee *technology services company executive*

Palatine
Bender, Virginia Best *computer scientist, educator*

Urbana
Han, Jiawei *computer scientist, educator*
Liebman, Judith Rae Stenzel *operations research educator*
Rotman, Joseph Jonah *mathematician, educator*
Williams, Martha Ethelyn *information science educator*

Westchester
Pavelka, Elaine Blanche *mathematics educator*

INDIANA

Fort Wayne
Beineke, Lowell Wayne *mathematics educator*

Gary
Keehn, Jeffrey James *mathematics educator*

Indianapolis
Elmore, Garland Craft *information science educator*

Lafayette
Comer, Douglas Earl *computer science educator, consultant*
Gautschi, Walter *mathematics educator*

Notre Dame
Pollak, Barth *mathematics educator*
Sommese, Andrew John *mathematics educator*

Syracuse
Metcalf, Philip Leslie *mathematics educator, career/technical coordinator*

West Lafayette
Moore, David Sheldon *statistics educator, researcher*
Price, Justin J. *mathematics educator*
Rice, John Rischard *computer scientist, researcher, educator*

IOWA

Ames
Dahiya, Rajbir Singh *mathematics educator, researcher*
David, Herbert Aron *statistician, educator*
Willis, Jerry Weldon *computer systems educator, writer*

Cedar Falls
Kashef, Ali Ebrahim *industrial technology educator*

Center Junction
Antons, Pauline Marie *mathematics educator*

Earlham
Duncan, John Wiley *information professional, retired air force officer*

Forest City
Kappos, Steven Wayne *secondary social studies educator*

Grinnell
Ferguson, Pamela Anderson *mathematics educator, educational administrator*

Hiawatha
Ashbacher, Charles David *computer programmer, educator, mathematician*

Iowa City
Atkinson, Kendall Eugene *mathematics educator*
Hogg, Robert Vincent, Jr., *mathematical statistician, educator*

Storm Lake
McDaniel, Timothy Elton *mathematics, statistics and business educator*

West Burlington
Polley, Michael Glen *mathematics educator*

KANSAS

Emporia
Emerson, Marion Preston *mathematics educator*

Lawrence
Porter, Jack Ray *mathematician, educator*

Manhattan
Ramm, Alexander G. *mathematics educator*

KENTUCKY

Lexington
Holsapple, Clyde Warren *decision and information systems educator*
Man, Chi-Sing *mathematics educator*
Mostert, Paul Stallings *mathematician, educator*

Louisville
Graham, James Henry *computer science and engineering educator, consultant*
Greaver, Joanne Hutchins *mathematics educator, author*

Richmond
King, Amy Cathryne Patterson *retired, mathematics educator, researcher*

LOUISIANA

Baton Rouge
Segars, Trudy W. *mathematics educator*

MAINE

Orono
Markowsky, George *computer science educator*

MARYLAND

Adamstown
Tidball, Charles Stanley *computer scientist, educator*

Adelphi
Kirwan, William English, II, *mathematics educator, university official, academic administrator*

Baltimore
Arsham, Hossein *operations research analyst*
Bausell, R. Barker, Jr., *research methodology educator*
Kosaraju, S. Rao *computer science educator, researcher*
Pittenger, Arthur O., Jr., *mathematics educator*
Sherman, Alan Theodore *computer science educator*

College Park
Schwartz, Richard Evan *mathematician, educator*

Columbia
Vassar, John Dixie, Jr., *technical consultant, military aviator*

Elkton
Fell, Michael John *mathematics educator*

Glenn Dale
Sahu, Atma Ram *mathematics educator, university administrator, consultant, researcher*

Hyattsville
Fortson-Rivers, Tina E. (Thomasena Elizabeth Fortson-Rivers) *information technology specialist*

Kensington
Lisle, Martha Oglesby *retired mathematics educator*

Perryville
Dunne, Judith Doyle *information scientist, educator*

Potomac
Crowson, Henry Lawrence *mathematician, educator*
Medin, Julia Adele *mathematics educator, researcher*

Rockville
Counihan, Darlyn Joyce *mathematics educator*
Long, Harvey Shenk *retired computer educational consultant*

Stevenson
Shearer, Vallory Ann *mathematics educator*

Towson
Shirley, Lawrence Hoyt *mathematician, educator*

MASSACHUSETTS

Boston
D'Agostino, Ralph Benedict *mathematician, statistician, educator, consultant*
Devaney, Robert L. *mathematician, educator*
Falb, Peter Lawrence *mathematician, educator, investment company executive*
Marolda, Maria Rizzo *mathematics educator*
Neilforoshan, Mohamad R. *computer science and information systems educator*
Taqqu, Murad Salman *mathematics educator*

Cambridge
Chernoff, Herman *statistics educator*
Dudley, Richard Mansfield *mathematician, educator*
Gagliardi, Ugo Oscar *systems software architect, educator*
Greenspan, Harvey Philip *applied mathematician, educator*
Helgason, Sigurdur *mathematician, educator*
Kac, Victor G. *mathematician, educator*
Kazhdan, David *mathematics educator*
Moses, Joel *computer scientist, educator*
Oettinger, Anthony Gervin *mathematician, educator*
Roberts, Edward Baer *technology management educator*
Rockart, John Fralick *information systems researcher*
Rubin, Donald Bruce *statistician, educator, research company executive*
Schmid, Wilfried *mathematics educator*
Singer, Isadore Manuel *mathematics educator*
Strang, William Gilbert *mathematics educator*
Stroock, Daniel Wyler *mathematician, educator*
Yau, Shing-Tung *mathematics educator*

Medford
Jacob, Robert Joseph Kassel *computer scientist, educator*

Norwell
Bowman, Marie Agnes *mathematics educator*

Orleans
Freeman, John Henry *mathematics educator*

Shrewsbury
Garabedian, Charles, Jr., *mathematician, educator*

Sudbury
Woldman, Evelyn Jandorf *computer information specialist, educator*

Waltham
Lian, Bong H. *mathematician, educator, mathematician, department chairman*

Weston
Berwick, Robert Cregar *computer science educator*

Westwood
Smith, Denis Joseph *mathematics educator*

Williamstown
Hill, Victor Ernst, IV, *mathematics educator, musician*
Morgan, Frank *mathematics educator*

Worcester
Kotzen, Marshall Jason *mathematics educator*

MICHIGAN

Ann Arbor
Behmer, Kevin Shea *mathematics educator*
Fulton, William *mathematics educator*

Hill, Bruce Marvin *statistician, scientist, educator*

Auburn Hills
Neumann, Charles Henry *mathematician, educator*

Bloomfield Hills
Greenwood, Frank *information scientist, educator*
Nuss, Shirley Ann *computer coordinator, educator*

Centreville
Carlisle, Maribeth Shirley *mathematics educator*

Detroit
Mordukhovich, Boris Sholimovich *mathematician, educator, researcher*
Rajlich, Vaclav Thomas *computer science educator, researcher, consultant*

East Lansing
Sledd, William Tazwell *mathematics educator*
Weng, John Juyang *computer science educator, researcher*

Kalamazoo
Targowski, Andrew Stanislaw *computer information educator, consultant*

Northville
Hansen, Jean Marie *math and computer educator*

Novi
Chow, Chi-Ming *retired mathematics educator*

Ypsilanti
Gledhill, Roger Clayton *statistician, engineer, mathematician, educator*
Randolph, Linda Jane *mathematics educator*

MINNESOTA

Caledonia
Eppelheimer, Linda Louise *software educator*

Duluth
Gallian, Joseph Anthony *mathematics educator*

Mankato
Hopkins, Layne Victor *computer science educator*
Mericle, Robert Bruce *mathematics educator*

Minneapolis
Bingham, Christopher *statistics educator*
Du, Ding-Zhu *mathematician, educator*
Garfield, Joan Barbara *statistics educator*
Serrin, James Burton *mathematics educator*

Northfield
Schuster, Seymour *mathematician, educator*
Steen, Lynn Arthur *mathematics educator*

Saint Cloud
Olagunju, Amos Omotayo *computer science educator, consultant*

Saint Paul
Geisser, Seymour *statistics educator*

MISSISSIPPI

Gulfport
West, Margaret Lynne *computer science and mathematics educator*

Long Beach
Miller, Diane Moon *data processing educator*
Miller, James Edward *computer scientist, educator*

MISSOURI

Columbia
Beem, John Kelly *retired mathematician, educator*

Joplin
Cassens, Barbara Ann *mathematics and computer educator, consultant*

Kansas City
Bodde, David Leo *technology educator*

Lees Summit
Kahwaji, George Antoine *computer and mathematics educator*

Moberly
Roads, Jane Elizabeth McNatt *mathematics educator*

Rolla
Sabharwal, Chaman Lal *computer science educator*

Saint Louis
Freese, Raymond William *mathematics educator*
Haskins, James Leslie *mathematics educator*
Tomazic, Terry John *research methodology educator, statistical consultant*

Salem
Pace, Karen Yvonne *mathematics and computer science educator*

Springfield
Hignite, Michael Anthony *computer information systems educator, researcher, writer, consultant*

Willard
Roth, Jay Brian *mathematics educator*

NEVADA

Henderson
Jackson, Robert Loring *science and mathematics educator, academic administrator*

Las Vegas
Bahorsky, Judy Ann Wong *computer specialist, learning strategist*
Berghel, Hal L. *computer science educator, columnist, author, consultant*
Blattner, Meera McCuaig *computer science educator*
Snyder, John Henry *computer science educator, consultant*

NEW HAMPSHIRE

Hanover
Lamperti, John Williams *mathematician, educator*

New Hampton
Lockwood, Joanne Smith *mathematician educator*

NEW JERSEY

Blackwood
Sperduto, Leonard Anthony *mathematics educator*

Cresskill
Jurasek, John Paul *mathematics educator, counselor*

Jersey City
Camacho, James, Jr., *mathematician, educator*
Mastro, Victor John *mathematician, educator*
Poiani, Eileen Louise *mathematics educator, college administrator, higher education planner*

Montclair
Stevens, John Galen *mathematics educator, consultant*

New Brunswick
Kulikowski, Casimir Alexander *computer science and engineering educator*

Newark
Leung, Joseph Y. *computer science educator, researcher*

Princeton
Chazelle, Bernard *computer science educator*
Cook, Perry Raymond *computer science educator*
Gunning, Robert Clifford *mathematician, educator*
Haberman, Shelby Joel *statistician, educator*
Kobayashi, Hisashi *computer scientist, dean*
Kohn, Joseph John *mathematician, educator*
Levin, Simon Asher *mathematician, ecologist, educator*
Livingston, Samuel Alton *statistician*
Tarjan, Robert Endre *computer scientist, educator*

Wayne
Sanok, Gloria *mathematics educator, author*

Weehawken
Metallo, Frances Rosebell *mathematics educator*

West Paterson
Metz, Philip John *mathematics educator*

NEW MEXICO

Albuquerque
Ihde, Mary Katherine *retired mathematics educator*

Hobbs
Fox, Susan Frances *mathematics educator, education educator*

NEW YORK

Albany
Murray, Neil Vincent *computer science educator*
Rosenkrantz, Daniel J. *computer science educator*

Bayside
Fabricant, Mona *mathematics and computer science educator*

Binghamton
Hilton, Peter John *mathematician, educator*
Klir, George Jiri *systems science educator*

Brockport
Michaels, John G. *mathematics educator*

Bronx
Fitting, Melvin Chris *computer scientist, educator*

Brooklyn
Bachman, George *mathematics educator*

Buffalo
Goodberry, Diane Jean (Diane Oberkircher) *mathematics educator, tax accountant*

Lawvere, F. William *mathematician, educator*
McConnell, Jeffrey Joseph *computer science educator, researcher*
Schroeder, Thomas Leonard *mathematics educator*
Seitz, Mary Lee *mathematics educator*

Corning
Peaslee, Jayne Marie *computer scientist, educator*

Forest Hills
Gebaide, Stephen Elliot *retired mathematics and computer science educator*
Mindin, Vladimir Yudovich *information systems specialist, chemist, educator*

Garden City
Kranzer, Herbert C. *mathematician, educator*

Ithaca
Nerode, Anil *mathematician, educator*

Johnstown
Prestopnik, Richard John *electronics and computer educator*

Kingston
Shaffer, Sheila Weekes *mathematics educator*

Long Island City
Goldstein, Katherine H. *technology educator, computer consultant*

Manhasset
Levit, Mikhail *mathematician, statistician, educator*

Middleport
Travers, Carol *mathematics educator*

Middletown
Edelhertz, Helaine Wolfson *mathematics educator*

New York
Anderson, Dennis *computer scientist information technology educator*
Chichilnisky, Graciela *mathematician, economist, writer, educator, writer*
Derman, Cyrus *mathematical statistician*
Gilmore, Jennifer A.W. *computer specialist, educator*
Gross, Jonathan Light *computer scientist, mathematician, educator*
Preiss, Mitchell Paul *mathematics educator*
Saul, Mark E. *mathematics educator, consultant*
Traub, J(oseph) F(rederick) *computer scientist, educator*
Wallace, Robert James *mathematics and science educator*

New York Mills
Blank, William Russell *mathematics educator*

Newark
Smith, Mary Beth *radiographic technology educator, musician*

Old Westbury
Gordon, Florence Shanfield *mathematics educator*

Red Hook
Strever, Martha May *mathematics educator*

Rochester
Alling, Norman Larrabee *mathematics educator*
Angel, Allen Robert *mathematics educator, author, consultant*
McNamara, Timothy James *mathematics educator*

Staten Island
Shullich, Robert Harlan *systems analyst*

Stony Brook
Laspina, Peter Joseph *computer resource educator*
Michelsohn, Marie-Louise *mathematician, educator*
Tucker, Alan Curtiss *mathematics educator*

Syracuse
Graver, Jack Edward *mathematics educator*
Tanner, Jane *mathematics educator*

Washingtonville
Perrego, Virginia *mathematics educator*

West Nyack
Bladel, Rita Catherine *mathematics educator*

NORTH CAROLINA

Asheville
Collins, George Edwin *computer scientist, mathematician, educator*

Chapel Hill
Calingaert, Peter *computer scientist, educator*
Coulter, Elizabeth Jackson *biostatistician, educator*
Weiss, Stephen Fredrick *computer science educator*

Charlotte
Nelson, Barbara Secrest *educational developer*
Royster, David Calvin *computer educator, mathematics educator, researcher*

Cullowhee
Willis, Ralph Houston *mathematics educator*

Davidson
Klein, Benjamin Garrett *mathematics educator, consultant*

Fayetteville
Hadley, Landon R. *mathematician, educator*

Gatesville
Cherry, Lawrence Edward, Jr., *computer programming educator*

Greensboro
Blanchet-Sadri, Francine *mathematician, educator*
Casterlow, Gilbert, Jr., *mathematics educator*
Kurepa, Alexandra *mathematician, educator*

Pine Knoll Shores
Thatcher, Muriel Burger *mathematics education educator, consultant*

Raleigh
Chukwu, Ethelbert Nwakuche *mathematics educator*
Fabrizio, Louis Michael *computer scientist, educator*
McRoy, Willie Clifford *information systems educator*
Peterson, Elmor Lee *mathematical scientist, educator*
Rhyne, Theresa-Marie *computer graphics and university executive*

West Jefferson
Merrion, Arthur Benjamin *mathematics educator, tree farmer*

OHIO

Akron
Kreider, Kevin Lee *mathematician, educator*

Berea
Little, Richard Allen *mathematics and computer science educator*

Bowling Green
Newman, Elsie Louise *mathematics educator*

Cincinnati
Wilsey, Philip Arthur *computer science educator*

Cleveland
Lyytinen, Kalle Juhani *computer scientist, educator*

Columbus
Burke, Janet Lois *business consultant, computer science educator*
Chandrasekaran, Balakrishnan *computer and information science educator*
Friedman, Avner *mathematician, educator*
Muller, Mervin Edgar *computer scientist, statistician, educator*
Santner, Thomas *statistician, educator*
Tian, Fei-Ran *mathematician, educator*

Dayton
Khalimsky, Efim *mathematics and computer science educator*

Defiance
Mirchandaney, Arjan Sobhraj *mathematics educator*

Mansfield
Gregory, Thomas Bradford *mathematics educator*

Minerva
Schoeppner-Grunder, Mary Catherine *mathematics educator*

Painesville
Taylor, Norman Floyd *computer educator, administrator*

Portsmouth
Hamilton, Virginia Mae *mathematics educator, consultant*

Saint Clairsville
Neff, Gary Veryl *mathematics educator, consultant*

Uniontown
Sama, Joy Lyn *mathematics educator*

Vermilion
Vance, Elbridge Putnam *mathematics educator*

Westerville
Reeves, Roy Franklin *mathematician, engineer, educator*

Wooster
Hales, Raleigh Stanton, Jr., *mathematics educator, academic administrator*

OKLAHOMA

Edmond
Rice, Earl Clifton *retired mathematics educator*

Norman
Apanasov, Boris N. *mathematics educator*
Provine, Lorraine *retired mathematics educator*
Reynolds, Anne Marie *mathematics educator*

Oklahoma City
Philipp, Anita Marie *computer sciences educator*
Tang, Irving Che-hong *mathematician, educator*

Stillwater
Lu, Huizhu *computer scientist, educator*
Mayfield, Blayne Eugene *computer science educator*
Nord, G. Daryl *computer science educator*

Tulsa
Thompson, Carla Jo Horn *mathematics educator*

OREGON

Corvallis
Parks, Harold Raymond *mathematician, educator*

Eugene
Kennevan, Walter James *computer science educator*
Mpinga, Derek Amos *mathematics educator*

Portland
Lambert, Richard William *mathematics educator*

Tualatin
Brown, Robert Wallace *retired mathematics educator*

PENNSYLVANIA

Abington
Ayoub, Ayoub Barsoum *mathematician, educator*

Allentown
Dunham, William Wade *mathematics educator*

Bethlehem
Schattschneider, Doris Jean *mathematics educator*

Conshohocken
Froman, Ann Dolores *computer education educator*

Coraopolis
Kohun, Frederick Gregg *information scientist, economist, educator*
Skovira, Robert Joseph *information scientist, educator*

Easton
Sites, John Milton *mathematics educator, computer consultant*

Hershey
King, Carolyn Marie *mathematics educator*

Indiana
Moore, Wayne Andrew *information specialist, educator*
Shepler, Jack Lee *mathematics educator*

Lancaster
Anderson, Jay Martin *computer scientist educator*

Marion Center
Bomboy, John David *mathematics educator*

Newtown Square
Speelhoffer, Thomas John Michael *mathematics and German language educator*

Philadelphia
Badler, Norman Ira *computer and information science educator*
Freyd, Peter John *mathematician, computer scientist, educator*
Kadison, Richard Vincent *mathematician, educator*
Porter, Gerald Joseph *mathematician, educator*
Scedrov, Andre *mathematics and computer science researcher, educator*
Sztandera, Les Mark *computer science educator*
Warner, Frank Wilson, III, *mathematics educator*
Zitarelli, David Earl *mathematics educator*

Pittsburgh
Byers, Mary Margaret (Peg Byers) *systems educator*
Carbo, Toni (Toni Carbo Bearman) *information scientist, educator*
Heath, David Clay *mathematics educator, consultant*
Shaw, Mary M. *computer science educator*

Reading
Rochowicz, John Anthony, Jr., *mathematician, mathematics and physics educator*

Swarthmore
Kelemen, Charles F. *computer science educator*

Villanova
Beck, Robert Edward *computer scientist, educator*

Wallingford
Morrison, Donald Franklin *statistician, educator*

RHODE ISLAND

Kingston
Ma, Yan *information science educator*

Providence
Dafermos, Constantine Michael *applied mathematics educator*
Freiberger, Walter Frederick *mathematics educator, actuarial science consultant, educator*
Hsieh, Din-Yu *applied mathematics educator*
Kushner, Harold Joseph *mathematics educator*
Mumford, David Bryant *mathematics educator*
Shu, Chi-Wang *mathematics educator, researcher*

SOUTH CAROLINA

Clemson
Hare, Eleanor O'Meara *computer science educator*

Florence
Croteau, Kevan Howard *computer science educator*
Strong, Roger Lee *retired mathematics educator*

Johns Island
Richbart, Carolyn Mae *mathematics educator*

Orangeburg
Champy, William, Jr., *mathematician, educator, researcher, scientist, writer, biologist, chemist, inventor, physicist*

Summerville
Worthy, Fred Lester *computer science educator*

TENNESSEE

Brownsville
Kalin, Robert *retired mathematics educator*

Chattanooga
Ebiefung, Aniekan Asukwo *mathematics educator and researcher*
Kennedy, Daniel *mathematics educator*

Dickson
Peterson, Bonnie Lu *mathematics educator*

Gallatin
Evans, Robert Byron *software engineer, educator*

Knoxville
Romeo, Joanne Josefa Marino *mathematics educator*
Sherman, Gordon Rae *computer science educator*

Martin
Gathers, Emery George *computer science educator*

Maryville
Deal, Barbara Pickel *mathematics educator*

Memphis
Hodges, Velma Quinn *mathematics educator*
Tan, Wai-Yuan *statistics educator, researcher*

Nashville
Cobb, Paul *mathematics educator*
Crooke, Philip Schuyler *mathematics educator*
Jonsson, Bjarni *mathematician, educator*
Rowan, William Hamilton, Jr., *computer science educator*
Williams, Marsha Rhea *computer science educator, researcher, consultant*

TEXAS

Abilene
Potter, Andrew Jay *mathematics educator*
Retzer, Kenneth Albert *mathematics educator, entrepreneur*

Austin
Liu, Min *technology educator*
Radin, Charles Lewis *mathematics educator, physicist*
Xin, Jack *mathematician, educator*

Cypress
Burghduff, John Brian *mathematics educator*

Denton
Renka, Robert Joseph *computer science educator, consultant*

Edinburg
Smith, Cynthia Marie *mathematics educator*

El Paso
Foged, Leslie Owen *mathematician, educator*
Gianelli, Victor F. *mathematics and physics educator*

Fort Worth
Doran, Robert Stuart *mathematician, educator*
Sullenberger, Ara Broocks *mathematics educator*

Houston
Fitzgibbon, William Edward, III, *mathematician, educator, academic administrator*
Freeman, Marjorie Schaefer *mathematician, educator*
Hodgess, Erin Marie *statistics educator*
Kennedy, Ken *computer science educator*
Parker, Norman Neil, Jr., *software systems analyst, mathematics educator*
Scott, David Warren *statistics educator*
Ward, Jo Alice *computer consultant, educator*

Irving
Conger, Sue Ann *computer information systems educator*

Kingsville
Morey, Philip Stockton, Jr., *mathematics educator*

Laredo
Mendiola, Anna Maria G. *mathematics educator*

Longview
McKinney, Brenda Jane *mathematics educator*

HIGHER EDUCATION: MATHEMATICS AND COMPUTERS

Mcallen
Cox, George Sherwood *computer science educator*

Plano
Benn, Douglas Frank *information technology and computer science executive*

Richardson
Van Ness, John Winslow *mathematics educator*

San Antonio
Hall, Douglas Lee *computer science educator*

Stephenville
Chilton, Bradley Stuart, Jr., *computer information systems educator*

UTAH

Draper
Averett, Robert Lee *information system professional, educator*

Ogden
Leali, Shirley A. *mathematician, educator*

Provo
Hansen, James Vernon *computer science, information systems educator*
Ivie, Evan Leon *computer science educator*

VIRGINIA

Arlington
Spresser, Diane Mar *mathematics educator*

Blacksburg
Good, Irving John *statistics educator, mathematician, philosopher of science*

Charlottesville
Martin, Nathaniel Frizzel Grafton *mathematician, educator*
Roberts, William Woodruff, Jr., *applied mathematics educator, researcher*
Simmonds, James Gordon *mathematician, educator*
Thomas, Lawrence Eldon *mathematics educator*

Chester
Jordan, Joseph Tandy *mathematics educator*

Fairfax
Palmer, James Daniel *information technology educator*
Polyak, Roman Aronovich *mathematics educator*

Newport News
Summerville, Richard M. *mathematician, academic administrator*

Radford
Carter, Edith Houston *statistician, educator*

Reston
Forster, Susan Bogart *computer educator*

Richlands
Witten, Thomas Jefferson, Jr., *mathematics educator*

Richmond
Charlesworth, Arthur Thomas *mathematics and computer science educator*

Round Hill
Bergeman, George William *mathematics educator, software author*

Spotsylvania
Lipscomb, Stephen Leon *retired mathematician*

Sweet Briar
Wassell, Stephen Robert *mathematics educator, researcher*

Virginia Beach
Cheng, Richard Tien-ren *computer scientist, educator*

Williamsburg
Rodman, Leiba *mathematician*
Zhang, Xiaodong *computer scientist, educator, researcher*

Yorktown
Risden, Nancy Dika *mathematics educator*

WASHINGTON

Bellevue
Eldenburg, Mary Jo Corliss *mathematics educator*

Kent
Personette, Louise Metzger (Sister Mary Roger Metzger) *mathematics educator*

Orcas
Greever, John *retired mathematics educator*

Seattle
Kevorkian, Jirair *applied mathematics, aeronautics and astronautics educator*
Klee, Victor La Rue *mathematician, educator*
Pyke, Ronald *mathematics educator*
Segal, Jack *mathematics educator*
Wellner, Jon August *statistician, educator*

WEST VIRGINIA

Elkins
Reed, Elizabeth May Millard *mathematics and computer science educator, publisher*

Martinsburg
Day, Michael Gordon *information technology executive, educator*

Morgantown
Holtan, Boyd DeVere *retired mathematics educator*

Princeton
Pratt, Carolyn Kay *retired language arts/mathematics educator*

Shepherdstown
Hendricks, Ida Elizabeth *mathematics educator*

War
Hill, Lansing Brent *mathematics educator*

WISCONSIN

Cumberland
Lindquist, Keith Nelson *mathematics educator*

Dodgeville
Fry, David Francis *computing educator*

Franklin
Bui, Ty Van *computer programmer, systems analyst*

Madison
Kurtz, Thomas Gordon *mathematics educator*

Mequon
Locklair, Gary Hampton *computer science educator*

Milwaukee
Simms, John Carson *logic, mathematics and computer science educator*
Teply, Mark Lawrence *mathematics educator*

TERRITORIES OF THE UNITED STATES

PUERTO RICO

Ponce
Valero, Hernando *statistics educator*

CANADA

ALBERTA

Calgary
Varadarajan, Kalathoor *mathmatics educator, researcher*

NEW BRUNSWICK

Sackville
Dekster, Boris Veniamin *mathematician, educator*

ONTARIO

Ottawa
Csörgő, Miklós *mathematics and statistics educator*
Dlab, Vlastimil *mathematics educator, researcher*

Toronto
Friedlander, John Benjamin *mathematician, educator*

QUEBEC

Montreal
Delfour, Michel *mathamatics/statistics educator*

St Irénée
Jean, Roger V. *mathematician, educator*

CHINA

Changchun Jilin
Bi, Shuwei *management information systems educator*

ENGLAND

Brighton
Coad, Derek Stephen *statistics educator*

FRANCE

Amiens
Myoupo, Jean Frédéric *computer science educator, researcher*

GREECE

Athens
Panaretos, John *mathematics and statistics educator*

JAPAN

Tokyo
Eto, Hajime *information scientist, educator*

LEBANON

Beirut
Jurdak, Murad Eid *mathematics educator*

ADDRESS UNPUBLISHED

Allgood, Marilyn Jane *mathematics educator*
Barat, Christopher Eugene *mathematician, educator*
Barrett, Lida Kittrell *mathematics educator*
Benson, Sharon Joan *mathematics educator*
Bentley, Donald Lyon *mathematics and statistics educator, minister*
Browder, Felix Earl *mathematician, educator*
Clark, Jeffrey William *mathematics educator, author*
Corbett, Lenora Meade *mathematician, community college educator*
Cover, Thomas M. *statistician, electrical engineer, educator*
Craff-Mendez, Katherine *systems analyst, college official*
Dunham, Barbara Jean *administrator*
Edwards, Elwood Gene *mathematician, educator*
Fishback, William Thompson *educator*
Fransen, Christine Irene *mathematics educator*
Fuller, Nancy MacMurray *mathematics educator, tutor*
Gacnik, Bonita L. *computer science, mathematics educator*
Gessaman, Margaret Palmer *mathematician, educator, retired dean*
Graham, Kirsten Rae *computer scientist, educator*
Greever, Margaret Quarles *retired mathematics educator*
Grenander, Ulf *mathematics educator*
Hudson, Carolyn Brauer *application developer, educator*
Hunte, Beryl Eleanor *mathematics educator, consultant*
Jacobson, Norman Maron *computer science educator*
Johnson, Deborah Crosland Wright *mathematics educator*
Jones, Anita Katherine *computer scientist, educator*
Juberg, Richard Kent *mathematician, educator*
Kent, Jack Thurston *retired mathematics educator*
Keyes, David Elliot *scientific computing educator, researcher*
Koo, Delia Z.F. *mathematics educator*
Kornecki, Andrew Jan *computer scientist, educator*
Krantz, Steven George *mathematics educator, writer*
Lamm, Harriet A. *mathematics educator*
Larson, Janice Talley *computer science programmer*
Lerner, Vladimir Semion *computer scientist, educator*
Levine, Maita Faye *mathematics educator*
Levy, Leslie Ann *application developer*
Low, Emmet Francis, Jr., *mathematics educator*
Mahoney, Linda Kay *mathematics educator*
Main, Myrna Joan *retired mathematics educator*
Maisel, Herbert *computer science educator*
McKellips, Terral Lane *mathematics educator, university administrator*
Merilan, Jean Elizabeth *statistics educator*
Murphy, Robin Roberson *computer science educator*
Oldani, Norbert Louis *mathematician, educator, composer*
Olshen, Richard A. *statistician, educator*
Owens, Julia Marie *mathematics educator*
Paul, Vera Maxine *mathematics educator*
Pizzuto, Debra Kay *mathematics educator*
Pustilnik, Seymour W. *mathematics and education educator*
Rabe, Laura Mae *mathematician, educator*
Ricca, RoseLinda Frances *mathematics educator*
Richgels, Glen William *mathematics educator*
Robold, Alice Ilene *retired mathematician, educator*
Shier, Gloria Bulan *mathematics educator*
Smith, Kathleen Ann *mathematics educator*
Spence, Dianna Jeannene *software engineer, educator*
Stone, Robert Christopher *computer scientist, educator*
Suleiman, Ibrahim *computer education educator*
Suppes, Patrick *philosophy, statistics, psychology educator and education*
Switzer, Paul *statistics educator*
Tan, Hui Qian *computer science and civil engineering educator*
Tobiassen, Barbara Sue *systems analyst consultant, educator, Peace Corps volunteer*
Tyrl, Paul *mathematics educator, researcher, consultant*
Vasily, John Timothy *information systems executive, state government official*
Vollan, Rodney R. *mathmatics educator, coach*
Wagner, Ellyn S(anti) *mathematics educator*
Wenger, John Childs *retired mathematics educator, labor union administrator*
Whitaker, Wilma Neuman *retired mathematics instructor*
Yackel, James William *mathematician, academic administrator*
Yopconka, Natalie Ann Catherine *computer specialist, educator, business owner*
Young, Sharon Laree *mathematics educator*
Zaslavsky, Claudia *mathematics education consultant, author*

HIGHER EDUCATION: MEDIA AND COMMUNICATIONS

UNITED STATES

ALABAMA

Adamsville
Hill, Bobby Nell *media specialist, elementary school educator*

ARIZONA

Tempe
Rankin, William Parkman *educator, former publishing company executive*

ARKANSAS

Fayetteville
Smith, Stephen Austin *communications educator*

Magnolia
Reppert, James Eugene *mass communications educator*

Paragould
Huffman, Kelley Raye *reporter and columnist, former elementary educator*

CALIFORNIA

Belvedere
Benet, Carol Ann Levin *journalist, teacher*

Fresno
Hart, Russ Allen *telecommunications educator*
Rehart, Burton Schyler *journalism educator, freelance writer*

Hollywood
McAdams, Frank Joseph, III, *communications educator*

Lake Elsinore
Corral, Jeanie Beleyn *journalist, school board administrator*

Monterey Park
Stapleton, Jean *journalism educator*

Oakland
Wood, Larry (Mary Laird) *journalist, author, university educator, public relations executive, environmental consultant*

Palos Verdes Peninsula
King, Nancy *communications educator*

San Diego
Borden, Diane Lynn *communications educator*

San Francisco
Hale, Cecil *communications educator, finance educator*
Risser, James Vaulx, Jr., *journalist, educator*
Smith, Miriam A. *broadcast and communications educator*

San Jose
Branch, Robert (Rob) Hardin *radio and television educator, broadcast executive*
Brown, Barbara Mahone *communications educator, poet, consultant*

Stanford
Roberts, Donald Frank, Jr., *communications educator*

Walnut
Tan, Colleen Woo *communications educator*

COLORADO

Denver
Barbour, Alton Bradford *human communication studies educator*
Brom, Libor *journalist, educator*
Dance, Francis Esburn Xavier *communication educator*

CONNECTICUT

Bristol
St. Onge, Barbara S. *media services coordinator, educator*

Cos Cob
Fishman, Claire *media specialist*

Torrington
Di Russo, Terry *communications educator, writer*

HIGHER EDUCATION: MEDIA AND COMMUNICATIONS

DISTRICT OF COLUMBIA

Washington
Brock, Gerald Wayne *telecommunications educator*
Hull, Marion Hayes *communications educator, researcher*
Mowlana, Hamid *international relations and communication educator*
Warren, Clay *communication educator*

FLORIDA

Gainesville
Hollien, Harry Francis *speech and communications scientist, educator*
Kelly, Kathleen S(ue) *communications educator*
Maple, Marilyn Jean *educational media coordinator*

Jacksonville
Koeppel, Mary Sue *communications educator*

Lake Worth
Asher, Kathleen May *communications educator*

Marianna
Connor, Catherine Brooks *educational media specialist*

Miami
Frank, Walter Monroe, Jr., *media specialist*
Welsh, Judith Schenck *communications educator*

Saint Augustine
Henson, (Betty) Ann *media specialist, educator*

Sanford
Scott, Mellouise Jacqueline *educational media specialist*

Tampa
White, Nancy G. *journalism educator*

GEORGIA

Athens
Agee, Warren Kendall *journalism educator*

Atlanta
Daughtry, Sylvia *journalist, educator*

Lizella
Habersham, Janice Johnson *media specialist, music educator*

HAWAII

Honolulu
Tehranian, Majid *political economy and communications educator*

ILLINOIS

Berwyn
Forst, Edmund Charles, Jr., *communications educator, administrator, consultant*

Evanston
Lavine, John M. *journalism educator, management educator*
Wills, Garry *journalist, educator*

Kenilworth
Ewing, Raymond Peyton *educator, author, management consultant*

Plainfield
Diercks, Eileen Kay *educational media coordinator, elementary school educator*

Urbana
Helle, Steven James *journalism educator, lawyer*
Meyer, Eric Kent *jouralist, educator, consultant*

INDIANA

Auburn
Record, Lincoln Fredrick *speech communications educator, communications consultant*

Franklin
Nuwer, Henry Joseph (Hank Nuwer) *journalist, educator*

Hammond
Fanno, Dave *English composition and speech communications educator*

KENTUCKY

Fort Knox
Barnes, Larry Glen *journalist, editor, educator*

Frankfort
Smith, Sherri Long *journalist, secondary education educator*

Prestonsburg
Bennin, Hope Elizabeth *communication educator*

LOUISIANA

Baker
Roberson, Patt Foster *mass communications educator*

MARYLAND

College Park
Beasley, Maurine Hoffman *journalism educator, historian*
Fink, Edward Laurence *communications educator*

MASSACHUSETTS

Boston
Bourne, Katherine Day *journalist, educator*
Klarfeld, Jonathan Michael *journalism educator*
Selig, Michael Emil *communications educator*

MICHIGAN

Ann Arbor
Beaver, Frank Eugene *communication educator, film critic and historian*
Eisendrath, Charles Rice *journalism educator, farmer, consultant*

East Lansing
Ralph, David Clinton *communications educator*

Midland
Linderman, Charlene Ruth *media specialist*
Messing, Carol Sue *communications educator*

Ypsilanti
Evans, Gary Lee *communications educator and consultant*

MINNESOTA

Bigfork
Carlson, David Charles *media specialist, secondary school educator*

Roseville
Arndt, Joan Marie *media specialist, educator*

Saint Joseph
Rowland, Howard Ray *mass communications educator*

Saint Paul
Burkart, Jeffrey Edward *communications educator*

MISSISSIPPI

Clinton
Fortenberry, Jack Clifton (Cliff Fortenberry) *mass communications educator*

MISSOURI

Columbia
Taft, William Howard *journalism educator*

Harrisonville
Vallee, Marie Lydia *library media specialist*

Kansas City
Williams, Randy G. *community relations executive, communication professional*

Marshall
Roberts, David Lowell *journalist, educator*

Springfield
Champion, Norma Jean *communications educator, state legislator*

MONTANA

Bozeman
O'Donnell, Victoria *communication educator*

NEBRASKA

Cozad
Peterson, Marilyn Ann Whitney *journalism educator*

Hastings
Bush, Marjorie Evelynn Tower-Tooker *educator, media specialist, librarian*

Omaha
Lipschultz, Jeremy Harris *communication educator*

York
Givens, Randal Jack *communications educator*

NEVADA

Fernley
Weniger-Phelps, Nancy Ann *media specialist, photographer*

Reno
Miller, Newton Edd, Jr., *communications educator*

NEW JERSEY

Cherry Hill
Gutin, Myra Gail *communications educator*

Lawrenceville
Sakson, Sharon R(ose) *journalist, writer, educator*

Madison
Goodman, Michael B(arry) *communications educator*

New Brunswick
Kubey, Robert William *media educator, developmental psychologist, television analyst and researcher*
Taliaferro, James Hubert, Jr., *communications educator*

Parsippany
Smay, Connie R. *educational media specialist, educator*

Pleasantville
DeCicco, James Joseph *media and technology supervisor*

Princeton
Sandman, Peter M. *risk communication consultant, speaker*

Trenton
Donahue, Donald Francis *media specialist*

Whippany
Morris, Patricia Smith *media specialist, writer, educator*

NEW MEXICO

Bosque
Alsbrook, James Eldridge *journalist, educator*

Las Cruces
Merrick, Beverly Georgianne *journalism, communications educator*

Silver City
Hall, Jean Quintero *communications and history educator*

NEW YORK

Brooklyn
De Lisi, Joanne *media consultant, educator*

Great Neck
Fiel, Maxine Lucille *journalist, behavioral analyst, lecturer*

Ithaca
Hardy, Jane Elizabeth *communications educator*

Long Beach
Robbins, Jeffrey Howard *media consultant, research writer, educator*

Massapequa
Colbourn, Frank Edwin *communications educator*

Melville
Hildebrand, John Frederick *newspaper columnist*

Moravia
Kennedy, Samuel Van Dyke, III, *journalist, educator*

New Paltz
Irvine, Rose Loretta Abernethy *retired communications educator, consultant*

New York
Cleveland, Ceil Margaret *writer, journalist, education administrator, English language educator*
Wolper, Allan *journalist, educator*

Oswego
Loveridge-Sanbonmatsu, Joan Meredith *communication studies and women's studies educator, poet*

Port Byron
Tomasso, Bernard Gerard *library media specialist*

Rochester
Prosser, Michael Hubert *communications educator*

NORTH CAROLINA

Battleboro
Hardy, Linda Lea Sterlock *media specialist*

Greensboro
McKissick-Melton, S. Charmaine *mass communications educator*
Smink, Mary Jane *graphic communications technology educator*

Raleigh
Entman, Robert Mathew *communications educator, consultant*
Kauffman, Terry *broadcast and creative arts communication educator, artist*

Spindale
Trautmann, Patricia Ann *communications educator, storyteller*

OHIO

Cincinnati
King, Margaret Ann *communications educator*

Columbus Grove
Thiede, Richard Wesley *retired communications educator*

Kirtland
Ryan, William Joseph *multimedia and distance education designer, information technology executive*

Wilberforce
Oluyitan, Emmanuel Funso *communications educator*

Willoughby
Corrigan, Faith *journalist, educator, historian*

OREGON

Bend
Loewenthal, Nessa Parker *intercultural communications consultant*

PENNSYLVANIA

Bethlehem
Friedman, Sharon Mae *science journalism educator*

Bloomsburg
Brasch, Walter Milton *journalist, educator*

East Stroudsburg
Gasink, Warren Alfred *speech communication educator*

Philadelphia
Lent, John Anthony *journalist, educator*

University Park
Benson, Thomas Walter *rhetoric educator, writer*

RHODE ISLAND

Providence
Olmsted, Audrey June *communications educator, department chairman*

SOUTH CAROLINA

Columbia
Dickey, Elizabeth Brown *journalism educator*
Stephens, Lowndes Frederick *journalism educator*

Inman
Holt, Kathryn Smith *media specialist*

Orangeburg
Creekmore, Verity Veirs *media specialist*

Simpsonville
Gilstrap, Leah Ann *media specialist*

SOUTH DAKOTA

Martin
Kampfe, Nancy Lee *communications educator*

TENNESSEE

Knoxville
Ambrester, Marcus LaRoy *communication educator, program administrator*
Ashdown, Paul George *journalist, educator*
Howard, Herbert Hoover *broadcasting and communications educator*
Siler, Susan Reeder *communications educator*

TEXAS

Abilene
Marler, Charles Herbert *journalism educator, historian, consultant*

Arlington
Mosley-Matchett, Jonetta Delaine *communications educator*

Austin
Danielson, Wayne Allen *journalism and computer science educator*
Rodden, John Gallagher *communications educator, writer*
Tankard, James William, Jr., *journalism educator, writer*

Beaumont
Baker, Mary Alice *communication educator, consultant*
Roth, Lane *communications educator*

Denton
Shelton, James Keith *journalism educator*

Houston
Taylor, James Sheppard *communications educator*

Stephenville
King, Clyde Richard *journalism educator, writer*

VERMONT

Randolph
Ryerson, Marjorie Gilmour *journalist, educator, poet, photographer*

HIGHER EDUCATION: MEDIA AND COMMUNICATIONS

VIRGINIA

Alexandria
Tarpley, James Douglas *journalism educator, magazine editor*
Yoder, Edwin Milton, Jr., *columnist, educator, editor, writer*

Arlington
Goodman, Mark *journalist, educator*

Hampton
Coombs, Vanessa Moody *journalism educator, lawyer*

Mc Lean
Newman, Mary Thomas *communications educator, management consultant*

Springfield
Rankin, Jacqueline Annette *communications expert, educator*

WASHINGTON

College Place
Harris, Pamela Maize *journalism educator*

WEST VIRGINIA

Beckley
Bush, Deborah Lee *communications technology educator*

WISCONSIN

Madison
Dunwoody, Sharon Lee *journalism and communications educator*
Rowe, Marieli Dorothy *media literacy education consultant, organization executive*

Menomonie
Cutnaw, Mary-Frances *emeritus communications educator, writer, editor, publisher*

WYOMING

Sheridan
Schatz, Wayne Ardale *district technology coordinator, computer educator*

INDONESIA

Surabaya
Tondowidjojo, John Vincent *communication educator, priest*

ADDRESS UNPUBLISHED

Disbrow, Lynn Marie *communication educator*
Green, Barbara *communications educator*
Harvey, Nancy Melissa *media specialist, art teacher*
Hill, Steven John *author, educator, political reformer, campaign manager*
Littlewood, Thomas Benjamin *retired journalism educator*
Main, Robert Gail *communications educator, training consultant, television and film producer, former army officer*
Mandell, Arlene Linda *communications educator*
Michel, Daniel John *broadcast educator, writer, photographer, artist*
Morgan, Anne Marie G. *broadcast journalist, educator*
Shreiner, Curt *educational technologist, consultant*
Witmer, Diane F. *communications educator*

HIGHER EDUCATION: PHYSICAL EDUCATION

UNITED STATES

ALABAMA

Birmingham
Huff, Sherri Lynn *physical education educator*

Tuscaloosa
Curtner-Smith, Matthew David *sport pedagogy educator*

ARIZONA

Holbrook
Rhyan, Jeanette Delores *physical education educator*

Phoenix
Jones, Lucia Jean *physical education educator*
Starks, Rosalyn June *physical education and health educator*

Scottsdale
Maier, William Otto *martial arts, yoga and pilates instructor, author, seminar leader, consultant*

Tempe
Hoke, Judy Ann *physical education educator*

ARKANSAS

Hot Springs National Park
Garner, Douglas Michael *gymnastics fitness center executive, team coach*

Russellville
Holeyfield, Mary Annette *health and physical education educator*
Jackson, Shelia Lucyle *physical education educator, consultant*

Strong
Nunnally, Dolores Burns *retired physical education educator*

CALIFORNIA

Alta Loma
Tolan, Vicki Irvena *physical education educator*

Bellflower
Raphael, Mary D. *physical education educator*

Carmel
Epstein-Shepherd, Bee *mental skills golf coach, hypnotist, professional speaker*

Clovis
Mort, Gary Steven *physical education educator*

Felton
Wughalter, Emily Hope *physical education educator*

Long Beach
Fornia, Dorothy Louise *physical education educator*

Newhall
Knutson, Richard Dean *physical education educator*

Pleasanton
Emery, Rita Dorothy *physical education educator*

Riverside
Schlax, Sharon Lynn Newell *physical education educator*

Sacramento
Fortunato, Joanne Alba *athletic director*

COLORADO

Colorado Springs
Badger, Sandra Rae *health and physical education educator*
Dudenhoeffer, Frances Tomlin *physical education educator*

Denver
Johnson, Mary Bettina Black *physical education educator, athletic trainer*

Greeley
Hilgenkamp, Kathryn Darline *exercise and sport psychologist, health educator*

Littleton
Lening, Janice Allen *physical education educator*

CONNECTICUT

Bozrah
Heinrich, Carl Chester *retired physical education*

Greenwich
Boutelle, Jane Cronin *fitness consultant*

Hamden
Barberi, Matthew *physical education and health educator*

Litchfield
Kennedy, Susan Orpha *education consultant, sports official, physical education educator*

New London
Pinhey, Frances Louise *retired physical education educator*

West Hartford
Ciotto, Carol Jean Miller *physical education educator*
Spencer, Priscilla James *physical education educator*

DELAWARE

Milton
Scott, Phyllis Wright *coach, music educator*

Newark
Cairns, Sara Albertson *physical education educator*
Wilson, Deborrah *physical education educator*

Wilmington
Miller, Christine Talley *physical education educator*

DISTRICT OF COLUMBIA

Washington
Brown, Jeanne Pinkett *physical education educator*
Chin, Allen E., Sr., *athletic administrator, educator*

FLORIDA

Daytona Beach
Wood, Katherine *physical education educator*

Gainesville
Singer, Robert Norman *motor behavior educator*

Hollywood
King, Alma Jean *former health and physical education educator*
Workman, Gayle Jean *physical education educator, educator*

Lady Lake
Hartzler, Genevieve Lucille *physical education educator*

Miami
Farmer, Hiram Leander *physical education educator*
Greenwood, Carl Michael *physical education educator*

Safety Harbor
Kennedy, Kay Frances *physical education educator, social studies educator*

Starke
Loper, George Wilson, Jr., *physical education educator*

GEORGIA

Atlanta
Thompson, Wallace Reeves, III, *physical education educator*

Augusta
Gustafson, Robert Paul *exercise science educator*

Macon
Wetmore, Renée Margaret *physical education educator*

Marietta
Devigne, Karen Cooke *retired amateur athletics executive*

Savannah
Knorr, Ginny Walton *health and physical education educator*

HAWAII

Waipahu
Stevens, Adele Amy Kubota *physical education educator*

IDAHO

Boise
Petlichkoff, Linda Marie *physical education educator*

Coeur D Alene
Harvey, JoAnn Marie *physical education specialist*
Kotnour, Mary Margaret *physical education educator*

ILLINOIS

Alsip
Fournier, Maureen Mary *physical education educator*

Chicago
Cannon, Bennie Marvin *physical education educator*
Jenkins, Sandra Marie *physical education educator, coach*

Deerfield
Mocivnik, Patricia Ann *physical education educator*

Elgin
Umbdenstock, Judy Jean *physical education educator, real estate agent, farmer, entrepreneur*

Erie
Latham, LaVonne Marlys *physical education educator*

Eureka
Schuster, Sandra Jean *women's basketball coach, educator*

Gifford
Kuntz, Becky Jo *physical education educator*

Glendale Heights
Spearing, Karen Marie *physical education educator, coach*

Highland Park
Mordini, Marilyn Heuer *physical education educator*

Libertyville
Trzyna, Chris *physical education educator*

Lincolnshire
Schauble, John Eugene *physical education educator*

Olympia Fields
Stratta, Terese Marie *physical education educator*

Saint Charles
Felt, Jennifer Ruth *elementary physical education educator*

Schaumburg
Pickett, Phyllis Asselin *physical education educator*

Sterling
Moran, Joan Jensen *physical education and health educator*

Wheaton
Miller, Lynn Breckenfelder *health and physical education educator*

INDIANA

Bloomington
Davis, Kimberly Jane *physical education educator*

Evansville
Nahrwold, Susan Norma *physical education educator*

Kokomo
Blackburn, Michael Lynn *athletic administrator*

Muncie
Shondell, Donald Stuart *physical education educator*

Munster
Pillarella, Deborah Ann *fitness program manager, elementary education educator, consultant*

North Manchester
Duchane, Kim Allen *health and physical education educator*

Oakland City
Schafer, Patricia Day *physical education educator*

Porter
Moffett, Karen Elizabeth *physical education educator, guidance counselor*

Rochester
Neff, Kathy S. *swimming and water safety educator*

IOWA

Decorah
Hoff, Betty Ann *physical education educator*

KANSAS

Overland Park
Voska, Kathryn Caples *consultant, facilitator*

KENTUCKY

Campbellsville
Morgan, Tim Dale *physical education educator*

Paducah
Ragland, Nancy Simmons *physical education educator*

Pippa Passes
Walford, Gerald Albert *physical education educator*

LOUISIANA

Glenmora
Mealer, Lynda Ream *physical education educator*

Grambling
Porter, Douglas Taylor *retired athletic administrator*

Lafayette
Perron, Anne Michelle *physical education educator*

MAINE

Bangor
Kelley, Barbara Bannin *physical education educator*

MARYLAND

Baltimore
Cannon, Bryan Cedric *physical education educator*

Bowie
Silva, Lawrence Kehinde *physical education educator*

PROFESSIONAL INDEX — HIGHER EDUCATION: PHYSICAL EDUCATION

Columbia
Welty, Gail Ann Harper *physical education educator*

Rockville
Offutt, Drew Griffith *physical education educator*

Westminster
Clower, Richard Allen *physical education educator*

MASSACHUSETTS

Andover
Brophy, Susan Dorothy *adapted physical education educator*

Berlin
White, Christine *physical education educator*

Bridgewater
Anderson, Marcia Kay *physical education educator*

Quincy
Lydon, Mary C. *physical education educator*

Wilmington
Hayes, Carol Jeanne *physical education educator*

MICHIGAN

Detroit
Roberts, Peter Allen *physical education educator*

MINNESOTA

Kenyon
Radtke, Peggy Ann *physical education educator*

Saint Cloud
Isberner, Brad Joseph *health and safety educator, coach*

Saint Paul
Swanson-Schones, Kris Margit *developmental adapted physical education educator*

MISSISSIPPI

Hattiesburg
Gangstead, Sandra Kay *physical education educator, administrator*

Itta Bena
Ware, William Levi *physical education educator, researcher*

MISSOURI

Kansas City
Hanover, R(aymond) Scott *tennis management professional*

Lees Summit
Ferguson, Julie Ann *physical education educator*

Warrensburg
Nelson, Jimmie Dirk *kinesiology administrator, educator, researcher*

MONTANA

Great Falls
Anderson, C(harles) Henry *physical education educator*

NEBRASKA

Hartington
Meyer, Betty Jean *physical education educator*

Indianola
Troester, Dennis Lee *physical education educator*

Lincoln
Mulvaney, Mary Jean *physical education educator, department chairman*

Omaha
Brennan, Stephen James *physical education educator, consultant*

NEVADA

Las Vegas
Allen, Vicki Lynette *physical education educator*
Holmes, David Leo *recreation and leisure educator*

NEW HAMPSHIRE

Canaan
Butler, Joan Marie *physical education educator*

Goshen
Wright, Lilyan Boyd *physical education educator*

NEW JERSEY

Blackwood
Merlino, Dani Michelle *physical education educator*

Cherry Hill
Forvour, Jack Edwin *adapted physical education educator, consultant*

Flemington
Castelgrant, Elizabeth Ann Saylor *physical education educator, consultant*

Montclair
Lucenko, Leonard Konstantyn *sport, recreation management, and safety educator, coach, consultant*

New Brunswick
Dougherty, Neil Joseph *physical education educator, safety consultant*

Newton
McCarthy, Mary Eleanor *elementary physical education educator*

Orange
Bas, Juan Reinerio Rader *physical education educator*

Ridgewood
Ross, James Robert *physical education educator*

Ringwood
Foreman, Robert Charles *physical education educator*

Rumson
Reiser, Walter Frederick *athletic director, athletic trainer*

Union
Darden, Joseph Samuel, Jr., *health educator*
Pasvolsky, Richard Lloyd *parks, recreation, and environment educator*

Wayne
Jable, John Thomas *physical education educator*

NEW MEXICO

Abiquiu
Howlett, Phyllis Lou *retired athletics conference administrator*

NEW YORK

Altamont
Kinnaird, Mary Ann *physical education educator*

Delmar
Collins, Sandra Dee *physical education educator*

Fallsburg
Carey, Janet L. *physical education educator*

Franklin Square
Vomacka, Jill Elizabeth *adapted physical education specialist*

Garden City
Berka, Marianne Guthrie *health and physical education educator*
Feingold, Ronald Sherwin *physical education educator*

Glasco
Sheehan, Dennis Michael *physical education educator*

Hamburg
Davis, Christine Dale *physical education educator*

Mohegan Lake
Ettinger, Jayne Gold *physical education educator*

New Hartford
Kelley, Sharon Lee *physical education educator*

New York
Katz, Jane *swimming educator*
Keigher, Sharon *physical education educator*

Newburgh
Orbacz, Linda Ann *physical education educator*

Port Jefferson Station
Schlessinger, Arthur Joseph *physical education educator*

Syracuse
Duerr, Dianne Marie *physical education educator, sports medicine consultant*

Troy
Rogan, Thomas Paul *physical education educator*

Utica
Trojan, Penelope Ann *physical education educator*

White Plains
Constantine, Gus *physical education educator, coach*
Williams, Ted Vaughnell *physical education educator*

Yorktown Heights
Bogdanoff, Stewart Ronald *physical education educator, coach*

NORTH CAROLINA

Asheville
Quinn, Barbara Ann *athletics administrator, educator*

Dana
Morgan, Lou Ann *physical education educator*

Trinity
Weeks, Marie Cook *health and physical education educator*

OHIO

Akron
Cai, X. Sean *physical education educator*

Cadiz
Hoffman, Barbara Jo *health and physical education educator, athletic director*

Cincinnati
Casselman, Sharon Mae *recreational specialist*
Turck, Marsha Ann *physical education educator*

Cleveland
Rubins, Alex *physical education educator*

Columbus
Cowardin, Dana Sue *physical education educator, consultant, coach*
Pastore, Donna Lee *physical education educator*

Dayton
Wetzel, Richard Dennis *physical education educator, administrator*

Parma
Esterhay, Judith M. *physical education educator*

OKLAHOMA

Tulsa
Huber, Fritz Godfrey *physical education educator, excercise physiologist*

PENNSYLVANIA

Altoona
Wright, Jerry Jaye *physical education educator*

Bethel Park
Bohn, James Francis *physical education educator*

Bradford
Ross, Jean Louise *physical education educator*

East Stroudsburg
Sheska, Jerome Wallace *physical education educator*

Furlong
Ide, John Edwin *physical education educator*

Harrisburg
DuComb, Suzanne Marie *health and physical education educator*
Farrell, Kelly Jean *health and physical education educator*

Hazleton
Jago, Deidre Ellen Berguson *kinesiology educator, tennis and volleyball coach*

Millersville
Kabacinski, Stanley Joseph *health and physical education educator, consultant, speaker*

Philadelphia
Fish, Elizabeth Ann *physical education educator*

Strattanville
Schirmer, David Wayne *coach*

West Chester
Matejkovic, Edward Michael *athletic director, coach*

TENNESSEE

Brentwood
Abernathy, Sue Eury *physical education educator*

Jackson
Nelson, Scott Lee *physical education educator*

Nashville
Griffith, Jerry Lynn *physical education educator*
Snoddy, Chris Raymond *athletic trainer*
Voight, Michael Lee *physical education educator*

TEXAS

Abilene
Curtis, Joyce Mae *physical education educator*

Austin
Abraham, Lawrence Dagger *kinesiology educator*
Zawadzki, Katherine Mary *physical education educator, coach*

Corpus Christi
Garza, Marguerite Scott *physical education educator*

Dallas
Hudel, Chestella Alvis *athletics educator*
Polansky, Barbara Carol Crosby *physical education educator*

Del Valle
Hallman, Victoria Stella *athletic director*

Denton
French, Ronald Wayne *physical education educator*

Houston
Spencer, Albert Franklin *physical education and education educator*

Lubbock
Reeve, Thomas Gilmour *physical education educator*
Wilson, Margaret Eileen *retired physical education educator*

San Angelo
Messbarger, Edward Joseph *physical education educator, university coach*

VERMONT

Jacksonville
Alfieri, Francis Joseph *physical education educator*

VIRGINIA

Alexandria
Gutmann, Kathryn Carol *physical education educator*

Chantilly
Hammerle, Holly Ann *health and physical education educator*

Charlottesville
Dodson, Claudia Lane *athletic administrator*

Fredericksburg
Lauer, Susan Parker *personal trainer, writer*

Lynchburg
Langhorne, Linda Kay *health and physical education teacher*

Norfolk
Hunter, David William *physical education educator*

Roanoke
Sandidge, June Carol *retired physical education educator*

WASHINGTON

Camas
Sundquist, Leah Renata *physical education specialist*

WISCONSIN

Madison
Larson, G. Steven *coach, athletic director*

Tomah
Powell, Sharon Joyce *retired physical education educator*

WYOMING

Evanston
Schrad, Roger William *elementary physical education educator, coach*

ADDRESS UNPUBLISHED

Boling, Robert Bruce *physical education educator*
Cauraugh, James H. *physical education educator*
Clarke, Peg *physical education educator*
Crocker, Evelyne Marie *retired physical education educator*
Davidson, Bonnie Jean *gymnastics educator, sports management consultant*
Davila, Rebecca Tober *health and physical education educator*
Haberl, Valerie Elizabeth *physical education educator, company executive*
Harding, F(red) Victor *fitness consultant*
Hicks, Ritchie B. *physical education educator*
Jones, Alpha Belle *physical education educator*
Kelly, Patricia Aline *physical education educator, coach*
Kluka, Darlene Ann *human performance educator, researcher*
Knechtges, Mary Kay *retired coach*
Lacko, J. Michelle *physical education, health and science educator*
Lueke, Donna Mae *yoga instructor, Reiki practitioner, instructor*
Manahan, Joan Elsie *health and physical education educator*
Mason, Linda *physical education educator, softball and basketball coach*
Molloy, Margot Katherine *secondary physical education educator*
Morrison, Craig Somerville *physical education educator*
Safrit, Margaret *physical education educator*
Santos, Robert David *health and fitness educator, consultant*

Seifert, Teresa diStefano *physical education educator*
Wilson, Barbara T. *retired physical education educator*
Zeigler, Robert G. *physical education educator emeritus*

HIGHER EDUCATION: PHYSICAL SCIENCES

UNITED STATES

ALABAMA

Auburn
Melius, Paul *biochemist, educator*
Vodyanoy, Vitaly Jacob *biophysicist, educator*

Birmingham
Elgavish, Gabriel Andreas *physical biochemistry educator*
Robinson, Edward Lee *retired physics educator, consultant*

Daphne
Baugh, Charles Milton *biochemistry educator, college dean*

Huntsville
Wright, John Collins *retired chemistry educator*

ALASKA

Anchorage
Ennis, William Lee *physics educator*

Fairbanks
Duffy, Lawrence Kevin *biochemist, educator*
Lingle, Craig Stanley *glaciologist, educator*

ARIZONA

Flagstaff
Young, Robert Donald *physicist, educator*

Mesa
Burgoyne, Edward Eynon *chemistry educator*

Phoenix
Bylsma, Carol Ann *environmental education and science education consultant*

Scottsdale
Kinsinger, Jack Burl *chemist, educator*

Tempe
Blankenship, Robert Eugene *biochemistry educator*
Juvet, Richard Spalding, Jr., *chemistry educator*

Tucson
Cameron, Alastair Graham Walter *astrophysicist, educator*
Falco, Charles Maurice *physicist, educator*
Magee, Wayne Edward *biochemistry educator, researcher*
Wehinger, Peter Augustus *astronomer, educator*
Wolff, Sidney Carne *astronomer, observatory administrator*

ARKANSAS

Fayetteville
Lacy, Claud Harold Sandberg *astronomer, educator*

Pine Bluff
Walker, Richard Brian *chemistry educator*

CALIFORNIA

Apple Valley
Mays, George Walter, Jr., *educational technology educator, consultant, tutor*

Arcata
Paselk, Richard Alan *chemist, educator*

Atherton
Coleman, Robert Griffin *geology educator*
Levinthal, Elliott Charles *physicist, educator*

Berkeley
Barnett, R(alph) Michael *theoretical physicist, educational agency administrator*
Bartlett, Neil *chemist, emeritus educator*
Berry, William Benjamin Newell *geologist, educator, former museum administrator*
Bukowinski, Mark Stefan Tadeusz *geophysics educator*
Calendar, Richard Lane *biochemistry educator*
Cohen, Marvin Lou *physics educator*
Derenzo, Stephen E. *physics educator, research scientist*
Hall, Lawrence John *physics educator*
Halpern, Martin Brent *physics educator*
Heathcock, Clayton Howell *chemistry educator, researcher*
Heiles, Carl Eugene *astronomer, educator*
Klinman, Judith Pollock *biochemist, educator*
Lipps, Jere Henry *paleontology educator*
Louie, Steven Gwon Sheng *physics educator, researcher*
Markowitz, Samuel Solomon *chemistry educator*
McKee, Christopher Fulton *physicist, educator, astronomer, educator*
Miller, William Hughes *theoretical chemist, educator*
Pines, Alexander *chemistry educator, researcher, consultant*
Ritchie, Robert Oliver *materials science educator*
Somorjai, Gabor Arpad *chemist, educator*
Strauss, Herbert Leopold *chemistry educator*
Strovink, Mark William *physics educator*
Trilling, George Henry *physicist, educator*
Valentine, James William *paleobiology educator, writer*

Bradbury
Greenstein, Jesse Leonard *astronomer, educator*

Camarillo
Leerabhandh, Marjorie Bravo *chemist, educator*

Chula Vista
Smith, Peggy O'Doniel *physicist, educator*

Claremont
Helliwell, Thomas McCaffree *physicist, educator*
Oxtoby, David William *college president, chemistry educator*

Costa Mesa
Bender, Edward Erik *geology educator, researcher*
Lorance, Elmer Donald *organic chemistry educator*

Davis
Cahill, Thomas Andrew *physicist, educator*
Day, Howard Wilman *geology educator*
Gunion, John Francis *physicist, educator*
Mukherjee, Amiya K. *metallurgy and materials science educator*
Nachtergaele, Bruno Leo Zulma *mathematical physics educator, researcher*

El Cerrito
Alpen, Edward Lewis *biophysicist, educator*

Fresno
Kauffman, George Bernard *chemistry educator*

Fullerton
Fearn, Heidi *physicist, educator*
Shapiro, Mark Howard *physicist, educator, academic dean, consultant*

Huntington Beach
Licata, David Paul *chemistry educator*

Irvine
Wallis, Richard Fisher *physicist, educator*

La Jolla
Kolodner, Richard David *biochemist, educator, geneticist*
Lauer, James Lothar *physicist, educator*
MacDougall, John Douglas *environmental scientist educator, science administrator, academic administrator*
Schimmel, Paul Reinhard *biochemist, biophysicist, educator*
Somerville, Richard Chapin James *atmospheric scientist, educator*
Wolynes, Peter Guy *chemistry researcher, educator*

Lafayette
Seaburg, Glen T. *chemistry educator*

Lakewood
Snow, James Harry *metallurgist, educator, aircraft planning executive*

Loma Linda
Slattery, Charles Wilbur *biochemistry educator*

Los Angeles
Cline, David Bruce *physicist, educator*
Coleman, Charles Clyde *physicist, educator*
Coleman, Paul Jerome, Jr., *physicist, educator*
Jordan, Thomas Hillman *geophysicist, educator*
Kunc, Joseph Anthony *physics and engineering educator, consultant*
Markland, Francis Swaby, Jr., *biochemist, educator*
McLean, Ian Small *astronomer, physics educator*
Olah, George Andrew *chemist*
Onak, Thomas Philip *chemistry educator*
Wright, Byron T. *physicist, educator*

Menlo Park
Winick, Herman *physicist, educator*

Monarch Beach
Marsi, Kenneth Larue *chemist, educator*

North Highlands
Buis, Patricia Frances *geology educator, researcher*

Oroville
Sincoff, Steven Lawrence *chemistry educator*

Palo Alto
Ernst, Wallace Gary *geology educator*
Schreiber, Everett Charles, Jr., *chemist, educator*

Pasadena
Allen, Clarence Roderic *geologist, educator*
Baldeschwieler, John Dickson *chemist, educator*
Barnes, Charles Andrew *physicist, educator*
Cohen, Marshall Harris *astronomer, educator*
Culick, Fred Ellsworth Clow *physics and engineering educator*
Dougherty, Dennis A. *chemistry educator*
Frautschi, Steven Clark *physicist, educator*
Hitlin, David George *physicist, educator*
Ingersoll, Andrew Perry *planetary science educator*
Kavanagh, Ralph William *physics educator*
Lewis, Nathan Saul *chemistry educator*
Marcus, Rudolph Arthur *chemist*
Politzer, Hugh David *physicist, educator*
Steidel, Charles C. *astronomy educator*
Stevenson, David John *planetary scientist, educator*
Stone, Edward C. *physicist, educator*
Thorne, Kip Stephen *physicist, educator*
Vogt, Rochus Eugen *physicist, educator*
Westphal, James Adolph *planetary science educator*
Zachariasen, Fredrik *physics educator*

Pomona
Aurilia, Antonio *physicist, educator*

Redondo Beach
Mulvey, Gerald John *meteorologist*

Riverside
Fung, Sun-Yiu Samuel *physics educator*
Green, Harry Western, II, *geology-geophysics educator*

Sacramento
Nussenbaum, Siegfried Fred *chemistry educator*

Salinas
Mercurio, Edward Peter *natural science educator*

San Diego
Fineman, Morton A. *chemistry and physics educator*

San Francisco
Batterman, Boris William *physicist, educator, academic director*
Dickinson, Wade *physicist, oil and gas company executive, educator*
Dill, Kenneth Austin *pharmaceutical chemistry educator*
Featherstone, John Douglas Bernard *biochemistry educator*
Marshall, Grayson William, Jr., *biomaterials scientist, health sciences educator*

San Luis Obispo
Grismore, Roger *physics educator, researcher*

Santa Barbara
Dunne, Thomas *geology educator*
Metiu, Horia Ion *chemistry educator*

Santa Clara
Lee, Chan-Yun *physicist, process engineer, educator*

Santa Cruz
Bunnett, Joseph Frederick *chemist, educator*
Flatté, Stanley Martin *physicist, educator*
Noller, Harry Francis, Jr., *biochemist, educator*

Selma
Hushek, Joseph Charles *chemistry educator*

Stanford
Bienenstock, Arthur Irwin *physicist, educator, federal official*
Brauman, John I. *chemist, educator*
Fetter, Alexander Lees *theoretical physicist, educator*
Harbaugh, John Warvelle *geologist, educator*
Harrison, Walter Ashley *physicist, educator*
Little, William Arthur *physicist, educator*
McConnell, Harden Marsden *biophysical chemistry researcher, chemistry educator*
Osheroff, Douglas Dean *educator, physicist, researcher*
Ross, John *physical chemist, educator*
Solomon, Edward Ira *chemistry educator, researcher*
Trost, Barry Martin *chemist, educator*
Wagoner, Robert Vernon *astrophysicist, educator*
Walt, Martin *physicist, consulting educator*
Wojcicki, Stanley George *physicist, educator*
Zare, Richard Neil *chemistry educator*

Tarzana
Nies, Kevin Allison *physics educator*

Weed
Ryan, Daberath *chemistry educator*

Woodland Hills
Sharma, Brahama D. *chemistry educator*

Woodside
Ashley, Holt *aerospace scientist, educator*

COLORADO

Boulder
Kapteyn, Henry Cornelius *physics and engineering educator*
Low, Boon Chye *physicist*
Ostrovsky, Lev Aronovich *physicist, oceanographer, educator*
Stern, Raul Aristide *physics educator, researcher*

Denver
Smith, Dwight Morrell *chemistry educator*

Englewood
Gabel, Connie *chemist, educator*

Fort Collins
Patton, Carl Elliott *physics educator*

Golden
Coffey, Mark William *theoretical physicist, applied mathematician*
Warme, John Edward *geology educator*

Lakewood
Oakley, David Sterling *physics educator, consultant*

CONNECTICUT

Danbury
Pastor, Stephen Daniel *chemistry educator, researcher*

Farmington
Glasel, Jay Arthur *biochemistry educator*

Groton
Prakash, Chandra *chemistry educator*

Hartford
Church, William Handy *chemistry educator*
Hammond, Charles Robert *astronomer, educator*
Moyer, Ralph Owen, Jr., *chemist, educator*

New Britain
Baskerville, Charles Alexander *geologist, educator*

New Haven
Berson, Jerome Abraham *chemistry educator*
Bromley, David Allan *physicist, engineer, educator*
Larson, Richard Bondo *astronomy educator*
Lichten, William L. *physics educator*
Mac Dowell, Samuel Wallace *physics educator*
Moore, Peter Bartlett *biochemist, educator*
Parker, Peter D.M. *physicist, educator, researcher*
Sandweiss, Jack *physicist, educator*
Shulman, Robert Gerson *biophysics educator*
Turekian, Karl Karekin *geochemistry educator*
Wolf, Werner Paul *physicist, educator*
Zeller, Michael Edward *physicist, educator*

New London
Brennan, Victoria Elizabeth *chemistry and biology educator*

Storrs Mansfield
Marcus, Harris Leon *materials science educator*

Woodbury
Skinner, Brian John *geologist, educator*

DELAWARE

New Castle
Bellenger, George Collier, Jr., *physics educator*
Bouchelle, Henry Ellsworth Wirt, III, *planetarium director, educator*

Newark
Theopold, Klaus Hellmut *chemistry educator*

Wilmington
Moore, Carl Gordon *chemist, educator*

DISTRICT OF COLUMBIA

Washington
Baker, D. James *oceanographic and atmospheric administrator*
Bates, Richard Doane, Jr., *chemistry educator, researcher*
El Khadem, Hassan Saad *chemistry educator, researcher*
Fogleman, Guy Carroll *physicist, mathematician, educator*
Giacconi, Riccardo *astrophysicist, educator*
Lehman, Donald Richard *physicist, educator, academic administrator*
Orbach, Raymond Lee *physicist, educator*
Pardavi-Horvath, Martha Maria *physicist, educator*
Perros, Theodore Peter *chemist, educator*
Venable, Demetrius D. *physics educator*

FLORIDA

Alachua
Carlisle, Casey Allen *chemist, educator*

Boca Raton
Finkl, Charles William, II, *geologist, educator*

Bonita Springs
Brown, Theodore Lawrence *chemistry educator*

Coral Gables
Einspruch, Norman Gerald *physicist, engineering educator*
Glaser, Luis *biochemistry educator*

Dade City
Burdick, Glenn Arthur *physicist, engineering educator*

Gainesville
Broyles, Arthur Augustus *physics educator, researcher*
Cohen, Robert Jay *biochemistry educator, researcher*
Cousins, Robert John *nutritional biochemist, educator*
Hanson, Harold Palmer *physicist, government official, editor, academic administrator*
Jacobs, Alan Martin *physicist, educator*
Jones, Kevin Scott *materials science educator*

Hollywood
Perlman, Barry Arnold *astronomy educator*

Marco Island
Foster, Edward John *engineer physicist*

Miami
Kowalska, Maria Teresa *research scientist, educator*
Millero, Frank Joseph, Jr., *marine and physical chemistry educator*

Ocala
Fredericks, William John *chemistry educator*

Orlando
Baker, Peter Mitchell *laser scientist, educator, science administrator*
Chow, Lee *physics educator*
Kolattukudy, Pappachan Ettoop *biochemist, educator*
Llewellyn, Ralph Alvin *physics educator*
Van Stryland, Eric William *physics educator, consultant*

Sanford
Dickison, Alexander Kane *physical science educator*

Tallahassee
Berg, Bernd Albert *physics educator*
Caspar, Donald L.D. *biophysics and structural biology educator*
Choppin, Gregory Robert *chemistry educator*
Mandelkern, Leo *biophysics and chemistry educator*
Pfeffer, Richard Lawrence *meteorology and geophysics educator*

Tampa
Binford, Jesse Stone, Jr., *chemistry educator*
Jones, William Denver *physicist, educator*

Titusville
McCord, Scott Anthony *chemistry educator*

GEORGIA

Atlanta
Anderson, Gloria Long *chemistry educator*
Bosah, Francis N. *molecular biochemist, educator*
Chen, Peter Conway *chemistry educator*
Hicks, Heraline Elaine *environmental health scientist, educator*
Kahn, Bernd *radiochemist, educator*
Long, Leland Timothy *geophysicist educator, seismologist*
Norton, Bryan G. *environmental scientist, educator, philosopher*
O'Shea, Donald C. *physicist, educator, optical engineer*
Strekowski, Lucjan *chemistry educator*

HAWAII

Honolulu
Tata, Xerxes Ramyar *physicist, educator*

IDAHO

Moscow
LeTourneau, Duane John *retired biochemist, educator*
Miller, Maynard Malcolm *geologist, educator, research institute director, explorer, legislator*
Renfrew, Malcolm MacKenzie *chemist, educator*
Shreeve, Jean'ne Marie *chemist, educator*

ILLINOIS

Argonne
Jonkouski, Jill Ellen *materials scientist, ceramic engineer, educator*

Bourbonnais
Reams, Max Warren *geology educator, researcher*

Carbondale
Smith, Gerard Vinton *chemistry educator*

Champaign
Treadway, William Jack, Jr., *biochemistry and chemistry educator*

Chicago
Blumberg, Avrom Aaron *physical chemistry educator*
Erber, Thomas *physics educator*
Halpern, Jack *chemist, educator*
Levi-Setti, Riccardo *physicist, director*
Tao, Mariano *biochemistry educator*
Trenary, Michael *chemist, educator*
Winston, Roland *physicist, educator*
Zhao, Meishan *chemical physics educator, researcher, writer*

Elmhurst
Betinis, Emanuel James *physics and mathematics educator*

Evanston
Basolo, Fred *chemistry educator*
Brown, Laurie Mark *physicist, educator*
Goldberg, Erwin *biochemistry educator*
Ibers, James Arthur *chemist, educator*
Lambert, Joseph Buckley *chemistry educator*
Oakes, Robert James *physics educator*
Olson, Gregory Bruce *materials science and engineering educator, academic director*
Poeppelmeier, Kenneth Reinhard *chemistry educator*
Shriver, Duward Felix *chemistry educator, researcher, consultant*
Silverman, Richard Bruce *chemist, biochemist, educator*
Vaynman, Semyon *materials scientist, educator*
Weertman, Johannes *materials science educator*
Weertman, Julia Randall *materials science and engineering educator*

Grayslake
Barrington, Leonard Barry *chemist, educator, writer*

Homewood
Parker, Eugene Newman *retired physicist, educator*

Milford
Coogan, Melinda Ann Strank *chemistry and biology educator*

Naperville
Rosenmann, Daniel *physicist, educator*
Sherren, Anne Terry *chemistry educator*

Normal
Lash, Timothy David *chemistry educator, researcher*

North Chicago
Neet, Kenneth Edward *biochemist, educator*
Walters, D. Eric *biochemistry educator*

Northfield
Shabica, Charles Wright *geologist, earth science educator*

Palos Heights
Van Kley, Harold *chemistry educator*

Peoria
Foster, Merrill White *geology and marine biology educator*

Rock Island
Anderson, Richard Charles *geology educator*

Skokie
Filler, Robert *chemist educator*

Urbana
Dickel, Hélène Ramseyer *astronomy educator*
Girolami, Gregory Scott *chemistry educator*
Govindjee, *biophysics, biochemistry, and biology educator*
Iben, Icko, Jr., *astrophysicist, educator*
Jackson, Edwin Atlee *physicist, educator*
Klein, Miles Vincent *physics educator*
Langenheim, Ralph Louis, Jr., *geology educator*
Mapother, Dillon Edward *physicist, university official*
Robinson, James Lawrence *biochemistry educator, researcher*
Rowland, Theodore Justin *physicist, educator*
Salamon, Myron Ben *physicist, educator, dean*
Satterthwaite, Cameron B. *physics educator*
Schlesinger, Michael Earl *atmospheric sciences educator*
Switzer, Robert Lee *biochemistry educator*

Wheaton
Wharton, William Raymond *physicist educator*

INDIANA

Bloomington
Murray, Haydn Herbert *geology educator*

Fort Wayne
Argast, Anne Scott *geology educator*

Goshen
Swartzendruber, Calvin Frederick *chemistry educator, chemical health official*

Indianapolis
Aprison, Morris Herman *biochemist, experimental and theoretical neurobiologist, emeritus educator*
Bein, Frederick L. *geography educator*
Malik, David Joseph *chemist, educator*
Snare, Leroy Earl *physicist, physics educator*

Lafayette
Brown, Herbert Charles *chemistry educator*

New Albany
Crump, Claudia *geography educator*

Notre Dame
Huber, Paul William *biochemistry educator, researcher*
Schuler, Robert Hugo *chemist, educator*
Trozzolo, Anthony Marion *chemistry educator*

Terre Haute
Guthrie, Frank Albert *chemistry educator*

West Lafayette
Chang, Ching-jer *medicinal chemistry educator*
Elmore, David *physicist, educator*
Judd, William Robert *engineering geologist, educator*
Rossmann, Michael George *biochemist, educator*

IOWA

Ames
Bakac, Andreja *chemist, educator*
Barnes, Richard George *physicist, educator*
Finnemore, Douglas Kirby *retired physics educator*
Kostić, Nenad Miodrag *chemist, educator*
Peterson, Francis *physicist, educator*

Ankeny
Schaefer, Joseph Albert *physics and engineering educator, consultant*

Cedar Falls
Walters, James Carter *geology educator, consultant*

Grinnell
Erickson, Luther Eugene *chemist, educator*
Swartz, James Edward *chemistry educator, dean, university administrator*

Indianola
Meints, Clifford L. *chemistry educator*

Iowa City
Baker, Richard Graves *geology educator, palynologist*
Conway, Thomas William *biochemist, educator*
Foster, Charles Thomas, Jr., *geology educator*
Koch, Donald LeRoy *retired geologist, state agency administrator*
Montgomery, Rex *biochemist, educator*

West Des Moines
Lynch, David William *physicist, retired educator*

KANSAS

Lawrence
Angino, Ernest Edward *retired geology and engineering educator*
Gerhard, Lee Clarence *geologist, educator*
Sanders, Robert B. *biochemistry educator, administrator*
Stella, Valentino John *pharmaceutical chemistry educator*

North Newton
Quiring, Frank Stanley *chemist, educator*

Topeka
Barton, Janice Sweeny *chemistry educator*

Wichita
Behrman, Elizabeth Colden *physics educator*

KENTUCKY

Lexington
Ehmann, William Donald *chemistry educator*
Holler, F. James *chemistry educator*
Liu, Keh-Fei Frank *physicist, educator*
Ng, Kwok-Wai *physics educator*
Schwert, George William, Jr., *biochemist, educator*

Louisville
Klinge, Carolyn Muriel *biochemist, educator*

Owensboro
Hoover, Donna Whitehouse *math and physics educator*

LOUISIANA

Baton Rouge
Kaiser, Mark John *research scientist, science educator*
Mc Glynn, Sean Patrick *physical chemist, educator*

Monroe
De Hon, René Aurel *geology educator*
Zander, Arlen Ray *retired physics educator*

New Orleans
Allen, Gary Curtiss *geology educator*
Perdew, John Paul *physics educator, condensed matter and density functional theorist*
Seab, Charles Gregory *astrophysicist, educator*

MAINE

Falmouth
Oates, Maureen Katherine *environmental educator*

Lewiston
Semon, Mark David *physicist, educator*

Orono
Otto, Fred Bishop *retired physics educator*

MARYLAND

Aberdeen Proving Ground
Bowlus, Dale Richard *environmental scientist, educator, consultant*

Baltimore
Albinak, Marvin Joseph *chemistry educator*
Beer, Michael *biophysicist, educator, environmentalist*
Chien, Chia-Ling *physics educator*
Englund, Paul Theodore *biochemist, educator*
Fulton, Thomas *theoretical physicist, educator*
Green, Robert Edward, Jr., *physicist, educator*
Haig, Frank Rawle *physics educator, clergyman*
Henry, Richard Conn *astrophysicist, educator*
Judd, Brian Raymond *physicist, educator*
Koski, Walter S. *chemistry educator, scientist*
Krolik, Julian Henry *astrophysicist, educator*
Lee, Yung-Keun *physicist, educator*
Margon, Bruce Henry *astrophysicist, educator*
Marsh, Bruce David *geologist, educator*
Palmer, C(harles) Harvey *physicist, educator*
Phillips, Owen Martin *oceanographer, geophysicist, educator*
Posner, Gary Herbert *chemist, educator*
Roseman, Saul *biochemist, educator*
Silverstone, Harris J. *chemistry educator*

Cabin John
Oertel, Goetz Kuno Heinrich *physicist, professional science administrator*

College Park
Dickerson, Russell Robert *atmospheric science and chemistry educator*
Fisher, Michael Ellis *mathematical physicist, chemist*
Grim, Samuel Oram *chemistry educator*
Redish, Edward Frederick *physicist, educator*
Skuja, Andris *physics educator*
Stith, James Herman *physics educator*
Wylie, Ann Gilbert *geology educator*

Crofton
Kniffen, Donald Avery *astrophysicist, educator, researcher*

Frostburg
Tam, Francis Man Kei *physics educator*

Greenbelt
Boldt, Elihu *astrophysicist, educator*

Parkton
Fitzgerald, Edwin Roger *physicist, educator*

MASSACHUSETTS

Amherst
Barnes, Ramon Murray *chemistry educator*
Marshall, Mark David *chemistry educator, researcher*

Boston
Brownell, Gordon Lee *physicist, educator*
Cohen, Saul G. *chemist, educator*
Edmonds, Dean Stockett, Jr., *physicist, educator, director*
Stanley, H(arry) Eugene *physicist, educator*
Vaughn, Michael Thayer *physicist, educator*

Cambridge
Becker, Ulrich J. *physics educator, particle physics researcher*
Boyle, Edward Allen *oceanography educator*
Bradt, Hale Van Dorn *physicist, x-ray astronomer, educator*
Burchfiel, Burrell Clark *geology educator*
Burke, Bernard Flood *physicist, educator*
Butler, James Newton *chemist, educator*
Canizares, Claude Roger *astrophysicist, educator*
Carter, Ashton Baldwin *physicist, educator, government agency executive*
Ceyer, Sylvia T. *chemistry educator*
Clark, George Whipple *physics educator*
Coleman, Sidney Richard *physicist, educator*
Dalgarno, Alexander *astronomy educator*
Dresselhaus, Mildred Spiewak *physics and engineering educator*
Ehrenreich, Henry *physicist, educator*
Feld, Michael Stephen *physics educator*
Feldman, Gary Jay *physicist, educator*
Frey, Frederick August *geochemistry researcher, educator*
Friedman, Jerome Isaac *physics educator, researcher*
Garland, Carl Wesley *chemist, educator*
Geller, Margaret Joan *astrophysicist, educator*
Georgi, Howard *physics educator*
Gingerich, Owen Jay *astronomer, educator*
Gordon, Roy Gerald *chemistry educator*
Gould, Stephen Jay *paleontologist, educator*
Greene, Frederick D., II, *chemistry educator*
Grindlay, Jonathan Ellis *astrophysics educator*
Herschbach, Dudley Robert *chemistry educator*
Huang, Kerson *physics educator*
Huchra, John Peter *astronomer, educator*
Jackiw, Roman *physicist, educator*
Jaffe, Arthur Michael *physicist, mathematician, educator*
Joss, Paul Christopher *astrophysicist, atmospheric physicist, educator*
Karplus, Martin *chemistry educator*
King, Ronold Wyeth Percival *physics educator*
Klemperer, William *chemistry educator*
Kleppner, Daniel *physicist, educator*
Lindzen, Richard Siegmund *meteorologist, educator*
Lomon, Earle Leonard *physicist, educator, consultant*
Lyon, Richard Harold *physicist educator*
Martin, Paul Cecil *physicist, educator*
Meselson, Matthew Stanley *biochemist, educator*
Molina, Mario Jose *physical chemist, educator*
Narayan, Ramesh *astronomy educator*
Negele, John William *physics educator, consultant*
Oppenheim, Irwin *chemical physicist, educator*
Parkinson, William Hambleton *physics, educator*
Paul, William *physicist, educator*
Pettengill, Gordon H(emenway) *physicist, educator*
Pritchard, David Edward *physics educator*
Rajur, Sharanabasava Basappa *chemistry educator, researcher*
Raymo, Maureen Elizabeth *geologist, researcher*
Redwine, Robert Page *physicist, educator*
Rice, James Robert *engineering scientist, geophysicist*
Rose, Robert Michael *materials science and engineering educator*
Sadoway, Donald Robert *materials science educator*
Schild, Rudolph Ernst *astronomer, educator*
Seyferth, Dietmar *chemist, educator*
Shapiro, Irwin Ira *physicist, educator*
Silvera, Isaac Franklin *physics educator*
Spaepen, Frans August *applied physics researcher, educator*
Stone, Peter Hunter *atmospheric scientist, educator*
Ting, Samuel Chao Chung *physicist, educator*
Tinkham, Michael *physicist, educator*

Wang, James Chuo *biochemistry and molecular biology educator*
Whitesides, George McClelland *chemistry educator*
Wiley, Don Craig *biochemistry and biophysics educator*
Wu, Tai Tsun *physicist, educator*

Framingham
Dawicki, Doloretta Diane *analytical chemist, research biochemist, educator*

Haverhill
DeSchuytner, Edward Alphonse *biochemist, educator*

Medford
Cavallaro, Mary Caroline *retired physics educator*
Chaisson, Eric Joseph *astrophysicist, science administrator, educator*
Thornton, Ronald *physicist, educator*

Natick
Kennedy, Dallas Clarence, II, *physicist, educator, writer*

Waltham
Deser, Stanley *physicist, educator*

Weston
Lin, Alice Lee Lan *physicist, researcher, educator*

Williamstown
Johnson, Markes Eric *geology educator*
Markgraf, J(ohn) Hodge *chemist, educator*
Pasachoff, Jay Myron *astronomer, educator*
Wobus, Reinhard Arthur *geologist, educator*

Woods Hole
Berggren, William Alfred *geologist, research micropaleontologist, educator*
Gagosian, Robert B. *chemist, educator*

MICHIGAN

Ann Arbor
Agranoff, Bernard William *biochemist, educator*
Ashe, Arthur James, III, *chemistry educator*
Atreya, Sushil Kumar *planetary-space science educator, astrophysicist*
Atzmon, Michael *materials scientist, educator*
Clarke, Roy *physicist, educator*
Drake, Richard Paul *physicist, educator*
Farrand, William Richard *geology educator*
Filisko, Frank Edward *physicist, educator*
Freese, Katherine *physicist, educator*
Gingerich, Philip Derstine *paleontologist, evolutionary biologist, educator*
Griffin, Henry Claude *chemistry educator*
Haddock, Fred(erick) T(heodore), Jr., *astronomer, educator*
Neal, Homer Alfred *physics educator, researcher, university administrator*
Pollack, Henry Nathan *geophysics educator*
Savit, Robert Steven *physics educator, consultant*
Steel, Duncan Gregory *physics educator*
Townsend, LeRoy B. *chemistry educator, university administrator, researcher*
van der Pluijm, Bernardus Adrianus (Ben van der Pluijm) *geologist, educator*

Belleville
Wilson, David James *chemistry researcher, educator*

Detroit
Gupta, Suraj Narayan *physicist, educator*
Yin, Fang-Fang *medical physicist, educator*

East Lansing
Austin, Sam M. *physics educator*
Pollack, Gerald Leslie *physicist, educator*

Holland
Williams, Donald Howard *chemist, educator, chemist, consultant*

Hudsonville
Hamelink, Jerry Lee *environmental research scientist, educator*

Kalamazoo
Askew, Thomas Rendall *physics educator, researcher, consultant*
Pancella, Paul Vincent *physics educator*

Midland
Dreyfuss, M(ax) Peter *research chemist, educator*

Romulus
Yussouff, Mohammed *retired physicist, educator*

University Center
Menard, Albert Robert, III, *physics educator*

MINNESOTA

Austin
Brown, Rhoderick Edmiston *biochemistry researcher, educator*
Schmid, Harald Heinrich Otto *biochemistry educator, academic director*

Duluth
Zhdankin, Viktor Vladimirovich *chemistry educator*

Marshall
Carberry, Edward Andrew *chemistry educator*

Minneapolis
Gasiorowicz, Stephen George *physics educator*
Johnson, Robert Glenn *geology and geophysics educator*
Marshak, Marvin Lloyd *physicist, educator*
Truhlar, Donald Gene *chemist, educator*
Wood, Wellington Gibson, III, *biochemistry educator*

Moorhead
Strong, Judith Ann *chemist, educator*

Northfield
Cederberg, James *physics educator*

Saint Paul
Perry, James Alfred *environmental scientist, consultant, science educator, director*
Van Pilsum, John Franklin *biochemist, educator*

MISSISSIPPI

Hattiesburg
Bedenbaugh, Angela Lea Owen *chemistry educator, researcher*
Hall, Margaret Jean (Margot Hall) *biochemistry educator*

Jackson
Leszczynski, Jerzy Ryszard *chemistry educator, researcher*

MISSOURI

Cape Girardeau
Holbrook, John Millard *geologist, educator*

Columbia
Kaiser, Edwin Michael *chemistry educator*
Pfeifer, Peter Martin *physics educator*
Plummer, Patricia Lynne Moore *chemistry and physics educator*
Randall, Linda Lea *biochemist, educator*

Kansas City
Durig, James Robert *chemistry educator*
Streng, William Harold *chemist, researcher, educator*
Wheeler, James Donlan *chemistry educator*

Rolla
Alexander, Ralph William, Jr., *physics educator*
Mc Farland, Robert Harold *physicist, educator*
Shrestha, Bijaya *nuclear scientist, electrical engineering educator*

Saint Louis
Bender, Carl Martin *physics educator, consultant*
Macias, Edward S. *chemistry educator, university official and dean*
Taylor, Morris Anthony *chemistry educator*
Walker, Robert Mowbray *physicist, educator*
Wrighton, Mark Stephen *chemistry educator*

Springfield
Toste, Anthony Paim *chemistry educator, researcher*

NEBRASKA

Fremont
Clements, Gregory Leland *physics educator*

Kearney
Underhill, Glenn Moris *physics educator, consultant*
Wubbels, Gene Gerald *chemistry educator*

Lincoln
Adams, (Alfred) Birk *biochemistry educator, nutritionist*
Diffendal, Robert Francis, Jr., *geologist, researcher, educator*
Jones, Lee Bennett *chemist, educator, university official*
Smith, Norman Dwight *geological sciences educator*
Starace, Anthony Francis *theoretical atomic physicist*

Omaha
Hulce, Martin Russell *chemistry educator*
Lovas, Sándor *chemist, researcher, educator*
Rea, Roger Uhl *chemistry educator, consultant*
Zepf, Thomas Herman *physics educator, researcher*

NEVADA

Las Vegas
Lepp, Stephen Henry *physicist, educator*
Nicol, Malcolm F. *physical chemistry educator*

Reno
Taranik, James Vladimir *geologist, educator*

NEW HAMPSHIRE

Berlin
Cabaup, Joseph John *geology educator*

Hanover
Doyle, William Thomas *physicist, retired educator*
Winn, John Sterling *chemist, educator*

NEW JERSEY

Columbia
Timcenko, Lydia Teodora *biochemist, chemist*

Jersey City
Weinrich, Marcel *physics educator*

New Brunswick
Gotsch, Audrey Rose *environmental health sciences educator, researcher*
Ho, Chi-Tang *food chemistry educator*

Paterson
Porter, Gary Francis *chemistry educator*

Pennington
Halasi-Kun, George Joseph *hydrologist, educator*

Piscataway
Idol, James Daniel, Jr., *chemist, educator, inventor, consultant*
Lebowitz, Joel Louis *mathematical physicist, educator*
Manowitz, Paul *biochemist, researcher, educator*
Robbins, Allen Bishop *physics educator*
Shatkin, Aaron Jeffrey *biochemistry educator*
Witz, Gisela *scientist, educator*

Princeton
Fisch, Nathaniel Joseph *physicist*
Groves, John Taylor, III, *chemist, educator*
Hopfield, John Joseph *biophysicist, educator*
Lieb, Elliott Hershel *physicist, mathematician, educator*
Ostriker, Jeremiah Paul *astrophysicist*
Royce, Barrie Saunders Hart *physicist, educator*
Smith, Arthur John Stewart *physicist, educator*
Spiro, Thomas George *chemistry educator*
Stix, Thomas Howard *physicist, educator*
Taylor, Edward Curtis *chemistry educator*
Torquato, Salvatore *materials science and chemistry educator*
Wheeler, John Archibald *physicist*
White, Roscoe Beryl *research physicist, educator*
Wightman, Arthur Strong *physicist, educator*
Wood, Eric Franklin *earth and environmental sciences educator*

Union
Zois, Constantine Nicholas Athanasios *meteorology educator*

NEW MEXICO

Albuquerque
Duncan, Irma Wagner *retired biochemist, museum educator*
Evans, Pauline D. *physicist, educator*

Las Vegas
Clark, Ronald Duane *chemistry educator*

Los Alamos
Brown, Lowell Severt *physicist, educator*

Santa Fe
Romanowski, Thomas Andrew *physics educator*
Whitten, David George *chemistry educator*

NEW YORK

Albany
Corelli, John Charles *physicist, educator*
Keyser, Daniel *atmospheric scientist, educator*
Kim, Jai Soo *physics educator*

Binghamton
Dickman, Steven Richard *geophysicist, educator*
Doetschman, David Charles *chemistry educator*
Nelson, Charles A. *physicist, educator*

Bronx
Thysen, Benjamin *biochemist, health science facility administrator, researcher*

Brooklyn
Armenakas, Anthony Emmanuel *aerospace educator*
Choudhury, Deo Chand *physicist, educator*
Friedman, Gerald Manfred *geologist, educator*
Karan, Hiroko Ito *organic chemistry educator*
Ma, Tsu Sheng *chemist, educator, consultant*

Buffalo
Anbar, Michael *biophysics educator*
Rashba, Emmanuel Iosif *physicist, educator*

Clinton
Ring, James Walter *physics educator*

Farmingdale
Makarowitz, Lloyd *physics educator*
Nolan, Peter John *physics educator*
Purandare, Yeshwant K. *chemistry educator, consultant*

Flushing
Coch, Nicholas K. *geologist, educator*
Finks, Robert Melvin *paleontologist, educator*

Fredonia
Barnard, Walther M. *geosciences educator*

Hamilton
Balonek, Thomas Joseph *physics and astronomy educator*
Selleck, Bruce W. *geologist, educator*

Horseheads
Josbeno, Larry Joseph *physics educator*

Ithaca
Bassett, William Akers *geologist, educator, retired*
Berkelman, Karl *physics educator*
Bethe, Hans Albrecht *physicist, educator*
McMurry, John Edward *chemistry educator*

Jamaica
Manche, Emanuel P. *chemistry educator*

New Hyde Park
Ronn, Avigdor Meir *chemical physics educator, consultant, researcher*

New Paltz
Lavallee, David Kenneth *chemistry educator, researcher*
Manos, Constantine Thomas *geologist, educator*

New York
Allison, Michael David *space scientist, astronomy educator*
Breslow, Ronald Charles *chemist*
Chan, Siu-Wai *materials science educator*
Cheng, Chuen Yan *biochemist, educator*
Chevray, Rene *physics educator*
Erlanger, Bernard Ferdinand *biochemist, educator*
Knowles, Richard James Robert *medical physicist, educator, consultant*
Koeppl, Gerald Walter *chemistry educator*
Krasna, Alvin Isaac *biochemist, educator*
Machlin, Eugene Solomon *metallurgy educator, consultant*
Marshall, Thomas Carlisle *applied physics educator*
Middleton, David *physicist, applied mathematician, educator*
Nakanishi, Koji *chemistry educator, research institute administrator*
Navratil, Gerald Anton *physicist, educator*
Pope, Martin *chemist, educator*
Roeder, Robert Gayle *biochemist, educator*
Stroke, Hinko Henry *physicist, educator*
Turro, Nicholas John *chemistry educator*

Niagara Falls
Bharadwaj, Prem Datta *physics educator*

Old Westbury
Li, Yongji *chemistry educator*

Oneonta
Helser, Terry Lee *biochemistry educator*
Hickey, Francis Roger *physicist, educator*
Merilan, Michael Preston *astrophysicist, educator, dean*
Pence, Harry Edmond *chemistry educator*

Oswego
Hyde, Kenneth Edwin *chemistry educator*

Palisades
Hayes, Dennis Edward *geophysicist, educator*
Kellogg, Herbert Humphrey *metallurgist, educator*
Sykes, Lynn Ray *geologist, educator*

Poughkeepsie
Beck, Curt Werner *chemist, educator*
Deiters, Sister Joan Adele *psychoanalyst, nun, chemistry educator*
Rossi, Miriam *chemistry educator, researcher*

Rochester
Cain, B(urton) Edward *chemistry educator*
Ferbel, Thomas *physics educator, physicist*
Li, James Chen Min *materials science educator*
McCrory, Robert Lee *physicist, mechanical engineering educator*
Salamone, Joseph Charles *polymer chemistry educator*
Smith, Harold Charles *biochemistry educator, academic administrator*
Wolf, Emil *physics educator*

Stony Brook
McCarthy, Robert Lane *physics educator*
Swanson, Robert Lawrence *oceanographer, academic program administrator*

Syracuse
Birge, Robert Richards *chemistry educator*
Pearse, George Ancell, Jr., *chemistry educator, researcher*
Schiff, Eric Allan *physics educator*

Troy
Krause, Sonja *chemistry educator*
Ohanian, Hans Christoph *physicist, author, educator*

NORTH CAROLINA

Chapel Hill
Buck, Richard Pierson *chemistry educator, researcher*
Eliel, Ernest Ludwig *chemist, educator*
Merzbacher, Eugen *physicist, educator*

Durham
Chao, James Lee *chemist, educator*
Joklik, Wolfgang Karl *biochemist, virologist, educator*
Wilder, Pelham, Jr., *chemist, pharmacologist, educator, academic administrator*

Greenville
Marks, Richard Henry Lee *biochemist, educator*
Toburen, Larry Howard *physicist, educator*

Raleigh
Arya, Satya Pal *meteorology educator*
Janowitz, Gerald Saul *geophysicist, educator*
McGregor, Ralph *textile chemistry educator, consultant, researcher, author*

Wilmington
Kelley, Patricia Hagelin *geology educator*

Winston Salem
Hinze, Willie Lee *chemistry educator, researcher*

PROFESSIONAL INDEX — HIGHER EDUCATION: PHYSICAL SCIENCES

OHIO

Akron
Gent, Alan Neville *physicist, educator*

Alliance
Rodman, James Purcell *astrophysicist, educator*

Bowling Green
Midden, William Robert *chemist, educator*

Canton
Arora, Sardari Lal *chemistry educator*

Cincinnati
Meal, Larie *chemistry educator, researcher, consultant*
Stricklin, Rebecca Ellen *chemistry educator*
Sullivan, James F. *physicist, educator*

Cleveland
Chamis, Christos Constantinos *aerospace scientist, educator*
Leventis, Nicholas *chemist, research scientist*
Rogers, Charles Edwin *physical chemistry educator*
Schuele, Donald Edward *physics educator*
Simha, Robert *chemistry educator, researcher*
Smith, Mark Anthony *biochemist, educator*

Columbus
Adelson, Edward *physicist, educator, musician*
Bergstrom, Stig Magnus *geology educator*
Jossem, Edmund Leonard *physics educator*
Mayer, Victor James *geologist, educator*
Newsom, Gerald Higley *astronomy educator*
Peterson, Bradley Michael *astronomy educator*
Wali, Mohan Kishen *environmental science and natural resources educator*
Wojcicki, Andrew Adalbert *chemist, educator*

Dayton
Huang, Mei Qing *physics educator, researcher*

Middletown
Marine, Susan Sonchik *analytical chemist, educator*

Oxford
Danielson, Neil David *chemistry educator*

Youngstown
Zitto, Richard Joseph *physics educator*

OKLAHOMA

Lawton
Koll, Kurtis James *physical and natural scientist, educator*

Norman
Cook, Paul Fabyan *chemistry educator*
Kessler, Edwin *meteorology educator, consultant*
Nelson, Donna Jean *chemistry educator, researcher*
Pigott, John Dowling *geologist, geophysicist, geochemist, educator, consultant*

Oklahoma City
Weigel, Paul Henry *biochemistry educator, researcher, consultant*

Seminole
Laule, Gerhard Helmut *chemistry educator, researcher*

Stillwater
Berlin, Kenneth Darrell Darrell *chemistry educator, consultant, researcher*

Tulsa
Anderson, David Walter *physics educator, consultant*
Blais, Roger Nathaniel *physics educator*

OREGON

Beaverton
Engelmann, Reinhart Wolfgang Hanns *physics educator*

Corvallis
Baird, William McKenzie *chemical carcinogenesis researcher, biochemistry educator*
Freeman, Peter Kent *chemist, educator*
Krueger, James Harry *chemistry educator*
Shoemaker, Clara Brink *retired chemistry researcher*

Eugene
Cina, Jeffrey A. *chemistry educator*
von Hippel, Peter Hans *chemistry educator, molecular biology researcher*

Portland
Farrell, David Henry *biochemistry and molecular biology educator*
Gard, Gary Lee *chemistry educator, researcher*
Takeo, Makoto *physics education educator*

PENNSYLVANIA

Abington
Schmiedekamp, Ann Marie Boudreaux *physicist, educator*

Ardmore
Stanley, Edward Alexander *geologist, forensic scientist, technical and academic administrator*

Berwyn
Devlin, Thomas McKeown *biochemist, educator*

Bethlehem
Lyman, Charles Edson *materials scientist, educator*
Zeroka, Daniel *chemistry educator*

Bryn Mawr
Crawford, William Arthur *geologist, educator*

Camp Hill
Zook, Merlin Wayne *meteorologist, educator*

Carlisle
Laws, Priscilla Watson *physics educator*

Clearfield
Haag, Harvey Eugene *physics educator*

Dallas
Rockensies, Kenneth Jules *physicist, educator*

East Stroudsburg
Bergo, Conrad Hunter *chemistry educator*

Harrisburg
Mowery, J. Ronald *geologist, physicist, educator*

Hazleton
Miller, David Emanuel *physics educator, researcher*

Indiana
Bencloski, Joseph W. *geography educator*

Johnstown
Brice, William Riley *geology educator, planetary science educator*

Lincoln University
Roberts, Lynn Ernest *theoretical physicist, educator*

Media
Camarda, Harry Salvatore *physics educator, researcher*

Monroeville
Bortz, Alfred Benjamin *science and technology educator, writer*

New Wilmington
Long, Kenneth Maynard *chemistry educator*

Philadelphia
Conover, Thomas Ellsworth *biochemistry educator*
Hameka, Hendrik Frederik *chemist, educator*
Klein, Michael Lawrence *research chemist, educator*
Kritchevsky, David *biochemist, educator*
MacDiarmid, Alan Graham *metallurgist, educator*
Malamud, Daniel *biochemistry educator*
Mitchell, Glenn M. *chemistry researcher, educator*
Narasimhulu, Shakunthala *biochemist, educator*
Prairie, Celia Esther Freda *biochemistry educator*
Steinberg, Richard Ira *physics educator*
Takashima, Shiro *biophysics educator*
Tao, Rongjia *physicist, educator*

Pittsburgh
Berry, Guy Curtis *polymer science educator, researcher*
Griffiths, Robert Budington *physics educator*
Kumta, Prashant Nagesh *materials science educator, engineering educator, consultant*
Matyjaszewski, Krzysztof *chemist, educator*
Pezacka, Ewa Hanna *biochemist, educator*
Yates, John Thomas, Jr., *chemistry educator, research director*

Swarthmore
Bilaniuk, Oleksa Myron *physicist, educator*

University Park
Allcock, Harry R. *chemistry educator*
Hardy, Henry Reginald, Jr., *physicist, educator*
Howell, Benjamin Franklin, Jr., *geophysicist, educator*
Komarneni, Sridhar *mineralogist, educator*
Song, Chunshan *chemist, chemical engineer, educator*

Waynesburg
Maguire, Mildred May *chemistry educator, magnetic resonance researcher*

RHODE ISLAND

Providence
Briant, Clyde Leonard *metallurgist, educator*
Greene, Edward Forbes *chemistry educator*
Lanou, Robert Eugene, Jr., *physicist, educator*
Levin, Frank S. *physicist, educator*
Rieger, Philip Henri *chemistry educator, researcher*
Stratt, Richard Mark *chemistry researcher, educator*
Tauc, Jan *physics educator*
Webb, Thompson *geological sciences educator, researcher*
Widgoff, Mildred *physicist, educator*

SOUTH CAROLINA

Aiken
Pirkle, William Arthur *geologist, educator*

Anderson
Molz, Fred John, III, *hydrologist, educator*

Charleston
Adelman, Saul Joseph *astronomy educator, researcher*
Coombs, Cassandra Runyon *geologist, educator*

Clemson
Krause, Lois Ruth Breur *chemistry educator*

Columbia
Paleologos, Evangelos *hydrologist, educator*
Preedom, Barry Mason *physicist, educator*

Rock Hill
Maheswaranathan, Ponn *physicist, educator, physicist, researcher*

TENNESSEE

Chattanooga
Gaudin, Timothy J. *paleontologist, biology educator*

Cookeville
Kumar, Krishna *retired physics educator*
Swartling, Daniel Joseph *chemistry educator, researcher*

Johnson City
McIntosh, Cecilia Ann *biochemist, educator*

Knoxville
Wunderlich, Bernhard *physical chemistry educator*

Lenoir City
Huheey, James Edward *chemist, herpetologist and educator*

Memphis
Dass, Chhabil *chemistry educator*
Fain, John Nicholas *biochemistry educator*
Lasslo, Andrew *medicinal chemist, educator*

Nashville
Hall, Douglas Scott *astronomy educator*
Hamilton, Joseph Hants, Jr., *physicist, educator*
Inagami, Tadashi *biochemist, educator*
Lukehart, Charles Martin *chemistry educator*

TEXAS

Arlington
Cuntz, Manfred *astrophysicist, researcher, educator*
Reaser, Donald Frederick *retired geology educator*
Willoughby, Sarah-Margaret C. *chemist, educator, chemical engineer, consultant*

Austin
Bash, Frank Ness *astronomer, educator*
Boggs, James Ernest *chemistry educator*
Folk, Robert Louis *geologist, educator*
Lundelius, Ernest Luther, Jr., *vertebrate paleontologist, educator*
Maxwell, Arthur Eugene *oceanographer, marine geophysicist, educator*
Reed, Lester James *biochemist, educator*
Sprinkle, James Thomas *paleontologist, educator*
Stewart, Kent Kallam *analytical biochemistry educator*
Swinney, Harry Leonard *physics educator*
Udagawa, Takeshi *physicist, educator*

Brenham
French, Kenneth Alfred *chemistry educator*

Brownsville
Tijerina, Raul Martin *physics and mathematics educator*

College Station
Eaton, Gordon Pryor *geologist, consultant*
McIntyre, Peter Mastin *physicist, educator*

Dallas
Bracks, Oscar, Jr., *physician, educator, nuclear chemist*
Cottam, Gene Larry *biochemistry educator*

Denton
Johnson, Mary Lynn *chemistry educator, consultant*
Saleh, Farida Yousry *chemistry educator*

El Paso
Wang, Paul Weily *materials science and physics educator*

Galveston
Bonchev, Danail Georgiev *chemist, educator*
Gorenstein, David G. *chemistry and biochemistry educator*

Houston
Askew, William Earl *chemist, educator*
Baker, Stephen Denio *physics educator*
Bennett, George Nelson *biochemistry educator*
Brooks, Philip Russell *chemistry educator, researcher*
Capuano, Regina Marie *hydrogeologist, geochemist educator*
Dasgupta, Amitava *chemist, educator*
De Bremaecker, Jean-Claude *geophysics educator*
Kinsey, James Lloyd *chemist, educator*
Lane, Neal Francis *physics educator, former government official*
Liang, Edison Parktak *astrophysicist, educator, researcher*
Margrave, John Lee *chemist, educator, university administrator*
Matthews, Kathleen Shive *biochemistry educator*
Reiff, Patricia Hofer *space physicist, educator*
Rudolph, Frederick Byron *biochemistry educator*
Sisson, Virginia Baker *geology educator*
Weinstein, Roy *physics educator, researcher*
Yang, Chao Yuh *chemistry educator*

Hurst
Benge, Raymond Doyle, Jr., *astronomy educator*

Laredo
Coats, Charles F. *physics and mathematics educator*

Plano
Broyles, Michael Lee *geophysics and physics educator*

Richardson
Rutford, Robert Hoxie *geologist, educator*
Urquhart, Sally Ann *environmental scientist, chemist, educator*

San Antonio
Ball, M(ary) Isabel *chemistry educator, dean*
Budalur, Thyagarajan Subbanarayan *chemistry educator*
Sutherland, Berry *geologist, educator*
Tsin, Andrew Tsang Cheung *cell biology and biochemistry researcher*
Walmsley, Judith Abrams *chemistry educator*

Seguin
Scheie, Paul Olaf *physics educator*

Southlake
Herrmann, Debra McGuire *chemist, educator*

Temple
Coulter, John Breitling, III, *biochemist, educator*

Vernon
Roberson, Mark Allen *physicist, educator*

UTAH

North Logan
Sunderland, Norman Ray (Norm Sunderland) *health physicist, nuclear engineer educator*

Orem
Benson, Alvin K. *physicist, geophysicist, consultant, educator*

Salt Lake City
Ernst, Richard Dale *chemistry educator*
Facelli, Julio Cesar *physics researcher, university administrator*
Miller, Jan Dean *metallurgy educator*
Olson, Ferron Allred *metallurgist, educator*
Parry, Robert Walter *chemistry educator*

VERMONT

Burlington
Wu, Junru *physics educator*

VIRGINIA

Alexandria
Goldstein, Jeffrey Jay *astrophysicist, educator*

Arlington
Dorman, Craig Emery *oceanographer, academic administrator*
Zirkind, Ralph *physicist, educator*

Charlottesville
Bloomfield, Louis Aub *physicist, educator*

Fairfax
Morowitz, Harold Joseph *biophysicist, educator*

Falls Church
Akkara, Joseph Augustine *chemist, educator*
Berg, Lillian Douglas *chemistry educator*

Gloucester Point
Schaffner, Linda Carol *biological oceanography educator*

Hampden Sydney
Joyner, Weyland Thomas *physicist, educator, business consultant*

Lexington
Spencer, Edgar Winston *geology educator*

Petersburg
Stronach, Carey Elliott *physicist, educator*

Radford
Whisonant, Robert Clyde *geology educator, scientist*

Richmond
Gipson, Jeffery *chemistry educator*

Roanoke
Al-Zubaidi, Amer Aziz *physicist, educator*

Salem
Fisher, Charles Harold *chemistry educator, researcher*

Williamsburg
Goodwin, Bruce Kesseli *retired geology educator, researcher*
Starnes, William Herbert, Jr., *chemist, educator*

WASHINGTON

Anacortes
Businger, Joost Alois *atmospheric scientist, educator*

HIGHER EDUCATION: PHYSICAL SCIENCES

Cheney
Whelton, Bartlett David *chemical and biochemical educator*

Ellensburg
Mitchell, Robert Curtis *physicist, educator*
Rosell, Sharon Lynn *physics and chemistry educator, researcher*

Pullman
Hinman, George Wheeler *physics educator*

Richland
Kouzes, Richard Thomas *physicist, educator*

Seattle
Andersen, Niels Hjorth *chemistry educator, biophysics researcher, consultant*
Anderson, Arthur G., Jr., *chemistry educator*
Baum, William Alvin *astronomer, educator*
Bodansky, David *physicist, educator*
Brown, Robert Alan *atmospheric science educator, research scientist*
Charlson, Robert Jay *atmospheric sciences educator, scientist*
Christian, Gary Dale *chemistry educator*
Dalton, Larry Raymond *chemistry educator, researcher, consultant*
Engel, Thomas *chemistry educator*
Evans, Bernard William *geologist, educator*
Fischer, Fred Walter *physicist, engineer, educator*
Fleagle, Robert Guthrie *meteorologist, educator*
Fortson, Edward Norval *physics educator*
Gerhart, James Basil *physics educator*
Gordon, Milton Paul *biochemist, educator*
Gouterman, Martin Paul *chemistry educator*
Hartmann, Dennis Lee *atmospheric science educator*
Henley, Ernest Mark *physics educator, university dean emeritus*
Hodge, Paul William *astronomer, educator*
King, Ivan Robert *astronomy educator*
Kwiram, Alvin L. *physical chemistry educator, university official*
Lord, Jere Johns *retired physics educator*
Lubatti, Henry Joseph *physicist, educator*
Rabinovitch, Benton Seymour *chemist, educator emeritus*
Reed, Richard John *retired meteorology educator*
Reinhardt, William Parker *chemical physicist, educator*
Stuiver, Minze *geological sciences educator*
Szkody, Paula *astronomy educator, researcher*
Thouless, David James *retired physicist, educator*

Spokane
Benson, Allen B. *chemist, educator, consultant*

Tacoma
Anderson, Charles Dean *chemistry educator*

Walla Walla
Wade, Leroy Grover, Jr., *chemistry educator*

WEST VIRGINIA

Huntington
Hubbard, John Lewis *chemist, educator, researcher*

WISCONSIN

Appleton
Cook, David Marsden *physics educator*

Cottage Grove
Hesse, Thurman Dale *welding and metallurgy educator, consultant*

La Crosse
Barmore, Frank Edward *physics educator*

Madison
Barger, Vernon Duane *physicist, educator*
Bentley, Charles Raymond *geophysics educator*
Churchwell, Edward Bruce *astronomer, educator*
Code, Arthur Dodd *astrophysics educator*
Cornwell, Charles Daniel *physical chemist, educator*
DeWerd, Larry Albert *medical physicist, educator*
Evenson, Merle Armin *chemist, educator*
Farrar, Thomas C. *chemist, educator*
Hokin, Lowell Edward *biochemist, educator*
Houghton, David Drew *meteorologist, educator*
Moore, John Ward *chemistry educator*
Skinner, James Lauriston *chemist, educator*
Wright, John Curtis *chemist, educator*

Menomonie
Richards, Hugh Taylor *physics educator*

Milwaukee
Baker, John Edward *cardiac biochemist, educator*
Karkheck, John Peter *physics educator, researcher*

Stoughton
Huber, David Lawrence *physicist, educator*

WYOMING

Laramie
Grandy, Walter Thomas, Jr., *physicist, educator*
Snoke, Arthur Wilmot *geology educator, researcher*

TERRITORIES OF THE UNITED STATES

PUERTO RICO

Mayaguez
Souto Bachiller, Fernando Alberto *chemistry educator*

CANADA

ALBERTA

Edmonton
Freeman, Gordon Russel *chemistry educator*
Harris, Walter Edgar *chemistry educator*
Kay, Cyril Max *biochemist, educator*
Sykes, Brian Douglas *biochemistry educator, researcher*

BRITISH COLUMBIA

Vancouver
Zakarauskas, Pierre *physicist, educator*

White Rock
Cooke, Herbert Basil Sutton *geologist, educator*

MANITOBA

Winnipeg
Barber, Robert Charles *physics educator*
Secco, Anthony Silvio *chemistry educator*

NOVA SCOTIA

Halifax
Jones, William Ernest *chemistry educator*

Wolfville
Bishop, Roy Lovitt *physics and astronomy educator*

ONTARIO

Guelph
Karl, Gabriel *physics educator*

Kingston
Szarek, Walter Anthony *chemist, educator*

London
Fyfe, William Sefton *geochemist, educator*

Mississauga
Percy, John Rees *astronomer, educator*

Ottawa
Kates, Morris *biochemist, educator*

Toronto
Packham, Marian Aitchison *biochemistry educator*

Waterloo
McBoyle, Geoffrey R. *geography educator*

QUEBEC

Montreal
Carignan, Claude *astronomer, educator*
Chan, Tak Hang *chemist, educator*
Michaud, Georges Joseph *astrophysics educator*

BELGIUM

Leuven
De Schryver, Frans Carl *chemistry educator*

FRANCE

Besancon
Boillat, Guy Maurice Georges *mathematical physicist*

Creteil
Renoux, André *physicist, educator*

Paris
Batamack, Patrice Theodore Desire *chemistry educator, researcher*

INDIA

Visakhapatnam
Kasipathi, Chinta *geologist, educator, consultant, researcher*

ISRAEL

Ariel
Meyerstein, Dan *college president, chemistry educator*

JAPAN

Suita
Akutsu, Hideo *biophysical chemist, educator*

NIGERIA

Port Harcourt, Post Office Choba
Ojinnaka, Chukwunonye Moses *chemistry educator*

POLAND

Gliwice
Soczkiewicz, Eugeniusz Stanisław *physicist, educator*

REPUBLIC OF KOREA

Pusan
Sung, Dae Dong *chemist, educator, dean*

ADDRESS UNPUBLISHED

Andersen, Hans Christian *chemistry educator*
Arbuckle-Keil, Georgia Ann *chemistry educator*
Arnett, Edward McCollin *chemistry educator, researcher*
Autin, Ernest Anthony, II, *chemist, educator, consultant*
Bartelt, John Eric *physics researcher and educator*
Bennett, William Ralph, Jr., *physicist, educator*
Betlach, Mary Carolyn *biochemist, molecular biologist*
Boudreau, Robert Donald *meteorology educator, retired*
Bundy, Hallie Flowers *biochemist, educator*
Carroll, Harvey Franklin *retired chemistry and nutrition educator*
Chu, Steven *physics educator*
Coletta, Nancy Joy *vision scientist, educator*
Cook, Desmond C. *physicist, educator, consultant*
Crabtree, Robert Howard *chemistry educator*
Curott, David Richard *physics educator*
Daves, Glenn Doyle, Jr., *science educator, chemist, researcher*
Devine, Katherine *environmental consultant, educator*
Earthman, James Calvin, Jr., *material sciences educator, consultant*
Epstein, Herman Theodore *biophysics educator*
Erlichson, Herman *physics educator*
Faber, Katherine Theresa *materials science educator*
Flynn, George William *chemistry educator, researcher*
Franz, Judy R. *physics educator*
Galli, John Ronald *physicist, educator*
Glesk, Ivan *physicist, educator, researcher*
Goldberger, Marvin Leonard *physicist, educator*
Goldfine, Howard *microbiology and biochemistry educator, researcher*
Griesé, John William, III, *astronomer, educator, mental health advocate*
Hall, Grace Rosalie *physicist, educator, writer*
Hardy, Ralph W. F. *biochemist, biotechnology executive*
Hemenway, Mary Kay *astronomer, educator*
Hibbs, Robert Andrews *analytical chemistry educator*
Ho, John Wing-Shing *biochemistry educator, researcher*
Ingle, James Chesney, Jr., *geology educator*
Kastner, Marc Aaron *physics educator*
Koster van Groos, August Ferdinand *geology educator*
Lederman, Leon Max *physicist, educator*
Levy, Gad *atmospheric scientist, educator, statistician*
Lightman, Alan Paige *writer, physicist, educator*
Lillegraven, Jason Arthur *paleontologist, educator*
Lingren, Wesley Earl *chemistry educator*
Loach, Paul Allen *biochemist, biophysicist, educator*
McKenna, Malcolm Carnegie *vertebrate paleontologist, curator, educator*
Mead, Kathryn Nadia *astrophysicist, educator*
Mendelson, Sol *physical science educator, consultant*
Mogil, H(arvey) Michael *meteorologist, educator*
Nagys, Elizabeth Ann *environmental issues educator*
Nevill, William Albert *chemistry educator*
Newton, Roger Gerhard *educator, physicist*
O'Brien, James Francis *chemistry educator*
Oort, Abraham Hans *meteorologist, researcher, educator*
Pytlinski, Jerzy Teodor *physicist, educator, research administrator*
Pytte, Agnar *physicist, former university president*
Rea, David K. *geology and oceanography researcher*
Richards, Paul Linford *physics educator, researcher*
Sehr, Sister Cecilia Anne *chemistry and physics educator*
Selbin, Joel *chemistry educator*
Setters, Paula Louise Henderson *physics educator*
Shockley, James Thomas *physics educator*
Sink, John Davis *chemist, clergyperson*
Stanley, George Dabney, Jr., *paleontology educator*
Steinlicht, Steven *astrologer, mystic, educator*
Stevenson, Paul Michael *physics educator, researcher*
Sullivan, Woodruff Turner, III, *astronomy educator, science historian, researcher, astrobiologist, gnomonicist*
Taylor, Hugh Pettingill, Jr., *geologist, educator*
Titus, Robert C. *geologist, educator*
Tubis, Arnold *physics educator*
Tuul, Johannes *physics educator, researcher*
Veronis, George *geophysicist, educator*
Vušković, Leposava *physicist, educator*
Wald, Francine Joy Weintraub (Mrs. Bernard J. Wald) *physicist, academic administrator*
Ward, Sandra June *physicist, researcher, educator*
Wellner, Marcel Nahum *physics educator, researcher*
Wilson, Kenneth Geddes *physics research administrator*
Zhou, Ming De *aeronautical scientist, educator*

HIGHER EDUCATION: SOCIAL SCIENCES

UNITED STATES

ALABAMA

Auburn
Whitten, David Owen *economics educator*

Birmingham
Morrisey, Michael A. *health economics educator*

Collinsville
Beasley, Mary Catherine *home economics educator, administrator, researcher*

Hartselle
Penn, Hugh Franklin, Jr., *psychology educator*

Huntsville
O'Reilly, Patty Mollett *psychometrist, consultant*

Montevallo
McChesney, Robert Michael, Sr., *political science educator*

Montgomery
Wendzel, Robert Leroy *political science educator*

Pell City
Passey, George Edward *psychology educator*

Phenix City
Greathouse, Patricia Dodd *retired psychometrist, counselor*

Tuscaloosa
Weaver, David *geography educator*

ALASKA

Anchorage
Fisher, Margaret Eleanor *psychologist, lawyer, arbitrator, mediator, educator*
Jones, Garth Nelson *business and public administration educator*
Obermeyer, Theresa Nangle *sociology educator*

Fairbanks
McBeath, Gerald Alan *political science educator, researcher*

ARIZONA

Gilbert
Metcalf, Virgil Alonzo *economics educator*

Green Valley
Leege, David Calhoun *political scientist, educator*

Phoenix
Beck, John Christen *sociologist, educator*
Lyon, William James *sociology educator*

Tempe
Montero, Darrel Martin *social worker, sociologist, educator*
Tracey, Terence John *psychology educator*
Uttal, William R(eichenstein) *psychology and engineering educator, research scientist*

Tucson
Berliner, David Charles
Snyder, Richard Gerald *research scientist, administrator, educator, consultant*

ARKANSAS

Fayetteville
Murray, Tracy *economics educator, consultant*
Purvis, Hoyt Hughes *political scientist, academic administrator, educator*

Jonesboro
Burns, John Luther *psychologist, educator*

Little Rock
Dykman, Roscoe Arnold *psychology educator*

Searcy
Hobby, Kenneth Lester *psychology educator*

CALIFORNIA

Bakersfield
Osterkamp, Dalene May *psychology educator, artist*

Berkeley
Breslauer, George William *political science educator*
Gilbert, Richard Joseph *economics educator*
Glenn, Evelyn Nakano *social sciences educator*
Hakansson, Nils Hemming *financial economics and accounting educator*
Jensen, Arthur Robert *psychology educator*
Keeler, Theodore Edwin *economics educator*
Lambert, Nadine Murphy *psychologist, educator*
Lee, Ronald Demos *demographer, economist, educator*
Letiche, John Marion *economist, educator*
McFadden, Daniel Little *economist, educator*
Norgaard, Richard Bruce *economist, educator, consultant*
Polsby, Nelson Woolf *political scientist, educator*
Quigley, John Michael *economist, educator*
Scotchmer, Suzanne Andersen *economics educator*
Shapiro, Carl *economics educator and consultant*
Ulman, Lloyd *retired social sciences educator*
Varian, Hal Ronald *economics educator*
Watts, Michael J. *geographer, educator*
Williamson, Oliver Eaton *economics and law educator*
Wolfinger, Raymond Edwin *political science educator*

Carlsbad
Fikes, Jay Courtney *anthropology educator, art dealer*

Claremont
Albaum, Jean Stirling *psychologist, educator*
Csikszentmihalyi, Mihaly *psychology educator*
Likens, James Dean *economics educator*

Costa Mesa
Coaty, Patrick Clark *social sciences educator*

Davis
Skinner, G(eorge) William *anthropologist, educator*

Fresno
O'Brien, John Conway *economist, educator, writer*

Healdsburg
Glad, Joan Bourne *retired clinical psychologist, educator*

Hermosa Beach
Wickwire, Patricia Joanne Nellor *psychologist, educator*

Irvine
Feldman, Martha Sue *political scientist, educator*
Huff, C(larence) Ronald *public policy and criminology educator*
Sperling, George *cognitive scientist, educator*

La Jolla
Cain, William Stanley *experimental psychologist, educator, researcher*
Coburn, Marjorie Foster *psychologist, educator*
Smith, Peter Hopkinson *political scientist, consultant, writer*

Laguna Beach
Dale, Leon Andrew *economist, educator*

Loma Linda
Betancourt, Hector Mainhard *psychology scientist, educator*

Los Altos
Carr, Jacquelyn B. *psychologist, educator*

Los Angeles
Acosta, Frank Xavier *psychologist, educator*
Arnold, Jeanne Eloise *anthropologist, educator*
Champagne, Duane Willard *sociology educator*
Dekmejian, Richard Hrair *political science educator*
Dosamantes-Beaudry, Irma *psychology educator*
Goldschmidt, Walter Rochs *anthropologist, educator*
La Force, James Clayburn, Jr., *economist, educator*
Landen, Sandra Joyce *psychologist, educator*
O'Neil, Harold Francis *psychologist, educator*
Raven, Bertram H(erbert) *psychology educator*
Sandler, Todd Michael *economist, educator, political scientist, educator*
Sears, David O'Keefe *psychology educator*
Wilcox, Rand Roger *psychology educator*

Lynwood
Avery, Ronald Dennis *school psychologist*

Madera
Glynn, James A. *sociology educator, author*

Malibu
Caldwell, Dan Edward *political science educator*

Menlo Park
Clair, Theodore Nat *educational psychologist*

Mill Valley
Harner, Michael James *anthropologist, educator, author*

Monterey
Boger, Dan Calvin *statistical and economic consultant, educator*

Monterey Park
Amezcua, Charlie Anthony *social science counselor*

Newhall
Sylvers, Arlene Marder *clinical psychologist*

Northridge
Harwick, Betty Corinne Burns *sociology educator*
Mitchell, Rie Rogers *psychologist, counselor, educator*

Oakland
Nathan, Laura E. *sociology educator*

Oceanside
Hertweck, Alma Louise *sociology and child development educator*
Hertweck, E. Romayne *psychology educator*

Orange
Booth, Donald Richard *economist, educator*

Pacific Palisades
Hoffenberg, Marvin *retired political science educator, consultant*

Palo Alto
Flanagan, Robert Joseph *economics educator*
Rosaldo, Renato Ignacio, Jr., *cultural anthropology educator*
Spangenberg, Ruth Beahrs *psychologist, educator*

Pasadena
Grether, David Maclay *economics educator*
Ledyard, John Odell *economics educator, consultant*
Scudder, Thayer *anthropologist, educator*

Placentia
Gobar, Alfred Julian *retired economic consultant, educator*

Pomona
Garrity, Rodman Fox *psychologist, educator*
Singer-Chang, Gail Leslie *social sciences educator, assistant dean for student affairs*

Rancho Cucamonga
Shields, Andrea Lyn *psychologist, educator*

Redondo Beach
McWilliams, Margaret Ann *home economics educator, author*
Naples, Caesar Joseph *law and public policy educator, lawyer, consultant*

Riverside
Calfee, Robert Chilton *psychologist, educational researcher*
Carpenter, Mark Warren *social sciences educator*
Rosenthal, Robert *psychology educator*
Turk, Austin Theodore *sociology educator*

Sacramento
Boylan, Richard John *psychologist, psychotherapist, researcher, anthropologist, educator*
Chapman, Loring *psychologist, physiology educator, neuroscientist*
Newland, Chester Albert *public administration educator*
Sherwood, Robert Petersen *retired sociology educator*

San Bernardino
Turpin, Joseph Ovila *counselor, educator*

San Clemente
Ditty, Marilyn Louise *gerontologist, educator*

San Diego
Berger, Bennett Maurice *sociology educator*
Blade, Melinda Kim *archaeologist, educator, researcher*
Heer, David Macalpine *sociology educator*
Hoston, Germaine Annette *political science educator*
Kiesler, Charles Adolphus *psychologist, academic administrator*

San Francisco
Butz, Otto William *political science educator*
Crittenden, Mary Rita *clinical psychology educator*
Warner, Rollin Miles, Jr., *economics educator, real estate broker*

Santa Barbara
Blum, Gerald Saul *psychologist, educator*
Davidson, Roger H(arry) *political scientist, educator*
Kendler, Howard H(arvard) *psychologist, educator*
Mack, Judith Cole Schrim *political scientist, educator*
Mayer, Richard Edwin *psychology educator*
Sherman, Alan Robert *psychologist, educator*

Santa Clara
Field, Alexander James *economics educator*

Santa Cruz
Pettigrew, Thomas Fraser *social psychologist, educator*
Pratkanis, Anthony Richard *social psychologist, educator*
Roby, Pamela Ann *sociology educator*
Rorer, Leonard George *psychologist, writer*
Tonay, Veronica Katherine *psychology educator*

Santa Monica
Wolf, Charles, Jr., *economist, educator*

Santa Rosa
Finley, Carmen Joyce *psychologist, former research administrator*

Somerset
Carr, Les *psychologist, educator*

Stanford
Arrow, Kenneth Joseph *economist, educator*
Damon, William Van Buren *developmental psychologist, educator, writer*
Enthoven, Alain Charles *economist, educator*
Fetterman, David Mark *anthropologist, education evaluator*
Fuchs, Victor Robert *economist, educator*
Hall, Robert Ernest *economics educator*
Holloway, David James *political science educator*
Krumboltz, John Dwight *psychologist, educator*
Lau, Lawrence Juen-Yee *economics educator, consultant*
Lazear, Edward Paul *economics and labor relations educator, researcher*
Lepper, Mark Roger *psychology educator*
Manley, John Frederick *political scientist, educator*
Noll, Roger Gordon *economist, educator*
Pearson, Scott Roberts *economics educator*
Roberts, Donald John *economics and business educator, consultant*
Scott, W(illiam) Richard *sociology educator*
Van Horne, James Carter *economist, educator*

Ventura
Bowles, Walter Donald *economist, educator*
Lipinski, Barbara Janina *psychologist, psychotherapist, educator, writer*

Victorville
Miller, David Julian *psychologist, educator*

Watsonville
Fobes, Jacqueline Theresa Mitchell *psychologist, educator*

COLORADO

Boulder
Linn, Robert Lee *educational researcher*
Owen-Riesch, Anna Lou *economics and history educator*
Zax, Jeffrey Stephen *economist, educator*

Colorado Springs
Standing Bear, Zugguelgeres Galafach *criminologist, forensic scientist, educator*

Denver
Delay, Eugene Raymond *psychologist, educator, researcher*
Kalamaros, Anastasia Ann *educational psychology educator*
Mills, Kathleen Claire *anthropology and mathematics educator*
Purcell, Kenneth *psychology educator, university dean*

Englewood
Make, Isabel Rose *multicultural studies educator, small business owner*

Littleton
Lohman, Loretta Cecelia *social scientist, consultant*

Nederland
Sutton, Philip D(ietrich) *psychologist, educator*

Pueblo
Alt, Betty L. *sociology educator*

CONNECTICUT

Branford
Blair, Harry Wallace *political science educator, consultant*

Fairfield
Meyer, Goldye W. *psychologist, educator*

Hartford
Behuniak, Peter *psychometrician, educational psychologist, educational consultant*

Milford
Haigh, Charles *criminal justice educator*

New Britain
Kim, Ki Hoon *economist, educator*

New Canaan
Thomas, Marianne Gregory *school psychologist*

New Haven
Alexander, Jeffrey Charles *sociology educator*
Brantl, Sister Charlesmarie *economics educator*
Brownell, Kelly David *psychologist, educator*
Chawarski, Marek Cezary *psychologist, researcher, educator*
Coe, Michael Douglas *anthropologist, educator*
Conklin, Harold Colyer *anthropologist, educator*
Dudley, Kathryn Marie *anthropology and American studies educator*
Ember, Melvin Lawrence *anthropologist, educator*
Hsiao, James Chingnu *economics educator*
Kaufman, Alan Stephen *psychologist, educator*
LaPalombara, Joseph *political science and industrial management educator*
Marks, Lawrence Edward *psychologist, educator*
Mayhew, David Raymond *political science educator*
McGuire, William James *social psychology educator*
Phillips, Peter Charles Bonest *economist, educator, researcher*
Ranis, Gustav *economist, educator*
Russett, Bruce Martin *political science educator*
Scarf, Herbert Eli *economics educator*
Schultz, T. Paul *economics educator*
Sternberg, Robert Jeffrey *psychology educator, researcher*
Sutterlin, James Smyrl *political science educator, researcher*
Westerfield, Holt Bradford *political scientist, educator*
Zigler, Edward Frank *psychologist, educator*

New London
Chrisler, Joan C. *psychologist, educator*

Norwalk
Rosado, Rodolfo Jose *psychologist, educator*

Salisbury
Bratter, Thomas Edward *psychologist, educator*

Storrs Mansfield
Brown, Scott Wilson *educational psychology educator*
Dewar, Robert Earl, Jr., *anthropologist, educator*
McEachern, William Archibald *economics educator*

Voluntown
Thevenet, Patricia Confrey *social studies educator*

DELAWARE

Dover
Bieker, Richard Francis *economics educator, consultant, program director*
Hoff, Samuel Boyer *political science educator*

Newark
Pika, Joseph A. *political scientist, educator, educational association administrator*
Scarpitti, Frank Roland *sociology educator*

Wilmington
Boston, Martha Bibee *psychologist, educator*

DISTRICT OF COLUMBIA

Washington
Adams, Arvil Van *economist, educator*
Albanese, Jay Samuel *criminologist, educator*
Arend, Anthony Clark *international relations educator*
Ashbrook, Arthur Garwood, Jr., *economist, educator*
Bergmann, Barbara Rose *economics educator*
Bloom-Feshbach, Sally *psychologist, educator*
Brzezinski, Zbigniew *political science educator, author*
Caldwell, Willard E. *psychologist, educator*
Charner, Ivan *educational sociologist*
Greenberg, Milton *political scientist, educator*
Kane, Michael Barry *social science research executive*
Keck, Lois T. *anthropology educator*
Kirkpatrick, Jeane Duane Jordan *political scientist, government official*
Lardy, Nicholas Richard *economist, educator*
LeoGrande, William Mark *political science educator, writer*
Lieber, Robert James *political science educator, writer*
Meepagala, Gaminie *economics educator*
Metz, Helen Chapin *retired Middle East analyst*
Miller, Margery Silberman *psychologist, speech pathologist, medical educator and administrator*
O'Connor, Karen *political science educator, researcher, writer*
Pasternack, Robert Harry *school psychologist*
Saunders, Mauderie Hancock *psychology educator*
Solomon, Elinor Harris *economics educator*
Steinberg, David Isaac *social sciences educator, consultant*
Whitehurst, Grover Jay *federal official, psychologist and educator*

FLORIDA

Coral Gables
Muller, Peter O. *geographer, educator*
Nijman, Jan *geographer, educator*

Fort Lauderdale
Collins, Ronald William *psychologist, educator*
Maxwell, Sara Elizabeth *psychologist, educator, speech pathologist, director*
Runo, Michael Joseph *psychologist, school system administrator*

Fort Myers
McDonald, Jacquelyn Milligan *parent and family studies educator*

Gainesville
Severy, Lawrence James *psychologist, educator*
von Mering, Otto Oswald *anthropology educator*
Wass, Hannelore Lina *educational psychology educator*

Jacksonville
Brady, James Joseph *economics educator*
Coffin, Bonnie Breanne *home economist, educator*
Ejimofor, Cornelius Ogu *political scientist, educator*
Libby, Ronald Theodore *political science educator, consultant, researcher*

Juno Beach
Penn, Sherry Eve *communication psychologist, educator*

Lakeland
Ratliff, Charles Edward, Jr., *economics educator*

Miami
Boyle, Judith Pullen *clinical psychologist, educator*
Chalfin, Susan Rose *psychologist, educator*
Fuertes, Raul A. *psychologist, educator*
Gamarra, Eduardo A. *political scientist, educator*
Humphries, Joan Ropes *psychologist, educator*
Salazar-Carrillo, Jorge *economics educator*

Ocala
Grissom, Robert Jesse, Sr., *criminal justice educator*

Ormond Beach
Boyle, Susan Jean Higle *social studies educator*

Palm City
Whichello, Carol *political scientist, educator, writer*

Palm Harbor
Eberts, John Jacob *social science educator, department chair*

Pensacola
Kernstock, Elwyn Nicholas *political science educator, author*

Saint Augustine
Armstrong, John Alexander *political scientist, educator*

Sarasota
Cramer, Stanley Howard *psychology educator, author*
Masters, John Christopher *psychologist, educator, writer*
Serrie, Hendrick *retired anthropology and international business educator*

Tallahassee
Benson, Bruce Lowell *economics educator*
Joiner, Thomas *psychology educator*
Serow, William John *economics educator*
Thompson, Gregory Lee *social sciences educator*
Whitney, Glayde Dennis *psychologist, educator, geneticist*

Tampa
Brady, Kathleen Deming *psychologist, occupational therapist, educator*
DeMarie, Darlene *psychology educator*
Jreisat, Jamil Elias *public administration and political science educator, consultant*
MacManus, Susan Ann *political science educator, researcher*
Mellish, Gordon Hartley *economist, educator*
Spielberger, Charles Donald *psychology educator, behavioral medicine, clinical and health psychologist*
Tykot, Robert Howard *social sciences educator, archaeologist*
Vanden, Harry Edwin *political science educator*

Venice
Cline, Paul Charles *political science educator, state legislator*

GEORGIA

Americus
Kooti, John G. *economist, educator*

Athens
Allsbrook, Ogden Olmstead, Jr., *retired economics educator*
Berger, Jane Mauldin *psychologist, educator*
Bullock, Charles Spencer, III, *political science educator, author, consultant*
Parker, Keith Dwight *sociology educator*
Pollack, Robert Harvey *psychology educator*
Turner, Steven Cornell *agricultural economics educator*

Atlanta
Endicott, John Edgar *international relations educator*
Frazer, Ricardo Amando *psychology educator*
Garland, LaRetta Matthews *nursing educator*
Kanfer, Ruth *psychologist, educator*
Knapp, Charles Boynton *economist, educator, university president*
Levy, Daniel *economics educator*
Thomas, Peter Charles *psychology educator*
Tillman, Mary Norman *urban affairs consultant*
Waugh, William Lee, Jr., *political science educator*

Carrollton
Aanstoos, Christopher Michael *psychology educator*

College Park
Ford, Vandelette *mental health educator*

Dahlonega
Friedman, Barry David *political scientist, educator*

Decatur
Bockwitz, Cynthia Lee *psychologist, psychology and women's studies educator*

Demorest
Vance, Cynthia Lynn *psychology educator*

Evans
Zachert, Virginia *psychologist, educator*

Fort Valley
Chandras, Kananur V. *psychology educator*

Kennesaw
Frank, Mary Lou Bryant *psychologist, educator*
Ziegler, Christine Bernadette *psychology educator, consultant*

Milledgeville
Isaac, Walter Lon *psychology educator*

Rome
Black, Suzanne Watkins DuPuy *psychology educator*

Savannah
Strauser, Edward B. *psychologist, educator*

Statesboro
Henry, Nicholas Llewellyn *public administration educator*
Lloyd, Margaret Ann *psychologist, educator*

Stockbridge
Grimes, Richard Allen *economics educator*

Union City
Croom, Beverly Jo *social science educator, retired*

Valdosta
Diamond, Pollyann Joyce Kirk *psychologist*

HAWAII

Hilo
Dixon, Paul William *psychology educator*

Honolulu
Au, Kathryn Hu-pei *educational psychologist*
Ishikawa-Fullmer, Janet Satomi *psychologist, educator*
Laney, Leroy Olan *economist, banker, educator*
Ogawa, Dennis Masaaki *American studies educator*

IDAHO

Boise
Caskey, Owen LaVerne *retired psychology educator*

Caldwell
Lonergan, Wallace Gunn *economics educator, management consultant*

ILLINOIS

Carbondale
Trescott, Paul Barton *economics educator*

Champaign
Gold, Paul Ernest *psychology educator, behavioral neuroscience educator*
Grinols, Earl Leroy, III, *economist, educator*
Lewis, R. Barry *archaeology educator*
Scott, Anna Marie Porter Wall *sociology educator*
Sprenkle, Case Middleton *economist, educator*

Charleston
Price, Dalias Adolph *geography educator*
Smith, Betty Elaine *geography educator*

Chicago
Anthony-Perez, Bobbie Cotton Murphy *psychology educator, researcher*
Becker, Gary Stanley *economist, educator*
Becker, Geraldine Ann *psychology educator*
Bidwell, Charles Edward *sociologist, educator*
Coase, Ronald Harry *economist, educator*
Fogel, Robert William *economist, educator, historian*
Harris, Chauncy Dennison *geographer, educator*
Kennedy, Eugene Cullen *psychology educator, writer*
Larson, Allan Louis *political scientist, educator, lay church worker*
Laumann, Edward Otto *sociology educator*
Lincoln, Bruce Kenneth *anthropology and history of religions educator*
Lipson, Charles Henry *political scientist, educator*
Lucas, Robert Emerson, Jr., *economist, educator*
Miller, Laura Ann *linguistic anthropologist, educator*
Moretti, Robert James *psychologist, educator*
Morewitz, Stephen John *behavioral scientist, consultant, educator*
Myerson, Roger Bruce *economist, game theorist, educator*
Newman, Amy Suzanne *psychologist, educator*
Nicholas, Ralph Wallace W. *anthropology educator*
Rosen, George *economist, educator*
Sah, Raaj *economist, advisor, educator*
Sanders, Jacquelyn Seevak *psychologist, educator*
Schwartz, Eliezer Lazar *psychologist, educator*
Shaw, Michael Lee *social studies educator*
Simons, Helen *school psychologist, psychotherapist, educator*
Simpson, Dick Weldon *political science educator*
Stocking, George Ward, Jr., *anthropology educator*
Sumner, William Marvin *anthropology and archaeology educator*
Sween, Joyce Ann *psychologist, evaluation methodologist*

Coal City
Vigna, Dean Joseph *social studies educator*

Darien
Klassek, Christine Paulette *behavioral scientist*

Dekalb
Lippold, Neal William *criminal justice educator*

Edwardsville
Lin, Steven An-Yhi *economics educator, consultant*

Evanston
Bienen, Henry Samuel *political science educator, university executive*
Braeutigam, Ronald Ray *economics educator*
Brown, James Allison *anthropology educator*
Gordon, Robert James *economics educator*
Mills, Edwin Smith *economics educator*
Mineka, Susan *psychology educator*
Moskos, Charles C. *sociology educator*

Galesburg
McAndrew, Francis Thomas *psychology educator*

Glen Ellyn
Frateschi, Lawrence Jan *economist, statistician, educator*

Glencoe
Warren, Elizabeth Curran *retired political science educator*

Huntley
Saporta, Jack *psychologist, educator*

Joliet
Holmgren, Myron Roger *social sciences educator*

Lockport
McIntyre, John Andrew *environmental and economic planner, geography educator*

Naperville
Galvan, Mary Theresa *economics and business educator*

Norridge
Berg, Evelynne Marie *geography educator*

Oak Park
Goldberg, Steven Edward *history and philosophy educator*

Palos Park
Peckenpaugh, Donald Hugh *psychologist, consultant, writer*

Peoria
Deissler, Janice Kay *home economics educator*

Rockford
Longhenry, John Charles *social studies educator, human resources specialis*

Saint Charles
Osowiec, Darlene Ann *clinical psychologist, educator, consultant*

Springfield
Phillips, John Robert *political scientist, educator*

Urbana
Baer, Werner *economist, educator*
Cunningham, Clark Edward *anthropology educator*
Gabriel, Michael *psychology educator*
Rich, Robert F. *law and political science educator*
Wei, Tam Dang *mental health specialist, educator*

Wheaton
Allen, Henry Lee *sociology educator, consultant*

INDIANA

Bloomington
Beckwith, Christopher Irving *social sciences educator, writer, composer*
DeWeese, Devin A. *history educator*
Hunt, Kevin Dean *anthropologist, educator*
Ingersoll, Gary Michael *educational psychologist*
Kane, Stephanie C. *social anthropologist, educator*
Moran, Emilio Federico *anthropology and ecology educator*
O'Meara, Patrick O. *political science educator*
Patrick, John Joseph *social sciences educator*
Risinger, C. Frederick *social studies educator*
Stryker, Sheldon *sociologist, educator*

Evansville
Barber, Charles Turner *political science educator*

Indianapolis
Namjoshi, Madhav *economist, educator*
Tomlinson, Susan Wingfield *social studies educator*

Lafayette
Schweickert, Richard Justus *psychologist, educator*

Muncie
Meyer, Fred Albert, Jr., *political science educator*
Warrner, Robert Andrew *social studies educator*

Notre Dame
Arnold, Peri Ethan *political scientist*
Bartell, Ernest *economist, educator, priest*

Despres, Leo Arthur *sociology and anthropology educator, academic administrator*
Dowty, Alan Kent *political scientist, educator*
Hallinan, Maureen Theresa *sociologist, educator*
Swartz, Thomas R. *economist, educator*
Walshe, Aubrey Peter *political science educator*

Ridgeville
Church, Jay Kay *psychologist, educator*

West Lafayette
Connor, John Murray *agricultural economics educator*
Gruen, Gerald Elmer *psychologist, educator*
Jagacinski, Carolyn Mary *psychology educator*
Knudsen, Dean DeWayne *sociology educator*
McGee, Reece Jerome *sociology educator emeritus*

IOWA

Ames
Brown, Frederick Gramm *psychology educator*
Harl, Neil Eugene *economist, lawyer, educator*

Dubuque
Jorgensen, Gerald Thomas *psychologist, educator, lawyer*

Grinnell
Caulkins, David Douglas *anthropology educator*

Iowa City
Block, Robert I. *psychologist, researcher, educator*
Forsythe, Robert Elliott *economics educator*
Fuller, John Williams *economics educator*
Hudson, John Boswell *sociologist, educator*
Kim, Chong Lim *political science educator*
Shannon, Lyle William *sociology educator*

Johnston
Boyle, John Daniel *school psychologist*

La Porte City
Wigg, Bruce Jay *social studies educator*

Mason City
Rosenberg, Dale Norman *retired psychology educator*

KANSAS

Emporia
Catlett, Robert Bishop *economics educator*

Larned
Strong, Mayda Nel *psychologist, educator*

Lawrence
Heller, Francis H(oward) *law and political science educator emeritus*

Lenexa
Ashe, Maude Llewellyn *home economics educator*

Lindsborg
Pierce, Gregory Lee *criminal justice educator*

Manhattan
Babcock, Michael Ward *economics educator*
Barkley, Andrew Paul *economics educator*
Kromm, David Elwyn *geography educator*
Murray, John Patrick *psychologist, educator, researcher*
Parish, Thomas Scanlan *human development educator*
Richter, William Louis *social sciences educator*
Thomas, Lloyd Brewster *economics educator*

Overland Park
Burger, Henry G. *vocabulary scientist, anthropologist, publisher*

Shawnee Mission
Gaar, Marilyn Audrey Wiegraffe *political scientist, educator, property manager*

KENTUCKY

Covington
Littleton, Nan Elizabeth Feldkamp *psychologist, educator*

Eddyville
Cooley-Parker, Sheila Leanne *psychologist, consultant, educator*

Independence
Hopgood, James F. *anthropologist, educator*

Lexington
Hultman, Charles William *economics educator*
Stilwell, William Earle, III, *psychology educator, retired military officer*

Louisville
Edgell, Stephen Edward *psychology educator, statistical consultant*

Richmond
Wright, Virginia Baxter *retired economics educator*

LOUISIANA

Baton Rouge
Cook, Timothy Edwin *political science educator*

Lake Charles
Middleton, George, Jr., *clinical child psychologist*

New Orleans
Balée, William L. *anthropology educator*
Brazier, Mary Margaret *psychology educator, researcher*
Izawa, Chizuko *psychologist, researcher*
Sarpy, Sue Ann Corell *environmental health sciences educator*
Taras, Raymond Casimer *political science educator*
Wolf, Thomas Mark *psychologist, educator*

Ruston
Sale, Tom S., III, *financial economist*

Shreveport
Gwin, Dorothy Jean Bird *psychology educator, college dean*
Pederson, William David *political scientist, educator*

MAINE

Brunswick
Beitz, Charles R. *political scientist, educator*

Kittery Point
Howells, William White *anthropology educator*

Lewiston
Kessler, Mark Allen *political scientist, educator*

Mount Desert
Elias, Merrill Francis *behavioral/cardiovascular epidemiology researcher*

Sargentville
Anderson, Janet Stettbacher *home economics educator*

South China
MacFarland, Mary Harris *home economics educator*

MARYLAND

Annapolis
Brann, Eva Toni Helene *archaeology educator*
Gurr, Ted Robert *political science educator, author*

Baltimore
Bucher, Richard David *sociology educator*
Cooper, Joseph *political scientist, educator*
Desoto, Clinton Burgel *psychologist, educator*
Dietze, Gottfried *political science educator*
Entwisle, Doris Roberts *sociology educator*
Green, Bert Franklin, Jr., *psychologist*
Howard, J. Woodford, Jr., *political science educator*
Hunt, Wayne Philip *psychologist, educator*
Karni, Edi *economics educator*
Kohn, Melvin L. *sociologist*
Laopodis, Nikifords-Themistocles *economic and business educator*
Maccini, Louis John *economic educator*
Mintz, Sidney Wilfred *anthropologist*
Money, John William *psychologist, educator*
Rose, Hugh *retired economics educator*
Stanley, Julian Cecil, Jr., *psychology educator*
Takacs, Wendy Emery *economics educator*
Young, Hobart Peyton *economist, mathematician, educator*

Bethesda
Duncan, Constance Catharine *psychologist, educator, researcher*
Guadagno, Mary Ann Noecker *social scientist, consultant*

Chestertown
McKillop, Kevin James, Jr., *psychology educator*

Chevy Chase
Linowes, David Francis *political economist, educator, corporate executive*

College Park
Dill, Bonnie Thornton *sociology educator*
Goode, B. Erich *sociologist, educator, retired criminologist*
Quester, George Herman *political science educator*
Schwedler, Jillian Marie *political science educator*
Sperling, Mindy Toby *social sciences and bilingual education educator*

Columbia
May, John Raymond *clinical psychologist*

Hagerstown
Thomas, Yvonne Shirey *family and consumer science educator*

Lutherville
Chait, Andrea Melinda *school psychologist*

Lutherville Timonium
Richmond, Lee Joyce *psychologist, educator*

Perryville
Thompson, Tracy Marie *social studies educator*

Potomac
Rotberg, Iris Comens *social scientist*
Wonnacott, Paul *economics educator*

Rockville
Niewiaroski, Trudi Osmers (Gertrude Niewiaroski) *social studies educator*

Saint Marys City
Hopkins, James Roy *psychology educator*

Wheaton
Ghosh, Arun Kumar *economics, social sciences and accounting educator*

MASSACHUSETTS

Amherst
Keen, Rachel *psychology educator*
Mills, Patricia Jagentowicz *political philosophy educator, writer*
Woodbury, Richard Benjamin *anthropologist, educator*

Beverly
Arnold, Gordon B. *social science educator*

Boston
Amy-Moreno de Toro, Angel Alberto *social sciences educator, writer, oral historian*
Buckner, John Crawford *psychologist, educator*
Dimmitt, Cornelia *psychologist, educator*
Gamst, Frederick Charles *social anthropologist*
Hammond, Norman David Curle *archaeology educator, researcher*
Manning, Peter Kirby *sociologist educator*
Newhouse, Joseph Paul *economist, educator*
O'Hern, Jane Susan *psychologist, educator*
Psathas, George *sociologist, educator*
Rossell, Christine Hamilton *political science educator*

Braintree
Salloway, Josephine Plovnick *psychologist, marriage and family therapist, mental health counselor, psychology educator, college counselor*

Bridgewater
Holton, Susan A. *psychology educator*

Brockton
O'Farrell, Timothy James *psychologist, educator*

Cambridge
Abt, Clark C. *social scientist, executive, engineer, publisher, educator*
Alt, James Edward *political science educator*
Bailyn, Lotte *psychology and management educator*
Campbell, John Young *economics educator*
Caramazza, Alfonso *psychology educator*
Dominguez, Jorge Ignacio *government educator*
Drago-Severson, Eleanor Elizabeth E. *developmental psychologist, educator, researcher*
Eckaus, Richard Samuel *economist, educator*
Feldstein, Martin Stuart *economist, educator*
Fisher, Franklin Marvin *economist*
Friedman, Benjamin Morton *economics educator*
Hardacre, Helen *university professor*
Johnson, Willard Raymond *political science educator, consultant*
Kagan, Jerome *psychologist, educator*
Kosslyn, Stephen M. *psychologist educator*
Laibson, David Isaac *economist, educator*
Langer, Ellen Jane *psychologist, educator, writer*
Mitten, David Gordon *classical archaeologist*
Moore, Sally Falk *anthropology educator*
Perkins, Dwight Heald *economics educator*
Rathjens, George William *political scientist, educator*
Rayman, Paula M. *economics educator*
Rogoff, Kenneth Saul *economics educator*
Siegel, Abraham J. *economics educator, academic administrator*
Taymor, Betty *political science educator*
Temin, Peter *economist, educator*
Viscusi, W(illiam) G. Kip *economics educator*
Weston, Kath *anthropology educator*
Whyte, Martin King *sociology and Chinese studies educator*
Zinberg, Dorothy Shore *science policy educator*

Chestnut Hill
Carfora, John Michael *economics educator, academic administrator*
Chester, Nia Lane *psychology educator*

Falmouth
Davidson, Florence Hickman *clinical psychologist, education consultant*

Framingham
Tischler, Henry Ludwig *sociology educator*

Haydenville
Shallcross, Doris Jane *creative behavioral educator*

Lexington
Chaskelson, Marsha Ina *neuropsychologist*
Collins, Allan Meakin *cognitive scientist, psychologist, educator*
Jordan, Judith Victoria *clinical psychologist, educator*
Papanek, Gustav Fritz *economist, educator*
Thernstrom, Abigail (Mann) *political scientist*

Lowell
Galizzi, Monica *economics educator*

Medford
Conklin, John Evan *sociology educator*
DeBold, Joseph Francis *psychology educator*
Luria, Zella Hurwitz *psychology educator*

Needham
Wegner, Kenneth Walter *psychology educator*

Newton
Murphy, Bianca Cody *psychology educator*

Newton Center
Adams, F. Gerard *economist, educator*

North Dartmouth
Barrow, Clyde Wayne *political scientist, educator*

Truro
Holt, Robert Rutherford *clinical psychology educator*

Waltham
Cecchetti, Stephen Giovanni *economics educator*
Flynn, Patricia Marie *economics educator*

Whitinsville
Plaud, Joseph Julian *psychology educator*

Williamstown
Cramer, Phebe *psychologist*
Crider, Andrew Blake *psychologist*
Solomon, Paul Robert *neuropsychologist, educator*

Worcester
Dyer-Cole, Pauline *school psychologist, educator*
Mathisen, Howard *psychologist, minister*
Upshur, Carole Christofk *psychologist, educator*

MICHIGAN

Ann Arbor
Arlinghaus, Sandra Judith Lach *mathematical geographer, educator*
Brace, C. Loring *anthropologist, educator*
Brown, Donald Robert *psychology educator*
Cohen, Malcolm Stuart *economist, business executive*
Courant, Paul Noah *economist, educator, academic administrator*
Eccles, Jacquelynne S. *psychology educator*
Haefner, Don Paul *retired psychology educator*
Hoffman, Lois Wladis *psychologist, educator*
House, James Stephen *social psychologist, educator*
Howrey, Eugene Philip *economics educator, consultant*
Jackson, James Sidney *psychology educator*
Kestenbaum, Lawrence *political science educator*
Kingdon, John Wells *political science educator*
Krahmalkov, Charles Richard *social sciences educator*
Markovits, Andrei Steven *political science educator*
Mizruchi, Mark Sheldon *sociology and business administration educator*
Parsons, Jeffrey Robinson *anthropologist, educator*
Shapiro, Matthew David *economist, educator*
Singer, J. David *political science educator*
Smith, Dean Gordon *economist, educator*
Stevenson, Harold William *psychology educator*
Tropman, John Elmer *social sciences educator*
Weisskopf, Thomas Emil *economics educator*
Whitman, Marina Von Neumann *economist, educator*

Auburn Hills
Etefia, Florence Victoria *school psychologist*

Big Rapids
Ball, Richard Everett *sociology educator*

Clifford
Staples, Lynne Livingston Mills *retired psychologist, educator, consultant*

Detroit
Shantz, Carolyn Uhlinger *psychology educator*

East Lansing
Finifter, Ada Weintraub *political scientist, educator*
Karon, Bertram Paul *psychologist, educator*
Lang, Marvel *urban affairs educator*
Manderscheid, Lester Vincent *agricultural economics educator*
Obst, Norman Philip *economist, educator*
Woodbury, Stephen Abbott *economics educator*

Farmington
Blum, Eleanor Goodfriend *social sciences educator*

Flint
Wall, Harriet Marie *psychology educator*

Grand Rapids
Yamazaki, Makoto *economics educator*

Harbor Springs
Ketcham, Warren Andrew *psychologist, educator*

Holland
Holmes, Jack Edward *political science educator*

Houghton
Reynolds, Terry Scott *social science educator*

Iron Mountain
Doehr, Ruth Nadine *home economics educator*

Kalamazoo
Sichel, Werner *economics educator*

Lansing
Heater, William Henderson *retired psychology educator*

Saint Clair Shores
Vogel, Sally Thomas *psychologist, social worker, educator*

Sault Sainte Marie
Johnson, Gary Robert *political scientist*

Ypsilanti
Blackwell, Thomas T. *leadership educator, consultant*
Friedman, Monroe *psychologist, educator*

MINNESOTA

Eden Prairie
Schaeffer, Brenda Mae *psychologist, author*

Edina
Gottesman, Irving Isadore *psychology educator*

Minneapolis
Bouchard, Thomas Joseph, Jr., *psychology educator, researcher*
Chipman, John Somerset *economist, educator*
Hansen, Jo-Ida Charlotte *psychology educator, researcher*
Johnson, Badri Nahvi *sociology educator, real estate business owner*
Kudrle, Robert Thomas *economist, educator*
Lewis, Stephen Richmond, Jr., *economist, educator, academic administrator*
Macmillan, Ross *sociology educator*
Mohring, Herbert *economics educator*
Nightingale, Edmund Joseph *clinical psychologist, educator*
Scoville, James Griffin *economics educator*
Ysseldyke, James Edward *psychology educator, dean*

Moorhead
Trainor, John Felix *retired economics educator*

Morris
Bina, Cyrus *economist, poet*

Rochester
Taylor, Jeffrey Lee *political science educator, author*

Round Lake
Spillers, Betsy Rose *history educator*

Saint Cloud
Frank, Stephen Ira *political science educator*
Tripp, Luke Samuel *educator*

Saint Paul
Fulton, Robert Lester *sociology educator*
Lanegran, David Andrew *geography educator*
Meissner, Ann Loring *psychologist, educator*

Saint Peter
Mc Rostie, Clair Neil *economics educator*

Upsala
Piasecki, David Alan *social studies educator*

Winona
Holm, Joy Alice *psychology educator, goldsmith, artist, art educator*

MISSISSIPPI

Clarksdale
Cline, Beth Marie *school psychologist*

Indianola
Gary, Toni Berryhill *psychology educator, psychotherapist*

Lorman
Kim, Young Jeh *political science educator*

Mississippi State
Wall, Diane Eve *political science educator*

Tupelo
Witty, Thomas Ezekiel, III, *psychologist, researcher*

University
Bomba, Anne Killingsworth *family relations and child development educator*

MISSOURI

Bolivar
Hood, Michael Lee *psychologist, clinical researcher, educator*

Columbia
Biddle, Bruce Jesse *social psychologist, educator*
Eastman, Harold Dwight *retired social studies educator, journalist*
Salter, Christopher Lord *geography educator*
Yarwood, Dean Lesley *political science educator*

Fayette
Carter, John Jefferson *government educator, author*

Florissant
Debo, Geraldine Virginia *social studies educator*

Fulton
Jefferson, Kurt Wayne *political science educator*

Jefferson City
Holland, Antonio Frederick *social and behavioral science educator*

Kansas City
Jagtiani, Julapa A. *economist, educator*

Lees Summit
Rethemeyer, Robert John *social studies educator*

Rolla
Haemmerlie, Frances Montgomery *psychology educator, consultant*

Saint Joseph
Boor, Myron Vernon *psychologist, educator*

Saint Louis
Berndt, Clarence Fredrick, Jr., *social studies educator*
De Voe, Pamela Ann *anthropologist, educator*
Greenbaum, Stuart I. *economist, educator*
Leven, Charles Louis *economics educator*
Lindsey, Linda Lee *sociology educator*
O'Connell, Daniel Craig *psychology educator*
Sargent, Lyman Tower *political science educator, academic administrator*
Smith, Arthur E. *counseling educator, vocational psychologist*
Swiener, Rita Rochelle *psychologist, educator*
Thompson, Vetta Lynn Sanders *psychologist, educator*
Weidenbaum, Murray Lew *economist, educator*

Springfield
Smith, Donald L. *social sciences educator*

Urbana
Frey, Lucille Pauline *social studies educator, consultant*

Warrensburg
Kemp, Arthur Derek *psychology educator*

MONTANA

Bozeman
Block, Richard Atten *psychology educator*
Gray, Philip Howard *former psychologist, writer, educator*

NEBRASKA

Lincoln
Auld, James S. *educational psychologist*
Deegan, Mary Jo *sociology educator*
Stoddard, Robert H. *geography educator*

NEVADA

Ely
Alderman, Minnis Amelia *psychologist, educator, small business owner*

Las Vegas
Meiner, Sue Ellen Thompson *gerontologist, nurse practitioner, nursing educator and researcher, legal nurse consultant*
Weeks, Gerald *psychology educator*

Yerington
Price, Judith Holm *educational psychologist*

Zephyr Cove
Hudzinski, Leonard Gerard *social sciences educator, researcher*

NEW HAMPSHIRE

Durham
Woodward, Robert Simpson, IV, *economics educator*

Hanover
Demko, George Joseph *geographer*
Kleck, Robert Eldon *psychology educator*
Masters, Roger Davis *government and neurotoxicology educator*
Rutter, Jeremy Bentham *archaeologist, educator*
Starzinger, Vincent Evans *political science educator*

Nashua
Flynn, William Berchman, Jr., *psychology educator, clinical psychologist*

Newport
Gibbs, Elizabeth Dorothea *developmental psychologist*

NEW JERSEY

Belmar
De Santo, Donald James *psychologist, educational administrator*

Camden
Van Til, Jon *sociology educator*
Yamada, Tetsuji *health economist, educator*

Dover
Seadler, Stephen Edward *social scientist*

East Brunswick
Johnson, Edward Elemuel *psychologist, educator*

Eastampton
Haws, Elizabeth Anne *education administrator, school psychologist*

Ewing
Robboy, Howard Alan *sociologist, educator*

Florham Park
Brodkin, Adele Ruth Meyer *psychologist*

Glassboro
Mukhoti, Bela Banerjee *economics educator*

Hackensack
Ciccone, Joseph Lee *criminal justice educator*

Jersey City
D'Amico, Thomas F. *economist, educator*

Lakewood
Quinn, Evelyn Saul *social work educator*

Mahwah
Frundt, Henry John *sociologist, educator*

Manasquan
Hanbury, Raymond Francis, Jr., *psychologist, consultant*

Montclair
Lang, Gerhard *psychology educator*

Montvale
Baba, Thomas Frank *corporate economist, economics educator*

Mountain Lakes
Loomis, Rebecca C. *psychology educator*

New Brunswick
Alexander, Robert Jackson *economist, educator*
Glickman, Norman Jay *economist, urban policy analyst*
Reock, Ernest C., Jr., *retired government services educator, academic director*
Tiger, Lionel *social scientist, anthropology consultant*

New Providence
Sinnott, William Michael *social studies educator*

Newark
Cheng, Mei-Fang *psychobiology educator, neuroethology researcher*
Holzer, Marc *public administrator educator*

Piscataway
Alderfer, Clayton Paul *organizational consultant, educator, writer, administrator*
McCrady, Barbara Sachs *psychologist, educator*
Zerubavel, Eviatar *sociologist, educator*

Princeton
Baumol, William Jack *economist, educator*
Benabou, Roland Jean-Marc *economist, educator*
Bradford, David Frantz *economist*
Chow, Gregory Chi-Chong *economist, educator*
Doig, Jameson Wallace *political science educator*
Fried, Eleanor Reingold *psychologist, educator*
Geertz, Clifford James *anthropology educator*
Girgus, Joan Stern *psychologist, university administrator*
Gordenker, Leon *political sciences educator*
Greenstein, Fred Irwin *political science educator*
Hirschman, Albert Otto *political economist, educator*
Hoebel, Bartley Gore *psychology educator*
Johnson-Laird, Philip Nicholas *psychologist*
Joyce, Carol Bertani *social studies educator*
Kateb, George Anthony *political science educator*
Kenen, Peter Bain *economist, educator*
Kuenne, Robert Eugene *economics educator*
Malkiel, Burton Gordon *economist, educator*
Manning, Winton Howard *psychologist, educational administrator*
Quandt, Richard Emeric *economics educator*
Reinhardt, Uwe Ernst *economist, educator*
Rosen, Harvey Sheldon *economics educator*
Rozman, Gilbert Friedell *sociologist, educator*
Shear, Theodore Leslie, Jr., *archaeologist, educator*
Sigmund, Paul Eugene *political science educator*
Tienda, Marta *demographer, educator*
Ullman, Richard Henry *political science educator*
Von Hippel, Frank Niels *public and international affairs educator*
Wallace, Walter L. *sociologist, educator*
Westoff, Charles Francis *demographer, educator*
Willig, Robert Daniel *economics educator*

Saddle River
Lasser, Gail Maria *psychologist, educator*

Teaneck
Westin, Alan Furman *political science educator*

Tinton Falls
Butler, Nancy Taylor *gender equity specialist, program director*

Trenton
Peroni, Peter A., II, *psychologist, educator*
Rusciano, Frank Louis *political science educator, consultant*

NEW MEXICO

Albuquerque
Basso, Keith Hamilton *cultural anthropologist, linguist, educator*
May, Philip Alan *sociology educator*

Bayard
Lopez, Linda Carol *social sciences educator*

Kirtland Afb
Tritten, James John *national security educator*

Portales
Shaughnessy, Michael Francis *psychology educator*

NEW YORK

Albany
Friedlander, Myrna Lois *psychologist, educator*
Justeson, John S. *anthropologist, educator*
Nathan, Richard P(erle) *political scientist, educator*
Sattinger, Michael Jack *economics educator, researcher*

Annandale On Hudson
Papadimitriou, Dimitri Basil *economist, college administrator*

Bearsville
Nell, Edward John *economist, educator*

Binghamton
Levis, Donald James *psychologist, educator*
Rightmire, George Philip *anthropology educator*

Bronx
Anarfi, Isaac Kwame *economic educator, researcher*
Battista, Leon Joseph, Jr., *economics educator*
Golland, Jeffrey H. *psychologist, psychoanalyst, educator*
Hooker, Olivia J. *psychologist, educator*
Kelly, Mary Susan *psychologist, educator*
Martinez-Tabone, Raquel *school psychologist supervisor*
Procidano, Mary Elizabeth *psychologist, educator*
Riddell, Alice Mary *drug prevention educator*

Brooklyn
Frantzve, Jerri Lyn *psychologist, educator, consultant*
Lieberman, Morris Baruch *psychologist, educator, researcher*
Martinez-Pons, Manuel *psychologist, educator*
Reinisch, June Machover *psychologist, educator*
Schuman, Elliott Paul *psychoanalyst, mediator, arbitrator, facilitator*
Spivack, Frieda Kugler *psychologist, administrator, educator, researcher*

Buffalo
Beck, J. Gayle *psychologist, educator*
Floss, Frederick George *economics and finance educator, consultant*
Hetzner, Donald Raymund *social studies educator, forensic social scientist*
Lamb, Charles Moody *political scientist, educator*
Levine, Murray *psychology educator*
Zagare, Frank Cosmo *political science educator*
Zarembka, Paul *economics educator*

Center Moriches
Schiavoni, Thomas John *social studies educator*

Chester
Tysvaer, Cynthia Kay *social studies educator*

Dobbs Ferry
Perelle, Ira B. *psychologist, educator*

Dryden
Baker, Lucille Stoeppler *sociology and anthropology educator*

Fishkill
Stein, Paula Nancy *psychologist, educator*

Flushing
Bodnar, Richard *psychology educator*
Lakah, Jacqueline Rabbat *political scientist, consultant*

Garden City
Michael, Suzanne *sociologist, educator*

Garrison
Murray, Thomas Henry *bioethics educator, writer*

Geneseo
Olczak, Paul Vincent *psychology educator*

Greenport
Watts, Harold Wesley *economist, educator*

Greenvale
Abdolali, Nasrin *political scientist, educator, consultant*
Araoz, Daniel Leon *psychologist, educator*

Hamilton
Blum, Lester *educator*
Johnston, Michael (William Johnston) *political science educator, university administrator*

Huletts Landing
Kapusinski, Albert Thomas *economist, educator*

Ithaca
Assie-Lumumba, N'Dri T. *Africana studies educator*
Bestor, Theodore Charles *anthropologist, educator*
Ehrenberg, Ronald Gordon *economist, educator*
LaDue, Eddy Lorain *economist, educator*
Lowi, Theodore J(ay) *political science educator*
Tomek, William Goodrich *agricultural economist*
Vanek, Jaroslav *economist, educator*

Jamaica
Ovedovitz, Albert Chester *economist, educator*

Levittown
Juszczak, Nicholas Mauro *psychology educator*

Manhasset
Pam, Eleanor *behavorial sciences educator*

Mexico
Sade, Donald Stone *anthropology educator*

Mount Vernon
Cammarosano, Joseph Raphael *economist, educator*

New City
Frawley-O'Dea, Mary Gail *clinical psychologist, psychoanalyst, educator*

New Paltz
Scott, Barbara Ann *sociology educator, feminist, peace activist*

New Rochelle
Grimes, Tresmaine Judith Rubain *psychology educator*

New York
Alland, Alexander, Jr., *anthropology educator*
Andersen, Susan Marie *educator, researcher, clinician, policy advisor*
Arther, Richard Oberlin *polygraphist, educator*
Betts, Richard Kevin *political science educator*
Bond, George Clement *anthropologist, educator*
Bowen, William Gordon *economist, educator, foundation administrator*
Brams, Steven John *political scientist, educator, game theorist*
Broisman, Emma Ray *economist, retired international official*
Chelstrom, Marilyn Ann *political education consultant*
Cohen, Stephen Frand *political scientist, historian, educator, author, broadcaster*
Cole, Jonathan Richard *sociologist, academic administrator*
Comitas, Lambros *anthropologist, educator*
Connelly, Matthew *history educator*
Dhrymes, Phoebus James *economist, educator*
Domowitz, Ian *economics educator*
Downie, David Leonard *political science educator*
Eisenstein, Hester *sociology educator*
Fancher, Edwin Crawford *psychologist, educator*
Fischbach, Ruth Linda *ethics educator, social scientist, researcher*
Franklin, Julian Harold *political science educator*
Galanter, Eugene *psychologist, educator*
Gans, Herbert J. *sociologist, educator*
Gerber, Gwendolyn Loretta *psychologist, educator*
Glanzer, Murray *psychology educator*
Glickman, Michael Richard *social studies educator*
Gross, Feliks *writer*
Heal, Geoffrey Martin *economics and business educator*
Holloway, Ralph Leslie *anthropology educator*
Jordan, Theresa Joan *psychologist, educator*
Kvint, Vladimir Lev *economist, mining engineer, finance educator*
Levin, Henry Mordecai *economist, educator*
Low, Setha Marilyn *anthropology and psychology educator, consultant*
Maldonado-Bear, Rita Marinita *economist, educator*
Miller, Cate *psychologist, educator*
Murphy, Austin de la Salle *economist, educator, banker*
Patrick, Hugh Talbot *economist, educator*
Peck, Fred Neil *economist, educator*
Robinson, Daniel N. *psychology and philosophy educator*
Schilling, Warner Roller *political scientist, educator*
Schneider, Greta *economist, speaker, author, security consultant*
Schwab, George David *social science educator, author*
Stiglitz, Joseph Eugene *economist, educator*
Sylla, Richard Eugene *economics educator*
Vitz, Paul Clayton *psychologist, educator*
Walter, Ingo *economics educator*
Watkins, Don Orra *public affairs educator*
Zimmerman, Barry Joseph *educational psychology educator, researcher*

Newburgh
Fallon, Rae Mary *psychology educator, early childhood consultant*

Old Westbury
Ozelli, Tunch *economics educator, consultant*

Oneonta
Malone, Laurence Joseph *economics educator, writer*
vom Saal, Walter *psychology educator*

Oswego
Roodin, Paul A. *psychology educator*

Plattsburgh
Smith, Noel Wilson *psychology educator*

Pleasantville
Robak, Rostyslaw Wsewolod *psychologist, educator*

Pomona
Gordon, Edmund Wyatt *psychologist, educator*

Potsdam
Chugh, Ram L. *economics educator*
Hanson, David Justin *sociology educator, researcher*

Poughkeepsie
Balderrama, Sylvia Ramírez *psychologist, educator*
Scileppi, John A. *psychologist, educator*

Ridge
Mooney, Vita Maria Elena *social studies educator, tax examiner*

Rochester
Buckingham, Barbara Rae *social studies educator*
Fenno, Richard Francis, Jr., *political scientist, educator*
Ossip-Klein, Deborah Jann *psychologist, educator*
Plosser, Charles Irving *economist, educator*

Rockville Centre
Flanagan, Rosemary *psychologist, educator*

Shoreham
Ciborowski, Paul John *counseling psychology educator*

Sleepy Hollow
Schippa, Joseph Thomas, Jr., *psychologist, educational consultant, hypnotherapist*

Staten Island
Grieve, William Roy *psychologist, educator, educational administrator, researcher*
Meltzer, Yale Leon *economist, educator*

Stony Brook
Stone, Elizabeth Cecilia *anthropology educator*

Syracuse
Fiske, Sandra Rappaport *psychologist, educator*
Griffith, Daniel Alva *geography educator*
Monmonier, Mark *geographer, graphics educator, essayist*
Wadley, Susan Snow *anthropologist*

Troy
Baron, Robert Alan *psychology and business educator, author*
Bayly, Patricia Anne *psychologist, educator*

Utica
Brown, Thomas Glenn *psychology educator*

West Seneca
Wolfgang, Jerald Ira *economic development educator*

Westbury
Kremin, Daniel Paul *clinical forensic psychologist*

Yonkers
Monegro, Francisco *psychology educator, alternative medicine consultant*

NORTH CAROLINA

Cary
Serafine, Mary Louise *psychologist, educator, lawyer*

Chapel Hill
Jones, Lyle Vincent *psychologist, educator*
Lowman, Robert Paul *psychology educator, academic administrator*
Page, Ellis Batten *psychologist, educator*
Smith, James Finley *economist, educator*
Stenberg, Carl W., III, *public administration educator, dean*
Steponaitis, Vincas Petras *archaeologist, anthropologist, educator*
Weinstein, Sidney *neuropsychologist*

Charlotte
Kidda, Michael Lamont, Jr., *psychologist, educator*
Webster, Murray Alexander, Jr., *sociologist, educator*

Davidson
Palmer, Edward L. *social psychology educator, television researcher, writer*

Durham
Boguslavsky, George William *psychologist, educator*
Bunch, Michael Brannen *psychologist, educator*
Diem, Gordon Neal *political science educator, video producer*
Holsti, Ole Rudolf *political scientist, educator*
Jenkins, Clara Barnes *psychology educator*
McClain, Paula Denice *political scientist, educator*
Tiryakian, Edward Ashod *sociology educator*

Greensboro
Gill, Diane Louise *psychology educator, university official*
Goldman, Bert Arthur *psychologist, educator*
Zopf, Paul Edward, Jr., *sociologist*

Greenville
Webster, Raymond Earl *psychology educator, director, psychotherapist*

Kernersville
Hall, Marvin *psychology educator, counselor*

Lillington
Wood, Maggie Ethel *social studies educator*

Raleigh
Allen, Steven Glen *economics and business educator*

Salisbury
Tseng, Howard Shih Chang *business and economics educator, investment company executive*

NORTH DAKOTA

Fargo
Query, Joy Marves Neale *medical sociology educator*

OHIO

Akron
Sam, David Fiifi *political economist, educator*

Athens
Brehm, Sharon Stephens *psychology educator, university administrator*
Rader, William Donald *economics educator, university administrator*

Berea
Miller, Dennis Dixon *economics educator*

Bluffton
Friesen, Ronald Lee *economics educator*

Bowling Green
Berger, Bonnie G. *sport psychologist, educator*

Cincinnati
Apostolides, Anthony Demetrios *economist, educator*
Stevens, Brenda Anita *psychologist, educator*
Warm, Joel Seymour *psychology educator*
Wenger, Lowell Edward *history educator*

Cleveland
Goldstein, Melvyn C. *anthropologist, educator*
Hill, Edward William *economics educator, urban and regional planner*

Columbus
Arnold, Kevin David *psychologist, educational researcher*
Beck, Paul Allen *political science educator*
Gouke, Cecil Granville *economist, educator*
Huber, Joan Althaus *sociology educator*
Ichiishi, Tatsuro *economics and mathematics educator*
Johnson, Neal Frederick *psychological scientist, educator*
Kehler, Abbejean *economist, educator*
Kessel, John Howard *political scientist, educator*
Krueger, Lester Eugene *psychology educator*
Leland, Henry *psychology educator*
Mueller, John Ernest *political science educator, dance critic and historian*
Namboodiri, Krishnan *sociology educator*
Randall, Alan John *environmental economics educator*
Tuckman, Bruce Wayne *educational psychologist, educator, researcher*

Findlay
Peters, Milton Eugene *educational psychologist*

Hamilton
New, Rosetta Holbrock *home economics educator, nutrition consultant*

Hudson
Reuter, Jeanette Miller *psychologist, educator*

Huron
Round, Alice Faye Bruce *school psychologist*

Kent
Los, Cornelis Albertus *financial economist, portfolio risk manager, educator*
McKee, David Lannen *economics educator*
Neal-Barnett, Angela Marie *psychology educator*

Kirtland
Skubby, Christopher Daniel *political science educator, social sciences educator, department chairman*

Marietta
Taylor, Michael Brooks *economist, educator*

Oberlin
Friedman, William John *psychology educator*

Oxford
Wagenaar, Theodore Clarence *sociology educator*
Wolfe, Christopher Randall *psychologist, researcher, educator*

Toledo
Attoh, Samuel Aryeetey *geographer, educator, planner*
Davis, David Howard *political science educator*
Heintz, Carolinea Cabaniss *retired home economics educator*

OKLAHOMA

Altus
Newman, Bruce Allan *political science educator*

Norman
Kondonassis, Alexander John *economist, educator*
Pruitt, Nancy Elizabeth *social science educator*

Oklahoma City
Craig, George Dennis *economics educator, consultant*
Rundell, Orvis Herman, Jr., *psychologist, educator*

Stillwater
Poole, Richard William *economics educator*

OREGON

Beaverton
Hughes, Laurel Ellen *psychologist, educator, writer*
Ricks, Mary F(rances) *archaeologist, anthropologist, consultant*

Corvallis
Bernieri, Frank John *social psychology educator*

Eugene
Upham, Steadman *anthropology educator, university dean, academic administrator*

Fairview
Blodgett, Forrest Clinton *economics educator*

Newberg
Adams, Wayne Verdun *pediatric psychologist, educator*

Portland
Davis, James Allan *gerontologist, educator*
Matarazzo, Ruth Gadbois *psychologist, educator*
Rufolo, Anthony Michael *economics educator*
Wineberg, Howard *social studies educator, researcher*

Talent
Diers, Carol Jean *psychology educator*

PENNSYLVANIA

Alburtis
Stafford, William Butler *retired psychology educator*

Allentown
Graham, Kenneth Robert *psychologist, educator*

Bala Cynwyd
Bersh, Philip Joseph *psychologist, educator*

Beaver
DeLuigi, Dominic Joseph *psychologist, educator*

Beaver Falls
Berkey, Julie Marie *school psychologist*

Bethlehem
Aronson, Jay Richard *economics educator, researcher, academic administrator*

Bloomsburg
Osunde, Egerton Oyenmwense *social studies and social sciences educator, curriculum studies educator*

Bridgeville
Moore, Daniel Edmund *psychologist, educator, retired educational administrator*

Bryn Mawr
Kline, Harriet Dennis *psychologist, school psychologist*

Buckingham
Callahan, Francis Patrick, Jr., *social studies educator*

Collegeville
Pierson, Ellery Merwin *retired psychometrist*

Coudersport
Kysor, Daniel Francis *psychologist*

Doylestown
Dimond, Roberta Ralston *psychology and sociology educator*

Edinboro
Stone, Alfred Ward *educator*

Elizabethtown
McDonald, W. Wesley *political science educator*

Elkins Park
Goode, Paul *psychologist, educator, consultant*

Erie
Kurre, James Anthony *economics educator*

Gettysburg
Heisler, Barbara Schmitter *sociology educator*
Plischke, Elmer *political science educator*

Greensburg
Gribschaw, Victoria Marie *social sciences educator, department chairman*

Huntingdon
Murray, Andrew *peace studies educator*

Johnstown
Teich, Alan Harvey *psychology educator, clinical psychologist*

Kutztown
Dougherty, Percy H. *geographer, educator, politician, planner*

Lancaster
Auster, Carol Jean *sociology educator*
Stephenson, Donald Grier, Jr., *government studies educator*

Lebanon
Sowers, Margaret Ann *home economics, family and consumer science educator*

Lincoln University
Gaymon, William Edward *psychology educator*

Moscow
Lisandrelli, Carl Albert *social studies educator*

Philadelphia
Cass, David *economist, educator*
Coché, Judith *psychologist, educator*
Cunningham, Jacqueline Lemmé *psychologist, educator, researcher*
Diebold, Francis X. *economist, educator*

Donaldson, Thomas *ethicist, educator*
Fox, Renée Claire *sociology educator*
Herbert, James Dalton *psychology educator*
Klausner, Samuel Zundel *sociologist, educator*
Klein, Lawrence Robert *economist, educator*
Kopytoff, Igor *anthropology educator*
Offenberg, Robert M. *educational psychologist*
Rosenberg, Robert Allen *psychologist, educator, optometrist*
Ruane, Joseph William *sociologist, educator*
Seligman, Martin E.P. *psychologist, educator*
Smith, Rogers Mood *political scientist, educator*
Snelbecker, Glenn Eugene *psychologist, educator*
Tokar, Bette Lewis *economics educator*
Van De Walle, Etienne *demographer*
Weiss, Mary Alice *insurance economics educator*

Pittsburgh
Eaton, Joseph W. *sociology educator*
Ginsburg, Mark Barry *comparative sociology of education educator*
Haney, Edward Francis *social studies educator, educator*
Holzner, Burkart *sociologist, educator*
Kenkel, James Lawrence *economics educator*
McCallum, Bennett Tarlton *economist, educator*
Perlman, Mark *economist, educator*
Perloff, Robert *psychologist, educator*
Tervo, Denise Ann *psychologist, educator*

Ridgway
Gladden, Kathleen Ann *anthropologist, educator*

Sayre
Tubbs, Stephen Walter *social studies educator*

Shippensburg
Loveland, Christine Ann *anthropology educator*

State College
Schaie, K(laus) Warner *human development and psychology educator*

Swarthmore
Keith, Jennie *anthropology educator and administrator, writer*
Marecek, Jeanne *psychologist, educator*

Tarentum
McGuire, Timothy William *economics and management educator*

University Park
Firebaugh, Glenn Allen *sociology educator*
Friedman, Robert Sidney *political science educator*
Marshall, Robert Clifford *economics educator*

Villanova
Hadley, Judith Marie *archaeologist, educator*
Langran, Robert Williams *political scientist, educator*
Lesch, Ann Mosely *political scientist, educator*
Malik, Hafeez *political scientist, educator*

Wayne
Stayton, William Ralph *psychologist, educator*

Waynesboro
Swartz, William Rick *school psychologist*

Wynnewood
Khouri, Fred John *political science educator*
Phillips, Almarin *economics educator, consultant*
Porter, Jack *psychologist, educator*

RHODE ISLAND

Kingston
Felner, Robert David *psychology educator, researcher, consultant*
Newman, Barbara Miller *psychologist, educator*
Seifer, Marc Jeffrey *psychology educator*

Providence
Anderson, James Alfred *psychology educator*
Church, Russell Miller *psychology educator*
Goldscheider, Frances K. *sociologist, educator*
Gould, Richard Allan *anthropologist, archaeologist, educator*
Grossman, Herschel I. *economics educator*
Heath, Dwight Braley *anthropologist, educator*
Hopmann, Philip Terrence *political science educator*
Jones, Ferdinand Taylor, Jr., *psychologist, educator*
Putterman, Louis G. *economics educator*
Ryder, Harl Edgar *economist, educator*
Siqueland, Einar *psychology educator*
Stein, Jerome Leon *economist, educator*
Stultz, Newell Maynard *retired political science educator*

Smithfield
Morahan-Martin, Janet May *psychologist, educator*

SOUTH CAROLINA

Charleston
Bowman, Daniel Oliver *psychologist*
Moore, William Vincent *political science educator*
Roper, Birdie Alexander *social sciences educator*

Chester
Platt, Leslie Oliver *psychologist*

Clemson
Curry, Linda Jean *social studies educator*

Columbia
Booth, Hilda Earl Ferguson *clinical counselor, Spanish language educator*

Kegley, Charles William, Jr., *political science educator, author*
Logan, Sandra Jean *retired economics and business educator*
Weber, Lynn *sociology educator*

Mc Cormick
Zeller, Michael James *psychologist, educator*

Surfside Beach
Parks, William Raymond, II, *criminal justice educator*

Williamston
Hawkins-Sneed, Janet Lynn *school psychologist, human resources administrator, small business owner*

SOUTH DAKOTA

Brookings
Gilbert, Howard Alden *economics educator*

Vermillion
Wang, X. T. (Xiaotian Wang) *psychologist, educator*

TENNESSEE

Chattanooga
Drennon-Gala, Donney Thomas *sociologist, educational consultant, writer*

Memphis
Daniel, Coldwell, III, *economist, educator*
Papachristou, Patricia Towne *economics educator*

Nashville
Fels, Rendigs *economist, educator*
Graham, George J., Jr., *political scientist, educator*
Kaas, Jon H. *psychology educator*
McCarty, Richard Charles *psychology educator, university dean*
Ridley, Carolyn Fludd *retired social studies educator*
Smith, Dani Allred *sociologist, educator*
Westfield, Fred M. *economics educator*
Young, Tommie Morton *social psychology educator, writer*

Oak Ridge
Colston, Freddie Charles *political science educator*
Johnson, Ruth Crumley *economics educator*

Sewanee
Mohiuddin, Yasmeen Niaz *economics educator*

TEXAS

Arlington
Bernstein, Ira Harvey *psychology educator*

Austin
Buss, David Michael *psychology educator*
Dalton, Caryl *school psychologist*
Glenn, Norval Dwight *sociologist, educator*
Holz, Robert Kenneth *retired geography educator*
Keith, Timothy Zook *psychology educator*
Lariviere, Richard Wilfred *university administrator, educator, consultant*
Magee, Stephen Pat *economics and finance educator*
Markman, Arthur Brian *psychology educator*
Pingree, Dianne *psychotherapist*

Bedford
Walther, Richard Ernest *psychology educator, library administrator*

Bellaire
Mayo, Clyde Calvin *organizational psychologist, educator*
Parker, Bonnie Gae *social science educator*

Borger
Kasch, Julia Ann *social sciences educator*

College Station
Greenhut, Melvin Leonard *economist, educator*
Knutson, Ronald Dale *economist, educator, academic administrator*

Corpus Christi
Cutlip, Randall Brower *retired psychologist, university president emeritus*

Dallas
Berkeley, Betty Life *gerontology educator*
Betts, Dianne Connally *economist, educator*
Kemper, Robert Van *anthropologist, educator, minister*
Kress, Gerard Clayton, Jr., *psychologist, educator*
Murphy, John Carter *economics educator*

Denton
Schumacker, Randall *educational psychologist*

El Paso
Himelstein, Philip Nathan *psychology educator*

Fort Worth
Durham, Floyd Wesley, Jr., *economist, educator*

Georgetown
Muir-Broaddus, Jacqueline Elizabeth *psychology educator*

Houston
Bailey, Ruth Janet *retired home economics educator*
Callender, Norma Anne *psychology educator, counselor*
Coker, Sally Jo (Bozeman) *sociology educator*
Cuthbertson, Gilbert Morris *political science educator*
Davidson, Chandler *sociologist, educator*
Foster, Dale Warren *political scientist, educator, management consultant, real estate broker, accountant*
Gouti, Sammy Yasin *psychologist, educator, television talk show host, psychotherapist, writer*
Martin, William C. *sociology educator, writer*
Perez, Francisco Ignacio *clinical psychologist, educator*
von der Mehden, Fred R. *political science educator*

Prairie View
French, Laurence Armand *social science educator, psychology educator*

Richardson
Beron, Kurt James *economics educator*
Berry, Brian Joe Lobley *geographer, political economist, urban planner*
Harpham, Edward John *political science educator, dean, writer, research*

San Antonio
Bellows, Thomas John *political scientist, educator*
Firestone, Juanita Marlies *sociology educator*
Harris, Richard John *social sciences educator*
Mott, Peggy Laverne *sociologist, educator*
Ribble, Ronald George *retired psychologist, educator, writer*
Salvucci, Richard Joseph *economics educator*
Truett, Dale Brian *economics/finance educator, consultant*
Truett, Lila Flory *economics educator*

San Marcos
Fletcher, John Lynn *political science educator*

Stafford
Greco, Janice Teresa *psychology educator*

Tomball
Kral, Nancy Bolin *political science educator*

Waco
Achor, Louis Joseph Merlin *psychology and neuroscience educator*
Sharp, Ronald Arvell *sociology educator*

Weatherford
Buckner-Reitman, Joyce *psychologist, educator*

UTAH

Logan
Van Dusen, Lani Marie *psychologist*

Ogden
Elliott, Harold Marshall *geography educator*

Sandy
Park, William Laird *agricultural economics educator, consultant, college associate dean*

VERMONT

Middlebury
Davis, Eric Lyle *political scientist, educator, college administrator*

VIRGINIA

Annandale
Atiyeh, Naim Nicholas *psychologist, educator*

Arlington
Bradburn, Norman M. *behavioral science educator*
Siddayao, Corazón Morales *economist, educator, consultant*
Weidemann, Celia Jean *social scientist, international business and financial development consultant*

Blacksburg
Morgan, George Emir, III, *financial economics educator*

Burke
Bayer, Ada-Helen *industrial organizational psychologist, educator*

Charlottesville
Cornell, Dewey Gene *psychologist*
Elzinga, Kenneth Gerald *economics educator*
Feigert, Frank Brook *retired political science educator, writer*
Moreno, Zerka Toeman *psychodrama educator*
Perdue, Charles L., Jr., *social sciences educator, language educator*
Reppucci, Nicholas Dickon *psychologist, educator*
Wagner, Roy *anthropology educator, researcher*
Whitaker, John King *economics educator*

Earlysville
Caplow, Theodore *sociologist, educator*

Eastville
Williams, Ida Jones *consumer and home economics educator, writer*

Fairfax
Dennis, Rutledge M. *sociology educator, researcher*
Williams, Thomas Rhys *anthropologist, educator*

Fredericksburg
Kilmartin, Christopher Thomas *psychology educator*

Herndon
Spragens, William Clark *public policy educator, consultant*

Lexington
Elmes, David Gordon *psychology educator*
Jarrard, Leonard Everett *psychologist, educator*
John, Lewis George *political science educator*

Lorton
Sun, Li-Teh *economics educator*

Mc Lean
Stevens, Richard Gordon *political scientist, educator*

Midlothian
Baretski, Charles Allan *political scientist, librarian, educator, historian, municipal official*
Prophett, Andrew Lee *political science educator*

Reston
Watson, William Downing, Jr., *economist, educator*

Richmond
Leary, David Edward *psychology educator*

Springfield
de Haan, Henry John *research psychologist*

WASHINGTON

Bellingham
Haensly, Patricia Anastacia *psychology educator*

Cheney
Bunting, David Cuyp *economics educator, consultant*

Everett
Van Ry, Ginger Lee *school psychologist*

La Conner
Knopf, Kenyon Alfred *economist, educator*

Longview
Weber, Dennis Paul *social studies educator*

Pullman
Rosa, Eugene Anthony *sociologist, environmental scientist, educator*

Seattle
Benezet, Louis Tomlinson *retired psychology educator, former college president*
Berninger, Virginia Wise *psychologist, educator*
Chirot, Daniel *sociology and international studies educator*
Fiedler, Fred Edward *organizational psychology educator, consultant*
Hirschman, Charles, Jr., *sociologist, educator*
Narver, John Colin *business administration educator emeritus*

Sequim
Guilmet, George Michael *cultural anthropologist, educator*

Spokane
McBride, Michael Joseph *psychology educator, administrator*

Vancouver
Craven, James Michael *economist, educator*

WEST VIRGINIA

Bethany
Cooey, William Randolph *economics educator*

Fairmont
Fulda, Michael *space policy researcher*

Morgantown
Jackson, Randall W. *geography educator*
McAvoy, Rogers *educational psychology educator, researcher*
Vargas, Julie S. *behaviorologist, educator*

Salem
Frasure, Carl Maynard *political science educator*

WISCONSIN

Beloit
Fitzsimmons, Robert William *social science educator*
Green, William *archaeologist*
Kreider, Leonard Emil *economics educator*

Eau Claire
Davidson, John Kenneth, Sr., *sociologist, educator, researcher, writer, consultant*

Green Bay
Laatsch, William *geography educator*

La Crosse
Morehouse, Richard Edward *psychology educator*

Madison
Andreano, Ralph Louis *economist, educator*
Ferree, Myra Marx *sociologist, educator*
Gernsbacher, Morton Ann *psychology educator*
Haller, Archibald Orben *sociologist, educator*
Hester, Donald Denison *economics educator*
Rice, Joy Katharine *psychologist, educational policy studies and women's studies educator*
Schmidt, John Richard *agricultural economics educator*

Middleton
Taylor, Fannie Turnbull *social education and arts administration educator*

Milwaukee
Warren, Richard M. *experimental psychologist, educator*

River Falls
LeCapitaine, John Edward *counseling psychology professor, researcher, writer*

Whitewater
Laurent, Jerome King *economics educator*
Refior, Everett Lee *labor economist, educator*

WYOMING

Laramie
Chai, Winberg *political science educator*

Powell
Brophy, Dennis Richard *psychology and philosophy educator, administrator, clergyman*

TERRITORIES OF THE UNITED STATES

PUERTO RICO

San Juan
Borges, Ingrid *industrial psychologist, trainer*
Díaz de Gonzalez, Ana María *psychologist, educator*
Rivera-Urrutia, Beatriz Dalila *psychology and rehabilitation counseling educator*

CANADA

ALBERTA

Calgary
Kelley, Jane Holden *archaeology educator*

BRITISH COLUMBIA

Vancouver
Olsen, Inger Anna *psychologist, educator*

ONTARIO

Guelph
Cronshaw, Steven Frank *psychology educator*

Lindsay
Montgomery, Tommie Sue *political scientist, educator*

London
Kuiper, Nicholas Ahlrich *psychology educator*

Ottawa
Dagum, Camilo *economist, educator*

QUEBEC

Montreal
Nayar, Baldev Raj *political science educator*

Quebec
Tremblay, Marc Adélard *anthropologist, educator*

CHINA

Dalian
Shum, Margaret *market economy educator*

INDONESIA

Jakarta
Tilaar, Henry A.R. *social planner educator*

ISRAEL

Haifa
Krau, Edgar *psychologist, scientist, educator, researcher*

ITALY

Rome
Celant, Attilio *geographer, educator*

SPAIN

Valencia
Casas-Pardo, Jose *economics educator*

SWITZERLAND

Geneva
Sidjanski, Dusan *economist, educator*

ADDRESS UNPUBLISHED

Adams, Robert McCormick *anthropologist, educator*
Adelman, Richard Charles *gerontologist, educator*
Alker, Hayward Rose *political scientist, educator*
Allen, John Lyndon *social studies educator*
Altshuler, Alan Anthony *political scientist, educator*
Andrain, Charles Franklin *political science educator*
Becker, Charles McVey *economics and finance educator*
Bert, Clara Virginia *retired home economics educator, school system administrator*
Briggs, Philip James *political science educator, author, lecturer, reviewer*
Buchin, Jean *psychologist, educator*
Buck, Jane Louise *psychology educator*
Burkholder, Grace Eleanor *archaeologist, educator*
Canipe, James Boyd *economics educator*
Carlson, Janet Frances *psychologist, educator*
Coats, Wendell John, Jr., *political science educator*
Collier, Ruth Berins *political science educator*
Colosimo, Mary Lynn Sukurs *psychology educator*
Conaway, Mary Ann *behavioral studies educator*
Cotten, Annie Laura *psychologist, educator*
Crumpton, Evelyn *psychologist, educator*
de Blij, Harm Jan *geography educator, editor*
Del Rosario, Rose Marie *clinical sociologist, educator, consultant*
De Mora, Juan Miguel *indologist, educator, writer*
Dobriansky, Lev Eugene *economist, educator, diplomat*
Dorman, Patricia M. *sociologist, educator*
Drummond, Dorothy Weitz *geography education consultant, educator, author*
Dwyer, Gerald Paul, Jr., *economist, bank executive*
Fritz, Jan Marie *planning educator, mediator, clinical sociologist*
Gischlar, Karen Lynn *psychologist*
Gorelick, Molly Chernow *psychologist, educator*
Gutmann, David Leo *psychology educator*
Hanushek, Eric Alan *economics educator*
Hartstein, Harold Herman *psychology educator, consultant*
Hayes, Mary Ann *social studies educator*
Helfgott, Roy B. *economist, educator*
Herod, Charles Carteret *Afro-American studies educator*
Hiler, Monica Jean *reading and sociology educator*
Humberd, Donna Sue *retired social studies educator*
Hume, Susan Rachel *finance and economics educator*
Ioffe, Grigory *geography educator, researcher*
Isaacs, Kenneth S(idney) *psychoanalyst, educator*
Jacobs, Grace Gaines *retired gerontologist, adult education educator*
Jones-Johnson, Gloria *sociologist, educator, consultant*
Joyce, Joseph Patrick *economist, educator*
Kahana, Eva Frost *sociology educator*
Kaye, Janet Miriam *psychologist, educator*
Kenyon, Daphne Anne *economics educator*
Koss, Mary Lyndon Pease *psychology educator, researcher*
Kramberg, Heinz-Gerhard *ecomomist, educator*
Kuecker, Liza Louise *sociology educator*
Leith, Karen Pezza *psychologist, educator*
Lipsitt, Lewis Paeff *psychology educator*
Lipson, Abigail *psychologist*
Lurensky, Robert Lee *economist, educator*
Martin, Catherine Elizabeth *anthropology educator*
McCormack, Marjorie Guth *psychology educator, career counselor, communications educator, public relations consultant*
McCoy, Patricia A. *clinical special educator, writer, art and culture critic*
McCutcheon, Ronald Eugene *social studies educator*
McDougal, Marie Patricia *retired educator, freelance writer and editor*
McGreevy, Mary Sharron *former psychology educator*
McHugh, Betsy Baldwin *sociologist, educator, journalist, business owner*
Miller, Elmer Schaffner *anthropologist, educator*
Morris, Jane Elizabeth *home economics educator*
Mruk, Christopher J. *psychologist, educator*
Mutalipassi, Louis Richard *psychologist, educator*
Norman, Donald Arthur *cognitive scientist*
Parker, Cynthia Mary *economist, educator*
Paupp, Terrence Edward *research associate, educator*
Pedersen, Knud George *economics educator, academic administrator*
Pollack, Gerald Alexander *economist, government official*
Ragusea, Stephen Anthony *psychologist, educator*
Rakove, Jack Norman *history educator*
Reynolds, Clark Winton *economist, educator*
Rickel, Annette Urso *psychology and psychiatry researcher, educator*
Schenkel, Susan *psychologist, educator, author*
Seltzer, Vivian Center *psychologist, educator*
Sharpe, William Forsyth *economics educator*
Smith, Verna Mae Edom (Vme Edom Smith) *sociology educator, freelance writer, photographer*
Solomon, Eldra Pearl Brod *psychologist, educator, biologist, writer*
Sorkin, Robert Daniel *psychologist, educator*
Steinhauser, Sheldon Eli *sociology and gerontology educator, diversity and development consultant*
Striker, Cecil Leopold *archaeologist, educator*
Thomson, Marjorie Belle Anderson *sociology educator, consultant*
Tobin, Ilona Lines *psychologist, marriage and family counselor, educator, media consultant*
Uselton, Darrell Brent *social sciences educator, researcher*
Voss, James Frederick *psychologist, educator*
Wallen, Lina Hambali *economics educator, consultant*
Wertlieb, Donald Lawrence *psychologist, educator*
Widman, Elizabeth Ann *home economics educator*
Wilkinson, Louise Cherry *psychology educator, dean*
Witte, Raymond Henry *psychologist, educator*
Zimet, Lloyd *sport psychologist, health planner, educator*
Zuckerman, Harriet *sociologist, educator*

HIGHER EDUCATION: VISUAL AND PERFORMING ARTS

UNITED STATES

ALABAMA

Andalusia
Rich, Lonnie Keven *art educator, artist*

Cullman
Schgier, Linda Priest *musician, educator*

Madison
Johnson, Kathy Virginia Lockhart *art educator*

Mobile
Atkinson, Alanna Beth *music educator*

Montgomery
French, Elizabeth Chamberlain *musician*

Normal
Hall, Doris Spooner *music educator*

Talladega
Lanier, Anita Suzanne *musician, piano educator*

Troy
Moffett, Thomas Delano *music educator*

Trussville
Best, Frederick Napier *artist, designer, educator*

ARIZONA

Chino Valley
Casey, Bonnie Mae *artist, educator*

Fountain Hills
Mantor-Clarysse, Justine Claire *fine arts educator*

Glendale
Drakulich, Martha *retired arts educator*

Gold Canyon
Braig, Betty *artist, educator*

Mesa
Lawes, Patricia Jean *art educator*

Peoria
Rebb, Karen Marlene *music educator*

Phoenix
Black, Barry Maitland *music educator, educator*
Cook, Douglas Neilson *theater educator, producer, artistic director*
Missal, Stephen Joseph *art educator, portraitist*

Sierra Vista
Boughan, Zanetta Louise *music educator*

Sun City
Blanchet, Jeanne Ellene Maxant *artist, educator, performer*

Tempe
Nagrin, Daniel *dancer, educator, choreographer, lecturer, writer*

Tucson
Conant, Howard Somers *artist, educator*
Cook, Gary Dennis *music educator*

ARKANSAS

Bella Vista
Veach, Patricia J. *music educator*

Huntsville
Musick, Pat *artist, sculptor, art educator*

Monticello
Ross, Elgenia Ruth Snipes *art educator*

Paragould
Stallings, Phyllis Ann *music educator*

Smackover
Ingram, Johnnye Hughes *artist, educator*

State University
Lindquist, Evan *artist, educator*

CALIFORNIA

Anaheim
Vidergar, Teresa *music educator, musician*

Antioch
Rios, Diego Marcial *artist, educator*

Atherton
Greenbaum, Vicky *music and English educator*

Belmont
Jacobson, Vera Lee *theater educator*

Berkeley
Kasten, Karl Albert *painter, printmaker, educator*
Moore, Frank James *artist, educator*
Polos, Iris Stephanie *artist, art educator*
Simpson, David William *artist, educator*

Bodega Bay
Fruiht, Dolores Giustina *artist, educator, poet*

Brea
Ellis, Cynthia Bueker *musician, educator*

Burlingame
Pollard, Jann Diann *fine artist, graphic artist, educator*

Calistoga
Sassoon, Janet *ballerina, educator*

Carmichael
Sahs, Majorie Jane *art educator*

Chico
Patton, Thomas Edward *artist, educator*
Taylor, Carolyn Kay *music educator*

Claremont
Benjamin, Karl Stanley *artist, art educator*
Lachowicz, Rachel *artist, art educator*

Clarksburg
Couzens, Julia *artist, educator*

Corona
Hagmann, Lillian Sue *violin instructor*

Cupertino
Fisher, Shirley Ida A. *photography and humanities educator*

Escondido
Carey, Catherine Anita *artist, art educator*

Fontana
Trotter, Gwendolyn Diane Nelson *choral and vocal educator, music publisher*

Fresno
Johnson, Edith Curtice *art education administrator*

Hayward
Jordahl, Kathleen Patricia (Kate Jordahl) *photographer, educator*

Hollywood
Pearlman, Alison *art educator*

Huntington Beach
Camp, Roger Ortho *fine arts educator, artist, photographer*

Kingsburg
Olson, Maxine Louise *artist, lecturer*

La Canada Flintridge
Drees, Elaine Hnath *artist and educator*

La Jolla
Bastien, Jane Smisor *music educator*
Hujsak, Ruth Joy *musician, educator*
Reynolds, Roger Lee *composer, educator*

Laguna Beach
Burchfield, Jerry Lee *artist, educator, author*

Laguna Hills
Walker, Virginia L. *art educator*

Laguna Woods
Saudek, Martha Folsom *artist, educator*

Loleta
Schoenfeld, Diana Lindsay *photographer, educator*

Long Beach
Kenneday, Elizabeth *fine arts educator*
Pizzo, Pia *artist, educator*

Los Altos
Alexander, Kathryn Jean (Kay Alexander) *retired art education consultant, art curriculum writer*
Sherwood, Patricia Waring *artist, educator*
Ward, Lillian Hazel *music educator*

Los Angeles
Ashforth, Alden *musician, educator*
Baca, Judith F. *art educator*
Chen, Edna Lau *art educator, artist*
Curran, Darryl Joseph *photographer, educator*
Dismukes, Valena Grace Broussard *photographer, former physical education educator*
Howe, John Thomas *film director, emeritus educator*
Schnitzler, Beverly Jeanne *designer, art educator, writer*
Stevens, Phyliss Elizabeth *fine art dealer, consultant, publisher, lecturer*
Termini, Olga Ascher *music educator, educator*

Manhattan Beach
Lee, Gloria Deane *artist, educator*

Mendocino
Dalglish, Meredith Rennels *artist, educator*

Merced
Barnett, Cheryl Lee *sculptor, educator*

Mill Valley
Jones, Pirkle *photographer, educator*

Moraga
Schumacher, Suzanne Lynne *artist, art educator*

Napa
Norman, Sheri Hanna *artist, educator, cartographer*

Northridge
Matsumoto, Shigemi *opera soprano, voice educator*

Oakland
DeFazio, Lynette Stevens *dancer, educator, choreographer, writer, actress*

Oceanside
Megill, David Wayne *music educator, author*

Ojai
Brookes, Mona E. *author, lecturer, art educator*

Palmdale
Handley, Sue Ann *professional quiltmaker, educator*

Palo Alto
Christiansen, Susan Putnam *artist, educator, consultant*
Kiser, Stephen *artist, educator*

Panorama City
Janis, Elinor Raiden *artist, educator*

Pasadena
Frodsham, Olaf Milton *music educator*
Sanchez, Pauline Stella *artist*

Paso Robles
Spencer, Harold Edwin *retired art educator, art historian, painter*

Pinole
Gerbracht, Robert Thomas (Bob Gerbracht) *painter, educator*

Pomona
Wilson, Stanley Charles *artist, educator, curator, art gallery director, consultant*

Rancho Cordova
Potterton, Barbara Alice *artist, educator, illustrator*

Redding
Ray, Helen Virginia *art educator*

Salinas
Rosen, Jacqueline I. *flutist, music educator*

San Diego
Farmer, Janene Elizabeth *artist, educator*
Nyiri, Joseph Anton *sculptor, art educator*
Pagan, Keith Areatus *music educator, academic administrator*
Russell, Louise Bernice *instructional designer*
Ward-Steinman, David *composer, music educator, pianist*

San Dimas
Wolfe, Edward William, II, *music educator, composer*

San Francisco
Babcock, Jo *artist, educator*
Beall, Dennis Ray *artist, educator*
Dickinson, Eleanor Creekmore *artist, educator*
Irwin, Michelle Kathleen *artist, educator*
Lamanet LaLonde, Shari *artist, art educator*
Lee, Patricia Taylor *pianist, music educator*
Schechter, Joel *magazine editor, writer, educator*

San Gabriel
Smith, June Sylvia Kolbe *artist, educator*

San Jose
Abbott, Barbara Louise *artist, educator*
Caywood, Barbara May *artist, educator*
Ellner, Josephine Helene *art educator*
Ellner, Michael William *art educator*
Gunther, Barbara *artist, educator*

San Luis Obispo
Dickerson, Colleen Bernice Patton *artist, educator*

San Marino
Santoso, Michelle Jo *music educator, pianist*

HIGHER EDUCATION: VISUAL AND PERFORMING ARTS

San Mateo
Chester, Sharon Rose *photographer, natural history educator, writer, illustrator*

Santa Barbara
Braiden, Rose Margaret *art educator, illustrator, calligrapher*
Cavat, Irma *artist, educator*
Decker, Beverly Anne *art educator, museum arts program director*

Santa Cruz
Leites, Barbara L. (Ara Leites) *artist, educator*

Santa Rosa
Conway, Lois Lorraine *piano teacher*

Santa Ynez
Rymer, Ilona Suto *artist, retired art educator*

Sebastopol
Snyder, Allegra Fuller *dance educator*

Sherman Oaks
Wood, David Laurence *artist, art educator, consultant*

Simi Valley
Brock, James Wilson *drama educator, playwright, researcher*

Sonora
Sharboneau, Lorna Rosina *artist, educator, author, poet, illustrator*

Stanford
Cohen, Albert *musician, educator*

Stockton
Tregle, Linda Marie *dance educator*

Studio City
Boyett, Joan Reynolds *arts administrator*
von Dassanowsky, Elfi (Elfriede Maria von Dassanowsky) *film producer, educator, opera singer*

Sugarloaf
Lytal, Patricia Lou *art educator*

Sylmar
Foster, Dudley Edwards, Jr., *musician, educator*
Scheib, Gerald Paul *fine art educator, jeweler, metalsmith*

Vacaville
Ford, John T., Jr., *art, film and video educator*

Van Nuys
Graham, Roger John *photography and journalism educator*

West Covina
Shiershke, Nancy Fay *artist, educator, property manager*

Westchester
Capetillo, Charlene Vernelle *music educator, special education educator*

Woodland Hills
Katz, Leon *theatre and drama educator*
Taylor, Rowan Shaw *music educator, composer, conductor*

COLORADO

Aurora
Countryman, L. Lynn Flieger *fine arts educator*
McKenney, Muriel Anita *art educator, engineer*

Boulder
Crites, Gayle *artist, educator*
Duckworth, Guy *musician, pianist, educator*
Lamun, JoAnne *theatre producer, writer, educator, director*

Colorado Springs
Borgen, Irma R. *music educator*
Leaf, John Brian *art instructor, elementary education educator*

Denver
McElhinney, James Lancel *artist, educator*
Ragland, Bob *artist, educator*

Englewood
Brennan, Joann *photographer, educator*

Fort Collins
Jacobs, Peter Alan *artist, educator*
Wilber, Clare Marie *musician, educator*

Golden
Acevedo, Angelique Marie *art educator*

Littleton
Hirokawa, Barbara Anne *art educator*
Keats, Donald Howard *composer, educator*
Nesheim, Dennis Warren *art educator, artist, writer, instructional materials producer, special education educator*

Ouray
Radovich, Donald *painter, illustrator, retired art educator*

Pritchett
Hall, Carol Ann *music educator*

Wiley
Dooley, Jennie Lee *art educator*

CONNECTICUT

Danbury
Jennings, Alfred Higson, Jr., *music educator, actor, singer*

Fairfield
Khachian, Elisa Arpenia *artist, educator*

Hartford
Shuler, Scott Corbin *art education administrator*

Monroe
Cote-Beaupre, Camille Yvette *artist, educator*
Wheatley, Sharman B. *art educator, artist*

Naugatuck
Chrzanowski, Rose-Ann Cannizzo *art educator*

New Britain
Kot, Marta Violette *artist, art educator*

New Haven
Bailey, William Harrison *artist, educator*
Bresnick, Martin *composer, educator*
Friedman, Erick *concert violinist, educator*
Garvey, Sheila Hickey *theater educator*
Papageorge, Tod *photographer, educator*
Tirro, Frank Pascale *music educator, author, composer*

Old Lyme
Hinman, Rosalind Virginia *storyteller, drama educator*

Pawcatuck
De Vore, Sadie Davidson *printmaker, art educator, artist*

Rocky Hill
Myers, Helen Priscilla *music educator*

Stamford
Preiss-Harris, Patricia *music educator, composer, pianist*

Storrs Mansfield
Jones, Clyde Adam *art educator, artist*

Trumbull
Hess, Terry Wichter *music educator, composer*

West Hartford
Levitz, I. S. *artist, educator, curator*

Westport
Wilk, Barbara *artist, educator*

Winsted
Firimita, Florin Ion *artist, educator, writer*

Woodbridge
Lytle, Richard *artist, educator*

DELAWARE

Lewes
Buchert, Stephanie Nicole *music educator*

Newark
Brown, Hilton *visual arts educator, artist, writer*

DISTRICT OF COLUMBIA

Washington
Giles, Patricia Cecelia Parker *retired art educator, graphic designer*
Hottendorf, Diane V. *dance educator*
Ihrie, John Richard, III, *art educator*
Robinson, Emma Hairston *artist, educator*

FLORIDA

Apopka
Almeida, Artie N. *music specialist*

Boca Raton
Dower Gold, Catherine Anne *music history educator*

Bonita Springs
McNamara-Ringewald, Mary Ann Thérèse *artist, educator*

Boynton Beach
Rabinof, Sylvia *pianist, composer, author, educator*

Bradenton
Bjorklund, Nancy Margarette Watts *music educator*
Voorhees, Stephanie Robin Faught *retired art educator*

Cape Coral
Wendel, Joan Audrey *music educator*

Coral Gables
Sackstein, Rosalina Guerrero *music educator, consultant*

Cortez
Fowler, Arden Stephanie *music educator*

Daytona Beach
Chesnut, Nondis Lorine *screenwriter, consultant, reading and language arts educator, instructor, counselor*
Knestrick, Janice Lee *art educator*
Rodriguez, Carmen Vila *artist, art educator, art historian*

Destin
Najarian, Betty Jo *music educator*

Eagle Lake
Londeree, Ramona Gayle *art educator*

Englewood
Brainard, Paul Henry *musicologist, retired music educator*
Dickson, Katharine Hayland *dance educator*

Eustis
Alfrey, Lydia Jean *musician educator*

Fort Lauderdale
Gillam, Paula Sample *artist, educator*
Moorhead, Rolande Annette Reverdy *artist, educator*

Fort Myers
Frank, Elizabeth Ahls (Betsy Frank) *art educator, artist*
Gorelik, Alla *piano educator*

Gainesville
Bodine, Willis Ramsey, Jr., *music educator, organist*
Klenk, Terry Allen *theater educator*
Paul, Ouida Fay *music educator*

Hollywood
Border, Gladys Louise *piano educator*

Jacksonville
Huber, Mary Susan *music educator*
Mikulas, Joseph Frank *graphic designer, educator, painter*

Key West
Mitchell, John Dietrich *theatre arts institute executive*

Kissimmee
Mastrangelo, Bobbi *artist, educator*

Melbourne
Failla, Sophia Lynn *artist, educator*

Melrose
Harley, Ruth *artist, educator*

Miami
Brant, Duane James *art educator*
Kitner, Jon David *art educator*
Tschumy, Freda Coffing *artist, educator*

Milton
Arnold, Margaret Morelock *music specialist, educator, performer*

Okeechobee
Chilcutt, Dorthe Margaret *art educator, artist*
Mercer, Frances deCourcy *artist, educator*

Orange Park
Walsh, James Anthony (Tony Walsh) *theater and film educator*

Osprey
Koenig, Peter Laszlo *artist, educator, curator, author*

Pinellas Park
Benedict, Gail Cleveland *music educator*

Saint Augustine
Quirke, Lillian Mary *retired art educator*
Solomon, James Emory *music educator*

Sarasota
Chase, Jeanne Norman *artist, educator*
Eginton, Margaret L. *movement educator, dancer, theater director*
Teller, Douglas H. *artist, educator*
Vasilaki, Linda Boozer *music educator*
Winterhalter, Dolores August (Dee Winterhalter) *art educator*

Shalimar
Sublette, Julia Wright *music educator, performer, adjudicator*

Tallahassee
Barrett-Hayes, Debra Paige *art educator*
Housewright, Wiley Lee *music educator*

Tampa
Cardoso, Anthony Antonio *artist, educator*
Manieri, Michele Dawn *musician, educator*
Nadrotoska, Barbara Anna *art educator*
Noyes, Debra Rose *dance educator*
Scialdo, Mary Ann *music educator, musician*

Tarpon Springs
Renee, Lisabeth Mary *art educator, artist, galley director*

Temple Terrace
Kashdin, Gladys Shafran *painter, educator*

Titusville
Davis, Thomas Paul *music educator, choral director*

West Palm Beach
Rander, JoAnn Corpaci *musician, music educator*

Yulee
Harper, Sheryl Ann *music educator*

GEORGIA

Athens
Edison, Diane *artist, educator, administrator*

Kent, Robert B. *artist, educator*
Pannell, Sylvia Jo Hillyard *drama/theatrical designer, educator*
Staub, August William *drama educator, theatrical producer, director*

Atlanta
Albrecht, Timothy Edward *musician, educator*
Greco, Anthony Joseph *artist, educator, administrator*
McLean, James Albert *artist, educator*
McRaney, James Thomas *choral music educator*
Rhodes, Ann Frances Bloodworth *artist, art history lecturer*

Bainbridge
Lucas, Tammi Michelle *music educator*

Carrollton
Barr, Mary Jeanette *art educator*

Cave Spring
Morrow, Winifred Bryant *artist, educator*

Columbus
Arnold, James Austin *music educator, director of bands, administrator*

Decatur
Cartman, Shirley Eleise *retired music educator*
Downs, Jon Franklin *drama educator, director, writer*
Morrison, Margaret L. *artist, educator, consultant*

Dunwoody
Clark, Faye Louise *drama and speech educator*

Gainesville
McCord, Gloria Dawn Harmon *music educator, choral director, organist*

Homer
Rylee, Gloria Genelle *music educator*

Lagrange
Greene, Annie Lucille *artist, retired art educator*

Lawrenceville
Hendrix, Jacquelyn McIntyre *elementary music educator*

Macon
Johnson, Bonnie Sue *piano educator*
Weaver, Jacquelyn Kunkel Ivey *artist, educator*

Marietta
Hutson, Jacquelyn Collins *pianist, educator*
Ramirez, Sandra Leigh *ceramic artist, potter, educator*
Stone, Cynthia Marie Beavers *dancing and gymnastics educator*

Rome
Potts, Glenda Rue *music educator*

Roswell
Devine, Libby *art educator, consultant*
Lackey, Deborah K. *art educator*

Stone Mountain
Bundy, Jane Bowden *artist, educator*

Thomaston
Pitts, Charles Carey *music educator*

Tucker
Johnson, Sherilyn Rae *music educator*

Waleska
Naylor, Susan Embry *music educator*

HAWAII

Ewa Beach
Kea, Jonathan Guy *instrumental music educator*

Honolulu
Betts, Barbara Stoke *artist, educator*
Preble, Duane *artist, art educator*
Sussman, Sharon Ann *art educator*

IDAHO

Boise
Baldassarre, Joseph Anthony *musician, musicologist, music educator*

Meridian
Shaffer, Mary Louise *art educator*

Middleton
Killmaster, John Henry, III, *artist, educator*

ILLINOIS

Aurora
Halfvarson, Lucille Robertson *music educator*
McCarthy, Mary Elizabeth (Beth) Constance *conductor, educator, music educator*

Chicago
Castillo, Mario Enrique *artist, educator*
Cole, Grace V. *painter, art educator*
Heider, Anne Harrington *music educator*
Howell, Pamela Catherine *vocal music educator*
Kenney, Estelle Koval *artist, educator*
Lazar, Ludmila *concert pianist, music educator, pedagogue*
May, Aviva Rabinowitz *music educator, linguist, musician*
Naudzius, Aldona Kanauka *pianist, music educator*

Novak, Marlena *artist, educator, writer, curator*
Smoller, Irene Mildred *artist, educator*
Wooten, Robert E. *musician, educator*
Wyszynski, Richard Chester *musician, writer, conductor, educator*

Country Club Hills
McClelland, Helen *music educator*

Dekalb
Mahmoud, Ben *artist, art educator*
Rollman, Charlotte *artist, educator*

East Saint Louis
Brown, Joan Renee *music educator*

Edwardsville
Anderson, Mary Jane *music educator*
Malone, Robert Roy *artist, art educator*

Elgin
Colpitts, Gail Elizabeth *artist, educator*
Dodohara, Jean Noton *music educator*

Elmhurst
Weber, John Pitman *artist, educator*

Eureka
West, Nancy Lee *music educator, performance artist, entertainer*

Evanston
Karlins, M(artin) William *composer, educator*

Glenview
Shineflug, Elizabeth (Nana) *theater educator, artistic director*

Highland Park
Slavick, Ann Lillian *retired art educator*

Joliet
Randolph, Sarah Ann Bush *music supervisor, computer coordinator*

Libertyville
Wyckoff, Alexander *stage designer, educator*

Lombard
Hudson, Samuel Campbell, Jr., *art educator, artist, sculptor, portraitist*

Oak Park
Mason, Barbara E. Suggs *educator*

Palatine
Anderson, Craig Allen *art educator*

Palos Hills
Porter, Joyce Klowden *theatre educator and director*

Pana
Waddington, Irma Joann *music teacher*

Park Forest
Cribbs, Maureen Ann *artist, educator*

Peoria
Price Boday, Mary Kathryn *choreographer, small business owner, educator*

Rantoul
Holmes, Lois Rehder *composer, piano and voice educator*

River Forest
Prendergast, Carole Lisak *musician, educator*

Rock Island
Maloon, Cleve Alexis *music educator*

Rockford
Heuer, Beth Lee *music educator, composer, arranger*

Westmont
Nyien, Patricia *music educator*

Wheaton
Lowrie, Pamela Burt *educator, artist*

INDIANA

Anderson
Olson, Carol Lea *lithographer, educator, photographer*

Bloomington
Connally, Sandra Jane Oppy *retired art educator, artist*

Evansville
Baker, Gloria Marie *visual artist, art educator*
Roth, Carolyn Louise *art educator*

Hanover
Nickels, Ruth Elizabeth *band director*

Indianapolis
Kleeman, Diane Elizabeth *music educator*
Lord, William Herman *performing arts educator, theatre consultant*
McIntyre, Lola Mazza *music educator*
Prince, Eileen Simkin *art educator*

Kokomo
Foust, Karen *art educator*

Muncie
Hunter, Miriam Eileen *artist, educator*

Nashville
Bartels, Patricia Rhoden *masters fine art educator*

West Lafayette
Bannatyne, Mark William McKenzie *technical graphics educator*

IOWA

Ames
Paschke, Teresa Ann *artist, educator*

Cedar Falls
Hedden, Debra Gordon *music educator*

Cedar Rapids
Carson, William Stuart *music educator, music administrator*

Des Moines
Erickson, Elaine Mae *composer, poet*

Iowa City
Mather, Betty Bang *musician, educator*

Iowa Falls
Sherve-Ose, Anne *music educator*

Le Grand
Hildebrandt, Willis Harvey *artist, educator*

KANSAS

Caldwell
Robinson, Alice Jean McDonnell *retired drama and speech educator*

Dodge City
Ross, Connie L. *music educator*

Gem
Ziegelmeier, Patricia Kay *music educator, executive secretary*

Independence
Delacour, JoNell *music educator*

Lawrence
Duerksen, George Louis *music educator, music therapist*
Tsubaki, Andrew Takahisa *theater director, educator*

Manhattan
Bailey, Sally Dorothy *drama therapist, playwright*
Kren, Margo *artist, art educator*

Olathe
Smith, Katheryn Jeanette *music educator*

Pratt
Shrack, Marsha Carol *art educator, gallery director*

Topeka
Menninger, Rosemary Jeanetta *art educator, writer*
Smith, Linda S. *music educator, musician*

KENTUCKY

Frankfort
Fletcher, Winona Lee *theater educator emeritus*
Kirstein, Janis Adrian *art educator*

Lexington
Boyer, Lillian Buckley *artist, educator*

Louisville
Murrell, Deborah Anne *music educator, speaker, writer*

LOUISIANA

Alexandria
Jeffress, Charles H. *retired art educator*

Baton Rouge
Bishara, Monica Stewart *art educator*
McCoy, Wesley Lawrence *musician, conductor, educator*
Wright, Erin Dean *graphic design educator*

Hammond
Hemberger, Glen James *university band director, music educator*

Lafayette
Stravinska, Sarah *dance educator*

Madisonville
Flattmann, Alan Raymond *artist, educator*

Metairie
deMoruelle, Charmaine *music educator*

Monroe
Sharp, Karen Dean *art educator*

New Orleans
Best, Susan Marie *artist, educator*

Sulphur
Barnes, Aleta Willis *communication and drama educator*

MAINE

Scarborough
Warg, Pauline *artist, educator*

Waterville
Desrosiers, Muriel C. *music educator, retired nursing consultant*

Wells
Hero, Barbara Ferrell *visual and sound artist, writer*

West Baldwin
Simmonds, Rae Nichols *musician, composer, educator*

MARYLAND

Annapolis
Smith Tarchalski, Helen Marie *piano educator*

Arnold
Kellogg-Smith, Peter *sculptor, educator*
Malmgren, Richard Axel, Jr., *art educator*

Baltimore
Carroll, Karen *art educator*
Hall, Marian M. *retired music educator*
Rauschenberg, Dale Eugene *music educator*

Bel Air
Delaney, Jean Marie *art educator*

Cabin John
Bergfors, Constance Marie *artist, educator*

Chevy Chase
Kranking, Margaret Graham *artist, educator*

College Park
Lapinski, Tadeusz Andrew *artist, educator*

Columbia
Blackwell, Camellia Ann *art educator*
Kurlander, Honey Wachtel *artist, educator*

Elkridge
Matthews, Lois Marr *musician, music educator*

Fort Washington
Hankerson, Charlie Edward, Jr., *music educator*

Frederick
Pope, Deanna L. T. *music educator*

Galena
Hunsperger, Elizabeth Jane *art and design consultant, educator*

Glen Burnie
Ruth, Shiela Grant *music educator*

Highland
Varga, Deborah Trigg *music educator, entertainment company owner*

Huntingtown
Jameson, Gary *art educator*

Olney
Mardis, Linda Keiser *educator, consultant, writer*

Reisterstown
Goethe, Elizabeth Hogue *music educator*

Rockville
Cain, Karen Mirinda *musician, educator*
Kurkul, Wenyi Wang *musician, educator, administrator*
Waidler, Beverly Mae *music teacher*

Saint Marys City
Froom, David *composer, music educator*

Silver Spring
Jones, Tina Charlene *music educator, genealogy and law researcher*

Takoma Park
McLain, Sandra Brignole *art educator*

Woodstock
Wells, Christine Valerie *music educator*

MASSACHUSETTS

Amherst
Anderson, Ronald Trent *artist, educator*

Beverly
Broudo, Joseph David *art educator*

Boston
Anderson, Jewelle Lucille *musician, educator*
Lesser, Laurence *musician, educator*
Weeks, Clifford Myers *musician, educational administrator*

Bridgewater
Nicholeris, Carol Angela *music educator, composer, conductor*

Brookline
Rizzi, Marguerite Claire *music educator*
Swirnoff, Lois *artist, color theorist*

Cambridge
Alcalay, Albert S. *artist, design educator*
Bakanowsky, Louis Joseph *visual arts educator, architect, artist*

Chicopee
Costanzo, Nanci Joy *art educator*

Falmouth
Powers, L. Lindley (L. Lindley) *communication and theatre arts educator*

Fitchburg
Lorenzen, Louis Otto *art educator*

Gloucester
Donnelly, Barbara *artist, educator*

Groton
Clark, Susan Frances *theater educator*

Lenox
Lindner, Erna Caplow *dance educator, choreographer, movement therapist*

Medford
Senelick, Laurence Philip *theatre educator, director, writer*

Natick
Morgan, Betty Mitchell *artist, educator*

Newtonville
Polonsky, Arthur *artist, educator*

Norfolk
Beard, Carol Elaine *art educator*

North Dartmouth
Lindenberg, Mary K. *artist*

Norwood
Howard, Doris Marie *fine arts educator*

Plymouth
Freyermuth, Virginia Karen *art educator*

Reading
Frey, Joanne Alice Tupper *art educator*

Rockport
Martin, Roger Hemenway *artist, educator*

Sheffield
Schmehl Morley, Susan Linda *fine arts educator, artist*

Sudbury
Aronson, David *artist, retired art educator*

Wayland
Dergalis, George *artist, educator*

Westfield
Conant, Patricia Carol *printmaker, educator*

Weston
Fine, Sally Solfisburg *artist, educator*
Rearick, Anne *photographer, educator*

Winchester
Neuman, Robert Sterling *art educator, artist*

Worthington
Schrade, Rolande Maxwell Young *composer, pianist, educator*

MICHIGAN

Ann Arbor
Woods, Leigh Alan *theatre educator*

Battle Creek
Cramer, Janis R. *educational art specialist, artist*
Matthews, Wyhomme S. *retired music educator, academic administrator*
Van Almen, Karen *art educator*

Beverly Hills
Tolias, Linda Puroff *music educator*

Bloomfield Hills
Burnett, Patricia Hill *portrait artist, author, sculptor, lecturer*

Brethren
Crandell, Deborah Lynne Kaskinen *art educator*

Cedar
Kunkel, Dorothy Ann *music educator*

Clinton Township
Zanni, Christina Marie *art educator*

Dearborn
Dzuiblinski, Gerard Arthur *theatre educator, artistic director*
Orlowska-Warren, Lenore Alexandria *art educator, fiber artist*

Detroit
Catchings, Yvonne Parks *artist, educator*

East Lansing
Wellman, William Walter *printing executive*
Whiting-Dobson, Lisa Lorraine *video production educator, producer, director*

Farmington Hills
Eisner, Gail Ann *artist, educator*
Goslin, Gerald Hugh *concert pianist, educator*

Flint
McGinnis, Tina Marie *art educator*

Glenn
Rizzolo, Louis B. M. *artist, educator*

Grand Blanc
Thompson, Thomas Adrian *sculptor*

Grand Rapids
Blovits, Larry John *retired art educator*

Holland
Van Noord, Diane C. *artist, educator*

Kalamazoo
Vander Weg, Phillip Dale *art educator, academic administrator, sculptor*

Lansing
Kluge, Len H. *director, actor, theater educator*

Lawton
Bowman, Jerry Wayne *artist, research scientist*

Midland
Belton, Betty Kepka *retired art educator, artist*

Monroe
Brodie, Catherine Anne *music educator*

Mount Pleasant
Craig, John Robert *broadcast and cinematic arts educator, researcher*
Orlik, Christina Bear *music educator*
Traines, Rose Wunderbaum *sculptor, educator*

Novi
Barr, David John *retired art educator*

Petoskey
Switzer, Carolyn Joan *artist, educator*

Plainwell
Flower, Jean Frances *art educator*

Royal Oak
Chambers-McCarty, Lorraine *painter, educator*

South Branch
Savard, Christine Elizabeth *music educator*

Williamston
Mehaffey, Mark Edward *retired art educator, artist*

MINNESOTA

Blue Earth
Ellingsen, Michael O. *music educator, theater educator*

Brainerd
Wannamaker, Mary Ruth *music educator*

Edina
Kirchner, Mary Katherine *singer, music educator*

Minneapolis
Fetler, Paul *retired composer*
Holen, Norman Dean *art educator, artist*
Nortwen, Patricia Harman *music educator*
Williamson, Dorothy June *art consultant, artist, educator, writer*

Moorhead
Ruzicka, Charles Edward *music educator, director*

Plymouth
Werden, David Ray *music educator*

Saint Cloud
Gainey, Kathryn O'Reilly *art education educator*

Saint Paul
Matteson, Clarice Chris *artist, educator*
Olson, Bettye Johnson *artist, retired educator*

Two Harbors
Gredzens, Sandra May Pillsbury *art educator*

MISSISSIPPI

Clinton
Eaves, Dorothy Ann Greene *music educator*

Florence
Forbes, Felicia René *art educator*

Grenada
Thomas, Ouida Power *music educator*

Jackson
Holly, Ellistine Perkins *music educator*
Howle, Martha Alice Turner *retired art educator*

Moss Point
Stephens, Cecile Higdon *artist, art educator*

Ocean Springs
Odom, Patricia Ann (Patt Odom) *artist, educator*

Raymond
Bee, Anna Cowden *dance educator*

MISSOURI

Ballwin
Rothermich, Gayla *music educator, director*

Blue Springs
Ennis, Calvin Joseph *art educator*

Bolivar
Gott, Wesley Atlas *art educator*
Hooper, William Loyd *music educator, university administrator*

Branson
Bradley, Leon Charles *musician, educator, consultant*

Brunswick
Riddle, Donald Ray, Sr., *retired art educator*

Chesterfield
Fowler, Marti *fine arts consultant*

Columbia
Leong, Proessor Lampo (Lanbo Liang) *artist, educator*

Foristell
Travis-Jaspering, Margaret Rose *artist, educator*

Hermann
Mahoney, Catherine Ann *artist, educator*

Iberia
Novak, Jaunita Kathyl *retired music educator*

Imperial
Enrico, Lisa Renee *music educator*

Jefferson City
Greene, Thomasina Talley *concert pianist, educator*

Kansas City
Bodinson, Nancy Sue *art educator*
Bransby, Eric James *muralist, educator*
Buford, Ronetta Marie *music educator*
Crist, William Gary *artist, retired educator*
Ethern, Aberdeen *music educator*
Hutson, Betty Switzer *art educator, artist*
Londré, Felicia Mae Hardison *theater educator*

Kirksville
Weerts, Richard Kenneth *music educator*

Liberty
Harriman, Richard Lee *performing arts association administrator, educator*

Platte City
Kalin, D(orothy) Jean *artist, educator*

Richmond Heights
Campbell, Abe William *music educator*

Saint Louis
Bradley, Marilynne Gail *advertising executive, advertising educator*
Dunivent, John Thomas *artist, educator*
Haley, Johnetta Randolph *musician, educator, university official*
Lipan, Petruta E. *semiotician, curator, artist*
Ott, Sabina *art educator*
Rosen, Adrienne *artist, educator*
Sago, Janis Lynn *photography educator*
Schindler, Laura Ann *piano teacher, accompanist*
Shucart, Evelyn Ann *artist, educator*
Waddington, Bette Hope (Elizabeth Crowder) *violinist, educator*

Springfield
Thompson, Wade S. *artist, art and design educator, administrator*

Warrensburg
McAdams, Charles Alan *music educator*
Resch, Rita Marie *music educator*

Webster Groves
Smith, Barbara Martin *art educator, artist*

MONTANA

Great Falls
Becker, Julia Margaret *artist, educator*

Miles City
Walden, Alice *artist, educator*

Shelby
Burns, Carolyn Diane *music educator*

NEBRASKA

Albion
Texley, Tamera Sue *musician, educator*

Chadron
Winkle, William Allan *music educator*

Lincoln
Janovy, Karen Anne Oneth *art museum educator, curator*

Mc Cook
Dernovich, Donald Frederick *artist, educator*

Omaha
Fareri, Veronica Helen *church musician, liturgist, educator*
Keiser, Catherine Ann *band director*

South Sioux City
Dailey, Michael Patrick *music educator*

NEVADA

Fallon
Venturacci, Toni Marie *artist, substitute educator*

Las Vegas
Bond-Brown, Barbara Ann *musician, educator*
Slade, Barbara Ann *art educator*

Mesquite
Alcorn, Karen Zefting Hogan *artist, art educator, journalist*

Reno
Hudson, Karen Ann Sampson *music educator*

NEW HAMPSHIRE

Hanover
Moss, Ben Frank, III, *art educator, painter*

Wolff, Christian *composer, music and classics educator*

Manchester
Joseph, Lynne Cathie *art educator*

Salem
Flanagan, Anne Patricia *art educator, artist*

Somersworth
Tully, Hugh Michael *music educator*

NEW JERSEY

Belmar
Swett, Stephen Frederick, Jr., *artist, educator*

Bridgewater
Patton, Diana Lee Wilkoc *artist, educator*

Cliffside Park
Perhacs, Marylouise Helen *musician, educator*

Cresskill
Smyth, Craig Hugh *fine arts educator*

Delran
Korba, Donna Marie *art educator*

Denville
Veech, Lynda Anne *musician, educator*

East Brunswick
Kupchynsky, Jerry Markian *orchestra conductor, educator*
Savio, Frances Margaret Cammarotta *music educator*

Elizabeth
Evans, Arthur Richard *visual arts educator*

Englewood
Valenti, Paula Anne (Pelak) *art educator, assistant principal*

Fair Lawn
Parker, Adrienne Natalie *art educator, art historian*

Freehold
Cheng, Grace Zheng-Ying *music educator*
Flynn, Pamela *artist, educator*

Glassboro
Wasserman, Burton *artist, educator*

Hightstown
Raichle, Elaine Lucas *retired art educator*

Holmdel
Slovik, Sandra Lee *retired art educator*

Little Silver
Sizer, Rebecca Rudd *performing arts educator, arts coordinator*

Lodi
Arella, Ann Marietta *music educator, vocalist*

Long Valley
Falk, Barbara Higinbotham *music educator*

Medford
Saltus, Phyllis Borzelliere *music educator*

Metuchen
Arbeiter, Joan *artist, educator*

Monmouth Junction
Kriegman, Susan L. *artist, educator*

Monroe Township
Liebson, Milt *sculptor, educator, author*

Montville
Garfinkel, Barbara Ann *pianist, educator, musicologist*

Morristown
Prince, Leah Fanchon *art educator and research institute administrator*

Newark
D'Astolfo, Frank Joseph *graphic designer, educator*

Oak Ridge
Bodek, Ruth Naomi *art educator*

Paramus
Teichman, Evelyn *antiques appraiser, educator, estate liquidator*

Perth Amboy
Richardson-Melech, Joyce Suzanne *music educator, singer*

Pomona
White, Wendel Alberick *art educator, artist, photographer*

Princeton
Boretz, Naomi Messinger *artist, educator*
Bunnell, Peter Curtis *photography and art educator, museum curator*
Orphanides, Nora Charlotte *ballet educator*
Vizzini, Carol Redfield *symphony musician, music educator*
Wilmerding, John *art history educator, museum curator*

Princeton Junction
Rose, Peggy Jane *artist, art educator, gifted education advocate*

Ridgewood
Riccio-Sauer, Joyce *art educator*

Rivervale
Moderacki, Edmund Anthony *music educator, conductor*

Shamong
Knight, Margaret Elizabeth *music educator*

Shrewsbury
Abel, Mary Elizabeth (Bette) *art educator, artist*

Somers Point
Hagerthey, Gwendolyn Irene *retired music educator*

Somerville
Dixon, Joanne Elaine *music educator*

Springfield
DeVone, Denise *artist, educator*

Tinton Falls
Polese, Mary Lucretia *art educator*

Toms River
Hughes, Frank Louis *high school band director*

Trenton
Chavooshian, Marge *artist, educator*
Goldstein, Howard *art educator*

Union
Korn, Neal Mark *painter, art educator*

Verona
Monks, Linda Ann *art educator*

Wayne
Law, Janet Mary *music educator*

Westwood
French, Phyllis Olivia *artistic director, dance instructor*

Wyckoff
Olejarz, Harold *art educator*

NEW MEXICO

Albuquerque
Antreasian, Garo Zareh *artist, lithographer, art educator*
Feinberg, Elen Amy *artist, educator*
Hovel, Esther Harrison *art educator*
Rice, Linda Angel *music educator*
Smyer, Myrna Ruth *drama educator*

Bernalillo
Pritchard, Betty Jean *retired art educator*

Farmington
Evans, Helen Ruth *music educator, pianist*

Gallup
Cattaneo, Jacquelyn Annette Kammerer *artist, educator*

Portales
Sikes, Juanita Lou *art educator*

Roswell
Peterson, Dorothy Hawkins *artist, educator*

Sandia Park
Weitz, Jeanne Stewart *artist, educator*

Santa Fe
Dean, Nat *artist, educator*
Herdman, Susan *art educator, artist*
Lippincott, Janet *artist, art educator*
Sauer, Jane Gottlieb *artist, educator*
Shubart, Dorothy Louise Tepfer *artist, educator*
Taylor, Beverly Lacy *musician, educator, stringed instrument restorer*

Silver City
McCray, Dorothy Westaby *artist, printmaker, educator*

NEW YORK

Albany
Herrick, Kristine Ford *graphic design educator*
Shankman, Gary Charles *art educator*

Amherst
Braun, Kazimierz Pawel *theatrical director, writer, educator*

Ardsley
Lysun, Gregory *artist, educator*

Bearsville
Jordan, John Lester (Gaudeamus) *artist*

Binghamton
Weissman, Ann Paley *art educator, artist, consultant*

Briarcliff Manor
Ostrofsky, Anna *music educator, violinist*

Bronx
Fiddle, Lorraine Anne *artist, art educator*
Pearlman, Barbara *artist, educator*
Ter-Abramyants, Lala Abramovna *artist, educator*
Trovato-Cantori, Lorraine Maria *art educator*
Tygiel, Marti (Martha Tygiel) *instrumental music educator*

PROFESSIONAL INDEX — HIGHER EDUCATION: VISUAL AND PERFORMING ARTS

Brooklyn
Amendola, Sal John *artist, educator, writer*
Borel, Ludmila Ivanovna *ballerina, educator*
Contino, Rosalie Helene *historian, playwright*
Dantzic, Cynthia Maris *artist, educator*
Dinnerstein, Simon Abraham *artist, educator*
Gianlorenzi, Nona Elena *painter, art dealer, educator*
Gordon, Edward Harrison *choral conductor, educator*
Hoyt, Ellen *artist, educator*
Plaut, Jane Margaret *art educator*
Scherer, Suzanne Marie *artist, educator*
Vidal, Maureen Eris *theater educator, actress*

Buffalo
Duling, Gretchen Anne *music educator*
Janiga, Mary Ann *art educator, artist*
Krims, Les *artist*
St. Pierre, Cheryl Ann *retired art educator*
Siskar, John Frederick *art educator*

Catskill
Petrosky, Regine *art educator*

Clifton Park
Orsini, Paul Vincent *music educator*

Cutchogue
Penney, Jacqueline *artist, educator*

Forest Hills
Baral, Lillian *artist, retired educator*

Fredonia
Booth, Robert Alan *artist, educator*

Great Neck
Shapiro, Dee *artist, educator*

Greenlawn
Starost, Diane Joan *music educator*

Hamilton
Loveless, James King *art educator*

Hempstead
Chapman, Ronald Thomas *musician, educator*
Graffeo, Mary Thérèse *music educator, performer*

Highland
Pritzker, Elisa *painter, sculptor, educator, theater director*

Ithaca
Arquit, Nora Harris *retired music educator, writer*
McCue, Arthur Harry *artist, educator*

Jackson Heights
Morrow, Nana Kwasi Scott Douglas *choreographer, writer, filmmaker, educator*
Schuyler, Jane *fine arts educator*

Larchmont
Demsky, Hilda Green *artist, secondary and college art educator*
Swire, Edith Wypler *music educator, musician, violist, violinist*

Manlius
Koch, Catherine Ann *music educator, musician*

Massapequa
Douglas, Mary Christine *artistic director, dance instructor*
Turk, Elizabeth Ann *music educator*

Massena
Schroll, Edwin John *retired secondary educator, stage director*

Melville
Sobol, Elise Schwarcz *music educator*

Millbrook
Flexner, Josephine Moncure *musician, educator*

New Rochelle
Adato, Linda Joy *artist, educator*
Metz, Roxie Anne *art educator*

New York
Baker, Ruth Baytop *music educator*
Bardos, Karoly *television and film educator, writer, director*
Braden, Martha Brooke *concert pianist, educator*
Cardullo, Robert James *theatre educator*
Carlson, Marvin Albert *theater educator*
Chwatsky, Ann *photographer, educator*
Cooper, Mark Frederick *artist, sculptor, art educator*
David, Don Raymond *artist, educator*
Donelian, Armen *pianist, composer, author*
Frankel, Gene *theater director, writer, producer, educator*
Friedman, Sally *artist, educator*
Gentile, Gloria Irene *computer designer, educator, watercolor artist*
Goldin, Leon *artist, educator*
Healy, Julia Schmitt *artist, educator*
Horowitz, Robert Aaron *art educator, researcher, music educator*
Kaish, Luise Clayborn *sculptor, former educator*
Kelley, Mike *artist*
Kurman, Juta *music educator*
Morgan, Jacqui *illustrator, painter, educator, writer*
Papi, Liza Renia *artist, writer, educator*
Pardee, Margaret Ross *violinist, violist, educator*
Pionk, Richard Cletus *artist, educator*
Richards, Bill Arthur *artist, educator*
Robbins, Carrie F(ishbein) *costume designer, educator*
Semmel, Joan *artist, educator*
Shane, Rita *opera singer, educator*
Sherman, Arthur *theater educator, writer, actor, composer, sculptor*
Southworth, Linda Jean *artist, critic, educator, poet*
Stoloff, Carolyn *artist, poet, educator*
Sullivan, Edward J. *fine arts educator*
Verona, Monica J. *concert pianist, educator*

Newburgh
Sabini, Barbara Dorothy *art educator, artist*

Newcomb
Chatzky, Herbert *music educator*

Niagara Falls
Kuciewski, Patrick Michael *music educator*

Northport
Wolf, Constance Sloggatt *artist, educator*

Nyack
Price, Helen (Lois) Burdon *artist, retired nurse educator*

Odessa
Stillman-Myers, Joyce L. *artist, educator, writer, illustrator, consultant*

Oswego
Baitsell, Wilma Williamson *artist, educator, lecturer*
Fox, Michael David *retired art educator*
Lisk, Edward Stanley *musician, educator, conductor*

Palisades
Porta, Siena Gillann *sculptor, educator*

Pawling
Utter, Donald L. *music educator*

Peekskill
Clark, William Roger *artist, educator*

Port Chester
Penney, Linda Helen *music educator*

Rhinebeck
Ewald, Wendy Taylor *photographer, writer, educator*

Riverhead
Talmage, Lisa Birnstein *music educator*

Rochester
Amy, Michaël Jacques *art historian, educator, art critic*
Kleper, Michael Laurence *graphic arts educator*
Wenger, Bruce Edward *art educator, educator*

Saratoga Springs
Porter, David Hugh *pianist, classicist, academic administrator, liberal arts educator*

Sparkill
Myers, Adele Anna *artist, educator, nun*

Syracuse
Belfort-Chalat, Jacqueline *art educator, sculptor*
Serafin, John Alfred *art educator*

Troy
Isaacs, Andrea *editor, publisher, dancer, choreographer, former educator*
Vamos, Igor *art educator*

Verona
Smith, Kathy Ann *music educator*

Westbury
Waterman, Dianne Corrine *artist, educator, writer, ministry leader*

Westhampton Beach
Costanzo, Frank Dennis *music educator*

Willow
Goetz, Mary Anna *artist, educator*

NORTH CAROLINA

Apex
Johnson, Leslie Diane Horvath *artist, graphic designer, small business owner, educator*

Brevard
Dillon, Doris (Doris Dillon Kenofer) *artist, art historian*

Chapel Hill
Hammond, David Alan *stage director, educator*
Parker, Scott Jackson *theatre manager*
Powell, Carolyn Wilkerson *music educator*

Charlotte
D'Amato, Frances Louise *art and psychology educator*
Iley, Martha Strawn *music educator*

Clarkton
Wuebbels, Theresa Elizabeth *art educator*

Creedmoor
Cross, June Crews *retired music educator*

Davidson
Jackson, Herb *artist, educator*

Eden
Sanders, Barbara Fayne *artist, educator*

Greensboro
Middleton, Herman David, Sr., *theater educator*
Russell, Peggy Taylor *soprano, educator*
Styles, Teresa Jo *producer, educator*

Greenville
Chamberlain, Charles Frank *retired artist, educator*
Laing, Penelope Gamble *art educator*
Wallin, Leland Dean *artist, educator*

King
Shanahan, Elizabeth Anne *art educator*

Leasburg
Treacy, Sandra Joanne Pratt *art educator, artist*

Lincolnton
Hallman, Patricia Ann *music educator*

Plymouth
Boyd, Mona Manning *music educator*

Raleigh
Garriss, Phyllis Weyer *music educator, performer*

Rougemont
Nilsson, Mary Ann *music educator*

Salisbury
Julian, Rose Rich *music educator, director*

Wilmington
Jones, Sarah Downing *visual arts educator*

Winston Salem
Stewart, Virginia L. Caudle *retired cosmetology educator*
Trautwein, George William *conductor, educator*

NORTH DAKOTA

Richardton
Miller, Jean Patricia Salmon *art educator*

OHIO

Alliance
Fugelberg, Nancy Jean *music educator*

Canton
Klotz, Leora Nylee *retired music educator, vocalist*

Centerville
Wasson-Shaw, Carol R. *music teacher*

Cincinnati
Bollen, Sharon Kesterson *artist, educator*
Brown, Lillie Harrison *music educator*
Cettel, Judith Hapner *artist, secondary school educator*
Strohmaier, Thomas Edward *designer, educator, photographer*

Cleveland
Pozo, Angelica *ceramic artist, educator*

Columbus
Landrum-Bittles, Jenita *artist, educator*
Reilly, Joy Harriman *theatre educator, playwright, actress, director*

East Cleveland
Soule, Lucile Snyder *pianist, music educator*

Fairfield
Huellemeier, Lori Ann *art educator*

Fredericktown
Boyd, Donald Edgar *artist, educator*

Geneva
Carrel, Marianne Eileen *music educator*

Lebanon
Coyan, Michael Lee *art and performing arts educator*

Middlefield
Jaite, Gail Ann *music educator*

Ottoville
Bowery, Warren E. *music educator*

Springfield
Patterson, Martha Ellen *artist, art educator*

Strongsville
Myers, Jack Fredrick *artist, educator, author*

Tipp City
Ahmed, Gail R. *music educator*

Wadsworth
Ross, Jane Arlene *music educator*

Walnut Creek
Lawrence, Alice Lauffer *artist, educator*

Warren
Starkey, Lucille A. *music educator*

Westerville
Lott, Vera Naomi *artist, educator*

Whitehall
Van Camp, Diana J. *music educator*

Willoughby
Baker, Charles Stephen *music educator*

Yellow Springs
Kadish, Katherine *artist, art educator*

Zanesville
Brown, Karen Rima *orchestra manager, Spanish language educator*

OKLAHOMA

Enid
Russell, Rhonda Cheryl *piano educator, recording artist*

Guthrie
Owens, Wallace, Jr., *art educator*

Lawton
Klein, Scott Richard *acting and directing educator*

Moore
Schonauer, Anne Miller *music educator*

Mounds
Fellows, Esther Elizabeth *musician, music educator*

Norman
Day, Adrienne Carol *artist, art educator*
Herstand, Theodore *theatre artist, educator*

Oklahoma City
Alaupovic, Alexandra Vrbanic *artist, educator*
Boston, Billie *costume designer, costume history educator*
Payne, Gareld Gene *vocal music educator, medical transcriptionist*
Rowan, Jo *ballerina, educator*
Twyman, Nita (Verita Twyman) *music educator*

Tulsa
Geary, Barbara Ann *recital and concert pianist, music educator*
Spencer, Winifred May *art educator*

Vinita
Castor, Carol Jean *artist, teacher*

OREGON

Corvallis
Hiratsuka, Yuji *artist, educator*

Eugene
Bailey, Exine Margaret Anderson *soprano, educator*
Bergquist, Peter *music educator emeritus*
Gourley, Paula Marie *art educator, artist, designer bookbinder, writer, publisher*

Medford
Schubert, Ruth Carol Hickok *artist, educator*

Portland
Berentsen, Kurtis George *music educator, choral conductor*
Blumberg, Naomi *symphony musician, educator*
Kaluza, Sheryle Siegfried *music educator, singer, songwriter*
Kuhns, Sally Nelson *trumpeter, music ensemble director, educator*
Robinson, Helene M. *retired music educator*

Roseburg
Ferguson, John Franklin *music educator*

Salem
Marshall, Cak (Catherine Elaine Marshall) *music educator, composer*

PENNSYLVANIA

Allentown
Battle, Turner Charles, III, *art educator, educational association administrator*
Beltzner, Gail Ann *music educator*

Ardmore
Rodriguez, Kathleen Moore *art educator*

Bethel Park
Culbertson-Stark, Mary *art educator*

Bryn Mawr
Goutman, Lois Clair *retired drama educator*

Cheyney
Ellis-Scruggs, Jan *theater arts educator*
Perlmutter, Dawn *art and philosophy educator, aesthetics researcher*

Clarion
Joslyn, Catherine Ruth *art educator, artist*

Downingtown
Crescenz, Valerie J. *music educator*

Edinboro
Weinkauf, David *film, animation, and photography educator*

Elkins Park
Simon, Marilyn Weintraub *art educator, sculptor*

Erie
Hamwi, Richard Alexander *art educator*
Wilson, Janet Marie *art educator*

Fairview
Krider, Margaret Young *art educator*

Hatboro
Carroll, Lucy Ellen *choral director, music coordinator, educator*

Haverford
Williams, William Earle *artist, educator, curator*

Havertown
Craley, Carol Ruth *art educator, academic administrator*

Hellertown
Conover, Annelle Elizabeth *music educator, educator*

Kutztown
Daub, Matthew Forrest *artist, educator*
Kuehne, Helenirene Anne *art educator*

Millersville
Bensur, Barbara Jean *art educator, researcher*

Monaca
Soltes, Joann Margaret *retired music educator, realtor*

Philadelphia
Fine, Miriam Brown *artist, educator, poet, writer*
Graffman, Gary *pianist, music educator*
Ingolfsson-Fassbind, Ursula G. *music educator*
Le Clair, Charles George *artist, retired university dean*
Spandorfer, Merle Sue *artist, educator, author*

Phoenixville
Allen, Carol Linnea Ostrom *art educator*
Landis, Linda Kay *music educator*

Pittsburgh
Bononi, Robert Andrew *music educator*
dePackh, Mary Fraser Carter *artist, retired educator*
Foucart Vincenti, Valerie *retired art educator*
Holland, Dena *ballet educator*
Marinelli, Donald *drama educator*

Reading
Horacek, Constance Heller *graphic designer, educator*

Saint Marys
Pontzer, Lynda Marie *art educator*

Saltsburg
Buseck, Larry Allen *music educator*

Scranton
McCusker, Sister Joan *music educator*

Shavertown
Motyka, Susanne Victoria *music educator*

Shickshinny
Bonham-Hontz, Nancy Lynne *art educator*
Luksha, Rosemary Dorothy *art educator*

Slippery Rock
Bruya, John Robert *art educator*

Spring Grove
Helberg, Shirley Adelaide Holden *artist, educator*

State College
Knight, Wanda Bridges *art educator*

Swarthmore
Devin, Lee (Philip Lee Devin) *dramaturg, author*

University Park
Van Dommelen, David B. *artist, educator*

Warminster
Koch, Nancy Joy *music educator, choral director, vocal coach*

Waverly
Tosti, Sally T. *artist, educator*

West Chester
Burton, John Bryan *music educator*
Pettigrew, Claire Rudolph *music educator*

Wilkes Barre
Joyce, Ann Iannuzzo *art educator*

RHODE ISLAND

Chepachet
Jubinska, Patricia Ann *ballet instructor, choreographer, artist, artist*

Cranston
Crooks, W. Spencer *artist, educator*

Greenville
Hopkins, Catherine Lee *music educator*

Pawtucket
Tetreault, Louis N. *art educator*

Portsmouth
Byassee, Margaret Foley *art educator, poet, vocalist*

Providence
Dempsey, Raymond Leo, Jr., *radio and television producer, moderator, writer*
Feldman, Walter Sidney *artist, educator*
Geisser, Peter James *artist, educator for hearing impaired*
Wilmeth, Don Burton *theatre arts educator, theatre historian, administrator, editor*

SOUTH CAROLINA

Anderson
Carroll, Edward Perry *instrumental music educator, conductor*
Williamson, Richard Anthony *music educator, conductor*

Central
Smith-Cox, Elizabeth Shelton *art educator*

Denmark
Oliver, David Francis *music educator, director*

Mc Cormick
Hofer, Ingrid *artist, educator*

Orangeburg
Kozachek, Janet Lynne *artist, educator*

Pendleton
Landreth, James Mack *elementary school music educator*

Rock Hill
Wishert, Jo Ann Chappell *music educator, elementary and secondary education educator*
Woods, Jeannie Marlin *theatre educator*

SOUTH DAKOTA

Brookings
Kinder, Karen DeAnn *art educator*

TENNESSEE

Chattanooga
Fouquet, Anne (Judy Fuqua) *musician, music educator*

Cookeville
McGhee, Katherine Elaine *art education educator*

Covington
Kinningham, Alan Goodrum *music educator, composer/arranger*

Hendersonville
Clark, Alan Martin *band director*

Johnson City
Jenrette, Thomas Shepard, Jr., *music educator, choral director*

Kingsport
Hyder, Betty Jean *art educator*

Knoxville
Jacobs, Kenneth A. *composer, educator*

Memphis
Bernstein, Janna S. Bernheim *art educator*
Crawford, Sheila Jane *elementary education librarian, reading consultant*
McPherson, Larry E(ugene) *photographer, educator*
Stark, Agnes Gordon *artist, educator*

Nashville
Hazlehurst, Franklin Hamilton *fine arts educator*
Lee, Douglas A. *music educator*
McKinney, Jane-Allen *artist and educator*
Montgomery, Dillard Brewster *musician, educator*
Roberts, Margaret Reynolds *art educator*
Warren, Jerry Lee *conductor, educator*

TEXAS

Arlington
Anderson, Jane Talley *artist, educator*
Witt, Anne Cleino *musician, education educator*

Austin
Hatgil, Paul Peter *artist, sculptor, educator*
Kennan, Kent Wheeler *composer, educator*
Mayer, Susan Martin *art educator*
Weismann, Donald Leroy *art educator, artist, filmmaker, writer*

Beaumont
Brailsford, June Evelyn *musician, educator*

Bellville
Wentworth, Bette Wilson *artist, educator*

Brenham
Brown, Marguerite Johnson *music educator*

Coleman
Needham, Judy Len *artist, art educator*

Corpus Christi
Allison, Joan Kelly *music educator, pianist*

Crystal City
Espinoza, Doris Loida *music educator, minister*

Dallas
Freiberger, Katherine Guion *composer, retired piano educator*
Hudgins, Louise Nan *art educator*
Johnson, Mary Elizabeth *music educator, pianist*
Palmer, Christine (Clelia Rose Venditti) *operatic singer, pianist, vocal educator*
Schulz, Sandra E. *art educator*
Varner, William Henry *music educator*

Denton
Bentley, Marji *music educator*
Davidson, Norma Lewis *concert violinist, composer, music educator, psychologist*

Desoto
Tyrer-Ferraro, Polly Ann *music instructor, software developer*

El Paso
Allaire-Curtis, Mary *dance instructor*

Euless
Leding, Anne Dixon *artist, educator*

Fort Worth
Rickett, Carolyn Kaye Master *artist, criminologist*
Schultz, Darrell Lee *art educator*

Frisco
de Veritch, Nina *cellist, music educator*

Garland
Syphers, Mary Frances *music educator*

Gonzales
Ince, Laurel T. *music educator*

Hallsville
Hutcherson, Donna Dean *retired music educator*

Harlingen
Godfrey, Aline Lucille *music specialist, church organist*

Houston
Auchter, Norma Holmes *musician, educator*
Baranovich, Diana Lea *music educator*
Jones, Florence M. *music educator*
Kenda, Juanita Echeverria *artist, educator*
King, Kay Wander *academic administrator, design educator, fashion designer, consultant*
Marion, Suzanne Margaret *music educator*
Perkyns, Jane Elizabeth *music educator, composer, actress*
Reid, Katherine Louise *artist, educator, author*
Rigsby, Carolyn Erwin *music educator*
Sing, Doris Anne *music educator*

Irving
Allen, Barbara Ann *musician, educator, personnel contractor*

Kerrville
Gold, Marlyn H. *art educator*

Lago Vista
Curtis, Mary Louise *artist, educator*

Lakehills
Spears, Diane Shields *artist, retired art academy administrator*

Lubbock
Mittler, Gene Allen *art educator*
van Appledorn, Mary Jeanne *composer, music educator, pianist*

Mcallen
Huber, Melba Stewart *dance educator and historian, dance studio owner, retailer*

Midland
Powers, Patricia Kennett *piano and organ educator*

Munday
Bennett, Rodney Dee *music educator*

Plano
Kuddes, Kathryn M. *fine arts director*

Redwater
Hammer, Richard Lee *music educator*

Rockwall
House, Robert William *music educator*

San Antonio
Broderick, James Allen *art educator*
Stephens, Martha Lockhart *writer, researcher*

Spring
Doyle, Joseph Francis, III, *art educator*
Mackay, Cynthia Jean *music educator*

Stephenville
Levisay, Leesa Dawn *music educator, composer*

Temple
Chamlee, Ann Combest *music educator*

Three Rivers
Barnes, Patricia Ann *art educator*

Tyler
Baker, Rebecca Louise *musician, music educator, consultant*
Hatfield, James Allen *theater arts educator, administrator*

UTAH

American Fork
Reinhold, Allen Kurt *graphic design educator*

Provo
Pratt, Rosalie Rebollo *harpist, educator*

Salt Lake City
Hayes, Elizabeth Roths *retired dance educator*
Kristensen, Kathleen Howard *music educator*
Romney-Manookin, Elaine Clive *music educator, composer*
Worthen, Ellis Clayton *retired fine arts administrator, educator*

Stansbury Park
Moyer, Linda Lee *artist, educator, author*

West Jordan
Strasburg, Linda Ann *corporate radio trainer, talk show host speaker*

VERMONT

East Calais
de Gogorza, Patricia *sculptor, educator*

Middletown Springs
Lloyd, Robert Andrew *art educator*

Woodstock
Gyra, Francis Joseph, Jr., *artist, educator*

VIRGINIA

Alexandria
Alderson, Margaret Northrop *arts administrator, educator, artist*
Erion, Carol Elizabeth *music educator*

Arlington
Mc Donald, Gail Faber *musician, educator*
Murphy, Donn Brian *theater educator*

Blacksburg
Dukore, Bernard Frank *theatre arts and humanities educator, writer*
Gablik, Suzi *art educator, writer*

Chantilly
Gunnerson, Debra Ann *piano teacher*

Charlottesville
Bishop, Ruth Ann *coloratura soprano, voice educator*
Chapel, Robert Clyde *stage director, theater educator*
Dass, Dean A. *artist, educator*
Ross, Walter Beghtol *music educator, composer*

Chincoteague Island
Payne, Nancy Sloan *retired visual arts educator*

Clifton Forge
Stump, Pamela Ferris *music educator*

Fairfax
Hilbrink, William John *violinist*
Negron, Jaime *performing arts center administrator, real estate agent*

Falls Church
Kotler, Wendy Illene *art educator, social studies educator, grants coordinator*

Fredericksburg
Herndon, Cathy Campbell *artist, educator*

Harrisonburg
Theodore, Crystal *artist, retired educator*

Herndon
Bergman, Richard Lee *secondary school educator, band director*

Lebanon
Fuller, Wrenda Sue *music and secondary school educator*

Lynchburg
Booth, Dirie Murphy Dee *music educator, church musician*
Troxel, Steven Richard *communication studies educator*

Midlothian
Sanders, Helen Caravas *art educator*

Mount Crawford
German, Lynne Cummings *music educator*

Newport News
Trachuk, Lillian Elizabeth *music educator*

Norfolk
Frieden, Jane Heller *art educator*

Oakton
Bealey, Laura Ann *artist, educator*
Drummond, Carol Cramer *voice educator, singer, artist, writer*

Richmond
Bray, Patricia Shannon *music educator, musician, small business owner*
Erb, James Bryan *music educator, conductor, musicologist*
Ferguson, Wanda Renee *art educator*
Greene, John Samuel, Jr., *art educator*

Salem
Crowder, Rebecca Byrum *music educator, elementary school educator*

Springfield
Eastman, Donna Kelly *composer, music educator*

Sweet Briar
Green, Jonathan David *music educator, composer, conductor*

Vienna
Kinsolving, Sylvia Crockett *musician, educator*

Virginia Beach
Stevens, Suzanne Duckworth *artist, educator*

Williamsburg
Coleman, Henry Edwin *art educator, artist*
Lashinger, Genrose Mullen *retired elementary school music educator*
Papenthien, Ruth Mary *fiber artist, retired educator*

WASHINGTON

Bellingham
Whyte, Nancy Marie *performing arts educator*

Bremerton
Wu, Ina Zhiqing *art educator*

East Wenatchee
Marion, Sarah Kathleen *music educator*

Longview
Williamson, Debra Faye *performing arts educator*

Mercer Island
Francis, Carolyn Rae *music educator, musician, author, publisher*

Olympia
Macduff, Ilone Margaret *music educator*

Port Angeles
Andrus, Joycelon Marie *art educator*

Pullman
Salusso, Carol Joy *apparel design educator, consultant*

Richland
Ristow, Gail Ross *art educator, paralegal, children's rights advocate*

Seattle
Brixey, Shawn Alan *digital media artist, media educator, director*
Brody, David *artist, educator*
Christenson, Charles Elroy *art educator*
Collier, Tom Ward *musician, educator*
Feldman, Roger Lawrence *artist, educator*
Hu, Mary Lee *artist, educator*
Humphries, Edna Bevan *music educator, choir director*
Lundin, Norman Kent *artist, educator*
Ozaki, Nancy Junko *performance artist, performing arts educator*
Tanzi, Ronald Thomas *artist, educator*

Spokane
Coffee, Gale Furman *musician, educator*
Pugh, Kyle Mitchell, Jr., *musician, retired music educator*

Stanwood
Finney, Linnea Ruth *tailor, accountant, writer*

Sumner
Poppe, Donna *music educator*

Tacoma
Ragan, Betty Sapp *artist, educator*

Tenino
Orsini, Myrna J. *sculptor, educator*

Vashon
Schwennesen, Carol Ann *artist, educator*

WEST VIRGINIA

Bluefield
Brown, Sheri Lynn *artist, poet, educator*

Charleston
Moore, Jeanne *retired art educator and administrator*

Institute
Moore, Mark Tobin *art educator, artist, retired museum curator*

Kermit
Jarvis, Teresa Lynn *art educator, artist*

Mannington
Reese, Katherine Rose *music educator*

Mount Gay
Earnest, C. Lynn *art educator, sculptor, artist*

WISCONSIN

Appleton
Amm, Sophia Jadwiga *artist, educator*

Coon Valley
Kluth, Irma Lee *music educator*

Delavan
Lepke, Charma Davies *musician, educator*

Eau Claire
Lawler, John Griffin *graphic designer, educator*

Green Bay
Meinel, Diane Hartwig *music educator*

Janesville
Detert-Moriarty, Judith Anne *graphic artist, educator, civic activist*

Madison
Knutson, Amanda *art educator, artist*
Schilling, Rhonda Christine *music educator*
Sproule, Deborah W. *art educator, artist*

Middleton
Semmes, Sally Peterson *choreographer, educator, performer*

New Richmond
Schwan, LeRoy Bernard *artist, retired art educator*

Oconomowoc
Driscoll, Virgilyn Mae (Schaetzel) *retired art educator, artist, consultant*

Oshkosh
Smith, Merilyn Roberta *art educator*

Racine
McPheron, JoAnn Marie *music educator, poet*
Schoening, Ruth Irene *retired music educator, musician*

River Falls
Hedahl, Gorden Orlin *theatre educator, university dean*

Stevens Point
Smith, David Lyle *art educator, artist*

Waukesha
Helgert, Mark James *music educator*

Waunakee
Brinkley, Phyllis *program artist, educator*

Wausau
Loftus, Stephen Edward *elementary art educator*

WYOMING

Lander
Bakke, Luanne Kaye *music educator*

Laramie
Griffin, Leah G. *art specialist*

TERRITORIES OF THE UNITED STATES

PUERTO RICO

San Juan
Luna Padilla, Nitza Enid *photography educator*

CANADA

ONTARIO

Toronto
Kramer, Burton *graphic designer, educator*

Waterloo
Urquhart, Tony *artist, educator*

QUEBEC

Montreal
Woszczyk, Wieslaw Richard *audio engineering educator, researcher*

Westmount
Gersovitz, Sarah Valerie *painter, printmaker, playwright*

BRAZIL

Uberlândia
Hinkle, Erika Galvão *art educator, digital artist*

ADDRESS UNPUBLISHED

Aasen-Hull, Audrey Avis *music educator*
Adams, Susan Lois *music educator*
Anderson, Isabel *artist, educator*
Andrade, Edna *artist, art educator*
Aschheim, Eve Michele *artist, educator*
Ascone, Teresa Palmer *artist, educator*
Astaire, Carol Anne Taylor *artist, educator*
Bailin, David William *artist, educator*
Barlow, Jean *art educator, painter*
Barnes, Robert Vincent *retired elementary and secondary school art educator*
Bartlett, Dolores Bre Veglieri (Doe Bartlett) *artist, educator*
Beach, David Williams *music educator, dean*
Beloff, Zoe *artist, educator*
Bennett, Dorothy Jean *art educator*
Bennett, Sharon Kay *music educator*
Benzle, Curtis Munhall *artist, art educator*
Berry, Nancy Westphal *art educator*
Bethlen, Ilona R. *designer, educator*
Bickley-Green, Cynthia Ann *art educator, artist*
Bishop, Delores Ann *artist, educator*
Blattner, Florence Anne *retired music educator*
Blees, Joan Margaret *music educator*
Boardman, Eunice *retired music educator*
Brady, Mary Rolfes *music educator*
Bronkar, Eunice Dunalee *artist, art educator*
Brooks, Lorraine Elizabeth *retired music educator*
Brooks-Turner, Myra *music educator*
Bryant, Daryl Leslie *painter, educator*
Callahan, Tanya Denise *art educator*
Carraher, Mary Lou Carter *art educator*
Castro-Pozo, Talía *dancer, educator*
Cecchi, David Robert *graphic designer*
Chee, Ann-Ping *music educator*
Chen, Judy Faye *music educator*
Cisler, Valerie Clare *music educator, pianist*
Clarke, Marie Elsie *apparel design educator*
Clem, Elizabeth Ann Stumpf *music educator*
Cohen, Shirley *musician, educator*
Coleman, Malcolm James, Jr., *band director, music educator, flute educator*
Cooper, Judith Kase *retired theater educator, playwright*
Coulter, Cynthia Jean *artist, educator*
Dailey, Irene *actress, educator*
David, Christine A. *artist, educator*
Davis-Townsend, Helen Irene *retired art educator*
de Barcza, Gladys Mary *art administrator*
Deller, Harris *artist, educator*
Dickau, Keith Michael (Mike Dickau) *artist, secondary school educator*
Downs, Kevin Ernest *screenwriter, film director, educator*
Egelson, Polly Seliger *artist, educator*
Enriquez, Nora Olague *artist, educator*
Epstein, David Mayer *composer, conductor, music theorist, educator*
Erbe, Yvonne Mary *music educator, marketing specialist, guidance counselor*
Fairleigh, James Parkinson *music educator*
Faust, John Joseph, Jr., *theatre educator, director*
Faxon, Alicia Craig *art educator, department chairman*
Fisch, Arline Marie *artist, educator*
Fischer, Mary Christine *artist, art and elementary education educator*
Flinn, Mary Agnes *artist, educator*
Fraser, Frederick Ewart *art educator*
Freier, Susan Marcie *violinist, music educator*
Fritz, Madeline Milidonis *art educator, professional artist*
Garniss, Joan Brewster *musician, educator*
Gazaway, Barbara Ann *music educator, art educator*
Goldblatt, Eileen Witzman *art director, director, management consultant*
Golden, Judith Greene *artist, educator*
Gordon, Marjorie *lyric coloratura soprano, opera producer, teacher*
Grames-Lyra, Judith Ellen *retired artist, building plans examiner*
Gray, Vicki Lou Pharr *music educator*
Grim, Ellen Townsend *artist, retired art educator*
Hall, Susan Laurel *artist, educator, writer*
Hamblen, Karen *art educator*
Hammond, Mary Sayer *art educator*
Haney, Marlene Carol *music educator*
Harlow, Elizabeth Mary *retired music educator*
Hartley, Corinne *painter, sculptor, educator*
Hawkins, Cynthia *artist, educator*
Hay, George Austin *actor, artist, musician, director*
Hecht, Irene *artist, educator*
Hecht, Sylvia Lillian *pianist, educator*
Heller, George Norman *music educator*
Heller, Jules *artist, writer, educator*
Higgins, Larkin Maureen *artist, poet, educator*
Hill, Willie L., Jr., *music educator*
Hilton, Jean Bull *musician*
Hoggard, Lara Guldmar *conductor, educator*
Holmes, Susan G. *music educator*
Hom, Mei Ling *artist, educator*
Hooper, Robert Alexander *television producer, international educator*
Hopkins, Robert Elliott *music educator*
Horsman, Lenore Lynde (Eleanora Lynde) *soprano, educator, actress*
Hosman, Sharon Lee *music educator*
Hull, Margaret Ruth *artist, educator, consultant*
Hume, Helen Duncan *art educator*
Hundley, Carol Marie Beckquist *music educator*
Indenbaum, Dorothy *musician, researcher*
Jackson, Lola Hirdler *art educator*
Jarcho, Judith Lynn *artist, art educator*
Jelsma, Elizabeth Barbara *music educator*
Jenkins, Marie Prescott *art and music educator*
Johnson, Carla Rae *sculptor, art educator*
Jones, Claire Burtchaell *artist, teacher, writer*
Joynes, Amelia C. *art educator*
Karnofsky, Mollyne *artist, poet*
Kasperbauer, Isabel Giles *art educator*
Kauffman, Kaethe Coventon *art educator, artist, author*
Kennedy, William Bruce *theatre educator, writer*
Kirsch, Roslyn Ruth *art educator, painter, printmaker*
Knieser, Catherine *music educator*
Koerber, Dolores Jean *music educator, musician*
Koplowitz, Stephan *choreographer*
Kousari, Ehsan O. *art educator*
Kunin, Jacqueline Barlow *art educator*
Langley, Joellen S. *music educator*
Lawrence, Lois Marie *art educator*
Lee, Anne *music educator*
Lee, Elizabeth A. *art educator*
Lee, Gwendolin Kuei *retired ballet educator*
Lehman, Paul Robert *retired music educator*
Lindsay, Carol Frances Stockton *art specialist*
Lipofsky, Marvin Bentley *art educator*
Livingstone, Trudy Dorothy Zweig *dancer, educator*
Madeira, Francis King Carey *conductor, educator*
Malachowski, Ann Mary *elementary and secondary art educator*
Malloy, Johnn Edward *media artist, writer*
Manuelian, Lucy Der *art educator, architecture educator*
Martin, Leonard Austin, II, *music educator*
McClain, Sylvia Nancy (Nancy Jo Grimm) *voice educator, vocalist*
McDaniel, Richard W. *artist, art educator*
McKennee, Arden Norma *art educator, retired, consultant*
McLean, Julianne Drew *concert pianist, educator*
McVicker, Jesse Jay *artist, educator*
Mezacapa, Edna S. *music educator, elementary school educator*
Moon, Spencer *author, program consultant, educator*
Morrison, Nancy Jane *art educator*
Moslak, Judith *retired music educator*
Myers, Carole Ann *artist, educator*
Nahumck, Nadia Chilkovsky *performer, dance educator, choreographer, author*
Nemiroff, Maxine Celia *art educator, gallery owner, consultant*
Neuls-Bates, Carol *business executive, musicologist*
Nolan, Patrick Joseph *screenwriter, playwright, educator*
Noll, Jeanne C. *retired music educator*
Olesen, Carolyn McDonald *dance educator, choreographer*
Olson, Joanne J. *artist, art educator*
Oritsky, Mimi *artist, educator*
Orscheln, Sheryl Jane *art educator*
Ortega, Ginka Gerova *concert flutist*
Owen, Carol Thompson *artist, educator, writer*
Oxell, Loie Gwendolyn *fashion and beauty educator, consultant, columnist*
Paddock, Sandra Constance *music educator*
Perkins, Leeman Lloyd *music educator, musicologist*
Psillos, Susan Rose *artist, educator*
Pyzow, Susan Victoria *artist, educator*
Quist, Jeanette Fitzgerald *television production educator, choreographer*
Ragland, Kathryn Marie *dancer, educator*
Richards, Ann *actress, poet*
Rifman, Eileen *music educator*
Robinson, Linda Schultz *art educator, artist*
Rohloff, Lori Luanne *artist, former special education educator*
Romano, Mena N. *artist, educator*
Rose, Kathy Lerner *artist*
Ross, Joan Stuart *artist, art educator*
Rothschild, Jennifer Ann *artist, educator*
Rowe, Bobby Louise *art educator*
Russo, Vincent Barney *music educator*
Rutland-Amagliani, Carol Elaine *music director, educator*
Schaefer, Nancy Turner *artist, educator*
Schafer, Ruth Erma *artist, educator*
Scott, Rosa Mae *artist, educator*
Sennett, Henry Herbert, Jr., *theatre arts educator and consultant*
Shaw, Gloria Doris *art educator*
Shea, Rosanne Mary *artist, art educator*
Smith, Cheryl Diane *music educator*
Snider, Patricia Faye *retired theater educator, small business owner*
Snowden, Ruth *artist, educator, legal secretary*
Stanley, Robert Anthony *artist, educator*
Starkweather, Teresa Madery *artist, educator*
Strong, Karin Hjort *artist, educator*
Swanson, Christine Mason *art educator*
Taylor, Margaret Turner *clothing designer, economist, writer, architectural designer*
Thompson, Lola May *music educator, volunteer*
Tishner, Keri Lynn *visual art education consultant*
Turner, Bonese Collins *artist, educator*
Uken, Marcile Rena *music educator*
Underwood, Martha Jane Menke *artist, educator*
Urista, Diane Jean *music educator, researcher*
Van Hooser, Patricia Lou Scott *art educator*
Vassil, Pamela *graphic designer, writer, administrator*
Verburg, JoAnn *artist, photography educator*
Vero, Radu *freelance medical and scientific illustrator, educator, writer, consultant*
Villella, Edward Joseph *ballet dancer, educator, choreographer, artistic director, performing arts administrator*
VonSchulze-Delitzsch, Marilyn Wandling (Lady VonSchulze-Delitzsch) *artist, writer*
Wagoner, Geraldine Vander Pol *music educator*
Wallach-Levy, Wendee Esther *astrophotographer*
Warberg, Willetta *concert pianist, writer, piano educator*
Weaver, Marie Antoinette *artist, educator*
Weiner-Heuschkel, Sydell *theater educator*
Wernick, Richard Frank *composer, conductor*
Wilde, John *artist, educator*
Wood, Vivian Poates *mezzo soprano, educator, writer*
Wright, Gladys Stone *music educator, composer, writer*
Wynn, Gaines Clore *artist, educator, museum consultant*
Zacher, Valerie Marie *art educator*
Zoritch, George *dance educator, choreographer*

LIBRARIES

UNITED STATES

ALABAMA

Albertville
Sheets, Dorothy Jane *retired school librarian and educator*

Auburn
Straiton, T(homas) Harmon, Jr., *librarian*

Hampton Cove
Harris, Marquita Bolden *school librarian*

Odenville
Whitten, Joseph Lee *retired school librarian, elementary educator*

Thomaston
Counselman, Anne *librarian*

ARIZONA

Davis Monthan Afb
Smail, Leslie Anne *librarian*

Phoenix
Bickford, David Lawrence *librarian, educator*

Tucson
Irwin, Mildred Lorine Warrick *library consultant, civic worker*
Skorupski, Diane Christine *school library media specialist*

LIBRARIES

ARKANSAS

Monticello
Guenter, Helen Marie Giessen *librarian, reading specialist*

CALIFORNIA

Berkeley
Buckland, Michael Keeble *librarian, educator*

Culver City
Souza, Blase Camacho *librarian, educator*

El Cerrito
Kao, Yasuko Watanabe *retired library administrator*
Smith, Eldred Reid *library educator*

Fullerton
Ayala, John *librarian, dean*

Los Angeles
Shank, Russell *librarian, educator*

Ontario
Dunn, Donald Jack *law librarian, law educator, dean, lawyer*

Riverside
Prosser, Michael Joseph *college librarian*

San Diego
Donley, Dennis Lee *school librarian*

San Jose
Woolls, Esther Blanche *library science educator*

Santa Rosa
Neuberg, Joel Gary *librarian*

Stanford
Rondestvedt, Karen Anne *librarian, educator*

Woodland Hills
Zeitlin, Eugenia Pawlik *librarian, educator, writer*

Yucca Valley
Vuncannon, Delcie Hobson *librarian, educator*

COLORADO

Aurora
Miller, Dorothea Helen *librarian, educator*

Boulder
O'Brien, Elmer John *librarian, educator*

Craig
Miller, Donna Pat *library administrator, consultant*

Denver
Hall-Ellis, Sylvia Dunn *library science educator, consultant*

Edwards
Chambers, Joan Louise *retired librarian, retired dean*

Fleming
Nichols, Lee Ann *library media specialist*

Golden
Mathews, E. Anne Jones *library educator and administrator, consultant*

Greeley
Seager, Daniel Albert *university librarian*

CONNECTICUT

Branford
George, Diane Elizabeth *school media specialist, educational technology and computer education educator*

Hartford
Posteraro, Catherine Hammond *librarian, gerontology educator*
Van Leer, Jerilyn Mosher *library media specialist*

Litchfield
Simko, Helen Mary *school library media specialist*

New Britain
Chasse, Emily Schuder *librarian, educator*

New Haven
Oliver-Warren, Mary Elizabeth *retired library science educator*

Southbury
Rorick, William Calvin *librarian, educator, portrait artist*

Trumbull
Birch, Grace Morgan *library administrator, educator*

DISTRICT OF COLUMBIA

Washington
Craig, Susan Lyons *library director*
McGuirl, Marlene Dana Callis *law librarian, educator*
Meyer, Margaret Vaughan *librarian, educator*
Preer, Jean Lyon *information science educator*
Rovelstad, Mathilde V(erner) *library science educator*
Segall, JoAnn Butters *retired school librarian*
Wand, Patricia Ann *librarian*

FLORIDA

Boca Raton
Kramer, Cecile E. *retired medical librarian*

Bradenton
Ehde, Ava Louise *librarian, educator*

Clearwater
Werner, Elizabeth Helen *librarian, language educator*

Fort Lauderdale
Riggs, Donald Eugene *librarian, university official*

Gainesville
DuPree, Sherry Sherrod *historian, religion consultant, writer*

Jacksonville
Farkas, Andrew *library director emeritus, educator, writer*

Melbourne
Regis, Nina *librarian, educator*

Orlando
Ahlers, Glen-Peter, Sr., *law library director, educator, consultant*

Palm Bay
Hoefer, Margaret J. *librarian*

Palm Harbor
Jones, Winona Nigels *retired library media specialist*

Saint Augustine
Sappington, Sharon Anne *retired school librarian*

Saint Petersburg
Kent, Allen *library and information sciences educator*

Sarasota
Clopine, Marjorie Showers *librarian*

Tallahassee
Hunt, Mary Alice *library science educator*
Manley, Walter Wilson, II, *lawyer, business educator*
Robbins, Jane Borsch *library science educator, information science educator*

Tampa
Luddington, Betty Walles *library media specialist*

GEORGIA

Atlanta
Drake, Miriam Anna *librarian, educator, writer*
Robison, Carolyn Love *retired librarian*

Barnesville
Adams, Cynthia Ann *librarian, media specialist, writing instructor*

Savannah
Ball, Ardella Patricia *library media educator*

Smarr
Evans, Rosemary King (Mrs. Howell Dexter Evans) *librarian, educator*

HAWAII

Aiea
Uyehara, Harry Yoshimi *library educator*

Hilo
Golian-Lui, Linda Marie *librarian*

IDAHO

Moscow
Abraham, Terry *school librarian*
Jankowska, Maria Anna *librarian, educator*

ILLINOIS

Aurora
Christiansen, Raymond Stephan *librarian, educator*

Carbondale
Matthews, Elizabeth Woodfin *law librarian, law educator*
Werlich, David Patrick *history educator*

Champaign
Krummel, Donald William *librarian, educator*

Chicago
Bodi, Sonia Ellen *library director, educator*
Choldin, Marianna Tax *librarian, educator*
Davis, Mary Ellen K. *library director*
Ford, Barbara Jean *library studies educator*
Gerdes, Neil Wayne *library director, educator*
Maloy, Frances *librarian*
Mikolyzk, Thomas Andrew *librarian*
Wright, Judith Margaret *law librarian, educator, dean*

Deerfield
Fry, Roy H(enry) *librarian, educator*

Dixmoor
Chapman, Mary Joyce *school librarian*

Evanston
Bjorncrantz, Leslie Benton *librarian*

Glen Ellyn
Hoornbeek, Lynda Ruth Couch *librarian, educator*

Hinsdale
Ferro-Nyalka, Ruth Rudys *librarian, educator*

Jacksonville
Gallas, Martin Hans *librarian*
Stevens, Mary Jo Thomas *librarian*

Lake Forest
Miller, Arthur Hawks, Jr., *librarian, archivist, educator*

Maywood
Ellington, Mildred L. *librarian*

Palos Park
Shumard, Ellen Blaine *school librarian, artist*

Robinson
Wolfe, Ellen Darlene *school librarian, elementary school educator*

Rockford
Traci, Kathleen Frances *library media specialist*

Saint Charles
Abraham, Robert Paul *secondary education administrator*
Babel, Rayonia Alleen *retired librarian, educator*

Urbana
Shtohryn, Dmytro Michael *librarian, educator*

Wauconda
Kramer, Pamela Kostenko *librarian*

INDIANA

Hammond
Marzocchi, Judith Ann *librarian*

Indianapolis
Fischler, Barbara Brand *librarian*
Guyonneau, Christine Huguette *librarian*

Lafayette
McKowen, Dorothy Keeton *librarian, educator, consultant*
Mobley, Emily Ruth *library dean, educator*

Muncie
Schull, Myra Edna *librarian*
Yeamans, George Thomas *librarian, educator*

Notre Dame
Hayes, Stephen Matthew *librarian*

Tipton
Gentry, Donna Jean *librarian*

West Lafayette
Markee, Katherine Madigan *librarian, educator*

IOWA

De Witt
Rittmer, Elaine Heneke *retired library media specialist*

Mount Vernon
Donham, Jean *library and information science educator*

Storm Lake
Klavano, Ann Marie *school librarian*

KANSAS

Arkansas City
Bachman, Neal Kenyon *librarian*

Burr Oak
Underwood, Deanna Kay *librarian*

Bushton
Cooper, Sharon Kay *school media specialist*

Olathe
Morrison, Ray Leon *library administrator, graduate education educator*

Pittsburg
Lee, Earl Wayne *library science educator*

Wichita
Woolf, Amy Kaspar *librarian, storyteller*

KENTUCKY

Burlington
Crouch, Arline Parks *librarian*

Frankfort
McDaniel, Karen Jean *university library administrator, educator*

Grayson
Waite, Lemuel Warren *library director*

Lexington
Levy, Charlotte Lois *law librarian, educator, consultant, lawyer*
Sineath, Timothy Wayne *library educator, university dean*

Louisville
Coalter, Milton J., Jr., *library director, educator*
Edwards, Grace Coleman *librarian*
Schneider, Jayne Bangs *school librarian*

Summer Shade
Smith, Ruby Lucille *retired librarian*

LOUISIANA

Arnaudville
LaGrange, Claire Mae *librarian*

Baton Rouge
Bensman, Stephen J. *school librarian, researcher*
Kelly, Mary Joan *librarian*

Covington
Stahr, Beth A. *academic librarian*

Franklinton
Dillon, Carol Jean *librarian, educator*

Lake Charles
Curol, Helen Ruth *librarian, English language educator*

Monroe
Martin, Diane Caraway *school librarian*
Smith, Donald Raymond *librarian*

New Orleans
Robinson, Cummie Adams *librarian, consultant*

Shreveport
Green, Rachael Paulette *librarian*

MAINE

Nobleboro
Fisher, Ellen Roop *retired librarian, educator*

MARYLAND

Annapolis
Werking, Richard Hume *librarian, historian, academic administrator*

Baltimore
Allen, Norma Ann *librarian, educator*
Follet, Robert Edward *music librarian*
McAdam, Paul Edward *retired library administrator*
Mc Cabe, Gerard Benedict *retired library administrator*

Bethesda
Lindberg, Donald Allan Bror *library administrator, pathologist, educator*

College Park
Wasserman, Paul *library and information science educator*

Columbia
Gruhl, Andrea Morris *librarian*

Easton
Bronson, John Orville, Jr., *retired librarian*

Fort Washington
Cross, Rita Faye *librarian, early childhood educator, writer*

Greenbelt
Moore, Virginia Bradley *librarian*

Rockville
Rankin, Rachel Ann *retired media specialist*

Towson
Tull, Willis Clayton, Jr., *librarian*

Upper Marlboro
Rough, Marianne Christina *librarian, educator*

MASSACHUSETTS

Amherst
Tenenbaum, Jeffrey Mark *academic librarian*

Boston
Hernon, Peter *library science educator*
Wendorf, Richard Harold *library director, scholar*

Brookline
Finkelstein, Norman Henry *librarian*

Concord
Bander, Edward Julius *law librarian emeritus, lawyer*

Lakeville
Grasela, James Walter *librarian*

Marshfield
Fife, Betty H. *retired librarian*

Needham
Mills, Elizabeth Ann *retired librarian*

Shrewsbury
Chang, Isabelle C. *librarian, educator, writer*

Springfield
Utley, F. Knowlton *library director, educator*

Wayland
Anderson, Monica Luffman *school librarian, educator, real estate broker*

MICHIGAN

Adrian
Dombrowski, Mark Anthony *librarian*

Ann Arbor
Dede, Bonnie Aileen *librarian, educator*
Dougherty, Richard Martin *library and information science educator*
Durrance, Joan C. *library and information science educator*
Sears, JoAnn Marie *academic librarian*

Detroit
Mika, Joseph John *library school director, educator, consultant*

East Lansing
Unsworth, Michael Edward *university librarian*

Grosse Pointe
Casey, Genevieve M(ary) *librarian, educator*

Kalamazoo
Grotzinger, Laurel Ann *librarian, educator*

Marquette
Henderson, Roberta Marie *librarian, educator*

Plymouth
deBear, Richard Stephen *library planning consultant*

MINNESOTA

Mankato
Descy, Don Edmond *educational technology educator, writer, editor*

Minneapolis
Howland, Joan Sidney *law librarian, law educator*

Northfield
Hong, Howard Vincent *library administrator, philosophy educator, editor, translator*

Winona
Sullivan, Kathryn Ann *librarian, educator*

MISSOURI

Brentwood
O'Neill, Kathryn J. *librarian, educator*

Kansas City
Pedram, Marilyn Beth *reference librarian*
Spalding, Helen H. *library director*

Moberly
Reynolds, Linda Kay *librarian*

Saint Louis
Collins, Margaret Elizabeth *librarian*
Heiser, Walter Charles *librarian, priest, educator*
Krasney, Rina Susan *school librarian*
Searls, Eileen Haughey *retired lawyer, librarian, educator*

Springfield
Bohnenkamper, Katherine Elizabeth *library science educator*

NEBRASKA

Omaha
Tollman, Thomas Andrew *librarian*

NEVADA

Henderson
Pavalon, Donna Mae *librarian*

Las Vegas
Gordon, Lee Diane *school librarian, educator*
Ramsey, Inez Linn *librarian, educator*

Reno
Arosio, Charlyne Mary *school librarian, educator*

NEW HAMPSHIRE

Exeter
Thomas, Jacquelyn May *librarian*

Hanover
Hunter, Marie Hope *library media generalist*

NEW JERSEY

Clifton
McCoy, Linda Korteweg *library director*

Lodi
Karetzky, Stephen *library director, educator, researcher*

Metuchen
Massey, Eleanor Nelson *school librarian, media specialist*

Monmouth Junction
Lawton, Deborah Simmons *library director, educational media specialist*

New Brunswick
Turock, Betty Jane *library and information science educator*

New Egypt
Nanna, Elizabeth Ann Will *librarian, educator*

Princeton
Fox, Mary Ann Williams *librarian*

Princeton Junction
Butorac, Frank George *librarian, educator*

Roselle
Riley, Barbara Polk *retired librarian*

Teaneck
Huang, Theresa C. *librarian*

NEW MEXICO

Albuquerque
Payne, Lucy Ann Salsbury *law librarian, educator, lawyer*
Wilkinson, Frances Catherine *librarian, educator*

Gallup
Sarath, Carol Ann *library/media coordinator*

Portales
Miller, Bettie Gene *librarian, educator*

NEW YORK

Albany
Aceto, Vincent John *librarian, educator*

Bohemia
Manley, Gertrude Ella *librarian, media specialist*

Bronx
Caffin, Louise Anne *library media educator*
Ostrow, Rona Lynn *librarian, educator*
Skurdenis, Juliann Veronica *librarian, educator, writer, editor*

Brooklyn
Clune, John Richard *library administrator*
Henderson, Janice Elizabeth *law librarian*
Langstaff, Eleanor Marguerite *retired library science educator*
Schneider, Adele Goldberg *librarian, educator*
Sharify, Nasser *educator, author, librarian*
Sicherman, Robbin Meryl *library media specialist*

Buffalo
Bobinski, George Sylvan *librarian, educator*
Peterson, Lorna Ingrid *library educator*

Hempstead
Freese, Melanie Louise *librarian, professor, assistant dean*

Ithaca
Hammond, Jane Laura *retired law librarian, lawyer*

Kings Point
Billy, George John *library director*

Larchmont
Courtney, Diane Trossello *library consultant*

Marlboro
Parker, Marion Hawkins *retired librarian*

New York
Barnett, Philip *science librarian, educator*
LeClerc, Paul *library director*
Little, Robert David *library science educator*
Melnick, Ralph *library director, secondary school educator*
Osten, Margaret Esther *librarian*
Tsai, Bor-sheng *educator*

Niagara Falls
Jessiman, Marilynn R. *library media specialist*

Penfield
Birkby, Paul Donald *library media specialist, consultant*

Pleasantville
Murdock, William John *librarian*

Port Washington
Futter, Joan Babette *former school librarian*

Rochester
Palvino, Nancy Mangin *retired librarian*

Sherrill
Rosendale, Suzanne Moore *library media specialist*

Staten Island
Auh, Yang John *librarian, educational administrator*
Ciolli, Antoinette *librarian, retired educator*

White Plains
Newman, Marie Stefanini *law librarian, educator*

Woodbury
Rosenthal, Marilyn *school librarian, educator*

NORTH CAROLINA

Asheboro
Talley, Doris Lanier *instructional technology specialist*

Asheville
Boyce, Emily Stewart *retired library and information science educator*

Cary
Rosar, Virginia Wiley *librarian*

Chapel Hill
Carpenter, Raymond Leonard *information science educator*
Gasaway, Laura Nell *law librarian, educator*
Kilgour, Frederick Gridley *librarian, educator*
Moran, Barbara Burns *librarian, educator*
Pruett, James Worrell *librarian, musicologist*

Davidson
Jones, Arthur Edwin, Jr., *library administrator, English and American literature educator*

Elm City
Smith, Sue Parker *media administrator*

Seymour Johnson A F B
Demark, Robin Kay *librarian*

NORTH DAKOTA

Minot
Iversen, David Stewart *librarian*

OHIO

Canton
Kilcullen, Maureen *librarian, educator*

Cincinnati
Bestehorn, Ute Wiltrud *retired librarian*
Everett, Karen Joan *retired librarian, genealogy educator*
Everson, Jean Watkins Dolores *librarian media technical assistant, educator*

Columbus
Branscomb, Lewis Capers, Jr., *librarian, educator*
Donovan, Maureen Hildegarde *librarian, educator*

Delaware
Schlichting, Catherine Fletcher Nicholson *librarian, educator*

Dublin
Meyer, Betty Jane *former librarian*

Middleburg Heights
Maciuszko, Kathleen Lynn *librarian, educator*

Middletown
Schaefer, Patricia Ann *retired librarian*

Northfield
Sleeman, Mary (Mrs. John Paul Sleeman) *retired librarian*

Oberlin
Greenberg, Eva Mueller *librarian*

Springfield
Beatty, Betty Joy *library educator*

OKLAHOMA

Bethany
Pelley, Shirley Norene *library director*

Dale
Capps, Larry Lynn *school librarian*

Midwest City
Saulmon, Sharon Ann *college librarian*

Norman
Carroll, Frances Laverne *librarian, educator*
Croft, Janet Brennan *academic librarian*
Lester, June *library information studies educator*

Tulsa
Clement, Evelyn Geer *library educator*

OREGON

Seaside
Bishop, Virginia Wakeman *retired librarian and humanities educator, small business owner*

PENNSYLVANIA

Audubon
Tanis, James Robert *library director, history educator, clergyman*

Bethel Park
Marrs, Sharon Carter *librarian*

Bloomsburg
Vann, John Daniel, III, *library consultant, historian*

Du Bois
Lee, Catherine A. *librarian, educator*

Fenelton
Anderson, Jane Louise Blair *librarian, horse breeder, poet*

Greencastle
Dietrich, Joyce Diane *librarian*

Johnstown
Berkebile, Mary Lou *librarian*

Lock Haven
Chang, Shirley Lin (Hsiu-Chu Chang) *librarian, educator*

Monroeville
Sehring, Hope Hutchison *library science educator*

Philadelphia
Mancall, Jacqueline Cooper *library science educator, information science educator*
Senecal, Kristin Schwartz *librarian*
Warner, Elizabeth Rose *librarian, educator*

Pittsburgh
Jenkins, Georgann Klaus *librarian*
Josey, E(lonnie) J(Unius) *librarian, educator, former state administrator*
Linke, Erika C. *academic librarian*

University Park
Joyce, William Leonard *librarian*

Wayne
Garrison, Guy Grady *librarian, educator*

Yardley
Morris, Cindra Ann *librarian, educator*

RHODE ISLAND

Kingston
Caldwell, Naomi Rachel *library and information scientist, educator*

Newport
Peterson, Lorraine Elizabeth *retired librarian, educator*

Providence
Monroe, William Scott *librarian*

SOUTH CAROLINA

Bluffton
Cann, Sharon Lee *retired health science librarian*

Charleston
Basler, Thomas G. *librarian, administrator, educator*
Devereaux, Evelyn Janine *librarian, civilian military employee*

Orangeburg
Caldwell, Rossie Juanita Brower *retired library service educator*

Rock Hill
Herring, Mark Youngblood *librarian, university dean*

SOUTH DAKOTA

Pierre
Miller, Suzanne Marie *state librarian*

TENNESSEE

Dresden
Powell, Wanda Garner *librarian*

Johnson City
Norris, Carol Brooks *librarian, educator*

Maryville
Tabor, Curtis Harold, Jr., *librarian, minister*

Nashville
Wilson, Carolyn Taylor *librarian*

TEXAS

Abilene
Specht, Alice Wilson *university libraries dean*

Aledo
Rowe, Sheryl Ann *librarian*

Austin
Covington, Veronica Pro *librarian, educator*
Davis, Donald Gordon, Jr., *librarian, educator, historian*
Howard, Carol Spencer *librarian, journalist*
Larson, Jeanette Carolyn *librarian*
Smith, Dorothy Brand *retired librarian*

Bellville
Borgeson, Earl Charles *law librarian, educator*

Dallas
Howell, Bradley Sue *librarian*
Roach-Reeves, Catharyn Petitt *librarian, educator*
Young, Julia Anne *librarian, elementary education educator*

LIBRARIES

Denton
Snapp, Elizabeth *librarian, educator*

Hale Center
Courtney, Carolyn Ann *school librarian*

Houston
Suter, Jon Michael *academic library director, educator*

Iowa Park
Harvill, Melba Sherwood *retired university librarian*

San Antonio
Frisch, Paul Andrew *librarian*
Hogan, Donna Helen *school librarian, educator*
Nance, Betty Love *librarian*

San Marcos
Fox, Frank G. *school librarian, writer*

Weimar
Rocha, Osbelia Maria Juarez *librarian, assistant principal*

Whitehouse
Brewer, Edith Gay *librarian, educator*

UTAH

Provo
Marchant, Maurice Peterson *librarian, educator*

VIRGINIA

Alexandria
Gray, Dorothy Louise Allman Pollet *librarian*

Burke
Emery, Vicki Morris *school library media administrator*

Dumfries
Gaudet, Jean Ann *retired librarian, educator*

Falls Church
Krug, Adele Jensen (Mrs. Walter John Krug) *library science educator*

Franklin
Culpepper, Jo Long *librarian*

Harrisonburg
Gill, Gerald Lawson *librarian*

Leesburg
Fall, Dorothy Eleanor *librarian*

Roanoke
Henn, Shirley Emily *retired librarian*

WASHINGTON

Ellensburg
Lindvig, Leona Mindell *librarian, educator*

Kirkland
Rosett, Ann Doyle *librarian*

Port Townsend
Hiatt, Peter *retired librarian studies educator*

Seattle
Boylan, Merle Nelson *librarian, educator*
Hazelton, Penny Ann *law librarian, educator*

Spokane
Bynagle, Hans Edward *library director, philosophy educator*
Murray, James Michael *librarian, law librarian, legal educator, lawyer*

WISCONSIN

Brillion
Kjelstrup, Cheryl Ann *librarian*

Osceola
Finster, James Robert *library media specialist*

MILITARY ADDRESSES OF THE UNITED STATES

EUROPE

Apo
Sokolowski, Denise Georgia *librarian, university administrator, educator*

EGYPT

Cairo
Wichman, Edna Carol *media specialist, librarian*

GERMANY

Hannover
Huthloff, Christa Rose *library and information science educator*

HONG KONG

Kowloon
Burton, Barry Lawson *librarian, educator*

NETHERLANDS

Tilburg
Kleijnen, Jack P. *simulation and information systems educator*

ADDRESS UNPUBLISHED

Bowden, Ann *bibliographer, educator*
Callard, Carole Crawford *librarian, educator*
Cammack, Ann *librarian, secondary school educator*
Citron, Beatrice Sally *law librarian, lawyer, educator*
Cochran, Carolyn *library director*
Curley, Elmer Frank *librarian*
Diehl, Carol Lou *library director, retired, library consultant*
Evans, Anaclare Frost *college librarian*
Fessler, Patricia Lou *retired library and media coordinator*
Flinner, Beatrice Jeffreys Allayaud *retired library and media sciences educator*
Folk, Judith Alynn *school librarian, educator*
Frederking, Kathy Hahn *elementary school librarian*
Garrett, Donna Irvin *librarian*
Goldenberg, Linda (Linda Atkinson) *librarian, author*
Greenberg, Hinda Feige *library director*
Gross, Dorothy-Ellen *library director, dean*
Hayden, Linda C. *librarian, educator*
Howell, Sharon S. *retired librarian*
Klatt, Melvin John *library consultant*
Knight, Margaret L. *librarian, educator*
Kraemer, Alfred Robert *school librarian*
Larson, Carole Allis *library and information scientist, educator*
Laurie, Alison Margaret *retired school librarian*
Leather, Victoria Potts *college librarian*
Mahood, Ramona Madson *library science educator, financial consultant*
Maltby, Florence Helen *library science educator*
Marquardt, Larry Dean *librarian*
McGrath, Anna Fields *retired librarian*
Meng, Guang Jun *librarian, educator*
Miller, Marilyn Lea *library science educator*
Moore, Penelope *retired school librarian*
Pierik, Marilyn Anne *retired librarian, piano teacher*
Poad, Flora Virginia *retired librarian and educator*
Roberts, Judith Marie *librarian, educator*
Rouse, Roscoe, Jr., *librarian, educator*
Slavens, Thomas Paul *library science educator*
Smith, Dentye M. *library media specialist*
Spaeth, C. Edmond *library media specialist*
Stallworth-Barron, Doris A. Carter *librarian, educator*
Storck, Thomas Charles Joliffe *author, librarian*
Toor, Ruth *librarian, consultant*
Trenery, Mary Ellen *librarian*
Trezza, Alphonse Fiore *librarian, educator*
Van Orden, Phyllis Jeanne *librarian, educator*
Wik, Jean Marie (Jean Marie Beck) *librarian, media specialist*
Williams, John Troy *librarian, educator*
Wilson, Patricia Potter *library science and reading educator, educational and library consultant*
Wingate, Bettye Faye *librarian, educator*
Wolf, Cynthia Tribelhorn *librarian, library educator*
Woods, Phyllis Michalik *librarian*

PRESCHOOL EDUCATION

UNITED STATES

ARIZONA

Phoenix
Whitlow, Donna Mae *daycare and primary school administrator*

Scottsdale
Spero, Diane Frances *school director*

CALIFORNIA

Anaheim
Goodspeed, Kathryn Ann *pre-school educator*

Davis
Green, Bonnie Jean *early childhood administrator*

Foster City
Danker, Mervyn Kenneth *director of education*

Hayward
Harris, Penelope Claire *preschool, daycare administrator, consultant*

Huntington Park
Johnson, Patricia Hardy *early childhood specialist pre-school provider*

La Mesa
Charleton, Margaret Ann *child care administrator, consultant*

Los Angeles
Money, Ruth Rowntree *infant development and care specialist, consultant*

COLORADO

Trinidad
Sandoval, Mona Lisa *daycare provider, educator*

CONNECTICUT

Harwinton
Patnode, Lynne Marie *childcare center owner*

FLORIDA

Bradenton
Jain, Mohinder (Mona Jain) *daycare administrator, educator*

Fort Pierce
Wilkins, Carolyn Noreen *early childhood educator*

Fort Walton Beach
Green, Vivian Louise *preschool program specialist*

Lake Worth
Gregorchik, Lameece Atallah *early childhood educator*

Palm Coast
Freifeld, Muriel Israel *early childhood consultant*

Spring Hill
Weber, Mary Linda *preschool educator*

Thonotosassa
Grant, Pauline Larry *retired daycare center director, consultant*

GEORGIA

Mableton
Harris, Paulette Collier *pre-school administrator, educator*

Macon
Williamson, Christine Wilder *preschool specialist, educational consultant, small business owner*

Statesboro
Diebolt, Monte Sue *daycare provider*

HAWAII

Honolulu
Kaiser-Botsai, Sharon Kay *early childhood educator*

ILLINOIS

Chicago
Bowman, Barbara Taylor *early childhood educator*

Des Plaines
Lakier, Thelma *child development specialist, librarian*

Murphysboro
Fark, Sandra Jean *preschool, daycare provider/administrator*

KANSAS

Kansas City
Williams, Shirley J. *daycare provider, educator, writer*

MASSACHUSETTS

Boston
Hilliard, Carol Searls *early childhood special education consultant*

MICHIGAN

Saint Clair Shores
Kavadas-Pappas, Iphigenia Katherine *preschool administrator, educator, consultant*

Sterling Heights
Pierson, Kathleen Mary *child care center administrator, consultant*

MINNESOTA

Albert Lea
Rechtzigel, Sue Marie (Suzanne Rechtzigel) *child care center executive*

Minneapolis
Jax, Christine *educational administrator, education educator*

Winona
Vickman, Patricia Ann *preschool educator*

NEW JERSEY

Beachwood
Newman, Justina Anne *nursery school administrator, consultant*

NEW YORK

Elmira
Kerr-Nowlan, Donna Courtney *pre-school administrator*

Hempstead
Chapman, Lenora Rosamond *day care provider, social service organization director*

Levittown
Dwyer, Mary Elizabeth *nursery school director*
Schettino, Maria Carmen *preschool educator*

New Rochelle
Vitale, Francis M. *preschool director*

New York
Stacknowitz, Janet *reading specialist*

Rockville Centre
Becker, Nettie *preschool administrator*

Schenectady
DeFilippo, Linda Kellogg *preschool educator*

OKLAHOMA

Tinker AFB
Scott, Carol Lee *child care educator*

Tulsa
Kukura, Rita Anne *pre-school educator*

PENNSYLVANIA

Hughesville
McCoy, Rhonda Luann *daycare administrator*

Manheim
Frederick, Susan Louise *preschool educator*

Philadelphia
Cooke, Sara Mullin Graff *daycare provider, kindergarten educator, medical assistant*
Davidson, Rhonda Elizabeth *preschool educator*

SOUTH CAROLINA

Aiken
Scurlock, Judy B. *early childhood educator*

Columbia
Tunstall, Dorothy Fiebrich *early childhood educator*

TEXAS

Fort Worth
Thomason, Deborah Lee *kindergarten educator*

Laredo
Engelhardt-Alvarez, Madeline *retired preschool administrator*

Southlake
Somerstein-Campbell, Jasmine Aurora Abrera *preschool administrator, educator*

VERMONT

Saint Albans
Johnson, Paula Bouchard *preschool administrator, educator, consultant*

VIRGINIA

Fredericksburg
Jenks-Davies, Kathryn Ryburn *retired daycare provider and owner, civic worker*

Richmond
Jones, Jeanne Pitts *pre-school administrator*

Warrenton
Haley, Jeanne Ackerman *preschool director*

WISCONSIN

Milwaukee
Schaub, Theresa Marie *early childhood educator*

Three Lakes
Bauknecht, Barbara Belle *retired pre-school educator*

MILITARY ADDRESSES OF THE UNITED STATES

EUROPE

Fpo
Chaiklin, Amy Lynn *childhood education program developer*

ADDRESS UNPUBLISHED

Baker, C. B. *retired day care director, organizer, communicator*
Heaton, Jean M. *early childhood educator*
Jenkins, Brenda Gwenetta *early childhood and special education specialist*
Kaspin, Susan Jane *child care specialist*
Meier, Enge *pre-school educator*
Pitera, Doreen Ann *pre-school educator*
Pugh-Marzi, Sherrie *daycare center administrator*
Salmon, Phyllis Ward *early education educator*
Yitts, Rose Marie *nursery school executive*

PRIMARY/ELEMENTARY/MIDDLE SCHOOL EDUCATION

UNITED STATES

ALABAMA

Albertville
Turley, Kathy Elaine *elementary school educator*

Anniston
Smith, Judith Day *early childhood educator*

Auburn
Chamberlain, Jennifer Ruth *elementary school educator*

Bessemer
Drysdale, Esther Ann *elementary school educator*
Stephens, Betsy Bain *retired elementary school educator*

Birmingham
Christman, Sharon Ann *elementary school educator*
Stith, Cheryl Diane Adams *elementary school educator*
Thomas, Theresa Brown *middle school educator*
Wood, Clinton Wayne *middle school educator*

Cherokee
McWilliams, Elizabeth Ann *elementary school educator*

Dothan
Fletcher, Sarah Lee *retired elementary school educator*

Enterprise
Harrison, Helen Ray Griffin *elementary school educator, volunteer*
Rikard, Yvonne H. *elementary educator*

Evergreen
Dailey, Marilyn *elementary education educator*

Florence
Brown, Jacqueline Reynell *primary school educator*
Simpson, Rita Ann *early childhood educator*

Greensboro
Crawford, Connie Allene *elementary education educator*

Hartselle
Smith, Pamela Rodgers *elementary education educator*

Homewood
Hart, Virginia Wade *elementary education educator*

Hoover
Parrish, Sherry Dye *elementary school educator*

Huntsville
Foster, Deborah Simmons *educator*
Hoppe, Lea Ann *elementary education educator*
Morgan, Beverly Hammersley *middle school educator, artist*
Ratchford-Merchant, Betty Jo *elementary education educator*
Turner, Mary Alice *elementary school educator*

Madison
Murphy, Randall Dee *middle school educator, administrator*

Millbrook
Hull, Mary Frances *elementary school educator*

Mobile
McGuire, Camille Hall *elementary education educator*
Parden, Cindy Maria *elementary school educator*
Street, Cecilia Regina *elementary school educator, administrator*

Montgomery
Brown, Joan Hall *elementary school educator*
Cox, Cathy A *elementary school educator*

Rainbow City
Browning, Leslie O. *middle school educator*

Scottsboro
McGill, Judy Annell McGee *early childhood and elementary educator*

Tuscaloosa
Christian, Marie Washington Roberts *retired elementary school educator*

Fields, Ruth Kinniebrew *secondary and elementary educator, consultant*
May, Katrina Forrest *elementary educator*

Warrior
James, Virginia Scott *elementary school educator*

ALASKA

Anchorage
Brunstad, Michael Lewis *elementary education educator*
Matsui, Dorothy Nobuko *elementary education educator*
Mitchell, Michael Kiehl *elementary and secondary education educator, minister*
Rampmeyer, Kimberly Kay *elementary education educator*
Skladal, Elizabeth Lee *retired elementary school educator*

Delta Junction
Aillaud, Cindy Lou Virginia *elementary education educator*

Tuntutuliak
Daniel, Barbara Ann *retired elementary school educator*

ARIZONA

Arizona City
Donovan, Willard Patrick *retired elementary education educator*

Chandler
Barnard, Annette Williamson *elementary school principal*

Cottonwood
Parrott, Sharon Lee *retired elementary school educator*

Douglas
Britton, Ruth Ann Wright *elementary educator*

Gilbert
Peoples, Esther Lorraine *elementary education educator, writer, publisher*
Tegovich, Elaine A. *elementary education educator*

Glendale
Bret, Donna Lee *elementary education educator*
Woods, Cyndy Jones *secondary educator, researcher*

Green Valley
Shafer, Susan Wright *retired elementary school educator*

Kingman
Gonzales, Eloise A. *elementary education educator*

Marana
Ruehle, Dianne Marie *retired elementary education educator*
Sederholm, Sarah Kathleen (Kathy Sederholm) *primary education educator*

Mesa
Carter, Sally Packlett *elementary education educator*
Lingle, Muriel Ellen *retired elementary education educator*

Page
Hoodenpyle, Sandra Kay *elementary education educator*

Phoenix
Davis, Colleen Teresa *elementary education educator, reading educator*
Peabody, Debbie Kay *elementary school educator*

Roll
Jorajuria, Elsie Jean *elementary education educator*

Safford
Riddlesworth, Judith Himes *elementary and secondary education educator*

Scottsdale
Esquer, Deborah Anne *elementary school educator*

Sells
Fire Thunder, Sondra Nadine *elementary educator*

Shonto
Haviland, Marlita Christine *elementary school educator*

Sierra Vista
Rosen, Sarah Ann *elementary education educator*

Snowflake
Dwornik, Lynda Bebee *elementary school educator*

Surprise
Bradford, Mariah *elementary school educator, consultant*
Marsh, Roberta Reynolds *elementary education educator, consultant*

Tempe
Scott, Judith Myers *elementary education educator*

Tucson
Arzoumanian, Linda Lee *early childhood educator*
Bowlan, Nancy Lynn *elementary and secondary school educator*
Jacobs, Dorothy Patricia *elementary education educator*
Johnstone, Craig S. *elementary education educator*

Yuma
Kuechel, Rebecca June *elementary education educator*

ARKANSAS

Barton
Murphree, Kenneth Dewey *elementary school educator*

Camden
Bradshaw, Otabel *retired primary school educator*

Cotter
Gordon, Joyce Anne *elementary education educator*

De Witt
McCoy, Carolyn Smith *middle school educator*

Dumas
Hudson, Joy Nuckols *retired elementary school educator*

Fayetteville
Jones, Susan Matthews *elementary education educator*

Fort Smith
Henry, Letus Kay *elementary education educator, hair designer*

Hindsville
Peirce, Carole *elementary school educator*

Hot Springs National Park
Trieschmann, Elizabeth Suzanne *elementary school educator*

Jonesboro
Mangrum, Debra Kirksey *elementary school educator*

Little Rock
Shirrell, Martha Huggins *elementary school educator*
Smith, Mary Scott *elementary school educator, education educator*
Willingham, Joyce Jarrett *elementary education educator, gifted education educator*

Prairie Grove
Dunn, Anne Ewald Nefflen *elementary education educator*

Rogers
Plitt, Doris Smith *elementary education educator*
Vesper, Rebecca Hessick *child development specialist, special education and parent educator*

Star City
Strain, Linda Rogers *elementary art educator*

CALIFORNIA

Aguanga
Mendoza, Peggy Ann Gilbert *elementary education educator, writer*

Alhambra
Austin, Elizabeth Ruth *retired elementary school educator*

Alta Loma
Haskvitz, Alan Paul *elementary education educator, consultant*

Anaheim
Jantolak, Laura Jean *elementary school educator*

Arcadia
Baltz, Patricia Ann (Pann Baltz) *elementary education educator*
Morton, Laurel Anne *elementary education educator*

Bakersfield
Kennedy, Joseph Paul, Jr., *retired elementary school educator*
Novak, Martha Lois *elementary education educator*

Banning
Finley, Margaret Mavis *retired elementary school educator*

Bay Point
Essary-Anderson, Catherine *elementary education educator*

Berkeley
Johnson, Mary Katherine (Katie Johnson) *elementary education educator*

Bloomington
Llanusa, Steven Michael *elementary education educator*

Blythe
Thomas, Marcella Elaine *elementary education educator*

Boulevard
Charles, Blanche *retired elementary education educator*

Brawley
Patterson, Melissa *elementary education educator*

Brentwood
Groseclose, Wanda Westman *retired elementary school educator*

Buena Park
Turkus-Workman, Carol Ann *elementary school educator*

Burbank
Godwin, Annabelle Palkes *retired early childhood education educator*

Burlingame
Clover, Haworth Alfred *elementary school educator, historian*

Camarillo
El Shami, Patricia Ann *elementary school tutor*

Carmichael
Green, Marjorie Joan *elementary education educator*

Carson
Garcia, Angélica María *elementary education educator*

Chatsworth
Wilson, Darlene Anderson *elementary school educator*

Colton
Slider, Margaret Elizabeth *elementary education educator*

Corcoran
Martines, Eugenia Belle *elementary school educator*

Corona
Clark, Nanci *elementary education educator*

Coronado
Heap, Suzanne Rundio *elementary school educator*

Coulterville
Henderson, Pamela Mason *elementary education educator*

Culver City
Hoge, Geraldine Rajacich *elementary education educator*

Cupertino
Axelson, Donna Irene *elementary education educator*

Davis
Ginosar, D. Elaine *elementary education educator*

Diamond Bar
Domeño, Eugene Timothy *elementary education educator, principal*

Elk Grove
Moe, Janet Anne *elementary school educator, church organist*

Fair Oaks
Lemke, Herman Ernest Frederick, Jr., *retired elementary education educator, consultant*

Fontana
Donica, Cheryl Marie *elementary education educator*
Rynearson, Patricia Heaviside *elementary school educator*

Fortuna
Fisher, Bruce David *elementary school educator, education educator*

Fremont
Ours, Marian Leah *elementary education educator*

Fresno
Girvin, Shirley Eppinette *retired elementary education educator, journalist*
Graves, Melissa June *elementary school educator*

Fullerton
Snider, Jane Ann *elementary school educator*

Gardena
Hite, Janet Sue *elementary education educator*

Granite Bay
Altman, Sally Lucile *middle school educator*

Grass Valley
Thomas, Frances Marguerite Lake *retired elementary school educator*

Hanford
Roberts, Sylvia Dale *elementary school educator*

Hemet
Jaynes, Cherie Lou *early childhood education educator*
Knapp, Lonnie Troy *elementary education educator*
Masters, Judith Anne *elementary school educator*
Tolliver, Edith Catherine *retired educator*

Highland
Dondalski, Linda *elementary education educator*

Hughson
Hailey, Kathleen Wilson *elementary education educator*

Inglewood
Guzy, Marguerita Linnes *middle school education educator*
Logan, Lynda Dianne *elementary education educator*

Inyokern
Norris, Lois Ann *elementary school educator*

Irvine
McCubbin, Sharon Anglin *elementary school educator*
Payne, Lisa Mossman *middle school educator*

La Mesa
Black, Eileen Mary *retired elementary school educator*

La Verne
Ebersole, Helen Brownsberger *elementary school educator*

Laguna Niguel
Gunning, Monica Olwen Minott *elementary educator*

Lake Elsinore
Wolsey, Thomas DeVere *middle school educator*

Lakeside
Walker, Wanda Medora *retired elementary school educator, consultant*

Lawndale
Ferguson, Martha Ann *elementary school educator*

Lemon Grove
MacIntyre, Patricia Colombo *middle school educator*

Lompoc
Maxwell, Marilyn Julia *retired elementary education educator*

Long Beach
Cook, Karla Joan *elementary education educator*
Fleming, Jane Williams *retired educator, writer*
Martinez, Patricia Ann *middle school educator, administrator*

Los Altos
Welsh, Doris McNeil *early childhood education specialist*

Los Angeles
Allums, Henriene *elementary education educator*
Ansley, Julia Ette *educator, poet, writer, consultant*
Calhoun, Ollie Arlene *elementary school educator*
Fitz-Carter, Aleane *elementary school educator, composer*
Grose, Elinor Ruth *retired elementary education educator*
Polon, Linda Beth *elementary school educator, writer, illustrator*
Saito-Furukawa, Janet Chiyo *primary school educator*
Villarreal, Sharon Marie *elementary education educator*
Wilson, Ira Lee *middle school educator*

Los Gatos
Hartinger, Patricia Bernardine *elementary school educator*

Menlo Park
Raffo, Susan Henney *elementary education educator*

Merced
Delgado, Theresa Michelle *middle school educator*

Mission Viejo
Quinn, Elizabeth R. *elementary education educator*

Modesto
Gilmore, Jennie Rae *elementary education educator*
Harrison-Scott, Sharlene Marie *elementary school educator*
Smith, Glenda Irene *elementary school educator*

Montebello
Bucey, Constance Virginia Russell *retired elementary school educator, education educator*
Cabrera, Carmen *secondary education educator*

Monterey
Vandevere, Joyce Ryder *retired educator, activist*

Moreno Valley
Moulthrop, Rebecca Lee Stilphen *elementary education educator*
Smith-Farnsworth, Sharon Anne *elementary education educator*

Newark
Palomino, Kristi Suzann *elementary school educator*

Newbury Park
Colby, Evelyn Jane *elementary school educator*

Oakland
Griffin, Betty Jo *elementary school educator*

Oceano
Montano, Robert Allen *elementary education educator*

Oceanside
Druhe Brandt, Iris Claire *retired elementary school educator*

Orange
Stuewe, Isabel *elementary school educator*

Oroville
Keena, Dolores May *retired elementary education educator*

Palm Desert
Porter, Priscilla *elementary education educator*

Palm Springs
Gill, Jo Anne Martha *middle school educator*
Owings, Thalia Kelley *elementary school educator*

Palo Alto
Collins, Margery Louise *elementary school educator*
Gist, Joseph Andrew, Jr., *retired elementary school educator*
Gong, Mamie Poggio *elementary education educator*

Pasadena
Peter, Kenneth Shannon *elementary school educator*

Penn Valley
Longan, Suzanne M. *retired elementary school educator*

Petaluma
Siebe, Carol Ann *elementary school educator*

Pomona
Amaya-Thetford, Patricia *elementary education educator*

Red Bluff
Hoofard, Jane Mahan Decker *retired elementary school educator*

Redondo Beach
Barrie, Joan Parker *elementary school educator*

Rialto
Jackson, Betty Eileen *music and elementary school educator*

Riverside
Lacy, Carolyn Jean *elementary education educator, secondary education educator*
Morris, Stephen Allen *elementary school educator*

Rohnert Park
Newcomb, Joan Leslie *elementary education educator*

Roseville
French, Leura Parker *secondary educator*

Sacramento
Amezcua, Esther Hernandez *elementary education educator*
Branch, Barbara Lee *elementary education educator*
Grimes, Pamela Rae *retired elementary school educator*
Zaidi, Emily Louise *retired elementary school educator*

San Andreas
Millsaps, Rita Rae *elementary school educator*

San Bernardino
Kaisershot, Edward Joseph *elementary education educator, coach*

San Diego
Conant, Kim Untiedt *elementary education educator*
Flint, Betty Ruth *elementary education educator*
Lomeli, Marta *elementary education educator*
Ulen, Gene Eldridge *elementary school educator*
Uribe, Jennie Ann *elementary school educator*

San Dimas
Lindly, Douglas Dean *elementary/middle school educator, administrator*

San Francisco
Clemens, Sydney Gurewitz *early childhood educator, consultant*
Thé, Hoang-Dinh *middle school educator*

San Jose
Arvizu, Charlene Sutter *elementary education educator*
Jordan, Bernice Bell *retired elementary school educator*

San Leandro
Chohlis, Dana Marie *educator, theatre director*

San Pablo
Colfack, Andrea Heckelman *elementary education educator*
Collier, Judith Brandes *elementary educator*

San Ramon
Kravitz, Michelle Rae *elementary educator*

Santa Clarita
Ungar, Roselva May *primary and elementary educator*

Santa Cruz
Mirk, Judy Ann *retired elementary educator*

Santa Rosa
Wilson, Margie Jean (Marjorie Wilson) *elementary school educator, writer*

Simi Valley
Brown, Melbourne Thomas, Sr., *elementary education educator*
Soukup, Deborah Craig *elementary education educator*

South Pasadena
Yett, Sally Pugh *elementary school educator, gifted and talented educator*

Stockton
Cobb, Judy Lynn *elementary educator*
Haines, Joybelle *retired elementary school educator*

Tarzana
Streeter, Patricia Ellen *elementary school educator*

Tehachapi
Sprinkle, Martha Clare *elementary school educator*

Temecula
Randall, John Albert, III, *elementary and secondary education educator*

Thousand Oaks
Wetherwax, Georgia Lee (Peg Wetherwax) *elementary education educator*

Torrance
Rex Ton, Sheila Ward *elementary school educator*

Truckee
Williams, Beverly Beatrice *retired elementary education educator*

Vallejo
Marshall, Roberta Navarre *middle school educator*
Pelkey, Teena Ferris *elementary education educator, consultant*

Ventura
Moffatt, Mindy Ann *elementary school educator, educational training specialist*
Renger, Marilyn Hanson *elementary education educator*

Visalia
Goulart, Janell Ann *elementary education educator*

Waterford
Larrick, Phyllis Dale *retired elementary school educator*

Wawona
Horner, Michelle *elementary school educator, principal*

West Hills
Burstein, Joyce Hope *elementary education educator*

Westlake Village
Steadman, Lydia Duff *symphony violinist, retired elementary school educator*

Yorba Linda
Sternitzke-Holub, Ann *elementary school educator*

Yuba City
Higdon, Bernice Cowan *retired elementary education educator*

COLORADO

Arvada
Lucas, Theresa Eileen *elementary education educator*
Nutting, Kathleen S. *elementary education educator*
Rusch, Pamela Jean *middle school educator*

Aurora
Berg, Karen Lynn Anderson *educator*
Fair, Mary Louise *retired elementary school educator*
Pearlman, Mitzi Ann *elementary education educator*
Young, Gordon *elementary education educator*

Calhan
Henderson, Freda LaVerne *elementary education educator*

Colorado Springs
Martin, Kathryn Linda Hain *middle school foreign language educator*
Ruch, Marcella Joyce *retired elementary school educator, biographer*

Cortez
Noland, Monica Gail *elementary school educator*

Creede
Carter, Shirley Raedelle *retired elementary school educator*

Denver
Erwin, Vicki Cornelius
Fielden, C. Franklin, III, *early childhood education consultant*
Lane, Peggy Lee *elementary school educator*

Ryman, Ruth (Stacie) Marie *primary education educator*
Shaeffer, Thelma Jean *primary school educator*

Englewood
Graves, Nada Proctor *retired elementary school educator*
Shields, Marlene Sue *elementary school educator*

Fort Collins
Hodge, Mary Thomas *elementary education educator*

Grand Junction
Born, Frances Emmary Hollick *middle school art educator*

Highlands Ranch
Erickson, Linda Rae *elementary school educator*

Lakewood
Milan, Marjorie Lucille *early childhood education educator*
Tucker, James Raymond *primary education educator*
West, Marjorie Edith *former elementary education educator*

Littleton
Houser, Cheryl Ann *elementary education educator*
Pardue, Karen Reiko *elementary education educator*
Rockwell, Kay Anne *elementary education educator*

Longmont
Blackwood, Lois Anne *elementary education educator*

Louisville
Zirakzadeh, Armando Ardeshir *elementary educator*

Pueblo
Lindskog, Marjorie Otilda *elementary school educator*
Woods, Alma Jean *elementary educator*

San Luis
Maldonado, Theresa Mary *elementary education educator*

Thornton
Piccolo, Jo Anne *elementary education educator, reading consultant*

Trinidad
Amari, Kathryn Jane *elementary education educator*
Palovich, Marilyn Lee *elementary education educator*

Wiggins
Kammerzell, Susan Jane *elementary school educator, music educator*

CONNECTICUT

Avon
Brennan, Barbara McCarthy *elementary education educator*

Branford
Bullard, Linda Lane *elementary school educator*

Bridgeport
Barrows, Francine Eleanor *early childhood educator*
Simone, Angela Paolino *elementary education educator*
Wiley, Shirley Ann *elementary school educator, musician*

Bristol
Roberts, Alida Jayne *elementary school educator*

Canterbury
Neborsky, Stephanie Joy *reading and language arts consultant, educator*

Coventry
Halvorson, Judith Anne (Judith Anne Devaud) *elementary education educator*

Danbury
Arbitelle, Ronald Alan *elementary school educator*

Enfield
Doty, Victoria Skower *elementary educator*

Fairfield
Kalapos, Felicia Zera *elementary school educator, writer*

Groton
Galbraith, Marian *elementary school educator*

Hartford
McKone, Mary Katherine *elementary school educator*

Higganum
Greene, Virginia Anne *elementary education educator*

Huntington
Piazza-Harper, Anna Frances *elementary education educator*

Milford
Jahnke, Susan Alice *primary education educator*

PROFESSIONAL INDEX — PRIMARY/ELEMENTARY/MIDDLE SCHOOL EDUCATION

Naugatuck
Stauffer, Elizabeth Clare *elementary school educator, music choral director, consultant*

New Britain
Johnston, James H. *elementary school educator*

New Hartford
Manzer, Rachael Lee Elizabeth *early childhood education educator*

New Haven
Walker-LaRose, Linda Waleska *elementary education educator*

Newtown
Corey, Susan Horn *elementary school educator, special education educator*

Northford
James, Virginia Stowell *retired elementary, secondary education educator*

Seymour
Cweklinsky, Judith Ann *elementary education educator*

Shelton
Choronzy, Sandra *elementary education educator*
Dunham, Lucia Ann Varanelli *elementary school educator*

South Glastonbury
Gardner, Judith Warren *retired elementary educator*

Suffield
Friedman, Dian Debra *elementary education educator*

Torrington
Theeb, Judith Ann *elementary school educator*

Trumbull
Herman, Elizabeth Mullee *elementary educator*

West Hartford
Collins, Carol Ann *primary education educator*
Gaumond, Lynn E. *elementary school educator*

West Haven
Farquharson, Patrice Ellen *primary school educator*

Westport
Jessep, Jane (Nordli) *elementary education educator*

Woodbury
Gaia, H. Veronika *middle school educator*

DELAWARE

Delmar
Czernik, Joanne *elementary and secondary education educator*

Millsboro
Derrickson, Shirley Jean Baldwin *elementary school educator*

New Castle
Morton, Hazel Caudle *elementary education educator*

Newark
Kessler, Betty Dean *academic administrator*

Ocean View
Parler, Anne Hemenway *elementary education educator, horse trainer*

Wilmington
Simkins, Sandra Lee *middle school educator*

DISTRICT OF COLUMBIA

Washington
Collins, Herbert, Jr., *retired elementary education educator*
Davis, Gladys Maria *early childhood educator*
Jones, Alice Samuels *elementary education educator, reading specialist*
Jones, Dorothy Jefferson *elementary education educator*
Robinson, Ruth Harris *elementary education educator*
Sharpe, Dorothy Jones *secondary education educator, researcher*

FLORIDA

Altamonte Springs
Huyett, Debra Kathleen *elementary education educator*

Apopka
Shepp, Judith Rosser *elementary education educator*

Belleview
Quinn, Martha Sue *elementary education educator*

Boca Raton
Knapp, Janis Ann *elementary school educator*
Rebel, Amy Louise *elementary education educator*
Rosen, Harriet R. *elementary school educator*

Cape Coral
Mac Master, Harriett Schuyler *retired elementary school educator*

Clermont
Stanton, Lea Kaye *elementary school educator, counselor*

Coconut Grove
Soto, Patricia McFarlane *elementary school educator*

Coral Springs
Caserta, Jean Kilsheimer *elementary education educator, family counselor*

Dade City
Marler, Addie Karen *elementary school educator*

Daytona Beach
Cool, Mary L. *education specialist*

Delray Beach
Hirsch, Leda Treskunoff *elementary school educator*
Jones, Myra Kendall *elementary school educator*

Deltona
Neal, Dennis Melton *middle school administrator*

Dunedin
Cappiello, Mimi *elementary school educator*

Fernandina Beach
Fishbaugh, Carole Sue *middle school educator*

Fort Lauderdale
Carton, Cristina Silva-Bento *elementary educator*
Friedman, Debra Reneé *elementary education educator*
Kearney, Bonnie Helen *elementary education educator*

Fort Myers
Frank, Mary Lou *retired elementary school educator*
Gerdes, Lillian Anna *elementary education educator*

Fort Walton Beach
Bautista, Kimberly Rae *elementary school educator*
Berry, Nancy June *elementary school educator*
Stevenson, Mary Eva Blue *retired elementary education educator*

Gainesville
Chapin, Kenneth Lee *middle school educator*
Ketts, Sharon Davis *elementary education educator*
Rosenberger, Margaret Adaline *retired elementary school educator, writer*

Goulds
Taylor, Millicent Ruth *elementary school educator*

Graceville
Collier, Evelyn Myrtle *elementary school educator*

Greensboro
Hoffman, Lynn Renee *elementary education educator*

Hernando
Brown, Martha Wolfe *elementary school educator*

Hialeah
Hernandez, Alicia C. *elementary school educator*
Laidler, Kaywesley Sneed *elementary school educator*

Holiday
Meyers, Beatrice Nurmi *retired primary school educator, director*

Hollywood
Bivens, Constance Ann *retired elementary education educator*
Budnik, Patricia McNulty *retired elementary education educator*

Howey In The Hills
Brown, Diana Hayes *elementary education educator*

Inverness
Hawk, Pauletta Browning *student elementary school educator*

Jacksonville
Alexander, Edna M. DeVeaux *elementary education educator*
Metzler, Mary Fink *elementary education educator*
Piotrowski, Sandra A. *elementary education educator*

Jupiter
Loper, Lucia Ann *retired elementary school educator*
Strom, Carla Castaldo *elementary education educator*

Kissimmee
Severance, Jeri-Lynne White *elementary school educator*
Toothe, Karen Lee *elementary and secondary school educator*

Lady Lake
Staub, Martha Lou *retired elementary education educator*

Lake Worth
Tanner, Debbie Stivland *elementary education educator*

Lantana
Valentine, Tara E. *early childhood educator*

Leesburg
Burns, Diane *elementary education educator*

Macclenny
Delifus, Patricia Tucker *elementary school educator*

Maitland
Rose, Mary Catherine *elementary educator*

Miami
Baker, Robert James *elementary education educator*
Banas, Suzanne *middle school educator*
Barker-Lashley, Anne Elizabeth *elementary education educator*
Berkell, Doris Audrey *elementary education educator*
Davis, Anthony Maurice *elementary education educator*
Dawkins, Debra *elementary school educator*
Heller, Beverly Buxbaum *elementary education educator*
Jones, Janice Cox *elementary school educator, writer*
La Villa, Silvia J. *early childhood educator*
Miller, Constance Johnson *educator*
O'Farrill, Francisca Josefina *early childhood educator*
Patrie, Cheryl Christine *elementary education educator*
Paulovkin, Joseph Matthew *middle school educator*
Vargas-Alcaro, Juana Amada *elementary education educator*

Mount Dora
Scharfenberg, Margaret Ellan *retired elementary school educator*

Naples
Finger, Iris Dale Abrams *elementary school educator*
Mahoney, Sheila Irene *middle school educator*
Post, Barbara Joan *elementary school educator*
White, Sallie Snow Wilber *retired elementary educator*

Navarre
Korn, Irene Elizabeth *retired elementary education educator, consultant*
McLaughlin, Carolyn Lucile *elementary school educator*

New Port Richey
Keller-Augsbach, Linda Jean *elementary school educator*

Nokomis
Smith, Pamela Jean *elementary education educator*

Orange Park
Oglesby, Beverly Clayton *kindergarten educator*
Tracanna, Kim *elementary and secondary physical education educator*

Orlando
Baggott, Brenda Jane Lamb *elementary educator*
Bradshaw, Elaine Reynolds *elementary school educator*
Hires, Claudia Manigault *retired elementary school educator*
Wright, Martha Helen *elementary education educator*

Osprey
Weathermon, Sidney Earl *elementary school educator*

Oviedo
Hallstrom, Victoria Jane *primary school educator, consultant*

Pace
Jackson, Ruth Naomi *primary school music educator*

Palatka
Pounds, Janice Jones *elementary education educator*

Palm Beach
Robb, Babette *retired elementary school educator*

Palm Harbor
Fanning, Wanda Gail *retired elementary school educator*

Parkland
Isenberg, Shelly Sconyers *elementary education educator*

Pembroke Pines
Allbee, Teresa Jo *elementary school educator*

Pensacola
Dorman, Jo-Anne *elementary school educator*
Dunkerley, Eileen Tomlinson *elementary education educator*
Samson, Valerie J. *elementary education educator*

Plantation
Ornstein, Libbie Allene *primary school educator*

Pompano Beach
Endahl, Ethelwyn Mae *elementary education educator, consultant*
Johnson, Dorothy Curfman *elementary education educator*

Port Charlotte
Carter, Gale Denise *elementary education educator*
Gravelin, Janesy Swartz *elementary education educator*
Norris, Dolores June *elementary school educator*

Port Orange
Snodgrass, Traci Morton *elementary education educator*

Port Saint Lucie
Cash, Lisa Freeman *elementary education educator*

Punta Gorda
McGregor, Janet Eileen *elementary school educator*

Rockledge
Sutton, Betty Sheriff *elementary education educator*

Saint Augustine
Sullivan, Mary Jean *elementary school educator*

Saint Cloud
Lawson, Mary Birchwood *elementary education educator*

Saint Petersburg
Gray, Geraldine Manning *retired elementary school educator*
McArdle, Barbara Virginia *elementary school educator*
Smith, Betty Robinson *elementary education educator*

Sarasota
Feldhusen, Hazel Jeanette *elementary education educator*
Powell, Susan Lynn *secondary educator*

Satellite Beach
Coleman, Julie Kathryn *elementary and secondary school educator*

Sebastian
Scott, Michelle Williams *elementary education educator*

Stuart
Harvin, Kay Kerce *elementary school educator*

Tallahassee
Cue, Louella Washington *elementary education educator*
Warner, Sylvia Claar *elementary school educator*

Tampa
Brookes, Carolyn *early childhood education educator*
Nevsimal, Ervin L. *elementary education educator*
Reese-Brown, Brenda *primary education educator*

Tierra Verde
Schmitz, Dolores Jean *primary education educator*

Titusville
Furci, Joan Gelormino *early childhood education educator*

West Palm Beach
Long, John Madison *elementary music educator*
Ward, Alice Faye *elementary education educator*

GEORGIA

Adel
Darby, Marianne Talley *elementary school educator*

Albany
Forsyth, Rosalyn Moye *middle school educator*
Ledwitch, Grace Evelyn *elementary school educator, principal*

Alpharetta
Willingham, Thornton *physical education specialist*

Athens
Delgado, Lisa James *elementary education educator*
Mixon, Deborah Lynn Burton *elementary school educator*
West, Marsha *elementary school educator*

Atlanta
Bullard, Judyann DePasquale *elementary education educator*
Coleman, Mattie Jones *primary education educator*
Falana-Green, Rosebud Dixon *elementary school educator*
Jackson, Ernestine Hill *elementary education educator*
Mock, Larry John *elementary education educator*
Wilson, Deborah Sue *elementary education educator*

Augusta
Jackson, Rosa M. *educator*
Martin, Willie Pauline *retired elementary school educator, illustrator*

Barnesville
Smith, Linda *middle school educator*

PRIMARY/ELEMENTARY/MIDDLE SCHOOL EDUCATION

Bonaire
Davis, Mary Hortman *elementary school educator*
Griffin, Barbara Conley *reading educator*

Brunswick
Hanson, Carol Hall *elementary school educator*

Buford
Carswell, Virginia Colby *retired primary school educator, special education educator*

Columbus
Cook, Mary Gooch *elementary school educator*
Montgomery, Anna Frances *elementary school educator*
Newsome, Patricia H. *retired elementary school educator*
Robbins, Brenda Sue *early childhood educator*

Dacula
Birge, Esther Bonita *elementary school educator*

Danielsville
Bond, Joan *retired elementary school educator*

Decatur
Keaton, Mollie M. *elementary school educator*

Douglasville
Rodgers, Sherry Hovious *elementary education educator*

Ellenwood
Weyand, Edwina Wicker *elementary school educator*

Fairburn
Smith, Jean Benzing *retired elementary and middle school educator*

Fayetteville
Harmon, Lelia Todd *elementary school educator*

Gainesville
Embry, Karen Thompson *elementary education educator*
Hollingsworth, Jane Cannon *art education educator*

Griffin
Reid-Pollard, Cheryl Ann *early childhood education specialist*

Hamilton
Prather, Rhonda Cliatt *elementary school educator*

Hoschton
Lutz, Wendy S. *elementary school educator*
Osburn, Ella Katherine *elementary education educator*

La Fayette
Hendrix, Bonnie Elizabeth Luellan *retired elementary school educator*

Lawrenceville
Crain, Mary Ann *elementary school educator*
Harris, Melba Iris *elementary education educator, secondary school educator, state agency administrator*

Lizella
Vogel, Diane Oscherwitz *primary education educator*

Lyons
Cancer, Cathy Lynn *elementary education educator*

Macon
Vance, Elizabeth Ann *retired elementary school educator*

Madison
Short, Betsy Ann *elementary education educator*

Manchester
Ellison, Betty D. *retired elementary educator*
McIntyre, Richard Rawlings, II, *elementary school educator*

Marietta
Ellerbee, Diane Turner *elementary school educator*
Laframboise, Joan Carol *middle school educator*
Siegel, Sharon Barbara *middle school educator*
Ward, Judith Ann Kitchens *elementary education educator*
York, Darryl Robert *health and physical education educator*

Midland
Bonham, Martha Dianne *elementary art educator, watercolorist*

Monroe
Marshall, Loretta *elementary education educator*

Morrow
Burroughs, Tammy Westberry *elementary education educator*
Smith-Jones, Mary Emily *elementary school physical education educator*

Newnan
Royal, Nancy B. *primary school educator*

Norcross
Burnett, Cassie Wagnon *middle school educator*
Holzer, Tamera Lee-Phillis *middle school educator*
Melson, René Harber *elementary school educator*

Patterson
Cunningham, Raymond Carol, Jr., *elementary school educator*

Ringgold
McKown, Melissa Anne *elementary school educator*

Roopville
Huckeba, Emily Causey *retired elementary school educator*

Roswell
Hoskinson, Carol Rowe *middle school educator*

Savannah
Jarnigan-Gray, Angela Renee *elementary school educator*
Polite, Evelyn C. *retired middle school educator, counselor, evangelist*

Senoia
Preece, Jim *elementary education educator, consultant*

Smyrna
Qualls, Sophronia Anita *elementary school educator*

Snellville
Magill, Dodie Burns *early childhood education educator*

Statesboro
Schriver, Martha Louise *middle school educator*

Thomaston
Brown, June Dyson *elementary education educator, administrator*

Tifton
Simpson, Juliette Rich *elementary educator*

Tucker
Noble, Nelda Kaye *elementary education educator*

Valdosta
Mayer, Katherine Gentz *elementary education educator*

Warner Robins
Owens, Helen Dawn *elementary school educator, reading consultant*

Watkinsville
Jackson, Sharon Broome *elementary educator*

Waycross
Hickox, Barbara Nodine *retired elementary school educator*

Waynesboro
Parris, Florence Mae *elementary education educator*

Willacoochee
Wingate, Ann *early childhood education educator*

Winder
Allen, B. Janice *elementary educator*
Ellington, Cynthia Hemphill *elementary education educator*

Woodstock
Baumann, Sara Margaret Culbreth *retired elementary school educator*

HAWAII

Eleele
Takanishi, Lillian K. *elementary school educator*

Hilo
Larson, Mary Bea *elementary education educator*

Honolulu
Eppling, Jacqueline Quon *elementary school educator*
Gonsalves, Margaret Leboy *elementary school educator*
Toyama, Jewel B.C. *elementary school educator, physical education educator*
Wee, Christine Dijos *elementary school educator*

Kailua Kona
Spitze, Glenys Smith *retired educator*

Kaneohe
Ing, Grace Sachiko Nakamura *elementary education educator*

Pearl City
Lee, Kenneth *secondary education educator*
Mokulehua, Jocelyn Kojima *elementary school educator*

IDAHO

Boise
Rumpeltes, Sherrie Jan *primary school educator, pre-school educator*
Wentz, Catherine Jane *elementary education educator*

Burley
Vargas, Teresa Marie Bradley *elementary school educator*

Chubbuck
Ward, Pamela Melczer *elementary school educator*

Coeur D Alene
Medved, Sandra Louise *elementary education educator*

Idaho Falls
Woodruff, Shirley *middle school educator*

Inkom
Wagner, Hazel Ann *primary and elementary school educator*

Meridian
Marsh, Lynn *elementary education educator*

Mountain Home A F B
Borchert, Warren Frank *elementary education educator*

New Plymouth
Matthews-Burwell, Vicki *elementary education educator*

Wendell
Anderson, Marilyn Nelle *elementary education educator, librarian, counselor*

ILLINOIS

Alexander
Eck, Gail Ann *elementary education educator*

Altamont
Zimmerman, Sally Gail *elementary education educator*

Andalusia
Gilliland, Diane *elementary school educator*
Gilliland, Rick E. *elementary education educator*

Anna
Wolfe, Martha *elementary education educator*

Barrington
Shuldes, L(illian) June *elementary school educator*

Belleville
Shepheard, Linda June *elementary school educator*

Bement
Vezina, Vicky Lynne *middle school educator*

Bloomington
Gregor, Marlene Pierce *primary education educator, elementary science consultant*
McNulty, Carol Jeanne *elementary education educator*

Buffalo Grove
Boesch, Deborah Ann *elementary school educator*
Sussman, Beverly Kall *elementary education educator*

Cahokia
Wade, Susan Kaye *elementary education educator*

Calumet City
Henke, Susan Kay *elementary education educator*

Carbondale
Gurley, Deborah Carlene *elementary school educator*

Chester
Gross, Melissa Kay *elementary education educator*

Chicago
Cintron, Judith *elementary education educator*
Cummings, Maxine Gibson *elementary school educator*
Dunlap, Patricia Pearl *elementary school educator*
Feig, Barbara Krane *elementary school educator, author*
Flynn-Franklin, Gertrude Elizabeth *elementary education educator, social worker*
Fruchter, Rosalie Klausner *elementary school educator*
Gasior, Dawn Marie *elementery education educator*
Harris, Shirley *elementary, secondary and adult education educator*
Holland, Jean *elementary education educator*
Howard, Janet *elementary education educator*
Long, Earline Davis *elementary education educator*
Miller, Judith Ann *elementary education educator*
Nero, Ellie Theresa *elementary education educator*
Perlman, Bella Beach *retired elementary school educator*
Spearman, David Leroy *elementary education educator, administrator*
Stelmack, Gloria Joy *elementary education educator*
Turner, Sadie Lee *elementary educator*
Weiman, Heidi *early childhood education educator*

Christopher
Eovaldi, Karen Ann *elementary education educator*

Cicero
Brusky, Linda L. *middle school mathematics and science educator*

Clarendon Hills
Gorski, Nancy Anne *elementary education educator*

Coal Valley
Cosentine, Sherry Lee *elementary education educator*

Downers Grove
LaRocca, Patricia Darlene McAleer *middle school mathematics educator*

Edgewood
Lewis, Linda Sue *elementary education educator*

Edwardsville
May, Mary Louise *elementary education educator*

Effingham
Pickett, Steven Harold *retired elementary school educator*

Elgin
Thompson, Phyllis Darlene *retired elementary school educator*

Elmhurst
Nega, Nancy Kawecki *middle school science educator*
Poltrock, Naomi Eunice *elementary education educator*

Forreston
Hall, Carol Beth *elementary school educator*

Frankfort
Ruggles, Barbara Ann *elementary education educator*

Galesburg
Kilpatrick, Jean Ann *elementary education educator*

Geneseo
Simonich, Sandra Sue *elementary education educator*

Geneva
Weigand, Jan Christine *elementary education educator, computer specialist*

Glenview
Corley, Jenny Lynd Wertheim *elementary education educator*

Godfrey
Gallagher, Kathryn Kasich *elementary school educator*

Granite City
Cassy, Catherine Mary *elementary school educator*

Hanover Park
Guest, James Donald *elementary education educator*

Hazel Crest
Chapman, Delores *elementary education educator*

Jacksonville
Anderson, Michael R. *elementary school educator, writer*

Joliet
Krieger, Dolores Esther *retired elementary education educator*

Kankakee
Dauphin, Sheryl Lynn *elementary school educator*

Kewanee
Lotspeich, Ellin Sue *elementary education educator*

Lake Zurich
Nemeth, Robert Fred *elementary school educator*

Lemont
Urban, Patricia A. *former elementary school educator*

Libertyville
Tremmel, Lynn Alison *elementary education educator*

Lisle
Huffman, Louise Tolle *middle school educator*

Manito
Summar, Sharon Kay *elementary school educator*

Markham
Peacock, Marilyn Claire *primary education educator*

Mason City
Breedlove, Jimmie Dale, Jr., *elementary education educator*

Mchenry
Carson, Linda Marie *elementary school educator*

Metamora
Crow, Mary Jo Ann *retired elementary education educator*

Moline
Lewis, Thomas Robert *elementary school educator*
Mitchell, Lucille Anne *retired elementary school educator*

Mount Prospect
Jacobsen, Charlene Marie *middle school music educator, band director*

Naperville
Jansz, Barbara Raymond *elementary education educator*

Normal
Ball, Linda Ann *primary school educator*
Glover, Peggy Ann *elementary education educator*

North Aurora
Butcher, Ann Patrice *elementary school educator*

Northbrook
Ament, Arlene Shub *middle school educator*

Oak Park
Williams, Patricia Marie *middle school educator, art educator*

Ottawa
Quinn, Christine Marie (Jensen) *elementary education educator*

Palos Park
Lawler, Susan George *elementary education educator*
Nicholls, Richard Allen *middle school social studies educator*

Pekin
Bogle, Janice L. *elementary and special education educator*
Herbstreith, Yvonne Mae *primary education educator*

Peoria
Borders, Carol Lee *primary school educator*
Nielsen, Eloise Wilma Soule *elementary education educator*

Peru
Sarver, Kathryn Margaret *elementary education educator*

Poplar Grove
Hullah, Ann Marie *elementary education educator*

Quincy
Brown, David Edward *elementary and environmental education educator*

Richton Park
Pierce, Mary E. *retired educator, public relations consultant*

Rockford
Babb, Margaret L. *elementary school educator*
Hart-Nolan, Elsie Faye *elementary education educator*
Johnson, Elizabeth Ericson *retired educator*
Rauch, Janet Melodie *elementary school educator*
Thompson, Margie Jane *retired elementary school educator*

Roselle
Gomopoulos, Mary *elementary school educator*

Roxana
Tucker, David Wayne *elementary school educator, antique dealer*

Schaumburg
Harmon, Nancy Jean *elementary school educator*

Springfield
Penning, Patricia Jean *elementary education educator*

Sycamore
Johnson, Yvonne Amalia *elementary education educator, science consultant*

Tinley Park
Henley, Gloria Jane *elementary education educator*

Trenton
Brown, Karen Lucille *elementary school educator*

Tuscola
Henderson, E. Suzanne *elementary school educator*

Urbana
Splittstoesser, Shirley O. *elementary school educator*

Vandalia
Keele, Kerry Leanne *elementary school educator, counselor*

Waukegan
Adams, Pamela Grace *primary school educator*

Western Springs
Delaney, Jane Ellen *elementary education educator*

Wheaton
Domeier, Sue Ann *elementary education educator*

Winnetka
McKee, Judith Nelson *elementary school educator*

Woodridge
Rathke, Barbara Joanne *elementary school educator*

Zion
Studebaker, Sally Jane *elementary education educator*

INDIANA

Anderson
Earnest, Linda Kay Hart *elementary education educator*

Avon
Alsop, Thomas Walter *secondary education educator*

Batesville
Volk, Cecilia Ann *elementary education educator*

Bloomington
Stone, Debra Lynn (Debbie Stone) *elementary education educator*

Brazil
Rector, Irene *retired elementary school educator*

Cayuga
Corey, Donald Edward *elementary education educator*

Churubusco
Deck, Judith Therese *elementary school educator*

Clay City
Neiswinger, Rhonda Jean *elementary school educator*

Connersville
Herald, Sandra Jean *elementary education educator*

East Chicago
Vis, Mary A. Murga *elementary education educator*

Evansville
Van Hoosier, Judy Ann *elementary education educator*

Fort Wayne
Cummins, Kathleen K. *retired elementary school educator*
Cutshall-Hayes, Diane Marion *elementary education educator*
Pease, Ella Louise *elementary education educator*
Stebbins, Vrina Grimes *retired elementary school educator, counselor*

Gary
Steele, Beverly J. *elementary school educator*
Thomas, Carolyn Harper *elementary educator*
Williams, Mary Elizabeth *elementary school educator*

Granger
Skale, Linda Dianne *retired elementary education educator*

Greenville
Hall, Susan Liddell *elementary education educator*

Highland
DeVaney, Cynthia Ann *elementary education educator, real estate broker*
Gregory, Marian Frances *retired elementary school educator, retired principal*

Indianapolis
Barcus, Mary Evelyn *primary school educator*
Crosier, Hazel Jane *primary education educator*
Grube, Linda Louise *elementary education educator*
Hefler, William Louis *elementary education educator*
Solomon, Marilyn Kay *educator, consultant*
Strauss, Diane Jayne *elementary school educator, small business owner*
Sullender, Joy Sharon *elementary school educator*
Watkins, Sherry Lynne *elementary school educator*

Jeffersonville
Fellows, Marilyn Kinder *elementary education educator*

Kokomo
Kirkpatrick, Holly Jean *elementary education educator, special education educator*

La Porte
Curtis, Gayle Lynne *elementary school educator, coach*
Heiden, Susan Jane *elementary education educator*
Serpe-Schroeder, Patricia L. *elementary education educator*

Lafayette
Schramm, Beatrice Griffin *retired teacher*

Lebanon
Ohmart, Sally Jo *elementary education educator*

Marion
Maddox, Nancy L *elementary school educator, special education educator*

Merrillville
Kamanaroff, Charlene *elementary education educator*
Magry, Martha J. *elementary education educator*

Monroeville
Geldien, Judith Ruth Motter *elementary educator*

Muncie
Dickson, Nancy Starr *retired elementary school educator*
Jarvis, Sara Lynn *elementary education educator*

Munster
Fies, James David *elementary education educator*

New Albany
Kaiser, Michael Bruce *elementary education educator*

New Haven
Smith, Barbara Ann *elementary education educator*

Newport
Weeks, Catherine Claire *elementary education educator*

North Webster
Pryor, Dixie Darlene *elementary education educator*

Poneto
McNamara-Needler, Tamara Sue *elementary education educator*

Portage
Zuick, Diane Martina *elementary education educator*

Richmond
Robinson, Dixie Faye *elementary and secondary school educator*

Shelbyville
Clark, Rose Sharon *elementary school educator*

South Bend
Emery, Margaret Ross *elementary school educator*
Knight, Ida Brown *retired elementary educator*
Mills, Nancy Anne *elementary education educator*

Spencer
Coley, Brenda Ann *elementary education educator*

Terre Haute
Nugent, Mary Katherine *elementary education educator*

Wheatfield
Woolever, Gail Waluk *elementary school educator, artist, secondary school educator*

Whiting
Kazragys, Linda Kayan Bublis *elementary school educator*

Williamsport
Baysinger, Jane Ann *elementary school music educator*

Zionsville
Rutledge, Marian Sue *middle school language arts and social studies educator*

IOWA

Albia
Putnam, Bonnie Colleen *elementary education educator*

Ames
Mattila, Mary Jo Kalsem *elementary and art educator*

Ankeny
Morley, Connie Ann *elementary school educator*

Boone
Zehr, Amy Jo Wurch *elementary education educator*

Burlington
Brocket, Judith Ann *elementary education mathematics educator*

Cedar Falls
Ehmen, James Edward *elementary education educator*

Charles City
Dunkel, Janet L. *middle school educator*

Charter Oak
Kutschinski, Dorothy Irene *elementary education educator*

Corydon
Snook, Beverly Jean *elementary school educator*

Council Bluffs
McMullen, Kristi Kay *elementary school educator*

Davenport
Corcoran, Janet Patricia *elementary school educator*
Currence, Glennda Kay *elementary education educator*

Des Moines
Mattern, David Bruce *elementary education educator*
Sly, Marilynn Jane *elementary education educator*

Dubuque
Collins, Barbara Louise *retired elementary school educator*

Eagle Grove
Manues, Patricia Ann *elementary education educator*
Tschetter, Lois Jean *retired elementary school educator*

Emmetsburg
Wells, Martha Johanna *elementary education educator*

Fort Dodge
Pratt, Diane Adele *talented and gifted education educator*

Fredericksburg
Moore, Myrna M. *elementary school educator*

Gilmore City
Worthington, Patricia *elementary education educator*

Harlan
Wilson, Annette Sigrid *elementary school educator*

Holstein
Radke, Beverly Ida *elementary education educator*

Keokuk
Fife-LaFrenz, Janet Kay *elementary school educator*

Kingsley
Hodnefield, Elaine Marie *elementary education educator*

Knoxville
Baker, Cynthia Joan *elementary education educator, historic site interpreter*
Dittmer, Linda Mae *elementary school educator*

Lisbon
Everly, Debra Goettsch *elementary educator*

New Hampton
Kennedy, Linda Marie *elementary school educator, curriculum director*

New Sharon
Sullivan, Mary Jane *elementary school educator*

Oakland
Brant, Raymond Dean *elementary education educator*

Prairie City
Hill, Pamela Jean *middle school educator*

Shenandoah
Beavers, Patsy Ann *elementary teacher*

Sioux Center
Schut, Donna Sue *elementary education educator*

Sioux City
Dillman, Kristin Wicker *elementary and middle school educator, musician*

Spirit Lake
Wilson, Wendy Melgard *kindergarten and special education educator*

Urbandale
Hewitt (Ver Hoef), Lisa Carol *elementary education educator*

Vinton
Ramsey, Ardeth Jane *retired elementary school educator*

Walnut
Myers, Gloria Jean *elementary education educator*

Waverly
Rose, Mary Mabel *elementary school educator*

KANSAS

Anthony
Carr, Cynda Annette *elementary education educator*

Baxter Springs
O'Neal, Vicki Lynn *elementary education educator*

Bonner Springs
Ringel, Karen Elaine (Killian) *elementary education educator*

Carbondale
McCollum, Susan *elementary school educator*

Clifton
Reed, Trudy Faye *elementary school educator*

Coffeyville
Roberson, Carolyn Rea *elementary school educator*

El Dorado
Flaming, Iretha Mae *elementary education educator*

Emporia
Cookson, Linda Marie *retired elementary education educator*

Grinnell
Heier, Marilyn Kay *retired elementary school educator*

Hays
Fleischacker, Donna M. *middle school educator*
Harman, Nancy June *elementary education educator, principal*
Miller, Elouise Darlene *primary education educator*

Hiawatha
Pennel, Marie Lucille Hunziger *retired elementary education educator*

Hutchinson
Green, Thereasa Ellen *elementary education educator*
Stevens, Leota mae *retired elementary education educator*

Kansas City
Merritt, Carol Ruth *middle school educator*

Kingman
Mason, Betty Rose *elementary school educator*

Liberal
Smothermon, Reba Maxine *elementary education educator*

Meade
Brannan, Cleo Estella *retired elementary education educator*

Norton
Roe, Enid Adrian Talton *retired elementary and special education educator*

Olathe
Stevens, Diana Lynn *elementary education educator*

Osawatomie
Poland, Donna Lee *elementary education educator*

Pomona
Gentry, Alberta Elizabeth *elementary education educator*

Salina
Demaree, Hilma Marie *elementary school educator*

Shawnee Mission
Crooks, Lisa Zahn *elementary education educator*
Steele, Dorothy Pauline *retired elementary education educator*

Smith Center
Wolfe, Mindy René *early childhood special education educator*

Topeka
Jennings, Nancy Ann *retired elementary education educator*

Wichita
Cox, Shirley Rose *elementary education educator*
Rudd, Darcie Kay *elementary education educator*
Van Arendonk, Susan Carole *elementary school educator*

KENTUCKY

Berea
Sparks, Larry Edward *elementary school educator*

Bowling Green
Gary, Janet Lynne Carlock *middle school educator*
Murrell, Estelle C. *elementary school educator*

Brandenburg
Carman, Darren L. *middle school educator*

Brooksville
King, Sharon A. *elementary school educator*

Campbellsville
Conner, Jeanette Jones *elementary school educator*

Covington
Tillar, Aimee Campbell *early childhood professional*

Ekron
Hamilton, Amelia Wentz (Amy Wentz) *elementary school educator*

Eubank
Buis, Dianna Lovins *elementary education educator, guidance counselor*

Fort Knox
Olive, Karl William *elementary education educator, secondary educator*

Frankfort
Jones, Connie Jeanne *primary school educator*

Guston
Yundt, Betty Brandenburg *elementary education educator*

Hustonville
Coffey, Donna Hoskins *middle school educator*

Independence
Boster, Judy Landen *primary school educator*

Inez
Fannin, Donald Ray *elementary school educator*

Letcher
Banks, Vina Michelle *primary education educator*

Lexington
Hodges, Joseph Marion *elementary school educator*
Manley, Margaret Edwards *primary education educator*

London
Ridner, Kathleen Rader *elementary education educator*

Louisville
Accordino, Barbara Lynn *elementary school educator*
Cecil, Bonnie Susan *elementary education educator*
Conely, Lois Ann *elementary education educator*
Embry, Julia Edwards *elementary education educator*
Goldstein, Irvin L. *elementary school educator*
Goodpaster-Troyer, Sheila Rogers *elementary education educator*

Madisonville
Aubrey, Sherilyn Sue *elementary school educator*
Sneed, Joanne Lawson *elementary school educator, author*

Maysville
Trimble, Garnet O'Cull *retired elementary music educator*

Middlesboro
Miracle, Donald Eugene *elementary school educator*

Mount Sterling
Farris, Marketta Blackburn *elementary educator*

Owensboro
Roberts, Sandra Miller *middle school language arts educator*

Partridge
Burton, Sharon K. *primary education educator*

Princeton
Holt, Linda Fitzgerald *elementary education educator*

Richmond
Rowlett, Jeannette Gail *elementary education educator*

Springfield
Ward, James Kenneth *primary school educator*

Stanford
Malone, Jennifer Carol Smith *primary school educator*

Tompkinsville
Pitcock, Linda Hart *middle school educator*

Wallins Creek
Hensley, Judith Victoria *elementary school educator*

Williamsburg
Ramey, Patricia Ann *elementary education educator*

Winchester
Dulin, Teresa Dianne *primary school educator*

LOUISIANA

Alexandria
Goldich, Sandra McGinty *secondary school educator, consultant*
Maples, Mary Lou *elementary education educator*

Baker
Welch, Brenda Roxson *elementary education educator*

Benton
Arnold, Deborah Lynne *elementary school educator*

Des Allemands
Jarrell, Roseann *elementary school educator*

Eunice
Moreau, Cindy Lynn *elementary education educator*

Golden Meadow
Guidry, Gaye Cheramie *elementary education educator*

Kenner
Cook, Willie Chunn *retired elementary school educator*

Lafayette
Andrew, Catherine Vige *elementary school educator*
Manuel, Nancy Williamson *elementary education educator, special education educator*

Lake Arthur
Dronet, Judy Lynn *elementary educator, librarian*

Lake Charles
Douglas, Wanda Sue Lenard *middle school educator*
Leder, Sandra Juanita *retired elementary school educator*

Mandeville
Lunn, Pamela Kellogg *elementary education educator*

Metairie
Caruso, Kay Ann Pete *elementary education educator*
Davis, Teri Cecilia *elementary education educator*

New Orleans
Abad, Rosario Dalida *elementary education educator*
Ross, Brenda Marie *elementary school educator*

Shreveport
Thomas, Bessie *primary education educator*
Wallace, Clinton John *middle school educator*

Westwego
Reyes, Shirley Norflin *computer learning center educator*

Winnsboro
Wilson, Rose Eaton *elementary education educator*

MAINE

Bar Harbor
Carman, John Herbert *elementary education educator*

Bar Mills
Burns, Maryann Margaret *elementary education educator*

Brunswick
Small, Helen Agnes *reading education specialist*

Lewiston
Dutile, Shelley Sue Reed *elementary school counselor*

New Gloucester
Wurtz, Betty Lou *retired educator*

Palermo
Robbins, Marjorie Jean Gilmartin *elementary education educator*

South Paris
Martin, Charles Seymour *middle school educator*

Waterville
Armstrong, Darlene L. *elementary education educator*

Westbrook
Corkery, Martha Gallagher *elementary education educator*

Yarmouth
Bissonnette, Jean Marie *retired elementary school educator, polarity therapist*

MARYLAND

Annapolis
Crawford, Genie Zorn *elementary school educator*
Vahsen, Faustena F. (Penny) *elementary education educator*

Baltimore
Boston, William Lawrence *elementary educator, administrator*
Brewer, Nevada Nancy *elementary education educator*
Gleichmann, Frances Evangeline *retired elementary educator*
Kemp, Suzanne Leppart *elementary education educator*
Logan-Generette, Charletta Lee *elementary education educator*
Webb, Myrtle Bailey *elementary school educator*

Bel Air
Nye, Daniel William *retired elementary school educator*

Berlin
Auxer, Cathy Joan *elementary school educator*

Bethesda
Hinzman, Susan Emmons *retired elementary school educator*

Brookeville
Rowe, Joseph Charles *elementary school educator, principal*

Capitol Heights
McKinney-Ludd, Sarah Lydelle *middle school education, librarian*

Catonsville
Smith, F. Louise *elementary school educator*

Clinton
Johns, Jayne Howell *elementary education educator, administrator, achievement specialist*

Cockeysville Hunt Valley
Allen, Barbara Jill *educator*

College Park
Stewart, Teresa Elizabeth *elementary school educator*

Columbia
Flack, Mignon Scott-Palmer *elementary school educator*

Delmar
Kheirme, Sharon Lynn *elementary educator*

Ellicott City
Powell, Lillian Marie *retired music educator*

Fallston
Orlando, Katherine Kay *elementary education educator*

Fort Washington
Birts, Kimberly Edwards *elementary educator*

Gaithersburg
Horman, Karen Loeb *elementary education educator*

Hagerstown
McCoy, Mildred Brookman *retired elementary education educator*

Hyattsville
Premužić-McChesney, Arianne Tamara Maria *elementary education educator*

Indian Head
Gebler, Mary Anne *elementary school educator*

Kensington
Hudson, Yvonne Morton *elementary education educator*

Landover
Dortch, Susan Madeline *elementary education educator*

Laurel
Langshine-Kistler, Donna *elementary education educator*

Mardela Springs
Harcum, Louise Mary Davis *retired elementary education educator*

Middletown
Smith, Karen Marie *middle school educator*

Mount Rainier
Steinbach, Donald Ervin *middle school educator*

Potomac
Ahmad, Sharmin *elementary education educator*

Rockville
Generlette, Bertram B. *elementary school educator*
Krear, Gail Richardson *elementary education educator, consultant*
Levine, Barbara Gershkoff *primary school educator, consultant*
Rosenberg, Judith Lynne *middle school educator*
Stenger, Judith Antoinette *middle school educator*

Salisbury
Johnston, Carolyn S. *elementary education educator, reading specialist*

Severna Park
Darden, Alverta Eleanor *elementary educator*

Silver Spring
Holcomb, Minnie Irby *elementary educator*

Towson
Myers, Debra Taylor *elementary school educator, writer*

Whaleyville
Truitt, Shirley Ann Bowdle *middle school educator*

Woodbine
LaMarca, Mary Margaret *elementary education educator*

MASSACHUSETTS

Amherst
Skolnick Rothenberg, Barbara *elementary education educator*

Andover
Loschi, Richard Paul *middle school educator*

Berlin
Nelson, Lynda P. *elementary education educator*

Beverly
Smith, Merelyn Elizabeth *elementary and middle school educator*

Bolton
Foster, Mary Jean Smith *elementary educator, reading specialist*

Boston
Pereira, Julio Cesar *middle school educator*
Pertuz, Marcia Jane *primary school educator*

Boxford
Guazzaloca, Edward Francis *elementary school educator*

Brookline
Weinstein, Rhonda Kruger *elementary mathematics educator, administrator*

Dunstable
Polaski, Anne Faith *elementary education educator*

PRIMARY/ELEMENTARY/MIDDLE SCHOOL EDUCATION

Framingham
LeDuc, Karen Lorain Leacu *elementary and middle school education educator*
Valakis, M. Lois *retired elementary school educator*

Gardner
Marceau, Judith Marie *retired elementary school educator, small business owner*

Lakeville
Chase, Karen Humphrey *middle school education educator*

Lexington
Levy, Steven Z. *elementary education educator*
Mack, Jane Louise *early childhood education educator, administrator*

Lowell
Hayes, Donald Paul, Jr., *elementary and secondary education educator*

Marshfield
Langefoss, Heather Smith *elementary education educator*

Maynard
Holway, Ellen Twombly Hay *primary education educator*

Nantucket
Grover-Moores, Mary Lea *elementary music education educator*

New Bedford
Gagnon, Marie Frances *elementary school educator*

North Andover
McGovern, Barbara Elizabeth Ann *elementary education educator*

North Easton
Olson, Priscilla Ann *elementary education*

Norton
Giordano, Diane E. *middle school educator*

Pembroke
Bailey, Kathleen Ellen *reading educator*

Plymouth
Taylor, Maryann Courtney *elementary education educator*

Quincy
Adams, Ronald G. *middle school educator*

Roxbury
Gamer, Frances *elementary school educator*

South Deerfield
Fritz, Nancy H. *educational researcher, administrator*

Southwick
MacEwan, Barbara Ann *middle school educator, historian*

Springfield
Chappell, Shirley Ann *elementary school educator*
Foster, Margaret Ann *elementary school educator*

Tyngsboro
Lee, Joan Roberta *elementary education educator*

Wakefield
Downey, Mary Ethel *elementary school educator*

West Roxbury
Roach, Maureen S. *primary school educator*

Wilbraham
Woloshchuk, Candace Dixon *secondary school educator, artist, consultant*

MICHIGAN

Alanson
Ginop, Anita Leuolla *elementary education educator*

Almont
Ferzacca, Pamela Ann *elementary education educator*

Ann Arbor
Murray, Barbara Ann Libs *elementary educator*
Tice, Carol Hoff *intergenerational specialist, consultant*

Auburn Hills
Schoff, Pamela Ann *elementary school educator*

Belmont
Delnick, Martha Joyce *retired elementary education educator*

Burton
Gillespie, Cornelia Messler (Connie Gillespie) *retired reading specialist*

Cadillac
Foley, David Ray *middle school educator*

Carson City
Richards, Patricia Fae *elementary education educator*

Charlotte
Blodgett, Juanita Rice *retired elementary school educator*

Chesterfield
Suchecki, Lucy Anne *elementary education educator*

Coloma
Groff, Charlotte Virginia *elementary education educator*

Dearborn
Meyer, Lisa Marie *elementary school educator*

Detroit
Hough, Cynthia Denise Cook *middle school educator*

East Lansing
Velicer, Janet Schafbuch *retired elementary school educator*

Escanaba
Bennett, Kathleen Marourneen *elementary school educator*

Farmington Hills
Hechler, Ellen Elissa *elementary education educator*

Fennville
Hagger, Bobbie *elementary education educator*

Flint
Edson, Ray Zachariah *middle school educator*

Galesburg
Hymer, Martha Nell *elementary education educator*

Gaylord
Magsig, Judith Anne *retired early childhood education educator*

Grand Ledge
Farnsworth, Judith Marie *elementary education educator*

Harrison Township
Kennard, Margaret Anne *middle school educator*

Holland
Hill, JoAnne Francis *retired elementary education educator*

Ida
McCully, Ruth Alida *elementary education educator*

Jackson
Straayer, Carole Kathleen *retired elementary education educator*
Wilcox, Charlene Deloris *elementary school educator*

Kalamazoo
Gray, Audrey Nesbitt *elementary education educator*
McCarthy, Catherine Therese *elementary educator*

Lake Orion
Leonard, Jacquelyn Ann *retired elementary school educator*

Marquette
Harrington, Lucia Marie *elementary education educator*
Jajich, James Gary *elementary and middle school educator*

Mount Morris
Bohms, Patricia Anne *elementary education educator*

Pontiac
Bond, Evelyn Roberta *elementary education educator*
Love, Sharon Irene *elementary education educator*

Port Huron
Larzelere, Michael Louis *elementary education educator*

Portage
Kim, Sonja Chung *elementary education educator*

Saginaw
Kinney, Yvonne Marie *primary grades educator*

Sparta
McDonald, Lois Alice *elementary school educator*

Spring Arbor
Dillman, Marie *elementary education educator, music educator*

Sterling Heights
Nierath, Debra Ann *elementary education educator*

Tawas City
Jacob, Elizabeth Ann *elementary education educator*

Warren
Duzyj, Doris Nachwostach *middle school educator, gifted and talented education consultant*

Willis
Washington, Adrienne Marie *elementary school educator*

Ypsilanti
Gerber, Lucille D. *elementary education educator*
Lewis-White, Linda Beth *elementary school educator*

Zeeland
Kaiser, Martha Winnifred *elementary school educator*

MINNESOTA

Albert Lea
Larson, Paul Theodore *elementary school educator*

Andover
Peterson, Jill Susan *elementary school educator*

Bemidji
DeKrey, Petra Jean Hegstad *elementary school educator*

Bloomington
Larson, Beverly Rolandson *elementary education educator*

Buffalo
Swanson, Fern Rose *retired elementary education educator*

Cannon Falls
Hjermstad, Roslyn *elementary educator*

East Grand Forks
Trembath, Marjorie Faye *elementary school educator*

Eden Prairie
Wilson, Marilyn Ione *retired educator*

Eden Valley
Kjar, Nancy *elementary school educator*

Fairmont
Millette, Robert Joseph *elementary education educator*

Fridley
Larson, Marilyn J. *retired elementary music educator*

Hopkins
Zins, Martha Lee *elementary education educator, media specialist*

Lakeland
Fisher, Pearl Beatrice *retired reading specialist educator*

Maple Grove
Gall, Patience Beth *elementary education educator*
Kirpes, Anne Irene *elementary education educator*

Minneapolis
Burroughs, Blanche Edwina *retired elementary school educator*
Kirschner, Ruth Brin *elementary education educator*
Knoell, Nancy Jeanne *kindergarten educator*
Nordgren, Lynn Lizbeth *elementary education educator, educational administrator*
Porter, Jeannette Upton *elementary education educator*
Roe, Leslie Eileen *elementary education educator*
Stark, Janice Ann *elementary education educator*
Wehrwein-Hunt, Jeri Lynn *elementary education educator*

Minnetonka
Vanstrom, Marilyn June Christensen *retired elementary education educator*
Wigfield, Rita L. *elementary education educator*

Oakdale
Siluk, Carol Linda *elementary school educator*

Perham
Kingsbury, Rex Alan *elementary education educator, administrator*

Red Lake Falls
Oakland, Velma LeAne *elementary school educator*

Richmond
Olson, Dorothy Bernice *retired elementary and secondary school educator*

Roseville
Mooney, Patricia Eileen *elementary school educator, coach*

Saint Paul
Bell, Joyce Anne *elementary school educator*
Hultman, Carol Linda *middle school education educator*
Stroud, Rhoda M. *elementary education educator*

Ulen
Harmon, Kay Yvonne *elementary education educator*

Winnebago
Willmert, Lois Ann *elementary education educator*

Winona
White, Marjorie Mary *retired elementary school educator*

MISSISSIPPI

Bay Saint Louis
Warren, Rita Robins *early childhood educator*

Biloxi
Manners, Pamela Jeanne *middle school educator*

Columbus
Himes, Rose Kendrick *elementary school educator*

Grenada
Marasalco, Lynne Callis *elementary education educator*

Gulfport
West, Eula Kirkpatrick *retired elementary education educator*

Jackson
Anglin, Linda McCluney *retired elementary school educator*
Bishop, Loraine Kelly *middle school educator*

Kiln
Jackson, Judith Ann *elementary education educator*

Laurel
Masters, Beda M. *elementary educator*

Long Beach
White, Edith Roberta Shoemake *elementary school educator*

Marietta
Bolen, Brenda Windham *elementary education educator*

Natchez
Profice, Rosena Mayberry *elementary school educator*

Noxapater
Sumner, Margaret Elizabeth *elementary school educator*

Starkville
Goodman, Ellen *elementary education educator*

Tupelo
Johnson, Ruth Allen *elementary school educator*

Walls
Rayford, Paula Judelle *elementary education educator*
Stanford, Amelia Jean *elementary education educator*

MISSOURI

Bellflower
Francis, Albert W. *elementary education educator*

Bethel
Coonrod, Delberta Hollaway (Debbie Coonrod) *retired elementary education educator, consultant, freelance writer*

Blue Springs
Hiles, Barbara Lynn *retired elementary school educator*
Peterson, Mary Kay *elementary education educator*

Bolivar
Casebeer, Deanna Fern Gentry *elementary education educator*
Lehman, Lisa Marie *elementary education educator*

Camdenton
Hosman, Sharon *elementary education educator*

Caruthersville
Joslin, Linda Joy Harber *elementary education educator*

Cassville
Sheats, Rachel Gay *computer and reading educator, videographer*

Chesterfield
Cox, Glenda Jewell *retired elementary school educator*

Columbia
Staley, Marsha Lynn *elementary school educator, principal*

Delta
Lee, Drenna O'Reilly *kindergarten educator*

Ewing
Lueckenhoff, Mark Albert *elementary school educator*

Excelsior Springs
Hewitt, June Ann *elementary education educator*

Fort Leonard Wood
Campbell, Sonya Beth *elementary school educator*

Gallatin
Wilsted, Joy *elementary education educator, reading specialist, parenting consultant*

Glencoe
Schick, Brian Keith *middle school educator*

Gower
Findley, Martha Jean *elementary education educator*

Hayti
Skelton, Diann Clevenger *elementary education educator*

Hollister
Head, Mary Mae *elementary education educator*

Houston
Ruckert, Rita E. *retired elementary education educator*

Independence
Marlow, Lydia Lou *elementary education educator*

Jefferson City
Bardwell, Rosemary Ann *elementary school educator*
Holzschuh, Susan Kay *elementary school educator*

Jennings
Robards, Bourne Rogers *elementary education educator*

Kansas City
Brown, Zania Faye *elementary education educator*
Fraker, Barbara J. *elementary education educator, school system administrator, middle school education educator*
Hilton, Linda Sue *elementary education educator*
Miller, Lawrence Donald *retired middle school educator*
Myers, Betty J. *retired elementary music specialist*
Slaughter, Rochelle Denise *elementary school educator*

Kirksville
Wachter-Ream, Therese *elementary school educator, supervisor*

Lees Summit
Hartnett, Gina Ann *elementary education educator*
Linder, Beverly L. *elementary school educator*

Lexington
Struchtemeyer, Carol Sue *middle school educator*

Marthasville
Ogle, Terri J. Bryant *elementary education educator*

Maryville
Strating, Sharon L. *elementary school educator, college instructor*

Mexico
Teague, Deborah Gant *elementary school educator*

Miller
Myers, Roberta Frances *retired elementary school educator*

Neosho
Ketcham, Madaline Sue *elementary school educator*
Kluth, Harriet Ann Hamlet *elementary education educator*

Nixa
Watts, Jackie Sue *elementary education educator*

Noel
Gilgen, Joy René *elementary education educator*

Owensville
Rademacher, Anna Mae *junior high school educator*

Pilot Grove
Betteridge, Elizabeth Ann *elementary education educator*

Poplar Bluff
Allen, Brenda Kay *elementary school educator*

Prairie Home
Bacon, Sherri Leah *elementary education educator*

Rich Hill
Laughlin, Jo Ann *elementary school educator*

Saint Charles
Dawson, Bruce Alan *elementary school educator, software designer*

Saint Joseph
Poloski, Patricia Elizabeth *elementary school educator*

Saint Louis
Gordon, Larry Dean *elementary education educator*
Kelly, Ann Terese *elementary education educator*
Kemna, Rita Marie *primary/elementary school educator*
Lackey, Kayle Diann *elementary school educator*
Laws, Karen Sue *elementary school educator*
Mohrmann, Rae Jeanne *retired elementary school educator*
Parks, Beatrice Griffin *elementary school educator*
Payuk, Edward William *elementary education educator*
Reid, Lorene Frances *middle school educator*

Schneider, Lois Alene *elementary education educator*
Watkins, Hortense Catherine *middle school educator*

Saint Peters
Bond, Karla Jo *educator*
Goodwin, Leslie Diane *elementary education educator*
Huckshold, Wayne William *elementary education educator*
Wilkison, Dennis Lyle *elementary education eductor*

Salem
Will, Anne Marilyn *elementary education educator*

Springfield
Groves, Sharon Sue *elementary education educator*

Stella
Davidson, Cynthia Ann *elementary school educator*

Washington
Tobben, Larry John *elementary education educator*

Webster Groves
Zimmerman, Harold Seymour *elementary school educator*

MONTANA

Antelope
Olson, Betty-Jean *retired elementary education educator*

Billings
Sleeth, Joan Marie *elementary school educator*

Butte
Lovell, Kathryn Sheehy *elementary education educator*
Sherrill, Barbara Ann Buker *elementary school educator*

Havre
Verploegen, Lorraine Jean *elementary school educator*

Kalispell
Ormiston, Patricia Jane *elementary education educator*

Lambert
Schields, Vickie Marie *elementary educator*

Lewistown
Edwards, Linda L. *former elementary education educator*

Missoula
Barnett, Mary Louise *elementary education educator*
Mercer, Chet Atom *retired elementary educator*

Sheridan
Wilson, L(etitia) Alexandra *elementary school educator*

NEBRASKA

Atkinson
Martens, Helen Eileen *elementary school educator*

Bellevue
Maye-Bryan, Mamie Ellene *elementary education educator*

Dakota City
Huff, Patsy Jo Hernandez *elementary education educator*

Daykin
Rife, Ronald Eugene *elementary education educator*

Elkhorn
Hays, Kathy Ann *elementary education educator*

Grand Island
Weseman, Vicki Lynne *elementary school educator*

Hastings
Menning, Barbara Susan *elementary school educator, language educator*

Hyannis
Wilder, Floydene *primary school educator*

La Vista
Phillips, Kimberly Kay *elementary school educator*

Lincoln
Mickens, Adeline *elementary education educator*
Tonack, DeLoris *elementary school educator*

Morrill
Steele, Sarah Jane *elementary school educator*

Ogallala
Barent, Barbara Ann *elementary education educator*

Omaha
Fyfe, Doris Mae *elementary school educator*
Juel, Twila Eileen *elementary education educator*

Plainview
Mauch, Jeannine Ann *elementary education educator*

Tecumseh
Johns, Karen Kay *elementary education educator*

Winnebago
Bauer-Sanders, Katherine Ann *primary school educator*

NEVADA

Carson City
Barbie, Cathy Therese *middle school educator*
Yeager, Carol Annette *instrumental music educator*

Fallon
Smith-Ansotegui, Susan Coonley *elementary school educator*

Las Vegas
Brooks, Shelley *middle school educator*
Cutrone, Dee T. *retired elementary education educator*
Cwerenz-Maxime, Virginia Margaret *primary and secondary education educator*
DelPrete, Agnes *elementary school educator*
Flemming, Naomi Verneta *elementary school educator*
Gaspar, Anna Louise *retired elementary school educator, consultant*
Gelfer, Jeffrey Ian *early childhood education educator*
Horner, Sandra Marie Groce (Sandy Heart) *educator, poet, songwriter, lyricist*
Johnson, Mary Elizabeth *retired elementary education educator*
Patricks, Edward John *elementary education educator*
Roselle, Cathy Colman *kindergarten education, educational consultant*
Ross, Janine *elementary education educator*

Minden
Pyle, David *elementary education educator*

North Las Vegas
Watson, Rebecca M. *elementary education educator*

Reno
Dale, Debra Eileen *elementary school educator*
Totten, Andrea Lee *elementary education educator*

NEW HAMPSHIRE

Bristol
Redman-Joyce, Ramona Lea *middle school art educator*

Campton
Benton, Geraldine Ann *preschool owner, director*

Concord
Colby, Virginia Little *retired elementary school educator*

Cornish
Oszajca, Sharon-Ann Elizabeth *elementary education educator*

Melvin Village
Farwell, Margaret Wheeler *elementary education educator*

Nashua
Purington, David W. *elementary education educator*

Raymond
Benz, Marilyn Christine *elementary education educator*

Rochester
Albert, Carole Annette *elementary school educator*

Salem
Shafer, Christine Mary *elementary school educator*

NEW JERSEY

Allendale
Miller, Mary Margaret *elementary education educator*

Atlantic City
Logan-Sutton, Floretta R. *elementary school educator*
Stuart, Eve Lynne *elementary education educator*

Bellmawr
Wilke, Constance Regina *elementary education educator*

Belmar
Petrovich, Dorothy *elementary school educator*

Berkeley Heights
Older, Richard Samuel *elementary school music educator*

Bogota
Oldenhage, Irene Dorothy *retired elementary school educator*

Branchville
Ansorge, Helen J. *retired elementary school*

Brigantine
Kickish, Margaret Elizabeth *elementary school educator*

Brookside
Esposito, Audrey Matthews *elementary school educator*

Browns Mills
Rakes, Randi Lee *elementary school educator, test developer*

Budd Lake
Shepherd, Deborah Gulick *elementary education educator*

Butler
Struble, Sandra Marie *reading specialist*

Cape May Court House
Dodson, Deborah Ann *elementary school educator*
Lare, Jayne Lee *elementary education educator*

Cherry Hill
Teare, Bernice Adeline *elementary school educator, reading specialist*

Chester
Fluker, Jay Edward *middle school visual arts educator*

Clifton
Charsky, Thomas Robert *elementary education educator*

Delaware
Hill-Rosato, Jane Elizabeth *elementary education educator*

East Orange
Clerkin, Lori Susan *primary school educator*
Hart, Cynthia Faye *elementary education educator*
Torkpo, Bettye Jewell *kindergarten educator*

Egg Harbor Township
Sheridan, Katharine Jane *elementary school educator*

Elmer
DuBois, Mary Lou Howell *elementary education educator*

Fair Lawn
Aitchison, Suann *elementary school educator*
Wallace, Mary Monahan *elementary and secondary schools educator*

Flemington
Andrews, Barbara Harcourt *retired elementary educator*

Freehold
Olbis, Karen *elementary education educator, musician, vocalist*

Hackensack
Kalisch, Kathryn Mary *elementary education educator*
Parisi, Cheryl Lynn *elementary school educator*

Harrington Park
Grantuskas, Patricia Mary *elementary education educator*

Hawthorne
Lawlor, Suzanne Kathryn *elementary school educator*

Highland Park
Broggi, Barbara Ann *elementary education educator, staff developer*

Highlands
Lofstrom, Arlene Katherine *primary school educator*

Hillside
Aragonés-Enda, Lillian Estella *elementary educator*

Ho Ho Kus
O'Loughlin, Judith Beryl *elementary and special education educator*

Hopatcong
Cullen, Lawrence David *elementary education educator*
Hill, Linda Marie Palermo *elementary school educator*
May, Eileen Marie *elementary education educator*
Tanella, Valerie Cagiano *elementary school educator*

Island Heights
MacDonald, Jane Cronin *elementary school educator, supervisor*

Jamesburg
Popowski, Mary Jean Nancy *elementary education educator*

Jersey City
DeBenedictis, JoAnne *elementary school educator*
Pesce, Phyllis Anne *elementary education educator*

Kearny
Meissner, Dorothy Theresa *reading specialist*

Leonia
Penin, Linda Margaret *elementary education educator*

PROFESSIONAL INDEX — PRIMARY/ELEMENTARY/MIDDLE SCHOOL EDUCATION

Linden
Shepard, Jeannie *elementary school educator*

Lindenwold
Brown, Kathleen *elementary school educator, consultant*

Livingston
Tamburro, Barbara Boscaino *educator*

Long Valley
Schlenner, Diane Marie *elementary school educator*

Lyndhurst
DeBellis, Francine Darnel *elementary education educator*

Madison
D'Amico, Beverly Ann *elementary education educator*

Manchester
Cohen, Marie Carol *elementary education educator*
Heale, Darryl Rhawn *elementary and secondary education educator*

Marlton
Benjamin, Leni Bernice *elementary education educator*

Mendham
Posunko, Barbara *retired elementary education educator*

Milltown
Temkin, Judith Celia *elementary school educator*

Morristown
Burton, Valerie Diane *elementary school educator*

Mount Arlington
Kinney, Dorothy Jean *retired elementary school educator*

Mount Holly
Mancini, Lois Jean *elementary education educator*

Mountain Lakes
King, Georgeann Camarda *elementary education educator*

Mullica Hill
Delia, Margaret M. *elementary education educator*

Neptune
Baccarella, Theresa Ann *primary school educator*

New Brunswick
Morrow, Lesley Mandel *literacy and elementary education educator*

Newark
Allwood, Rhonda Marie *middle school educator*

North Bergen
Zondler, Joyce Evelyn *kindergarten educator*

Northfield
Watkins, Joan Frances *retired elementary school educator*

Nutley
Colarusso, Roger Michael, Sr., *middle school educator*

Ocean City
Guokas, Joan Ellen (Mrs. Matthew Guokas Sr.) *retired elementary educator*

Parsippany
Maness, Mildred *reading specialist*

Paterson
Harrell, Constance Loress *elementary education educator*

Pemberton
Orosz, Patricia Ann *elementary education educator*

Pennsauken
Curry, Emma Beatrice *elementary school educator*

Phillipsburg
Stull, Frank Walter *elementary school educator*

Pleasantville
Mora, Benedetto P. *elementary school administrator*

Princeton
Williams, Bertha Elizabeth Griffin *elementary education educator*

Raritan
Boyle, Thomas Francis *educational administrator*

Ridgewood
Walczak, Ann Marie *elementary education educator*

River Edge
Meldonian, Susan Lucy *elementary education educator*

Roselle
Bizub, Barbara L. *elementary school educator*

Saddle River
Lehmann, Doris Elizabeth *elementary education educator*

Scotch Plains
Johnson, Valerie Anne *elementary education educator*

South Bound Brook
Simpson-Steeber, Marybeth *elementary school educator*

South Plainfield
Steele-Hunter, Teresa Ann *elementary education educator*

South River
Cole, Marianne Lee *secondary education educator*

Sparta
Harrison, Alice Kathleen *retired elementary educator*

Summit
Williams, Sandra Castaldo *elementary school educator*

Toms River
Finale, Frank Louis *elementary school educator, writer*

Trenton
Smallwood, Robert Albian, Jr., *secondary education educator*
Telencio, Gloria Jean *elementary education educator*

Union City
Bozoyan, Sylvia *elementary school educator*
Ortizio, Debra Louise *elementary education educator*

Voorhees
Carter, Catherine Louise *retired elementary and middle school educator*

Wayne
Pulhamus, Marlene Louise *retired elementary school educator*

Weehawken
Edwards, Maureen Susan *elementary school educator*

West Paterson
Marren, Maryann Fahy *primary school educator*

West Windsor
Newman, Rochelle Beverly *middle school educator*

Westfield
Ruvolo, Barbara *elementary education educator*

Westmont
Danner, Charles L. *elementary education educator*

Westwood
Wright, Norman Albert, Jr., *middle school educator*

Willingboro
Denslow, Deborah Pierson *primary education educator*

Woodbridge
Stankewicz, Mary Christine *middle school educator*

Woodbury
Banks, Theresa Ann *retired elementary education educator*

NEW MEXICO

Alamogordo
Lee, Joli Fay Eaton *elementary education educator*
McFadin, Helen Lozetta *retired elementary education educator*

Albuquerque
Bailey, Virginia Hurt *elementary education educator*
Beahm, John Metz *middle school educator*
Benson, Sharon Stovall *primary school educator*
Betts, Dorothy Anne *elementary school educator*
Blottner, Myra Ann *retired elementary school educator*
Cass, Barbara Fay *elementary school educator*
Paler, Peggy Louise D'Arcy *elementary education educator, education educator*
Stepetic, Mary Lorraine *elementary school educator*

Carlsbad
Gossett, Janine Lee *middle school educator*

Crownpoint
Tolino, Arlene Becenti *elementary education educator*

Gallup
Swain, Melinda Susan *elementary education educator*

Laguna
Ray, Rebecca Ann *elementary school educator*

Loco Hills
Sánchez, Frank Perez *elementary education educator*

Los Alamos
Benjamin, Susan Selton *elementary school educator*

Rio Rancho
Meyerson, Barbara Tobias *elementary school educator*

Ruidoso
Coe, Elizabeth Ann *retired elementary education educator*
Stover, Carolyn Nadine *middle school educator*

Santa Fe
Torres, Gilbert Vincent *retired elementary education educator*

Shiprock
Atcitty, Fannie L. *elementary school educator, education educator*

Silver City
Moses-Foley, Judith Ann *elementary school educator*

NEW YORK

Albany
Chonski, Denise Theresa *primary school educator, artist*

Alfred Station
Huntington, Mary C. *elementary school educator*

Amityville
Gicola, Paul *middle school science educator, administrator*

Babylon
Schwarz, Barbara Ruth Ballou *elementary school educator*

Beacon
Stokes, Catherine Ann *elementary education educator*

Binghamton
Beach, Beth *elementary educator*
Holder, Kathleen *elementary education educator*

Bluff Point
Fitch, Linda Bauman *elementary school educator*

Bolton Landing
Andersen, Deborah Jean *elementary education educator*

Bronx
Dukette, Ann Marie *elementary education educator, reading specialist*
Hadley-Banahene, Sara Singletary *elementary education educator*
Milano, MaryAnn T. *elementary school educator*
Murray, Phyllis Cynthia *educator*
O'Gorman, Tara Ann *elementary education educator*
Ukponmwan, Lucy *elementary education educator*
Williams, Lovie Jean *elementary education educator*

Brooklyn
Allotta, Joanne Mary *elementary education educator*
Arcuri, Leonard Philip *elementary education educator*
Merola, Josephine *elementary education educator*
Thoering, Robert Charles *elementary education educator*
Troy, Charles David *secondary social studies educator*
Williams, Ethel Coger *elementary education educator*

Buffalo
Keller-Mathers, Susan *elementary educator, adult education educator*
Wilbur, Barbara Marie *elementary education educator*

Catskill
Tompkins, Sharon Lee *primary education educator*

Cedarhurst
Van Raalte, Polly Ann *reading and writing specialist, photojournalist*

Centerport
Mallett, Helene Gettler *retired elementary education educator*

Central Islip
Gillespie, Eileen Rose *elementary education educator*
Griffith, Philip Arthur *elementary school educator*
Rodriguez, Teresa Ida *elementary education educator, educational consultant*
Vereline, Catherine *elementary school educator, administrator*

Cicero
Crabtree, Robert Allen *elementary education educator*

Clifton Park
Murphy, Mary Patricia *elementary education educator*

Cold Spring
Battersby, Katherine Sue *elementary school educator*

Commack
Bernstein, Judi Ellen *elementary school educator*

Corinth
Kipp, Beverly J. *elementary and secondary education educator*
Winslow, Norma Mae *elementary education educator*

Cornwall
Ryan, Sarah (Sally Ryan) *retired secondary education educator*

Cortland
Wood, Barbara Lynn *elementary education educator*

Cortlandt Manor
Valentini, Anna Maria *elementary education educator, reading specialist*

Coxsackie
Amado, Lisa *elementary education educator*

Dix Hills
Somerville, Daphine Holmes *retired elementary education educator*
Virostko, Joan *elementary school educator*

Dolgeville
Klump, Jane F. Harrad *elementary school educator*

Dunkirk
Miller, Gail Ann *elementary school educator*

East Berne
Lounsbury, Helen Marie *education educator, consultant*

East Williston
Abernethy, Ann Lawson *retired elementary education educator*

Eden
Gephart, Michele Marie *elementary education educator*

Endicott
Wells, Sharon A(nn) *primary education educator*

Fairport
Gorzka, Margaret Rose *elementary education educator*
Holtzclaw, Diane Smith *elementary education educator*
Radell, Carol K. *elementary school educator*

Farmingdale
Nelson, Barbara Ann *elementary education educator*

Fresh Meadows
Sperling, Marylin Kurlan *early childhood education educator*

Garden City
Weinrich, Gloria Joan Castoria *retired elementary education educator*

Greenvale
Megay-Nespoli, Karen Patricia *elementary school educator*

Greenwood
Rollins, June Elizabeth *elementary education educator*

Harrison
Northcutt, Marie Rose *elementary, secondary, & special education educator*

Hewlett
Santopolo, Beth Franklin *elementary education educator*

Hicksville
Kruse, Nancy Clarson *retired elementary school educator*
Moshoyannis, Phillip Demetri Alexander *educator*
Reedy, Catherine Irene *elementary school educator*

Hilton
Ratigan, Hugh Lewis *middle school and elementary school educator*

Holland Patent
Giacobbe, Anna Gretchen Steinhauer *elementary education educator*

Hopewell Junction
Coppola, Patricia L. (Scheffel) *elementary school educator*
Hsieh, Hazel Tseng *retired elementary and secondary educator*

Houghton
Kingdon, Mary Oneida Grace *retired elementary education educator*

Huntington Station
Boxwill, Helen Ann *primary and secondary education educator*

Islip
Stein, Belle Weiss *retired elementary educator*

Jamaica
Malewitz, Joan *elementary school educator, library and information scientist*

Jeffersonville
Hoering, Helen G. *elementary educator*

Jordan
Fixler, Michael H. *elementary education educator*

Kendall
Rak, Linda Marie *elementary education educator, consultant*

Lindenhurst
Gentile, Patricia M. *elementary education educator*

Long Beach
Thompson, Dorothy Barnard *elementary school educator*

Lynbrook
Pagillo, Carl Robert *elementary school educator*

Massapequa
McCann, Susan Lynn *elementary education educator*
Pullen, Kathryn Ann Link *elementary education educator*

Medford
Young-Oskey, Susan Marie *elementary education educator*

Middle Island
Ferrara, Frank Gregory *middle school educator*

Middleport
Blumrick, Carol Susan *elementary school educator*

Middletown
Byrne, Mary Margaret (Meg Byrne) *elementary education educator*
Moore, Virginia Lee Smith *elementary education educator*
Teabo-Sandoe, Glenda Patterson *elementary education educator*

Monsey
Schaefer, Rhoda Pesner *elementary school educator*

Moravia
Kinney, Patricia May *elementary art educator*

Mount Vernon
Guzman-Smith, Marilyn Elizabeth *elementary school educator*

Nanuet
Miney, Maureen Elizabeth *middle school educator*

New Windsor
Saunders, Joanne Hines *elementary educator*

New York
Crocetti, Gino *elementary and secondary education educator*
Lewis, Enid Selena *elementary school educator, special education educator*
Lloyd, Jean *early childhood educator*
Prutzman, Penelope Elizabeth *elementary school educator*
Reissman, Rose Cherie *elementary education educator*

Newburgh
Conner, Susan *elementary educator*

Niagara Falls
Colpoys-Coia, Patricia Ann *elementary school educator*

Oceanside
Behar, Lisa Denise *elementary and secondary educator*

Oneida
Moller, Jacqueline Louise *elementary education educator*

Oriskany
Hinderling, Karen Marie Cianfrocco *elementary education educator*
Jacobson, Karen *retired elementary school educator*

Ossining
Perlman, John Niels *retired elementary school educator, poet*

Owego
Slater, Rebecca Ann *elementary educator*

Patchogue
Fritz, Mary Noonan *elementary school educator, consultant*
Orlowski, Karel Ann *elementary school educator*

Peekskill
Wiggins, Ida Silver *elementary school educator*

Port Jefferson
Ecker, Allison Joanna *elementary education educator*

Porter Corners
Schwartzbeck, Patricia Ann *retired elementary school educator*

Poughkeepsie
Currie, Stephen *educator, writer*

Ransomville
Mayer, George Merton *retired elementary education educator*

Riverhead
Passanante, Patricia Marie *middle school educator*

Rochester
Campbell, Alma Jacqueline Porter *elementary education educator*
Rissone, Donna *educator, financial executive*
Stone, Gail Ann *elementary and secondary education educator*

Rockville Centre
Smyth, Anne *elementary school educator*

Rotterdam Junction
Cox, Paulyn Mae *retired elementary school educator*

Saint James
Van Dover, Karen *middle and elementary school educator, curriculum consultant, language arts specialist, lecturer*

Schoharie
Stiver, Patricia Abare *elementary education educator*

Seaford
Schlossberg, Fred Paul *elementary education educator*

Shelter Island
Clark, Wendy Rodgers *elementary school educator*

Shoreham
Reynolds, Carolyn Mary *elementary education educator*

Slate Hill
O'Connor, Kathryn MacVean *elementary educator*

Staten Island
Lockhart, Patricia Ann *elementary school educator*
Mercaldo, David *elementary school educator, writer*

Stony Brook
Arloff, William John *elementary education educator*

Syosset
Magrino, Lisa Ann *elementary education educator*

Syracuse
Giacchi, Judith Adair *elementary education educator*

Thendara
Hiltebrant, Jane *elementary education educator*

Thiells
DiRubbo, Dana Dawn *elementary school educator*

Troy
Hyde, Frances Elizabeth *elementary school educator*

Tuxedo Park
Groskin, Sheila Marie Lessen *primary school educator*

Uniondale
Jones, Barbara Ann *elementary education educator*

Vestal
Staby, Dorothy Louise *elementary school educator*

Victor
Abbott, Susan Alicia *elementary education educator*

Wading River
Kretschmer, Ingrid Butler *elementary school educator*

Wallkill
Chumas, Linda Grace *elementary school educator*

Warsaw
McKeown, Laurie Anne *elementary school educator*

Wellsville
Dahlgren, Denis Andrew *elementary education educator*

West Leyden
Kornatowski, Susan Carol *elementary education educator*

Westbury
Neziri, Maria G. De Lucia *elementary school educator*

White Plains
Barrow, Marie Antonette *elementary school educator*
Peck, Alexander Norman *elementary education educator*

Whitesboro
Voce, Joan A. Cifonelli *retired elementary school educator*

Williamsville
Vanderwerf, Mary Ann *elementary school educator, consultant*

Windsor
Snyder, Henry Allen *elementary education educator*

Woodside
Burchell, Jeanne Kathleen *primary school educator*

Yorktown Heights
Gould, Betty Chaikin *elementary school educator*
Piteo, Carol Ann *elementary education educator*

NORTH CAROLINA

Angier
Raynor, Wandra Adams *middle school educator*

Asheboro
Seitz, Sharon Elizabeth *elementary school educator*

Beaufort
Macartney, Norman Scarborough *retired middle school educator*

Belmont
Abernathy, Dixie Friend *elementary education educator*

Bladenboro
Walters, Cathryne Brunson *primary school educator*

Boone
Austin, Roberta Jones *elementary school educator*
Phipps, Susan *retired elementary school educator*

Chapel Hill
Stewart, Sarah *elementary school educator*

Charlotte
Eppley, Frances Fielden *retired secondary education educator, author*
Gilbert, Montine Fox (Tina Gilbert) *elementary and middle school educator*
Phillips, Sandra Allen *retired primary school educator*

Dallas
Fruits, Cheryl Ann *elementary education educator*
Green, Gayla Maxine *elementary school educator*

Dobson
Brame, Patti Thomas *middle school educator*
Smith, Richard Jackson *elementary education educator*

Dunn
Overton, Elizabeth Nicole *elementary school educator, aerobics instructor*

Durham
O'Briant, Margaret Denny *retired elementary school educator*

Elizabeth City
Morring, Dorothy Wilson *elementary education educator*

Fayetteville
Bryant, Evelyn Christine *elementary education educator*
Jordan, Karla Salge *early childhood education educator*
Lydon, Kerry Raines *elementary school educator*

Gastonia
Bell, Sharon Teresa Echerd *elementary physical education specialist*

Goldsboro
Bryan, Gina Gray *middle school educator*
Yelverton, Deborah Sue *middle school art educator*

Greensboro
Cardwell, Jessie Womack *elementary education educator*
Godfrey, Eutha Marek *elementary school educator, consultant*
Goulder, Debra Kriegsman *elementary education educator*
White, Gladys Hope Franklin *reading specialist*

Hamlet
Ritter, Elizabeth Carroll *elementary education educator*

Harrells
Spivey, Sarah Eakins *retired elementary school educator*

High Point
Blue, Rhonda Holmes *kindergarten educator*
Howard, Lou Dean Graham *elementary education educator*

Kings Mountain
Harris, Audrey Leonhardt *middle school educator*

Liberty
Link, Eleanor Ann *elementary education educator*

Matthews
Kocsis, Joan Bosco *elementary education educator, administrative assistant, assistant principal*

Monroe
Rorie, Nancy Catherine *retired elementary and secondary school educator*

Mooresville
Neill, Rita Jarrett *elementary school educator*

Mount Airy
Short, Linda Matthews *retired elementary education educator*

Powellsville
Lassiter, Bettie Watford *retired elementary education educator*

Raleigh
Kabis, Rebecca Sloop *elementary education educator*
Kinlaw, Hilda Hester *primary education educator*

Rocky Point
Moore, Wanda Johnson *elementary education educator*

Rural Hall
McDermon, Linda Garrett *elementary school educator*

Rutherfordton
Metcalf, Ethel Edgerton *retired elementary school educator*

Shelby
Edgar, Ruth R. *retired elementary school educator*
Grigg, Kathy Austell *elementary education educator*

Southern Pines
Brown, Carol Ann *elementary education educator*

Thomasville
Winters, Cynthia Saintsing *middle school education educator*

Waxhaw
Kornman, Elsie Fry *retired elementary education educator*

Weaverville
Atkins, Patricia Hollar *primary school educator*

Whitakers
Fleming, Janice J. *elementary education educator*

Wilson
Howell, Maria DeLane *elementary physical education educator*

Winston Salem
Jarrell, Iris Bonds *elementary school educator, business executive*

Yanceyville
Bowen, Audrey Lynn Harris *elementary education educator*

NORTH DAKOTA

Beulah
Maize, Linda Lou *elementary education educator*

Cooperstown
Surerus, Dorothea Kae *elementary education educator*

Fargo
Morey, Charlotte Ann *elementary school educator, music educator*
Wegenast, Judy H. *elementary school educator, consultant*

Jamestown
Thompson, Vicki Lyn *elementary school educator*

Mandan
Nider, Michael Edward *elementary school educator*

Mercer
Ketterling, Melissa Cary *elementary school educator*

Minot
Jermiason, John Lynn *elementary school educator, farmer, rancher*

Minot Afb
Jacobs-Ciranni, Mary Lauralee *elementary education educator*

Zahl
Anfinson, Donna Mae *elementary school educator, home economics educator*

OHIO

Akron
Childs, Sally Johnston *elementary and secondary education administrator*
Phillips, Dorothy Ormes *elementary education educator*

Andover
Mathay, John Preston *elementary education educator*

Anna
Thompson, Virigina A. *elementary education educator*

PROFESSIONAL INDEX   1419   PRIMARY/ELEMENTARY/MIDDLE SCHOOL EDUCATION

Arcanum
Pitzer, Elizabeth Ann *elementary school educator*

Ashland
Kerr, Margaret Ann *elementary education educator*

Athens
Gallaway, Gladys McGhee *elementary education educator*

Avon Lake
Mick, Deborah West Fairchild *elementary education educator*

Bellefontaine
Sheeley, Sharon Kay *elementary education educator*

Bergholz
Goddard, Sandra Kay *elementary education educator*
McElwain, Edwina Jay *retired elementary school educator*

Bucyrus
Frey, Judith Lynn *elementary education educator*

Cambridge
Greenwood, David Wilbur *elementary education educator*

Canton
Herritt, David R. *elementary education educator*
Peterson, Mary Elizabeth *retired elementary school educator*

Cardington
Dye, Sally Ann *middle school educator*

Castalia
Kishman, Rachel Tressler *elementary education educator*

Chesterland
Alves, Elizabeth Martha Hagerty *elementary education educator*

Cincinnati
Campbell, Patricia Elaine *elementary education educator*
Croskery, Beverly Ann *education consultant*
Fischer, Patricia Ann *middle school educator*
Hall, Madelon Carol Syverson *elementary education educator*
Jordan, Mary Lee *retired elementary education educator*
Kamp, Cynthia Lea *elementary education educator*
Sanford, Wilbur Lee *retired elementary education educator*
Skilbeck, Carol Lynn Marie *elementary educator and small business owner*
Smith, Joyce Camille *elementary education educator*
Yates, Patricia Ann Thompson *elementary school educator*

Circleville
Martin, Rebecca J. *elementary school educator*

Cleveland
Knieriem, Beulah White *retired elementary school educator, minister*
Queen, Joyce Ellen *elementary school educator*
Schubert, Janet Lee *middle school educator*
Sherrill, Gladys Marie *elementary education educator*
Smith, Beverly Harriett *elementary school educator*
Stewart, Zelma Brown *elementary school educator*
Thomas, Faye Evelyn J. *elementary and secondary school educator*
White-Ware, Grace Elizabeth *elementary school educator, secondary school educator*

Columbus
Ennis, Lori Lee *elementary education educator*
Evans, David Charles *retired elementary educator*
Foucht, Joan Lucille *retired elementary school educator, retired counseling administrator*
Mathis, Lois Reno *retired elementary education educator*
Oxley, Margaret Carolyn Stewart *elementary education educator*

Copley
Cox, Hillery Lee *retired primary school educator*

Cortland
Lane, Sarah Marie Clark *elementary education educator*

Curtice
Cashen, Elizabeth Anne *elementary school educator*

Cuyahoga Falls
Spencer, Heather Leigh *middle school language educator*

Cygnet
Bowsher, Laura Kay *elementary education educator*

Delaware
Beery, Pamela Elayne *intermediate school educator*

Dublin
Bordelon, Carolyn Thew *elementary school educator*

East Cleveland
England, Diana Whitten *elementary education educator*
Wilson, Katie Jean *elementary education educator*

Elyria
Hughes, Kenneth G. *elementary school educator*
Sweda, Linda Irene *elementary school educator*

Euclid
Keay, Charles Lloyd *elementary school educator*

Fairborn
Seymour, Joyce Ann *elementary school educator*

Fairfield
Parsons, Mary Louise Britton *elementary educator*

Gahanna
Chappell, Michelle R. *elementary education educator*
Rush, Mary Beth *elementary education educator*

Gates Mills
O'Malley, Mary Kay *elementary education educator*
Svets, Gayle Ann *elementary education educator*

Greenville
Mardin-Burchett, Karen Joan *elementary education educator*

Hilliard
Packard, Linda Lee *elementary education educator*

Hudson
Hallenbeck, Linda Sue *elementary school educator*

Jackson Center
Wical, Barbara Lou *elementary school educator*

Kettering
Hoffman, Sue Ellen *elementary education educator*
Martin, Margaret Gately *elementary school educator*

Lancaster
Young, Nancy Henrietta Moe *retired elementary education educator*

Lorain
Comer, Brenda Warmee *educator, real estate company executive*
Strick, Cynthia Lee *elementary education educator*
Wittlinger, Cheryl A. *elementary education educator*

Magnolia
Zimmerman, Judith Rose *elementary art educator*

Maineville
Cook, Janice Eleanor Nolan *retired elementary school educator*

Mansfield
Kee, Shirley Ann *retired elementary education educator*

Marietta
Fredericks, Margaret Matterson *elementary education educator*

Marion
Badertscher, Doris Rae *elementary education educator*
Lynch, Patricia Marie *elementary education educator*
Uresti, Ronda VeVerka *elementary bilingual education educator*

Massillon
Jones, Bonnie Jill *elementary education educator*
McCoy, David Brion *middle school educator*

Medina
DeMars, Judith M. *elementary educator*

Mesopotamia
Newcomb, Kathy Rae *elementary education educator*
Newcomb, Thomas Lee *elementary school educator*

Milan
Steris, Cheryl Lynn *elementary school educator, reading coordinator*

Millersburg
Yoder, Anna A. *elementary school educator*

Minerva
Koniecko, Mary Ann *elementary education educator*

Minford
Williams, Paula Marie Shuter *elementary education educator*

Mogadore
Kelly, Janice Helen *elementary school educator*

Mount Vernon
Martin, Carolyn Frances *elementary education educator*

Munroe Falls
Clawson, Judith Louise *middle school educator*

New Bremen
Wierwille, Marsha Louise *elementary education educator*

New Carlisle
Perrin, Nancy Ann *elementary music educator*

Newark
Simpson, Linda Sue *elementary educator*

North Olmsted
Kross, Betty Ann *elementary education educator*

Orwell
Strong, Marcella Lee *music specialist, educator*

Ottoville
Hanneman, Darlene Marie *elementary school educator*

Painesville
Refe, Sandra M. *retired elementary school educator*

Parma
Romeo, William Joseph *middle school educator*
Scheffel, Donna Jean *elementary school educator*
Tener, Carol Joan *retired secondary education educator*

Paulding
Moore, Pamela Rae *elementary school educator*

Pickerington
Young, Glenna Asche *elementary education educator*

Plain City
Brown, D. Robin *elementary school educator*

Port Clinton
Taylor, Jane Ellen *elementary educator*

Portsmouth
Billiter, Freda Delorous *retired elementary education educator*

Racine
Manuel, Jenny Lynn *elementary education educator*

Richmond
Martin, Clara Rita *elementary educator*

Shaker Heights
Breland, Kathleen Sylvia *elementary education educator*

Sheffield Lake
McHenry, Timothy Howard *elementary education educator*

Sidney
Schlagetter, Jeanne Louise *elementary education educator*

South Euclid
Conrad, Sister Linda *elementary school educator*

Southington
Kirk, Cheryl Linda *elementary education educator*

Springboro
Ramey, Rebecca Ann *elementary education educator*

Strongsville
Shambaugh, Catherine Anne *elementary education educator*

Sylvania
Stout, Linda Kay *elementary education educator*

Toledo
Braithwaite, Margaret Christine *retired elementary education educator*
Ingle, Kay Sue *elementary education educator*

Upper Sandusky
Case, Penny Lu *elementary education educator*
Schmidt, Janis Ilene *elementary education educator*

Vincent
Meek, Barbara Susan *elementary education educator*

Washington Court House
Perrill, Rebecca Lauran *elementary educator*

Wellston
Loxley, Kathryn *retired elementary school educator*
McCall-Smith, Catherine Ann *elementary school educator*

Westfield Center
Spinelli, Anne Catherine *elementary education educator*

Willoughby
Grossman, Mary Margaret *elementary education educator*
Kerkel, Lynn *retired middle school educator*

Willowick
VanArnhem, Sylvia *elementary education educator*

Wintersville
Shields, Carla Faye *elementary school educator*

Wooster
Shepherd, Mary Anne *elementary education educator*

Youngstown
Crenshaw, Loretta Ann *retired elementary education educator*

Zanesville
Jones, Marlene Wiseman *elementary education educator, reading specialist*

OKLAHOMA

Ada
Frye, Linda Beth (Linda Beth Hisle) *elementary, secondary education educator*
Gray, Edna Jane *elementary education educator*
Groves, Noralene Katherine *elementary school educator*
West, Mildred Marie *elementary education art educator*

Anadarko
Mashaw, Dawn Ella *elementary school educator, consultant*

Bartlesville
Sauter, Marsha Jeanne *elementary school educator*
Woodruff, Wanda Lea *elementary education educator*

Chickasha
Smith-Willoughby, Dolores Anne *educator, computer consultant*

Claremore
Shrum, Alicia Ann *elementary school educator, librarian*

Earlsboro
Duncan, Glenda Julaine *elementary education educator*

Elk City
Redd, Betty *retired elementary school educator*

Enid
Brown, Delores Jean *retired elementary school educator*
Mabry, Betsy *elementary education educator*
McGuire, JoAnn Michele *elementary education educator*

Grove
McFarland, Carmen Renea *elementary education educator, counselor, music educator*

Jenks
Majors, Sandra Marie *elementary school educator*

Lawton
Calaway, James *elementary education educator*
Gardner, Carol Elaine *elementary school educator*

Mcalester
Moore, Primus Monroe, Jr., *elementary educator, counselor, administrator*

Midwest City
Davis, K. Jean *elementary school educator*

Norman
Huntington, Penelope Ann *middle school educator*
Smith, Patricia Ann *middle school educator*
Zapffe, Nina Byrom *retired elementary education educator*

Oklahoma City
Fischer, Gayle *elementary education educator*
Graves, Virginia Beth *elementary education educator*
Mankins, Donna Kay *primary school educator*
Noakes, Betty LaVonne *retired elementary school educator*
Regier, Elaine Roxanne *elementary school educator, school librarian*
Shirey, Margaret (Peggy Shirey) *elementary school educator*

Seminole
Bennett, Delores Elaine (Dee Bennett) *elementary education educator*

Skiatook
Dunham, Mary Helen *elementary education educator*

Tahlequah
McClure, Veronica Ann *elementary education educator*

Tulsa
Brewer, Marjorie Joy *elementary school educator*
Knaust, Clara Doss *retired elementary school educator*
Smith, Penny *middle school educator*

Warr Acres
Weir, Richard Dale *elementary education educator*

Woodward
Selman, Minnie Corene Phelps *elementary school educator*

OREGON

Cottage Grove
Miller, Joanne Louise *middle school educator*

Eagle Point
Blanchard, Shirley Lynn *primary school educator, consultant*

Florence
Devereux, Barbara L. *elementary school educator*

Grants Pass
Christensen, James Arthur *middle school educator*

Lake Oswego
Lenderman, Joanie *elementary school educator*

Mcminnville
McGillivray, Karen *retired elementary school educator*

Portland
Franklin, Dolores Roberts *elementary education educator*
Frolick, Patricia Mary *retired elementary school educator*
Hatt, Barbara Ann *elementary and secondary school educator*
Kuney, Gary Wallace *elementary school educator, real estate agent*
Qutub, Carol Hotelling *elementary education educator*
Rosenfeld, Sandra Kaye *elementary school educator*
Wilson, Catherine Phillips *elementary education educator*

Roseburg
Northcraft, Shirley Louise *elementary school educator*
Tilson, Daniel *elementary education educator*

Salem
Page, Cheryl Miller *elementary school educator*

Sandy
Thies, Lynn Wapinski *elementary education educator*

Waldport
Hockett, Lorna Dee *elementary education educator*

PENNSYLVANIA

Allentown
Zellner, Kenneth Kermit *elementary education educator*

Allison Park
Guffey, Barbara Braden *elementary education educator*

Altoona
Killian, William Clarence *elementary education educator*
Vreeland-Flynn, Tracy Lynn *elementary education educator*

Aston
Clark, Marveta Yvonne *elementary education educator, consultant, writer*

Athens
Luther-Lemmon, Carol Len *elementary school educator*

Bally
Kelsch, Joan Mary *elementary education educator*

Barto
Desko, Brenda K. *elementary education educator*
Isett, Deborah Michele Gunther *elementary education educator*

Beaver
Helmick, Gayle Johnston *elementary education educator*
Kaufman, Mary Susan *elementary education educator*

Bensalem
Klingerman, Karen Nina *elementary school educator, teacher consultant, course coordinator*

Berwyn
Mariani, Marcia Anne *health and physical education educator*

Bethel Park
Douds, Virginia Lee *elementary education educator*

Boswell
Markferding, Gail Maureen *elementary school educator*

Bradford
Sanderson, Deborah Shirley *elementary education educator, writer*

Bridgeville
Lucatorto, Helen Ann *elementary education educator*

Brodheadsville
Weinman, David Peter *elementary education educator*

Bryn Mawr
Worrall, Charles Harrison *elementary education educator*

Butler
Grinder, MaryJo I. *elementary education educator*

Cambridge Springs
Grinarml, Sandi Molnar *elementary education educator*

Carnegie
Whitfield, Tammy J. *elementary school educator, director*

Chalfont
Tomlinson, Juliette Shell *elementary school educator*

Chester
Jackson, Cynthia Marie *elementary school educator*

Chester Springs
Davish, Noreen Rowland *elementary education educator, music educator*

Christiana
Fitzgerald, Susan Helena *elementary educator*

Clairton
Cooper, Angela B. *elementary education educator*

Coatesville
Berkeihiser, Virginia Marie *elementary education educator*
Rodkey, Frances Theresa *elementary school educator*
Walker, Marie Fuller *elementary education educator*

Dayton
Patterson, Madge Lenore *elementary education educator*

Dillsburg
Holmes, David James *elementary school educator*

Downingtown
Getz, Michael David *elementary school educator*

Doylestown
Carney-Dalton, Pat *elementary education educator*

East Stroudsburg
Shoemaker, Patricia Washabaugh *reading specialist*

Edinboro
Curry-Carlburg, Joanne Jeanne *elementary education educator*

Elizabeth
Cornell, Marsha R. *elementary education educator*

Elkland
Button, Carol Drusilla *elementary education educator*

Evans City
Micco, Tammy Lynn *elementary education educator*

Fairless Hills
Webb-Kershaw, Marianne Elizabeth *elementary education educator*

Flourtown
Lambert, Joan Dorety *elementary education educator*

Fredericktown
Hess, Dolores J. *elementary education educator*

Freedom
Blaney, M. Kathleen *elementary education educator*

Gilbert
Mack, Cindy Steigerwalt *early childhood educator*

Greencastle
Manifold, Rebecca March *elementary school art educator*

Greensburg
Neff, Mary Ellen Andre *retired elementary school educator*
Olenick, Sandra Leigh *elementary education educator*

Hanover
Goldstein, Sharon Louise *elementary education educator*

Harleysville
Freudig, David Wayne *elementary educator*

Harrisburg
Pringle, Rebecca *elementary school educator*

Hatfield
Madden, Theresa Marie *elementary education educator*

Hermitage
Havrilla, John William *middle school educator*

Hershey
Cook, Christine *elementary education educator*

Honesdale
Carrick, Elaine Leet *kindergarten educator*

Hummelstown
Moffett, Dawn Schulten *retired elementary education educator*
Nagle, Donna Paar *middle school art educator*

Hunlock Creek
Zimmerman, Anita Eloise *elementary education educator*

Indiana
Kulis, Ellen Mae *elementary education educator*

Irwin
Slebodnik, Tressa Ann *retired elementary education educator*

Johnsonburg
Kirkpatrick, Anne Mary *elementary education educator*

Johnstown
Lovingood, Rebecca Britten *elementary school educator*

Kersey
Meredith, Tia Kathryn Johnson *elementary school educator*

Kutztown
Laub, Mary Lou *elementary education educator*

Lafayette Hill
Slagle, Robert Lee, II, *elementary and secondary education educator*

Lake Ariel
Casper, Marie Lenore *middle school educator*

Lake City
Hudak, Sharon Ann. *elementary education educator*

Lancaster
Fleming, Susan Elaine *elementary school educator*
Kane, Edward Joseph *elementary and secondary school educator*
Linton, Joy Smith *primary school educator*
Minney, Barbara Ann *elementary educator and administrator*

Langhorne
Weinstein, Eileen Ann *elementary education educator*

Lansdale
Rosen, Bonnie *elementary school principal, consultant*

Lebanon
Balthaser, Gerda Haas *elementary school educator*

Levittown
Rogers, Lavancha Jayne *elementary school educator*
Upton, Lorraine Frances *elementary education educator*

Lewisburg
Roberts, Ruth W. *retired elementary school educator*

Lock Haven
Moyer, Anna Blackburn *retired secondary and elementary school educator*

Macungie
Kocian, Nancy Jane *elementary education educator*

Manheim
Geib, Violet M. *elementary education educator*

Mc Murray
Giarrusso, Alena Louisa *elementary education educator*

Media
Devine, Kathleen Anne *elementary school educator*

Millersburg
Kirkwood, Nancy Lynne *elementary education educator*

Millersville
Mallery, Anne Louise *elementary education educator, consultant*

Milton
Jarrett, Craig Allen *elementary school educator*

Minersville
Murray, Teresa Marie *elementary education educator*

Monaca
Grivna, Doris M. *elementary education educator*

Monroeville
Baker, Faith Mero *retired elementary education educator*

Myerstown
Robson, Barbara S. *elementary education educator*

Nazareth
Brackbill, Nancy Lafferty *elementary education educator*

Nescopeck
Shiner, Nikki Rae *elementary education educator*

New Brighton
Bucci, Mary Ruth *primary education educator*

New Castle
Denniston, Marjorie McGeorge *retired elementary school educator*

New Freedom
Spicer, Barbara Jean Wentz *elementary school educator*

New Wilmington
Magyary, Cynthia Marie *elementary school educator, music educator*

Newtown
Duncan, Stephen Robert *elementary education educator*

Newville
Rand, Sharon Kay *elementary education educator*

Norristown
Chung, Ann Jane Zane Macdonald *early childhood education educator, counselor*
McDaniel, Brian Edwin *elementary school educator*

Oakdale
Gilden, Robin Elissa *elementary education educator*

Philadelphia
Gillison, Jeanette Scott *elementary school educator*
Gusoff, Patricia Kearney *retired elementary education educator*
Johnson, Shari *early childhood educator*
Landis, Jean Myer *elementary education educator*
Mason, Loretta Yvonne *elementary education educator*
McCafferty, Eileen Patricia *elementary school educator*
Peirce, Donald Oluf *retired elementary education educator*
Williams, Juanita Lundy *elementary education educator*

Philipsburg
Reiter, Daisy K. *retired elementary education educator*

Phoenixville
Harkin, Ann Winifred *elementary school educator, psychotherapist*
Wright, Jean Norman *elementary education educator*

Pittsburgh
Cohen, Luisa Faye *primary education educator*
Dehouske, Ellen Jane *early childhood education educator, consultant*
Eckert, Jean Patricia *elementary education educator*
Heitzenroder, Wendy Roberta *elementary school educator*
Hlawati, Joyce F. *elementary education educator*
McLaughlin, Virginia Barlow *elementary educator, reading specialist*
Packard, Rochelle Sybil *elementary school educator*
Pattak, Kathy Kramer *elementary physical education educator*
Patton, Nancy Matthews *elementary education educator*
Spohn, Janice *elementary education educator, consultant*
Sullivan, Loretta Roseann *elementary education educator*
Warner, Judith (Anne) Huss *elementary school educator*
Williams, Nathaniel, Jr., *elementary education educator*

Pottstown
Fake, Ingrid Christine *middle school educator*

Red Lion
Collier, Linda Arlene *kindergarten educator*

Riegelsville
Robbins, Arlene Agnes *elementary education educator*

Russellton
Curtis, Paula Annette *elementary and secondary education educator*

Sayre
Cron, Juanita Marlene *elementary education educator*

Scottdale
Sember, June Elizabeth *retired elementary education educator*

Scranton
Bianca, Joanne Marie *elementary and early childhood educator*
Drozdik Seasock, Lora Marie *elementary education educator*

Shillington
Sweatlock, Suzanne Marie *primary education educator*
Weller, Rita Barbara Shepley *elementary education educator*

Shohola
Williams, Carolyn Woodworth *retired elementary education educator, consultant*

Solebury
Gilleo, Sandra V. *elementary education educator*

Thorndale
Ciarlone, Patricia Ann *elementary education educator*

Titusville
Campasino, Ellen Marie *elementary school educator*
Dawes, Sharon Kay *elementary school educator*

Vandergrift
Quader, Patricia Ann *elementary education educator*

Warminster
Chandler, Victoria Jane *elementary school educator, writer*

West Chester
Bove, Patrice Magee *elementary education educator*
Morgan, John David *middle school educator*

West Lawn
Shirk, Sharon L. *elementary education educator*

Wexford
Hutchinson, Barbara Winter *elementary school educator*

Windber
Baltzer, Patricia Germaine *elementary school educator*

York
Coffman, (Anna) Louise M. *retired elementary education educator*
Owens, Marilyn Mae *elementary school educator, secondary school educator*

RHODE ISLAND

Newport
Flowers, Sandra Joan *elementary education educator*

North Scituate
Nardacci, Martha Joyce *elementary education educator*

Providence
Newman, Janet Elaine *elementary education educator*

Warwick
Artesani, Maryann *elementary education educator*
Polselli, Linda Marie *elementary education educator*

SOUTH CAROLINA

Aiken
Lehrhaupt, Karen *elementary and secondary education educator*
Santos, Karey Michale *elementary school educator*

Belton
O'Dell, Bernice Vinson (Kathy O'Dell) *elementary school educator*

Bennettsville
Best, Carolyn Anne Hill *elementary school educator*
Rankin, Martha Miller Cottingham (Marty Rankin) *elementary school educator*

Columbia
Pettus, Karen Rosenbalm *elementary education educator*
Pfefferkorn, Laura Bigger *middle school educator*

Conway
Johnson-Leeson, Charleen Ann *former elementary school educator, insurance agent, insurance consultant, regional executive assistant*

Darlington
Farmer, Jane Warner *elementary education educator*

Easley
Cole, Lois Lorraine *retired elementary school educator*

Elgin
Peake, Frank *middle school educator*

Fairforest
Parker, Cheri Ann *elementary education educator*

Gaffney
Suttle, Helen Jayson *retired education educator*

Greenville
Drummond, Julia Elaine Butler *retired middle school educator*
Frampton, Lisa *elementary education educator*

Hilton Head Island
Exley, Winston Wallace *middle school educator*

Iva
Burton, Amy June *retired elementary education educator*

Kingstree
Davis, Michelle Marie *elementary education educator*

Leesville
Covington, Tammie Warren *elementary education educator*

Lexington
Floyd, Ann R. *elementary education educator*

Manning
Frierson, Marie Holmes *middle school educator*

Moore
Simmons, Sharon Dianne *elementary education educator*

North Myrtle Beach
Hilliard, Linda Walters *primary education educator*

Pawleys Island
Spencer, Gayle *elementary school educator*

Society Hill
King, Amanda Arnette *elementary school educator*

Spartanburg
Gardner, Teresa Gabrels *elementary education educator*
Hatley, Amy Bell *elementary education educator, broadcast journalist*
Hightower, Mary Lou Swartz *elementary education educator*

Sumter
Blair, Charlie Lewis *elementary school educator*

Timmonsville
Temoney, Verneda Daniels *elementary education educator*

Union
Lorenz, Latisha Jay *elementary education educator*

Wedgefield
Mingo, Joe Louis *elementary school educator*

Westminster
Duncan, Gwendolyn McCurry *elementary education educator*

SOUTH DAKOTA

Buffalo
Helms, Carol Dorothy *elementary education educator*

Chamberlain
Harmon, Heather Catharine *elementary school educator*

Letcher
Selchert, Dianne Kay *elementary school educator*

Meadow
Rosenau, Ruth Elizabeth *retired elementary and secondary school educator*

Mission
Nelson, Sarah Ellen *elementary music educator*

Pierre
Benson, Bernice LaVina *elementary education educator*

Rapid City
Ankrum, Dorothy Darlene *elementary education educator*

Sioux Falls
Ashworth, Julie *elementary education educator*
Sanford, Delores Mae *retired elementary school educator, assistant principal*

Vermillion
Milton, Leonharda Lynn *elementary and secondary school educator*

TENNESSEE

Alcoa
Widner, Nelle Ousley *retired elementary education educator*

Antioch
Saviste, Tami Rae *early childhood educational specialist*

Ashland City
Roehrich, Cheryl Brinkley *elementary education educator*

Birchwood
Lowrance, Rita Gale Hamrick *elementary school educator*

Bristol
Thomas, Barbara Wayne *elementary school educator*
Weeden, Debbie Sue *early childhood education educator*

Chattanooga
Harris, Harriett Smitherman *retired elementary school educator*
Nunley, Malinda Vaughn *retired elementary school educator*

Cleveland
Goff, Nadine Farabee *elementary education educator*

Collierville
Kent, Catharine Hazen *elementary education educator*
Seed, Allen H. *elementary and secondary education educator, science educator*

Columbia
Bone, Rosemary Cook *elementary education educator*

Cookeville
Lankford, Mary Anne *elementary school educator*

Cordova
Conrow, Mary Frances *retired elementary education educator, real estate broker*

Crossville
Hooks, Vandalyn Lawrence *former elementary school educator*
Moore, Harold Blaine *middle school educator*

Elkton
Newman, Sharon Lynn *elementary education educator*

Ethridge
Calvert, Jacqueline Claire *elementary education educator*

Henderson
Guinn, Mary Ann *elementary education educator*

Hermitage
Quaintance, Alice Lynn *elementary school media specialist*

Jacksboro
Ford, Ruth Alice *elementary education educator*

Jellico
Chitwood, Helen Irene *elementary education educator*

Kingsport
Carico, Opal Lee *retired elementary school educator*

Knoxville
Ratliff, Eva Rachel *elementary education educator*
Reynolds, Megan Beahm *primary and elementary education educator*
Walsh, Joanne Elizabeth *retired elementary school educator, librarian*

Lawrenceburg
Pinckley, Frances Ann *middle school language arts educator*

Linden
Yarbro, Billy Ray *elementary school educator, basketball coach*

Lookout Mountain
Jones, Alma Arlene *elementary education educator*

Luray
Connor, Nancy King *elementary school educator*

Maryville
Effler, Wilma Jean *elementary education educator*

Mc Donald
Lawson, Billie Katherine *elementary school educator*

Mc Minnville
Henry, Mary Lou Smelser *elementary education educator*

Memphis
Allison, Helen Thomas *retired primary school educator, author*
Donahue, Joan Elizabeth *elementary school educator*
Eller, Linda Sadler *elementary school educator, district administrator, technology specialist*
Hord, Pauline Jones *primary school educator*
Young, Irma Jean *elementary education educator*

Mount Juliet
Holloway, Susan Master *elementary education educator*

Murfreesboro
Paraiso, Johnna Kaye *elementary education educator*

Nashville
Chambers, Carol Tobey *elementary school educator*
Greene, Lydia Abbi Jwuan *elementary education educator*
Jackson, Patricia Marie *retired elementary education educator*
Williams, Mary Helen *elementary education educator*

Newport
Runnion, Cindie J. *elementary school educator*

Oliver Springs
Heacker, Thelma Weaks *retired elementary school educator*

Pleasant View
Hampton, Margaret Ann Barnes *elementary education educator*

Portland
Miller, Sandra Perry *middle school educator*

Saint Andrews
Warner, Wayne Henry *elementary and secondary educator*

Smyrna
Faules, Barbara Ruth *retired elementary education educator*

Sparta
Langford, Jack Daniel *elementary school educator*

TEXAS

Allen
Perez, Renae Lewis *elementary education educator*

Arlington
Randle, Rolinda Carol *elementary education educator*

Atascosa
Hale, Nancy Annette *kindergarten educator*

Austin
Boehm, P. Diann *elementary education educator*
Gregory, Marilyn *primary school educator*
Hardin, Sheryl Dawn *elementary education educator*
Lafferty, Joyce G. Zvonar *retired middle school educator*
Piper, Susie E. *elementary and secondary school educator, counselor, writer*

Azle
Koym, Zala Cox *elementary education educator*

Brenham
Dawson, Cathy Jayne *elementary school educator*

Cedar Hill
Kramer, Judith Ann *elementary education educator*

Channelview
Vlach, Rose Anne *elementary school teacher*
Wallace, Betty Jean *elementary school educator, lay minister*

Childress
Simmons, Lorna Womack *elementary school educator, educator*

Comanche
Droke, Edna Faye *elementary school educator, retired*

Conroe
Gray, Janet Ethel *elementary educator*
Munguia, Gay Yaeger *elementary school educator, secondary school educator*

Coppell
Myers, Carol Ann *elementary education educator*
Smothermon, Peggi Sterling *middle school educator*

Corpus Christi
Chodosh, Robert Ivan *retired middle school educator, coach*
Salinas, Sonia *elementary school educator*

Dallas
Herold-Joven, Emma Lee *elementary education educator*
Ingram, Sandy Goggans *elementary school educator*
Lopez, Francisca Uy *elementary education educator*
Montgomery, Doris Stroustrup Henriksen *primary school educator*
Qualls, June Carol *elementary school educator*
Robbins, Jane Lewis *elementary school educator*
Savannah, Mildred Thornhill *public school educator*
Thomas, Sarah Elaine *elementary music educator*
Wrucke-Nelson, Ann C. *elementary education educator*

Decatur
Acker, Linda Brown *middle school educator*
Jordan, Linda Susan Darnell *elementary school educator*

Denton
McAlister, Janice Marie *elementary educator, radio announcer*
Palermo, Judy Hancock *elementary school educator*

Denver City
Garate, Rebecca *elementary school bilingual educator*

Dilley
McMillian, Marilyn Lindsey *elementary educator, health, home economics*

El Paso
Malone, Debra Beatrice *elementary education educator*
Samaniego, Julia Rose *elementary educator*

Euless
Warwick, Sharon Brenda *elementary art educator*

Floresville
Alvarez, Olga Mendoza *elementary school educator*
Vontur, Ruth Poth *retired elementary school educator*

Flower Mound
L'Huillier, Valerie Elizabeth *elementary education educator*

Fluvanna
Jackson, Rebecca M. *elementary education educator, English as a second language educator*

Fort Worth
Booghrey, LaWanda *elementary school educator*
Diffily, Deborah Lynn *early childhood education educator*
Scott-Wabbington, Vera V. *elementary school educator*

Friendswood
Kennedy, Priscilla Ann *elementary school educator*

Gainesville
Dietz, David W. *elementary education educator*

Galveston
Hawkins, Ida Faye *elementary school educator*

Garland
Chenault, Sheryl Ann *elementary education educator*
Knox, Dianne Medlin *mathematics educator*

Gladewater
Cox-Beaird, Dian Sanders *middle school educator*

Gonzales
Brooks, Gerldine McGlothlin *elementary school educator*

Grand Prairie
Scott, Dorothy Elaine *elementary education educator*

Hawkins
Lewis, Annice Moore *middle school language arts educator*

Henderson
Rhoades, Eva Yvonne *retired elementary school educator*

Houston
Banks, Evelyn Yvonne *middle school educator*
Berti, Margaret Ann *early childhood education educator*
Boney, Norma Marie Davis *elementary school educator*
Bustamante, Dolores Morales *elementary education educator*
Crenshaw, Corinne Burrowes *kindergarten educator*
Ehlinger, Janet Ann Dowling *elementary school educator*
Fizer, Marilyn Dahle *elementary education educator*
Fuller, Theodore, Jr., *elementary education educator*
Hines, Constance Faye *elementary education educator*
Jimmar, D'Ann *elementary education educator, fashion merchandiser*
Johnson, Judy Dianne *elementary education educator*
Krouse, Jenny Lynn *elementary school educator*
LeBoff, Barbara *educator*
Lewis, Cleotrice O. Ney Tillis *retired elementary education educator*
Paul, Alida Ruth *arts and crafts educator*
Petrillo, Anna *elementary school educator*
Pinson, Artie Frances *retired elementary educator*
Pittman, Katherine Anne Atherton *elementary education educator*
Roos, Sybil Friedenthal *retired elementary school educator*
Trichel, Mary Lydia *middle school educator*
Walker, Sammie Lee *retired elementary education educator*

Huntington
Smith, Joan Colvin *elementary education educator, principal*

Hurst
Kaspar, Lori Jayne *elementary school educator*
Kidwell, Georgia Brenner *elementary education educator*

Irving
Clark, Priscilla Alden *retired elementary education educator*
McCloskey, Ann Frances *elementary and secondary music educator*

Johnson City
Pollock, Margaret Landau Peggy *elementary school educator*

Katy
Gould, Sandra Joyce *elementary education educator*

Killeen
Marshall, Shirley Elizabeth *elementary educator*

Laredo
Charles, Joseph Glenn *middle school educator*
Condon, Maria del Carmen *retired elementary school educator*
Heimes, Charmaine Marie *elementary school educator, poet, writer*

Leander
Almour, Vicki Lynn *elementary education educator*

Lewisville
Fisher, Janine Galmiche *educator, counselor*

Livingston
Oliver, Debbie Edge *elementary education educator*

Longview
Anderson, Linda Kay *elementary education educator*
Northcutt, Kathryn Ann *elementary school and gifted-talented educator, reading recovery educator*

Los Fresnos
Olivárez, Celinda *elementary education educator*

Lubbock
Huggins, Cannie Mae Cox Hunter *retired elementary school educator*
Mitchell, Paula Kay *elementary education educator*
Nelson, Toza *retired elementary school educator, church administrator*

Luling
Perryman, Billy Pat *elementary educator*

Manor
Chew, Lynda Casbeer *elementary school educator*

Marfa
Chambers, Johnnie Lois (Tucker Chambers) *elementary school educator, rancher*

Mathis
Jimenez, Praxesdis *middle school educator*
Leija, Anita Leija *elementary school educator*

Mercedes
Alaniz, Theodora Villarreal *elementary education educator*

Mesquite
Andrews, Mary June *elementary education educator*

Mineola
Tabor, Beverly Ann *retired elementary school educator*

New Braunfels
Dunn, Charlotte Valborg Lund *elementary education educator*
Williams, Vickie Glyn *elementary and special education educator, administrator*

Odessa
Miller, Ana Marie *elementary education educator*
Stone, Hazel L. *educator*

Pampa
Auwen, Judith K. *elementary education educator*

Paris
Cox, Sandy Gail *elementary education educator*

Pasadena
Hall, Georganna Mae *elementary school educator*

Plainview
Gaston, Bonnie Faye James *elementary education educator*

Plano
Haggard, Geraldine Langford *primary school educator, adult education educator, consultant*
McWilliams, Chris Pater Elissa *elementary school educator*
Tipping, Sharon Rutledge *elementary school educator*
Toney, Barbara Chadwick *elementary education educator*

Port Aransas
Cook, Marilyn Jane *elementary school educator*
Goodwin, Mary McGinnis *secondary education educator*

Red Oak
Wittsche, Valerie Josephine *elementary education educator, special education educator*

Roscoe
Beeks, Cheryl Elaine *elementary school educator*

Rosebud
Warren, Ernestine Hill *elementary education educator, mayor*

San Antonio
Arnold, Marie Collette *elementary school educator*
Contie, Mary Margarita *primary education educator, consultant*
Dahl, Cathy Davenport *elementary educator*
Garner, Jo Ann Starkey *retired elementary and special education educator*
Gómez, Mary Alice *bilingual elementary educator*
Haggard, Victoria Marie *elementary education educator, secondary education educator*
Hernandez, Mary Antonieta *retired elementary education educator*
Lloyd, Susan Elaine *middle school educator*
Madrid, Olga Hilda Gonzalez *retired elementary education educator, association executive*
Massey, Patti Chryl *elementary school educator*
Maxwell, Diana Kathleen *early childhood education educator*
McBee, Lucy Armijo *retired elementary education educator, administrator, singer, actress, writer*

Menchaca
Menchaca, Robert *elementary education educator*
Norwood, Carole Gene *retired middle school educator*
Potts, Martha Lou *elementary education educator*
Salisbury, Margaret Mary *retired public school educator*
Speer, Glenda O'Bryant *middle school educator*
Swinney, Phyllis Marie *elementary education educator*
Tarte, Teresa Michelle *elementary education educator*
Tomkewitz, Marie Adele *elementary school educator*
Wimpee, Mary Elizabeth *elementary school educator*

San Marcos
Barragán, Celia Silguero *elementary school educator*
Clayton, Katy *elementary education educator*
Guettner, Pamela Rea *elementary school educator*

Seguin
Hastings, Evelyn Grace *retired elementary school educator*

Spring
Joseph, Jeneen Kay *elementary education educator*

Sugar Land
Duvall, Cathleen Elaine *elementary education educator, consultant*
Finney, Patricia Ann *elementary education educator*
Ramos, Rose Mary *elementary school educator*

Temple
Kreitz, Helen Marie *retired elementary education educator*
Staten, Donna Kay *elementary school educator*

Terrell
Root, Elaine Harper *elementary education educator*

Texas City
Davis, Robert Edgar *elementary school educator*

The Colony
Roberts, Ginny Barkley *middle school language arts educator*

Throckmorton
Balthrop, Cynthia Diane *elementary school educator*

Trinity
Chavez, Dorothy Vaughan *elementary school educator, environmental educator*

Troy
Mosley, Linda Carol *elementary school educator*

Vidor
Morgan, Rosetta Richardson *elementary education educator*

Waco
Symank, Oleta Marlene *elementary school educator*

Weatherford
Estes, Carolyn Ann Hull *retired elementary school educator*
Miller, Dixie Davis *elementary school educator*

Whiteface
Lamb, Stacie Thompson *elementary school educator*

UTAH

Kaysville
Johnson, Charles N. *elementary education educator*

Orem
Bowman, Naoma Susann *elementary school educator*

Provo
Whatcott, Marsha Rasmussen *elementary education educator*

Salt Lake City
Nielsen, Cherie Sue *elementary educator*
Smith, J(ames) Scott *elementary education educator*

VERMONT

Burlington
Miller, Jane Cutting *elementary education educator*

East Barre
Badeau, Carlene Dianna *elementary education educator*

Ludlow
Davis, Vera *elementary school educator*

Manchester Center
Waldinger Seff, Margaret *special elementary education educator*

Moretown
Hartshorn, Brenda Bean *elementary education educator*

Shelburne
Myers, David Alan *middle school music educator*

South Burlington
Kenyon, Judith *primary school educator*

South Hero
Bisson, Roger *middle school educator*
Thompson, Ellen Ann *elementary education educator*

VIRGINIA

Alexandria
Abernathy, Mary Gates *elementary school educator*
Johnson, Marlys Marlene *elementary school educator*

Altavista
Shelton, Deborah Kay *elementary education educator*

Amherst
Campbell, Catherine Lynn *elementary school educator*

Arlington
Neel, Barbara Anne Spiess *elementary school educator, artist*
Simms, Frances Bell *retired elementary education educator*

Bedford
Henry, Nancy Sinclair *middle school educator*
Robertson, Sylvia Douglas *middle school educator*
Sweeney, Garnette Grinnell *elementary education educator*

Broadway
Hutchens, Joan Reid *elementary school educator, reading specialist, consultant*

Chesapeake
Belson, Carolyn Barwick *elementary education educator*
Clarkson, Phyllis Owens *early childhood educator*
Lewter, Helen Clark *elementary education educator, retired*
Nicely, Denise Ellen *elementary education educator*

Chester
Spindler, Judith Tarleton *elementary school educator*

Christiansburg
Patty, Anna Christine *tax specialist*

Cobbs Creek
Lawson, Janice Rae *retired elementary education educator*

Emporia
Bottoms, Brenda Pinchbeck *elementary education educator*

Evington
Fortune, Laura Catherine Dawson *elementary school educator*

Fairfax
Graves, Dana Louise *elementary school educator*
McAllister, Rena Farrell *elementary educator*

Front Royal
Foster, Pamela Lynn *elementary education educator*

Gainesville
Pemberton, Melissie Collins *retired elementary education educator*

Gloucester
Smith, Susan K. *elementary education educator*

Harrisonburg
McCormick, Linda Yancey *elementary education educator*

Haysi
Deel, George Moses *elementary school educator*

Heathsville
Sisson, Jean Cralle *retired middle school educator*

Keysville
Keeling, Rita D. *elementary educator*

Lansdowne
Green, May Clayman *early childhood educator and administrator*

Lynchburg
Hudson, Katherine Ruth McClain *elementary school educator*

Manassas
McKoy, Phyllis Cofield *elementary school educator*

Mechanicsville
Henshaw, William Raleigh *retired middle school educator*
Long, Patricia Gavigan *elementary education educator, English language educator*

Midlothian
Smith, Alma Davis *elementary education educator*

Williams, Dorothy Putney *middle school educator*

Moneta
Wiatt, Carol Stultz *elementary education educator*

Natural Bridge Station
Locher, Elizabeth Aiken *elementary education educator, reading specialist*

Newport News
Winkle, Susan Renee *elementary education educator*

Norfolk
Oberne, Sharon Brown *elementary education educator*
Russell, Susan Webb *elementary and middle school education educator*
Winslow, Janet Lucas *elementary education educator*

Oakton
Hu, Sue King *elementary and middle school educator*

Orange
Daniel, Daniele Mallison *elementary school educator*

Petersburg
Johnson, Alice Jean Shumate *elementary education educator*

Poquoson
Moore, Sandra Bucher *mathematics educator*
Tuck, Carolyn Weaver *middle school educator*

Richmond
Fleisher, Paul *elementary education educator*
Kvetko, Nell Patterson *elementary school educator*
Mason, Vivian Lee Conway *elementary education educator*
Minor, Marian Thomas *elementary and secondary school educational consultant*

Roanoke
Denton, Judy Holley *elementary education educator*

Spotsylvania
Westwood, Geraldine E. *elementary school educator*

Spring Grove
Davis, Shirley Stancil *retired elementary education educator*

Springfield
Insalaco-De Nigris, Anna Maria Theresa *middle school educator*

Stafford
Garrison, Anne-Marie Dickinson *middle school educator*
Lambert, Linda Margaret *reading specialist*

Suffolk
Harrell, Florence Louise *elementary education educator*
Parker, James Fletcher *middle school educator*

Unionville
Highland, Phyllis Antoinette *elementary education educator*

Vinton
Louthian, Brenda Jennings *elementary music educator*

Virginia Beach
Jones, Robert Clair *middle school educator*
Kawczynski, Diane Marie *elementary and middle school educator, composer*
Lang, Vicki Scott *primary school educator*
LeGeyt, Patricia Ann *elementary education educator*
Rhodes, Betty Moore *elementary education educator*
Von Mosch, Wanda Gail *middle school educator*

Warrenton
Norskog, Eugenia Folk *elementary education educator*

West Point
Jenkins, Bonnie Buch *elementary education educator*

West Springfield
Sproul, Joan Heeney *elementary school educator*

Williamsburg
Aldrow-Liput, Priscilla Reese *retired elementary education educator*

Winchester
Lightner, Patricia Payne *elementary education educator*

Woodbridge
Packard, Mildred Ruth *middle school educator*

Yorktown
Rogers, Sheila Wood *elementary and secondary school educator*

WASHINGTON

Auburn
Butz, Gloria K. *elementary education educator*

Bellevue
Egashira, Susan Lea *elementary education educator*

Bremerton
Shelton, Elizabeth Anne *elementary school educator*

Brush Prairie
Piper, Christine Marie *elementary education educator*

Federal Way
Hogan, Nancy Kay *elementary education educator*

Issaquah
Newbill, Karen Margaret *elementary school educator, education educator*

Kennewick
Fontana, Sharon Marie *early childhood education educator*
Knight, Janet Ann *elementary education educator*

Kent
Hickey, Shirley Louise Cowin *elementary education educator*

Oak Harbor
Porter, Edith Priscilla *elementary school educator*

Pullman
Paznokas, Lynda Sylvia *elementary and middle school education educator*

Seatac
Sheely, Cindy Jean *elementary education educator*

Seattle
Edwards, Margery Faye *alternative elementary/middle school educator, real estate investor*
Halferty, Frank Joseph *middle school music educator*

Sequim
McGee, Jane Marie *retired elementary school educator*

Shelton
Deyette, Jennifer Lee *middle school educator*

Silverdale
Moore, Julie Kay *middle school educator*

Spanaway
Koyama, Sheila H. *elementary educator*

Spokane
Linn, Diana Patricia *elementary education educator*

Sumner
Wickizer, Cindy Louise *retired elementary school educator*

Vancouver
Ghormley, William Frederick *elementary school educator, music educator*
Soltero, Mary Ann *elementary education educator*

Yakima
Dorsett, Judith A. *elementary education educator*
Walker, Lorene *retired elementary school educator*

WEST VIRGINIA

Buckhannon
Simmons, Diana A. *elementary education educator*

Bunker Hill
Palmer, Barbara Louise Moulden *elementary education educator*

Cameron
Fullerton, Nancy Lee *elementary school and music educator*

Dunbar
Given, Melissa Ann *elementary school educator, educational consultant*

Fairmont
Tarley, Joanna Jane *elementary school educator*

Harpers Ferry
Bailey, Nancy Joyce *elementary school educator*
Blue, Kathy Jo *elementary school educator*

Huntington
Cole, Patricia Aluise *elementary school educator*

Madison
Jarussi, Patricia Lillian *elementary education educator*

Morgantown
Bennett, Mildred Lorline *elementary school educator*
Jones, Julia Pearl *retired elementary school educator*
Robertson-Thorn, Karen *middle school educator*

Mullens
Lee, Debora Ann *elementary school educator, reading specialist*

Nitro
Lucas, Panola *elementary education educator*

Parkersburg
Meadows, Lois Annette *elementary education educator*

Philippi
McLean, Gloria Dawn *elementary education educator*

Shady Spring
Reed, Cathy Lorraine *elementary education educator*

Sharples
Moxley, Jacqulyn Catherine *elementary education educator*

Spencer
Williams, Carol Kunz *elementary education educator*

Squire
Dishman, Roberta Crockett *retired elementary education educator*

Wellsburg
Price, Verla Blanche *elementary education educator*

Weston
Rastle, Maxine Shiflet Cole *retired elementary school educator*
Sumpter, Sonja Kay *elementary school educator*

WISCONSIN

Ashland
Malyuk, Patricia L. *elementary school educator*

Balsam Lake
Bergstrand, Laura Joyce *elementary education educator*

Clayton
Kuntz, Karen Frances *preschool education educator*

Clinton
Wildermuth, Anita Jean *elementary school art educator*

Crivitz
Gerhart, Lorraine Pfeiffer *reading specialist, educator*

Cross Plains
Rodenschmit, Helen Juliana *elementary education educator*

De Forest
O'Neil, J(ames) Peter *computer software designer, educator*

Eagle
Whitney, Cynthia Jeanne *elementary school educator*

Eau Claire
Kozbial, Richard James *retired elementary education educator*

Elkhorn
Reinke, Doris Marie *retired elementary education educator*
Townsend, Barbara Louise *reading specialist, elementary school educator*

Fish Creek
Zvara, Christine C. *middle school education educator*

Fond Du Lac
Fett, Diane P. *child development specialist*

Hartford
Zanchetti, Pamela Joan *elementary education educator*

Janesville
Ream Dravus, Angela Marie *elementary education educator*

Kenosha
Helman, Iris Barca *elementary school educator, consultant*

Malone
Tyunaitis, Patricia Ann *elementary school educator*

Mequon
Dohmen, Mary Holgate *retired primary school educator*

Milwaukee
Carter, Martha Eloise *retired curriculum specialist, reading consultant*
Martin, Mabel Joyce *early childhood educator*
Reed, John Kennedy Emanuel *elementary school teacher*
Rozman, Kevin Michael *middle school arts educator*
Weiner, Wendy L. *elementary education educator, writer*
Williams, Maxine Eleanor *retired elementary school educator*

Neenah
Gorsalitz, Jeannine Liane *elementary school educator*

New Richmond
Zuberbier, Jo Ann *elementary school educator*

Oak Creek
Udziela, Loretta Ann *elementary education educator*

Oshkosh
Gumz, Carol Ann *elementary education educator*
Ristow, Thelma Frances *elementary educator*

Port Washington
Pelczynski, Suzette Elizabeth *elementary school educator*

Racine
Zuhlke, Marybeth *curriculum consultant, educator, coordinator*

Reedsville
Schutte, Pamela Kay *elementary school educator*

Sheboygan
Oyler, Bertha Jeanne *elementary school educator*
Roelse, Lori Ann *elementary school educator*

Slinger
Giordano, Lois Lydia *elementary school educator, consultant, writer*

Stoddard
Hollenbeck, Sue J. *elementary education educator*

Verona
Hoffmeister, Ann Elizabeth *elementary education educator*

Washington Island
Small, Gloria Jean *retired elementary school educator*

Waukesha
Hanko, Mary Ellen *elementary education educator*
Winkelman, Mary Lynn *middle school educator*

West Bend
Christianson, Marcia LaRaye *middle school educator*

Wisconsin Dells
Kolumba, Kim Dale *elementary education educator, speech and language pathologist*

Wisconsin Rapids
McGrath, Cheryl Julia *elementary education educator*
Olson-Hellerud, Linda Kathryn *elementary school educator*

WYOMING

Casper
Junge, Cheryl Marie *elementary education educator*
Wilkes, Shar (Joan Charlene Wilkes) *elementary education educator*

Cheyenne
Reynolds, Glenda Carol *elementary school educator*
Richardson, Earl Wilson *elementary education educator, retired*

Gillette
Peters, Sue Ellen *elementary school educator*

Jackson
Ward, Adrienne Baptiste Brown *elementary school educator, writer*

Laramie
McBride, Judith *elementary education educator*
Schmitt, Diana Mae *elementary education educator*

TERRITORIES OF THE UNITED STATES

GUAM

Hagatna
Flores, Christina Rosalie *elementary education art educator*

PUERTO RICO

Cabo Rojo
Rivera-Martinez, Socorro *retired elementary school educator, assitant principal*

San Juan
Rodriguez, Gladys Montalvo *elementary education educator*
Vázquez-Camuñas, Maribel *elementary school educator, educator*

VIRGIN ISLANDS

St Thomas
Davis, Jacquelyn Delores *elementary education educator*

MILITARY ADDRESSES OF THE UNITED STATES

EUROPE

Fpo
Grossenbacher, Katherine Ann *elementary education educator*

CAPE VERDE

Santa Catarina
Kern, Jean Glotzbach *elementary education educator, gifted education educator*

LITHUANIA

Vilnius
Robertson, Suzanne Marie *primary education educator*

ADDRESS UNPUBLISHED

Abell, Dawn Gabbitas *elementary school, high school educator, administrator*
Adams, Nancy Calhoun *elementary education educator*
Adams, Renee Bledsoe *retired elementary school educator*
Adamson, Jane Nan *retired elementary school educator*
Adams-Passey, Suellen S. *elementary education educator*
Addicott, Beverly Jeanne *retired elementary school educator*
Akana, Keith Kalani *elementary education educator, consultant*
Aldridge, Linda Ann *retired elementary education educator, librarian*
Alfano, Edward Charles, Jr., *elementary education educator*
Almeida, Evelyn *retired elementary education educator*
Anderson, Donna Elaine *elementary and secondary school educator*
Andrews, Carol *primary education educator*
Applin, Catherine Balash *primary school educator, consultant*
Aretz, Barbara Jane *reading specialist, educator*
Arnold, Ruth Ann *elementary education educator*
Arri, Michele Renee *elementary school educator*
Ataie, Judith Garrett *middle school educator*
Austin, Linda R. Compton *elementary education educator*
Axlund, Mary Kate *middle school education educator*
Babcock-Nice, Michele Elizabeth *elementary school educator*
Baghaei-Rad, Nancy Jane Bebb *elementary educator*
Baker, Carol Ann *elementary school educator*
Baker, Katherine June *elementary school educator, minister, artist*
Baker, Margery Louise *elementary education educator*
Ball, Margie Barber *elementary school educator*
Baral, Wanda *elementary school educator*
Bates Stoklosa, Evelynne (Eve Bates Stoklosa) *educational consultant, educator*
Beck, Barbara Nell *elementary school educator*
Becker, Eleen Marie *secondary education educator*
Becton, Amy Earle *elementary school educator*
Belanger, Cherry Churchill *elementary school educator*
Bell, Loretta Mae *elementary education educator*
Belval, Josephine Antanette *retired elementary school educator*
Beresford, Wilma *retired elementary and gifted education educator*
Bernstein, Eva Gould *retired elementary education educator, reading specialist*
Bertrand, Annette Maria *elementary education educator*
Bigelow, Sharon Lee *elementary school educator*
Billups, Nelda Joyce *elementary educator*
Birman, Linda Lee *retired elementary school educator*
Black, Recca Marcele *educator*
Blackburn, Lou Jean *elementary school educator*
Blakley, Earnestine *elementary education educator*
Bland, Sarah Bell *retired elementary school educator*
Bloodworth, Gladys Leon *elementary school educator*
Boesch, Diane Harriet *retired elementary education educator*
Bono, Charlene Cecilia *elementary school educator*
Borchers, Mary Amelia *middle school educator*
Boswell, Tommie C. *retired middle school educator*
Boudreaux, Susan Castro *elementary school educator*
Bozzomo, Winifred Kathryn *elementary education educator*
Brace, Joan Elaine *elementary education educator*
Bridges, Christine E. *elementary education educator*
Brisko, Cynthia Bell *primary education educator*
Brown, Beulah Louise *retired elementary educator*
Brown, Diana L. *elementary education educator*
Brown, Elmira Newsom *retired elementary school educator*
Brown, Julia Anne *elementary school educator*
Brown, Linda M. *elementary education educator*
Brown, Raquel Lynn *elementary school educator*
Brown-Ekue, Mavis Icilda *elementary education educator*
Brown-Zekeri, Lolita Molanda *elementary school educator*
Brull, Carol Jean *elementary school educator*
Bryant, Gwendolyn Lana *elementary education educator*
Bullock, Molly *retired elementary school educator*
Bunker, Debra J. *elementary education educator*
Burbridge, Ann Arnold *music educator, choir director*
Burgess, Nancy Jo *elementary education educator*
Burgoyne, Barbara Elizabeth *elementary education educator*
Burton, Sharon Ilene *elementary educator*
Bush, Sandi Tokoa *elementary school educator*
Caldwell, Jo Ann Kennedy *elementary educator*
Calhoun, Joan Marie *elementary education educator, resource specialist*
Callan, Richard John *elementary school educator*
Campbell, Sarah *elementary school educator, special education educator*
Campos, Jeri LaRuth *elementary education educator*
Carlson, Nora *elementary school educator*
Carr, Bessie *retired middle school educator*
Casey, Darla Diann *elementary school educator*
Cepielik, Elizabeth Lindberg *elementary school educator*
Cheoros, Edith Marie *elementary school educator*
Clark, Barbara June *elementary education educator*
Clark, Linda Jane *elementary school educator*
Cleary, Frances Marie *retired elementary school educator*
Click, Gail Irene *middle school educator*
Cobert, Katharine Jones *elementary education educator*
Coleman, Gary William *retired elementary school educator*
Coleman, Kimberly Marie *elementary educator, special education educator*
Coluccio, Josephine Catherine *primary and elementary school educator*
Conley, Patsy Gail *retired elementary education educator*
Cormican, M. Alma *elementary education educator*
Crouse, Carol K. Mavromatis *elementary education educator*
Cucciniello, Dawn Grace *elementary and secondary school educator*
Curnyn, Kathleen Marie *elementary school educator*
Dattilo, Linda Kathleen *elementary education educator*
Davis, Anna Jane Ripley *elementary education educator*
Davis, Diann Holmes *elementary school educator*
Davis, Helen R. *elementary and middle school educator*
Day, Afton J. *elementary school educator, administrator*
De Lancey, Patricia A. *elementary education educator*
Detwiler, Christina LeFevre *elementary school educator*
Devoe, Dorothy S. *elementary school educator*
Dibert, Rosalie *elementary school educator*
Dirks, Sandra L. *elementary school educator*
Donaldson, Wilma Crankshaw *elementary education educator*
Doviak, Ingrid Ellinger *elementary school educator*
Dubois, Nancy Q. *elementary school educator*
Ducote, Deborah M. *elementary education educator, reading specialist*
Duffey, Rosalie Ruth *elementary school educator*
Duncan, Debra Lynn *elementary education educator*
Duncan, Margaret A. *elementary education educator*
Dye, Linda Kaye *elementary school educator*
Eaton, Dorel *elementary school educator*
Eirich (Stein), Genevieve Theresa *reading specialist, elementary school educator*
Ertl, Rita Mae *elementary education educator*
Essa, Lisa Beth *elementary school educator*
Evans, Edith Todd *elementary education educator*
Evans, Valerie Elaine *elementary education educator*
Feldman, Lillian Maltz *early childhood education consultant*
Feuer-Stern, Barbie Shnider *elementary and secondary school educator*
Filomeno, Linda Jean Harvey *elementary education educator*
Flaks, J. Margot *retired elementary school educator*
Folz, Kathleen Louise *elementary education educator*
Ford, Barbara Foreman *middle school educator*
Forney, Ronald Dean *elementary school educator, consultant, educational therapist*
Fugazzi, Haven Hardin *elementary education educator*
Gallatin, Nancy Mae *retired elementary education educator*
Galliher, Clarice A. Andrews *secondary education educator*
Garabedian, Betty Marie *retired elementary school educator*
Gelder, Donna Rae *elementary school educator, retired*
Gillin, Carol Ann *middle school educator*
Glasscock, Elizabeth Anne (Libby Glasscock) *kindergarten educator, adjunct college instructor*
Goff, Renee Rosenstock *middle school educator*
Goffe, Esther *elementary school educator*
Goldinger, Shirley Anne *elementary education educator*
Gonzales, Judith Anne *retired elementary school educator*
Good, Linda Lou *elementary education educator*
Goode, Janet Weiss *elementary school educator*
Graupner, Sheryll Ann *elementary education educator*
Gray, Denise Deanne *elementary school educator*
Greeley, Patricia E. *elementary school educator*
Green, Mildred Simpson *retired elementary school educator*
Greenberg, Ina Florence *retired elementary education educator*
Griffin, Gloria Jean *retired elementary school educator*
Grove, Myrna Jean *elementary education educator*
Groves, Bernice Ann *elementary school educator*
Hankins, Mary Denman *elementary school educator*
Hardage, Page Taylor *elementary education educator*
Harrington, James L., Jr., *elementary school educator*
Harris, Ann *elementary school teacher*
Harris, Delmarie Jones *elementary education educator*
Hartman, Elizabeth Diane *retired elementary education educator*
Harvey, Judith Gootkin *elementary school educator, real estate agent*
Hauser, Dennis James *technology educator*
Hays, Kay Ann *elementary counselor, educational diagnostician*
Hebert, Christine Anne *elementary education educator*
Hegel, Pamela Rene *elementary school educator*
Helton, Thelma Ann *elementary education educator*
Henjum, Kay Dee *elementary education educator*
Henkel, Cynthia Leigh *elementary education educator*
Hereford, Pamela Ann *elementary school educator*
Herndon, Eloise J. *retired elementary educator*
Herold, Rochelle Snyder *early childhood educator*
Herzog, Carol Jean *elementary school educator*
Heskett, Luvina Hylton *retired elementary education educator*
Hibbs, Dawn Wilcox *elementary school educator*
Hillery, Susie Moore *retired elementary school educator*
Hoffman, H(oward) Carl *retired elementary school educator*
Holguin, Kathryn Rae *elementary school educator*
Holt, Jana Sue *middle school educator*
Holt, Sandra Grace *middle school educator*
Holthaus, Joan Marie *elementary school educator*
Holtkamp, Susan Charlotte *elementary education educator*
Horstmann, Jane Kristi *elementary school educator*
Horton-Wright, Alma Irene *retired elementary school educator*
Howell, Elizabeth Adell *elementary and junior high school education educator*
Hudson, Elizabeth Mae *elementary education educator*
Huffman, Carol Koster *retired elementary school educator*
Hummel, Marilyn Mae *elementary education educator*
Hurlbut, Geraldine *retired elementary education educator*
Hutchison, Brenda Lee *elementary education educator*
Jacobs, Linda Rotroff *elementary school educator*
James, Nancy Irene *elementary education educator*
Jimenez, Jacquelyn *elementary education educator*
Jinkerson, Maxine Louise *gifted education educator*
Johnson, Carolyn Louise *elementary education educator*
Johnson, Kirsten Denise *elementary education educator*
Johnson, LaVerne St. Clair *retired elementary school educator*
Johnson, Monica Lynn *elementary education educator*
Johnson-MIller, Charleen V. *teacher coordinator*
Jones, Arneitha R. *middle school educator*
Jones, Linda Jackson *professional educator*
Joyner, Nina Womble *elementary education educator*
Kachur, Betty Rae *elementary education educator*
Kalman-Coburn, Elaine Priscilla *elementary school educator*
Karber, Johnnie Faye *elementary education educator*
Keane Hernandez, Noreen B(ernadette) *elementary education educator*
Keebler, Lois Marie *elementary school educator*
Keller, Toni L. *elementary education educator*
Kestner, Cheryl Lynn *elementary school educator*
Kiehlbauch, Sheryl Lynn *elementary education educator*
Kincanon, Gary Lee *elementary school educator*
King-Garner, Miria *elementary education educator*
Kirsch, Mary Anne Gwen *elementary education educator*
Klauck, Judith Lynn *middle school educator*
Klein, Elayne Margery *retired elementary education educator*
Kolb, Dorothy Gong *elementary education educator*
Koleilat, Betty Kummer *middle school educator, mathematician*
Kosa, Jaymie Reeber *middle school educator*
Krainski, Joanna Donna *middle school educator*
Kristensen, Marlene *early childhood education educator*
Krulik, Gloria Lee Ancell *guidance counselor, educator, retired*
Lambrix, Winifred Marie McFarlane *retired elementary education educator*
Lansing, Kathy Ann *elementary school educator*
La Sala, Carolann Marie *elementary, secondary and academic administrator, educator*
Lauck, Lynne Ruth *retired elementary and secondary school educator*
Lauzon, Laura M. *middle school educator*
Leavitt, Maura Lynn *elementary education educator*
Leban, Celeste Casdia *elementary school educator*
Legington, Gloria R. *middle school educator*
Leovy, Janet Seitz *elementary education educator*
leRoux, Betty Von Moore *elementary education educator*
Lipka, Rita Ann *retired elementary education educator*
Lockette, Daphney D. *elementary education educator*
Loring, Mildred Rogers *retired elementary educator, reading specialist*
Love, Sara Elizabeth *retired elementary school educator*
Lowenberg, Georgina Grace *retired elementary school educator*
Lubetzky, Carole Diane *elementary education educator, math-science specialist*
Lumb, Sandra Jayne *elementary school educator*
Lynam, Gloria *elementary school educator*
Lynch, Laura Ellen *elementary education educator*
Martinez, Nancy Marie *elementary education educator*
Mason, Margaret Crather *elementary school educator*
Matera, Frances Lorine *elementary school educator*
Mathews, Dona June *elementary educator*
May, Beverly *elementary school educator*
McCann, Diana Rae *elementary education educator*
McCann, Joyce Jeannine *retired elementary education educator*
McCarthy, Joanne Mary *reading specialist*
McCullough, Deanna Carolyn *elementary education educator*
McFarland, Mary A. *elementary and secondary school educator, administrator, consultant*
McKinsey, Lynn *elementary education educator*
McLaughlin, Constance Nethken *middle school science educator*
McNully, Lynnette Larkin *elementary education educator*
Meagher, Joan Cecelia *elementary education educator*
Meek, Amy Gertrude *retired elementary education educator*
Meltzer, E. Alyne *elementary school educator, social worker, volunteer*
Mendon, Karen Jeanette *middle school education educator*
Menestrina, Angel *elementary school educator*
Messerschmidt, Joyce Irene *retired elementary school educator*
Meyer, Frances Margaret Anthony *elementary and secondary school educator, health education specialist*
Middleton, Gregory Alfonso *elementary school educator*
Miller, Kim Zaneski *elementary education educator*
Miller, Marian Roberta *elementary education educator*
Miller, Roberta Doris *elementary school educator*
Millman, Marilyn Estelle *elementary school educator*
Mindlin, Paula Rosalie *retired reading educator*
Moore, Marsha Lynn *elementary school educator, counseling administrator*
Moore, Robert Paul *elementary school educator*
Morgan, Joyce Elizabeth *elementary school educator*
Mott, Mary Elizabeth *retired educational administrator*
Muskopf, Margaret Rose *elementary school educator*
Myers, Lee Edward *elementary education educator*
Myers, Shelley Lynn *elementary education educator*
Nader, Suzanne Nora Beurer *elementary education educator*
Nelson, Patricia Lynn *early childhood educator*
Neunzig, Carolyn Miller *elementary, middle and high school educator*
Newton, Janna Sue *elementary education educator*
Nisbett, Wilma Constance *elementary education educator*
Nobles, Darlene Adele *elementary education educator*
Nordyke, Robyn Lee *primary school educator*
O'Brien-Crothers, Janice Louise *elementary education educator*
O'Driscoll, Marilyn Lutz *elementary school educator*
Ofstad, Evelyn Larsen Boyl *retired primary school educator, radio announcer, video producer*
Oglesby, Jerri Burdette *elementary education educator*
Oldham, Elaine Dorothea *retired elementary and middle school educator*
Olive, Alicia Norma Johnson *retired elementary school educator*
Otwell, Donna Sharon *history educator*

Owens, Sue Gaston *middle school educator*
Parrish, Alma Ellis *elementary school educator*
Peacock, Janie Joan *retired elementary school educator*
Peters, Patricia L. *elementary education educator*
Pippin, James Adrian, Jr., *middle school educator*
Plaisted, Carole Anne *elementary education educator*
Plants, Walter Dale *retired elementary school educator, minister*
Poinsett-White, Sadie Ruth *retired elementary education educator*
Pope, Sarah Ann *retired elementary education educator*
Post, Rose Elizabeth *retired elementary education educator*
Profaizer, Josephine E. *elementary education educator*
Quast, Pearl Elizabeth Kolb *retired elementary school educator*
Ranada, Rose Marie *retired elementary education educator*
Ranks, Anne Elizabeth *retired elementary and secondary education educator*
Reece, Geraldine Maxine *elementary education educator*
Reese, Madge Eleanor Read *elementary education educator*
Regenauer, Carol McCurdy *elementary education educator, consultant*
Reinalda, David Anthony *elementary education educator*
Reinertsen, Gloria May *elementary education educator*
Reynolds, Betty Ann *elementary education educator*
Rhodes, Anna Margaret *retired elementary school educator and school system administrator*
Rhodes, Judith Kay *elementary education educator*
Rice-Dietrich, Therese Ann *elementary education educator*
Rich, Cynthia Gay *elementary education educator*
Richardson, Sandra Lorraine *retired elementary school educator*
Rickard, Carolyn Lucille *retired elementary school educator*
Riggs, Sonya Woicinski *elementary education educator*
Robertson, Mary Virginia *retired elementary education educator*
Robles, Rosalie Miranda *elementary education educator*
Robotin, Barbara Zielinski *elementary school educator*
Rodgers, Geraldine Ellen *retired elementary school educator*
Rogers, Olivia Johnson *elementary school counselor*
Romick, Joyce Trudeau *elementary school educator*
Roth, Evelyn Austin *retired elementary school educator*
Roth, Michelle Lynn *computer educator*
Roth, Sharon A. *elementary school educator, consultant*
Ryan, Ellen Marie *elementary education and gifted education educator*
Said, Phyllis Dianne *elementary school educator*
Sanders, Trisha Lynn *middle school educator*
Sannito, Judith Ann *elementary education educator*
Savercool, Susan Elisabeth *elementary school educator*
Scaffidi-Wilhelm, Gloria Angelamarie *elementary education educator*
Schleede, Lori Geraine *primary education educator*
Schlesinger, Carole Lynn *elementary education educator*
Schmidt, Carolyn Lea *elementary school educator*
Schmitt, Phyllis Mary *elementary education educator*
Schneider, Carolyn Alice Brauch *elementary education educator*
Schneider, Mary Louise *retired elementary education educator*
Shadler, Barbara Gordon *reading specialist*
Sheerin, Marilyn Rita *elementary school educator*
Shell, Mary Belinda Johnson *elementary school educator*
Shepard, Anna Richardson *elementary educator, tutoring company executive*
Smalls, Peggy Ann *educational consultant, retired elementary educator*
Smith, Ann Elizabeth *elementary school educator*
Smith, Debbie Ilee Randall *elementary school educator*
Smith, Martha Virginia Barnes *retired elementary school educator*
Smith, Melanie Maxted *secondary education educator*
Smith, Patricia Ann Hoehn *elementary school educator, music educator*
Sneed, Alberta Neal *retired elementary education educator*
Snyder, Martha Jane *elementary school educator, consultant*
Sockey, Felicia Willene *elementary school educator*
Solloway, Mary Elise *elementary educator*
Spoor, Kathrine Sue *elementary education educator*
Starnes, Susan Smith *elementary education educator*
Starr, Ila Mae *elementary school educator*
Stefanelli, Lisa Eileen *elementary education educator*
Stokely, Joan Barbara *retired elementary school educator*
Stoll, Sarah May Reichert *elementary school educator*
Sugnet, Linda A'Brunzo *elementary education educator*
Sullivan, Marissa M. *elementary school educator*
Surber, Regina Brammell *early childhood education educator, administrator*
Svaldi, Kathleen Alice *elementary education educator*
Sweezy, Melanie Elizabeth *elementary school educator*
Talbot, Kathleen Mary *elementary education educator*
Terpening, Alice Margaret *elementary school educator*
Therrien, Anita Aurore *elementary school educator*
Thomas, Sharyn Lee *elementary education educator*
Thomson, Mabel Amelia *retired elementary school educator*
Timmons, Sharon L. *retired elementary education educator*
Tobias, Tom, Jr., *retired elementary school educator*
Travis, Laura Rose *elementary education educator*
Trelfa, Eugenia Marie *elementary school educator*
Tucker, Ruth M. *elementary education educator*
Tudor, Mary Louise Drummond *retired elementary school educator*
Vallat, Louise Marie *elementary school educator, poet*
Vandevender, Barbara Jewell *elementary education educator, farmer*
Verbish, Deborah Louise *elementary school educator*
Vogel, Ruth Anne *retired elementary school educator*
Vorous, Margaret Estelle *primary, secondary and middle school educator*
Vorous, Patricia Ann Marie *elementary school educator*
Wadley, Cynthia Ann (Cynde) *elementary school educator*
Wagner, Marilyn Faith *retired elementary school educator*
Wagner-Serwin, Dorothy Elizabeth *elementary education educator*
Watson, Marilyn Kaye *elementary education educator*
Webb, Beverly A. *elementary and secondary education educator*
Weiss, Elinor *elementary education educator*
Wendt, Marilynn Suzann *elementary school educator, principal*
Wilce, Joan Hubbell *elementary education educator*
Williams, Elaine Engster *primary education educator*
Wilson, Cheryl Yvonne *elementary school educator, secondary school educator*
Wimmer, Kathryn *retired elementary school educator*
Witt, Judith Anne *elementary education educator*
Wolfe, Elizabeth Anne *elementary education educator*
Woodruff, Mary Brennan *elementary education educator*
Woolworth, Susan Valk *primary school educator*
Worrell, Betty Cartrette *elementary school educator*
Wright, Kathi Brown *elementary educator*
Wright, Ruth P. *primary education educator, photographer, writer*
Wyman, Viola Bousquet *elementary educator*
Wymer, Barbara Sue *elementary educator*
Yates, Margery Gordon *elementary education educator*
Young, Margaret Chong *elementary education educator*
Young, Susan Eileen *elementary education educator*
Zahner, Dorothy Simkin *elementary education educator*
Zeilinger, Elna Rae *elementary educator, gifted-talented education educator*
Zimmerman, Victoria Annmarie *elementary education educator, administrator*

PRIVATE/PAROCHIAL SCHOOL EDUCATION

UNITED STATES

CALIFORNIA

Anaheim
Surprenant, Faith Elsie *parochial school educator*

Northridge
Dubin, Susan Helen *private school educator, storyteller*

Ojai
Shagam, Marvin Hückel-Berri *private school educator*

Temecula
Palafox, Mari Lee *private school educator*

COLORADO

Denver
Kinney, Dick Joseph *private school educator, coach*

CONNECTICUT

Fairfield
Howell, Karen Jane *private school educator*

Hartford
Brown, Nora M. *private school educator*

Naugatuck
Connolly, Mary Christine *parochial school educator*

DELAWARE

Hockessin
Alexander, Michele Yermack *private school educator*

Newark
Pozzi, Debra Elizabeth *private school art educator*

DISTRICT OF COLUMBIA

Washington
Curtis, Martha Louise *parochial school social studies educator, administrator*
Kyhos, M. Gaither Galleher *private school educator*

FLORIDA

Lecanto
Mathia, Mary Loyola *parochial school educator, nun*

Plantation
Giese, Sally Jean *parochial school educator*

Tampa
Hoover, Betty-Bruce Howard *private school educator*

GEORGIA

College Park
Ferguson, Wendell *private school educator*

Roswell
Thacker, Janice Dee *parochial school art educator*

Uvalda
Hierholzer, Connie McArthur *parochial school educator*

ILLINOIS

Chicago
Iwanski, Mary *parochial school educator*
O'Rourke, Suzan Marie *secondary education educator*

Orland Park
Dahlberg, Patricia Lee *parochial school educator*

KANSAS

Coffeyville
Brittain, Sister Janelle Ann *parochial school educator*

LOUISIANA

Natchitoches
Wolfe, George Cropper *retired private school educator, artist, writer*

MAINE

Cumberland Center
Thompson, Deborah Carpenter *private school educator*

MARYLAND

Baltimore
Ivey, Christyne Gloria *private school administrator*
Tamplin, Mary Ranke *secondary education educator*

Kensington
Miles, Eileen Fitz *private school educator*

MINNESOTA

New Prague
Deutsch, Judith Marie *elementary education educator*

MISSOURI

Saint Louis
Truitt, William Harvey *private school educator*

NEBRASKA

Daykin
Schoenbeck, Audrey Kay *parochial school educator*

NEW JERSEY

Edison
Renzulli, Mary Ann *parochial education educator*

Lakewood
Rodgers, Dianna Sue *private school educator*

Montclair
Coffin, Charlsa Lee *director, writer, artist*

NEW YORK

Bronx
Francois, Joseph Rufus *parochial school educator*

Brooklyn
Weaver, Jane Marie *parochial school educator*

Glendale
Stahl, Diane Irene *parochial school educator*

Laurelton
Reid Figueroa, Marcella Inez *educator, minister*

New York
Oreskes, Susan *private school educator*

Old Westbury
Christofides, Fotine *parochial school educator*

Seaford
Moore, Sister Mary Francis *parochial school educator*

White Plains
Manzione, Arthur P. *parochial schools administrator*

NORTH CAROLINA

Carrboro
Generous, William Thomas, Jr., (Tom Generous) *educator, coach*

High Point
Clark, Carol Ruth Jones *secondary education educator*

OHIO

Cincinnati
Backherms, Kathryn Anne *parochial school educator*

OKLAHOMA

Oklahoma City
Waldo, Catherine Ruth *private school educator*

PENNSYLVANIA

Gettysburg
Dixon, Virginia Julia *parochial school computers educator*

Greensburg
Haigh, Cindy Lou *private/parochial school physical education educator*

Langhorne
Koach, Lynne M. *private school educator*

Lower Burrell
Rose, Robert Henry *arts education administrator*

Mc Keesport
Regina, Marie Antoinette *parochial school educator*

Merion Station
Pearcy, Lee Theron *secondary education educator, writer*

Norristown
Nelson, Dawn Marie *middle school language arts educator*

Pittsburgh
Dobos, Sister Marion *parochial school educator*

Scottdale
Kropff, Patricia Ann *private school educator*

TENNESSEE

Columbia
Kirk, Deborah Dianne *private school educator, curriculum developer*

Johnson City
Roark, Edith Humphreys *private school language arts educator, reading specialist*

Knoxville
Mankel, Francis Xavier *former principal, priest*

Sewanee
Cameron, Douglas Winston *parochial education educator, writer*

Tullahoma
Kaczorek, Sharon Caps *parochial school educator*

PRIVATE/PAROCHIAL SCHOOL EDUCATION

TEXAS

Fort Worth
Von Rosenberg, Gary Marcus, Jr., *parochial school educator*

Galveston
Heins, Sister Mary Frances *private school educator, nun*

Harlingen
Perez, Mary Angelica *bilingual specialist, educational administrator*

VIRGINIA

Mc Lean
Salopek, Jennifer Jackson *private/parochial school administrator*

Norfolk
Sebren, Lucille Griggs *retired private school educator*

WISCONSIN

Mequon
Bell, Scott William *private school educator, principal*

TERRITORIES OF THE UNITED STATES

PUERTO RICO

Bayamon
Bonilla, Daisy Rose *parochial school English language educator*

Caguas
Ortiz, Víctor Raúl *parochial school educator*

VIRGIN ISLANDS

Charlotte Amalie
Parker, Diana Marie *parochial school educator, administrator*

ADDRESS UNPUBLISHED

Duff, Sheryl Kay *parochial school educator*
Greco, Joseph M *parochial school educator*
Hammond, Vernon Francis *school administrator*
Profit, Pamela Ann *middle school educator*
Root, Janet Greenberg *private school educator*
Simones, Marie Dolorosa *parochial school educator, nun*
Veneziano, David Alexander *parochial school educator*
White, Leslie Miles *parochial school educator*

SCHOOL ADMINISTRATION

UNITED STATES

ALABAMA

Birmingham
Branham, Grady Eugene *principal*
Left, Joan Marilyn *principal*

Elberta
Raley, Hope Miller *educational administrator*

Mobile
Copeland, Lewis *principal*
Wright, John Harrison, Jr., *retired headmaster*

Rainsville
Boland, Felicia Carol *principal*

Talladega
Paris, Virginia Hall (Ginger Paris) *principal*

ALASKA

Fairbanks
Doran, Timothy Patrick *educational administrator*

ARIZONA

Glendale
Avila, Lidia D. *principal*

Globe
Scholl, Glen *principal*

Green Valley
Carpenter, John Everett *retired principal, educational consultant*

Mesa
Philbrick, Douglas Robert *principal, librarian, educator, mental health professional*
Young, Daniel Edwin *principal*

Page
Hart, Marian Griffith *retired reading educator*

Phoenix
Daggett, Barbara Dalicandro *secondary education director*
Puchi, Linda Carol *elementary school principal*

Scottsdale
Cianfarano, Sam Anthony, Jr., *principal, educator*

Tempe
Mayer, Elizabeth Billmire *educational administrator*

Tucson
Brousseau, Georgia Cole *school principal*
Gallagher, Rosanna Bostick *elementary educator, administrator*
Larson, L. Jean *educational administrator*

ARKANSAS

Booneville
Dyer, V. Jeffrey *educational administrator*

Clinton
Gammill, Stephen Mark *school administrator*

Little Rock
O'Neal, Nell Self *retired principal*

Newark
Webb, Mary Ann *principal*

Sherwood
Vogler, Diane Clark *elementary school principal*

Springdale
Hill, Peggy Sue *principal*

West Helena
Ross, Donna Faye *educational administrator*

CALIFORNIA

Arcadia
Meysenburg, Mary Ann *principal*

Auberry
Reberg, Rosalie *principal*

Baldwin Park
Lopez-Reid, Norma Alicia *elementary school prinicpal*

Beverly Hills
Leeds, Margaret Ann *assistant principal*

Calabasas
Dworkoski, Robert John *headmaster*

Carlsbad
Clark, Violet Cathrine *retired school administrator, volunteer*

Carmichael
Carey, Richard Gwynn *principal*

Chula Vista
Hanson, Eileen *principal*
Steele, Nancy Eden Rogers *nonprofit corporation executive, former educator*

Culver City
Maxwell-Brogdon, Florence Morency *school administrator, educational adviser*

Encino
O'Riley, Karen E. *principal*

Fresno
Simuns, Judith Mata *elementary school vice-principal*

Gustine
Larsen, Karen Lynn *principal*

La Verne
Coray, Jeffrey Warren *assistant principal, instructor*

Lakewood
Kulesza, Carol May *principal, elementary school educator*

Long Beach
Duke, Phyllis Louise Kellogg Henry *school administrator, management consultant*

Los Angeles
Crede, Carol Ann Johnson *principal*
Lucente, Rosemary Dolores *retired educational administrator, consultant*
Steinberg, Warren Linnington *school principal*

Mill Valley
Maubert, Jacques Claude *retired school superintendent*

Monterey
Oder, Broeck Newton *school emergency management consultant*

Montrose
Zawacki, Gail Marie *religious studies educator, school principal*

Palm Desert
Baxter, Betty Carpenter *educational administrator*

Palm Springs
Aikens, Donald Thomas *educational administrator, consultant*

Poway
Shippey, Lyn *reading center director*

Ramona
Van Zant, Susan Lucille *principal*

Red Bluff
Kennedy, James William, Jr., (Sarge Kennedy) *special education administrator, consultant*

Redondo Beach
Sims, Dayla Dianne *elementary school principal*

Riverside
Rucker-Hughes, Waudieur Elizabeth *educator*

Rolling Hills Estates
Rarewala, Kathleen Agnes Berti *educational director*

Rosemead
Hansen, Robert Dennis *educational administrator*

Salinas
Trujillo, Michael Joseph *elementary school principal*

San Diego
James, Helen Foster *education director*
Maurer, Lawrence Michael *acting school administrator, educator*
McBrayer, Sandra L. *educational director, homeless outreach educator*

San Jose
Charest, Gabrielle Marya *educational administrator*
Collett, Jennie *principal*
Meegan, Brother Gary Vincent *school administrator, music educator*
Ridgley, Frances Aroc *principal*

San Leandro
Loeffler, Garry Antone *principal, municipal official*

San Lorenzo
Glenn, Jerome T. *secondary school principal*

San Mateo
Mark, Lillian Gee *educational administrator*

Stockton
Hitchcock, Susan Y. *school administrator, city council member*

Torrance
Dickerson, Joe Bernard *principal, educator*

Ventura
McElroy, Charlotte Ann *principal*
Williamson, John Henry, III, *school administrator*

Watsonville
Desimone, Richard Louis *principal*

COLORADO

Aurora
Kreisman, Dea Ann *principal*

Broomfield
Palmreuter, Kenneth Richard Louis *principal*

Denver
Gibson, Elisabeth Jane *retired principal*
Graham, Judith Kay *principal*
Tillapaugh, Thomas Allan *school administrator*

Englewood
Smith, Kathleen Dana *principal, consultant*

Grand Junction
Bergen, Virginia Louise *principal, language arts educator*
Moberly, Linden Emery *educational administrator*

Hotchkiss
Perry, Jeanne Elyce *principal*

Monte Vista
Gabaldon, Paul James *high school principal*
Tillman, John Lee *principal*

CONNECTICUT

Branford
Milgram, Richard Myron *music school administrator*

Brookfield
Eberhard Asch, Theresa J. *retired assistant principal*

East Hampton
Huelsmann, Richard Thaddeus *educator*

Farmington
Karlsrud, Gary Michael *administrator, consultant*

Glastonbury
Hatch, D. Patricia P. *principal*

Manchester
Mulhollen, Michael Edward *education director*

New Haven
Cappelli, Mary Antoinette *principal*

Ridgefield
Lindsay, Dianna Marie *educational administrator*

Trumbull
Nevins, Lyn (Carolyn A. Nevins) *educational supervisor, trainer, consultant*

Wolcott
Farrell, Brian E. *special education supervisor*
Gerace, Robert F. *secondary school principal*

DELAWARE

Bear
McLain, William Tome *principal, educator*

Lewes
Lane, William Harry, Jr., *principal*

DISTRICT OF COLUMBIA

Washington
Burgin, Walter Hotchkiss, Jr., *educational administrator*
Dixon, Michel L. *educational administrator*
Martas, Julia Ann *special education administrator*
Tainatonga, Rosie R. *director*
Thompson, Bernida Lamerle *principal, consultant, educator*

FLORIDA

Bell
Durham, Guinevere McCabe *educational administrator, writer, consultant*

Belle Glade
Grear, Effie Carter *educational administrator*

Boca Raton
Bittner, Barbara Newman *educational administrator*
Tennies, Robert Hunter *headmaster*

Boynton Beach
Costa, Terry Ann *principal*
Cotton, John Pierce *principal*

Cape Coral
Lane, William C., Jr., *principal*

Clearwater
Youngberg, Robert Stanley *principal, consultant*

Edgewater
Kennedy, Mary Patt *principal*

Fort Lauderdale
Ginn, Vera Walker *director*
Gonsher, Wendy *educational administrator*

Fort Myers
Pouliot, Assunta Gallucci *retired business school owner and director, consultant*
Tyrer, John Lloyd *retired headmaster*

Gainesville
Gets, Lispbeth Ella *educational administrator*

Goulds
Cooper, Kenneth Stanley *principal, educator, finance company executive*

Jacksonville
Lichtward, Fred *headmaster*

Jupiter
McGee, Lynne Kalavsky *principal*

Kissimmee
Kandrac, Jo Ann Marie *school administrator*

Largo
Gall, Keith M. *director*

Marco Island
Henry, Sally *assistant principal*

Miami
Carbia, Jose Eliseo *elementary school principal, educator*
Halberg, F. David *principal*
Lopez, Maria Elena Chelala *principal, educator*
Young, Freddie Gilliam *educational administrator*

Miramar
Stephens, Sallie L. *retired assistant principal, commissioner*

Oak Hill
Smith, Mary Frances *school administrator*

Orlando
Qadri, Yasmeen *educational administrator, consultant*

Panama City
Shumate, Gloria Jones *retired education administrator*

Pensacola Beach
Longacre, Linda S. *school administrator*

Saint Augustine
Horn, Patricia Solomon *technology coordinator*

PROFESSIONAL INDEX — SCHOOL ADMINISTRATION

Sanford
Collins, Connie Woods *educational administrator*

Tallahassee
Daniels, Irish C. *principal*

Tampa
Castellano, Sandra Lorrain *principal*

West Palm Beach
Russell, Joyce Weber *principal*

GEORGIA

Athens
Cole, David Akinola *educational administrator, educator*

Atlanta
Bailey, Mary Jolley *eucational administrator*
Cleghorn, Gwendolyn Michael *principal, educator*
Lee-Willingham, Anita Marie *school system liaison*

Bonaire
Cherry, Carol Lynn *principal*

Cartersville
Wheeler, Susie Weems *retired educator*

Douglas
Pugh, Joye Jeffries *educational administrator*

Franklin
Lipham, William Patrick *principal, educator*

Gainesville
Martin, James Harbert *school administrator, retired Air Force officer*

Hahira
Webb, Lyndal Miller *principal*

Harlem
Lewis, Ellen Clancy *assistant principal*

Madison
Allen, Betty Jean *assistant principal*

Nahunta
Thrift, Sharron Woodard *director*

Norcross
Wingate, Thomas Marie Joseph *assistant headmaster*

Pembroke
Butler, Janet Babington *assistant principal*

Rome
Morgan, Sylvia Denise (Mrs. Harold Morgan) *school administrator, poet*

Roswell
Hopping, Janet Melinda *principal*

Thomson
Sapough, Roy Sumner, Jr., *educational administrator*

White
Curry, James Linton, Jr., *school administrator*

HAWAII

Honolulu
Hee, Vivian Sanae Mitsuda *principal*

Waialua
Krause-Diaz, Mary Jean *educational administrator*

IDAHO

Mccall
Erekson, Laurie Ida *school administrator*

ILLINOIS

Calumet City
Palagi, Robert Gene *college administrator*

Champaign
Gomez, Terrine *school director*

Chicago
Anderson, Rudolph Valentino, Jr., *principal*
Carlson, Karen Glinert *principal*
Coy, Patricia Ann *special education director, consultant*
Culverwell, Rosemary Jean *principal, elementary education educator*
Esenberg, Robert Thomas *principal*
Felton, Cynthia *educational administrator*
Hernandez, Flavia *bilingual school principal*
Howell, Lynnette *elementary school principal*
Jordan, Mark D. *school administrator*
Kloc, Emily Alvina *retired elementary school principal*
Martin, Barbara Jean *elementary school principal*
Mosley, Elaine Christian Savage *principal, chief education officer, consultant*
Perry, Edna Burrell *retired elementary school principal*
Wooten-Bryant, Helen Catherine *principal*

Deerfield
Meyer, Mara Ellice *special education consultant, principal*

Des Plaines
Coburn, James LeRoy *educational administrator*

Downers Grove
Ward, William Allen *principal, district curriculum coordinator*

East Alton
McGill, Clyde Woodrow *principal*

Edwardsville
Kovarik, M. Leora *elementary principal*

Elgin
Welu, Suzanne Marie *special education administrator*

Evanston
Krugly, Andrew *elementary school principal*
Musiala, Rosalie *principal, educator*

Frankfort
Shultz, Kenneth Lowell *athletic director*

Grayslake
Choice, Priscilla Kathryn Means (Penny Choice) *educational director, international consultant*

Harwood Heights
O'Mara, Kevin Joseph *principal*

Joliet
Scott, Linda Ann *principal, elementary education educator*

Kankakee
Peters-Lambert, Betty A. *assistant principal*

Kildeer
Muffoletto, Mary Lu *retired school program director, consultant, editor*

Lake Forest
Bransfield, Joan *principal*
DuBose, Cornelius Bates *educational director*

Lansing
Helming, Scott Bryon *principal*

Lincolnshire
Martin, John Driscoll *school administrator*

Macon
Gatchel, Dennis LeRoy *assistant principal*

Maywood
Libka, Robert John *educational director, consultant*

Midlothian
Cagala, M. Therese *assistant principal*

Mount Carmel
Weir, Darlene *principal*

Mundelein
Carroll, Robert C. *principal*

Naperville
Murphy, Paul Irwin *special education administrator*

Norridge
Karlin, Bernard Richard *retired educational administrator*

North Chicago
Johnson, Lucille Merle Brown *elementary school principal*

O Fallon
Grimmer, Dennis L. *principal*

Oak Brook
Baar, John Greenfield, II, *assistant principal*

Oakland
Greenwood, Sheila Lynn *principal, coach*

Ottawa
Benning, Joseph Raymond *principal*

Palatine
Wallace, Marilyn Jean *academic director*

Peoria
Wortham, Maxine Alline *early childhood education executive director*

Rockford
Matthews, Katherine Jean *principal*

Rockton
Cunningham, Judy Evalyn *elementary school administrator, educator*

Wheaton
Jones, Larry Dee *principal*

Winnetka
Schwartz, Daniel Joel *education administrator*

Zion
Baule, Steven Michael *principal*

INDIANA

Brownsburg
Doss, Richard *principal*

Carmel
Brooks, Patricia Scott *principal*

Cloverdale
Schwartz, Susan Lynn Hill *principal*

Evansville
Schultz, John Edward *principal*

Indianapolis
Brash, Susan Kay *principal*
Cilella, Mary Winifred *director*
Galbraith, Bruce W. *educational administrator*
Stockard, Robert Thomas *secondary school administrator*
Wynn, Sherri Lorraine *educational administrator*

Jamestown
Waymire, John Thomas *principal*

Kokomo
Stevens, Rebecca Sue *retired religious education administrator*

Monticello
McTaggart, Patrick William *principal*

Pendleton
Phenis-Bourke, Nancy Sue *educational administrator*

IOWA

Cedar Rapids
Plagman, Ralph *principal*
Williams, Colin Dale *principal*

Des Moines
Cordaro, Joseph Frank *school principal*

Hastings
Schumacher, Jeffrey David *principal*

Johnston
Henkenius, Cheryl Greiman *educational administrator*

Waterloo
Kober, Arletta Refshauge (Mrs. Kay L. Kober) *supervisor*

KANSAS

Auburn
Good, Martha Gail *educational administrator*

Colby
Sharp, Glenn (Skip Sharp) *college administrator*

Dodge City
Sapp, Nancy L. *educational administrator*

Effingham
Figgs, Linda Sue *educational administrator*

Emporia
Torrens, Peggy Jean *technical school coordinator*

Goddard
Wasinger, Michaelita Jean *principal, educator*

Hutchinson
Hope, Linda Ruth *principal*

Mulvane
George, Donald Richard *retired principal*

Shawnee Mission
Koster-Peterson, Lois Mae *educational administrator*

Ulysses
Palmer, Barbara Jean *special education administrator*

KENTUCKY

Fort Mitchell
McQueen, Pamela *principal*

Owensboro
Gray, Arthur Michael *elementary principal*

Pleasureville
Spears, Robert Keith *principal*

LOUISIANA

Baton Rouge
Voorhies, Melinda J(acque) *principal*
Warner, Walter John *educational administrator*

Denham Springs
Perkins, Arthur Lee, Sr., *retired principal, real estate broker, insurance agent*

Houma
Lemoine, Pamela Allyson *principal*

Independence
Vaccaro, Nick Anthony *principal*

Mansfield
Smelley, Joyce Marie *special education supervisor*

Metairie
Buetow, Paul Elmer *principal*
Gennaro, Glenn Joseph *principal*
Johnson, Beth Michael *school administrator*
Piper, Claudia Rosemary *assistant principal*

Monroe
Jones, Emma Jean *principal*

New Orleans
Falkner, David A. *principal, educator*
Hassenboehler, Donalyn *principal*
McMahon, Maeve *middle school administrator*
Recasner, Tony *director*
Reddix, Rowena Pinkie *retired elementary school principal*

Pride
Jones, LaCinda *assistant principal*

Saint Francisville
Edwards, Joyce Ann *principal*

Shreveport
Prothro, Marilyn Smith *assistant principal*

Westwego
Chimento, Cindy Brown *principal*

Zachary
Hull, Donnie Faye *special education director, educator*

MAINE

Caribou
Belanger, Madeline *principal*
McElwain, Franklin Roy *educational administrator*

Millinocket
Steeves, Eric William *school administrator*

MARYLAND

Baltimore
Adams, Gail Jackson *educational administrator*
Allen, Elizabeth Jean Jackson *associate headmaster, language arts specialist, educator*
Buser, Carolyn Elizabeth *correctional education administrator*
Hall, Merrill Souel, III, *head master*
Johnson, Flora Gilchrist *school principal*
Nwofor, Ambrose Onyegbule *vocational assessment evaluator*
Reid, Lauretta Glasper *retired principal*

Bel Air
Hagenbuch, Stephen Lee *principal*

Bethesda
Lasinski, Kathleen Zellmer *elementary principal*

Cumberland
Jancuk, Kathleen Frances *educational administrator*

Eldersburg
Bastress, Robert Lewis *principal*

Fort Washington
Johns, Christine Michele *elementary school principal*

Hagerstown
Myers, Robert True *educational administrator*
Palmisano, Sister Maria Goretti *principal*

Hyattsville
Moylan, John L. *secondary school principal*
Williams, Gladys Tucker *elementary school principal*

La Plata
Merrick, Barbara Barnhart *school administrator*

Prince Frederick
Karol, Victoria Diane *educational administrator*

Salisbury
Wright, Melva Polk *school administrator*

Severna Park
Picken, Edith Daryl *school administrator*

Silver Spring
Jackson, Mary Jane McHale Flickinger *principal*

Takoma Park
Goode, Anne *early childhood education administrator*

Towson
Hoch, David Allen *athletic director*

MASSACHUSETTS

Andover
Faris, Anne Marie *secondary education dean*

Auburn
DeFrino, Anthony M. *middle school administrator*

Boston
Blaine, Henri Remi *cosmetology school administrator*
DiFranza, Virginia *principal*
Meier, Deborah *principal*
Yarborough, Nellie Constance *principal, minister*

Housatonic
Charpentier, Gail Wigutow *private school executive director*

Indian Orchard
Daley, Veta Adassa *educational administrator*

Marlborough
Pronovost, Stephen H. *principal*

New Bedford
Stankiewicz, Angela L. *principal elementary school*

Newton
Quarcoo, Marilynne Smith *principal*

Newton Centre
Best, Paul Allen *education executive*

Quincy
Short, Janet Marie *principal*

Salem
LaValley, Thomas Richard *principal*

Springfield
Flink, Charles Lawrence *education director*
Mantoni, Philip Joseph *principal*
Vella, Sandra Rachael *principal*

Westford
Scuzzarella, Carla Ann *dean*

Worcester
Sinkis, Deborah Mary *principal*

MICHIGAN

Bloomfield Hills
Johnson, Carol J. *principal*

Brighton
Jensen, Baiba *principal*

Clarkston
Mousseau, Doris Naomi Barton *retired elementary school principal*

Clinton Township
Syropoulos, Mike *retired school system director*

Commerce Township
Boynton, Irvin Parker *retired educational administrator*

Detroit
Ayala, Rowena Winifred *retired principal*
Mitchell, Connie *director*

Fennville
Kelley, Marie Elaine *retired director*

Flint
Duckett, Bernadine Johnal *retired elementary principal*
Simmons, Robert Randolph *principal*

Mount Pleasant
Lippert, Robert J. *administrator and culinary arts educator, consultant*

Oak Park
Beyerlein, Susan Carol *educational administrator*

Portage
Rainey, John Mark *administrator*

Rockford
Duzan, Dee *elementary school principal*

Saint Clair Shores
Skoney, Sophie Essa *educational administrator*

Sterling Heights
Walby, Sandra Lee *principal*

Troy
Feldkamp, James Norbert *athletics, physical education director*

Walled Lake
Peal, Christopher John *educational administrator*

Westland
Mullinix, Barbara Jean *special services director*

MINNESOTA

Minneapolis
Griffin, Shannon *middle school principal*

Owatonna
Larson, Diane LaVerne Kusler *principal*

MISSISSIPPI

Columbus
Fant, Joseph Lewis, III, *academic administrator, retired army officer*

Jackson
Summers, Tracy Yvonne *assistant principal*

Rolling Fork
Kyzar, Ollie Jeanette *assistant principal*

MISSOURI

Bronaugh
Phillips, Patricia Anna *principal, educator*

Columbia
Wheeler, Otis V., Jr., *public school principal*

Florissant
Barnes, Rebecca Marie *assistant principal*

Bartlett, Robert James *principal*
Earle, James Anthony *education consultant*

High Ridge
Cowell, Robert Samuel *school principal*

Independence
Starks, Carol Elizabeth *retired principal*

Kansas City
Doyle, Wendell E. *retired band director, educator*
Gibbons, Dona Lee *principal*
Maxwell, Delores Young *elementary school principal*
Stubbs, Marilyn Kay *education administrator*

Saint Louis
Gilligan, Sandra Kaye *private school director*
O'Neill, Sheila *principal*

Seymour
Wallace, Dorothy Alene *special education administrator*

Springfield
Allcorn, Terry Alan *principal, educator*
Huffman, Kevin Dale *principal*

MONTANA

Billings
Evans, Judith Christien Lunbeck *elementary school principal*

Victor
Stewart, JoAnne *director*

NEBRASKA

Omaha
Kolowski, Richard L. *principal*

NEVADA

Las Vegas
Gerye, Robert Allen *secondary school administrator*
Joyce, Phyllis Norma *educational administrator*
Russo, Angela Brown *assistant principal*

Reno
Cathey-Gibson, Sharon Sue Rinn *school principal, college administrator*
Clarke, Janice Cessna *principal*

NEW HAMPSHIRE

Hudson
Blanchard, Glenn Robert *principal*

Lyman
Kaplan, Frada M. *retired principal, special education educator*

Nashua
Tremblay, Mary Denise *administrator, educator*

Walpole
Harris, Grant Warren *principal*

Wilton
Potter, Robert Wallace, Jr., *assistant principal, educator*

NEW JERSEY

Asbury Park
Avella, John Thomas *educational administrator*

Bloomfield
Rivera, Ruth Ellen *special services director*

Camden
Smith, Cherylynne Diane *middle school principal*

Clifton
Haefeli, Lillian Reardon *school administrator*

Clinton
Beebe, Jane Gertrude Albright *headmaster*

Englishtown
Jones, Sarah Lucille *supervisor, consultant*

Farmingdale
DiDonato, Diane Carmen *principal*

Freehold
Foster, Delores Jackson *retired elementary school principal*

Frenchtown
Fogelson, Brian David *educational administrator*

Glen Rock
Keenaghan, Patricia Anne *principal, educator*

Hackensack
Cicchelli, Joseph Vincent *principal*

Hackettstown
Sheninger, Arthur Wayne *retired principal*

Hammonton
Ranere, Barbara Phylis *elementary principal*

Hillsborough
Weicksel, Charlene Marie *principal*

Jersey City
Barrett, Kathleen Anne *assistant principal*

Lincroft
Pollock, William John *secondary school administrator*

Livingston
Cosmas, Stella Anatolitou *principal*

Monroe Township
Barberi, Lynn Claire Fenelli *principal*

New Brunswick
Cawley, Sister Maureen Ann *school principal*

Pleasantville
Jenkins-Smith, Effie Sharon *educational administrator*

Pomona
Gasbarro, Norman John, Jr., *educational administrator*

Randolph
Helfant, Mariann Theresa *school administrator*

Toms River
Dougherty, John Kevin *secondary school administrator*

NEW MEXICO

Albuquerque
Bass, Martha Postlethwaite *high school principal*

Artesia
Flores, Sylvia A. *principal*

Aztec
Scandary, Robert Glenn *administrator*

Gallup
Maikowski, Thomas Robert *educational director, priest*

Rio Rancho
Baehr, Catherine Marie *principal*

Smith Lake
Hansen, Harold B., Jr., *principal*

NEW YORK

Amsterdam
Hoffman, James David *secondary instruction and personnel director*

Bronx
Cutié, David Alan *school principal*

Brooklyn
Edelstein, Brenda *school administrator*
Meade, Dorothy Winifred *retired educational administrator*
Wapner, Myrna *retired principal*
Williams, Gloria M. *assistant principal*

Buffalo
Singletary, James, Jr., *school board administrator*

East Aurora
Weidemann, Julia Clark *retired principal, educator*

Elmont
Cowan, Dennis Lloyd *educational administrator*

Garden City
Okulski, John Allen *principal*

Howard Beach
Watnick, Rochelle *principal*

Jamaica
Davis-Jerome, Eileen George *principal, educational consultant*
Jackson, Sheila Bernice *principal*
Mangru, Basdeo *secondary education educator*

New York
Howard, David *educational administrator*
Kozlowski, Cheryl M. *principal*
Page, Tammy *assistant principal*
Palmeri, Marlaina *school executive*
Pigott, Irina Vsevolodovna *educational administrator*
Tinker, Thomas Eaton *headmaster*

Newburgh
Irish, Robert Michael *principal*
Joyce, Mary Ann *principal*
Weiss, Barry Ronald *education administrator*

Rochester
Scalise, Francis Allen *admnstrator, consultant*

Saratoga Springs
Wallner, Ludwig John *principal*

Smithtown
Pelcyger, Iran *retired principal*

Southold
Butz, Mary *principal*

Staten Island
Brady, Christine Ellen *education coordinator*
Greco, Donna *educational administrator*

Valatie
Opela, Marian Meade *principal, consultant*

West Seneca
Peters, Barbara Agnes *principal*

NORTH CAROLINA

Asheville
Sgro, Beverly Huston *day school administrator, educator, state official*

Charlotte
Clark, Ann Blakeney *educational administrator*

Clyde
Rogers, Frances Nichols *assistant principal*

Cramerton
Renfro, Anna Sturgis *principal*

Faison
Bell, Ruby Aycock *educational administrator*

Greensboro
McCauley, Alfreda Ellis *elementary school principal*

New Bern
Gilbert, Nan Varley *retired principal*

Rosman
Dutton, Sharon Gail *retired elementary school educator*

Salisbury
Hall, Telka Mowery Elium *retired educational administrator*

Turkey
Chavious, Marian Delorese *assistant principal*

Weldon
Stephenson, Mary U. *principal, educational administrator*

Winston Salem
Hitch, Chris Dooley *principal*

NORTH DAKOTA

Bismarck
Stastney, Agnes Florence *principal*

OHIO

Akron
Kodish, Arline Betty *principal*
Stroll, Beverly Marie *elementary school principal*

Bath
Bowman-Dalton, Burdene Kathryn *education testing coordinator, computer consultant*

Brunswick
Sutter, Mark Robert *school administrator*

Canton
Steele, Robert B. *director vocational education*

Chagrin Falls
Robertson, Linda F. *educational admnstrator*

Cincinnati
Briggs, Henry Payson, Jr., *headmaster*
Harte, Sandra Wiswell *principal*

Cleveland
Pettiegrew, Henry *assistant principal*
Prater-Fipps, Eunice Kay *educational administrator*

Columbus
Blankenship, Dolores Moorefield *principal, music educator, retired*
Jones, Wilbert *school principal*

Dublin
Keck, David Michael *school administrator*

Fairview Park
Flynn, Patricia M. *director, special education educator, gifted and talented educator*

Fremont
Schueler, Jan Frances Menier *early childhood special education administrator*

Garrettsville
Spiker, George David *principal*

Greenfield
Bishop, Bonnie *principal*

Harrison
Zigler, Ted Alan *principal*

Hudson
Seiberling, Daniel R. *principal*

Louisville
Shadle, Donna A. Francis *principal*

Maple Heights
Watts, Willie Cephus, Jr., *elementary school principal*

New Albany
Partlow, Madeline *principal*

Oberlin
Fastenau, Frederick Henry, III, *principal*

PROFESSIONAL INDEX — SCHOOL ADMINISTRATION

Peninsula
Brobeck, David George *middle school administrator*

Plymouth
Hartman, Ruth Campbell *director, educator*

Portsmouth
Turner, Elvin L. *retired educational administrator*

Shaker Heights
Trefts, Joan Landenberger *retired educator, administrator*

Strongsville
Simon, Linda Day *assistant principal*

Toledo
Rabideau, Margaret Catherine *retired media center director*

OKLAHOMA

Lawton
McKeown, Rebecca J. *principal*

Norman
Jones, Charlotte *principal*

Pauls Valley
Pesterfield, Linda Carol *retired school administrator, educator*

Ponca City
Gallagher, Gary W(ayne) *educational services executive*

Tulsa
Christopher, Michael Mayer *secondary education development director*

Yukon
Somerville, Carolyn Johnson *educational administrator*

OREGON

Gresham
Harris, Michael Hatherly *educational administrator*

Portland
Campbell, William Joseph *academic director*
Harris, Linda Jean *principal*
Shaff, Beverly Gerard *education administrator*

West Linn
Newman, Sharon Ann *principal*

PENNSYLVANIA

Cambridge Springs
Learn, Richard Leland *corrections classification program manager*

Canonsburg
Mascetta, Joseph Anthony *principal*

Center Valley
Kelley-Brockel, Kathleen Frances *principal*
Siegfried, Christine Louise *principal*

Easton
Hughes, Michael P. *principal*

Emmaus
Torma, Denise M. *assistant principal*

Folsom
White, Barbara Cloud *principal, educator*

Gibsonia
Pysch, Richard Lawrence *principal*

Harrisburg
Brown, John Walter *vocational education supervisor*

Hershey
Fillgrove, Kevin *principal*
Ruth, Edward B. *supervisor*

Hollidaysburg
McCall, Linda Agnes *assistant principal*
Robinson, Gary David *principal*

Homestead
King, Richard Wayne *principal*

Johnstown
Alcamo, Frank Paul *retired educational administrator*

King Of Prussia
Adiletto, John J., Jr., *principal*

Kutztown
Watrous, Robert Thomas *academic director*

Lansdale
Cotter, Vincent F. *assistant principal*

Luzerne
Skierkowski, Sister Teresa Marie *educational administrator*

Meadville
Dixon, Armendia Pierce *school program administrator*

Moon Township
Hayes, Diane Elizabeth *principal*

Northampton
Greenleaf, Janet Elizabeth *principal*

Philadelphia
Alper, Steven Ira *principal*
Rice, Carrie Sottile *public relation director, retired principal*

Pittsburgh
Christiano, Paul P. *academic administrator, civil engineering educator*
Dempsey, Jacqueline Lee *special education director*
Losacco, Lesley Herdt *supervisor, educator*

Saltsburg
Pidgeon, John Anderson *headmaster*

Solebury
Sellers, Susan Taylor *principal*

Tyrone
Spewock, Theodosia George *principal, reading specialist, educator*

West Chester
Ray, E. Denise *assistant principal*

RHODE ISLAND

Barrington
Graser, Bernice Erckert *elementary school principal, educational consultant, psychologist*

Newport
Segerson, Michael P(eter) *elementary school administrator*

Providence
Munir, Yusuf *vocational education administrator*
Stevos, Joyce Louise *education director*

SOUTH CAROLINA

Charleston
Sarasohn, Evelyn Lois Lipman *principal*

Estill
Exum, Cynthia Phillips *headmaster*

Greenville
Jones, Robert Thaddues *principal*

Greer
Southerlin, Kenneth Gowan *principal*

Landrum
Summers, Janie I. *elementary school principal*

Little River
Sarvis, Elaine Magann *retired assistant principal*

Mauldin
Norris, Joan Clafette Hagood *retired assistant principal*

Simpsonville
Webster, Edward Glen *principal, school system administrator*

Spartanburg
Moore, Charles Gerald *educational administrator*

York
Clinch, Nicholas *assistant principal*

SOUTH DAKOTA

Mitchell
Schilling, Katherine Lee Tracy *retired principal*

TENNESSEE

Brownsville
Scott-Wilson, Susan Rice *vice principal*

Chattanooga
Rende, Toni Lynn *principal, counselor*

Columbia
Cantrell, Sharron Caulk *principal*

Crossville
Baas, Robert Miller *school administrator*

Dickson
Thomas, Janey Sue *elementary school principal*

Dunlap
Carr, Marsha Hamblen *elementary school principal*

Goodlettsville
Vatandoost, Nossi Malek *art school administrator*

Johnson City
Cross, James Millard *assistant principal*

Jonesborough
Broyles, Ruth Rutledge *retired principal*

Kingsport
Davis, Tammie Lynette *assistant principal*

Kingston
Oran, Geraldine Ann *assistant principal*

Knoxville
Moor, Anne Dell *education director*

Lebanon
Toombs, Cathy West *assistant principal*

Mc Minnville
Ferrell, Eva Boiko *principal*

Murfreesboro
Doyle, Delores Marie *retired principal*

Pinson
Bailey, James Andrew *principal*

Pleasant View
Dyce, Mickey *principal*

Whiteville
Allen, Yvonne *principal*

TEXAS

Aledo
Lindsay, John, IV, *principal*

Amarillo
Stapleton, Claudia Ann *school director*

Austin
Kane, Ruth Anne *principal, educator*

Bellaire
Carbon, Clinton LeRoy *headmaster*

Boerne
Daugherty, Linda Hagaman *private school executive*

Brookshire
Bauer, Laurie Koenig *educational administrator*

Carrollton
Maher, Sheila *secondary school principal*

Corpus Christi
Pérez-Gonzalez, Esmeralda *principal, educator*

Dallas
Russell, S. G., III, (Jacky Russell) *principal*

Denton
McDonald-West, Sandi MacLean *headmaster, consultant*

Garland
Strozeski, Michael Wayne *director research*
Wetzel, Joe Steven *principal*

Grapevine
Hirsh, Cristy J. *principal*

Houston
Bowden, Nancy Butler *school administrator*
Davis, Bruce Gordon *retired principal*
Gaelens, Albert Robert *educational administrator, priest*
Thorne, Joye Holley *special education administrator*

Littlefield
Driskell, Charles Mark *principal*

Lubbock
Hisey, Lydia Vee *educational administrator*

Mesquite
Slejko, Linda Marie *principal*

Midland
Hall, Linda Norton *principal, reading specialist*
McAfee, John Wilson, Sr., *retired principal*

Midlothian
Van Amburgh, (Brenda) Elizabeth *principal*

Missouri City
Hill, Anita Pamela *secondary school administrator*

Mount Pleasant
Jenkins, Beverly Ann *education specialist*

Paige
Trevino, Jerry Rosalez *retired secondary school principal*

Portland
Mircovich, Karen S. *principal*

Prairie View
Clark, Sharon Enid *principal*

San Antonio
Ahart-Walls, Pamela *elementary school principal*
Crews, Cinda Melane *assistant principal*
Drennan-Taylor, Joan Marie *director*
Harmon, William Francis *principal*
Lackan, Siewchan *principal, school system administrator*
Paloczy, Susan Therese *elementary school principal*

San Diego
Pena, Modesta Celedonia *retired principal*

Sugar Land
Thompson, Alice Mae Broussard *special education administrator*

Texarkana
Hill, Imogene Penton *school administrator*

Trophy Club
Hardy, Vicki *elementary school principal*

Woodway
Mulholland, Barbara Ann *school director*

UTAH

Provo
Densley, Colleen T. *principal*

Salt Lake City
Cannell, Cyndy Michelle *elementary school principal*
Thatcher, Blythe Darlyn *assistant principal*

VERMONT

Arlington
Miller, Jean Ellen *academic development director*

Poultney
Pentkowski, Raymond J. *principal*

Strafford
Williams, William Magavern *headmaster*

VIRGINIA

Alexandria
Dubin, Martin Steven *principal*
Wilson, Kathy *principal*

Arlington
Myers, Marjorie Lora *elementary school principal*

Dahlgren
Bales, Ruby Jones *retired elementary school educator and principal*

Fairfax
Tucker, Calanthia Rallings *school administrator*

Lexington
Mutispaugh, Mary Jane *principal*

Lynchburg
Herndon, Merle Puckette *principal*
Sprouse, Cheryl Lynne *principal*

Martinsville
McCraw, John Randolph, Jr., *assistant principal*

Nottoway
Bradley, Douglas Oliver *school principal*

Petersburg
Franklin, Virgil L. *school administrator, education educator*

Portsmouth
Williams, Lena Harding *educational administrator*

Richmond
Ragland, Ines Colom *principal*
Slonaker, Celester Lee *principal*

Vienna
Tordiff, Hazel Midgley *education director*

Virginia Beach
Richardson, Daniel Putnam *director, educator*

Waynesboro
Tynes, Theodore Archibald *educational administrator*

Williamsburg
Sebastian, Lucia Villa *principal*

Yorktown
Davis, Margaret Dinan *assistant principal, educator*

WASHINGTON

Bremerton
Goux, Clarajane Teal *retired special services director, educator*

Everett
Brynildsen-Smith, Kristine Ann *principal*

Fairchild Air Force Base
Munn, Eufemia Tobias *elementary school principal*

Gig Harbor
Minnerly, Robert Ward *retired headmaster*

Kent
Bolonesi, Naomi Grant *principal*
Johnson, Dennis D. *elementary school principal*

Moses Lake
Debenedetti, P(atrick) J(ohn) *director*

Port Angeles
Kane, Patrick J. *high school principal*

Renton
Schoenrock, Cheri Michelle *principal*

Richland
Piippo, Steve *director*

Seattle
Mitchell, Gloria Jean *principal, educator*

Spokane
Danke, Virginia *educational administrator, travel consultant*

Yakima
Cook, Kay Ellen *remedial programs coordinator*

SCHOOL ADMINISTRATION

WEST VIRGINIA

Bud
Garretson, Richard A. *principal*

Rowlesburg
Forrester, Donald Dean *educational administrator*

WISCONSIN

Chippewa Falls
Popple, Patricia Jane Ehlers *retired principal*

Clinton
Nodorft, Rebecca Ann *school administrator*

Eau Claire
Shaw, Bonita Lynn *school administrator*

Janesville
Thomas, Margaret Ann *educational administrator, art educator*

Kenosha
Tacki, Bernadette Susan *principal*

Manitowoc
Clark, James Alan *principal*

Milwaukee
Fair, Jerald Duane *principal*
Hatton, Janie R. Hill *principal*
Spann, Wilma Nadene *retired principal*

New Berlin
Dehli-Young, Gregory Lawrence *educational administrator*

Norwalk
Le Jeune, Jean Maria *administrator, educator*

West Allis
Nowak, Mary Leonarda *school administrator, principal*

Wrightstown
Leonard, Mary Beth *principal*

TERRITORIES OF THE UNITED STATES

AMERICAN SAMOA

Pago Pago
Faleali'i, Logoleo T. V. *educational services administrator*

FEDERATED STATES OF MICRONESIA

Chuuk
Marcus, Mariano Nakamura *secondary school principal*

GUAM

Barrigada
Pascual, Matilda Pereda *vocational program coordinator*

Tamuning
Sarmiento, Sister Mary Kathleen *principal*

PUERTO RICO

Adjuntas
Altieri Rosado, José Aníbal *principal*

San Juan
Cintrón-Ferrer, Carmen Rhode *educational director*
Santiago, Juan Jose *secondary school president*

VIRGIN ISLANDS

St Thomas
Lindo, Sandra Marcele *elementary school administrator*

MEXICO

Chihuahua
Alvarez, Blanca Magrassi *educational director, psychotherapist*

CHILE

Santiago
Strommen, Clifford H. *headmaster*

ENGLAND

Northampton
Rees, Brian *headmaster*

JAPAN

Fujisawa-shi
Kano, Hisao *director*

ADDRESS UNPUBLISHED

Barrow, Joseph Carlton *elementary school principal*
Betts, Elaine Wiswall *retired headmistress*
Bivens, Lynette Kupka *director*
Black, David R. *superintendent*
Blackwell, Jacqueline Pflughoeft *school district administrator*
Blecke, Arthur Edward *retired principal*
Borntrager, John Sherwood *principal*
Brackenhoff, Lonnie Sue *principal*
Brammer, Elizabeth Hedwig *administrator*
Brown, Lillie McFall *elementary school principal*
Cattando-Held, Donna *school director*
Chadwell, Jim F. *principal*
Chase, Barbara Landis *school administrator*
Cline, Pauline M. *educational administrator*
Coleman, Barbara Helene *educational administrator*
Cruce, Carol Ann *retired principal*
Doyle, Denise Elaine *principal*
Faverty, Patrick William *educational administrator*
Gentilcore, Eileen Marie Belsito *elementary school principal*
Gentilcore, John C. *principal*
Gentile, Joseph F. *principal*
Glasgow, Karen *principal*
Grier, Dorothy Ann Pridgen *secondary education specialist*
Hamler, Shelley Jefferson *administrator*
Handly-Johnson, Patricia *school administrator, school psychologist, educational consultant*
Harris, Cynthia Viola *principal*
Harrison, Earl Grant, Jr., *educational administrator*
Hartnett, Kathleen Mary *coordinator special education*
Haupt, Patricia A. *principal*
Hensley, Patricia Drake *principal*
Hestad, Marsha Anne *educational administrator*
Hoffman, Judy Greenblatt *preschool director*
Houseman, Ann Elizabeth Lord *educational administrator, state official*
Inglett, Betty Lee *retired director*
Jandris, Thomas Paul *program director*
Jones, Lillian Barnes *elementary school principal*
Kasberger-Mahoney, Elvera A. *educational administrator*
Keller, Janice Gail *principal*
Kryzak, Linda Ann *educational administrator*
LeSage, Janet Billings *elementary school principal*
Lynch, Sister Elizabeth *elementary school principal*
Lyon, Barbara Brooks *educational administrator*
Major, Patrick Webb, III, *principal*
Manuel, Ralph Nixon *former private school executive*
Mazur, Deborah Joan *assistant principal*
McCalla, Sandra Ann *educational administrator*
McIntosh, Carolyn Meade *retired educational administrator*
Merritt, Loretta Gaetana *principal, primary education educator*
Mosca, Christopher Patrick *principal*
Munsterman, Ingrid Anita *assistant principal*
Nance, Katherine Roark *principal*
Newman, Rebecca K. *principal*
Norman, Arlene Phyllis *principal*
O'Donnell, Brother Frank Joseph *principal*
Parry-Gill, Barbara Drepperd *retired educational administrator*
Pasic, Mary Rose *principal*
Paulino, Sister Mary McAuley *principal*
Perry, Donald E. *principal*
Piperato, David F. *principal*
Polston, Barbara Jean *principal, educational psychologist*
Rittel, Kathleen Ann Maurer *former assistant principal and school system administrator, middle school educator*
Robbins, Frances Elaine *educational administrator*
Ronco, Wilma Lilley *chief operating officer*
Sartorius, Gregg Steven *educational administrator*
Seay, Greg Wayne *principal*
Seeligson, Molly Fulton *professional life coach, education consultant, academic administrator*
Simmons, Lynda Merrill Mills *retired principal*
Snow, Sue *principal*
Soinski Opaskar, Gail V. *secondary school administrator*
Steele, Antonio L. *retired principal, educator*
Stokes, Rosa *educational administrator*
Van der Tuin, Mary Bramson *headmistress*
Wall, Julia Ann Wilhite *educational administrator, consultant*
Waskow, Joyce Ann *school administrator*
Wells-Carr, Elizabeth Antoinette *educational leadership trainer*
Whidden, Nancy Prince *principal*
Whitaker, Linda M. *principal*
White, Annette Jones *retired early childhood educator, administrator*

SCHOOL SYSTEM ADMINISTRATION

UNITED STATES

ALABAMA

Abbeville
Messick, Richard Douglas *educational administrator*

Athens
Ruth, Betty Muse *school system administrator*

Guntersville
Patterson, Harold Dean *retired superintendent of schools*

Mobile
Byrd, Gwendolyn Pauline *school system superintendent*

Montgomery
Richardson, Edward R. *school system administrator*

ALASKA

Anchorage
Comeau, Carol Smith *school system administrator*

Juneau
Gilley, Edward Ray *school system administrator*

Manokotak
Ward, Charles Cecil *educational administrator*

ARIZONA

Chandler
VanderVeen, Joseph Richard *special education administrator*

Mesa
Ramirez, Janice L. *assistant school superintendent*

Morristown
Rosehnal, Mary Ann *educational administrator*

Phoenix
Horne, Thomas Charles *school system administrator*

Whiteriver
Clark, John Munro *school system administrator*

Yuma
Thompson, Lynn Kathryn Singer *educational administrator*

ARKANSAS

Cherry Valley
Smith, Don Edward *school system administrator*

Fort Smith
Gooden, Benny L. *school system administrator*

Little Rock
Branon, M. Susan *school system administrator*
Simon, Raymond Joseph *school system administrator*
Wilhoit, Gene *school system administrator*
Young, Linda Irene *school district administrator*

North Little Rock
Holcomb, Beverly J. *educational administrator*

White Hall
Scott, Vicki Sue *school system administrator*

CALIFORNIA

Anaheim
Jackson, David Robert *school system administrator*

Apple Valley
Grunert, David Lloyd *school administrator*

Bakersfield
Olsen, Carl Franklin *school superintendent*

Berkeley
Bodenhausen, Judith Anne *school system administrator*
Rice, Robert Arnot *school administrator*

Camarillo
Knapp-Philo, Joanne *school system administrator*

Concord
Thall, Richard Vincent *school system administrator*

Corcoran
Roberts, Alice Noreen *educational administrator*

Del Mar
Sullivan, Romaine Brust *school system administrator*

El Centro
Kussman, Eleanor (Ellie Kussman) *retired educational superintendent*

Hollister
Turpin, Calvin Coolidge *retired university administrator, educator*

Inglewood
Kimble, Bettye D. *retired educational administrator*

Kelseyville
Berry, John Joseph *educational administrator*

La Canada Flintridge
Lamson, Robert Woodrow *retired school system administrator*

Lemon Grove
Mott, June Marjorie *school system administrator*

Long Beach
Shipley, Marilyn Elizabeth *school system administrator*

Los Angeles
Avila, Marvin Arthur *assistant principal student services*
Mull, Jocelyn Bethe *school system administrator*
Zamir, Frances Roberta (Frances Roberta Weiss-Swede) *educational compliance specialist*

Moraga
Sibitz, Michael William *school system administrator*

Newport Beach
Dean, John F. *retired school system administrator*

Oakland
Adwere-Boamah, Joseph *school district administrator*

Orange
Carriere, Brother William Joseph *school system administrator*

Oxnard
Rosales, Sandra Johnson *school system administrator*

Penn Valley
Nehls, Robert Louis, Jr., *school system financial consultant*

Redlands
Gogolin, Marilyn Tompkins *language pathologist, retired educational administrator*

Redwood City
Jones, Brenda Gail *school district administrator*

Riverside
Williams, Pamela R. *elementary school administrator*

Ross
Matan, Lillian Kathleen *educator, designer*

Sacramento
Law, Nancy Enell *school system administrator*
O'Connell, Jack *school system administrator*
Walls, Herbert LeRoy *school system administrator*

San Francisco
Ackerman, Arlene *school system administrator*
Fleishhacker, David *school administrator*

San Jose
Cryer, Rodger Earl *educational administrator*

Santa Barbara
Cirone, William Joseph *educational administrator*

Santa Clara
Abdaljabbar, Abdalhameed A. *educational administrator*

Santa Rosa
Foster, Lucille Caster *school system administrator, retired*

West Covina
Adler, Laurel Ann *educational administrator, consultant*

Whittier
Hurley, Eileen Beverly *school system administrator*

COLORADO

Boulder
Scrogan, Len Craig *school district administrator*
Sirotkin, Phillip Leonard *education administrator*

Broomfield
Yocum, Charleen Elaine *educational administrator, counselor*

Colorado Springs
Gossman, Jane McMinn *school system administrator*

Denver
Bautista, Michael Phillip *school system administrator*
Bosworth, Bruce Leighton *school administrator, educator, consultant*
Moloney, William J. *school system administrator*

Greeley
Townsend, Susan Louise *elementary school administrator*

Littleton
Rothenberg, Harvey David *educational administrator*

Rangely
Mullen, Robert Charles *school system administrator*

Westminster
Reed, John Howard *school administrator*

CONNECTICUT

Bloomfield
D'Annolfo, Suzanne Cordier *educational administrator, educator*

Glastonbury
Roy, Kenneth Russell *school system administrator, educator*

Hamden
Norberg-Caliendo, Lynda Joy *school system administrator*

Hartford
Hay, Leroy E. *school system administrator*

Ridgefield
Wallace, Ralph *superintendent*

Storrs Mansfield
MacDonald, John Thomas *educational administrator*

Stratford
Rozarie, Vera Jean *school district administrator*

Trumbull
Norcel, Jacqueline Joyce Casale *educational administrator*

DELAWARE

Milford
Walls-Culotta, Sandra L. *educational administrator*

New Castle
Martin, Jean Ann *retired school system administrator, educator*

DISTRICT OF COLUMBIA

Washington
Andell, Eric *school system administrator, judge*
Bader, Rochelle Linda (Shelley Bader) *educational administrator*
Spillane, Robert Richard *school system administrator*
Vance, Paul L. *school system administrator*

FLORIDA

Boca Raton
Leary, William James *educational administrator*

Brooksville
Tucker, John Curtis *school system administrator*

Coral Gables
Campbell, Shannon *school executive director*

Crawfordville
Black, B. R. *retired educational administrator, consultant*

Gainesville
Benedict, Gary Clarence *school system administrator, psychotherapist, educator*

Hialeah
Agrawal, Piyush C. *school system administrator*

Jupiter
Moseley, Karen Frances Flanigan *educational consultant, retired school system administrator, educator*

Miami
Cortes, Carol Solis *school system administrator*
de Arteaga-Morgan, Ivette *school administrator*
Exelbert, Michael Mark *educational administrator*
Geis, Tarja Pelto *educational coordinator, consultant, counselor, teacher, professor*
Kaplan, Betsy Hess *school board member*

Naples
Marcy, Jeannine Koonce *retired educational administrator*

Ocala
DeLong, Mary Ann *educational administrator*

Okeechobee
Raulerson, Phoebe Hodges *school superintendent*

Orange Park
Miller, Martin Eugene *school system consultant, negotiator, lobbyist*

Palm Beach Gardens
Orr, Joseph Alexander *educational administrator*

Plantation
Till, Franklin L. *school system administrator*

Port Charlotte
Whittaker, Douglas Kirkland *school system administrator*

Punta Gorda
Klarik, Bela William James Clark *retired school system administrator*

Saint Petersburg
Gregg, Kathy Kay *school system administrator*

Sanford
Luna, Charaline *superintendent*

Tallahassee
Horne, James *school system administrator*

Tamarac
Sherman, Mona Diane *school system administrator*

Tampa
Battle, Lucy Troxell (Mrs. J. A. Battle) *retired middle school administrator*

Tavares
Harper, Jane Walker *educational administrator*

GEORGIA

Auburn
Clines, Cindy Collins *elementary school administrator, educator*

Bremen
McBrayer, Laura Jean H. *school media specialist*

Brunswick
Rice, Cathy Sue Harrison *educational administrator*

Buchanan
Boatwright, Janice Ellen Willis *school system administrator*

Cartersville
Barnett, Harold Thomas *school system superintendent*

Columbus
Korcha, Lynda Lee *school system administrator*

Decatur
Baker, Stephen Monroe *school system administrator*
DiSalvo, Melinda Long *school system administrator*
Fletcher, Regina Roberson *school system administrator*
Schwartz, Jerrold Bennett *school system administrator*

Elberton
Wheeler, Timothy Arneal *assistant superintendent*

Jonesboro
Johnson, Philip Calvin *school administrator*

Lithonia
Mabry, Cathy Darlene *elementary school administrator*

Milledgeville
West, D(ruey) Tom, Jr., *school administrator*

Ocilla
Miller, Mavis Moss *school administrator, social worker*

Saint Marys
Durr, Marguerite Denise *school system administrator*

Valdosta
Evans, Marie Annette Lister *school system administrator*
Scruggs, Betty Joyce Clenney *public school administrator*

HAWAII

Honolulu
Hamamoto, Patricia *school system administrator, educator*
Ramler, Siegfried *educator*

Kaneohe
Inamine, Sharon Ogawa *elementary school administrator*

IDAHO

Boise
Howard, Marilyn *school system administrator*

New Plymouth
Horton, Nadine Rose *school system administrator*

ILLINOIS

Arlington Heights
Placek-Zimmerman, Ellyn Clare *school system administrator, educator, consultant*

Bolingbrook
Taylor, Lynda Dora *school administrator, principal*

Chicago
Ciszek, Sister Barbara Jean *educational administrator*
Cooper, Jo Marie *elementary school principal*
Roberts, Jo Ann Wooden *school system administrator*
Standberry, Herman Lee *school system administrator, educational consultant*

Dekalb
Healey, Robert William *school system administrator*

Downers Grove
DeJulio, Ellen Louise *special education administrator*

East Saint Louis
Wright, Katie Harper *educational administrator, journalist*

Elgin
Patterson, Paul M. *school administrator*

Granite City
Humphrey, Owen Everett *retired education administrator*

Jacksonville
Johns, Beverley Anne Holden *special education administrator*

Kankakee
Green, Kay Suzanne *school system administrator*

Kewanee
Golby, James L. *school system administrator*

Knoxville
Johnson, Robert Oliver, Jr., *school system administrator*

Murphysboro
Brewer, Donald Louis *school superintendent*

Naperville
Nylander, Donna Marie *educational administrator*
Scullen, Thomas G. *superintendent*

O Fallon
Bradley, Thomas Michael *school system administrator*

Park Ridge
Millies, Palma Suzanne *school system administrator*

Patoka
Borgmann, Norma Lee *school superintendent*

Peoria Heights
Bergia, Roger Merle *school system administrator*

River Forest
Smith, Curtis Alfonso, Jr., *university administrator*

Schaumburg
Hlousek, Joyce B(ernadette) *school system administrator*

Skokie
Arandia, Carmelita S. *school administrator*

Springfield
Taylor, Mary Kathleen *school system administrator*

Swansea
Chambers, Jerry Ray *school system administrator*

University Park
Peterson, Kenneth Allen, Sr., *superintendent, retired*

Wheaton
Potter, Janice Baber *retired school superintendent, educator*

INDIANA

Brownsburg
Ward, Marvin Ted *school system administrator*

Cannelton
Moore, Larry Glenn *school system administrator*

Hammond
Watson, Steven Ellis *school district administrator*

Indianapolis
Boatright, Gregory Bruce *school system administrator, educator*
Reed, Suellen Kinder *school system administrator*

Lafayette
Troutner, Joanne Johnson *school technology administrator, educator, administrator, consultant*

Linden
Lefebvre, Gren Gordon *school superintendent*

Logansport
Thacker, Jerry Lynn *school administrator*

Pierceton
Hill, John Edward *school system administrator*

IOWA

Calmar
Wede, Richard J. *school superintendent*

Council Bluffs
Howsare, Galen Glenn *school system administrator*

Des Moines
Davilla, Donna Elaine *school system administrator*
Stilwill, Ted *school system administrator*

Dubuque
Toale, Thomas Edward *school system administrator, priest*

Urbandale
Racki, Joan *educational administrator*

KANSAS

Easton
Willson, Charles Emery *school system administrator*

Pittsburg
Dobrauc, Patricia Cecilia *school board executive*

Shawnee Mission
Barton, Betty Louise *school system administrator*

Wichita
Willon, Mychael Cole *school system administrator, educator*

KENTUCKY

Harlan
Greene, James S., III, *school administrator*

Lexington
Lewis, Richard Jeffrey *special education administrator*

Murray
Herndon, Donna Ruth Grogan *educational administrator*

LOUISIANA

Baton Rouge
Picard, Cecil *school system administrator*

Hahnville
Smith, Raymond Kermit *former educational administrator*

Hammond
Bender, Victor M. *educational administrator*

Lafayette
Ventress, Mary Ellen *school system administrator*

New Orleans
Burns, Mary W. *school system administrator*
Jones, John Anderson, Jr., *retired school system administrator*

Reserve
Becnel, Albert Thomas *retired educational administrator*

Shreveport
Fair, Darlene Ann *school system administrator*

Sicily Island
Dale, Sam E., Jr., *retired educational administrator*

MAINE

Fairfield
Mitchell-Donar, Susan Nancy *school system administrator*

Falmouth
Taub, Larry Steven *education administrator*

North Yarmouth
Fecteau, Rosemary Louise *educational administrator, educator, consultant*

MARYLAND

Annapolis
Smith, Eric J. *school system administrator*

Baltimore
Grasmick, Nancy S. *school system administrator*
Levine, Robert Joseph *secondary school administrator*
Wortham, Deborah Lynne *school principal*

Chestertown
Miller, Frances Elizabeth *assistant superintendent*

College Park
Hey, Nancy Henson *educational administrator*

Cumberland
Shelton, Bessie Elizabeth *school system administrator*

Frederick
Klein, Elaine Charlotte *school system administrator*

Laurel
Wales, Patrice *school system administrator*

Potomac
Au, Mary Lee *school system administrator*
Schuessler, Isabelle Sweeny *school administrator*

Rockville
Rohr, Karolyn Kanavas *school system administrator*

Silver Spring
Bonner, Bester Davis *school system administrator*
Fromberg, Jean Stern *school system administrator*

Upper Marlboro
Traynor, Barbara Mary *school system administrator*

MASSACHUSETTS

Athol
Grout, Coral May *school system administrator, consultant*

Boston
Rittner, Carl Frederick *educational administrator*
Tewhey, Karen Marie *special education and mental health administrator*

Danvers
Clark, Sharon Jackson *private school administrator*

Dennis
Wadsworth, Christopher *school system administrator, director*

Kingston
Squarcia, Paul Andrew *school superintendent*

Lynn
Astuccio, Sheila Margaret *educational administrator*

Plymouth
Goggin, Joan Marie *school system administrator*

Taunton
Croteau, Gerald A., Jr., *retired school system administrator*

Tewksbury
DeAngelis, Michele F. *school system administrator*

Wareham
Gustafson, Deborah Lee *educational administrator, educator*

Whitman
Delaney, Matthew Michael *school administrator, fine arts educator*

Worcester
Bowen, Alice Frances *school system administrator*

MICHIGAN

Alma
Moerdyk, Charles Conrad *school system administrator*

Armada
Kummerow, Arnold A. *superintendent of schools*

Brighton
Carter, Pamela Lee *program administrator*

Coloma
Tallman, Clifford Wayne *retired school system administrator, consultant*

Detroit
Brynski, Christina Halina *school system administrator, consultant, educator*
Burnley, Kenneth Stephen *school system administrator*

Fort Gratiot
Mueller, Don Sheridan *retired school administrator*

Monroe
Kelly, Judith Johanna Cova *elementary language arts consultant*

Saint Clair Shores
Welch, Robert Dinwiddie *retired school administrator*

Warren
Weigle, Michaeline Joanne *school system administrator*

Ypsilanti
Ellis, Katherine Ann *school administrator*

MINNESOTA

Annandale
Schilplin, Yvonne Winter *educational administrator*

Eden Prairie
McCoy, Gerald Leo *superintendent of schools*

Minneapolis
Morrow, Dennis Robert *school system administrator, consultant*

Osseo
Ramsey, Marl *retired school system administrator*

Richfield
Devlin, Barbara Jo *school district administrator*

MISSISSIPPI

Grenada
Colbert, Beatrice Halfacre *special education administrator*

Iuka
Barnes, Betty Jean *educational administrator*

Jackson
McLin, Hattie Rogers *school system administrator*

Meridian
Phillips, Patricia Jeanne *retired school system administrator*

Oxford
Boyd, Richard Alfred *school system administrator*

Tupelo
Daniels, Bruce Eugene *school system administrator*
Rupert, Daniel Leo *education and educational technology consultant*
Smith, Sarah Sterdivant *educational administrator, educational consultant*

Walls
Williams, H. Leon, Sr., *school system administrator, minister*

Yazoo City
Cartlidge, Shriley Ann Bell *school administrator*

MISSOURI

Chesterfield
Moore, Benjamin *educational administrator*

Columbia
Steeno, Paula Herrick *special education administrator*

Ironton
Dillard, Lisa Reichert *assistant superintendent*

Joplin
Pulliam, Frederick Cameron *educational administrator*

Kansas City
Horsely, Willie Woodruff *educational administrator*

Saint Louis
Bloomberg, Terry *early childhood education administrator*
Green, Rose Mary *school system administrator*
Morice, Linda Kay *school system administrator*
Ramming, Michael Alexander *retired school system administrator*
Stodghill, Ronald *school system administrator*

MONTANA

Havre
Windel, Robert Eugene *school system administrator*

Poplar
Birrer, Michael Floyd *school system administrator*

NEBRASKA

Lincoln
Christensen, Douglas D. *school system administrator*
Hopkins, Barbara Jo Glass *school system administrator*
Powers, David Richard *educational administrator*

Norfolk
Mortensen-Say, Marlys *school system administrator*

NEVADA

Carson City
McLaughlin, Jack M. *superintendent*

Las Vegas
Ananias, José *retired school system administrator*
Ozi, Elizabeth *private school administrator*

NEW HAMPSHIRE

Berlin
Cascadden, Corinne Elizabeth *elementary school administrator*

North Haverhill
Charpentier, Keith Lionel *school system administrator*

Tilton
Schultz, Judith *educational administrator, consultant*

NEW JERSEY

Basking Ridge
Lachenauer, Robert Alvin *retired school superintendent*

Bergenfield
Alfieri, John Charles, Jr., *educational administrator*

Bloomfield
Chagnon, Joseph V. *school system administrator*

Browns Mills
Di Nunzio, Dominick *educational administrator*

Cherry Hill
Tackett, William Edward *school system administrator*

Cliffside Park
Colagreco, James Patrick *school superintendent*

East Brunswick
Charatz, Pearl Eileen *educational administrator*

Farmingdale
Munger, Janet Anne *education administrator*

Hamburg
Kane, James Patrick *superintendent, educator*

Howell
Borowick, Bernadine Ann *school system administrator*
Vetere, Laura Ann *school system administrator, educator*

Jackson
Ranone, John Louis *school board executive*

Jersey City
Miller, Adele Engelbrecht *educational administrator*

Lindenwold
Kish, Elissa Anne *educational administrator, consultant*

Little Falls
Nash, James John *superintendent*

Medford
Galbraith, Frances Lynn *educational administrator*

Midland Park
Dunn, Patricia Ann *school system administrator, English language educator*

Morristown
Venezia, William Thomas *school system administrator, counseling consultant*

New Brunswick
Miskiewicz, Susanne Piatek *educational administrator*

New Milford
Dexheimer, Richard Joseph *school system administrator*

Newark
Flagg, E(loise) Alma Williams *educational administrator*

Newton
Clymer, Jerry Alan *educational administrator*

Nutley
Hirsch, Barbara *school administrator*

Penns Grove
Graham, Albert Darlington, Jr., *educational administrator*

Piscataway
French, Kathleen Patricia *educational administrator*

Plainsboro
Hunter, Alyce *school system administrator*

Rutherford
Sarsfield, Luke Aloysius *school system administrator*

Skillman
Messner, Richard Stephen *school system administrator*

Teaneck
Dewey, Ralph Jay *school system administrator*

Waldwick
Lynch, Carol *director special services, psychologist*

West New York
Cave, Lillian JoAnn *school system administrator*

West Orange
Vernon, Arthur *educational administrator*

Westfield
Fitts, Leonard Donald *educational administrator*

Woodbridge
Chesky, Pamela Bosze *school system administrator*

NEW MEXICO

Albuquerque
Miller, Mickey Lester *retired school administrator*
Ward, Katherine Marie *retired school administrator*

Artesia
Sarwar, Barbara Duce *education consultant*

Las Cruces
Elliott, Richard L. *school administrator*

Placitas
Owings, Suzann M. *school system administrator, educator*

NEW YORK

Albany
Enokian, Ralph Avedis *school administrator, retired*
Lobosco, Anna Frances *state program development specialist*
Mills, Richard P. *school system administrator*
Van Amburgh, Robert Joseph *school system administrator*

Belmont
Feldbauer, James Frederick *retired school system administrator*

Bridgehampton
Edwards, John W. *school superintendent*

Brooklyn
Ierardi, Eric Joseph *school system administrator*
McIver, Anne Pooser *school system administrator*

Buffalo
Swanson, Austin Delain *educational administration educator*

Canandaigua
Eckert, Nancy Ruscio *school system administrator*

Cicero
Manning, J. Francis *school administrator*

Craryville
Paciencia, David A. *school superintendent*

Elmira
Burke, Rita Hoffmann *educational administrator*

Floral Park
Goldstein, George A. *school system administrator*

Glendale
Piro, Joseph Martin *school system administrator*

Holbrook
Bartley, Mary Lou Ruf *school administrator*

Holland
Loockerman, William Delmer *educational administrator, retired*

Kings Park
LoPresti, Marilyn Angela *school system administrator*

Krumville
Nagi, Catherine Raseh *retired educational administrator, financial planner*

Long Beach
Koehler, Sister Patricia *elementary school administrator*

Marcy
Rishel, Kenn Charles *school superintendent*

New York
Borkon, Doris *educational administrator, entrepreneur*
Hickey, Catherine Josephine *school system administrator*
Schloss, Martin *educational administrator*

Newburgh
Saturnelli, Annette Miele *school system administrator*

Niagara Falls
Bundy-Iannarelli, Barbara Ann *educational administrator*

Northport
Weaver, Eric James *educational administrator*

Patchogue
Fogarty, James Vincent, Jr., *special education administrator, educator*

Pelham
Zehner, Jeanne Madelyn *school system administrator*

Port Jefferson Station
Shockley, Alonzo Hilton, Jr., *school system administrator*

Poughkeepsie
Rhodes, Geraldine Bryan *secondary school administrator*

Rochester
Woods, John Joseph *school system administrator*

Sands Point
Fuchsberg Fishman, Adele Raquel *school district administrator*

Saranac Lake
Szwed, Beryl J. *school system administrator, mathematics educator*

Schoharie
Giangreco, Carmine Charles *superintendent*

Shoreham
Christina, Barbara Ann *bilingual education administrator*

Staten Island
Dobis, Joan Pauline *education administrator*

Syosset
Streitman, Jeffrey Bruce *education administrator*

PROFESSIONAL INDEX — SCHOOL SYSTEM ADMINISTRATION

Syracuse
Ariola, Marie J. *school system administrator, principal*
DeSiato, Donna Jean *school system administrator*

Tillson
Whittington-Couse, Maryellen Frances *education administrator, organizational specialist, consultant*

Webster
Cupini, Mariellen Louise *school district administrator*

Woodmere
Fowler, Charles William *school administrator*

Youngstown
Polka, Walters S. *school superintendent*

NORTH CAROLINA

Ahoskie
Brett, Mauvice Winslow *retired educational administrator, consultant*

Charlotte
Randolph, Elizabeth S. (Mrs. John Daniel Randolph) *former educational administrator*

Durham
Bunting, Carolyn Ellen *educational consultant, writer*

Gastonia
McGlohon, Reeves *education administrator*

Greensboro
Schappell, Lola Irene Hill *school system administrator*
Wright, John Spencer *school system administrator*

Hazelwood
Lowder, Mary Katherine *school system administrator*

Hendersonville
Burnham, Tom *school system administrator*

High Point
Farlow, Joel Wray *school system administrator*

Liberty
Feaster, Charlotte Josephine S. *school administrator*

Raleigh
Dornan, John Neill *public policy center professional*

Wilson
Hardy, Patti Sanders *school system administrator*

Winston Salem
Liner, Ronald Sims *middle school administrator*

NORTH DAKOTA

Bismarck
Sanstead, Wayne Godfrey *school system administrator*

Fargo
Yliniemi, Hazel Alice *educational administrator*

Walhalla
Dahl, Merlin Hugh *school system administrator*

OHIO

Avon Lake
Gwiazda, Caroline Louise *school system administrator*

Bainbridge
Thompson, Dorothy Mae *school system administrator, real estate manager*

Bay Village
Woods, Dennis Craig *school superintendent*

Bowling Green
Pendleton, Marie Pearson *school administrator, educator*

Canton
Griffin, Connie May *school system administrator*

Chillicothe
Atwood, Joyce Charlene *curriculum and instruction administrator, consultant*

Cincinnati
Brinkmeyer, Mary Foss *school system administrator*

Cleveland
Gronick, Patricia Ann Jacobsen *school system administrator*
Hardman, Corlista Helena *school system administrator, educator*

Columbus
Stearns, Wanda June *state and federal programs supervisor*
Zelman, Susan Tave *school system administrator*

Dayton
Brown, Nancy Miller *school system administrator*

Reno, Lee Curtis *school system administrator, consultant*

East Cleveland
Corley, Myrna Loy *school system administrator*

Euclid
Gallagher, Janice Mori *school administrator*

Jefferson
Crepage, Richard Anthony *school system administrator*

Liberty Center
Jones, Marlene Ann *retired education supervisor*

Mansfield
Ash, Thomas Phillip *superintendent of schools*
Ogden, William Michael *school system administrator*

Newark
Fortaleza, Judith Ann *school system administrator*

Oregon
Crain, John Kip *school system administrator*

Port Clinton
Ewersen, Mary Virginia *educator, poet*
Phillips, Margaret *retired school system administrator*

Tipp City
Bristow, Carolyn Luree Cummings *library media specialist*

Wauseon
McNulty, Roberta Jo *educational administrator*

Westerville
Husarik, Ernest Alfred *educational administrator*

OKLAHOMA

Bartlesville
Chambers, Imogene Klutts *school system administrator, financial consultant*

Oklahoma City
Garrett, Sandy Langley *school system administrator*
Mason, Betty G(wendolyn) Hopkins *school system administrator*

Ponca City
Surber, Joe Robert *assistant superintendent*

Pryor
Burdick, Larry G. *school system administrator*

Sapulpa
Barnes, Paulette Whetstone *school system administrator*

Shawnee
Hill, Bryce Dale *school administrator*

Tulsa
Buthod, Mary Clare *school administrator*

OREGON

Bend
Nelson, Douglas Michael *school system administrator, educator*

Hillsboro
Moore, Melvin G. *school system administrator*

Salem
Castillo, Susan *school system administrator*

Sunriver
Schade, Wilbert Curtis *education administrator*

PENNSYLVANIA

Boyertown
Kuser, Edwin Charles *educational administrator, retired*

Downingtown
Watto, Dennis Paul *school system administrator, researcher, writer*

Doylestown
Thomas, Ellen Louise *school system administrator*

Everett
Vollbrecht, Edward Alan *school superintendent*

Hanover
Clark, Sandra Marie *school administrator*

Harrisburg
Phillips, Vicki L. *school system administrator*

Horsham
Strock, Gerald E. *school system administrator*

Kennett Square
Gring, Stephen Robert *educational administrator*

Kingston
Marko, Andrew Paul *school system administrator*

Maple Glen
Taddei, Edward P. *school system administrator*

Mount Joy
Lawrence, James David *school system administrator*

New Hope
Knight, Douglas Maitland *educational administrator, optical executive, writer*

Norristown
Del Collo, Mary Anne Demetris *school administrator*

Palmyra
Summers, Dale Edwards *school system administrator, education educator*

Pittsburgh
Roppa, Kathleen Marie *educational administrator*
Smartschan, Glenn Fred *school system administrator*
Tesfarmariam, Bernice Jefferson *school administrator, counselor*

Scottdale
Lee, John Lawrence, Jr., *educational administrator*

Scranton
Connolly, Ruth Ann *school system administrator*
Williams, John Ralph *school superintendent*

Shillington
Becker, Sandra Louise *education technical specialist*

Warminster
Ciao, Frederick J. *school system administrator, educator*

West Chester
Schantz, Allen Ray *retired school administrator*

RHODE ISLAND

Portsmouth
Mello, Michael William *educational administrator*

Providence
McWalters, Peter *school system administrator*

South Kingstown
Zarrella, Arthur M. *superintendent of schools*

SOUTH CAROLINA

Aiken
Brooks, Joseph Russell *educational administrator*

Clio
McLeod, Marilynn Hayes *retired educational administrator, farmer*

Greenville
Dozier, Herbert Randall *school system administrator*

Lake City
Hawkins, Linda Parrott *school system administrator*

Spartanburg
Gray, Nancy Ann Oliver *college administrator*

Sumter
Kieslich, Anita Frances *school system administrator*

Union
Morgan, June Smith *elementary education director*

Walhalla
Kelley, John H. *school system administrator*

SOUTH DAKOTA

Bison
Soehren, Sharon Kaye *school district administrator*

TENNESSEE

Hendersonville
Glover, Nancy Elliott *elementary school administrator*

Knoxville
Bernards, Pamela J. *school system administrator*
Morgan, Sherry Rita Guy *school system administrator*

Memphis
Hirsch, Callie Clark *instructional facilitator*
Thompson, Rex Allen *school business administrator*

Newport
Ball, Travis, Jr., *educational consultant, editor*

Powell
Holmes, Margaret Lester *school system technology coordinator*

Selmer
Prather, Sophie S. *educational administrator*

Shelbyville
Austin, Margaret Cully *school administrator*

TEXAS

Austin
Auvenshine, Anna Lee Banks *school system administrator*
Hetzler, Susan Elizabeth Savage *educational administrator*

Burnet
Gurno, Mary Ann *school system administrator*

Copperas Cove
Barnes, Sara Lynn *school system administrator*

Corpus Christi
Gutierrez, Arturo Luis *school system administrator*

Dallas
Davis, Patricia Ann *school system administrator*
Hopkins, Zora Clemons *training and development specialist*

El Paso
Gordon, Erline Schecter *educational administrator*

Houston
Comeaux, Tina Boissey *school board executive, civic worker*
Friedrich, Katherine Rose *educational researcher*
Goode, James Cleveland *educational administrator*

Keller
McCown, Gloria Booher *school system administrator*

Killeen
Hallbauer, Celinda *school system administrator, music educator*

Longview
White, Raye Mitchell *educational administrator*

Lufkin
Strohschein, Helen Frances *educational administrator*

Moody
Judah, Frank Marvin *retired school system administrator*

Mumford
Bienski, Pete Joseph, Jr., *school superintendent*

Nacogdoches
Isabell, Gene Paul, Sr., *school district administrator*

Paris
Stegall, Diane Joyce *school system administrator*

Pearland
Smith, Annie Lee Northern *retired school system administrator*

Plano
McWilliams, Mary Ann *school administrator*

Rockdale
Estell, Dora Lucile *retired educational administrator*

San Antonio
Middleton, Richard A. *school system administrator*
O'Neill, Mary Boniface *alternative education administrator*

San Marcos
Byrom, Jack Edwards *private school administrator*

Sour Lake
Tule, Sharon Burchard *school system administrator*

Temple
Andrews, George Arthur *school administrator*

Texarkana
Palmer-Callicott, Deborah Dawn *educational examiner*

Tyler
Lawson, Billy Joe *educational administrator*

Victoria
Boatman, Helen Adell *school district administrator*

Weatherford
Westbrook, Juanita Jane *school administrator*

UTAH

Salt Lake City
Laing, Steven O. *school system administrator*

Sandy
Pierce, Ilona Lambson *educational administrator*

VERMONT

Montpelier
Larsen, David Carl *school system administrator*

Swanton
Chaim, Linda Susan *special education administrator*

SCHOOL SYSTEM ADMINISTRATION

VIRGINIA

Abingdon
Luker, Jean Knarr *school system administrator*

Alexandria
Anderson, Ann Davis *reading curriculum specialist*
Gil, Libia Socorro *school system administrator*
Jarrard, James Paul *school program administrator*

Arlington
Houston, Paul David *school association administrator*
Tafoya, Joe *school system administrator*

Blacksburg
King, Stephen Emmett *educational administrator*

Chesterfield
Copeland, Jean Parrish *school system administrator, school board executive*
Hill, Ida Johnson *education consultant, technologist, administrator*

Clifton
Latt, Pamela Yvonne *school system administrator*

Fairfax
Dantzler, Joyce Elston *school system administrator, educator*

Falls Church
Todd, Shirley Ann *school system administrator*

Mc Lean
Laine, Elaine Frances *school system administrator*

Norfolk
Steele, James Eugene *retired school system administrator*

Portsmouth
Trumble, Richard Dwain *superintendent, consultant*

Roanoke
Johns, Dolores Yuille *educational administrator*

Stevensville
Baytops, Joy L. *gifted education administrator, consultant*

Surry
Rollings, Martha Anderson *retired school system administrator*

WASHINGTON

Olympia
Bergeson, Teresa *school system administrator*

Renton
Walker, Roberta Smyth *school system administrator*

Ridgefield
Franks, Lou Ella *school system administrator, educator*

Seattle
Maurer, Barbara Glee *educational administrator*
Silver, Michael *school superintendent*

Yakima
Eastwood, Patricia J. *school system administrator*
Hornstein, Pamela Kathleen *educational administrator, educator*

WEST VIRGINIA

Charleston
Arrington, Carolyn Ruth *education consultant*
Simmons, Virginia Gill *educational administrator*
Stewart, David *school system administrator*

Dunbar
Nichols, Charles Edward *secondary education administrator*

Huntington
De Fazio, Jack Joseph *school system administrator, coach*

New Cumberland
Chandler, Charles Lee, Jr., *school system administrator*

WISCONSIN

Cedarburg
Mielke, Jon Alan *elementary school administrator*

Laona
Sturzl, Alice A. *school library administrator*

Madison
Burmaster, Elizabeth *school system administrator*

Manitowoc
Gaus, Lynn Shebesta *school administrator*
Staniszewski, Sue Ann Kober *special education administrator*

Shorewood
Lietz, Jeremy Jon *educational administrator, writer*

Silver Lake
Hellum, Perry K. *school system administrator*

Walworth
Sissons, John Roger *educational administrator*

TERRITORIES OF THE UNITED STATES

AMERICAN SAMOA

Pago Pago
Sataua, Sili K. *school system administrator*

NORTHERN MARIANA ISLANDS

Saipan
Inos, Rita Hocog *school system administrator*

PUERTO RICO

Ceiba
DeMaio, Dorothy Walters *tutorial school administrator, consultant*

Sabana Seca
Sierra Millán, Daniel *school administrator*

San Juan
Rey-Hernandez, Cesar A. *school system administrator*

ENGLAND

Egham
Kittell, Andrew John *educational administrator*

ADDRESS UNPUBLISHED

Amie, Barbara E. *school system administrator*
Angiuli, Rosemarie *special education administrator*
Armstrong-Law, Margaret *school administrator*
Baldassare, Louis J. *former school superintendent, educational consultant*
Bellum, Fred Lewis *school system administrator, retired*
Bennett, Elsie Margaret *music school administrator*
Bertram, Joan M. *school system administrator*
Black, Georgia Ann *educational administrator*
Blazey, Judith Leiston *school district administrator*
Blount, Peter Allen *educational administrator, educator, researcher*
Bowens, Gloria Furr *educational administrator*
Brown, David Richard *school system administrator, minister*
Burns, Brenda Carolyn *retired special education administrator, chemical dependence counselor*
Caldwell, William Edward *educational administration educator, arbitrator*
Carrell, Heather Demaris *school system administrator*
Case, Elizabeth Joy *special education administrator*
Charney, Carolyn Jean *school administrator, elementary education educator*
Childers, Lawrence Jeffrey *superintendent, personnel director*
Cioffi, Eugene Edward, III, *retired educational administrator*
Cline, Janet E. Safford *school district administrator, desktop publisher*
Davis, Hiram Joe *public school administrator*
Delahanty, Rebecca Ann *school system administrator*
Dohrenwend, Sandra Blackman Masterman *superintendent*
Downen, Thomas William *retired school system administrator*
Dresbach, Mary Louise *state educational administrator*
Dunham, Rebecca Betty Beres *school administrator*
Duplessis, Audrey Joseph *school system administrator*
Dworkin, Irma-Theresa *school system administrator, researcher, secondary school educator*
Eads, Albert E., Jr., *school system administrator*
Edwards, Lynn A. *retired school system administrator*
Fafoglia, Barbara Ann *school administrator*
Farrar, Richard Bartlett, Jr., *school system administrator*
Gitner, Deanne *retired school system administrator*
Green, Patricia Pataky *school system administrator, consultant*
Hageman, Richard Philip, Jr., *educational administrator*
Hall, Lorene Mary *elementary school administrator*
Harper, Janet Sutherlin Lane *retired educational administrator, writer*
Haynes, Michael Scott, Sr., *resource specialist*
Henley, Robert Lee *school system administrator*
Hester, Gerald LeRoy *retired school system administrator*
Holmes, Erline Morrison *retired educational administrator, consultant*
Jernigan, Sharon Reynolds *school system administrator, educator*
Lawrence, Linda Hiett *retired school system administrator, writer*
Maney, Daniel B. *elementary administrator*
Maurer, Beverly Bennett *school administrator*
Maxwell, Mary Ellen *school system administrator*
McAbeer, Sara Carita *school administrator*
McConner, Stanley Jay, Sr., *school system administrator*
Medalie, Marjorie Lynn *educational administrator, consultant*
Moffett, Kenneth Lee *superintendent schools*
Nicholson, Theodore H. *educational administrator*
O'Rourke, Joan B. Doty Werthman *retired school system administrator*
Padilla, Elsa Norma *retired school system administrator*
Papin, Nancy Sue *educational computer coordinator*
Perry, Glen Joseph *school system administrator, educator*
Pickerign, Roger *superintendent*
Piper, Fredessa Mary *school system administrator*
Piper, Margarita Sherertz *retired school administrator*
Powell, Linda *school system administrator*
Rains, Hazel Grace *curriculum director*
Ray, Shirley Dodson *educational administrator, consultant*
Ritchie, Anne *educational administrator*
Roberts, Kathleen Mary *school system administrator, retired*
Rodriguez-Roig, Aida Ivelisse *school system administrator*
Rowley, Charlene Marie *educational administrator*
Salagi, Doris *educational administrator, retired*
Scholl, Allan Henry *retired school system administrator, educational consultant*
Schrage, Rose *educational administrator*
Shugart, Jill *retired school system administrator, educational consultant*
Sikorski, Lorena L. *school system administrator*
Smith, Doris Victoria *educational agency administrator*
Smith, Howard Ray *school system administrator*
Sommer, Barbara *school administrator*
Stellar, Arthur Wayne *educational administrator*
Tankersley, Melissa Maupin *educational administrator*
Tignor, George *school system administrator*
Tzimopoulos, Nicholas D. *educational administrator*
Valentine, Charles Francis *educational administrator*
Violenus, Agnes A. *retired school system administrator*
Williams, Harriette Flowers *retired school system administrator, educational consultant*
Wilson, Carolyn Ross *retired school administrator*

SECONDARY SCHOOL EDUCATION

UNITED STATES

ALABAMA

Bessemer
Clarke, McKinley A. *secondary school educator*
Thompson, Lula Averhart *retired educator*

Centre
Martin, Wilma Irish *secondary education educator*

Cottondale
Blackshear, Helen Friedman *retired educator*

Daphne
Henson, Pamela Taylor *secondary education educator*
Skinner, Mary Jane Pickens *secondary education educator*

Decatur
Davis, Marian Bloodworth *secondary school educator*

Eclectic
Tracy, Patricia Ann Koop *secondary school educator*

Eufaula
Mims, Paula Cain *secondary education educator*

Foley
Wood, Linda Sherrill *secondary education educator*

Gadsden
Crow, Jo Ann *secondary education educator*

Huntsville
Billings, Nancy Carter *secondary education educator*
Evans, Darrell J. *higher education educator*
Leslie, Lottie Lyle *retired secondary education educator*
Mitcham, Patricia Ann Hamilton *educator*
Tucker, Eunice Jones *retired secondary education educator*
Vought, Barbara Baltz *secondary school educator*

Jackson
Stringer, Rebecca Huggins *secondary education educator*

Mobile
Floyd, Cinthia Ann *secondary school educator, coach*

Ozark
Anderson, John Henderson *retired secondary education educator, retired army officer*

Selma
Moore, Jean Moore *secondary education educator*

Tuscaloosa
Smith, Lois Colston *secondary school educator, educator*

ALASKA

Anchorage
Anthony, Susan *secondary education educator*
Bowie, Phyllis *secondary education educator*
Collins, Michael Paul *secondary school educator, earth science educator, consultant*
Rude, Phyllis Aileen *retired secondary school educator*
Wedel-Cowgill, Millie Redmond *secondary school educator, performing arts educator*
Young, Bettye Jeanne *retired secondary education educator*

Homer
Wolfe, Steven Albert *secondary education educator*

North Pole
Martin, Dorothy Sue *secondary education educator, counselor*

ARIZONA

Chinle
Reed, Leonard Newton *secondary school educator*

Mesa
Klopper, Stephanie Rudolph *secondary education educator*
Yates, Cheryl Ann *home economist, educator*

Phoenix
Bobbitt, Helen Davis *secondary school educator*
Buehler, Marilyn Kay Hasz *secondary education educator*
Price, Beverly Bruns *secondary education educator*
Stanford, Janine Lynette *secondary school educator*
Thompson, Bonnie Ransa *education consultant*
Wood, Barbara Butler *secondary language arts and television production educator*

Prescott
Baca, Sherry Ann *secondary school educator*
Waterer, Bonnie Clausing *retired secondary school educator*

San Manuel
Hawk, Dawn Davah *secondary education educator*
Hawk, Floyd Russell *secondary school educator*

Scottsdale
Phillips, Wanda Charity *secondary education educator, writer*

Sun Lakes
Middleton, Mary *secondary education educator*

Tucson
Fountain, Linda *secondary education educator*
Freiman, Lela Kay *retired secondary school educator*
Schumacher, Mary Lou *secondary education educator*
Sigafus, Evelyn *secondary school educator*
Watts, Lou Ellen *elementary education educator*

ARKANSAS

Beebe
Linder Ward, Debra Susan *secondary school educator*

Booneville
Demchik, Virginia Carol *secondary education educator*

Fort Smith
Maness, Jeanie Jones *secondary education educator, mathematics educator*

Gentry
Ward, Sharon Dee *secondary school educator*

Hot Springs National Park
Irwin, Sara *retired secondary school educator*

Jonesboro
Nelsen, Evelyn Rigsbee Seaton *retired educator*

Little Rock
Williams, Karmen Petersen *secondary school educator*

Monticello
Akin, Barbara Jean *secondary educator*

PROFESSIONAL INDEX — SECONDARY SCHOOL EDUCATION

Newark
Lindsey, Stacey Jean *secondary education educator*

Pine Ridge
Hays, Annette Arlene *secondary school educator*

Rector
Simmons, Rebecca Ann *secondary education educator*

Sheridan
Oates, Edith Lunsford *secondary education mathematics educator*

Stamps
Moore-Berry, Norma Jean *secondary school educator*

Van Buren
Breeden, Betty Loneta *secondary school educator*

CALIFORNIA

Antioch
Thomson, Sondra K. *secondary school educator*

Aptos
Allen, Harold (Jim) *secondary school English educator*

Arcadia
Endrusick, Rose Marie *secondary school educator*

Baldwin Park
Pinheiro, Aileen Folson *secondary education educator*

Benicia
Dunaway, Phillip Lee, Jr., *secondary school education educator*

Berkeley
Davis, Maggie L. *elementary teacher*
McPhail-Geist, Karin Ruth *secondary school educator, real estate agent, musician*

Brentwood
Stillwell, Valorie Celeste *secondary school mathematics educator*

Burbank
Dorobek, Carroll Frances *retired secondary school educator*

Cerritos
Robinson, Terence Vachel *secondary education educator*

Chatsworth
Miller, Robert Steven *secondary school educator*

Chino
Outen, Dawn *secondary education educator*

Colton
Zuccarelli, Sharron Adele *educator*

Corona
Steiner, Barbara Anne *secondary school educator*

Corte Madera
Dalpino, Ida Jane *retired secondary education educator*

Costa Mesa
Fones, Monty Garth *secondary school educator*

Cupertino
Lyon, Mary Lou *educator*

Danville
Sekera, Cynthia Dawn *secondary education educator*

El Monte
Gabriel, Barbara Jamieson *secondary school educator*

Encinitas
Ringstrom, James Rodney *retired secondary school educator*

Encino
O'Connor, Patricia Ranville *secondary and special education educator*

Escondido
Hannam-Oosterbaan, Maria Gertrude *educator*

Eureka
Smith, Roger Lewis *mathematics educator secondary school*

Felton
Blocher, Paul Thomas *secondary education educator*

Fillmore
Bereki, Debra Lynn *secondary education educator*

Folsom
Sarraf, Shirley A. *secondary school educator*

Fremont
Creger, John Holmes *secondary school educator, writer*
Sousa, Joseph Philip *secondary education educator*

Fresno
Nickel, Rosalie Jean *reading specialist*

Gardena
Staton, Shelley Victoria *secondary education educator*

Goleta
Hopkins, Shirley May *former educator, real estate broker*

Hayfork
Viel, Dori Michele *secondary education educator*

Huntington Beach
Davidson-Shepard, Gay *secondary education educator*

Indio
Houghton, Robert Charles *secondary education educator*

Inglewood
Cato, Gloria Maxine *retired secondary education educator, school program administrator*

La Canada Flintridge
Rieger, Bin Hong *secondary school educator*

La Jolla
North, Kathryn E. Keesey (Mrs. Eugene C. North) *retired secondary school educator*

La Mirada
Krotinger, Sheila M. *educator*

La Palma
Akubuilo, Francis Ekenechukwu *secondary school educator*

La Puente
Slakey, Stephen Louis *secondary school educator*

La Quinta
Tebbs, Carol Ann *secondary education educator, academic administrator*

Laguna Beach
Mirone-Bartz, Dawn *secondary school and community college educator*

Lake Elsinore
Wilson, Sonja Mary *retired secondary school educator, poet*

Lemoore
Krend, William John *secondary education educator*

Livermore
Fong, Nelson S. *secondary education educator*

Long Beach
Dublin, Stephen Louis *secondary school educator, singer, musician*
Lofland, Patricia Lois *secondary school educator, travel company executive*
Springer, Wilma Marie *retired secondary school educator*
Wheeler, Diana Jean Miller *secondary education educator*
Writer, Sharon Lisle *secondary education educator*

Los Angeles
Clayton, Ina Smiley *retired secondary education educator*
Gobus, Barbara Chatterton *secondary education educator*
Lee, Jennifer Morita *secondary school educator*
Mallard, Jacqueline *secondary education educator*
Miller, Webster Theodis *retired secondary education educator*
Moriuchi, K. Derek *secondary school educator*
Stevens, Gerald D. *secondary education educator, consultant*
Wagner, Ruth Joos *secondary school educator*
Zexter, Eleanor M. *secondary education educator*

Los Banos
Ellington, Karen Renae *secondary education resource specialist*

Los Gatos
Ferrari, L. Katherine *speaker, consultant, entrepreneur*

Mission Viejo
McGinnis, Joan Adell *retired secondary school educator*

Modesto
Anderson, Carol Elaine *primary and secondary school educator*
Naeve, Catherine Ann *secondary education educator*

Mojave
Shelby, Tim Otto *secondary education educator*

Mountain View
Craig, Joan Carmen *secondary school educator, drama teacher*

Norwalk
McCamly, Jerry Allen *secondary education educator*

Oak Park
Forman, Judith Avis *retired secondary school educator*

Oakland
Isaac Nash, Eva Mae *educator*
Krause, Marcella Elizabeth Mason (Mrs. Eugene Fitch Krause) *retired secondary education educator*
Napier, Beth *secondary education educator*

Oceanside
Johnson, Karen Elaine *secondary school educator, tax specialist*

Ojai
Benton, Gladys Gay *educator, musician*

Ontario
Kennedy, Mark Alan *secondary school educator*
Peters, Jacqueline Mary *secondary education educator*

Orange
Gray, Sandra Rae *retired secondary school educator*

Oroville
Tamori, David Isamu *secondary education educator*

Oxnard
Hamm, George Ardeil *retired secondary education educator, hypnotherapist, consultant*

Palm Desert
Bratrud, Linda Kay *secondary education educator*
Furr, Cyndi J. *secondary school educator*

Pasadena
Stolper, Edward Manin *secondary education educator*

Paso Robles
Gruner, George Richard *retired secondary education educator*

Placerville
Miller, Edna Rae Atkins *secondary school educator*

Pleasanton
Aladeen, Lary Joe *secondary school educator*

Pomona
Demery, Dorothy Jean *secondary school educator*

Rancho Cordova
Hendrickson, Elizabeth Ann *retired secondary education educator*

Redlands
Healy, Daniel Thomas *secondary education educator*

Riverside
Barton, Lauralee Griffin *secondary school educator*

Rocklin
Hyde, Geraldine Veola *retired secondary school educator*

Sacramento
Nelson, Susannah Marie *secondary school educator, literature educator*
Wise-Johnson, Kimberly Ann *middle school educator*

San Diego
Heeter, Norma Jean *secondary school educator*
Idos, Rosalina Vejerano *secondary school educator*
Williams, Carolyn *secondary school educator*
Woodford, Mary Imogene Steele *secondary school educator*

San Dimas
Bettencourt, Don *educator*
Cameron, Judith Lynne *secondary education educator, hypnotherapist*

San Francisco
Finocchiaro, Penny Morris *secondary school educator*
Weed-Wolnick, Patricia Hurley *secondary education educator*

San Gabriel
Tomich-Bolognesi, Vera *secondary school educator*

San Jose
Dampier, Frances May *secondary school educator*
Edwards, Dianne Carol *retired secondary school educator*
Elsorady, Alexa Marie *secondary education educator*
Pflughaupt, Jane Ramsey *secondary school educator*
Rose, Virginia Shottenhamer *secondary school educator*

San Luis Obispo
Kulp, Bette Joneve *retired educator, wallpaper installation business owner*

San Pedro
Gaines, Jerry Lee *retired secondary education educator*
Matich, Matthew P. *alternative secondary school English educator*

Santa Ana
Watts, Judith-Ann White *secondary school educator*

Santa Maria
Dunn, Judith Louise *secondary school educator*

Saratoga
Wood, Gladys Blanche *retired secondary education educator, journalist*

Silverado
Mamer, James Michael *secondary education educator*

Stanton
Durham, Martha L. *retired secondary school educator*

Stockton
Klinger, Wayne Julius *secondary education educator*

Temple City
Provenzano, Maureen Lynn *secondary school educator*

Thousand Oaks
Conaway, Patricia Louise *secondary education English educator*
Rosenberg, Sheila Rae *secondary education educator*

Torrance
McNamara, Brenda Norma *secondary school educator*

Turlock
Antoniuk, Verda JoAnne *secondary school educator*

Twentynine Palms
Clemente, Patrocinio Abiola *secondary education educator*

Vallejo
Baker, Christine Marie *secondary education educator*
Kobak, Theresa Bernice *secondary education educator*
Murillo, Carol Ann *secondary school educator*

Valley Center
Whitten, Laura A. *secondary school educator*

Van Nuys
Altshiller, Arthur Leonard *secondary education educator*

Walnut
Spencer, Constance Marilyn *secondary education educator*

Walnut Creek
Carver, Dorothy Lee Eskew (Mrs. John James Carver) *retired secondary education educator*

West Covina
Wagner, Frances Rita *secondary school educator*

West Hills
McNutt, Margaret H. Honaker *secondary school educator*

Woodland Hills
Swaim, Ruth Carolyn *secondary education educator*
Tapper, Lance Howard *secondary education educator*

Yorba Linda
Lunde, Dolores Benitez *retired secondary education educator*

COLORADO

Aurora
Bowdish, Colette Elizabeth *educator*
Kellogg Fain, Karen *retired history and geography educator*
Matthews, Barbara Lee *teacher, consultant*
Shearer, Carolyn Juanita *secondary school educator*

Boulder
Frender, Gloria G. *secondary school educator*
Knierim, Willis M. *secondary school educator*

Broomfield
Rodriguez, Linda Takahashi *secondary school educator, administrator*

Cheyenne Wells
Palmer, Rayetta J. *technology coordinator, educator*

Colorado Springs
Thompson, William Joseph *secondary school educator, coach*

Denver
DePew, Marie Kathryn *retired secondary school educator*
Goss, Patricia Elizabeth *secondary education educator*
Johnston, Calvin George *secondary education educator*
Mirich, David Gage *secondary education language educator*

Englewood
Nelson, Barbara Louise *secondary education educator*
Whiteaker, Ruth Catherine *retired secondary education educator, counselor*

Evergreen
Berger, Sue Anne *secondary education educator, chemist*

Highlands Ranch
Barenz, John Richard *secondary education educator*
Landis, Sharyn Branscome *educator*
Pond, Barbara Weller *secondary school educator*

Lafayette
London, Douglas *English educator*

Lakewood
Nesmith, Sara *secondary education educator and counselor*

Littleton
Kennedy, Jack *secondary education journalism educator*

Longmont
Wetzbarger, Donna Kay *secondary education educator*

Loveland
Lee, Evelyn Marie *elementary and secondary education educator*

Parker
Crowley, Judith Diane *secondary educator*

Pueblo
Tipton, Karen *middle school educator*
Vest, Rosemarie Lynn Torres *secondary school educator*

Westminster
Selle, Eleanor Blake *secondary education educator*

Yuma
Pfalmer, Charles Elden *secondary school educator*

CONNECTICUT

Avon
Schwartz, Janet Singer *secondary school educator*

Branford
Thomas, Lisa Francine *secondary school educator, assistant principal*

Bridgeport
Pitzschler, Kathryn Van Duren *secondary school educator*

Dayville
Ames, Sandra Cutler *secondary education educator*

East Haven
Dayharsh, Virginia Fiengo *secondary school educator*

Glastonbury
Juchnicki, Jane Ellen *secondary education educator*

Greenwich
Karraker, David Franklin *secondary educator, reading consultant*

Hamden
Brown, Jay Marshall *retired secondary school educator*
Loro, Lauren Marguerite *secondary education educator*
Sola, Janet Elaine *secondary school educator*

Hartford
Rodriguez-Acevedo, Felix Manuel *secondary school educator*
Skerker, Arthur J. *secondary education educator*

Hebron
Lawson, Patricia Gilly *secondary education English educator*

Kensington
Colaiacovo, Christine Mary *secondary school educator*

Manchester
Cazenave, Anita Washington *secondary school educator*

Meriden
Brandt, Irene Hildegard *retired secondary education educator*

Milford
Palochko, Eleanor LaRivere *retired secondary education educator*
Sullivan, Christine Anne *secondary school educator*

New Canaan
Norman, Christina Reimarsdotter *secondary education language educator*

North Stonington
Keane, John Patrick *retired secondary education educator*

Norwalk
Wiggins, Charles *secondary education educator*

Orange
Schwartz, Arlene Harriet *secondary school educator*

Plantsville
Bailey, Bette Ann Patricia *secondary school language arts educator*

Prospect
Straka, Robert John, Jr., *music educator, band director*

Shelton
Bonina, Sally Anne *secondary school educator*

Simsbury
Barnicle, Stephan Patrick *secondary school educator*
DiCosimo, Patricia Shields *secondary school educator*

Southington
Gurga, Rosemary *secondary foreign language educator*

Suffield
Savoie, Ronald E. *secondary educator*

Waterbury
Head, Lillie Jewel *secondary physical education educator*

West Haven
Yeager, Louise Barbara Lehr *secondary education educator*

Wethersfield
Gaudreau, Gayle Glanert *computer resource educator*

Wilton
Gonzalez, Eleanor Morodo *secondary educator*

Windsor
Archibald, Jane Martyn *secondary education educator*

Windsor Locks
Coelho, Sandra Signorelli *secondary school educator, consultant*

DELAWARE

Dover
Braverman, Ray Howard *secondary school educator*
Ferrari, Mercedes V *secondary education educator*

Hockessin
Hounsell, Jillann Cusick *secondary education educator*

Newark
Phillips, Richard A. *English educator*

Wilmington
Renshaw, John Hubert *retired secondary education educator*
Smith, June Ellen *secondary and special education educator*
Wasson, Ellis Archer *history educator*

DISTRICT OF COLUMBIA

Washington
Carter, Dorothy Annis *secondary school educator*
Covington, Eileen Queen *secondary education educator*
Fink, Kristin Danielson *secondary education educator*
Isaacs, Kathleen Taylor *secondary education educator*
Johnson-Brock, Lether Sheree *secondary education educator*
Spencer, Constance Jane *reading educator, consultant*

FLORIDA

Altamonte Springs
Poland, Phyllis Elaine *secondary school educator, consultant*

Babson Park
Reeb, W. Suzanne *retired middle school educator*

Boynton Beach
Kobliner, Richard *secondary school educator*

Casselberry
Breneman, Carol Lou *secondary school educator*

Cocoa
Delisio, Sharon Kay *secondary school educator, school administrator*

Dania
Fernander, Karen Geneine *secondary school educator*

Daytona Beach
Manthey, Robert Wendelin *retired secondary school educator*

Deltona
Venuti, Ruth Louise *secondary school educator, counselor*

Dunedin
Gamblin, Cynthia MacDonald *mathematics educator, lobbyist*

Fort Lauderdale
Fershleiser, Steven Buckler *secondary education educator*
Yaxley, Jack Thomas *secondary education educator*

Fort Pierce
Sampson, Bonita Lippard *health occupations educator*

Fort Walton Beach
Register, Annette Rowan *reading educator*

Gainesville
Kirkland, Nancy Childs *secondary education educator, consultant*
Saucerman, Alvera Adeline *secondary school educator*

Green Cove Springs
Yelton, Eleanor O'Dell *retired reading specialist*

Hernando
Saxe, Thelma Richards *secondary school educator, consultant*

Holmes Beach
Vergason, Glenn A. *special education educator, researcher*

Homestead
Brammer, Barbara Allison *secondary school educator, consultant*

Jacksonville
Brown, Beverly Jean *educator*
Colby, Lestina Larsen *secondary education educator*
Olin, Marilyn *secondary school educator*
Simms, Jacqueline Kamp *secondary education educator*

Jay
Cloud, Linda Beal *retired secondary school educator*

Kissimmee
Evans-O'Connor, Norma Lee *secondary education educator, consultant*

Lady Lake
Head-Hammond, Anna Lucille *retired secondary education educator*

Lakeland
Mooney, Burton Lee *secondary school educator, editor*
Osthoff, Pamela Bemko *secondary education educator*
Wetzel-Tomalka, Mary Margerithe *retired secondary educator*

Land O Lakes
Curbow, Deborah Elizabeth *secondary education educator*
Isenbarger, Rosalie Adams *retired secondary school educator*

Lecanto
Walker, Mary Diane *secondary school educator*

Lutz
Pfeuffer, Dale Robert *secondary school social studies educator*

Marco Island
Petry, Barbara Louise Cross *elementary educator*

Melbourne
Stark, Norman *secondary school educator*

Merritt Island
Young, Nancy M. *retired secondary school educator, artist*

Miami
Bachmeyer, Steven Allan *secondary education educator*
Love, Mildred Allison *retired secondary school educator, historian, writer, volunteer*
Riecken, Ellnora Alma *retired music educator*
Warren, Emily P. *retired secondary and adult school educator*

Middleburg
Castile, Nora Faye Parks *retired secondary education educator*

Miramar
Dennis, Doretha B. *secondary education educator*

New Smyrna Beach
Shaffer, Joye Coy *reading specialist*

Niceville
Schlitt, Jean Wanamaker *secondary school educator*

Ocala
Ovrebo, Judith *retired physical education educator*
Tait, Patricia Ann *secondary education educator*
Westbrook, Rebecca Vollmer *secondary school educator*

Ocoee
Mabie, Susan (Susse Mabie) *secondary education educator*

Okeechobee
Brown, Radie Lynn *secondary school educator*

Orange Park
Ratzlaff, Judith L. *retired secondary educator*

Orlando
Hardesty, Stephen Don *secondary education educator*

Palm Beach Gardens
Dorris, Peter George *secondary mathematics educator*

Pensacola
Abercrombie, Charlotte Manning *reading specialist, supervisor*

Perry
Tuttle, Donna Lynn *secondary school educator*

Pinellas Park
Pellegrino, Nancy Davis *middle school educator*

Pompano Beach
Phillips-Scheuerman, Elizabeth Snedeker *educator*

Port Charlotte
Hixson, Doris Kennedy *retired secondary school educator*

Sanford
Williams, Andrew D. *secondary school educator*

Sarasota
Holland, Martha King *primary and secondary education educator*
Russell, Margaret Jones (Peg Russell) *secondary school educator, retired writer*
Tatum, Joan Glennalyn John *secondary educator*
Williams, Julia Rebecca Keys *secondary school educator*

Sebastian
Kirk, Aida Montequin *secondary education Spanish and home economics educator*

Tallahassee
Crew, Andrew Jackson *retired secondary school educator, band director*

Tampa
Sanchez, Mary Anne *retired secondary school educator*
Scudder, Sallie Elizabeth *secondary education educator*

Valrico
Benjamin, Sheila Pauletta *secondary education educator*
McKinley-Payton, Linda Jo *educator*

Weeki Wachee
Jernstrom, Joan *retired secondary school educator*

Winter Springs
Warner, Maureen Joan *secondary education educator, English*

GEORGIA

Albany
Paschal, James Alphonso *counselor, educator secondary school*
Robbins, Christopher Mark *English educator*

Athens
Coley, Linda Marie *retired secondary school educator*
Marable, Robert Blane *secondary school educator, agricultural studies educator*
Speering, Robin *educator, computer specialist*

Atlanta
Maddox-Adams, Sherry *secondary school educator*
McQueen, Sandra Marilyn *educator, consultant*

Austell
Vance, Sandra Johnson *secondary school educator*

Baxley
Williams, Sonia Kay *retired secondary school educator*

Brunswick
Pittman, Catherine Sylvia *secondary school educator*
Talbott, Mary Ann Britt *secondary education educator*

Canton
Bragg, Rick Arlen *secondary education educator*

Carrollton
Kielborn, Terrie Leigh *secondary education educator*

Chamblee
Lass, Teresa Lee *secondary school and special education educator*

Chatsworth
Witherow, Jimmie David *secondary school educator*

Columbus
Averill, Ellen Corbett *secondary education science educator, administrator*
Edmondson, Michael Herman *secondary school educator*
Salamanca, Merlina Espiritu *secondary education educator*

Cordele
Spires, Denise Tate *secondary education educator*

Dallas
Calhoun, Patricia Hanson *secondary education educator*

PROFESSIONAL INDEX — SECONDARY SCHOOL EDUCATION

Douglasville
Hall, Mary Hugh *retired secondary school educator*
Yates, Brenda H. Carroll *secondary school educator*

Evans
Shrader, Lynne Ann *secondary school educator, coach*

Gainesville
Clark, Debbie Suzanne *secondary school educator*
Fish-Lacey, Helen Therese *educator, author*

Georgetown
Swinson, Sue Whitlow *secondary education educator*

Griffin
Champion, Ann Louverta *secondary school educator*
Hobbs, Alton Dwayne *secondary education educator*

Hazlehurst
Howard, Kathy *secondary education educator*

Jesup
Childers, Anita Flowers *language arts educator*

Jonesboro
Blevins, Andrea Elizabeth *secondary education educator*

Lilburn
Wagner, Douglas Alan *secondary school educator*

Macon
Parrish, Carmelita B. *retired secondary school educator*
Smith, Constance Lewis *secondary school educator*

Marietta
Goodrum, Marlene Roach *secondary school educator*
Matias, Patricia Trejo *secondary education educator*
Norman, Peggy Rocker *retired secondary school educator*
Oliver, Ann Breeding *secondary education educator*
Ramsey, Virginia Carol Marshall *middle school educator*
Rickard, Ruth Ann (Toni Rickard) *secondary school educator*

Millwood
King, Mary Ann *secondary education educator*

Monroe
Lynch, Lillian *retired secondary education educator*

Moultrie
Wright, Kathy Diane *secondary school educator*

Nashville
Parker, Skeeter *secondary school educator*

Newnan
Watkiss, Regina (Regina Monks) *secondary school educator*

Peachtree City
Wilde, Mary *secondary education educator*

Ringgold
Mullis, Lelia Christie *retired secondary school educator*

Riverdale
Lambert, Ethel Gibson Clark *secondary school educator*

Rockmart
Vinson, Victoria Dean *middle school educator*

Roswell
Steine, Lynette Hazel Anne *secondary school educator, educator*

Saint Marys
Hall, Lois Bremer *retired educator, volunteer*

Savannah
Presley, Susan Franklin *secondary school educator, department chairman*

Sharpsburg
Skinner, Lynn Strickland *secondary school mathematics educator*

Stockbridge
Sprayberry, Roslyn Raye *retired secondary school educator*

Suwanee
Gerson, Martin Lyons *secondary school educator*

Toccoa
Lyles, Adele Hemphill *secondary school educator*

Valdosta
Barrett, Patricia Louise *mathematician, educator*

Watkinsville
Kennon, Pamela Canerday *secondary school educator*

Woodstock
Brennan, Ann Richard *secondary education educator*

HAWAII

Honolulu
Keaulana, Jerald Kimo Alama *secondary education educator*
Migimoto, Fumiyo Kodani *retired secondary education educator*

Kailua Kona
Diama, Benjamin *retired educator, artist, composer, writer*

Lihue
Shigemoto, April Fumie *secondary school English language educator*

Pearl City
Rhinelander, Esther Richard *secondary school educator*

IDAHO

Boise
Ferguson, Bettie Jean *secondary education educator*

Idaho Falls
Winston, Jane Kay *secondary education educator, artist*

Lewiston
Marshall, Josie *secondary school educator*

Meridian
Ascuena, Vikki Pepper *secondary school educator*

Preston
Harrold, Merry Ellenor *retired secondary education educator*

Shelley
Thompson, Sandra Jane *secondary school educator*

ILLINOIS

Arcola
Eskridge, Judith Ann *educator, administrator*

Athens
Curry, John Wesley *secondary school educator*

Aurora
Settles, William Frederick *secondary and university educator, administrator*
Sloan, Michael Lee *secondary education educator*

Barrington
Hicks, Jim *secondary education educator*
Riendeau, Diane *secondary school educator*
Scranton-Kraemer, Lynda Kay *secondary education educator*

Batavia
Flannigan, Sandra F. *secondary education educator*

Beecher
Termuende, Edwin Arthur *retired chemistry educator*

Belleville
Frerker, Jeffrey Carl *secondary education educator*

Bethalto
Sabaj, Nancy J. *secondary school educator*

Bradley
Anderson, Janice Lee Ator *secondary education mathematics educator*
Williams, Renee Lynn *secondary mathematics educator*

Calumet City
Housinger, Margaret Mary *math and computer science educator*

Centralia
Williams, Denise *secondary education educator*

Chicago
Anderson, Lorraine *secondary education educator*
Arnold-Massey, Helen Phyllis *health education educator, motivational speaker*
Chippas, Denyse Leilani *secondary mathematics educator, travel agent*
Coleman, Roy Everett *secondary education educator, computer programmer*
Crockett, George Ephriam *secondary education educator*
Davis, Sylvester, Jr., *secondary education educator*
Diaz-Gemmati, Griselle Maritza *secondary education educator*
Drechney, Michaelene *secondary education educator*
Einoder, Camille Elizabeth *retired secondary education educator*
Gajic, Ranka Pejovic *educator*
Hawkins, Loretta Ann *retired secondary school educator, playwright*
Jones-Bland, Valerie Quinetta Brewer *secondary education educator*
Mason, Gregory Wesley, Jr., *secondary education educator*
McDowell, Orlando *secondary education educator*
Petitan, Debra Ann Burke *educator, education counselor, design engineer, writer, author*
Petrak, Cliff Matthew *secondary school educator*

Wallace, Helen Marie *secondary school educator, coach, dean*
Wham, David Buffington *secondary school educator*
Wyndewicke, Kionne Annette (Annette Johnson Moorer) *reading educator*

Chicago Heights
Dutko, Cara Marie *secondary school educator*

Clinton
Gruber, Donald David *secondary education educator, graphic artist*

Collinsville
Bucher, Dorothy Ann *secondary education English educator*
Taake, Karen Reneé *secondary education educator*

Darien
Meyer, James Philip *secondary school educator, social studies educator*

Decatur
Brooks, Leanne Ruth Hurt *secondary school educator*

Des Plaines
Mueller, Susan Gahagan *secondary school educator*

Dolton
Hahn, Gerald Eugene *industrial education educator*

East Moline
Eis, Loryann Malvina *secondary education educator*

Edinburg
Jones, Kenneth D. *secondary education educator, coach*

Edwardsville
Potthast, Ray Joseph *secondary education educator*

Elgin
Aydt, Mary I. *secondary school educator*

Evanston
Doud, Dennis Adair *secondary education educator*

Evergreen Park
Bucinski, Janice Kay *secondary education educator*
Sochacki, Tina Marie *secondary education educator*

Frankfort
Ferreira, Daniel Alves *secondary education Spanish language educator*

Galesburg
Wiegand, Julie Wilds *secondary school educator*

Glenview
Rosenthal, Hilary *secondary school educator*

Grayslake
Watt, Glenn A. *secondary school educator*

Harvey
Jackson, Richard Perry *secondary school educator*

Hoffman Estates
Albamonte, Mary Kay *secondary education educator*
Schmitz, Alice J. *secondary education educator*
Starzynski, Christine Joy *secondary education educator*

Homer
Gilhaus, Barbara Jean *secondary education home economics educator*

Homewood
Schillings, Denny Lynn *retired history educator, educational and grants consultant*

Kankakee
Flanigan, Annette Lipscomb *secondary education educator*
Frogge, James Lewis *secondary school educator*

Lincolnshire
Nehring, Lisa Marie *secondary school educator*
Rauch, Catherine Kerkes *secondary school educator*
Zimmermann, Pamela Semmens *secondary education educator*

Loves Park
Whinna, George Waltman Roper, III, *secondary education educator*

Machesney Park
Cain, Sandra Kay *secondary school educator*

Morton Grove
Mohrdieck, William Allen *mathematician, educator*

Murphysboro
Hall, James Robert *secondary education educator*

Naperville
Burton, Kay Fox *retired secondary education educator, guidance counselor*
Johnson, Herman *secondary education educator*
Martin, Joan Ellen *secondary education educator*
PoPolizio, Vincent *retired secondary education educator*
Rosenthal, Edward Leonard *secondary school educator*

Nokomis
Schneider, Janice Kay *secondary education educator*

Northbrook
Middleton, Deborah O *secondary educator, reading specialist*

O Fallon
Herrington, James Patrick *secondary education educator*

Olney
Saul, Barbara Ann *English studies educator*

Pekin
Strifler, Pete *secondary education educator*

Peoria
Gasparovich, Sandra *educator*

Perry
Woods, Gwendolyn Annette *retired secondary education educator*

Princeton
Weber, Lynne Suzanne *elementary education educator*

Quincy
Bohne, Jeanette Kathryn *retired mathematics and science educator*

River Grove
Brown, Carlos *secondary education educator, psychology educator*
Stein, Thomas Henry *social science educator*

Rockford
Austin, Jane Stewart *educator*
Burdick, Larry Eldon *retired science educator*
Steely, Allen Merle *secondary school educator*
Whitsell, Doris Benner *retired educator*

Rockton
Hollerith, Charles, III, *secondary school educator*

Rolling Meadows
Peekel, Arthur K. *secondary school educator*

Roscoe
Zapke, Clifford F. *secondary education educator*

Roselle
Umlauf, Karen Elizabeth *educator*

Rossville
Tracy, Christina L. *secondary school educator*

Schaumburg
MacDonald, William Burke *secondary education educator, education consultant*

Shelbyville
Storm, Sandy Lamm *secondary education educator*

Skokie
Sloan, Judi C. *former physical education educator*

Springfield
Aiello, Elizabeth Blackwell *secondary school educator*

Tinley Park
Baker, Betty Louise *retired secondary education educator*

Urbana
Rogers, Paula Ann *secondary school educator*

Vernon Hills
Anderson, Lee *secondary school educator*
Kotecki, Joanna Krystyna Emerle *middle school educator*

West Chicago
Kosek, Wayne Richard *secondary education educator*

Westchester
Lisenko, Emilie Dierking *secondary school educator*

Winnetka
Huggins, Charlotte Susan Harrison *secondary school educator, author, travel specialist*

Woodstock
Totz, Sue Rosene *secondary school educator*

INDIANA

Auburn
Gearhart, Marilyn Kaye *mathematics and biology educator*

Butler
Bowman, Connie Jo *secondary education educator*

Cicero
Lay, Andrew Sean *secondary school educator, elementary school educator*

Columbus
Robbins, Mary Ann *secondary school educator*

Crawfordsville
Mosbaugh, Gary Ray *agriculturist, educator*

Elkhart
Preheim, John S. *secondary education educator*

Elwood
Barnett, Marilyn Doan *secondary education business educator*

Fort Branch
Bertram, Michael Wayne *secondary education educator*

Fort Wayne
Daniels, Mark Lee *secondary education educator*

Fortville
Demegret, A. Jean Hughes *secondary education educator, artist*

Gary
Hogan, Linda Rae *educator*
Wells, Charles Robert *secondary education educator*

Hammond
Fehring, Mary Ann *secondary education educator*
Woodson, Adrianne Marie *secondary school educator and coordinator*

Indianapolis
Fischer, Joseph Edward *secondary school mathematics educator*
Guffin, Jan Arlen *secondary education educator*
Russell, Charles E. *secondary school educator*
Woody, John Frederick *retired secondary education educator*

Kokomo
Friedrich-Fox, Marilyn Dale *secondary school educator*

Kouts
Miller, Sarabeth *secondary education educator*

Lafayette
Fernandez, Martin Andrew *secondary school educator*
Hill, Rebecca Sue Helm *secondary education educator*

Marion
Philbert, Robert Earl *secondary school educator*

Merrillville
Roberts, Samuel Alden *secondary school educator*

Monroeville
Sorgen, Elizabeth Ann *retired educator*

New Albany
Rea, Patrick Shaw *secondary school educator*

New Castle
Griffith, John Scott *secondary school educator*

New Harmony
Koch, Jane Ellen *secondary school educator*

Notre Dame
Green, Catherine Gertrude *retired secondary school educator, education educator*

Plainfield
Lucas, Georgetta Marie Snell *retired educator, artist*

Plymouth
Jurkiewicz, Margaret Joy Gommel *secondary education educator*

Richmond
Porter, Patrick Kevin *secondary education educator, administrator*
Routson, Susan Hutchins *secondary school educator, consultant, peer counseling specialist*

Upland
Harbin, Michael Allen *religion educator, writer*

Whiteland
Hadley, Robert Clinton *secondary art educator*

Winslow
McKinney, Shannon J. *retired secondary school educator*

IOWA

Bettendorf
Brugge, Diane Elizabeth *secondary education educator*

Burlington
Lundy, Sherman Perry *secondary school educator*
Noll, Laurie Jane *secondary school educator*

Cedar Rapids
Thompson-Stanton, Mary Jean *secondary educator*

Clinton
Winkler, Joann Mary *secondary school educator*

Corydon
Olson, Diane Louise *secondary education educator*

Denison
Lewis, Phyllis Marie North *retired secondary school educator*

Des Moines
Paterik, Frances Sue *secondary school educator, actress*

Early
Myers, Kenneth L(eRoy) *secondary education educator*

Grimes
Harper, Karen Beidelman *secondary special education educator*

Harlan
Madson, Paulette Kay *secondary school educator*

Lockridge
Wolfe, Eva Agnes *retired educator*

Marshalltown
Peterson, Donald Dean *secondary school educator*

Newton
Ponder, Marian Ruth *retired mathematics educator*

Ottumwa
Mefford, Naomi Ruth Dolbeare *secondary education and elementary education educator*

Pella
Schulte, Matthew Lee *secondary school educator*

Remsen
Hamil, Lynn Ray *secondary education educator*

Sioux City
Mounts, Nancy *secondary education educator*

Traer
Holmes-Ehlers, Valerie Lynn *secondary school educator*

West Des Moines
Holderness, Susan Rutherford *at-risk educator*

Woodward
Jenkins, Alice Marie *secondary school educator*

KANSAS

El Dorado
Cahalen, Shirley Leanore *retired secondary education educator*

Galena
Clyburn, Michael Lee *secondary school educator*

Gardner
Dymacek, Billy Joe *retired secondary school educator*

Hays
Boldra, Sue Ellen *social studies educator, business owner*

Horton
Radford, Virginia Rodriguez *retired secondary education educator, librarian*

Macksville
Rohr, Brenda Ann *band and vocal director*

Madison
Flock, Carol Ann *secondary education educator*

Meade
Coles, Lori Jane *secondary school educator*

Olathe
Haas, Kay Bushman *secondary school English educator*
Williams, Carol Marie *secondary school educator*

Overland Park
Kagan, Gloria Jean *secondary education educator*

Rossville
Wiebers, Dawn Rae *secondary education educator*

Shawnee
Klein, Georgia Ann *retired secondary school educator*

Shawnee Mission
Foreman, Mary Lu *educator*
Stilwell, Connie Kay *secondary school educator*

Sublette
Swinney, Carol Joyce *secondary education educator*

Topeka
Bolejack, Shelly Bess *secondary education educator*
Wilson, Peggy Jo *secondary education educator*

Uniontown
Conard, Norman Dale *secondary education educator*

KENTUCKY

Butler
Mudd, Sheryl Kay *secondary school educator, guidance counselor*

Columbia
Brown, Billy Charlie *secondary school educator*

Corbin
Osborne, Martha P. *secondary education educator*

Edmonton
Bunch, Kathy Lynn *secondary education educator*

Elizabethtown
Sweat, Nora Ellen *home economics educator*

Fairdale
Steffen, Pamela Bray *secondary school educator*

Fordsville
Upchurch, Sally Ann *school counselor*

Fort Thomas
Yelton, Dianne Burgess *secondary school educator*

Frankfort
Vincent, Phyllis Mattingly *secondary music educator*

Lexington
Barren, Michael Joseph *secondary education educator, coach*
Casey, Elberta *secondary education educator*
Lyon, Marina *secondary school educator, translator*
Norman, Charlene Wilson *secondary school educator*
Walters-Parker, Kimberly Kay *secondary school educator*

Louisville
Baugh, Ivan Wesley *retired educator, computer consultant*
Bratton, Ida Frank *retired secondary school educator*
Watts-Wilson, Denise *secondary school educator*

Mount Washington
Williams, Kathryn Sanders *elementary education administrator*

Murray
Russell, Mary Ann *secondary school educator*

Owensboro
Martin, Barbara Ann *secondary education educator*
Melhiser, Myrna Ruth *secondary education educator*

Russell Springs
Ackerman, Anthony Wayne *secondary school educator, band director*

Vanceburg
Phillips, Susan Diane *secondary school educator*

LOUISIANA

Baton Rouge
Harrelson, Clyde Lee *retired secondary school educator*
Kennedy, Melba Faulkner *secondary education educator*
Wilson, Beverly Mangham *secondary education educator, artist*
Wilson, Roosevelt Ledell *secondary education educator*

Boutte
Breaux, Marion Mary *secondary education educator*

Destrehan
Greene, Glen Lee *secondary school educator*

Grant
Leger, Pamela Denise *secondary education educator*

Jennings
Romine, Donna Mae *gifted and talented program educator*

Lafayette
Colbert-Cormier, Patricia A. *secondary school educator*
Rieck, William Albert *secondary school educator and administrator, professor*

Lake Charles
Dronet, Virgie Mae *educational technology educator*
Earhart, Lucie Bethea *volunteer, former secondary school educator*

Mandeville
Arrowsmith, Marian Campbell *secondary education educator*

Metairie
Moak, Mary Jane *secondary education art educator*

New Orleans
Leonard, Barbara Ballard *retired secondary school educator*
Ross, Kathleen *elementary and secondary school educator, author*
Sneed, Barbara Lynn Follins *retired secondary school educator, counselor*

Scott
Resweber, Ellen Campbell *retired secondary education educator*

Shreveport
Smith, Harriet Gwendolyn Gurley *secondary school educator, writer*

Slidell
Sanders, Georgia Elizabeth *secondary school educator*

Edmonton
Schmit, Sharyn Kearney *secondary school educator*

Westwego
Brehm, Loretta Persohn *secondary art educator, librarian, consultant*

MAINE

Ashland
Morrow, David Andrew *secondary education educator*

Fryeburg
Farnham, Dawn Marie *secondary education educator*

South Thomaston
Buffington, Audrey Virginia *educator, consultant, author*

MARYLAND

Annapolis
Calvin, Teresa Ann B. *secondary education educator*

Arnold
Eriksson, Barbara Dunlap *secondary education educator*

Baltimore
Bowser, Geneva Beatrice *secondary school educator, principal*
Giza, Marie Theresa *elementary school educator, secondary school educator*
Taylor, Janet Winona Mills *secondary school educator*
Wallis, Sandra Rhodes *educator*

Brandywine
Rottier, Kathleen Louise *secondary education educator*

Clarksville
Peirce, James Walter *secondary school educator, historian, educator*

Cobb Island
Rudy, Linda Mae *secondary school educator*

Columbia
Davis, Janet Marie Gorden *secondary education educator*
Gross, Linda Maria *secondary school educator*
Hartman, Lee Ann Walraff *educator*

Ellicott City
Fox, Joan Marie *educator*
Wheltle, Margaret Maie *secondary school educator*

Fort Washington
Capitol-Jefferson, Viola Whiteside *secondary education art educator*
Jones, Kenneth Don *secondary education educator*

Frederick
Brauer, Ethel May *secondary education educator*

Germantown
Stroud, Nancy Iredell *retired secondary school educator, freelance writer, editor*

Hanover
BoodhooSingh, Yasmin Shanta *secondary education educator*
Schmidt, Sandra Jean *secondary school educator*

Lanham Seabrook
Campion, Thomas Clifford *secondary school educator*

Laurel
Montgomery, Rose Ellen Gibson *secondary education educator, organist*

Lusby
Ladd, Culver Sprogle *secondary school educator*

Queenstown
Ryans, Reginald Vernon *music education educator, special education educator*

Randallstown
Hood-Mincey, Hollie Nannette *secondary education educator*

Salisbury
Merritt, Carole Anne *secondary school educator*

Silver Spring
Geiger, Anne Ellis *secondary education educator*
McGinn, Cherie M. *secondary education educator*
McLurkin-Harris, Kimberly Elana *secondary education educator*

Suitland
Speier, Peter Michael *mathematics educator*

Towson
Baltzley, Patricia Creel *secondary mathematics educator*

Union Bridge
Rau, Alice Marie *secondary school mathematics educator*

Upper Marlboro
Newsome, Sandra Singleton *elementary education educator, assistant principal*

Street, Patricia Lynn *secondary education educator*

Waldorf
Hastings, Lee L. *secondary education educator*
Robey, Sherie Gay Southall Gordon *secondary education educator, consultant*

MASSACHUSETTS

Agawam
Schilling-Nordal, Geraldine Ann *retired secondary school educator*

Amherst
Trimarchi, Ruth Ellen *educator, researcher, community activist*

Belchertown
Psyris, Thomas George *secondary education educator, consultant*

Beverly
Farrar, David Conrad *secondary school educator, coach*
Hart, Claire-Marie *educator*

Boston
Estabrooks, Gordon Charles *secondary education educator*

Brewster
Milano, Heather Casey *retired secondary education educator*

Bridgewater
Thompson, Andrew Ernest *secondary school educator*

Cambridge
Hamilton, Sharon (Saros) *secondary education English educator*

Concord
Lilien, Elliot Stephen *secondary education educator*

Easthampton
Metras, Gary (leo) *English educator*

Fairhaven
Goes, Kathleen Ann *secondary education educator, choral director*
Rose, Anita Carroll *retired educator*

Fall River
Horvitz, Susan Smith *educator*

Fitchburg
Sullivan, Sally Anne *secondary education educator*

Framingham
Hodgins, Beatrice Davis *educator*

Gardner
Coulter, Sherry Parks *secondary education educator*

Grafton
Tite, John Gregory *secondary school educator*

Haverhill
Charlesworth, Marion Hoyen *secondary education educator*

Holyoke
Parker, Judith Ann Kelley *secondary school educator*

Hudson
Sullivan, J. Bryan *secondary education educator*

Lenox
Vincent, Shirley Jones *secondary education educator*

Leominster
Vogel, Gloria Jean Hilts *secondary school educator*

Lexington
Della Penna, Joan Frances *secondary educator*
McFarland, Philip James *educator, writer*

Mansfield
Iovieno-Sunar, Mary Susan *secondary education educator*

Monson
St. Louis, Paul Michael *foreign language educator*

New Bedford
Romano, Donna Marie *secondary school educator*

Newbury
Hamond, Karen Marie Koch *secondary education educator*

Norwood
Reilley, Margaret Randall *secondary school educator*

Peabody
Costa, Donna Marie *secondary education educator*

Reading
Terilli, Joseph Anthony *secondary education educator*

Sharon
Johnson, Addie Collins *secondary education educator, former dietitian*

Somerset
Camara, Pauline Francoeur *secondary school educator, principal*
Perry, Robert *fine arts and performing arts educator*

South Dartmouth
Hindle, Peter Gage *retired secondary mathematics educator*

South Egremont
Avin, Dorothy Elizabeth Clark *retired educator, artist*

Spencer
Higgins, Jane Edgington *secondary school educator*

Springfield
Knowles, Elizabeth Anne *educator, counselor, assisstant principal*
Miller, Leroy Paul, Jr., *secondary English educator*
St. Laurent, Patricia Rose *secondary parochial school educator*

Turners Falls
Finley-Morin, Kimberley K. *educator*

Walpole
Marshall, Virginia Mary *library media specialist, educator*

Waltham
Mc Menimen, Kathleen Brennan *secondary education educator*

West Falmouth
Vaccaro, Martha Walsh *secondary school educator*

Westfield
Dunphy, Maureen Milbier *reading educator*

Westwood
Rayen, James Wilson *art educator, artist*

Worcester
Robinson, Evelyn Edna *educator*

MICHIGAN

Alpena
Lancour, Karen Louise *secondary education educator*

Ann Arbor
Beutler, Suzanne A. *retired middle school educator, artist*
Eiseman, Timothy William *art and history educator*
Ross, Theresa Mae *secondary school educator*

Bloomfield Hills
Wermuth, Mary Louella *secondary school educator*

Cedar Springs
Thomas, Judith Lynn *retired secondary school educator*

Dearborn
LeVasseur, Susan Lee Salisbury *secondary education educator*

Dearborn Heights
Johns, Diana *secondary education educator*

Detroit
Ellison, James Morton *secondary education educator*
Johnson, Sylvia S. *retired secondary school educator*
Snow, Velma Jean *secondary education educator*

Grand Rapids
Garofalo, Vincent James *secondary education educator*

Grosse Pointe
Gruenwald, Barbara Savage *secondary school art educator, art coordinator*

Gwinn
Lasich, Vivian Esther Layne *secondary education educator*

Huntington Woods
Logan, Linda Mary *art education educator*

Jenison
Roberts-Harvey, Bonita *elementary education educator*

Kalamazoo
Cody, Frank Joseph *secondary school educator*
Gordon, Alice Jeannette Irwin *secondary and elementary education educator*
Ransford, Sherry *secondary education educator*

Lansing
Marazita, Eleanor Marie Harmon *retired secondary education educator*

Lawrence
Bourg, Louise Janette *retired secondary school educator*

Leroy
David, Gloria Elaine *secondary education educator*

Milford
Black, Denise Louise *secondary school educator*

Monroe
Siciliano, Elizabeth Marie *secondary school educator*

Novi
Lorenz, Sarah Lynne *secondary education educator*

Pontiac
Anderson, Anita A. *secondary education educator*
McClellan, Thomas James *math and science educator*

Remus
Turnbull, R. Craig *secondary school educator*

Rockford
Bakita, Sue Jo *secondary education educator*
Teliczan, Casimir Joseph *secondary school educator*

Rogers City
Kosiara, Michael Anthony *secondary education educator*

Royal Oak
Pike, Charlene Helen *retired secondary school educator*

Saginaw
Blue, Robert Lee *secondary education educator*

Stanton
Winchell, George William *curriculum and technology educator*

Sturgis
Brenneman, Mary Beth *secondary educator*

Temperance
Jan, Colleen Rose *secondary education educator*

Trenton
Dillon, Karen Lee *secondary school educator*

Union City
Stanton, Dennis Joe *secondary school educator*

Utica
Olman, Gloria *secondary education educator*

Warren
Cutter, Jeffrey S. *secondary education educator, music educator*
Quay, Gregory Harrison *retired secondary school educator*

MINNESOTA

Bloomington
Allen, Mary Louise Hook *secondary education educator*
Kuntz, Lila Elaine *secondary business education educator*

Eden Valley
Stringer, Patricia Anne *retired secondary educator*

Grand Rapids
King, Sheryl Jayne *secondary education educator, counselor*

Kelliher
Hughes, Patricia E. *secondary education educator*

Mankato
Korpal, Charyl Elaine *secondary education educator*
Seiler, Mark William *technology education educator*

Minneapolis
Eckberg, E. Daniel *secondary education educator*
Fruen, Lois *secondary education educator*
Wilhelm, Gretchen *retired secondary school educator, volunteer*

Monticello
Sonbuchner, Gail Murphy *secondary special education educator*

Moorhead
Emmel, Bruce Henry *retired secondary education mathematics educator*

Preston
Hokenson, David Leonard *secondary school educator*

Rosemount
Bohan, Wanda M. *secondary school educator*
Trygestad, JoAnn Carol *secondary education educator*

Saginaw
Stauber, Marilyn Jean *retired secondary and elementary school*

Saint Cloud
Wertz, John Alan *retired secondary school educator*

Saint Paul
Gabrick, Robert William *secondary education educator*
Tobias, Richard Charles *retired secondary educator, consultant*

Waubun
Sullivan, Kathleen M. Skaro *secondary education educator*

MISSISSIPPI

Ackerman
Coleman, Frances McLean *secondary school educator*

Belmont
Wright, Joan McAnally *English educator*

Biloxi
Cadney, Carolyn *secondary education educator*

Brandon
Streit, Karen Crossno *secondary school educator, curriculum writer*

Clinton
Whitlock, Betty *secondary education educator*

Crystal Springs
Conley, Bobbie Jean *English educator*

Forest
Knowles, Carolyn Sue Edwards *secondary education educator*

Indianola
Crigler, Sammie Mae *secondary school English language educator*

Jackson
Bender, Susan Arlyce *secondary school educator, educational consultant*
Collins, Deloris Williams *secondary school educator*
Cora, Spiro Pete *retired secondary education educator*
Harris, Josephine Stevenson *health educator*

Meridian
Hoskins, Mable Rose *secondary education educator, English language educator*
Reed, Vanessa Regina *secondary education educator*

Natchez
Barfield, Cynthia Marie *secondary school educator*

Nettleton
Hairald, Mary Payne *vocational education educator, coordinator*

Ocean Springs
Kennedy, Cynthia Lynn Thian *secondary educator*

Olive Branch
Mullins, Sharon Goudy *secondary education educator*

Sallis
Perteet, Icy D. *secondary education educator*

Starkville
Hunt, Pamela Stafford *retired secondary school educator*

MISSOURI

Blue Eye
Erickson, Dorothy Louise *counselor, secondary school teacher*

Blue Springs
Shover, Joan *retired secondary school educator*

California
Wood, Mary Marie *secondary education educator*

Columbia
Bay, Marjorie Seaman *secondary school educator*

Deepwater
Baskins, Tamara Anne *secondary school educator*

Defiance
Zutter-Brock, Pamela Jean *secondary school educator*

Florissant
Carman, Robert Eugene *secondary school educator*

Kansas City
Custer, Sharon Lynnette *secondary school educator*
Hoffer, Sharon Marie *secondary education educator*
Price, Mona Renita *music educator, school administrator*
Thomas, Larry Wayne *secondary school educator*
Trotter, Betty Lou *retired secondary school educator*

Kirkwood
Hoglen, Jewel Pamela *retired secondary school educator*

Lees Summit
Rethemeyer, Kay Lynn *secondary school educator*
Reynolds, Tommy *secondary school educator*

Macks Creek
Kinney, Mary May *secondary education educator*

Maryland Heights
Schmoeker, Peter Frank *secondary school educator*

Ravenwood
Henry, Kila Ann *secondary educator*

Saint Charles
Dencker, Linda Craven *secondary school educator*

Saint James
Jenkins, James Boswell *secondary educator*

Saint Louis
Burmeister, Virginia Elizabeth *retired secondary educator*
Grant, Michele Byrd *secondary school educator*
Greminger, Michael Leo *secondary education educator*
Irving, Brenda A. *secondary education educator*
Jordan, Julia Crawford *secondary education educator*
Marshall, C. Christine *secondary education educator*
Pfefferkorn, Michael Gene, Sr., *secondary school educator, writer*
Pfefferkorn, Sandra Jo *secondary school educator*
Richards, Amy Kathleen Burr *secondary school educator*
Schoeneberg, Joyce Eileen *secondary school biology educator*
Williams, Nellie James Batt *secondary education educator*

Sainte Genevieve
Cantu, Dino Antonio *secondary education history educator*
Fluegge, Glenn William *secondary education educator*

Salem
Dent, Catherine Gale *secondary education educator*

Shelbina
Harvey, Denise Elaine *secondary education educator*

Waynesville
Learmann, Judith Marilyn *secondary school educator*

MONTANA

Billings
McDonald, Jacquie Gay *secondary school educator*

Gardiner
Barber, Shannon Michelle *secondary school educator*

Hardin
Alvarado, Rebecca Jane *secondary education educator*

Helena
Duff, Gary Nolan *secondary education educator*

Lodge Grass
Anderson, Della Jean *secondary school educator*

Polson
Hermes, Dean Walter *secondary education educator*

Superior
Tull, Steven Gerald *secondary education educator*

NEBRASKA

Alliance
Schlenker, Shirley May *secondary education educator*

Fremont
Samson, Wanda Kay *secondary school educator, consultant*

Gering
Harvey, Karon Lee *secondary education educator*

Grand Island
Zichek, Shannon Elaine *retired secondary school educator*

Hastings
Devine, Hazel Bernice *retired secondary school educator*
Kort, Betty *secondary education educator*

Lincoln
Epp, Dianne Naomi *secondary educator*

Omaha
Deeths, Lenore Clair *retired secondary education educator*
Garofolo, Ronald Joseph *secondary education drafting and architecture educator*
Konwinski, Maureen Kavanaugh *secondary school educator*
Krecklow, Douglas Earl *secondary education educator, coach*
Lenners, Colleen Renee *secondary education educator*

Stuart
Larabee, Brenda J. *secondary education educator*

NEVADA

Carson City
Keller, Charles Dale *secondary school educator*

Elko
Lovell, Walter Benjamin *secondary education educator, radio broadcaster*

Fernley
Fletcher, Charles *secondary school educator*

Las Vegas
Garn, Susan Lynn *middle school art educator*
Holmes, BarbaraAnn Krajkoski *secondary education educator*
Phillips, Karen *secondary education educator*
Salazar, Pamela Sue *secondary education educator*
Shriner, Joan Ward *secondary school educator*
Smith, Janice Alfreda *secondary school educator*

Minden
Tyndall, Gaye Lynn *secondary education educator*
Zabelsky, William John *choral and band director*

Sparks
Salls, Jennifer Jo *secondary education educator, consultant*

NEW HAMPSHIRE

Alton Bay
Scott, Susan Shattuck *secondary education educator*

Concord
Denham, Robin Richardson *secondary school educator*

Exeter
McLaughlin, Anne Elizabeth *secondary education educator*

Farmington
Meyers, James B. *secondary education educator*

Goffstown
Glines, Jon Malcolm *secondary education educator*

Nashua
Johnson, Arthur V., II, *secondary education educator*
Provencher, Jeanne Stansfield *secondary education educator*

North Haverhill
Brown, Susan Elizabeth S. *secondary school educator*

Northwood
Chatfield, Scott Patrick *secondary school art educator*

Penacook
Hynes, Judith Anne *secondary education educator*

NEW JERSEY

Barnegat
Prisbell, Kathleen Frances *middle education educator, language arts*

Beach Haven
Prevot, Nancie Louise *middle school educator*

Berkeley Heights
Shaffer, Gail Dorothy *secondary education educator*

Brick
Beebe, John Drew, Sr., *secondary education educator*

Bridgewater
Ford, Frederic Hugh *secondary school educator*
Mack, Robert William *secondary school educator*

Caldwell
Lamb, Wendy Karen Laurent *secondary school mathematics educator*

Cedar Grove
Nash, Annamarie *secondary education educator*

Cherry Hill
La Paglia, Umberto *secondary education educator, retired*

Clifton
Roberts, Robert Charles *secondary school educator*

Cresskill
Del Vecchio, Elizabeth Ann *secondary education educator*

East Brunswick
Haupin, Elizabeth Carol *retired secondary school educator*

East Hanover
Tamburro, Peter James, Jr., *secondary school educator*

East Orange
Jones-Gregory, Patricia *secondary art educator*

Garfield
Kobylarz, Joseph Douglas *secondary education educator*

Glassboro
Detofsky, Louis Bennett *secondary education educator*

Highland Park
Hawkins, Calvin Mae *secondary education educator*

Hightstown
Miller, Mary Kathleen *secondary education educator*
Septer, Elizabeth Byrnside *secondary education educator*

Lake Hiawatha
Schonfeld, Rudolf Leopold *secondary school educator*

Lawrenceville
Stehle, Edward Raymond *secondary education educator, school system administrator*

Linwood
Rogers, Debra Lynn *secondary school educator, artist*

Manahawkin
Rahn, James Robert *secondary school educator*

Marlton
Cheney, Eleanora Louise *retired secondary education educator*

Matawan
Lynch-Firca, Diana Joan *secondary education educator*

Mays Landing
McGonigal, Shirley Joan O'Hey *secondary education educator*

Mendham
Posunko, Linda Mary *retired elementary education educator*

Middletown
Gilberti, Judith Anne *secondary education educator*

Monroeville
Stubbs, Barbara Joan *secondary education educator*

Mount Laurel
Haines, Lisa Ann *secondary school educator*

Newton
MacMurren, Margaret Patricia *secondary education educator, consultant*

North Bergen
Rovere, Robert John *secondary school language educator*

Ocean
Petruski, Mary Theresa *secondary school educator*

Old Tappan
Gaffin, Joan Valerie *secondary school educator*

Parlin
Hanns, Christian Alexander *vocational and educational consultant*

Pleasantville
London, Charlotte Isabella *secondary education educator, reading specialist*

Pompton Lakes
Brolsma, Catherine *secondary education educator, educational administrator*

Pompton Plains
Graf, John Christian, Jr., *secondary education educator*

Ramsey
Suchy, Martin Raymond *secondary education educator*

Ridgefield Park
Finch, Carol Anne *former secondary education educator*

Robbinsville
Buono, Frederick J. *secondary school educator*

Rockaway
Allen, Dorothea *secondary education educator*

Roselle
Meister, Karen Olivia *educator*

Roselle Park
Zahumeny, Janet Mae *secondary education educator*

Salem
Enns, Ann Wilson *retired mathematics educator*

Scotch Plains
Refinski, Joseph Anthony *secondary education educator*

Sewell
Letki, Arleen *secondary school educator*

Somerdale
Morgan, Mary Anne *secondary education educator*

Stanhope
Scala, John Charles *secondary education educator, astronomer*

Stone Harbor
Macconi, Mary Davis *secondary education educator*

Teaneck
Baldwin, Dorothy Leila *secondary school educator*
Mahoney, Maureen E. *retired secondary education educator*
Walker, Lucy Doris *secondary school educator, writer*

Toms River
Gluck, Lucille Gindoff *educator*

Trenton
Stefane, Clara Joan *business education secondary educator*

Union City
Makar, Nadia Eissa *secondary education educator, educational administrator*
Sullivan, Kathleen Ann *secondary education educator*

Vernon
Megna, Steve Allan *secondary school educator*
Zweier, Richard Joseph, Jr., *secondary school educator, education supervisor*

Wayne
Benedict, Theresa Marie *retired secondary education mathematics educator*
SchoenGood, Jo-Ann *physical education and health educator*

West Milford
Adams, Catherine Horn *secondary school educator*

Woodbridge
Sabo, Mary Jane *secondary school educator*
Strack, Sharon Ann *educator, musician*

NEW MEXICO

Albuquerque
Graff, Pat Stuever *secondary education educator*
Greene, Linda Kay *retired secondary school educator*
Henke, Ana Mari *secondary education educator*
McCutcheon, Randall James *secondary school educator*
Sanders, Roberta Mae *secondary school educator*
Trunk, James Francis *secondary school educator*

Artesia
Horner, Elaine Evelyn *secondary education educator*

Farmington
Salazar, Gumercindo Prudencio *mathematics educator*

Las Cruces
Bird, Mary Francis *secondary education educator*
Cothrun, Thomas Keith *secondary education educator*
Evans, Eloise Swick *retired educator, writer*
Thayer, Michael J. *secondary education educator*

NEW YORK

Albany
Fadeley, Eleanor Adeline *secondary education educator*
Quackenbush, Roger E. *retired secondary school educator*
Trapasso, Joseph Angelo *secondary school educator, coach*

Babylon
Vaswani, Sheila Ann *secondary education educator*

Bedford
Kluge, Steve *secondary education educator*

Bellmore
Harris, Ira Stephen *secondary education educator, administrator*

Bethpage
Leone, Michele Castaldo *secondary education educator*

Bohemia
Ortiz, Germaine Laura De Feo *secondary education educator, counselor*

Brentwood
Koretzki, Paul Richard *secondary education educator, coach*

Bronx
Payson, Martin Saul *secondary school educator, mathematician*
Reichert, Marlene Joy *secondary school educator, writer*

Bronxville
Flam, Bernard Vincent *retired secondary education educator*
Hamilton, Barbara *secondary school educator*

Brooklyn
Avraham, Regina *retired secondary education educator*

Buffalo
Alderdice, Douglas Alan *secondary education educator*
Amato, Rosalie *educator*
Vitagliano, Kathleen Alyce Fuller *secondary education educator*

Camillus
Davis, Lynn Harry *secondary education educator*

Cape Vincent
Uhlig, Ruth Angus *secondary school educator*

Center Moriches
Flynn-Trace, Patricia M. *secondary education educator*

Centereach
Hoeffner, Balbina Thecla *retired secondary education educator*

Centerport
Rogers, Ailene Kane *retired secondary school educator*

Coopers Plains
Wilson, Louise Astell Morse *home economics educator*

Cortland
Valentine, Gordon Carlton *retired secondary school educator*

Delmar
Davies, Jo Ann *retired secondary school educator*
Quackenbush, Cathy Elizabeth *secondary school educator*

Dobbs Ferry
Lesack, Beatriz Díaz *secondary education educator*

Downsville
Hornick, Susan Florence Stegmuller *secondary education educator, fine arts educator, curriculum specialist, artist*

East Islip
Cullen, Valerie Adelia *secondary education educator*

East Meadow
Beyer, Norma Warren *secondary education educator*
Kalin, Karin Bea *retired secondary school educator, consultant*

East Northport
Zimmer, Stuart *retired secondary school educator*

Elma
Eschner, Joan Elizabeth Michael *elementary education mathematics educator*

Elmont
Pilkington, Frances Jean *secondary school educator*

Endicott
Goodwin, Charles Hugh *technology education educator*

Fairport
Lavoie, Dennis James *secondary education educator*
Wiener, David L. *secondary education educator*

Farmingdale
Setteducati, Anthony David *secondary/elementary educator, English*

Flushing
Roberts, Kathleen Joy Doty *secondary education educator*

Frankfort
Conigilaro, Phyllis Ann *retired elementary education educator*

Freeport
Martorana, Barbara Joan *secondary school educator*

Garden City
Gorin, Robert Murray, Jr., *history educator*

Goshen
Kiernan, Deirdre *secondary education educator*

Grahamsville
Stratton, Charlotte Ethel *retifed secondary education educator*

Great Neck
Feiler Goldstein, Paulette *secondary education educator, researcher*
McAleer, Kathy M. *secondary school educator, language educator*

Hamburg
Cichocki, Sharon Ann *secondary education educator*
Witt, Dennis Ruppert *secondary school mathematics educator*

Harrisville
Seelman, Jannet Genevieve *secondary school educator*

Hempstead
Grinage, Debra L. *secondary education educator*
Jackson, Alethea White *secondary educator*

Hicksville
O'Flaherty, Lucy Louise *secondary education educator*

Hilton
Scutt, Ed *English language educator*

Holbrook
Senholzi, Gregory Bruce *secondary school educator*

Hopewell Junction
Cznarty, Donna Mae *secondary education educator*

Horseheads
Hamilton, Lois Ann *math educator, consultant*
Mortimer, Garth Eugene *mathematics educator*

Hudson Falls
Richard, Peter Wayne *math educator*

Huntington
Lucca, Carole Celiberti *secondary school educator*

Island Park
Estevez, Elia *secondary education mathematics educator*

Jackson Heights
McFadden, Barbara *secondary education educator*

Kingston
Bruck, Arlene Forte *secondary education educator*

Lake Grove
Matthews, Dianne Ferne *mathematics educator*

Larchmont
Gallaher, Carolyn Combs *secondary education educator*

Lindenhurst
DeLuca, Albert R., Jr., *secondary education educator*

Liverpool
Williams, John Alan *secondary school educator, coach*

Lockport
Leader, Bruce Robert *secondary education educator*

Long Eddy
Van Swol, Noel Warren *secondary education educator and administrator*

Lowville
Beagle, Charlotte Ann *secondary education educator*

Malone
Quesnel, Elizabeth Dimick *secondary school educator*

Marcellus
DeForge, Katherine Ann *secondary education educator*

Medina
Berger, Frank Raymond *secondary education educator, county legislator*

Middletown
D'Agostino, Gloria M. *secondary school educator*
McCord, Jean Ellen *secondary art educator, coach*

New Rochelle
Capasso, Frank Louis *secondary school educator*
Donahue, Richard James *secondary school educator*
Reddington, Mary Jane *retired secondary school educator*

New York
Cymet, David *secondary education educator*
Dimino, Sylvia Theresa *elementary and secondary educator*
Ekstrom, Katina Bartsokas *secondary education educator, artist*
Feld, Steve *data coordinator*
Hayes, Joyce Merriweather *secondary education educator*
Rutigliano, Antonio *secondary school and college educator*
Silverman, Martin Morris Bernard *secondary education educator*

Newburgh
Spielhagen, Frances Rose *secondary school educator*

Niskayuna
Bish, L. Ann *retired secondary school educator*

North Massapequa
Kriegstein, Helene Lesly *secondary education educator*

Northville
Wolf, Kelly *secondary school educator*

Norwich
Birmingham, Kathleen Christina *secondary school educator*

Old Westbury
van Wie, Paul David *secondary school educator, historian, educator*

Oneonta
Nassau, Carol Dean *educator*

Palmyra
Rose, Donna Marie *secondary education educator, farmer*

Peekskill
Mason, Rebecca Sussa *retired secondary education educator*
Risoli, Allison Lee *secondary school educator*

Piermont
Dusanenko, Theodore Robert *retired math educator, county official*

Potsdam
Rudiger, Lance Wade *secondary school educator*

Rensselaer
Kennedy, Linda Louise *secondary education educator*

Ridgewood
Giambalvo, Vincent Salvatore *secondary education educator*

Rochester
Cantore Green Oehler, Jean *secondary education educator*
Grant, Marilynn Patterson *secondary educator*
Hurt, Davina Theresa *educator*

Rock Hill
Williams, Annemarie Hauber *secondary education educator*

Roslyn Heights
Jordan, Patricia James *secondary education educator*

Sag Harbor
Sendlenski, Linda Stachecki *secondary education educator*

Saint Johnsville
Sweet, Johanna Mae *secondary school educator*

Saratoga Springs
Ratzer, Mary Boyd *secondary education educator, librarian*

Sea Cliff
Martin, David S. *retired secondary school educator, administrator*

Sidney
Haller, Irma Tognola *secondary education educator*

Suffern
Riba, Netta Eileen *retired secondary school educator*

Syracuse
Shoemaker, Pamela Jean *educator*

Tonawanda
Krucenski, Leonard Joseph *secondary education educator*

Union Springs
Eldred, Thomas Gilbert *secondary education educator, historian*

Van Hornesville
Bronner, Debra Ann *secondary school educator*

Verona
Bly, James Lee *secondary education educator*

Wallkill
Leopold, Richard William *middle school educator*

Wantagh
Stern, Jeannette Anne *secondary school educator*

Warwick
Volpe, Ellen Marie *secondary school educator*

Watertown
Smith, Marcia Jeanne *secondary school educator*

West Hempstead
Natale, Marlene Elvira *secondary school educator*

West Islip
Housman, B. Jane *secondary education educator*

West Nyack
Coffey, Kimberly E. *secondary school educator*
Kanyuk, Joyce Stern *secondary art educator*

Williamson
Ross, Kathleen Marie Amato *retired secondary school educator*

Williamsville
Coniglio, Charles, Jr., *secondary education educator*

Woodmere
Seyfert, Wayne George *secondary education educator, anatomy educator*

Yonkers
Schrader, Diana Lee *secondary education educator*
Tuly, Charles A. *mathematics and computer science educator*
Weston, Francine Evans *secondary education educator*

NORTH CAROLINA

Asheboro
Lineberry, Paul F., Jr., *secondary education music educator*

Asheville
Bryson, Paula Kay *secondary school educator*
Carver, M. Kyle *secondary education educator*
Pickard, Carolyn Rogers *secondary school educator*

Benson
Aranda, Evelyn Bonner *secondary educator*

Biscoe
McIlvaine, William L. *secondary school educator*

Clyde
Parris, Donna Sands *secondary educator*

Durham
Bell, Judith Carolyn Ott *interdisciplinary educator*
Britton, Charles Valentine *secondary education educator*

Graham
Lancaster, Carolyn Hohn *secondary school educator*

Greensboro
Bynum, Magnolia Virginia Wright *retired secondary school educator*
Oliver, Donna H. *secondary education educator*

Hallsboro
Barefoot, Anne Farley *secondary education educator, consultant*

Haw River
Harrison, Carla Isley *secondary education educator*

Hillsborough
Dula, Rosa Lucile Noell *retired secondary education educator*

La Grange
Kennedy, Marian Elizabeth *secondary school educator*

Laurinburg
Snead, Eleanor Leroy Marks *secondary school educator*

Lexington
Murphy, Suellen *home economics educator*

Raleigh
Jarrett, Polly Hawkins *secondary education educator, retired*
Jividen, Loretta Ann Harper *secondary school educator*

Roxboro
Stockstill, James William *secondary school educator*

Shelby
Weathers, Gerald Lee *secondary school educator, educator*

Spruce Pine
Rensink, Jacqueline Biddix *secondary school educator*

Sylva
Montague, Mary Ellen *retired secondary school educator, small business owner*

Waynesville
Boyd, Charles Lee *horticulture educator*

Winston Salem
O'Bryant, Cecyle Arnold *secondary English language educator*
Williams, Frances Elizabeth *retired secondary education educator*

NORTH DAKOTA

Bismarck
Ketterling, Debra M. *secondary school educator*

Golden Valley
Nordgren, Mary Kathleen *secondary school educator*

Grand Forks
Mondry, Diane *secondary school educator*

Mandan
Schroeder, Henry Nick *secondary education educator*

Northwood
Braaten, Linda Marie Skurdell *secondary education educator*

Valley City
Legge, Jean Mary *secondary school educator*

West Fargo
Cwikla, Rich I. *secondary education educator*

OHIO

Ashville
Schilling, Eydie Anne *science educator, consultant*

Beachwood
Sneiderman, Marilyn Singer *secondary and elementary school educator*

Beloit
Plano, Sandra Kay *secondary school educator*

Brunswick
Zahs, David Karl *secondary school educator, educational administrator*

Bryan
Mabus, Barbara Jean *secondary science educator*

Bucyrus
Bowlby, Linda Arlene *secondary school educator*

Chillicothe
Ray, Dennis Robert *secondary school educator*

Cincinnati
Benavides, Marian Terry *secondary education educator*
Capps, Dennis William *retired secondary school educator, artist*
Clutter, Timothy John *secondary language arts educator*
Hadley, Donna Louise Barnes *retired secondary education educator*
Hess, Marcia Wanda *retired secondary school educator*
Johnson, Betty Lou *secondary education educator*
Thompson, Adrienne *secondary school educator*
Wentsler, Gertrude Josephine *secondary school educator*

Cleveland
Kennedy, Frederick Morgan *retired secondary school educator*
Nickerson, Gary Lee *secondary school educator*

Columbus
Benton-Borghi, Beatrice Hope *secondary education educator, author, publisher*
Jackson, John Charles *retired secondary education educator, writer*
Marcus, Lola Eleanor *elementary and secondary education educator*
Silverstein, Linda Lee *secondary school educator*

Dayton
Taylor, Elisabeth Coler *retired secondary school educator*
Wagner, Samuel, V, *secondary school English language educator, college counselor*

East Palestine
Gregory, Judith Mary *secondary education educator*

Eastlake
Kerata, Joseph J. *secondary education educator*

Elyria
Kennard, Emily Marie *secondary school art educator, watercolor artist*

Euclid
Clements, Mary Margaret *retired educator*

Fairborn
Russell-Rader, Kathleen *secondary school educator*

Huber Heights
Behler, Philip Keifer *secondary education educator*

Hudson
Radie, Christine Jo *middle school educator*

Jamestown
Liem, Darlene Marie *secondary education educator*

Kent
Fultz, John Howard *retired middle school educator*
McClure, Michael Jay *secondary education educator*

Kettering
Denlinger, Vicki Lee *secondary school physical education educator*
Taylor, Billie Wesley *retired secondary education educator, investor*

Kings Mills
Hill, Sandra Kay *secondary educator, librarian*

Lakewood
Fritsch, Carla E. *secondary education educator*

Massillon
Walker, James William *secondary education educator, freelance writer*

Mc Connelsville
Retton, Sandra Jo *physical education educator, coach*

Mentor
Shaffer, Becky Marie *secondary mathematics educator*

Mount Gilead
Brucker, Robin Rae *secondary education art educator*

Mount Vernon
Shriver, William Russell *secondary educator*

Napoleon
Gribler, Jeffery Lynn *secondary education educator*

New Middletown
Ade, Barbara Jean *secondary education educator*

New Philadelphia
Doughten, Mary Katherine (Molly Doughten) *retired secondary education educator*
Goforth, Mary Elaine Davey *secondary education educator*

Newark
Williams, Gale Cady *secondary education educator*

Newton Falls
Baker, Don Forrest *secondary educator*

Niles
Bako, Phyllis Jean (Phyllis Jean Blott) *art educator, consultant*

Oberlin
Zinn, Mary Farriss *educator*

Oxford
Dizney, Robert Edward *retired secondary education educator*

Painesville
Blyth, Ann Marie *secondary education educator*

Parma
McFadden, Nadine Lynn *secondary education Spanish educator*

Perrysburg
Zuchowski, Beverly Jean *chemistry educator*

Pickerington
Collins, Arlene *secondary education educator*

Port Clinton
Randels, David George *secondary school educator*

Saint Paris
Ward, Marcia Balmut *secondary education educator*

Strongsville
Dillon, Frederick L. *secondary education mathematics educator*

Tiffin
Hart, Gary Charles *secondary school educator*

Toledo
Berson, Michael Jay *secondary education educator*
Binkley, Jonathan Andrew *secondary education educator, government educator*

Uniontown
Whited, Linda Lee *secondary school English language educator*

University Heights
Mahon, Marinna Fairbank *secondary education educator, writer, consultant*

Vandalia
Schaefer, Sandra Ellen *secondary education educator*

Waterford
Montgomery, Gretchen Golzé *secondary education educator*

West Chester
Garland, Connie Jo *secondary health and physical education educator*

Westerville
Anderson, Jane Ellsworth *secondary school educator*

Xenia
Willis, Douglas MacArthur *secondary education educator, consultant*

Youngstown
Coleman, Esther Mae Glover *retired secondary school educator*
Rupert, William Alphonse *secondary school educator, counselor*

Zanesville
Lineweaver, Paul Kelton *retired secondary education educator*

OKLAHOMA

Durant
Weiner, Kathy Carole *secondary educator*

Edmond
Chase, Eugene Thomas *secondary school educator*
Helie, Robert Alden *secondary education educator*
Zabel, Vivian Ellouise *secondary education educator*

Enid
Dyche, Kathie Louise *secondary school educator*
Toews, Charlotte Louise *secondary school educator*

Hammon
Bottom, Doris Allene *secondary school educator*

Kingfisher
Schieber, Christiana Elizabeth *secondary education educator*

Norman
Hamilton, Donna Martha *secondary education educator*

Oklahoma City
Brady-Black, Wandalene *secondary school educator*

Paden
Adams, Darlene Agnes *secondary education educator*

Ponca City
Poole, Richard William, Jr., *secondary school educator*

Wilburton
Johnston, Joyce Ashmore *secondary education educator*

OREGON

Ashland
Baird, Susan Elizabeth *secondary education educator, writer*

Beaverton
Duncan, Richard Fredrick, Jr., *secondary education educator, travel consultant*

Bend
Forbes Johnson, Mary Gladys *retired primary education educator*

Cannon Beach
Wismer, Patricia Ann *retired secondary education educator*

Florence
de Sá e Silva, Elizabeth Anne *secondary school educator*

Grants Pass
Agricola, Dianne G. *secondary education educator, tutor*

Hillsboro
Cleveland, Charles Sidney *secondary education educator*

Madras
Hillis, Stephen Kendall *secondary education educator*

Monmouth
Dunn, Doris Marjory *retired educator, volunteer*

Ontario
Gaskill, John William *secondary school educator*

Portland
Darling, Lynda Karen *secondary education educator*

Sisters
Keppler, Donald John *secondary education educator*

Springfield
Rasmussen, Ellen L. *secondary school educator*

Tillamook
Voges, Alice Furby *retired secondary school educator, real estate agent*

Yamhill
Close, Beverly Jean *secondary education educator*

PENNSYLVANIA

Allentown
Buenaflor, Judith Luray *secondary education educator*

Annville
Kreiser, Raymond Michael *secondary school educator*

Ashland
Lucas, Harry David *secondary education educator*

Biglerville
Marks, Nora Maralea *retired secondary school educator*

Bloomsburg
Traugh, Donald George, III, *secondary education educator*

Brownsville
Dryburg, Ann *secondary education educator*

Chester
McFarland, Ella Mae Gaines *secondary school educator, elementary school educator*

Chester Springs
Kulp, Jonathan B. *retired secondary school educator*

Claridge
Perich, Terry Miller *secondary school educator*

Clarks Summit
Hatton, Brenda Nafzinger *secondary education educator*

Clymer
Busovicki, John Francis *secondary education educator*

Cochranton
Miller, Carl F. *secondary school educator*

Columbia
McTaggart, Timothy Thomas *secondary education educator*

Coraopolis
Fryz, Betty Farina *educator*

Dallas
Hunter, Todd Lee *secondary school music educator*

Darragh
Ferens, Marcella *secondary school educator, business executive*

Davidsville
Bowman, Jan Marie Albright *secondary English educator*

Downingtown
Valentin, Joan Marie *secondary school educator*

Doylestown
Somers, Sarah Pruyn *retired elementary school educator*

Du Bois
Kearney, Linda Lee *secondary education educator*

Exeter
Stocker, Joyce Arlene *retired secondary school educator*

Exton
DeBernardis, Bruce *secondary education educator*
Shollenberger, Sharon Ann *secondary school educator*

Fairless Hills
Glasheen, Gloria D. *secondary school educator*
Hess, Frances Elizabeth *retired secondary school educator, retired director*

Freeport
Dillen, William C., Jr., *secondary school educator*

Gettysburg
Sommers, Barbara Jean *secondary educator*

Hamburg
Weiss, Gerald Francis, Jr., *secondary education educator, coach*

Hanover
Toft, Thelma Marilyn *secondary school educator*

Harleysville
Johnson, Andrew W. *secondary education educator*

Hellertown
Eckert, Sandra Lynn *secondary education art educator*

Hershey
Hortman, David Jones *secondary education educator*

Hollidaysburg
Bradley, Audrey Laverne *secondary school educator*

Johnstown
Jones, Thomas William *secondary education educator, consultant*
Lindberg, Stephen *secondary education educator*

Kennett Square
Brigman, Dorothea Jane Pengelly *secondary and elementary education educator*
Eaton, Jana Sackman *secondary school educator*

King Of Prussia
Hawes, Nancy Elizabeth *mathematics educator*
Olexy, Jean Shofranko *English language educator*

Lancaster
Albright, Annarose M. *secondary school educator*

Lansford
Heffelfinger, Karan Annice *home economics educator*

Lock Haven
Bowers, Gloria Mills *secondary education art educator*

Mc Murray
Cmar, Janice Butko *home economics educator*

Mechanicsburg
Rudolph, Robert Norman *secondary school educator, adult education educator*

New Castle
Roux, Mildred Anna *retired secondary school educator*

New Holland
Good, Joanna Christina *retired secondary education educator*

New Stanton
Maxin, Alice J. *educator, labor relations specialist, presenter, facilitator*

Newtown Square
LeDonne, Deborah Jane *secondary education educator*

Northampton
Bartholomew, Gordon Wesley *health and physical education educator*

Palmyra
Miller, John Patrick *secondary education educator*

Patton
Pompa, Louise Elaine *secondary school educator*

Philadelphia
Lynch, William Francis, Jr., *secondary mathematics educator*
Rains, Muriel Barnes *retired secondary school educator, real estate agent*
Shakespeare, Edward Oram, III, *retired secondary school educator*
Simms, Amy Lang *writer, educator*
Snyder, Donald Carl, Jr., *secondary education educator*

Philipsburg
Shore, Shirley Walther *retired secondary school educator*

Pine Grove
Brand, Patricia Elizabeth *secondary education educator, librarian*

Pittsburgh
Bowers, Linda Herald *secondary education educator*
Carney, Ann Vincent *retired secondary education educator*
Carter-Jones, Sheila Lorraine *secondary school educator*
Wilson, Mark Moffett *secondary school educator*

Pittston
Schillaci, Patricia Ann *secondary school educator*

Plains
Elias, Joseph *secondary school educator*

Port Royal
Krow, Joyce Anne *secondary education eductor*

Punxsutawney
Graffius, Richard Stewart, II, *middle school educator*

Quakertown
Houston, Tracy Anne *secondary education educator*

Red Lion
Van Kouwenberg, Martha Nester *secondary education educator*

Ridgway
Hanes, Sandra Jean *secondary education educator*

Ridley Park
Brittell-Whitehead, Diane Peeples *secondary education educator, addiction counselor*

Sharon Hill
Poynton, John Thomas *secondary school educator*

Shiremanstown
Bouvier, Janet Laubach *secondary education educator*

State College
Link, Phoebe Forrest *educator, author*

Swiftwater
Braithwaite, Barbara J. *secondary school educator*

Troy
Lane, Carol Ann *secondary school educator*

Upper Darby
Leiby, Bruce Richard *secondary education educator, writer*

Warminster
Bonner, Mary Christine *secondary education educator, school system administrator*

Wayne
Ashley, Sheila Starr *retired educator, translator*

Waynesburg
Hatfield, Janice Lee (Ford) *secondary education educator*

West Chester
Hammonds, Jay A. *retired secondary education educator, administrator*

West Mifflin
DiCioccio, Gary Francis *secondary education educator*

Wexford
Bogos, Frances Lee *secondary school educator*

Willow Grove
Hoffman, Timothy James *secondary education educator*

RHODE ISLAND

Lincoln
Brites, José Baptista *secondary education educator, writer, artist*

Middletown
Yates, Elsie Victoria *retired secondary school educator*

Newport
Wood, Berenice Howland *retired secondary school educator*

North Kingstown
Sironen, Lynn Jane *secondary school educator*

North Providence
Markey, Mary Helen *secondary education educator*

Providence
Sweeney, Judith Kiernan *secondary education educator*

Rumford
Forrest, Kathleen *secondary education educator*

Warwick
Izzi, John *educator, author*

Westerly
Crowley, Cynthia Johnson *secondary school educator*

Woonsocket
Stubbs, Donald Clark *retired secondary school educator*

SOUTH CAROLINA

Aiken
Kanne, Elizabeth Ann Arnold *retired secondary school educator*
Salter, David Wyatt *secondary school educator*

Beaufort
Jenkins, Margie Kline *secondary school educator*
Shaw, Danny Wayne *educational consultant, musician*

Bowman
Glover, Deloris Dickson *history educator*

Columbia
Bernhagen, Debbie Anne *middle school educator*
Fields, Harriet Gardin *counselor, educator, consultant*

Darlington
Harrison, Valerie E. *English language educator*

Fort Mill
Honeycutt, Brenda *secondary education educator*

Greenwood
Williams, Sylvester Emanual, III, *secondary school educator, consultant*

Hartsville
Ingram, Gladys Almenas *secondary school educator*

Hemingway
Mitchum, Margaret Elaine *secondary educator*

Hilton Head Island
Fleischman, Kathryn Agnes *secondary education educator*

Hopkins
Hollingsworth, William Robert, Jr., *secondary education educator*

Marion
Kirkpatrick, Donald Robert *secondary school educator*

Myrtle Beach
Stanley, Denise Rose *secondary school educator*

Piedmont
Duncan, Donna Fowler *secondary school educator*

Rock Hill
Yeager, Bernice Whittaker *elementary and secondary school educator*

Spartanburg
Agnew, Janet Burnett *secondary education educator*
Jones, Virginia Allen *secondary education educator, site director*

Sumter
Wilder, Dorothy Ann *secondary school educator*

Walterboro
Turner, Catherine McDonald *middle school principal*

West Columbia
Williams, Sabrina Rose Hancock *middle school education educator*

SOUTH DAKOTA

Groton
Nelson, Dorene *secondary education educator*

North Sioux City
Rasmussen, Jerry William *secondary school educator*

Rapid City
Tays, Glenny Mae *retired secondary educator, adult education educator*

Spearfish
Thie, Genevieve Ann Robinson *retired secondary school educator*

Watertown
Meyer, Todd Kent *secondary school educator*

TENNESSEE

Apison
Lockerby, William H. *secondary education educator, administrator*

Benton
Pippenger, Wilma Jean *secondary school educator, principal*

Big Sandy
Hancock, Sandra Olivia *secondary school educator, elementary school educator*

Brentwood
Head, Anita Nix *secondary educator*

Clarksville
Myers, Linda Shafer *secondary educator*

Dyersburg
Robertson, Wanda Sue *secondary school educator*

Hendersonville
Phillips, Jeffrey Taylor *secondary school music educator*

Holladay
Allen, Wanda Ruth *secondary school educator*

Humboldt
Moore, Alice Cravens *retired secondary school educator*

Jackson
Hearn, Beverly Jean *secondary education educator, librarian*

Jonesborough
Range, Denver Hal *educator*

Kingston
Lannom, Julie Conway Hudson *secondary education educator*

Madison
Harvey, Donald Leroy *secondary education educator*

Memphis
Sigler, Lois Oliver *retired secondary school educator*
Watson, Ada *secondary education educator*

Nashville
Brewer, Carol Dean Coaker *secondary school English language educator*
Collins, Joe Lena *retired secondary school educator*

Paris
Brashear, Joy Ramona *secondary school educator*

Soddy Daisy
Watson, James Stanley *secondary education educator*

White House
Tomkins, Susan Gail *secondary education educator*

TEXAS

Abilene
Boyd, Cindy June *secondary mathematics educator, consultant*
Crymes, Mary Cooper *secondary school educator*

Alvin
Roberson, Deborah Kay *secondary school educator*

Austin
Lehmann-Carssow, Nancy Beth *secondary school educator, coach*

Baytown
Black, Sarah Joanna Bryan *secondary school educator*

Bedford
Zamorano, Wanda Jean *secondary education educator*

Boerne
Goode, Bobby Claude *retired secondary education educator, writer*

Brownsville
Santa-Coloma, Bernardo *secondary school educator, counselor*

Buda
Howell, Richard C. *secondary education educator*

Channelview
Courville, Susan Kay *secondary education educator*

Cleburne
Wall, Carlon Earl *secondary education educator*

Copperas Cove
Wagner, Susan Elizabeth *secondary school educator*
Wright, David Ray *secondary school educator*

Corpus Christi
Falkner, Ann Coody *secondary school educator*

Cypress
Wacker-B., Deborah *secondary Spanish and special education educator*

Dallas
Allen, Linda *secondary education educator*
Chapman, Kathy *secondary school educator*
Dumerer, Lorraine JoAnne Lori *social studies educator, clinician, consultant*
Harbaugh, Lois Jensen *secondary education educator*
Lindsey, Tanya Jamil *secondary education administrator*
Marks, Ann Thrasher *secondary and special education educator*
Matsumura, Donna Shigeko *secondary education English educator*
McCartor, Sheila Smith *secondary school educator*
Owen, Carolyn Sutton *educator*
Poindexter, Barbara Glennon *secondary school educator*
Reed, Timothy Max *secondary education educator*
Reynolds, Annette *secondary school educator*
Shaw, Laquetta Aveitte *computer specialist*
Swinton, Gwendolyn Delores *secondary education educator*
Yarbrough, John William *secondary school educator*

Decatur
Antoine, Terry Wayne *secondary school educator*

Denton
McAfee, Jill Randolph *secondary education educator*

Dickinson
Rubach, Jimmy Dale *vocational services educator*

Dripping Springs
Palmer, Dow Edward, Jr., *secondary educator*

Eagle Pass
Sumpter, Maria Elvira *secondary school educator*

Edgewood
Cates, Sue Sadler *educational diagnostician*

El Paso
Glover, Cindy *secondary school educator*
Jaraba, Martha E. (Betty Jaraba) *secondary school educator*
Kvapil, Donna Lee *secondary school educator*
Pena, Diana C. *mathematics educator*

Euless
Holbrook-Bryant, Jean Carroll *music educator, band director*
Kaufman, Susan Nanette Bland *secondary school educator*

Farmers Branch
Chambliss, Charlotte Marie *secondary education educator*

Farwell
Franse, Jean Lucille *secondary school educator*

Flatonia
Koudelka, George John *retired music educator*

Fort Worth
Braudaway, Gary Wayne *secondary school educator, administrator*
Cox, Alma Tenney *retired English language and science educator*
Zaslavsky, Robert *secondary school educator*

Garland
Foster, Rebecca Anne Hodges *secondary school educator*

Goree
Presnall, Bobby Joe *retired math educator*

Grand Prairie
Craig, Larry Vernon *secondary school educator*

Grapevine
Carter, Terri Gay Manns *Latin language educator*
Kraft, Karen Ann *secondary school educator*

Haltom City
Deering, Brenda Florine *secondary education educator*

Harker Heights
Unwin, Cynthia Girard *secondary education educator*

Henderson
Knapp, Virginia Estella *retired secondary education educator*

Houston
Darst, Mary Lou *secondary school educator*
Dent, Leanna Gail *secondary art educator*
Fisher, Janet Warner *secondary school educator*
Hitchman, Cal McDonald, Sr., *secondary education educator*
Maddox, Iris Carolyn Clark *secondary education educator*

Pennell, Linda Bennett *secondary school educator*
Rice, Emily Joy *retired secondary school and adult educator*
Robinson, Esther Martin *secondary school educator*
Schell, Mary Elizabeth *secondary education educator*
Sharp, Douglas Andrew *secondary school educator, educator*
Singleton, Robert *secondary school educator*
Timme, Kathryn Pearl *secondary education educator*
Whiting, Martha Countee *retired secondary education educator*
Woodward, Katherine Anne *secondary education educator*

Irving
McVay, Barbara Chaves *secondary education mathematics educator*
Rutledge, Deborah Jean *secondary school educator, music educator*

Kerrville
Ashley, Marjorie *retired secondary school educator*

Kingsville
Wiley, Millicent Yoder *realtor, pianist, accompanist, retired secondary school educator*

Klein
Slater, Joan Elizabeth *secondary education educator*

La Porte
Zimmer, Greta Gay *secondary school educator*

Lake Creek
Smith, Shirley Ann Nabors *retired secondary school educator*

Lampasas
Bear, Robert Emerson *secondary school educator*

League City
Morrell, Janine Marjorie Dacus *secondary education educator*

Leonard
Bonner, Brenda Carol *secondary school English educator*

Littlefield
Buckley, Myrna J. *secondary school educator*

Longview
Thompson, Jeanie Waller *secondary school educator*

Mabank
Beets, Hughla Fae *retired secondary school educator*

Magnolia
Esmond, Cheri Sue *secondary school educator*

Mart
Mathews, B. J. *secondary education educator*

Mc Kinney
Smith, Doris Wilma Dunn *retired mathematics and science educator, writer, poet, speaker*

Mcallen
Gonzalez, Rolando Noel *secondary school educator, religion educator, photographer*
Ramirez, Leo Armando *secondary school educator*

Mercedes
Schroll, Mark *research and development electronics educator*

Mesquite
Patrick, Pamela Ann *research consultant*

New Braunfels
Stephenson, Judyth Ann *secondary school educator*

Odessa
MacDonald, Karen Hope Cowart *educator, reading specialist*
Rasor, Doris Lee *retired secondary education educator*

Pasadena
Bezdek, Donna Anne *secondary school educator*

Perryton
Doerrie, Bobette *secondary education educator*

Plano
Gideon, Sharon Lee *secondary education educator*
Welsh, Sharon A. *elementary and secondary school educator*

Port Arthur
Davis, Beatrice Anna Kimsey *educator, civic worker*

Ranger
Morris, Michael Dale *athletic director, educator*

Rhome
Brammer, Barbara Rhudene *retired secondary education educator*

Richardson
Harp, Rose Marie *secondary education educator*
Shoffstall, Susan Diane *secondary school educator*

Young, Malcolm Eugene, Jr., *social studies secondary educator*

Rockwall
Keggereis, Norma Jean *music educator, composer, arranger, arranger, vocalist, keyboard artist*

Rusk
Hendrick, Zelwanda *drama and psychology educator*

San Antonio
Cox, Joanne Furtek *secondary school educator*
Irwin, Margaret Lynn *secondary education educator*
Kelly, Mae Baker *secondary education educator*
Ledvorowski, Thomas Edmund *secondary education educator*
Logan, Linda Jo *secondary school educator*

San Marcos
Schiflett, Peggy L. Kucera *secondary school educator, consultant*

Santa Fe
Meier, Sheila Rosalind *secondary school educator*

Seagraves
McAdoo, Carolyn *secondary school business educator*

Sherman
Jarma, Donna Marie *secondary education educator*

Spade
Davis, Thomas Pinkney *secondary school educator*

Spring
McClure, Michael Craig *secondary education administrator*
Ortmann, David C. *secondary school educator*

Stephenville
Sims, Larry Kyle *secondary school educator*

Talpa
Russell, Nedra Joan Bibby *secondary school educator*

The Woodlands
Butler, Mary Margaret *secondary education educator*
Emmons, Janet Galbreath *secondary education educator*
Sharman, Diane Lee *secondary school educator*

Tomball
Barron, Sandra McWhirter *library media specialist*

Tyler
Waller, Wilma Ruth *retired secondary education educator and librarian*

Waco
Emanuel, Gloria Page *secondary school educator*
Hollingsworth, Martha Lynette *secondary school educator*

Waller
Powell, Linda Stermer *mathematics educator secondary schools*

UTAH

Kaysville
Dickson, Marjorie Wagers Thatcher *secondary school educator*

Provo
Bangerter, Vern *secondary education educator*

Salem
Hahn, Joan Christensen *retired secondary education educator, travel agent*

Salt Lake City
Folland, Sharon Kay *secondary education educator*

VERMONT

Burlington
Allard, Judith Louise *secondary education educator*
Ferrari, Dennis M. *secondary education educator*

Middlebury
Forman, Michele *secondary school educator*

Plainfield
Oravec, Edward Paul *secondary school educator*

Saint Albans
Lazarnick, Sylvia *secondary education educator*

South Burlington
Sorrell, Ann Jean *secondary education educator*

VIRGINIA

Alexandria
Brown, Ann Herrell *secondary school educator*

Arlington
Finta, Frances Mickna *secondary school educator*
Leibensperger, Philip Wetzel *secondary education educator*

Welsford, James Joseph *secondary school educator*

Ashland
Stevenson, Carol Wells *secondary education educator*

Blacksburg
Wall, Robert Thompson *secondary school educator*

Charlottesville
Greville, Florence Nusim *secondary school educator, mathematician*
Norcross, Barbara Breeden *retired educator*

Chesapeake
Carson, Michael *secondary school educator, music educator*
Mizelle, Teresa Kay *secondary education educator*
Russell, Leonia Lavern *mathematics educator*
Spady, Benedict Quintin *secondary education educator*

Fairfax
Rendine, Maria Farese *secondary education educator*

Fishersville
Geiman, Stephen Royer *secondary school educator, coach*

Fredericksburg
Dameron, Betty Coffey *secondary education educator*

Galax
Key, Rita Kay *secondary education educator*

Goochland
Clay, John Harris, Jr., *secondary school educator*

Great Falls
Andrews, Betty Bauserman *retired secondary school educator, property manager*

Hampton
Fox, Margaret Louise *retired secondary education educator*

Harrisonburg
Emswiller, Ella Mae Custer *retired secondary school educator*

Hillsville
Becker, Elizabeth Anne *secondary education educator*

Lynchburg
Sullivan, Gregory Paul *secondary education educator*

Mc Lean
DeMott, Sara (Sally) Louise *secondary school educator*
Michalowicz, Karen Dee *secondary education educator*

Midlothian
Smoots, Rene Wagner *secondary school educator*

Moseley
Leslie, Lynn Marie *secondary education educator*

Norfolk
Gatje, George Carlisle *retired secondary education educator*

Orange
Reith, Linda Jo *secondary school educator*

Petersburg
Miles, Ruby Williams *secondary education educator*

Portsmouth
Butts, Georgia Lebrendelle *secondary education educator*
White, Mary George *business, economics educator*

Powhatan
Leighty, Diane Carol *secondary education educator*

Reston
Grefe, Jean Butler *secondary education art educator*

Richmond
Mottley, Melinda *secondary education educator*

Roanoke
Bersch, Martha Ratledge *secondary education educator*
Coleman, Sallye Terrell *retired social studies educator*
Price, Leroy Vernon *secondary school educator*

South Hill
Brooks, Arlene Sheffield *secondary education educator*
Taylor, Jean Mull *home economics educator, secondary educator*

Vienna
Cramer, Roxanne Herrick *retired gifted and talented education educator*
Duffield, Eleanor McAlpin *secondary education educator*

Virginia Beach
Monroe, Katherine Diane Osborne *secondary education educator*

Waller, Neola Shultz *secondary school educator*

Williamsburg
Bell, Christine Marie *secondary educator*
Smith, James Brown, Jr., *secondary school educator*
Williams, Ruth Elizabeth (Betty Williams) *retired secondary school educator*

Winchester
Aikens, Elaine Bower *secondary school educator*
Pleacher, David Henry *secondary school educator*

WASHINGTON

Auburn
Irwin, Deborah Jo *secondary education educator, flutist*

Bellevue
Wallentine, Mary Kathryn *secondary educator*

Benton City
Dobson, Andrea Carole *secondary school educator*

Brush Prairie
Bates, Margaret Habecker *secondary educator*

Enumclaw
Goff, Thomas M. *secondary education educator*

Everett
Callaghan, Mary Anne *secondary school educator*

Issaquah
Inman, Ana M. Jimenez *secondary education educator*

Kennewick
Thomas, Alta Parker *retired secondary school educator*

Kent
Armstrong, Leslie Ann Cronkhite *educational visual arts specialist, graphic artist*

Lacey
Cofer, Suzanne Marie *secondary school educator*
Kuniyasu, Keith Kazumi *secondary education educator*

Lynnwood
Ransons, Ellen Frances *high school administrator*

Mabton
Bazaldua, Christina Jo *secondary education educator*

Mercer Island
Van Valin, Sharon Frances *secondary school educator*

Mount Vernon
Blue, Nancy Ann *retired home economics educator*

Prosser
Boyle, Steven Leonard *secondary school educator*
Deffenbaugh, Kay Anne *secondary education art educator*

Seattle
Beaumonte, Phyllis Ilene *retired secondary school educator*
Brink, Dean Clifford *secondary school educator*
Drew, Jody Lynne *secondary education educator*
Voegtlin-Anderson, Mary Margaret *secondary school educator, music educator*

Shoreline
Rubinstein, Robin Levine *secondary school educator*

Spanaway
Paris, Kathleen *secondary school educator*
Parker, Lynda Christine Rylander *secondary education educator*
Roberts-Dempsey, Patricia E. *secondary school educator*

Spokane
Gerard, Susan Jane *secondary education educator*
Lemaitre, Louis Antoine *secondary education educator*

Sunnyside
Aiken, Dorothy Louise *secondary educator*

Tacoma
Murphy, David Bruce *secondary education educator*
Sedgwick, Thomas Farrington *secondary school educator*

Washougal
Nesmith, Susanna Kathleen *secondary educator*

Yakima
Mills, Carol Jane *secondary education educator*

WEST VIRGINIA

Blount
Keller, Nancy Camille *secondary educator*

Charleston
Frostick, Robert Maurice *secondary education educator*

Clarksburg
Leuliette, Connie Jane *secondary educator*

Elizabeth
Lipps, Deloris Jean *secondary school educator*
Lydon, Patricia Diane *secondary education educator*

Fairmont
Stalder, Florence Lucille *secondary education educator*

Inwood
Lambert, Delores Elaine *secondary education educator*

Martinsburg
Mauck, Elaine Carole *retired secondary education educator*
Wendel, Joseph Arthur *retired secondary education educator*

Milton
Roebuck, Judith Lynn *retired secondary school educator*

Morgantown
Rosenbluth, Gwen Socol *secondary educator*

New Martinsville
Francis, Elizabeth Romine *secondary school educator, theater director*

Point Pleasant
Williamson, Judy Darlene Greenlee *secondary school educator, librarian*

Ripley
Riffe, Stacy Christine *secondary school educator*

Vienna
Acree, Wilma Katheryn *retired secondary school educator*

Wheeling
Welker, William Andrew *reading specialist*

WISCONSIN

Brookfield
Gradeless, Donald Eugene *secondary education educator*
Zimmerman, Jay *secondary education educator*

Columbus
Schellin, Patricia Marie Biddle *secondary school educator*

Hartland
Nelson, Katherine MacTaggart *secondary school educator*

Kenosha
Levis, Richard George *secondary school educator*

Kiel
Madigan, Sharon May *physical education and health educator*

Madison
Nicka, Betty Lou *secondary education educator*

Manitowoc
Schuh, Martha Schuhmann *mathematics educator*

Merrill
Gravelle, John David *secondary education educator*

Milwaukee
Bolz, Sarah Jane *mathematics educator*
Eastern, Cynthia Renee *secondary education educator*

Montello
Ellenbecker, Catherine Riedl *secondary art educator, web developer*

Mount Calvary
Krieg, Jeffrey James *secondary education educator*

Mukwonago
Sidie, Steven L. *secondary school educator*

Nekoosa
Ramirez, Mary Catherine *retired secondary school educator*

Oconomowoc
Reich, Rose Marie *retired art educator*

Oshkosh
Herzog, Barbara Jean *secondary school educator, administrator*

Port Washington
King, Eileen Elizabeth *secondary education educator*

Saint Croix Falls
Finster, Diane L. Stelten *secondary school educator, media specialist, home economics educator*

Schofield
Plein, Kathryn Anne *retired secondary school educator*

Sheboygan
Fritz, Kristine Rae *secondary education educator*
Glanert, Karen Louise *secondary education educator*

Twin Lakes
Fleischer, John Richard *retired secondary education educator*

Wales
Schneider, Kathleen Ann *secondary school educator*

Waterford
Jerome, James John *secondary education educator*

Waukesha
Leekley, Marie Valpoon *secondary education educator*

WYOMING

Afton
Hoopes, Farrel G. *secondary education educator*

Casper
Matteson, Barbara Ann Vance *secondary education educator*

Cheyenne
Weigner, Brent James *secondary education educator*

Gillette
Buus, Linda Lee Pannetier *secondary education educator*
Cummings, Judy Annette *retired secondary education educator*

Green River
Albers, Dolores M. *secondary education educator*

Jackson
Gagnon, Margaret Ann Callahan *secondary education educator*

Lander
Willoughby, Julia Ann *secondary school educator*

Wheatland
Morrison, Samuel Ferris *secondary school educator*

TERRITORIES OF THE UNITED STATES

GUAM

Hagatna
Alano, Ernesto Olarte *secondary education educator*

MARSHALL ISLANDS

Majuro
Boucher, Raymond Joseph *retired secondary school educator*

PALAU ISLAND

Palau
Olkeriil, Lorenza *English language educator*

PUERTO RICO

Carolina
Higuera-Pereda, Mercedes *secondary education educator*

Ceiba
Washburn, Richard Wilbur *secondary education educator*

Guayama
Sanftner, Tammy Jean *secondary school educator*

Humacao
Delgado-Rodriguez, Manuel *secondary school educator*

VIRGIN ISLANDS

Frederiksted
Birbahadur, Dindial *secondary educator*
Petrait, Brother James Anthony *secondary education educator, clergy member*

SPAIN

Tacoronte
Kardas, Sigmund Joseph, Jr., *secondary education educator*

ADDRESS UNPUBLISHED

Ackert, Mary Ann *secondary school educator*
Albers, Edward James, Sr., *retired secondary school educator*
Allen, Charlotte *secondary education educator*
Anderson, Iris Anita *retired secondary education educator*
Anderson, Marilyn June *retired secondary school educator*
Anuebunwa, Cynthia Statham *secondary education educator*
Armstead, Tressa Maddux *secondary school educator*
Attig, John Clare *secondary education educator, consultant*
Baglos, Robert Joseph *secondary school educator*
Baird, Donald Robert *retired secondary school educator*
Baldwin, Marie Hunsucker *retired secondary school educator*
Ball, Brenda Joyce Sivils *secondary education educator*
Barber, Norma Ann *secondary education educator*
Barrett, Evelyn Carol *retired secondary education educator*
Battenfeld, John Leonard *secondary school educator, journalist, editor, education educator*
Beery, Barbara Faye *secondary school educator*
Bell, Elva Glenn *retired secondary school educator, retired counseling administrator, interpreter*
Benanti, Nerina Spotti *secondary school educator*
Benson, Joan Dorothy *secondary school educator*
Berendsen, Sallyann Lawrence *secondary education educator*
Beyersdorf, Marguerite Mulloy *retired secondary school educator*
Biebl, Patricia Ann *secondary education educator*
Boland, Margaret Frances *secondary education educator*
Bordonaro, Josephine Frances *retired secondary school educator*
Bourque, Boyd D. *secondary education educator*
Boyenga, Cindy A. *secondary education educator*
Brandt, B. Shirley Boschee *secondary education educator*
Brown, Rubye Golsby *secondary education educator, artist*
Burns, Marie T. *retired secondary education educator*
Bursley-Hamilton, Susan *secondary school educator*
Butler-Nalin, Kay *secondary school educator*
Campbell, Susan Carrigg *secondary education educator*
Carter, Evelyn Adkins *secondary education educator*
Carter, Julia Marie *secondary education educator*
Causey, Susan Marie *retired health educator*
Chajet, Lori Menschel *secondary education educator*
Chatman, Eleanor Louise *secondary school educator*
Chaudoir, Jean Hamilton (Jean Hamilton) *educator*
Childers, Pamela Barnard *secondary school educator*
Childers, Robert L. *secondary education educator*
Churukian, George Allen *retired education educator*
Chyu, Chi-Oy Wei *secondary school educator*
Clark, Claudia J. *educational administration, speech, language and learning disabilities professional*
Cohen, Shirley Mason *educator, writer, civic worker*
Costantini, William Joseph *secondary school educator, computer consultant*
Cutting, Edith Elsie *retired secondary education educator, writer*
Darensbourg, Cynthia Pepin *elementary and secondary school educator*
Davis, Sue Ellen H. *elementary and secondary music educator*
Davison, Helen Irene *secondary education educator, counselor*
DeBord, Marilyn Anne *retired secondary school educator*
De Long, Katharine *retired secondary education educator*
Denton, Joan Cameron *reading consultant, former educator*
Derrickson, Denise Ann *secondary school educator, educator*
Diamond, Richard *retired secondary education educator*
Dierksen, Kathryn Zimmerman *secondary education educator*
DiSalle, Michael Danny *secondary education educator*
Dombroski, Richelle Bragg *secondary education educator*
Donkle, Priscilla P. *secondary school educator*
Doud, Guy R. *motivational speaker, former secondary education educator*
Douglas, Mary Younge Riley *secondary education educator*
Douglas, Roxanne Grace *secondary school educator*
Duckworth, Paula Oliver *secondary school educator, freelance artist, writer, photographer*
Dunn, Helen Elizabeth *retired secondary school educator*
DuVall, Patricia Arlene *secondary education educator*
Edwards, Jack Lee *retired secondary school educator*
Enfield, Susan Ann *secondary school educator*
Evans, Michael Duane *middle school educator*
Eyster, John W. *secondary school educator*
Faherty, Patricia Bernadette *secondary education educator*
Fahrlander, Phillip Raymond *retired secondary school educator, music educator*
Faucette, Merilon Cooper *retired elementary educator*
Fedeli, Shirley Ann (Martignoni) *secondary school educator*
Fernandez-Arrondo, Maria del Carmen *secondary education educator*
Fields, Keith Allen *secondary education educator*
Fincher, Margaret Ann *retired secondary school educator*
Flusche, Joanne Martini *secondary education educator*
Forte, Virginia Frances *secondary educator*
Fuller, Maxine Compton *retired secondary school educator*
Galdi-Weissman, Natalie Ann *secondary education educator*
Garr, Wanda Faye *secondary education educator*
Geary, Allyson *secondary education educator*
Gemming, Mary Frances *college educator, writer, astrologer*
Genovese, Lawrence Matthew *secondary education educator*
Gerber, Sandra Lee *secondary education educator*
Godwin, Sandra Donna *secondary school educator*
Goff, Jane E. *secondary school educator*
Goldsborough, Edmund Lee, III, *retired secondary school educator*
Goron, Mara J. *social studies educator, assistant principal*
Graham, Sylvia Swords *secondary school educator, retired*
Grant, Miriam Rosenbloum *secondary school educator, journalist*
Green, Jerilyn D. *secondary school educator*
Greene, Katherine Margaret *secondary education educator, mathematics educator*
Gregoire, Sister Therese Germaine *retired secondary education educator*
Griffin, Laura Mae *retired elementary and secondary school educator*
Grimme, A. Jeannette *retired educator, community activist*
Grine, Florence May *secondary education educator*
Gruber, Sharon Doris *former secondary education educator*
Gudnitz, Ora M. Cofey *secondary education educator*
Gustafson, Sandra Lynne *retired secondary school educator*
Haeberle, Rosamond Pauline *retired educator*
Hancock, Priscilla Tedesco *retired education educator*
Hannewald, Norman Eugene *secondary school educator*
Hansbury, Vivien Holmes *elementary and secondary school educator, consultant*
Hauseman, Rosemary *secondary education educator*
Hawkins, Jacquelyn *elementary and secondary education educator*
Haynes, Eileen B. *secondary school art and photography educator*
Hedges, Norma Ann *retired secondary education educator*
Henderson, Catherine Lynn *retired secondary education educator, writer*
Henderson, Jean Woodburn *retired secondary education educator*
Hoeveler, Diane Long *English educator, researcher, writer*
Hoft, Ed. D. Lynne A. *elementary and secondary school educator, differentiation specialist, educational consultant*
Hull, Louise Knox *retired elementary educator, administrator*
Hulsey, Rachel Martinez *secondary school educator, columnist*
Iadipaolo, Donna Marie *educator, writer, director, artist, performer*
Jacobe, Carol Ann *secondary school educator*
Jefferson, Kathleen Henderson *retired secondary education educator*
Jenkins, Jacqueline Ann Moore *secondary education educator*
Kannady, Pam *secondary school educator*
Katz, Alan Martin *secondary education educator*
Kazmarek, Linda Adams *secondary education educator*
Ketron, Carrie Sue *secondary school educator*
Kilmer, Joseph Charles *secondary school educator*
Kimball, Mary Holt *retired secondary school educator*
Kluge, Cheryle Darlene Jobe *secondary education educator*
Knight, Rebecca Jean *secondary education educator*
Konior, Jeannette Mary *secondary school educator*
Krish, Raymond Peter *computer technology coordinator, educator*
Kushinka, Joyce Williams *secondary education educator, retired*
Langgood, Judith Ann *secondary level art educator*
Lee, Everyisch Hienrik *secondary and adult education educator*
Leibow, Lois May *secondary education educator*
Leistner, Mary Edna *retired secondary education educator*
Lindenmeyer, Mary Kathryn *secondary education educator, psychologist*
Locklear, Brenda Louise *mathematics educator*
Lundgren, Leonard, III, *retired secondary education educator*
Lynch, Rosemary G. *secondary school educator*
Lyne, Dorothy-Arden *educator*
Mack, Sandra Lee *secondary school educator*
Maclise, James Raymond *secondary school and education educator, writer*
Manera, Elizabeth Sturgis *education educator emeritus*

SECONDARY SCHOOL EDUCATION

Marlow, Marcia Marie *secondary school educator, publishing executive*
Marshall, Navarre *retired education educator*
Mason, Johanna Hendrika Anneke *retired secondary education educator*
McCall, Patricia Alene *secondary music education educator*
McClaron, Louisianna Clardy *retired secondary school educator*
McCrae, Linda Reed *secondary education educator*
McHale, Carol Ann *secondary education educator*
McMahon Mastroddi, Marcia A. *secondary education educator, artist*
McMorrow, Margaret Mary (Peg McMorrow) *retired secondary school educator*
McMullen, Jennifer Anne *secondary school educator*
Merrell, Jo Ann *secondary education educator, writer*
Meyer, Robert Lee *secondary education educator*
Miaskiewicz, Theresa Elizabeth *secondary education educator*
Miller, Linda Karen *retired secondary school educator, social studies educator, law educator*
Miner, Mary Elizabeth Hubert *retired secondary school educator*
Mintz, Patricia Pomboy *secondary education educator*
Mohr, Barbara Jeanne *secondary school educator*
Moormann, Vikki Patricia *secondary education educator*
Morales, Sandra Lee *secondary school educator*
Morgan, Rhelda Elnola *secondary school educator*
Murray, Dorothy Speicher *retired secondary school educator*
Nance, Mary Joe *retired secondary school educator*
Nappi, Marie Teresa *secondary school mathematics educator*
Neal, Teresa Schreibeis *secondary education educator*
Needham, Lillie Dulcenia *secondary education educator, business educator*
Newton, Elizabeth Purcell *counselor, consultant, author*
Nichols, Sandra Jean *reading specialist*
North, Anita *secondary education educator*
Owen, Virginia Bonnie *secondary school educator*
Pappas, John George *secondary school educator*
Parker, George Ernest *secondary mathematics educator*
Parsons, Harriet Jean *mathematics educator*
Parsont, Mina Rainès-Lambé *retired language educator*
Paterson, Patricia McDonnough *secondary school educator, sports official*
Patrizio, Liliana *educator*
Patterson, Myrna Nancy *secondary education educator*
Peebles, Ruth Addelle *secondary education educator*
Pennacchio, Linda Marie *secondary school educator*
Perger, Donna Spagnoli *retired secondary school mathematics educator*
Perry, Joyce Fitzwilliam *secondary school educator*
Peschel, Jo Ann *secondary school educator*
Peterson, Dan *secondary school educator*
Peterson, Ginger *secondary education educator*
Petoskey, Thomas W. *secondary school educator*
Petrou, Judith Ellen *retired secondary school educator*
Pickett, Wendy Lynn *secondary education educator*
Pinto, Rosalind *retired educator, civic volunteer*
Pitrelli, Ellen Jane *secondary school educator*
Platis, James George *secondary school educator*
Platti, Rita Jane *secondary school educator, draftsman, writer, inventor*
Porter, Nancy Kay H. *retired secondary school educator*
Powell, Patricia Ann *secondary school educator*
Price, Sandra Hoffman *secondary school educator*
Quarles, Peggy Delores *secondary school educator*
Rago, Dorothy Ashton *retired educator*
Ratliff, Lois L. *secondary school educator*
Raucci, Frances Lucille *secondary education educator*
Reeves, Lucy Mary *retired school educator*
Revor, Barbara Kay *secondary school educator*
Ricks, Mae Lois *secondary education educator*
Rivera-Ramirez, Ana Rosa *secondary school educator*
Roberts, Maura M. *retired secondary school educator*
Robinson, Nancy Diane *secondary school educator*
Rodgers, Lois Eve *secondary school educator*
Roop, Karen Danstedt *elementary and secondary school educator*
Rosof, Patricia J.F. *retired secondary education educator*
Ross, Ann Dunbar *secondary school educator*
Rouse, Elaine Burdett *retired secondary school educator*
Rudowski, Michael Henry *secondary school educator*
Russo-Rumore, Nancy *retired secondary education educator*
Sachitano, Sheila Marie *secondary school educator, small business owner*
Sagginario, Joan Theresa Vetere *elementary and secondary education educator*
Sanders, Gladys Nealous *retired secondary school educator*
Saunders, Karen Estelle *secondary school educator*
Sbuttoni, Karen Ryan *reading specialist*
Scarborough, Ann Barlow *secondary school educator*
Schopp, James A. *secondary education educator*
Schrenker, Virginia McCrary *math and Latin educator*
Schumacher, Cynthia Jo *retired elementary and secondary education educator*
Seguin, Lillian Angelin *secondary school educator, mathematics educator*
Seldomridge, Deborah McBee *secondary education educator*
Sellers, Annette Cabaniss *secondary education educator*
Sessler, Jane Virginia *retired secondary school educator*
Sestini, Virgil Andrew *retired biology educator*
Shahandeh, Arousha *secondary school educator*
Shanahan, Eileen Frances *secondary education educator*
Shin, Edward Sung-Shik *bilingual education educator*
Shoun, Ellen Llewellyn *retired secondary school educator*
Simkins, Gregory Dale *secondary education educator*
Singerman, Dona Fatibeno *reading specialist*
Slavin, Susan Ann *secondary educator*
Smith, Christine Jean *secondary school educator*
Soliday, Michael David *secondary school and special educator*
Spencer, Rex LeRoy *retired secondary school educator*
Stanford, Kathleen Theresa *secondary school educator*
Stauffer, Louise Lee *retired secondary school educator*
Steinberg, Joan Emily *retired middle school educator*
Stewart, David Leslie *secondary education educator*
Street, Lela Kathryn *retired secondary education educator*
Suarez, Elisabeth Clemence *counselor educator*
Sullivan, Faith Helen *secondary education educator, writer*
Suppa-Friedman, Janice DeStefano *secondary school educator, consultant*
Surma, Jane Ann *secondary education educator*
Sutro, Edmund J. *secondary school educator, consultant*
Tabandera, Kathlynn Rosemary *secondary education educator*
Tarbi, William Rheinlander *secondary education educator, curriculum consultant, educational technology researcher*
Thompson, Ana Calzada *secondary education educator, mathematician*
Thueme, William Harold *secondary school educator, travel coordinator*
Todd, Joan Abernathy *secondary school educator*
Todd, William Eric *secondary school educator*
Toop, Gillian V. *retired secondary school educator*
Turner, Elizabeth Robinson *secondary education educator*
Tussing, Lewis Benton, III, (Tony Tussing) *secondary education educator, coach*
Usher, Nancy Spear *retired language arts educator*
Veal, Laura *secondary school educator*
Veverka, Ruth Tonry *retired secondary school educator*
Vickers, Mark Stephen *business educator, travel industry executive, sculptor, painter*
Von Burg, Frederick E., Sr., *secondary school educator, writer*
Wade, June Booth *secondary school educator*
Washburn, Harriet Caroline *secondary education educator*
Wasiuk, Kathleen Page *secondary education educator*
Wean, Karla Denise *secondary school educator*
Westerberg, Mary L. *retired secondary school educator*
Whittington-Brown, Vanessa Elizabeth *educator*
Williams, Cheryl A. *secondary education educator*
Williams-Monegain, Louise Joel *retired science educator, ethnographer*
Woltering, Margaret Mae *retired secondary school educational consultant*
Wright, Ethel *secondary education educator*
Yablun, Ronn *secondary education educator, small business owner*
Yoder, Myron Eugene *secondary school educator*
Zabilka, Ivan L. *secondary education educator*
Ziegler, Mark Douglas *secondary school educator*

VOCATIONAL SCHOOL EDUCATION

UNITED STATES

ALABAMA

Phenix City
Jinright, Noah Franklin *vocational school educator, security executive*

ALASKA

Barrow
Trainor, Jerry Allen *vocational education professional*

ARIZONA

Sun Lakes
Dean, Charles Thomas *industrial arts educator, academic administrator*

ARKANSAS

Fort Smith
Hoppes, Gary Jon *vocational educator, management consultant*

CALIFORNIA

Lafayette
Dietz, Donald Arthur *vocational education educator*

Lakewood
De Lorca, Luis E. *public school administrator, educator, speaker*

Palmdale
Bowen, Jimmie Carl *vocational education educator*

San Quentin
Anderson, Douglas Sanford *vocational supervisor*

Stockton
Fish, Tom *vocational school educator*

COLORADO

Denver
Whatley, Lisa *vocational school administrator*

Westminster
Eaves, Stephen Douglas *vocational administrator, educator, consultant*

FLORIDA

Deland
Fritch, Ronald J. *vocational education educator*

Gainesville
Oppenheim, Paul *vocational educator*

Spring Hill
Rojas, Victor Hugo Macedo *retired vocational education educator*

GEORGIA

Atlanta
Dorsey, J(onnie) Naomi *vocational education educator, consultant*

Gainesville
Lipscomb, Shirley Ruth *vocational education educator*

Valdosta
Bridges, James A. *vocational school educator*

ILLINOIS

Chicago
Blumenthal, Carlene Margaret *vocational-technical school and language arts educator*
Johnson, Mary Ann *vocational school owner*

Highland Park
Gordon, Paul *metallurgical educator*

INDIANA

Franklin
Bender, Larry Wayne *vocational educator*

Merrillville
Protho, Jessie *educator*

KANSAS

Olathe
Tremain, Richard Dean *vocational educator*

KENTUCKY

Georgetown
Stephenson, Joseph Anderson *vocational school educator*

Louisville
Broady, Fannie Marie *vocational school educator*

Russell Springs
Dennison, Patricia Davis *vocational education educator, nurse*

MARYLAND

Bel Air
Phillips, Bernice Cecile Golden *retired vocational education educator*

MASSACHUSETTS

Chicopee
Anderson, Nancy Elaine *home economics educator*

Kingston
Rispettoso, George Alphonse *vocational educator, diesel technology consultant*

Raynham
Myers, Russell Davis *retired technical school educator*

MICHIGAN

Lawrence
Fudge, Mary Ann *vocational school educator*

MINNESOTA

Edina
Meyer, Warren George *vocational educator*

Lakeland
Helstedt, Gladys Mardell *vocational education educator*

Minnetonka
Moon, James Russell *technology education educator*

MISSISSIPPI

Batesville
Neal, Joseph Lee *vocational school educator*

Pascagoula
McKee, Ronald Gene *vocational education educator*

Starkville
Knight, Aubrey Kevin *vocational education educator*

MISSOURI

Sedalia
Noland, Gary Lloyd *vocational school educator, administrator*

West Plains
Smith, Brenda Marie *vocational home economics educator*

NEVADA

Las Vegas
Skoll, Pearl A. *retired mathematics and special education educator*

NEW JERSEY

Hackensack
Daut, Eleanor Gilmore *vocational education educator*

NEW YORK

Millwood
Durst, Carol Goldsmith *food studies educator*

New York
Lazarus-Franklin, Paula Guillermina *vocational services administrator*

Rochester
Lang, Harry George *vocational education researcher*

Sanborn
Schmidt-Bova, Carolyn Marie *career and technical school administrator*

NORTH CAROLINA

Clinton
Terry, George Marshall *vocational studies educator*

OHIO

Athens
Johnson, Jeannette Selby *vocational education educator*

Cincinnati
Patterson, Claire Ann *career techincal educator*

Columbus
Armes, Walter Scott *vocational school administrator*

Jackson
Clark, M. Juanita *vocational education evaluator*

Milford
Mechlem, Daphne Jo *vocational school educator*

Perrysburg
Carpenter, J. Scott *vocational educator*

Zanesville
Irvin, Helen Arlene *vocational education educator*

OKLAHOMA

Bartlesville
Risner, Anita Jane *vocational school educator*

Fort Cobb
Rexroat, Vicki Lynn *occupational child development educator*

Norman
Stover, Curtis Sylvester *retired vocational school educator*

Oklahoma City
Menz, Pamela *adult and vocational education educator*

Pawhuska
Holloway, Sharon Kay Sossamon *vocational/secondary school educator*

Stigler
Slusser, Brett William *vocational education educator*

OREGON

Portland
Bennett, Charles Leon *vocational and graphic arts educator*
Fan, Lee Siu *business executive and vocational training program administrator*
Lynch, Nita Marie Smith *vocational curriculum developer, ballroom dancer*

PENNSYLVANIA

East Pittsburgh
Miller, Colleen *vocational rehabilitation specialist, career counselor*

Philadelphia
Carr, Gwenn Claire *instructional technology consultant, educator*
Hughes, Robert Joseph *vocational school educator*

Wernersville
Himmelberger, Richard Charles *vocational school educator*

TENNESSEE

Memphis
Booth, Linda Leigh *vocational school educator*

Nashville
Fondaw, Elizabeth Louise *vocational school educator*

TEXAS

Houston
Little, H. Maurice *vocational educator*

Rockport
Stone-Magner, Rose Marie *vocational educator*

WASHINGTON

Spokane
Howell, Donald James *vocational school administrator*

WEST VIRGINIA

Barboursville
Lucas, Carol McCann *vocational education educator*

Morgantown
Drvar, Margaret Adams *vocational education educator*

WISCONSIN

Eau Claire
Brill, Donald Maxim *educator, writer, researcher*

Manitowoc
Butler, Robin Erwin *retired vocational technical educator, consultant*

Milwaukee
Fonner, Kelly S. *educational technologist, consultant*

TERRITORIES OF THE UNITED STATES

PUERTO RICO

San Juan
Rodríguez-Samalot, José Angel *vocational education administrator*

ADDRESS UNPUBLISHED

Becker, Walter Heinrich *vocational educator, planner*
Frierson, Jimmie Lou *retired vocational education educator*
Heidt-Dunwell, Debra Sue *vocational education educator*
Kretzmar, Mary Lynn *vocational education and sign language interpreter, educator*
Russell, Judy Elaine *consumer science and health educator*